6th Edition

CHILTON'S IMPORT CAR REPAIR MANUAL 1975-81

Editorial Director	Alan F. Turner
Managing Editor	Kerry A. Freeman, S.A.E.
Senior Editor	Richard J. Rivele, S.A.E.
Service Editors	Martin Gunther
	Carl Canfield
	Lance Ealey
	Dean Morgantini
	Ron Webb
Editorial Production	Dru Brown
	Donna Fisher
	Robin Small Miller
	Margaret Stoner
Production Manager	Warren Owens
Assistant Production Manager	Timothy Frelick
Production Assistant	Nancy A. Hassler
OFFICERS	
President	William A. Barbour
Executive Vice President	James Miades
Vice President & General Manager	John P. Kushnerick

CHILTON BOOK COMPANY
Chilton Way, Radnor, Pa. 19089

Manufactured in USA

ISBN 0-8019-7029-6
Library of Congress Catalog
Card No. 78-20243

234567890 0987654321

Acknowledgments

CHILTON BOOK COMPANY
expresses appreciation to the following
for their cooperation and technical assistance

AB Volvo, Gotenberg, Sweden
American Honda Motor Company, Moorestown, N.J.
A Pierburg Auto- & Luftfahrt/Geratebau KG (Zenith Carburetors), Neuss-Rhein, Germany
Arnolt Corporation (Solex Carburetors), Warsaw, Indiana
BMW of North America, Inc., Montvale, N.J.
Buick Motor Division, General Motors Corporation (Opel), Flint, Michigan
Champion Spark Plug Company, Toledo, Ohio
Chrysler Motors Corporation, Detroit, Michigan
Fiat Motors of North America, Inc., Montvale, New Jersey
Ford Motor Company, Dearborn, Michigan
Jaguar, Rover, Triumph, Ltd., Leonia, New Jersey
Lincoln-Mercury Division, Ford Motor Company (Capri), Dearborn, Michigan
Mazda Motors of America, Incorporated, Compton, California
Mercedes-Benz of North America, Incorporated, Montvale, New Jersey
Nissan Motor Corporation of USA, Carson, California
Peugeot, Inc., Clifton, New Jersey
Porsche-Audi, Division of Volkswagen of America, Incorporated, Englewood Cliffs, New Jersey
Renault, Inc., Englewood Cliffs, New Jersey
Robert Bosch Corporation, Long Island City, New York
SAAB-Scania, New Haven, Connecticut
Subaru of America, Incorporated, Pennsauken, New Jersey
Toyo Kogyo, Ltd., Hiroshima, Japan
Toyota Motor Sales, U.S.A. Incorporated, Torrance, California
Volkswagen of America, Incorporated, Englewood Cliffs, New Jersey
Volvo Incorporated, Rockleigh, New Jersey

Contents

Safety Notice

Proper service and repair procedures are vital to the safe, reliable operation of all motor vehicles, as well as the personal safety of those performing repairs. This manual outlines procedures for servicing and repairing vehicles using safe effective methods. The procedures contain many NOTES, CAUTIONS and WARNINGS which should be followed along with standard safety rocedures to eliminate the possibility of personal injury or improper service which could damage the vehicle or compromise s safety.

It is important to note that repair procedures and techniques, tools and parts for servicing motor vehicles, as well as the skill d experience of the individual performing the work vary widely. It is not possible to anticipate all of the conceivable ways or ons under which vehicles may be serviced, or to provide cautions as to all of the possible hazards that may result. and accepted safety precautions and equipment should be used when handling toxic or flammable fluids, and safety other protection should be used during cutting, grinding, chiseling, prying, or any other process that can cause moval or projectiles.

ocedures require the use of tools specially designed for a specific purpose. Before substituting another tool or you must be completely satisfied that neither your personal safety, nor the performance of the vehicle will b d.

SPECIFICATIONS

INDEX

BEFORE SERVICING, SEE THE SAFETY NOTICE ON THE CONTENTS PAGE

INTRODUCTION

The Audi, produced by Auto Union of Germany and distributed in the United States by Porsche Audi, a division of Volkswagen of America, has been available in the United States since 1970. Three models, the Super 90, Super 90 station wagon (Variant), and the 100 LS, were initially imported using one basic engine. A 1760 cc slanted four-cylinder, OHV engine was used. Displacement has since been increased to 1871 cc. The Super 90 was dropped in 1972, after an estimated 4500 sales. The 100 was introduced in 1972, to replace the Super 90 as a lower cost alternative to the 100 LS. The top of the line 100 GL, with automatic transmission as standard equipment, was added in 1973. The only 100 series car available in 1974 was the 100 LS. Production of the 100 series was ended in 1976. In mid-1973, a new smaller car, the Fox, was introduced. It had a 1471 cc overhead camshaft engine and shares many of the familiar Audi features such as MacPherson strut suspension and front-wheel drive. The Fox engine was enlarged to 1588 cc in 1975.

The 5000 series was introduced in 1978 as the world's first 5 cylinder gasoline powered car. The 5 cylinder engine is developed directly from the Fox 4 cylinder.

In 1979, Audi introduced a diesel version of the 5000 which had all the amenities of the gasoline engine model, plus the advantage of a high mileage, low maintenance diesel engine. The 5000 diesel is available only with a five speed manual transmission, while the 1979 gasoline engine 5000 changed its standard transmission from the four speed to the five speed with the automatic still available as an option.

For 1980, Audi introduced two new models, the 5000 Turbo and the entirely new 4000. The turbocharged 5000 has four wheel disc brakes, beefier suspension, an automatic transmission and is the new 'flagship' of the Audi line. The 4000, which takes the place of the discontinued Fox, looks somewhat like a scaled down version of the 5000. Audi offers two choices of engines in the 4000 body style, a four cylinder, overhead camshaft engine with fuel injection or the five cylinder from the 5000. The four cylinder model comes with rack and pinion steering, independent suspension, front disc brakes, rear drum brakes and a four speed manual transmission. The five cylinder 4000 has an automatic transmission. Both models are front engine, front wheel drive.

SERIAL NUMBER IDENTIFICATION

Vehicle

100 Series and 5000

The chassis number is on the plate on top of the instrument panel, clearly visible through the driver's side of the windshield. It is also stamped into the upper right corner of the firewall. The vehicle identification plate is mounted on the right wheel housing. The chassis number follows the words "Fahrgest.-Nr." on this plate.

4000 Series

The vehicle identification number (VIN) is located on the left (driver's side) windshield pillar and in the engine compartment on the ledge.

Fox

The chassis number is on a plate on the left windshield pillar, clearly visible through the driver's side of the windshield. It is also stamped into the top center of the firewall. The vehicle identification plate is on the right wheel housing. The chassis number follows the words "Fahrgest.-Nr." on this plate.

Engine

100 Series and 5000

The engine number is stamped on the left side of the engine block (clutch housing).

In addition to the engine number, an engine code number is also stamped on the starter end of the cylinder block, just below the cylinder head. This number indicates the exact cylinder bore of the particular engine.

4000 Series

The engine number is located on the left side of the cylinder block, below the cylinder head and next to the distributor.

Fox

The engine number is stamped on the left side of the engine block, just above the fuel pump.

In addition to the engine number, an engine code number is also stamped into the left front side of the cylinder block, just above the water pump. This number indicates the exact cylinder bore of the particular engine.

GENERAL ENGINE SPECIFICATIONS

Year and Model	Engine Cu In. Displacement	Fuel Delivery	SAE Horsepower @ rpm	SAE Torque @ rpm (ft-lbs)	Bore x Stroke (in.)	Compression Ratio	Normal Oil Pressure (psi) ①
1975-76 100	114.2 (1,871 cc)	F.I.	92 @ 5,500	106 @ 3,300	3.31 x 3.32	8.0:1	14-85
1975 Fox	97 (1,588 cc)	F.I.	81 @ 5,800 (79 Calif.)	99 @ 3,300	3.13 x 3.15	8.0:1	9-100
1976-80 Fox and 4000 4-cyl	97 (1,588 cc)	F.I.	79 @ 5,500	89 @ 3,300	3.13 x 3.15	8.0:1	64-74
1977-81 5000 and 4000 5-cyl	130.78 (2,144 cc)	F.I.	103 @ 5,500 (100 Calif.)	110 @ 4,000	3.13 x 3.15	8.0:1	14-85
1979-81 5000 turbo	130.78 (2144)	F.I.	130 @ 5,400	142 @ 3,000	3.12 x 3.40	7.0:1	N.A.

GENERAL ENGINE SPECIFICATIONS

Year and Model	Engine Cu In. Displacement	Carburetor Type	SAE Horsepower @ rpm	SAE Torque @ rpm (ft-lbs)	Bore x Stroke (in.)	Compression Ratio	Normal Oil Pressure (psi) ①
1979-81 5000 diesel	121 (1986)	F.I.	67 @ 4,800	84.4 @ 3,000	3.09 x 3.40	23.0:1	28 @ 2,000
1981 4000 4-cyl	105 (1,715)	F.I.	74 @ 5,000	89.6 @ 3,000	3.13 x 3.40	8.0:1	64-74

① At idle and 5000 rpm
F.I. Fuel injection

TUNE-UP SPECIFICATIONS

Year and Model	Engine Cu In. Displacement	Spark Plugs Type	Spark Plugs Gap (in.)	Distributor Point Dwell (deg)	Distributor Point Gap (in)	Ignition Timing (deg) MT	Ignition Timing (deg) AT	Intake Valve Opens (deg)	Pressure Fuel Pump (psi)	Idle Speed (rpm) MT	Idle Speed (rpm) AT	Valve Clear (in.) ① In	Valve Clear (in.) ① Ex	% CO @ Idle
1975 100 LS	114.2 (1,871 cc)	N7Y	0.035	47-53	0.016	6A @ idle	6A @ idle	5B	66.8-75.3	850-1000	850-1000	0.004-0.006	0.014-0.016	1.5/1.0 (Cal.)
1976 100	114.2 (1,871 cc)	N7Y	.027-.035	44-50	0.016	6A	6A	5B	4.8-5.4	850-1000	850-1000	0.008-0.010	0.016-0.018	0.9 (Fed.) 0.5 (Cal.)
1975 Fox	97 (1,588 cc)	N8Y	0.028	47-53	0.016	3A @ idle 1000	3A @ idle 1000	4B	66.8-85.3	900-950	900-950	0.008-0.012	0.016-0.020	1.0
1976-78 Fox	97 (1,588 cc)	N8Y	0.028	44-50	0.016	3A @ idle	3A @ idle	4B	4.8-5.4	850-1000	850-1000	0.008-0.012	0.016-0.020	1.0AT (Fed.) 1.5MT (Fed.) 0.5 (Cal.)
1977-81 5000 and 4000 5-cyl	130.78 (2,144 cc)	N8Y	0.035	Electronic		3A idle	—	6B	64-74	850-1000	850-1000	0.008-0.012	0.016-0.020	0.9 (Fed.) 0.3 (Cal.)
1980-81 5000 turbo	130.78 (2,144 cc)	N8Y	0.030	Electronic		—	21B@ 3000	—	72-82	—	880-1000	0.008-0.012	0.016-0.020	0.4-1.2
1980-81 4000 49 states	③	N8Y	0.028	44-50	0.016	3A idle	3A idle	4B	4.8-5.4	850-1000	850-1000	0.008-0.012	0.016-0.020	0.4-0.6
1980-81 4000 California	③	N8GY	0.032	Electronic		3A idle	3A idle	4B	4.8-5.4	880-1000	880-1000	0.008-0.012	0.016-0.020	②

NOTE: The underhood specifications sticker often reflects tune-up specification changes made in production. Sticker figures must be used if they disagree with those in this chart.

① Set hot; warm for Fox
② Check underhood label for specifications
③ 1980: 97 cid (1,588 cc)
1981: 105 cid (1,715 cc)
AT Automatic transmission
MT Manual transmission

DIESEL TUNE-UP SPECIFICATIONS

Model/ Year	Engine Displace Cu. In. (cc)	Warm Valve Clear (in) In	Warm Valve Clear (in) Ex	Intake Valve Opens (deg)	Injection Pump Setting (deg)	Injection Nozzle Pressure (psi) New	Injection Nozzle Pressure (psi) Used	Idle Speed (rpm)	Com-pression Pressure (psi)
1979-81 Diesel	121 (1986)	.008-.012	.016-.020	NA	Align Marks	1849	1706	720-880	398-483

FIRING ORDERS

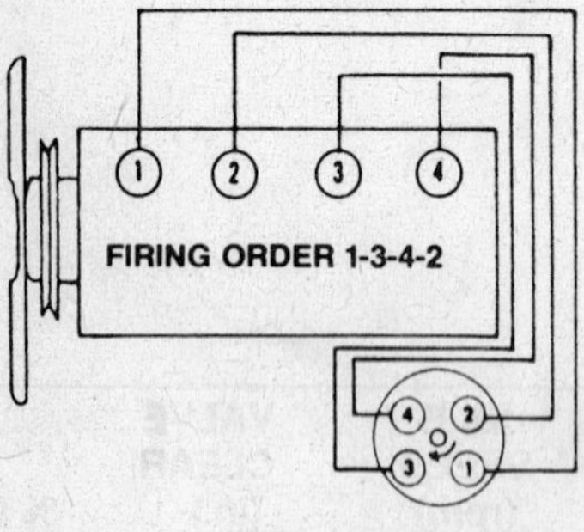

100 Series

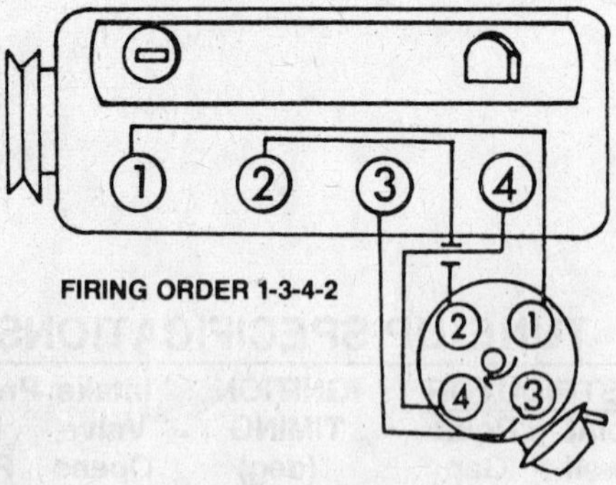

Fox and 4000, 4 cyl

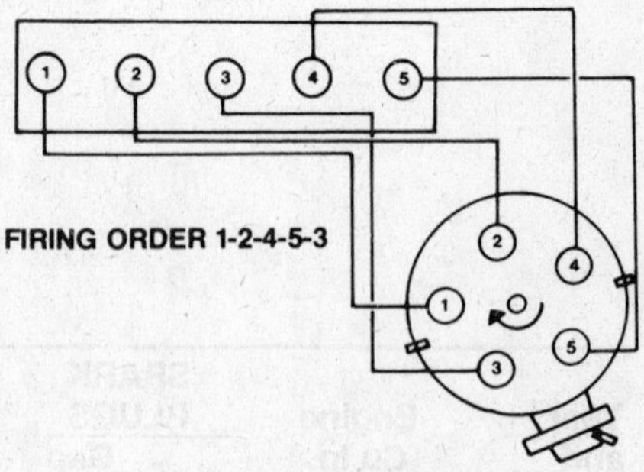

4000 and 5000, 5 cyl

CRANKSHAFT AND CONNECTING ROD SPECIFICATIONS

All measurements are given in inches

Model	Crankshaft: Main Brg. Journal Dia. ①	Crankshaft: Main Brg. Oil Clearance	Crankshaft: Shaft End-Play	Crankshaft: Thrust on No.	Connecting Rod: Journal Diameter ①	Connecting Rod: Oil Clearance	Connecting Rod: Side Clearance
100	2.3622	0.0020-0.0040	0.003-0.007	3	1.8898	0.001-0.003	0.004-0.009
Fox	2.1260	0.0010-0.0030	0.003-0.007	3	1.8110	0.0011-0.0034	0.010
5000 and 4000 5-cyl	2.2834②	0.0006-0.0030	0.003-0.007	4	1.8110③	0.0006-0.0020	0.016
4000 4-cyl	2.1587	0.0010-0.0030	0.0030-0.0070	3	1.8387	0.0011-0.0034	0.015

① Standard size
② Diesel: 2.3187
③ Diesel: 1.9107

VALVE SPECIFICATIONS

Model	Seat Angle (deg)	Face Angle (deg)	Stem to Guide Clearance (in.) Intake	Stem to Guide Clearance (in.) Exhaust	Stem Diameter (in.) Intake	Stem Diameter (in.) Exhaust
100	45	45° 15′	0.001	0.002	0.3507	0.3499
Fox & 4000	45	45	0.001-0.002	0.001-0.002	0.3140	0.3130
5000 (all)	45	45	0.039① Max.	0.051 Max.	0.3140	0.3130

NOTE: Valve guides are removable.
① Diesel: 0.051

CAPACITIES

Model	Crankcase (qts) With Filter	TRANSMISSION (pts) Manual	TRANSMISSION (pts) Automatic	Drive Axle (pts) ①	Gasoline Tank (gals)	Cooling System (qts)
100, 100LS, 100GL	4.3	4.2	12.5 fill 6.0 change	3	15.3	8
Fox and 4000 4-cyl	3.2 ⑥	3.4	12.5 fill 6.4 change	2.1	③	④
5000 and 4000 5-cyl	5.3 ⑦	5.2②	11.2 fill 6.4 change	2.2 ⑧	19.8 ⑨	⑤

① Only with automatic transmission.
② 1980-81: 5.5
③ Fox: 12.0
4000: 15.9
④ Fox: 6.3
4000: 7.4
⑤ 5000: 8.6
5000 turbo: 10.0
5000 diesel: 9.9
4000: 8.5
⑥ 1981: 3.7
⑦ 1981: 4.8
⑧ 4000: 1.6
⑨ 4000: 15.9

PISTON AND RING SPECIFICATIONS

All measurements in inches

Model	Piston Clearance	RING GAP Top Compression	RING GAP Bottom Compression	RING GAP Oil Control	RING SIDE CLEARANCE Top Compression	RING SIDE CLEARANCE Bottom Compression	RING SIDE CLEARANCE Oil Control
100	0.0010	0.039	0.039	0.039	0.0060	0.0060	0.0060
Fox & 4000	0.0010	0.039	0.039	0.039	0.0060	0.0060	0.0060
5000 & 4000 5-cyl	0.0012	0.010-0.020	0.010-0.020	0.010-0.020	0.0008-0.0030	0.0008-0.0030	0.0008-0.0030
5000 Diesel	0.0011	0.012-0.020	0.012-0.020	0.010-0.016	0.0020-0.0035	0.0020-0.0030	0.0010-0.0020

NOTE: Three oversizes of pistons are available to accommodate overbores up to 0.040 in.

TORQUE SPECIFICATIONS

All readings in ft. lbs.

Model	Cylinder Head Bolts	Rod Bearing Bolts ①	Main Bearing Bolts	Crankshaft Pulley Bolt	Flywheel To Crankshaft Bolts	MANIFOLD Intake	MANIFOLD Exhaust
100	65	25-31	58 ②	130-180	65	18	18
Fox & 4000	48-60 cold ③ 56-67 warm ④	25-33	47	58	36	18	17
5000 & 4000 5-cyl	54 cold 61 warm	36	47	253	54	18	18
5000 Diesel	65	33	47	253	54	—	18

① Use new bolts
② 24 on bearing cap no. 5
③ 1976 54 cold
61 warm
④ With Polygon head bolts tighten to 55 ft. lbs. with engine cold. Then tighten bolts ¼ turn (90°) more

TORQUE SEQUENCES

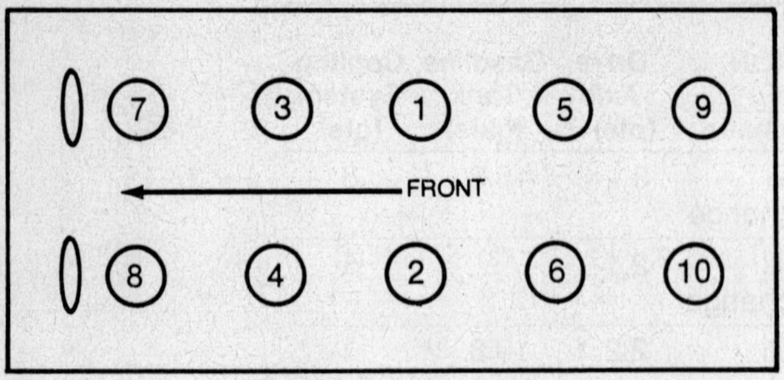

100 series cylinder head

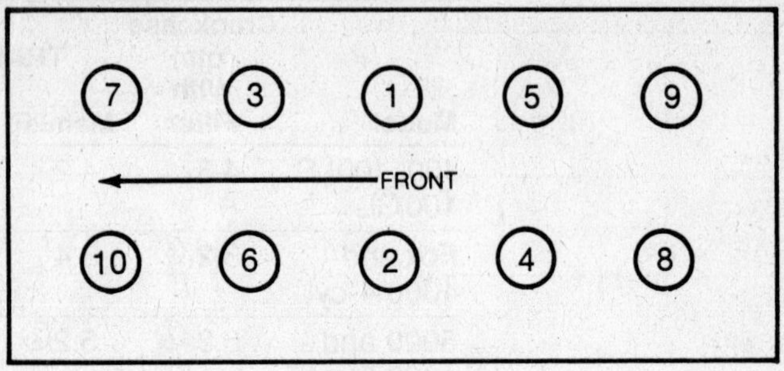

Fox cylinder head

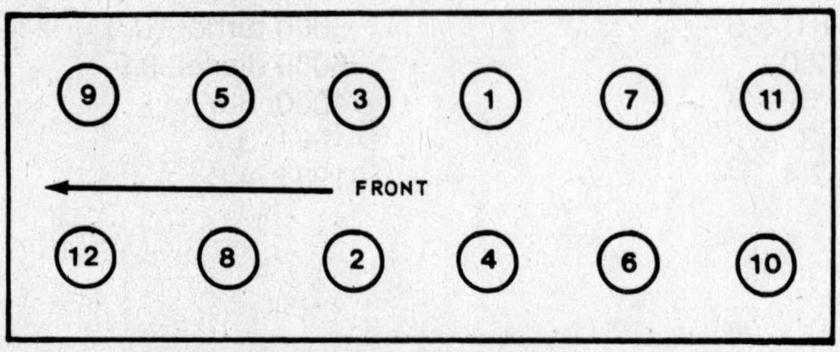

4000 and 5000 cylinder head—5 cyl

ALTERNATOR AND REGULATOR SPECIFICATIONS

	ALTERNATOR		REGULATOR	
Model	Part No. or Manufacturer	Output (amps.)	Part No. or Manufacturer	Volts
100 Series	Bosch K1 14V 55A 20	55	Bosch AD 1/14V or EE 14V (integral)	13.9-14.8
Fox and 4000 4-cyl	Bosch K1 14V 55A	55	Bosch EF 14V (integral)	13.5-14.5
5000 and 4000 5-cyl	Audi 063-903-017	75	Audi (integral) 063-903-803	13.8-14.7

BATTERY AND STARTER SPECIFICATIONS

All cars use 12 volt, negative ground electrical systems

		STARTER					
	Battery Amp Hour	LOCK TEST		NO LOAD TEST			Min. Brush Length
Model	Capacity	Amps	Volts	Amps	Volts	rpm	(in.)
100	45/55	250-300	7	30-55	11.5	6000-9000	0.47
Fox & 4000	45/54	250-300	7	30-55	11.5	6000-9000	0.5
5000	63 ①	—	8	—	—	—	—

—Not available
① Diesel battery 88 amps

BRAKE SPECIFICATIONS

All measurements given are in. unless noted

Model	Lug Nut Torque (ft. lb.)	Master Cylinder Bore	BRAKE DISC ③		BRAKE DRUM			MINIMUM LINING THICKNESS	
			Minimum Thickness	Maximum Run-Out	Diameter	Max. Machine O/S	Max. Wear Limit	Front	Rear
100, 100LS	85	0.813 ①	0.36 ②	0.002	7.870	7.890	7.910	0.078	0.098
Fox & 4000	65	0.825	0.413 ②	0.002	7.870	7.890	7.910	0.078	0.098
5000 & Diesel	80	0.875	0.807	0.004	10.157	9.005	9.094	0.078	0.098
5000 turbo	80	0.875	0.807	0.002	9.645 ④	0.335 ⑤	0.002 ⑥	0.551	0.472

NOTE: Minimum lining thickness is as recommended by the manufacturer. Due to variations in state inspection regulations, the minimum allowable thickness may be different than recommended by the manufacturer.

① 0.874 —1975-77
② With ventilated discs —0.768 after refinishing 0.728 in. —discard thickness
③ Federal law requires that the minimum rotor thickness be stamped in the disc
④ Rear disc diameter
⑤ Rear disc min. thickness
⑥ Rear disc max. runout

WHEEL ALIGNMENT

Model	CASTER		CAMBER		Toe-in (in.)	WHEEL PIVOT RATIO	
	Range (deg)	Pref Setting (deg)	Range (deg)	Pref Setting (deg)		Inner Wheel	Outer Wheel
1975-76 100LS	0°11′N to 0°29′P	0°0′	0°20′N to 0°20′P	0°	0.00	20	19°40′ to 20°20′
1975-76 100 LS, Power Steering	0°19′P to 0°59′P	0°39′	0°20′N to 0°20′P	0°	0.00	20	19°40′ to 20°20′
1975-77 Fox	0 to 1P	0°30′P	0°5′P to 0°55′P ③	0°30′P ②	0.00-0.08	20	18°36′ to 19°36′
1977-81 5000 & Diesel	5/6N to 1/2P	1/6N	1N to 0	1/2N	1/8 out to 1/16 in	—	—
1978 Fox	0 to 1P	1/2P	0 to 1P	1/2P	1/16 to 1/8 ①	20	18°36′ to 19°36′
5000 turbo	30′P to 1°50′P	1°10′P	1°N to 0	30′N	5′P to 10′N	—	—
4000 (all)	0-1°P	30′P	1°10′N to 10′N	40′N	0-20′P	—	—

N Negative
P Positive
—Not Available

① Toe-out
② 0°30′N (Rear wheel) not adjustable
③ In-0° (Rear wheel) not adjustable

TUNE-UP PROCEDURES

All the tune-up steps should be followed, as each adjustment complements the effects of the other adjustments. If the tune-up specifications sticker in the engine compartment disagrees with the Tune-up Specifications Chart, the sticker figures must be followed.

Spark Plugs

1. Disconnect each spark plug wire by pulling on the rubber cap, not on the wire.
2. Wipe the wires clean with a cloth dampened in kerosene and wipe them dry. If the wires appear to be cracked, they should be replaced.
3. Blow or brush the dirt away from each of the spark plugs.
4. Remove each spark plug with a spark plug socket. Be careful that the socket is all the way down on the plug to prevent it from slipping and cracking the porcelain insulator.
5. Evaluate the condition of the plugs. In general, a tan or medium gray color on the business end of the plug indicates normal combustion conditions. Refer to the Tune-Up Specifications Chart for the proper spark plug type.

Gap the spark plugs with a wire gauge

6. If the plugs are to be reused, file the center and side electrodes with a small, fine file. It is often suggested that plugs be tested and cleaned on a service station sandblasting machine; however, this piece of equipment is becoming rare. Check the gap between the two electrodes with a spark plug gap gauge. The round wire type is the most accurate. If the gap is not as specified, use the adjusting device on the gap gauge to bend the outside electrode to correct. Be careful not to bend the electrode too far, because excessive bending may cause it to weaken and possibly fall off into the engine. This would require cylinder head removal to reach the broken piece, and could result in cylinder wall and ring damage.
7. Clean the plug threads with a wire brush. Crank the engine with the starter to blow out any dirt particles from the cylinder head threads.
8. Put a drop of oil on the threads and screw the plugs in finger tight. Tighten them with the plug socket. If a torque wrench is available, tighten them to 22 ft/lbs.
9. Reinstall the wires. If there is any doubt as to their proper locations, refer to "Firing Order."

Breaker Points and Condenser

The condenser should be replaced each time the points are replaced. After every breaker point adjustment or replacement, the ignition timing must be checked and, if necessary, adjusted. No special equipment other than a feeler gauge is required for point replacement or adjustment, although a dwell meter should be used to ensure the accuracy of the adjustment.

1. Detach the two spring clips securing the distributor cap. Remove the cap.
2. Clean the cap inside and out. Check for cracks and carbon paths. A carbon path shows up as a dark line, usually from one of the cap sockets or inside terminals to a ground. Check the condition of the button inside the center of the cap and the four inside terminals. Replace the cap if necessary.
3. Pull the rotor up and off the shaft. Clean off the metal end if it is burned or corroded. Replace the rotor if necessary. Remove the dust cap, if there is one.
4. The manufacturer states that the points must be replaced, not reconditioned. Experience also shows that it is more economical and reliable in the long run to replace the point set while the distributor is open, than to have to do this at a later (and possibly more inconvenient) time.
5. Pull off the flat plug terminal on the wire from the point set. Remove the point set hold-down screw, being very careful not to drop it into the inside of the distributor. If this happens, the distributor will probably have to be removed to get at the screw. If the screw is lost elsewhere, it must be replaced with one that is no longer than the original to avoid interference with distributor workings. Remove the point set.
6. Remove the condenser by removing the screw and pulling the assembly out. Detach the lead from the coil. The condenser, wire, flat plug connection, and plastic sealing boot are a single assembly.
7. Install the new condenser, attaching the lead to the coil.
8. Apply a small amount of high melting point grease to the pivot side of the point set rubbing block.
9. Replace the point set and tighten the screw tightly. Replace the flat plug terminals.
10. Check that the contacts meet squarely. If they do not, bend the tab supporting the fixed contact.
11. Turn the engine until a high point on the cam that opens the points contracts the rubbing block on the point arm. This is easier if the spark plugs have been removed.
12. There is a screwdriver slot and two raised lugs near the contacts. Insert a screwdriver and lever the points open or closed until they appear to be open about the correct gap.
13. Insert the correct size feeler gauge and adjust the gap with the screwdriver until you can push the gauge in and out between the contacts with a slight drag but without moving the point arm. Another check is to try the gauges 0.001-0.002 in. larger and smaller than the setting size. The larger one should disturb the point arm, whereas the smaller one should not drag at all. Tighten the point set hold-down screw snugly. Recheck the gap, because it often changes when the screw is tightened.
14. After all the point adjustments are complete, pull a white business card through (between) the contacts to remove any traces of oil. Oil will cause rapid point burning.
15. Replace the dust cap.
16. Push the rotor firmly down into place. It will go on only one way. If it is not installed properly, it will probably break when the starter is operated.
17. Replace the distributor cap and install the spring clip.
18. Check the dwell with a meter. Dwell can be checked with the engine running or cranking. Decrease dwell by increasing the

Breaker point installation

(c)—Lead to coil
(g)—Vacuum line connection
(m)—Flat plug wire ter minal
(n)—Raised lugs
(o)—Screw-driver slot
(p)—Hold-down screw

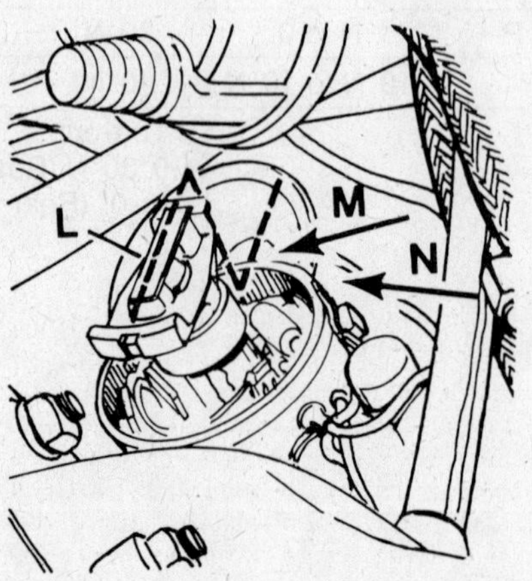

The distributor rotor (L) aligned with the No. 1 cylinder mark (M) on the rim of the distributor body. The dust cap is removed

point gap; increase by decreasing the gap. Dwell angle is simply the number of degrees of distributor shaft rotation during which the points stay closed. Theoretically, if the point gap is correct, the dwell should also be correct or nearly so. However, dwell is a more accurate setting. If dwell varies more than 3 degrees from idle speed to 2500 engine rpm, the distributor is worn.

NOTE: Some tachometers, dwell meters, and oscilloscopes will not work with the capacitive discharge ignition system. Some may be damaged. Check with the manufacturer of your test equipment if there is any doubt.

19. Start the engine. If it won't start, check:
   a. That all the spark plug wires are in place.
   b. That the rotor has been installed.
   c. That the wire inside the distributor is connected.
   d. That the points open and close when the engine turns.
   e. That the gap is correct and the hold-down screw is tight.
   f. That the condenser lead to the coil is attached.

20. After the first 200 miles on a new set of points, the point gap often closes up due to initial rubbing block wear. For best performance, recheck the gap or dwell at this time.

21. Since changing the point gap affects the ignition timing setting, the timing should be checked and adjusted if necessary after each point replacement or adjustment.

Electronic Ignition

With the exception of the Fox and the 1980 4000 (49 state), all gasoline engined Audis from 1978 are equipped with electronic ignition. Audi has used two different types of electronic ignition systems from 1978-80. The 5000 has used an electronic ignition system that consisted of a distributor with an impulse generator, an ignition coil and an electronic control unit. As of 1981, all Audis use an electronic ignition system with a Hall generator instead of an impulse generator. The Hall generator was also used on the 4000 (Calif.), the 5000 turbo and the 4000 (5 cyl.) in 1980.

Because no points or condenser are used and the dwell is determined by the control unit, no adjustments are necessary. Ignition timing is checked in the usual way, but unless the distributor has been distrubed it is unlikely to change.

Service consists of an inspection of the distributor cap, rotor and ignition wires. In addition, the air gap between the impulse rotor and the permanent magnet should be checked periodically. The air gap on the models equipped with a Hall generator is not adjustable.

AIR GAP ADJUSTMENT

1978-79 5000 Series

1. Release the two clips with a screwdriver and remove the distributor cap.
2. Remove the ignition rotor (not the impulse rotor) by pulling straight up.
3. Rotate the engine by the starter or by turning a wrench on the crankshaft pulley bolt and align the impulse rotor tooth with the tooth on the permanent magnet.
4. Using a non-metallic gauge, the gap should measure 0.010 in. (.25 mm). If adjustment is necessary, carefully bend the tooth on the impulse rotor until the proper gap is achieved.

Ignition Timing

STATIC

A basic timing adjustment can be made in the following manner. Turn the engine until the basic ignition timing mark is aligned with the ignition timing pointer and the distributor rotor points towards the No. 1 cylinder mark on the rim of the distributor body. Timing marks are on the flywheel on the 4000, 5000 and Fox, and the crankshaft pulley on the other models. This will put No. 1 cylinder at TDC (0° T). Connect a 12 volt test lamp between the ignition coil terminal, No. 1 connected to the distributor clockwise until the lamp goes out. Turn the distributor counterclockwise until the lamp just lights, and tighten the clamp on the distributor at that point. The ignition timing is now approximately set. As soon as possible, check the adjustment with a timing light.

100 series timing marks

DYNAMIC

To check with a timing light, connect a timing light to No. 1 cylinder and connect a tachometer.

NOTE: Some tachometers, dwellmeters, and oscilloscopes will not work with the capacitive discharge ignition system. Some may be damaged. Check with the manufacturer of your test equipment if there is any doubt.

Loosen the distributor clamp screw until it is just possible to turn the distributor by hand. Run the engine at idle speed and point the timing light at the pulley (flywheel on the 4000, 5000 and Fox). Turn the distributor until the specified notch (on the flywheel or pulley) aligns with the pointer. Disconnect the vacuum hoses and on the 1981 models the idle stabilizer must be bypassed. To bypass the idle stabilizer, disconnect its two electrical leads and plug them together. This must be

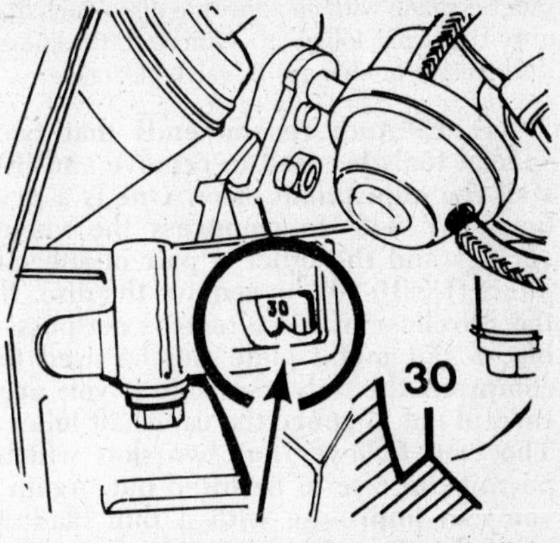

Fox timing marks—5000 series similar

done with the ignition turned off or it could ruin the entire system. Check the timing at 2500, 2750 or 3000 rpm if specified. Adjust as necessary.

NOTE: Timing should always be checked both at idle and at 2500, 2750 or 3000 rpm if specified.

Valve Lash

100 Series

The valve clearance should be adjusted in firing order, with the engine at operating temperature. See the specifications for the proper clearances. Remove the air filter and rocker cover. Set the engine at TDC on No. 1 cylinder by aligning the 0° T mark on the crankshaft pulley with the timing cover pointer and aligning the distributor rotor with the No. 1 cylinder mark on the rim of the distributor body. Turn the engine in the normal direction of rotation. The valve clearance of cylinder No. 1 should be adjusted when the valves of No. 4 cylinder overlap, i.e. when both arms move in opposite directions simultaneously. When this occurs, the exhaust valve is closing and the intake opening.

Adjust as follows:

1. Valve clearance of cylinder No. 3 at overlap of cylinder No. 2
2. Valve clearance of cylinder No. 4 at overlap of cylinder No. 1
3. Valve clearance of cylinder No. 2 at overlap of cylinder No. 3

When making adjustments, tighten the self-locking adjustment nut until it is just possible to remove the feeler gauge.

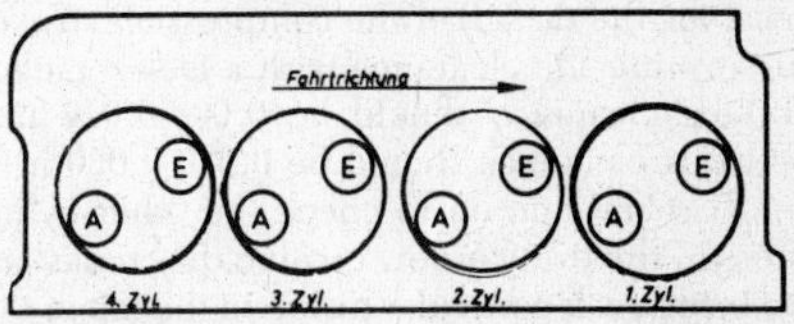

100 Series valve location: "A" equals intake; "E" equals exhaust. The arrow points forward.

4000 and 5000

Audi recommends checking the valve clearance at 1000 miles and then every 15,000 miles thereafter. The overhead cam acts directly on the valves through cam followers which fit over the springs and valves. Adjustment is made with an adjusting disc which fits into the cam follower. Different thickness discs result in changes in valve clearance.

NOTE: Audi recommends that two special tools be used to remove and install the adjustment discs. One is a pry bar (VW 546) to compress the valve springs and the other a pair of special pliers (US 10-208) to remove the disc. If the purchase of these tools is not possible, a flat metal plate can be used to compress the valve springs if you are careful not to gouge the camshaft lobes. The cam follower has two slots which permit the disc to be lifted out. Again, you can improvise with a thin bladed screwdriver. An assistant to pry the spring down while you remove the disc would be the ideal way to perform the operation if you must improvise your own tools.

Valve clearance is checked with the engine moderately warm (coolant temperature should be about 95° F (35° C).

1. Remove the accelerator linkage, the upper drive belt cover and any hoses or lines which may be in the way.

2. Remove the cylinder head cover. Valve clearance is checked in the firing order (1-3-4-2 for the 4000 and 1-2-4-5-3 for the 5000 series engines) with the piston of the cylinder being checked at TDC of the compression stroke. Both valves will be closed at this position and the cam lobes will be pointing straight up.

NOTE: When adjusting the clearances on the diesel engine, the pistons must not be at TDC. Turn the crankshaft ¼ turn past TDC so that the valves do not contact the pistons when the tappets are depressed.

3. Turn the crankshaft pulley bolt with a socket wrench to position the camshaft for checking.

CAUTION

Do not turn the camshaft by the camshaft mounting bolt, this will stretch the drive belt. When turning the crankshaft pulley bolt, turn it clockwise only.

4. With the No. 1 piston at TDC (½ turn past for the diesel) of the compression stroke, determine the clearance with a feeler gauge. Intake clearance should be 0.008-0.012 in., exhaust clearance should be 0.016-0.020 in.

5. Continue on to check the other cylinders in the firing order, turning the crankshaft to bring each particular piston to the top of the compression stroke (¼ turn for the diesel). Record the individual clearances as you go along.

6. If measured clearance is within tolerance levels (0.002 in.), it is not necessary to replace the adjusting discs.

7. If adjustment is necessary, the discs will have to be removed and replaced with thicker or thinner ones which will yield the correct clearance. Discs are available in 0.002 in. increments from 0.12 in. to 0.17 in.

NOTE: The thickness of the adjusting discs are etched on one side. When installing, the marks must face the cam followers. Discs can be reused if they are not worn or damaged.

8. To remove the discs, turn the cam followers so that the grooves are accessible when the pry bar is depressed.

9. Press the cam follower down with the pry bar and remove the adjusting discs with the special pliers or the screwdriver.

10. Replace the adjustment discs as necessary to bring the clearance within the 0.002 in. tolerance level. If the measured clearance is larger than the given tolerance, remove the existing disc and insert a thicker one to bring the clearance up to specification. If it is smaller, insert a thinner one.

11. Recheck all valve clearances after adjustment.

12. Install the cylinder head cover with a new gasket.

13. Install the accelerator linkage, the upper drive belt cover and any wires or lines which were removed.

Fox

The valve clearances should be checked in firing order, with the engine at normal operating temperature.

1. Remove the camshaft cover and the distributor cap.

2. Set the engine at TDC on No. 1 cylinder by aligning the 0° T mark on the flywheel with the pointer and aligning the distributor rotor with the No. 1 cylinder mark on the rim of the distributor body.

NOTE: Always turn the crankshaft in the normal direction of rotation. There is a hole in the body behind the front license plate through which a wrench can be used on the crankshaft.

3. The valve clearances of cylinder No. 1 should be checked when the valves of No. 4 cylinder overlap, i.e. when both No. 4 cylinder valves move in opposite directions simultaneously. You may have to move the crankshaft slightly to find this position. When this happens, the exhaust valve is closing and the intake opening. Check and note the clearance of both the intake and exhaust valves for No. 1 cylinder. Use a feeler gauge between each valve tappet and camshaft lobe.

4. Turn the crankshaft 180° (90° at the distributor rotor) in the normal direction of rotation. Check and note the valve clearances of cylinder No. 3 at the overlap position of cylinder No. 2.

5. Turn the crankshaft 180°. Check and note the valve clearances of cylinder No. 4 at the overlap position of cylinder No. 1.

6. Turn the crankshaft 180°. Check and note the valve clearances of cylinder No. 2 at the overlap position of cylinder No. 3.

7. Now the crankshaft has been turned two complete revolutions (one for the distributor rotor) and all the valve tappet to camshaft lobe clearances have been noted. Compare the noted clearances with those listed in the Tune-Up Specifications Chart. Normal wear usually results in the clearances becoming too small. Adjustment is made by replacing the tappet clearance disc in the top of each tappet. These are available in 26 sizes ranging from 3.0 mm (0.119 in.) to 4.25 mm (0.166 in.) in increments of 0.05 mm (0.002 in.). The thickness of each disc is marked on the bottom.

NOTE: If a valve clearance deviates 0.-002 in. or less from the specified clearance, it need not be adjusted.

8. To remove a tappet clearance disc, turn the cylinder to TDC and press down the tappet so that the disc can be lifted out. Audi dealers have special tools that make this operation much easier. Once the disc is removed, check its size and determine what size will be needed to produce the required adjustment.

NOTE: Before depressing the tappets, turn them so their openings are at right angles to the camshaft.

9. Install the required disc and turn the tappet back to its normal direction. When all the clearances have been corrected, check them again to catch any possible error caused by worn discs.

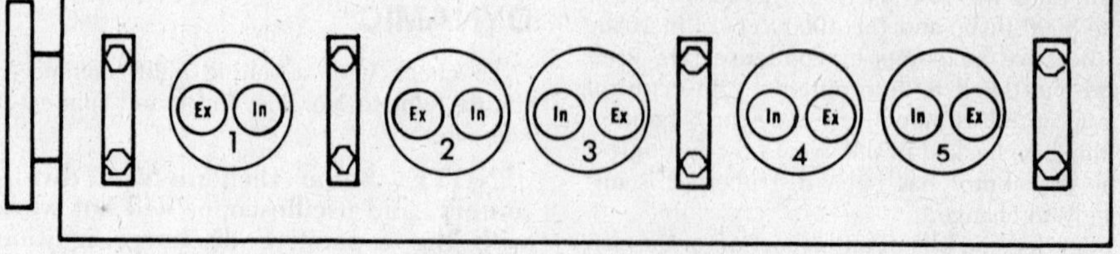

5000 series valve location

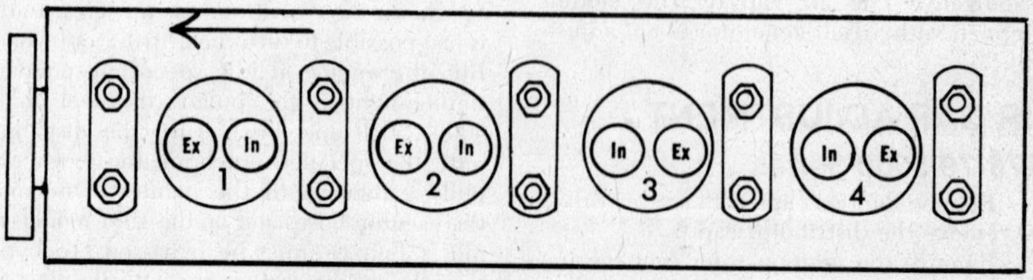

Fox valve location. The arrow points forward.

Idle Speed Adjustment

100 Series and Fox

1. Operate engine at normal operating temperature.
2. With high beams on and A/C on, ignition timing set to 3A with vacuum hose connected, adjust idle to 850-1000 rpm.

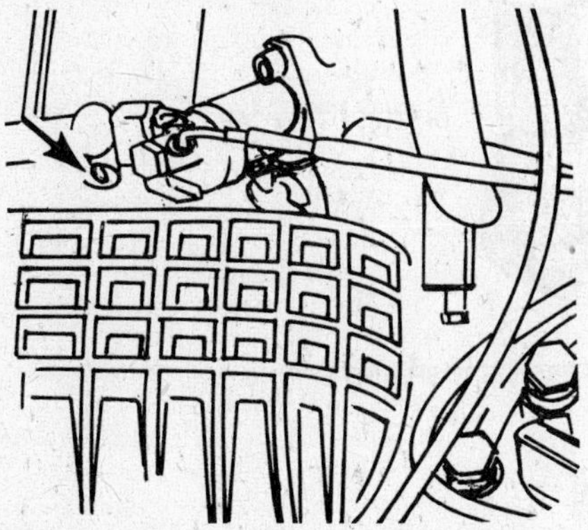

Idle speed adjustment point—Fox with fuel injection

4000 and 5000 Except 5000 Turbo and Calif. Models

NOTE: The timing must be set to specifications before adjusting the idle speed.

1. Connect a dwell/tachometer according to the manufacturer's instructions.
2. Run the engine until the oil temperature is above 140° F (60° C). The radiator fan must come on at least once.

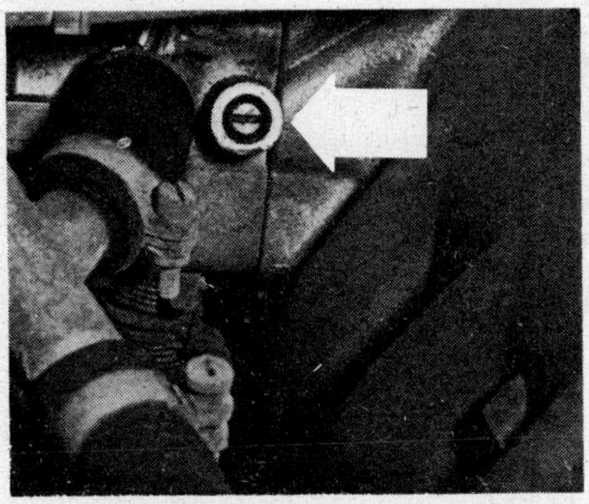

Idle speed adjustment, 5000

3. Turn the headlights on the high beam.
4. Disconnect the PCV valve.
5. Locate the idle adjusting screw in the throttle valve housing on the back of the intake manifold and adjust the idle to specifications.

NOTE: The radiator fan must not run while adjusting the idle.

6. Adjust the % CO.

4000 and 5000 Calif. Models and 5000 Turbo

NOTE: The timing must be set to specifications before adjusting the idle speed.

1. Connect a dwell/tachometer according to the manufacturer's instructions.
2. Turn off all electrical accessories.
3. Run the engine until the oil temperature is above 175° F (80° C). The radiator fan must come on at least once.
4. Turn the ignition off.
5. Disconnect the PCV valve.
6. Disconnect the plug for the oxygen sensor wire by the manifold.
7. Unplug both wire leads at the idle stabilizer and connect them together.
8. Start the engine.
9. Locate the idle adjusting screw in the throttle valve housing on the back of the intake manifold and adjust the idle to specifications.

NOTE: The radiator fan must not run while adjusting the idle.

10. Turn off the engine and reconnect the PCV valve, the oxygen sensor wire and the idle stabilizer.
11. Recheck the idle speed. If it has changed, the idle stabilizer will probably require replacement.
12. Adjust the % CO.

5000 Diesel

1. Connect a dwell/tachometer according to the manufacturer's instructions.
2. Run the engine until the oil temperature reaches 122-158° F (50-70° C).
3. Turn the idle speed control knob on the instrument panel counterclockwise until it stops.
4. Locate the idle speed adjusting screw on the injection pump and adjust the idle to specifications.
5. Lock the screw and seal it with paint.

CO Adjustment

4000 and 5000

NOTE: An exhaust gas analyzer or a CO meter will be required for this procedure. These are not common, everyday tools; adjustment of the CO is impossible without one of them. If you do not have access to these tools you will have to have the adjustment made by your dealer or a service station. If you do have one of them, please read on.

1. The ignition timing and the idle speed must be properly adjusted before proceeding.
2. Disconnect the PCV valve.
3. Turn the headlights on high beam (all but 5000 Turbo and Calif. cars).

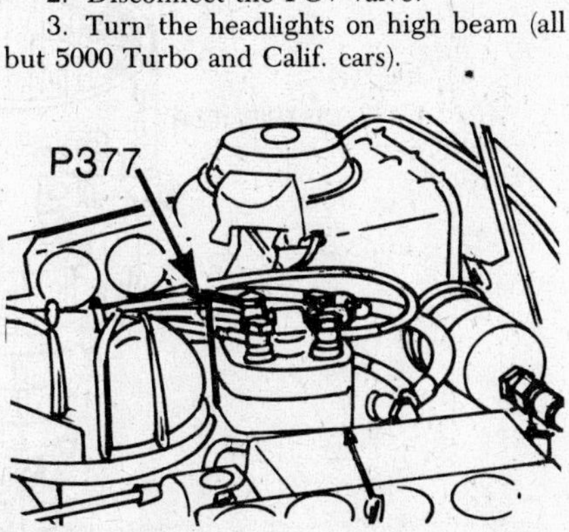

CO adjusting tool and locations—Fox with fuel injection

CO adjusting point, 5000

4. Turn off the ignition and disconnect the oxygen sensor wire and bypass the idle stabilizer as detailed in the "Idle Speed Adjustment" section (5000 Turbo and all Calif. cars only).
5. Hook the exhaust gas analyzer to the tailpipe on all 5000 models or the CO meter to the probe receptacle on all 4000 models. The probe receptacle is located on the front of the exhaust manifold.

NOTE: The hoses must fit snugly so that there is no exhaust leakage or you will get an improper reading.

6. Remove the plug from the fuel distributor and insert the Special Tool P377.

NOTE: While adjusting the CO, the radiator fan must not come on.

7. Adjust % CO to the proper level by turning the Special Tool clockwise to raise % CO or counterclockwise to lower % CO.

CAUTION

When adjusting CO, do not push the adjusting tool down. Do not accelerate the engine with the tool in place. Remove the tool after each adjustment and accelerate the engine briefly before reading the % CO. Always adjust CO from lean to rich.

8. Reconnect the PCV valve (all but 5000 Turbo and Calif. cars).
9. Readjust the idle speed if necessary (all but 5000 Turbo and Calif. cars).

The remainder of this procedure deals only with the 5000 Turbo and any Calif. cars.

10. Readjust the idle speed if necessary.
11. Reconnect the oxygen sensor wire and check that the % CO is still at the proper level.
12. Remove the exhaust gas analyzer or the CO meter, reconnect the PCV valve and adjust the idle speed if necessary.
13. Turn the ignition off and reconnect the idle stabilizer.
14. Start the engine and check the ignition timing.
15. Load the engine by switching on all electrical accessories and check that ignition timing advances. If not, the idle stabilizer will probably require replacement.

ENGINE ELECTRICAL

Distributor

REMOVAL AND INSTALLATION

100 Series and Fox

Remove thd air cleaner. Pry back the retaining clips and remove the distributor cap. Mark the relationship between the distributor body and the engine block. Make a mark on the distributor body to denote the position of the rotor tip. Disconnect the wiring at the ignition coil. Detach the vacuum line, being careful not to damage the plastic tube. Remove the bolt at the retaining clamp and pull the distributor from the housing. If the distributor is difficult to remove, the rubber seal is probably sticking. Carefully pry the distributor loose with a screwdriver.

Distributor installation is the reverse of removal. When installing the 100 series distributor, the projections on the shaft, at the bottom of the distributor, must engage the slots in the oil pump driveshaft. Turn the rotor slightly until the two engage. The projections and grooves have been milled off center, making it impossible to install the distributor incorrectly.

The gear-driven Fox distributor has a slot at the bottom which mates with a dog on top of the oil pump driveshaft. Lubricate the seal with a small amount of oil before installation. Align the marks made on removal, then tighten the clamp bolt.

Tach. Conv. Chart.

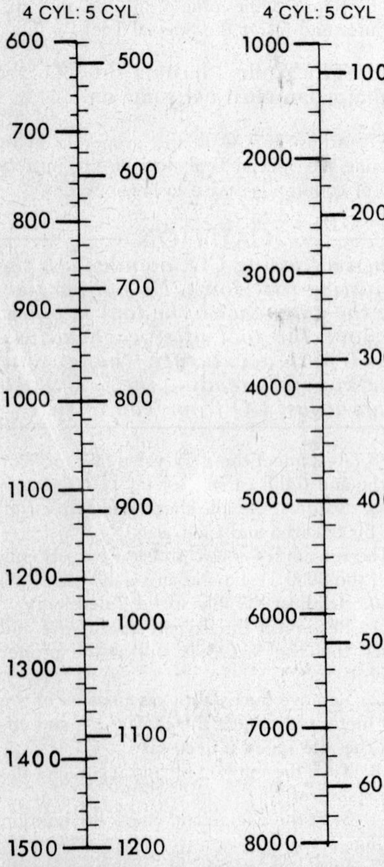

Use this chart to convert the 4-cylinder tachometer reading to the true idle speed on 5-cylinder 5000 models

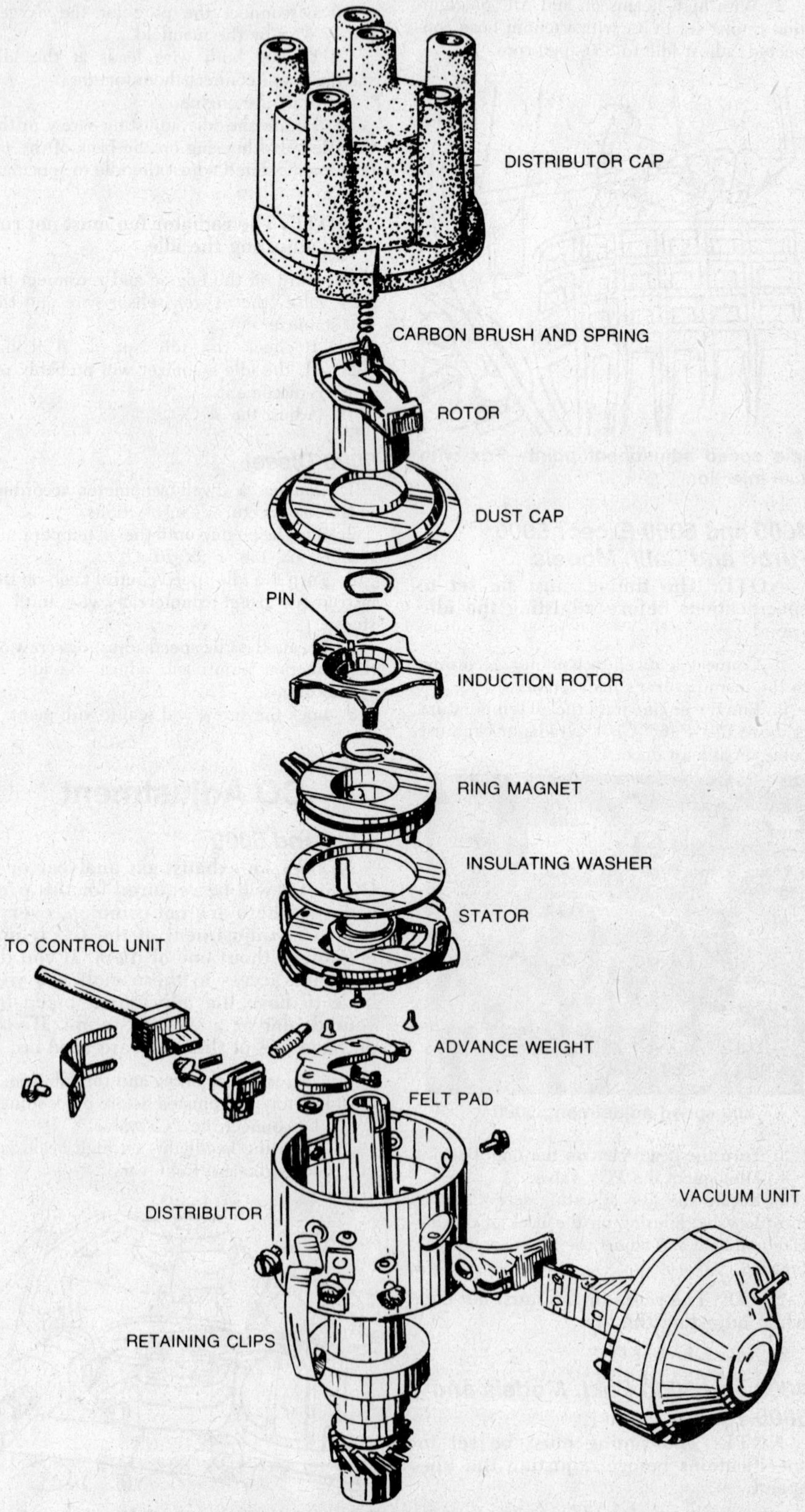

Exploded view of electronic distributor—5000 model shown

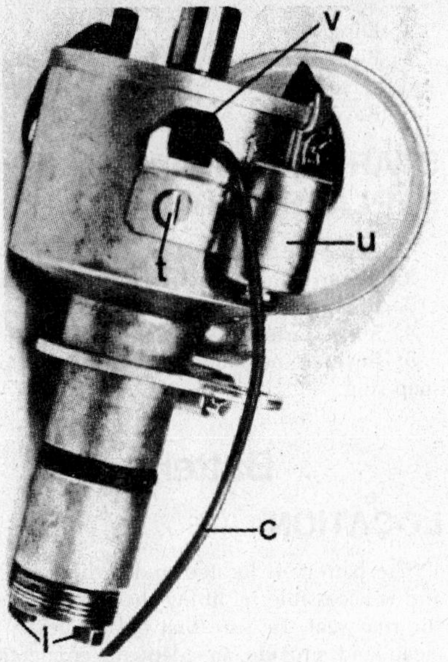

(c)—Green condenser lead
(t)—Condenser clamp screw
(u)—Condenser
(v)—Plastic boot

100 series distributor removed from the engine. The projections (1) engage the slots in the oil pump driveshaft.

NOTE: If the engine has been turned while the distributor was out, or if a new distributor is being installed, refer to the Static Ignition Timing procedure.

4000 and 5000

REMOVAL

1. Disconnect the wiring harness connector and any other connectors from the distributor cap.
2. Remove the static shield.
3. Disconnect and note the position of the vacuum lines.
4. Undo the two retaining spring clips and remove the distributor cap.
5. Note the position of the rotor in relation to the base. Scribe a mark on the base of the distributor and on the engine block to facilitate reinstallation. Align the marks with the direction the metal tip of the rotor is pointing. Note the approximate position of the vacuum advance unit in relation to the engine.
6. Remove the distributor hold-down bolt and clamp.
7. Lift the distributor assembly from the engine.

INSTALLATION

1. Insert the distributor shaft and assembly into the engine.
2. Line up the marks on the distributor and on the engine with the metal tip of the rotor.
3. Make sure the vacuum advance unit is pointed in the same direction as it was pointed originally. If the marks on the distributor and the engine are lined up properly, this will be done automatically.
4. Install the distributor hold-down clamp and bolt.
5. Install and secure the distributor cap.
6. Install the vacuum lines in their original places.
7. Install the static shield.
8. Install the wiring harness connector and any other connectors previously removed.
9. Start the engine. Adjust the dwell angle (breaker point ignitions) and set the ignition timing.

NOTE: If the crankshaft has been turned or the engine has been disturbed in any manner (i.e. disassembled and rebuilt) while the distributor was removed, or if the marks were not drawn, it will be necessary to initially time the engine. Follow the procedure given below.

1. It is necessary to place the No. 1 cylinder in the firing position to correctly install the distributor. To locate this position, the ignition timing marks on the flywheel and the clutch housing are used.
2. Remove the spark plug from the No. 1 cylinder. Turn the crankshaft until the piston in the No. 1 cylinder is moving up on the compression stroke. This can be determined by placing your thumb over the spark plug hole and feeling the air being forced out of the cylinder. Stop turning the engine when the timing mark on the flywheel is aligned with the lug on the flywheel housing.
3. Remove the upper drive belt cover.
4. Align the mark on the camshaft sprocket with the upper edge of the drive belt cover or with the upper edge of the cylinder head cover gasket.
5. Align the oil pump drive pinion lug so that it is parallel to the crankshaft (4000 only).
6. Oil the distributor housing lightly where it bears on the cylinder block.
7. Install the distributor so that the rotor, which is mounted on the shaft, points to the mark on the distributor housing for the No. 1 cylinder.
8. When the distributor shaft has reached the bottom of the hole, move the rotor back and forth slightly until the drive lug on the oil pump shaft enters the slots cut into the end of the distributor shaft, and the distributor assembly slides down into place (4000 only).
9. Clean the distributor cap and check for signs of cracking or carbon tracks. Replace the cap and continue from Step 6 of the installation procedure, engine undisturbed.

Alternator

ALTERNATOR PRECAUTIONS

All Audi models are equipped with alternators. When performing any service to the alternator or alternator system the following precautions should be observed.

A. Leads or cables to any part of the charging circuit should be disconnected only after the engine has been switched off and has stopped running.

B. When working on the electrical system, always disconnect the lead from the negative battery terminal.

C. When performing tests with the engine running, the battery must always be connected.

D. Temporary connections should never be made to the alternator. Always make firm connections.

The alternator warning light on the instrument panel should go out when the engine reaches idle speed, or shortly after.

REMOVAL AND INSTALLATION

1. Disconnect the battery ground strap.
2. Disconnect all the leads to the alternator, tagging them first. Various arrangements of plug-in or bolt-on connections have been used. On some models the wiring may be unplugged from the back of the alternator; on others, it must be unplugged at the voltage regulator on the right front wheel-housing.

NOTE: Current models have a voltage regulator built into the alternator.

3. Remove the belt tensioning bolt from the slotted adjusting bracket.
4. Remove the drive belt.
5. Unbolt and remove the alternator.

To install the unit:

6. Install the hinge bolts. On 100 series models, make sure that the head of the rear bolt is to the rear of the car.
7. Install the drive belt and the belt tensioning bolt.
8. Adjust the belt tension.
9. Replace all the electrical connections, making sure that they are installed in their original locations.
10. Connect the battery ground strap.

BELT TENSION ADJUSTMENT

The alternator drive belt is correctly tensioned when the longest span of belt between pulleys can be depressed about ½ in., by moderate thumb pressure. To adjust, loosen the slotted adjusting bracket bolt on the alternator. If the alternator hinge bolts are very tight, it may be necessary to loosen them slightly to move the alternator. Move the alternator in or out by hand to get the correct tension, then tighten the adjusting bolt.

NOTE: Be careful not to overtighten the belt, as this may damage the alternator bearings.

Regulator

The earlier models have a voltage regulator on the right front wheelhousing in the engine compartment. If there is none there, as on current models, it is built into the alternator.

REMOVAL AND INSTALLATION

To remove the regulator, disconnect the battery ground cable, disconnect the three-pronged plug, and unscrew the unit from the wheelhousing. Be careful to make a good ground connection on reinstallation. The manufacturer does not recommend any adjustments to the regulator.

Starter

REMOVAL AND INSTALLATION

100 Series

Disconnect the battery ground lead. Remove the oil filter.

NOTE: When the oil filter is removed, a certain amount of oil will escape.

Disconnect both leads from the upper terminal of the solenoid. Remove the open cable shoe lead from he lower solenoid terminal. The screw need only be slightly opened to permit removal. Unbolt the starter from the mounting flanges and remove it forward.

Installation is the reverse of removal. Be sure that all leads are positioned correctly and are not pinched. If necessary, replace the lower mounting bolt with the head to the front of the car. Thoroughly clean the seal and oil filter sealing surface. Lightly lubricate both surfaces and tighten the oil filter to approximately 14-18 ft/lbs or about one turn by hand. Replace the oil that escaped and run the engine, checking the filter for leaks.

CAUTION

Some starters are equipped with an additional terminal (16) which is under full battery voltage, with a direct connection to the ignition coil. This connection bridges the ignition coil series resistor to create higher ignition voltage.

Fox, 4000 and 5000

1. Disconnect the battery ground lead.
2. Remove snap-ring from armature shaft.
3. Remove the mounting bolt at the engine block on all other models.
4. Disconnect the three starter wires.
5. Remove the mounting bolts and nuts and the starter.
6. Reverse the procedure for installation.

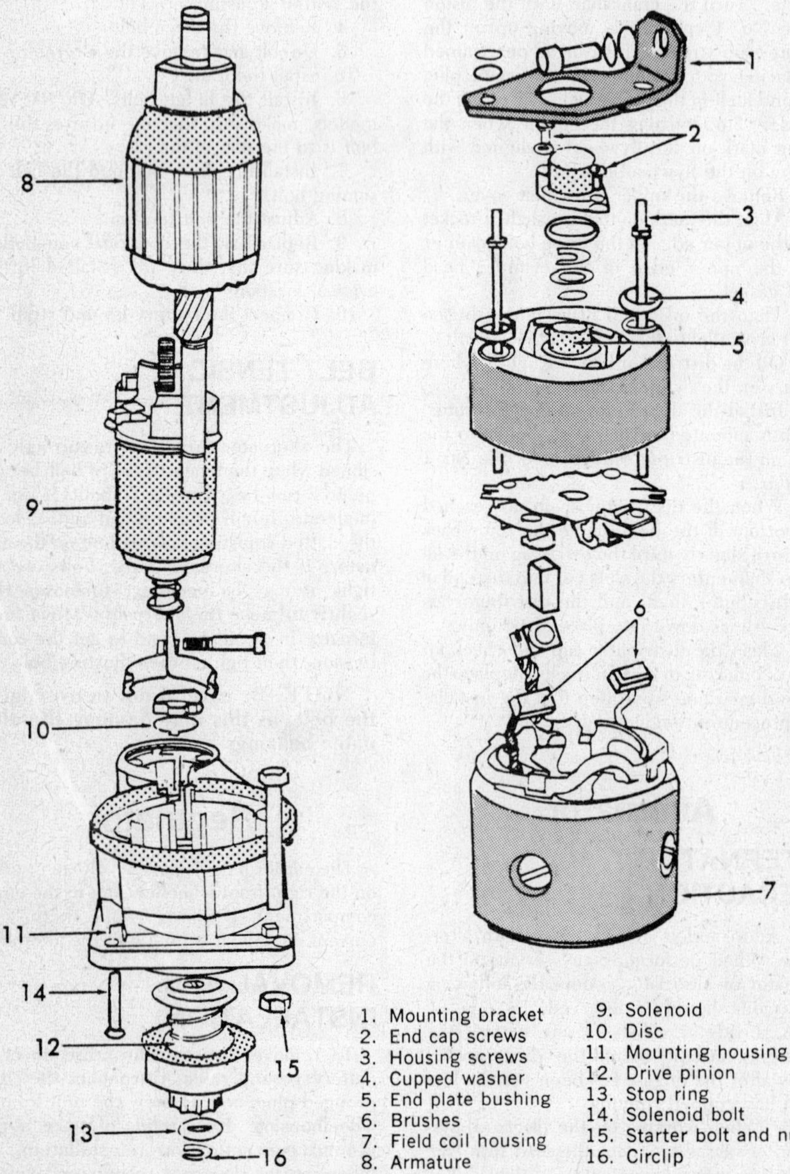

1. Mounting bracket
2. End cap screws
3. Housing screws
4. Cupped washer
5. End plate bushing
6. Brushes
7. Field coil housing
8. Armature
9. Solenoid
10. Disc
11. Mounting housing
12. Drive pinion
13. Stop ring
14. Solenoid bolt
15. Starter bolt and nut
16. Circlip

Exploded view of typical starter

STARTER DRIVE REPLACEMENT

1. Remove starter.
2. Remove snap ring from armature shaft.
3. Remove stop ring.
4. Slide starter drive from shaft.
5. Reverse the above to install. Use a new snap-ring.

Battery

LOCATION

The battery is located under the rear seat and is accessible by lifting the front edges of the rear seat. Be sure that the terminals are clean and provide an adequate connection. The terminals should be coated (lightly) periodically with grease to prevent corrosion.

Water should be added only to bring the solution level up to the bottom of the cell filler well, but not above.

ENGINE MECHANICAL

Engine Removal and Installation

100 Series

The transmission and engine must be lowered from the car as a unit. The following procedure is for manual transmission cars; see Automatic Transmission Removal and Installation for details on items that must be disconnected on the automatic transmission.

1. Remove the hood (only if using a hoist to remove the engine).
2. Unbolt and remove the apron just below the front bumper.
3. Remove the negative connection from the battery. Remove the air cleaner and carburetor breather hose at the air filter. Drain the coolant. Disconnect all hoses between the radiator and engine and the heater and engine. Disconnect the fuel hose at the fuel pump and plug the end of the line. Remove the power brake unit vacuum hose at the intake manifold.
4. Disconnect the speedometer cable at the transmission, the clutch cable at the mount and the gearshift linkage at the transmission.
5. Disconnect the accelerator linkage at the carburetor, mounting point, and connecting rod, and remove the throttle shaft.
6. Separate the brake line at the body mount and plug the line to prevent loss of fluid.
7. Remove the guard plate from the right engine mount.
8. Disconnect the following electrical wir-

ing from the engine and transmission: ignition leads, idle cut-off valve (if installed), temperature switch, four pole plug of regulator, oil pressure switch, starter connections, backup light switch and ground leads.

9. Remove the radiator and the fan support together with the fan and stop pad.

NOTE: This operation is only necessary if working with a frame contact hoist or in a pit where the opening in the pit is not large enough to permit lowering the engine with the fan attached. If the opening is large enough, unscrew the stop only.

10. Remove the front exhaust pipe at the exhaust manifold and at the primary muffler.

11. Unbolt the driveshaft flange at the brake disc. Do not lose the thin insulator from between the brake disc and the flange. Turn the driveshaft flange slightly in the direction of the wheel and wire it to the upper wishbone.

12. Detach the stabilizer from the lower wishbone, left and right.

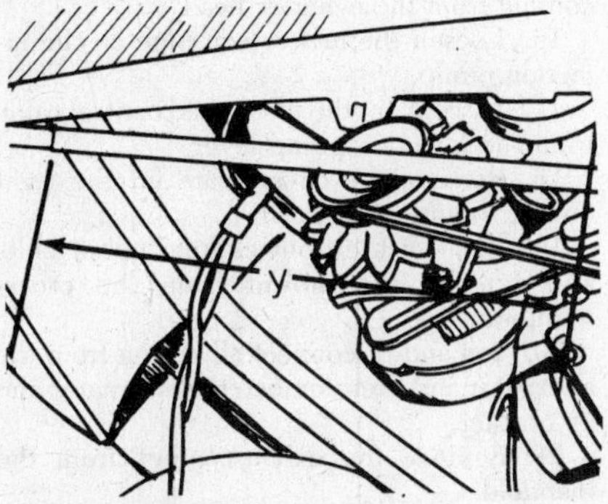

When installing the 100 series engine, the distance (y) between the pulley and the front of the side member must be the same on both sides. Maximum deviation is .08 inch

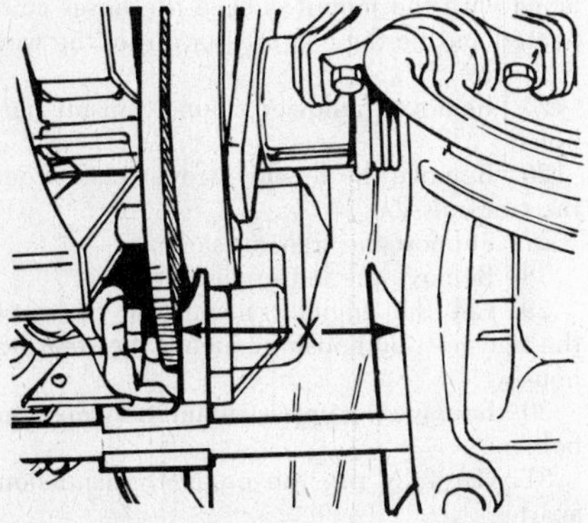

When installing the 100 series engine, the distance (x) between the brake discs and the control arms must be the same on both sides. Maximum deviation is .08 inch

13. Position the jack or lifting apparatus and lift the weight from the engine mounts. Remove the bolts retaining the rear crossmember to the body. Remove the retaining nut at the right engine/transmission mount. Note the position of the washers and sleeve on the right engine/transmission mount.

14. Remove the retaining nut from the left engine/transmission mount, but do not move the locknut. Lower the engine/transmission unit from the car.

15. Installation procedures are the reverse of removal. The engine and transmission unit must be aligned in such a way that the same distance between brake disc and wishbone exists on each side. The distance between the pulley and front end of the side-member must also be the same on each side. After installation, bleed the brakes.

Fox, Manual Transmission, Without A/C

This procedure explains how to lift the engine out of the chassis. If the car has air-conditioning, it will be necessary to lower the engine, transmission, and front suspension from the car as a unit.

1. Remove the hood and disconnect the battery ground cable. Detach the starter wires.
2. Remove the air cleaner.
3. Disconnect the accelerator linkage and the fuel cutoff solenoid wire.
4. Disconnect the ignition coil primary and secondary wires, the oil pressure sending unit, and the coolant temperature sending unit.
5. Loosen the clutch cable adjusting nuts and disconnect the cable. Disconnect the fuel line at the pump. Unplug the alternator.
6. Remove the grille.
7. Remove the bolts holding the panel.

On air-conditioned models, it is necessary to lower the engine, transmission, and front suspension from the car as a unit.

1. Raise the car, allowing the front wheels to hang down. Disconnect the battery ground cable.
2. Drain the coolant.
3. Disconnect all connections between engine, transmission, and body as explained for models without A/C.
4. Remove the radiator.
5. Disconnect the gearshift rod coupling at the transmission.
6. Detach the front engine mount at the engine block.
7. Use a removal tool to separate the tie rod ends from the steering levers.
8. Push the brake pedal down about 1½ in. and fasten it in place to keep the system from draining. Disconnect and plug the brake lines at the brackets on the wheel housing.
9. Attach a framework to keep the assembly steady to a sturdy floor jack and clamp it to the crossmember. Lift slightly and disconnect both coil spring units from the wheel housings. Unbolt the crossmember.
10. Disconnect the backup light switch wire and lower the engine, transmission, and front suspension assembly.
11. On installation, tighten the coil spring units to the body to 16 ft/lbs, and the crossmember to the body to 33 ft/lbs.

4000 4 Cylinder Engine

NOTE: Though not necessary, removal of the hood will make engine removal easier. Be sure to mark the location of each hood hinge to facilitate reinstallation.

1. Disconnect the negative battery cable. Steps 2 through 13 refer to cars equipped with air conditioning.
2. Remove the two clips on the top of the grille. Remove the screw on the bottom and remove the grille.
3. Loosen the right and left sides of the condenser and tilt it away from the radiator.
4. Remove the air duct from the throttle valve housing.
5. Remove the hose from the air duct to the auxiliary air regulator.
6. Remove the fuel distributor, the air flow sensor, the fuel injectors and the air cleaner as one unit.

NOTE: Leave all fuel lines connected; protect injectors and cold start valve with caps.

7. Remove the front engine mount bolts and remove the mount.
8. Loosen the nuts on the outer half of the crankshaft pulley and remove the V/belt.
9. Discharge the refrigerant.
10. Remove all lines from the compressor and plug all open connections.
11. Remove the crankcase ventilation hose from the valve cover.
12. Move the air conditioning hoses away from the engine.
13. Remove the mounting bolts (2 upper and 3 lower) and remove the compressor.
14. Open the heater control valve all the way (cold position).
15. Remove the cap on the expansion tank and drain the coolant as described in Chapter 1.
16. Remove the upper and lower radiator hoses from the radiator.
17. Disconnect the plug from the radiator fan.
18. Disconnect the plug from the radiator thermoswitch.
19. Remove the radiator rubber mounts and remove the radiator complete with the fan and the fan shroud.
20. Disconnect the clutch cable.
21. Tag and disconnect all wiring from the engine.
22. Remove the control pressure regulator (above the oil filter) leaving all the fuel lines connected.
23. Remove the air hose from the back of the alternator if so equipped.
24. Unplug the blue wire from the alternator at the plug located between the battery and the rear of the engine.
25. Remove the charcoal filter hose at the intake air duct.
26. Remove the heater hoses.
27. Remove the throttle cable.
28. Tag and remove all vacuum hoses.
29. Pull out the fuel injectors and remove the cold start valve from the top of the intake manifold.

NOTE: Leave all fuel lines connected; protect the injectors and the cold start valve with caps.

30. Remove the hose running from the auxiliary regulator to the air duct.
31. Remove the three upper engine/transmission bolts.
32. Remove the right and left engine mount nuts.

33. Remove the exhaust pipe attaching bolts from the manifold and remove the exhaust pipe.
34. Remove the cover plate bolts and remove the cover plate.
35. Remove the front engine mount bolts and remove the mount.
36. Tag and disconnect the starter cables and remove the starter.
37. Remove the two lower engine/ transmission bolts.
38. Loosen the right and left engine mount nuts on the sub-frame.
39. Remove the bolt from the front exhaust pipe support.
40. Support the transmission.
41. Lift the engine until the weight is taken off of the engine mounts and carefully pry the engine and transmission apart.
42. Remove the engine.

Proceed in the reverse order for installation and note the following:

1. Tighten the engine/transmission bolts to 40 ft/lbs.
2. Tighten the bolt for the front exhaust pipe support to 18 ft/lbs.
3. Tighten the starter bolts to 14 ft/lbs.
4. Hand-tighten the front engine mount bolts.
5. Tighten the front cover plate bolts to 7 ft/lbs.
6. Hand-tighten the right and left engine mount nuts.
7. Tighten the cold start valve bolts, the control pressure regulator bolts and the radiator mounting bolts to 7 ft/lbs.

NOTE: Tighten the engine and sub-frame mounting bolts while the engine is running at idle. Tighten the front engine mount bolts to 18 ft/lbs and the right and left engine mount bolts to 25 ft/lbs.

4000 (5 Cyl.), 5000 Turbo and 5000 Except Diesel

1. Disconnect the negative battery cable.
2. Open the heater control valve all the way (cold position).
3. Remove the cap on the expansion tank and drain the coolant.
4. Remove all radiator and heater hoses.
5. Remove the control pressure regulator.

CAUTION

Do not disconnect any fuel lines.

6. Remove the cold start valve.
7. Pull out the fuel injectors and lay them aside.

NOTE: Protect the fuel injectors and the cold start valve with caps.

8. Loosen the air duct and vacuum hoses from the throttle valve assembly.
9. Remove the air cleaner cover with the filter.
10. Pull the hood latch cable guide off of its bracket.
11. On cars equipped with air conditioning, remove the two clips on the top of the grille and the screw on the bottom and remove the grille, then loosen the condenser mounting bolts and tilt it away from the radiator.
12. Remove the power steering pump leaving the hose connected.
13. Remove the vacuum amplifier.
14. Remove the ignition coil.
15. Remove the EGR control valve.
16. Remove the windshield washer reservoir from its holder.
17. Remove the power steering reservoir from its holder.
18. Remove the distributor cap, the rotor and the ignition wires.

NOTE: Tape the distributor dust cap on to prevent it from falling off.

19. On cars equipped with a manual transmission, take off the circlip and remove the throttle cable.
20. On cars equipped with an automatic transmission, remove the throttle pushrod.
21. Disconnect the oil pressure and the water temperature senders.
22. On air-conditioned cars, remove the compressor mounting bolts. Leaving the hoses connected, tie back the compressor with wire.
23. Remove the exhaust pipe-to-manifold bolts.
24. Remove the exhaust pipe support bracket from the transmission.
25. Remove the front engine mount bolts and remove the mount.
26. Tag and disconnect all wires from the starter and remove the starter.
27. Tag and disconnect all wires leading from the alternator and remove the alternator.
28. On cars equipped with an automatic transmission, remove the torque converter mounting bolts from the drive plate. This can be done through the starter hole.
29. Remove the lower engine/transmission bolts.
30. Support the transmission.
31. Remove the upper engine/transmission bolts.
32. Remove the left bracket.
33. Loosen the right engine bracket from the right engine mount.
34. Lift the engine until the V-belt pulley is behind the grille opening.
35. Carefully detach the engine from the transmission.
36. Remove the engine completely, turning it to the right as you lift it out.

Proceed in the reverse order for installation and note the following:

1. Tighten the engine/transmission bolts to 43 ft/lbs.
2. Tighten the bolt for the exhaust pipe support bracket to 22 ft/lbs.
3. Tighten the torque converter to drive plate bolts to 4 ft/lbs.
4. Tighten the starter bolts to 14 ft/lbs.
5. Hand tighten all engine mount bolts.
6. Tighten the air conditioner mounting bolt to 29 ft/lbs.
7. Tighten the power steering pump bolts and the control pressure regulator bolts to 14 ft/lbs.

NOTE: Tighten the engine and sub-frame mounting bolts while the engine is running at idle. Tighten all bolts to 32 ft/lbs.

5000 Diesel

1. Disconnect the negative battery cable.
2. Remove the air cleaner.
3. Remove the cover plates underneath the engine and the transmission.
4. Remove the front grille.
5. Remove the windshield washer reservoir from its holder.
6. Remove the hydraulic fluid reservoir from its holder.
7. Pull the hood latch cable guide out of its bracket.
8. Remove the cap on the expansion tank and drain the radiator as described in Chapter 1.
9. Remove all radiator and heater hoses.
10. Remove the V-belt for the power steering pump and remove the power steering pump with the hoses connected.
11. On cars equipped with air conditioning, loosen the condenser mounting bolts and tilt it away from the radiator.
12. Remove the auxiliary radiator.
13. Remove the fuel filter and plug the fuel lines.
14. Detach the accelerator cable.
15. Tag and disconnect all electrical wiring coming from the cylinder head.
16. Loosen the fuel return pipe on the injection pump.
17. Disconnect the idle speed control cable from the injection pump lever.
18. Remove the cover plate for the right engine mount.
19. Remove the front engine mount bolts and remove the mount from the crossmember.
20. Tag and disconnect all wiring from the alternator and then remove the alternator and its bracket.
21. Remove the exhaust pipes from the manifold.
22. Remove the exhaust pipe support bracket from the transmission.
23. Tag and disconnect all wiring from the starter and remove the starter.
24. On cars equipped with air conditioning, remove the compressor mounting bolts along with the mount. Leave the hoses connected and tie the compressor out of the way with wire.
25. Remove the lower engine/transmission bolts.
26. Remove the flywheel cover plate from the transmission.
27. Support the transmission.
28. Remove the left engine bracket.
29. Lift the engine/transmission up until the transmission housing touches the steering housing.
30. Remove the upper engine/transmission bolts.
31. Carefully pry the engine/transmission apart.
32. Turn the engine to the right and lift up at the same time.
33. Turn the engine 90 degrees and lift it completely out.

Proceed in the reverse order for installation and note the following:

1. Tighten the engine/transmission bolts to 43 ft/lbs.
2. Tighten all engine mount bolts to 33 ft/lbs.
3. Tighten the exhaust pipe-to-manifold bolts to 22 ft/lbs.

Cylinder Head

REMOVAL AND INSTALLATION

100 Series

1. Drain the coolant from the radiator. Disconnect the spark plug wires.
2. Remove the sheet metal cover from the exhaust manifold. Remove the intake and exhaust manifolds.
3. Disconnect the hose from the thermostat housing.
4. Remove the valve cover. Loosen the valve rocker arm adjusting nuts and remove the pushrods. Note their original locations; they must all go back in the same place.
5. Loosen the cylinder head bolts in the same order as shown for tightening. Remove the bolts. A metric Allen wrench is required for the head bolts.

NOTE: Later model Fox cars come equipped with a new type head bolt. These bolts have a 12 point recessed "polygon" head. The manufacturer states that these bolts require no retorquing during their service life. These bolts may be used as replacements on older engines, but only in complete sets.

NOTE: Do not loosen the head bolts until the engine has thoroughly cooled.

6. Remove the head. It if sticks, operate the starter to loosen it by compression or rap it upward with a soft hammer. Do not force anything between the head and block. Check the head for warpage.
7. Reinstallation of the head is made easier by the use of guide studs installed in opposite corners of the block. These can be made by cutting the heads off two bolts of the same size as the head bolts.
8. Put the gasket in place on the block.
9. Guide the cylinder head into place.
10. Coat the head bolt threads with a graphite lubricant. Install them finger tight.
11. Tighten the bolts in the sequence shown in four stages until the proper torque is reached. The bolts should be torqued again after the first 500-1000 miles.
12. Install the pushrods in their original locations. Make a preliminary valve lash adjustment.
13. Replace the valve cover, using a new gasket. Replace the manifolds. Connect the coolant hoses and the spark plug wires.
14. Refill the cooling system.
15. Run the engine until it reaches normal operating temperature, watching for leaks. Make a final valve adjustment with the engine warm.
16. On overhaul, if the rocker studs and pushrod guide plates have been removed, the guides must be aligned so that the pushrods will not contact them. The cylinder head must be heated to 248° F in an oven in order to install or remove the valve guides.

Fox

1. Disconnect the battery ground cable.
2. Drain the coolant. Disconnect the hoses.
3. Unbolt the exhaust pipe from the manifold.
4. Disconnect the electrical wires. Detach the accelerator linkage.
5. Remove the alternator belt and the timing belt.
6. Loosen the cylinder head bolts in the reverse of the order shown for tightening. Remove the bolts. A metric Allen wrench is required for the head bolts.

CAUTION

Don't loosen the head bolts until the engine is thoroughly cool. Don't loosen the camshaft bearing cap nuts.

7. Remove the head. If it sticks, loosen it by compression or rap it upward with a soft hammer. Do not force anything between the head and block. Check the head for warpage.

CAUTION

Do not attempt to remove the camshaft from the head without checking the Camshaft Removal and Installation procedure. Special tools are required.

8. On installation, make sure that the head gasket is installed with the word OBEN up and to the left side of the engine. Put the head in place and install the right front and left rear head bolts first.
9. Tighten the bolts in the sequence shown in four stages until the proper torque is reached. The bolts should be torqued again after the first 300 miles.
10. On overhaul, valve guides must be pressed out or in from above. The cylinder head must be heated to 176-212° F in an oil bath or an oven to install new valve guides.

NOTE: New cylinder head bolts and a new, soft head gasket are available to correct coolant leakage problems. The new bolts are marked 12.9 and should be torqued to normal specifications. Anytime there is a leakage problem, both the head and block should be checked for warpage.

11. Make sure to align the timing belt and sprockets as explained under Timing Belt Removal and Installation.

CAUTION

Do not attempt to start the engine until you are sure of this alignment.

For cylinder head overhaul, see the Engine Rebuilding section of this manual.

4000 and 5000 Except Diesel

NOTE: Cylinder head removal should not be attempted unless the engine is cold.

1. Disconnect the negative battery cable.
2. Drain the cooling system.
3. Disconnect the air duct from the throttle valve assembly on all models except the 5000 Turbo. On the Turbo, remove the hose which runs between the air duct and the turbocharger.
4. Disconnect the throttle cable from the throttle valve assembly.

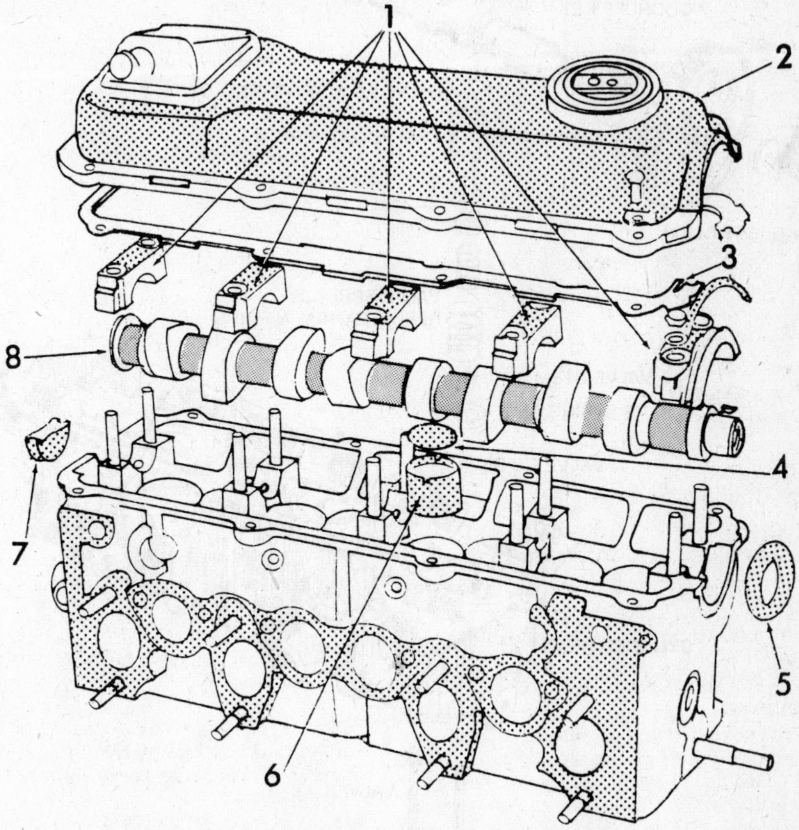

1. Camshaft bearing caps 2. Camshaft cover 3. Gasket 4. Valve adjusting disc 5. Oil seal 6. Cam follower 7. End plug 8. Camshaft

Fox cylinder head and camshaft

5. Remove the air duct for the injector cooling fan on the 5000 Turbo.
6. Clean and remove the fuel injectors and all other fuel lines.

NOTE: Protect the fuel injectors and the cold start valve with caps.

7. Tag and disconnect all vacuum and PCV lines.
8. Remove the hose which runs from the intake manifold to the turbocharger on the 5000 Turbo.
9. Tag and disconnect all electrical lines leading to the cylinder head.
10. Unbolt and remove the intake manifold.
11. Disconnect all radiator and heater hoses where they are attached to the cylinder head. Position them out of the way.
12. Tag and remove all spark plug wires and then remove the spark plugs.
13. For all models but the 4000, remove the distributor. To aid in reinstallation, scribe a mark on the body of the distributor and the cylinder head.
14. Unbolt and separate the exhaust manifold from the exhaust pipe.

NOTE: Exhaust pipe detachment differs slightly on the 5000 Turbo. First the exhaust pipe must be unbolted from the turbocharger and then it must be unbolted from the wastegate, towards the rear of the engine.

15. Disconnect the EGR valve and the oxygen sensor (4000 (5 cyl), 5000 Turbo and all 1979-81 Calif. models) from the exhaust manifold.
16. Remove the heat deflector shield on the 4000 models.
17. Unbolt and remove the oil lines (2) from the turbocharger.
18. Unbolt and remove the exhaust manifold.

NOTE: When removing the exhaust manifold on the 5000 Turbo, the manifold, turbocharger and wastegate should all be removed as one unit.

19. Remove the air hose cover from the back of the alternator (if so equipped) on the 4000.

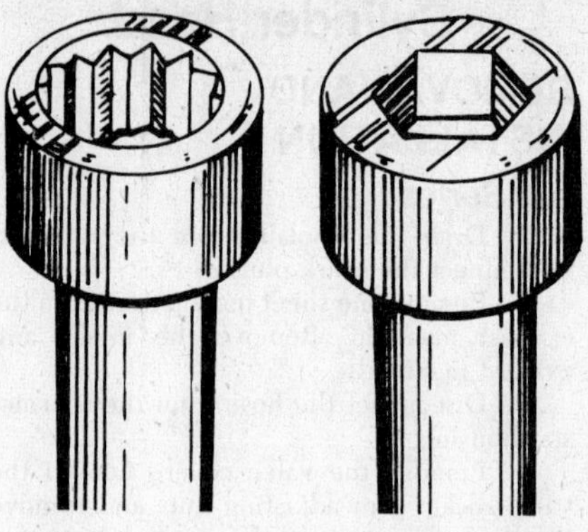

Left, new style, right old style Fox head bolts

20. Tag and disconnect all wires coming from the back of the alternator and then remove the alternator and the V-belt.
21. On all models but the 4000, disconnect and plug the hoses coming from the power steering pump.
22. Remove the power steering pump and the V-belt.
23. Remove the drive belt cover and the drive belt.
24. Remove the cylinder head cover.
25. Loosen the cylinder head bolts in the reverse order of the tightening sequence.
26. Remove the bolts and lift the cylinder head straight off.

CAUTION

If the head sticks, loosen it by compression or rap it upward with a soft rubber mallet. Do not force anything between the head and the engine block to pry it upward; this may result in serious damage.

27. Clean the cylinder head and engine block mating surfaces thoroughly and then install the new gasket without any sealing compound. Make sure the words TOP or OBEN are facing up when the gasket is installed.
28. Place the cylinder head on the engine block and install bolts No. 8 and 10 first. These holes are smaller and will properly locate the gasket and the head on the engine block.
29. Install the remaining bolts. Tighten them in three stages.

CAUTION

Do not retorque the cylinder head bolts at the 1000 mile maintenance nor at the 1000 mile interval following repairs.

30. Installation of all other components is in the reverse order of removal.

5000 Diesel

NOTE: Cylinder head removal should not be attempted unless the engine is cold.

1. Disconnect the negative battery cable.
2. Drain the cooling system.
3. Remove the air cleaner.

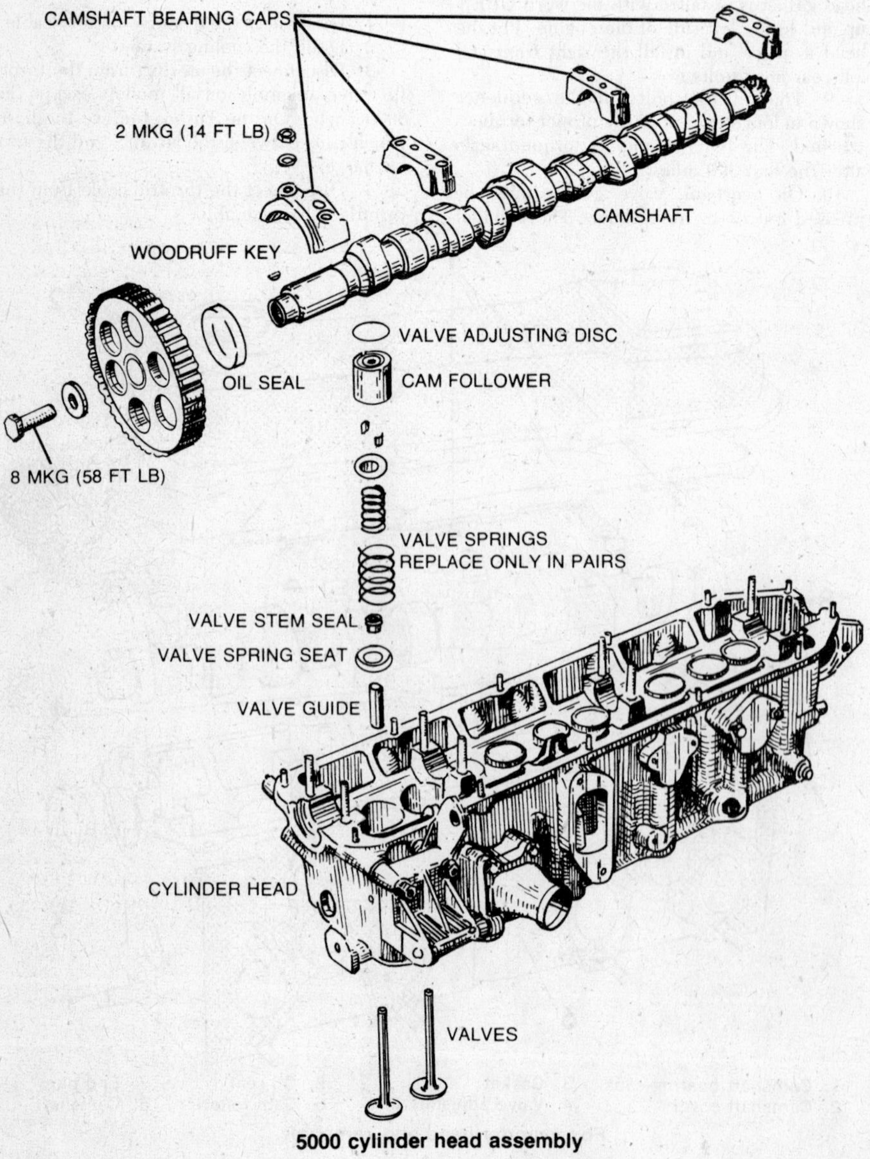

5000 cylinder head assembly

4. Clean and disconnect the fuel (injector) lines.
5. Tag and disconnect all electrical wires and leads.
6. Disconnect and plug all lines coming from the brake booster vacuum pump and remove the pump.
7. Unbolt and remove the intake manifold.
8. Disconnect and plug all lines coming from the power steering pump and remove the pump and V-belt.
9. Separate the exhaust pipe from the exhaust manifold and then remove the manifold.
10. Disconnect all radiator and heater hoses where they are attached to the cylinder head and position them out of the way.
11. Remove the drive belt cover and the drive belt.
12. Remove the injection pump belt cover and remove the belt.
13. Remove the PCV hose.
14. Remove the cylinder head cover.
15. Loosen the cylinder head bolts in the reverse order of the tightening sequence shown in the illustration.
16. Remove the bolts and lift the cylinder head straight off.

CAUTION

If the head sticks, loosen it by compression or rap it upward with a soft rubber mallet. Do not force anything between the head and the engine block to pry it upward; this may result in serious damage.

17. Clean the cylinder head and engine block mating surfaces thoroughly and then install the new gasket without any sealing compound. Make sure the words TOP or OBEN are facing up when the gasket is installed.

NOTE: Depending upon piston height above the top surface of the engine block, there are three gaskets of different thicknesses which can be used. Be sure that the new gasket has the same number of notches and the same identifying number as the one being replaced.

18. Place the cylinder head on the engine block and install bolts No. 8 and 10 first. These holes are smaller and will properly locate the gasket and the head on the engine block.
19. Install the remaining bolts. Tighten them in three stages (see "Torque Specifications" Chart) using the sequence shown in the illustration.
20. Installation of all other components is in the reverse order of removal.
21. After reassembly, start the engine and let it run until it reaches normal operating temperature (when the radiator fan switches on). Stop the engine, remove the cylinder head cover and check to see that all bolts are still at the proper tightness.
22. After 1000 miles, remove the cylinder head cover and loosen the cylinder head bolts 30 degrees (⅓ of a turn). Then retorque them to the proper specifications. This is done one bolt at a time, in the proper sequence.

Intake Manifold

REMOVAL AND INSTALLATION

All Except 4000 and 5000

1. Drain the coolant.
2. Remove the air cleaner.
3. Disconnect the coolant hoses from the manifold and the automatic choke. Remove the wire from the electric choke.
4. Disconnect the vacuum hose and the lead to the idle cutoff valve. Detach the fuel line and the accelerator linkage.
5. Remove the manifold nuts and the manifold support.
6. Pull the manifold off the studs. If it sticks, rap it with a soft hammer. Do not force anything between the manifold and the cylinder head. Discard the gaskets.
7. Installation is the reverse of the removal procedure. New gaskets must be used. Tighten the nuts to 18 ft/lbs. After refilling the cooling system, start the engine and check for leaks.

4000 and 5000 Except Diesel

1. Disconnect the negative battery cable.
2. Drain the cooling system.
3. Disconnect the air duct from the throttle valve assembly on all models but the 5000 Turbo. On the Turbo, remove the hose which runs between the air duct and the turbocharger.
4. Disconnect the throttle cable from the throttle valve assembly.
5. Remove the air duct for the injector cooling fan on the Turbo.
6. Clean and remove the fuel injectors.
7. Disconnect the cold start valve.

NOTE: Protect the fuel injectors and the cold start valve with caps.

8. Tag and disconnect all vacuum and PCV lines.
9. Tag and disconnect all electrical lines leading to the cylinder head.
10. Remove the hose which runs from the intake manifold to the turbocharger on the Turbo.
11. Remove the auxiliary air regulator.
12. Remove the manifold.
13. Installation is in the reverse order of removal.

5000 Diesel

1. Disconnect the negative battery cable.
2. Drain the cooling system.
3. Remove the air cleaner.
4. Disconnect and plug all lines coming from the brake booster vacuum pump and remove the pump.
5. Disconnect the PCV line.
6. Remove the manifold.
7. Installation is in the reverse order of removal.

Exhaust Manifold

REMOVAL AND INSTALLATION

All Except 4000, 5000 and 5000 Turbo

1. Disconnect the heated air intake hose from the manifold.
2. Unbolt the exhaust pipe from the manifold.
3. Remove the sheet metal cover.
4. Remove the manifold nuts. Pull the manifold off the studs. If it sticks, rap it with a soft hammer. Do not force anything between the manifold and the cylinder head. Discard the gaskets.
5. Installation is the reverse of the removal procedure. New gaskets must be used. If the gaskets are the type with round openings, they must be installed with the beaded side outward from the head and the notched edge down. Gaskets with oval openings must be installed with the beaded edge outward from the head. Tighten the manifold nuts to the specified torque. Torque the front exhaust pipe flange nuts to 18-22 ft/lbs, in steps. A new gasket should also be used between the exhaust pipe and the manifold.

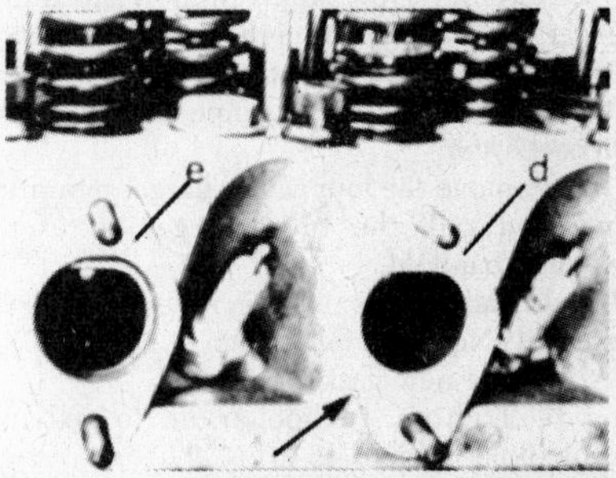

100 series exhaust manifold gaskets. (d) is the type with the oval opening which must be installed with the notched side down. (e) has a round opening. Both types must have the beaded edge around the opening facing outward.

4000 and 5000 Except 5000 Turbo

Although it is not imperative to remove the intake manifold in order to remove the exhaust manifold, you may find that it makes everything more accessible.

1. Unbolt and separate the exhaust pipe from the exhaust manifold.
2. Disconnect the EGR valve and the oxygen sensor (4000 5 cyl and all 1979-81 Calif. models) from the manifold.
3. Remove the heat deflector shield on the 4000.
4. Remove the manifold.
5. Installation is in the reverse order of removal.

NOTE: Always replace old gaskets.

5000 Turbo

1. Remove the hose which runs between the air duct and the turbocharger.
2. If the intake manifold has not been removed, disconnect the hose which runs from the intake manifold to the turbocharger.
3. Unbolt the exhaust pipe from the bottom of the turbocharger.
4. Unbolt the exhaust pipe from the wastegate on the rear of the manifold.
5. Disconnect the EGR valve and the oxygen sensor from the manifold.
6. Remove the oil lines (2) from the turbocharger.
7. Remove the manifold.

NOTE: The manifold, the turbocharger and the wastegate can all be removed as one unit.

8. Installation is in the reverse order of removal.

Turbocharger

REMOVAL AND INSTALLATION

1. Removal of the intake manifold (as detailed earlier) is not absolutely necessary but will greatly aid in the accessibility of all related nuts and bolts.
2. Loosen the hose clamps and remove the hose which leads to the intake manifold.
3. Loosen the hose clamps and remove the hose which leads to the air cleaner.
4. Unbolt the oil supply (upper) and return (lower) lines and position them out of the way.
5. Remove the four exhaust pipe mounting nuts and pull the exhaust pipe away from the turbocharger.
6. Remove the four turbocharger mounting nuts and pull the turbocharger off of the exhaust manifold.
7. Installation is in the reverse order of removal. Note the following:
   a. Use new gaskets.
   b. Tighten turbocharger to exhaust manifold bolts to 43 ft/lbs.
   c. Tighten turbocharger to exhaust pipe bolts to 22 ft/lbs.

Turbocharger Wastegate

REMOVAL AND INSTALLATION

1. As suggested in the turbocharger removal procedure, intake manifold removal is a prudent idea for wastegate accessibility.
2. Remove the wastegate to exhaust pipe connecting tube (three bolts top and three bolts bottom).
3. Remove the mounting bolt for the tube leading from the wastegate to the exhaust manifold.
4. Remove the vacuum line from the end of the wastegate.
5. Remove the four mounting bolts and remove the wastegate from the exhaust manifold.
6. Installation is in the reverse order of removal.

Timing Chain Cover

REMOVAL AND INSTALLATION

100 Series

1. Place the car on a lift or pit.
2. Remove the apron under the front bumper.
3. Have an assistant place the car in first gear and hold the brake on. Remove the crankshaft pulley nut. On cars with automatic transmission the nut can be removed by affixing a heavy wrench and rapping the wrench with a hammer. The nut must be unscrewed in the opposite direction of normal engine rotation.
4. Loosen the fan and alternator adjustments and remove the belts.
5. Remove the pulley, rapping it with a soft hammer if necessary. Be careful not to lose the shaft key.
6. Drain the oil.
7. Remove first the oil pan, then the timing chain cover.
8. Reverse the procedure to install, using new gaskets. Timing chain cover bolt torque is 7 ft/lbs.

TIMING CHAIN COVER OIL SEAL REPLACEMENT

100 Series

Current models have the lip retaining the oil seal in the cover to the inside. Thus the oil seal is pressed in from the front of the cover. Older models have the retaining lip toward the outside of the cover; the seal is pressed in from the inside of the cover. The result of this is that the oil seal may be replaced with the cover in place on the current models, while on older models the cover must be removed to replace the seal. The only way to determine which cover is installed is by inspection, after removing the crankshaft pulley. Virtually all US models use the current type. The seal can be replaced without removing the engine.

To replace either type:

1. Remove the timing chain cover on older models. Follow Steps 1-6 of the "Timing Chain Cover Removal and Installation" procedure for current models.
2. Carefully pry out the old seal with a screwdriver, being careful not to damage the housing.
3. Apply grease between the lips of the seal and apply a little oil to the outside edge.
4. On older models press in the seal from the inside of the cover. Press or drive it in with a seal installer or a suitable improvised tool, until it bottoms on the retaining lip. If there is no retaining lip, press the seal in until it is flush with the inside of the cover.
5. On current models, press or drive the seal in with the metal side out until it bottoms on the retaining lip. A good way to do this is to tighten a flat plate against the seal with the pully retaining nut.
6. Reverse the procedure followed in Step 1 to reassemble the engine.

Timing Chain and Tensioner

REMOVAL AND INSTALLATION

100 Series

1. Remove the timing chain cover.
2. All engines have a hydraulic chain tensioner. Bend open the lock plate, unscrew the chain tensioner plug, insert a Phillips screwdriver and turn counterclockwise. If this is not done, the chain tensioner will fly apart as it is removed. On some models, the tensioner

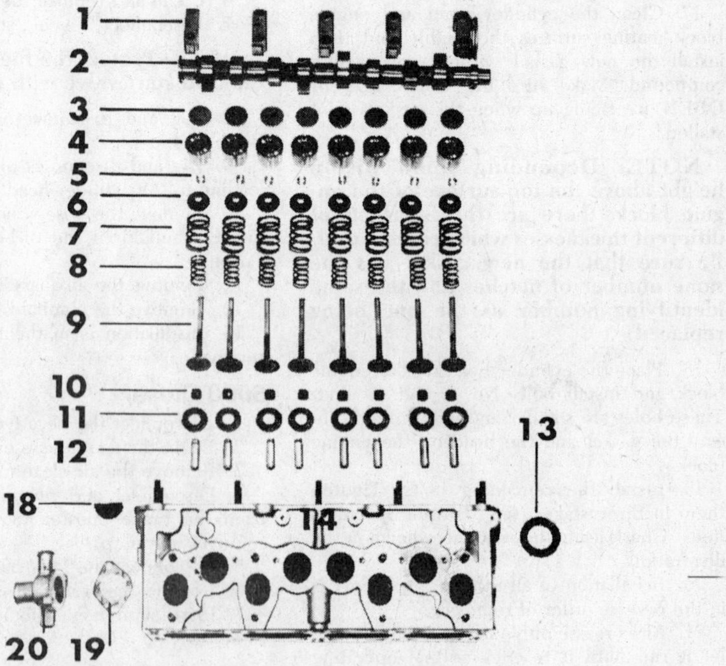

1. Bearing cap
2. Camshaft
3. Tappet clearance disc
4. Tappet
5. Lock
6. Spring retainer
7. Outer spring
8. Inner spring
9. Valve
10. Valve seal
11. Spring retainer
12. Valve guide
13. Shaft seal
14. Cylinder head
18. Plug
19. Gasket, water adapter
20. Water adapter

Details of the Fox cylinder head and valve train

must be held together while it is removed. Unbolt and remove the tensioner.

3. Remove the camshaft sprocket retaining bolt. Some way to keep the sprocket from turning will have to be devised.

4. Remove the camshaft sprocket, chain, and crankshaft sprocket together, using a puller on the crankshaft sprocket. Be careful not to lose the key for the crankshaft sprocket.

5. On reinstallation, heat the crankshaft sprocket to 140° F in an oven. Do not heat it with a flame, as it will be warped. Install the shaft key and slide the sprocket into place until it rests against the stop.

6. Align the No. 1 cylinder mark on the distributor body rim with the rotor. Set No. 1 cylinder precisely at top dead center. Place the camshaft sprocket on the camshaft and align the sprocket punch mark with the notch in the chain guide rail.

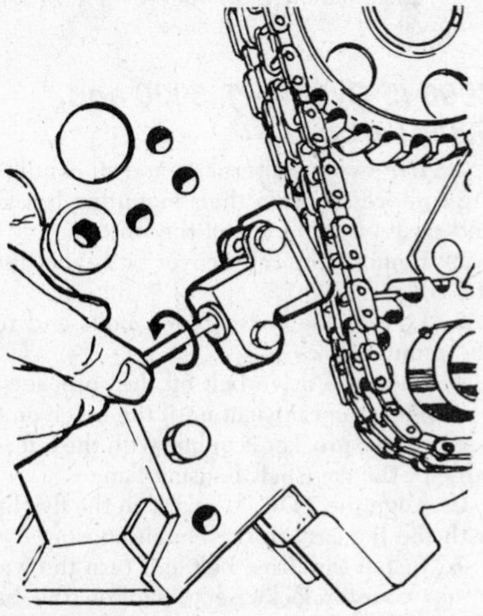

Use a Phillips screwdriver, as shown, to prevent the 100 series chain from coming apart when it is removed

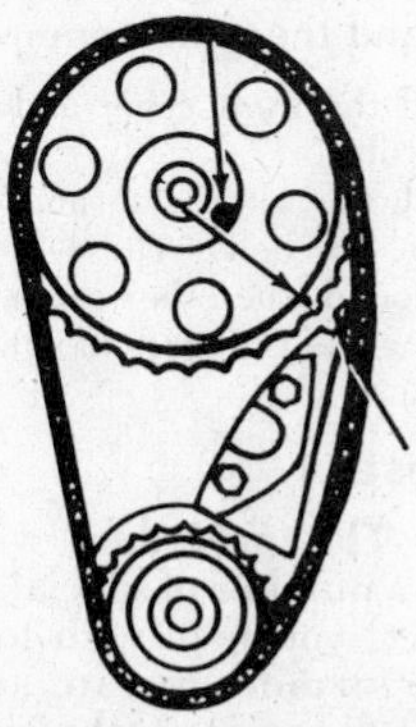

100 series timing chain alignment. The arrows show the camshaft sprocket punch mark, the notch in the chain guide rail, and the dowel which aligns the camshaft sprocket and camshaft.

7. Remove the camshaft sprocket, being careful not to turn the camshaft.

8. Place the timing chain over the crankshaft sprocket and place the camshaft sprocket in the chain, so that the camshaft sprocket can be installed without moving either the camshaft or the crankshaft.

NOTE: The factory specifies that timing chains with indented links should not be reused. They must be replaced with a straight-link chain.

9. Torque the camshaft sprocket to bolt to 58 ft/lbs.

10. Assemble and install the chain tensioner, torquing the bolts to 9 ft/lbs. Turn the chain plunger clockwise to release it. Current production models have a self-releasing chain tensioner. Make absolutely sure that the hydraulic chain tensioner is free to move. Install the tensioner plunger and lock plate.

11. Replace the timing cover.

Timing Belt Cover

REMOVAL AND INSTALLATION

4000 (4 Cylinder)

1. Loosen the alternator adjusting bolts. Pivot the alternator over and slip the V-belt off.

2. If equipped with air conditioning, loosen the compressor mounting bolts and slip off the V-belt.

3. Unscrew the retaining nuts and remove the upper timing belt cover. Take care not to lose any of the washers or spacers.

4. Using the large bolt on the crankshaft sprocket, turn the engine until the No. 1 cylinder is at TDC of the compression stroke. At this point, both of the valves will be closed and the 0 mark on the flywheel will be aligned with the pointer on the clutch housing.

5. Unscrew the crankshaft pulley retaining bolts (4) and then loosen the crankshaft sprocket bolt.

NOTE: To remove the crankshaft sprocket bolt you will need a friend. Put the car in 4th gear and apply the brake, this will enable you to loosen the bolt.

6. Remove the crankshaft pulley.

7. Unscrew the water pump pulley retaining bolts (3) and remove the pulley.

8. Unscrew the retaining nuts and remove the lower timing belt cover. Take care not to lose any of the washers or spacers.

9. Installation is in the reverse order of removal.

4000 (5 Cylinder), 5000 and 5000 Turbo

1. Loosen the alternator adjusting bolts and remove the V-belt.

2. Loosen the power steering pump adjusting bolts and remove the V-belt.

3. If equipped with air conditioning, loosen the compressor adjusting bolts and remove the V-belt.

4. Unscrew the retaining nuts and remove the timing belt cover. Take care not to lose any of the washers or spacers.

5. Installation is in the reverse order of removal.

5000 Diesel

There are two drive belts on the 5000 Diesel; one at the front of the engine and one at the rear, therefore there are two covers to remove. The front cover is removed in the same manner as the gasoline engined 5000's with two exceptions, the cover has an upper and a lower half. To remove the upper half, follow the procedure for the 5000 and 5000 Turbo. To remove the lower half, use the following procedure.

1. Remove the upper cover.

2. Unscrew the crankshaft pulley retaining bolts and remove the pulley.

3. Unscrew the retaining nuts and remove the lower cover.

4. Installation is in the reverse order of removal.

To remove the rear timing belt cover, use the following procedure.

1. Remove the outside half of the vacuum pump pulley and remove the V-belt.

2. Unscrew the retaining bolts and remove the rear timing belt cover. Take care not to lose any of the washers or spacers.

3. Installation is in the reverse order of removal.

Timing Belt

REMOVAL AND INSTALLATION

Fox

1. Remove the grille.

2. Remove the alternator belt and the timing belt cover.

3. Loosen the belt tensioner locknut and turn the tensioner counterclockwise (facing it) to release the belt tension.

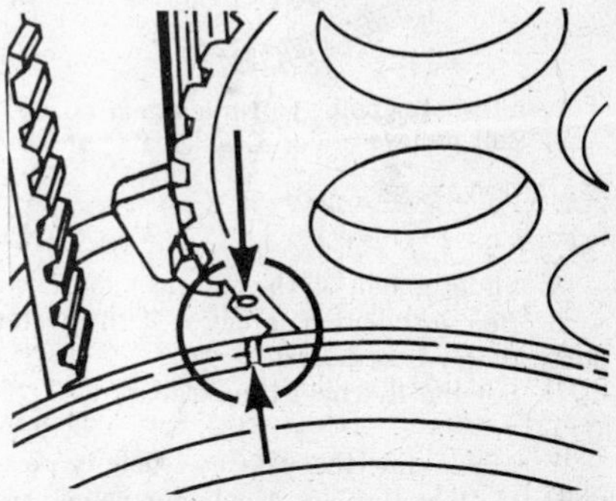

Fox crankshaft pulley and intermediate sprocket for timing belt installation. With the pulley and sprocket as shown, No. 1 piston should be at TDC and the distributor rotor aligned with the No. 1 cylinder notch

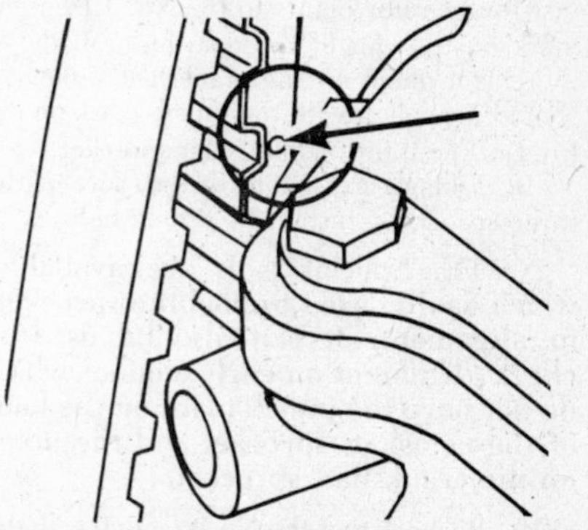

Fox camshaft sprocket aligned for timing belt installation. With the sprocket as shown, No. 4 cylinder valves should be in the overlap position

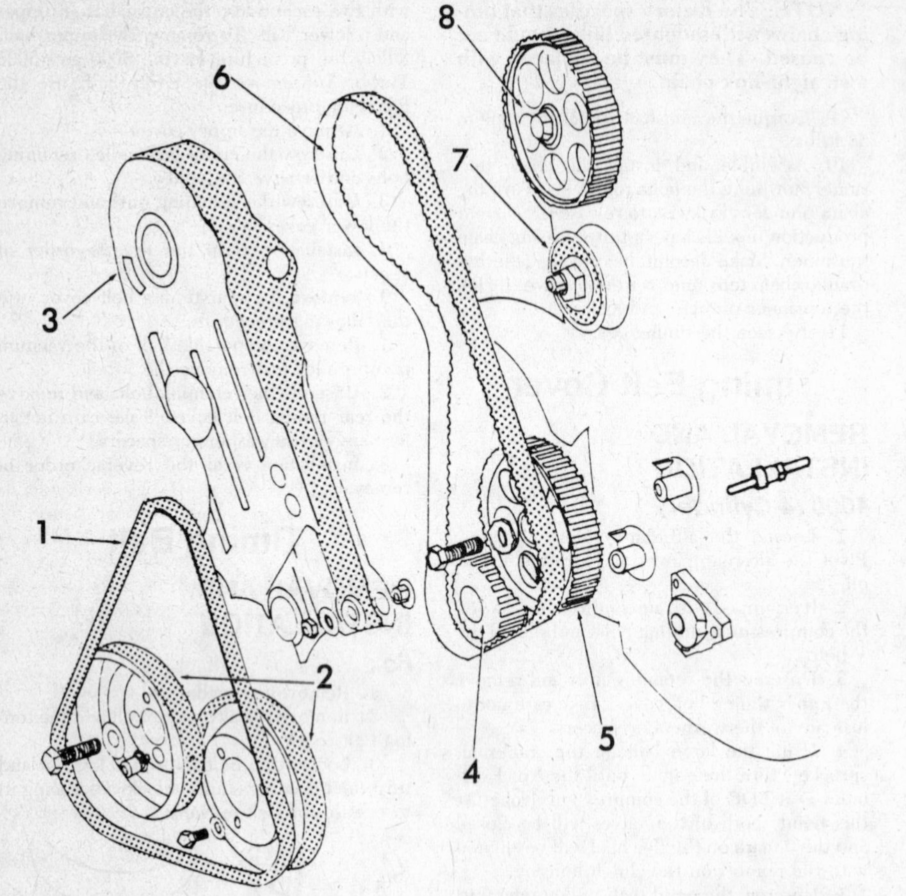

1. Alternator belt 2. Belt pulleys 3. Timing gear cover 4. Crankshaft sprocket 5. Intermediate sprocket 6. Drive belt 7. Tensioner 8. Camshaft sprocket

Fox timing belt

4. Slidethe belt off the camshaft sprocket.
5. Belt installation is easier if the water pump pulley is removed.
6. Set the flywheel timing mark at TDC (0° T).
7. Make sure that the camshaft is positioned so that the No. 4 cylinder values are overlapping; i.e. the exhaust valve is opening and the intake closing. If there is a punch mark on the back of the camshaft sprocket, align it with the camshaft cover gasket(left side).
8. Turn the intermediate shaft so that the distributor rotor points to the No. 1 cylinder mark on the rim of the distributor body. If there is a notch on the crankshaft pulley, it should now align with the punch mark on the front of the intermediate shaft sprocket.
9. Taking care not to disturb any of the three sprockets, install the timing belt.

NOTE: Special tools are available, which can be used to hold the sprockets in alignment. It can also be used to check alignment on early engines which do not have the punch mark on the back of the camshaft sprocket and the notch on the crankshaft sprocket.

10. Recheck that the No. 1 (and 4) cylinder is at TDC, that the camshaft is in the No. 4 cylinder overlap position, and that the distributor rotor is in the No. 1 cylinder firing position.
11. Turn the belt tensioner clockwise (facing it) until it is just possible to turn the longest span of belt about 90° with your thumb and forefinger. Lock the tensioner in place.

NOTE: It is not necessary to recheck the belt tension during the normal life span of the belt (about 60,000 miles).

12. Again recheck the alignment as in Step 10 and replace the belt cover, water pump pulley, alternator belt, and grille. Check the ignition timing when the job is complete.

4000 (4 Cylinder)

1. Remove the upper and lower timing belt covers.
2. While holding the large hex nut on the tensioner pulley, loosen the smaller pulley lock nut.
3. Turn the tensioner counterclockwise to relieve the tension on the timing belt.
4. Carefully slide the timing belt off of the three sprockets and remove the belt.
5. Using the large bolt on the crankshaft sprocket, turn the engine until the No. 1 cylinder is at TDC of the compression stroke. At this point, both valves will be closed and the 0 mark on the flywheel will be aligned with the pointer on the clutch housing.
6. Check that the timing mark on the rear face of the camshaft sprocket is aligned with the upper edge of the rear timing belt cover. If it's not, turn the sprocket until they align.
7. Replace the crankshaft pulley and check that the notch on the pulley is aligned with the mark on the intermediate shaft sprocket. If not, turn them until they align.

CAUTION

If the timing marks are not correctly aligned with the No. 1 piston at TDC of the compression stroke and the belt is installed, valve timing will be incorrect. Poor performance and possible engine damage can result from the improper valve timing.

8. Remove the crankshaft pulley. Observe its location on the crankshaft sprocket so that it can be replaced in the same position.
9. Slide the timing belt back onto the sprockets and check for the proper tension (see "Tension Adjustment").
10. Installation is in the reverse order of removal.

4000 (5 Cylinder), 5000 and 5000 Turbo

1. Remove the alternator and air conditioning compressor from their mounting brackets and position them out of the way.
2. Remove the front cover bolts and lift off the cover.
3. Loosen the water pump bolts and turn the pump clockwise.
4. Slide the drive belt off the sprockets.
5. Turn the camshaft until the notch on the back of the sprocket is in line with the left side edge of the camshaft housing flange.
6. Align the TDC "0" mark on the flywheel with the lug cast on the clutch housing.
7. Install the drive belt and turn the water pump counterclockwise to tighten the belt. Tighten the water pump bolts to 14 ft/lbs.

NOTE: The belt is correctly tensioned when it can be twisted 90° with the thumb and index finger along the straight run between the camshaft sprocket and the water pump.

8. Install the front cover and tighten the bolts to 7 ft/lbs.
9. Install the alternator and compressor and tighten the belts. These belts are correctly tensioned when they can be depressed ½ inch along their longest straight run.

5000 Diesel

NOTE: This procedure will require the use of a number of special tools. Due to this fact, you may wish to have the work performed by an authorized Porsche/Audi service technician.

1. Remove all V-belts on the front of the engine.
2. Remove the outside half of the vacuum pump pulley and remove the V-belt.
3. Remove the front timing belt covers.
4. Remove the rear timing belt cover.
5. Remove the cylinder head cover.
6. Using the large bolt on the crankshaft sprocket, turn the engine until the No. 1 cylinder is at TDC of the compression stroke. At this point, both of the valves will be closed and the mark on the flywheel will be aligned with the pointer on the clutch housing.

7. Align the marks on the injection pump sprocket mounting plate.

8. Using special tool 2064 (a pin), lock the injection pump sprocket in place so that it cannot move and change the valve timing.

9. Using special tool 3036, hold the remaining (inside) half of the vacuum pump pulley and the injection pump drive sprocket in place. Remove the center retaining bolt and take off the pulley half and the drive sprocket along with the timing belt.

10. Using special tool 2084 to hold the crankshaft pulley in place, attach special tool 2079 to a ratchet and *loosen* the crankshaft pulley center bolt.

11. Attach special tool 2065A to the rear of the camshaft so that it will not move and alter the valve timing.

12. Loosen the adjusting bolts (2) on the water pump and turn it counterclockwise to relieve the tension on the timing belt.

13. Unbolt and remove the crankshaft pulley and slide the timing belt off of the sprockets.

To install the front timing belt:

14. Check that the No. 1 cylinder is still at TDC and the mark on the flywheel is still aligned with the pointer on the clutch housing.

15. Loosen the camshaft sprocket bolt approximately 1 turn and lightly tap the gear loose from the camshaft with a rubber mallet.

16. Install the timing belt and check the tension (see "Tension Adjustment").

17. Tighten the camshaft sprocket bolt to 33 ft/lbs and remove special tool 2065A.

To install the rear timing belt:

18. Install the injection pump drive sprocket along with the timing belt.

19. Check that the No. 1 cylinder is still at TDC.

20. Tighten the injection pump drive sprocket retaining bolt until it is just possible to turn the sprocket by hand.

21. Check for proper tension (see "Tension Adjustment").

22. Retighten the retaining bolt to 7 ft/lbs.

23. Attach the rear timing belt cover and the outside half of the vacuum pump pulley along with the V-belt and check for proper tension.

24. Remove special tool 2064 from the injection pump.

25. Check the injection timing, and adjust if necessary.

26. Installation of the remaining components is in the reverse order of removal.

TENSION ADJUSTMENT

4000 (4 Cylinder)

1. Holding the large bolt on the tensioner pulley, loosen the small nut and turn the tensioner clockwise to tighten and counterclockwise to loosen.

2. The belt is correctly tensioned when it can be twisted 90 degrees with the thumb and forefinger, midway between the camshaft and the intermediate shaft drive sprockets.

4000 (5 Cylinder), 5000 and 5000 Turbo

1. Loosen the water pump adjusting bolts (2) and turn the pump clockwise to tighten and counterclockwise to loosen.

2. The belt is correctly tensioned when it can be twisted 90 degrees with the thumb and forefinger, midway between the camshaft drive sprocket and the water pump.

5000 Diesel

NOTE: Special tool VW210 will be required for this procedure.

Tension adjustment on the front timing belt is performed in the same manner as with the other five cylinder engines. Deflection is also checked in the same position, but with the special tool VW210 rather than your fingers. Proper tension is achieved when the scale reads 12-13.

Tension on the rear timing belt is also checked with VW210, in between the two drive sprockets. The scale should read between 12 and 13. To adjust the tension, loosen the injection pump mounting bracket bolts and move the pump toward the engine to loosen and away from the engine to tighten.

Timing Gears

REMOVAL AND INSTALLATION

4000 and 5000

All of the drive sprockets are located by keys on their respective shafts and each is retained by a bolt. To remove any or all of the sprockets, first remove the timing belt covers and belts and then use the following procedure.

1. Remove the center retaining bolt for the particular drive sprocket.
2. Gently pry the sprocket off of the shaft.
3. If the sprocket is stubborn in coming off, use a gear puller. Don't hammer on the sprocket as you may crack it.
4. Remove the sprocket being careful not to lose the key.
5. Installation is in the reverse order of removal.

NOTE: Always check valve timing after removing the drive sprockets.

Camshaft

REMOVAL AND INSTALLATION

100 Series

This operation requires that the engine be removed from the car and rather extensively disassembled.

1. Remove the timing chain and tensioner.
2. Remove the cylinder head.
3. Remove the tappets (valve lifters). A special tool is used to lift them out. Keep them in order so they can be replaced in their original locations.
4. Remove the distributor.
5. Remove the oil pump.
6. Unbolt and remove the camshaft locating plate.
7. Carefully guide the camshaft out of the block, being cautious not to bang the lobes into the bearings. This is a lot easier if a bolt is threaded into the front of the camshaft for use as a handle.
8. On reinstallation, oil the camshaft bearing surfaces. Insert the camshaft carefully.
9. Install the locating plate, torqueing the bolts to 18 ft/lbs.
10. Check the camshaft end-play in and out of the block, using a dial indicator. If it exceeds 0.004 in., install a new locating plate.
11. The rest of the reassembly procedure is the reverse of disassembly. Make sure to align the chain and sprockets as explained under Timing Chain and Tensioner Removal and Installation. Check the ignition timing when the job is complete.

Fox

NOTE: The manufacturer says that the camshaft must not be removed unless a special removal tool is used. This device bolts to the cylinder head and presses down on the camshaft at two places: between the lobes for cylinder 3 and between the lobes for cylinder 2. The following alternate procedure may be used, but great caution must be exercised. The alternate procedure is not recommended by the manufacturer.

1. Remove the timing belt.
2. Remove the camshaft sprocket.
3. Remove the air cleaner.
4. Remove the camshaft cover.
5. Unscrew and remove the No. 1, 3, and 5 bearing caps (No. 1 is at the front).
6. Unscrew the No. 2 and 4 bearing caps, diagonally and in increments.
7. Lift the camshaft out of the cylinder head.
8. Lubricate the camshaft journals and lobes with assembly lube or gear oil before installing it in the cylinder head.
9. Replace the camshaft oil seal with a new one whenever the cam is removed.
10. Install the No. 1, 3, and 5 bearing caps and tighten the nuts to 14 ft/lbs. The caps should be installed so they read right side up from the driver's seat.
11. Install the No. 2 and 4 bearing caps and diagonally tighten the nuts to 14 ft/lbs.

NOTE: If checking end play, install a dial indicator so that the feeler touches the camshaft snout. Endplay should be no more than 0.006 in.

12. Replace the seal in the No. 1 bearing cap. If necessary, replace the end plug in the cylinder head.
13. Install the camshaft cover.
14. Install the camshaft pulley and the timing belt.
15. Check the valve clearance.

4000 (4 Cylinder)

1. Remove the timing belt.
2. Remove the PCV line.
3. Remove the cylinder head cover.
4. Remove the camshaft drive sprocket.
5. Unscrew and remove the Nos. 1, 3 and 5 bearing caps (No. 1 is at the front of the engine).
6. Diagonally loosen bearing caps Nos. 2 and 4.
7. Remove the camshaft from the cylinder head.

8. Remove the camshaft journals, lobes, bearing shells and the contact faces of the caps with assembly lube or gear oil before reinstallation.

9. Replace the camshaft oil seal. If necessary, replace the end plug also.

10. Install the Nos. 1, 3 and 5 bearing caps and tighten the nuts to 14 ft/lbs.

NOTE: Tighten the bearing caps diagonally. Observe off center bearing position; numbers on bearing caps are not always on the same side.

11. Install the Nos. 2 and 4 bearing caps and tighten the nuts to 14 ft/lbs.

12. Replace the seal in the No. 1 bearing cap.

13. Installation of the remaining components is in the reverse order of removal.

NOTE: Always recheck the valve clearance after the camshaft has been removed.

4000 (5 Cylinder), 5000 and 5000 Turbo

1. Remove the camshaft cover.
2. Remove the drive belt and camshaft sprocket.
3. Remove bearing caps 2 and 4.
4. Diagonally loosen bearing caps 1 and 3.
5. Lift out the camshaft.
6. When installing, lightly oil the camshaft and bearings with clean engine oil.
7. Position the caps on the same journals from which they were removed.
8. Lightly tighten the nuts of caps 2 and 4.
9. Tighten all nuts to 14 ft/lbs.
10. Install the drive belt and sprocket and the camshaft cover. The sprocket bolt is torqued to 58 ft/lbs; the cover bolts to 7 ft/lbs.

5000 Diesel

1. Remove the front and rear timing belts.
2. Remove the cylinder head cover.
3. Remove the camshaft drive sprocket.
4. Remove the injection pump drive sprocket.
5. Set cylinder No. 1 to TDC of the compressor stroke.
6. Remove bearing caps Nos. 1 and 4.
7. Diagonally loosen bearing caps Nos. 2 and 3 and remove.
8. Remove the camshaft from the cylinder head.
9. Lubricate the camshaft journals, lobes, bearing shells and the contact faces of the caps with assembly lube or gear oil before reinstallation.
10. Replace both camshaft oil seals.

NOTE: The cam lobes for the No. 1 cylinder must face upward.

11. Install bearing caps Nos. 2 and 3, tightening alternately and diagonally.
12. Install bearing caps Nos. 1 and 4.
13. Replace the seal in the No. 1 bearing cap.
14. Installation of the remaining components is in the reverse order of removal.

NOTE: Always recheck the valve clearance after the camshaft has been removed.

Pistons and Connecting Rods

100 Series

The connecting rods must be installed in the engine with the grooved side toward the camshaft. New connecting rod bolts must always be used. Both the pistons and the piston pins must be heated to 140° F in an oven in order to install the pins. Three oversizes of pistons are available to accommodate overbores up to 0.004 in.

Fox 4000 and 5000 (Gasoline Engines)

The pistons must be installed in the block with the arrow at the edge of the crown facing to the front of the car. The connecting rod and cap alignment casting grooves must face the intermediate shaft. New connecting rod bolts must always be used. The pistons must be heated to 140° F in an oven before the piston pins can be pressed in. Three piston oversizes are available to accommodate overbores up to 0.040 in.

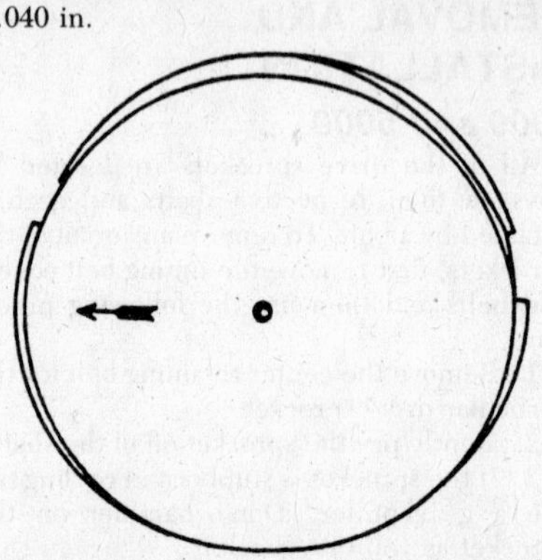

Arrow on pistons must face forward

5000 Diesel

The same basic procedures apply for the diesel engine as the gasoline engine. The one important difference is that whenever new pistons are installed, the piston projection must be checked.

A spacer (Special Tool VW 385/17) and a bar with a micrometer (Special Tool VW 385/7) are necessary and should be set up as shown, to measure the maximum amount of piston projection above the top surface of the engine block. After ascertaining the projection height, select a new gasket from the following chart.

Piston Height In. (mm)	Identification Notches In Gasket	Part Number
0.026-0.031 (0.67-0.80)	1	069 103 383
0.032-0.035 (0.81-0.90)	2	069 103 383A
0.036-0.040 (0.91-1.02)	3	069 103 383B

When installing the connecting rods on the diesel engine, the forged marks on the bearing caps and on the bottom of the rods should be facing the right side of the engine.

ENGINE LUBRICATION

Oil Pan

REMOVAL AND INSTALLATION

100 Series

1. Raise and support the car.
2. Remove the apron under the front bumper for better access.
3. Remove the radiator mounting bolts and press the radiator up out of the brackets.
4. Drain the oil.
5. Loosen and remove the Allen head bolts holding the pan. Tap it lightly with a soft hammer to break it loose. Remove the pan.
6. Clean the pan out thoroughly while it is off the engine.
7. Install new gaskets at either end of the oil pan. Apply a very thin coat of adhesive to them. Attach the pan rail gaskets to the block, using a slight amount of adhesive at both ends and in the middle. Put a tiny amount of adhesive at the extreme ends of the gaskets, adjacent to the rear main bearing cap and the timing cover. Stick on the small gasket segment below the starter.
8. Torque the larger pan bolts to 11 ft/lbs and the rest to 6 ft/lbs.
9. The rest of the installaton is the reverse of removal. Fill the crankcase and run the engine, checking for leaks.

Fox

The front crossmember has to be lowered to remove the oil pan.

1. Raise the car, allowing the front wheels to hang down. Drain the oil.
2. Disconnect the engine vacuum line from the power brake vacuum line T fitting. Pull the vacuum line from the cylinder head on automatic transmission cars.
3. Support the rear of the engine at the cast lifting eye in the cylinder head.
4. From underneath, unbolt the lower left and right engine mounts. Carefully and evenly loosen and remove the four crossmember to body bolts and lower the crossmember.
5. Remove the pan bolts. Tap it lightly with a soft hammer to break it loose. Remove the pan and clean it out thoroughly while it is off the engine.
6. On installation, use a new gasket wih no sealer. Torque the pan bolts in a criss-cross pattern, in steps, to 6 ft/lbs. Torque the crossmember bolts to 33 ft/lbs.

4000 and 5000

1. Raise and support the vehicle.
2. Drain the oil.
3. Remove the oil pan bolts while supporting the pan.

NOTE: To remove the two bolts at the rear of the oil pan on the diesel engine, turn the flywheel so that the recesses are pointing down. This will afford you access to the two bolts.

4. Lower the pan from the engine. Discard the gasket.
5. Coat both sides of a new gasket with sealer and install the gasket and oil pan.
6. Torque the bolts to 7 ft/lbs.

Rear Main Bearing Oil Seal Replacement

When this seal fails, the usual result is oil leakage onto the clutch. This, or course, causes clutch slippage or failure to disengage.

100 Series

This repair requires that the engine be removed from the car and extensively disassembled.

1. Remove the engine.
2. Remove the transmission (and clutch) from the engine.
3. Remove the flywheel. Some method of preventing the flywheel from turning will have to be devised.

NOTE: Mark the relationship between the flywheel and crankshaft to preserve balance.

4. Remove the oil pan.
5. Unbolt and remove the rear main bearing cap.
6. The circular seal may now be removed.
7. Press the new seal evenly into place with the sealing lip toward the front of the engine. This is rather difficult without special seal installing tools.
8. Torque the bearing cap to specifications.
9. The remainder of the procedure is the reverse of disassembly. Make sure to align the flywheel marks made in Step 3.

Fox

1. Remove the engine. Refer to the Engine Removal and Installation procedures.
2. Remove the transmission (and clutch) from the engine.
3. Remove the flywheel. Some method of preventing the flywheel from turning will have to be devised.

NOTE: Mark the relationship between the flywheel and crankshaft to preserve balance.

4. The circular seal may now be removed by placing a suitable tool under the sealing lip or behind the support ring carefully. Be very cautious not to damage the seal bearing surface.
5. Press the new seal evenly in place. This is rather difficult without special seal installing tools.
6. The remainder of the procedure is the reverse of removal. Make sure to align the flywheel marks made in Step 3.

4000 and 5000

The rear main oil seal is located at the rear of the engine block. It can be found in a housing behind the flywheel. To replace the seal, it is necessary to remove the transmission.

1. Remove the transmission.
2. Unscrew the six bolts and remove the flywheel.
3. Using special tool VW2086 or a suitable tool, pry the old seal out of its housing.
4. To install, lightly oil the replacement seal then press it into place using a canister top or other circular piece of flat metal.

CAUTION

Be careful not to damage the seal or score the crankshaft.

5. Install the flywheel and the transmission.

Oil Pump

REMOVAL AND INSTALLATION

100 Series

1. Remove the distributor. Remove the oil pan.
2. Disconnect the oil line from the block and the pump.
4. Place No. 1 cylinder on Top Dead Center. This can be done by turning the engine with a finger held over the No. 1 spark plug hole. When compression is felt, turn the engine to align with 0° T mark on the crankshaft pulley with the timing pointer.
5. On replacement, turn the pump until the wide segment of the pump driveshaft faces forward. Turn the shaft 15 degrees counterclockwise and slide the oil pump shaft into the gear teeth of the camshaft.
6. Install the spacer under the pump and mounting bolt and tighten the bolt finger tight.
7. Put the oil line in place. Turn the pump or add extra gaskets at either end of the oil line to prevent any strain on the line.
8. Torque the pump mounting bolt to 18 ft/lbs and the oil line bolts to 7 ft/lbs. Use the lock plates to hold the oil line bolts.
9. Align the distributor rotor with the No. 1 cylinder notch in the rim of the housing. Insert the distributor with the vacuum unit parallel to the engine block and pointing to the rear of the engine. When installing the distributor, wiggle the rotor back and forth to allow the shaft projections to engage the oil pump driveshaft slots. Tighten the distributor mounting bolt.
10. Replace and fill the oil pan.
11. Start the engine and watch for oil leaks. If it won't start, check the basic ignition timing. If it does start, check the final ignition timing with a timing light.

Fox

To remove the pump, remove the oil pan and the pump mounting bolts. Pull the pump straight down. Pump bolt torque is 13-16 ft/lbs.

4000

1. Drain the oil and remove the oil pan.
2. Remove the oil pump mounting bolts and pull the pump down and out of the engine.
3. Unscrew the two bolts and separate the pump halves.
4. Clean the lower half in solvent.
5. To remove the oil strainer for cleaning, bend out the metal rim of the oil strainer cover plate and remove it.
6. Examine the gears and the driveshaft for any wear or damage. Replace them if necessary.
7. Reassemble the pump halves.
8. Prime the pump with oil and install in the reverse order of removal.

5000

1. Loosen and remove crankshaft bolt.
2. Remove the drive belt guard.
3. Loosen the water pump bolts and turn the pump body clockwise.

The wide part of the 100 series oil pump driveshaft must face forward on installation.

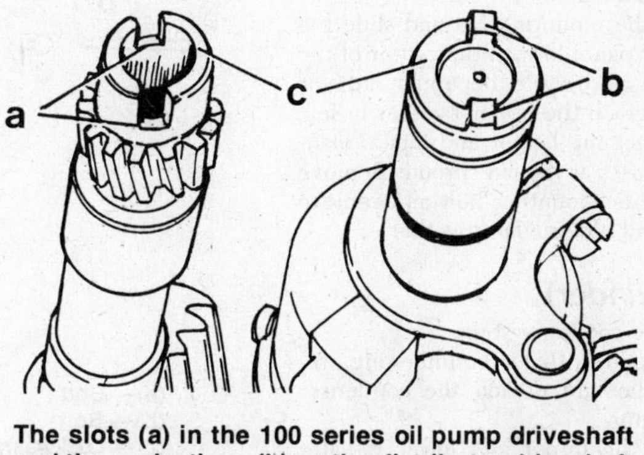

The slots (a) in the 100 series oil pump driveshaft and the projections (b) on the distributor driveshaft are offset. (c) indicates the wide segment of each shaft. The shafts can mate in only one way.

4. Remove the drive belt and V-belt pulley with the drive belt sprocket.
5. Remove the dipstick and drain the engine oil.
6. Remove the front bolts on the sub frame and remove the oil pan.
7. Remove the oil suction pipe from the base of the oil pump and bracket to the engine block.
8. Remove the oil pump bolts and remove the oil pump from the front of the engine.

ENGINE COOLING

The radiator drain plug is at the bottom, adjacent to the lower hose on all models. The engine drain plug is at the front, adjacent to the alternator except on the Fox. There is a breather plug in the upper heater hose, near the firewall on 100 series cars. The breather plug must be used to remove air from the system, when the engine is first started after refilling.

Radiator

REMOVAL AND INSTALLATION

100 Series

1. Drain the coolant.
2. Remove the upper radiator hose.
3. Detach the mounting strut at the top of the radiator, and swing it forward.
4. Detach the lower radiator hose. Detach the fan thermostatic switch.
5. Unbolt the radiator mountings.
6. Lift the radiator out.
7. To install, reverse the removal procedures. Make sure that the rubber sealing strips between the radiator and radiator cowl are in place.

Fox

1. Drain the coolant. Remove the grille.
2. Remove the bolts holding the panel at the side of the radiator through the grille opening.
3. Disconnect the lower radiator hose and the radiator fan switch at the bottom of the radiator. Remove the lower radiator panel and the lower radiator mounting nuts.
4. Loosen the mounting bar and slide the upper radiator panel toward the center of the car to remove it. Unbolt the upper radiator mounts and detach the upper radiator hose.
5. Disconnect the heater and intake manifold coolant hoses at the fan shroud. Remove the radiator side mounting bolt and remove the radiator and electric fan together.

4000 (4 Cylinder)

1. Drain the cooling system.
2. If equipped with air conditioning, remove the grille and detach the condenser from the radiator.
3. Remove the upper and lower radiator hoses, the expansion tank supply hose and the expansion tank vent hose. Being careful not to crimp them, tie all hoses back out of the way.

100 series engine block coolant drain plug

Radiator drain plug; 100, 100 LS, and 100 GL shown

NOTE: All disconnections should be done at the radiator-end of the particular hose.

4. Disconnect the wiring at the temperature switch (two switches if air conditioning) and the rear of the fan motor.
5. Unscrew the fan shroud retaining bolts and remove the fan, motor and shroud as one assembly.
6. Unscrew the radiator retaining bolts and remove the radiator.
7. Installation is in the reverse order of removal.

4000 (5 Cylinder) and 5000

1. Drain the cooling system.
2. Remove the three pieces of the radiator cowl and fan motor assembly. Take care in removing the fan motor connectors to avoid bending them.
3. Remove the upper and lower radiator hoses and the coolant tank supply hose.
4. Disconnect the coolant temperature switch located on the lower right side of the radiator.
5. Remove the radiator mounting bolts and life out the radiator.
6. Installation is the reverse of removal. Torque radiator mounting bolts to 14 ft/lbs and cowl bolts to 7 ft/lbs.

The 5000 Diesel is equipped with an auxiliary radiator which must also be removed. To remove the auxiliary radiator:

1. Remove the grille and detach the condenser (air conditioning only).
2. Remove all hoses from the auxiliary radiator.
3. Remove the radiator retaining bolts and remove the radiator.
4. Installation is in the reverse order of removal.

Water Pump

REMOVAL AND INSTALLATION

100 Series

1. Loosen the adjustment and remove the water pump drive belt.
2. Drain the coolant.
3. Remove the alternator pivot bolt at the front.
4. Loosen the clamp and pull the lower hose off the pump.
5. Remove the thermostat housing.
6. Unbolt the fan pulley. The pulley may be prevented from turning by wedging a

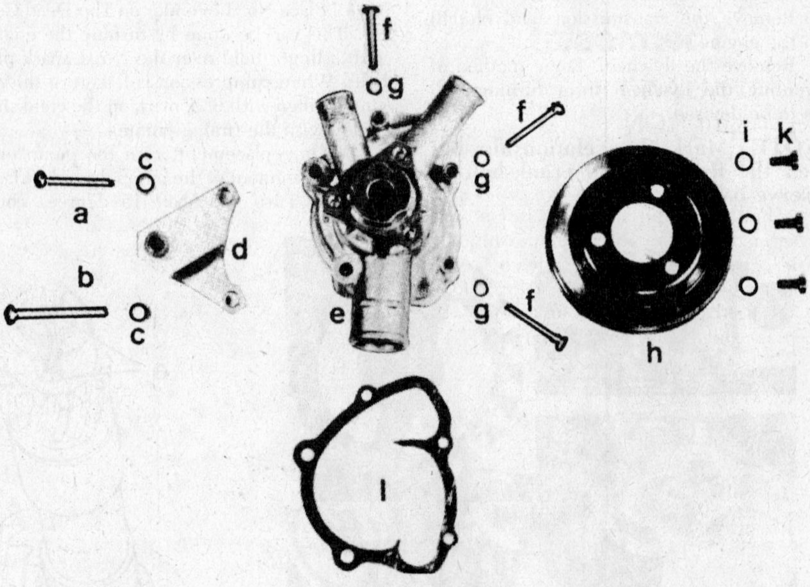

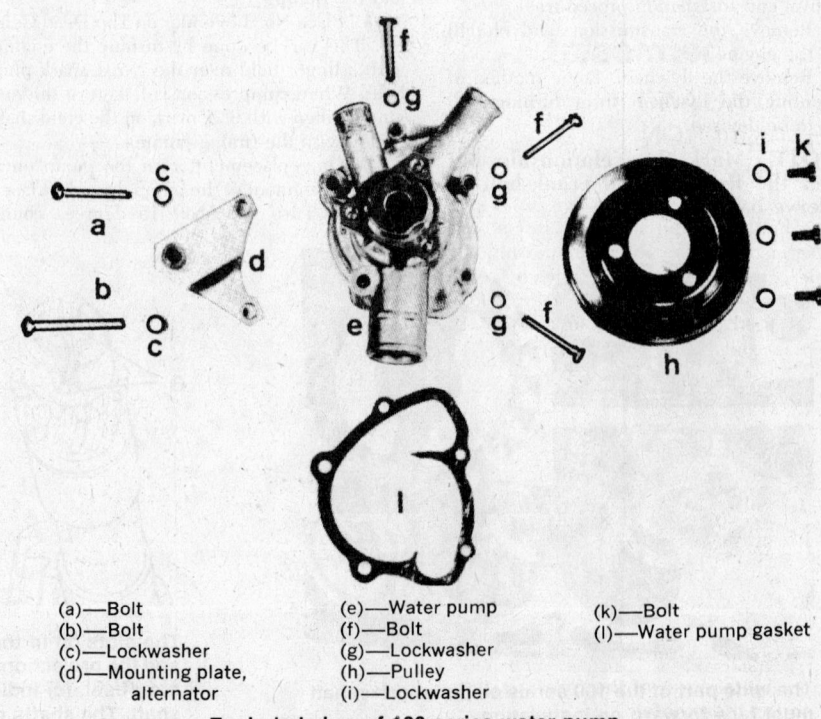

(a)—Bolt
(b)—Bolt
(c)—Lockwasher
(d)—Mounting plate, alternator
(e)—Water pump
(f)—Bolt
(g)—Lockwasher
(h)—Pulley
(i)—Lockwasher
(k)—Bolt
(l)—Water pump gasket

Exploded view of 100 series water pump

screwdriver between the pulley hub and one of the bolts.

7. The pulley may be carefully pried off the hub with two large screwdrivers.

8. Loosen the clamp and pull the upper hose off the pump.

9. Remove the five bolts and remove the pump.

10. Reverse the procedure for installation, using new gaskets and adjusting the alternator drive belt tension. Pump mounting bolt torque is 15 ft/lbs for the large bolts, and 9 ft/lbs for the small ones. Thermostat housing bolt torque is 15 ft/lbs. Pulley bolt torque is 7 ft/lbs.

Fox

1. Drain the coolant.
2. Remove the alternator.
3. Remove the timing belt cover.
4. Loosen the clamps and detach the hoses from the pump.
5. Unbolt the pump, turn it slightly, and lift it out.
6. On installation, use a new pump to block seal and torque the pump bolts to 14 ft/lbs.

4000 and 5000

1. Drain the cooling system.
2. Remove the V-belts, timing belt covers and timing belts as outlined earlier in this section.
3. On the 4000, unscrew the water pump pulley retaining bolts (3) and remove the pulley.
4. On the 4000, unscrew the intermediate shaft drive sprocket retaining bolt and remove the sprocket.
5. Unscrew the water pump retaining bolts and remove the pump from its housing on the 4000 or from the engine block on all other models.
6. Always replace the old gasket with a new one.
7. Installation is in the reverse order of removal.

Thermostat

REMOVAL AND INSTALLATION

100 Series and Fox

1. Drain the coolant from the radiator.
2. The thermostat is inside a cast housing on the engine or the water pump, connected to the upper radiator hose. Unbolt the cover and remove the gasket and the thermostat.
3. Some thermostats have an arrow on the bar which should also point at the projection.

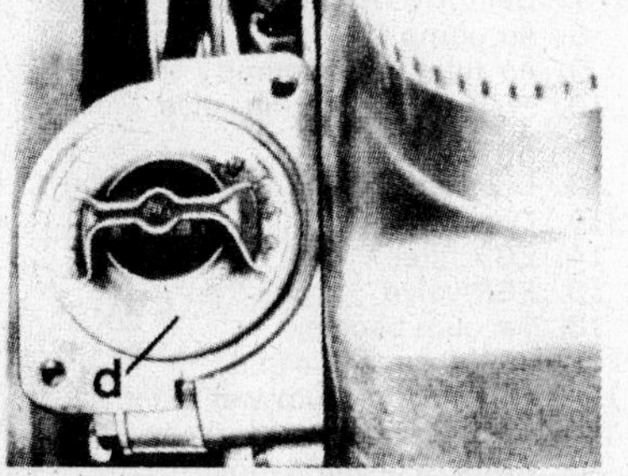

Correct installation of the front mounted 100 series thermostat

In any case, the bar should be up. The housing bolts should be torqued to 7 ft/lbs. Always use a new gasket.

4000 (4 cylinder)

The thermostat is located in the lower radiator hose neck on the bottom of the water pump housing.

1. Drain the cooling system.
2. Remove the two retaining bolts from the lower water pump neck.

NOTE: It is not necessary to disconnect the lower radiator hose.

3. Move the neck, with the hoses attached, out of the way.
4. Carefully pry the thermostat out of the water pump housing.

4000 (5 Cylinder), 5000

The thermostat is located in the lower radiator hose neck, on the left side of the engine block, behind the water pump housing.

Follow Steps 1-3 of the 4000 procedure.

1. Carefully pry the thermostat out of the engine block.
2. Install a new O-ring on the water pump neck.

Thermostat housing—5000

3. Install the thermostat.

NOTE: When installing the thermostat, the spring end should be pointing toward the engine block.

4. Reposition the water pump neck and tighten the retaining bolts.

Belt Tension Adjustment

1. Loosen the two bolts holding the fan housing to the fan support arm.

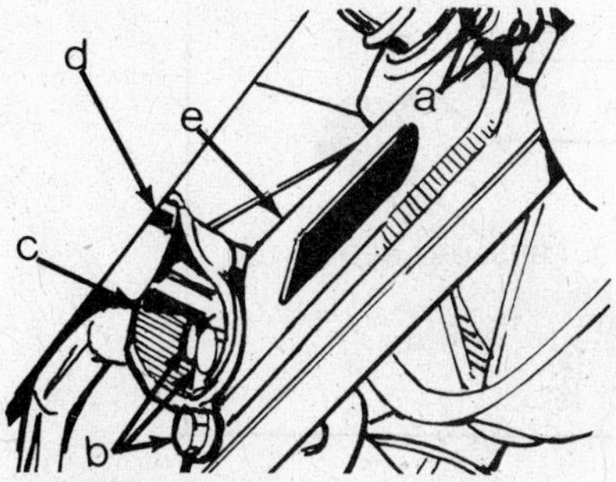

(a) Bolts-adjusting (b) Mounting bolts (c) Pad (d) Stop (e) Fan support

Radiator fan belt tension is adjusted with bolts

2. Move the fan and housing out to tighten the belt. The belt is correctly tensioned when the longest span of belt between pulleys can be depressed about ½ in. by moderate thumb pressure.
3. Tighten the bolts.

EMISSION CONTROLS

Several emission control devices are used to control different sources of emissions. Engine crankcase emissions are controlled by routing them directly into the carburetor air cleaner or into the fuel vapor control system, which is connected to the air cleaner.

Fuel vapor emissions from the carburetor float bowl and the fuel tank are handled by the fuel vapor control system. The system has an activated carbon container in the engine compartment to store vapors until they can be drawn in through the air cleaner and burned.

100 Series

The 100, 100LS, and 100GL use certain basic equipment to control exhaust emissions. The parts of the system are: a triple port intake manifold.

The triple port intake manifold has a separate intake for water, used to preheat the manifold. The preheating and the conduction of the fuel/air mixture from each stage separately leads to more complete combustion and a lower level of exhaust emissions.

The distributor uses both centrifugal and vacuum advance mechanisms.

All 100 series models are equipped with a capacitive discharge ignition system. This system reduces the normal decline in ignition system performance between tune-ups, keeping exhaust emissions at a minimum. It does this primarily reducing the electrical load on the breaker points and supplying very high voltage to the spark plugs.

NOTE: Some tachometers, dwell meters, and oscilloscopes will not work with this system. Some may be damaged. Check with the manufacturer of your best equipment if there is any doubt.

1975-76 models have the Audi continuous fuel injection system and the air injection system. California models only have a catalytic converter in the exhaust system.

Fox

The Fox uses emission control systems very similar to those on the 100 series. The fuel evaporation control system differs only in that it does not require a fuel recirculation line.

All models have the Audi continuous fuel injection system. California models only have a catalytic converter in the exhaust system.

4000 and 5000

A closed, positive crankcase ventilation system (PCV) is employed on all 4000 and 5000 models. This system cycles incompletely burned fuel which works its way past the piston rings back into the intake manifold for

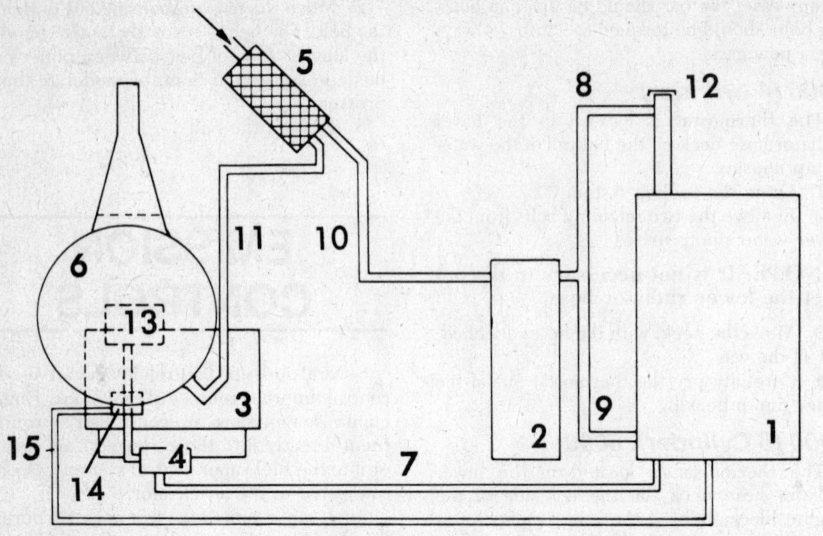

1. Fuel tank
2. Vapor expansion container
3. Engine
4. Fuel pump
5. Activated carbon container
6. Air cleaner
7. Fuel line from tank to pump
8. Breather line from neck to expansion container
9. Breather line from tank to expansion container
10. Breather line to carbon container
11. Line from carbon
11. Line from carbon container to air cleaner
12. Non-vented tank filler cap
13. Carburetor
14. Fuel return valve
15. Line from return valve to tank

Fuel vapor emission control system—typical

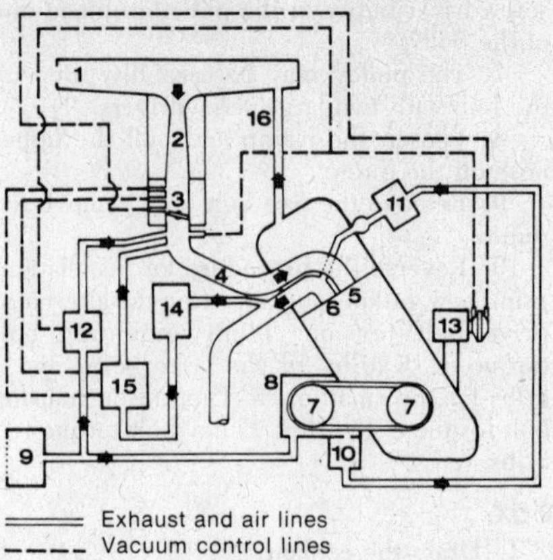

1. Air cleaner
2. Carburetor venturi
3. Throttle valve
4. Intake manifold
5. Cylinder head intake port
6. Cylinder head exhaust port
7. Belt drive for air pump
8. Air pump
9. Air pump filter
10. Pressure relief valve
11. Check valve
12. Diverter valve
13. Distributor
14. EGR filter
15. EGR valve
16. Crankcase ventilation

Emission control schematic for Fox

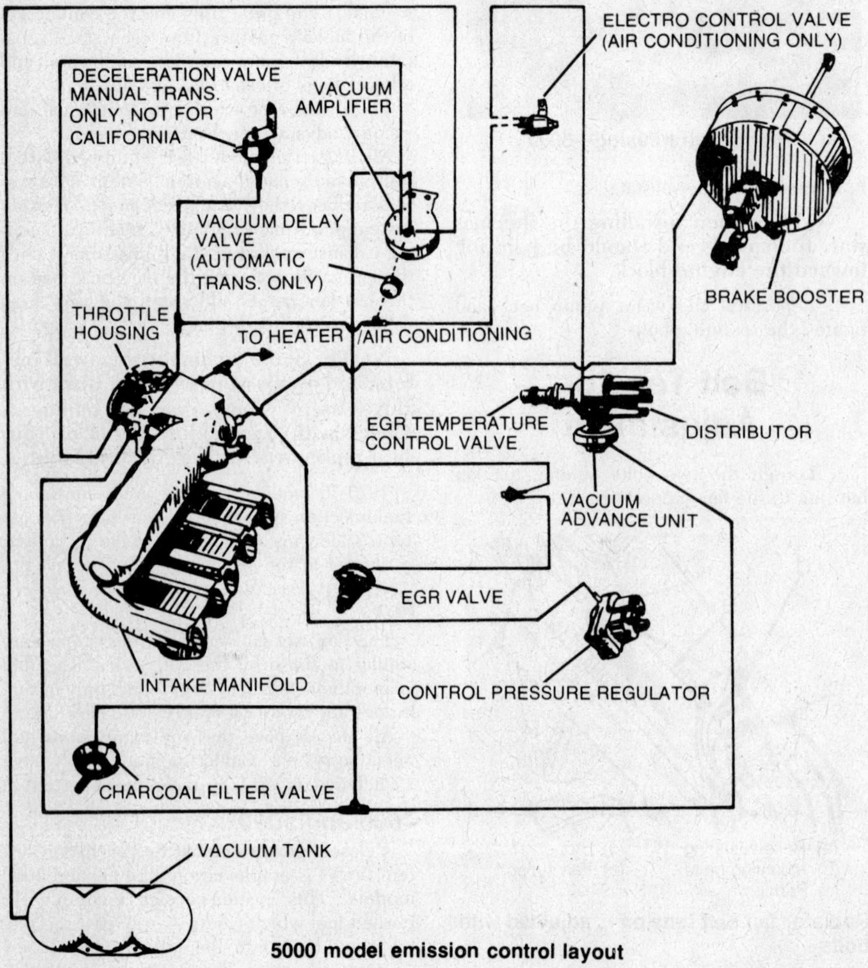

5000 model emission control layout

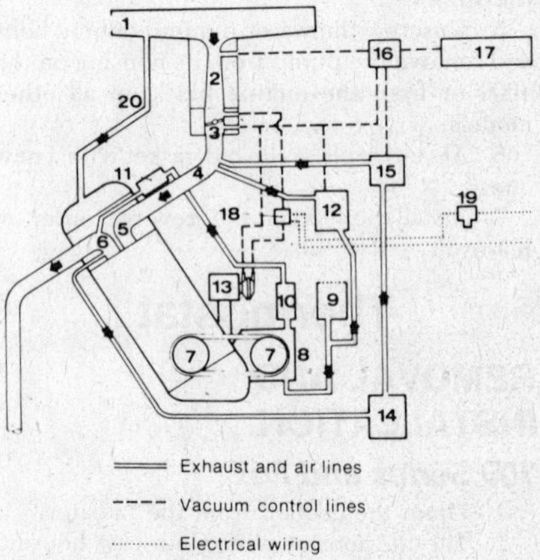

1. Air cleaner
2. Carburetor venturi
3. Throttle valve
4. Intake manifold
5. Cylinder head intake port
6. Cylinder head exhaust port
7. Belt drive for air pump
8. Air pump
9. Air filter for air pump
10. Pressure regulating valve
11. Check valve
12. Diverter valve
13. Distributor
14. EGR filter
15. EGR valve
16. Vacuum booster
17. Vacuum reserve
18. Solenoid vacuum valve
19. Temperature switch for cooling circuit
20. Crankcase ventilation

Emission control schematic for 100 LS

reburning with the fuel/air mixture. The oil filler cap is sealed and the air is drawn from the top of the crankcase into the intake manifold through a valve with a variable orfice (commonly known as a PCV valve).

The evaporative emission control system on these models includes: a sealed filler cap, a gravity vent valve, an activated charcoal canister, a charcoal canister control valve and a fuel pump check valve. All models are equipped with a dual diaphragm distributor. The purpose of the distributor is to reduce exhaust emissions during idling.

All Audis, with the exception of the 5000 Turbo, the 4000 5 cylinder and any 1979 and later car built for use in California are equipped with an EGR system to control part throttle exhaust emissions. Audi uses a vacuum operated EGR valve controlled primarily by a connection near the throttle plate where the vacuum is only present at part throttle. The EGR system also includes a temperature valve (two on cars equipped with air conditioning) which acts on engine coolant temperature, a vacuum amplifier that acts basically like a relay and a deceleration valve (found only on certain models) that aids in the fuel/air mixture adjustment on deceleration.

To aid in the reduction of exhaust emissions a catalytic converter is built into the exhaust system. There are two types of catalytic converters used: An oxidizing type and a three way type. The oxidixing type is used on the 1978 5000 (Calif.), the 1979-81 5000 (49 state) and the 1980-81 4000 (49 state). The three way type is used on the 5000 Turbo and the 4000 5 cylinder.

FUEL SYSTEM

Fuel Pump

REMOVAL AND INSTALLATION

100 Series

The fuel pump is on the left side of the engine, in front of the distributor.

1. Disconnect the hoses from the pump. Plug the inlet hose.
2. Remove the mounting bolts and pull out the pump.
3. When replacing the pump, use a new insulator. No other gaskets are required.

1975-77 Fox

The fuel pump is on the left side of the engine, in front of distributor.

1. Disconnect the hoses from the pump. Plug the inlet hose.
2. Remove the mounting bolts and remove the pump with the plastic insulator.
3. Reverse the procedure on installation.

1978-79 Fox

An electric pump is located on a bracket in the right rear wheel well.

1. Disconnect and plug the hoses.
2. Remove the mounting bolts and lift off the pump.
3. Installation is the reverse of removal.

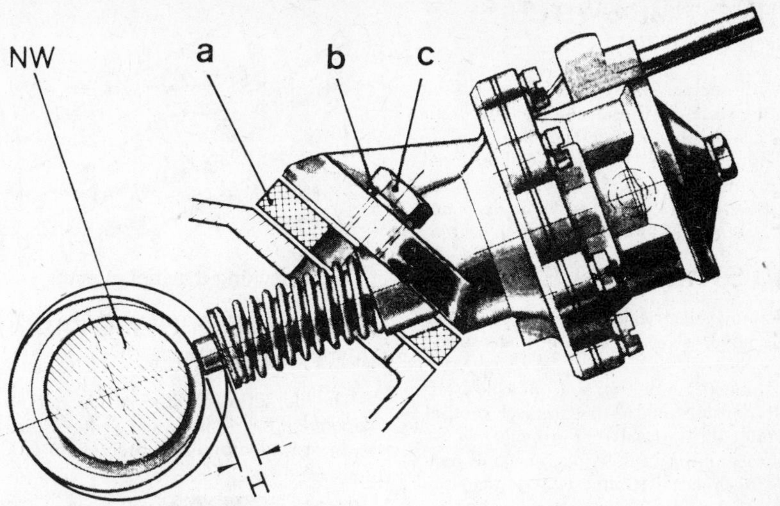

100 series fuel pump. (NW) is the camshaft, (a) is the insulator, (b) is the lockwasher and (c) is the mounting bolt

4000 and 5000

An electric pump is used, mounted on a bracket near the right rear wheel well.

1. Disconnect the battery ground.
2. Clean all fuel and electrical connections.
3. Disconnect the pump wiring.
4. Disconnect the fuel lines.
5. Unbolt and dismount the pump.
6. Installation is the reverse of removal. Torque the mounting bolts to 14 ft/lbs.

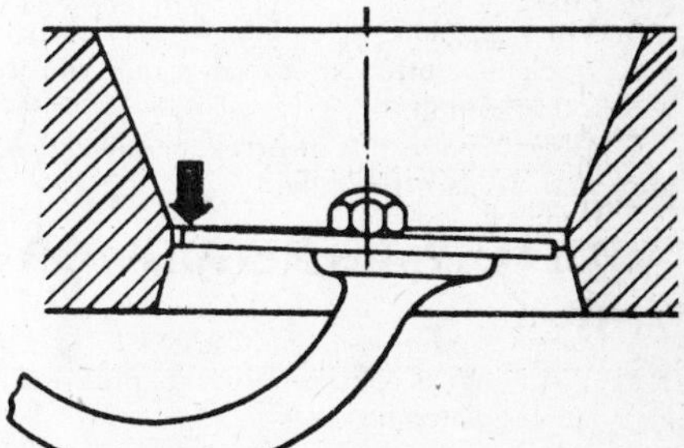

Sensor plate rest position

Fuel Injection

SENSOR PLATE POSITION ADJUSTMENT

1. Loosen fuel line-to-control pressure regulator connection at fuel distributor.
2. Upper edge of sensor plate must be flush with edge of air cone. Adjust if too high. Plate may be lower, but not by more than .019".
3. To adjust, remove air flow sensor with upper part of air cleaner.
4. Remove air filter.
5. Adjust spring stop by bending wire bracket.
6. Check and adjust idle, if necessary.

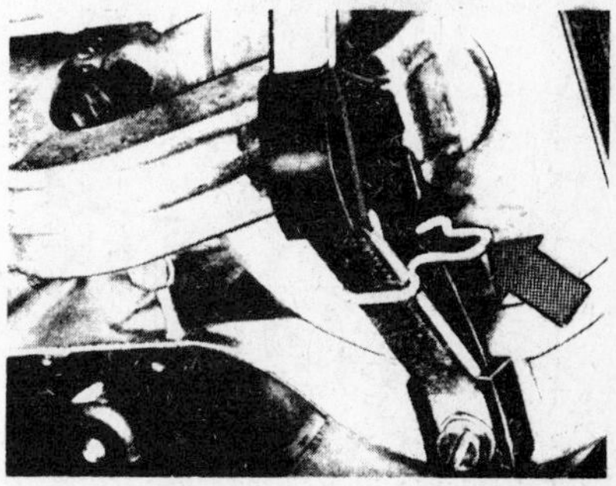

Adjustment point on wire bracket—bend here

CONTROL PRESSURE TEST-ENGINE COLD

1. Connect a pressure gauge in-line from fuel distributor to control pressure regulator.
2. Remove electrical connector from regulator.
3. Run engine at idle for no more than one minute.
4. Note control pressure. At room temperature, pressure should be 18-24 psi.

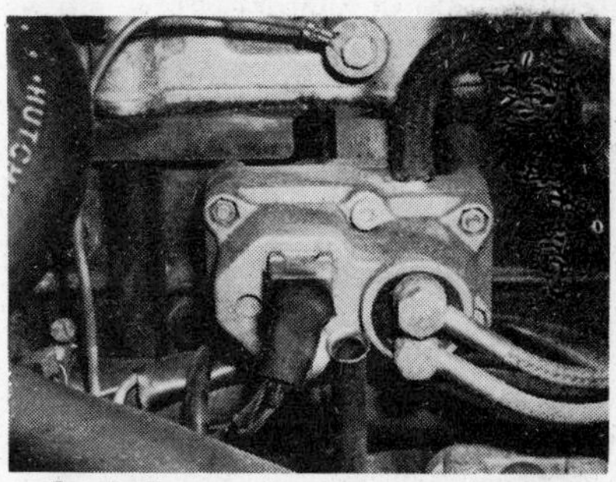

Control pressure regulator—5000

FUEL PUMP DELIVERY CHECK

1. Connect ground wire to #1 coil terminal.
2. Remove fuel return line and hold it in a measuring flask.
3. Crank engine for 30 seconds. Delivery reading must be 24 ounces. If less, replace the pump.

THERMO-TIME SWITCH CHECK

1. With engine cold, remove harness plug from cold start valve and connect test light across harness plug connectors.
2. Connect jumper wire from coil terminal #1 to ground.
3. Operate starter. If test light does not light for about 8 seconds, replace the switch.

COLD START VALVE CHECK

1. Remove electrical connector from valve.
2. Remove valve and hold in a measuring flask.
3. Connect jumper wire from cold start valve to coil terminal #15. Connect another wire from cold start valve to ground.
4. Run pump by removing relay and connecting terminals L13 and L14 on plate. (8 amp fuse should be connected in jumper wire.)
5. Turn on ignition switch and observe spray pattern. Pattern should be cone-shaped and steady.
6. Turn ignition off and wipe nozzle dry with a clean cloth. No drops should form within one minute.
7. If spray pattern is incorrect or leakage is observed, replace the valve.

AUXILIARY AIR REGULATOR CHECK

1. With engine cold, remove and plug auxiliary air regulator hose.
2. Run engine at idle; after 5 minutes the gate valve must be closed.

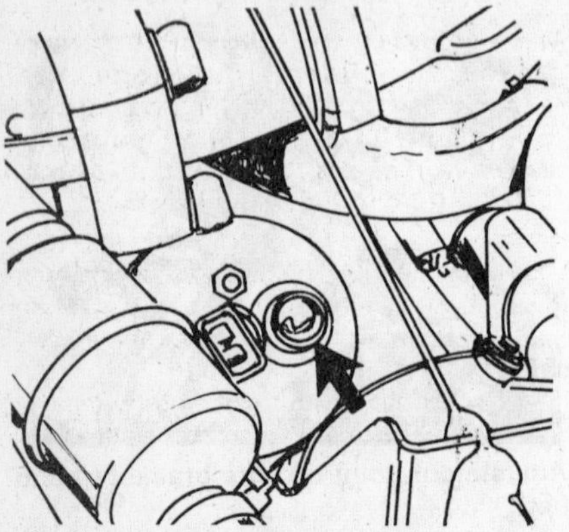

Auxiliary air regulator—arrow shows gate valve

INJECTOR REMOVAL, TESTING AND INSTALLATION

1. Remove injector from engine, but leave it connected to the fuel line.
2. Point injector into measuring flask and operate starter for 15 seconds. Spray should be even and conical.
3. Turn off ignition. Injector should not drip.
4. Moisten rubber seal on injector with fuel.
5. Press injectors fully into seat.

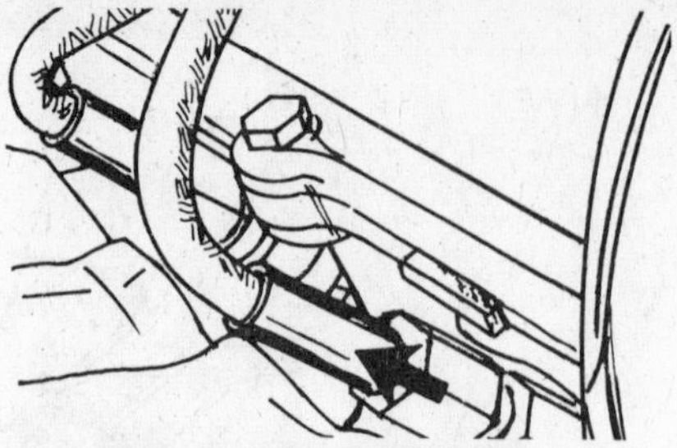

Checking the fuel injector

FUEL FILTER REMOVAL AND INSTALLATION

The fuel filter is bolted in-line and must be uncoupled for replacement. Filter is installed with arrows pointing in direction of flow.

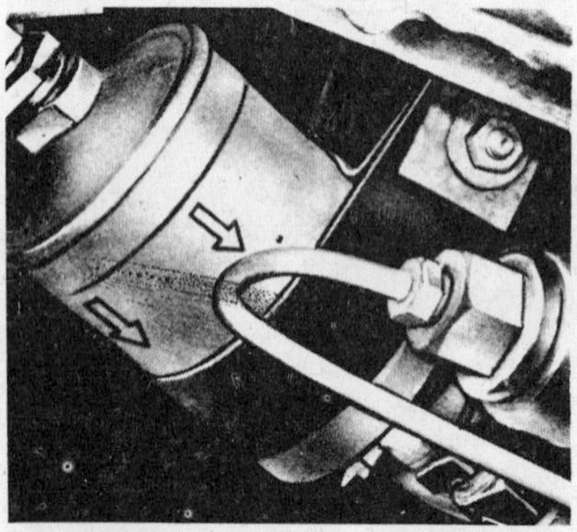

Installing the fuel filter, except 5000.

Fuel filter—5000

Fox fuel pump connections

FUEL DISTRIBUTOR REMOVAL AND INSTALLATION

1. Clean and remove fuel lines at distributor.
2. Remove retaining bolts and carefully lift out distributor. Take care not to drop control piston.
3. If control plunger has been removed, moisten with fuel before installing and insert small shoulder first.
4. Reinstall distributor using new O-rings.

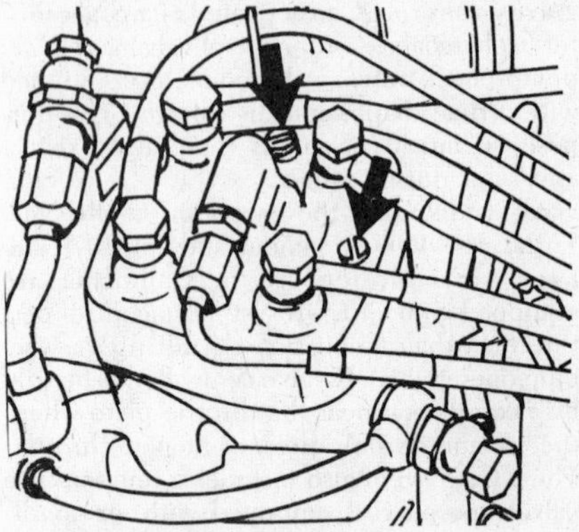

Fuel distributor attaching screws

FUEL PUMP CHECK VALVE REPLACEMENT

1. Remove right rear wheel.
2. Remove gas tank filler cap.
3. Clean and disconnect fuel line connections.
4. Remove screw connector, which contains check valve, and replace using a new seal.
5. Torque connector to 14-18 in/lbs.
6. Reconnect fuel line using new seals.

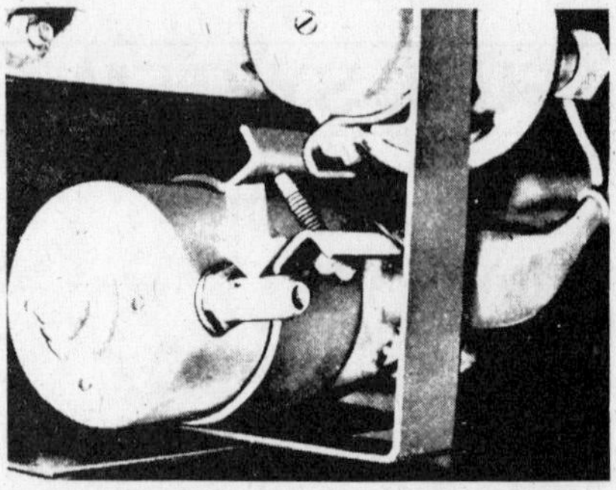

Fox fuel pump check valve locations

MANUAL TRANSMISSION

The transmission is combined with the differential in a transaxle.

REMOVAL AND INSTALLATION

100 Series

The engine/transaxle unit must be removed from the car as explained under "Engine Removal and Installation." Then the transmission can simply be unbolted from the engine and slid back. On replacement, tighten the bolts to 54, 33, and 18 ft/lbs, respectively, for the three sizes of bolts.

Fox

The transaxle can be lowered from the car, leaving the engine in place.

1. Disconnect the battery ground cable. Raise the car on a chassis lift.
2. Detach and wire up the entire exhaust system.
3. Release the lockplates and remove the axle shaft bolts. Wire the shafts up.
4. Use pliers to unscrew the speedometer cable nut.
5. Support the transaxle. Remove the engine to transaxle bolts and the clutch guard plate.
6. Remove the lock wire and unscrew the gearshift rod coupling square headed bolt. Pull off the gearshift rod.
7. Disconnect the gearshift strut at the transmission and unbolt the small crossmember at the rear of the transmission.
8. Disconnect the backup light and seat belt system wires at the transmission.
9. Separate the transaxle from the engine and lower it. Reverse the procedure on installation. Torque the engine to transaxle bolts to 40 ft/lbs and the axle shaft bolts to 28 ft/lbs.

4000

This procedure can be performed with the engine installed.

1. Disconnect the negative battery cable.
2. Unplug the two electrical connectors for the back-up lights. They can be found between the ignition coil and the fuel distributor filter.
3. Remove the upper engine/transmission bolts.
4. Using special tool 3016 or a pair of pliers, detach the speedometer cable where it attaches to the transaxle.
5. Detach the clutch cable from the clutch lever.
6. Unbolt the exhaust pipe from the exhaust manifold.
7. Unscrew the three mounting bolts and remove the center engine mount.
8. Unbolt the front exhaust pipe from the support bracket and then unbolt it from the catalytic converter (muffler on Canadian models).
9. Unscrew the six screws and remove the left halfshaft from the transaxle. Wire the halfshaft up and out of the way. Repeat the procedure for the right halfshaft.

CAUTION

When wiring the halfshaft, tighten the wire only enough so as to relieve any downward pressure on them.

10. Remove the cover plate.
11. Tag and disconnect all wires leading to the starter and remove the starter.
12. Remove the bolt from the shift rod coupling.
13. Pry off the linkage coupling.
14. Pull the shift rod coupling off of the shift rod.
15. Loosen the left (chassis) bolt on the rear transmission support. Remove the two bolts (some models have one) from the right (transmission) side of the support and pivot the support out of the way.
16. Remove the rubber mounting block.
17. Unscrew three bolts and remove the front transmission support.
18. Remove the lower engine/transmission bolts.
19. Carefully pry the transmission apart from the engine and remove it.
20. Installation is in the reverse order of removal.

Note the following:

a. Make sure that all engine/transmission mounts are correctly aligned and free of tension.

b. Check for proper adjustment of the gear shift lever.

c. Secure the bolt on the shift rod coupling with wire.

d. Tighten the engine/transmission bolts to 40 ft/lbs.

e. Tighten the halfshaft to drive flange bolts to 33 ft/lbs.

f. Tighten the subframe to body bolts to 51 ft/lbs.

g. Tighten the front transmission support to transmission bolts to 18 ft/lbs.

h. Tighten the rubber mount to body bolts to 29 ft/lbs (new mount, 80 ft/lbs).

i. Tighten the rubber mount to transmission bolts to 40 ft/lbs.

j. Tighten the rubber mount to crossmember bolts to 18 ft/lbs.

5000

The manual transaxle may be remove with the engine in place.

1. Disconnect the battery ground.
2. Remove the air filter (Diesel only).
3. Remove the windshield washer bottle.
4. Remove the upper engine-transmission bolts.
5. Raise and support the car.
6. Disconnect the speedometer cable at the engine.
7. Disconnect all wires and hoses connected to the transaxle.
8. Drive out the clutch slave cylinder lockpin and remove the slave cylinder. Leave the hydraulic line connected.
9. Support the engine, either from above with a hoist or from below with a jack.
10. Remove the heat shield.
11. Remove the lower engine/transmission splash shield (Diesel only).
12. Disconnect the exhaust pipe from the manifold.
13. Remove the right side guard plate.
14. Disconnect the driveshafts from the flanges and support them out of the way with wires.
15. Disconnect the backup light switch.
16. Pry off the shift and adjusting rods.
17. Remove the lower engine-transmission bolts.
18. Remove the starter.
19. Remove the subframe skid plate.
20. Install a jack under the transmission and lift it slightly.
21. Remove both transmission to subframe bolts.
22. Remove the right side transmission bracket.
23. Slide the transmission back off the locating dowels and remove it from the car.
24. When installing, place the driveshafts on top of the subframe; tighten the lower bolts first, then tighten the transmission bracket, subframe and upper bolts. Driveshaft bolts are torqued to 32 ft/lbs; transmission bracket bolts to 29 ft/lbs; subframe support bolts to 29 ft/lbs; subframe to body bolts to 80 ft/lbs and the transmission to engine bolts to 40 ft/lbs.

Install all other parts in reverse order of removal.

LINKAGE ADJUSTMENT

100 Series

1. Slide the seats all the way back and set the handbrake.
2. Remove the six sheet metal screws which secure the console. Unscrew the shift knob and lift off the console.
3. The shift lever bracket has a spring-loaded ball which should engage the groove in the long shift rod when the transmission is in Neutral.
4. To adjust, loosen the four bolts which hold the shift lever bracket to the floor and move the bracket to the front or rear. Tighten the bolts and recheck the adjustment. There is an adjustable linkage rod above the rear of the transmission for easier adjustment.

When adjusting the 100 series manual transmission floorshift linkage, the spring loaded ball should engage the slot (n) in the shift rod (33) when the transmission is in neutral. If it does not, loosen the bolts (8) and move the bracket.

5. If the long shift rod has a rubber damper apparatus in the middle, make sure that it is in good condition and not causing any unnecessary play.
6. Grease the moving parts lightly.
7. Replace the console and the shift knob.

Fox

1. Remove the rubber boot at the base of the shift lever.
2. Loosen the two bolts at the base of the lever and move the lever to the far right of the Neutral slot against the stop. Tighten the bolts.
3. If there is a problem with the lever sticking or jamming, loosen the two shift gate bolts from under the car and adjust the gate backward or forward. Tighten the bolts.

4000

NOTE: This procedure will require Special Tool VW 3014.

1. Place the shift lever in the Neutral position.
2. Working under the car, loosen the clamp nut on the shift rod.

3. Inside the car, remove the shift knob and the boot. It is not necessary to remove the console.

4. Align the holes in the shifter base with the holes in the bearing plate directly below it and tighten the bolts.

5. Install the Special Tool VW 3014 with the locating pin toward the front.

6. Push the shift lever to the left side of the tool cutout and tighten the lower knurled knob to secure the tool.

7. Move the top slide of the tool to the left side stop and tighten the upper knurled knot.

8. Push the shift lever into the right cutout of the slide. Align the shift rod and the shift finger under the car and tighten the clamp nut.

9. Remove the special tool.

10. Place the shift lever in the first gear position. Press the lever to the left side against the stop. Release the lever; it should spring back ¼ to ½ in. If not, move the lever housing slightly sideways to correct. Check that all gears can be engaged easily.

5000

1. Remove the gear shift boot.
2. Position the shift lever in neutral.
3. The seam on the plastic stop bracket should line up with the center hole in the curved stop plate. If not, proceed below:
4. Loosen the four bolts at the base of the shifter.
5. Align the holes in the shifter base with the holes in the bearing plate directly below it.
6. Tighten the bolts.
7. Loosen the clamp between the front and rear shift rods.
8. Make certain that the front shift rod is in the neutral position.

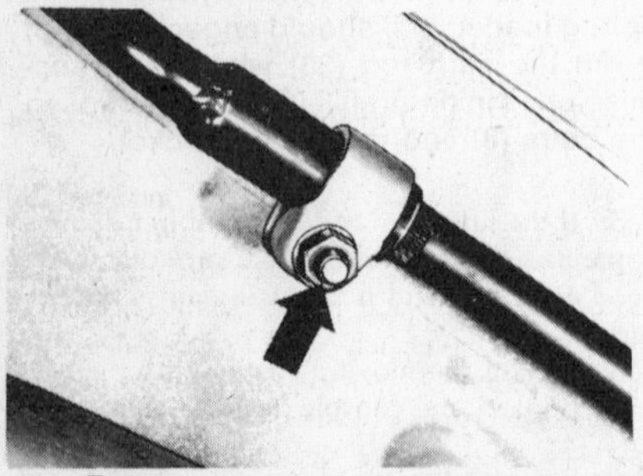

Front-to-rear rod clamp—5000

9. Clamp the shifter securely in the neutral position and tighten the shift rod clamp.

10. Release the shifter and check its operation in all gears.

11. Install the shifter boot, making sure that the top of the boot is in contact with the shift knob.

Shifter base plate bolts—5000

CLUTCH

REMOVAL AND INSTALLATION

100 Series

1. Remove the engine and transaxle as a unit.
2. Separate the engine and transaxle.
3. Mark the relationship of the pressure plate to the flywheel.
4. Unbolt the pressure plate from the flywheel, loosening the bolts alternately a little bit at a time to prevent warpage.
5. To install the clutch, place the driven plate on the pressure plate, making sure that it is facing the right way.
6. Hold the clutch assembly against the flywheel, aligning the marks in Step 3, and insert a dummy shaft through the pressure plate and the driven plate into the crankshaft pilot bearing.

Before removing the pressure plate bolts (a) mark the pressure plate (b) and the flywheel as shown at the arrow. The dummy shaft (d) is used to center the driven plate (clutch disc) on reinstallation.

7. Install the pressure plate bolts finger tight. Then tighten the bolts evenly, in rotation, to avoid distortion. Torque the bolts to 24-27 ft/lbs. Remove the dummy shaft.
8. The clutch release bearing in the front of the transmission housing should be checked before reassembly. It is retained by two springs.
9. Bolt the transaxle back to the engine. Bolt torque is 54, 33, and 18 ft/lbs, respectively, for the three sizes of bolts.
10. Replace the engine/transaxle unit in the car. Check the clutch adjustment.

Fox, 4000 and 5000

1. Remove the transaxle.
2. Mark the relationship of the pressure plate to the flywheel (only if it is to be reused).
3. Unbolt the pressure plate from the flywheel, loosening the bolts alternately, a little at a time, to prevent warpage.
4. To install the clutch, place the driven plate on the pressure plate, making sure that it is facing the right way.
5. Hold the clutch assembly against the flywheel, aligning the marks made in Step 2 and the three dowel pins on the flywheel with the pressure plate, and insert a dummy shaft through the pressure plate and the driven plate into the crankshaft pilot bearing.
6. Install the pressure plate bolts finger tight. Then tighten the bolts evenly, in rotation, to avoid distortion. Torque the bolts to 24 ft/lbs. Remove the dummy shaft.

Clamping the shifter in neutral—5000

Plastic stop bracket alignment on the 5000 shift control

7. The clutch release bearing in the front of the transaxle should be checked before reassembly. It is retained by two springs.

8. Replace the transaxle. Torque the engine-to-transaxle bolts to 40 ft/lbs and the axle shaft to 28 ft/lbs.

PEDAL FREE-PLAY ADJUSTMENT

100 Series and Fox

The pedal free-play is adjusted at the clutch end of the cable. Free-play is the distance that the pedal travels from the released position to the point at which clutch spring pressure can be felt. This can be measured by placing a yardstick alongside the clutch pedal. Play should be 0.6-0.8 in.

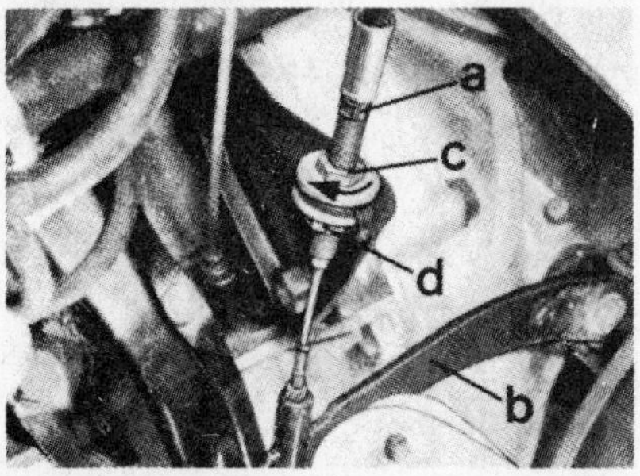

Clutch adjustment point on the 100 series and Fox. (a) is the clutch cable, (b) is the clutch lever, (c) and (d) are the adjusting nuts

1. On the 100, loosen the upper cable nut. Turn both nuts clockwise to reduce play, and counterclockwise to increase. After the adjustment is made, tighten the upper nut to lock the cable in place.

2. The total pedal travel on the 100 series should be at least 6.1 in. If it is not adequate, the pedal pivot can be loosened and moved up.

4000

Free-play is the distance that the pedal travels from the released position to the point at which clutch spring pressure can first be felt. This can be measured by placing a yardstick alongside the clutch pedal. Free-play should be ⅝ of an inch, measured at the pedal.

1. Locate the clutch cable bracket by the oil filter.

2. Loosen the upper cable nut.

3. Turn both nuts clockwise to reduce pedal free-play or counterclockwise to increase it.

4. When adjustment is correct, tighten the upper nut to lock the cable in position.

PEDAL HEIGHT ADJUSTMENT

5000

The clutch pedal should be at rest ⅜ inch above the brake pedal. To adjust the pedal height, remove the cotter pin holding the clutch master cylinder clevis to the pedal, loosen the locknut on the clevis shaft and turn the shaft to give the required pedal height. Tighten the locknut and install the clevis on the pedal.

Clutch Cable

REMOVAL AND INSTALLATION

1. Loosen the adjustment.

2. Disengage the cable from the clutch arm.

3. Unhook the cable from the pedal. Remove the threaded eye from the end of the cable. Remove the adjustment nut(s).

4. Remove the C-clip which holds the outer cable at the adjustment point. Remove all the washers and bushings, first noting their locations.

5. Pull the cable out of the firewall toward the engine compartment side.

6. Install and connect the new cable. Adjust the pedal free-play.

AUTOMATIC TRANSMISSION

The Audi automatic transmission is a hydraulically operated three-speed unit, with a torque converter.

REMOVAL AND INSTALLATION

100 Series

The automatic transmission can be disconnected from the engine and removed with the engine in the car.

1. Drain the transmission. Remove the grille and front apron. The engine must be mounted to the frame in some manner or suspended on a lift or jack to prevent it from falling from the mounts when the mounts are disconnected.

2. Loosen the brake pipe lines from the brake hoses and plug the ends of the brake hoses.

3. Disconnect the accelerator linkage.

4. Remove the front exhaust pipe.

5. Remove the oil filter and starter.

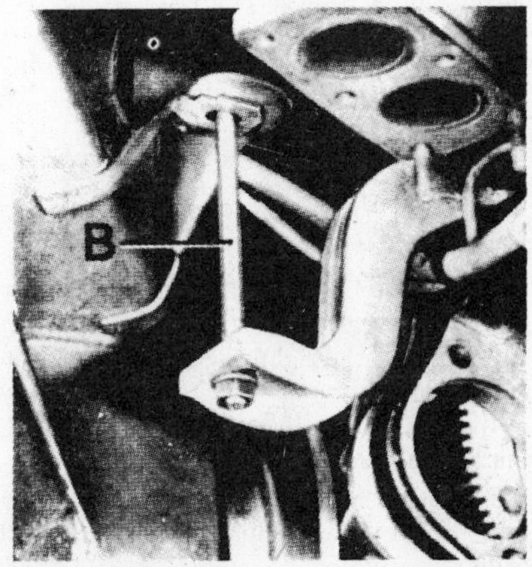

Insert bolts (B) through each engine mount to support the 100 series engine. Note that the starter has been removed for access to the torque converter bolts

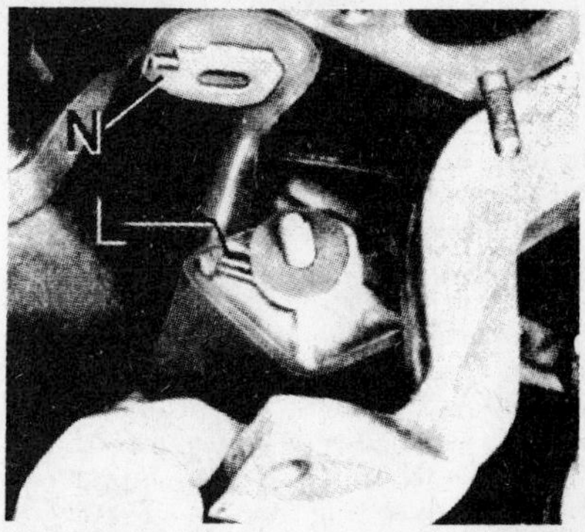

Be sure that the projection (N) engages the groove (L) of the 100 series mount

6. Disconnect both driveshafts and suspend them from the upper wishbones. Disconnect the stabilizer bar at both lower wishbones.

7. Unbolt the holder for the selector cable at the transmission. Remove the selector cable from the lever at the transmission. Remove the selector cable holder.

8. Disconnect the crossmember at the engine mounting and at the support. Place a jack or support under the transmission.

9. Remove the guard and disconnect the left and right engine mounts. Be careful not to alter the position of the left mount, which is fixed by means of locknuts.

10. Insert bolts (⅜ in. x 8 in.) through each side in place of the engine mounts. Lower the complete power plant until the unit rests on the bolts.

11. Disconnect the transmission vacuum hose at the vacuum unit or at the T adaptor.

12. Unbolt the torque converter Allen bolts by working through the hole for the starter.

13. Unbolt the engine-to-transmission connections and remove the transmission. Secure the torque converter in the transmission with a strap.

14. To install the transmission, reverse the removal procedure, noting the following: Lift the transmission and bolt it to the engine. Lift both the engine and transmission and install the selector lever holder. When installing the engine mounts, be sure that the projection engages the groove of the mount. After installing the engine and transmission assembly, check the alignment of the unit. Refer to "Engine Installation." Torque converter bolt torque is 22 ft/lbs. Transmission-to-engine bolt torque is 54, 33, and 18 ft/lbs, respectively, for the three bolt sizes. Refill the transmission.

Fox

The transaxle can be lowered from the car, leaving the engine in place.

1. Disconnect the battery ground cable.

2. Raise and support the car.

3. Remove the lockplates and remove the axle shaft bolts. Wire the shafts up.

4. Disconnect the vacuum hose. Remove the torque converter guard plate. Disconnect the kickdown switch wire.

5. Unscrew the speedometer cable nut.

6. Support the transaxle.

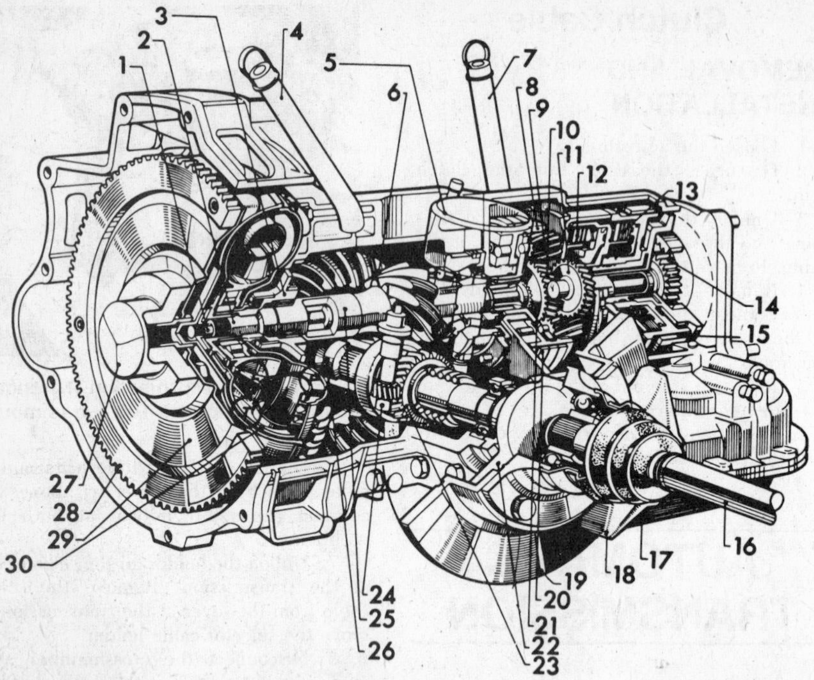

1. Pump shaft
2. Turbine shaft
3. Stator support
4. Oil filler tube, differential
5. Governor
6. Drive pinion
7. Filler tube, planetary gear
8. Annulus
9. Small planetary gear
10. Large sun gear
11. Large planetary pinion
12. Forward clutch
13. Direct and reverse clutch
14. Oil pump
15. 2nd gear brake band
16. Driveshaft
17. Oil pan
18. Brake caliper
19. Brake disc
20. Ist gear and reverse brake band
21. Planetary gear carrier
22. Stub axle
23. Impeller, governor and speedometer
24. Speedometer pinion shaft
25. Drive pinion shaft
26. Differential
27. Crankshaft, engine
28. Gear ring
29. Drive plate
30. Torque converter

(P)—Impeller
(L)—Stator
(T)—Turbine

Cross-section of the 100 series automatic transmission (transaxle)

7. Remove the upper engine-to-transaxle bolts.
8. Remove the starter and remove the three torque converter bolts through the starter opening.
9. Unbolt the small crossmember at the rear of the transmission.
10. Lower the transaxle slightly.
11. Detach the shift linkage cable at the transmission.
12. Remove the lower engine-to-transaxle bolts.
13. Separate the transaxle from the engine and lower it. Secure the torque converter in the transmission with a strap. Reverse the procedure on installation. Torque the engine-to-transaxle bolts to 40 ft/lbs and the torque converter bolts to 20-23 ft/lbs. New torque converter bolts and washers must be used. Torque the axle shaft bolts to 28 ft/lbs.
14. Check the shift linkage adjustment.

5000

1. Disconnect the battery ground.
2. Remove the windshield washer bottle.
3. Drain the cooling system.
4. Remove the hoses from the transmission cooler.
5. Remove the upper end of the accelerator linkage rod.
6. Disconnect the speedometer cable at the bell housing.
7. Remove the upper engine-to-transmission bolts.
8. Raise and support the car.
9. Using a chain hoist or jack, support the engine and raise it just enough to take the weight off of the mounts.
10. Remove the skid plate from the subframe.
11. Disconnect the exhaust pipe from the transmission and the manifold.
12. Remove the right driveshaft guard plate.
13. Remove the right and left driveshafts.
14. Remove the starter.
15. Remove the selector lever cable and holder from the transmission.
16. Remove the lower accelerator linkage rod.
17. Remove the accelerator cable from the transmission support.
18. Remove the right side guard plate from the subframe.
19. Remove both transmission mounts from the subframe.
20. Rotate the torque converter and remove each bolt as it appears in the starter opening.
21. Place a jack under the transmission and raise it slightly.
22. Remove the lower engine-to-transmission bolts.
23. Remove the rear subframe mounting bolts.
24. Swing both driveshafts rearward out of the way.
25. Separate the transmission from the engine and carefully lower the transmission on the jack.
26. Installation is the reverse of removal.

CAUTION

Be sure that the torque converter is fully seated on the one-way clutch support. When the converter is properly seated, the distance between the converter cover nose and the end of the bell housing should be 0.393 (10 mm) inch.

27. Install the lower engine-to-transmission bolts first, then the transmission-to-subframe bolts.
28. Observe the following torques: converter bolts 22 ft/lbs; transmission-to-engine bolts 40 ft/lbs; starter bolts 40 ft/lbs; subframe to body 80 ft/lbs.
29. Adjust the throttle kickdown switch.

PAN REMOVAL AND INSTALLATION

The automatic transmission fluid should be changed and the pan cleaned out every 20,000 miles. The interval should be shortened to 12,000 miles under severe use such as city driving or trailer towing.

To change the fluid:

1. Run the engine in Neutral for a minute or two.
2. Make sure that the vehicle is parked on level ground. Stop the engine.
3. Place a pan of at least four quarts capacity under the transmission.
4. Remove the plug from the transmission bottom pan, after wiping the area clean.
5. Remove the starter on the 100 series.
6. Remove and clean out the pan.
7. Replace the pan, using a new gasket. Torque the bolts to 7 ft/lbs. Wait ten minutes and retorque the bolts.
8. Clean off the plug, particularly the threads, and replace it.
9. Replace the starter on the 100 series.
10. Pour in five pints of fluid through the dipstick filler tube. The proper transmission fluid is Dexron® or Dexron® II.
11. Start the engine and shift through all the lever positions.
12. The level should reach the tip of the dipstick. Add fluid until the level reaches this point.
13. Take a short test drive. Fill the transmission until the level is between the marks on the dipstick. Retorque the bolts.

NOTE: If the transmission is overfilled, the excess must be drained.

KICKDOWN SWITCH

100 Series and Fox Models

The kickdown switch is mounted behind the accelerator pedal. With the ignition switch on, the switch should make an audible click when the pedal is pressed all the way down.

The transmission should downshift when

the accelerator is depressed to the wide open throttle position at speeds between 39 and 65 mph for second gear, and 16 and 36 mph for first gear.

5000

1. Position the accelerator pedal in the fully released position.
2. Check the distance between the pedal lower edge and the pedal stop. Clearance should be 3.0 inches.
3. If not, loosen the lockbolt which holds the cable at the pedal and place the pedal to give the three inch clearance. Tighten the lockbolt.

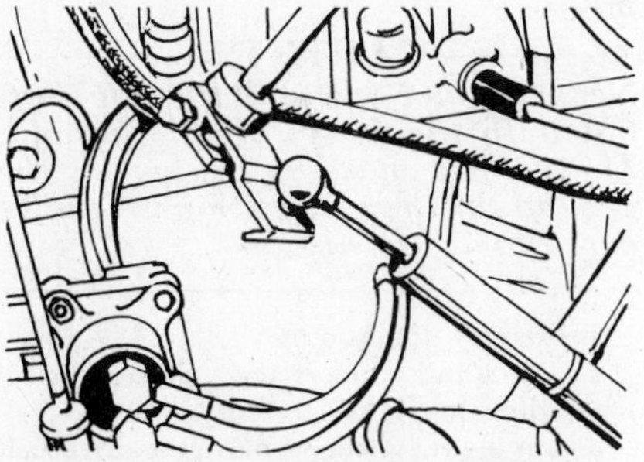

Kickdown detent linkage—5000

4. Press the pedal to the full throttle position but not into the kickdown detent. The kickdown take-up spring should not be compressed and the throttle valve should be wide open.
5. Adjust the shift linkage.

NEUTRAL SAFETY SWITCH ADJUSTMENT

The neutral safety switch prevents the engine from being started with the transmission in any position other than Park or Neutral. It also activates the backup lights. The switch is at the base of the shift lever, inside the floorshift console.

To replace or adjust the switch:

1. Remove the four screws which hold the console to the floor.
2. Shift into Neutral. Remove the two screws which hold the shift position indicator plate to the console. Remove the shift knob and the console.
3. Disconnect the switch electrical leads. These are: red/black—neutral safety; black—backup lights; blue/red—backup lights. The backup light wires are at the front.
4. Remove the two switch retaining screws. Remove the switch.
5. Install the new switch so that the neutral safety switch contacts are together.
6. Install the electrical connectors. Hold the footbrake while making sure that the engine will start only in Neutral and Park. Make sure that the backup lights operate only in Reverse. If the switch does not operate properly, it may have to be moved on its slotted mounting bracket.
7. Replace the console cover.

SHIFT LINKAGE ADJUSTMENT

The function of this adjustment is to make sure that the transmission is fully engaged in each shift position. If this is not done, the transmission may be only partially engaged in a range position. This would result in severe damage due to slippage.

1. Place the selector lever in Park.
2. Loosen the cable clamp nut at the transmission end. On the Fox, remove the rubber cover from the bottom of the shifter (underneath the car) and loosen the cable clamp screw.
3. Press the selector lever on the transmission back to the stop.
4. Tighten the clamp nut or screw.

VACUUM MODULATOR ADJUSTMENT

100 Series

The vacuum modulator, on the rear of the transmission, regulates the firmness and timing of shifts in relation to speed and throttle opening. A leaking modulator will result in transmission fluid being sucked into the engine through the vacuum modulator and burned. This will produce a smoky exhaust and a continually low transmission fluid level. The modulator must be adjusted any time it, or its seal, has been replaced. This adjustment is also necessary if the gearshift timing is incorrect.

1. Disconnect and plug the vacuum hose at the modulator.
2. Remove the test plug from the right side of the transmission. Connect a pressure gauge with a scale up to 150 psi.
3. Place the selector lever in Neutral and idle the engine at 1000 rpm. Adjust the modulator until the gauge shows 48.4 psi. Stop the engine.

Automatic transmission test gauge connections (Bs)

4. Remove the gauge and replace the plug and vacuum line.
5. The transmission should upshift with wide open throttle from First to Second gear at 19-21 mph, and from Second to Third at 54-58 mph.

BAND ADJUSTMENTS

100 Series

SECOND GEAR BAND

1. Loosen the locknut.
2. Tighten the adjusting screw to 87 in/lbs.
3. Loosen the adjusting screw and retighten to 44 in/lbs.
4. Turn the adjusting screw out 1¾-2 turns.
5. Tighten the locknut.

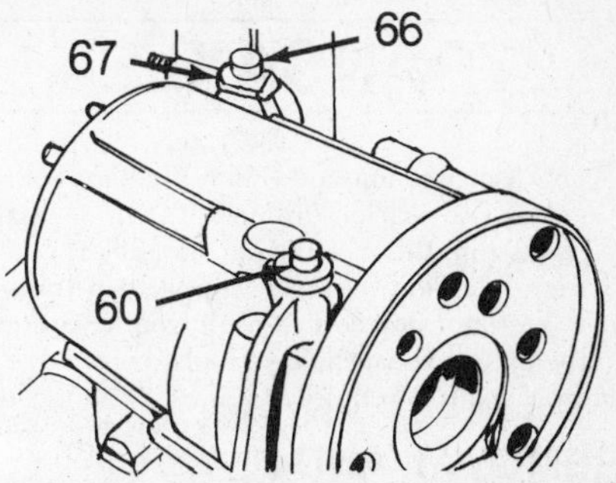

Automatic transmission second gear band adjusting screw and locknut (66) and (67). First gear band adjusting screw and locknut (60)

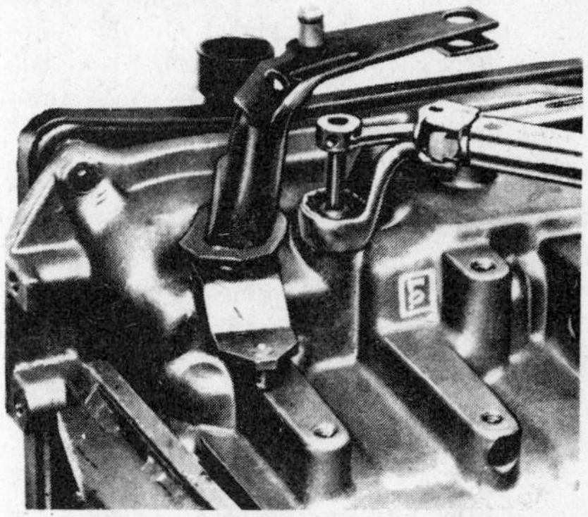

Second gear band adjustment

FIRST GEAR BAND

1. Loosen the locknut.
2. Tighten the adjusting screw to 87 in/lbs.
3. Loosen the adjusting screw and retighten to 44 in/lbs.
4. Turn the adjusting screw out 3¼-3¾ turns.
5. Tighten the locknut.

Fox

FIRST GEAR BAND

1. Loosen locknut.
2. Tighten first gear band adjusting screw to 7 ft/lbs.
3. Loosen adjusting screw and retighten to 3.5 ft/lbs.
4. Back off screw 3.25 to 3.5 turns and tighten locknut.

SECOND GEAR BAND

1. Loosen locknut.
2. Tighten adjusting screw to 7 ft/lbs.
3. Loosen screw and retighten to 3.5 ft/lbs.
4. Back off screw exactly 2.5 turns and tighten locknut.

NOTE: Transmission must be horizontal when adjusting bands or bands may jam.

5000

SECOND GEAR BAND

1. Loosen the locknut.
2. Tighten the adjusting screw to 7 ft/lbs.
3. Loosen the adjusting screw and retighten it to 4 ft/lbs.
4. Loosen the screw exactly 2½ turns.
5. Hold the screw and tighten the locknut.

TRANSAXLE

The transmission and differential are combined in a transaxle. On models with manual transmission, the transmission and differential share a common lubricant supply. No transaxle overhaul procedures are given here due to the extensive specialized tools, knowledge, and procedures required.

REMOVAL AND INSTALLATION

100 Series

The transaxle is removed from the car in unit with the engine. See "Engine Removal and Installation" for details. On the automatic, it is possible to remove the transaxle only, leaving the engine in place. See "Automatic Transmission Removal and Installation" for details.

Fox, 4000 and 5000

The transaxle can be removed from the car alone, leaving the engine in place. See Transmission Removal and Installation for details.

DRIVE AXLES

Each front wheel drive axle shaft has two Rzeppa constant velocity joints. These joints can handle lateral movement caused by suspension travel, as well as steering movements.

Driveshafts

REMOVAL AND INSTALLATION

100 Series

NOTE: A small puller or press is required for this job.

The steering knuckles must be removed along with the shafts.

1. Support the vehicle and remove the wheels. Let the front suspension hang free.
2. Have an assistant hold the brakes. Unbolt the driveshaft from the transmission stub axle and brake disc. There should be an insulator between the driveshaft and brake disc.
3. Remove the cotter pin and the castellated nut from the steering tie rod end. Press out the tie rod end from the steering knuckle arm. A small puller or press is required to free the tie rod end.
4. Remove the two steering knuckle mounting bolts.
5. Remove the steering knuckle and driveshaft assembly.
6. Reverse the procedure for installation. Torques are:
7. Check the wheel alignment.

Fox

1. With the wheels on the ground, remove the front wheel spindle nut.

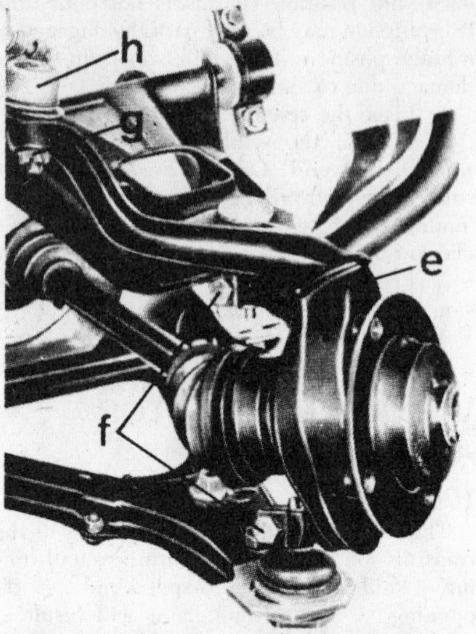

The castellated nut (g) and the cotter pin must be removed before pulling out the tie rod end (h) from the 100 series steering knuckle (e). (f) indicates the steering knuckle mounting bolts.

2. Unbolt the inner driveshaft coupling. If you are removing the right shaft, disconnect the front exhaust pipe at the manifold and the support on the transaxle. Push the inner end of the shaft up and let it rest on the transaxle.
3. Turn the steering wheel all the way in the direction of the side you are working on. Pull the driveshaft out of the steering knuckle.
4. Only the outer joint is available for replacement. If the inner joint is damaged, a new driveshaft must be installed. The outer joint can be removed by removing the snapring (inboard side) and hitting the axle end with a soft hammer.
5. On Installation, torque the driveshaft coupling bolts to 25 ft/lbs.

4000

CAUTION

Never remove or install the axle nut with the wheel off the ground. The vehicle must be resting on the ground for these operations.

1. Remove the axle nut.
2. Unbolt and remove the six halfshaft retaining bolts from the drive flange.
3. Mark the position of the ball joint on the control arm, remove the two retaining nuts and remove the ball joint.

NOTE: On cars with manual transmissions, remove only the right side ball joint.

4. Pull the pivot mounting outward and remove the halfshaft.
5. Installation is the reverse of removal.
6. Tighten the ball joint to control arm nuts to 47 ft/lbs.
7. Always replace the self-locking axle nut with a new one and tighten to 167 ft/lbs.
8. Check for proper camber adjustment.

5000

CAUTION

Never remove or install the axle shaft nut with the wheel off the ground. The vehicle must be resting on the ground for these operations. A puller is required for this job.

1. Remove the axle nut.
2. Raise and support the vehicle and remove the wheels.
3. On the right side, remove the driveshaft skid plate.
4. Disconnect the axleshaft from the transmission.
5. Using a 4-armed puller mounted on the wheel hub, press the axleshaft out of the hub.
6. Guide the inside end of the shaft up over the transmission and out of the hub.
7. When installing a shaft, make certain that the splines are clean and free of grease. Apply a ⅛ inch bead of RTV silicone sealant around the leading edge of the splines. Allow it to harden at least one hour. Torque the shaft-to-transmission bolts to 32 ft/lb and the axleshaft nut to 203 ft/lb.

DRIVESHAFT OVERHAUL

100 Series

This operation requires the use of a press or puller setup. It is necessary in order to replace the rubber boots.

1. Clamp the steering knuckle in a vise.
2. Remove the cotter pin. Unscrew the castellated nut and reverse it on the threads to protect them from damage.
3. Press the driveshaft from the steering knuckle. Steps 4-8 cover steering knuckle service.
4. Press out the wheel hub from the steering knuckle.

Applying RTV sealant to the shaft splines on a 5000

5. Remove the spacer, Nilos ring, and ball bearing inner race.
6. Drive the outer ball bearing race from the knuckle. Remove the internal snap-rings, using snap-ring pliers, and press out the second ball bearing outer race.
7. Replace the snap-rings. Press in the outer races. Fill the space between the races with high melting point wheel bearing grease.
8. Place the spacer and Nilos ring in the wheel hub. Press on the ball bearing inner race and install a new spacer bushing. Place the hub in the steering knuckle and press in the second ball bearing inner race.
9. Remove both rubber boot clamps and slide the boots off the joints.
10. Clamp the inner driveshaft in a vise. Spread the snap-ring in the joint and have an assistant hit the outer end of the shaft with a soft hammer. A "powerful" blow is required.
11. Drive the joint housing off the inner shaft, using the soft hammer.
12. Pull off the rubber boots.

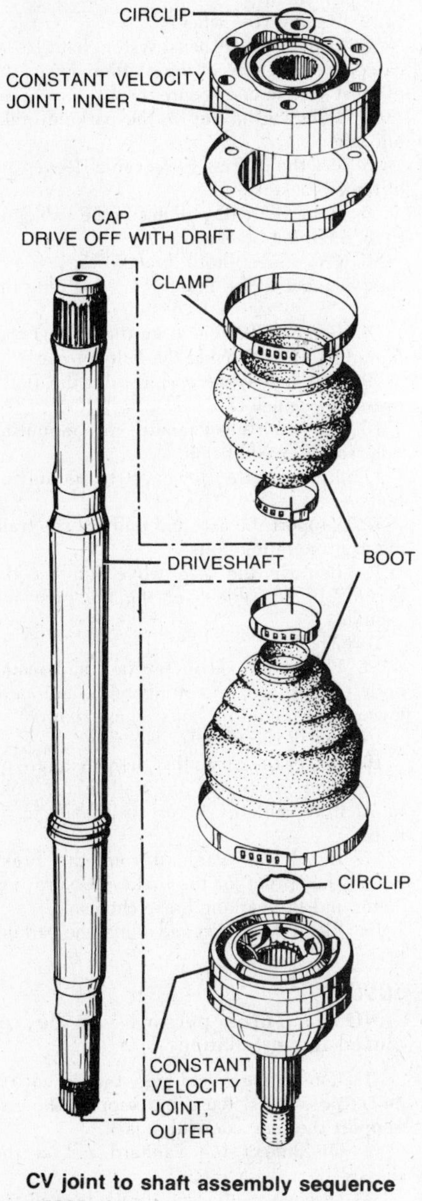

CV joint to shaft assembly sequence —5000

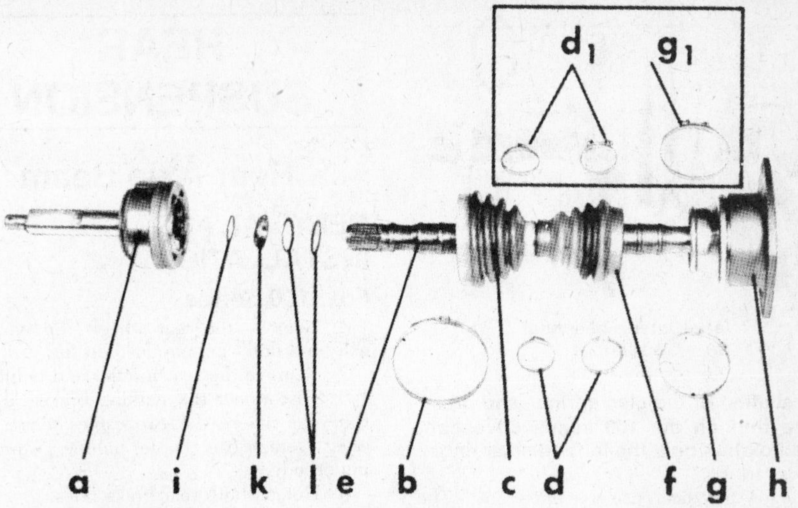

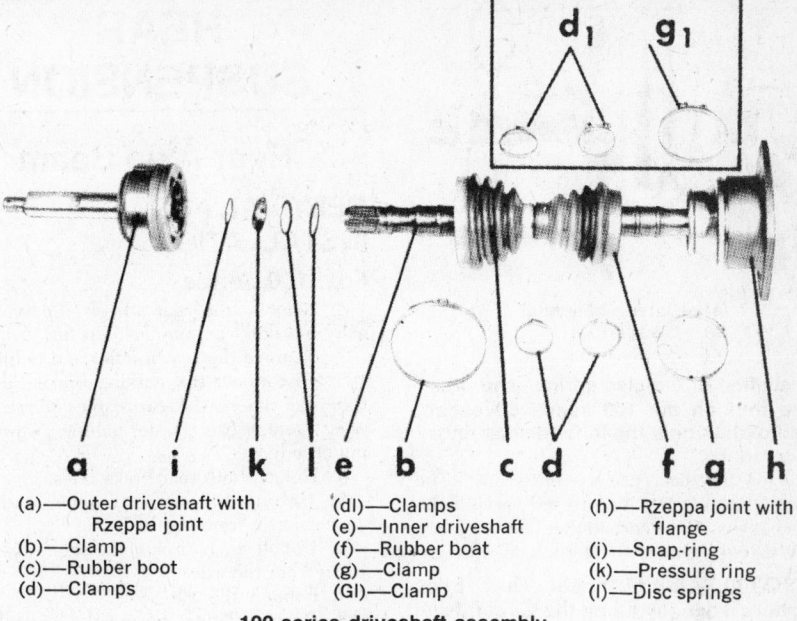

(a)—Outer driveshaft with Rzeppa joint
(b)—Clamp
(c)—Rubber boot
(d)—Clamps
(dl)—Clamps
(e)—Inner driveshaft
(f)—Rubber boat
(g)—Clamp
(Gl)—Clamp
(h)—Rzeppa joint with flange
(i)—Snap-ring
(k)—Pressure ring
(l)—Disc springs

100 series driveshaft assembly

13. Clean the joint with alcohol and air dry.
14. Install new rubber boots.
15. Place two new disc springs on the inner shaft with their concave side out. Install a pressure ring with the convex side out.
16. Place a new snap-ring in the joint. Place the ends in the machined groove.
17. Slide the joint onto the inner shaft, so that the snap-ring begins to go into place. Drive the joint in to place, hitting the outer end of the driveshaft with a soft hammer. The snap-ring should snap into place. The outer end of the shaft may also be pounded on with a wooden block.
18. Fill each joint with 60 cc of Molykote grease or its equivalent.
19. Put the rubber boots in place. Install the boot clamps, making sure that the free-ends trail in the normal direction of rotation.
20. Grease and install the spacer and Nilos ring. Press the driveshaft into the wheel hub. Adjust the hub nut so that there is 0.002-0.003 in. wheel bearing play, measured with a dial indicator at the outer edge of the wheel hub.

Fox, 4000 and 5000

NOTE: This procedure requires the use of a bench press.

1. Working at the transmission end, remove the circlip.
2. Mount the assembly in a bench press and press off the inner constant velocity joint.
3. Unclamp and remove the driveshaft boot.
4. Remove the circlip from the inside of the outer constant velocity joint and drive it off the shaft with a few taps of a brass drift against the hub.

NOTE: Be careful not to lose the thrust washer or dished washer on the 4000.

5. Place the outer CV joint on a clean work surface, mark the position of the hub in relation to the cage and housing and remove the balls one at a time.
6. Turn the cage until the two rectangular slots are level with the joint edge and remove the cage and hub.
7. Turn the hub until one segment can be inserted into the rectangular hole in the cage and tilt it out.

NOTE: A cooling fin ring is installed on the left and right inner CV joint on late model 5000 cars with manual transmission. Late model 5000 series cars with automatic transmission have the cooling fin ring on the right side only.

8. Place the inner CV joint on a clean work surface and pivot the hub and cage out of the outer ring. Pull out the balls.
9. Align the grooves in the hub and cage and pull the hub from the cage.
10. When assembling the outer CV joint, never replace one or some of the balls. Always replace all of the balls as a set. Force about one ounce of EP chassis lube into each side of the joint. When assembling the inner joint, push the balls into the cage before installing cage and hub into the joint. Note that the chamfer on the inside edge of the ball hub must face the contact shoulder of the axleshaft. The cage and ball assembly must be inserted vertically into the outer ring of the joint. Make certain that a wide ball-groove in the outer ring of the joint, and a narrow groove in the hub are aligned when the hub is pivoted into the joint. When pivoting the ball hub and cage into the joint, work the hub outward until the balls are spaced to fit in the grooves. Press the cage firmly into position so that the hub can pivot back into the joint when the balls are seated. The joint is correctly assembled when the hub can be moved in and out over a full range of axial movement using only hand pressure. Force 2 ounces of EP chassis lube into the joint.
11. The outer CV joint may be tapped into

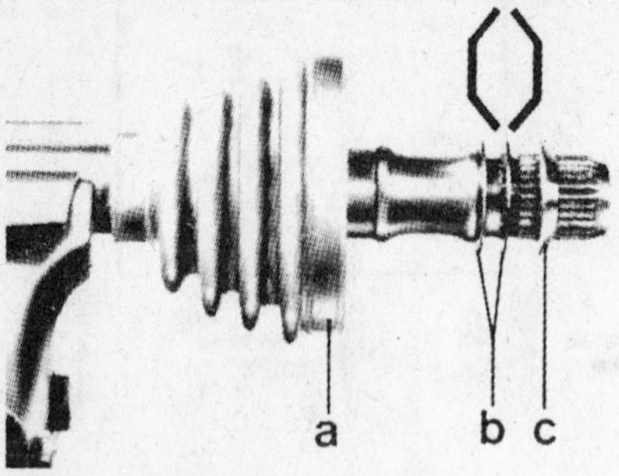

(a)—Outer rubber boot
(b)—Disc springs
(c)—Pressure ring

Installation of the disc springs and pressure ring on the 100 series driveshaft. The Fox has only the inner disc spring.

place on the shaft using a brass drift. The inner CV joint must be pressed on with the bench press. Make certain that both joints are fully seated before installing the circlips.

NOTE: Don't forget the three washers when installing the CV joints on the 4000. The dished washers should have the dish side facing the joint. The thrust washer should have the side without the lip closest to the joint.

REAR SUSPENSION

Rear Axle Beam

REMOVAL AND INSTALLATION

Fox, 100 Series

1. Remove the rear wheels. Support the axle, but don't put any load on the springs.
2. Remove the rear muffler and tailpipe.
3. Disconnect the parking brake cable at the yoke where the two cables merge into one. Detach the cable holders from the underbody.
4. Detach both rear brake lines.
5. Unbolt the control arms and the diagonal arm from the body.
6. Unbolt the bottom of the shock absorber struts from the axle.
7. Remove the axle.
8. On installation, torque the control arm to body bolts to 32 ft/lbs and the diagonal arm to body bolts to 61 ft/lbs. Torque the lower shock absorber strut to axle bolts to 43 ft/lbs. Bleed the brakes.

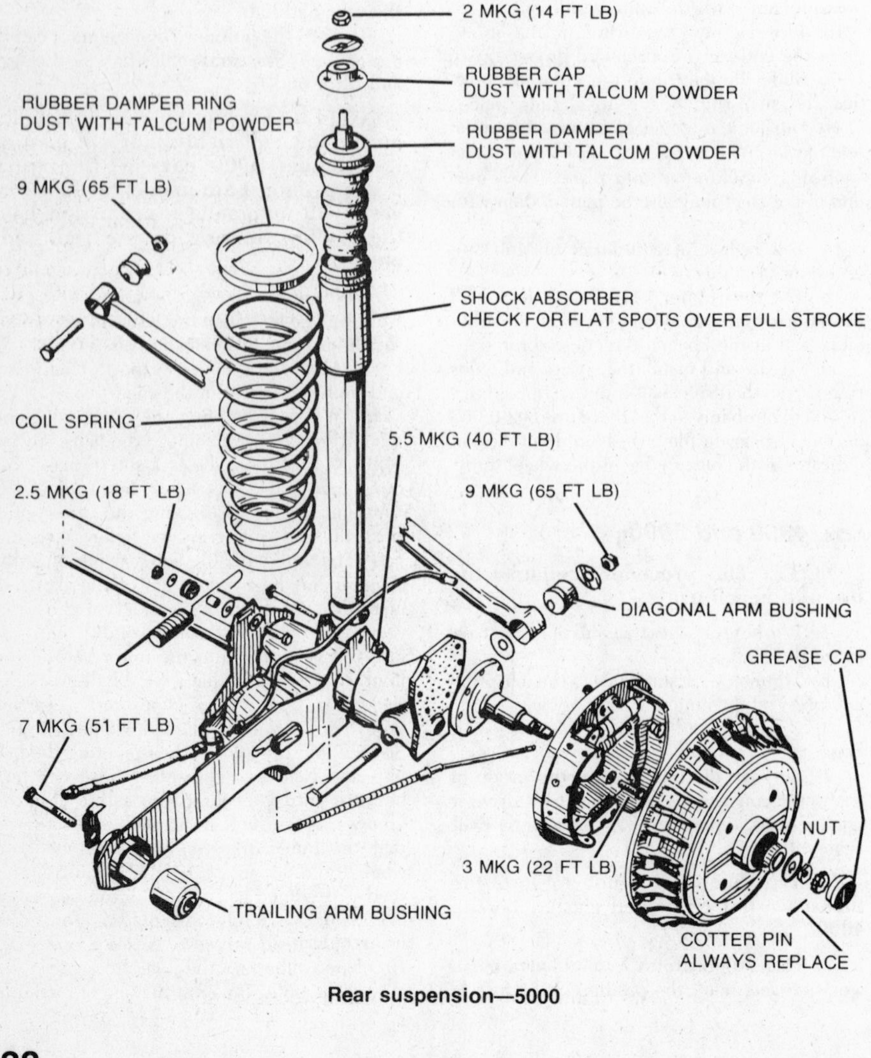

Rear suspension—5000

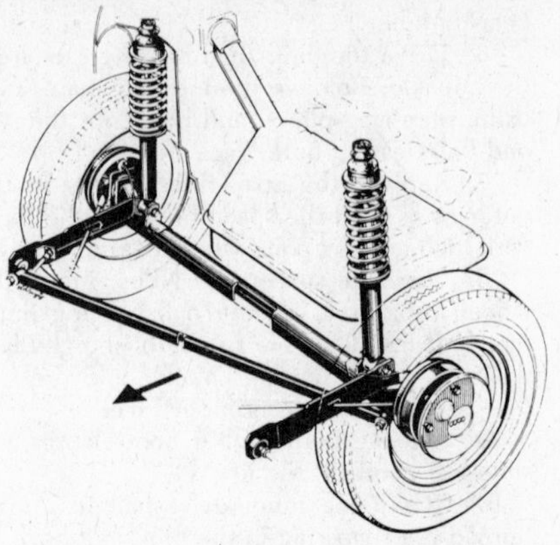

Rear suspension, Fox and 100 series

4000

1. Raise the rear of the car and support it with jack stands.
2. Remove the wheels.
3. Unhook the exhaust system hangers located at either side of the muffler, lower the exhaust system and secure it.
4. Remove the nut on the parking brake equalizer bar.
5. Pry the parking brake cable sleeves out of their brackets.
6. Remove both parking brake cables at their retaining brackets.
7. Disconnect both brake hoses where they connect to the brake lines and plug the lines.
8. Remove the nuts from the trailing arm mounting bolts, leaving the bolts in place.
9. Disconnect the spring from the brake pressure regulator.
10. Remove the Panhard rod mounting bolt from the axle beam.
11. Remove the lower strut mounting bolts.
12. Support the axle and pull out the trailing arm mounting bolts.
13. Remove the axle while guiding the parking brake cable over the tail pipe and muffler.

To install:

14. Place the axle in position and install both trailing arm mounting bolts and both lower strut mounting bolts. Hand tighten.
15. Install the wheels.
16. Lower the car so that the wheels are on the ground and tighten the trailing arm bolts to 72 ft/lbs and the lower strut bolts to 51 ft/lbs.
17. Install the Panhard rod, the brake hoses, the spring for the brake pressure regulator and the parking brake cables.
18. Bleed the brakes and adjust the parking brake.

5000

NOTE: Three persons will be required for installation.

1. Loosen the wheel lugs, but do not remove the wheels. Raise and support the car. Support the rear axle with a jack.
2. Disconnect the Panhard rod at the chassis.
3. Disconnect the right brake hose at the chassis.

4. Disconnect the brake pressure regulator spring.
5. Disconnect the left brake hose at the chassis.
6. Remove the right fuel tank retaining strap.
7. Remove the parking brake from the guide on the fuel tank.
8. Loosen the left side parking brake cable bolt.
9. Loosen the parking brake compensator and disconnect the cable.
10. Remove the exhaust system from the car.
11. Disconnect the shock absorbers at the upper end.
12. Lower the axle on the jack until the springs are clear.
13. Remove the springs and the rear wheels.
14. Remove the trailing arm mounting bolt and lower the axle from the car.
15. Place the axle in position on the jack.
16. Install the trailing arm bolts lightly.
17. Install the wheels.
18. Install both rear springs at the same time while raising the axle into position.
19. Connect the shock absorbers.
20. Installation of the remaining parts is the reverse of removal.
21. Torque the shock absorber upper bolts to 14 ft/lbs; the Panhard rod-to-chassis bolt to 65 ft/lbs; the trailing arm bolts to 51 ft/lbs.
22. Bleed the brakes.

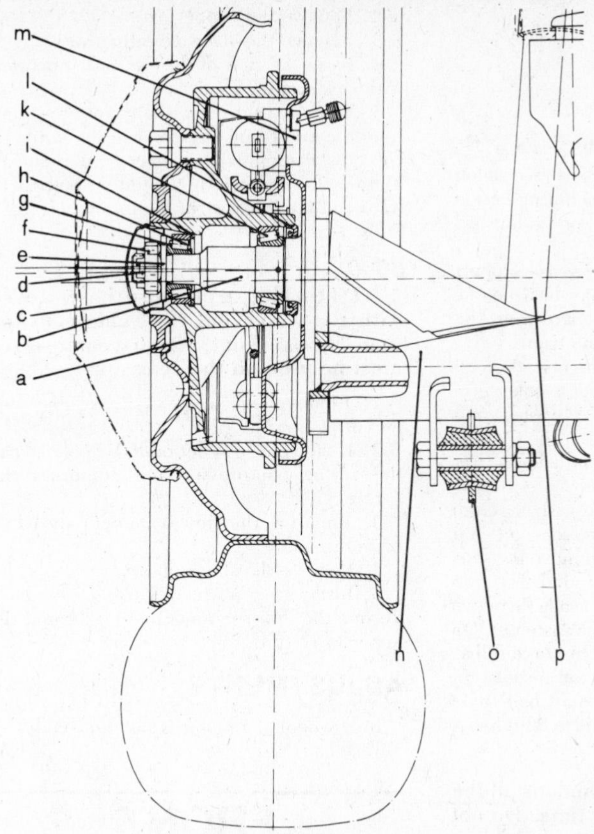

(a)—Brake drum
(b)—Rear stub axle
(c)—Cap
(d)—Cotter pin
(e)—Nut

(f)—Castellated nut
(g)—Washer
(h)—Roller bearing
(i)—Snap-ring
(k)—Roller bearing

(l)—Shaft seal
(m)—Brake assembly
(n)—Rear axle
(o)—Suspension arm
(p)—Shock absorber

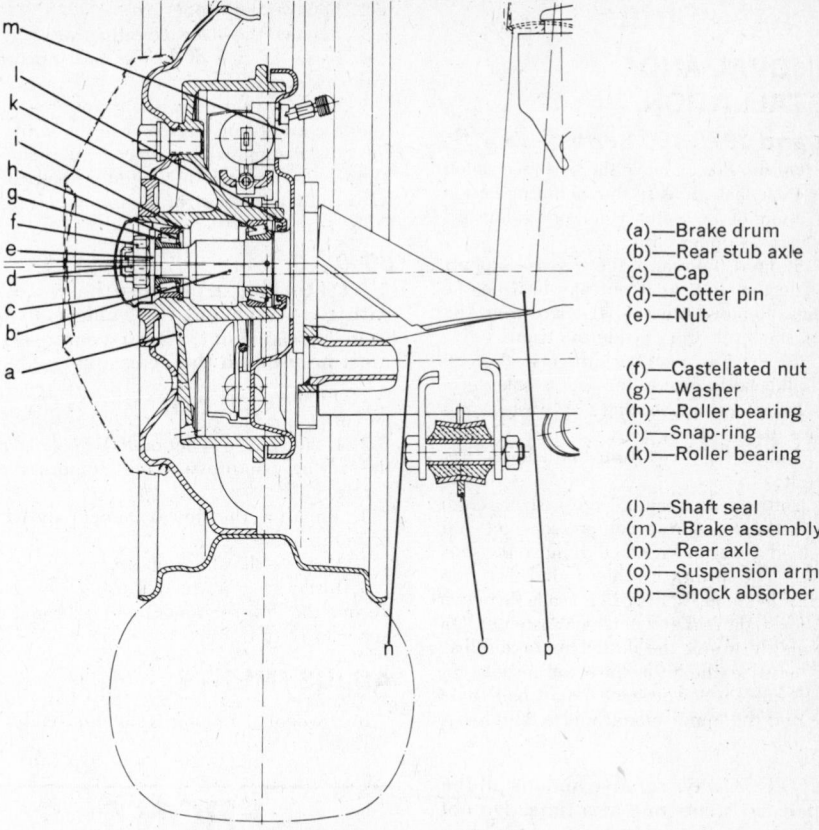

Rear wheel bearing and stub axle assembly

Wheel Bearings and Stub Axles

REMOVAL AND INSTALLATION

1. Depress the brake pedal approximately 1.2 in. and hold it in that position to close the master cylinder compensating bore.
2. Detach the brake lines on both sides and plug the lines.
3. Pry off the grease cap and remove the cotter pin, castellated nut, and washer. Remove the wheel and brake drum.
4. Remove the bearing inner race from the brake drum.
5. Carefully (the spring can fly out) pry out the brake shoe retaining spring. Remove the brake shoes complete with pressure rod and spring, bottom bracket first. Disconnect the handbrake cable.
6. Unbolt the rear stub axle and brake backing plate.
7. Pry out the shaft seal (which should be replaced) and remove the inner race of the roller bearing.
8. Drive the roller bearing outer race from the brake drum. Remove the snap-ring and drive the outer roller bearing race from the drum.
9. Replace the snap-ring and drive in the outer race of the outer roller bearing.
10. Press in the outer race of the inner roller bearing.
11. Lightly coat the inner race of the inner roller bearing with wheel bearing grease and push it into the outer race.
12. Drive a new shaft seal into position (the open side of the seal should face the roller bearing). Fill the space between the two roller bearings with approximately 10 oz. of wheel bearing grease.
13. Coat the inner race of the outer roller bearing with grease and install the inner race.
14. Replace the stub axle and brake backing plate with the groove in the stub axle facing upward. Bolt torque is 14-15 ft/lbs for 8G bolts and 22 ft/lbs for 10K bolts.
15. Assemble the brake shoes, connect the handbrake cable, and insert the brake shoes on the bottom bracket first, then at the wheel cylinder. Replace the retaining spring.
16. Replace the brake drum and wheel, special washer, nut, castellated nut, and a new cotter pin. Wheel bearing play should be 0.001-0.002 in. It can be measured with a dial indicator. Fill the dust cap with approximately 10 oz. of wheel bearing grease and replace it.

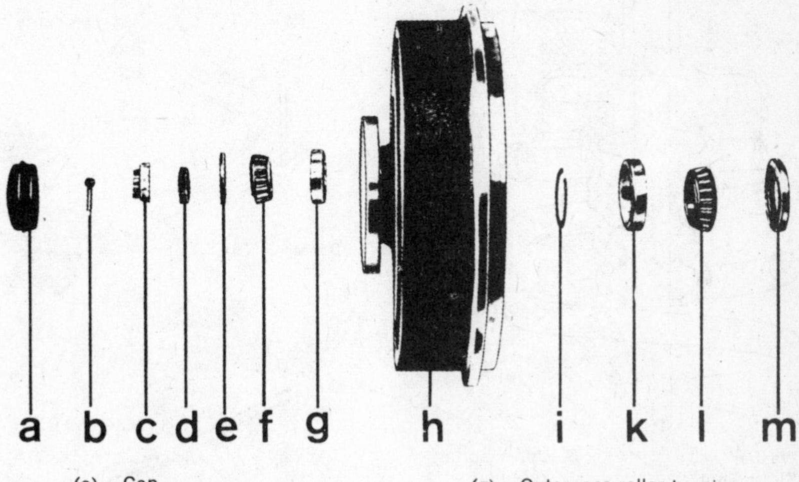

(a)—Cap
(b)—Cotter pin
(c)—Castellated nut
(d)—Nut
(e)—Washer
(f)—Inner race roller bearing
(g)—Outer race roller bearing
(h)—Brake drum
(i)—Snap-ring
(k)—Outer race roller bearing
(l)—Inner race roller bearing
(m)—Shaft seal

Rear brake drum and wheel bearing components

Struts

REMOVAL AND INSTALLATION

Fox and 1975 100 Series

1. On the Fox, remove the bottom cushion of the rear seat. Release the mounting tabs at the bottom of the seatback and pull it forward to detach its upper clips.
2. Support the rear of the chassis. Support the axle too, but don't put any load on the springs. Remove the rubber guard from the top of the strut, from inside the trunk.
3. On the Fox, peel back the insulation on the bulkhead to expose the access hole.
4. Remove the mounting nut, washer, and rubber disc.
5. Unbolt the strut from the axle and remove it.
6. You can disassemble these struts carefully without a spring compressor, but you will need a special wrench to remove the slotted nut. The springs are color coded. The stop pad inside the top of the coil is available in two sizes for slight rear end height adjustment. On reassembly, torque the slotted nut to 11 ft/lbs.
7. Reverse the procedure for installation and torque the lower strut mount bolt to 43 ft/lbs and the upper mount nut to 23 ft/lbs.

4000

NOTE: Always remove and install the suspension struts one at a time. Do not allow the rear axle to hang in place as this may cause undue damage to the brake lines.

1. With the car at ground level, open the trunk and remove the sheet metal trim from around the shock tower.
2. Remove the rubber cap.
3. Remove the strut mounting nut.
4. Raise the rear of the car and support it with jack stands.
5. Remove the lower strut mounting bolt from the axle beam and remove the strut.
6. Installation is the reverse of removal. Torque the upper strut mounting bolt to 14 ft/lbs and the lower strut mounting bolt to 43 ft/lbs.

5000

NOTE: The struts must be removed with the weight on the vehicle on the rear wheels. If not, a spring compressor must be used on the rear springs.

1. Remove the upper shock absorber mounting nut.
2. If the vehicle is not on its wheels, install the spring compressor and compress the spring.
3. Remove the lower shock absorber mounting nut.
4. Remove the shock absorber.
5. Installation is the reverse of removal. Torque the lower mounts to 40 ft/lbs and the upper to 14 ft/lbs.

ADJUSTMENTS

Rear wheel alignment is not adjustable.

FRONT SUSPENSION

The 100 series use MacPherson strut type spring and shock absorber units with upper and lower control arms (wishbones) and having a cross-chassis stabilizer bar connecting the two lower control arms.

The Fox, 4000 and 5000 also use MacPherson struts. The strut unit, steering arm, and steering knuckle are all combined in one assembly; there is no upper control arm. The system is designed with negative roller-radius; this stabilizes the car when different retarding forces are applied to the front wheels, as would happen if one front tire were on wet pavement and the other on dry.

NOTE: Exercise extreme caution when working with the front suspension. Coil springs and torsion bars are under great tension and can cause severe injury if released suddenly.

MacPherson Strut

REMOVAL AND INSTALLATION

100 Series

1. Support the vehicle and remove the wheels. Let the front suspension hang free.
2. Unbolt the strut unit from the upper control arm.
3. Inside the engine compartment, remove the three nuts which hold the top of the strut unit. Do not remove the nut and locknut in the center.
4. Pull the unit down and pull the top out through the wheel opening. It may be necessary to pull the steering knuckle down a bit for clearance.
5. It is not recommended that the strut unit be disassembled unless the necessary special tools to do this safely are available. The units should be serviced in pairs to maintain

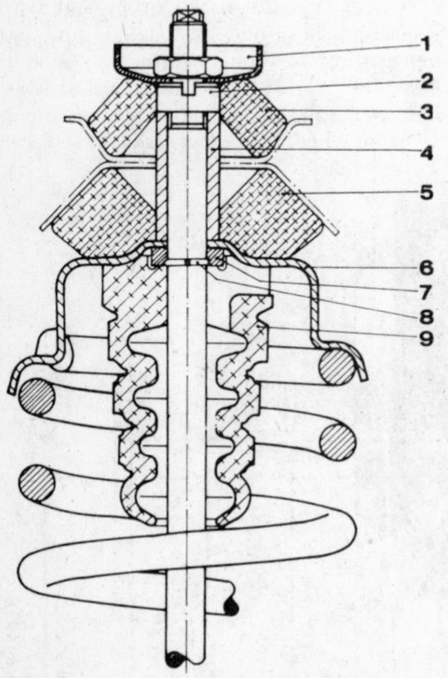

1. Washer
2. Slotted nut
3. Rubber disc
4. Spacer
5. Larger rubber disc
6. Upper spring retainer
7. Ring
8. Snap ring
9. Stop pad

Details of the upper part of the spring/shock strut used on the Fox and 100 series

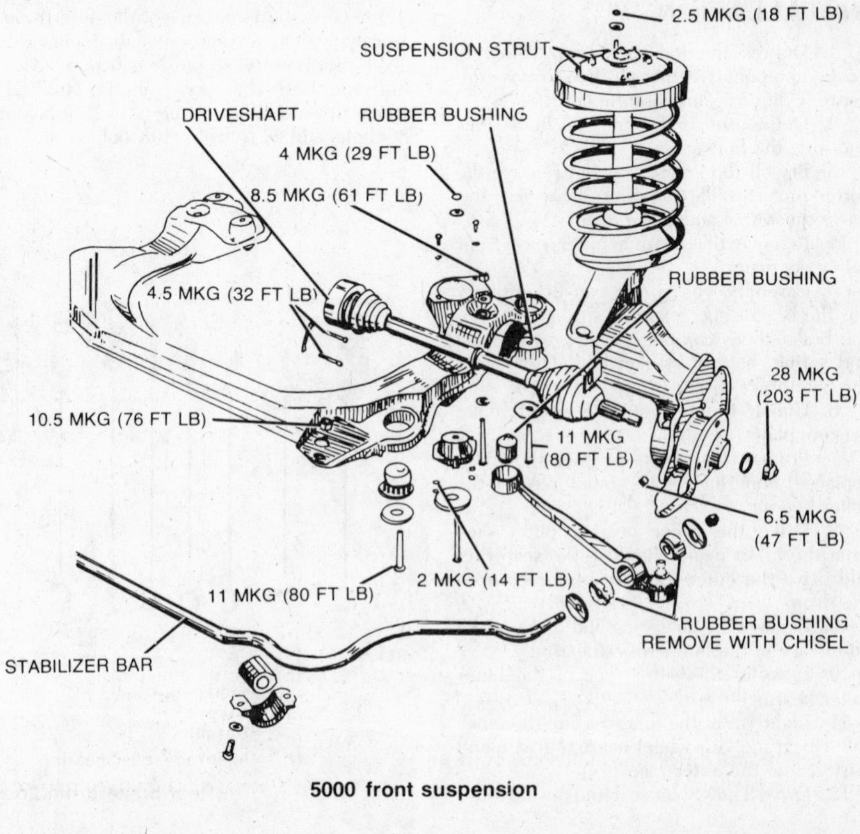

5000 front suspension

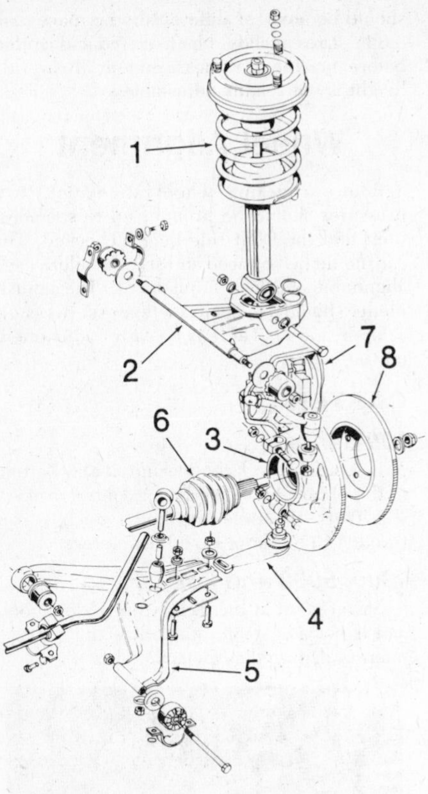

1. Coil spring
2. Upper control arm
3. Steering knuckle
4. Lower ball joint
5. Lower control arm
6. Driveshaft
7. Caliper
8. Disc

100 series front suspension

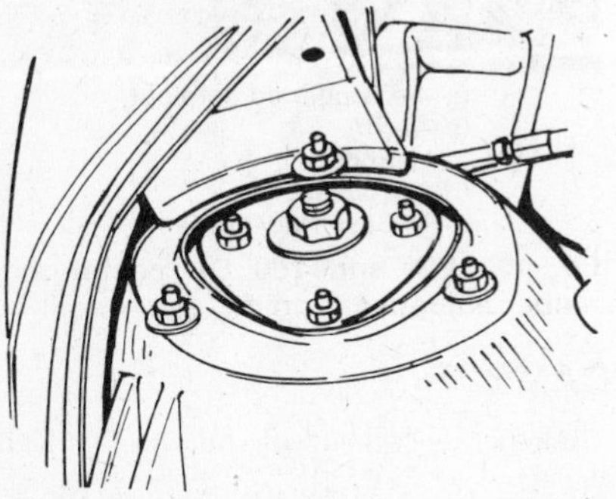

Front strut upper mounting nut—5000

equal shock absorbing qualities and ride height. Spacers are available to correct ride height. The strut unit must be disassembled to install these. The proper ride height with standard size tires is 8.2-8.7 in., measured from the floor to the 0.32 in. diameter hole in the front bearing shell of the lower control arm inner pivot.

6. When replacing the strut unit, torque the three bolts and nuts, which hold the upper end of the strut to the body, to 13-15 ft/lbs, and the lower end to 62-69 ft/lbs. The torque for the shock absorber to spring retaining nut is 18-26 ft/lbs.

7. Check the wheel alignment.

Fox

1. With the car resting on its wheels, remove the axle nut.
2. Raise the car and remove the wheels.
3. Unbolt the brake caliper, remove the brake line clip, and rest the caliper on the lower control arm.
4. Remove the bolt holding the steering knuckle to the lower control arm.
5. Detach the steering arm from the tie rod end.
6. Unbolt the stabilizer bar pivots from the lower control arm. Disconnect the lower control arm from the steering knuckle by removing the bolt at the ball joint.
7. Remove the strut mounting nuts in the engine compartment and remove the strut.
8. It is not recommended that the strut unit be disassembled unless the necessary special tools to do this safely are available. The units should be serviced in pairs to maintain equal shock qualities and ride height.
9. When replacing the strut unit, use a new nut and bolt to attach the lower control arm to the steering knuckle. Torque the strut to body bolts to 16 ft/lbs, the control arm to steering knuckle bolt to 16 ft/lbs, the brake caliper mounting bolts to 43 ft/lbs, and the stabilizer bar pivots to 7 ft/lbs.
10. Torque the axle nut to 180 ft/lbs and check the wheel alignment.

4000 and 5000

1. With the car on the ground, remove the front axle nut and loosen the wheel bolts.
2. Raise and support the front of the car and remove the wheels.
3. Remove the brake caliper mounting bolts and the brake line bracket. Remove the brake caliper with the line still attached to it and wire it out of the way.
4. Remove the wheel bearing housing/ball joint clamp bolt.
5. Remove the retaining nut and press of the tie rod end.
6. Unscrew the retaining bolt and remove move the stabilizer bar end clamps. Pivot the stabilizer bar downward. (4000 only).
7. Remove the two center stabilizer bar clamps and then unbolt it from the lower control arm. Remove the stabilizer bar (5000 only).
8. Pry the lower control arm down and remove the ball joint from the wheel hub.
9. Remove the halfshaft from the wheel hub.
10. While holding the shock absorber piston rod with an internal socket wrench, remove the retaining bolt and then remove the strut assembly (4000 only).
11. Remove the spring strut cover (5000 Turbo) and remove the three strut retaining nuts, then remove the strut assembly (5000 series only).
12. Installation is in the reverse order of removal. Note the following:
    a. When installing the stabilizer bar on the 4000, the positioning is correct if the clamps are difficult to install in the rubber bushings. Attach the clamps loosely, take a short test drive to bring the bushings into the correct position and then tighten to 18 ft/lbs.
    b. Tighten the ball joint bolt to 36 ft/lbs on the 4000 and 47 ft/lbs on the 5000.
    c. Tighten the axle nut to 167 ft/lbs on the 4000, 202 ft/lbs on the 5000 Turbo and 203 ft/lbs on all other 5000 models.

Upper Control Arm and Ball Joint

REMOVAL AND INSTALLATION

100 Series

NOTE: A press is needed for ball joint installation.

1. Remove the MacPherson strut unit.
2. Remove the upper control arm to steering knuckle bolt.

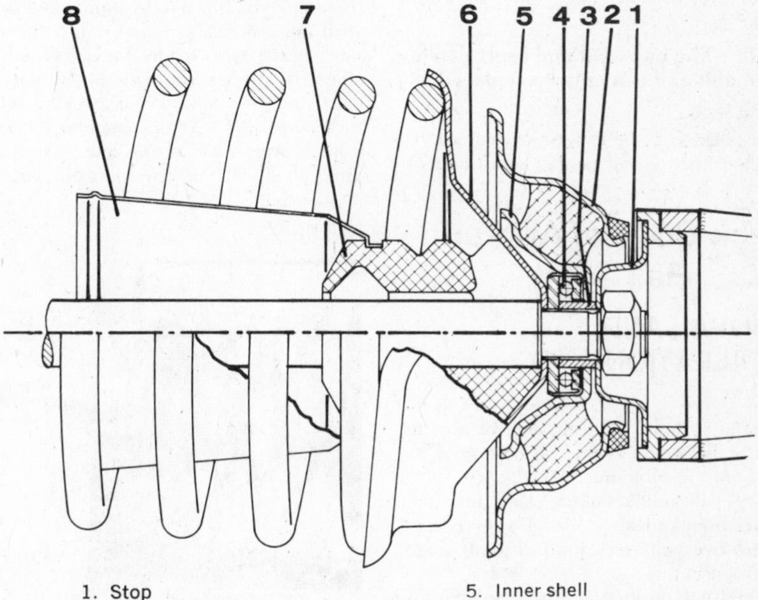

1. Stop
2. Outer shell
3. Spacer
4. Grooved ball bearing
5. Inner shell
6. Upper spring retainer
7. Stop pad
8. Guard

Details of the upper part of the Fox front spring/shock strut

3. Pull the control arm up so that the control arm upper joint comes loose from the steering knuckle.
4. Remove the four mounting bolts and the control arm.

NOTE: Upper ball joint is a press fit and may be replaced at this time.

5. Reverse the procedure for installation.

Lower Control Arm and Ball Joint

REMOVAL AND INSTALLATION

100 Series

1. Raise the vehicle and let the suspension hang free. Remove the wheels.
2. Remove the stabilizer bar. It may be necessary to move the exhaust pipe.
3. Support the lower control arm. Remove the lower control arm to steering knuckle bolt. Let the arm down to pull the joint loose from the steering knuckle.
4. Unbolt the bearing bolts and remove the control arm.

NOTE: To remove lower ball joint, remove retaining ring & nut and pull bad joint from joint plate.

5. Reverse the procedure for installation.

5000

1. Remove the ball joint clamp nut.
2. Pry the control arm down and out of the clamp.
3. Remove the nut on the end of the stabilizer bar.
4. Loosen the control arm to subframe mounting bolts and then pull the control arm off of the end of the stabilizer bar.
5. Remove the bolts and remove the control arm.

NOTE: The ball joint and control arm are one unit and can only be replaced as a unit.

6. Installation is the reverse of removal.
7. Check the toe and camber adjustments.

Track Control Arm and Ball Joint

REMOVAL AND INSTALLATION

Fox

1. Remove bolts securing control arm to subframe. Before removing ball joint, mark its position on the subframe.
2. Pull ball joint retaining clamp and pull ball joint from knuckle.
3. Remove bolts securing ball joint flange to control arm.
4. To install, position new ball joint on control arm and tighten bolts to 45 ft/lbs.
5. Install control arm in reverse of above. Torque control arm-to-subframe bolts to 32 ft/lbs.

Ball Joints

REMOVAL AND INSTALLATION

4000

1. Mark the position of the ball joint flange on the lower control arm.
2. Remove the ball joint retaining clamp nut and pull the ball joint/control arm down and out of the retaining clamp.
3. Unscrew the two ball flange retaining nuts and remove the ball joint.
4. Installation is the reverse of removal. Tighten the clamp nut to 47 ft/lbs and tighten the ball joint flange nuts to 47 ft/lbs.

Lower Control Arm

REMOVAL AND INSTALLATION

4000

1. Raise the front of the car and support it with jack stands.
2. Remove the ball joint as detailed earlier.
3. Unbolt the end of the stabilizer bar and pull it down.
4. Remove the two control arm-to-subframe bolts and remove the control arm.
5. Installation is in the reverse order of removal. Check control arm bushings for cracking or undue wear. Tighten the control arm to subframe bolts to 43 ft/lbs and the stabilizer bar mounting bolts to 18 ft/lbs.

Adjustments

RIDE HEIGHT

100 Series

The suspension strut units must be removed and be disassembled and new springs or spacers installed to adjust ride height on these models. It is not recommended that the strut unit be disassembled unless the necessary special tools to do this safely are available. The proper front ride height with standard size tires is 8.2-8.7 in., measured from the floor to the 0.32 in. diameter hole in the front bearing shell of the lower control arm inner pivot. The measurements on both sides should be alike, or different by no more than 0.3 in. The car should be bounced and settled before making the measurement. Rear ride height is not readily adjustable.

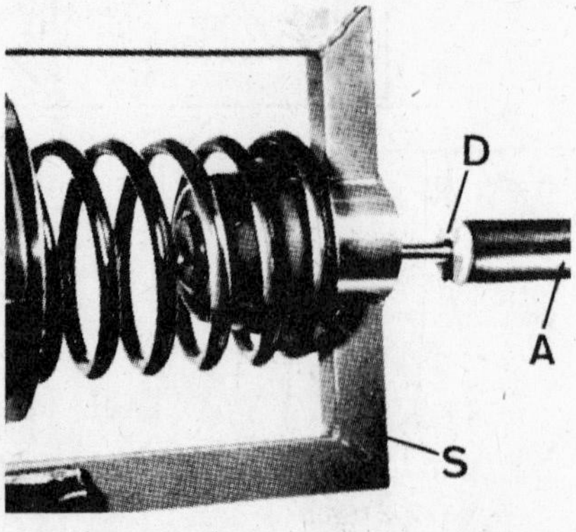

100, 100 LS, and 100 GL ride height is adjusted by inserting spacers (D) on the strut unit (A). (S) is the special strut compressor

Wheel Alignment

Before checking wheel alignment, tire pressures should be brought up to specifications and the front ride height checked. The car should be bounced and settled before each alignment check or adjustment. The adjustments should be made in this order: caster, camber, toe-in. There is no caster adjustment on the Fox.

CASTER

100 Series

1. Loosen the large locknut at the bottom of the outer end of the lower control arm.
2. Turn the eccentric bolt, which passes through the locknut, to adjust caster.

4000, 5000 and Fox

Caster is set at the factory on these models and is not adjustable other than the replacement of damaged suspension parts.

(a)—Camber adjustment
(b)—Nut
(c)—Bolt
(d)—Locknut
(e)—Caster adjustment

100, 100 LS, and 100 GL caster and camber adjustment points

CAMBER

Camber is checked with the wheels straight ahead.

100 Series

1. Loosen the nut (on the top) on the bolt that passes through the outer end of the lower control arm.
2. Loosen the bolt (on the bottom) inboard of the nut loosened in Step 1.
3. Adjust camber by turning the large nut on top of the bolt loosened in Step 2.
4. Tighten the bolt and nut to 32 ft/lbs.

Fox

1. Loosen the two nuts holding the ball joint to the lower control arm.
2. Push the ball joint in or out to adjust the camber. Dealers have a special tool to lever the ball joint in or out, using the holes in the control arm.
3. Tighten the nuts to 47 ft/lbs.

4000

1. Loosen both ball joint flange mounting bolts on the control arm.

2. Using the special tool US 4490, or by just moving the ball joint with your hands, adjust the camber to specifications.

5000

1. Loosen the spring strut plate mounting bolts.
2. Attach a socket wrench to the top piston rod nut and move the assembly in the slots until the camber is correct.
3. Tighten all bolts.

TOE-IN

Toe-in is checked with the wheels straight ahead.

1. Toe-in can be determined by measuring and comparing the distance between the center of the tire tread, front and rear, or by measuring and comparing the distance between the inside edges of the wheel rims, front and rear. If the wheel rims are used as the basis of measurement, the car should be rolled forward slightly and a second set of measurements taken. This avoids any error induced by bent wheels. If at all possible, a toe-in gauge should be used; it will give a much more accurate measurement.
2. Toe-in is adjusted at the steering tie rods at either end of the steering rack on the 100 Series. Loosen the clamp. Loosen the clip for the rubber boot at the end of the rack and slide the boot back. On the Fox, simply loosen the clamp and locknut on the adjustable left tie rod.
3. Turn both rods to lengthen or shorten them an equal amount. If the tie rods are not adjusted equally, the steering wheel will be crooked and the turning arcs of the front wheels will be changed. On the Fox, only the left tie rod is adjustable. If the steering wheel is crooked, it must be removed and repositioned.
4. Tighten the clamps and replace the boots.

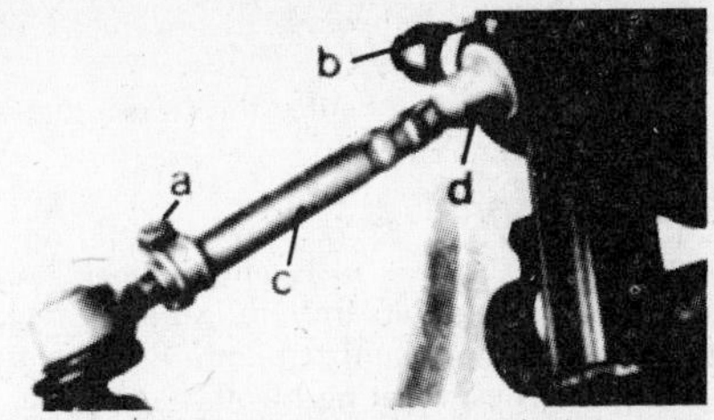

100 series toe-in is adjusted by loosening nut (a) on each tierod (c) and pushing back the rubber boot and clamp (b) in order to use a wrench on the flat surfaces.

STEERING

The steering is a rack and pinion type. The steering geometry is designed to give a variable ratio effect, giving faster steering response as the steering wheel is turned toward either right or left lock. The steering column and linkage is arranged so as to break away and telescope safely in an accident, rather than penetrating into the passenger compartment.

1. Cotter pin
2. Tie-rod
3. Axle driveshaft
4. Circlip
5. Retainer nut
6. Brake caliper
7. Wheel bearing
8. Hub
9. Brake disc
10. Axle nut

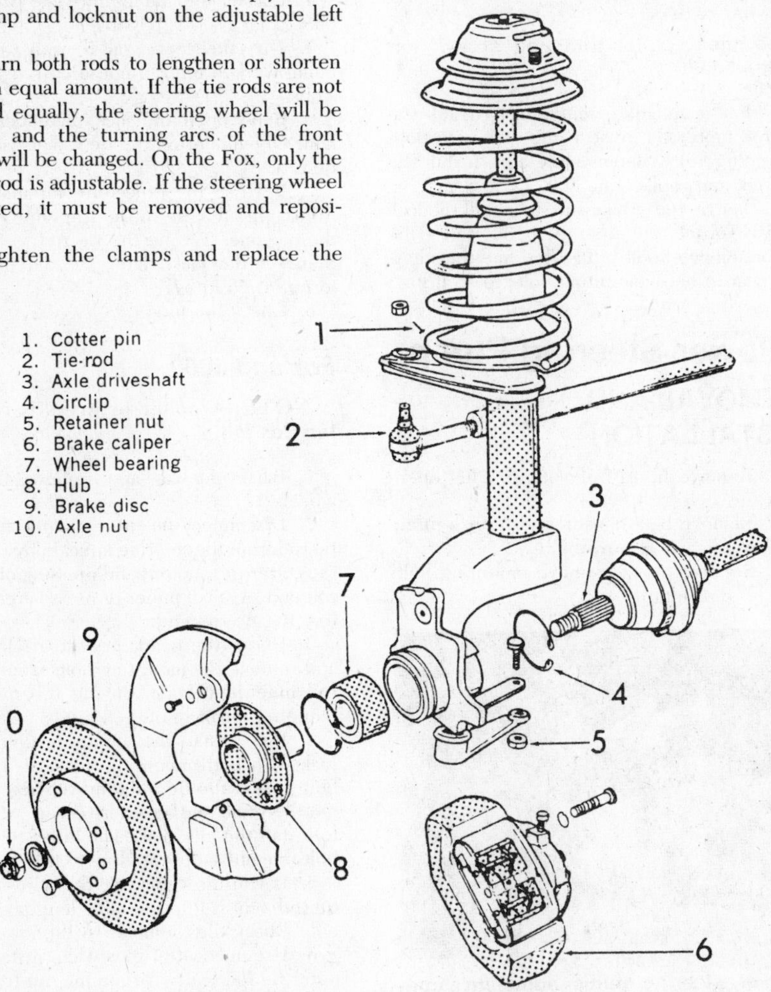

Exploded view of the Fox front suspension

Steering Wheel

REMOVAL AND INSTALLATION

1. Center the wheel. Disconnect the battery ground cable.
2. Pry off the wheel pad (horn button).
3. Unbolt and remove the wheel. A steering wheel puller should not be necessary.
4. On installation, torque the bolt to 36 ft/lbs (100 series, Fox and 5000) and 29 ft/lbs (4000 and 5000 Turbo). Do not pound on the wheel, as the collapsible column may be damaged.

Turn Signal and Headlight Dimmer Switch Replacement

100 Series

1. Remove the steering wheel.
2. Disconnect the battery ground cable.
3. Remove the wire from the horn contact ring. Remove the two screws and the horn contact ring.
4. Remove the screws which hold the column casing at the top and just below the instrument panel.
5. Remove the casing. Be careful to note the arrangement of any springs and washers removed from the top of the column.
6. The switch may now be disconnected, unscrewed, and removed. The wires are color coded for ease of replacement.

Fox

1. Disconnect the battery ground cable.
2. Remove the steering wheel.
3. Remove the screws in the top of the switch housing, lift off the housing and unplug the connectors, and remove the switch housing along with the wiper and turn signal levers.

4000 and 5000

1. Disconnect the negative battery cable.
2. Remove the steering wheel.
3. Remove the screws and remove the steering column cover on the 4000.
4. Remove the steering column switches. On the 4000, remove the three screws and pull the switches off enough to unplug the electrical connectors. On the 5000, insert a screwdriver into the slot on the bottom of the switch housing, loosen the screw and pull the housing off enough to unplug the electrical connectors.
5. Installation is in the reverse of removal.

Ignition and Steering Lock Switch

REMOVAL AND INSTALLATION

100 Series

To perform this operation, proceed with Steps 1-5 of "Turn Signal and Headlight Dimmer Switch Replacement." The lock switch is clamped to the steering column with

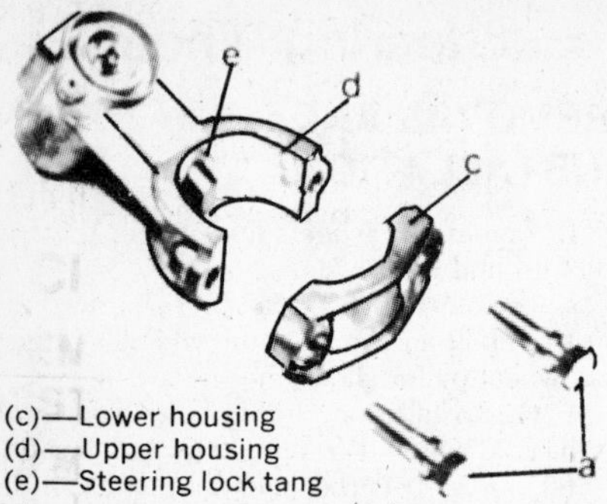

(c)—Lower housing
(d)—Upper housing
(e)—Steering lock tang

The ignition and steering lock switch is held in place by two bolts (a) whose heads shear on installation to deter theft

special bolts whose heads shear off on installation. These must be drilled out in order to remove the switch. When replacing the unit, make sure that the lock tang is aligned with the slot in the steering column.

4000

1. Disconnect the negative battery cable.
2. Remove the steering wheel, the steering column covers and the steering column switches.
3. Pry the lock washer off the steering column and discard it.
4. Remove the spring and pull off the contact ring.
5. Unplug the electrical connector.
6. Unscrew the retaining bolt and slide the ignition switch/steering lock assembly off of the steering column tube.
7. Installation is in the reverse order of removal. Replace the old lock washer with a new one.

Fox and 5000

1. Remove the column shroud for access to the screws.
2. Drill out the special shear bolt heads.

CAUTION

These bolts also support the steering column. Support the column while removing the bolts.

3. On installation, make sure the two projections on the lock clamp assembly engage the two depressions in the columns. Tighten the new bolts until their heads shear off.

Steering Gear

REMOVAL AND INSTALLATION

100 Series, Manual Steering

1. Point the front wheels straight ahead. Disconnect the steering column from the firewall.
2. Disconnect the steering shaft from the steering gear.
3. Disconnect the ends of the steering tie rods from the steering knuckles by removing the cotter pins and nuts and pressing out the tie rod ends. A small puller or press is required to free the tie rod ends.
4. Unbolt the steering gear from the firewall. Slide the unit toward the right and pull it up and out through the engine compartment.
5. On installation, center the steering gear and the steering wheel.

Fox and 5000

1. Pry off the lock plate and remove both tie rod mounting bolts from the steering rack, inside the engine compartment. Pry the tie rods out of the mounting pivot.
2. Remove the lower instrument panel trim.
3. Remove the shaft clamp bolt, pry off the clip, and drive the shaft toward the inside of the car with a brass drift.
4. Remove the steering gear mounting bolts at both ends. There is a single bolt at the right end.
5. Turn the wheels all the way to the right and remove the steering gear through the opening in the right wheel housing.

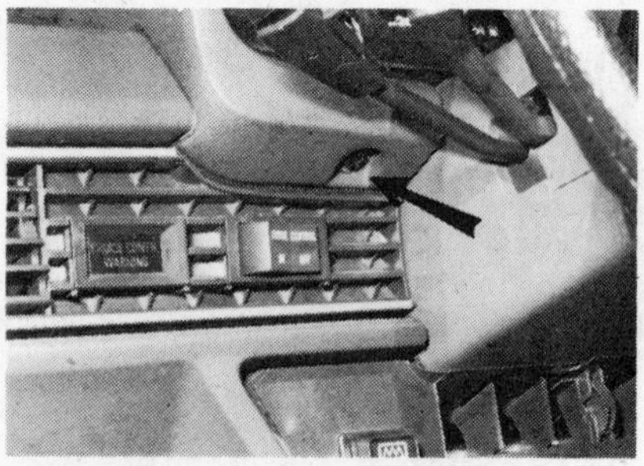

Instrument panel trim pad screw, left side—5000

6. For installation, temporarily install the tie rod mounting pivot to the rack with both mounting bolts. Remove one bolt, install the tie rod, and replace the bolt. Do the same on the other tie rod. Make sure to install the lock plate. Torque the tie rod to 39 ft/lbs, the mounting pivot bolt to 15 ft/lbs, and the steering gear to body mounting bolts to 15 ft/lbs.

Power Steering Pump

REMOVAL AND INSTALLATION

1. Remove hoses from pump. Plug openings.
2. Remove belt adjusting bolt, push pump to one side and remove belt.
3. Support pump, remove mounting bolts and lift out pump.

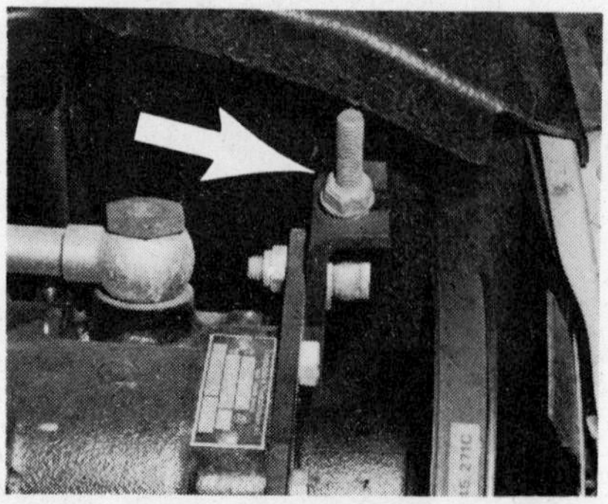

Power steering pump adjusting bolt—5000

Steering Linkage

TIE ROD REMOVAL AND INSTALLATION

100 Series

NOTE: A puller or press is required for this job.

1. Jack up the car and remove the wheels.
2. Disconnect the end of the steering tie rod from the steering knuckle by removing the cotter pin and nut and pressing out the tie rod end. A small puller or press is required to free the tie rod end.

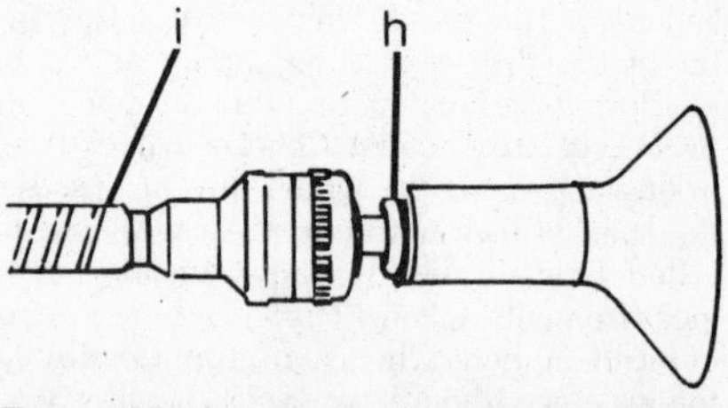

The nut (h) is loosened to remove the tie rod (i) from the 100 series steering gear

3. The steering gear boots can be replaced with no further disassembly at this point.
4. Loosen the clamp and slide the rubber boot as far back as possible.
5. Turn the steering all the way to the side being worked on. Do not force it against the stops.
6. Bend open the lock plate behind the knurled cylinder on the tie rod. Unscrew the tie rod.
7. Reverse the procedure for installation. Adjust the new tie rod to the same length as the old one. Torque the tie rod to 51 ft/lbs, then set the lock plate. Tie rod outer end torque is 26 ft/lbs.
8. Check the toe-in.

Fox and 5000

NOTE: A puller or press is required for this job.

1. Raise the car and remove the front wheels.
2. Disconnect the outer end of the steering tie rod from the steering knuckle by removing the cotter pin and nut and pressing out the tie rod end. A small puller or press is required to free the tie rod end.
3. Under the hood, pry off the lock plate and remove the mounting bolts from both tie rod inner ends. Pry the tie rod out of the mounting pivot.
4. First install the mounting pivot to the rack with both mounting bolts. Remove one bolt, install the tie rod, and replace the bolt. Do the same on the other tie rod. Make sure to install the lock plate The inner tie rod end bolts should be torqued to 40 ft/lbs.
5. If you are replacing the adjustable left tie rod, adjust it to the same length as the old one. Check the toe-in when the job is done.
6. Use new cotter pins when installing the outer tie rod ends. Torque the nut to 22 ft/lbs on the Fox and 4000 and 43 ft/lbs on the 5000.

BRAKES

All models have dual circuit hydraulic brakes with front disc brakes and rear drum brakes. (The 5000 Turbo utilizes disc brakes at all four wheels.) All models have a brake pad lining thickness warning light. The 5000 brakes are nearly identical to those used on the Fox.

Adjustment

FRONT DISC BRAKES

The front disc brakes are self-adjusting.

REAR DRUM BRAKES

100 Series, Fox and 1978 5000

The rear drum brakes must be adjusted periodically, or whether free travel is one third or more of the total pedal travel.

1. Raise the rear of the car.
2. Block the front wheels and release the parking brake. Step on the brake pedal hard to center the linings.
3. On the 100 series and Fox turn the front adjusting nut on the brake backing plate until the wheel can't be rotated forward by hand. On the 5000, remove the rubber plug and turn the adjuster with a screwdriver to lock the wheel.

When adjusting the rear brakes, turn adjustin nuts (A) toward (a) to tighten and (b) to loosen

4. Loosen the adjusting nut until the wheel can be turned freely without drag.
5. Repeat Steps 3 and 4 for the rear adjusting nut on the 100 and Fox.
6. Repeat Steps 3, 4, and 5 for the other rear wheel.
7. Step on the brake pedal hard and make sure the wheels still rotate without drag.

4000 and 5000 Except 1978 5000

The rear drum brakes are equipped with automatic adjusters actuated by the parking brake mechanism (as are the rear disc brakes on the 5000 Turbo). No periodic adjustment of the rear brakes is necessary if this mechanism is working properly. If the brake shoe to drum clearance is incorrect and applying the parking brake a few times does not adjust it properly, the parts will have to be disassembled for repairs.

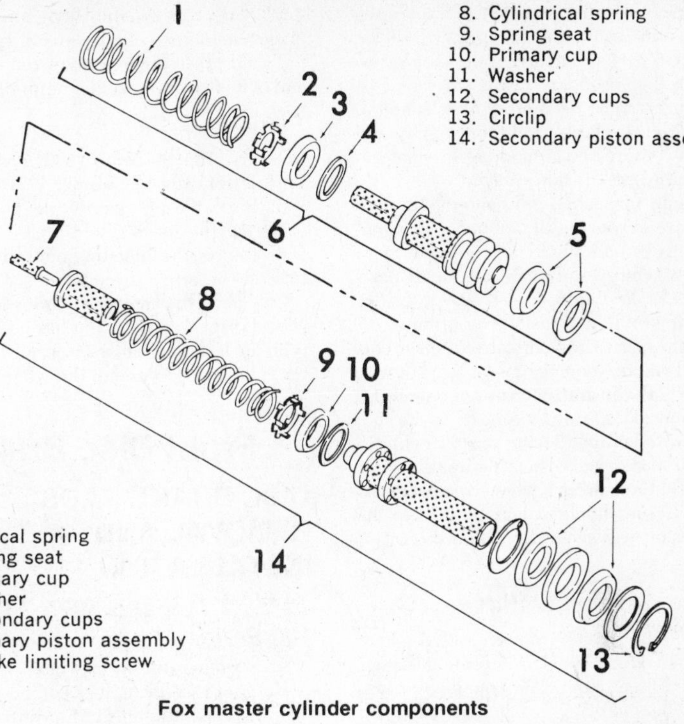

1. Conical spring
2. Spring seat
3. Primary cup
4. Washer
5. Secondary cups
6. Primary piston assembly
7. Stroke limiting screw
8. Cylindrical spring
9. Spring seat
10. Primary cup
11. Washer
12. Secondary cups
13. Circlip
14. Secondary piston assembly

Fox master cylinder components

Master Cylinder

REMOVAL AND INSTALLATION

1. Have an assistant hold the brake pedal down about 1½ in. Disconnect the brake lines nearest the firewall.
2. Hold a container under the fitting disconnected in Step 1 and have the assistant release the pedal. The contents of the reservoir will drain into the container. Discard the used fluid.
3. Disconnect the other brake line.
4. Disconnect the stoplight switch from the master cylinder.
5. Unbolt and remove the master cylinder from the power brake unit. Be careful not to lose the sealing ring between the two units.
6. Installation is the reverse of removal. Master cylinder bolt torque is 17 ft/lbs. Fill and bleed the system. There should be a pedal free-play of 0.2 in. It can be adjusted on the linkage, inside the car.

OVERHAUL

1. Clean the outside of the master cylinder.
2. Remove the brake fluid reservoir, un-

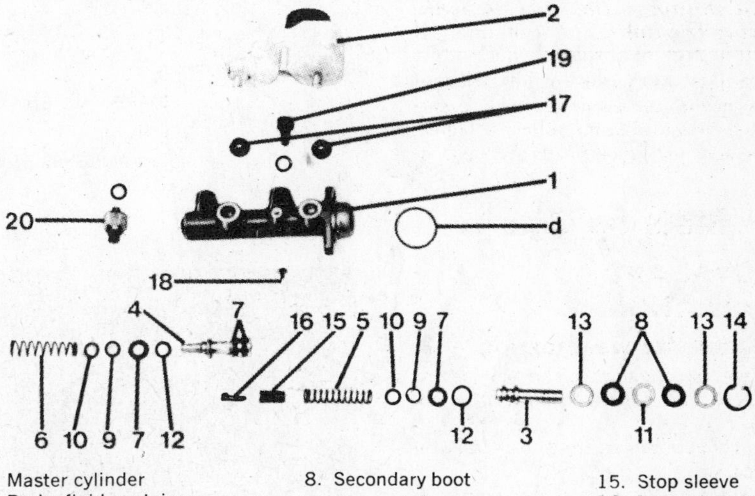

1. Master cylinder
2. Brake fluid container
3. Primary piston
4. Secondary piston
5. Primary spring
6. Secondary spring
7. Primary boot
8. Secondary boot
9. Support ring
10. Spring retainer
11. Intermediate ring
12. Filler disc
13. Stop disc
14. Snap-ring
15. Stop sleeve
16. Inner stop screw
17. Container plug
18. Outer stop screw
19. Pressure valve
20. Brake light switch

Exploded view of the 100 series master cylinder

screw the brake light switch, remove the snap-ring and dismantle the unit. It will be necessary to partially unscrew the stop screw to remove the secondary piston.

3. All parts must be thoroughly cleaned in alcohol or clean brake fluid only. Dry the parts with compressed air and be sure that the compensating port is not plugged.

4. Visually inspect all components. Replace any that are suspect. Rubber boots and container plugs should always be replaced.

5. On assembly, lubricate all metal parts with clean brake fluid.

6. Preassemble and install the piston.

7. Be sure that the boots are installed correctly and are not damaged.

8. Check the pistons for ease of operation. If the pistons do not return quickly to the stop screw or disc, dismantle the master cylinder and lightly polish the cylinder surface.

9. Further assembly is the reverse of disassembly. Grease should not be applied to the pushrod, as it will swell the rubber boots.

Bleeding

The hydraulic system must be bled whenever the pedal feels spongy, indicating that air has entered the system. The system must also be held whenever any component has been disconnected or there has been a leak.

1. Clean off the top of the master cylinder. Check that the fluid level in each reservoir is between the marks.

2. Attach a hose to the bleeder valve at the first wheel to be bled. Mechanics customarily start at the wheel farthest from the master cylinder and work closer. Some 100 Series cars with automatic transmissions and inboard brakes have three bleeder screws on each front brake caliper. On these cars, the bleeding sequence should be: upper right front, upper left front, lower outer right front, lower inner right front, lower outer left front, lower inner left front, left rear, and right rear. Pour a few inches of brake fluid into a clear container and stick the end of the tube below the surface.

NOTE: The tube and container of brake fluid are not absolutely necessary, but this is a very sloppy job without them.

3. Open the bleed valve about ½ turn. Have a helper slowly depress the pedal. Close the valve just before the pedal reaches the end of its travel. Have the helper let the pedal back up.

4. Check the fluid level. If the reservoir runs dry, the procedure will have to be restarted from the beginning.

5. Repeat Step 3 until no more bubbles come out the hose.

6. Repeat the bleeding operations, Steps 3 to 5, at the other three wheels.

7. Check the master cylinder level again.

8. If repeated bleeding has no effect, there is an air leak, probably internally in the master cylinder or in one of the wheel cylinders.

Front Disc Brakes

DISC BRAKE PADS REMOVAL AND INSTALLATION

1975-77 Fox and 1975-76 100 Series

1. Remove the front wheel.

2. Pull the spring locks off the pad retaining pins. Push the pins out toward the outside of the car. Remove the cross spring and lining wear elements.

NOTE: If the pads have worn excessively causing the lining wear elements to break, they must be replaced along with their wiring up to the firewall connector. The right connector is behind the battery.

3. Pull out the inner pad. A special hook tool is available to do this.

4. Press the caliper toward the outside of the car until the outer pad is free to be pulled out.

5. Drain off some of the brake fluid from the master cylinder, since pressing the piston back to install the new pads will cause the brake fluid level to rise in the reservoir and possibly overflow.

6. Press the piston back all the way into the cylinder.

NOTE: If you don't have a piston depressing tool, be extremely careful not to scratch the cylinder wall.

7. Check the piston alignment. It should be at an angle of 20°. If not, it must be rotated.

8. Install the new pads. Be careful that cylinder dust cup isn't damaged.

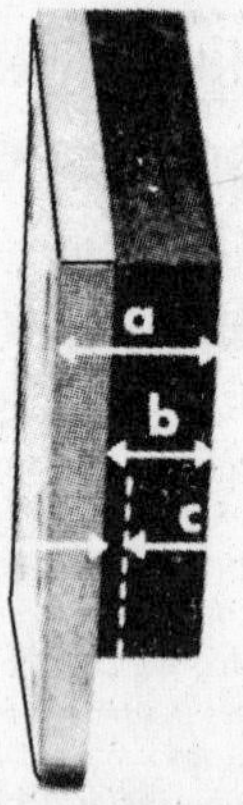

(a) is the thickness of the new pad and the backplate (b) is the thickness of the new pad, and (c) is the minimum safe pad thickness, 0.08 in.

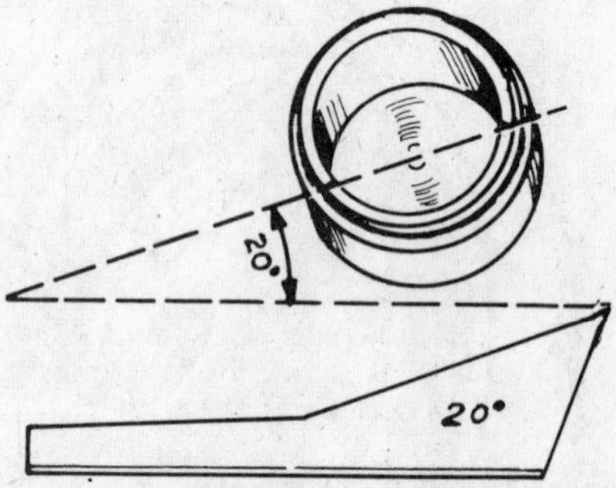

The pistons must be aligned at 20° in the caliper

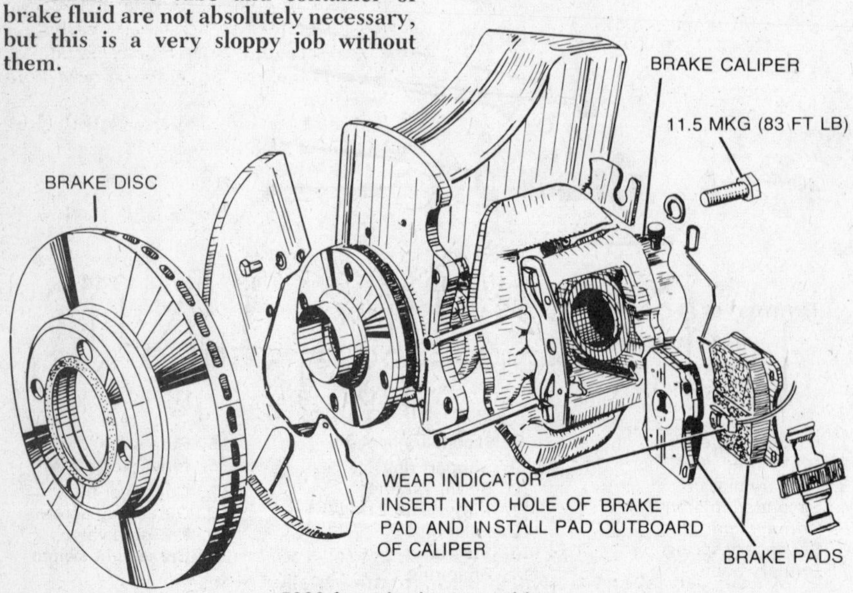

5000 front brake assembly

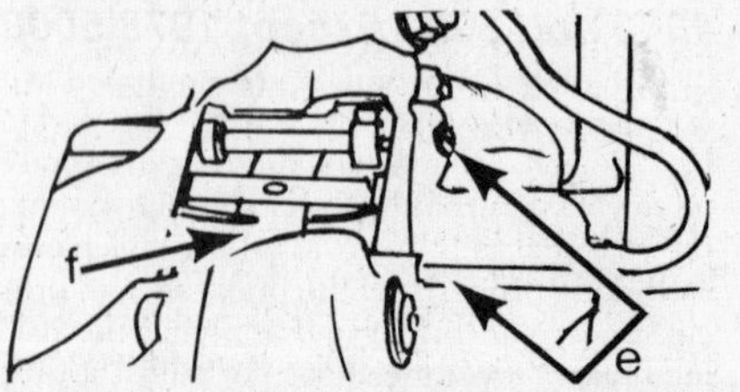

(e) is the pad retaining pins and (f) is the cross spring

9. Install a new cross spring. Install a new lining wear element, if the old one was broken. Replace the retaining pins and spring locks.

10. Replace the wheel.

1978-79 Fox

1. Raise and support the car.
2. Remove the wheel assembly.
3. Press the caliper, by hand, outward to depress the piston.

NOTE: About ½ inch of fluid should be removed from the master cylinder to avoid spillover.

4. Remove the lower caliper mounting bolt. While removing the bolt, hold the guide pin with an open-end wrench.
5. Swing the caliper up and lift out the pads. Make sure the pads are marked for installation if the old pads are being reused.
6. Installation is the reverse of removal. Torque the lower caliper bolt to 25 ft/lbs. Depress the brake pedal firmly several times to adjust the brakes, before moving the car.

If the Fox brake lining wear elements (arrows) have broken off, they must be replaced when new pads are installed

4000 and 5000 Turbo

1. Raise the front of the car and support it with jack stands.
2. Remove the wheels.
3. Using a squeeze bulb or kitchen baster, siphon about ½ an inch of brake fluid out of the master cylinder reservoir.
4. Grasp the caliper from behind and pull it toward you. This will push the piston back into the caliper cylinder.
5. Hold the guide-pin head with an open end wrench and remove the lower brake caliper cylinder bolt.
6. Pivot the caliper cylinder on the upper mounting bolt and swing it upward.

NOTE: If the brake pads are to be reused, mark each one to prevent changing inside to outside or from one caliper to the other.

7. Lift out the brake pads.
8. Install the new brake pads (don't forget the inner heat shield on the Turbo).
9. Swing the caliper down into position and tighten it to 25 ft/lbs using a new self-locking bolt.
10. Top off the master cylinder reservoir.

NOTE: After installation of new brake pads, depress the brake pedal firmly several times before driving to permit the pistons and brake pads to adjust to the brake disc.

5000 and 5000 Diesel

1. Loosen the lug bolts and raise and support the car.
2. Remove the wheel.
3. Detach the wear indicator connector.
4. Remove the pad retaining clips and drive out the retaining pins.
5. Pull out the inner pad.
6. The outer pads are secured by a notch at the top of the pad. To remove them, press the floating frame and cylinder outward.
7. Before installing new pads, remove about ½ inch of fluid from the reservoir. Drive the piston back into the caliper with a C-clamp. Install the pads, wear indicator, retaining pins and clips.
8. Depress the pedal firmly several times before moving the vehicle.

DISC BRAKE CALIPERS REMOVAL AND INSTALLATION

Fox, 1975-76 100 Series, 5000 and 5000 Diesel

1. Remove the wheel.
2. Disconnect the brake line from the caliper.
3. Unbolt the caliper from the steering knuckle.
4. On installation, torque the caliper mounting bolts to 43 ft/lbs. Bleed the brakes.

4000 and 5000 Turbo

1. Remove both brake caliper cylinder mounting bolts and remove the cylinder.

NOTE: If the caliper is being removed for overhaul purposes, disconnect and plug the brake line. If you do not intend to overhaul the caliper, position it out of the way and tie it up so it is not hanging by the brake line.

2. Remove the brake pads.
3. Unscrew the two mounting bolts and remove the brake pad carrier.
4. Installation is in the reverse order of removal.
5. Bleed the brakes if necessary.

Fox, 1975-76 100 Series and 5000 and 5000 Diesel

1. Remove the caliper.
2. Pry the mounting frame off the floating frame.
3. Pry the brake cylinder and guide spring off the floating frame.
4. Remove the clamp and dust cup from the cylinder.
5. Pull the piston out of the cylinder. If it won't come out, you can apply air pressure through the brake line connection.

CAUTION

When forcing the piston out with air pressure, make sure to hold it face down on the bench so that the piston doesn't fly out.

6. Pull the seal out of the cylinder. Be extremely careful not to damage the cylinder wall.
7. Clean the piston and cylinder in alcohol. They may not be refinished; replace them if damaged.
8. Coat the cylinder and piston parts with clean brake fluid. Install the piston with a new seal and dust cup. Make sure that the piston face is installed at a 20° angle. See "Brake Pad Replacement."

4000 and 5000 Turbo

1. Remove the caliper assembly and clean it of all mud and dust.
2. Remove the dust cap from the brake caliper cylinder.
3. Pull the piston out of the brake cylinder. If the piston can't be pulled out, apply compressed air to a brake line fitting.

NOTE: When forcing the piston out of the cylinder with air pressure, make sure to hold it face down against a table or bench so that the piston doesn't end up on the other side of the room.

4. Pull the seal out of the cylinder. Be extremely careful not to damage the cylinder wall.
5. Clean the piston and the cylinder in alcohol. If either is scratched, rusted or otherwise damaged, it must be replaced.
6. Slide the dust cap onto the inside end of the piston.
7. Coat the cylinder and piston with clean brake fluid. Install the seal.

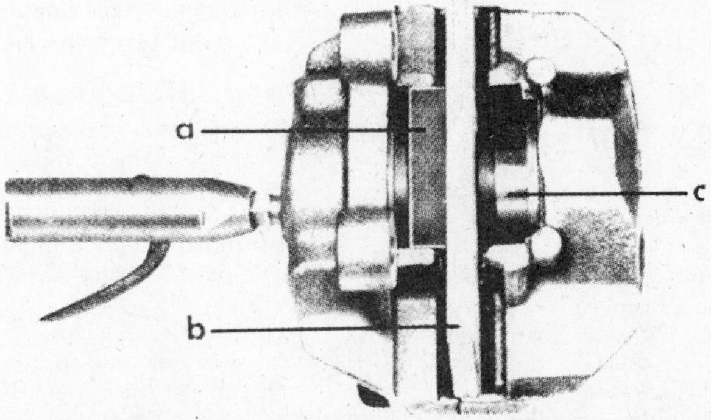

Air pressure is used to remove the piston (c) from the caliper. An old pad (a) and a piece of wood (b) are installed in the caliper

8. Install the piston and insert the inner lip of the dust cap into the groove in the brake cylinder wall.

9. Press the piston into the brake cylinder as far as it will go. The outer lip of the dust cap must slip into the groove in the piston.

10. Installation of the remaining components is in the reverse order of removal.

11. Bleed the brakes.

BRAKE DISC REMOVAL AND INSTALLATION

All Models

1. Jack up the car and remove the wheel.
2. Unbolt and set aside the caliper. Don't disconnect the brake line. Don't let the caliper hang on the brake line.
3. Remove the screw and take off the disc. Be very careful not to touch the disc surface with greasy fingers.
4. Installation is the reverse of removal.

INSPECTION

Fox, 1975-76 100 Series

Maximum permissible disc runout is 0.002 in. The disc may be machined but minimum safe thickness is 0.43 in. The original thickness is 0.46 in. Maximum permissible thickness variation is 0.001 in.

4000

The original disc thickness 0.472 in. (12 mm). The disc should not be ground to less than 0.413 in. (10.5 mm).

5000

Maximum runout is 0.004 in. The original thickness is 0.866 in. The minimum thickness after machining is 0.807 in. Maximum thickness variation is 0.008 in.

FRONT WHEEL BEARINGS REMOVAL AND INSTALLATION, ADJUSTMENT

There is no front wheel bearing adjustment. The bearing is pressed into the steering knuckle. Axle nut torque is 180 ft/lbs for the 100 series and Fox, 167 ft/lbs for the 4000, 203 ft/lbs for the 5000 and 5000 Diesel and 202 ft/lbs for the 5000 Turbo. The axle nut should be tightened only with the wheels resting on the ground.

Rear Drum Brakes

BRAKE DRUMS REMOVAL AND INSTALLATION

1. Jack up the car and remove the wheel. Release the parking brake.
2. Pry off the grease cap.
3. Remove the cotter pin and the nuts.
4. Pull off the brake drum by hand, making sure that the washer and roller bearing don't fall out. If the drum is held by the brakes, back off on the brake adjustment.
5. On reinstallation, tighten the nut to force the brake drum into place, then loosen it until there is 0.001-0.002 in. bearing play measured with a dial indicator.

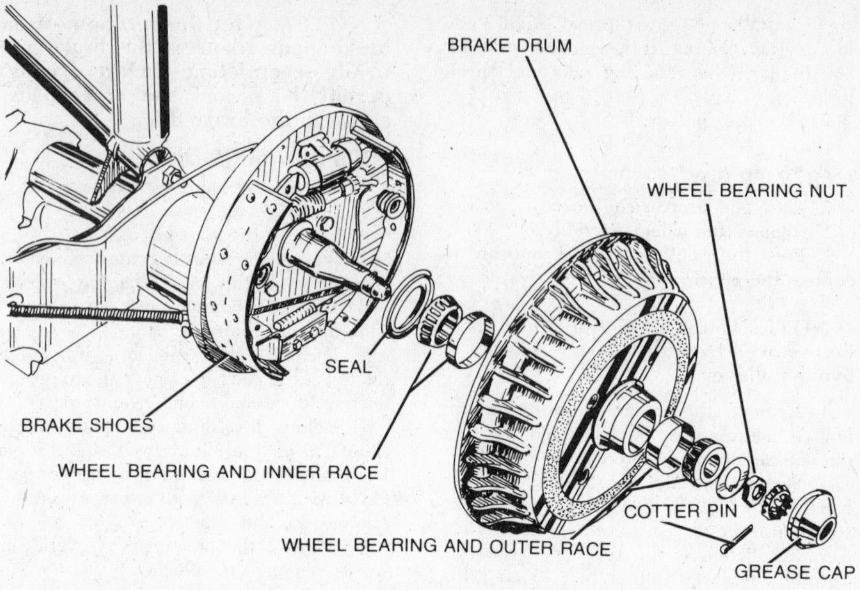

Rear brake components—5000 model shown, Fox similar

6. Replace the castellated nut and install a new cotter pin.
7. Fill the grease cap with about 10 oz of wheel bearing grease.
8. Adjust the brakes if necessary.

BRAKE SHOES REMOVAL AND INSTALLATION

100 Series

1. Remove the brake drum.
2. Remove the big retaining spring at the bottom. Be careful it doesn't fly out.
3. Disconnect the parking brake cable and pull the shoes from the wheel cylinder.
4. Remove the shoes.
5. Reverse the procedure for installation, making sure that the front and rear shoes are not interchanged.

Fox and 1978 5000

1. Remove the brake drum.
2. Use brake pliers to remove the lower spring, on Fox or the upper spring on the 5000.
3. Turn the washers to release the shoe retaining springs.
4. Disconnect the parking brake cable by pressing the spring toward the front of the car and unhooking the cable from the lever.
5. Reverse the procedure for installation.

4000 and 1979 and Later 5000

1. Raise the rear of the car and support it with jack stands.
2. Remove the wheels and then remove the brake drums.
3. Use brake pliers to unhook the upper and lower return springs and the adjusting wedge spring.
4. Turn and remove the caps to release the brake shoe retaining springs.
5. Disconnect the parking brake cable by pushing the spring toward the front of the car and unhooking the cable from the brake lever.
6. Unhook the tensioning spring and remove the pushrod.

To install:

7. Install the tensioning spring and position the brake shoe on the pushrod.
8. Insert the adjusting wedge with the lug facing the backing plate.
9. Position the remaining brake shoe with the brake lever onto the pushrod and connect the upper return spring.
10. Hook the parking brake cable back onto the brake lever.
11. Position the tops of the brake shoes in the wheel cylinder pistons and connect the lower return spring.
12. Lift the brake shoes onto the lower support and connect the adjusting wedge spring.
13, Install the brake shoe retaining springs and their caps.
14. Installation of the remaining components is in the reverse order of removal.
15. Depress the brake pedal once firmly to set the brake shoes.

WHEEL CYLINDERS REMOVAL AND INSTALLATION

1. Remove the brake shoes.
2. Depress the brake pedal about 1½ in. to block the master cylinder compensating port and prevent leakage. Secure the pedal in this position.
3. Disconnect the brake line and plug the opening.
4. Remove the two mounting screws from the backing plate.
5. Remove the cylinder.
6. Reverse the procedure for installation.

OVERHAUL

1. Clean the outside of the cylinder, using alcohol or clean brake fluid.
2. Remove the rubber boots and disassemble the cylinder.
3. Clean all parts in alcohol.
4. Air dry all parts.

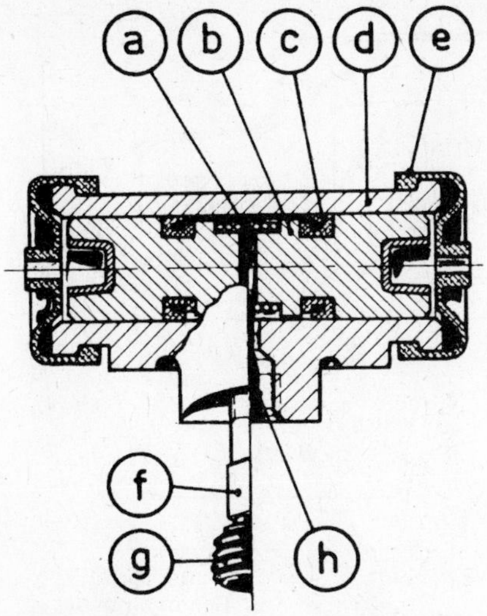

(a)—Spring
(b)—Piston
(c)—Grooved cup
(d)—Cylinder
(e)—Cap
(f)—Bleeder valve
(g)—Dust cap
(h)—Brake line connection

Cross-section of a rear wheel cylinder

5. If there are any pits or roughness inside the cylinder, it must be replaced.
6. Replace the piston if it is scratched or damaged in any way.
7. Lubricate all internal parts with clean brake fluid and reassemble the cylinder. Replace all rubber parts.
8. Make sure that the cylinder slides freely. If it does not, disassemble the cylinder and polish the inside of the cylinder lightly by revolving the cylinder around a piece of crocus cloth held by a finger. Do not polish the cylinder in a lengthwise direction. Clean the cylinder again after polishing. Air dry.
9. Replace the boots.
10. Replace the cylinder and tighten the bolts evenly. Bleed the system after it is reassembled.

REAR WHEEL BEARINGS REMOVAL AND INSTALLATION, ADJUSTMENT

Refer to "Rear Suspension—Wheel Bearings and Stub Axle Removal and Installation" for these procedures.

Parking Brake

ADJUSTMENT

100 Series, Fox and 1978 5000

The handbrake (parking brake) must be adjusted periodically to compensate for lining wear and cable stretching. The adjuster is at the cable junction, under the center of the car.

1. Block the front wheels. Raise and support the rear of the vehicle. Do not use a jack under the rear axle tube.
2. Pull the brake up to the first notch.
3. If the wheels will not rotate freely, loosen the adjusting nut.

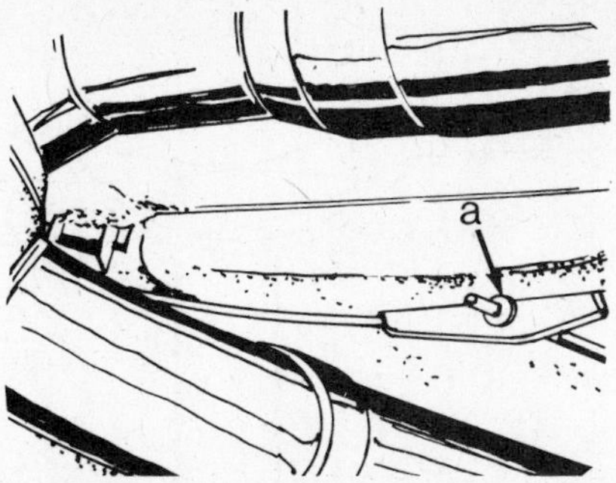

(a) indicates the adjusting point for one piece rear handbrake cables used on most models

4. Tighten the adjusting nut until neither wheel can be turned by hand.
5. Check that there is no drag when the brake handle is fully released.

4000 and 1979 and Later 5000

NOTE: Because of self-adjusting rear brakes, adjustment is only necessary after replacement of any of the brake components.

1. Raise the rear of the car and support it with jack stands.
2. Release the parking brake lever.
3. Depress the brake pedal once.
4. Pull the parking brake lever onto the second tooth in the 4000 and the third tooth in the 5000.
5. Tighten the adjusting nut on the parking brake cable equalizer bar until the wheels can just be turned by hand.
6. Release the lever and check that both wheels rotate freely.
7. Turn the ignition switch on and check that the brake warning light comes on when the parking brake lever is pulled up to the first tooth and goes out when it is released.

CABLE REMOVAL AND INSTALLATION

100 Series and Fox

1. Jack up the rear of the car. Do not place a jack under the axle tube on the 1973 100 Series.
2. Block the front wheels and release the handbrake.
3. Remove the rear brake shoes.
4. Remove the cable adjusting nut(s) and detach the cable guides from the floor pan.
5. Replace the cable and brake shoes. Check the parking brake adjustment.

4000 and 5000

1. Raise and support the rear of the car. Release the parking brake.
2. Remove the rear brake drums on all but the 5000 Turbo.
3. Disconnect the cable from the shoe assembly by pushing the spring forward and removing the cable from the adjusting arm on all but the 5000 Turbo.
4. Pull the parking brake cable out of its retaining clip on the caliper (5000 Turbo only).
5. Remove the cable compensating spring.
6. Back off the equalizer nut and guide the cable through the trailing arms and supports.
7. Installation is the reverse of removal.

NOTE: When installing the parking brake cables on the 5000 Turbo, the long cable goes on the left side and the short one goes on the right side. The cable coupling should connect the two cables on the right side of the equalizer bar.

8. Adjust if necessary.

CHASSIS ELECTRICAL

Heater

REMOVAL AND INSTALLATION

100 Series

To remove either the heater blower or the core, it is necessary to remove the heater unit from the car and disassemble it.

1. Drain the coolant, disconnect the battery, and remove the lower instrument panel trim and center shelf.
2. Remove the breather screw from the hose inside the engine compartment, being careful not to damage the firewall seal.
3. Detach both heater hoses.
4. Disconnect the cables that control the foot area heater flaps, the windshield flap and the heater valve.
5. Remove the plug connector from the heater controls and the lead from terminal 15 of the emergency warning light switch.
6. From the passenger compartment unbolt the heater and pull it down.
7. Installation is the reverse of removal.

NOTE: When installing the cables, place the heater levers in the Off position. Place the leg of the spring clip in the mount and install the spring clip. The cable sleeve must protrude at least 0.2 in. beyond the spring clip.

4000

1. Disconnect the negative battery cable.
2. Drain the engine coolant.

NOTE: Save the coolant for reuse.

3. Trace the heater hoses coming from the firewall and disconnect them. One leads to the back of the cylinder head and the other leads to the heater valve located above and behind the oil filter.
4. Detach the cable for the heater valve.
5. Remove the center console.
6. Remove the left and right covers below the instrument panel.
7. Pull off the fresh air/heater control knobs.
8. Pull off the trim plate.
9. Remove the screws (2) for the controls.
10. Remove the center cover mounting screws (2 top and 2 bottom) and remove the cover.
11. Detach the right, left and center air ducts.

12. Remove the heater housing retaining spring.

13. Remove the cowl for the air plenum which is located under the hood and in front of the windshield.

14. Remove the heater housing mounting screws (4) and remove the heater housing. The mounting screws are under the hood where the air plenum was.

15. Installation is in the reverse order of removal. Be sure to replace all sealing material.

5000

WITH OR WITHOUT FACTORY INSTALLED A/C

NOTE: Blower or core removal requires removal and disassembly of the entire unit.

1. Disconnect the battery ground.
2. Drain the cooling system.

CAUTION

If the vehicle is equipped with air conditioning, the A/C system must be discharged. This procedure should be left to a trained technician.

3. Discharge the air conditioning system.
4. Disconnect the:
   a. Temperature sensor connector.
   b. Evaporator/heater connector clamp.
   c. Temperature control cable.
   d. Fresh air door vacuum hose.
5. Disconnect the main harness connector.
6. Loosen the case retaining strap.
7. Remove the coolant hoses at the heater core tubes.

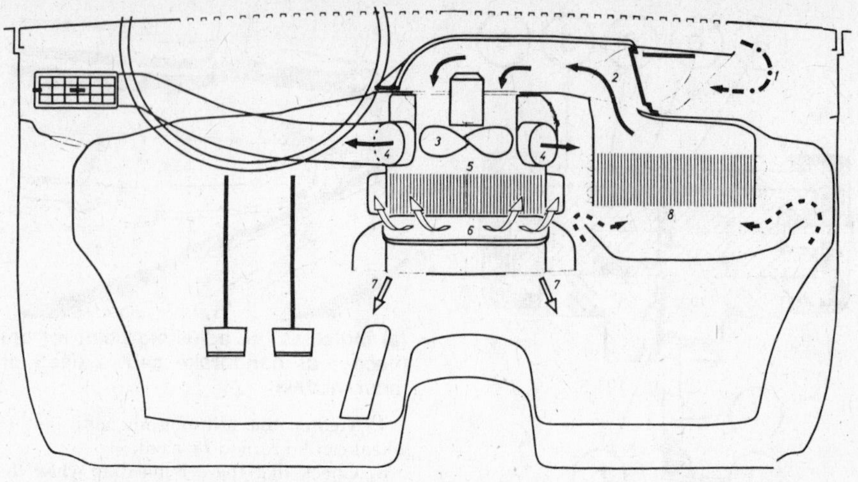

1. Fresh air inlet with control flap (opens with heater on)
2. Dry air flap (opens with A/C on)
3. Heater—A/C blower
4. Air outlets for ends of instrument panel
5. Heater core
6. Center air outlet
7. Floor air outlet
8. Evaporator

Fox heater system (models with A/C)

8. Remove the yellow, green and red vacuum hoses from the heater case.
9. Remove the air duct hoses.
10. Remove the heater case mounting screws (two in the passenger compartment, one in the engine compartment). On A/C equipped cars, remove the four evaporator housing mounting screws in the passenger compartment.
11. Support the heater/evaporator unit and pull it away from the firewall.
12. Remove the control cable grommet to facilitate case removal.

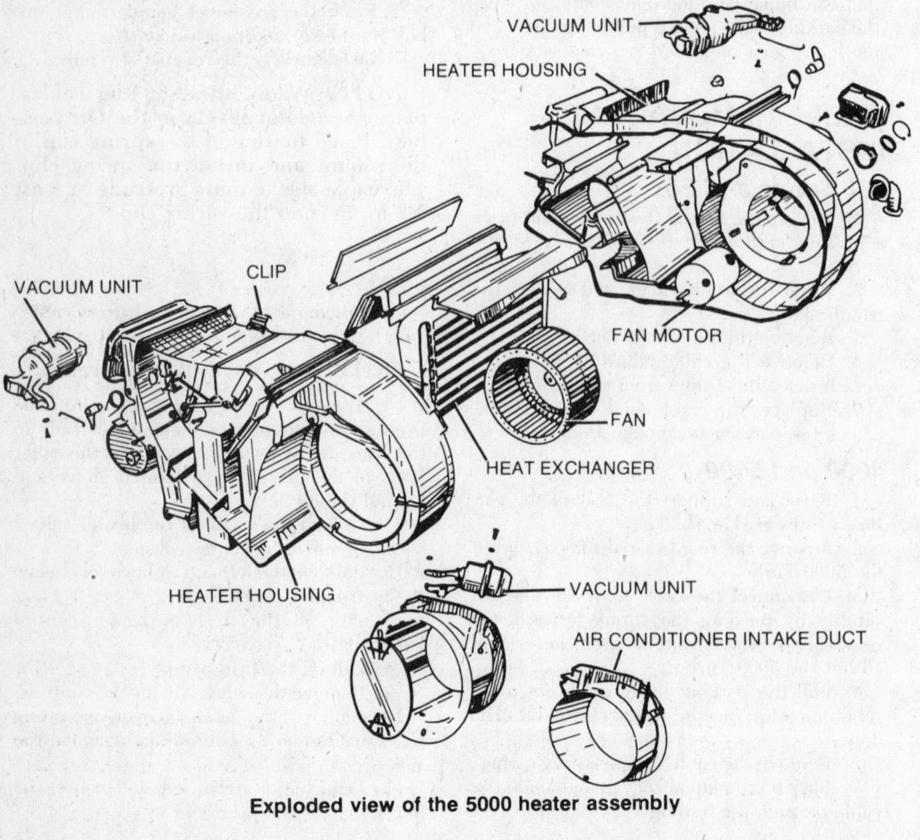

Exploded view of the 5000 heater assembly

13. The case halves may be separated by removing the clips at the top and bottom with a screwdriver.
14. Installation is the reverse of removal. Replace all sealing material. Evacuate, charge and leak test the system. This last procedure should be performed by a trained technician.

Fox

The heater must be removed and disassembled to service the heater of the core.

1. Remove the windshield washer container. Remove the ignition coil.
2. Disconnect the two hoses from the heater core connections at the firewall.
3. Unplug the electrical connector.
4. Remove the heater control knobs on the dash.
5. Remove the controls from the dash complete with brackets.
6. Pull the cable connection off the electric motor.
7. Disconnect the cable from the lever on the round knob.
8. Using a screwdriver, pry the retaining clip off the fresh air housing (the front portion of the heater).
9. Remove the fresh air housing complete with the controls.
10. Detach the left and right air hoses.
11. Lower the heater assembly.
12. Pull out the two pins and remove the heater cover. Unscrew and remove the fan motor.
13. Separate the heater halves to remove the heater core.
14. Installation is the reverse of removal.

Radio

The radio is usually a dealer installed or aftermarket unit. Thus no specific removal and installation procedures can be given. The following information applies generally to all car radios.

Care should be taken during installation to avoid reversing the ground and power leads. Reversal of these leads will cause serious

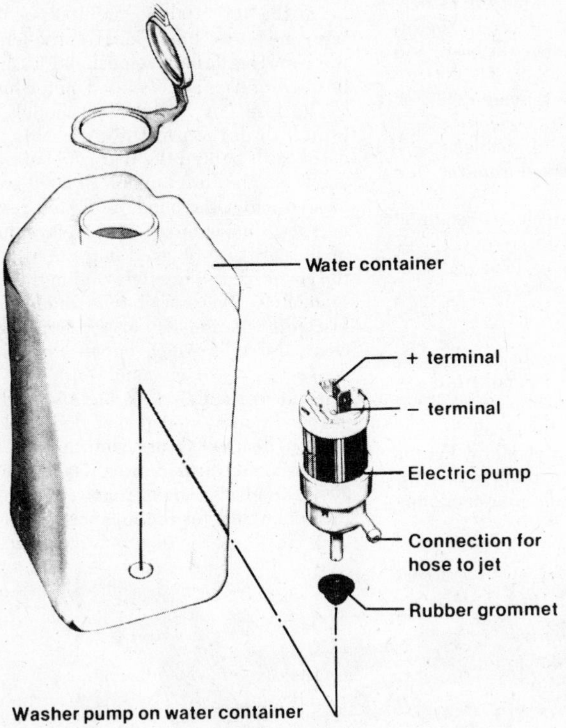

Washer pump on water container

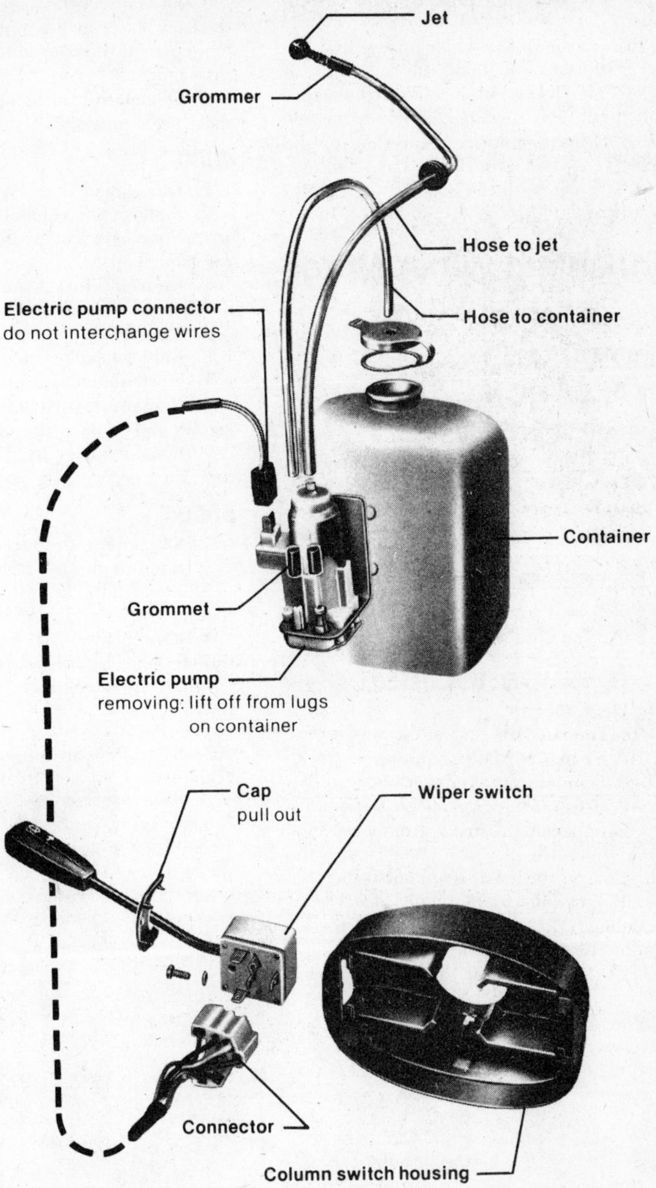

Fox windshield washer system

damage to the radio. The power lead usually has an in-line fuse.

If the speaker needs replacement, it should be replaced with one of the same impedance, measured in ohms. Mismatched impedance can cause rapid transistor failure as well as poor radio performance. This should also be taken into consideration when adding a second speaker.

The radio should never be operated without a speaker connected or with the speaker leads shorted. This will result in transistor failure.

ANTENNA TRIMMER ADJUSTMENT

The antenna trimmer should be adjusted whenever the radio, antenna cable, or antenna is replaced, or when reception is poor.

1. Tune the radio to a weak station at about 14 on the AM band.
2. Adjust the antenna to the normal height, or to 31 in. for FM receivers.
3. Turn the trimmer screw to get the maximum volume. The screw is usually on the back or side of the radio case, in the dial, or sometimes hidden behind one of the the dial knobs.

Wiper Motor

REMOVAL AND INSTALLATION

100 Series

The motor can be removed from inside the engine compartment.

1. Disconnect the battery negative terminal.
2. Remove the right and left knee padding.
3. From the engine compartment, pull out the rubber grommet to give the wiring harness more play. Pull out the wiper switch and remove the leads.
4. Bend open the metal tabs holding the wiring harness and remove the harness which runs below the spray jets, together with the spray jet line.
5. Loosen the nut and pry off the lever for the linkage.
6. Remove the motor and harness.
7. Reverse the procedure for installation.

Wiper Linkage

REMOVAL AND INSTALLATION

100, 100LS, 100GL

The linkage can be removed from inside the engine compartment.

1. Remove the windshield wiper arms from the studs by prying off the cap and removing the retaining nut. Remove the lower nut, washer and seal from the recess in the body.
3. Remove the mounting screws in the en-

gine compartment and tilt the wiper base to remove.

4. Installation of the wiper linkage and the motor is done by reversing the removal procedures. The lever connected to the wiper motor should be installed at approximately 90° to the front and rear centerline of the vehicle. The wiper arm blades have different angles. The arm with the blade at the greater angle is installed on the driver's side.

Windshield Wiper Motor and Linkage

REMOVAL AND INSTALLATION

Fox, 4000, and 5000

1. Pry off wiper arms and remove nuts from studs in cowl.
2. Remove brace-to-body screws.
3. Disconnect multiple connector at wiper motor.
4. Remove motor mounting screw, and pry off connecting rod.
5. Remove linkage followed by motor.

Instrument Cluster

REMOVAL AND INSTALLATION

100 Series

1. Disconnect the battery ground cable.
2. Remove the screws which hold the padding on top of the instrument panel. Remove the padding.
3. Remove the nuts at the rear of the instrument cluster and remove the cover.
4. Pull the cluster out toward the driver's seat.
5. Pull off the electrical connections and unscrew the speedometer cable.
6. Remove the instrument cluster. It may be further disassembled as necessary.

Fox

1. Disconnect the battery ground cable.
2. Remove the lower instrument panel trim.
3. Disconnect the speedometer cable from the back of the speedometer. Detach the electrical plug at the back of the fuel and temperature gauge.
4. Detach the spring at either end and pull the cluster forward.

4000

1. Disconnect the negative battery cable.
2. Remove the retaining screws for the instrument cluster cover. Remove the cover and the trim strip.
3. From the top of the instrument cluster, remove the four multi-point connectors.
4. Unscrew the speedometer cable.
5. Remove each switch panel from the side of the instrument cluster.
6. Remove the instrument cluster retaining screws and remove the cluster.
7. Installation is in the reverse order of removal.

5000

1. Disconnect the negative battery cable.
2. Remove the instrument panel trim.
3. Remove the instrument cluster cover retaining screws and remove the cover.
4. Loosen the instrument cluster retaining screws and slide it forward enough to remove the multi-point connectors and the speedometer cable.
5. Remove the cluster retaining screws and remove the cluster.
6. Installation is in the reverse order of removal.

Fuse Box Location

On the 100, 100LS, and 100GL, the fuse box is near the clutch pedal on the left side of the car. The flasher, windshield washer, and headlight relays are mounted on the fuse box.

The fuse box for all 4000 models can be found underneath the left side of the dashboard, behind the rear panel of the package tray. The fuse box for all 5000 models is located under the hood, at the left rear of the engine compartment. The relays for both models are also plugged into the fuse box. In the cover of each fuse box (and in the Owner's Manual) is a chart which tells which circuit the fuse protects and its correct amperage. The chart also tells which circuit the relays are connected to. Each model also uses in-line fuses for certain circuits: fuel pump, battery, air conditioning and power door locks (if so equipped), 4000; air conditioning, power windows, and heated seats, 5000; glow plug, 5000 Diesel; cigar lighter, power windows and the cooling fan for the injectors, 5000 Turbo.

Fuse box—5000

SPECIFICATIONS

INDEX

BEFORE SERVICING, SEE THE SAFETY NOTICE ON THE CONTENTS PAGE

INTRODUCTION

BMW cars are produced by the Bavarian Motor Works in Munich, West Germany.

The company was formed in 1916 to manufacture aircraft engines and has the distinction of manufacturing the first aircraft jet engine.

Beginning in 1923, BMW began to produce motorcycles, followed by automobiles in 1928.

Both 4 cylinder and 6 cylinder engines are used in the BMW vehicles, with fuel injection offered on most models as standard equipment.

SERIAL NUMBER IDENTIFICATION

Manufacturer's Plate

The manufacturer's plate is located in the engine compartment on the right side inner fender panel or support, or on the right side of the firewall.

Chassis Number

The chassis number can be found in the engine compartment on the right inner fender support or facing forward on the right side of the heater bulkhead. A label is also attached to the upper steering column cover inside the vehicle.

Engine Number

The engine number is located on the left rear side of the engine, above the starter motor.

Under hood serial number location—typical

Engine serial number location

GENERAL ENGINE SPECIFICATIONS

Year	Model	Engine No. Cyl.—Displacement cu. in. (cc)	Carburetor or Injection Type	SAE Horsepower @ rpm	SAE Torque @ rpm (ft. lbs.)	Bore X Stroke (in.)	Compression Ratio	Oil Pressure @ rpm (psi)
1975-76	2002	4-121 (1990)	Solex 32/32 DIDTA	98 @ 5500	106 @ 3500	3.504 x 3.150	8.3:1	57 @ 4000
1977-79	320i	4-121 (1990)	Bosch K-Jetronic mechanical injection	110 @ 5800	112 @ 3750	3.504 x 3.150	8.2:1	57 @ 4000
1977-79	530i 630CSi	6-182 (2985)	Bosch L-Jetronic electronic injection	176 @ 5500	185 @ 4500	3.504 x 3.150	8.1:1	71 @ 6000
1978-79	733i	6-196 (3210)	Bosch L-Jetronic electronic injection	177 @ 5200	195 @ 4000	3.504 x 3.386	8.4:1	71 @ 6000
1975-76	3.0Si	6-182 (2985)	Bosch electronic injection	200 @ 5500	200 @ 4000	3.504 x 3.150	9.5:1	71 @ 6000
1978-79	633CSi	6-196 (3210)	Bosch L-Jetronic electronic injection	176 @ 5500	195 @ 4000	3.504 x 3.150	8.4:1	71 @ 6000

GENERAL ENGINE SPECIFICATIONS

Year	Model	Engine No. Cyl.— Displacement cu. in. (cc)	Carburetor or Injection Type	SAE Horsepower @ rpm	SAE Torque @ rpm (ft. lbs.)	Bore X Stroke (in.)	Compression Ratio	Oil Pressure @ rpm (psi)
1980-81	320i	4-108 (1766)	Bosch K-Jetronic mechanical injection	101 @ 5800	100 @ 4500	3.504 x 2.795	8.8:1	57 @ 4000
1980-81	528i	6-170 (2788)	Bosch L-Jetronic electronic injection	169 @ 5500	170 @ 4500	3.390 x 3.150	8.2:1	71 @ 4000
1980-81	633CSi	6-196 (3210)	Bosch L-Jetronic electronic injection	174 @ 5200	188 @ 4200	3.504 x 3.386	8.0:1	71 @ 6000
1980-81	733i	6-196 (3210)	Bosch L-Jetronic electronic injection	177 @ 5500	196 @ 4000	3.504 x 3.386	8.4:1	71 @ 6000

TUNE-UP SPECIFICATIONS

Year	Model	SPARK PLUGS Type	SPARK PLUGS Gap (in.)	DISTRIBUTOR Dwell (deg.)	DISTRIBUTOR Point Gap (in.)	IGNITION TIMING (deg.) ③ MT	IGNITION TIMING (deg.) ③ AT	Intake Valve Opens (deg.)	Fuel Pump Pressure (psi)	IDLE SPEED (rpm) MT	IDLE SPEED (rpm) AT	Cold Valve Clearance (in.)
1975-76	2002	Bosch W175T30, W200T30, WG190T30; Champion N-8Y, N-9Y, N-11Y; NGK BP-6ES	.026	62	.016	1600 rpm ①	1600 rpm ①	4B	4.3	900	900	.007
1977-79	320i	Bosch W145T30	.026	62	.016	25B @ 2200 (2400)	25B @ 2200 (2400)	4B	64-74	950	950	007
1977-79	530i	Bosch W145T30	.026	38	.015	22B @ 1700 (2700)	22B @ 1700 (2700)	26B	35	950	950	.011
1978-79	733i	Bosch W145T30; Champion N-10Y	.026	Electronic		22B @ 2400 (2750)	22B @ 2400 (2750)	26B	43	950	950	.011
1975-76	3.0Si	Bosch W145T30, W175T30; Champion N-11Y, N-9Y	.026	38	.015	22B @ 1700	22B @ 1700	26B	30	900	900	.011
1977-79	630CSi	Bosch W145T30; Champion N-10Y	.024	38	.015	22B @ 1700 (2700)	22B @ 1700 (2700)	—	36.3	950	950	.012

TUNE-UP SPECIFICATIONS

Year	Model	SPARK PLUGS Type	Gap (in.)	DISTRIBUTOR Point Dwell (deg.)	DISTRIBUTOR Point Gap (in.)	IGNITION TIMING (deg.) ③ MT	IGNITION TIMING (deg.) ③ AT	Intake Valve Opens (deg.)	Fuel Pump Pressure (psi)	IDLE SPEED (rpm) MT	IDLE SPEED (rpm) AT	Cold Valve Clearance (in.)
1978-79	633CSi	Bosch W145T30; Champion N-10Y	.024	Electronic		22B @ 2400 (2750)	22B @ 2400 (2750)	14B	28.5	950	950	.012
1980-81	320i	Bosch WR9DS	.024	Electronic ②		25B @ 2200	25B @ 2200	4B	64-74	850	900	.007
1980-81	528i	Bosch WR9DS	.024	Electronic ②		22B @ 2100	22B @ 2100	26B	35	900	900	.011
1980-81	633CSi	Bosch WR9DS	.024	Electronic ②		22B @ 1650	22B @ 1650	—	35	900	900	.011
1980-81	733i	Bosch WR9DS	.024	Electronic ②		22B @ 1650	22B @ 1650	26B	35	900	900	.011

① Align steel ball in flywheel with pointer on flywheel housing window at specified speed

② Air gap 0.012-0.028″
Dwell 42° ± 10° @ 15 rpm
52° ± 5° @ 4500 rpm

③ Figures in parentheses are for California

B Before top dead center (TDC)

FIRING ORDERS

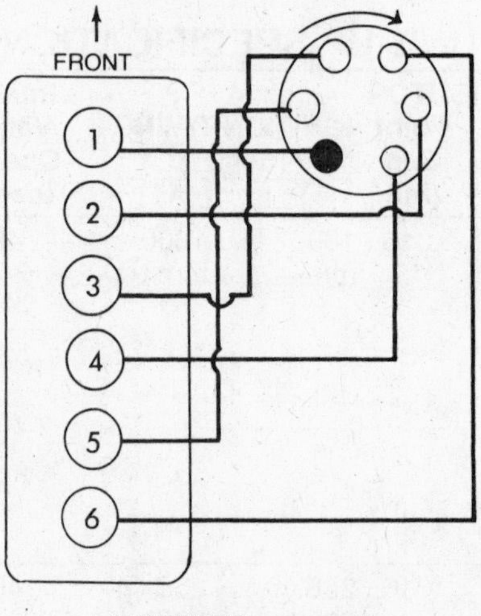

6 CYLINDER
FIRING ORDER 1-5-3-6-2-4

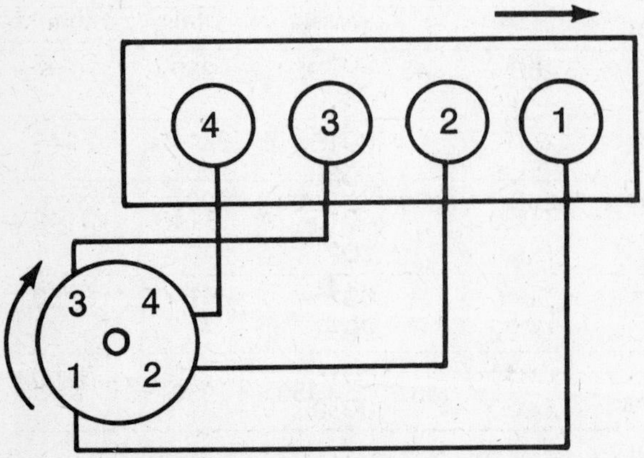

1975-79 4 cylinder firing order 1-3-4-2

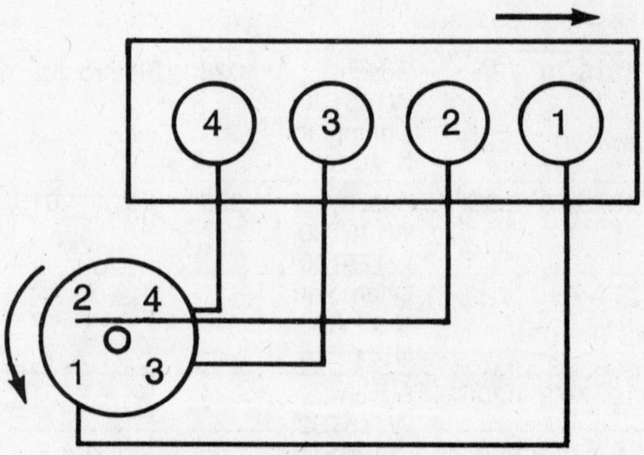

1980-81 4 cylinder firing order 1-3-4-2

CAPACITIES

Year	Model	Engine Crankcase (qts) With Filter Change	Engine Crankcase (qts) Without Filter Change	Transmission, Refill After Draining (pts) Manual	Transmission, Refill After Draining (pts) Automatic	Drive Axle (pts)	Gasoline Tank (gals)	Cooling System (qts)
1975-76	2002, 2002tii	4.5	4.25	2.8	3.6	1.9	13.5	7.0
1977-79	320i	4.25	4.0	2.2	4.2	2.0	15.9	7.4
1977-79	530i, 630CSi	6.1	5.25	2.3	4.2	3.4	16.4	12.7
1978-79	733i, 633CSi	6.1	5.25	2.4	4.8	4.0	22.5	12.7
1975-76	3.0S, 3.0Si	5.3	5.0	2.5	3.8	3.4	16.5	12.7
1980-81	320i	8.5	8.0	3.2	12.0	2.0	15.3	7.4
1980-81	528i	6.0	5.0	2.3	15.0	3.4	16.4	12.7
1980-81	633CSi	6.1	5.3	2.3	15.0	3.4	16.5	12.7
1980-81	733i	6.1	5.3	2.3	15.0	4.0	22.5	12.7

CRANKSHAFT AND CONNECTING ROD SPECIFICATIONS

(Measurements in inches)

Year	Model	Crankshaft Main Bearing Journal Diameter	Crankshaft Main Bearing Oil Clearance	Shaft End-Play	Thrust on No.	Journal Diameter	Connecting Rod Oil Clearance	Side Clearance
1975-76	2002, 2002tii	2.1654	.0012-.0028	.003-.007	3	1.8898	.0009-.0027	.0016
1977-81	320i	2.1653	.0012-.0027	.003-.007	3	1.8898	.0009-.0031	.0015
1977-81	528i, 530i, 630SCi	2.3622	.0011-.0027	.003-.007	4	1.8897	.0009-.0027	.0016
1978-81	733i, 633CSi	2.3622	.0012-.0027	.003-.007	4	1.8898	.0009-.0031	.0015
1975-76	3.0S, 3.0Si	2.3622	.0012-.0028	.003-.007	4	1.8898	.0013-.0027	.0016

VALVE SPECIFICATIONS

Year	Model	Seat Angle (deg.)	Face Angle (deg.)	Spring Pressure (lbs.) @ in.	Spring Free Height (in.)	Stem to Guide Clearance (in.) Intake	Stem to Guide Clearance (in.) Exhaust	Stem Diameter (in.) Intake	Stem Diameter (in.) Exhaust
1975-76	2002, 2002tii	45	45½	64 @ 1.48	1.71	.0010-.0020	.0015-.0030	.3149	.3149
1977-81	320i	45	45½	64 @ 1.48	1.71 or 1.81 ①	.0010-.0020	.0015-.0030	.3149	.3149
1977-81	528i, 530i, 630CSi	45	45⅓	64 @ 1.48	1.71	.0010-.0021	.0015-.0027	.3149	.3149
1978-81	733i, 633CSi	45	45½	64 @ 1.48	1.71 or 1.81 ①	.0010-.0022	.0016-.0027	.3150	.3150
1975-76	3.0S, 3.0Si	45	45⅓	64 @ 1.48	1.71	.0010-.0020	.0015-.0030	.3150	.3150

① A dimension of 1.81 applies to some springs depending on the original manufacturer

PISTON AND RING SPECIFICATIONS
(Measurements in inches)

Year	Model	Piston to Bore Clearance	Ring Gap Top Compression	Ring Gap Bottom Compression	Ring Gap Oil Control	Ring Side Clearance Top Compression	Ring Side Clearance Bottom Compression	Ring Side Clearance Oil Control
1975-76	2002, 2002tii	.002	.012-.020	.008-.016	.010-.016	.002-.003	.001-.002	.001-.002
1977-81	320i	.002	.012-.018	.008-.016	.010-.020	.002-.004	.002-.003	.001-.002
1977-81	528i, 530i 630CSi	.002	.012-.020	.008-.015	.010-.016	.002-.003	.001-.002	.001-.002
1978-81	733i, 633CSi	.002	.012-.018	.008-.016	.010-.020	.002-.004	.002-.003	.001-.002
1975-76	3.0S, 3.0Si	.002	.012-.020	.008-.016	.010-.016	.002-.003	.001-.002	.001-.002

TORQUE SPECIFICATIONS
(Measurements in inches)

Year	Model	Cylinder Head Bolts	Connecting Rod Bearing Bolts	Main Bearing Bolts	Crankshaft Bolt	Flywheel Bolts	Exhaust Manifold Bolts
1975-76	2002, 2002tii	49-52	38-41	42-46	101-108	72-83	22-24
1977-81	320i	49-52	38-41	42-45	101-108	72-83	22-24
1977-81	528i, 530i, 630CSi	53-56	38-40	42-46	320-330	72-83	22-24
1978-81	733i, 633CSi	56-59	38-40	42-45	320-330	72-83	22-24
1975-76	3.0S, 3.0Si	53-55	38-41	42-46	174-188 ① 318-333	72-83	22-24

① Higher figure is with collar nut

TORQUE SEQUENCES

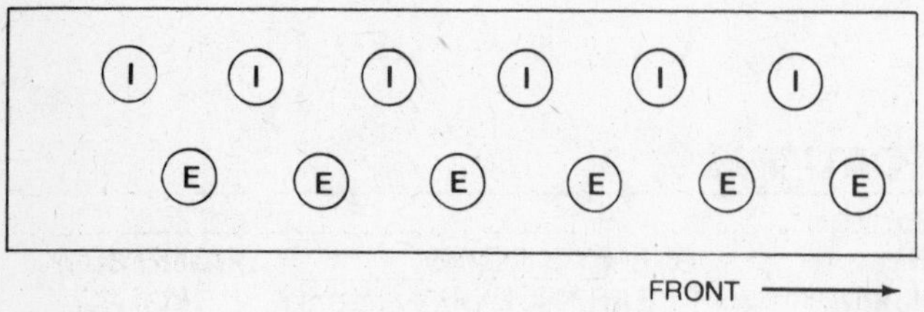

6-cylinder valve location

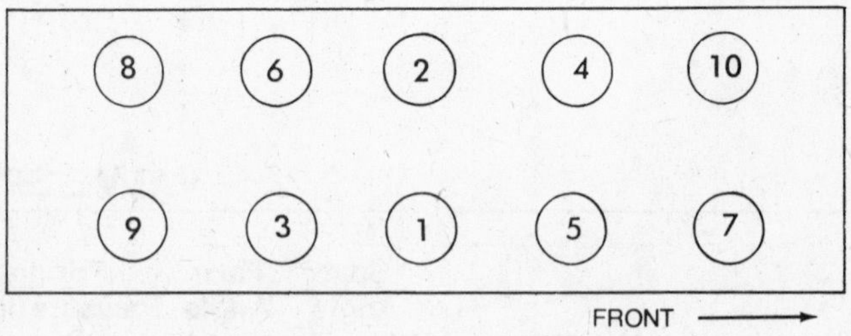

4-cylinder head torque sequence

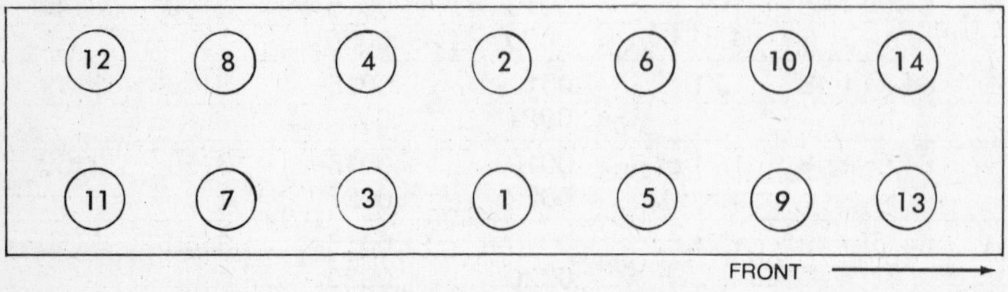

6-cylinder head torque sequence

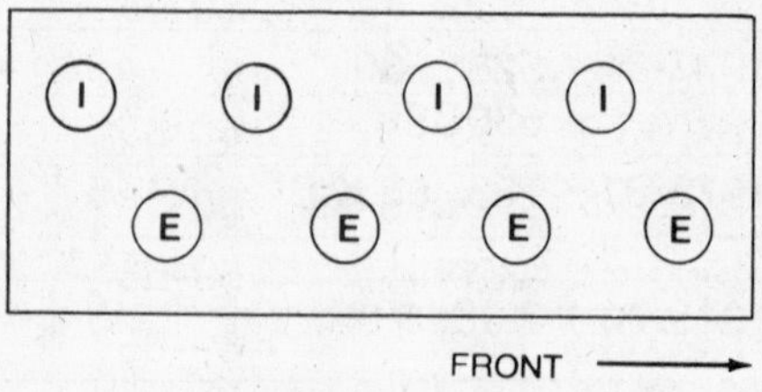

4-cylinder valve location

BATTERY AND STARTER SPECIFICATIONS

Year	Model	Battery (12 Volt, Negative Ground) Ampere Hour Capacity	Bosch Model or Part No.	STARTER NO-LOAD TEST Amps	Volts	rpm
1975-76	2002, 2002tii	44	GF(R)12V1 hp 0031 311 016	210	9.6	1300
1977-81	320i	55	GF(R)12V1.0 hp 0 001 311 045	210	9.6	1300
1977-81	528i, 530i, 630CSi, 633CSi	55 ①	GF12V1.2 hp	270	9.1	10,000
1978-81	733i	66	GF12V1.8 hp 0 001 311 042	340	9.1	10,000
1975-76	3.0S, 3.0Si	55	GF12V1.2 hp	270	9.1	10,000

① 633CSi—65 amp hour

ALTERNATOR AND REGULATOR SPECIFICATIONS

Year	Model	ALTERNATOR Bosch Model or Part No.	ALTERNATOR Maximum Output (Amps)	REGULATOR Bosch Model or Part No.	REGULATOR Regulated Voltage @ 68°F
1975-76	2002	K1/14V/45/24	45	AD1/14V or ADN1/14V ①	13.5-14.2
1977-81	320i	K1/14V/55A 0 120 489 608	55	0 192 052 004	13.9-14.3
1977-81	528i, 530i, 633CSi	14V/55A	55	AD1/14V	13.5-14.2
1978-81	733i, 630CSi	14V/65A 0 120 489 619	65	EE14/V3 0 192 052 006	13.5-14.2
1975-76	3.0Si	14/55A	55	ADN1/14V ① or AD1/14V	13.5-14.2

① With radio noise suppression

BRAKE SPECIFICATIONS

(Measurements in inches)

Year	Model	Lug Nut Torque (ft. lbs.)	Master Cylinder Bore	DISC Minimum Thickness	DISC Maximum Runout (installed)	DRUM Diameter	DRUM Maximum Machined Oversize	MINIMUM LINING THICKNESS Front	MINIMUM LINING THICKNESS Rear
1975-76	2002	59-65	.813	.354	.008	9.06	9.10	.08	.12
1977-79	320i	59-65	.812	.827	.008	9.84	9.89	.12	.12
1977-79	530i, 633CSi	59-65	.936	.460F/.334R	.008	—	—	—	—
1978-79	733i	60-66	.874	.827	.006	—	—	—	—
1975-76	3.0S, 3.0Si	60-66	.874	.827F/.709R	.008	—	—	—	—
1980-81	320i	59-65	.812	.827	.008	10.00	10.04	—	—
1980-81	528i	59-65	.936	.840F/.340R	.008	—	—	—	—
1980-81	633CSi	59-65	.936	.840F/.720R	.008	—	—	—	—
1980-81	733i	60-66	.874	.840F/.360R	.008	—	—	—	—

WHEEL ALIGNMENT

Year	Model	FRONT SUSPENSION Caster (deg.)	FRONT SUSPENSION Camber (deg.)	FRONT SUSPENSION Toe-In (in.)	Steering Axis Inclination (deg.)	REAR SUSPENSION Camber (deg.)	REAR SUSPENSION Toe-In (in.)
1975-76	2002, 2002tii	4P	½P	.07	8½P	2N	.06
1977-81	320i	8⅔P	0	.07	10½P	2N	.04
1977-79	530i	7⅔P	½P	.07	8½P	2N	.04
1978-81	733i	9P	0	.03	11½P	1½N	.08
1973-76	3.0S, 3.0Si	9⅔P	½P	.07	8½P	2N	.04
1980-81	528i	7⅔P	0	.06	8½P	2N	.04
1980-81	633CSi	7⅔P	0	.06	8P	2N	.04

TUNE-UP PROCEDURES

Breaker Points and Condenser

REPLACEMENT

1. Remove the distributor cap, rotor and the point guard, if equipped.
2. Disconnect the primary wire at the inner side of the distributor body terminal.
3. Remove the point set retaining screw and lift the point set from the breaker plate.

NOTE: Some distributors have the condenser mounted on the outside of the distributor body, while others have the condenser mounted inside the housing. The condenser lead will either be attached to the distributor outside terminal or to the inside terminal. Disconnect the condenser lead wire if necessary to replace the point set or condenser.

4. To install the new point set, clean the old grease from the cam and distributor plate. Put a small amount of special cam lubricant on the distributor cam and install the point set and condenser in the reverse of the removal.
5. Align the point faces to meet squarely and "bump" the engine until the rubbing block is on the high point of the distributor cam.
6. Adjust the point gap by moving the point set until feeler gauge of the specified size can be inserted in the gap.
7. Tighten the retaining screw and recheck the gap.
8. Start the engine and check the dwell.

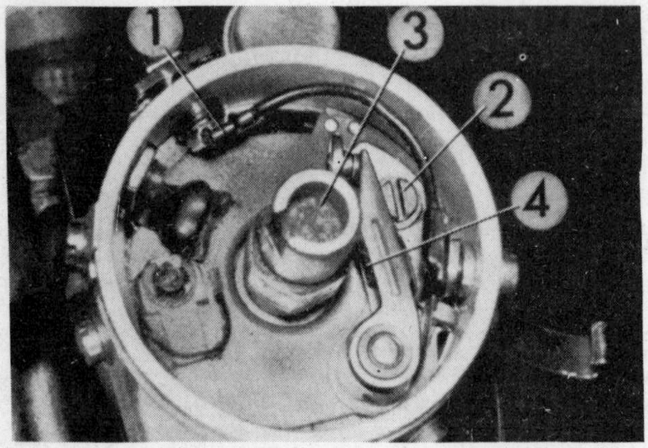

1. Flat connector
2. Point retaining screw
3. Felt pad
4. Rubbing block

Breaker point and condensor location—typical

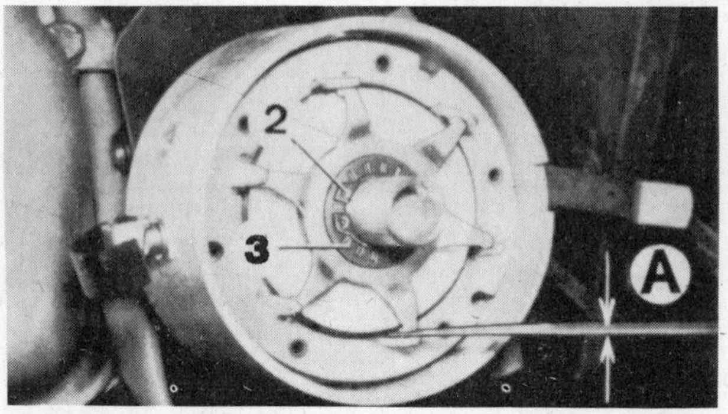

2. Circlip
3. Expander

Measuring rotor to stator clearance (A)

Electronic Ignition

Breaker points and condensers are not used with the electronic ignition. The air gap between the rotating teeth and the stator teeth can be checked with a brass or plastic feeler gauge. No adjustment is possible. If the gap is not as specified, the unit should be replaced.

CAUTION

All repair work to the electronic ignition system should be done with the engine stopped and the ignition switch Off.

Ignition Timing

The engine should be at normal operating temperature. Adjust the idle speed. Connect a timing light to the No. 1 spark plug wire and start the engine. Align the marks on the flywheel with the bell housing indicator, by rotating the distributor body. Tighten the distributor body clamp.

NOTE: The flywheel mark is either a pressed-in steel ball or a long tapered peg on the side of the starter ring gear.

Valve Clearance

All BMW engines are equipped with a chain driven, overhead camshaft, operating

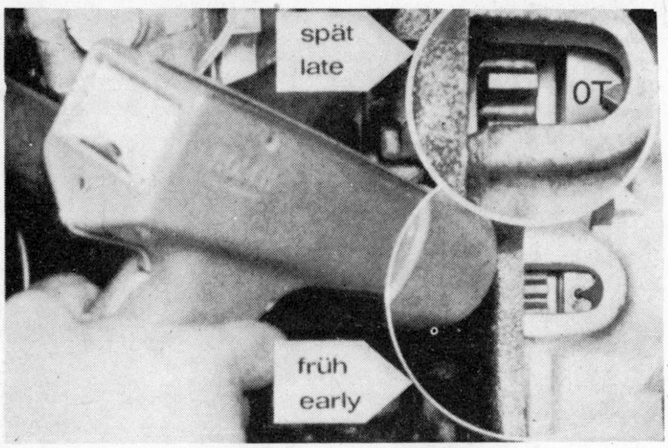

Ignition timing marks at flywheel

Adjusting of engine valve clearance with bent rod after loosening the locknut (1)

the intake and exhaust valves through rocker arm linkage.

NOTE: The valves must be adjusted cold.

1. Remove the rocker cover.
2. Rotate the engine until Number One cylinder is at TDC on compression stroke.

NOTE: Locate Number One cylinder firing position by the distributor rotor to cap position, or by observing the valve action in the opposite cylinder. Refer to following charts.

Cylinder Firing-Piston at TDC	Exhaust Valve Closing, Intake Valve Opening On Opposite Cylinder
6 cylinder	
1	6
5	2
3	4
6	1
2	5
4	3
4 cylinder	
1	4
3	2
4	1
2	3

3. Measure the valve clearance between the valve stem end and the rocker arm on the Number One cylinder. (Refer to the specifications for valve clearances).
4. Adjust the clearance by loosening the locknut on the rocker arm and turning the eccentric with a bent rod inserted through a hole provided on the surface of the eccentric.
5. When the proper clearance is obtained, tighten the locknut and recheck the valve clearance. Complete the adjustment on both valves.
6. Rotate the engine crankshaft to the next cylinder in the firing order, adjust the valves and repeat the procedures until all the valves are adjusted.
7. Replace the rocker cover, using a new gasket.

Carburetor

IDLE SPEED AND MIXTURE ADJUSTMENT

Models 2002 and 2002A 1975-76

1. The engine should be at normal operating temperature.
2. Turn the idle mixture screw until the engine runs erratically.
3. Adjust the idle mixture screw until the engine reaches the highest idle speed and runs smoothly.
4. Readjust the idle speed (with the idle speed screw) to specifications as necessary.

Idle speed adjustment screw (1) and mixture adjustment screw (2) location—2002 and 2002A

Fuel Injection

2002 Tii

1. Run the engine to normal operating temperature.
2. Before starting the engine, check the projection of the regulating cone of the warm-up runner. Projection must be 0.35-0.39 inch. The enrichment lever-to-collar nut distance should be 0.157 inch. The covered Grub screw should be in full contact with the stop-screw.

NOTE: If these specifications cannot be obtained, further checks must be made. Refer to the carburetor and fuel injection section.

3. Adjust the idle speed to specifications by turning the outer screw on the throttle shaft control synchronizer. A locknut holds the screw in place.
4. The CO level should range between .2-3%. If a correction is needed, detach the cover from the throttle shaft control synchronizer and turn the inner screw clockwise to lessen the CO emission. Reset the idle if necessary.

530i

1. Run engine to normal operating temperature.
2. Disconnect the hose from the collector to the charcoal filter. Do not plug the line.

NOTE: The hose is located between the first and second air induction tubes.

3. Disconnect the air pump hose at the air pump and plug the line.
4. Adjust the idle speed by turning the screw on the side of the throttle housing.
5. The CO level should be between 1.5-3.0% at idle speed.
6. If necessary, adjust the CO to specifications with the idle air screw located on the air volume control, by turning the screw to the left or right.
7. Reconnect the hoses.

320i

1. Run the engine to normal operating temperature.
2. Adjust the engine idle speed with the screw located near the throttle valve linkage.
3. Detach the exhaust check valve and plug the hose.
4. To adjust the CO, remove the plug from the fuel distributor and with a special wrench, adjust the CO level to a maximum of 2.0% for the 49 state vehicles or 3.5% for the California cars.
5. Reconnect the exhaust check valve hose and check the idle speed.

733i, 630i and 633i

1. Run the engine to normal operating temperature.
2. Disconnect the throttle housing-to-

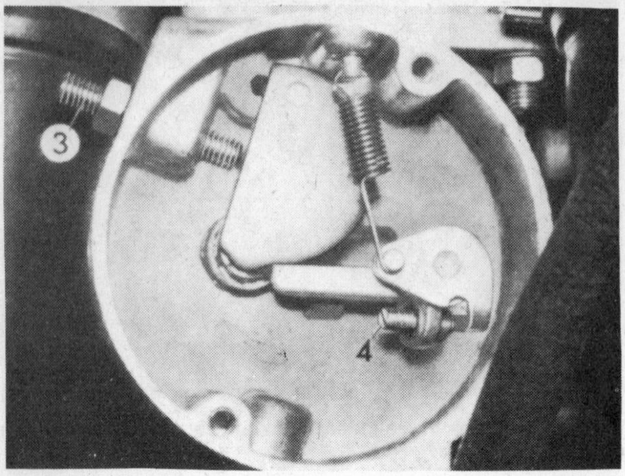

Adjusting idle speed screw (3) and CO adjusting screw (4)—2002Tii

1. Threaded pin
2. Stop screw

A. Projection of warm-up runner
B. Distance between enrichment lever to collar nut

Adjustment location of the enrichment system—2002Tii

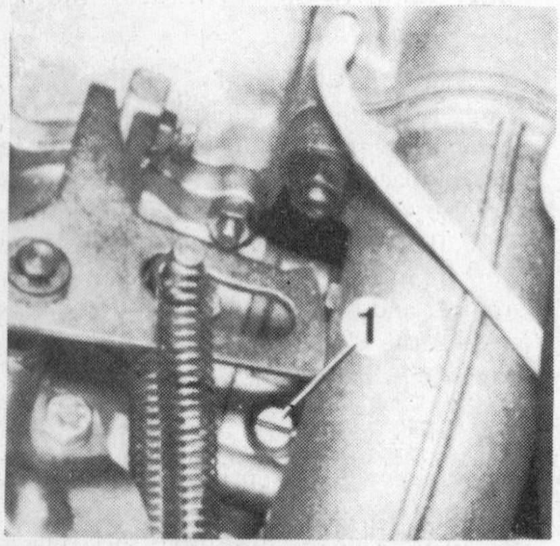

Idle speed screw location—320i

activated carbon filter hose. Disconnect and plug the air hose at the air pump.

3. Adjust the idle speed to specifications with the idle adjusting screw, located in the side of the throttle housing.

4. Adjust the CO to 1.5-3.0% at idle. Remove the cap from the air flow sensor and with the aid of a special tool, or short screwdriver, turn the bypass air screw located in the air flow sensor, until the CO level is as specified.

5. Reconnect the 2 hoses.

ENGINE ELECTRICAL

Distributor

REMOVAL AND INSTALLATION

1. Remove the distributor cap.
2. Disconnect the electrical wiring and vacuum hose.
3. Rotate the engine so that the rotor points to the notch on the distributor housing rim. The notch represents No. 1 cylinder.
4. Check that No. 1 piston is at TDC. The flywheel steel ball should be aligned with the indicator on the bell housing, or if the engine is equipped with a mark on the balancer, the mark should be aligned with the cast tab on the timing housing cover.
5. Remove the distributor clamp bolt and remove the distributor.
6. When the distributor is removed, the shaft and rotor will move counterclockwise. Mark the housing at this point for ease of installation.
7. Installation is the reverse of removal. Adjust the ignition timing.

NOTE: If the engine is cranked while the distributor is removed, the timing marks must be realigned and the No. 1 piston must be set at TDC, on the compression stroke.

CAUTION

Late model vehicles with electronic ignition are equipped with TDC position transmitters, which are used with the electronic test equipment. Do not damage or misalign the transmitters at the timing housing cover.

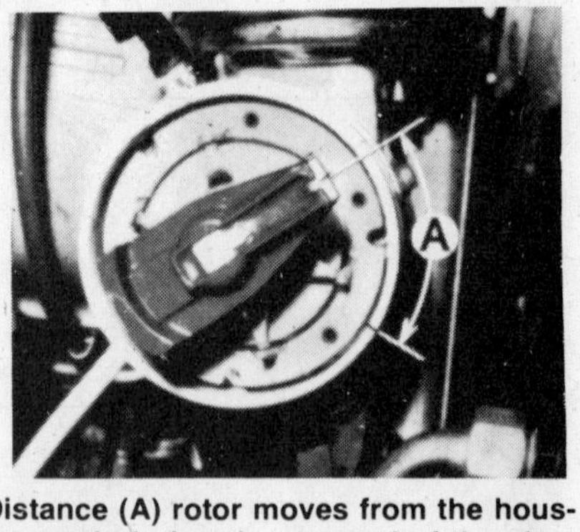

Distance (A) rotor moves from the housing mark during the removal of the electronic distributor

Adjusting CO level with special tool. Hole plug shown—320i

Remove plus (3) and use special tool 13-1-060 or equivalent to adjust the CO level with the screw in the bottom of the air intake sensor—530i, 630i, 633i and 733i

Aligning rotor with the mark on the conventional distributor housing before removing the distributor

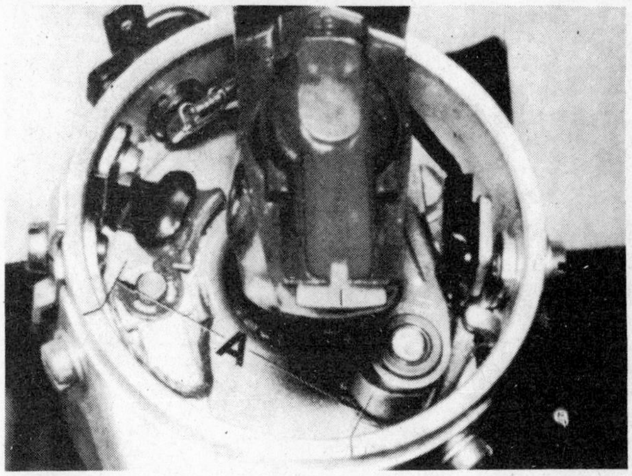

Distance (A) rotor moves from the housing mark during the removal of the conventional distributor—typical

Alternator

REMOVAL AND INSTALLATION

1. Disconnect the battery ground cable.
2. Disconnect the wires from the rear of the alternator, marking them for later installation.
3. Loosen the adjusting and pivot bolts, and remove the alternator.

NOTE: Early model vehicles use a voltage regulator mounted on the firewall or the inner fender panel. Later model vehicles use a voltage regulator mounted on the rear of the alternator as part of the brush holder.

4. Installation is the reverse of removal. Adjust the belt tension to approximately ⅜ in., measured between the balancer and the alternator pulley.

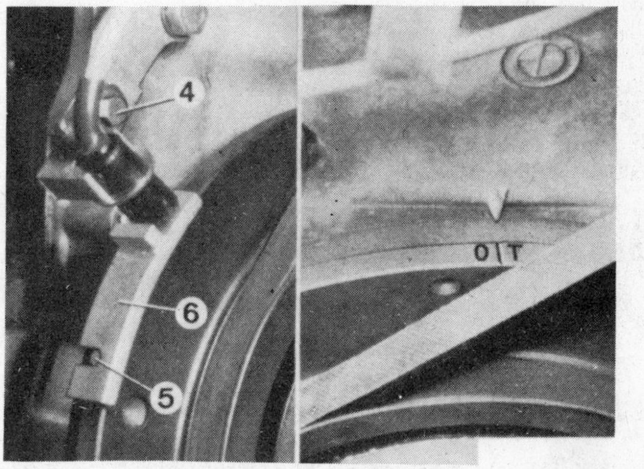

4. Transmitter and holder
5. Contact pin
6. Gauge

O/T = TDC

Electronic transmitter being gauged into position (left), and TDC mark on the balancer (right)

Starter

REMOVAL AND INSTALLATION

1. Disconnect the battery ground cable.

Exploded view of alternator housing (2), diode plate (9), stator (10), washer (11) and insulator (12)

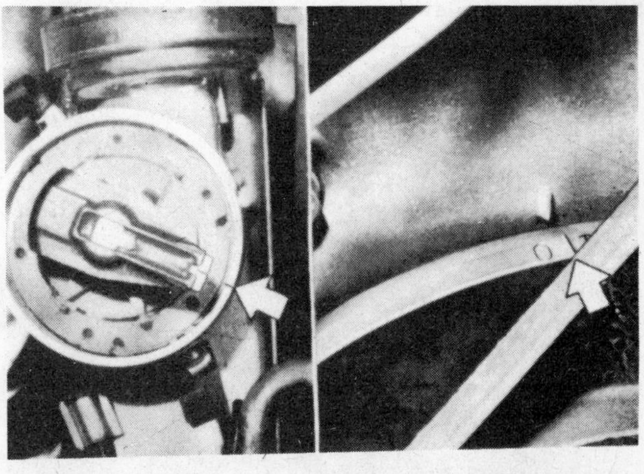

Alignment of the rotor with the electronic distributor housing and alignment of the balancer pulley TDC mark with the timing housing lug, before distributor removal

Removal of the voltage regulator and brush holder assembly—typical

2. On fuel injection models, you may have to remove No. 6 intake tube for clearance.
3. Remove the starter solenoid wire leads, marking them for later installation.
4. Unbolt and remove the starter.

NOTE: Remove the accelerator cable holder on automatic transmission equipped vehicles.

5. Installation is the reverse of removal.

STARTER DRIVE GEAR REPLACEMENT

The starter must be disassembled to replace the starter drive. A circlip retains the drive gear on the armature shaft and must be removed before the drive gear can be replaced.

Disassembled view of starter brush plate—typical

Exploded view of rotor assembly and bearing housing

Battery

The battery is located in the engine compartment and can be removed after disconnecting the 2 battery cables and removing the hold-down clamp.

ENGINE MECHANICAL

Engine

REMOVAL AND INSTALLATION

2002 and 2002A

The engine can be removed with or without the transmission, except for the 2002Tii, which can only be removed separately.

1. Scribe the hood hinge locations and remove the hood.
2. Remove the air cleaner assembly, drain the cooling system, disconnect the hoses and remove the radiator.
3. Remove the battery for safety reasons.
4. Disconnect all electric wiring and tag them for later reference.
5. Disconnect the fuel and vacuum lines. Tag the vacuum lines.
6. On 2002Tii, disconnect the fuel injection lines and wiring. Tag the wires for later reference.
7. Disconnect the accelerator linkage.
8. Raise and support the vehicle. Remove the clutch linkage with the pushrod attached.
9. Remove the slave cylinder from the clutch housing, leaving the pressure line attached.
10. Remove the driveshaft and disconnect the exhaust pipe from the exhaust manifold.

If desired, the transmission can be removed at this point, if the engine is to be removed separately. On the 2002Tii, the transmission must be removed.

11. Loosen the rear transmission crossmember, disconnect the electric wires from the transmission and lower the vehicle.
12. Support the engine with a lifting device, and remove the rear crossmember.
13. Remove the engine mounts and lift the engine from the compartment with the transmission attached.
14. Installation is the reverse of removal. Connect all wiring, hoses and switches in their original positions.

3.0 CARBURETED MODELS

1. Scribe the hood hinge locations and remove the hood. Disconnect and remove the battery.
2. Remove the air cleaner and hoses.
3. Drain the cooling system, disconnect the hoses and remove the radiator.
4. Remove the windshield washer reservoir and the fan.
5. Disconnect the electrical wiring from

Removal of starter solenoid

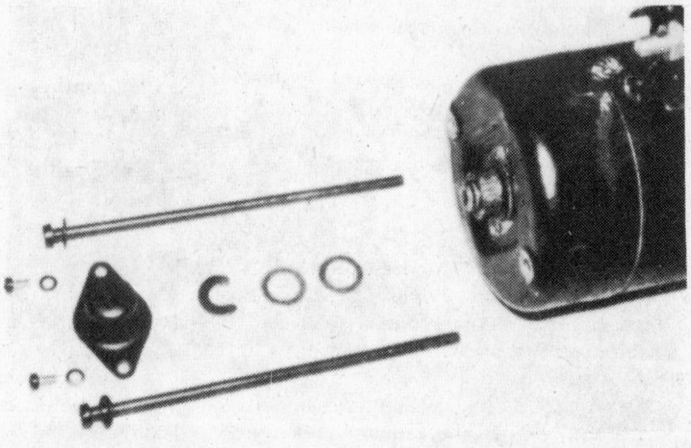

Disassembled view of end cap, retainer clip and through-bolts of starter—typical

Removal and/or installation of four cylinder engine—typical

Removal and/or installation of six cylinder engine—typical

the engine components, tagging them for later installation.

6. Disconnect the accelerator linkage and unbolt the exhaust pipe from the exhaust manifold.

7. Remove the front lower apron and loosen both engine mount retaining nuts.

8. On vehicles with power steering, remove the pump from the mounting brackets and move the pump out of the way. Do not remove the lines.

9. Raise and support the vehicle.

10. Remove the transmission. (Refer to the transmission removal and installation.)

11. On manual transmission cars, remove the slave cylinder from the clutch housing, leaving the pressure hose attached.

12. Lower the car and attach a lifting sling to the engine.

13. Be sure that all wires, hoses and linkages are disconnected and remove the engine.

14. Installation is the reverse of removal. Be sure all bolt and clip connections are secure and all fluids are filled before starting the engine.

FUEL INJECTION MODELS

Follow the engine removal and installation procedures for carburetor equipped models. The following procedures pertain specifically to fuel injection models.

1. Separate the electrical connection for the fuel injection wire loom by removing the 3 retaining screws.

2. Remove the wire leads from the relays, sensors, and switches. Mark the wire connections for installation.

3. Remove the transmission if equipped with an automatic transmission. If equipped with a manual transmission, the engine can be removed with the transmission attached.

320i

1. Raise and support the vehicle. Remove the transmission. (Refer to the transmission removal and installation). Remove the exhaust pipe from the exhaust manifold.

2. Remove the hood, after scribing the hinge locations.

3. Drain the cooling system, disconnect the hoses and remove the radiator. Remove the intake air panel.

4. Disconnect and tag the lines to the injector valves.

5. Disconnect all electrical wires from the engine, marking them for installation.

6. Disconnect all fuel and vacuum lines and mark them for installation.

7. Disconnect the accelerator cable. Disconnect the battery cables and remove the battery.

8. Attach a lifting sling to the engine. Remove the retaining nuts from the left and right engine mounts and the upper engine damper, located on the left side of the engine.

9. Carefully raise and remove the engine.

10. Installation is the reverse of removal.

530i

1. Raise and support the vehicle and remove the transmission. Remove the exhaust pipe from the exhaust manifold. (Refer to the transmission removal and installation.)

2. Remove the power steering pump and place it out of the way along the inner fender panel. Leave the hoses attached.

3. Lower the vehicle, scribe the hood hinge location and remove the hood.

4. Remove the air cleaner with the duct work attached. Disconnect and remove the air volume control.

5. Disconnect and remove the battery.

6. Disconnect all electrical wires and connectors. Mark the wires and connectors for installation.

7. Disconnect all vacuum hoses, marking them for installation.

8. Drain the cooling system, disconnect the hoses and remove the radiator.

9. Disconnect the accelerator linkage.

10. Install a lifting sling on the engine.

11. Remove the left and right engine mount retaining nuts and washers.

12. Carefully lift the engine from the engine compartment.

13. Installation is the reverse of removal.

630i

1. Raise and support the vehicle and remove the transmission. Remove the exhaust pipe from the exhaust manifold and reactor.

2. Remove the power steering pump and place it out of the way. Leave the hoses attached.

3. If equipped with air conditioning, remove the compressor and place it aside. Do not remove the hoses.

4. Scribe the hood hinge locations and remove the hood.

5. Drain the cooling system, disconnect the hoses and remove the radiator.

6. Remove the air cleaner housing at the wheelhouse.

7. Remove the electrical wires and connectors from the engine components. Tag the wires and connectors.

NOTE: The fuel injection control box is located either in the glove box or behind the right side kick panel. Remove the plug and thread the wire and connector through the hole in the firewall and into the engine compartment.

8. Install a lifting sling on the engine.

9. Remove the right and left engine mount retaining nuts and washers.

10. Remove the engine.

11. Installation is the reverse of removal.

733i

1. Raise and suport the vehicle and remove the transmission. Remove the exhaust pipe from the exhaust manifold and reactor.

2. Remove the clutch housing from the engine.

3. Remove the power steering pump and place it out of the way. Do not disconnect the hoses.

4. If equipped with air conditioning, remove the compressor and place it out of the way. Do not disconnect the hoses.

5. Remove the damper bracket from the crankcase and lower the vehicle.

6. Scribe the hood hinge locations and remove the hood.

7. Drain the cooling system, disconnect the hoses and remove the radiator.

8. Remove the windshield washer reservoir and the air filter housing located on the inner fender panel.

9. Remove the electrical wiring from the engine components. Tag all wires.

10. Disconnect and remove the battery.

11. Remove and tag all vacuum hoses.

NOTE: Some vacuum hoses are color coded.

12. Disconnect the throttle linkage.

13. Remove the right kick panel from the passenger compartment, remove the fuel injection control unit wire connector and thread

the connector and wire through the hole in the firewall.

14. Attach a lifting sling to the engine. Remove the left and right engine mount retaining nuts and washers. Lift the engine from the engine compartment.

15. Installation is the reverse of removal.

Cylinder Head

REMOVAL AND INSTALLATION

2002, 2002A, 2002Ti and 320i

1. Remove the air cleaner and disconnect the breather tube. On fuel injection engines, remove the intake manifold.
2. Disconnect the battery ground cable and drain the cooling system.
3. Remove the choke cable, if equipped.
4. Disconnect the throttle linkage. Pull the torsion shaft towards the firewall until the ball is free of the torsion shaft.
5. Remove and tag the vacuum hoses.
6. Disconnect the coolant hoses from the cylinder head.
7. Disconnect the electrical wiring and connectors from the cylinder head and engine components.
8. Remove the cylinder head cover and the front upper timing case cover.
9. Rotate the engine until the distributor rotor points to the notch on the distributor body edge and the timing indicator points to the first notch on the belt pulley 320i, or second notch for the 2002, 2002A and 2002Ti models. No. 1 piston should now be at TDC on its firing stroke.
10. Remove the timing chain tensioner piston by removing the plug in the side of the block.

CAUTION

The plug is under heavy spring tension.

11. Open the lockplates, remove the retaining bolts and remove the timing chain sprocket from the camshaft.

NOTE: The dowel pin hole on the camshaft flange should be in the 6 o'clock position while the notch at the top of the cam flange should be aligned with the cast projection on the cylinder head and in the 12 o'clock position for proper installation.

12. Remove the exhaust pipe from the exhaust manifold and remove the dipstick holder.
13. Unscrew the cylinder head bolts in the reverse of the tightening sequence and remove the cylinder head.
14. Installation is the reverse of removal but note the following points.
    a. Tighten the cylinder head bolts in three stages, following the illustrated sequence. Adjust the valves, start the engine and bring to normal operating temperature. Stop the engine and allow it to cool to approximately 95° F (35° C). Retorque the cylinder head bolts to specifications and readjust the valves.

NOTE: The cylinder head bolts should be retorqued after 600 miles (1000 km) of driving.

    b. Check the projection of the cylinder head dowel sleeve in the cylinder block mating surface. Maximum height is 0.20 in.
    c. Match the cylinder head gasket to the cylinder block and head to verify coolant flow passages are correct.
    d. Adjust timing and idle speed.
    e. Bleed the cooling system. Set heater valve to the warm position and fill cooling system. Run the engine to normal temperature and when thermostat has opened, release the pressure cap to the first position. Squeeze the upper and lower radiator hoses in a pumping effect, to allow trapped air to escape through the radiator. Recheck coolant level and close the pressure cap to its second catch position.

3.0, 530i, 630i, 633i and 733i

NOTE: Small variances may be encountered among models due to model changes, difference in electrical wiring, vacuum hoses and fuel line routings, but all are basically alike.

1. Disconnect the battery ground cable.
2. Disconnect the wire connectors. Loosen the clamps and remove the air flow sensor with the air filter on the fuel injected models, or remove the air cleaner from carburetor equipped models.

Alignment of dowel pin (1) with the sprocket and upper bolt hole and cylinder head cast tab—six cylinder engines

3. Disconnect the rocker cover vent hose, ignition line tube and electrical wiring.
4. Remove the rocker cover.
5. Drain the cooling system and remove the coolant hoses.

NOTE: Do not interchange the heater hoses.

6. Rotate the engine so that the distributor rotor points to the notch on the distributor body edge and the timing indicator points to the notch on the belt pulley. This will place number one piston at TDC on its firing stroke.
7. Remove the upper timing housing cover after removing the distributor and thermostat housing.
8. Remove the timing chain tensioner piston.

CAUTION

The retaining plug is under heavy spring tension.

9. Open the camshaft sprocket bolt lockplates and remove the bolts. Remove the sprocket.

Alignment of dowel pin hole and camshaft flange notch with the cast projection of the cylinder head—four cylinder engine

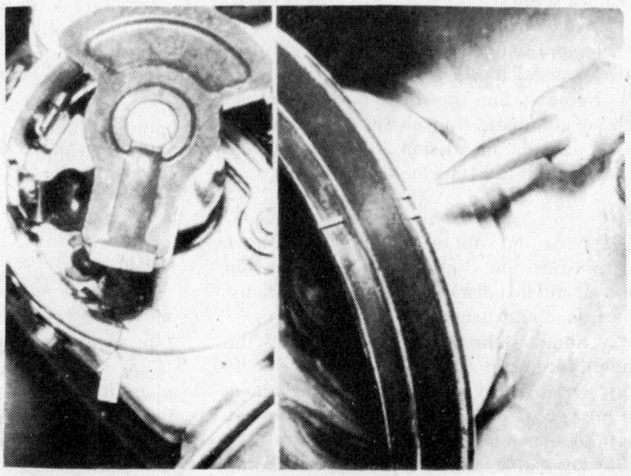

Alignment of distributor rotor and belt pulley notch—typical

Timing chain tensioner plug removal or installation—typical

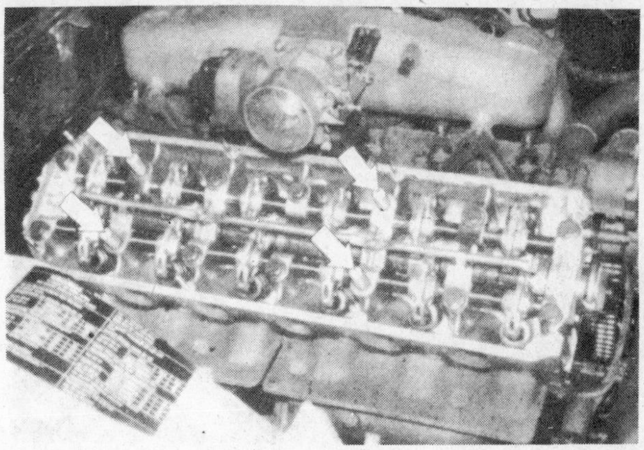

Installation of locating pins in the cylinder head bolt bores to prevent rocker shafts from turning—six cylinder engines

NOTE: For installation purposes, the sprocket dowel pin should be located at the lower left, between 7 and 8 o'clock, while the upper bolt bore must align with the threaded bore of the camshaft and the cylinder head cast tab, visable through the two bores, when at the 12 o'clock position.

10. Remove and tag the electrical wiring and connectors.
11. Remove and tag the vacuum lines.
12. Remove the intake tube at No. 6 cylinder (530i only).
13. Remove the wiring harness by pulling it upward through the opening in the intake neck.
14. Disconnect the fuel lines.
15. Remove the exhaust system completely (630i), or disconnect the exhaust line at the exhaust manifold. Remove the exhaust filter.
16. Remove the cylinder head bolts in the reverse order of the tightening sequence and install locating pins in four head bolt bores to prevent the rocker shafts from turning.
17. Remove the cylinder head.
18. Installation is the reverse of removal. Note the following points.
    a. Tighten the cylinder head bolts in three stages, following the illustrated sequence. Adjust the valves, start the engine and bring it to normal operating temperature. Stop the engine and allow it to cool to approximately 95° F (35° C). Retorque the cylinder head bolts to specifications and readjust the valves.

NOTE: The cylinder head bolts should be retorqued after 600 miles (1000 km) of driving.

    b. Check the projection of the cylinder head dowel sleeve in the cylinder block mating surface. Maximum height is 0.20 in. (5.0 mm).
    c. Match the cylinder head gasket to the cylinder block and head to verify that the coolant flow passages are correct.
    d. Adjust the timing and idle speed.
    e. Bleed the cooling system. Set the heater valve in the Warm position and fill the cooling system. Start the engine and bring to normal operating temperature. A venting screw is located on the top of the thermostat housing. Run the engine at fast idle and open the venting screw until the coolant comes out free of air bubbles. Close the bleeder screw and refill the reservoir with coolant.

CYLINDER HEAD OVERHAUL

Refer to the Engine Rebuilding section for general procedures.

Intake Manifold

REMOVAL AND INSTALLATION

2002, 2002A and 2002Ti

1. Remove the air cleaner.
2. Remove and tag the fuel lines, vacuum lines and electrical wiring.
3. Drain the cooling system.
4. Disconnect the manual choke control cable. On the 2002A, disconnect the wire connector to the choke cover.
5. Disconnect the accelerator linkage. On 2002A, disconnect the linkage at the ball socket.
6. Disconnect the coolant lines to the manifold.
7. Disconnect the dipstick support.
8. Remove the intake manifold.
9. Installation is the reverse of removal. Use new gaskets.

NOTE: The 2 front or rear intake tubes can be removed and installed on the 2002Ti engine (four carburetors), by separating the connecting rod between the middle carburetors and removing the front or rear section as desired by using the above procedure as a guide.

3.0 S

FRONT INTAKE MANIFOLD

1. Drain the cooling system.
2. Remove the air filter.
3. Disconnect and tag all fuel and vacuum lines.
4. Disconnect the throttle linkage bar and connecting bar and remove the bearing block.
5. Disconnect the manual choke cable.
6. Remove the coolant hoses to the manifold or carburetor.
7. Remove the dipstick support.
8. Remove the intake manifold with the carburetor attached.
9. Installation is the reverse of the removal. Use new gaskets.

REAR INTAKE MANIFOLD

1. Drain the cooling system.
2. Disconnect the battery ground cable.
3. Remove the air filter.
4. Disconnect and tag all fuel and vacuum lines.
5. Disconnect the accelerator thrust bar and bearing block.

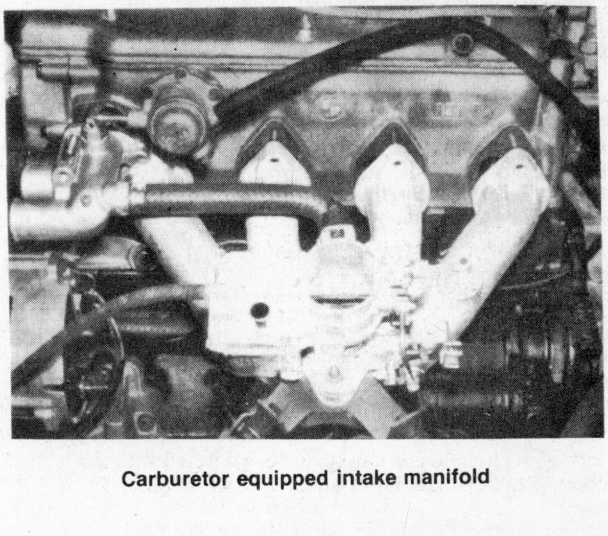

Carburetor equipped intake manifold

Induction resonator pipe—secured with clamps

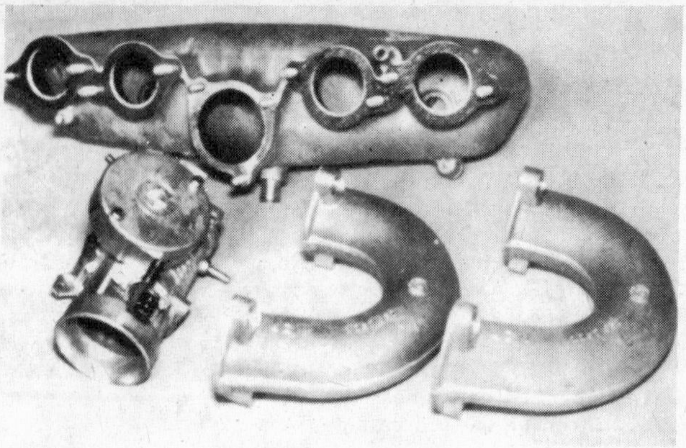

Induction system with induction tubes secured with nuts and washers

6. Disconnect the electrical wire from the choke cover. Remove the choke cover with the coolant lines attached.
7. Disconnect the heater hoses from the manifold base.
8. Remove the intake manifold with the carburetor attached.
9. Installation is the reverse of the removal. Use new gaskets.

2002 Tii

WITH INDUCTION RESONATOR PIPES (SECURED WITH CLAMPS)

1. Remove the air filter.
2. Remove and tag the fuel lines, starter valve cable, vacuum hoses and all induction resonator pipes.
3. Disconnect the throttle return spring and remove the injection pipe from No. One cylinder. Remove the injector valve.
4. Remove the bracket bolts at the throttle housing.
5. Remove the vacuum hose, auxiliary air hose and injection pipe from No. Four cylinder.
6. Remove the air collector from the cylinder head.
7. Installation is the reverse of removal.

WITH INDUCTION MANIFOLDS (SECURED WITH NUTS AND WASHERS)

1. Remove the air filter.
2. Remove the fuel line, fuel return line, starter valve cable and vacuum hose from the air tube assembly.
3. Remove the bracket bolts on the throttle housing.
4. Remove the air collector support bolts at the top engine cover area.
5. Remove the nuts and washers from the bottom of the induction manifolds.
6. Remove the air collector together with the induction manifolds and the throttle housing.
7. Installation is the reverse of removal.

INTAKE PIPE (ALL FUEL INJECTED 2002Tii)

1. After removing the air collector, induction resonator pipes or the induction manifolds as outlined preceding, remove all of the remaining injection pipes from the injection valves.
2. Disconnect the coolant hoses and electrical connections at the thermostat housing switches.
3. Remove the retaining nuts and washers from the cylinder head studs and remove the intake pipe. The injector valves can be removed before or after the removal.
4. Installation is the reverse of removal. Use new gaskets and place them on the intake opening properly so as not to interfere with the air flow.

3.0 CSi

NOTE: Combine the 2 next 2 operations to remove both front and rear intake manifolds.

FRONT INTAKE MANIFOLD

1. Remove the air cleaner.
2. Drain the cooling system.
3. Remove the intake air collector and the 3 front intake pipes.
4. Remove the pressure regulator and support from the intake manifold.
5. Disconnect the coolant hoses from the thermostat housing and the wiring from the coolant switches.
6. Remove the flat plugs from the injection valves by carefully pulling upward.
7. Remove the first three injection valves from the manifold.

NOTE: Leave the circular pipe connected.

8. Remove the retaining bolts from the intake manifold and remove it from the cylinder head.
9. Installation is the reverse of removal. Use new injection valve sealing rings.

REAR INTAKE MANIFOLD

1. Disconnect the battery ground cable.
2. Remove the air cleaner.
3. Remove the intake air collector and the 3 rear intake pipes.
4. Remove the pressure regulator and support from the intake manifold.
5. Remove the flat plugs from the injection valves by carefully pulling upwards.
6. Remove the three rear injector valves.

NOTE: Leave the circular pipe connected.

7. Remove and tag the electrical flat plugs and connectors from the end of the wire loom, routed through the intake manifold.
8. Carefully pull the wire loom upward through the hole in the intake manifold.
9. Remove the intake manifold from the cylinder head.
10. Installation is the reverse of removal. Always renew the injection valve sealing rings.

REAR INTAKE MANIFOLD

1. Disconnect the battery ground cable.
2. Remove the air cleaner.
3. Remove the intake air collector and the 3 rear intake pipes.
4. Remove the pressure regulator and support from the intake manifold.
5. Remove the flat plugs from the injection valves by carefully pulling upwards.
6. Remove the three rear injector valves.

NOTE: Leave the circular pipe connected.

7. Remove and tag the electrical flat plugs and connectors from the end of the wire loom, routed through the intake manifold.
8. Carefully pull the wire loom upward through the hole in the intake manifold.
9. Remove the intake manifold from the cylinder head.
10. Installation is the reverse of removal. Always renew the injection valve sealing rings.

320i

1. Remove the air cleaner and drain the cooling system.
2. Disconnect the accelerator cable and remove the vacuum hoses from the air collector. Tag the hoses.
3. Remove the injection line holder from No. 4 intake tube.
4. Remove the No. 3 intake tube and disconnect the vacuum and coolant lines from the throttle housing.
5. Disconnect the hoses at the EGR valve and remove the wire plugs at the temperature timing switch.
6. Remove the cold start valve from the air collector.
7. Disconnect the vacuum hose and electrical connections at the timing valve.
8. Disconnect the remaining intake tubes at the collector. Disconnect the collector brackets at the engine and remove the collector.
9. Remove the air intake tubes from the manifold and remove the injector valves.
10. Remove the intake manifold.

11. Installation is the reverse of removal.

530i, 630i and 733i

NOTE: Slight variations may exist among models due to model changes and updating but basic removal and installation remains the same.

1. Disconnect the battery ground cable and drain the cooling system.
2. Disconnect the wire harness at the air flow sensor. Remove the air cleaner and sensor as an assembly.
3. Remove the tag and vacuum hoses and electrical plugs. Disconnect the accelerator linkage from the throttle housing.
4. Disconnect the coolant hoses from the throttle housing.
5. Working from the rear of the collector housing, disconnect the vacuum lines, and starting valve connector, fuel line and air line. Tag the hoses and lines for ease of assembly.
6. Remove the EGR valve and line.
7. Remove all intake pipes.
8. Remove the air collector housing from the engine.
9. Disconnect the plugs at the injector valves and remove the valves.
10. Disconnect the wire plugs at the coolant temperature sensor, the temperature time switch and the temperature switch.
11. Pull the wire loom upward through the opening in the intake manifold neck.
12. Remove the coolant hoses from the intake neck.
13. Remove the retaining bolts or nuts and remove either front, rear or both intake manifold necks.
14. Installation of the manifolds is the reverse of removal. Use new gaskets on the manifolds and air intake tubes.

Exhaust Manifold

REMOVAL AND INSTALLATION

2002 Series

1. Loosen the exhaust system supports.
2. Separate the exhaust pipe from the exhaust manifold and remove the hot air guide sleeve.
3. Remove the retaining nuts and washers from the exhaust manifold studs and remove the manifold from the cylinder head.
4. Installation is the reverse of removal. Tighten the clamps holding the exhaust pipes last to avoid having an exhaust system vibration during operation.

3.0 Series

NOTE: Each exhaust manifold can be removed separately after the exhaust pipes are disconnected.

1. Remove the air cleaner and manifold cover plate.
2. On automatic transmission equipped vehicles, detach the oil filler pipe at the rear of the cover plate.
3. Disconnect the exhaust pipe from the manifold sections.
4. Remove the retaining nuts and washers and remove the exhaust manifolds from the cylinder head.
5. Installation is the reverse of removal.

320i, 530i, 630i, 633i and 733i

The exhaust manifolds are referred to as exhaust gas recirculation reactors. Refer to the Emission Control section for operation.

The removal and installation procedures are basically the same for all models. The four cylinder manifold (used on the 320i model), is a one piece, one outlet unit, while the six cylinder manifold assembly consist of a two piece, double outlet to the exhaust pipe. One piece can be replaced independently of the other.

1. Remove the air volume control and if necessary, air cleaner.
2. Disconnect the exhaust pipe at the reactor outlet(s).
3. Remove the guard plate from the reactor(s).
4. Disconnect the air injection pipe fitting, the EGR counterpressure line, EGR pressure line and any supports.

NOTE: An exhaust filter is used between the reactor and the EGR valve and must be disconnected. Replace the filter if found to be defective.

5. Remove the retaining bolts or nuts at the reactor and remove it from the cylinder head.
6. Installation is the reverse of removal. Use new gaskets.

Timing Chain

REMOVAL AND INSTALLATION

All Engines

1. Rotate the crankshaft to set No. 1 piston at TDC, at the beginning of its compression stroke.
2. Remove the distributor (6-cylinder engines only).
3. Remove the cylinder head cover, air injection pipe and guard plate.
4. Drain the cooling system and remove the thermostat housing.
5. Remove the upper timing housing cover.
6. Remove the timing chain tensioner piston.

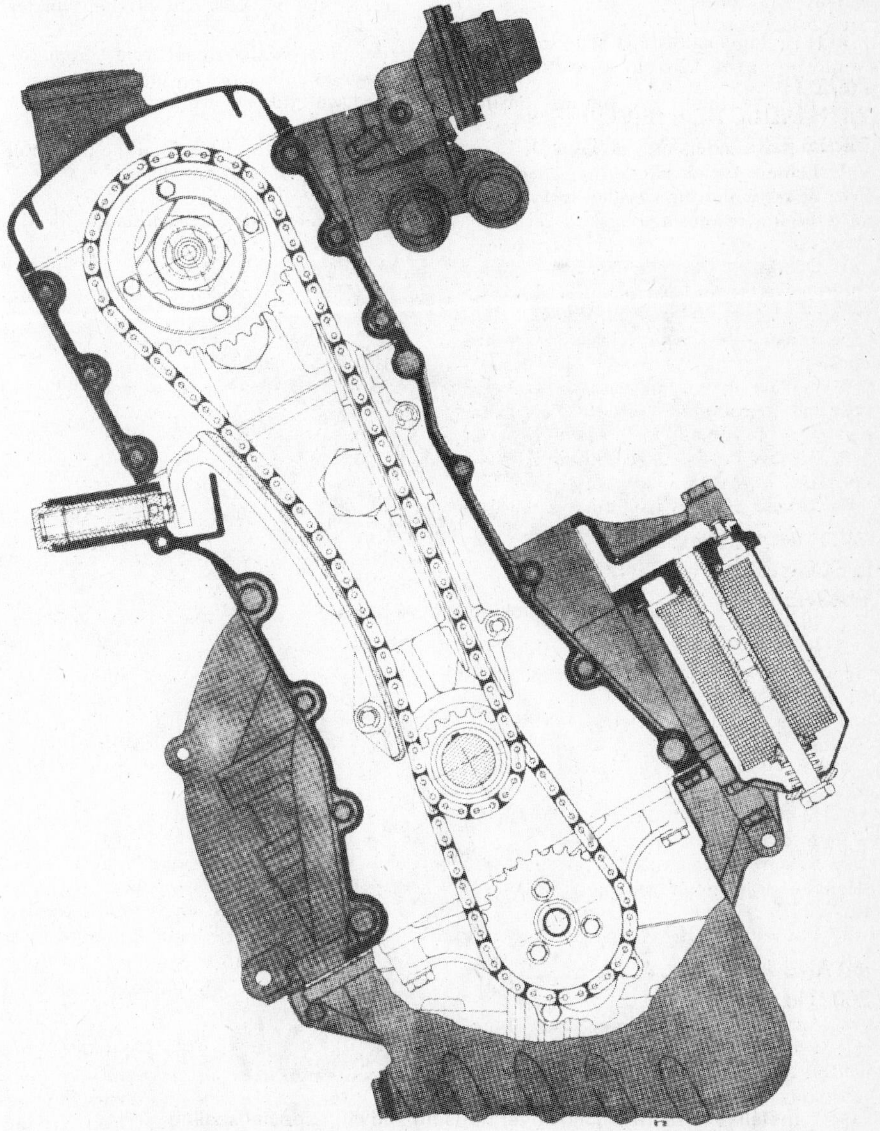

Typical timing chain arrangement—four cylinder engine illustrated

Location of upper (4) and lower (3) guide rail retainers

Removal of guide rail from lower (5) pivot pin

NOTE: The piston is under heavy spring tension.

7. Remove the drive belts and fan.

8. Remove the flywheel guard and lock the flywheel with a locking tool.

9. Remove the vibration damper assembly.

NOTE: The crankshaft Woodruff key should be in the 12 o'clock position.

10. Remove the lower timing housing cover screws and the front oil pan screws. Loosen the remaining oil pan screws.

11. Loosen the oil pan-to-timing housing cover gasket with a thin bladed tool and remove the timing housing cover.

12. Open the camshaft lockplates, remove the bolts and remove the camshaft sprocket.

13. On 4-cylinder engines:

a. Remove the bottom circlip holding the chain guide rail to the block. Loosen the upper pivot pin until the guide rail rests against the forward part of the cylinder head gasket.

b. Remove the timing chain from the sprockets and remove the guide rail by pulling downward and swinging the rail to the right.

c. Remove the chain from the guide rail and remove it from the engine.

14. On 6-cylinder engines:

a. Remove the chain from the lower sprocket, swing the chain to the right front and out of the guide rail and remove the chain from the engine.

15. Installation is the reverse of removal, but note the following:

16. Be sure that No. 1 piston remains at the top of its firing stroke and the key on the crankshaft is in the 12 o'clock position.

17. On 4-cylinder engines:

a. Position the camshaft flange so that the dowel pin bore is located at the 6 o'clock position and the notch in the top of the flange aligns with the cast tab on the cylinder head.

b. Position the chain in the chain guide rail and move the rail upward and to the left, engaging the lower locating pivot pin and threading the upper pivot pin into the block. Install the circlip on the lower guide pin.

c. Engage the chain on the crankshaft sprocket and fit the camshaft sprocket into the chain.

d. Align the gear dowel pin to the camshaft flange and bolt the sprocket into place. Use new lockplates and secure the bolt heads.

18. On 6-cylinder engines:

a. Position the camshaft flange so that the dowel pin bore is between the 7 and 8 o'clock position and the upper flange bolt hole is aligned with the cast tab on the cylinder head.

b. Position the chain on the guide rail and swing the chain inward and to the left.

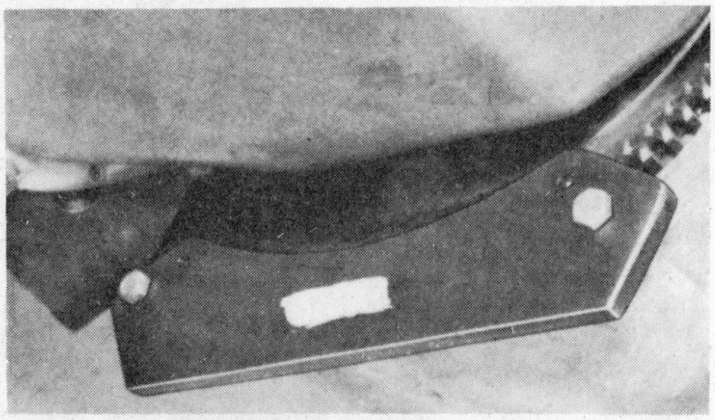

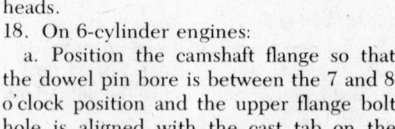

Flywheel locking tool in place

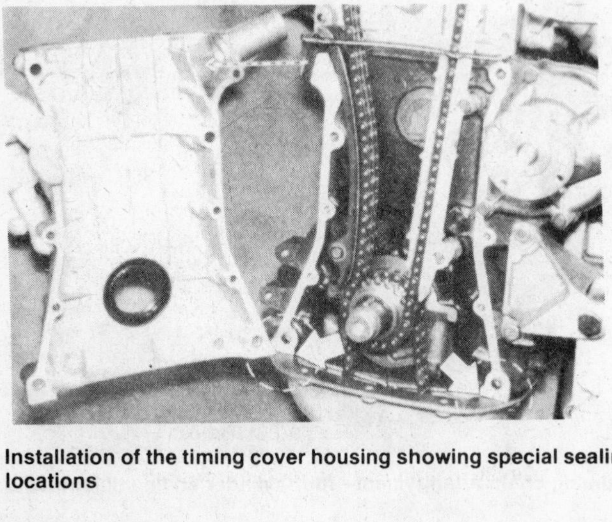

Installation of the timing cover housing showing special sealing locations

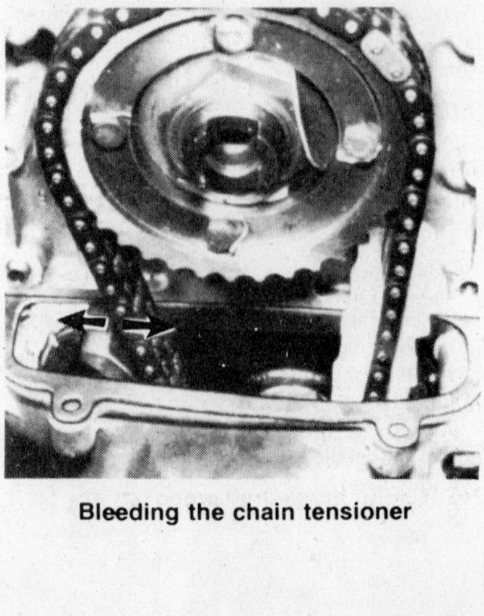

Bleeding the chain tensioner

c. Engage the chain on the crankshaft gear and install the camshaft sprocket into the chain.

d. Align the gear dowel pin to the camshaft flange and bolt the sprocket into place.

19. Install the chain tensioner piston, spring and cap plug, but do not tighten.

20. To bleed the chain tensioner, fill the oil pocket, located on the upper timing housing cover, with engine oil and move the tensioner back and forth with a screwdriver until oil is expelled at the cap plug. Tighten the cap plug securely.

21. Complete the assembly in the reverse order of removal. Check the ignition timing and the idle speed. Be sure the flywheel holder is removed before any attempt is made to start the engine.

Timing Housing Cover Oil Seal

REMOVAL AND INSTALLATION

1. Position the No. 1 piston at TDC on the beginning of its compression stroke.
2. Remove the flywheel guard and lock the flywheel with a locking tool.
3. Remove the drive belts and the fan.
4. Remove the retaining nut and remove the vibration damper from the crankshaft.

NOTE: The Woodruff key should be at the 12 o'clock position on the crankshaft.

5. Remove the seal from the timing housing cover.
6. Using a special seal installer or equivalent, lubricate and install the seal in the cover.

NOTE: If the balancer hub has serious scoring on the sealing surface, position the seal in the cover so that the sealing lip is in front of or behind the scored groove.

7. Lubricate the balancer hub and install it on the crankshaft, being careful not to damage the seal.
8. Complete the assembly, using the reverse of the removal procedure. Be sure to remove the flywheel locking tool before attempting to start the engine.

Camshaft

REMOVAL AND INSTALLATION

1. Remove the oil line from the top of the cylinder head.

NOTE: Observe the location of the seals when removing the hollow oil line studs. Reinstall the seals in the same position.

2. Remove the cylinder head.
3. Adjust the valve clearance to the maximum clearance on all rocker arms.
4. Remove the fuel pump and pushrod on carbureted engines.
5. On 4-cylinder engines:

a. Special tools (6025-1 for carbureted engines or 6025-2 for fuel injected engines) or their equivalent, are used to mold the rocker arms away from the camshaft lobes.

NOTE: The tool 6025-2 or its equivalent, must be used on fuel injection engines to avoid distorting the valve heads.

On 6-cylinder engines:

a. A special tool (11-2-060) or its equivalent, is used to hold the rocker arms away from the camshaft lobes. When installing the tool, move the intake rocker arms of No. 2 and 4 cylinders, forward approximately ¼ in. and tighten the intake side nuts to avoid contact between the valve heads.

6. Remove the camshaft.

On 4-cylinder engines:

a. Remove the guide plate retaining bolts and move the plate downward and out of the slots on the rocker arm shafts.

b. Carefully remove the camshaft from the cylinder head.

On 6-cylinder engines:

a. Rotate the camshaft so that the two cutout areas of the camshaft flange are horizontal and remove the retaining plate bolts.

b. Carefully remove the camshaft from the cylinder head.

c. The flange and guide plate can be removed from the camshaft by removing the lockplate and nut from the camshaft end.

7. Install the camshaft and associated components in the reverse order of removal, but observe the following:

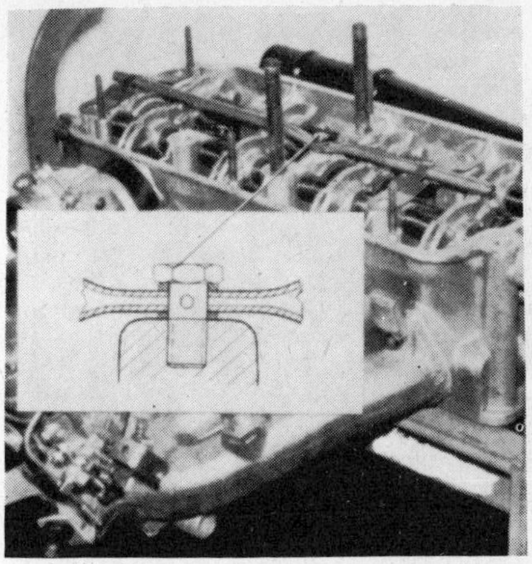

Location of seals at hollow oil line stud

a. After installing the camshaft guide plate, the camshaft should turn easily. Measure and correct the camshaft end play.

b. The camshaft flange must be properly aligned with the cylinder head before the sprocket is installed. Refer to the disassembly procedure.

c. Install the oil tube hollow stud washer seals properly, one above and one below the oil pipe.

d. Adjust the valves.

Rocker Arms and Shaft

REMOVAL AND INSTALLATION

1. Remove the cylinder head.
2. Remove the camshaft.
3. Slide the thrust rings and rocker arms rearward and remove the circlips from the rocker arm shafts.
4. On 4-cylinder engines:

a. Remove the distributor flange from the rear of the cylinder head.

b. Using a long punch, drive the rocker arm shaft from the rear to the front of the cylinder head.

NOTE: Be sure all circlips are off the shaft before attempting to drive the shaft from the cylinder head.

Position of crankshaft woodruff key (1)

Circlip location on the rocker arm shaft

Rocker arm shaft locking bolt (2) location—six cylinder engine

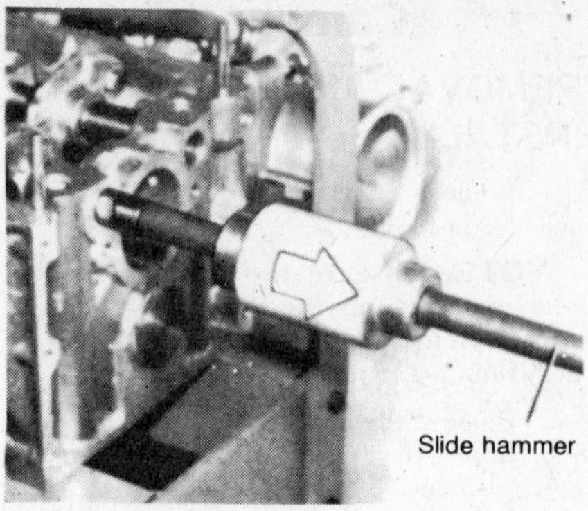

Use a slide hammer tool to remove the rocker arm shaft

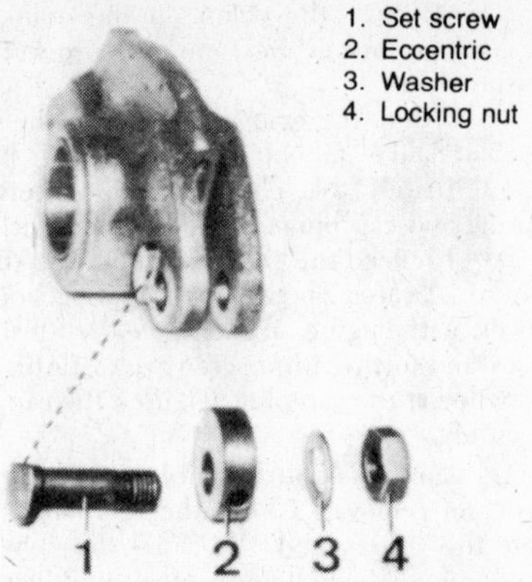

Rocker arm valve adjusting mechanism

c. The intake rocker shaft is not plugged at the rear, while the exhaust rocker shaft must be plugged. Renew the plug if necessary, during the installation.

5. On 6-cylinder engines:

a. Unscrew the rocker shaft locking bolts from the cylinder head.

b. Install a threaded slide hammer into the ends of the front rocker shafts and remove the shafts from the cylinder head.

NOTE: Be sure all circlips have been removed from the rocker shafts before removal.

c. Remove the end cover from the rear of the cylinder head.

d. Install a threaded slide hammer into the ends of the rear rocker shafts and remove.

NOTE: Be sure all circlips have been removed from the rocker shafts before removal.

6. The rocker arms, springs, washers, thrust rings and shafts should be examined and worn parts replaced. Special attention should be given to the rocker arm cam followers. If these are loose, replace the arm assembly.

The valves can be removed, repaired or

Removing the rocker arm shaft with special tool—four cylinder engine

Removal of the distributor flange—four cylinder engine

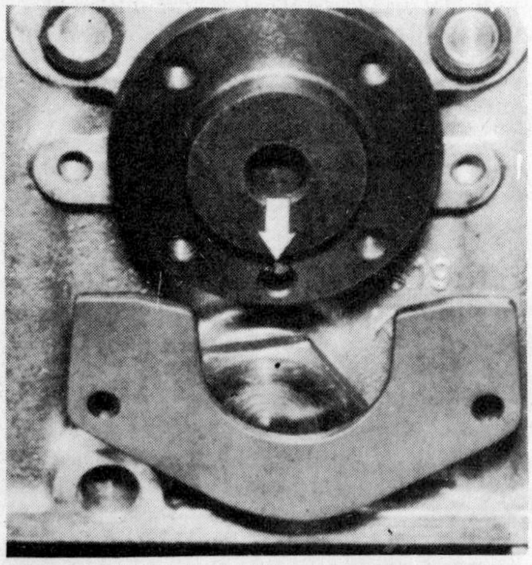

Removal of camshaft and rocker arm retainer plate from the cylinder head, showing the dowel pin hole on four cylinder engine

3. Spring
4. Washer
5. Rocker arm
6. Thrust ring

Installed position of rocker arm components

Use locating pins to retain rocker arm shaft when the head bolts are removed

Proper piston ring installation—typical

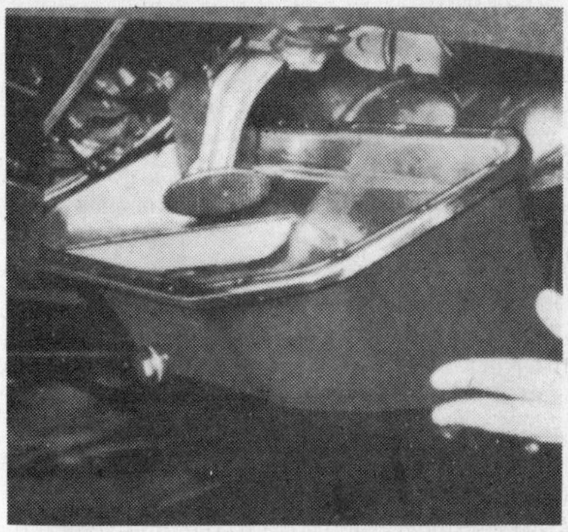

Removal of engine oil pan—typical

replaced, as necessary, while the shafts and rocker arms are out of the cylinder head.

7. Installation is the reverse of removal. Note the following procedures:
   a. Design changes of the rocker arms and shafts have occurred with the installation of a bushing in the rocker arm and the use of two horizontal oil flow holes drilled in the rocker shaft for improved oil supply. Do not mix the previously designed parts with the later designed parts.
   b. When installing the rocker arms and components to the rocker shafts, install locating pins in the cylinder head bolt bores to properly align the rocker arm shafts.
   c. Install sealer on the rocker arm shaft locking bolts and rear cover.
   d. On the 4-cylinder engines, position the rocker shafts so that the camshaft retaining plate ends can be engaged in the slots of shafts during camshaft installation.
   e. Adjust the valve clearance.

Pistons and Connecting Rods

REMOVAL AND INSTALLATION

The pistons and connecting rods may be removed from the engine after the cylinder head, oil pan and oil pump are removed. The connecting rods and caps are marked for each cylinder with No. 1 cylinder at the sprocket end of the engine.

Location of piston in the cylinder bore with ring gaps located 180° apart

All reference numbers on the pistons and connecting rods must be located on the same side, with the arrow on the piston top facing the front of the engine. Measurement, ring fitting and installation procedures are outlined in the Engine Rebuilding section.

ENGINE LUBRICATION

Oil Pan

REMOVAL AND INSTALLATION

2002 Series

1. Raise and support the vehicle. Drain the engine oil.
2. Remove the front stabilizer bar, if equipped.
3. Remove the oil pan retaining bolts and loosen the pan from the engine block.
4. Disconnect the left and right engine supports.
5. Lower the vehicle and attach a lifting sling and raise the engine slightly.
6. Rotate the crankshaft so that the No. 4 piston is at TDC.
7. Remove the oil pan toward the front.
8. Reverse the procedure to install the oil pan using a new gasket.

3.0 and 530i

1. Raise and support the vehicle. Drain the engine oil.
2. Remove the front lower apron (3.0) and remove the stabilizer bar.
3. Loosen the alternator (remove the alternator on 530i) and remove the power steering pump, but do not disconnect the hoses.
4. Remove the lower power steering bracket bolt and loosen the remaining bolts (remove the remaining bolts on 530i) enough to remove the oil pan retaining bolts.
5. Loosen the engine support bracket.
6. Remove the oil pan bolts and loosen the oil pan from the engine block.
7. Rotate the crankshaft until the No. 6 crankpin is above the bottom of the engine block.
8. Lower the front of the oil pan, turn the rear of the pan towards the support bracket and remove the pan.
9. Reverse the procedure to install the oil pan, using new gaskets.

320i

1. Raise and support the vehicle. Drain the engine oil.
2. Loosen the steering gear bolts and pull the steering box off the front axle carrier.
3. Remove the oil pan bolts and separate the pan from the engine block.
4. Swing the oil pan downward while rotating the crankshaft to allow the pan to clear the crankpin and remove the pan toward the front.
5. Reverse the procedure to install the oil pan, using new gaskets.

630i

1. Raise and support the vehicle. Drain the engine oil.
2. Remove the front stabilizer bar.
3. Disconnect the wire terminal at the oil level switch.
4. Disconnect the power steering pump, but do not disconnect the hoses. Loosen all the power steering bracket bolts, and remove the bottom bolt.
5. Remove the engine oil pan bolts, separate the oil pan from the engine block and lower the front of the pan.
6. Rotate the crankshaft until the No. 6 crankpin is above the bottom of the engine block.
7. Lift the engine slightly at the clutch

housing while removing the pan to the right side.

8. Reverse the procedure to install the oil pan, using new gaskets.

733i

1. Raise and support the vehicle. Drain the engine oil.
2. Remove the power steering pump, but do not disconnect the hoses.
3. Remove the lower power steering bracket bolt. Loosen the upper bracket bolts in order to move the bracket away from the oil pan.
4. Disconnect the oil level switch wire terminal.
5. Remove the oil pan bolts and separate the oil pan from the engine block.
6. Disconnect the left and right engine mounts.
7. Remove the engine vibration damper.
8. Lower the vehicle and remove the fan housing from the radiator.
9. Attach a lifting sling and raise the engine until the oil pan can be removed.
10. Reverse the procedure to install the oil pan, using new gaskets.

Rear Main Bearing Oil Seal

REMOVAL AND INSTALLATION

The rear main bearing oil seal can be replaced after the transmission, clutch/flywheel or the converter/flywheel has been removed from the engine.

Removal and installation, after the seal is exposed, is as follows.

1. Drain the engine oil and loosen the oil pan bolts.
2. Remove the two rear oil pan bolts.
3. Remove the end cover housing from the engine block and remove the seal from the housing.
4. Install a new seal into the end cover housing with a special seal installer or equivalent.

NOTE: Fill the cavity between the sealing lips of the seal with grease before installing.

5. Using a new gasket, install the end cover on the engine block and bolt it into place.
6. Reverse the removal procedure to complete the installation.

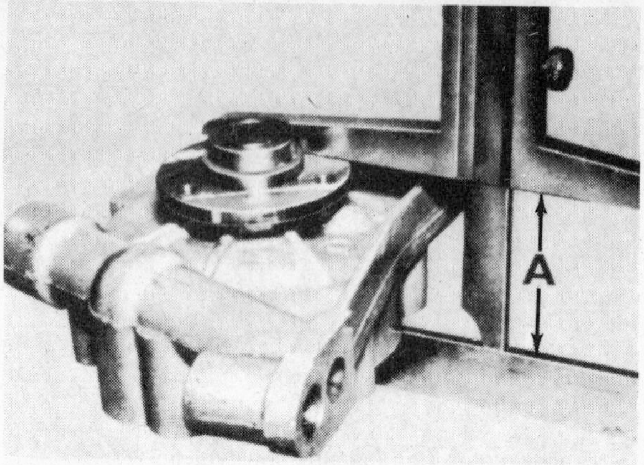

Measuring clearance (A) between hub and inner rotor

Oil Pump

REMOVAL AND INSTALLATION

1. Remove the oil pan.
2. Remove the bolts retaining the sprocket to the oil pump shaft and remove the sprocket.
3. On 4-cylinder engines:
   a. Remove the oil pump retaining bolts and lower the oil pump from the engine block.
   b. Note the location of the O-ring seal, between the housing and the pressure safety line.
   c. Be sure that the oil bore in the shim is correctly positioned during the oil pump installation.
4. On 6-cylinder engines:
   a. Remove the oil pump retaining bolts and lower the oil pump from the engine block.

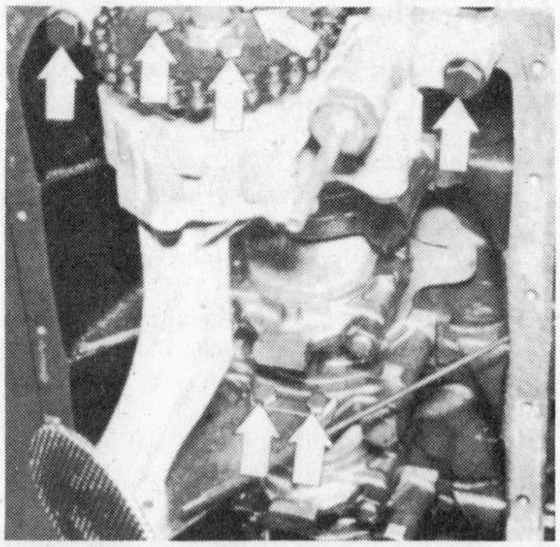

Oil pump bolt locations—4-cylinder shown but typical of 6-cylinder

Measuring inner rotor-to-outer rotor clearance

Rear main bearing oil seal and end cover housing showing special sealing locations

Measuring outer rotor-to-pump body clearance

b. Do not loosen the chain adjusting shims from the two mounting locations.

5. Install the oil pump in the reverse order of removal. On 6-cylinder engines, add or subtract shims between the oil pump body and the engine block to obtain a slight movement of the chain under light thumb pressure.

Important: When used, the two shim thicknesses must be the same. Tighten the pump holder at the pick-up end after shimming is completed to avoid stress on the pump.

ENGINE COOLING

Bleeding the Cooling System

With Bleeder Screw on Thermostat Housing

Set the heater valve in the WARM position, start the engine and bring it to normal operating temperature. Run the engine at fast idle and open the venting screw on the thermostat housing until the coolant comes out free of air bubbles. Close the bleeder screw and refill the cooling system.

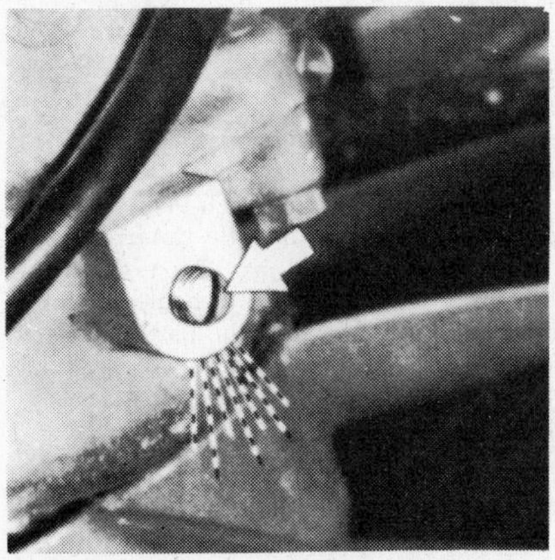

Bleeding of the cooling system with bleeder screw

Without Bleeder Screw

Fill the cooling system, place the heater valve in the WARM position, close the pressure cap to the second (fully closed) position. Start the engine and bring to normal operating temperature. Carefully release the pressure cap to the first position and squeeze the upper and lower radiator hoses in a pumping action to allow trapped air to escape through the radiator. Recheck the coolant level and close the pressure cap to its second position.

Radiator

REMOVAL AND INSTALLATION

The radiator can be removed after draining the cooling system, removing of the coolant hoses, disconnecting of the automatic transmission oil cooler lines, disconnecting of the temperature switch wire connectors and removing the shroud from the radiator core. Remove the radiator retaining bolts and life the radiator from the vehicle.

NOTE: The 2002 series may be equipped with an air preheater unit for the air cleaner that will have to be removed before the radiator can be taken from the vehicle.

The shroud will remain in the vehicle, resting on the fan. The radiator is installed in the reverse order of removal. Fill and bleed the cooling system.

Thermostat

REMOVAL AND INSTALLATION

The thermostat will be located near the water pump, either on the cylinder head or intake manifold on some models and will be located between two coolant hose sections on other models.

The removal and installation of the thermostat is accomplished in the conventional manner.

Water Pump

REMOVAL AND INSTALLATION

1. Drain the cooling system and remove the radiator.
2. Remove the fan blades, loosen the drive belts and remove as necessary.
3. Remove the belt pulley from the pump flange and disconnect the coolant hoses.
4. Remove the retaining bolts and remove the water pump from the engine.
5. The installation is in the reverse of the removal procedure. Use a new gasket and bleed the cooling system.

Belt Tension Adjustment

The fan belt tension is adjusted by moving the alternator on the slack adjuster bracket. The belt tension is adjusted to a deflection of approximately ½ in. under moderate thumb pressure in the middle of its longest span.

Measuring belt deflection

EMISSION CONTROLS

The BMW emission controls are composed of three major systems to control engine emissions of hydrocarbons (HC), carbon monoxide (CO), and oxides of nitrogen (NOx).

The 3 systems are (1) Crankcase Emissions Control System, (2) Exhaust Emission Control System and (3) Evaporative Emission Control System.

Differences may exist between the systems used on California models or Federal models depending upon the year of production and the vehicle model.

The Emission Control Information Label attached to the vehicle should be consulted before any repairs or specification changes are made to the engine.

Crankcase Emission Control System

This system is considered a "sealed" system. No fresh air is allowed to enter the crankcase and the blow-by emissions are routed to the air cleaner or air collector and blended with the air/fuel mixture to be burned through normal combustion.

TESTING

The Crankcase Emission Control System is virtually maintenance free. The connecting tube from the top engine cover to the air cleaner or air collector should be inspected during the routine maintenance services and replaced if cracked, distorted or plugged.

With the engine operating and the connecting tube disconnected, a vacuum should be noted at the air cleaner or air collector side of the hose. If vacuum is not present, an air leak or plugged air induction system may be the cause.

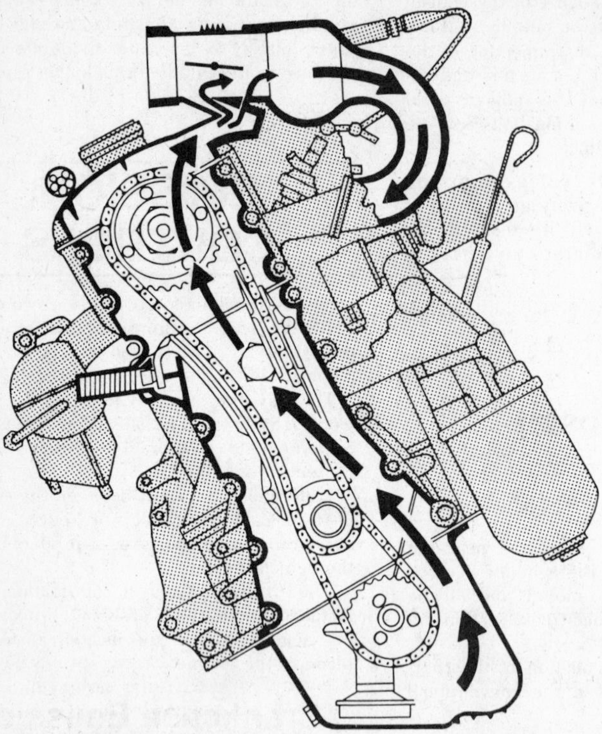

Crankcase emission control system (with Electronic Fuel Injection)

Air Injection System

The Air Injection system is used to add oxygen to the hot exhaust gases in the Thermal Reactor which replaces the exhaust manifold. The introduction of fresh air (oxygen) aids in more complete combustion of the air/fuel mixture lessening the hydrocarbons and the carbon monoxide emissions. A belt driven air pump is used to force air into the exhaust system, through a series of valves and tubing.

TESTING

2002 and 3.0

AIR PUMP

Remove the air return pipe and hold the palm of the hand over the pressure regulating valve unit while increasing the engine speed. The excess pressure valve must open between 1700 and 2000 rpm. If the valve opens early, replace the valve. If the valve opens at a higher rpm, replace the air pump.

BELT ADJUSTMENT

The air pump drive belt should have a deflection of no more than ⅜ in. measured in the middle of its longest span, when properly adjusted.

CONTROL VALVE

The control valve should be replaced if the carburetors are difficult to adjust or if the engine backfires when the throttle is released.

CHECK VALVE

The check valve should be replaced if air can be blown through the valve in both directins. Air should move towards the manifold only.

BLOW-IN PIPES

The exhaust manifold must be removed to expose the blow-in pipes. The pipes can be replaced by unscrewing them from the manifold and screwing in new ones.

320i, 530i, 630i, 633i and 733i

AIR PUMP

Disconnect the outlet hose and start the engine. The air velocity should increase as the engine speed increases. If not, the air pump drive belt could be slipping, the check valve or the air pump may be defective and would have to be adjusted or replaced.

BLOW-OFF VALVE

If backfiring occurs when releasing the accelerator or the air pump seems to be overloading, the blow-off valve may be defective.

The valve must release and blow-off during a coasting condition and the internal safety valve must open at 5 psi. The vacuum line must have suction when the engine is running and must allow the air to be blown off when reattached to the valve at idle.

ELECTRIC CONTROL VALVE–WHITE CAP

This control valve governs the blow-off valve and must be open at temperatures below 113° F (45° C) and closed above 113° F (45° C) of the coolant.

With the coolant temperatures above 113° F (45° C), the ignition switch on and the engine off, disconnect both vacuum hoses, attach a test hose to one nipple and blow air into the valve. The valve is functioning properly if air cannot flow through the valve. Turn the ignition switch off and blow into the valve again. Air should flow through the valve.

CHECK VALVE

The check valve must be replaced if air can be blown through the valve in both directions. Air should move towards the reactors only.

BLOW-IN PIPES

The air enters above the reactors, directly into the exhaust ports, behind the exhaust valves. The pipes can be replaced by removing the distribution tube assembly.

THERMAL REACTOR

The reactors have a double casing and has internally vented flame deflector plates. Spontaneous combustion, due to high temperatures, and the introduction of oxygen into

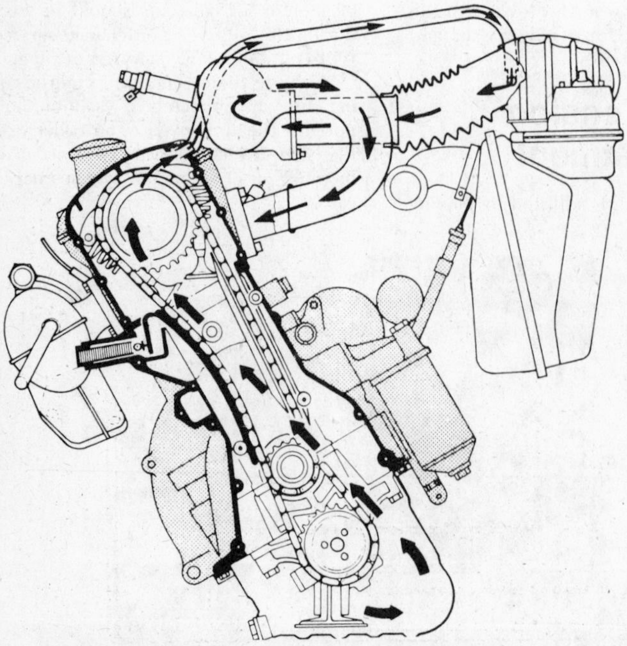

Crankcase emission control system (with Continuous Fuel Injection)

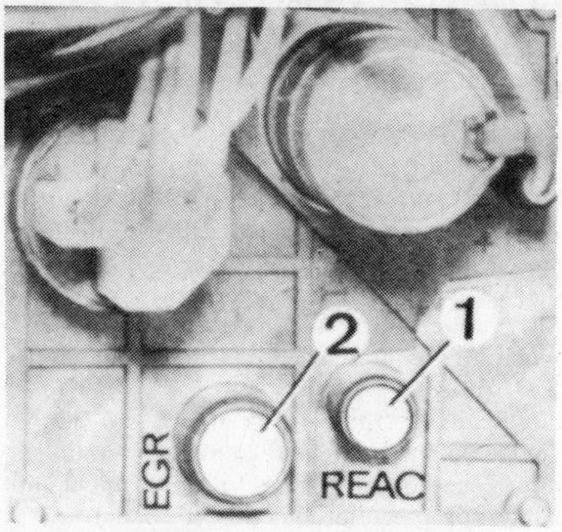

Triggering device with REACTOR (1) and the EGR (2) resetting buttons shown

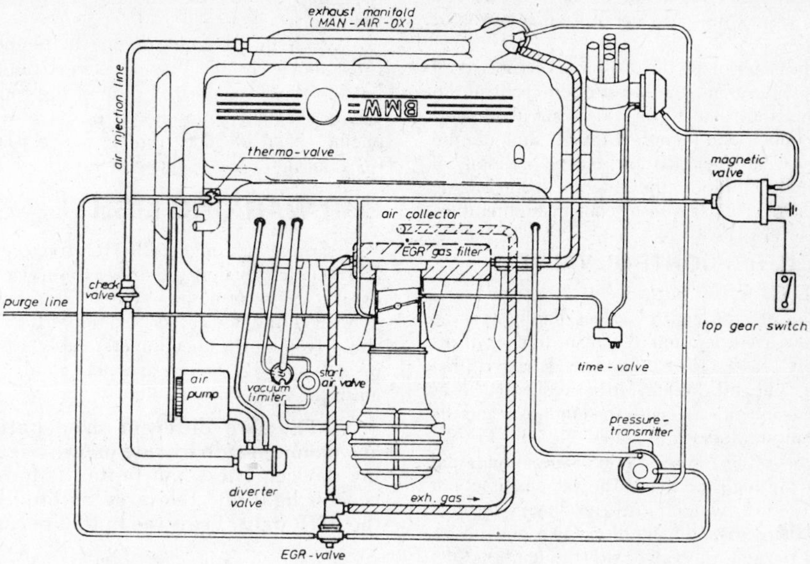

Typical exhaust emission control system—four cylinder engine

the exhaust gas flow maintains the after-burning of the gases.

A warning light marked "Reactor" alerts the driver to have the unit inspected for external heat damage every 25,000 miles. A triggering device, located behind the dash and operated by the speedometer cable, can be reset to open the electrical contacts and extinguish the warning light.

NOTE: Two different sized buttons are mounted side by side on the trigger-ing device. The small button is for the reactor and the large button is for the EGR valve. Press the button to reset.

Exhaust Gas Recirculating System

The EGR valve is vacuum operated by the position of the carburetor throttle plate in the throttle bore during vehicle operation. A metered amount of exhaust gas enters the combustion chamber to be mixed with the air/fuel blend. The effect is to reduce the peak combustion temperatures, which in turn reduces the amount of nitrous oxides (NOx), formed during the combustion process.

EGR VALVE–TESTING

2002 and 3.0

Remove the air filter and adjust the engine idle to 900 rpm. Remove the vacuum line from the valve and using an engine vacuum source, attach the hose to the vacuum nipple. The engine speed should drop 500-600 rpm if the valve is operating properly. If little or no change of engine speed is noted, the recirculation pipes, the cyclone filter or the EGR valve may be plugged or defective.

320i, 530i, 630i, 633i and 733i

The EGR valve is vacuum controlled from a pressure transmitter which regulates the amount of vacuum applied to the valve from

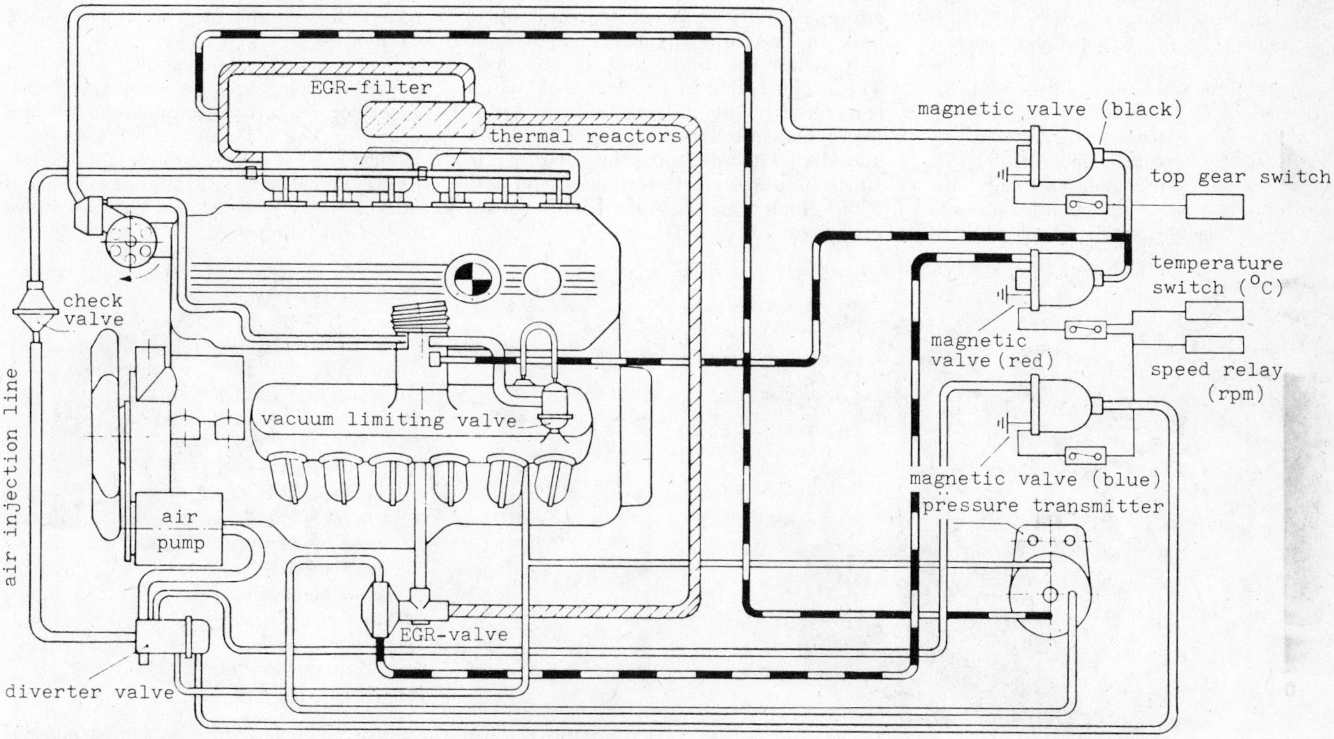

Typical exhaust emission control system—six cylinder engine (black magnetic valve and high gear switch used on California and High-Altitude version with manual transmission)

signals originating at the intake manifold and from a back-pressure signal from the exhaust system.

The interior of the EGR valve consists of two diaphragms, the lower one to control the amount of exhaust gas to be recirculated and the upper one to interrupt or shut off the exhaust gas recirculation under conditions of idle, deceleration, full engine load, engine speed over 3750 rpm or coolant temperature below 113° F.

ELECTRIC CONTROL VALVE–RED CAP

The electric control valve should stop the EGR valve operation at coolant temperatures below 113° F (45° C), and speeds above 3000 rpm. Tag and disconnect both vacuum hoses at the control valve with the engine off and the coolant temperature below 113° F (45° C). Connect a test hose to one of the nipples and blow through the hose. The valve is functioning properly when there is air flowing through the valve with the ignition OFF and no air flow through the valve with the ignition ON.

Connect the vacuum hoses to the valve and operate the engine until the coolant is heated over 113° F (45° C). Disconnect the hoses and check for air flow through the valve. Air should now flow through the valve.

COOLANT TEMPERATURE SWITCH AND CONTROL RELAY

1. With the coolant temperature below 113° F (45° C), turn the ignition ON, but do not start the engine. Remove the wire plug at the control valve and connect a test lamp to the plug.
   a. The test lamp should light. If the test lamp does not light, connect the test lamp to ground. If the lamp now operates, the ground wire to the control valve has an open circuit.
   b. If the test lamp still does not light, disconnect the wire terminal at the coolant temperature switch and connect it to ground. If the test lamp still does not light, replace the control valve.
2. With the coolant temperature above 113° F (45° C), turn the ignition switch ON but do not start the engine. Disconnect the wire terminal plug at the control valve and connect a test lamp. The lamp should be off. If the lamp is on, the coolant temperature switch or control relay is defective.
3. With the engine running at temperatures above 113° F (45° C), connect the test light to the disconnected plug of the control valve. The test lamp should be on over an engine speed of 3000 rpm. If the test lamp does not light, the speed switch is defective.

EGR WARNING LIGHT

A warning light marked EGR is triggered at 25,000 miles, to alert the driver to service the exhaust gas recirculation system filter.

A triggering device, located under the dash and driven by the speedometer cable, can be reset to open the electrical contacts and extinguish the EGR warning light.

NOTE: Two different sized buttons are mounted side by side on the triggering device. The small button is for the reactor light and the large button is for the EGR light. Press the button to reset.

Distributor Advance/Retard Units

A vacuum advance and retard unit is attached to the distributor and is controlled by engine vacuum. The advance can be checked with a strobe light and increasing the engine speed while observing the action of the timing mark during the increase in engine speed. The retard side can be checked at idle by removing the retard vacuum line and noting the increase in engine speed of at least 300 rpm.

NOTE: Models 733i, 633i, 320i California and High Altitude vehicles equipped with manual transmissions, have the vacuum advance in operation only when the high gear is engaged. This is controlled by an electrical switch connected to the shifting linkage. Automatic transmission 633i for California and High Altitude, have the vacuum advance inoperative. Late model 530i and 630i vehicles are equipped with a vacuum retard unit only.

ELECTRIC CONTROL VALVE TEST *(Black Cap)–California Equipment Only*

This control valve stops the retard distributor control over speeds of 3000 rpm.

Remove the outer hose (to distributor) and start the engine. At engine rpm lower than 3000 rpm, vacuum should be present in the distributor retard unit hose and not present when the engine speed is increased above 3000 rpm.

Disconnect the wire terminal end at the control valve and have the engine operating at idle. Connect a test lamp to the terminal and check for presence of current. If current is present, the speed switch is defective.

Increase the engine speed to 3000 rpm or above, and the test lamp should light. If the test lamp does not light, the speed switch is defective.

Carburetor Dashpot

A dashpot is used to slow the carburetor throttle return while the vehicle engine is above 1800 rpm. An electrically controlled set of relays and magnetic switches are used to direct engine vacuum to release the dashpot at engine speeds under 1800 rpm.

DASHPOT TEST

Operate the engine at 2500 rpm and slowly decrease the speed to approximately 1800 rpm. The dashpot plunger should contact the throttle linkage at the 1700-1900 rpm mark (2002-1550 minimum). Adjust the dashpot plunger if necessary.

The plunger must be free of the throttle linkage under 1700 rpm minimum (2002-1550 minimum) when the engine vacuum is directed through the magnetic valve to the dashpot.

If no vacuum is present at the dashpot hose under 1700 rpm, check the engine speed relay connector. Remove the terminal end from the magnetic valve and increase the engine speed to 2000 rpm. If voltage is present at the terminal, the magnetic switch is defective and if no voltage is present, the speed sensitive relay must be replaced.

2. Red 3. Blue

Electronic control valves with attaching bolt locations

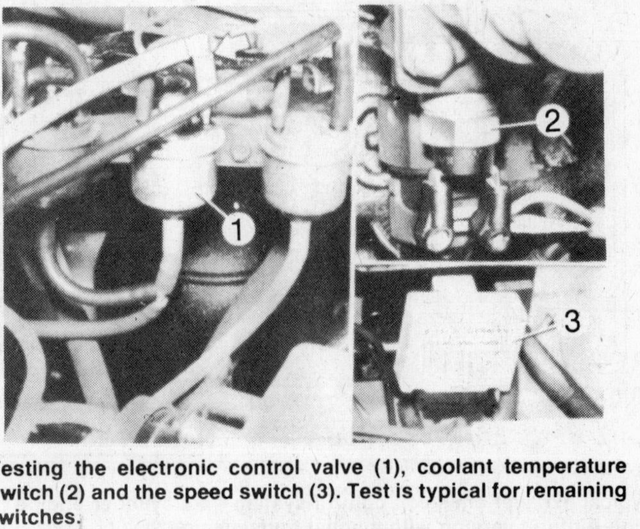

Testing the electronic control valve (1), coolant temperature switch (2) and the speed switch (3). Test is typical for remaining switches.

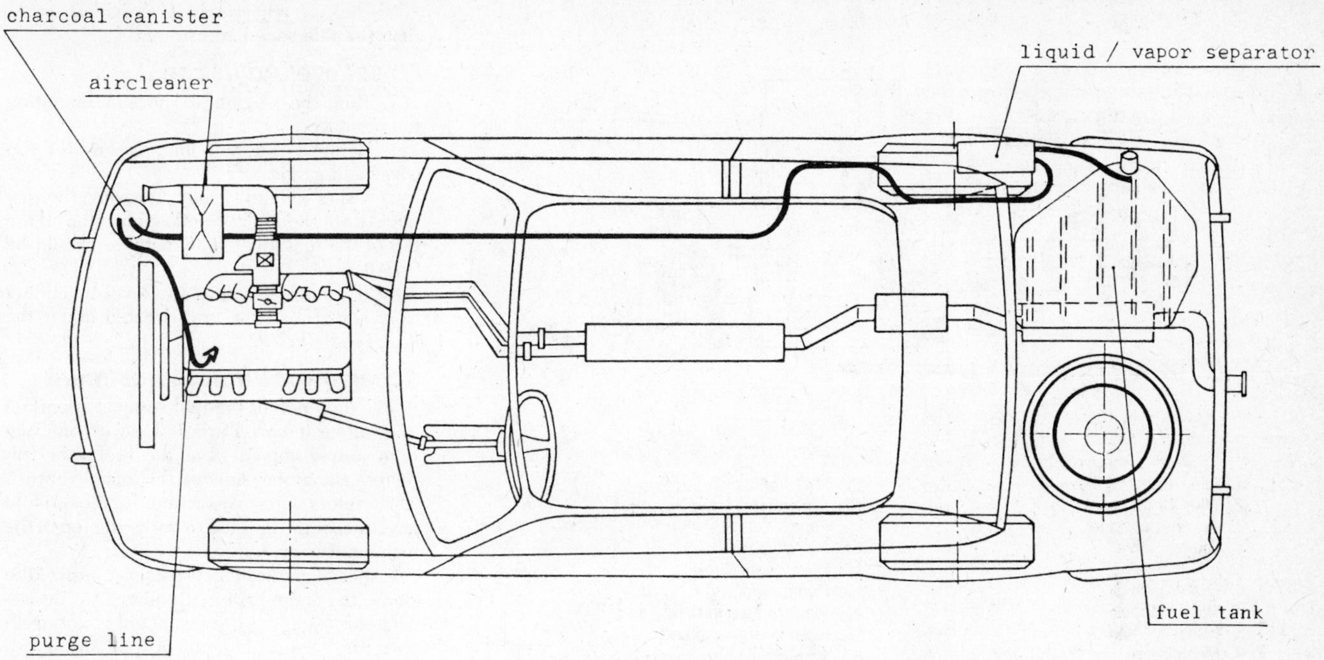

Typical evaportive control system—six cylinder engine illustrated

Evaporative Control System

This system is designed to collect and store the raw gasoline vapors (hydrocarbons) and to direct the vapors into the engine along with the air/fuel mixture when the engine is operating.

A maintenance free vapor storage tank is located in the trunk while an activated carbon filter canister is mounted in the engine compartment.

MAINTENANCE

The only repairs or checks that can be made are to maintain the hoses and to change the canister unit if it becomes saturated with raw gasoline.

FUEL SYSTEM

Fuel Pump

A diaphragm type fuel pump is located on the cylinder head and is operated by the camshaft, through a pump plunger rod. A fuel filter is located in the fuel pump while an in-line filter is located in the fuel line between the fuel pump and the carburetors.

REMOVAL AND INSTALLATION

Carburetor Equipped Models

1. Remove the air cleaner.
2. Remove and plug the fuel lines.
3. Remove the retaining bolts and separate the pump from the insulator block and cylinder head. Do not lose or shorten the pump rod.
4. Install the pump in the reverse order of removal.

Fuel Injection Models

The fuel pump is an electrical unit, delivering fuel through a pressure regulator, to a fuel distributor or a ring-line for the injection valves. The fuel pump is mounted under the vehicle, near the fuel tank, or in the engine compartment.

1. Disconnect the electrical connector.
2. Remove the fuel lines and plug the ends.
3. Remove the retaining bolts and remove the pump and expansion tank as an assembly.
4. The pump can be separated from the expansion tank after removal.
5. Installation is the reverse of removal.

Carburetors

2002 and 2002A

These carburetors are single-barrel down-

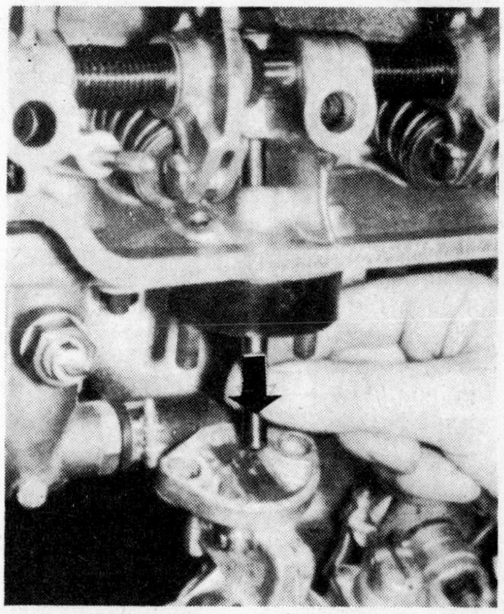

Removal of mechanical fuel pump and plunger rod

Electric fuel pump assembly—typical

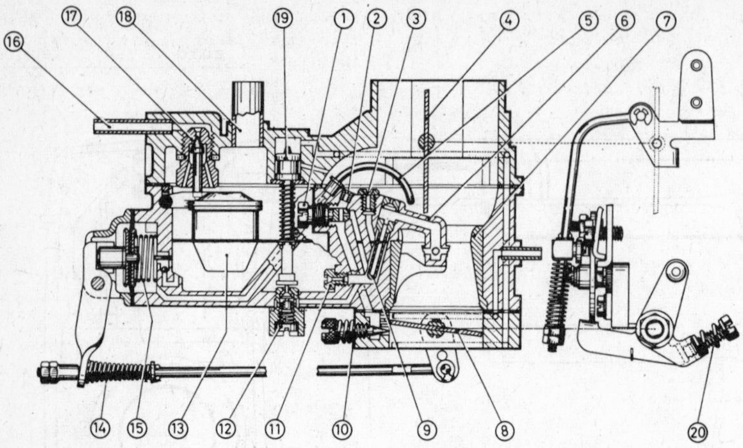

1. Idler jet
2. Idler air jet
3. Air regulating jet
4. Starter valve
5. Injection pipe
6. Outlet pipe
7. Venturi tube
8. Butterfly valve
9. Mixer pipe
10. Idling mixture regulating screw
11. Main jet
12. Enrichment valve
13. Float
14. Pump lever
15. Diaphragm spring
16. Pump diaphragm
17. Float needle valve
18. Float chamber bleed
19. Vacuum plunger
20. Idling speed adjusting screw

Exploded view of Solex 40PDSI carburetor (with manual choke)

draft units with a manually operated choke (2002 with 40PDSI) or an automatic choke (2002A vehicles with 40PDSIT).

Removal and Installation

1. Remove the air cleaner, fuel hoses, accelerator linkage and choke cable (if equipped).
2. Remove the carburetor retaining nuts and washers and remove the carburetor from the manifold.

NOTE: The cooling system will have to be partiallly drained on the model 2002A.

3. Using a new gasket, install the carburetor on the manifold using the reverse of the removal procedure.

Throttle Linkage Adjustment

The accelerator linkage shaft extends from the firewall, engages in the carburetor throttle lever and is fastened with a spring clip.

No linkage adjustment is provided, other than the idle speed adjustment.

Float Level Adjustment

1. Run the engine to normal operating temperature.
2. Remove the fuel line, carburetor top cover and gasket.
3. Using a depth gauge, measure the distance from the top of the float chamber to the top of the fuel level. The distance should be 0.70-0.75 in.
4. If necessary, adjust the level by adding to or subtracting the seals located under the float needle valve.

Accelerator Pump Adjustment

The direction of the fuel spray is important to avoid hesitation. Carburetors with one vacuum nipple should have the fuel spray directed along the side of the main venturi. Carburetors with two vacuum nipples should have the spray directed to strike the top of the main venturi.

A special carburetor test stand is utilized to gauge the amount of fuel injected by the accelerator pump. If the test stand is not available, the desired amount of fuel can be adjusted by moving the pump rod on the pump lever. Shorten the lever to increase the amount of fuel and lengthen the lever to decrease the amount.

Choke Adjustment

MANUAL CHOKE (40 PDSI)

1. Pull the choke cable to stop No. 2.
2. Adjust the choke valve clearance to 0.209 ± 0.012 inch, by loosening the cable retaining screw and moving the cable.

NOTE: Be sure the choke valve will close completely when the choke cable is fully pulled. The outside cable housing may have to be readjusted.

AUTOMATIC CHOKE (40PDSIT)

1. Be sure the choke valve shaft will rotate freely in its bore and that the choke cap aligning notch is aligned with the lug on the choke valve housing.
2. Depress the accelerator to allow the choke valve to close under spring tension.

NOTE: The choke valve should close if the ambient temperature is below 68° F (20° C).

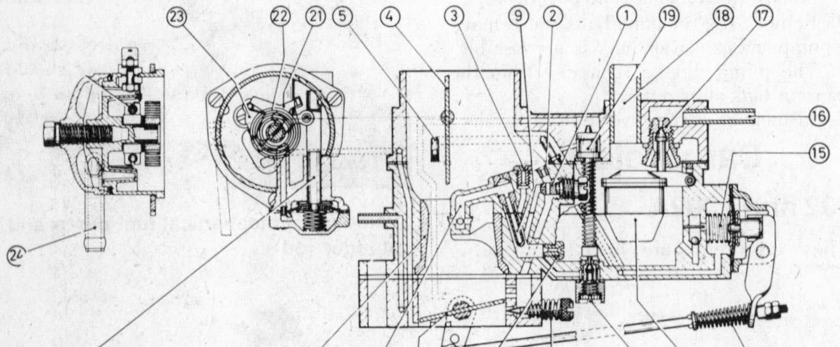

1. Idler jet
2. Idler air jet
3. Air regulating valve
4. Starter valve
5. Injection pipe
6. Outlet pipe
7. Venturi tube
8. Butterfly valve
9. Mixer pipe
10. Idling mixture regulating valve
11. Main jet
12. Enrichment valve
13. Float
14. Pump lever
15. Diaphragm spring
16. Pump diaphragm
17. Float needle valve
18. Float chamber bleed
19. Vacuum plunger
20. Pull rod
21. Carrier lever
22. Bi-metallic spring
23. Stepped disc
24. Hot water connection

Exploded view of Solex PDSIT carburetor (With automatic choke)

Depressing the choke rod to its stop—Solex 40PDSIT

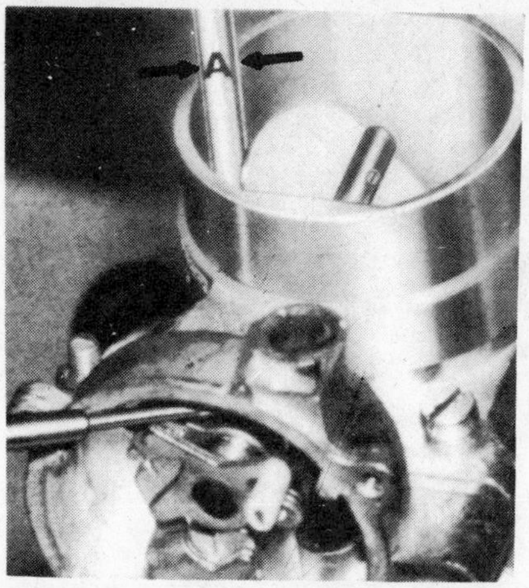

Measuring clearance (A) between choke valve and throttle bore—Solex 40PDSIT

3. If adjustment is needed, remove the choke cap with the water hoses attached.

4. Depress the choke rod (the vertical shaft inside choke housing) downward to its stop and check the choke valve clearance between the choke valve and the throttle bore. The gap should be 0.251-0.267 in.

5. An adjusting screw and locknut is located under the choke housing and controls the height of the choke rod. Loosen the locknut and move the screw in or out to change the choke valve gap.

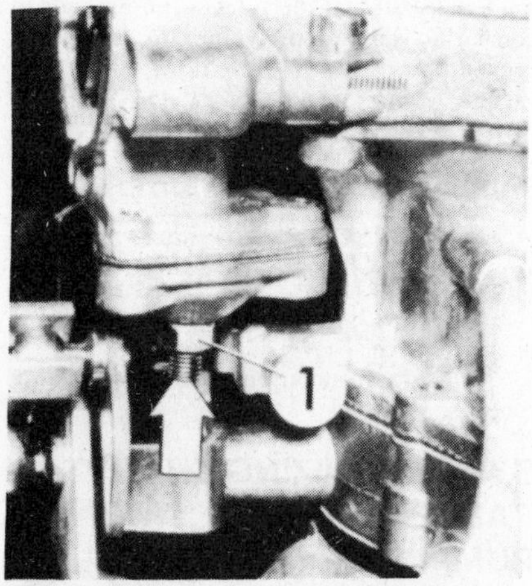

Adjusting screw (1) location for adjustment of choke rod—Solex 40PDSIT

6. Reposition the choke cover on the carburetor. Be sure the choke arm engages the coil spring loop in the choke cover. Align the notch on the cover with the lug on the choke housing.

7. Connect the heating coil wire terminal to the housing.

NOTE: Current flow should be approximately 1 amp at 12 volts.

8. Adjust the fast idle speed to 2000-2200 rpm with the engine at normal operating temperature.

9. With the choke valve set at a gap of 0.25 inch, adjust the choke connector rod nuts to set the fast idle. Shorten the rod to reduce the rpm and lengthen the rod to increase the rpm.

Fuel Injection Systems Model 2002Tii

The Kugelfischer fuel injection system consists basically of mechanical type fuel injectors, engine driven injector pump, cold start valve, and electrically controlled switches and sensors.

WARM-UP SENSOR

Adjustment

NOTE: The warm-up sensor adjustment must be made before the engine is warmed up.

1. Remove the air filter housing.

2. Press out the air regulator cone with a screwdriver, until special tool 6073 or equivalent can be inserted in the groove of the air regulator cone.

3. A distance of 0.102 ± 0.012 in. should exist between the grub screw and the stop screw (distance A). Adjustments can be made at the plate nut (1).

4. After the engine is at normal operating temperature, the air regulator valve cone must project 0.35-0.39 in. (distance A). The plate washer must project above the lever by 0.157 in. (distance B) and the grub screw must be in full contact with the stop screw.

5. If these specifications are not obtained, the warm up sensor must be replaced.

Removal and Installation

1. Drain the coolant and remove the air filter.

2. Disconnect the coolant hoses and the auxiliary air hose.

3. Disconnect the return spring and remove the warm-up sensor while disconnecting the accelerator linkage.

4. After installation, adjust the sensor as previously outlined and adjust the idle speed.

START VALVE

Testing

1. Remove the start valve from the throttle valve section.

2. Turn the ignition switch to ON to obtain fuel pressure from the pump, but do not start the engine.

3. Connect a positive current jumper wire to the "SV" connection of the time switch.

4. If fuel is ejected from the start valve, the valve and the feed pipe are considered to be good.

NOTE: The valve must not drip fuel with the current OFF.

THERMO-TIME SWITCH

Testing

1. Remove the wire terminal from the thermo-time switch.

2. Connect a test lamp to a positive terminal and the "W" terminal of the thermo-time switch.

3. The lamp should light at coolant temperature below 95° F (35° C).

4. Leave the test lamp attached to the "W" terminal and connect a positive jumper wire to terminal "G".

5. The internal bi-metal control should open after a short time and the light should then go out. If not, replace the thermo-time switch.

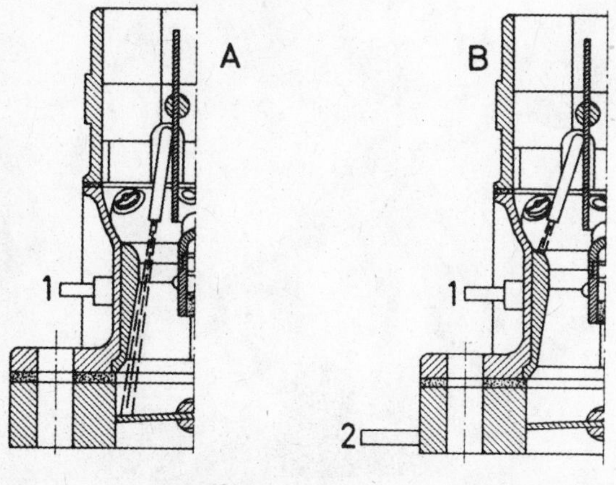

Difference in accelerator pump spray between one (A) and two (B) vacuum nipple equipped carburetors

1. Grub screw
2. Stop screw

A. Projection distance of air regulator cone ab ove valve body

B. Projection distance of plate washer above lever

Checking warm-up sensor when engine is at normal operating temperature

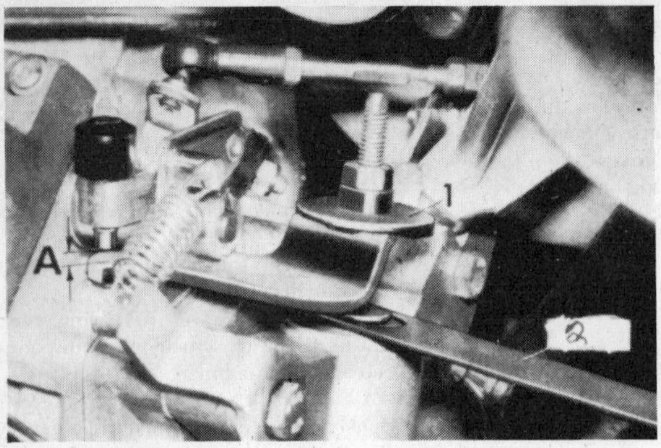

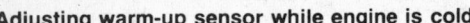

1. Plate nut
2. Special tool to lift air regulator cone
A. Clearance between grub screw and stop screw

Adjusting warm-up sensor while engine is cold

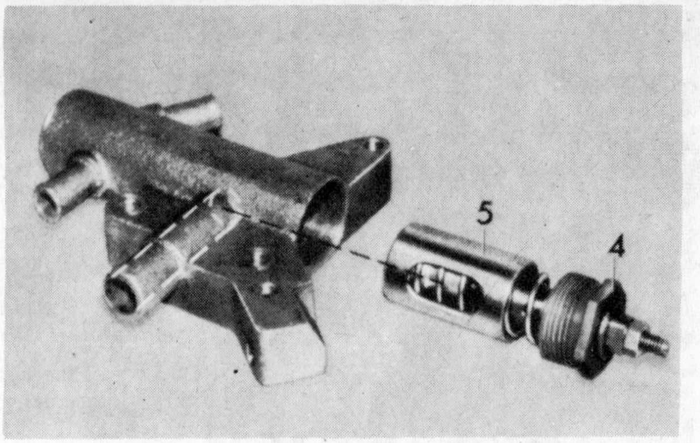

4. Closure nut
5. Valve sleeve

Exploded view of warm-up sensor

TIME SWITCH

Testing

1. Remove the time switch from the firewall.
2. Connect a test lamp between ground and the "SV" terminal of the time switch.
3. Remove the No. 4 wire from the ignition coil and actuate the starter. The test lamp should go out after a short time.

NOTE: The injection time period of start valve is as follows:

At 4° F (−20° C)	*9 to 15 seconds*
At 32° F (0° C)	*4 to 10 seconds*
A 95° F (35° C)	*1 second*

4. Remove the terminal plug from the thermo-time switch. Actuate the starter; the light should go on for one second and then go out.

5. Connect a test lamp between the "TH" terminal and ground. The test lamp must light up as long as the starter is actuated.

INJECTOR PUMP

Removal and Installation

1. Drain the cooling system and remove the air cleaner.
2. Remove all injection lines and fitting rings for the fuel hoses.

NOTE: Plug the pressure valves after removing the lines.

3. Remove the fuel return line, oil feed hose, water hoses and mounting for the engine oil dipstick. Remove the coolant hose and auxiliary air hose from the warm-up unit.
4. Remove the upper dust cap and disconnect the connecting link from the pump lever.
5. Rotate the engine so that the No. 1 piston is at TDC on its compression stroke. The notch in the cogged belt pulley must point to the cast mark in the pump body.
6. Remove the pulley with a puller and remove the cogged belt.
7. Remove the bolts holding the pump to the timing case cover, pull the injection pump from the cover until the intermediate shaft can be lifted out at the warm-up sensor housing. Remove the pump.
8. The injection pump can be installed using the reverse of the removal procedure.

COGGED BELT

Removal and Installation

1. Remove the front air filter hood and the upper dust cover on the pump assembly.
2. Rotate the engine so that the No. 1 piston is at TDC on its compression stroke. The crankshaft pulley must point to the mark on the dust cap and the pump pulley must align with the casting mark on the pump body.
3. Loosen the alternator and remove the belt.
4. Mark the V-pulley on the crankshaft and remove the retaining bolts from the pulley.
5. Remove the pulley and do not turn the engine, due to the pulley fitting at 180°.
6. Loosen the upper dust cover bolt, remove all other retaining bolts for the lower dust cover and remove the cogged belt by pulling the dust cover to the front and pulling the cogged belt out between the hub and the front dust cover.
7. Be sure of the pulley alignment for both the crankshaft and the injector pump and reverse the removal procedure to install the cogged belt.

INJECTION VALVE

Removal and Installation

1. Disconnect the feed line to the injector with fitting wrenches to avoid damage to the threaded areas.
2. Unscrew the injector valve from the induction sleeve.
3. During installation, use new sealing rings.

SYNCHRONIZING THROTTLE VALVE WITH INJECTION PUMP

1. The connecting rod must be adjusted to 3.346 in. (85 mm) (distance A).

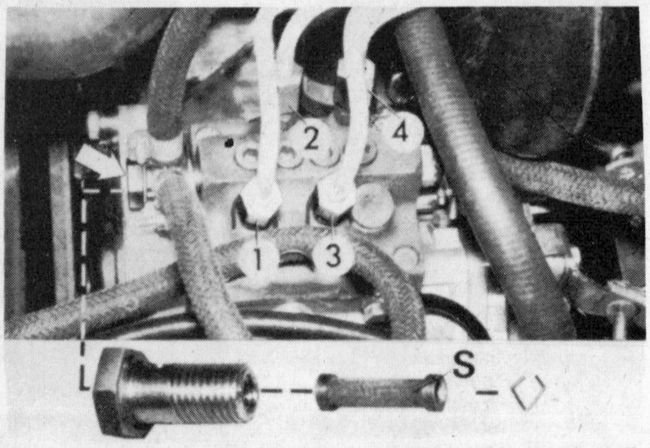

Injector lines-to-cylinder numbering sequence from the fuel distributor head. Location of fuel filter (S) is in the hollow fuel line bolt.

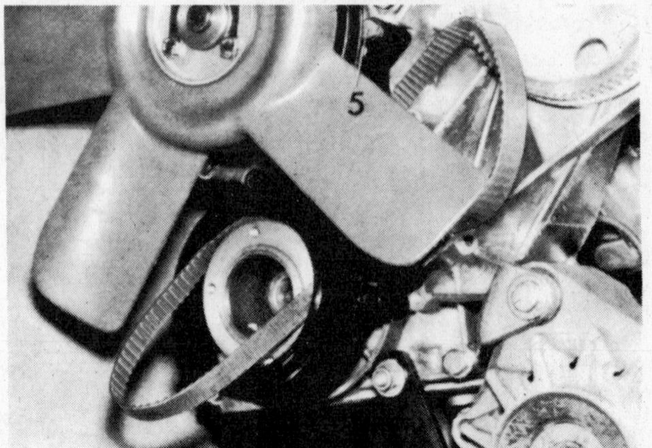

Removal of cogged belt through the lower front dust cover

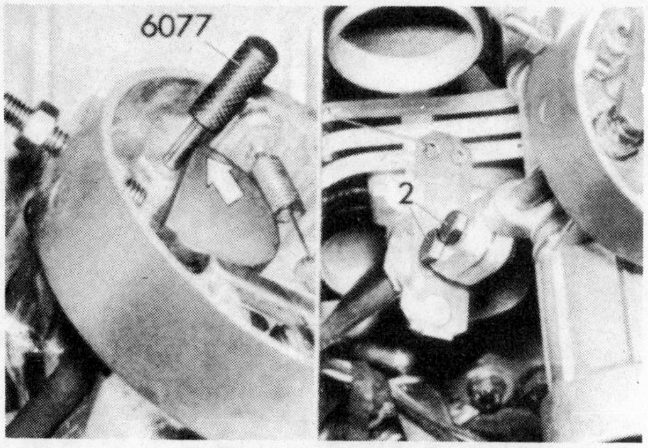

Use of special pin tool (6077) and throttle shaft clamping bolts (2)

Adjustment of full load setting with special tool 6075 and stop screw (3)

NOTE: A special tool is available for this measurement procedure.

2. Remove the throttle housing cover, loosen the adjusting screw until it is no longer in contact with the eccentric. Loosen the throttle shaft clamping screws.
3. Using special tool 6075 or equivalent, secure the regulating lever in the bore of the pump housing through the upper slotted hole.
4. Insert special tool 6077 or equivalent into the hole in the throttle valve base and press the eccentric against the tool. Tighten the throttle shaft clamping screws.
5. Remove the two special tools or equivalents from the throttle shaft housing. The synchronization is correct when the eccentric partially overlaps the tool bore.
6. Adjust the idle speed.
7. Using the special tool 6075 or equivalent, secure the regulating lever in the lowest slot in the pump housing and adjust the stop screw in a position in which the pump lever is just contacted.

320i

The Bosch Continuous Fuel Injection System (K-Jetronic) consists basically of mechanical type fuel injectors, a fuel distributor unit, operated by a sensor plate, and control valve. Electrical and vacuum operated regulators and switches complete the assembly. An electrical control box is not used.

BASIC THROTTLE SETTING

1. Disconnect the accelerator cable and loosen the throttle stop screw.
2. Adjust the distance between the throttle lever and the stop screw to 0.039-0.058 in. clearance.
3. Loosen the throttle lever clamping screw and position the throttle valve in the housing to zero play. Tighten the clamping screw.
4. Tighten the throttle stop screw one complete turn and lock it in place.
5. Adjust the accelerator cable to the throttle lever and attach.

AUXILIARY AIR REGULATOR

1. Disconnect the electrical terminal plug

Alignment of crankshaft pulley and injector pump timing marks

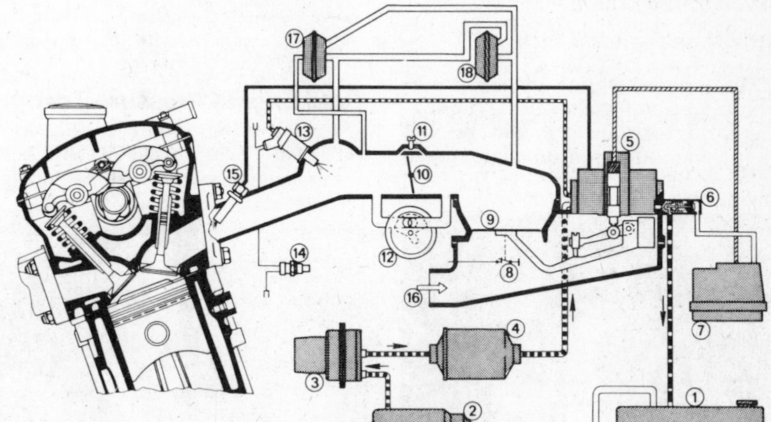

1. Fuel tank
2. Fuel delivery pump
3. Pressure reservoir
4. Fuel filter
5. Fuel distributor
6. System pressure regulator
7. Warm-up regulator
8. Safety switch
9. Sensor plate
10. Throttle valve
11. Idle adjusting screw
12. Auxiliary air regulator
13. Start valve
14. Thermo timing valve
15. Injection valves
16. Air inlet
17. Vacuum regulator
18. Auxiliary air valve

Injection press.
System pressure
Return
Control pressure

Bosch K-Jetronic® Fuel Injection System

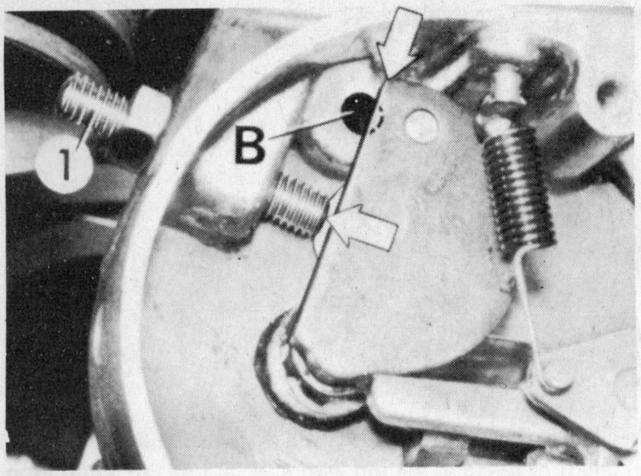

Eccentric overlap of tool bore (B) and idle adjustment screw (1)

Sensor plate (7) positioning in venturi with adjusting spring (9). Position A is allowable clearance from the top of the venturi

and the two air hoses at the auxiliary air regulator.

2. Voltage must be present at the terminal plug with the ignition switch ON.

3. Check the air bore of the regulator. With the engine temperature approximately 68° F (20° C), the air bore should be half open.

4. Connect the terminal plug and the two air hoses to the auxiliary air regulator.

5. Start the engine and the auxiliary air regulator bore should close within five minutes of engine operation by the cut-off valve.

MIXTURE CONTROL UNIT AND SENSOR PLATE ADJUSTMENT

NOTE: 49 state and California control units are not interchangeable.

1. Remove the air intake cowl at the mixture control unit and throttle housing.

2. Turn the ignition ON for approximately five seconds, and during this time, slowly raise the sensor plate with a magnet. Turn the ignition switch OFF.

NOTE: The amount of resistance should be constant when raising the sensor and no resistance should be felt when pushing the sensor plate down quickly.

3. The sensor plate should be flush or 0.019 in. (0.5 mm) below the beginning of the venturi taper. If necessary to adjust, remove the mixture control from the intermediate housing and bend the spring accordingly. Center the sensor plate in the bore by loosening the center plate screw. Tighten when aligned.

NOTE: With the sensor plate too high, the engine will run on and with the sensor plate too low, poor cold and warm engine start-up will result.

4. If the sensor plate movement is erratic, the control piston can be sticking. Remove the fuel distributor and inspect the control piston for damage and replace as necessary.

CAUTION

Do not drop the control valve.

SYSTEM PRESSURE TESTING

Install a shut-off valve and an oil pressure gauge between the control pressure line and the fuel distributor, with the pressure gauge next to the fuel distributor.

Cold Engine Pressure Test

1. Disconnect the terminal plug at the mixture control unit to avoid excessive heat.

2. Open the valve for oil flow and turn on the ignition switch to operate the fuel pump, but do not start the engine.

3. Control pressures depend upon the engine coolant temperature. At a temperature of 50° F (10° C), oil pressure should be 10-11 psi and at 77° F (25° C), oil pressure should be 22.0 psi. At coolant temperature of 104° F (40° C), the pressure should be over 29.4 psi.

NOTE: Oil pressure too low—warm-up regulator defective. Oil pressure too high—fuel return flow insufficient or defective warm-up regulator.

4. Turn the ignition OFF.

Warm Engine Control Pressure

1. Open the shut-off valve for oil flow. Disconnect the mixture control terminal plug and turn the ignition ON to start the fuel pump. Do not start the engine.

2. The control pressure should be 48-54 psi after three minutes, with the engine coolant at operating temperature. If the control pressure does not rise, check the wire plug terminal for current at the warm-up regulator. If current is present, the heating coil may be defective and would necessitate the replacement of the warm-up regulator.

TEST WITH ENGINE OPERATING

1. Connect the wire plugs to the auxiliary

Fuel distributor control valve (12) and seal (11)

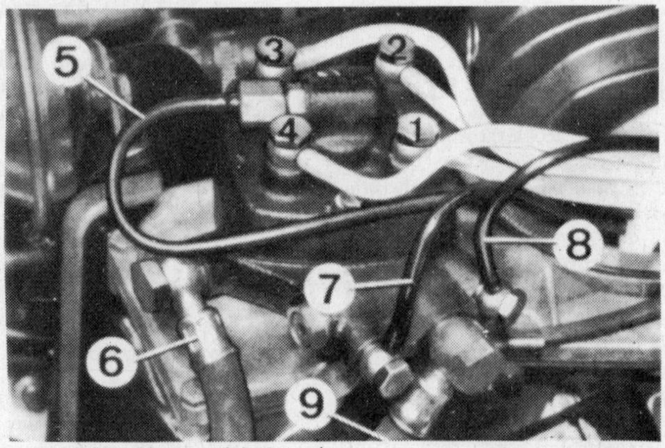

1,2,3,4—Hoses to injector valves
5. To warm-up regulator
6. Fuel filter outlet
7. To warm-up regulator
8. To start valve
9. To fuel tank

Fuel distributor hose schematic

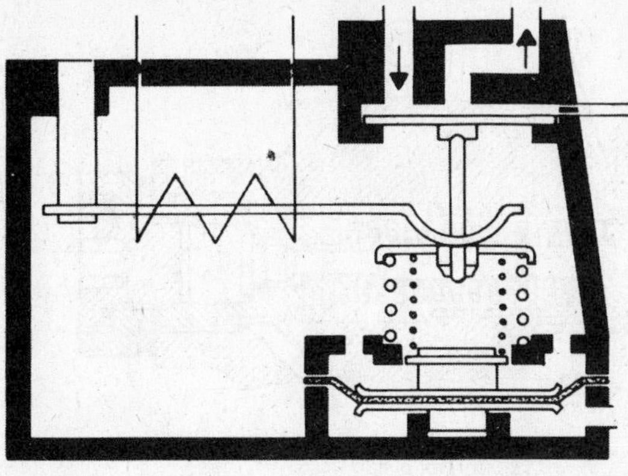

Cross-section of warm-up valve. "A" represents opening of valve—large opening on cold engine and small opening on hot engine

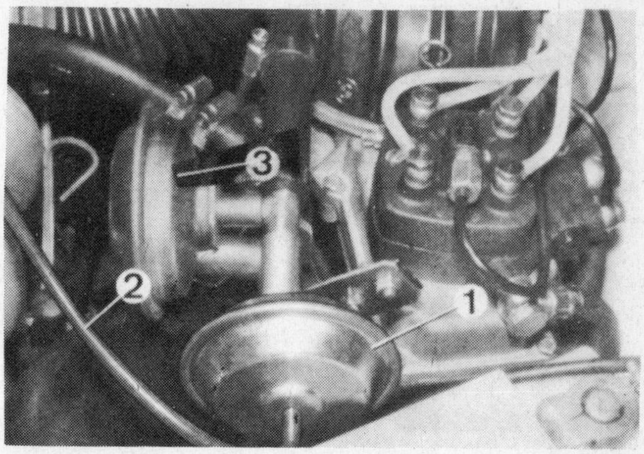

Location of vacuum regulator (1), vacuum control line (2) and auxiliary air valve (3)

air regulator and to the mixture control unit. Install the air intake cowl.

2. With the engine running at idle speed, the control pressure should be 48-54 psi.

COLD OR WARM ENGINE SYSTEM PRESSURE

1. Close the pressure shut-off valve with the engine stopped and disconnect the mixture control unit terminal plug.
2. Turn the ignition ON, but do not start the engine.
3. The speed control pressure must be 64-74 psi.
4. Turn the ignition OFF and if the pressure is not within specifications, one of the following defects may be the cause:

If the pressure is too low;

a. Leakage at the fuel lines or connections.
b. Fuel filter clogged.
c. Engine overruns.
d. Defective fuel pump.
e. Pressure adjustment incorrect.

If the pressure is too high:

a. Fuel return flow is restricted.
b. Incorrect pressure regulator setting.
c. Control piston stuck.

NOTE: Shims may be used to change the pressure.

Shim thickness changes will vary the pressure as follows:

0.004 inch=.85 psi
0.020 inch=4.3 psi

5. The transfer valve of pressure regulator must open at 50-57 psi.

CUT-OFF PRESSURE–CHECKING FOR LEAKAGE

1. Open the pressure shut-off valve and turn the ignition ON.
2. Disconnect the wire plug at the mixture control unit and then reconnect the plug. Turn the ignition OFF.
3. Cut-off pressure must not drop below 24 psi after several minutes.
4. If the pressure drops too early, one of the following may be leaking.
   a. Pressure regulator O-ring.
   b. Warm-up regulator or supply line.
   c. Fuel pump check valve.
   d. Pressure reservoir.
5. Remove the pressure gauge and shut-off valve and reconnect the pressure line.

VACUUM REGULATOR

Testing

The coasting vacuum regulator must be open to supply air behind the throttle valve, through the by-pass bore, when the vehicle is coasting.

1. Disconnect the vacuum hose and plug the end.
2. Increase the engine speed to 3000 rpm and release the throttle. The engine speed should drop quickly.
3. Connect the vacuum hose to the regulator valve and again increase the engine speed.
4. Release the throttle. The engine speed should drop slowly if the regulator is functioning properly.

AUXILIARY AIR VALVE

Testing

The auxiliary air valve is good, if after starting the engine, the rpm is higher than normal idle for a brief period of time.

TEMPERATURE TIMING SWITCH

The purpose of the timing switch is to control the cold start valve during the initial start-up of the engine, in relationship to the coolant temperature. The opening time is a maximum of 8 seconds at a temperature of −4° F (−20° C). The off temperature is 95° F (35° C).

Testing

1. Disconnect the terminal plug from the switch.
2. Connect a test lamp from the positive battery terminal to the "W" post on the temperature timing switch.

Disconnecting air hose and electrical connection (5) from the auxiliary air regulator

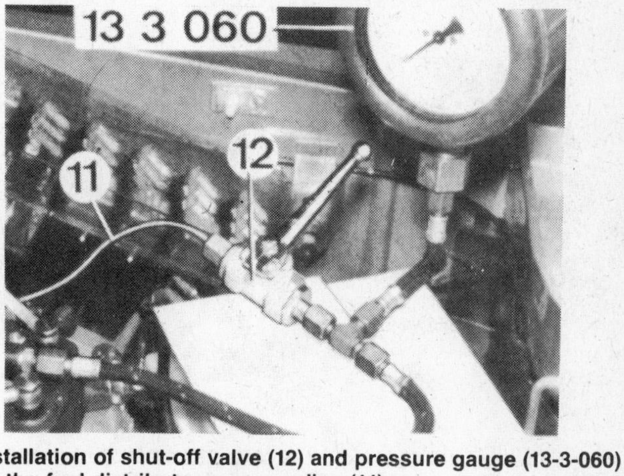

Installation of shut-off valve (12) and pressure gauge (13-3-060) on the fuel distributor pressure line (11)

Testing temperature timing switch (19) with terminals G and W shown

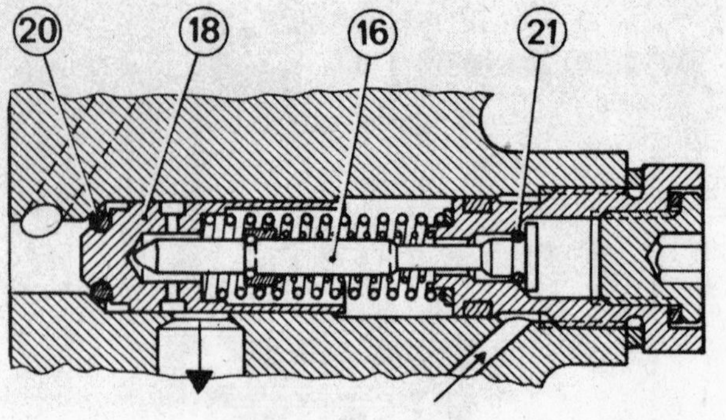

16. Transfer valve
18. Control piston
20 & 21. "O" ring

Exploded view of pressure valve

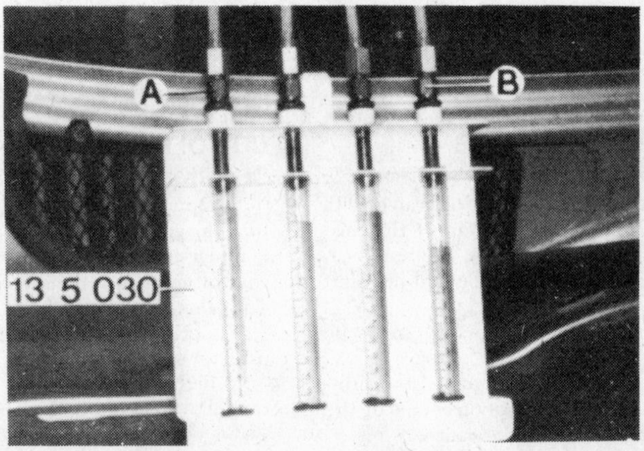

Use of special tool (13-5-030) to measure fuel discharge to determine good injector valve (A)

3. The test lamp should be on at coolant temperatures below 95° F (35° C) and go out above temperatures of 95° F (35° C).

COLD START VALVE

The purpose of the cold start valve is to inject added fuel into the induction system as dictated by the temperature timing switch.

Testing

1. Disconnect the plug terminal from the temperature timing switch and connect the contact "W" wire (brown/black) to ground.
2. Disconnect terminal #50 wire from the solenoid.
3. Remove the cold start valve from the induction header.
4. Connect the relay terminal C87 to a positive battery connector.
5. The cold start valve should eject fuel. If not, it should be replaced.

INJECTION VALVES

The injection valves must open at a minimum oil pressure of 47 psi minimum.

Testing

1. Connect a pressure valve and shut-off valve in the pressure line to the fuel distributor, with the pressure gauge on the fuel distributor side of the shut-off valve.
2. Open the shut-off valve, remove the injectors from the intake manifold and turn the ignition switch ON.
3. Disconnect the terminal plug from the mixture control unit.
4. Lift the sensor plate for a maximum of 4 seconds.
5. The pressure should not drop more than 4 psi. If the pressure drops more than the specifications, the fuel filter is clogged, fuel pump rate is inadequate or the fuel tank is empty.

INJECTOR VALVE COMPARISON

When the engine is operating erratically, with the compression and the air induction systems good, the injector valves should be tested with the use of a special tool (13-5-030) or equivalent.

Testing

1. The tool consists of scaled measuring tubes. Insert each injector valve into one of the tubes and secure. Disconnect the wire terminal plug from the mixture control valve, turn the ignition switch ON. Lift the sensor plate so that the injectors will fill the tubes with fuel.
2. Empty the tubes and again fill the tubes

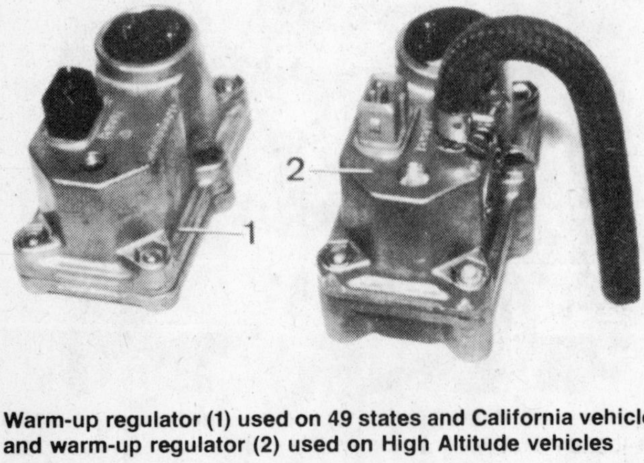

Warm-up regulator (1) used on 49 states and California vehicles and warm-up regulator (2) used on High Altitude vehicles

Pulling sensor plate (7) upward to test injector valves

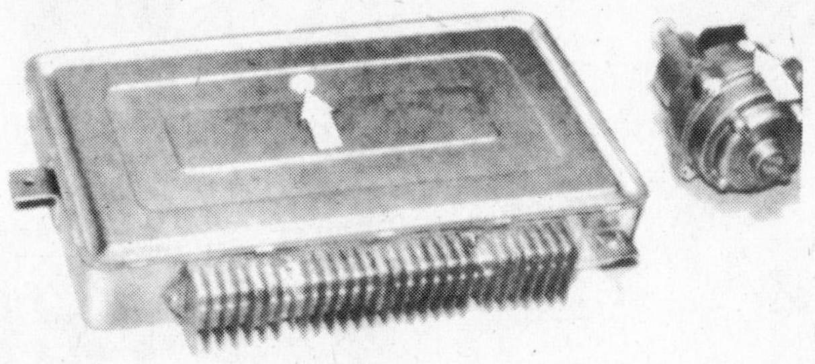

Control unit and pressure sensor identification

with fuel until the 0.9 cu. in. (15 cc) mark is reached on one tube. Compare the difference between the tubes for the fuel levels. The difference should not be over 15%.

3. If the fuel level difference is over 15% between tubes, exchange a good injector valve with a questionable one and repeat the test.

4. If the questionable injector valve flow rate remains the same, the valve is defective and must be replaced. If the injector valve flow rate is normal, the fuel distributor unit is defective and must be replaced.

FUEL PUMP SAFETY WIRING

When the engine is stopped, power to the fuel pump is cut-off by the ground contact switch, located beneath the sensor plate. As soon as the engine is cranked, the sensor plate is moved and the switch contacts are opened and allow current to flow to the fuel pump.

3.0Si, 530i, 630i, 633i and 733i

The Bosch L-Jetronic fuel injection system is electronically controlled to regulate the fuel supply in relation to the air flow. An air flow meter, located in the air intake chamber, converts angular movement of an air baffle plate into a voltage signal, which is sent to the control unit.

As the engine begins its revolution, twin contacts, located 180 degrees apart in the base of the distributor, trigger current impulses to the control unit at one impulse per crankshaft rotation.

After computation of the signals, a command signal is sent from the control unit to the electromagnetic injector valves, which are wired in a parallel circuit, causing them to open simultaneously. To obtain smooth combustion, half the total fuel volume necessary for the engine cycle, is injected per half rotation of the camshaft, which corresponds to each rotation of the crankshaft.

Automatic cold start and warm-up devices are incorporated in the system to give better driveability and engine operation during the initial start and warm-up period, when added fuel is needed.

CONTROL UNIT

Removal and Installation

3.0Si

1. Remove the rear seat and remove the control unit from the floor panel.
2. Open the wire connector clamp and pull out the cover slide.
3. Carefully remove the connector from the control unit.
4. During the installation, a matched pressure sensor should be replaced also. Random pairing can result in excessive fuel consumption and poor engine operation.
5. Permissible combinations are:

Pressure sensor	Control unit
a. With-out paint dot	With-out paint dot
b. Blue dot	Blue dot
c. Red dot	Red dot

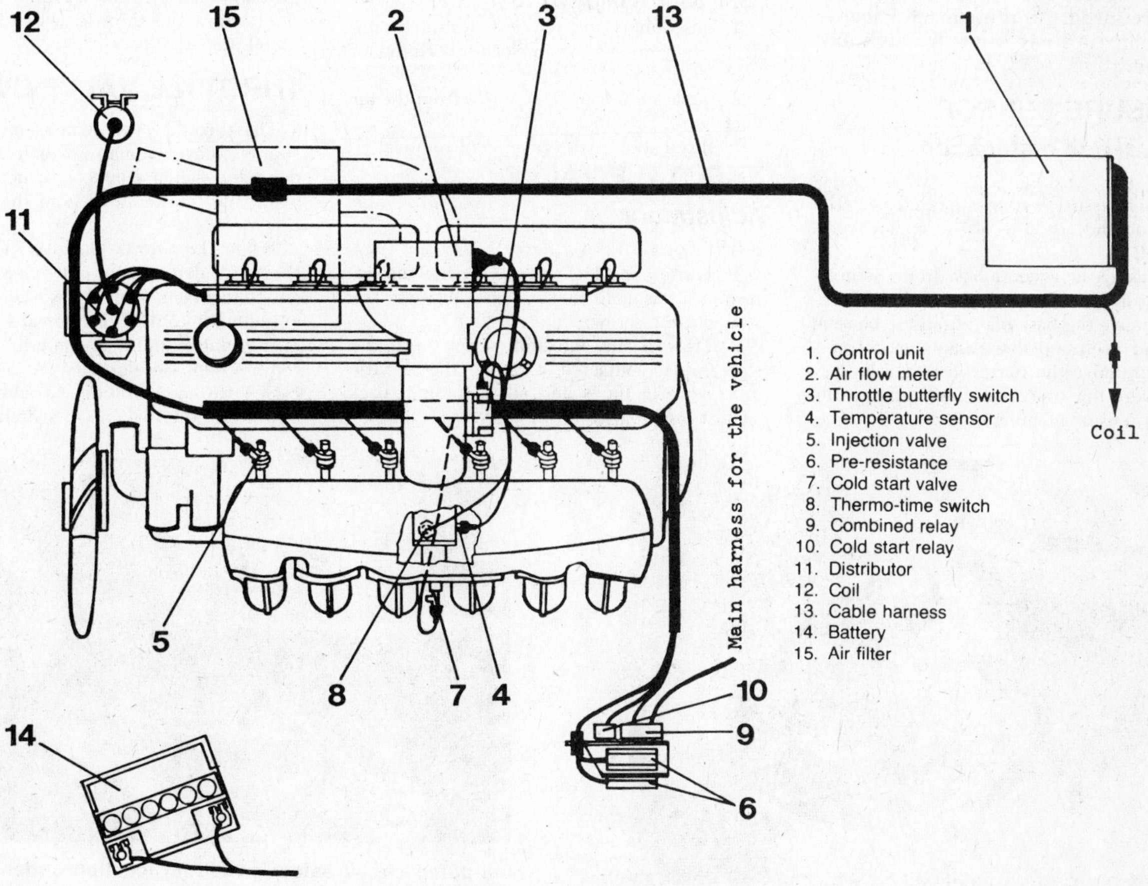

Bosch L-Jetronic® Fuel Injection System

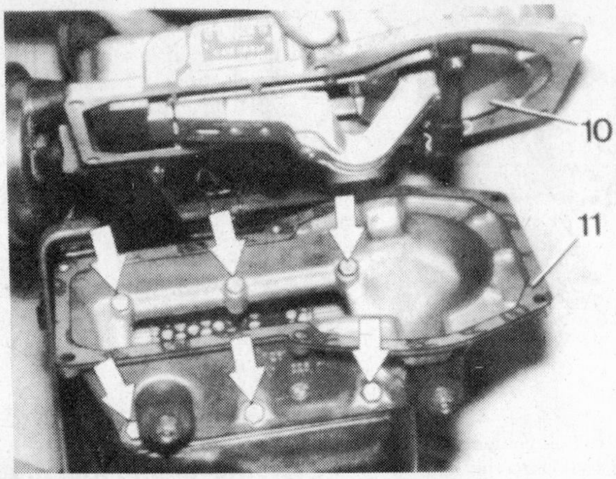

Mixture control unit upper section (10) separated from the lower section (11). Arrows indicate bolts to remove to separate the lower section from the air cleaner housing

1. Lock nut
2. Adjusting screw
3. Throttle lever stop

Throttle valve adjustment—3.0Si

530i, 630i, 633i AND 733i

1. The control unit is located behind the glove box on models 530i, 630i and 633i, and behind the right side cowl cover on the 733i.
2. Push the lock lug towards the wire loom or press the circlip rearward and pull the multiple terminal plug to the right. Disconnect the individual plug, if connected.
3. Remove the control unit from the body.
4. When installing the control box, connect the individual connector if the vehicle is to be used in high altitude operation.

NOTE: When the individual connector circuit is complete, the fuel injection time is reduced, resulting in a 6% leaner air/fuel mixture necessary for high altitude operation.

PRESSURE SENSOR

Removal and Installation

3.0Si

1. The pressure sensor is located near the firewall on the left side of the engine compartment.
2. Remove the vacuum hose from the pressure sensor.
3. Remove the base plate from the bearing block and if equipped with automatic transmission, remove the starter locking relay.
4. Invert the base plate and remove the pressure sensor retaining bolts.
5. Install the pressure sensor in the reverse order.

NOTE: Refer to the Steps 4 and 5 under the 3.0Si control unit removal and installation for proper part replacement.

530i, 630i, 633i AND 733i

The pressure sensor is an integral part of the air flow sensor unit and cannot be replaced separately.

AIR FLOW SENSOR

Removal and Installation

533i, 630i, 633i AND 733i

1. Disconnect the multiple terminal connector and remove the air cleaner with the air duct.
2. Separate the air flow sensor from the air duct.
3. Installation is the reverse of removal.

THROTTLE VALVE

Adjustment

3.0Si

1. Loosen the locknut and loosen the adjusting screw until there is play between the stop and the screw.
2. Tighten the adjusting screw until the stop is just contacted. Operate the throttle lever several times and allow to snap back against the stop by spring pressure.
3. Tighten the adjusting screw one full turn and lock the screw with the locknut.

530i, 630i, 633i AND 733i

1. Loosen the throttle lever clamp screw and the throttle stop screw.
2. Press the throttle valve closed and tighten the throttle stop screw until the clearance between the roller and the gate is approximately 0.020-0.040 in. (clearance A).
3. Tighten the throttle lever clamp screw. Tighten the throttle stop screw one complete turn and lock with the locknut.
4. Adjust the throttle switch and the idle speed.

THROTTLE VALVE SWITCH

The throttle valve switch cuts off the fuel supply to avoid engine overrunning. This is done by switch contacts, which are closed when the thottle valve is in the idling position.

When the throttle valve is moved 2°, the throttle valve switch movement opens the cut-off contacts and closes the acceleration enrichment control. Electrical impulses sent to the control unit determine the fuel quanity required for acceleration. A second switch closes the acceleration enrichment circuit only when the fuel cut-off switch is open.

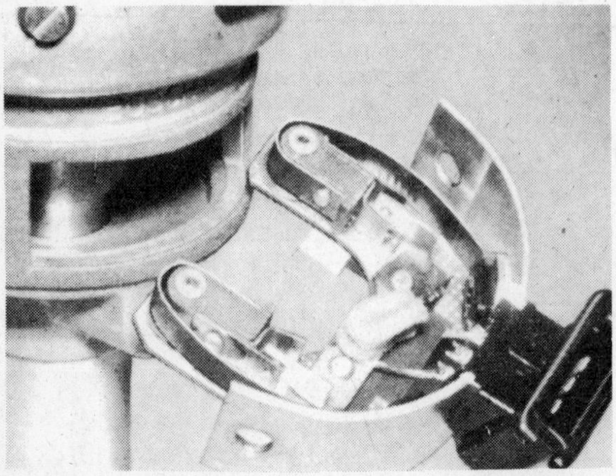

Twin electrical contact location on distributor

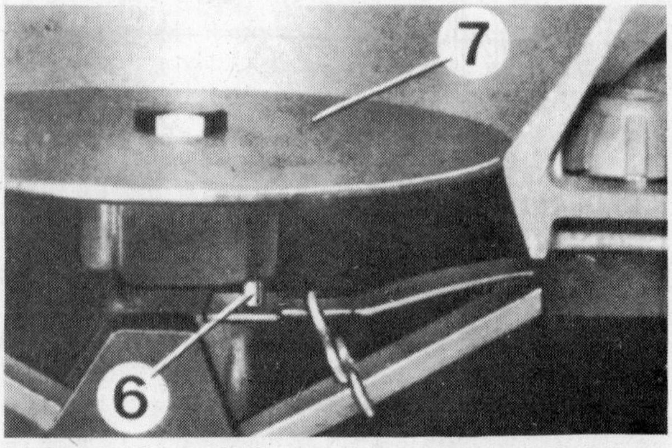

Fuel pump circuit safety switch (6) location under the sensor plate (7)

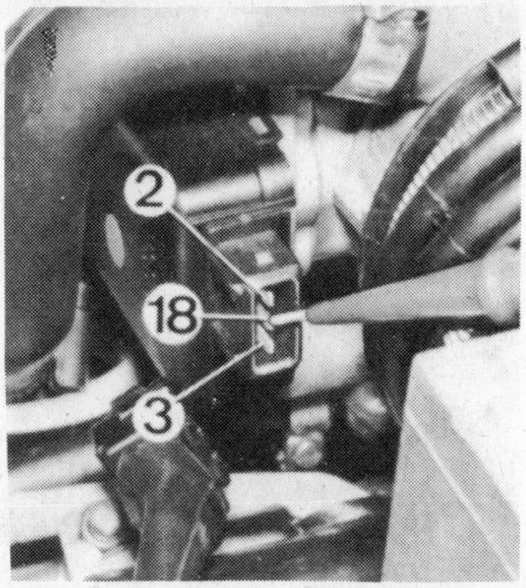

Testing throttle valve switch—530i, 630i, 633i and 733i. Terminals 2, 3 and 18 are shown.

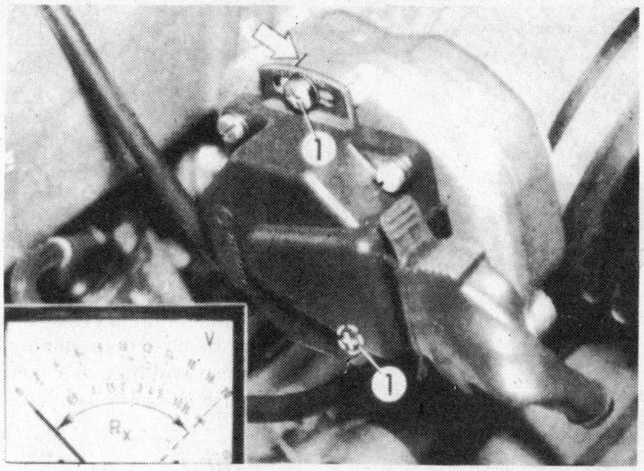

Adjustment of throttle switch—3.0Si (ohmmeter dial shown)

Removal and Installation

3.0Si, 530i, 630i, 633i AND 733i

1. Remove the terminal plug from the throttle valve switch.
2. Remove the switch retaining screws and remove the switch from the throttle shaft.
3. To install the switch, engage the throttle shaft into the switch orifice. Install the retaining screws and terminal plug.

Adjustment

3.0Si

1. Disconnect the electrical terminal plug from the throttle valve switch and loosen the switch retaining screws.
2. Connect the leads of a calibrated ohmmeter to terminals #17 and #45 of the throttle valve switch.
3. Rotate the switch until the meter needle moves to O resistance.
4. Mark the housing opposite the center indicator on the switch scale.
5. Rotate the switch clockwise 2° as indicated on the scale.

NOTE: The scale is graduated in ½° increments.

6. As the switch is rotated, the meter needle should move to infinity as the switch contacts open.
7. Rotate the switch counterclockwise to the original scale to housing mark. The meter needle should return to O resistance.
8. Lock the switch in place with the retaining screws and attach the wire terminal plug.

530i, 630i, 633i AND 733i

1. Connect an ohmmeter lead to terminals #18 and #2 of the throttle switch, after removing the terminal plug.
2. At idle position of the throttle, the meter needle should read O resistance.
3. Connect the meter leads to terminals #2 and #3.
4. With the throttle wide open, the meter needle should be at O resistance.
5. The switch can be moved for small adjustments. If adjustments are unattainable, replace the switch.

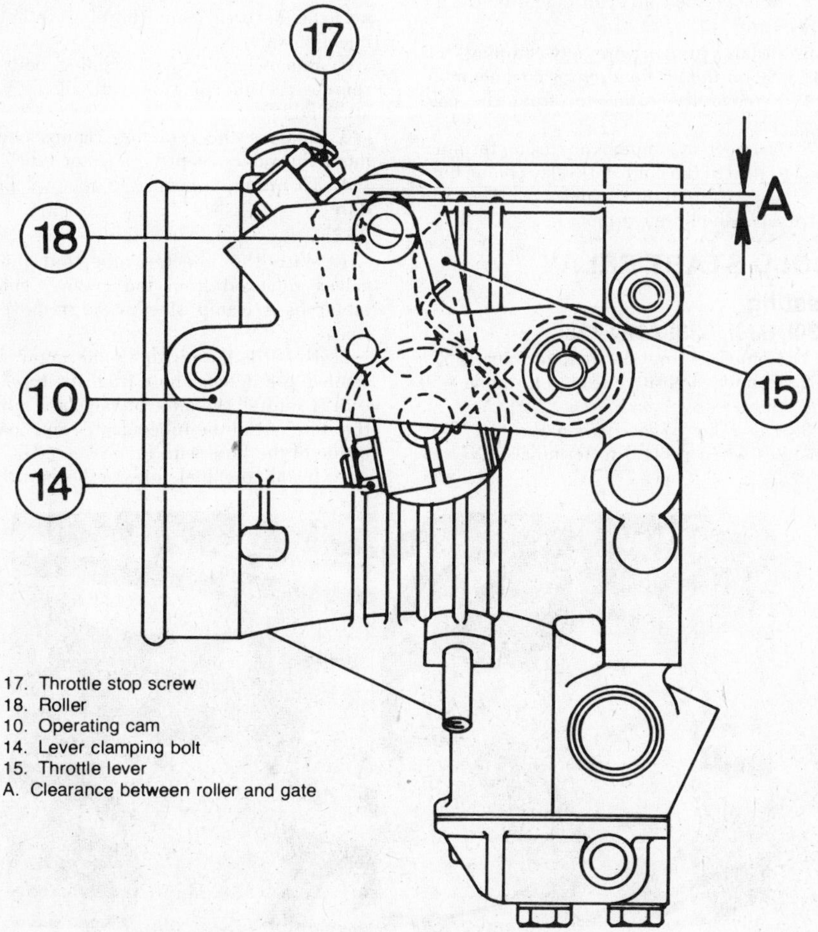

17. Throttle stop screw
18. Roller
10. Operating cam
14. Lever clamping bolt
15. Throttle lever
A. Clearance between roller and gate

Throttle lever adjustment—530i, 630i, 633i and 733i

AIR INTAKE TEMPERATURE SENSOR

Removal and Installation

3.0Si

The temperature sensor can be unscrewed from the air collector after disconnecting the electrical plug.

Testing

The desired resistance is listed in the following chart depending on temperature readings.

Degrees F (C)	Resistance (Ohms)
14 (−10)	9.6
32 (0)	6.4
50 (+10)	4.3
68 (20)	3.0
86 (30)	2.1
104 (40)	1.5
122 (50)	1.0
140 (60)	0.79

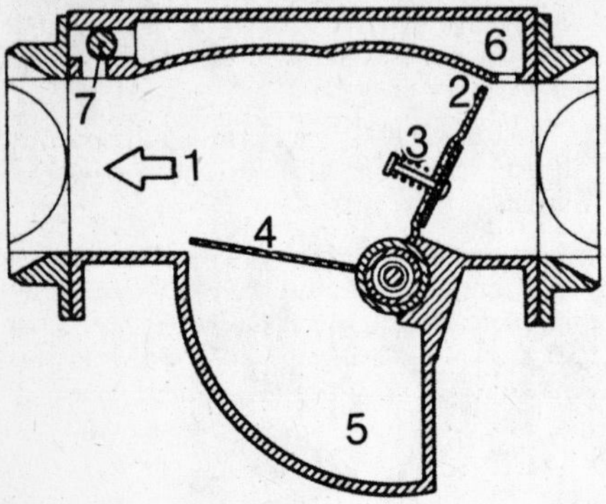

1. Air direction
2. Baffle plate
3. Check valve
4. Compensation valve
5. Damper valve chamber
6. By-pass circuit
7. By-pass adjusting screw

Cross-section of air flow sensor

NOTE: Allowable variation of resistance ± 10%.

COOLANT TEMPERATURE SENSOR

Removal and Installation

ALL MODELS

Disconnect the electrical terminal plug and unscrew the coolant temperature sensor.

Testing

3.0Si

The desired resistance is noted in the following chart depending on the temperature reading.

Degrees F (C)	Resistance (Ohms)
14 (−10)	9.2
32 (0)	5.9
50 (+10)	3.7
68 (20)	2.5
86 (30)	1.7
104 (40)	1.2
122 (50)	0.84
140 (60)	0.60
158 (70)	0.43
176 (80)	0.32
194 (90)	0.25
212 100)	0.20

530i, 630i, 633i AND 733i

The coolant temperature sensor can be checked with a test lamp. The circuit should open at temperatures above 113° F (45° C) and closed below 113° F (45° C.).

TEMPERATURE TIMING SWITCH

Removal and Installation

530i, 630i, 633i AND 733i

Partially drain the coolant and disconnect the electrical connector plug. Unscrew the temperature timing switch. After installation, bleed the cooling system.

Testing

With the use of a test lamp, the switch can be tested at various temperatures for continuity. The opeating time is eight seconds at −4° F (−20 C) and declines to 0 seconds at +59° F (−15 C).

COLD START VALVE

Removal and Installation

ALL MODELS

1. Remove the electrical connector and the fuel line to the valve.
2. Remove the retaining bolts and pull the valve assembly from the air collector.
3. Replace the rubber sealing ring during installation.

Testing

3.0Si

The cold start valve should only receive current when the starter or the timer switch is in operation. The use of a test lamp on the terminal end of the starter valve and to ground, will indicate current presence to the switch when starting. The current should stop flowing no longer than eight seconds after the starter is stopped. The temperature timing switch is operable under temperatures of 41° F (5° C).

530i, 630i, 633i AND 733i

1. Remove the cold start valve from the air collector but do not remove the fuel hose or the electrical connector.
2. Remove the connector plug from the air flow sensor.
3. Install a jumper wire between plug #36 and #39 on the air flow sensor connector.
4. Remove the connector from the cold start relay.
5. Connect a jumper wire from terminal #87 to #30 of the cold start relay connector.
6. Turn the ignition switch ON. The cold start valve should eject fuel.

COLD START RELAY

Testing

530i, 630i, 633i AND 733i

1. Connect a ground wire to terminal #85.
2. Connect a positive lead to terminal #30 and #86 C.
3. The relay is good when the test lamp operates when probed to terminals #87 and #86.

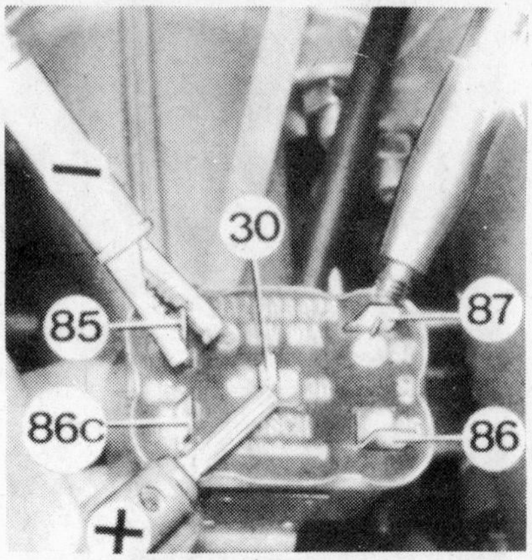

Testing cold start relay

INJECTION VALVES

Removal and Installation

3.0Si

1. Remove the electrical plug from the injection valves.
2. Loosen and remove the injection valve from the ring line.
3. Remove the retaining bolts and pull the injector from the manifold.
4. To install, replace the rubber ring and do not damage the nozzle jet during the installation.

530i, 630i AND 633i

1. With the air collector removed, disconnect the electrical connector plugs from the 6 injection valves.
2. Remove the valve retaining bolts and remove the injector tube with all the valves attached.
3. Remove the retaining clamps and remove the valves from the injector tube.
4. To install, reverse the removal procedure.

733i

1. With the injector tube and injector valves removed from the engine, cut the metal hose clamp sleeve and remove the sleeve.
2. Heat the hose with a soldering iron and remove the injector hose from the tube.
3. To install the injector valve assembly on the tube, clean the tube adapter and coat the inside of the hose with fuel.
4. Install the fuel injector hose with the

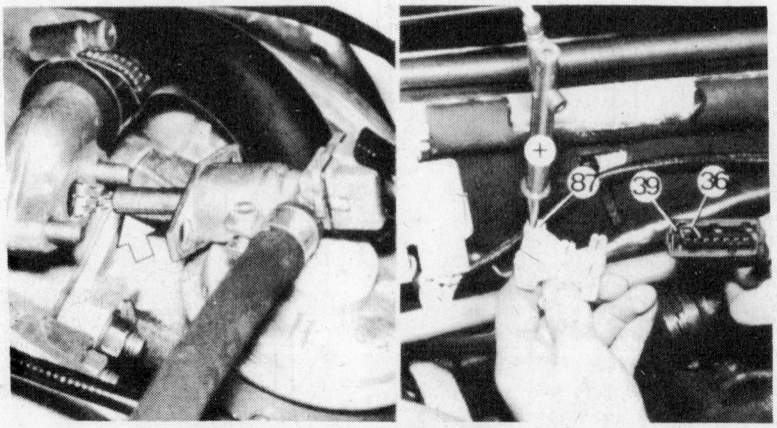

Testing cold start valve—terminals numbered

1. Support plate
2. Rubber ring
3. Cup flange
4. Rubber ring

Injector valve and sealing components

hose sleeve on the injector tube and push against the stop, with the electrical terminal facing up.

5. Complete the installation in the reverse of the removal procedure.

MANUAL TRANSMISSION

REMOVAL AND INSTALLATION

All Models

1. On 4 cylinder engines remove all transmission mounting bolts which are accessible from above.
2. On 4 cylinder engines remove the exhaust pipe support bracket and separate the pipe from the exhaust manifold.
3. On all 6 cylinder engines except model 733i, remove the entire exhaust system. On model 733i disconnect the exhaust pipe from the support bracket only.
4. Disconnect the propeller shaft at the transmission. On model 733i use a special clamping tool.
5. Remove the heat guard and center bearing, then remove the propeller shaft.
6. Remove the selector lever and circlip.
7. Disconnect the back-up switch connector and the speedometer cable.
8. Remove the slave cylinder from the transmission.
9. Support the transmission and disconnect the crossmember at the body. On models 530i and 3.0 loosen the rubber bearing on the gearbox.
10. On 4 cylinder models remove the remaining transmission mounting bolts and pull out the transmission toward the rear.
11. On 6 cylinder models lower the transmission to the front axle carrier and disconnect the transmission at the clutch housing. Remove from the rear.

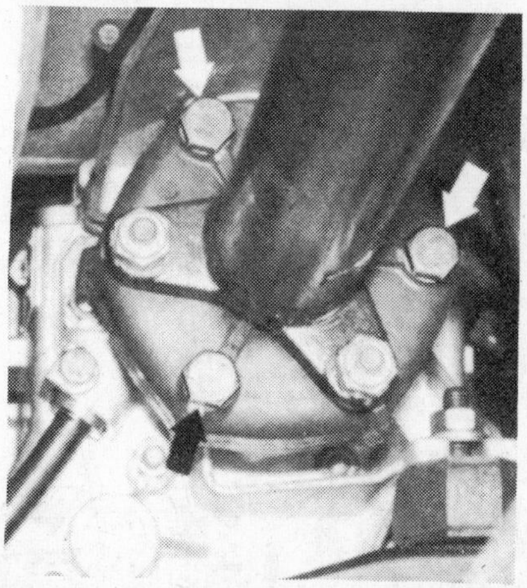

Disconnecting driveshaft at transmission

NOTE: On 3.0 pull the gearbox out slightly and lift the spring over the spherical pin collar.

12. Installation is the reverse of removal. Install the exhaust suspension without twisting. When installing the propeller shaft, preload the center bearing by (0.078 in.) in the forward direction. Install the clutch slave cylinder with the bleed screw facing down.

CLUTCH

REMOVAL AND INSTALLATION

All Models

1. Remove the clutch housing.
2. Prevent the flywheel from turning, using a locking tool.
3. Loosen the mounting bolts one after another gradually to relieve tension from the clutch.
4. Remove the mounting bolts, clutch, and drive plate.
5. To install, reverse the removal procedure. Torque the clutch mounting bolts to 16-17 ft/lbs.

Clutch Master Cylinder

REMOVAL AND INSTALLATION

All Models

1. Remove the necessary trim panel or carpet.
2. On model 320i, disconnect the accelerator cable and pull it forward out of the engine firewall.
3. Disconnect the pushrod at the clutch pedal.
4. Remove enough brake fluid from the tank until the level drops below the refill line.
5. Disconnect the windshield washer fluid tank without removing the hoses on model 733i.

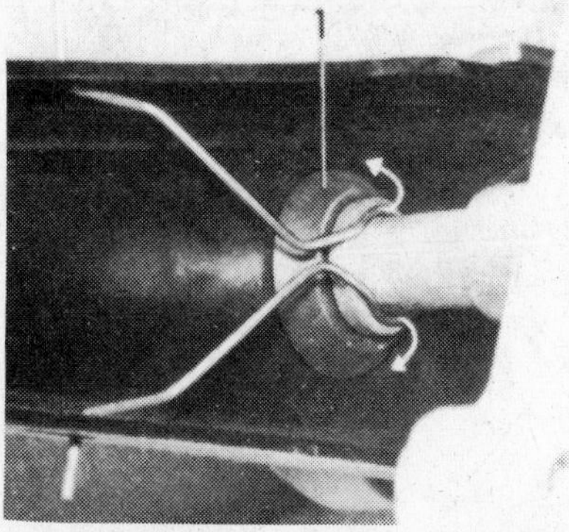

On model 3.0, lift spring over spherical pin collar. During installation angular seal (1) must be between spherical pin and throwout arm

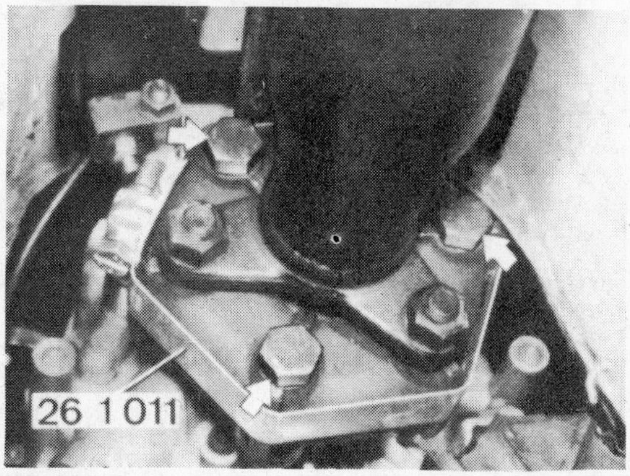

On model 3.0 use special clamping tool for removal of coupling bolts

6. Disconnect the lines and retaining bolts and remove the master cylinder from the firewall.

7. Installation is the reverse of removal. Bleed the system and adjust the pedal travel with the pushrod to 6 in.

Clutch Slave Cylinder

REMOVAL AND INSTALLATION

All Models

1. Remove enough brake fluid from the reservoir until the level drops below the refill line connection.
2. Remove the circlip or retaining bolts depending on the model.
3. Disconnect the line and remove the slave cylinder.
4. Installation is the reverse of removal. Bleed the system.

Bleeding Clutch Hydraulic System

All Models

1. Fill the reservoir.
2. Connect a bleeder hose from the bleeder screw to a container filled with brake fluid so that air cannot be drawn in during bleeding procedures.
3. Pump the clutch pedal about 10 times then hold it down.
4. Open the bleeder screw and tighten when no more air bubbles escape.
5. Release the clutch pedal and repeat the above procedure until no more air bubbles can be seen.

AUTOMATIC TRANSMISSION

REMOVAL AND INSTALLATION

All Models

1. Disconnect the accelerator cable.
2. On the 4 cylinder engine remove all of the transmission mounting bolts which are accessible from above.
3. Detach the oil filler neck and drain the oil.
4. On 4 cylinder engines remove the exhaust pipe support bracket and separate the pipe from the exhaust manifold.
5. On all 6 cylinder engines except model 733i, remove the entire exhaust system.
6. Detach the oil cooler lines from the transmission.
7. Disconnect the propeller shaft at the transmission. On model 733i, use special clamping tool.
8. Disconnect the speedometer cable.

Remove the 4 torque convertor retaining bolts

9. Remove the heat guard and center bearing and bend down and pull off the propeller shaft.
10. Remove the cover and remove the four bolts that attach the torque converter to the drive plate. Turn the engine for this procedure.
11. Support the transmission and disconnect the crossmember at the body.
12. Remove the remaining transmission mounting bolts.
13. Separate the transmission from the engine and take off the torque converter at the same time.

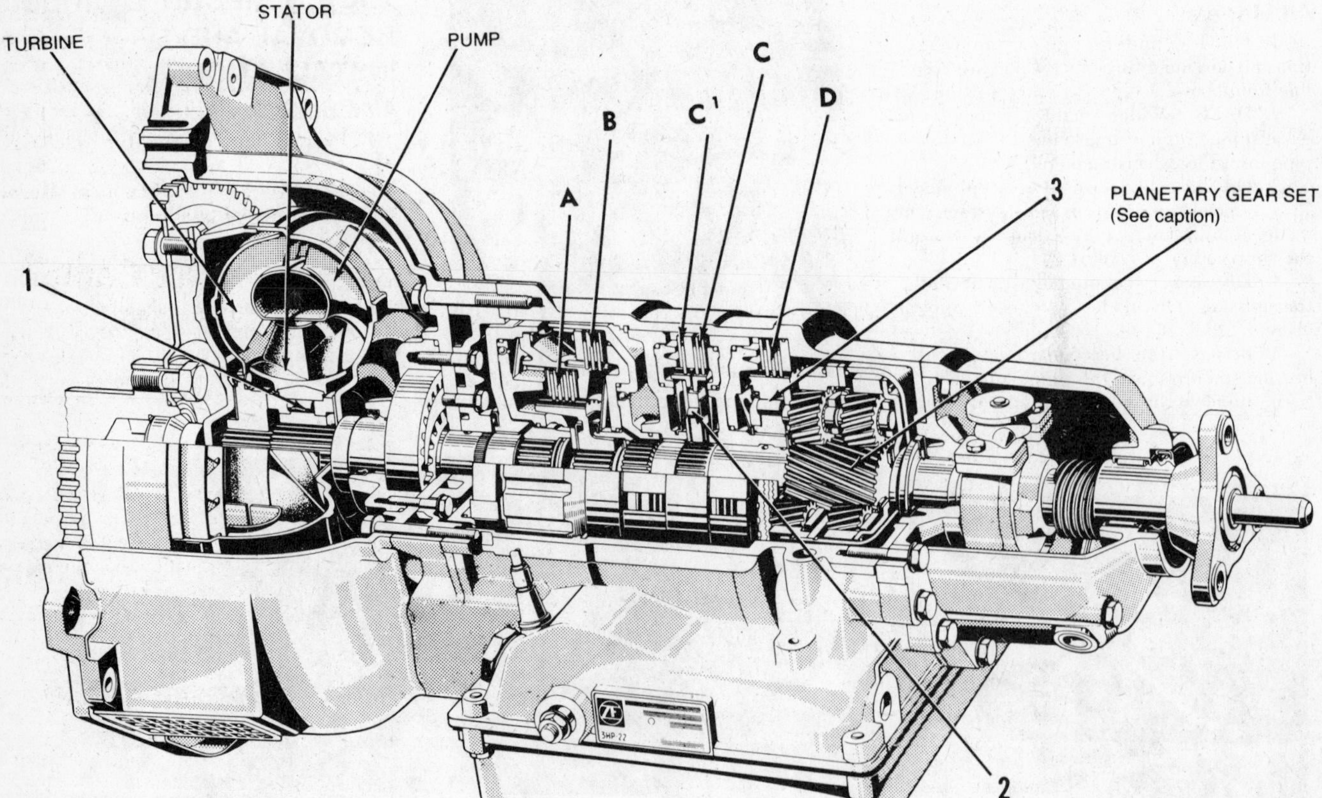

Typical automatic transmission cross section showing clutch identification—trans. model 3HP-12 uses Simpson planetary gear set, trans. model 3HP-22 uses Ravigineaux planetary gear set

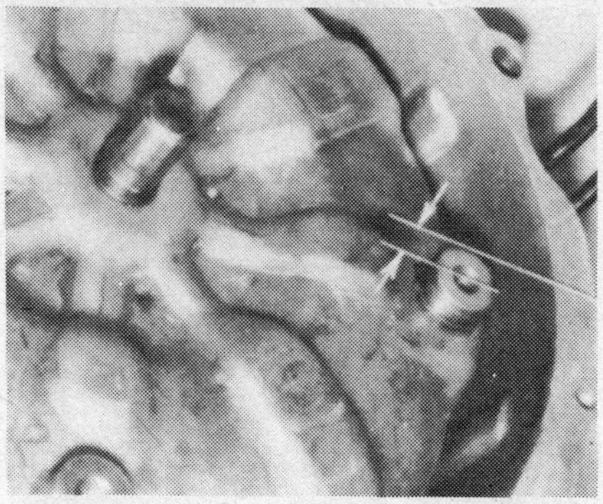

The torque converter is installed correctly if the drive shell mounting parts are located underneath the converter housing

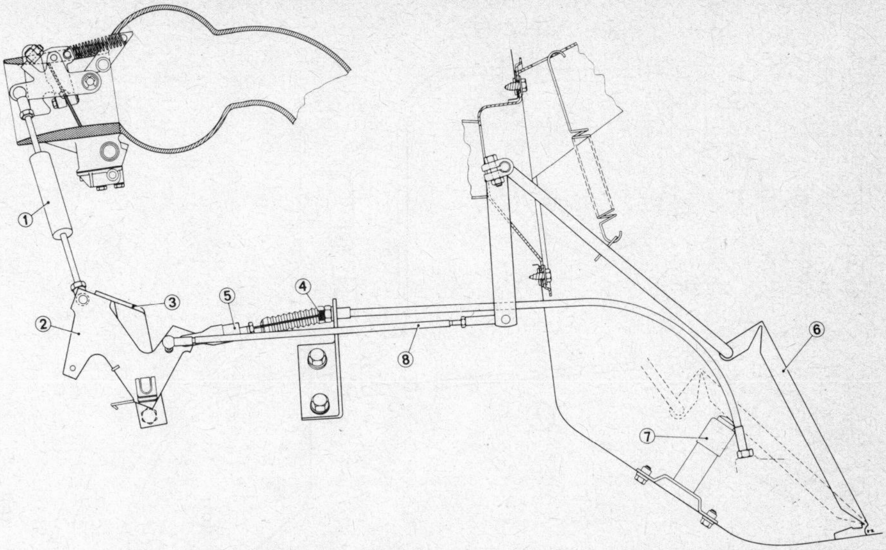

Accelerator linkage and accelerator cable adjustment—530i, 3.0

14. Installation is the reverse of removal. Install the exhaust suspension without twisting. When installing the propeller shaft preload the center bearing by 0.08 in. in the forward direction. Make sure the torque converter is positioned correctly before installing.

Selector Lever Adjustment

All Models

1. Detach the selector rod (1) at the selector lever lower section (2).
2. Move the selector lever (3) on the transmission to position 0.
3. Press the selector lever (4) against the stop (5) on the shift gate.
4. Adjust the length of the selector rod (1) until the pin (6) aligns with the bore in the selector lever lower section (2). Shorten the selector rod length by: 1 turn—320i, 630csi, 733i; 2-2½ turns—530i; 3 turns—2002, 3.0.

NOTE: If equipped with air conditioning on the 4 cylinder models, plates (7) must be installed between the bearing bracket and float plate and selector rod (1) must be attached in bore (K) of selector level (3).

Accelerator Linkage Adjustment

2002

1. Remove the air cleaner.
2. Remove the accelerator cable.
3. Press the accelerator pedal down to the kick down stop into the full acceleration position. In this position the throttle valve must be fully open and not extend beyond the vertical position. When adjusting, bend the stop.
4. Adjust the length of the accelerator linkage using the eye bolt.

Accelerator Linkage and Accelerator Cable Adjustment

530i and 3.0

1. Synchronize the idle speed with the engine at operating temperature.
2. Detach linkage (1).
3. Detach the accelerator cable at the operating lever (2).
4. Adjust linkage (1) so that the operating lever (2) rests on stop (3).

NOTE: Make sure that linkage (1) is not pulled down into the kickdown position.

5. The swivel joint (5) must align with the hole in the operating lever (2) leaving a play (0.009-0.019 in.) between nipple (4) and the end of the cable sleeve.
6. The accelerator must not sag. Press lever (6) against the acceleration stop (7) and adjust linkage (8) until the distance between nipple (4) and the end of the cable sleeve is 1.456 in. When in kickdown, the nipple (4) must be at least 1.69 in. from the end of the cable sleeve.

NOTE: If the idle speed is altered, repeat the above procedure.

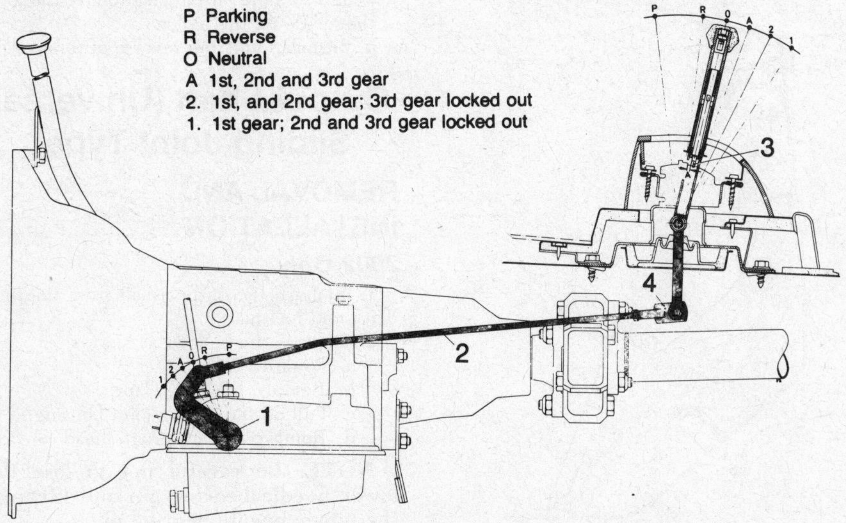

Selector lever adjustment—typical all models

Accelerator Cable Adjustment

2002

Remove the accelerator cable from the rotary shaft.

2. Press down the accelerator linkage to the full acceleration position.
3. Pull the accelerator cable to determine the full acceleration position. The holes in the fork head must now coincide with the hole on the rotary selector so that the bearing pin can be inserted with correct alignment.
4. Turn the fork head to adjust the cable length.

Accelerator Cable Adjustment

630 csi and 733i

1. Adjust play (S) to 0.010-0.030 in. with nuts when in Neutral.
2. Press the accelerator pedal against the stop.

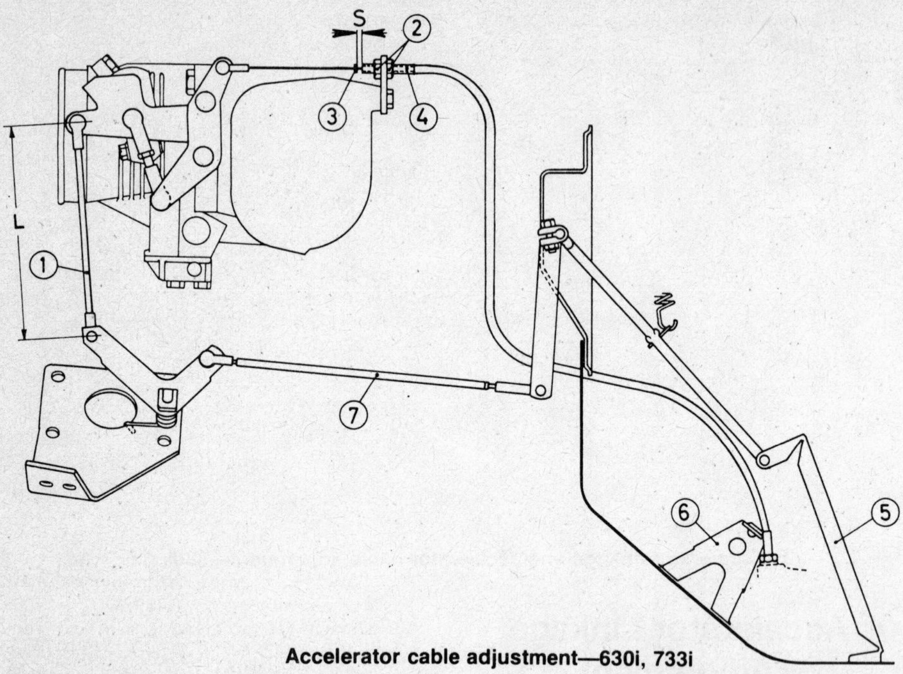

Accelerator cable adjustment—630i, 733i

3. Adjust the pressure rod (7) until the distance from the seal (3) to the end of the cable (4) is 630i—(1.732-2.008 in.), 733i—(1.722-2.057 in.).

Accelerator Cable Adjustment

320i

1. Adjust the accelerator cable at nuts (1) until the accelerator cable eye (2) has a play of 0.008 in.-0.012 in.

2. Depress the accelerator pedal (3) to the full throttle stop screw (4).

3. There must be 0.020 in. play between the operating lever (5) and stop nut (6).

4. Adjust by the full throttle stop screw (4).

Transmission Cable Adjustment

320i

NOTE: The accelerator cable must be correctly adjusted.

1. With the transmission in the Neutral position, adjust play (A) to 0.010-0.030 in. with the screw (7).

2. Depress the accelerator pedal (3) to kickdown stop; play (A) must now be 1.712-2027". Make corrections with screw (4).

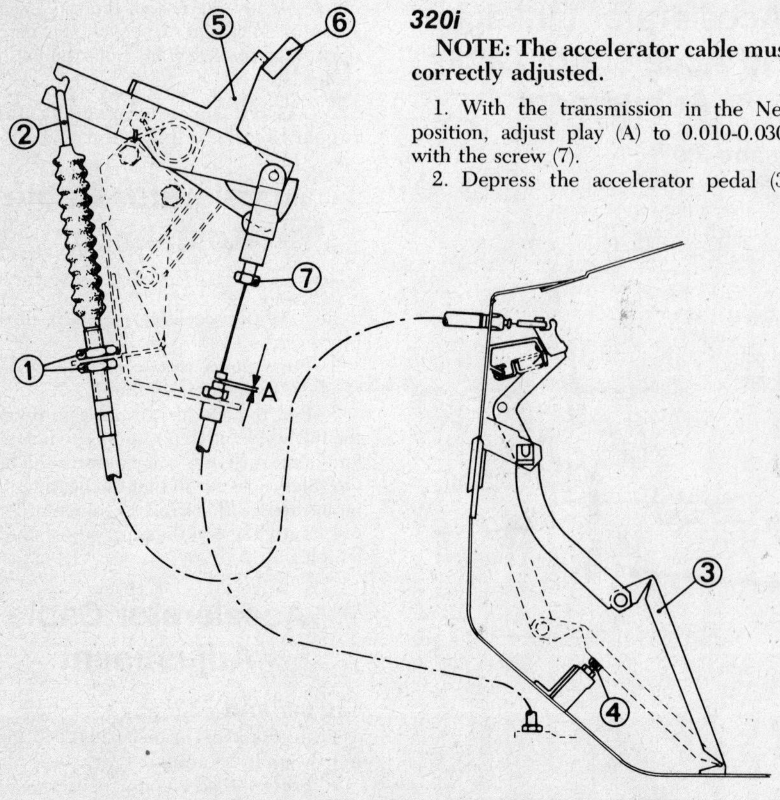

Accelerator cable and transmission cable adjustment—320i

DRIVE AXLES

Final Drive

REMOVAL AND INSTALLATION

All Models

1. Disconnect the universal shaft.

NOTE: On 2002, if equipped with a joint disc, the plate remains on the shaft.

2. Disconnect the output shaft and tie it up overhead.

3. Detach the self aligning support at the final drive on 320i.

4. Disconnect the final drive from the rear axle carrier.

5. On 2002 disconnect the transverse bracket, on all other models loosen the rubber mounting screw and remove the final drive.

6. Installation is the reverse of removal.

Output Shaft (Constant Velocity Type)

REMOVAL AND INSTALLATION

All Models

1. Detach the output shaft at the final drive and drive flange.

2. On 733i, support the control arm if the spring strut and shock absorber are detached.

3. On 630i, the spring strut serves as a retaining strap and the trailing arm must be supported if the spring strut is detached.

4. Replace the bellows as follows:
   a. Take off the sealing cover.
   b. Remove the circlip.
   c. Remove the clamp.
   d. Press the output shaft out of the joint then slide off the bellows.

5. Installation is the reverse of removal.

Output Shaft (Universal Sliding Joint Type)

REMOVAL AND INSTALLATION

2002 Only

1. Remove the output shaft from the final drive and halfshaft.

2. Replace the bellows as follows:
   a. Drain the oil.
   b. Remove the hose claps.
   c. Pull off the sliding joint housing.
   d. Remove the mushroom head caps.

NOTE: Be careful not to lose the lower needle bearing pin and lift over the upper needle bearing pin.

3. To install, reverse the above.

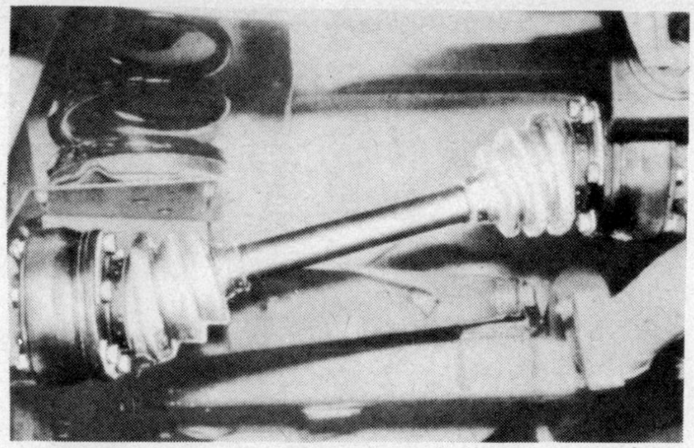

Constant velocity type output shaft

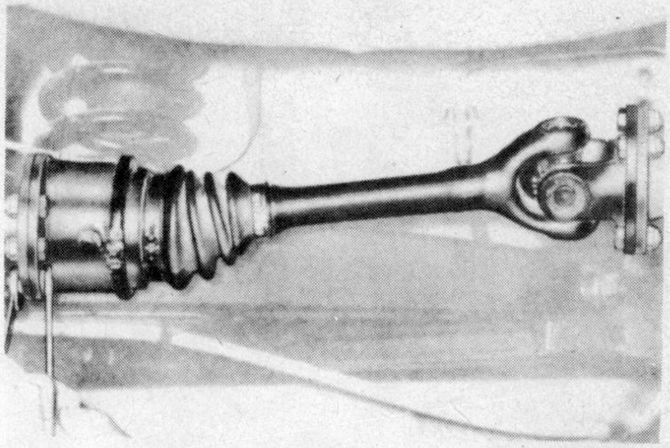

Output shaft (universal sliding joint type)

NOTE: If the bore in the joint yoke is distorted, the complete output shaft must be replaced.

Driveshaft

REMOVAL AND INSTALLATION

All Models

1. On 530i, 630i, remove the entire exhaust system.
2. On 2002 remove the primary muffler from the exhaust pipe.
3. On 3.0 remove the primary and main mufflers.
4. On 320i, detach the outer pipe at the manifold and support it at the transmission.
5. Remove the heat shield if so equipped.
6. Disconnect the propeller shaft at the transmission.

NOTE: On 733i, install a special clamping tool (BMW-261011) or equivalent around the coupling and remove the bolts.

7. Loosen the center bearing.
8. On 733i, with manual transmissions, loosen the crossmember and push the left end forward.
9. Bend the propeller shaft down and pull out.
10. Installation is the reverse of removal.
11. The propeller shaft is balanced in line and must only be renewed as a complete assembly.
12. Align the driveshaft with a gauge (BMW-21-1-000) or equivalent by moving the center bearing sideways or by placing washers underneath the center bearing.
13. On 733i, remove the special coupling tool only after the nuts have been tightened to prevent stress on the coupling.
14. Preload the center bearing by 0.078 in. in the forward direction.

Center Bearing

REMOVAL AND INSTALLATION

3.0, 630i, 530i and 733i

1. Bend down the driveshaft and pull it out of the centering pin on the transmission (Refer to Driveshaft Removal and Installation).
2. Loosen the threaded bushing.
3. Mark the driveshaft position on slide with a punch mark and pull the front half of the propeller shaft out of the slide.
4. Remove the circlip and dust guard.
5. Using a standard puller remove the center bearing without the dust guard.
6. Use a puller and remove the grooved ball bearing in the center bearing.
7. Installation is the reverse of removal. Drive the center bearing onto the grooved ball bearing with tool (BMW-24-1-050) or equivalent.

320i

1. With the propeller shaft removed, mark the shafts location to the coupling.

Preload center bearing in the forward direction

Preload center bearing—(A) = 0.08 in.

Checking alignment of driveshaft

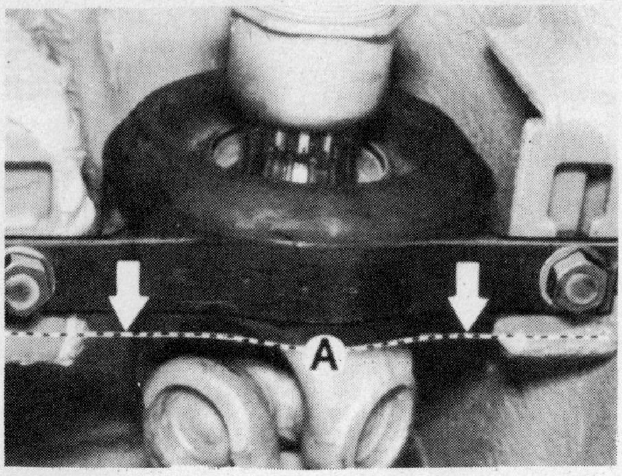

Preload the bearing in the forward direction—A=(0.078 in)

Remove circlip (2) and dust guard (3)

2. Remove the circlip and pull out the propeller shaft.
3. Using a standard puller remove the center bearing without its dust cover.
4. Drive the grooved ball bearing out of the center bearing.
5. Installation is the reverse of removal.

2002

1. With the propeller shaft removed, remove the coupling nut.
2. Using a standard puller, pull off the center bearing without the dust guard.
3. Remove the grooved ball bearing with a puller.
4. Installation is the reverse of removal.

Centering Ring

REMOVAL AND INSTALLATION

3.0 and 2002

1. Press off the sealing cap.
2. Lift out the circlip.
3. Take out the ball cup, centering ring, disc and spring.
4. Installation is the reverse of removal. Fill the centering assembly with approximately 6g (0.2 oz.) of grease.

All Models Except 3.0 and 2002

1. Fill the center with grease and using a 14mm (0.551") dia. mandrel, drive out the ring.
2. Installation is the reverse of removal.

NOTE: The shaft ring faces out.

Rear Axle Shaft, Wheel Bearings and Seals

REMOVAL AND INSTALLATION

6 Cylinder Models

1. Remove the wheel.
2. Loosen the brake caliper and leave the brake line connected.
3. Remove the brake disc.
4. Remove the driving flange as follows:
   a. Disconnect the output shaft.
   b. Remove the bookplate.
   c. Loosen the collared nut and pull off the drive flange.
5. Tighten the collared nut and drive off the rear axle shaft.
6. Drive off the wheel bearings and seals toward the outside.
7. Installation is the reverse of removal.

4 Cylinder Models

1. Remove the wheel.
2. Remove the cotter pin from the castellated nut.

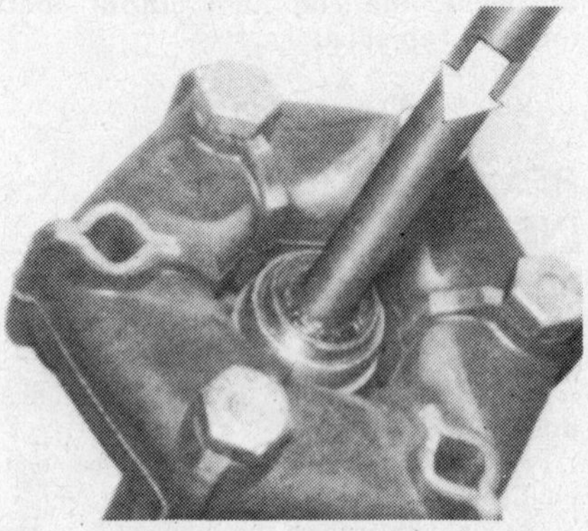
Driving out the center ring—all models except 3.0, 2002

3. Apply the handbrake.
4. Loosen the castellated nut.
5. Release the handbrake.
6. Remove the brake drum.
7. Pull off the drive flange with a puller.
8. Disconnect the output shaft and tie it up.
9. Drive out the halfshaft with a plastic hammer using the castellated nut to protect the end of the shaft.
10. Drive out the bearing and sealing ring.
11. Take out the spacer sleeve and shim.
12. Installation is the reverse of removal.

Drive center bearing onto grooved ball bearing

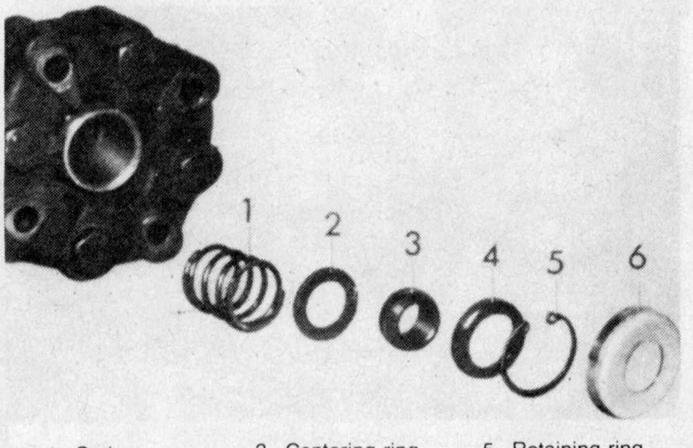

1. Spring
2. Washer
3. Centering ring
4. Ball socket
5. Retaining ring
6. Sealing cap

Remove centering ring and ball socket—3.0, 2002

Oil seal faces outward (A=0.19 in)—all models except 3.0, 2002

Wheel bearing with rear axle shaft removed—6 cylinder models

Driving out rear axle shaft—4 cylinder models

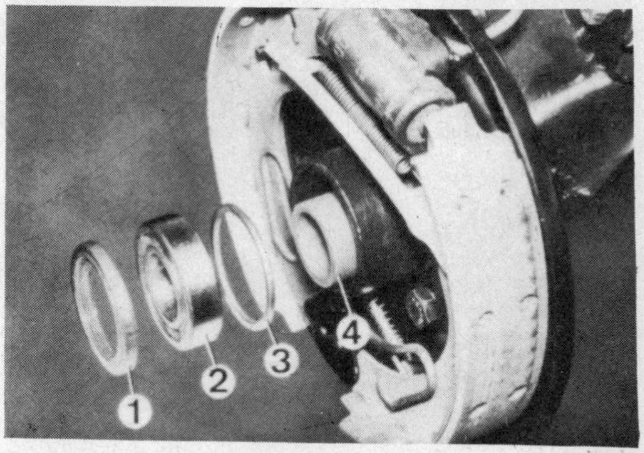

Rear axle shaft seal (1), bearing (2), ring (3), spacer (4)

REAR SUSPENSION

Coil Spring, Shock Absorber, Strut Assembly

REMOVAL AND INSTALLATION

All Models Except 2002

1. On model 733i remove the rear seat and back rest.
2. Jack up the car and support the control arms.

CAUTION

The coil spring, shock absorber assembly acts as a strap so the control arm should always be supported.

3. Disconnect the lower shock retaining bolt.
4. Disconnect the upper strut retaining nuts at the wheelbase and remove the assembly.
5. Using the appropriate spring compressor compress the coil spring far enough to remove the centering cup, then release the coil spring and separate the spring, boot and shock absorber.

Shock Absorber

REMOVAL AND INSTALLATION

2002

1. Jack up the car and support the control arm.
2. Remove the safety cap and remove the upper shock retaining nut.
3. Remove the lower shock retaining nut.
4. Press the shock together and remove.
5. Installation is the reverse of removal.

Coil Spring

REMOVAL AND INSTALLATION

2002

1. Remove the shock absorber.
2. Remove the rear wheel.
3. Unbolt the stabilizer from the trailing arm.
4. Disconnect the output shaft from the half-shaft and tie it up.

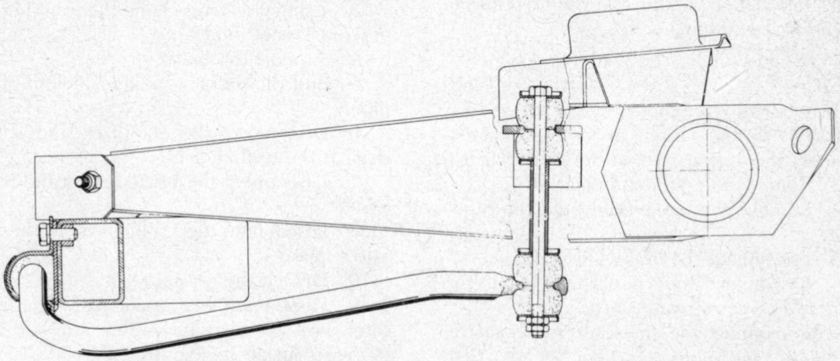

Output shaft detached and tied up for coil spring removal—2002

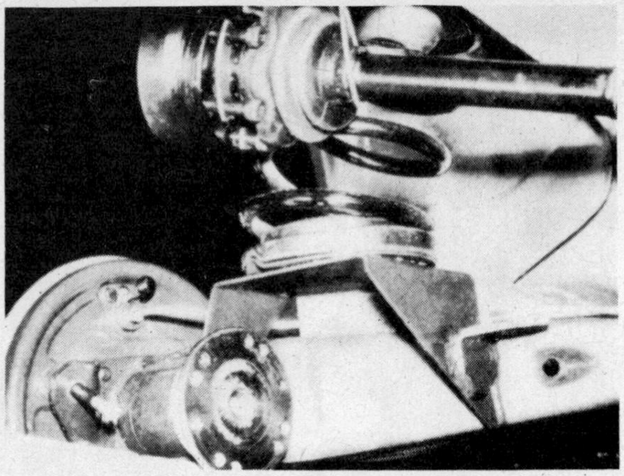

Stabilizer bar—2002 shown; others similar

5. Slowly lower the supported trailing arm with the jack and take out the coil spring.

Stabilizer

REMOVAL AND INSTALLATION

All Models

1. Remove the stabilizer from the trailing arm.
2. Disconnect the stabilizer on the crossmember.
3. Check the rubber bushings for wear and replace as necessary.

Rear Control Arm

REMOVAL AND INSTALLATION

530i

1. Remove the parking brake lever.
2. Plug the front hose to prevent loss of brake fluid in the reservoir.
3. Support the body.
4. Disconnect the brake line at the brake hose.
5. Disconnect the driveshaft.
6. Disconnect the stabilizer and coil spring at the control arm.
7. Disconnect the control arm at the axle carrier.
8. Installation is the reverse of removal. Bleed brake system.

733i

1. Remove rear wheel.
2. Pull up the parking brake lever and disconnect the output shaft at the drive flange.
3. Remove the parking brake lever.
4. Remove the brake fluid from the reservoir.
5. Disconnect the brake line.
6. Disconnect the control arm from the rear axle carrier.
7. Disconnect the shock absorber and remove the control arm.
8. Installation is the reverse of removal. Bleed the brake system.

Trailing Arm

REMOVAL AND INSTALLATION

2002

1. Remove the coil spring.
2. Release the handbrake cable at the handbrake lever.
3. Disconnect the stabilizer on the trailing arm.
4. Separate the brake hose from the pipe line and cap the hose to protect against dirt.
5. Disconnect both trailing arm mountings and remove the trailing arm.
6. Installation is the reverse of removal. Bleed the brake system.

3.0

1. Remove the handbrake lever.
2. Remove brake fluid from the reservoir.
3. Support the body.
4. Remove the wheel.
5. Pull the handbrake cable out of the protective tube.
6. Disconnect the brake hoses.
7. Remove the output driveshaft.
8. Remove the spring strut shock absorber from the trailing arm.
9. Remove the trailing arm from the axle support.

630

1. Remove the parking brake lever.
2. Remove the rear wheel.
3. Using vise grips clamp the front hose to prevent loss of fluid.
4. Support the body.
5. Pull the parking brake cable out of the pipe.
6. Disconnect the stabilizer and spring strut at the trailing arm.
7. Disconnect the brake line at the brake hose.
8. Disconnect the trailing arm at the rear axle support.
9. Detach the output shaft.
10. Disconnect the brake pad wear indicator wire at the right trailing arm and take the wire out of the clamps.
11. Installation is the reverse of removal. Bleed the system.

320

1. Disconnect the parking brake cable at the parking brake lever.
2. Detach the output shaft at the rear axle shaft.
3. Remove the wheel.
4. Disconnect the coil spring/shock absorber strut at the trailing arm.
5. Support the trailing arm.
6. Disconnect the brake hose at the pipe and plug the end of the hose to prevent dirt from entering.
7. Disconnect the stabilizer at the trailing arm and remove both trailing arm mounting bolts.
8. Installation is the reverse of removal. Bleed the brake system.

FRONT SUSPENSION

Strut Assembly

REMOVAL AND INSTALLATION

2002

1. Raise the vehicle and support safely. Remove the wheel.
2. Disconnect the angle bracket from the strut assembly.
3. Disconnect the caliper, leaving the brake line attached. Tie the caliper to the vehicle body so that the weight is not supported by the brake hose.
4. Disconnect the lower arm from the axle beam.
5. Remove the lockwire and disconnect the track rod arm from the strut assembly.
6. Remove the three retaining nuts and detach the strut assembly at the wheelhouse.
7. Installation is the reverse of removal.

320i

1. Raise the vehicle and support safely. Remove the wheel.
2. Detach the bracket at the strut assembly.

Angle bracket retaining bolt—2002

3. Disconnect and suspend the brake caliper with a wire from the vehicle body. Do not disconnect the brake line.

4. Remove the cotter pin and castle nut. Press the tie rod off the steering knuckle.

5. Remove the three retaining nuts and detach the strut assembly at the wheel house.

6. Installation is the reverse of removal.

3.0

1. Raise the vehicle and support safely. Remove the wheel.

2. Disconnect the brake caliper and suspend from the vehicle body with a wire. Do not remove the brake hose.

3. Disconnect the angle bracket from the strut assembly.

4. Remove the lock wire and disconnect the track rod arm from the strut assembly.

5. Remove the three retaining nuts and detach the strut assembly at the wheel house.

6. Installation is the reverse of removal.

530i and 630i

1. Raise the vehicle and support safely. Remove the wheel.

2. Disconnect the bracket at the strut assembly.

3. Disconnect the brake caliper and suspend from the vehicle body with wire. Do not remove the brake hose.

4. Remove the lock wire and disconnect the tie rod arm at the strut assembly.

5. Remove the three retaining nuts and detach the strut assembly at the wheelhouse.

6. Installation is the reverse of removal.

733i

1. Raise the vehicle and support safely. Remove the wheel.

2. Disconnect the vibration strut from the control arm.

3. Disconnect the bracket and clamps from the strut assembly.

4. Disconnect the wire connection and press out the wire from the clamp on the spring strut tube.

5. Remove the brake caliper and suspend it from the vehicle body with a wire. Do not remove the brake hose.

6. Disconnect the tie rod from the shock absorber.

7. Remove the three retaining nuts and

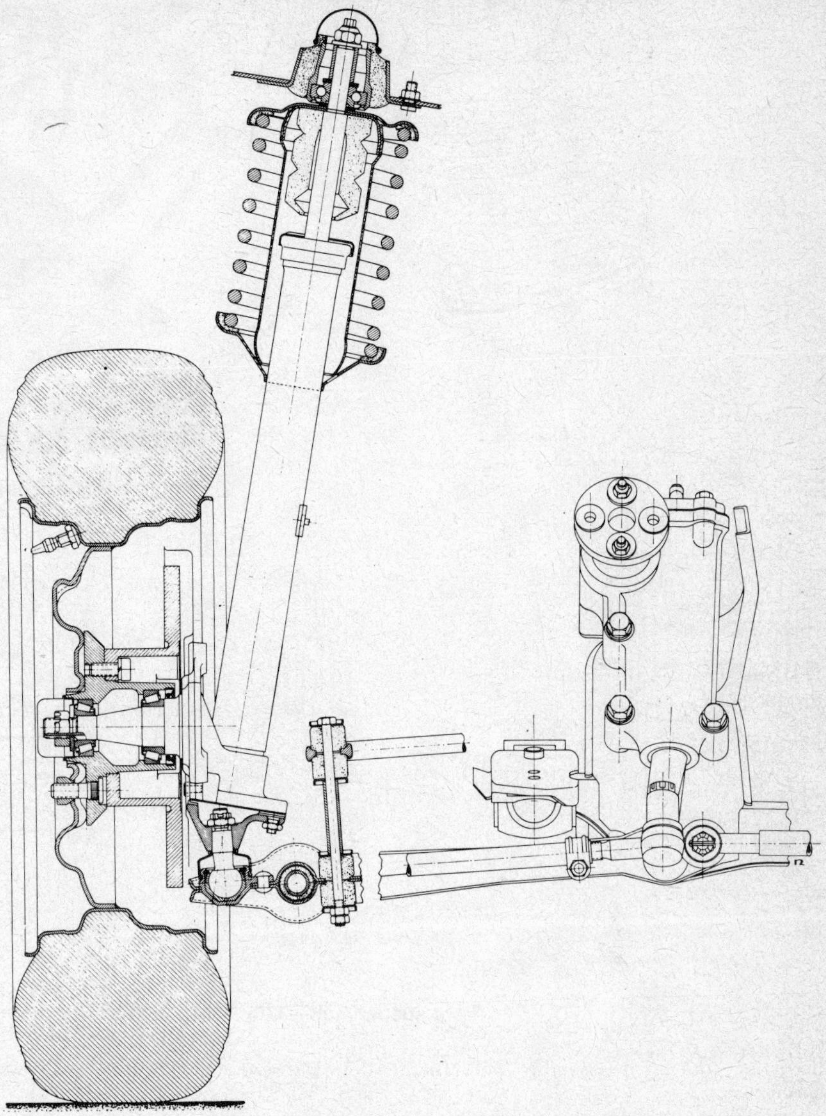

Front suspension—2002

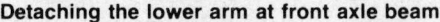

1. Spacer ring 2. Washer 3. Wishbone

Detaching the lower arm at front axle beam

Lock wire location at strut assembly

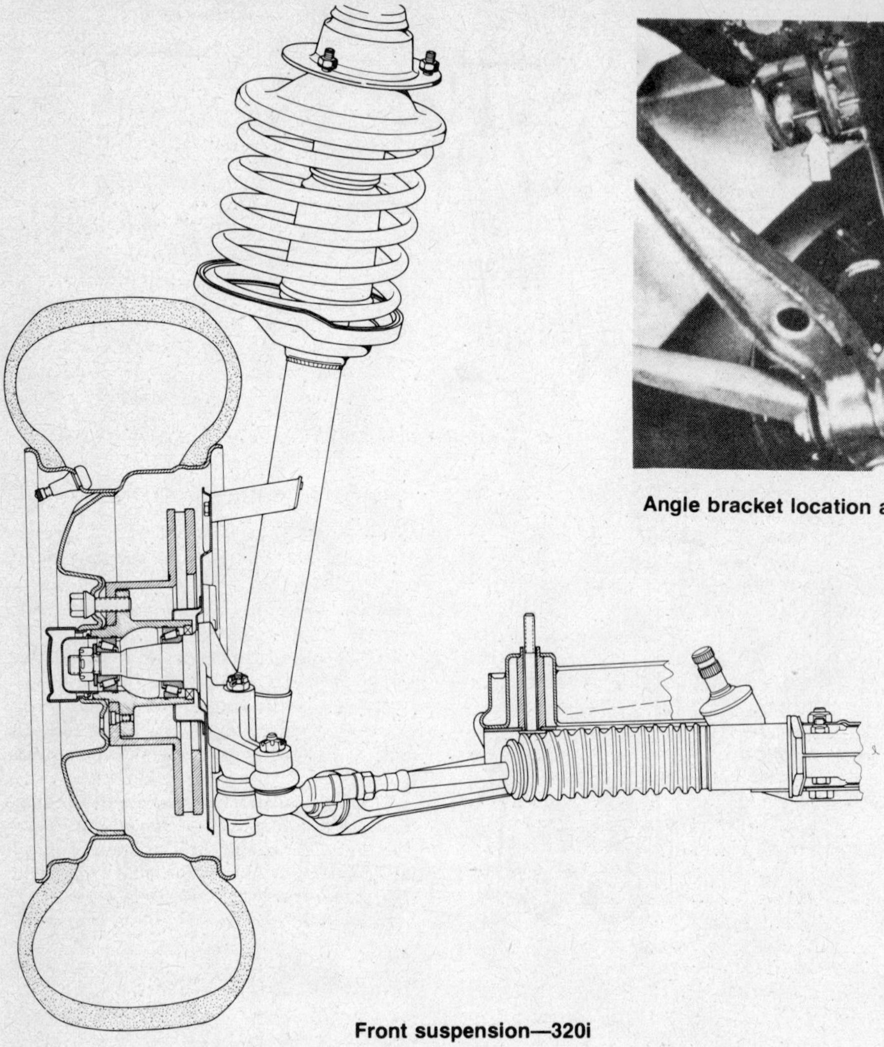

Front suspension—320i

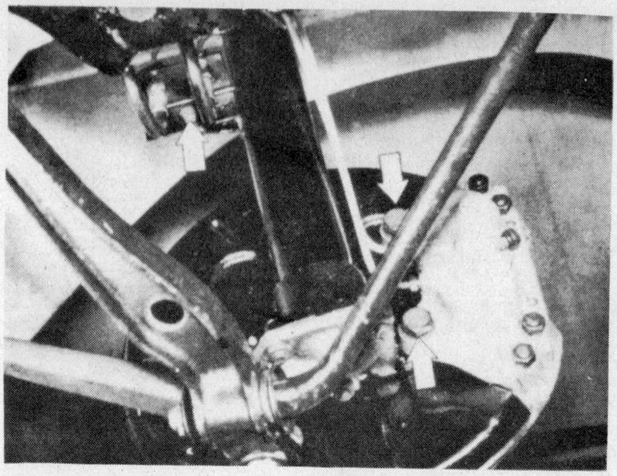

Angle bracket location and caliper retaining nuts—3.0

Bracket retaining bolt—320i

disconnect the strut assembly from the wheelhouse.

8. Installation is the reverse of removal.

Coil Spring and Shock Absorber

REMOVAL AND INSTALLATION

All Models

1. Remove the strut assembly.
2. Compress the coil spring with a spring compressor tool.
3. Remove the locknut and remove the retaining plate, or cap and washers, if equipped. Remove the coil spring.
4. Remove the threaded ring and pull out the shock absorber.
5. Installation is the reverse of removal.

Control Arm

REMOVAL AND INSTALLATION

530i and 630i

1. Raise the vehicle and support safely. Remove the wheel.
2. Disconnect the stabilizer at the control arm.
3. Remove the tension strut nut on the control arm.
4. Disconnect the control arm at the front axle support and remove it from the tension strut.
5. Remove the lock wire, remove the bolts and take the control arm off the spring strut.

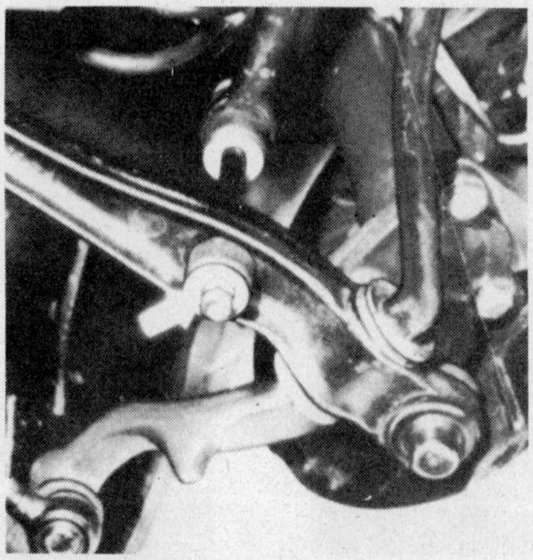

Stabilizer-to-control arm attaching nut —530i, 630i

6. Remove the cotter pin and nut.
7. Using special tool BMW 007-500 or equivalent, pull the guide joint from the tie rod arm.
8. Installation is the reverse of removal.

320i

1. Disconnect the stabilizer at the control arm.
2. Disconnect the control arm at the front axle support.
3. Remove the cotter pin and castle nut.
4. Press the control arm off the steering knuckle with special tool BMW 31-1-100 or equivalent.
5. Installation is the reverse of removal.

733i

1. Raise the vehicle and support safely. Remove the wheel.
2. Disconnect the vibration strut from the control arm.
3. Disconnect the control arm from the axle carrier.
4. Disconnect the tie rod arm from the shock absorber.
5. Remove the cotter pin and castle nut. Press off the control arm with special tool BMW 31-1-110 or equivalent.
6. Installation is the reverse of removal.

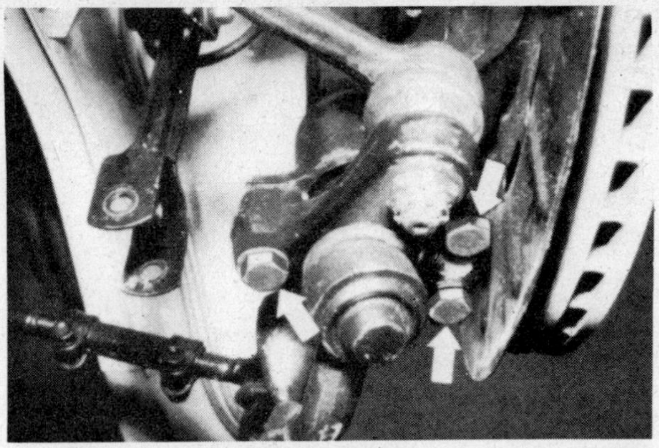

Tie rod arm-to-shock absorber retaining bolts—733i

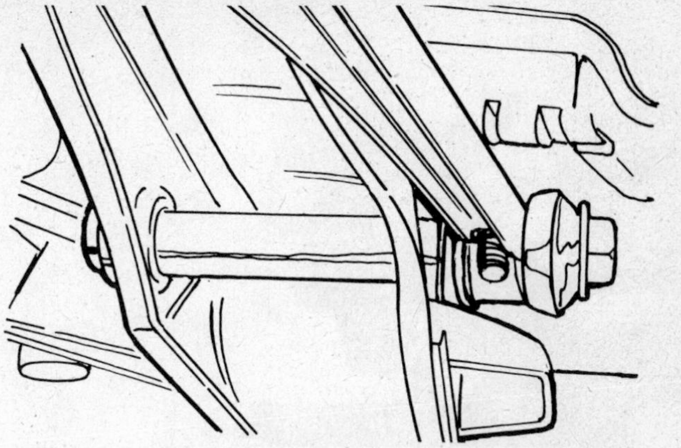

Lower control arm spacer ring in axle carrier—3.0

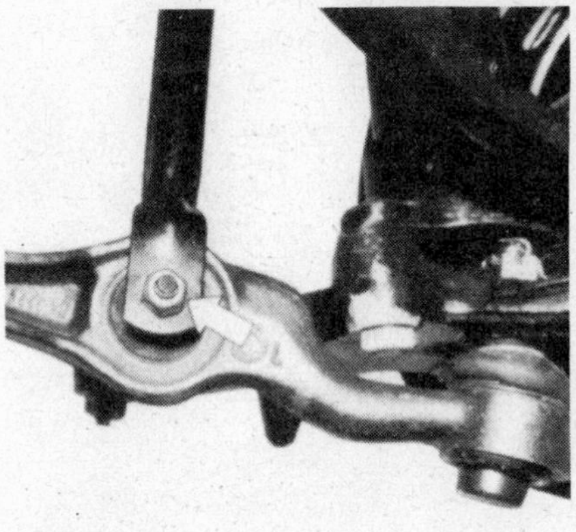

Vibration strut attaching bolt—733i

Control Arm (Wishbone)

REMOVAL AND INSTALLATION

3.0

1. Raise the vehicle and support safely. Remove the wheel.
2. Remove the lock wire and disconnect the track rod arm from the strut assembly.
3. Press the guide joint out of the track rod arm.
4. Disconnect the lower arm from the axle carrier.
5. Disconnect the trailing link from the lower arm.
6. Installation is the reverse of removal.

2002

1. Raise the vehicle and support safely. Remove the wheel.
2. Disconnect the trailing link at the lower arm.
3. Disconnect the lower arm from the front axle beam and push off at the trailing link.
4. Remove the cotter pin and castle nut. Press off the track rod at the track rod arm with special tool BMW 00-7-500 or equivalent.
5. Remove the lock wire and nuts. Remove the track rod arm with the lower arm.
6. Remove the cotter pin and nut. Press off the track rod arm from the guide joint with special tool BMW 00-7-500 or equivalent.
7. Installation is the reverse of removal.

Ball Joint

REMOVAL AND INSTALLATION

2002

1. Remove the lower control arm assembly and lock in a vise.
2. Drill out the rivet heads and drive the rivets out, using a suitable punch.
3. Replace the ball joint, using nuts and bolts.
4. Reassemble the lower control arm in the reverse of the removal.

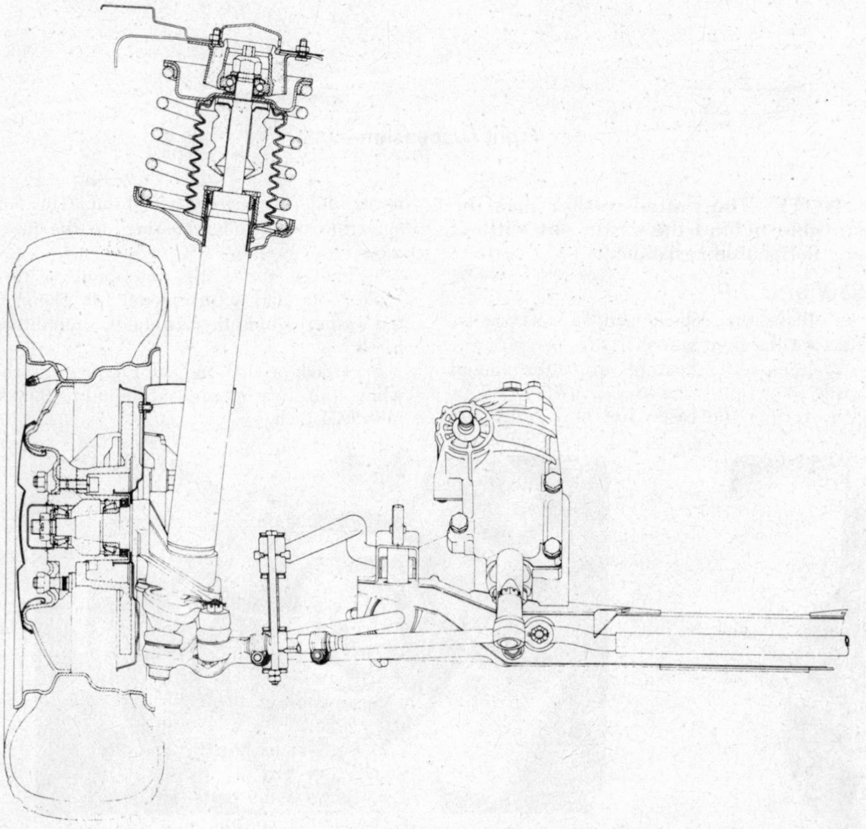

Front suspension assembly—520i

Drilling out ball joint rivet heads

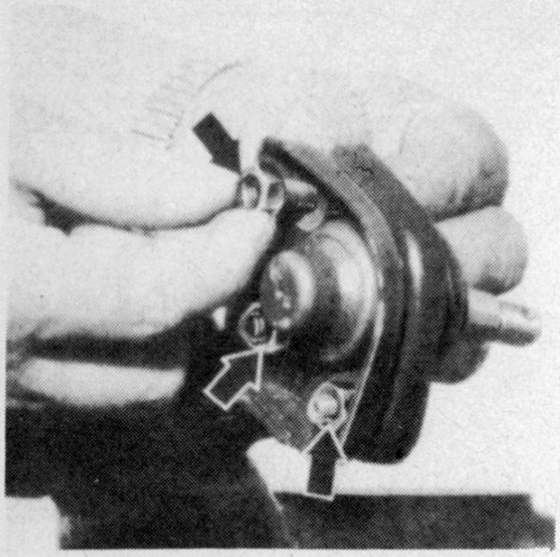

Replace rivets with nut and bolt

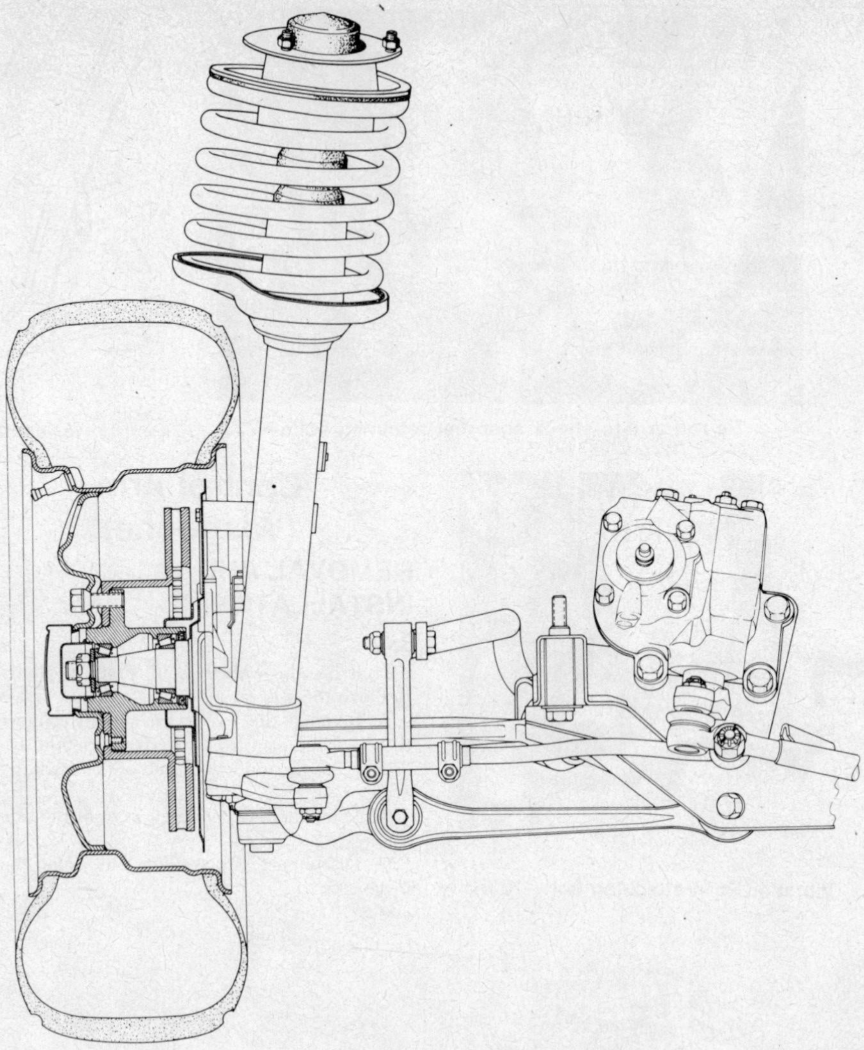

Front suspension—733i

Front Suspension Alignment

CASTER AND CAMBER

Caster and camber are not adjustable, except for replacement of bent or worn parts.

TOE-IN ADJUSTMENT

Toe-in is adjusted by changing the length of the tie rod and tie rod end assembly. When adjusting the tie rod ends, adjust each by equal amounts (in the opposite direction) to increase or decrease the toe-in measurement.

Front Wheel Bearing Adjustment

2002, 320i, 630i and 733i

1. Raise the vehicle and support safely. Remove the front wheels.
2. Remove the bearing cap, cotter pin and loosen the castle nut on the spindle.
3. Tighten the castle nut to 22-24 ft/lbs (30-33 n/m), while turning the hub continuously. After the proper torque is attained, rotate the hub at least two more turns.

NOTE: This aligns the tapered bearings to the inner races.

4. Loosen the castle nut until a slight play is present on the bearings. Retighten the nut to a maximum of 2 ft/lbs (3 n/m) and turn back to the nearest hole and insert the cotter pin.

NOTE: The slotted washer must be movable behind the castle nut without any noticeable resistance.

530i and 3.0

1. Raise the vehicle and support safely. Remove the front wheels.
2. Remove the bearing cap, cotter pin and castle nut.
3. Torque the castle nut to 7 ft/lbs (9.5 n/m), while turning the wheel hub. This will align the taper roller bearings to the inner races.
4. Loosen the castle nut about ⅓ turn Model 530i, and ¼ turn model 3.0. The slotted washer behind the castle nut, should turn freely.
5. Attach a dial indicator gauge to the wheel hub. Bearing preload should be 0.0008 to 0.0024 inch.

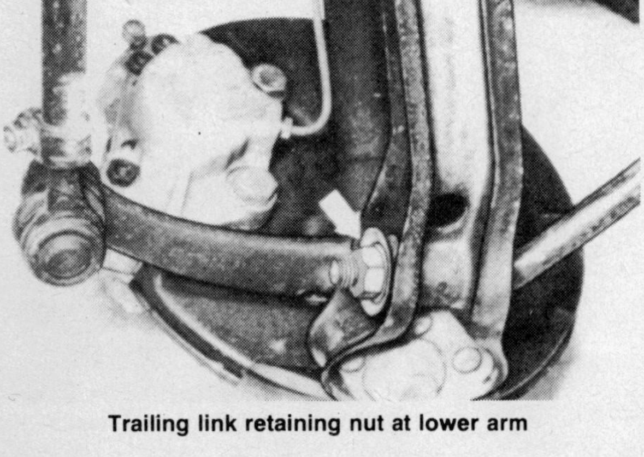

Trailing link retaining nut at lower arm

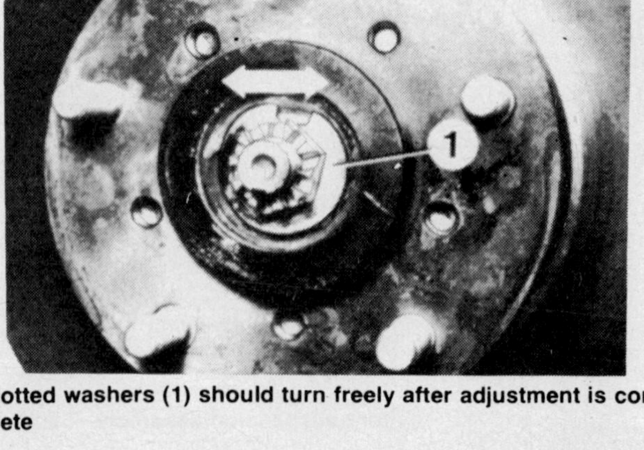

Slotted washers (1) should turn freely after adjustment is complete

STEERING

Steering Wheel

REMOVAL AND INSTALLATION

All Models

NOTE: Remove and install steering wheel in straight ahead position.

1. Remove steering wheel pad.
2. Unscrew retaining nut and remove the wheel.
3. Installation is the reverse of removal.

Turn Signal/Dimmer Switch and Wiper Switch

REMOVAL AND INSTALLATION

All Models Except 3.0

1. Disconnect negative battery terminal.
2. Remove steering wheel.
3. Remove lower steering column casing.
4. On 2002, remove upper steering column surround and leave choke cable attached.
5. Disconnect fuel relay/plate plug.
6. Installation is the reverse of removal.

Turn signal switch adjustment

NOTE: When installing turn signal switch, steering wheel is pointed in the straight ahead position, turn signal lever is in centered position and adjust play "A" to about 3 mm.

7. On 320i make sure to connect the ground strap.

3.0 Turn Signal and Headlight Dimmer Switch

1. Disconnect negative battery terminal.
2. Remove steering wheel.
3. Remove lower steering column casing.
4. Remove lower center left section of instrument panel housing.
5. Installation is the reverse of removal.

NOTE: When installing turn signal switch, steering wheel is pointed in the straight ahead position, turn signal lever is in the centered position and adjust play "A" to about 3 mm.

Ignition Switch

REMOVAL AND INSTALLATION

All Models

1. Disconnect negative battery terminal.
2. Remove lower steering column casing.
3. On model 3.0 remove lower center left instrument panel trim.
4. Unscrew set screw and remove switch.
5. Disconnect central fuse/relay plate plug.
6. Installation is the reverse of removal.

NOTE: Turn ignition key all the way back and set the switch at the "O" position before installing. Marks on the switch must be opposite each other.

Manual Steering Gear

REMOVAL AND INSTALLATION

320i

1. Loosen front wheels.
2. Remove cotter pin and castle nut.

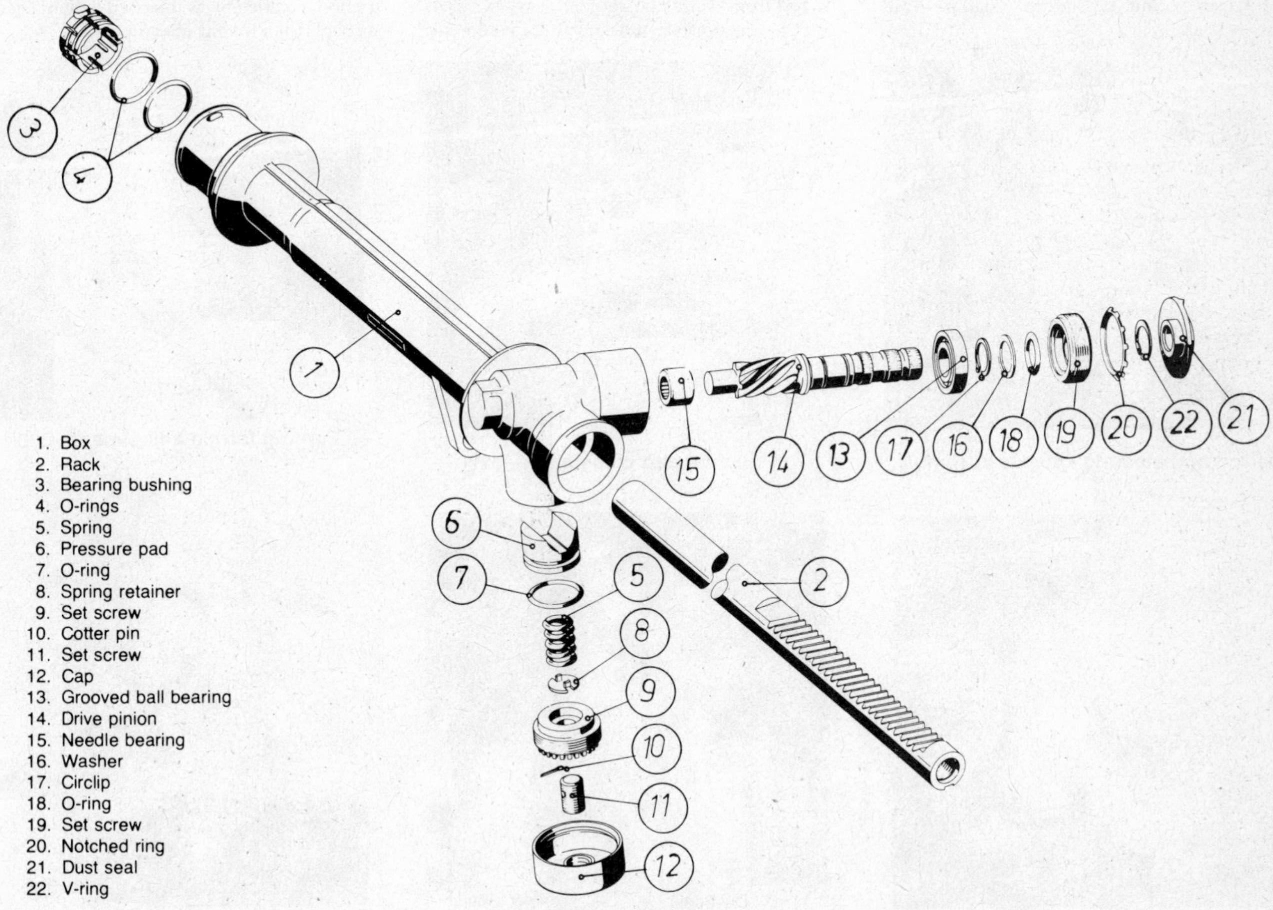

Steering gear—typical

3. Press tie rods off steering knuckles.
4. Detach steering at front axle support.
5. Pull steering gear off steering spindle.
6. Installation is the reverse of removal.

NOTE: Turn steering wheel until wheels point straight ahead. Mark on dust seal must be between marks on gear box.

2002 and 3.0

1. Loosen bolt connecting coupling flange to steering column, remove bolt attaching flange to steering box.

NOTE: On model 2002, do not reuse self locking nuts.

2. Remove castle nut and press off left track rod from center track rod.
3. Press the center track rod from the steering drop arm.
4. Detach and remove steering box from front axle beam.
5. Installation is the reverse of removal.

NOTE: Steering wheel must be in the straight ahead position and the markings on the steering box and the pitman shaft must align.

ADJUSTMENT

320i

1. Remove steering gear from car.
2. Clamp special tool 32-1-100, or equivalent in a vise and place steering gear assembly into the tool.
3 Unscrew nut on steering damper and slide it back.
4. Remove cap and unscrew socket head cap about ½ inch.
5. Pressure pad adjustment:
   a Remove cotter pin. Tighten set screw with special tool 32-1-040, or equivalent, and a torque wrench, to 4 ft/lbs. Loosen set screw by one full castle slot to align the cotter pin bore.
   b. Use special tools 32-1-000 and 00-2-000 or equivalent to move rack to the left and right over the entire stroke and check for sticking and hooking. If this is the case loosen set screw by one more castle slot and insert cotter pin.
   c. Repeat test. If there is still sticking or hooking replace rack, drive pinion or the entire steering gear. Never loosen screw by 2 castle slots regardless of circumstances.
6. Turning torque adjustment:
   a. Move rack to center position. Place special tools 00-2000 and 32-1-000 or equivalent on the drive pinion, check the turning torque. If it is not between 7.8 and 11.2 ft/lbs, adjust the set screw.
   b. Turn to the right to increase friction, and turn to the left to decrease friction.
   c. Install cap.

2002 and 3.0

1. Remove air intake filter on model 2002.
2. Position front wheels straight ahead.
3. Marking on worm shaft must be in alignment with marking on steering box.
4. Remove castle nut and press left-hand tie rod from center tie rod.
5. Remove castle nut and press center tie rod from drop arm with special tool 7009, or equivalent.
6. Remove steering wheel center and install friction gauge.
7. Turn the steering wheel one turn to the left from the straight ahead position. In this position the worm cannot be pressed one-sided into its bearing by the steering roller shaft, which might indicate absence of play.
8. Turn adjustment screw until specified friction coefficient is reached when passing through the straight ahead position.

Adjusting friction coefficient—2002 and 3.0

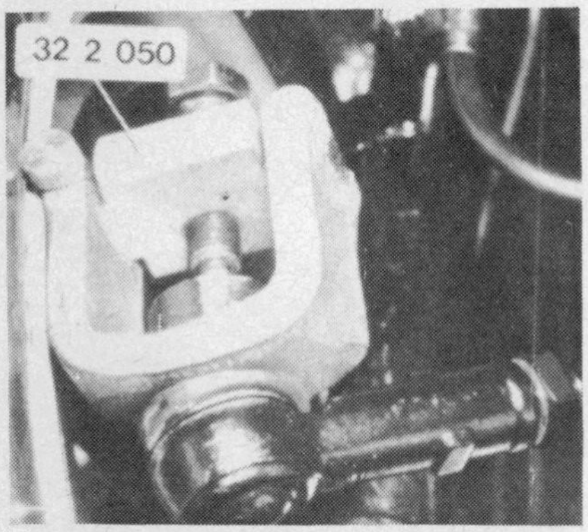

Tie rod and steering knuckle assembly

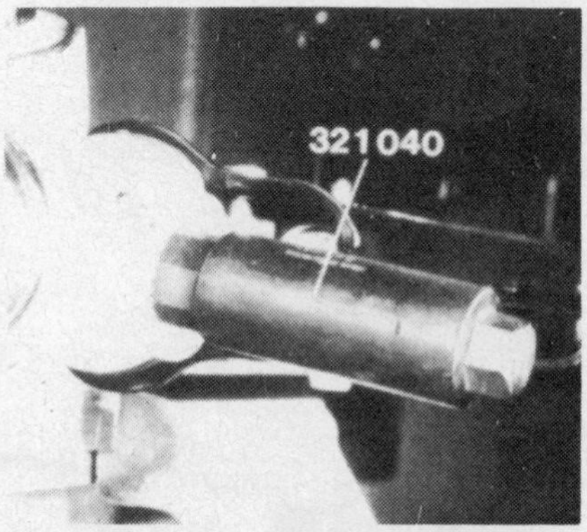

Pressure pad adjustment—320i

Turning torque adjustment—320i

Steering adjustment 320i

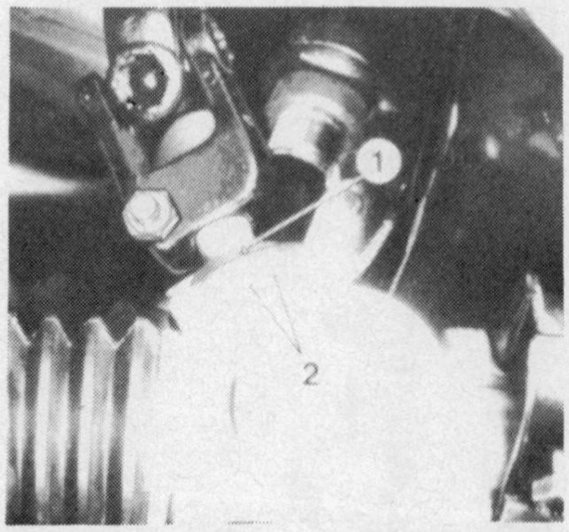

1. Dust seal 2. Alignment marks

Steering gear box alignment

Pressure pad adjustment—320i

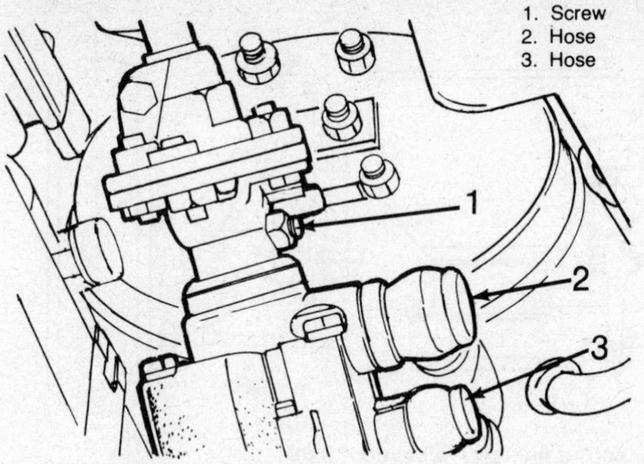

1. Screw
2. Hose
3. Hose

Coupling flange and steering box

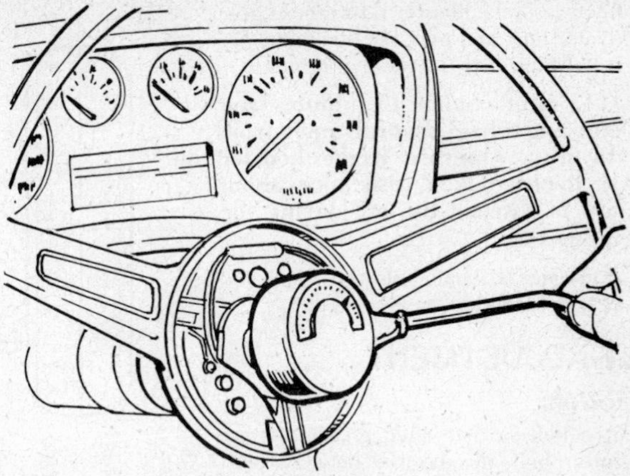

Friction gauge installation

Power Steering

REMOVAL AND INSTALLATION

All Models

1. Turn steering to left lock.
2. Drain steering fluid.
3. Remove cotter pin and loosen castle nut.
4. Press center tie rod off steering drop arm.
5. Remove screw and slide coupling flange with steering column upward.
6. Disconnect hoses at steering gear and plug the openings.
7. Detach and remove steering gear at front axle carrier.
8. Installation is the reverse of removal.

NOTE: System must be bled and the front wheels must be in the straight ahead position. Marks on the housing and propeller shaft must align. Use new self locking nuts on all models except model 3.0.

ADJUSTMENT

All Models

1. Remove steering wheel center.
2. With front wheels in straight ahead position remove cotter pin and loosen castle nut. On 630i models, wheels are turned to the right lock.
3. Press center tie rod off steering drop arm.
4. Turn steering wheel to the left about one turn. Install a friction gauge and turn the wheel to the right, past the point of pressure and the gauge should read 10.4 in/lbs.
5. To adjust, turn steering wheel about one turn to the left. Loosen counter nut and turn the adjusting screw until specified friction is reached when passing over point of pressure.

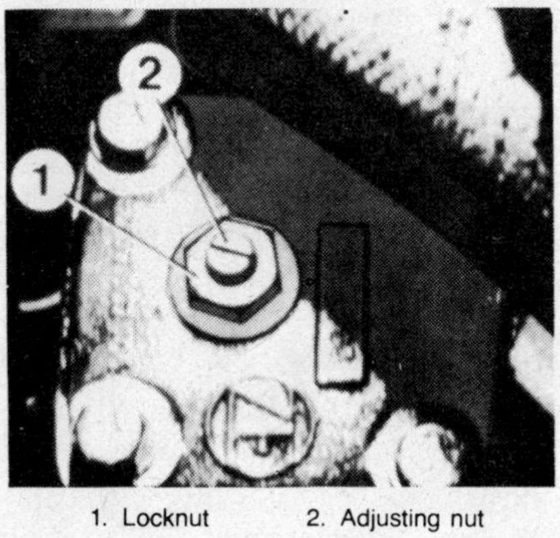

1. Locknut 2. Adjusting nut

Power steering adjustment

Power Steering Pump

REMOVAL AND INSTALLATION

Models 530i, 630i and 3.0

1. Detach steering pump hoses.
2. Remove bolts from the brackets holding the front and rear of the pump.
3. Installation is the reverse of removal.

NOTE: Bleed the system and torque the hose connections to 35 ft/lbs.

733i

1. When the pump is damaged the pressure control regulator must also be replaced.
2. Discharge the hydraulic accumulator, by depressing the brake pedal with the force required for full stop breaking (about 20 times).
3. Detach hoses at pump.
4. Remove bolts from the brackets holding the pump in place.

1. Drive shaft
2. Shaft seal
3. Circlip
4. Ball bearing
5. Snap rings
6. Bearing sleeve
7. Dowel pin
8. Drive end face plate
9. Rotor set
10. Cover end face plate
11. O-ring
12. O-ring
13. Spring
14. Cover
15. Hook snap ring
16. Spring
17. Valve piston assembly

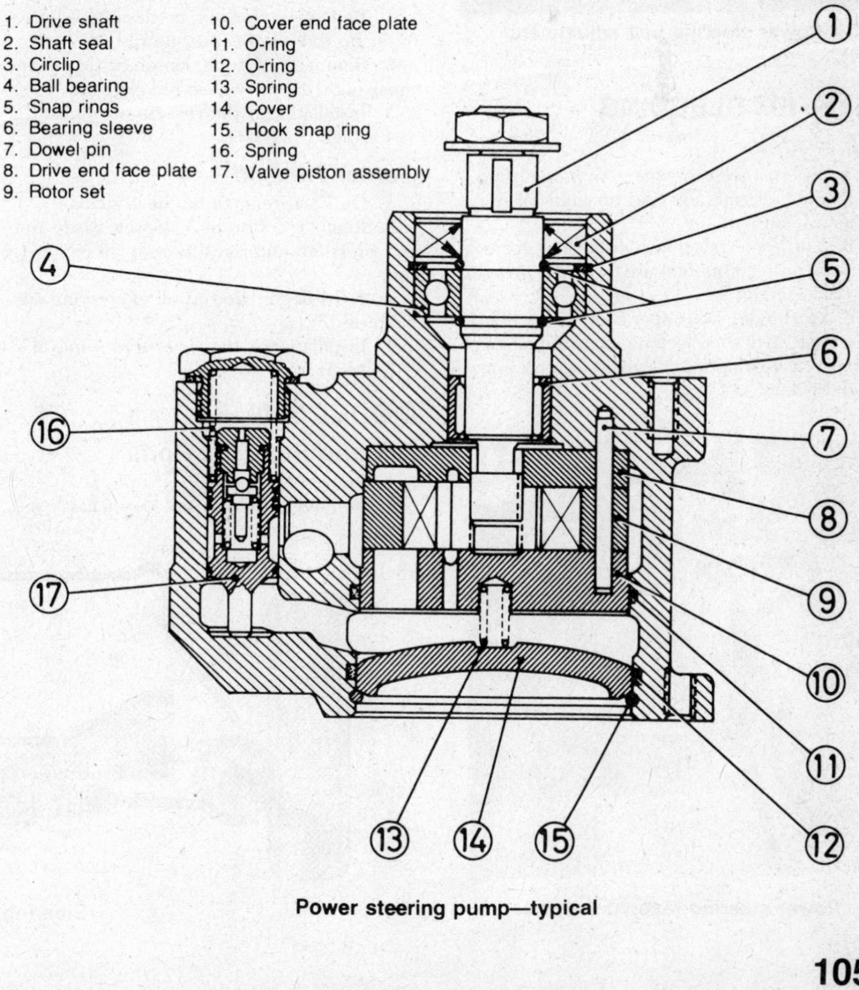

Power steering pump—typical

5. Remove brake booster return hose from accumulator tank and plug the opening.
6. Installation is the reverse of removal.

NOTE: Run engine 10 minutes and turn steering wheel several times from stop to stop. Operate brake booster quickly, to obtain hard resistance, about 10 times to discard the oil leaving the return hose.

7. Stop engine, drain oil from tank and connect booster return hose on tank.

BELT ADJUSTMENT

All Models

Tighten belt so that when pressure is applied to the belt, the distance between both belt pulleys is 5 to 10 mm.

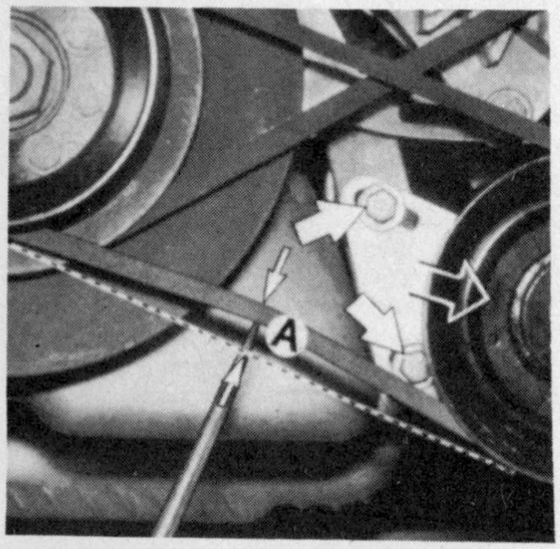

Power steering belt adjustment

SYSTEM BLEEDING

All Models

1. Fill reservoir to edge with proper fluid.
2. Start engine and add oil until oil level remains constant.
3. Turn steering wheel from lock to lock quickly until air bubbles are no longer present in the reservoir.
4. On model 733i, operate brake pedal to discharge hydraulic accumulator until oil level stops rising or noticeable resistance on brake pedal is felt.

Power steering reservoir—typical

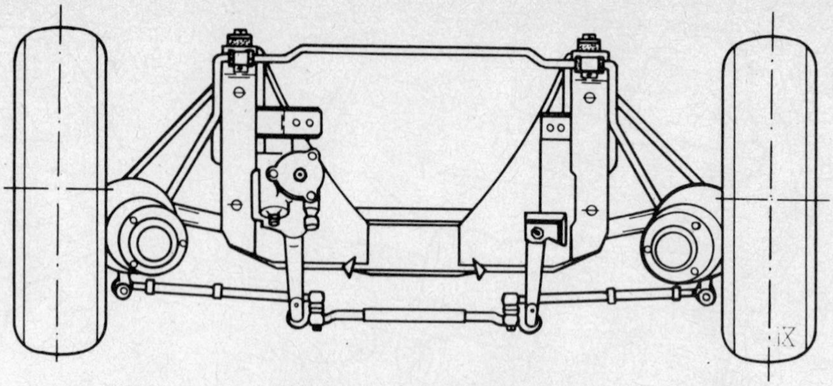
Steering linkage—all except 320i

Steering Linkage

ALL MODELS EXCEPT 320i

Tie Rod Arm

1. Remove front wheel.
2. On model 2002, detach stabilizer from wishbone. Detach wishbone at front axle beam. Detach trailing link from wishbone.
3. Remove cotter pin and castle nut.
4. Press outer tie rod off tie rod arm, and press stabilizer off control arm.
5. Remove lock wire and detach tie rod arm at shock absorber.
6. Press tie rod arm off control arm.
7. Installation is the reverse of removal.

Outer Tie Rod

1. Remove cotter pin, castle nut and press outer tie rod off of center tie rod.
2. Remove cotter pin, loosen castle nut and press outer tie rod off tie rod arm.
3. Installation is the reverse of removal.
4. Align front axle.

Center Tie Rod

1. On 733i, remove the heat guard.
2. Remove cotter pins, loosen castle nuts and press left and right tie rods off center tie rod.
3. Press center tie rod off of steering control arm.
4. Installation is the reverse of removal.
5. Align front axle.

MODEL 320i

Left and Right Tie Rods

1. Loosen the wheel.
2. Remove cotter pin and loosen castle nut.

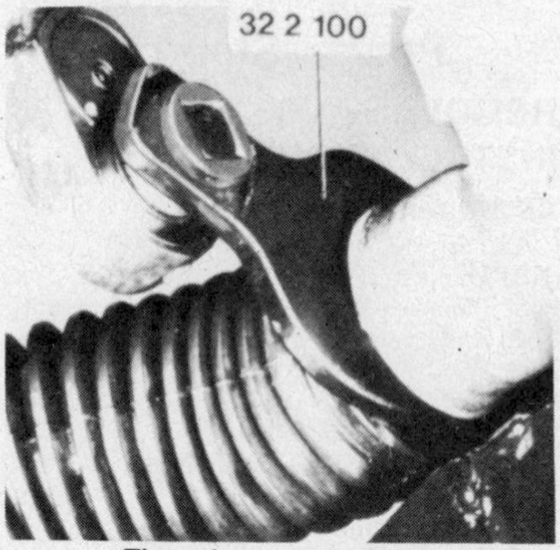

Tie rod removal—320i

3. Press tie rod off steering knuckle.
4. Detach strap, slide back bellows and bend open lock plate.
5. Detach tie rod at rack.
6. Installation is the reverse of removal.

BRAKE SYSTEM

All BMW models incorporate dual, fluid-circuit, tandem arrangement master cylinders in their brake systems, which are similar to one another in design and function. However, even though they are similar to one another, they are not identical to one another in design or function.

By dual circuit, tandem arrangement we

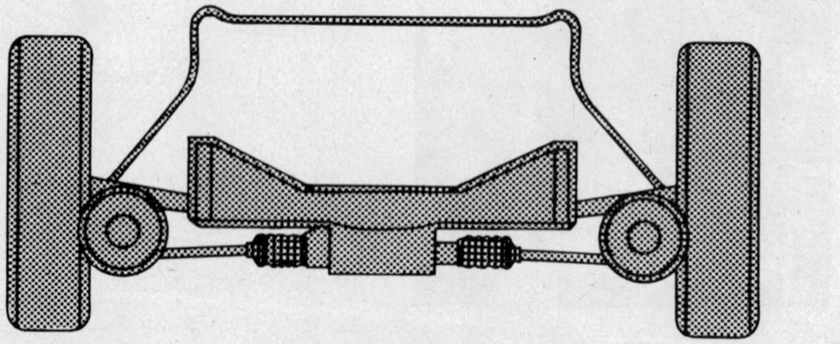
Steering linkage—320i

mean that the master cylinder is comprised of two (dual) integrally joined fluid chambers (each supplying a predetermined combination of wheel brakes) which are positioned one in front of the other (tandem).

Two variations of the standard dual circuit system are the double dual circuit system and the diagonally split, dual circuit system.

In the case of the standard dual circuit system, one chamber supplies the front brakes while the other chamber supplies the rear brakes. In the case of the double dual circuit system, one chamber supplies the circuit to the front brakes while the other supplies a circuit to the front and rear brakes combined. In the case of the diagonally split, dual circuit system, one chamber supplies the left front and right rear brakes while the other chamber supplies the right front and left rear brakes.

A brief list of brake-system-according-to-model follows.

Models 2002, 2002tii: Standard dual circuit; (front) Ate four piston, fixed caliper discs with automatic pad wear compensation, (rear) internal-expanding drums with self-centering leading and trailing shoes, (park) mechanical, acting on rear wheels.

Model 320i: Standard dual circuit; (front) Ate caliper type disc brakes with automatic adjustment for pad wear, (rear). Inside shoe brakes with simplex shoes, (park) mechanical, with action on rear wheels. Model 530i: Double Dual Circuit; (front) Ate four piston with fixed caliper discs and automatic adjustment, (rear) Ate two piston, fixed caliper discs with automatic adjustment, (park) Duo servo drums.

Models 630i, and 633i: Double dual circuit brakes with brake pressure booster and governor, and brake pad wear indicator, (front) Ate four piston caliper disc brakes with automatic adjustment, (rear) Ate two piston caliper disc brakes with automatic adjustment, (park) Dual hydraulic drum brakes with cable operation on rear wheels only.

Model 733i: Diagonally split, dual circuit brake system with hydraulic brake pressure boost and mutual hydraulic pump for brakes and steering as well as pressure accumulator for brakes including brake fluid reservoir. Equipped with an indicator for brake fluid level and brake pad wear, (front) Ate four piston caliper disc brakes with automatic adjustment, (rear) Ate two piston caliper disc brakes with automatic adjustment, (park) Dual power drum brakes with bowden cable acting on the rear wheels.

NOTE: In the hydraulically boosted power brake system, pressure developed in the booster is transferred to the standard master cylinder which is bolted to the booster unit.

The hydraulic pressure to the power booster is regulated between the power steering pump and the power booster by a pressure control regulator. The fluid is pumped through the regulator at an approximate flow rate of 7 quarts per minute, and into a fluid accumulator where it is stored (charged) at 510-810 psi. This charge is sufficient to operate the brake system several times if the power steering pump fails. When the reserve pressure is depleted the brake system will remain operational, however, considerably more force will be required to stop the vehicle.

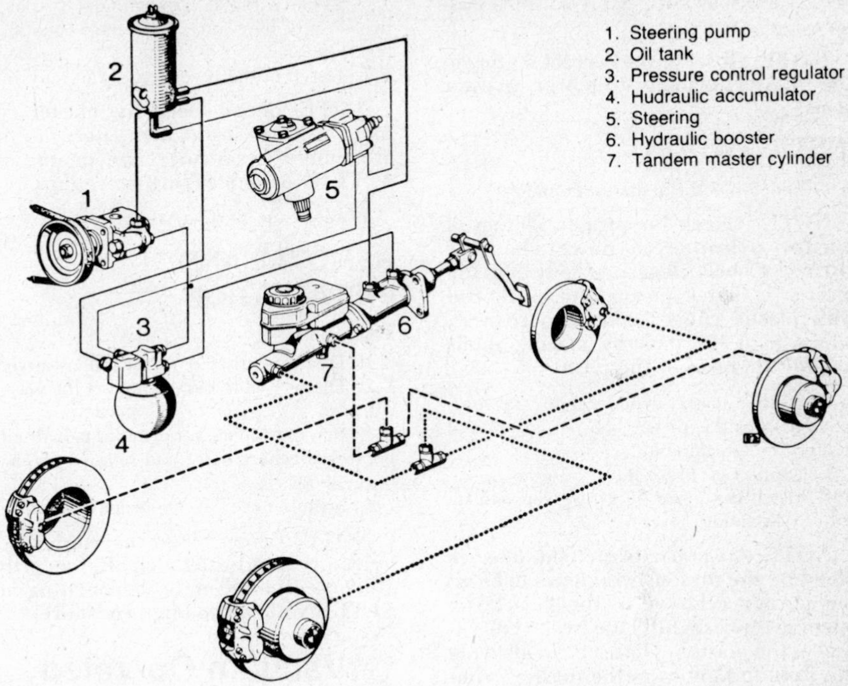

Diagonally split, dual circuit brake system—733i

Models 3.0S and 3.0Si: Double dual circuit brakes; (front) Ate four piston fixed caliper disc brakes with automatic pad wear compensation, (rear) Ate two piston fixed caliper disc brakes with automatic pad wear compensation, (park) Duo-servo drums with leading and trailing shoe drum brakes.

Bleeding the Brake System

All Models

The manufacturer recommends bleeding the brake system in the conventional manner.

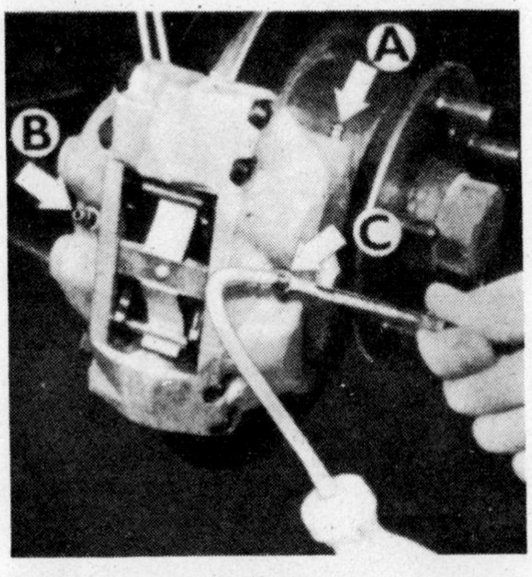

Bleeding through four piston caliper in the order illustrated—A, B, and then C

NOTE: On vehicles equipped with four piston, fixed calipers begin by bleeding through the highest bleed screw (farthest from the ground) proceed by bleeding through the inboard screw (closest to the centerline of the vehicle) complete the procedure by bleeding through the outboard screw.

Master Cylinder

REMOVAL

2002, 2002tii, 530, 630, 633i, 3.0S and 3.0Si

1. Remove the air cleaner if necessary.
2. Drain and disconnect the brake fluid reservoir from the master cylinder. The brake fluid reservoir will be mounted in one of two ways: (1) assembled directly on top of the master cylinder; it is removed by tilting the reservoir to one side and lifting it off of the master cylinder, or (2) the reservoir is mounted in the engine compartment where it is attached to the inner fender sheet metal by means of attaching bolts; carefully disconnect hoses leading to the master cylinder and allow the reservoir to drain.

CAUTION

Exercise extreme care in handling brake fluid near painted surface of vehicle as fluid will destroy the paint finish if allowed to come into contact with it.

3. Disconnect all brake lines from the master cylinder.
4. Remove the master cylinder to power

booster attaching nuts, and remove the master cylinder.

NOTE: Observe the correct seating of the master cylinder-to-power booster seals.

INSTALLATION

1. Bench-bleed the master cylinder.

NOTE: Check for proper seating of master cylinder to power booster O-ring. Check clearance between the master cylinder piston and push rod with plastic gauge, and, if necessary, adjust to 0.002 inch by placing shims behind the head of the push rod.

2. Position master cylinder onto studs protruding from the power booster; install and tighten the attaching nuts.
3. Connect all brake lines.
4. Install the brake fluid reservoir and fill with brake fluid.

NOTE: An alternate method to bench bleeding the master cylinder is to bleed the master cylinder in the vehicle by opening (only slightly) the brake line fitting at the master cylinder, and allowing the fluid to flow from the master cylinder into a container. however, this method should be considered as an ALTERNATE METHOD ONLY as it is more difficult to control the fluid leaving the master cylinder during bleeding, thereby increasing the chance of accidentally splashing brake fluid onto the painted surface of the vehicle.

5. Bleed the brake system.

REMOVAL AND INSTALLATION

320i

1. Remove the fuel mixture control unit.
2. Disconnect the hose at the clutch connection.
3. Drain and disconnect the brake fluid reservoir.
4. Disconnect the brake lines from the master cylinder.
5. Working from the underside of the left-side inner fender panel (wheel opening area) remove the two master cylinder support bracket attaching nuts.
6. Remove the master cylinder to power booster attaching nuts, and remove the master cylinder.
7. Install in the reverse order of removal.

NOTE: Bench bleed the master cylinder prior to installation. Refer to the aforementioned note concerning an ALTERNATE bleeding procedure.

8. Bleed the brake system.

REMOVAL AND INSTALLATION

733i

1. Drain and disconnect the fluid reservoir.
2. Disconnect the brake lines at the master cylinder.
3. Remove the master cylinder to hydraulic booster attaching bolts, and remove the master cylinder.
4. Install in the reverse order of removal.

NOTE: Bench bleed the master cylinder prior to installation. Refer to the aforementioned note concerning an ALTERNATE bleeding procedure.

Vacuum Operated Power Brake Booster

REMOVAL AND INSTALLATION

2002, 2002tii and 320i

1. Remove the master cylinder.
2. Disconnect the vacuum line at the power booster.
3. Remove the brake pedal apply-rod to power booster push rod pin.
4. Remove the power booster attaching nuts, and remove the power booster.
5. Install in the reverse order of removal.

NOTE: If the original power booster unit is to reused, remove the dust boot and clean the silencer and filter. Position the slots in the silencer 180 degrees away from the slots in the filter.

6. Adjust the extended visible length of the brake light switch head to 0.20-0.24 inch.

REMOVAL AND INSTALLATION

530i, 630i and 633i

1. Remove the coolant reservoir.
2. Remove the master cylinder.
3. Disconnect the vacuum hose at the power booster.
4. Disconnect the power booster apply rod at the brake pedal.
5. Remove the power booster attaching bolts.
6. Remove the power booster.
7. Install in the reverse order of removal.

NOTE: If the original power booster unit is to be reused, remove the dust boot and clean the silencer and filter. Position the slots in the silencer 180 degrees away from the slots in the filter.

8. Adjust the brake pedal distance to 9.055-9.450 inches. Adjust the stop light switch distance to 0.197-0.237 inch.

REMOVAL AND INSTALLATION

3.0S and 3.01Si

1. Remove the air cleaner.
2. Remove the battery.
3. Loosen the power steering fluid reservoir, and secure it out of the way.
4. Remove the hose between the radiator and the coolant overflow reservoir.
5. Remove the master cylinder.
6. Disconnect the vacuum hose at the power booster.
7. Remove the lower left instrument panel housing, and secure it out of the way.
8. Remove the power booster apply-rod pin at the brake pedal.
9. Remove the power booster to support bracket attaching nuts, and remove the power booster.
10. Install in the reverse order of removal.

NOTE: If the original power booster unit is to be reused, remove the dust boot and clean the silencer and filter. Position the slots in the silencer 180 degrees away from the slots in the filter.

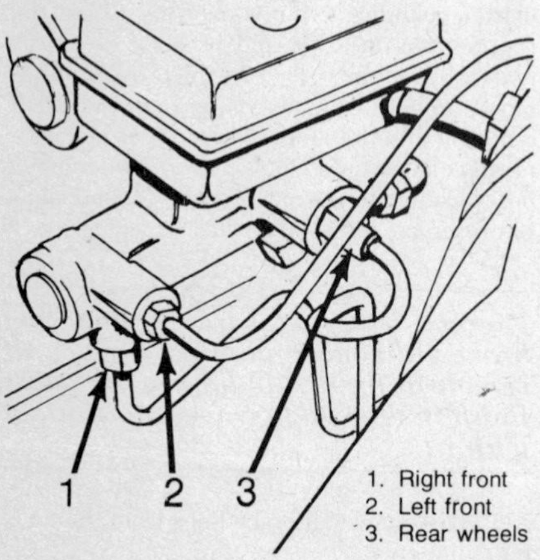

1. Right front
2. Left front
3. Rear wheels

Master cylinder—320i

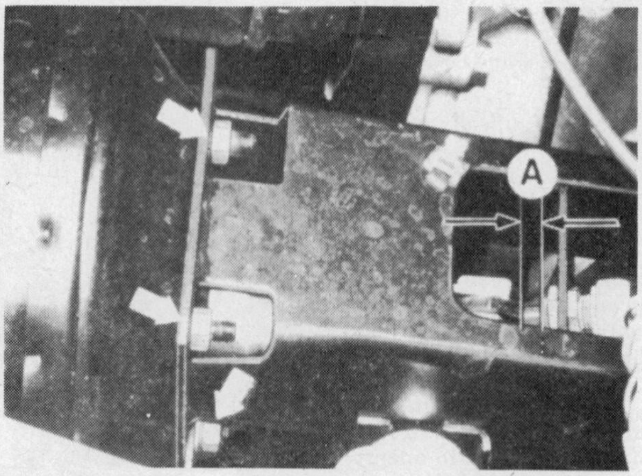

A. 0.20-0.24 inch

Brake light switch adjustment—2002 series

11. Adjust the power booster apply-rod length to 14.5 inches.
12. Adjust the brake pedal-to-bulk head distance to 9.65 inches.
13. Adjust the extended visible length of the brake light switch head (plunger) to 0.24-0.28 inch.

Hydraulically Operated Power Brake Booster

REMOVAL AND INSTALLATION

733i

1. Release the pressure in the hydraulic accumulator by operating the brake pedal (with the engine not running) with a force equivalent to that necessary to bring the vehicle to a full and complete stop.
2. Remove the lower left instrument panel trim.
3. Disconnect the power booster apply-rod at the brake pedal.
4. Remove the master cylinder.
5. Disconnect the fluid lines at the brake booster.
6. Remove the power booster to pedal base assembly attaching bolts, and remove the power booster.
7. Install in the reverse order of removal.
8. Adjust the distance between the brake pedal and the bulk head to 9.882-10.236 inches.
9. Adjust the extended visible length of the brake light switch head (plunger) to 0.197-0.237 inch.

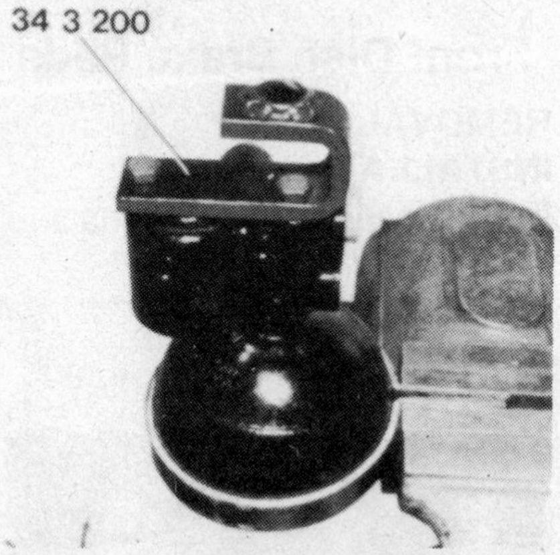

Removing the pressure control regulator

Hydraulic Accumulator

REMOVAL AND INSTALLATION

733i

1. Release the pressure in the hydraulic accumulator by operating the brake pedal (with the engine not running) with a force equivalent to that necessary to bring the vehicle to a full and complete stop.
2. Disconnect the electrical lead at the indicator switch.
3. Disconnect the hydraulic fluid lines from the pressure control regulator:

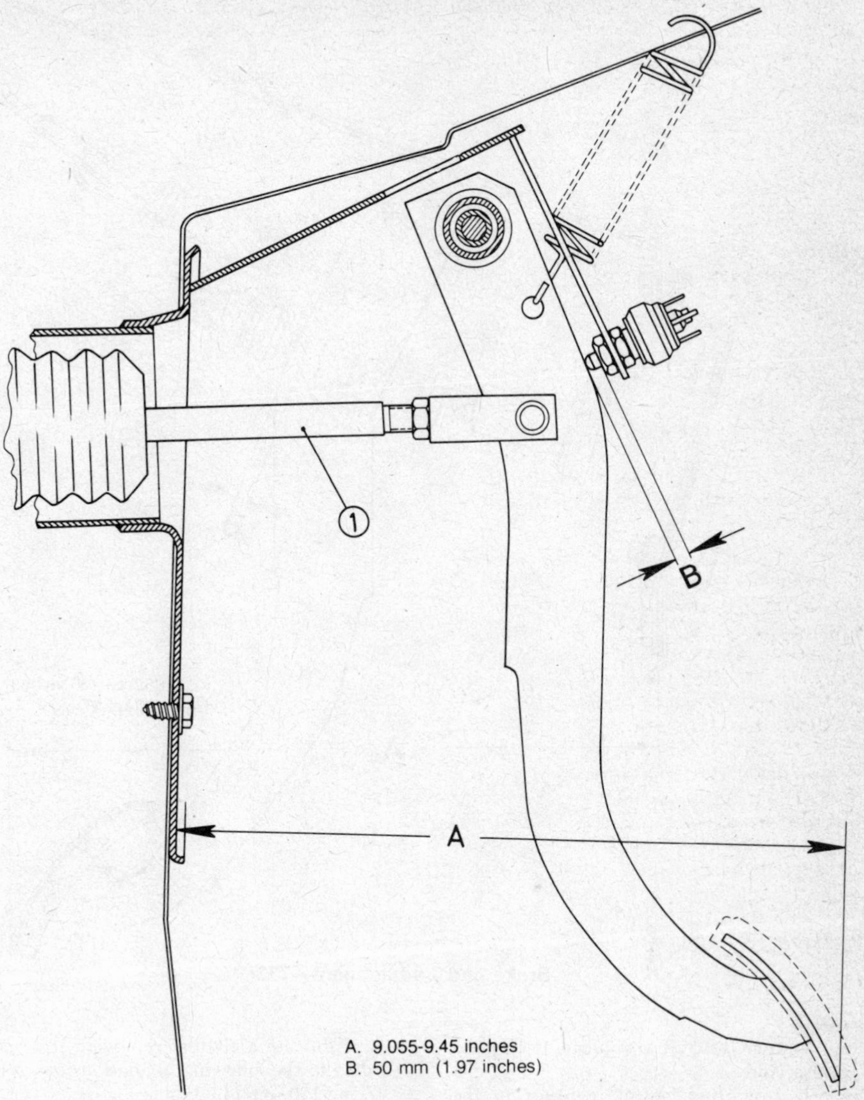

A. 9.055-9.45 inches
B. 50 mm (1.97 inches)

Brake pedal adjustment 530i, 630i, and 633i

1. From the control regulator to the fluid reservoir
2. From the control regulator to the power steering gear box
3. From the control regulator to the power steering pump
4. From the control regulator to the power brake booster

Pressure control regulator—733i

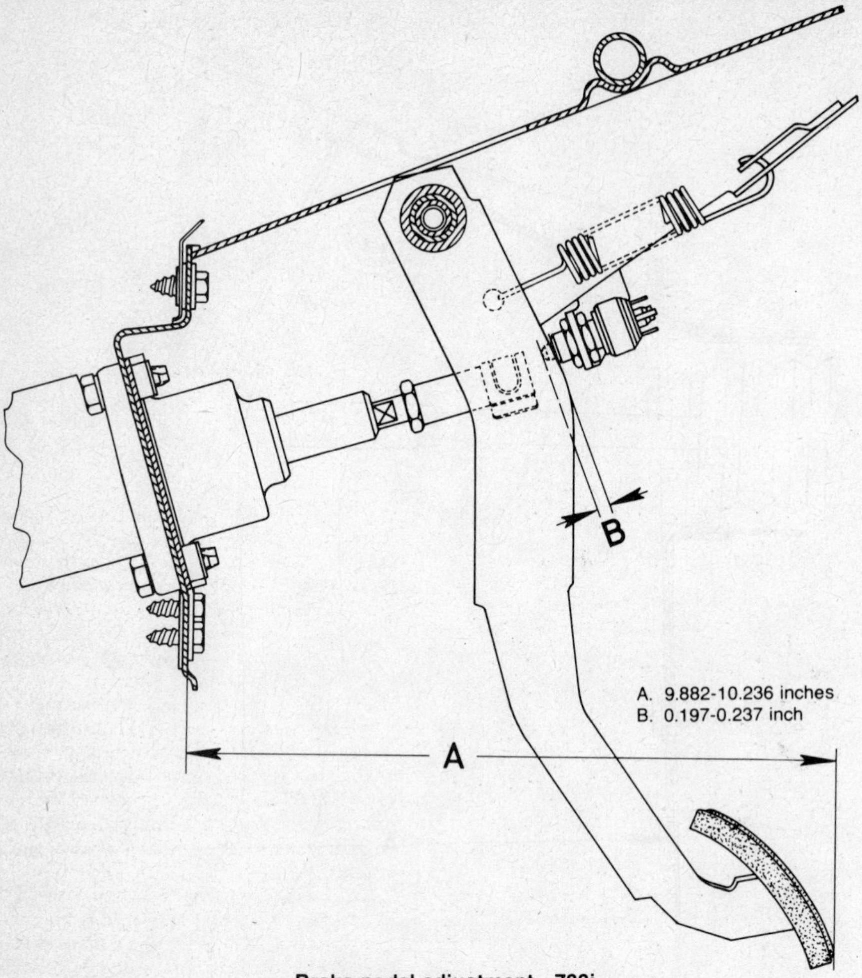

Brake pedal adjustment—733i

a. from the control regulator to the fluid reservoir.

b. from the control regulator to the power steering gear box.

c. from the control regulator to the power steering pump.

d. from the control regulator to the power brake booster.

4. Fabricate a circular removing strap according to the following dimensions:

   a. 110 mm (4.33 inches)
   b. 50 mm (1.97 inches)
   c. 5 mm (0.197 inch)

5. Place the removing strap around the accumulator and clamp the ends of the strap in a vise, thereby locking the accumulator, so as to prevent the accumulator from turning when torque is applied to the pressure control regulator.

6. Install BMW special tool 34-3-200 or an equivalent removing device directly on the pressure control regulator, and turn the regulator free from the accumulator.

7. Install in the reverse order of removal.

CAUTION

When connecting the fluid lines to the pressure control regulator be certain that all lines are clean and free from dirt. The presence of foreign particles trapped in the fluid circuit can seriously impair the functioning of the pressure control regulator, thereby causing failure of power assistance to the steering and brake systems.

8. Fill the fluid reservoir with type A power steering fluid to a level approximately ⅜ inch below the top edge of the reservoir. Start the engine; and, while the engine is running, add fluid to the reservoir, if necessary, in order to maintain the level at the full mark.

9. Turn the steering wheel from stop to stop, until air bubbles stop rising in the reservoir.

10. Stop the engine.

11. Operate the brake pedal until the fluid level in the reservoir stops rising, or until there is noticeable resistance at the brake pedal.

12. Check the fluid level in the reservoir. Correct the level to approximately ⅜ inch below the top edge of the reservoir.

Front Disc Brake Pads

REMOVAL AND INSTALLATION

2002, 2002tii, 320i, 530i, 3.0S and 3.0Si

1. Support the front of the vehicle in a raised position.
2. Remove the front wheels.

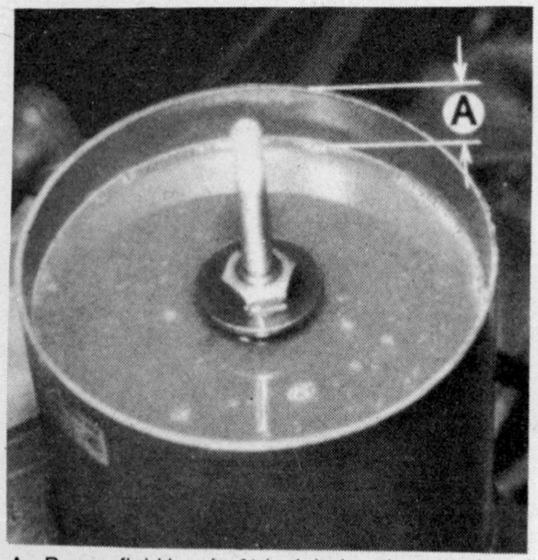

A. Proper fluid level—⅜ inch below the top edge of the reservoir

Power steering/brakes fluid reservoir—733i

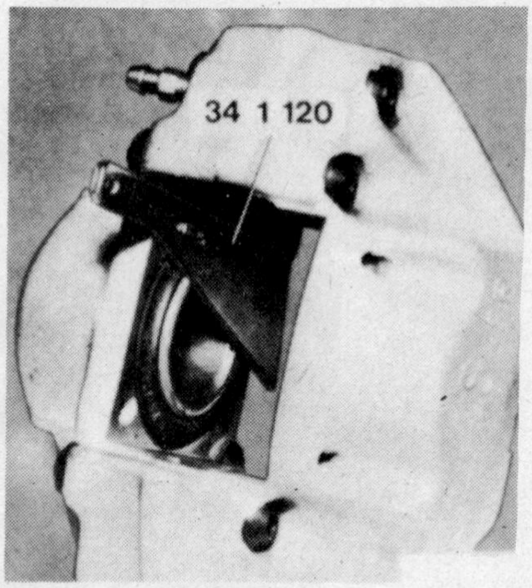

Checking the 20 degree position of the caliper—320i

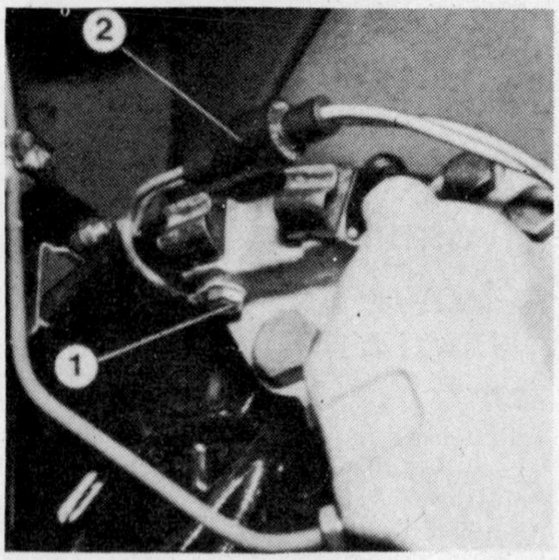

1. Ground wire
2. Connector

Location of the electrical connector for pad wear indicator

3. Drive the support pins out of the calipers.
4. Remove the cross-springs (anti-rattle spreader springs). Note the correct position of the cross-spring prior to removal. Replace if necessary.
5. Attach A BMW special hook tool 34-1-010 or an equivalent pad removal tool to the brake pad, and pull the pad out and away from the caliper.
6. Using a cylindrical brush, clean the pad guide surface of the caliper assembly.
7. Press the caliper piston into the caliper up to the stop with a BMW special tool 34-1-050 or an equivalent tool.
8. Check the 20 degree position of the caliper piston with a BMW special gauge 34-1-000 or an equivalent gauge. The 20 degree stop must face the incoming brake disc (Model 210i).
9. Install in the reverse order of removal.

REMOVAL AND INSTALLATION

630i, 633i and 733i

1. Support the front of the vehicle in a raised position.
2. Remove the front wheels.
3. Disconnect the electrical connector for the pad wear indicator, and pull the wires out of the clamp.
4. Drive the support pins out of the calipers.
5. Remove the cross-springs (anti-rattle spreader springs). Note the correct position of the cross-spring prior to removal. Replace if necessary.
6. Attach a BMW special hook tool 34-1-010 or an equivalent pad removal tool to the brake pad, and pull the pad out and away from the caliper.
7. Using a cylindrical brush, clean the pad guide surface of the caliper assembly.
8. Press the caliper piston into the caliper up to the stop with a BMW special tool 34-1-050 or an equivalent tool.
9. Install in the reverse order of removal.

NOTE: When replacing the front brake pads, be sure to install a new wear indicator in the front left side of the right brake pad.

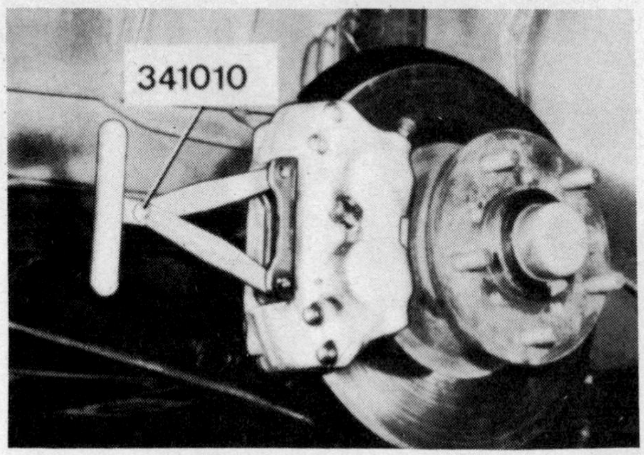

Removing front disc pads

Front Brake Caliper

REMOVAL AND INSTALLATION

All Models

1. Support the front of the vehicle in a raised position, and remove the front wheels.
2. Remove the brake pads.
3. Disconnect the brake lines at the caliper, and cap the lines to prevent brake fluid from escaping.

CAUTION

If fluid appears to be contaminated, discolored, or otherwise unusual in appearance, viscosity, or smell, then allow the fluid to drain from the uncapped brake lines, and flush the system.

4. Remove the caliper to steering knuckle attaching bolts, and remove the caliper.
5. Install in the reverse order of removal.
6. Torque the caliper to steering knuckle attaching bolts to 58-70 ft/lbs.

OVERHAUL (FOUR PISTON)

2002tii, 530i, 630i, 633i, 3.0S and 3.0Si

1. Remove the protective-dust-boot snap-ring and remove the dust boot.
2. Using a BMW special tool 34-1-050 or an equivalent piston pressing device, press one piston into the caliper cylinder to the fully retracted position, and lock into place.
3. Insert a piece of hardwood, plastic, or any material of similar consistency, approximately 0.31 inch thick, between the secured piston and the opposing piston.
4. Apply compressed air through the threaded bare line port and into the circuit which controls the locked piston, thereby forcing the opposed piston out of the cylinder.
5. Remove the piston pressing tool, and plug the open cylinder bore with an Ate sealing plate and clamp or any similar sealing device.
6. Insert the protective block of wood between the remaining piston and the caliper housing, and, again, apply compressed air through the threaded brake line port and into the circuit which controls the remaining piston, thereby forcing the piston out of the cylinder.

CAUTION

Apply compressed air through the circuit which corresponds with the piston to be removed. DO NOT apply compressed air to the other circuit unless the corresponding pistons are protected with the piece of wood previously mentioned.

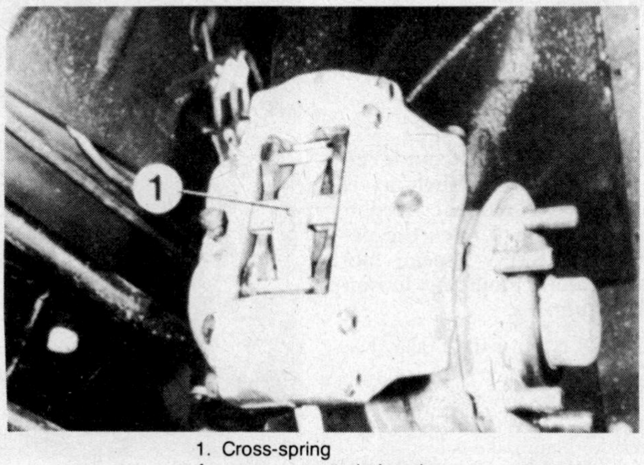

1. Cross-spring
Arrows—support pin location

Removing caliper support pins and cross spring

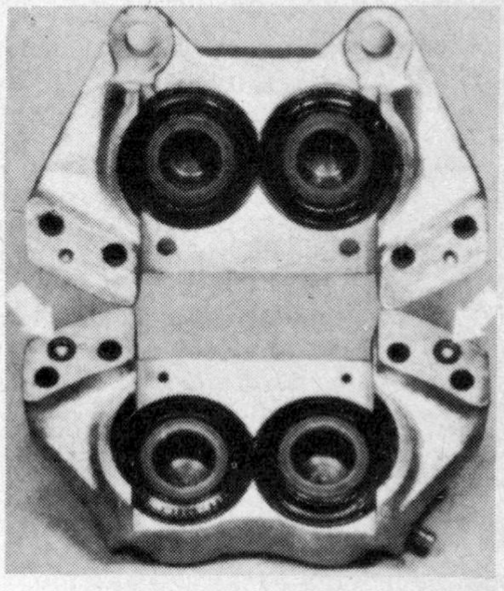

Separated caliper halves—typical

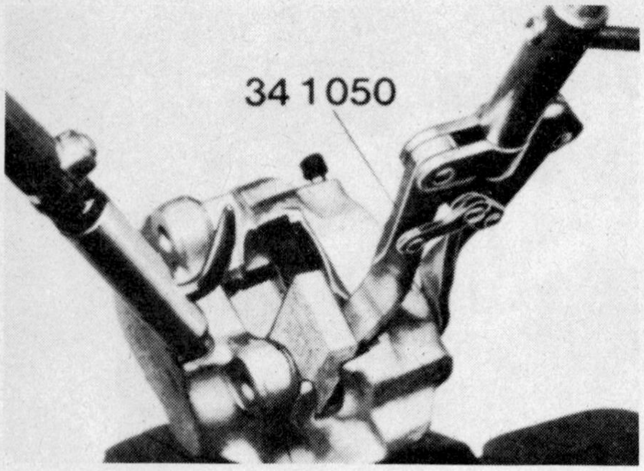

Removing the caliper piston with compressed air

1. Snap-ring
2. Dust boot

Removing dust boot and snap-ring from caliper piston

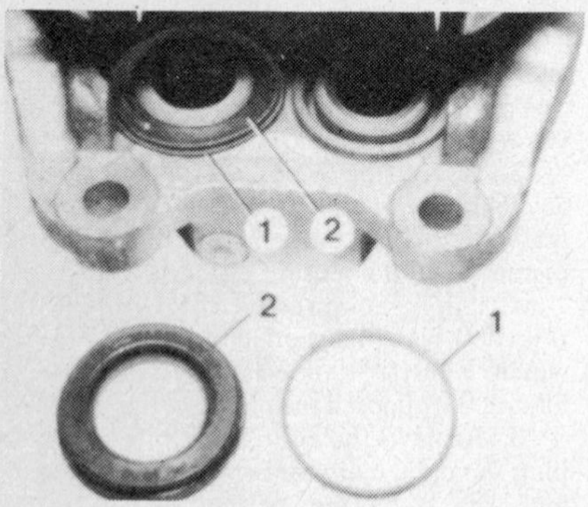

1. Snap-ring
2. Dust boot

Piston dust boot and snap-ring removed—733i

7. Repeat Steps 2 through 6 for the remaining pistons.
8. Carefully remove the piston O-ring.
9. Examine the pistons and cylinder bores for a scoring or binding condition. Replace if necessary.

NOTE: The manufacturer specifically advises against machining either the piston or the cylinder bore. The recommended extent of overhaul should include only the examination of parts and/or the replacement of the dust boot and piston O-ring.

The caliper halves should not be separated. An exception to this would be a problem involving a piston which is jammed in the cylinder bore. In this case it may be necessary to separate the cylinder halves in order to free the piston from the cylinder bore.

10. Lubricate the piston, cylinder wall, and piston O-ring with brake fluid prior to assembly.
11. Assemble in the reverse order of disassembly.
12. Adjust the 20 degree position of the caliper piston with a BMW special gauge 34-1-000 or an equivalent gauge. The 20 degree step must face the incoming brake disc.

OVERHAUL

733i

The procedure for overhauling the four piston caliper on the 733 model is the same in all respects as the procedure for overhauling the four piston caliper on the 2002, 2002i, etc., models with one major distinction. There is only one brake line to the caliper which attaches to a single line port as opposed to two brake lines with two brake line ports on the 2002 models. Because of the dual circuit arrangement on the 2002 models it is possible to isolate two of the four pistons, thus facilitating piston removal. The circuits to the pistons on the 733 model can not be isolated, and it is for this reason that it is easier to remove two pistons at a time.

Instead of locking only one piston, two pistons (side by side) are locked into position in the cylinder bores, while the two opposed pistons are removed. A special sealing plate will be needed to seal the two open cylinder bores. Proceed as though overhauling a model 2002 four piston caliper.

OVERHAUL

320i

The caliper used on the Model 320i is similar in construction to the standard four piston caliper, however, it is comprised of only two pistons. Proceed as though overhauling a four piston caliper.

Rear Drum Brakes

REMOVAL AND INSTALLATION

2002, 2002tii, 320i, 3.0S and 3.0Si

1. Support the rear of the vehicle in a raised position.
2. Remove the brake drum.

NOTE: If difficulty is encountered while removing the drum, such as is caused by excessive wear of the friction surface of the drum, turn back the eccentric nut using a BMW special tool 6038 or an equivalent tool, and loosen the handbrake cable.

3. Disconnect and remove the brake shoe spring.
4. Pull the brake shoes out and away from the wheel cylinders.
5. Disconnect the handbrake cable.
6. Remove the brake shoes.
7. Install in the reverse order of removal.

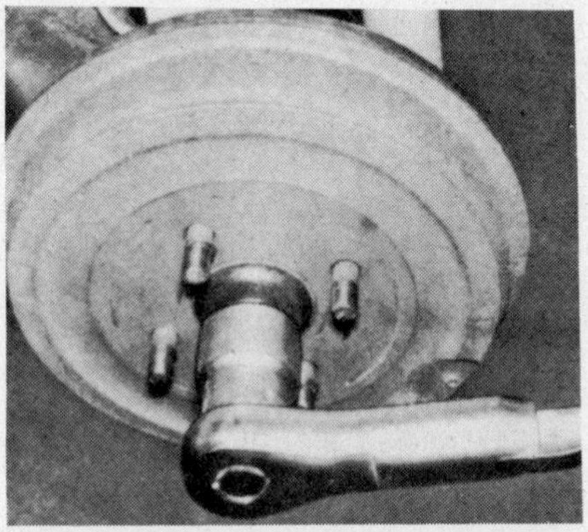

Remove brake drum—4 cylinder models

Location of eccentrics for brake adjustment on drum brakes

Adjustment eccentrics turned to outside position

Location of eccentric adjustment nut—2002 series

1. Cylinder
2. Spring
3. Piston seals
4. Pistons
5. Dust caps
6. Bleeder valve
7. Dust cap

Typical wheel cylinder

NOTE: Be certain that the brake shoe spring is located behind the support plate.

Connect the long end of the handbrake spring between the handbrake actuator and brake shoe.

Rear Disc Brake Pads

REMOVAL AND INSTALLATION

530i, 3.0S and 3.0Si (Models 630i, 633i, and 733i Similar)

1. Support the rear of the vehicle in a raised position, and remove the rear wheels.
2. Drive out the retaining pins.
3. Remove the cross springs (anti-rattle clips).
4. Using a BMW special hook tool 34-1-010 or an equivalent tool, pull the pads out and away from the caliper.
5. Using a BMW special tool 34-1-050, press the piston into the caliper to the fully retracted position.
6. Check the 20 degree position of the caliper piston with a BMW special gauge 34-1-000 or an equivalent gauge. The 20 degree step must face the incoming brake disc.
7. Install the new brake pads in the reverse order of removal.

NOTE: On 630i, 633i, and 733i models be sure to install a new brake pad wear indicator in the left brake pad on the right side rear brake.

Rear Wheel Cylinder

REMOVAL AND INSTALLATION

2002, 2002i, 320i, 3.0S and 3.0Si

1. Remove the rear brake drum.
2. Loosen the wheel cylinder bleeder screw. DO NOT remove the bleeder screw.
3. Disconnect the brake line from the wheel cylinder.
4. Turn the brake shoe adjusting cams as far to the outside as possible.
5. Remove the wheel cylinder attaching bolts, and remove the wheel cylinder.
6. Install in the reverse order of removal.

OVERHAUL

The wheel cylinders are overhauled in the conventional manner.

Rear Brake Caliper

The rear disc brake system is similar in design and function to the front disc brake system. Refer to the removal/installation and overhaul procedures for front disc brakes.

Parking Brake (Vehicles Equipped with Rear Disc Brakes)

REMOVAL AND INSTALLATION

530i, 630i, 633i, 733i, 3.0S and 3.0Si

1. Remove the rear caliper.
2. Remove the rear brake disc.
3. Remove the bottom return spring.
4. Using BMW special tool 34-4-000, turn the retaining springs 90 degrees, and remove the springs.
5. Pull the brake shoes apart at the bottom, and lift them out.
6. Install the new brake shoes in the reverse order of removal.

Parking Brake

ADJUSTMENT

Vehicles Equipped with Rear Drum Brakes

1. Support the rear of the vehicle in a raised position.
2. Fully release the handbrake.
3. While rotating the tire and wheel assembly, turn the left hand eccentric adjustment nut counterclockwise and the right-hand eccentric adjustment nut clockwise until the brake shoes are tight against the drum and the wheel will no longer rotate.
4. Loosen the eccentric nuts by ⅛ of a turn, so that the wheel is just able to turn.
5. Push up the rubber sleeve on the handbrake lever until the locknut is visible.
6. Loosen the locknut.
7. Pull up on the handbrake lever for a distance of five notches. Measure the distance between the middle of the handle and propeller shaft tunnel. This distance should be approximately 4.5± 0.2 inches.
8. Tighten the adjustment nut until the wheels are locked, and retighten the locknut.
9. Release the handbrake. Make sure that the wheels turn freely when the handbrake is released.

Vehicles Equipped with Rear Disc Brakes

The procedure for adjusting the handbrake on vehicles equipped with rear disc brakes is

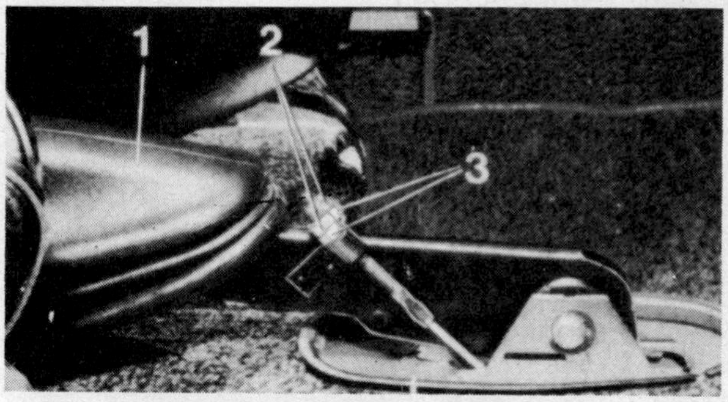

1. Rubber boot
2. Locknut
3. Adjustment nut

Handbrake assembly

similar to the procedure for adjusting the handbrake on vehicles equipped with rear drum brakes with one exception.

The mechanism for adjusting the brake shoes is a star-wheel type adjuster. Insert a screwdriver through the 0.6 inch hole, and turn the adjusting star-wheel until the brake disc can no longer be moved. Proceed as though adjusting the handbrake on vehicles equipped with rear drum brakes.

CHASSIS ELECTRICAL

Heater Assembly

REMOVAL AND INSTALLATION

2002 and 2002tii (320i similar)

1. Disconnect the battery ground.
2. Move the selector lever to the WARM position.
3. Drain the cooling system.
4. Loosen the hose clamp, and remove the heater core return hose.
5. Disconnect the heater hose between the hot water control valve and the engine.
6. Remove the package tray.
7. Remove outer tube casing.
8. Remove the lower center trim panel.
9. Remove the left side outer trim panel.
10. Remove the upper section of the steering tube casing.
11. Remove the heater control knobs.
12. Remove the heater control trim panel.
13. Remove the right side trim panel.
14. Disconnect the heater electrical lead.
15. Remove the heater housing retaining nuts.
16. Disconnect the left side distribution duct, and move the steering tube outer casing retaining bracket out of the way.
17. Remove the glove box lower trim panel.
18. Disconnect the left side distribution duct, and lift out the heater housing.
19. Remove the housing rivets.
20. Remove the housing clamps, and separate the housing halves.
21. Disconnect the bowden cable from the hot water control valve.
22. Remove the hot water control valve and hose from the water valve bracket on the heater housing.
23. Remove the rubber sleeves from the heater core inlet and outlet tubes.
24. Disconnect the electrical leads at the blower motor.
25. Disconnect the electrical leads at the blower resistor in the heater housing.
26. Open the blower motor support clamps, and remove the blower motor and fan as an assembly.
27. Install in the reverse order of removal.
28. Check operation of the heater controls. Adjust if necessary.

REMOVAL AND INSTALLATION

530i (630i and 633i similar)

1. Remove the center tray.
2. Remove the glove box.
3. Disconnect the battery ground.
4. Push the selector lever to the WARM position.
5. Drain the coolant.
6. Disconnect the heater hoses from the heater core, and remove the rubber seal.
7. Remove the lower instrument panel center trim.
8. Disconnect the heater controls at the instrument panel.
9. Disconnect the control shafts at the joints.
10. Disconnect the multiple electrical connector at the heater.
11. Remove the instrument panel center cover.
12. Working from inside the engine compartment, remove the upper section of the fire shield.
13. Remove the heater assembly retaining nuts, and lift out the heater.
14. Open the heater housing clips, and separate the housing halves.
15. Disconnect the electrical leads at the blower motor, and remove the motor.
16. Install in the reverse order of removal.

Heater assembly—530i

REMOVAL AND INSTALLATION

733i

1. Drain the coolant from the system.
2. Discharge the refrigerant from the air conditioner.
3. Remove the instrument trim panel.
4. Remove the cowl fresh air grille.
5. Remove the heater assembly cover attaching screws, and remove the cover.
6. Disconnect the heater hoses at the heater core.
7. Disconnect the vacuum lines at the heater.
8. Bend open the heater duct mounting clamp.
9. Disconnect the central electrical lead.
10. Pull the duct cover downward, and remove it.
11. Remove the center strut attaching bolts (4).
2. Remove the insulation from the refrigerant lines.
13. Disconnect the refrigerant lines from the evaporator.
14. Disconnect the evaporator drain tube.
15. Remove the heater assembly retaining bolts, and remove the heater.
16. Install in the reverse order of removal.

REMOVAL AND INSTALLATION

3.0S and 3.0Si

1. Drain the coolant from the system.
2. Disconnect the heater hoses from the heater core, and remove the rubber seal.
3. Remove the fresh air outlet grille cover.

Coupe only:

a. Remove the heater control cover.
b. Disconnect the air distribution hoses from the discharge nozzles.
c. Remove the intermediate distribution duct.

4. Remove the buttons from the control levers.
5. Remove the threaded knobs for the left instrument panel trim strip.
6. Remove the rear switch plate.
7. Remove the front switch plate.
8. Remove the heater retaining nuts.
9. Tilt the heater and switch plate inwards, and remove the heater.
10. Remove the heater cover plate.
11. Remove the blower motor mesh grid.
12. Disconnect the electrical leads at the blower motor.
13. Remove the blower motor attaching screws, and lift out the blower motor.
14. Remove the blower motor-to-mounting retaining clips, and remove the blower motor and fan assembly.
15. Install in the reverse order of removal.

Radio

REMOVAL AND INSTALLATION

3.0 and 2002

1. Disconnect negative battery terminal.
2. Remove screws from both sides of the radio housing. On model 2002 remove the lower steering column shroud.
3. Detach antenna wire, ground wire, speaker wire and radio power source.
4. Installation is the reverse of removal.

Windshield Wiper Motor

The electric wiper motor assembly is located under the engine hood, at the top of the cowl panel. A few models have covers over the wiper motor assembly, while others have the motors exposed. Link rods operate the left and right wiper pivot assemblies from a drive crank bolted to the wiper motor output shaft.

REMOVAL AND INSTALLATION

2002

1. Remove the drive crank retaining nut and washer.
2. Remove the wiper motor retaining screws.
3. Remove the electrical connector and remove the wiper motor from the vehicle.
4. The installation is in the reverse of the removal procedure.

3.0

1. Remove the cover for the heater unit on the cowl panel (except coupes).
2. Remove the crank arm retaining nut and washer.
3. Remove the wiper motor retaining screws, tilt the motor downward and remove.
4. Disconnect the electrical contact plug from the wiper motor.
5. The installation is in the reverse of the removal procedure.

NOTE: The complete wiper motor, pivot assemblies and linkage can be removed as a unit, if necessary.

320i, 530i, 630i and 63i

1. Remove the cowl cover to expose the wiper motor (320i and 530i).
2. Disconnect the wiper motor crank arm from the motor output shaft.
3. Remove the motor retaining screws and disconnect the electrical connector.
4. Remove the wiper motor from the vehicle.
5. Reverse the procedure to install the motor.

733i

1. Remove the cowl fresh air intake grill and tilt rearward.
2. Remove the cover from the windshield wiper motor and remove the electrical plugs.
3. Remove the left and right wiper arms. Loosen the left and right pivot bearings.
4. Turn the rubber pad at the motor, counterclockwise and disconnect the right wiper linkage.
5. Remove the motor bracket retaining screws. Separate the spacers and remove the wiper motor assembly.

NOTE: Do not lose the shims.

6. The wiper motor can be removed from the bracket after the removal.
7. Reverse the removal procedure to install.

Windshield Wiper Switch

All Models

The wiper switch is located on the steering column and in most cases the steering wheel will have to be removed, along with the lower steering column trim panels, to gain access to the switch.

After the retaining screws and electrical connectors are removed, the switch can be lifted from the plate of the steering column.

CAUTION

To avoid possible electrical short-circuits, the negative battery cable should be removed before the repairs are attempted.

Windshield Washer Motor

The windshield washer motor is attached to the washer reservoir and controlled from the wiper switch. A double motor is present on some models to pump the washer solution to both the windshield washers and to the headlamp cleaners.

To remove the washer pump, the reservoir should be removed from the vehicle to avoid damage to the reservoir.

A delaying relay is used on some models, to control the spraying of the washer solution for a period of five seconds, stop briefly and then recycle.

Ignition Switch

REMOVAL AND INSTALLATION

2002

1. Disconnect the negative battery cable.
2. Remove the lower center fascia trim panel.
3. Turn the ignition switch to the "HALT" (stop) position.
4. Remove the machine screws from the ignition/starter switch and disconnect the electrical leads.
5. Remove the switch from the steering column side bracket.
6. Reverse the removal procedure to install the switch. During the installation, the arrow must point to the ball with the switch in the "HALT" (stop) position and the locating lug in the slot of the steering lock.

3.0, 320i, 530i, 630i, 633i and 733i

1. Remove the negative battery cable.
2. Remove the lower steering housing cover.
3. Remove the left lower center instrument trim panel, if necessary.
4. Align the switch to housing marks, remove the switch retaining screw and pull the switch outward and away from the steering column.
5. Disconnect the electrical wiring connectors.
6. Reverse the removal procedure to install the ignition switch. Be sure the marks are aligned.

Instrument Cluster

REMOVAL AND INSTALLATION

2002

1. Disconnect the negative battery cable.
2. Remove the lower steering column trim panel.
3. Remove the lower center instrument trim panel.
4. Remove the knurled nuts from the rear of the instrument cluster.
5. Disconnect the speedometer cable from the cluster.
6. Remove the cluster from the dash and remove the wire connector plug.
7. The installation is in the reverse of the removal procedure.

3.0

1. Disconnect the negative battery cable.
2. Remove the instrument panel trim cover.
3. Remove the radio speaker grill and unscrew the cluster retaining screw.
4. Remove the speedometer cable and remove the electrical wire connectors.
5. Remove the instrument cluster from the dash.
6. Reverse the removal procedure to install the cluster.

320i

1. Disconnect the negative battery cable.
2. Remove the steering wheel assembly.

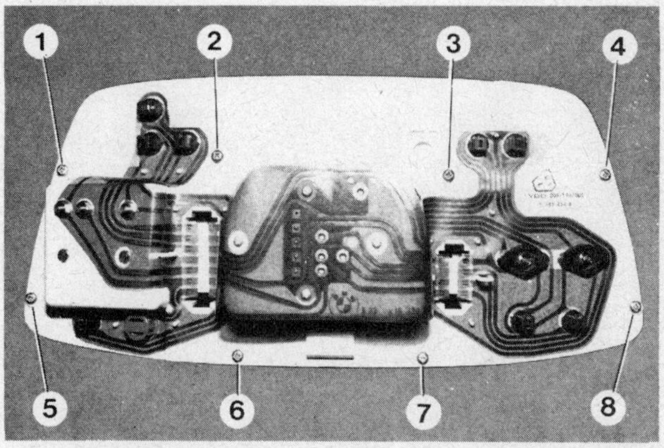

Typical instrument panel removal and installation numbers indicate screw locations

3. Remove the bottom center instrument trim panel.
4. Disconnect the speedometer cable, loosen the knurled nut and pull the instrument assembly outward.
5. Remove the electrical plugs and wires.
6. Remove the instrument cluster from the dash.
7. Reverse the removal procedure to install.

530i

1. Remove the negative battery cable.
2. Remove the lower instrument trim panel.
3. Disconnect the speedometer cable.
4. Loosen the knurled nuts on the cluster back.
5. Loosen the steering column to dash screws.
6. Pull the instrument cluster outward and remove the electrical wires and connectors.
7. Remove the cluster from the dash panel.
8. Reverse the removal procedure to install the cluster.

630i and 633i

1. Disconnect the negative battery cable.
2. Remove the steering wheel assembly.
3. Remove the bottom center instrument trim panel.
4. Remove the cover from the "INQUIRY" unit.
5. Remove the three retaining screws and remove the "INQUIRY" printed circuit board.
6. Remove the light switch, leaving the wiring connected.
7. Remove the left air control knob and remove the bezel cover.
8. Remove the fog lamp switch and leave the wiring attached.
9. Remove the screws from the instrument cluster and loosen the steering column control base screws.
10. Disconnect the speedometer cable.
11. Push downward on the upper section casing and the steering column, so that the instrument cluster can be removed at an angle. Disconnect the electrical wiring and connectors.
12. Reverse the removal procedure to install the instrument cluster.

733i

1. Remove the negative battery cable from the battery post.
2. Remove the instrument panel trim section at the left bottom of the dash.
3. Remove the upper bezel retaining screws.
4. Loosen the steering column control and pull the steering housing all the way out.
5. Pull the instrument cluster outward, remove the electrical wires and plugs, after removal of the speedometer cable.
6. Turn the cluster assembly towards the right rear and pull it away from the dash.
7. The installation is in the reverse of the removal procedure.

Fuse Box Locations

The fuse box is located behind the left glove box door on the model 3.0 and under the engine hood on the left side, near the upper strut housing or near the battery, on the remaining models.

Various relays are also mounted on the fuse box for easy accessibility.

SPECIFICATIONS

INDEX

BEFORE SERVICING, SEE THE SAFETY NOTICE ON THE CONTENTS PAGE

INTRODUCTION

The Capri, imported from 1970 through 1978, is a product of Ford of Europe. There are two basic Capri body styles. The first was made through 1974. The 1974 models were sold through the 1975 model year; there was no 1975 model. The Capri II was introduced in 1976. The 1977 model was sold through the 1978 model year; there was no 1978 model. Importation was stopped after 1978.

SERIAL NUMBER IDENTIFICATION

Engine

NOTE: Engine type can be determined by using the Vehicle Identification Plate.

Engine Identification

No. of Cyl.	Displace. (cc)	Type	Engine Model Code
4	2000	OHC	NB, NA, N
4	2300	OHC	YA
6	2600	OHV	UX
6	2800	OHV	PX

VEHICLE IDENTIFICATION PLATE

The vehicle identification plate is located on the right-side front fender apron in the engine compartment. This plate gives details of the engine, axle, body and transmission. The vehicle identification number is also visible through the driver's side of the windshield.

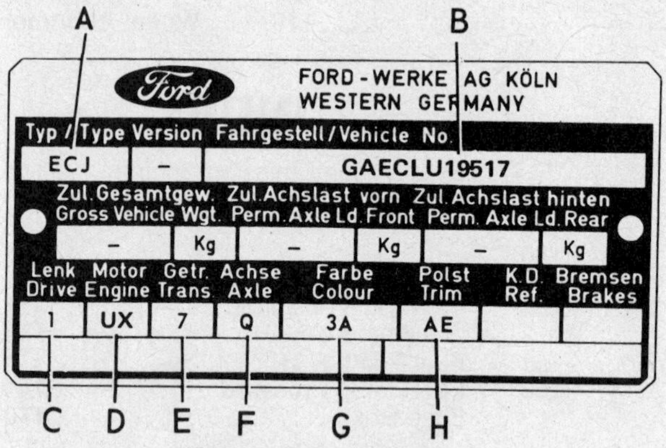

1975 Vehicle I.D. plate

A) Body Type
ECJ—Tudor Coupe

B) Vehicle Number
consists of eleven symbols
G A E C K U 78175
1) G—assembled in Germany
2) A—denotes Cologne Plant
B—denotes Genk Plant
3) model type (EC-Capri)
4) year and month of manufacture, first letter—year, second—month: L-1971, M-1972, K-1973, P-1974
5) serial number

C) Drive code
1—left hand drive

D) Engine code
L1. L4—1600 cc
NB, NA, N—2000 cc
UX—2600 cc
P—2800 cc

E) Transmission code
5, B—manual shift
7, C—automatic

F) Rear Axle Code
V, C—3.89:1
Q, S—3.44:1
R—3.22:1

G) Paint code
1—Sapphire Metallic
3—Silver Fox Metallic
6—Evergreen Metallic
7—Tawny Metallic
J—Sunset
T—Yellow
B—Ermine White
A—Vinyl Roof Black

H) Trim code
AE—Black
FE—Marquis Blue
JE—Tan
KE—Parchment

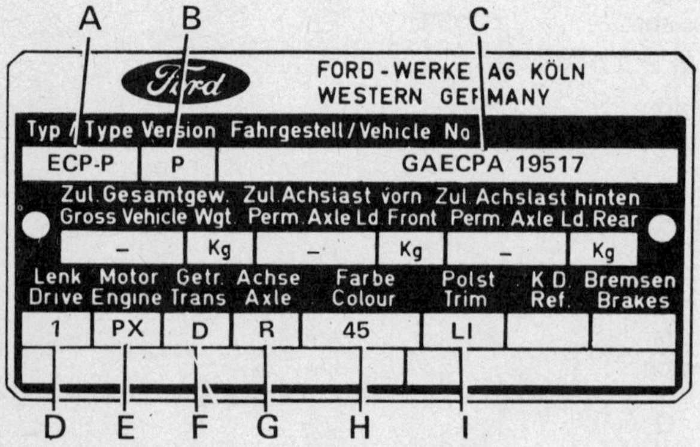

1976-77 Vehicle I.D. plate

A. Body Type
ECP—three door hatchback

B. Version
P—decor option
D—standard
T—Ghia

C. Vehicle number
GAECPA19517
G—built in Germany
A—Cologne assembly plant
EC—model type
PA—assembly code
first letter—year; second letter—month
Sequence number—a five digit code ranging from 00001-99999

D. Drive code
I—left hand drive

E. Engine code
YA-2300
PX-2800

F. Transmission code
B—4sp.
D—automatic

G. Rear axle code
S—3.44:1
R—3.22:1
L—3.09:1

H. Paint code
B5—White 691
T5—Yellow 779
J5—Orange 913
05—Dk. red 979
35—Silver met. 888
45—Bronze met. 884B
15—Med. blue met. 859
55—Lt. green met. 924

I. Trim code
AA—black vinyl
LA—saddle vinyl
KA—lt. tan vinyl
AI—black cloth
LI—saddle cloth
KI—lt. tan cloth

GENERAL ENGINE SPECIFICATIONS

Year/ Model	Engine Displacement cu. in. (cc)	Carburetor Type	Horsepower @ rpm	Torque @ rpm (ft. lbs.)	Bore x Stroke (in.)	Compression Ratio	Oil Pressure @ rpm (psi)
1975	122 (2000)	Motorcraft 2V	100 @ 5600	120 @ 3600	3.575 x 3.029	8.2:1	35 @ 1500
1975	170 (2800)	Motorcraft 2V	105 @ 4600	140 @ 3200	3.660 x 2.700	8.2:1	40 @ 1500
Capri II	140 (2300)	Motorcraft 2V	88 @ 5000	116 @ 2600	3.781 x 3.126	8.4:1	50 @ 2000
Capri II	170 (2800)	Motorcraft 2V	105 @ 4600	140 @ 3200	3.660 x 2.700	8.2:1	40 @ 1500

TUNE-UP SPECIFICATIONS

Year/ Model	Engine Displacement (cc)	SPARK PLUGS Type	Gap (in.)	DISTRIBUTOR Point Dwell (deg)	Point Gap (in.)	IGNITION TIMING (deg) ④ MT	AT	Intake Valve Opens (deg)	Fuel Pump Pressure (psi)	Compression Press. (psi)	IDLE SPEED (rpm) MT	AT	VALVE CLEARANCE (in.) ② In	Ex
1975	2000	AGR-32	0.034	37-41	0.025	6B	10B	24B	3½-4½	①	750	650	0.008	0.010
1975	2800	AGR-42	0.034	37-41	0.025	③	③	20B	3½-4½	①	③	③	0.014	0.016
Capri II	2300	③	③	Electronic		③	③	22	3½-4½	①	③	③	—	—
Capri II	2800	③	③	Electronic		③	③	20	3½-4½	①	③	③	0.014	0.016

NOTE: The underhood specifications sticker often reflects tune-up specification changes made in production. Sticker figures must be used if they disagree with those in this chart.
① Lowest 75 per cent of the highest
② Cold
③ See engine compartment sticker
④ With the vacuum lines disconnected and plugged
MT Manual transmission
AT Automatic transmission
—Not applicable

FIRING ORDERS

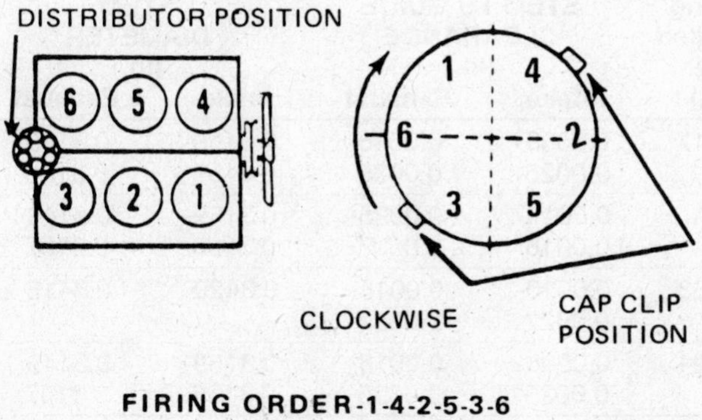

V6 engine

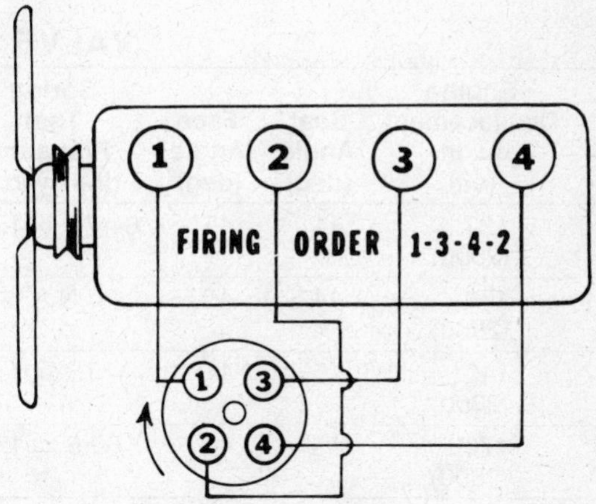

2000 cc engine

FIRING ORDER

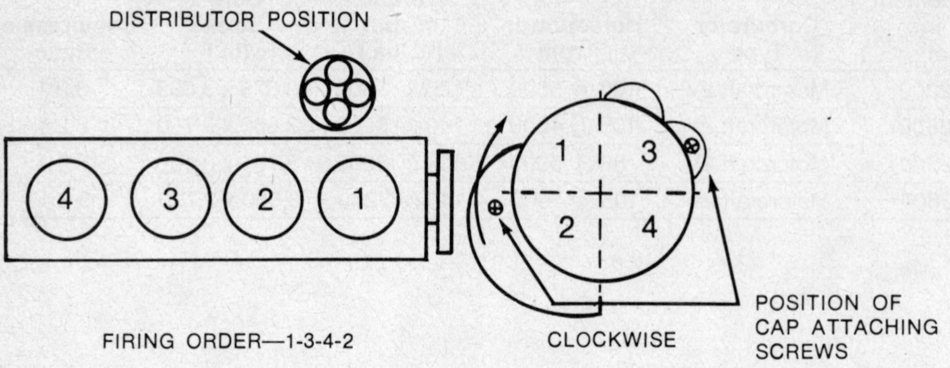

2300 cc engine

CAPACITIES

Year/ Model		Engine Crankcase Refill After Draining (qt) With filter	Engine Crankcase Refill After Draining (qt) Without filter	Transmission Refill After Draining (pt) Manual 4 speed	Automatic (total cap.) C3, C4	Automatic (total cap.) Borg Warner	Differential (pt)	Fuel Tank (gal)	Cooling (qt)
1975	2000	4	3.5	2.8	12.5	13.5	2.3	12	8.1
1975	2800	4.5	4	2.8	14.4	13.5	2.3	12	10.8
Capri II	2300	5	4	2.8	16	—	2.3	15	7.6
Capri II	2800	5	4.5	2.8	16	—	2.3	15	8.5

—Not applicable

VALVE SPECIFICATIONS

Year/ Model	Engine Displacement cu. in. (cc)	Seat Angle (deg)	Face Angle (deg)	Spring Test Pressure (lbs @ in.)	Spring Installed Height (in.)	Stem to Guide Clearance (in.) Intake	Stem to Guide Clearance (in.) Exhaust	Stem Diameter (in.) Intake	Stem Diameter (in.) Exhaust
1975	122 (2000)	44	45	64-73 @ 1.417	1.417	0.0008-0.0025	0.0018-0.0035	0.3159-0.3167	0.3149-0.3156
1975	170 (2800)	44.5	45.5	N.A.	N.A.	0.0015-0.0018	0.0025-0.0027	0.3159-0.3166	0.3149-0.3157
Capri II	140 (2300)	45	44	75 @ 1.56	1.563	0.0010-0.0027	0.0015-0.0032	0.3420	0.3415
Capri II	170 (2800)	45	44	66.5 @ 1.59	1.594	0.0008-0.0025	0.0018-0.0035	0.3159-0.3166	0.3149-0.3157

N.A. Not available

CRANKSHAFT AND CONNECTING ROD SPECIFICATIONS

All measurements are given in inches

Year/ Model	Engine Displacement (cu. in.)	CRANKSHAFT Main Brg Journal Dia	Main Brg Oil Clearance	Shaft End-Play	Thrust on No.	CONNECTING ROD Journal Diameter	Oil Clearance	Side Clearance
1975	122 (2000)	2.2432-2.2440	0.0006-0.0016	0.003-0.011	3	2.0464-2.0472	0.0006-0.0026	0.004-0.011
1975	170 (2800)	2.2437-2.2441 ① 2.2433-2.2437 ②	0.0006-0.0019	0.004-0.008	3	2.1256-2.1260 ① 2.1252-2.1256 ②	0.0006-.0021	0.004-0.011
Capri II	140 (2300)	2.3982-2.3990	0.0008-0.0026	0.004-0.008	3	2.0465-2.0472	0.0008-0.0015	0.004-0.011
Capri II	170 (2800)	2.433-2.441	0.0006-0.0019	0.004-0.008	3	2.1252-2.1260	0.0006-0.0021	0.004-0.011

① Red
② Blue

PISTON AND RING SPECIFICATIONS

All measurements in inches

Year/ Model	Engine Displacement Cu. In. (cc)	Piston Clearance	RING GAP Top Compression	Bottom Compression	Oil Control	RING SIDE CLEARANCE Top Compression	Bottom Compression	Oil Control
1975	122 (2000)	0.001-0.002	0.015-0.023	0.015-0.023	0.016-0.055	0.0019-0.0038	0.0019-0.0038	SNUG
1975	170 (2800)	0.001-0.003	0.015-0.023	0.015-0.023	0.015-0.055	0.0020-0.0033	0.0020-0.0033	SNUG
Capri II	140 (2300)	0.001-0.002	0.010-0.020	0.010-0.020	0.015-0.055	0.0020-0.0040	0.0020-0.0040	SNUG
Capri II	170 (2800)	0.0011-0.0019	0.015-0.023	0.015-0.023	0.015-0.055	0.0020-0.0033	0.0020-0.0033	SNUG

TORQUE SPECIFICATIONS

All readings in ft. lbs.

Year/ Model	Engine Displacement Cu. In.	Cylinder Head Bolts	Rod Bearing Bolts	Main Bearing Bolts	Crankshaft Bolt	Flywheel-to-Crankshaft Bolts	MANIFOLDS Intake	Exhaust
1975	122 (2000)	65-80	29-34	65-75	39-43	47-51	12-15	12-15
1975	170 (2800)	65-80	21-25	65-75	31-36	47-52	15-18	15-18
Capri II	140 (2300)	80-90	30-36	80-90	80-114	54-64	14-21	16-23
Capri II	170 (2800)	65-80	21-25	65-75	92-103	47-52	15-18 ①	16-23

① Stud: 10-12

TORQUE SEQUENCES

Cylinder Head

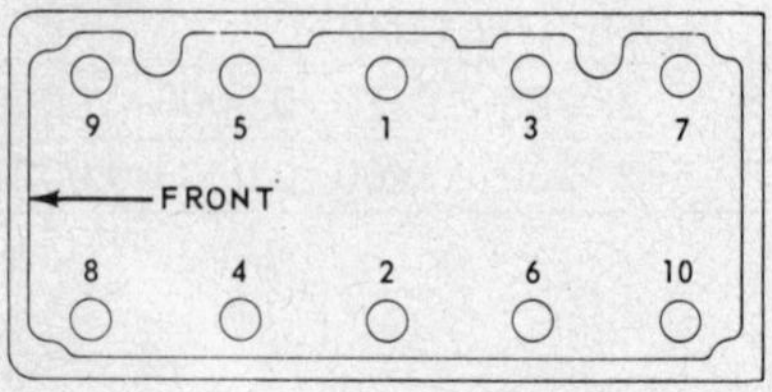

2000 and 2300 cc engines

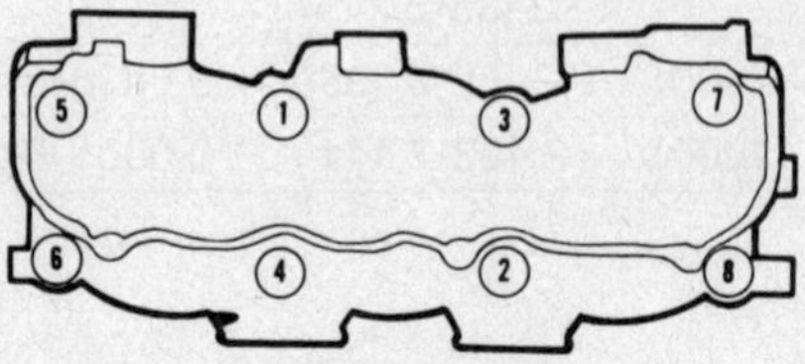

2800 cc engine

Exhaust Manifold

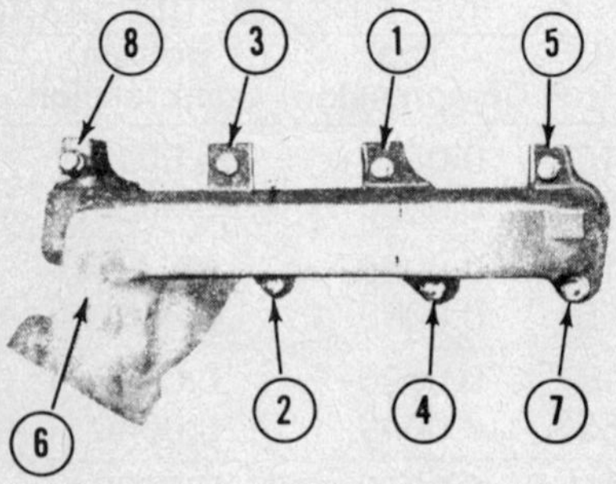

2000 cc engine

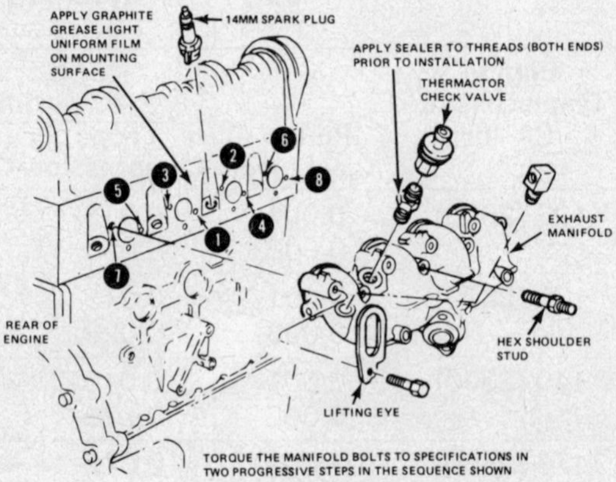

2300 cc engine

Intake Manifold

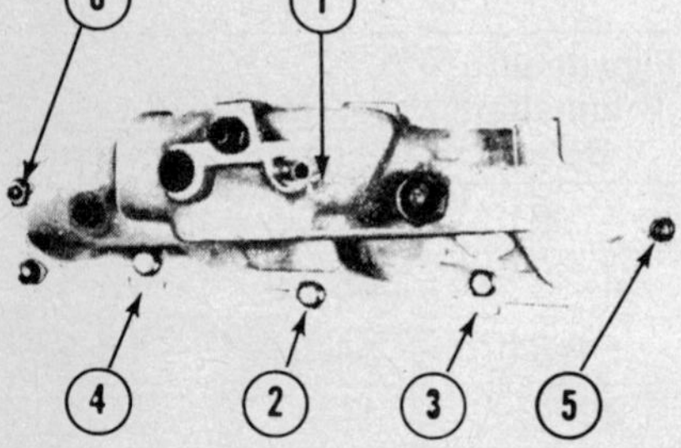

2000 cc engine

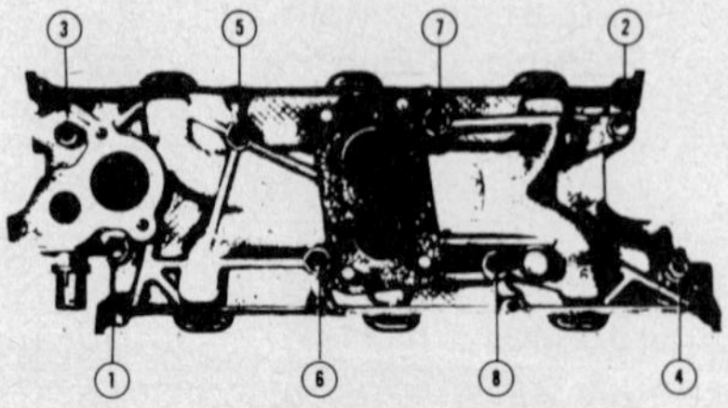

2800 cc engine

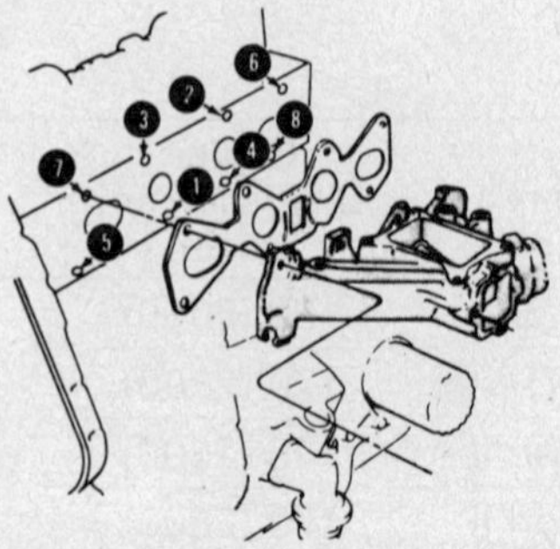

2300 cc engine

ALTERNATOR AND REGULATOR SPECIFICATIONS

		ALTERNATOR			REGULATOR						
						FIELD RELAY			REGULATOR		
Year	Model	Part No. or Manufacturer	Field Current @ 12 v	Output (amps)	Part No. or Manufacturer	Air Gap (in.)	Point Gap (in.)	Volts to Close	Air Gap (in.)	Point Gap (in.)	Volts @ 75°
1975-77	2000, 2800	Bosch K-1	—	35 ①	—	Not adjustable					13.7-14.4

① 55 Amps w/AC

BATTERY AND STARTER SPECIFICATIONS

All cars use 12 volt, negative ground electrical systems

			LOCK TEST			STARTER NO LOAD TEST				
Year	Model	Battery Amp Hour Capacity	Amps	Volts	Torque (ft. lbs.)	Amps	Volts	rpm	Brush Spring Tension (oz)	Min. Brush Length (in.)
1975-77	170 (2800)	66	Not Recommended			54	N.A.	N.A.	42	0.375

BRAKE SPECIFICATIONS

All measures given are (in.) unless noted

				BRAKE DISC		BRAKE DRUM			MINIMUM LINING THICKNESS	
Year	Model	Lug Nut Torque (ft. lb.)	Master Cylinder Bore	Minimum Thickness	Maximum Run-Out	Diameter	Max. Machine O/S	Max. Wear Limit	Front	Rear
1975-77	2000, 2800	50-55 ①	0.813	0.45	0.0035	9.0	9.05	9.06	1/8	1/32 above rivets

NOTE: Minimum lining thickness is as recommended by the manufacturer. Due to variations in state inspection regulations, the minimum allowable thickness may be different than recommended by the manufacturer.
① Aluminum wheels 90-100 ft. lbs.

WHEEL ALIGNMENT

Year	Caster (deg)	Camber (deg)	Toe-In (in)	King Pin Inclination (deg)
1975	½P to 1½P	½N to ½P	0 to 1/4	7½ to 8½
1976-77	1P to 2¼P	¾P to 2¼P	0 to 9/32	7½ to 8½

N Negative
P Positive

TUNE-UP PROCEDURES

Breaker Points and Condenser

The point set and condenser should be replaced as a unit. Whenever the points are adjusted, the ignition timing should be checked since adjusting the points will change the timing.

Release the clips which secure the distributor cap. Remove the cap and the rotor. Inspect the inside of the distributor cap for cracks or excessive wear and also check the rotor for burning or excessive wear.

REMOVAL AND INSTALLATION

When replacing the points and condenser, special care should be taken to prevent dropping any of the attaching screws into the distributor or on the ground. To remove the points and condenser follow this procedure:

1. Remove the screws which retain the points and condenser.
2. Remove the condenser and distributor wires.
3. Remove the points and condenser.
4. Apply a small amount of heat-resistant white grease to the distributor cam.
5. Replace the points and condenser.
6. Replace the screws, being careful not to strip the threads.
7. Replace the condenser and distributor wires.
8. Adjust the points.

BREAKER POINT ADJUSTMENT

Rotate the engine until the rubbing block of the points is on a high point of the distributor cam.

CAUTION

The 2000 cc engine must be rotated only clockwise. Insert the correct size feeler gauge between the contacts and adjust them to the proper gap.

(See "Tune-Up Specifications Chart.")

Slightly loosen the attaching screws, insert a screwdriver in the notch on the breaker plate, and twist the screwdriver to open or close the points to the proper gap. The feeler

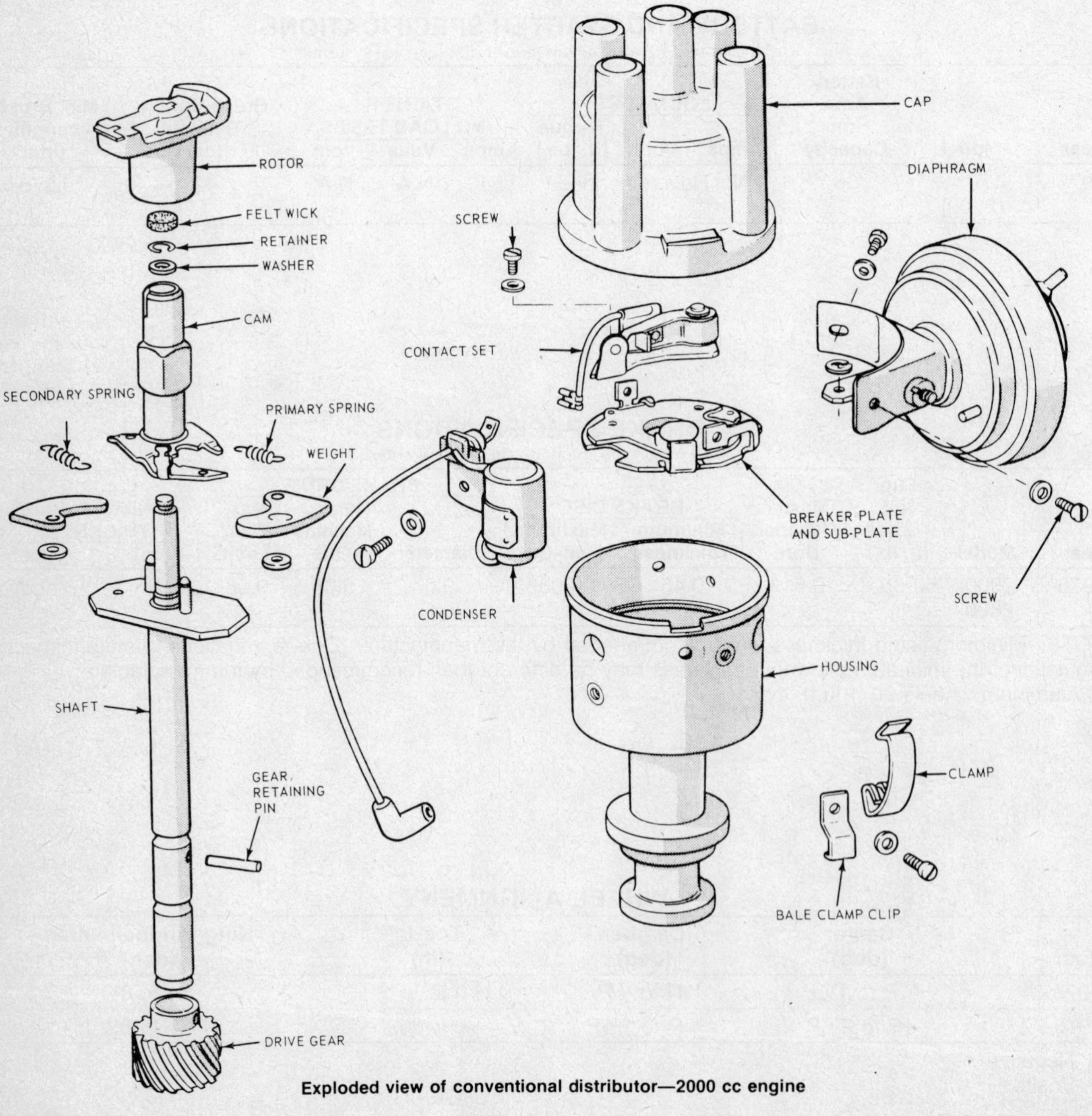

Exploded view of conventional distributor—2000 cc engine

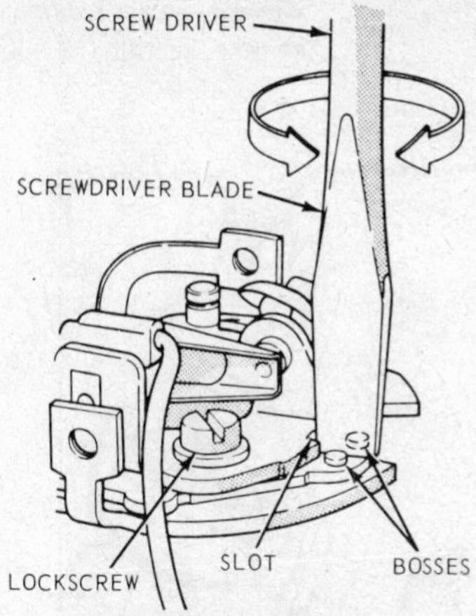

Adjusting the point gap

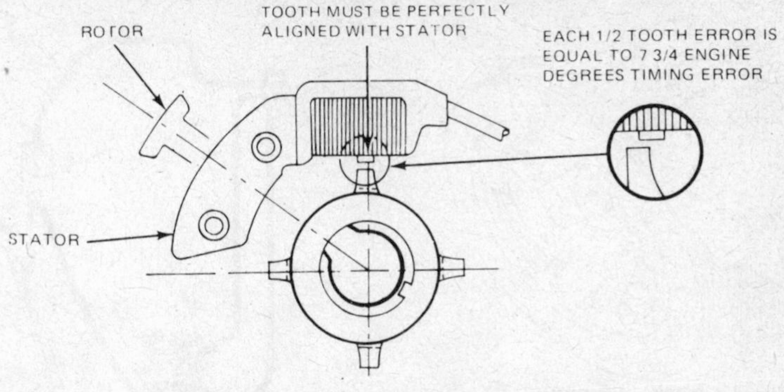

Distributor rotor position for static timing

gauge should have a slight drag on it at the proper gap. Retighten the attaching screws. Replace the rotor, aligning the tab inside the rotor with the notch on the distributor shaft. Replace the distributor cap and snap the retaining clips into place.

Dwell Angle

The dwell angle is the angle that the distributor cam rotates while the breaker points are closed. This is a more precise adjustment than point gap. To adjust the dwell angle, connect a dwell meter between the primary lead (the distributor wire terminal on the coil) and ground. Start the engine and observe the dwell angle on the meter. Refer to the "Tune-up Specifications Chart" for the proper dwell angle. If it is necessary to adjust the angle, adjust it by opening or closing the point gap as previously described. Remove the dwell meter and replace the distributor cap.

Ignition Timing

Set the dwell angle before setting the timing. Disconnect and plug the vacuum lines. Locate the timing mark on the pulley and the pointer on the engine block. Clean the pointer and the timing mark. Mark the correct timing position on the pulley with a piece of chalk or paint. (See the "Tune-up Specifications Chart.") Install a timing light and set the idle at 600 rpm. Loosen the distributor

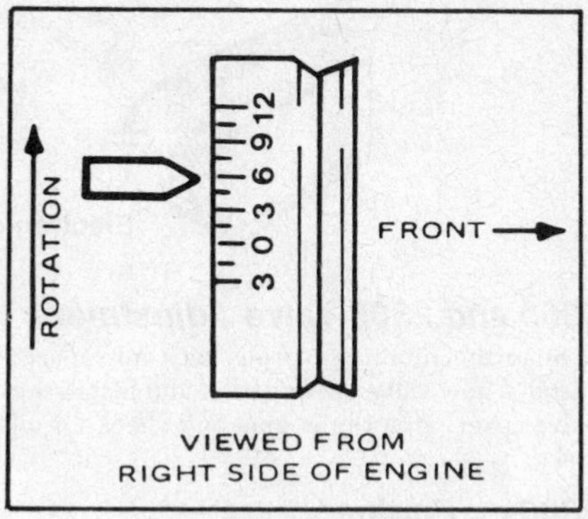

Timing marks 2300 cc engine

locknut at the base of the distributor. Adjust the ignition timing to the proper specifications by turning the distributor. (Align the pointer and the mark.) On the 2000, 2300 and V6 engines, turn the distributor clockwise to advance timing. Make sure that the locknut is retightened and the vacuum lines are reconnected.

BREAKERLESS IGNITION SYSTEM–CAPRI II

There are no points or condenser to replace, and no adjustments to be made other than timing. An occasional check of the rotor and cap contacts for excessive burning and pitting should be performed.

Ignition timing can be performed in the same manner as with older point type systems.

Valve Lash Adjustment

VALVE ARRANGEMENT

2000, 2300 cc Engines

Front
—— E-I-E-I-E-I-E-I

2800 cc Engine

Right Bank I-E-I-E-E-I
Front
——
Left Bank I-E-E-I-E-I

2000 cc Engine

The valves should be set when the engine is cold. Remove the valve cover. Rotate the engine by turning the bolt on the crankshaft pulley clockwise.

CAUTION

Do not turn the pulley counterclockwise; the timing belt may slip and alter the valve timing.

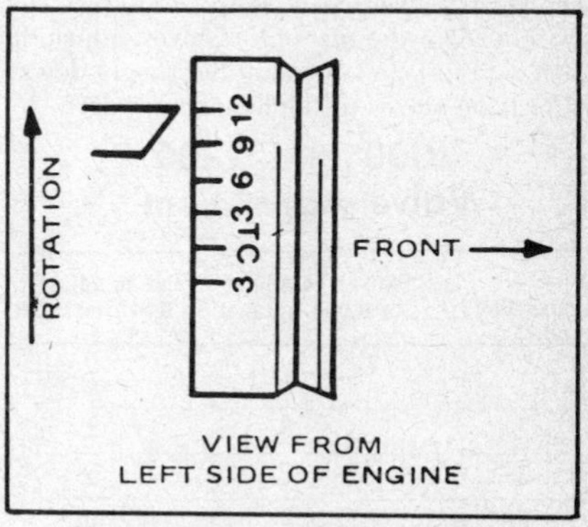

Timing marks—2800 cc engine

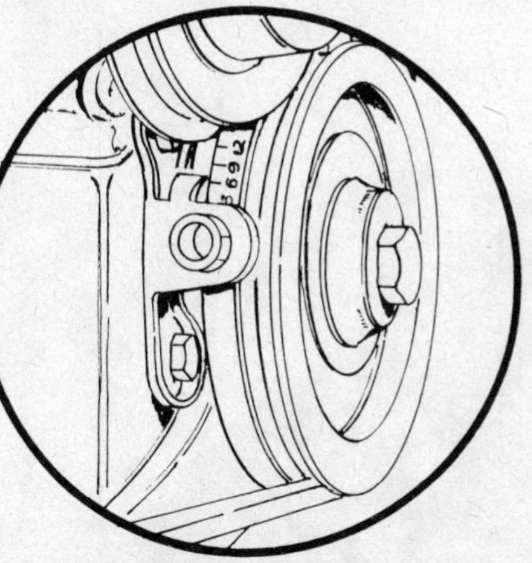

Timing mark—2000 cc engine

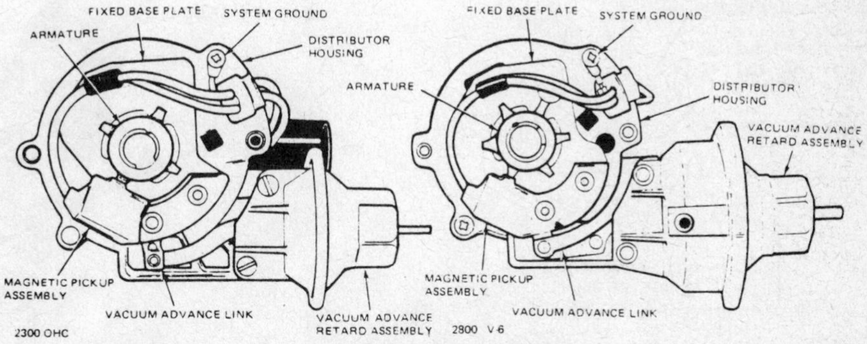

Electronic ignition distributor

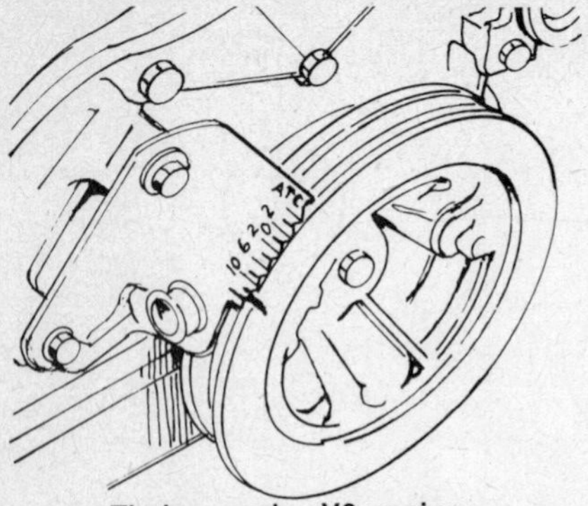

Timing mark—V6 engine

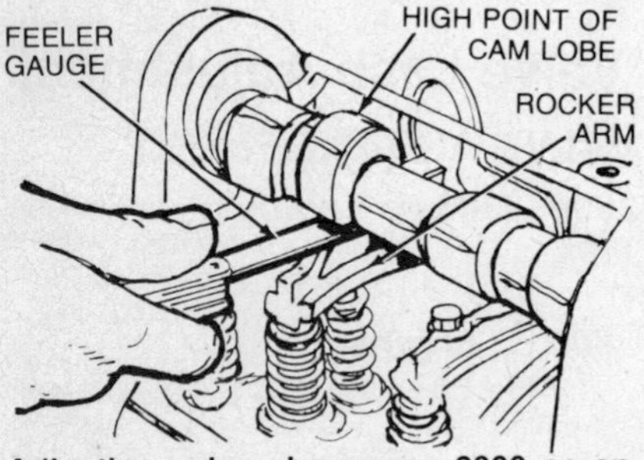

Adjusting valve clearance—2000 cc engine

Rotate the engine until the high point of the number 1 cam lobe is pointing straight down. Remove the number 6 and 7 rocker arm retaining springs by inserting a screwdriver under the spring at the rocker arm and snapping the spring off. Loosen the locknut. Adjust the clearance between the cam lobe and the rocker arm with a feeler gauge. Turn the adjustment screw in or out to obtain the proper clearance. Retighten the locknuts when the adjustment is complete. Repeat the procedure for the rest of the valves, adjusting each with its cam lobe pointing straight down. Adjust the valves in the following order:

2000 and 2300 Valve Adjustment

Valve Open	Valves to Adjust to 0.008 (intake)	Valve to Adjust to 0.010 (exhaust)
1	6	7
2	8	3
3	2	5
6	4	1

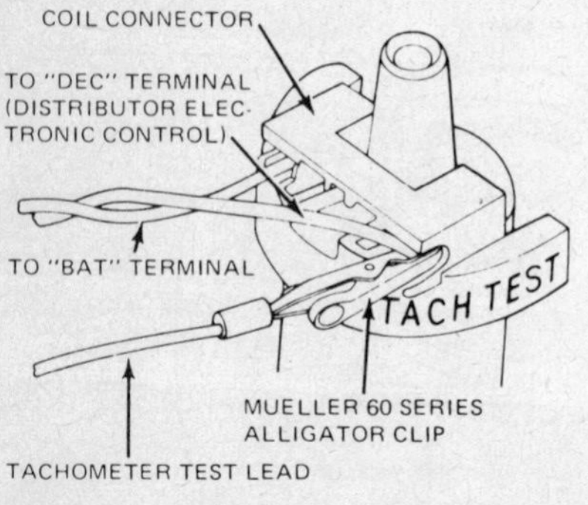

Electronic ignition tachometer connections

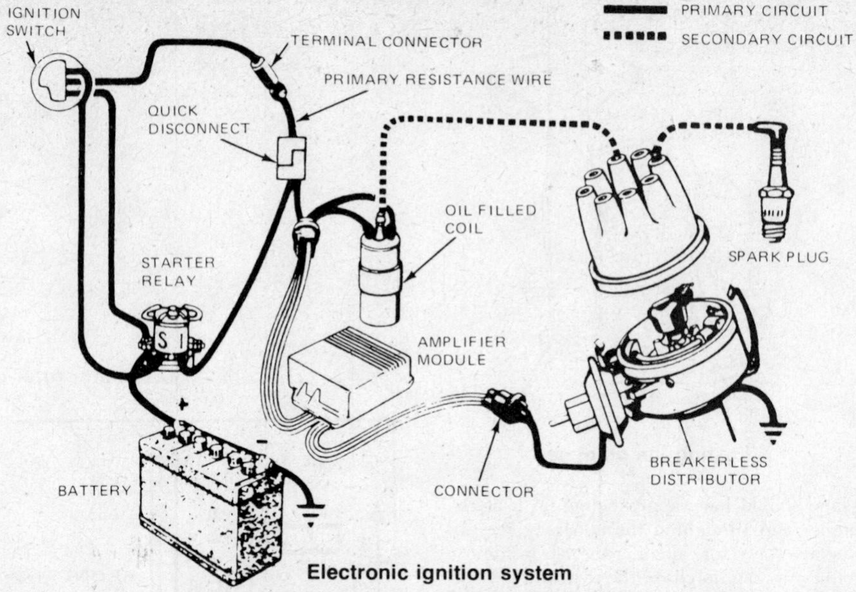

Electronic ignition system

2000 and 2300 Valve Adjustment

Snap the retaining spring back into place. Install a new valve cover gasket and install the valve cover. Run the engine and check for oil leaks.

2300 cc Engine

This engine employs hydraulic valve lifters. No periodic adjustment is necessary. To check valve lash: use the special tool available from Ford, or its equivalent and depress the cam follower until the lash adjuster is completely collapsed. Insert the proper feeler gauge (.008 int.; .010 exh) between the base circle of the cam and the follower. This should be done when the camshaft is in a position with the base circle of the lobe facing the follower. If the clearance is excessive, remove the follower and check for damage. If the follower is okay, check the spring assembled height to make sure the valve is not sticking. If the spring height is okay, check the camshaft lobe for excessive wear.

Replace damaged or worn parts as necessary.

V6 Engine

If some component of the valve system is replaced, the valves must be set cold before starting the engine. If the valves are set for a tune-up, adjust them hot and running. When setting the valves of the cold engine, rotate the engine so that No. 1 cylinder is at top dead center (TDC). Remove the valve covers. Both valves should be closed and the timing pointer and pulley mark aligned. Adjust the valves in the rest of the cylinders in firing order (1-4-2-5-3-6). This can be done by turning the crankshaft 120 degrees clockwise each time. After two full revolutions, each cylinder will have been at TDC once. To adjust the valves

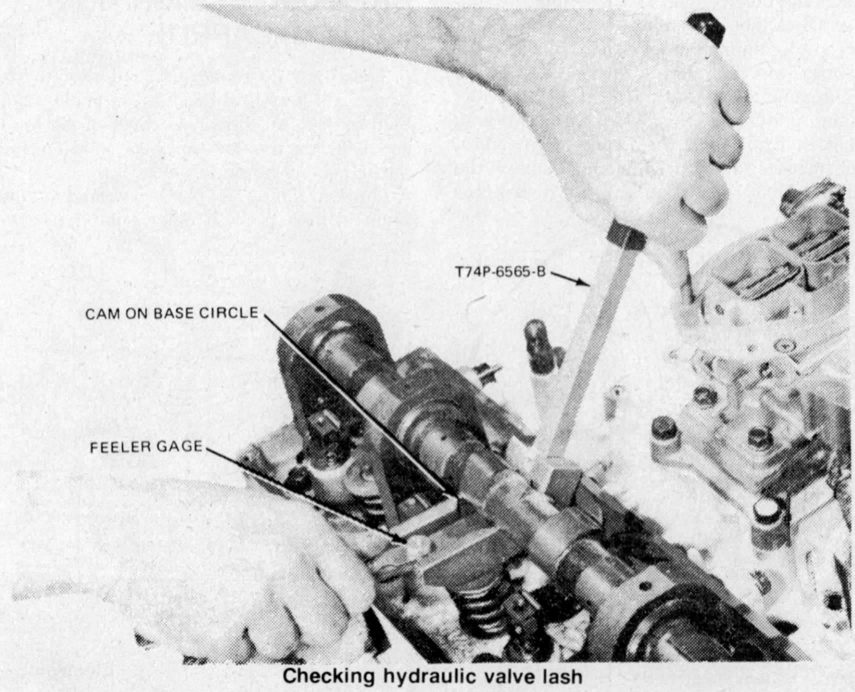

Checking hydraulic valve lash

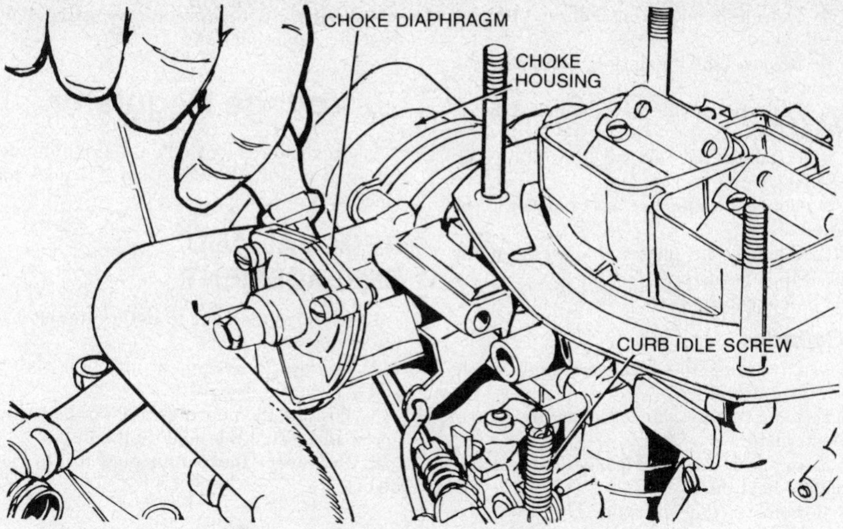

Setting curb idle—2000 cc and V6 engines

when the engine is hot, run the engine until it reaches operating temperature. With the engine running at idle speed, insert a feeler gauge between the valve stem and rocker arm and adjust the valve. After adjusting each valve recheck the valve clearance.

Carburetor

IDLE SPEED AND MIXTURE

1. Remove the air cleaner.
2. Connect a tachometer.
3. Allow the engine to run until it reaches operating temperature.
4. Check the ignition timing as in the previous section, and make sure it is set to proper specifications.
5. Disconnect the hose which runs from the carburetor to the decel valve (if equipped) and plug the decel valve fitting.
6. Place the car in Drive, if the car is equipped with an automatic transmission, and in neutral if it has a manual transmission.
7. Set the idle speed to the speed listed in the "Tune-up Specifications Chart" by using the curb idle screw. This reading must be taken with the air cleaner connected.
8. Turn the idle mixture screw to the right or left to obtain the smoothest idle.

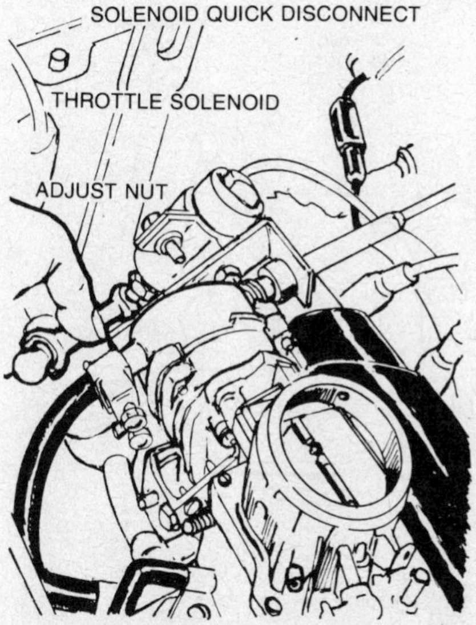

Throttle solenoid adjustment and solenoid lead disconnected

ENGINE ELECTRICAL

Distributor

REMOVAL AND INSTALLATION

The distributor is located on the left side of the 2000 cc and 2300 cc engines, and at the rear of the V6 engine.

Before removing the distributor, match mark the distributor body and engine block with chalk or paint. Remove the distributor cap and mark the distributor body to show the direction in which the rotor is pointing. This will ensure correct distributor installation and timing.

Remove the vacuum lines and the locknut and retainer. Do not crank the engine while the distributor is removed. Install the distributor by aligning the rotor marks and the distributor marks. The cam will turn slightly to the left or right, depending on the engine. To compensate for this, determine the direction that the cam turns and align the rotor slightly before the mark, then insert the distributor. Reconnect the wires and locknut. Attach a timing light and set the ignition timing to the proper specifications.

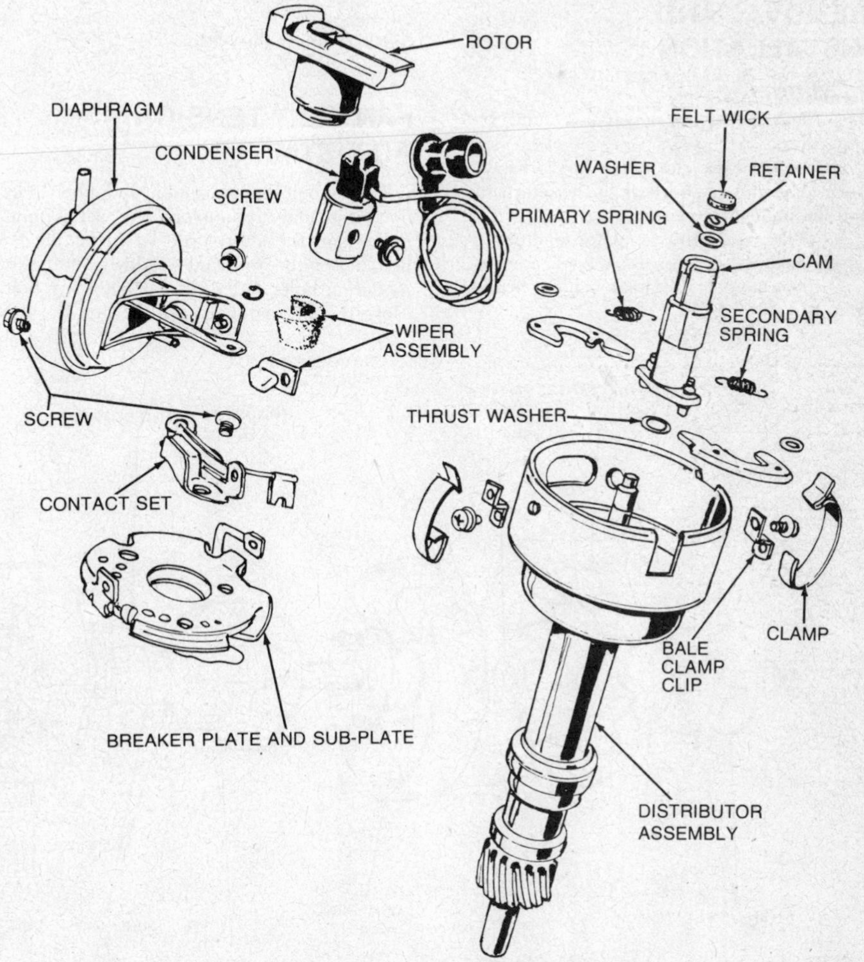

V6 distributor components; 2000 cc is similar

If the engine has been turned while the distributor was out, install in the following manner. Find top dead center (TDC) of the compression stroke of the number one (No. 1) cylinder. The exact location of TDC can be found by aligning the timing mark on the crankshaft pulley with the pointer on the engine block. Install the distributor so the rotor is pointing to the No. 1 spark plug wire on the distributor cap and the points are just opening. Again, use a timing light to set the timing to the proper specifications.

Alternator

ALTERNATOR PRECAUTIONS

When servicing an alternator or a circuit incorporating one, the following precautions should be observed:

1. The alternator is used on a negative ground system only.
2. When installing a battery, connect the positive cable first, then connect the negative (ground) cable.
3. Never disconnect the battery while the engine is running.
4. Remove the molded connections from the alternator when you are welding.
5. Never attempt to polarize the alternator.

REMOVAL AND INSTALLATION

4 Cylinder

1. Disconnect the negative (ground) battery cable.
2. Remove the clip which holds the wire plug connector to the rear of the alternator, and disconnect the wiring plug.
3. Disconnect the regulator-to-alternator wiring at the alternator.
4. Disconnect the heater hose bracket from the alternator.
5. Loosen the mounting bolts and remove the alternator.
6. Remove the mounting bolts and the alternator.
7. Position the alternator and install the mounting bolts.
8. Install the fan belt and adjust it to ½ in. free-play.
9. Connect the heater hose bracket to the alternator.
10. Connect the plug and the clip at the rear of the alternator.
11. Connect the battery.

6 Cylinder

1. Disconnect the negative (ground) cable from the battery.
2. Remove the connectors at the rear of the alternator.
3. Remove the air cleaner and exhaust manifold heat duct.
4. Remove the adjusting bolt from the rear of the alternator.
5. Remove the mounting bolts. Slide the alternator back and away from the mounting bracket and lift it out between the battery and the exhaust manifold.
6. Position the alternator to the mounting bracket and install the mounting bolts.
7. Install the fan belt and adjust it to ½ in. free-play.
8. Connect the multiple connectors to the rear of the alternator.
9. Install the heat duct and the air cleaner.
10. Connect the battery.

FAN BELT TENSION ADJUSTMENT

The fan belt free movement should be ½ in. measured midway between the water pump pulley and the alternator. To adjust the fan belt, loosen the front and rear lower alternator mounting bolts and the front adjusting bolt. Move the alternator to give the belt the correct tension. Retighten the adjusting bolt, then the mounting bolts.

Voltage Regulator

The regulator is located on the right fender apron. It is not adjustable and if it does not function properly it should be replaced.

REMOVAL AND REPLACEMENT

1. Unplug the wiring from the alternator to the regulator.
2. Remove the regulator attaching screws and remove the regulator.
3. Position the new regulator on the fender apron and install the mounting bolts.
4. Reconnect the wiring plug to the regulator.

Starter

REMOVAL AND INSTALLATION

4 Cylinder

1. Disconnect the battery ground cable.
2. Disconnect the wires at the solenoid.
3. Remove the attaching screws and then the starter.
4. Reverse the procedure to install the starter.

6 Cylinder

1. Disconnect the battery ground cable.
2. Jack up the front of the car, block the rear wheels, and support the car with jackstands.
3. Disconnect the battery cable and the two push-on wire connectors from the solenoid.
4. Remove the mounting bolts and the starter.
5. Reverse the procedures to install the starter.

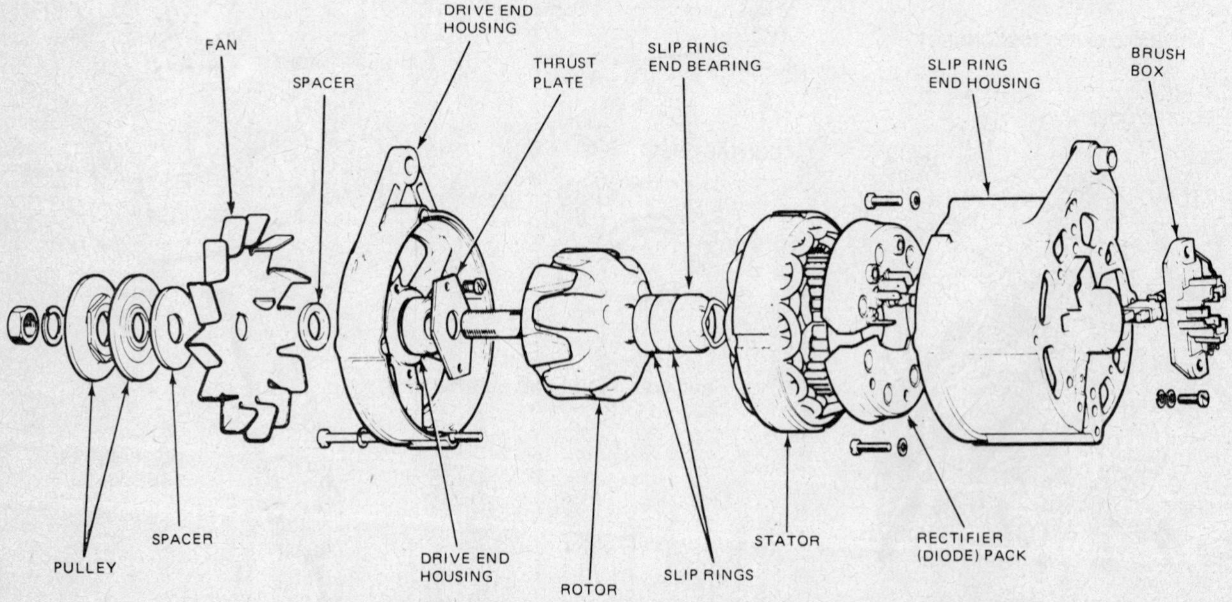

Exploded view—Bosch 35/55 ampere alternator

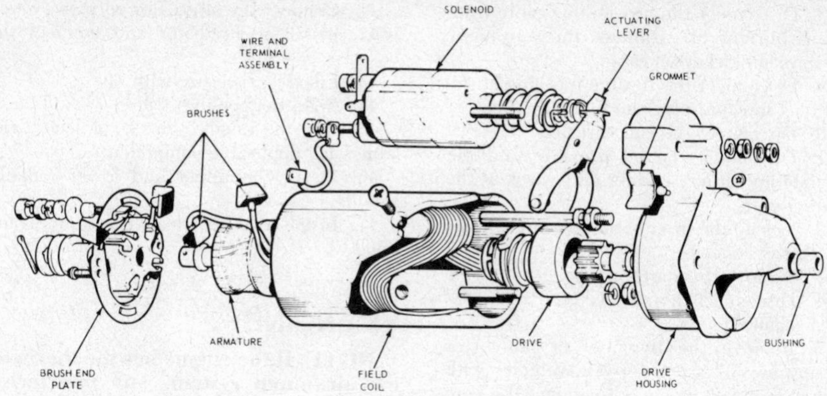

Lucas starter—disassembled

STARTER DRIVE REPLACEMENT

1. Remove the starter from the engine.
2. Detach the field winding cable and remove the solenoid.
3. Remove the engaging lever guide screw.
4. Remove the end plate through bolts.
5. Remove the drive end plate.

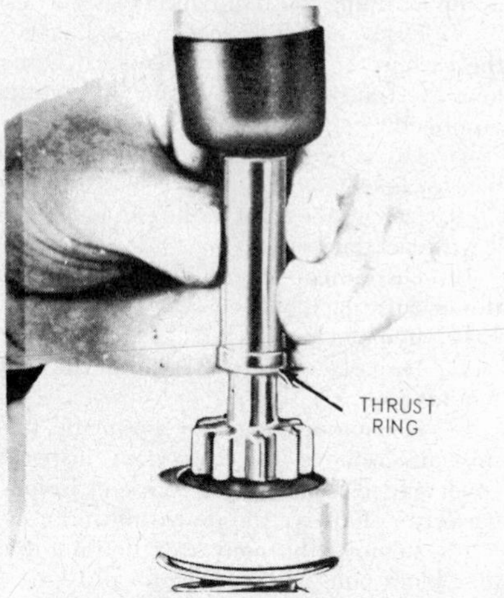

Thrust ring installation

6. Press the stop-ring toward the pinion.
7. Remove the snap-ring.
8. Remove the stop-ring and the starter drive gear.
9. Put silicone grease on the armature shaft thread and the starter drive gear engaging ring. Install the stop-ring and snap-ring on the armature shaft.
10. Press the snap-ring in the groove of the shaft.
11. Press on the stop-ring.
12. Install the engaging lever on the engaging ring and install the drive end plate.
13. Attach the engaging fork to the guide screw.
14. Install the steel washer, and then the rubber washer, with the tap pointing toward the armature.
15. Install the housing and rubber washer.
16. Insert the end plate bolts.
17. Hook the solenoid to the engaging fork and attach the screws.
18. Connect the field winding cable.

STARTER SOLENOID REPLACEMENT

1. Remove the starter.
2. Disconnect the field winding cable from the solenoid.
3. Unscrew the mounting bolts and remove the solenoid.
4. Link the new solenoid to the engaging lever and install the two screws.
5. Connect the field winding cable to the solenoid.
6. Seal the joints and screw heads with lacquer.

ENGINE MECHANICAL

Design

2000 cc ENGINE

The 2000 cc engine is a four-cylinder inline engine with an overhead camshaft. The camshaft is mounted on the top of the cylinder head in three bearings and opens the valves by means of rocker arms. The overhead cam eliminates the need for valve lifters and pushrods. The cylinder head and engine block are made of cast iron, while the intake manifold is aluminum.

The pistons are made from an aluminum alloy with steel struts. The cast iron crankshaft is supported by five main bearings. The camshaft is driven at one-half engine speed by a rubber belt. Since the camshaft is mounted on the top of the engine, the oil pump, fuel pump, and distributor must be driven by an auxiliary shaft on the camshaft belt.

2300 cc ENGINE

The 4 cylinder 2300 cc overhead cam engine is of lightweight iron construction. The crankshaft is supported on five main bearings and the camshaft by four. Main, connecting rod, camshaft and auxiliary shaft bearings are all replaceable.

The camshaft is driven from the crankshaft by a cogged belt, which also operates the auxiliary shaft, and thusly the oil pump, fuel

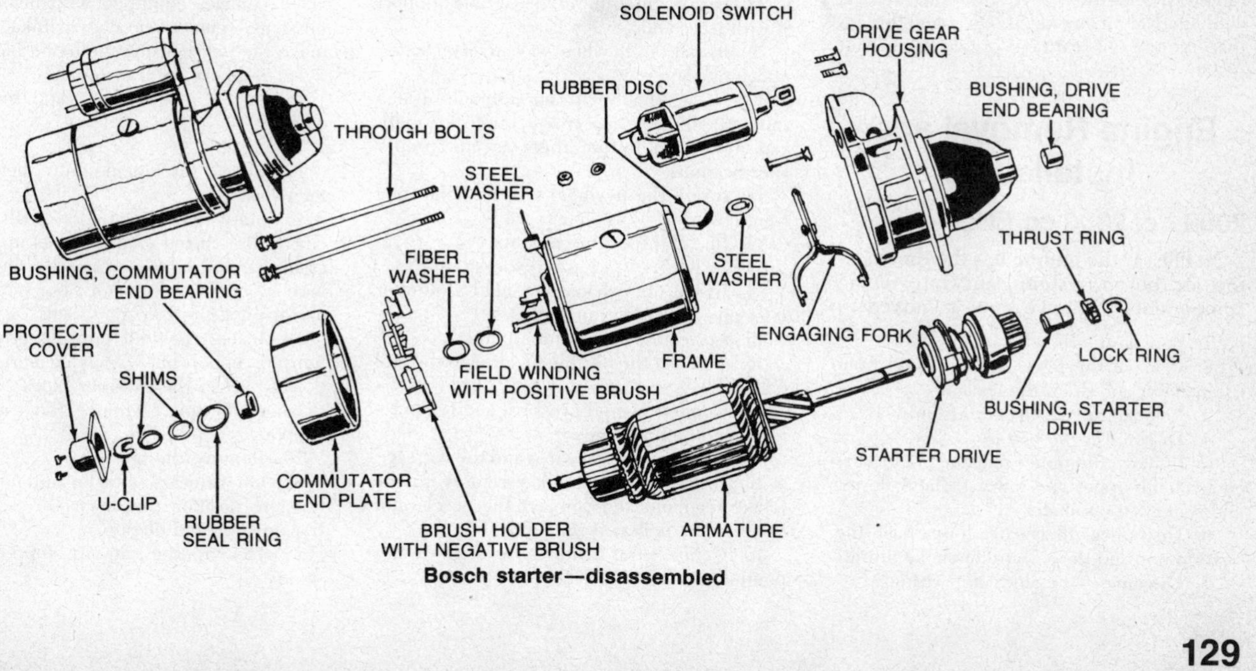

Bosch starter—disassembled

pump and distributor. Belt tension is maintained by a pre-loaded and locked idler pulley bearing on the outside of the belt.

Water pump and fan are separately driven from the crankshaft by a conventional V-belt which also drives the alternator.

Hydraulic adjusters are used on the valve train. These units are placed at the fulcrum point of the cam followers. Their action is similar to lifters in an OHV engine. The head is drilled to supply oil to these units.

Although similar in design to the 2000 cc the 2300 cc is different in detail and few parts will interchange. A set of metric tools is needed for service.

V6 ENGINE

The 2800 cc engine is a V6 overhead valve design. The cylinder heads and engine block are made of cast iron. Four main bearings support the crankshaft. The distributor and the oil pump are driven by an eccentric at the front of the camshaft. The connecting rods are forged steel with replaceable copper-lead alloy insert bearings. The intake manifold is made from aluminum and has individual passages to the openings in the cylinder heads. The V6 has a full pressure lubrication system fed by a rotor type oil pump mounted at the rear of the crankcase.

Engine Cautions

Metric and standard thread bolts are mixed throughout the engine and transmission. Since some of the metric threads are very similar to the standard threads, caution should be used when installing or removing bolts.

Metric bolts and screws will have the letters "M" or "ISOM" embossed on the head. Metric nuts will have the letter "M" on the sides.

If any repair operation requires the removal of any component of the air conditioning system, do not disconnect any of the lines of the system. If it is impossible to move the component out of the way with the lines attached, have the air conditioning system evacuated by a trained serviceman.

When installing nuts or bolts (refer to the torque specification chart), oil the threads with lightweight engine oil. Do not oil threads that require oil-resistant or water-resistant sealers.

Engine Removal and Installation

2000 cc, 2300 cc ENGINES

NOTE: If the engine has the thermactor air pump system, any interfering components will have to be removed.

1. Remove the hood.
2. Remove the lower splash shield from the radiator and drain the coolant.
3. Remove the air cleaner assembly.
4. Disconnect the battery.
5. Remove the upper radiator shield, disconnect the upper and lower radiator hoses, and remove the radiator.
6. Disconnect the heater hoses from the water pump and the carburetor choke fitting.
7. Disconnect the alternator wiring.
8. Disconnect the accelerator cable from the carburetor. Disconnect the automatic transmission kickdown cable.
9. Disconnect the flexible fuel line at the fuel tank line and plug the fuel tank line.
10. Disconnect the coil wires.
11. Disconnect the oil pressure and the water temperature sending unit wires at the sending units.
12. Jack up the front of the car and support it with jackstands.
13. Remove the starter motor.
14. Disconnect the muffler pipe at the exhaust manifold.
15. Remove the flywheel or converter housing lower front cover. On vehicles with automatic transmissions, disconnect the converter from the flexplate. Remove the converter housing-to-cylinder block lower attaching screws.
16. Mark the flywheel and torque converter so they can be correctly mated during installation.
17. Support the transmission.
18. Disconnect the motor mounts at the underbody bracket.
19. Lower the car to the ground.
20. Attach a chain hoist and remove the engine.

To install:

21. Place a new gasket over the exhaust inlet pipe.
22. Lower the engine into the engine compartment.
23. Line up the dowel pins on the rear face of the cylinder block with the corresponding holes in the flywheel or converter housing. Make sure that the studs in the exhaust manifold are aligned with the holes in the muffler inlet pipe. Line up the engine mount studs.
24. On a vehicle with a manual transmission, start the transmission shaft into the clutch disc. If the engine hangs up after the shaft enters, turn the crankshaft slowly until the shaft spline meshes with the clutch disc splines.
25. Install the flywheel or converter housing upper attaching screws.
26. Remove the chain hoist.
27. Remove the transmission support.
28. Jack up the front of the car and support it with jackstands.
29. Install the flywheel or converter lower attaching capscrews.
30. On a vehicle with an automatic transmission, install the converter-to-flexplate capscrews and torque them to the proper specifications.
31. Install the flywheel converter housing front cover.
32. Install the engine mounts.
33. Install the starter and wires.
34. Install the exhaust manifold-to-muffler inlet pipe retaining nuts.
35. Lower the car to the ground.
36. Connect the flexible fuel line to the fuel tank line.
37. Connect the oil pressure and temperature sending unit wires.
38. Connect the coil wires and the battery.
39. Install the bellcrank assembly to the intake manifold and connect the accelerator cable to the bellcrank assembly.
40. Connect the heater hose to the water pump and choke housing.
41. Connect the alternator wires.
42. Install the radiator and connect the hoses.
43. Fill the crankcase with oil.
44. Refill the cooling system.
45. Run the engine, check for leaks, and adjust any applicable components.
46. Install the upper and lower radiator shields.
47. Install the air cleaner assembly and hood.

V6 ENGINE

NOTE: If the engine has the thermactor air pump system, any interfering components will have to be removed.

1. Remove the hood.
2. Disconnect the battery and drain the cooling system.
3. Remove the air cleaner assembly and remove the radiator hoses.
4. Remove the fan shroud attaching bolts and position the shroud over the fan. Remove the radiator and shroud.
5. Remove the alternator and bracket and remove the alternator ground wire.
6. Disconnect the fuel line from the fuel pump and plug the fuel tank line.
7. Disconnect the accelerator linkage at the carburetor and intake manifold. Disconnect the transmission downshift linkage if so equipped.
8. Disconnect the coil wires and the brake booster lines.
9. Jack up the front of the car and support it with jackstands.
10. Disconnect the muffler inlet pipes at the exhaust manifold.
11. Remove the starter.
12. Disconnect the engine from the motor mounts.
13. If equipped with an automatic transmission, remove the converter inspection cover and disconnect the flywheel from the converter. Remove the downshift rod.
14. Remove the converter housing-to-engine block bolts and the adaptor plate-to-converter housing bolt.

On vehicles equipped with manual transmissions, remove the clutch linkage and remove the bell housing-to-engine block bolts.

15. Support the transmission.
16. Install a chain hoist and remove the engine.

To install:

17. Lower the engine into the compartment.
18. Start the transmission shaft into the clutch disc. If the engine hangs up, turn the crankshaft until the gear meshes. On a vehicle with an automatic transmission, start the converter pilot into the crankshaft.
19. Install the bell housing or converter housing upper bolts, making sure that the dowel pins in the cylinder block engage the flywheel housing. Remove the transmission support.
20. Remove the hoist.
21. On vehicles with an automatic transmission, position the downshift cable on the transmission and engine.
22. Jack up the car and support it with stands.

23. On a vehicle with an automatic transmission, position the transmission linkage bracket and install the remaining converter housing bolts. Install the adaptor plate-to-converter housing bolt. Install the converter-to-flywheel nuts and install the inspection cover.

On a vehicle with a manual transmission, remove the pilot studs, and then install the lower bell housing bolts, and connect the clutch linkage to the engine block.

24. Install the starter and connect the wires.

25. Connect the muffler inlet pipes at the exhaust manifold.

26. Install the front motor mounts.

27. Lower the car to the ground.

28. Install the wires to the coil, and connect the wires to the temperature sending unit and the oil pressure sending unit. Connect the brake booster line.

29. Install the accelerator linkage and connect the downshift rod if so equipped. Connect the vacuum lines. Connect the fuel tank line at the fuel pump.

30. Connect the ground wire at the cylinder block. Install the heater hoses at the water pump and cylinder block.

31. Install the alternator and bracket. Connect the alternator ground wire to the cylinder block. Install the fan belts and adjust them to the proper specifications.

32. Position the fan shroud over the fan. Install the radiator and connect the hoses. Install the fan shroud attaching bolts.

33. Refill the cooling system. Fill the crankcase with oil. Adjust the transmission downshift linkage if so equipped.

34. Run the engine and check for leaks.

35. Install the air cleaner assembly and adjust any applicable components.

36. Install the hood.

Cylinder Head

NOTE: To prevent distortion or warping of the cylinder head, allow the engine to cool completely before removing the head bolts.

REMOVAL AND INSTALLATION

2000 cc, 2300 cc Engines

1. Drain the cooling system.
2. Remove the air cleaner assembly.
3. Remove the valve cover.

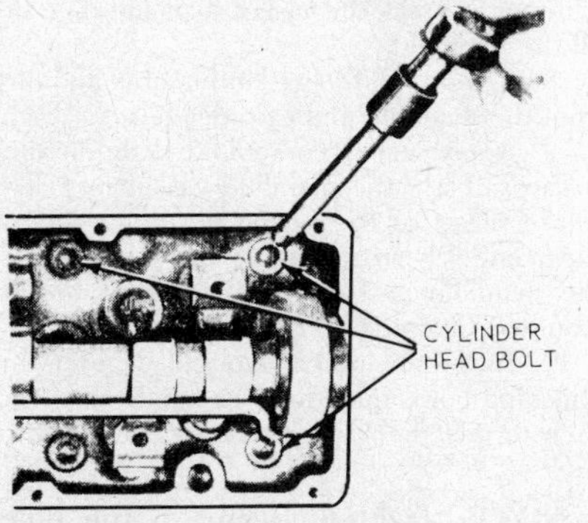

Removing or installing cylinder head bolts—2000 cc engine

4. Remove the exhaust manifold. (See the Exhaust Manifold Removal procedures.)

5. Remove the intake manifold, carburetor, and the decel valve as an assembly. (See the Intake Manifold Removal procedures.)

6. Remove the camshaft drive belt cover. Note the location of the belt cover attaching bolts that have rubber grommets.

7. Loosen the drive belt tensioner and remove the drive belt.

8. Remove the water outlet elbow from the cylinder head with the hose attached.

9. Using an Allen socket, remove the cylinder head bolts. (This tool is available at automotive stores and parts houses.)

10. Lift the cylinder head and camshaft assembly from the engine.

11. Remove all the gasket material and carbon from the top of the engine block and pistons and from the bottom of the cylinder head.

12. Place a new cylinder head gasket on the engine block and position the cylinder head on the engine.

NOTE: If you encounter difficulty in positioning the cylinder head on the engine block, it may be necessary to install guide studs in the engine block to correctly align the head on the block.

13. Tighten the head bolts in sequence, and in steps, to 65-80 ft/lbs for the 2000 cc, and 80-90 ft/lbs for the 2300 cc with a torque wrench.

14. Install the camshaft drive belt. (See the Camshaft Drive Belt Installation procedures in the following sections.)

15. Install the camshaft drive belt cover with its attaching bolts. Make sure that the rubber grommets are installed on the bolts. Tighten them to 6-13 ft/lbs.

16. Install the water outlet elbow and a new gasket.

17. Install the intake and exhaust manifolds. (See the Intake and Exhaust Manifold Installation sections.)

18. Adjust the valve clearance.

19. Install the valve cover and air cleaner assembly.

20. Fill the cooling system.

V6 Engine

1. Remove the air cleaner assembly and disconnect the battery and accelerator linkage. Drain the cooling system.

2. Remove the distributor cap with the spark plug wires attached. Remove the distributor vacuum line and the distributor. Remove the hose from the water pump to the water outlet which is on the carburetor.

3. Remove the valve covers, fuel line and filter, carburetor, and the intake manifold.

4. Remove the rocker arm shaft (by loosening two bolts at a time, in sequence) and oil baffles. Remove the pushrods, keeping them in the proper sequence for reinstallation in their original positions.

5. Remove the exhaust manifold, referring to the appropriate procedures.

6. Remove the cylinder head retaining bolts and remove the cylinder heads and gaskets.

CAUTION

Do not lay the cylinder head flat on its surface.

7. Remove all gasket material and carbon from the engine block and cylinder heads.

8. Place the head gaskets on the engine block.

NOTE: The left and right gaskets are not interchangeable. They are marked "front" and "top."

9. Install guide studs in the engine block. Install the cylinder head assemblies on the engine block one at a time. Tighten the cylinder head bolts in sequence, and in steps, to 65-80 ft/lbs.

10. Install the intake and exhaust manifolds.

11. Install the pushrods in the proper sequence. Install the oil baffles and the rocker arm shaft assemblies. Adjust the valve clearances.

12. Install the valve covers with new gaskets.

13. Install the distributor and set the ignition timing.

14. Install the carburetor and the distibutor cap with the spark plug wires.

15. Connect the accelerator linkage, fuel line, with fuel filter installed, and distributor vacuum line to the carburetor. Fill the cooling system.

CYLINDER HEAD OVERHAUL

The procedure for the 2000 cc and 2300 cc engines is the same as for OHV engines with this exception; if the camshaft is removed from the cylinder head, it must be installed along with the camshaft thrust plate and the camshaft drive gear and attaching bolt. The cylinder head must be removed to remove the camshaft.

For cylinder head overhaul, see the Engine Rebuilding Section of this Manual.

Rocker Shaft

DISASSEMBLY AND ASSEMBLY

V6 Engines

1. Remove the air cleaner assembly and any interfering emission control equipment.

2. Disconnect the spark plug wires and

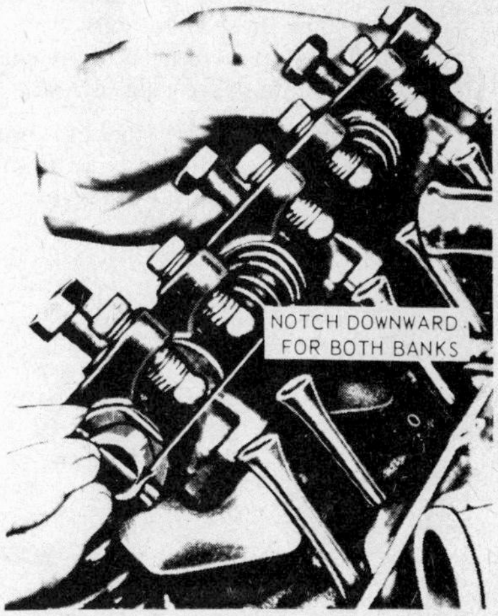

Removing rocker arm shaft assembly—V6 engine

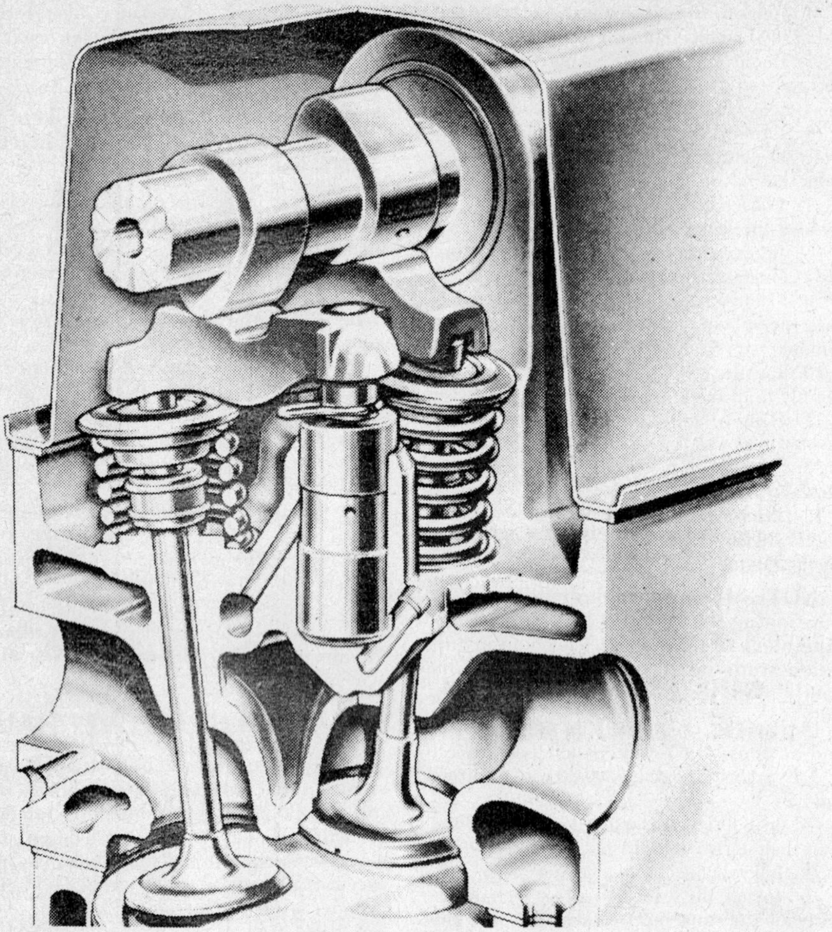

Valve train—four cylinder—typical

move them aside. Disconnect the throttle rod if necessary.

3. Remove the rocker arm cover and its gasket.

4. Remove the rocker arm attaching bolts (by loosening two bolts at a time, in sequence) and lift off the rocker arm assembly.

5. Remove the pin from one end of the shaft and slip off the spring washer from the shaft. The supports, springs, and rocker arms may now be removed.

6. Check the shaft and its component parts for excessive wear or damage. Replace any parts that show these conditions.

7. Clean the component parts of the shaft assembly in a suitable degreasing solvent.

NOTE: Ordinarily, the rocker shaft itself is not cleaned. If there is an insufficient amount of engine oil being circulated through the rocker arm assembly, however, the inside of the shaft should be cleaned in this manner.

Remove the plugs in the rocker shaft ends by drilling a hole in one plug. Insert a long rod through the drilled hole and knock out the opposite plug. Remove the drilled plug in the same manner. Clean the shaft in a degreasing solvent and replace the plugs.

8. Assemble the rocker arm shaft. The cotter pins should be installed with their heads up.

9. Replace the rocker assembly on the cylinder head. Make sure that the notch on the end of the rocker shaft is down. Install the attaching bolts hand tight and then torque them down evenly to 43-49 ft/lbs.

10. Adjust the valve clearances. (Be sure to set the valves when cold and then again, when hot.)

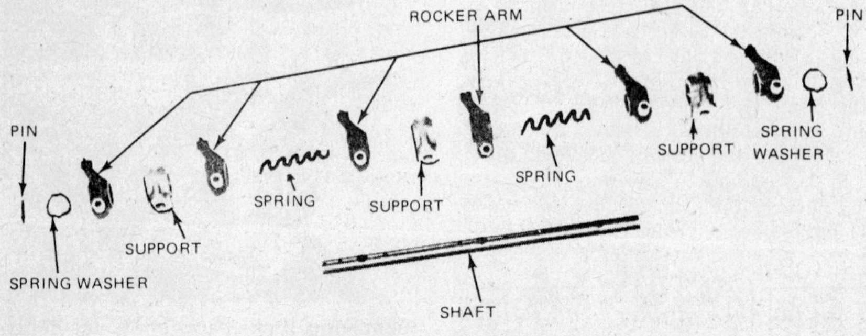

V6 rocker shaft assembly

11. Clean the cylinder head and valve cover of any dirt or gasket material and replace the valve cover.

12. Replace the spark plug wires.

Intake Manifold

REMOVAL AND INSTALLATION

4 Cylinder Engines

1. Remove the air cleaner assembly.

2. Disconnect the fuel line from the carburetor. Remove the carburetor.

3. Disconnect the vacuum lines at the intake manifold. On 2300 cc, disconnect the water lines at the manifold.

4. Disconnect the crankcase ventilation hose at the intake manifold.

5. Remove the intake manifold attaching bolts and remove the manifold, carburetor, and decel valve from the studs, as an assembly.

6. Clean all dirt and gasket material from the surfaces on the cylinder head and intake manifold.

7. Position a new gasket and the manifold on the studs. Torque the bolts and nuts to 12-15 ft/lbs for the 2000 cc and 14-21 for the 2300 cc.

8. Connect the crankcase ventilation hose to the manifold.

9. Connect the distributor vacuum lines to the manifold.

10. Connect the fuel line to the carburetor.

11. Install the air cleaner assembly.

V6 Engine

1. Remove the air cleaner assembly and disconnect the battery.

2. Disconnect the throttle cables.

3. Drain the cooling system. Disconnect and remove the hose from the water outlet to the radiator and the hoses and the line from the water outlet to the water pump.

4. Remove the distributor cap and spark plug wires as an assembly. Disconnect the distributor wire and the vacuum line.

5. Mark the position of the distributor and remove it.

6. Remove the fuel line and filter between the fuel pump and the carburetor and then remove the rocker arm covers.

7. Remove the intake manifold bolts and nuts. Tap the manifold lightly with a plastic hammer to break the gasket seal; and then lift off the manifold.

8. Remove all the gasket material and dirt from the manifold and cylinder heads.

9. Apply sealing compound to the joining surfaces. Place the manifold gasket in place. (Make sure that the tab on the right bank of the cylinder head gasket fits into the cutout of the manifold gasket.) Apply sealant to the manifold retaining bolt bosses.

10. Install the intake manifold. Tighten the attaching bolts until they are hand tight, and then torque them, in sequence, to 15-18 ft/lbs.

NOTE: Tightening one of the bolts with a torque wrench will require a "crow's foot." This tool can be obtained

from an automatic supply house or parts store.

11. Install the distributor so the rotor is pointing to the mark made previously.
12. Connect the distributor wire and vacuum line.
13. Install the carburetor, fuel line, fuel filter, and the rocker arm covers.
14. Install the distributor cap and wires.
15. Install and adjust the carburetor linkage.
16. Install the air cleaner assembly and air cleaner tube to the carburetor. Connect the battery.
17. Fill the cooling system. Adjust the ignition timing.

Exhaust Manifold

REMOVAL AND INSTALLATION

4 Cylinder Engines

1. Remove the air cleaner.
2. Remove the two attaching nuts from the top of the exhaust manifold shroud.
3. Disconnect the two attaching nuts from the muffler inlet pipe. If engine is equipped with thermactor, disconnect the line at the check valve.
4. Remove the manifold attaching nuts and remove the manifold from the cylinder head.
5. This manifold does not use a gasket. When installing the manifold, smear a light coat of graphite grease on the mating surfaces of the exhaust manifold.
6. Position the manifold on the guide studs and install the attaching bolts hand tight, then torque them in sequence to 12-15 ft/lbs for the 2000 cc and 16-23 ft/lbs for the 2300 cc.
7. Install a new exhaust pipe gasket and install the two nuts.
8. Position the exhaust manifold shroud on the manifold and install the two nuts.
9. Install the air cleaner.

V6 Engine

1. Remove the air cleaner.
2. Remove the four attaching nuts from the exhaust manifold shroud (right side only).
3. Disconnect the attaching nuts from the muffler inlet pipe.
4. Remove the exhaust manifold attaching nuts and remove the manifold.
5. These manifolds do not use gaskets. When installing the manifold, smear a light coat of graphite grease on the mating surfaces.

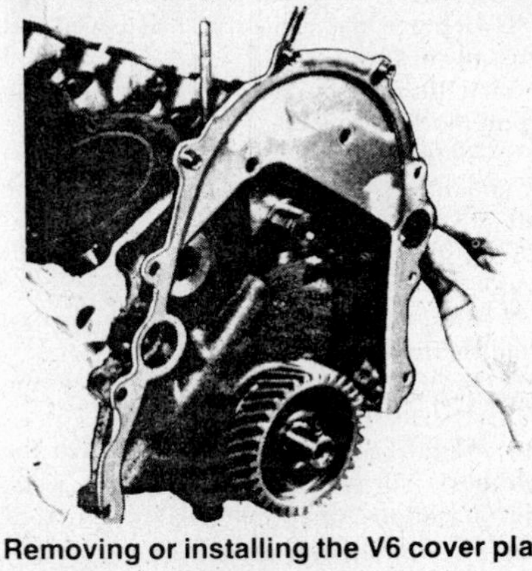

Removing or installing the V6 cover plate

6. Position the manifold on the studs and install the bolts hand tight then torque them evenly to 15-18 ft/lbs.
7. Install a new inlet pipe gasket and the attaching nuts.
8. Position the exhaust manifold shroud on the manifold and install the attaching nuts (right side).

Timing Gear Cover

NOTE: These procedures apply to the V6 engines only.

REMOVAL AND INSTALLATION

V6 Engine

1. Remove the oil pan as described in a following section.
2. Remove the radiator and any other necessary parts to allow clearance.
3. Remove the alternator and drive belts. Remove the water pump and water lines.
4. Remove the fan.
5. Remove the crankshaft pulley with a puller and, if necessary, remove the guide sleeves from the cylinder block.
6. Remove the front cover retaining bolts and remove the front cover. If the front cover plate gasket needs replacement, remove the two screws and the plate to replace the gasket.
7. To install, reverse the procedures, cleaning all surfaces of gasket material and installing new gaskets and sealing compound.

Removing or installing the V6 guide sleeves

NOTE: If the guide sleeves were removed, install them with new seal rings but do not use sealing compound.

OIL SEAL REPLACEMENT

V6 Engine

Remove the front cover as previously described. Support the front cover and drive out the seal with a socket of a suitable size. To install the new seal, support the cover and drive the new seal in with a socket.

Timing Chain, Gears, and Tensioner

REMOVAL AND INSTALLATION

V6 Engine

1. Drain the cooling system.
2. Remove the timing chain cover as previously described.

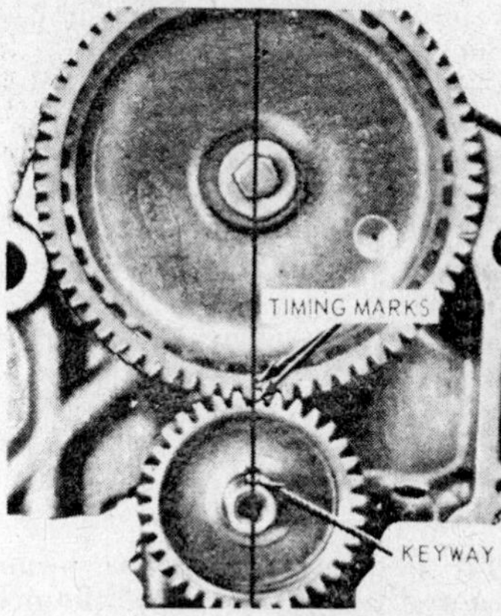

Aligning timing marks—V6 engine

3. Remove the crankshaft gear with a puller. Remove the key from the crank shaft.
4. Remove the bolt and washer which hold the camshaft gear, then pry the camshaft gear from the camshaft. Pry off the gear carefully. Do not push the camshaft toward the rear of the engine or you might knock out the oil plug at the rear of the engine. Remove the thrust plates, spacer, and key.
5. Place the spacer and thrust plate on the camshaft. Install the key in the camshaft. Align the keyway in the gear with the key and press the gear onto the shaft, making sure that it seats tight against the spacer.
6. Camshaft end-play should be 0.001-0.004 in; it can be corrected by replacing the thrust plate. Position the crankshaft key, align the keyway and press on the gear, making sure the timing marks are aligned.
7. Install the timing chain cover and fill the cooling system.
8. Set the ignition timing.

Timing Belt Cover, Belt, and Tensioner

REMOVAL AND INSTALLATION; TENSIONER ADJUSTMENT

4 Cylinder Engine

1. Remove the camshaft drive belt cover.

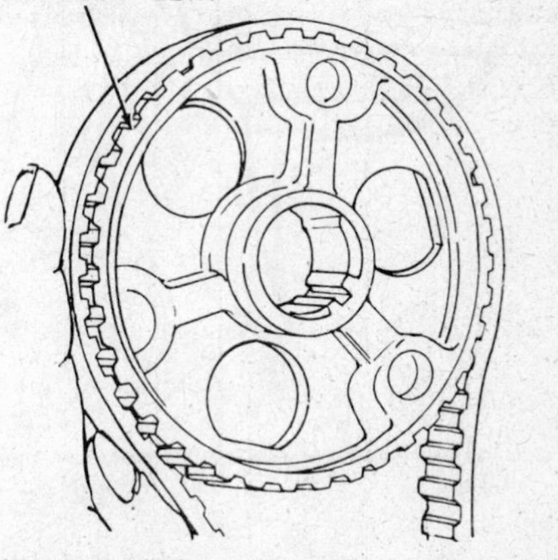

Incorrect fitting of camshaft drive belt sprocket—2000 cc engine

2. Remove the distributor cap and position it out of the way.

3. Using a large socket and a breaker bar, turn the bolt on the crankshaft pulley in a clockwise direction until the following conditions exist.

a. The timing pointer on the front of the engine is aligned with the O or V mark on the pulley.

b. The pointer on the camshaft sprocket is aligned with the ball in the belt guide plate.

c. The distributor rotor is aligned with the timing mark on the upper lip of the distributor housing.

NOTE: If the drive belt has slipped and is out of timing, disregard the preceding operations.

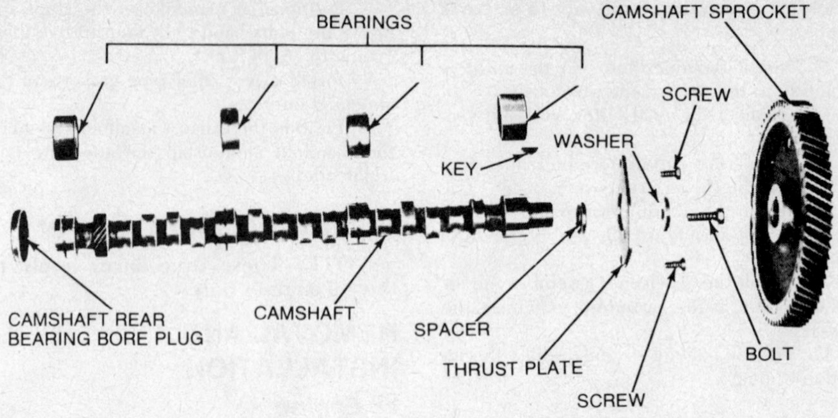

Camshaft and related parts—V6 engine

4. Loosen the drive belt tensioner bolt and move the tensioner as far to the left as possible. Tighten the tensioner adjustment bolt. This will remove the preload of the tensioner from the belt.

5. Remove the belt from the pulleys.

6. If the timing marks on the camshaft, crankshaft, and distributor were not aligned before the belt was removed, align them at this time. Turn the crankshaft (A), camshaft (B), or the auxiliary shaft (C) until the components are in the positions described in Step 3.

7. Install the belt on the three sprockets, making sure the cogs on the belt fully engage the slots in the sprockets.

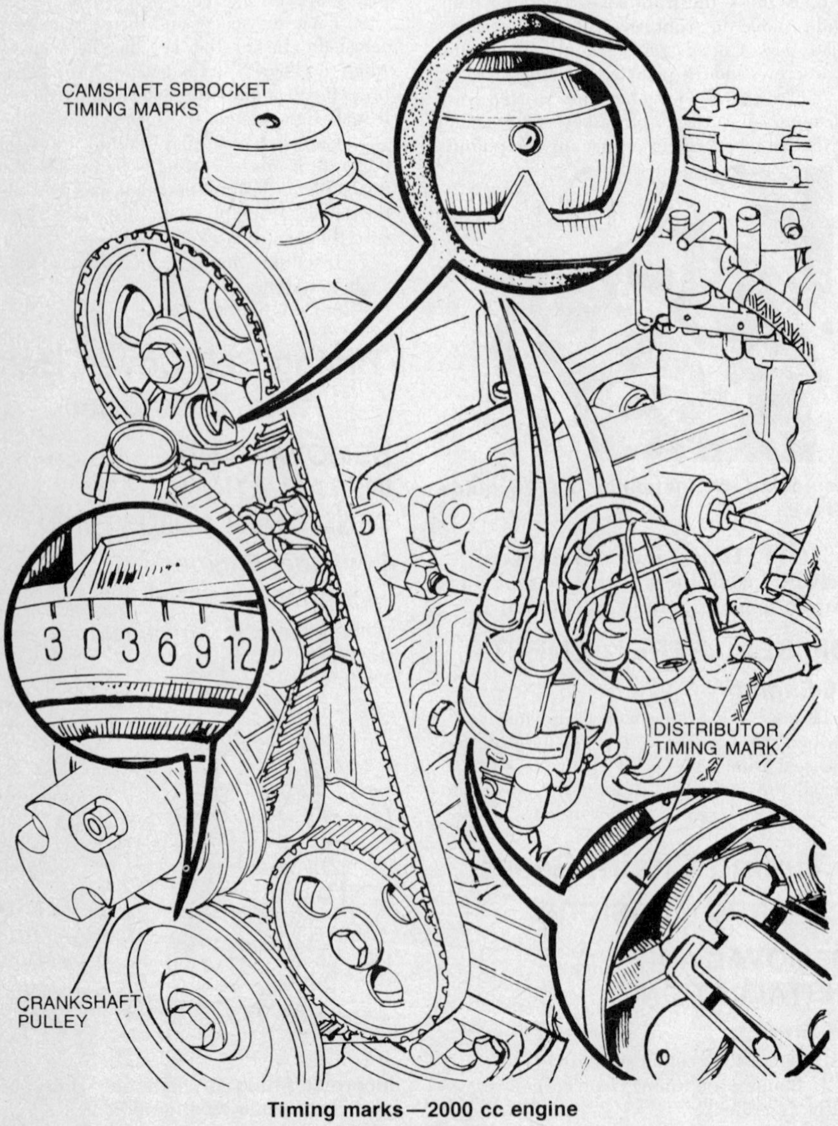

Timing marks—2000 cc engine

8. Loosen the tensioner adjustment bolt and allow the full spring pressure of the tensioner to force the tensioner against the belt.

9. Using a socket and breaker bar on the crankshaft pulley bolt, turn the crankshaft two complete turns in a clockwise direction to remove all slack from the belt. Tighten the tensioner adjustment pivot bolt to 32-26 ft/lbs.

10. Continue to turn the crankshaft until the three marks described in step 3 of the belt removal procedure are aligned. If the belt has slipped, remove the belt and repeat the installation procedure.

11. Install the distributor cap and the drive belt cover.

On vehicles where the timing belt has jumped engine timing without a known cause, e.g., foreign material, snow or ice, behind the belt, or a loose tensioner, remove the camshaft sprocket from the engine. Wrap the drive belt around the sprocket for at least 300 degrees (300°). Visually check to make sure that each cog of the belt is properly seated in the valley between the teeth on the camshaft sprocket.

Auxiliary Shaft

REMOVAL AND INSTALLATION

4 Cylinder Engine

1. Remove the camshaft drive belt cover.
2. Remove the drive belt and auxiliary shaft sprocket.
3. Remove the distributor and fuel pump.
4. Remove the auxiliary shaft cover and thrust plate.
5. Withdraw the auxiliary shaft from the engine block.
6. Slide the auxiliary shaft into the housing and insert the thrust plate to hold the shaft.
7. Install a new gasket and auxiliary shaft cover.
8. Fit a new gasket to the fuel pump and install the fuel pump.
9. Insert the distributor and install the auxiliary shaft sprocket.
10. Align the timing marks and install the drive belt.
11. Install the drive belt cover.
12. Set the ignition timing.

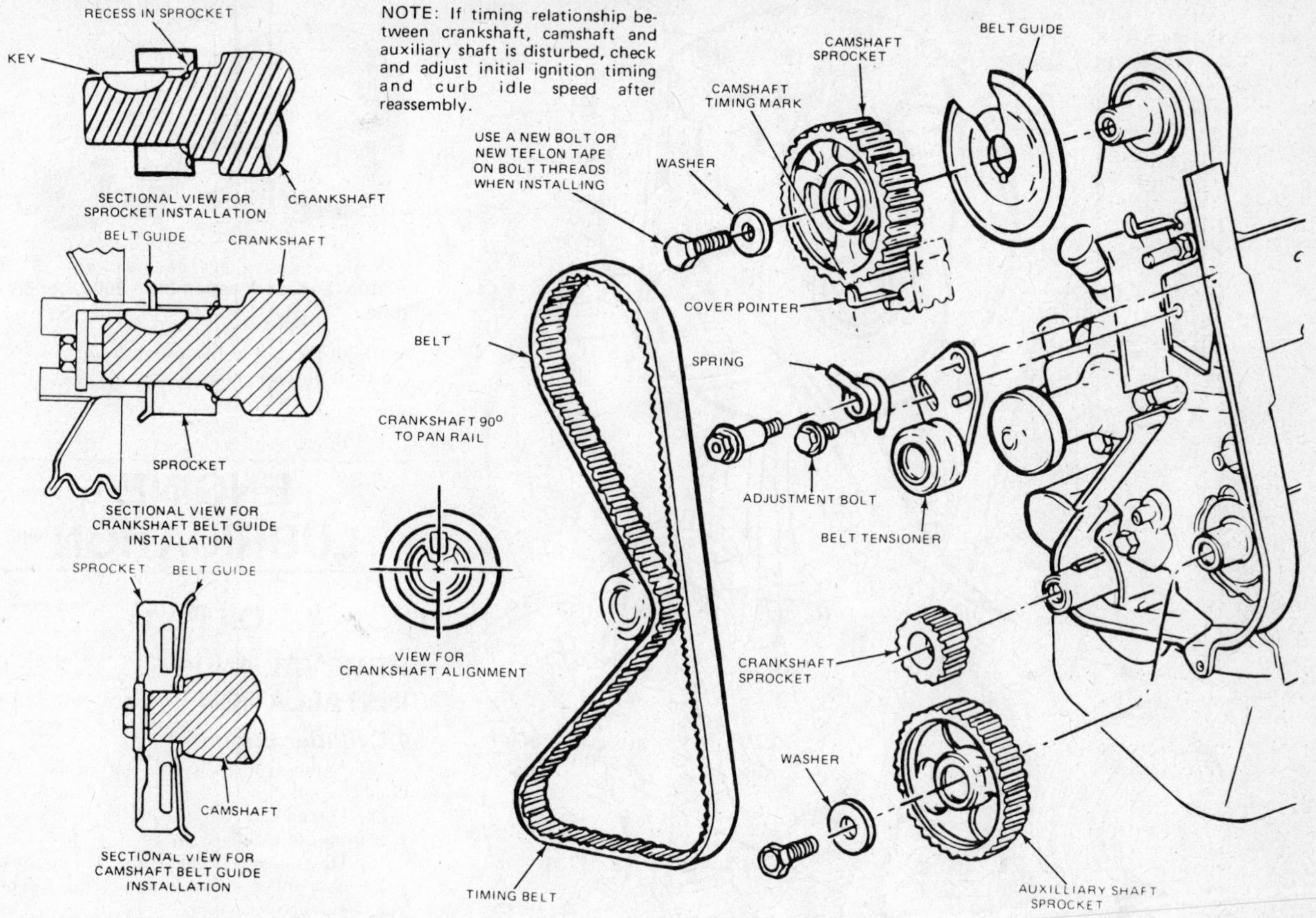

Camshaft drive belt assembly and components

Camshaft and/or Valve Lifters

REMOVAL AND INSTALLATION

4 Cylinder Engine

The camshaft is mounted on the cylinder head. The bearings are mounted in carriers that are an integral part of the cylinder head. On 2000 cc engines the bearings and their journals have a progressively larger diameter from front to rear; therefore, the cylinder head must be removed and the camshaft must be removed from the rear. The opposite is true on 2300 cc engines.

1. Remove the cylinder head.
2. Remove the rocker arms.
3. Remove the camshaft drive gear attaching bolt and washer, and remove the gear and belt guide plate.
4. Remove the camshaft thrust plate from the rear of the cylinder head.
5. Carefully slide the camshaft out of the rear of the cylinder head.

To install, reverse the procedures.

V6 Engine

1. Drain the cooling system.
2. Remove the radiator, fan, spacer, water pump pulley, and belt.
3. Remove the distributor cap, with the spark plug wires attached. Remove the distributor vacuum line, distributor, alternator, rocker arm covers, fuel line and filter, carburetor, and intake manifold.
4. Remove the rocker arm and shaft assemblies. Lift out the pushrods and mark them so they can be replaced in the same location.
5. Remove the oil pan.
6. Remove the timing chain cover and water pump as an assembly.
7. Remove the camshaft gear retaining bolt and slide the gear off the camshaft. Remove the camshaft thrust plate.
8. Remove the valve lifters from the engine block with a magnet. Lifters should be identified to permit installation in the same location.
9. Carefully pull the camshaft from the engine block, avoiding damage to the camshaft bearings. Remove the key and spacer ring.
10. Coat the camshaft with a cam lubricant or heavy engine oil.
11. Install the camshaft, carefully avoiding damage to the bearings.

NOTE: When installing the camshaft, do not push it hard into the engine. There is an oil plug at the rear of the engine block called the "bore plug". If the camshaft is forced into the engine, it could push this plug out, resulting in oil leaking on the clutch and pressure plate.

12. Install the spacer ring with the chamfered side toward the camshaft. Insert the camshaft key. Install the thrust plate. Camshaft end-play should be 0.001-0.004 in. The spacer ring and thrust plate are available in two sizes for adjustment.
13. Align the timing marks and install the camshaft timing gear. Install the retaining washer and bolt.
14. Install the valve lifters.
15. Install the timing cover and water pump.
16. Install the belt drive pulley and secure it with the washer and retaining bolt.
17. Install the oil pan.
18. Install the pushrods in the same locations from which they were removed. Install the intake manifold.
19. Install the oil baffles and rocker arm shaft assemblies. Adjust the valves to the cold setting.
20. Install the water pump pulley, fan spacer, fan and belt, carburetor, fuel line and filter, alternator, distributor cap, and wires.
21. Fill the cooling system.
22. Install the rocker arm covers but not permanently. Run the engine, check for leaks, and set the ignition timing.
23. Set the valves at their hot setting. Install the valve covers permanently.

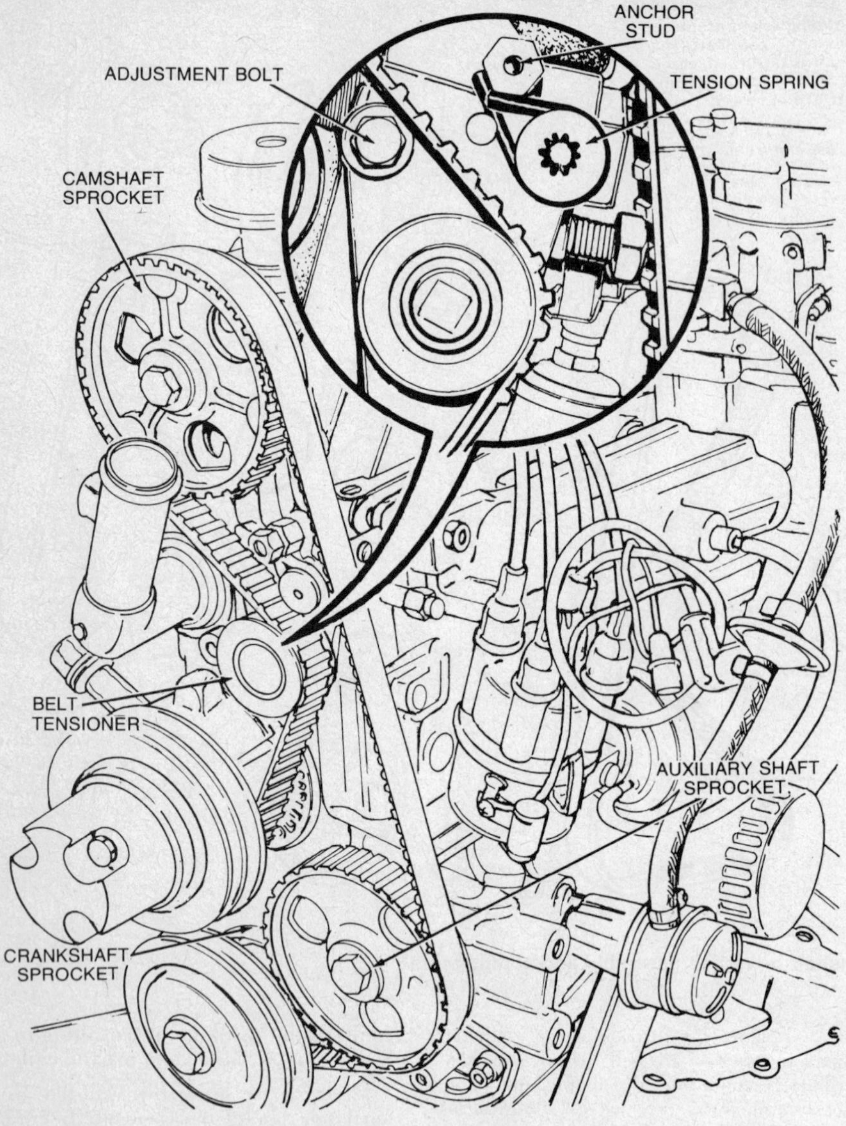

Camshaft drive train—2000 cc engine

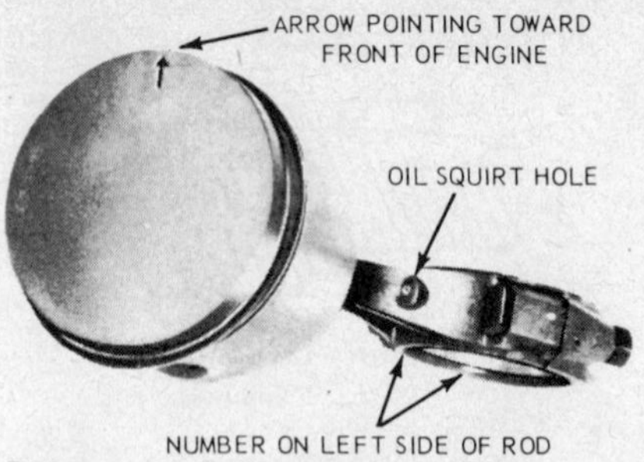

Piston and rod assembly—2000 cc engine

Pistons and Connecting Rods

IDENTIFICATION AND POSITIONING

4 Cylinder Engine

Install the pistons in the same cylinders from which they were removed. The connecting rod and bearing caps are numbered on the left side from one to four, beginning at the front of the engine. The numbers on the connecting rods and bearing cap must be on the same side when installed in the cylinder bore.

Install the pistons with the arrow or notch on the top facing toward the front of the engine.

V6 Engine

Pistons must be installed in the same cylinders from which they were removed. The connecting rod and bearing caps are numbered from one to three in the right bank and from four to six in the left bank, beginning at the front of the engine. The numbers on the connecting rod and bearing cap must be on the same side when installed in the cylinder bore.

Install the pistons with the indentation notch on the top of the piston facing toward the front of the engine.

ENGINE LUBRICATION

Oil Pan

REMOVAL AND INSTALLATION

4 Cylinder Engine

1. Remove the dipstick and drain the crankcase oil.
2. Disconnect the steering shaft connection from the rack and pinion.
3. Disconnect the rack and pinion from the crossmember and move it forward to provide clearance.
4. Remove the flywheel housing inspection cover.
5. Remove the oil pan attaching bolts and also remove the pan.
6. Clean the gasket mounting surfaces on the pan and block.
7. Coat the block surfaces and oil pan mounting surfaces with an oil-resistant sealer and position the pan gasket on the engine block. There is a two piece gasket.
8. Coat the oil pan front seal and the front cylinder cover with a sealer, and position the seal on the front cover. Coat the rear oil pan

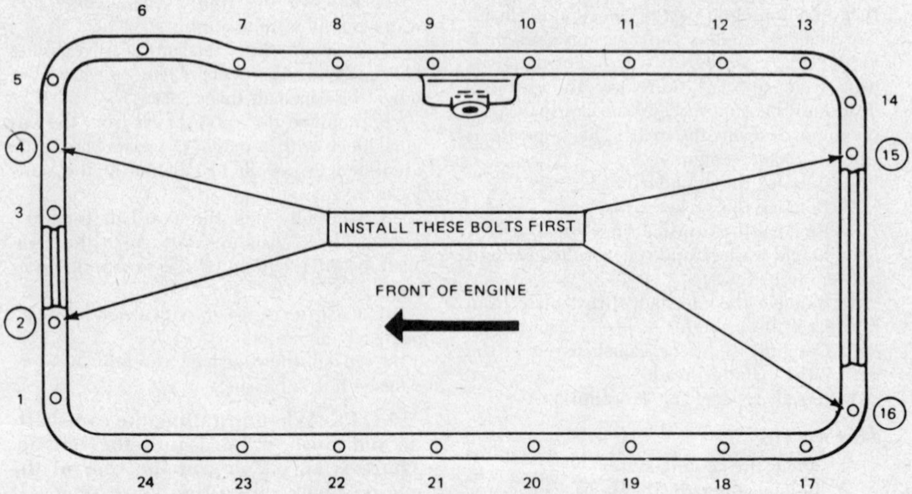

V6 oil pan tightening sequence

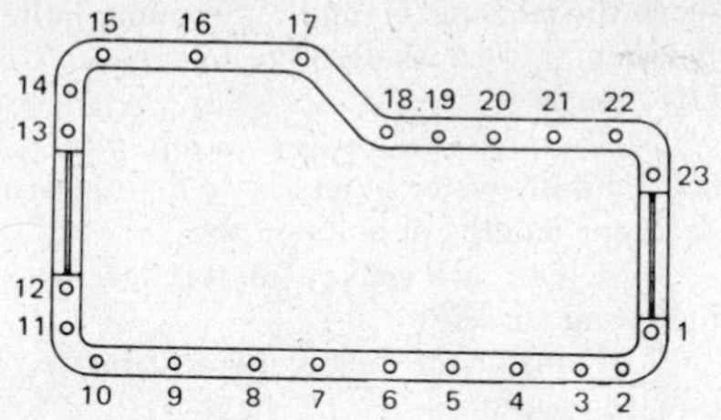

4 cylinder OHV oil pan tightening sequence

seal with sealer and install the seal in the rear main bearing cap.

9. Position the oil pan on the engine and tighten the bolts finger tight.

10. Tighten the bolts in sequence to 7-9 ft/lbs for M6 bolts and 11-13 ft/lbs for M8 bolts.

11. Install the flywheel housing inspection cover.

12. Connect the rack and pinion to the crossmember, and the steering shaft to the rack and pinion.

13. Install the dipstick and fill the crankcase with oil.

14. Run the engine and check for leaks.

V6 Engine

1. Remove the dipstick. Remove the fan shroud and position it over the radiator. Disconnect the battery ground wire and loosen the alternator bracket and adjusting bolts.

2. Raise the vehicle and drain the oil.

3. Remove the splash pan and starter.

4. Remove the engine front support nuts. Raise the engine and place wood blocks between the engine supports and the chassis.

5. Remove the clutch or converter housing cover.

6. Remove the oil pan retaining bolts and the pan.

7. Clean the surfaces of the oil pan and the engine block. Coat the block surface and the oil pan gasket with sealer. Position the pan gasket on the engine block.

8. Position the oil pan front seal on the cylinder front cover. Position the oil pan rear seal on the rear main bearing cap.

9. Position the oil pan on the engine block and install two front and two rear bolts. Install the rest of the bolts. Torque the bolts in steps (2-4 ft/lbs, then 5-7 ft/lbs).

10. Replace the converter housing or clutch cover.

11. Remove the wood blocks and install the support nuts.

12. Replace the starter and splash shield.

13. Lower the car. Position the alternator and tighten the bolts. Adjust the belt tension and connect the battery cable.

14. Install the fan shroud.

15. Install the dipstick. Fill the crankcase with oil. Run the engine and check for leaks.

CRANKSHAFT REAR OIL SEAL

Removal and Installation

2000 cc, V6

1. Remove the transmission assembly. Remove clutch pressure plate and clutch disc, if so equipped.

2. Remove flywheel, flywheel housing and rear plate.

3. Use an awl to punch two holes in the crankshaft rear oil seal. Punch the holes on opposite sides of the crankshaft and just above the bearing cap to cylinder block split line. Install a sheet metal screw in each hole. Use two large screwdrivers or small pry bars and pry against both screws at the same time to remove the crankshaft rear oil seal. It may be necessary to place small blocks of wood against the cylinder block to provide a fulcrum point for the pry bars. Use caution throughout this procedure to avoid scratching or otherwise damaging the crankshaft oil seal surface.

4. Clean the oil seal recess in the cylinder block and main bearing cap. Inspect and clean the oil seal contact surface on the crankshaft.

5. Coat the oil seal to cylinder block surface of the oil seal with oil. Coat the seal contact surface of the oil seal and crankshaft with Lubriplate. Start the seal in the recess and install it. Drive the seal into position until it is firmly seated.

6. Install rear plate, flywheel housing, and flywheel. Tighten flywheel bolts to specifications.

7. Install clutch disc and clutch pressure plate, if so equipped. Align clutch disc before tightening pressure plate retaining screws.

2300 cc

1. Remove the oil pan.

2. Loosen all the main bearing cap bolts, thereby lowering the crankshaft slightly but not more than 1/32 in.

3. Remove the rear main bearing cap, and remove the oil seal from the bearing cap and the cylinder block. Install a small sheet metal screw in one end of the cylinder block half of the seal, and pull on the screw to remove the seal.

4. Clean the seal grooves in the cap and block with a brush and solvent. Dry the area thoroughly. No solvent should come in contact with the seal.

5. Dip the seal halves in clean engine oil.

6. Carefully install the upper seal (block half) into its groove with the undercut side of the seal toward the front of the engine, by rotating it on the seal journal of the crankshaft until about 3/8 in. protrudes below the parting

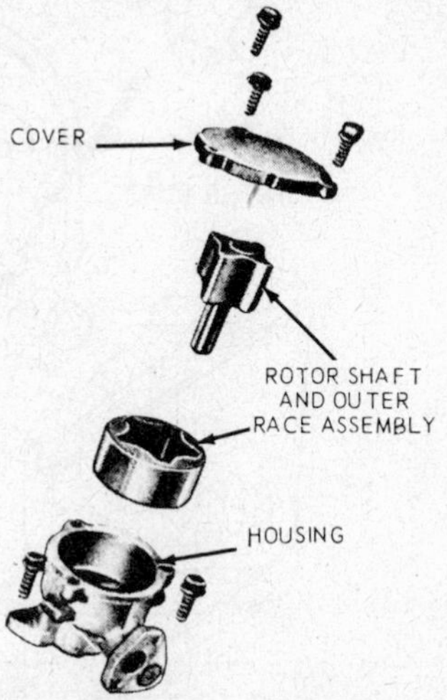

Exploded view of oil pump—2000 and 2300 cc engines

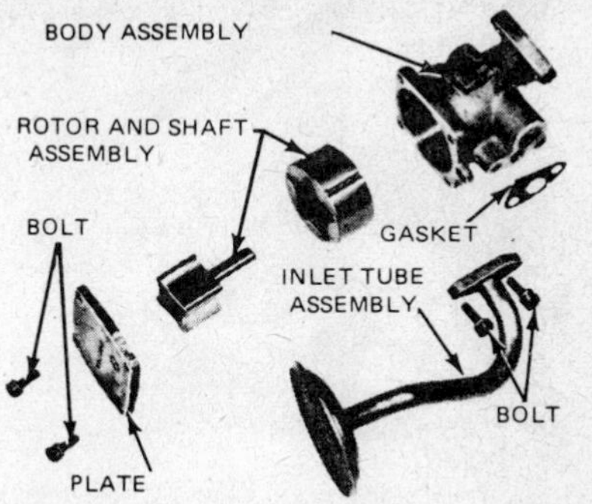

Exploded view of oil pump—2600 and 2800 cc engines

surface. Be sure that no rubber has been shaved off. Wipe all oil from the mating surface of the bearing cap and cylinder block.

7. Tighten the bearing cap bolts to specifications.

8. Install the lower seal in the rear main bearing cap with the undercut side of the seal toward the front of the engine. Allow the seal to protrude about 3/8 in. above the parting surface to mate with the upper seal when the cap is installed.

NOTE: Install the seals so that the locating tab faces the rear of the engine.

9. Apply a small amount of sealer to the mating surface of the bearing cap. No sealer compound should come in contact with the rubber seals when the bearing cap is installed and tightened.

10. Install the oil pump (if removed) and oil pan. Fill the crankcase with oil, and operate the engine, checking for leaks.

Oil Pump

REMOVAL AND INSTALLATION

4 Cylinder Engine

The oil pump is mounted on the bottom of the engine block and is enclosed by the oil pan. To remove the pump, remove the oil pan, the attaching bolts, and the pump. When installing, use a new gasket and fill the pump with oil to prime it.

V6 Engine

Remove the oil pan and remove the bolt that retains the oil pick-up screen to the main bearing cap. Remove the oil pump retaining bolts. Lift off the oil pump and pull out the oil

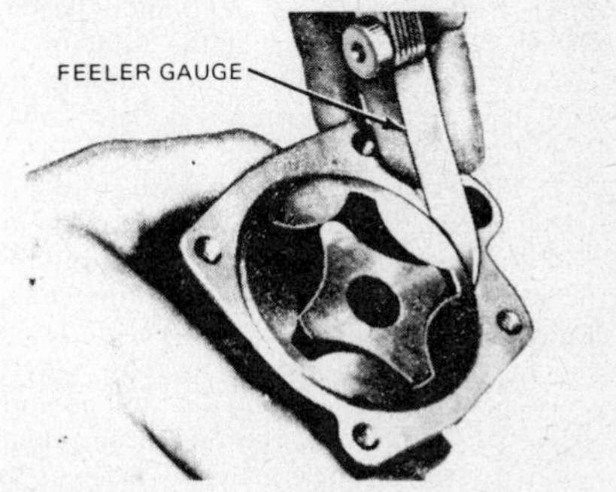

Checking oil pump outer race to housing clearance

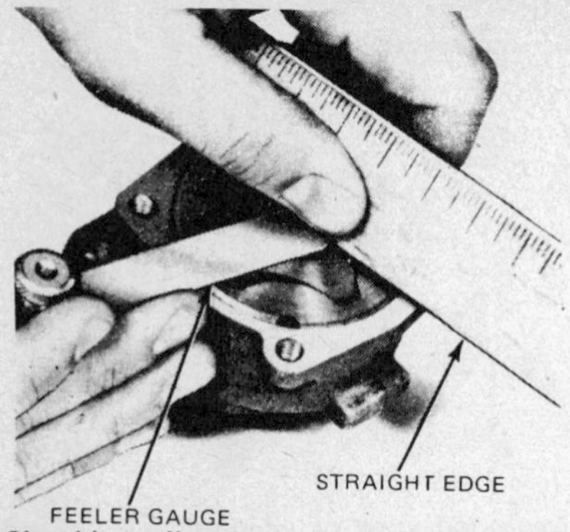

Checking oil pump rotor end clearance

pump driveshaft. When installing the pump, insert the driveshaft into the engine block with the pointed end facing inward. Use a new gasket and fill the pump with oil to prime it.

CHECKING CLEARANCES

Inspect the inside of the oil pump housing, the outer race, and the rotor, for wear or damage. Measure the outer race-to-housing clearance.

With the rotor assembly installed in the housing, place a ruler over the rotor assembly and the housing. Check the clearance between the ruler and the rotor outer race.

Oil Pump Clearance Specifications

Model	Outer Race-to-Housing	Rotor Assembly End Clearance
2000, 2600	0.005-0.011	0.001-0.004
2300	0.001-0.007	0.001-0.004
2800	0.006-0.012	0.001-0.004

ENGINE COOLING

The four cylinder engines employ a pressurized cooling system with the pump fan assembly bolted to the front face of the cylinder block. Coolant is circulated from the base of the radiator up through the water pump and into the cylinder block. The coolant circulates through the engine block and cylinder head to the thermostat, located at the front of the cylinder head. It then returns to the top radiator tank, flows down the radiator tubes, and is cooled by passing air.

The V6 system has a three-stage system which uses a centrifugal type water pump with the thermostat located in the water inlet housing at the lower left corner of the engine front cover. In the first stage, coolant flow to the radiator is blocked off to allow a quick warmup. In the second, normal temperature stage, some coolant is returned from the engine directly through a bypass hose to the water pump. In the third, overheat stage, the bypass hose is blocked off by the thermostat so that all coolant must circulate through the radiator.

NOTE: On the V6 it may be necessary to disconnect the heater hose from the water outlet on top of the engine while filling the radiator. When water comes from both the hose and the outlet, the system is free of air.

Radiator

REMOVAL AND INSTALLATION

1. Remove the radiator upper splash shield. Unbolt the shroud and place it over the fan.
2. Place a drain pan under the radiator, remove the cap, open the drain plug, and drain the radiator.
3. Disconnect the upper and lower radiator hoses.
4. Disconnect the automatic transmission cooling lines from the radiator, if so equipped.
5. Remove the retaining screws and lift out the radiator.
6. Reverse the procedures to install.
7. Refill the cooling system with antifreeze solution.
8. Run the engine, with the cap off and heater on, to relieve any air pockets, then install the radiator cap, run the engine, and check for leaks.

Water Pump

REMOVAL AND INSTALLATION

1. Drain the cooling system.
2. Disconnect the lower radiator hose and heater hose from the water pump.
3. Remove the alternator belt. Remove the fan shroud.
4. Remove the fan attaching bolts and remove the fan, spacer, and water pump pulley. Remove the camshaft drive belt cover from OHC engines.
5. Remove the water pump attaching bolts and the water pump. Note that there are different lengths of bolts on the V6.
6. Clean all gasket material from all mounting surfaces.
7. Transfer the heater hose fitting to the new water pump.
8. Coat the new gasket with sealer and position the pump and gasket on the engine.
9. Install the pump mounting bolts. Install the camshaft drive belt cover on 4 cylinder engines.
10. Install the fan, spacer, and water pump pulley.
11. Install the alternator belt. Install the fan shroud.
12. Connect the heater and radiator hoses.
13. Fill the cooling system, run the engine, and check for leaks.

Thermostat

All thermostats installed in these engines start to open at 185-192° F.

REMOVAL AND INSTALLATION

4 Cylinder Engine

1. Drain the cooling system.
2. Remove the thermostat housing attaching bolts.
3. Lift the thermostat housing from the engine and remove the retaining ring, thermostat, and seal from the engine.
4. Clean all gasket material from the engine and thermostat housing.
5. Assemble the thermostat, seal, and retaining ring to the housing.
6. Install the housing bolts and tighten them.
7. Fill the cooling system.

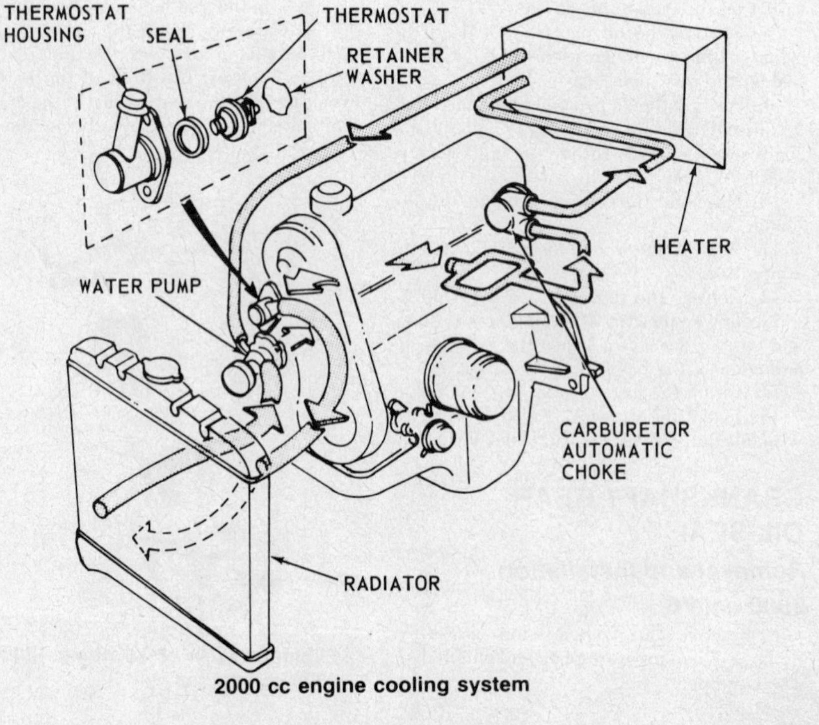

2000 cc engine cooling system

V6 Engine

1. Drain the cooling system.
2. Disconnect the radiator and heater hose from the thermostat housing cover.
3. Remove the three screws which hold the thermostat housing to the water pump. Pull the housing cover away from the water pump and remove the thermostat.
4. Clean the thermostat housing cover and water pump surfaces of all gasket material.
5. Position the thermostat in the water pump and install a new gasket and thermostat housing cover.
6. Connect the radiator and heater hoses. Fill the cooling system, run the engine, and check for leaks.

EMISSION CONTROLS

PCV Valve (Positive Crankcase Ventilation Valve)

The PCV valve is located in the oil separator on 4 cylinder engines. On the V6 engine the PCV valve is located at the left front of the intake manifold and screws out.

TESTING

With the engine running, remove the PCV valve from its mounting. Block off the end of the valve with your finger. You should feel a vacuum when the valve is blocked. Another test is to remove the valve (engine stopped) and shake it. There will be a clicking sound if the valve is free.

Decel Valve

The decel valve is mounted on the intake manifold, adjacent to the carburetor. The purpose of this valve is to meter an additional amount of fuel and air to the engine during deceleration. During deceleration, the manifold vacuum forces the diaphragm assembly in the decel valve against the spring which in turn raises the decel valve. With the valve now open, existing manifold vacuum pulls a metered amount of fuel and air from the carburetor and travels through the valve body assembly into the intake manifold. The decel valve remains open and continues to feed additional fuel and air for a specified time.

TESTING

To prevent unnecessary replacement of the decel valve, the following test should be performed. If the decel valve is found to be out of adjustment, the complete adjustment procedure should be performed before the valve is replaced.

Idle speed and initial ignition timing settings are detailed for all engines on the emission sticker located in the engine compartment.

1. Run the engine until it reaches operating temperature and then turn it off.
2. Connect a tachometer and timing light to the engine.
3. Disconnect both distributor vacuum lines and plug the intake manifold line.
4. With the engine running at the idle

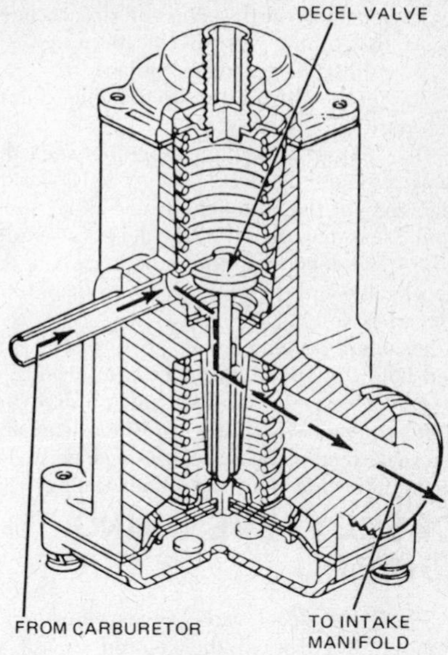

SECTIONAL VIEW
(VALVE SHOWN IN OPEN POSITION)

Decel valve

Decel Valve Timing Chart

Engine	Valve Timing
2000 (manual trans)	2.5-3.5 sec
2000 (auto. trans)	1.5-3.5 sec
2600 (manual trans)	1.5-3.5 sec
2600 (auto. trans)	1.5-3.5 sec
All 1974 models	2-5 sec

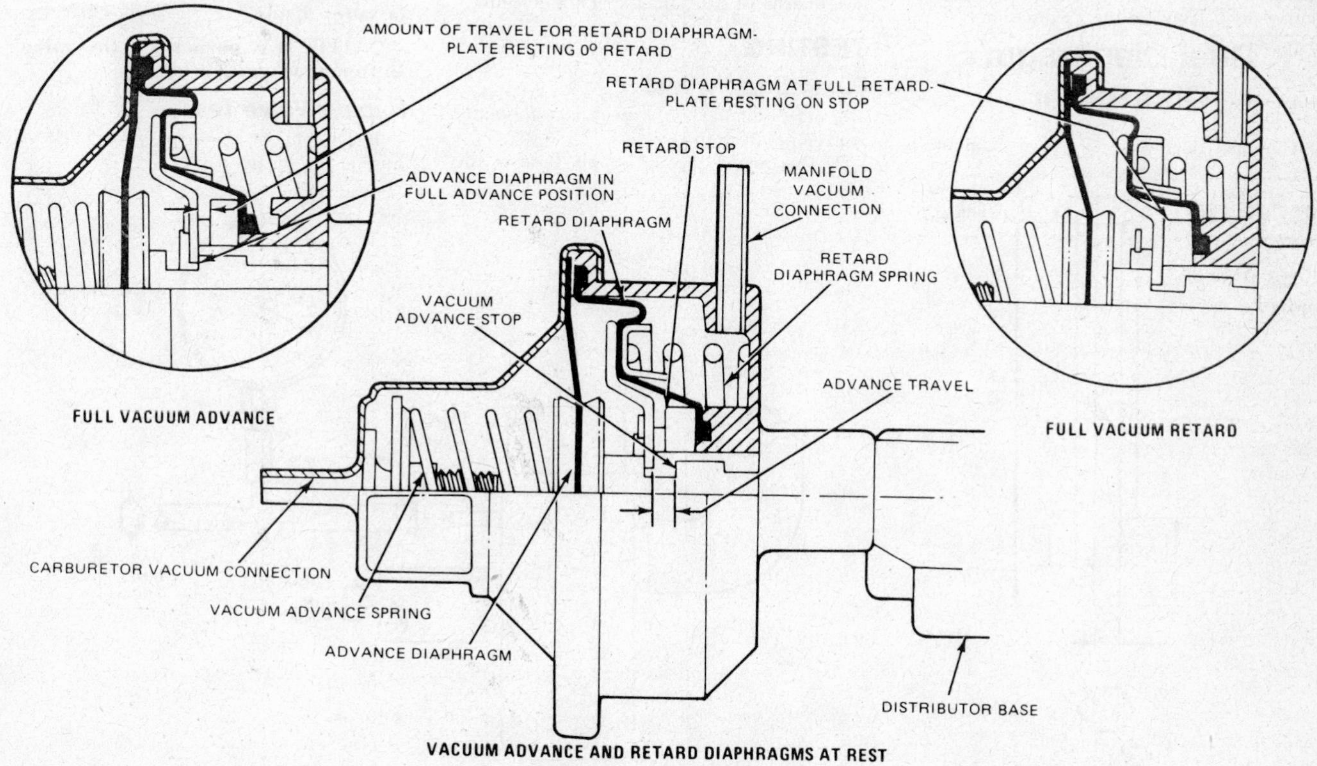

Dual vacuum diaphragm

speed specified on the emission decal, check to see that timing is to specifications.

5. Adjust the timing as required.

6. Set the idle limiter cap to the maximum rich position.

7. Connect a vacuum gauge between the carburetor and the decel valve. The ID (inside diameter) of the connections and pipes must not be less than the ID of the decel valve inlet tube. The length of the tube between the decel valve and the vacuum gauge should not exceed 60 in.

8. Increase the engine speed to 3000 rpm and hold this speed for about two seconds.

9. Release the throttle and observe the time interval between the throttle release and a zero (0) reading on the vacuum gauge. Refer to the following chart for proper timing.

DECEL VALVE TIMING CHART

10. If the decel valve needs adjustment, remove and discard the colored cap (if so equipped) for access to the nylon adjuster. Use the tool shown in the illustration to adjust the decel valve. This tool can be made by grinding down a ⅜ in. allen wrench to the dimensions shown.

11. Insert the tool into the decel valve nylon adjusting screw. To increase the valve timing, back out the screw (counterclockwise). To decrease the valve timing, turn the adjusting screw inward (clockwise). One turn of the adjuster in either direction will increase or decrease the valve timing approximately ½ second.

12. Snap in a new colored cap in the top of the decel valve, if so equipped.

13. Remove the vacuum gauge and connect the tube between the carburetor and the decel valve. Remove the tachometer and the timing light. Connect the vacuum lines.

Dual Diaphragm Distributor

The dual diaphragm is a two-chambered housing which is mounted on the side of the distributor. The outer side of the housing is a distributor vacuum advance mechanism. The vacuum advance is connected to the carburetor by a vacuum hose. The purpose of the vacuum advance is to advance the ignition timing according to the conditions under which the engine is operating.

The second side of the dual diaphragm has been added to the older type of distributor to help control engine exhaust emissions at idle and on deceleration. This inner side of the diaphragm is connected by a vacuum hose to the intake manifold. When the engine is idling, intake manifold vacuum is high and the carburetor vacuum is low. Under these conditions, intake manifold vacuum, applied to the inner side of the dual diaphragm, retards the ignition timing to promote more complete combustion of the air-fuel mixture in the engine combustion chambers.

Testing and adjustments of these distributors requires the use of an off-the-car distributor machine.

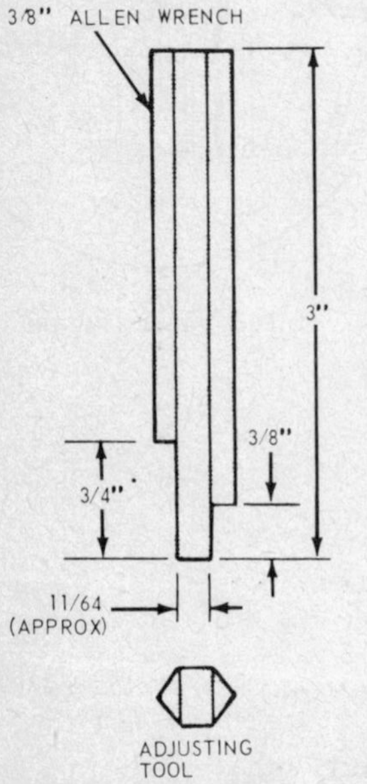

Decel valve adjusting tool

Thermactor (Air Pump) System

The Thermactor system is used on all models to reduce carbon monoxide and hydrocarbon content of exhaust gases. It does this by injecting air into the hot exhaust gases as they leave the combustion chamber. A belt-driven air pump with a centrifugal filter fan on the intake forces the air through external air passages on the 4 cylinder, and internal passages on the V6. A vacuum-operated bypass valve dumps excess air during deceleration to prevent backfiring in the exhaust manifold. A check valve in the system prevents reverse flow of exhaust gases in case of pump failure.

TESTING

Pump Supply Test

1. The engine should be at normal operating temperature.

2. Disconnect the air supply hose at the check valve. If there are two check valves, clamp a plug in the end of one hose.

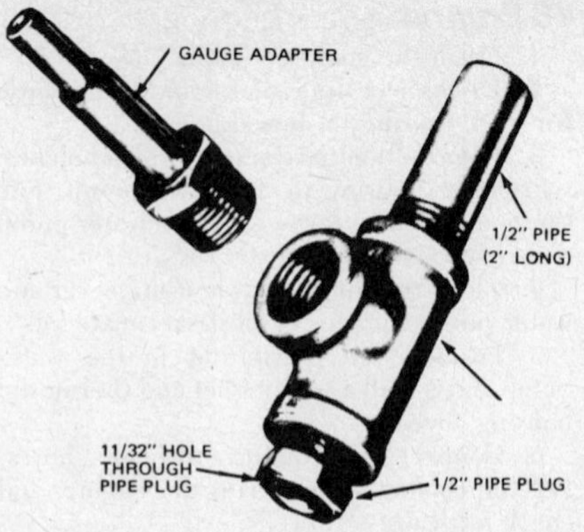

Thermactor system test gauge adapter

3. Clamp an adapter and pressure gauge into the air supply hose.

4. Start the engine and slowly increase its speed to 1500 rpm.

5. Air pressure should be 1 psi or more. If not, the pump must be replaced.

Check Valve Test

1. The engine should be at normal operating temperature.

2. Disconnect the air supply hose at the check valve. If there are two, disconnect them both.

3. The valve plate inside the valve body should be lightly against the seat, and away from the air or exhaust manifold.

4. Depress the valve plate with a screwdriver. It should return freely to the seat when released.

5. Leave the hose or hoses off and start the engine. Increase speed slowly to 1500 rpm.

6. Feel for exhaust gas leakage at the valve or valves. Replace any leakers.

NOTE: It is normal for the valve to flutter or vibrate at idle speed.

Bypass Valve Test

1. Disconnect the bypass to check valve hose at the bypass valve.

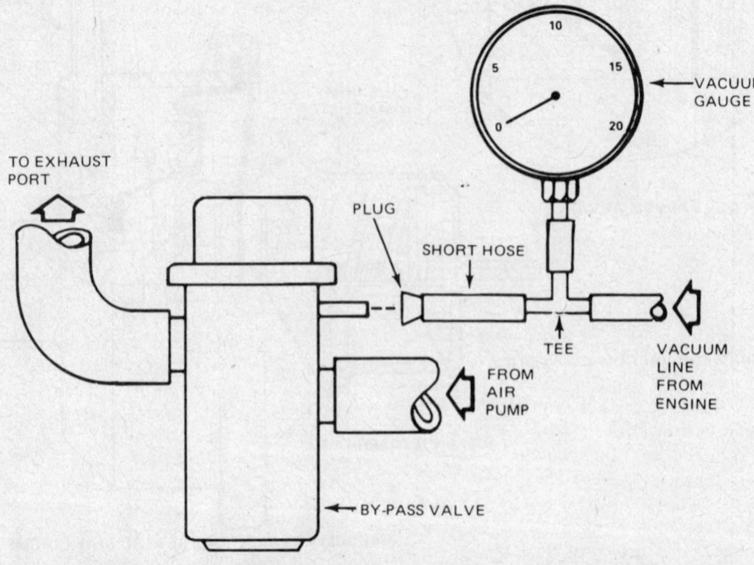

Vacuum gauge hookup for Thermactor system bypass valve test

2. Start the engine and let it idle.
3. Air should be coming from the hose.
4. Pinch the vacuum line to the bypass valve shut for 5-8 seconds.
5. Air flow through the bypass valve should stop for a while when you release the vacuum hose. No time length is specified.
6. Check the bypass valve for leaks:
a. Tee a vacuum gauge into the bypass valve vacuum hose.
b. Plug the end of the hose.
c. Note the gauge reading with the engine running.
d. Remove the plug and connect the vacuum hose to the bypass valve. Check the vacuum reading after 60 seconds.
e. If readings c. and d. differ, replace the bypass valve.

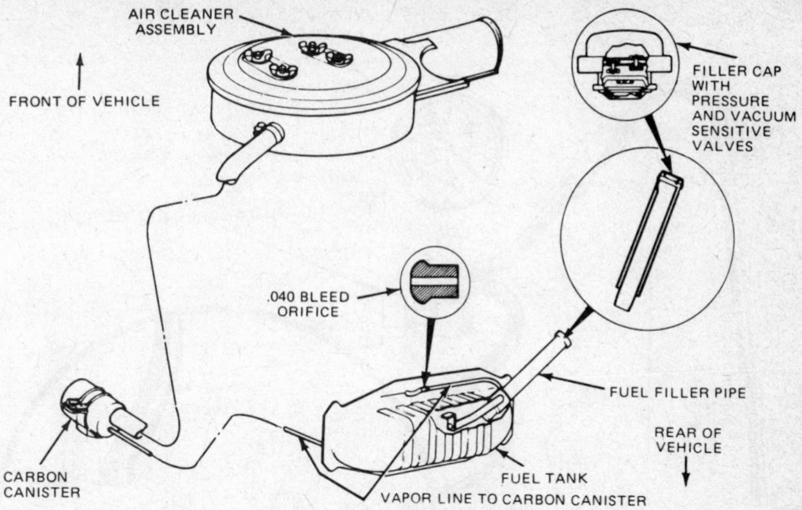

V6 fuel evaporative system

EGR (Exhaust Gas Recirculation) System

The EGR system is used on all models to reduce combustion temperatures and production of oxides of nitrogen by introducing a small volume of exhaust gas into the combustion chamber. The vacuum operated EGR valve is mounted on a spacer plate under the carburetor. The amount of exhaust gas recirculated and when it is recirculated are controlled by engine vacuum and temperature. A venturi vacuum amplifier is used to operate the EGR valve with manifold vacuum, under the control of carburetor vacuum.

SYSTEM TEST

1. With the engine running at normal operating temperature, about 8 in. Hg vacuum should be sufficient to open the EGR valve.
2. If the valve is operating properly, the engine should slow and idle roughly when the valve is opened at idle.
3. A rough idle may be caused by an EGR valve or gasket that isn't sealing properly.

Evaporative Emission System

This emission system is designed to limit the emission of fuel vapors into the atmosphere and prevent raw gas from escaping from the fuel tank. The system consists of four components: the fuel tank; a pressure-sensitive and vacuum-sensitive fuel tank cap; a restrictor in the vapor line; and a vapor-absorbing charcoal canister.

This system allows fuel vapors to escape but prevents liquid gasoline from escaping. The fuel vapors enter the vapor separator outlet hose to the charcoal canister which is mounted in the engine compartment. The vapors enter the canister, pass through a charcoal filter, and then exit through a hole in the bottom. As the vapors pass through the charcoal they are cleansed of hydrocarbons so the air that passes from the canister is free of pollutants.

When the engine is running, vacuum from the carburetor draws fresh air into the charcoal canister. As the entering air passes through the charcoal in the canister, it picks up the hydrocarbons that were deposited by the gasoline vapors. This gas mixture is then carried to the carburetor where it combines with incoming air and enters the combustion chambers of the engine to be burned.

Heated Air Intake Duct

The heated air intake portion of the air cleaner consists of a thermostat and a spring-loaded temperature control door in the snorkel of the air cleaner. The temperature control door is located between the end of the air cleaner snorkel, which draws in air from the engine compartment, and the duct that carries heated air up from the exhaust manifold. When the temperature under the hood is below 85° F (100° on the V6), the temperature control door blocks off under-hood air from entering the air cleaner and allows only heated air from the exhaust manifold to be drawn into the air cleaner. When the temperature under the hood rises above 110° F (135° F on the V6), the temperature control door blocks off heated air from the exhaust manifold and allows only under-hood air to be drawn into the air cleaner. Between 90 and 110° (135°) F, a mixture of heated and underhood air is provided. By controlling the temperature of the engine intake air this way, exhaust emissions are lowered and fuel economy increased.

TESTING

4 Cylinder Engine

1. With the engine cold and the temperature under the hood below 85° F, check the position of the temperature door in the air cleaner. It should be in the up (open) position, blocking off underhood air.
2. Remove the air cleaner from the car. Immerse the air cleaner duct assembly in water, raise the water temperature to 85° F, and allow the temperature to stabilize for five minutes. The flap should be open to hot air. Now raise the temperature to 110° F stabilize. The temperature control door should be in the down position, blocking off the heated air from the exhaust manifold.

If the temperature door does not react in this manner, and the door is not binding, replace the valve and duct assembly.

V6 Engine

1. With the engine cold and the underhood temperature less than 100° F, the valve plate should be in the heat on position.
2. Immerse the duct assembly in water, raise the temperature to 100° F, and allow the temperature to stabilize for five minutes. The valve should still be in the heat on position.
3. Now raise the temperature to 135° F and stabilize. The valve plate should be in the heat off position. Replace the duct and valve assembly if large variations from the specified temperatures were found.

FUEL SYSTEM

FUEL FILTER REPLACEMENT

1. Remove air cleaner.
2. Loosen the clamps securing the fuel filter to the fuel line hoses.
3. Remove the fuel filter and discard the clamps.
4. Install a new filter using new clamps.
5. Crimp clamps securely, start engine and check for leaks.
6. Install air cleaner.

Fuel Pump

A single-action fuel pump is used on all models. The fuel pump is on the left side of the engine and is actuated by an eccentric on the auxiliary shaft on OHC engines or a rod driven by the camshaft (V6).

TESTING

Pressure Test

Disconnect the fuel line from the carburetor and attach a pressure tester to the line. Idle the engine and note the reading on the tester. The readings should be 3.5-5.5 psi.

Capacity Test

Disconnect the fuel line from the carbure-

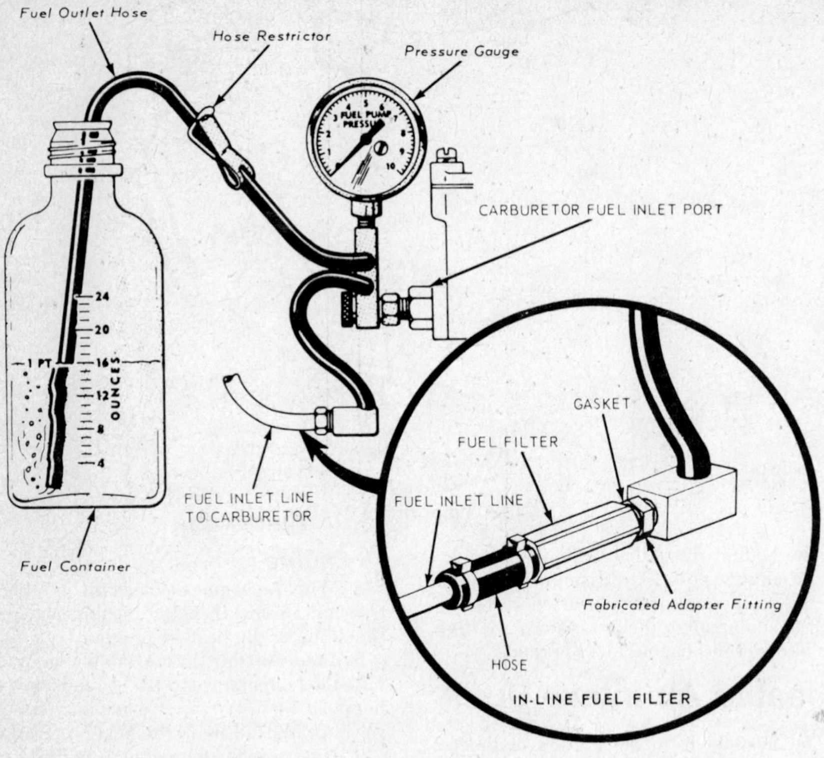

Fuel pump pressure and capacity test

tor and insert it into a one quart container. Crank the 2000 cc and 2300 cc engines for 35-43 seconds, and the V6 engine for 15 seconds (25 starting 1976). The bottle should be half-full (one pint).

REMOVAL AND INSTALLATION

1. Disconnect the inlet line and outlet fuel lines at the fuel pump.
2. Remove the fuel pump retaining bolts and remove the pump and gasket. Discard the gasket.
3. Remove all the gasket material from the engine block and pump mounting surface. Apply oil-resistant sealer to both sides of the new gasket. Position the gasket on the fuel pump flange and hold the pump in position against the engine block.

NOTE: Make sure the rocker arm or rod is riding on the camshaft eccentric.

4. Press the pump tightly against the engine block, install the retaining bolts and tighten them securely.
5. Connect the fuel lines. Start the engine and check for leaks.

Carburetors

The 2000, 2300 and 2600 cc engines are equipped with a model 5200 two barrel carburetor. The 2800 cc engines are equipped with a model 2150 carburetor. 1977 California 2800 cc engines use a 2700 VV (variable venturi) carburetor. On the 2bbl carburetor, the primary venturi is smaller than the secondary venturi. The two are connected by mechanical linkage and, when the primary throttle plate opens approximately 45° the secondary plate begins to open.

REMOVAL AND INSTALLATiON

1. Remove the air cleaner.
2. Remove the bolt that attaches the choke water housing to the carburetor and remove the water cover with its hoses attached. Detach the electrically assisted choke wire.
3. Note the location of all fuel lines and vacuum hoses that attach to the carburetor, then disconnect them from the carburetor.
4. Disconnect the throttle linkage from the carburetor.
5. Disconnect the throttle solenoid wire at the push-on connection.
6. Remove the four nuts that attach the carburetor to the intake manifold.
7. Inspect the carburetor base gasket. If it is damaged in any way, replace it. Clean any foreign matter from the base of the carburetor.
8. Position the carburetor on the intake manifold and tighten the nuts.
9. Connect the vacuum lines and the fuel lines to the carburetor.
10. Connect the throttle linkage to the carburetor.
11. Connect the water housing to the carburetor.
12. On those models equipped with a

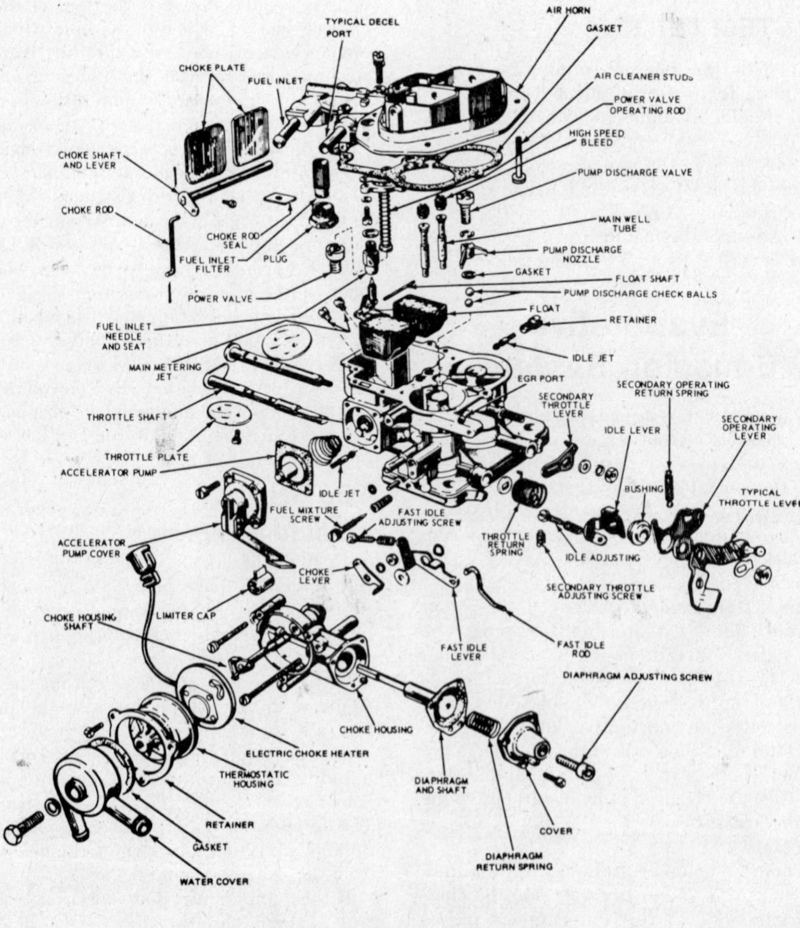

Exploded view of 5200 carburetor

throttle solenoid, connect the lead wire at the push-on connector.

13. Replace any coolant that was lost in the removal of the water hoses.

OVERHAUL

Efficient carburetion depends greatly on careful cleaning and inspection during overhaul since dirt, gum, water, or varnish in or on the carburetor parts are often responsible for poor performance.

Overhaul your carburetor in a clean, dust-free area. Carefully disassemble the carburetor, referring often to the exploded views. Keep all similar and lookalike parts segregated during disassembly and cleaning to avoid accidental interchange during assembly. Make a note of all jet sizes.

When the carburetor is disassembled, wash all parts except diaphragms, electric choke units, pump plunger, and any other plastic, leather, fiber, or rubber parts) in clean carburetor solvent. Do not leave parts in the solvent any longer than is necessary to sufficiently loosen the deposits. Excessive cleaning may remove the special finish from the float bowl and choke valve bodies, leaving these parts unfit for service. Rinse all parts in clean solvent and blow them dry with compressed air or allow them to air dry. Wipe clean all cork, plastic, leather, and fiber parts with a clean, lint-free cloth.

Blow out all passages and jets with compressed air and be sure that there are no restrictions or blockages. Never use wire or similar tools to clean jets, fuel passages, or air bleeds. Clean all jets and valves separately to avoid accidental interchange.

Check all parts for wear or damage. If wear or damage is found, replace the defective parts. Especially check the following:

1. Check the float needle and seat for wear. If wear is found, replace the complete assembly.
2. Check the float hinge pin for wear and the float(s) for dents or distortion. Replace the float if fuel has leaked into it.
3. Check the throttle and choke shaft bores for wear or an out-of-round condition. Damage or wear to the throttle arm, shaft, or shaft bore will often require replacement of the throttle body. These parts require a close tolerance of fit; wear may allow air leakage, which could affect starting and idling.

NOTE: Throttle shafts and bushings are not included in overhaul kits. They can be purchased separately.

4. Inspect the idle mixture adjusting needles for burrs or grooves. Any such condition requires replacement of the needle, since you will not be able to obtain a satisfactory idle.
5. Test the accelerator pump check valves. They should pass air one way but not the other. Test for proper seating by blowing and sucking on the valve. Replace the valve if necessary. If the valve is satisfactory, wash the valve again to remove breath moisture.
6. Check the bowl cover for warped surfaces with a straightedge.
7. Closely inspect the valves and seats for wear and damage, replacing as necessary.
8. After the carburetor is assembled, check the choke valve for freedom of operation.

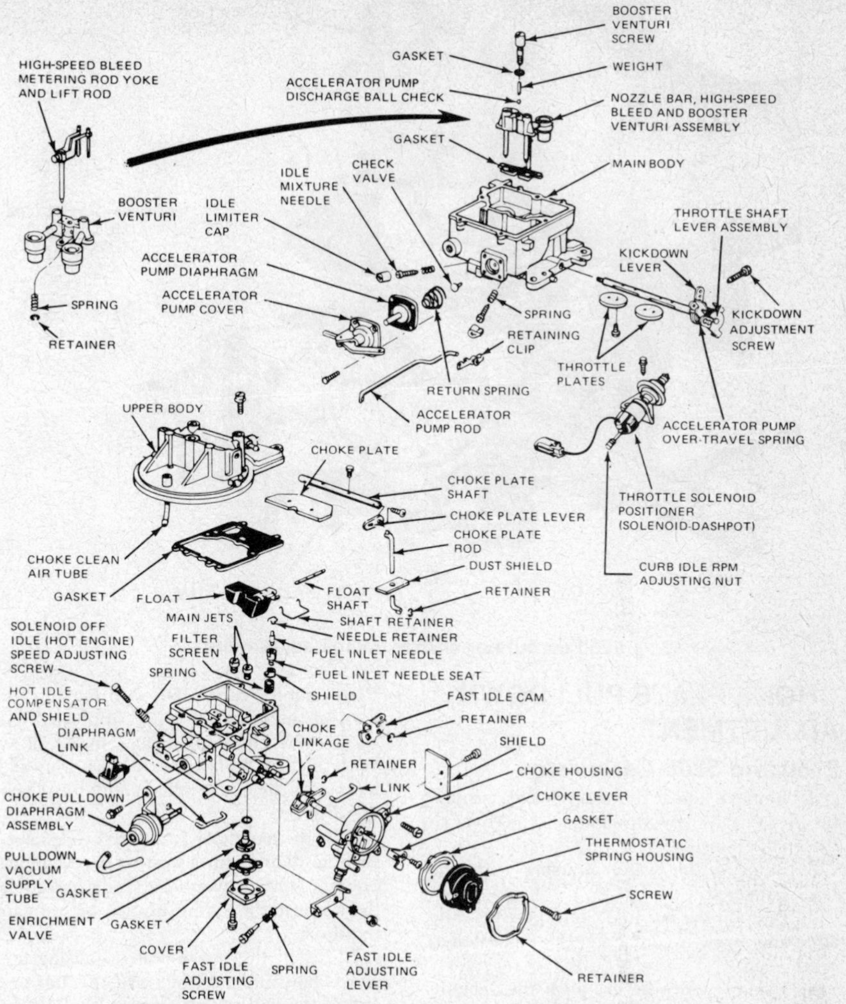

Exploded view of 2150 carburetor used on Capri II V6

Carburetor overhaul kits are recommended for each overhaul. These kits contain all gaskets and new parts to replace those that deteriorate most rapidly. Failure to replace all parts supplied with the kit (especially gaskets) can result in poor performance later.

After cleaning and checking all components, reassemble the carburetor, using new parts and referring to the exploded view. When reassembling, make sure that all screws and jets are tight in their seats, but do not overtighten, as the tips will be distorted. Tighten all screws gradually, in rotation. Do not tighten needle valves into their seats; uneven jetting will result. Always use new gaskets. Be sure to adjust the float level when reassembling.

CHOKE UNLOADER ADJUSTMENT

5200 Carburetor

1. Hold the carburetor throttle lever in the wide-open position.
2. Insert a 0.256 in. drill bit into the air horn of the carburetor.
3. Apply light pressure to the choke plate to remove all slack.
4. With the drill bit against the carburetor wall, the bottom of the choke plate should just contact the drill. If it does not, bend the tab on the fast idle lever where it contacts the fast idle cam to correct it.

AUTOMATIC CHOKE ADJUSTMENT

2150 and 5200 Carburetor

1. Loosen the three screws that attach the choke water housing to the choke housing.
2. Turn the choke water housing as required to align the index mark on the water housing with the specified mark on the choke housing. If the choke cap setting is index, align the notch on the water cover with the large index mark in the center of the top of the choke housing. If the choke setting is one lean, align the notch on the water cover with the first notch to the left of the large index mark on the choke housing.

Choke Specifications

Model	Carburetor	Setting
2000, 2600	Manual	1 Lean
2000, 2600	Automatic	Index
All 1974 and Later Models	See Engine Compartment Sticker	

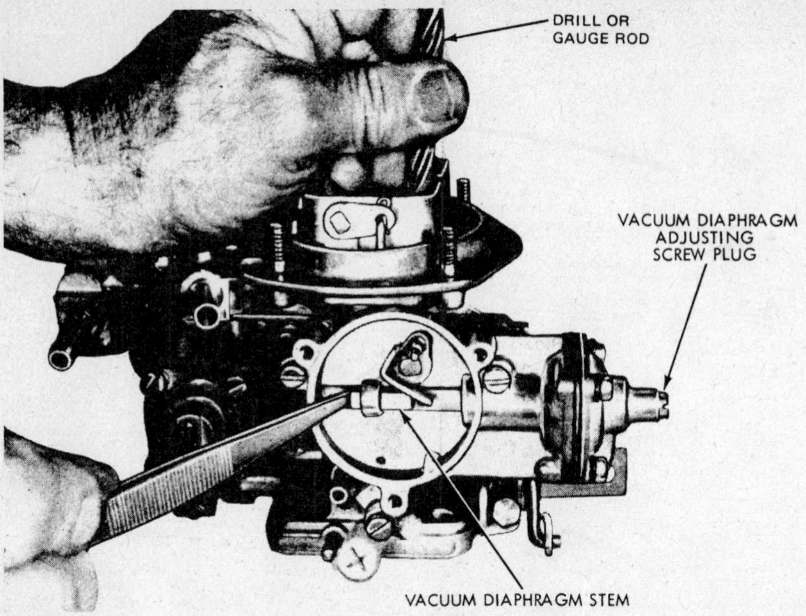

5200 carburetor choke linkage adjustment

CHOKE PLATE PULLDOWN ADJUSTMENT

2150 and 5200 Carburetor

1. Remove the three screws from around the choke water cover that attach the cover to the choke housing.
2. Remove the water housing with the hoses attached.
3. Position the fast idle cam so the fast idle adjusting screw is contacting the highest step on the cam.
4. Using a screwdriver, push the vacuum diaphragm stem back into the diaphragm housing until it stops. Hold the stem in this position.
5. Insert a $^1/_4$ in. ($^{13}/_{64}$ in. for 1976-77 5200; $^9/_{64}$ in. for 1976-77 2150) drill bit into the air horn of the carburetor and apply light pressure to the choke plate to remove all slack. With the drill bit against the air horn wall, the bottom of the choke plate should just contact the drill bit.
6. If the clearance is incorrect, remove the vacuum diaphragm adjusting screw plug and insert a screwdriver into the exposed hole, then adjust the screw inward or outward as required.
7. Install the choke water housing on the choke housing, making sure the tab on the end of the coil spring engages the slot in the choke housing shaft.
8. Install the three choke water housing attaching screws and tighten them finger-tight. Adjust the automatic choke as previously described.

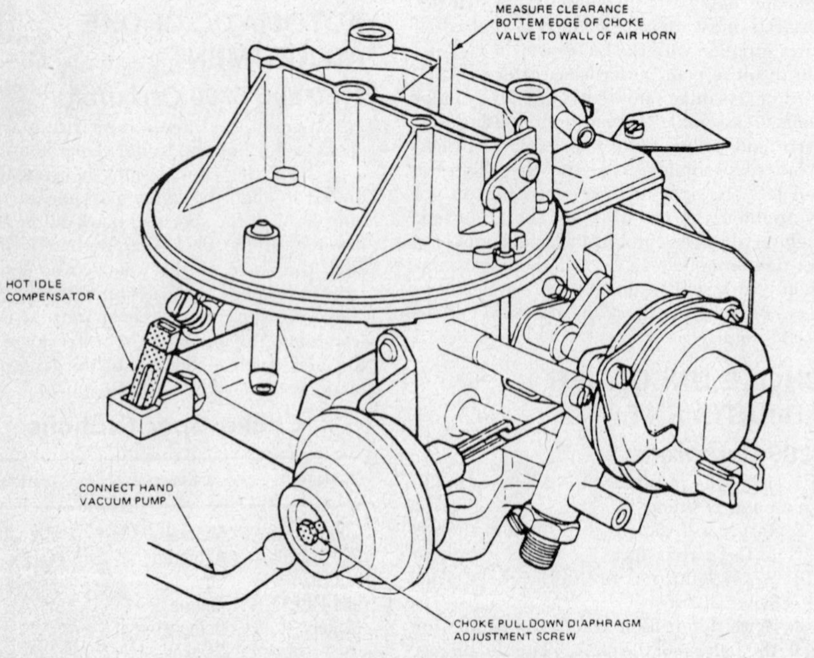

Adjusting choke plate pull-down—2150

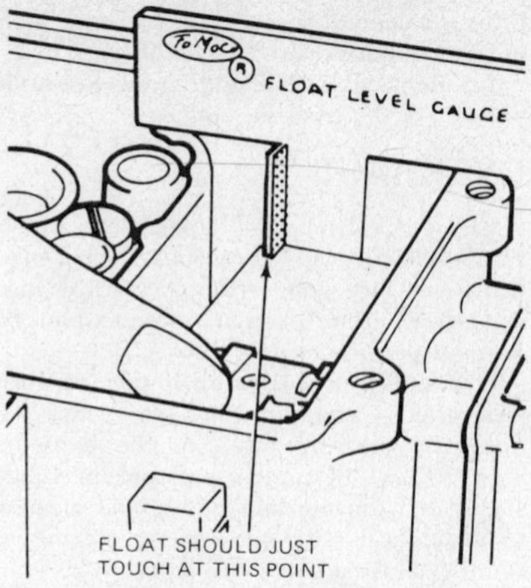

Dry float level adjustment—2150

FLOAT LEVEL ADJUSTMENTS

2150 Carburetor

A two stage adjustment procedure is necessary.

1. Remove and invert the air horn. With the inlet needle seated, check the distance between the top surface of the main body gasket and the top of the float. Setting should be ⅜″.
2. Bend float tab, if necessary, to adjust.
3. Replace air horn and operate engine to normal operating temperature. Place vehicle on as flat a surface as possible.
4. Stop engine and remove the air horn attaching screws.
5. Start engine and remove air horn.
6. While the engine is idling, use a standard depth scale to measure the vertical distance from the top of the machined surface of the carburetor main body to the level of the fuel in the bowl. The measurement must be made at least ¼″ away from any vertical surface. Setting should be ¾″.
7. If adjustment is necessary, stop engine and bend tab on float to adjust.

5200 Carburetor

1. Remove the air cleaner.
2. Disconnect the fuel and decel valve hoses from the carburetor.
3. Remove the small clip that attaches the choke rod to the choke plate shaft and disconnect the rod from the shaft.

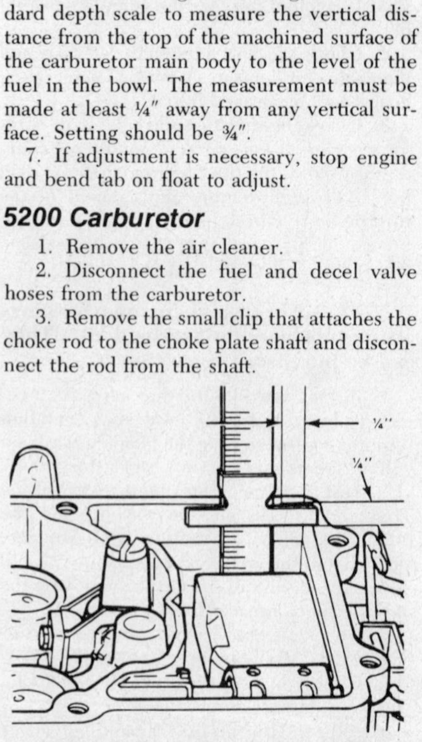

Wet float level adjustment—2150

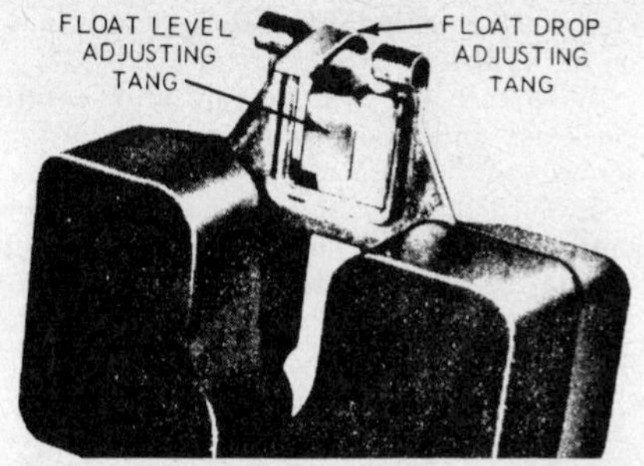

5200 carburetor float drop adjustment

4. Remove the screws that attach the upper body of the carburetor to the main body of the carburetor and carefully lift the upper body off the main body. Be careful not to tear the upper body gasket.

5. Turn the carburetor upper body upside down and measure the clearance between the bottom of each float and the bottom of the carburetor upper body. The clearance should be 0.420 in. (0.460 for the 1976-77 2300 cc).

6. If the clearance is incorrect, bend the float lever adjusting tang to correct it.

NOTE: Both floats must be adjusted to the same clearance.

7. With the upper body still in the inverted position, measure the clearance between the tang on the rear of the float mounting bracket and the bumper spring on the float pivot pin. The clearance should be 0.020-0.050 in. If the clearance is incorrect, bend the float drop tang to adjust it.

8. Position the upper body and gasket of the main body of the carburetor and connect the choke rod to the choke plate lever. Install the choke rod attaching clip in the hole in the rod.

9. Install the upper body attaching screws.

10. Connect the fuel and decel valve hoses to the carburetor.

11. Install the air cleaner.

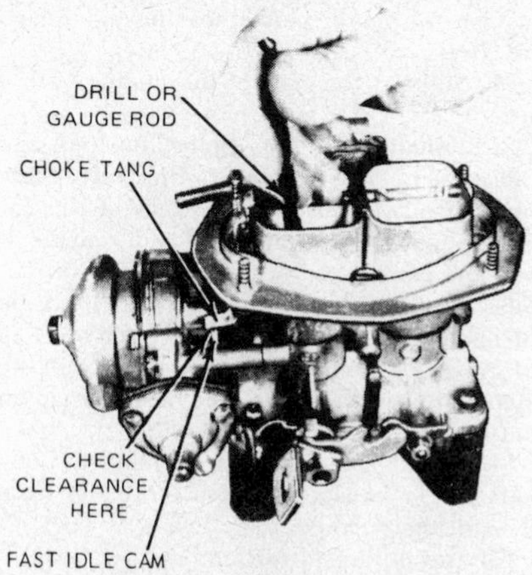

5200 carburetor fast idle

FAST IDLE CAM CLEARANCE

2150 & 5200 Carburetor

1. Place a 3/32 (5/32 for 1975) drill bit between the lower edge of the choke plate and the air horn wall.

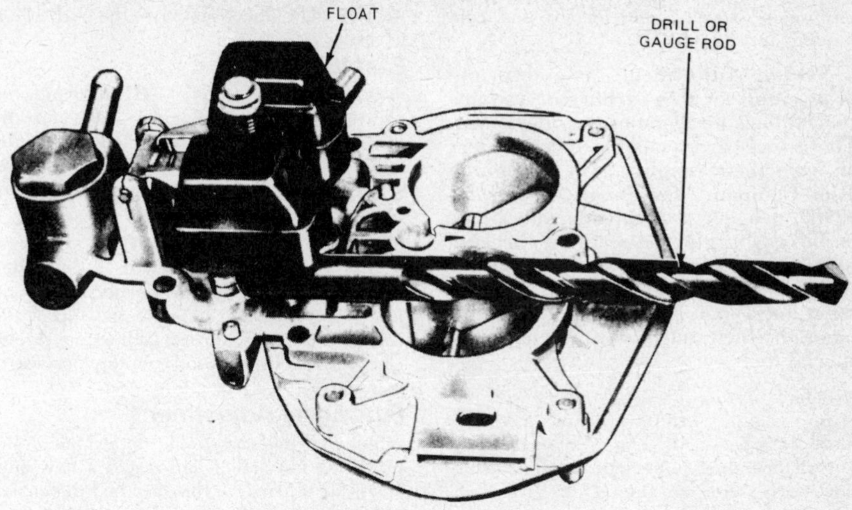

5200 carburetor float level adjustment

2. Set the fast idle screw on the second step of the fast idle cam and measure the clearance between the choke lever tang and the arm on the fast idle cam.

3. The clearance should be about 1/8 in.

4. If the clearance is excessively large or small, bend the choke lever tang up or down. Don't bend it any more than necessary; it can break off.

FAST IDLE ADJUSTMENT

All idle & mixture adjustments are to be made with the artificial enrichment procedure. This procedure is impractical for all but Ford dealers.

2700VV CARBURETOR ADJUSTMENTS

For 1977, Ford's new 2700VV (Variable Venturi) carburetor is on California cars with the V6 engine. Since the design of this carburetor differs considerably from the other carburetors in the Ford lineup, an explanation of the differences in both theory and operation of this carburetor is presented here.

In exterior appearance, the variable venturi carburetor is similar to conventional carburetors and, like a conventional carburetor, it uses a normal float and fuel bowl system. However, the similarity ends there. In place of a normal choke plate and fixed area venturis, the 2700VV carburetor has a pair of small oblong castings in the top of the upper carburetor body where you would normally expect to see the choke plate. These castings slide back and forth across the top of the carburetor in response to fuel/air demands. Their movement is controlled by a spring-loaded diaphragm valve regulated by a vacuum signal taken below the venturis in the throttle bores. As the throttle is opened, the strength of the vacuum signal increases, opening the venturis and allowing more air to enter the carburetor.

Fuel is admitted into the venturi area by means of tapered metering rods that fit into the main jets. These rods are attached to the venturis, and, as the venturis open or close in response to air demand, the fuel needed to maintain the proper mixture increases or decreases as the metering rods slide in the jets. In comparison to a conventional carburetor with fixed venturis and a variable air supply, this system provides much more precise control of the fuel/air supply during all modes of operation. Because of the variable venturi principle, there are fewer fuel metering systems and fuel passages. The only auxiliary fuel metering systems required are an idle trim, accelerator pump (similar to a conventional

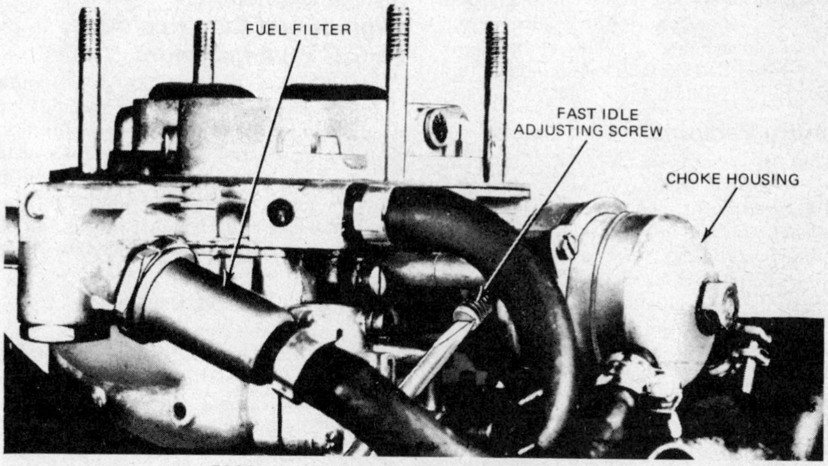

5200 carburetor fast idle adjustment

carburetor), starting enrichment, and cold running enrichment.

NOTE: Adjustment, assembly and disassembly of this carburetor require special tools for some of the operations. These tools are available from dealers or from their supplier, The Owatonna Tool Company, Owatonna Minnesota, 55060. Do not attempt any operations on this carburetor without first checking to see if you need the special tools for that particular operation. The adjustment and repair procedures given here mention when and if you will need the special tools.

Before making any adjustments with the engine running, set the parking brake and block the wheels. Make sure the engine is at normal operating temperature and that any power accessories are turned off.

Curb Idle Speed

Adjust the curb idle speed as you would on a conventional carburetor. Check the emission control sticker under the hood for the proper idle speed.

Internal Vent Adjustment

This adjustment must be checked whenever the curb idle speed is adjusted. After you have set the curb idle, place a .010 in. feeler gauge between the accelerator pump stem and the pump operating link. Turn the adjusting nut until there is just a slight drag when the gauge is removed.

Cold Enrichment Metering Rod

NOTE: This procedure requires special tools.

Remove the choke cap, after noting its position so that you will be able to return it to the correct setting. Install a dial indicator with the tip of the indicator on the top of the enrichment rod and adjust the dial to zero. The cold enrichment rod is seated by installing the stator cap as a weight. After installing the cap in place of the choke cap, raise it slightly and let it drop. This should seat the cold enrichment rod. The dial indicator should still read zero. If it does not, repeat the procedure. Remove the stator cap and re-install it in the choke cap's original position. The index mark on the stator cap should be in the same relative position as the index mark on the choke cap. The dial indicator should now read 0.125 in. If it does not, turn the adjusting nut clockwise to increase or counterclockwise to decrease rod height. Reinstall the choke cap in its original position.

Control Vacuum

You will need a tachometer, a vacuum gauge and some allen wrenches for this adjustment. With the engine at curb idle and a tachometer hooked up, turn the venturi valve diaphragm adjusting screw clockwise until the valve is completely closed. Connect a vacuum gauge to the vacuum tap on the venturi valve cover. Turn the venturi bypass adjusting screw to reach the specified vacuum (5 in. H_2O). Then turn the venturi valve diaphragm adjusting screw counterclockwise until the vacuum drops to the specified setting. In order to get the vacuum to drop, you must rev the engine once or twice. After you get the vacuum right, check and reset the curb idle if necessary.

Fast Idle Speed

Wit the engine idling, EGR disconnected and the vacuum line plugged, make sure the fast idle lever is on the specified step of the fast idle cam. Turn the fast idle adjusting screw clockwise to increase speed and counterclockwise to decrease speed.

Idle Mixture Adjustment

Idle trim is adjusted with a $^{3}/_{32}$ allen wrench. Remove the air cleaner cover and locate the adjusting holes in the top of the carburetor. Turn the air adjusting screws clockwise to enrichen and counterclockwise to lean out.

Fuel Level Adjustment

Remove the carburetor upper body. Remove the old gasket and install a new one. Fabricate a gauge to the specified dimension of $^{13}/_{64}$ in. Turn the upper body upside down and place the fuel level gauge on the cast surface, not on the gasket. Measure the vertical distance from the cast surface to the bottom of the float. If it needs adjustment, bend the float operating lever away from the fuel inlet needle to decrease the setting and toward the needle to increase the setting.

Float Drop Adjustment

You will need to fabricate a gauge for this adjustment, also. With the upper body in the upright position, measure the distance between the cast surface of the upper body and the bottom of the float. It should be $1^{15}/_{32}$ in. To adjust, bend the stop tab on the float lever away from the hinge pin to increase the setting and toward the hinge pin to decrease the setting.

Control Vacuum Regulator (CVR) Adjustment

NOTE: The cold enrichment metering rod adjustment must be set before making this adjustment.

Cycle the throttle to set the fast idle speed cam and then rotate the choke cap 180 degrees clockwise (rich). Press down on the CVR rod. If it moves downward, it is not seated and must be adjusted. To adjust, turn the rod clockwise until the adjusting nut just begins to rise. Then turn the adjusting screw clockwise in ¼ turn increments until the rod is fully seated (no down travel). Reset the choke cap to the original setting.

High Speed Cam Positioner (H.S.C.P.) Adjustment

Holding the throttle closed, place the H.S.C.P. in the corner of the specified cam step (counting the highest step as the first). Place the fast idle lever in the corner of the H.S.C.P. Remove the diaphragm cover and turn the assembly clockwise until it just bottoms on the casting, then turn it back until the vacuum port and diaphragm hole line up. Reinstall the cover.

Fast Idle Cam Setting

1. Remove the choke cap.
2. Place the fast idle lever in the corner of the specified step of the fast idle cam (counting the highest step as the first) with the high cam speed positioner retracted.
3. Hold the throttle lightly closed with a rubber band to maintain cam position. This step is not required if the adjustment is done on the vehicle.
4. Install the stator cap and rotate clockwise until lever contracts the adjusting screw.
5. Turn the fast idle cam adjusting screw until the index mark on the stator cap lines up with the specified notch on the choke casting.
6. Remove the stator cap and reinstall the choke cap.

MANUAL TRANSMISSION

REMOVAL AND INSTALLATION

1. Disconnect the ground cable from the battery.
2. Raise the car and support it with jackstands.
3. Disconnect the shift levers. Remove the shifter.
4. Remove the four bolts joining the driveshaft to the rear axle pinion. Also remove the two bolts securing the center bearing carrier to its bracket. Remove the driveshaft. Install a dummy yoke in the transmission to prevent oil loss if the oil has not been drained.
5. Remove the clip and the speedometer cable from the transmission.
6. Disconnect the exhaust pipe(s) from the exhaust manifold.
7. Move the clutch release lever boot and free the clutch operating cable from the lever.
8. Remove the starter motor attaching bolts and move the starter to one side.
9. Remove the bolts holding the clutch housing to the engine.
10. Remove the bolts holding the lower dust cover from the clutch housing and detach the cover.
11. Support the rear of the engine with a jack.
12. Remove the four bolts attaching the transmission crossmember to the body. Slide the transmission toward the rear of the car while supporting its weight, and remove it from the car.
13. Position the transmission assembly on the engine. Make sure that the clutch housing fully engages the dowel pins on the rear of the engine. Install the bolts attaching the clutch housing to the engine.
14. Install the four crossmember-to-body bolts and lockwashers. Remove the jack from beneath the engine.
15. Install the starter motor.
16. Replace the lower dust cover.
17. Coat the ball on the end of the clutch cable with chassis grease and install the clutch cable to the clutch release lever. Adjust the cable. (See the clutch section.) Locate the boot in the release lever opening.
18. Install the shift rods to the shifter, if so equipped.
19. Connect the exhaust pipe(s) to the exhaust manifold.

20. Install the speedometer cable and secure it with the retaining clip.

21. Install the driveshaft, aligning the mating marks. Replace the four nuts and bolts at the rear axle pinion. Locate the center bearing carrier in position and attach it to its bracket with the two bolts.

22. Refill the transmission if the oil was drained.

23. Remove the jackstands and lower the car to the ground. Check the transmission and the clutch for proper operation.

LINKAGE ADJUSTMENT

1. Make an alignment pin out of 3/16 in. rod stock.
2. Place the gearshift lever in neutral and raise the car off the ground.
3. Remove the spring retainers and disconnect the shifter rods from the transmission shift levers.
4. Insert the alignment pin in the shift levers.
5. Place all the transmission shift levers in the neutral position.
6. Adjust the length of the shifter rods so they fit into the holes in the transmission shift levers. Install the shifter rods and the spring retainers.
7. Remove the alignment pin and lower the car to the ground. Check the transmission for proper operation.

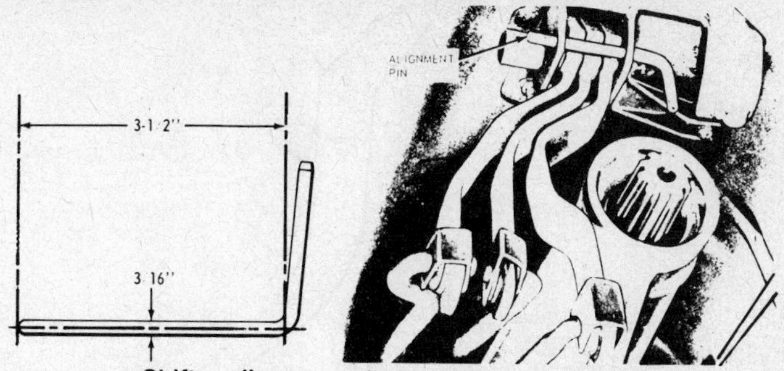

Shifter alignment pin for 2000, 2300, and V6

CLUTCH

REMOVAL AND INSTALLATION

1. Remove the transmission from the car.
2. Loosen each of the pressure plate-to-flywheel attaching bolts gradually to relieve the spring pressure.
3. If the same pressure plate is being used again, match-mark it with the flywheel so it may be installed in its original position.
4. Remove the clutch disc and the pressure plate from the car.
5. Position the pressure plate and the clutch disc on the flywheel and install the attaching bolts by hand, but do not tighten them with a wrench.
6. Install a clutch (dummy or pilot) shaft to the center of the clutch disc.
7. Tighten the pressure plate attaching bolts evenly to 12-15 ft/lbs.
8. Remove the dummy shaft.
9. Install the transmission.

CLUTCH ADJUSTMENT

2000

1. Loosen the locknut (2000 cc only) and position the clutch pedal back against the stop on the pedal bracket. Pull the outer cable forward. Turn the adjusting nut as necessary to obtain a clearance of 0.125-0.145 in. be-

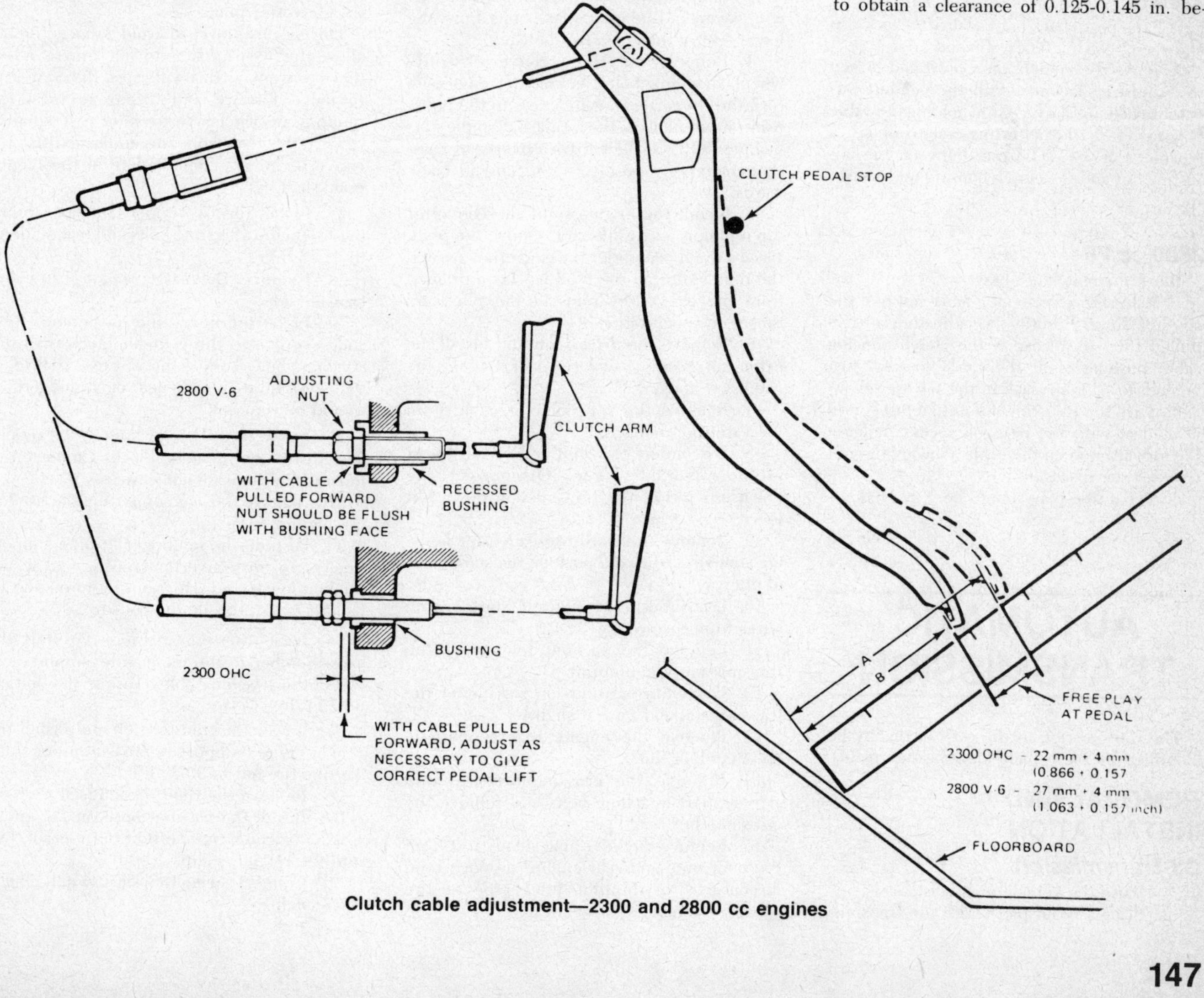

Clutch cable adjustment—2300 and 2800 cc engines

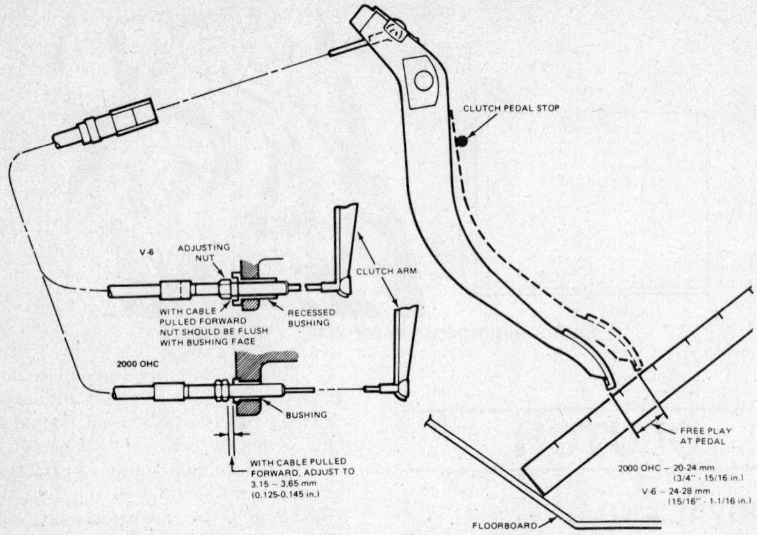

Clutch cable adjustment—2000 and 2600 cc engines

tween the nut and the clutch housing on the 2000 cc. With this setting, clutch pedal free-play should be ¾-15/16 in. pedal free-play.

2. Lock the locknut but do not overtighten it.

3. Lubricate the pedal end of the clutch cable.

2300 cc

Pull the pedal back hard against its backstop and secure with a block of wood.

1. Raise the vehicle on a hoist and loosen the adjusting locknut. Pull the conduit forward to take up slack. While holding the cable forward, turn the adjusting nut to obtain a clearance of 3.15-3.65 mm between the adjusting nut and the clutch housing cable bushing.

2800 cc V6

Block the clutch as above.

1. Raise the vehicle on a hoist and pull the conduit foward until the adjusting nut is pulled from its recess in the clutch housing cable bushing. Pull the cable forward just enough to take up slack in the release lever.

2. Turn the adjusting nut until it just comes in contact with the hexagon recess. Release the forward pull on the cable allowing the nut to enter the recess.

3. Pedal free-play should be 29/32-17/32.

AUTOMATIC TRANSMISSION

The transmission in the car can readily be identified by the vehicle identification plate.

REMOVAL AND INSTALLATION

C3 Transmission

1. Raise the vehicle on a hoist.

2. Place a drain pan under the transmission fluid pan. Starting at the rear of the pan and working toward the front, loosen the attaching bolts and allow the fluid to drain. Then remove all of the pan attaching bolts except two at the front, to allow the fluid to further drain. After all the fluid has drained, install two bolts on the rear side of the pan to temporarily hold it in place.

3. Remove the converter drain plug access cover and adapter plate bolts from the lower end of the converter housing.

4. Remove the three converter-to-flywheel attaching bolts. Crank the engine to turn the converter to gain access to the bolts, using a wrench on the crankshaft pulley attaching bolt. On belt driven overhead camshaft engines, never turn the engine backwards.

5. Crank the engine until the converter drain plug is accessible and remove the plug. Place a drain pan under the converter to catch the fluid. After all the fluid has been drained from the converter, reinstall the plug and torque to specification.

6. Remove the drive shaft and install the extension housing seal replacer tool in the extension housing.

7. Remove the speedometer cable from the extension housing.

8. Disconnect the shift rod at the transmission manual lever. Disconnect the downshift rod at the transmission downshift lever.

9. Remove the starter-to-converter housing attaching bolts and position the starter out of the way.

10. Disconnect the neutral start switch wires from the switch.

11. Remove the vacuum lines from the transmission vacuum unit.

12. Position a transmission jack under the transmission and raise it slightly.

13. Remove the engine rear support-to-crossmember nut.

14. Remove the crossmember-to-frame side support attaching bolts and remove the crossmember.

15. Remove the inlet pipe steady rest from the inlet pipe and rear engine support; then disconnect the muffler inlet pipe at the exhaust manifold and secure it.

16. Lower the jack under the transmission and allow the transmission to hang.

17. Position a jack to the front of the engine and raise the engine to gain access to the two upper converter housing-to-engine attaching bolts.

18. Disconnect the oil cooler lines at the transmission. Plug all openings to keep out dirt.

19. Remove the lower converter housing-to-engine attaching bolts.

20. Remove the transmission filler tube.

21. Secure the transmission to the jack with a safety chain.

22. Remove the two upper converter housing-to-engine attaching bolts. Move the transmission to the rear and down to remove it from under the vehicle.

23. Torque the converter drain plug to specification if not previously done.

24. Position the converter to the transmission making sure the converter hub is fully engaged in the pump gear.

25. With the converter properly installed, place the transmission on the jack and secure with safety chain.

26. Rotate the converter so the bolt drive lugs and drain plug are in alignment with their holes in the flywheel.

27. With the transmission mounted on a transmission jack, move the converter and transmission assembly forward into position being careful not to damage the flywheel and the converter pilot.

During this move, to avoid damage, do not allow the transmission to get into a nosed down position as this will cause the converter to move forward and disengage from the pump gear. The converter must rest squarely against the flywheel. This indicates that the converter pilot is not binding in the engine crankshaft.

28. Install the two upper converter housing-to-engine attaching bolts and torque them to 28-38 ft/lb.

29. Remove the safety chain from the transmission.

30. Insert the filler tube in the stub tube and secure it to the cylinder block with the attaching bolt. Torque the bolt to 7-10 ft/lb. If the stub tube is loosened or dislodged, it should be replaced.

31. Install the oil cooler lines in the retaining clip at the cylinder block. Connect the lines to the transmission case.

32. Remove the jack supporting the front of the engine.

33. Position the muffler inlet pipe support bracket to the converter housing and install the four lower converter housing-to-engine attaching bolts. Torque the bolts to 28-38 ft/lb.

34. Raise the transmission. Position the crossmember to the frame side supports and install the attaching bolts. Torque the bolts to 48-52 ft/lb.

35. Lower the transmission and install the rear engine support-to-crossmember nut. Torque the nut to 30-35 ft/lb.

36. Remove the transmission jack.

37. Install the vacuum hose on the transmission vacuum unit. Install the vacuum line into the retaining clip.

38. Connect the neutral start switch plug to the switch.

39. Install the starter and torque the attaching bolts to 20-25 ft/lb.

40. Install the three flywheel-to-converter attaching bolts.

Flywheel assemblies used with C3 Automatic Transmissions are designed with a pilot hole to be sure of proper flywheel-to-converter alignment. Prior to installing the transmission to the engine, the flywheel must be indexed with the pilot hole, in the six o'clock position.

When assembling the flywheel to the converter, first install the attaching bolt through the pilot hole and torque to 27-37 ft/lb. Install the remaining two bolts and torque to 30-35 ft/lb.

If the first bolt is not installed in the pilot hole, a misalignment of the flywheel holes and the mating converter weld nuts may occur. This misalignment will cause difficulty in installing the remaining bolts, crossthreaded bolts, or interference between flywheel and bolt threads. Any of these conditions will result in improperly torqued flywheel-to-converter attaching bolts, which may contribute to transmission or flywheel failures.

41. Install the converter drain plug access cover and adapter plate bolts. Torque the bolts to 5-7 ft/lb.

42. Connect the muffler inlet pipe to the exhaust manifold.

43. Connect the transmission shift rod to the manual lever.

44. Connect the downshift rod to the downshift lever.

45. Connect the speedometer cable to the extension housing.

46. Install the drive shaft. Torque the companion flange U-bolt attaching nuts to 17-23 ft/lb.

47. Adjust the manual and downshift linkage as required.

48. Lower the vehicle. Fill the transmission to the proper level with the specified fluid.

Pour in five quarts of fluid; then run the engine and add fluid as required.

49. Check the transmission, converter assembly and oil cooler lines for leaks.

C4 Transmission

1. Raise the car on a lift.

2. Drain the fluid from the transmission. Place a pan under the transmission. Loosen the transmission pan attaching bolts and allow the fluid to drain. After some fluid has drained remove all the bolts and remove the pan.

3. Remove the ground cable from the battery at the engine block. Disconnect the starter cable from the starter. Remove the starter attaching bolts and remove the starter.

4. Remove the access cover from the lower part of the converter housing.

5. Remove the nuts which hold the converter to the flywheel. You must rotate the flywheel in order to gain access to the bolts. To rotate the flywheel, place a socket on the crankshaft pulley bolt and turn it.

6. Cars equipped with a V6 engine have a drain plug on the converter. Rotate the flywheel as previously described to gain access to the converter plug. Remove the plug and drain the fluid. Replace the plug after draining the fluid.

7. Mark the driveshaft for correct alignment when installing.

8. Remove the bolts which hold the driveshaft center bearing to the body.

9. Lower the driveshaft assembly and remove it from the car.

10. Remove the speedometer cable from the tailshaft.

11. Disconnect the shift cable from the lever on the transmission.

12. Remove the shift cable bracket from the converter housing.

13. Disconnect the downshift cable from the transmission downshift lever bracket.

14. Disconnect the neutral safety switch wires and the connectors from the switch.

15. Remove the vacuum line from the modulator on the transmission.

16. Support the transmission with a transmission jack and then remove the crossmember bolts and the crossmember.

17. Disconnect the transmission fluid cooler lines at the transmission.

18. Remove the transmission filler tube.

19. Secure the transmission to the jack with a chain.

20. Remove the converter housing attaching bolts. Move the transmission to the rear and down in order to remove it.

21. To install, move the transmission into position. The converter must rest squarely against the flywheel.

22. Install the converter housing to engine attaching bolts and tighten them to 23-33 ft/lbs. Remove the chain from the transmission.

23. Install the transmission filler tube.

24. Install the transmission fluid cooler lines to the transmission.

25. Position the crossmember to the frame and install the bolts.

26. Install the flywheel-to-converter nuts and tighten them to 23-28 ft/lbs.

27. Remove the transmission jack. Install the vacuum hose to the modulator.

28. Connect the neutral safety switch.

29. Connect the downshift cable to the downshift bracket. Connect the shift cable bracket to the converter housing.

30. Connect the downshift cable to the lever on the transmission.

31. Connect the speedometer cable to the tailshaft.

32. Install the driveshaft and align the marks. Install the center driveshaft bearing.

33. Install the converter housing access cover. Install the starter and the starter cable. Install the battery ground cable.

34. Lower the car to the ground and fill the transmission to the correct level with the proper fluid.

Borg-Warner Transmission

1. Remove the transmission dipstick and disconnect the downshift valve cable.

2. Raise the car on a hoist and remove the transmission pan drain plug and drain the fluid.

3. Mark the driveshaft with paint, for correct alignment when installing. Remove the bolts from the flange.

4. Remove the bolts which hold the driveshaft center bearing to the body.

5. Lower the driveshaft assembly and remove it from the car.

6. Disconnect the exhaust pipe bracket from the transmission. Loosen the exhaust pipe and move it to one side.

7. Remove the speedometer cable from the transmission.

8. Disconnect the starter wires and remove the starter.

9. Remove the torque converter front cover. Remove the cap screws which hold the flex plate to the converter.

10. Disconnect the linkage control cable at the transmission. Disconnect the neutral safety switch wires.

11. Place a transmission jack under the transmission, and secure the transmission to the jack with a chain.

12. Remove the four engine mount to body bolts.

13. Remove the converter housing bolts. Remove the transmission filler tube. Using a bar, apply pressure to the converter to prevent the converter from coming off the transmission when the assembly is removed.

14. Lower the transmission and converter assembly and remove it from the car.

15. To install, raise the transmission into position and install five of the six housing attaching bolts. Position the rear engine support to the body and install the bolts.

16. Remove the chain from the transmission.

17. Install the bolts which hold the flex plate to the converter. Install the converter front cover.

18. Install the starter and connect the wires.

19. Install the exhaust pipe bracket to the transmission.

20. Install the speedometer cable. Install the manual linkage control cable.

21. Connect the wires to the neutral safety switch. Install the driveshaft, aligning the marks then install the retaining bolts. Position the center bearing to the body and install the holding bolts.

22. Lower the car to the ground and install the downshift cable.

23. Fill the transmission to the proper level with specified transmission fluid.

24. Adjust the downshift cable.

PAN REMOVAL & INSTALLATION

C4 Transmission

1. Raise the car on a hoist.

2. Place a drain pan under the transmission.

3. Starting at the rear of the pan and working toward the front, loosen the attaching bolts and allow the transmission fluid to drain.

4. Remove the bolts and the pan.

5. Remove all gasket material from the pan and the transmission mounting surface.

6. Apply gasket sealer to the oil pan and position the gasket on the pan.

7. Position the pan on the transmission and install the bolts hand-tight.

8. Torque the bolts evenly to 12-16 ft/lbs. Fill the transmission to the proper level with the specified fluid.

Borg-Warner Transmission

Follow the previous procedures for removal and installation. The fluid can be removed through the drain plug. The torque for the pan bolts is 8-13 ft/lbs.

PAN REMOVAL AND FILTER SERVICE

C3 Transmission

1. Loosen the pan attaching bolts to drain the fluid from the transmission.
2. When the fluid has stopped draining from the transmission, remove and thoroughly clean the pan and the screen. Discard the pan gasket. Remove and clean filter screen in solvent and blow it dry.
3. Place a new gasket on the pan, and install the pan on the transmission.
4. Add three quarts of fluid to the transmission through the filler tube.
5. Run the engine at idle speed for about two minutes, and then run it at fast idle speed (about 1200 rpm) until it reaches its normal operating temperature. Do not race the engine.
6. Shift the selector lever through all the positions, place it at P, and check the fluid level. The fluid level should be above the ADD mark. If necessary, add enough fluid to the transmission to bring the level between the ADD and FULL marks on the dipstick. Do not overfill the transmission.

FILTER SERVICE

C4 Transmission

Remove the transmission pan. Remove the screws attaching the filter screen to the transmission. Wash the filter in a solvent and blow it clean of solvent with an air gun. Install the filter screen and replace the oil pan.

NOTE: Cleaning the filter screen is not a regular maintenance procedure. It should be cleaned when the oil pan has been removed for other service procedures.

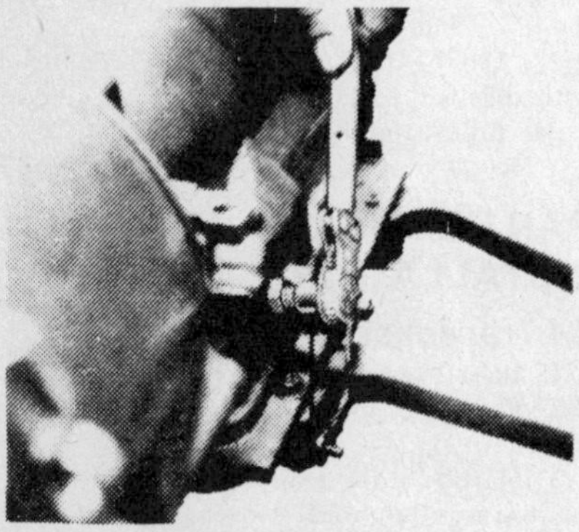

C3 front band adjustment

FRONT BAND ADJUSTMENT

C3 Transmission

1. Remove the downshift rod from the transmission downshift lever.
2. Clean all dirt from the band adjusting screw area. Remove and discard the locknut.
3. Install a new locknut on the adjusting screw and torque to 18-23 ft/lb.
4. Back off the adjusting screw exactly one and a half turns.
5. Hold the adjusting screw from turning and torque the locknut to 23 ft/lb.
6. Install the downshift rod on the transmission downshift lever.

INTERMEDIATE BAND ADJUSTMENT

C4 Transmission

1. Wipe the area clean around the adjusting screw on the side of the transmission.
2. Remove the adjusting screw locknut and discard it.
3. Install a new locknut on the adjusting screw but do not tighten it.
4. Tighten the adjusting screw to exactly 10 ft/lbs.
5. Back off the adjusting screw exactly 1¾ turns.

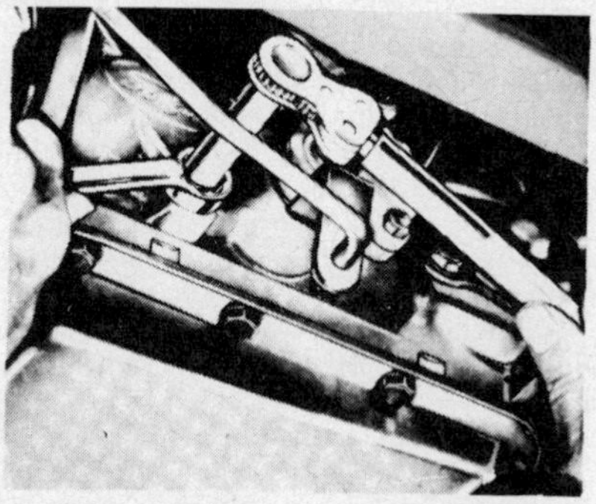

Adjusting intermediate band—C4 automatic transmission

6. Hold the adjusting screw so that it does not turn and tighten the locknut to 35-45 ft/lbs.

NOTE: The tools used in the illustration of band adjustment are: a torque wrench, an extension, and an allen socket.

Borg-Warner Transmission

1. Drain the transmission fluid. Remove the pan.
2. Remove the servo rear mounting bolt, the two fluid transfer tubes, and the cam plate.
3. Pull out on the servo actuating lever and insert a ¼ in. spacer between the adjusting screw and the servo piston stem.
4. Tighten the adjusting screw to 10 in/lbs.
5. Hold the adjusting screw stationary and position the one-way clutch spring two threads away from the actuating lever with the long leg of the spring to the rear. Now install the cam plate, being careful to engage the leg of the spring in the ramp.

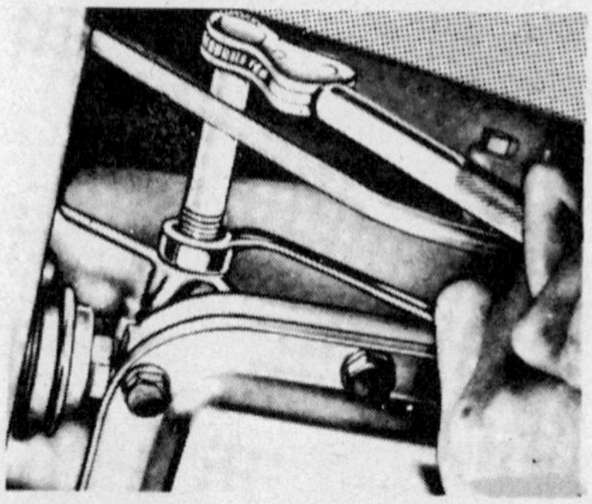

Adjusting low-reverse band—C4 automatic transmission

6. Install the two fluid transfer tubes. Install the pan with a new gasket.
7. Refill the transmission.

LOW-REVERSE BAND ADJUSTMENT

C4 Transmission

1. Wipe the area clean around the adjustment screw on the side of the transmission.
2. Remove the adjusting screw locknut and discard it.
3. Install a new locknut but do not tighten it.
4. Tighten the adjusting screw to exactly 10 ft/lbs.
5. Back off the adjusting screw exactly three full turns.
6. Hold the adjusting screw so that it does not turn and tighten the locknut to 35-45 ft/lbs.

Borg-Warner Transmission

1. Snap out the woodgrain panel at the rear of the console. Remove the two screws and slide the plastic cross panel forward to remove.
2. Lift up the rear corners of the handbrake boot and remove the two screws. Pry up the rear edge of the front woodgrain panel and remove the center retaining screw. Remove the two screws, one on each side of the lower forward console edge, and remove the console. Pull the carpet back on the right.
3. If there isn't an access hold, cut one.
4. Loosen the locknut and tighten the adjusting screw to 10 ft/lbs. Back off the adjusting screw one complete turn.

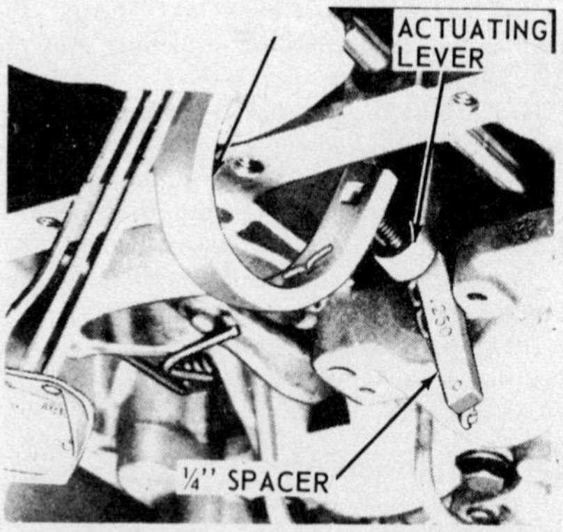

Borg Warner automatic intermediate band adjustment. The U-shaped device is a special wrench

5. Tighten the locknut to 25-30 ft/lbs without disturbing the adjusting screw.
6. Plug the hole in the transmission tunnel and replace the carpet and console.

SHIFT LINKAGE ADJUSTMENT

1. Position the transmission selector lever in the Drive position.
2. Raise the car and remove the clevis pin and disconnect the cable and the bushing from the transmission.
3. Move the transmission lever to the Drive position, which is the third detent from

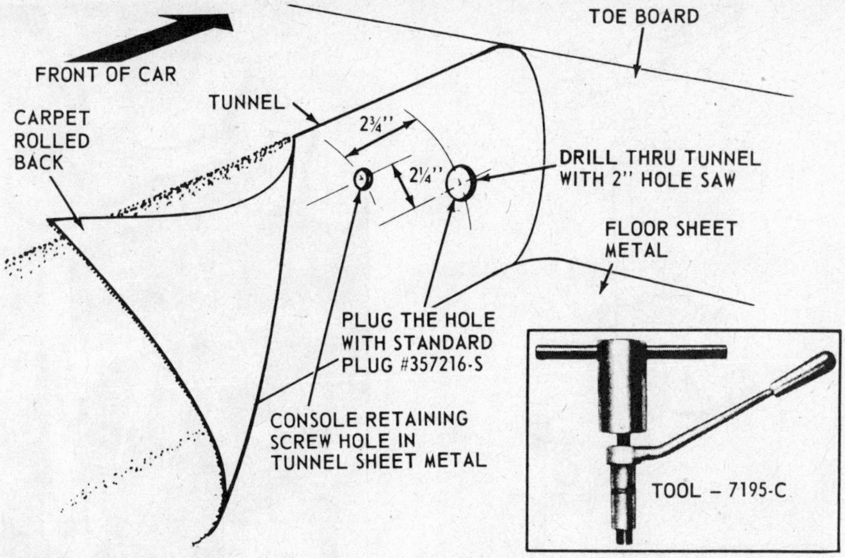

Dimensions for cutting access hole in floor sheet metal to gain access for low-reverse band adjustment on Borg Warner transmission

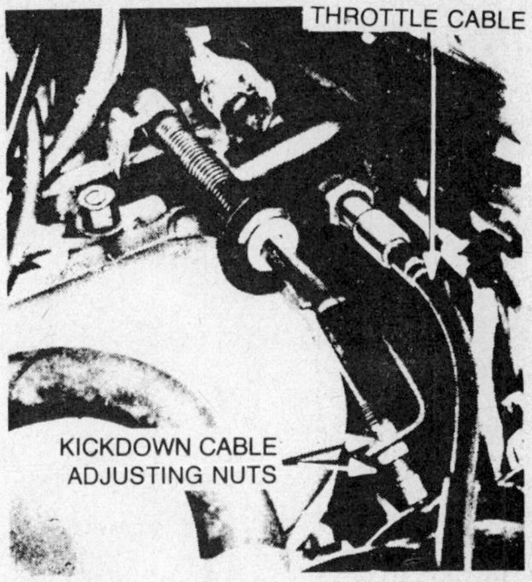

C4 automatic transmission kickdown linkage adjustment nuts

the back of the transmission on the C4. It is the third detent from the front on the C3.

4. With the transmission selector lever and the transmission lever in the Drive positions, adjust the cable length until the clevis pin holes in the transmission lever and the end of the cable are aligned.

5. Connect the cable, lower the car, and check the operation of the transmission in each selector lever position.

DOWNSHIFT LINKAGE ADJUSTMENT

C3 Transmission

The transmission kick-down cable is adjusted by varying the position of the cable housing in its mounting bracket. To adjust:

1. Hold the accelerator pedal in full throttle position with a suitable wedge.

2. Place the transmission lever in full kick-down position.

3. Loosen the top nut and adjust bottom nut to give a 0.020 to 0.080 inch clearance between the carburetor linkage kick-down lever and the throttle operating shaft. Tighten the top nut.

4. Remove the weight from the accelerator and operate the linkage several times to be sure that wide open throttle and full transmission kick-down can be achieved.

C4 Transmission

1. Press the gas pedal to the floor to completely open the throttle.

2. Position the kick-down cable so that the tang just contacts the throttle shaft.

3. If an adjustment is required, loosen the two kick-down cable adjusting nuts at the bracket and move the cable as required. Tighten the adjusting nuts.

Borg-Warner Transmission

The downshift valve control cable governs the transmission control pressure which, in turn, determines the shift points. It also manually downshifts the transmission at full throttle.

NOTE: This procedure is recommended only for service personnel skilled in automatic transmission adjustment. The instructions must be followed exactly.

1. Connect a tachometer to the engine.

2. Attach a pressure gauge to the control pressure take-off at the rear of the transmission.

3. Allow the engine to warm up (in Neutral) to normal operating temperature.

4. Apply the parking brake and block the wheels securely. Do not stand in front of the car.

5. Adjust the idle speed to 630-680 rpm in Drive. The pressure should be 50-65 psi.

6. Apply the footbrakes and increase the engine speed 500 rpm above idle, in Drive. The pressure should increase 15-20 psi over idle.

CAUTION

Do not operate the engine at this speed, in Drive, for more than 20 seconds. If the engine speed exceeds 500 rpm over idle speed, release the accelerator and let the engine idle before restarting the test. Do not perform the test repeatedly.

7. Adjust the downshift valve control cable to get the pressures specified in Steps 5 and 6.

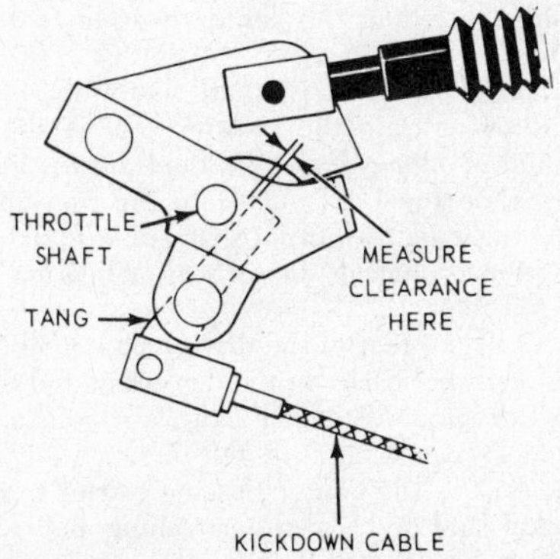

C4 automatic transmission kickdown linkage adjustment

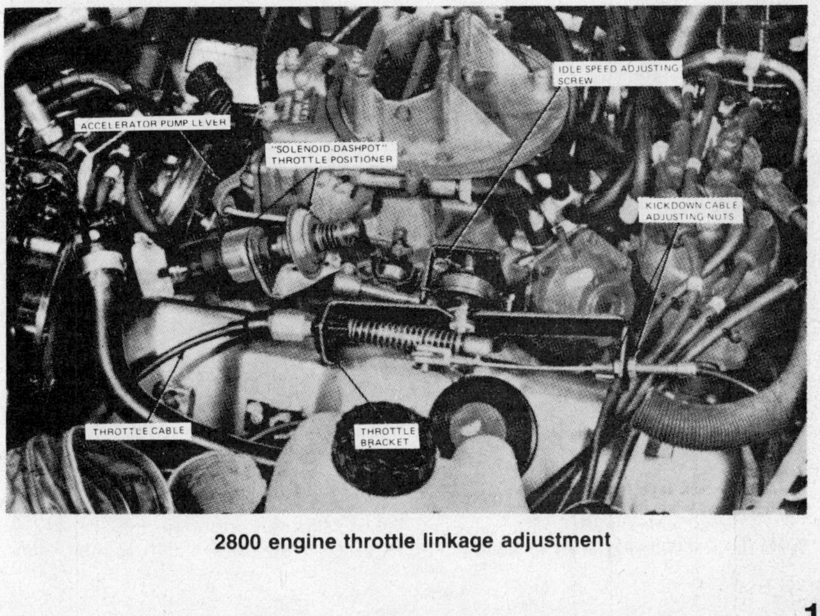

2800 engine throttle linkage adjustment

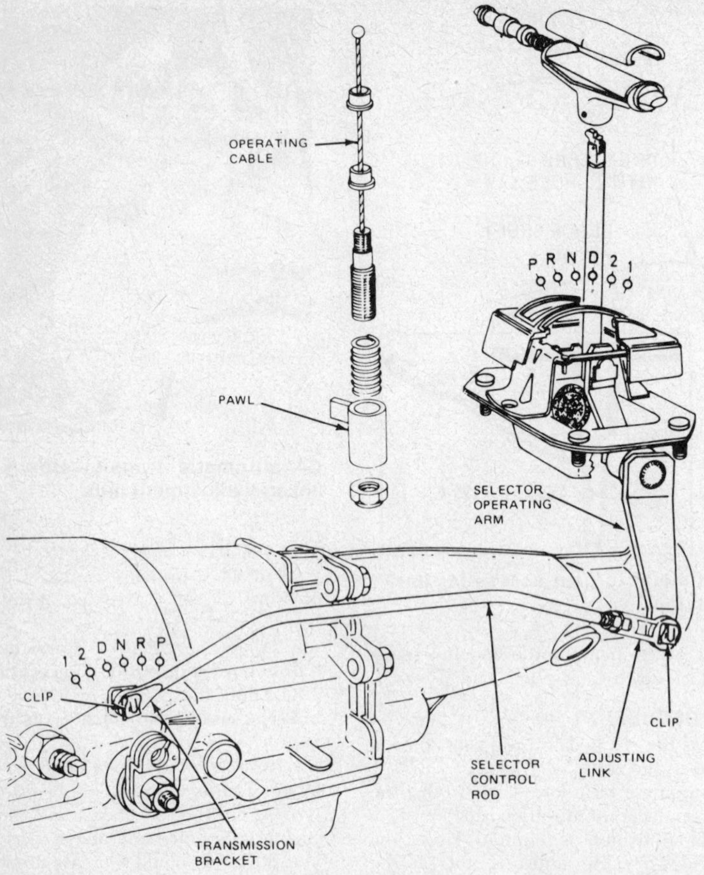

Automatic transmission manual linkage control—Capri II

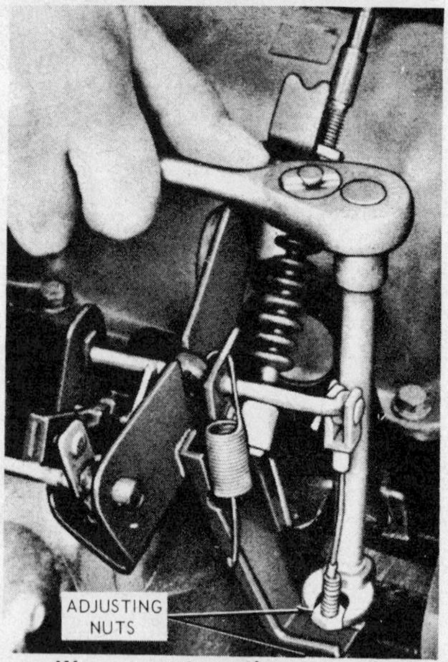

Borg Warner automatic transmission downshaft cable adjustment

NEUTRAL SAFETY SWITCH REMOVAL AND INSTALLATION, ADJUSTMENT

C3 Transmission

1. Raise car on hoist.
2. Disconnect cable connector from switch.
3. Use a thin wall socket to remove the neutral start switch and O-ring.
4. Install new O-ring and neutral start switch. Tighten switch to specified torque.
5. Install cable connector.
6. Check the operation of the switch in each detent position. Check to see the backup light operates in reverse only. The engine should start only with the transmission selector lever in N (neutral) and P (park).

C4 Transmission

1. Remove the downshift cable from the transmission downshift lever.
2. Remove the transmission downshift outer lever retaining nut and lever. It may be necessary to apply penetrating oil to the lever shaft and nut in order to remove the nut and lever.
3. Remove the neutral safety switch attaching bolts.
4. Disconnect the multiple wire connector. Remove the switch.
5. Install the new switch on the transmission. Install the attaching bolts.
6. With the transmission lever in neutral, rotate the switch and insert a gauge pin (No. 43 drill) into the gauge pin hole.
7. Tighten the switch attaching bolts to 4-8 ft/lbs and remove the gauge pin.
8. Install the outer downshift lever and attaching nut, and install the downshift cable to the downshift lever.
9. Install the switch wires. Connect the multiple wire connector. Check the operation of the switch in each lever position. The engine should start only with the transmission lever in the Neutral or Park position.

Borg-Warner Transmission

1. Place the transmission lever in Drive.
2. Raise the car and disconnect the four leads from the neutral safety switch.
3. Loosen the locknut using a $^{11}/_{16}$ in. "crow's foot" and unscrew the switch from the transmission. Remember the number of turns required to remove it.
4. Screw the new switch in about the same number of turns as required to remove the old one. Back out a couple of turns.
5. Connect a battery powered test light across the backup light terminals (the two big ones).
6. Screw the switch in until the test light goes out. Make a mark on the switch and transmission case at this point.
7. Connect the test light to the two small terminals, the starter terminals.
8. Screw in the switch until the test light lights. Mark this position.
9. Unscrew the switch to a point halfway between the marks made in Steps 6 and 8. Tighten the locknut and connect the leads.
10. Check that the engine will start only with a transmission in Neutral or Park. Have an assistant check the backup lights.

DRIVE AXLE

Driveshaft and Universal Joints

The Capri uses a one-piece driveshaft with two serviceable universal joints. There is no center bearing.

Driveshaft

REMOVAL AND INSTALLATION

1. Mark the driveshaft and the rear axle pinion flange for correct realignment when installing and then remove the four attaching bolts and lockwashers.
2. Remove the two bolts and the lockwashers securing the center bearing to the body.
3. Lower the driveshaft assembly and withdraw it from the transmission. A slight amount of oil may leak from the transmission.
4. Slide the front yoke into the transmission, engaging the output shaft splines, taking care not to damage the oil seal or bearing in the tail shaft.
5. Lift the rear of the driveshaft assembly, and align the marks on the driveshaft and the rear axle pinion flange. Fit the four bolts and the lockwashers, and tighten them.
6. Secure the center bearing carrier to its bracket and tighten the attaching bolts to 13-17 ft/lbs.
7. Check the level of the transmission lubricant.

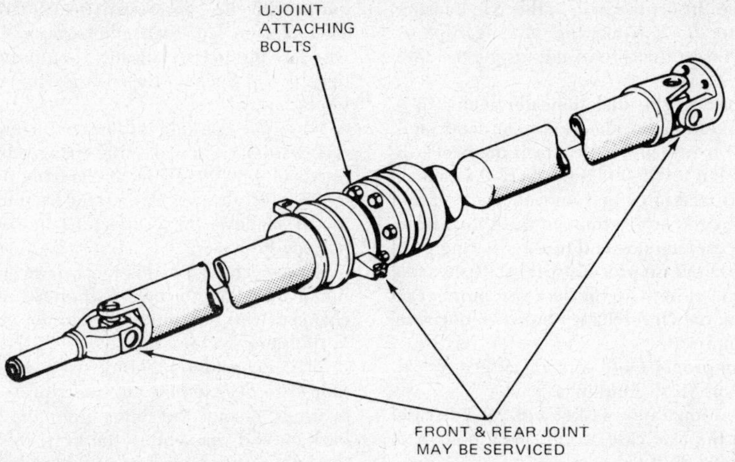

The constant velocity center universal joint is to be serviced by replacement of the complete assembly

UNIVERSAL JOINT OVERHAUL

NOTE: This procedure is for service replacement. Original equipment retainers are pressed in with a preload and staked in place.

1. Remove the driveshaft.
2. Position the driveshaft assembly in a vise.
3. Remove the snap-rings which retain the bearing caps.
4. Using a suitably sized socket or an arbor press, drive one of the bearing caps in toward the center of the universal joint. This will force the opposite bearing cap out.
5. As each bearing cap is pressed or punched far enough out of the universal joint assembly so that it is accessible, grip it with a pair of pliers and pull it from the driveshaft yoke. Drive or press the spider in the opposite direction in order to make the opposite bearing cap accessible and pull it free with a pair of pliers. Use this procedure to remove all bearings from the universal joints.
6. After removing the bearings, lift the spider from the yoke.
7. Thoroughly clean the yoke areas on the driveshaft.

CAUTION

Use extreme care when installing a new bearing into position. A heavy jolt can cause one or more of the needle bearings to fall out of place which will stop the cap from sitting properly on the spider.

8. Start a new bearing into the yoke.
9. Position the spider in the yoke and press or drive the new bearing cap ¼ in. below the surface of the yoke.
10. With the bearing cap in position, install a new snap-ring.
11. Start a new bearing cap into the opposite side of the yoke.
12. Press or drive the bearing cap until the opposite bearing—which you have just installed—contacts the inner surface of the snap-ring.
13. Install a new snap-ring on the second bearing cap.
14. Position the slip yoke on the spider and install new bearings and snap-rings.
15. Check the reassembled joints for freedom of movement. Never install a driveshaft in a car if there is any binding in the universal joints.

Center Bearing

REMOVAL AND INSTALLATION

1. Remove the driveshaft.
2. Mark the center universal yoke and the front universal yoke for correct realignment when installing. On the constant velocity center universal joint, mark the two halves of the joint housing before removing the six bolts to separate the halves. Bend back the locktab in the center of the universal yoke and loosen the retaining bolt. Remove the U-shaped plate and separate the two halves of the driveshaft.
3. Remove the driveshaft and the bearing assembly from the rubber insulator.
4. Bend back the tabs securing the rubber insulator into its carrier and then remove the insulator.
5. Remove the bearing and the protective caps from the driveshaft with a puller.
6. Drive the ball bearing and the protective caps onto the driveshaft.
7. Insert the rubber insulator into its carrier with boss upward. Bend the tabs on the carrier back over the beaded edge of the rubber insulator.
8. Slide the carrier and the rubber insulator over the bearing assembly.
9. Screw the retaining bolt with a new locktab onto the end of the front driveshaft, leaving enough space to allow for the U-shaped plate.
10. Align the mating marks on the two universal joint yokes and assemble the driveshaft. Insert the U-shaped plate, with the smooth surface toward the bolt under the retaining bolt head and tighten the bolt to 25-30 ft/lbs. Bend the locktab up.
11. Install the driveshaft.

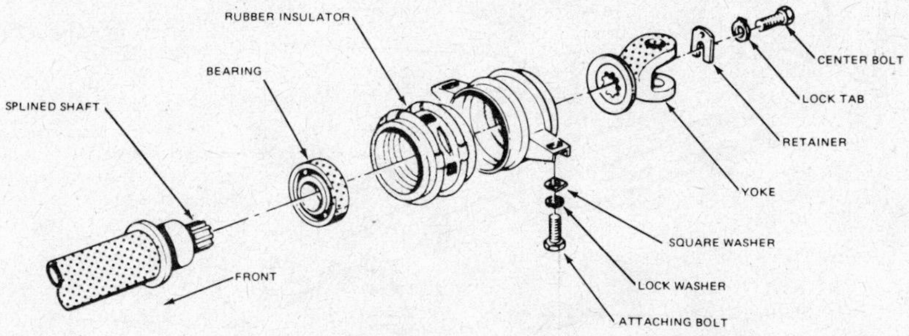

Details of the center driveshaft bearing

Axle Shaft and/or Bearing Replacement

REMOVAL AND INSTALLATION

1. Jack up the rear of the car and support it with jackstands.
2. Remove the wheel, brake drum securing screw, and the brake drum. Be sure that the parking brake is released.
3. Remove the bolts that secure the bearing retaining plate to the backing plate. These bolts are accessible through holes in the axle shaft flange.
4. Pull the axle and bearing assembly out of the axle housing with a slide hammer.
5. Loosen the inner retaining ring by nicking it deeply with a chisel in several places. It will then slide off easily.
6. Press off the bearing and seal assembly and install the new one by pressing it into position.
7. Press on the new retainer.
8. Assemble the shaft and the bearing in the housing.
9. Install the retaining nuts, drum, wheel, and tire.

Differential

REMOVAL

1. Jack up the car and pull the axle shafts.
2. Mark the driveshaft and pinion flanges for realignment. Remove the four bolts and washers, the ten retaining bolts, the cover, the gasket, and drain the axle.
3. Match mark and remove the differential bearing caps. Using two pry bars, remove the differential.

OVERHAUL

1. Pull off the bearings from each side of the differential assembly. Remove the shims.
2. Unscrew the ring gear retaining bolts

and remove the ring gear from the differential assembly.

3. Drive out the locking pin which secures the differential pinion shaft in the differential case. Remove the pinion shaft, differential pinions, differential side gears and adjusting shims.

4. Hold the drive pinion flange and remove the nut. Pull off the pinion flange using a puller. Remove the pinion and bearing spacer from the pinion.

5. Press off the large roller bearing from the pinion shaft, remove the spacer shim from the pinion shaft.

6. Remove the small tapered roller bearing together with the oil seal from the axle housing.

7. Drive the bearing races out from the axle housing.

8. Install the pinion bearing races, pulling them squarely into position.

9. To determine total side play of the differential case in the housing, press the taper roller bearings on the differential case without shims. Install pressure blocks into the axle tubes and install the differential into the housing. Install the bearing caps, tighten, loosen, then retighten finger tight. Mount a dial indicator gauge on the axle housing so the feeler contacts the side of the ring gear and the dial reads zero. By moving the differential, the total side play can be measured. Record this measurement. Remove the differential and pressure blocks.

10. To determine the thickness of the pinion bearing spacer, use the trial and error method. Install the pinion with a selected spacer, small taper bearing, drive pinion flange, and the old self-locking nut. Tighten the nut to 72-87 ft/lbs and rotate the pinion several times using an in/lbs torque wrench. If the rotating torque required is too high, the spacer is too thin, and should be replaced with a thicker one. If the torque is too low, a thinner spacer should be used. Correct torque is 13-19 in/lbs. Remove the old nut. To check the spacer thickness, use the method described in "Pinion Mesh Markings."

11. Make sure that the new oil seal has grease between the two sealing lips and is coated with sealing compound on the other side. Install it with a new self locking nut and torque to 72-87 ft/lbs.

12. Remove the differential case bearings. Position the shims as indicated by the total side play figure, one half of the required amount on each side, on the differential case. Press the taper roller bearings on the differential case. Insert the case in the axle housing and center it. Position the bearing caps as marked. Insert the screws and torque to 43-49 ft/lbs.

13. Position the dial indicator feeler in a vertical position on one ring gear tooth and check the tooth flank backlash. If the backlash is not within 0.005-0.009 in. (0.12-0.22 mm.) the differential must be removed again. If the backlash is too large, remove the shims from the ring gear face side and transfer to ring gear back side. Reverse procedure if backlash is too small. Do not increase or decrease number of shims, but only interchange between one side and the other.

14. For proper tooth contact pattern check, see "Pinion Mesh Markings."

15. Position a new gasket and the axle case cover on the axle case, secure with bolts and torque to 22-29 ft/lbs.

16. Install the driveshaft, axles and wheels.

Differential Specifications

	2000	2600	2300 & 2800
Axle Ratio	3.44:1	3.22:1	3.08:1
No. teeth in pinion	9	9	11
No. teeth in ring gear	31	29	34
Oil capacity	2.3	2.3	2.3
Side gear play	0.004-0.006		
Bearing pre-load	0.0012-0.0031		
Backlash	0.047-0.086		

Pinion Mesh Markings

The following method of determining the relative position of the ring gear and pinion, and whether or not they are in proper mesh, will prove satisfactory for all pinion and ring gears. This should be followed by a final check, even when the pinion depth has been determined by special tools. Assemble the pinion in the housing, without preload, and tighten the pinion nut until a preload of about 10 in/lbs is developed on the bearings to insure that they are completely free of end play.

This, of course, is not the final bearing preload setting, but is a good one for checking the pinion mesh markings.

Install the differential assembly and adjust it to provide from 0.004-0.008 in. backlash of the ring gear, measured at the rim of the gear.

Paint five or six of the ring gear teeth with red lead and, while a helper brakes the ring gear with a piece of wood, slowly turn the pinion until the ring gear makes at least one full revolution. The mesh of the pinion with the ring gear will be indicated as a mark in the red lead on the ring gear teeth. Compare this mark with the accompanying illustrations. The caption on each photograph explains whether the mark indicates the pinion is too deep or too shallow, the ring gear too close or too far away.

When the marking is found to be improper, it is customary to make trial changes in increments of 0.005-0.007 in. If changing the shim 0.005-0.007 throws the marking from too deep to too shallow, the proper distance is about halfway between.

If, after changing this increment of shims, the mark still indicates that more must be changed, it is advisable to continue changing in the same increments.

While considerable time is generally required to disassemble the unit, press off the bearings, change the shims, press the bearing back on and reassemble the unit, this is still the only positive method of determining that the differential will operate quietly after it is finally installed in the car.

REAR SUSPENSION

The rear axle is suspended by two three leaf springs with a stabilizer bar. Sealed, hydraulic shock absorbers are positioned between the rear axle and the reinforced mountings on the floor pan. The shock absorbers are staggered on the axle. The right-hand shock absorber axle mounting is located in front of the rear axle and the left-hand shock is mounted to the rear of the axle.

Springs

REMOVAL AND INSTALLATION

1. Block each front wheel.

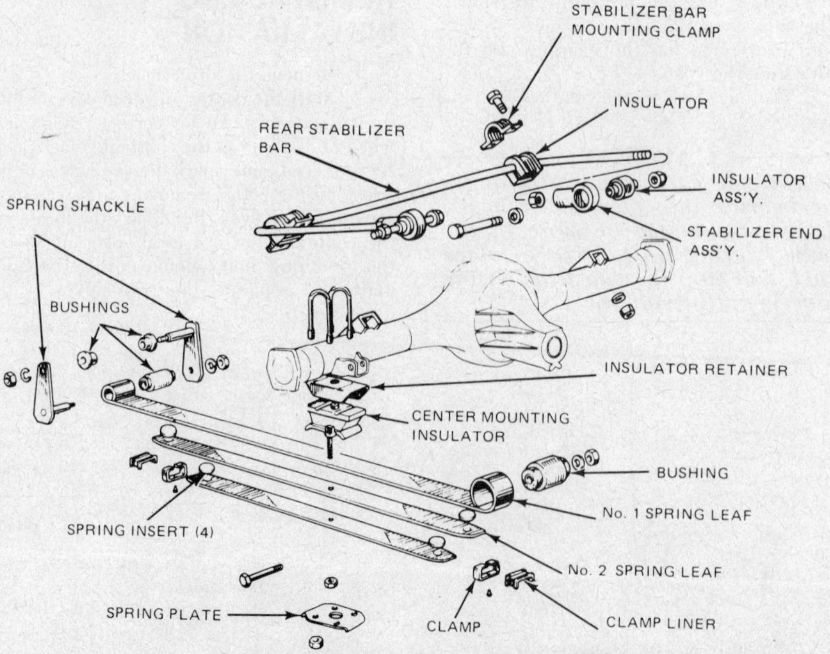

An exploded view of the rear suspension

2. Jack up the rear of the car and support it with jackstands.

3. Position a jack under the rear axle and extend it sufficiently to support the axle.

4. Remove the rear shackle nuts and the washers and then detach the combined shackle bolt and the place assemblies. Remove the two rubber bushings.

NOTE: Skip steps 5-10 if you are not replacing the bushings.

5. Unscrew the nut from the front mounting bracket and then withdraw the thru-bolt.

6. Remove the U-bolts and then the attaching plate.

7. Remove the spring assembly.

8. Remove the insulator sleeve and the retaining plate from the spring.

9. Pull the bushings out of the spring eyes.

10. Press in the bushings in the front and the rear eyes.

11. Position the front of the spring in its body mounting bracket. Install the thru-bolt and loosely assemble the nut and washer.

12. Position the rubber insulator sleeve around the spring and then place the retainer plate over the insulator.

13. Position the spring assembly to the axle and install the U-bolts, plate, and the nuts. Tighten the nuts initially to about 5 ft/lbs to compress the rubber insulators.

14. Place the spring into position and assemble the rear shackle bolt and plate assemblies. Install the nuts and washers but do not tighten them.

15. Remove the jack supporting the rear axle.

16. Lower the car to the ground.

17. Tighten the U-bolts, front hanger nuts, and the axle shackle nuts. Refer to the following chart for torque specifications.

Shock Absorbers

REMOVAL AND INSTALLATION

1. Remove the two rear seat attaching bolts and remove the rear seat.

2. Unscrew the seat belt retaining bolt from the upper end of the B post. Remove belt.

3. Remove the B post trim.

4. Remove the upper quarter window trim.

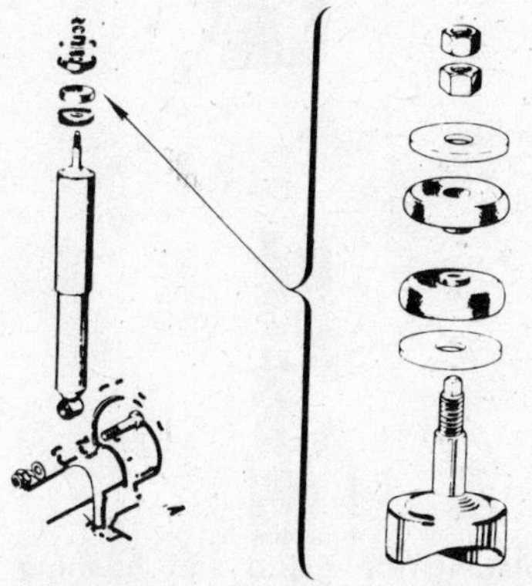

Rear shock absorber assembly

5. Remove two screws at the rear end of the rocker panel and pull off the door weatherstrip in the side trim area.

6. Remove the side trim panel and remove the luggage compartment carpet.

7. Tilt the rear seat back rest forward and remove the rear panel trim and the side panel.

8. Remove the two nuts from the top of the shock absorber and lift off the top steel washer and the rubber bushing.

9. Raise the car on a hoist.

10. Remove the lower end of the shock absorber from the bracket on the axle by removing the nut, lock washer and bolt. Remove the shock absorber from the car.

11. Remove the rubber bushing and steel washer from the top of the shock absorber.

12. Assemble the large steel washer and the rubber bushing to the top of the shock absorber.

13. Extend the shock absorber upward and pass it through the mounting hole in the body. Position the rubber bushing to the mounting hole in the body. Position washer and nut on the piston rod but do not tighten.

14. Position the lower end of the shock absorber in the bracket on the axle. Install the bolt, lock washer and nut. Tighten to 40-45 ft/lbs.

15. Lower the car to the ground.

16. Tighten the shock absorber upper attaching nut to 15-20 ft/lbs. Install the lock nut and tighten securely.

17. Replace the rear panel, and side trim panel. Replace the luggage compartment carpet.

18. Replace the side trim panel, fit the door weatherstrip in place and attach the rocker panel.

19. Replace the upper quarter window and B post trim.

20. Replace the seat belt attachment at the B post and fit the rear seat.

Stabilizer Bar

REMOVAL AND INSTALLATION

1. Raise and safely support the rear of the car.

2. Disconnect the parking brake primary cable from the relay lever on the rear axle.

3. Push the stabilizer bar back for access and unbolt the clamps from the axle.

4. Remove the bar.

5. On installation, if the bushing fittings at the end of the bar have been disturbed, check, that the lever arm length of the bar is correct on both sides. Adjust by screwing the bushing fittings in or out. Tighten the locknuts.

6. Locate the bar on the axle and position the bushing fittings in the frame channels. Install the bolt heads inside the frame. Replace the plain washers and self-locking nuts loosely.

7. Hold the bar in place and start the retaining clamp bolts. Lower the car to rest on its wheels. Torque the clamp bolts to 29-37 ft/lbs. Tighten the bushing fitting pivot bolts to 33-37 ft/lbs.

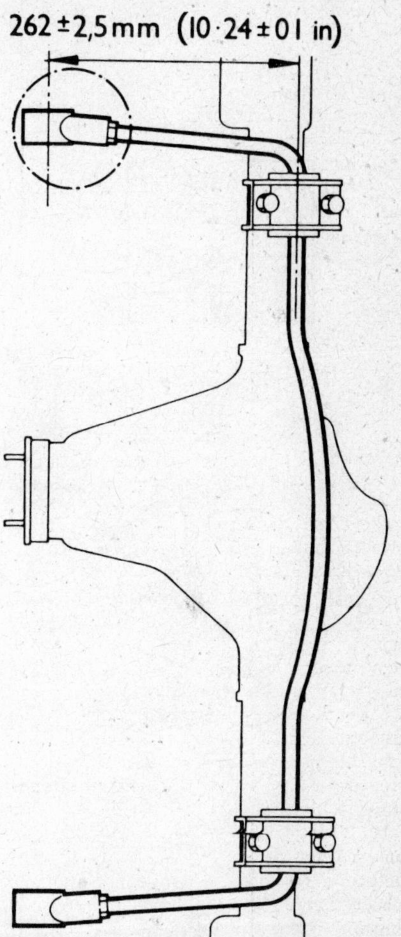

Stabilizer bar lever arm length should be adjusted to the dimension shown

FRONT SUSPENSION

This independent front suspension uses MacPherson struts. These units combine vertically mounted shock absorbers surrounded by coil springs. Side-to-side movement of each front wheel is controlled by a track control arm, and fore and aft movement is controlled by the stabilizer bar.

Downward movement of the wheel is limited by a rebound stop inside the shock absorber, and the upward movement by the spring reaching its limit of compression and by a rubber bumper around the suspension unit piston rod.

Front suspension geometry figures (i.e. camber, caster, and the kingpin inclination angles) are set when the car is manufactured and are not adjustable. Toe-in, however, is adjustable.

Strut Assembly

REMOVAL AND INSTALLATION

1. Jack up the front of the car and support it with jackstands.

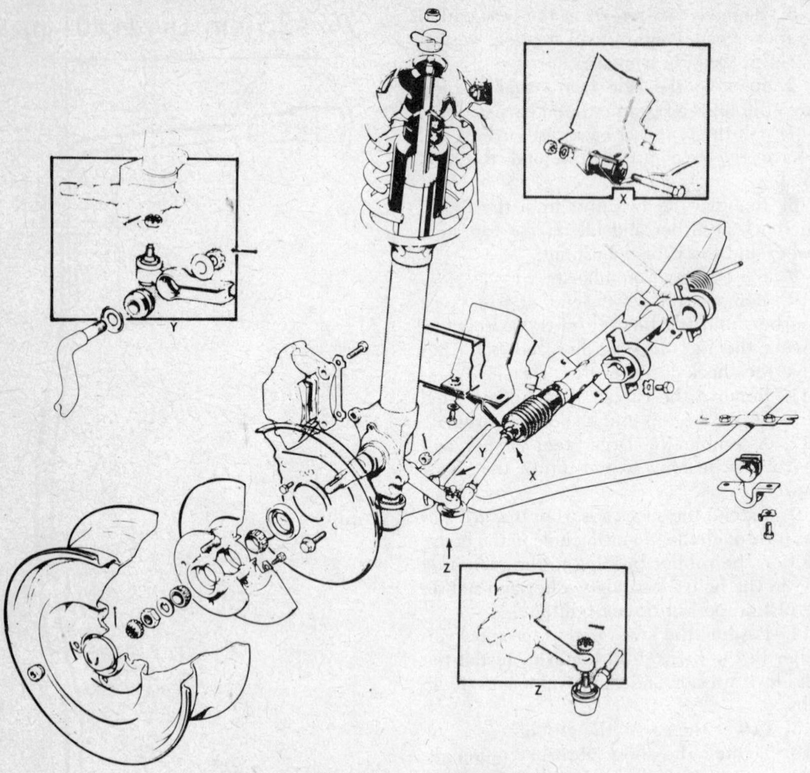

Front suspension—exploded view

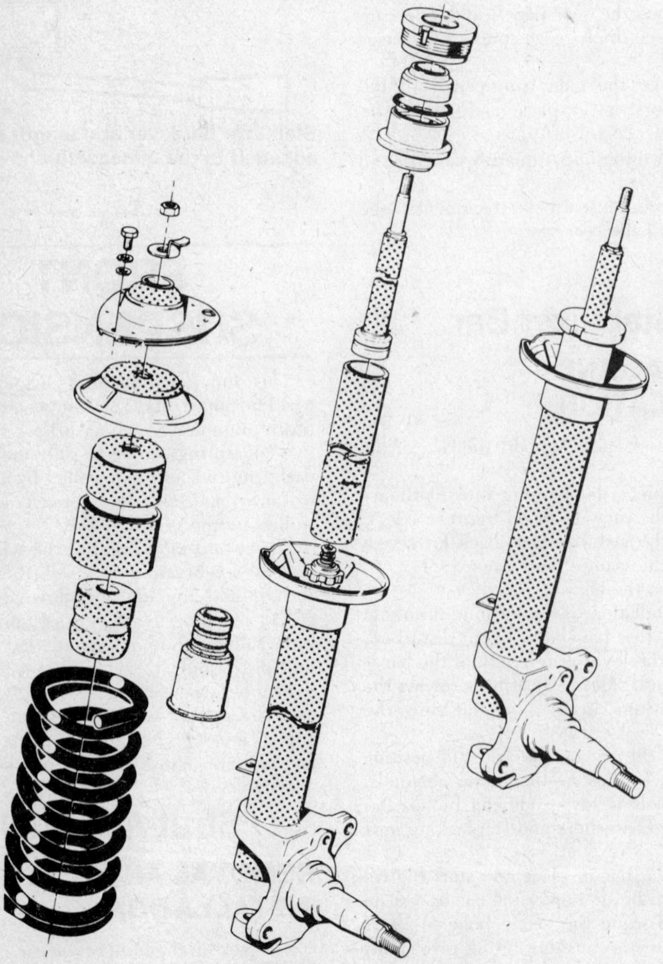

Strut assembly—exploded view

2. Remove the wheel.
3. Remove and plug the brake line.
4. Position a jack under the track control arm and jack up the suspension unit.
5. Remove the cotter pin and unscrew the castle nut holding the connecting rod end to the steering arm. Using a ball joint separator, separate the joint. Remove the jack from under the control arm.
6. Remove the cotter pin and unscrew the castle nut holding the track control arm to the base of the suspension unit and disconnect the track control arm.
7. Remove the three bolts holding the top mount assembly to the side apron panel and remove the suspension assembly from the car, complete with the disc brake caliper.
8. Lift the suspension assembly into position and secure it with the three bolts through the side apron panel, to the top mount assembly. Tighten the bolts to 15-18 ft/lbs.
9. Assemble the track control arm ball stud to the base of the suspension unit and tighten the securing nut to 30-35 ft/lbs. Install a new cotter pin.
10. Install the connecting rod end to the steering arm and tighten the castle nut to 18-22 ft/lbs. Install a new cotter pin.
11. Remove the brake line plug and install the brake line.
12. Bleed the brakes.
13. Replace the wheel and lower the car.

Disassembly and Assembly

1. Install adjustable spring retainers, to the front spring.

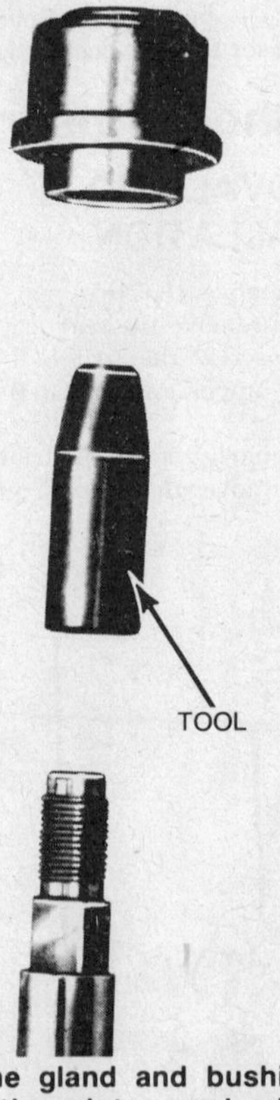

Replacing the gland and bushing assembly on the piston rod with the bushing guide tool

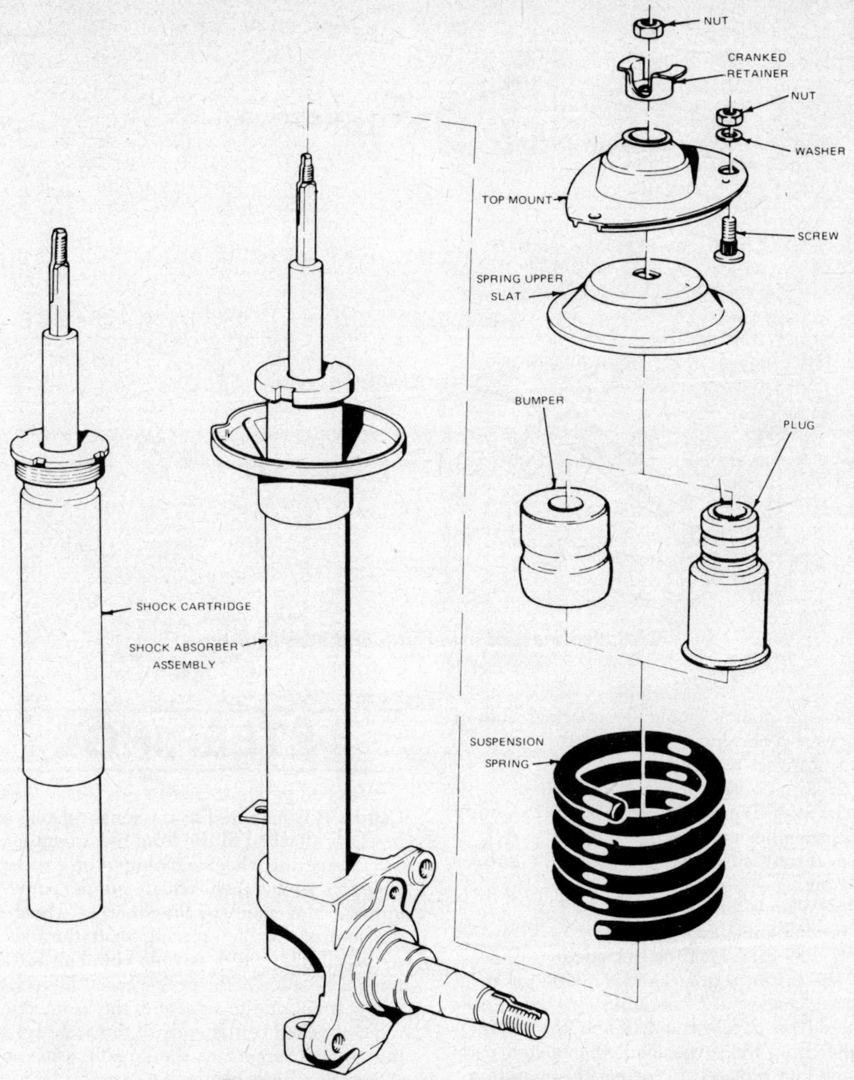

Exploded view of front strut assembly

2. Remove the piston rod nut by forcing the nut collar out of the piston rod keyway with a small punch. Remove and discard the nut.

3. Remove the cranked retainer.

4. Remove the top mount and lift off the spring upper seat, suspension spring and the rubber bumper.

5. Using a suitable wrench, remove shock cartridge.

6. Screw the shock cartridge into the top of the outer casing. Using a suitable wrench, tighten it securely to 55-60 ft/lbs.

7. Install the suspension spring, rubber bumper, plug, and the spring upper seat.

8. Assemble the top mount and the cranked retainer. Install a new collared piston rod nut and tighten to 5-10 ft/lbs. Do not bend the nut collar into the piston rod keyway at this time.

9. Remove adjustable spring retainers from the front spring.

10. Loosen the piston rod nut and retighten to 28-32 ft/lbs when the suspension unit is assembled into the car and the car is on the ground. When tightening the piston rod nut, the wheels must be in the straight-ahead position and the cranked retainer must face inwards, i.e. towards the engine.

11. After retightening the piston rod nut, force its collar into the piston rod keyway with a small punch.

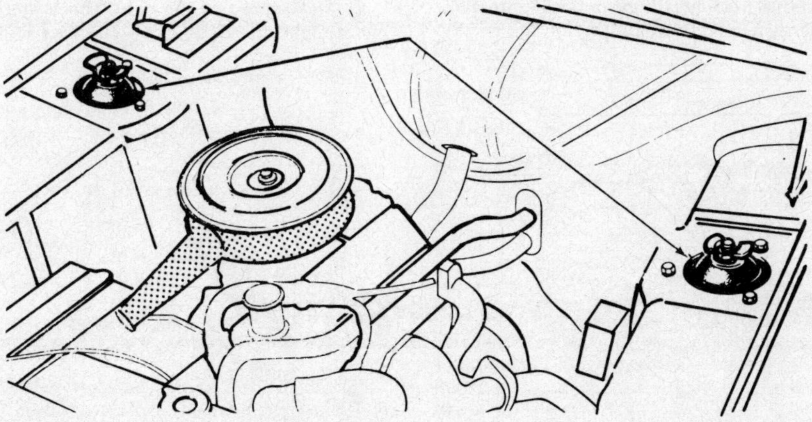
Cranked retainers

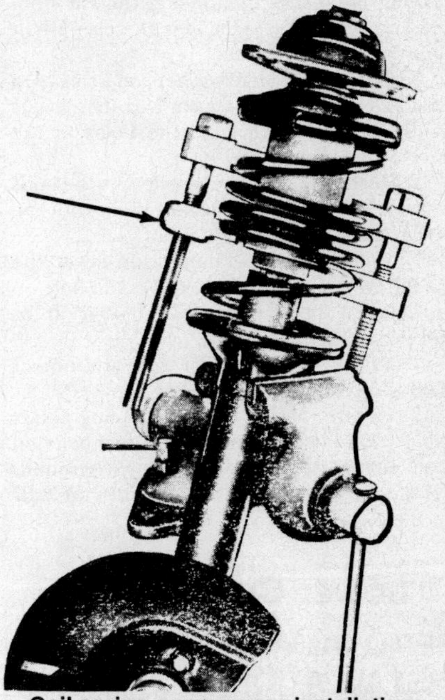
Coil spring compressor installation

Coil Springs

REMOVAL AND INSTALLATION

1. Remove the strut assembly and install a spring compressor.
2. Unscrew the piston rod nut and remove the cranked retainer.
3. Detach the top mount and lift off the spring upper seat, and the spring.
4. Mount the spring in a vise and remove the compressor.
5. Install the new spring in a vise and install the spring compressor. Replace the spring on the strut.
6. Install the rubber bumper and the upper seat.
7. Replace the cranked retainer and the piston rod nut. See the section on strut assembly for the proper torque and procedures when installing the piston rod nut.

Stabilizer Bar

REMOVAL AND INSTALLATION

1. Jack up the front of the car and support it with jackstands.

2. Remove the two attachment clamps from the front of the stabilizer bar after bending back the locktabs and removing the four bolts.

3. Remove the cotter pins and unscrew the stabilizer bar nuts which hold the ends of the stabilizer bar to the track control arm. Remove the nuts and pull off the large washers.

4. Pull the stabilizer bar forward and remove it.

5. Remove the sleeve and the large washer from each end of the stabilizer bar.

6. Remove the stabilizer bar mounting bushings.

7. Install the stabilizer bar mounting bushing by sliding them along the bar from one end until they are under the clamp bolt holes in the body bracket.

8. Assemble a large washer and a sleeve to each end of the stabilizer bar and then insert the stabilizer bar through the holes in the track control arms.

9. Assemble the large washers to the ends of the stabilizer bar and secure them with the castle nuts.

10. Remove the jackstands and lower the car to the ground. Tighten the castle nuts on the ends of the stabilizer bar to 15-45 ft/lbs and install the cotter pins.

11. Install the stabilizer bar attachment clamps.

12. Secure the bar to the mounting points using two new lockwashers and two bolts on each clamp. With the car on the ground, tighten the bolts to 15-18 ft/lbs. Turn the tabs on the lockwashers.

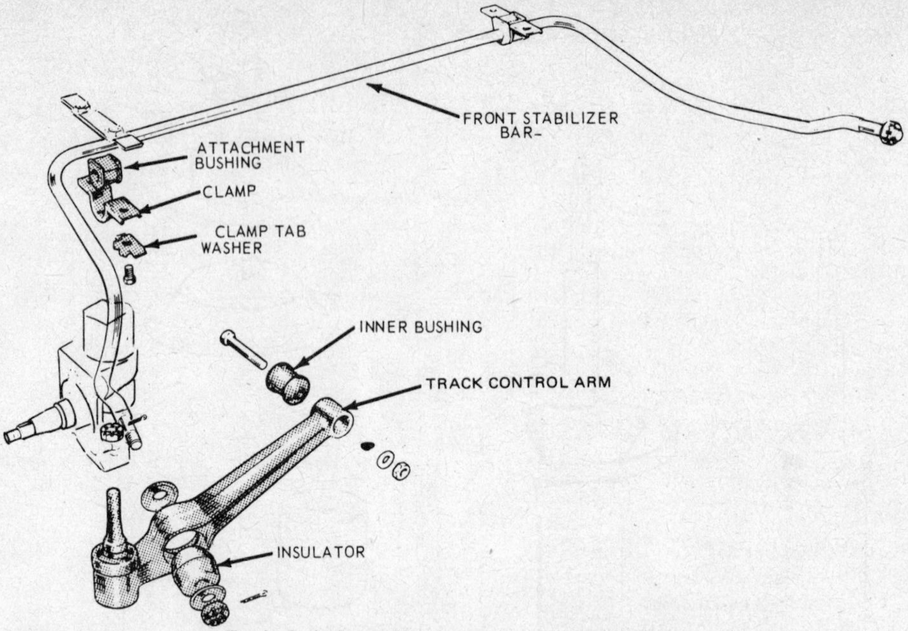

Exploded view of lower arm and stabilizer bar

Lower Control Arm

REMOVAL AND INSTALLATION

1. Jack up the front of the car and support it with jackstands.

2. Remove the cotter pin and unscrew the castle nut holding the control arm to the stabilizer bar. Pull off the large dish washer.

3. Remove the self-locking nut and the flat washer from the rear of the lower control arm pivot and release the inner end of the control arm.

4. Remove the cotter pin and unscrew the nut securing the control arm ball joint to the base of the strut unit and then separate the joint.

5. Assemble the control arm ball stud to the base of the strut unit, and tighten it to 30-35 ft/lbs. Install a new cotter pin.

6. Position the control arm so that it is in place over the stabilizer bar and then secure the inner end. Slide the pivot bolt into position from the front and install the flat washer and the self-locking nut from the rear. Tighten the nut to 22-27 ft/lbs with the car resting on its wheels.

7. Assemble the dished washer to the end of the stabilizer bar. Install the castle nut, lower the car to the ground, and tighten the nut to 15-45 ft/lbs. Install a new cotter pin.

Front-End Alignment

Before any alignment checks are made, the following points should be checked and, if necessary, corrected.

1. Correct tire inflation.
2. Front wheel bearing adjustment.
3. Stabilizer bar brackets to body crossmember nuts for tightness.
4. Front suspension springs for proper seating.
5. Wheels for trueness.
6. Ball joints for wear.
7. The car should be unloaded.

The caster, camber, and the king pin inclination angles are not adjustable, but they should be checked and, when the readings differ from those specified, the related parts should be replaced to correct the condition.

TOE-IN ADJUSTMENT

Toe-in is the difference of the distance between the centers of the front and rear, of the front wheels. Toe-in is necessary to compensate for the tendency of the wheels to deflect toward the rear while in motion. Toe-in is adjusted by changing the length of the tie rod ends. When adjusting the tie rod ends, adjust each equal amounts (in the opposite direction) to increase or to decrease the toe-in.

STEERING

Rack and pinion steering gear is used on all Capris. It is mounted in rubber insulators on brackets attached to the front crossmember.

The steering wheel is mounted on a collapsible can, so that it will collapse under a heavy impact. Movement of the steering wheel is transmitted by the steering shaft through a universal joint and a flexible coupling to the pinion. Rotation of the pinion cases the rack to move from side-to-side and the connecting rods, attached to the ends of the rack, transmit this movement to the spindle arms and cause the wheels to turn.

The steering gear holds three tenths (0.3) of a pint of SAE 90 hypoid oil. Never fill the gear completely with oil. This would result in a buildup of pressure which could burst or blow off the bellows in the gear.

Steering Wheel

REMOVAL AND INSTALLATION

1. Make sure that the front wheels are facing straight ahead. Remove the two screws

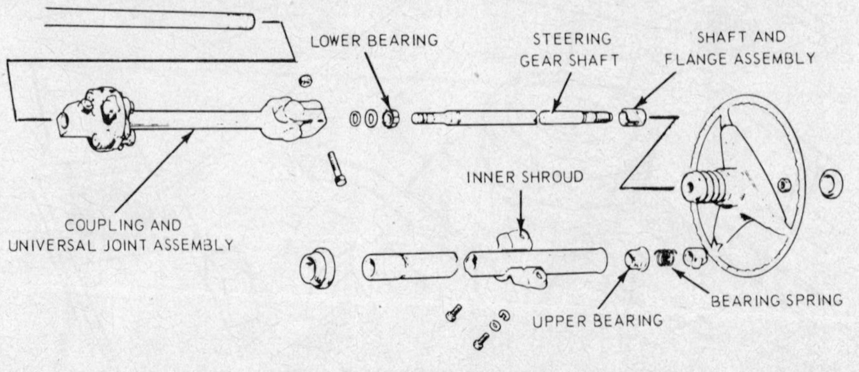

Steering column details

holding the steering column shroud and remove the lower half. Pull off the upper shroud.

2. Pry out the steering wheel center emblem. Matchmark the steering shaft and wheel so they can be correctly realigned.

3. Remove the steering wheel retaining nut and then pull the steering wheel off the steering shaft by hand.

4. Align the steering wheel in the correct position and push it onto the shaft. Be sure that the turn signal cancelling cam is in the groove on the underside of the wheel.

5. Install the steering wheel retaining nut and tighten it to 25-30 ft/lbs.

6. Install the steering wheel center. Replace the shrouds, if removed.

Turn Signal Switch

REMOVAL AND INSTALLATION

1. Disconnect the battery ground cable.

2. Remove the steering column shroud screws and remove the lower shroud half. Pull sharply up to release the upper shroud half.

3. Remove the switch retaining screws, disconnect the electrical plug, and remove the switch.

4. On reinstallation, connect the electrical plug and screw the switch in place.

5. Replace the shroud halves.

6. Connect battery.

Ignition Switch and Lock

SWITCH REMOVAL AND INSTALLATION

1. Disconnect the negative cable from the battery.

2. Remove the screws securing the steering column shroud. Remove the lower half of the shroud and release the shroud upper half retaining lug from its spring clip on the steering column by pulling sharply upward.

3. Be sure that the ignition key is in the 0 position.

4. Remove the screws holding the lower left dash trim panel. Pull the trim panel forward and down and remove the connector from the hazard warning flasher switch. Remove the trim panel from the dash.

5. Disconnect ignition wires at the connector.

6. Remove the screws securing the ignition switch to the lock and withdraw the switch.

7. Position the switch to the lock, being sure that the key remains in the 0 position and is correctly inserted.

8. Engage and tighten the switch retaining screws.

9. Connect ignition wires at the connection.

10. Position the lower left dash trim panel under the dash panel and connect the hazard warning flasher switch. Press the trim panel into its location and install and tighten the screws.

11. Mount the upper and lower halves of the steering column shroud and secure with screws.

12. Connect the battery negative cable and check the operation of the switch.

LOCK REMOVAL AND INSTALLATION

1. Disconnect the negative cable from the battery.

2. Remove the screws holding the steering column shroud. Remove the lower half of the shroud and release the shroud upper half retaining lug from its spring clip on the steering column by pulling sharply upward.

3. Remove the screws holding the left and right lower dash trim panels and lower the panels.

4. Remove the screws holding the turn signal switch. Move the switch out of the way.

5. Disconnect the ignition wires at the connector.

6. Remove the screws holding the steering column to the dash.

7. Turn the steering column to gain access to the headless bolts.

8. Remove lock from steering column by drilling out headless bolts or removing bolts with a screw extractor.

9. Position the new lock assembly, with the key in the lock, to the steering column.

10. Withdraw the lock to allow the pawl to enter the steering shaft.

11. Locate the loose half of the clamp to the lock, engage the shear head bolts and tighten evenly until the bolt heads shear off. While tightening the bolts, check the pawl for free operation.

12. Reconnect the ignition wires at the connector.

13. Turn the steering column in the correct position. Install the screws holding the steering column.

14. Install the turn signal switch.

15. Install the lower dash trim panels.

16. Install the upper and lower halves of the steering column shroud.

17. Connect the battery ground cable.

Steering Gear

REMOVAL AND INSTALLATION

Manual Steering

1. Set the steering wheel so the front wheels are facing straight ahead.

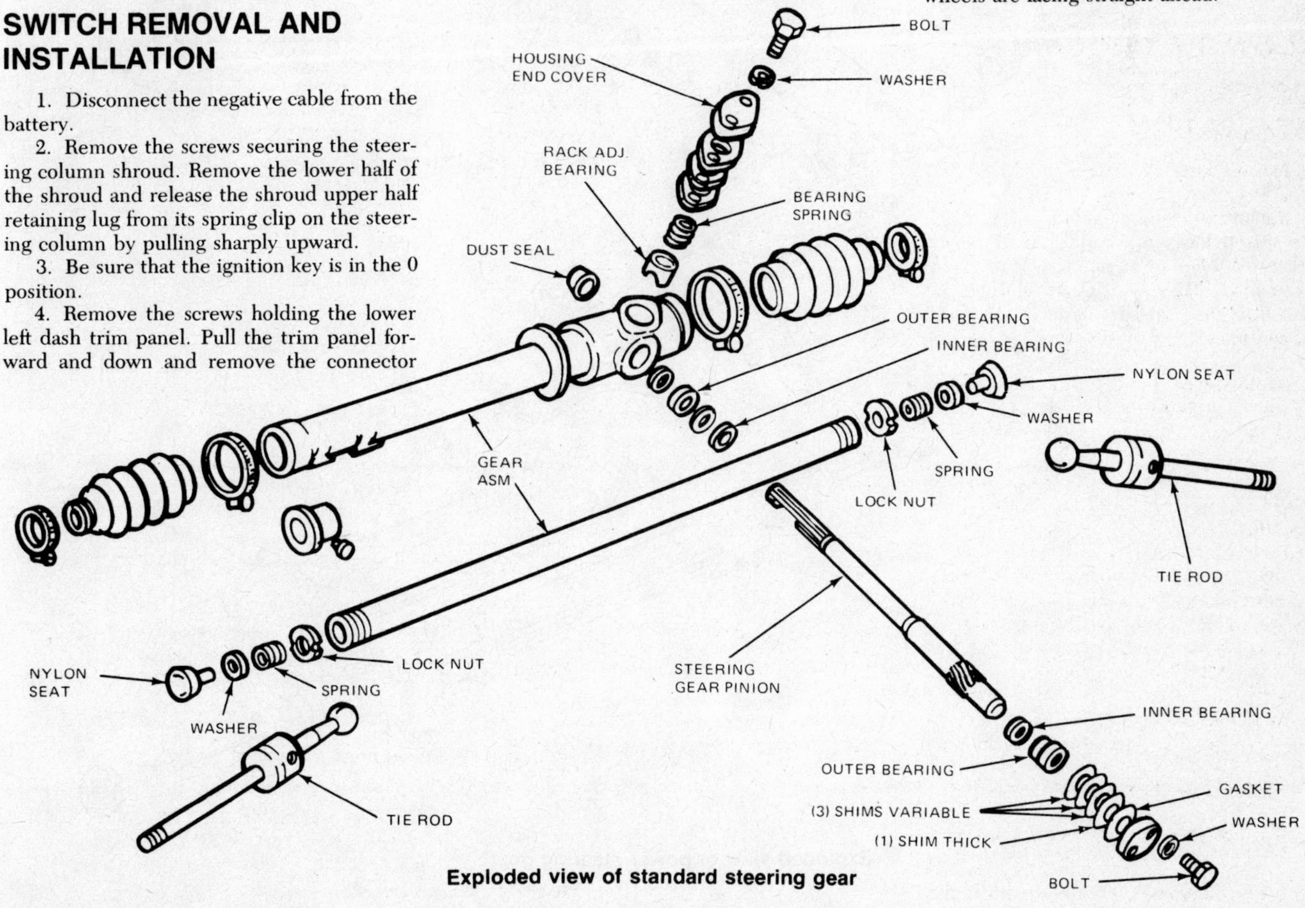

Exploded view of standard steering gear

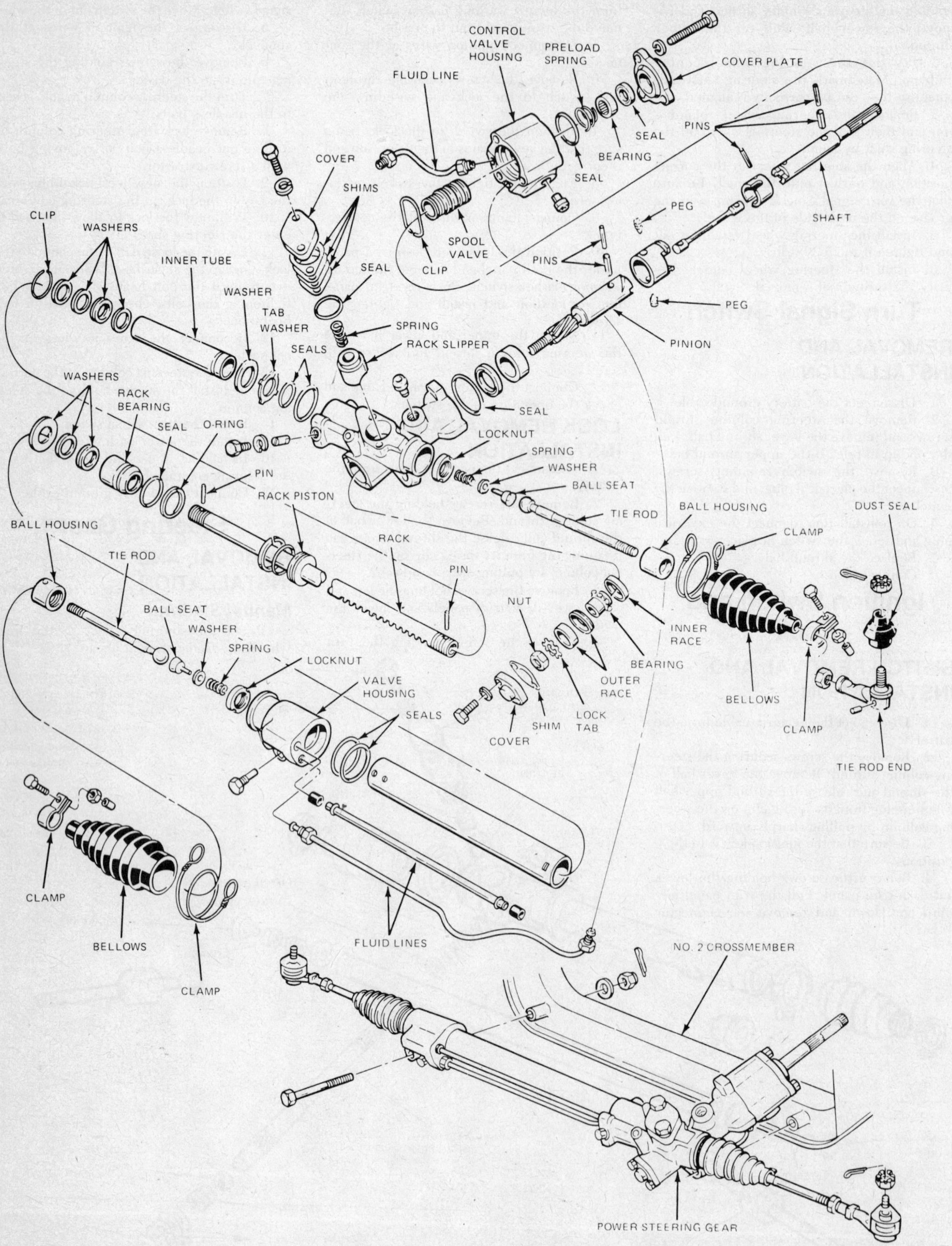

Exploded view of power steering gear

2. Jack up the front of the car and support it with jackstands.

3. Remove the nut and the bolt retaining the flexible coupling to the pinion splines.

4. Bend back the locktabs and remove the screws holding the steering gear to the mounting brackets on the crossmember. Remove the screws, locking plates, and the U-clamps.

5. Remove the cotter pins and slacken the castle nuts securing the connecting rod ends to the spindle arms.

6. Using a ball joint separator tool, separate the connecting rod ends from the spindle arms. Remove the castle nuts and withdraw the steering gear from the car. It may be necessary to turn one wheel to the stop to permit the steering gear assembly to be moved sideways enough to allow the other end to clear the stabilizer bar.

7. Remove the connecting rods and the locknuts. Note the number of turns required to unscrew them.

8. Replace the locknuts and the connecting rod ends; screw them in the same number of turns required to take them out.

9. Make sure the steering wheel is aligned straight ahead.

10. Set the steering gear in the straight ahead position.

11. Position the steering gear and align the mating splines on the flexible coupling and the pinion shaft.

12. Secure the steering gear assembly to its mounting brackets on the crossmember. Tighten the screws to 15-18 ft/lbs.

13. Assemble the connecting rod ends to the spindle arms. Install the castle nuts and tighten them to 18-22 ft/lbs. Install new cotter pins.

14. Tighten the flexible coupling-to-pinion shaft securing bolt to 12-15 ft/lbs.

15. Remove the jackstands and lower the car to the ground.

16. Check the front end wheel alignment. Check the position of the steering wheel.

Power Steering

1. Disconnect negative battery cable.

2. Raise car on hoist and remove engine splash shield if equipped.

3. Disconnect fluid pipes from rack and drain power steering fluid.

4. Remove steering coupling lower clamp bolt.

5. Disconnect tie rod ends from steering arm.

6. Remove the two steering rack mounting bolts and remove rack from vehicle.

7. Remove tie rod ends from track rods. Count number of turns required to disengage threads and note the number for assembly purposes.

8. Install tie rod ends on tie rods. Screw on each tie rod end the same number of turns as required to remove it.

9. Position steering rack into vehicle and locate pinion in steering coupling. Ensure bolt hole in steering coupling aligns with flat on steering pinion shaft.

10. Secure steering rack to crossmember with the two bolts.

11. Install steering coupling lower clamp bolt. Be sure coupling segments are all in same plane. Align as necessary by sliding coupling up or down on pinion shaft.

12. Connect tie rod ends to steering arms, and connect fluid lines to rack. Torque pressure lines 19 to 23 ft/lbs and return lines 12 to 15 ft/lbs.

13. Install engine splash shield, if equipped.

14. Check and adjust front wheel toe-in.

15. Connect negative cable battery, fill power steering reservoir, and bleed system.

16. Lower car from hoist.

Power Steering Pump

REMOVAL AND INSTALLATION

1. Open hood and disconnect negative cable from battery.

2. Raise car on hoist.

3. Remove engine splash shield, if so equipped.

4. Loosen alternator mounting bolts (2300 cc) or idler pulley bolts (2800 cc) and remove drive belt.

5. Disconnect fluid lines and drain fluid.

6. On 2300 cc engines disconnect fuel pump from engine. Do not disconnect fuel pump lines, but move pump away from power steering pump mounting bolts.

7. Remove power steering pump (2300 cc). On 2800 cc equipped cars remove the pump and bracket assembly.

8. Remove pulley from pump and pump from adaptor bracket, if so equipped.

9. Secure pump properly to bracket.

10. Install pulley on pump.

11. Install pump (2300 cc) and bracket assembly.

12. Reinstall fuel pump on 2300 cc engines.

13. Connect power steering fluid lines. Torque pressure lines to 19 to 23 ft/lbs. and return lines to 12 to 15 ft/lbs.

14. Install drive belts and adjust tension. Cooling.

15. Install engine splash shield, if so equipped.

16. Lower hoist and fill reservoir with power steering fluid. Bleed system.

17. Connect negative battery cable and close hood.

AIR BLEEDING

1. Open hood and check the fluid level. If the fluid is low, add power steering fluid to maximum level.

2. After adding fluid, allow fluid to stand for two minutes. Start car and run engine to 1500 rpm.

3. Slowly turn steering wheel from lock to lock. At the same time check fluid level, add fluid until lever is steady and air bubbles no longer appear.

4. Check pipe connections, bellows, valve body and pump for leaks and repair.

5. Close hood.

MANUAL STEERING GEAR ADJUSTMENTS

Support Yoke and Pinion Bearing Pre-Load

1. Carefully mount the steering gear in a vise (with protected jaws), so that the pinion is horizontal and the rack pre-load cover plate is on top.

2. Remove the two screws attaching the rack pre-load cover plate to the housing.

3. Lift off the cover plate, shim pack and gasket. Withdraw the spring and support yoke.

4. Remove the two screws attaching the pinion bearing pre-load cover plate to the housing.

5. Lift off the cover plate, shim pack and gasket.

6. Position shim pack and pinion cover plate on bearing and install the retaining screws. The shim pack must be made up of at least three shims. One shim must be 0.093 inch thick and positioned immediately next to plate.

7. Tighten the cover retaining screws then loosen until the plate just touches shim pack.

8. Using feeler gages, measure the gap between the cover plate and the steering gear housing. The gap should measure 0.011 to 0.013 inches. (To confirm that the cover plate has been pulled down evenly by the retaining screws, take feeler gage measurements adjacent to each screw.)

9. If the gap measured exceeds 0.011 to 0.013 inches the shim pack must be made smaller. If the gap is smaller than specification, the shim pack must be made larger. The shim pack must still use a 0.093 inch thick shim, positioned next to plate.

10. Remove the cover plate, assemble the shim pack and reinstall the cover plate. Install

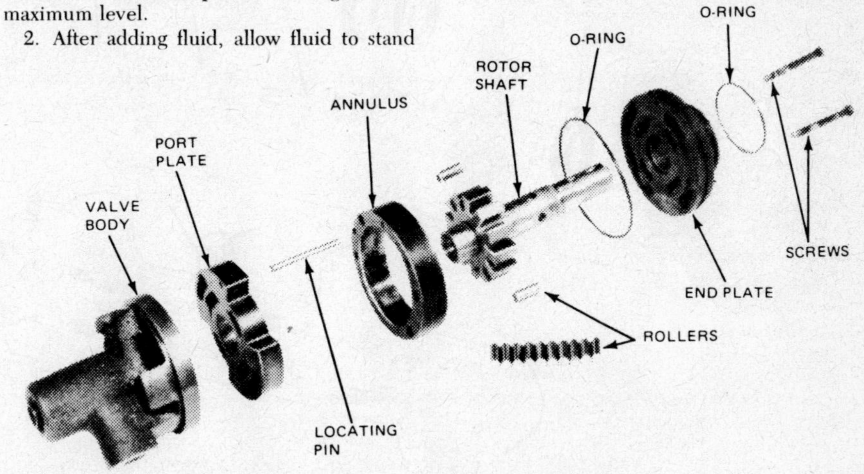

Exploded view of power steering pump

the attaching screws, using sealer on the threads, and tighten to 6-8 ft/lbs.

11. Set the support yoke adjustment. For the spring to exert the correct pressure on the support yoke, it is necessary for the distance between the underside of the cover plate and the top of the support yoke to be accurately set to 0.0005-0.0035 inch.

12. Assemble the support yoke to the rear of the rack and push it fully into position. Using a straight edge and feeler gages, measure the distance between the top of the support yoke and the surface of the steering gear housing at the cover plate. Note this dimension.

13. Assemble a shim pack (including two gaskets which must sandwich the shim pack), the thickness of which is 0.0005-0.0035 inch greater than the dimension obtained in the previous paragraph.

It is most important that the dimension is correctly set. If it is not, it may result in a knocking noise from the steering gear or heavy steering effort.

14. Install the spring into the recess in the support yoke.

15. Position the shim pack and gaskets and replace the cover plate.

16. Assemble the attaching screws to the cover plate, using sealer on the threads. Tighten the screws to 6-8 ft/lbs.

17. Install an in/lbs torque wrench to the splined end of the pinion shafts.

18. Determine the torque required to start the pinion rotating. This should be 10-18 in/lbs. If the actual torque is not within the prescribed limits, the adjustment is incorrect (check the shimming) or there is some malfunction within the gear assembly (tight bearings, damaged gear teeth, lack of lubricants, etc.) which is increasing the friction level.

BRAKES

All Capris are equipped with floating caliper type disc brakes on the front wheels and conventional drum brakes on the rear. A twin-reservoir hydraulic system is used to operate the brakes. This provides separate hydraulic circuits for the front and rear brakes. If one circuit fails, the driver is still able to stop the car by using the other system.

All models use a floor-mounted handbrake which is located between the front seats. This parking brake operates through a two-cable linkage and its operation causes the self-adjusting mechanism in the rear brakes to operate.

A power brake vacuum booster is installed in the engine compartment. The booster operates through a rod and clevis assembly which is attached to the brake pedal at one end and the brake master cylinder at the other end.

Adjustment

The front disc brakes are not adjustable. The rear drum brakes are self adjusting.

Hydraulic System

MASTER CYLINDER

Removal and Installation

1. Siphon the fluid from the reservoir.
2. Disconnect the brake lines from the master cylinder.
3. Remove the master cylinder-to-brake booster retaining nuts.
4. Lift the master cylinder away from the brake booster, being careful not to damage the vacuum seal.
5. Position the master cylinder, including the fluid seal, correctly onto the pushrod and hold it in position. With the cylinder in this position, screw in all union nuts of the brake lines a few turns.
6. Connect the master cylinder to the brake booster and tighten the nuts.
7. Connect the brake lines.
8. Fill the reservoir with heavy-duty brake fluid designated for disc brake systems. Bleed the entire brake system.
9. Check the operation of the brakes.

Overhaul

1. Remove the master cylinder.
2. Remove the reservoir from the cylinder assembly. Remove the rubber plugs.
3. Loosen the stopscrew at the center of the cylinder.
4. Push the piston inward and, using snap-ring pliers, remove the cylinder retaining snap-ring.
5. Remove the stopwasher and the primary piston assembly from the first chamber.
6. Press the secondary piston assembly out of the second chamber of the cylinder with compressed air.
7. Clean the master cylinder and the pistons with commercial alcohol or methylated spirit. Blow the parts dry with moisture-free air. Master cylinders with scored or otherwise damaged surfaces must not be reused.
8. Lightly coat the inner surfaces, pistons, and cups with brake fluid.
9. Assemble the piston of the second chamber with the filler washer, cups, pressure disc, pressure spring, and spring seat, and carefully insert the piston into the cylinder. Press the piston inward slightly and screw in the stopscrew, with the seal. Release the piston and let it contact the stopscrew.
10. Assemble the piston of the first chamber. Do not overtighten the retainer screw.
11. Insert the piston and press it in slightly. Don't move the piston against the stopscrew until the chambers have been filled with fluid. Install the rubber plug and the reservoir.

PRESSURE DIFFERENTIAL VALVE AND SWITCH

Removal and Installation

1. Disconnect the five brake lines from the ports on the valve and the switch assembly. Plug the end of the lines from the master cylinder.
2. Disconnect the wire from the switch.
3. Unscrew the bolt securing the assembly

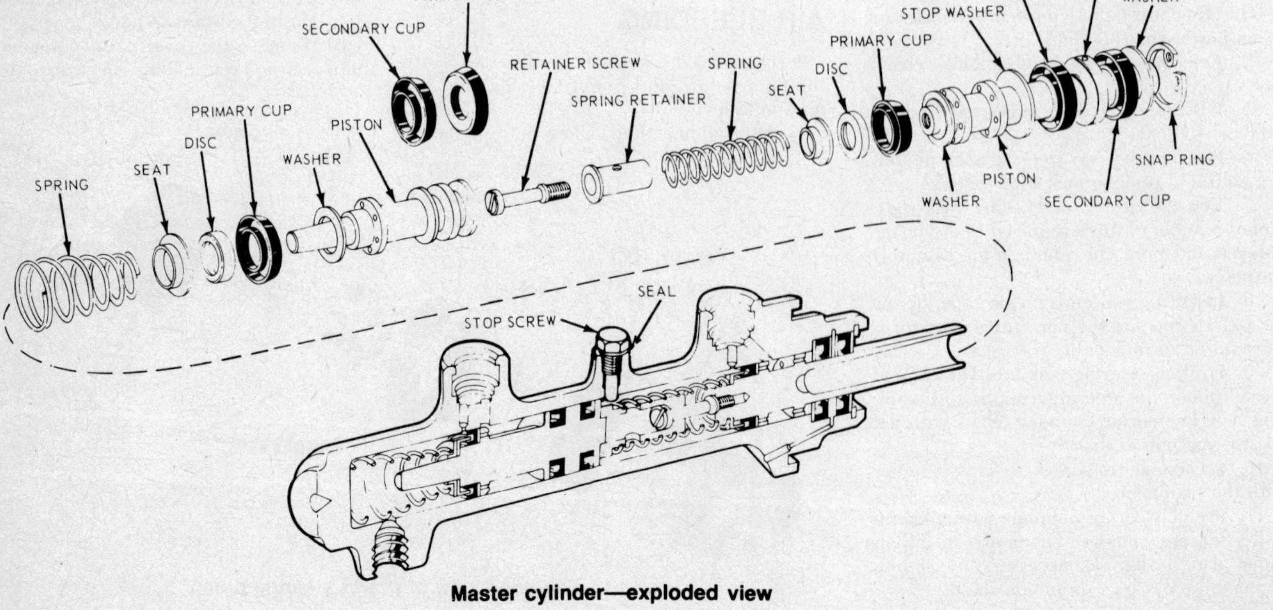

Master cylinder—exploded view

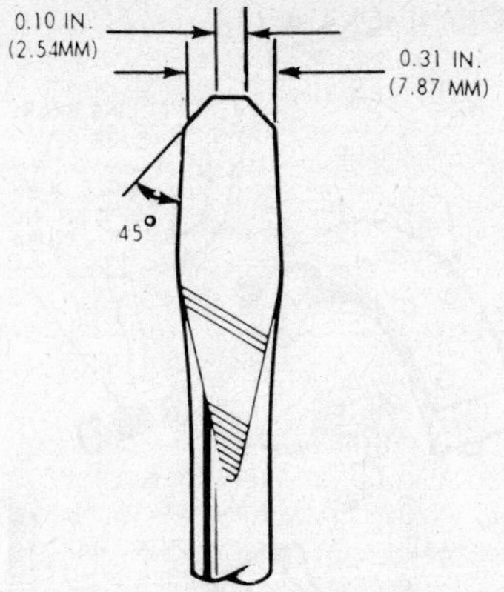

Piston centralizing tool

to the rear of the engine compartment. Remove the assembly.

4. Position the assembly in place on the firewall and loosely install the attaching bolt.

5. Connect the hydraulic lines. Tighten the attaching bolt.

6. Connect the wiring to the switch.

POWER BRAKE BOOSTER

Removal and Installation

1. Remove the brake pushrod clevis pin from the brake pedal and remove the pin.

2. Remove the master cylinder retaining nuts and position the master cylinder assembly away from the brake booster.

3. Remove the vacuum hose from the brake booster.

4. Remove the brake booster-to-dash panel retaining screws and remove the brake booster assembly and seal.

5. Remove the retaining bracket and the gasket from the brake booster.

6. Assemble the brake booster retaining bracket with a new gasket to the brake booster.

7. Position the booster assembly and the bracket onto the bolts protruding through the dash panel. Use a new gasket. Connect the pushrod with the clevis pin to the brake pedal.

8. Install and tighten the bracket retaining screws. Connect the vacuum hose to the booster.

9. Position the master cylinder assembly with a new seal ring on the booster and tighten the master cylinder-to-booster retaining nuts.

BLEEDING

1. Make sure that the master cylinder is full with brake fluid.

2. Remove the rubber dust cap from the right front bleed valve on the rear of the backing plate.

3. Install a box wrench on the bleed valve. Push a piece of rubber tubing over the bleeder until it is flush with the wrench. Place the other end of the tube in a glass jar that contains a small amount of brake fluid. During the bleeding operation the end of the tube must always be kept in the brake fluid.

Start with the right-front wheel then bleed the left-front, left-rear, and the right-rear, in that order.

NOTE: The Capri II doesn't have a right rear bleeder valve.

4. Unscrew the bleed valve about half a turn, then depress the brake pedal fully, release it, and allow it to return to its normal position. Brake fluid and/or air bubbles should have been pumped into the jar; if not, unscrew the valve further.

5. Pause for about five seconds to allow the master cylinder to be refilled with fluid.

6. Continue to depress the brake pedal, pausing after each return stroke of the brake pedal, until the fluid entering the jar is free of air bubbles.

NOTE: Check the master cylinder periodically during bleeding, making sure not to let it run out of fluid.

7. Press the pedal to the floor and tighten the bleed valve. Remove the tool from the pressure valve.

Front Brakes

DISC BRAKE PAD INSPECTION

An inspection of the pad contact surface should be routinely made. Check for scoring or cracking, glazing or signs of abnormal or uneven wear. Also check for signs of oil or grease contamination.

If any of the above are found, discard the shoes and replace with a new set on both sides.

DISC BRAKE PADS

Removal and Installation

1. Jack up the front of the car and support it with jackstands.

2. Remove the front wheels.

3. Pull out the retaining clips and retaining pins, and remove the brake pads from the caliper. Remove the brake pad tension springs and shims. (It may be necessary to use a pair of thin-nosed pliers.) Remove the master cylinder reservoir cap and siphon off a third of the fluid in the reservoir.

4. Push the pistons into their bores with a screwdriver.

5. Place the brake pad tension springs on the brake pads and shims. Install new brake pads and shims. The shims must be installed with the arrows up.

6. Install the retaining pins and clips. Refill the reservoir to the proper level.

7. Operate the brake pedal several times to bring the pads into correct adjustment.

8. Install the wheel and lower the car to the ground.

DISC BRAKE CALIPERS

Removal and Installation

1. Jack up the front of the car and support it with jackstands. Remove the wheels.

2. Remove the retaining pins and lift out the brake pads. If you plan to overhaul the calipers, press on the brake pedal to force the pistons out.

3. Remove the brake line from the rear of the caliper and install a plug into each open end.

4. Bend back the locktabs and remove the two caliper retaining bolts and the caliper assembly.

5. Replace the caliper assembly, using a new locking plate, and tighten the retaining bolts to 45-50 ft/lbs. Bend up the locktabs.

6. Install the brake lines. Install the brake pads and bleed the brakes.

Overhaul

The caliper is made in two paired halves, which are bolted together. Under no circumstances should the halves be separated.

1. Remove the caliper assembly.

2. Partially remove the piston from one cylinder bore. Remove the securing circlip and also the sealing bellows from its location in the lower part of the piston skirt. Remove the piston.

3. Pull the sealing bellows from its location in the annular ring machined in the cylinder bore. Remove the piston sealing ring.

4. Repeat these operations for the other cylinders.

5. Wash the pistons and the piston bores in commercial alcohol, methylated spirits, or brake fluid.

6. Check the pistons and their bores for score marks or other imperfections.

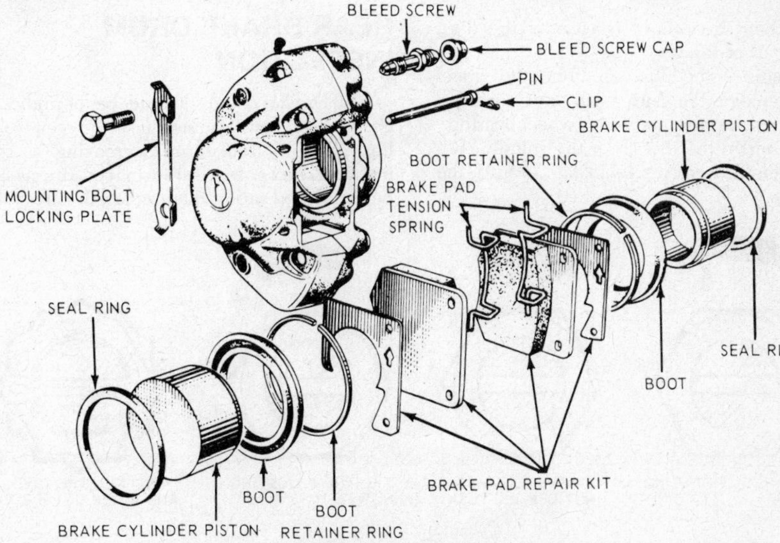

Caliper assembly—exploded view

7. Assemble a piston seal in the groove of the piston bore.
8. Install the rubber bellows to the cylinder, with the lip that is turned outward installed in the groove provided in the cylinder.
9. Lubricate the piston with clean brake fluid. Place the piston—crown first—through the rubber sealing bellows and into the cylinder.
10. When the piston is located in the cylinder, install the inner edge of the bellows in the groove in the piston skirt.
11. Push the piston as far down in the cylinder as possible.
12. Secure the sealing bellows to the caliper with the circlip.
13. Install the caliper assembly.
14. Bleed the brakes.

ROTOR (DISC) INSPECTION

Routinely check the surface of the rotors for signs of heat checking (bluish tints), uneven wear, waviness or grooving and scoring. See the brake specifications chart at the beginning of this section for wear limits. In most instances rotors can be resurfaced rather than replaced.

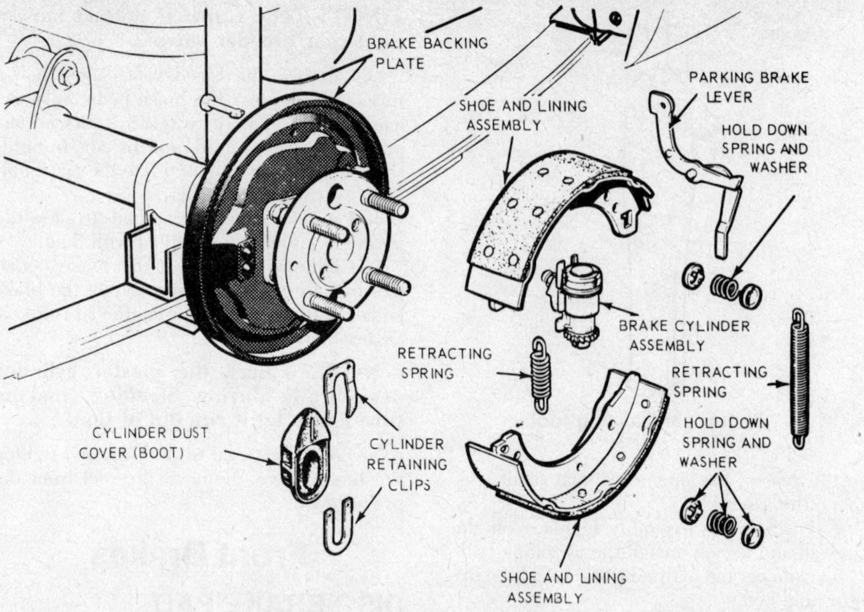

Rear brake—exploded view

BRAKE DISC

Removal and Installation

1. Jack up the front of the car and support it with jackstands.
2. Remove the front wheels.

NOTE: In order to remove the disc, the caliper must be removed.

3. Loosen, but do not remove, the upper caliper attaching bolt.
4. Remove the lower attaching bolt. When the caliper is removed from the disc, it must be wired out of the way of the disc. Also, the brake pads will fall out if they are not held in place when the caliper is removed. Insert a small piece of wood or fold a piece of heavy cardboard to fit between the shoes to hold them in place.
5. Hold the caliper in place and remove the upper attaching bolt.
6. Slide the caliper off the brake disc, inserting a piece of wood between the brake pads.
7. When the caliper is clear of the disc, wire it out of the way.
8. Remove the dust cap from the wheel hub. Remove the cotter pin, nut retainer, nut, thrust washer, and outer wheel bearing.
9. Remove the disc from the spindle. Reverse the procedures to install. Adjust the bearings.

WHEEL BEARINGS

1. Remove the wheel cover and dust cap.
2. Jack up the car.
3. Remove the cotter pin, nut retainer, adjusting nut, washer, and bearing.
4. Wash all parts in a solvent.
5. Hand-pack the wheel bearing with wheel bearing grease.
6. Reassemble, reversing the removal procedure.

NOTE: When installing the cotter pin it may be necessary to move the nut retainer in various positions on the nut to allow the cotter pin to go through the hole in the axle.

7. Torque the adjusting nut to 17-20 ft/lbs while turning the disc. Back the nut off one-half turn then tighten it hand-tight or 10-15 in/lbs. Install the nut retainer and cotter pin.

Rear Brakes

REAR BRAKE DRUM INSPECTION

Rear brake drums should be periodically checked for signs of abnormal or uneven wear, heat checking (bluish tints), grooving or scoring, and cracks. In most instances, drums can be resurfaced rather than replaced. Check the brake specifications at the beginning of this section for wear limits.

BRAKE DRUMS

Removal and Installation

1. Place blocks under the front wheels. Jack up the rear of the car and support it with jackstands.
2. Remove the wheel. Make sure that the parking brake is fully released.
3. Remove the screw holding the brake drum to the half-shaft and remove the brake drum by pulling it off the lugnut studs.
4. Inspect the inside of the drum. It should be smooth with no ridges and with no excessive glazing. If any of these conditions are excessively severe, the brake should be taken to a machine shop and turned down.
5. Replace the drum and install the holding screw. Install the tire and lower the car to the ground.

BRAKE SHOES

Removal and Installation

Remove and replace only one side at a time. This will allow you to see how to replace parts by referring to the side that is still intact as a reference.

1. Jack up the rear of the car and support it with jackstands. Remove the rear wheels and remove the brake drums (as previously described).
2. Using a brake spring tool remove the shoe hold down springs by turning the top washer on each shoe ¼ turn and pull off the washer and the spring.
3. Disengage each shoe from its slot and remove it from the wheel cylinder. Remove the shoes. To prevent the piston from falling out of the wheel cylinder, it should be held in place with a clip or a rubber band around the cylinder.
4. Remove the retracting spring from the brake shoes.
5. Assemble the retracting springs between the two shoes on the drum side of the

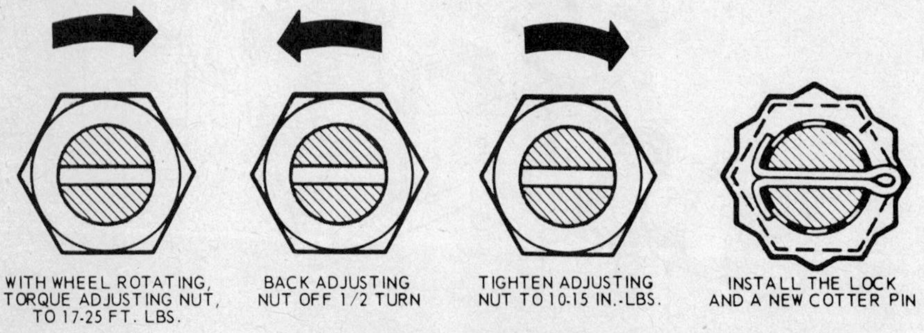

Front wheel bearing adjustment

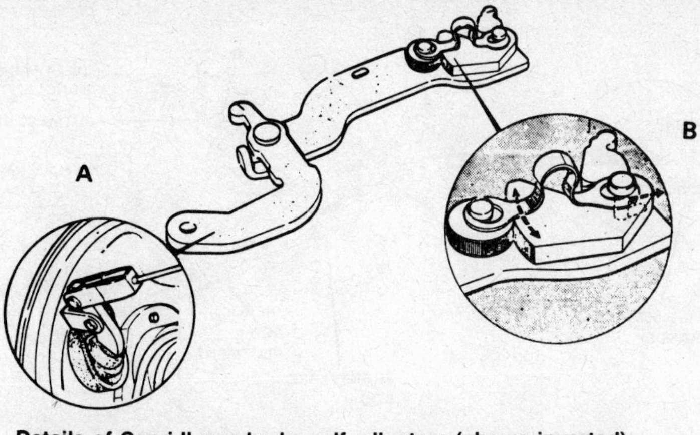

Details of Capri II rear brake self adjusters (shown inverted)

shoes. Apply white grease on the brake shoe support pads, brake shoe pivots, and to the adjustment wheel threads of the wheel cylinder.

6. Fit the shoe assembly to the backplate with the hold-down springs and washers.

7. Check to see that the shoes are seated firmly and that the springs are not binding. Reset the self adjusting unit by prying the adjusting arm away from the serrated wheel with a screwdriver and gently pushing the arm toward the backing plate. Make sure the lever returns to the fully off position. Install the brake drum and the holding screw.

8. Operate the parking brake lever at the backplate for as long as necessary to adjust the brakes, until the clicking stops. Make sure that the lever returns to the fully off position.

9. Install the wheel. Remove the jackstands and lower the car to the ground. Check the operation of the brakes on a road test.

WHEEL CYLINDERS

Removal and Installation

1975

1. Remove the brake line (two on the right side) from the rear of the backplate and install plugs.
2. Remove the spring pin and the clevis pin from the handbrake link on the inside of the brake plate.
3. Pry the rubber boot on the rear of the wheel cylinder away from the brake plate and remove it. Pull off the two U-shaped retainers that hold the cylinder to the brake plate.
4. Remove the wheel cylinder and the parking brake link.
5. Install the parking brake link and the wheel cylinder in the hole in the brake plate. Make sure that the pivot on the parking brake link is correctly located in the slot in the wheel cylinder body.
6. Secure the wheel cylinder to the brake plate using the U-shaped retainers.
7. Install the rubber boot over the wheel cylinder and the parking brake link. Make sure that the wheel cylinder can slide in the carrier plate. Lubricate with waterproof grease. Check the parking brake link and see that it operates properly.
8. Connect the parking brake linkage to the parking brake link using a clevis pin, and retain it in position with the spring clip.
9. Remove the plug and connect the brake line to the wheel cylinder. Bleed the brake system.

1976–77

1. Remove the wheel and drum.
2. Remove the brake shoes.
3. Disconnect, but don't pull away the brake line.
4. Remove the wheel cylinder bolts and lockwashers and remove it.
5. Position the cylinder and start the tubing connection.
6. Fasten the cylinder down.
7. Tighten the tubing connection.
8. Replace and adjust the shoes.
9. Replace the drums and bleed the brakes.

Overhaul

1975

1. Remove the wheel cylinder.
2. Remove the boot retainer, pry off the boot, and withdraw the piston—complete with seal—from the wheel cylinder bore.
3. Detach the seal from the piston.
4. Remove the return spring from the cylinder bore.
5. Remove the adjustment wheel and the screw assembly from the other end of the wheel cylinder.
6. Wash all parts in commercial alcohol or brake fluid, inspect them for wear or damage, and replace any necessary parts.
7. Dip the piston and seal in brake fluid and then reassemble them. Install the seal to the piston with the flat face of the seal adjacent to the piston rear shoulder.
8. Install the return spring in the wheel cylinder.
9. Dip the piston and the seal assembly in brake fluid and insert them into the cylinder bore, seal end first.
10. Install the dust cover on the wheel cylinder and then install the retainer.
11. Replace the adjustment wheel and screw the assembly into the wheel cylinder. Turn the rachet wheel until it is flush with the shoulder of the slot head bolt. Replace the cylinder.

1976–77

1. Remove the two rubber dust covers.
2. Slide out the piston assemblies from each end.
3. Remove the spring.
4. Wash all parts in alcohol or brake fluid, inspect them for wear or damage, and replace any necessary parts.

NOTE: Rebuilding kits are usually available for wheel cylinders.

5. Install new seals on the pistons. Slide one piston into place. Insert the spring and the second piston from the other end.
6. Replace the dust covers.

Parking Brake

CABLE REMOVAL AND INSTALLATION

1975

1. Place blocks in front and back of the front wheels. Jack up the rear of the car and support it with jackstands. Release the parking brake.
2. Unscrew the nuts holding the end of the primary brake cable to the relay lever on the rear of the axle housing.
3. Remove the primary cable from the end of the parking brake lever by removing the spring and the clevis pin.
4. Free the cable from its guides on the underbody and then remove it from under the car.
5. Attach the cable to the end of the parking brake lever by installing the clevis pin and securing it with the spring clip.

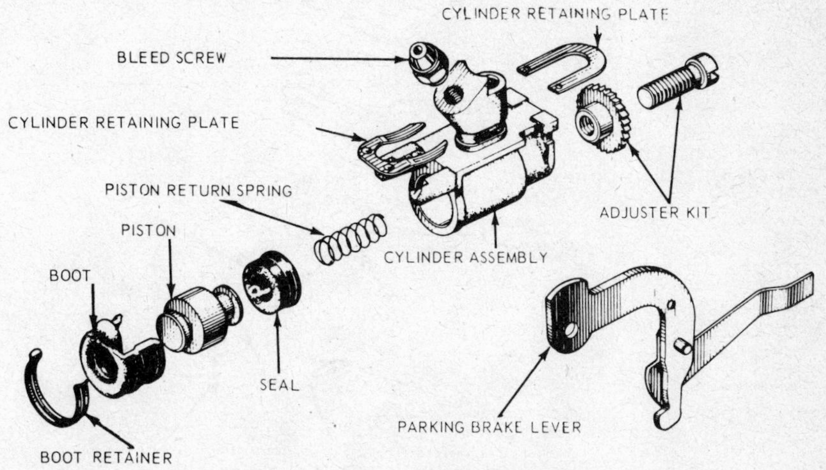

Wheel cylinder—exploded view

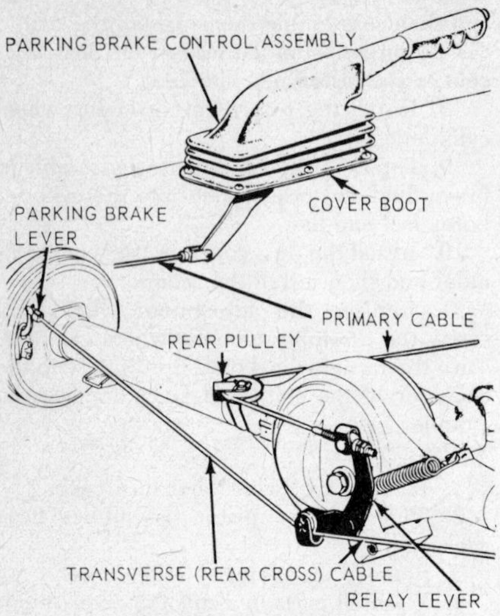

Capri parking brake

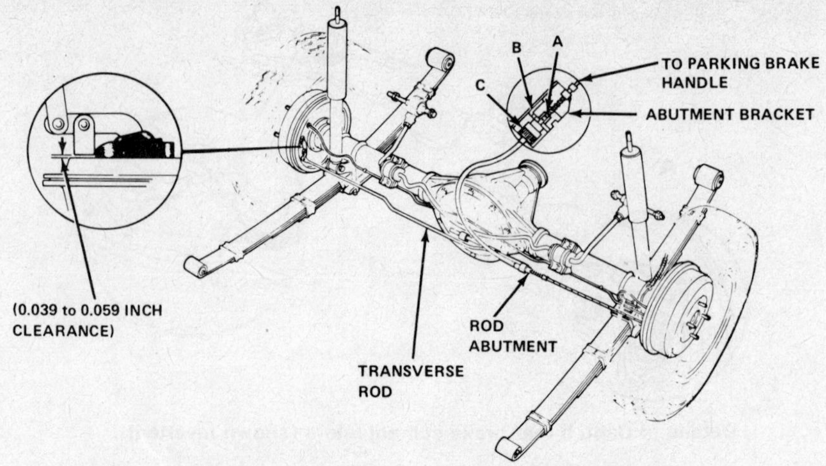

Capri II parking brake system details

6. Apply grease to the cable guides and thread the cable through the guides.

7. Connect the cable to the relay lever by threading it through the pivot pin, installing the spacer, and securing it with the two nuts. Adjust the cable.

8. Remove the jackstands and lower the car to the ground. Remove the blocks from the front wheels.

Capri II

1. Release the parking brake.

2. Remove the spring clip and clevis pin holding the cable to the handle.

3. Remove the spring clip and clevis pin holding the cable to the right rear brake lever.

4. Remove the clip holding the cable to transverse rod. Slide the cable clear of the rod bracket.

5. Slide the cable, adjusting nut, and guide clear of the abutment bracket and remove.

6. Reverse the procedure for installation. Grease the pivot points. Adjust the parking brake.

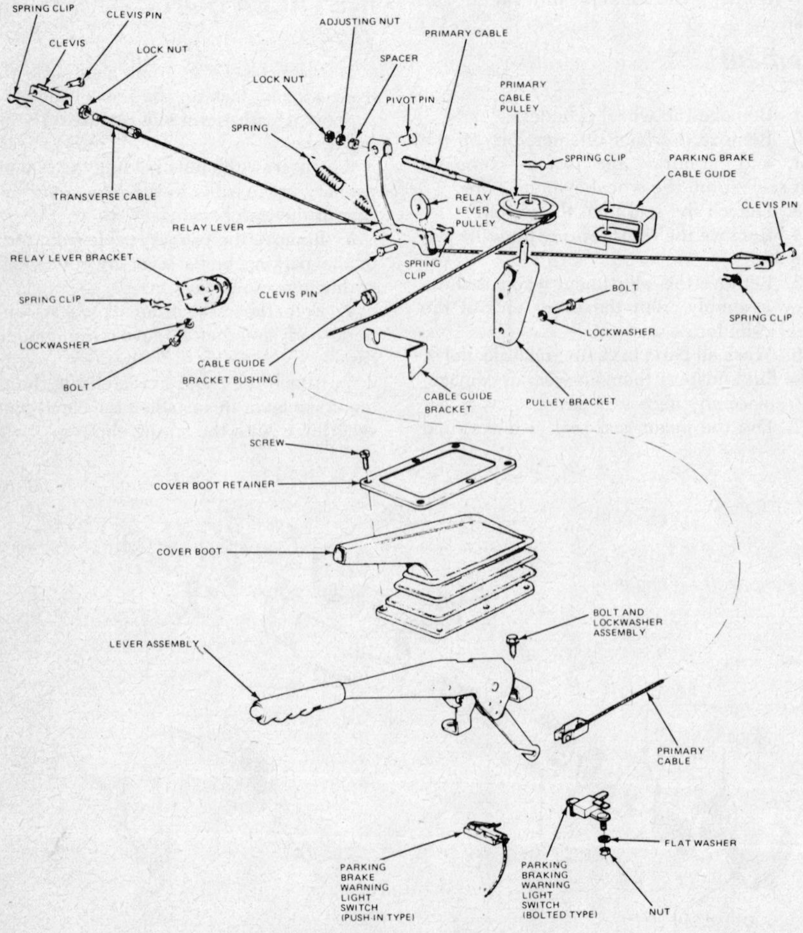

Capri parking brake system details

ADJUSTMENT

1975

1. Block the front wheels of the car. Jack up the rear of the car and support it with jackstands.

2. Adjust the length of the primary cable by tightening or loosening the adjusting nut on the relay lever so the cable has no slack.

3. Adjust the length of the transverse cable so that the cable has no slack in it. Do this by adjusting the nut on the end of the cable adjacent to the right-hand rear brake.

Remove the jackstands and lower the car to the ground. Remove the blocks from the front wheels. Check the operation of the parking brake.

Capri II

1. Raise and support the rear axle. Block the front wheels.

2. Check the clearance between each brake lever abutment (stop) and the backing plate. It should be 0.039-0.059 in.

3. To adjust, engage the keyed cable sleeve into the abutment slot and turn the adjuster nut to remove cable slack.

CHASSIS ELECTRICAL

Heater Assembly

REMOVAL AND INSTALLATION

Non A/C

1. Remove the lower dash trim panel and the glove box. To do this, the steering column shroud, ashtray, hazard flasher switch, and turn signal switch must be removed.

2. Remove the four-speed shift knob. Remove the screws for the center console. Pry the rear console panel up and remove the two screws. Pry up the clock panel and disconnect the electrical connections. Remove the main screw at the rear end of the area under the

clock panel. Slide the plastic brace forward below the parking brake lever and remove it. Lift the console out.

3. Drain the coolant, with the heater controls on.
4. Disconnect the hoses from the heater core and detach the gasket.
5. Disconnect the right and left vent and defroster ducts from the heater assembly.
6. Disconnect the control cables from the heater and water valve.
7. Unscrew the seat belt buzzer and let it hang.
8. Disconnect the wiring harness connector from the heater blower.
9. Remove the wiper motor bracket.
10. Remove the heater assembly bolts and remove the unit.
11. On installation, replace the heater assembly and the wiper motor bracket.
12. Install the left vent and defroster ducts.
13. Connect the blower wiring.
14. Connect the control cables. Adjust the upper lever in the WARM position and the lower in the OFF position.
15. Install the right vent and defroster ducts.
16. Replace the gasket and heater hoses.
17. Fill the cooling system.
18. Replace the console, shift knob, glove box, and lower dash trim panel.

With Factory-Installed A/C

CAUTION

This operation requires discharging the A/C system. This should not be attempted by untrained personnel.

The assembly to be removed in this procedure is the evaporator case assembly.

1. Discharge the system.
2. Disconnect the refrigerant lines from the evaporator core and the heater hoses from the heater core in the engine compartment.
3. Remove the glove box and the lower right trim panel. Remove the control head assembly and lower instrument panel.
4. Disconnect the vacuum hoses from the evaporator case.
5. Disconnect the temperature control cable from the blend door operating lever.
6. Remove the evaporator case bolts beside the outside/recirculation air control door.
7. Remove the air conditioning and heater ducts.
8. Disconnect the blower lead plug from the blower motor resistor.
9. Remove the three evaporator attaching nuts from the engine compartment. Rotate the evaporator assembly down and away from the firewall and out from under the instrument panel.
10. Reverse the procedure for installation. Recharge the air conditioning system.

Heater Blower

REMOVAL AND INSTALLATION

Non A/C

1. Remove the heater assembly and separate the two halves of the heater.

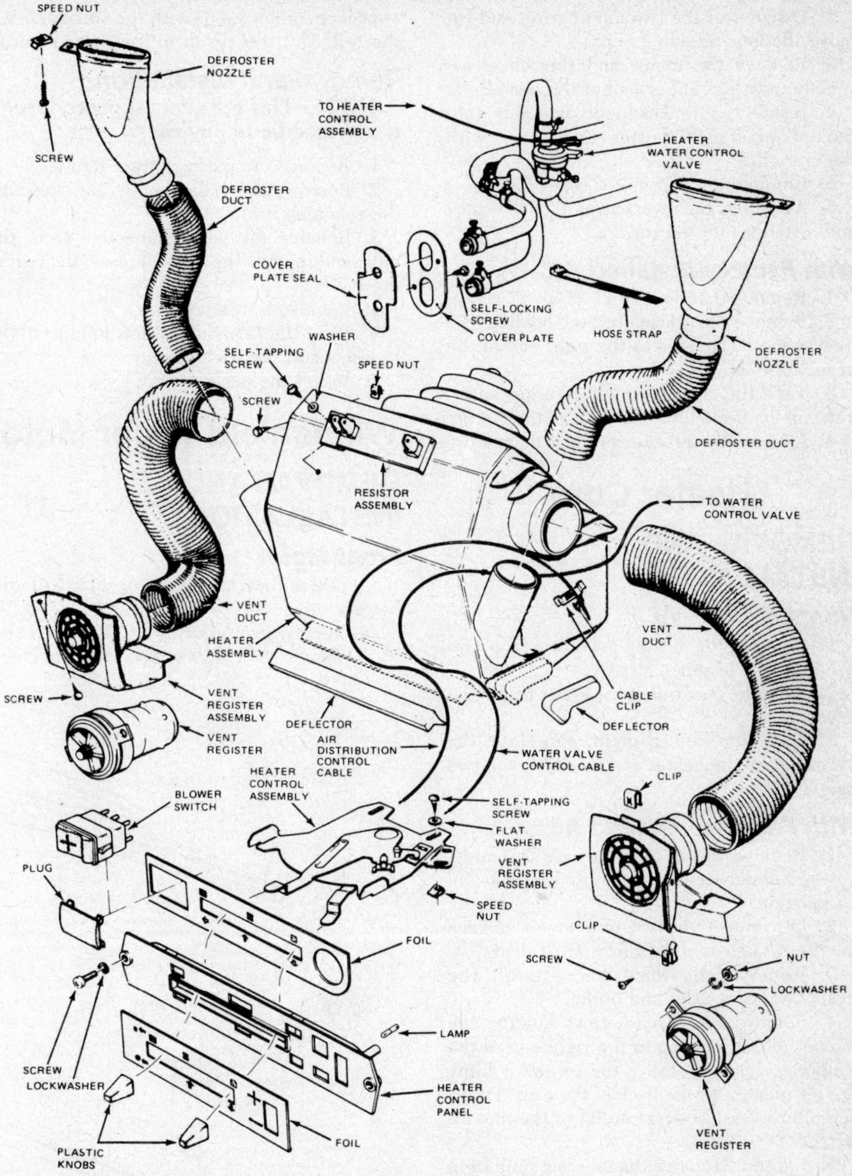

1975 Capri heating and ventilation system, without factory-installed A/C

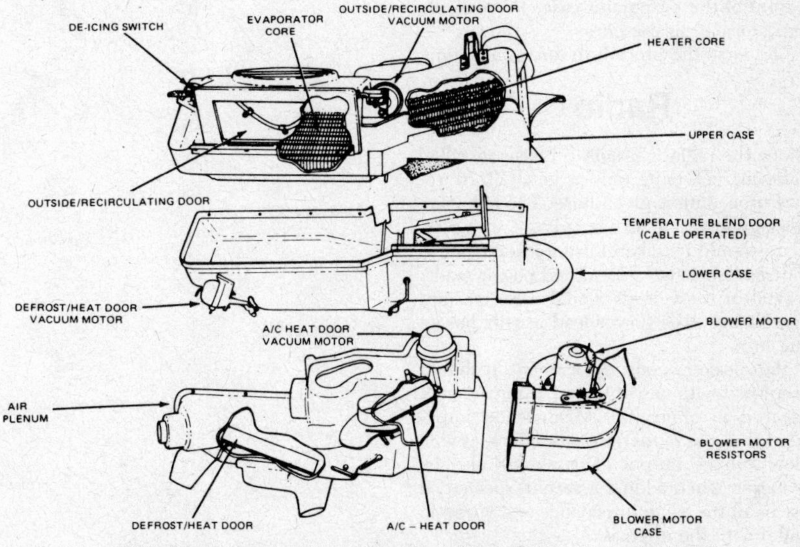

1975 Capri evaporator case assembly—factory installed A/C

2. Disconnect the two motor wires and remove the four retaining clips.
3. Remove the motor and the wheel assembly from the upper half of the heater.
4. Install the replacement assembly into the upper half of the heater and secure it with the four clips.
5. Connect the two motor wires.
6. Assemble the two halves of the heater and install it into the car.

With Factory-Installed A/C

1. Remove the glove box.
2. Remove the three screws holding the blower motor housing to the right end of the evaporator case.
3. Take the blower motor housing apart. Take off the three nuts and remove the motor.
4. Reverse the procedure for installation.

Heater Core

REMOVAL AND INSTALLATION

Non A/C

1. Remove the heater assembly, the two halves of the heater.
2. Slide the core out of the lower half of the heater.
3. Slide the replacement core into the lower half of the heater and assemble the two heater halves.

With Factory-Installed A/C

1. Remove the evaporator case assembly, covered under Heater Assembly Removal and Installation.
2. Disconnect the vacuum motor linkage for the A/C-Heat and Defrost/Heat doors.
3. Remove the foam pad around the evaporator core inlet and outlet.
4. Remove the three screws holding the blower motor housing to the right end of the evaporator case. Remove the screws holding the air plenum to the back of the case. Disassemble the case, being careful of the moulding.
5. Carefully remove the de-icing bulb from in front of the evaporator core.
6. Remove the core mounting screws from the front of the evaporator case. Remove the evaporator and heater cores.
7. Reverse the procedure for installation.

Radio

Since the radio is usually a dealer installed or aftermarket unit, only a generalized removal procedure is given here. The following applies generally to all car radios.

Care should be taken during installation to avoid reversing the ground and power leads. Reversal of these leads would cause serious radio damage. The power lead usually has an inline fuse.

If the speaker needs replacement, it should be replaced with one of the same impedance, measured in ohms (Ω). Mismatched impedance can cause rapid transistor failure as well as low volume output. This should also be considered when adding a second speaker; it must be of the same impedance and wired in parallel with the original.

The radio should never be operated without a speaker connected or with the speaker leads shorted. This will result in transistor failure.

Removal and Installation

NOTE: This is a general procedure; it is not specific to any car.

1. Remove the package tray, if any.
2. Remove the radio knobs and unscrew the retaining nuts.
3. Remove the wire connectors from the radio and remove the brackets from the rear of the radio.
4. Remove the radio.
5. Place the radio in position and install the brackets and the wiring connectors.
6. Install the package tray.

Windshield Wiper Motor

REMOVAL AND INSTALLATION

Front Motor

1. Disconnect the negative cable from the battery.
2. Remove wiper arms and blades.
3. Remove the screws securing the steering column shroud. Remove the lower half of the shroud and release the shroud upper half retaining lug from its spring clip on the steering column by pulling sharply upward.
4. Remove retaining screws and pull lower dash panel assembly clear of dash panel.
5. Disconnect cigar lighter wiring and remove panel assembly from vehicle.
6. Remove instrument cluster bezel.
7. Remove instrument cluster.
8. Remove glovebox catch striker and glovebox assembly. Disconnect glovebox light wiring.
9. Disconnect heater control cables from heater controls.
10. Disconnect left-side defroster tube connector from heater and remove connector and tube.
11. Disconnect and remove left-side face-level vent tube.
12. Disconnect wiring at heater and wiper motor.
13. Remove left defroster vent retaining screw and remove vent.
14. Remove wiper spindle retaining nuts and motor bracket retaining screw and remove motor and linkage assembly from vehicle.

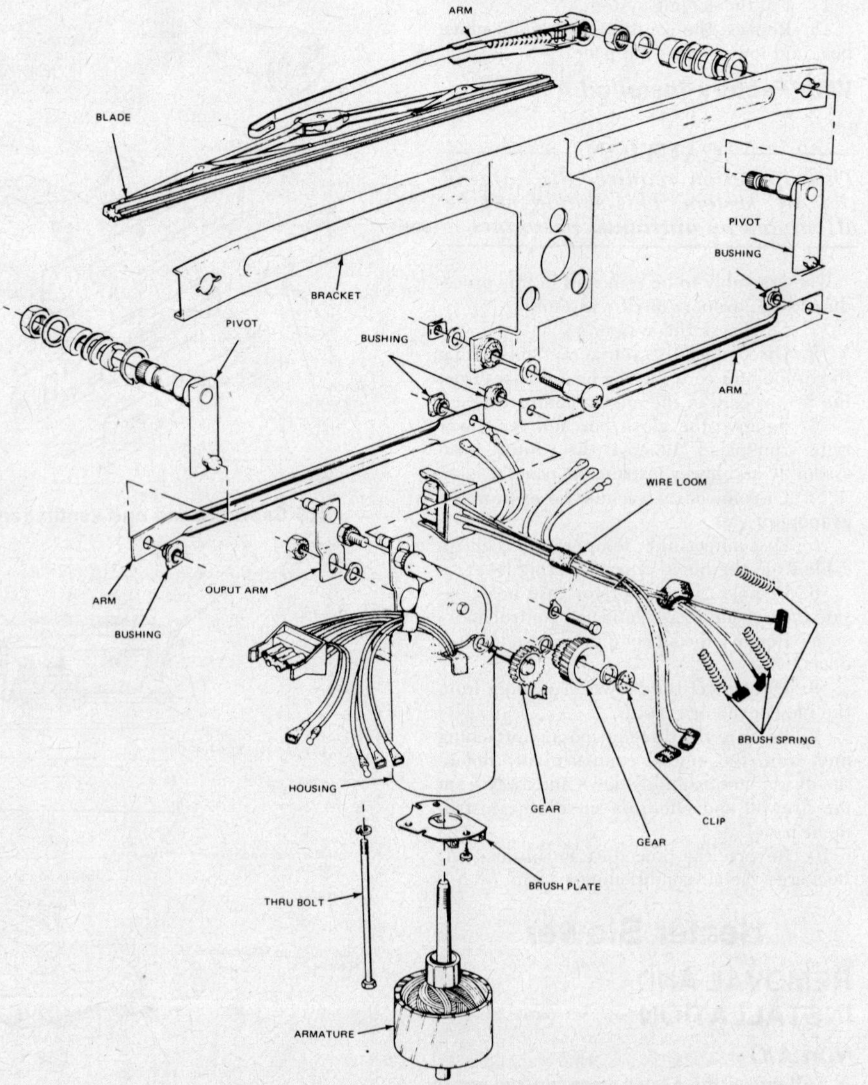

Windshield wiper system components

15. Separate motor from linkage.
16. Attach motor to linkage.
17. Install wiper motor and linkage assembly. Secure with spindle retaining nuts and motor bracket retaining screw.
18. Install left side defroster vent.
19. Reconnect wiper motor and heater wiring.
20. Install left side face-level vent tube.
21. Reconnect left side defroster vent tube to vent and connect defroster tube connector to heater box.
22. Connect and adjust heater control cables.
23. Install glovebox and glovebox catch striker. Reconnect glovebox light wiring.
24. Install instrument cluster.
25. Install instrument cluster bezel.
26. Reposition lower dash insulator panel and cover panel assembly. Connect cigar lighter wiring and install panel.
27. Install steering column shroud.
28. Install wiper arms and blades.
29. Connect negative battery cable and check wiper operation.

Rear Wiper Motor

1. Disconnect the negative cable from the battery.
2. Remove wiper arm and blade.
3. Open tailgate and remove tailgate trim panel.
4. Disconnect wiring at wiper motor.
5. Remove wiper spindle retaining nut, three motor bracket retaining screws and remove motor and linkage assembly from bracket.
6. Remove drive spindle nut and three retaining bolts and remove motor from bracket.
7. Remove linkage from bracket. Remove snap-ring at wiper spindle end.
8. Install linkage on bracket. Secure with snap-ring.
9. Install motor on bracket.
10. Install wiper motor and bracket on tailgate and reconnect wiper motor wiring. To avoid water leaks the position of the bracket may be altered by adjusting bracket arm and tightening nut.
11. Install wiper arm and blade.
12. Reconnect negative battery cable.
13. Check wiper operation.
14. Replace tailgate trim panel.

Instrument Cluster

REMOVAL AND INSTALLATION

Non A/C

1. Disconnect the battery ground cable.
2. Remove the steering column shroud and the ashtray.
3. Unfasten the hazard warning switch and disconnect its connector.
4. Unfasten the turn signal switch and let it hang.
5. Remove the lower trim panel screws. Pull the panel forward and down to disconnect the lighter and clock. Remove the trim panel.
6. Pull off the panel illumination control knob.

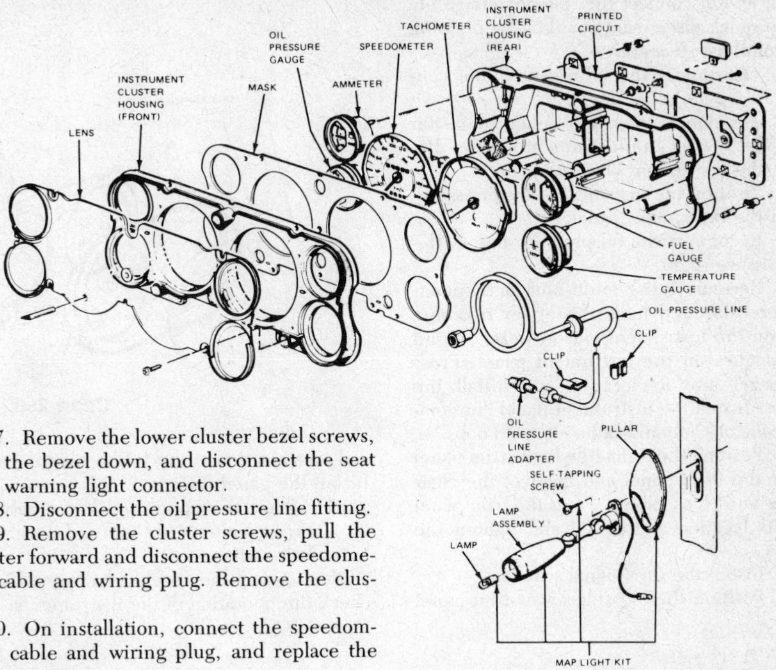

Optional and V6 Capri instrument cluster

7. Remove the lower cluster bezel screws, pull the bezel down, and disconnect the seat belt warning light connector.
8. Disconnect the oil pressure line fitting.
9. Remove the cluster screws, pull the cluster forward and disconnect the speedometer cable and wiring plug. Remove the cluster.
10. On installation, connect the speedometer cable and wiring plug, and replace the cluster screws.
11. Connect the oil pressure line.
12. Connect the seat belt warning wire.
13. Hook the upper bezel retaining clips behind the tongues on the instrument panel. Push the bezel in and install the screws.
14. Replace the panel illumination control knob.
15. Put the lower trim panel in place and connect the lighter and clock. Install the panel screws.
16. Install the turn signal switch, hazard warning switch, ashtray, steering column shroud, and battery ground cable.

W/Factory A/C

1. Disconnect the negative cable from the battery.
2. Remove the screws securing the steering column shroud; remove the lower half of the shroud upper half retaining lug from its spring clip on the steering column by pulling sharply upward.
3. Withdraw the hazard flasher switch and disconnect the wiring at the cable connector.
4. Remove the screws holding the turn signal switch. Release the switch and leave it hanging in the wiring harness.
5. Pull out the instrument panel illumination control knob and radio control knobs. Remove the lower screws securing the instrument cluster bezel, release the bezel from its upper location by pulling downward, and disconnect the seat belt warning light at the connector.
6. Remove the screws securing the instrument cluster assembly to the instrument

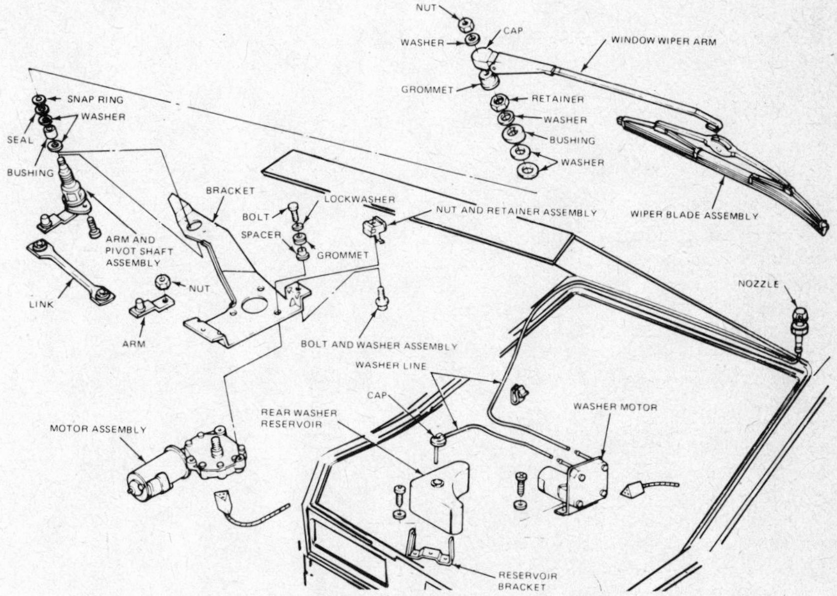

Rear window wiper assembly—Capri II

panel, and disconnect the speedometer cable at the quick disconnect coupling by pressing the coupling off-center.

7. Disconnect the oil-pressure line coupling.

8. Disconnect the multi-plug connector from the rear of the instrument cluster. Remove the instrument cluster assembly.

9. Position the instrument cluster assembly in the instrument panel.

10. Reconnect the oil pressure line to the oil pressure gage.

11. Reconnect the multi-plug and speedometer cable and hook the upper retaining clips on the instrument cluster bezel behind the tongues on the instrument panel. Press the bezel into its location and install the screws. Install the instrument panel illumination control knob and radio control knobs.

12. Position the right-side lower trim panel under the dash panel and connect the cigar lighter and clock cables. Press the trim panel into its location and install and tighten the screws.

13. Install the turn signal switch.

14. Position the left-side lower trim panel and connect the wiring to the hazard switch. Install the panel screws.

15. Mount the upper and lower halves of the steering column shroud and secure the lower half with screws.

16. Connect the negative battery cable and check the operation of the instruments.

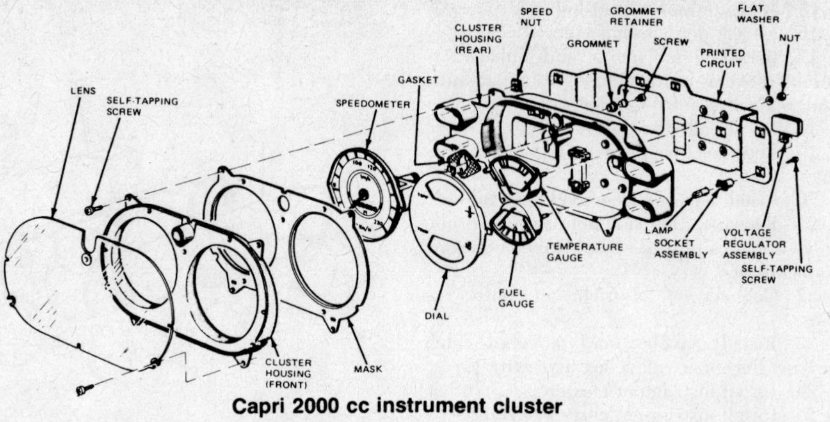

Capri 2000 cc instrument cluster

Fuse Box Location

The fuse box is under the hood in front of the left hood hinge. Amp ratings for each fuse are marked on the clear plastic inner fuse box cover. There are 8 and 16 Ampere fuses.

SPECIFICATIONS

INDEX

BEFORE SERVICING, SEE THE SAFETY NOTICE ON THE CONTENTS PAGE

INTRODUCTION

The Colt and Challenger are manufactured by Mitsubishi Heavy Industries, Ltd., and have been sold and serviced in the United States through Dodge dealers.

The Arrow, Champ, Lancer, and Sapporo are also Mitsubishi built cars, and have been sold and serviced in the United States through Plymouth dealers.

SERIAL NUMBER IDENTIFICATION

Vehicle Number

The vehicle identification plate is mounted on the instrument panel, adjacent to the lower corner of the windshield on the driver's side, and is visible through the windshield. The thirteen digit vehicle number is composed of a seven digit identification code, and a six digit sequential number.

Serial number location

Engine Number

The engine model number is embossed on the lower left side of the block.

Beginning 1978, the engine model number is stamped near the serial number on the upper right front side of the engine block. The serial number is stamped on a pad at the upper right front of the engine, adjacent to the exhaust manifold.

Engine model number

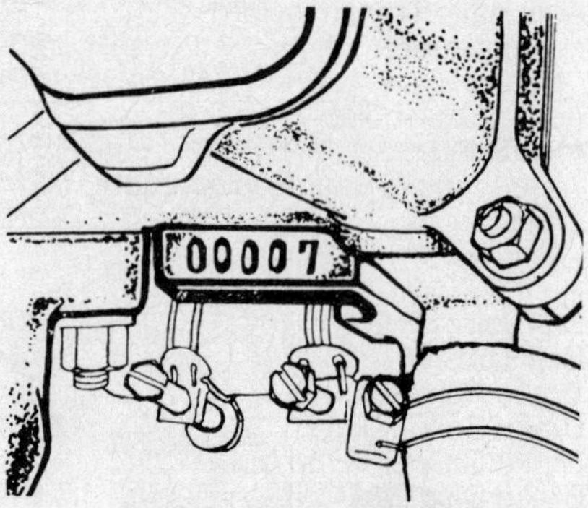

Engine number location

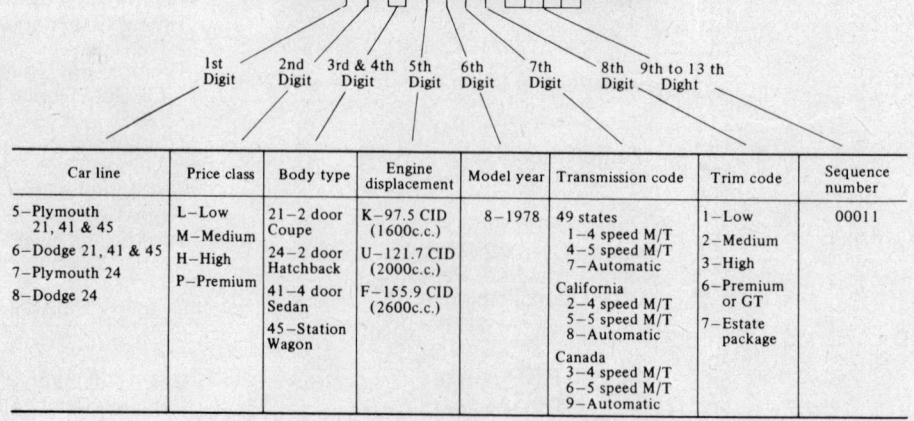

Vehicle Identification Plate

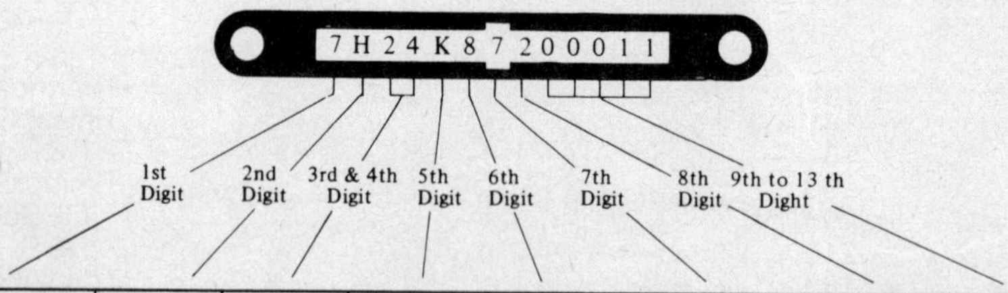

Car line	Price class	Body type	Engine displacement	Model year	Transmission code	Trim code	Sequence number
5–Plymouth 21, 41 & 45	L–Low	21–2 door Coupe	K–97.5 CID (1600c.c.)	8–1978	49 states	1–Low	00011
6–Dodge 21, 41 & 45	M–Medium	24–2 door Hatchback	U–121.7 CID (2000c.c.)		1–4 speed M/T	2–Medium	
7–Plymouth 24	H–High	41–4 door Sedan	F–155.9 CID (2600c.c.)		4–5 speed M/T	3–High	
8–Dodge 24	P–Premium	45–Station Wagon			7–Automatic	6–Premium or GT	
					California	7–Estate package	
					2–4 speed M/T		
					5–5 speed M/T		
					8–Automatic		
					Canada		
					3–4 speed M/T		
					6–5 speed M/T		
					9–Automatic		

Vehicle I.D. plate—typical

GENERAL ENGINE SPECIFICATIONS

Year	Engine Displacement cu. in. (cc)	Carburetor Type	Horsepower @ rpm	Torque @ rpm (ft. lbs.)	Bore x Stroke (in.)	Compression Ratio	Oil Pressure (psi)
1975	97.5 (1600)	1 x 2 bbl	79 @ 5300	86 @ 3000	3.03 x 3.39	8.5:1	57-71
	121.7 (2000)	1 x 2 bbl	89 @ 5200	105 @ 3000	3.31 x 3.54	8.5:1	57-71
1976 ①	97.5 (1600)	1 x 2 bbl	83 @ 5500	89 @ 3500	3.03 x 3.39	8.5:1	57-71
	121.7 (2000)	1 x 2 bbl	96 @ 5500	109 @ 3500	3.31 x 3.54	8.5:1	50-64
1977-78 ①	97.5 (1600)	1 x 2 bbl	83 @ 5500	89 @ 3500	3.03 x 3.39	8.5:1	57-71
	97.5 (1600) ②	1 x 2 bbl	83 @ 5500	89 @ 3500	3.03 x 3.39	8.5:1	50-64
	121.7 (2000) ②	1 x 2 bbl	96 @ 5500	109 @ 3500	3.31 x 3.54	8.5:1	50-64
1979-81	86.0 (1400)	1 x 2 bbl	70 @ 5200	78 @ 3000	2.91 x 3.23	8.8:1	50-64
	97.5 (1600)	1 x 2 bbl	77 @ 5200	87 @ 3000	3.03 x 3.39	8.5:1	50-64
	121.7 (2000)	1 x 2 bbl	93 @ 5200	108 @ 3000	3.31 x 3.54	8.5:1	50-64
	155.9 (2600)	1 x 2 bbl	105 @ 5000	139 @ 2500	3.59 x 3.86	8.2:1	50-64

① California emission:
97.5 (1600) MT: 80 @ 5500 HP
87 @ 3500 torque
AT: 78 @ 5500 HP
83 @ 3500 torque
121.7 (2000) All: 93 @ 5500 HP
106 @ 3500 torque
② Silent shaft
MT—Manual transmission
AT—Automatic transmission

TUNE-UP SPECIFICATIONS

When analyzing compression test results, look for uniformity among cylinders, rather than specific pressures.

Year	Engine Displace. cu. in. (cc)	SPARK PLUGS Type	SPARK PLUGS Gap (in.)	DISTRIBUTOR Point Dwell (deg)	DISTRIBUTOR Point Gap (in.)	IGNITION TIMING (deg) MT	IGNITION TIMING (deg) AT	Intake Valve Opens (deg) BTDC	Fuel Pump Pressure (psi)	Idle Speed (rpm)	VALVE CLEAR (in) In.	VALVE CLEAR (in) Ex.
1975	97.5 (1600)	BP6ES	0.030	49-55	0.018-0.022	5A	5A	32 M 22 A	3.7-5.1	800-900	0.006 hot	0.010 hot
	121.7 (2000)	BP6ES	0.030	49-55	0.018-0.022	5A	5A	20	3.7-5.1	800-900	0.006 hot	0.010 hot
1976	97.5 (1600)	BPR6ES	0.030	49-55	0.018-0.022	TDC	TDC	32M 22 A	3.7-5.1	900-1000 M 800-900 A	0.006 hot	0.010 hot
	121.7 (2000)	BPR6ES	0.030	49-55	0.018-0.022	3B	3B	20	3.7-5.1	900-1000 M 800-900 A	0.006 hot	0.010 hot
1977-78	97.5 (1600)	BPR6ES	0.030	49-55	0.018-0.022	5B ②	5B ②	24 M 19 A	3.7-5.1	①	0.006 hot	0.010 hot
	121.7 (2000)	BPR6ES	0.030	49-55	0.018-0.022	5B ②	5B ②	24	4.6-6.0	③	0.006 hot	0.010 hot
	155.9 (2600)	BPR6ES	0.039-0.043	52 ±3	0.018-0.021	7B	7B	25	4.6-6.0	④	0.006 hot	0.010 hot ⑤

TUNE-UP SPECIFICATIONS

When analyzing compression test results, look for uniformity among cylinders, rather than specific pressures

Year	Engine Displace. cu. in. (cc)	SPARK PLUGS Type	SPARK PLUGS Gap (in.)	DISTRIBUTOR Point Dwell (deg)	DISTRIBUTOR Point Gap (in.)	IGNITION TIMING (deg) MT	IGNITION TIMING (deg) AT	Intake Valve Opens (deg) BTDC	Fuel Pump Pressure (psi)	Idle Speed (rpm)	VALVE CLEAR (in) In.	VALVE CLEAR (in) Ex.
1979-81	86.0 (1400) ⑧	BPR6ES-11	0.039-0.043	52 ±3	0.018-0.021	5B	—	18	3.7-5.1	700	0.006 hot	0.010 hot ⑤
	97.5 ⑧ (1600)	BPR6ES-11	0.039-0.043	52 ±3	0.018-0.021	5B ⑥	5B ⑥	20	3.7-5.1	650 M 700 A	0.006 hot	0.010 hot ⑤
	121.7 (2000)	BPR6ES	0.039-0.043	Electronic		5B	5B	25	4.6-6.0	650 M 700 A	0.006 hot	0.010 hot ⑤
	155.9 (2600)	BPR6ES	0.039-0.043	Electronic		7B ⑦	7B ⑦	25	4.6-6.0	④	0.006 hot	0.010 hot ⑤

NOTE: The underhood specifications sticker often reflects tune-up specification changes made in production. Sticker figures must be used if they disagree with those in this chart.

① Fed.: 800-900
Alt.: 900-1000
Calif.: 900-1000 man.
800-900 auto.

② Altitude (TDC)
Calif.: 5A

③ Fed.: 900-1000 man.
800-900 auto.
Calif.: 900-1000

④ Fed.: 850 ± 50 rpm—both MT and AT
Calif. & High Alt.: 700 ± 50 rpm—MT
Calif.: 750 ± 50 rpm—AT

⑤ Jet valve clearance: 0.006 inch

⑥ High altitude only: 10B

⑦ Actual timing with dual diaphragm advance, Calif.: 3 ATDC
High Alt.—2 BTDC

⑧ 1980 California cars and all 1981 cars: electronic

TDC Top dead center

B Before top dead center

FIRING ORDERS

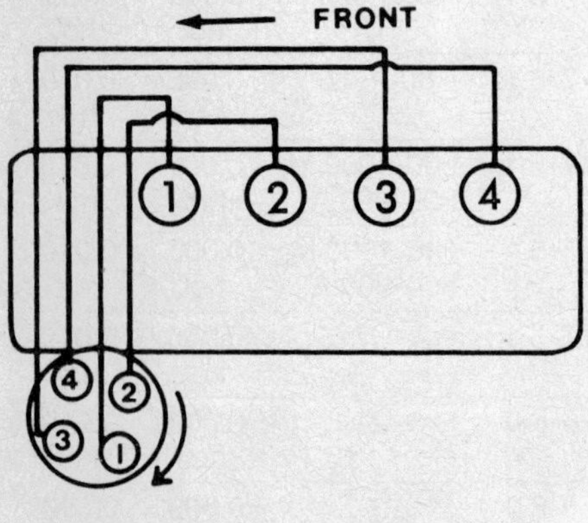

1400 cc and 1600 cc engines

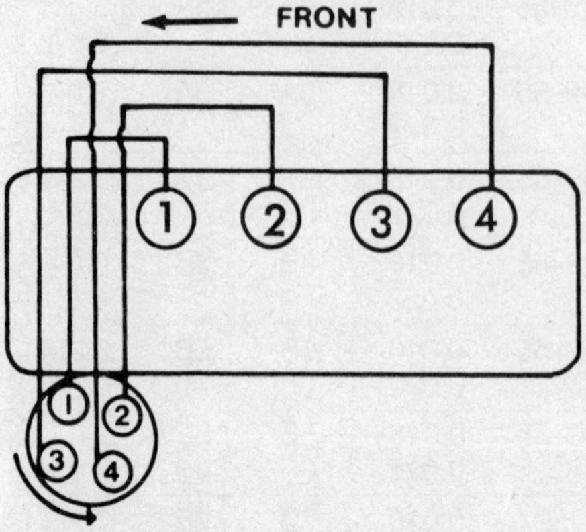

1975 2000 cc engine

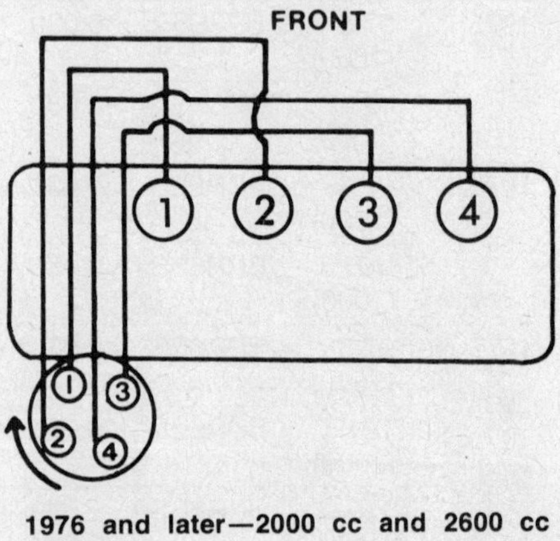

1976 and later—2000 cc and 2600 cc engines

VALVE SPECIFICATIONS

Year	Engine Displacement cu. in. (cc)	Seat Angle (deg)	Face Angle (deg)	Spring Test Pressure (lbs @ in.)	Spring Installed Height (in.)	STEM TO GUIDE CLEARANCE (in.)		STEM DIAMETER (in.)	
						Intake	Exhaust	Intake	Exhaust
1975	97.5 (1600)	45	45	59-65 @ 1.470	1.47	0.0010-0.0022	0.002-0.0033	0.315	0.315
	121.7 (2000)	45	45	55-62 @ 1.600	1.47	0.0010-0.00	0.002-0.0033	0.315	0.315
1976-81	86.0 (1400)	45	45	69 @ 1.417	1.417	0.0012-0.0024	0.0020-0.0035	0.315	0.315
	97.5 (1600)	45	45	61 @ 1.470	1.47	0.0010-0.0022	0.002-0.0033	0.315	0.315
	121.7 (2000)	45	45	61 @ 1.590	1.59	0.0010-0.0022	0.002-0.0033	0.315	0.315
	155.9 (2600)	45	45	61 @ 1.59	1.59	0.0012-0.0024	0.0020-0.0035	0.315	0.315
1978-81	Jet valve	45	45	5.5 @ .846	.846	—	—	0.1693	

CAPACITIES—REAR WHEEL DRIVE CARS

Year	Model	Engine Displacement (cc)	ENGINE CRANKCASE (qts)		TRANSMISSION (qts)			Drive Axle (pts)	Gasoline Tank (gals)	COOLING SYSTEM (qts)	
			With Filter	Without Filter	Manual 4-spd	Manual 5-spd	Automatic			W/AC	W/O AC
1975	All	1600	4.2	3.7	1.8	—	6.8	1.2	13 ①	6.4	6.4
		2000	5.0	4.5	—	2.4	6.8	1.2	13 ①	8.0	8.0
1976	All	1600	4.2	3.7	1.8	2.1	6.8	1.2	13 ①	7.7	7.7
		2000	4.5	4.0	—	2.4	6.8	1.2	13 ①	9.5	9.5
1977	All	1600	4.2	3.7	1.8	2.1	6.8	1.2	②	7.7	7.7
		2000	4.5	4.0	—	2.4	6.8	1.2	②	9.5	9.5
1978	All	1600	4.2	3.7	1.8	2.1	6.8	1.2	15.8	7.7	7.7
		2000	4.5	4.0	—	2.4	6.8	1.2	15.8	9.5	9.5
		2600	4.5	4.0	—	2.4	6.8	1.2	15.8	9.7	9.7
1979-81⑥	All	1600	4.2	3.7	—	2.1	7.2	1.2	③	7.7	7.7
		2000	4.5	4.0	—	2.4	7.2	1.2	③	9.5	9.5
		2600	4.5	4.0	—	2.4	7.2	1.4 ④	③⑤	9.5	9.5

① Station wagon: 11 gallons
② Coupe, Sedan and Hatchback: 13.2 gallons
Hard top: 13.5 gallons
Station wagon: 11.1 gallons
③ Colt Coupe, Sedan, and Arrow: 13.2
Challenger and Sapporo: 15.8
Sta. Wgn.: 14.0 (1979) 13.2 (1980)
④ 1981: 2.7
⑤ 1981: 15.8
⑥ 1600: 1979-80
2000: 1979
2600: 1979-81

CAPACITIES—FRONT WHEEL DRIVE CARS

Year	Model	Engine Displacement (cc)	Engine Crankcase (qts) With Filter	Engine Crankcase (qts) W/O Filter	Transaxle (qts) Manual 4-spd	Transaxle (qts) Manual Twin Stick	Transaxle (qts) Automatic	Gasoline Tank (gals)	Cooling System (qts) W/AC	Cooling System (qts) W/O AC
1979	All	1400	3.7	3.17	2.2	2.2	—	10.6	—	5.2
		1600	4.2	3.67	2.2	2.2	—	10.6	6.9	6.9
1980	All	1400	3.7	3.17	2.3	2.3	—	10.6	—	4.7
		1600	4.2	3.67	2.3	2.3	6.0	10.6	4.7	4.7
1981	All	1400	3.7	3.17	2.4	2.4	—	10.6 ①	—	5.0
		1600	4.2	3.67	2.4	2.4	6.0	10.6 ①	5.0	5.0

① RS, LS: 13.2

CRANKSHAFT AND CONNECTING ROD SPECIFICATIONS

All measurements are given in inches

Year	Engine Displace. (cu. in.)	Crankshaft Main Brg. Journal Dia.	Crankshaft Main Brg. Oil Clearance	Crankshaft Shaft End-Play	Crankshaft Thrust on No.	Connecting Rod Journal Diameter	Connecting Rod Oil Clearance	Connecting Rod Side Clearance
1975-76	97.5	2.2441	0.0006-0.0031	0.002-0.007	3	1.7717	0.0004-0.0028	0.004-0.010
	121.7	2.5984	0.0008-0.0028	0.002-0.007	3	2.0866	0.0006-0.0025	0.004-0.010
1977-81	86.0	1.8898	0.0008-0.0028	0.002-0.007	3	1.6535	0.0004-0.0024	0.004-0.010
	97.5	2.2441	0.0008-0.0028	0.002-0.007	3	1.7717	0.0004-0.0028	0.014-0.010
	121.7	2.5984	0.0008-0.0028	0.002-0.007	3	2.0866	0.0008-0.0028	0.004-0.010
	155.9	2.5984	0.0008-0.0028	0.002-0.007	3	2.0866	0.0008-0.0028	0.004-0.010

PISTON AND RING SPECIFICATIONS

All measurements in inches

Year	Engine Displace. cu. in. (cc)	Piston Clearance	Ring Gap Top Compression	Ring Gap Bottom Compression	Ring Gap Oil Control	Ring Side Clearance Top Compression	Ring Side Clearance Bottom Compression	Ring Side Clearance Oil Control
1975	97.5 (1600)	0.0008-0.0016	0.0008-0.0169	0.0008-0.0169	0.006-0.014	0.0012-0.0028	0.0008-0.0024	0.0010-0.0030
	121.7 (2000)	0.0008-0.0016	0.0118-0.0197	0.0098-0.0177	0.010-0.018	0.0012-0.0028	0.0008-0.0024	0.0008-0.0026
1976-81	86.0 (1400) 97.5 (1600)	0.0008-0.0016	0.008-0.016	0.008-0.016	0.008-0.020	0.0012-0.0028	0.0008-0.0024	—
	121.7 (2000) 155.9 (2600)	0.0008-0.0016	0.010-0.017	0.010-0.017	0.008-0.035	0.0024-0.0039	0.0008-0.0024	—

TORQUE SPECIFICATIONS

All readings in ft. lbs.

Year	Engine Displace. (cu. in.)	Cylinder Head Bolts	Rod Bearing Bolts	Main Bearing Bolts	Crankshaft Pulley Bolt	Flywheel to Crankshaft Bolts	MANIFOLD Intake	MANIFOLD Exhaust
1975-76	97.5	51-54 (cold) 58-61 (hot)	23-25	36-39	43-50	83-90	11-14	11-14
	121.7	65-72 (cold) 72-77 (hot)	33-35	54-61	80-93	83-90 ③	11-14	11-14
1977-81	86.0, 97.5	51-54 (cold)	24-25	37-39	44-50 ①④	94-101 ②	11-14	11-14
	121.7	65-72 (cold)	33-34	55-61	80-94	94-101 ②	11-14	11-14
	155.9	65-72 (cold)	33-34	55-61	80-94	94-101 ②	11-14	11-14

① 1600 cc w/silent shaft —44-50 ft. lbs.
② AT drive plate —84-90 ft. lbs.
③ 1976 2000 cc —94-101 ft. lbs.
④ 86.0: 37-43

TORQUE SEQUENCES

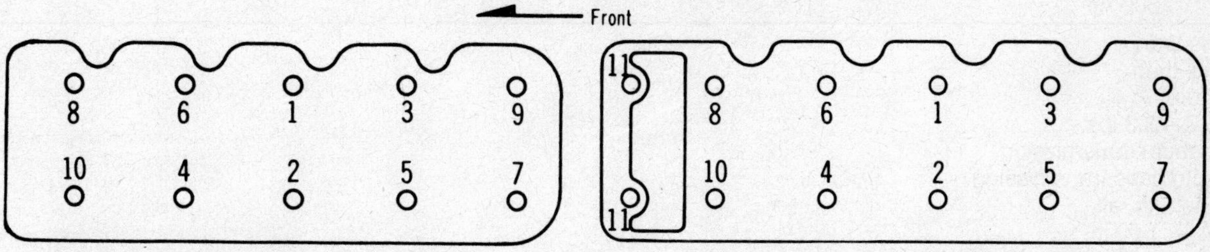

86.0 CID (1400 cc) and 97.5 CID (1600 cc) engines

121.7 CID (2000 cc) and 155.9 CID (2600 cc) engines

Head bolt tightening sequence

ALTERNATOR, REGULATOR AND BATTERY SPECIFICATIONS

Year	Engine	ALTERNATOR Rated Output	ALTERNATOR Rotation (Viewed from Pulley)	REGULATOR ③ No Load Adjusted Voltage	REGULATOR ③ Cover Temperature	CHARGING LIGHT RELAY Off Voltage	CHARGING LIGHT RELAY On Voltage	Battery Capacity Ampere-Hour
1975	All	45A @ 12V	Clockwise	14.3 to 15.8V	68° F-20° C	4.2 to 5.2V	0.5 to 3.0V	60
1976	All	45A @ 12V	Clockwise	14.2 to 15.3V	68° F-20° C	4.2 to 5.2V	0.5 to 3.0V	60
1977	All	45A @ 12V	Clockwise	14.5 to 15.3V	68° F-20° C	4.2 to 5.2V ②	0.5 to 3.0V ②	60
1978-81	1400, 1600	45A @ 12V	Clockwise	14.5 to 15.3V	68° F-20° C	4.0 to 5.8V	0.5 to 3.5V	①
	2000, 2600	50A @ 12V	Clockwise	14.5 to 15.3V	68° F-20° C	4.2 to 5.2V	0.5 to 3.0V	①

① Coupe 1600 MT: 45 A.H.
AT: 60 A.H.
Sedan all models: 60 A.H.
Hatchback 1600 MT, AT: 60 A.H.
2000 MT: 45 A.H.
AT: 60 A.H.
Station wagon 1600 MT, AT: 60 A.H.
2000, 2600 All: 65 A.H.
② 1600 W/SS, off voltage: 4.0 to 5.8V
on voltage: 0.5 to 3.5V
③ All models are equipped with sealed voltage regulators which cannot be adjusted if the readings vary from the specifications.

STARTER SPECIFICATIONS

Year	Engine (cc) and Transmission	NO LOAD TEST Amp ①	NO LOAD TEST Volts	NO LOAD TEST rpm ②	LOAD TEST Amp ①	LOAD TEST Volts	LOAD TEST Torque ②③	LOAD TEST rpm ②	STALL TEST Amp ①	STALL TEST Volts	STALL TEST Torque ③	Brush Spring Tension (lbs.)
1975	1600 MT	53	10.5	5000	150	8.6	—	1600	400	6.0	7	3.5
	1600 AT, 2000 MT	55	11.0	6500	150	9.6	—	2200	560	6.0	11	3.5
	2000 AT	62	11.0	4500	200	9.2	—	1600	730	6.0	18	3.5
1976-77	1600 MT	53	10.5	5000	150	8.6	2.53	1600	400	6.0	6.73	2.4 ④
	1600 AT 2000 MT	55	11.0	6500	150	9.6	2.24	2200	560	6.0	10.85	2.4 ④
	2000 AT	62	11.0	4500	200	9.2	3.83	1600	730	6.0	18.08	2.4 ④
1978-81	1400, 1600 MT	53	10.5	5000	150	8.6	2.53	1600	400	6.0	6.73	3.3
	1600 AT 2000 MT	55	11.0	6500	150	9.6	2.24	2200	560	6.0	10.85	3.3
	2000 AT 2600 All	62	11.0	4500	200	9.2	3.83	1600	730	6.0	18.08	3.3

① Less than
② More than
③ Ft. lbs.
④ 1977—3.3 lbs.
MT: Manual transmission
AT: Automatic transmission
Brush length, all
Max.: 669 in.
Min.: .453 in.
Pinion drive to stopper gap, all: 0 to .079 in.

BRAKE SPECIFICATIONS—REAR WHEEL DRIVE CARS

All measurements given are in. unless noted

Year	Lug Nut Torque ft. lbs.	Master Cylinder Bore	Brake Disc Thickness Max.	Brake Disc Thickness Min.	Brake Disc Runout	Brake Drum Diameter	Brake Drum Maximum	Brake Drum Maximum Wear	Lining Thickness Front Max.	Lining Thickness Front Min. ⑦	Lining Thickness Rear Max.	Lining Thickness Rear Min. ⑦
1975	51-58	①	0.510	0.450	0.006	9.0	9.060	9.079	0.38	0.08	0.017	0.04
1976	51-58	②	0.510	0.450	0.006	9.0	9.060	9.079	0.38	0.08	0.17	0.04
1977	51-58	13/16	0.510	0.450	0.006	9.0	9.060	9.079	0.38	0.08	0.17	0.04
1978-81	51-58	13/16	0.510 ③⑧	0.450 ④⑨	0.006	9.0	9.060	9.079	0.38 ⑤	0.08 ⑥	0.157	0.04

① 1600 engine equipped: 11/16 in.
2000 engine equipped: 13/16 in.
② Vehicles without power brakes: 11/16 in.
Vehicles with power brakes: 13/16 in.
③ Station wagon: max. 0.490 in.
④ Station wagon: min. 0.430 in.
⑤ Station wagon: 0.41 in.
⑥ Station wagon: 0.04 in.
⑦ Due to variations in state inspection regulations, the minimum allowable lining thickness may be different from that recommended by the manufacturer.
⑧ 1980-81—0.380
⑨ 19800-81—0.08

BRAKE SPECIFICATIONS—FRONT WHEEL DRIVE CARS

All measurements given are in. unless noted

Year	Lug Nut Torque ft. lbs.	Master Cylinder Bore	Brake Disc Thickness Max.	Brake Disc Thickness Min.	Brake Disc Runout	Brake Drum Diameter	Brake Drum Maximum	Brake Drum Maximum Wear	Lining Thickness Front ② Max.	Lining Thickness Front ② Min.	Lining Thickness Rear ② Max.	Lining Thickness Rear ② Min.
1979	51-58 ①	13/16	0.510	0.450	0.006	7.0	7.060	7.079	0.382	0.08	0.201	0.04
1980-81	51-58 ①	13/16	0.510	0.450	0.006	7.1	7.160	7.200	0.382	0.08	0.201	0.04

① Aluminum wheels: 58-72

② Due to variations in state inspection regulations, the minimum allowable lining thickness may be different from that recommended by the manufacturer.

WHEEL ALIGNMENT—REAR WHEEL DRIVE CARS

Year	Model	Caster (degrees)	Camber (degrees)	Toe-in (in.)	Steering Angle Inner Wheel (degrees)	Steering Angle Outer Wheel (degrees)	King Pin Angle
1975-76	All	1 1/4° ± 1/2°	5/6° ± 1/2	0.08 to 0.23	39	30 1/2	7°
1977	Coupe Sedan Hatchback	2°05′ ± 1/2°	1° ± 45′	0.08 to 0.23	35	30	8°53′
	Hardtop Station Wagon	1°9′ ± 1/2°	51′ ± 1/2°	0.08 to 0.23	39	30 1/2	9°
1978	All exc. Sta. Wgn.	2°05′ ± 1/2°	1° ± 1/2°	0.08 to 0.24	35	36	9°
	Station Wagon	2°38′ ± 1/2°	1°28′ ± 1/2°	0.08 to 0.35	39	30 1/2	8°25′
1979	Colt Coupe & Sedan, Arrow	2°05′ ± 30′	1° ± 30′	0.08 to 0.24	35	30	9°01′
	Challenger & Sapporo	2°38′ ± 30′	1°28′ ± 30′	0.08 to 0.35	37	32	8°52′
	Colt Sta. Wagon	2°38′ ± 30′	1°28′ ± 30′	0.08 to 0.35	39	30°30′	8°52′
1980	Arrow	2°05′ ± 30′	1° ± 30′	0.08 to 0.24	35	30	9°01′
	Challenger & Sapporo	2°38′ ± 30′	1°14′ ± 30′	0.08 to 0.35	37	32	8°52′
	Colt Sta. Wagon	2°38′ ± 30′	1°14′ ± 30′	0.08 to 0.35	37	32	8°52′
1981	Challenger, Sapporo	2°40′	1°10′	0 to 0.28	37	32	9°30′

WHEEL ALIGNMENT—FRONT WHEEL DRIVE CARS

Year	Model	Caster (degrees)	Camber (degrees)	Toe-in (in.)	Steering Angle Inner Wheel (degrees)	Steering Angle Outer Wheel (degrees)	King Pin Angle (degrees)
1979-81	All	50′ ± 20′	30′ ± 30′	0.16 in to 0.08 out	35°40′	29°17′	12°42′

TUNE-UP PROCEDURES

All 1975-78 models use a breaker point type ignition system. In 1979 an electronic ignition system was introduced and used on various models through 1980. All 1981 models use electronic ignition.

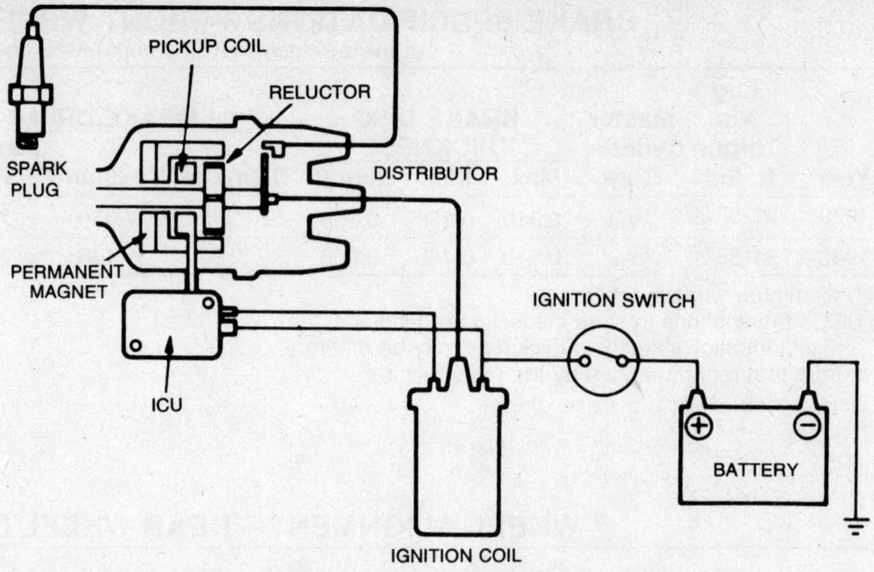

Typical electronic ignition circuit

Breaker Points and Condenser

Snap off the two retaining clips on the distributor cap. Remove the cap and examine it for cracks, deterioration, or carbon tracking. Replace the cap, if necessary, by transferring one wire at a time from the old cap to the new one. Examine the rotor for corrosion or wear. Check the points for pitting and burning. Slight imperfections on the contact surface may be filed off with a point file (fine emery paper will also do), but it is best to replace the breaker point set when tuning. Always replace the condenser when you replace the point set.

To replace the breaker points:

1. Remove the rotor.
2. Observe which screws retain the ground and primary wires. Remove the two retaining screws and lift out the lubricator wick plate and the point set.
3. Install the new point set, making sure that the pin on the bottom engages the hole in the breaker plate.
4. Install the lubricator wick plate, primary and ground wires, and then the two retaining screws (hand-tight).
5. Turn the fan belt or crankshaft pulley until the breaker arm rubbing block is on the high point of one of the cam lobes.

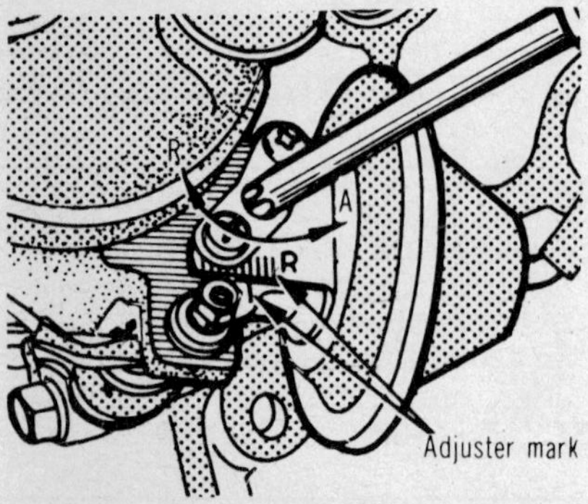

Vacuum advance adjustment

6. The correct size feeler gauge should just slip through the points. If the gap is incorrect, adjustment is made by inserting a screwdriver in the slot and pivoting it to correct the gap.
7. When the gap is correct, tighten the two retaining screws.
8. Lubricate the distributor cam wick with engine oil or silicone grease.
9. Install the rotor and distributor cap.
10. Check the dwell angle and the ignition timing as outlined in the following sections.
11. The condenser is mounted on the outside of the distributor. Undo the mounting screw and the terminal screw to replace the condenser.

Dwell Angle

The dwell angle or cam angle is the number of degrees that the distributor cam rotates while the points are closed. There is an inverse relationship between dwell angle and point gap. Increasing the point gap will decrease the dwell angle and vice versa. Checking the dwell angle with a meter is a far more accurate method of measuring point opening then the feeler gauge method.

After setting the point gap to specification with a feeler gauge check the dwell angle with a meter. Attach the dwell meter according to the manufacturer's instruction sheet. The negative lead is grounded and the positive lead is connected to the primary wire that runs from the coil to the distributor. Start the engine, let it idle and reach operating temperature, and observe the dwell on the meter. The reading should fall within the allowable range. If it does not, the gap will have to be reset.

Electronic Ignition System

This system consists of the battery, ignition switch, breaker (point-less type), electronic control unit, spark plugs and wiring. Primary circuit is switched by the electronic control unit responding to timing signals produced by a magnetic pick-up (which replaces the breaker points). Any malfunction in this system should be serviced by a qualified serviceman. The only adjustment necessary is ignition timing, dwell is adjusted electronically. Plug wires, distributor cap and rotor are inspected and serviced as on breaker type distributors.

Ignition Timing

CAUTION

When performing this or any other adjustment with the engine running, be very careful of the fan belt and pulley.

Ignition timing should always be checked as a part of any tune-up. Timing is checked after the points have been adjusted or replaced. An accurate stroboscopic timing light is a necessity for timing the engine.

1. Attach the timing light according to the manufacturer's instructions.
2. Locate the timing tab on the engine near the crankshaft pulley. Mark the "T" or appropriate line (according to the tune-up specifications), and the notch in the crankshaft pulley with chalk so that they will be more visible.
3. Disconnect and plug the hose to the vacuum advance unit on the distributor if it is a single unit i.e. one vacuum hose. (See paragraph below if distributor has two vacuum hoses.)
4. Start the engine and allow it to reach normal operating temperature.
5. Shine the timing light at the crankshaft pulley marks. The marked line should align with pulley notch.

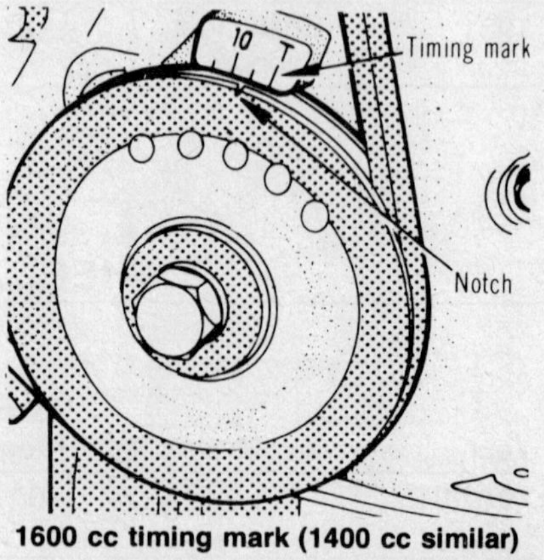

1600 cc timing mark (1400 cc similar)

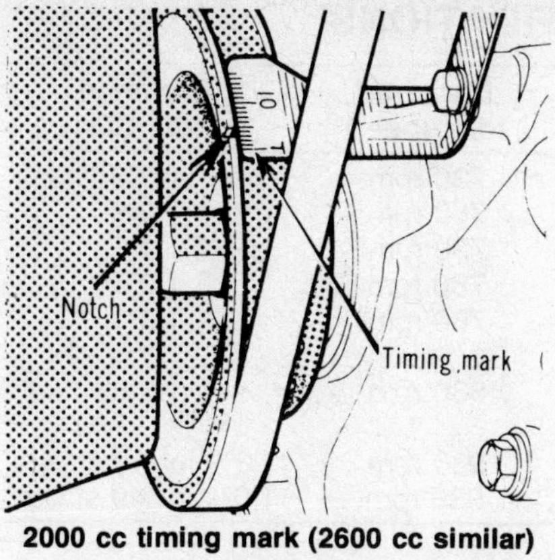

2000 cc timing mark (2600 cc similar)

6. If the marks do not align, loosen the distributor mounting nut and rotate it slowly to align the timing marks.

7. Tighten the mounting nut when the ignition timing is correct.

Some of these models are equipped with vacuum advance/retard distributors. Vacuum retard functions at idle to retard the spark. Basic timing is checked by removing the rubber plug from the vacuum advance/retard unit on the distributor. Check and adjust basic timing with the vacuum advance line connected. Replace the rubber plug and check the retarded timing. Adjustment, if necessary, is made by a Phillips screw on the vacuum advance assembly. Loosen the two screws that mount the advance to the distributor. Slowly turn the Phillips screw and check the timing mark with the timing light. Tighten the mounting screws and recheck the timing.

Valve Adjustment

THROUGH 1977

Valve clearance is adjusted with the engine stopped. When adjusting the valves cold, for example after an engine rebuild, proceed as follows:

1. Adjust the valves in the firing order 1-3-4-2.
2. Turn the crankshaft pulley to bring the piston to TDC of the compression stroke on the cylinder being adjusted.
3. Loosen the two rocker adjusting screw locknuts.
4. Using a 0.003 in. feeler gauge for the intake and a 0.007 in. gauge for the exhaust, turn the adjusting screw until the clearance is correct.
5. Tighten the locknuts to 7-9 ft/lbs.

The normal valve clearance adjustment, or final adjustment after the above initial cold adjustment, is performed as follows:

1. Run the engine until it reaches normal operating temperature and then turn it off.
2. Undo the wing nut and remove the air cleaner. Pull the large crankcase ventilation hose off of the front of the air cleaner. Disconnect the two smaller hoses, one goes to the rear of the rocker arm cover and one to the intake manifold.
3. Loosen and remove the nuts and one bracket which attach the air cleaner to the rocker arm cover.
4. Lift the bottom housing of the air cleaner off of the carburetor and, with it, the hose coming up from the exhaust manifold heat stove.
5. Unsnap the spark plug wires from their clips on the rocker arm cover.
6. Loosen and remove the two rocker arm cover bolts. The rear bolt is a crankcase ventilation fitting, so you will have to use a deep socket or a box wrench.
7. Carefully lift the rocker arm cover off the cylinder head. Using a 5/16 in. Allen socket (1600 cc) or regular socket (2000 cc) and torque wrench, make sure that the cylinder head bolts are all tightened to 58-62 ft/lbs on 1600 cc engines. 72-79 ft/lbs on 2000 cc engines.
8. Valves for each cylinder are adjusted in the firing order: 1-3-4-2.
9. Turn the crankshaft pulley to bring the piston to TDC of the compression stroke. Both valves will be closed at this point and the rocker arms will be resting on the "heel" of the camshaft lobe (the round side, not the egg-shaped side).
10. Loosen the two rocker arm adjusting screw locknuts.
11. Using the correct thickness feeler gauge, turn the adjusting screw until the gauge just snaps through the valve stem and the rocker arm.
12. Proceed to adjust the valves of each cylinder in the firing order. Remember to bring each piston to TDC of its compression stroke.

CAUTION

The importance of correctly setting the valve clearance cannot be overemphasized. Loose valve clearances will result in excessive wear and valve train clatter; tight valve clearances will result in valve seat burning.

13. Apply non-hardening sealer to the rocker arm cover gasket. Replace the gasket if its condition is at all questionable.
14. Install the cover, hoses, spark plug wires, and air cleaner in the reverse order of removal. Tighten the rocker arm cover bolts to 4-5 ft/lbs.
15. Start the engine and check for leaks.

1978-81

A jet valve has been added to the combustion chamber (on USA models). Its adjuster is on the intake valve rocker arm. The jet valve must be adjusted *before* the intake valve.

1. Bring the selected cylinder to its firing position at TDC.
2. Back off the intake valve adjusting screw two or more turns.
3. Loosen the jet valve locknut and turn the jet adjusting screw counterclockwise to obtain 0.006 inch clearance between the jet valve and the adjusting screw.
4. Tighten the locknut and recheck the clearance.
5. Adjust the intake valve clearance. Adjust the exhaust valve clearance.
6. The sequence of adjustment can be found by turning the engine in the normal direction of rotation and watching the exhaust valves. The following chart gives the sequence.

Exhaust Valve Closing	Adjust
No. 1 cylinder	No. 4 cylinder valves
No. 2 cylinder	No. 3 cylinder valves
No. 3 cylinder	No. 2 cylinder valves
No. 4 cylinder	No. 1 cylinder valves

Carburetor

IDLE SPEED ADJUSTMENT

1975-77

1. Warm the engine to normal operating temperature.
2. Disconnect the air shut-off solenoid electrical plug. This is located under the air control valve which is on the left-side of the engine. This equipment is part of the air injection system.
3. Adjust the idle speed to 900 rpm on manual transmission cars or 800 rpm on automatic transmission cars. Do this with the carburetor idle speed adjusting screw (B) on manual cars. Be careful that the screw doesn't contact the throttle arm. Use the throttle positioner screw (C) on automatic cars.
4. Connect the air shut-off solenoid.
5. On manual cars, adjust engine speed to 1000 rpm with screw B. On automatic cars, set the engine speed to 900 rpm with screw C.
6. On automatic cars only, remove the rubber plug from the vacuum unit on the distributor. Adjust the idle speed to 800 rpm with screw band, reinstall the rubber plug.
7. Race the engine to about 2500 rpm a few times and observe that it returns to normal idle speed.

1978-81

1. Have the engine at normal operating temperature.
2. Position the manual altitude compensator knob (if equipped) with the lugs and the slot in a vertical position for altitudes over 4000 ft. and the lugs and the slot in a horizontal position for less than 4000 ft.

NOTE: Some model carburetors have a tamperproof, sealed, idle mixture screw. These cannot be adjusted except by an authorized garage.

3. Adjust the engine speed and idle CO concentration to the enriched idle speed and enriched idle CO as specified in the following chart.

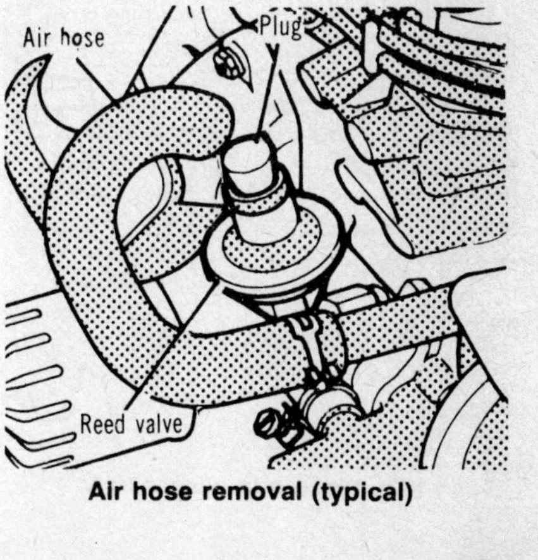

Air hose removal (typical)

ENGINE IDLE AND CO ADJUSTMENT SPECIFICATIONS

Engine	Transmission	Curb idle speed	Curb idle CO	Enriched idle speed	Enriched idle CO
97.5 CID (1600 cc)	Manual	650±50 rpm	Below 0.1%	730 rpm	1.0%
97.5 CID (1600 cc)	Automatic	700±50 rpm	Below 0.1%	780 rpm	1.0%
121.7 CID (2000 cc)	Manual	650±50 rpm	Below 0.1%	730 rpm	1.0%
121.7 CID (2000 cc)	Automatic	700±50 rpm	Below 0.1%	780 rpm	1.0%
155.9 CID (2600 cc) for California	Manual	700±50 rpm	Below 0.1%	780 rpm	1.0%
155.9 CID (2600 cc) for California	Automatic	750±50 rpm	Below 0.1%	830 rpm	1.0%
155.9 CID (2600 cc)	Manual	850±50 rpm	Below 0.1%	930 rpm	1.0% for 49 states
155.9 CID (2600 cc)	Automatic	850±50 rpm	Below 0.1%	930 rpm	1.0% for 49 states

4. Reset the engine speed to curb idle specifications by adjusting the idle mixture adjusting screw.
5. With the adjustment complete, the engine should run smoothly.
6. If the adjustment procedure does not bring the CO concentration and speed to specifications, reset the idle mixture adjusting screw or repeat Steps 3 through 5.
7. When the adjustment is completed, install the limiter cap on the idle mixture adjusting screw, so that adjustment of 180 degrees is possible, clockwise (lean) from the throttle body stop lug.

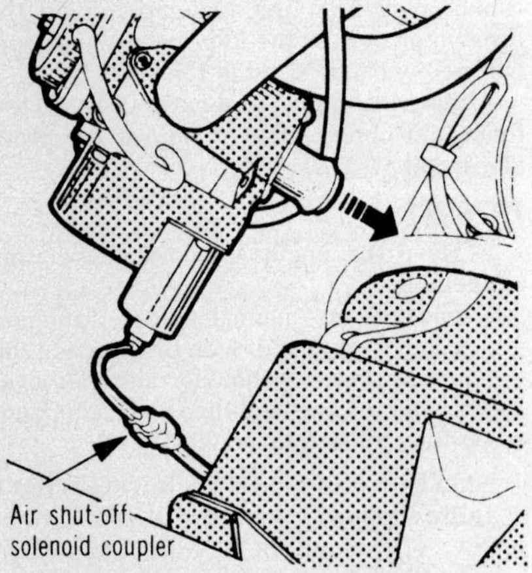

Air shut-off solenoid coupler

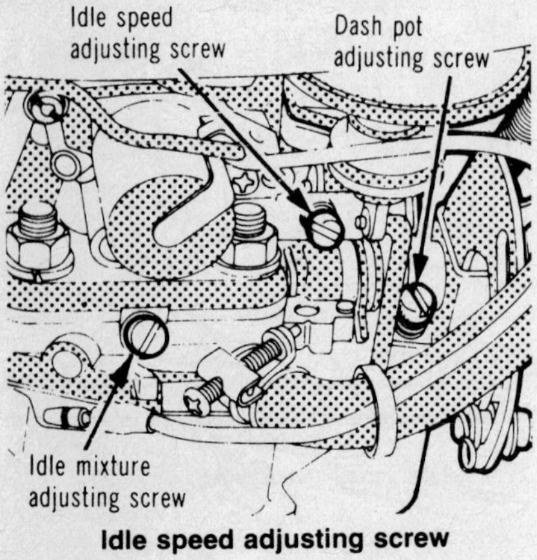

Idle speed adjusting screw

ENGINE ELECTRICAL

Distributor

REMOVAL AND INSTALLATION

1975

1. Remove the distributor cap and the vacuum hoses and remove the distributor.
2. To install adjust the alignment mark of the timing adjuster to the center position. One division of the timing adjuster equals 4° of the crankshaft angle.
3. Set No. 1 cylinder at TDC and align the timing marks.
4. On the 1600 cc engine, the lug at the lower end of the distributor shaft fits the groove in the upper end of the oil pump driveshaft. The groove should be parallel with the crankshaft center line.
5. Adjust the distributor position so the stud will be at the center of the oblong hole in the distributor flange.

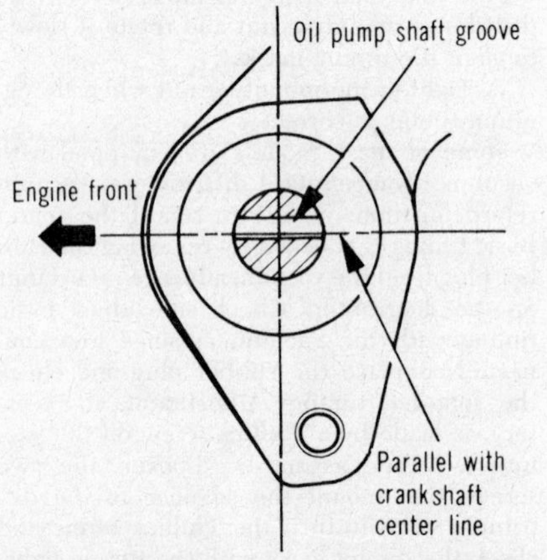

Positioning the oil pump driveshaft groove—2000 cc

1976-81

1. Remove the distributor cap and disconnect the primary wire.
2. Disconnect the vacuum hoses.
3. Remove the distributor mounting nuts and remove the distributor assembly.
4. Turn the crankshaft until No. 1 piston is at TDC on the compression stroke, and the

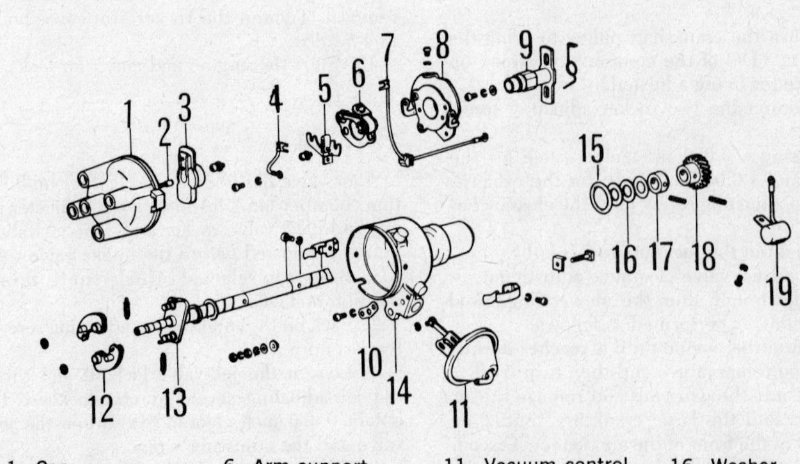

1. Cap
2. Carbon
3. Rotor
4. Ground wire
5. Cam felt
6. Arm support
7. Lead wire
8. Breaker base
9. Cam
10. Locking plate
11. Vacuum control
12. Governor weight
13. Shaft
14. Housing
15. O-ring
16. Washer
17. Thrust collar
18. Gear
19. Condenser

Exploded view of the distributor

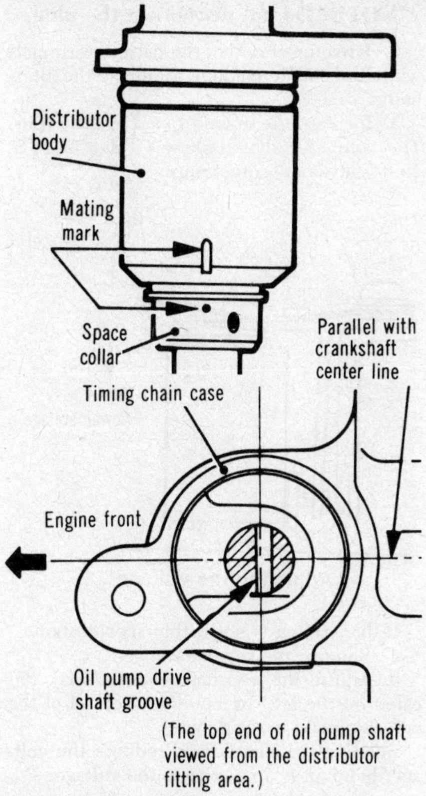

Distributor installation 1975-77 1600 cc

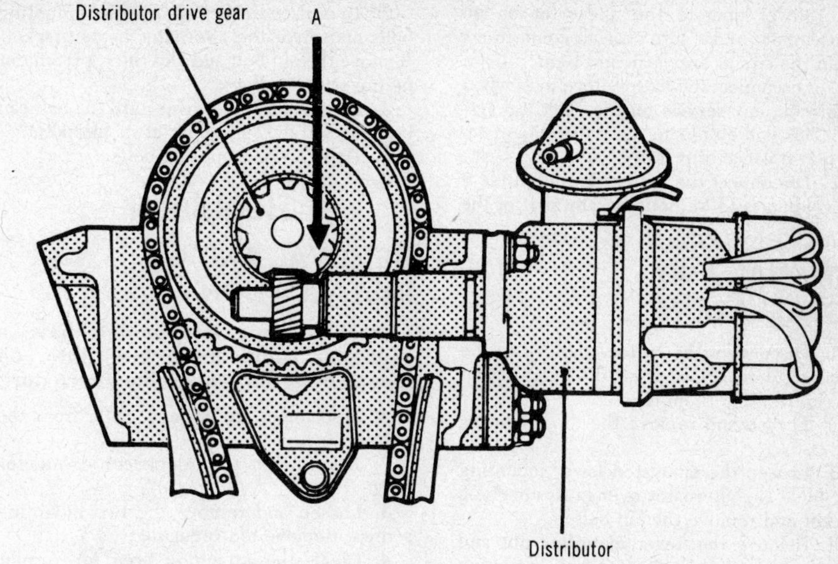

Distributor installation—cylinder head mounted distributors

notch on the crankshaft pulley is aligned with the timing mark "T".

1400 AND 1600 CC ENGINE (STANDARD)

a. Turn the oil pump driveshaft groove to the vertical position (1975-77).

b. Align the mating marks on the lower end of the distributor body with that of the spacer (1976); or with the mating mark on the distributor driven gear (1978-81).

c. (1978-81). Align the mating marks on the distributor attaching flange with the center of the distributor installing stud and install the distributor into the cylinder head.

1600 CC W/SILENT SHAFT, 2000 CC AND 2600 CC ENGINES

a. Align the mating marks of the distributor housing with the distributor driven gear.

b. Install the distributor into the cylinder head so that the mating marks are in an upright position.

5. Adjust the breaker points and install the distributor cap and primary wire.

6. Install the vacuum hoses and adjust the ignition timing to specifications.

Alternator

ALTERNATOR PRECAUTIONS

All Colts and Arrows are equipped with alternators. There are several precautions which must be strictly observed in order to avoid damaging the unit. They are:

1. Reversing the battery connections will result in damage to the diodes.
2. Booster batteries should be connected from negative to negative, and positive to positive.
3. Never use a fast charger as a booster to start the car.
4. When servicing the battery with a fast charger, always disconnect the car battery cables.
5. Never attempt to polarize an alternator.
6. Avoid long soldering times when replacing diodes or transistors. Prolonged heat is damaging to alternators.
7. Do not use test lamps of more than 12 volts (V) for checking diode continuity.
8. Do not short across or ground any of the terminals on the alternator.
9. The polarity of the battery, alternator, and regulator must be matched and considered before making any electrical connections within the system.

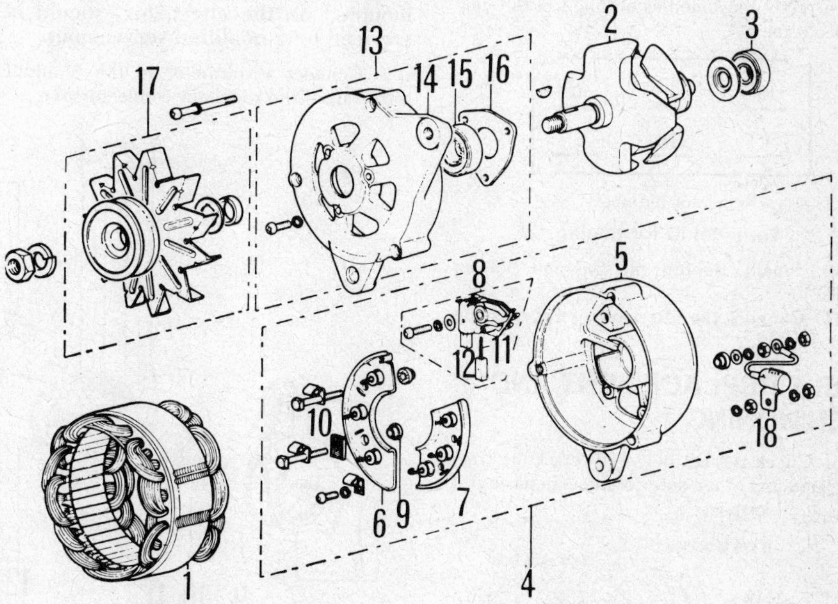

1. Stator
2. Rotor
3. Ball bearing
4. Rear bracket assembly
5. Rear bracket
6. Heat sink complete (+)
7. Heat sink complete (−)
8. Brush holder assembly
9. Insulator
10. Insulator
11. Brush spring
12. Brush
13. Front bracket assembly
14. Front bracket
15. Ball bearing
16. Bearing retainer
17. Pulley
18. Condenser

Exploded view of the alternator

10. Never operate the alternator on an open circuit. Make sure that all connections within the circuit are clean and tight.

11. Disconnect the battery terminals when performing any service on the electrical system. This will eliminate the possibility of accidental reversal of polarity.

12. Disconnect the battery ground cable if arc welding is to be done on any part of the car.

REMOVAL AND INSTALLATION

1. Disconnect the battery cables and the alternator wires. Note or tag the wires so that you can reinstall them correctly.
2. Loosen and remove the top mounting bolt.
3. Loosen the elongated lower mounting nut. Slide the alternator over in its attaching bracket and remove the fan belt.
4. Remove the lower mounting nut and bolt, being sure not to lose any mounting shims.
5. Remove the alternator.

NOTE: Remember when installing the alternator that it is not necessary to polarize the system.

6. Trial fit the alternator on the engine. The shims are installed on the inside of both alternator mounting legs. Add more shims, if necessary, for a tight fit.
7. Install the lower mounting bolt and nut. Do not completely tighten it yet.
8. Fit the fan belt over the alternator and crankshaft pulleys.
9. Loosely install the top mounting bolt and pivot the alternator over until the fan belt is correctly tensioned as outlined in the next procedure.

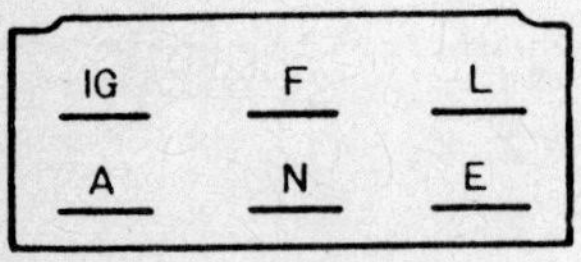

Regulator terminals

Terminal ID for testing

10. Finally tighten the top and bottom bolts.
11. Connect the alternator wires and the battery cables.

BELT REPLACEMENT AND TENSIONING

1. Check the fan belt(s) for cracking, fraying, and any other deterioration. Replace it if it is at all suspect.

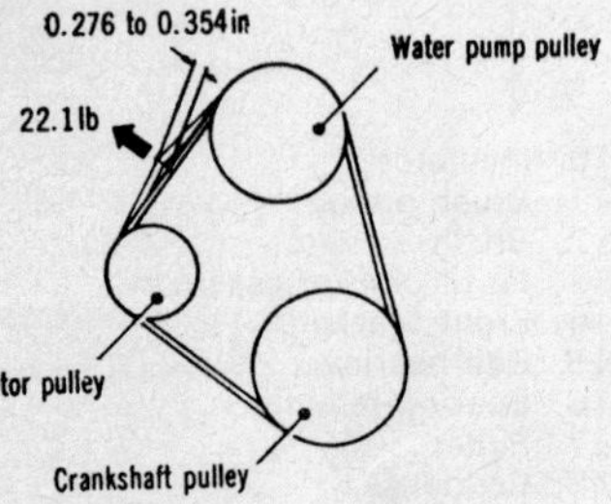

Belt tension adjustment

2. To replace the belt, loosen the mounting bolts and pivot the alternator in its bracket. Remove the old belt and slip the replacement belt over the pulleys.
3. Pry the alternator over until the belt can be deflected 9/32-11/32 in. at its midpoint.
4. Tighten the mounting bolts.

Regulator

REMOVAL AND INSTALLATION

NOTE: Some late models have a regulator (solid state) built into, on mounted on the rear of the alternator.

1. Disconnect the ground cable from the battery.
2. Disconnect the electrical connector plug.
3. Loosen and remove the two mounting screws. Remove the regulator.
4. Clean the attaching area for proper grounding of the regulator.
5. Install the regulator. Do not overtighten the mounting screws or you will distort the case.
6. Connect the electrical plug and the battery cable.

CAUTION

Never operate the engine with the regulator disconnected.

VOLTAGE CHECK AND ADJUSTMENT

NOTE: Later model cars having a solid state regulator built into, or mounted on the alternator, should be serviced by a qualified serviceman.

1. Connect a voltmeter to the A and E terminals of the regulator connector plug.

NOTE: Do not disconnect the plug.

2. Disconnect one of the battery terminals while the engine is idling to unload the alternator.
3. Increase the engine speed to 2000 rpm. The voltmeter should show a value of 14.3-15.8 V at room temperature.

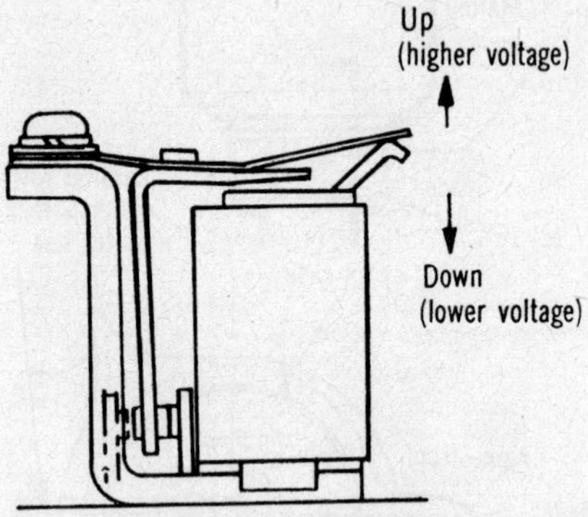

Adjusting the voltage

If the reading is not within specifications:

4. Remove the regulator cover.
5. Adjust the constant voltage relay (located on the left) by bending the end of the coil side plate up or down.

Bending the plate down reduces the voltage, bending it up increases the voltage.

6. The field relay is adjusted in the same manner as the voltage relay.

Starter

REMOVAL

1. Disconnect the battery ground cable and the starter motor wiring.
2. Loosen the two starter attaching bolts and remove the starter motor.

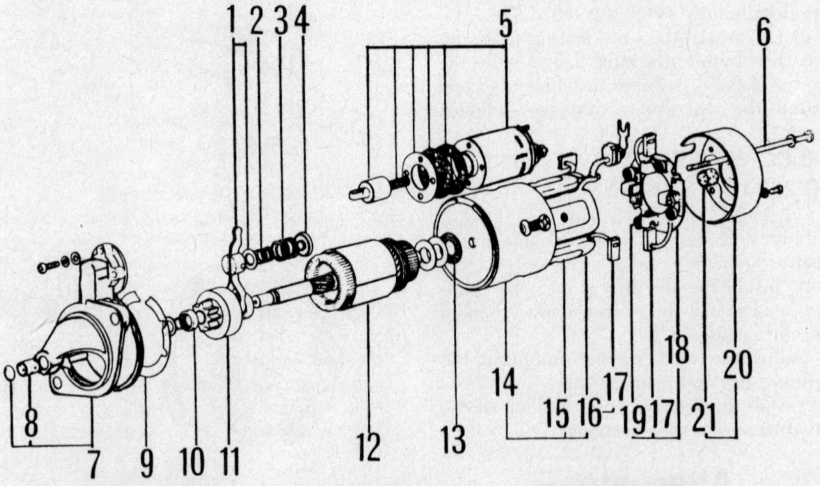

1. Lever assembly
2. Lever spring (A)
3. Lever spring (B)
4. Spring retainer
5. Electromagnetic switch
6. Through bolt
7. Front bracket
8. Front bracket bearing
9. Plate
10. Stop ring
11. Overrunning clutch
12. Armature
13. Insulating washer
14. Yoke assembly
15. Pole piece
16. Field coil
17. Brush
18. Brush holder
19. Brush spring
20. Rear bracket
21. Rear bracket bearing

Exploded view of starter

NOTE: With air conditioning or large steering gear box, disconnect the pitman arm from the starter motor attaching bolts and remove the starter from under the car.

INSTALLATION

1. Position the starter in the housing opening.
2. Install the attaching bolts and tighten evenly to avoid binding.
3. Install the starter wiring and connect the battery cable.

ENGINE MECHANICAL

Engine/Transmission Removal–Except Front Wheel Drive

The engine and transmission must be removed as a unit.

1. Remove the hood. Remove the bridge panel and grille. Drain and remove the radiator. Remove the battery.
2. Disconnect the ground strap, ignition coil wiring and vacuum and fuel solenoid valves.
3. Disconnect the following: alternator, starter, transmission switch, back-up light switch, temperature gauge and oil pressure gauge.
4. Disconnect all hoses and remove the air cleaner.
5. Disconnect all carburetor linkage. Remove the heater hose.
6. Unbolt the exhaust pipe at the manifold flange and disconnect the muffler pipe bracket at the transmission.
7. Remove the hose between the fuel filter and the fuel pump return line.
8. Remove the vacuum hose from the purge control valve.
9. Disconnect the speedometer cable backup light and distributor switches.
10. Disconnect the clutch cable and shaft lever.
11. Remove the cross shaft and control rod from the bracket under the transmission. On automatic transmission, remove the tie rod.
12. Remove the leatherette cover inside the car and remove the shifter assembly.
13. Attach a hoist and remove weight from the engine mounts. Remove the attaching bolts from the engine mounts and lift the engine upward and forward.
14. Installation is the reverse of removal.

FRONT-WHEEL DRIVE MODELS

The factory recommends that the engine and transaxle be removed as a unit.

REMOVAL

1. Disconnect the battery cables (ground cable first) remove battery hold-down and battery. Remove the battery tray.
2. Remove the air cleaner assembly. Disconnect the purge control vacuum hose from the purge valve. Remove the purge control valve mounting bracket. Remove the windshield washer reservoir, radiator tank and carbon canister.
3. Drain the coolant from the radiator. Remove the radiator assembly with the electric cooling fan attached. Be sure to disconnect the fan wiring harness and the transmission cooler lines (if equipped with automatic trans.).
4. Disconnect the following cables, hoses and wires from the engine and transaxle: clutch, accelerator, speedometer, heater hose, fuel lines, PCV vacuum line, high-altitude compensator vacuum hose (Calif. models), bowl vent valve purse hose (U.S.A. models), inhibitor switch (auto. trans), control cable (auto. trans.), starter, engine ground cable, alternator, water temperature, ignition coil, water temperature sensor, back-up light (man. trans.) and oil pressure wires.
5. Remove the ignition coil. The next step will be to jack up the car. Before you do this, look around and make sure all wires and hoses are disconnected.
6. Jack up the front of the car after you block the rear wheels. Support the car on jack stands. Remove the splash shield (if equipped).
7. Drain the lubricant out of the transaxle.
8. Remove the right and left driveshafts from the transaxle and support them with wire. Plug the transaxle case holes so dirt cannot enter.

CAUTION

The driveshaft retainer ring should be replaced whenever the shaft is removed.

9. Disconnect the assist rod and the control rod from the transaxle. If the car is equipped with a range selector, disconnect the selector cable.
10. Remove the mounting bolts/bolt from the front and rear roll control rods.
11. Disconnect the exhaust pipe from the engine and secure it with wire.
12. Loosen the engine and transaxle mounting bracket nuts.
13. Lower the car.
14. Attach a lifting device and a shop crane or chain hoist to the engine. Apply slight lifting pressure to the engine. Remove the engine and transaxle mounting nuts and bolts.
15. Make sure the rear roll control rod is disconnected. Lift the engine and transaxle from the car.

CAUTION

Make sure the transaxle does not hit the battery bracket when the engine and transaxle are lifted.

INSTALLATION

1. Lower the engine and transaxle carefully into position and loosely install the mounting bolts. Temporarily tighten the front and rear roll control rods mounting bolts. Lower the full weight of the engine and transaxle onto the mounts and tighten the nuts and bolts. Loosen and retighten the roll control rods.
2. The rest of the engine installation is the reverse of the removal. Make sure all cables, hoses and wires are connected. Fill the radiator with coolant, the transaxle with lubricant. Adjust the clutch cable and accelerator cable. Adjust the transaxle control rod. Take another check on everything you have done. Start the engine and check for leaks.

Intake Manifold

REMOVAL AND INSTALLATION

CAUTION

The intake manifold is cast aluminum.

1. Remove the air cleaner.
2. Disconnect the fuel line and EGR lines on models so equipped.
3. Disconnect the throttle positioner solenoid and fuel cut-off solenoid wires.
4. Disconnect the accelerator linkage and, if equipped with automatic transmission, the shift cables at the carburetor.
5. Drain the coolant.
6. Remove the water hose from carburetor and cylinder head.
7. Remove the heater and water outlet hoses.
8. Disconnect the water temperature sending unit.
9. Remove the manifold and carburetor.
10. Installation is the reverse of removal.

Exhaust Manifold

REMOVAL AND INSTALLATION

1. Remove the carburetor air cleaner assembly.
2. Remove the manifold heat stove and hose. Disconnect the EGR lines and reed valve, if equipped.
3. Disconnect the exhaust pipe bracket from the engine block.
4. Remove the exhaust pipe flange bolts. (One bolt and nut may have to be removed from under the car).
5. Remove the manifold flange stud nuts and remove the manifold from the cylinder head.
6. Installation is the reverse of removal. Port liner gaskets may be used along with the exhaust manifold gaskets on some engine models.

Cylinder Head

The timing chain and gear must be removed and hung on wire except on 1400 cc engines where only the timing belt needs to be removed. 1400 and 1600 cc engines require a 5/16 in. Allen socket; 2000 engines are hex head.

CAUTION

Never remove the cylinder head unless the engine is absolutely cold; the cylinder head could warp.

REMOVAL

1. Disconnect the battery ground cable, remove the air cleaner assembly, and the attached hoses.
2. Drain the coolant, remove the upper radiator hose, and the heater hoses.
3. Remove the fuel line, disconnect the accelerator linkage, distributor vacuum lines, purge valve, and water temperature gauge wire.
4. Remove the spark plug wires and the fuel pump. Remove the distributor, where necessary.
5. Disconnect the exhaust pipe from the exhaust manifold flange.

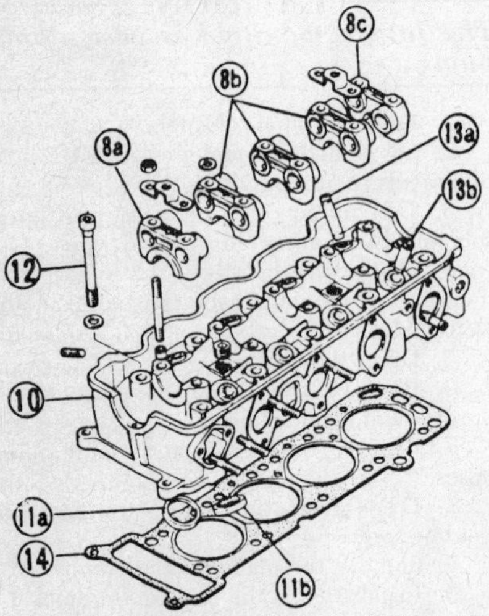

8a. Camshaft bearing cap
8b. No. 2, 3 and 4 caps
8c. Camshaft bearing cap (rear)
10. Cylinder head
11a. Intake valve seat ring
11b. Exhaust valve seat ring
12. Cylinder head bolt
13a. Exhaust valve guide
13b. Intake valve guide
14. Cylinder head gasket

Exploded view of the cylinder head

6. Remove the exhaust manifold assembly.
7. Remove the intake manifold and carburetor as a unit.
8. Turn the crankshaft to put No. 1 piston at TDC on the compression stroke.

NOTE: During the following procedures, do not turn the crankshaft after locating TDC.

1400 cc ENGINE

a. Remove the timing belt cover. Be sure that the knockout pin is at 12 o'clock and the cam sprocket mark and cylinder head pointer are aligned at 3 o'clock.
b. Loosen the timing belt tensioner mounting. Move the tensioner toward the water pump and secure it in that position. Remove the timing belt from the pulley.
c. Remove the rocker arm cover.

NOTE: The cam pulley need not be removed.

1975-76 1600 cc ENGINE–STANDARD

a. Remove the rocker arm cover.
b. Position the crankshaft sprocket dowel pin between 1 and 2 o'clock, with the crankshaft pulley notch aligned with the timing mark "T" at the front of the timing chain case.
c. Match-mark the timing chain and the timing mark on the camshaft sprocket with white paint. Lock the chain to the sprocket with mechanics wire.
d. Remove the sprocket from the camshaft.

1977-81 1600 cc ENGINE–WITH OR WITHOUT SILENT SHAFT

a. Align the timing mark on the upper under cover of the timing belt with that of the camshaft sprocket.
b. Match-mark the timing belt and the timing mark on the camshaft sprocket with a felt tip pen.
c. Remove the sprocket and insert a 2 inch piece of timing belt or other material between the bottom of the camshaft sprocket and the sprocket holder on the timing belt lower front cover, to hold the sprocket and belt so that the valve timing will not be changed.
d. Remove the timing belt upper under cover and the rocker arm cover.

1975 2000 cc ENGINE

a. Remove the rocker arm cover.
b. Position the camshaft sprocket dowel pin at the 12 o'clock position with the crankshaft pulley notch aligned with the TDC or "T" mark on the timing indicator scale.
c. Match the timing chain and the timing mark on the camshaft sprocket with white paint. Lock the chain to the sprocket with mechanics wire.
d. Remove the sprocket from the camshaft.

1976-81 2000 cc and 2600 cc ENGINES

a. Remove the rocker arm cover.
b. Position the camshaft sprocket dowel pin at the 12 o'clock position with the crankshaft pulley notch aligned with the timing mark "T" at the front of the timing chain case.
c. Match the timing chain with the timing mark on the camshaft sprocket.
d. Remove the camshaft sprocket bolt, distributor, gear and the sprocket from the camshaft.

9. Loosen and remove the cylinder head bolts in two or three stages to avoid cylinder head warpage.
10. Remove the cylinder head from the engine block.

INSTALLATION

1. Clean the cylinder head and block mating surfaces, and install a new cylinder head gasket.
2. Position the cylinder head on the engine block, engage the dowel pins front and rear, and install the cylinder head bolts.
3. Tighten the head bolts in three stages and then torque to specifications.
4. Install the timing belt upper under cover on the 1977-81 1600 cc engine.
5. Locate the camshaft in original position. Pull the camshaft sprocket and belt or chain upward, and install on the camshaft.

NOTE: If the dowel pin and the dowel pin hole does not line up between the sprocket and the spacer or camshaft, move the camshaft by bumping either of the two projections provided at the rear of No. 2 cylinder exhaust cam of the camshaft, with a light hammer or other tool, until the hole and pin align. Be certain the crankshaft does not turn.

6. Install the camshaft sprocket bolt and the distributor gear, and tighten. (The gear is used on 1976-81 2000 cc and 2600 cc engines).
7. Install the timing belt upper front cover and spark plug cable support.
8. Apply sealant to the intake manifold gasket on both sides. Position the gasket and install the intake manifold. Tighten the nuts to specifications.

CAUTION

Be sure that no sealant enters the jet air passages, when equipped.

9. Install the exhaust manifold gaskets and the manifold assembly. Tighten the nuts to specifications.
10. Connect the exhaust pipe to the exhaust manifold and install the fuel pump. Install the purge valve.
11. Install the water temperature gauge wire, heater hoses and the upper radiator hose.
12. Connect the fuel lines, accelerator linkage, vacuum hoses, and the spark plug wires.
13. Fill the cooling system and connect the battery ground cable. Install the distributor.
14. Temporarily adjust the valve clearance to the cold engine specifications.

Cold Engine Specifications	
Jet Valve—If equipped	.003 in. (.07 mm)
Intake Valve	.003 in. (.07 mm)
Exhaust Valve	.007 in. (.17 mm)

15. Install the gasket on the rocker arm cover and temporarily install the cover on the engine.
16. Start the engine and bring it to normal operating temperature. Stop the engine and remove the rocker arm cover.
17. Adjust the valves to hot engine specifications.

Hot Engine Specifications	
Jet Valve—If equipped	.006 in. (.15 mm)
Intake Valve	.006 in. (.15 mm)
Exhaust Valve	.010 in. (.25 mm)

18. Reinstall the rocker arm cover and tighten securely.
19. Install the air cleaner, hoses, purge valve hose, and any other removed unit.

Camshaft and Rocker Arm

ALL EXCEPT 1400 CC ENGINE

Removal and Installation

The camshaft and rocker arms are best removed after the cylinder head has been removed from the engine block.

1. Match-mark the rocker arm bearing caps to the cylinder head.
2. Remove the bearing cap bolts from the cylinder head, but do not remove them from the bearing caps and shafts. Lift the rocker arm assembly from the cylinder head.
3. Remove the camshaft from the bearing saddles.

NOTE: On some engines, a distributor drive gear and spacer are used on the front of the camshaft.

4. The valves, valve springs, and valve guide seals can now be removed from the cylinder head.

NOTE: Refer to the cylinder head overhaul procedures in the General Information Section. Valve guides are a shrink fit, with oversize guides available. Valve seats are replaceable, with oversize seats available.

5. The rocker arm assembly can be disassembled by the removal of the bolts from the bearing caps and shafts.

NOTE: a. Keep the rocker arms and springs in proper order. The left and right springs have different tension ratings and free lengths.
b. Observe the location of the mating marks of the right and left rocker arm shaft in relation to the front bearing cap mating marks.

6. Observe the mating marks and reassemble the units in the reverse order of the removal.

1400 CC ENGINE

Removal and Installation

1. Remove the cylinder head rear cover.
2. Remove the camshaft thrust case tightening bolt, located on top of the rear mounting boss.
3. Carefully slide the camshaft and thrust case (attached to the rear of the cam) out the rear of the cylinder head.
4. Installation is the reverse of removal. Coat all parts with clean engine oil prior to installation.

Jet Valves–1978-81

The jet valve can be removed from the cylinder head with the rocker arm either in place or removed. Care must be exercised not to twist the socket while removing or replacing the valve, so as not to break it. Torque the valve to 13.5 to 15.5 ft/lbs.

Timing Gear Cover, Chain, Counterbalance Shafts, and Tensioner

NOTE: The timing chain case is cast aluminum, so exercise caution when handling this part.

The following outlines are the recommended removal and installation procedures for the timing chain or belt. Some modifications to the procedures may be necessary due to added accessories, sheet-metal parts, or emission control units and connecting hoses.

REMOVAL–CHAIN EQUIPPED

1600 cc Engine–Standard (1975-77)
2000 cc Engine–Standard (1975)

1. Drain the coolant and remove the radiator. Disconnect the battery ground cable.
2. Remove the alternator and accessory belts.
3. Rotate the crankshaft to bring No. 1 piston to TDC on the compression stroke, by aligning the notch on the crankshaft pulley with the "T" mark on the timing indicator scale.
4. Remove the crankshaft pulley and bolt.

NOTE: Do not move the crankshaft when removing the pulley. If the crankshaft is turned, return the shaft to the original position as in Step 3.

5. Remove the crankshaft pulley and bolt.
6. Remove the fan blades and the water pump assembly.
7. Remove the cylinder head assembly.

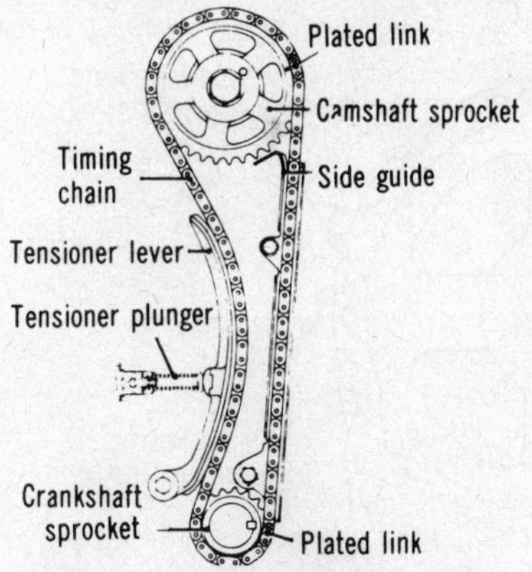

1600 cc timing chain and tensioner

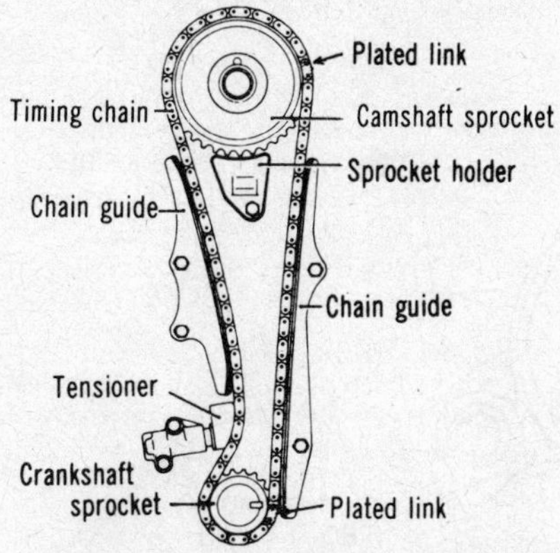

2000 cc timing chain and tensioner

8. Raise the car and support it safely.
9. Drain the engine oil and remove the oil pan, oil pressure switch, oil filter, and oil pump.

NOTE: Undercar splash pans may have to be removed to gain access to the oil pan.

10. Remove the chain tension holder, spring, and plunger, on the right side of the chain cover.
11. Remove the timing chain cover from the engine block.
12. Remove the oil slinger and crankshaft gear from the crankshaft. Do not loose the Woodruff key from the crankshaft.
13. Remove the crankshaft and camshaft sprockets with the chain attached, from the engine block.
14. If needed, remove the chain tensioner lever and side guide.

INSTALLATION

1. If removed, install the chain tensioner lever and the side guide, with the jet of the guide toward the chain and sprocket meshing point.
2. Be sure the No. 1 piston is at TDC. Using a new gasket, install the cylinder head assembly.
3. Rotate the camshaft until the dowel pin is between the 1 and 2 o'clock position on the 1600 cc engines, and the 12 o'clock position on the 2000 cc engines.
4. Position the crankshaft sprocket and the camshaft sprocket so that the punch marks on the sprockets align with the chrome or buff plated links of the timing chain.
5. Install the Woodruff key on the crankshaft and while holding the timing chain and sprockets in position, install the sprockets onto the camshaft and the crankshaft.
6. If the dowel pin does not align with the hole in the camshaft sprocket, bump the camshaft on the projections provided to align the two. Install the camshaft sprocket bolt and torque to 36 to 43 ft/lbs.

NOTE: The chain must be fitted in the guide groove and against the tensioner lever.

7. Install the Woodruff key, crankshaft gear with the "F" mark toward the front on 1600 cc engines, and with the "C" or "A" mark toward the front on the 2000 cc engine. The oil slinger must be installed with its concave side facing the front of the engine.
8. Install a new gasket and seal on the front timing cover case and install the case on the engine block. Torque the bolts to 11 to 13 ft/lbs.
9. Install the tensioner lever plunger and spring into the case and torque to 29 to 36 ft/lbs.

CAUTION

Because the timing chain is supported and stretched by the tensioner lever, it is important to align the marks on the sprockets and chain.

10. Install the oil screen and oil pump.
11. Install the oil pan, oil filter, and the oil pressure gauge sender. Fill the oil pan.
12. Reinstall any splash pans and lower the car to the floor.
13. Align the oil pump shaft in a vertical position on the 1600 cc engine and in a horizontal position on the 2000 cc engine. Align the distributor marks to fire No. 1 cylinder, and install the distributor.
14. Install the crankshaft pulley and torque the bolt to 43 to 50 ft/lbs.

15. Install the water pump, fan blades, alternator and belt. Adjust the belt.

16. Install the radiator, add coolant to the system, and connect the battery ground cable.

17. Refer to the Cylinder Head Installation Section and adjust the valves as for a cold engine. Temporarily install the rocker arm cover, start the engine, and warm it up.

18. Stop the engine and remove the rocker arm cover. Adjust the valves to the hot specifications.

REMOVAL–BELT EQUIPPED

1400 cc Engine (1979-81)

REMOVAL

1. Turn the engine until No. 1 piston is on TDC with the timing marks aligned.

2. Disconnect the ground (negative) battery cable.

3. Remove the fan drive belt, the fan blades, spacer and water pump pulley.

4. Remove the timing belt cover.

5. Loosen the timing belt tensioner mounting bolt and move the tensioner toward the water pump. Temporarily secure the tensioner.

6. Remove the crankshaft pulley and slide the belt off of the camshaft and crankshaft drive sprockets.

7. Inspect the drive sprockets for abnormal wear, cracks or damage and replace as necessary. Remove and inspect the tensioner. Check for smooth pulley rotation, excessive play or noise. Replace tensioner if necessary.

INSTALLATION

1. Reinstall the tensioner, if it was removed, and temporarily secure it close to the water pump.

2. Make sure that the timing mark on the camshaft sprocket is aligned with the pointer on the cylinder head and that the crankshaft sprocket mark is aligned with the mark on the engine case (see illustration).

3. Install the timing belt on the crankshaft sprocket.

4. Install the belt counterclockwise over the camshaft sprocket making sure there is no play on the tension side of the belt. Adjust the belt fore and aft so that it is centered on the sprockets.

5. Loosen the tensioner from it's temporary position so that the spring pressure will allow it to contact the timing belt.

6. Rotate the crankshaft two complete turns in the normal rotation direction to remove any belt slack. Turn the crankshaft until the timing marks are lined up. If the timing has slipped, remove the belt and repeat the procedure.

7. Tighten the tensioner mounting bolts, slotted side (right) first then the spring side.

8. Once again rotate the engine two complete revolutions until the timing marks line up. Recheck the belt tension.

NOTE: When the tension side of the timing belt and the tensioner are pushed in horizontally with a moderate force (about 11 lbs.) and the cogged side of the belt covers about a quarter of an inch of the tensioner right side mounting bolt head, (across flats) the tension is correct.

9. Reinstall the timing belt cover, the water pump pulley, spacer, fan blades and drive belt.

10. Connect the battery ground cable.

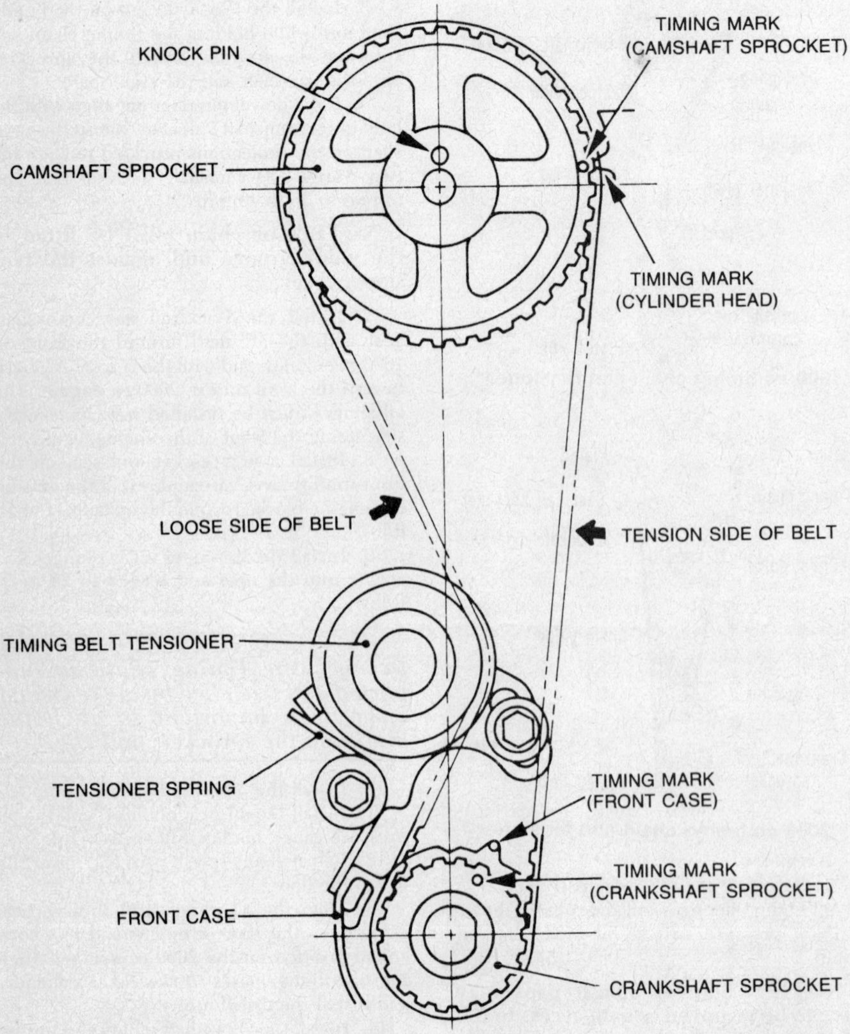

Belt driven cam—1400 cc shown

1600 cc Engine–Standard (1978-81)

1600 cc Engine–W/Silent Shaft (1977-81)

1. Drain the coolant and remove the radiator. Disconnect the battery cable.

2. Remove the alternator and accessory belts.

3. Rotate the crankshaft to bring No. 1 piston to TDC on the compression stroke. Align the notch on the crankshaft pulley with the "T" mark on the timing indicator scale and the timing mark on the upper under cover of the timing belt with the mark on the camshaft sprocket. Mark and remove the distributor.

5. Remove the crankshaft pulley and bolt.

6. Remove the fan blades.

7. Remove the timing belt covers, upper front and lower front.

8. Remove the crankshaft sprocket bolt.

9. Loosen the tensioner mounting nut and bolt. Move the tensioner away from the belt and retighten the nut to keep the tensioner in the off position. Remove the belt.

10. Remove the camshaft sprocket, crankshaft sprocket, flange, and tensioner.

11. Silent shaft engines:

a. Loosen the counterbalance shaft sprocket mounting bolt.

b. Remove the belt tensioner and remove the timing belt.

c. Remove the crankshaft sprocket (inner) and counterbalance shaft sprocket.

d. Remove the upper and lower under timing belt covers.

12. The water pump or cylinder head may be removed at this point, depending upon the type of repairs needed.

13. Raise the front of the car and support it safely. Remove any interfering splash pans.

14. Drain the oil pan and remove the pan from the block.

15. Remove the oil pump sprocket and cover.

NOTE: On the silent shaft engines, remove the plug at the bottom of the left side of the cylinder block and insert a screwdriver to keep the left counterbalance shaft in position while removing the sprocket nut.

16. Remove the front cover and oil pump as a unit, with the left counter shaft attached, if equipped.

17. Remove the oil pump gear and left counterbalance shaft.

NOTE: To aid in removal of the front cover, a driver groove is provided on the cover, above the oil pump housing. Avoid prying on the thinner parts of the housing flange or hammering on it to remove the case.

18. Remove the right counterbalance shaft from the engine block.

INSTALLATION–STANDARD ENGINE

1. Install a new front seal in the cover. Install a new gasket on the front of the cylinder block, and using a seal protector on the front of the crankshaft, install the front cover on the engine block.

2. Tighten the front case mounting bolts to 11 to 13 ft/lbs.

3. Install the oil screen, and using a new gasket, install the oil pan. Tighten bolts to 4.5 to 5.5 ft/lbs.

4. If the cylinder head and/or water pump had been removed, reinstall them, using new gaskets.

5. Install the upper and lower under covers.

6. Install the spacer, flange and crankshaft sprocket and tighten the bolt to 43.5 to 50 ft/lbs.

7. Align the timing mark on the crankshaft sprocket with the timing mark on the front case.

8. Align the camshaft sprocket timing mark with the upper under cover timing mark.

9. Install the tensioner spring and tensioner. Temporarily tighten the nut. Install the front end of the tensioner spring (bent at right angles) on the projection of the tensioner and the other end (straight) on the water pump body.

10. Loosen the nut and move the tensioner in the direction of the water pump. Lock it by tightening the nut.

11. Ensure that the sprocket timing marks are aligned, and install the timing belt. The belt should be installed on the crankshaft sprocket, the oil pump sprocket, and then the camshaft sprocket, in that order, while keeping the belt tight.

12. Loosen the tensioner mounting bolt and nut and allow the spring tension to move the tensioner against the belt.

NOTE: Make sure the belt comes in complete mesh with the sprocket by lightly pushing the tensioner up by hand toward the mounting nut.

13. Tighten the tensioner mounting nut and bolt.

NOTE: Be sure to tighten the nut before tightening the bolt. Too much tension could result from tightening the bolt first.

14. Recheck all sprocket alignments.

15. Turn the crankshaft through a complete rotation in the normal direction.

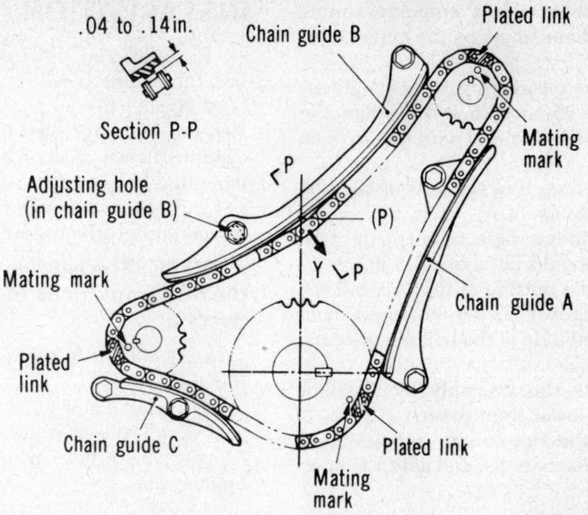

Silent shaft balancing system

CAUTION

Do not turn in a reverse direction or shake or push the belt.

16. Loosen the tensioner bolt and nut. Retighten the nut and then the bolt.

17. Install the lower and upper front outer covers.

18. Install the crankshaft pulley and tighten the bolts to 7.5 to 8.5 ft/lbs.

19. Install the alternator and belt and adjust. Install the distributor.

20. Install the radiator, fill the cooling system, and inspect for leaks.

INSTALLATION–W/SILENT SHAFT

CAUTION

To be assured that the phasing of the oil pump sprocket and the left counterbalance shaft is correct, a screwdriver or a metal rod should be inserted in the plugged hole on the left side of the cylinder block. If it can be inserted more than 2⅜ inches, the phasing is correct. If the tool can only be inserted approximately one inch, turn the oil pump sprocket through one turn and realign the timing marks. Keep the screwdriver or metal rod inserted until the installation of the timing belt is completed. Remove the tool from the hole and install the plug, before starting the engine.

1. Install a new front seal in the cover. Install the oil pump drive and driven gears in the front case, aligning the timing marks on the pump gears.

2. Install the left counterbalance shaft in the driven gear and temporarily tighten the bolt.

3. Install the right counterbalance shaft into the cylinder block.

4. Install an oil seal guide on the end of the crankshaft, and install a new gasket on the front of the engine block for the front cover.

5. Install a new front case packing, if equipped.

6. Insert the left counterbalance shaft into the engine block and at the same time, guide the front cover into place on the front of the engine block.

7. Insert a screwdriver at the bottom of the left side of the block and hold the left counterbalance shaft and tighten the bolt. Install the hole plug.

8. Install an O-ring on the oil pump cover and intall it on the front cover.

9. Tighten the oil pump cover bolts and the front cover bolts to 11 to 13 ft/lbs.

10. Install the oil screen, and using a new gasket, install the oil pan.

11. Install the water pump and/or the cylinder head, if removed previously.

12. Install the upper and lower under covers.

13. Install the spacer on the end of the right counterbalance shaft, with the chamfered edge toward the rear of the engine.

14. Install the counterbalance shaft sprocket and temporarily tighten the bolt.

15. Install the inner crankshaft sprocket and align the timing marks on the sprockets with those on the front case.

16. Install the inner tensioner (B) with the center of the pulley on the left side of the mounting bolt and with the pulley flange toward the front of the engine.

17. Lift the tensioner by hand, clockwise, to apply tension to the belt. Tighten the bolt to secure the tensioner.

18. Check that all alignment marks are in their proper places and the belt deflection is approximately ¼ to ½ inch on the tension side.

NOTE: When the tensioner bolt is tightened, make sure the shaft of the tensioner does not turn with the bolt. If the belt is too tight there will be noise, and if the belt is too loose, the belt and sprocket may come out of mesh.

19. Tighten the counterbalance shaft sprocket bolt to 22 to 28.5 ft/lbs.

20. Install the flange and crankshaft sprocket. Tighten the bolt to 43.5 to 50.5 ft/lbs.

21. Install the camshaft spacer and sprocket. Tighten the bolt to 44 to 57 ft/lbs.

22. Align the camshaft sprocket timing mark with the timing mark on the upper inner cover.
23. Install the oil pump sprocket, tightening the nut to 25 to 28.5 ft/lbs. Align the timing mark on the sprocket with the mark on the case.
24. Refer to Step 9 of the belt installation for the standard engine.
25. If the timing belt is correctly tensioned, there should be about 0.5 in. clearance between the outside of the belt and the edge of the belt cover. This is measured about halfway down the side of the belt opposite the tensioner.
26. Complete the assembly by installing the upper and lower front covers.
27. Install the crankshaft pulley, alternator, and accessory belts, and adjust to specifications.
28. Install the radiator, fill the cooling system, and start the engine.

REMOVAL–CHAIN EQUIPPED

2000 cc Engine–W/Silent Shaft (1976-81)

2600 cc Engine–W/Silent Shaft (1978-81)

1. Drain the coolant and remove the radiator. Disconnect the battery ground cable.
2. Remove the alternator and accessory belts.
3. Rotate the crankshaft to bring No. 1 piston to TDC, on the compression stroke.
4. Mark and remove the distributor.
5. Remove the crankshaft pulley.
6. Remove the water pump assembly.
7. Remove the cylinder head, if necessary.
8. Raise the front of the car and support it safely.
9. Drain the engine oil and remove the oil pan and screen.
10. Remove the timing case cover.
11. Remove the chain guides, Side (A), Top (B), Bottom (C), from the "B" chain (outer).
12. Remove the locking bolts from the "B" chain sprockets.
13. Remove the crankshaft sprocket, counterbalance shaft sprocket and the outer chain.
14. Remove the crankshaft and camshaft sprockets and the "A" (inner) chain.
15. Remove the camshaft sprocket holder and the chain guides, both left and right. Remove the tensioner spring and sleeve from the oil pump.
16. Remove the oil pump by first removing the bolt locking the oil pump driven gear and the right counterbalance shaft, and then remove the oil pump mounting bolts. Remove the counterbalance shaft from the engine block.

NOTE: If the bolt locking the oil pump driven gear and the counterbalance shaft is hard to loosen, remove the oil pump and the shaft as a unit.

17. Remove the left counterbalance shaft thrust washer and take the shaft from the engine block.

INSTALLATION

1. Install the right counterbalance shaft into the engine block.
2. Install the oil pump assembly. Do not lose the Woodruff key from the end of the counterbalance shaft. Torque the oil pump mounting bolts to 6 to 7 ft/lbs.
3. Tighten the counterbalance shaft and the oil pump driven gear mounting bolt.

NOTE: The counterbalance shaft and the oil pump can be installed as a unit, if necessary.

4. Install the left counterbalance shaft into the engine block.
5. Install a new O-ring on the thrust plate and install the unit into the engine block, using a pair of bolts without heads, as alignment guides.

CAUTION

If the thrust plate is turned to align the bolt holes, the O-ring may be damaged.

6. Remove the guide bolts and install the regular bolts into the thrust plate and tighten securely.
7. Rotate the crankshaft to bring No. 1 Piston to TDC.
8. Install the cylinder head, if removed.
9. Install the sprocket holder and the right and left chain guides.
10. Install the tensioner spring and sleeve on the oil pump body.
11. Install the camshaft and crankshaft sprockets on the timing chain, aligning the sprocket punch marks to the plated chain links.
12. While holding the sprocket and chain as a unit, install the crankshaft sprocket over the crankshaft and align it with the keyway.
13. Keeping the dowel pin hole on the camshaft in a vertical position, install the camshaft sprocket and chain on the camshaft.

NOTE: The sprocket timing mark and the plated chain link should be at the 2 to 3 o'clock position when correctly installed.

CAUTION

The chain must be aligned in the right and left chain guides with the tensioner pushing against the chain. The tension for the inner chain is predetermined by spring tension.

14. Install the crankshaft sprocket for the outer or "B" chain.
15. Install the two counterbalance shaft sprockets and align the punched mating marks with the plated links of the chain.
16. Holding the two shaft sprockets and chain, install the outer chain in alignment with the mark on the crankshaft sprocket. Install the shaft sprockets on the counterbalance shaft and the oil pump driver gear. Install the lock bolts and recheck the alignment of the punch marks and the plated links.
17. Temporarily install the chain guides, *Side* (A), *Top* (B), and *Bottom*(C).
18. Tighten *Side* (A) chain guide securely.
19. Tighten *Bottom* (B) chain guide securely.
20. Adjust the position of the *Top* (B) chain guide, after shaking the right and left sprockets to collect any chain slack, so that when the chain is moved toward the center, the clearance between the chain guide and the chain links will be approximately $9/64$ inch. Tighten the *Top* (B) chain guide bolts.
21. Install the timing chain cover using a new gasket, being careful not to damage the front seal.
22. Install the oil screen and the oil pan, using a new gasket. Torque the bolts to 4.5 to 5.5 ft/lbs.
23. Install the crankshaft pulley, alternator and accessory belts, and the distributor.
24. Install the oil pressure switch, if removed, and install the battery ground cable.
25. Install the fan blades, radiator, fill the system with coolant and start the engine.

Piston Identification

On 1975 models the pistons are designated by a letter into three weight groups, A, B and C. Always replace a piston with another from the same weight group. On 1976-81 models the pistons are stamped with a size mark.

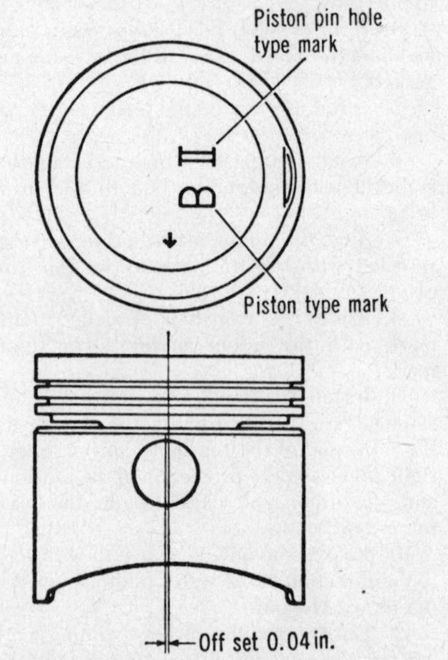

Piston weight designation through 1975

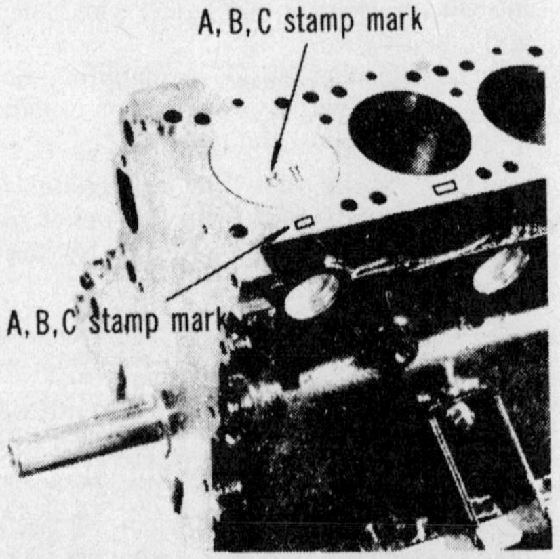

Cylinder block and piston designation through 1975

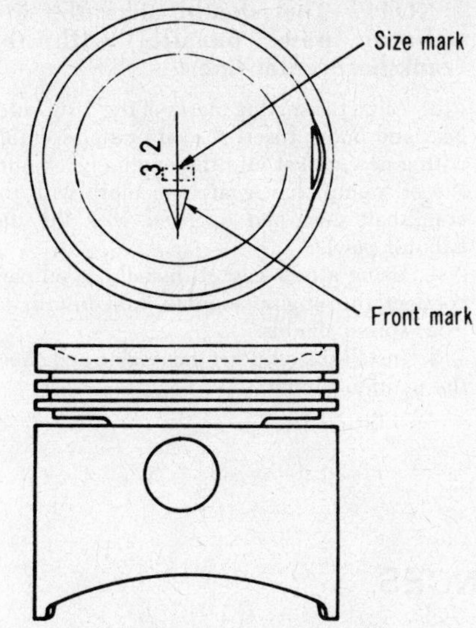

1976 and later piston identification

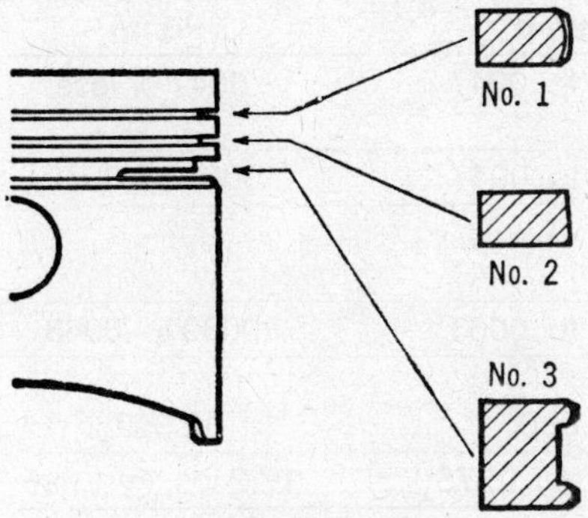

Piston ring installation

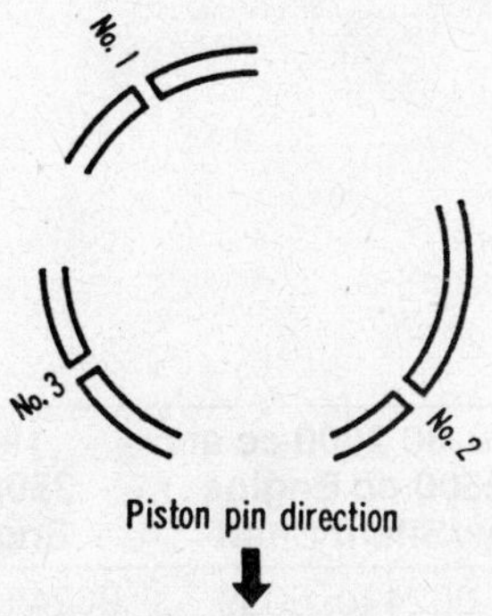

Ring end gap positioning

When replacing the piston and connecting rod assembly always direct the front mark on the piston head toward the front of the engine.

PISTON SIZE MARKINGS

Size	Size Mark
S.T.D.	None
.010 in. O.S.	25
.020 in. O.S.	50
.030 in. O.S.	75
.039 in. O.S.	100

ENGINE LUBRICATION

Oil Pan

REMOVAL AND INSTALLATION

The engine must be raised off its mounts for the pan to clear the suspension crossmember. However, on front wheel drive models there is usually enough room without raising the engine.

1. Remove the underbody splash shield.
2. Unbolt the left and right engine mounts (except front wheel drive).
3. Jack up the engine under the bell housing (except front wheel drive).
4. Remove the oil pan.
5. Installation is the reverse of removal.

Rear Main Oil Seal

REPLACEMENT

The rear main oil seal is located in a housing on the rear of the block. To replace the seal, remove the transmission and do the work from underneath the car (except front wheel drive models) or remove the engine and do the work on the bench.

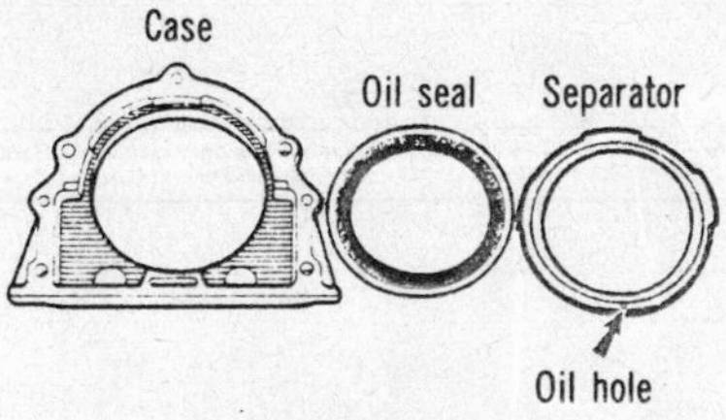

Rear main oil seal

1. Remove the housing from the block.
2. Remove the separator from the housing.
3. Pry out the oil seal.
4. Lightly oil the replacement seal. The oil seal should be installed so that the seal plate fits into the inner contact surface of the seal case. Install the separator wih the oil holes facing down.

Oil Pump

1400 cc ENGINE

1979-81 (Timing Belt)

A gear driven oil pump is mounted in the front case and driven directly by the crankshaft.

1600 cc ENGINE

1975-77 Standard–(Timing Chain)

A rotor type oil pump is located in the timing chain case and driven by a crankshaft gear.

1975-81 Standard–(Timing Belt)

A rotor type oil pump is located on the lower left side of the front case, driven by the timing belt.

2000 cc ENGINE

1975 Standard Engine

A rotor type oil pump is under the timing case, inside the oil pan.

1976-80 W/Silent Shaft

A gear type oil pump is on the front of the right counterbalance shaft, driven by the timing chain.

2600 cc ENGINE

1978-81 W/Silent Shaft

A gear type oil pump is on the front of the right counterbalance shaft, driven by the timing chain.

OIL PUMP REMOVAL AND INSTALLATION

1400 cc Engine

1978-81 (TIMING BELT)

1. Remove the timing belt. See timing belt removal section.
2. Remove the engine oil pan and oil screen.
3. Remove the front case assembly (seven bolts).

The oil pump is mounted in the rear of the front case. Turn the front case over and remove the oil pump cover. Service as required.

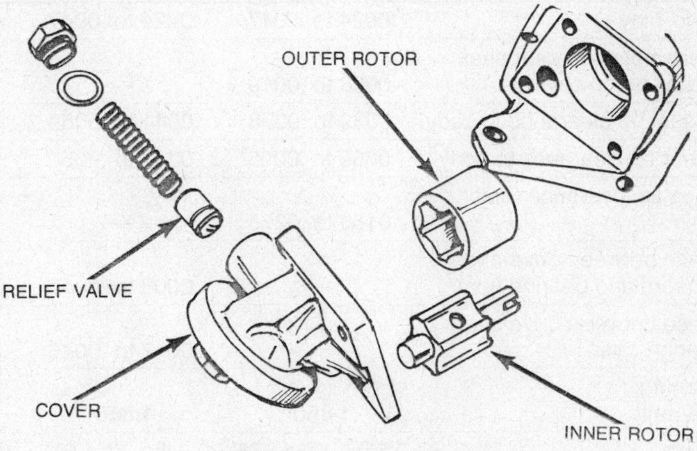

Exploded view of oil pump

All Other Engines

To remove the rotor type pumps that are located behind the front timing cover, refer to the Timing Gear Cover, Chain, Counterbalance Shaft and Tensioner Section and follow the procedure to remove the pump.

To remove the oil pumps that are located in the oil pan, the following procedures should be followed.

REMOVAL

1. Place No. 1 piston at TDC on the compression stroke.
2. Loosen the left and right engine mounts and raise the engine off the mount brackets.
3. Remove the front splash shields. Drain the oil and remove the oil pan.
4. Remove the screen and the oil pump from the engine block.

INSTALLATION

1. Be sure that No. 1 piston is still on the compression stroke.
2. Remove the distributor cap and make sure the rotor is pointing to the No. 1 position.

NOTE: This should align the distributor pawl parallel with the crankshaft center line.

3. Align the mating marks of the distributor gear and body. Insert the oil pump assembly with a new gasket into the engine block until the oil pump shaft gear is in mesh with the crankshaft gear and engaged with the distributor pawl.
4. Using a new gasket, install the oil pan, connect the engine mounts, and install the front splash shields.
5. Install the oil, start the engine and check the ignition timing.

TROCHOID TYPE OIL PUMP CLEARANCES

All measurements in inches

Measurement Point	1979-81 1400 cc Engine	1975-77 1600 cc Engine Standard—Pump in Timing Cover	1978-81 1600 cc Engine Standard—Separate Pump	1975 2000 cc Engine Standard—Separate Pump
Inner rotor to outer rotor clearance	—	.0047 or less	.0016 to .0047	.0047 or less
Rotor to cover end-play	.0016 to .0039	.0008 to .0039	.0024 to .0047	.0008 to .0079
Outer rotor to chain case clearance	.0039 to .0079	.0039 to .0063	—	—
Drive shaft to cover clearance	—	—	.0039 to .0063	.0039 to .0063
Relief spring				
Free length	1.850	2.352	1.850	2.352
Tension	9.5 lbs @ 1.575	17.2 lbs. @ 1.696	9.5 lbs. @ 1.575	17.2 lbs. @ 1.696

GEAR TYPE OIL PUMP CLEARANCES

All measurements in inches

Measurement Point	1977-81 1600 cc Engine w/Silent Shaft	1976 2000 cc Engine w/Silent Shaft	1977 2000 cc Engine w/Silent Shaft	1978-80 2000 cc and 2600 cc Engine w/Silent Shaft	1981 2600 cc Engine
Gear end-play	.0024 to .0047	.0024 to .0047	.0024 to .0047	.0024 to .0059	.0024 to .0047
Clearance between gear shaft end and oil pump cover	.0008 to .0019	—	—	—	—
Driven gear tip clearance to body	.0039 to .0078	.0041 to .0059	.0041 to .0059	.0041 to .0059	.0043 to .0059
Drive gear tip clearance to body	.0059 to .0098	.0041 to .0059	.0041 to .0059	.0041 to .0059	.0043 to .0059
Maximum tip clearance (both gears)	.0158 to .0275	—	—	—	—
Clearance between drive and driven gears and bearing front	—	.0008 to .0047	.0008 to .0018	.0008 to .0018	.0008 to .0020
Clearance between drive gear and bearing gear	—	.0017 to .0026	.0017 to .0026	.0017 to .0026	.0016 to .0028
Relief spring					
Free length	1.850	1.850	1.850	1.850	1.850
Tension	9.5 lbs. @ 1.575	9.5 lbs. @ 1.575	9.5 lbs. @ 1.575	9.5 lbs. @ 1.575	9.5 lbs @ 1.575

COOLING SYSTEM

Radiator

REMOVAL AND INSTALLATION

1. Remove the splash panel from the bottom of the car. Drain the radiator by opening the petcock. Remove the shroud on models so equipped.
2. Disconnect the radiator hoses at the engine. On automatic transmission cars, disconnect and plug the transmission lines to the bottom of the radiator.
3. Remove the two retaining bolts from either side of the radiator. Lift out the radiator. On front wheel drive models, disconnect the electric fan wiring harness. Do not remove the fan motor, blades or bracket—remove as a unit with the radiator.
4. Install the radiator in the reverse order of removal. Tighten the retaining bolts gradually in a criss-cross pattern.

Water Pump

REMOVAL

1. Drain the cooling system.
2. Remove the fan shroud and radiator if necessary for working room.
3. Remove the alternator and accessory belts.
4. Remove the fan blades and/or automatic hub, if equipped.
5. Remove the water pump assembly from the timing chain case or the cylinder block.

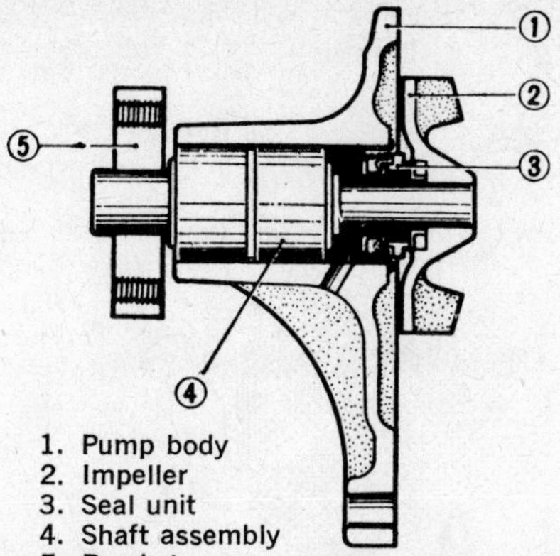

1. Pump body
2. Impeller
3. Seal unit
4. Shaft assembly
5. Bracket

Cross-section of the water pump

INSTALLATION

1. Install the water pump to the timing chain case or the engine block and tighten the bolts securely.
2. Install the fan blades and/or the automatic clutch fan hub.
3. Install the alternator and accessory belts and adjust as necessary.
4. Install the fan shroud and the radiator, if removed.
5. Fill the cooling system, start the engine, and check for coolant leakage.

Thermostat

REMOVAL AND INSTALLATION

The thermostat is located in the intake manifold under the upper radiator hose.

1. Drain the coolant below the level of the thermostat.
2. Remove the two retaining bolts and lift the thermostat housing off the intake manifold with the hose still attached.

NOTE: If you are careful, it is not necessary to remove the upper radiator hose.

3. Lift the thermostat out of the manifold.
4. Install the thermostat in the reverse order of removal. Use a new gasket and coat the mating surfaces with sealer.

EMISSION CONTROLS

Crankcase Emission Control System

A closed-type crankcase ventilation system is used to prevent engine blow-by gases from escaping into the atmosphere.

A hose connects the rear of the rocker arm cover and the intake manifold. A small fixed orifice is located in the intake manifold or on the rocker arm cover. Some later models have replaced the orifice with a PCV valve.

A larger hose is connected from the front of the rocker arm cover to the air cleaner assembly. Under light to medium carburetor throttle opening, the blow-by gases are drawn through the fixed orifice or PCV valve. Under heavy acceleration, both the fixed orifice or PCV valve and the large hose route the gases into the engine.

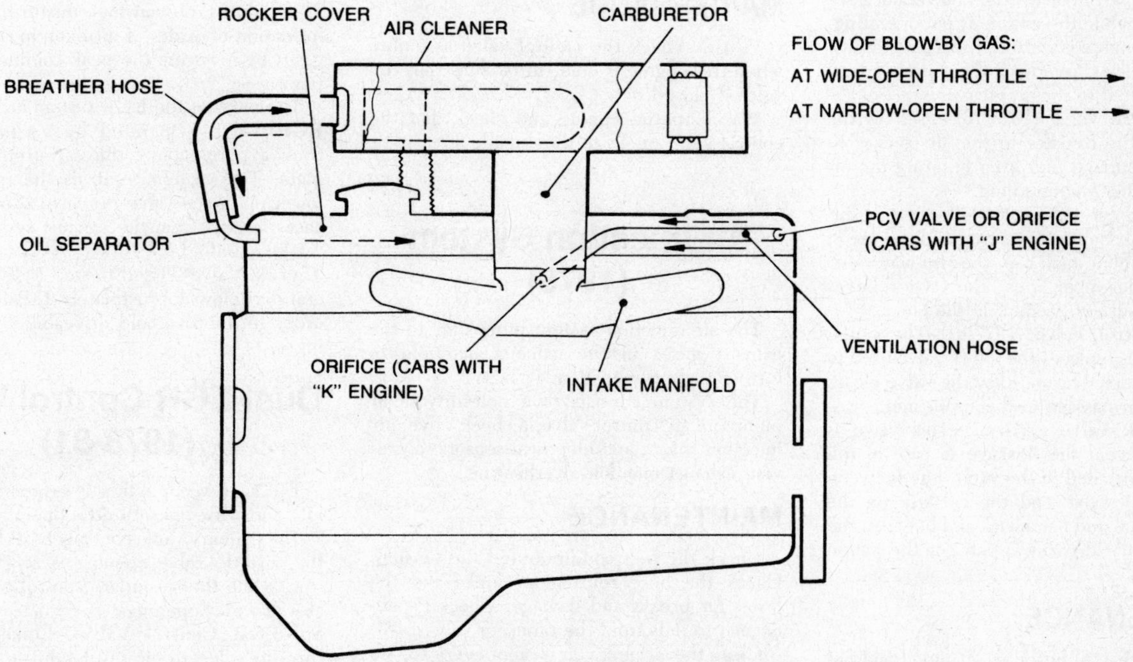

Late model crankcase ventilation system (typical)

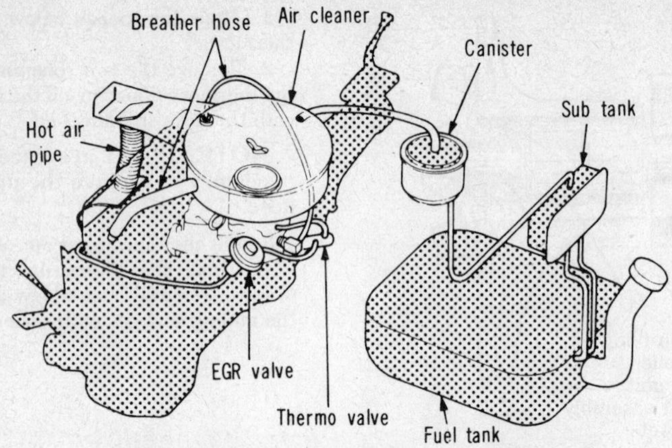

1975 and later—typical emission controls

Maintenance required is to regularly check the breather hose condition, clean the orifice or PCV valve (replace if clogged) and clean the steel wool filter, in the air cleaner.

Fuel Evaporation Control System (1975-81)

This system is designed to prevent hydrocarbons from escaping into the atmosphere from the fuel tank, due to normal evaporation.

The parts of the system are as follow:

Separator Tank–Located near the gasoline tank, used to accommodate expansion, and to allow maximum condensation of the fuel vapors.

Bowl Vent System (1980-81)–Controls carburetor bowl vapors between canister and carburetor.

Carbon Element (1980-81)–Element is located in air cleaner to store vapors generated in the carburetor. Replace if clogged or dirty.

Canister–Either one or two, located in the engine compartment to trap and retain gasoline vapors while the engine is not operating. When the engine is started, fresh air is drawn into the canister, removing the stored vapors, and is directed to the air cleaner.

Vapor Check Valve (1975-76)–Used in the hose from the canister to the air cleaner to prevent vaporized fuel from entering the air cleaner during engine idling.

Two-Way Valve (1977-1981)–Because of different methods of tank venting and the use of a sealed gasoline tank cap, the two-way valve is used in the vapor lines. The valve relieves either pressure or vacuum in the tank.

Purge Control Valve (1977-81)–The purge control valve replaces the check valve used in previous years. During idle, the valve closes off the vapor passage to the air cleaner.

Fuel Check Valve (1976-81)–This valve is used to prevent fuel leakage in case of roll over. It is installed in the vapor line between the two-way valve and the canister on the coupe, sedan, and hatchback and between the separator and the two-way valve on the station wagon.

MAINTENANCE

Be sure that all hoses are clamped and not dry-rotted or broken. Check the valves for cracks, signs of gasoline leakage, and proper operating condition.

The canister air filter (if equipped) should be inspected and changed at least every 24,000 miles.

Heated Air Intake System

All models are equipped with a temperature regulated air control valve in the air cleaner snorkel.

When the underhood air temperature is 41 degrees or lower, the air control valve allows preheated air to flow through the heat cowl of the exhaust manifold, via a flexible hose, to the air cleaner and into the carburetor.

When the underhood temperature is 108 degrees or above, the air flow is directed through the air cleaner snorkel.

At intermediate temperatures, the carburetor intake air is a blend of the direct underhood and preheated air.

MAINTENANCE

Visually check the control valve assembly when the engine is cold, to be sure that the valve is closed.

Warm up the engine and check that the control valve opens to the outside air.

Air Injection System (1975)

The air injection system pumps air to the exhaust gases in the exhaust manifold to further their combustion.

The system consists of a belt driven air pump, an air control valve, a check valve, air injection tubes, and electrical sensors to prevent exhaust manifold overheating.

MAINTENANCE

Check the belt condition and the tension. Check the hose routing for kinks and the hoses for breaks and damage. Check for abnormal sounds from the pump or valves.

Clean the air pump air cleaner every 12,000 miles and replace it every 24,000 miles.

Secondary Air Supply System (1976-81)

This system supplies air for the further combustion of unburned gases in the thermal reactor (if equipped) or exhaust manifold and consists of a reed valve, air hoses, and air passages built into the cylinder head.

The reed valve is operated by exhaust pulsations in the exhaust manifold. It draws fresh air through the air cleaner and supplies it to the exhaust ports.

MAINTENANCE

Check for damage to the air hoses and air pipes. Make sure the air passages are open in the head.

PULSE AIR FEEDER SYSTEM (1981)

This system supplies "secondary air" into the exhaust system between the front and rear catalytic converters to promote oxidation of exhaust emissions in the rear converter. The system consists of a main reed valve, a sub-reed valve, air hoses and crankcase passages.

The main reed valve is actuated by pressures created by No. 3 piston. The sub-reed valve is actuated by exhaust pulsations. Fresh air is drawn through the air cleaner.

INSPECTION

Remove the hose connecting the "reed valve" at the air cleaner. Start the engine and check for vacuum in the hose. Check the hose for leaks if no vacuum is felt.

Exhaust Gas Recirculation System

The EGR system recirculates part of the exhaust gases into the combustion chambers. This dilutes the air/fuel mixture, reducing formation of oxides of nitrogen in the exhaust gases by lowering the peak combustion temperatures.

The parts of the EGR system are:

EGR Valve—Operated by vacuum drawn from a point above the carburetor throttle plate. The vacuum controls the raising and lowering of the valve pintle to allow exhaust gases to pass from the exhaust system to the intake manifold.

Thermo Valve—Used to stop EGR valve operation below approximately 131 degrees, in order to improve cold driveability and starting.

Dual EGR Control Valve (1978-81)

The EGR vacuum flow is suspended during idle and wide open throttle operation.

The primary valve controls EGR flow when the throttle valve opening is relatively narrow, while the secondary control valve operates at wider openings.

Sub-EGR Control Valve—Linked to the throttle valve to closely modulate the EGR gas flow.

EGR Maintenance Warning Light (1977-81)

A light in the speedometer assembly to alert the driver to the need for EGR system maintenance.

This device has a mileage sensor to light the visual signal at 15,000 mile intervals.

Upon completion of the required EGR system maintenance, the warning light can be turned off by resetting the switch. It is in the speedometer cable, under the instrument panel.

MAINTENANCE

1. Check all vacuum hoses for cracks, breakage and correct installation.
2. Check EGR valve operation by applying vacuum to the EGR valve vacuum nipple with the engine idling. The idle should become rough.
3. Check the passages in the cylinder head and intake manifold for clogging. Clean as necessary.
4. Cold start the engine. The EGR port nipple should be open. When the coolant is warmed to over 131 degrees, the port should be closed.

Thermal Reactor (1975-77 California and High Altitude)

This unit is used to further the combustion of the exhaust gases. It consists of a shell and a core with heat insulation material between, mounted at the exhaust manifold.

MAINTENANCE

1. Listen for any abnormal sound from the reactor.
2. Check for cracks and damage.
3. Check the thermal reactor flange on the cylinder head for warpage.

NOTE: The thermal reactor must be replaced when defective. It cannot be disassembled.

Catalytic Converter (1978-81)

This unit or units (two used in 1981) replaces the thermal reactor. It is filled with catalyst to oxidize hydrocarbons and carbon monoxide in the exhaust gases.

MAINTENANCE

1. Check the core for cracks and damages.
2. If the idle carbon monoxide and hydrocarbon content exceeds specifications and the ignition timing and idle mixture are correct, the converter must be replaced.

Jet Air System (1978-81)

A jet air passage is provided in the carburetor, intake manifold, and cylinder head to direct air to a jet valve, operated simultaneously with the intake valve.

On the intake stroke, jet air is forced into the combustion chamber because of the pressure difference between the ends of the air jet passage.

This jet of air produces a strong swirl in the combustion chamber scavenging the residual gases around the spark plug.

The jet air volume lessens with increased throttle opening. It is at a maximum at idle.

MAINTENANCE

NOTE: Refer to Valve Lash Adjustment for adjusting jet valve clearance.

No maintenance is required, other than clearance adjustment during valve adjustment. The valve can be removed from the cylinder head for service or replacement.

Ignition Timing Control System (1975-81)

When the engine is idling or operating at low speeds under light load or deceleration, the exhaust gas temperature is low, resulting in incomplete combustion of the air/fuel mixture. To prevent this, ignition timing is retarded under these conditions to maintain high exhaust gas temperature.

The units in the Ignition Timing Control system are as follow:

Dual-diaphragm distributor–This distributor has both retard and advance mechanisms operated by vacuum.

Thermo valve–This valve is used to protect the engine from overheating. When coolant temperature reaches 203 degrees, the advance unit is allowed to operate, causing an increase in engine speed and a decrease in coolant temperature.

Single diaphragm distributor–This distributor has a single diaphragm vacuum advance unit, which advances the ignition timing as engine vacuum dictates. The single diaphragm distributor must not be interchanged with the dual diaphragm distributor. The distributor operating curves are different and would cause increased emissions. A thermo valve is *not* used with this type of distributor.

MAINTENANCE

Distributor maintenance is at tune-up intervals.

Orifice Spark Advance Control (1977)

The OSAC valve is located in the vacuum line between the distributor and the carburetor. Its function is to delay vacuum advance during medium to high speed operation, when high vacuum would be present. It is used only with the single diaphragm distributor.

MAINTENANCE

No maintenance is required.

Deceleration Device (1975, 1977-81)

Closing of the throttle valve on deceleration is delayed in order to burn the air/fuel mixture more thoroughly. A vacuum controlled dashpot, attached to the carburetor linkage is used.

A servo valve detects intake manifold vacuum and closes if vacuum exceeds a preset value. Since the air in the dashpot diaphragm chamber can not escape, the throttle linkage opening is temporarily retained. If the vacuum is below the preset value, the servo valve opens and the dashpot works normally.

MAINTENANCE

Inspect the hoses for breaks and damage, and the valve body for cracks.

ADJUSTMENT

1. Have the engine running, brakes locked, and a tachometer attached.
2. Push the dashpot rod, connected to the carburetor arm, upward and into the dashpot until it stops.
3. Note the rpm at the dashpot stop and adjust to the following specifications. Note the time required between suddenly releasing the dashpot rod and the return to normal curb idle.
4. The specifications are as follow: 1980
   a. 1600 cc engine–Calif. and H/Alt.
   Set Speed–1900 ± 100 rpm
   Required Time–3 to 6 Sec.
   b. 2000 cc engine–Calif.
   Set Speed–1500 ± 100 rpm
   Required time–3 to 6 Sec.
   c. 1400 cc & 1600 cc engines–49 States, 2000 cc engine–49 States
   Set Speed–2000 ± 100 rpm
   Required Time–3 to 6 Sec.
   d. All engines: 1981
   Set Speed–2000 ± 100 rpm

Mixture Control Valve (1977-81)

This control valve is used to supply additional air into the intake manifold to decrease manifold vacuum during deceleration, and is activated by the intake manifold vacuum level.

Manual Altitude Compensation System (1977-81)

An off-on valve is used to increase the air supply to the carburetor to lean the mixture and decrease the EGR flow for high altitude operation.

MAINTENANCE

The required maintenance is to inspect any vacuum hoses and routing for kinks, breakage and cracks. The off-on valve should be on for high altitude and off for driving under 4000 ft.

FUEL SYSTEM

Fuel Filter

REPLACEMENT

All models use an in-line filter which should be replaced every 12,000 miles.

Mechanical Fuel Pump

REMOVAL AND INSTALLATION

1. Remove the fuel lines.
2. Unbolt the pump mounting bolts, and remove the pump, insulator, and gasket.
3. Coat both sides of a new insulator and gasket with sealer, and install the pump in the reverse order of removal.

TESTING

Disconnect the fuel line from the carburetor and attach a pressure tester to the end of the line. Crank the engine. The tester should show 3.7-5.1 psi.

Electric Fuel Pump

1975 models are equipped with an electric fuel pump mounted in the trunk on sedans and hardtops and in the left rear wheel housing on station wagons.

REMOVAL AND INSTALLATION

1. Disconnect the battery ground cable.
2. Disconnect the fuel lines.
3. Disconnect all electrical connections.
4. Remove the pump.
5. Installation is the reverse of removal.

TROUBLESHOOTING

If the fuel pump doesn't work:
1. Check the fuse.
2. Check all wiring connections.
3. Check the control relay which is located in the engine compartment, next to the ignition coil. If the engine starts when the ignition switch is turned to "START" but stops when it is turned to "ON", the relay is defective.

Carburetors

REMOVAL AND INSTALLATION

1. Remove the solenoid valve wiring.
2. Disconnect the air cleaner breather hose, air duct and vacuum tube.
3. Remove the air cleaner.
4. Remove the air cleaner case.
5. Disconnect the accelerator and shift cables (automatic transmission) at the carburetor.
6. Disconnect the purge valve hose; remove the vacuum compensator, and fuel lines.
7. Drain the coolant.
8. Remove the water hose between the carburetor and the cylinder head.
9. Remove the carburetor.
10. Installation is the reverse of removal.

OVERHAUL

Efficient carburetion depends greatly on careful cleaning and inspection during overhaul, since dirt, gum, water, or varnish in or on the carburetor parts are often responsible for poor performance.

Overhaul your carburetor in a clean, dust-free area. Carefully disassemble the car-

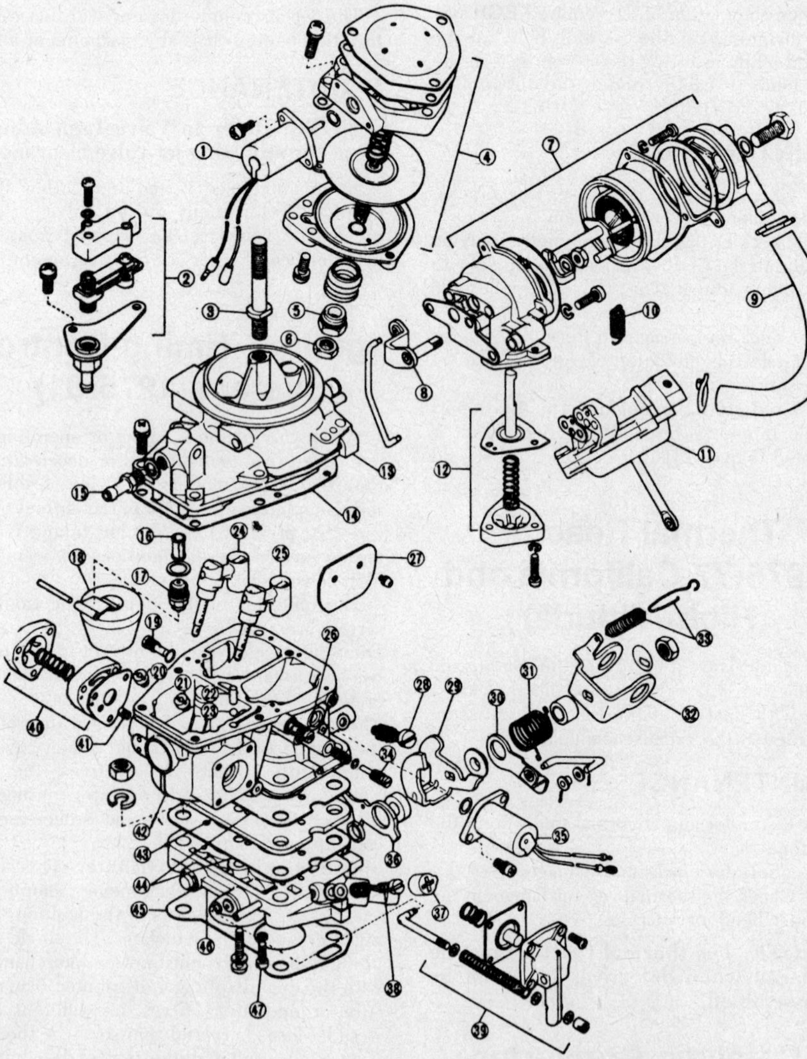

1. Throttle positioner solenoid
2. Compensator
3. Stud
4. Throttle positioner
5. Adjusting nut
6. Locknut
7. Auto-choke
8. Choke shaft
9. Water hose
10. Return spring
11. Depression chamber
12. Piston chamber
13. Float chamber cover
14. Float chamber packing
15. Fuel joint
16. Filter
17. Needle valve
18. Float
19. Secondary pilot jet
20. Secondary main jet
21. Primary main jet
22. Pump weight
23. Steel ball
24. Inner secondary venturi
25. Inner primary venturi
26. Primary pilot jet
27. Choke valve
28. Throttle stop screw
29. Abatement plate
30. Lever
31. Lever spring
32. Throttle lever
33. Throttle return spring
34. By-pass screw
35. Fuel cut solenoid
36. Intermediate lever
37. Idle limiter
38. Pilot screw
39. Accelerator pump
40. Enrichment body assembly
41. Enrichment jet
42. Main body
43. Insulator
44. Throttle chamber packing
45. Carburetor gasket
46. Throttle body
47. Throttle stop screw

Exploded view of the carburetor

buretor, referring often to the exploded views. Keep all similar and lookalike parts segregated during disassembly and cleaning to avoid accidental interchange during assembly. Make a note of all jet sizes.

When the carburetor is disassembled, wash all parts (except diaphragms, electric choke units, pump plunger, and any other plastic, leather, fiber, or rubber parts) in clean carburetor solvent. Do not leave parts in the solvent any longer than is necessary to sufficiently loosen the deposits. Excessive cleaning may remove the special finish from the float bowl and choke valve bodies, leaving these parts unfit for service. Rinse all parts in clean solvent and blow them dry with compressed air or allow them to air dry. Wipe clean all cork, plastic, leather, and fiber parts with a clean, lint-free cloth.

Blow out all passages and jets with compressed air and be sure that there are no restrictions or blockages. Never use wire or similar tools to clean jets, fuel passages, or air bleeds. Clean all jets and valves separately to avoid accidental interchange.

Check all parts for wear or damage. If wear or damage is found, replace the defective parts. Especially check the following:

1. Check the float needle and seat for wear. If wear is found, replace the complete assembly.
2. Check the float hinge pin for wear and the float(s) for dents or distortion. Replace the float if fuel has leaked into it.
3. Check the throttle and choke shaft bores for wear or an out-of-round condition. Damage or wear to the throttle arm, shaft, or shaft bore will often require replacement of the throttle body. These parts require a close tolerance of fit; wear may allow air leakage, which could affect starting and idling.

NOTE: Throttle shafts and bushings are not included in overhaul kits. They can be purchased separately.

4. Inspect the idle mixture adjusting needles for burrs or grooves. Any such condition requires replacement of the needle, since you will not be able to obtain a satisfactory idle.
5. Test the accelerator pump check valves. They should pass air one way but not the other. Test for proper seating by blowing and sucking on the valve. Replace the valve if necessary. If the valve is satisfactory, wash the valve again to remove breath moisture.
6. Check the bowl cover for warped surfaces with a straightedge.
7. Closely inspect the valves and seats for wear and damage, replacing as necessary.
8. After the carburetor is assembled, check the choke valve for freedom of operation.

Carburetor overhaul kits are recommended for each overhaul. These kits contain all gaskets and new parts to replace those that deteriorate most rapidly. Failure to replace all parts supplied with the kit (especially gaskets) can result in poor performance later.

After cleaning and checking all components, reassemble the carburetor, using new parts and referring to the exploded view. When reassembling, make sure that all screws and jets are tight in their seats, but do not overtighten as the tips will be distorted. Tighten all screws gradually, in rotation. Do not tighten needle valves into their seats; uneven jetting will result. Always use new gaskets. Be sure to adjust the float level when reassembling.

THROTTLE LINKAGE ADJUSTMENT

1975-77

Throttle linkage is adjusted at the clamp which joins the accelerator pedal rod to the carburetor rod. With the carburetor throttle valves closed, (engine at normal operating temperature), the distance between the top of the clamp and the toe-board should be about 1.4 inches. The distance between the end of the connecting rod to the toe-board should be a minimum of 0.4 inch, and the clearance between the stopper bolt and the pedal lever should be 0 to 0.8 inch.

1978-81

Adjust the stopper bolt to a distance of .75 ± 0 to 0.4 inch from the inside of the bolt holding bracket, to the contact point of the pedal lever, while holding the carburetor throttle plates closed. The yoke at the carburetor end of the accelerator rod is serrated to allow the yoke to be loosened and moved so that a minimal readjustment of the stopper adjusting bolt is needed to give the proper throttle release and opening.

FLOAT AND FUEL LEVEL ADJUSTMENT

A sight glass is fitted at the float chamber and the fuel lever can be checked without disassembling the carburetor. Normal fuel level is within the level mark on the sight glass.

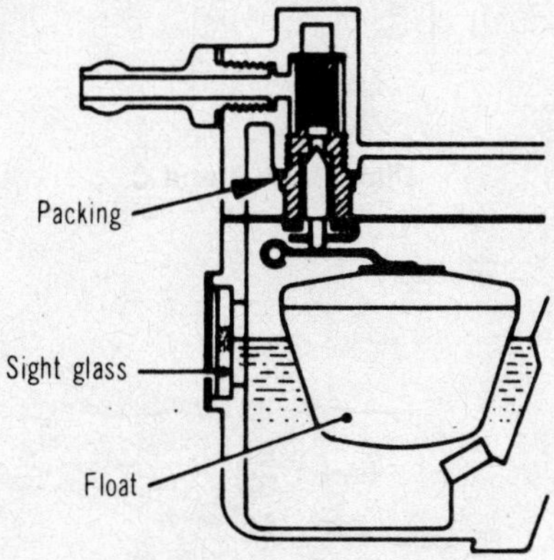

Float level adjustment

The fuel level adjustment is corrected by increasing or decreasing the number of needle valve packings. The float level may be off 0.160 inch, above or below the level mark and the operation of the engine would not be affected.

FAST IDLE ADJUSTMENT

1. Start the engine and open the throttle valve about 45 degrees. Manually close the choke valve and slowly return the throttle valve to the stop position.
2. With a tachometer, check that the fast idle speed is 2000 rpm or lower. (Not less than 1700 rpm). Adjust the speed as necessary with the fast idle speed screw.
3. Cold start the engine and check the automatic choke and fast idle operation.

AUTOMATIC CHOKE ADJUSTMENT

The choke case has five small projections. Align the center projection with the yellow punch mark of the bimetal case.

MANUAL TRANSMISSION

Four and Five Speed

REMOVAL AND INSTALLATION EXCEPT FRONT WHEEL DRIVE

1. Disconnect the battery ground cable, remove the air cleaner and the starter.
2. Remove the top transmission mounting bolts from the bell housing.
3. From inside the car, raise the console assembly, if equipped, or the carpet and remove the dust cover retaining plate at the shift lever.
4. Place the four speed transmission in second gear and the five speed transmission in first gear. Remove the control lever assembly.
5. Raise the car and support it safely. Drain the transmission. Disconnect the speedometer and the backup light switch.
6. Remove the driveshaft, exhaust pipe, and the clutch cable.
7. Support the transmission and remove the engine rear support bracket.
8. Remove the bell housing cover and bolts, move the transmission rearward, and lower it carefully to the floor. Remove the transmission from under the car.
9. To install the transmission, reverse the removal procedure. Make sure the transmission is in the proper gear before installing the gear shift lever.

FRONT WHEEL DRIVE MODELS

TRANSAXLE REMOVAL–MANUAL

1. Disconnect the battery ground (negative) cable.
2. Disconnect from the transaxle; the clutch cable, speedometer cable, backup light harness, starter motor and the four upper bolts connecting the engine to the transaxle.
3. Jack up the car and support on jack stands.
4. Remove the front wheels. Remove the engine splash shield.
5. Remove the shift rod and extension. It may be necessary to remove any heat shields that interfere with your progress.
6. Drain the transaxle fluid.
7. Remove the right and left driveshafts from the transaxle case.

a. Remove center cap (front wheel hub) and nut.

b. Remove ball joint and strut bar from lower control arm.

c. Insert pry bar between transaxle case and double off-set joint; move bar to the right to remove the left driveshaft, left to remove the right driveshaft.

CAUTION

Pry on the rib only of the transaxle. Do not insert the pry bar too deeply causing damage to the oil seal. Always replace the DOJ retainer ring each time the driveshaft is removed from the transaxle case.

d. Use an axle shaft puller to force the driveshaft out of the front hub. Be careful not to prevent the spacer from falling out of place.

8. Disconnect the range selector cable (if equipped). Remove the engine rear cover.

9. Support the weight of the engine from above (chain hoist). Support the transaxle and remove the remaining lower mounting bolts.

10. Remove the transaxle mount insulator bolt.

11. Remove (slide away from the engine) and lower the transaxle.

12. To install reverse the removal procedure. Be sure to connect all controls and wiring. Use new retaining rings when installing the driveshafts.

CLUTCH

Clutch Cable

REMOVAL AND INSTALLATION

1. Loosen the cable adjusting wheel inside the engine compartment.
2. Loosen the clutch pedal adjusting bolt locknut and loosen the adjusting bolt.
3. Remove the cable end from the clutch throwout lever.
4. Remove the cable end from the clutch pedal.
5. Installation is the reverse of removal.

NOTE: Lubricate the cable with engine oil and after installation, install pads isolating the cable from the intake manifold and from the rear side of the engine mount insulator on coupe, sedan, and hatchbacks only.

ADJUSTMENT

1. Adjust the clutch pedal height by the adjusting bolt to the distance shown in the following specifications. (Dimension A.)
2. Draw the outer cable from the cable holder on the toe-board and adjust its free-play by means of the adjusting nut. (Dimension D.)
3. Check clutch pedal free-play, (Dimension C), and the correct pedal stroke distance, (Dimension B), as outlined in the following specifications.

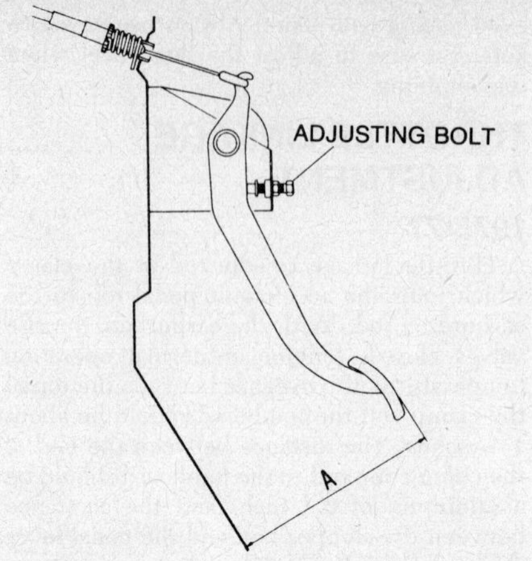

Measure dimension A between these points

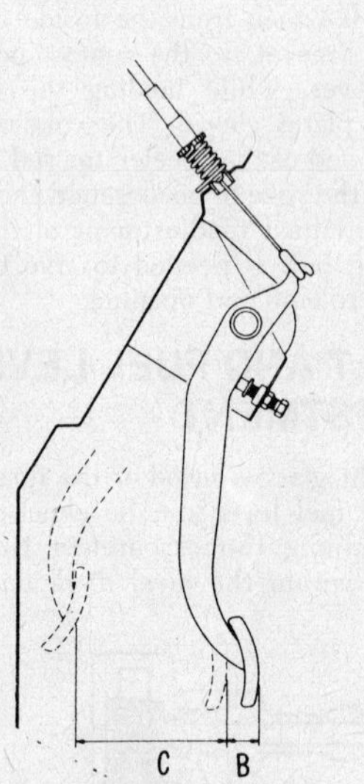

Dimension B and C

CLUTCH DISC REPLACEMENT

1. Remove the transmission as outlined in the Manual Transmission Removal and Installation section.

NOTE: It is recommended that a clutch aligning tool be inserted in the clutch hub to prevent dropping of the clutch disc during disassembly.

2. Remove pressure plate bolts, pressure plate and clutch disc.
3. From inside the transmission bell housing, remove the return spring clip and remove the release bearing assembly.
4. If necessary, remove the release control lever and spring pin with a $^{3}/_{16}$ inch punch.

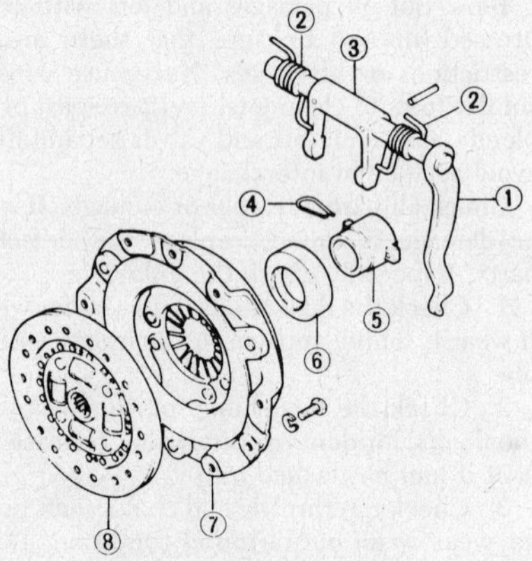

1. Clutch control shaft
2. Return spring
3. Clutch shift arm
4. Return clip
5. Release bearing carrier
6. Release bearing
7. Pressure plate assembly
8. Clutch disc

Exploded view of the clutch

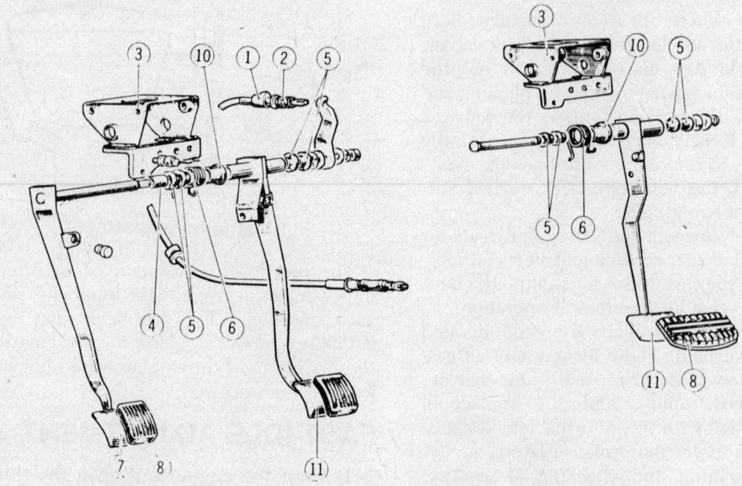

1. Clutch cable
2. Spring
3. Pedal support
4. Spacer
5. Bushing
6. Spring
7. Clutch pedal
8. Pedal pad
10. Silencer
11. Brake pedal

Clutch pedal components

CLUTCH ADJUSTMENT SPECIFICATIONS—FRONT WHEEL DRIVE CARS

	1979-81
Pedal upper face from toe board	7.1 to 7.3
Pedal stroke	5.7
Clearance between adjusting nut & cable	0.20-0.24

CLUTCH AND PEDAL ADJUSTMENT SPECIFICATIONS—REAR WHEEL DRIVE CARS

	Dimension	1975-77	1978	1979	1980	1981
Pedal height from toe board	A	6.5 to 6.7 inch	6.8 inch	6.8 ⑤	6.8 ⑤	7.1
Pedal stroke	B	5.1 inch ①	5.5 inch ②	5.5 ②	5.9	5.8
Clutch pedal free-play	C	0.8 to 1.4 inch	0.8 to 1.2 inch ③	0.6-0.08 ⑥	0.6-0.8 ⑥	0.6-0.8
Adjusting nut to cable holder clearance	D	0.2 to 0.24 inch	0.2 to 0.24 inch ④	.12 to .16	0.12-0.16	0.12-0.16
Clearance between release bearing face and pressure plate	E	0.080 inch	0.080 inch	—	—	—

① 1977 Coupe, Sedan and Hatchback: 5.9 inch
② 2600 cc engine: 5.9 inch
③ Station wagon: 0.4 to 0.6 inch
④ Station wagon w/2000 cc engine: 0.14 to 0.18 inch
⑤ 2600 cc engine: 7.2
⑥ Arrow: 0.8-1.2

Remove the control lever shaft assembly and clutch shift arm, two felt packings and two return springs.

5. Installation is the reverse of removal.

NOTE: Upon assembly—
a. Apply grease to the inside surface of the bushings and oil seal lips.
b. Apply grease in the clutch hub splines and main drive gear splines.
c. Apply grease to the inside of the release bearing carrier grooves.
d. Apply oil to the two felt packings.

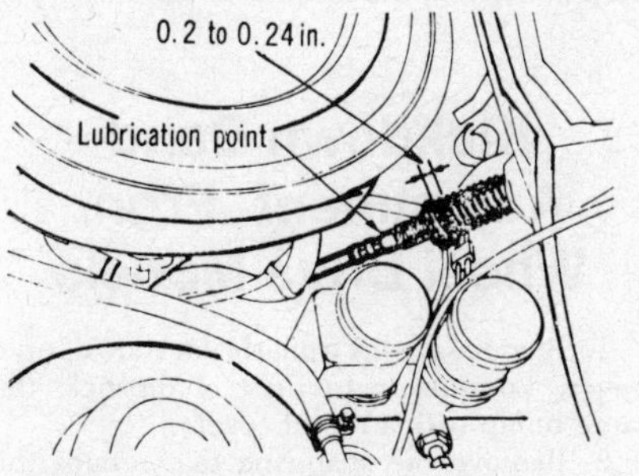

Clutch lubrication and adjustment

AUTOMATIC TRANSMISSION

1975-76 97.5 CID cars use a Borg-Warner aluminum case 3-speed. All others use a Chrysler Torque Flite.

Rear Wheel Drive Models

REMOVAL AND INSTALLATION

Borg-Warner

The exhaust system must be removed from the connecting pipe to the muffler.

1. Remove the air cleaner, battery with cables, starter, and the upper bolts which attach the engine to the transmission.
2. Drain the transmission. Remove the speedometer cable and driveshaft.
3. Remove the exhaust system from the connecting pipe rearward to the muffler.
4. Remove the transmission oil lines.
5. Remove the control rod.
6. Remove the bell housing cover. Rotate the torque converter and remove the four exposed bolts.
7. Place a jack under the transmission.
8. Remove the insulator attaching bolts, ground cable, and spacer. Remove the insulator.
9. Remove the torque converter housing to engine bolts and pull out the transmission.
10. To install the transmission, reverse the removal procedure.

TorqueFlite

The transmission and converter must be removed as an assembly; otherwise, the converter drive plate, pump bushing, or oil seal may be damaged. The drive plate will not support a load; therefore, none of the weight of the transmission should be allowed to rest on the plate during removal.

1. Disconnect battery ground cable, drain the transmission, and remove cooler lines at transmission.
2. Remove starter and cooler line bracket.
3. Rotate crankshaft clockwise and remove bolts attaching torque converter to drive plate.
4. Remove the driveshaft.
5. Disconnect gearshift rod and torque shaft.
6. Disconnect throttle rod from lever at the left side of transmission. Remove linkage bellcrank from transmission if so equipped.
7. Remove the oil filler tube and speedometer cable.
8. Support the rear of the engine with jack.
9. Raise transmission slightly.
10. Remove crossmember.
11. Remove all bell housing bolts.
12. Carefully work transmission converter assembly rearward off engine block dowels and disengage converter hub from end of crankshaft. Attach a small C-clamp to edge of bell housing to hold converter in place during transmission removal.
13. Remove transmission.
14. Installation is the reverse of removal.

Front Wheel Drive Models

TRANSAXLE REMOVAL

NOTE: The transaxle and converter must be removed and installed as an assembly.

1. Disconnect the battery ground (negative) cable.
2. Disconnect the throttle control cable at the carburetor and the manual control cable at the transaxle.
3. Disconnect from the transaxle; the inhibitor switch (neutral safety) connector, fluid

cooler hose and the four upper bolts connecting the engine to the transaxle.

4. Jack up the car and support on jack stands.

5. Remove the front wheels. Remove the engine splash shield.

6. Drain the transaxle fluid.

7. Remove the right and left driveshafts from the transaxle case. Refer to Step 7 in the manual transaxle removal for procedure.

8. Disconnect the speedometer cable. Remove the starter motor.

9. Remove the lower cover from the converter housing. Remove the three bolts that connect the converter to the engine drive plate.

NOTE: Never support the full weight of the transaxle on the engine drive plate.

10. Turn and force the converter back and away from the engine drive plate.

11. Support the weight of the engine from above (chain hoist). Support the transaxle and remove the remaining mounting bolts.

12. Remove the transaxle mount insulator bolt.

13. Remove (slide away from the engine) and lower the transaxle and converter as an assembly.

14. To install reverse the removal procedure. Be sure to connect all controls, wiring and hoses. Use new retaining rings when installing the drive axles.

Pan and Filter

REMOVAL AND INSTALLATION

Borg-Warner

1. Raise and support vehicle.

2. Remove pan bolts in a criss-cross fashion allowing fluid to drain at the same time.

3. Remove gasket and magnet. The magnet is used to pick up metallic foreign objects.

4. Install magnet and new gasket and attach pan, tightening bolts in a criss-cross pattern to 6-9 ft/lbs. Refill with Dexron® type fluid.

TorqueFlite

1. Raise and support vehicle.

2. Loosen the pan bolts from one end to the other allowing the fluid to drain out.

3. Unbolt the old filter from the pan.

4. Clean the pan and install a new filter. Tighten filter bolts to 35 in/lbs.

5. Install the pan and new gasket. Torque pan bolts to 6-9 ft/lbs.

6. Add four quarts of Dexron® fluid, start the engine and move the lever through all positions, pausing momentarily in each. Add enough fluid to bring the level to the full mark on the dipstick.

Front Wheel Drive Models

1. Raise and support the vehicle.

2. Loosen and remove the transmission pan drain plug and the differential drain plug.

3. Remove the pan to install a new filter. Clean the pan and reinstall with a new gasket.

4. Add four quarts of Dexron® II fluid through the dipstick after replacing the two (2) drain plugs. Start the engine and move selector lever through all positions; allow engine to run for at least two minutes.

5. Add sufficient fluid to bring level up to the lower dipstick. Recheck after transmission is at normal operating temperature.

Front Band Adjustment–Borg-Warner

1. Remove the transmission pan.

2. Loosen the locknut and move the servo lever out of the way.

3. Insert a 0.25 in. feeler gauge between the servo piston pin and the adjusting screw.

4. Torque the servo screw to 10 in/lbs.

5. Tighten the locknut and remove the feeler gauge.

Rear Band Adjustment–Borg-Warner

This screw is located on the right-hand outer wall of the transmission case. Loosen the locknut. Tighten the nut to 10 ft/lbs. Loosen the nut ¾ turn. Tighten down the locknut.

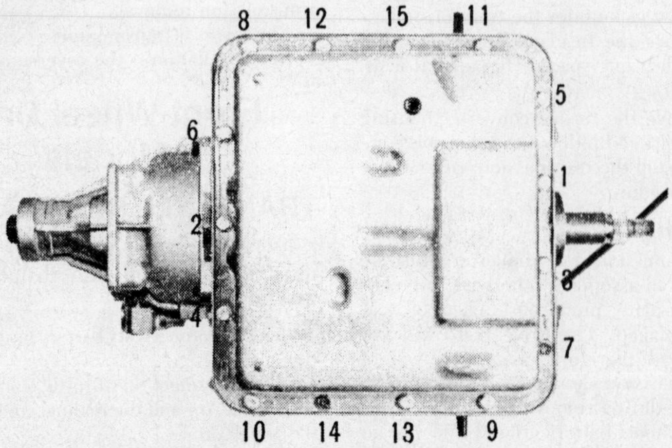

Fluid pan removal sequence—Borg-Warner

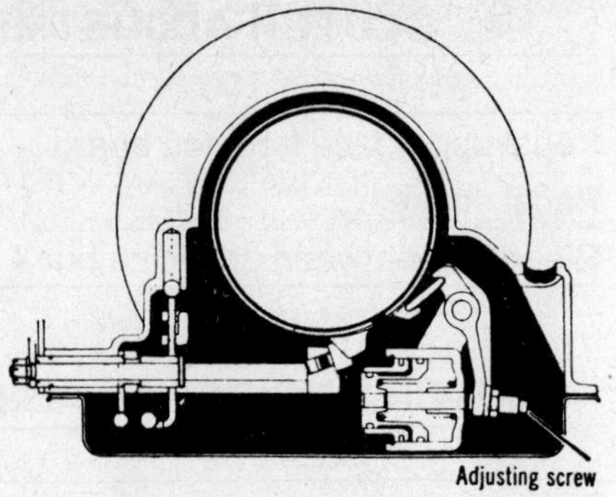

Front band adjusting screw location, Borg-Warner

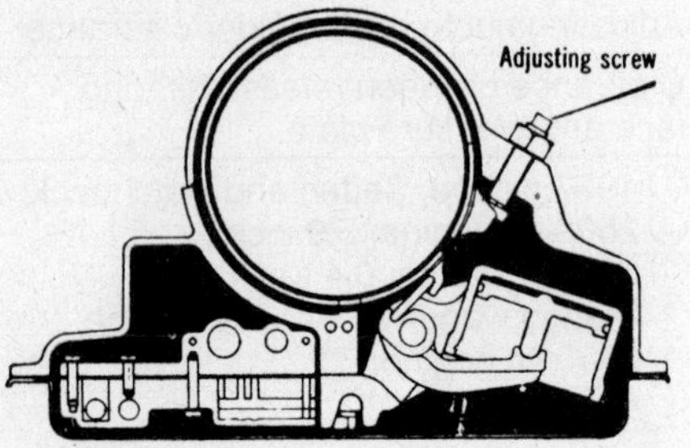

Rear band adjusting screw location, Borg-Warner

Kickdown Band–TorqueFlite

The kickdown band adjusting screw is located on the left side of the transmission case.

1. Loosen locknut and back off approximately 5 turns. Test adjusting screw for free turning in the transmission case.

2. Tighten the adjusting screw to 72 in/lbs.

3. Back off adjusting screw 3 turns from Step 2. Tighten the locknut to 35 ft/lbs.

Kickdown Band Adjustment–Front Wheel Drive Models

1. Remove all dirt from the kickdown servo cover. Location is to right of dipstick; the large bump with a round cover.

2. Remove the snap-ring that retains the cover. Use a pair of pliers that fit into the notches of the cover and remove.

3. Loosen the locknut. Hold the kickdown servo piston from turning and tighten the adjusting screw to 7 ft/lbs, then back it off. Repeat the tightening and backing off two times. This will assure the seating of the kickdown band on the drum.

4. Tighten the adjusting screw to 3.5 ft/lbs and back off 3.5 turns (counterclockwise).

5. Hold the adjusting screw and tighten the locknut to 12 ft/lbs.

6. Install a new cover seal ring "D"-shaped section in the groove. Install the servo cover and snap-ring.

Kickdown Switch—Borg-Warner

The kickdown switch is located on the carburetor and is operated when the throttle valve is opened fully by the accelerator pedal and linkage.

1. To inspect the kickdown switch, a test lamp is used to check that electrical current is flowing through the switch, with the throttle valve wide open.
2. If there is no current indication, adjust the switch. If no current is indicated with the switch plunger completely depressed, replace the switch.
3. If current flows through the switch but the kickdown is still inoperative, the internal solenoid on the valve body may be defective. A clicking noise should be heard if the solenoid is working normally.

Modulator Valve Adjustment—Borg-Warner

1. Install a vacuum gauge in the line from the engine to the transmission modulator valve.
2. Remove the pipe plug from the left rear of the transmission case and install a 0 to 300 psi pressure gauge.
3. Start the engine and allow it to warm up to normal operating temperature.
4. Apply the hand brake and chock the wheels. Place the selector lever in the R position.
5. With a 17.7 in. Hg reading, the oil control pressure should be 55 to 68 psi.
6. Increase the engine speed until the vacuum gauge reads 12 in. Hg. The pressure gauge should read 92 to 98 psi.
7. An engine stall vacuum reading of 2 in. Hg should result in a pressure reading of 160 to 195 psi.

NOTE: Do not hold the stall test longer than 10 seconds. Return the selector lever to the N position and increase the engine speed to cool both the transmission and the engine. Wait approximately two minutes between tests, if a repeat is necessary.

8. If line pressure is below the specified value, remove the modulator vacuum line and turn the adjusting screw clockwise.
9. If the line pressure is above the specified value, remove the modulator vacuum line and turn the adjusting screw counterclockwise.

NOTE:
a. One turn of the modulator screw causes a change of pressure of approximately 10 psi.
b. Do not adjust line pressure in any forward range. Use R position only.

10. Remove the vacuum and pressure gauges.

Neutral Start Switch Adjustment—Borg-Warner

1. Place the selector lever in N position.
2. Lock the switch with a screw so that when the pin at the forward end of the rod assembly is near the crest of the pawl of the detent plate, the switch should be at the forward end of the N range.
3. Tighten the neutral start switch screw. A clearance of .059 inch should be present between the switch and the selector lever.
4. Check switch operation by attempting to start the engine in gears other than the P and N positions. Make sure that the backup lights operate with the lever in the R position.

Inhibitor Switch Adjustment—Front Wheel Drive Models

1. Place the control lever in the "N" position.
2. Make sure the short end of the manual control lever covers the switch body flange. Loosen the switch mounting bolts (2) and adjust switch as necessary. Tighten the bolts.
3. Check the switch operation by a attempting to start engine in gears other than the P and N positions.

Low & Reverse Band—TorqueFlite

1. Raise vehicle, drain transmission fluid and remove the pan.
2. This transmission has an Allen socket adjustment screw at the servo end of lever. After removing the locknut this screw is tightened to 41 in/lbs torque them backed off 7½ turns. Tighten locknut to 30 ft/lbs.
3. Reinstall the pan.

Neutral Safety Switch—TorqueFlite

1. When testing the safety switch, check to see if the switch has been properly installed. Move the selector lever into N position and adjust the switch by moving it so that the pin on the forward end of the rod assembly will be in the position near the lobe of detent plate and that this position will be at the front end of the range of N connection of the switch. Temporarily tighten the attaching screws. After adjusting the selection lever clearance to 0.059 in. securely tighten the screws.
2. Test the continuity of the switch circuit by using a test light with switch connector disconnected.

Shift Linkage Adjustment—TorqueFlite

To adjust the shift linkage, the control cover must be removed.

REMOVAL AND INSTALLATION, 1975

1. Remove the shift handle assembly from the lever.
2. Take the position indicator assembly out upward.

Remove the position indicator lamp.

3. Disconnect the control rod from the arm.

Remove the lever bracket assembly.

4. Installation is the reverse of removal. If the proper turning effort (13-29 in/lbs) is not obtained, adjust it by using a selective wave-washer of proper size.

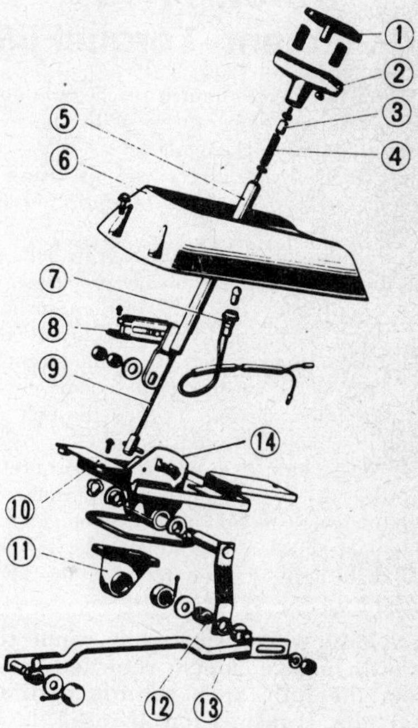

1. Push button
2. Shift handle
3. Rod adjusting nut
4. Rod return spring
5. Selector lever assembly
6. Position indicator assembly
7. Indicator lamp socket assembly
8. Inhibitor switch
9. Shift lever rod
10. Shift lever bracket assembly
11. Lever bracket cover
12. Transmission control arm
13. Transmission control rod

Exploded view of Torqueflite automatic transmission control

CAUTION

When the turning effort at the pivot A is checked, the pin at the forward end of the rod assembly must not slide with the detent plate. If the arm is loose, the bushing should be replaced.

CONTROL ROD ADJUSTMENT, 1975

Adjust the rod adjusting nut at the top end of the selector lever assembly so that when the selector lever is in N position, the nut may be flush with the bottom of the lever notch.

To connect the control rod to the selector lever assembly, first make certain that the selector lever is held in N position, and then move the control rod 3 detent stops from L position to place transmission in N neutral.

CONTROL ROD ADJUSTMENT, 1976-81

The control rod is adjusted at the transmission control lever with the control rod adjusting nuts.

Throttle Rod Adjustment–TorqueFlite

Warm the engine until it reaches the normal operating temperature. With the carburetor automatic choke off the fast idle cam, adjust the engine idle speed by using a tachometer. Then make the throttle rod adjustment.

1. Install each linkage. Loosen its bolts so that the rods B and C can slide properly.
2. Lightly push the rod A or the transmission throttle lever and the rod C toward the idle stopper and set the rods to idle position. In this case the carburetor automatic choke must be fully released. Tighten the bolt securely to connect the rods B and C.
3. Make sure that when the carburetor throttle valve is wide-open, the transmission throttle lever smoothly moves from idle to wide-open position (operating angle; 45°-54°) and that there is some room in the lever stroke.

NOTE: Make sure that when the throttle linkage alone is returned slowly from the fully open throttle position, that the transmission throttle lever completely returns to the idle position by spring force.

DRIVE AXLE

Driveshafts and U-Joints

The driveshaft and U-joints are of conventional design and construction. Driveshaft length differs between the manual and automatic transmission equipped vehicles.

Dynamic Damper

Transmission mounted dynamic dampers are used on all automatic transmission cars from 1975 to 1977.

Beginning 1977, dampers are installed on some models with the five speed transmission.

The dynamic damper units are not interchangeable.

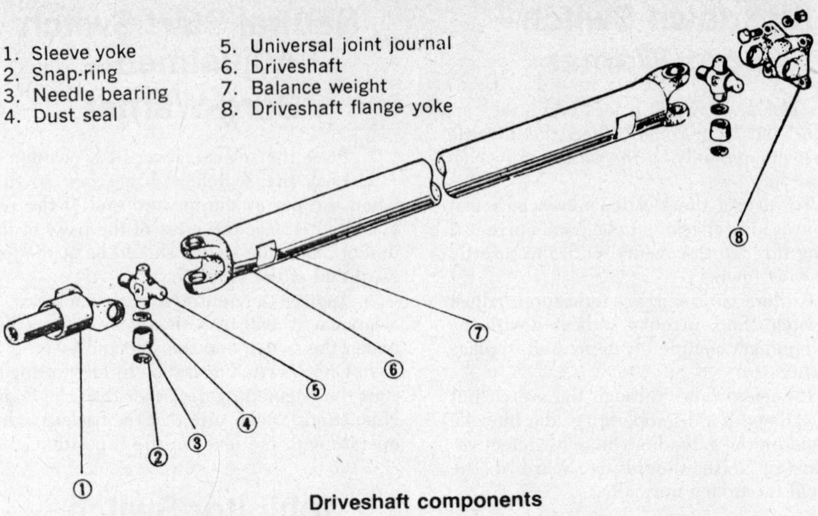

Driveshaft components

Driveshaft

REMOVAL AND INSTALLATION

1. Matchmark the rear flange yoke and the differential pinion flange.
2. Remove the bolts from the rear flange. Remove the driveshaft by pulling it from the rear of the transmission extension housing.

NOTE: Place a container under the transmission extension housing to collect any oil leakage when the driveshaft is removed.

3. To install the shaft, align the front sleeve yoke with the splines of the transmission output shaft, and push the driveshaft into the extension housing.

NOTE: Be careful not to damage the rear transmission seal lip upon installation.

4. Align the matchmarks on the rear yokes, install the bolts, and tighten securely.
5. Inspect the oil level of the transmission.

U/JOINT OVERHAUL

1. Remove the bearing retainer snap-rings from the flange yoke.
2. With a vise and suitable sockets, force one needle bearing cup outward from the yoke, using the cross as a ram.
3. Grasp the protruding bearing with pliers or vise grips and remove it from the yoke.
4. Reverse the sockets and again using the cross as a ram, force the opposite bearing outward from the yoke and remove it with pliers or vise grips.
5. Follow the same procedure to remove the remaining bearing in the yoke.
6. To install, place the cross in the yoke and start a bearing cup into the yoke collar, engaging the cross arm.
7. With the aid of a vise, force the bearing cup into the yoke collar until it bottoms. Install the opposite bearing cup in the same manner.

NOTE: Sockets may be used to force the bearing cup inward so that the retaining snap-rings can be installed.

8. Different thickness snap-rings are used to control the clearance between the bearing and the snap-ring.
9. Install a snap-ring and measure the clearance with a feeler gauge. Replace the snap-ring with one of the proper thickness to have a total clearance tolerance of .000 to .001 inch.

Snap ring selection range
No color-0.0504 inch
Yellow-0.0561 inch
Blue-0.0528 inch
Purple-0.0539 inch

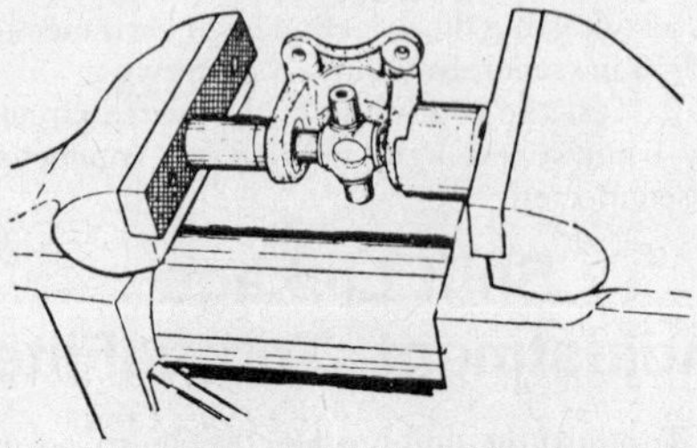
U-joint bearing removal

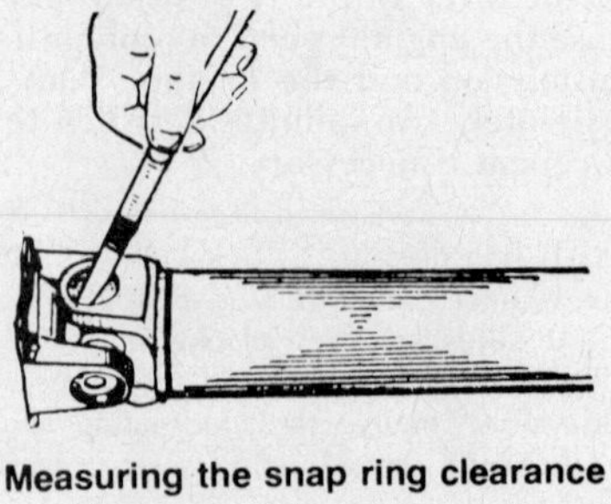
Measuring the snap ring clearance

NOTE: When snap-rings are installed, press each bearing towards the opposite side to measure the maximum clearance.

Drive Axle

Front Wheel Drive Models

1. Remove the hub center cap and loosen

the driveshaft (axle) nut. Loosen the wheel lug nuts.

2. Lift the car and support it on jack stands. Remove the front wheels. Remove the engine splash shield.

3. Remove the lower ball joint and strut bar from the lower control arm.

4. Drain the transaxle fluid.

5. Insert a pry bar between the transaxle case (on the raised rib) and the driveshaft double off-set joint case (DOJ). Do not insert the pry bar too deeply or you will damage the oil seal. Move the bar to the right to withdraw the left driveshaft; to the left to remove the right driveshaft.

6. Plug the transaxle case with a clean rag to prevent dirt from entering the case.

7. Use a puller-driver mounted on the wheel studs to push the driveshaft from the front hub. Take care to prevent the spacer from falling out of place.

8. Assembly is the reverse of removal. Insert the driveshaft into the hub first, then install the transaxle end.

NOTE: Always use a new DOJ retaining ring every time you remove the driveshaft.

U-JOINT OVERHAUL

NOTE: The Birfield joint (wheel side) cannot be rebuilt. It must be replaced with the axle, however a boot kit is available.

1. Remove the boot band from double off-set joint (DOJ) and slide the boot away from the joint.

2. Remove the circlip from the DOJ with a flat-blade screwdriver. Remove the drive-shaft from the DOJ and wipe off the grease.

3. Remove the snap-ring that retains the inner race. Remove the inner race, cage and balls as an assembly.

4. Clean the inner race, cage and balls without disassembly.

5. Remove the Birfield joint boot, clean grease away and inspect the joint for wear; check the splines on both ends of the shaft for wear.

6. Check the DOJ for rust, damage or wear to the outer race, inner race, cage and balls. If any parts show wear, replace with the necessary kit. It is a good idea to at least replace the boots. Kits available are; Drive-shaft and Birfield joint, Double offset joint, Birfield boot kit and DOJ boot kit.

7. To reassemble: Tape the ends of the splines to prevent damage to the boots when they are installed.

8. Apply gear oil to the shaft and slide the new boots on. If you are not installing a kit, apply an amount of grease equal to the amount you wiped away.

9. Installation of the old parts is the reverse of removal after you have regreased them. To install the DOJ kit, use the grease supplied with the kit and apply an amount to the inner race and cage. Install the inner race and cock slightly.

10. Apply grease to the balls and install them in the cage. Place the inner race on the driveshaft and install the snap-ring. Apply grease to the outer race and install. Install the boots and bands.

11. Install the driveshaft using a new retainer ring on the DOJ side.

FRONT WHEEL DRIVE MODELS

FRONT HUB AND WHEEL BEARINGS

1. Remove driveshaft and front brake assembly.

2. Disconnect tie rod end and strut.

3. Remove hub and knuckle as an assembly.

4. Remove front hub from knuckle. It may be necessary to drive out the hub with a soft (plastic) hammer.

5. Remove disc rotor from hub.

6. The oil seal and the inner and outer bearings may now be serviced. Refer to the front wheel bearing section.

7. Assembly is the reverse of removal.

REMOVAL AND INSTALLATION

Leaf Spring Type

1. Raise and support the car safely.
2. Remove the rear wheels.
3. Remove the driveshaft.
4. Disconnect all rear brake lines.
5. Remove the rear U-bolts and the shock absorbers.
6. Remove the spring shackle pin nuts and the shackle plate. With the axle housing resting on the jack, remove the rear springs.
7. To replace the axle assembly, reverse the removal procedure. Bleed the brakes.

Coil Spring Type

1. Raise the car and support it safely.
2. Remove the rear wheels and the driveshaft.
3. Disconnect the parking brake cable and the hydraulic brake hose.
4. Remove the shock absorbers from the rear housing.
5. Lower the housing and remove the coil springs.
6. Position the housing and remove the lower and upper control arms and the assist link.
7. Guide the housing from under the car with the aid of a helper.
8. Installation is the reverse order of removal.
9. Bleed the brakes thoroughly.

Rear Axle Shaft

REMOVAL AND INSTALLATION

1. Remove the rear wheels and the brake backing plate.
2. The axle shaft may be pulled out manually or with a slide hammer.
3. Installation is the reverse of removal.
4. Bleed the brakes.

Axle Shaft Bearing/Oil Seal

REMOVAL AND INSTALLATION

NOTE: Front wheel drive models use an inner and outer bearing contained in the rear brake drum hub. Refer to front wheel bearing servicing, in the brake section, for removal and installation.

1. Remove the axle shaft.
2. Grind a small notch on the inner bearing retainer and split the retainer at that point with a chisel.

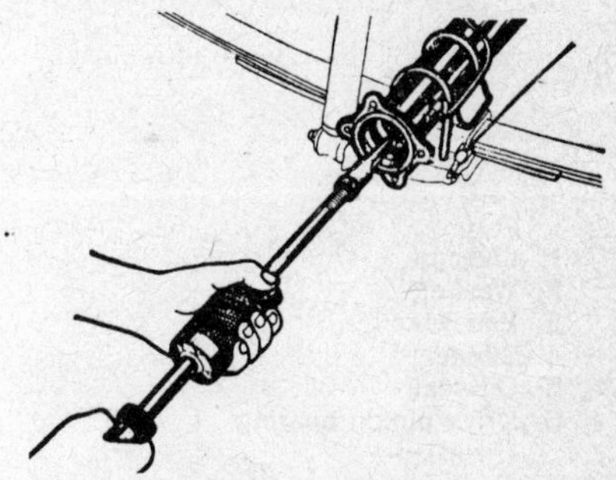

Oil seal removal

3. Remove the bearing with a puller.
4. The oil seal can be removed after the axle shaft is removed.
5. Install the outer bearing retainer (raised surface facing the wheel hub), axle shaft bearing and retainer. Using packing, set the clearance between the outer bearing retainer and the bearing to 0.00-0.01 in.

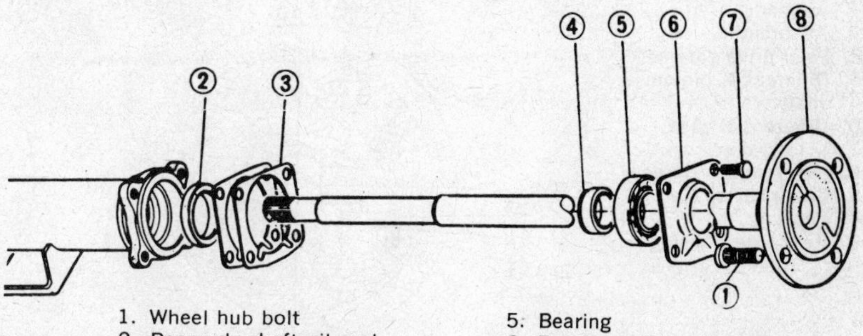

1. Wheel hub bolt
2. Rear axle shaft oil seal
3. Packing
4. Bearing retainer (inner)
5. Bearing
6. Bearing retainer (outer)
7. Bearing retainer bolt
8. Rear axle shaft

Exploded view of axle shaft

Power Train

FRONT WHEEL DRIVE MODELS

The power train of the manual transaxle consists of three shafts including an input shaft assembly, an intermediate shaft assembly, an output shaft assembly and a differential assembly.

The automatic transaxle consists of a torque converter, fully automatic three speed transmission, transfer gearing and a differential assembly.

Both the manual and automatic transaxles, combined with the four cylinder engine, make a very compact front wheel drive system.

Transaxle removal is described in a previous section. Repairs to the transaxle, other than routine maintenance, should be done by a qualified repair shop.

Differential

REMOVAL AND INSTALLATION

1. Drain the oil.
2. Remove the driveshaft.
3. Pull out both axle shafts to disengage the axle shafts from the differential gears. They need only be pulled out about 2 in.
4. Unbolt and remove the differential carrier.
5. Installation is the reverse of removal.

OVERHAUL

1. Remove the bearing cap and pry the differential from the carrier.
2. Remove the differential side bearings. Be sure to keep the right and left bearing shims separated.
3. Remove the ring gear.
4. Drive out the pinion shaft lockpin from the rear of the ring gear, and remove the pinion shaft.
5. Remove the pinions and side gears with spacers. Note the position of the side gear spacers.
6. Hold the end yoke and remove the pinion nut.
7. Remove the end yoke.
8. Tape the drive pinion shaft with a plastic faced mallet and remove the drive pinion with the adjusting shim, rear inner race, spacer and preload adjusting shim.
9. Remove the front pinion bearing outer race and oil seal.
10. Remove the pinion bearing rear outer race.

NOTE: If the unit is to be assembled using no replacement parts, the same spacers and shims can generally be used. If either pinion bearing or ring gear and drive pinion are being replaced, new shims should be used. Only replace the drive pinion and ring gear in matched sets.

Pinion Depth Chart

Example:	
Dimension 1	0.863 in.
Dimension 2 (includes 0.004 in.)	—0.774 in.
	0.089 in.
Minus 0.009-0.012 in. in clearance	—0.011 in.
Thickness of thrust washer required	0.078 in.

Thrust washer identification (in.)

A—0.078	C—0.093
B—0.085	D—0.100

11. Assemble the side gears in the differential case. Install the thrust washers in the same place as they were installed.
12. With washers, insert both differential gears at the same time to mesh with the side gears. Insert the pinion shaft.
13. Measure the backlash of the differential gears and side gears. The backlash should be (1972-73) 0.003-0.005 in. (1975-77) 0-.003 in. and can be adjusted with the use of spacers listed below.
14. Align the pinion shaft hole with the case and drive the lockpin in.
15. Install the ring gear.
16. To assemble the drive pinion, press the front and rear outer races into the gear carrier.

1. Locknut
2. Washer
3. End yoke
4. Slinger
5. Oil seal
6. Drive pinion bearing (front)
7. Gear carrier
8. Carrier cap
9. Preload adjusting shim
10. Drive pinion spacer
11. Drive pinion bearing (rear)
12. Drive pinion adjusting shim
13. Side bearing
14. Side bearing adjusting shim
15. Differential pinion
16. Differential pinion washer
17. Air breather
18. Final drive gear set
19. Differential pinion shaft
20. Differential case
21. Lockwasher
22. Differential side gear
23. Side gear spacer
24. Packing
25. Rear axle housing

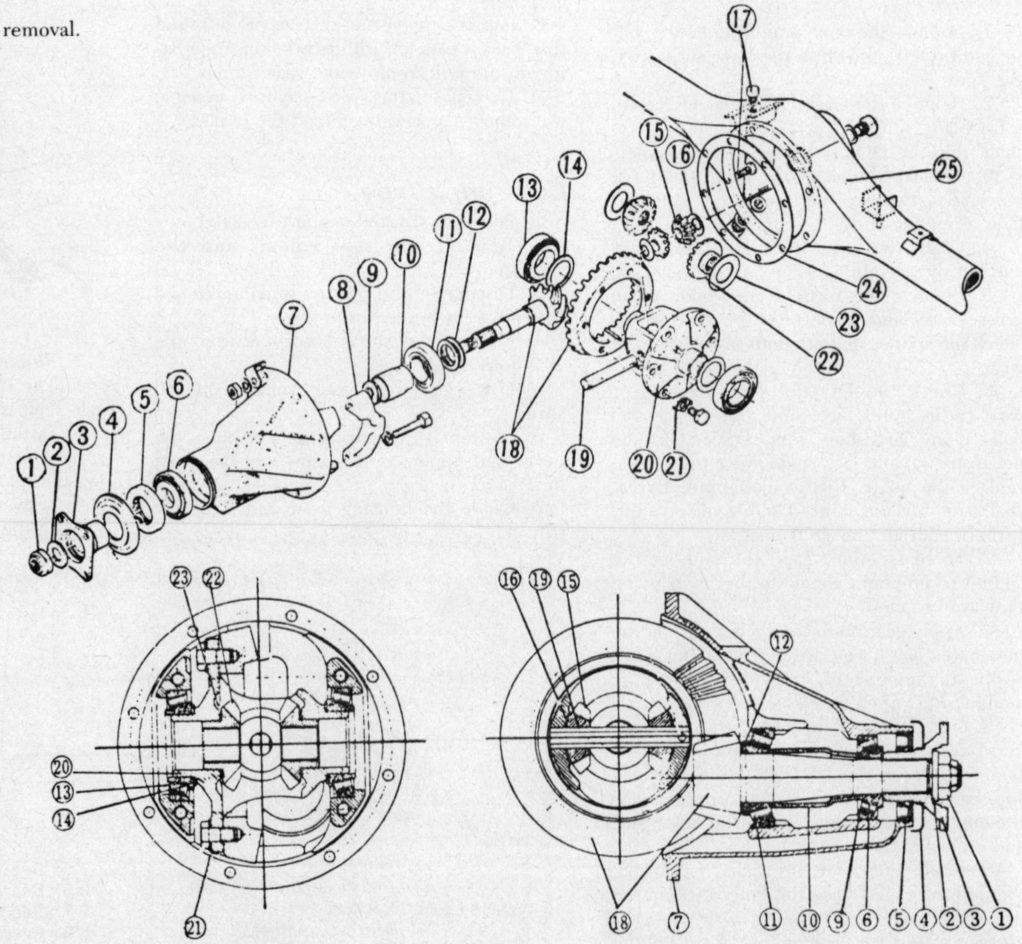

Exploded view of differential

17. Insert a shim between the drive pinion and rear bearing. If the original gear set is being replaced, the original shims may be used. If a new gear set is being installed, calculate the shim dimension in the following manner. Assuming the pinion height before disassembly is correct, subtract the new pinion variation marking (on the pinion head) from the old pinion variation marking. If the answer is positive, add shims in the corresponding amount. If the answer is negative, subtract shims in the corresponding amount. This will produce a reasonable starting point for assembly. If the shim choice is proved incorrect, the entire pinion must be disassembled, and the shim changed accordingly. The etched marking on the face of the pinion represents a positive or negative variation from the standard in millimeters.

18. Assemble the front bearing, end yoke, pinion spacer and washer and torque the pinion nut gradually. Torque the pinion nut constantly checking the preload, until a preload of 6-9 in/lbs is reached (without the oil seal).

Shims are available in the following sizes:

19. Remove the end yoke and insert the bearing preload adjusting shim between the pinion spacer and the bearing and torque the pinion nut to 8-11 in/lbs of preload with oil seal.

The pinion nut torque should be 100-145 ft/lbs.

20. Install each side bearing into the differential case without the adjusting shim.

21. Install the differential case assembly on the gear carrier and measure the clearance between the side bearing outer race and the gear carrier.

22. The thickness of the shim on each side is determined by the following formula:

Side Gear Spacers

Part No.	Thickness of spacer (in.)	
		0
MA180860	0.0394	
		−0.0028
		−0.0031
MA180861	0.0394	
		−0.0067
		−0.0071
MA180862	0.0394	
		−0.0098
MA180876	0.0394	+0.0063
		−0.0035
MA180875	0.0394	+0.0031
		−0.0004

PINION BEARING PRELOAD SHIMS

Part No. A-type differential	Part No. B-type differential	Thickness (in.)
MB044435	MB092130	.0118
MA180828	MB092131	.0787
MA180829	MB092132	.0799
MA180830	MB092133	.0811
MA180831	MB092134	.0823
MA180832	MB092135	.0835
MA180833	MB092136	.0846
MA180834	MB092137	.0858
MA180835	MB092138	.0870
MA180836	MB092139	.0882
MA180837	MB092140	.0894
MA180838	MB092141	.0906
MA180839	MB092142	.0917

PINION HEIGHT ADJUSTING SHIMS

Part No.	Thickness of Shim ① (in.)
MA180842	0.0543 ± 0.0004
MA180843	0.0555 ± 0.0004
MA180844	0.0567 ± 0.0004
MA180845	0.0579 ± 0.0004
MA180846	0.0591 ± 0.0004
MA180847	0.0603 ± 0.0004
MA180848	0.0614 ± 0.0004
MA180849	0.0626 ± 0.0004
MA180850	0.0638 ± 0.0004
MA180851	0.0650 ± 0.0004
MA180852	0.0118 ± 0.0005

① $\frac{\text{Measures clearance} + 0.004\text{ in.}}{2}$ =

thickness of shims on one side

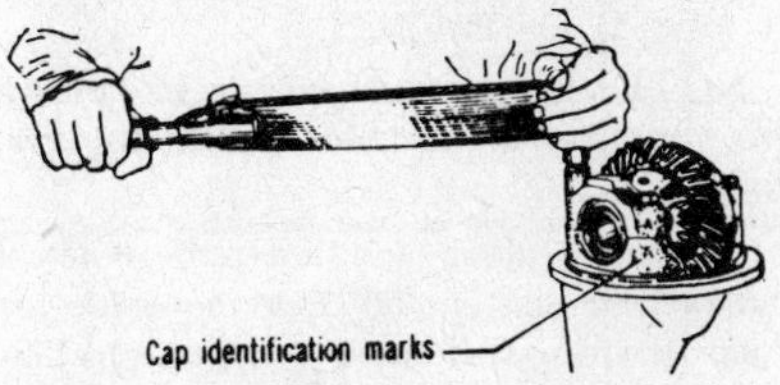

Bearing cap identification marks

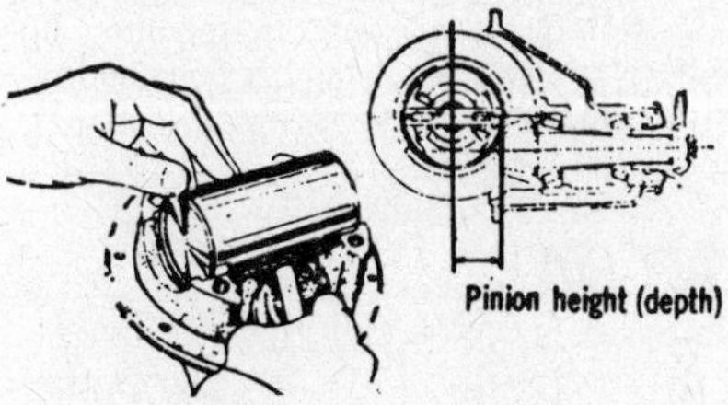

Measuring pinion height

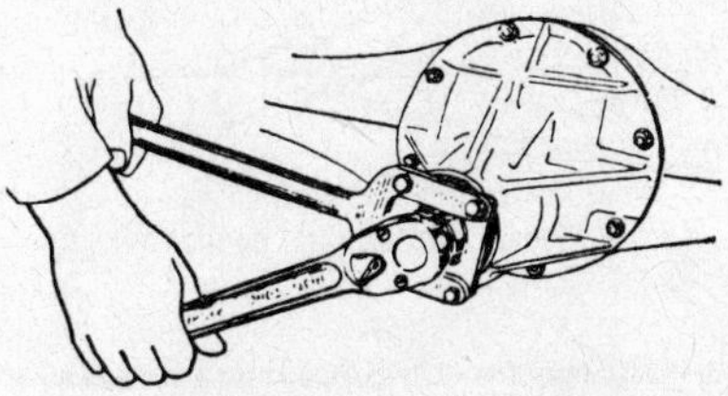
Removing the end yoke

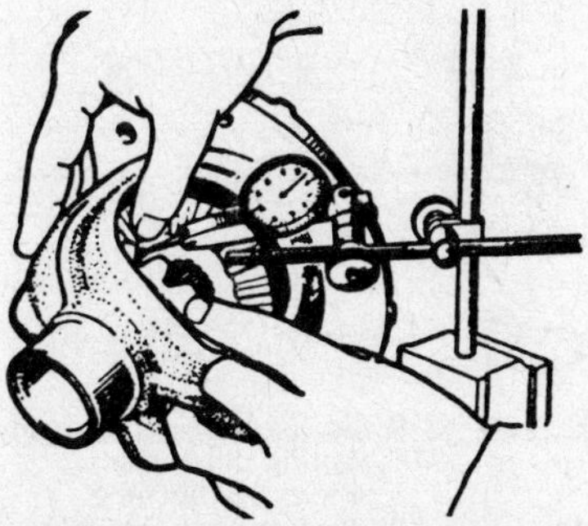
Checking pinion gear and side gear backlash

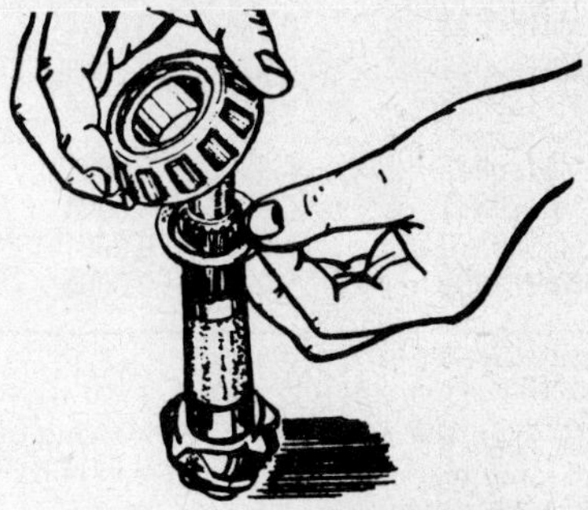
Pinion height shim installation

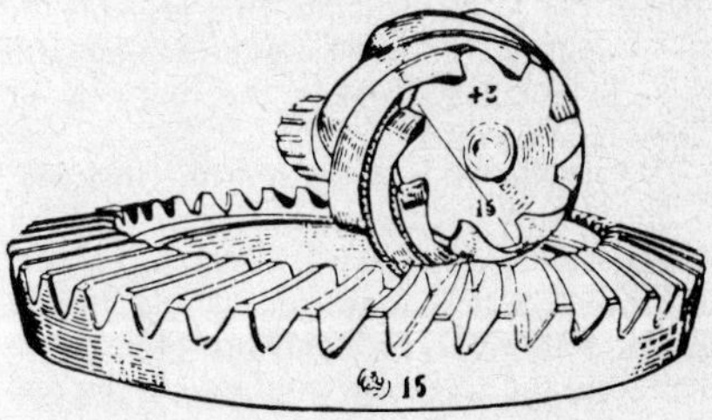
Pinion and ring gear markings

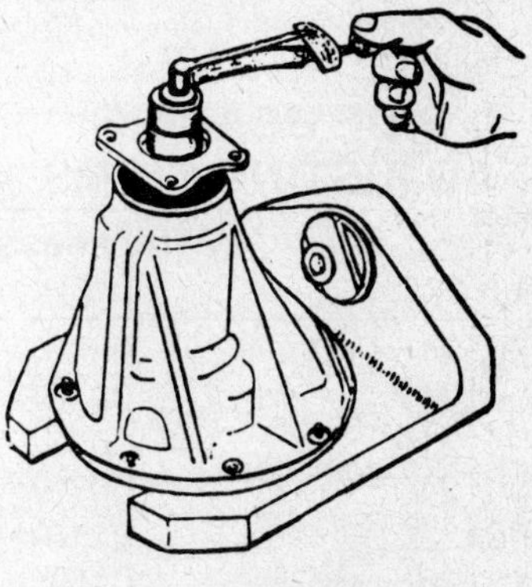
Measuring pinion preload

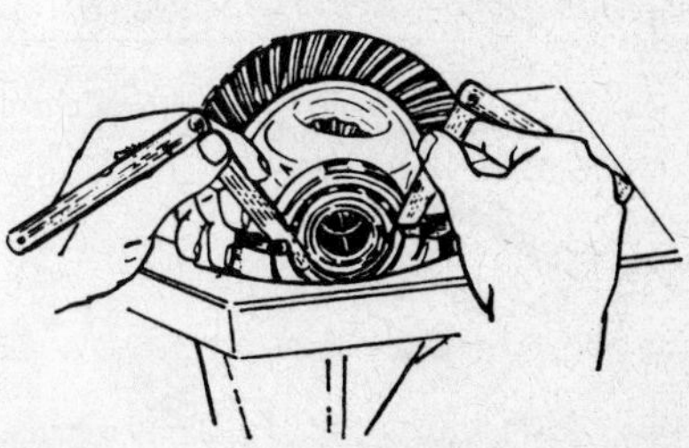
Measure the side bearing-to-carrier clearance

The 0.004 in. dimension is added as the side bearing preload (0.002 in. on each side). Side bearing preload shims are available in the following sizes:

SIDE BEARING PRELOAD SHIMS

Part No.	Shim thickness (in.)
MA180828	0.0787 ± 0.0004
MA180829	0.0799 ± 0.0004
MA180830	0.0811 ± 0.0004
MA180831	0.0823 ± 0.0004
MA180832	0.0835 ± 0.0004
MA180833	0.0846 ± 0.0004
MA180834	0.0858 ± 0.0004
MA180835	0.0870 ± 0.0004
MA180836	0.0882 ± 0.0004
MA180837	0.0894 ± 0.0004
MA180838	0.0906 ± 0.0004
MA180839	0.0917 ± 0.0004

23. Align the gear carrier and bearing cap positioning marks and torque the cap bolts to 25-29 ft/lbs.
24. Install a dial indicator and measure ring gear run-out. If the run-out exceeds 0.002 in., change the position of the ring gear on the differential carrier by 90°. If the run-out still exceeds 0.002 in., replace the ring gear or differential carrier.
25. Measure the backlash of the ring gear at four points, 90° apart. Ring gear backlash should not exceed 0.000-0.002 in. If the measured backlash is greater than the specification, shift shims in a corresponding thickness from the ring gear tooth side to the rear of the ring gear. If backlash is less than specified, shift shims from the rear side of the ring gear to the tooth side. Side gear adjusting shims are available in the following sizes:

SIDE BEARING ADJUSTING SHIMS

Part No.	Thickness (in.)
MB001216	.0020
MB001217	.0028
MB001218	.0039
MB001219	.0079
MB001220	.0118
MB132038	.0157
MB132039	.0197
MB001221	.0276

26. Make a ring gear tooth pattern check.

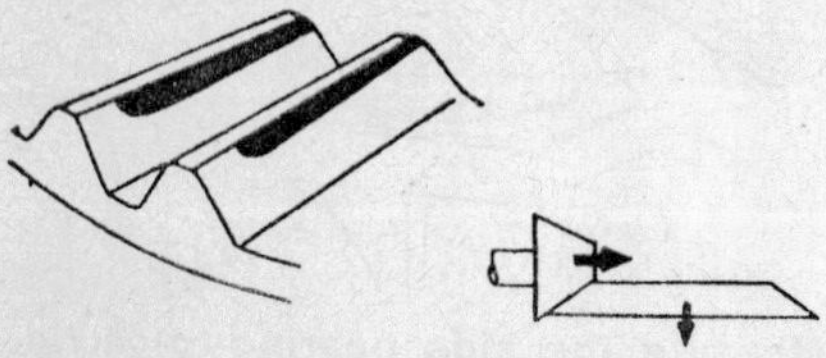

Face contact

Proper tooth contact

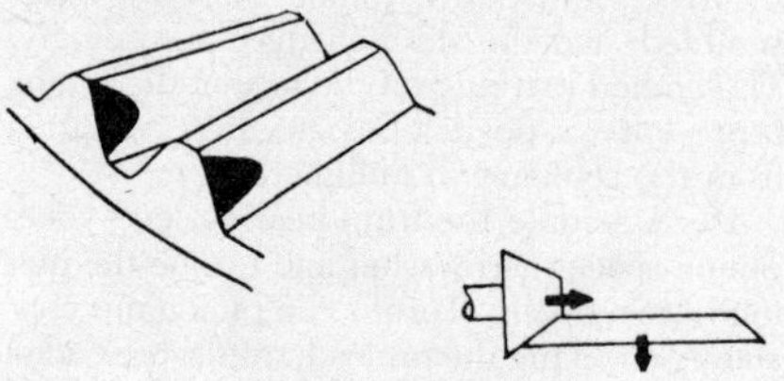

Heel contact

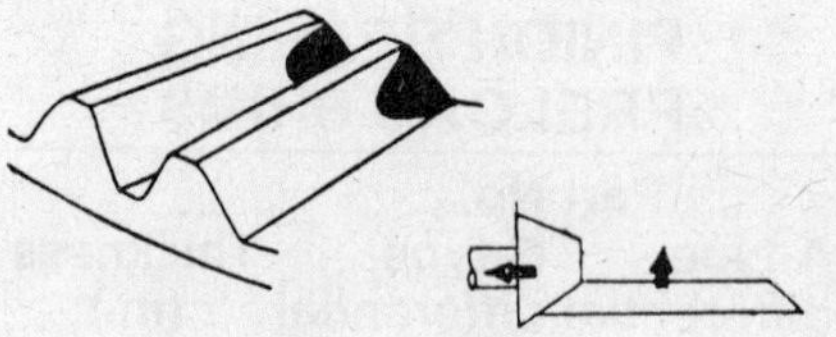

Toe contact

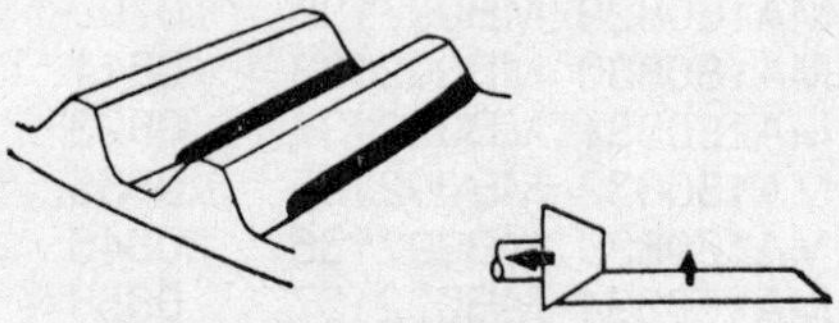

Flank contact

REAR SUSPENSION

Leaf Springs

REMOVAL AND INSTALLATION

1. Remove the hub cap or wheel cover. Loosen the lug nuts.
2. Raise the rear of the car. Install a stand at the exact point of the sill shown in the drawing. Two dimples locate the support point on the sill flange.

CAUTION

Damage to the unit body can result from installing a stand at any other location.

3. Disconnect the lower mounting nut of the shock absorber.
4. Remove the four U-bolt fastening nuts from the spring seat.

NOTE: It's not necessary to remove the shock absorber, leave the top connected.

5. Place a floor jack under the rear axle and raise it just enough to remove the load from the springs. Remove the spring pad and seat.
6. Remove the two rear shackle attaching nuts and remove the rear shackle.
7. Remove the front pin retaining nut. Remove the two pin retaining bolts and take off the pin.

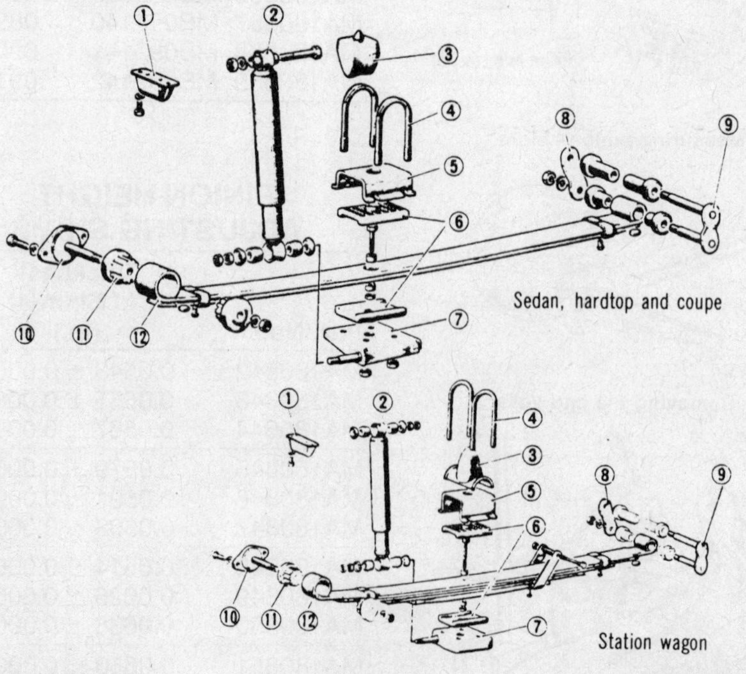

1. Carrier bumper
2. Shock absorber
3. Rubber cushion
4. Spring U-bolt
5. Pad bracket
6. Pad
7. U-bolt seat
8. Shackle plate
9. Spring shackle assembly
10. Spring pin assembly
11. Front eye bushing
12. Leaf spring assembly

Colt rear suspension (Arrow similar)

8. Remove the spring.

NOTE: It is a good safety practice to replace used suspension fasteners with new parts.

9. Install the front spring eye bushings from both sides of the eye with the bushing flanges facing out.
10. Insert the spring pin assembly from the body side and fasten it with the bolts. Temporarily tighten the spring pin nut.
11. Install the rear eye bushings in the same manner as the front, insert the shackle pins from the outside of the car, and temporarily tighten the nut after installing the shackle plate.
12. Install the pads on both sides of the spring, aligning the pad center holes with the spring center bolt collar, and then install the spring seat with its center hole through the spring center collar.
13. Attach the assembled spring and spring seat to the axle housing with the axle housing spring center hole meeting the spring center bolt and install the U-bolt nuts. Tighten the nuts to 33-36 ft/lbs.
14. Tighten the lower shock absorber nut to 12-15 ft/lbs on all models.
15. Lower the car to the floor, jounce it a few times, and then tighten the spring pin and shackle pin nuts to 36-43 ft/lbs.

Coil Springs

REMOVAL AND INSTALLATION

1. Raise and support the car safely allowing the rear axle to hang unsupported.
2. Place a jack under the rear axle, and remove the bottom bolts or nuts of the shock absorbers.
3. Lower the rear axle and remove the left and right coil springs.
4. Installation is the reverse of removal.

Shock Absorbers

REMOVAL AND INSTALLATION

1. Remove the hub cap or wheel cover. Loosen the lug nuts.
2. Raise the rear of the car. Support the car with jack stands.

NOTE: The body sill is marked with two dimples to locate the support position. Never place a stand anywhere but between these marks or you'll damage the body.

3. Remove the upper mounting bolt and nut.
4. While holding the bottom stud mount nut with one wrench, remove the locknut with another wrench.
5. Remove the shock absorber.
6. Check the shock for:
   a. Excessive oil leakage, some minor weeping is permissable;
   b. Bent center rod, damaged outer case, or other defects;
   c. Pump the shock absorber several times, if it offers even resistance on full strokes it may be considered serviceable.
7. Install the upper shock mounting nut and bolt. Hand tighten the nut.
8. Install the bottom eye of the shock over the spring stud. Tighten the lower nut to 12-15 ft/lbs.
9. Finally, tighten the upper nut to 47-58 ft/lbs on all models except station wagons, which are tightened to 12-15 ft/lbs.

FRONT SUSPENSION

Strut

REMOVAL AND INSTALLATION EXCEPT FRONT WHEEL DRIVE

1. Remove the front wheel and caliper. Remove the front hub with disc and dust cover.
2. Disconnect the stabilizer linkage and the lower arm. Remove the strut assembly, knuckle arm and strut insulator retaining bolts and remove the strut assembly from the wheelhouse.
3. Installation is the reverse of removal.

Front Suspension Torque Specifications

Description	Torque
Bolts retaining strut assembly to wheelhouse	7-10 ft lbs.
Bolts retaining strut assembly to knuckle arm	29-36 ft lbs.

FRONT WHEEL DRIVE MODELS

1. Jack up and support the front of the car.
2. Remove the front wheel. Remove the brake line from the strut.
3. Remove the four upper and two lower mounting nuts/bolts and remove the strut.
4. Installation is the reverse of removal. Be sure to bleed the brakes after installation.

FRONT SUSPENSION TORQUE SPECIFICATIONS—REAR WHEEL DRIVE CARS

Description	Torque (ft. lbs.)
Bolts retaining strut assembly to wheelhouse	7-10
Bolts retaining strut assembly to knuckle arm	29-36

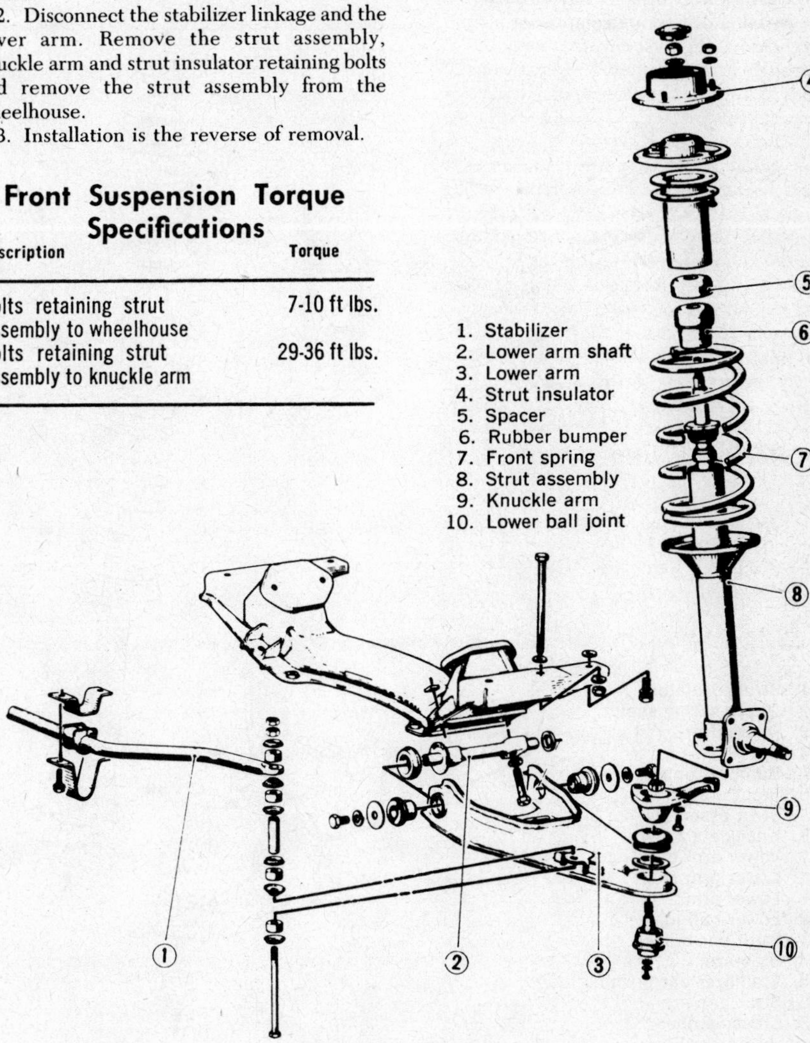

Colt front suspension

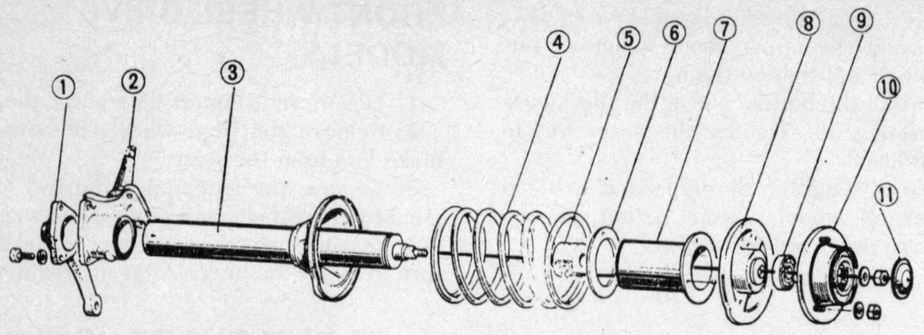

1. Knuckle arm
2. Knuckle
3. Strut sub-assembly (shock absorber)
4. Front suspension spring
5. Rubber bumper
6. Dust cover plate
7. Dust cover
8. Upper spring seat
9. Ball bearing
10. Insulator
11. Dust cover

Exploded view of the front suspension strut

Spring

REMOVAL AND INSTALLATION

The strut assembly must be removed to the bench.

1. Clamp the strut assembly in a vise.
2. Install a coil spring compressor.
3. Remove the dust cover.
4. Remove the insulator.
5. Remove the spring.
6. Installation is the reverse of removal. Align the spring seat upper assembly with the indentation on the piston rod and the D-shaped hole.

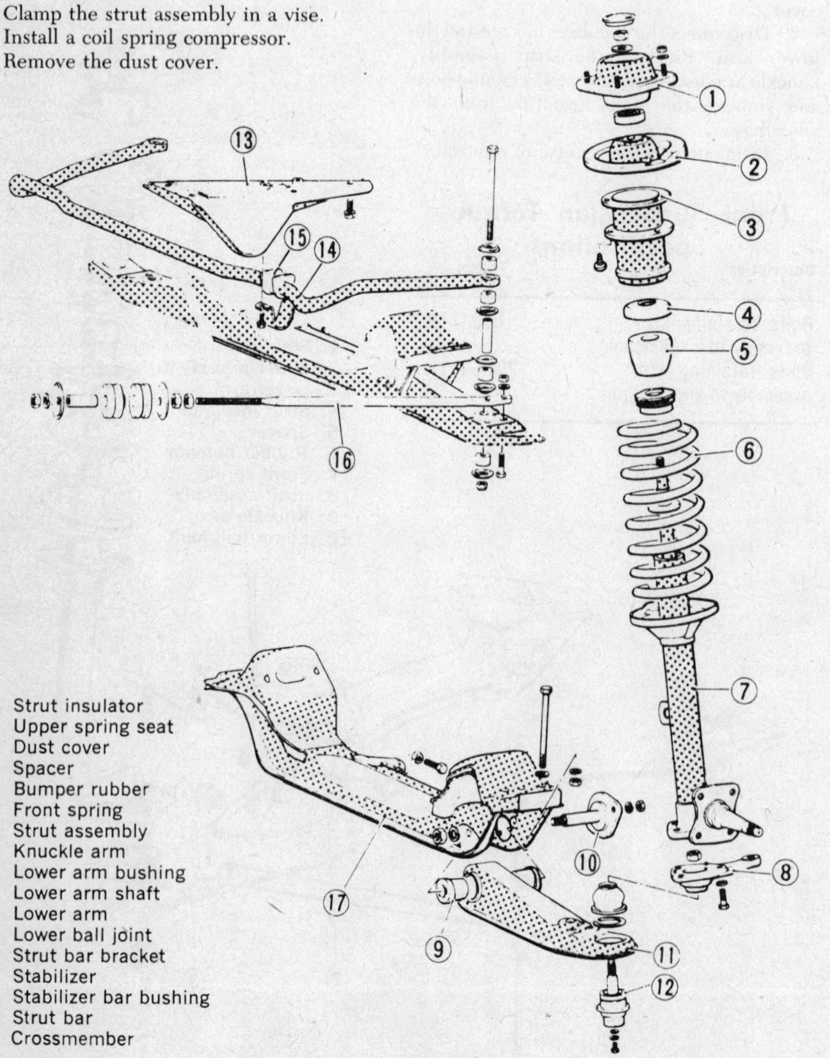

1. Strut insulator
2. Upper spring seat
3. Dust cover
4. Spacer
5. Bumper rubber
6. Front spring
7. Strut assembly
8. Knuckle arm
9. Lower arm bushing
10. Lower arm shaft
11. Lower arm
12. Lower ball joint
13. Strut bar bracket
14. Stabilizer
15. Stabilizer bar bushing
16. Strut bar
17. Crossmember

Arrow front suspension

Ball Joint

REMOVAL AND INSTALLATION

NOTE: The ball joint on front wheel drive models may be replaced by removing the mounting nut from the front hub, separating the stud from the hub and removing the two control arm mounting nuts and bolts. Installation is reverse of removal.

1. Remove the strut assembly and tie rod.
2. Remove the lower arm ball joint dust seal by prying up the dust seal ring evenly with a screwdriver.
3. Remove the snap-ring using snap-ring pliers.
4. Using a ball joint remover and installer tool, press off the ball joint.
5. To install the ball joint, press the ball joint properly into the burred hole, with the ball joint and lower arm mating marks aligned.

Lower Control Arm

REMOVAL AND INSTALLATION

EXCEPT FRONT WHEEL DRIVE

1. After disconnecting the stabilizer ring from the lower arm, remove the strut assembly.
2. Disconnect the steering knuckle arm and the tie rod ball joint.
3. Using the knuckle arm puller, disconnect the knuckle arm and the lower arm ball joint.
4. Remove the bolts holding the lower arm to the sub-frame, and remove the lower arm assembly.

Installation is the reverse of removal.

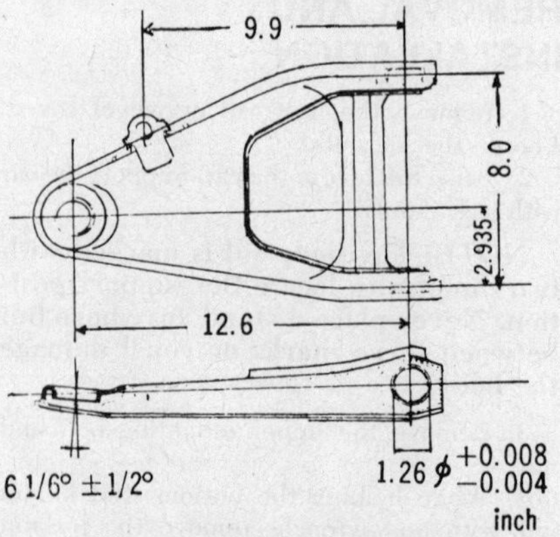

Alignment of the lower arm

FRONT WHEEL DRIVE MODELS

1. Remove lower ball joint (two bolts) and strut bar (two bolts) from the lower control arm.

NOTE: It is not necessary to remove the ball joint from the front hub.

2. Remove inner mounting nut and bolt and remove control arm. Installation is the reverse of removal.

Front End Alignment

CASTER AND CAMBER

Caster is preset at the factory. It requires adjustment only if the suspension and steering linkage components are damaged, in which case, repair is accomplished by replacing the damaged part. A slight caster adjustment can be made by moving the nuts on the front anchors of the strut bars.

TOE-IN

Toe-in is the difference in the distance between the front wheels, as measured at both the front and the rear of the front tires.

Toe-in is adjusted by turning the tie rod turnbuckles as necessary. The turnbuckles should always be tightened or loosened the same amount for both tie rods; the difference in length between the two tie rods should not exceed 0.2 in. On the Challenger and Sapporo, only the left tie rod is adjustable.

STEERING

Steering Wheel

REMOVAL AND INSTALLATION

1. Pry off the steering wheel center foam pad.
2. Remove the steering wheel retaining nut.

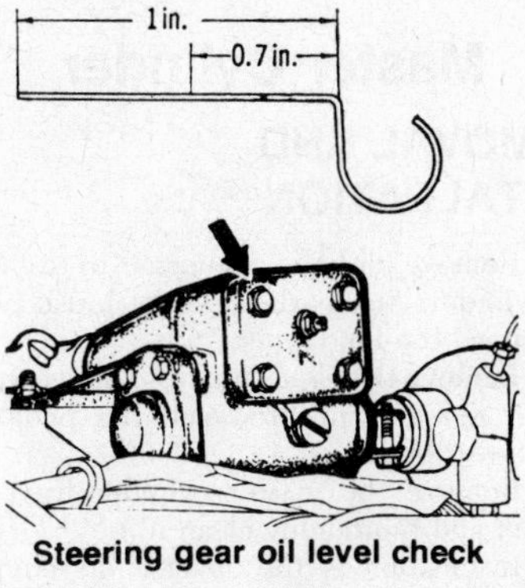

Steering gear oil level check

3. Using a steering wheel puller, remove the wheel.
4. Be sure the front wheels are in a straight ahead position. Reverse the removal procedure.

Manual Steering Gear

REMOVAL AND INSTALLATION

1. Remove the clamp bolt connecting the steering shaft with the steering gear housing mainshaft. Check for or make mating marks for the assembly.
2. Using appropriate pullers, disconnect the pitman arm and the relay rod at the linkage connection.
3. Remove the gearbox from the frame by removal of the attaching bolts.
4. Remove the pitman arm from the cross shaft. Check for mating marks.
5. Installation is the reverse of removal.

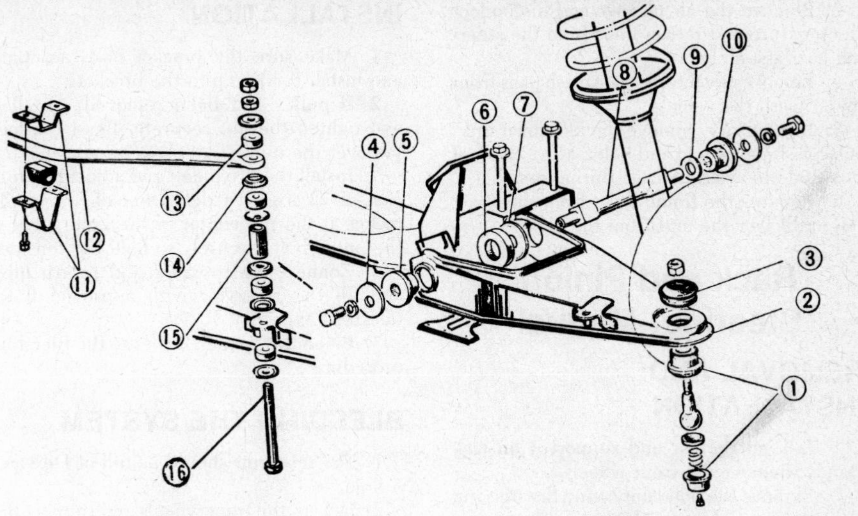

1. Joint assembly
2. Lower arm
3. Joint cover
4. Washer
5. Bushing (front)
6. Stopper rubber
7. Stopper washer
8. Lower arm shaft
9. Spacer
10. Bushing (rear)
11. Stabilizer fixture
12. Stabilizer
13. Rubber bushing
14. Seat
15. Collar
16. Stabilizer bolt

Lower arm

ADJUSTMENT

1. Measure the mainshaft preload with an inch pound torque wrench. The allowable torque is 3-4.8 in/lbs.
2. The preload torque is corrected by reducing or increasing the number of shims under the end plate.
3. Seat the cross shaft and bearings by turning the steering mainshaft and the adjusting bolt two or three times.
4. Tighten the adjusting bolt to obtain zero free-play with the cross shaft in the center position. Tighten the locknut on the adjusting bolt.

Power Steering Gear

Beginning 1978, power steering became available with the 2600 cc engine.

The power steering consists of a belt driven pump, a separate fluid reservoir, pressure and return lines, and a steering gear assembly with an integral control valve.

REMOVAL

1. Matchmark and disconnect the steering shaft from the gearbox main shaft.
2. Disconnect the tie rod end and pitman arm from the relay rod.

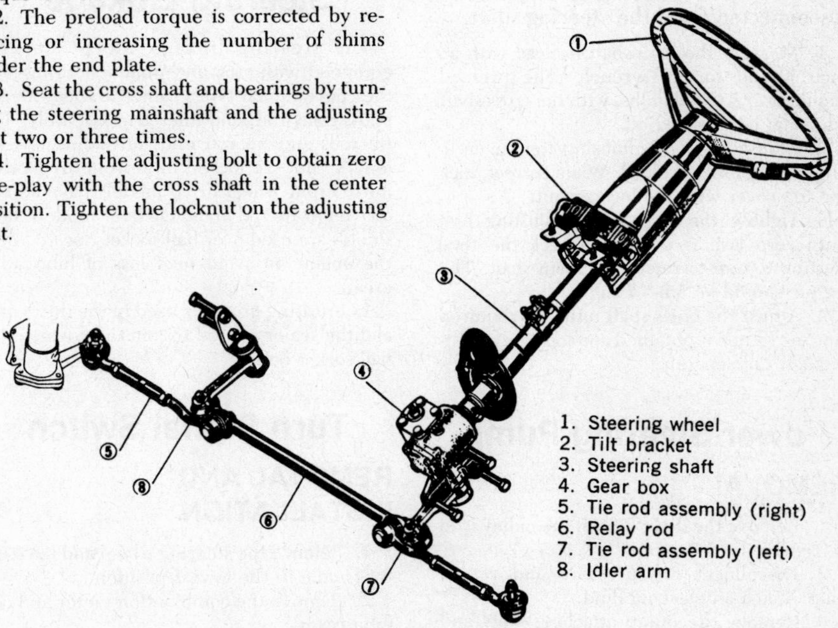

1. Steering wheel
2. Tilt bracket
3. Steering shaft
4. Gear box
5. Tie rod assembly (right)
6. Relay rod
7. Tie rod assembly (left)
8. Idler arm

Steering system

3. Remove the air cleaner and disconnect the pressure and return lines from the steering gear assembly.
4. Remove any interfering splash pans from underneath the vehicle.
5. If necessary, remove the kickdown linkage splash pan shield and bolts. Move the fuel line aside to avoid damage during removal.
6. Remove the frame bolts from the gearbox and lower the unit from the vehicle.

Rack and Pinion Steering–Manual

REMOVAL AND INSTALLATION

1. Jack up the car and support it on jack stands. Remove the front wheels.
2. Remove the bolt connecting the steering shaft universal joint with the steering gear. Before removing the bolt, mark its location and be sure the wheels are pointed straight.
3. Remove the tie rod ends from the hub knuckles. Disconnect mounting bolts (four) located near the inner tie rods on the crossmember.
4. Installation is the reverse of removal.

INSTALLATION

1. Installation is the reverse of removal.
2. Fill the reservoir with Dexron® A fluid and air bleed the system. (Refer to the bleeding procedure).
3. Start the engine and inspect for leakage.

CAUTION

When installing the pressure and return hoses, be careful not to twist or strip the fittings and pipes. Route the lines so as not to interfere with adjacent parts.

ADJUSTMENT

NOTE: The steering gear must be disconnected from the steering shaft.

1. Measure the mainshaft preload with an inch pound torque wrench. The preload should be 3.5 to 6.9 in/lbs, with the cross shaft adjusting bolt backed off.
2. Adjust the valve housing top cover to obtain the proper preload. When correct, lock the top cover with the locking nut.
3. Tighten the cross shaft adjusting bolt until zero lash is present. Check the total starting torque to rotate the main shaft. The torque should be 5.2-8.7 in/lbs.
4. Adjust the cross shaft until the required starting torque is obtained and lock the adjusting bolt nut securely.

Power Steering Pump

REMOVAL

1. Remove the drive belt. If the pulley is to be removed, do so now.
2. Disconnect the pressure and return lines. Catch any leaking fluid.
3. Remove the pump attaching bolts and lift the pump from the brackets.

INSTALLATION

1. Make sure the bracket bolts are tight and install the pump to the brackets.
2. If pulley had been removed, install it and tighten the nut securely. Bend the lock tab over the nut.
3. Install the drive belt and adjust to a tension of 22 lbs at a deflection of .28 to .39 inches at the top center of the belt. Tighten the pump bolts securely to hold the tension.
4. Connect the pressure and return lines and fill the reservoir with approved fluid. (Dexron® type A.)
5. Bleed the system. (Refer to the Bleeding procedure.)

BLEEDING THE SYSTEM

1. The reservoir should be full of Dexron® A fluid.
2. Jack up the front wheels and support the vehicle safely.
3. Turn the steering wheel fully to the right and left until no air bubbles apear in the fluid. Maintain the reservoir level.
4. Lower the vehicle and with the engine idling, turn the wheels fully to the right and left. Stop the engine.
5. Install a tube from the bleeder screw on the steering gear box to the reservoir.
6. Start the engine, turn the steering wheel fully to the left and loosen the bleeder screw.
7. Repeat the procedure until no air bubbles pass through the tube.
8. Tighten the bleeder screw and remove the tube. Refill the reservoir as needed, and check that no further bubbles are present in the fluid.

CAUTION

An abrupt rise in the fluid level after stopping the engine is a sign of incomplete bleeding. This will cause noise from the pump or control valve.

Steering Linkage

The steering linkage except on cars equipped with rack and pinion steering is of the conventional type, using tie rods, tie rod ends, relay rod, and idler arm assembly. The tie rods and tie rod ends are adjustable for length, and are locked in position by locking nuts. Front wheel drive models have adjustable outer tie rod ends. On later models, heat shields are used over ball sockets located near the engine to avoid heat loss of lubricating grease.

Lubricating grease is used in the dust cover and the sealer is used to join the cover to the ball socket body.

Turn Signal Switch

REMOVAL AND INSTALLATION

1. Remove the steering wheel and have the tilt handle in the lowest position.
2. Remove the combination meter and column cover.
3. Remove the connectors from the column switch, and the column switch from the column tube.

NOTE: Early models may have the turn signal and hazard switches mounted on a base plate. Removal of the attaching screws will allow these switches to be removed without removal of the remaining switches.

4. Switch installation is the reverse of removal. Be sure that the switch is centered in the column or self-cancelling will be affected.

Ignition Lock and Switch

REMOVAL AND INSTALLATION

1. Cut a notch in the lock bracket bolt head with a hacksaw.
2. Remove the bolt and lock.
3. Remove the column cover and unbolt and remove the ignition switch.
4. Install both lock and switch in reverse of removal.

NOTE: When installing lock, the bolt should be tightened until the head is crushed. When installing switch, install the switch bolt loosely and insert and work the key a few times to make sure everything checks out before tightening the bolt.

BRAKES

Adjustment

The front disc brakes require no periodic adjustment. All models have self adjusting rear brakes.

Master Cylinder

REMOVAL AND INSTALLATION

1. Remove all lines connected to the master cylinder. Slowly depress the brake pedal to remove the fluid.
2. Remove the clevis pin from between the master cylinder pushrod and the pedal on non-power brakes.
3. Remove the master cylinder from the firewall and thoroughly clean it.
4. Installation is the reverse of removal. Bleed the brakes.

OVERHAUL

Refer to the exploded view. Do not disassemble the primary piston.

Combination Valve

The combination valve has three functions:
a. rear brake pressure control
b. warning light control
c. differential failure control

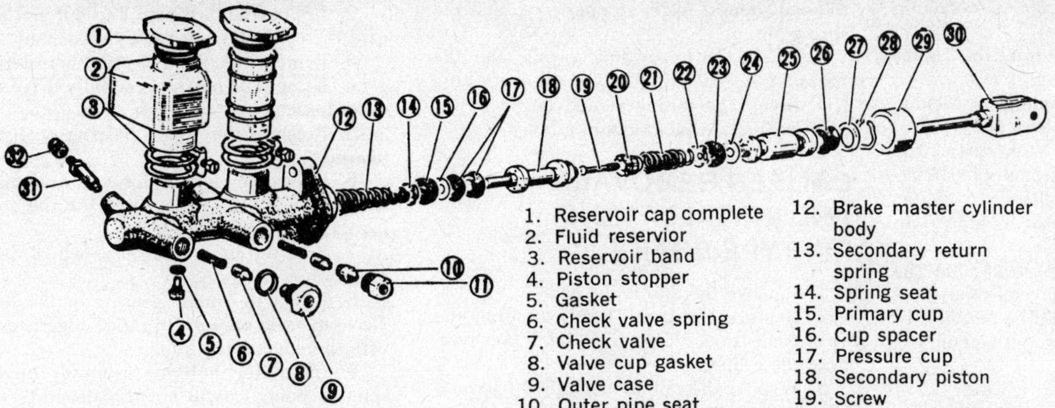

1. Reservoir cap complete
2. Fluid reservior
3. Reservoir band
4. Piston stopper
5. Gasket
6. Check valve spring
7. Check valve
8. Valve cup gasket
9. Valve case
10. Outer pipe seat
11. Check valve cap
12. Brake master cylinder body
13. Secondary return spring
14. Spring seat
15. Primary cup
16. Cup spacer
17. Pressure cup
18. Secondary piston
19. Screw
20. Spring seat (B)
21. Primary return spring
22. Spring seat (A)
23. Primary cup
24. Cup spacer
25. Primary piston
26. Secondary cup
27. Piston stopper
28. Stopper ring
29. Master cylinder boots
30. Pushrod assembly

Exploded view of master cylinder

REMOVAL AND INSTALLATION

NOTE: The valve should not be disassembled. If it is faulty, replace it.

1. Disconnect and plug brake lines at the valve.
2. Remove the valve.
3. Install the valve and tighten the attaching bolts to 6-9 ft/lbs. Tighten the brake tube nuts to 9-12 ft/lbs.

System Bleeding

1. Check the master cylinder fluid level.
2. Remove the cap from the bleeder screw of the wheel farthest from the master cylinder.

NOTE: Some 1976 and later models don't have a bleeder fitting on the left rear brake. Both rear brakes must be bled at the right brake.

3. Connect a length of rubber tubing to the screw and place the other end in a jar half full of clean brake fluid.
4. Pump the brake pedal until no bubbles are visible in the container.
5. Hold the pedal in the depressed position and tighten the screw. Replace the cap and proceed to each wheel in turn.

NOTE: Periodically check the master cylinder during the bleeding operation to check the fluid level does not go too low. If it does, air will enter the master cylinder and it will have to be bled as well.

Front Disc Brakes

Sliding caliper type disc brakes are used on station wagons, Challenger, and Sapporo. All others have pin type brakes.

BRAKE PAD REMOVAL AND INSTALLATION–PIN TYPE BRAKE

1. Remove the wheel.
2. Remove the protector.
3. Holding the center of the clip detach it

1. Pin retaining clip
2. Pad retaining pin
3. Connector bolt
4. Gasket
5. Connector
6. Gasket
7. Caliper seal
8. Bleeder cap
9. Bleeder screw
10. Cross-spring
11. Pad shim
12. Retaining ring
13. Dust seal
14. Front brake piston
15. Piston seal
16. Caliper (outer)
17. Caliper (inner)
18. Pad assembly

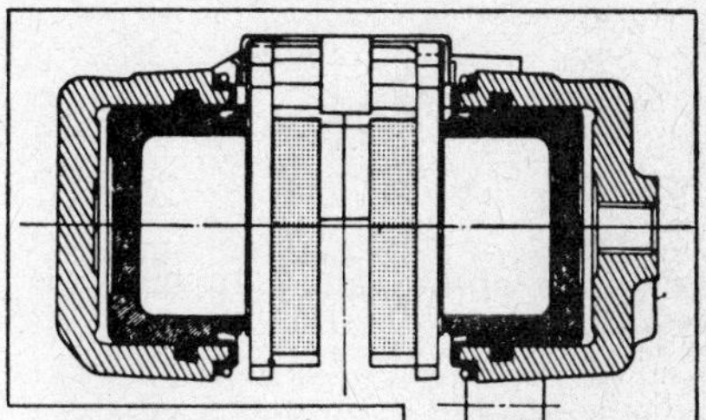

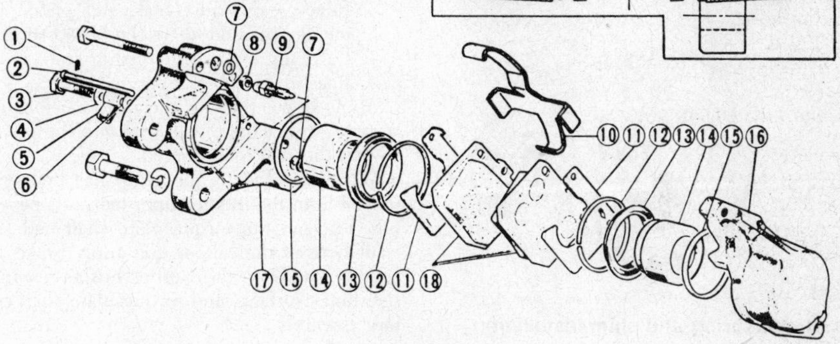

Early disc brake

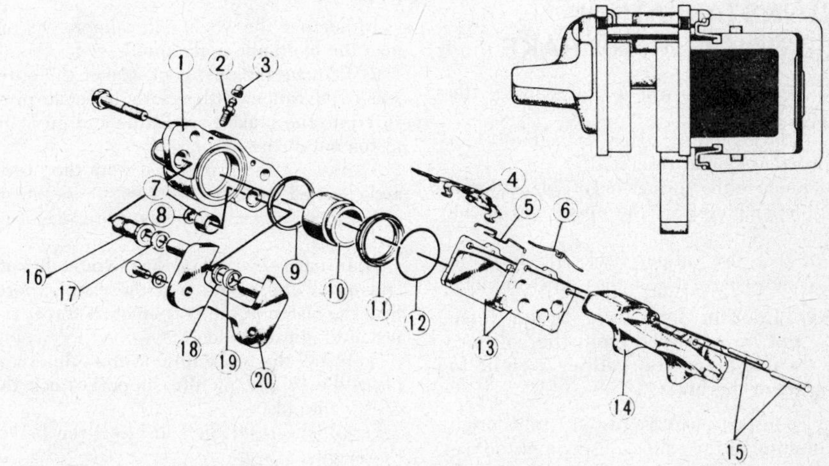

1. Inner caliper
2. Bleeder screw
3. Bleeder screw cap
4. Pad protector
5. Spring
6. Clip
7. Torque plate pin cap
8. Cap plug
9. Piston seal
10. Piston
11. Dust seal
12. Retaining ring
13. Pad assembly
14. Outer caliper
15. Pad retaining pin
16. Torque plate pin bushing
17. Spacer
18. Wiper seal retainer
19. Wiper seal
20. Torque plate

Pin type disc brakes

from the pad and its ends from the retaining pins. Remove the clip.

4. Pull the retaining pins from the caliper assembly. Remove the spring.

5. Remove the pad by holding the backing plate area of the pad with pliers.

6. To replace the brake pad, spread the piston and insert the pad through the shim.

7. Install the spring and clip.

8. Install the pad protector in proper direction.

9. Check the brake drag torque after the brakes have been applied several times on a test drive. The torque should be 39 in/lbs or less, measured at a wheel mounting bolt.

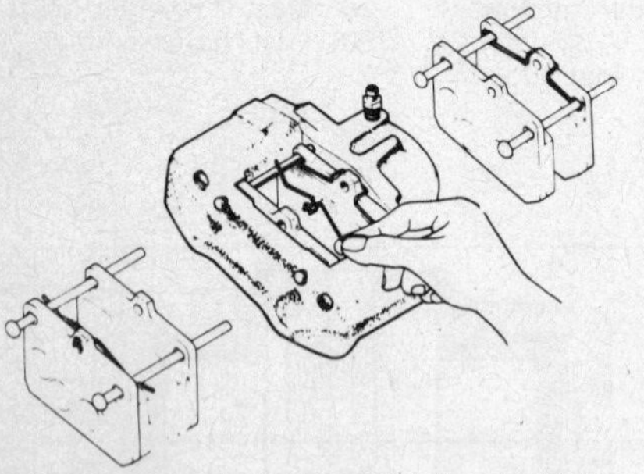

Disc brake spring and clip installation—pin type

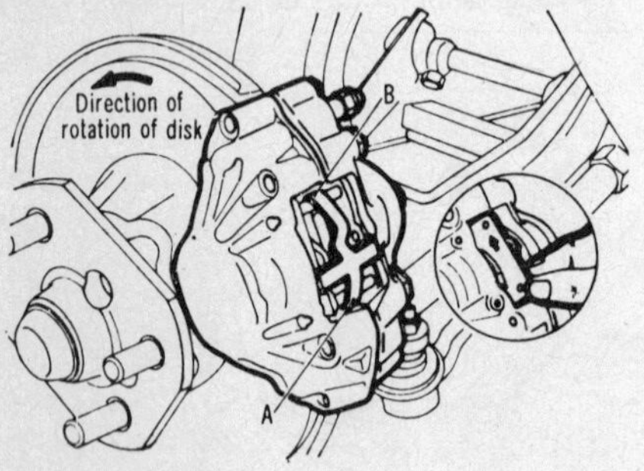

Cross-spring and shim installation

BRAKE PAD REMOVAL AND INSTALLATION–SLIDING CALIPER BRAKE

1. Remove the wheel and expose the caliper.

2. Remove approximately ½ the fluid from the master cylinder reservoir.

3. Remove the spring (spigot) pin and pull the stopper plug from the upper end of the caliper.

4. Move the caliper back and forth to loosen and remove it from the caliper support.

NOTE: The hydraulic brake hose need not be removed from the caliper, but do not allow the caliper weight to hang from the hose.

5. To install, push the piston into its original position in the caliper, using a piston expander tool or a hammer handle.

NOTE: The bleeder may have to be opened to allow the piston to bottom.

6. Install the pads, pad clip B, and pad clips inner and outer.

7. Slip the caliper over the pads and install the pad support plate, stopper plug, and the spring pin.

8. Check the brake drag torque after the brakes have been applied several times on a test drive. The torque should be 26 in/lbs, measured at a wheel mounting bolt.

CALIPER REMOVAL AND INSTALLATION–PIN TYPE BRAKE

1. Remove the disc brake pad.

2. Remove the brake hose clip from the strut area, then disconnect the brake hose from the caliper.

3. Remove the caliper assembly by loosening torque plate and adapter mounting bolts.

4. Installation is the reverse of removal. If the brake pedal stroke is excessively long, remove the brake pad and replace it with a piece of metal about the same size. Press the piston into the caliper about ⅛ in. Reinstall the brake pad and pump the pedal several times. Repeat until the pedal stroke is normal.

CALIPER OVERHAUL–PIN TYPE BRAKE

1. Remove the caliper.

2. Separate the two caliper halves.

3. Remove the dust seal, and piston by applying compressed air to the hose fitting.

4. Carefully remove the piston seal.

5. Reassemble the caliper.

Apply brake fluid to the piston before assembly. Insert the piston seal into the piston so that the seal isn't twisted.

Whenever the torque plate has been removed from the inner caliper half, it is necessary to clean the torque plate shaft and the shaft bore of the caliper and apply brake assembly grease to the rubber bushing, wiper seal inner surface, and torque plate shaft before assembly.

CALIPER OVERHAUL–SLIDING CALIPER BRAKE

1. Remove the wheel and caliper. Disconnect the hydraulic brake line.

2. Remove the dust boot. Cover the outer side of the caliper with a cloth, inject air pressure into the brake hose fitting and push the piston out of the caliper.

3. Remove the piston seal from the piston and clean all parts.

4. Hone the caliper piston bore, if necessary.

5. Install a new seal on the piston, lubricate and install the piston into the caliper bore. Seat the piston at the bottom of its travel and install the dust shield.

6. Install the brake hose to the caliper and place the caliper on the support. Lock the caliper into place.

7. Fill the reservoir and bleed the brakes thoroughly.

BRAKE DISC AND WHEEL BEARING

Removal and Installation

1. Remove the caliper.

2. Pry off the dust cap. Tap out and discard the cotter pin. Remove the locknut.

3. Remove the brake disc and wheel hub.

4. Using a brass drift, carefully drive the outer bearing race out of the hub.

5. Remove the inner bearing seal and bearing.

6. Check the bearings for wear or damage and replace them if necessary. Drift the bearing race into place in the hub.

7. Pack the inner and outer wheel bearings with grease.

8. Install the inner bearing in the hub. Drive the seal on until its outer edge is even with the edge of the hub.

9. Install the hub/disc assembly on the spindle, being careful not to damage the oil seal.

10. Install the outer bearing, washer, and spindle nut. Adjust the bearing.

Adjustment

1. Tighten the spindle nut to 15 ft/lbs and then loosen it.

2. Tighten the nut to 4 ft/lbs.

3. Install the cap on the nut. Do not back off the nut more than 15° for cotter pin hole-to-slot alignment.

Rear Drum Brakes

BRAKE SHOE AND WHEEL CYLINDER REMOVAL AND INSTALLATION

1975-81 Rear Wheel Drive

1. Remove the wheel and the brake drum.

2. Disconnect the strut to shoe spring and shoe return spring (upper) end hook from the trailing shoe.

3. Remove the brake shoe assembly together with the shoe return spring.

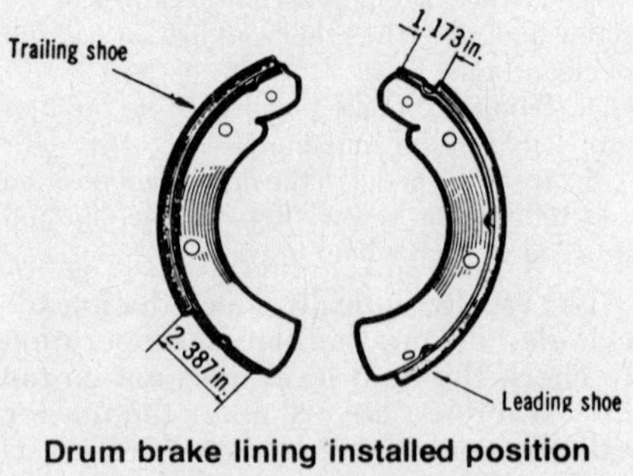

Drum brake lining installed position

4. Pull the adjusting lever toward the center of the brake while holding the adjusting latch downward. Remove the leading shoe assembly.

5. Remove the strut to shoe spring and the shoe return spring (upper).

6. The wheel cylinder can be removed from the backing plate.

7. Remove the parking brake extension lever and strut from the backing plate, if necessary.

On installation:

1. Install the parking brake extension lever and strut, if previously removed.

2. Install the wheel cylinder, if removed.

3. Lubricate the contact surfaces on the backing plate, wheel cylinder piston ends, anchor plate shoe contact surfaces, and the parking brake strut joints and contact surfaces.

4. Install the adjusting lever and latch spring assembly on the leading shoe.

NOTE: The adjusting lever and the latch spring are different for right and left.

5. Install the brake shoes in position on the backing plate with the upper and lower springs in place. Install the top shoe to shoe spring. Make sure the top web of the shoe is in the slot of the wheel cylinder piston and the bottom of the shoe web is against the anchor block with the lower shoe to shoe spring in place.

6. Set the amount of engagement of the adjusting lever with the strut, by pulling the adjusting lever fully toward the center of the brake.

7. Install the strut to shoe spring to the strut.

NOTE: The strut to shoe springs differ in color from side to side; left–white and right–neutral color.

8. Return the adjusting lever until it touches the shoe rim.

9. Bleed the brake system. Maintain the reservoir level.

10. The lining to drum clearance is automatically adjusted by applying the brakes several times. The adjuster is designed to operate when approximately .003 inch of lining wear occurs.

1979-81 Front Wheel Drive Models

1. Remove the wheel and the brake drum.
2. Remove the lower clip spring and the large shoe return spring. Remove the shoe to shoe lower spring and the two hold-down springs.
3. Remove the shoes and the adjuster as an assembly. Disconnect the parking brake cable from the shoe lever.
4. The wheel cylinder can now be removed by disconnecting the brake line and removing the two mounting bolts.
5. Release spring pressure on the adjuster and turn the star wheel in. Reinstall the adjuster between the new brake shoes, connect the parking brake cable and reverse the removal procedure to replace the brakes.
6. Make sure the parking brake adjustment is not interfering with the adjuster, back off on the hand brake adjustment if necessary.
7. The shoe adjustment is made by pulling and releasing the parking brake and depressing and releasing the brake pedal. If the wheel cylinders have been replaced or rebuilt, be sure to bleed the brake system. Adjust the parking brake lever after all other system service is completed.

Rear Disc Brakes

SLIDING CALIPER TYPE

The caliper support is mounted on the rear axle housing. The support consists of an anti-rattle spring used to keep the caliper "floating", and a stopper plate installed between

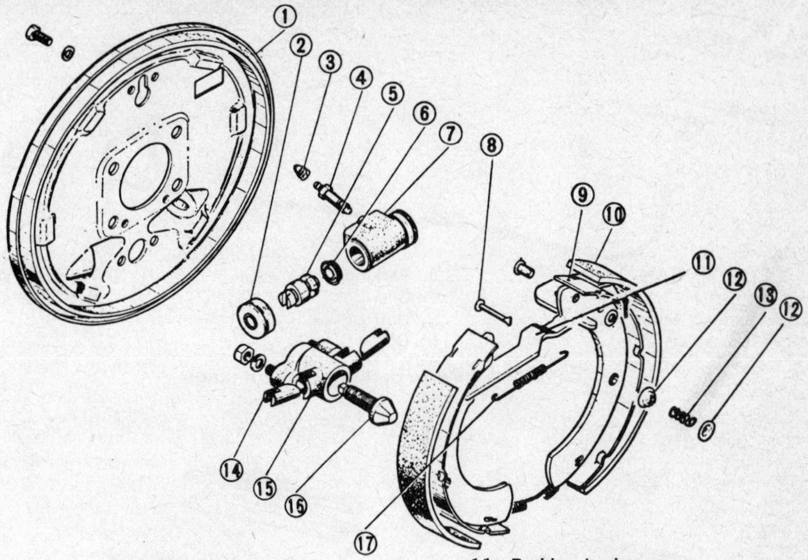

1. Backing plate
2. Wheel cylinder boot
3. Bleeder screw cap
4. Bleeder screw
5. Wheel cylinder piston
6. Piston cup
7. Wheel cylinder body
8. Shoe hold-down spring pin
9. Brake shoe assembly
10. Brake lining
11. Parking brake extension lever
12. Shoe hold-down spring seat
13. Shoe hold-down spring
14. Slack adjuster anchor
15. Slack adjuster body
16. Slack adjuster
17. Shoe return spring

Exploded view of the rear brakes

the caliper body and the support on which the caliper body slides. The rear caliper has the parking brake mechanism, which contains an automatic adjuster to keep the parking brake stroke constant, built into the caliper.

BRAKE PAD REPLACEMENT

1. Remove the rear wheel and the caliper dust cover.
2. Disconnect the parking brake cable.
3. Remove the spring pin and stopper plug.
4. Move the caliper back and forth to loosen, then remove the caliper from the support.

NOTE: The brake hose need not be disconnected, however, do not suspend the weight of the caliper from the hose.

5. Take time to examine the location of the various clips and springs. Remove the pads from the support. Do not mix up the inner and outer clips, they must be installed in the same location.

6. Set the caliper piston by pushing in while turning clockwise (use a special tool). Install new pads into the support and reinstall the caliper.

CALIPER OVERHAUL–REAR DISC BRAKES

1. Remove caliper from support after disconnecting the brake hose.
2. Remove the clevis pin connecting the parking brake lever.
3. Remove the ring that retains the lever cap and remove the cap. Remove the lever assembly.
4. Remove the automatic adjuster spindle by turning.
5. Remove the piston boot and the piston. Remove the seal from the piston and clean all parts.
6. Hone the caliper bore.
7. Install a new piston seal on the piston, lubricate and install into caliper. Seat the piston and install the dust shield (boot). Lubricate and install the adjuster spindle.

NOTE: When installing the adjuster spindle the spring washers must be in the proper direction, i.e. the first, nearest the piston, must curve toward the piston; the second, away from the piston; the third, toward and so on. It may be necessary to apply pressure while installing the lever cap and retaining ring.

Install the parking brake lever assembly by reversing the removal procedure.

8. Install the caliper, connect the brake hose and bleed the brakes.

REAR DISC ROTOR REPLACEMENT

1. Remove caliper, brake pads and support.
2. Remove retaining bolts.
3. Remove rotor. Installation is reverse of removal.

Parking Brake

ADJUSTMENT

1975-76

1. Release the brake cable.

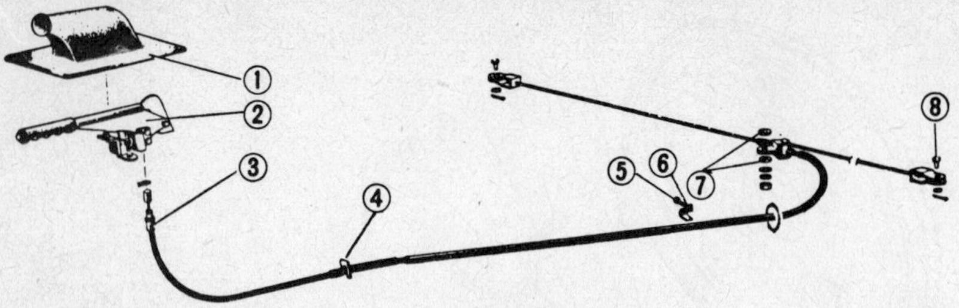

1. Parking brake lever cover
2. Parking brake lever assembly
3. Parking brake cable
4. Clip
5. Bolt
6. Clip
7. Bushing
8. Clevis pin

Exploded view of parking brake linkage

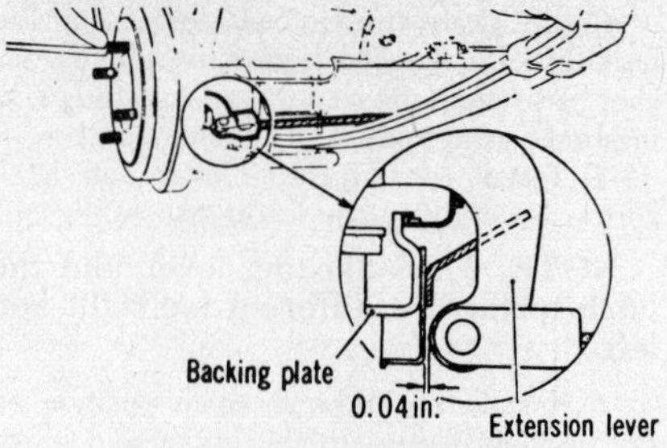

Parking brake adjustment

2. Loosen the adjusting nuts on either side of the cable.
3. Move the cable lever to each side and tighten the nuts to the tension.
4. Cable tightening should provide back plate and extension lever clearance of *less* than 0.04 in.
5. Be certain the drum does not contact the lining. Standard parking brake lever travel is 10 notches.

1977-79 Coupe, Sedan, and Hatchback

1. Release the parking brake.
2. Adjust the extension lever to backing plate clearance to .008-.080 inch, by moving the adjustment nut on the cable.
3. Check the brake lever free stroke. Brake drag should occur at 6 to 8 notches.

1977-79 Station Wagon

1. Release the parking brake.
2. Adjust the extension lever to stopper clearance to 0.100 inch by loosening both cable lever attaching bolts and adjusting nut. Move the cable lever to the right. Set the left cable first and then the right.
3. Check the brake lever free stroke. Brake drag should occur at 5 to 7 notches.

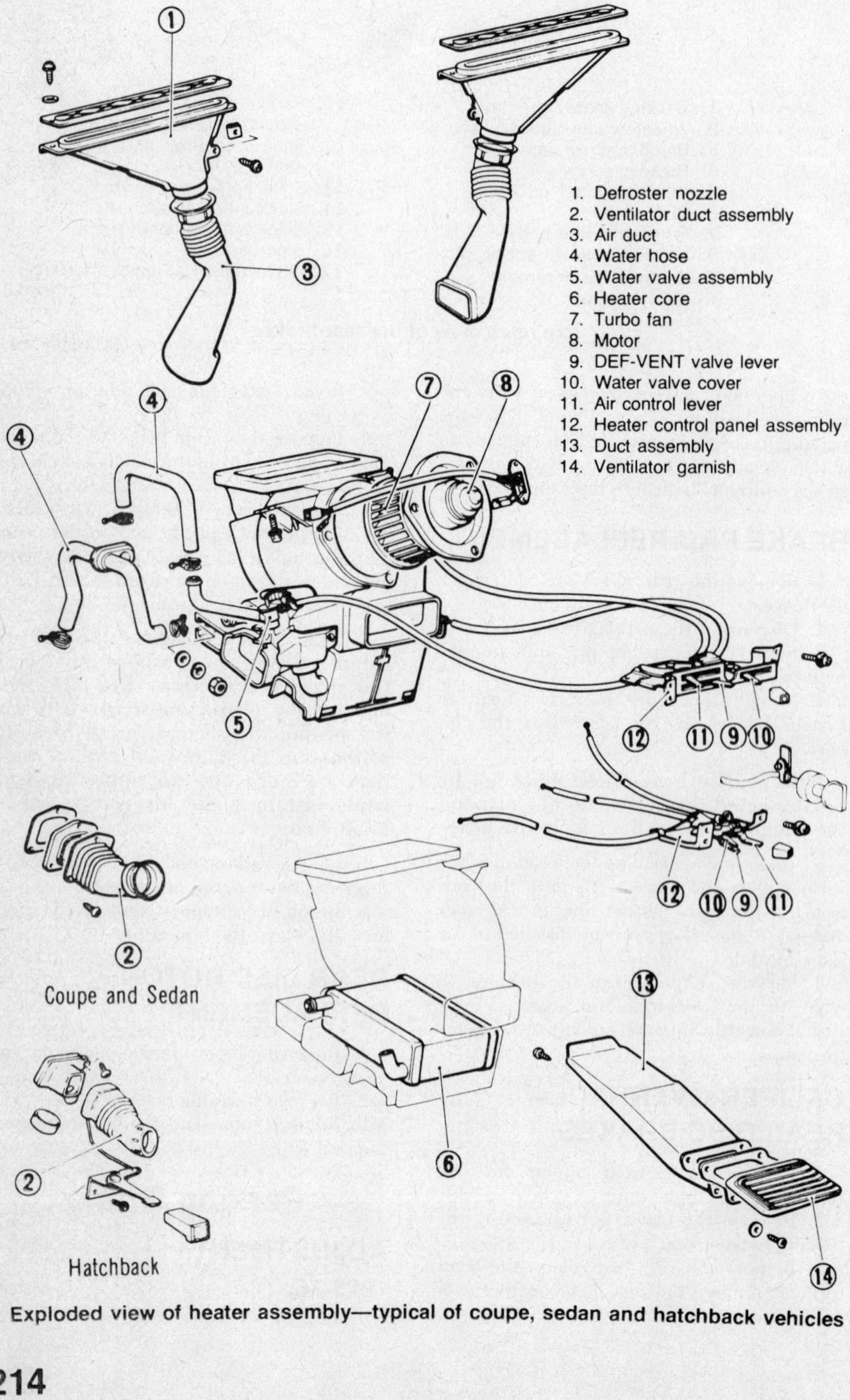

1. Defroster nozzle
2. Ventilator duct assembly
3. Air duct
4. Water hose
5. Water valve assembly
6. Heater core
7. Turbo fan
8. Motor
9. DEF-VENT valve lever
10. Water valve cover
11. Air control lever
12. Heater control panel assembly
13. Duct assembly
14. Ventilator garnish

Exploded view of heater assembly—typical of coupe, sedan and hatchback vehicles

CHASSIS ELECTRICAL

Heater Blower Motor

REMOVAL AND INSTALLATION

1975-76

The heater is located directly under the center of the dashboard.

1. Unplug the two electrical leads from the motor.
2. Remove the three retaining screws and remove the motor.
3. Install the motor in the reverse order of removal.

1977-81 Coupe, Sedan, and Hatchback

1. Remove the instrument cluster (coupe and sedan). Remove the instrument cluster and the glove box (hatchback).
2. Remove the heater control bracket assembly.

3. Remove the motor assembly and disconnect the wire connection.
4. (Coupe and sedan) Remove the motor in a horizontal position while holding the control bracket down.
5. (Hatchback) Remove the motor through the glove box opening.
6. Installation is the reverse of removal.

1977-81 Station Wagon

1. Remove the instrument cluster and the meter cluster.
2. Disconnect the wiring to the motor.
3. Remove the motor assembly.
4. Installation is reverse of removal.

Heater Unit

NOTE: The 1975-76 models use an air conditioner evaporator and blower unit that is not integral with the heating system. To remove the heater assembly, it may be necessary to first remove or loosen various parts of the air conditioner unit.

REMOVAL AND INSTALLATION

1975-81 Coupe, Sedan and Hatchback

1. Drain the cooling system.
2. Disconnect the battery ground cable.
3. Place the water valve in the OFF position.
4. Remove the under tray, defroster nozzle and console box.
5. Disconnect each heater control wire and connectors at the heater assembly.
6. Disconnect the water hoses, heater duct and wiring harness.
7. Remove the heater assembly.
8. Installation is the reverse of removal.

1974-81 Hardtop and Station Wagon

1. Drain the cooling system.
2. Remove the glove box, instrument cluster and console assembly.
3. Disconnect the heater control wires at the heater box.
4. Remove the heater control assembly.
5. Disconnect all heater hoses and air ducts.
6. Remove the heater assembly.
7. The installation is in the reverse of the removal procedure.

NOTE: Upon removal of the heater control box, the heater core is removable. Replace all gaskets and insulation in its proper place.

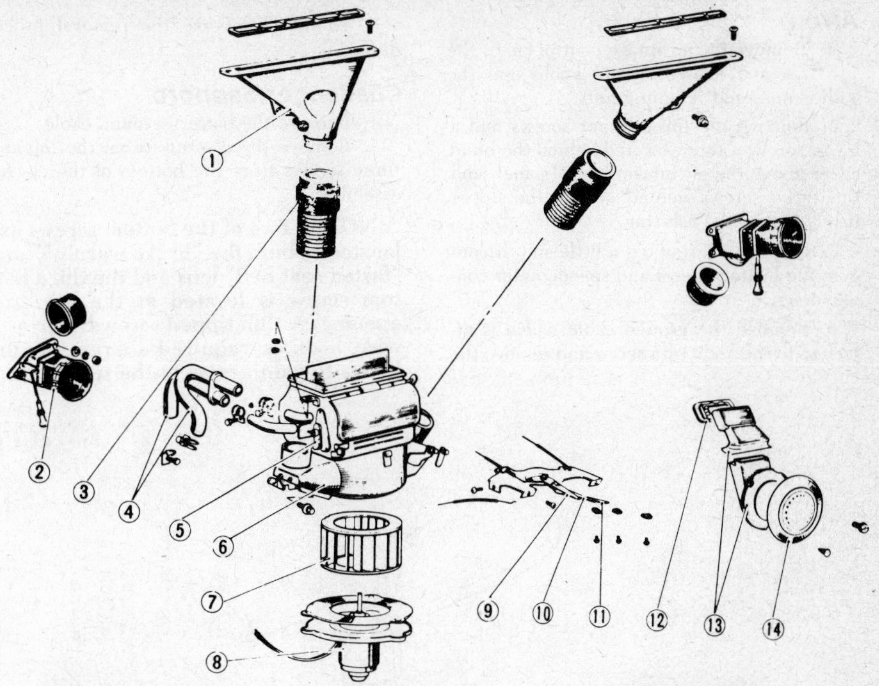

1. Defroster nozzle
2. Ventilator duct assembly
3. Air duct
4. Water hose
5. Water valve assembly
6. Heater assembly
7. Turbo fan
8. Motor
9. Heater-defroster lever
10. Water valve lever
11. Air control lever
12. Valve (Hardtop)
13. Duct assembly (Hardtop)
14. Ventilator garnish (Hardtop)

Exploded view of heater assembly—typical of hardtop and station wagon vehicles

Windshield Wipers

MOTOR AND LINKAGE

Removal and Installation

NOTE: The wiper motor may be located on either the right or left side of the front deck, depending upon the year and model. A wiper removing hole is provided to gain access to the linkage for removal purposes.

1. Remove the wiper arms. Remove the arm shaft locknuts and push in the shafts. Disconnect the electrical wiring.
2. Remove the bolts holding the motor bracket to the body and pull the wiper assembly outward and away from the body.
3. Hold the motor shaft and the linkage at right angles to each other and disconnect them. Remove the motor.
4. The linkages can be pulled from the opening in the front deck.
5. The installation is in the reverse of the removal, being sure to insert the linkage shaft bracket positioning boss positively in the hole provided in the body before tightening the wiper shaft nut.
6. Locate the wiper blades in the stopped position approximately ½ to ¾ inch above the bottom moulding or sealer of the windshield.

Radio

REMOVAL AND INSTALLATION

Colt

1. Remove glove box then loosen the knobs and attaching nuts on the front of the radio.
2. Remove speaker, antenna, and power wires from the back of the radio. Remove the radio attaching bracket and take out the radio.
3. Installation is the reverse of removal.

Arrow

1. Remove the instrument cluster.
2. Remove the radio knobs from the radio panel.
3. Remove the nuts from behind the knobs, the screw from the bracket and remove the radio (AM radio). Remove the bolts from under the brackets and remove the radio (AM/FM radio).

NOTE: The AM radio circuit fuse block is located on the right rear side of the radio, the AM/FM circuit fuse block is installed in the line with the power cable.

Instrument Cluster

REMOVAL AND INSTALLATION

Colt

NOTE: Disconnect the battery ground cable before cluster removal.

1. Loosen screws at the upper and lower part of the instrument cluster. Loosen the screws holding the heater control knobs, ash tray, and cigarette lighter from their respective brackets. Remove blind cover on the right side of the glove box and remove the attaching screws on the right side of the cluster.
2. Remove the harness cover at the bottom of the instrument panel and disconnect lighting switch and the instrument panel harness.
3. Pull the instrument panel cluster a little toward you, disconnect multiple connector, antenna feeder, speaker connector, heater fan connector and meter cables and then remove instrument cluster assembly.
4. Installation is the reverse of removal.

After the instrument cluster has been installed, draw out the meter cables as long as the marking tape can be seen from the engine compartment.

Arrow

1. Remove the air intake control knob, the ash tray and heater control knobs and the radio knobs and retaining nuts.

2. Remove the three upper screws and a lower screw, a screw located behind the blind cover above the air intake control panel, and the three screws behind and in the upper inside part of the ash tray.

3. Pull the ash tray out a little and disconnect the heater, meter and speedometer connectors.

4. Remove the ground cable which is attached to the body by a screw and remove the cluster.

5. To install reverse the removal procedure.

Challenger/Sapporo

1. Remove the battery ground cable.

2. Remove three screws from the top and three screws from the bottom of the cluster assembly.

NOTE: Two of the bottom screws are located behind the "brake warning" and "fasten seat belt" lens and the third bottom screw is located at the ash tray opening. A thin tipped screwdriver or a wire hook is required to remove the lenses to gain access to the screws.

3. Move the instrument cluster away from the dash and disconnect the meter connections, heater fan connections, speedometer cable and any other connector or ground cables.

4. Remove the cluster assembly from the dash.

5. Installation is the reverse of removal.

1978-81 Station Wagon

The instrument cluster hood is removed separately to expose the instrument cluster attaching screws. Remove the screws, attaching wires and cables, and remove the cluster from the dash. Install in the reverse of the removal procedure.

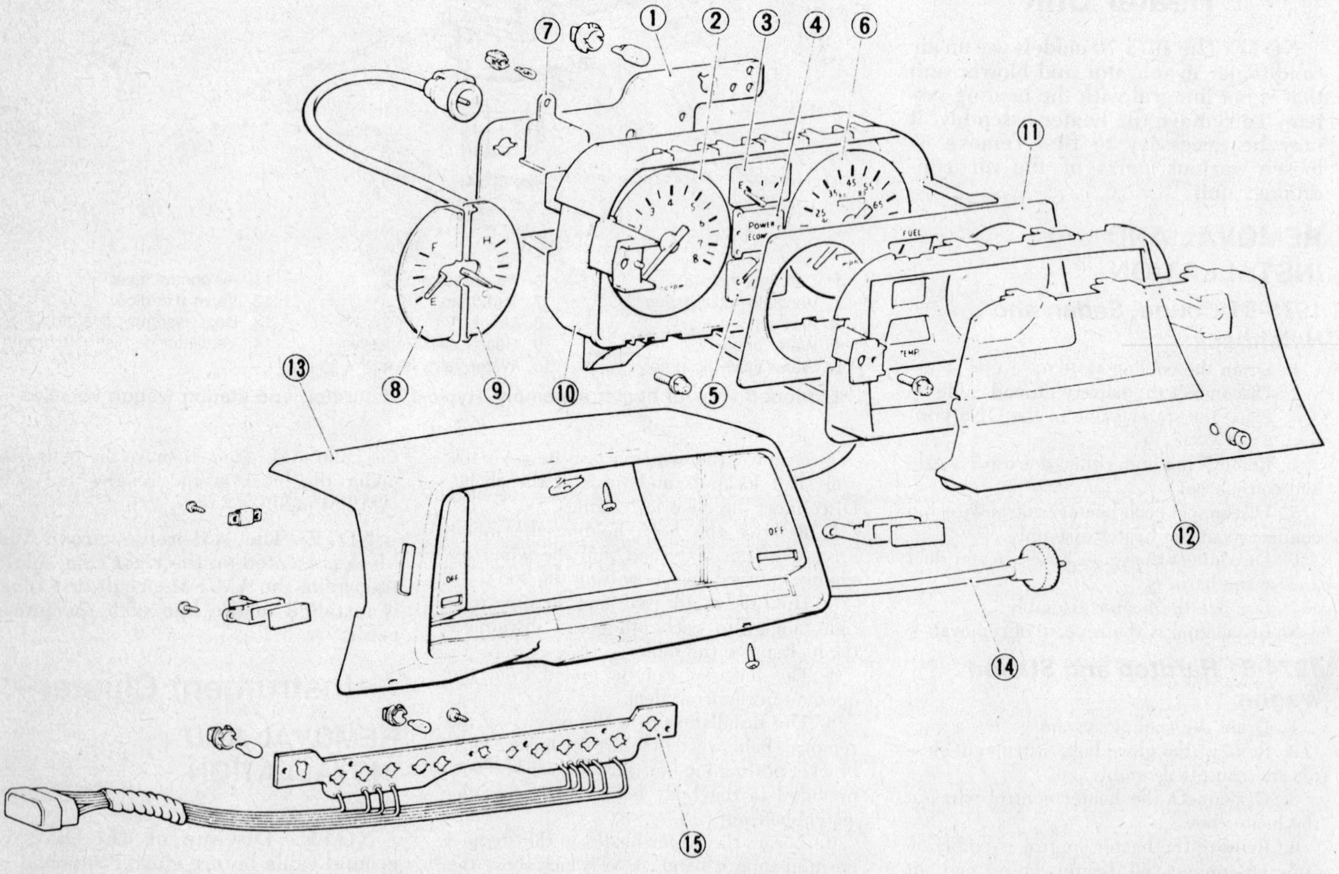

1. Printed circuit board
2. Tachometer
3. Fuel gauge
4. Select indicator
5. Temperature gauge
6. Speedometer
7. Chime
8. Fuel gauge
9. Temperature gauge
10. Instrument cluster case
11. Instrument cluster panel
12. Instrument cluster glass
13. Instrument cluster hood
14. Speedometer cable
15. Printed circuit board (for indicator)

Instrument cluster arrangement

SPECIFICATIONS

INDEX

BEFORE SERVICING, SEE THE SAFETY NOTICE ON THE CONTENTS PAGE

INTRODUCTION

Nissan Motor Company Limited, the producer of Datsun vehicles, was established in 1933. Nissan was Japan's first mass producer and exporter of cars and trucks. Datsun's rise to second place in imported car sales was based primarily on three models: the pick-up, the original 510, and the 240Z sports car. The pick-up has been the best selling truck of its type ever since its introduction, the 510 offered a host of usually expensive European features at an affordable Japanese price, and the 240Z similarly offered outstanding performance and style at moderate cost. Datsun has always been active in motorsports, consistently winning international rallies in Europe and Africa, and SCCA championships in this country.

SERIAL NUMBER IDENTIFICATION

Engine Number

The engine number is stamped on the right side top edge of the cylinder block. The engine serial number is preceded by the engine model code.

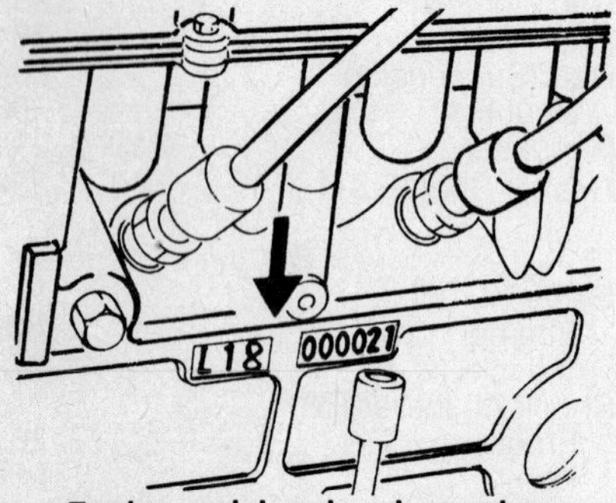

Engine serial and code number

ENGINE I.D. TABLE

Number of Cylinders	Displacement cu. in. (cc)	Type	Engine Model Code
4	119.1 (1952)	OHC	L20B
4	85.24 (1397)	OHV	A14
6	146 (2393)	OHC	L24
6	168 (2753)	OHC	L28
4	75.48 (1237)	OHV	A12A
4	90.80 (1488)	OHV	A15
4	119.1 (1952)	OHC	Z20S, Z20E

Chassis Number

The chassis number is on the firewall under the hood. On pickups, it is on top of the right frame member, in the engine compartment. Late model vehicles also have the chassis number on a plate attached to the top of the instrument panel on the driver's side. The chassis serial number is preceded by the model designation.

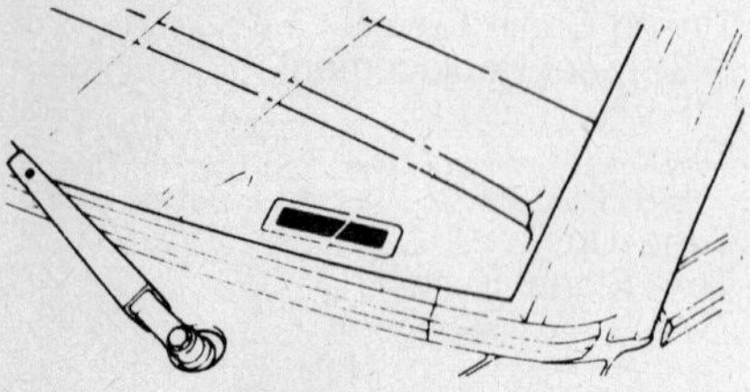

VIN location

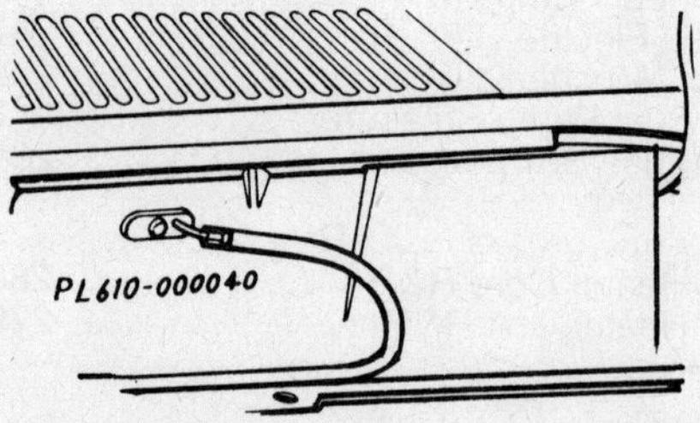

Chassis number location for all models except pickup

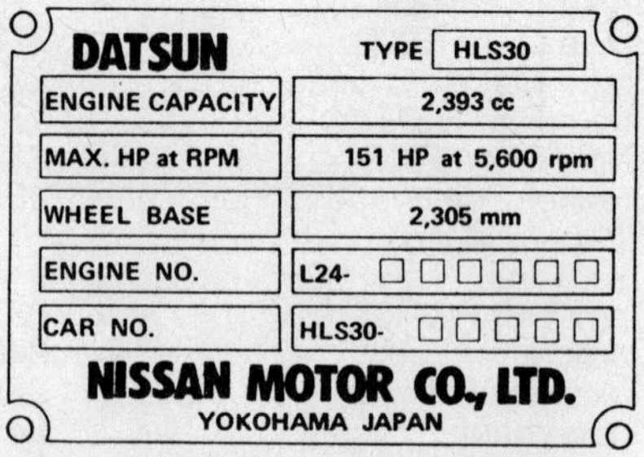
DATSUN
TYPE HLS30
ENGINE CAPACITY
2,393 cc
MAX. HP at RPM
151 HP at 5,600 rpm
WHEEL BASE
2,305 mm
ENGINE NO.
L24-
CAR NO.
HLS30-
NISSAN MOTOR CO., LTD.
YOKOHAMA JAPAN

Vehicle identification plate

VEHICLE IDENTIFICATION PLATE

The vehicle identification plate is attached to the hood ledge or the firewall. This plate is mounted on the right front suspension strut housing on the 240Z and 260Z, on the left hood ledge panel at the back of the strut housing on the 280Z and on the right side of the firewall, behind the battery, on the 280ZX. The identification plate gives the vehicle model, engine displacement in cc., SAE horsepower rating, wheelbase, engine number, and chassis number.

GENERAL ENGINE SPECIFICATIONS

Year	Model	Type (Model)	Engine Displacement cu. in. (cc)	Carburetor Type	Horsepower (SAE) @ rpm	Torque @ rpm (ft. lbs.)	Bore x Stroke (in.)	Compression Ratio	Normal Oil Pressure (psi)
1975	610 Sedan 610 Hardtop 610 Wagon	OCH 4 (L20B)	119.1 (1952)	Dual throat downdraft	110 @ 5600	112 @ 3600	3.35 x 3.39	8.5:1	50-57
	710 Sedan 710 Hardtop 710 Wagon	OCH 4 (L20B)	119.1 (1952)	Dual throat downdraft	100 @ 5600	100 @ 3600	3.35 x 3.39	8.5:1	50-57

GENERAL ENGINE SPECIFICATIONS

Year	Model	Type (Model)	Engine Displacement cu. in. (cc)	Carburetor Type	Horsepower (SAE) @rpm	Torque @rpm (ft. lbs.)	Bore x Stroke (in.)	Com-pression Ratio	Normal oil Pressure (psi)
	B210 Sedan, Coupe	OHV 4 (A14)	85.24 (1397)	Dual throat downdraft	78 @ 6000	75 @ 4000	3.09 x 3.03	8.5:1	43-50
1975-78	280Z	OHC 6 (L28)	168 (2753)	F.I.	170 @ 5600	177 @ 4400	3.39 x 3.11	8.3:1	50-57
1976	610	OHC 4 (L20B)	119.1 (1952)	Dual throat downdraft	112 @ 5600	108 @ 3600	3.35 x 3.39	8.5:1	50-57
1976-77	710	OHC 4 (L20B)	119.1 (1952)	Dual throat downdraft	110 @ 5600	112 @ 5600	3.35 x 3.39	8.5:1	50-57
1976-78	B210	OHV 4 (A14)	85.2 (1397)	Dual throat downdraft	80 @ 6000	83 @ 3600	2.99 x 3.03	8.5:1	43-50
	F10	OHV 4 (A14)	85.2 (1397)	Dual throat downdraft	80 @ 6000	83 @ 3600	2.99 x 3.03	8.5:1	43-50
1977-78	200SX	OHC 4 (L20B)	119.1 (1952)	Dual throat downdraft	97 @ 5600	102 @ 3200	3.35 x 3.39	8.5:1	50-57
	810	OHC 6 (L24)	146 (2393)	Electronic fuel injection	154 @ 5600	155 @ 4400	3.27 x 2.90	8.6:1	50-57
1978	510	OHC 4 (L20B)	119.1 (1952)	Dual throat downdraft	97 @ 5600	102 @ 3200	3.35 x 3.39	8.5:1	50-57
1979	200SX, 510	OHC 4 (L20B)	119.1 (1952)	Dual throat downdraft	92 @ 5600	107 @ 3200	3.35 x 3.39	8.5:1	50-57
	280ZX	OHC 6 (L28)	168 (2753)	F.I.	135 @ 5200	144 @ 4400	3.39 x 3.11	8.3:1	50-57
1979-80	810	OHC 6 (L24)	146 (2393)	Electronic fuel injection	120 @ 5200	125 @ 4400	3.27 x 2.90	8.9:1	50-60
	310	OHV 4 (A14)	85.2 (1397)	Dual throat downdraft	65 @ 5600	75 @ 3600	2.99 x 3.03	8.9:1	43-50
	210	OHV 4 (A12A)	75.5 (1237)	Dual throat downdraft	58 @ 5600	67 @ 3600	2.95 x 2.75	8.5:1	43-50
		OHV 4 (A14)	85.3 (1397)	Dual throat downdraft	65 @ 5600	75 @ 3600	2.99 x 3.03	8.5:1	43-50
		OHV 4 (A15)	90.8 (1488)	Dual throat downdraft	67 @ 5200	80 @ 3200	2.99 x 3.23	8.9:1	43-50
1980	200SX	OHC 4 (Z20E)	119.1 (1952)	Electronic fuel injection	100 @ 5200	112 @ 3200	3.35 x 3.39	8.5:1	50-60
	510	OHC 4 (Z20S)	119.1 (1952)	Dual throat downdraft	92 @ 5200	112 @ 2800	3.35 x 3.39	8.5:1	50-60
	280ZX	OHC 6 (L28)	168 (2753)	F.I.	132 @ 5200	144 @ 4000	3.39 x 3.11	8.3:1	50-57

NOTE: Specifications given are for United States except California.

TUNE-UP SPECIFICATIONS

When analyzing compression test results, look for uniformity among cylinders, rather than specific pressures

Year	Model	SPARK PLUGS Type	SPARK PLUGS Gap (in.)	DISTRIBUTOR Point Dwell (deg)	DISTRIBUTOR Point Gap (in.)	IGNITION TIMING (deg) MT	IGNITION TIMING (deg) AT	Fuel Pump Pressure (psi)	IDLE SPEED (rpm) MT	IDLE SPEED (rpm) AT (1)	VALVE CLEARANCE (in.) In	VALVE CLEARANCE (in.) Ex	Percentage of CO at Idle
1975	B210 (Federal)	BP5ES	0.031-0.035	49-55	0.017-0.022	10B	10B	3.8	700	650	0.041 hot	0.014 hot	2.0
	610 (Federal)	BP6ES	0.031-0.035	49-55	0.017-0.022	12B	12B	3.8	750	650	0.010 hot	0.012 hot	2.0
	710 (Federal)	BP6ES	0.031-0.035	49-55	0.017-0.022	12B	12B	3.8	750	650	0.010 hot	0.012 hot	2.0
	B210 (California)	BP6ES	0.031-0.035	Electronic	(2)	10B	10B	3.8	750	650	0.014 hot	0.014 hot	2.0
	710, 610 (California)	BP6ES	0.031-0.035	Electronic	(2)	12B	12B	3.8	750	650	0.010 hot	0.012 hot	2.0
1975-76	280Z	BP6ES	0.028-0.031	Electronic	(2)	7B (9)(13)	7B (9)(13)	164-178	800	700	0.010 hot	0.012 hot	2.0
1976	B210 (Federal)	BP5ES	0.031-0.035	49-55	0.017-0.022	10B	10B	3.8	700	650	0.014 hot	0.014 hot	2.0
	B210 (California)	BP5ES	0.031-0.035	Electronic	(2)	10B	10B	3.8	700	650	0.014 hot	0.014 hot	2.0
	610, 710 (Federal)	BP6ES	0.031-0.035	49-55	0.018-0.022	12B	12B	3.8	750	650	0.010 hot	0.012 hot	2.0
	610, 710 (California)	BP6ES	0.039-0.043	Electronic	(2)	12B	12B	3.8	750	650	0.010 hot	0.012 hot	2.0
	F10 (Federal)	BP5ES	0.031-0.035	49-55	0.018-0.022	10B	—	3.8	700	—	0.014 hot	0.014 hot	2.0
	F10 (California)	BP5ES	0.031-0.035	Electronic	(2)	10B	—	3.8	700	—	0.014 hot	0.014 hot	2.0
1977	B210 (Federal)	BP5ES	0.039-0.043	49-55	0.018-0.022	10B	8B	3.8	700	650	0.014 hot	0.014 hot	2.0
	B210 (California)	BP5ES	0.039-0.043	Electronic	(2)	10B	10B	3.8	700	650	0.014 hot	0.014 hot	2.0
	710 (Federal)	BP6ES	0.039-0.043	49-55	0.018-0.022	12B	12B	3.8	750	650	0.010 hot	0.012 hot	2.0
	710 (California)	BP6ES	0.039-0.043	Electronic	(2)	12B	12B	3.8	600	600	0.010 hot	0.012 hot	1.0
	F10 (Federal)	BP5ES	0.039-0.043	49-55 (2)	0.018-0.022 (2)	10B	—	3.8	700	—	0.014 hot	0.014 hot	2.0
	200SX (Federal)	BP6ES	0.039-0.043	49-55	0.018-0.022	10B (3)	12B	3.8	600	600	0.010 hot	0.012 hot	1.0
1977-78	280Z	BP6ES-11 (14)	0.039-0.043	Electronic	(2)	10B	10B	164-178	800	700	0.010 hot	0.012 hot	2.0
	F10 (California) (1978 Federal)	BP5ES	0.039-0.043	Electronic	(2)	10B	—	3.8	700	—	0.014 hot	0.014 hot	2.0
1977-79	200SX (1977 California)	BP6ES	0.039-0.043	Electronic	(2)	9B (3)	12B	3.8	600	600	0.010 hot	0.012 hot	1.0
1978	B210 (except FU)	BP5ES	0.039-0.043	Electronic	(2)	10B	8B (9)	3.9	700	650	0.014	0.014	2.0
	B210 (FU model)	BP5EQ	0.043-0.051	Electronic	(2)	5B	—	3.9	700	—	0.014	0.014	1.0
1977-80	810	BP6ES	0.039-0.043	Electronic	(2)	10B	10B	3.6 EFI	700	650	0.010 hot 0.008 cold	0.012 hot 0.010 cold	1.0/0.5 Cal.

TUNE-UP SPECIFICATIONS

When analyzing compression test results, look for uniformity among cylinders, rather than specific pressures

Year	Model	SPARK PLUGS Type	SPARK PLUGS Gap (in.)	DISTRIBUTOR Point Dwell (deg)	DISTRIBUTOR Point Gap (in.)	IGNITION TIMING (deg) MT	IGNITION TIMING (deg) AT	Fuel Pump Pressure (psi)	IDLE SPEED (rpm) MT	IDLE SPEED (rpm) AT ①	VALVE CLEARANCE (in.) In	VALVE CLEARANCE (in.) Ex	Percentage of CO at Idle
1978-79	510	BP6ES	0.039-0.043	Electronic	②	12B ④	12B	3.8	600	600	0.010 hot	0.012 hot	1.0
1979	210	BP5ES ⑪	0.039-0.043 ⑫	Electronic	②	10B ⑥⑩	8B ⑥	3.8	700	650	0.014 hot	0.014 hot	2.0
	310	BP5ES	0.039-0.043	Electronic	②	10B ⑥	—	3.8	700	—	0.014 hot	0.014 hot	2.0
	280ZX	BP6ES-11 ⑯	0.039-0.043	Electronic	②	10B	10B	171	800	700 ⑮	0.010 hot	0.012 hot	2.0
1980	210	BP5ES	0.039-0.043	Electronic	②	10B ⑤	8B	3.8	700	650	0.014 hot	0.014 hot	2.0
	310	BP5ES	0.039-0.043	Electronic	②	8B	—	3.8	750	—	0.014 hot	0.014 hot	2.0
	200SX	BP6ES	0.031-0.035	Electronic	②	8B ⑦	8B ⑦	⑧ EFI	700	700	0.012 hot	0.012 hot	1.3
	510	BP6ES	0.031-0.035	Electronic	②	8B ⑦	8B ⑦	3.8	600	600	0.012 hot	0.012 hot	1.5
	280ZX	BP6ES-11	0.039-0.013	Electronic	②	10B	10B	171	700	700	0.010 hot	0.012 hot	1.5

NOTE: Emission control requires a very precise approach to tune-up. Timing and idle speed are peculiar to the engine and its application, rather than to the engine alone. Data for the particular application is on a sticker in the engine compartment on all late models. If the sticker disagrees with this chart, use the sticker figure. The results of any adjustments or modifications should be checked with a CO meter. On many 1980 cars, CO levels are not adjustable.

NOTE: FU models are Hatchbacks with 5-speed transmissions sold in the U.S.A. except for California.

① In Drive
② Electronic ignition—reluctor gap: 0.008-0.016 in. (1975-78); 0.012-0.020 in. (1979-80)
③ California models: 12B
④ 1979 Federal: 11B
⑤ A14 engine: 8B
⑥ California models: 5B
⑦ California models: 6B
⑧ At idle: 3.0 psi
Accelerator fully depressed: 3.7 psi
⑨ California: 10B
⑩ FU model: 5B
⑪ FU model: BP5EQ
⑫ FU model: 0.043-0.051 in.
⑬ 13B with engine cold on dual reluctor models
⑭ Canada: BR6ES
⑮ Non-Calif. models with converter: 700
⑯ Canada: BR6ES-11
EFI: electronic fuel injection
CO levels are not adjustable.

FIRING ORDERS

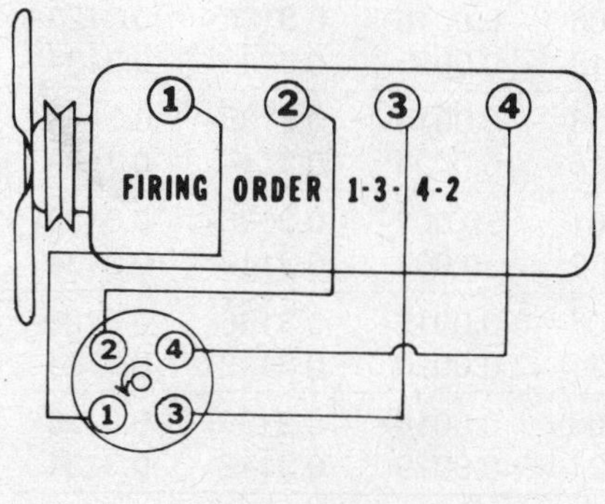

L20B engine

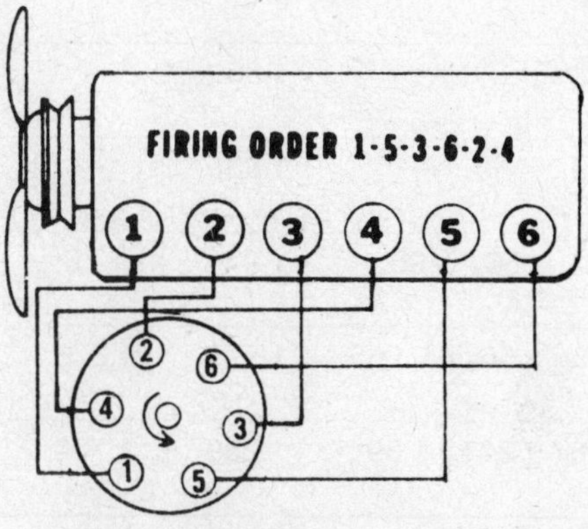

L24, L28 engines

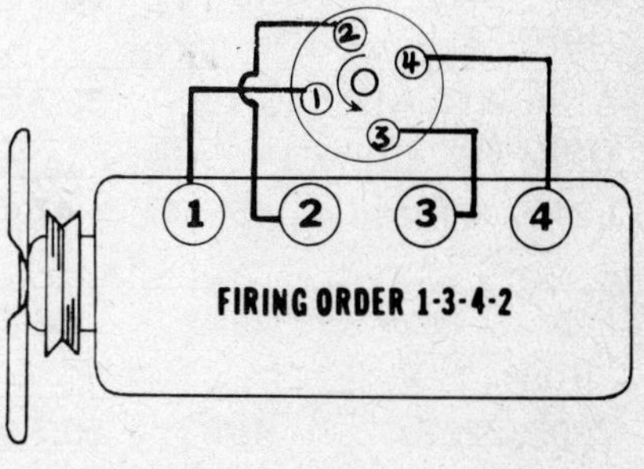

A14 and 15 engines

CAPACITIES

Year	Model	Engine Crankcase: With Filter	Engine Crankcase: Without Filter	Transmission (pts): 4-Spd	Transmission (pts): 5-Spd	Transmission (pts): Automatic (Total Capacity)	Drive Axle (pts)	Gas Tank (gals)	Cooling System (qts)
1975	B210	4.2	3.7	2.7	—	11.4	1.89	11.5	6.25 ④
	610	4.5	4.0	4.25	—	11.8	1.75/2.75 (wagon)	14.5/13.7 (wagon)	7.25
	710	5.0	4.5	4.25	—	11.8	2.75	13.2/11.8 (wagon)	7.25
1975-76	280Z	5.0	4.25	3.13	—	11.8	2.75	17.25	10.00 ⑥
1976	610	4.5	4.0	4.25	—	11.8	1.75/2.2 (wagon)	14.5/13.75 (wagon)	7.25
1976-77	710	4.5	4.0	4.25 ①	—	11.8	2.75	13.25/11.8 (wagon)	7.25
1976-78	B210	3.8	3.4	2.75	3.6	11.8	1.8	11.5	6.25 ④
	F10	3.6	3.2	4.90	4.9	—	—	10.6/9.1 (wagon)	7.00
1977-78	810	6.0	5.5	3.60	—	11.8	2.75/2.2 (wagon)	15.9/14.5 (wagon)	11.0
1977-78	280Z	5.0	4.25	3.63	—	11.8	2.75	17.25	11.0
1977-79	200SX	4.5	4.0	—	3.6	11.8	2.75	15.9	7.90
1978-79	510	4.5	4.0	3.6	3.6	11.8	2.4	13.2	9.40
1979-80	210	②	—	③	2.5	11.8	1.8	13.25	6.25 ④
	310	3.4	2.8	4.9	4.9	—	—	13.25	6.25
	810	5.9	5.25	3.7	4.25	11.8	2.0	15.9/14.5 (wagon)	11.00
1979-80	280ZX	4.75	4.25	3.63	—	11.8	2.75	21.12	11.12
1980	510	⑤	—	3.15	3.6	11.8	2.4	13.25	9.25
	200SX	4.4	4.1	—	4.25	11.8	2.4	14/15.9 (hatchback)	10

① 3.6 pts., 1977
② A12A, A14 engines: 3.46 qts.
A15 engine: 3.25 qts.
③ A12A engine: 2.5 pts.
A14 engine: 2.75 pts.
④ Automatic transmission: 6 qts.
⑤ L20B engine: 4.5 qts.
Z20S engine: 4.65 qts.
⑥ 1976: 11.00

VALVE SPECIFICATIONS

Model	Seat Angle (deg)	Spring Test Pressure lbs @ in.: Outer	Spring Test Pressure lbs @ in.: Inner	Free Length (in.): Outer	Free Length (in.): Inner	Stem to Guide Clearance (in.): Intake	Stem to Guide Clearance (in.): Exhaust	Stem Diameter (in.): Intake	Stem Diameter (in.): Exhaust
L20B	45° ②	47 @ 1.58	27 @ 1.38	1.97	1.77	0.0008-0.0021	0.0016-0.0029	0.3136-0.3142	0.3128-0.3134
A14 (1975-78)	45°	52.7 @ 1.52	—	1.83	—	0.0006-0.0018	0.0016-0.0028	0.3138-0.3144	0.3128-0.3134
A12A, A14, A15 (1979-80)	45°30′	52.7 @ 1.19	—	1.83	—	0.0006-0.0018	0.0016-0.0028	0.3138-0.3144	0.3128-0.3134
L24	45°	47 @ 1.57	56 @ .96	1.97	1.76	0.001-0.002	0.002-0.003	0.3136-0.3142	0.3128-0.3134
L28	45°	108 @ 1.16	56 @ 0.965	1.575	1.378	0.0008-0.0021	0.0016-0.0029	0.3136-0.3142	0.3128-0.3134
Z20E, Z20S	45°	50.7 @ 1.58	24 @ 1.39	1.959	1.736	0.0008-0.0021	0.0016-0.0029	0.3136-0.3142	0.3128-0.3134

① Valves closed ② 45°30′, 1975 710 ③ 45°30′, 1979-80 810

CRANKSHAFT AND CONNECTING ROD SPECIFICATIONS

	CRANKSHAFT				CONNECTING ROD BEARINGS		
Engine Model	Main Brg. Journal Dia.	Main Brg. Oil Clearance	Shaft End-Play	Thrust on No.	Journal Diameter	Oil Clearance	Side Clearance
L20B	2.333-2.360	0.0008-0.002	0.002-0.007	3	1.9660-1.9670	0.001-0.002	0.008-0.012
L24	2.1631-2.1636	0.001-0.003	0.002-0.007	center	1.9670-1.9675	0.001-0.002	0.008-0.012
L28 (1975-78)	2.1631-2.1636	0.0008-0.0028	0.002-0.007	center	1.9670-1.9675	0.0010-0.0022	0.0079-0.0118
A14 (1975-78)	1.966-1.967	0.0008-0.002	0.002-0.006	3	1.7701-1.7706	0.0008-0.002	0.008-0.012
A12A, A14, A15 (1979-80)	1.9666-1.9671	0.001-0.0035	0.002-0.0059	3	1.7701-1.7706	0.0012-0.0031	0.008-0.012
Z20S, Z20E	2.1631-2.1636	0.0008-0.0024	0.002-0.0071	3	1.967-1.9675	0.001-0.0022	0.008-0.012
L28 (1979-80)	2.1631-2.1636	0.0008-0.0026	0.002-0.007	center	1.9670-1.9675	0.0009-0.0026	0.0079-0.0118

PISTON AND RING SPECIFICATIONS

All measurements in inches

		RING GAP			RING SIDE CLEARANCE		
Engine Model	Piston Clearance	Top Compression	Bottom Compression	Oil Control	Top Compression	Bottom Compression	Oil Control
L24	0.001-0.002	0.009-0.015	0.006-0.012	0.006-0.012	0.002-0.003	0.001-0.003	0.001-0.003
L28 (1975-76)	0.001-0.0018	0.0091-0.0150	0.0059-0.0118	0.0059-0.0118	0.0018-0.0031	0.0012-0.0028	0
L28 (1977-78)	0.001-0.0018	0.0098-0.0157	0.0118-0.0197	0.0118-0.0354	0.0016-0.0029	0.0012-0.0028	0
L20B	0.001-0.002	0.010-0.016	0.012-0.020	0.012-0.035	0.002-0.003	0.001-0.003	0
A14 (1975-78)	0.0009-0.002	0.008-0.014	0.006-0.012	0.012-0.035	0.002-0.003	0.001-0.002	Combined ring
A12A, A14, A15 (1979-80)	0.001-0.002	0.008-0.014	0.006-0.012	0.012-0.035	0.002-0.003	0.001-0.002	0
Z20E, Z20S	0.001-0.002	0.0098-0.016	0.006-0.012	0.012-0.035	0.002-0.003	0.001-0.0025	0
L28 (1979-80)	0.001-0.0018	0.0098-0.0157	0.0118-0.0197	0.0118-0.0354	0.0016-0.0029	0.0012-0.0025	0

TORQUE SPECIFICATIONS

All readings in ft. lbs.

						MANIFOLDS	
Engine Model	Cylinder Head Bolts	Main Bearing Bolts	Rod Bearing Bolts	Crankshaft Pulley Bolt	Flywheel to Crankshaft Bolts	Intake	Exhaust
L24	51-61	33-40	33-40	101-116	94-108	④	④
L20B	51-61	33-40	33-40	87-116	101-116	9-12	9-12
L28	54-61	33-40	27-31	94-108 ②	94-108	③	③
A12A, A14, A15	51-54	36-43	23-27	108-145	58-65 ①	11-14	11-14
Z20E, Z20S	51-58	33-40	33-40	87-116	101-116	12-15	12-15

① 1975-78 A14: 54-61 ft. lbs.
② 1977-78: 87-116; 1979-80: 101-116
③ 8 mm bolts: 10-13; 10 mm bolts: 25-36
④ 8 mm bolts: 11-18; 10mm bolts: 25-33; 8 mm nut: 9-12

TORQUE SEQUENCES

Cylinder Head

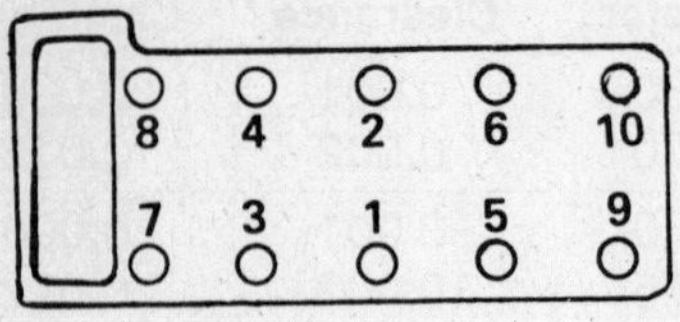

L20B engine

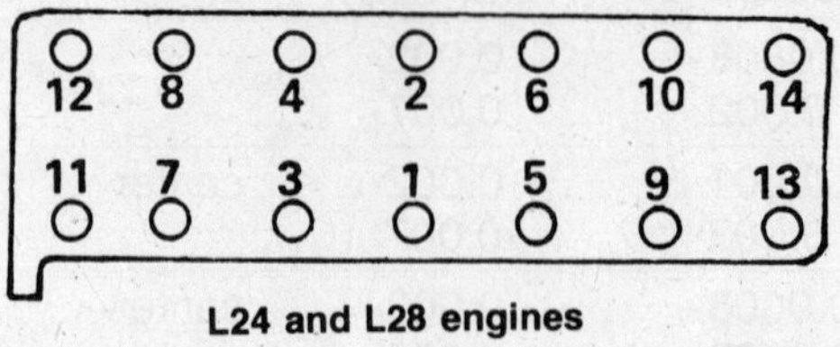

L24 and L28 engines

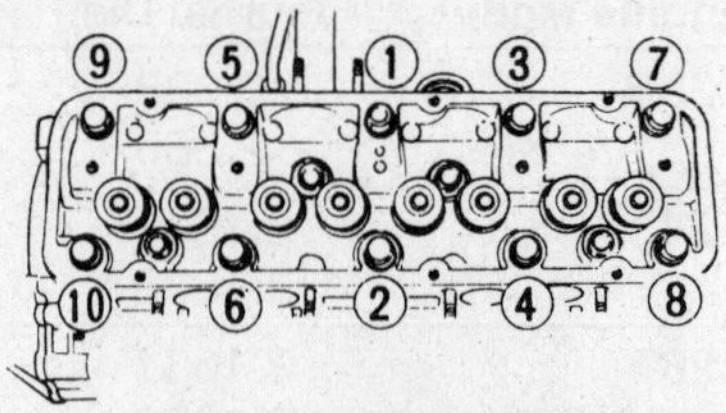

A14 and 15 engines

ALTERNATOR AND REGULATOR SPECIFICATIONS

Model	Year	Alternator Identification Number	Rated Output @ 5000 rpm (amps)	Output @ 2500 rpm (not less than) (volts)	Brush Length (in.)	Brush Spring Tension (oz.)	Regulated Voltage (volts)
B210	1975-76	LT150-19	50	37.5	0.295	9.0-12.2	14.3-15.3
	1977	LT150-26	50	37.5	0.295	9.0-12.2	14.3-15.3
	1978	LR150-36 ①	50	40	0.295	9.0-12.2	14.3-15.3
810	1977	LT160-39	60	40	0.310	9.0-12.2	14.3-15.3
	1978-79	LR160-42 ①	60	40	0.280	8.99-12.17	14.4-15.0
	1980	LR160-42B ①	60	50	0.295	8.99-12.17	14.4-15.0
710	1975	LT150-13	50	37.5	0.571	8.80	14.3-15.3
	1976	LT150-13	50	37.5	0.295	9.0-12.2	14.3-15.3
	1977	LT150-25	50	37.5	0.295	9.0-12.2	14.3-15.3
610	1975-77	LT150-13	50	37.5	0.310	9.0-12.2	14.3-15.3
200SX	1977-79	LR150-35 ①	50	40	0.295	8.99-12.17	14.4-15.0
	1980	LR160-47 ①	60	45	0.295	8.99-12.17	14.4-15.0
510	1978-79	LR150-35 ①	50	40	0.295	8.99-12.17	14.4-15.0
		LR160-47 ①③	60	41	0.295	8.99-12.17	14.4-15.0
	1980	LR150-52 ①	50	40	0.295	8.99-12.17	14.4-15.0
210	1979-80	LR150-36 ①	50	40	0.295	8.99-12.17	14.4-15.0
F-10	1976-77	LT150-26	50	37.5	0.295	9.0-12.2	14.3-15.3
	1978	LR150-36 ①	50	40	0.295	8.99-12.7	14.3-15.3
		LR160-46 ①②	60	45	0.295	8.99-12.17	14.4-15.0
310	1979-80	LR160-46 ①	60	40	0.295	8.99-12.17	14.4-15.0
280Z	1975-77	LT160-23	60	45	0.310	9.0-12.2	14.3-15.3
280ZX	1978	LT160-42 ①	60	45	0.280	8.99-12.17	14.4-15.0
	1979-80	LR160-42B ①	60	50	0.276	8.99-12.17	14.4-15.0

① Uses integral voltage regulator
② With air conditioning
③ Optional

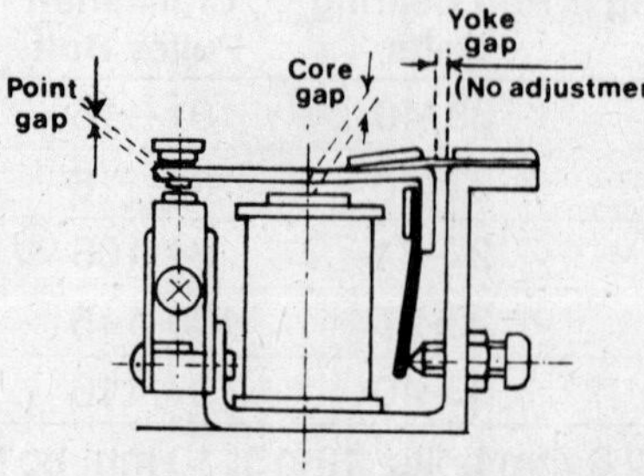

Regulator and charge indicator relay

BATTERY AND STARTER SPECIFICATIONS

All cars use 12 volt, negative ground electrical systems

			STARTER							
			LOCK TEST			NO LOAD TEST				
Year	Model	Battery Amp Hour Capacity	Amps	Volts	Torque (ft. lbs.)	Amps	Volts	rpm	Brush Spring Tension (oz.)	Min. Brush Length (in.)
All	610, 710	50, 60	430 MT	6.0	6.3	60	12	7000	49-64	0.47
			540 AT	5.0	6.0	60	12	6000	49-64	0.47
All	F10	60	Not Recommended			60	12	7000	49-64	0.47
All	B210	60	420	6.3	6.5	60	12	7000	49-64	0.47
			Not Recommended			60	12	6000	29	0.37
			Not Recommended			100	12	4300 RG	56-70	0.43
1975-77	280Z	65	Not Recommended			60	12	5000	56.4	0.43
1978	280Z	65	Not Recommended			100	12	4300	63.4	0.43
1977-79	200SX	60	Not Recommended			60 MT	12	7000	49-64	0.47
			Not Recommended			60 AT	12	6000	49-64	0.47
			Not Recommended			100 RG	12	4300	56-70	0.43
1978	510	60	Not Recommended			60 MT	12	7000	49-64	0.47
			Not Recommended			60 AT	12	6000	49-64	0.47
			Not Recommended			100 RG	12	4300	56-70	0.43
1979	280ZX	60 ①	Not Recommended			100	12	4300	63.4	0.43
1980	280ZX	60 ①	Not Recommended			100	11	3900	63.4	0.43
1979-80	510	60	Not Recommended			60 MT	11.5	7000	50-64	0.47
			Not Recommended			60 AT	11.5	6000	50-64	0.47
			Not Recommended			100 RG	11	3900	56-70	0.43
All	210, 310	60	Not Recommended			60	11.5	7000	50-64	0.47
			Not Recommended			100 RG	11	3900	56-70	0.43
1977-79	810	60	Not Recommended			100 RG	12	4300	56-70	0.43
1980	200SX	60	Not Recommended			60 MT	11.5	7000	50-64	0.47
			Not Recommended			60 AT	11.5	6000	50-64	0.47
			Not Recommended			100 RG	11	3900	56-70	0.43
	810	60	Not Recommended			100 RG	11	3900	56-70	0.43

① Canada and optional in USA: 70 amps
MT: Manual Transmission
AT: Automatic Transmission
RG: Reduction Gear type starter

BRAKE SPECIFICATIONS

All measurements given are in inches unless noted

				BRAKE DISC		DRUM		MINIMUM LINING THICKNESS	
Model	Year	Lug Nut Torque (ft. lbs.)	Master Cylinder Bore	Minimum Thickness	Maximum Run-Out	Diameter	Max. Wear Limit	Front	Rear
510	1978-80	58-72	0.8125	0.331	0.0047	9.000	9.060	0.080	0.059
810	1977-80	58-72	0.8125	0.413	0.0059	9.000	9.060	0.080	0.059
B210	1975-78	58-65	0.750	0.331	0.0047	8.000	8.051	0.063	0.059
610	1975	58-65	0.750	0.331	0.0048	9.000	9.055	0.063	0.059
	1976-77	58-65	0.750	0.331	0.0048	9.000	9.055	0.079	0.059
710	1975	58-65	0.750	0.331	0.0047	9.000	9.055	0.039	0.059
	1976-77	58-65	0.750	0.331	0.0047	9.000	9.055	0.079	0.059
200SX	1977-79	58-65	0.750	0.331	0.0047	9.000	9.060	0.059	0.059
	1980	58-72	0.8750	③	④	—	—	0.079	0.079
F-10	1977-78	58-65	0.750	0.337	0.0059	8.000	8.050	0.063	0.039
210	1979-80	58-65	0.8125	—	—	8.000	8.050	—	—

BRAKE SPECIFICATIONS

All measurements given are in inches unless noted

Model	Year	Lug Nut Torque (ft. lbs.)	Master Cylinder Bore	Brake Disc: Minimum Thickness	Brake Disc: Maximum Run-Out	Drum: Diameter	Drum: Max. Wear Limit	Minimum Lining Thickness: Front	Minimum Lining Thickness: Rear
280Z	1974-76	58-65	0.8748	0.413	0.0039	9.000	9.055	0.079	0.059
	1977-78	58-65	0.8750	0.413	0.0039	9.000	9.060	0.079	0.059
280ZX	1979-80	58-72	0.9375	0.709 ①	0.0039 ②	—	—	0.080	0.080
310	1979-80	58-72	0.8125	0.339	0.0047	8.000	8.050	0.079	0.059

NOTE: Minimum lining thickness is as recommended by the manufacturer. Due to variation in state inspection regulations, the minimum allowable thickness may be different than recommended.

① Rear disc: 0.339
② Rear disc: 0.0059
③ Front disc: 0.413; Rear disc: 0.339
④ Front disc: 0.0047; Rear disc: 0.0059
— Not applicable

WHEEL ALIGNMENT SPECIFICATIONS

Year	Model	Caster: Range (deg)	Caster: Preferred Setting (deg)	Camber: Range (deg)	Camber: Preferred Setting (deg)	Toe-In (in.)	Steering Axis Inclination (deg)	Wheel Pivot Ratio (deg): Inner Wheel	Wheel Pivot Ratio (deg): Outer Wheel
1975	610	1°15′-2°15′	1°50′	1°15′-2°45′	2°	0.43-0.55	5°55′-7°25′	32-33	29°30′-31°30′
	610 Station Wagon	1°15′-2°15′	1°50′	1°30′-3°00′	2°15′	0.43-0.55	5°45′-7°15′	32-33	29°30′-31°30′
	710	1°10′-2°40′	1°55′	1°25′-2°55′	2°10′	0.32-0.43	6°25′	32-33	29°30′-31°30′
1975-78	B210	1°00′-2°30′	1°45′	0°25′-1°55′	1°10′	0.08-0.16	7°32′-9°02′	37-39	31-33
	280Z	2°3′-3°33′	—	0°18′-1°48′	—	0-0.12	11°14′-12°44′	33°54′-34°54′	32°6′-34°6′
	280Z 2+2	2°3′-3°33′	—	0°21′-1°51′	—	0-0.12	11°14′-12°44′	36°18′-37°18′	34°24′-36°24′
1976-77	610, 710	1°-2°35′	1°45′	1°15′-2°45′	2°	①	6°15′-7°45′	32°-33°	29°30′-31°30′
1976-78	F10	20′-1°50′	—	0°50′-2°20′	—	②	9°15′-10°45′	36°30′-39°30′	31°-34°
1977-79	200SX	1°05′-2°35′	—	0°20′-1°50′	—	0.08-0.16	7°20′-8°20′	34°-36°	29°-31°
1977-80	810	1°10′-2°40′	—	0°-1°30′	—	0.0-0.08	7°10′-8°40′	36°-40°	29°-33°
1978-80	510 Sedan, Hatchback	1°05′-2°35′	—	−15′ to 1°15′	—	0.04-0.12	8°05′-9°35′	40°-42°	32°30′-36°30′
	510 Station Wagon	55′-2°25′	—	0°5′-1°35′	—	0.04-0.12	7°45′-9°15′	40°-42°	32°30′-36°30′
1979-80	210 Sedan, Hatchback	1°40′-3°10′	—	0°-1°30′	—	0.04-0.12	7°50′-9°20′	38°-42°	31°30′-35°30′
	210 Station Wagon	1°55′-3°25′	—	0°-1°30′	—	0.04-0.12	7°50′-9°20′	38°-42°	31°30′-35°30′
	310	25′-1°55′	—	0°15′-1°45′	—	0.0-0.08	11°10′-12°30′	36°30′-39°30′	29°30′-32°30′
	280ZX	4°10′-5°40′	—	−35′-+0.55′	—	0.04-0.12	8°35′-10°5′	33°30′-37°30′ ③	29°-33° ④
1980	200SX	1°45′-3°15′	—	−40′-+50′	—	0.0-0.08	7°25′-8°55′	33°-35°	27°-29°

① 0.16-0.24 Radial tires
0.24-0.31 Bias tires
② 0-0.79 Radial tires
0.20-0.28 Bias tires
③ With power steering: 32°-36°
④ With power steering: 24°30′-28°30′
— Information not applicable

OIL PUMP SPECIFICATIONS

Engine	Pump Type	Clearance Between Inner and Outer Rotor (in.)	Tip Clearance—Gear or Rotor to Cover or Outer Rotor (in.) (max.)	Clearance Between Outer Rotor and Body (in.)	Maximum Oil Pressure (psi)	Minimum Oil Pressure (psi) at Idle	Relief Valve Spring Free Length (in.)	Relief Valve Opening Pressure (psi)
L24	Rotor	0.002-0.005	0.005	0.006-0.008	54-60	14-17	2.24	54.0-59.7
L20B	Rotor	0.001-0.003	0.005	0.006-0.008	71	11	2.067	50
A14, A12A, A15	Rotor	0.002-0.0047	0.0047	0.0059-0.0083	54-74	11	1.7122	54-60
L28	Rotor	—	0.0047	0.0059-0.0083	80	—	2.067	—

— Not applicable

TUNE-UP PROCEDURES

Spark Plugs

Number the spark plug wires and clean any foreign material from around the spark plugs prior to removing them. Use a spark plug socket with a rubber insert to remove the plugs. This will prevent cracking the porcelain insulator. Each spark plug should be individually inspected and, if necessary, replaced. Refer to the Troubleshooting Section for an analysis of plug tip conditions. Clean reusable spark plugs and file the center electrode flat. Adjust the spark plug gap, according to the Tune-Up Specifications chart, wih a wire type feeler gauge. Lightly oil the threads and torque the spark plugs to 11-15 ft/lbs.

Breaker Points and Condenser

Either single points or dual points systems may be used. Dual points are serviced in the same manner as single points, with the exception of setting dwell, which is covered later.

1. Release the distributor cap clips and remove the cap.
2. Remove the distributor rotor by pulling straight up. Replace it if the contact tip is burned or corroded. Do not file the tip.
3. Inspect the points; if they are burned, worn, or corroded, replace them.
4. Use a magnetic screwdriver to remove the points hold-down screws. On distributors with the condenser mounted inside, the points screws also retain the condenser. Remove the points (and condenser, if inside). Loosen the screw in the side of the distributor to allow the points wire to slip out.
5. On dual points distributors and single points distributors with the condensers mounted outside the distributor, remove the condenser lead screw(s) and remove the condenser(s). On dual points models, note the locations of the condensers; they have different electrical capacities, and replacements must be installed in the same relationship.
6. Place a dab of grease on the distributor points cam and spread it around evenly. Do not use oil.
7. Install the new points and condenser(s). Tighten the condenser mounting screws, but leave the points screws slightly loose.
8. Check that the points meet squarely. The fixed point can be bent slightly if necessary.
9. Adjust the point gap. The rubbing block of the points must be on one of the high points of the distributor cam. The engine can be rotated with a wrench on the crankshaft pulley bolt (sparkplugs removed) or bumped around with the starter. Insert a flat feeler gauge of the correct thickness (see the specifications chart) between the points. Adjust the gap until the feeler gauge slides through with a slight drag.
10. Tighten the points hold down screws and recheck the adjustment. When the gap is correct, pull a matchbook cover or business card through (between) the points to clean them. Install the rotor and cap, and set the dwell and ignition timing.

Dwell Angle

1. Hook up a dwell meter according to the manufacturer's instructions. Zero the meter needle if necessary. Start the engine and read the dwell on the meter. If the dwell is correct, shut off the engine and remove the meter.
2. If the dwell requires adjustment, shut off the engine, remove the distributor cap, and adjust the point gap. Open the point gap to decrease dwell, close the gap to increase dwell.
3. Replace the cap and start the engine. Check the dwell, and repeat the process as necessary.

If the distributor has two sets of points, proceed as follows:

1. Unplug the distributor from the engine wiring harness.
2. Connect the two black wires with a jumper wire. This activates the advanced set of points.
3. Check and adjust the dwell of the advanced set of points.
4. Take one end of the jumper wire from the distributor side of the plug. Connect the black wire in the engine harness to the yellow wire from the distributor. This activates the retarded set of points.
5. Check and adjust the dwell of the retarded set of points.
6. Reconnect the plug.

Solid State Breakerless Ignition

AIR GAP

Through 1978

Reluctor air gap should be checked periodically. Standard air gap is 0.012-0.016 in. for both single and dual gap distributors. If the gap is incorrect, adjustment may be made by loosening the pick-up coil screws and inserting a feeler gauge.

NOTE: The use of a non-magnetic feeler gauge such as plastic or brass, is recommended for accurate gapping.

Remove the rubber cap from the tip of the rotor shaft. Add grease if necessary. The reluctor cannot be removed. To remove the pick-up coil, take out the two pick-up coil assembly and core screws clamping the primary wire. Reverse the sequence to install.

1979

1979 models use a ring-type pick-up instead of the arm type used in earlier years. There is no provision for air gap adjustment.

Ignition Timing

Timing settings for each model are given in the Tune-Up Specifications Chart.

NOTE: Datsun does not give ignition timing adjustments for 1980 and later California Datsuns. The procedure has been discontinued.

All Except 1975-76 280Z

1. Set the dwell to the proper specification.
2. Locate the timing marks on the crankshaft pulley and the front of the engine.
3. Clean off the timing marks so that you can see them.
4. Use chalk or white paint to color the mark on the crankshaft pulley and the mark on the scale which will indicate the correct timing when aligned with the notch on the crankshaft pulley.
5. Attach a tachometer to the engine.
6. Attach a timing light to the engine, according to the manufacturer's instructions.
7. Leave the vacuum line connected to the distributor vacuum diaphragm on all models except the 1979 210 wagons with automatic transmission, the A15 engine and 1980 and later A series engines; disconnect and plug the hose on those models.
8. Check to make sure that all of the wires clear the fan and then start the engine. Allow the engine to reach normal operating temperature.
9. Adjust the idle to the correct setting.
10. Aim the timing light at the timing marks. If the marks that you put on the pulley and the engine are aligned when the light flashes, the timing is correct. Turn off the engine and remove the tachometer and the timing light. If the marks are not in alignment, proceed with the following steps.
11. Turn off the engine.
12. Loosen the distributor lockbolt just enough so that the distributor can be turned with a little effort.
13. Start the engine. Keep the wires of the timing light clear of the fan.
14. With the timing light aimed at the pulley and the marks on the engine, turn the distributor in the direction or rotor rotation to retard the spark, and in the opposite direction of rotor rotation to advance the spark. Align the marks on the pulley and the engine with the flashes of the timing light. Tighten the hold-down bolt.

NOTE: See the "Emission Controls" section for adjustment of phase difference on dual point models.

1975-76 280Z

1. Connect a timing light and tachometer to the engine. Clean the timing scale and pulley notch; repaint the marks if necessary.
2. On all models (except California), disconnect the red temperature switch and ground the *harness* end of the wire with a jumper. Make sure that *all* wires are out of the way of the engine fan and other rotating parts.
3. Start the engine and operate it at idle speed. If the car has an automatic transmission, securely apply the parking brake and put the transmission in drive.
4. Verify that the idle speed is approximately correct as shown in the "Tune-Up" chart. If not, adjust it until it is correct as described in the carburetor adjustment section of this chapter.

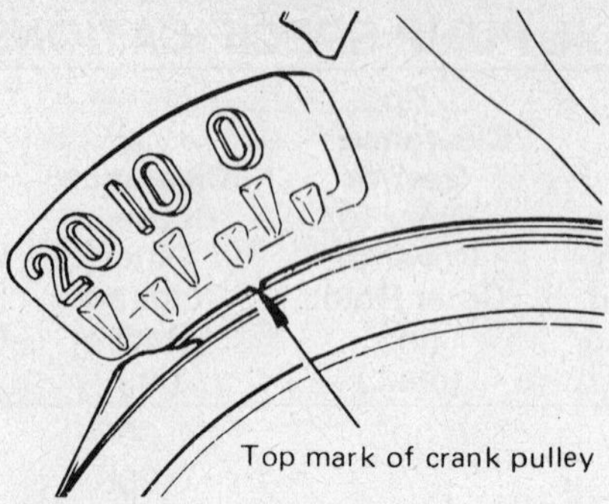

Timing marks typical of 4-cylinder engines

5. Carefully keeping the wires away from all rotating parts, aim the light at the timing marks. Compare the indication with the specified timing.
6. If the timing is not correct, stop the engine and loosen the nut which holds the distributor clamped in position (it is on the front of the clamp).
7. Then, restart the engine (putting an automatic transmission back in drive).
8. Slowly rotate the distributor back and forth until the timing is correct.
9. Stop the engine and tighten the clamp nut, being careful not to disturb the setting.
10. Recheck the timing and readjust it as necessary.
11. Run a jumper wire across the two terminals of the connection to the temperature switch. On all models (except California), disconnect the temperature switch wire.
12. Again check the timing exactly as described above. It should be 7 degrees retarded. If the timing is incorrect, adjust the phase difference as follows:
    a. Loosen the set screws which hold the adjuster plate in position and turn the plate using the notch in the adjuster plate. Timing is retarded by turning the plate counterclockwise. The edge of the distributor is marked in graduations which equal 4 degrees of crankshaft rotation each.
    b. Recheck the ignition timing. Repeat the adjustment and check until retard timing is within specification.
    c. Make sure to disconnect all jumper wires and securely reconnect all disturbed ignition wiring.

Valve Lash

Models B210, F10, 210, 310

1. Run the engine until it reaches normal operating temperature. Oil temperature, not water temperature, is critical to valve adjustment. With this in mind, make sure the engine is fully warmed up since this is the only way to make sure the parts have reached their full expansion. Generally speaking, this takes around fifteen minutes. After the engine has reached normal operating temperature, shut it off.
2. Purchase a new valve cover gasket before removing the valve cover. The new silicone gasket sealers are just as good or better if you can't find a gasket.
3. Note the location of any hoses or wires which may interfere with valve cover removal, disconnect them and move them aside. Then, remove the bolts which hold the valve cover in place.
4. After the valve cover has been removed, the next step is to get the number one piston at TDC on the compression stroke. There are at least two ways to do it; you can bump the engine over with the starter or turn it over by using a wrench on the front pulley attaching bolt. The easiest way to find TDC is to turn the engine over slowly with a wrench (after first removing No. 1 plug) until the piston is at the top of its stroke and the TDC timing mark on the crankshaft pulley is in alignment with the timing mark pointer. At this point, the valves for No. 1 should be closed.

NOTE: Make sure both valves are closed with the valve springs up as high as they will go. An easy way to find the compression stroke is to remove the distributor cap and see toward which spark plug lead the rotor is pointing. If the rotor points to number one spark plug lead, number one cylinder is on its compression stroke. When the rotor points to number two spark plug lead, number two cylinder is on its compression stroke, etc.

5. With No. 1 piston at TDC of the compression stroke, check the clearance on valves Nos. 1, 2, 3 and 5 (counting from the front to the rear).
6. To adjust the clearance, loosen the locknut with a wrench and turn the adjuster with a screwdriver while holding the locknut. The correct size feeler gauge should pass with a slight drag between the rocker arm and the valve stem.
7. Turn the crankshaft one full revolution to position the No. 4 piston at TDC of the compression stroke. Adjust valves Nos. 4, 6, 7 and 8 in the same manner as the first four.
8. Replace the valve cover.

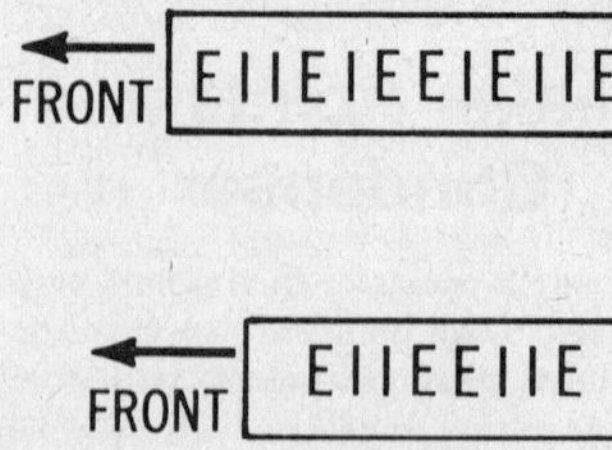

Valve order: 6 cylinder (top), 4 cylinder (bottom)

1975–79 510, 610, 710, 1977–79 200SX, 1975–81 280Z, 280ZX

1. The valves are adjusted with the engine at normal operating temperature. Oil temperature, and the resultant parts expansion, is much more important than water temperature. Run the engine for at least fifteen minutes to ensure that all the parts have reached their full expansion. After the engine is warmed up, shut it off.
2. Purchase either a new gasket or some

silicone gasket seal before removing the camshaft cover. Note the location of any wires and hoses which may interfere with cam cover removal, disconnect them and move them aside. Then remove the bolts which hold the cam cover in place and remove the cam cover.

3. Place a wrench on the crankshaft pulley bolt and turn the engine over until the valves for No. 1 cylinder are closed. When both cam lobes are pointing up, the valves are closed. If you have not done this before, it is a good idea to turn the engine over slowly several times and watch the valve action until you have a clear idea of just when the valve is closed.

4. Check the clearance of the intake and exhaust valves. You can differentiate between them by lining them up with the tubes of the intake and exhaust manifolds. The correct size feeler gauge should pass between the base circle of the cam and the rocker arm with just a slight drag. Be sure the feeler gauge is inserted *straight* and not on an angle.

5. If the valves need adjustment, loosen the locking nut and then adjust the clearance with the adjusting screw. You will probably find it necessary to hold the locking nut while you turn the adjuster. After you have the correct clearance, tighten the locking nut and recheck the clearance. Remember, it's better to have them too loose than too tight, especially exhaust valves.

6. Repeat this procedure until you have checked and/or adjusted all the valves. Keep in mind that all that is necessary is to have the valves closed and the camshaft lobes pointing up. It is not particularly important what stroke the engine is on.

7. Install the cam cover gasket, the cam cover and any wires and hoses which were removed.

Model 810

1977 810 engines must be "overnight" cold before the valves can be adjusted. They must not be operated for about eight hours before adjustment. 1978-80 810 engines are adjusted hot.

NOTE: Skip steps 7 and 8 if you have a 1978-80 810; complete steps 7 and 8 if you have a 1977 810.

1. Note the locations of all hoses or wires that would interfere with valve cover removal, disconnect them and move them aside. Then, remove the six bolts which hold the valve cover in place.

2. Bump one end of the cover sharply to loosen the gasket and then pull the valve cover off the engine vertically.

3. Crank the engine with the starter until both No. 1 cylinder valves (No. 1 is at the front) are closed (the lobes are pointed upward), and the timing mark on the crankshaft pulley is lined up approximately as it would be when the No. 1 spark plug fires.

4. Adjust the No. 1 cylinder intake valve to 0.008 in. (0.20 mm). First loosen the pivot locking nut and then insert the feeler gauge between the cam and cam follower. Adjust the pivot screw until there is a slight pull on the gauge when it is inserted *straight* between the cam and follower. Then, tighten the locking nut, recheck the adjustment, and correct as necessary.

5. Repeat the procedure for the No. 1 cylinder exhaust valve, but use a 0.010 in. (0.25 mm) gauge.

You can differentiate between the intake and exhaust valves by lining them up with the tubes of the intake and exhaust and exhaust manifolds.

6. Repeat Steps 4 and 5 for the other cylinders, going in the firing order of 1-5-3-6-2-4. Turn the engine ahead ⅓ turn before adjusting the valves for each cylinder so that the lobes will point upward.

7. Reinstall the valve cover gasket and hoses, start the engine, and operate it until it is fully warmed up.

8. Repeat the entire valve adjustment procedure using the gauges specified in the "Tune-Up" chart, but do not loosen the locking nuts unless the gauge indicates that adjustment is required.

9. When all valves are at hot specifications, clean all traces of old gasket material from the valve cover and the head. Install the new gasket in the valve cover with sealer and install the valve cover. Tighten the valve cover bolts evenly in several stages going around the cover to ensure a good seal. Reconnect all hoses and wires securely and operate the engine to check for leaks.

1980 and Later 510 and 200SX with Z20 Engines

1. The valves must be adjusted with the engine warm, so start the car and run the engine until the needle on the temperature gauge reaches the middle of the gauge. After the engine is warm, shut it off.

2. Purchase either a new gasket or some silicone gasket sealer before removing the camshaft cover. Counting on the old gasket to be in good shape is a losing proposition; always use new gaskets. Note the location of any wires and hoses which may interfere with cam cover removal, disconnect them and move them to one side. Remove the bolts holding the cover in place and remove the cover. Remember, the engine will be hot, so be careful.

3. Place a wrench on the crankshaft pulley bolt and turn the engine over until the first cam lobe behind the camshaft timing chain sprocket is pointing straight down.

NOTE: If you decide to turn the engine by "bumping" it with the starter, be sure to disconnect the high tension wire from the coil(s) to prevent the engine from accidentally starting and spewing oil all over the engine compartment.

CAUTION

Never attempt to turn the engine by using a wrench on the camshaft sprocket bolt; there is a one to two turning ratio between the camshaft and the crankshaft which will put a tremendous strain on the timing chain.

4. See the illustration marked "Primary adjustment" and adjust valves (1), (4), (6), and (7) to 0.012 in. using a flat-bladed feeler gauge. The feeler gauge should pass between the valve stem end and the rocker arm screw with a very slight drag. Insert the feeler gauge *straight*, not at an angle.

5. If the clearance is not within specified value, loosen the rocker arm lock nut and turn the rocker arm screw to obtain the proper clearance. After correct clearance is obtained, tighten the lock nut.

6. Turn the engine over so that the first cam lobe behind the camshaft timing chain sprocket is pointing straight up and adjust the valves marked (2), (3), (5), and (8) in the "Secondary adjustment" illustration. They, too, should have a clearance of 0.012 in.

7. Install the cam cover gasket, the cam cover and any wires and hoses which were removed.

Carburetor

IDLE SPEED AND MIXTURE ADJUSTMENT (CARBURETED ENGINES)

NOTE: 1980 and later model Datsuns require a CO meter to adjust their mixture ratios, therefore, no procedures concerning this adjustment are given. Also, many California model Datsuns have a plug over their mixture control screw. It is suggested that in both of these cases, mixture adjustment be left to a qualified technician.

1. Start the engine and allow it to run until it reaches normal operating temperature.

2. Allow the engine idle speed to stabilize by running the engine at idle for at least one minute.

3. If it hasn't already been done, check and adjust the ignition timing to the proper setting.

4. Shut off the engine and connect a tachometer.

5. Disconnect and plug the air hose between the three way connector and the check valve, if equipped. On 1980 and later models, disconnect the air induction hose and plug the pipe. With the transmission in Neutral, check the idle speed on the tachometer. If the reading is correct, continue onto Step 6 for 1975-79 models. For 1980 and later and certain California models, proceed to Step 8 below if the idle is correct. If not, turn the idle speed adjusting screw clockwise with a screwdriver to increase idle speed or counterclockwise to decrease it.

6. With the automatic transmission in Drive (wheels blocked and parking brake on) or the manual transmission in Neutral, turn the mixture screw out until the engine rpm start to drop to an overly rich mixture.

7. Turn the screw in past the starting point until the rpm start to drop due to an overly lean mixture. Turn the mixture screw in until the idle speed drops 60-70 rpm with manual transmission, or 15-25 rpm with automatic transmission (in Drive) for 1975-76 B 210, 610, and 710, and 1975-77 Pick-up; 35-45 rpm with manual transmission or 10-20 with automatic for 1977-78 B 210; 35-45 rpm (all transmissions) for 1977-78 F 10; or 45-55 rpm for all 1977 710, and 1978-79 510, 200 SX, and Pick-up. If the mixture limiter cap will not allow this adjustment, remove it, make the adjustment, and reinstall it. Go on to Step 8 for 1975-79 model.

8. Install the air hose. If the engine speed increases, reduce it with the idle speed screw.

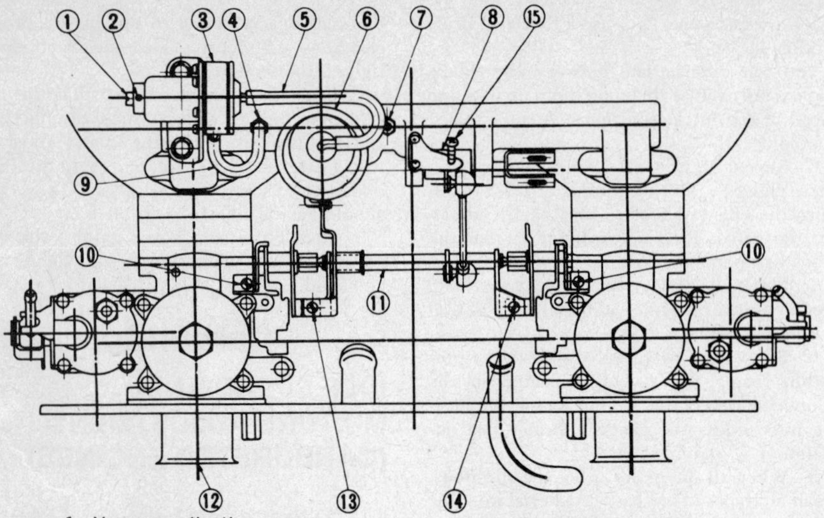

1. Vacuum adjusting screw
2. Lock screw
3. Control valve
4. Connector-control valve
5. Vacuum tube-servo diaphragm
6. Throttle positioner servo diaphragm
7. Connector-anti-backfire valve
8. Auxiliary throttle shaft
9. Vacuum tube-control weights
10. Throttle adjusting screw
11. Throttle shaft
12. Air cleaner air horn
13. Positioner adjusting screw
14. Balance screw
15. Fast idle setting screw

Late Hitachi/SU throttle linkage

Hitachi/SU carburetor mixture adjusting nut

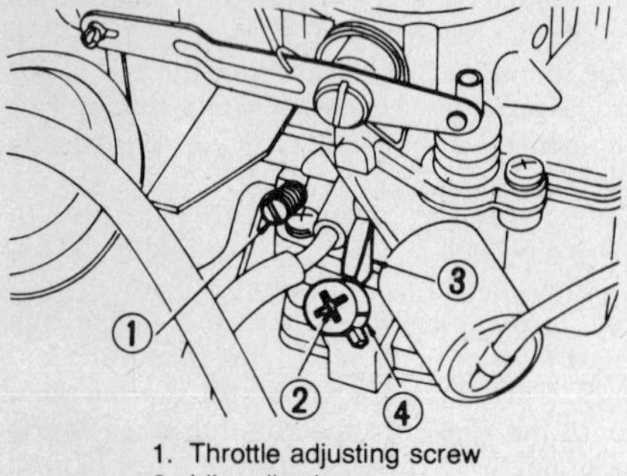

1. Throttle adjusting screw
2. Idle adjusting screw
3. Stopper
4. Idle limiter cap

Downdraft carburetor idle adjustment screw

Fuel Injection

IDLE SPEED

To adjust the mixture controls on these units requires a CO meter and several special Datsun tools, therefore we will confine ourselves to idle speed adjustment.

1. Start the engine and run it until the water temperature indicator points to the middle of the temperature gauge. It might be quicker to take a short spin down the road and back.
2. Open the engine hood. Run the engine at about 2,000 rpm for a few minutes with the transmission in Neutral and all accessories off. If you have not already done so, check the ignition timing and make sure it is correct.

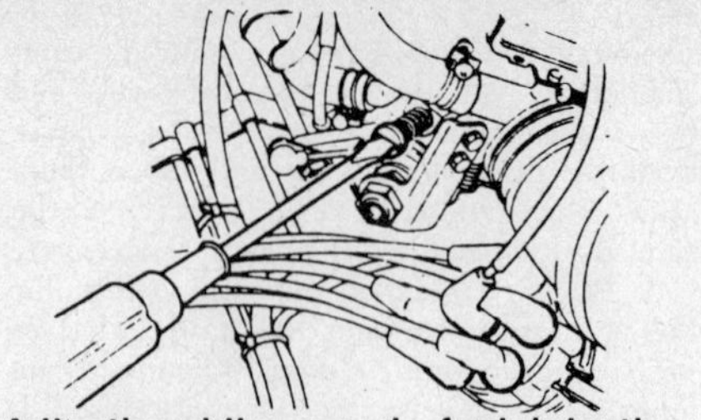

Adjusting idle speed—fuel injection models

Hook up a tachometer. For automatic transmission, set parking brake, block wheels and set shift selector in Drive position.

3. Run the engine at idle speed and disconnect the hose from the air induction pipe, then plug the pipe. Allow the engine to run for about a minute at idle speed.
4. Check the idle against the specifications given earlier in this chapter. Adjust the idle speed by turning the idle speed adjusting screw. Turn the screw clockwise for slower idle speed and counterclockwise for faster idle speed.
5. Connect hose and disconnect the tachometer. If idle speed increases, adjust it with the idle speed adjusting screw.

ENGINE ELECTRICAL

Distributor

REMOVAL AND INSTALLATION

When removing the distributor for any rea-

1. Cap
2. Rotor head
3. Rollpin
4. Reluctor
5. Pick-up coil
6. Contactor
7. Breaker plate assembly
8. Packing
9. Rotor shaft
10. Governor spring
11. Governor weight
12. Shaft assembly
13. Cap setter
14. Vacuum controller
15. Housing
16. Fixing plate
17. O-ring
18. Collar

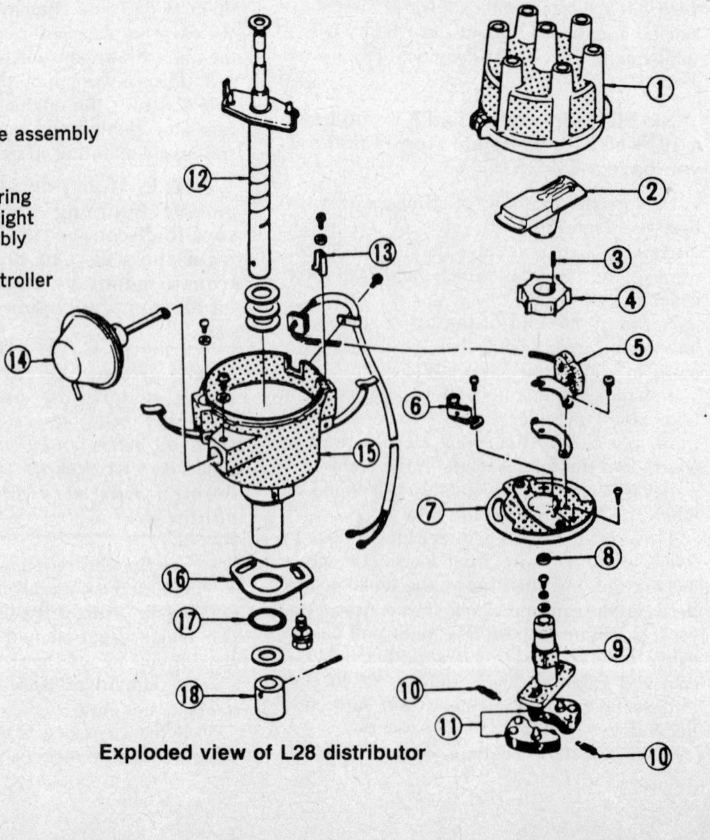

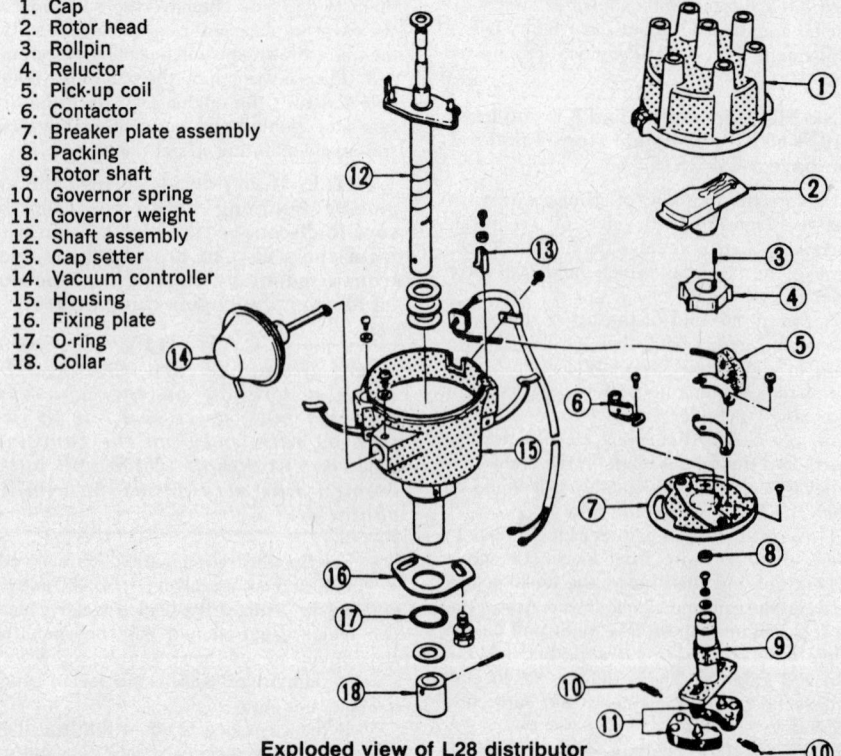

Exploded view of L28 distributor

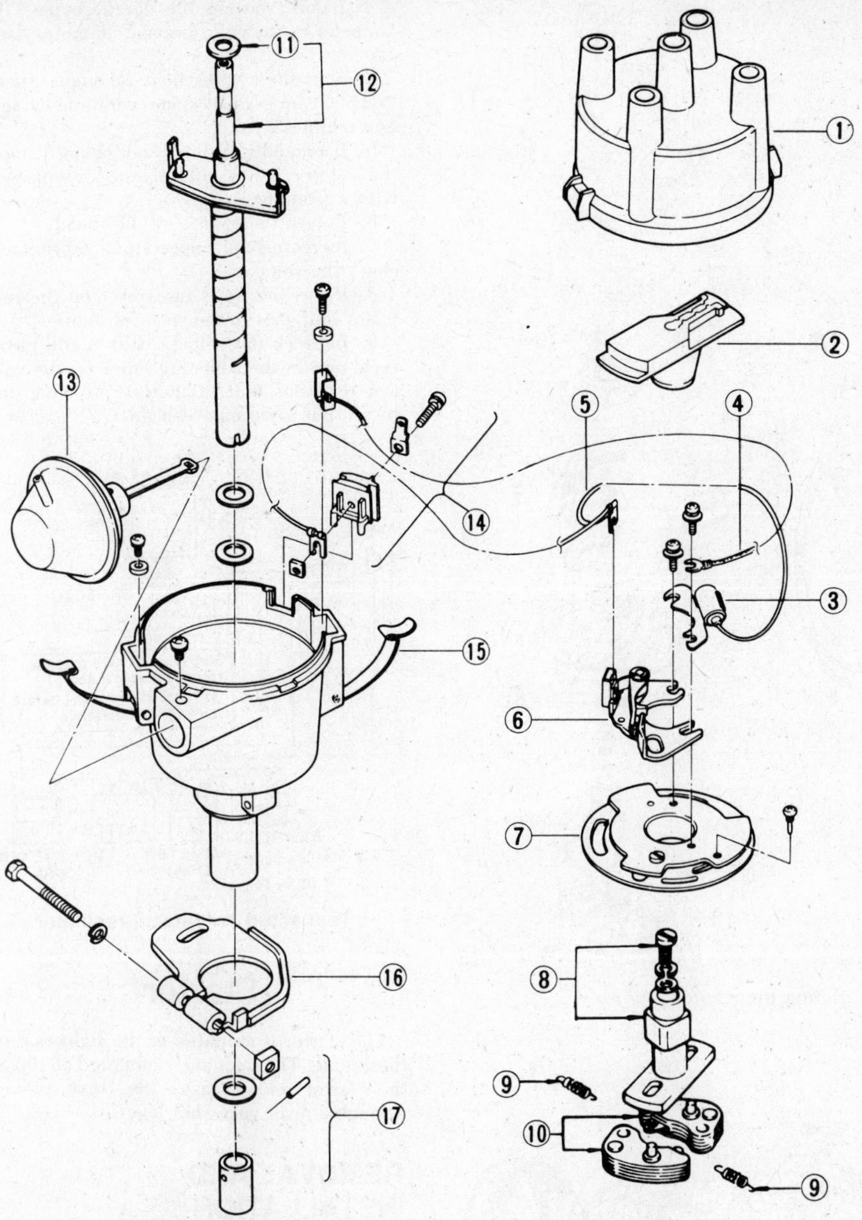

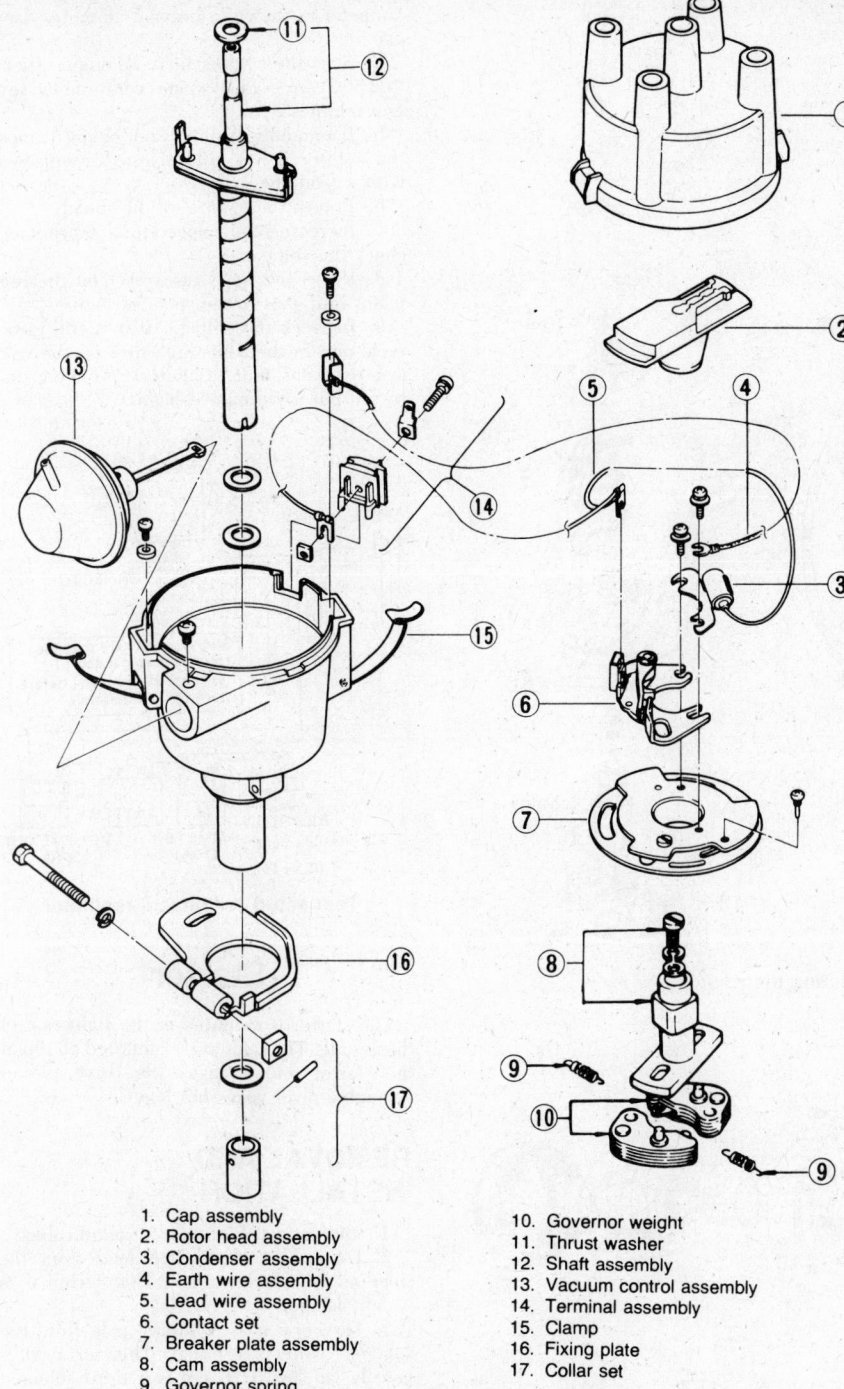

1. Cap assembly
2. Rotor head assembly
3. Condenser assembly
4. Earth wire assembly
5. Lead wire assembly
6. Contact set
7. Breaker plate assembly
8. Cam assembly
9. Governor spring
10. Governor weight
11. Thrust washer
12. Shaft assembly
13. Vacuum control assembly
14. Terminal assembly
15. Clamp
16. Fixing plate
17. Collar set

Typical points–type distributor

son, note the location of the rotor and mark the relationship of the distributor body to the engine. The distributor can then be replaced precisely in its original location, if the engine has not been turned. If the engine has been turned while the distributor was removed, or the distributor location was not marked, proceed as follows: Find top dead center of the compression stroke of No. 1 cylinder by holding a finger to the spark plug and rotating the engine. Compression pressure will force the finger from the hole. The exact location top of top dead center can then be found by use of the crankshaft pulley timing marks. Install the distributor so that the rotor is pointing at the No. 1 spark plug wire and the points are just opening. The ignition wires may now be installed in the distributor cap, following the firing order in the direction of rotation. Set the timing to specifications.

Alternator

An alternator is used on all models. The following precautions must be observed to prevent alternator and regulator damage:

1. Be absolutely sure of correct polarity when installing a new battery, or connecting a battery charger.
2. Do not short across or ground any alternator or regulator terminals.
3. Disconnect the battery ground cable before replacing any electrical unit.
4. Never operate the alternator with any of the leads disconnected.
5. When steam cleaning the engine, be careful not to subject the alternator to excessive heat.
6. When charging the battery, remove it from the car or disconnect the alternator output terminal.

REMOVAL AND INSTALLATION

1. Disconnect the battery ground.
2. Disconnect lead wires from alternator.
3. Remove adjusting bolt and slip off belt.
4. Support unit and remove mounting bolts.
5. Reverse the above to install.

BELT TENSION ADJUSTMENT

The correct belt tension for all alternators gives about ½ in. play on the longest span of the belt.

1. Loosen the alternator pivot and mounting bolts.
2. Pry the alternator toward or away from the engine until the tension is correct. Use a hammer or wooden prybar.
3. When the tension is correct, tighten the bolts and check the adjustment. Be careful not to overtighten the belt, which will lead to bearing failure.

Regulator

ADJUSTMENT

NOTE: 1978 and later models are equipped with electronic voltage regulators integral with the alternator. No adjustments are necessary or possible.

1. Connect an ammeter, voltmeter, fully charged battery, and resistor as shown.
2. Since this regulator is temperature compensated, the temperature of the regulator cover must be noted. Regulated voltage varies with ambient temperature.

VOLTAGE SPECIFICATIONS

Ambient Temperature (°F)	Regulated Voltage
14	14.6-15.6
32	14.5-15.5
50	14.3-15.3
68	14.2-15.2
86	14.0-15.0
104	13.9-14.9

1. Cap assembly
2. Rotor head assembly
3. Roll pin
4. Reluctor
5. Pick-up coil
6. Contactor
7. Breaker plate assembly
8. Packing
9. Rotor shaft
10. Governor spring
11. Governor weight
12. Shaft assembly
13. Cap setter
14. Vacuum controller
15. Housing
16. Fixing plate
17. Collar

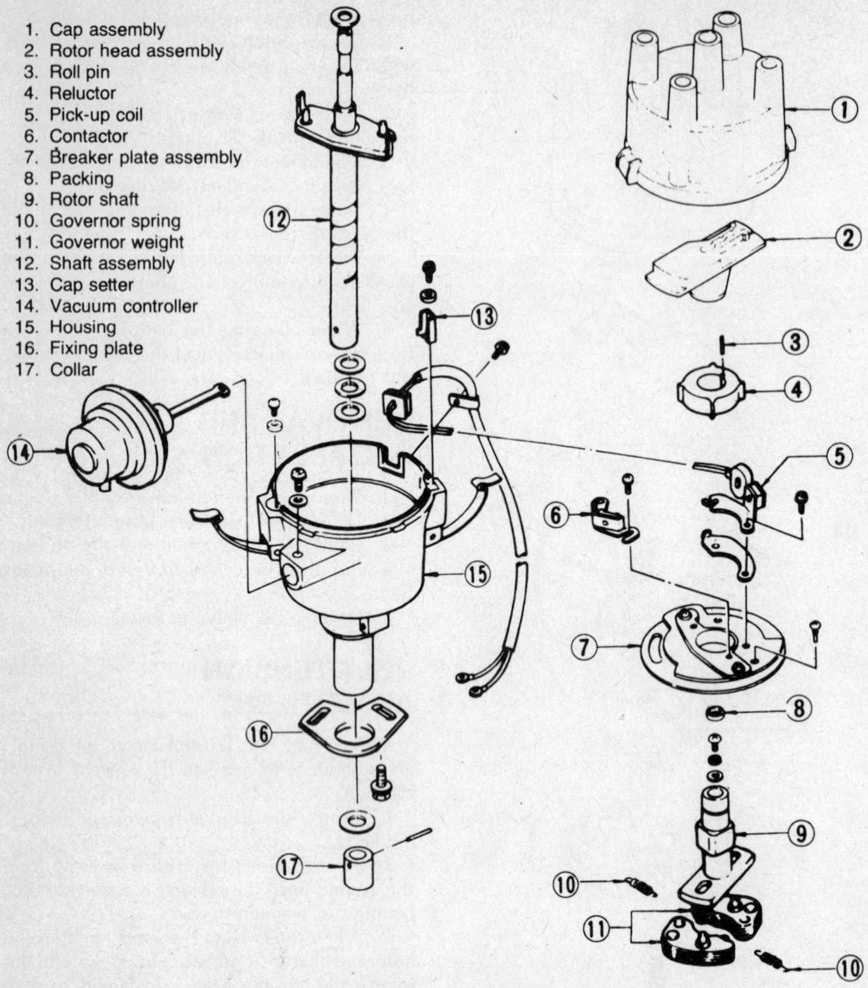

1977 arm–type electronic ignition distributor

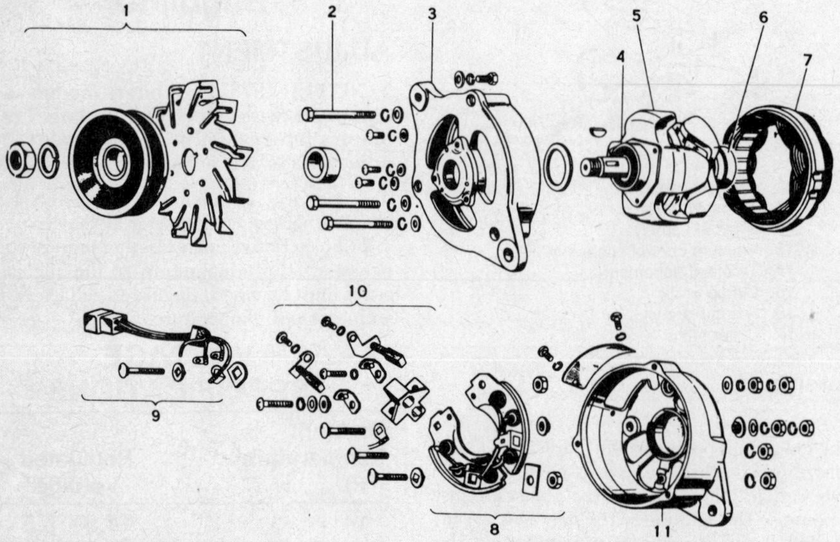

1. Pulley assembly
2. Through bolt
3. Front cover
4. Front bearing
5. Rotor
6. Rear bearing
7. Stator
8. Diode plate assembly
9. Lead wire assembly
10. Brush assembly
11. Rear cover

Hitachi alternator, exploded view

3. Before starting the check, bypass the ammeter as shown to prevent ammeter damage.

4. Start the engine, increase engine speed to 2,500 rpm gradually, and continue for several minutes.

5. If ammeter reading is not below 5 amps, the battery is not fully charged. Replace it with a good one.

6. Return the engine to idle speed.

7. Increase engine speed to 2,500 rpm and check the voltage.

8. If the voltage is incorrect, set the regulator unit gaps to the specified figures.

9. Recheck the voltage. If it is still incorrect, turn in the adjusting screw on the voltage regulator unit to increase voltage, and turn it out to decease voltage.

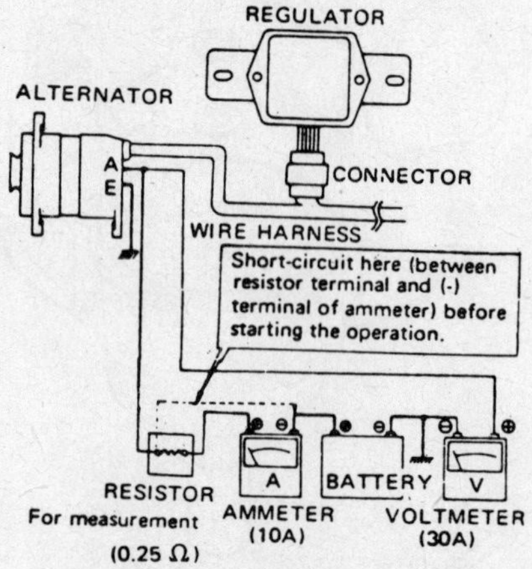

Test setup for Hitachi regulator

Starter

The starter is mounted at the right rear of the engine. The solenoid is mounted on top of the starter and engages the drive pinion through a pivot yoke shift lever.

REMOVAL AND INSTALLATION

1. Disconnect the battery ground cable.
2. Disconnect the switch lead from the solenoid switch terminal. This terminal is usually labeled S.
3. Disconnect the battery cable from the solenoid battery terminal. This terminal is usually labeled B. There is a third solenoid terminal, labeled M, connected to the starter motor.
4. Remove both starter mounting bolts. Pull the starter assembly forward and out.
5. Reverse the procedure to install.

STARTER DRIVE REPLACEMENT

1. Remove the solenoid.
2. Remove the dust cover, E-ring and thrust washer.
3. Remove the brush holder assembly screws.
4. Remove the two through-bolts and the rear cover.

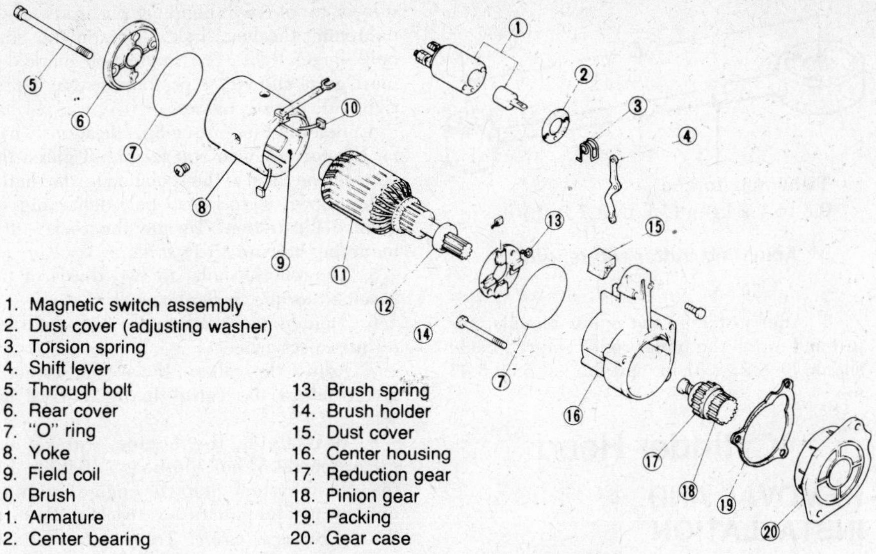

1. Magnetic switch assembly
2. Dust cover (adjusting washer)
3. Torsion spring
4. Shift lever
5. Through bolt
6. Rear cover
7. "O" ring
8. Yoke
9. Field coil
10. Brush
11. Armature
12. Center bearing
13. Brush spring
14. Brush holder
15. Dust cover
16. Center housing
17. Reduction gear
18. Pinion gear
19. Packing
20. Gear case

Exploded view—reduction-type starter

5. Remove the brushes and brush holder.
6. Disengage the yoke and remove the armature assembly.
7. Remove the retaining clip, collar and drive gear.
8. Reverse the above for installation.

Battery

All Datsun models are equipped with a 12-volt battery. The battery is located under the hood in all models. To gain access to the battery in the 280Z coupe, first open the hood, then the inspection flap in the fender. The inspection flap must be closed before the hood.

ENGINE MECHANICAL

Datsun engines are all inline, with either four or six cylinders. Some have overhead valves with a rocker arm arrangement and others have a single overhead camshaft. Refer to the Engine Identification Chart for identification of engines by model, number of cylinders, displacement, and camshaft location. Engines are referred to by model designation codes throughout this section.

All Models Except F-10 and 310

It is best to remove the engine and transmission as a unit.

1. Mark the location of the hinges on the hood. Unbolt and remove.
2. Disconnect the battery cable. Remove the battery on the 220E California models with air conditioning.
3. Drain the coolant and automatic transmission fluid.
4. Remove the grille on 510, 610, and 710 models. Remove the radiator after disconnecting the automatic transmission coolant tubes.
5. Remove the air cleaner.
6. Remove the fan and pulley.
7. Disconnect:
   a. water temperature gauge wire
   b. oil pressure sending unit wire
   c. ignition distributor primary wire
   d. starter motor connections
   e. fuel hose
   f. alternator leads
   g. heater hoses
   h. throttle and choke connections
   i. engine ground cable
   j. thermal transmitter wire—B210, 280Z
   k. fuel cut-off switch wire—B210
   l. vacuum cut solenoid wire—B210

NOTE: A good rule of thumb when disconnecting the rather complex engine wiring of today's cars is to put a piece of masking tape on the wire and on the connection you removed the wire from, then mark both pieces of tape 1, 2, 3, etc. When replacing wiring, simply match the pieces of tape.

CAUTION

On models with air conditioning, it is necessary to remove the compressor and the condenser from their mounts. DO NOT ATTEMPT TO UNFASTEN ANY OF THE AIR CONDITIONER HOSES.

8. Disconnect the power brake booster hose from the engine.
9. Remove the clutch operating cylinder and return spring.
10. Disconnect the speedometer cable from the transmission. Disconnect the backup light switch and any other wiring or attachments to the transmission. On cars with the L20B engine, disconnect the parking brake cable at the rear adjuster.
11. Disconnect the column shift linkage. Remove the floorshift lever. On the Z 20 and B 210 models, remove the boot, withdraw the lock pin, and remove the lever from inside the car.
12. Detach the exhaust pipe from the exhaust manifold. Remove the front section of the exhaust system.
13. Mark the relationship of the driveshaft flanges and remove the driveshaft.
14. Place a jack under the transmission. Remove the rear crossmember. On B210 models, remove the rear engine mounting nuts.
15. Attach a hoist to the lifting hooks on the engine (at either end of the cylinder head). Support the engine.
16. Unbolt the front engine mounts. Tilt the engine by lowering the jack under the transmission and raising the hoist.
17. Reverse the procedure to install the engine.

F10 and 310

It is recommended that the engine and transmission be removed as a unit. If need be, the units may be separated after removal.

1. Mark the location of the hinges on the hood. Remove the hood by holding at both sides and unscrewing bolts. This requires two people.
2. Remove the battery and drain radiator coolant.
3. Remove the air cleaner and disconnect the accelerator wire from the carburetor.
4. Disconnect the following wires and hoses:

   Ignition wire from the coil to the distributor

   Ignition coil ground wire and the engine ground cable

   Disconnect the block connector from the distributor

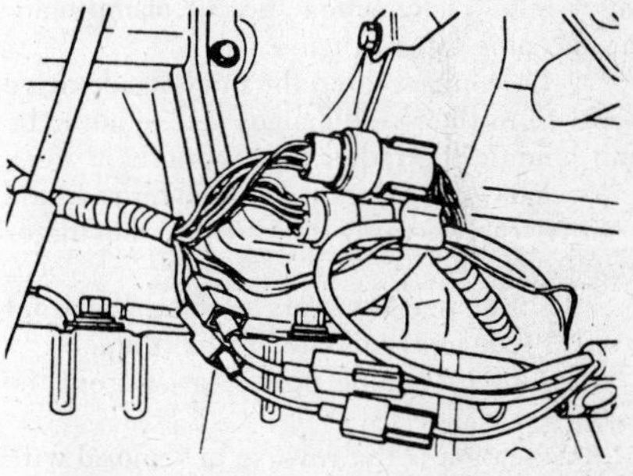

Engine harness connector—F-10

   Remove fusible links

   Unplug all engine harness connectors

   Remove the fuel and fuel return hoses

   Disconnect the upper and lower radiator hoses

   Detach the heater inlet and outlet

   Remove the Master-Vac vacuum hose

   Disconnect the carbon canister hoses and the air pump air cleaner hose

5. Remove the air pump air cleaner.

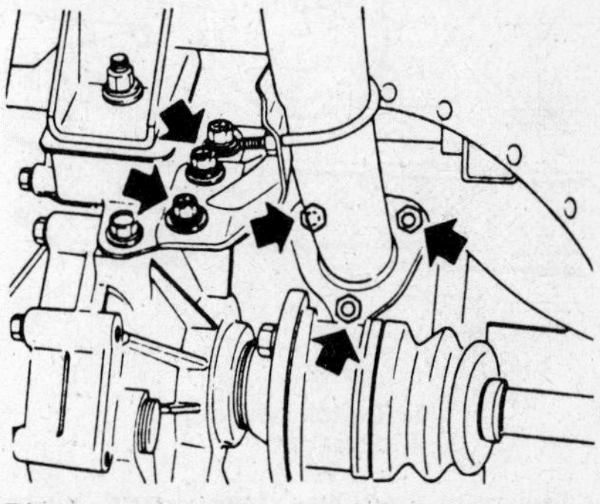

Disconnecting the front exhaust pipe—F-10

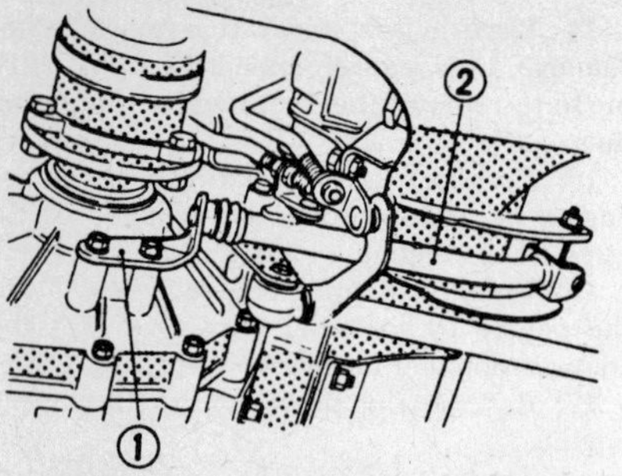

1. Link support
2. Radius link

Removing radius link support—F-10

6. Remove the carbon canister.
7. Remove the auxiliary fan and the washer tank.
8. Remove the grille and radiator with the fan assembly.
9. Remove the clutch cylinder from the clutch housing.
10. Remove both buffer rods (do not alter the length of the rods) and disconnect the speedometer cable.
11. Remove the spring pins from the transmission gear selection rods.
12. Attach suitable engine slingers to the block and attach chain or cable. Keep the lifting source slack at this point.
13. Disconnect the exhaust pipe at both the manifold connection and the clamp holding the pipe to the engine.
14. Disconnect the right and left side drive shafts from their side flanges and remove the bolt holding the radius link support.
15. Lower the shifter and selector rods and remove the securing bolts from the motor mounts.
    a. Remove the nuts holding the front and rear motor mounts to the frame.
16. Lift the engine up and away from the car.

Installation is the reverse of removal with the following cautions and observations.

1. When lowering the engine into the car and onto the frame, make sure to keep it as level as possible.
2. Check the clearance between the frame and clutch housing and make sure that the engine mount bolts are seated in the groove of the mounting bracket.
    a. Distance"H" should be 0.394-0.472 in.

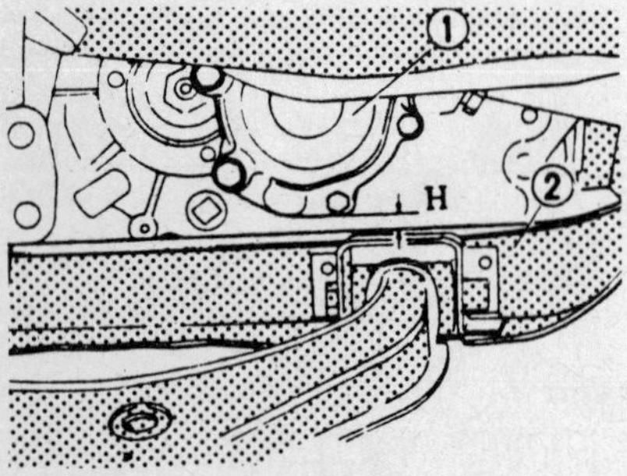

1. Clutch housing
2. Sub-frame

Clearance between frame and clutch housing

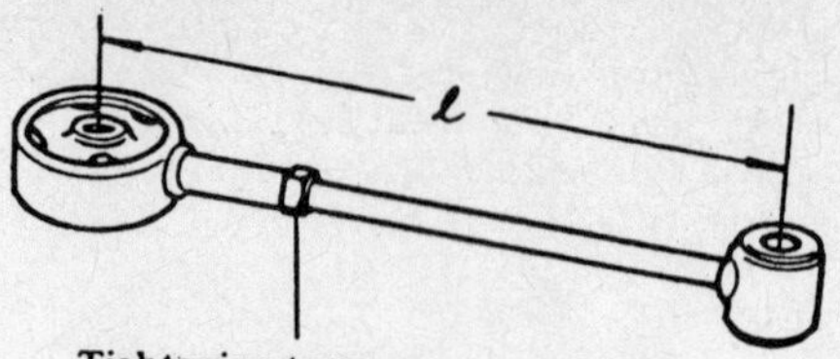

Tightening torque
0.8 to 1.2 kg-m (5.8 to 8.7 ft-lb)

Adjusting buffer rod length

3. After installing the motor mounts, adjust and install the buffer rods. The right side should be 8.23-8.31 in. and the left 5.39-5.47 in.

Cylinder Head

REMOVAL AND INSTALLATION

NOTE: To prevent distortion or warping of the cylinder head, allow the engine to cool completely before removing the head bolts.

FOR OVERHAUL SEE THE ENGINE REBUILDING SECTION

A14 and A15 Overhead Valve Engines

To remove the cylinder head on OHV engines:

1. Drain the coolant.
2. Disconnect the battery ground cable.
3. Remove the upper radiator hose. Remove the water outlet elbow and the thermostat.
4. Remove the air cleaner, carburetor, rocker arm cover, and both manifolds.
5. Remove the spark plugs.
6. Disconnect the temperature gauge connection.
7. Loosen the rocker arm adjusting nuts and turn the adjusting screws out to disengage the push rods. Loosen the rocker shaft bolts evenly and remove the rocker shaft assembly. Remove the push rods, keeping them in the same order for reassembly.
8. Remove the head bolts and remove the head. Rap the head with a mallet to loosen it from the block. Remove it and discard the gasket.

To replace the cylinder head on OHV engines:

1. Make sure that head and block surfaces are clean. Check the cylinder head surface with a straightedge and a feeler gauge for flatness. If the head is warped more than 0.003 in., it must be trued. If this is not done, there will probably be a leak. The block surface should also be checked in the same way. If the block is warped more than 0.003 in., it must be trued.
2. Install a new head gasket. Most gaskets have a TOP marking. Make sure that the proper head gasket is used so that no water passages are blocked off.
3. Install the head. Install the pushrods in their original locations. Install the rocker arm assembly. Loosen the rocker arm adjusting screws to prevent bending pushrods when tightening the head bolts. Tighten the head bolts finger tight. The single bolt marked T must go in the No. 1 position on the center right side of the engine.
4. Refer to the Torque Specifications Chart for the correct head bolt torque. Tighten the bolts to one third of the specified torque in the order shown in the head bolt tightening sequence illustration. Torque the rocker arm mounting bolts to 15-18 ft/lbs.
5. Tighten the bolts to two thirds of the specified torque in sequence.
6. Tighten the bolts to the full specified torque in sequence.
7. Adjust the valves. If no cold setting is given, adjust the valves to the normal hot setting.
8. Reassemble the engine. Intake and exhaust manifold bolt torque is 7-10 ft/lbs. Fill the cooling system. Start the engine and run it until normal temperature is reached. Remove the rocker arm cover. Torque the bolts in sequence once more. Check the valve clearances.
9. Retorque the head bolts after 600 miles of driving. Check the valve clearances after torquing, as this may disturb the settings.

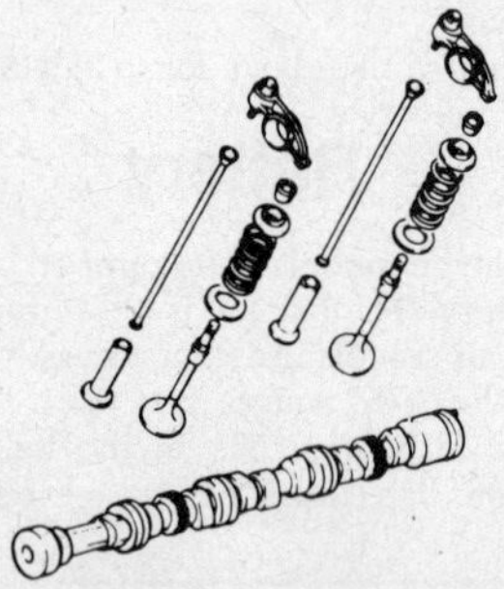

Pushrod, cam and valve assemblies—A series engines

L20B Overhead Camshaft Engines

1. Crank the engine until the No. 1 piston is TDC of the compression stroke and disconnect the negative battery cable, drain the cooling system and remove the air cleaner and attending hoses.
2. Remove the alternator.
3. Disconnect the carburetor throttle linkage, the fuel line and any other vacuum lines or electrical leads, and remove the carburetor.
4. Disconnect the exhaust pipe from the exhaust manifold.
5. Remove the fan and fan pulley.
6. Remove the spark plugs.
7. Remove the rocker cover.
8. Remove the water pump.
9. Remove the fuel pump.
10. Remove the fuel pump drive cam.
11. Mark the relationship of the camshaft sprocket to the timing chain with paint or chalk. If this is done, it will not be necessary to locate the factory timing marks. Before removing the camshaft sprocket, it will be necessary to wedge the chain in place so that it will not fall down into the front cover. The factory procedure is to wedge the timing chain

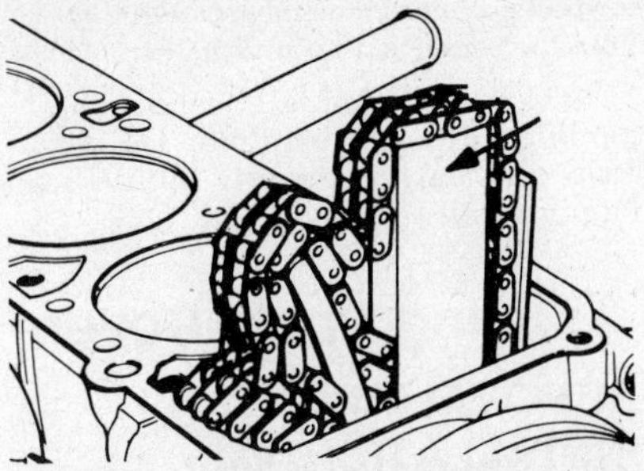

On overhead cam engines, the wedge shown by the arrow can be used to prevent the timing chain from slipping off the crankshaft sprocket.

in place with the wooden wedge shown here. The problem with this procedure is that it may allow the chain tensioner to move out far enough to cock itself against the chain. If this happens, you'll find that the chain won't go back over the sprocket after you've put the sprocket back on. In this case, you'll have to remove the front cover and push the tensioner back. After you've wedged the chain, unbolt the camshaft sprocket and remove it.

12. Loosen and remove the cylinder head bolts. You will need a 10 mm allen wrench to remove the head bolts. Keep the bolts in order since they are different sizes. Lift the cylinder head assembly from the engine. Remove the intake and exhaust manifolds as necessary.

13. Thoroughly clean the block and head mating surfaces. Check for warpage; see the preceding A-series engine section for instructions. Install a new head gasket on the block. Do not use sealer on the gasket.

14. With the crankshaft turned so that the No. 1 piston is at TDC of the compression stroke (if not already done so as mentioned in Step 1), make sure that the camshaft sprocket timing mark and the oblong groove in the plate are aligned.

15. Place the cylinder head in position on the cylinder block, being careful not to allow any of the valves to come in contact with any of the pistons. Do not rotate the crankshaft or camshaft separately because of possible damage which might occur to the valves.

16. Temporarily tighten the two center right and left cylinder head bolts to 14.5 ft/lbs.

17. Install the camshaft sprocket together with the timing chain to the camshaft. Make sure the marks you made earlier line up with each other. If you get into trouble, see "Timing Chain Removal and Installation" for timing procedures.

18. Install the cylinder head bolts. Note that there are two sizes of bolts used; the longer bolts are installed on the driver's side of the engine with a smaller bolt in the center position. The remaining small bolts are installed on the opposite side of the cylinder head.

19. Tighten the cylinder head bolts in three stages: first to 29 ft/lbs, second to 43 ft/lbs, and lastly to 47/62 ft/lbs.

Tighten the cylinder head bolts on all models in the proper sequence.

20. Install and assemble the remaining components of the engine in the reverse order of removal. Adjust the valves. Fill the cooling system; start the engine and run it until normal operating temperature is reached. Retorque the cylinder head bolts to specification, then readjust the valves. Retorque the head bolts again after 600 miles, and recheck the valves at that time.

L24, L28 Overhead Cam Engines

1. Crank the engine until the No. 1 piston is at TDC of the compression stroke, disconnect the battery, and drain the cooling system.

2. Remove the radiator hoses and the heater hoses. Unbolt the alternator mounting bracket and move the alternator to one side.

3. If the car is equipped with air-conditioning, unbolt the compressor and place it to one side. *Do not disconnect the compressor lines. Severe injury could result.*

4. Remove the fan and the fan pulley. Remove the power steering pump.

5. Remove the water pump. Remove the spark plug leads from the spark plugs.

6. Remove the cold start valve and the fuel pipe as an assembly. Remove the throttle linkage.

7. Remove all lines and hoses from the intake manifold. Mark them first so you will know where they go.

8. Unbolt the exhaust manifold from the exhaust pipe. The cylinder head can be removed with both the intake and exhaust manifolds in place.

9. Remove the camshaft cover.

10. Mark the relationship of the camshaft sprocket to the timing marks chain with paint. There are timing marks on the chain and the sprocket which should be visible when No. 1 piston is at TDC, but the marks are quite small and not particularly useful.

11. Before removing the camshaft sprocket, it will be necessary to wedge the chain in place so that it will not fall down into the front cover. The factory procedure is to wedge the timing chain in place with the wooden wedge shown here. The problem with this procedure is that it may allow the chain tensioner to move out far enough to cock itself against the chain. If this happens, you'll find that the chain won't go back over the sprocket after you've put the sprocket back on. In this case, you'll have to remove the front cover and push the tensioner back. After you've wedged the chain, unbolt the camshaft sprocket and remove it.

12. Remove the cylinder head bolts. They require an allen wrench type socket adapter. Keep the bolts in order as two different sizes are used.

13. Lift off the cylinder head. You may have to tap it *lightly* with a hammer.

14. Clean the block and head mating surfaces thoroughly and check for warpage according to the procedure described in the A-series engine section. Install a new head gasket on the block and lower the head into position.

15. Install a new head gasket and place the head in position on the block.

16. Install the head bolts in their original locations.

17. Torque the head bolts in three stages: first to 29 ft/lbs, then to 43 ft/lbs, then to 62 ft/lbs.

18. Reinstall the camshaft sprocket in its original location. The chain is installed at the same time as the sprocket. Make sure the marks you made earlier line up. If the chain has slipped, or the engine has been disturbed, correct the timing as described under "Timing Chain Removal and Installation."

19. Reinstall all ancillary parts, coolant, etc.

20. Adjust the valves.

21. After 600 miles of driving, retorque the head bolts and readjust the valves.

Z20E, Z20S, Overhead Camshaft Engine

1. Complete steps 1 through 5 under L24 Overhead Camshaft Engine. Observe the following note for step 5.

NOTE: The spark plug leads should be marked, however it would be wise to mark them yourself, especially the dual spark plug California models.

2. Disconnect the throttle linkage, the air cleaner or its intake hose assembly (fuel injection). Disconnect the fuel line, the return fuel line and any other vacuum lines or electrical leads. On the Z20S, remove the carburetor to avoid damaging it while removing the head.

NOTE: A good rule of thumb when disconnecting the rather complex engine wiring of today's automobiles is to put a piece of masking tape on the wire or hose and on the connection you removed the wire or hose from, then mark both pieces of tape 1, 2, 3, etc. When replacing wiring, simply match the pieces of tape.

3. Remove the EGR tube from around the rear of the engine.

4. Remove the exhaust air induction tubes from around the front of the engine on Z20S engines and from the exhaust manifold on Z20E engines.

5. Unbolt the exhaust manifold from the exhaust pipe. On the Z20S, remove the fuel pump.

6. On the Z20E, remove the intake manifold supports from under the manifold. Remove the PCV valve from around the rear of the engine if necessary.

7. Remove the spark plugs to protect them from damage. Remove the valve cover.

8. Mark the relationship of the camshaft sprocket to the timing chain with paint or chalk. If this is done, it will not be necessary to locate the factory timing marks. Before removing the camshaft sprocket, it will be necessary to wedge the chain in place so that it will not fall down into the front cover. The factory procedure is to wedge the timing chain in place with the wooden wedge shown here. The problem with this procedure is that it may allow the chain tensioner to move out far enough to cock itself against the chain. If this happens, you'll find that the chain won't go back over the sprocket after you've put the sprocket back on. In this case, you'll have to remove the front cover and push the tensioner back. After you've wedged the chain, unbolt the camshaft sprocket and remove it.

9. Working from both ends in, loosen the cylinder head bolts and remove them. Remove the bolts securing the cylinder head to the front cover assembly.

10. Lift the cylinder head off the engine block. It may be necessary to tap the head lightly with a copper or brass mallet to loosen it.

To install the cylinder head:

11. Thoroughly clean the cylinder block and head surfaces and check both for warpage. See A12, etc. Overhead Valve Engines cylinder head removal section for procedure. (Step 1 of assembly process).

12. Fit the new head gasket. Don't use sealant. Make sure that no open valves are in the way of raised pistons, and do not rotate the crankshaft or camshaft separately because of possible damage which might occur to the valves.

13. Temporarily tighten the two center right and left cylinder head bolts to 14 ft/lbs.

14. Install the camshaft sprocket together with the timing chain to the camshaft. Make sure the marks you made earlier line up with each other. If you get into trouble, see "Timing Chain Removal and Installation" for timing procedures.

15. Install the cylinder head bolts and torque them to 20 ft/lbs, then 40 ft/lbs, then 58 ft/lbs in the order shown in the illustration.

16. Assemble the rest of the components in the reverse order of disassembly.

NOTE: It is always wise to drain the crankcase oil after the cylinder head has been installed to avoid coolant contamination.

VALVE GUIDE REPLACEMENT

When replacing cylinder head valve guides, be sure that the guide height above the top of the cylinder head surface is as follows.

VALVE GUIDE HEIGHT SPECIFICATIONS

Engine	Guide Height (in.)
L24	0.409-0.417
A12A	0.709
L20B, Z20S, Z20E	0.417
L28	0.409-0.417
A14, A15	0.728

Rocker Shaft Removal and Installation

A14, 15 Engines

1. Remove rocker cover.
2. Loosen rocker adjusting bolts and push adjusting screws away from pushrods.
3. Unbolt and remove rocker shaft assembly.
4. To install, reverse the above. Tighten rocker shaft bolts to 14-18 ft/lbs in a circular sequence. Adjust the valves.

Intake and Exhaust Manifolds

REMOVAL AND INSTALLATION

The intake and exhaust manifolds share a common gasket. Therefore, whenever it is necessary to remove either manifold, both manifolds must be removed in order to provide access to the gasket. The gasket must be replaced whenever the manifolds are removed, to prevent air leaks and burned valves.

A14, 15, 20B and Z20S

1. Drain the cooling system on later models with a preheated intake manifold.
2. Disconnect all hoses from the air cleaner and remove the air cleaner.
3. Disconnect and tag all hoses from the intake manifold.
4. Disconnect and tag all linkage, dashpot and bracket if equipped, fuel lines, and hoses from the carburetor. The carburetor may be removed at this time if desired.
5. Remove the EGR control valve and tube.
6. Disconnect the exhaust pipe from the manifold at the flange.
7. Unbolt and remove the manifolds as an assembly. The manifolds may be separated after removal.
8. Use a new gasket on installation. Install the manifolds on the engine. Torque the bolts to specification in a circular pattern, working from the inner to outer bolts. On later L20B engines, be sure that the stud bolt is installed in the center of the outermost guide hole (at the #4 cylinder) in the manifold. The remainder of installation is the reverse of removal.

Fuel Injected L24, 28 and Z20E

1. Drain the cooling system.
2. Remove the air regulator hoses which attach to the rocker cover, three-way connector, and air regulator, as an assembly.
3. Remove the cold start valve and fuel pipe as an assembly.
4. Remove the EGR valve, vacuum switching valve, and hoses as an assembly.
5. Remove the BPT valve control tube from the intake manifold.
6. Remove the throttle chamber, together with the dash pot and BCDD.
7. Remove the fuel pipe, pressure regulator, cold start valve, injector, canister control vacuum tube, and canister purge hose as an assembly.

NOTE: Unfasten the clip securing the fuel inlet hose to the injector. Do not pull, twist, or bend the fuel inlet hose during removal.

8. Remove the PCV valve hose, small heat shield plate, and EGR tube.
9. Remove the intake manifold and large heat shield plate as an assembly.
10. Unbolt the exhaust pipe from the manifold, and remove the exhaust manifold from the engine.
11. Use new gaskets upon installation. Torque the intake and exhaust manifold bolts to specification in a circular pattern, working from the center out toward the ends.

NOTE: 1979 and later models have a modified exhaust manifold. Do not use 1978 and earlier gaskets on 1979 and later models.

Timing Chain Cover

REMOVAL AND INSTALLATION, OIL SEAL REPLACEMENT

A14 and A15 Overhead Valve Engines

1. Remove the radiator. Loosen the alternator adjustment and remove the belt. Loosen the air pump adjustment and remove the belt on engines with the air pump system.
2. Remove the fan and unbolt and remove water pump.
3. Bend back the lock tab from the crankshaft pulley nut. Remove the nut with a heavy wrench. Rap the wrench with a hammer. The nut must be unscrewed opposite normal engine rotation. Pull off the pulley.
4. It is recommended that the oil pan be removed or loosened before the front cover is removed.
5. Unbolt and remove the timing chain cover.
6. Replace the crankshaft oil seal in the cover. Most models use a felt seal.
7. Reverse the procedure to install, using new gaskets. Apply sealant to both sides of the timing cover gasket. Front cover bolt torque is 4 ft/lbs, water pump bolt torque is 7-10 ft/lbs, and oil pan bolt torque is 4 ft/lbs.

L20B, L24, L28, Z20E and Z20S Overhead Cam Engines

NOTE: It may be necessary to remove the cylinder head to perform this operation if you cannot cut the front of the head gasket cleanly as described in Step 10. If so, you will need a new head gasket.

1. Disconnect the negative battery cable from the battery, drain the cooling system, and remove the radiator together with the upper and lower radiator hoses.
2. Loosen the alternator drive belt adjusting screw and remove the drive belt. Remove the bolts which attach the alternator bracket to the engine and set the alternator aside out of the way.
3. Remove the distributor.
4. Remove the oil pump attaching screws, and take out the pump and its drive spindle.
5. Remove the cooling fan and the fan pulley together with the drive belt.
6. Remove the water pump.
7. Remove the crankshaft pulley bolt and remove the crankshaft pulley.
8. Remove the bolts holding the front cover to the front of the cylinder block, the four bolts which retain the front of the oil pan to the bottom of the front cover, and the two bolts which are screwed down through the front of the cylinder head and into the top of the front cover.

9. Carefully pry the front cover off the front of the engine.

10. Cut the exposed front section of the oil pan gasket away from the oil pan. Do the same to the gasket at the top of the front cover. Remove the two side gaskets and clean all of the mating surfaces.

11. Cut the portions needed from a new oil pan gasket and top front cover gasket.

12. Apply sealer to all of the gaskets and position them on the engine in their proper places.

13. Apply a light coating of grease to the crankshaft oil seal and carefully mount the front cover to the front of the engine and install all of the mounting bolts.

Tighten the 8 mm bolts to 7-12 ft/lbs and the 6 mm bolts to 3-6 ft/lbs. Tighten the oil pan attaching bolts to 4-7 ft/lbs.

14. Before installing the oil pump, place the gasket over the shaft and make sure that the mark on the drive spindle faces (aligned with) the oil pump hole. Install the oil pump so that the projection on the top of the shaft is located in the exact position as when it was removed or in the 11:25 o'clock position with the piston in the No. 1 cylinder placed at TDC on the compression stroke, if the engine was disturbed since disassembly. Tighten the oil pump attaching screws to 8-10 ft/lbs. See "Oil Pump Removal and Installation."

Timing Chain and Camshaft

REMOVAL AND INSTALLATION

A14 and A15 Overhead Valve Engines

This operation can only be performed with the engine out of the car.

1. Remove the engine.
2. Remove the rocker cover and rocker shaft assembly.
3. Remove the pushrods.
4. Invert the engine.
5. Remove the timing chain cover.
6. Remove the chain tensioner.
7. Remove the camshaft sprocket retaining bolt.
8. Remove the camshaft sprocket, crankshaft sprocket, and timing chain as an assembly. Be careful not to lose the shims (if present) and oil slinger from behind the crankshaft sprocket.
9. Remove the distributor, and distributor drive spindle. Remove the oil pump and pump driveshaft.
10. Unbolt and remove the camshaft locating plate. Remove the camshaft carefully. The engine must be inverted to prevent the lifters from falling down into the engine. If the lifters must be removed, remove the oil pan and remove them after withdrawing the camshaft. Keep the lifters in order and return them to their original positions.
11. The camshaft bearings can be pressed out and replaced. They are available in undersizes, should it be necessary to regrind the camshaft journals. The bearings must be line-bored after installation.
12. Coat the bearings and camshaft with engine oil. Reinstall the camshaft. If the locating plate has an oil hole, it should be to the right of the engine. The locating plate is marked with the word LOWER and an arrow. The engine locating plate bolt torque is 3-4 ft/lbs. Be careful to engage the drive pin in the rear end of the camshaft with the slot in the oil pump driveshaft.
13. Camshaft end-play can be measured after temporarily replacing the camshaft sprocket and securing bolt.

If end-play is excessive, replace the locating plate. They are available in several sizes.

CAMSHAFT END-PLAY SPECIFICATIONS

Engine	Camshaft End-Play (in.)
A12A	0.001-0.003
A14, A15	0.0004-0.002
L20B, Z20S, Z20E	0.0031-0.0150
L28	0.0031-0.0150

14. If the crankshaft or camshaft has been replaced, install the sprockets temporarily and make sure that they are parallel. Adjust by shimming under the crankshaft sprocket.
15. Assemble the sprockets and chain, aligning them.
16. Turn the crankshaft until the keyway and No. 1 piston is at top dead center. Install the sprockets and chain. The oil slinger behind the crankshaft sprocket must be replaced with the concave surface to the front. If the chain and sprocket installation is correct, the sprocket marks must be aligned between the shaft centers when No. 1 piston is at top dead center. Engine camshaft sprocket retaining bolt torque is 33-36 ft/lbs.
17. The rest of the reassembly procedure is the reverse of disassembly. Engine chain tensioner bolt torque is 4-6 ft/lbs.

Timing Chain and Tensioner Removal and Installation

L20B, L24, L28, Z20E and Z20S Overhead Cam Engines

1. Before beginning any disassembly procedures, position the No. 1 piston at TDC on the compression stroke.
2. Remove the front cover as previously outlined. Remove the camshaft cover.
3. With the No. 1 piston at TDC, the timing marks on the camshaft sprocket and the timing chain should be visible. Mark both of them with paint. Also mark the relationship of the camshaft sprocket to the camshaft. At this point you will notice that there are three sets

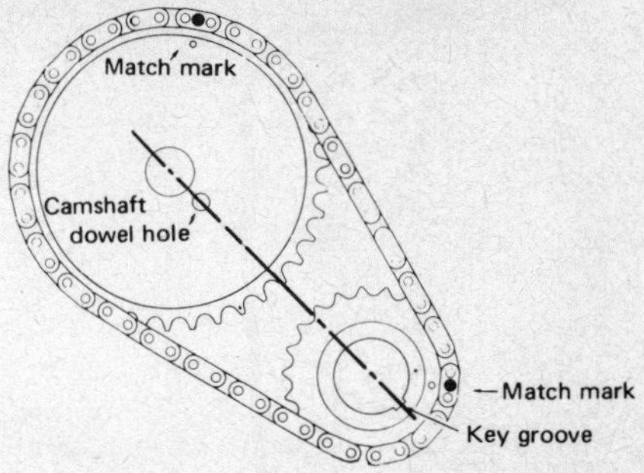

A14 and 15 sprocket and timing chain assembly

of timing marks and locating holes in the sprocket. They are for making adjustments to compensate for timing chain stretch. See the following "Timing Chain Adjustment" for more details.

4. With the timing marks on the cam sprocket clearly marked, locate and mark the timing marks on the crankshaft sprocket. Also mark the chain timing mark. Of course, if the chain is not to be re-used, marking it is useless.
5. Unbolt the camshaft sprocket and remove the sprocket along with the chain. As you remove the chain, hold it where the chain tensioner contacts it. When the chain is removed, the tensioner is going to come apart. Hold on to it and you won't lose any of the parts. There is no need to remove the chain guide unless it is being replaced.
6. Install the timing chain and the camshaft sprocket together after first positioning the chain over the crankshaft sprocket. Position the sprocket so that the marks made earlier line up. This is assuming that the engine has not been disturbed. The camshaft and crankshaft keys should both be pointing upward. If a new chain and/or gear is being installed, position the sprocket so that the timing marks on the chain align with the marks on the crankshaft sprocket and the camshaft sprocket (with both keys pointing up). The marks are on the right-hand side of the sprockets as you face the engine. If you must turn either the crankshaft or camshaft sprocket, be careful that the valves do not contact the tops of the pistons.

Engines, except the L24 and L28, have 44 pins between the mating marks of the chain and sprockets when the chain is correctly installed. The L24 and L28 engines have 42 pins between the timing marks in all years. The Z20E and Z20S engines do not use the pin counting method for finding correct valve timing. Instead, position the key in the crankshaft sprocket so that it is pointing upward and install the camshaft sprocket on the camshaft with its dowel pin at the top using the number 2 mounting hole and timing mark. The painted links of the chain should be on the right-hand side of the sprockets as you face the engine. See the illustration. The factory refers to the pins as links, but in American terminology this is incorrect. Count the pins. There are two pins per chain link. *This is an important step. If you do not get the exact number of pins between the timing marks, valve timing will be incorrect.*

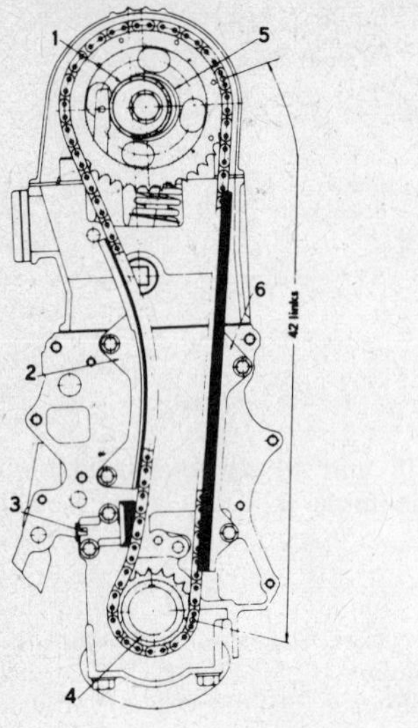

1. Fuel pump drive cam
2. Chain guide
3. Chain tensioner
4. Crankshaft sprocket
5. Camshaft sprocket
6. Chain guide

Camshaft chain installation—OHC Engines

7. Install the chain tensioner. Install the remaining components in the reverse order of disassembly.

The camshaft can be removed from the cylinder head with the head either in place on the engine or removed. To remove the camshaft:

1. Remove the camshaft cover or cylinder head. Remove the camshaft sprocket. Remove the rocker arm springs.
2. Loosen the rocker pivot locknuts and remove the rocker arms by pressing down the valve springs.
3. Remove the camshaft locating plate.
4. Withdraw the camshaft carefully. Do not remove the camshaft bearings. If these bearings are removed, an alignment boring procedure will be required to properly realign them.

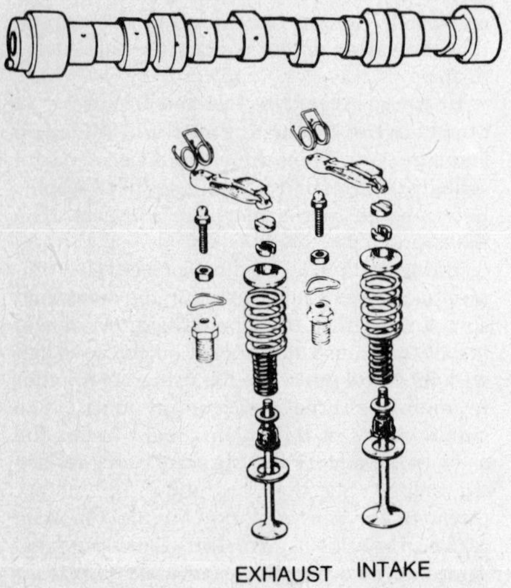

Cam and valve assemblies—L series engines

To replace the camshaft:

5. Coat the bearings and camshaft with engine oil and carefully slide the cam into the head. Install the retaining plate with the oblong groove in the plate facing out toward the front of the car.
6. Check camshaft end-play. It should be 0.003-0.015 in. Adjust by replacing the locating plate.
7. Replace the sprocket, torquing the bolt to 87-116 ft/lbs.
8. Install the rocker arms, pressing down the valve springs with a screwdriver. Install the rocker arm springs.
9. Adjust the valves.

TIMING CHAIN ADJUSTMENT

L20B, L24, L28, Z20E and Z20S

When the timing chain stretches excessively, the valve timing will be adversely affected. There are three sets of holes and timing marks on the camshaft sprocket. The first two are used for the four cylinder engines, and the third one is only of use for the L24 engine.

If the stretch of the chain roller links is excessive, adjust the camshaft sprocket location by transferring the set position of the camshaft sprocket from the factory position of No. 1 to one of the other positions as follows:

1. Turn the crankshaft until the No. 1 piston is at TDC on the compression stroke. Examine whether the camshaft sprocket location notch is to the left of the oblong groove on the camshaft retaining plate. If the notch in the sprocket is to the left of the groove in the retaining plate, then the chain is stretched and needs adjusting.
2. Remove the camshaft sprocket together with the chain and reinstall the sprocket and chain with the locating dowel on the camshaft inserted into either the No. 2 or 3 hole of the sprocket (depending on whether the engine is a four or six cylinder). The timing mark on the timing chain must be aligned with the mark on the sprocket. The amount of modification is 4 degrees of crankshaft rotation for each mark.
3. Recheck the valve timing as outlined in Step 1. The notch in the sprocket should be to the right of the groove in the camshaft retaining plate.
4. If and when the notch cannot be brought to the right of the groove, the timing chain is worn beyond repair and must be replaced.

Pistons and Connecting Rods

On all engines, it is advisable to mark the connecting rods on removal so that they will be reinstalled in the same cylinder, facing in the same direction. On early engines with a clamp bolt at the top of the connecting rod, the clamp bolt must face toward the camshaft side of the engine. The oil hole at the bottom of the connecting rod must face to the right side. F marks or notches on the tops of the pistons must be at the front of the piston when installed.

ENGINE LUBRICATION

Oil Pump

REMOVAL AND INSTALLATION

1975 and Later A14, A15 Engines

The oil pump is mounted on the right side of the engine.

1. Drain the oil.
2. Remove the front stabilizer.
3. Remove the splash shield.
4. Unbolt and withdraw the pump from the side of the engine.
5. Prime the pump. Reverse the procedure to install. Torque the pump mounting bolts to 9-11 ft/lbs.

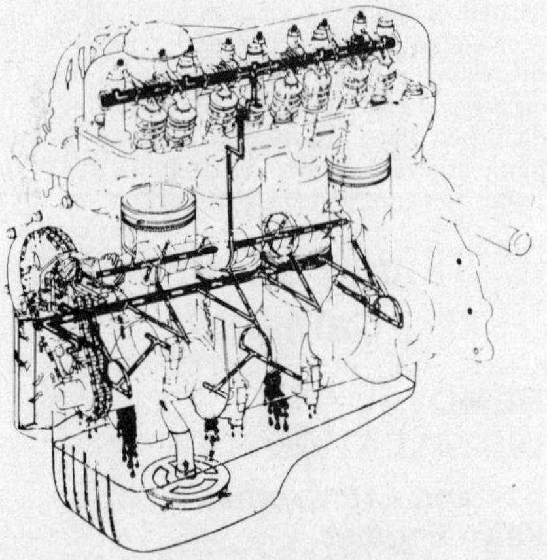

A series engine lubrication circuit

1975–79 L20B, L24, L28 Engines

These oil pumps are mounted at the bottom of the engine front cover.

1. Remove the distributor.
2. Drain the oil.
3. Remove the front stabilizer.
4. Remove the splash shield.
5. Unbolt and remove the oil pump.
6. Before replacing the pump, prime the pump and position No. 1 cylinder at top dead center. Install the oil pump with the spindle punch mark toward the front. The projection on top of the drive spindle must be in the 11:25 o'clock position, viewed from above. Torque the mounting bolts to 11-15 ft/lbs.
7. Install the distributor with the rotor pointing to the No. 1 spark plug lead in the cap.
8. Reverse the rest of the removal procedure.

1980 and Later L28E, L24, L20B, Z20S, Z20E Engines

1. Drain the oil from the oil pan.
2. Turn the crankshaft so that the No. 1 piston is at top dead center on its compression stroke.
3. Remove the distributor cap and mark the position of the distributor rotor in relation to the distributor base with a piece of chalk.

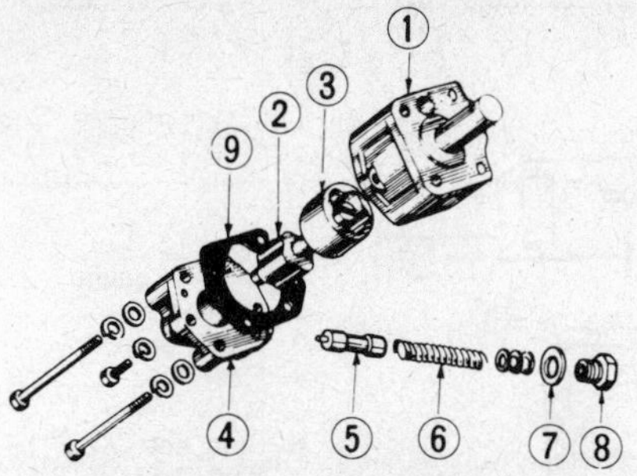

Oil pump, OHC Engines

1. Pump body
2. Inner rotor and shaft
3. Outer rotor
4. Pump cover
5. Pressure regulator valve
6. Valve spring
7. Washer
8. Cap
9. Gasket

Oil pump, OHC Engines

4. Remove the front stabilizer bar, if so equipped.
5. Remove the splash shield.
6. Remove the oil pump body with the drive spindle assembly.
7. To install, fill the pump housing with engine oil, align the punch mark on the spindle with the hole in the oil pump. The No. 1 piston should be at top dead center (TDC) on its compression stroke.
8. With a new gasket placed over the drive spindle, install the oil pump and drive spindle assembly, making sure the tip of the drive spindle fits into the distributor shaft notch securely. The distributor rotor should be pointing to the match mark you made earlier.

NOTE: Great care must be taken not to disturb the distributor rotor while installing the oil pump, or the ignition timing may be wrong.

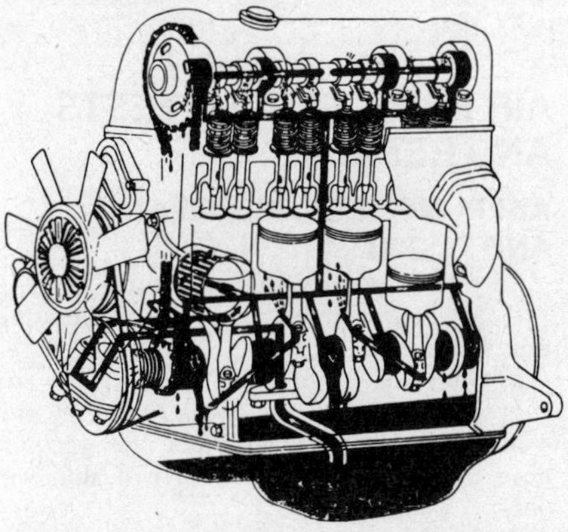

L series engine lubrication circuit

9. Assemble the remaining components in the reverse order of removal.

INSPECTION

The pump can readily be disassembled and checked for wear. Refer to the Oil Pump Specifications Chart for clearances. The rotor pump used on J engines has a chamfered edge on the outer rotor. On reassembly, the chamfer must be toward the base of the pump body.

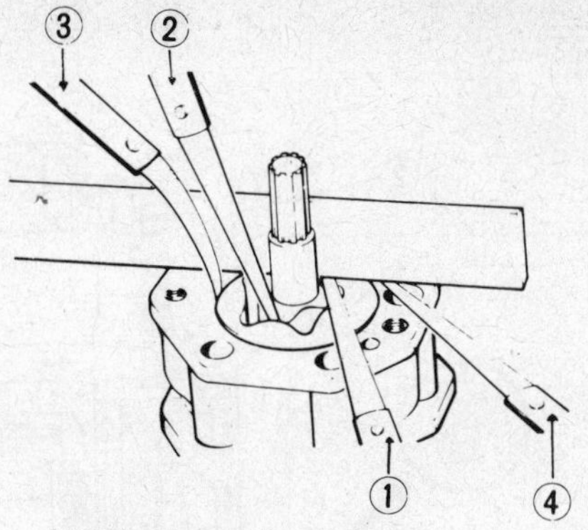

1. Side clearance
2. Tip clearance
3. Outer rotor to pump body clearance
4. Rotor to cover clearance

Clearance to be checked in rotor oil pumps

ENGINE COOLING

Water Pump

REMOVAL AND INSTALLATION

1. Drain the engine coolant.
2. Loosen the bolts retaining the fan shroud to the radiator and remove the shroud.
3. Loosen the belt, then remove the fan and pulley from the water pump hub.
4. Remove the bolts retaining the pump and remove the pump together with the gasket from the front cover.
5. Remove all traces of gasket material and install the pump in the reverse order. Use a new gasket and sealer. Tighten the bolts uniformly.

Thermostat

REMOVAL AND INSTALLATION

The engine thermostat is housed in the water outlet casting on the cylinder head.

1. Drain the coolant.
2. Remove the upper radiator hose and unbolt the water outlet elbow.
3. The thermostat may now be removed.
4. Reverse the removal procedure to replace the thermostat. When installing be sure that the side with the spring faces into the engine. Use a new gasket.

THERMOSTAT SPECIFICATIONS

Engine	Opening Temperature of Thermostat (°F)	Full Opening of Thermostat (in.)
All	183	0.315 @ 203°F

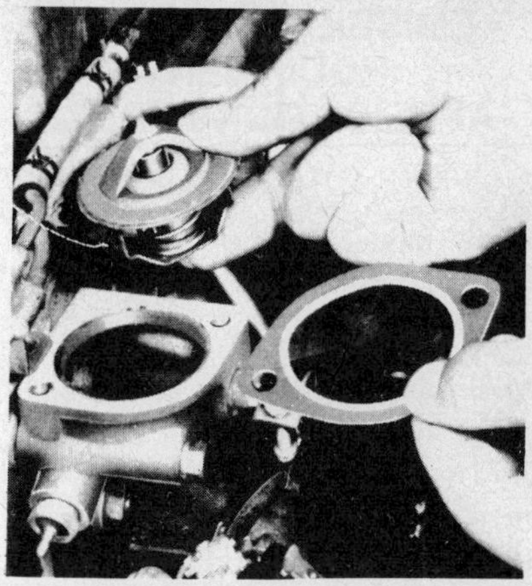

Correct thermostat installation

Radiator

REMOVAL AND INSTALLATION

To remove the radiator:

1. Drain the coolant.
2. Disconnect the upper hose, lower hose, and expansion tank hose.
3. Disconnect the automatic transmission oil cooler lines after draining the transmission. Cap the lines to exclude dirt.
4. If the fan has a shroud, unbolt the shroud and move it back, hanging it over the fan.
5. Remove the radiator mounting bolts and radiator.
6. Reverse the procedure to replace the radiator. Fill the automatic transmission to the proper level. Fill the cooling system.

EMISSION CONTROLS

Various systems are used to control crankcase vapors, exhaust emissions, and fuel vapors. The accompanying chart shows the systems used with various models and engines.

Crankcase Ventilation System

The closed crankcase ventilation system is used to route the crankcase vapors to the intake manifold (carburetor equipped) or throttle chamber (fuel injected), to be mixed and burned with the air/fuel mixture.

An air intake hose is connected between the air cleaner assembly or the throttle chamber, and the valve cover. A return hose is connected between a steel net baffle on the side of the crankcase to the intake manifold or throttle chamber, with a metering positive crankcase ventilation (PCV) valve in the hose.

To test the system, allow the engine to idle. With the PCV valve removed from the hose, a

EMISSION CONTROL EQUIPMENT APPLICATIONS TABLE

Year	Model	Engine	Emission Control Systems
1975	B210	A14	1, 3, 4, 5, 6, 7
1975	710	L20B	1, 3, 4, 5, 6, 7
1975	610	L20B	1, 3, 4, 5, 6, 7
1976-1977	610	L20B	1, 3, 4, 6, 7, 8, 9, 10, 11
1976-1977	710	L20B	1, 3, 4, 6, 7, 8, 9, 10, 11
1976-1978	B210	A14, A15	1, 3, 4, 6, 7, 8, 10, 11
	280Z	L28	1, 6, 7, 9, 11, 12
1977-1978	280Z	L28	1, 6, 7, 9, 12
1977-1978	F-10	A14	1, 3, 4, 6, 7, 8, 10, 11
1978-1980	510	L20B	1, 3, 4, 6, 7, 8, 9
1978-1980 ①	810	L24	1, 3, 6, 7, 9, 13, 17, 18
1978-1980	200SX	L20B	1, 3, 4, 6, 7, 8, 9
1979-1980	210	A12A	1, 3, 5, 6
		A14	1, 5, 8
		A15	10, 13, 14
1979-1980	310	A14	1, 3, 5, 6, 8, 10, 14, 17
1979-1980	280ZX & L28		1, 3, 5, 6, 8, 10, 13, 17, 18

1. Closed crankcase ventilation system
2. Not used
3. Air pump system
4. Engine modification system
5. Fuel vapor control system
6. Exhaust gas recirculation system
7. Catalytic converter California cars only
8. Early fuel evaporation system
9. Boost controlled deceleration device
10. High altitude compensator—California option
11. TCS—manual transmission exc. California
12. Floor temperature sensing device
13. Spark timing control & 280ZX
14. Air induction system—49 states
15. Catalytic converter—50 states
16. Catalytic converter—49 states
17. 3 way catalytic converter w/exhaust sensor (California only)
18. Electronic fuel injection

① 1979-80: All 810 models are equipped with catalytic converter

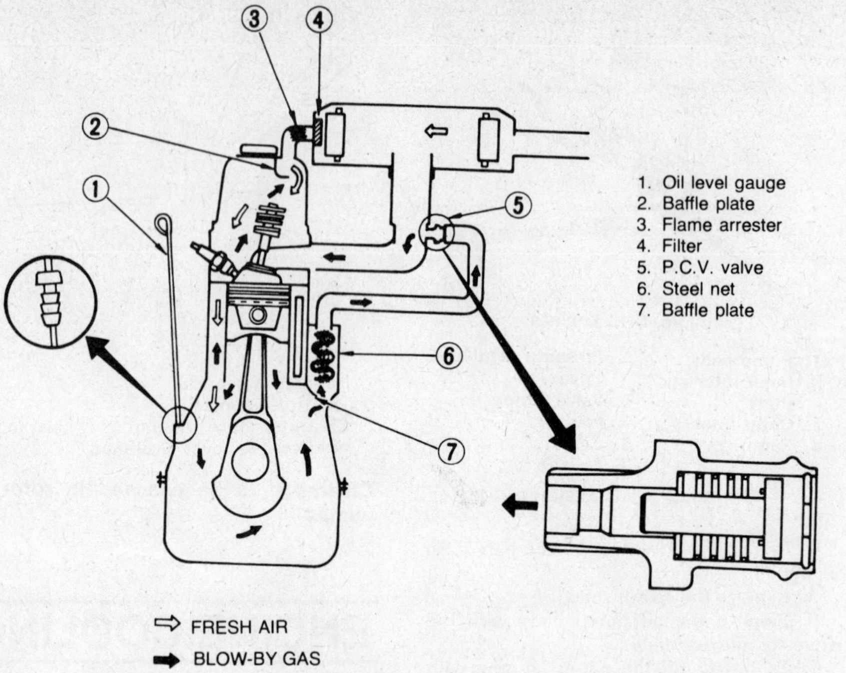

PCV valve air flow

hissing sound should be heard, and vacuum should be felt when you cover the engine side of the valve with your finger. The PCV valve should be replaced at regular intervals of 24,000 miles.

Air Injection Reactor System

In this system, an air injection pump, driven by the engine, compresses, distributes, and injects filtered air into the exhaust port of each cylinder. The air combines with unburned hydrocarbons and carbon monoxide to produce harmless compounds. The system includes an air cleaner, the belt driven air pump, a check valve, and an anti-backfire valve.

The air pump draws air through a hose connected to the carburetor air cleaner or to a separate air cleaner. The pump is a rotary vane unit with an integral pressure regulating valve. The pump outlet pressure passes through a check valve which prevents exhaust gas from entering the pump in case of insufficient pump outlet pressure. An anti-backfire valve admits air from the air pump into the intake manifold on deceleration to prevent backfiring in the exhaust manifold.

In 1976 California models utilized a secondary system consisting of an air control valve which limits injection of secondary air and an emergency relief valve which controls the supply of secondary air. This system protects the converter from overheating. In 1977 the function of these two valves was taken by a single combined air control (C.A.C.) valve.

All engines with the air pump system have a series of minor alterations to accommodate the system. These are:

1. Special close-tolerance carburetor. Most engines, except the L16, require a slightly rich idle mixture adjustment.
2. Distributor with special advance curve. Ignition timing is retarded about 10° at idle in most cases.
3. Cooling system changes such as larger fan, higher fan speed, and thermostatic fan clutch. This is required to offset the increase in temperature caused by retarded timing at idle.
4. Faster idle speed.
5. Heated air intake on some engines.

The only periodic maintenance required on the air pump system is replacement of the air filter element and adjustment of the drive belt.

AIR PUMP SYSTEM TESTS AND REPAIRS

AIR PUMP TEST, REMOVAL AND INSTALLATION

To test air pump output pressure:

1. The engine must be at normal operating temperature.
2. Stop the engine. Disconnect the air supply hose from the check valve at the exhaust manifold. Disconnect the vacuum hose from the air control valve (Calif. cars only).
3. Start the engine. Check the pump pressure output at 1,500 rpm. With an L24, or L28 engine, the pressure should be 0.063 in. (16 mm.) Hg or more. 1975 and later L20B, A14 and A15, Z20S, L20B engines should have at least 3.94 in. Hg pressure.
4. If air pressure is not as specified, disconnect the air hose at the anti-backfire valve. Plug the hose opening and repeat the pressure test.
5. At 1500 rpm, close the hole of the gauge with a finger. If leaking air is felt at the relief valve, replace the relief valve.
6. Replace the pump if it does not show proper pressure.

To remove and replace the air pump:
1. Disconnect the hoses from the pump.
2. Remove the bolt holding the pump to the belt adjustment arm or adjusting bracket.
3. Unbolt the pump from the mounting bracket. Remove the belt.
4. Remove the pump from the car.
5. Reverse the procedure to install, adjusting the belt to have about ½ in. play under thumb pressure at the longest span between pulleys.

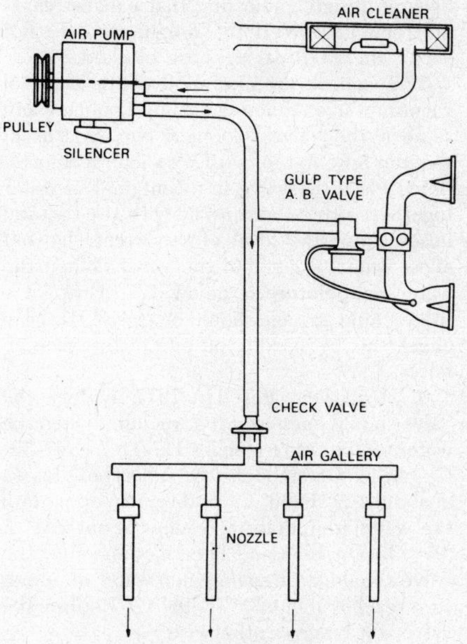

Air pump system

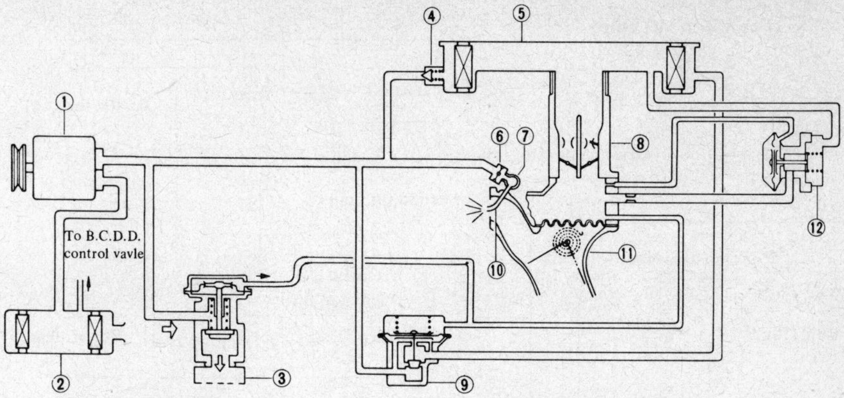

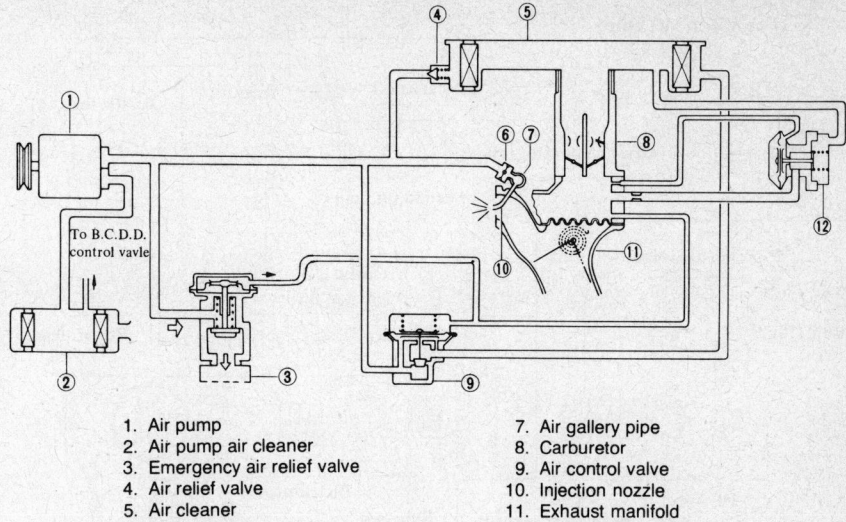

1. Air pump
2. Air pump air cleaner
3. Emergency air relief valve
4. Air relief valve
5. Air cleaner
6. Check valve
7. Air gallery pipe
8. Carburetor
9. Air control valve
10. Injection nozzle
11. Exhaust manifold
12. Anti-backfire valve

Air pump system schematic—typical

CHECK VALVE TEST, REMOVAL AND INSTALLATION

To test the check valve action:
1. The engine must be at normal operating temperature.
2. Stop the engine. Disconnect the air supply hose from the check valve at the exhaust manifold.
3. The valve plate inside the valve body should be lightly positioned against the valve seat away from the air distributor manifold.
4. Insert a small screwdriver into the valve and depress the valve plate. The plate should reset freely when released.
5. Start the engine. Increase the idle speed to 1500 rpm and check for exhaust leakage. Valve pulsation or vibration at idle is a normal condition.

To remove and replace the check valve.
1. Remove the check valve from the air gallery pipe, holding the air gallery flange with a wrench.
2. On reinstallation, the proper torque is 65-76 ft/lbs.

AIR CONTROL VALVE TEST, REMOVAL AND INSTALLATION

1. Warm engine to normal operating temperature.
2. Check all hoses for leaks.
3. Disconnect the outlet side hose of the valve and check for air flow. If no air is felt, replace the valve.
4. Disconnect the vacuum hose from the valve. If air flow from the air hose stops, the valve is working correctly, if air flow continues, replace the valve.
5. To replace valve, disconnect hoses and remove from bracket.

EMERGENCY AIR RELIEF VALVE TEST, REMOVAL AND INSTALLATION

1. Warm engine to normal operating temperature.
2. Check all vacuum hoses for leaks.
3. Run engine at 2000 rpm and check for air flow at outlet port of valve. If no air is felt, the valve is normal.
4. Disconnect the vacuum hose from the valve. Run engine at 2000 rpm and check for air at the outlet port of the valve. If air is felt, the valve is normal.
5. To remove valve, remove hoses and disconnect valve from mounts.

ANTI-BACKFIRE VALVE TEST, REMOVAL AND INSTALLATION

To test the anti-backfire valve:
1. The engine must be at normal operating temperature.
2. Disconnect the air hose from the air cleaner at the anti-backfire valve. Plug the hose.
3. Open and close the throttle rapidly. Air flow should be felt at the valve for 1-2 seconds on deceleration. If no air flow is felt or flow is felt continuously for more than 2 seconds, replace the valve.

To remove the anti-backfire valve, simply disconnect the hoses.

Air Induction System

This system is used on models 210, 310 and 810 models made in USA and Canada except California, models 200SX and 510 in all of USA and model 280ZX in USA except California.

The system is designed to send fresh air into the exhaust manifold without the need of an air pump, utilizing a vacuum caused by exhaust pulsation in the exhaust manifold. The fresh air promotes burning of hot HC and Co gases which otherwise would escape the combustion process.

The only periodic maintenance required is the replacement of the air induction filter, installed at the dust side of the air cleaner at 24,000 mile or 30 month intervals.

Exhaust Gas Recirculation System (EGR)

Oxides of nitrogen (NO_x) are formed in the engine under conditions of high temperature and high pressure. Elimination of one of these two conditions reduces the formation of NO_x. Exhaust gas recirculation is used to reduce combustion temperatures in the engine.

1975–78 280Z
1979 and Later 280ZX

Only models sold in California have EGR in 1975 and 1976. All 1977-79 models have EGR, and all 1980 and later models sold in Canada and for 49 State use in the U.S. have EGR; 1980 and later models sold in California do not have the system.

An EGR valve is mounted on the intake manifold. The exhaust gas is drawn from the exhaust manifold, through the EGR valve, and into the intake manifold. The EGR valve is closed when the engine is idling; exhaust gas recirculation would cause a rough idle. As the throttle is opened, vacuum is applied to the EGR valve vacuum diaphragm. When the vacuum reaches about 2 inches of mercury (in. Hg) the diaphragm moves against spring pressure and is fully open at 8 in. Hg of vacuum. As the diaphragm moves up, it pulls the EGR valve pintle from its seat, allowing exhaust gas to be pulled into the intake manifold by intake vacuum. The valve closes at full throttle, when EGR is not needed, as a means of improving fuel economy.

1975-76 models have an electrically operated solenoid valve mounted on the EGR valve. The vacuum signal to the EGR valve must travel through the solenoid valve. The solenoid valve prevents EGR when the engine is cold. 1975-76 models use a temperature switch installed in the engine coolant outlet housing; as long as engine coolant tem-

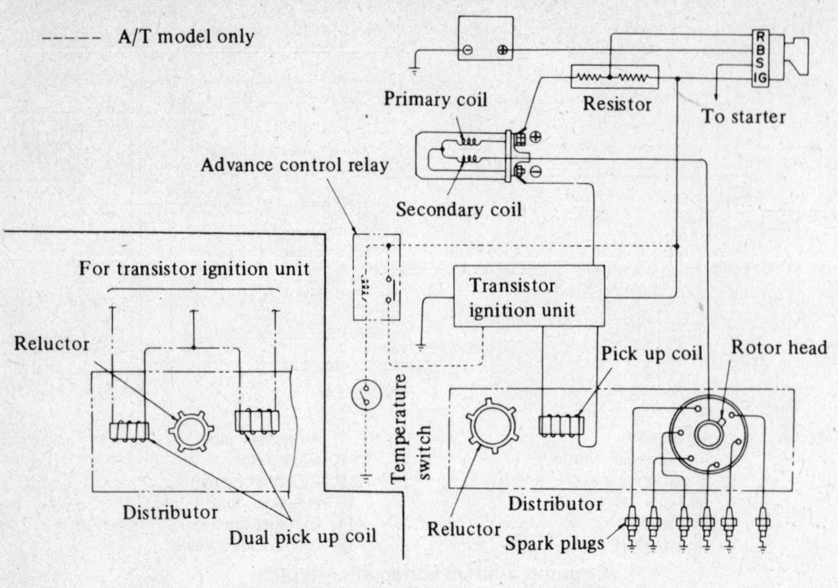

Breakerless distributor system, 280Z

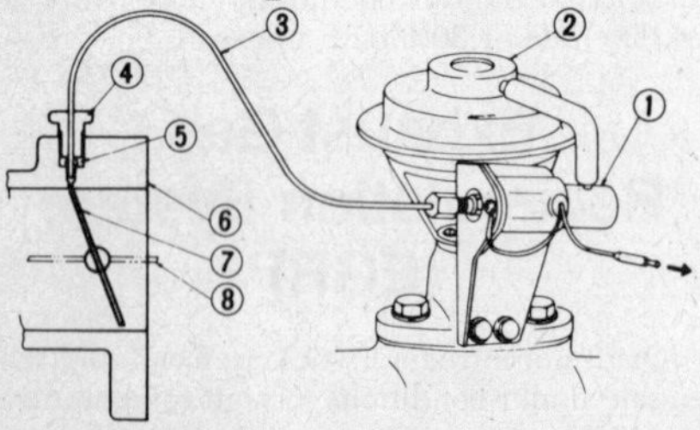

1. Solenoid valve
2. EGR valve
3. EGR vacuum tube
4. Attaching nut
5. Sealing nut
6. Rear carburetor
7. Throttle valve
8. Throttle valve fully open

L24 EGR system

peratures remain below approximately 122° F (50° C) the solenoid valve blocks vacuum to the EGR valve. When the temperature of the engine coolant, or the passenger compartment, reaches normal operating temperature, the solenoid is deactivated and intake manifold vacuum is allowed to act upon the EGR valve diaphragm and exhaust gas recirculation takes place.

On 1977 and later models, a thermal vacuum valve (TVV) controls the application of vacuum to the EGR valve. When the engine coolant reaches a predetermined temperature, the TVV opens and allows vacuum to be routed to the EGR valve. Below the predetermined temperature, the TVV closes and blocks vacuum to the EGR valve.

All 1977-78 models, all 1979 U.S. models, and all 1980 and later 49 State U.S. models have a back pressure transducer (BPT) valve installed between the EGR valve and the thermal vacuum valve. The BPT valve has a diaphragm raised or lowered by exhaust back pressure. The diaphragm opens or closes an air bleed, which is connected into the EGR vacuum line. High pressure results in higher levels of EGR, because the BPT diaphragm is raised, closing off the air bleed, which allows more vacuum to reach and open the EGR valve. Thus, the amount of recirculated exhaust gas varies with exhaust pressure.

1977-78 models sold in California, 1979 models with a catalytic converter, and 1980 and later 49 State models have a vacuum delay valve (VDV) installed in the line between the thermal vacuum valve and the EGR valve. The valve delays rapid drops in vacuum in the EGR signal line, thus effecting a longer EGR time.

INSPECTION

1975-76

Inspect the individual components as follows.

1. Remove the EGR valve from the intake manifold.
2. Apply 6.0 in. Hg of vacuum to the EGR valve vacuum connection. The valve should open. Pinch off the connection with the vacuum still applied. The valve should remain in the raised position for at least 30 seconds.
3. Inspect the EGR valve for any signs of warpage or damage, and replace as necessary.
4. Clean the EGR valve seat with a brush and compressed air.
5. Connect the solenoid to a 12 volt DC power source. The solenoid should click when power is applied. If the valve clicks, it is considered to be working properly.
6. Check the temperature switch by removing it from the engine (drain the engine coolant first) and placing it in a container of water together with a thermometer. Connect a self-powered test light to the temperature switch electrical leads. Heat the water. The switch should conduct current when the water temperature is below 122° F (50° C) on 1975-76 models. The switch should stop conduction somewhere between 134-145° F (57-63° C). Replace the switch if it behaves otherwise.

1977 and Later

1. Remove the EGR valve. Apply enough vacuum to the EGR valve vacuum connection to raise the diaphragm and open the valve. Pinch off the vacuum connection. The valve should remain open for at least thirty seconds. If not, the diaphragm is leaking and the valve must be replaced.
2. Check the valve for damage (warpage, cracks, etc.) and replace as necessary.
3. Clean the valve seat with a wire brush and compressed air.
4. Install the EGR valve on the engine. Start the engine and allow it to idle. With the engine idling, reach up under the EGR valve and raise the diaphragm by pushing it upwards with your fingers. Wear a glove to protect your hand if the engine is hot. When the diaphragm is raised, the engine idle should become rough, indicating that exhaust gases are recirculating. If the roughness does not occur, the EGR passages are blocked.
5. To check the operation of the thermal vacuum valve, drain the engine coolant and remove the valve. Connect two lengths of vacuum hose to the two TVV vacuum connections. Place the valve in a container of water together with a thermostat, with the vacuum hoses above the level of the water. Do not allow water to get into the valve. When the water temperature is below 177° F (47° C), the vacuum passage should be closed. You can check this by sucking on one of the vacuum hoses.
6. Heat the water. On 1977 models, the valve should open (conduct vacuum) when the water temperature reaches 117-127° F (47-53° C). On 1978-80 models, the valve should open at about 122° F (50° C), and remain open until the water temperature reaches about 203° F (95° C). On 1978 and later models only, the valve should close again when water temperature reaches about 208° F (98° C). Replace the valve if it behaves otherwise.
7. To test the BPT valve installed on some 1977 and later models, disconnect the two vacuum hoses on the valve. Plug one of the ports. While applying pressure to the bottom of the valve, apply vacuum to the unplugged port and check for leakage. If any exists, replace the valve.
8. To check the delay valve installed on some 1977 and later models, remove the valve and blow into the side which connects to the EGR or BPT valve. Air should flow. When air is applied to the other side, air flow resistance should be greater. If not, replace the valve.

All Models Except 280Z and 280ZX

An EGR valve is mounted on the center of the intake manifold. The recycled exhaust gas is drawn into the bottom of the intake manifold riser portion through the exhaust manifold heat stove and EGR valve. A vacuum diaphragm is connected to a timed signal port at the carburetor flange.

As the throttle valve is opened, vacuum is applied to the EGR valve vacuum diaphragm. When the vacuum reaches about 2 in. Hg, the diaphragm moves against spring pressure and is in a fully up position at 8 in. Hg of vacuum. As the diaphragm moves up, it opens the exhaust gas metering valve which allows exhaust gas to be pulled into the engine intake manifold. The system does not operate when the engine is idling because the exhaust gas recirculation would cause a rough idle.

On 1975 and later models, a thermal vacuum valve inserted in the engine thermostat housing controls the application of the vacuum to the EGR valve. When the engine coolant reaches a predetermined temperature, the thermal vacuum valve opens and allows vacuum to be routed to the EGR valve. Below the predetermined temperature, the thermal vacuum valve closes and blocks vacuum to the EGR valve.

All 1978-79 models and the 1980 and later 210, 510 (Canadian), 200SX (Canadian), 310 and 810 have a BPT valve installed between the EGR valve and the thermal vacuum valve. The BPT valve has a diaphragm which is raised or lowered by exhaust back pressure. The diaphragm opens or closes an air bleed, which is connected into the EGR vacuum line. High pressure results in higher levels of EGR, because the diaphragm is raised, closing off the air bleed, which allows more vacuum to reach and open the EGR valve. Thus, the amount of recirculated exhaust gas varies with exhaust pressure.

The 1980 and later 510 (USA), 200SX (USA), 310 (California), and 210 (California) use a VVT valve (venturi vacuum transducer valve) instead of the BPT valve. The VVT valve monitors exhaust pressure and carburetor vacuum in order to activate the diaphragm which controls the throttle vacuum applied to the EGR control valve. This system expands the operating range of the EGR unit, as well as increasing the EGR flow rate as compared to the BPT unit.

Many 1975 and later Datsuns are equipped with an EGR warning system which signals via a light in the dashboard that the EGR system may need service. The EGR warning light should come on every time the starter is engaged as a test to make sure the bulb is not blown. The system uses a counter which works in conjunction with the odometer, and lights the warning signal after the vehicle has traveled a pre-determined number of miles.

To reset the counter, which is mounted in the engine compartment, remove the grommet installed in the side of the counter and insert the tip of a small screwdriver into the hole. Press down on the knob inside the hole. Reinstall the grommet.

TEST

1. Remove the EGR valve and apply enough vacuum to the diaphragm to open the valve.
2. The valve should remain open for over 30 seconds after the vacuum is removed.
3. Check the valve for damage, such as warpage, cracks, and excessive wear around the valve and seat.
4. Clean the seat with a brush and compressed air and remove any deposits from around the valve and port (seat).
5. To check the operation of the thermal vacuum valve, remove the valve from the engine and apply vacuum to the ports of the valve. The valve should not allow vacuum to pass.
6. Place the valve in a container of water with a thermometer and heat the water. When the temperature of the water reaches 134°-145° F, remove the valve and apply vacuum to the ports; the valve should allow vacuum to pass through it.
7. To test the BPT valve installed on 1978 and later models, disconnect the two vacuum hoses from the valve. Plug one of the ports. While applying pressure to the bottom of the valve, apply vacuum to the unplugged port and check for leakage. If any exists, replace the valve.
8. To test the check valve installed in some 1978 and later models, remove the valve and blow into the side which connects to the EGR valve. Air should flow. When air is applied to the other side, air flow resistance should be greater. If not, replace the valve.
9. To check the VVT valve which replaces the BTP valve on some 1980 and later models, disconnect the top and bottom center hoses and apply a vacuum to the top hose. Check for leaks. If a leak is present, replace the valve.

Early Fuel Evaporation System (E.F.E.)

The 1975-79 A-series and all L-series engines use a system much akin to the old style exhaust manifold heat riser. In this system, a control valve is welded to the valve shaft and installed on the exhaust manifold through bushing. This heat control valve is actuated by a coil spring, thermostatic spring and counterweight which are assembled on the valve shaft projecting at the rear outside of the manifold. The counterweight is secured to the shaft with a key, bolt and snap-ring. A chamber between the intake and exhaust manifolds above the manifold stove heats the air-fuel mixture by means of exhaust gases. This results in better atomization and lower HC content.

The 1980 and later carbureted engines use coolant water heat instead of exhaust gas heat to pre-warm the fuel mixture. This system should be trouble-free.

TESTING

1. Run engine and visually check for movement.
2. In cold weather, the counterweight will move counterclockwise until it reaches the stop pin. As the engine warms up the counterweight gradually moves down.
3. As engine speed increases, the flow of exhaust gases causes the counterweight to move clockwise. When the heat control valve is full open the counterweight should again be in contact with the stop pin.

Check for bent stop pin, broken heat valve key, axial clearance between heat control valve and manifold of 0.028"0.059", and cracks or flaking at the heat control valve weld.

Boost Control Deceleration Device (BCDD)/Throttle Opener Control System (TOCS)

The Boost Control Deceleration Device (BCDD) used on the L-series and non-fuel injected Z-series engines, and the Throttle Opener Control System (TOCS) used on A-series engines (except 1980 and later California) both accomplish the same purpose: to reduce hydrocarbon emissions during coasting conditions.

High manifold vacuum during coasting prevents the complete combustion of the air/fuel mixture because of the reduced amount of air. This condition will result in a large amount of HC emission. Enriching the air/fuel mixture for a short time (during the high vacuum condition) will reduce the emission of the HC.

However, enriching the air/fuel mixture with only the mixture adjusting screw will cause poor engine idle or invite an increase in the carbon monoxide (CO) content of the exhaust gases. The BCDD consists of an independent system that kicks in when the engine is coasting and enriches the air/fuel mixture, which reduces the hydrocarbon content of the exhaust gases. This is accomplished without adversely affecting engine idle and the carbon monoxide content of the exhaust gases.

The TOCS system used on 1980 A-series non-California models achieves the same end as the BCDD system but uses a slightly different method. The system consists of a servo diaphragm, vacuum control valve, throttle opener solenoid valve, speed detecting switch

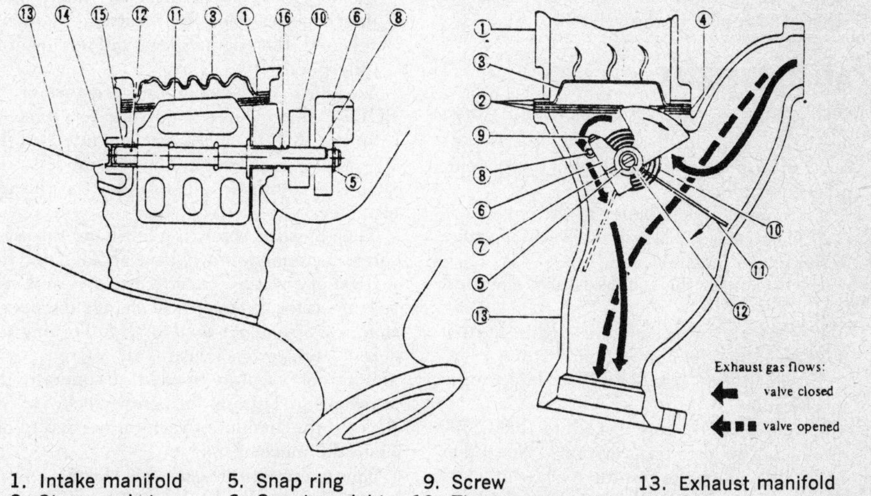

1. Intake manifold	5. Snap ring	9. Screw	13. Exhaust manifold
2. Stove gasket	6. Counterweight	10. Thermostat spring	14. Cap
3. Manifold stove	7. Key	11. Heat control valve	15. Bushing
4. Heat shield plate	8. Stopper pin	12. Control valve shaft	16. Coil spring

Early Fuel Evaporation (EFE) system

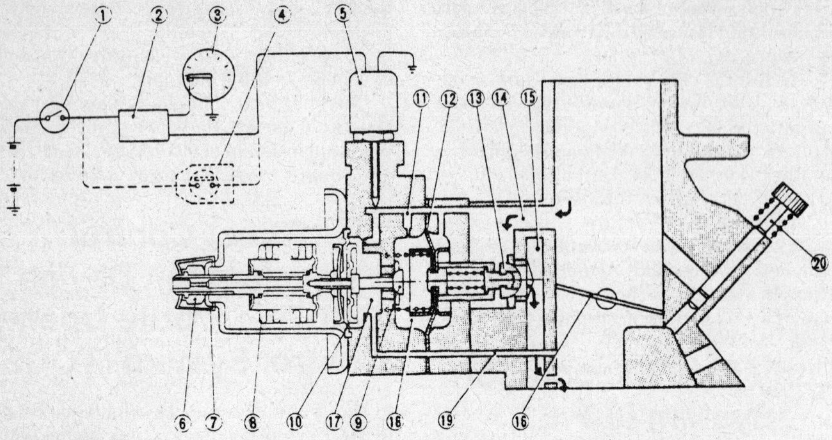

1. Ignition switch
2. Amplifier
3. Speed detecting switch Blow 10 M.P.H.: ON (For M/T)
4. Inhibitor switch "N" or "P" position: ON (For A/T)
5. Vacuum control sólenoid valve
6. Adjusting nut
7. Lock spling
8. Altitude corrector
9. Vacuum control valve
10. Diaphragm I
11. Air passage
12. Diaphragm II
13. Air control valve
14. Air passage
15. Air passage
16. Throttle valve
17. Vacuum chamber I
18. Vacuum chamber II
19. Vacuum passage
20. Idle speed adjusting screw

BCDD sectional view

and amplifier on manual transmission models. Automatic transmission models use an inhibitor and inhibitor relay in the place of the speed detecting switch and amplifier. At the moment when the manifold vacuum increases, as during deceleration, the vacuum control valve opens to transfer the manifold vacuum to the servo diaphragm chamber, and the carburetor throttle valve opens slightly. Under this condition, the proper amount of fresh air is sucked into the combustion chamber. As a result, a more thorough ignition takes place, burning much of the HC in the exhaust gases.

1980 and Later Z20E Engine (200SX)

This engine uses a simplified version of the boost control system. In place of the BCDD (see above) is a vacuum control valve which works on manifold vacuum. Service is restricted to replacing the valve.

ADJUSTMENT

Normally, the BCDD never needs adjustment. However, if the need should arise because of suspected malfunction of the system, proceed as follows:

1. Connect a tachometer to the engine.
2. Connect a quick-response vacuum gauge to the intake manifold.
3. Disconnect the solenoid valve electrical leads.
4. Start and warm up the engine until it reaches normal operating temperature.
5. Adjust the idle speed to the proper specification.
6. Raise the engine speed to 3000-3500 rpm under no-load (transmission in Neutral or Park), then allow the throttle to close quickly. Take notice as to whether or not the engine rpm returns to idle speed and if it does, how long the fall in rpm is interrupted before it reaches idle speed.

At the moment the throttle is snapped closed at high engine rpm the vacuum in the intake manifold reaches between -23 to -27.7 in. Hg and then gradually falls to about -16.5 in. Hg at idle speed. The process of the fall of the intake manifold vacuum and the engine rpm will take one of the following three forms:

a. When the operating pressure of the BCDD is too high, the system remains inoperative and the vacuum in the intake manifold decreases without interruption just like that of an engine without a BCDD.

b. When the operating pressure is lower than that of the case given above, but still higher than the proper set pressure, the fall of vacuum in the intake manifold is interrupted and kept constant at a certain level (operating pressure) for about one second and then gradually falls down to the normal vacuum at idle speed.

c. When the set of operating pressure of the BCDD is lower than the intake manifold vacuum when the throttle is suddenly released, the engine speed will not lower to idle speed.

To adjust the set operating pressure of the BCDD, remove the adjusting screw cover from the BCDD mechanism mounted on the side of the carburetor. On 810 models, the BCDD system is installed under the throttle chamber.

The adjusting screw is a left-hand threaded screw. Late models may have an adjusting nut instead of a screw. Turning the screw ⅛ of a turn in either direction will change the operation pressure about 0.79 in. Hg. Turning the screw counterclockwise will increase the amount of vacuum needed to operate the mechanism. Turning the screw clockwise will decease the amount of vacuum needed to operate the mechanism.

The operating pressure for the BCDD on most models should be between -19.9 to -22.05 in Hg. The decrease in intake manifold vacuum should be interrupted at these levels for about one second when the BCDD is operating correctly.

Don't forget to install the adjusting screw cover after the system is adjusted.

ADJUSTMENT–TOCS

Adjustment procedures for TOCS are the same as those for BCDD. Observe the following pressures.

When snapping the throttle closed as described in Step 6 for BCDD, the vacuum in the intake manifold should reach -23.6 in. Hg or above and then gradually decreases to idle lever.

The operating pressure of the TOCS should be -22.05±0.79 in. Hg.

Turning the adjusting screw clockwise raises the vacuum level. Turning the screw counterclockwise lowers the vacuum level.

NOTE: When adjusting the TOCS, turn the adjusting nut in or out with the lock spring in place. Always set the lock spring properly to prevent changes in the set pressure.

Evaporative Emission Control System

These systems include the positive-seal fuel tank cap and vapor vent line of the earlier system. Additionally, a carbon canister, vacuum signal line, and canister purge line are used. The canister stores fuel vapors until vacuum pressure in the vacuum signal line forces a purge control valve to open. This admits fuel vapor from the canister into the intake manifold to be burnt with the incoming charge. The only maintenance required with this system is to change the carbon canister filter, located in the bottom of the canister, once every two years, and to periodically check the lines for leaks or obstructions.

Automatic Temperature Controlled Air Cleaner

This system is used on all Datsun models, except the 810, 280Z, 280ZX and the 200SX.

The rate of fuel atomization varies with the temperature of the air that the fuel is being mixed with. The air/fuel ratio cannot be held constant for efficient fuel combustion with a wide range of air temperatures. Cold air being drawn into the engine causes a denser and richer air/fuel mixture, inefficient fuel atomization, and thus, more hydrocarbons in the exhaust gas. Hot air being drawn into the engine causes a leaner air/fuel mixture and more efficient atomization and combustion for less hydrocarbons in the exhaust gases.

The automatic temperature controlled air cleaner is designed so that the temperature of the ambient air being drawn into the engine is automatically controlled, to hold the temperature of the air and, consequently, the fuel/air ratio at a constant rate for efficient fuel combustion.

A temperature sensing vacuum switch controls vacuum applied to a vacuum motor operating a valve in the intake snorkle of the air cleaner. When the engine is cold or the air being drawn into the engine is cold, the vacuum motor opens the valve, allowing air heated by the exhaust manifold to be drawn into the engine. As the engine warms up, the temperature sensing unit shuts off the vacuum applied to the vacuum motor which allows the valve to close, shutting off the heated air and allowing cooler, outside (under hood) air to be drawn into the engine.

TESTING

When the air around the temperature sensor of the unit mounted inside the air cleaner housing reaches 100° F, the sensor should block the flow of vacuum to the air control valve vacuum motor. When the temperature around the temperature sensor is below 100° F, the sensor should allow vacuum to pass onto the air valve vacuum motor thus blocking off the air cleaner snorkle to under hood (unheated) air.

When the temperature around the sensor is above 118° F, the air control valve should be completely open to under hood air.

If the air cleaner fails to operate correctly, check for loose or broken vacuum hoses. If the hoses are not the cause, replace the vacuum motor in the air cleaner.

Dual Spark Plug Ignition System

The California model Z-series engine has two spark plugs per cylinder. This arrangement allows the engine to burn large amounts of recirculated exhaust gases without effecting performance. In fact, the system works so well it improves gas mileage under most circumstances.

Both spark plugs fire simultaneously, which substantially shortens the time required to burn the air/fuel mixture when exhaust gases (EGR) are not being recirculated. When gases are being recirculated, the dual spark plug system brings the ignition level up to that of a single plug system which is not recirculating exhaust gases.

ADJUSTMENT

The only adjustments necessary are the regular tune-up and maintenance procedures outlined in the tune-up section.

SPARK TIMING CONTROL SYSTEM

The spark timing control system has been used in different forms on Datsuns since 1972. The first system, Transmission Controlled Spark System (TCS) was used on most Datsuns through 1979. This system consists of a thermal vacuum valve, a vacuum switching valve, a high gear detecting switch, and a number of vacuum hoses. Basically, the system is designed to retard full spark advance except when the car is in high gear and the engine is at normal operating temperature. At all other times, the spark advance is retarded to one degree or another.

The 1980 and later Spark Timing Control System replaces the TCS system. The major difference is that it works solely from engine water temperature changes rather than a transmission-mounted switch. The system includes a thermal vacuum valve, a vacuum delay valve, and attendant hoses. It performs the same function as the earlier TCS system; to retard full spark advance at times when high levels of pollutants would otherwise be given off.

INSPECTION AND ADJUSTMENTS

Normally the TCS and Spark Timing Control systems should be trouble-free. However, if you suspect a problem in the system, first check to make sure all wiring (if so equipped) and hoses are connected and free from dirt. Also check to make sure the distributor vacuum advance is working properly. If everything appears all right, connect a timing light to the engine and make sure the initial timing is correct. On vehicles with the TCS system, run the engine until it reaches normal operating temperature, and then have an assistant sit in the car and shift the transmission through all the gears slowly. If the system is functioning properly, the timing will be 10 to 15 degrees advanced in high gear (compared to the other gear positions). If the system is still not operating correctly, you will have to check for continuity at all the connections with a test light.

To test the Spark Timing Control System, connect a timing light and check the ignition timing while the temperature gauge is in the "cold" position. Write down the reading. Allow the engine to run with the timing light attached until the temperature needle reaches the center of the gauge. As the engine is warming up, check w ith the timing light to make sure the ignition timing retards. When the temperature needle is in the middle of the gauge, the ignition timing should advance from its previous position. If the ignition timing does not change, replace the thermal vacuum valve.

Mixture Ratio Rich-Lean and EGR Large-Small Exchange System

This system controls the air-fuel mixture ratio and the amount of recirculated exhaust gas on 1980 California A series engines (manual transmission models only) in accordance with the engine coolant temperature and car speed. The system consists of a vacuum switching valve, a power valve, a speed detecting switch located in the speedometer, a speed detecting switch amplifier and a water temperature switch.

When the coolant temperature is above 122° F and the car is traveling at least 40 miles per hour, the vacuum switching valve is on and acts to lean down the fuel mixture. It also allows a small amount of EGR to be burned on manual transmission cars. When the coolant temperature is above 122° F but the vehicle is traveling less than 40 miles per hour, the vacuum switching valve is off and allows the mixture to richen. It also allows a large amount of EGR to be burned in manual transmission models. When coolant temperature is below 122° F the vacuum switching valve is always on and acts to lean down the fuel mixture.

TESTING

Warm up the engine and jack up the drive wheels of the vehicle. Support the raised end of the car on jack stands and chock the wheels still on the ground. Start the engine and shift the transmission into TOP speed and maintain a speedometer speed higher than 50 mph. Pinch the hose running from the vacuum switching valve to the air cleaner and see if the engine speed decreases and operates erratically. Shift the transmission into 3RD speed and run the car at a speed lower than 30 mph. Disconnect the vacuum hose running between the vacuum switching valve and the power valve, by detaching it at the power valve and blocking its open end with your finger. The engine should operate erratically. If the expected engine reaction in both of these tests does not happen, check all wiring connections and hoses for breaks and blockage.

Mixture Ratio Feedback System

The need for better fuel economy coupled to increasingly strict emission control regulations dictate a more exact control of the engine air/fuel mixture. Datsun has developed a Mixture Ratio Feedback System in response to these needs. The system is installed on all 1980 and late 280ZX and 810 models sold in California.

The principle of the system is to control the air/fuel mixture exactly, so that more complete combustion can occur in the engine, and more thorough oxidation and reduction of the exhaust gases can occur in the catalytic converter. The object is to maintain a stoichiometric air/fuel mixture, which is chemically correct for theoretically complete combustion. The stoichiometric ratio is 14.7:1 (air to fuel). At that point, the converter's efficiency is greatest in oxidizing and reducing HC, CO, and NOx into CO_2, H_2O, O_2, and N_2.

Components used in the system include an oxygen sensor, installed in the exhaust manifold upstream of the converter; a three-way oxidation-reduction catalytic converter; an electronic control unit, which is part of the electronic fuel injection control unit; and the fuel injection system itself.

The oxygen sensor reads the oxygen content of the exhaust gases. It generates an electrical signal which is sent to the control unit. The control unit then decides how to adjust the mixture to keep it at the correct air/fuel ratio. For example, if the mixture is too lean, the control unit increases the fuel metering to the injectors. The monitoring process is a continual one, so that fine mixture adjustments are going on at all times.

The system has two modes of operation: open loop and closed loop. Open loop operation takes place when the engine is still cold. In this mode, the control unit ignores signals from the oxygen sensor and provides a fixed signal to the fuel injection unit. Closed loop operation takes place when the engine and catalytic converter have warmed to normal operating temperature. In closed loop operation, the control unit uses the oxygen sensor signals to adjust the mixture; the burned mixture's oxygen content is read by the oxygen sensor, which continues to signal the control unit, and so on. Thus, the closed loop mode is an interdependent system of information feedback.

Mixture is, of course, not readily adjustable in this system. All system adjustments require the use of a CO meter; thus, they should be entrusted to a qualified dealer with access to the equipment and special training in the system's repair. The only regularly scheduled maintenance is replacement of the oxygen sensor at 30,000 mile intervals. This procedure is covered in the following section.

It should be noted that proper operation of the system is entirely dependent on the oxygen sensor. Thus, if the sensor is not replaced at the correct interval, or if the sensor fails during normal operation, the engine fuel mixture will be incorrect, resulting in poor fuel economy, starting problems, or stumbling and stalling of the engine when warm.

OXYGEN SENSOR INSPECTION AND REPLACEMENT

An exhaust gas sensor warning light will illuminate on the instrument panel when the car has reached 30,000 miles. This is a signal that the oxygen sensor must be replaced.

Note that the warning light is not part of a repeating system; that is, after the first 30,000 mile service, the warning light will not illuminate again. However, it is important to replace the oxygen sensor every 30,000 miles, to ensure proper monitoring and control of the engine air/fuel mixture.

The oxygen sensor can be inspected using the following procedure:

1. Start the engine and allow it to reach normal operating temperature.
2. Run the engine at approximately 2,000 rpm under no load. Block the front wheels and set the parking brake.
3. An inspection lamp has been provided on the bottom of the control unit, which is located in the passenger compartment on the driver's side kick panel, next to the clutch or brake pedal. If the oxygen sensor is operating correctly, the inspection lamp will go on and off more than 5 times in 10 seconds. The inspection lamp can be more easily seen with the aid of a mirror.
4. If the lamp does not go on and off as specified, the system is not operating correctly. Check the battery, ignition system, engine oil and coolant levels, all fuses, the fuel injection wiring harness connectors, all vacuum hoses, the oil filler cap and dipstick for proper seating, and the valve clearance and engine compression. If all of these parts are in good order, and the inspection lamp still does not go on and off at least 5 times in 10 seconds, the oxygen sensor is probably faulty. However, the possibility exists that the malfunction could be in the fuel injection control unit. The system should be tested by a qualified dealer with specific training in the Mixture Ratio Feedback System.

To replace the oxygen sensor:

1. Disconnect the negative cable from the battery.
2. Disconnect the sensor electrical lead. Unscrew the sensor from the exhaust manifold.
3. Coat the threads of the replacement sensor with a nickel base anti-seize compound. Do not use other types of compounds, since they may electrically insulate the sensor. Install the sensor into the manifold. Installation torque for the sensor is 29-36 ft/lbs (4.0-5.0 kg-m). Connect the electrical lead. Be careful handling the electrical lead; it is easily damanged.
4. Connect the negative battery cable.

After the first 30,000 mile replacement, the warning lamp harness connector should be unplugged to extinguish the lamp. The connector is located under the right side of the instrument panel; the harness wire color is green with a yellow stripe.

Catalytic Converter

All 1975 and later models sold in California, some 1979 models sold in the other 49 States of the U.S., and all 1980 and later models sold in the U.S. and Canada have a catalytic converter, which is a muffler-shaped device installed into the exhaust system. The converter is filled with a monolithic substrate coated with small amounts of platinum and palladium. Through catalytic action, a chemical change converts carbon monoxide and hydrocarbons into carbon dioxide and water. All 1980 and later 280ZX and 810 models sold in California have a three-way catalytic converter. Platinum, palladium, and rhodium are used in an oxidation-reduction process which acts on all three major constituents of exhaust pollution; HC and CO and oxidized in the usual manner into H_2O and CO_2, and oxides of nitrogen are reduced to free hydrogen and nitrogen (H_2 and N_2 respectively).

1975-78 models (all California models) have a floor temperature warning system, consisting of a temperature sensor installed onto the floor of the car above the converter; a relay, located under the passenger seat; and a light, installed on the instrument panel. The lamp illuminates when floor temperatures become abnormally high, due to converter or engine malfunction. The light also comes on when the ignition switch is turned to Start, to check its operation. 1979 and later models do not have the warning system.

1980 and later 280ZX and 810 California models have an oxygen sensor warning light on the dashboard, which illuminates at the first 30,000 mile interval, signaling the need for oxygen sensor replacement. The oxygen sensor is part of the Mixture Ratio Feedback System, described in this section. The Feedback System uses the three-way converter as one of its major components.

No regular maintenance is required for the catalytic converter system, except for periodic replacement of the Air InductionSystem filter on some 1980 and later models. The Air Induction System is described earlier in this section. The Air Induction System is used to supply the catalytic converter with fresh air; oxygen present in the air is used in the oxidation process.

REMOVAL AND INSTALLATION

1. Apply the parking brake.
2. Disconnect the temperature sensor connectors (1975-78 Calif.) and pull the connectors outside of the floor.
3. Block the wheels.
4. Jack and support the car.
5. Remove the temperature sensor protector (1975-78 Calif.)
6. Remove the catalytic converter shield.
7. Unbolt and remove the catalytic converter. Handle the converter gently; it is very delicate.
8. Installation is the reverse of removal.

FLOOR TEMPERATURE WARNING SYSBEM

1975-78 California Models

This system employs temperature sensors to warn of impending catalytic converter overheating. The system consists of a floor sensor located in the luggage compartment, a floor sensor relay located under the front passenger seat and a warning lamp located on the left side of the instrument panel.

TESTING

Lamp should light when ignition is turned to ON.

To test sensor, wait until floor temperature is below 80° F. Then heat floor area around sensor to 239° F. Light should come on.

FUEL SYSTEM

Mechanical Fuel Pump

The mechanical fuel pump is driven from the engine camshaft on all engines. It is mounted on the side of the engine on OHV engines and on the side of the cylinder head on OHC engines. The pump is on the right side of all engines.

REMOVAL AND INSTALLATION

1. Disconnect the inlet and outlet lines from the pump.
2. Remove the mounting bolts.
3. Remove the pump and discard the gasket.
4. Lubricate the pump rocker arm, rocker arm pin, and lever pin before reinstallation.
5. Bolt the pump into position, using a new gasket.
6. Connect the fuel lines.

FUEL PUMP TESTS

Static Pressure Test

1. Disconnect fuel line at carburetor.
2. Attach adapter and tee to fuel line and connect a pressure gauge.
3. Run engine at varying speeds. Pressure should remain constant, 3-4 psi.

Capacity Test

1. With static pressure within specifications, disconnect fuel line at carburetor.
2. Fuel in bowl should be sufficient to start and run engine at 1000 rpm for one minute. Fuel delivery should be 600 cc in one minute.

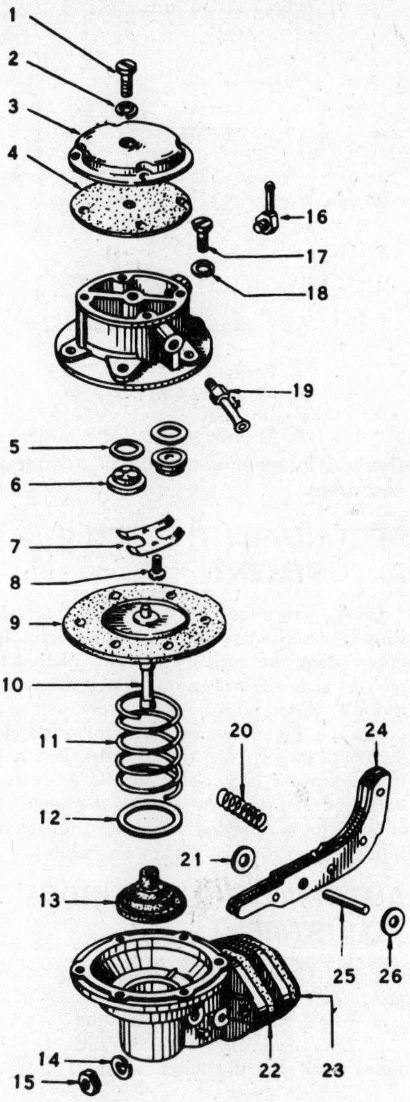

1. Screw
2. Lockwasher
3. Cover
4. Cover gasket
5. Packing
6. Valve
7. Valve retainer
8. Valve retainer screw
9. Diaphragm
10. Pull rod
11. Spring
12. Seal washer
13. Seal
14. Lockwasher
15. Nut
16. Elbow
17. Screw
18. Lockwasher
19. Connector
20. Spring
21. Rocker arm slide spacer
22. Spacer
23. Gasket
24. Rocker arm
25. Pin
26. Rocker arm slide spacer

Mechanical fuel pump

Electric Fuel Pump

DESCRIPTION

1975 and Later 280Z, 280ZX

The electric pump used on 260Z models is a transistorized plunger type which force feeds the conventional mechanical fuel pump in order to minimize the chances of vapor lock or other fuel deficiency problems. The pump is located in the corner where the differential mounting member intersects the side member. The 1975 and later Z and ZX models are equipped with one electric fuel pump mounted near the fuel tank and the right rear wheel.

1977 and Later 810 and 200SX

The fuel injected 810 and 200SX use an electric fuel pump mounted near the fuel tank on the 810 and near the center of the car on the 200SX. The pump is of wet type construction. A vane pump and roller are directly coupled to a motor filled with fuel. A relief valve in the pump is designed to open when the pressure in the fuel line rises over 64 psi. Normal operating pressure is 36-43 psi. The pump is automatically activated when the ignition switch is turned to the "start" position. If the engine stalls for some reason, the fuel pump is cut off even though the ignition switch remains in the "on" position.

PRESSURE TEST

1975-78 280Z

1. Reduce the fuel line pressure to zero, following Steps 1-3 of the pump removal and installation procedure.
2. Connect a pressure gauge into the fuel line in the engine compartment between the fuel tube and the fuel filter outlet hose.
3. Disconnect the wire from the "S" terminal of the starter motor solenoid.
4. Connect the negative battery cable.
5. Turn the ignition key to Start.
6. Pressure should be approximately 36.3 psi (2.55 kg/cm^2).
7. If not, replace the pressure regulator (see the replacement procedure following) and repeat the tests. If the pressure is still not correct, check all fuel lines for kinks or blockage, and replace the pump as necessary.

1979 and Later 280ZX

1. Reduce the fuel pressure to zero. For 1979 models, follow Steps 1-3 of the 1975-79 fuel pump replacement procedure. For 1980 and later models, follow Step 1 of the 1980 fuel pump replacement procedure.
2. On 1979 models, connect the negative battery cable.
3. Connect a fuel pressure gauge into the fuel line in the engine compartment between the fuel pipe and the fuel filter outlet hose.
4. Start the engine and read the fuel pressure. It should be approximately 30 psi (2.1 kg/cm^2) at idle, and approximately 37 psi (2.6 kg/cm^2) at any speed above idle.
5. If the pressure is incorrect, replace the pressure regulator, following the replacement procedure given later in this chapter. After replacement of the regulator, repeat the pressure test. If still incorrect, check the fuel lines for kinks or blockage, and replace the pump as necessary.

1977 and Later 810 and 200SX

1. Fuel pressure must be reduced to zero.
2. Connect a fuel pressure gauge between the fuel feed pipe and the fuel filter outlet.
3. Start the engine and read the pressure. It should be 30 psi at idle, and 37 psi at the moment the accelerator pedal is fully depressed.
4. If pressure is not as specified, replace the pressure regulator and repeat the test. If the pressure is still incorrect, check for clogged or deformed fuel lines, then replace the fuel pump.

FUNCTIONAL TEST

1975-78 280Z

1. Disconnect the cable from the "S" terminal of the starter motor solenoid.
2. Unplug the cold start valve wiring harness connector.
3. Turn the ignition key to Start. You should be able to hear the fuel pump running. If not, check the wiring circuits and fuses. If the circuits and fuses are in order, replace the pump.

1979 and Later 280ZX

1. Disconnect either the wire to the alternator "L" terminal, or the oil pressure switch connector.
2. Turn the ignition key to Start. You should be able to hear the fuel pump running. If not, check the wiring circuits and fuses; if they are in order, replace the fuel pump.

1977 and Later 810 and 200SX

Fuel pressure must be reduced to zero before tests are made.

On 1977-79 810's, disconnect the ground cable from the battery. Disconnect the cold start valve wiring harness at the connector. Connect two jumper wires to the terminals of the cold start valve. Touch the other ends of the jumpers to the positive and negative terminals of the battery for a few seconds to release the pressure.

For 1980 and later 810's and 200SX's, start the engine, disconnect the harness connector of fuel pump relay-2 while the engine is running. After the engine stalls, crank it over two or three times to make sure all of the fuel pressure is released.

NOTE: If the engine will not start, remove the fuel pump relay-2 harness connector and crank the engine for about 5 seconds.

REMOVAL AND INSTALLATION

1975-79 280Z and 280ZX

1. Disconnect the battery ground cable.
2. Disconnect the wiring harness to the cold start valve.
3. Using two jumper wires from the battery, energize the cold start valve for two or three seconds to relieve pressure in the fuel system.

CAUTION

Be careful not to short the two jumpers together.

4. Jack up the rear of the car and safely

support it on stands. Have a can and a rag handy to catch any spilled fuel.

5. Clamp the hose between the fuel tank and the fuel pump.

6. Loosen the hose clamps on the fuel lines at both ends of the pump and remove the lines from the pump.

7. Remove the two retaining screws and remove the fuel pump bracket.

8. Disconnect the fuel pump harness connector. On 280Z models, roll back the carpet behind the passenger seat to reach the connector. On 280Z 2+2 models, remove the rear seat and remove the harness cover. Disconnect the wiring. On ZX models, remove the mat in the luggage compartment, and disconnect the harness connector at the rear of the compartment.

9. Pull the harness through the rubber grommet in the floor and remove the fuel pump.

10. Install the fuel pump in the reverse order of removal.

1980 and Later 280ZX

1. Reduce the fuel line pressure to zero: start the engine and remove the fuel pump relay #2 while the engine is running. After the engine stalls, crank the engine with the starter two or three times. Turn the ignition off.

2. Disconnect the negative battery cable.

3. Remove the luggage compartment mat. Disconnect the fuel pump harness wiring at the connector at the rear of the compartment. Push the wires and grommet through the floor.

4. Raise and support the rear of the car.

5. Clamp the hose between the fuel tank and the pump.

6. Loosen the fuel line clamps and disconnect the hoses from the pump. Have a metal container ready to catch the fuel which will spill from the lines.

7. Remove the bolts which secure the pump bracket to the body and remove the pump.

8. Installation is the reverse.

1977 and Later 810 and 200SX

1. Reduce the fuel pressure to zero. See procedures under the "Testing" section, above.

2. Disconnect the electrical harness connector at the pump. The 810 pump is located near the fuel tank. The 200SX pump is located near the center of the car.

3. Clamp the hose between the fuel tank and the pump to prevent gas from spewing out from the tank.

4. Remove the inlet and outlet hoses at the pump. Unclamp the inlet hose and allow the fuel lines to drain into a suitable container.

5. Unbolt and remove the pump. The 200SX pump and fuel damper can be removed at the same time.

6. Installation is the reverse of removal. Use new clamps and be sure all hoses are properly seated on the fuel pump body.

Carburetors

The carburetor used is a two-barrel downdraft type with a low-speed (primary) side and a high-speed (secondary) side.

All models have an electrically-operated anti-dieseling solenoid. As the ignition switch is turned off, the valve is energized and shuts off the supply of fuel to the idle circuit of the carburetor.

REMOVAL AND INSTALLATION

1. Remove the air cleaner.
2. Disconnect the fuel and vacuum lines from the carburetor.
3. Remove the throttle lever.
4. Remove the four nuts and washers retaining the carburetor to the manifold.
5. Lift the carburetor from the manifold.
6. Remove and discard the gasket used between the carburetor and the manifold.
7. Install the carburetor in the reverse order of removal, using a a new carburetor base gasket.

FUEL LEVEL ADJUSTMENT

All Nihonkikaki (Nikki) carburetors have a glass float chamber side cover marked with a fuel level line. Fuel level is adjusted by bending the float seat tab with the float cover removed and inverted, and the float fully raised.

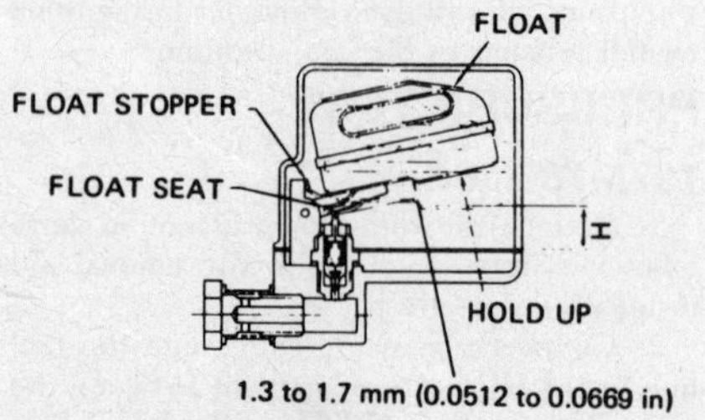

Hitachi downdraft carburetor float level adjustment

THROTTLE LINKAGE ADJUSTMENT

On all models, make sure the throttle is wide open when the accelerator pedal is floored. Some models have an adjustable accelerator pedal stop to prevent strain on the linkage.

DASHPOT ADJUSTMENT

A dashpot is used on carburetors of cars with automatic transmission as means of slowly closing the throttle valve to prevent stalling. It is also used in later years as an emission control device on models with either automatic or manual transmissions. The dashpot should be adjusted to contact the throttle lever on deceleration at approximately 1900-2100 rpm for manual transmissions, or 1600-1800 rpm for automatic transmission with the L series engines, or 2000-2300 rpm for all models of the A series engine. The 1980 and later Z20S engine's dashpot contact point should be between 1400-1600 rpm for automatic transmissions.

NOTE: Before attempting to adjust the dashpot, make sure the idle speed, timing and mixture adjustments are correct.

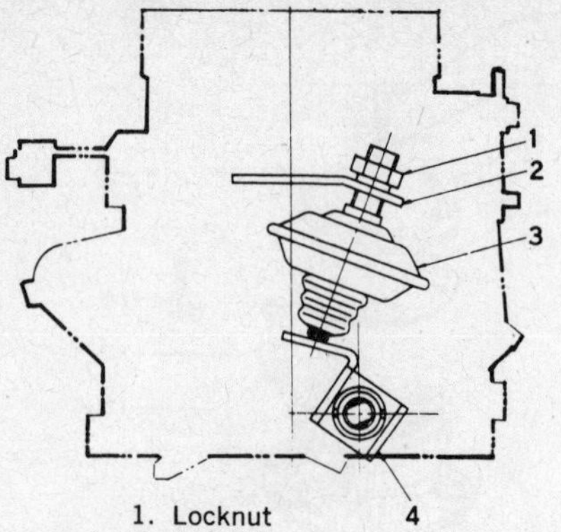

1. Locknut
2. Mounting arm
3. Dashpot
4. Throttle lever

Dashpot installation on Hitachi downdraft carburetor

SECONDARY THROTTLE ADJUSTMENT

On the two stage carburetors used on Datsuns, the secondary throttle plate begins to open when the primary throttle plate has opened to an angle of approximately 50° (from the fully closed position). This works out to a clearance measurement of approximately 0.28-0.32 in. between the throttle valve and the carburetor body. This can be measured with a drill bit of the correct diameter. If adjustment is required, bend the connecting link between the two linkage assemblies.

AUTOMATIC CHOKE INDEX ADJUSTMENT

1. Start engine and close choke valve completely.
2. Check for choke valve binding.
3. Loosen choke cover screws and set cover index mark at center notch only.
4. Tighten screws.

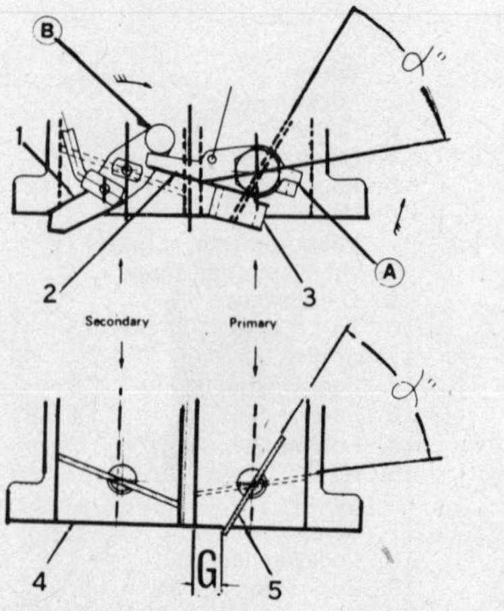

1. Connecting lever
2. Return plate
3. Adjusting plate
4. Secondary throttle chamber
5. Primary throttle valve

a. Primary throttle opening in degrees

G. Primary throttle opening in inches

Measurement of point at which secondary throttle starts to open, Hitachi downdraft carburetor

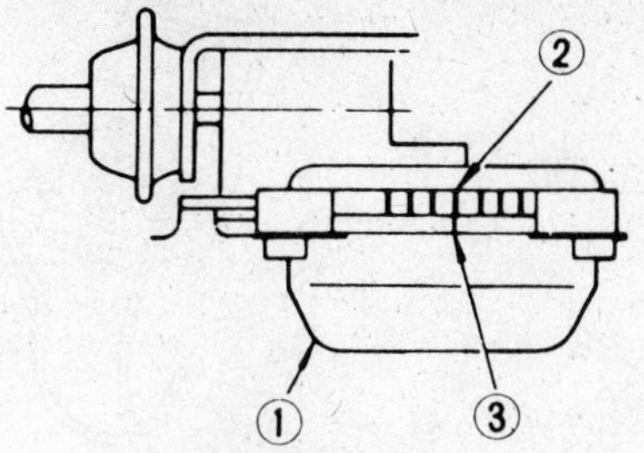

1. Thermostat cover
2. Thermostat housing
3. Groove

Choke index setting

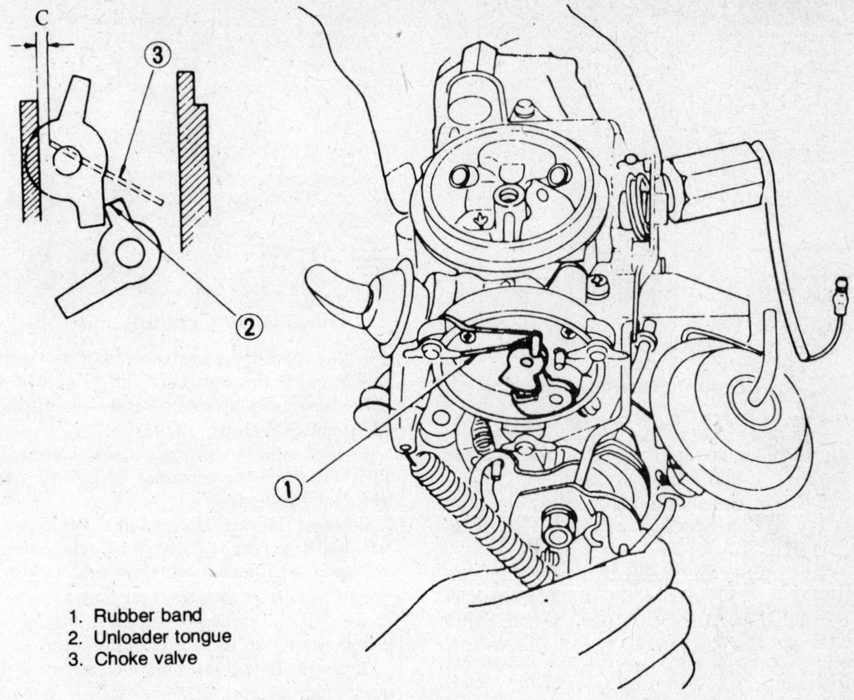

1. Rubber band
2. Unloader tongue
3. Choke valve

Choke unloader adjustment

CHOKE UNLOADER ADJUSTMENT

1. Close choke valve completely.
2. Hold choke valve by stretching a rubber band between choke shaft lever and carburetor.
3. Pull throttle lever until it completely opens.
4. Adjust gap between the choke plate and the carburetor body to:

A-series engines:

1973-77: 0.0791 in.
1978-80: 0.0929 in. except:
1978-80: Non-Cal. 5 speed hatchback 210, B210 and 1980 Canada manual trans. A12A: 0.0854 in.

L-series engines, 1980 Z20S engine:

1973-74: 0.173 in.
1975-77: 0.096 in., except:
1977 710: 0.0807-0.1122 in.
1978-80: 0.0807-0.1122 in.

OVERHAUL

Carburetor overhaul involves separating the major components, removing and blowing out all jets, blowing out all passages, washing the parts in a safe solvent, and reassembling with new gaskets. After overhaul, the idle mixture and speed must be adjusted. Carburetor overhaul kits are available and generally contain complete instructions, a full set of gaskets, a new float needle valve and accelerator pump parts.

Overhaul your carburetor in a clean, dust-free area. Carefully disassemble referring often to the exploded views. Keep all similar and lookalike parts apart during disassembly and cleaning to avoid accidental interchange during assembly. Make a note of all jet sizes.

When the carburetor is disassembled, wash all parts (except diaphragms, electric choke units, pump plunger, and any other plastic, leather, fiber, or rubber parts) in clean carburetor solvent. Do not leave parts in the solvent any longer than is necessary to sufficiently loosen the deposits. Excessive cleaning may remove the special finish from the float bowl and choke valve bodies, leaving these parts unfit for service. Rinse all parts in clean solvent and blow them dry with compressed air or allow them to air dry. Wipe clean all cork, plastic, leather, and fiber parts with a clean, lint-free cloth.

Blow-out all passages and jets with compressed air and be sure there are no restrictions or blockages. Never use wire or needles to clean jets, fuel passages, or air bleeds. Clean all jets and valves separately to avoid accidental mixing.

Check all parts for wear or damage. If any is found, replace the defective parts. Especially check the following:

1. Check the float needle and seat for wear. If wear is found, replace the complete assembly.
2. Check the float hinge pin for wear and the float(s) for dents or distortion. Replace the float if fuel has leaked into it.
3. Check the throttle and choke shaft bores for wear or an out-of-round condition. Damage or wear to the throttle arm, shaft, or shaft bore will often require replacement of the throttle body. These parts require a close tolerance; wear may allow air leakage, which could affect starting and idling.

NOTE: Throttle shaft and bushings are not included in overhaul kits. They can be purchased separately.

4. Inspect the idle mixture adjusting needles for burrs or grooves. This type of wear requires replacement to obtain a satisfactory idle.
5. Test the accelerator pump check valves. They should pass air one way but not the other. Test for proper seating by applying a vacuum to the valve. Replace if necessary. If the valve is satisfactory, wash the valve again to remove breath moisture.
6. Check the bowl cover with a straight edge for warped surfaces.
7. Closely inspect the valves and seats for wear and damage, replacing as necessary.
8. After the carburetor is assembled, check the choke valve for free movement.

Carburetor overhaul kits are recommended for each overhaul. These kits contain all gaskets and new parts to replace those that deteriorate most rapidly. Failure to replace all parts supplied with the kit (especially gaskets) may result in poor performance later.

After cleaning and checking all components, reassemble the carburetor, using new parts and referring to the exploded view. When reassembling, make sure all screws and jets are tight. Do not overtighten or you may distort the tips. Tighten all screws gradually, in rotation. Do not tighten needle valves into their seats; uneven jetting will result. Always use new gaskets. Be sure to adjust the float level when reassembling.

Fuel Injection

The fuel injection system is an electronic type, using various types of sensors to convert engine operating conditions into electrical signals. The informaton generated is fed to a control unit, giving it the right figures to set the injector open-valve period.

CAUTION

The 1979 and later Electronic Control Unit must not be installed on 1978 or earlier models. Damage to the ECU will result. A special adapter harness must be used with the factory EFI analyzer when testing the 1979 and later ECU.

CHECKING FUNCTIONAL PARTS

For the processes described you will need a small testing light and an ohmmeter. Be sure the car's battery is fully charged before making test.

Control Unit

1. Connect the testing lamp to the harness-side connector of the injector.

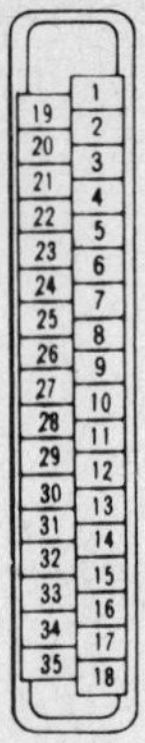

EFI connector numbering

2. Crank the engine. If the light flashes due to the pulse voltage applied to the injector, the control unit is operating.

Because two different transistors are used in the system, you will have to test both the No. 1 and 4 cylinders.

To confirm your findings, remove the connector on the coolant sensor. The installed testing lamp should flash more brightly. It is only necessary to run this test on the No. 1 or No. 4 cylinders.

Checking Potentiometer

CAUTION

Before checking the air flow meter, remove the battery ground cable.

1. Remove the air flow meter.
2. Measure the resistance between terminals 8 and 6, through 1978, or 33 and 34 for 1979 and later models. It should be 180 ohms through 1978, 100-400 ohms thereafter.

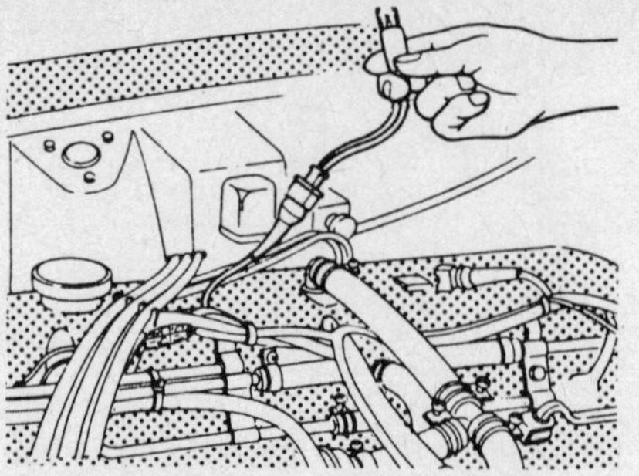

Checking control unit

3. Measure the resistance between terminals 8 and 9 through 1978, or 34 and 35 for 1979. Resistance should be 100 ohms through 1978, 200-500 ohms, 1979.
4. For models through 1978: Connect a 12-volt battery to terminal 9 (positive) and terminal 6 (negative).

Connect the positive lead of a volt meter to terminal 8 and the negative lead to terminal 7.

Reaching into the air flow meter, slowly open the flap so that the bolt flow slowly decreases. If the indicator varies suddenly, the problem may be in the potentiometer.

5. For 1979 and later models: Slide the flap open and measure the resistance between terminals 32 and 34. Resistance other than zero or infinity is correct.

Air Flow Meter Insulation Check

Connect an ohmmeter to any one terminal on the flow meter. Touch the flow meter body with the other connector. If any continuity is indicated, the unit is out of order.

Checking Flap

Reach into the air flow meter with your fingers. If the flap opens and closes smoothly, without binding, the mechanical portion of the unit is working.

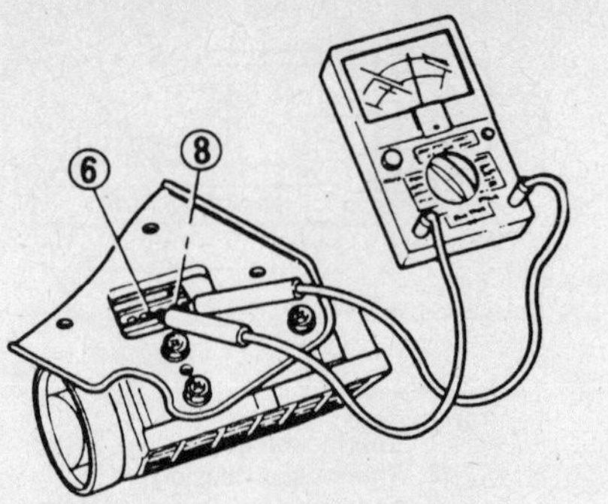

Measuring terminal resistance

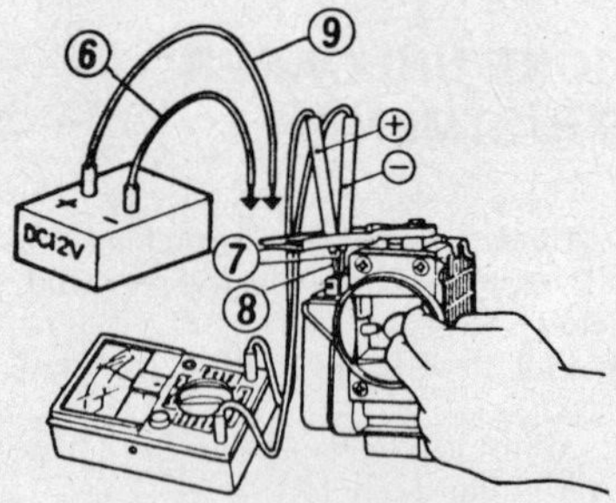

Checking terminal voltage variation

Air Temperature Sensor

NOTE: This test applies to all except 1980 and later California 810.

CHECKING CONTINUITY

1. Disconnect the battery ground cable.

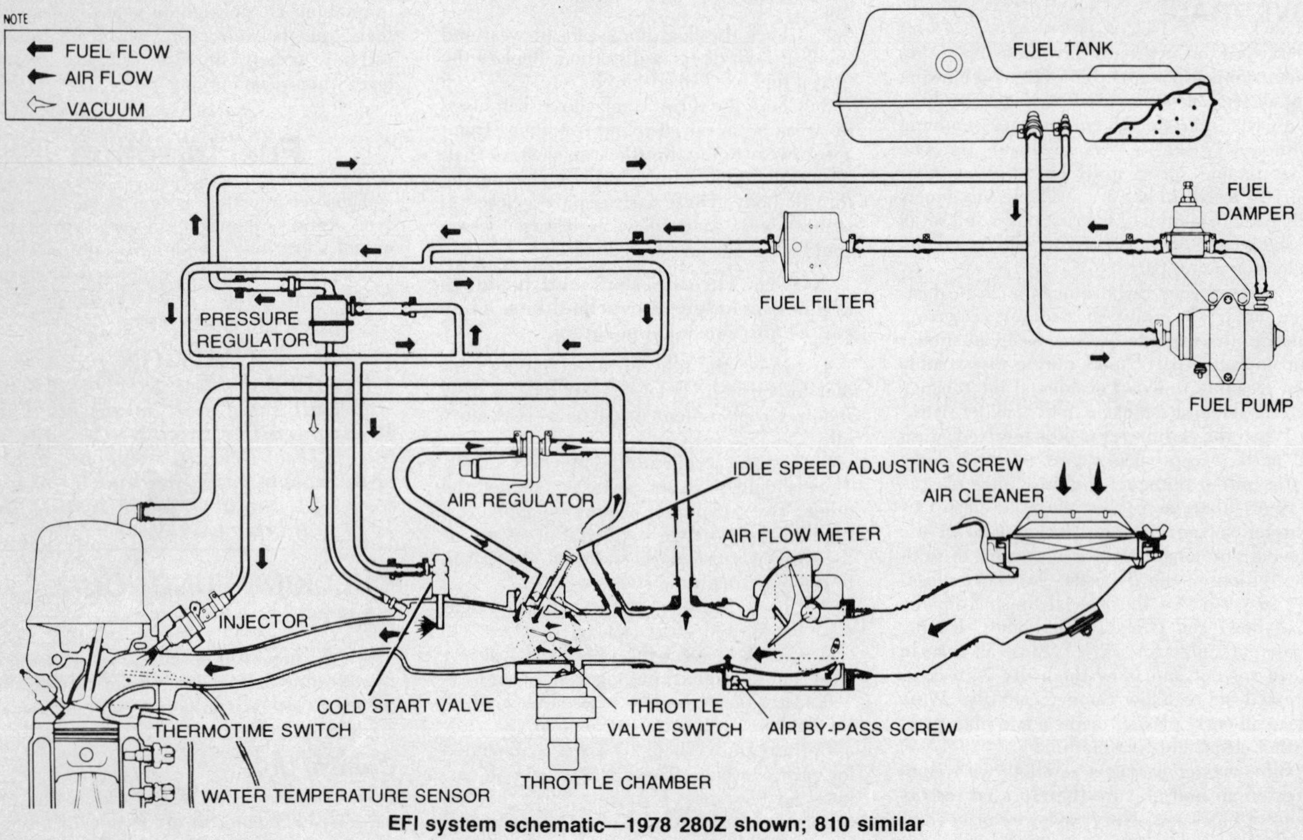

EFI system schematic—1978 280Z shown; 810 similar

2. Remove the air flow meter.

3. Check the temperature of your surroundings and make note of it.

4. Connect an ohmmeter to terminals 27 and 6 through 1978, or 25 and 34 for 1979 and later, on the air flow meter connector and check the resistance indicated. Make note of it.

The resistance values should be as indicated in the chart. Should the test results vary far from the ranges provided, replace the air temperature sensor and air flow meter as a unit.

AIR FLOW METER RESISTANCE SPECIFICATIONS

Air Temperature °C (°F)	Resistance (kΩ)
−30 (−22)	20.3 to 33.0
−10 (−14)	7.6 to 10.8
10 (50)	3.25 to 4.15
20 (68)	2.25 to 2.75
50 (122)	0.74 to 0.94
80 (176)	0.29 to 0.36

INSULATION RESISTANCE

Connect an ohmmeter to terminal 27 of the air flow meter through 1978, or terminal 25 for 1979 and later models, and touch the body with the other connector. Should continuity be indicated, replace the unit.

Water Temperature Sensor

NOTE: 1980 and later 810's and 280ZX's are equipped with cylinder head temperature sensors rather than water temperature sensors. However, the test is the same for both units.

This test may be done either on or off the vehicle. The test should be done with the coolant both hot and cold.

1. Disconnect the battery ground cable.

2. Disconnect the water temperature sensor harness.

3. Place a thermometer in the coolant when the engine is cold. Make note of the indication.

4. Read the resistance indicated on the meter and compare it wih the chart for temperature/resistance values.

WATER TEMPERATURE SENSOR RESISTANCE SPECIFICATIONS

Cooling Water Temperature °C (°F)	Resistance (kΩ)
−30 (−22)	20.3 to 33.0
−10 (−14)	7.6 to 10.8
10 (50)	3.25 to 4.15
20 (68)	2.25 to 2.75
50 (122)	0.74 to 0.94
80 (176)	0.29 to 0.36

To measure the coolant temperature and resistance values when hot:

1. Connect the water temperature sensor harness.

2. Connect the battery ground cable.

3. Warm the engine and disconnect the harness and battery cable.

4. Read the sensor resistance as described in the cold process.

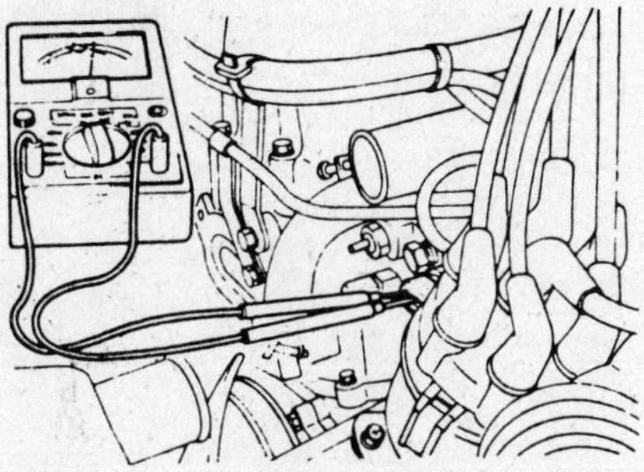

Resistance test of the water temperature sensor

SENSOR CHECK OFF THE ENGINE

1. Remove the sensor and dip the unit into water maintained at 68°F. Read the resistance.

2. Heat the water to 176°F and check the resistance.

In either type of check, should the resistance be far outside the ranges provided, replace the sensor unit.

SENSOR INSULATION CHECK

This check is done on the engine.

1. Disconnect the battery ground cable.

2. Disconnect the sensor harness connector.

3. Connect an ohmmeter to one of the terminals on the sensor and touch the engine block with the other. Any indication of continuity indicates need to replace the unit.

Thermotime Switch–810 and 280ZX

1. Disconnect the ground cable from the battery.

2. Disconnect the electric connector of the thermotime switch and measure the resistance between terminal No. 46 and the switch body.

The resistance should be zero with water temperatures less than 57° F.

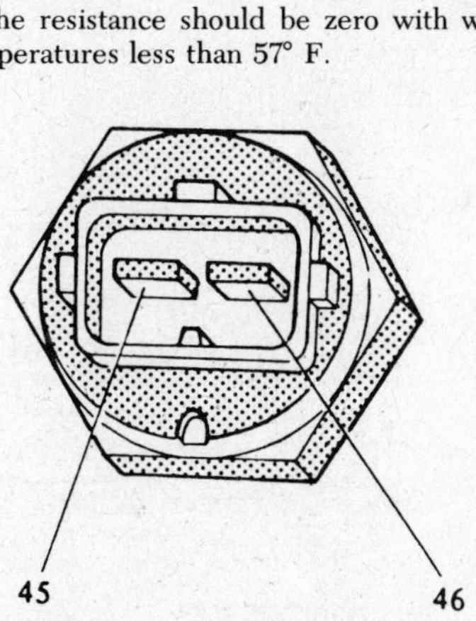

Terminals—thermotime switch

The resistance should be zero or infinite with temperatures of 57° to 72° F.

The resistance should be infinite with a temperature of 72° F.

3. Measure the resistance between terminal No. 45 and the switch body.

70-86 ohms through 1977 .... OK
51-62 ohms, 1978 .... OK
40-70 ohms, 1979 and later .... OK

Any different reading than shown indicates replacement.

Cold Start Valve–810 and 280ZX

Steps 1 and 2 are for models through 1978 only.

1. Disconnect the lead wire from the "S" terminal of the starter motor.

2. Turn the ignition switch to START and make sure the fuel pump is working. You should be able to hear it.

3. Disconnect the ground cable from the battery.

4. Remove the screws holding the cold start valve to the intake manifold and remove the valve.

5. Disconnect the start valve electrical connector.

6. Put the start valve into a large glass container and plug the neck of the jar.

7. For models through 1978, connect the ground cable of the battery and turn the ignition switch to START. The valve should not inject fuel.

For 1979 and later models, disconnect the connector at the oil pressure switch, or the connector alternator "L" terminal; turn the ignition switch to ON. The valve should not inject fuel.

8. Turn the switch to OFF and connect a jumper wire between the valve and the battery terminals. Leave the valve in the jar.

At this point, the valve should inject fuel. If not, proceed to the next step for models through 1977 only. For 1978 and later models, replace the valve.

9. With the ignition switch in the START position, and the jumper wire installed as described, check for fuel flow. If the fuel is injected to the jar, the unit is operating. If not, replace.

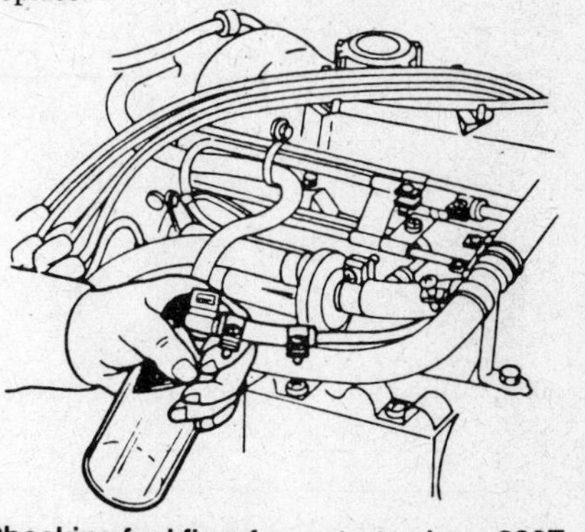

Checking fuel flow from start valve—280Z

Fuel Injection Relay

1. Disconnect the ground cable from the battery.

2. Remove the relay from the automobile.

MAIN RELAY CHECK

For models through 1977: Connect a battery (12-volt) between the positive (86c) ter-

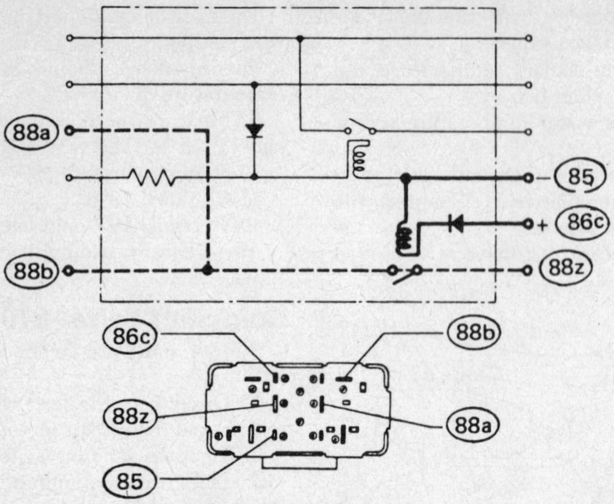

Checking main relay

minal and the negative (85). Clicks should be heard and continuity indicated between terminals 88z and 88a, and between 88z and 88b.

Connect the battery (12-volt) between positive (85) and negative (86c) terminals. No clicks should be heard.

If the results are not as described in the two tests, the unit is faulty.

For 1978 models:

Disconnect the battery ground cable. Remove the relay. Test for continuity as follows for 810 models:

Between terminals 71 and 72: Yes
Between terminals 43 and 70: No
Between terminals 10 and 77: No

Apply 12 v d.c. between terminals 71 and 72 and test for continuity between terminals 43 and 70, and 10 and 77. Continuity should exist. If not, replace the relay.

For 1978 280Z models, the procedure is the same as for the 810, but the terminals are different:

Between terminals 74 and 73: Yes
Between terminals 43 and 72: No
Between terminals 10 and 71: No

Apply 12 v d.c. between terminals 74 and 73. Test for continuity between terminals 43 and 72: and 10 and 71. If no continuity exists, replace the relay.

For all 1979 and later models:

Test as for 1978. The terminals are:

Between terminals 4 and 5: Yes
Between terminals 1 and 3: No
Between terminals 2 and 6: No

Apply 12 v d.c. between terminals 4 and 5. Test for continuity between 1 and 3, and 2 and 6. If no continuity exists, replace the relay.

Fuel Pump Relay

For models through 1977:

1. Make sure there is continuity between terminals 88d and 88c and between 86a and 86.
2. Connect a 12-volt battery to positive (86a) and negative (85) terminals. Clicks should be heard and there should be continuity between 88y and 88d.
3. Connect the battery to positive (85) and negative (86a) terminals. No clicks should be heard.
4. If the test results are not as outlined, the relay is faulty.

Tests on the fuel pump control relay and pump relay cannot be performed on 1978 and later models without special equipment.

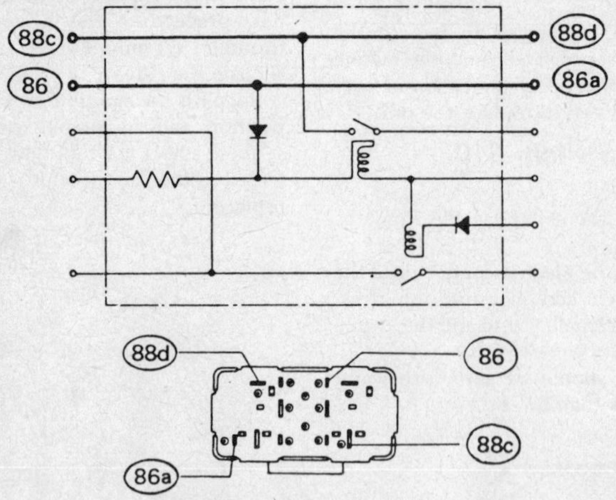

Fuel pump relay (1)

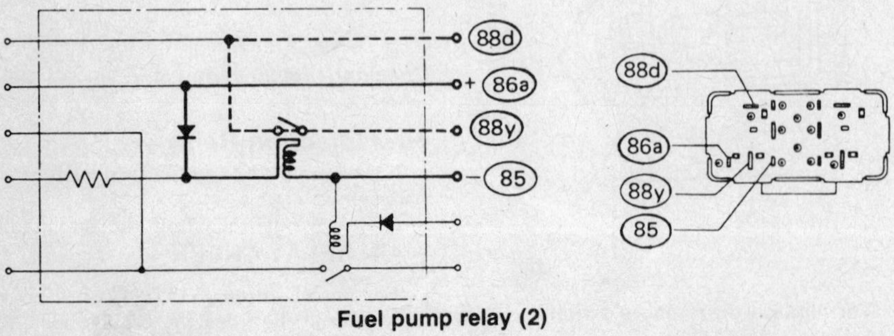

Fuel pump relay (2)

Throttle Valve Switch

Dsiconnect the ground cable from the battery.

Remove the throttle valve switch connector.

IDLE SWITCH

This applies to models through 1978 only.

1. Connect an ohmmeter between terminals 2 and 18.
2. If continuity is indicated when the throttle valve is in the IDLE position, and does not exist when the valve opens about 4° the switch is normal.

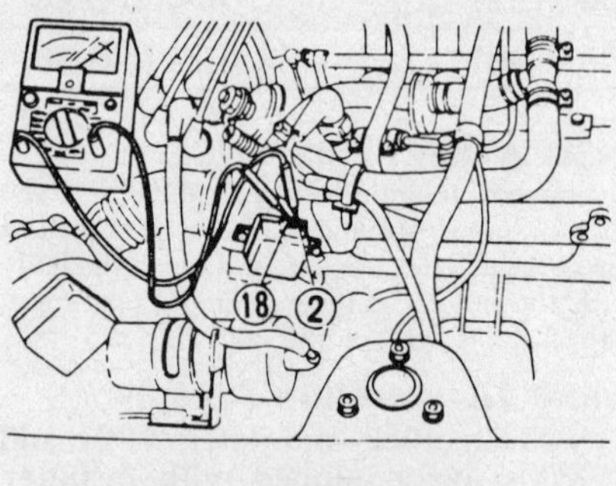

Idle switch check

FULL SWITCH CHECK

This applies to models through 1978 only.

1. Connect an ohmmeter between terminals 3 and 18.
2. Gradually open the throttle valve and read the indication when the valve is open about 34°. If the indication is higher at all settings other than 34°, the full switch is operating properly.

THROTTLE VALVE SWITCH INSULATION

Connect an ohmmeter between body metal and terminals 2, 3 and 18 through 1978, or 29, 24, and 30 for 1979. Meter reading should be infinite.

Dropping Resistor

Disconnect the ground cable from the battery.

Disconnect the 4-pin and 6-pin connectors from the injection system harness and conduct resistance checks between the following points.

43/1 and No. 41-# 4 cylinder
43/1 and No. 40-# 3 cylinder
43/1 and No. 38-# 2 cylinder
43/1 and No. 37-# 1 cylinder

The resistance readings should be approximately 6 ohms.

Also conduct checks between:

43/2 and No. 56-# 6 cylinder

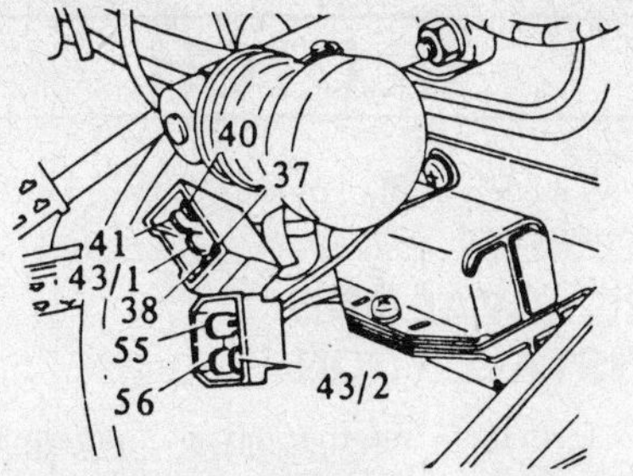

Dropping resistor terminal numbers

43/2 and No. 55-# 5cylinder
The resistance should again be 6 ohms.

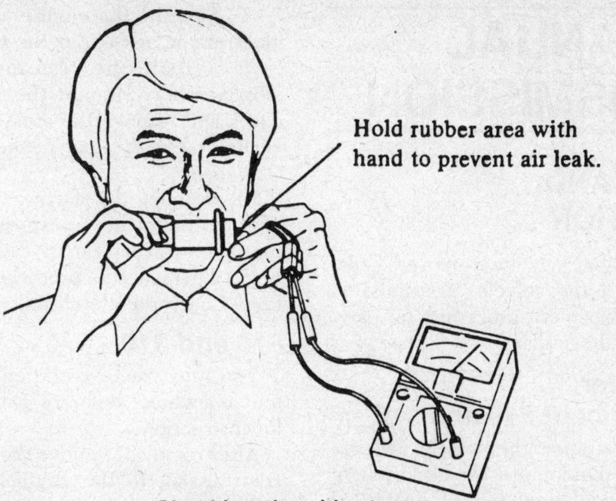

Checking the altitude switch

Altitude Switch (California Models Only)

The altitude switch is not used on 1979 models.

Disconnect the ground cable from the battery and remove the switch from the automobile.

Attach an ohmmeter to the connector and blow or suck through the discharge port. If a click is heard and continuity exists, the switch is in good order.

There is no adjustment possible on the switch. Should it be found to be defective, replace the unit.

Fuel Pump

Refer to the Electric Fuel Pump procedures at the beginning of the Fuel System Section.

Injector

For continuity, remove the ground cable from the battery and disconnect the electrical connectors from the injectors.

Check for continuity readings between the two terminals. If there is no indication, the injector is faulty.

Check the injectors for sound as follows:

If the engine is running, run it at idle and place a screwdriver tip against each injector and your ear to the handle to check for operating sounds. If there is low sound from any injector, it is faulty.

If the engine is not running, disconnect the connector of the cold start valve and crank the engine. Check for sounds as described.

If there are low sounds from any injector, that injector is faulty.

If there is no sound from all the injectors, check the harness. If the harness is normal, check the operation of the control unit.

If sounds are heard from numbers 1, 2 and 3 injectors or numbers 4, 5, or 6, replace the control unit.

Air Regulator

Hold the rubber tubing between the throttle chamber and the air regulator with your fingers and squeeze. The engine speed should be reduced.

If it does not, remove the hoses from both ends of the regulator and check to see if the valve opens. The opening should be as indicated by the gray area in the illustration.

Disconnect the regulator electrical connector and check for continuity, it should exist. If not, the regulator is faulty.

To open the valve, pry with a screwdriver and then close. If the operation is smooth, the valve is operating correctly. Any binding indicates replacement.

Throttle Chamber

1. Remove the throttle chamber.
2. Check to see that the idle adjust screw moves smoothly and adjust the throttle valve to the fully closed position.
3. Move the dash pot rod to see if it moves smoothly and also check the movement of the throttle valve.
4. Check the bypass port for obstacles and dirt. Do not touch the EGR vacuum port screw.

Because of the sensitivity of the air flow meter, there cannot be any air leaks in the fuel system. Even the smallest leak could unbalance the system and affect the performance of the automobile.

During every check, pay attention to hose connections, dipstick and oil filler cap for evidence of air leaks. Should you encounter any, take steps to correct the problem.

Fuel Hoses

Check hoses for leaks or looseness. Retighten connection and replace as necessary.

1. Air cleaner element
2. Air duct (air cleaner to AFM)
3. Air duct (AFM to throttle chamber)
4. Flange (throttle chamber to intake manifold)
5. Co'd start valve mounting surface
6. Blind plug (E.G.R.),
7. Injector mounting surface in intake manifold
8. Cylinder head mounting surface in intake manifold
9. Hose (throttle chamber to 3-way connector), both sides
10. Hose (3-way connector to rocker cover), both sides
11. Hose (3-way connector to air regulator), both sides
12. Hose (air regulator to throttle chamber connector), both sides
13. Throttle chamber connector mounting surface
14. Hose (pipe connector to P.C.V. valve), both sides
15. Distributor vacuum line
16. E.G.R. vacuum line
17. Canister vacuum and purge line
18. Automatic transmission vacuum line
19. Cooler vacuum line

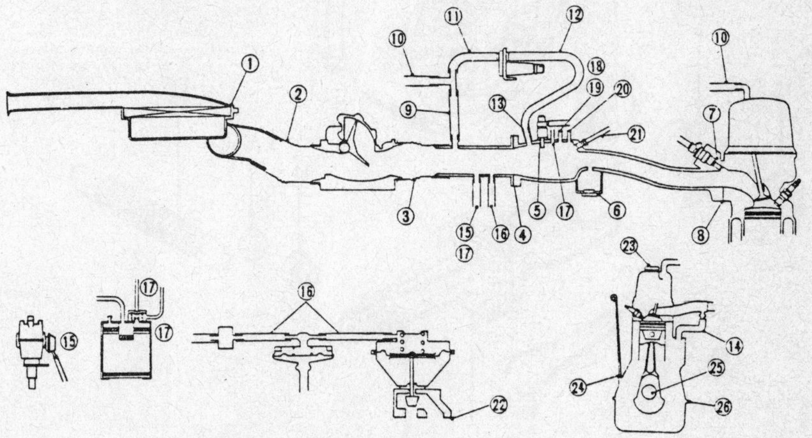

20. Master-Vac line
21. Pressure regulator vacuum line
22. E.G.R. valve mounting surface
23. Oil filler cap
24. Oil level gauge
25. Oil seal (on front and rear of crankshaft)
26. Oil pan gasket mounting surface.

Air leak check points in the intake system

MANUAL TRANSMISSION

REMOVAL AND INSTALLATION

The transmission may be removed separately from under the vehicle. Transmission removal and replacement procedure for early models is generally similar.

1975 and Later
All Models except F10 and 310

1. Raise and support the vehicle. Disconnect the battery. Disconnect the backup light switch on all models and neutral switch, if equipped.
2. On the Z and ZX, remove the exhaust system. On models with the A14 or L20B engine, disconnect the exhaust pipe from the manifold. On the 280Z and 280Z and the 1980 200SX, disconnect the accelerator linkage. Remove the bent shield plate on the 280Z and ZX.
3. Unbolt the driveshaft at the rear and remove. If there is a center bearing, unbolt it from the crossmember. Seal the end of the transmission extension housing to prevent leakage.
4. Disconnect the speedometer drive cable from the transmission.
5. Remove the shift lever.
6. Remove the clutch operating cylinder from the clutch housing.
7. Support the engine with a large wood block and a jack under the oil pan.
8. Unbolt the transmission from the crossmember. Support the transmission with a jack and remove the crossmember.
9. Lower the rear of the engine to allow clearance.
10. Remove the starter.
11. Unbolt the transmission. Lower and remove it to the rear.
12. Reverse the procedure for reinstallation. Check the clutch linkage adjustment.

F10 and 310

You must remove the engine/transmission unit as a whole. Refer to "Engine Mechanical" for instructions.

After removal, remove the bolts holding the transmission to the engine and separate by pulling the transmission towards the clutch housing.

NOTE: The clutch assembly will remain attached to the engine.

Installation is the reverse of removal. The bolts holding the transmission should be torqued to 10 to 13 ft/lbs.

CAUTION

If the clutch has been removed, it will have to re-aligned and when connecting driveshafts, insert O-rings between differential side flanges and drive shafts.

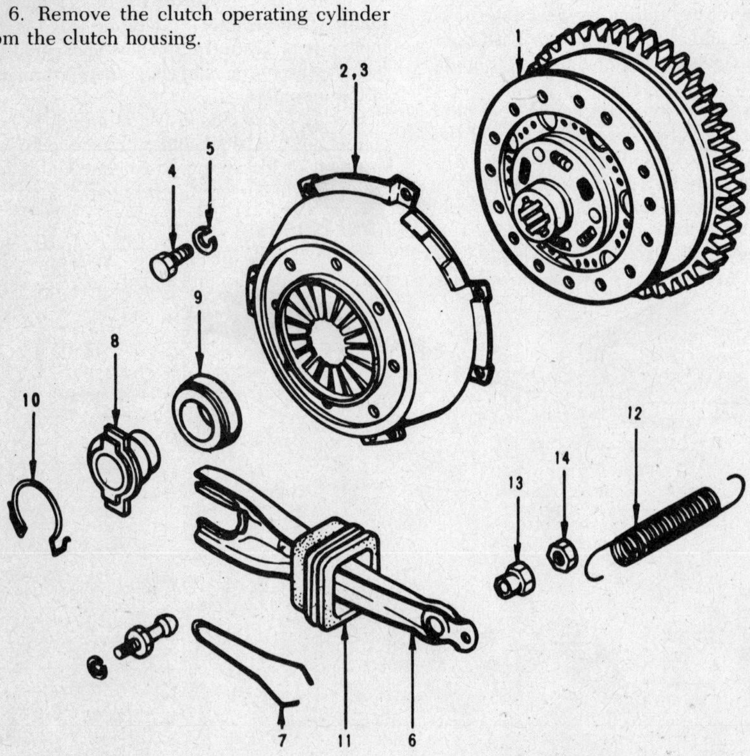

1. Disc
2, 3. Clutch cover assembly with pressure plate
4. Bolt
5. Lockwasher
6. Withdrawal lever
7. Retainer spring
8. Bearing sleeve
9. Release bearing
10. Bearing sleeve holder spring
11. Dust cover
12. Return spring
13. Withdrawal lever push nut
14. Locknut

Diaphragm spring clutch—510 shown

CLUTCH

All models in all years use diaphragm spring pressure plates.

REMOVAL AND INSTALLATION

1. Remove the transmission from the engine.

L24 clutch release mechanism. (1) is the withdrawal lever, (2) is the return spring and (3) is the release bearing

2. Insert a clutch aligning bar or similar tool all the way into the clutch disc hub. This must be done so as to support the weight of the clutch disc during removal. Mark the clutch assembly-to-flywheel relationship with paint or a center punch so that the clutch assembly can be assembled in the same position from which it is removed.
3. Loosen the bolts in sequence, a turn at a time. Remove the bolts.
4. Remove the pressure plate and clutch disc.
5. Remove the release mechanism. Apply multi-purpose grease to the bearing sleeve inside groove, the contact point of the withdrawal lever and bearing sleeve, the contact surface of the lever ball pin and lever. Replace the release mechanism.
6. Inspect the pressure plate for wear, scoring, etc., and reface or replace as necessary. Inspect the release bearing and replace as necessary. Apply a small amount of grease to the transmission splines. Install the disc on the splines and slide back and forth a few times. Remove the disc and remove excess grease on hub. Be sure no grease contacts the disc or pressure plate.
7. Install the disc, aligning it with a splined dummy shaft.
8. Install the pressure plate and torque the bolts to 11-16 ft/lbs.
9. Remove the dummy shaft.
10. Replace the transmission.

F10 Transaxle Clutch

REMOVAL

Because of the unique configuration of the F10 and 310 transmission/drive shaft system (transaxle), the transmission is impossible to remove from the car without removing the engine.

Due to this problem, Datsun has made provisions for clutch service through an access plate (cover) on the top of the housing. The engine and transmission need not be removed to permit repair or replacement.

NOTE: The clutch cover and pressure plate are balanced as a unit. If replacement is necessary, replace both parts.

1. Disconnect the following cables, wires and hoses:
   - Battery ground cable
   - Fresh air duct
   - Engine harness connectors on the clutch housing
   - Ignition wire between the coil and the distributor
   - Carbon canister hoses
2. Remove the inspection plate from the top of the clutch housing and remove the six bolts holding the clutch cover.

NOTE: In order to reach all six bolts, you are going to have to jack up the car and, as you loosen the bolts, rotate the right front wheel with the car in top gear. This will rotate the clutch cover.

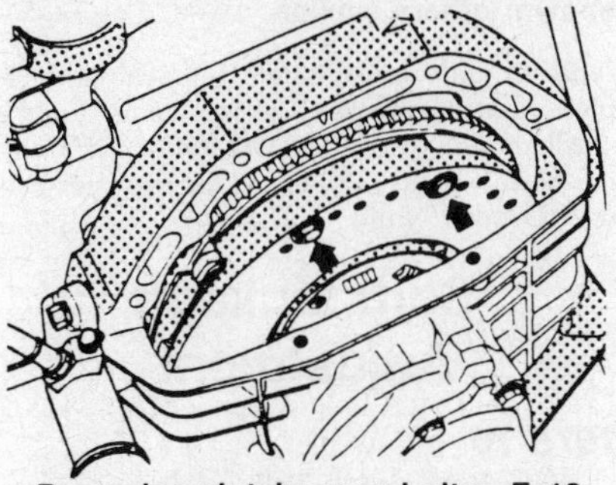

Removing clutch cover bolts—F-10

CLUTCH PEDAL SPECIFICATIONS

Model	Pedal Height Above Floor (inches)	Pedal Free Play (inches)
B210	6.02	0.04-0.12
210 (1980)	5.75	0.04-0.20
310	7.29	0.04-0.20
710	7.09	0.04-0.20
810	6.90	0.04-0.20
F-10	6.90	0.23-0.55
200SX	7.60	0.04-0.12
510	6.50	0.04-0.20
280Z (1975)	8.78	0.071-0.173
280Z (1976-79)	8.78	0.039-0.197
280ZX (1980)	7.99	0.04-0.20

CAUTION

Be sure to loosen the bolts evenly in order.

3. Rotate the steering wheel all the way to the right and remove the inspection plate inside the right wheel well.
4. Disconnect the withdrawal lever and remove the six bolts on the bearing house. Reaching through the wheel well inspection hole, pull out the primary drive gear assembly.
5. After removing the drive gear, go back to the engine compartment and lift the clutch cover and disc assembly out through the open section of the clutch housing. You may also remove the diaphragm at the same time.
6. Remove the strap holding the pressure plate to the clutch cover and remove the clutch from the center.

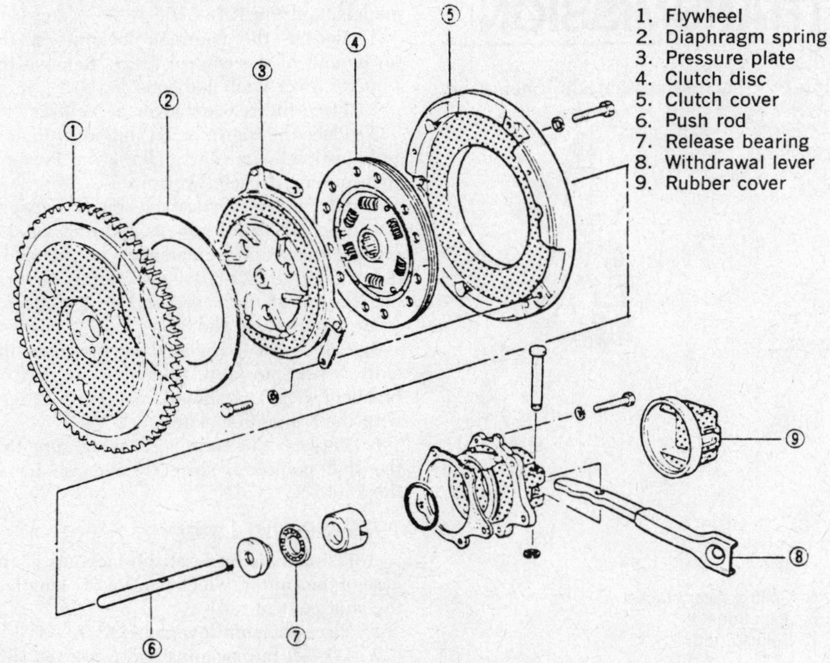

F-10 clutch components

NOTE: This strap must be replaced in the same position it had before removal. Mark the relative position before removal. Installing it out of position will cause an imbalance.

INSTALLATION

Installation is the reverse of removal. But, you must observe the following:

1. Paying particular attention to the alignment marks, reassemble the disc and cover to the pressure plate. Tighten the strap bolts to 5-6 ft/lbs.
2. Put the diaphragm spring and cover assembly onto the flywheel and screw the bolts in with your fingers.

NOTE: These bolts should remain loose enough to shift the assembly when installing the drive gear. There are a pair of aligning pins on the flywheel.

3. Install the drive gear assembly by aligning the disc hub with the gear spline. After alignment, tighten the cover bolts to 5-7.2 ft/lbs.

Clutch Linkage

ADJUSTMENT

Refer to the Clutch Specifications Chart for clutch pedal height above floor and pedal free-play.

All models have a hydraulically operated clutch. Pedal height is usually adjusted with a stopper limiting the upward travel of the pedal. Pedal free-play is adjusted at the master cylinder pushrod. If the pushrod is nonadjustable, free-play is adjusted by placing shims between the master cylinder and the firewall. On a few models, pedal free-play can also be adjusted at the operating (slave) cylinder pushrod. Pushrods are available in three lengths for the F-10 and 310.

HYDRAULIC SYSTEM BLEEDING

Bleeding is required to remove air trapped in the hydraulic system. This operation is

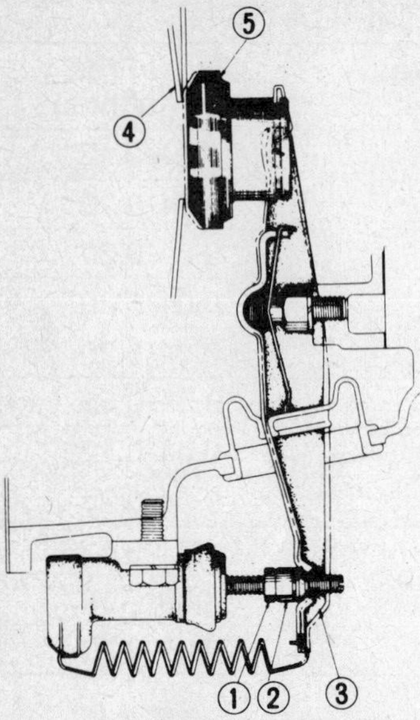

1. Locknut
2. Adjusting nut
3. Withdrawal lever
4. Diaphragm spring
5. Release bearing

Details of the clutch operating cylinder and withdrawal lever for the 280Z. Free play is adjusted at this point

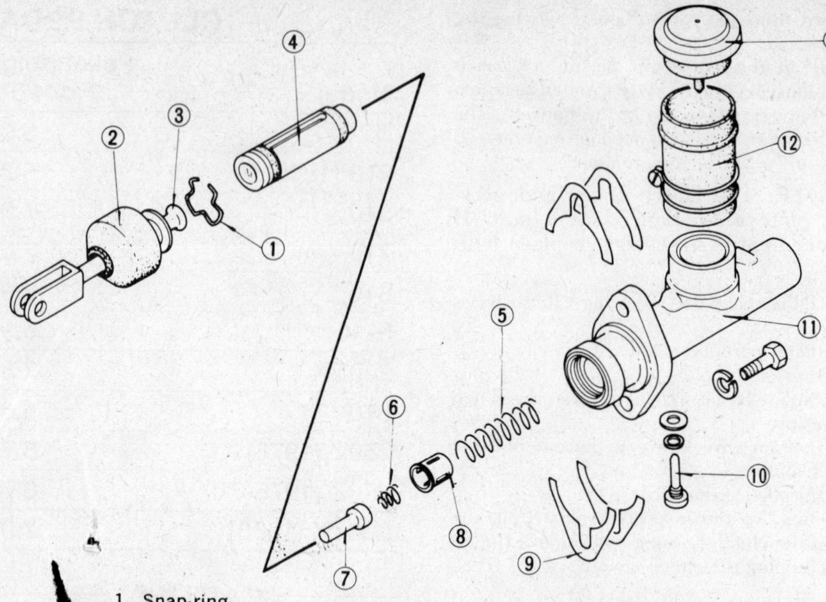

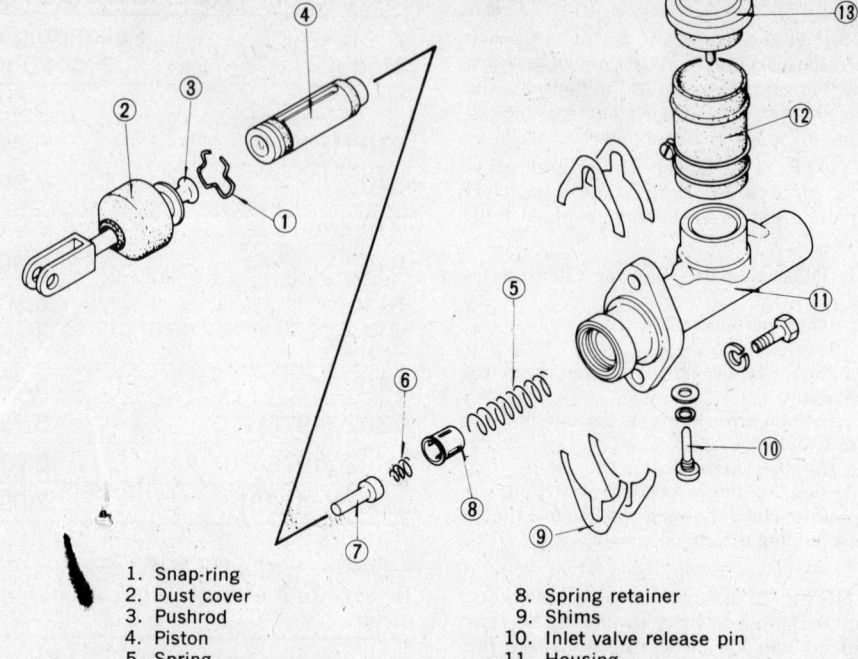

1. Snap-ring
2. Dust cover
3. Pushrod
4. Piston
5. Spring
6. Inlet valve spring
7. Inlet valve
8. Spring retainer
9. Shims
10. Inlet valve release pin
11. Housing
12. Fluid reservoir
13. Reservoir cap

Clutch master cylinder—B210 shown; others similar

necessary whenever the system has been leaking or dismantled. The bleed screw is usually located on the clutch operating (slave) cylinder.

1. Remove the bleed screw dust cap.
2. Attach a tube to the bleed screw, immersing the free end in a clean container of brake fluid.
3. Fill the master cylinder with fluid.
4. Open the bleed screw about ¾ turn.
5. Depress the clutch pedal quickly. Hold it down. Have an assistant tighten the bleed screw. Allow the pedal to return slowly. Bleeder screw torque: 5-6 ft/lbs.
6. Repeat steps 2 and 5 until no more air bubbles are seen in the fluid container.
7. Remove the bleed tube. Replace the dust cap. Refill the master cylinder.

HYDRAULIC SYSTEM REPAIRS

Clutch master and slave cylinders are repaired in much the same way as are brake master and wheel cylinders. Bleeding is required whenever the clutch hydraulic system has been dismantled.

AUTOMATIC TRANSMISSION

Only external transmission adjustments and repairs, and transmission removal and replacement, are covered in this book.

All models use a JATCO automatic transmission, model 3N71B. This transmission uses Dexron® fluid.

Shift Linkage Adjustment

1975-78

This adjustment is only necessary on the 1975-78 B210, 1978 200SX, all 610 and 710 models, and the 1978 510.

1. Loosen the trunnion locknuts at the lower end of the control lever. Remove the selector lever knob and console.
2. Place the selector lever in Neutral.
3. Place the transmission shift lever in neutral position by pushing it all the way forward, then pulling it back two stops.
4. Check the vertical clearance between the top of the shift lever pin and transmission control bracket. The clearance ("B") should be 0.1-1.1 mm (0.020-0.059 in.). Adjust by turning the nut at the lower end of the selector lever compression rod.
5. Check the horizontal clearance of the shift lever pin and transmission control bracket ("C"). This should be 1.0 mm. Adjust with the trunnion locknuts.
6. Replace the console, making sure that the shift pointer is correctly aligned. Install the knob.

1979-80 and Later

Adjustment is made at the locknuts at the base of the shifter, which control the length of the shift control rod.

1. Place the shift lever in "D".
2. Loosen the locknuts and move the shift lever until it is firmly in the "D" range, the

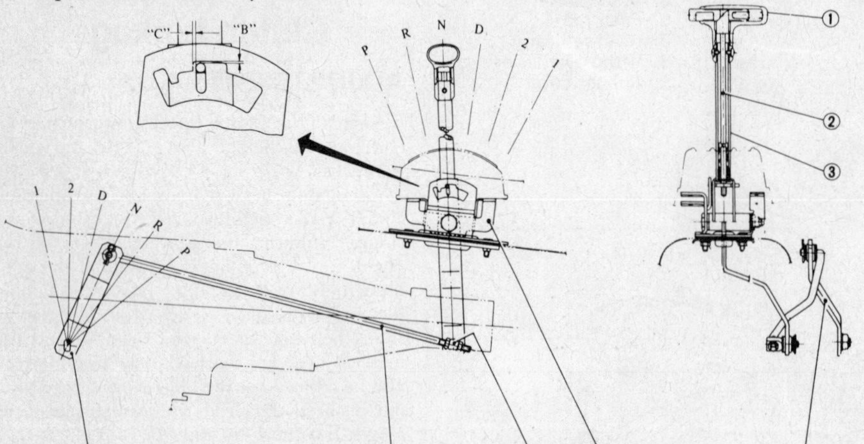

1. Control lever knob
2. Pusher
3. Control lever assembly
4. Selector range lever
5. Control lever bracket
6. Joint trunnion
7. Selector rod

Automatic transmission floor shift adjustment—1975-78

pointer is aligned, and the transmission is in "D" range.

3. Tighten the locknuts.

4. Check the adjustment. Start the car and apply the parking brake. Shift through all the ranges, starting in "P". As the lever is moved from "P" to "1", you should be able to feel the detents in each range. If proper adjustment is not possible, the grommets are probably worn and should be replaced.

Downshift Solenoid Check

The solenoid is controlled by a downshift switch on the accelerator linkage inside the car. To test the switch and solenoid operation:

1. Turn the ignition on.
2. Push the accelerator all the way down to actuate the switch.
3. The solenoid should click when actuated. The solenoid is screwed into the outside of the case. If there is no click, check the switch, wiring, and solenoid.

To remove the solenoid, first drain 2-3 pints of fluid, then unscrew the unit.

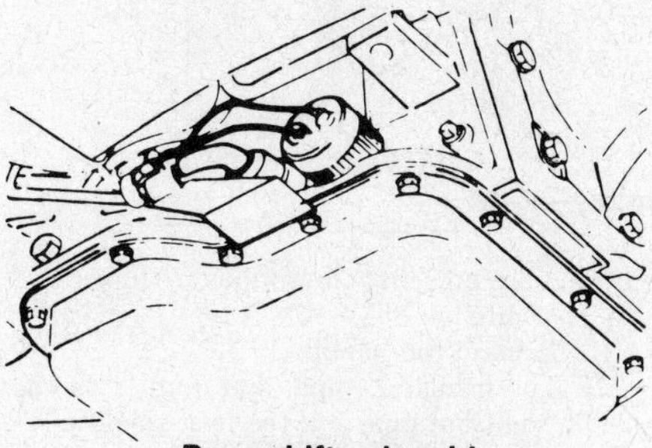

Downshift solenoid

Neutral Safety and Backup Light Switch Adjustment

The switch unit is bolted to the left side of the transmission shift lever. The switch prevents the engine from being started in any transmission position except Park or Neutral. It also controls the backup lights.

1. Remove the transmission shift lever retaining nut and the lever.
2. Remove the switch.
3. Remove the machine screw in the case under the switch.
4. Align the switch to the case by inserting a 0.059 in. diameter pin through the hole in the switch into the screw hole. Mark the switch location.
5. Remove the pin, replace the machine screw, install the switch as marked, and replace the transmission shift lever and retaining nut.
6. Make sure while holding the brakes on, that the engine will start only in Park or Neutral. Check that the backup lights go on only in reverse.

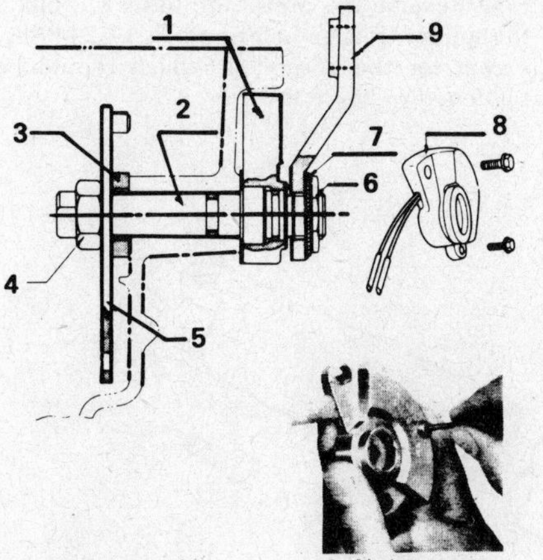

1. Neutral safety switch
2. Manual shaft
3. Washer
4. Nut
5. Manual plate
6. Nut
7. Washer
8. Neutral safety switch
9. Transmission shift lever

Neutral safety and back-up light switch —JATCO transmission

Transmission Removal and Installation

1. Disconnect the battery cable.
2. Remove the accelerator linkage.
3. Detach the shift linkage.
4. Disconnect the neutral safety switch and downshift solenoid wiring.
5. Remove the drain plug and drain the torque converter. If there is no converter drain plug, drain the transmission. If there is no transmission drain plug, remove the pan to drain. Replace the pan to keep out dirt.
6. Remove the front exhaust pipe.
7. Remove the vacuum tube and speedometer cable.
8. Disconnect the fluid cooler tubes.
9. Remove the driveshaft and starter.
10. Support the transmission with a jack under the oil pan. Support the engine also.
11. Remove the rear crossmember.
12. Mark the relationship between the torque converter and the drive plate. Remove the four bolts holding the converter to the drive plate through the hole at the front, under the engine. Unbolt the transmission from the engine.
13. Reverse the procedure for installation. Make sure the drive plate is warped no more than 0.020 in. Torque the drive plate-to-torque converter and converter housing-to-engine bolts to 29-36 ft/lbs. Drive plate-to-crankshaft bolt torque is 101-116 ft/lbs.
14. Refill the transmission and check the fluid level.

TRANSAXLE

Shift Linkage Adjustment

F-10 4 Speed

1. Loosen control lever adjusting nuts.
2. Measure the initial clearance between the case cover and the shift lever when the shift lever is pushed completely into the case cover.
3. Relocate the shift lever to increase the clearance by 8 mm. Move shift lever fully downward (hand lever in 4th gear).
4. Push select lever fully upward so that hand lever guide plate touches detent pin.
5. Turn upper adjusting nut until it contacts trunnion plate then back off one full turn.
6. Tighten lower adjusting nut.

F-10 5 Speed

1. Loosen all 4 locknuts and move shift lever completely into transmission case, then back out 8 mm.
2. Move shift lever down so that gears are in 3rd position.
3. Push select lever fully down so that hand lever guide plate touches detent pin.
4. Turn selector shaft upper adjusting nut until it touches the trunnion plate. Then turn it one complete turn more and tighten lower nut.
5. Place hand lever in neutral and adjust hand lever to detent gap to one to two millimeters. Tighten lock nuts.

310 4 and 5 Speed

Adjustment can be made by adjusting the select lever.

1. Loosen the adjusting nuts at each end of the control rod lever near the bottom of the linkage.
2. Set the shift control lever in the Neutral position.
2. Fully push the shift lever (transmission side) in the direction P1, as shown in the illustration. On the four speed transmission, pull the lever back about 8 mm (0.31 in.). On the five speed, pull the shift lever back 11.5 mm (0.453 in.). With the select lever held in the above position, move the shift lever in direction P2, which engages third gear on four speed transmissions and second gear on five speed transmissions.
4. Push the control rod select lever as far as it will go in direction P3, then turn the upper adjusting nut until it touches the trunnion. Turn the nut a quarter turn more, and lock the select lever with the other adjusting nut.
5. Operate the shift control lever in the car to see if it shifts smoothly through the gears.

DRIVE AXLE

Driveshaft and U-Joints

F-10 Halfshafts

The F-10 front wheel drive halfshafts (driveshafts) have constant velocity joints at each end. They are joined to the hubs by splines, and bolted to the output flanges of the transaxle.

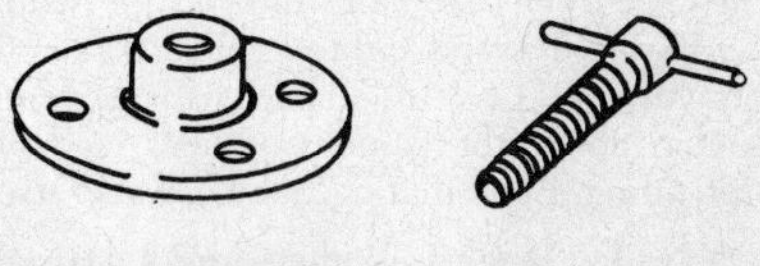

Special Datsun tool ST35100000 for removing driveshaft

Removal

1. Raise the car and support it. Remove the front wheels and tires.
2. Remove the cotterpin and take off the locknut from the driveshaft while holding the wheel hub.
3. Install a driveshaft remover (screw type), remove the bolts holding the driveshaft and pull the shaft. The shaft may be removed from under the engine compartment.

NOTE: When removing, do not damage the seal on the knuckle.

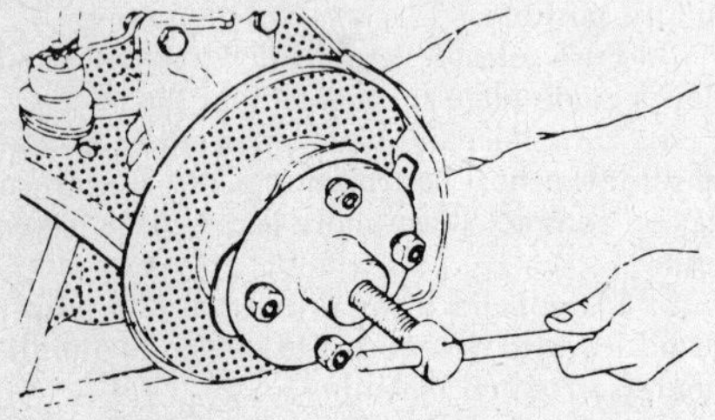
Removing driveshaft

Disassembly

1. Place the driveshaft in a "soft" vise and straighten and remove boot band, then remove the dust cover from the joint outer ring and slide back.
2. Pry off the clip with a screwdriver and pull out the outer ring (with flange).
3. Wipe the grease from the ball cage and drive out the ball bearings. Turn the cage half a turn and remove from the inner ring.
4. Pry off the retaining ring and remove the inner ring. It is easily removed by tapping with a mallet. Then remove the dust cover.

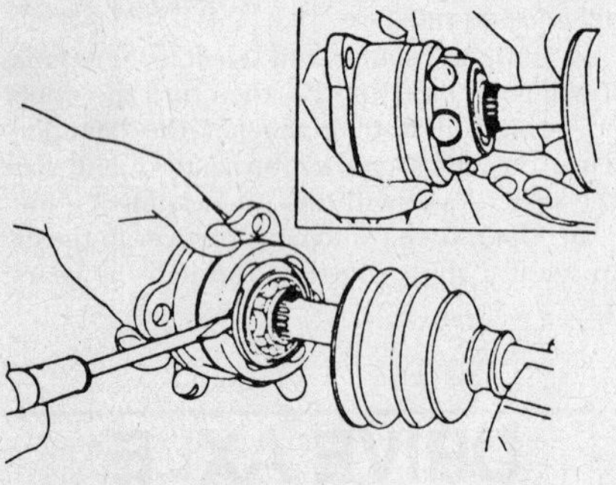
Removing the clip and outer ring

Inspection

Clean all parts with a safe solvent and dry with compressed air. Check all the parts for wear, deformation, rust, burn or excessive play. Replace any part that seems damaged.

Assembly

Assembly is the reverse procedure, with the following steps added:

To securely fasten the dust cover, wrap a band around it and tighten with pliers and a screwdriver. Lock the band with a punch, leaving about the same length as its width protruding. Bend that portion back over itself:

NOTE: Renew grease and take care not to allow any dirt inside the dust cover.

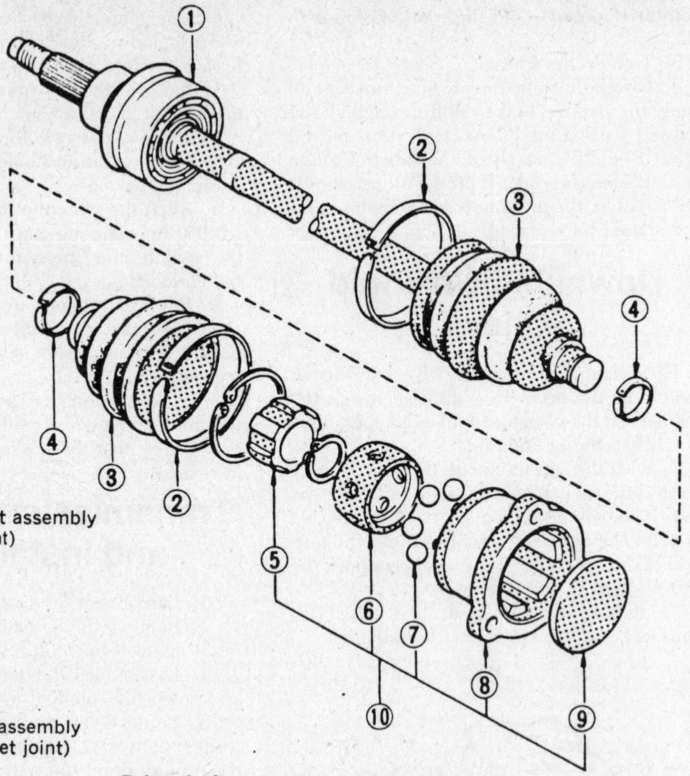

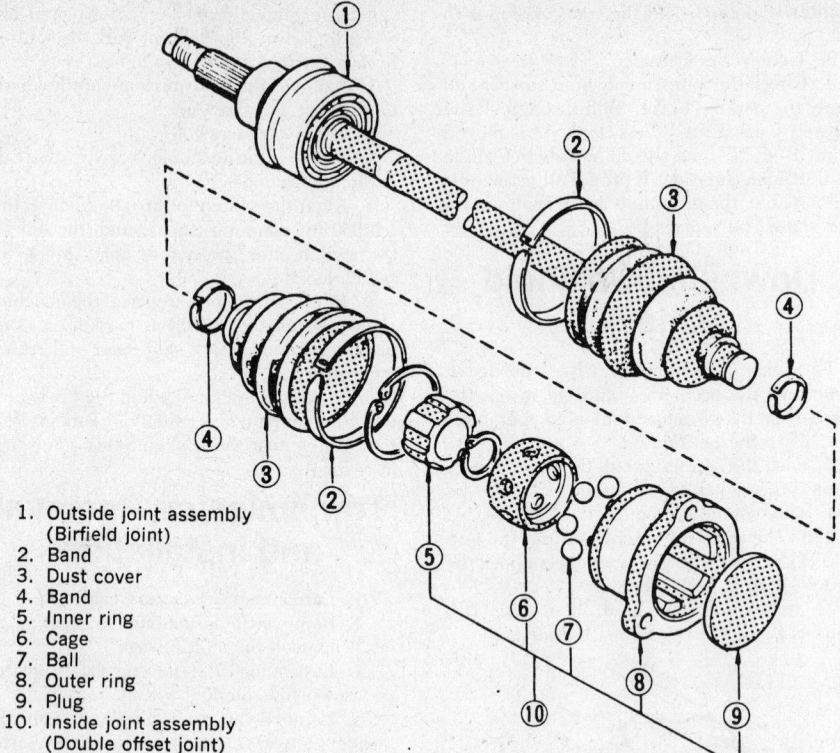

1. Outside joint assembly (Birfield joint)
2. Band
3. Dust cover
4. Band
5. Inner ring
6. Cage
7. Ball
8. Outer ring
9. Plug
10. Inside joint assembly (Double offset joint)

Driveshaft assembly—F-10

Installation

Installation is the reverse of removal. Add the following steps to your procedure:

Do not damage the grease seal.

Lubricate the grease seal lip with grease.

Install an O-ring on the flange surface of the double offset joint.

Be sure that the drive shaft thread is clear of the hub before tightening.

If the fit seems to be tight, lightly hammer the flange surface until threads are exposed. Torque hub nut to 87-145 ft/lbs and shaft bolts to 28-36 ft/lbs.

REMOVAL AND INSTALLATION

510, 610 Sedan, 710, B210, 200SX with Automatic Transmission, 280Z and ZX

These driveshafts are the one piece type with a U-joint and flange at the rear, and a U-joint and a splined sleeve yoke which fits into the rear of the transmission, at the front. The U-joints must be disassembled for lubrication at 24,000 mile intervals if no grease fittings are present. The splines are lubricated by transmission oil.

1. Release the handbrake.
2. The insulator, pipe, and muffler on the 280Z; the front pipe and the heat shield plate must come off on 280ZX models sold in California.
3. Matchmark the flanges on the driveshaft and differential so that the driveshaft can be reinstalled in its original orientation; this will help maintain driveline balance.
4. Unbolt the rear flange.
5. Pull the driveshaft down and back.
6. Plug the transmission extension housing.
7. Reverse the procedure to install, oiling the splines. Flange bolt torque is 17-24 ft/lbs, except for the Z models, which should be tightened to 25-33 ft/lbs.

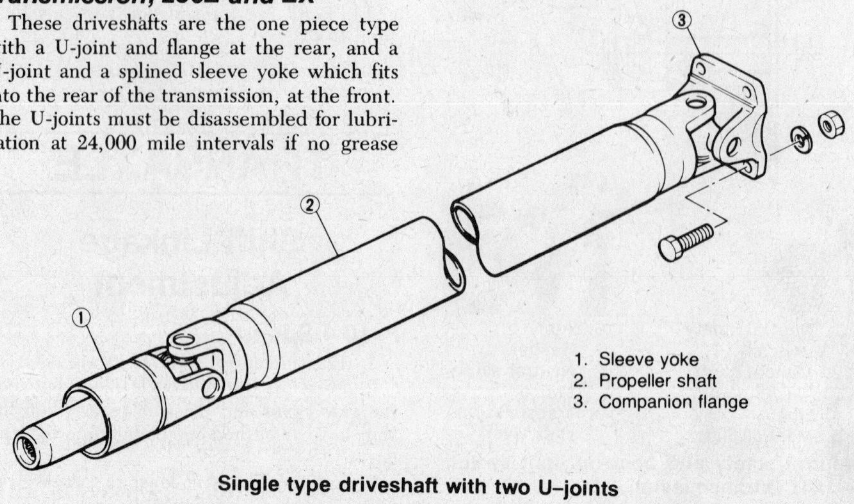

1. Sleeve yoke
2. Propeller shaft
3. Companion flange

Single type driveshaft with two U-joints

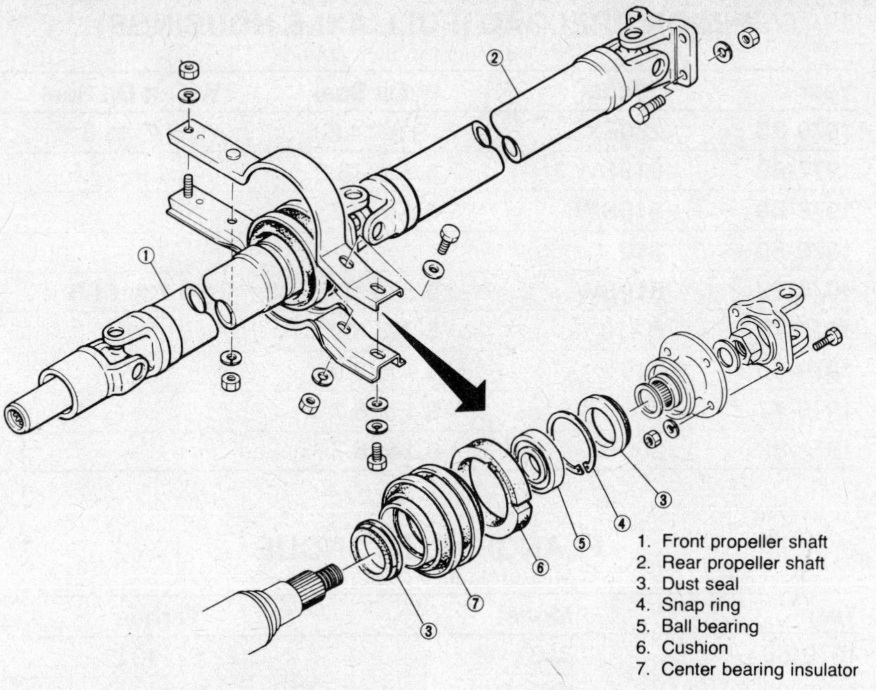

Two piece driveshaft with center bearing and three U–joints

610 Wagon, 200SX with Manual Transmission, 810

These models use a driveshaft with three U-joints and a center support bearing. The driveshaft is balanced as an assembly. It is not recommended that it be disassembled.

1. Mark the relationship of the driveshaft flange to the differential flange.
2. Unbolt the center bearing bracket.
3. Unbolt the driveshaft flange from the differential flange.
4. Pull the driveshaft back under the rear axle. Plug the rear of the transmission to prevent oil or fluid loss.
5. On installation, align the marks made in Step 1. Torque the flange bolts to 17-24 ft/lbs. Center bearing bracket bolt torque is 26-35 ft/lbs on the 610.

U-JOINT OVERHAUL

Disassembly

1. Mark the relationship of all components for reassembly.
2. Remove the snap-rings. The snap-rings seat in the needle bearing races.
3. Tap the yoke with a soft hammer to release one bearing cap. Be careful not to lose the needle rollers.
4. Remove the other bearing caps. Remove the spiders from the yokes.

Inspection

1. Spline backlash should not exceed 0.0197 in.
2. Driveshaft runout should not exceed 0.015 in.
3. On units with snap-rings seated in the needle bearing races, different thicknesses of snap-rings are available for U-joint adjustment. Play should not exceed 0.0008 in. Use snap-rings of equal thickness on each side of the U-joint to maintain balance.
4. U-joint spiders must be replaced if their bearing journals are worn more than 0.0059 in. from their original diameter.

Assembly

1. Place the needle rollers in the races and hold them in place with grease.
2. Put the spider into place in its yokes.
3. Replace all seals.
4. Tap the races into position and secure with the snap-rings.

Differential

All models have solid rear drive axles except all 610 and 810 sedans, and all Z models, which have independent rear suspension with the differential carrier solidly mounted.

SOLID REAR AXLE

Axle Unit Disassembly

1. Remove the rear axle assembly from the vehicle. Disconnect the brake lines at the wheel cylinders.
2. Remove the handbrake linkage.
3. Drain the oil.
4. Unbolt the backing plate from the axle housing. Pull the axle shaft and backing plate out with a slide hammer.
5. From the rear of the backing plate, press off the bearing collar or cut it off with a cold chisel. The collar should not be reused. Pull out the bearing.

NOTE: Some units use a locknut instead of a bearing collar.

6. Unbolt and pull out the differential carrier from the axle housing.

Axle Unit Assembly

1. Use a new gasket between the axle housing and differential carrier. Torque the bolts to 14-18 ft/lbs in a diagonal pattern.
2. Install the grease catcher, bearing spacer, bearing packed with grease, and new bearing collar onto the axle shaft. The seal side of the wheel bearing must face the wheel. Coat the oil seal lips with grease. Press on the bearing collar.
3. Adjust the axle end-play by using shims between the backing plate and axle housing. Specified end-play is 0.004 in. for the B210, 0.004-0.018 in. for the 610 and 710, 0.008-0.020 in. for 810 wagon, 0.003-0.017 for 200SX, 210, and 1978-79 510.
4. Specified bolt torque for the brake backing plate is 16-20 ft/lbs for the 610 and 710, and 16-20 ft/lbs for all other models.
5. Refill the unit with oil. See the Capacities Chart.

Differential Overhaul

Two types of differential pinion bearing preload adjustment are used on the solid axles. One type uses a collapsible sleeve; the other uses selective washers and a non-collapsible sleeve. In other aspects, including selection and placement of shims for pinion depth, ring gear backlash and side carrier preload, the procedures are the same.

DISASSEMBLY

1. Remove the side bearing caps, marking their locations for reassembly. Remove the differential assembly from the carrier.
2. Pull off the side bearings. Do not mix left and right side parts.
3. Flatten the lock tabs and unbolt the ring gear, loosening the bolts diagonally.
4. Drive out the pinion shaft lock pin from left to right. Remove the pinion shaft and pinions, side gears, and thrust washers. Separate these parts by original location.
5. Remove the drive pinion nut and pull off the flange. Tap the drive pinion back with a soft hammer and remove it with the rear bearing inner race, bearing spacer, and adjusting washer.
6. Remove and discard the oil seal. Remove the front bearing inner race.
7. Pull out the front and rear bearing outer races.

INSPECTION

1. Wash all parts in a safe solvent. Oil the bearings immediately.
2. Ring and pinion gears must be replaced only in pairs. If the ring gear is warped more than 0.002 in., replace it.
3. Check all parts for wear or distortion. Replace any suspected bearings.

ASSEMBLY

1. Assemble the pinions, side gears, pinion shaft, and thrust washers in the case. Clearance between the side gears and thrust washers should be 0.004-0.008 in. Thrust washers are available in various thicknesses for adjustment.
2. Drive in and peen over the lock pin.
3. Bolt on the ring gear using new lock tabls. Tighten the bolts diagonally.
4. Press the side bearing inner races onto the differential case without shims.
5. The drive pinion height is adjusted with shims behind the rear bearing race. Dealers have special tools for making this measurement.

Standard pinion height is measured from

the axle centerline to the pinion face. The deviation of the drive pinion from standard size is marked on the pinion face with + for larger and − for smaller. There is usually an M mark on pinions graded in hundredths of a millimeter. If no standard pinion height is specified, the adjustment must be made by use of special tools or by comparing the marks on the old and new drive pinion and adjusting the original shim pack to suit.

6. Press in the drive pinion rear bearing outer race and shims. Press in the front bearing outer race. Press the rear bearing inner race onto the drive pinion.

7. Install the drive pinion and collapsible spacer or the selected washer and spacer into the differential carrier. The front bearing inner race and the flange should be installed.

Pinion face marking, B210 is shown

Tighten the flange nut until the torque required to turn the shift (bearing preload) is:

PINION PRELOAD

PINION PRELOAD (FULL AXLE HOUSINGS)

Measurement in inch pounds

Year	Model	W/Oil Seal	W/Out Oil Seal
1979-80	280ZX	9.5-14.8	8.7-11.3
1977-80	810SW	6.9 to 13.9	6.1 to 13.0
1978-80	510SW	6.1 to 8.7	—
1979-80	310	—	—
1975-77	610SW	9.5 to 12.2	8.7 to 11.3
1975-78	B210	5.2 to 6.9	—
1979-80	210	6.1 to 8.9	—
1975-77	710	6.1 to 8.7	—
1977-80	200SX	6.1 to 8.7	—

8. Check the drive pinion height again.

9. Torque the flange nut to the specified torque.

FLANGE NUT TORQUE

FLANGE NUT TORQUE

Measurement in foot pounds

Year	Model	Torque
1979-80	310	87-101
1977-80	810SW	94 to 130
1978-80	510SW	101 to 217
1975-77	610SW	101 to 123
1975-78	B210	101 to 217
1979-80	210	101 to 217
1975-77	710	101 to 123
1977-80	200SX	101 to 217
1979-80	280ZX	25-33

10. Make sure that pinion bearing preload is as in Step 7. If it is excessive, a new spacer or washer must be installed.

11. If the cotter pin does not align, replace the nut and retorque. Do not overtorque.

12. The required side bearing adjusting shim thickness can be determined by the use of the following formulae:

Side Bearing Dimensions

$T_1 = (A - C + D - H') \times 0.01 + 0.20 + E$

$T_2 = (B - D + H') \times 0.01 + 0.09 + F$

a. T_1 is the required shim thickness on the left side.

b. T_2 is the required shim thickness on the right side.

c. A is the figure marked on the left side bearing housing of the gear carrier.

d. B is the figure marked on the right side bearing housing of the gear carrier.

e. C and D are figures marked on the differential case.

f. E and F are differences in the width of the left and right side bearings against the standard width.

g. H′ is the figure marked on the ring gear.

NOTE: Because the markings on the parts are in metric figures, it is advisable to use them to compute shim thicknesses, converting to inches as necessary when completed.

13. Locate and substitute the figures in the formulae.

NOTE: If the values for A, B, C, D and H′ are not given, regard them as zero.

14. Place the determined side bearing adjusting shims on the differential case and press the side bearings in place.

15. Install the differential case assembly into the gear carrier and install the caps and bolts.

NOTE: After the assembly, make sure the preload and backlash are correct. It may be necessary to readjust.

16. If the backlash is too small, decrease the thickness of the left shim and increase the thickness of the right shim by the same amount.

17. If the preload does not agree with the specifications, adjust it with the side bearing shims.

18. Check the tooth contact pattern of the ring gear and pinion gear by painting the ring gear teeth with a suitable mixture to produce a contact pattern.

19. Rotate the pinion through several revolutions in both the forward and the reverse directions so that a definite pattern is made on the ring gear teeth.

20. If the tooth contact is proper and no adjustment is needed, clean the paint mixture from the ring and pinion teeth. The installation of the carrier assembly is in the reverse of the removal.

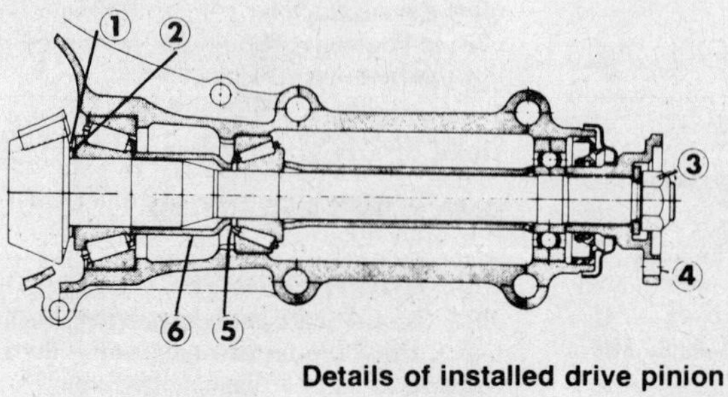

1. Pinion bearing adjusting washer
2. Pinion height adjusting shims
3. Pinion nut
4. Pinion flange
5. Pinion bearing adjusting washer
6. Pinion bearing adjusting spacer

Details of installed drive pinion

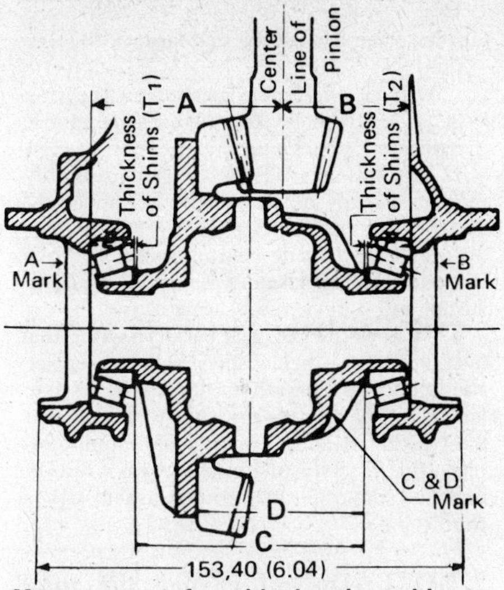

Measurement for side bearing shims, B210

Final Drive Unit—Independent Rear Suspension

REMOVAL AND INSTALLATION

280Z

1. Chock the front wheels. Raise and support the rear of the vehicle.
2. Remove the main muffler.
3. Unbolt the driveshaft.
4. Loosen the transverse link spindle inner bolts (on the front of the front differential mounting crossmember) enough to free the crossmember.
5. Unbolt the axle shafts.
6. Support the differential unit with a jack.
7. Remove the two mounting nuts from the rear of the rear differential mounting crossmember.
8. Remove the four nuts from the bottom of the front crossmember.
9. Lower the front crossmember and final drive unit together.
10. Unbolt the front crossmember from the differential unit.
11. Reverse the procedure to install. Tighten the transverse link spindle inner bolts with the vehicle lowered to the ground and with two 150 lb. passengers.

610 Sedan

1. Chock the front wheels. Raise and support the rear of the vehicle.
2. Disconnect the handbrake rear cable driveshaft, and axle shafts.
3. Support the differential unit with a jack.
4. Unbolt the differential rear mounting crossmember from body.
5. Remove the four bolts holding the differential to the rear suspension crossmember.
6. Remove the differential to the rear.
7. Support the rear suspension crossmember with stands to prevent damage to the insulators.
8. Unbolt the differential rear mounting crossmember from the differential.
9. Reverse the procedure to install. Pry the differential unit into position.

280ZX and 810 Sedan

1. Jack up the rear of the car and drain the oil from the differential.
2. Disconnect the driveshaft.
3. Disconnect the halfshafts.
4. Remove the side flange fixing bolts, and disconnect the flange yokes together with the halfshafts. Support the case with a jack.
5. Remove the four bolts retaining the case to the suspension carrier.
6. Pull the case backwards on the jack until clear of the car.
7. After the case is removed, support the suspension on a stand to prevent damage.
8. Installation is the reverse. Tighten the rear cover-to-insulator nuts to 65-87 ft/lbs, the case-to-suspension bolts to 43-58 ft/lbs, and the side flange and driveshaft bolts to 36-43 ft/lbs.

RING GEAR BACKLASH

DISASSEMBLY

1. Drain the oil and remove the rear cover.
2. Clamp the housing down securely.
3. Check the toothe contact pattern with red lead.
4. Check the backlash between the ring and pinion with a dial indicator and record.
5. If the tooth contact pattern or gear backlash is incorrect, make sure that runout at the rear of the ring gear does not exceed 0.002 in.
6. Remove the flanges.

NOTE: The model R160 and R180 side flanges are retained by bolts and removed during the differential removal procedure. The R200 side flanges are removed from the assembly after differential removal. The flanges are retained by circlips within the side gears and must be pried out.

7. Unbolt and pull off the side retainers. Note the original locations of retainers and shims.
8. Remove the differential assembly from the carrier.
9. Remove the bearing outer races from the side retainers with an oil seal puller.
10. Hold the drive pinion flange and loosen the nut. Tighten the nut to 123-145 ft/lbs and check the torque required to turn the drive pinion and record. Remove the nut and pull off the flange.
11. Press the drive pinion from the gear carrier with the front and rear bearing inner races, bearing spacers, and adjusting washers. Press out the front pilot bearing.
12. Press the drive pinion from the rear bearing.

NOTE: If the tooth contact pattern and backlash was correct in Steps 3 and 4 and the original ring gear, carrier, drive pinion, rear bearing, and washers are to be reused, it is not necessary to remove the rear bearing.

13. Press the front and rear bearing outer races from the carrier.
14. Pull off the right differential side gear. Spread the lock straps, loosen and remove the ring gear bolts in a diagonal pattern. Remove the ring gear and pull off the left differential side gear. Do not mix right and left side parts.
15. Punch out the pinion shaft lock pin

RING GEAR BACKLASH SIDE BEARING WIDTH AND PRELOAD

Measurement in inches and inch-pounds

Year	Model	Backlash	BEARING STANDARD Width	(mm)	Side Carrier Preload ①
1977-80	310	.0024-.0059	—	—	—
	810SW	.0059-.0079	0.7874	(20.00)	10.0-17.0
1978-80	510SW	.0039-.0059	0.7280	(18.50)	7.8-14.8
1975-77	610SW	.0059-.0079	0.7874	(20.00)	7.7-12.8
	280ZX, R180,	.0039-.0079	0.7870	(20.00)	—
	R200	.0051-.0071	0.8270	(21.00)	—
1975-78	B210	.0039-.0059	0.6890	(17.50)	5.1-6.2
1979-80	210	.0039-.0059	0.7280	(18.50)	7.8-14.8
1975-77	710	.0039-.0059	0.7280	(18.50)	5.7-10.8
1977-80	200SX	.0039-.0059	0.7280	(18.50)	7.8-14.8

① Measured at companion flange bolt hole

from the ring gear side. Remove the shaft, differential gears, and thrust washers. Note the original location of all parts.

16. To replace the front oil seal, pull off the seal retainer and pull out the seal. Apply grease between the lips of the new oil seal and drive it into place. Replace the retainer.

NOTE: The front oil seal can be replaced with the differential mounted on the vehicle, after the driveshaft and flange are removed.

17. To replace the side oil seals, pull out the seal and drive in the new one, applying grease between the seal lips.

NOTE: The side oil seals can be replaced with the differential mounted on the vehicle, after the axle shafts, flanges, and retainers are removed.

Assembly

1. Wash all parts in a safe solvent and oil the bearings immediately.
2. Install the side and pinion gears into the differential case. Replace the pinion shaft. Check the clearance between the side gears and thrust washers. It should be 0.004-0.008 in. Various thicknesses of thrust washers are available for adjustment.
3. Drive in the pinion shift lock pin. Stake the end of the pin with a punch.
4. Install the ring gear to the differential assembly. Use new lock straps under the bolts. Torque the bolts to 51-58 ft/lbs in a diagonal pattern, tapping the bolt heads lightly before final torquing.
5. Before pressing on new differential side bearings, check bearing width. Standard width is 0.787 in.
6. Press the front and rear drive pinion bearing outer races into the gear carrier.
7. Drive pinion bearing preload turning torque should be 6-9 in/lbs, with the pinion flange nut torqued to 123-145 ft/lbs and without the oil seal on R160 and R180 differentials; it should be 9.5-15.0 in/lbs with the oil seal installed on the R200 (pinion flange nut torqued to 137-159 ft/lbs). This is normally checked and adjusted with special tools.
8. Special tools are required to make the drive pinion height adjustment. The height is adjusted by a washer and shims between the rear bearing and the drive pinion gear. The deviation of the drive pinion from standard size, in hundredths of a millimeter, is marked on the pinion face with + for larger and − for smaller. If the drive pinion is replaced, compare the old and new marks and adjust the shim pack to suit.
9. Install the drive pinion, front pilot bearing, and oil seal. Replace the flange and torque the bolt to 123-145 ft/lbs.
10. Side bearing shims are selected by these formulae:

Model R160 and R180:

$T_1 = (A+C+G_1-D) \times 0.01 + 0.76 - E$

$T_2 = (B+D+G_2) \times 0.01 + 0.76 - F$

a. T_1 is the required thickness of the right side retainer shim;

b. T_2 is the required thickness of the right side retainer shim;

c. A and B are the figures marked on the gear carrier;

d. C and D are the figures marked on the differential case;

e. E and F are the differences in width of the left or right side bearings against the standard width (20.00 mm);

f. G_1 and G_2 are the figures marked on the left and right side retainers.

NOTE: It is advisable to use the metric figures and convert to inches as necessary after making calculations.

Side Bearing Dimensions—280Z

Figure	Location
A,B	on gear carriers
C,D	on differential case
E,F	difference from standard size (20 mm.) of bearing
G	on side retainers
H	on ring gear

Model R200:

$T_1 = (A-C+D-H') \times 0.01 + E + 2.05$

$T_2 = (B-D+H') \times 0.01 + F + G + 1.95$

a. T_1, T_2, A, B, C, D, E, F are the same as for the R160 and R180 differentials, except that the standard width is 21.00 mm.

b. G is the difference in thickness of the side spacer against the standard width (8.10 mm).

c. H' is the figure marked on the ring gear. See the note above about using metric figures.

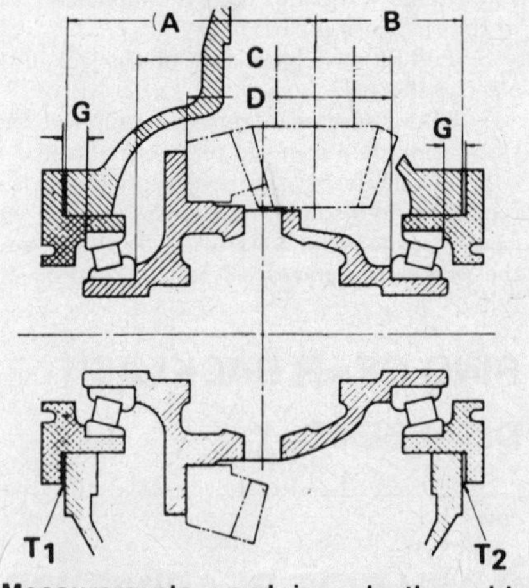

Measurements used in selecting side bearing shims

11. Install the differential case assembly into the carrier and install the left and right side bearing preload washer.
12. Drive the side bearing spacer in place between the right side washer and housing. Install and tighten the bearing caps.
13. Check the ring gear backlash with a dial indicator. If it is below specifications, replace the left adjusting washer with a thinner one, and the right adjusting washer with a thicker one. If the reading is over specifications, replace the left adjusting washer with a thicker one and the right adjusting washer with a thinner one.

NOTE: Do not change the total thickness of the washers.

14. Check and adjust the tooth contact pattern as necessary (outlined in the solid axle procedure).
15. Install the side flanges on the carrier and make sure the circlip is engaged in the groove in the side flange (model R200).
16. Install the side flange yokes and tighten the retaining bolts (R160 and R180).
17. Install the differential assembly.

Axle Shafts–Independent Rear Suspension

Wheel Bearing, Seal, and Axle Shaft Service

1. Jack up and support the rear of the car.
2. Remove the wheel and brake drum.
3. Disconnect the axle driveshaft from the axle shaft at the flange.
4. Remove the wheel bearing locknut while holding the axle shaft outer flange from turning.
5. Pull out the axle shaft with a slide hammer. Remove the spacer and inner flange.
6. Drive the inner wheel bearing and oil seal out toward the center of the car.
7. Press or pull the out wheel bearing from the axle shaft.

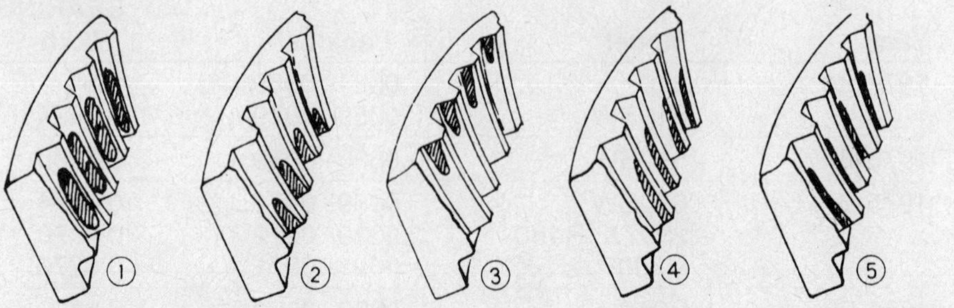

1. Correct tooth contact
2. Short toe contact; move ring gear away from pinion.
3. Short heel contact; move ring gear toward pinion.
4. Contact too high and narrow; pinion should be moved toward center of axle.
5. Contact too low and narrow; pinion should be moved away from center of axle.

Ring gear tooth contact patterns

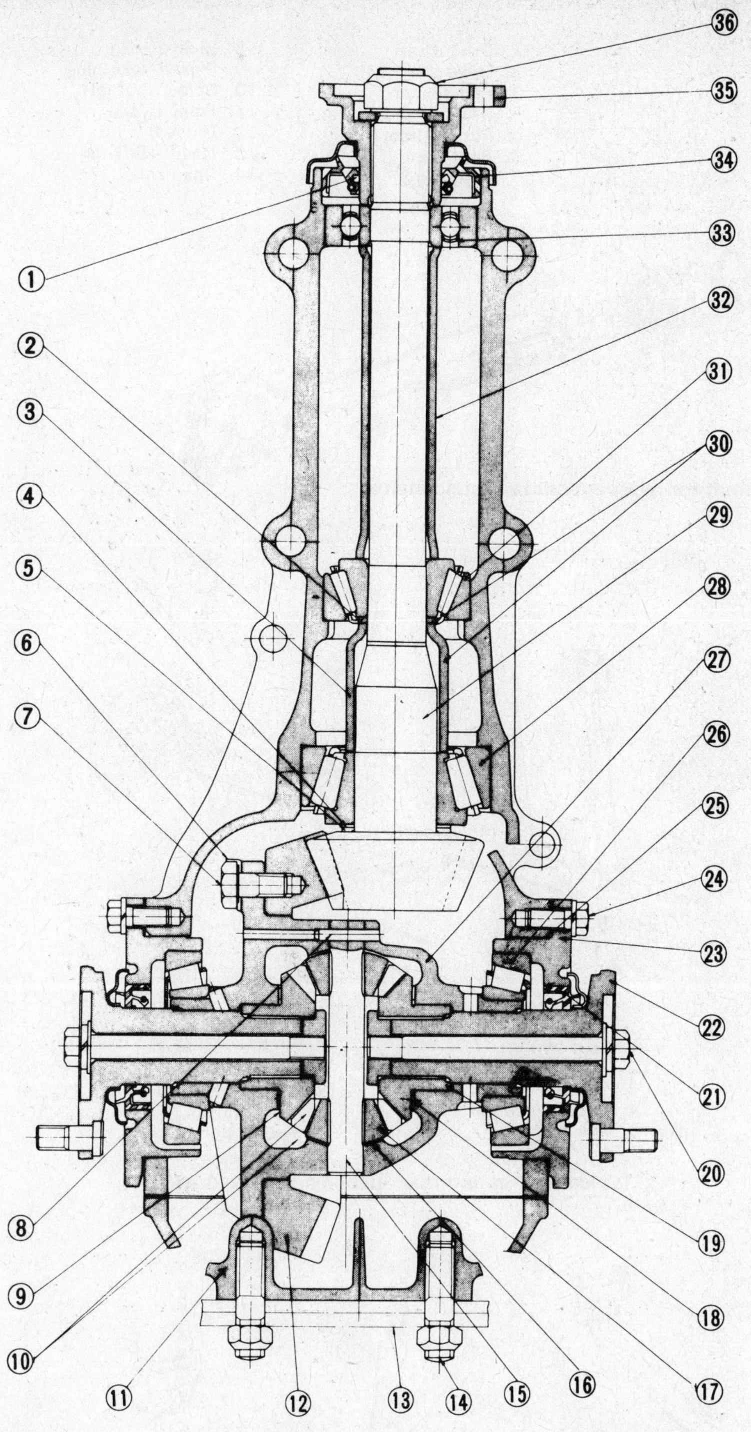

1. Oil seal
2. Pinion bearing adjusting washer
3. Pinion bearing adjusting spacer
4. Pinion height adjusting shims
5. Pinion height adjusting washer
6. Lock strap
7. Ring gear retaining bolt
8. Pinion shaft lock pin
9. Side gear thrust washer
10. Side gear
11. Rear cover
12. Ring gear
13. Differential mount
14. Nut
15. Pinion shaft
16. Thrust washer
17. Pinion gear
18. Thrust washer
19. Side gear
20. Side flange bolt
21. Oil seal
22. Side flange
23. Side retainer
24. Bolt
25. O-ring
26. Side bearing
27. Differential gear case
28. Drive pinion rear bearing
29. Drive pinion
30. Pinion bearing preload adjusting spacer and washer
31. Pinion front bearing
32. Front pilot bearing spacer
33. Front pilot bearing
34. Oil seal
35. Drive pinion flange
36. Drive pinion nut

Details of independent rear suspension differential assembly

8. Pack the wheel bearings with grease. Coat the seal lip.

9. Reinstall the wheel bearings. Install the outer bearing on the axle shaft so the side with the seal will be toward the wheel. Always press or drive on the inner bearing race.

10. The spacer may be reused if it is not collapsed or deformed. The distance piece must always carry the same mark, A, B, or C, as the bearing housing.

11. Fill the area illustrated with grease.

12. Replace the axle shaft and flange. Tighten the bearing locknut to the specified torque.

13. The torque required to start the axle shaft turning should be 3.9 in/lbs or less. This is a 28.7 oz or less pull at the hub bolt. Axle shaft end-play, checked with a dial indicator, should be 0-0.006 in.

14. If the turning torque or axle shaft play is incorrect, disassemble the unit and install a new distance piece.

Halfshafts

The axle halfshafts must be removed and disassembled to lubricate the ball splines every 30,000 miles. Handle the shaft carefully; it is easily damaged. No repair parts for the shafts are available. If a shaft is defective in any way, it must be replaced as an assembly.

To disassemble:

1. Remove the U-joint spider from the differential end of the shaft.
2. Remove the snap-ring and sleeve yoke plug.
3. Compress the shaft and remove the snap-ring and stopper.
4. Disconnect the boot and separate the shaft carefully so as not to lose the balls and spacer.
5. Pack about 0.35 oz of grease into the ball grooves. Also pack about 1.23 oz of grease into the area illustrated.
6. Twisting play between the two shaft halves should not exceed 0.004 in. Check play with the shaft completely compressed.
shaft completely compressed.
7. While reassembling, adjust the U-joint side play to 0.001 in. or less by selecting suitable snap-rings. Four different thicknesses are available for adjustment. Axle shaft flange nut torque is 36-43 ft/lbs.

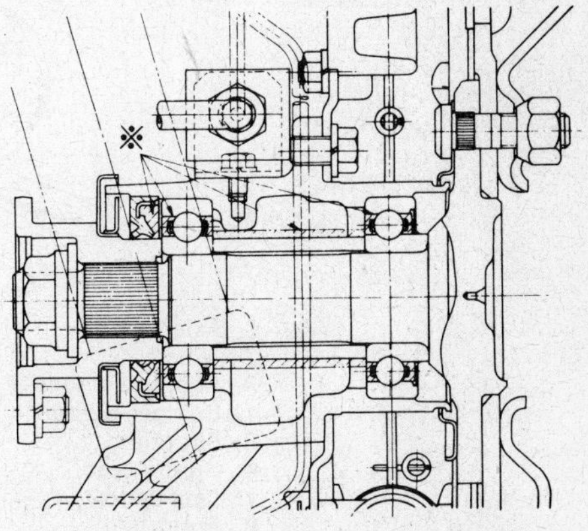

* indicates areas to receive grease

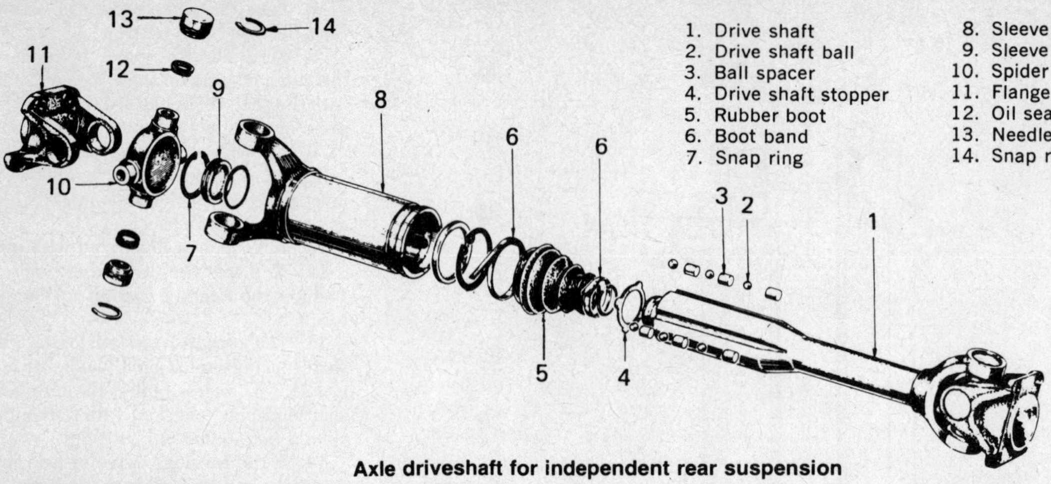

Axle driveshaft for independent rear suspension

REAR SUSPENSION

Leaf Spring Type

B210, 200SX, 710, AND 510, F-10 AND 610 WAGONS

Spring Removal and Installation

1. Raise the rear axle until the wheels hang free. Support the car on stands. Support the rear axle with a jack.
2. Unbolt the bottom end of shock absorber.
3. Unbolt the axle from the spring leaves. Unbolt and remove the front spring bracket. Lower the front of the spring to the floor.
4. Unbolt and remove the spring rear shackle.
5. Before reinstallation, coat the front bracket pin, bushing, shackle pin, and shackle bushing with a soap solution.
6. Reverse the procedure to install. The front pin nut and the shock absorber mounting should be tightened before the vehicle is lowered to the floor.

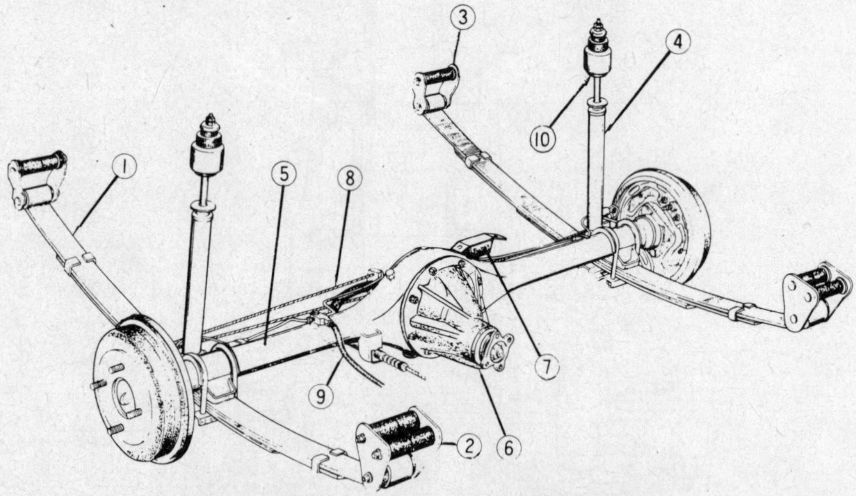

Typical leaf spring rear suspension—B210 shown

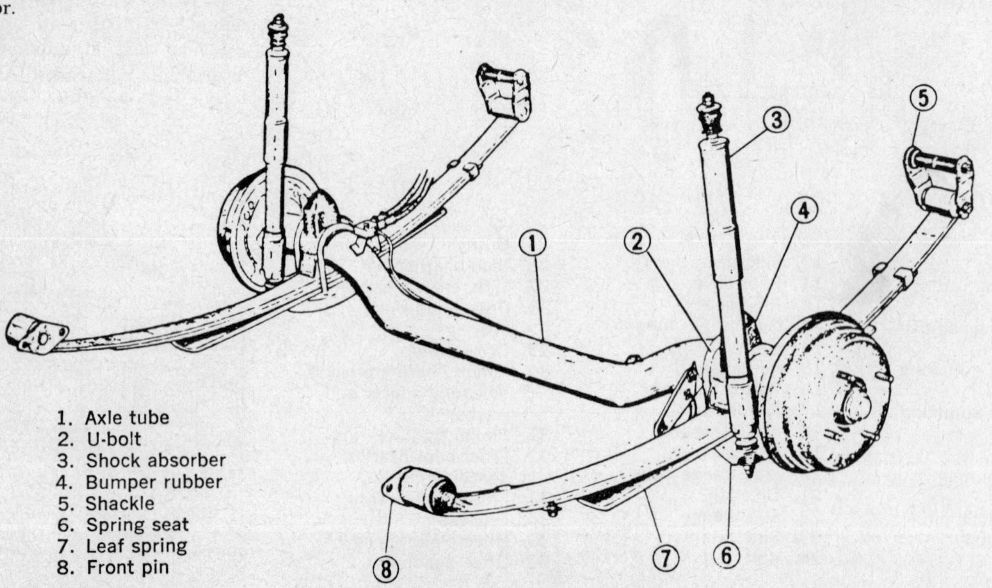

F–10 wagon rear suspension

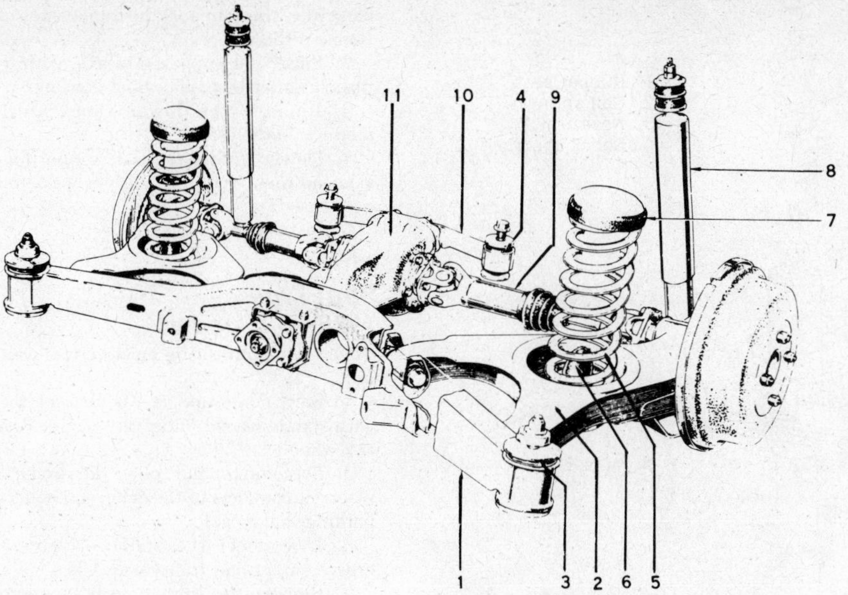

1. Suspension member
2. Suspension arm
3. Member mounting insulator
4. Differential mounting insulator
5. Coil spring
6. Bumper rubber
7. Spring seat
8. Shock absorber
9. Drive shaft
10. Differential mounting member
11. Differential carrier

Sedan independent rear suspension

Shock Absorber Removal and Installation

To remove the rear shock absorbers, simply unbolt the lower and upper ends. The upper nuts are under the rear seat back on the B210 sedans, on the top of the frame on the 200SX attached to the underbody on the 710, 510 and 610, and accessible through the trunk, under cover panels on the F-10. The shock absorbers are not serviceable and should be replaced if defective.

Coil Spring Type

Three types of coil spring suspension are used: Trailing arm independent suspension (F-10 sedan and hatchback, all 610 sedan, 810 sedan, and 280ZX), four bar link solid axle (1978-79 510 sedan, all 210), and MacPherson strut type independent suspension (1975-78 Z).

CAUTION

Coil springs are under considerable tension, and can exert enough force to cause serious injury. Exercise extreme caution when working on them, especially when disassembling strut or shock absorber and spring units (810, Z and ZX).

SPRING REMOVAL AND INSTALLATION

Trailing Arm Type 610, F-10 and 310

1. Jack up and support the rear of the car. Remove the wheels.
2. Disconnect the parking brake cable on the 610.
3. Disconnect the axle halfshaft flange nuts on the wheel side, on 610.
4. Support the arm with a jack and remove the lower shock mount. Carefully lower the jack until spring tension is released, and remove the spring.
5. Installation is the reverse.

810 and 280ZX

The shock absorber and spring must be removed as a unit.

1. block the front wheels. Raise the rear of the car until the suspension hangs free and support the car with stands under the frame members.
2. Remove the upper shock absorber mounting nuts (inside the trunk on the 810, or under covers in the cargo compartment in the ZX).
3. Disconnect the lower end of the shock and remove the assembly.
4. The spring can be removed with the use of a coil spring compressor once the assembly is removed from the car.
5. Installation is the reverse. Install the top end of the unit first.

Four Bar Link 210 and 510

1. Block the front wheels. Raise the rear of the car enough to allow the suspension to

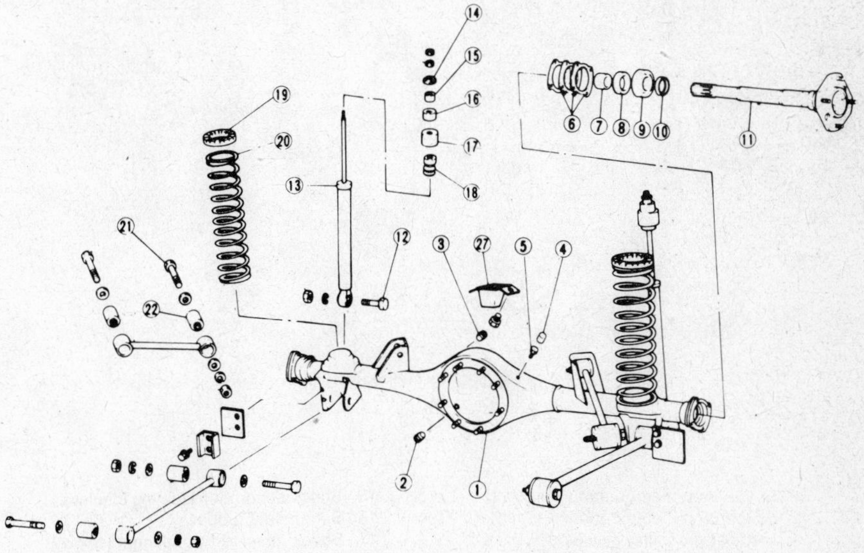

1. Rear axle case
2. Drain plug
3. Filler plug
4. Breather cap
5. Breather
6. Rear axle case end shim
7. Bearing collar
8. Oil seal
9. Rear axle bearing
10. Bearing spacer
11. Rear axle shaft
12. Shock absorber lower end bolt
13. Shock absorber assembly
14. Special washer
15. Shock absorber mounting bushing
16. Shock absorber mounting bushing
17. Bound bumper cover
18. Bound bumper rubber
19. Shock absorber mounting insulator
20. Coil spring
21. Upper link bushing bolt
22. Upper link bushing

Four link rear suspension

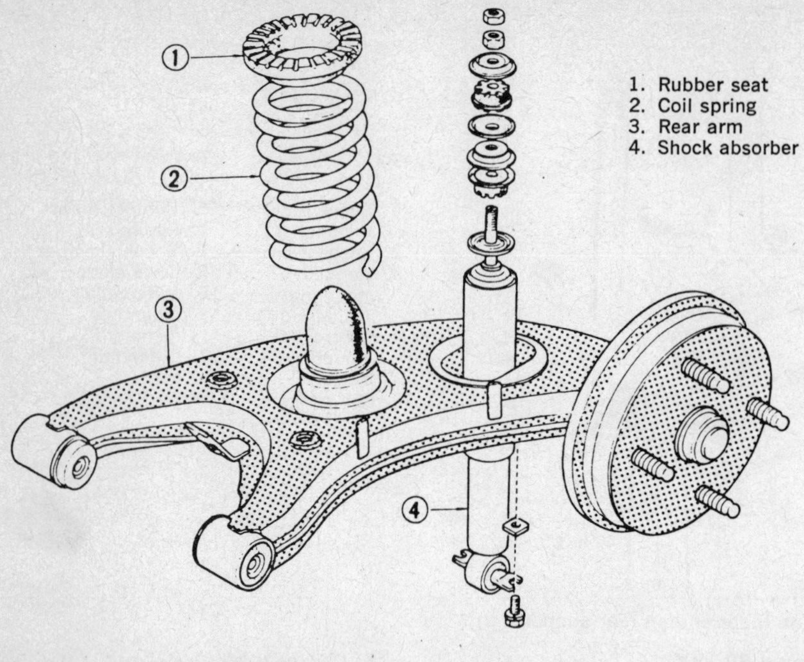

Shock absorber and coil spring—310 and F-10 sedan and hatchback

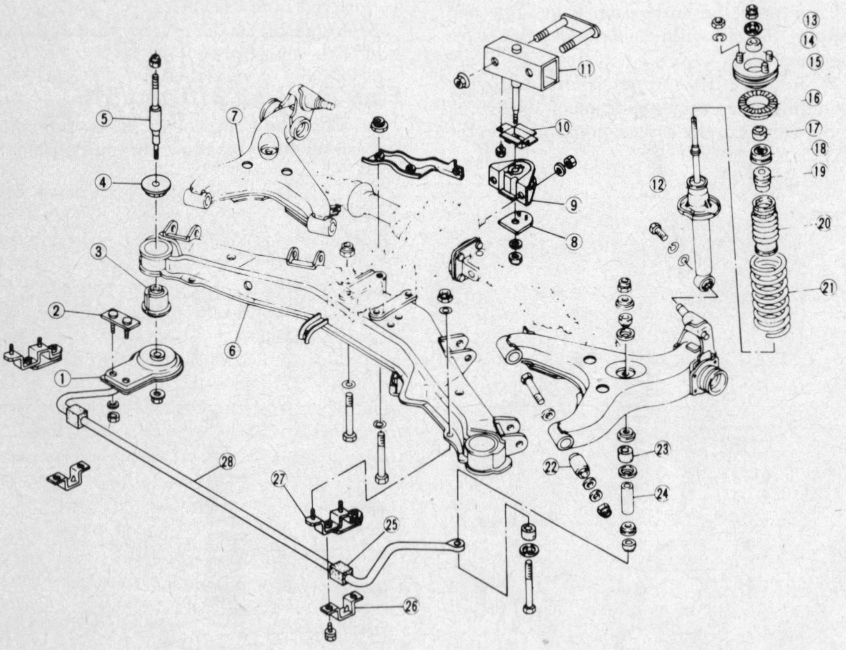

1. Suspension member mounting stay
2. Suspension member mounting bolt
3. Member mounting insulator
4. Member mounting upper stopper
5. Suspension mounting bolt
6. Suspension member assembly
7. Suspension arm assembly
8. Differential mounting plate
9. Differential mounting insulator
10. Differential mounting adapter plate
11. Differential mounting bracket
12. Shock absorber assembly
13. Special washer
14. Shock absorber mounting bushing A
15. Shock absorber mounting insulator
16. Spring seat rubber
17. Shock absorber mounting bushing B
18. Bound bumper cover
19. Bound bumper
20. Dust cover
21. Coil spring
22. Suspension arm bushing
23. Stabilizer bushing
24. Stabilizer collar
25. Stabilizer mounting bushing
26. Stabilizer mounting clip
27. Stabilizer mounting bracket
28. Rear stabilizer

280 ZX and 810 sedan independent rear suspension

hang free, then support the frame with stands. Remove the wheels.

2. Raise and support the axle with a jack placed under the differential housing.
3. Remove the lower shock absorber mounts (both sides).
4. Slowly lower the jack supporting the axle and remove the springs when the tension is released.
5. Installation is the reverse.

Strut Type 1975-78 Z Models

The strut and spring must be removed as a unit.

1. Raise and support the rear of the car with stands placed under the frame. Remove the wheels.
2. Disconnect and plug the brake hose where it connects to the tube; disconnect the parking brake cable.
3. Disconnect the stabilizer bar at the crossmember and transverse link.
4. Remove the transverse link outer spindle nuts and spindle bolt. Pull the spindle out and separate the transverse link and strut.
5. Disconnect the outer end of the halfshaft.
6. Place a jack under the lower end of the strut. Remove the upper mounting nuts of the strut inside the cargo compartment. Carefully and slowly lower the jack until all spring tension is released, and remove the strut.
7. The strut can be removed from the spring with a coil spring compressor of the proper type.
8. Installation is the reverse. The spindle is installed with the shorter length (measured from the locking bolt notch) toward the front. Be certain to bleed the brakes after installation.

SHOCK ABSORBER REMOVAL AND INSTALLATION

Trailing Arm and Four Bar Link Type All 510, 610, 210

1. Open the trunk and remove the upper shock absorber mounting nuts.
2. Remove the lower mounting nuts on the suspension arm or axle.
3. Remove the shock. Installation is the reverse.

F-10 and 310 Sedan and Hatchback

1. Raise and support the rear of the car.
2. Remove the wheels.
3. Support the rear arm with a jack at the lower end.
4. Remove the upper and lower shcok mounting nuts.
5. Slowly and carefully lower the jack and remove the shock.
6. Installation is the reverse.

810 and 280ZX

See the coil spring removal procedure.

Strut Type

See the coil spring removal procedure.

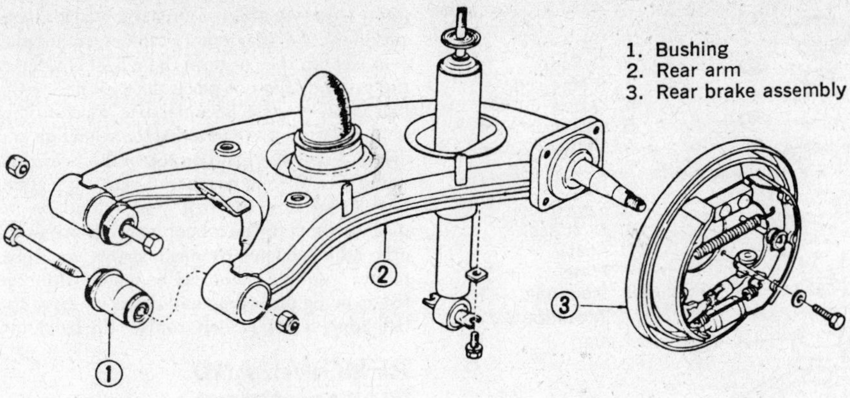

1. Bushing
2. Rear arm
3. Rear brake assembly

Rear arm—F-10 sedan and hatchback

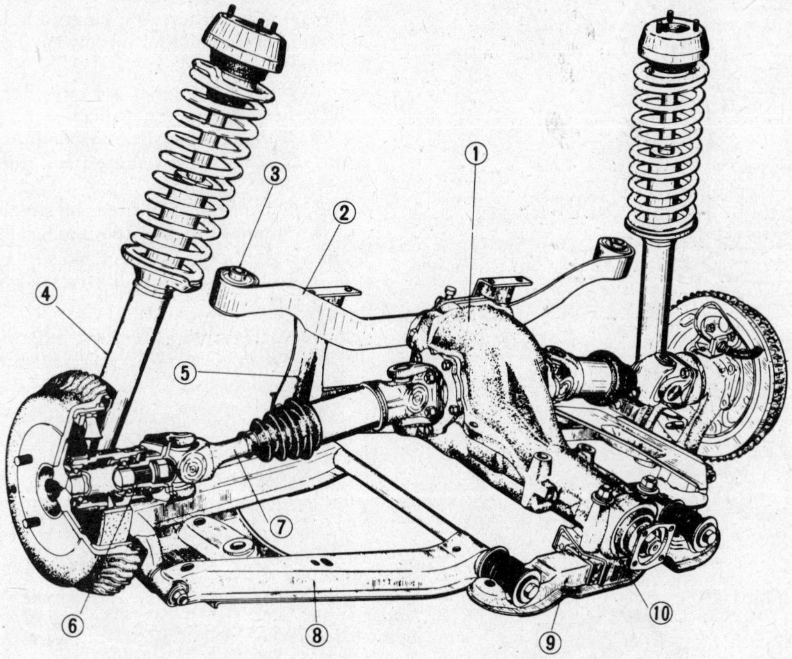

1. Differential carrier
2. Differential case mount rear member
3. Differential case mount rear insulator
4. Strut assembly
5. Link mount brace
6. Rear axle shaft
7. Drive shaft
8. Transverse link
9. Differential case mount front member
10. Differential case mount front insulator

Z car independent rear suspension

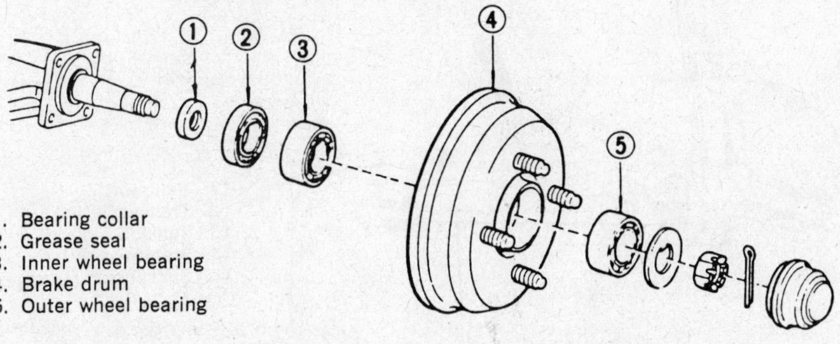

1. Bearing collar
2. Grease seal
3. Inner wheel bearing
4. Brake drum
5. Outer wheel bearing

F-10 rear brake drum and bearing assembly

Rear Wheel Bearings

ADJUSTMENT

F-10 and 310

The rear wheel bearings on the F-10 and 310 are adjusted in the same manner as front wheel bearings. Use this procedure for all F-10 and 310 models.

1. Raise and support the rear of the car.
2. Remove the wheel.
3. Remove and discard the cotter pin.
4. Tighten the wheel bearing lock nut to 18-22 ft/lbs(F-10) 29-33 ft/lbs (310).
5. Rotate the drum back and forth a few revolutions to snug down the bearing.
6. On the F-10, loosen the locknut, then tighten handtight.
7. On the 310, after turning the wheel, recheck the torque of the nut then loosen it 90° from its position.
8. Check the drum rotation. If it does not move freely, check for dragging brake shoes, or dirty bearings.
9. Align the cotter pin hole in the spindle with that in the locknut, and install a new cotter pin.
10. Turn the nut slightly clockwise on the F-10 to align the holes. On the 310, tighten the nut no more than 15° to align the holes.

FRONT SUSPENSION

This independent front suspension uses MacPherson struts. Each strut combines the function of coil spring and shock absorber. The spindle is mounted to the lower part of the strut which has a single ball joint. No upper suspension arm is required in this design. The spindle and lower suspension transverse link (control arm) are located fore and aft by the tension rods to the front part of the chassis on most models. Compression rods, which run rearward, are used on the 280Z. A cross-chassis sway bar is used on all models.

Strut

REMOVAL AND INSTALLATION

All Models

1. Jack up the car and support it safely. Remove the wheel.
2. Disconnect and plug the brake hose.
3. Disconnect the tension rod (compression rod on the "Z" series) and stabilizer bar from the transverse link.
4. Unbolt the steering arm.
5. Place a jack under the bottom of the strut.
6. Open the hood and remove the nuts holding the top of the strut.
7. Lower the jack slowly and cautiously until the strut assembly can be removed.
8. Reverse the procedure to install. The self locking nuts holding the top of the strut must be replaced.

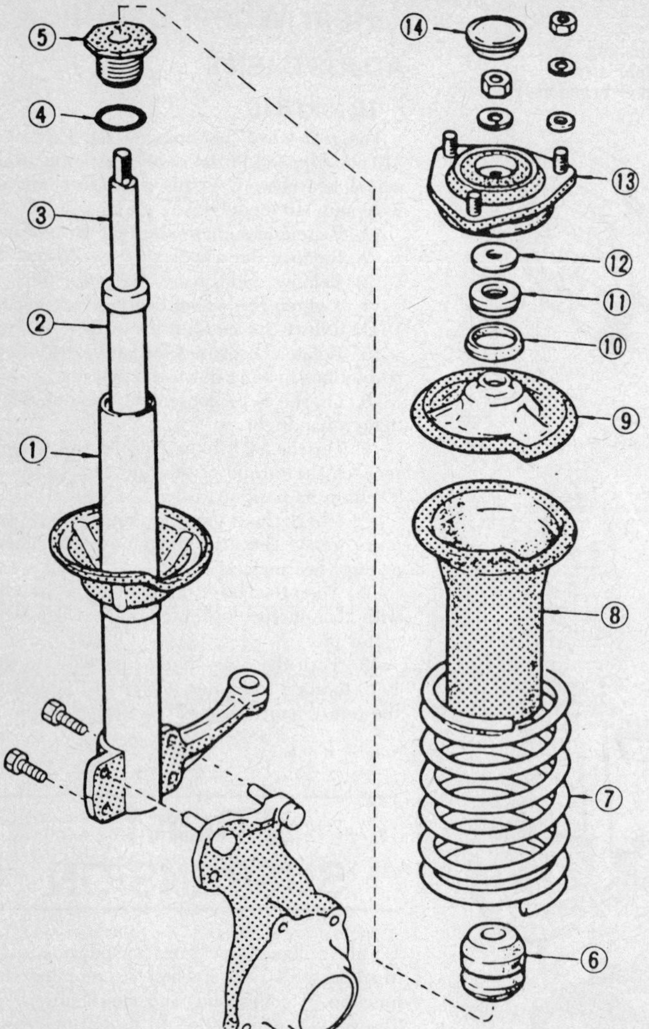

1. Strut
2. Cylinder
3. Piston rod
4. O-ring
5. Gland packing
6. Bumper rubber
7. Coil spring
8. Dust cover
9. Spring seat
10. Dust seal
11. Seat
12. Plate
13. Mounting insulator
14. Cap

Suspension strut—F-10 and 310

Coil Spring

REMOVAL AND INSTALLATION

All Models

CAUTION

Coil springs are under considerable tension, and can exert enough force to cause serious injury. Disassemble struts only if proper tools are available, and use extreme caution.

Coil springs on all models may be removed from the strut with the aid of a coil spring compressor. The strut must be removed prior to spring removal.

Ball Joint

INSPECTION

The lower ball joint should be replaced when play becomes excessive. Datsun does not publish specifications for this, giving instead a rotational torque figure for the ball joint. However, this requires removal for measurement. An effective way to determine play is to jack up the car until the wheel is clear of the ground. Do not place the jack under the ball joint; it must be unloaded. Place a long bar under the tire and move the wheel up and down. Keep one hand on top of the tire while doing this. If ¼ in. or more of play exists at the top of the tire, the ball joint should be replaced. Be sure the wheel bearings are properly adjusted before making this measurement. A double check can be made: while the tire is being moved up and down, observe the ball joint. If play is seen, replace the ball joint.

REMOVAL AND INSTALLATION

All Models Except F-10

The ball joint should be greased every 30,000 miles. There is a plugged hole in the bottom of the joint for installation of a grease fitting.

1. Raise and support the car so the wheels hang free. Remove the wheel.
2. Unbolt the tension rod (compression rod on "Z" series) and stabilizer bar from transverse link.
3. Unbolt the strut from the steering arm.
4. Remove the cotter pin and ball joint stud nut. Separate the ball joint and steering arm.
5. Unbolt the ball joint from the transverse link.
6. Reverse the procedure to install a new ball joint. Grease the joint after installation.

F-10

1. Raise the car and support with safety stands. Remove the wheel and tire.

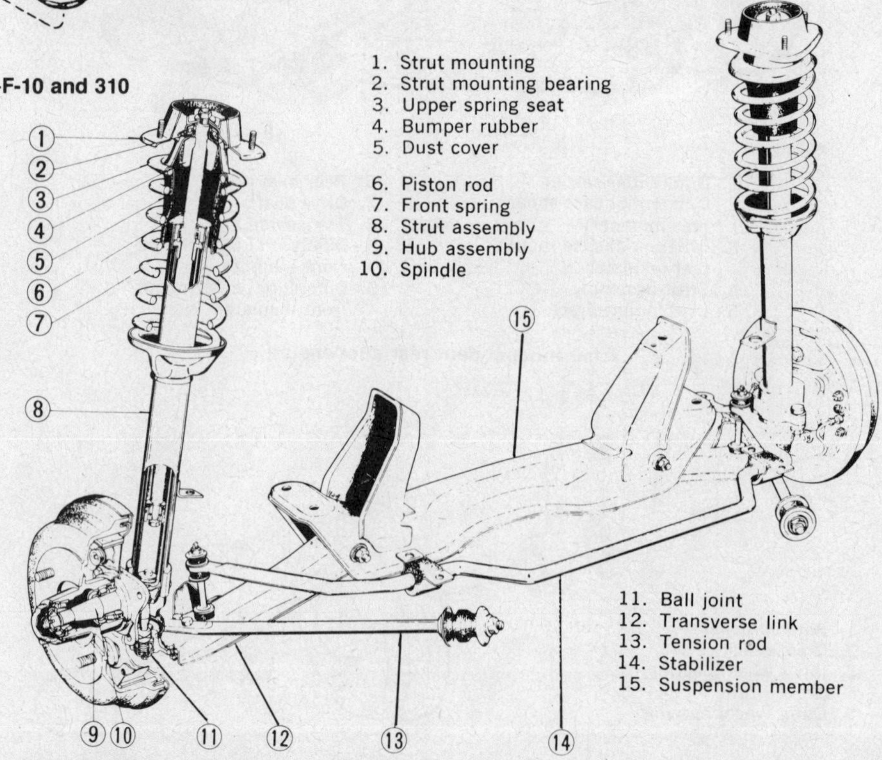

1. Strut mounting
2. Strut mounting bearing
3. Upper spring seat
4. Bumper rubber
5. Dust cover
6. Piston rod
7. Front spring
8. Strut assembly
9. Hub assembly
10. Spindle
11. Ball joint
12. Transverse link
13. Tension rod
14. Stabilizer
15. Suspension member

B210 strut-type front suspension. On the 280Z, the tension rods are replaced by compression rods running to the rear

2. Remove the nut holding the ball stud to the knuckle and force out the stud with a ball joint fork, being careful not to damage the ball joint dust cover.

3. Remove the ball joint bolts and ball joint.

310

1. Jack up the car and support it on stands.
2. Remove the wheel.
3. Remove the driveshaft.
4. Separate the ball joint from the steering knuckle with a ball joint remover, being careful not to damage the ball joint dust cover if the ball joint is to be used again.
5. Remove the other ball joint from the transverse link and remove the ball joint.

Installation is the reverse of removal. Tighten the ball stud attaching nut (from ball joint to steering knuckle) to 22-29 ft/lbs, and the ball joint to transverse link bolts to 40-47 ft/lbs.

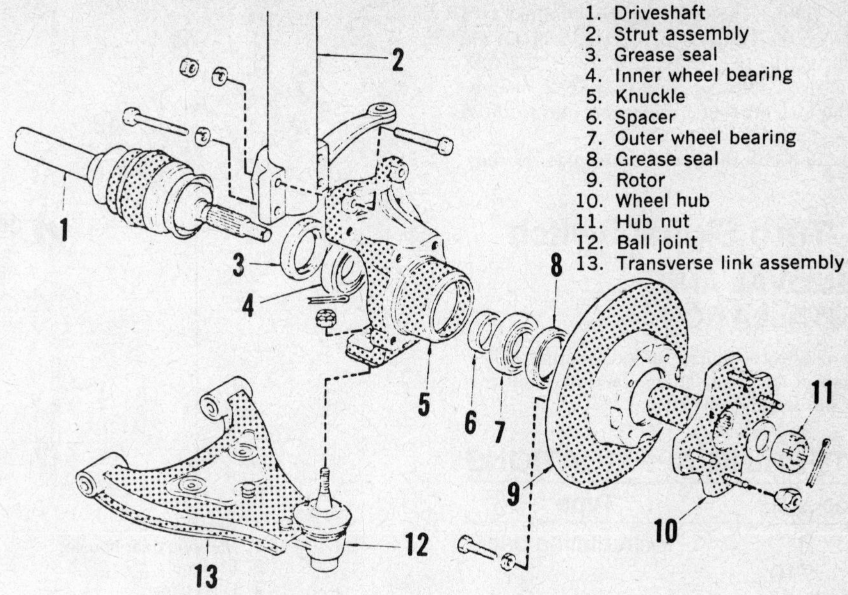

Wheel hub and knuckle—F-10 and 310

Lower Control Arm (Transverse Link) and Ball Joint

REMOVAL AND INSTALLATION

You'll need a ball joint remover for this operation.

1. Jack up the vehicle and support it with jackstands; remove the wheel.
2. Remove the splash board, if so equipped.
3. Remove the cotter pin and castle nut from the side rod (steering arm) ball joint and separate the ball joint from the side rod. You'll need either a fork type or puller type ball joint remover.
4. Separate the steering knuckle arm from the MacPherson strut.
5. Remove the tension rod and stabilizer bar from the lower arm. The F-10 and 310 do not have tension rods. On Z models through 1978, remove the compression rod.
6. Remove the nuts or bolts connecting the lower control arm (transverse link) to the suspension crossmember on all models.
7. On the 810, to remove the transverse link (control arm) on the steering gear side, separate the gear arm from the sector shaft and lower steering linkage; to remove the transverse link on the idler arm side, detach the idler arm assembly from the body frame and lower steering linkage.
8. Remove the lower control arm (transverse link) with the suspension ball joint and knuckle arm still attached.

Installation is the reverse of removal with the following notes.

9. When installing the control arm, temporarily tighten the nuts and/or bolts securing the control arm to the suspension crossmember. Tighten them fully only after the car is sitting on its wheels.
10. Lubricate the ball joints after assembly.

Wheel Alignment

Caster and camber angles cannot be adjusted except by replacing worn or bent parts. Suspension height is adjusted by replacing the front springs. Various springs are available for adjustment. Toe-in is adjusted by changing the length of the steering side-rods. The length of these rods should always be equal. Steering angles are adjusted by means of a stop bolt on each steering arm.

Wheel Bearing Adjustment

All Models Except F-10

1. Raise and support the front of the car or truck.
2. Remove the wheel and tire, hub cap, and cotter pin. Discard the cotter pin. Remove the adjusting cap over the wheel bearing nut.
3. Remove the brake pads on disc brake models. Check to make sure the shoes are not dragging on models with drum brakes.
4. Loosen the wheel bearing nut, then retighten to 18-22 ft/lbs on all models except the 1978-79 510 and 1979 210, which should be tightened to 22-25 ft/lbs.
5. Rotate the hub a few times in both directions to seat the bearings. Retighten the nut to the torque given in Step 4.
6. Loosen the nut 60° on all models except the 1978-79 510 and 1979 210; back off the nut 90° on those models.
7. Install the adjusting cap and a new cotter pin. It is permissible to loosen the nut 15° to allow the holes to align, on all models except the 1978-79 510 and 1979 210. On those models only, tighten the nut up to 15°.
8. Temporarily install the wheel and tire, and spin the wheel. There should be no roughness or binding, and there should be negligible axial play. If excessive play exists, readjust the bearings. If roughness is present, clean and repack, or replace, the bearings.
9. Remove the wheel and tire and install the brake pads (disc brakes). If the brake shoes were backed off (drum brakes), readjust. Install the wheel and tire and lower the vehicle.

STEERING

Steering Wheel

REMOVAL AND INSTALLATION

1. Position the wheels in the straight-ahead direction. The steering wheel should be right-side up and level.
2. Disconnect the battery ground cable.
3. Look at the back of your steering wheel. If there are countersunk screws in the back of the spokes, remove the screws and pull off the horn pad. Some models have a horn wire running from the pad to the steering wheel. Disconnect it.

There are three other types of horn buttons or rings on Datsuns. The first simply pulls off. The second, which is usually a large, semi-triangular pad, must be pushed up, then pulled off. The third must be pushed in and turned clockwise.

4. Remove the rest of the horn switching mechanism, noting the relative location of the parts. Remove the mechanism only if it hinders subsequent wheel removal procedures.
5. Match-mark the top of the steering column shaft and the steering wheel flange.
6. Remove the attaching nut and remove the steering wheel with a puller.

CAUTION

Do not strike the shaft with a hammer, which may cause the column to collapse.

7. Install the steering wheel in the reverse order of removal, aligning the punch marks. Do not drive or hammer the wheel into place, or you may cause the collapsible steering column to collapse; in which case you'll have to buy a whole new steering column unit.

8. Tighten the steering wheel nut to 14-18 ft/lbs on the 1976-77 F-10, 22-25 ft/lbs on the 1200, B210, 1978 F-10, 310, 1977-79 200SX and 36-51 ft/lbs on the 1975-76 Z models. Tighten all other steering wheel nuts to 28-36 ft/lbs.

9. Reinstall the horn button, pad, or ring.

Turn Signal Switch

REMOVAL AND INSTALLATION

Follow procedures under Steering Wheel Removal and Installation. Remove shell covers and remove switch.

STEERING APPLICATIONS

Model	Type
510, 610, 521, 710, B210, 210, 200SX, 810, 280ZX ①	Recirculating ball
280Z F-10 280ZX ② 310	Rack and pinion

① Power steering
② Manual steering

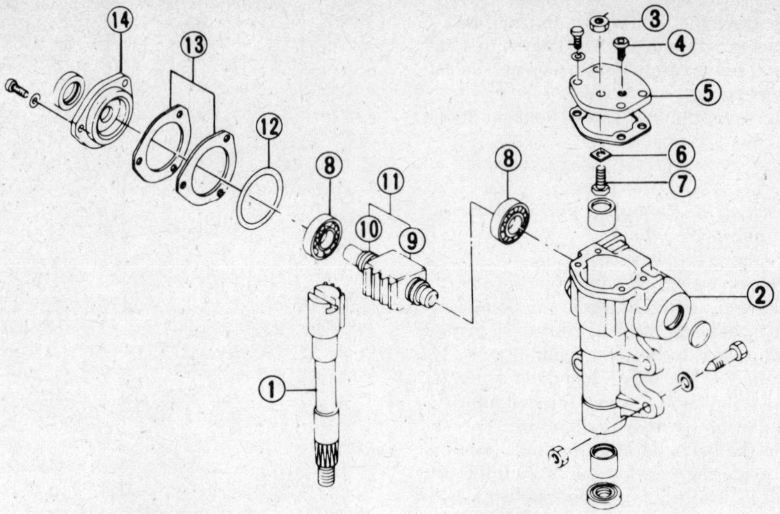

1. Sector shaft
2. Steering gear housing
3. Lock nut
4. Filler plug
5. Sector shaft cover
6. Sector shaft adjusting shim
7. Sector shaft adjusting screw
8. Worm bearing
9. Ball nut
10. Worm shaft
11. Steering worm assembly
12. "O" ring
13. Worm bearing shim
14. Rear cover

Recirculating ball steering gear

Steering Gear

ADJUSTMENT

Worm and Roller Adjustment

The backlash adjusting screw is located next to the filler plug on the steering gear box cover.

1. Disconnect the drag link from the steering arm.
2. Loosen the locknut and turn the adjusting screw in clockwise until the mechanism binds.
3. Back off the screw until the unit operates smoothly. Tighten the locknut.
4. Check free-play at the end of the steer-

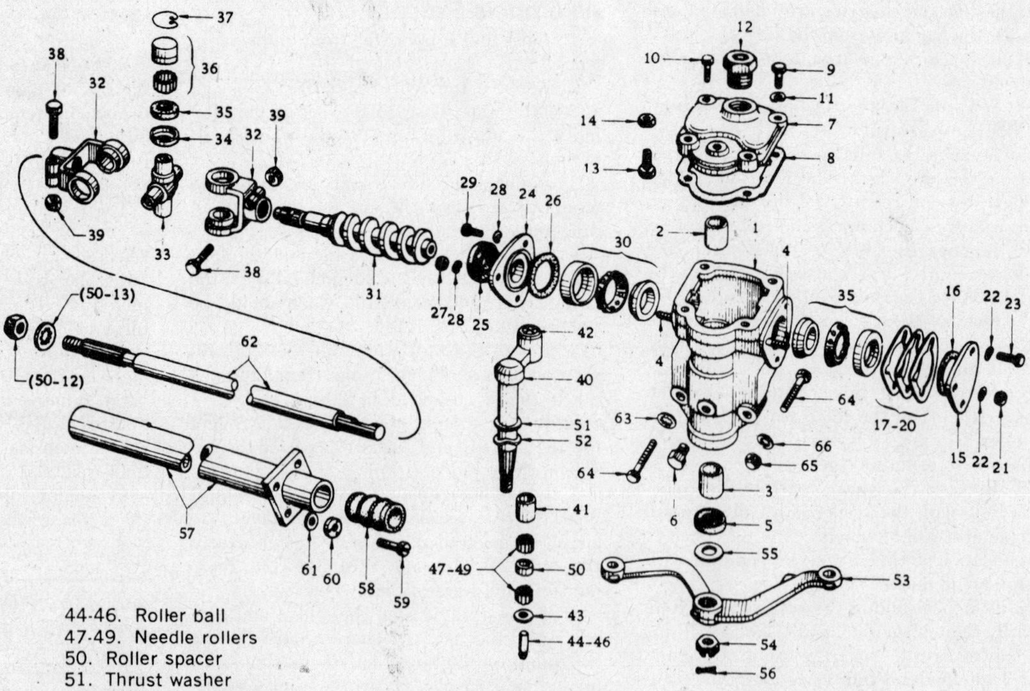

1. Steering gear housing
2. Bushing
3. Bushing
4. Stud
5. Oil seal
6. Drain plug
7. Cover
8. Gasket
9. Bolt
10. Bolt
11. Lockwasher
12. Filler plug
13. Adjusting screw
14. Locknut
15. Cover
16. O-ring
17-20. Shims
21. Nut
22. Lockwasher
23. Bolt
24. Rear cover
25. Oil seal
26. O-ring
27. Nut
38. Lockwasher
29. Bolt
30. Bearing
31. Worm gear
32. U-joint yoke
33. U-joint spider
34. Oil seal retainer
35. Oil seal
36. Bearing
37. Snap-ring
38. Bolt
39. Nut
40. Rocker shaft (lever)
41. Needle roller race
42. Roller ball pug
43. Needle roller cover
44-46. Roller ball
47-49. Needle rollers
50. Roller spacer
51. Thrust washer
52. Shaft adjusting thrust washer
53. Steering arm
54. Nut
55. Washer
56. Cotter pin
57. Steering column
58. Column bushing
59. Bolt
60. Lockwasher
61. Washer
62. Steering shaft
63. Lockwasher
64. Mounting bolt
65. Nut
66. Lockwasher

Cam and lever steering gear

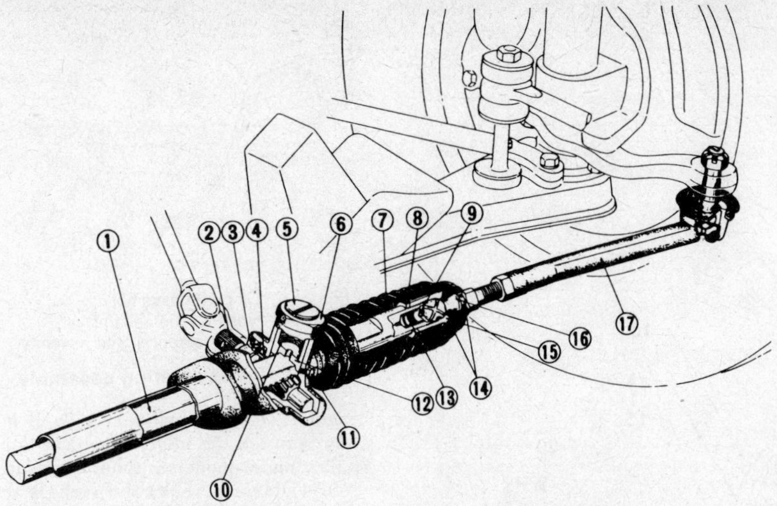

1. Rack
2. Pinion
3. Oil seal
4. Pinion bearing
5. Retainer adjusting screw
6. Locknut
7. Boot
8. Locknut
9. Side rod spring seat
10. Retainer spring
11. Filler plug
12. Retainer
13. Side rod inner spring
14. Dust cover clamp
15. Side rod inner socket
16. Ball stud
17. Side rod

Rack and pinion steering gear, left side shown

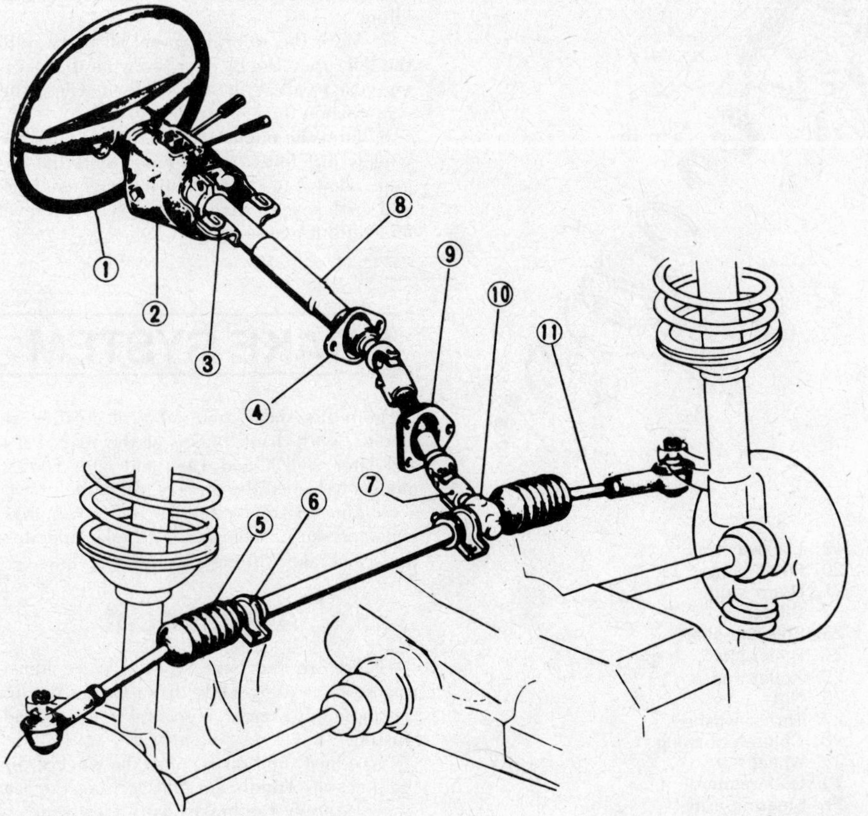

1. Steering wheel assembly
2. Steering column cover
3. Upper clamp
4. Lower clamp
5. Steering gear boot
6. Steering clip
7. Column lower joint assembly
8. Steering column assembly
9. Column hole cover assembly
10. Steering gear assembly
11. Side rod assembly

Typical rack and pinion steering gear

ing arm, with the steering gear in the central (straight ahead) position. Free-play should be 0-0.008 in.

5. Check the force required to turn the steering wheel with a spring scale attached to the wheel rim. It should be 1.1-1.5 lbs.

6. Replace the drag link.

7. Maximum permissible play at the steering wheel rim is 1-1.4 in.

Cam and Lever Adjustment

The adjusting screw is adjacent to the filler plug on the steering gear box cover.

1. Disconnect the steering linkage ball stud from the steering arm.
2. Loosen the locknut and tighten the adjusting screw until there is no steering arm free-play in the straight ahead position.
3. Tighten the locknut. Replace the steering linkage.
4. Maximum permissible play at the steering wheel rim is 0.98-1.38 in.

Recirculating Ball Adjustment

The adjusting screw is adjacent to the filler plug on the steering gear box cover.

1. Disconnect the steering gear arm from the steering linkage.
2. Adjust the backlash at the steering center point so that play at the end of the steering gear arm is 0-0.004 in.
3. Tighten the adjusting screw $^1/_8$-$^1/_6$ turn more and tighten the locknut.
4. Reconnect the steering linkage. Specified linkage stud nut torque is 40-55 ft/lbs for the 510, B210, 610 and 40-72 for the 610 1975 and later, 710.
5. Maximum free-play at steering wheel rim should be 0.98-1.18 in for the 510, and 1-1.4 in. for all other models.

Steering Lock

The steering lock/ignition switch/warning buzzer switch assembly is attached to the steering column by special screws whose heads shear off on installation. The screws must be drilled out to remove the assembly. The ignition switch is on the back of the assembly, and the warning switch on the side. The warning buzzer, which sounds when the driver's door is opened with the steering unlocked, is located behind the instrument panel.

Power Steering Pump

REMOVAL AND INSTALLATION

1. Disconnect and plug the hoses at the pump.
2. Disconnect the pump mounting bolts and remove the drive belt.
3. Remove the pump. Installation is the reverse. Adjust the belt tension after installation, and fill and bleed the system.

BELT TENSION ADJUSTMENT

1. Loosen the tension adjustment and mounting bolts.
2. Move the pump toward or away from the

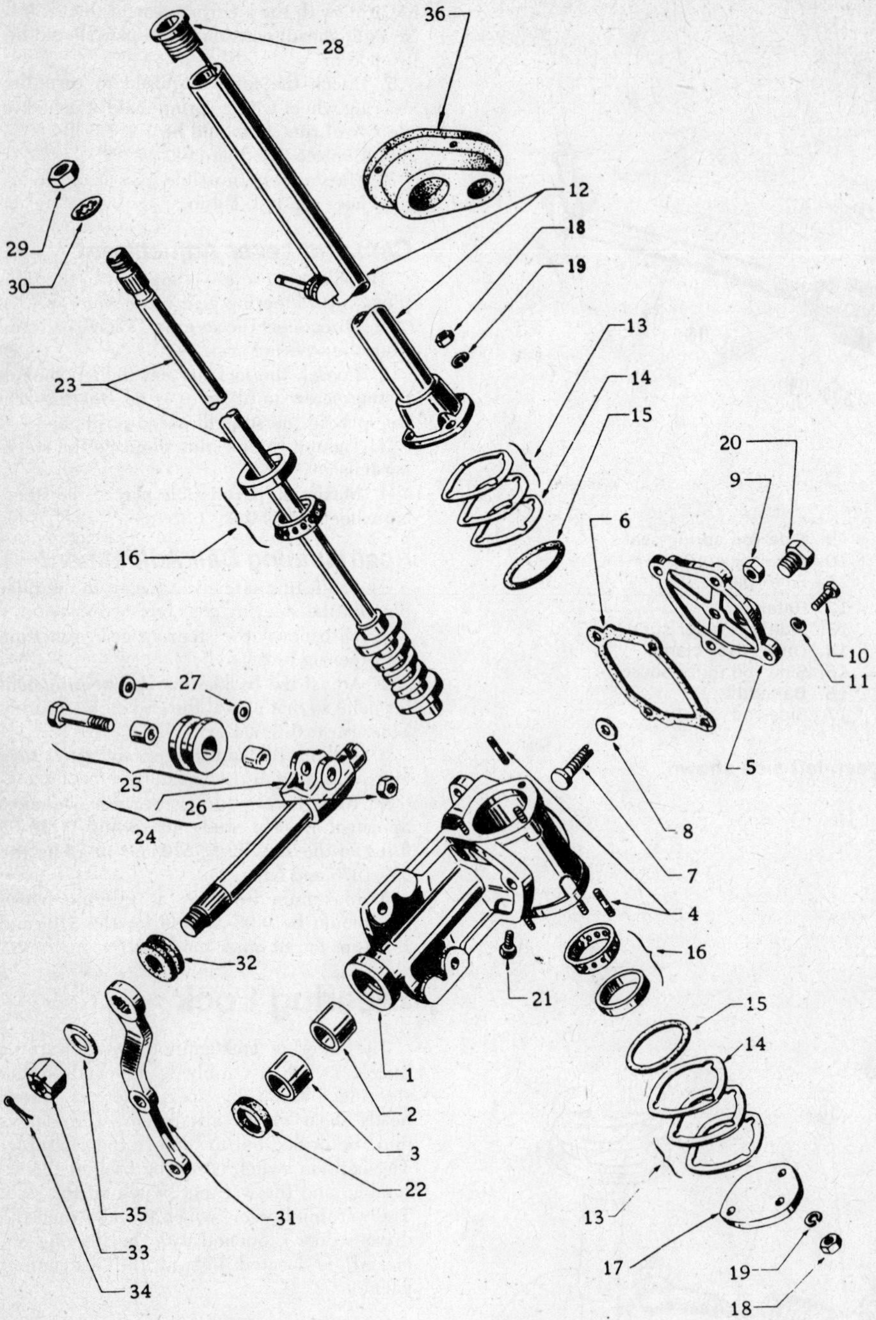

1. Steering gear housing
2. Upper bushing
3. Lower bushing
4. Stud
5. Cover
6. Gasket
7. Adjusting screw
8. Adjusting shim
9. Locknut
10. Bolt
11. Lockwasher
12. Steering column
13. Worm bearing shim
14. Shims
15. O-ring
16. Worm bearing
17. Cover
18. Nut
19. Lockwasher
20. Filter plug
21. Drain plug
22. Oil seal
23. Steering shaft
24. Roller shaft
25. Roller and pin
26. Nut
27. Thrust washers
28. Column bushing
29. Wheel nut
30. Lockwasher
31. Steering arm
32. Dust seal
33. Nut
34. Cotter pin
35. Washer
36. Rubber grommet

Worm and roller steering gear

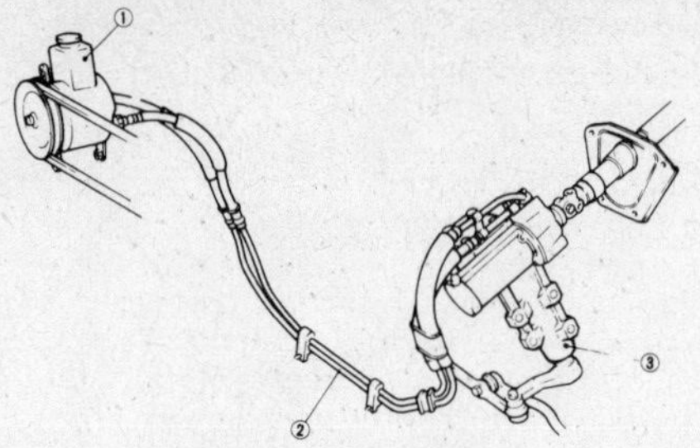

1. Oil pump assembly
2. Hose & tube assembly
3. Power steering gear assembly

Power steering assembly

engine so that the belt deflects ¼-½ in. midway between the idler pulley and the pump pulley under moderate thumb pressure.

3. Tighten the bolts and recheck the tension adjustment.

SYSTEM BLEEDING

1. Fill the pump reservoir and allow to remain undisturbed for a few minutes.
2. Raise the car until the front wheels are clear of the ground.
3. With the engine off, quickly turn the wheels right and left several times, lightly contacting the stops.
4. Add fluid if necessary.
5. Start the engine and let it idle.
6. Repeat Steps 3 and 4 with the engine idling.
7. With the steering wheel all the way to the left, open the bleeder screw on the steering gear to allow the air to bleed. Close the screw when fluid is expelled.
8. Stop the engine, lower the car until the wheels just touch the ground. Start the engine, allow it to idle, and turn the wheels back and forth several times. Check the fluid level and refill if necessary.

BRAKE SYSTEM

Front disc brakes are used on all current car models, with drum brakes at the rear. 1979 and later 280ZX and 1980 and later 200SX models have rear disc brakes. All models have a vacuum booster system to lessen required pedal pressure. The parking brake operates the rear brakes through a cable system.

Adjustment

There are four basic types of brake adjusting systems used. Only drum brakes require periodic adjustment; disc brakes are self-adjusting.

To adjust the brakes, raise the wheels, disconnect the handbrake linkage from the rear wheels, apply the brakes hard a few times to center the drums, and proceed as follows:

BOLT ADJUSTER

Turn the adjuster bolt on the backing plate until the wheel can no longer be turned, then back off until the wheel is free of drag. Repeat the procedure on the other adjuster bolt on the same wheel. Some models may have only one adjuster bolt per wheel.

BOLT ADJUSTER WITH CLICK ARRANGEMENT

The adjuster is located on the backing plate. The adjustment proceeds in clicks or notches. The wheel will often be locked temporarily as the adjuster passes over center for each click. Thus the adjuster is alternately hard and easy to turn. When the wheel is fully locked, back off 1-3 clicks.

STAR WHEEL ADJUSTER

Remove the rubber boot from the backing plate. Insert a screwdriver through the adjusting hole to engage the toothed wheel. Turn the adjuster teeth down until the wheel is locked, then push them up about 12 notches so that the wheel is free of drag.

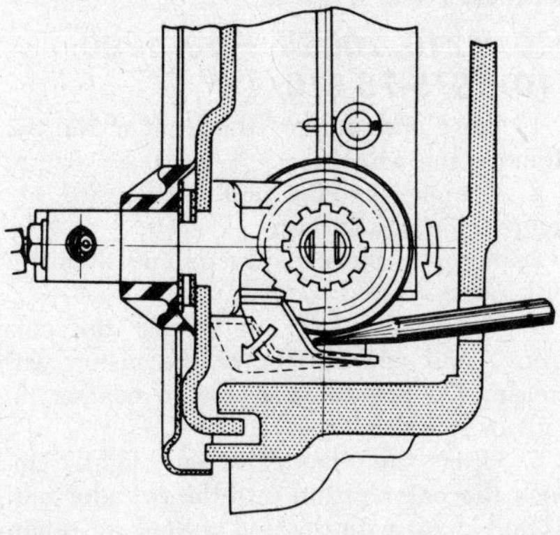

Loosening the "Z" series rear brake adjuster

SELF-ADJUSTING

No manual adjustment is required. The self-adjusters operate whenever the hand or foot brakes are used.

After Adjustment

After adjusting the brakes, reconnect the handbrake linkage. Make sure that there is no rear wheel drag with the handbrake released. Loosen the handbrake adjustment if necessary.

Master Cylinder

REMOVAL AND INSTALLATION

Clean the outside of the cylinder thoroughly, particularly around the cap and fluid lines. On ZX models, remove the heatshield plate. Disconnect the fluid lines and cap them to exclude dirt. On models with a fluid level gauge, disconnect the electrical connector. Remove the clevis pin connecting the pushrod to the brake pedal arm inside the vehicle. This pin need not be removed on models with the vacuum booster. Unbolt the master cylinder from the firewall and remove. If the pushrod is not adjustable, there will be shims between the cylinder and the firewall. These shims, or the adjustable pushrod, are used to adjust brake pedal free-play. After installation, bleed the system and check the pedal free-play. The 1980 and later 200SX's pushrod is not adjustable, as the rod between the brake booster and the master cylinder is secured by adhesion. After installation, bleed the system and check the pedal free-play.

NOTE: Ordinary brake fluid will boil and cause brake failure under the high temperatures developed in disc brake systems. Special fluid meeting DOT 3 or 4 specifications for disc brake systems must be used.

PEDAL ADJUSTMENT

Before adjusting the pedal, make sure that the wheelbrakes are correctly adjusted.

Adjust the pedal free-play by means of an adjustable pushrod or shims between the master cylinder and the firewall. Adjust the pedal height by means of the pedal arm stop pad. Free-play should be approximately 0.04-0.20 in. on all models. Pedal height (floorboard to pedal pad) should be approximately 6 in. on all B210s, 1978-80 510s and 1980 and later 200SX and 210 models; 7 in. on all 200SX, 610, 710, 810 and F-10 models; and 8 in. on all Z models.

OVERHAUL

The master cylinder can be disassembled using the illustrations as a guide. Clean all parts in clean brake fluid. Replace the cylinder or piston as necessary if clearance between the two exceeds 0.006 in. Lubricate all parts with clean brake fluid on assembly. Master cylinder rebuilding kits, containing all the wearing parts, are available to simplify overhaul. Master cylinders are supplied to Datsun by two manufacturers: Nabco and Tokico. Parts between these manufacturers are not interchangeable. Be sure you obtain the correct rebuilding parts for your master cylinder.

Bleeding

Bleeding is required whenever air in the hydraulic fluid causes a spongy feeling pedal and sluggish response. This is almost always the case after some part of the hydraulic system has been repaired or replaced.

1. Fill the master cylinder reservoir with the proper fluid. Special fluid is required for disc brakes.
2. The usual procedure is to bleed at the points furthest from the master cylinder first.
3. Fit a rubber hose over the bleeder screw. Submerge the other end of the hose in clean brake fluid in a clear glass container. Loosen the bleeder screw.
4. Slowly pump the brake pedal several times until fluid free of bubbles is discharged. An assistant is required to pump the pedal.
5. On the last pumping stroke, hold the pedal down and tighten the bleeder screw. Check the fluid level periodically during the bleeding operation.
6. Bleed the front brakes in the same way as the rear brakes. Note that some front drum brakes have two hydraulic cylinders and two bleeder screws. Both cylinders must be bled.
7. Check the fluid level in the master cylinder periodically during the bleeding procedure, and refill as necessary. Do not allow it to run dry.
8. Check that the brake pedal is now firm. If not, repeat the bleeding operation.

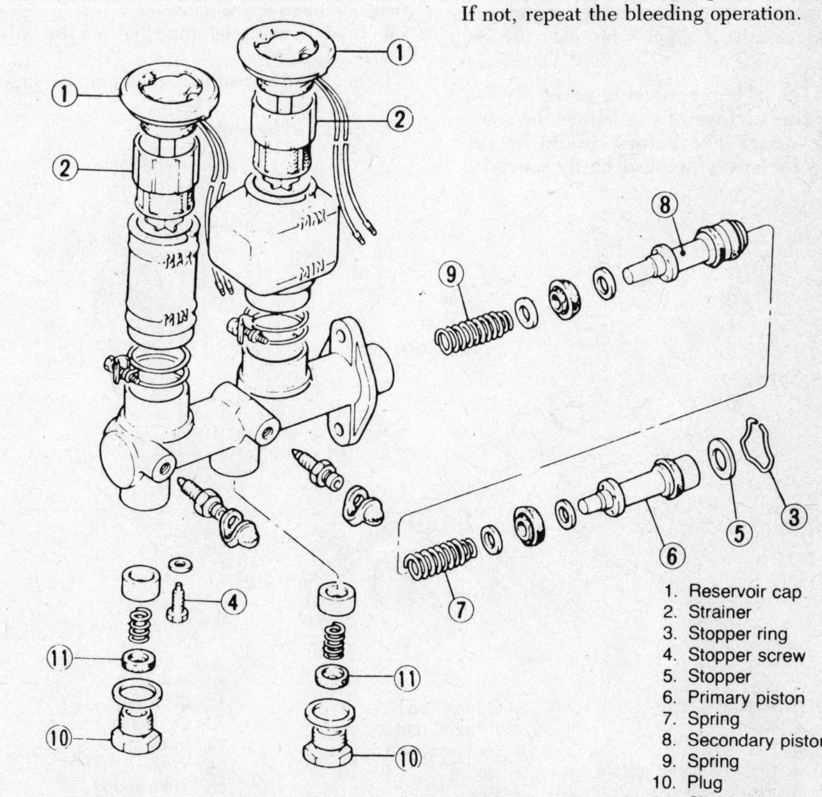

1. Reservoir cap
2. Strainer
3. Stopper ring
4. Stopper screw
5. Stopper
6. Primary piston
7. Spring
8. Secondary piston
9. Spring
10. Plug
11. Check valve

Exploded view of typical master cylinder

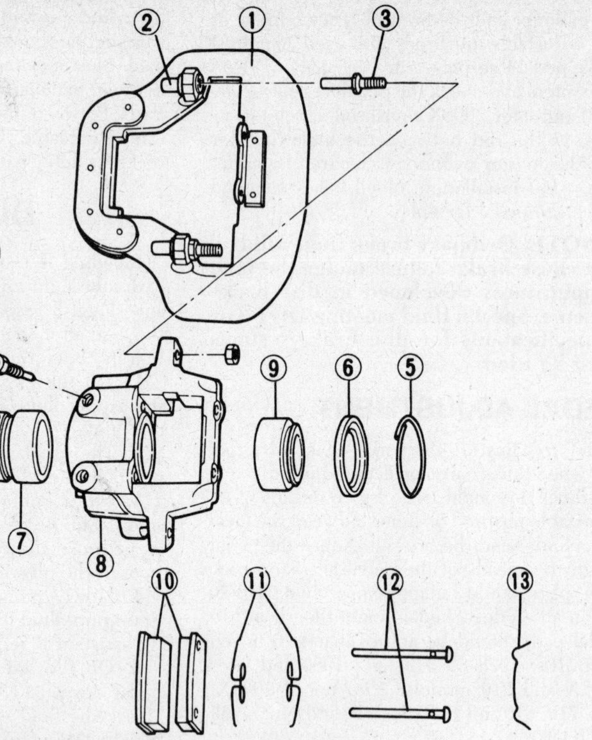

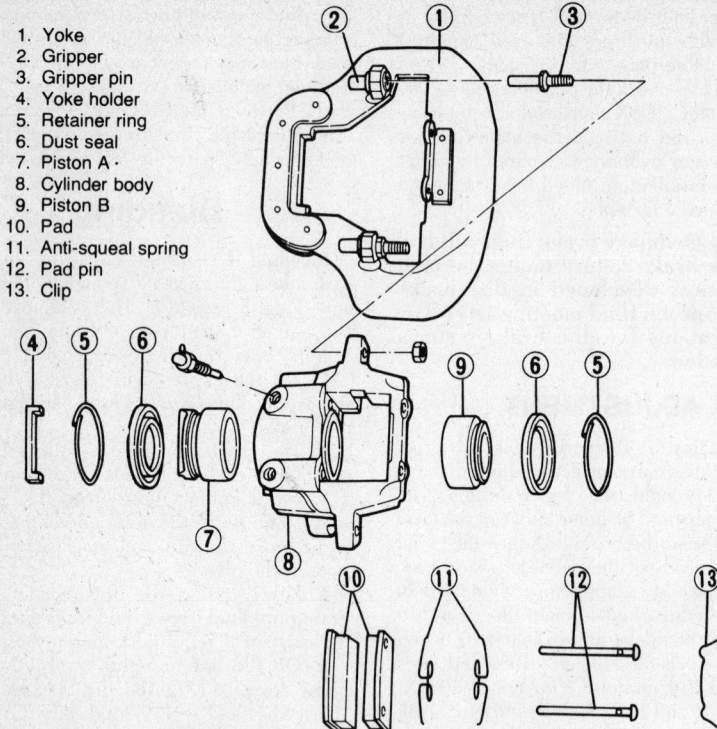

1. Yoke
2. Gripper
3. Gripper pin
4. Yoke holder
5. Retainer ring
6. Dust seal
7. Piston A ·
8. Cylinder body
9. Piston B
10. Pad
11. Anti-squeal spring
12. Pad pin
13. Clip

N32 disc brake; N20, N22A, N34L similar

Front Disc Brake Pads Removal and Installation

All four front brake pads must always be replaced as a set. Several grades of pads are available for most models for road use, or racing.

NOTE: When replacing pads, always check the surface of the rotors for scoring or wear. The rotors should be removed for resurfacing if badly scored.

TYPES N20, N22A, N32, AND N34L

1975-77 710, 1978-79 and Later 510 and all 810

1. Raise and support the front of the car or truck. Remove the wheels.
2. Remove the retaining clip from the outboard pad.
3. Remove the pad pins retaining the anti-squeal springs.
4. Remove the pads.
5. To install, open the bleeder screw slightly and push the outer piston into the cylinder until the dust seal groove aligns with the end of the seal retaining ring, then close the bleed screw. Be careful, because the piston can be pushed too far, requiring disassembly of the caliper to repair. Install the inner pad.
6. Pull the yoke to push the inner piston into place. Install the outer pad.
7. Lightly coat the areas where the pins touch the pads, and where the pads touch the caliper (at the top) with grease. Do not allow grease to get on the pad friction surfaces.
8. Install the anti-squeal springs and pad pins. Install the clip.
9. Apply the brakes a few times to seat the pads. Check the master cylinder level; add fluid if necessary. Bleed the brakes if necessary.

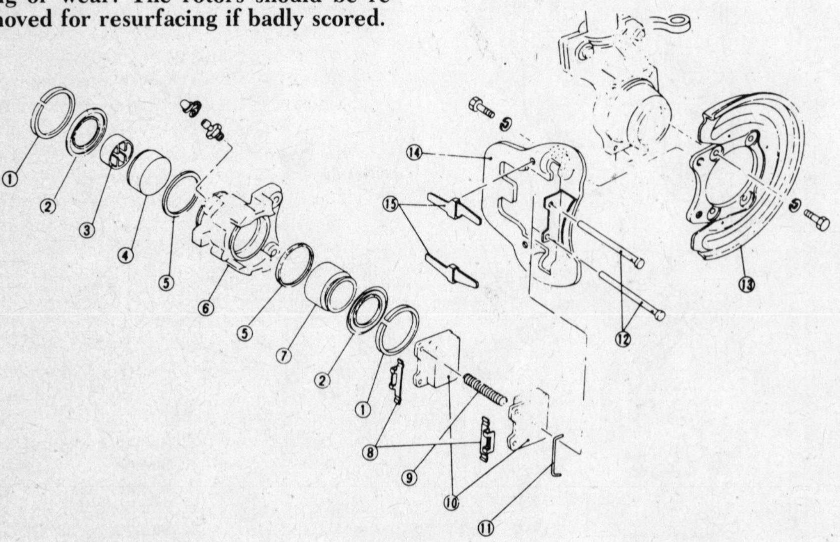

1. Retaining ring
2. Boot
3. Bias ring
4. Piston A (inner piston)
5. Piston seal
6. Cylinder body
7. Piston B (outer piston)
8. Hanger spring
9. Spring
10. Pad
11. Clip
12. Clevis pin
13. Buffle plate
14. Yoke
15. Yoke spring

Typical Annette disc brake

ANNETTE TYPE

210, B210, 200SX, F-10, 1200, 310, 1975-76 610

1. Raise and support the front of the car. Remove the wheels.
2. Remove the clip, pull out the pins, and remove the pad springs.
3. Remove the pads by pulling them out with pliers.
4. To install, first lightly coat the yoke groove and end surface of the piston with grease. Do not allow grease to contact the pads or rotor.
5. Open the bleeder screw slightly and push the outer piston into the cylinder until its end aligns with the end of the boot retaining ring. Do not push too far, which will require caliper disassembly to correct. Install the inner pad.
6. Pull the yoke toward the outside of the car to push the inner piston into place. Install the outer pad.
7. Apply the brakes a few times to seat the pads. Check the master cylinder and add fluid if necessary. Bleed the brakes if necessary.

S16 GIRLING-SUMITOMO TYPE

1975-78Z

1. Raise and support the front of the car.
2. Remove the hairpin clips, retaining pins, anti-squeal spring, and the pads and shims.
3. To install, open the bleeder screw slightly and press the pistons into the caliper.
4. Apply a light coat of grease to the sliding surfaces of the caliper and both sides of the shim. The shim should only be greased along the round cut-out which fits around the piston.
5. Install the pads and shims. The arrow on the shim must point in the direction of forward rotor rotation. Install the anti-squeal springs, the pins, and the pin clips.
6. Apply the brakes a few times to seat the pads. Check the master cylinder level, and add fluid if necessary. Bleed the brakes if necessary.

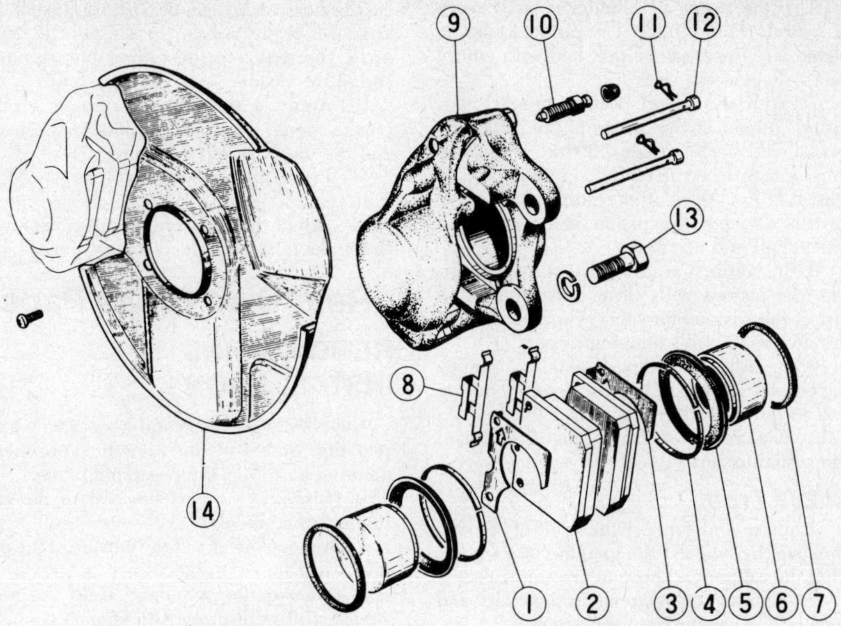

1. Anti-squeal shim, right
2. Pad
3. Anti-squeal shim, left
4. Retaining ring
5. Dust cover
6. Piston
7. Piston seal
8. Anti-squeal spring
9. Caliper assembly
10. Bleeder
11. Clip
12. Retaining pin
13. Caliper fixing bolt
14. Baffle plate

S-16 Girling-Sumitomo front disc brake

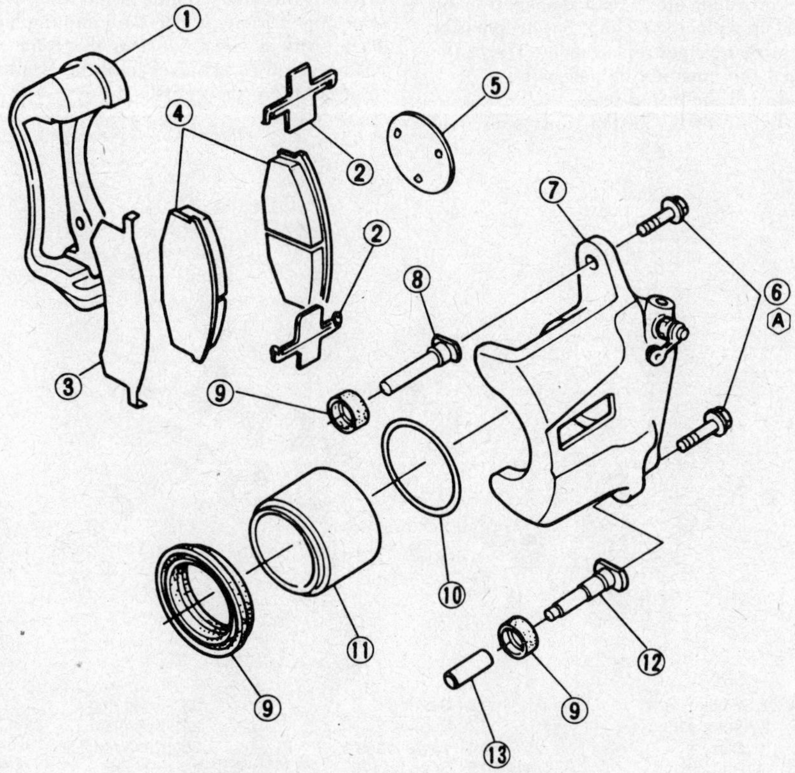

1. Torque member
2. Pad retainer
3. Outer shim
4. Pad
5. Inner shim
6. Pin bolt
7. Cylinder body
8. Main pin
9. Dust seal
10. Piston seal
11. Piston
12. Sub pin
13. Rubber seal

A—16-23 ft. lbs.

280 ZX CL28V front disc brake

CL28V TYPE

280ZX

1. Raise and support the front of the car. Remove the wheels.
2. Remove the lower pin bolt which retains the caliper to the torque member.
3. Rotate the caliper upward out of the way, exposing the pads. Do not try to move the caliper sideways.
4. Remove the pad retainers, inner and outer shims, and pads.
5. To install, clean the piston end and pin bolts.
6. Install a new inner pad. Rotate the caliper back down into place, slightly open the bleeder screw, then, with a long bar, lever the caliper to the outside to press the piston into place. Rotate the caliper back up out of the way.
7. Lightly coat the sliding surfaces of the torque member with grease. Install a new outer pad and inner and outer shims. Install the pad retainers; be careful not to install upside down.
8. Rotate the caliper down and install the pin bolt (torque to 16-23 ft/lbs.)
9. Apply the brakes a few times to seat the pads. Check the master cylinder level, and add fluid if necessary. Bleed the brakes if necessary.

Calipers and Brake Discs

OVERHAUL

Types N20, N22A, N32, N34L

1. With the vehicle supported safely and the front wheels off, remove the brake fluid tube from the caliper assembly.
2. Remove the caliper from the knuckle assembly by removing the mounting bolts, located at the rear of the caliper, and lifting the caliper from the rotor.
3. Remove the pads from the caliper (refer to the pad removal procedure).
4. Remove the gripper pin attaching nuts and separate the yoke from the cylinder body.
5. Remove the yoke holder from the piston and remove the retaining rings and dust seals from the ends of both pistons.
6. Apply air pressure *gradually* into the fluid chamber of the caliper, to force the pistons from the cylinders.
7. Remove the piston seals.
8. Inspect the components for damage or excessive wear. Replace or repair as needed.
9. To assemble, install the piston seals in the cylinder bore. Lubricate seals and pistons.
10. Slide the "A" piston into the cylinder, followed by the "B" piston so that its yoke groove coincides with the yoke groove of the cylinder.
11. Install the dust seal and clamp tightly with the retaining ring.
12. Install the yoke holder on the "A" piston and install the gripper to yoke.

NOTE: The use of soapy water will aid in the installation of the gripper pins.

13. Support the end of "B" piston and press the yoke into the yoke holder.

14. Install the pads, anti-squeal springs, pad pins and retain with the clip.
15. Tighten the gripper pin attaching nuts to 12-15 ft/lbs and install the caliper on the spindle knuckle. Torque the caliper mounting bolts to 53-72 ft/lbs.
16. Bleed the system, check the fluid level, install the wheels and lower the vehicle.

Annette Type

1. Remove the pads.
2. Disconnect the brake tube.
3. Remove the two bottom strut assembly installation bolts to provide clearance.
4. Remove the caliper assembly mounting bolts.
5. Loosen the bleeder screw and press the pistons into their bores.
6. Clamp the yoke in a vise and tap the yoke head with a hammer to loosen the cylinder. Be careful that primary piston does not fall out.
7. Remove the bias ring from primary piston. Remove the retaining rings and boots from both pistons. Depress and remove the pistons from the cylinder. Remove the piston seal from the cylinder carefully with the fingers so as not to mar the cylinder wall.
8. Remove the yoke springs from the yoke.
9. Wash all parts with clean brake fluid.
10. If the piston or cylinder is badly worn or scored, replace both. The piston surface is plated and must not be polished with emery paper. Replace all seals. The rotor can be removed and machined if scored, but final thickness must be at least 0.331 in. Runout must not exceed 0.001 in.
11. Lubricate the cylinder bore with clean brake fluid and install the piston seal.
12. Insert the bias ring into primary piston so that the rounded ring portion comes to the bottom of the piston. Primary piston has a small depression inside, while secondary does not.
13. Lubricate the pistons with clean brake fluid and insert into the cylinder. Install the boot and retaining ring. The yoke groove of the bias ring of primary piston must align with the yoke groove of the cylinder.
14. Install the yoke springs to the yoke so the projecting portion faces to the disc (rotor).
15. Lubricate the sliding portion of the cylinder and yoke. Assemble the cylinder and yoke by tapping the yoke lightly.
16. Replace the caliper assembly and pads. Torque the mounting bolts to 33-41 ft/lbs. Rotor bolt torque is 20-27 ft/lbs. Strut bolt torque is 33-44 ft/lbs. Bleed the system of air.

S16 Girling–Sumitomo Type

The caliper halves must not be separated. If brake fluid leaks from the bridge seal, replace the caliper assembly.

1. Remove the pads.
2. Disconnect the brake line and caliper mounting bolts.
3. Remove the retaining ring and dust seal. Hold the piston in one side and force the other out with air pressure. Remove the other piston.
4. Remove the piston seal from the cylinder carefully with your fingers so as not to mar the cylinder wall.
5. Wash all parts with clean brake fluid.
6. If the piston or cylinder is badly worn or scored, replace both. The piston surface is plated and must not be polished with emery paper. Replace all seals.
7. With the wheel bearing properly adjusted, runout at the center of the rotor surface should be less than 0.006 in. The rotor can be resurfaced if scored, but must be at least 0.413 in. thick after resurfacing.
8. Lubricate the piston seal with clean brake fluid and install it.
9. Install dust seals on the pistons, lubricate the pistons with clean brake fluid, and install the pistons into the cylinders. Clamp the dust seals with retaining rings.
10. Reinstall the caliper assembly. Mounting bolt torque is 53-71 ft/lbs. Rotor mounting bolt torque is 28-38 ft/lbs.
11. Replace the pads and brake line. Bleed the system of air.

CL28V Type

1. Raise and support the front of the car. Remove the wheels. Remove the brake hose. Plug the caliper and hose to prevent leakage.
2. Remove the two mounting bolts and remove the caliper from the spindle.
3. Remove the two pin bolts.
4. Separate the caliper from the torque member.
5. Remove the pad retainers and pads.
6. Apply compressed air to the fluid inlet and remove the pistons and dust seals. Remove the piston seals.
7. Check the caliper bore for scoring, wear, corrosion, etc. Minor damage can be cleaned up with crocus cloth, but deep pits or wear warrant caliper replacement. The piston is plated and must not be polished.
8. Install the piston seals.
9. Lubricate the piston, dust seals, and caliper bore with clean brake fluid. Install the dust seal to the piston, then install the other lip of the seal into the caliper bore groove. Install the piston.
10. Apply a thin coat of grease to the torque member (where it contacts the pads) and the pin bushings and pins.
11. Install the pin bolts, tightening to 53-72 ft/lbs.
12. Install the pads and retainers. Connect the brake hose and bleed the system.

Rear Disc Brake Pads

REMOVAL AND INSTALLATION

The 280ZX and 1980 and later 200SX have rear disc brakes of the Annette type, incorporating a cam-operated parking brake.

1. Raise and support the rear of the car. Remove the wheels.
2. Remove the clip at the outside of the pad pins.
3. Remove the pad pins. Hold the anti-squeal springs in place with your finger.
4. Remove the pads.
5. To install, first clean the end of the piston with clean brake fluid.
6. Lightly coat the caliper-to-pad, the yoke-to-pad, retaining pin-to-bracket surfaces with grease. Do not allow grease to get on the rotor or pad surfaces.
7. Push the piston into place with a screwdriver by pushing in on the piston while at the same time turning it clockwise into the bore. Then, with a lever between the rotor and yoke, push the yoke over until the clearance to install the pads is equal.

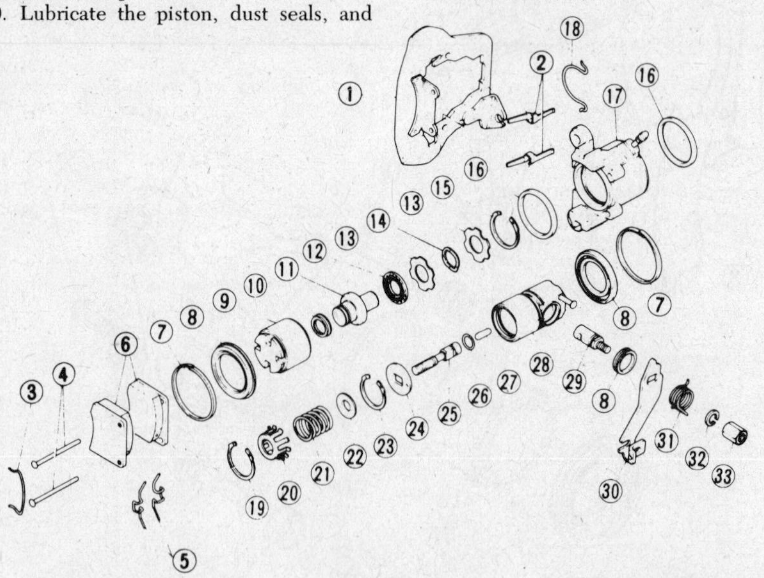

1. Yoke
2. Yoke spring
3. Clip
4. Pad pin
5. Anti-squeal spring
6. Pad
7. Retaining ring
8. Dust seal
9. Outer piston
10. Oil seal
11. Adjusting nut
12. Bearing
13. Spacer
14. Wave washer
15. Snap ring B
16. Piston seal
17. Cylinder body
18. Retainer
19. Snap ring A
20. Spring cover
21. Spring
22. Spring seat
23. Snap ring C
24. Key plate
25. Push rod
26. "O" ring
27. Strut
28. Inner piston
29. Cam
30. Toggle lever
31. Spring
32. Washer
33. Nut

280 ZX Annette AN14H rear disc brake

8. Install the shims and pads, anti-squeal springs and pins. Install the clip. Note that the inner pad has a tab which must fit into the piston notch. Therefore, be sure that the piston notch is centered to allow proper pad installation.

9. Apply the brakes a few times to center the pads. Check the master cylinder fluid level and add if necessary.

Caliper Overhaul

1. Disconnect the brake hose from the caliper. Plug the hose and caliper to prevent fluid loss.
2. Disconnect the parking brake cable.
3. Remove the mounting bolts and remove the caliper from the suspension arm.
4. Remove the pads.
5. Stand the caliper assembly on end, large end down, and push on the caliper to separate it from the yoke.
6. Remove the retaining rings and dust seals from both pistons.
7. Push in on the outer piston to force out the piston assembly. Remove the piston seals.
8. Remove the yoke spring from the yoke.
9. Disengage the piston assembly by turning the outer piston counterclockwise.
10. Disassemble the outer piston by removing the snap ring.
11. Disassemble the inner piston by removing the snap ring. This will allow the spring cover, spring, and spring seat to come out. Remove the inner snap ring to remove the key plate, push rod, and strut.
12. To install, assemble the pistons in reverse order of disassembly. Apply a thin coat of grease to the groove in the push rod, its O-ring, the strut ends, oil seal, piston seal, and the inside of the dust seal.
13. Install the piston seals. Apply a thin coat of grease to the sliding surfaces of the piston and caliper bore. Install the pistons into the caliper. Install the retainers onto the dust seals.
14. Install the yoke springs on the yoke.
15. Lightly coat the yoke and caliper body contact surfaces, and the pad pin hole, with silicone grease. Assemble the yoke to the caliper.
16. Install the pads.
17. Install the caliper to the suspension arm (28-38 ft/lbs). Connect the parking brake cable. Connect the brake hose. Apply the brakes a few times to center the pads. Bleed the system.

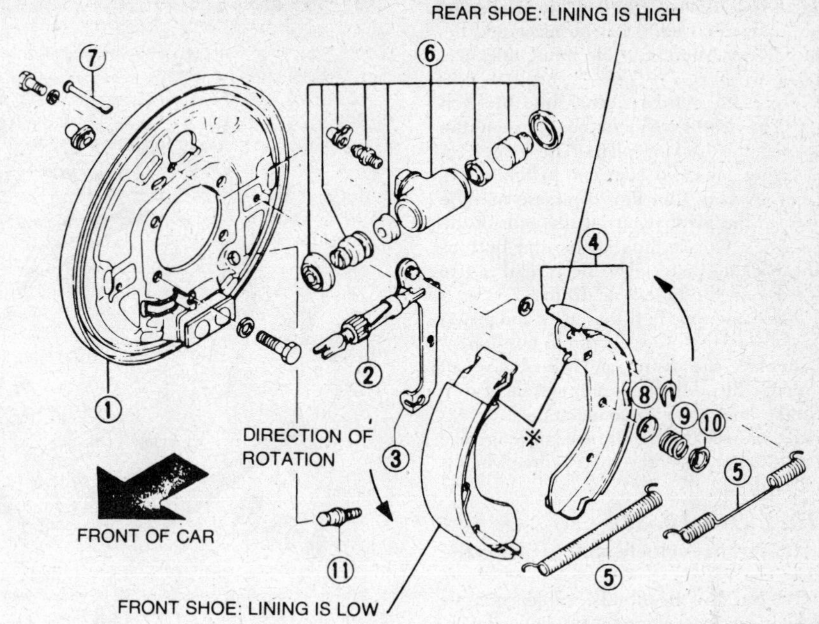

1. Brake disc
2. Adjuster
3. Lever
4. Brake shoe assembly
5. Return spring
6. Wheel cylinder
7. Anti-rattle pin
8. Spring seat
9. Anti-rattle spring
10. Retainer
11. Stopper assembly

*Adjuster location hole

810 sedan rear drum brake

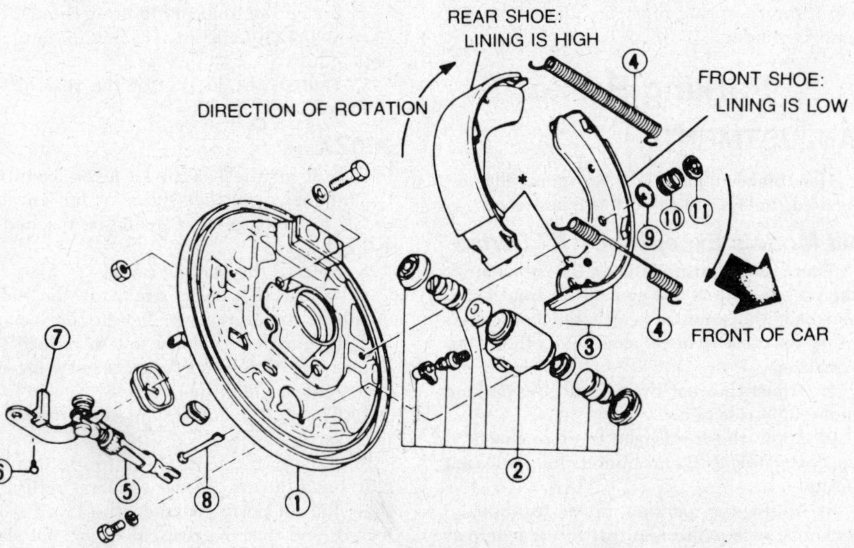

1. Brake disc
2. Wheel cylinder assembly
3. Brake shoe assembly
4. Return spring
5. Adjuster assembly
6. Stopper pin
7. Stopper
8. Anti-rattle pin
9. Spring seat
10. Anti-rattle spring
11. Retainer

200 SX rear drum brake

Drum Brakes

All models except the 280ZX and the 1980 and later 200SX have rear drum brakes. Each rear brake assembly has two brake shoes and a single hydraulic cylinder which is free to slide back and forth in a slot in the brake backing plate. On some models the hydraulic cylinder is bolted and the adjuster slides.

Brake parts are supplied to Datsun by two manufacturers: Tokico and Nabco. These parts are not interchangeable. Be sure you get the correct parts for your model.

DRUM, LINING AND WHEEL CYLINDER REPLACEMENT

510, 610, 710, 810 and 1977-79 200SX Rear

1. Raise the vehicle and remove the wheels.
2. Release the parking brake. Disconnect the cross rod from the lever of the brake cylinder. Remove the brake drum. Place a heavy rubber band around the cylinder to prevent the piston from coming out.
3. Remove the return springs and shoes.
4. Clean the backing plate and check the wheel cylinder for leaks. To remove the wheel cylinder, remove the brake line, dust cover, plates, and adjusting shims. Clearance between the cylinder and the piston should not exceed 0.006 in.
5. The drums must be machined if scored

or out of round more than 0.002 in. The drum inside diameter should not be machined beyond 9.04 in. Minimum safe lining thickness is 0.059 in.

6. Hook the return springs into the new shoes. The springs should be between the shoes and the backing plate. The longer return spring must be adjacent to the wheel cylinder. A very thin film of grease may be applied to the pivot points at the ends of the brake shoes. Grease the shoe locating buttons on the backing plate, also. Be careful not to get grease on the linings or drums.

7. Place one shoe in the adjuster and piston slots, and pry the other shoe into position.

8. Replace the drums and wheels. Adjust the brakes. Bleed the hydraulic system of air if the brake lines were disconnected.

9. Reconnect the handbrake, making sure that it does not cause the shoe to drag when it is released.

B210, 210, F-10, 310

1. Raise the vehicle and remove the wheels.

2. Loosen the handbrake cable, remove the clevis pin from the wheel cylinder lever, disconnect the handbrake cable, and remove the return pull spring.

3. Remove the brake drum, shoe retainers, return springs, and brake shoes. Loosen the brake adjusters if the drums are difficult to remove. Place a heavy rubber band around the cylinder to prevent the piston from coming out.

4. Clean the backing plate and check the wheel cylinder for leaks. To remove the wheel cylinder, remove the brake line, dust cover, plates, and adjusting shims. Clearance between cylinder and piston should not exceed 0.006 in.

5. The drums must be machined if scored or out of round more than 0.001 in. The drum inside diameter must not be machined beyond 8.04 in. Minimum safe lining thickness is 0.059 in. (0.039 in.-F-10).

6. Follow Steps 6-9 for 510 Rear.

280Z Rear

1. Raise and support the vehicle. Remove the wheel.

2. Remove the brake drum. If it is difficult to remove, on models through 1976, remove the wheel cylinder lever handbrake clevis pin. Remove the brake drum adjusting hole plug and pry the adjusting lever away from the adjusting wheel with a screwdriver inserted through the adjusting hole. Turn the adjusting wheel down with the screwdriver to loosen the brake shoes. Remove the brake drum. For 1977-78 models, fully apply the handbrake, push or tap the cotter pin out and remove the stop from the parking brake lever on the rear of the drum; then release the parking brake and remove the drum.

3. Remove the brake shoe retainers and springs. Remove the shoes and return springs. Place a heavy rubber band around the cylinder to prevent the piston from coming out.

4. Clean the backing plate and check for wheel cylinder leaks. To remove the wheel cylinder, detach the brake tube and dust cover, drive the lock plate out toward the front, pull the adjusting plate to the rear, and remove the cylinder. Clearance between the cylinder and piston should not exceed 0.006 in.

5. The drums should be machined if scored or out of round more than 0.002 in. The drum inside diameter should not be machined beyond 9.04 in. Minimum safe lining thickness is 0.060 in.

6. On reassembly, apply a very light film of grease to all sliding surfaces. Be careful not to get any on the linings or drums. The wheel cylinder must be free to slide. The longer black return spring must be adjacent to the wheel cylinder.

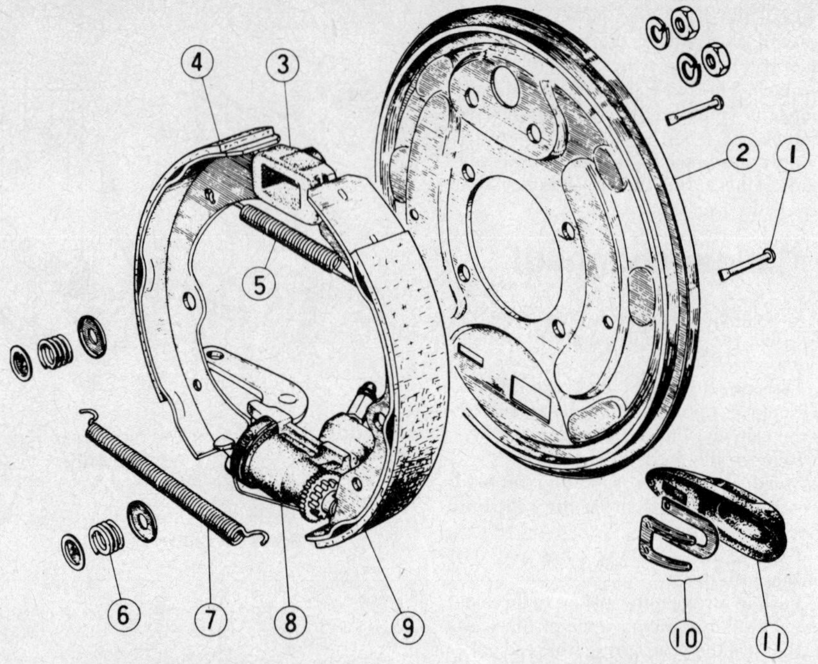

1. Anti-rattle pin
2. Brake backing plate
3. Anchor block
4. After shoe assembly
5. Return spring
6. Anti-rattle spring
7. Return spring
8. Wheel cylinder
9. Fore shoe assembly
10. Retaining shim
11. Dust cover

Z car rear drum brake

Parking Brake

ADJUSTMENT

Handbrake adjustments are generally not needed, unless the cables have stretched.

All Models Except the "Z" Series

There is an adjusting nut on the cable under the car, usually at the end of the front cable and near the point at which the two cables from the rear wheels come together (the equalizer).

1. Adjust the rear brakes with the parking brake fully released.

2. Apply the handbrake lever so that it is approximately 3-3½ in. from its fully released position.

3. Adjust the parking brake turnbuckle, locknuts, or equalizer so that the rear brakes are locked.

4. Release the parking brake. The wheels should be free to turn. If not, loosen the parking brake adjuster until the wheels turn with no drag.

280Z

The driveshaft must be removed to gain access to the adjusting nut on the front linkage rod.

1. Release the handbrake fully and block the vehicle wheels.

2. Loosen the locknut at the rear of the front rod.

3. Measure the dimension between the wheel cylinder lever pin hole centers and their respective buffer plates.

4. Rotate the front rod to bring the dimension to 0.453-0.492 in. (11.5-12.5 mm) on both sides.

5. Tighten the locknut at the rear of the front rod.

280ZX

1. Pull up the handbrake lever, counting the number of ratchet clicks for full engagement. Full engagement should be reached in 4-6 notches.

2. Release the parking brake.

3. Adjust the lever stroke at the cable equalizer under the car: loosen the locknut and tighten the adjusting nut to reduce the number of ratchet clicks necessary for engagement. Tighten the locknut.

4. Check the adjustment and repeat as necessary.

5. After adjustment, check to see that the rear brake levers (at the calipers) return to their full off positions when the lever is released, and that the rear cables are not slack when the lever is released.

6. To adjust the warning lamp, bend the warning lamp switch plate down so that the light comes on when the lever is engaged one notch.

CHASSIS ELECTRICAL

Heater Unit

REMOVAL AND INSTALLATION

610

1. Disconnect the battery ground cable.
2. Drain the coolant.
3. Detach the coolant inlet and outlet hoses.
4. Remove the center ventilator grille from the bottom of the instrument panel.
5. Remove the heater duct hose.
6. Detach the defroster hose from each side of the heater unit.
7. Disconnect the control cables.
8. Disconnect the wires at the connectors.
9. Remove the bolt at each side of the unit and the one on the top for 1973 models and two on each side for 1974-76 models.
10. Remove the unit.
11. Reverse the procedure for installation. Run the engine for a few minutes with the heater on to make sure the system is filled with coolant.

B210

1. Disconnect battery ground strap.
2. Drain engine coolant.
3. Remove the defroster hose from both sides of heater unit.
4. Disconnect electrical wires from heater unit.
5. Remove clamps and disconnect water hose from right side of heater.
6. Remove one attaching bolt from each side of the unit and one at the top center and remove unit by pulling forward and out.
7. Reverse procedure for installation.

710

1. Disconnect battery ground strap.
2. Drain engine coolant. Disconnect the heater hoses at the firewall (engine compartment side).
3. Remove intake duct hose and defroster duct from both sides of heater unit. Remove console box if so equipped.
4. Disconnect electrical wires at connectors.
5. Loosen retaining clamps and remove control cables.
6. Remove two bolts on each side of unit and one on top. Remove unit from vehicle.
7. Install in reverse of the above.

280Z

1. Disconnect battery ground and drain coolant.
2. Remove console box by removing the five attaching screws.
3. Remove the four attaching screws and lift off finisher. Disconnect wires.
4. Remove attaching screws and lift out three way duct to instrument panel.
5. Remove the control cables at the intake duct, water cock and floor mode doors.
6. Disconnect defroster ducts and two right side heater hoses from the unit.

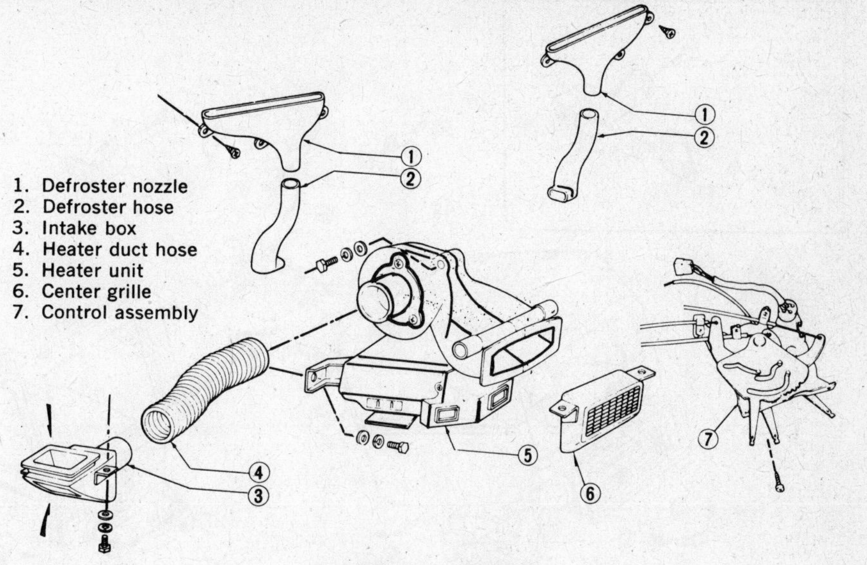

610 heater installation

7. Remove heater control and vent ducts from the unit.
8. Remove two bolts retaining the unit to the dash panel from inside the passenger compartment and two bolts retaining the unit to the firewall from the engine compartment.
9. Move heater unit to the right and out.
10. Reverse the above for installation.

F-10

1. Disconnect battery ground cable and drain coolant.
2. Disconnect inlet and outlet hoses and remove defroster hoses from each side of the heater unit.
3. Remove the cable retaining clamps for the heater valve, floor door and intake door.
4. Disconnect electrical connectors. Remove the four unit retaining screws and remove the heater unit.

Installation is the reverse of removal.

1977-79 200SX

1. Disconnect the battery ground cable. Drain the coolant. Disconnect the heater hose clamp at the engine.
2. Inside the car, disconnect the electrical connectors at each side of the instrument panel.
3. Remove the instrument panel: Remove the steering column covers; disconnect the speedometer cable and radio antenna cable; disconnect all electrical connectors; remove the steering column clamp bolts; remove the package tray; remove the bolts attaching the panel to the side brackets; remove the right windshield pillar moulding and remove the panel bolt there; remove the panel moulding; remove the panel bolts and remove the panel.
4. Remove the defroster hoses. Remove the coolant hoses.
5. On air conditioned models, disconnect

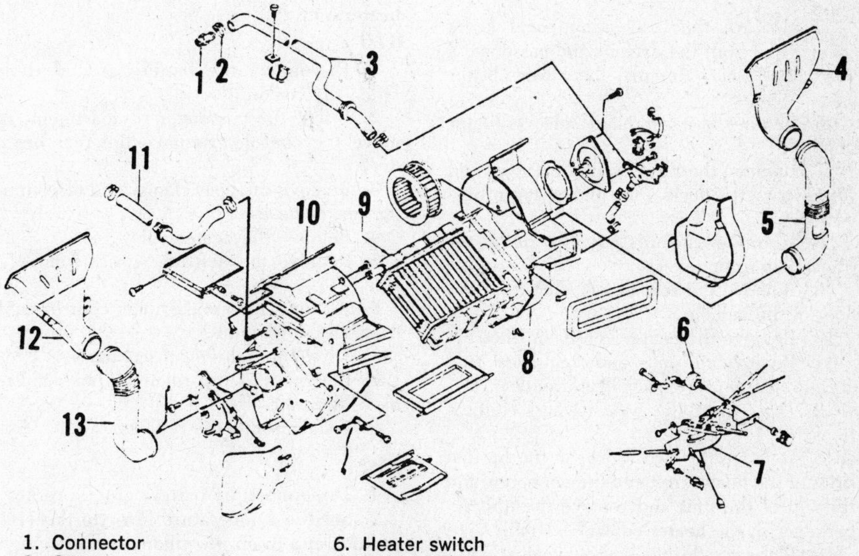

1. Connector
2. Clip
3. Heater hose (inlet)
4. Defroster nozzle (R.H.)
5. Defroster duct (R.H.)
6. Heater switch
7. Heater control
8. Heater case (R.H.)
9. Heater core
10. Heater case (L.H.)
11. Heater hose (outlet)
12. Defroster nozzle (L.H.)
13. Defroster duct (L.H.)

F–10 heater construction

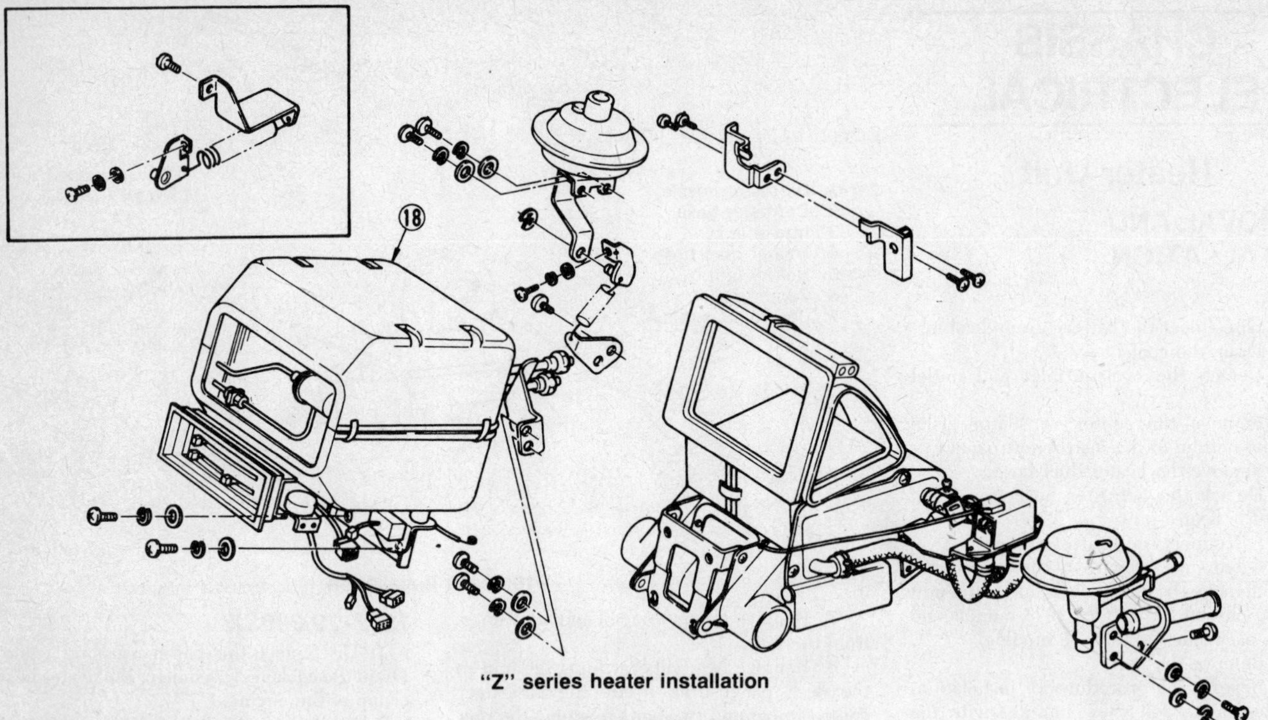

"Z" series heater installation

the electrical wires between the heater and a/c unit.

6. Remove the three bolts and heater.

7. Installation is the reverse.

1980 and Later 200SX

1. Set the TEMP lever to the HOT position and drain the coolant.

2. Disconnect the heater hoses from the driver's side of the heater unit.

3. At this point the manufacturer suggests you remove the front seats. To do this, remove the plastic covers over the ends of the seat runners, both front and back, to expose the seat mounting bolts. Remove the bolts and remove the seats.

4. Remove the console box and the floor carpets.

5. Remove the instrument panel lower covers from both the driver's and passenger's sides of the car. Remove the lower cluster lids.

6. Remove the left hand side ventilator duct.

7. Remove the radio, sound balancer and stereo cassette deck. (See below for procedures).

8. Remove the instrument panel-to-transmission tunnel stay.

9. Remove the rear heater duct from the floor of the vehicle.

10. Remove the center ventilator duct.

11. Remove the left- and right-hand side air guides from the lower heater outlets.

12. Disconnect the wire harness connections.

13. Remove the two screws at the bottom sides of the heater unit and the one screw and the top of the unit and remove the unit together with the heater control assembly.

Installation is the reverse of removal.

NOTE: You may be able to skip several of the above steps if only certain components of the heater unit need service.

1978 and Later 510, 210

1. Disconnect the ground cable at the battery. Drain the coolant.

2. Remove the console.

3. Remove the driver's side of the instrument panel. See the section following.

4. Remove the heater control assembly: remove the defroster ducts, door cables at the doors, harness connector, and control assembly.

5. Remove the radio.

6. Disconnect the heater ducts, side defrosters, and center vent duct,

7. Remove the screws attaching the defroster nozzle to the unit. Disconnect the blower wire, and the heater hoses.

8. Remove the retaining bolts and the heater unit.

810

1. Disconnect the battery ground cable. Drain the coolant.

2. Inside the passenger compartment, remove the console. Remove the rear heater duct.

3. Remove the hose clamps and disconnect the heater hoses.

4. Remove the heater duct.

5. Remove the defroster hoses from each side.

6. Remove the intake door control cable from the blower box.

7. Disconnect the electrical harness.

8. Remove the unit retaining bolts and remove the unit.

9. Installation is the reverse.

310

1. Disconnect the battery ground cable.

2. Set the temperature lever to the HOT position and drain the engine coolant.

3. Remove the instrument panel assembly. See the following section for instructions.

4. Disconnect the control cables and rod from the heater unit. Disconnect the heater motor harness.

5. Disconnect the inlet and the outlet heater hoses from the engine compartment.

6. Remove the two lower and three upper bolts attaching the heater and blower units to the vehicle. The air conditioning unit is on the passenger's side of the vehicle. It does not have to be removed to remove the heater and blower units.

7. Remove the heater and blower units.

8. Installation is the reverse of removal.

280ZX

1. Disconnect the battery ground cable.

2. Set the temperature lever to maximum heat and drain the coolant.

3. Inside the passenger compartment remove the instrument panel lower covers, floor nozzles, defroster ducts, console, and center vent.

4. Remove the glove compartment.

5. Remove the heater duct.

6. Disconnect the control cables and rod from the unit.

7. Remove the control assembly.

8. Disconnect heater hoses from unit.

9. Remove the blower: disconnect the wire harness, the control cable clip and cable, then remove the retaining bolts and remove the blower.

10. Remove the heater unit attaching bolts and remove the unit.

Heater Core

REMOVAL AND INSTALLATION

610 and 710

The heater unit need not be removed to remove the heater core. It must be removed to remove the blower motor.

1. Drain the coolant.

2. Detach the coolant hoses.
3. Disconnect the control cables on the sides of the heater unit.
4. Remove the clips and the cover from the front of the heater unit. Remove the console if so equipped.
5. Pull out the core.
6. Reverse the procedure for installation. Run the engine with the heater on for a few minutes to make sure the system fills with coolant.

B210, F-10

1. Remove heater from car.
2. Remove clip and slide hose from cock.
3. Pry off five clips and separate left and right sides of heater case.
4. Lift out heater core.

280Z

1. Remove heater from car.
2. Loosen clamp on heater cock side.
3. Remove screws retaining heater cock and remove from case.
4. Loosen clamp on core side and disconnect hose.
5. Remove E-ring from floor door operating rod.
6. Remove five screws and take off side cover. Pull out heater core with the floor door open.
7. Assemble in reverse of the above.

1977-79 200SX

1. Remove the heater unit.
2. Remove the control lever assembly. Remove the knobs, disconnect the lamp wire, remove the center vent (4 screws), disconnect the fan wires, remove the clips and cables, remove the retaining screws and the unit.
3. Disconnect the hose from the heater cock.
4. Remove the connecting rod (with bracket) from the air door.
5. Remove the clips on each side of the box, split the box, and remove the core.

1980 and Later 200SX

1. Remove the heater unit as described earlier.
2. Remove the hoses from the heater core and remove the core.
3. Installation is the reverse of removal.

1978 and Later 510, 210

1. Remove the heater unit.
2. Disconnect the inlet and outlet hoses.
3. Remove the case clips and split the case. Remove the core.

810

1. Remove the heater unit.
2. Remove the center vent cover and heater control assembly, loosening the clips and screws.
3. Remove the screws securing the door shafts.
4. Remove the clips from the case and split the case. Remove the core.

280ZX

1. Remove the heater unit.
2. Remove the water cock.
3. Remove the case clips and split the heater case. Remove the core.

310

1. Remove the heater unit from the vehicle.
2. Disconnect the inlet and outlet hoses from the core if you have not done so already.
3. Remove the clips securing the case halves and separate the halves.
4. Remove the heater core.
5. Installation is the reverse of removal.

Radio

REMOVAL AND INSTALLATION

610, 710, 280ZX and F-10

1. Detach all electrical connections.
2. Remove the radio knobs and retaining nuts.
3. Remove the mounting screws, tip the radio down at the rear, and remove.
4. Reverse the procedure for installation.

B210, 1978-79 510, 1977-79 200SX, 810, 210

1. Remove the instrument cluster.
2. Detach all electrical connections.
3. Remove the radio knobs and retaining nuts.
4. Remove the rear support bracket.
5. Remove the radio.
6. Reverse the procedure for installation.

1980 and Later 200SX

1. Disconnect the battery. Before removing the radio (audio assembly), you must remove the center instrument cluster which holds the heater controls, etc. Remove the two side screws in the cluster. Remove the heater control and the control panel. Remove the two bolts behind the heater control panel and the two bolts at the base of the cluster. Pull the cluster out of the way after disconnecting the lighter wiring and any other control cables.
2. Remove the radio knobs and fronting panel.
3. Remove the five screws holding the radio assembly in place.
4. Remove the radio after unplugging all connections.
5. Installation is the reverse of removal.

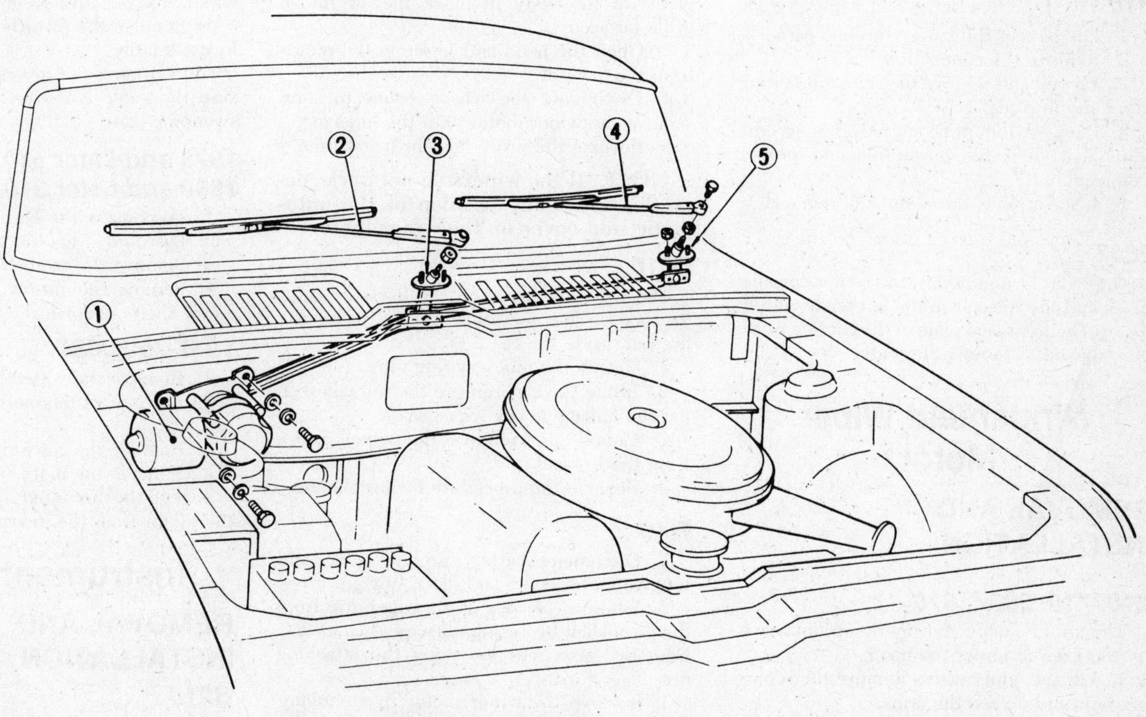

1 Wiper motor
2 Wiper arm
3 Pivot
4 Wiper arm
5 Pivot

610 wiper installation

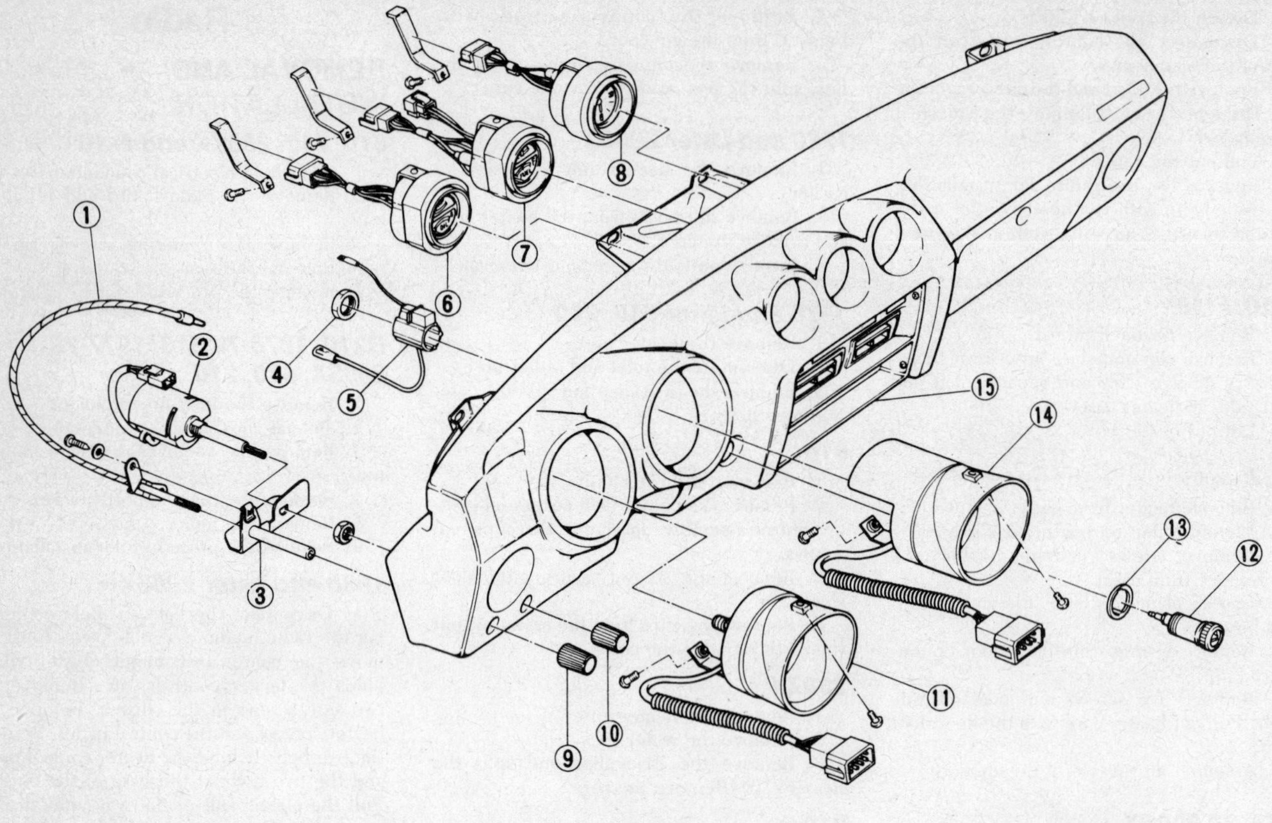

1. Trip meter reset cable
2. Rheostat
3. Bracket
4. Cigarette lighter retaining nut
5. Cigarette lighter housing
6. Oil/Temp gauge
7. Volt/Fuel gauge
8. Clock
9. Trip meter knob
10. Rheostat knob
11. Speedometer
12. Cigarette lighter
13. Escutcheon
14. Tachometer
15. Panel

280 Z instrument panel and gauges

310

1. Disconnect the battery ground cable.
2. Remove the center bezel.
3. Loosen and remove the screws retaining the radio in place.
4. Remove the radio and disconnect the antenna feeder cable, power lines and speaker connections.
5. Installation is the reverse of removal.

280Z

The radio is mounted in the center console panel and the speaker in the left fender inner panel. The front face plate of the console must be removed to remove the radio.

Windshield Wiper Motor

REMOVAL AND INSTALLATION

610, 710, 280Z, 810

The wiper motor and operating linkage is on the firewall under the hood.

1. Lift the wiper arms. Remove the securing nuts and detach the arms.
2. Remove the nuts holding the wiper pivots to the body. Remove the air intake grille for access.
3. Open the hood and unscrew the motor from the firewall.
4. Disconnect the wiring connector and remove the wiper motor with the linkage.
5. Reverse the procedure for installation.

NOTE: If the wipers do not park correctly, adjust the position of the automatic stop cover on the wiper motor.

B210

The wiper motor is on the firewall under the hood. The operating linkage is on the firewall inside the car.

1. Detach the motor wiring plug.
2. Inside the car, remove the nut connecting the linkage to the wiper shaft.
3. Unbolt and remove the wiper motor from the firewall.
4. Reverse the procedure for installation.

F-10

1. Disconnect battery ground cable and remove meter cover and glove box.
2. Remove the base of the wiper arm from the pivot shaft by raising the wiper blade away from the glass and loosening the attaching nut.
3. Remove the wiper motor by removing the ball joint connecting the motor shaft to the wiper link. Remove the motor from the dash.
4. Remove the pivot bolts and remove the link assembly.

Installation is the reverse of removal. Make sure the angle is correct to obtain the right sweeping zone.

1978 and Later 510, 210, 280ZX, 1980 and Later 310, 200SX

1. Disconnect the battery ground cable.
2. Disconnect the electrical connector.
3. Remove the motor attaching bolts.
4. Remove the nut securing the arm to the motor shaft. Remove the motor.

1977-79 200SX

1. Remove the wiper arms.
2. Disconnect the motor electrical connector.
3. Remove the cowl top grille.
4. Remove the motor retaining bolts.
5. Pull the motor out a little and disconnect the motor from the linkage.

Instrument Cluster

REMOVAL AND INSTALLATION

B210

1. Disconnect the battery negative lead.

2. Depress the wiper, light switch, and choke knobs, turning them counterclockwise to remove.
3. From the rear, disconnect the lighter wire. Turn and remove the lighter outer case.
4. Remove the radio and heater knobs.
5. Remove the shell cover from the steering column.
6. Remove the screws which hold the instrument cluster to the instrument panel. Pull out the cluster.
7. Disconnect the wiring connector. Disconnect the speedometer cable by unscrewing the nut at the back of the speedometer.
8. Individual instruments may be removed from the rear of the cluster.

610, 710

1. Disconnect the battery ground cable.
2. Remove the four screws and the steering column cover.
3. Remove the screws which attach the cluster face. Two are just above the steering column, and there is one inside each of the outer instrument recesses.
4. Pull the cluster lid forward.
5. Disconnect the multiple connector.
6. Disconnect the speedometer cable.
7. Disconnect any other wiring.
8. Remove the cluster face.
9. Remove the odometer knob if the vehicle has one.
10. Remove the six screws and the cluster.
11. Instruments may now be readily replaced.
12. Reverse the procedure for installation.

620

1. Disconnect the battery ground cable.
2. Remove the three cluster face retaining screws from inside the instrument recesses.
3. Remove the cluster face retaining screw from underneath the instrument panel.
4. Pull the cluster face outward.
5. Disconnect the speedometer cable and the multiple electrical connector. Disconnect any other wiring. Remove the four screws which hold the cluster to the cluster face. Remove the cluster.
6. Reverse the procedure for installation.

F-10

1. Disconnect the battery ground cable and remove all knobs, nuts and exposed screws.
2. Remove the ashtray and the retaining screws. Pull the panel downward and forward. Disconnect the cigarette lighter connector. Remove panel.

Installation is the reverse of removal.

210

1. Disconnect the battery ground cable.
2. Remove the steering wheel.
3. Remove the steering column cover.
4. Remove the illumination control rheostat.
5. Pull off the heater control knob and remove control panel. Remove the screw attaching the panel to the instrument panel.
6. Pull off the radio knobs; remove the nuts and washers.
7. Remove the ash tray and ash tray holder.
8. Remove the cluster lid screws.
9. Disconnect the electrical connectors.
10. Remove the cluster lid.
11. Remove the cluster gauge screws.
12. Disconnect the speedometer cable by pushing and turning the cap counterclockwise.
13. Disconnect the cluster wires and remove the instrument cluster.

1978 and Later 510

1. Disconnect the battery ground cable.
2. Remove the steering column covers. Disconnect the hazard warning switch connector.
3. Remove the wiper switch. Pull out the ash tray, remove the heater control knobs, and remove the heater control plate by inserting a screwdriver into the fan lever slit and levering the plate out.
4. Remove the finish plate to the left of the glove compartment.
5. Pull off the radio knobs and remove the nuts and washers.
6. Remove the choke and side defroster knobs.
7. Remove the cluster lid screws.
8. Disconnect the electrical connectors.
9. Remove the cluster lid.
10. Remove the instrument cluster retaining screws. Disconnect the speedometer cable by pushing and turning counterclockwise.
11. Disconnect the instrument cluster wire connectors and remove the cluster.

1 Cluster lid
2 Meter assembly
3 Instrument mounting lower bracket
4 Instrument pad
5 Ventilation grille
6 Defogger nozzle
7 Instrument garnish
8 Radio
9 Speaker
10 Ventilation duct
11 Package tray
12 Glove box
13 Glove box lid
14 Ash tray
15 Ash tray cover

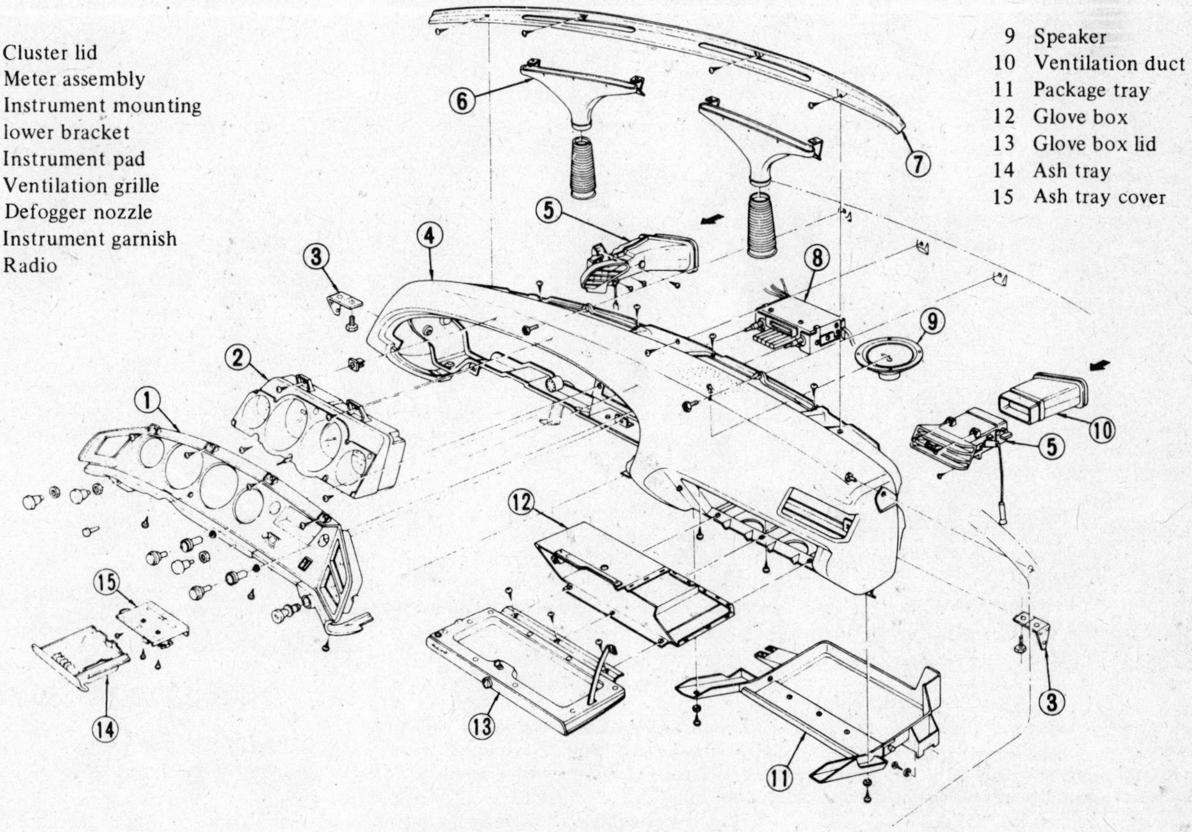

200SX instrument panel and gauges

810

1. Disconnect the battery ground cable.
2. Remove the radio and choke knobs.
3. Remove the ash tray.
4. Remove the steering column covers.
5. Disconnect the harness connectors.
6. Remove the cluster lid retaining screws and remove the cluster lid.
7. Disconnect the speedometer cable by pushing and turning counterclockwise. Remove the retaining screws for the instrument cluster and remove the cluster.

1977-79 200SX

1. Remove the instrument panel as outlined in the Heater Unit Removal section.
2. Remove the steering wheel and steering column covers.
3. Remove the instrument panel knobs: push and turn counterclockwise to remove the head lamp switch, instrument illumination rheostat, windshield wiper knob; pull off the radio knobs; remove the trip meter knob by turning counterclockwise. Remove the nuts and washers under the radio and wiper knobs.
4. Remove the screws securing the cluster lid.
5. Pull the cluster lid forward and disconnect the wiring connectors. Remove the lid.
6. Remove the instrument cluster retaining screws and pull the cluster out a little.
7. Disconnect the speedometer cable and wires, then remove the instrument cluster.

280ZX

1. Disconnect the battery ground cable.
2. Remove the steering wheel.
3. Remove the steering column cover.
4. Remove the instrument panel lower cover on the left side.

FUSE BOX LOCATION CHART

Model	Fuse Box Location	Fusible Link Location
310	Under dash at extreme right	Right fender area of eng. comp.
610	Below hood release knob	Adjacent to battery
710	Engine compartment, right rear	Relay bracket right front of engine compartment
280ZX 280Z, 810	Under dash at extreme right	Right rear of engine compartment ①
B210, 210	Above brake light switch	Engine compartment below voltage regulator
F-10, 510	Under dash at extreme left	Off of (+) cable on battery

① A fusing link for the fuel injection is in (+) battery cable

5. Disconnect the speedometer cable at the intermediate connection.
6. Remove the combination switch.
7. Remove the cluster retaining screws, pull out slightly and disconnect the electrical connectors. Remove the instrument cluster.

1980 and Later 200SX

1. Disconnect the battery ground terminal.
2. It may be necessary to remove the steering wheel and covers to remove the instrument cluster.
3. Remove the screws holding the cluster lid in place and remove the lid.
4. Remove the five bolts holding the cluster in place and pull the cluster out, then remove all connections from its back. Make sure you mark the wiring to avoid confusion during reassembly.

310

1. Disconnect the battery terminals.
2. Remove the steering wheel and the steering column covers.
3. Remove the instrument cluster lid by removing its screws.
4. Remove the instrument cluster screws, pull the unit out and disconnect all wiring.

Instruments

REMOVAL AND INSTALLATION

280Z

The speedometer and tachometer are both attached at the rear with two wingnuts. Access is from under the instrument panel. After the wingnuts are removed, the instrument can be pulled out through the instrument panel. The other three gauge units are held to brackets by slotted head hex bolts. To gain access, the center console panel must be removed.

SPECIFICATIONS

INDEX

BEFORE SERVICING, SEE THE SAFETY NOTICE ON THE CONTENTS PAGE

SERIAL NUMBER IDENTIFICATION

Vehicle and Engine

The vehicle serial number is stamped on a metal plate located on the left front corner of the instrument panel, visible through the windshield. The serial number is also stamped on a non-removable rib or bulkhead of the body.

An identification plate, mounted on the engine compartment wall, (front trunk XI/9), carries the chassis number and the spare parts ordering number. The engine number is stamped on a pad on the engine block.

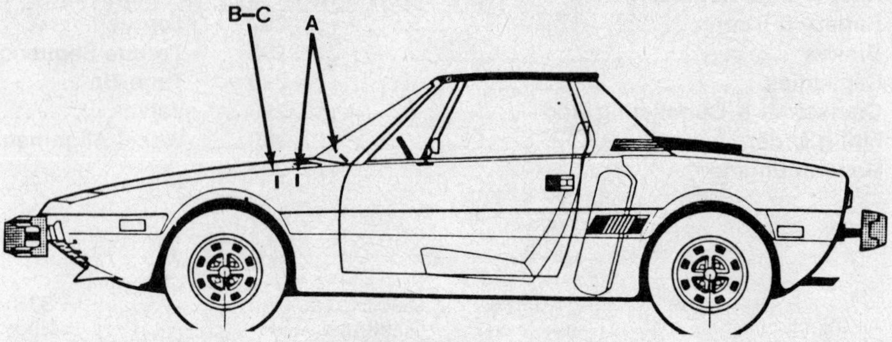

Fiat X1/9 Identification Locations
A—Chassis type and serial number
B—Identification plate
C—Engine type and serial number

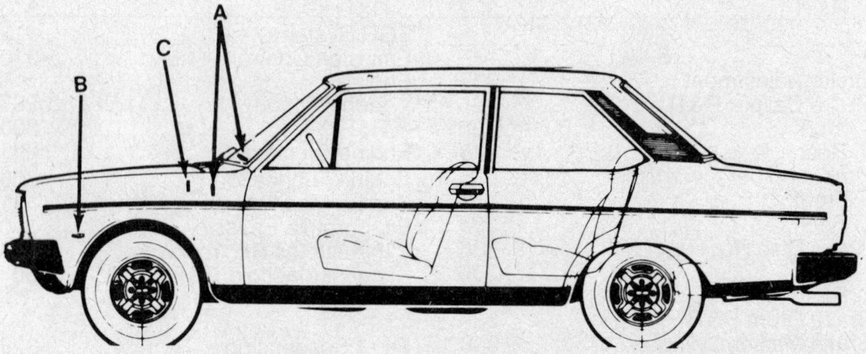

Fiat 131 and Brava Identification Locations
A—Chassis type and serial number
B—Engine type and serial number
C—Identification plate

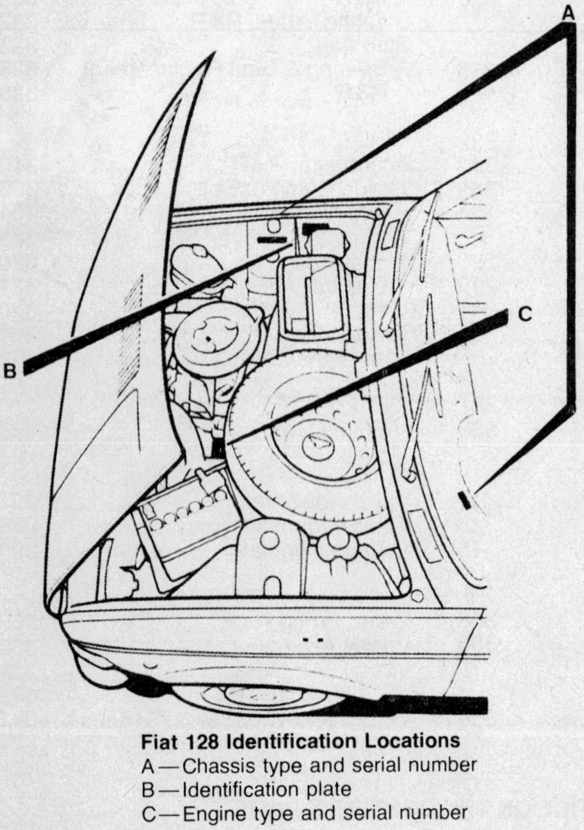

Fiat 128 Identification Locations
A—Chassis type and serial number
B—Identification plate
C—Engine type and serial number

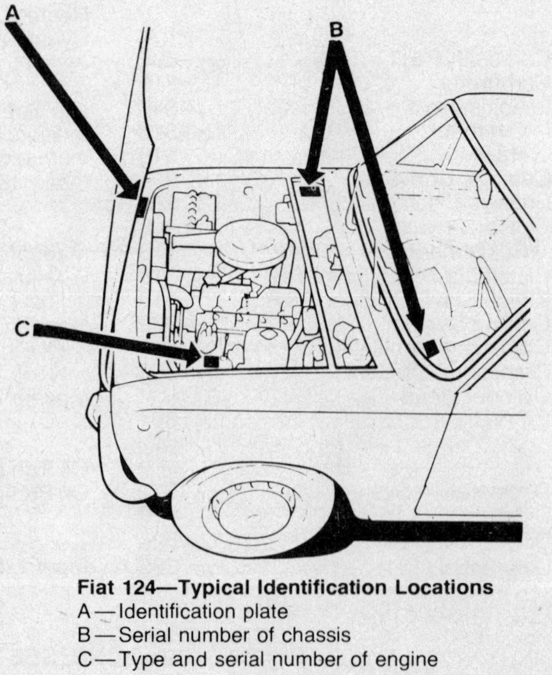

Fiat 124—Typical Identification Locations
A—Identification plate
B—Serial number of chassis
C—Type and serial number of engine

ENGINE IDENTIFICATION

Year	Model	Displacement (cc)	Engine Serial Prefix
1975	128 all types—49 states	1290	128 A1 040 5
	128 all types—California	1290	128 A1 031 5
	X1/9	1290	128 AS 031 5
	131 all types—49 states	1756	132 A1 040 5
	131 all types—California	1756	132 A1 031 5
	24 Sport Coupe, Spider—49 states	1756	132 A1 040 5
	124 Sport Coupe, Spider—California	1756	132 A1 031 5
1976	128 all types—49 states	1290	128 A1 040 6
	128 all types—California	1290	128 A1 031 6
	X1/9—49 states	1290	128 AS 031 6
	X1/9—California	1290	128 AS 031 5
	131 all types—49 states	1756	132 A1 040 5
	131 all types—California	1756	132 A1 031 5
	124 Sport Spider—49 states	1756	132 A1 040 5
	124 Sport Spider—California	1756	132 A1 031 5
1977-81	128 all types-49 states	1290	128 A1 040 6
	128 all types—California	1290	128 A1 031 6
	X1/9—49 states	1290	128 AS 031 6
	X1/9—California	1290	128 AS 031 5
	Brava, 131—manual trans., 49 states	1756	132 A1 040 6
	Brava, 131—auto. trans., Calif.	1756	132 A1 040 5
	Brava, 131—manual trans., Calif.	1756	132 A1 031 6
	Brava, 131—auto trans., Calif.	1756	132 A1 031 5
	124 Sport Spider—49 states	1756	132 A1 040 6
	124 Sport Spider—California	1756	132 A1 031 6
	Brava, Spider—49 states	1995	132 C2 040
	Brava, Spider—California	1995	132 C2 031
	Strada	1498	138 A2 040

GENERAL ENGINE SPECIFICATIONS

Year	Model	Displacement (cc)	SAE net Horsepower @ rpm	Torque (ft. lbs.) @ rpm	Bore & Stroke (in.)	Compression ratio
1975-77	128 all types—49 states	1290	62 @ 6000	67 @ 4000	3.39 x 2.19	8.5:1
	128 all types—California	1290	61 @ 5800	67 @ 4000	3.39 x 2.19	8.5:1
	X1/9	1290	61 @ 5800	67 @ 4000	3.39 x 2.19	8.5:1
	131 all types—49 states	1756	86 @ 6200	90 @ 2800	3.31 x 3.12	8.0:1
	131 all types—California	1756	83 @ 5800	89 @ 2800	3.31 x 3.12	8.0:1
	① 124 Sport Cpe., Spider—49 states ②	1756	86 @ 6200	90 @ 2800	3.31 x 3.12	8.0:1
	① 124 Sport Cpe., Spider—Calif. ②	1756	83 @ 5800	89 @ 2800	3.31 x 3.12	8.0:1
1978-79	128—all w/SE	1290	62 @ 6000	67 @ 4000	3.39 x 2.19	8.5:1
	w/CC	1290	61 @ 5800	67 @ 4000	3.39 x 2.19	8.5:1
	X1/9—w/SE	1290	61.5 @ 5800	67 @ 4000	3.39 x 2.19	8.5:1
	w/CC	1290	61 @ 5800	67 @ 4000	3.39 x 2.19	8.5:1
	124 Spider—w/SE	1756	86 @ 6200	90 @ 2800	3.31 x 3.12	8.0:1
	w/CC	1756	83 @ 6200	89 @ 2800	3.31 x 3.12	8.0:1

GENERAL ENGINE SPECIFICATIONS

Year	Model	Displacement (cc)	SAE net Horsepower @ rpm	Torque (ft. lbs.) @ rpm	Bore x Stroke (in.)	Compression ratio
1978-79	131—all, Brava—all w/SE	1756	86 @ 6200	90 @ 2800	3.31 x 3.12	8.0:1
	w/CC	1756	83 @ 6200	89 @ 2800	3.31 x 3.12	8.0:1
1979-81	X1/9	1500	66 @ 5250	75.9 @ 4000	3.40 x 2.52	8.5:1
	Brava & Spider 2000	2000	80 @ 5000 ③	100 @ 3000 ④	3.31 x 3.54	8.1:1
	Strada	1498	65 @ 5100	75 @ 2900	3.40 x 2.52	8.5:1

① Starting serial numbers: 0213370 Coupe; 0063308 Spider
② Sport Coupe not sold in 1976-77
③ W/F.I.: 102 @ 5500
④ W/F.I.: 110 @ 3000
TC—Twin Cam
SE—Standard exhaust
CC—Catalytic Converter
Prod—Production

TUNE-UP SPECIFICATIONS

Year	Model	Displacement (cc)	SPARK PLUG Type ⑬	SPARK PLUG Gap (in.)	POINTS Gap (in.)	POINTS Dwell (deg.)	Ignition Timing (deg.)	Idle Speed (rpm)	VALVE LASH Intake (in.)	VALVE LASH Exh. (in.)	Intake Valve Opens (deg.)	Mixture (% CO)
1975-77	128 49 states	1290	Champion N9Y	.023	.016	55	TDC	850	.012	.016	10B	1±0.5 ③
	128 California	1290	Champion N9Y	.023	.016	55	TDC	825	.012	.016	10B	3±0.5 ③
	X1/9	1290	Champion N9Y	.023	.016	55	TDC ②	825	.012	.016	10B	3±0.5 ③
	131 49 states	1756	Champion N9Y	.023	.016DP	55	TDC	MT-850 AT-725	.018	.020	5B	MT-0.5±0.2 AT-0.7±0.2
	131 California	1756	Champion N9Y	.023	.016DP	55	TDC	MT-825 AT-725	.018	.020	5B	3±0.5
	124 Sport Cpe., Spider—49 states ⑭	1756	Champion N7Y ④	.023	.016DP	55	TDC	850	.018	.020	5B	0.5±0.2
	124 Sport Cpe., Spider—Calif. ⑭	1756	Champion N7Y ④	.023	.016DP	55	TDC	825	.018	.020	5B	3±0.5
1978	128 all	1290	⑤	.023	.015-.017	52-58	TDC ⑧	800-850	.011-.014	.015-.018	10B	1.5-2.5%
	X1/9	1290	⑥	.027-.031	.015-.017	52-58	TDC ⑧	800-850	.016-.019	.018-.021	5B	1.5-2.5
	124 Spider	1756	⑤	.023-.027	.015-.017 ⑦	52-58	TDC ⑧	800-850	.016-.019	.018-.021	5B	1.5-2.5
	131 all	1756	⑥	.027-.031	.015-.017	52-58	TDC ⑧	800-850	.016-.019	.018-.021	5B	1.5-2.5
	Brava all	1756	⑥	.027-.031	.015-.017	52-58	TDC ⑧	800-850 ⑨	.018	.020	5B	1.5-2.5

TUNE-UP SPECIFICATIONS

Year	Model	Displace-ment (cc)	SPARK PLUG Type ⑬	SPARK PLUG Gap (in.)	POINTS Gap (in.)	POINTS Dwell (deg.)	Ignition Timing (deg.)	Idle Speed (rpm)	VALVE LASH Intake (in.)	VALVE LASH Exh. (in.)	Intake Valve Opens (deg.)	Mixture (% CO)
1979-81	X1/9	1500	⑥	.029	Electronic		800-900	5° BTDC ①	.011-.014	.015-.018	5B	1.0 to 2.0
	Brava, Spider	1995	⑥	.029	Electronic		800-900 ⑪	10° BTDC ⑩	.016-.019	.018-.021	5B	1.0 to 2.5
	Super Brava	1995	⑥	.029	Electronic		800-850 ⑨	5° BTDC ⑫	.016-.019	.018-.021	5B	1.5 to 2.5

NOTE: The underhood specifications sticker often reflects tune-up specification changes made in production. The sticker specifications must be used if they disagree with those in the chart.

① At 800 to 850 rpm
② 10 BTDC on 1976-77 California models
③ 1976-77 models 2% CO ± 0.5
④ 1977 models—N9Y plugs or equivalent
⑤ Regular
Bosch W175T30
Marelli CW7LP
Champion N9Y
AC 42 XLS
⑥ Resistor
Bosch W175TR30
Marelli CW7LPR
Champion RN9Y
AC R42 XLS
⑦ Starting point gap—.012-.019 inch
⑧ w/auto trans—5 BTDC
⑨ w/auto trans—700-750 rpm
⑩ w/MT at 800 to 850 rpm
w/AT at 700 to 750 rpm
⑪ w/AT at 700 to 800 rpm
⑫ 0° BTDC on standard transmission with no catalytic converter
⑬ Original equipment spark plugs; similar characteristic plugs of different manufacture may be used without damage to the engine
⑭ Sport Coupe not available in 1976-77
DP Dual point distributor; see text for explanation
MT Manual transmission
AT Automatic transmission

FIRING ORDERS

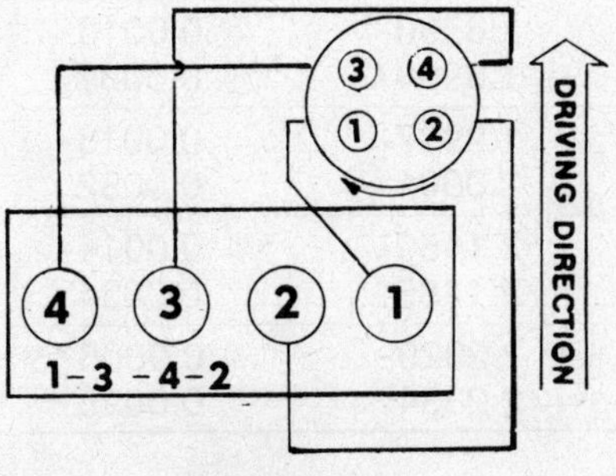

1975-79 128

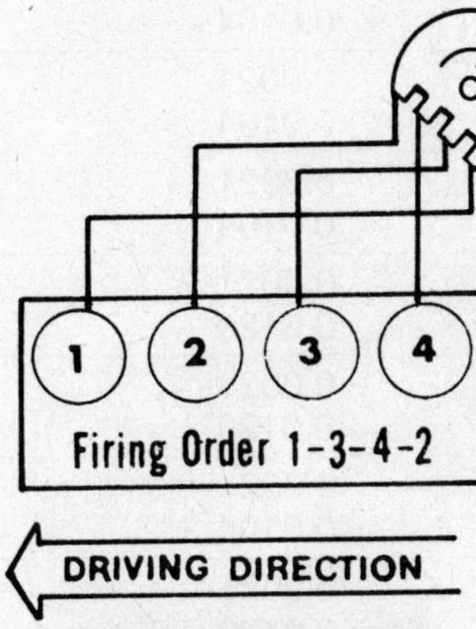

1975-79 124 Sport Spider
1975 and later 131
1979 and later Brava

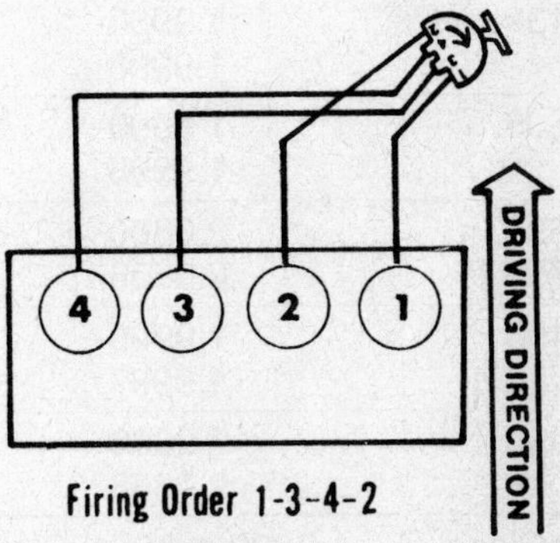

1975-81 X1/9

CAPACITIES

Year	Model	Engine Disp. (cc)	Crankcase (qts) With Filter	Crankcase (qts) Without Filter	Trans-axle (pts)	Transmission Manual (pts)	Transmission Automatic (pts)	Rear Axle (pts)	Fuel Tank (gals)	Cooling System (qts)
1975-79	128 Sedan, Wagon	1116, 1290	4.5	4.5	6.6	—	—	—	9.5	6.8
	128 SL, 3P	1290	4.5	4.5	6.6	—	—	—	12.5	7.0
1975-81	X1/9	1290	4.5	4.5	6.6	—	—	—	12.7	11.6
		1498	—	4.5	—	7.0	—	—	12.2	11.6
1975-79	124 Special Sedan and Wagon	1438	4.0	3.5	—	2.8	6.0	2.8	Sed. 10.3 Wag. 12.5	8.0
	124 TC Sedan and and TC Wagon	1592	4.5	4.0	—	3.0	6.0	2.8	Sed. 9.6 Wag. 11.4	8.0
	124 Sport Coupe and Spider	1608, 1592, 1756	4.5	4.0	—	3.5	—	2.8	11.4	8.0 ①
	131 Sedan and Wagon Brava Sedan, Wagon	1756	4.5	4.0	—	3.8	6.0 ②	2.8	12.2	8.0
1980-81	Brava	1995	5.5	4.3	—	3.5	60	2.8	12.2	8.5
	Spider	1995	5.5	4.3	—	3.5	60	2.8	11.4	8.0
1980-81	Strada	1498	4.75	3.75	7.0	—	—	—	12.1	7.5

① 1975-77 models; 8.8 qts.
② 12 pints to refill after total disassembly and rebuild
Sed. Sedan
Wag. Wagon

CRANKSHAFT AND CONNECTING ROD SPECIFICATIONS

(All measurements in inches)

Engine Displacement (cc)	Crankshaft Main Bearing Journal Dia.	Crankshaft Main Bearing Oil Clearance	Crankshaft End-Play	Crankshaft Thrust on No.	Connecting Rod Journal Dia.	Connecting Rod Oil Clearance
1116	1.9990-1.9998	0.0019-0.0037	0.0021-0.0104	5	1.7913-1.7920	0.0014-0.0034
1290	1.9994-2.0002	0.0016-0.0033	0.0021-0.0104	5	1.7913-1.7920	0.0014-0.0034
1438	1.9990-1.9998	0.0019-0.0037	0.0021-0.0104	5	1.7916-1.7924	0.0010-0.0029
1608	1.9990-1.9998	0.0020-0.0037	0.0021-0.0120	5	1.8990-1.8994 ①	0.0018-0.0032
1592, 1756	2.0860-2.0868	0.0020-0.0037	0.0021-0.0120	5	1.9997-2.0001 ②	0.0018-0.0032
1498	1.9990-1.9997	0.0019-0.0037	0.0021-0.0104	—	2.1459-2.1465	0.0014-0.0034
1995	2.0860-2.0868	0.0012-0.0030	0.0021-0.0120	—	2.2329-2.2334	0.0008-0.0025

① Class "A", 1.8990-1.8994; Class "B", 1.8986-1.8990 in.
② Class "A", 1.9997-2.0001; Class "B", 1.9993-1.9997 in.

VALVE SPECIFICATIONS

Engine Displacement (cc)	Seat Angle (deg)	Face Angle (deg)	Spring Test Pressure (lbs. @ in.) Inner	Spring Test Pressure (lbs. @ in.) Outer	Stem to Guide Clearance (in.) Intake	Stem to Guide Clearance (in.) Exhaust	Stem Diameter (in.) Intake	Stem Diameter (in.) Exhaust
1116, 1290, 1498	45	45.5	32.7 @ 1.220	75.5 @ 1.417	0.0012-0.0026	0.0012-0.0026	0.3139-0.3146	0.3139-0.3146
1438	45	45.5	30.6 @ 1.173	63.5 @ 1.327	0.0008-0.0021	0.0010-0.0023	0.3143-0.3149	0.3142-0.3148
1608, 1592, 1756, 1995	45	45.5	32.7 @ 1.220	85.5 @ 1.417	0.0012-0.0026	0.0012-0.0026	0.3139-0.3146	0.3139-0.3146

PISTON AND RING SPECIFICATIONS

Engine Displacement (cc)	Piston Clearance	Ring Gap Top Compression	Ring Gap Top Oil Control	Ring Gap Bottom Oil Control	Ring Side Clearance Top Compression	Ring Side Clearance Top Oil Control	Ring Side Clearance Bottom Oil Control
1116	0.0020-0.0028	0.0118-0.0177	0.0079-0.0138	0.0079-0.0138	0.0018-0.0030	0.0006-0.0022	0.0008-0.0020
1290	0.0028-0.0035	0.0118-0.0176	0.0118-0.0176	0.0098-0.0157	0.0018-0.0030	0.0016-0.0028	0.0012-0.0024
1438	0.0024-0.0031	0.0118-0.0176	0.0079-0.0138	0.0079-0.0138	0.0018-0.0030	0.0012-0.0028	0.0012-0.0024
1592	0.0025-0.0033	0.0118-0.0176	0.0079-0.0138	0.0079-0.0138	0.0018-0.0030	0.0011-0.0027	0.0011-0.0024
1608, 1756	0.0016-0.0024	0.0118-0.0176	0.0079-0.0138	0.0079-0.0138	0.0018-0.0030	0.0011-0.0027	0.0011-0.0024
1498	0.0011-0.0019	0.0118-0.0177	0.0118-0.0177	0.0098-0.0157	0.0018-0.0030	0.0016-0.0028	0.0011-0.0024
1995	0.0016-0.0024	0.0118-0.0177	0.0118-0.0177	0.0098-0.0157	0.0018-0.0030	0.0011-0.0027	0.0011-0.0024

TORQUE SPECIFICATIONS

(All readings in ft. lbs.)

Displacement (cc)	Cylinder Head Bolts	Rods Bearing Bolts	Main Bearing Bolts	Crankshaft Pulley Bolt Chart	Flywheel to Crankshaft Bolts	Manifolds Intake	Manifolds Exhaust
1116	61	40	61	101	61	22	22
1290, 1498	69	36	58	101	61	22	22
1438	58	36	58	87	61	18	18
1608	61	36	58	87	61	18	18
1592,	54	47 ②	83 ①	87	61	18	18
1756	61	—	—	—	—	—	—
1995	61	54	83	181	105	18	18

① Smaller front main bearing cap bolt—58 ft. lbs.
② 1977 and later 131 models—36 ft. lbs.

TORQUE SEQUENCES

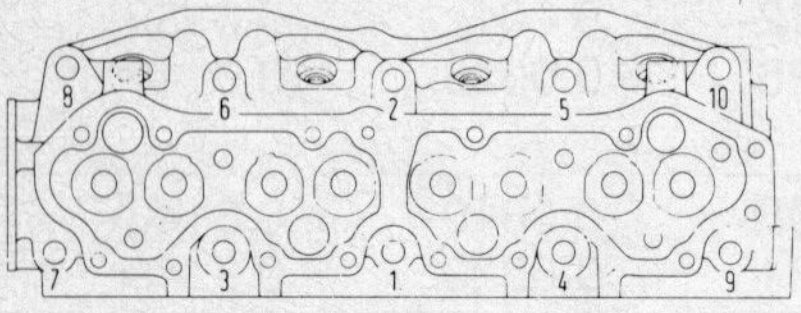

128, X1/9

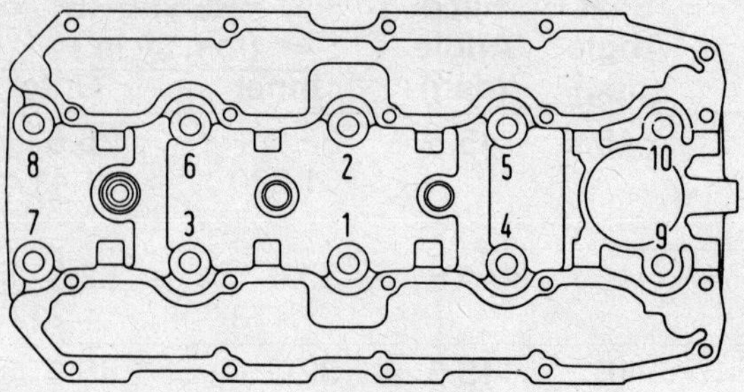

124, 131, Brava

ALTERNATOR AND REGULATOR SPECIFICATIONS

		ALTERNATOR			REGULATOR						
						1st STAGE		2nd STAGE			
Year	Model	Part No. or Manufacturer	Output Current @ 14v	Max. Output (amps)	Part No. or Manufacturer	Testing Current (amps)	Regulating Voltage (volts)	Testing Current (amps)	Regulating Voltage (volts)	Contact Gap (in.)	Armature to Core Gap (in.)
1975-79 1975-81 1980-81	128, X1/9 Strada	Marelli A124-14V 60A Variant 1 ①	60	70	Marelli RC2/12E ①	40-45 ①	13.7-14.2	10-14	14.2	.018	.059 ③
1975-79 1979-81	124 Spider 2000	Fiat A12M 124/12/42M	42	53	Marelli RC2/12B	25-35	13.5-14.0	2-12	14.2	.018	.059 ③
1975-78 1975-81	131 Brava, Strada	Marelli A-124-14V-44A ②	43	53	Marelli RC2/12D ②	25-35 ②	13.5-14.0	10-14	14.2	.018	.059 ③

① X1/9 not equipped with A/C uses Marelli A124-14V-44A alternator and Marelli RC2/12D regulator with 1st stage testing current of 25-35 amps

② 131 models equipped with A/C use Marelli A124-14V-60A alternator and Marelli RC2/12E regulator with 1st stage testing current of 40-45 amps

③ 1978-80 models use electronic non-adjustable regulators

BATTERY AND STARTER SPECIFICATIONS

All cars use 12 volt, negative ground electrical systems

			STARTER							
			LOCK TEST			NO LOAD TEST				
Year	Model	Battery Amp Hour Capacity	Amps	Volts	Torque (ft. lbs.)	Amps	Volts	rpm	Brush Spring Tension (oz.)	Manufacturer or Part No.
1975-79 1975-81	128, X1/9	50 ①	370	8.3	7.9	35	11.7	7000	40	Fiat E84-0.8/12 Variant 1
1975-81	All except 128, X1/9	60	530	7	12.6	28	12	5200	35	Fiat E100-1.3/12

① X1/9—60 amp hour battery

BRAKE SPECIFICATIONS

All measurements given are in inches unless noted

Year	Model	Lug Nut Torque (ft. lbs.)	Master Cylinder Bore	Brake Disc Minimum Thickness	Brake Disc Maximum Run-Out	Brake Drum Diameter	Brake Drum Max. Machine O/S	Brake Drum Max. Wear Limit	Minimum Lining Thickness Front	Minimum Lining Thickness Rear
1975-79 1980-81	128 Strada	50	0.75	Regrind 0.368 Wear limit 0.354	0.006	7.2929- 7.3043	7.3234- 7.3358	7.3554	0.08	0.06
1975-78 1979-81	124 Spider 2000	51	0.75	Regrind front—0.368 rear—0.371 Wear limit 0.354	0.006	— ①	—	—	0.08	0.08
1975-81	131, Brava Sedan, Wagon	51	0.75	Regrind 0.368 Wear limit 0.354	0.006	8.9882- 9.000	9.0182- 9.0300	9.0551	0.06	0.18
1975-81	X1/9	50	0.75	Regrind 0.368 Wear limit 0.354	0.006	— ①	—	—	0.08	0.08

① Disc brakes on four wheels

WHEEL ALIGNMENT SPECIFICATIONS

(Applies only to unladen vehicle)

Year	Model	Caster Front (deg)	Camber Front (deg)	Camber Rear (deg)	Toe-In Front (in.)	Toe-In Rear (in.)
1975-81 1979-81	128 Sedan, Wagon Strada	1 1/6P to 2 1/6P ④	1 1/6P to 2 1/6P	2/3N to 1/3P ① 1/6N to 1 1/6P ②	−0.120+0.040 ⑤	+0.059+0.217
1975-81	128SL, 3P	1 1/6P to 2 1/6P	1/2P to 1 1/2P ③	2/3N to 1 2/3N	−0.060+0.100	+0.079+0.236
1975	124 Sport Coupe	2 1/2P to 3 1/2P	1/4N to 1/2P	Fixed	+0.200+0.360	Fixed
1975-78 1979-81	124 Sport Spider Spider 2000	2 2/3P to 3 2/3P	1/3N to 2/3P	Fixed	+0.160+0.320 ⑥	Fixed
1975-81	X1/9	6 1/2P to 7 1/2P	0 to 1N	1 1/6N to 2 1/6N	+0.080+0.240	+0.360+0.510
1975-78 1979-81	131 Sedan, Wagon Brava Sedan, Wagon Brava, Super Brava	3 1/4P to 4 1/4P	1/4P to 1 1/4P	Fixed	+0.236+0.393 ⑥	Fixed

NOTE: Toe-in = + sign
Toe-out = − sign

① Sedan
② Wagon
③ 1974 models; 5/6P to 1 1/2P
④ Strada 1 1/2P to 2 1/2P
⑤ Strada 10.157 —10.314
⑥ 1979-81 Spider 2000 & Brava + 0.157 to + 0.315
P Positive
N Negative

TUNE-UP PROCEDURES

Spark Plugs

Spark plugs should be cleaned and re-gapped at 6000 mile intervals, and replaced every 12,000 miles.

Since all late model Fiat engines use aluminum alloy cylinder heads, care should be exercised to prevent damage to the spark plug threads. When reinstalling used plugs, clean the threads and lightly oil the threads. Do not overtighten the spark plugs. Thread the plugs into the head by hand until tight, and then torque to specifications (see chart) using a torque wrench of known accuracy. All that is necessary is to seat the plug snugly against the head, forming a good compression seal.

If cross-threaded or stripped threads are encountered, see the engine rebuilding section at the end of this book.

Breaker Points and Condenser

NOTE: 1979 2000 cc models have electronic ignition, eliminating the breaker points and condenser. Ignition timing (10°B) is checked in the usual manner. On 1979-1980-1981 models no timing adjustment is necessary unless distributor has been removed.

Electronic Ignition Test

1. Set key to ON position.
2. Check that voltage at primary coil terminal equals battery voltage.
3. Repeat test at tachometer coil terminal. Voltage should be within 0.3 of battery voltage.
4. If not, check coil primary winding for open circuits.
5. Resistance across low coil terminals should be 0.8 ohms.

NOTE: Do not remove ignition cables with engine running or while attempts are made at starting. Do not ground tachometer lead.

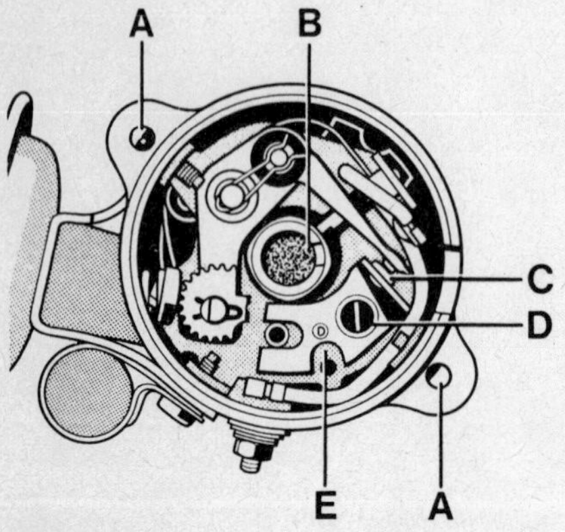

B. Lubricating wick
C. Contact gap
D. Adjusting screw
E. Adjusting slot

Ignition points—1975 and later 128, X1/9

ELECTRONIC IGNITION TEST SPECIFICATIONS

Pick up coil resistance — wires from terminal 7 and 31d of module	890 to 1285 ohms
Pick up insulator—wire from terminal 7 to the distributor body	∞
Primary input —positive coil terminal to ground	6 volts or more
Control module ground — negative battery terminal to module support mount	0.2 ohms or less
Coil primary resistance — disconnect primary coil wires	1.1 to 1.7 ohms
Primary resister —disconnected	0.85 to 0.95 ohms
Coil secondary resistance to primary	6,000 to 10,000 ohms
Stator pole to reluctor gap	0.3 to 0.5 mm (.011 to .019 in.)
Control module —check only after all other components have checked out good	Disconnect the coil tower wire. Position wire 5mm —¼ in. from ground. Rotate the engine manually and observe spark as each tooth passes the pick up.

Ignition Distributor Test

1. With key in OFF position remove connector from module.
2. Place ohmmeter leads on module connector.
3. Reading should be 700-800 ohms.
4. Remove distributer cap and check rotor arm resistance.
5. Should be about 5000 ohms.

NOTE: If above tests indicate proper results module is at fault.

Breaker points should be inspected and re-gapped at 6000 mile intervals, and replaced with the condenser(s) every 12,000 miles.

REMOVAL AND INSTALLATION

128 and X1/9

NOTE: On the X1/9, Fiat recommends servicing the points and condenser with the distributor removed. See "Distributor Removal and Installation" in the Engine Electrical section.

1. Unsnap the two distributor cap clasps and remove the cap with high tension wires connected. On some models, the cap is retained by two screws that stay with the cap.
2. Pull straight up and remove the rotor. At this time, it is good practice to apply a few drops of light (10W) oil to the lubricating wick at the top of the distributor shaft.
3. Disconnect the breaker points lead and condenser lead at the primary connection. Remove the condenser bracket retaining screws, and replace the condenser. Remove the breaker point retaining screws (and wire clip on 1975-79 128 and X1/9 models) and remove the points. Apply a light film of silicone based grease to the distributor cam lobes. Wipe off any excess.
4. Install new breaker points and condenser. To adjust point gap, rotate the crankshaft pulley until the breaker point rubbing block rests on the high point of the distributor cam lobe. Slightly loosen the breaker points retaining screw and insert the proper sized feeler gauge between the point contacts. Move the fixed arm in or out to obtain the specified clearance. Tighten the retaining screw.
5. Connect the electrical leads for the breaker points and condenser. Install the cap and rotor.
6. Check dwell angle and ignition timing.

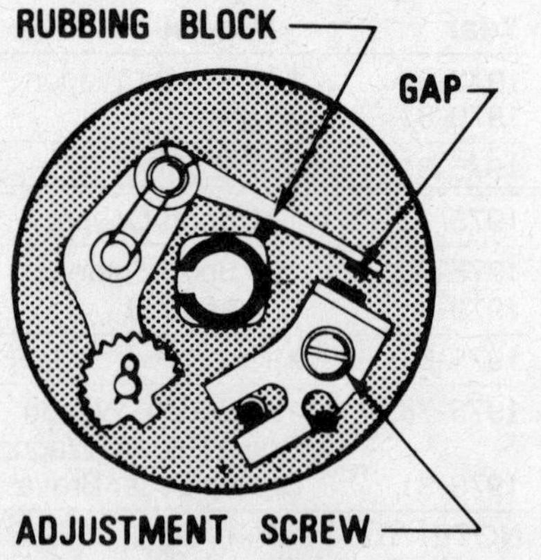

1975-79 X1/9, 128—Setting point gap—typical

131, 1975-79 124 Sport Coupe and Spider (1756 cc)

NOTE: These models are equipped with a dual point distributor. The dual point sets do not operate simultaneously; one set is used for starting, and the other for running. The starting set provides 10 degrees of additional spark advance during starter cranking. The running set returns the spark timing to Top Dead Center. On 1975-79 models with automatic choke, the starting set is actuated by coolant temperatures of 36-46° F or less. On both systems, the starting set cuts out and the running set takes over when full cold oil pressure is reached.

1. Remove the two distributor cap retaining screws. The screws will stay with the cap. Remove the cap.
2. Pull straight up and remove the rotor. Apply a few drops of light (10W) oil to the lubricating wick atop the distributor shaft.
3. Crank the engine over, or rotate the crankshaft pulley by hand or push the car in 4th gear, until both point sets open with their rubbing blocks on the high points of the distributor cam lobes. Disconnect both breaker

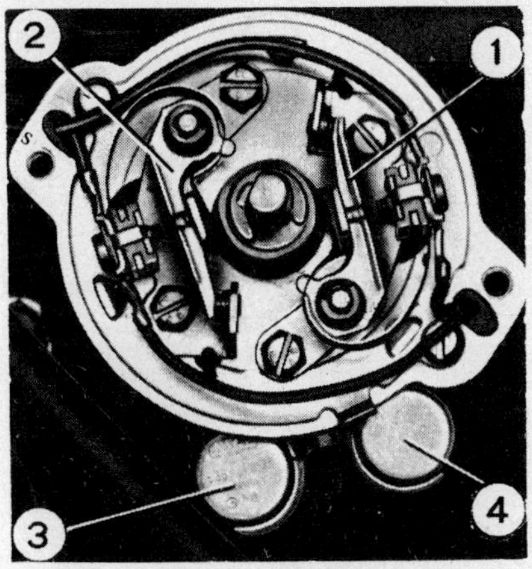

1. Main breaker points
2. Auxiliary breaker points
3. Capacitor, main breaker points
4. Capacitor, auxiliary breaker points

Ignition points—1975-79 124 Sport Spider and Coupe, 1975-78 131

point leads and condenser leads at the primary connections. Remove and replace both point sets and condensers. Apply a light film of silicone based grease to the distributor cam lobes. Wipe off any excess.

4. Adjust the point gap for both breaker point sets by inserting the feeler gauge between the point contacts; 0.012-0.019 in. for the starting set, and 0.014-0.017 in. for the running set. The running points are connected to the green wire and the starting points are connected to the green/black wire. If the points need adjustment, insert a screwdriver in the adjusting slot and twist it one way or the other to change the gap.

NOTE: For longer service, set the gap to the maximum specification, as the rubbing block will wear down in service and slowly close the gap.

5. Install the rotor. Install the distributor cap.
6. Check dwell angle and ignition timing.

Dwell Angle

Dwell angle is not applicable on electronic ignition.

Dwell angle is the amount of degrees of distributor shaft rotation that the points remain closed (making contact). Increasing the point gap decreases dwell, while decreasing the point gap increases dwell. Dwell angle may be checked with the engine running, or with the engine cranking over at starter speed. With a running engine, the dwell angle reading should be fairly constant. When the engine is being cranked over, the dwell angle reading will fluctuate between zero and the maximum figure for that angle.

Dwell angle should always be checked after adjusting or installing new points. Using a dwell meter of known accuracy, connect the negative lead to a good ground (such as an engine bolt) and the positive lead to the primary distributor connection at the coil (the small wire that leads from the distributor to the coil). On 128 and X1/9 models, disconnect and plug the vacuum retard signal line at the distributor.

NOTE: Leave the line connected on high altitude versions.

On all models with dual points, both sets must be checked separately. To check the running set of points, first locate the ignition mode selector relay. Trace the wires from the distributor until you locate it. Usually, it is located on the passenger's side fender well. Remove the relay from the plug and connect a jumper wire between the Power side and the Running side as shown in the illustration. Connect the dwell-meter positive lead to the green disributor lead. Crank the engine and check the dwell. If the dwell needs adjusting, remove the distributor cap and adjust the point gap. To check the dwell on the starting set of points, leave one end of the jumper wire on the power side of the relay and connect the other end to the Starting side as shown. Connect the dwell meter positive lead to the green/black lead at the distributor. Crank the engine and check the dwell.

On all other Fiat models, dwell is adjusted in the normal manner. Simply connect the dwell meter positive lead to the distributor primary wire and the negative lead to a good ground. When adjusting the dwell, remember that increasing the point gap decreases the dwell, while decreasing the point gap increases dwell.

Once you have set the dwell, the ignition timing must be checked. A 1° increase in dwell results in the ignition timing being retarded 2° and vice versa.

Ignition Timing

Fiat recommends that the ignition timing be checked at 6000 mile intervals, or whenever the breaker points, dwell angle setting, or distributor body is disturbed. All timing checks are made with the engine warmed to operating temperature, and idling in neutral (manual transmission cars) or Drive (automatic equipped cars). Timing on models with electronic ignition is checked in the usual way.

124 WAGON, 124 SPORT COUPE AND SPIDER (SINGLE POINT MODELS)

1. The first step in timing the engine is to locate the timing marks. The marks are located on the front cover. There will be three of them and, in accordance with Fiat practice, the longest mark is TDC. Find the correct mark and highlight it with chalk or luminous paint. Find the reference mark on the crank pulley and mark it also.
2. Connect the timing light according to the manufacturer's instructions.

A = 10° (Adv.)
B = 5° (Adv.)
C = 10° (TDC)

Timing marks—124 Sport Coupe, Spider and 131

3. Start the engine and let it warm up. Check the idle speed and make sure it is correct before setting the timing.
4. Aim the timing light at the marks on the front cover and the crank pulley. The marks should coincide. If the marks are not aligned with the timing light flashes, turn off the engine.
5. Loosen the distributor hold-down bolt and turn the distributor to alter the timing. To retard the spark, turn the distributor slightly in the direction of distributor rotor rotation. To advance the spark, turn the distributor slightly in the direction opposite that of distributor rotation. Tighten the hold-down nut.
6. Restart the engine and check the timing. If the timing marks are still not aligned, repeat the previous step. If you have never performed this operation, you'll discover that it takes a bit of practice to get it right.
7. After you have the timing set correctly, recheck the idle speed as it may have changed.

128 AND X1/9

1. 1975 and later 128's and X1/9's are equipped with two sets of timing marks—one set is in the conventional position on the front cover and the other set is located on the flywheel, visible through a small opening in the bellhousing. Early 128's and X1/9's had only the front cover timing marks, which are fairly difficult to see. On 1975 and later 128's,

remove the spare tire and you'll see the marks.

2. Locate the correct mark and highlight it with paint or chalk. If you're timing the engine through the bellhousing, tap the engine over with the starter or turn it over by hand until you can find the punch mark on the flywheel. Put a spot of paint or chalk on it.

3. Connect the timing light according to the manufacturer's instructions.

4. Start the engine and let it warm up. Check the idle speed and make sure it is correct before setting the timing.

A = 0° (Adv.)
B = 5° (Adv.)
C = 10° (T.D.C.)

Timing marks on flywheel—1975 and later 128

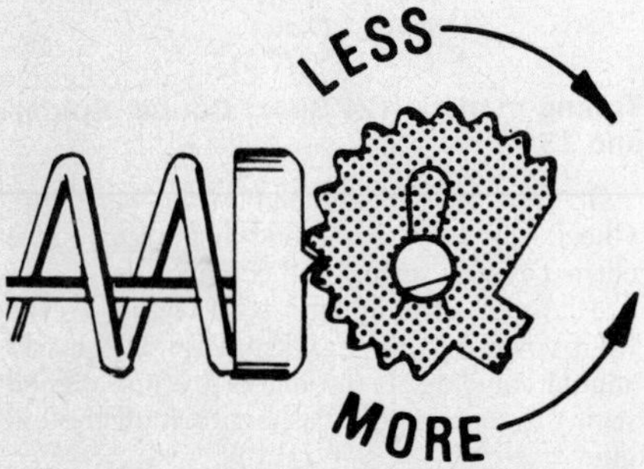

Adjusting retard with the distributor eccentric star wheel—X1/9, 128

5. Disconnect the vacuum line from the distributor and plug it. Remember this is a vacuum *retard*, not a vacuum advance.

6. Aim the timing light at the marks. The marks should coincide. Keep in mind that with the vacuum line disconnected, the timing should be 10° BTDC. If the timing needs adjusting, stop the engine, loosen the distributor hold-down clamp and turn the distributor in the engine.

7. Reconnect the vacuum retard line. The timing should now be TDC. You may have to mark the timing marks with different paint colors to distinguish between them.

8. If the retard mechanism has not provided approximately 10 degrees retard, stop the engine and remove the cap and rotor. Depress the retard follower cap and rotate the eccentric star wheel to change the amount of retard. Counterclockwise equals more retard and clockwise equals less retard.

NOTE: On high altitude versions, simply leave the vacuum line connected and time the engine. There is no need to check the ignition retard.

9. After the timing is set, recheck the idle speed as it may have changed.

ALL DUAL POINT MODELS

1. Locate the timing marks on the front cover and mark them with paint. Mark the pulley also. The longest mark is TDC and the shortest mark is 10° BTDC. The middle mark is 5 ° BTDC.

2. Start the engine and let it warm up. Check to make sure the idle is correct before setting the timing.

3. Locate the ignition mode selector relay. This is generally found on the passenger's side fender well. Remove the top of the relay and connect a jumper wire (with blade ends) between the Power and Running terminals.

4. Connect the timing light according to the manufacturer's instructions.

5. Start the engine and aim the timing light at the marks. The TDC mark on the front cover and the reference mark on the pulley should coincide. If they don't, stop the engine, loosen the distributor hold-down clamp and rotate the distributor as necessary to obtain a reading of TDC. Tighten the hold-down clamp once you get the timing right.

6. Shut the engine off and connect the Starting and Power terminals in the relay block. Start the engine and check the timing. It should now be 10° BTDC. If it isn't, adjust the amount of advance by changing the dwell angle of the starting points. If the timing is less than 10° BTDC, increase the point gap. If it's more than 10° BTDC, decrease the point gap.

7. Once you have the starting timing correct, remove the jumper wire and replace the relay.

8. Check and reset the idle speed if necessary.

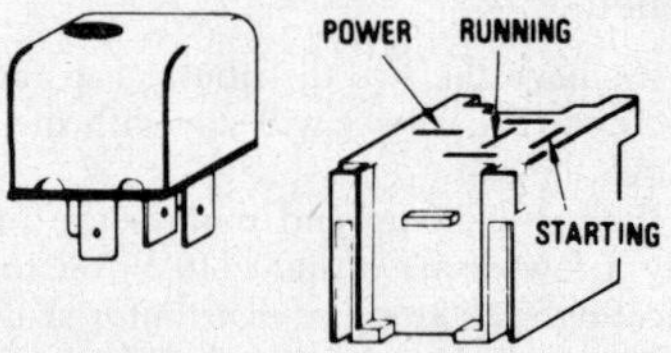

Locate ignition mode selector relay and terminal position on plastic base 1975-79 124, 131, Brava

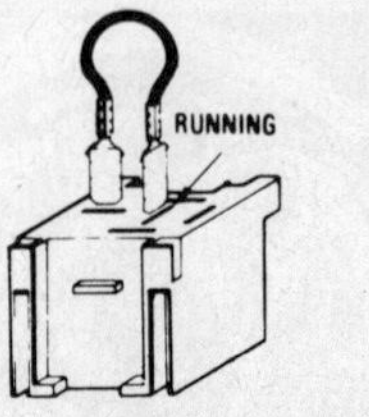

Jumper wire in power to running position

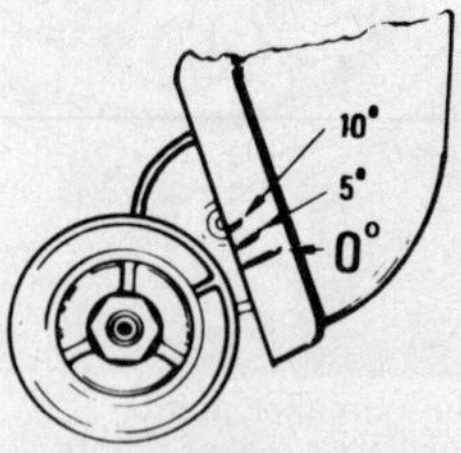

Timing marks aligned with the running points—1975-79 124, 131, Brava

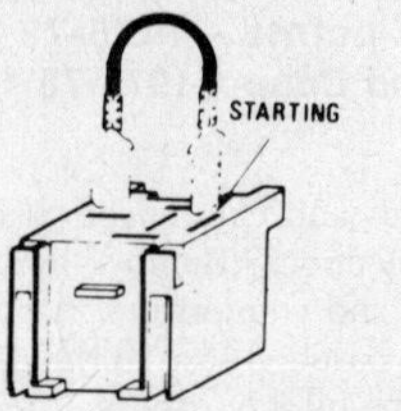

Jumper wire in power to starting position

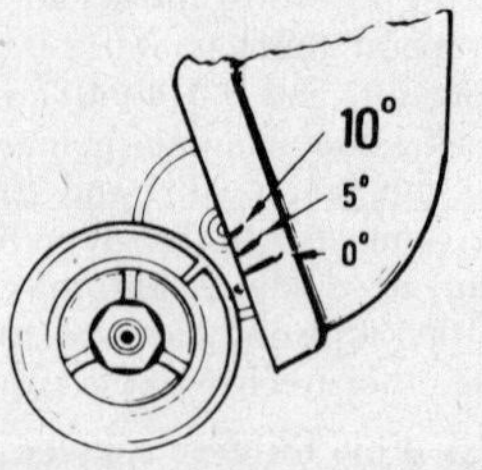

Timing marks advanced 10 degrees with the starting points—1975-79 124, 131, Brava

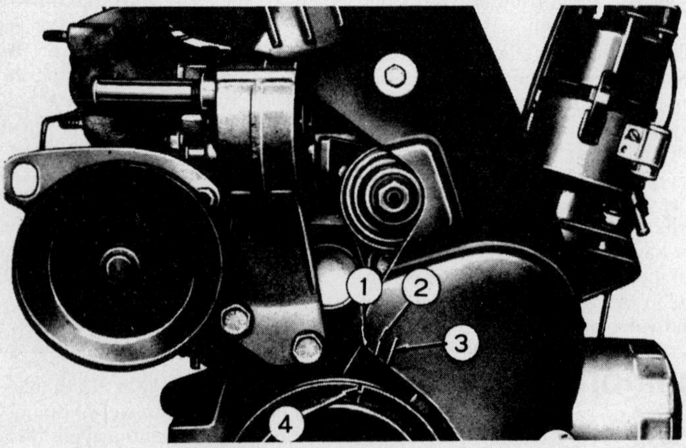

1. 10° BTDC
2. 5° BTDC
3. 0° TDC
4. Timing mark on the crankshaft pulley

Timing marks—128, X1/9

Valve Clearance Adjustment

Valve clearance should be checked every 12,000 miles—sooner if the head is removed or if excessive valve train noise is noticed. On both single and double overhead cam engines (128, X1/9, 131, 124 Sport, valve clearance is adjusted by the thickness of the Shim (plate) between the cam lobe and tappet bucket, requiring special service tools.

128, X1/9, 131 and 124 Sport

NOTE: Special tools required for this job include a tappet depressor tool #A 60421 (128, X1/9), or #A 60422 (124, 131), a pair of curved tip needle nose pliers (such as #A 87001), a lever #A 60443 (Twin cam only), and a compressed air source and air chuck to blow out the old adjusting shim.

NOTE: The engine must be cold for a valve clearance check.

1. Remove the retaining screws and remove the camshaft cover.
2. Turn the crankshaft until the lobe controlling the tappet being checked is pointing upward and is at a right angle to the tappet plate.

NOTE: To simplify crankshaft rotation on the 128 and X1/9, place the transmission in 4th gear and raise the car so that the right front wheel on the 128, or right rear wheel on the X1/9, is free to rotate. Turn the free wheel to rotate the engine to the valve adjustment positions.

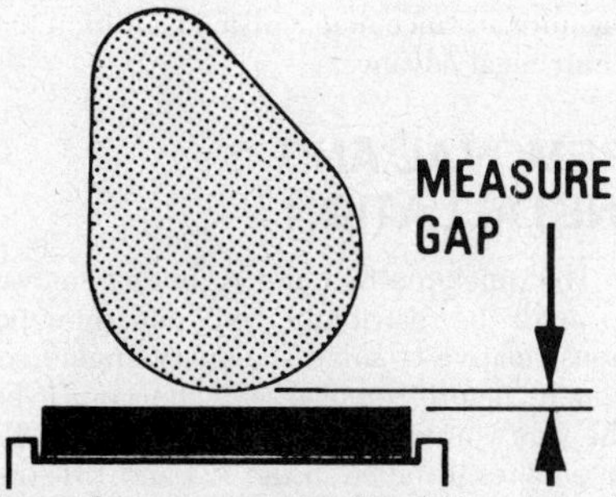

Measuring gap on overhead cam lobe to tappet plate

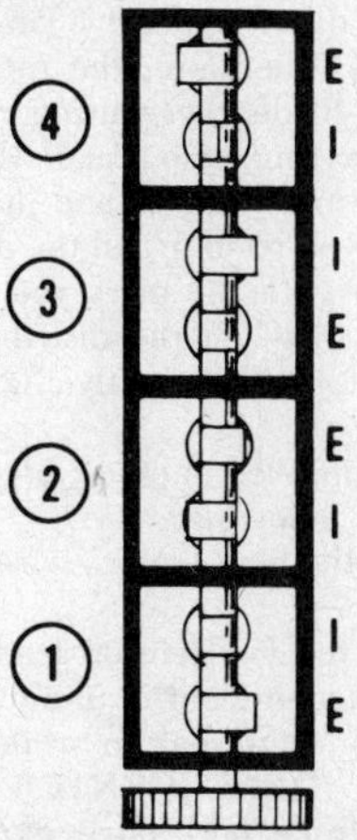

Single overhead cam—Cylinder and valve location

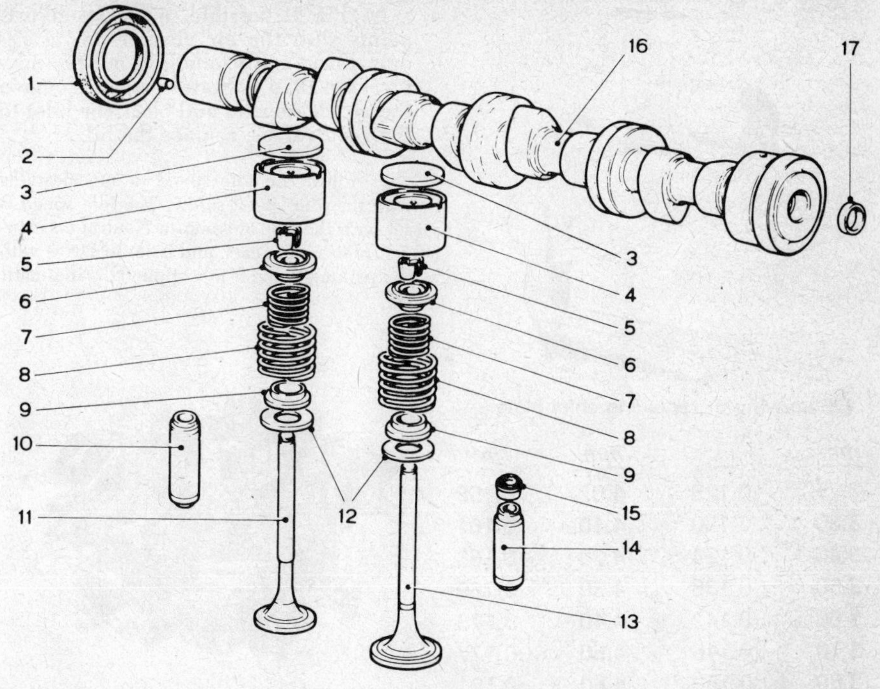

1. Seal
2. Dowel
3. Plates of adjusting valve clearance
4. Tappets
5. Locks
6. Upper cups
7. Inner spring
8. Outer springs
9. Lower cups
10. Exhaust valve guide
11. Exhaust valve
12. Flat washer
13. Intake valve
14. Intake valve guide
15. Oil seal
16. Camshaft
17. Welch plug

Exploded view of single overhead cam valve mechanism—typical

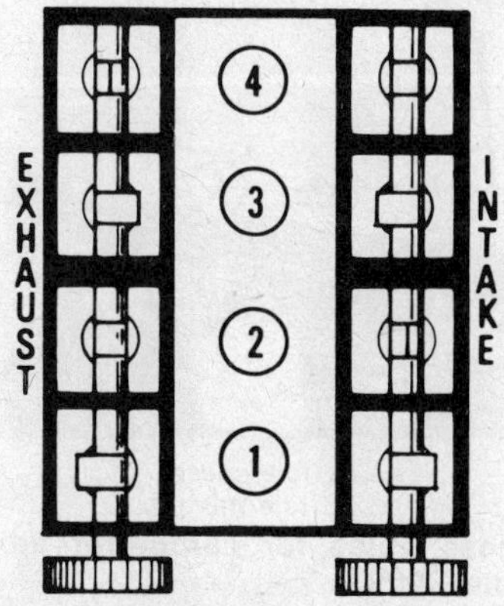

Double overhead cam—Cylinder and valve location

3. Measure the clearance between the tappet plate and the camshaft lobe with a feeler gauge.
4. If the clearance is not at the proper specification, a tappet plate of the required thickness will have to be installed.
5. To remove the old tappet plate (shim), the tappet must be depressed and held in that position. On the 128 and X1/9, this is accomplished with special tool #A 60421 (see illustration). However, on the 124 and 131 twin cam engines, this is a two step process. First, depress the tappet with special lever #60443 or rotate the camshaft until the lobe depresses the tappet. Then, install the tappet clamping tool #60422 which will keep the tappet depressed. If you rotated the camshaft to depress the tappet, rotate it again to give clearance for plate removal. Finally, using com-

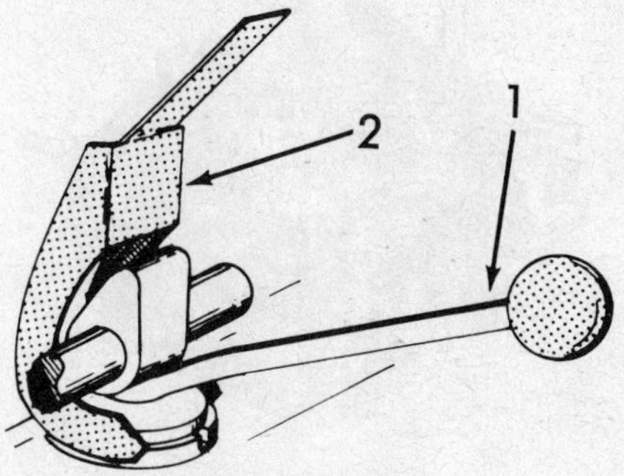

1. Depress Tappet
2. Tappet retaining tool

Preparing to change shim plate—Double overhead cam type

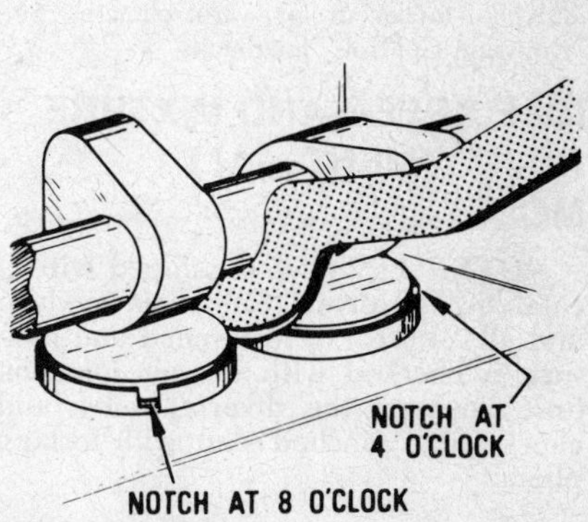

Preparing to change shim plate—Single overhead cam type

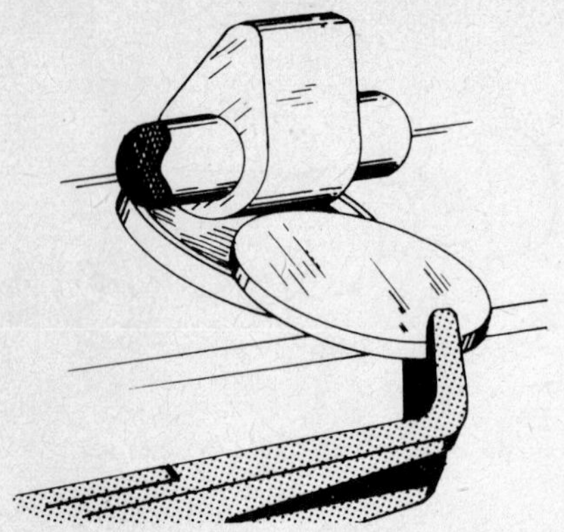

Removing or replacing shim plate

mm	in.	mm	in.
3.25	0.128	4.02	0.158
3.30	0.130	4.10	0.161
3.40	0.134	4.20	0.165
3.50	0.138	4.30	0.169
3.60	0.142	4.40	0.173
3.70	0.146	4.50	0.177
3.80	0.150	4.60	0.181
3.90	0.154	4.70	0.185
4.00	0.157	4.80	0.189

Valve shim size

pressed air through the notch in the tappet or needle nose pliers, or both, remove the old plate.

6. Install a new tappet plate after determining its thickness by comparing it to the clearance measurement taken in Step 3.

Tappet clearance adjustment plates are available in a range of thicknesses from 0.146 in. to 0.185 in. with a difference between each plate of 0.002 in.

The thickness of the plate is shown on one of the plate's flat sides. This side should be installed facing the tappet. It is recommended that the plate's thickness be checked to make sure that it is actually the thickness specified.

Carburetor

Often mistaken for an improperly adjusted carburetor is an incorrectly adjusted air cleaner climatic setting. This adjustment provides warmed intake air for cold climates and cool intake air for warm climates. See "Emission Controls" for details.

IDLE SPEED AND MIXTURE ADJUSTMENT—ALL MODELS

NOTE: On models equipped with a catalytic converter (California models, and all X1/9 cars), idle speed and mixture is checked with the air injection hose between the diverter valve and check valve pinched shut with locking pliers.

1. Start the engine and warm to operating temperature (176° F min.). Make sure the choke plate is open.

NOTE: If possible, make all adjustments with the air cleaner on, as removal may artificially lean out the mixture. On 1979 49 State versions, remove the air cleaner lid and block the inlet to the reed valves; replace the lid.

2. Adjust the idle speed to specifications with the idle speed screw. The idle speed is set with the transmission in Neutral on manual transmission cars, and is set in Drive with the parking brake firmly applied on automatic cars.

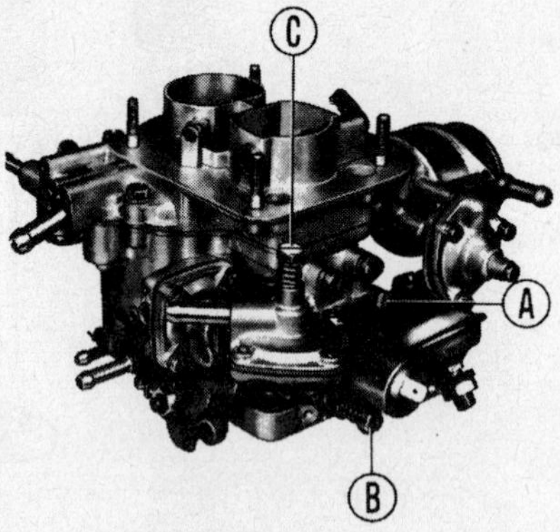

A. Idle speed screw
B. Idle mixture screw
C. Fast idle screw (Air conditioned cars only)

Idle speed and mixture—128, X1/9

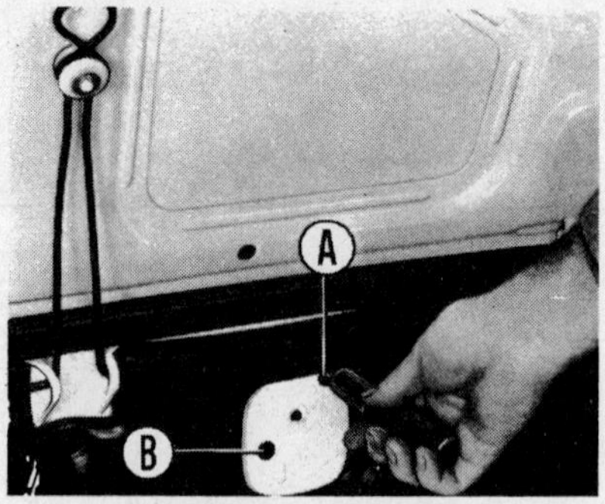

A. Idle speed
B. Idle mixture

Access holes for carburetor adjustments—X1/9

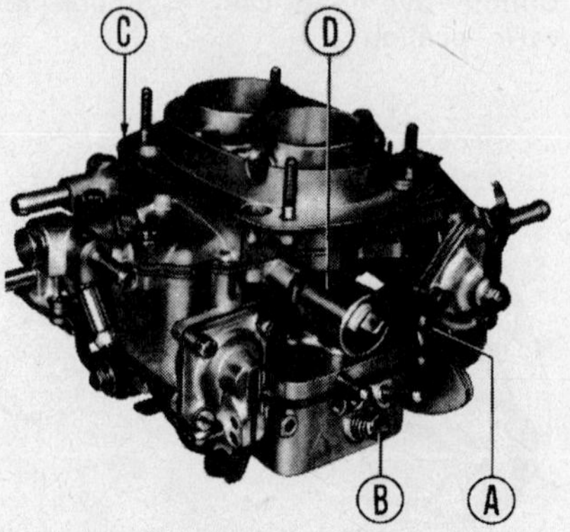

A. Idle speed screw C. Fast idle screw
B. Idle mixture screw D. Idle stop solenoid

Idle speed and mixture adjustments—1975 and later 124, 131, Brava

3. Adjust the idle mixture(% CO) to specifications (see "Tune-up" chart) with the idle mixture metering screw.

NOTE: Fiat recommends the use of a carbon monoxide (CO) meter for setting the mixture. However, if one is not available, a satisfactory setting should be found by first screwing the mixture screw all the way in until it lightly sets, and then backing it out about 2 to 3½ turns. This will get you in the ballpark, and then you can adjust the mixture for the highest possible rpm within that range. Screw clockwise to lean (decrease CO), and counterclockwise to richen (increase CO).

4. After adjusting mixture, recheck idle speed and adjust if necessary.

ENGINE ELECTRICAL

Distributor

All Fiat distributors use a centrifugal ignition advance system which advances spark timing in direct proportion to increasing engine rpm. In addition, 128 and X1/9 models with the Ducellier distributor utilize a vacuum retard system which retards the ignition timing about 10° under high vacuum situations such as idling and deceleration. 1979 2000 cc models with electronic ignition have a vacuum advance mechanism in addition to the centrifugal advance.

REMOVAL AND INSTALLATION

The quick method of distributor removal is to mark the distributor body and rotor positions relative to some stationary engine component before removal, and then put it back the way you found it. However, on the 1756 cc engines installed in the 124 and 131 (these are the ones with the distributor located at the right rear of the engine above the exhaust manifold), the distributor drive gear is helical (slanted drive). Therefore, the rotor will rotate about 30-40 degrees during removal or installation. For this reason, mark the position of the rotor before removal and just after removal. When you go to install the distributor, align the rotor with the mark you made just after removal so when the distributor is installed, the rotor will correctly align with the first mark.

The Fiat approved method of distributor removal is the following:

1. Remove the high tension wires from the distributor.
2. Remove the low tension leads and disconnect the vacuum control (if equipped).
3. Rotate the crankshaft to bring No. 1 cylinder to TOP DEAD CENTER (TDC) of compression stroke (both valves closed). Align the timing marks.
4. Remove the distributor clamp bolt at the

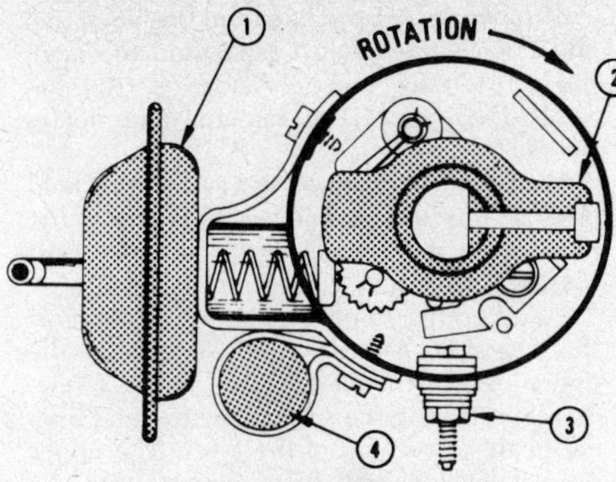

1—Vacuum retard
2—Rotor toward #4 terminal
3—Primary lead facing grille
4—Condenser

Single point distributor

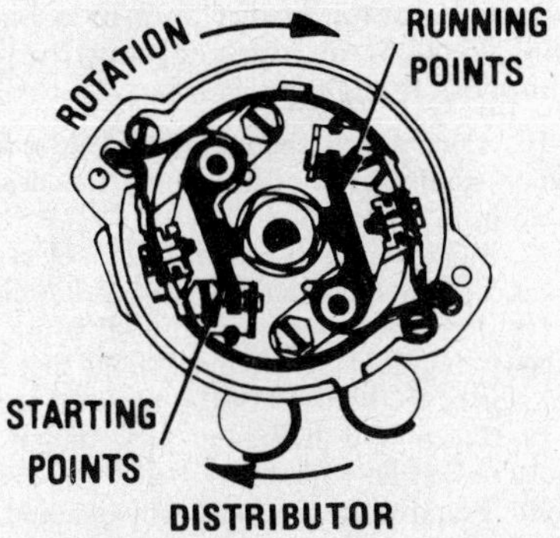

Double point distributor

base of the distributor and remove the distributor from the engine. To install:

5. Position the distributor rotor opposite the No. 1 contact in the cap. At this point the contact breaker points are about to open.
6. Fit the distributor into its housing and tighten the clamp bolt.
7. Replace the distributor cap and connect the spark plug wires in the correct firing order.
8. Check the ignition timing with a timing light and the point dwell with a dwell meter.

Alternator

ALTERNATOR PRECAUTIONS

Certain precautions should be observed when working on this, or any other AC charging system.

1. Never switch battery polarity.
2. When installing a battery, connect the ground cable last.
3. Never disconnect the battery while the engine is running.
4. If the molded connector is disconnected from the alternator, do not ground the hot wire.
5. Never run the alternator with the main output cable disconnected.
6. Never electric weld around the vehicle, without disconnecting the alternator.
7. Never apply any voltage, other than battery voltage, when testing.
8. Never apply more than 12 volts to jump a battery for starting purposes.

REMOVAL AND INSTALLATION

NOTE: Disconnect the battery first.

The alternator is removed by disconnecting the electrical leads and unscrewing the nut on the upper bracket and the screw which attaches the bracket to the engine. Remove the two nuts of the lower brackets, fan, generator and water pump belt. Installation is the reverse of removal.

Voltage Regulator

Only the electro-mechanical regulator mounted separately from the alternator is adjustable.

ADJUSTMENTS

Cut-out

1. Measure the air gap for the cut-out relay between the clapper and the edge of the core nearest the contacts.
2. Make the cut-in adjustment with the unit at 65-95° F.
3. Adjust by bending the spring tension arm until the points close at the proper specification.
4. Check the reverse current by connecting a two-way ammeter in series with the battery lead to the regulator.
5. Run the alternator to 4500 rpm and gradually reduce speed, noting the reverse current at the point where the contacts open. (See specifications for the proper amperage.)
6. The range between cut-in and cut-out action can be adjusted by enlarging or reducing the air gap.

Starter

REMOVAL AND INSTALLATION

Front Engine Models

1. Jack up the car and place jack stands beneath the frame.
2. Disconnect the battery positive terminal to prevent accidental shorting.
3. Remove the exhaust manifold and muffler to provide clearance.
4. Disconnect the wires from the starter, tagging each wire to facilitate later identification.
5. Remove the mounting bolts and pull the starter from the housing.
6. Installation is the reverse of removal.

Rear Engine Models

1. Raise the car at the rear and set it on two stands at the control arms.
2. Disconnect the battery (positive) cable to prevent shorting.
3. Disconnect and remove the lower linings of the compartment.
4. If necessary, remove the exhaust manifold and muffler.
5. Disconnect the wires from the starter motor and tag each wire to facilitate later identification.
6. Remove the mounting bolts and the starter.
7. Installation is the reverse of removal.

OVERHAUL

The starter can be broken down into the following subassemblies: solenoid, commutator end head, frame, armature, drive and pinion end head.

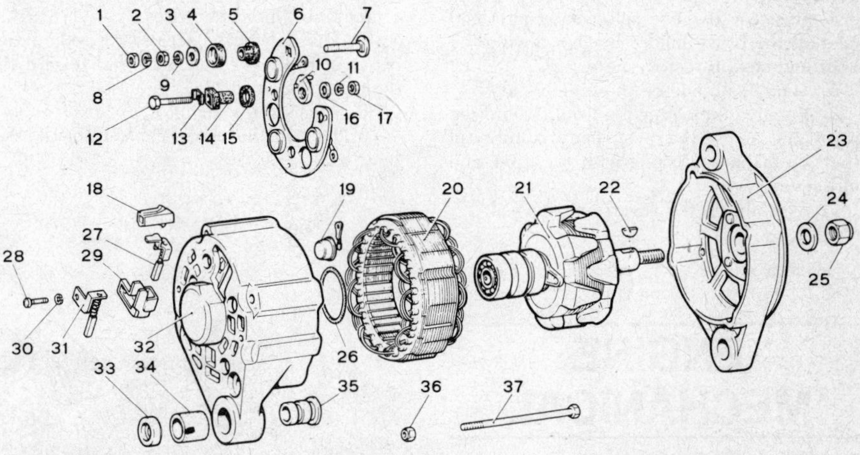

1-2. Nuts
3. Flat washer
4-5. Positive clamp insulators
6. Positive diode plate
7. Screw, positive clamp
8-9. Spring washers
10. Diode terminal connector insulator
11. Spring washer
12. Screw, positive diode plate, diode terminals and stator phases ends attachment
13. Plate
14-15. Insulators
16. Flat washer
17. Nut
18. Insulated connector for charge indicator blade plug
19. Negative diode
20. Stator
21. Rotor
22. Key
23. Drive end frame
24. Spring washer
25. Pulley nut
26. Rubber seal, bearing outer race
27. Positive brush
28. Screw
29. Brush holder
30. Spring washer
31. Negative brush
32. Diode end frame
33-34-35. Rubber bushing components
36. Nut
37. Through-bolt

Fiat A 12M 124/12/41M alternator—all 124; others similar

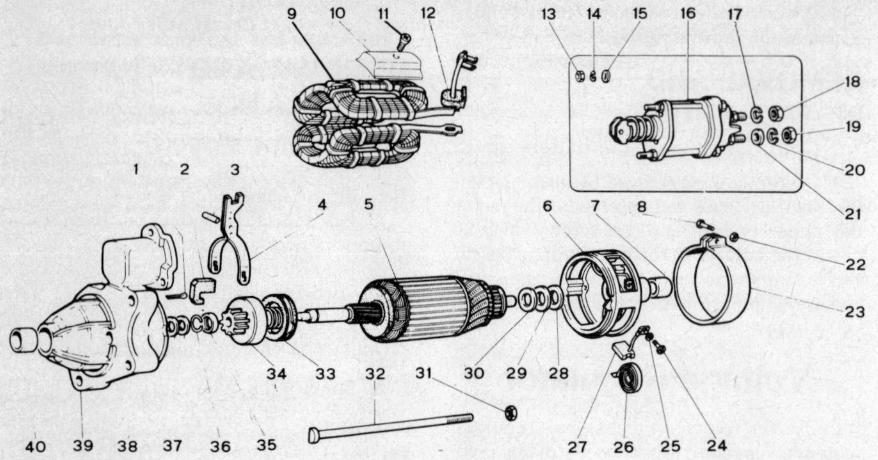

1. Split pin
2. Rubber pad
3. Lever pivot pin
4. Starter drive pinion shifter fork
5. Armature
6. Commutator end head
7. Bushing
8. Protection band screw
9. Field winding
10. Pole shoe
11. Pole shoe attaching screw
12. Grommet
13. Nut, solenoid to drive end head
14. Lock washer
15. Plain washer
16. Solenoid assembly
17. Lock washer
18. Nut, current lead clamping
19. Nut, field winding terminal
20. Lock washer
21. Plain washer
22. Nut, protection band screw
23. Commutator end head protection band
24. Screw, brush terminal clamping
25. Lock washer
26. Brush spring
27. Brush
28-29. Plain washers
30. Fibre thrust washer
31. Thru-bolt nut
32. Starter thru-bolt
33. Starter drive sleeve
34. Drive pinion
35. Stop ring
36. Snap ring
37-38. Plain washers
39. Drive end head
40. Bushing

Fiat E84—0.8/12 starter—all 128, X1/9; other similar

1. To disassemble, disconnect the starter motor lead from the solenoid and remove the solenoid.
2. Remove the brush cover and disconnect the brush holder.
3. Lift the brushes slightly and retain them in their holders by arranging springs against their sides.
4. Unscrew the two self-locking nuts and take off the brush holder bracket, saving the fiber and steel thrust washers.
5. Slide the frame off the pinion end.
6. Remove the cotter pin from the linkage pivot and remove the pivot. The armature can then be taken out, along with the drive and fork lever.
7. Assembly is the reverse of removal.

ENGINE MECHANICAL

Engine Removal and Installation

All 124 Models and 131

1. Removal of 124 sedan and sports car engines is facilitated by removing the radiator and the transmission. Proceed as follows:
2. Jack up the car and place it on jack stands.
3. Drain the radiator, auxiliary tank, block and heater system by first moving the heater lever to far right, then opening the radiator drain cock and removing the plug on the right-hand side of the block.
4. Speed drainage by removing the radiator and auxiliary tank caps.
5. Disconnect the battery leads.
6. Then disconnect the ignition coil, generator, starter, low oil pressure and water temperature indicator wires.
7. Disconnect the accelerator rod, sliding it out of the lever ball joint end toward the dash.
8. Remove the air filter.
9. Detach the choke cable from the carburetor.
10. Disconnect the line from the fuel pump and detach the exhaust pipe from the manifold.
11. Disconnect the radiator and heater hoses.
12. Remove the upper two screws that hold the radiator to the body, then remove the radiator by sliding it from the lower support bracket.
13. Working from inside the car, remove the gearshift lever by pressing down the upper part of the sleeve and, with a screwdriver, releasing the spring ring from its seating in the lower part of the lever. The upper part of lever can then be slipped from the lower part.
14. Remove the transmission cover.
15. From under the car, disconnect the driveshaft spider and transmission mainshaft from the universal.

NOTE: This is facilitated by placing a 5 inch diameter hose clamp or a band, Tool A70025, on the coupling itself to compress it slightly.

16. Disconnect speedometer cable from the transmission and disconnect the flexible cable from the clutch fork.
17. Remove the flywheel cover, electrical ground cable and exhaust pipe bracket clip.
18. Remove the heat shield from the exhaust manifold and the three bolts that hold the starter to the front of the transmission.
19. Position a hydraulic jack under the transmission for support.
20. Remove the four bolts which mount the transmission to the crankcase.
21. Remove the crossmember that holds the transmission to the car floor.
22. Supporting the transmission jack, move it toward the rear of the car so as to withdraw the clutch shaft from the pilot bushing and clutch hub.
23. Lower the jack and pull the transmission from under the car.
24. Remove the starter from the engine compartment.
25. Using a chain hoist, pass the rear sling under the crankcase and the front sling under the thermostat housing.

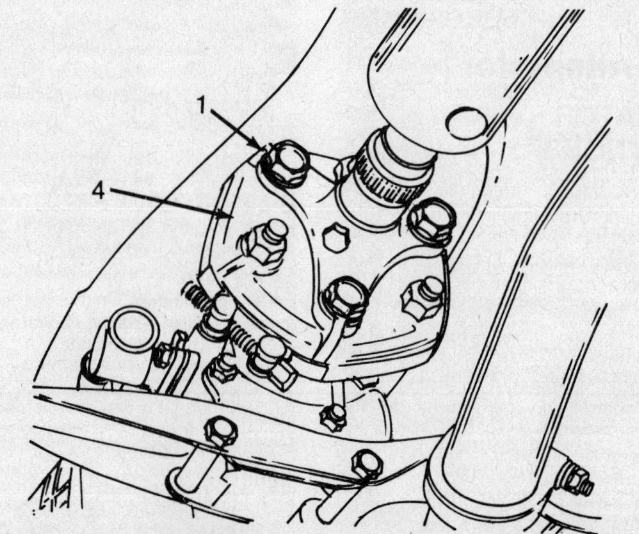

A clamp holds universal (4) together, while removing driveshaft screws (1) and transmission spider screws

26. Supporting the engine with a hoist, remove the front mounts and lift the engine clear.

27. Installation is the reverse of removal.

128

1. Place the car on jack stands and be sure the car is in a stable position before removal.

2. Raise the hood and unhook the stay rod. Place covers on the fenders.

3. Loosen the wing nut and remove the spare tire.

4. Take off the lower guards.

5. Drain the water from the radiator, supply tank, cylinder block and passenger compartment heating sysem in the following way:

a. Completely lower the heater lever inside the car.

b. Open the cock at the bottom of the radiator and remove the radiator cap.

c. Open the cock at the inner side of the engine block and take the cap off the supply tank to help water drainage.

6. Disconnect the battery cables.

7. Disconnect the primary and secondary wires from the coil to the distributor.

8. Disconnect the wires from the generator.

9. Disconnect the wires from the starter, the oil pressure sending unit, and the water temperature sending unit.

10. Disconnect the air cleaner.

11. Disconnect the linkage and choke wire from the carburetor.

12. Disconnect the fuel inlet hose from the fuel pump.

13. Disconnect the exhaust pipe from the manifold.

14. Remove the two rubber hoses from the union with the thermostat to the radiator.

15. Disconnect the water inlet and outlet hoses from the engine to the passenger compartment heater.

16. Disconnect the speedometer drive from the transmission housing by unscrewing the retaining ring.

17. Remove the adjustable rod of the flexible cable from the clutch release lever by unscrewing the locknut and nut.

18. Detach the anti-roll bar by removing the screws which clamp the brackets and insulators to the body. Then unscrew the nuts which fasten the ends to the control arms.

19. Remove the exhaust pipe support bracket from the transmission housing.

20. Disconnect the rod from the gearshift control lever.

21. Remove the ground strap from the transmission housing.

22. Take off the left-hand wheel. Unscrew the left tie rod-to-steering nut and disconnect the ball joint.

23. Remove the shock absorber from the pillar.

24. Unscrew the constant-speed joint nuts from both front wheels.

25. From above the car, working in the engine compartment, disconnect the reaction strut.

26. Hook up the engine and put the cable under light tension. Then, working from above, unscrew the engine to body clamping bolt and, from below, detach the crossmember from the underbody.

27. Work the shaft of each constant-speed joint out of its seat in the pillars and secure the axle shafts with wire to prevent them from coming away from their seats in the differential.

28. Using a hoist lower the engine group to remove.

29. Install in the reverse order.

X1/9

1. Disconnect the battery and drain the cooling system.

2. Remove the air cleaner assembly.

3. Disconnect the air pump inlet hose and outlet hose from the pump.

4. Disconnect the heater return hose at the coupling joint and disconnect the heater hose from the pump.

5. Disconnect the wires from the alternator.

6. Remove the two bolts retaining the louvered protection panel below the carbon trap in the rear firewall.

7. Disconnect the choke linkage from the carburetor.

8. Disconnect the vacuum hoses from the base of the carburetor. Disconnect the electrical leads from the solenoid and the carburetor vent hose from the carburetor.

9. Disconnect the coil wires at the distributor. Disconnect the leads from the oil pressure and water temperature sending units. Disconnect the electrical wires from the starter.

10. Remove the clamp securing the fuel lines to the firewall and disconnect the fuel supply and return lines from the firewall.

11. Remove the stopbolt from the accelerator cable, slide the seal off the cable, remove the retainer clip from the cable sheath and remove the cable from the support.

12. Remove the bolts securing the coolant expansion tank, top and bottom, and lift the tank, allowing the water to drain into the engine. Disconnect the hoses from the tank at the thermostat and remove the tank.

13. Remove the hoses from the thermostat.

14. Remove the cotter pin holding the slave cylinder pushrod to the clutch shaft. Loosen the two bolts securing the slave cylinder to the transmission. Open the bleeder screw of the slave cylinder and allow the pushrod to retract. Swing the slave cylinder out of the way.

15. From underneath the vehicle, remove the remaining bolt holding the louvered panel and remove the panel from the firewall. Remove the heat shield located behind the alternator. Remove the three panels from the bottom of the engine compartment and the panel in board of each rear wheel.

16. Drain the transmission/differential lubricant.

17. Disconnect the electrical connectors for the seatbelt interlock system and the back-up lights. Remove any clamps as necessary to allow the wires to be removed with the engine.

18. Disconnect the speedometer cable from the differential and secure the cable out of the way.

19. Remove the bolts retaining the gearshift linkage to the shifting tube. Loosen the bolt at the transmission end of the flexible link and swing the link to one side.

20. Remove the bolts holding the ground strap to the body.

21. Straighten the lock-tabs on the exhaust manifold flange. Remove the four nuts and lock-tab plates. Remove the 2 bolts from the upper bracket at the left end of the muffler. Remove the two nuts retaining the center support of the muffler to the crossmember and remove the muffler assembly. Remove the two nuts and bolt retaining the upper bracket to the differential case and remove the bracket.

22. Remove the three bolts securing the axle boots retaining ring on the right and left sides and slide the boots away from the differential, draining excess oil.

23. Remove the handbrake cable bracket at the forward end of each suspension control arm.

24. Take note of and record the number of shims at each suspension control arm mounting point.

25. Remove the four bolts and nuts plus the shims holding the control arms to the body and swing the control arms downward out of their brackets. Move the control arms away from the differential until the axles are free of the differential. Secure the axle assemblies to the control arms.

NOTE: If necessary, the entire suspension assemblies may be removed at this time by removing the wheels and brake calipers and the three nuts securing the top of the shock absorbers.

26. Straighten the lock-tabs on the two bolts on each end of the lower crossmember and loosen the bolts. Lower the vehicle until the engine is resting on a support.

CAUTION

Support the engine in such a manner so as not to damage the oil pan or any cast aluminum parts.

Remove the bolts from the lower crossmember.

27. From the top of the engine compartment, disconnect the engine torque rod from the bracket on the engine.

28. Remove the bolt from the engine mount, raise the car slightly and rock the engine/transmission assembly in order to clear the front engine mount.

29. Carefully raise the vehicle while supporting the engine.

30. Install the engine in the reverse order of removal.

Cylinder Head

REMOVAL AND INSTALLATION

124 and 131 DOHC Engine

1. There are two versions of the Fiat Twin-Cam engine—early and late. The early models lasted up till about 1973 and then they were replaced in 1974 by the late version of the motor. The early engine has the distributor mounted low on the block on the left-hand (driver's) side. Later engines (known as the 132 series) have the distributor mounted high on the block next to the right-

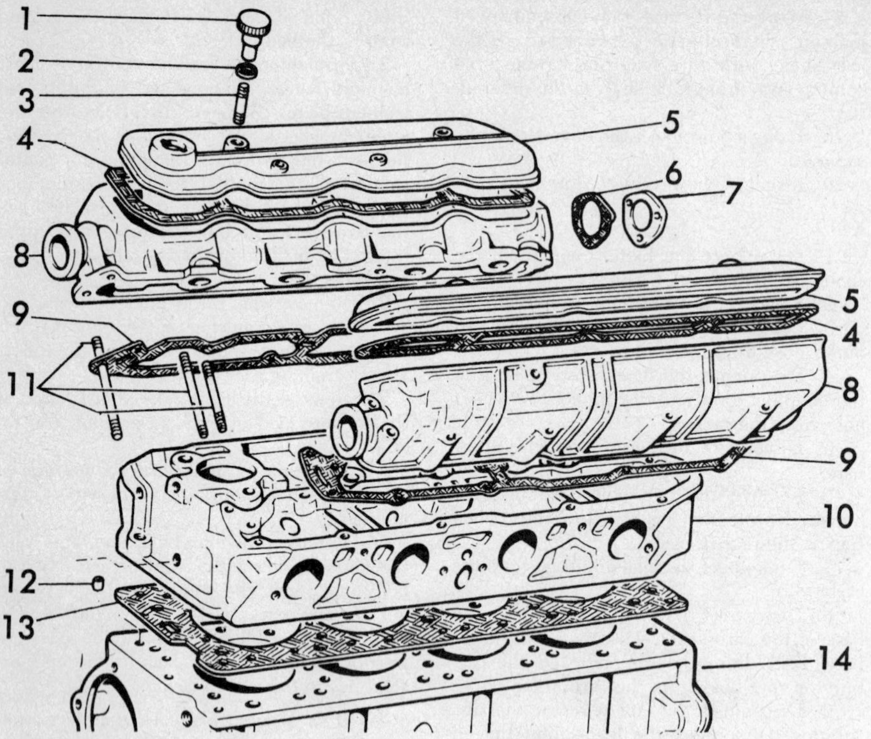

1. Knob
2. Washer
3. Stud
4. Cover gasket
5. Cover
6. End cover gasket
7. End cover
8. Cam housing
9. Cam housing gasket
10. Cylinder head
11. Studs
12. Locating dowel
13. Head gasket
14. Engine block

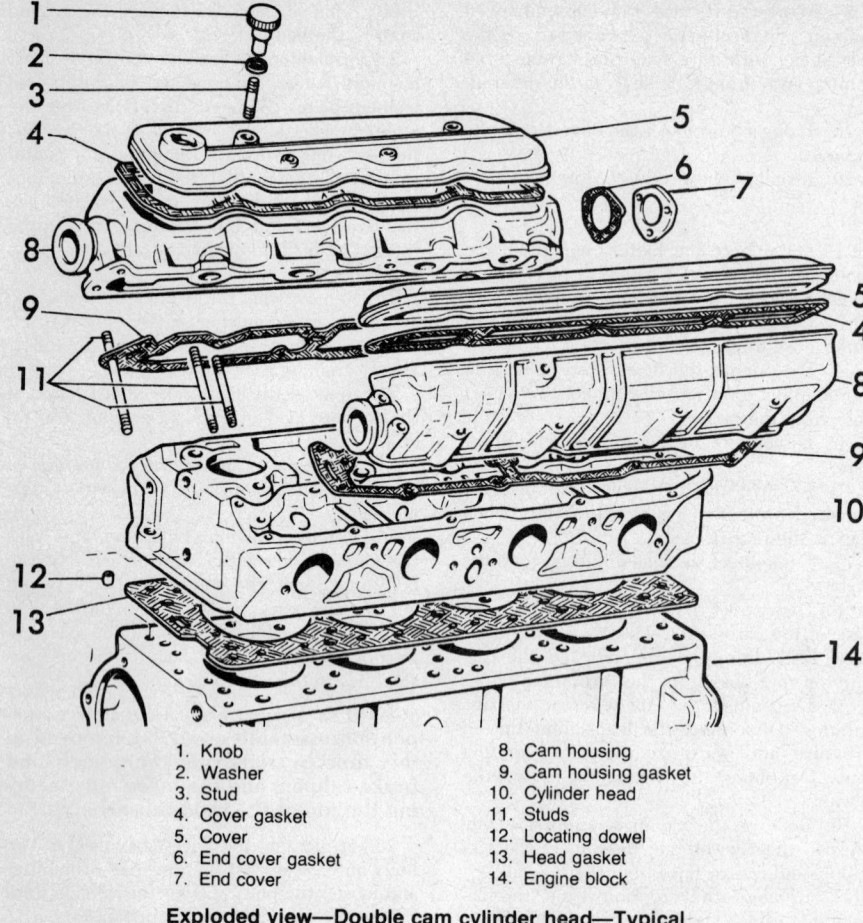

Exploded view—Double cam cylinder head—Typical

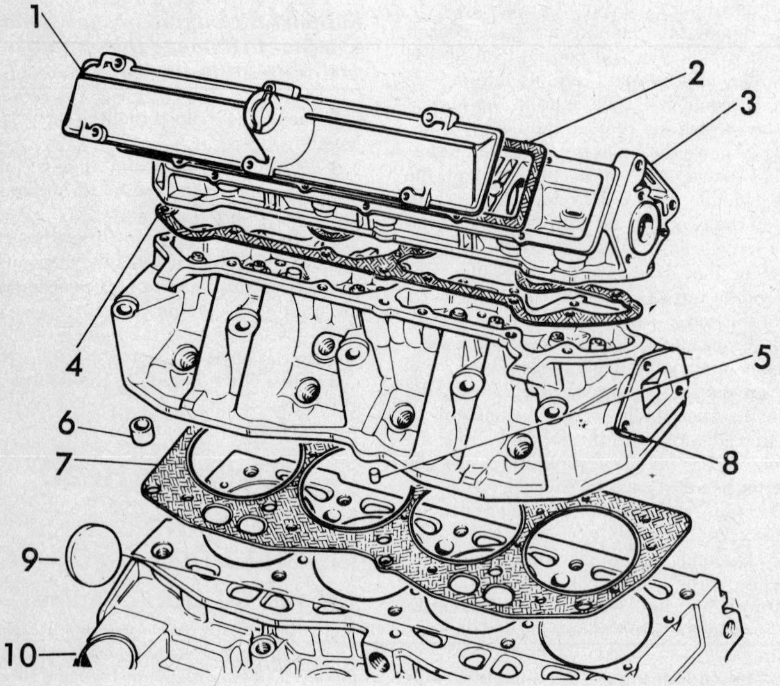

1. Cover
2. Cover gasket
3. Cam housing
4. Cam housing gasket
5. Locating dowel
6. Bushing
7. Cylinder head gasket
8. Cylinder head
9. Welsh plug
10. Engine block

Exploded view—Single cam cylinder head—Typical

hand cam cover. Although the procedure for both of these engines is essentially the same, Fiat altered the procedure slightly when they changed to the later engines.

2. Before beginning any dismantling procedures, it's helpful to find the valve timing marks first. Turn the engine over until the timing mark on the crank pulley is aligned with the TDC mark on the front cover, and the rotor is pointing at No. 1 cylinder in the distributor cap (early models) or No. 4 in the cap (late models). At this point, you should be able to see the marks on the cam housings in line with the holes in the cam gears (late models only). The timing pointer for the early engines isn't visible until you remove the front cover.

3. Drain the cooling system and disconnect the upper radiator hose.

4. Remove the air cleaner.

5. Disconnect all linkage and hoses from the carburetor and cylinder head.

6. Remove the carburetor and intake manifold as an assembly.

7. Disconnect the exhaust manifold from the side of the cylinder head.

8. Remove the timing belt shroud from the front of the engine.

9. Loosen the timing belt tensioner (idler) and remove the timing belt from the camshaft drive pulleys.

10. Remove the spark plug wires from the spark plugs.

11. Unscrew the cylinder head attaching bolts and carefully lift off the cylinder head. Lift the head straight up so as not to damage any of the open valves.

12. Clean the mating surfaces of all gasket material.

13. Before placing the cylinder head on the block, make sure the reference marks on the intake and exhaust cam gears are aligned with the fixed pointers on the front of the cylinder head on early engines. On late engines, make sure the holes in the cam gears are aligned with the marks on the cam housings. Once the timing marks are aligned, avoid turning the camshafts until the drive belt has been installed.

14. Carefully place the cylinder head on the block. Do not allow any of the open valves to contact the block.

15. Install the cylinder head bolts and tighten to specifications in the proper sequence.

16. Install the belt on the crankshaft pulley, auxiliary shaft pulley, intake camshaft pulley, exhaust cam pulley and the tensioner.

17. The Fiat recommended procedure for tightening the belt on the early models is to attach a spring scale to the upper right arm of the drive belt idler pulley. Apply a load of sixty pounds to the belt and tighten the idler pulley attaching nut. On the later engines, allow the tensioner to remove the play from the belt.

18. Check the belt tension after turning the crankshaft two or three times.

19. Check for proper valve timing by checking the timing marks. Refer to Timing Belt Removal and Installation if you get in trouble. Assemble the remaining components in the reverse order of removal.

128 SOHC Engine

NOTE: The aluminum cylinder head sometimes seizes on 128 and X1/9 models. To remove the head, remove all nuts and washers, then saturate the area around the studs with penetrating oil and allow to soak overnight. Before reassembly, clean all oil from the studs and housings and apply anti-seize compound.

1. Drain the cooling system.
2. Remove the spare tire from the engine compartment.
3. Remove the air cleaner.
4. Disconnect the spark plug cables.
5. Disconnect the accelerator control linkage from the carburetor.
6. Disconnect the fuel line and the choke control cable from the carburetor.
7. Disconnect the temperature sending unit electrical lead.
8. Disconnect the heater inlet hose, the upper and lower radiator hoses, and the coolant pump delivery hose from the thermostat housing.
9. Disconnect the exhaust pipe from the manifold and remove the bracket.
10. Remove the belt guard cover, working from below the vehicle to get at the lower screw after removing a guard. 1977 and later models have a two-piece cover.
11. Loosen the belt tensioner pulley retaining nut and remove the belt from the camshaft sprocket.
12. Unscrew the belt guard lower screw.
13. Remove the shroud by unscrewing the set screws.
14. Disconnect the reaction rod from the bracket in the cylinder head.
15. Remove the cylinder head retaining screws and nuts and remove the cylinder head along with the intake and exhaust manifolds, carburetor, and the camshaft housing. Removal of these parts is best performed with the cylinder head out of the vehicle.
16. Install the cylinder head, with the intake and exhaust manifolds, carburetor and camshaft housing assembled to it, in the reverse order of removal. Tighten the cylinder head bolts in the proper sequence in two stages; 29 ft/lbs the first time and to specifications the second time.

X1/9

See the note preceding the 128 cylinder head removal section before beginning.

1. Drain the cooling system and disconnect the battery.
2. Remove the air cleaner assembly.
3. Disconnect the fuel hoses from the carburetor and pull the two hoses out of the bracket on the camshaft cover.
4. Disconnect the accelerator linkage leading from the carburetor at the camshaft.
5. Disconnect the spark plug cables from the spark plugs.
6. Disconnect the distributor vacuum hose from the fitting in the cylinder head.
7. Remove the stop-bolt from the accelerator cable.
8. Slide the seal off of the cable and remove the clip retaining the cable to the camshaft cover. Remove the cable.
9. Disconnect the expansion tank hose, water pump inlet and outlet hoses, and the water pump-to-union hose.
10. Remove the bolt retaining the engine torque rod in its bracket and move the rod out of the way.
11. Disconnect the hose from the exhaust shroud.
12. Disconnect the electrical leads of the thermostatic switch on the carburetor.
13. Disconnect the evaporative hose from the carburetor.
14. Remove the air pump hoses.
15. Disconnect the muffler from the exhaust manifold flange.
16. Remove the bolts and washers attaching the timing cover. 1977 and later covers are two-piece. The earlier covers are often broken during removal. If so, replace with the later version.
17. Remove the lower right shield from under the engine.
18. Remove the alternator and the drive belt.
19. Remove the air pump.
20. Loosen the nut on the timing belt tensioner pulley and remove the timing belt.
21. Remove the lower bolt through the belt guard.
22. Remove the cylinder head attaching bolts and nuts and lift the cylinder head straight up and off of the engine. The carburetor and intake and exhaust manifolds are removed with the cylinder head as an assembly and removed from the cylinder head on the work bench.
23. Install the cylinder head in the reverse order of removal. Tighten the cylinder head bolts in the proper sequence. The valve timing is adjusted in the same manner as for the 128.

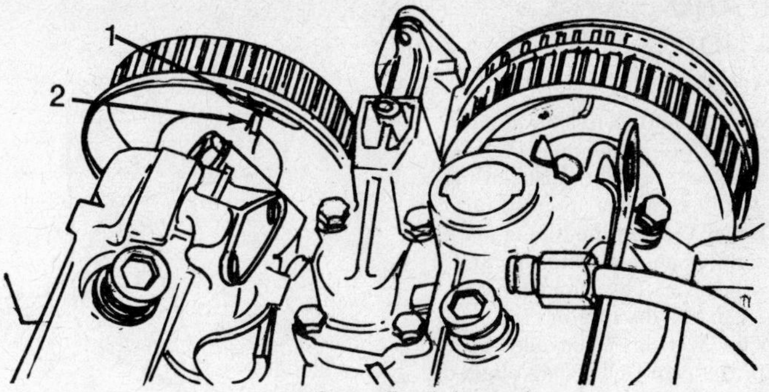

1—Cam pulley timing marks
2—Cam housing timing marks

Timing marks on cam pulleys and cam housings—DOHC 1608 and 1756 cc engines

CYLINDER HEAD OVERHAUL

See Engine Rebuilding Section.

Intake and Exhaust Manifolds

REMOVAL AND INSTALLATION

1. Remove the air cleaner.
2. Remove the fuel line, all vacuum lines, coolant lines (128 and X1/9), and accelerator linkage from the carburetor.
3. The carburetor can be removed at this point or removed after the manifold is removed from the vehicle.
4. Disconnect the exhaust pipe from the manifold. This is not necessary if removing just the intake manifold on DOHC engines.
5. Remove the manifold retaining bolts from the cylinder head and remove the manifold from the engine.
6. Install the manifold(s) in the reverse order of removal, tighten the retaining bolts to specification in an alternating sequence starting at the center and working toward the ends.

Timing Gear Cover

REMOVAL AND INSTALLATION

131 and 124 OHC

The valve mechanism drive belt cover on these engines is removed by simply removing the retaining screws and lifting the cover from the engine. Install in reverse order.

128 and X1/9

Removal of the timing belt cover on these engines is quite difficult because of the lack of space, particularly on the X1/9. There are only three bolts, but reaching them is a chore. Cover breakage on the early models is quite common. 1977 and later covers are two piece for this reason.

1. On 128 models, loosen the right engine mount and jack the engine up slightly.
2. On X1/9 models, there is no room to jack the engine. Remove the bolts that retain the belt cover and work the cover loose. There is no easy way to do this.
3. On 128 models, remove the bolts and tilt the cover up and out. If the engine is jacked up far enough, the cover should come out intact.
4. Installation is the reverse.

Timing Chain or Belt

NOTE: On those engines with belt-driven camshafts, Fiat recommends that the timing belt not be reused. Anytime belt tension is relieved, the timing belt must be replaced. The belt should also be replaced every 25,000 miles.

REMOVAL AND INSTALLATION

124 and 131 DOHC

1. This precedure applies to later engines which have the distributor mounted high on the right-hand cam cover. Before dismantling anything, turn the engine over by hand until No. 4 cylinder is on TDC and the timing mark on the crank pulley is aligned with the TDC mark on the timing cover. The rotor should be pointing at No. 4 in the distributor cap.

2. At this point, you should be able to see that the holes in the cam pulleys are aligned with the small cast fingers on the cam housing.

3. If the car is equipped with air-conditioning, remove the compressor drive belt.

4. Partially drain the cooling system and remove the upper radiator hose.

5. Remove the thermostat housing.

6. Remove the timing belt cover.

7. Remove the drive belt for the air pump. Remove the alternator drive belt.

8. Loosen the nut on the belt tensioner. Loosen the bolt for the spring support. Pry the tensioner away from the belt and remove the belt.

9. Install a new belt. Allow the tensioner to remove the play from the belt, and tighten the tensioner and the spring support. Rotate the engine a couple of times and recheck the belt tension.

10. Loosely install the belt cover and check to make sure all the valve timing marks line up.

11. If the valve timing is correct, reinstall the timing belt cover.

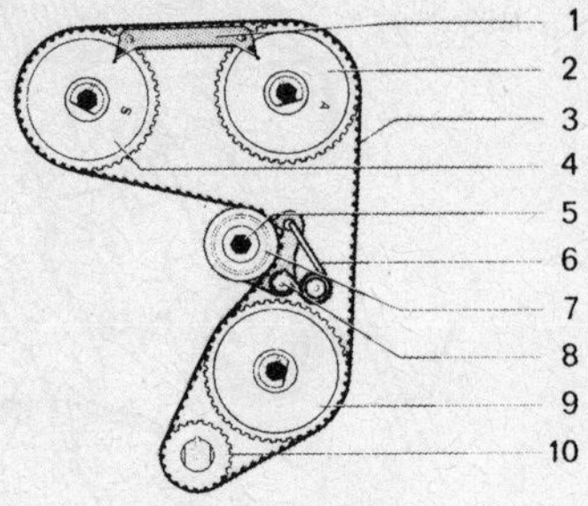

1. Valve timing pointers
2. Intake camshaft drive pulley
3. Timing belt
4. Exhaust camshaft/distributor drive pulley
5. Roller retaining nut
6. Tensioner spring
7. Tensioner roller
8. Tensioner retaining screw
9. Oil pump drive pulley
10. Crankshaft pulley

124, 131, Brava Twin Cam engine cam drive

12. Reinstall the remaining components in the reverse order of removal.

128 SOHC

1. Remove the timing gear cover. The lower retaining screw of the cover must be removed from under the car after removing the right side guard.

2. Check the valve timing by aligning the timing mark on the camshaft sprocket with the fixed mark on the engine and making sure that the timing mark on the crankshaft sprocket is simultaneously aligned with its fixed index mark.

3. Remove the water pump and generator drive belt.

4. Loosen the tensioner pulley retaining nut and relieve the spring action to remove the timing belt.

5. Install the new belt, making sure the belt and sprocket teeth engage perfectly.

6. Tighten the tensioner pulley nut to 33 ft/lbs.

X1/9

1. Turn the crankshaft until no. 4 piston is at TDC of the compression stroke. The timing mark on the front (right) crankshaft pulley should be at TDC and the camshaft timing pulley mark should be aligned with the cast finger of the support, visible through the hole in the camshaft cover.

NOTE: Throughout this entire procedure remember that if the camshaft is turned independently of the crankshaft the valves may hit the pistons causing damage.

2. Remove the bolts attaching the timing cover, remove the right guard from under the engine, remove the lower bolt retaining the timing cover and remove the cover.

3. Loosen the alternator and remove the alternator water pump drive belt.

4. Remove the drive pulley from the crankshaft.

5. Loosen the air pump and remove the drive belt.

Install timing belt (3) with camshaft gears at top (exhaust left, intake right) locked by tool (4) and positioned with reference marks opposite pointers on (1). Idler pulley (8), locked by screws (7 and 9), exerts tension on belt. Auxiliary drive gear is held in place by (6).

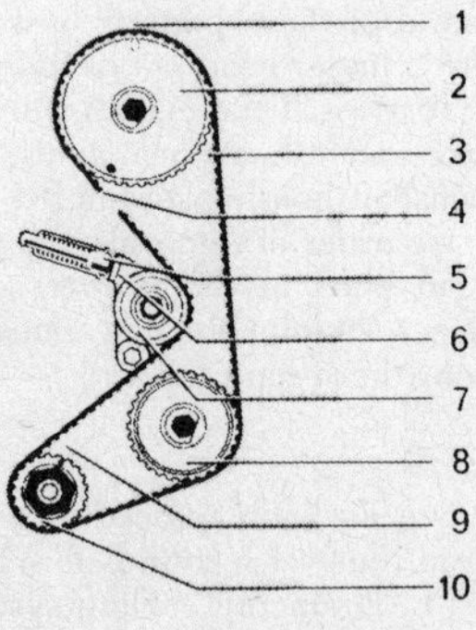

1. Camshaft timing reference mark (engine on car)
2. Camshaft drive pulley
3. Toothed timing belt, driving the camshaft and pulley 8
4. Camshaft timing reference mark (engine on bench)
5. Idler pulley tensioner
6. Idler pulley support
7. Idler pulley
8. Drive pulley for oil pump and ignition distributor
9. Reference mark for pulley 10 setting
10. Crankshaft sprocket

128, X1/9 engine valve gear drive

6. Remove the camshaft cover. Check and make sure the cam lobes of No. 4 cylinder are pointing up.

7. Remove the distributor.

8. Loosen the idler pulley locknut, push it on the support and tighten the locknut. Remove the timing belt, starting at the idler pulley.

9. Install the new timing belt, starting at the crankshaft. Twist the belt gently into position around the crankshaft pulley. Do not kink the belt.

10. Slip the belt over the camshaft pulley. The camshaft pulley may have to be turned slightly to align the slots with the belt cogs.

11. Install the belt over the idler pulley last.

12. Loosen the idler pulley locknut and retighten after tension is on the belt. Turn the crankshaft of the engine one half of a turn in the direction of normal rotation by either pushing the car with it in fourth gear or bumping the starter.

13. Release the idler pulley locknut to make sure all slack is removed from the belt and then retighten the locknut.

14. Continue to turn the crankshaft of the engine in the direction of normal rotation by either method mentioned in Step 12 until No. 4 piston reaches TDC of the compression stroke (one and one-half turns).

NOTE: Never push the car backward in gear or allow the engine to rock backward while pushing the car. Slack will develop in the belt, allowing the belt to jump timing.

15. Position the belt cover on the engine and check to make sure the crankshaft timing mark is at TDC and that the camshaft mark is aligned with the pointer. Tighten the tensioner pulley nut to 32 ft/lbs.

16. Install the pulley on the crankshaft.

17. Install the drive belt on the air pump.

18. Install the drive belt for the water pump and the alternator. Adjust the belt tension.

19. Install the timing gear cover.

20. Install the lower right guard.

21. Install the camshaft cover.

22. Install the distributor. The rotor should be pointing toward No. 4 cylinder spark plug tower of the distributor cap.

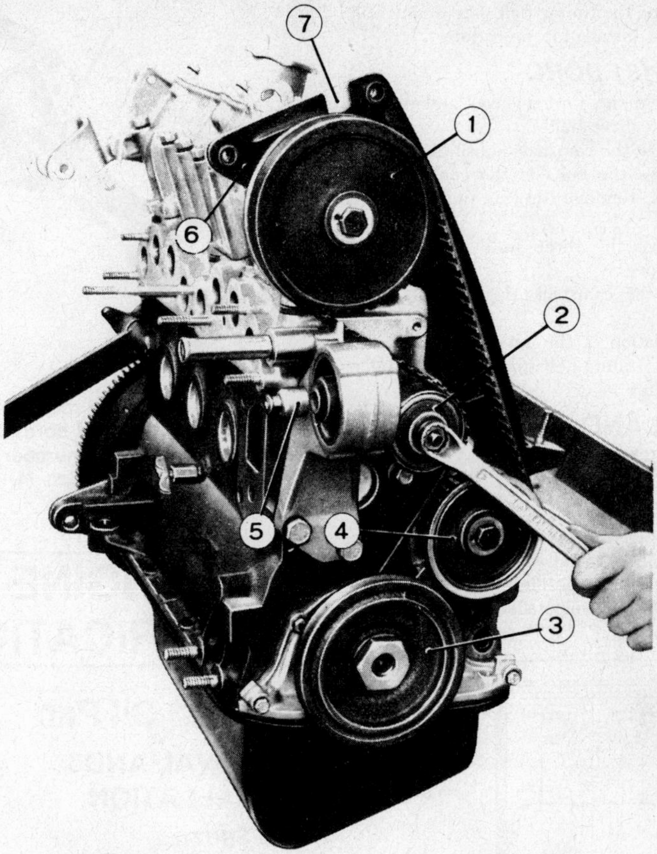

1. Camshaft sprocket
2. Tensioner pulley
3. Drive pulley
4. Auxiliary shaft sprocket
5. Tensioner
6. Belt guard
7. Bracket

Removing the belt tensioner pulley nut

Camshafts(s)

REMOVAL AND INSTALLATION

128 and X1/9 SOHC

1. Remove the camshaft drive belt.

2. Remove the camshaft carrier attaching bolts and remove the camshaft carrier assembly from the engine.

3. Remove the camshaft drive sprocket.

4. Remove the camshaft thrust plate from the opposite end (opposite the belt end) of the camshaft carrier.

5. Carefully slide the camshaft out of the camshaft carrier.

6. Install the camshaft in the reverse order of removal, making sure the valve timing marks on the camshaft sprocket and the crankshaft sprocket are properly aligned be-

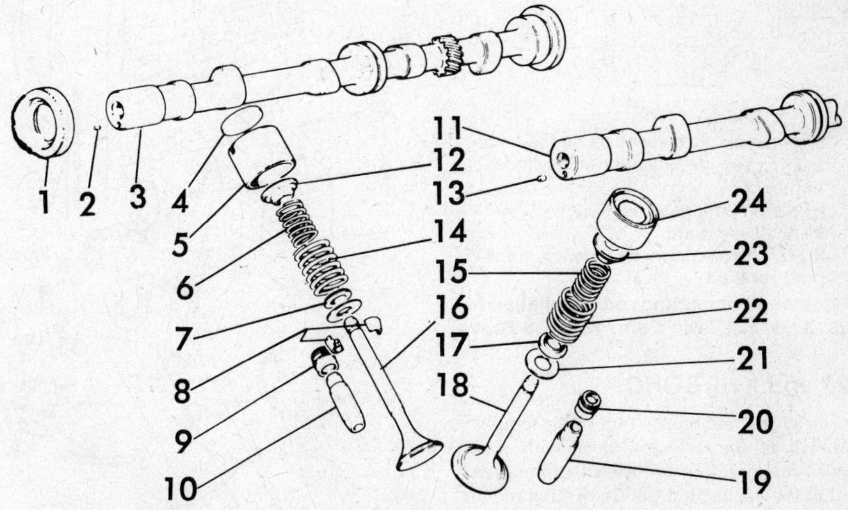

1. Camshaft seal
2. Exhaust camshaft dowel
3. Exhaust camshaft
4. Tappet plate
5. Exhaust valve tappet
6. Exhaust valve inner spring
7. Lower cup
8. Locks
9. Exhaust valve oil seal
10. Exhaust valve guide
11. Intake camshaft
12. Upper cup
13. Dowel
14. Exhaust valve outer spring
15. Intake valve inner spring
16. Exhaust valve
17. Lower cup
18. Intake valve
19. Intake valve guide
20. Oil seal
21. Washer
22. Intake valve outer spring
23. Upper cup
24. Intake valve tappet

124, 131, Brava Twin Cam valve mechanism

fore installing the timing belt. See timing belt removal and installation procedure.

124 and 131 DOHC

1. Remove the timing cover and remove the camshaft drive belt.
2. Remove the camshaft housings.
3. Remove the bolts in the center of the cam pulleys. Remove the cam pulleys with a gear puller.
4. Remove the three nuts retaining the front cam covers.
5. Slide the camshafts out from the cam housings.
6. Installation is the reverse of removal. Refer to the timing belt removal and installation procedure.

PISTON AND CONNECTING ROD IDENTIFICATION AND POSITIONING

If the connecting rod and piston assemblies are going to be reinstalled in the engine, they should be clearly identified during disassembly so they can be reinstalled in their original positions.

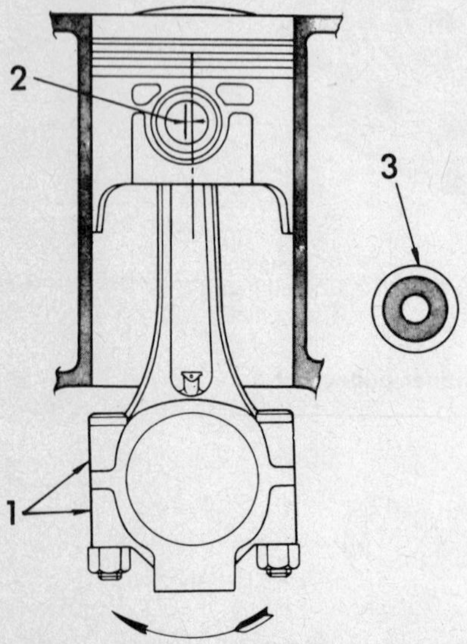

1. Location of the connecting rod and bearing cap identification and cylinder number
2. Piston pin offset 0.08 in.
3. Auxiliary shaft

NOTE: **Arrow shows direction of crankshaft rotation**

Piston and connecting rod installation for 128, X1/9, 124 Twin Cam, 131, and Brava

128 and X1/9 SOHC

The piston and connecting rod assembly is installed in the cylinder block with piston identification letter toward the timing belt end of the engine and the connecting rod and cap identification numbers facing away from the auxiliary shaft.

124, 131 DOHC

The piston and connecting rod assemblies are installed with the piston identification letter facing toward the front of the engine and the connecting rod and cap identification numbers facing away from the auxiliary shaft.

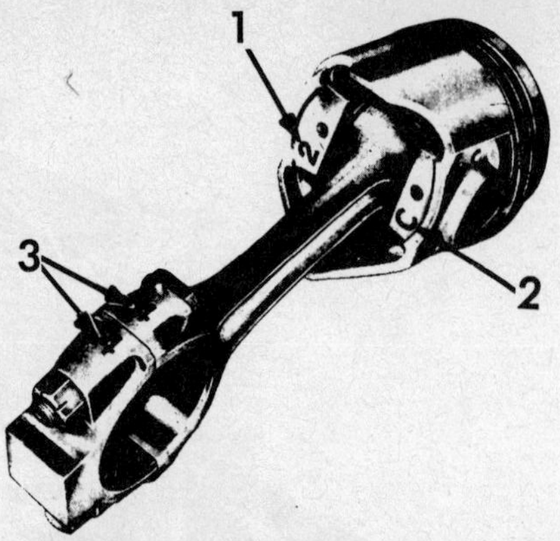

128, X1/9 piston and rod assemblies are marked for (1) size of bore, (2) wrist pin size, and (3) cylinder number. Metal may be removed from areas (1) and (2) to equalize rod weights

ENGINE LUBRICATION

Oil Pan

REMOVAL AND INSTALLATION

124 Sedan

1. Raise the car in the air and support it with jack stands.
2. Drain the oil from the engine.
3. Unbolt the motor mounts.
4. Fiat uses a special tool to hold the engine up in the chassis while removing the pan. Jack up the engine and support it securely.
5. With the engine in the air to provide clearance, remove the retaining bolts and remove the oil pan. The pan will have to be tilted to be removed.
6. Installation is the reverse of removal.

124 Coupe and Spider and 131

1. Drain the engine oil.
2. Raise the car in the air and support it securely.
3. The engine will have to be raised about six inches in the chassis in order for the oil pan to be removed. Unbolt the motor mounts and raise the engine up about six inches.
4. You will have to facricate some way of holding the engine in the air while removing the oil pan. Remove the oil pan bolts and remove the pan.
5. Installation is the reverse of removal.

128 and X1/9

1. Raise the car in the air and support it securely. Drain the engine oil.
2. The oil pan can be removed from the bottom only if the engine is supported with a hoist or other lifting device which will allow the engine mounting crossmember and splash shields to be removed.
3. If a hoist is available, raise the engine high enough to take the strain off, and remove the crossmember and splash shields. The crossmember holds the engine up, so be careful.

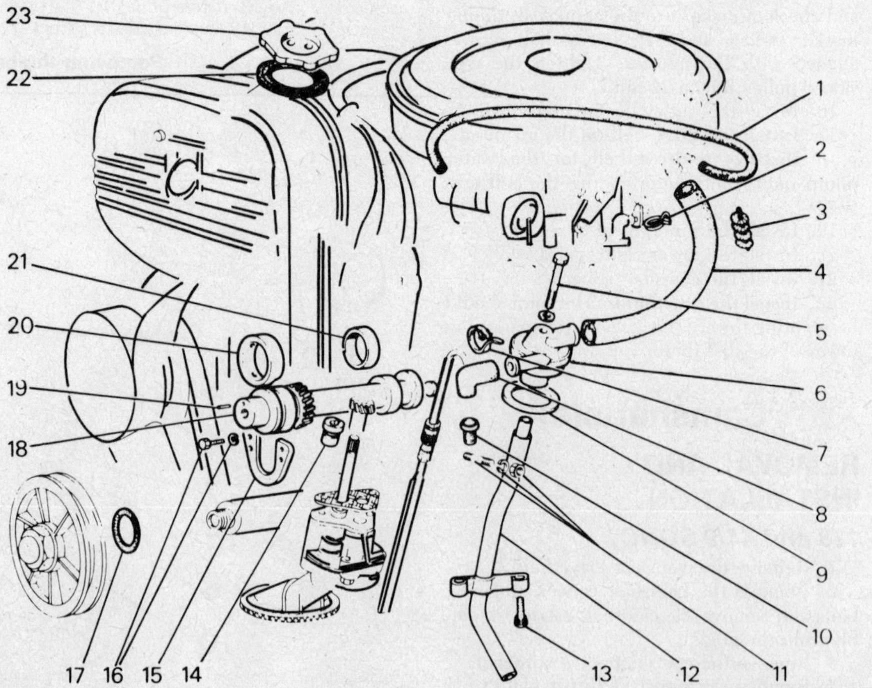

1. Blow-by gas and oil vapor hose
2. Collar
3. Flam trap
4. Breather hose
5. Bolt and washer
6. Breather
7. Collar
8. Hose
9. Seal
10. Vapor return connection
11. Stud, lockwasher, and nut
12. Breather tube
13. Bolt
14. Gear bushing
15. Retaining plate
16. Bolt and lockwasher
17. Spring washer
18. Auxiliary shaft
19. Dowel
20. Front bushing
21. Rear bushing
22. Seal
23. Oil filler cap

124, 131, Brava Twin Cam engine lubrication components

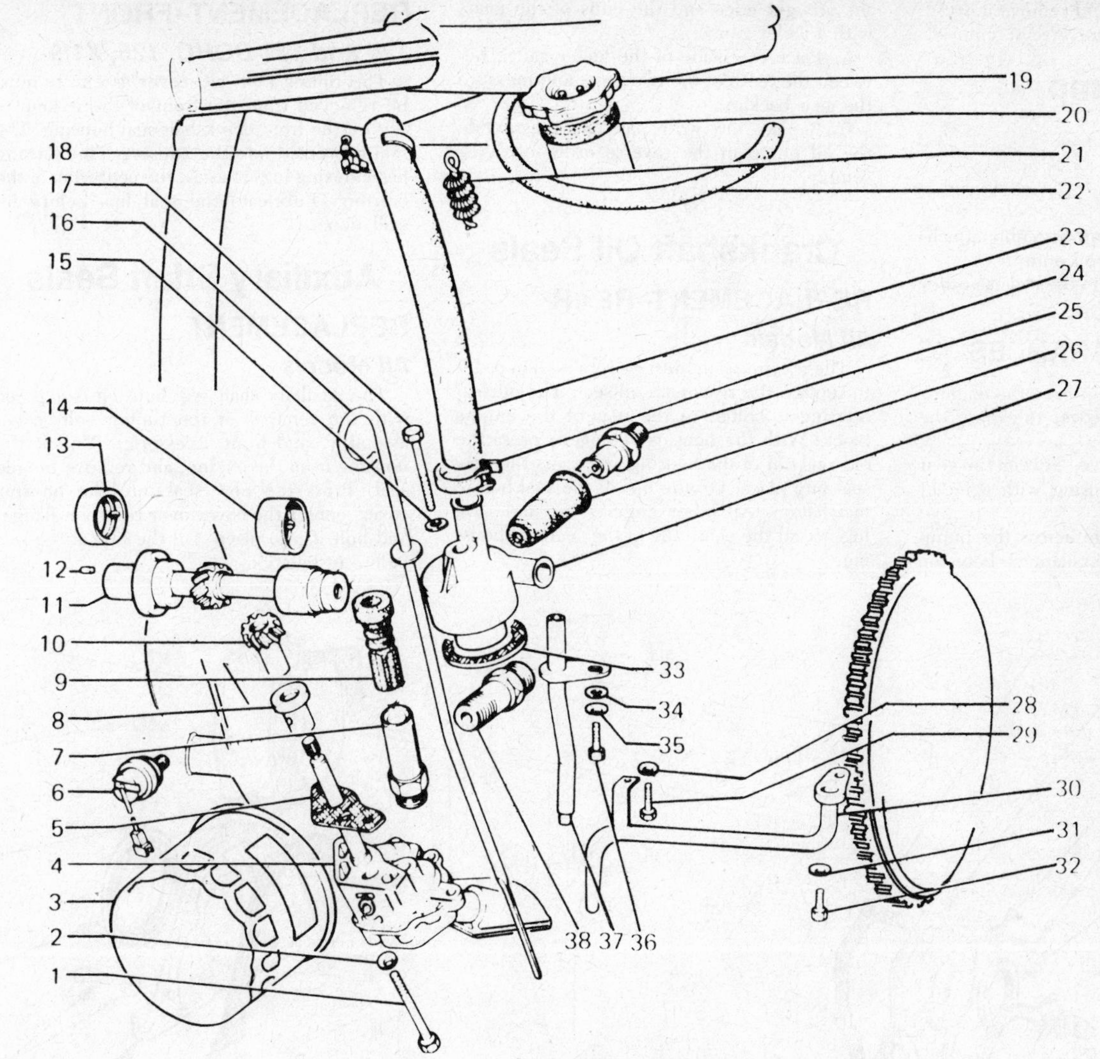

1. Bolt
2. Washer
3. Filter
4. Oil pump
5. Gasket
6. Sending unit
7. Pipe
8. Bushing
9. Seal
10. Gear
11. Shaft
12. Pin
13. Bushing
14. Bushing
15. Washer
16. Dip stick
17. Bolt
18. Clamp
19. Oil cap
20. Gasket
21. Flame trap
22. Hose
23. Hose
24. Clamp
25. Switch
26. Boot
27. Boot
28. Washer
29. Bolt
30. Pipe
31. Washer
32. Bolt
33. Gasket
34. Washer
35. Lockwasher
36. Bolt
37. Pipe
38. Connector

128, X1/9 engine lubrication components

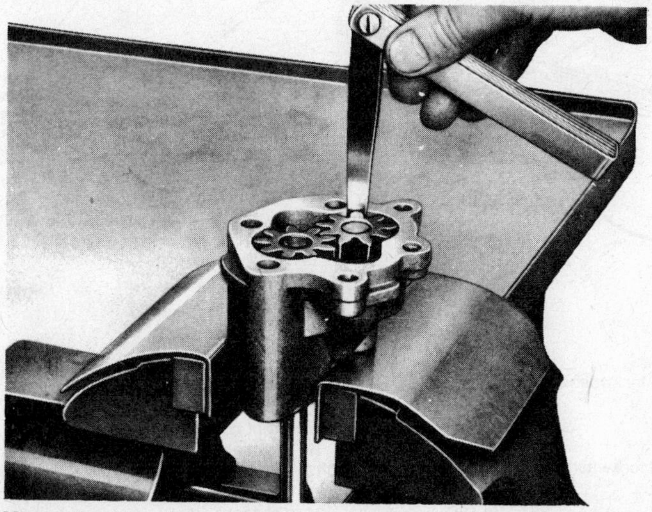

Measuring the clearance between the gear and housing of the oil pump

Measuring the clearance between the ends of the gears and a straight edge

4. Unbolt the oil pan and remove it.
5. Installation is in the reverse of removal.

Oil Pump

REMOVAL AND INSTALLATION

1. Remove the oil pan.
2. Remove the oil pump assembly attaching bolts and remove the oil pump.
3. Install the oil pump in the reverse order of removal.

CHECKING CLEARANCES

1. Remove the oil pump from the engine.
2. Remove the pump cover to expose the oil pump gears.
3. Measure the clearance between the gear teeth and the pump housing with a feeler gauge.
4. Place a straight edge across the pump housing and measure the clearance between the straight edge and the ends of the gears with a feeler gauge.
5. Place the blade of the feeler gauge between the teeth of the two gears and measure the gear backlash.
6. Replace any worn part and reassemble the oil pump in the reverse order of disassembly.

Crankshaft Oil Seals

REPLACEMENT–REAR

All Models

The transmission must be removed in order to replace the rear main oil seal. The oil seal housing is bolted to the rear of the engine block. With the housing removed, press the old seal out of the housing and press the new seal into place. Oil the lips of the seal before installation. All other engines use indexing lugs to aid the centering of the seal and housing.

REPLACEMENT–FRONT

124 and 131 DOHC, 128, X1/9

The timing belt and cover assembly must be removed from the front of the engine to expose the front crankshaft seal housing. The seal is pressed into the housing. The housing has indexing lugs to assist the centering of the housing. Lubricate the seal lips before installation.

Auxiliary Shaft Seals

REPLACEMENT

All Models

The auxiliary shaft seal housing is exposed with the removal of the timing belt, cover assembly, and front accessories. Unbolt the housing from the engine, and remove the old seal. Press the new seal into the housing cover, center the cover over the shaft flange, and bolt it into place. Oil the lips of the seal before installation.

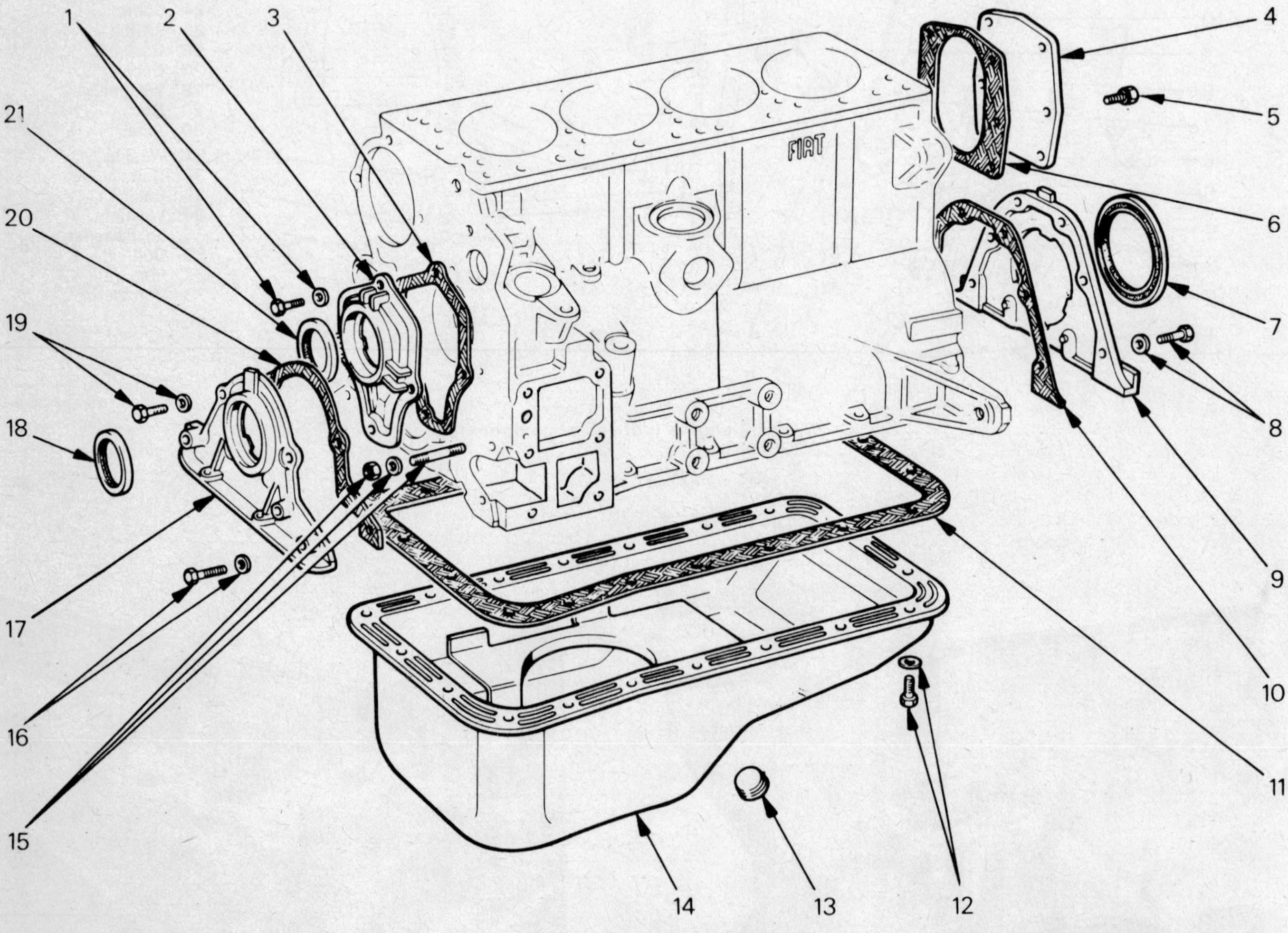

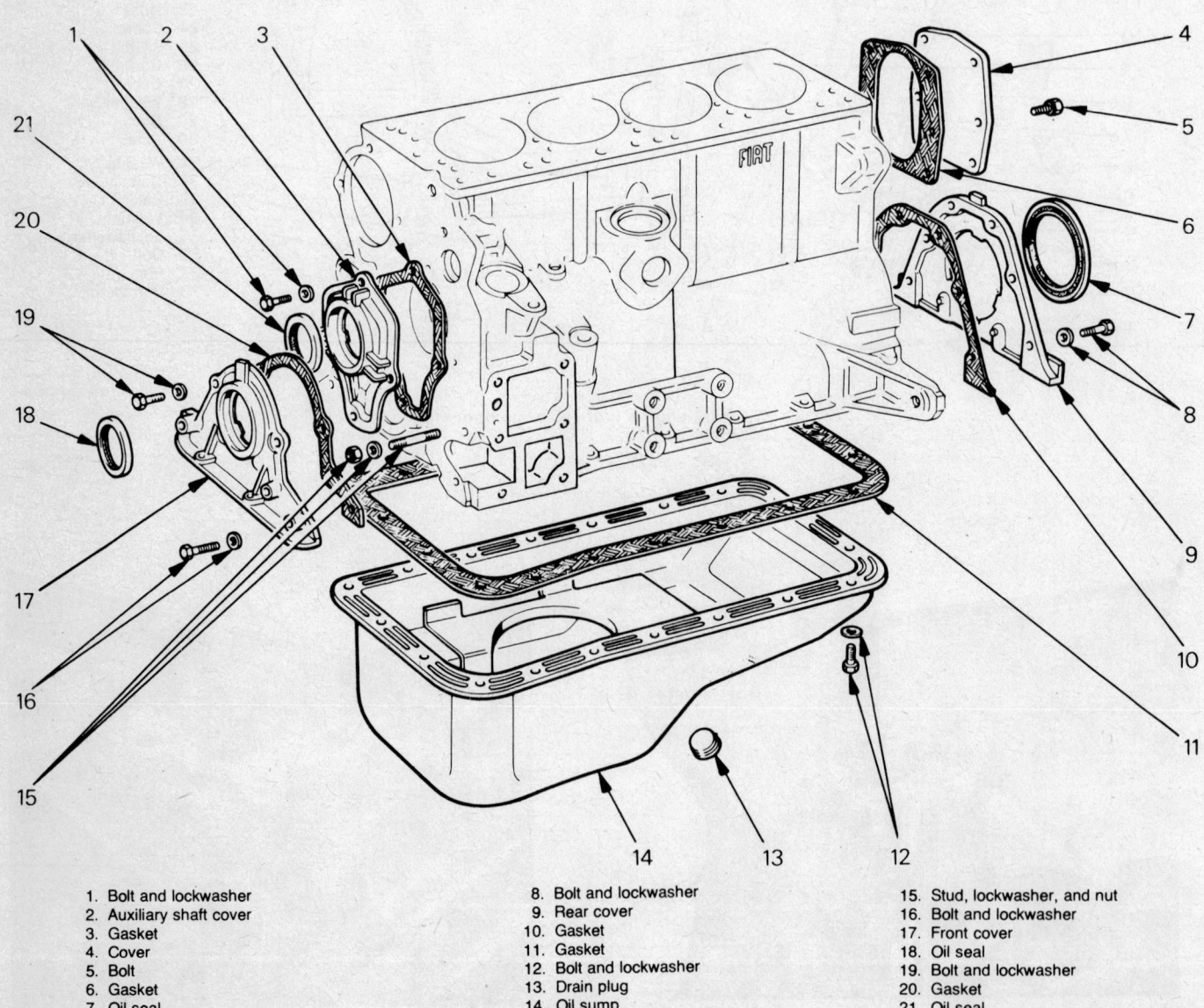

1. Bolt and lockwasher
2. Auxiliary shaft cover
3. Gasket
4. Cover
5. Bolt
6. Gasket
7. Oil seal
8. Bolt and lockwasher
9. Rear cover
10. Gasket
11. Gasket
12. Bolt and lockwasher
13. Drain plug
14. Oil sump
15. Stud, lockwasher, and nut
16. Bolt and lockwasher
17. Front cover
18. Oil seal
19. Bolt and lockwasher
20. Gasket
21. Oil seal

Oil pan and crankshaft seal locations—typical

ENGINE COOLING

Radiator

REMOVAL AND INSTALLATION

124, 131

1. Open the petcock at the bottom of the radiator and drain the coolant from the radiator and cylinder block.
2. Remove the hose which connects the radiator and thermostat cover.
3. Remove the hose which connects the radiator and water pump.
4. Remove the pipe which connects the radiator to the auxiliary tank.
5. When equipped with automatic transmission disconnect oil lines.
6. Unbolt and remove the radiator.
7. Installation is the reverse of removal.

128

1. Drain the radiator and the cylinder block.
2. Disconnect the thermal fan switch and the fan relay switch.
3. Disconnect the hose running from the radiator to the expansion tank.
4. Remove the hoses running from the thermostat union to the radiator.
5. Remove the screws that attach the top part of the radiator to the brackets fitted on the body, together with the rubber pads, washers, and spacers.
6. Slide the radiator, fan, and shroud out of the top of the engine compartment.
7. Installation is the reverse of removal.

X1/9

1. Drain the cooling system.
2. Remove the three lower screws securing the grille to the crossrail.
3. Remove the four nuts retaining the guard plate to the body and remove the plate.
4. Disconnect the hoses at the radiator.
5. Disconnect the electrical connector for the fan motor and the wires from the thermostatic switch.
6. Remove the bolt and nut holding the bottom crossrail at each side and remove the crossrail.
7. Lower the radiator out from under the car, being careful of the fan.
8. Install the radiator in the reverse order of removal. The radiator must be bled after it is refilled with coolant. The bleeder valve is on the top of the radiator, accessible through the trunk once the radiator is in place. Start the car and check for leaks. Turn on the heater. Connect a pressure tester to the radiator and pump in no more than 11 psi of air. Open the bleeder valve and repeat the operation until all air is removed from the system.

1. Fan motor
2. Fan
3. Washer
4. Nut
5. Plate
6. Washer
7. Lockwasher
8. Nut
9. Gasket
10. Conveyor
11. Washer
12. Lockwasher
13. Nut
14. Nut
15. Lockwasher
16. Washer
17. Nut
18. Relay
19. Thermostatic switch
20. Gasket
21. Lockring
22. Spacer

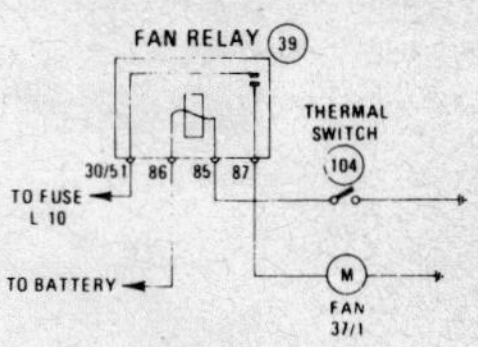

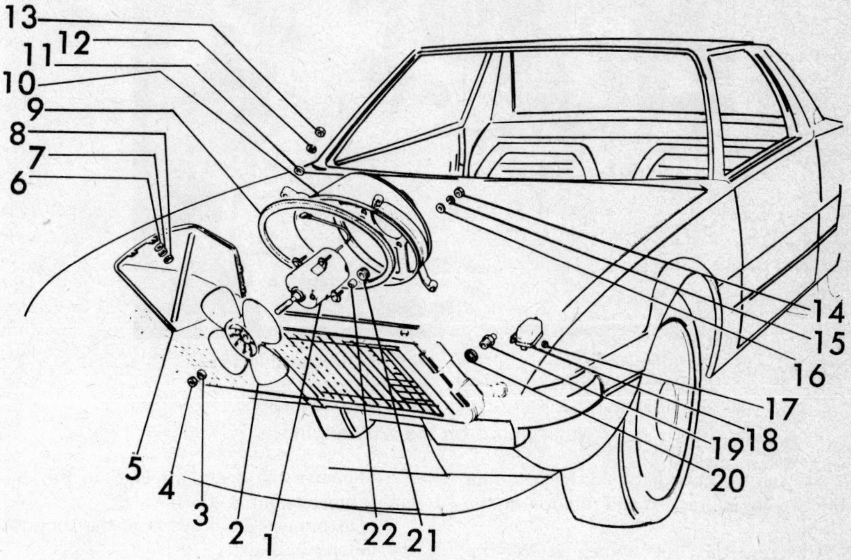

X1/9 electric cooling fan installation

Water Pump

REMOVAL AND INSTALLATION

124 and 131

1. If necessary, remove the radiator from the vehicle.
2. Unbolt and remove the fan from the water pump flange.
3. Remove the hose which connects the water pump and radiator.
4. Remove the water pump from the mounting.
5. Installation is the reverse of removal.

128

1. Remove the spare wheel.
2. Place protective coverings on the fenders.
3. Drain the water from the cooling system.
4. Disconnect the hot air hose and the accelerator rod from the shroud.
5. Remove the shroud.
6. Disconnect the passenger compartment heater water delivery and return hoses.

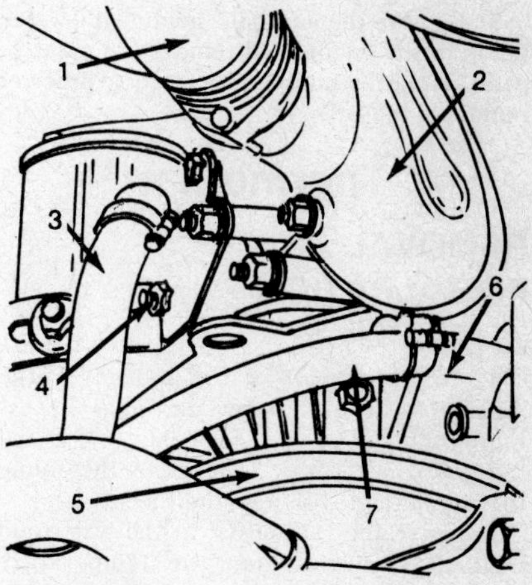

1. Hot air hose
2. Shroud
3. Water return hose from passenger compartment heater
4. Generator bracket to pump housing attachment nuts
5. Vee belt
6. Water pump
7. Water delivery hose to passenger compartment heater

Water pump removal—128

RADIATOR COOLING FAN

Model	Engine cc	How Driven
128 Sedan and Wagon	1116	Fan operated by electric thermostat
X1/9, 128 Coupe and Strada	1290	Fan operated by electric thermostat
124 Sedan and Wagon	1438	Fan operated by water pump shaft
124 Sedan and Wagon	1592	Fan operated by electric thermostat
124 Coupe and Spider	1608	Fan operated by electric thermostat
124 Spider, 131 and Brava	1756	Fan operated by electric thermostat

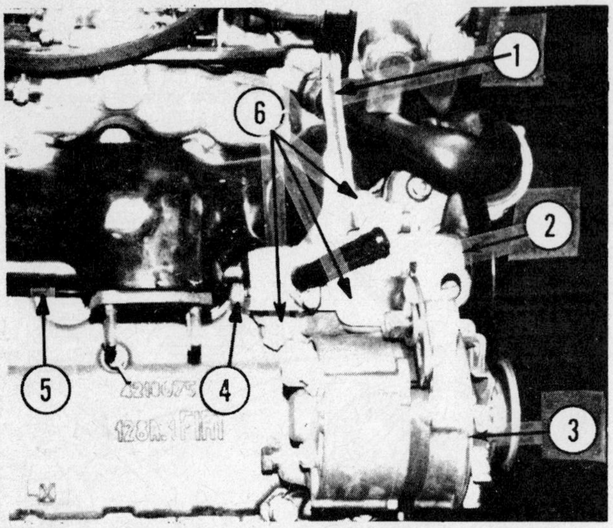

1. Support bracket
2. Water pump
3. Alternator
4. Water pipe attaching screw
5. Water pipe
6. Water pump attaching screws

Water pump on the X1/9 engine

7. Slacken the nuts that hold the generator on the two lower brackets and remove the top bracket.

8. Unscrew the nuts which attach the pump to the crankcase and slide off the pump assembly.

9. Installation is the reverse of removal.

X1/9

1. Drain the cooling system.
2. Remove the protection panels from the bottom right side of the engine.
3. Remove the alternator and drive belt.
4. Disconnect the hoses from the water pump.
5. Remove the three nuts and washers retaining the heater hose pipe to the pump.
6. Remove the bolt holding the support for the air pump to the water pump.
7. Remove the four bolts holding the water pump to the engine and remove the pump.
8. Install the pump in the reverse order of removal.

Thermostat

REMOVAL AND INSTALLATION

124 and 131

1. Drain off part of the coolant in the radiator (to a level below the inline bypass thermostat).
2. Disconnect the 3 hoses to the inline thermostat and withdraw the thermostat.

Immerse the thermostat in the water and heat the water. When the temperature reaches 185-192° F, the thermostat valve should begin to open. The valve should be completely open when the water temperature reaches 212° F. If the thermostat does not meet specifications, it is defective and must be replaced.

3. Installation is the reverse of removal.

128 and X1/9

1. Drain the water from the cooling system.
2. Remove the spare wheel from the engine compartment on the 128.
3. Disconnect the hoses from the thermostat union.
4. Unscrew the attachment screws and remove the union, compete with the thermostat.
5. Unscrew the union cover and slide out the thermostat and its seal.
6. Installation is the reverse of removal.

EMISSION CONTROLS

APPLICATION

Crankcase Ventilation System—All models
Evaporative Control System—All models
Engine Modification System—All models
Deceleration Throttle Positioner System—All 124, 131
Air Injection System—All 1974-79 models
Exhaust Gas Recirculation System—1975-79 124, 131, 1979 X1/9
Catalytic Converter System—1975-79 California models—All 1975-79 X1/9 models (50 states)

Crankcase Ventilation System

This is a closed system in which all crankcase vapors are drawn into the engine's combustion chambers to be consumed, rather than being vented to the atmosphere.

During idle and part-throttle engine operation, intake vacuum draws the vapors from the crankcase and a connecting hose (with a flame trap) conveys them to the air cleaner and into the carburetor.

During full-throttle engine operation, the crankcase vapors are conveyed directly to the intake manifold downstream of the carburetor by an additional smaller diameter hose; this part of the circuit is controlled by a valve which is activated by the throttle mechanism of the carburetor.

MAINTENANCE

Every 12,000 miles, this blowby gas and oil vapor recirculation system, including the carburetor, vent valve and flame trap must be cleaned and flushed with solvent.

Evaporative Emission Control

This system is designed to prevent the escape of raw fuel vapors into the atmosphere—that is, in effect, a "sealed" fuel system.

The fuel tank is of the "limited filling" type—that is, it maintains a volume of air space which is normally slightly pressurized. The tank and filler cap are non-vented. Fuel vapors originating in the fuel tank are conveyed to the separator; this component passes vapors but is designed to return liquid fuel to the tank. The vapors are then conveyed to a three-way valve. With the fuel tank slightly pressurized, fuel vapors are passed through this valve to the active carbon trap and become absorbed there.

As the engine is operated, intake manifold vacuum is applied to the trap. This draws warm air from a collector, normally near the exhaust manifold, into the trap and up through the carbon trap; the warm air regenerates the carbon, purifying it and releasing the fuel vapors to be drawn into the intake manifold.

MAINTENANCE

It is recommended that the components of the system be visually inspected periodically in order to determine that all units and hoses are intact and hose connections are secure. Replace the charcoal canister every 25,000 miles.

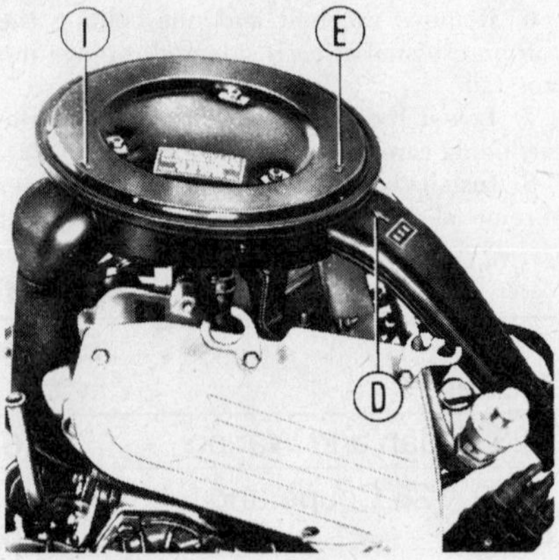

Warm climate—Align arrow "D" with reference "E"
Cold climate—Align arrow "D" with reference "I"

Air cleaner climatic adjustment—1975-77 128, 1975-77 124 Sport and 131

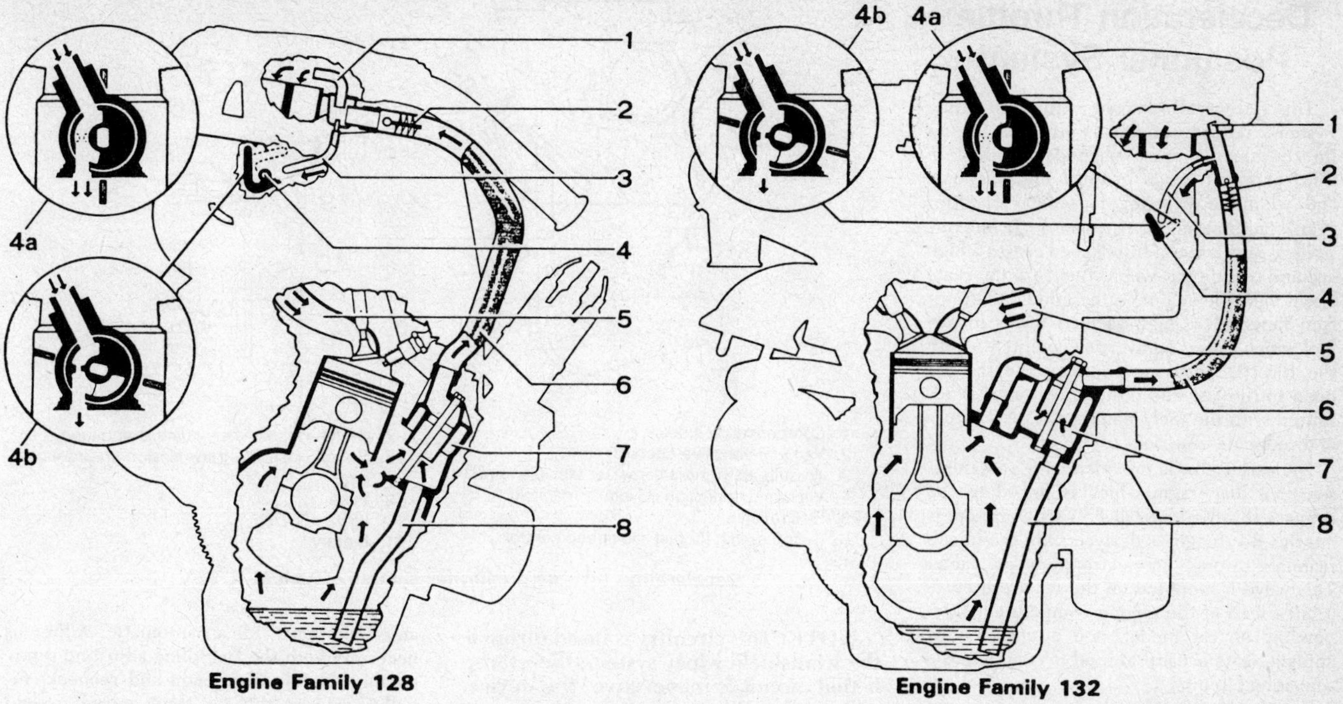

1. Emission feedback line to air cleaner
2. Flame trap
3. Air cleaner-to-control valve line
4. Control valve
4a. Control valve in engine beyond idle condition
4b. Control valve in engine idling condition
5. Intake manifold
6. Sump-to-air cleaner line
7. Cyclone liquid/vapor separator
8. Oil drain line into sump

Crankcase emission control system for the 128 and 132 engine families

Engine Modification System

This system is a catch-all for all the emission control features and components that do not fall under any of the other headings. Basically, it consists of a leaner, more carefully controlled carburetor; a recalibrated distributor that brings in the ignition advance at a higher rpm; a revised camshaft and valve timing; and a lower compression ratio.

To help the engine burn the leaner air/fuel mixture, a climatic setting is provided on the air cleaner (all models except X1/9). In cold weather, the air cleaner can be adjusted to draw in only exhaust manifold heated intake air, providing for better fuel atomization and overall better driveability when cold. In warm climates, the air cleaner can be adjusted to draw in only cool (ambient) intake air.

An idle stop solenoid is used on the carburetor linkage to prevent dieseling or "running on" after the key is shut off. The solenoid cuts off the fuel supply to the engine, closing the throttle plate completely.

MAINTENANCE

The only maintenance item is the air cleaner climatic setting. In temperate zones, the setting is adjusted in spring and autumn. Adjust the air intake as per the following illustrations:

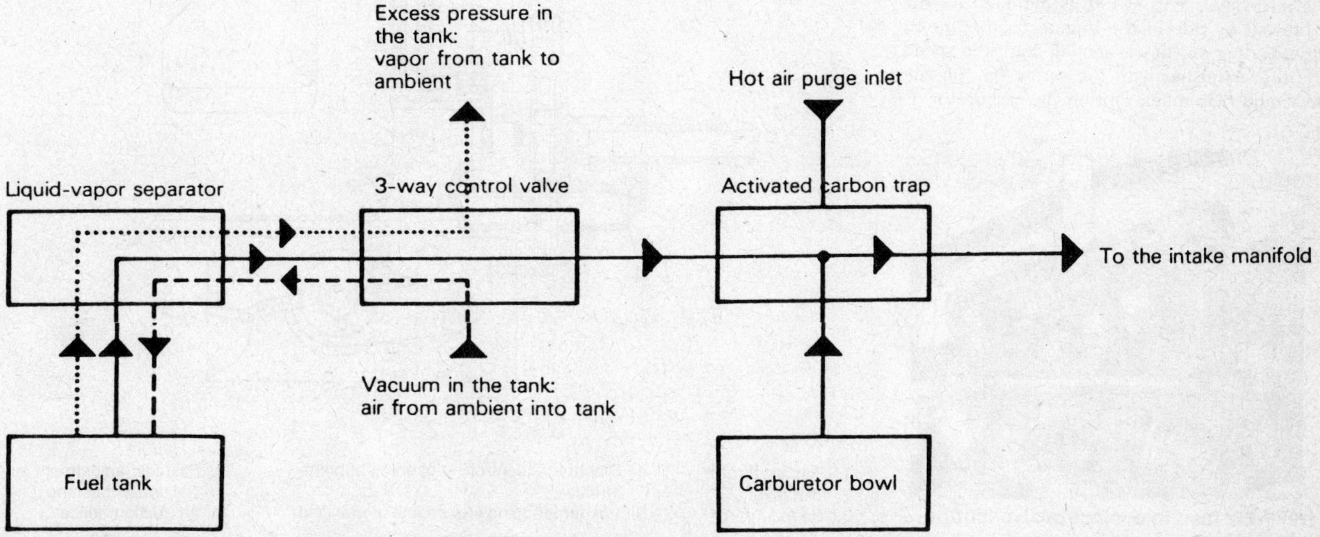

Typical fuel evaporation emission control system

Deceleration Throttle Positioner System

This system, also known as the Fast Idling System, reduces emissions by holding the throttle slightly open when decelerating in third or fourth gears (manual transmission), and when decelerating in second or third gears (automatic transmission). If uncontrolled, deceleration from speed causes a high vacuum condition when the throttle plate closes with the engine in the middle to upper rpm range. This high vacuum draws in raw fuel which causes an overrich condition. With the throttle positioner holding the throttle open to the fast idle position, extra air is admitted with the fuel, leaning out the mixture and reducing emissions.

The carburetor is provided with a vacuum-sensitive diaphragm which is linked to the primary throttle plate shaft. Vacuum to operate this diaphragm is derived from the intake manifold through an electropneumatic valve. This valve is mounted on the vehicle firewall or side wall of the engine compartment, depending on car model, and is operated by applying an electrical ground to complete the activating circuit.

Switch "A" is fitted to the transmission, and is closed (activating the circuit) when 3rd or 4th gears are engaged.

Switch "B" is fitted at the clutch pedal and is connected in series with switch "A". It is closed when the pedal is released and opens as the pedal is depressed. Thus, with 3rd or 4th gear engaged and the clutch pedal released, both switches are closed and the electrovalve is energized. Under such conditions, manifold vacuum is applied to the diaphragm keeping the throttle plate from returning completely to the closed or idle position. If the transmission is in a position other than 3rd or 4th gears (opening switch "A") or the clutch pedal is depressed regardless of conditions existing in the transmission (opening switch "B"), the activating circuit is broken and the device is rendered inoperative.

In order to be able to check and/or adjust the fast idle setting, pushbutton switch "C" is provided to manually ground, or activate, the electrovalve. This switch is mounted on the firewall or side of the engine compartment, depending on the car model. Fast idle speed is then adjusted with the screw "G" on the vacuum diaphragm unit on the carburetor.

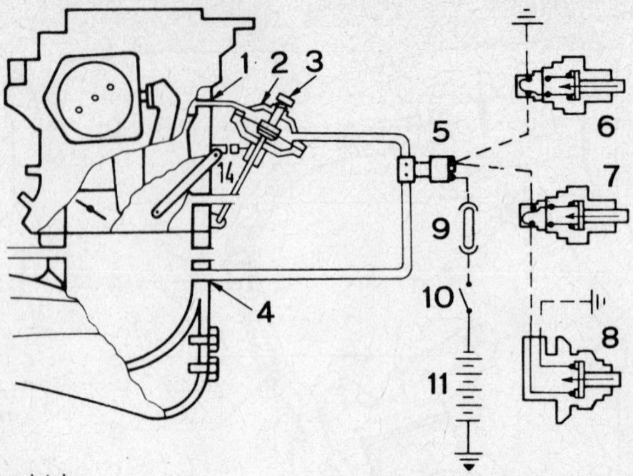

1. Compensating intake
2. Vacuum-sensitive capsule
3. Throttle adjustment screw for fast idle speed
4. Vacuum connection on intake manifold
5. Electrovalve
6. Button switch for fast idle speed control
7. Switch closed when clutch is engaged
8. Switch closed by transmission on 3rd-4th gear
9. Fuse
10. Ignition switch
11. Battery

Deceleration throttle positioner system—Typical

NOTE: This circuitry is fused through the windshield wiper system; therefore, if that circuit is inoperative, the device will not function.

MAINTENANCE

The only adjustment on the system is the fast idle speed, which can be checked after setting normal idle speed and mixture. With the engine warm and idling in neutral, depress and hold down the fast idle electrovalve button (located inside the engine compartment on the firewall, radiator support or fender apron) while accelerating the engine to approximately 2500 rpm. This will activate the system and simulate a deceleration condition. While still depressing the button, allow the engine speed to decrease to the fast idle speed; 1600 rpm on a manual transmission car and 1300 rpm with an automatic. Adjust as necessary with the fast idling adjusting screw on the fast idle diaphragm and recheck. Finally, release the pushbutton switch and check that the engine speed returns to normal idle speed, within 1-3 seconds.

Air Injection System

All Fiats are equipped with this system (also known as a thermal reactor system) to control emissions. A belt-driven air pump delivers filtered air to the exhaust ports. Here, the additional oxygen supplied by the vane type pump reacts with the uncombusted fuel mixture, promoting an afterburning effect in the hot exhaust manifold. To prevent a damaging reverse flow in the air injection manifold when exhaust gas pressure exceeds air supply

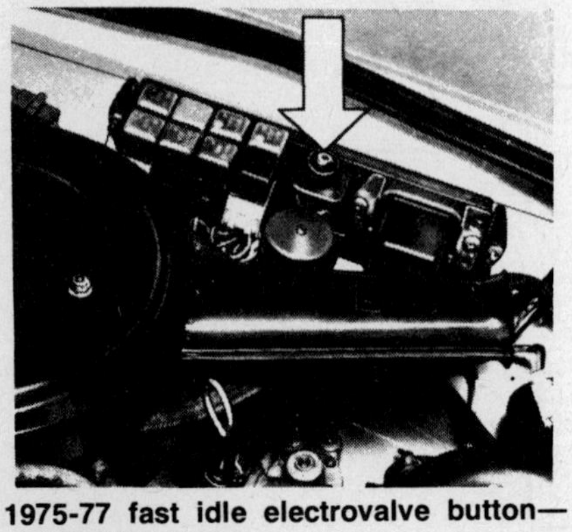

1975-77 fast idle electrovalve button—124 Spider shown

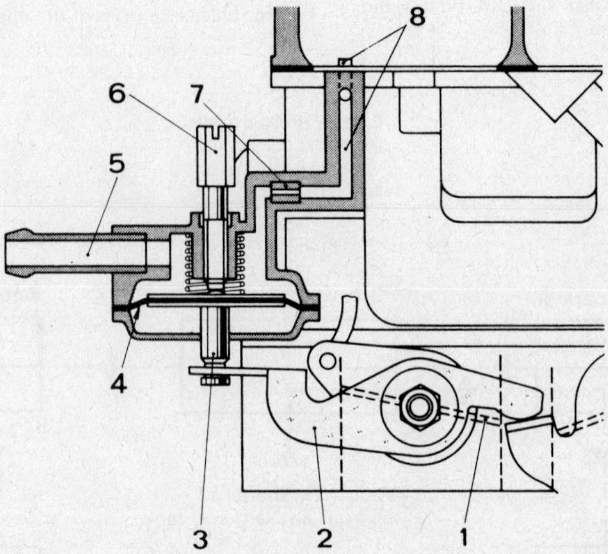

1. Primary throttle
2. Idler lever
3. Tie rod
4. Diaphragm controlling opening of primary throttle
5. Vacuum tapping line on intake manifold
6. Fast idle adjustment screw
7. Calibrated bushing
8. Air suction orifice

Cross section of fast idle adjusting screw and vacuum control

pressure, a non-return check valve is used. Also, to prevent backfiring in the exhaust system during deceleration, a diverter valve is used to divert pump air to the atmosphere under these conditions. The diverter valve also serves to cutout the air pump air during cold temperature starts.

MAINTENANCE

On 128 and X1/9 models with the Bosch or Nippondenso air pump, replace the air pump filter cartridge at 12,000 mile intervals; sooner if the car is driven in dusty areas. On 124 and 131 models with the Saginaw air pump, the filter is integral with the pump and does not require servicing.

Air pump belt tension cannot be adjusted when the toothed belt is used (v-belts are adjustable). Replace belt if worn. Average belt life should be 25,000-35,000 miles.

Exhaust Gas Recirculation System

All 124 and 131 models are equipped with an Exhaust Gas Recirculation (EGR) System to control nitrogen oxide emissions. The system recirculates a small portion (about 10%) of the exhaust manifold into the intake mixture during part-throttle conditions. Since the exhaust gases contain little oxygen, they cannot burn when fired, thereby lowering the peak combustion chamber temperatures and reducing NOx. To ensure good driveability of the car, an EGR valve is used to prevent exhaust gas recirculation during periods of idling or wide open throttle, and is used to meter the degree of recirculation during part-throttle applications, depending on engine load. A thermostatic switch cuts out recirculation when the engine is cold (catalytic converter models only). Also, on 1977 and

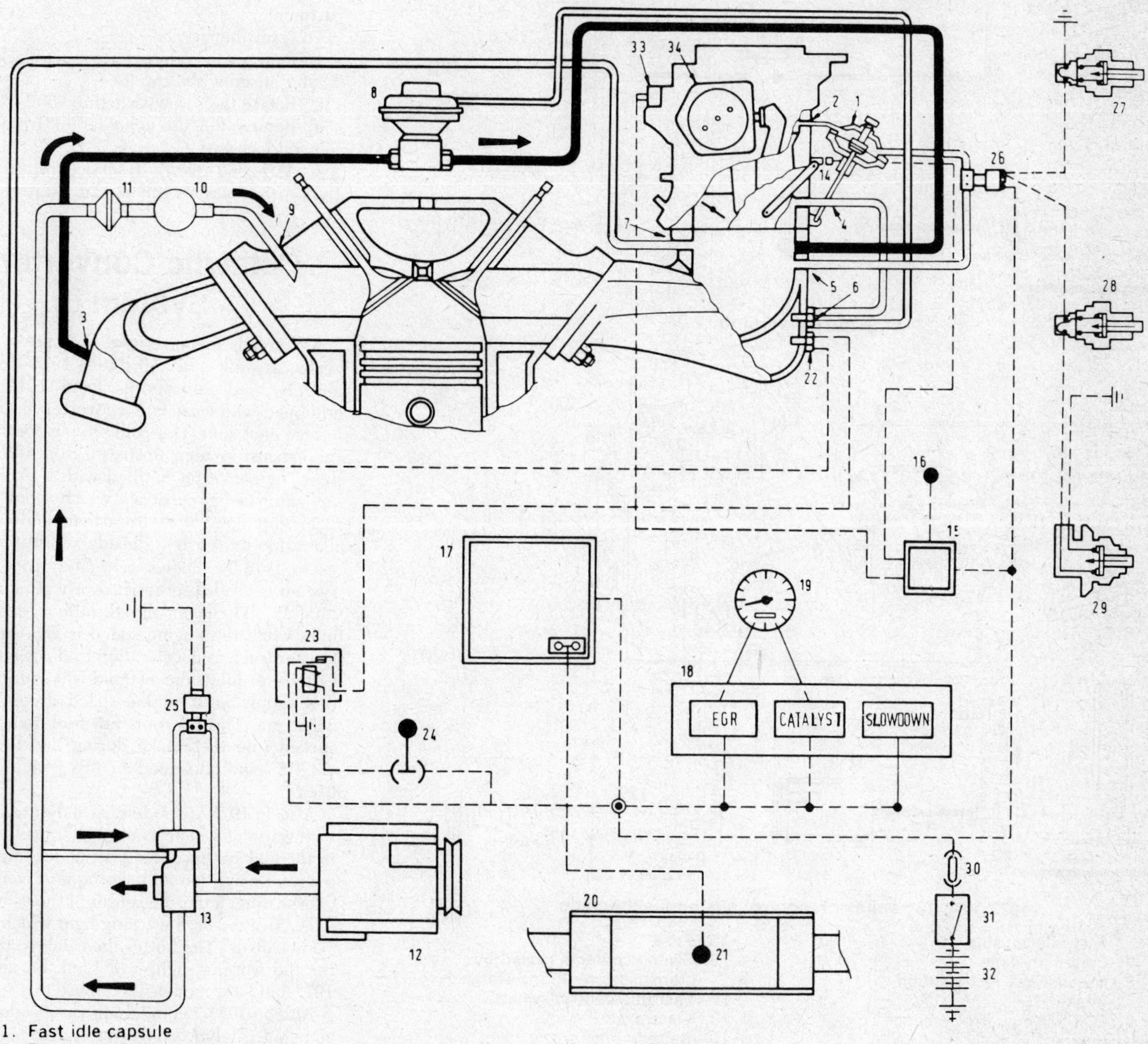

1. Fast idle capsule
2. Continuity hole
3. Exhaust gas recirculation intake
4. EGR valve control vacuum intake
5. Fast idle valve control vacuum intake
6. EGR valve control thermovalve
7. Diverter valve control vacuum intake
8. EGR valve
9. Air injector
10. Air injection manifold
11. Check valve
12. Air injection pump
13. Diverter valve
14. Inhibitor switch
15. Tachymetric switch (operates at 2650 ± 50 rpm)
16. From ignition coil
17. Control unit
18. Warning device panel
19. Odometer
20. Catalytic converter
21. Thermocouple
22. Thermoswitch
23. Magnetic reversing switch
24. Gearshift lever (switch open with transmission in neutral)
25. Electrovalve (normally closed)
26. Electrovalve
27. Fast idle control switch
28. Switch closed when clutch is engaged
29. Switch contacts closed by transmission on 3rd-4th gear
30. Fuse
31. Ignition contact matched switch
32. Battery
33. Idle stop solenoid
34. Automatic choke system

1975–76 124, 131 emission control systems schematic

later models, recirculation is prevented when 5th gear is engaged.

On 1975-76 models only, an odometer actuated EGR service reminder system is used. At 25,000 mile intervals, the system will light an "EGR" service warning lamp on the dash. Beginning with the 1977 model year, the EGR system has been "recertified" for 50,000 miles eliminating the need for the 25,000 mile service reminder system.

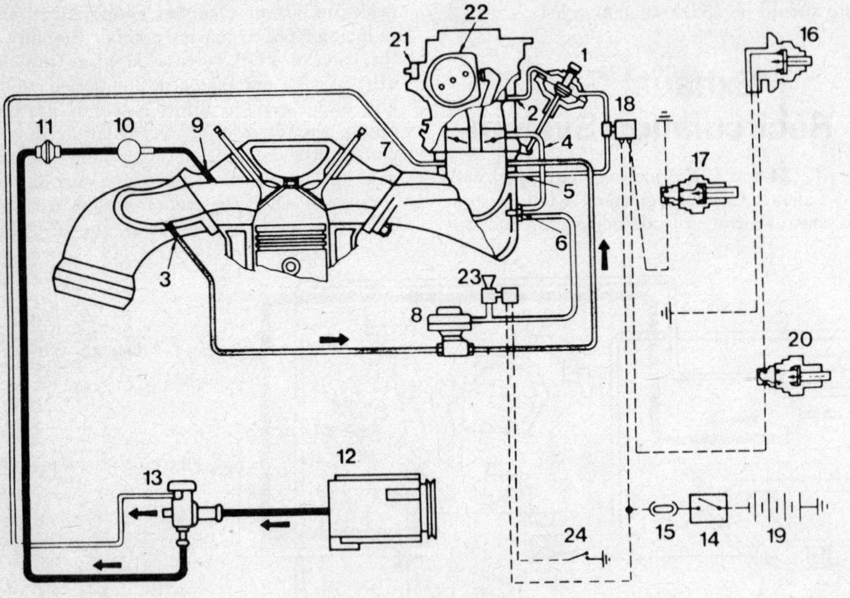

Standard version

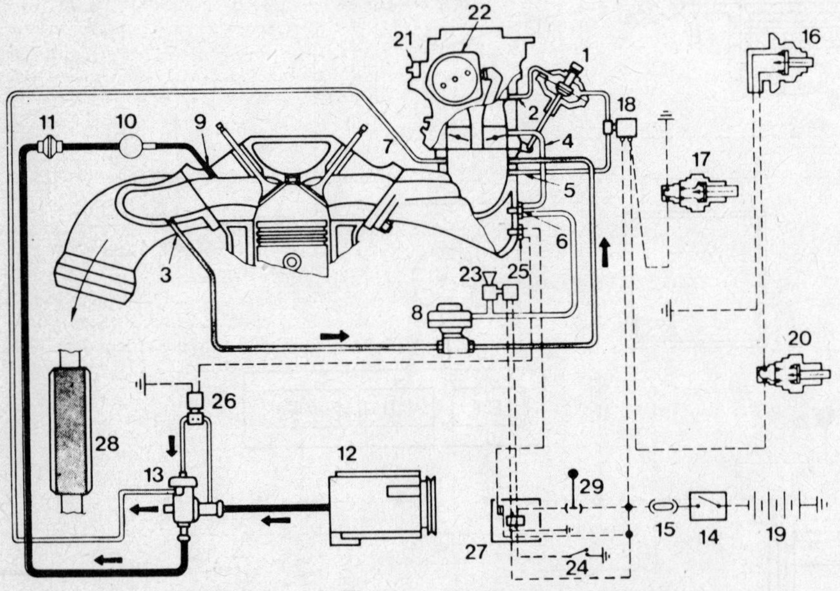

1977 124, 131 emission control systems schematic

1. Fast idle capsule
2. Continuity hole
3. Exhaust gas recirculation intake
4. EGR valve control vacuum intake
5. Fast idle valve control vacuum intake
6. EGR valve control thermovalve
7. Diverter valve control vacuum intake
8. EGR valve
9. Air injector
10. Air injection manifold
11. Check valve
12. Air pump
13. Diverter valve
14. Ignition contact matched switch
15. Fuse
16. Switch contacts closed by transmission on 3rd-4th gear
17. Fast idle control switch
18. Electrovalve
19. Battery
20. Switch closed when clutch is engaged
21. Idle stop solenoid
22. Automatic choke system
23. Electrovalve
24. Transmission switch (closed with 5th gear engaged)
25. Thermoswitch
26. Electrovalve
27. Magnetic reversing switch
28. Catalytic converter
29. Gear shift lever (switch open with transmission in neutral)

MAINTENANCE

On 1975-76 models, check the vacuum lines for leaks or cracks every 25,000 miles. Also check the EGR valve and exhaust gas line for deposits, particularly if a steady diet of leaded fuel is used. Clean with a bristle bore brush, or replace as necessary. 1977 and later models have no regularly scheduled EGR maintenance specified.

On 1975-76 models with the EGR service reminder system, the warning light is extinguished by resetting the odometer counter, located on the firewall of the engine compartment.

To reset the switch:

1. Remove the odometer counter lockwire (5) and unscrew the cap (6).
2. Rotate the screw switch to "50".
3. Replace the fuse in holder (6). Install the cap and lockwire.
4. At 50,000 mile EGR service, repeat Step 1 and rotate screw back to "25". Repeat Step 3.

Catalytic Converter System

All models manufactured for sale in California, as well as all (50 states) 1975-76 X1/9 models, and all models from 1979, are equipped with a catalytic converter to further reduce emissions. The converter is located in the exhaust system, upstream from the muffler. The converter is filled with a platinum/palladium pellet substrate which rapidly oxidizes emissions of hydrocarbons and carbon monoxide into carbon dioxide and water.

On 1975-76 models, a catalyst protection system is used to prevent overheating of the catalyst. Whenever the throttle is released fully while the engine speed is 2650 rpm or greater (such as deceleration from speed), the carburetor idle stop solenoid will shut off the fuel supply until engine speed drops below 2650 rpm. This prevents raw fuel from being sucked into the intake during deceleration. On 1977 and later models, this system is not used.

Also on 1975-76 models, a catalyst temperature warning system is used. If a malfunction in the fuel system should occur, leading to an overrich condition and subsequent converter overheating, a thermo sensor in the converter will activate a dash warning light which reads "slow down." The hotter the catalyst, the faster the warning light will blink on and off. 1977 and later models do not use this system.

Also on 1975-76 models only is an odometer actuated catalytic converter replacement reminder system. Identical to the EGR service reminder, at 25,000 mile intervals, a dash warning light will display "catalyst", indicating that it's time to replace the converter. Beginning with the 1977 model year, the converter has been re-certified for 50,000 miles or more, with no regularly scheduled replacement intervals.

MAINTENANCE

On 1975-76 models, replace the converter

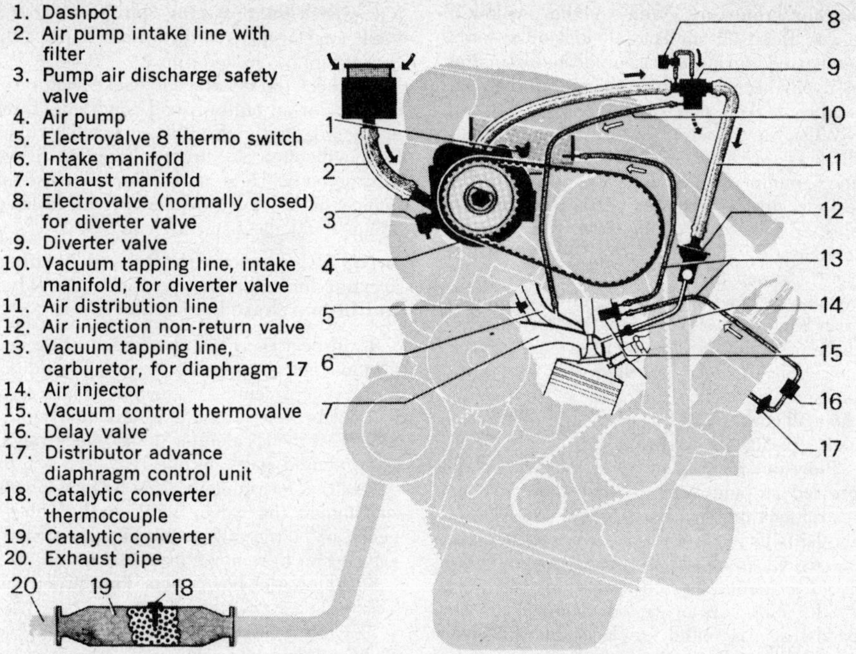

1. Dashpot
2. Air pump intake line with filter
3. Pump air discharge safety valve
4. Air pump
5. Electrovalve 8 thermo switch
6. Intake manifold
7. Exhaust manifold
8. Electrovalve (normally closed) for diverter valve
9. Diverter valve
10. Vacuum tapping line, intake manifold, for diverter valve
11. Air distribution line
12. Air injection non-return valve
13. Vacuum tapping line, carburetor, for diaphragm 17
14. Air injector
15. Vacuum control thermovalve
16. Delay valve
17. Distributor advance diaphragm control unit
18. Catalytic converter thermocouple
19. Catalytic converter
20. Exhaust pipe

1975–79 128, X1/9 emission control systems schematic

at 25,000 mile intervals, and reset the odometer switch. The switch, and resetting procedure is the same as that listed under EGR Maintenance. 1977 and later models do not require replacement of the converter in normal service.

FUEL SYSTEM

Mechanical Fuel Pump

A mechanical type fuel pump is used on the 1977 and later 124 Spiders. The pump is located on the engine block and is driven by the auxiliary shaft. A pushrod (X1/9) or pump lever (124) riding on the camshaft or auxiliary shaft eccentric operates the fuel pump diaphragm.

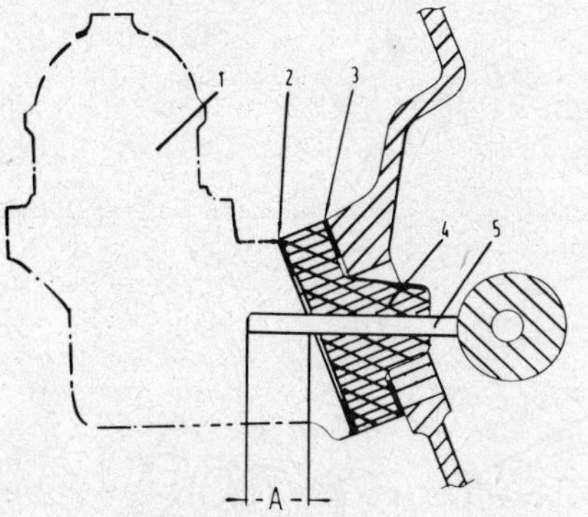

1. Pump
2. Gasket between pump and support
3. Gasket between support and crankcase
4. Insulating support
5. Rod

Adjusting fuel pump pushrod projection X1/9

REMOVAL AND INSTALLATION

X1/9 and 124

1. Remove and plug the fuel lines leading to the fuel pump.
2. Remove the mounting nuts and carefully remove the fuel pump from the block (or crankcase).
3. If the pump is equipped with a pushrod, remove the pushrod, gasket and insulator from the mounting.

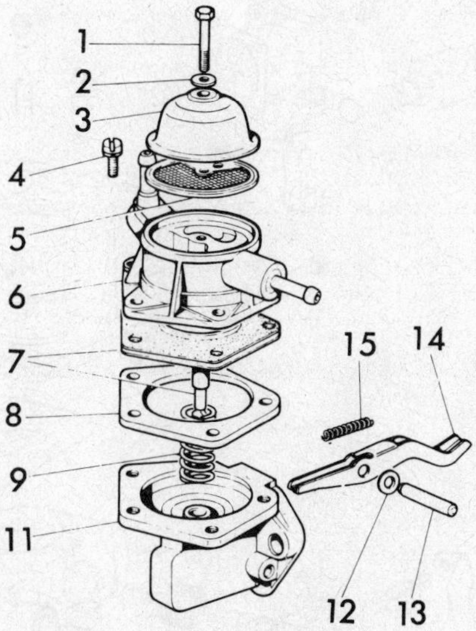

1. Screw
2. Lockwasher
3. Cover
4. Screw
5. Filter
6. Upper body
7. Diaphragm
8. Spacer
9. Spring
11. Lower body
12. Flat washer
13. Pivot pin
14. Operating lever
15. Spring

Mechanical fuel pump—124

4. Installation is the reverse of removal. Perform the following additional steps on the 128 and X1/9.
   a. Before replacing the fuel pump, adjust the projection of the pump pushrod.
   b. Fit the insulating spacer to its seat with a gasket.

NOTE: On the X1/9 and 128, the outer gasket used must be 0.012 in. In all cases, adjust pushrod projection only with the inner gasket thickness.

   c. Slide in the pushrod. The projection of the pushrod should be 0.59-0.61 in. on the X1/9 and 128. If the projection is not within specified limits, adjust the projection by replacing the inner gasket with another.

X1/9 and 128 service gaskets are available in the following thicknesses: 0.012 in., 0.027 in., and 0.047 in.

SERVICE

Sludge deposited in the fuel chamber or on the filter may be removed with the pump cover off. Intake and outlet valves should be inspected and replaced if damaged. Check springs for good condition.

Control mechanism for the intake chamber diaphragm should be washed in kerosene and lightly lubricated with thin oil. Lightly coat new fuel pump seals with grease before assembly. If a new diaphragm is to be installed, soak it in kerosene for a few minutes before assembly.

Electric Fuel Pump

An electric fuel pump is used on the later 128, 131, and all 1975-76 124 Sport Coupe and Spider models. On the 128, the pump is located beneath the floor pan, near the fuel tank. On 124 and 131 models, the pump is located inside the luggage compartment. The fuel pump is activated by a relay located in the engine compartment. The system is also protected by an 8 amp fuse located in the fuse box.

NOTE: If the fuel pump stops, check the relay and the fuse box before attempting any repairs.

REMOVAL AND INSTALLATION

1. Jack up the rear of the car and place it on stands allowing room to work on the pump.
2. Remove the hot wire from the pump.
3. Remove the ground wire. (If applicable.)
4. Before removing the gas inlet line, find something to stop the gas from flowing. A small piece of hose with the end pinched or with a bolt in the end will do. Or pinch shut the lines.
5. Remove the gas lines.
6. Remove the fuel recirculating lines.
7. Remove the mounting screws and the pump.

124 and 131

It is located in the luggage compartment. Use the Steps 2-7 given above for the 128.

Carburetor

REMOVAL AND INSTALLATION

1. Disconnect the accelerator rod, sliding it out of the lever ball joint end toward the dashboard.
2. Remove the air filter.
3. Disconnect the fuel line.
4. Disconnect all of the vacuum lines.
5. Remove the mounting bolts or nuts.
6. Remove the carburetor and gasket.
7. Installation is the reverse of the above procedure.

OVERHAUL

All Types

Efficient carburetion depends greatly on careful cleaning and inspection during overhaul, since dirt, gum, water, or varnish in or on the carburetor parts are often responsible for poor performance.

Overhaul your carburetor in a clean, dust-free area. Carefully disassemble the carburetor, referring often to the exploded views. Keep all similar and look-alike parts segregated during disassembly and cleaning to avoid accidental interchange during assembly. Make a note of all jet sizes.

When the carburetor is disassembled, wash all parts (except diaphragms, electric choke units, pump plunger, and any other plastic, leather, fiber, or rubber parts) in clean carburetor solvent. Do not leave parts in the solvent any longer than is necessary to sufficiently loosen the deposits. Excessive cleaning may remove the special finish from the float bowl and choke valve bodies, leaving these parts unfit for service. Rinse all parts in clean solvent and blow them dry with compressed air or allow them to air dry. Wipe clean all cork, plastic, leather, and fiber parts with a clean, lint-free cloth.

Blow out all passages and jets with compressed air and be sure that there are no restrictions or blockages. Never use wire or similar tools to clean jets, fuel passages, or air bleeds. Clean all jets and valves separately to avoid accidental interchange.

Check all parts for wear or damage. If wear or damage is found, replace the defective parts. Especially check the following:

1. Check the float needle and seat for wear. If wear is found, replace the complete assembly.
2. Check the float hinge pin for wear and the float(s) for dents or distortion. Replace the float if fuel has leaked into it.
3. Check the throttle and choke shaft bores for wear or an out-of-round condition. Damage or wear to the throttle arm, shaft, or shaft bore will often require replacement of the throttle body. These parts require a close tolerance of fit; wear may allow air leakage, which could affect starting and idling.

NOTE: Throttle shafts and bushings are not included in overhaul kits. They can be purchased separately.

4. Inspect the idle mixture adjusting needles for burrs or grooves. Any such condition requires replacement of the needle, since you will not be able to obtain a satisfactory idle.
5. Test the accelerator pump check valves. They should pass air one way but not the other. Test for proper seating by blowing and sucking on the valve. Replace the valve if necessary. If the valve is satisfactory, wash the valve again to remove breath moisture.
6. Check the bowl cover for warped surfaces with a straightedge.
7. Closely inspect the valves and seats for wear and damage, replacing as necessary.
8. After the carburetor is assembled, check the choke valve for freedom of operation.

Carburetor overhaul kits are recommended

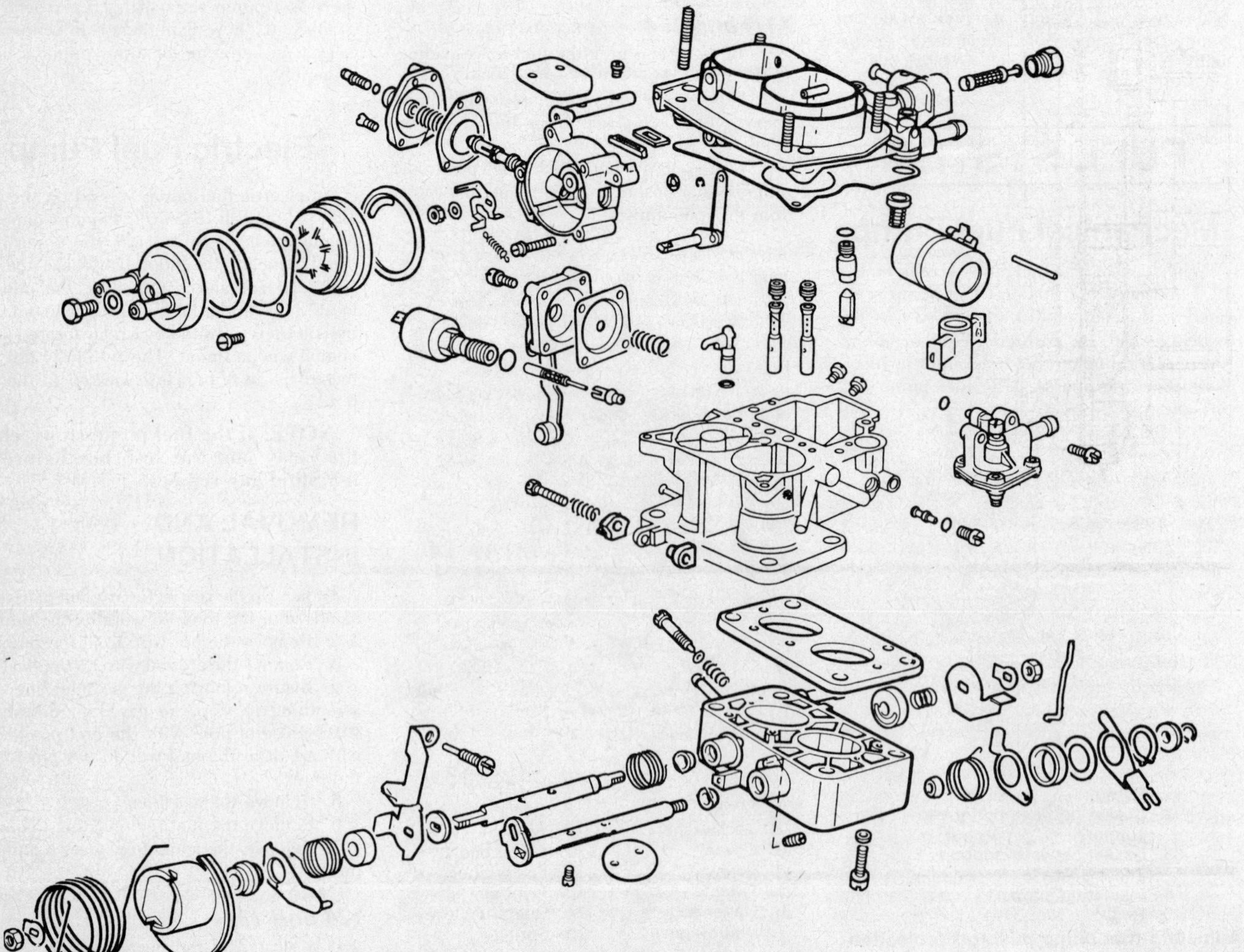

Exploded view of Weber 32 ADFA—1975–77 124, 131

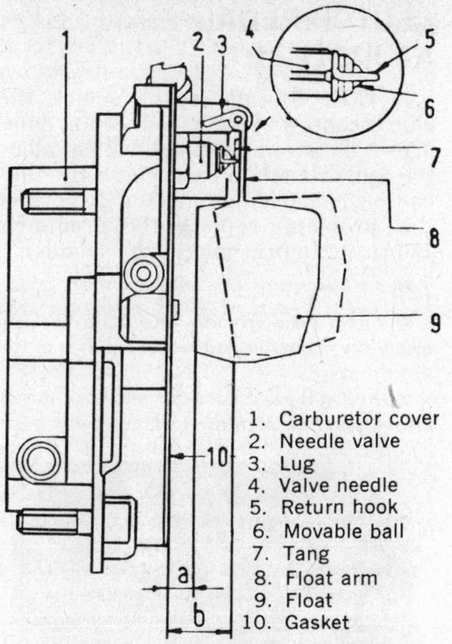

a = 0.236 in. (6mm) = distance between float and cover with gasket, in vertical position
b = 0.590 in. (15mm) = maximum distance of float from cover face with gasket
b-a = 0.354 in. (9mm) = float travel

Float level adjustment—1975-77 128, X1/9

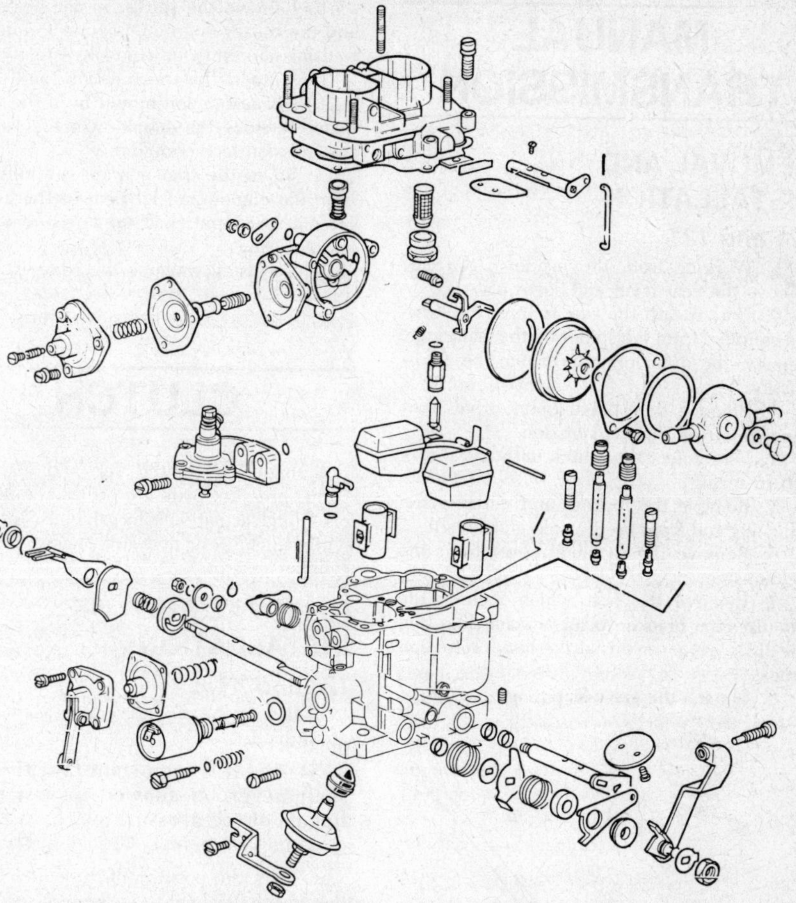

Exploded view of Weber 32 DATRA—1975-77 128, X1/9

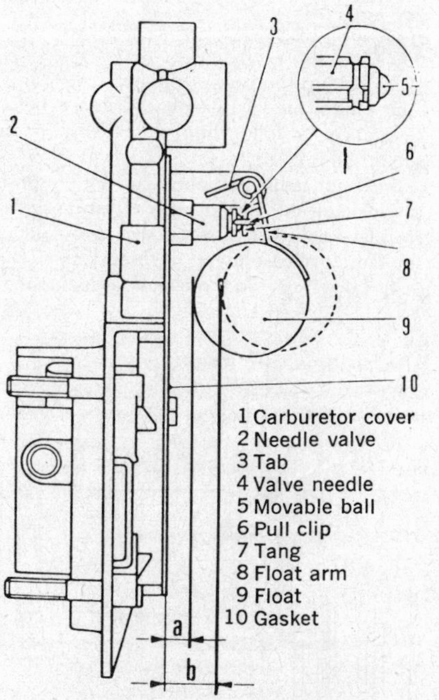

a = 6 mm (.236 in.) = distance between float and cover with gasket, in vertical position
b = 14 mm (.551 in.) = maximum distance of float from cover face, with gasket
b-a = 8 mm (.315 in.) = float travel

Float level adjustment—1975-77 124, 131

for each overhaul. These kits contain all gaskets and new parts to replace those that deteriorate most rapidly. Failure to replace all parts supplied with the kit (especially gaskets) can result in poor performance later.

Some carburetor manufacturers supply overhaul kits of three basic types: minor repair; major repair; and gasket kits.

After cleaning and checking all components, reassemble the carburetor, using new parts and referring to the exploded view. When reassembling, make sure that all screws and jets are tight in their seats, but do not overtighten as the tips will be distorted. Tighten all screws gradually, in rotation. Do not tighten needle valves into their seats; uneven jetting will result. Always use new gaskets. Be sure to adjust the float level when reassembling.

THROTTLE LINKAGE ADJUSTMENT

All Fiat models use cable type throttle linkage. Adjustments can be made at the carburetor by loosening the hold-down screw of the eye in which the cable slides. Proper adjustment will allow the gas pedal to be fully released from the floor boards and at the same time the carburetor will be in the fully-closed position.

NOTE: If the gas pedal suddenly becomes sloppy, before checking the adjustment be sure that the cable housing is securely mounted.

FLOAT LEVEL ADJUSTMENT

1. Remove the air horn section of the carburetor from the rest of the carburetor assembly.
2. Check to make sure that the needle valve is screwed all the way into its seat. Make sure that the float is not dented or punctured and can turn freely on its hinge.
3. Holding the air horn assembly so that the float hangs vertically, the distance between the top side of the float and the cover with the gasket in place should be 0.236 in.
4. Holding the air horn assembly in the normal horizontal position, the float should drop so that the maximum distance between the end of the float and the cover mating surface with the gasket in place is distance "b" (see illustrations). Total float travel is b-a.
5. To adjust the float level, carefully bend the tang of the float that attaches to the needle valve.

FAST IDLE SPEED ADJUSTMENT

See the "Deceleration Throttle Positioner Maintenance" portion of the Emission Control section.

MANUAL TRANSMISSION

REMOVAL AND INSTALLATION

124 and 131

1. Working from the inside of the car, remove the gear lever and cover plate.
2. Underneath the car, remove the flexible coupling from the spider on the mainshaft. Remove the drain plug and drain the transmission.
3. Remove the speedometer drive from the support on the transmission.
4. Disconnect the clutch withdrawal fork return spring.
5. Remove the locknut and unscrew the adjusting rod from the flexible clutch cable.
6. Remove the flywheel cover from the bellhousing.
7. Remove the bolt which secures the exhaust pipe bracket to the transmission. On the 131, remove the driveshaft protection bracket.
8. Detach the exhaust piping.

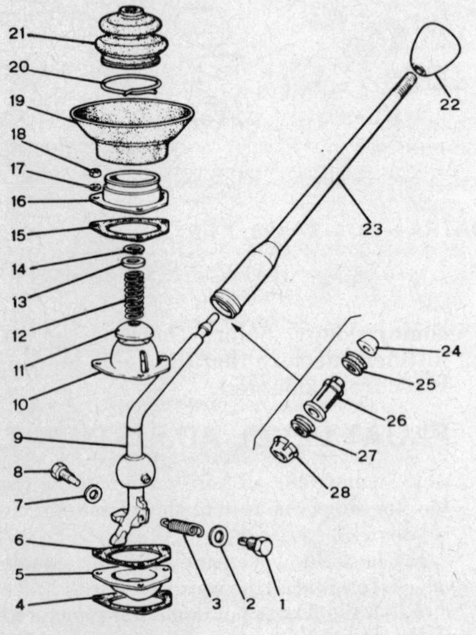

1. Gear lever return spring anchor screw
2. Flat washer
3. Lever return spring
4. Gasket
5. Socket plate
6. Gasket
7. Flat washer
8. Gear lever stop screw
9. Lower part of gear lever with ball
10. Upper socket plate
11. Dome washer
12. Spring
13. Cup washer
14. Retaining snap-ring
15. Gasket
16. Flange
17. Spring washer
18. Nut
19. Grommet
20. Spring clip
21. Rubber boot
22. Knob
23. Upper part of gear lever
24. Shoulder block
25. Rubber bushings
26. Spacer
27. Rubber bushings
28. Spring-ring

Exploded view of 124 4-speed shifter assembly

9. Remove the starter motor heat shield and the starter motor. Disconnect clutch and transmission emission control switch wires.
10. Support the transmission, and disconnect the transmission mount from the underbody. Remove the 4 bolts which secure the transmission to the engine.
11. Move the transmission carefully away from the engine and lower it to the ground. Do not rest input shaft on clutch disc or release bearing.
12. To install, reverse the removal procedure.

CLUTCH

A single, dry clutch disc and diaphragm spring pressure plate are utilized on all models. Clutch actuation is by cable, except on the X1/9, which uses a hydraulic master and slave cylinder system.

REMOVAL AND INSTALLATION

128 and X1/9

1. Jack up the car and remove the transaxle as outlined:

NOTE: It is important that the input shaft never be allowed to rest on the fingers of the pressure plate, as the fingers may be bent.

2. Mark the position of the clutch in relation to the flywheel to facilitate assembly.
3. Remove the bolts (in stages) which secure the clutch cover to the flywheel. The bolts should be removed evenly to prevent distortion of the clutch.
4. Remove the pressure plate and clutch disc.
5. Check the condition of the pilot bushing which is pressed into the crankshaft. If necessary, replace the bushing. Installation of the clutch is the reverse of removal. Use an old input shaft or wooden dummy shaft to center the clutch disc. Tighten the clutch cover bolts diagonally, in rotation, to 11 ft/lbs.

124 and 131

1. Jack up the car and remove the transmission.
2. Before removing the clutch, mark the position of the clutch in relation to the flywheel to facilitate reassembly (if the clutch is to be reused).
3. Remove the bolts which secure the clutch cover to the flywheel. Remove them in stages to prevent distortion.
4. Remove the pressure plate and clutch.
5. Before reinstallation, check the pilot bushing in the crankshaft for wear, replacing as necessary.
6. Install the clutch using an alignment tool or an old input shaft to center the clutch disc. A wooden dummy shaft cut to the proper size will also work. Be careful not to get oil or grease on the clutch disc during installation.
7. With the clutch disc centered, tighten the cover bolts diagonally, in rotation, to 22 ft/lbs.
8. Install the transmission.

CLUTCH PEDAL ADJUSTMENT

NOTE: On all models check the clutch control cable grommet for damage. A damaged grommet will not allow the cable sheath to react correctly, thus causing a clutch malfunction. To correct this problem, replace the grommet. Lubricate to prevent clutch "shudder".

128

1. Open hood, remove the spare tire and locate the cable nut and locknut shown in the illustration.
2. Adjust the nut until the pedal has one in. of free-play. Tighten the locknut.

1. Cable
2. Nut and locknut for adjusting the tie-rod
3. Forked lever

Clutch free play adjusting location—128

X1/9

1. Jack up the rear of the car.
2. Clutch pedal free-play (distance before resistance is felt when depressing pedal) should be 1.25 in.
3. If not, adjust as necessary by loosening the locknut and turning the adjusting nut on the slave cylinder pushrod where it contacts the clutch release lever. Tighten locknut.
4. Lower car and recheck adjustment. If

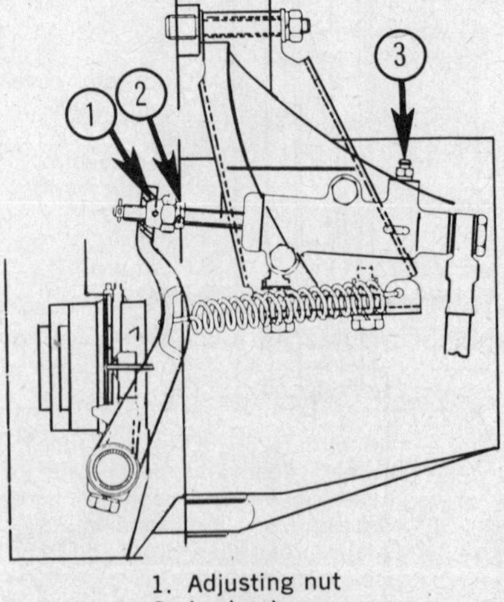

1. Adjusting nut
2. Locknut
3. Bleed nipple

Clutch free play adjusting location—X1/9

slave cylinder does not operate at all, check for air in system and bleed circuit.

131

1. Recheck adjustment.
2. Clutch adjustment is not required. Automatic wear adjustment. No pedal free travel.

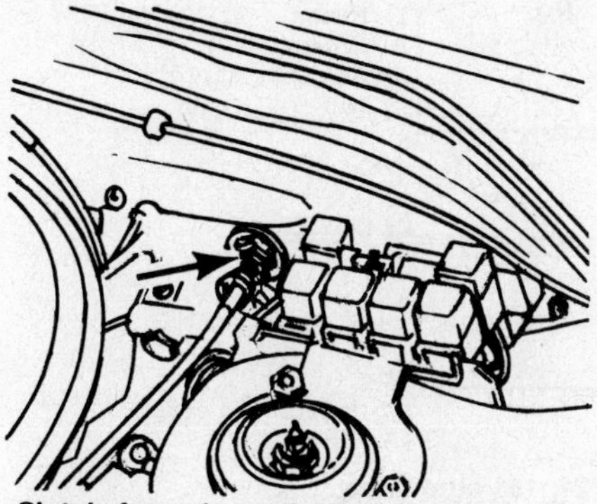

Clutch free play adjusting location—131 and Brava

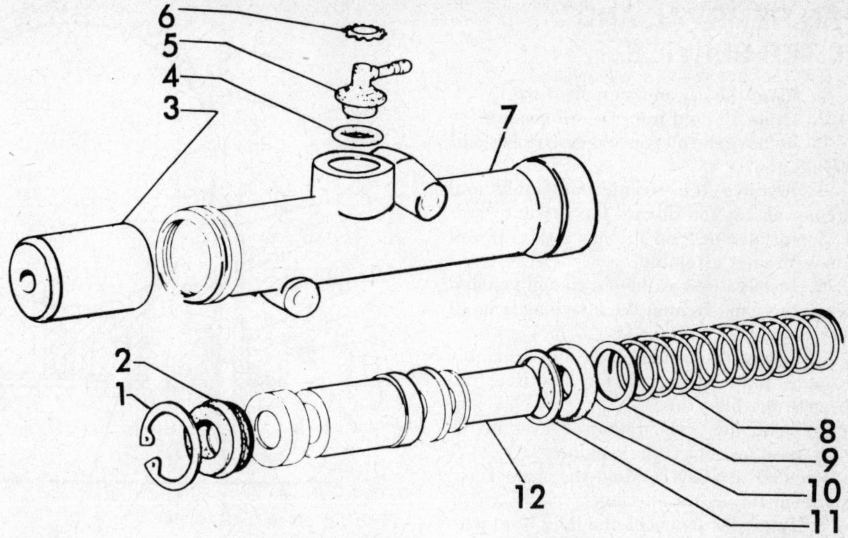

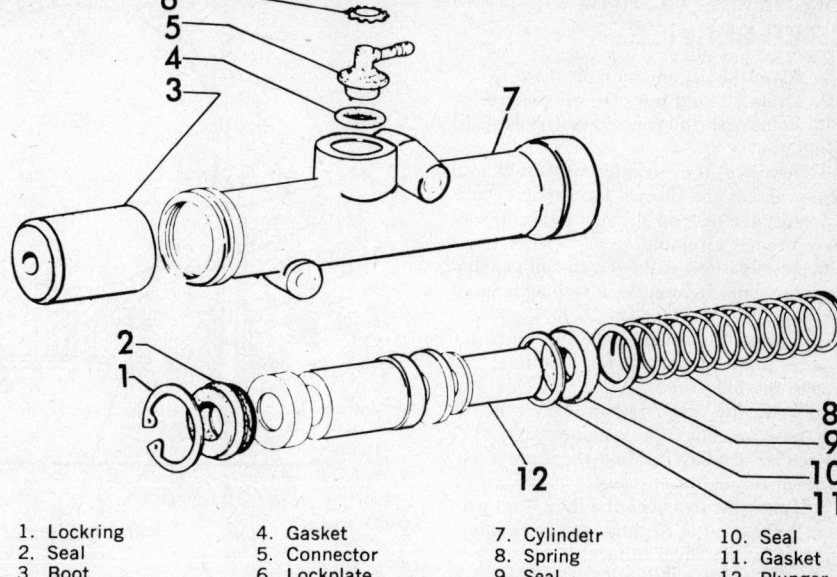

1. Lockring	4. Gasket	7. Cylindetr	10. Seal
2. Seal	5. Connector	8. Spring	11. Gasket
3. Boot	6. Lockplate	9. Seal	12. Plunger

Exploded view of clutch master cylinder—X1/9

124

1. Jack up the front of the car.
2. Adjustment is made at the cable nut at the clutch release lever as shown in the illustration.
3. Adjust the pedal travel to 0.98 in.

Clutch Master Cylinder

REMOVAL AND INSTALLATION

X1/9

NOTE: The upper steering column assembly must first be removed to gain access to the clutch master cylinder.

1. Disconnect the battery.
2. Remove the five screws retaining the steering column upper and lower trim halves.
3. Disconnect the column wiring (three connectors and one wire).
4. Remove the two nuts and two bolts retaining the upper column assembly to the underside of the dashboard. Support the column and steering wheel assembly and pull it straight back and out, disconnecting it from the steering box shaft. Remove the complete column and steering wheel assembly from the car.
5. Place absorbant rags over the driver's side floor carpets. Locate the master cylinder up over the clutch pedal. Disconnect and plug the fluid line to the slave cylinder.
6. Remove the two retaining bolts. Pull the cylinder out far enough to disconnect and plug the fluid line to the reservoir. Pull the cylinder off the pushrod. Remove from car.
7. Reverse Steps 1-6 to install. Refill the fluid reservoir and bleed the hydraulic system.

Clutch Slave Cylinder

REMOVAL AND INSTALLATION

X1/9

1. Disconnect and plug the fluid line banjo connector from the rear of the slave cylinder.
2. Remove the cotter pin from the end of the slave cylinder pushrod.
3. Disconnect the release arm return spring.
4. Remove the two slave cylinder retaining bolts and remove the cylinder.
5. Reverse Steps 1-4 to install, using new copper gaskets at the fluid line banjo connector. Bleed the hydraulic system. Adjust clutch pedal free-play, if necessary.

Hydraulic System Bleeding

X1/9

1. Connect a bleeder hose to the slave cylinder bleeder nipple. Place the other end of the hose in a container partially filled with brake fluid. Make sure the hose end is immersed in fluid.
2. Fill up the clutch fluid reservoir with clean brake fluid. Open the bleeder nipple screw.
3. Have an assistant pump the clutch pedal until all air bubbles stop coming out of the hose. Periodically check the reservoir level so that it doesn't run dry.
4. When all air is expelled, close the nipple screw and remove the hose. Discard the old clutch (brake) fluid. Refill the reservoir and check clutch operation.

AUTOMATIC TRANSMISSION

The automatic transmission available in the 124 and 131 series is the GM/Adam Opel Trimatic. It is a three-speed unit with a variable torque multiplication ratio of between 2.4 to 1 and 1 to 1.

1. Spring	4. Housing	7. Boot	10. Seal
2. Washer	5. Bleeding screw	8. Seal	11. Bushing
3. Lockring	6. Rod	9. Piston	

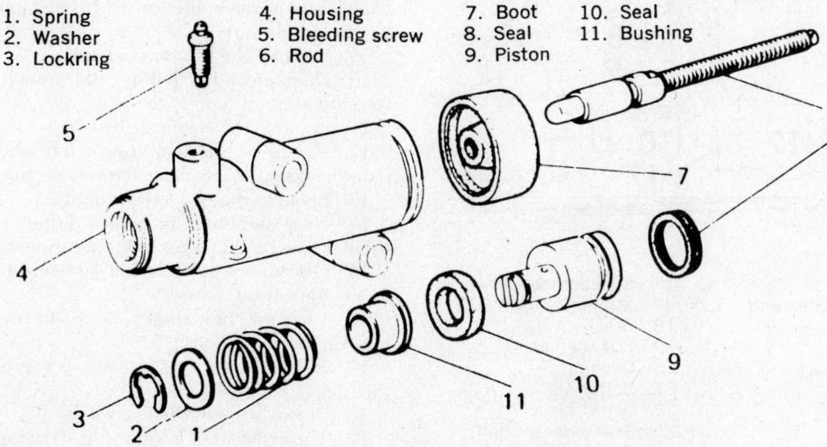

Exploded view of clutch slave cylinder—X1/9

PAN REMOVAL AND FILTER SERVICE

1. Raise the car and support it safely.
2. Drain all fluid from the oil pan.
3. Remove the oil pan and gasket. Discard the old gasket.
4. Remove the strainer assembly and strainer gasket and discard the gasket.
5. Install a new oil strainer gasket. Install a new strainer assembly.
6. Install a new gasket on the oil pan and install the pan. Tighten the attaching bolts to 7-10 ft/lbs.
7. Lower the car and add approximately three (3) pints of transmission fluid (Dexron) through the filler tube.
8. With the manual control lever in the Park position, start the engine. DO NOT RACE THE ENGINE. Move the manual control lever through each range.
9. Immediately check the fluid level with the selector lever in Neutral, engine running, and vehicle on a level surface.
10. Add additional fluid to a level between the MIN and MAX marks on the dipstick. Do not overfill.

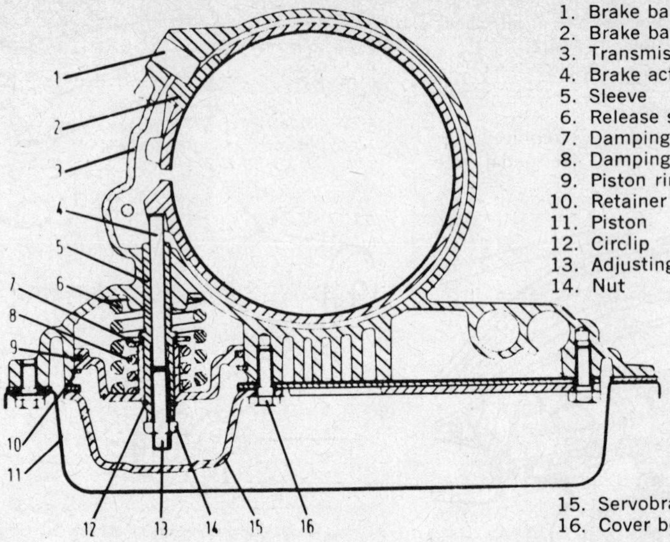

Band adjustment—124, 131 automatic

BAND ADJUSTMENT

1. Drain the transmission.
2. Remove the pan and gasket.
3. Remove the servo brake band cover.
4. Loosen the locknut for the servo brake adjusting screw.
5. Tighten the adjusting screw to 40 *inch pounds*. Then, back off the adjusting screw five full turns.
6. Without disturbing the adjustment, tighten the locknut to 12-15 ft/lbs.
7. Install the servo brake band cover, using a new gasket. Tighten to 17-19 ft/lbs.
8. Install the pan and gasket. Tighten to 7-10 ft/lbs.
9. Fill the transmission with Dexron automatic transmission fluid. Follow Steps 7-10 under "Pan Removal and Filter Service."

GEAR SELECTOR LINKAGE ADJUSTMENT

1. With the engine off, place the shift lever in Drive.
2. Jack up the front of the car and support with jack stands.
3. Disconnect the shifter tie rod at the relay lever (shift lever).
4. Move the cross shaft actuating lever (shift lever on transmission) to the Drive position, which is third detent from the front.
5. Without disturbing either of the two levers, try to insert the end of the shifter tie rod into the relay lever. If necessary, loosen the adjusting nut and rotate until the tie rod end will just slip into the eye of the relay lever. Then, tighten the adjusting nut. Connect the tie rod to the relay lever using a new circlip.
6. Remove the jack stands and lower the car. Check shifter operation.

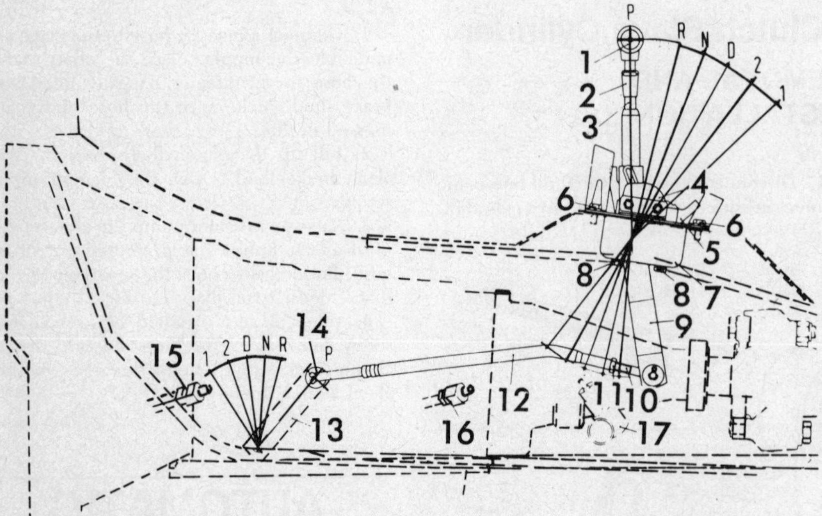

1. Upper handle
2. Lower handle
3. Selector lever
4. Starter inhibitor switch
5. Gear selector
6. Bolt
7. Support
8. Bracket bolt
9. Relay lever
10. Tie rod adjustable end
11. Adjusting nut
12. Tie rod
13. Cross shaft actuating lever
14. Flat washer
15. Oil union
16. Oil union
17. Speedometer drive support
18. Bracket
19. Flat washer
20. Bushing
21. Cotter pin
22. Cotter pin
23. Gear selector bolt

Shift lever linkage adjustment—124, 131, Brava automatic

TRANSAXLE

REMOVAL AND INSTALLATION

128

1. Disconnect the battery.
2. Remove the spare tire.
3. Remove the speedometer drive.
4. Disconnect the flexible cable adjusting rod from the clutch release lever and unhook the return spring.
5. Unscrew the guard-to-body nut.
6. Unscrew the transmission-to-crankcase attachment screws and nuts, accessible from above.
7. Attach the engine support crosspiece.
8. Remove the hub caps from the front wheels and unscrew the constant speed joint-to-wheel hub nuts.
9. Remove the left front wheel.
10. Disconnect the left tie rod from the steering arm.
11. Remove the stabilizer bar.
12. Unscrew the two lower left shock absorber-to-pillar attaching screws and nuts.
13. Remove the two lower guards.
14. Unscrew the nuts which fasten the exhaust clamping bracket to the transmission.
15. Disconnect the gearshift and selection lever control rod.
16. Unscrew the starter motor-to-transmission assembly bolts.
17. Remove the engine support crossmember.
18. Remove the flywheel cover.
19. Unscrew the remaining transmission-to-engine attachment screws.

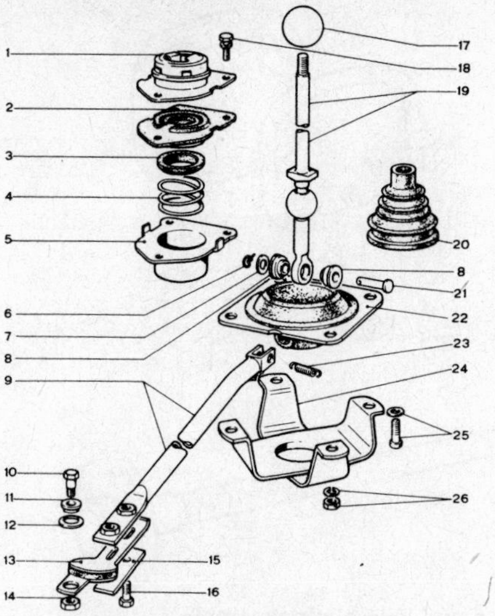

1. Guide plate
2. Upper socket
3. Lower socket
4. Spring
5. Support
6. Cotter pin
7. Flat washer
8. Bushings
9. Rod
10. Screw
11. Bushing
12. Spring washer
13. Flexible rod
14. Nut
15. Plate
16. Screw
17. Knob
18. Screw
19. Lever
20. Dust boot
21. Pin
22. Guard and boot
23. Return spring
24. Guard
25. Screw and washer
26. Nut and spring washer

Gear shift mechanism for 128; X1/9 similar

20. Disconnect the ground cable from the transmission assembly.
21. Using wire, fix the axle shafts complete with constant-speed joints, to the transmission in order to prevent them from coming away from their seats in the differential.
22. Remove the transmission-differential assembly from beneath the car using a hydraulic jack.
23. Installation is the reverse of removal.

X1/9

1. Remove the air cleaner and the carburetor cooling duct.
2. Disconnect the battery cables from the battery.
3. Disconnect the clutch slave cylinder from the clutch linkage, remove the two slave cylinder attaching bolts and move the cylinder out of the way.
4. Support the engine and remove the nuts and bolts holding the transmission to the crankcase that are accessible from above.
5. Raise the vehicle and remove the rear wheels.
6. Remove the three lower guards on the left side.
7. Mark the position of the shift tube where it is connected to the gearshift flexible link.
8. Remove the two bolts holding the flexible link to the shift tube, loosen the bolt at the transmission end of the link and swing the link out of the way.
9. Disconnect the electrical connector for the backup lights and remove the clamp securing the wires to the body.
10. Disconnect the connector for the seat belt system in the transmission. The connector is located inboard and forward of the transmission near the engine water hoses.
11. Remove the starter from the transmission.
12. Disconnect the ground strap.
13. Remove the exhaust pipe.
14. Remove the hub nuts holding the constant speed joints to the wheel hubs.
15. Remove the two bolts and nuts securing the suspension control arms to their supports. Pull the hub off the constant speed joints and attach the axle shafts to the transmission with wire to prevent them from coming out.
16. Remove the flywheel cover.
17. Remove the crosspiece supporting the engine.

CAUTION

Make sure that the engine is properly supported from above.

18. Remove the remaining nuts and bolts securing the transmission to the engine.
19. Remove the transmission/differential from below the vehicle. Use a hydruaulic jack to support the assembly.
20. Install the transmission/differential in the reverse order of removal.

SHIFT LINKAGE ADJUSTMENT

128 and X1/9

1. Place the transmission in Neutral.
2. Loosen the two adjustment screws at the transmission end of the shift rod.
3. Place the gear shift lever in the neutral position (centered and straight up and down) and tighten the two adjusting screws at the transmission end of the shift rod. The holes in the flexible shift rod are slotted to allow for adjustment.

DRIVE AXLE

Driveshaft and U-Joints

124 AND 131

Fiat 124 and 131 driveshafts are in two parts; a splined tubular front piece connected to the transmission through a flexible spider coupling and a solid rear piece, connected to the front piece by a universal joint and to the rear axle by a universal joint.

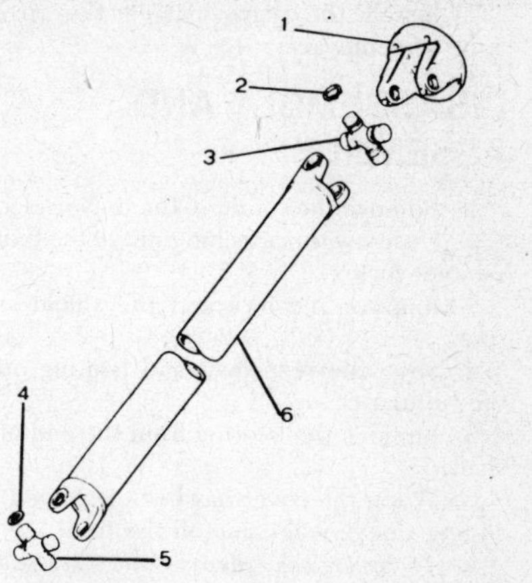

1. Fork connecting rear prop shaft to drive pinion sleeve
2. Spider snap ring
3. Spider assy.
4. Snap ring
5. Spider assy.
6. Rear prop shaft

124, 131, Brava driveshaft rear section

REMOVAL AND INSTALLATION

NOTE: Special tool A.70025 or a 5 in. diameter screw type hose clamp is required to remove the sleeve of the front shaft.

1. Install the special tool or 5 in. diameter hose clamp and unscrew the 3 self-locking nuts and withdraw the bolts.
2. Remove the retaining clip of the brake hose from the rear shaft cover and disconnect the hose from the rear brake pipe.
3. Release the brake pipe from the two clips on the rear shaft cover.
4. Disconnect the rear shaft cover from the differential.
5. Disconnect the handbrake return spring from the central support.
6. Unscrew the nuts holding the central support to the body and slide the shafts toward the front to remove.

1. Flexible coupling
2. Bushing
3. Sleeve
4. Lubrication fitting
5. Slotted sleeve and spring
6. Seal
7. Resilient pad
8. Yoke
9. Nut
10. Disc
11. Lock ring
12. Ball bearing

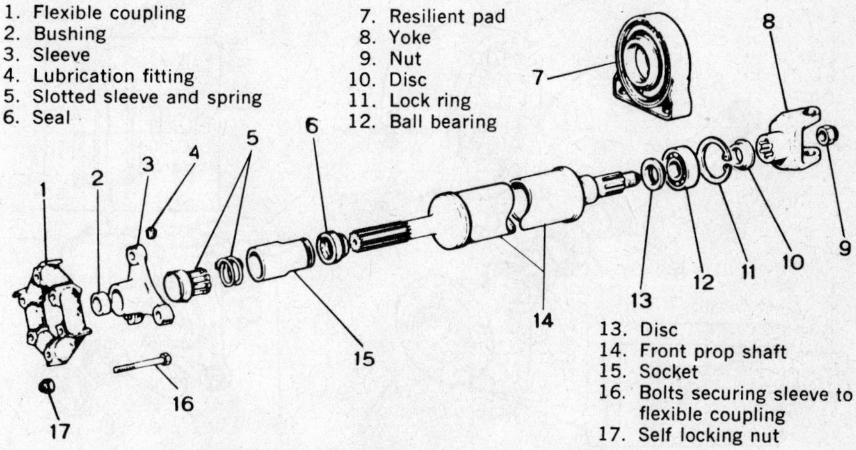

13. Disc
14. Front prop shaft
15. Socket
16. Bolts securing sleeve to flexible coupling
17. Self locking nut

124, 131, Brava driveshaft front section (except automatic)

7. Install the driveshaft in the reverse order of removal.

DISASSEMBLY AND ASSEMBLY

1. Remove the spider of the universal joint.
2. Unscrew the attaching nut of the universal joint fork.
3. Remove the fork and the shield snap-ring.
4. Slide the rear shaft and bearing out of the tubular cover.
5. Remove the bearing from the end of the shaft.
6. When the cover has been removed, the sliding sleeve will come off the front.
7. To assemble, reverse the disassembly procedure using grease to lubricate the couplings.

NOTE: The universal joint fork nut must be tightened to 69 ft/lbs and then staked with a center punch.

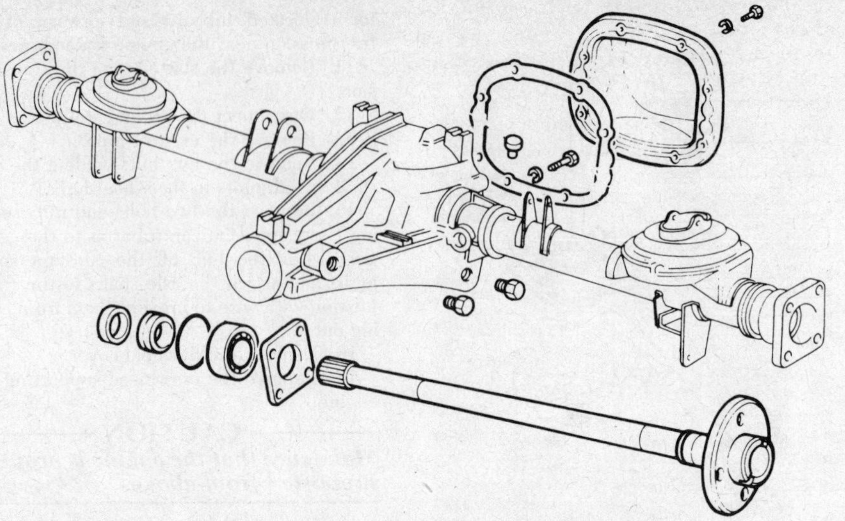

131 and Brava rear axle and axle shaft assembly

U-JOINT OVERHAUL

NOTE: It is best to use a small press when working with U-joints although a vise can be used in a pinch. It is very easy to crush the needle bearings during installation, so be careful during overhaul.

1. Mark the driveshaft halves so you can put them together in the same way they were taken apart.
2. See "Driveshaft Removal and Installation" and remove the shaft.
3. Remove the snap-rings which retain the cups.
4. Press the joint toward the center. This will make one of the cups accessible with pliers.
5. Remove the cup, turn the shaft over and press out the other side.
6. Press the other two cups out in the same manner and remove the joint.
7. Before installing the new joint, clean the shaft surfaces where the cups are pressed through and be sure to check the snap-ring groove for burrs as the snap-rings must seat perfectly.
8. Insert the first cup in its seat and press it through until it is flush with the shaft.
9. Remove all of the cups from the joint and insert the joint through the hole opposite the installed cup, then slide the joint into the cup making sure that the needle bearings stay in order.
10. Insert the second cup in its seat and press it halfway into the shaft.
11. Carefully move the joint from side-to-side until it reaches the point where the joint is making contact with the needle bearings in both cups, then press them together driving the second cup in far enough to insert the snap-ring.
12. Insert the ring, turn the shaft over and press the cup in and insert the other ring.
13. Use the same procedure to connect the shaft halves observing the marks made in Step 1.
14. It is best to have someone assist you in connecting the shafts together because of the weight and awkwardness of the assembly.

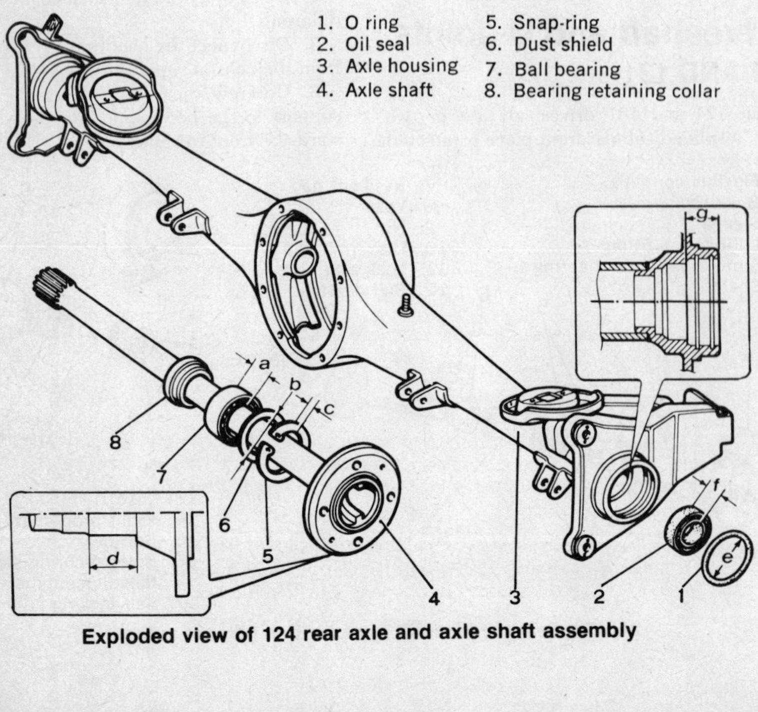

Exploded view of 124 rear axle and axle shaft assembly

Axle Shafts

REMOVAL AND INSTALLATION

124

1. Jack up the rear of the car. Remove the wheels. Remove the caliper support bracket assembly without disconnecting the brake fluid lines.
2. Remove the snap-ring which retains the bearing dust cover.
3. Using a slide hammer, remove the axle shaft, complete with snap-ring, dust cover, bearing and bearing retained collar.
4. Extract the shaft oil seal and O-ring.

NOTE: Always use a hydraulic press to remove the axle shaft bearing retaining collar.

5. Fit the oil seal and O-ring to the housing.
6. Insert the complete axle shaft and fit the snap-ring to the housing.
7. Fit the brake disc to the axle shaft hub with two centering screws.
8. Fit the caliper support bracket and caliper assembly to the axle.
9. Fit the wheel and lower the car to the ground.

131

1. Jack up the rear of the car and block the front wheels. Release the parking brake. Remove the rear wheel.
2. Remove the two brake drum retaining bolts and pull off the drum.
3. Working through the axle shaft flange, remove the four backing plate bolts.
4. Attach a slide hammer to the axle shaft flange and pull out the axle shaft, bearing and retainer.

NOTE: Do not stretch or bend brake line.

5. Remove and replace the oil seal in the axle housing.

6. Check that the axle bearing is tight against its retainer and axle shaft shoulder. If replacement is necessary, press off the retainer with an arbor press. Never reuse the retainer. To install the new retainer, heat to 578° F and press on so that the bearing inner race is locked between the retainer and axle shaft shoulder.

7. Install the axle shaft assembly. Install the backing plate bolts, brake drum, and wheel.

128

1. Drain the transmission oil.
2. Unscrew the oil seal boot at the transmission.
3. Remove the outer clamps on the boot at the constant-speed joint and pull back both boots enough to uncover both joints.
4. Clean the grease off both joints.
5. Open the sealing ring on the constant-speed joints and remove the shaft ends from their seats in the joint.
6. Turn the car wheels to enable the shafts to be fully removed from their seats in the differential.

NOTE: Some early cars are equipped with twin type axle shafts. If it becomes necessary to replace one of these shafts it can be replaced with the later integral type shaft.

7. Installation is the reverse of the removal procedure, bearing the following in mind.
8. When each axle shaft end has been inserted into the constant-speed joint, check that the snap-ring is lying in its axle shaft groove.

CAUTION

Make sure that the axle shaft snap-ring is, in fact, lying in its groove. Move the shaft inward and outward a few times; this operation is necessary as correct ring setting is vital.

9. Grease the constant-speed joint sockets and the protection boot. No more than 3 oz of grease should be used.

X1/9

1. Remove the wheel/tire assembly.
2. Remove the two bolts and nuts securing the shock absorber to the pillar.
3. Remove the nut holding the ball joint of the control arm in the pillar and remove the ball joint from the pillar.
4. Remove the nut retaining the strut ball joint to the pillar and remove the ball joint from the pillar.
5. Drain the transmission.
6. Remove the three bolts and washers retaining the oil seal boot to the differential.
7. Pull the axle shaft and wheel hub from the differential.
8. Remove the brake caliper and support bracket from the pillar.
9. Remove the bolts securing the retaining plate and brake rotor to the hub and remove the plate and rotor.
10. Remove the clamp retaining the boot to the constant-speed joint and pull the boot back to uncover the joint. Clean the grease off of the joints.
11. Remove the lock-ring from the constant-speed joints, using a pair of pliers.
12. Remove the axle shaft from the constant-speed unit.
13. Install the axle shaft in the reverse order of removal. After installing the axle shaft in the constant-speed joint and installing the snap-ring in the groove of the axle shaft, make sure the snap-ring is properly seated by moving the shaft in and out. Grease the constant-speed joint with no more than 3 ozs of grease.

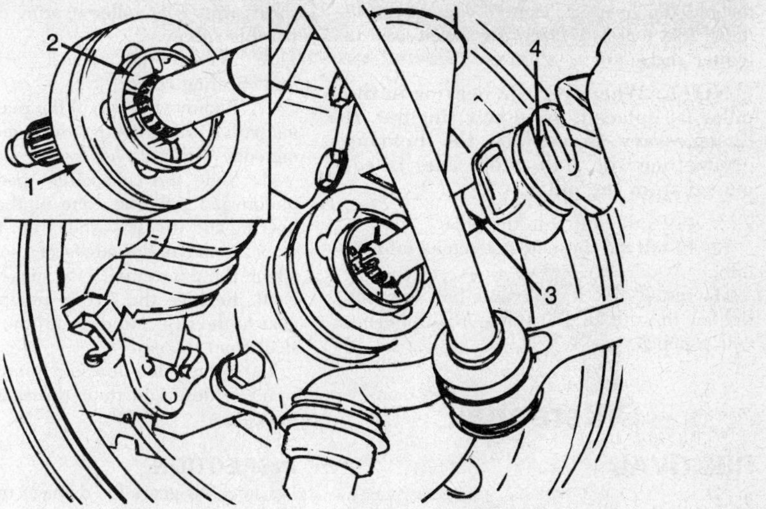

1. Constant-speed joint
2. Sealing ring
3. Axle shaft
4. Boot

Removing axle shaft for constant-speed joint—128

Stub Axle

128

1. Raise and support the front of the car.
2. Remove the wheel.
3. Disconnect the shock absorber from the steering knuckle.
4. Disconnect the brake caliper from the steering knuckle.
5. Remove the brake disc and mounting plate from the hub.
6. Disconnect the tie rod from the steering knuckle.
7. Disconnect the anti-roll bar from the control arm.

NOTE: When removing the anti-roll bar from the control arms, make sure to take note of the number of adjustment shims inserted between the ends of the bar and the control arm bushings so they can be replaced in their original positions.

8. Disconnect the control arm from the body.
9. If necessary, remove the control arm from the steering knuckle.
10. Remove the stub axle from the steering knuckle with a press.
11. Install the stub axle in the reverse order.

X1/9

1. Remove the axle shaft.
2. Remove the hub and pillar assembly from the car.
3. Remove the hub nut and washer.
4. Pull the constant-speed joint out of the hub.
5. Press the hub from the pillar.
6. Remove the ring nut securing the bearing in the pillar and remove the bearing from the pillar.
7. Install the new bearing in the pillar.
8. Screw the *new* ring nut into the pillar

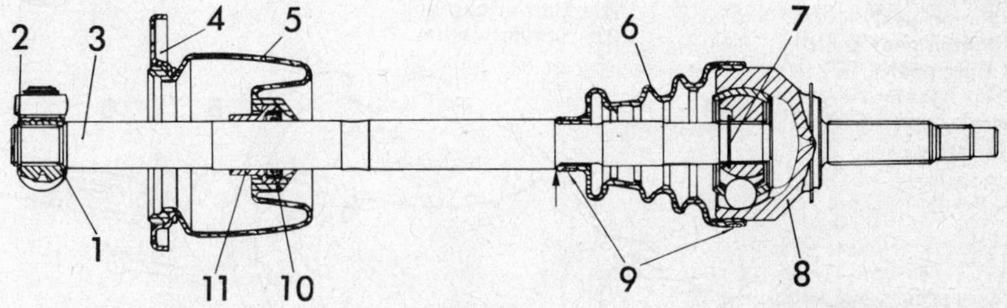

1. Tripod joint
2. Circlip
3. Axle shaft
4. Flange
5. Oil seal boot
6. Boot
7. Snapring
8. Constant-speed joint
9. Boot clamps
10. Sealing ring
11. Bushing

The arrow indicates the shoulder with which the boot (6) should be in contact after installation

Left axle shaft assembly—128

to hold the bearing. Tighten the nut to 43 ft/lbs. Fiat tool A.57123 is the socket used to tighten the nut.

NOTE: Whenever the bearing in the pillar is replaced, use a new ring nut. It is necessary to replace the bearing every time the hub (stub axle) is removed from the pillar.

9. Press the hub into the pillar.
10. Install the constant-speed joint into the hub.
11. Install the washer and hub nut and tighten the nut to 100 ft/lbs. Stake the nut with a punch.

Differential

REMOVAL

124

To remove only the differential, use the following procedure.

1. Unscrew the drain plug in the lower part of the axle housing and drain the gear oil.
2. Jack the rear of the car and remove the rear wheels. Disconnect the driveshaft.
3. Withdraw the axle shafts far enough to disengage them from the side gears.
4. Unbolt and remove the differential from the housing.

DISASSEMBLY

1. Matchmark the bearing caps and bosses. Remove the bolts and lockplates from the bearing caps. The lockplates hold the bearing adjusters in place.
2. Remove the caps, adjuster rings and rolller bearing cups.
3. Withdraw the differential case from the carrier, complete with gears, ring gear and bearing cones.
4. Turn the carrier upside down and by locking the pinion, unscrew the pinion nut.
5. Withdraw the pinion, complete with thrust ring, rear roller bearing cone and collapsible spacer.
6. Remove the oil seal, oil slinger and front bearing cone.
7. Remove the cup of the rear roller bearing with a drift. Remove the front roller bearing cone with a driver.
8. Slide the collapsible spacer from the pinion and pull the cone of the rear roller bearing and thrust washer from the pinion.
9. Remove the cones of the bearings in which the differential case runs.
10. Remove the screws retaining the ring gear to the case and drift out the pinion gears shaft from the case.
11. Rotate the side and pinion gears and remove these and their thrust washers from the case.

INSPECTION

Check all gears for damage or wear. Very slight wear damage can be corrected with very fine abrasive paper. Inspect the side gear thrust washers. If the thrust washers are only slightly defective polish them. Be sure that the case and carrier are not cracked.

ASSEMBLY

Assemble the side gears and thrust washers in the case. Insert the pinion gears through the opening in the case and engage them with the side gears. Align the holes in the pinion gears with the holes in the case and insert the pinion gears shaft. Check the axial play in each side gear. The play should be 0.004 in. max. If the side gear play is excessive, replace the thrust washers with thicker ones, to bring the axial play within specifications. Service thrust washers are supplied in the following sizes: 0.070 in., 0.072 in., 0.074 in., 0.076 in., 0.078 in., 0.080 in. and 0.082 in. If the thrust washers were changed, measure the clearance again. If new thrust washers fail to bring the clearance within specifications, the side gears are excessively worn and must be replaced. Fit the ring gear to the case and torque the bolts to 72 ft/lbs. Fit the cones of both roller bearings with a driver of proper size.

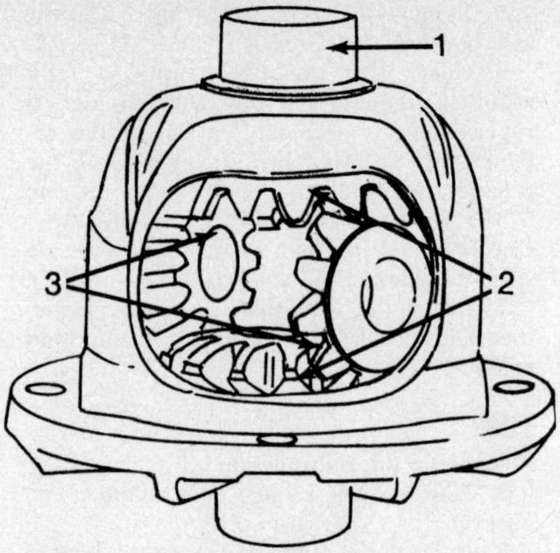

1. Differential case
2. Side gears
3. Pinion gears

Arrange the pinion gears as shown in the figure and push them into place by rolling them on the side gear.

Assembly of side gears in the differential case

At this point, assembly of the pinion requires a trial and error method to determine the thickness of the pinion thrust washer, which controls pinion and ring gear mesh, compensating for differences in machining between pinion and carrier. Assemble several thrust washers of varying thicknesses: 0.100 in., 0.102 in., 0.104 in., 0.106 in., 0.108 in., 0.110 in., 0.112 in., 0.114 in., 0.116 in., 0.118 in., 0.120 in., 0.122 in., 0.124 in ., 0.126 in., 0.128 in., 0.130 in. and 0.132 in.

Arrange the pinion gears as shown in the figure and push them into place by rolling them on the side gear.

If the pinion, ring gear, pinion bearings and differential carrier are not changed, the same

1. Spacer
2. "U" joint sleeve
3. Oil seal
4. Front roller bearing
5. Rear roller bearing
6. Pinion shaft rear roller bearing thrust washer
7. Side gear thrust washer
8. Side gear
9. Pinion gear
10. Pinion gear shaft
11. Ring gear
12. Differential case
13. Differential case roller bearing
14. Bearing adjuster ring
15. Locking plate bolt
16-17. Locking plates
18. Bolt fixing ring gear to differential case
19. Bevel pinion
20. Carrier cap bolt
21. Spring washer
22. Gasket
23. Differential carrier to axle housing bolt
24. Differential carrier
25. Collapsible spacer
26. Oil slinger
27. Plain washer
28. Bevel pinion nut

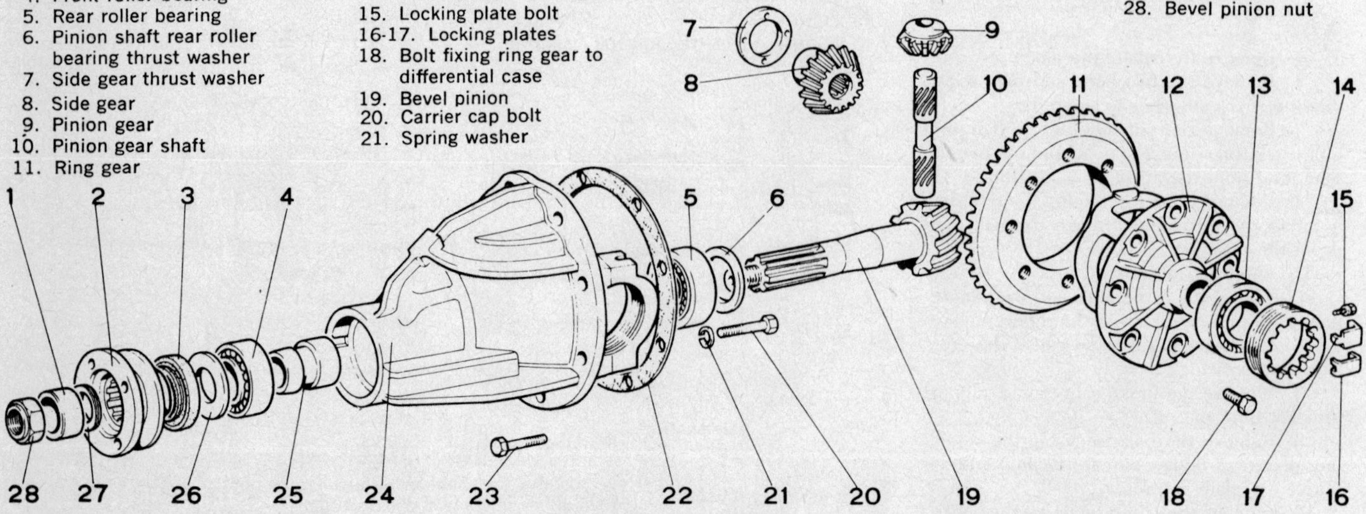

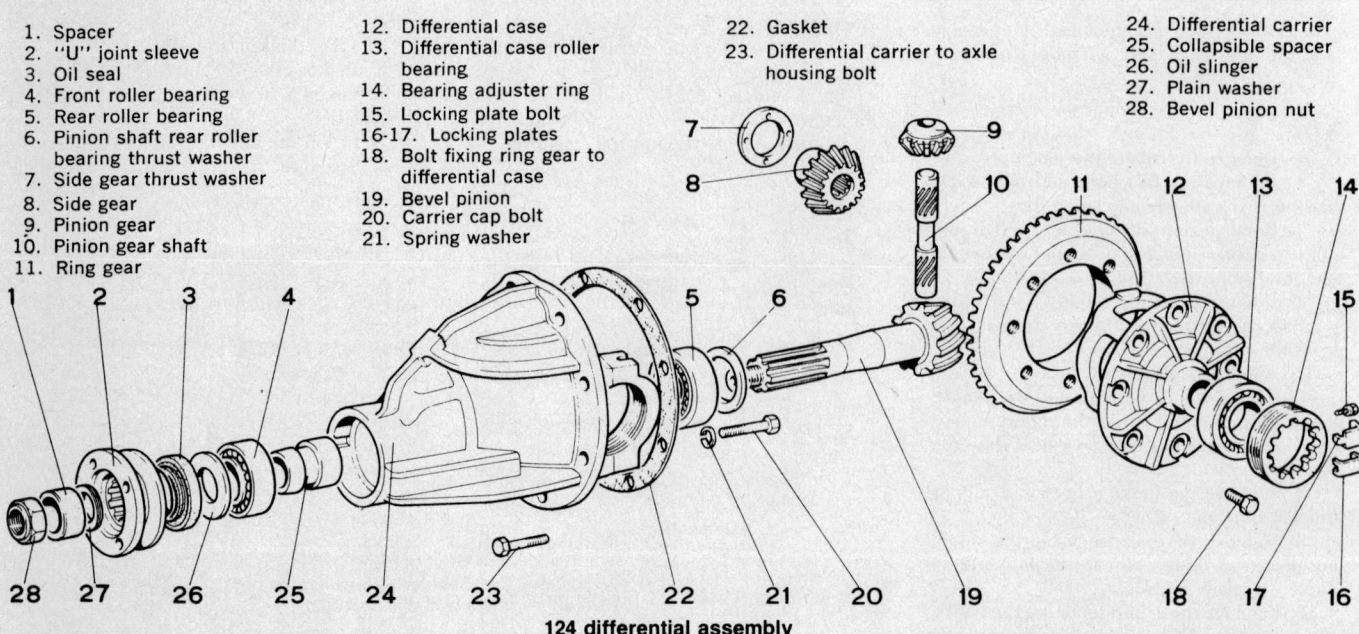

124 differential assembly

124 Differential Specifications

Pinion nut torque	87-166 ft. lbs.
Pinion turning torque	14-17 inch pounds
Bearing preload	
Differential cap spread	0.0055-0.0071 in.①
Side gear axial clearance	0.004 in. max.
Pinion and ring gear backlash	0.0031-0.0051②
Oil	
Type	Fiat W 90/M
Quantity	1 pt. 26 oz.

① 124 Sport Spyder, Sport Coupe 0.0063-0.0059 in.
② 124 Sport Spyder, Sport Coupe 0.0039-0.0078 in.

collapsible spacer and pinion thrust washer may be reused. However, if any of those parts are installed new, the thrust washer and collapsible spacer will have to be replaced with new parts.

By comparing the number stamped on the pinion and ring gear (old or new gear sets), a reasonable determination of thrust washer thickness can be made. The number, stamped on the pinion and preceded by a (+) or (−) sign, is the difference, in hundredths of a millimeter, between the actual fitting clearance and the nominal fitting clearance. Select a thrust washer thought to be of nearly proper size (or as close to the proper size as possible). Assemble the pinion, rear roller bearing cone and collapsible spacer, and insert the pinion assembly in the carrier. Fit the front roller bearing cone, the oil seal, oil slinger, spacer U-joint sleeve, washer, and pinion nut through the front of the carrier.

The pinion bearings are preloaded in the following manner. Clamp the pinion and torque the pinion nut to 87-166 ft/lbs., constantly checking the rotational torque. The rotational torque of the pinion must be between 14-17 inch/pounds.

NOTE: If the tightening torque is exceeded, the collapsible spacer will have to be replaced. If the proper rotational torque cannot be obtained, the spacer will have to be removed and replaced with another.

Fit the differential case into the carrier, complete with bearing outer races. Fit the two bearing retaining and adjusting rings and bring them into light contact with the bearings. Fit the bearing caps and torque the bolts to 36.0 ft/lbs. Temporarily adjust the ring gear and pinion backlash to 0.0031-0.0051 in. Alternately, tighten the two bearing adjusting rings the same number of turns, until the differential case bearing cap divergence measures 0.0055-0.0071 in. The ring gear backlash must remain as set.

Using a dial gauge, adjust the ring gear backlash to 0.0032-0.0051 in. It is important that if one adjuster ring is turned, the other be turned an equal amount in an opposite direction, ensuring that the preload is not altered.

Coat the ring gear with red lead and check the tooth contact pattern. Depending on the results of this test, the pinion thrust washer may have to be replaced with another of different thickness, either thicker of thinner, depending on the direction in which the pinion must be moved. Bear in mind that if this operation is necessary, the entire process will have to be repeated.

131

DISASSEMBLY

NOTE: A case spreader is required to remove the carrier assembly.

1. Drain the lubricant.
2. Pull out the axle shafts.
3. Position a case spreader on the axle housing. Matchmark the carrier bearing caps and bosses. Remove carrier bearing bolts, washers and caps. Spread case and remove carrier, bearings and shims, noting position of bearing outer races and shims.
4. Lock pinion flange and remove pinion nut and washer. Remove flange.
5. Remove oil seal and plate from pinion shaft.
6. Push out pinion shaft.
7. Remove front and rear pinion bearing outer rings.
8. Press off rear pinion bearing. Keep shims in order.
9. Pull off carrier bearings. Keep outer race, caps and shims from same side in order.
10. Remove bolts retaining ring gear to carrier.
11. Drift out pinion shaft from carrier. Remove pinion side gears and thrust washers.

ASSEMBLY

1. Position thrust washers under side gears. Install side gears in carrier.
2. Mesh pinion gears with side gears and rotate until aligned with hole for pinion shaft. Install pinion shaft in carrier.
3. Check that the rotating torque required to turn one side gear while holding the other is 22-36 ft/lbs. If not, adjust thrust washer thickness. Washers are available in sizes from 0.0709 in. to 0.0817 in., in increments of 0.002 in.
4. Install rear bearing outer race in case.
5. Install front bearing outer race in case.
6. Install ring gear on carrier. Tighten bolts to 72 ft/lbs.
7. Press bearings into carrier. If reusing old bearings, install in original position.
8. To determine drive pinion shim thickness, proceed as follows:

Check marking on old pinion and measure shim thickness. Add shim thickness to marking on old pinion (in hundreths of a millimeter) to obtain nominal dimension. If old pinion marking is + 10 and old shim thickness is 2.90 mm, nominal dimension is 3.00 mm. So, if the new pinion marking is +20, then required shim thickness is 2.80 mm.

9. Position shim on drive pinion and press bearing onto pinion shaft.
10. Install drive pinion in case. Install collapsible spacer, front pinion bearing and plate on pinion. Install a new oil seal in case.
11. Position U-joint flange, washer and nut on pinion. Oil pinion bearings and tighten flange nut so that rotating torque is 14-18 *inch/pounds.*
12. If reusing old bearings, outer races and shims, install spreader on case. Spread case and install carrier with outer races and shims in their original positions. Install caps. Tighten bolts to 36 ft/lbs and check backlash.
13. If using new bearings or carrier, position carrier and outer race assembly in case. Install an equal amount of shims at either side; sufficient to remove any end-play. Install cap bolts and washers and tighten.
14. To measure backlash, a dial indicator is used. Block the drive pinion flange from turning. Move ring gear one way as far as it will go and zero the indicator. Then, move it the other way as far as it will go and check the reading. If reading is not 0.003-0.005 in., adjust shim size accordingly.
15. If using new bearings or carrier, increase size of each shim by 0.002 in. Install case spreader and spread case. Install carrier bearing outer races and shims. Remove the spreader. Install bearing caps in original positions and tighten bolts to 36 ft/lbs.
16. Install rear cover with new gasket. Tighten bolts to 18 ft/lbs. Install axle shafts. Fill with lubricant.

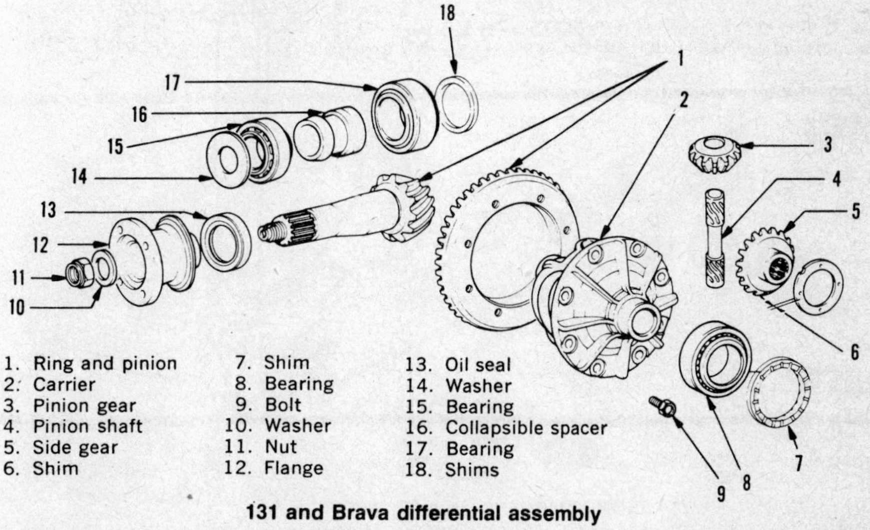

1. Ring and pinion
2. Carrier
3. Pinion gear
4. Pinion shaft
5. Side gear
6. Shim
7. Shim
8. Bearing
9. Bolt
10. Washer
11. Nut
12. Flange
13. Oil seal
14. Washer
15. Bearing
16. Collapsible spacer
17. Bearing
18. Shims

131 and Brava differential assembly

REAR SUSPENSION

REMOVAL AND INSTALLATION

128

1. Jack up the rear of vehicle and place safety stands underneath.
2. Remove the rear wheels.
3. Plug the outlet hole of the brake fluid reservoir.
4. Detach the flexible brake fluid hose from the metal pipe.
5. Release the handbrake relay lever and detach the cable from the shoe control levers on the brake backing plate.
6. Disconnect the braking regulator torsion bar from the left control arm.
7. Place a hydraulic jack under the control arm, raise the suspension, and detach the shock absorbers inside the luggage compartment. Remove the jack.
8. Detach the rubber pads which attach the leaf spring to the control arms.
9. Unscrew the nuts that attach the swivels of the control arms to the screws which pass through the plate that mounts the suspension to the body.
10. Attach the control arm to the body by passing the two screws through the plate. Finger tighten the nuts.
11. Reattach the rubber pads used to anchor the leaf spring.
12. Link the braking regulator torsion bar to the left control arm.
13. Slip the bottom rubber bushing onto the top stud of the shock absorber. Apply a hydraulic jack under the suspension and lift the whole assembly to enable the top stud of the shock absorber to be inserted into the special hole provided in the luggage compartment.
14. Mount the top rubber bushings, the retainer cap, and the self-locking nut to the top stud of the shock absorber.
15. Tighten the shock absorber nuts.
16. Reattach the handbrake control cable to the lever on the brake backing plate and reconnect the brake fluid hose and metal pipe to each other.
17. Restore the brake fluid and bleed the system.

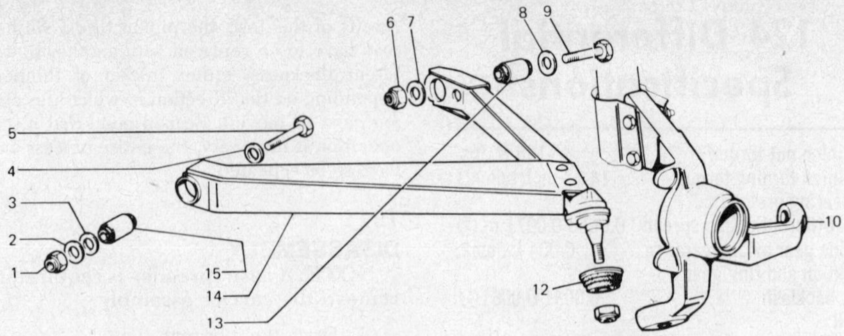

1. Nut
2. Washer
3. Washer
4. Washer
5. Bolt
6. Nut
7. Washer
8. Washer
9. Bolt
10. Pillar
12. Boot
13. Bushing
14. Control arm
15. Bushing

Exploded view of the rear control arm assembly for an X1/9

X1/9

1. Remove the wheel.
2. Disconnect the flexible brake tube from the caliper if the caliper is to be removed with the suspension assembly or, in order to save from bleeding the brake hydraulic system, remove the caliper from the suspension assembly and support with heavy gauge wire attached to the body.
3. Disconnect the parking brake cable from the caliper, depending on whether or not it is being removed from the vehicle.
4. Remove the exhaust pipe.
5. Note the number of shims and their position on the control arm. Remove the nut, washer, and bolt attaching the control arm to the bracket at the front of the suspension. Allow the shims to remain between the arm and bracket.
6. Remove the nut, washer, and bolt securing the arm to the bracket at the rear of the suspension. Take note to the number of shims and their position. Allow the shims to remain between the arm and bracket.
7. Remove the hub nut and washer.
8. Remove the three nuts and washers securing the top of the shock absorber.
9. Slide the suspension assembly off of the constant-speed joint shaft. Position the axle shaft so that it will not come out of the differential.

To install the suspension assembly:

10. Install the shims in their original positions and loosely attach the arm to the brackets.
11. Raise the assembly and mount the hub to the constant-speed joint.
12. Insert the upper attachment of the shock absorber in the holes in the body and install the three attaching nuts and spring washers.
13. Place the washer on the axle shaft and thread a new hub nut onto the shaft. Tighten the nut to 101 ft/lbs and stake the nut.

NOTE: Always use a new hub nut.

14. Install the exhaust pipe.
15. Install the wheel.
16. Lower the car to the ground.
17. With the vehicle laden (two people sitting inside), tighten the control arm attaching nuts to 72 ft/lbs. Tighten the three upper shock absorber attaching nuts to 43 ft/lbs.

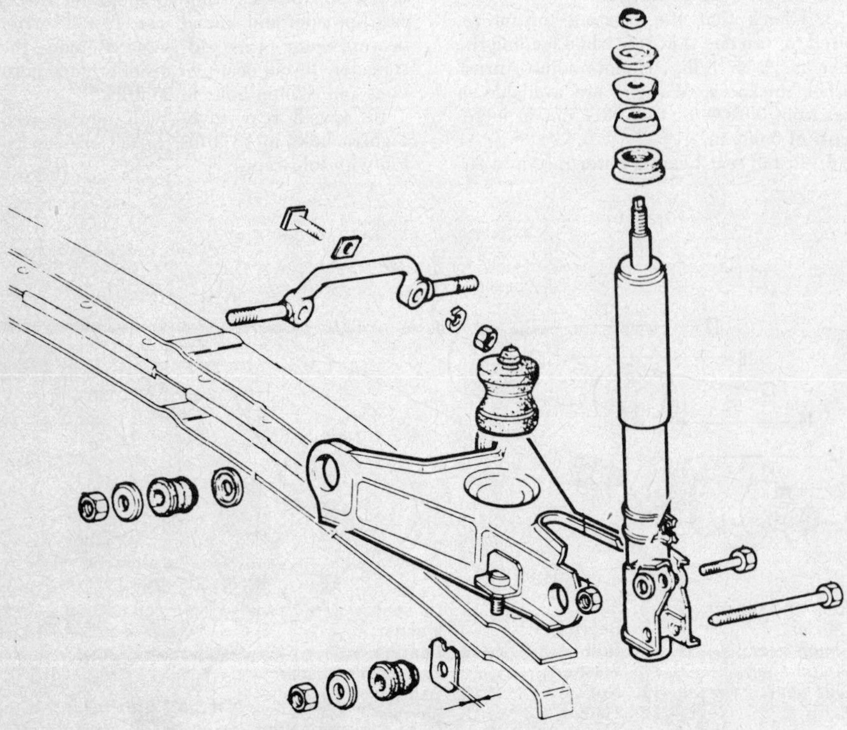

128 rear suspension components

124 and 131

1. Jack up the rear of the car. Remove the rear wheels after placing the car on jack stands.

2. Disconnect the driveshaft.
3. Disconnect the brake lines.
4. Disconnect the handbrake cables.
5. Free the cables from their clips on the body.
6. Disconnect the shocks from inside the trunk. On 131 wagons, disconnect the shocks from their upper mounts, beneath the car.
7. Disconnect the two stabilizer bar links.
8. Disconnect the brake regulator link.
9. Support the rear axle with a hydraulic jack.
10. Disconnect the anchor rods and the sway bar.
11. Remove the assembly by lowering the jack.
12. Remove the stabilizer bar brackets and the bar.
13. Remove the shocks at the spring mounts, or lower attachment (131 wagon).
14. Remove the anchor rods and sway bar from the axle.

NOTE: Do not tighten any bolts during assembly unless otherwise instructed. Bolts should be tightened in sequence with the vehicle on a level surface.

15. Connect the anchor rods and the sway bar to the housing.
16. Bolt the shocks to the spring seats or lower mount (131 wagon), and tighten them.
17. Bolt up the stabilizer bar with its links, but do not tighten it completely.
18. Seat the springs with pads to the axle plates.
19. Place the jack in position.
20. Connect the axle to the body, but do not fully tighten the anchor rods to their brackets.
21. Connect the stabilizer bar links to the housing, but do not tighten fully.
22. Connect the brake regulator rod to the housing.
23. Tighten the shocks at the luggage compartment, or upper mount (131 wagon).
24. Install the driveshaft and tighten.
25. Install brake lines and handbrake cables.
26. Bleed the brake system.
27. Install the wheels. Lower the vehicle and torque the wheels to 51 ft/lbs.
28. Tighten the nuts on the pivot bolts.

NOTE: The following bolts should be tightened in the order in which they appear. They should be gradually loaded until the specified torque is obtained.

a. Anchor rod-to-the housing (124)—72 ft/lbs.
b. Sway bar-to-the axle (124)—72 ft/lbs.
c. Stabilizer bar links-to-axle—25 ft/ lbs.
d. Reaction strut nuts (131)—58 ft/lbs.
e. Transverse strut nuts (131)—58 ft/ lbs.

NOTE: The above procedure prevents the rubber bushings from being unduly stressed.

ADJUSTMENTS

128

Rear wheel camber and toe-in are adjusted at the lower control arm-to-body attaching bolts by means of shims. To increase the negative camber angle, add an equal number

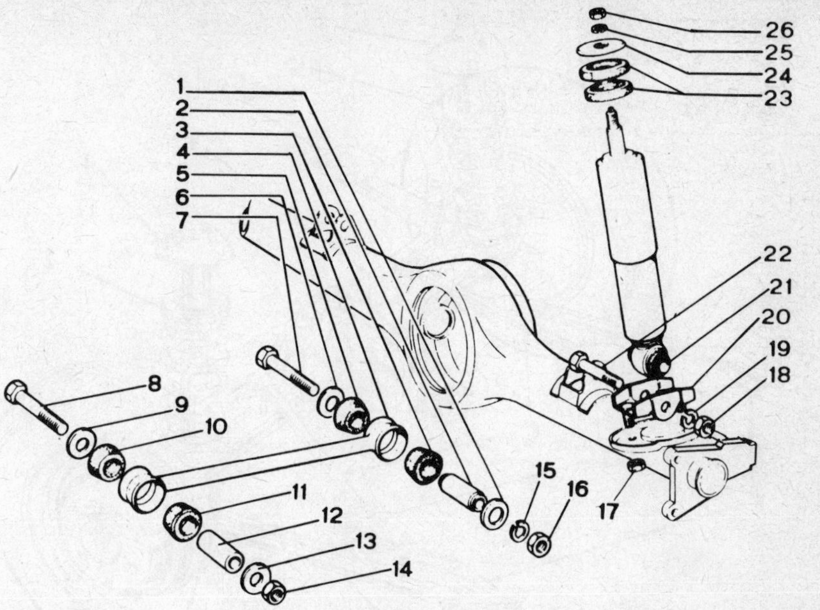

1. Flat washer
2. Spacer
3. Rubber bushing
4. Upper side rod
5. Rubber bushing
6. Flat washer
7. Bolt anchoring upper side rod to axle housing
8. Bolt anchoring upper side rod to body
9. Flat washer
10. Rubber bushing
11. Rubber bushing
12. Spacer
13. Flat washer
14. Nut
15. Lock washer
16. Nut
17. Nut
18. Nut
19. Lock washer
20. Lower bracket
21. Shock absorber, complete
22. Bolt fixing shock absorber to lower bracket
23. Rubber bushing
24. Upper cup
25. Lock washer
26. Nut

124 rear suspension shock absorbers

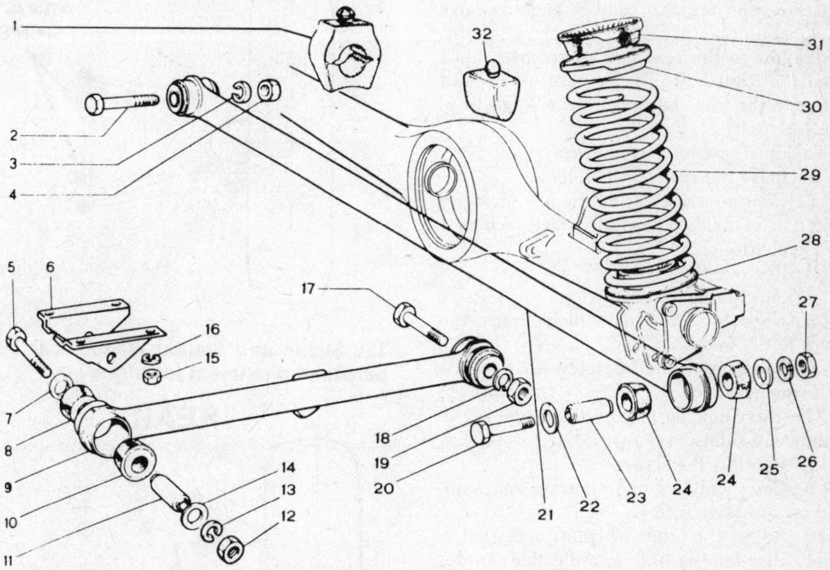

1. Rubber pad
2. Bolt anchoring cross rod to body
3. Lock washer
4. Nut
5. Bolt anchoring lower side rod to bracket 6
6. Bracket
7. Flat washer
8. Rubber bushing
9. Lower side rod
10. Rubber bushing
11. Spacer
12. Nut
13. Lock washer
14. Flat washer
15. Nut
16. Lock washer
17. Bolt anchoring lower side rod to axle housing
18. Lock washer
19. Nut
20. Bolt anchoring cross rod to axle housing
21. Cross rod
22. Flat washer
23. Spacer
24. Rubber bushings
25. Flat washer
26. Lock washer
27. Nut
28. Lower ring-pad
29. Coil spring
30. Upper seating ring
31. Upper rubber ring-pad
32. Rubber buffer

124 rear suspension rods and springs

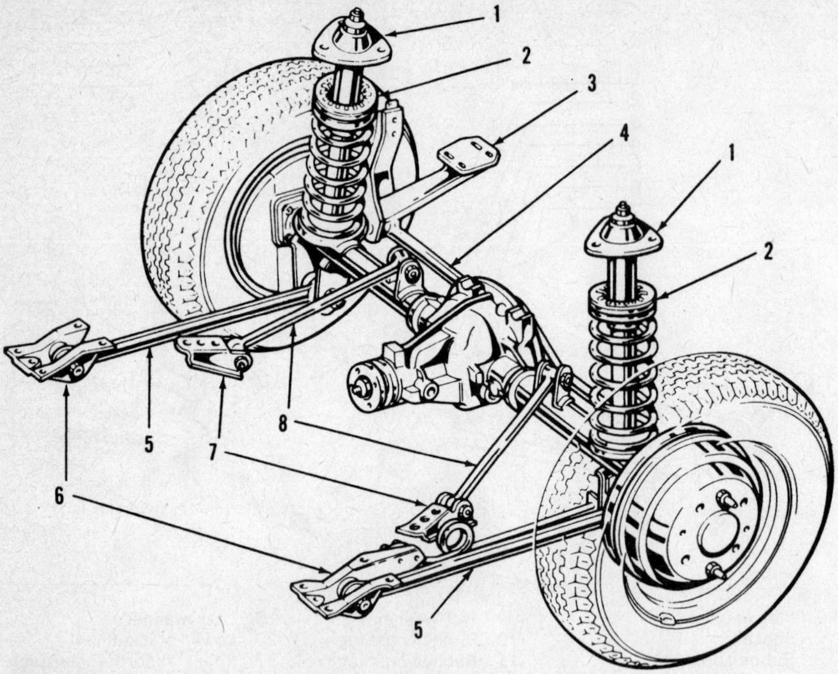

1. Shock absorber
2. Coil spring
3. Transverse strut support
4. Transverse strut
5. Lower reaction strut
6. Lower reaction strut support
7. Upper reaction strut support
8. Upper reaction strut

131 and Brava rear suspension

of shims. To decrease the negative camber angle, remove an equal number of shims. To decrease the negative camber angle remove an equal number of shims. To increase toe-in, add shims to the rear bolt or remove shims from the front bolt. To decrease toe-in, add shims to the front bolt or remove shims from the rear bolt.

To adjust, proceed as follows:

1. Raise the rear of the vehicle.
2. Compress one end of the leaf spring to shift it from the flexible guide which anchors it to the control arm.
3. Remove the guide.
4. Slowly release the spring.
5. Unscrew the nuts which attach the pivot to the body.
6. Partly remove the screw to free the adjustment shims.
7. Carry out the required variation in the number of shims.
8. Reinsert the screw.
9. Carry out this operation on both control arm-to-body screws.
10. Adjust the other wheel as necessary.
11. Reassemble the two flexible guides which anchor the leaf spring to the control arms and tighten the attachment nuts to 22 ft/lbs.

X1/9

Toe-in is adjusted by turning the reaction rod, thus lengthening or shortening the rod to the desired toe-in specification. Toe-in with the vehicle unladen should be between + 0.360 and + 0.510 in.

Camber should be −1°10′ to −2°10′.

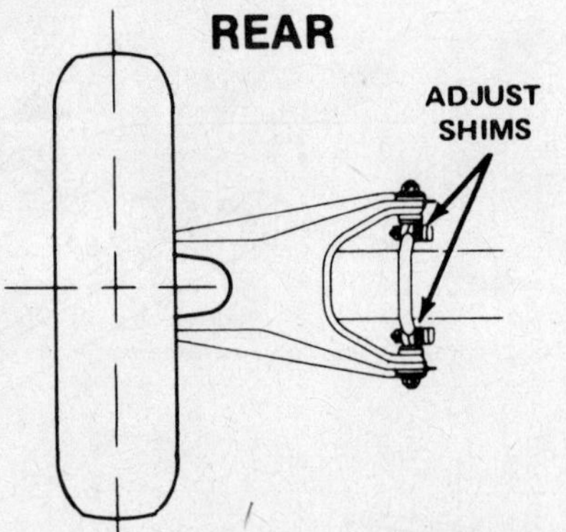

128 Sedan and Station Wagon rear suspension adjustment locations

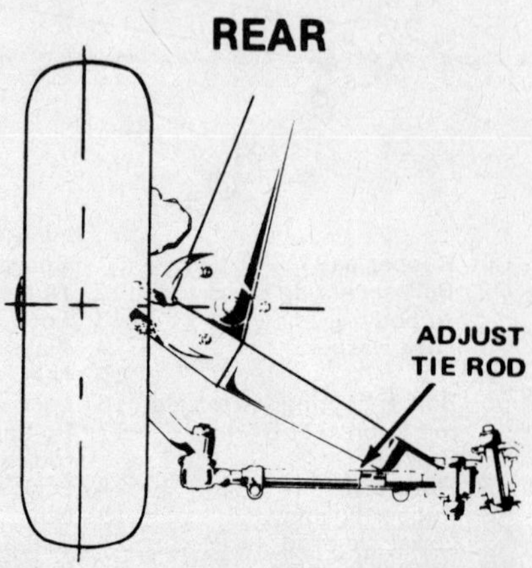

X1/9 rear suspension adjustment locations

FRONT SUSPENSION

The 124 model range is equipped with parallel upper and lower control arm front suspension. A coil spring is located between the control arms, along with a shock absorber. The steering knuckles are located in ball joints. A stabilizer bar is used on all models.

The 128, 121 and X1/9 are equipped with MacPherson front suspension. The suspension strut acts as shock absorber, suspension (with a concentric coil spring), and upper locating member. A control arm is located at the bottom of the steering knuckle. A stabilizer bar is used on all models.

REMOVAL AND INSTALLATION

124

1. Support the front of the car with safety stands.
2. Remove the front wheels.
3. Remove the shock.
4. Using a spring compressor, compress the spring until it no longer exerts pressure on the control arm.
5. Disconnect the stabilizer bar at the lower control arm.
6. Disconnect the brake hoses.
7. Disconnect the tie rod at the steering knuckle arm.
8. Unscrew the fixing nut and remove the pivot bolt to allow the control arm to separate from the body.
9. Remove the nuts which secure the lower control arm to the crossmember. Be sure to mark the number of shims removed and from which stud they were removed.
10. The assembly can now be removed and disassembled.

NOTE: Shims are located between the body and the pivot bar to which the control arm is mounted.

11. Install the stabilizer bar to the body.
12. Insert the shims and install the wishbone assembly, bolting the lower ocntrol arm to the crossmember.
13. Insert the spring with tool attached into its seat in the control arm.
14. Compress the spring until its height will allow you to connect the upper control arm.
15. Connect the upper control arm, but do not tighten it fully.
16. Connect the stabilizier bar to the control arm.
17. Connect the tie-rod to the steering arm.
18. Connect the brake lines.
19. Bleed the brake system.
20. Seat the spring by unloading the compressor.
21. Remove the compressor and install the shock.
22. Install the tires, lower the car and torque the wheels to 50 ft/lbs.
23. With the vehicle on a level surface, gradually tighten the following bolts in the

order in which they appear and to the proper specification.

a. Nut on the pin connecting the upper control arm to the body—72 ft/lbs.

b. Nuts retaining the lower control arm to the crossmember—43 ft/lbs.

c. Nuts fixing the lower control arm to the pin—72 ft/lbs.

128

1. Loosen the front wheel stud bolts.
2. Loosen the front wheel hub nuts.
3. Place the vehicle on jack stands.
4. Remove the front wheels.
5. Unscrew the nuts which attach the brake caliper to the pillar and secure the caliper to the body.
6. Unscrew the nut which attaches the tie rod ball joint to the steering arm and then remove the swivel with a puller.
7. Unscrew the nut which attaches the end of the anti-roll bar to the control arm.
8. Detach the control arm from the body.
9. Remove the hub nut.
10. Release the top attachment of the shock absorber by unscrewing the 3 mounting nuts in the engine compartment and slide the suspension assembly off the constant-speed joint shaft and support the axle shaft in such a way as to prevent it from slipping out of the differential.
11. Attach the anti-roll bar to the body.

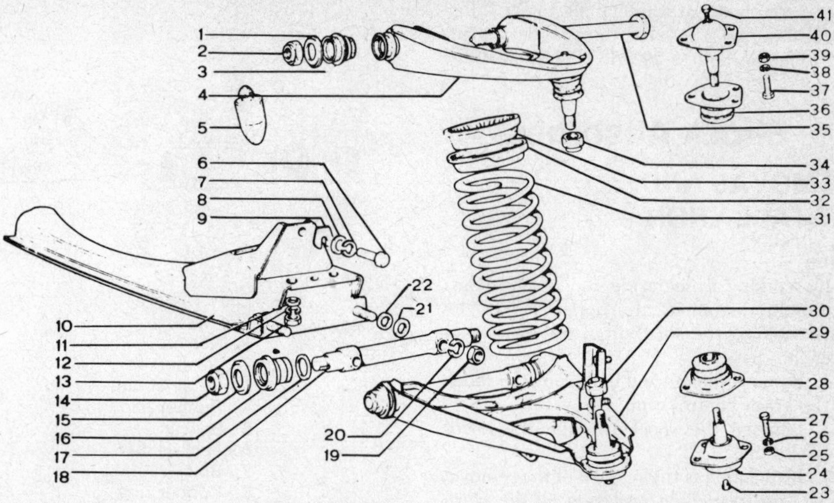

1. Cup
2. Nut fixing upper control arm to body
3. Resilient bushing
4. Upper control arm
5. Buffer
6. Bolt
7. Spring washer
8. Flat washer
9. Tab strip
10. Crossmember
11. Flat washer
12. Spring washer
13. Nut
14. Nut fixing pivot bar 18 to lower control arm
15. Cup
16. Resilient bushing
17. Flat washer
18. Pivot bar
19. Nut fixing lower control arm to crossmember 10
20. Spring washer
21. Flat washer
22. Tab strip
23. Plug
24. Lower ball joint
25. Nut
26. Spring washer
27. Bolt
28. Seal
29. Lower control arm
30. Self-locking nut fixing steering knuckle to lower control arm
31. Spring
32. Spring seat
33. Rubber pad
34. Self-locking nut fixing steering knuckle to upper control arm
35. Bolt
36. Seal
37. Bolt
38. Spring washer
39. Nut
40. Upper ball joint
41. Plug

Exploded view of 124 front suspension

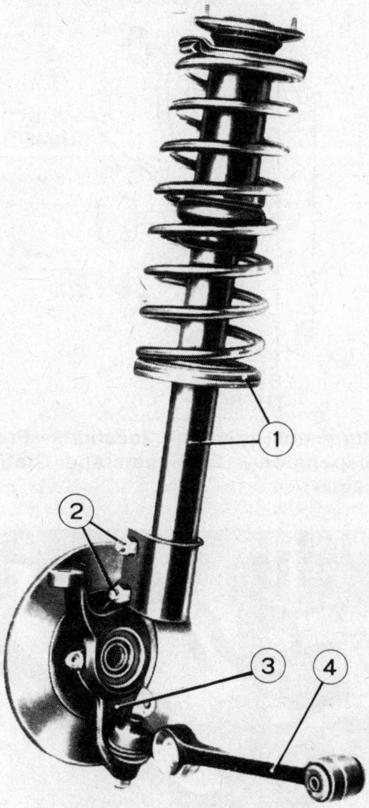

1. Shock absorber and spring
2. Screws and nuts attaching the shock absorber to the pillar
3. Pillar
4. Control arm

Left front suspension assembly—128; 131 and Brava similar

12. Take up each completely reassembled control arm and mount the hub on the shaft of the constant-speed joint. At the same time, insert the upper attachment of the shock absorber into the holes provided in the body and secure it with the nuts and the spring washers.
13. Place a flat washer on the shaft of the constant-speed joint and screw up the attachment nut.
14. Grease the rubber bushings in the anti-roll bar-to-control arm joint.
15. Using as many shims as were present on disassembly, reattach the end of the anti-roll bar and its flexible pads to the control arm and reinstall the latter on the body.
16. Attach the tie rod to the steering arm and tighten the nut to 58 ft/lbs.
17. Remount the brake caliper onto the brake disc.

X1/9 and 131

1. Remove the wheel and tire.
2. If the brake caliper is to be removed with the suspension, disconnect the flexible brake line from the caliper and plug it. If the caliper need not be removed from the vehicle, remove it from the suspension and support it with a length of heavy gauge wire.
3. Disconnect the stabilizer strut (sway bar) from the suspension.
4. Remove the bolt holding the control arm to the body mount.
5. Remove the nut holding the tie rod ball joint to the steering arm and remove the ball joint.
6. Support beneath the steering knuckle. Disconnect the top of the shock absorber by removing the three nuts and washers.
7. Lower the suspension strut assembly out of the car.
8. Install the suspension assembly in the reverse order. Tighten the attaching nuts and bolts with the vehicle under a load. Tighten the knuckle-to-tie rod attaching nut to 58 ft/lbs; the control arm-to-lower pillar attaching nut to 51 ft/lbs (X1/9) 58 ft/lbs (131); the con-

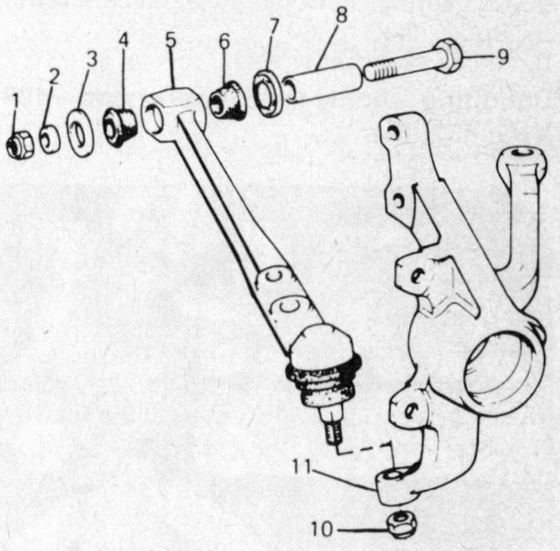

1. Nut
2. Washer
3. Washer
4. Rubber bushing
5. Control arm
6. Rubber bushing
7. Washer
8. Spacer
9. Bolt
10. Nut
11. Pillar

Exploded view of the front control arm assembly for an X1/9

trol arm-to-body attaching bolt to 29 ft/lbs (X1/9) 65 ft/lbs (131); and the stabilizer strut bar attaching bolt to 29 ft/lbs (X1/9) 43 ft/lbs (131).

Shock Absorber

REMOVAL AND INSTALLATION

124

1. Working from inside the engine compartment, disconnect the upper end of the shock holding the shank from turning with a wrench.
2. Remove the nut and bolt fixing the shock to the lower control arm.
3. Remove the shock through the lower control arm.
4. Installation is the reverse of the removal procedure to include replacing all the worn bushings and washers.

131, 128 and X1/9

NOTE: A coil spring compressor is required.

1. Detach the shock at the top by unscrewing the three nuts that attach it to the body.
2. Jack up the front of the car and support beneath the subframe with jack stands. Remove the wheel.
3. Remove the two bolts retaining the lower end of the strut to the knuckle or pillar.

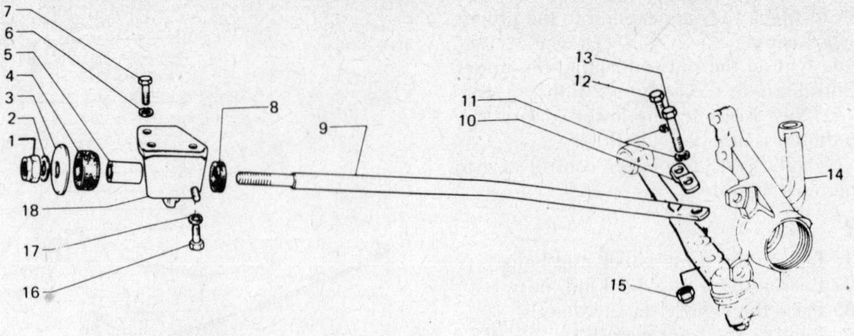

1. Nut
2. Washer
3. Retainer cup
4. Rubber pad
5. Spacer
6. Lockwasher
7. Bolt
8. Rubber ring
9. Reaction strut bar
10. Lockplate
11. Lockwasher
12. Bolt
13. Bolt
14. Pillar
15. Nut
16. Bolt
17. Washer
18. Body support

Exploded view of the front reaction strut bar assembly for an X1/9

1. Coil spring check plate clearance screws
2. Upper check plate
3. Shock absorber wrench

Unbolting shock from spring cap—128, X1/9, 131, Brava

4. Remove the shock and coil spring (strut assembly).
5. Using a spring compressor, compress the spring making sure that the compressor is installed properly.

CAUTION

Be sure that the lips of the compressor are gripping the spring firmly. If the spring should escape, great damage or injury could result.

6. Unscrew the pad mounting nut and release the spring compressor. Remove the spring.
7. Remove the old shock, insert the new one and reverse the removal procedure. With the suspension loaded, torque the lower strut attaching bolts to 36 ft/lbs.

Adjustments

CAMBER

124

Camber angle adjustments are made by changing the number of shims under the two bolts that hold the lower control arm to the frame crossmember. Camber is increased by removing shims and reduced by adding shims. Add or remove the same number for each bolt, otherwise caster will be affected.

X1/9, 131 and 128

Camber cannot be adjusted and is built into the suspension. Replace weak, worn, or damaged springs or other suspension components to gain the proper camber measurement.

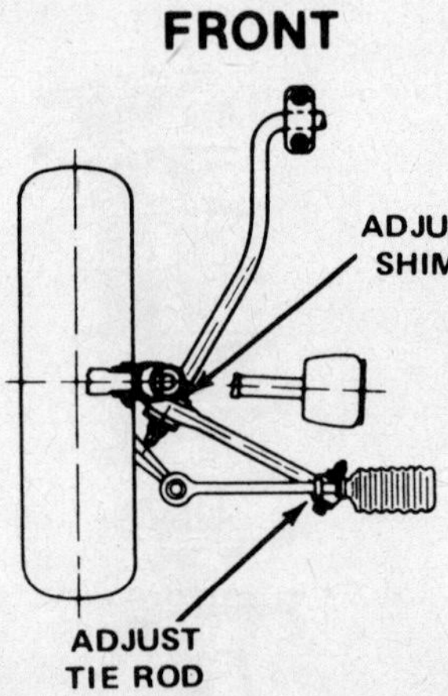

Alignment adjusting locations—Front suspension—128 Sedan and Station Wagon

Removing front shock upper attachment—128, X1/9, 131, Brava

1. Screws and nuts attaching the lower end of the shock absorber to the pillar

Removing front shock lower attachment-128, X1/9, 131, Brava

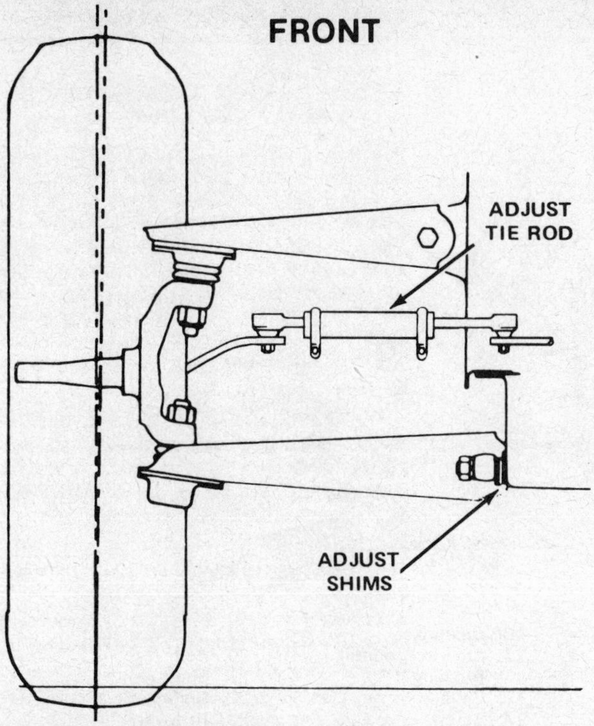

Alignment adjusting locations—Front suspension 124 Sedan and Station Wagon

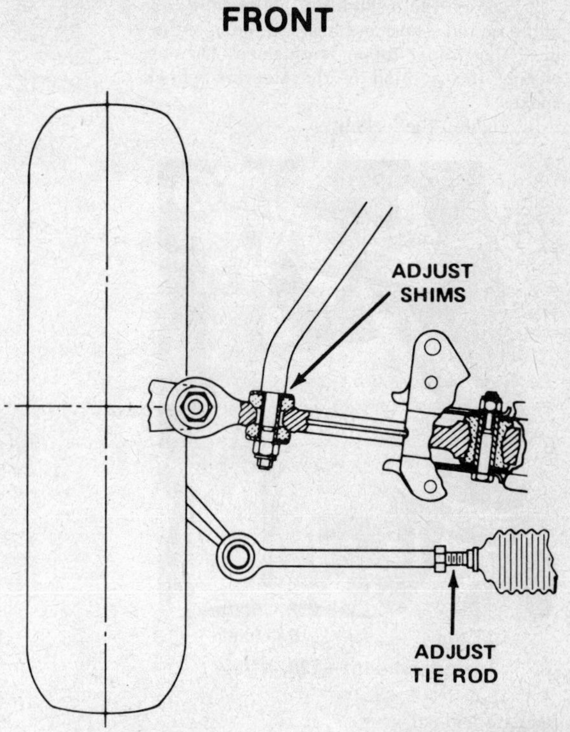

Alignment adjusting locations—Front suspension 131 and Brava

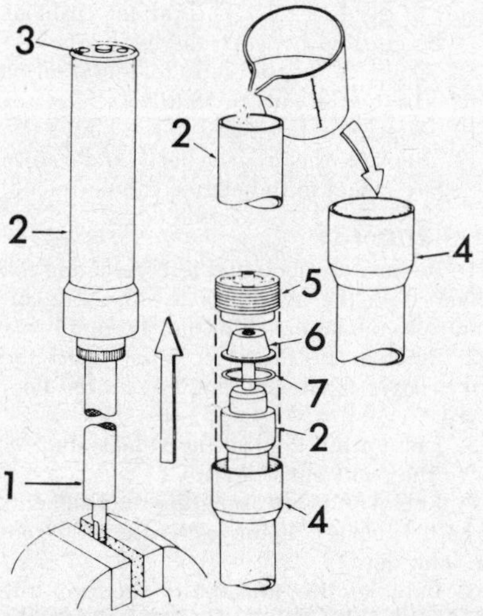

1. Stem
2. Inner cylinder
3. Valve
4. Outer cylinder
5. Threaded plug
6. Cap
7. Ring seal

Place stem (1) of inner cylinder (2) in vise. Extend cylinder. Carefully and gently tape around and under valve (3) to remove it. Pour fluid into cylinder (2) until full. Add remaining fluid to outer cylinder (4). Install valve (3) by carefully tapping it around edge. Insert cylinder (2) into cylinder (4). Assemble absorber using new ring seal (7) and Cap (6). Screw threaded plug (5) on absorber.

Refilling X1/9, 128, 131, and Brava shock inserts

CASTER

124

Caster angle is increased by moving these shims from the front bolts to the rear and decreased by moving them from the rear bolt to the front.

131

Caster is adjusted by adding or removing shims between the sway bar and lower support (control) arm.

128

If the caster angles are incorrect, the necessary corrections must be made by varying the number of shims inserted between the end of the anti-roll bar and the rubber pad of the control arm. The angle is reduced by about 15 minutes for each extra shim.

1. Raise the front of the vehicle on a pneumatic jack.
2. Remove the nut which anchors the anti-roll bar to the control arm.
3. Disconnect the control arm from the body.
4. Withdraw the end of the anti-roll bar from the control arm.
5. Add or remove as many shims as necessary to correct the caster angle.
6. Reassemble the various components. Lower the vehicle and rock it a few times to settle down the suspension before tightening the two attachment nuts to their correct torque values.

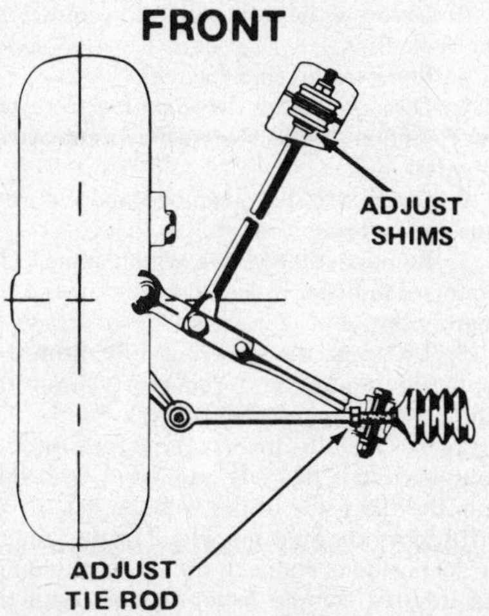

Alignment adjusting locations—Front suspension—X1/9

X1/9

Caster is adjusted on the X1/9 by adding or subtracting shims between the front reaction struts and body-end supports.

TOE-IN

124, 850

Toe-in is adjusted by loosening the clamp bolts and turning sleeves to lengthen or shorten the left and right-hand tie rods. Turn the sleeves in opposite directions and to an equal extent. After adjusting, make sure the gaps in the sleeves and clamps are on the same side and flush.

X1/9 and 128

1. Set the wheels straight ahead. Make sure the spokes on the steering wheel are positioned properly.

2. Loosen the locknut on the inboard end of the tie rod sleeve and turn the rod in or out until the proper toe-in is obtained. Do not change the position of the steering wheel spokes.

3. Tighten the locknut.

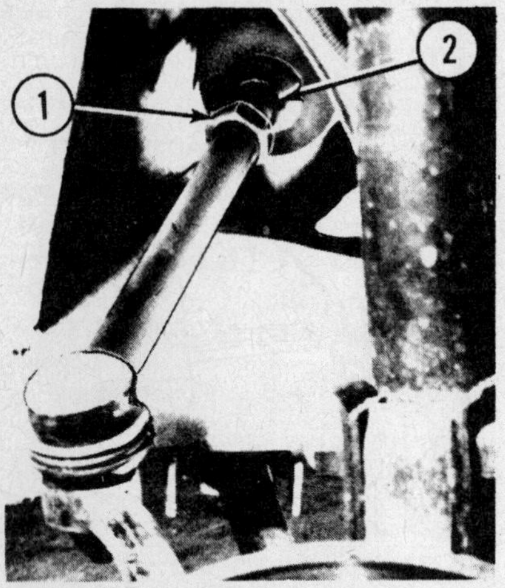

1. Nut 2. Ball joint

Toe adjustment—128, X1/9

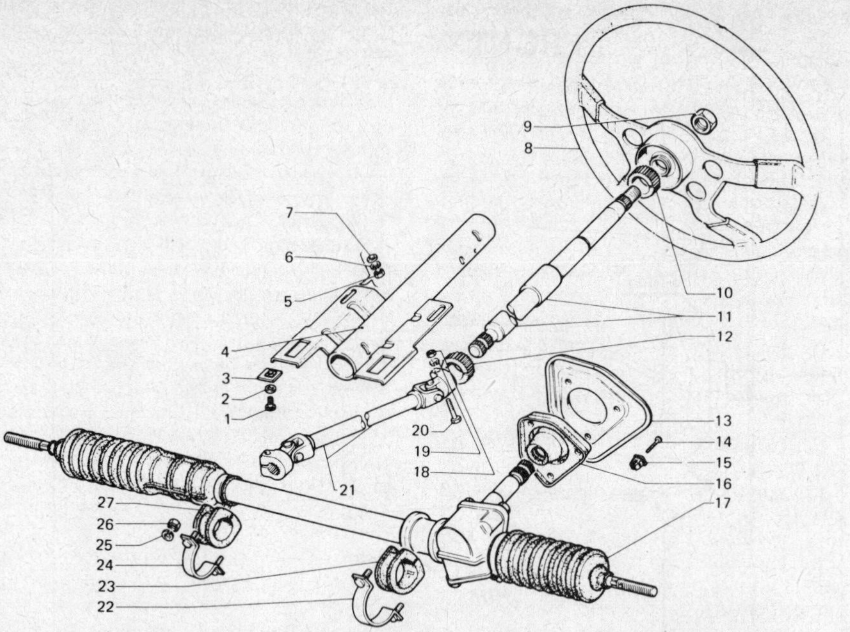

1. Bolt
2. Washer
3. Retainer
4. Support
5. Nut
6. Lockwasher
7. Washer
8. Steering wheel
9. Nut
10. Bushing
11. Steering column
12. Bushing
13. Cover
14. Screw
15. Pad
16. Gasket
17. Steering box
18. Nut
19. Lockwasher
20. Bolt
21. Shaft
22. Clamp
23. Pad
24. Clamp
25. Lockwasher
26. Nut
27. Pad

Exploded view of the steering column and steering gear of the X1/9

131

131 toe-in is adjusted in the same manner as the 128 and X1/9, except that the outboard locknut is loosened to rotate the tie rod.

NOTE: Lubricate the steering rod boot so it doesn't tear.

STEERING

Steering Wheel

REMOVAL AND INSTALLATION

128, X1/9 and 131

1. Disconnect the battery. Remove the screws attaching the horn button cover.
2. Remove the screws holding the steering column masking sleeves and remove the sleeves.
3. Unscrew the steering wheel attaching nut and remove the steering wheel.
4. Install in the reverse order.

124

1. Disconnect the battery. Pry off the horn button by inserting a screwdriver between the button and the wheel hub.
2. Disconnect the horn wire at the button.
3. Unscrew and remove the steering wheel attaching nut and remove the steering wheel from the shaft.
4. Install the steering wheel in the reverse order.

TURN SIGNAL SWITCH

1. Remove horn button and steering wheel.
2. Disconnect switch wiring. Remove shroud.
3. Remove attaching clamp and slide off switch.
4. Installation is the reverse of removal.

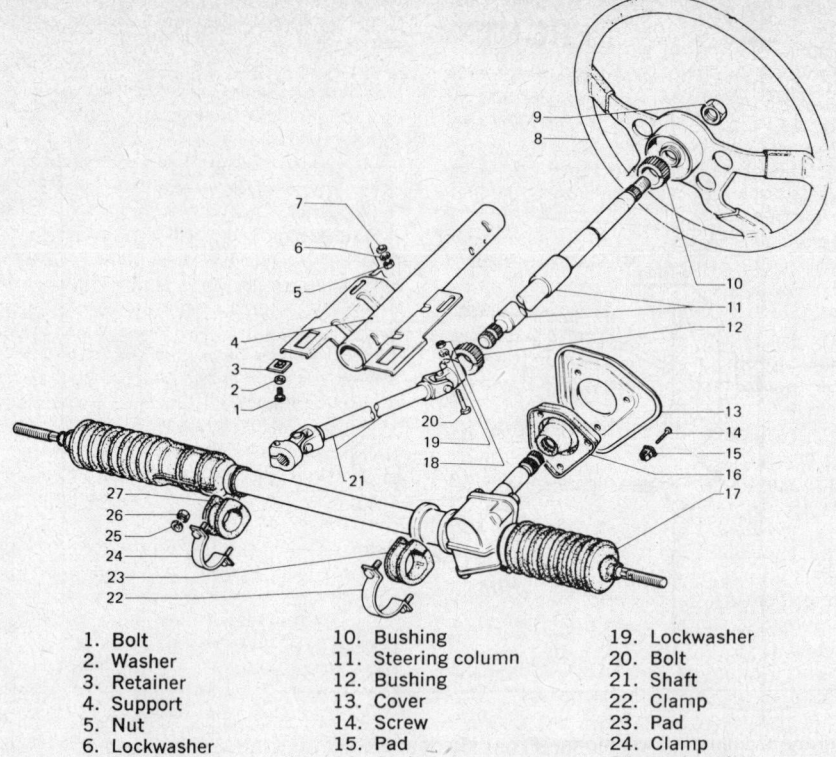

Steering Gear

REMOVAL AND INSTALLATION

128

1. Disconnect the battery leads.
2. Rest the front of the car on stands.
3. Unscrew the stud bolts and remove the front wheels.
4. Remove the spare wheel.
5. Disconnect the drive pinion from the lower section of the steering column at the universal joint.
6. Using a puller, remove the tie rods from the steering arms.
7. Remove the screws which attach the top guard in order to facilitate removal of the steering box.
8. Unscrew the steering box from the mounting bracket and remove it from the right-side of the vehicle.
9. To install, insert the steering box (complete with tie rods and filled with oil), from the right-side of the vehicle.
10. With the steering wheel in the straight ahead position, connect the drive pinion to the steering column lower section, with the universal joints.
11. Mount the assembly on the body by means of the brackets. The rubber cushions must be inserted between the two parts.
12. Connect the tie rods to the steering arms. Torque the nuts to 58 ft/lbs.
13. Attach the top guard to the body.
14. Replace the front wheels and return the spare wheel to the engine compartment.

X1/9 and 131

1. Remove the bolt and nuts retaining the universal on the bottom of the steering column to the pinion shaft of the steering box.
2. Remove the three screws securing the gasket cover to the steering box on the floor boards.
3. Jack up the front of the vehicle and remove the two front wheels.
4. Remove the nuts securing the ball joints in both knuckles. Remove the tie rods from the knuckles.
5. Remove the four bolts securing the steering box to the body and remove the steering box from the vehicle.
6. Install the steering box in the reverse order of removal.

Power Steering

1. Remove nut on tie rod.
2. Remove ball joint from steering knuckle.
3. Repeat for other side.
4. Remove hoses and allow box to drain.
5. Remove bolt and nut on steering shaft.
6. Remove bolt holding left side of box.
7. Remove 2 bolts holding right side.
8. Remove steering box from car.
9. Install steering box in reverse order of removal.
10. Fill with Dexron ATF fluid.

Power Steering Pump Removal

1. Disconnect both lines going to the pump.
2. Allow to drain.
3. Remove tensioner bolt and mounting bolt.
4. Remove belt.
5. Remove pump.
6. Install in reverse order of removal.

124

1. Disconnect the battery.
2. Remove the horn button and emblem cover.
3. Remove the steering wheel retaining nut and pull the steering wheel from the shaft, using a wheel puller.
4. Remove the turn signal switch half covers and unscrew the retaining collar of the turn signal switch. This is located on the bracket which fixes the steering column to the body.
5. Disconnect the steering column bracket from the ignition switch (threaded ring) and remove the retaining collar of the turn signal switch.
6. Remove the screw which clamps the steering column to the worm shaft and remove the steering column from inside the car.

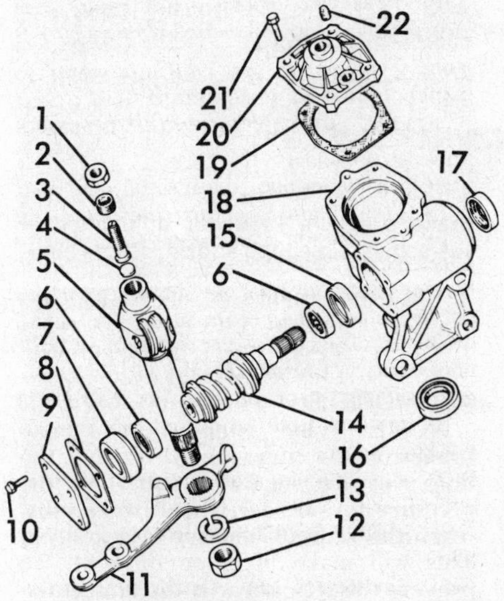

1. Adjusting screw nut
2. Screw ring
3. Adjusting screw
4. Plug
5. Roller shaft
6. Ball bearings
7. Bearing retainer
8. Shims
9. Worm screw thrust cover
10. Cover screws
11. Pitman arm
12. Nut, pitman arm to roller shaft
13. Washer
14. Worm screw
15. Bearing retainer
16. Roller shaft seal
17. Steering column seal
18. Steering gear housing
19. Gasket
20. Steering housing upper cover
21. Upper cover screws
22. Oil filter plug

Exploded view of newer type 124 steering gear

7. Unscrew the nuts which fix the left-hand steering arm and intermediate arm pins.
8. Remove the pins with an appropriate puller.
9. Remove the steering box from the body by removing the 3 mounting screws.

NOTE: Shims can be placed on the steering box bolts to ensure proper alignment.

Note the number and placement of such shims.

10. Drain the oil from the steering box.
11. Using a puller, remove the drop arm from the roller shaft.
12. Remove the roller shaft cover, complete with roller shaft adjusting screw, adjusting disc, lockwasher and locknut.
13. Remove the roller shaft assembly from the steering box.
14. Remove the worm shaft thrust cover and the front bearing adjusting shims.
15. Turn the worm shaft to withdraw the front roller bearing.
16. Use a puller and remove the outer race of the rear roller bearing.
17. Remove the worm and shaft from the steering box along with the inner race of the inner roller bearing.

ADJUSTMENTS

124

1. Measure the amount of free-play in the steering wheel by moving it back and forth until the wheels will not respond. At this point whatever movement is left in the wheel is free-play.
2. To adjust this condition, loosen the locknut and turn the adjusting screw in.
3. Gradually adjust the free-play out of the steering wheel until it becomes minimal.
4. Tighten the locknut while holding the adjustment screw in place.

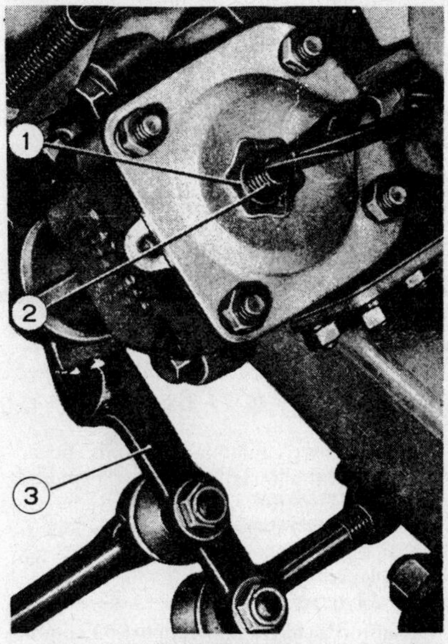

1. Lockwasher
2. Adjusting screw
3. Drop arm

Adjusting worm and roller clearance—124

NOTE: Serious damage may result from turning the adjustment screw in too far. A small amount of free-play should remain to insure against this condition.

128, X1/9 and 131

Adjustments to the steering gear are not necessary during normal service. Adjustments are performed only as part of overhaul.

BRAKES

Adjustment

REAR DRUM BRAKES

1. Jack up the car and it on stands.
2. Push the brake pedal to lock the shoes against the drum.
3. Rotate the adjustment nuts outward until locked.
4. Rotate them back about 20° and be sure that the wheels turn freely.

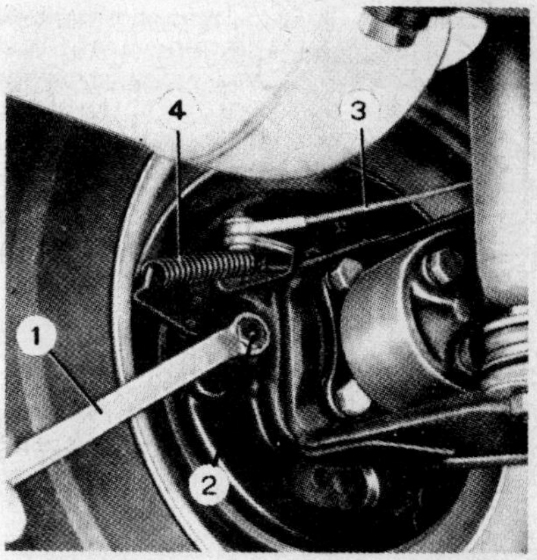

1. Wrench
2. Brake shoe actuating cam nut
3. Handbrake control cable
4. Brake shoe actuating lever return sprin[g]

Adjusting the rear drum brakes

Master Cylinder

REMOVAL AND INSTALLATION

124 and 131

1. Remove the reservoir cover and plug the fluid outlet port.
2. Disconnect the pipe between the reservoir and master cylinder.
3. Remove the 3 brake lines from the master cylinder.
4. Unbolt the master cylinder from the firewall, or power booster (124, 131).
5. Reverse the removal procedure to install the master cylinder. Bleed the system after installation.

X1/9

1. Remove the steering column as follows:

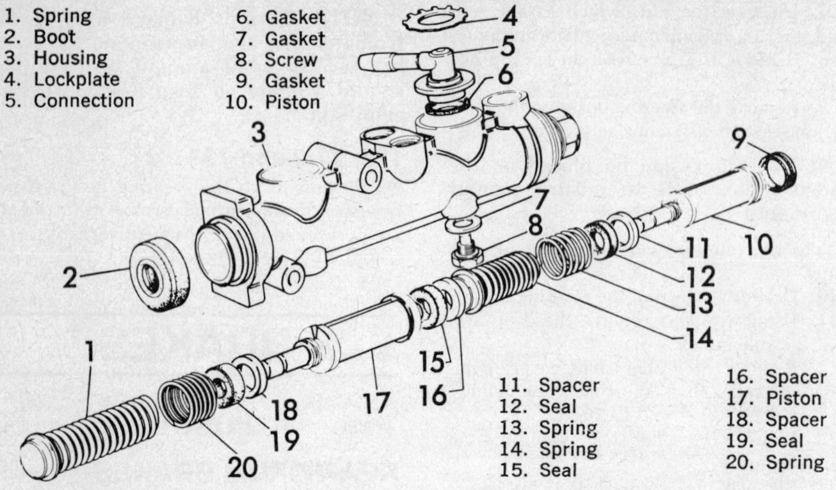

Exploded view of master cylinder—X1/9 shown; others similar

a. Disconnect the battery.

b. Remove the five screws holding the steering column cover halves and remove the covers.

c. Disconnect the three electrical connectors and one wire.

d. Remove the two nuts and washers holding the column to the top of the dashboard.

e. Remove the two bolts and washers holding the column to the bottom of the dashboard.

f. Slide the shaft off of the steering box shaft and remove the column from the vehicle.

2. Disconnect the hoses from the master cylinder reservoir.
3. Remove the nuts and washers holding the master cylinder to its support.
4. Pull the master cylinder off of the actuating rod. Remove the hoses from the master cylinder and switch assembly.
5. Remove the master cylinder from the vehicle and drain the fluid into an appropriate container.
6. Install the master cylinder and steering column in the reverse order of removal and bleed the brake hydraulic system.

128

1. Remove the spare wheel from the engine compartment.
2. Remove the fluid reservoir cover and plug the outlet to the master cylinder in order to keep the reservoir from draining.
3. Disconnect the reservoir-to-master cylinder tubes.
4. Disconnect the fluid delivery tubing to the front and rear brakes, removing the fastening screws.
5. Remove both nuts and spring washers which secure the master cylinder to the power booster and remove the master cylinder.
6. Installation is the reverse of removal.

OVERHAUL

All Models

1. Disconnect the fluid inlet connector from the cylinder.
2. Remove the boot from its groove in the cylinder body.
3. Back out the set screws and the end plug.
4. Remove from the cylinder body the piston return springs, cups, seal rings, and spacers.
5. Check the valve carriers, reaction springs, and rubber seal rings.
6. Inspect the cylinder bore for pits or roughness. If this condition exists, hone the bore to prevent excessive wear of seals or fluid loss.

NOTE: If the cylinder bore is badly scored or corroded, the cylinder body must be replaced.

7. Be sure to lubricate all parts with clean brake fluid.
8. Assembly is the reverse of disassembly.

Brake Pressure Regulator

This device, located near the rear axle is used on 124, 128 and 131 models only. It serves to adjust hydraulic line pressure to prevent rear wheel lock-up under hard braking. An important safety factor, the pressure regulator will apply a reduced line pressure to the rear brakes (roughly half that of the front brakes) when the rear suspension is off-loaded. A torsion bar, anchored to the rear axle, senses suspension angle, and transmits this mechanically to the pressure regulator valve. The result is straight line stopping and more even braking effect.

ADJUSTMENT

The pressure regulator need only be adjusted upon initial installation, or if its mounting bolts become loose in service. By loosening the mounting bolts, the regulator may be pivoted to adjust the travel of the torsion bar.

124, 131 and 128

1. Raise rear of car and support on stands.
2. Disconnect regulator torsion bar (E) at axle connecting link (G).
3. Pivot axle end of the torsion bar to distance "X" from the rubber buffer resting surface.
4. Lift dust boot (C) and check that regulator piston (D) contacts other end of torsion bar.
5. If not, loosen regulator mounting screws (A+B) and pivot regulator until piston just grazes torsion bar.
6. Then tighten the mounting screws and connect the torsion bar. On the 128, torque the bolts to 14 ft/lbs. Distance "X" is:

5.78 in.—124 Special Sedan and 124 Sport Coupe
5.0 in.—124 Wagon
3.74 in.—124 Sport Spider
12.0 in.—131 Sedan
12.25 in.—131 Wagon
2.126 in.—128 All

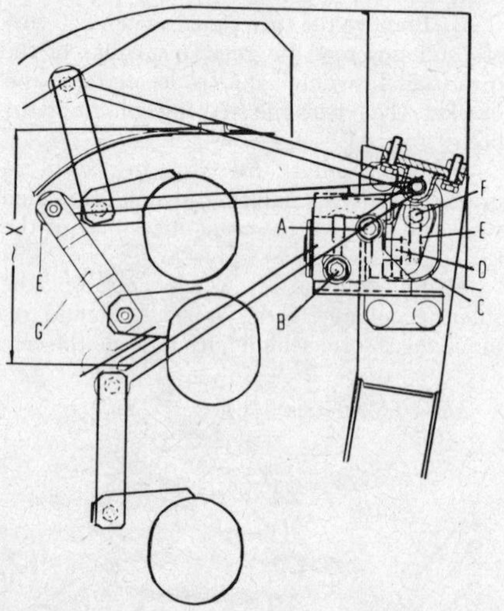

Brake pressure regulator adjustment—124 sedan and coupe shown; others similar

Bleeding

ALL MODELS

NOTE: When bleeding the rear brakes on 124, 128 and 131 models, the line pressure regulator will limit the pressure to the rear wheel brake units when the rear suspension is jacked up. This will make bleeding difficult. To prevent this, temporarily disconnect the regulator torsion bar from the rear axle link and tie it up to simulate normal suspension height. This will allow full pressure to the rear brakes and speed up bleeding.

1. Fill the reservoir and hydraulic system with brake fluid.
2. Clean all dirt from the bleeder screws and remove the protective caps.
3. Install a bleeder hose over the fitting in the brake caliper or the wheel cylinder and submerge the other end of the bleeder hose in a clean jar half-filled with brake fluid.
4. Loosen the bleeder screw a few turns and have a helper press the brake pedal down quickly, allowing it to return slowly.
5. Do this procedure several times until no more air bubbles escape from the rubber hose.
6. Keeping the brake pedal depressed, remove the bleeder hose and tighten the bleeder screw.

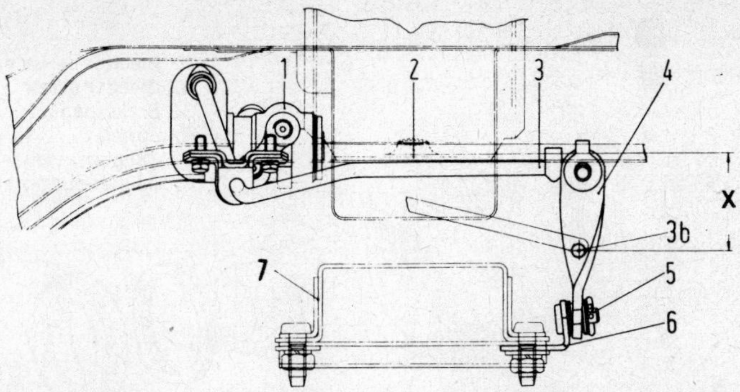

1. Pressure regulator
2. Rubber buffer seat
3. Torsion bar
3B. Torsion bar end, anchor pin side
4. Torsion bar to control arm link
5. Torsion bar link to control arm link
6. Link anchor pin support
7. Control arm

Brake pressure regulator—128 models

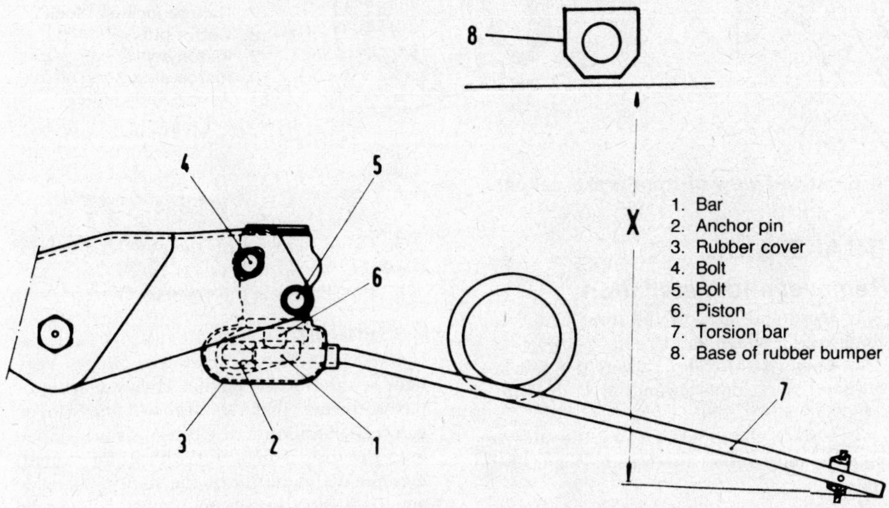

1. Bar
2. Anchor pin
3. Rubber cover
4. Bolt
5. Bolt
6. Piston
7. Torsion bar
8. Base of rubber bumper

Brake pressure regulator—131, Brava models

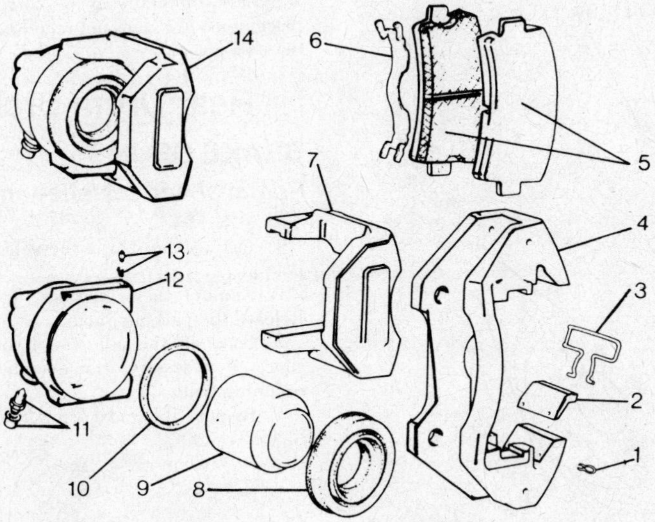

1. Cotter pin
2. Caliper locking block
3. Spring
4. Caliper support bracket
5. Brake pads
6. Brake pad retainer spring
7. Cylinder housing
8. Dust boot
9. Piston
10. Piston seal
11. Bleeder screw and dust cap
12. Cylinder
13. Spring and attaching
14. Assembled caliper assembly

Front brake caliper assembly on the X1/9

7. Clean the bleeder screw and refit the protective cap.
8. Repeat Steps 2, 3, 4 and 5 on the other wheels. Make sure that the reservoir is full after each wheel cylinder is bled.

Front Disc Brakes

BRAKE PADS

Removal and Installation

1. Remove the caliper from the mounting brackets. It is not necessary to disconnect the hose from the caliper; suspend it from the body with a length of wire. Do not allow it to hang by the hose.
2. Note the position of the tensioner springs on the pads. Remove the springs and pads.
3. Inspect the pad thickness. It must be at least $^1/_{16}$ inch. Replace pads in sets only.
4. Installation is the reverse.

BRAKE CALIPERS

Removal and Installation

ALL MODELS

1. Jack up the car, put it on stands, and
2. Plug the outlet port of the brake fluid reservoir.
3. Disconnect the brake hose from the caliper by unscrewing the junction.
4. Remove the cotter pins, which hold the locking blocks in place.
5. Drive the locking blocks out from between the mounting bracket and the caliper with a punch.
6. Pull the caliper free from the bracket.
7. Installation is the reverse. Push the piston back into the caliper with a C-clamp if necessary. Drive the locking blocks into place and retain with new cotter pins. Bleed the system after installation.

Overhaul

124, 128 and 131

1. Remove the dust boot.
2. Direct a jet of air into the fluid inlet coupling to remove the piston from the caliper cylinder. Catch the piston with a rag or a block of wood.
3. Remove the seal with a piece of wood. Do not use a screwdriver or punch.

NOTE: When pistons are removed, piston seals always must be changed.

4. Wash all parts in hot water and dry them with compressed air.
5. Fit the piston seal to the caliper cylinder. Lubricate the seal and the piston with brake fluid.
6. Insert the piston and push it to the far end of the cylinder.
7. Fit the dust boot, making sure that the lip enters the undercut in the caliper body.

X1/9

1. Remove the dust boot.
2. Depress the dowel holding the caliper cylinder to the caliper support bracket with a thin drift or rod.
3. Separate the cylinder from the support bracket.
4. Apply compressed air to the brake hose port and blow the piston out of the cylinder.

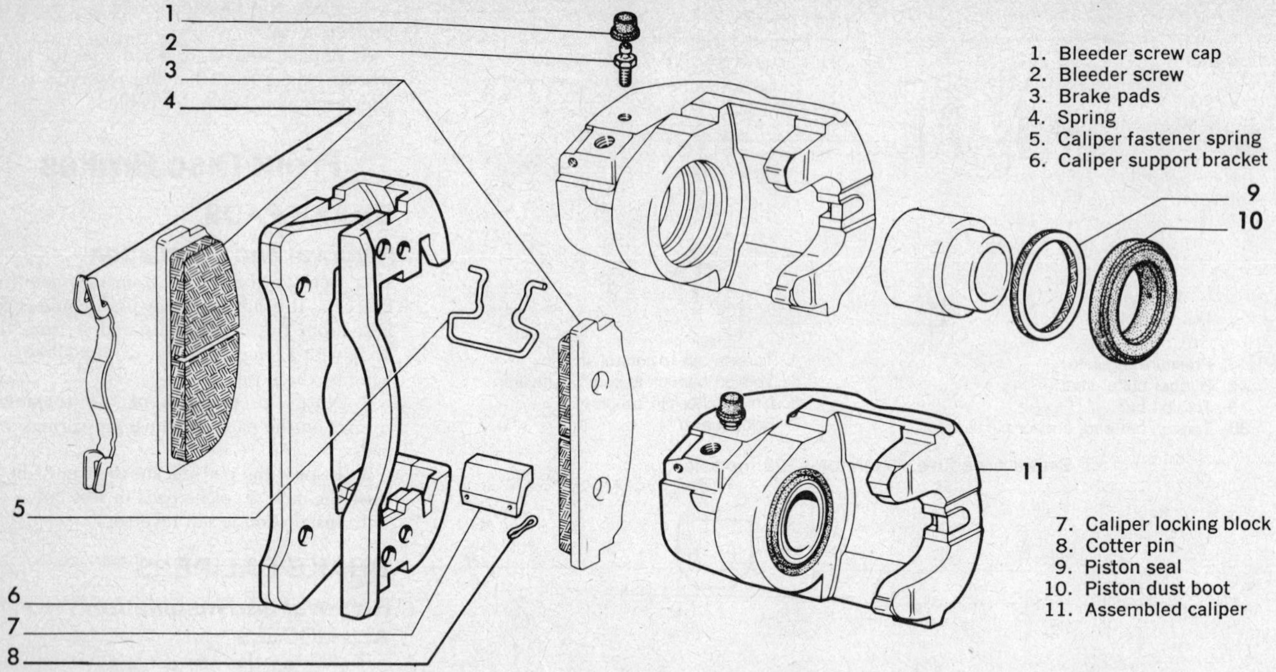

Exploded view of front brake caliper

Catch the piston with a rag. Remove the piston seal with a piece of wood. Do not use a screwdriver or punch.

5. Check the piston and caliper cylinder for scoring or binding. The cylinder bore can be refinished by honing.

6. Clean and flush the parts with clean brake fluid. Make sure that all metal particles are removed from the cylinder bore.

7. Assemble the caliper in the reverse order of removal, keeping the parts liberally coated with clean brake fluid.

BRAKE DISC

Removal and Installation

1. Raise and support the front of the car. Remove the wheel and tire.
2. Remove the caliper from the bracket. Suspend the caliper from the body with a length of wire.
3. Unbolt the bracket from the steering knuckle and support the assembly out of the way.
4. Remove the two bolts securing the disc to the wheel hub.
5. Using a brass drift, remove the disc from the hub.
6. Installation is the reverse.

Inspection

Check the discs for scoring or pitting. Very light scoring is acceptable. Heavy scoring or pitting means that the disc will have to be replaced. Minimum disc thickness is stamped onto the disc. To check the discs for runout, mount a dial indicator on the steering knuckle and turn the disc. Runout must not exceed 0.006 in. Be sure the wheel bearings are properly adjusted before making this measurement. Runout may be corrected by replacement. Fiat does not recommend that the discs be ground.

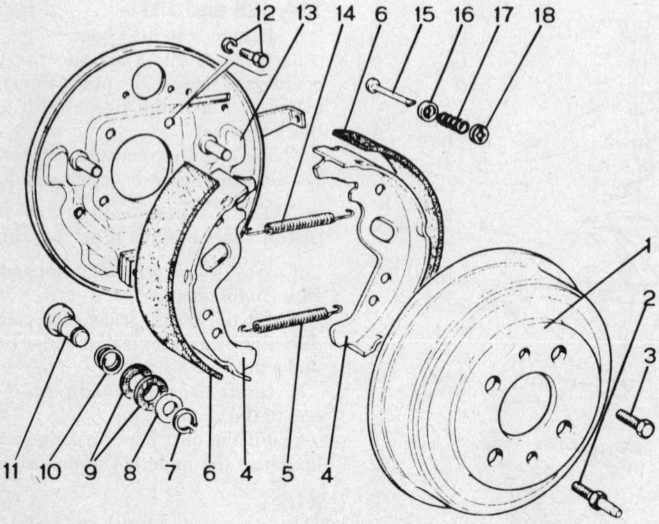

1. Brake drum
2. Drum attaching screw wheel location dowel
3. Brake drum attaching screw
4. Shoe side
5. Lower shoe return spring
6. Brake linings
7. Snap ring
8. Plain washer
9. Friction washers
10. Spring
11. Casing
12. Screw and washer
13. Brake backing plate
14. Upper shoe return spring
15. Pivot pin
16. Inner cup
17. Shoe guide spring
18. Outer cup

Rear brake assembly—128

Rear Drum Brakes

BRAKE DRUMS

Removal and Installation

128 and 131

1. Jack up the rear of the vehicle and support it.
2. Remove the wheel and tire assembly. Release the parking brake.
3. Back off the adjustment of the brake shoes, if necessary. Remove the two drum retaining bolts.
4. Remove the brake drum from the hub or

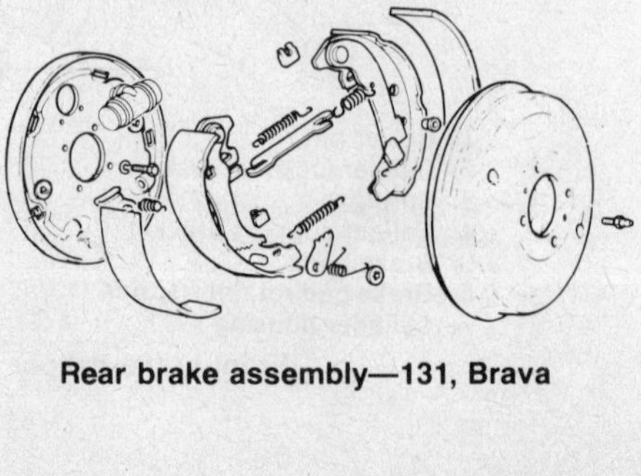

Rear brake assembly—131, Brava

axle shaft flange by pulling it straight out and off the locating dowels.

5. Install in the reverse order.

Inspection

After the brake drum has been removed from the vehicle, it should be inspected for runout, severe scoring, cracks, and the proper inside diameter.

Minor scores on a brake drum can be removed with fine emery cloth, provided that all grit is removed from the drum before it is installed on the vehicle.

A badly scored, rough, or out-of-round (runout) drum can be ground or turned on a brake drum lathe. Do not remove any more material from the drum than is necessary to provide a smooth surface for the brake shoe to contact. The maximum diameter of the braking surface is shown on the inside of each brake drum. Brake drums that exceed the maximum braking surface diameter shown on the brake drum, either through wear or refinishing, must be replaced. This is because after the outside wall of the brake drum reaches a certain thickness (thinner than the original thickness) the drum loses its ability to dissipate the heat created by the friction between the brake drum and the brake shoes, when the brakes are applied. Also, the brake drum will have more tendency to warp and/or crack.

BRAKE SHOES

Removal and Installation

ALL MODELS

1. Always leave the brake shoes on the other side of the vehicle intact for a reference.
2. Remove the brake drums.
3. Using pliers or a brake spring removal tool, remove the retaining springs from the shoes.
4. Remove the retaining springs and clips.
5. Disconnect the handbrake cable from the brake shoe link.
6. Remove the shoes from the backing plate.
7. Installation is the reverse.

WHEEL CYLINDERS

Overhaul

ALL MODELS

NOTE: When overhauling a wheel cylinder still on the backing plate, take care not to get brake fluid on the linings.

1. Jack up the car and place it on stands.

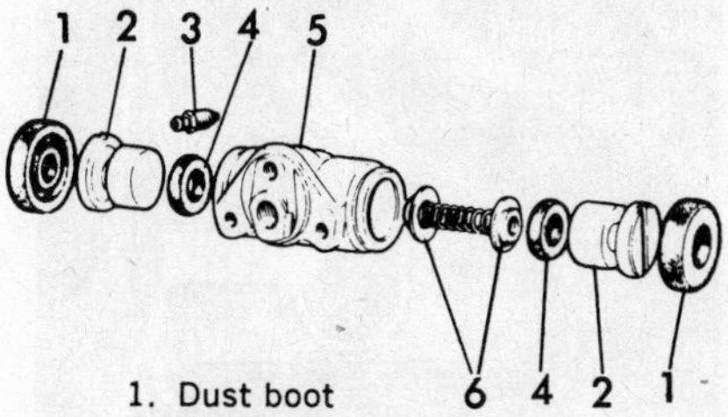

1. Dust boot
2. Pistons
3. Bleeder screw
4. Seal rings
5. Cylinder body
6. Backing washers and piston reaction spring

Rear wheel cylinder

2. Remove the wheels and brake drums. Release the upper shoe springs and tilt the shoes away from the wheel cylinder.
3. Unfasten and remove the rubber boots from the ends of the wheel cylinder.
4. The plunger, valve rings and cups on the end of the reaction spring will be pushed out by the expansion of the spring.
5. Check the condition inside of the cylinder.

NOTE: The cleaning process is only to smooth the inside surface of the cylinder. Do not try to remove deep pits or grooves by honing.

7. Valve rings should be replaced and all parts lubricated, with clean brake fluid.
8. Assembly is the reverse of the disassembly procedure.

Rear Disc Brakes

BRAKE PADS

Removal and Installation

124 and X1/9

Follow the procedure given in the "Front Disc Brakes" section.

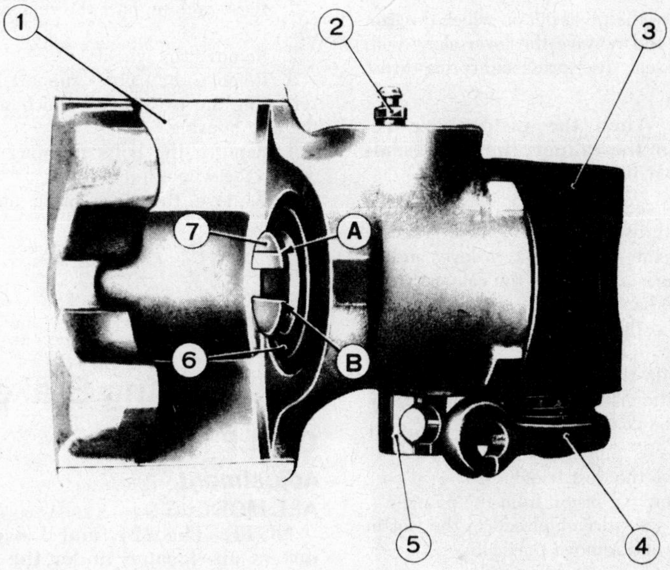

1. Caliper body
2. Bleed connection
3. Gaiter
4. Hand brake cam lever
5. Hand brake cable anchorage
6. Piston protection boot
7. Piston

A. Reference mark
B. Slot engaging friction pad rib

Rear brake caliper—124

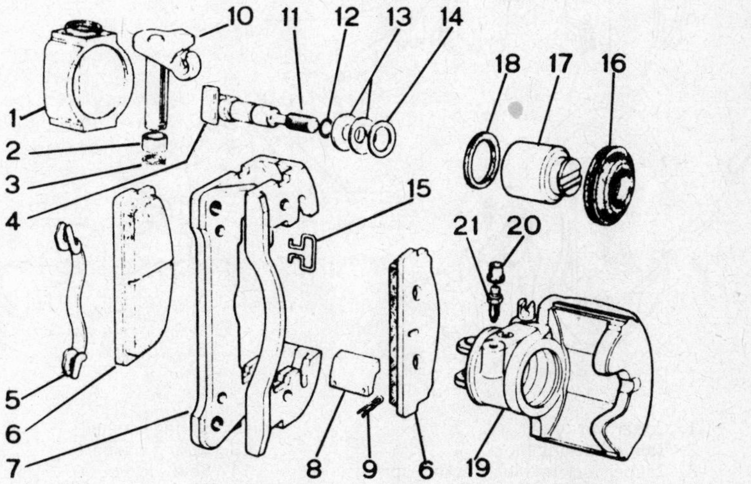

1. Boot over hand brake lever end
2. Bushing
3. Snap ring
4. Pawl
5. Friction pad locking spring
6. Friction pad
7. Caliper bracket
8. Caliper locking block
9. Cotter pin
10. Hand brake cam lever
11. Self-adjusting plunger
12. Plunger sealing ring
13. Disc springs
14. Disc spring thrust washer
15. Flat radial spring
16. Boot
17. Piston
18. Piston seal
19. Caliper body
20. Cap for bleed connection
21. Bleed connection

Rear brake assembly—124

BRAKE CALIPERS

Removal and Installation

124 and X1/9

Follow the procedure given for the front brake calipers. Remember to reconnect the handbrake cable to the cam levers.

Overhaul

124

1. Remove the dust boot and unscrew the piston from the handbrake plunger.
2. To do this, insert a screwdriver into the slot in the head of the piston.
3. Remove the seal and the handbrake gaiter.
4. Remove the pivot pin on which the cam lever turns and remove the lever along with the plunger seal, disc spring and spring thrust washer.

NOTE: When the pistons are removed from the caliper, the piston seals always must be changed.

5. Fit the self-adjusting plunger with seal, spring and thrust washer.
6. Install the handbrake cam lever and fit the pivot pin in the fork of the caliper body.
7. Fit the handbrake lever gaiter.
8. Replace the rubber piston seal in the caliper body.
9. Screw in the piston until it is properly seated and the mark cut in the piston is opposite the bleed connection.

X1/9

1. Remove the dust boot.
2. Unscrew the piston from the plunger.
3. Use a screwdriver placed in the slot in the plunger and remove the seal.
4. Remove the lock ring from the handbrake shaft and remove the shaft.
5. Remove the handbrake plunger together with the plunger pawl, seal and spring washers.
6. The cylinder bore can be refinished by honing. Flush all metal particles out of the cylinder bore with clean brake fluid. Replace all worn or damaged parts.
7. Assemble the caliper in the reverse order of removal, keeping all of the parts liberally coated with clean brake fluid.

BRAKE DISCS

Removal and Installation

1. Raise and support the rear of the vehicle.
2. Remove the wheel.
3. Remove the caliper support bracket by removing the two screws which secure it to the axle housing.
4. Remove the bolts retaining the brake disc to the wheel hub.
5. Remove the disc, using an ordinary drift.
6. Install the disc in the reverse order of removal.

Inspection

See the front disc inspection section.

Parking Brake

CABLE

Adjustment

ALL MODELS

NOTE: The 124, and 128 cable adjusters are located under the car. The 131 models have the adjuster located on the underside of the handbrake lever. The X1/9 adjuster is located on the underside of the car underneath an access plate.

1. Disengage the handbrake cable, using the lever.
2. Pull the lever up three or four notches.

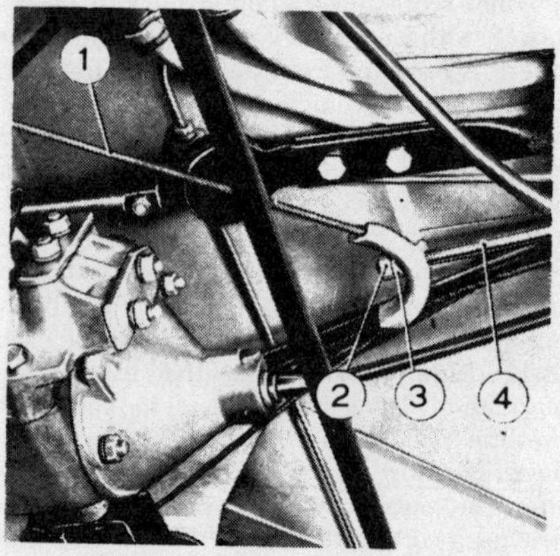

1. Parking brake control cable
2. Locknut
3. Adjusting nut
4. Threaded tensioner

Parking brake adjustment—124

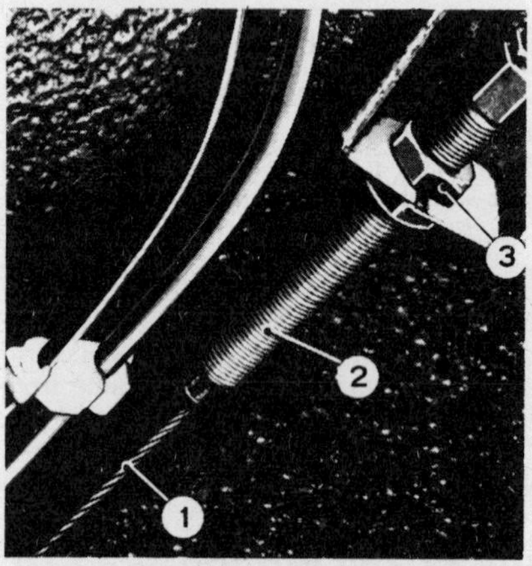

1. Main cable
2. Threaded tensioner
3. Adjusting nut and locknut

Parking brake adjustment—128

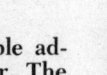

Parking brake adjustment access window—X1/9

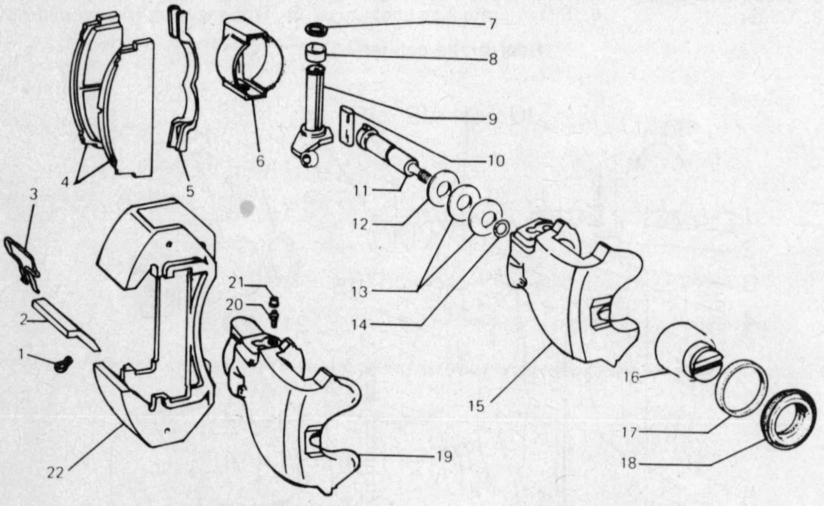

1. Cotter pin
2. Caliper locking block
3. Caliper locking block locking spring
4. Brake pads
5. Brake pad retaining spring
6. Rubber boot
7. Snap ring
8. Spacer
9. Handbrake
10. Pawl
11. Plunger
12. Spring washer
13. Spring washers
14. Seal
15. Caliper cylinder
16. Piston
17. Piston seal
18. Dust boot
19. Assembled caliper
20. Bleeder screw
21. Bleeder screw dust boot
22. Support bracket

Rear brake caliper assembly on the X1/9

3. Loosen the locknut on the tensioner and turn the adjusting nut until the cable is stretched and the wheels are locked.
4. Tighten the locknut.
5. The cable is correctly tensioned when the car is held by a movement of the lever through 3 notches.
6. Release the lever and check that the wheels are free to turn.

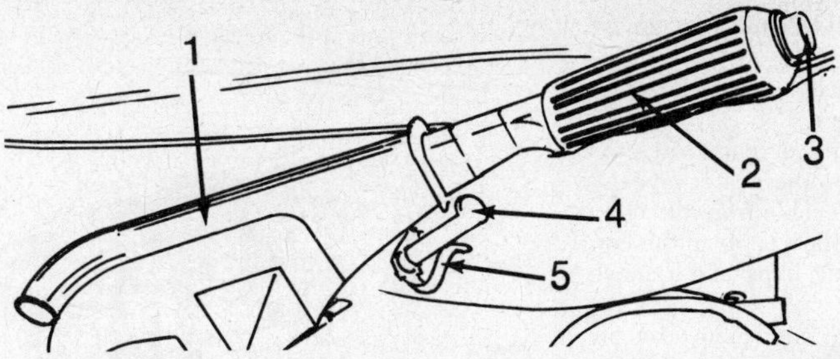

Parking brake adjustment—131, Brava models

Wheel Bearings

PACKING AND ADJUSTMENT

128

1. Remove the wheel, caliper, disc, and plate.
2. Remove the hub nut and discard.
3. Remove the tie rod end, shock absorber bolts, and lower ball joint spindle from the knuckle pillar.
4. Slide the knuckle pillar from the constant-speed joint.
5. Remove the bearing retainer ring or retaining nut from the pillar.
6. Press the old bearing out of the bearing cavity.
7. Clean the bearing with solvent.
8. If possible, blow dry with air.

NOTE: Do not spin the bearing around on your finger with an air blast; hold the bearing from spinning with your finger.

9. Insert a finger full of grease into your left palm and with your right hand, dip the bearing into the grease. Allow the grease to seep between the rollers.
10. Continue packing until the grease has tightened the bearing considerably.

NOTE: The easiest way to insert the grease is between the race and the roller housing from the wide side of the taper until it begins to come out of the thin side.

11. Press the new or repacked bearing into the bearing cavity.
12. Reinstall the snap ring or retaining nut. Torque the retaining nut to 44 ft/lbs. Stake to the knuckle pillar.
13. Complete the assembly in the reverse of removal. Torque the hub attachment nut to 100 ft/lbs and stake the collar of the nut.

X1/9

1. Jack up the front end of the vehicle and remove the wheel.
2. Disconnect the brake calipers and support bracket from the steering pillar.
3. Remove the bolt and centering stud holding the brake rotor and plate and remove the rotor and plate.
4. Remove the nut securing the tie rod to the pillar and remove the ball joint from the pillar.
5. Remove the nut holding the control arm to the pillar and remove the control arm ball joint from the pillar.
6. Remove the two nuts and bolts holding the shock absorbers to the pillar and remove the pillar from the vehicle.
7. Remove the nut and washers holding the hub to the pillar and press the hub out of the pillar.
8. Remove the ring nut holding the bearing in the pillar and pull the bearing out of the pillar.

NOTE: The removal and installation of the bearing is facilitated by using special Fiat tools A.57123 socket to remove the bearing ring nut and 8015 bearing puller/installer to remove and install the bearing.

9. Clean the bearing and pack it with grease as outlined for the 128.
10. Install the new bearing.
11. Screw a *new* ring nut into the pillar. Tighten the nut to 43 ft/lbs. Always use a new ring nut.
12. Stake the ring nut with a punch.
13. Install the hub in the pillar and press it into place with a press. Install the two washers and a nut and tighten the nut to 100 ft/lbs. Stake the nut with a punch.
14. Install the steering pillar to the car in the reverse order of removal.

124 and 131

NOTE: A puller is required to remove the wheel hub.

1. Raise and support the front of the car. Remove the wheel, caliper assembly, disc and plate.
2. Remove the hub nut and discard.
3. Remove the hub from the spindle using a puller.
4. The inner and outer bearings can be driven or pressed from the hub and new or repacked ones installed. Pack the bearings and the area between the bearings with grease.

NOTE: Some replacement bearings are of the sealed type and do not require lubrication. Follow the package instructions.

5. Install the hub on the spindle and tighten the new hub nut to 15 ft/lbs while turning the hub back and forth.
6. Back off the nut and retighten to 5 ft/ lbs.
7. Back the nut off 30 degrees and check the hub end play. It should measure between 0.001 and 0.004 inch.
8. Stake the nut to the spindle and reverse the removal process to complete assembly.

CHASSIS ELECTRICAL

Heater Assembly

REMOVAL AND INSTALLATION

124

1. Drain the engine cooling system and the heater radiator.

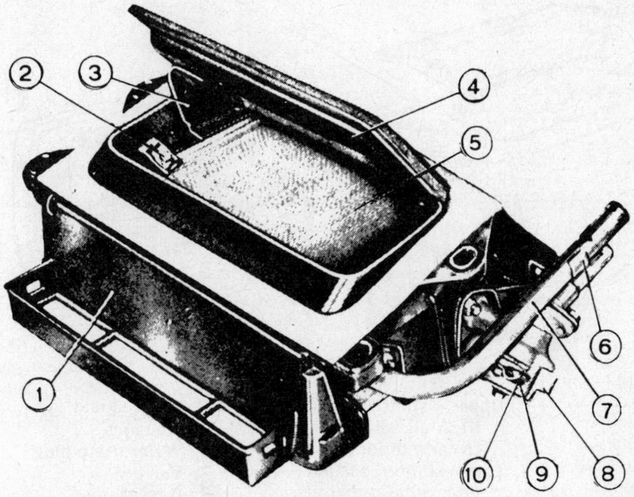

1. Heater core housing
2. Operating cable clip
3. Support
4. Air inlet shutter
5. Heater core
6. Inlet pipe
7. Outlet pipe
8. Water valve lever
9. Water valve
10. Water valve operating cable clamp

Heater core housing—124

2. The lower heater lever must be moved to the right.

3. Loosen the hose clips on the flow and return pipes to the heater.

4. From the engine compartment, remove the rubber seals on the heater pipes.

5. Remove the valve cable from the clip.

6. Disconnect the yellow cable to the fan.

7. Release the spring clips and remove the fan housing.

8. Lower the radiator and remove the air intake shutter control cable.

9. Remove the heater from the car.

10. Installation is the reverse of removal. Be sure that the gasket between fan and body is positioned correctly. Run the engine and fill the radiator.

128

1. Completely drain the cooling system.

2. Loosen the clips which retain the inlet and outlet hoses.

3. Remove the screw and nut from the air shutter actuating rod.

4. Remove the air conveyor.

5. Slide out the radiator housing spring clips.

6. Withdraw the outside shutter actuating rod.

7. Remove the heater valve control cable.

8. Remove the heater core.

9. Remove the fan housing attaching nuts.

10. Disconnect the cables which feed the motor at the fan switch.

11. Installation is the reverse of removal.

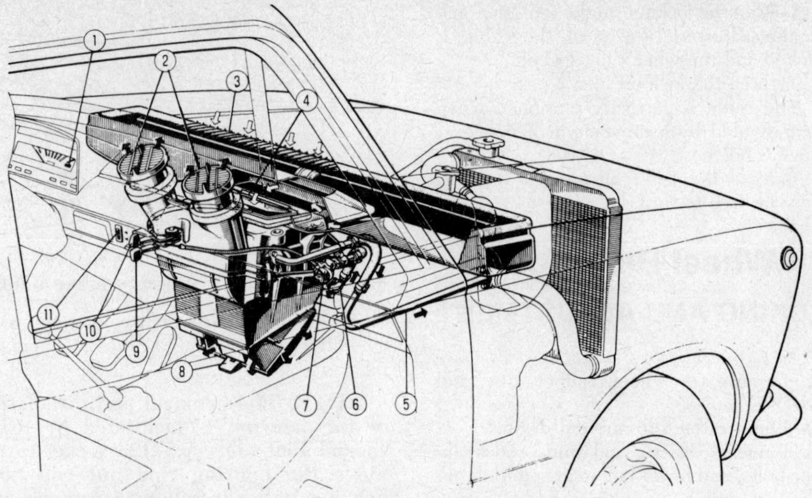

1. Engine temperature warning light
2. Air adjuster
3. Air intake slots
4. Air intake shutter
5. Heater water return line
6. Heater water delivery line
7. Heater water control valve
8. Shutter
9. Lever operating valve (7)
10. Lever to control air shutter (4)
11. Heater fan switch

Heater system—124

NOTE: Be sure to check all hoses and clamps and the drain cock and gaskets before reinstalling the heater core. Heater disassembly is done easily by removing or prying out the case clips. The electric fan is also mounted with clips.

X1/9

1. Drain the cooling system. Make sure you have drained it thoroughly, or there will be water left in the heater radiator.

2. The heater assembly is located behind the console in the center of the car. Remove the console.

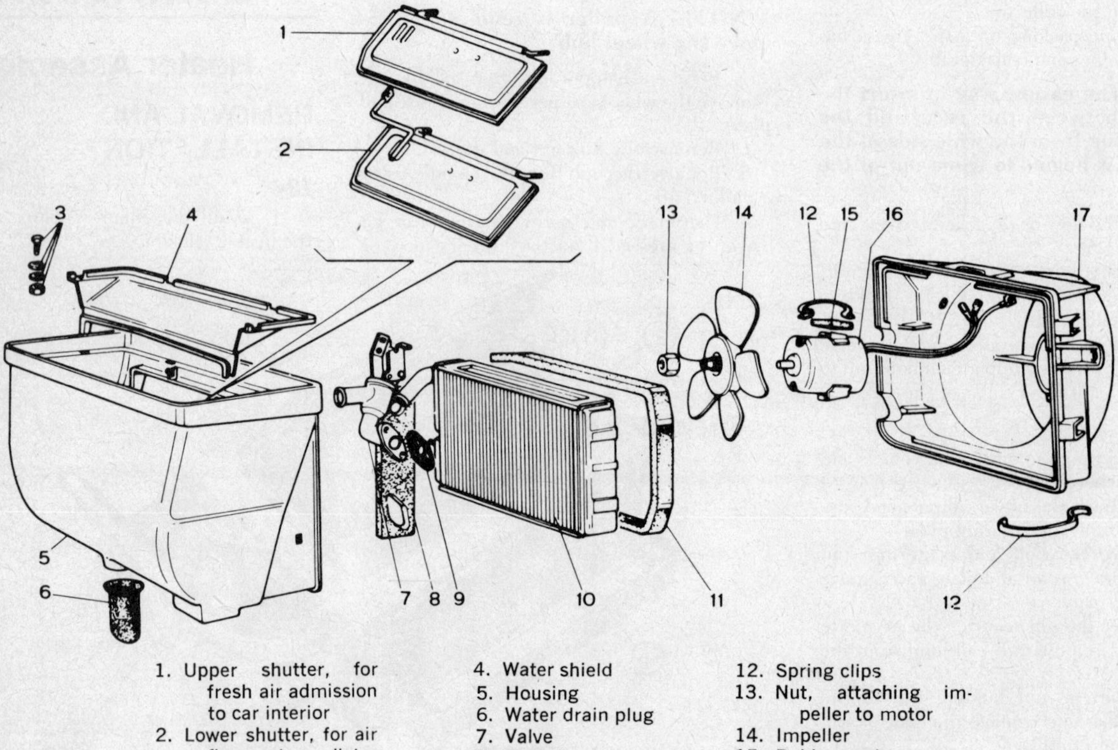

1. Upper shutter, for fresh air admission to car interior
2. Lower shutter, for air flow onto radiator (10)
3. Attaching screw, washers and nut
4. Water shield
5. Housing
6. Water drain plug
7. Valve
8. Gasket
9. Gasket
10. Radiator
11. Gasket
12. Spring clips
13. Nut, attaching impeller to motor
14. Impeller
15. Rubber pad
16. Motor
17. Fan housing

Starting from car with chassis No. 215963 a grid has been added to the heater housing

Heater assembly components—128

3. Remove the hoses from the heater assembly.
4. The heater assembly box is a two piece unit which is held together with clips. Remove all attached components and remove the heater assembly.
5. Installation is the reverse of removal.

131

1. Drain the cooling system. Make sure you have drained it thoroughly or there will be water left in the heater radiator.
2. The heater assembly is located in the center of the dashboard behind the console (if equipped).
3. Remove all hoses and control cables from the heater. The heater is a two piece unit, held together with clips. Remove the heater assembly.
4. Installation is the reverse of removal.

Windshield Wiper Motor

REMOVAL AND INSTALLATION

124

The windshield wiper motor is removed from the engine compartment side in the following manner:
1. Unscrew the left-hand spacer nut and remove the left-hand wiper blade and arm.
2. Remove the retaining nuts from the bracket and pull the motor back slightly.
3. Remove the clip connecting the right half-link to the motor and remove the motor.
4. Installation is the reverse of removal.

128

1. Remove the wiper blades and arms.
2. Back out the attaching nuts and remove the wiper blade pivot spacers.
3. Remove the spare wheel.
4. Remove the speedometer cable clip from the body.
5. Remove the screws which attach the wiper assembly to the mounting bracket.
6. Disconnect the connector block and remove the unit completely.
7. Installation is the reverse of removal.

X1/9

1. The X1/9 wiper motor is located on the driver's side under a screen on the cowling.
2. Remove the cowl screen. The wiper motor and linkage will then be visible.
3. Unbolt the wiper motor to remove it.
4. Installation is the reverse of removal.

131

1. The wiper motor is located under a plastic cover on the firewall.
2. Remove the plastic cover. The wiper motor should now be visible.
3. Unbolt and remove the motor.
4. Installation is the reverse of removal.

Instrument Cluster

REMOVAL AND INSTALLATION

124 Spider

1. Unscrew the 4 mounting screws securing the cluster.

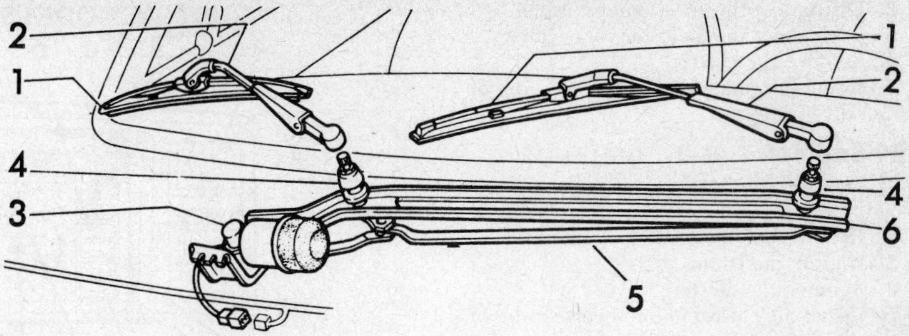

1. Wiper blade
2. Wiper arm
3. Wiper motor
4. Wiper arm transmission
5. Linkage
6. Bracket, mounting

Exploded view—124 model wiper assembly

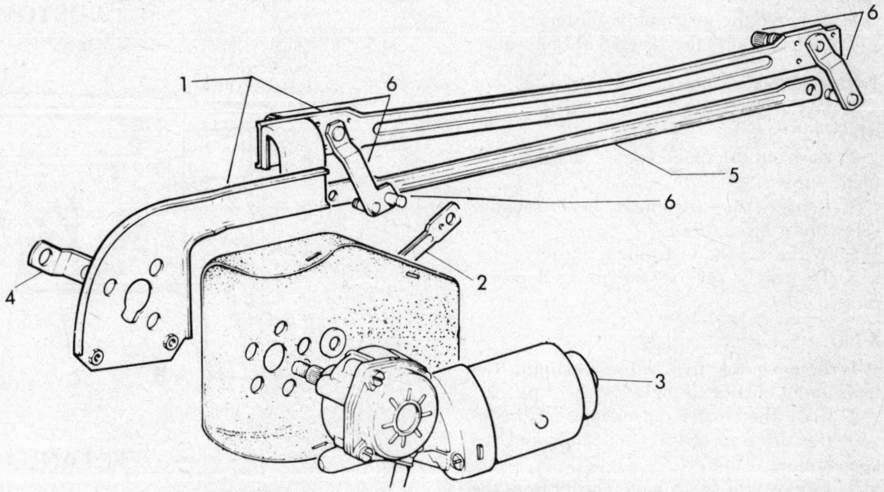

1. Bracket, mounting
2. Motor drive arm
3. Wiper motor
4. Bracket lug
5. Connecting link
6. Wiper transmission and drive arm

Exploded view—128 model (Sedan and Station Wagon)

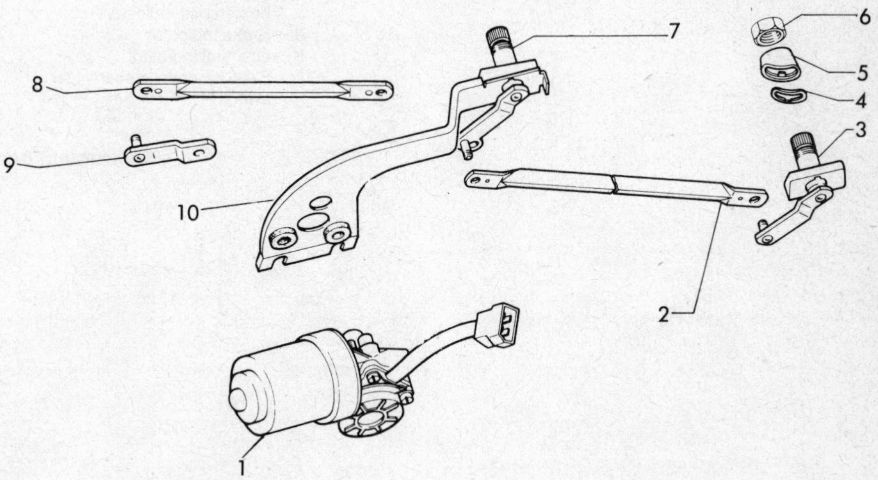

1. Wiper motor
2. Connecting link
3. Right Wiper transmission
4. Washer
5. Spacer
6. Nut
7. Left Wiper transmission
8. Drive link
9. Motor drive arm
10. Bracket, mounting

Exploded view—X1/9—Wiper assembly

2. Disconnect the speedometer cable.
3. Disconnect the 5 cluster connectors.
4. Remove the cluster.
5. Install the cluster in the reverse order of removal.

124 Special

1. Depress spring (A) from the front of the panel.
2. Remove the speedometer cable.
3. Unplug the connectors.
4. Remove the cluster.
5. Install the cluster in the reverse order of removal.

131

1. Remove the screws which hold the instrument cluster to the panel.
2. Pull the cluster out a short way and disconnect the electrical connections and the speedometer cable.
3. Remove the instrument cluster.
4. Installation is the reverse of removal.

128 Sedan

1. Open the hood and remove the spare wheel.
2. Back out the speedometer cable retainer plate screw.
3. Remove the instrument cluster retainer screw from inside the car.
4. Withdraw the instrument cluster.
5. To install, reverse the removal procedure.

X1/9

1. Remove the five screws retaining the instrument cluster to the instrument panel.
2. Slide the cluster out enough to disconnect the three electrical connectors and the speedometer cable.
3. Remove the instrument cluster from the instrument panel.
4. Install the instrument cluster in the reverse order of removal.

CUSTOM MODELS WITH LUXURY PACKAGES

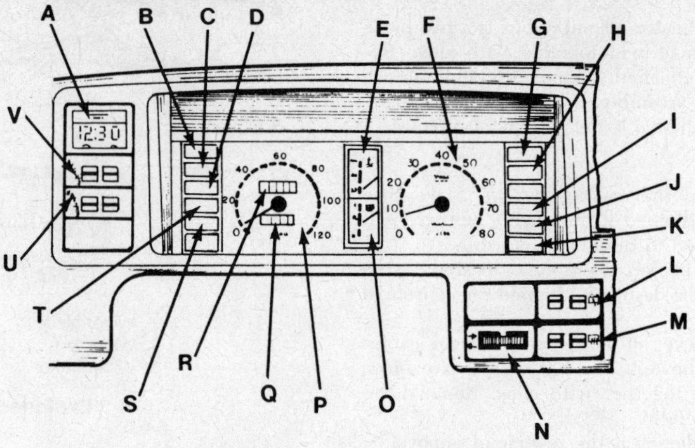

CUSTOM MODELS

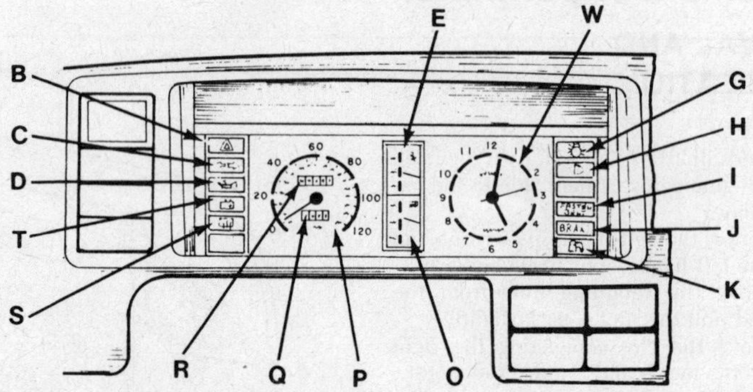

STANDARD MODEL

A. Digital Clock
B. Hazard indicator
C. Turn indicator
D. Low oil indicator
E. Coolant temp. gauge
F. Tachometer
G. Lights indicator
H. High beam indicator
I. Fasten belt indicator
J. Brake indicator
K. Low fuel indicator
L. Rear window washer/wiper switch
M. Rear window defogger switch
N. Panel light rheostat
O. Fuel gauge
P. Speedometer
Q. Trip recorder
R. Odometer
S. Rear window defogger indicator
T. Battery charge indicator
U. Hazard switch
V. Outer lighting switch
W. Quartz clock

Instrument panel arrangements

SPECIFICATIONS

INDEX

BEFORE SERVICING, SEE THE SAFETY NOTICE ON THE CONTENTS PAGE

INTRODUCTION

The Ford Fiesta manufactured in West Germany by the Ford-Werke, is imported by the Ford Motor Co. dealer network. The Fiesta is sold only as a three door sedan. There are decor, Sport, and Ghia trim options. 1980 marks the end of Fiesta production.

VEHICLE IDENTIFICATION PLATE

The vehicle identification plate is riveted on the panel above the right front headlight, just under the hood.

The eleven digit number is composed of a six digit identification code and a five digit serial number.

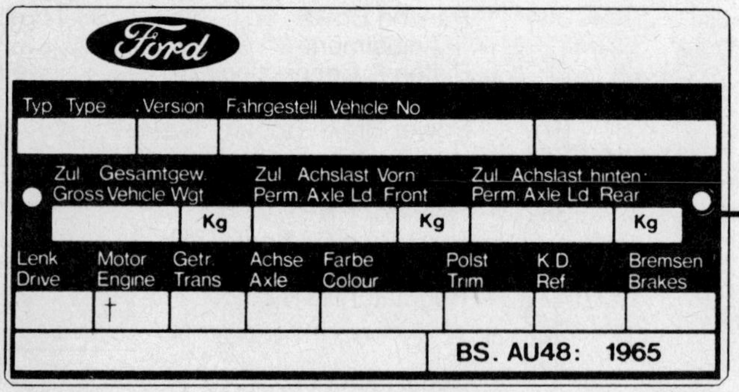

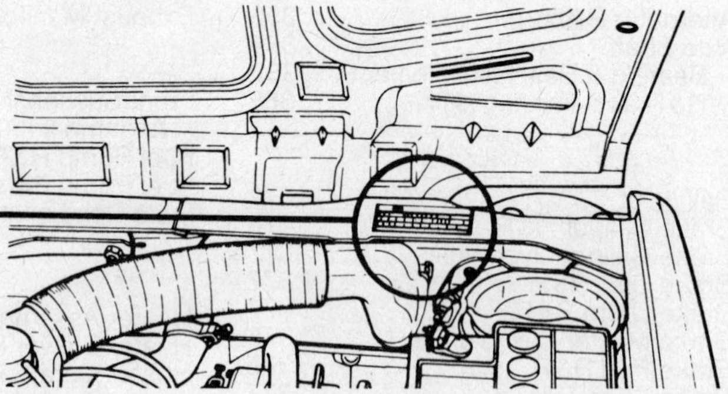

VIN plate location

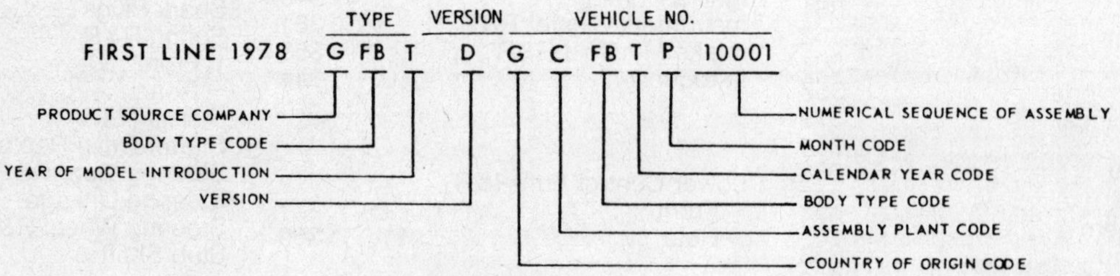

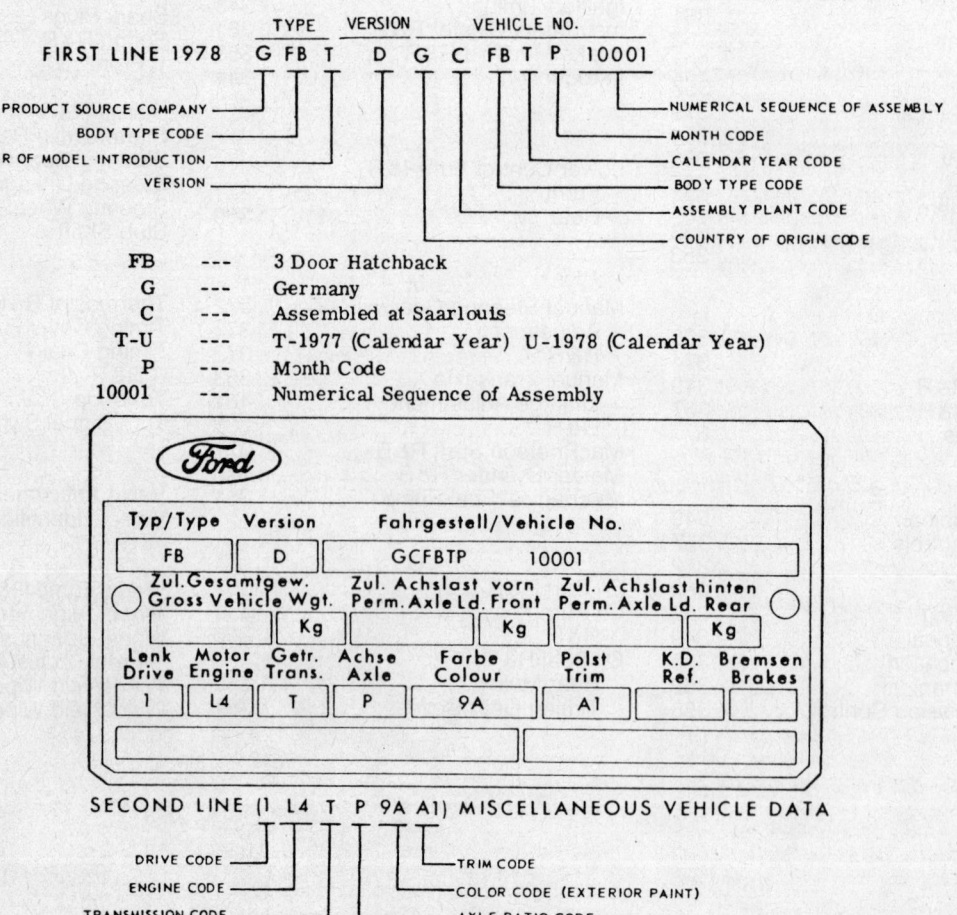

FB	---	3 Door Hatchback
G	---	Germany
C	---	Assembled at Saarlouis
T-U	---	T-1977 (Calendar Year) U-1978 (Calendar Year)
P	---	Month Code
10001	---	Numerical Sequence of Assembly

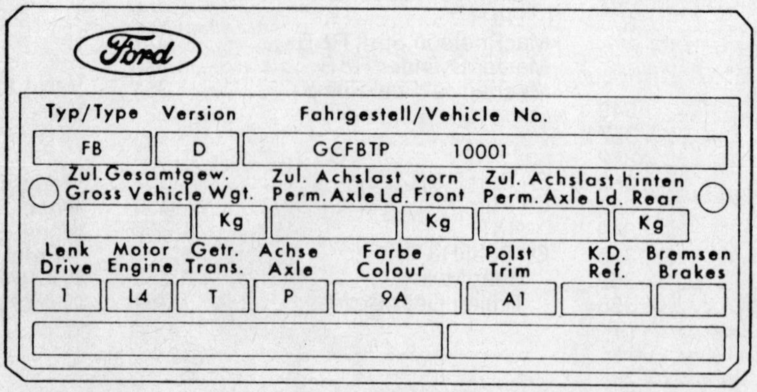

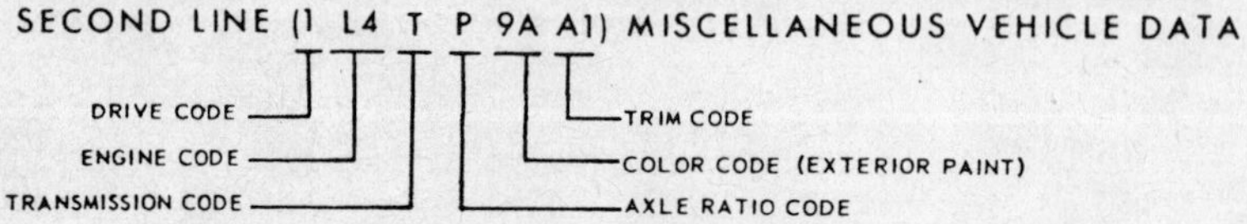

VIN plate general information

GENERAL ENGINE SPECIFICATIONS

Year	Engine Displacement Cu. In. (cc)	Carburetor No. of Bbls.	Horsepower @ rpm	Torque @ rpm (ft. lbs.)	Bore X Stroke (in.)	Compression Ratio	Oil Pressure (psi)
1978-80	97.5 (1600 cc)	2V	65 @ 5000	82 @ 3200	3.188 x 3.056	8.6	24-45 @ 2000 rpm

TUNE-UP SPECIFICATIONS

Year	Engine Displacement Cu. In. (cc)	SPARK PLUG Type	SPARK PLUG Gap (in.)	DISTRIBUTOR Point Dwell (deg.)	DISTRIBUTOR Point Gap (in.)	IGNITION TIMING (deg.) MT	IGNITION TIMING (deg.) AT	Intake Valve Opens BTDC (deg.)	Fuel Pump Pressure (psi)	VALVE CLEARANCE (in.) In.	VALVE CLEARANCE (in.) Ex.	Idle Speed (rpm)
1978-80	97.5 (1600 cc)	AWRF-32	.050	Electronic Dura-Spark II		12° BTDC	—	29	3.5 @ 700 rpm	0.008-.010 (cold)	.021 ① (cold)	②

① 0.018 in. Hot ② See underhood sticker

FIRING ORDER

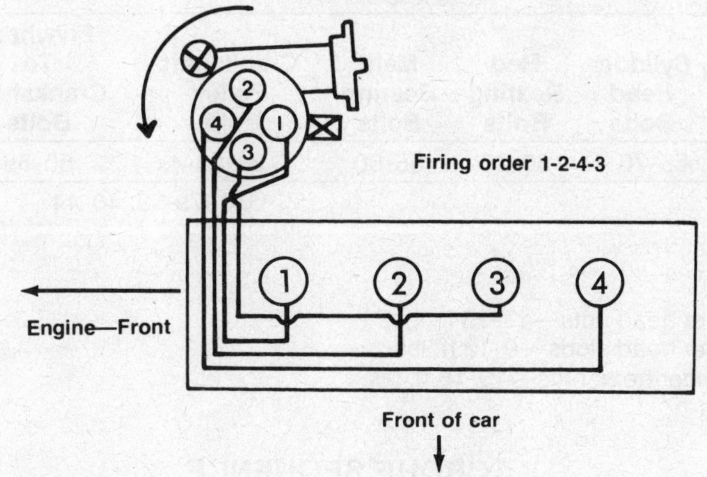

CAPACITIES

Year	Engine Displacement Cu. In. (cc)	ENGINE CRANKCASE (qts.) With Filter	ENGINE CRANKCASE (qts.) W/Out Filter	TRANSAXLE ASSEMBLY (pts.) MT	TRANSAXLE ASSEMBLY (pts.) AT	Gasoline Tank (gal.)	COOLING SYSTEM (qts.) W/AC	COOLING SYSTEM (qts.) W/O AC
1978-80	97.5 (1600 cc)	3.5	3.0	5	—	10	6.6	6.6

VALVE SPECIFICATIONS

Year	Engine Displacement Cu. In. (cc)	Seat Angle (deg.)	Face Angle (deg.)	Spring Test Pressure (lbs. @ in.)	Spring Installed Height (in.)	STEM TO GUIDE CLEARANCE (in.) Intake	STEM TO GUIDE CLEARANCE (in.) Exhaust	STEM DIAMETER (in.) Intake	STEM DIAMETER (in.) Exhaust
1978-80	97.5 (1600 cc)	45	45	42 @ 1.263 104 @ .952	$1^1/_4$-$1^9/_{32}$	0.0008-0.0027	0.0017-0.0036	0.3098-0.3105	0.3089-0.3096

CRANKSHAFT MAIN AND CONNECTING ROD BEARING SPECIFICATIONS

Year	Engine Displacement Cu. In. (cc)	MAIN BEARING Journal Diameter (in.)	MAIN BEARING Oil Clearance (in.)	MAIN BEARING Shaft End-Play (in.)	MAIN BEARING Thrust Taken on No.	CONNECTING ROD BEARING Journal Diameter (in.)	CONNECTING ROD BEARING Oil Clearance (in.)	CONNECTING ROD BEARING Side Clearance (in.)
1978-80	97.5 (1600 cc)	2.1253-2.1261	0.0005- ② 0.0015	0.003-0.011 ①	3	1.9368-1.9376	0.0004-0.0015	0.004-0.010

① Controlled by half-circled thrust washers
② 1979-80: 0.0004-0.0015

PISTON AND RING SPECIFICATIONS
(All measurements given in inches)

Year	Engine Displacement Cu. In. (cc)	Piston Clearance (in.)	RING GAP (in.) Top Compression	RING GAP (in.) Bottom Compression	RING GAP (in.) Oil Control	RING SIDE CLEARANCE (in.) Top Compression	RING SIDE CLEARANCE (in.) Bottom Compression	RING SIDE CLEARANCE (in.) Oil Control
1978-80	97.5 (1600 cc)	0.0009-0.0017	0.009-0.017	0.009-0.017	0.009-0.014	0.0016-0.0036	0.0016-0.0036	0.0018-0.0038

TORQUE SPECIFICATIONS
(All readings in ft. lbs.)

Year	Engine Displacement Cu. In. (cc)	Cylinder Head Bolts	Rod Bearing Bolts	Main Bearing Bolts	Crankshaft Pulley Bolts	Flywheel To Crankshaft Bolts	MANIFOLD Intake	MANIFOLD Exhaust
1978-80	97.5 (1600 cc)	65-70 ①	30-35	55-60	24-28 ④	50-55	12-15 ②	9-12 ③

① Step 1—5 ft. lbs.
Step 2—20-30 ft. lbs.
Step 3—50-55 ft. lbs.
Step 4—65-70 ft. lbs.
② Intake manifold to cylinder head nuts—12-15 ft. lbs.
Intake manifold to cylinder head studs—9-12 ft. lbs.
③ Exhaust manifold to cylinder head nuts—15-18 ft. lbs.
④ 1979-80: 40-44

TORQUE SEQUENCE

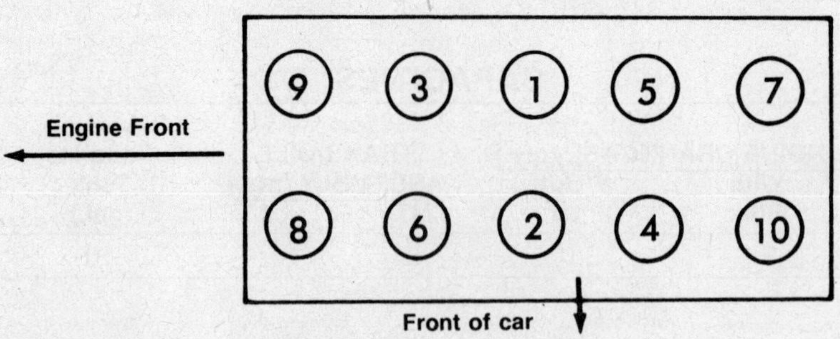

STARTER SPECIFICATIONS

Year	Engine Displacement Cu. In. (cc)	NO-LOAD TEST Amps	NO-LOAD TEST Volts	NO-LOAD TEST rpm	LOAD TEST Amps	LOAD TEST Volts	LOAD TEST rpm	LOCK TEST Amps	LOCK TEST Volts	LOCK TEST Torque (ft. lbs.)	Brush Spring Tension (lbs.)	Brush Minimum Length (in.)
1978-80	97.5 (1600 cc)	—	—	—	—	—	—	350	12	6.9	2.0-2.7	.39

BATTERY, ALTERNATOR AND REGULATOR SPECIFICATIONS

Year	Engine Displacement Cu. In. (cc)	Battery④ Capacity (amp. hr.)	ALTERNATOR Field Current @ 12V	ALTERNATOR Rated Output (amps.)	Brush Spring Tension (oz.)	Brush Minimum Length (in.)	REGULATOR Type	REGULATOR Voltage Setting
1978-80	97.5 (1600 cc)	35	—	40	—	—	Electro-mechanical	14V
		43 ①	29	60 ②	—	0.3125	Electro-mechanical	14V
			29	55 ③	10.6-14.1	0.200	Integral	13.7-14.4V

① Heavy duty
② With rear window defogger
③ With air conditioning
④ Located in engine compartment

BRAKE SPECIFICATIONS

(All measurements in inches unless noted)

Year	Engine Displacement Cu. In. (cc)	Wheel Lug Nut Torque (ft. lbs.)	Master Cylinder Bore	BRAKE DISC Max. Thickness	BRAKE DISC Min. Thickness	BRAKE DISC Max. Runout	BRAKE DRUM Diameter	BRAKE DRUM Max. Machine	BRAKE DRUM Wear Limit	LINING THICKNESS MINIMUM Front	LINING THICKNESS MINIMUM Rear
1978-80	97.5 (1600 cc)	52-74	—	0.390	0.340	0.006	7.00	①	①	0.060	0.060

NOTE: Minimum lining thickness is as recommended by the manufacturer. Due to variation in state inspection regulations, the minimum allowable thickness may be different than recommended by the manufacturer.
① Refer to state inspection regulations

WHEEL ALIGNMENT SPECIFICATIONS

Year	Engine Displacement Cu. In. (cc)	CASTER ① Range (deg.)	CASTER ① Pref. Setting (deg.)	CAMBER ① Range (deg.)	CAMBER ① Pref. Setting	Toe Adjustment (In or Out)	Steering Axis Inclination	Standard Tire Size
1978-80	97.5 (1600 cc)	−0°25′-+1°20′	+0°20′	+3°15′-+1°15′	+2°15′	Out 0.10±0.04 in. ($^{13}/_{64} \pm ^{3}/_{64}$)	—	155SR12

① Maximum variation—LH side to RH side 1°15′

TUNE-UP PROCEDURES

NOTE: Refer to the Emission Control Sticker for the required specifications.

Distributor

The Fiesta uses the Dura-Spark II solid state ignition system which eliminates the conventional contact point and condenser set. The gap between the magnetic pickup assembly and the armature is preset and no attempt should be made to change it.

Spark Plug and Coil Wires

Inspect all wiring for cracks, fraying, loose connections and other damage. Measure the secondary cable resistance, which should not exceed 4100 ohms per foot of cable.

NOTE: Be sure the ignition switch is in the OFF position, because any movement of the distributor armature spoke past the pick-up coil will cause high voltage to occur in the coil secondary circuit.

NOTE: If a high tension lead was disconnected from the coil, spark plug or distributor cap, silicone grease must be applied to the boot before reconnection.

Ignition Coil

Inspect the ignition coil for cracks and carbon traces on both the primary and secondary sides. The primary resistance should be between 1.0 to 2.0 ohms, while the secondary resistance should be between 7700 and 9300 ohms. The primary circuit resistance (ignition switch to control module) should range from 1.05 to 1.15 ohms.

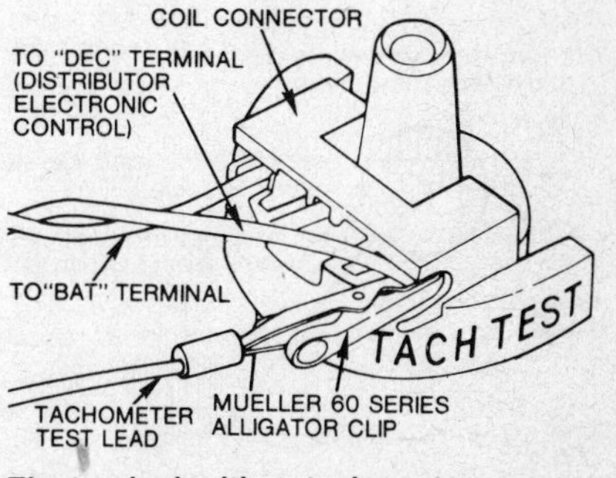

Electronic ignition tachometer connection

Spark Plugs

Remove the spark plugs and inspect them. If reusable, a sand blaster cleaner or equivalent can be used to remove the accumulated carbon. Do not prolong the cleaning operation. After cleaning, inspect the spark plugs for cracked or broken insulators, badly pitted electrodes or other signs of failure. If the spark plugs are to be reused, lift the ground electrode slightly and file both the ground and the center electode as flat as possible without removing much metal from the contact surfaces. Using a round wire gauge, gap the spark plug, both new or used, to the correct specifications.

Rotor and Distributor Cap

Inspect for excessive burning and pitting of the cap segments and eroding of the rotor end.

Do not remove excessive metal from the rotor or cap segments by filing.

Filters

Inspect and replace filters for the air and fuel supplies and for the emission control units as necessary.

Ignition Timing

Use the following procedures for the adjustment of ignition timing.

STATIC

1. Place a white mark on the proper degree line on the front cover and the crankshaft damper as per the specification given on the engine sticker.
2. Align the two marks by rotating the engine crankshaft.
3. Loosen the distributor hold-down bolt and rotate the distributor so that the rotor points to the No. 1 cylinder tower of the distributor cap.
4. By moving the distributor body, align the armature squarely with the lug on the magnetic pick up coil, and tighten the distributor hold-down bolt. Verify that the distributor body has not moved.

NOTE: An error of ½ a tooth is equal to 7¾ engine degrees timing error.

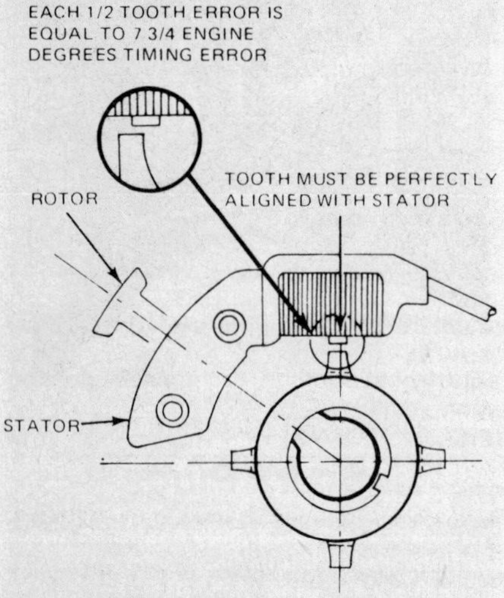

Distributor armature and stator lug alignment

DYNAMIC

1. Place a white mark on the proper degree line on the front cover and the crankshaft damper as per the specification given on the engine sticker.
2. Disconnect and plug the distributor vacuum line.
3. Connect a timing light to the No. 1 spark plug cable.

NOTE: A special timing light may be necessary for this type system. Inductive pickup type lights may work satisfactorily if an insulated standoff, such as a piece of split vacuum hose, is placed around the spark plug wire.

4. Start the engine and adjust the idle to specifications. Inspect the timing mark location with the timing light.
5. If the timing is within ±2 degrees of specifications, do not reset, but if the timing is off more than ±2 degrees, reset by loosening the distributor hold down bolt and moving the distributor body to correct the timing alignment and retighten the distributor hold-down bolt.
6. Recheck the ignition timing mark alignment after the hold-down bolt is tightened.

MONOLITHIC

The monolithic system uses a timing bracket to accept an electronic probe that is connected to digital read-out equipment, which determines the timing electronically. This timing system is used by the manufacturer at the time of assembly. Tool manufacturers have this type of test equipment available.

Valve Adjustment

The valves should be checked with the engine at normal operating temperature. The clearance should be checked by inserting a feeler gauge between the valve stem and the rocker arm, with the cam lobe at its lowest point.

The following chart gives the sequence for valve adjustment.

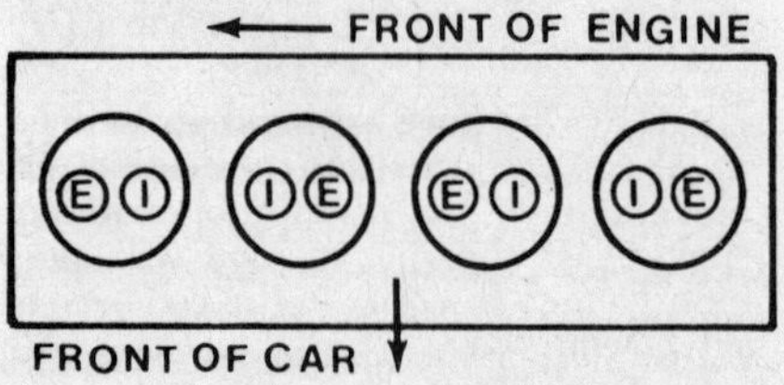

Valve arrangement in cylinder head
Front of engine
1-2-3-4-5-6-7-8

VALVE ADJUSTMENT SEQUENCE CHART

The adjusting screws are self-locking.

Carburetor

All specifications for carburetor adjustments are on the engine emission sticker.

CURB IDLE SPEED ADJUSTMENT

1. Have the engine at normal operating temperature, apply the parking brake and chock the wheels.
2. Disconnect the engine electric fan temperature switch wires, located on the thermostat housing. Use a jumper wire and connect the two wires so that the fan will run continuously.
3. Remove the air cleaner assembly from the engine and check the throttle linkage for freedom of movement.
4. Remove the Spark Delay Valve from the vacuum advance hose, if equipped, and connect a jumper hose between the two hoses.
5. Disconnect the fuel decel valve hose, if equipped, and plug the hose.
6. If equipped with a ported vacuum switch (PVS) to control the exhaust gas recirculation valve (EGR), disconnect the EGR valve by removing and plugging the vacuum hose at the EGR-PVS. If the engine is *not* equipped with an EGR-PVS unit, *do not* disconnect the EGR valve.
7. Attach a tachometer and run the engine for 15 seconds at 2500 rpm.
8. Allow engine to return to idle and to stabilize.
9. If the curb idle speed is incorrect, adjust.
10. If you are unable to obtain the specified curb idle speed, check the dashpot, if equipped, for hanging or misadjustment.
11. Reinstall the air cleaner and recheck the curb idle speed.

NOTE: Final curb idle speed reading must be taken with the air cleaner assembly installed.

12. Stop the engine and reinstall the radiator fan temperature switch wires.

PROPANE ENRICHMENT IDLE FUEL MIXTURE ADJUSTMENT

NOTE: Ford Motor Co. recommends the use of propane gas to adjust the idle fuel mixture. The equipment necessary is not readily available to the general

VALVE ADJUSTMENT SEQUENCE

Rotate engine to fully open these valve numbers	1 + 6	2 + 4	3 + 8	5 + 7
to check valve clearances of these valves	3 + 8	5 + 7	1 + 6	2 + 4

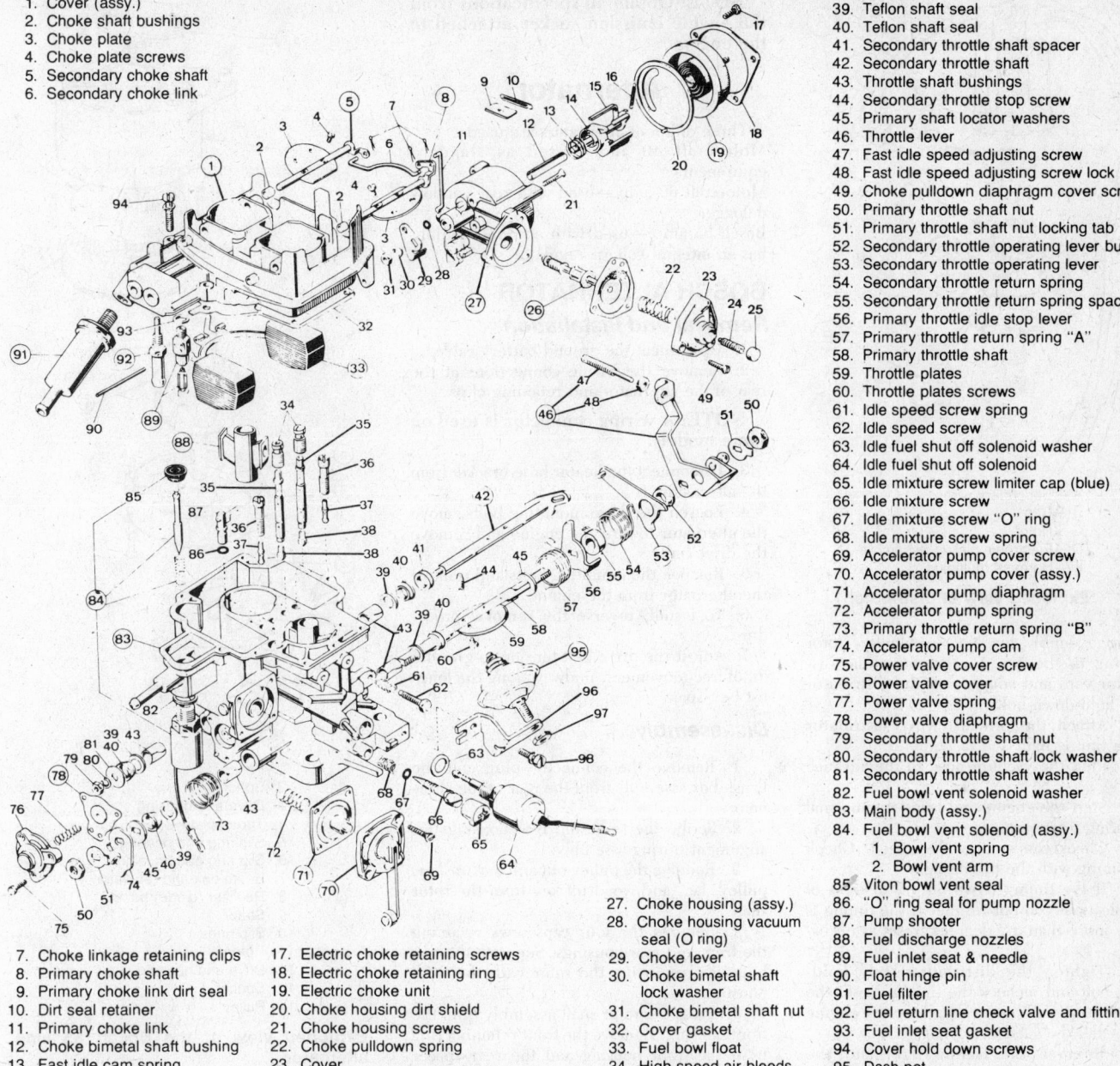

1. Cover (assy.)
2. Choke shaft bushings
3. Choke plate
4. Choke plate screws
5. Secondary choke shaft
6. Secondary choke link

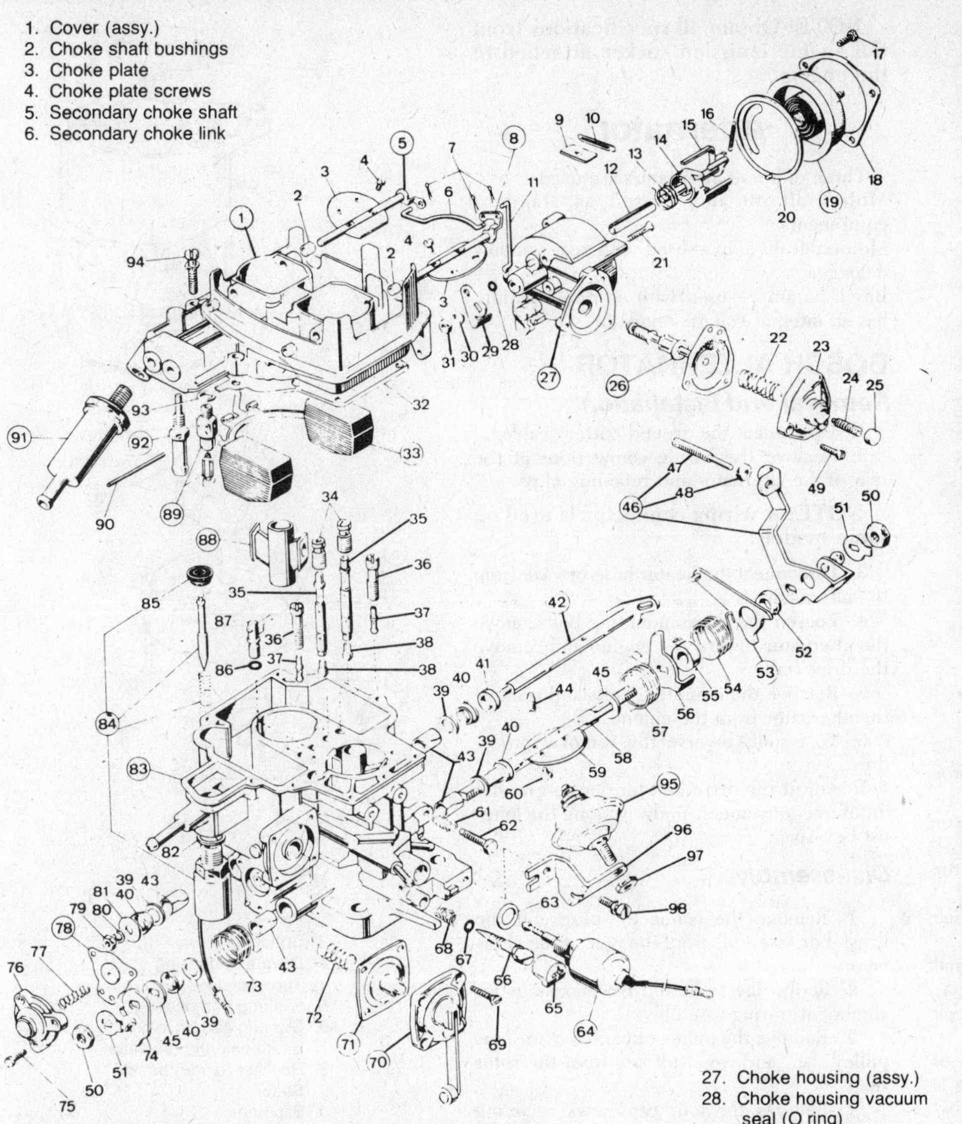

7. Choke linkage retaining clips
8. Primary choke shaft
9. Primary choke link dirt seal
10. Dirt seal retainer
11. Primary choke link
12. Choke bimetal shaft bushing
13. Fast idle cam spring
14. Choke bimetal lever
15. Choke bimetal shaft
16. Choke assist spring
17. Electric choke retaining screws
18. Electric choke retaining ring
19. Electric choke unit
20. Choke housing dirt shield
21. Choke housing screws
22. Choke pulldown spring
23. Cover
24. Choke pulldown adjusting screw
25. Choke pulldown adjusting screw seal
26. Choke pulldown diaphragm assembly
27. Choke housing (assy.)
28. Choke housing vacuum seal (O ring)
29. Choke lever
30. Choke bimetal shaft lock washer
31. Choke bimetal shaft nut
32. Cover gasket
33. Fuel bowl float
34. High speed air bleeds
35. Well tubes
36. Idle jet holder
37. Idle jet
38. Main jet
39. Teflon shaft seal
40. Teflon shaft seal
41. Secondary throttle shaft spacer
42. Secondary throttle shaft
43. Throttle shaft bushings
44. Secondary throttle stop screw
45. Primary shaft locator washers
46. Throttle lever
47. Fast idle speed adjusting screw
48. Fast idle speed adjusting screw lock nut
49. Choke pulldown diaphragm cover screw
50. Primary throttle shaft nut
51. Primary throttle shaft nut locking tab
52. Secondary throttle operating lever bushing
53. Secondary throttle operating lever
54. Secondary throttle return spring
55. Secondary throttle return spring spacer
56. Primary throttle idle stop lever
57. Primary throttle return spring "A"
58. Primary throttle shaft
59. Throttle plates
60. Throttle plates screws
61. Idle speed screw spring
62. Idle speed screw
63. Idle fuel shut off solenoid washer
64. Idle fuel shut off solenoid
65. Idle mixture screw limiter cap (blue)
66. Idle mixture screw
67. Idle mixture screw "O" ring
68. Idle mixture screw spring
69. Accelerator pump cover screw
70. Accelerator pump cover (assy.)
71. Accelerator pump diaphragm
72. Accelerator pump spring
73. Primary throttle return spring "B"
74. Accelerator pump cam
75. Power valve cover screw
76. Power valve cover
77. Power valve spring
78. Power valve diaphragm
79. Secondary throttle shaft nut
80. Secondary throttle shaft lock washer
81. Secondary throttle shaft washer
82. Fuel bowl vent solenoid washer
83. Main body (assy.)
84. Fuel bowl vent solenoid (assy.)
    1. Bowl vent spring
    2. Bowl vent arm
85. Viton bowl vent seal
86. "O" ring seal for pump nozzle
87. Pump shooter
88. Fuel discharge nozzles
89. Fuel inlet seat & needle
90. Float hinge pin
91. Fuel filter
92. Fuel return line check valve and fitting
93. Fuel inlet seat gasket
94. Cover hold down screws
95. Dash pot
96. Dash pot mounting bracket
97. Dash pot adjusting lock nut
98. Dash pot mounting bracket screw

Exploded view of the carburetor

public. This procedure should not be attempted without the required equipment.

ENGINE ELECTRICAL

Distributor

REMOVAL

1. Rotate the engine so that the timing marks are aligned at 12 degrees BTDC with No. 1 piston is on its firing stroke.

2. Remove the distributor cap, primary wire, vacuum line and distributor hold-down bolt.

3. Note the position of the rotor in relationship to the distributor body and pull the distributor up from the engine block.

INSTALLATION

1. Be certain that the engine has not moved from its previous position.

NOTE: If the engine crankshaft has been turned while the distributor is out of the engine, locate No. 1 piston on its firing stroke by removing No. 1 spark plug and holding a finger over the hole. Rotate the engine in its normal rotation until compression build-up can be felt; align the timing marks at 12 degrees BTDC.

2. Install a new O-ring on the distributor body. Align the projecting side of the drive gear retaining pin with the boss in the distributor body.

3. Install the distributor in the engine block so that the vacuum advance unit is parallel to the engine centerline. Install the distributor hold-down bolt loosely.

4. Align the armature lug to the lug on the

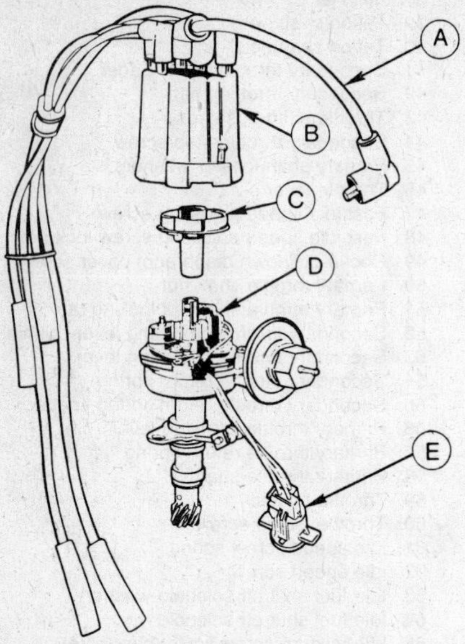

A—Secondary wires
B—Cap
C—Rotor
D—Electronic pickup assembly
E—Harness multiplug

Exploded view of distributor

pickup assembly for No. 1 cylinder (rotor pointing to the No. 1 segment in the distributor cap) and snug down the distributor body hold-down bolt.

5. Attach the primary wire, distributor cap, a timing light and tachometer.
6. Plug the vacuum hose to the advance unit.
7. Start the engine and bring it to normal operating temperature.
8. Check the engine idle speed. Check the timing with the timing light.
9. If the timing is within ±2 degrees of specifications, do not retime. If the timing is off by more than ±2 degrees, reset as necessary.
10. Tighten the distributor body hold-down bolt and recheck the timing. Reset the curb idle speed if necessary. Stop the engine and install the vacuum advance hose.
11. Remove the timing light and the tachometer.

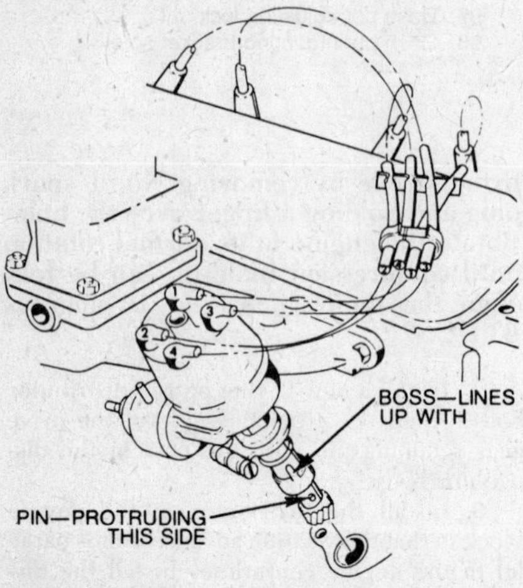

Aligning distributor body to shaft before installation

NOTE: Obtain all specifications from the engine emission sticker attached to the engine.

Alternator

Three different alternators are used.
Motorcraft 40 amp.—used as standard equipment.
Motorcraft 60 amp.—used with rear window defogger.
Bosch 55 amp.—used with air conditioning, has an integral voltage regulator.

BOSCH ALTERNATOR

Removal and Installation

1. Disconnect the ground battery cable.
2. Remove the wiring connections at the rear of the alternator and retaining clips.

NOTE: A wiring connector is used on some models.

3. Disconnect the heater hose bracket from the alternator.
4. Loosen the three mounting bolts, move the alternator toward the engine and remove the drive belt.
5. Remove the mounting bolts and remove the alternator from the engine.
6. To install, reverse the removal procedure.
7. Adjust the drive belt tension to give 0.5 in. of free movement, midway along the longest belt span.

Disassembly

1. Remove the connector plug and the brush box assembly from the rear of the alternator.
2. Scribe the front and rear housings for alignment during assembly.
3. Remove the pulley nut and lockwasher, pulley, fan, and woodruff key from the rotor shaft.
4. Remove the four capscrews retaining the front and rear housings. Separate the two housings, removing the rotor with the front housing.
5. Press the rotor shaft assembly from the front housing. Remove the front retaining ring from the front housing and the rear spacer from the rotor shaft.
6. Remove the retaining plate screws, plate and front bearing from the front housing.
7. With the aid of a puller, remove the rear rotor shaft bearing.
8. Remove the four diode plate to rear housing screws and remove the diode and stator plate assembly.

CAUTION

Do not lose the spring washer, in the rear housing bearing bore.

9. If necessary, unsolder the stator to diode connections for further testing or replacement.
10. Assembly is the reverse of disassembly.

CAUTION

Use a pair of pliers as a heat sink to prevent damage to the diodes when soldering or unsoldering.

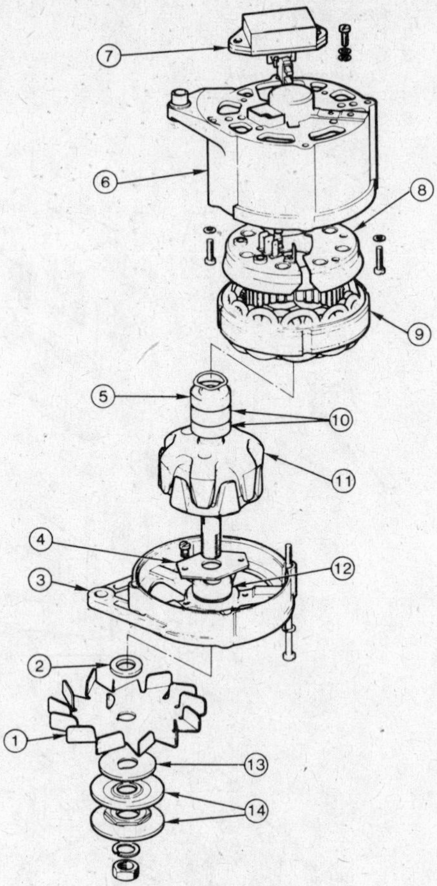

1. Fan
2. Spacer
3. Drive end housing
4. Thrust plate
5. Slip ring end bearing
6. Slip ring end housing
7. Brush box and regulator
8. Rectifier (diode) pack
9. Stator
10. Slip rings
11. Rotor
12. Drive end housing
13. Spacer
14. Pulley

Exploded view of the Bosch 55 amp alternator

NOTE: When assembling the front and rear housings, be sure the scribed lines are aligned.

MOTORCRAFT ALTERNATOR

Removal and Installation

1. Disconnect the negative battery cable.
2. Remove the drive belt by loosening the alternator mounting bolts and moving the alternator toward the engine.
3. Remove the wiring connections at the rear or side. (Mark the wires for proper reinstallation).
4. Remove the mounting bolts and lift the alternator from the engine brackets.
5. To install the alternator, reverse the removal procedure.
6. Adjust the belt tension to give 0.5 inch

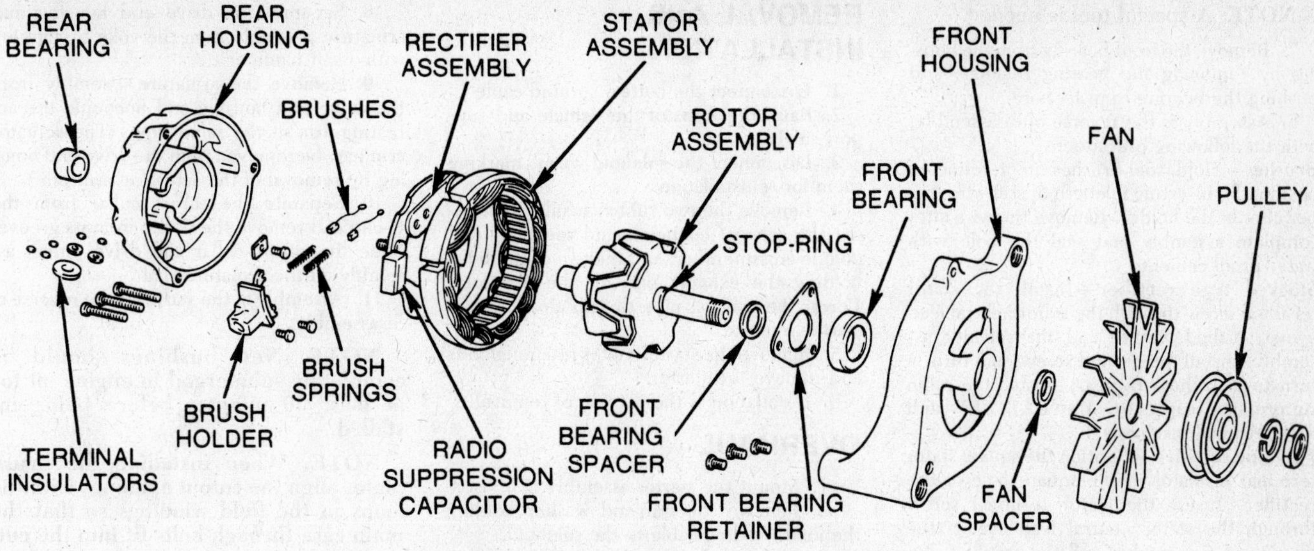

Exploded view of Motorcraft alternator— typical

of free movement, midway along the longest belt span.

Disassembly and Assembly

1. Scribe a mark on both the front and rear housings for alignment during reassembly.
2. Remove the through bolts and separate the front and rear housings.
3. Remove the terminal insulators and housing from the stator and rectifier assembly.

NOTE: If the alternator has an integral regulator, remove it at this time.

4. Press the rear housing bearing from the bearing bore.
5. Remove the rectifiers from the stator as follows:

Stacked type rectifier—Remove the stator terminal screw and ground screw by turning them ¼ turn to unlock them from the rectifier. Unsolder the leads of the stator from the rectifier.

Flat type rectifier—Remove the stator terminal screw by pressing it straight out of the rectifier.

CAUTION

Do not turn the screw or remove the ground screws.

6. Separate the rotor, fan, and pulley from the front housing by removing the front nut.

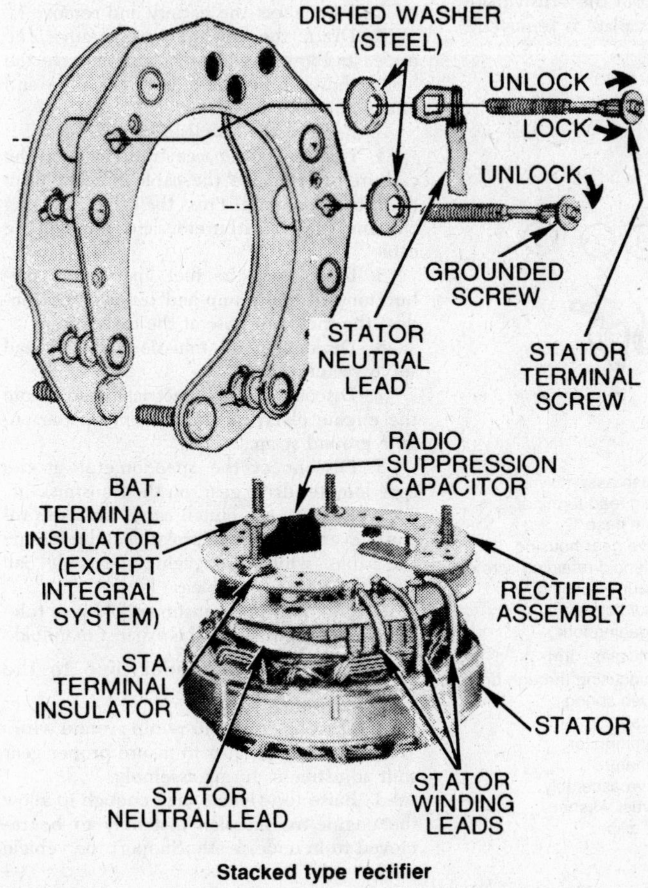

Stacked type rectifier

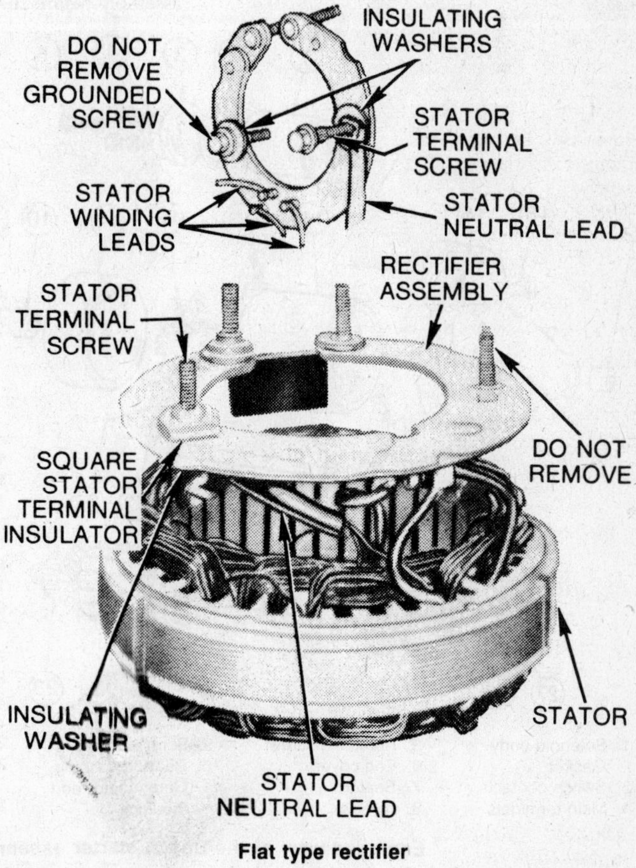

Flat type rectifier

NOTE: A special tool is needed.

7. Remove the front bearing from the housing by removing the bearing retainer, and pushing the bearing from its bore.

8. Assembly is the reverse of disassembly, with the following precautions.

Brushes—Hold the brushes in a retracted position by inserting a length of stiff wire (paper clip) in the holder. Remove the wire after complete assembly and seal the hole with water-proof cement.

Stacked type rectifier—Install the stator terminal screw through the stator neutral lead eyelet, dished washer and the rectifier assembly. Install the ground screws and turn ¼ turn to lock them in place. Install the radio suppression capacitor, the *BATTERY* and *STA* terminal insulators.

Flat type rectifier—Position the square stator terminal insulator in the square hole of the rectifier. Insert the stator terminal screw through the stator neutral lead eyelet, the fiber insulating washer and the rectifier. Rotate the screw until the serrations engage the rectifier and the screw shank. Press the screw in place. Install the radio suppression capacitor and the *BAT* terminal insulator.

Terminal insulators—Make sure all terminal insulators are seated in their recesses. Add the colored insulators to the protruding terminals. *STA*/Black colored, *BAT*/red colored, and *FLD*/orange colored.

Starter

A Bosch positive engagement type starter is used. It has an integral solenoid on top of the starter motor. A separate starter relay is not used.

REMOVAL AND INSTALLATION

1. Disconnect the battery ground cable.
2. Raise the front of the vehicle and support safely.
3. Disconnect the solenoid wires, marking them for reinstallation.
4. Remove the two rubber insulators holding the exhaust connection to the body and engine crossmember, and the two clamp bolts holding the exhaust pipe to the manifold. Lower the exhaust pipe to gain clearance for starter removal.
5. Remove the starter motor retaining bolts and remove the starter.
6. Installation is the reverse of removal.

OVERHAUL

1. Mount the starter assembly in a vise.
2. Remove the nut and washer holding the field winding cable to the solenoid.
3. Remove the three solenoid mounting screws and guide the solenoid yoke away from the drive end housing and solenoid armature. Unhook the solenoid armature from the actuating lever.
4. Remove the commutator end housing cap, seal and screws.
5. Remove the C-clip and shims from the armature end.
6. Remove two nuts and washer from the studs and remove the commutator end housing.

NOTE: Some Bosch starters use screws instead of nuts and studs.

7. Remove brushes from the brush plate assembly before the brush plate is removed.

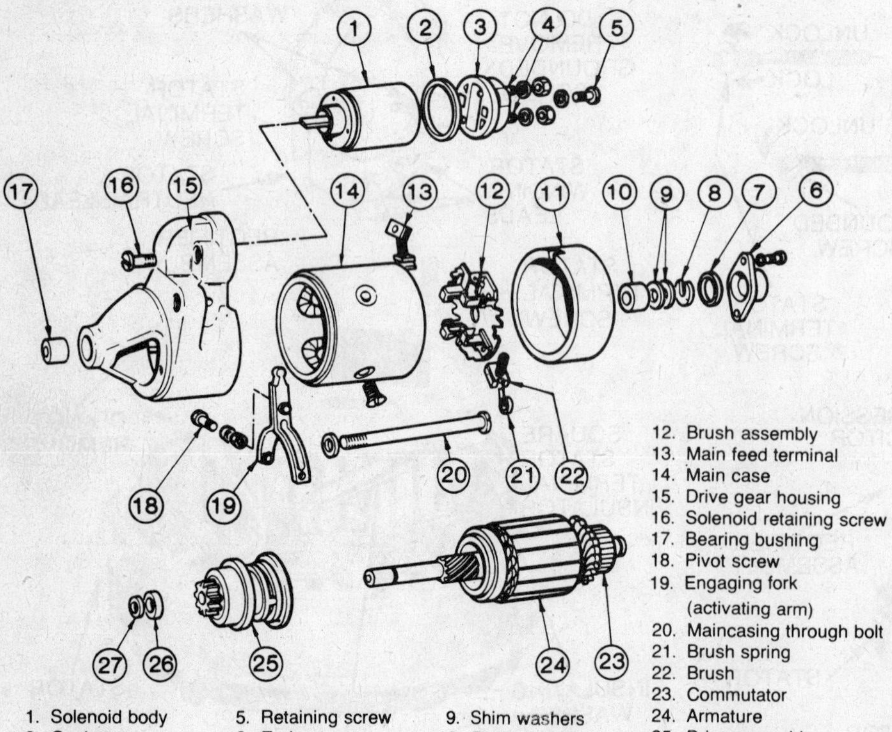

1. Solenoid body
2. Gasket
3. Switch contacts
4. Main terminals
5. Retaining screw
6. End cover
7. Seal
8. "C" clip
9. Shim washers
10. Bearing bushing
11. Commutator end housing
12. Brush assembly
13. Main feed terminal
14. Main case
15. Drive gear housing
16. Solenoid retaining screw
17. Bearing bushing
18. Pivot screw
19. Engaging fork (activating arm)
20. Maincasing through bolt
21. Brush spring
22. Brush
23. Commutator
24. Armature
25. Drive assembly
26. Thrust washer
27. "C" clip

Exploded view of the Bosch starter assembly

8. Separate the drive end housing and armature assembly from the yoke by tapping with a soft hammer.
9. Remove the armature assembly from the drive end housing and uncouple the actuating arm at the same time. (The actuator arm may be removed from the drive end housing by removal of the actuating arm pin.)
10. Separate the thrust collar from the C-clip and remove the C-clip from its groove. Slide the thrust collar and drive pinion assembly off the armature shaft.
11. Assembly of the starter is the reverse of disassembly.

NOTE: New bushings should be completely submerged in engine oil for at least 30 minutes before being installed.

NOTE: When installing the brush plate, align the cutout openings with the loops in the field windings so that the main case through bolts fit into the cutouts.

ENGINE MECHANICAL

Engine/ Transmission

REMOVAL AND INSTALLATION

1. Disconnect the battery and remove it.
2. Drain the coolant and remove the upper and lower radiator hoses. Remove the heater hoses from the side water pipe and intake manifold connector.
3. Remove the air cleaner assembly.
4. Disconnect the accelerator cable at the carburetor. Remove the cable bracket from the intake manifold. Press the cable retaining clip out of the carburetor and remove the cable.
5. Disconnect the fuel line at the carburetor and fuel pump and remove. Disconnect the fuel vent hose at the carburetor.
6. Disconnect all emission control and servo vacuum hoses.
7. Disconnect the electrical leads from the engine electrical units. Remove the engine ground strap.
8. Disconnect the speedometer at the speedometer drive gear, on the transmission.
9. Remove the clutch cable from the release lever by briefly depressing and releasing the cable, while disengaging the cable ball from the slot on the release lever.
10. Remove the exhaust manifold heat tube and the inlet pipe from the exhaust manifold.

NOTE: Wire the inlet pipe to the body.

11. Disconnect the air pump ground wire.
12. Engage 4th gear to insure proper gear shift adjustment during assembly.
13. Raise the vehicle high enough to allow the engine/transmission assembly to be removed from underneath. Support the vehicle safely.

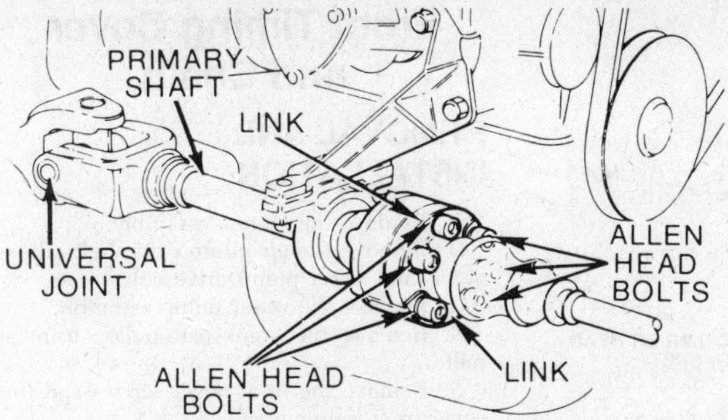

Right-hand driveshaft connection

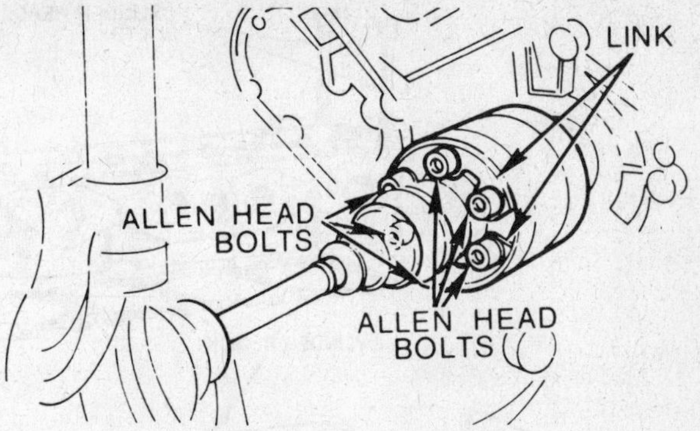

Left-hand driveshaft connection

14. Loosen the clamp bolt and remove the gear selector rod. Unhook the spring between the selector rod and the longitudinal body member.

15. Loosen the mounting nuts on the stabilizer rubber insulators and engine mounts. Loosen the stud lock nut and remove the stud from the transmission. (An Allen wrench is needed to remove the stud.)

16. Remove the complete exhaust system as a unit, after removing the rubber mounting brackets.

17. Remove the shifter tower from the floor pan. Rotate the gear selector rod with the stabilizer half way around. Hang it on a wire to avoid dropping the rod to the floor.

18. Disconnect the starter leads and the alternator leads.

19. Disconnect the left axle driveshaft at the coupling with the stubshaft, by removing the six Allen headed bolts.

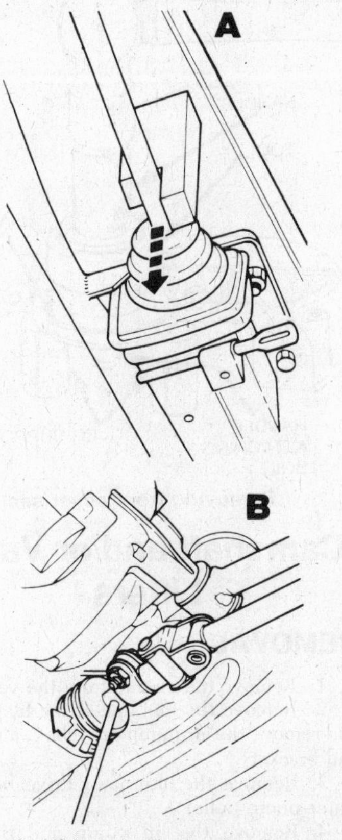

A—Lock shift lever in 4th gear. Install spacer.
B—Rotate shift shaft against stop.

Installing shift lever rod

20. Disconnect the right driveshaft at the inner constant velocity joint by removing the six allen headed bolts.

21. Support the engine/transmission assembly on a jack and remove the engine mounts;

a. Remove the right front upper engine mounting rubber insulator.

b. Remove the engine to body bracket in the engine compartment.

c. Remove the left engine mount.

d. Remove the bottom engine mounting strap.

22. If the vehicle is on a hoist, raise the hoist and lift the vehicle off the engine/transmission assembly. If the vehicle is on stands, lower the engine/transmission assembly from under the vehicle.

23. Installation of the engine/transmission assembly is the reverse of removal. The following precautions must be noted.

a. Be sure that the front mount rubber insulators are parallel to the engine front and do not distort when tightening the attaching nuts.

b. Be sure that the shift selector is still in the 4th gear position when installing the shift rod.

c. Use a 0.16 in. arbor to lock the shift lever in the 4th gear position in the shift tower, and a 2.76 in. spacer between the floor pan and selector rod. Rotate the shift shaft clockwise until it is stopped by the spacer. Tighten the selector rod locating bolt in this position.

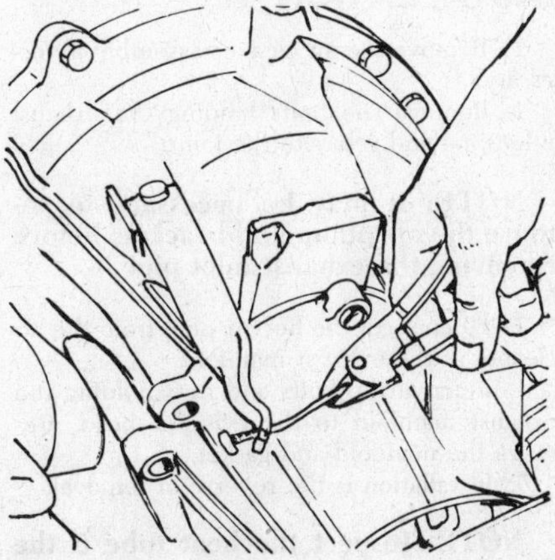
Removing or installing clutch cable in the clutch release lever

d. The clutch cable need not be adjusted since the Fiesta is equipped with an automatic clutch adjuster. Refer to the clutch section for information.

e. The accelerator cable must be routed over the air cleaner spout to prevent damage and to prevent ignition interference.

Cylinder Head

REMOVAL AND INSTALLATION

1. Remove the air cleaner assembly.

2. Remove the fuel line from the fuel pump to the carburetor.

3. Drain the coolant from the radiator and the engine block.

4. Disconnect the spark plug wires and tie them out of the way. Disconnect the fan switch wires and the temperature sending switch wire.

5. Remove the heater and vacuum hoses at the intake manifold. Disconnect the hoses at the choke housing.

6. Disconnect the exhaust inlet pipe and cover the pipe opening to avoid loss of nuts or bolts.

7. Disconnect the throttle linkage and vacuum hoses at the carburetor.

8. Disconnect and remove the air pump and brackets from the cylinder head.

9. Remove the thermostat and housing.

10. Remove the rocker arm cover and the rocker arm assembly.

11. Lift the push rods out of the head, while keeping them in proper order.

12. Remove the cylinder head bolts and lift the cylinder head off the engine block.

13. Installation is the reverse order of removal. Note the following during installation.

a. Clean the gasket sealing area and measure the flatness. Warpage should not exceed 0.0015 in. in a twelve inch span.

b. Tighten the cylinder head bolts in sequence in the increments listed in the specifications.

c. Adjust the valves.

Intake Manifold

REMOVAL AND INSTALLATION

1. Remove the carburetor air cleaner assembly.

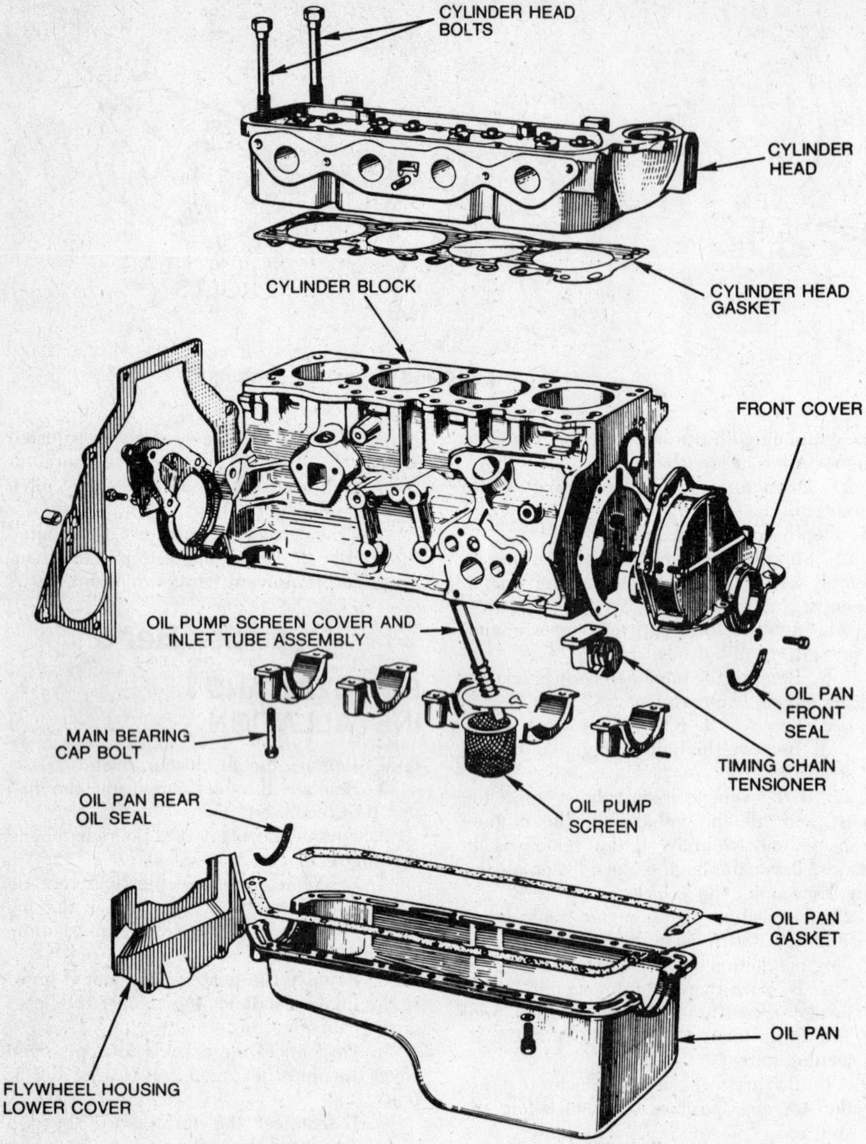

Exploded view of engine block, head and oil pan assembly—external parts

2. Drain the cooling system.
3. Disconnect the accelerator cable from the carburetor throttle lever.
4. Disconnect the fuel line and the vacuum line at the carburetor.
5. Disconnect the fan switch wires; remove the thermostat and housing.
6. Disconnect the water outlet hose and the crankcase ventilation hose from the manifold.
7. Remove the decel valve to carburetor pipe, if equipped, from the carburetor.
8. Remove the manifold attaching bolts and nuts and remove the manifold from the cylinder head.
9. Installation of the intake manifold is the reverse of removal and the following recommendations should be observed.
   a. Clean the gasket surface of all old material.
   b. Apply waterproof sealer to both sides of the manifold gasket at the water ports.
   c. Tighten all nuts and bolts to the proper torque specifications.

Exhaust Manifold

REMOVAL AND INSTALLATION

1. Remove the air cleaner assembly if necessary.
2. Remove the bolts holding the exhaust inlet pipe and separate the joint.

NOTE: It may be necessary to remove the air pump and brackets before removing the exhaust inlet pipe.

3. Disconnect the hot air pipe from the air cleaner at the exhaust manifold.
4. Remove the bolts and nuts holding the exhaust manifold to the cylinder head. Remove the manifold and gasket.
5. Installation is the reverse of removal.

NOTE: Inspect the heat tube if the manifold is to be reinstalled. Replace if needed.

Front Timing Cover and Chain

REMOVAL AND INSTALLATION

1. Remove the engine assembly.
2. Remove the air pump drive belt, alternator, and water pump drive belt.
3. Remove the water pump assembly.
4. Remove the crankshaft pulley using a puller.
5. Remove the front cover screws and the cover from the engine.
6. Remove the crankshaft oil slinger, camshaft sprocket retainer and bolts.
7. Remove the timing chain tensioner and bolts.
8. Remove the camshaft sprocket and timing chain.
9. Installation is the reverse of removal. Note the following during installation.
   a. Align the camshaft and crankshaft sprocket timing marks opposite each other and along the camshaft and crankshaft center lines.
   b. Install a new front cover oil seal.
   c. Install the front cover gasket with oil resistant sealer at the ends and if necessary, on portions of the oil pan gasket.
   d. The cover is properly positioned by the centering lug and the pulley.

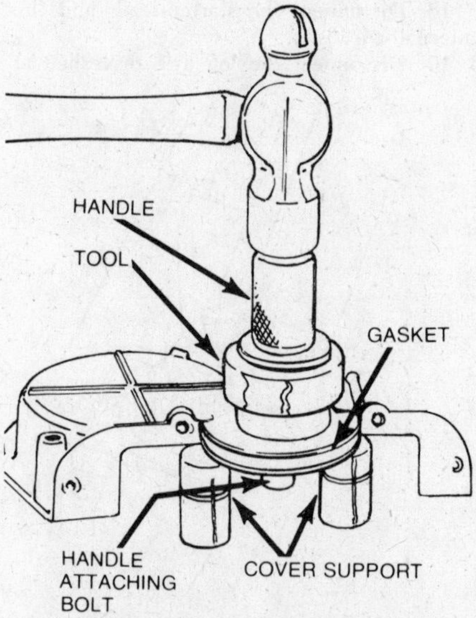

Removing front cover seal

Camshaft and/or Valve Lifters

REMOVAL

1. Remove the engine from the vehicle.
2. Remove the fuel line at the fuel pump and remove the air pump drive belt, air pump and brackets.
3. Remove the alternator drive belt and water pump pulley.
4. Remove the oil pump and the fuel pump.
5. Remove the rocker arm cover from the head.

6. Remove the distributor from the engine.
7. Remove the rocker arm retaining bolts and lift out the rocker arm assembly.
8. Lift the pushrods from the engine and keep them in order.
9. Remove the oil pan and gasket, dipstick and with a puller, the crankshaft pulley.
10. Remove the front cover, crankshaft oil slinger, and the timing chain tensioner assembly.
11. Remove the timing chain and the camshaft sprocket.
12. Remove the camshaft thrust plate and remove the camshaft from the engine block, being careful not to damage the cam bearings.
13. Remove the valve tappet assemblies from their bores in the engine block.

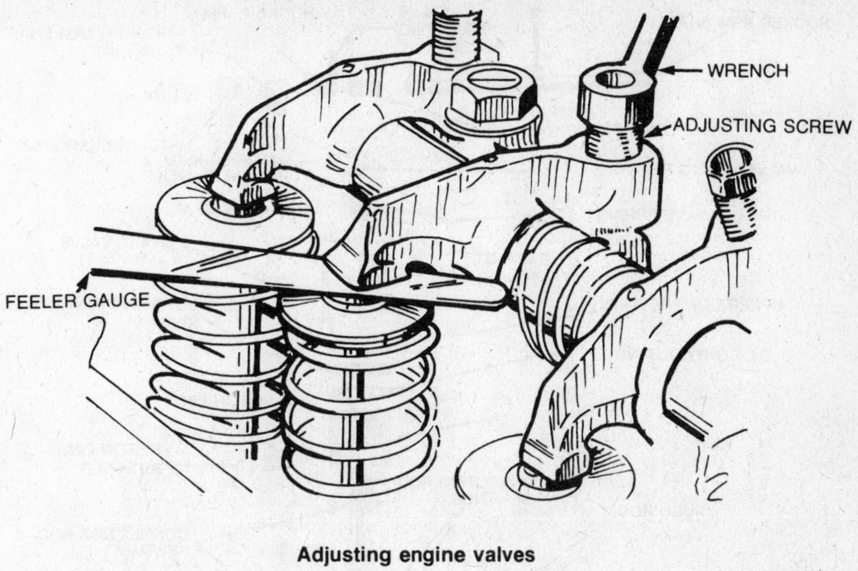

Adjusting engine valves

INSTALLATION

1. Install the valve tappets in the engine block.
2. Carefully install the camshaft into the engine block so as not to damage the camshaft bearings.
3. Install the thrust plate into the camshaft groove and install the retaining bolts.
4. Measure the free play between the thrust plate and the camshaft flange. Clearance should be between 0.0025 and 0.0075 in.
5. Align the timing marks on the crankshaft and camshaft gears and install the timing chain.
6. Install the tensioner arm on the pivot pin and install the timing chain tensioner.
7. Install the crankshaft oil slinger and the front cover, using new gaskets.
8. Install the oil pan, using new gaskets and oil resistant sealer at all joints.
9. Install the dipstick.
10. Install the crankshaft pulley and tighten to specifications.
11. Install and time the distributor.
12. Install the oil pump, using a new gasket. Install a new oil filter.
13. Install the fuel pump to the engine block, using a new gasket.
14. Install the pushrods into their original positions.
15. Install the rocker arm shaft assembly.
16. Adjust the valve clearances to specifications, following the chart in the tuneup section.
17. Install the water pump pulley, vacuum lines, fuel lines, and drive belts. Adjust as necessary.
18. Install the engine into the vehicle.
19. Start the engine and check for any oil or water leaks.
20. Readjust the valves to normal operating temperature specifications. Install the rocker arm cover.
21. Complete the installation of removed and disconnected units and hoses.
22. Complete the installation by checking the ignition timing, carburetor air/fuel mixture, and idle speed adjustment.

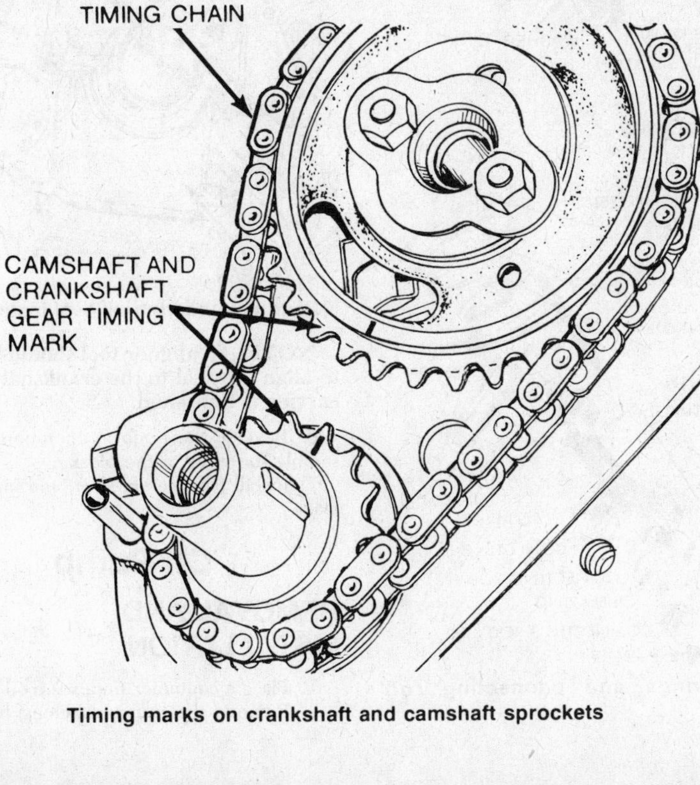

Timing marks on crankshaft and camshaft sprockets

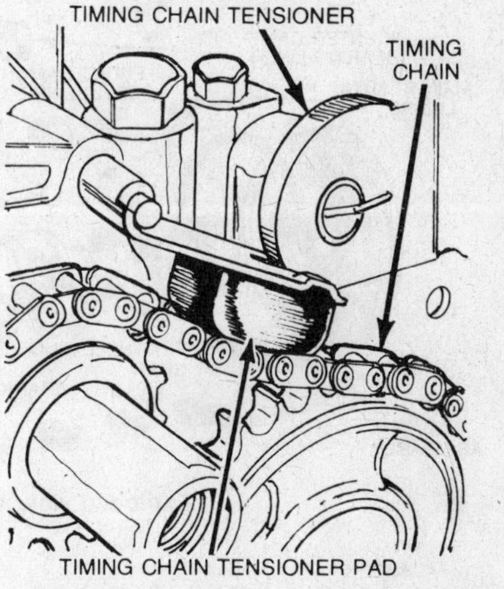

Timing chain tensioner in position

Pistons and Connecting Rods

REMOVAL

1. Remove the cylinder head assembly and oil pan assembly.
2. Inspect the connecting rods to make sure that all rods have been numbered correctly. The numbers should be stamped on the camshaft side of the large end.
3. Remove the ring ridge at the top of the cylinder bore, if present, to avoid ring and piston damage upon removal.
4. Loosen the connecting rod cap bolts and lightly tap the caps to loosen. Remove the caps and push the connecting rod and piston assembly upward out of the cylinder bore.
5. Refer to the Engine Rebuilding Section

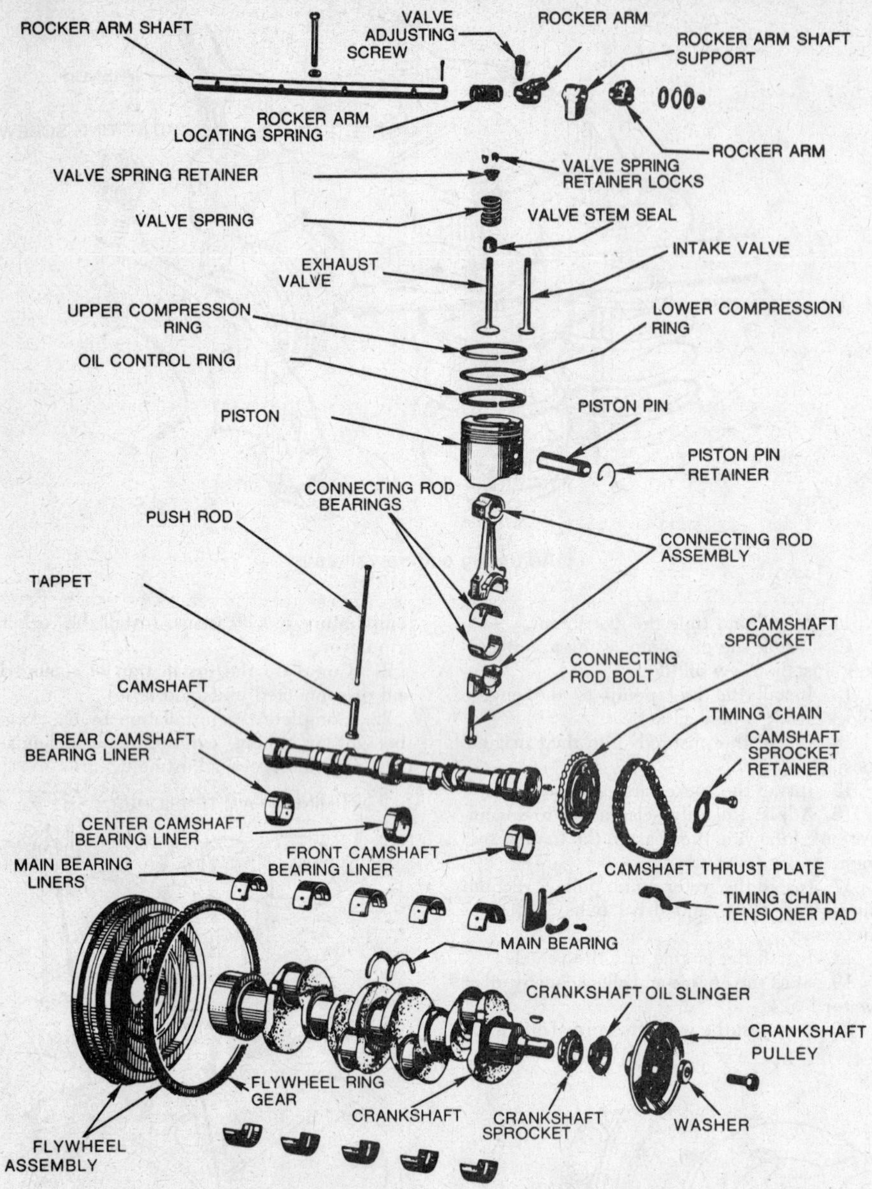

Exploded view of engine internal parts

for piston ring installation, cylinder bore examination and reconditioning, and piston selection.

INSTALLATION

1. Check the ring gaps in the cylinder bores and the piston ring to piston groove clearance as outlined in the engine rebuilding section.
2. Assemble a preheated piston to a connecting rod with the "Front" markings on the connecting rod on the same side as the arrow on the piston crown. Retain the wrist pins with snap rings.
3. Install the rings on the pistons with the oil control ring gap to the rear and the top and second compression ring gaps at 180 and 90 degree angles.
4. Compress the rings with a ring compressor tool, align the piston in the cylinder bore so that the arrow on the piston crown is pointing to the front, and tap the piston assembly into the cylinder bore.

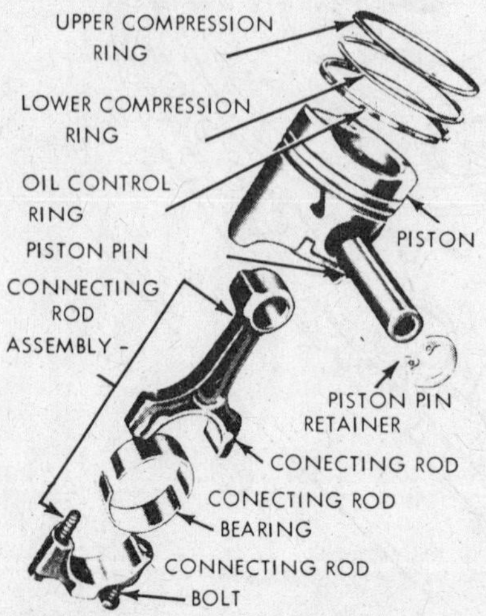

Piston, rings and connecting rod assembly

NOTE: Dip the piston assembly into an oil filled container before compressing the rings. Make sure the cylinder walls and connecting rod journals are clean and oiled before installation of the piston/rod assembly.

5. Align the connecting rod to the crankshaft rod journal and install the bearing as outlined in the Engine Rebuilding Section. Tighten the cap bolts to specifications.

ENGINE LUBRICATION

Crankshaft Rear Main Bearing Oil Seal

REMOVAL AND INSTALLATION

1. Remove the engine from the vehicle.
2. Remove the pressure plate and clutch plate.
3. Remove the flywheel, oil pan, and gaskets.
4. Remove the rear oil seal carrier from the rear of the engine block.
5. Install the new oil seal in the carrier and using a new gasket, install the carrier on the engine block.

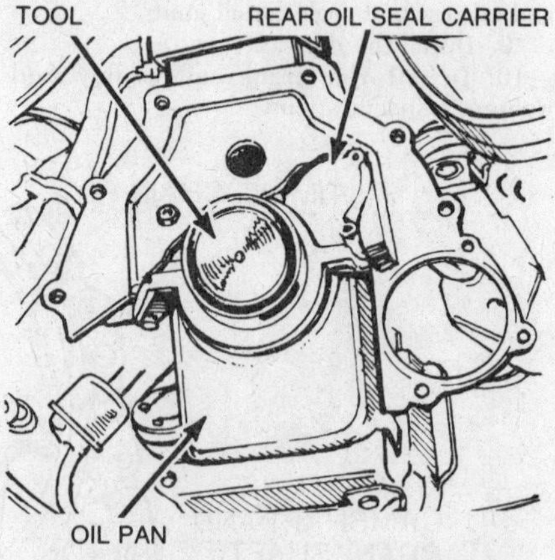

Rear main bearing oil seal installation

NOTE: An aligner tool should be used to align the seal to the crankshaft as the carrier is tightened.

6. Reverse the removal operation to reassemble the units to the block.
7. Install the engine, start, and inspect for leaks.

Oil Pump

REMOVAL AND INSTALLATION

1. Place a container under the oil pump.
2. Remove the pump attaching bolts and

remove the oil pump with filter attached, from the engine.

3. Separate the oil filter from the pump.
4. Installation is the reverse of removal. Use a new oil filter.

Oil Pan

REMOVAL AND INSTALLATION

1. Raise the vehicle and support safely.
2. Drain the oil pan and remove the dipstick.
3. Disconnect the battery ground cable.
4. Disconnect the throttle linkage from the carburetor.
5. Disconnect the steering cable from the rack and pinion unit.
6. Remove the rack and pinion unit from the crossmember and move it forward to provide oil pan removal clearance.
7. Remove the starter motor.
8. Remove the lower flywheel cover.
9. Remove the oil pan bolts and remove the oil pan assembly.

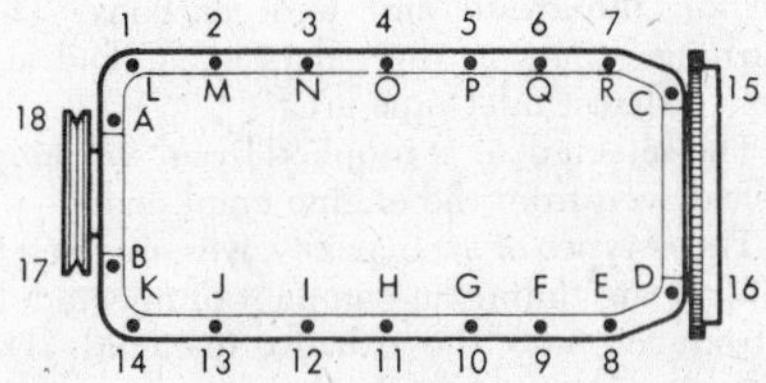

Oil pan bolt tightening sequence—follow alphabetical first, then numerical

10. Installation is the reverse of removal. Note the following:
    a. Clean the inlet screen and tube assembly.
    b. Clean the seal retainer grooves in the front cover and the rear main bearing cap.
    c. Install the gasket to the engine block with an oil resistant sealer.
    d. Apply oil resistant sealer to the end joints of the gasket and end seals.

CAUTION

When installing the oil pump, prime it by filling the inlet or outlet port with engine oil and rotating the pump by hand. This will prevent damage when the engine is started.

ENGINE COOLING

Radiator

REMOVAL AND INSTALLATION

1. Drain the cooling system.
2. Remove the top and bottom hoses. Remove the expansion tank tube from the radiator filler neck.
3. Disconnect the wire loom connection from the fan motor and unclip the loom from the shroud clip.

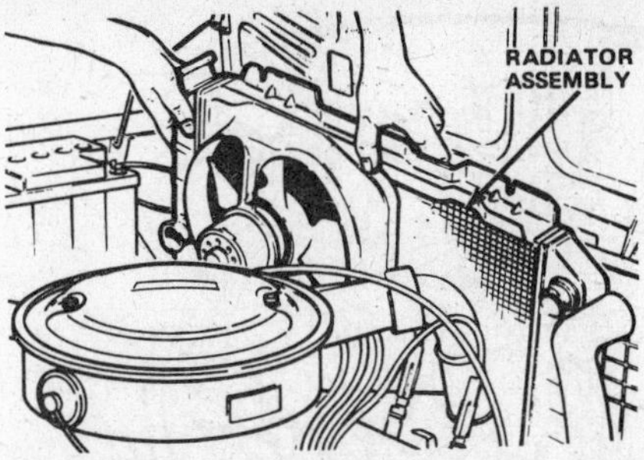

Removing or installing radiator shroud/fan assembly

4. Remove the two lower radiator attaching bolts from the front of the vehicle.
5. Remove the two upper radiator attaching bolts from inside the engine compartment.
6. Remove the radiator assembly with the shroud and fan attached.
7. Installation is the reverse of removal.

Water Pump

REMOVAL AND INSTALLATION

1. Disconnect the battery ground cable and drain the cooling system.
2. Loosen the three pump pulley bolts while the belts are still attached.
3. Remove the air pump belt and air pump brackets and loosen the alternator bolts.
4. Move the alternator toward the engine and remove the drive belt.
5. Remove the lower hose from the water pump, the three pump pulley bolts, and the pulley.
6. Remove the three pump body retaining bolts and the pump assembly.
7. Installation is the reverse of removal. Note the following:
    a. Clean the old gasket from the sealing surface; use a new gasket and a waterproof sealer.
    b. The air pump pivot bolt may have a nut welded to the bracket or a loose nut.

Thermostat

The thermostat housing is on the front top of the engine secured by two bolts. Two different length housings are used, short for regular duty and long for air conditioning.

EMISSION CONTROLS

The engine tune-up and emission control information is on a sticker located in the engine compartment or on the engine. This information is critical to the proper adjustment of the engine and emission system.

NOTE: It is suggested that the sticker information be copied and saved with the owners manual and other important papers.

Two emission control systems are used for the Fiesta engine, one for 49 states and High Altitude, and one for California.

Catalytic Converter

The catalytic converter is installed in the exhaust system to change most exhaust gases into carbon dioxide and water vapor. Unleaded fuel only is to be used with the catalytic converter. Two lengths of converters are used, short for 49 states and High Altitude, and long for California.

Exhaust Gas Recirculation System

The EGR system is used to re-introduce metered amounts of exhaust gases into the

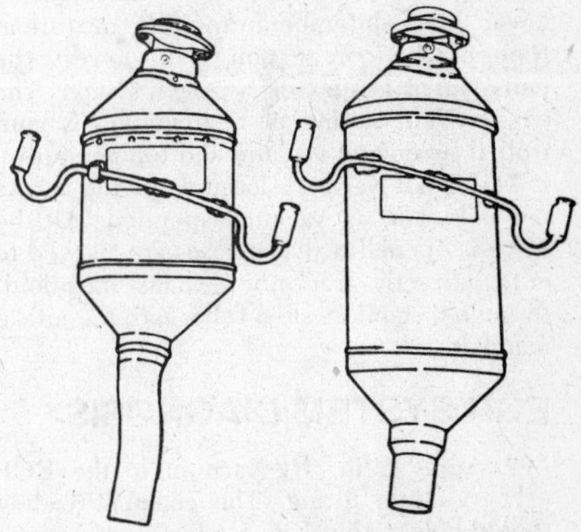

49 States **California**

Two types of catalytic converters used on Fiesta

A—Impeller
B—Seal
C—Bearing shaft
D—Pump body
E—Pump pulley hub

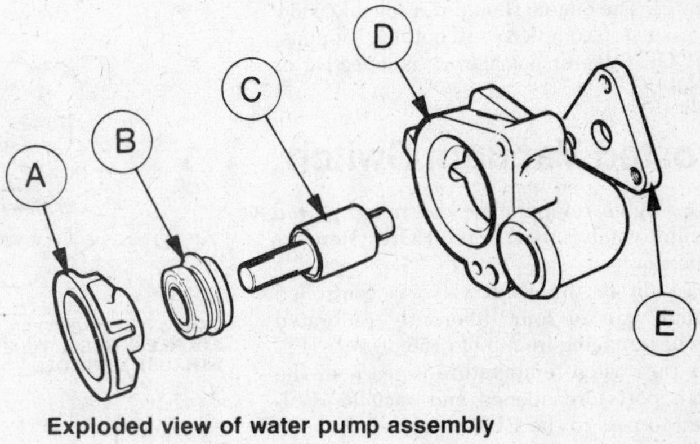

Exploded view of water pump assembly

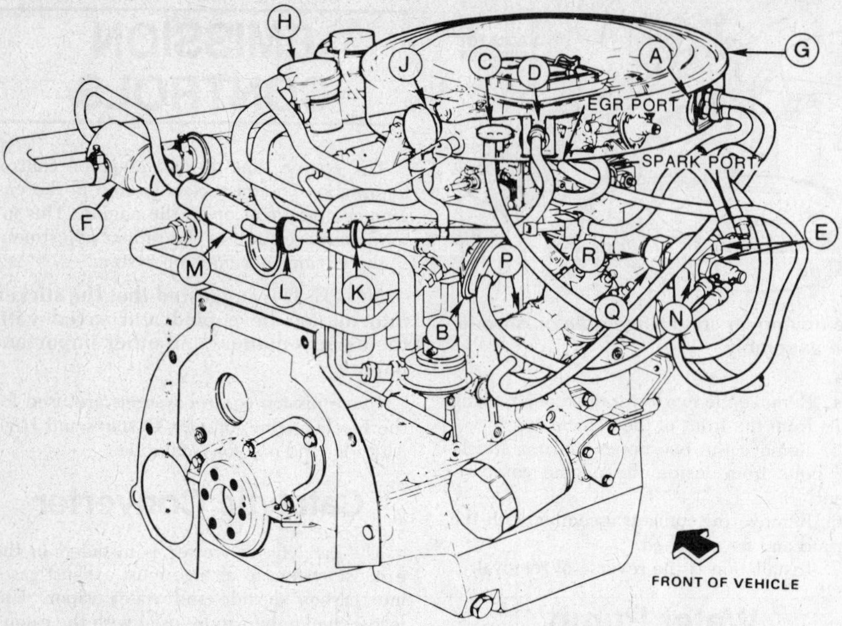

A—TVS switch (normally closed)
B—EGR valve
C—Air cleaner bimetal sensor
D—TVS switch (normally open)
E—Ported vacuum switch (PVS) (2 required)
F—Valve assembly (air bypass)
G—Air cleaner assembly
H—Oil filler cap assembly
J—Valve assembly (vacuum vent)
K—Check valve
L—Delay valve
M—Vacuum reservoir
N—Fitting (PVS valve)
P—Distributor
Q—Adapter (PVS fitting)
R—Adapter (PVS fitting)

California emission controls

air/fuel mixture in the intake manifold to lower the peak temperature of the mixture at time of the combustion. This lowers the emission of Oxides of Nitrogen (NOx). The amount and timing of recirculation is controlled by engine vacuum and temperature.

The EGR valve is located on the intake manifold and is vacuum operated. As the valve is opened, exhaust gases are allowed to enter directly from the exhaust manifold, through a stainless steel tube, into the intake manifold.

EGR SYSTEM DIAGNOSIS

1. Apply 8 in. Hg vacuum to the EGR valve vacuum fitting. The vacuum reading should hold within 1 in. Hg for a minimum of 30 seconds.

2. With the engine at idle, apply at least 8 in. Hg vacuum to the EGR valve. The valve stem or pintle should move to the full extent of travel. The engine should run roughly, slow down, or stop completely. If nothing happens, the EGR valve or passageway is defective or blocked.

Ported Vacuum Switch

An engine temperature controlled ported vacuum switch is used in the EGR system for California.

Vacuum to the EGR valve is controlled through one of four differently calibrated switches, ranging from 90 to 155 degrees (F).

As the switch temperature is reached, the switch ports are opened and vacuum is allowed to pass to the EGR valve.

PORTED VACUUM SWITCH DIAGNOSIS

1. Cold start the engine and check for vacuum at the EGR valve. None should be present.

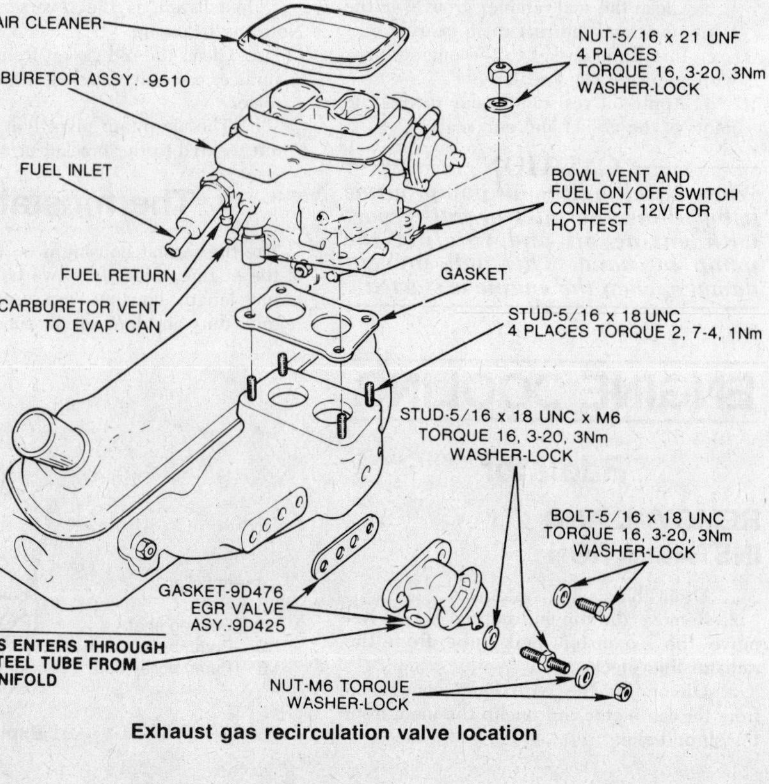

Exhaust gas recirculation valve location

2. Allow the engine to warm up to normal operating temperature and recheck for vacuum at the EGR valve. Vacuum should be present at light to medium throttle opening.

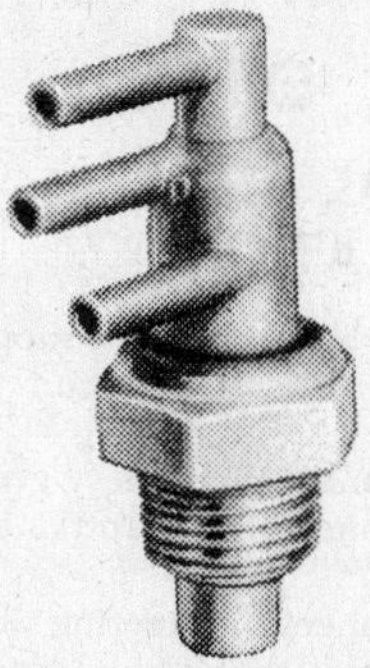

Ported vacuum switch—typical

Thermactor System

The Thermactor system injects fresh air into the stream of hot exhaust gases leaving the combustion chambers, to further burn carbon monoxide and hydrocarbons. This burning occurs in the exhaust manifold and front exhaust inlet pipe area.

The injected air is supplied by an air pump, belt driven from the engine crankshaft.

Three types of air bypass valves are used to control the timing and amount of injected air introduced into the exhaust manifold. The bypass valves are controlled by engine vacuum and internal spring tension.

Two of the bypass valves use a one nipple vacuum control port and have a normally closed internal valve. The third type uses double nippled vacuum control ports and has an internal timed air bypass valve which is normally open.

All bypass valves have a relief valve to exhaust excessive injected air when the demand from the engine is low.

BYPASS VALVE DIAGNOSIS

Normally Closed Bypass Valve

1. Remove the bypass outlet hose. Start the engine and increase the engine speed to 1500 rpm.
2. The air should be felt and heard at the bypass valve outlet.
3. Remove the vacuum hose and plug it. Again increase the engine speed to 1500 rpm.
4. There should be virtually no air flow felt or heard from the bypass valve outlet. The air should be exhausted from the end of the valve silencer cover.

Timed Bypass Valve With Vacuum Vent

1. Remove the air outlet hose from the bypass valve.
2. Cap the bypass valve vacuum vent nipple (top). Remove or circumvent any restrictions or delaying devices in the sensing vacuum hose (bottom).
3. Start the engine and increase the speed to 1500 rpm.
4. Air should be felt and heard from the bypass valve air outlet.
5. Pinch off the sensing vacuum hose to simulate the air bypass cycle. Release the pinched hose.
6. Air flow through the bypass hose should diminish or stop and then resume its normal air flow.
7. Remove the cap from the vacuum vent nipple (upper) and leave the nipple open.
8. Increase the engine speed to 1500 rpm. The air should be discharged through the exhaust port. Air should not be felt or heard at the bypass valve air outlet.

Vacuum Vent Valve

The vacuum vent valve is used to deactivate the Thermactor system after a period of idling.

Vacuum is applied to both sides of the vent valve, causing a dump valve to seat and allowing vacuum to be applied to the system.

At idle, the vacuum is stopped at one side of the valve, allowing the dump valve to leave its

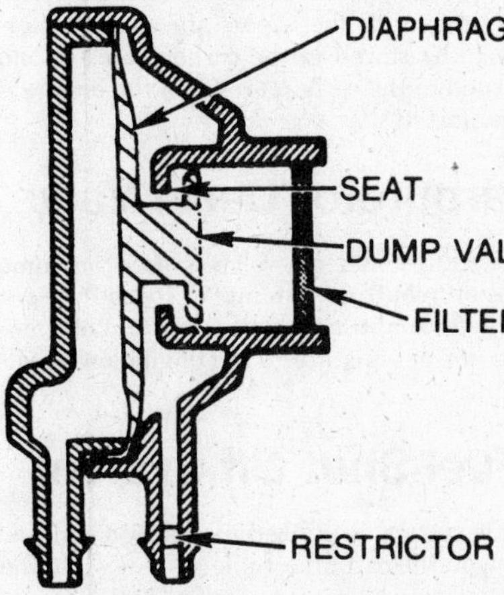

Vacuum vent valve cross section

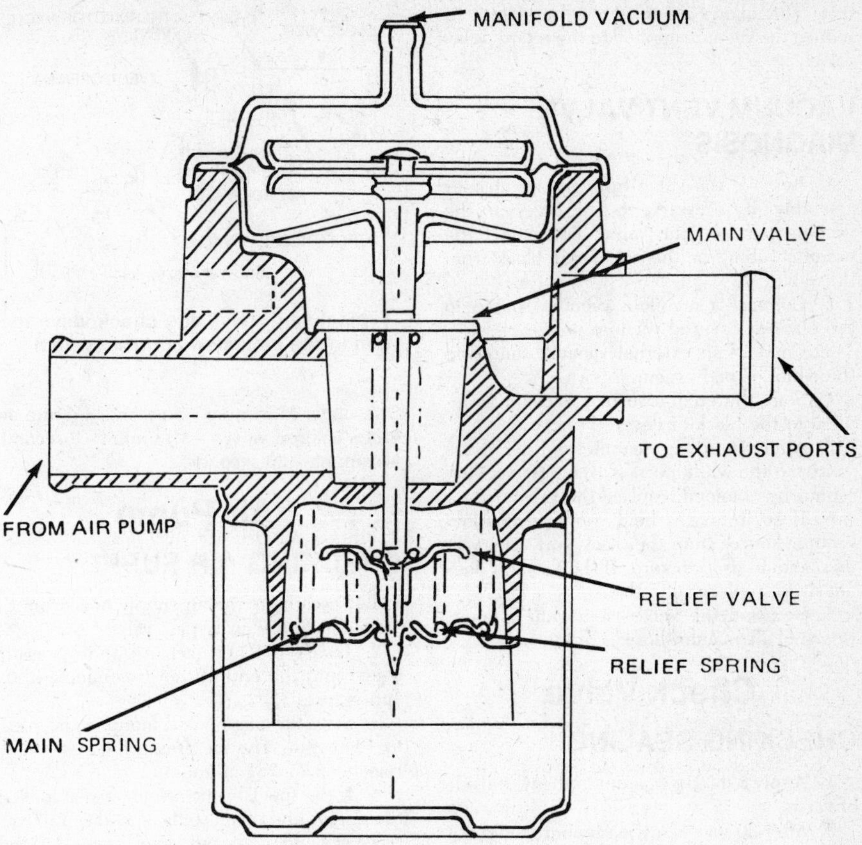

One nipple vacuum control bypass valve—typical

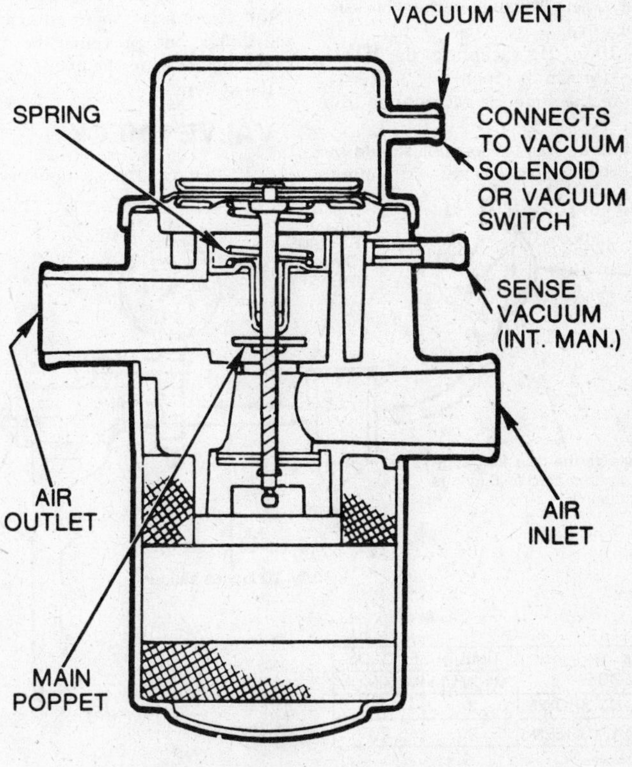

Two nipple vacuum control bypass valve—typical

seat. This allows air to enter the system to reduce the vacuum applied to the retard delay valve.

VACUUM VENT VALVE DIAGNOSIS

1. Remove the valve from the air cleaner assembly, if necessary, to gain access to the vacuum ports on the valve. Disconnect the vacuum tubing or the connector block from the valve.
2. Connect a manifold vacuum source to the black or covered vacuum port.
3. Connect an external vacuum source to the white or body vacuum port.
4. Start the engine so that vacuum is applied to the black or covered port.
5. Apply 10 in. Hg vacuum from an outside source to the white port. If 10 in. Hg vacuum cannot be obtained, replace the valve.
6. If 10 in. Hg is held, remove manifold vacuum source from the black port. The vacuum should drop to zero. If the vacuum does not drop, replace the valve.
7. Reinstall the valve on the air cleaner. Reinstall all vacuum hoses.

Check Valve

CHECKING SEALING

1. Apply 5 in. Hg vacuum to the white side of valve.
2. After 30 seconds, the vacuum should not be less than 4 in. Hg.
3. If the vacuum reading is less, replace the valve.

Vacuum Delay Valve

1. Install a vacuum gauge to the white side of the delay valve.
2. Apply 10 in. Hg vacuum to the "Dist." side of valve (brown or green).
3. Measure the time for gauge to go from zero to 8 in. Hg.
4. The time interval in seconds should be: White and brown colored valves—Minimum - 2 seconds, Maximum - 5 seconds. White and green colored valves—Minimum - 9 seconds, Maximum - 20 seconds.

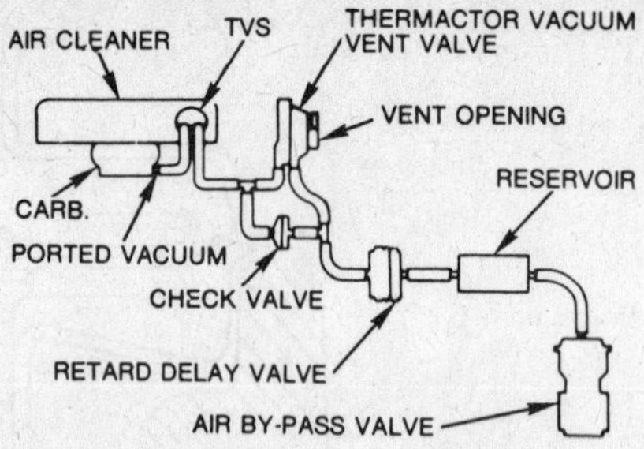

Typical vent valve and check valve location in the emission control system

Air Pump

CHECKING AIR SUPPLY

1. Disconnect the air supply hose from the air pump to the air bypass valve.
2. Insert a Thermactor pump pressure gauge into the end of the disconnected hose and secure.
3. Start the engine and increase the speed to 1000 rpm. The air pressure gauge should register 2.25 PSI minimum.
4. If the special gauge is not available, start the engine and increase the speed to 1500 and place a hand over the open hose. Air flow should be felt and heard.

Exhaust Check Valve

This valve is located between the bypass valve and the exhaust port drillings and allows the Thermactor air to enter the exhaust port drillings but prevents the reverse flow of exhaust gases in the event of a malfunction of the system.

VALVE CHECK

1. Remove the air delivery hose from the valve and by using a probe, make sure the check valve operates.
2. Push down on the check valve. When released, spring tension should return the valve to its seat.
3. If the valve does not return, replace the valve.

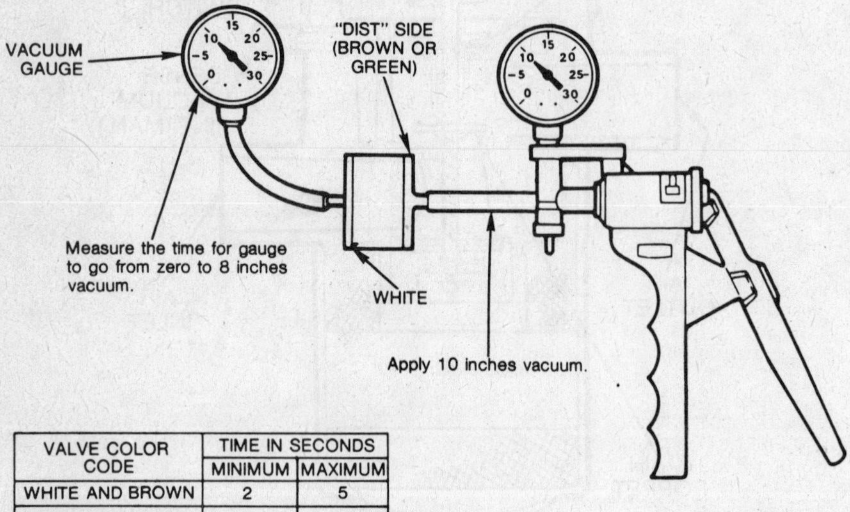

VALVE COLOR CODE	TIME IN SECONDS	
	MINIMUM	MAXIMUM
WHITE AND BROWN	2	5
WHITE AND GREEN	9	20

Testing vacuum delay switch

Temperature Vacuum Switch

This switch is mounted on the air cleaner assembly and is opened by the temperature increase as the engine warms up.

CHECKING TEMPERATURE VACUUM SWITCH

1. Install a hand vacuum pump to the engine port side of the switch.
2. Cool the TVS to 40 degrees or less.
3. The valve should close.

Oil Filler and Breather Cap

Fresh air is drawn into the engine air cleaner assembly and routed to the oil filler and breather cap, where it passes through a one-way valve, an outlet, and on to the crankcase.

The fresh air is mixed with the blow-by gases and is routed internally to the valve cover to be drawn upward into the filler and breather cap.

The gases are further routed through a metered orifice and into the intake manifold.

At times of low fresh air intake, the gas pressure closes the fresh air intake valve to avoid spilling oil laden fumes into the air cleaner assembly. A second valve is opened within the filler and breather cap, and the gases are directed into the intake manifold system through the metered orifice.

Fuel Inlet Bowl Vent System

The float bowl has a dual venting system through a solenoid valve, located on the carburetor. With the ignition on, the vapors are vented internally into the air cleaner. With the ignition off, the vapors are vented externally to be stored in the carbon canister and returned to the carburetor when the engine is again started.

Carburetor Decel Valve

A carburetor decel valve is used on some emission control systems to permit more complete combustion by the addition of a metered air/fuel mixture to the engine on deceleration.

Fuel Shut Off System

This system is utilized to close off the fuel supply to the carburetor idle system when the ignition switch is turned off. This prevents dieseling or running on.

FUEL SYSTEM

Fuel Pump

A single action mechanical fuel pump is attached to the engine block, under the intake manifold. It is operated by the engine camshaft.

If any problem is suspected with the fuel pump, both the pressure and the volume output should be tested.

The minimum volume should be a pint in 38 seconds, at an engine speed of 500 rpm. Pressure should be 3.5 lbs. at 700 rpm.

REMOVAL AND INSTALLATION

1. Disconnect the battery ground cable.
2. Disconnect the inlet and outlet hoses from the fuel pump ports.
3. Remove the two retaining bolts and remove the pump from the engine block.
4. To install the pump, clean the gasket surface and install a new gasket.
5. Position the pump on the engine block so that the pump arm contacts the camshaft.
6. Install the retaining bolts and tighten securely.
7. Connect the inlet and outlet lines to the pump ports.
8. Connect the battery cable, start the engine and check for leakage.

NOTE: If the air cleaner assembly was removed, place the accelerator cable on top of the fresh air intake tube on installation.

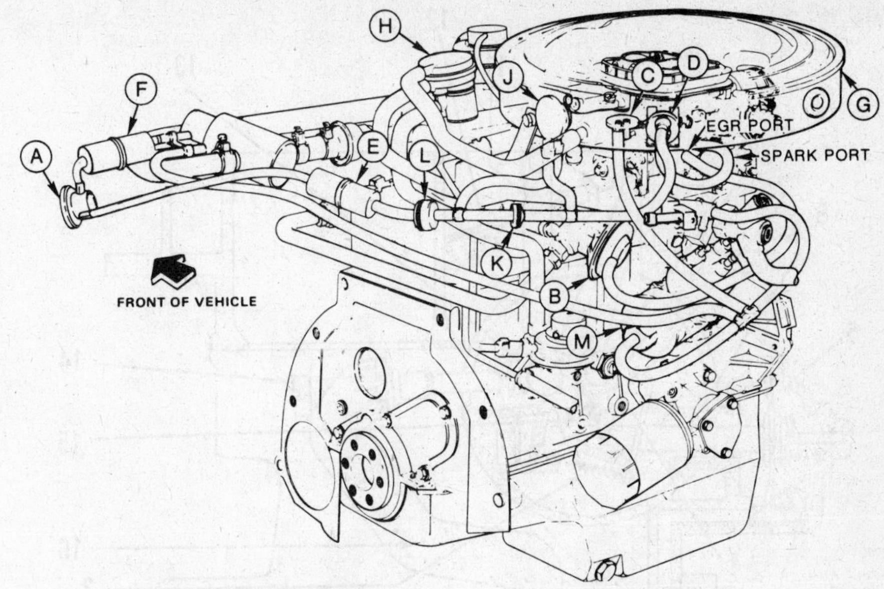

A—Thermactor idle vacuum valve (TIV)
B—Exhaust gas recirculation (EGR) valve
C—Bimetal sensor
D—TVS switch (normally open)
E—Vacuum reservoir
F—Valve assembly (air bypass)
G—Air cleaner assembly
H—Oil filter cap assembly
J—Valve assembly (vacuum vent)
K—Check valve
L—Delay valve
M—Distributor

Typical hose arrangement to check fuel pump pressure and volume

Carburetor

The carburetor is a Weber model 740, two venturi, two stage design. The primary and secondary bores are of equal size.

The primary side is operated by the accelerator linkage, while the secondary side is operated by mechanical linkage from the primary throttle linkage. The secondary is preset to start to open after the primary throttle plate has opened approximately 45 degrees.

The vacuum supply ports for the emission control units are on the primary side of the carburetor.

REMOVAL AND INSTALLATION

1. Remove the carburetor air cleaner assembly.
2. Disconnect the fuel shut off solenoid wire and the electric choke wire.
3. Disconnect the fuel line from the fuel filter.

NOTE: Have a container or shop rags to catch any leakage. Plug the hose end.

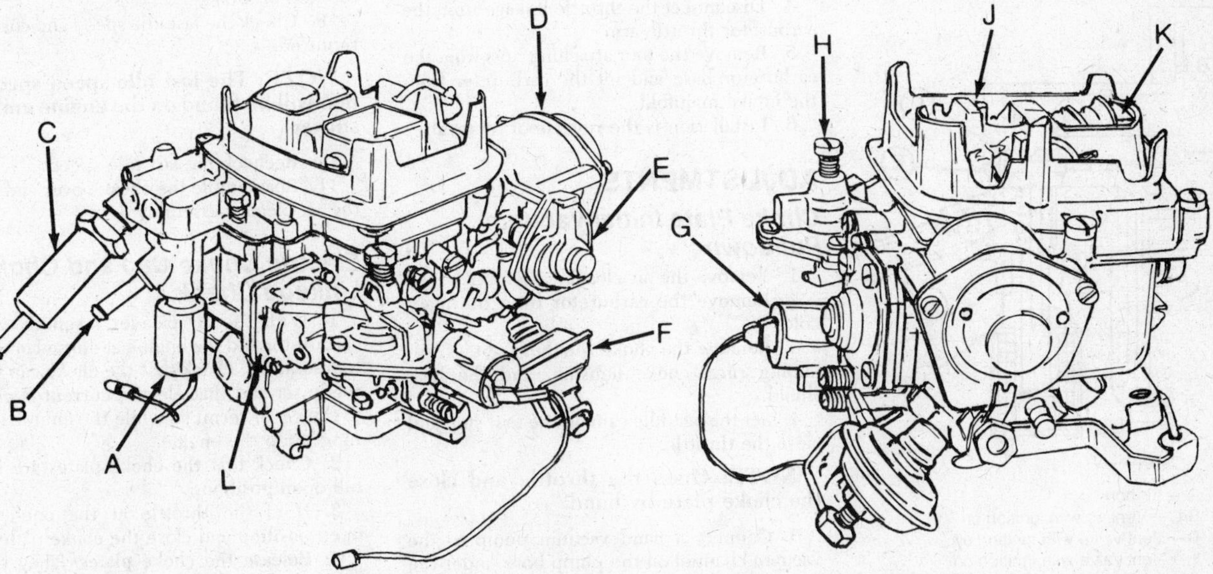

A—Vent solenoid
B—Vent connection (external)
C—Fuel filter
D—Electric choke
E—Choke pulldown diaphragm
F—Dash pot
G—Fuel shutoff solenoid
H—Throttle Modulator (A/C only)
J—Primary venturi
K—Secondary venturi
L—Accelerator pump

Carburetor external components

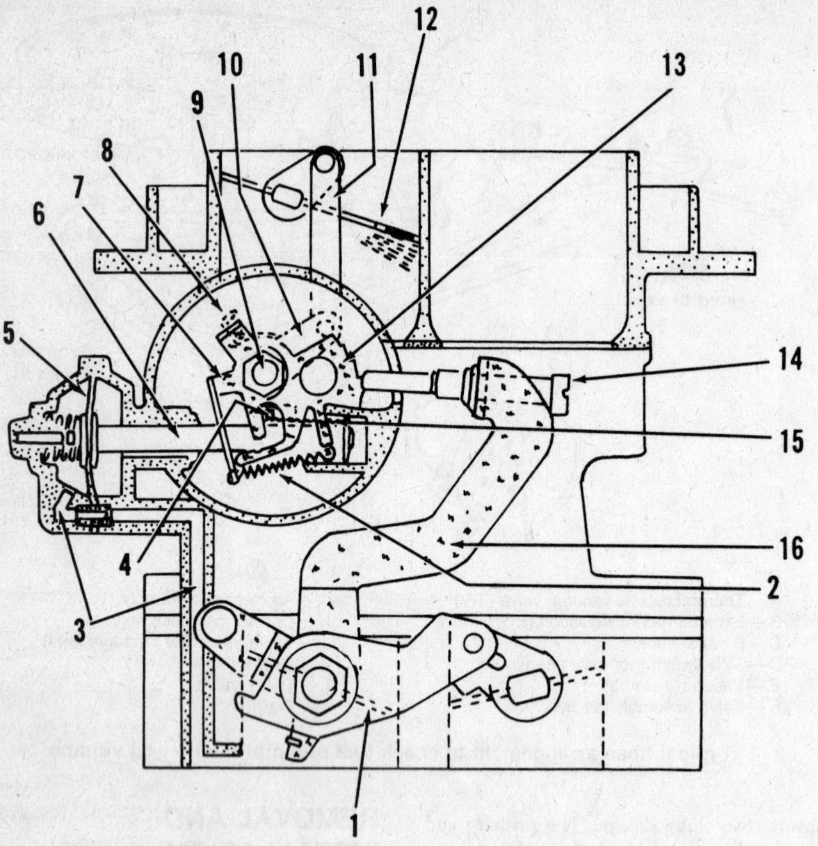

1. Primary throttle valve
2. Cam return spring
3. Vacuum passage
4. Bushing
5. Vacuum diaphragm device
6. Rod
7. Choke valve opening lever
8. Bi-metal spiral spring
9. Choke valve control shaft
10. Lever
11. Throttle valve rod
12. Choke throttle valve
13. Choke fast idle adjustment cam
14. Choke fast idle adjustment screw
15. Spring
16. Throttle operating lever

Exploded view of choke mechanism—typical

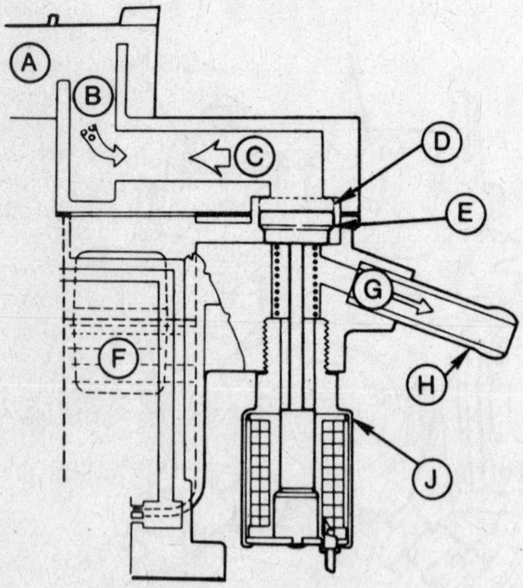

A—Air horn
B/C—Venting with ignition on
D—Vent valve with ignition off
E—Vent valve with ignition on
F—Float
G—Venting with ignition off
H—Connection for canister
J—Solenoid

Cross section of fuel inlet bowl vent valve

4. Disconnect the throttle linkage from the carburetor throttle arm.
5. Remove the four attaching nuts from the carburetor base and lift the carburetor from the intake manifold.
6. Installation is the reverse of removal.

ADJUSTMENTS

Choke Plate Initial Vacuum Pulldown

1. Remove the air cleaner assembly.
2. Remove the carburetor from the manifold.
3. Remove the choke retaining screws, retaining ring, choke housing, and the heat shield.
4. Set the fast idle cam on the first step and close the throttle.

NOTE: Open the throttle and close the choke plate by hand.

5. Connect a hand vacuum pump to the vacuum channel on the pump bore under the base of the carburetor. Pump to attain 17 in. Hg.
6. Check the clearance of the choke plate to the air horn. It should be between .110 to .178 in.

NOTE: Light thumb pressure may be needed to assist in closing the choke plate.

NOTE: The modulator spring should not be compressed.

7. To adjust the clearance, rotate the vacuum diaphragm adjusting screw, located under a seal on the diaphragm, in or out as required.

NOTE: A new seal should be installed after the adjustment has been made.

8. Reassemble the choke cover, reinstall the carburetor on the manifold and install the air cleaner assembly.

Fast Idle Speed Adjustment

1. Warm up the engine, remove the air cleaner assembly and attach a tachometer.
2. Disconnect the electrical leads from the radiator temperature fan switch and connect the two leads with a jumper wire so that the fan will run continuously.
3. If there is a spark delay valve in the distributor advance line, disconnect it and install a jumper hose.
4. Disconnect the decel valve hose, if any, at the carburetor and plug the hose.
5. If the vehicle is equipped with the EGR-PVS system, disconnect and plug the EGR vacuum line.

NOTE: If the vehicle is not equipped with the EGR-PSV system, do not disconnect the EGR valve.

6. Turn off all accessories.
7. Remove the electric choke cap unit after noting and marking the setting and the bi-metal spring to choke lever relationship. Start the engine.
8. Set the choke linkage so that the fast idle screw is against the shoulder of the highest step of the cam.
9. Check the fast idle speed and correct as required.

NOTE: The fast idle speed specification will be found on the engine emission sticker.

10. Recheck the fast idle speed.
11. Reassemble the choke cover and install the air cleaner assembly.

Electric Choke Cap and Choke Linkage Check

1. With the air cleaner assembly off the carburetor and the engine at normal operating temperature, check that the choke cap is correctly set and that electric current is present to the cover terminal while the engine is running. Stop the engine.
2. Check that the choke plates are in the full open position.
3. Hold the throttle at the one-quarter open position and close the choke plates.
4. Release the choke plates. They should rotate to the full open position.
5. If the choke plates do not open properly or there is binding, the linkage or the electric heating components may be worn or damaged.

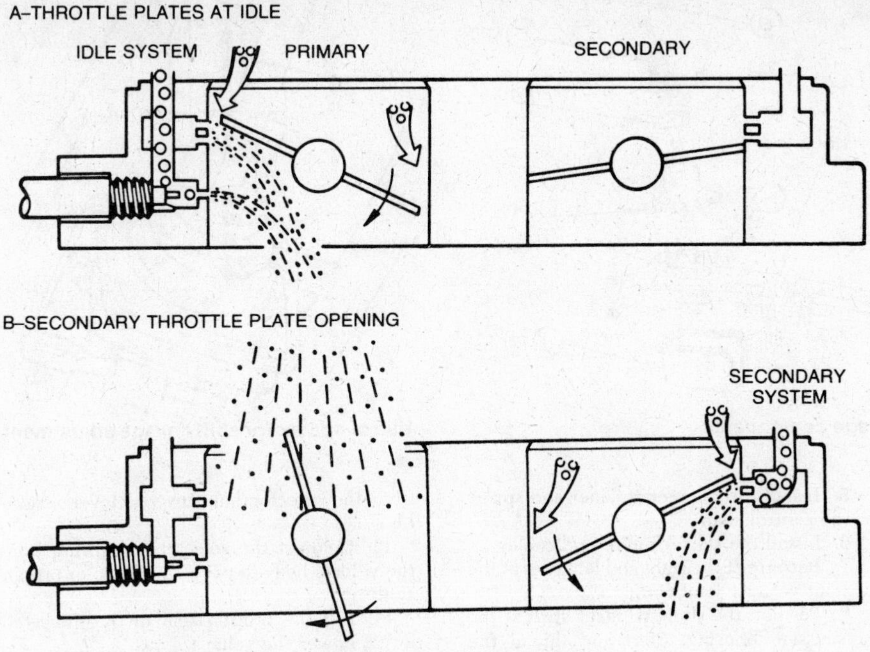

Carburetor flow schematic

Accelerator Cable

REMOVAL

1. Remove the battery ground cable and the air cleaner assembly.
2. Remove the lower insulator panel and disconnect the accelerator cable from the pedal shaft.
3. Punch out the firewall grommet to detach the cable from the firewall.

NOTE: The grommet will be broken and cannot be reused.

4. Disconnect the accelerator cable from the carburetor linkage and detach the cable.
5. Remove the retaining clip, depress the retaining pegs, and twist the cable from the bracket.

INSTALLATION

1. Route the inner cable through the firewall and connect it to the pedal shaft.
2. Install a new cable grommet into the firewall and push the cable through the grommet.
3. Install the cable into the bracket at the carburetor end.

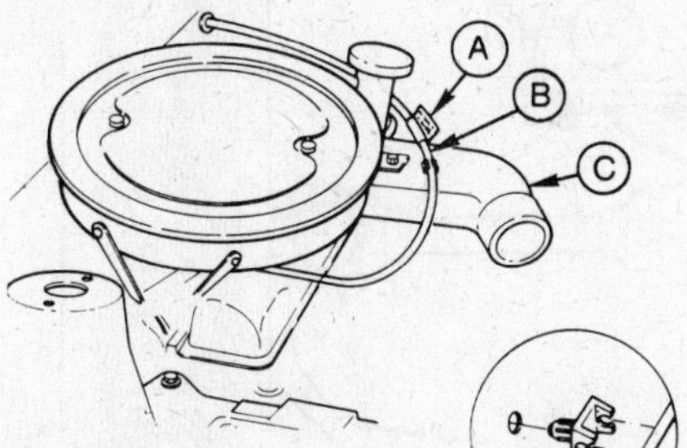

A—Decal
B—Accelerator cable
C—Spout

Accelerator cable routing over air intake spout of air cleaner

4. Connect the cable to the carburetor linkage and adjust to give full throttle opening when the accelerator pedal is fully depressed.
5. Refit the lower insulator panel.
6. Install the air cleaner assembly. Route the accelerator cable over the air intake spout and retain it with a clip.
7. Reinstall the battery ground cable.

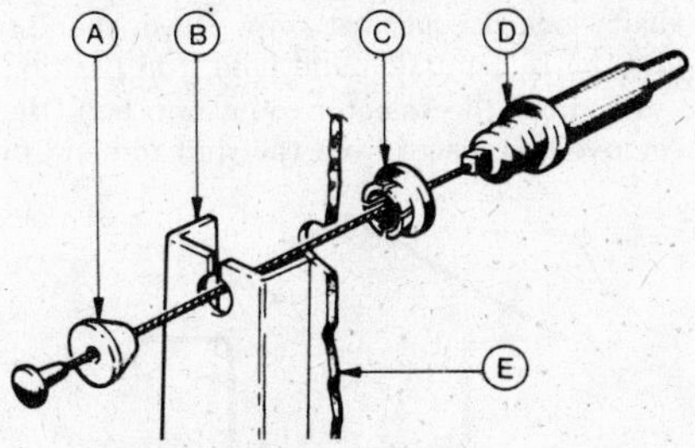

A—Inner cable grommet
B—Pedal shaft
C—Outer cable grommet
D—Outer cable
E—Engine compartment rear bulkhead

Exploded view of accelerator cable routed through firewall

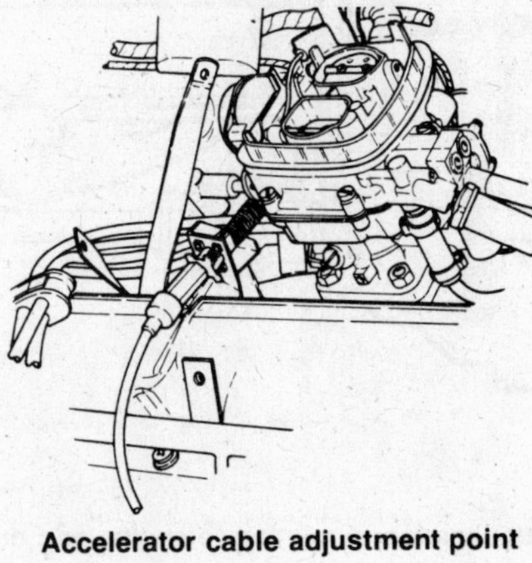

Accelerator cable adjustment point

MANUAL TRANSAXLE

REMOVAL

1. Disconnect the battery ground cable.
2. Install an engine support in the engine compartment to hold the engine during transmission removal.
3. Disconnect the speedometer cable at the transaxle assembly.
4. Disconnect the clutch cable from the clutch release lever by pulling the cable from the slot in the release lever.
5. Remove the four upper transmission flange bolts.
6. Jack up the vehicle and support it safely. Drain the transmission oil by removing the plunger-retainer. Do not lose the spring.

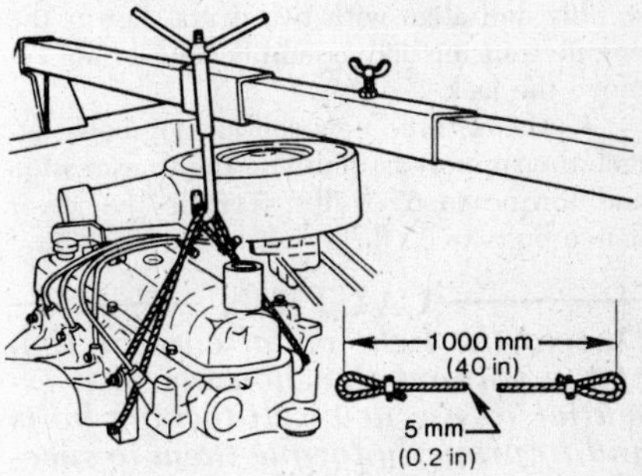

Suggested Ford type engine holding support

7. Be sure the transmission is in fourth gear. Remove the shift rod spring from the body to the rod.
8. Loosen the clamping screw and remove the shift rod from the selector shaft. Remove the stabilizer mechanism from the transmission.
9. Loosen the locknuts and remove the stabilizer bar stud from the transmission housing with an Allen wrench.
10. Remove the six Allen headed screws from the left drive shaft at the coupling of the inner constant velocity joint and stub shaft and separate the coupling.
11. Separate the right axle assembly from the inner constant velocity joint by removing the six Allen headed screws.
12. Disconnect the starter cable and remove the starter motor.
13. Place a jack under the transmission assembly.
14. Remove the lower flange bolts from the transmission housing.
15. Remove the bolts from the engine mounting member and remove it from the vehicle.
16. Remove the transmission from the vehicle.

INSTALLATION

1. Lubricate the splines of the driveshaft and differential gear. Align the engine adapter plate to the engine guide bushing.
2. Install the transmission to the engine

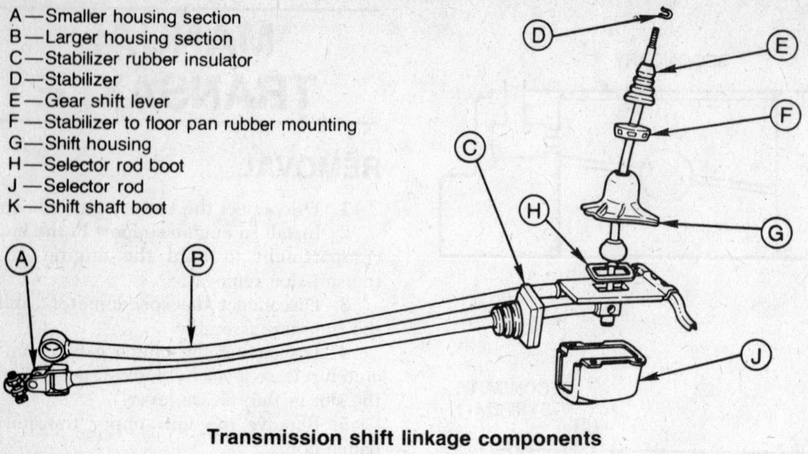

Transmission shift linkage components

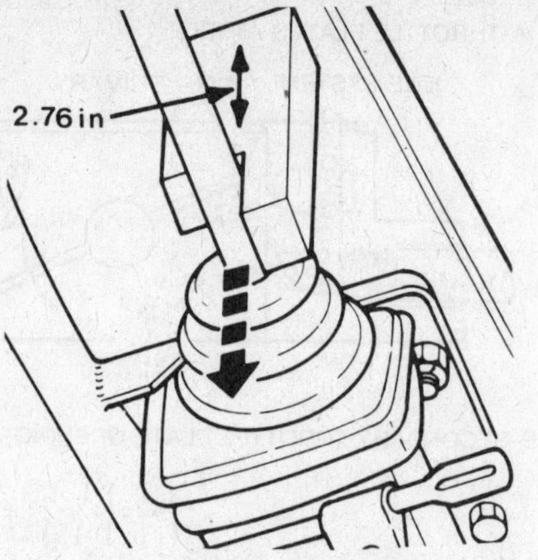

Use of spacer for shift linkage adjustment

block and secure with two flange bolts, lightly tightened.

3. Install the upper and lower support assembly and align with two drifts. Lower the engine/transmission assembly, but do not remove the jack.

4. Using three new self-locking bolts, attach the support assembly to the transmission and torque to 65 ft./lbs. Torque the lower flange bolts to 30 ft./lbs.

CAUTION

Due to the light metal construction of the transmission housing, it is essential to use new self-locking bolts and to properly torque them to specifications.

NOTE: Relieve some of the weight of the transmission/engine assembly to aid in the installation of the bolts, and then remove the jack.

5. Install the plunger retainer and spring for the control shaft.

6. Install the starter motor and cables.

7. Reconnect the right and left axles at the constant velocity joint couplers.

8. Position the shift stabilizer strut at the transmission housing. Start and thread the Allen screw into the housing until it bottoms. Thread the inner lock nut to the rubber and lock with the outer nut.

9. Check that the transmission is still in fourth gear and install the gear selector rod to the gear shift shaft.

10. Align the holes in the selector housing and the end of the gear lever. Lock it into position with a 0.160 inch pin.

11. Place a 2.76 inch spacer between the floor pan and the selector rod. Rotate the shift shaft clockwise until it stops. Push the shaft into the transmission and hold it in position.

12. Lock the selector rod clamp bolt, then remove the spacer from the shift rod and pin from the selector housing/gear lever assembly.

13. Connect the selector rod spring from the vehicle body to the rod. Check for proper shifting.

14. Fill the transmission to the indicated level. Lower the vehicle.

15. Install the top transmission flange bolts and torque to 30 ft/lbs.

16. Connect the clutch cable to the clutch release lever. No adjustment is necessary.

17. Install the speedometer driven gear and connect the battery ground lead to the battery.

18. Remove the engine lifting support bar.

CLUTCH

The clutch assembly is comprised of a pressure plate, clutch disc, release bearing and

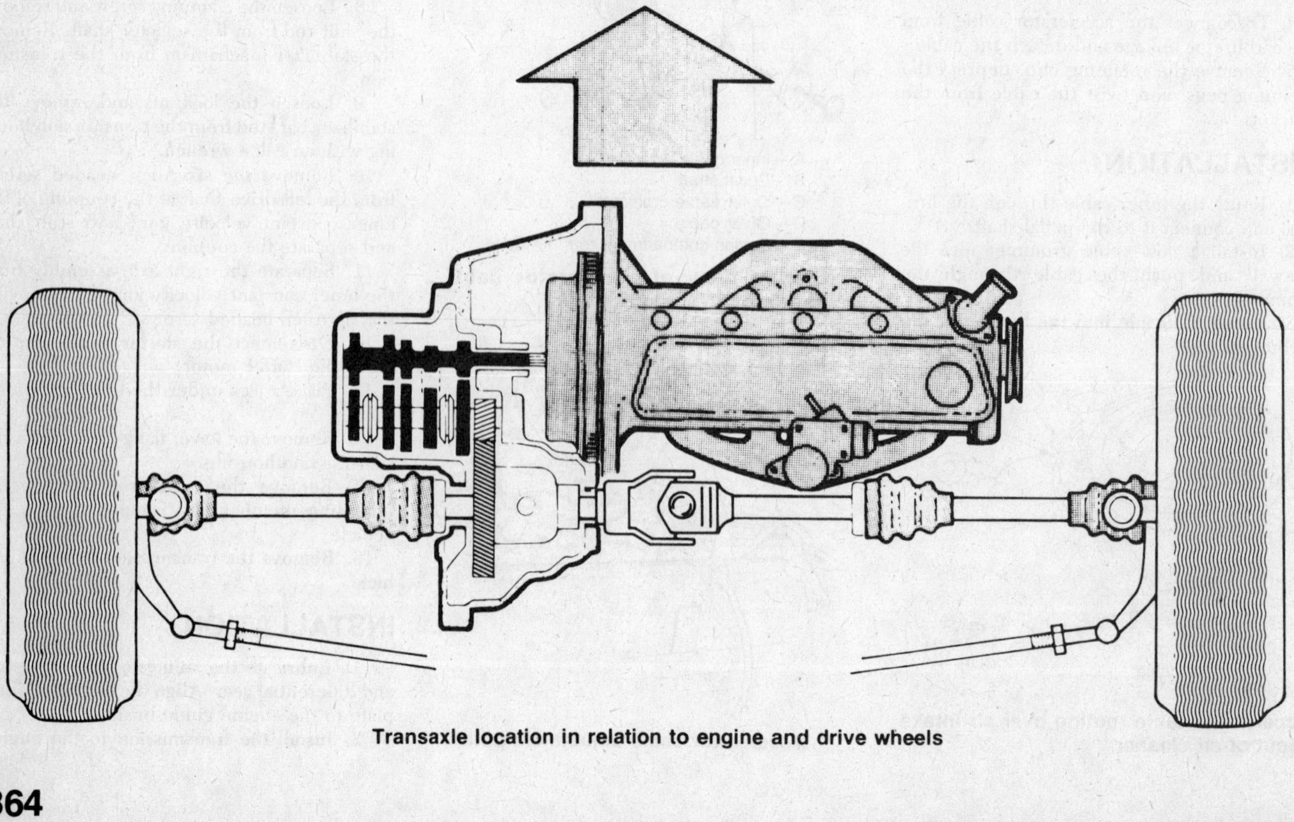

Transaxle location in relation to engine and drive wheels

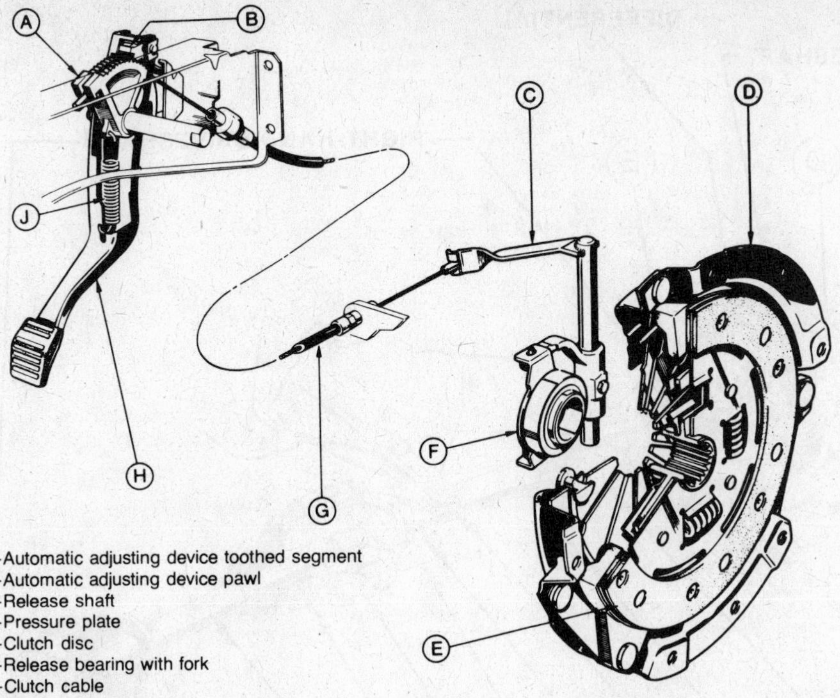

A—Automatic adjusting device toothed segment
B—Automatic adjusting device pawl
C—Release shaft
D—Pressure plate
E—Clutch disc
F—Release bearing with fork
G—Clutch cable
H—Clutch pedal
J—Toothed segment tension spring

Exploded view of clutch assembly and operating mechanism

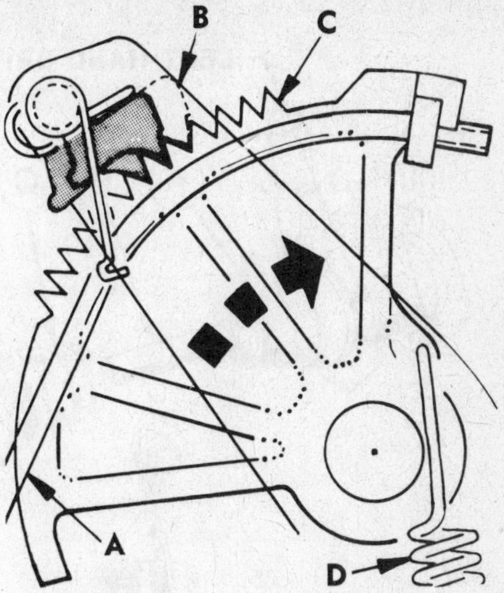

A—Clutch cable
B—Pawl
C—Toothed segment
D—Tension spring

Operation of automatic clutch cable adjuster

automatically adjusted clutch cable. A pilot shaft bushing is not used.

REMOVAL AND INSTALLATION

1. Expose the clutch assembly by removal of the transaxle or the engine.
2. Remove the pressure plate bolts from the flywheel, loosening the bolts a few turns at a time in rotation, and remove the clutch/pressure plate assembly.
3. To install, position the clutch/pressure plate assembly on the flywheel and center the clutch plate with special tool T77F-7137A or equivalent.

NOTE: The flat side of the disc must face the flywheel side.

4. Tighten the pressure plate bolts to 13 ft/lbs and remove the centering tool.
5. Install the engine or transaxle.

Clutch Cable

REMOVAL

1. Disconnect the clutch cable from the clutch release lever.
2. Remove the dash left lower insulating panel from inside the car.
3. Disconnect the clutch cable from the clutch pedal. Pull the clutch pedal to the rear to release the adjusting pawl from the toothed segment. Rotate the toothed segment forward and unhook the cable from the segment. The toothed segment will swivel backward.
4. Pull the cable outward through the recess between the pedal and the automatic adjusting unit and then remove the cable assembly from the engine compartment side.

INSTALLATION

1. Insert the clutch cable through the firewall and between the pedal and the automatic adjusting device.
2. Swivel the toothed segment rearward and connect the cable to the segment.
3. Connect the cable to the release lever at the transaxle housing.
4. Operate the clutch pedal several times to make sure the automatic adjusting mechanism is operating correctly.
5. Install the insulation panel.

Automatic Self-Adjuster

The clutch pedal linkage is kept automatically adjusted by the action of a ratchet device attached to the clutch pedal pivot.

As clutch wear develops into cable slack and as the pedal is depressed, the pawl moves over the toothed segment in stages and engages the next tooth in line to maintain a predetermined tension of the clutch cable.

DRIVE AXLES

Right and left intermediate driveshafts of equal length are used to transfer the power to the front wheels.

The right shaft assembly uses a primary shaft support bearing to control the rotating whipping action of the driveshafts and the constant velocity U-joint.

Left Drive Axle

REMOVAL

1. Remove the wheel center cap and re-

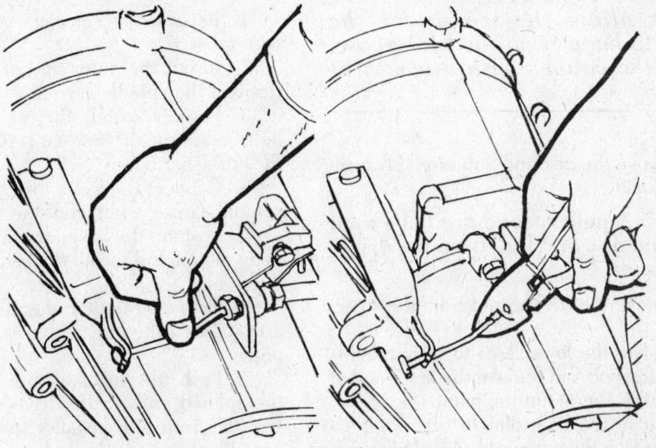

Connecting and disconnecting the clutch cable

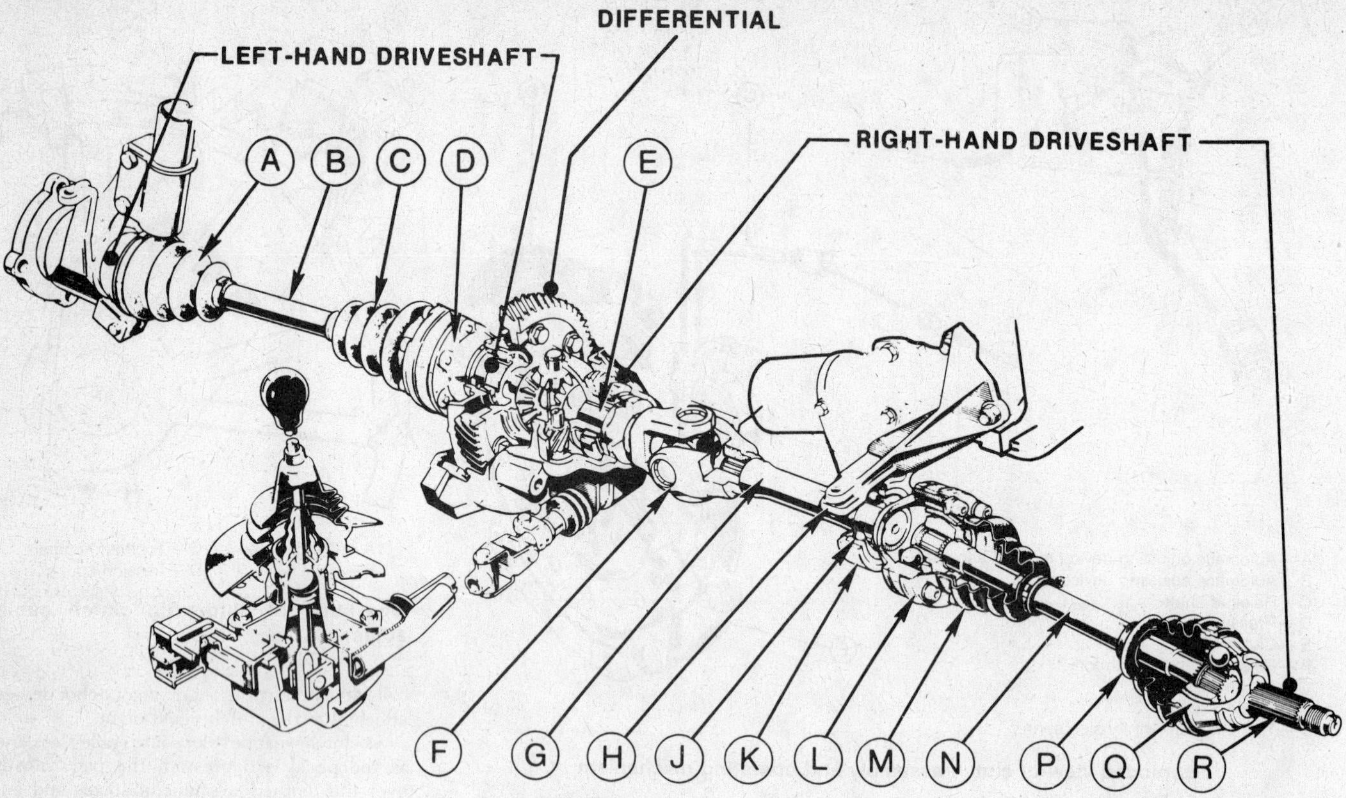

A—Left hand outer C.V. joint
B—Left hand intermediate driveshaft
C—Left hand inner C.V. joint
D—Left hand stubshaft
E—Right hand stubshaft
F—Universal joint
G—Primary shaft
H—Primary shaft bearing support bracket
J—Primary shaft support bearing
K—Primary shaft support bearing housing
L—Right-hand inner C.V. joint
M—Bellows
N—Right-hand intermediate driveshaft
P—Bellows
Q—Right-hand outer C.V. joint
R—Spindle shaft

Exploded view of driveshaft and differential assembly

move the hub retaining nut and washer. Loosen the wheel lug bolts.

2. Raise the front of the car and support it safely. Remove the wheel and tire assembly.

3. Remove the six Allen headed bolts and washers from the constant velocity joint to the stub shaft flange.

4. Remove the brake caliper retaining bolts and lift the caliper free of the support.

CAUTION

Do not allow the weight of the caliper to hang from the brake hose. Secure the caliper with a length of wire.

5. Remove the disc and hub assembly from the driveshaft.

NOTE: A puller may have to be used to pull the disc and hub from the driveshaft splines.

6. Remove the tie rod end from the steering arm.

7. Remove the lower arm to body mounting retaining bolt and remove the inner end of the arm from the mounting point.

8. Remove the ball joint to carrier clinch bolt and detach the outer end of the lower arm assembly.

CAUTION

Do not strain the tie-bar forward mounting by pushing the rear end of the bar downward.

9. Remove the driveshaft assembly from the spindle carrier and the vehicle.

INSTALLATION

1. Repack the constant velocity U-joint with grease.

2. Install the outer end of the driveshaft through the spindle carrier.

3. Loosely install the six Allen headed bolts securing the constant velocity joint to the stub shaft.

4. Connect the lower arm ball joint to the spindle carrier and install the clinch bolt.

5. Position the lower arm inner end to the body mount and install the retaining bolt and nut.

6. Connect the tie rod end to the steering arm, tighten the nut, and install a new cotter pin.

7. Push the hub and disc assembly onto the splined end of the drive shaft by hand. Use the front hub installer special tool or its equivalent to pull the hub and disc onto the driveshaft to its normal position.

CAUTION

Do not attempt to drive the hub and disc onto the driveshaft; the constant velocity joint can be damaged.

8. Install a new hub retaining nut and washer and snug them on the driveshaft threads.

9. Reinstall the brake caliper and tighten the bolts securely.

10. Tighten the six Allen headed bolts to 28-32 ft/lbs.

11. Install the wheel and lower the vehicle to the ground.

12. Tighten the wheel lug bolts.

13. Torque the hub retaining nut to 180 to 200 ft/lbs and stake the nut to the slot of the driveshaft.

14. Install the wheel center cap.

Right Drive Axle

REMOVAL

1. Remove the wheel center cap and the hub retaining nut and washer. Loosen the wheel lug bolts.

NOTE: The hub retaining nut and washer may be removed by an alternate method with the wheels off the ground. Install two lug bolts, and while holding

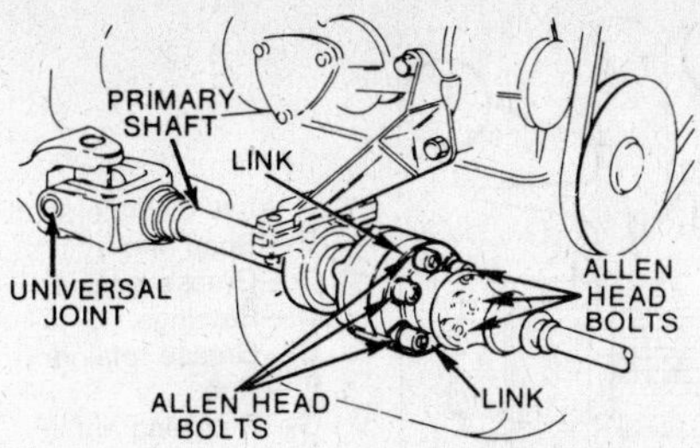

Right side driveshaft coupling

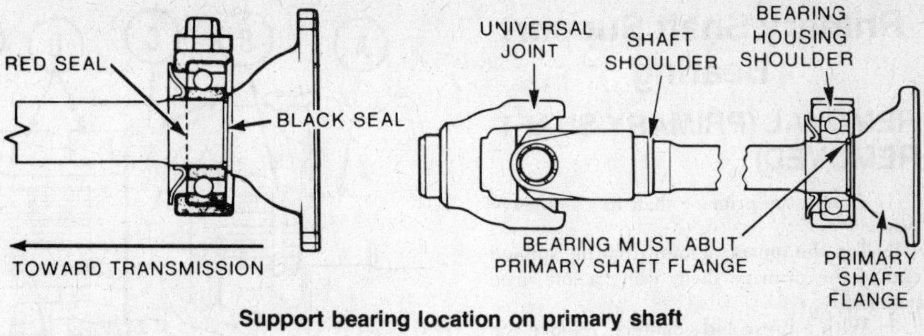

Support bearing location on primary shaft

the brake pedal on, loosen and remove the retaining nut. Release the foot brake and remove the wheel lug bolts.

2. Raise the front of the car and support it safely. Remove the wheel.
3. Remove the six Allen headed bolts from the inner constant velocity joint to the primary shaft flange.
4. Remove the bolts holding the primary shaft bearing housing to the bracket. Allow the primary shaft and bearing assembly to rest clear of its location.
5. Remove the driveshaft assembly from the spindle carrier and the vehicle.

INSTALLATION

1. Repack the constant velocity joint with grease.
2. Insert the driveshaft through the spindle carrier.
3. Loosely install the six Allen headed bolts to secure the constant velocity joint to the primary shaft flange.
4. Align the primary shaft bearing housing to the support bracket and install the two bolts.
5. Loosely install a new hub retainer nut and washer on the driveshaft.
6. Torque the six Allen headed bolts to 28 to 32 ft/lbs.
7. Install the wheel and lower the vehicle to the ground. Fully tighten the lug bolts.
8. Torque the hub retaining nut to 180 to 200 ft/lbs and stake the nut to the slot of the driveshaft.
9. Install the center cap.

Primary Driveshaft

REMOVAL

1. Raise the front of the car and support it safely.
2. Remove the six Allen headed bolts from the constant velocity joint to primary shaft flange.

CAUTION

Support the intermediate driveshaft with wire to avoid unnecessary strain on the universal joint.

3. Remove the primary shaft bearing housing bolts and guide the primary shaft and constant velocity joint from the stub shaft.

Levering left stub axle shaft from transaxle housing

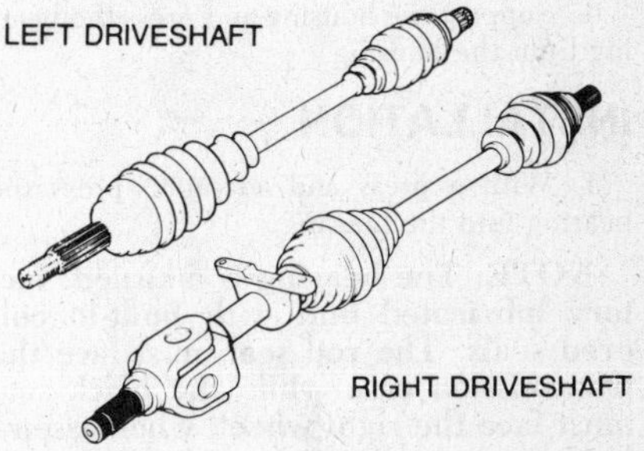

Bellow location on right and left drive shafts

4. Loosen the bolts holding the bearing bracket to the engine.

NOTE: It is necessary to loosen the bearing bracket to avoid any stress or misalignment during assembly.

INSTALLATION

1. Repack the constant velocity joint with grease.
2. Align and install the primary shaft and constant velocity joint assembly into the stub shaft.
3. Attach the bearing housing to the support bracket and install the two bolts.
4. Align the constant velocity joint to the primary shaft flange and install the six Allen headed bolts. Torque the bolts to 28 to 32 ft/lbs.
5. Tighten the bearing support bracket at the engine and lower the vehicle to the ground.

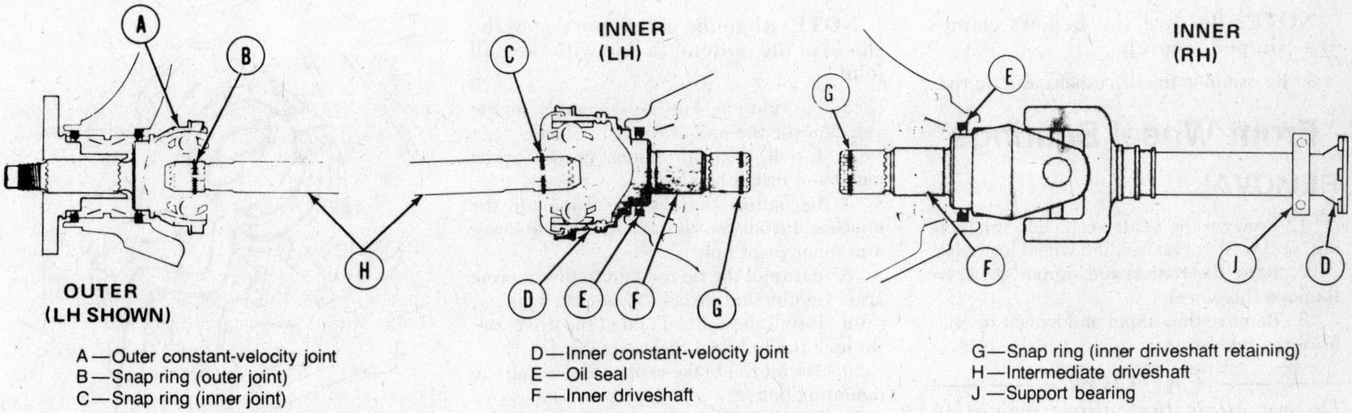

Driveshaft retaining ring locations

Primary Shaft Support Bearing

REMOVAL (PRIMARY SHAFT REMOVED)

1. Clamp the primary shaft in a soft jawed vise.
2. Tap the universal joint from the splined end of the primary shaft, using a soft faced hammer.
3. With a press and adapters, remove the bearing and housing from the driveshaft.
4. Support the housing and press the bearing from the housing.

INSTALLATION

1. With a press and adapters, press the bearing into the housing.

NOTE: The bearing is a sealed, factory lubricated unit with built-in colored seals. The red seal must face the transmission case while the black seal must face the right wheel, when assembled.

2. Press the bearing and housing assembly onto the driveshaft followed by the dirt shield.

NOTE: Be sure the bearing seats to the shoulder on the shaft flange.

3. Tap the universal joint in place on the splined end of the primary shaft with a soft faced hammer.

Bellows

REMOVAL

1. Separate the driveshafts as in the driveshaft removal procedure.
2. Remove the clamps from the bellows and slide the bellows on the shaft to expose the retaining ring for the constant velocity joint.
3. Remove the retaining ring and constant velocity joint, allowing the bellows to be slipped from the driveshaft.

INSTALLATION

1. Install the bellows on the shaft.
2. Install the coolant velocity joint and retaining ring. Clamp the bellows in the proper position.

NOTE: Be sure the bellows clamps are crimped securely.

3. Reassemble the driveshafts as required.

Front Wheel Bearings

REMOVAL

1. Remove the center cap, hub retaining nut, and washer. Loosen the wheel lug bolts.
2. Raise the vehicle and support it safely. Remove the wheel.
3. Remove the caliper and hang it by wire from the body.

CAUTION

Do not allow the caliper weight to hang from the brake hose.

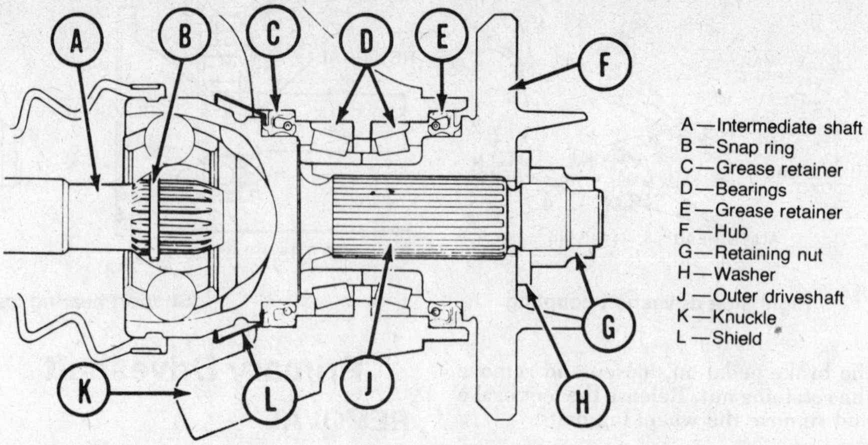

Front wheel bearings and grease retainer locations

4. Remove the hub and disc assembly.

NOTE: A puller may be needed to remove the hub from the shaft.

5. Remove the tie rod end from the steering arm.
6. Remove the lower arm to body mounting retaining bolt and pull down the inner end of the arm.
7. Separate the ball joint from the knuckle by removal of the ball joint clinch bolt.
8. Remove the top mount to apron panel retaining bolts.
9. Support the driveshaft at the outer constant velocity joint and pull the knuckle clear of the driveshaft and out of the vehicle.
10. Mount the unit in a vise or other support, and carefully remove the dust shield from the groove in the knuckle.
11. Using a slide hammer and seal remover, remove the inner and outer grease retainers and bearings.
12. Drive out the bearing cups.

INSTALLATION

1. Install new bearing cups into the knuckle. Make sure the cups are properly seated.
2. Pack the new bearings with grease and install them in their races.
3. Using a seal driver, install the grease retainers.
4. Gently tap the disc shield into position in the groove on the inner face of the knuckle.

NOTE: Align the cutout portion of the shield at the bottom, in line with the ball joint.

5. Position the knuckle assembly in the vehicle over the end of the driveshaft.
6. Install the top mount in the apron panel and install two bolts.
7. Reconnect the lower ball joint to the knuckle. Install the clinch bolt and the lower arm inner pivot bolt.
8. Reinstall the tie rod end to the steering arm. Tighten and install a new cotter pin.
9. Install the splined end of the driveshaft through the hub and disc assembly.
10. Mount the brake caliper and install the mounting bolts.
11. Install the wheel, snug the lug bolts, and lower the vehicle to the ground.
12. Securely tighten the lug bolts and torque the hub retaining nut to 180 to 200 ft/lbs. Stake the retaining nut to the slot in the driveshaft.

Stub Shaft

REMOVAL

1. Raise the vehicle and support it safely.
2. Remove the six Allen headed bolts from the left driveshaft inner constant velocity joint to left stub shaft flange.

NOTE: Support the intermediate driveshaft with a wire to the vehicle underbody to avoid unnecessary strain to the constant velocity joint.

3. Place a container under the stub axle to be removed, and lever the stub axle out of the differential side gear.

NOTE: Tapping the lever with a hammer may be necessary to overcome the retainer ring resistance.

4. Using a seal remover tool, remove the seal from the transaxle housing.
5. Disconnect the right intermediate driveshaft from the primary driveshaft by removing the six Allen headed bolts.

NOTE: Support the intermediate driveshaft by wire.

6. Remove the two bolts securing the pri-

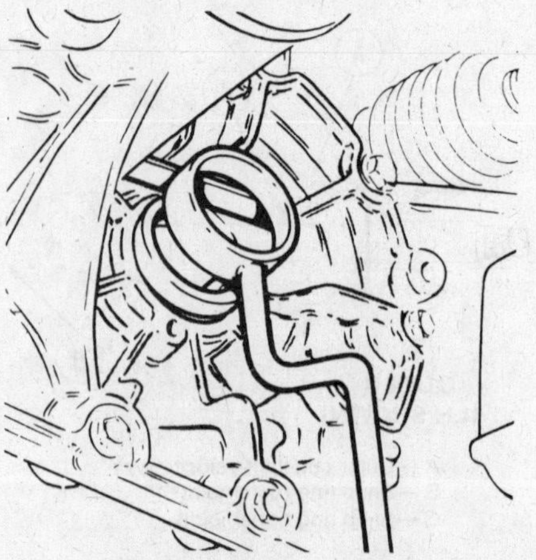

Stub shaft seal removal

mary shaft bearing housing to the bracket and relocate the shaft from the stub shaft.

7. Loosen the bearing support bracket at the engine block.

NOTE: It is necessary to loosen the bearing bracket to avoid any stress or misalignment during assembly.

8. Insert a long slender drift or other tool through the differential at the left stub shaft opening and force the right stub shaft out by firm blows.

NOTE: Do not allow the stub shaft to drop.

9. Remove the right oil seal from the transaxle housing with a seal remover tool.

INSTALLATION

1. Install new left and right oil seals in the transaxle housing.
2. Install a new retaining ring on the stub axle shafts.

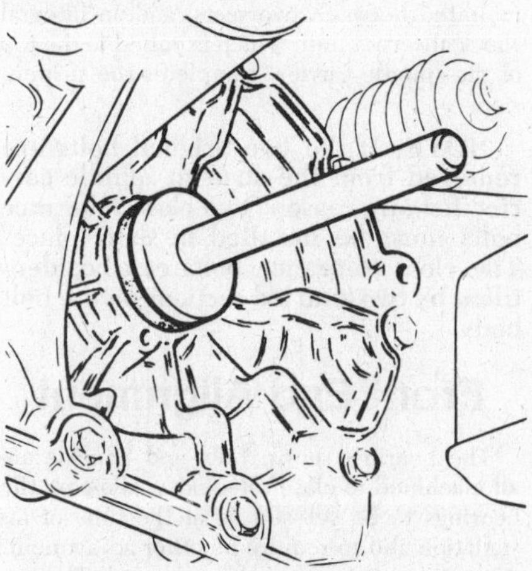

Stub shaft seal installation

3. Beginning at either side, position a stub axle into the transaxle opening. With the aid of a soft faced hammer, bump the stub axle into place. Repeat the process with the second stub axle shaft.

NOTE: The stub shaft will be felt to snap into place as the retaining ring mates with the inner face of the differential side gears.

4. Repack the constant velocity joint with grease. Align the primary shaft and universal joint assembly to the stub shaft and slide it into position.
5. Align the bearing housing to the support bracket. Install the bolts.
6. Align the inner right constant velocity joint and secure it with the six Allen headed bolts. Torque to 28 to 32 ft/lbs.

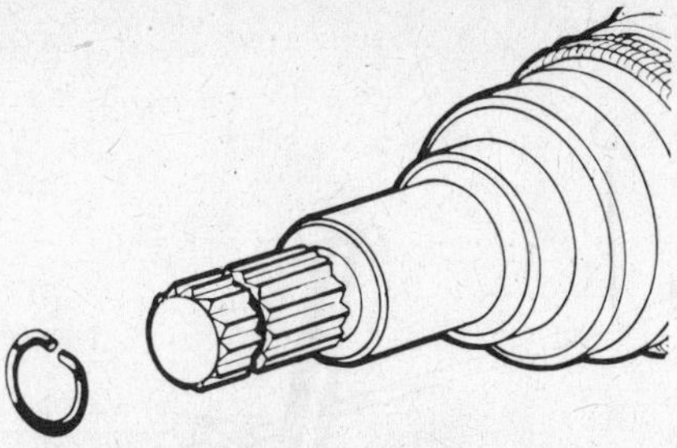

Left stub shaft retaining ring location

7. Align the left side constant velocity joint to the left side stub shaft and secure with the six Allen headed bolts. Torque to 28 to 32 ft/lbs.
8. Tighten the bearing support bracket to the engine block, add transmission oil as necessary, and lower the vehicle to the floor.

REAR SUSPENSION

The rear axle is of tubular construction. Coil springs, a Panhard (transverse) rod, shock absorbers, and lower control arms are used to stabilize the axle assembly to the vehicle body. A stabilizer bar is used as an option to help control the roll effect on turns.

Rear Axle and Suspension Assembly

REMOVAL

1. Loosen the rear wheel lug bolts, raise the car and support it safely both front and rear. Remove the wheels.
2. Loosen the exhaust pipe at the exhaust manifold. Release the pipe from the rear supports and lower the exhaust system.
3. Disconnect the handbrake cable from the adjuster. Remove the hydraulic lines at the axle.
4. Remove the Panhard (transverse) rod bolts from both the body and the axle. Remove the rod.
5. Position a jack under the center of the axle and remove the lower arm bolts from the body bracket.
6. Remove the two stabilizer bar to body bracket retaining nuts, if any.
7. Raise the tailgate and parcel tray, remove the plastic caps, and detach the shock absorber upper mounting nuts and washers. Note the location of the rubber insulators.

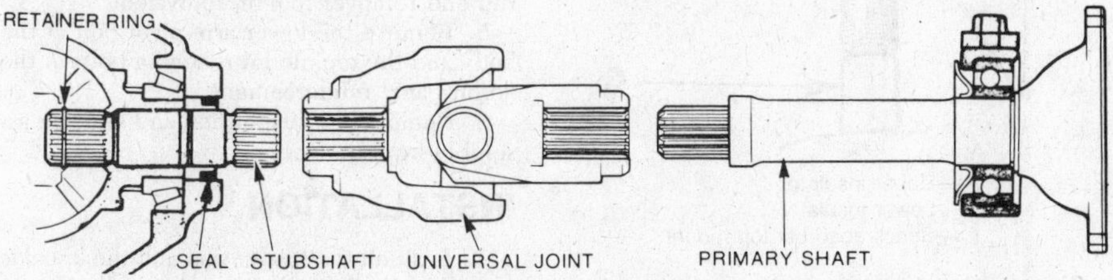

Exploded view of right stub shaft, universal joint, and primary shaft

8. Lower the axle assembly and remove it from under the vehicle.

INSTALLATION

1. Position the rear assembly under the vehicle. Position the springs and insulator pads and raise the assembly to the vehicle body. Connect the lower arms to the body.
2. Connect the shock absorbers at the upper mounts and replace the plastic caps.
3. Connect the stabilizer bar to body brackets and install the retaining nuts.
4. Connect the Panhard (transverse) rod to the body and axle and tighten securely.
5. Connect the brake lines at the axle.
6. Connect the handbrake cable at the adjuster.

NOTE: Refer to the brake section for handbrake adjustment and hydraulic system bleeding.

7. Mount the exhaust system to the rear supports and secure the pipe at the exhaust manifold.
8. Install the wheels, lower the vehicle to the floor, tighten the lower arms and the wheel lug bolts.

Rear Springs

Rear spring removal requires the same procedures as removal of the rear axle and suspension assembly.

Installation is the reverse of removal.

NOTE: During the installation of the springs, be sure the spring tang end butts are on the axle spring seats.

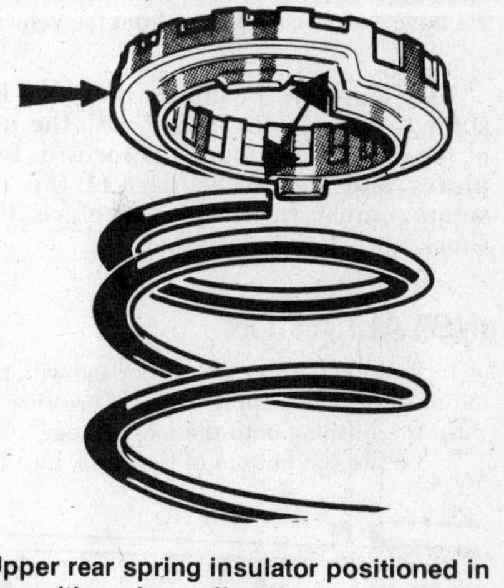

Upper rear spring insulator positioned in line with spring coil end

Lower Arms

The lower arms are removed by supporting the rear axle and removing the front and rear attaching bolts. Reinstall the arms in the reverse of the removal.

Shock Absorbers

REMOVAL

1. Loosen the rear wheel lug bolts, raise the vehicle and support it safely. Remove the wheel.

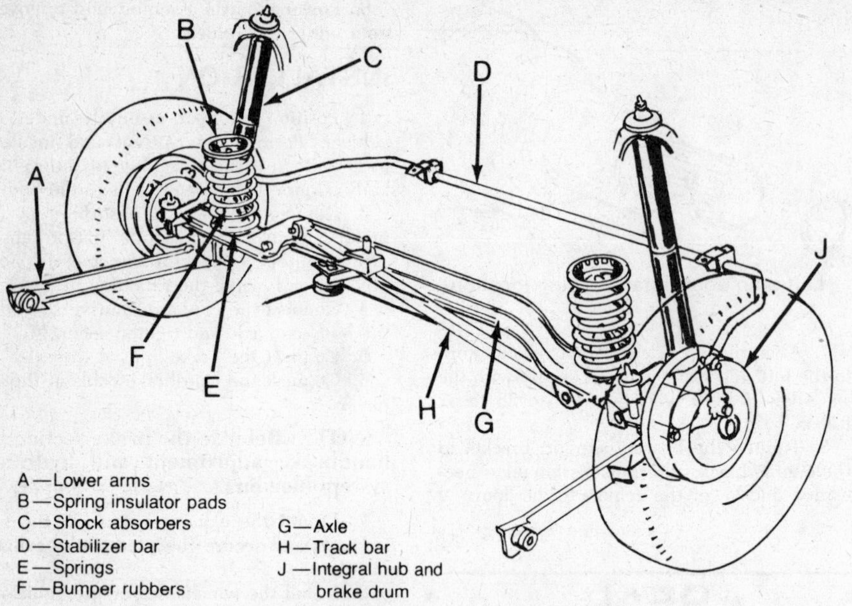

A—Lower arms
B—Spring insulator pads
C—Shock absorbers
D—Stabilizer bar
E—Springs
F—Bumper rubbers
G—Axle
H—Track bar
J—Integral hub and brake drum

Rear axle and suspension assembly

2. Position a jack under the rear axle to spring tension.
3. Remove the plastic cap from the inner upper fender panel and remove the nut and washer assembly from the shock absorber upper mount. Note the positioning of the insulator for installation.
4. Remove the bolt from the lower shock mounting.
5. With the aid of a lever, remove the shock absorber arm from the locating peg. Remove the shock absorber from the vehicle.

NOTE: New bushings may be installed in the lower mount with the use of lubricant. The top insulator is in two pieces and the lower part of the insulator must be in place before the shock absorber is installed.

INSTALLATION

1. Position the shock absorber and with the aid of a flat lever, apply a steady pressure to push the bushing onto the locating peg.
2. Locate the bottom of the shock into the mount and install the bolt and nut. Tighten securely.
3. With the top insulator properly positioned, install the upper mounting nut and washer. Reinstall the plastic cap on the inner fender panel.
4. Replace the wheel, lower the vehicle to the floor and tighten the wheel lug bolts.

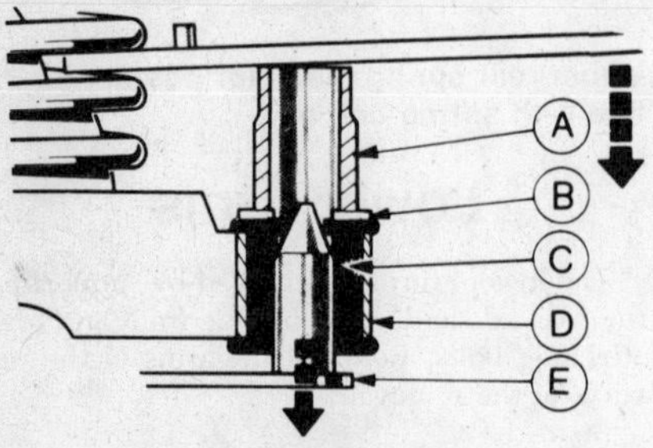

A—Hollow tube or socket
B—Washer
C—Rubber bushing
D—Rubber bushing housing
E—Peg base

Installing bushing over shock absorber locating peg with a flat lever and socket

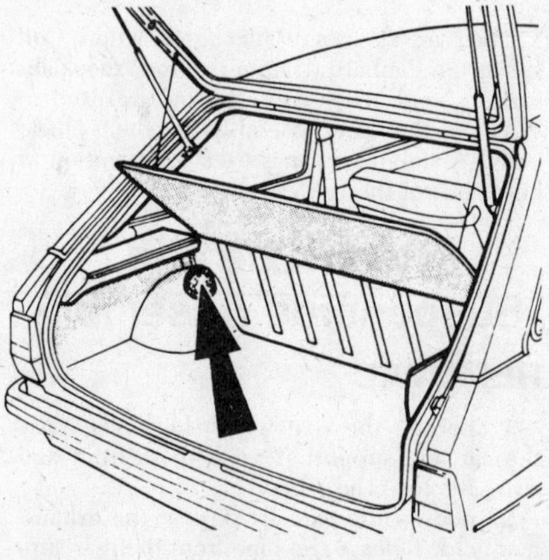

Location of upper shock mount—left side shown

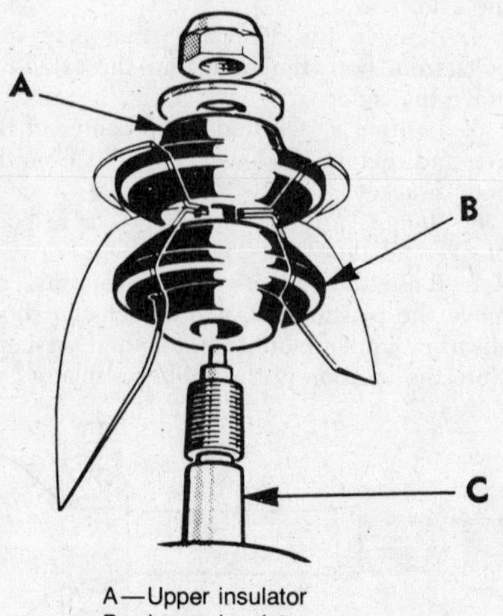

A—Upper insulator
B—Lower insulator
C—Shock absorber top mount

Shock absorber upper mounting insulators

FRONT SUSPENSION

The front suspension used on the Fiesta is of the MacPherson strut design. A conventional lower control arm with a bolt on ball joint is used, attached to a spindle carrier by the ball joint spindle and retained by a clinch bolt. A rubber top mount, a coil spring mounted between two seats, and an integral shock absorber unit, which is bolted to the top of the spindle carrier, completes the suspension.

NOTE: If the two original bolts are removed from the strut to spindle carrier for any reason, two close tolerance bolts must be installed in their place. The close tolerance bolts can be identified by two knurled sections on the bolt body.

Front End Alignment

The bearings, cups, hub, and knuckle are all machined to close tolerances, allowing the bearings to be self-setting at the time of installation and to require no other adjustment. A retaining nut and washer are used. The nut is retained to the driveshaft by staking.

Rever to the Drive Axle section for bearing, cup, or seal replacement procedures.

Suspension and Spindle Carrier Assembly

REMOVAL

1. Loosen the wheel lug bolts, raise car and support safely. Remove the road wheels.
2. Disconnect the flexible brake hose and plug the end to prevent fluid loss.
3. Remove the tie bar mounting bracket from the body.
4. Remove the tie rod end cotter pin and retaining nut. Remove the tie rod end from the steering arm with the use of a special tie rod end remover tool or equivalent.
5. Remove the lower arm pivot bolt at the body and the top mount retaining bolts at the apron panel reinforcement.
6. Remove the suspension and knuckle assembly from the vehicle.

INSTALLATION

1. Position the suspension and the knuckle assembly in the vehicle and install the top mount bolts.

2. Connect the lower arm to the body bracket.
3. Connect the tie rod end to the steering arm and install the nut and new cotter pin.
4. Connect the tie bar mounting bracket to the body reinforcement.
5. Connect the brake flexible hose and bleed the affected brake.
6. Install the wheels, lower the vehicle to the floor and tighten the wheel lug bolts.

Suspension Strut

REMOVAL

1. Loosen the wheel lug bolts, raise the front of the vehicle, and support it safely. Remove the wheel.
2. Remove the suspension strut to spindle carrier retaining bolts.
3. Remove the two top mounted apron panel retaining bolts and remove the suspension strut assembly from the vehicle.

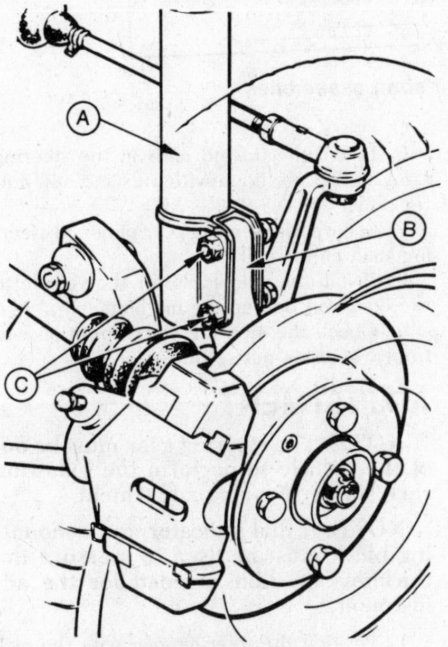

A—Front suspension strut
B—Knuckle
C—Strut to knuckle retaining nuts and bolts

Front suspension strut retaining bolt location

INSTALLATION

1. Position the suspension assembly into the vehicle and secure the top mount to the apron panel by the retaining bolts.
2. Install two close tolerance bolts to retain the suspension strut to the spindle carrier, replacing the regular production bolts removed.

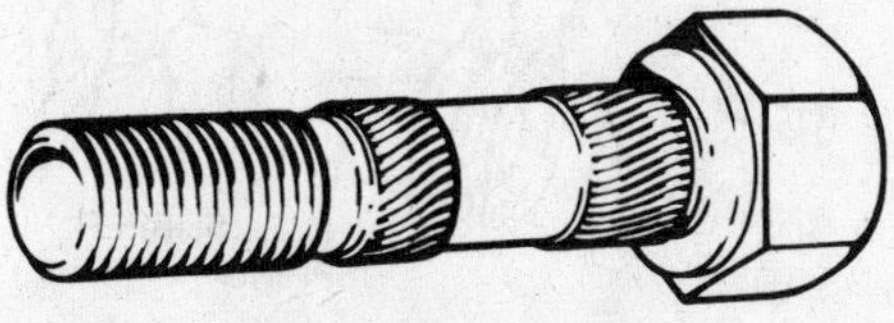

Close tolerance bolts

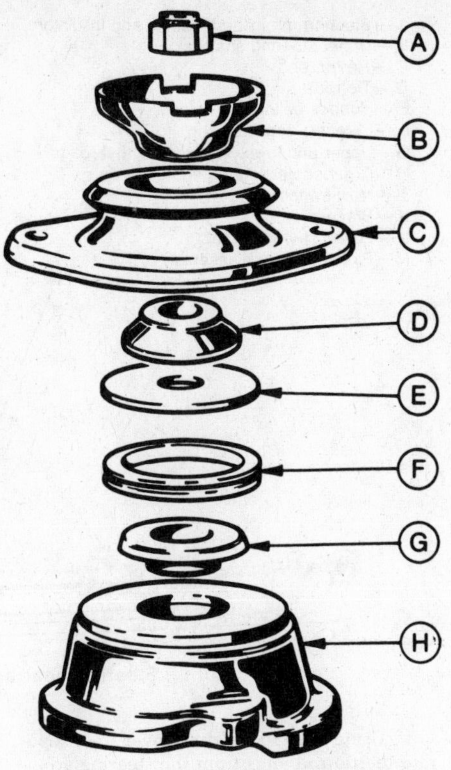

A—Nut
B—Retainer
C—Top mount
D—Spacer
E—Thrust washer
F—Rubber seal
G—Phenolic resin bearing
H—Upper spring seat

Top strut mount components

NOTE: The close tolerance bolts can be identified by two knurled sections on the bolt body.

3. Mount the wheel, lower the vehicle to the floor, and tighten the wheel lug bolts.

NOTE: It is advisable to check the wheel toe-out setting.

DISASSEMBLY (UNIT REMOVED FROM VEHICLE)

1. Install a spring compressor tool to the coil spring and compress the spring to relieve the tension from the top mount assembly.
2. Remove the top mount retaining nut while holding the top of the piston rod with a 6 mm Allen wrench in the socket provided.
3. Disassemble the top mount assembly and separate the spring from the strut assembly.

CAUTION

The spring will be under much more tension than normal while the compressor tool is in place. If the spring is not to be replaced and the compressor tool is left on the spring, locate the spring in a safe place until ready for use.

ASSEMBLY

1. Install the spring over the strut assembly.

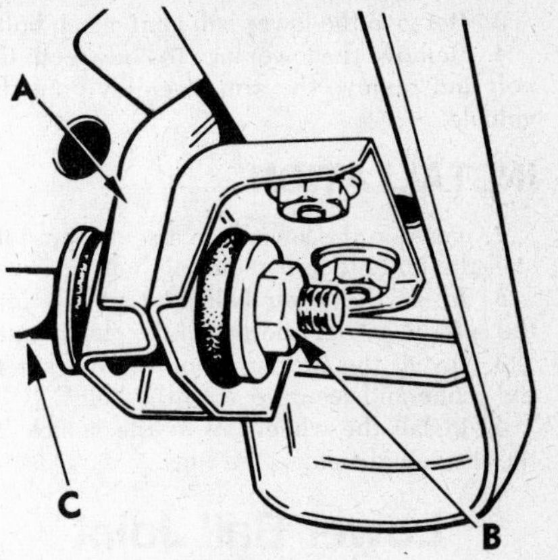

A—Mounting bracket
B—Retaining nut
C—Tie bar

Front tie bar body mount assembly

2. Assemble the top mount components to the strut.
3. Install the top mount retaining nut, and tighten it while holding the strut piston with the Allen wrench.
4. Release the spring compressor tool and check that the spring ends seat correctly in the top and bottom spring seats.

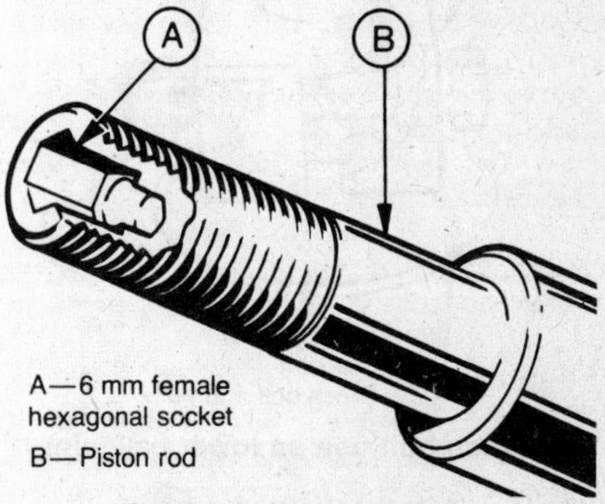

A—6 mm female hexagonal socket
B—Piston rod

Strut top piston socket

Lower Control Arm

REMOVAL

1. Loosen the wheel lug bolts, raise the vehicle and support it safely. Remove the wheel.
2. Remove the tie-bar to body mount bracket assembly.

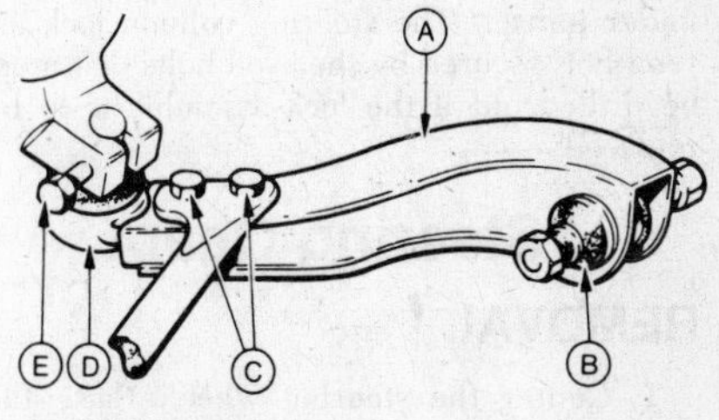

A—Lower arm
B—Lower arm bushing
C—Tie bar and ball joint to lower arm retaining bolts
D—Lower arm ball joint
E—Ball joint to knuckle clinch bolt

Lower arm components

3. Remove the lower ball joint clinch bolt.
4. Remove the lower arm to body retaining bolt and remove the arm assembly from the vehicle.

INSTALLATION

1. Position the lower arm assembly and install the body to arm retaining bolt.
2. Insert the lower ball joint spindle into the spindle carrier and install the clinch bolt.
3. Install the tie bar mounting bracket to the frame and secure it with the bolts.
4. Install the wheel, lower the vehicle to the floor, and tighten the lugs.

Lower Ball Joint

REPLACEMENT (VEHICLE RAISED OFF FLOOR)

The lower ball joint can be replaced by removing the clinch bolt holding the ball joint spindle to the spindle carrier and the two tie bar retaining bolts. Position the new ball joint and install the retaining bolts and the clinch bolt. The toe-out setting should be checked to complete the repairs.

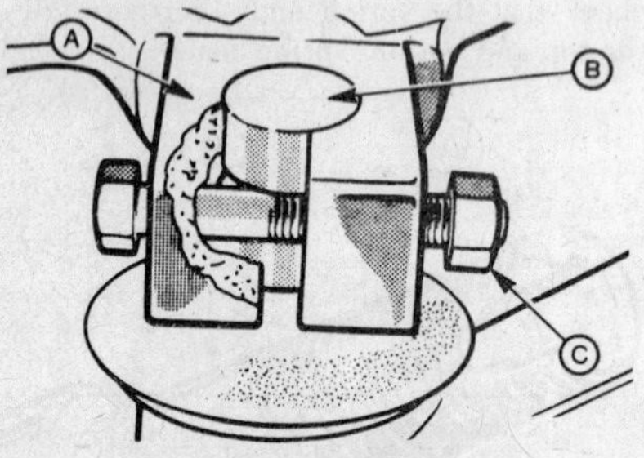

A—Knuckle body
B—Ball joint
C—Clinch bolt and nut

Clinch bolt use on lower ball joint

STEERING

The steering system is comprised of a rack and pinion unit, mounted to the engine compartment rear firewall, with tie rods linked to the steering arms of the spindle carrier.

The steering column assembly is a two piece tubular shaft type, designed to collapse under impact. The steering column lock assembly is secured by shear-off bolts that must be drilled out if the lock assembly is to be replaced.

Steering Gear

REMOVAL

1. Center the steering wheel. Raise the front of the vehicle and support it safely. Remove the front wheels.
2. Remove the clinch bolt holding the steering gear pinion to the lower steering shaft.
3. Remove the left and right tie rod end retaining cotter pins and nuts.

A—Steering mounting brackets and insulators
B—Upper steering shaft
C—Tie rod ends
D—Tie rods
E—Rubber bellows
F—Steering gear housing
G—Upper and lower steering shaft shrouds
H—Collapsable steering shaft coupling
J—Multi-switches
K—Brace
L—Lower steering shaft
M—Pinion and rack assembly

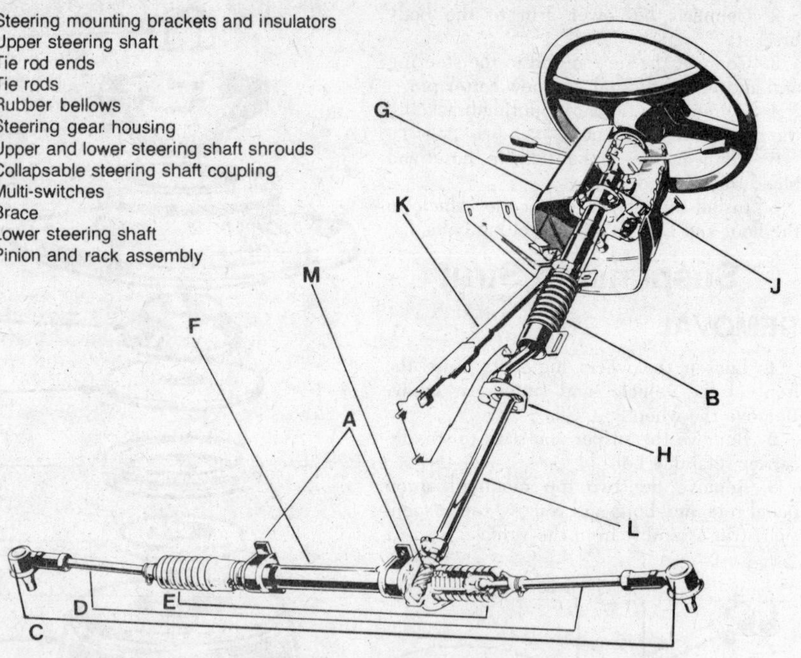

Steering gear and shaft assemblies

4. Using a tie rod end remover tool, separate the tie rod ends from the steering arms.
5. Straighten the lock tabs on the steering gear retaining bolts and clamps and remove.
6. Carefully remove the steering gear from the vehicle. Remove the rack clamp insulators.

NOTE: If the tie rod ends are removed, count the number of turns necessary to disconnect them.

INSTALLATION

1. Install the tie rod ends using the same number of turns required to remove each.
2. Install the rack clamp mounting insulators.
3. Set the steering wheel and steering gear in the straight ahead position.
4. Locate the steering gear in the vehicle and engage the steering gear pinion to the steering shaft. Install the clamp and clinch bolt loosely.
5. Install the clamps over the insulators and install the retaining bolts with new lock tabs. Secure the bolts and bend the lock tabs over the bolt heads.

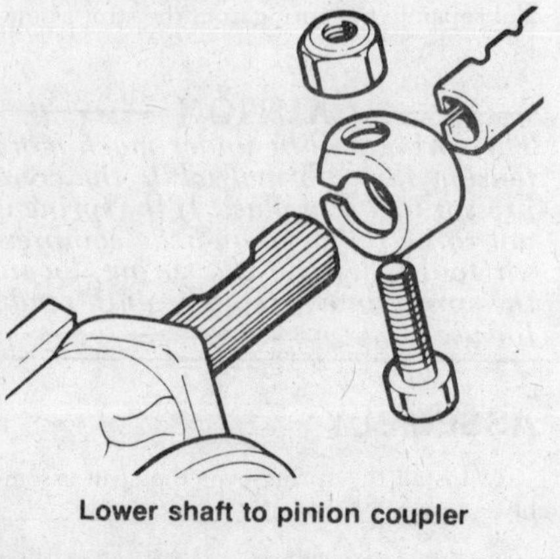

Lower shaft to pinion coupler

6. Install the tie rod ends in the steering arms and secure them with nuts and new cotter pins.
7. Secure the steering gear pinion to steering shaft clinch bolt.
8. Install the wheels, lower the vehicle to the floor and tighten the lug bolts.
9. Check the steering wheel position and front wheel toe-out setting.

ADJUSTMENT

NOTE: The steering gear must be out of the vehicle to perform the following rack slipper bearing adjustment.

NOTE: A dial indicator and a mounting block must be used to measure the thickness of shims needed for the adjustment.

1. Position the steering gear with the rack slipper bearing cover plate facing up.
2. Remove the cover plate, shim pack and gasket from the housing.
3. Place the dial indicator in the mounting block and zero the gauge. Remove the gauging discs and position the base of the tool against the slipper. The dial reading will indicate the thickness of the shim pack needed between the slipper and the outer cover.
4. Assemble the shim pack as per the dial indicator reading and preload by adding a 0.002 to 0.005 inch shim.

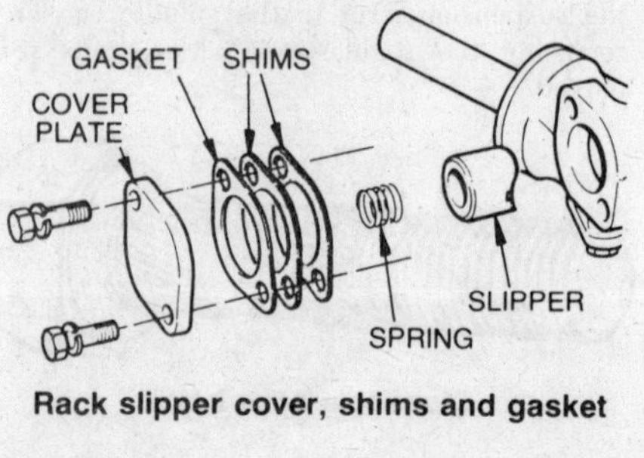

Rack slipper cover, shims and gasket

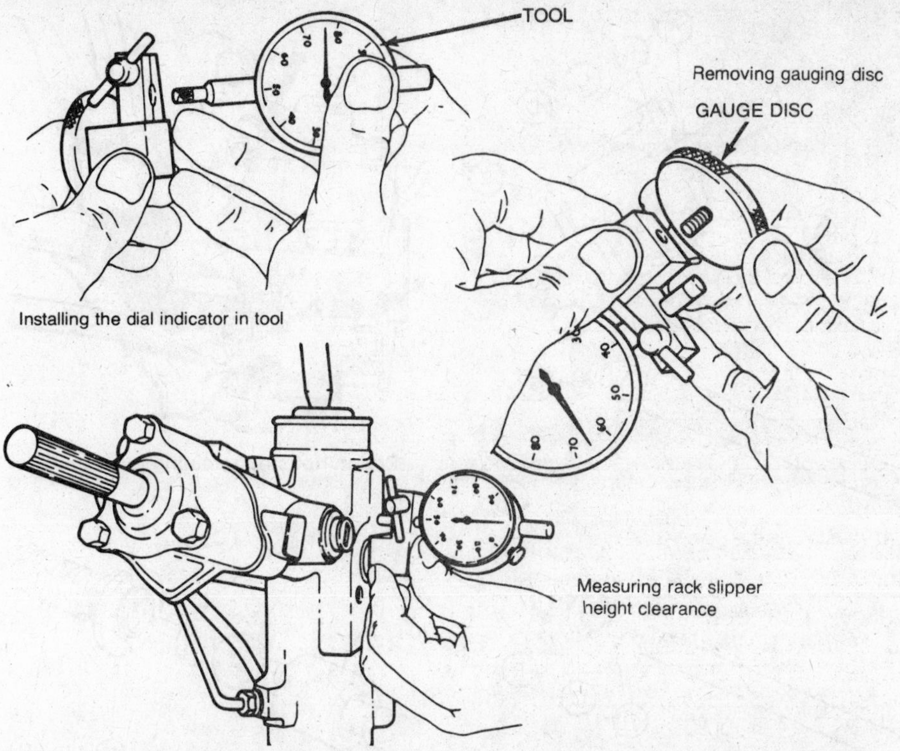

Use of dial indicator and mounting tool to measure rack slipper height clearance

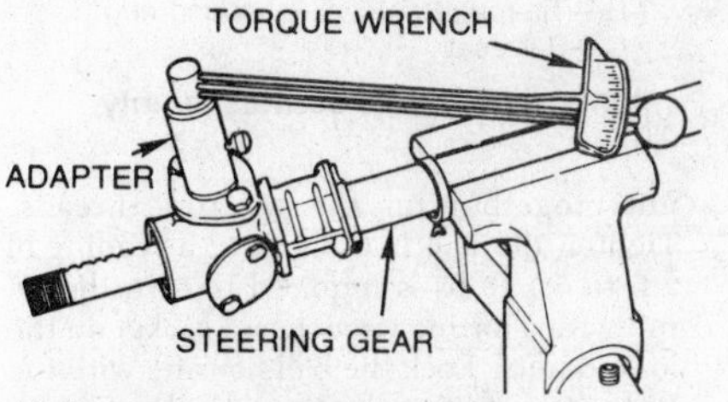

Using torque wrench to determine steering gear pinion resistance

5. Install the cover plate, the corrected shim pack and gasket on the gear housing.
6. Using an inch pound torque wrench, rotate the steering gear pinion at approximately 4 rpm. The torque reading should be in a range of 5 to 18 in/lbs.

Steering Wheel

REMOVAL AND INSTALLATION

1. Pry out the center steering wheel insert.
2. Remove the steering wheel retaining nut and lift the steering wheel from the shaft.

NOTE: Observe any match marks for alignment during installation.

3. Installation is the reverse of removal.

Combination Column Switch

REMOVAL AND INSTALLATION

1. Disconnect the ground battery cable.
2. Remove the steering wheel assembly and the turn signal direction indicator cam from the steering shaft.
3. Remove the steering column upper and lower shrouds.
4. Remove the attaching screws for the multi-lever switches and remove the wiring retaining clip from the column tube.
5. Disconnect the wiring at the terminal connectors.
6. Installation of the switches is the reverse of removal.

Ignition Switch

REMOVAL

1. Disconnect the battery ground cable.

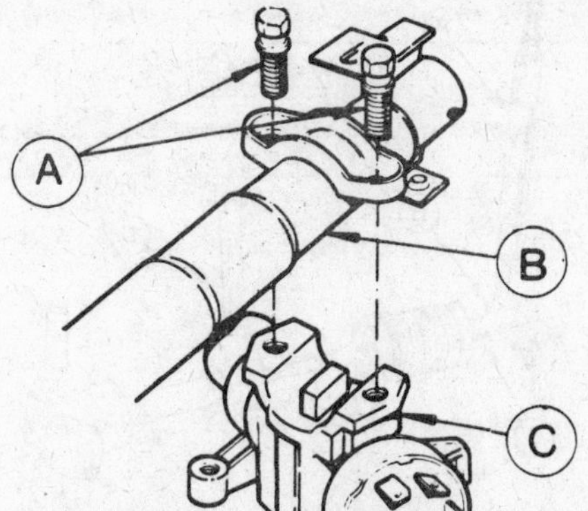

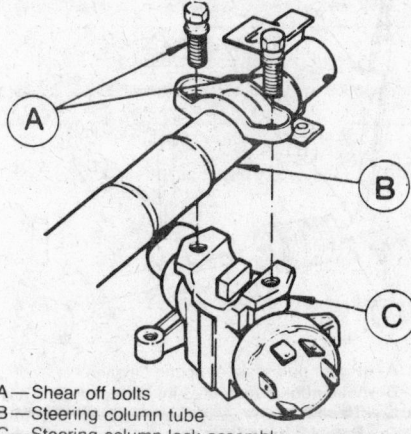

A—Shear off bolts
B—Steering column tube
C—Steering column lock assembly

Ignition switch location and shear-off bolts

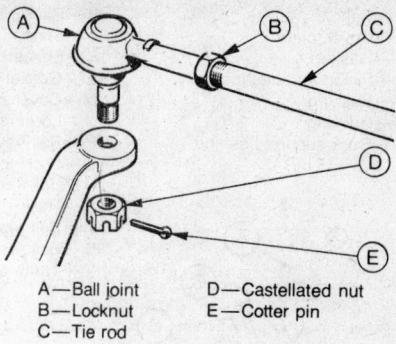

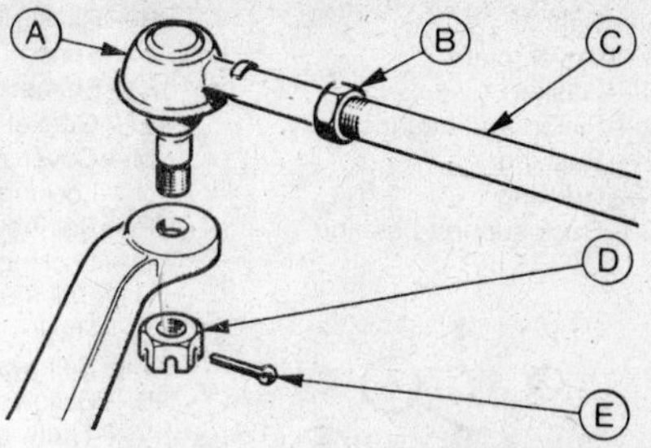

A—Ball joint
B—Locknut
C—Tie rod
D—Castellated nut
E—Cotter pin

Tie rod end assembly

2. Remove the upper and lower steering column shrouds.
3. Disconnect the ignition switch multi-wire plug.
4. Center punch and drill out the two lock retaining bolts and remove the ignition switch.

INSTALLATION

1. Position the ignition switch on the steering column and install new shear bolts.
2. Tighten the shear bolts until the heads break off.
3. Attach the ignition switch multi-wire plug.
4. Install the column upper and lower shrouds.
5. Connect the battery ground cable and check the ignition switch operation.

Steering Linkage

TIE ROD END REMOVAL AND INSTALLATION

The tie rod end is removed from the steering arm by removal of the cotter pin and castellated nut from the tie rod end spindle. Use a tie rod end removal tool to separate the tie rod end from the steering arm. Install the tie rod end using the same number of turns that were necessary to remove it.

TIE ROD REMOVAL AND INSTALLATION

Pins secure the tie rod ball joint housing and locknut and must be drilled out before the locknut can be loosened.

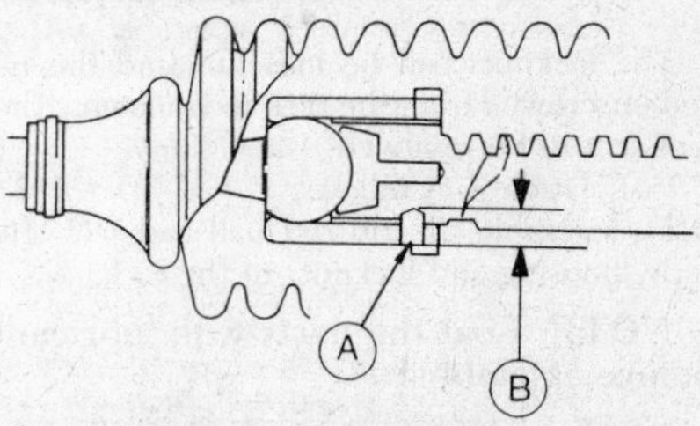

A—4.0 mm (5/32 in) dia. locking pin hole
B—Maximum depth 9.5 mm (0.4 in) deep

Drilling lock pin from locknut/ball housing

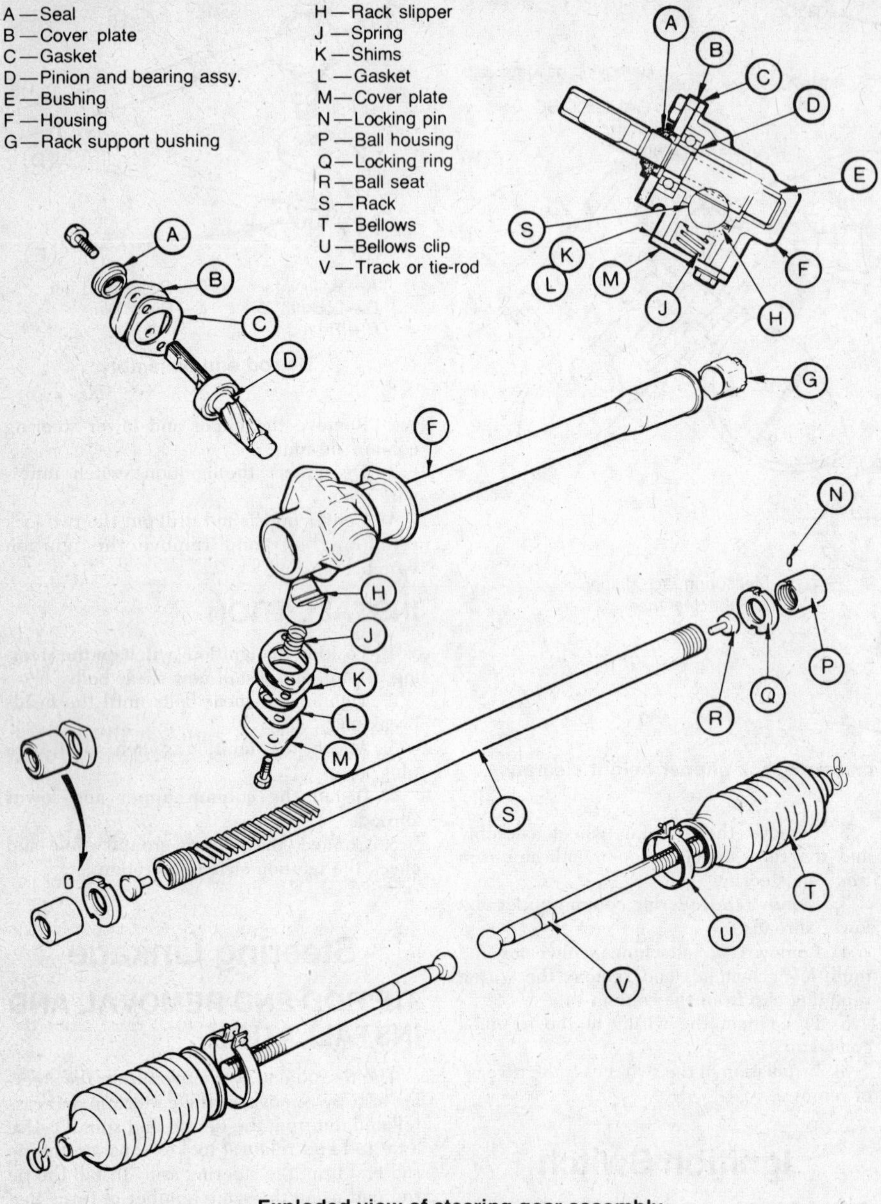

A—Seal
B—Cover plate
C—Gasket
D—Pinion and bearing assy.
E—Bushing
F—Housing
G—Rack support bushing
H—Rack slipper
J—Spring
K—Shims
L—Gasket
M—Cover plate
N—Locking pin
P—Ball housing
Q—Locking ring
R—Ball seat
S—Rack
T—Bellows
U—Bellows clip
V—Track or tie-rod

Exploded view of steering gear assembly

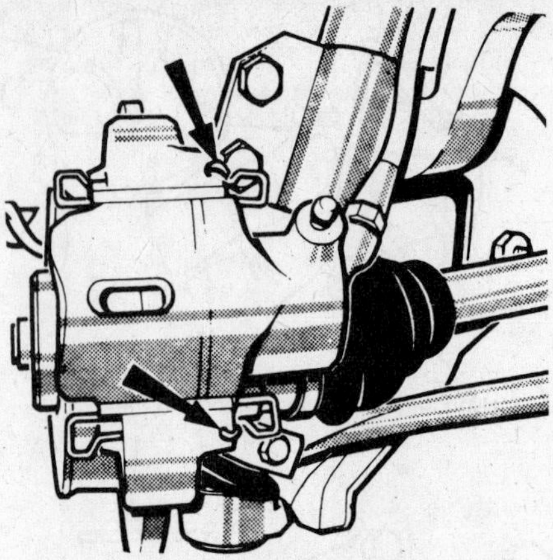

Piston housing retaining pin location

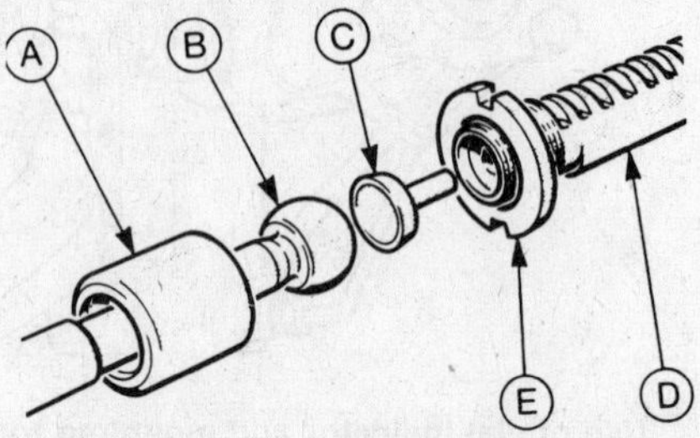

A—Housing
B—Tie-rod
C—Ball seat
D—Rack
E—Locking ring

Inner tie rod ball seat assembly

CAUTION

A 5/32 inch diameter drill bit with a 0.400 inch depth stop must be used. Do not drill deeper than 0.400 inch. A special tool is available for use in the drilling operation.

The locknuts can be loosened and the tie rod unscrewed from the rack rod, allowing the ball seat to be removed.

Installation is as follows:

1. Assemble the tie rod ball and seat, tie rods, housing and locknuts to the rack.

NOTE: Coat the parts with lubricant before assembly.

2. Adjust the tie rod movement resistance by tightening the housing and locknuts and measuring the resistance by one of the following methods:

a. Remove the tie rod end and lock two nuts together on the tie rod threads. Tighten the ball housing until a reading of 2.6 to 5.1 ft/lbs is required to turn the tie rod with a torque wrench and socket on the locked nuts. Lock the ball housing with the locknut and rotate the tie rod at least seven times. Recheck the resistance to verify that it still remains within specifications. Remove the two locknuts and reinstall the tie rod end.

b. With a piston pull gauge attached to the tie rod approximately ¼ in. from the end, measure the effort required to move the tie rod. The reading should be 5.1 lbs. Lock the ball housing with the locknut and recheck the effort.

3. Center punch and drill a hole on the housing to locknut mating faces, using a 5/32 inch drill bit with a stop adjusted to 0.400 inch. Drill a new hole, even if the old hole lines up.

4. Install new retaining pins in the drilled holes and retain them by peening over the surrounding metal with a punch.

5. Install the rack bellows and retain them in position with clamps.

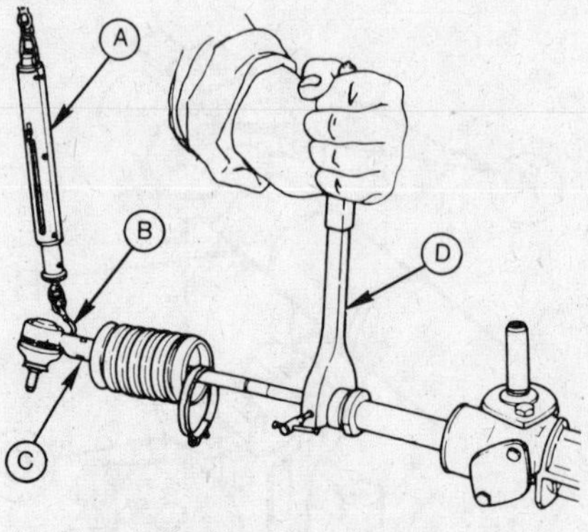

A—Piston pull scale or spring balance
B—Wire hook 6 mm (0.25 in) from end of tie rod
C—Tie-rod
D—Ball joint housing spanner

Checking tie rod movement effort with a scale gauge

BRAKE SYSTEM

The Fiesta is equipped with a dual hydraulic brake system, using disc brakes on the front wheels and drum brakes on the rear wheels.

The hydraulic system is split diagonally, so that one front and the opposite rear brake are in one circuit, while the remaining front and opposite rear brakes are in the second circuit.

Any brake imbalance created is overcome by the front suspension design.

A power brake unit is available as an option.

Master Cylinder

REMOVAL

1. Disconnect the battery ground cable.
2. Remove the brake fluid from the master cylinder reservoir and detach the pressure lines from the cylinder body.

NOTE: Install plugs in the fluid line ports to avoid leakage.

3. Remove the switch wires from the brake differential pressure valve.
4. Remove the spring clip, clevis pin and bushing from the pedal and master cylinder pushrod.
5. Remove the attaching nuts and washers from the studs and remove the master cylinder from the firewall.

INSTALLATION

1. Position the master cylinder on the firewall and secure with the nuts and washers.
2. Remove the plugs from the fluid line ports. Attach the fluid lines to the cylinder body and tighten securely.
3. Install the clevis pin and bushing in the brake pedal, connect the master cylinder pushrod, and secure with the spring clip.
4. Fill the master cylinder reservoir with brake fluid and bleed the system.
5. Connect the battery ground cable and road test the vehicle.

Brake System Bleeding

The following is the Ford Motor Co. approved method of brake system air bleeding for the Fiesta.

1. Raise the front and rear of the vehicle and support it safely.

CAUTION

Keep the car level.

2. Check that both reservoir sections are filled with brake fluid.
3. Remove the rubber dust shield from the bleed nipple of the left front wheel. Install a bleed tube on the nipple with the other end in a glass jar containing brake fluid.

CAUTION

During the bleeding operation, the end of the tube must be kept immersed in the fluid.

4. Position the glass jar at least 12 inches *above* the bleed nipple to insure that the bleed nipple is subjected to fluid pressure and to prevent air leaking past the threads of the nipple.
5. Open the bleed nipple, depress the brake pedal fully, and allow it to return to the off position. Two people are needed to do this.

NOTE: The fluid and/or air will be pumped into the jar.

6. Wait for approximately 3-5 seconds between pedal strokes to allow the cylinder to refill. Keep depressing the brake pedal and releasing it until the fluid entering the glass jar is clean and free of air. Tighten the bleeder nipple.
7. Repeat steps 3 to 6 for the right front brake cylinder.
8. Bleed each rear brake the same as the front.

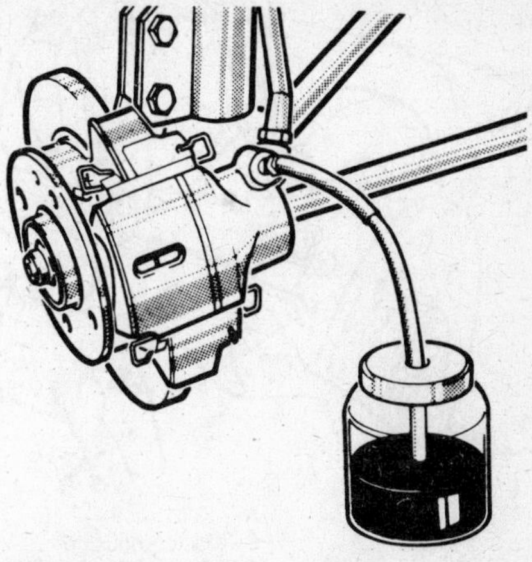

Use of bleed tube and glass jar to bleed brake system

NOTE: During the bleeding operation, the master cylinder reservoir must be kept filled.

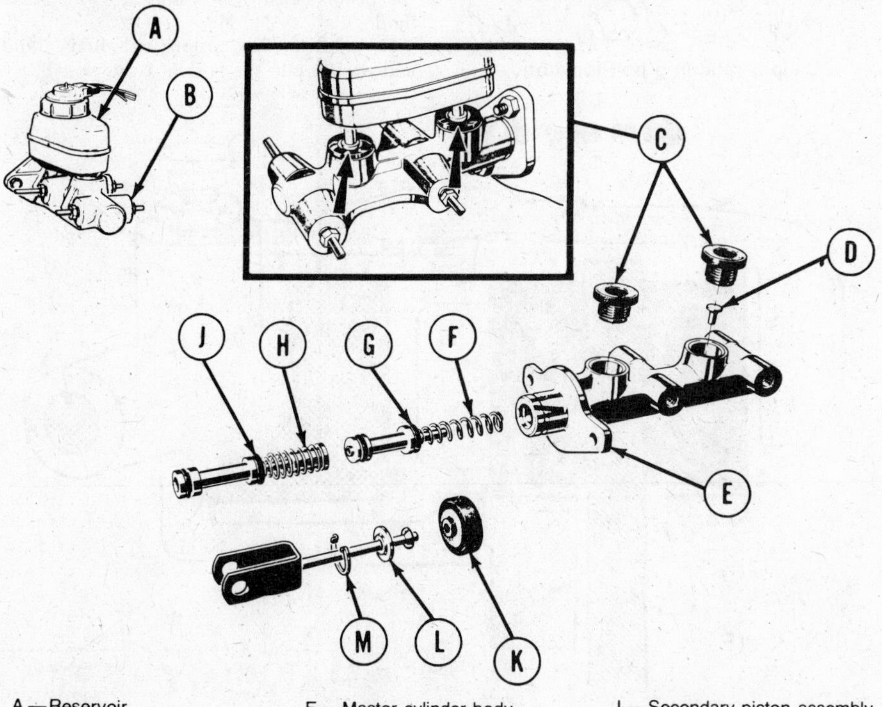

A—Reservoir
B—Master cylinder assembly
C—Rubber seals
D—Check valve
E—Master cylinder body
F—Primary return spring
G—Primary piston assembly
H—Secondary return spring
J—Secondary piston assembly
K—Boot
L—Operating rod seal
M—Snap ring

Exploded view of master cylinder

Power Brake Servo

REMOVAL

1. Follow the procedure for removal of the master cylinder.
2. Remove the spring clip and clevis pin securing the actuating rod to the brake pedal.
3. Disconnect the vacuum hose from the vacuum valve at the servo unit.
4. Remove the four nuts and washers retaining the servo unit to the firewall studs.

INSTALLATION

1. Secure the power brake servo to the firewall studs with the retaining nuts and washers.
2. Install the vacuum hose to the vacuum valve nipple.
3. Install the clevis pin in the actuating rod and pedal. Retain the pin with the spring clip.
4. Reinstall the master cylinder to the power brake servo unit. Bleed the hydraulic system.

Front Brake Pads

REMOVAL

1. Loosen the wheel lug bolts, raise the front of the car, and support it safely. Remove the wheels.
2. Remove the retaining pins, apply pressure to the piston housing, against the tension springs, and remove the key.
3. Remove the caliper piston housing and suspend it from the vehicle body by a wire.

NOTE: Do not allow the caliper to hang from the flexible brake hose.

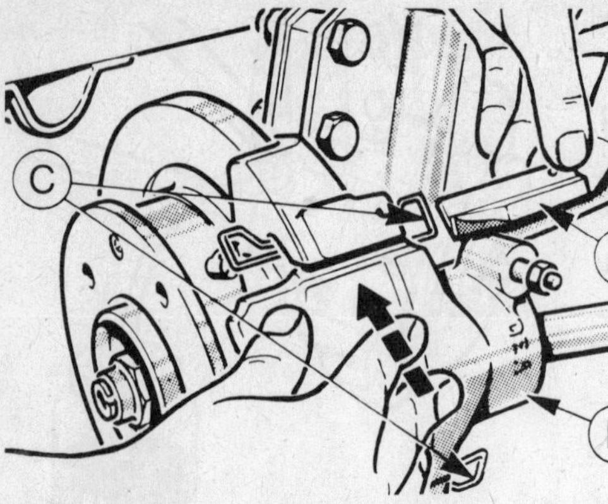

A—Key
B—Piston housing
C—Caliper tension springs

Removing or installing keys between piston housing and pad housing

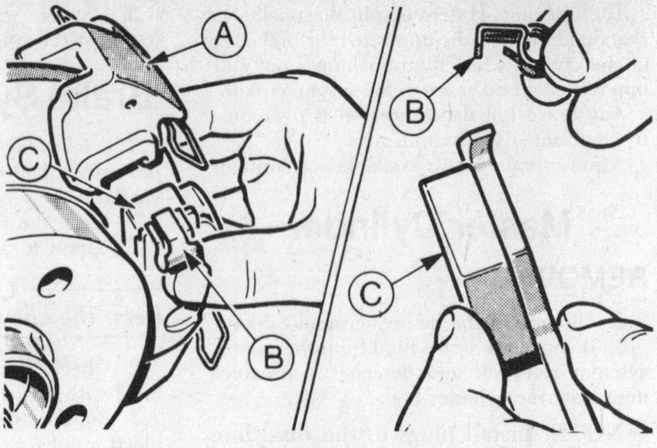

A—Pad housing
B—Anti-rattle clip
C—Brake pad

Fitting anti-rattle clips on brake pads

4. Remove the disc pads and anti-rattle clips from the piston housing.
5. Repeat the operation on the opposite side.

INSTALLATION

1. Push the piston into its bore by applying pressure to the face of the piston.

NOTE: It may be necessary to remove a small portion of brake fluid from the master cylinder reservoir to accommodate the displaced fluid.

2. Install new disc pads and new anti-rattle clips into the pad housing.

NOTE: The anti-rattle clips must be placed at the top of the brake pad.

3. Install the caliper piston housing so that it is mounted above the tension springs.
4. Apply pressure against the caliper tension spring and slide in a new key. Align the retaining pin holes in the key and piston housing.
5. Install new retaining pins from the disc side and secure.
6. Repeat the operation on the opposite side. Operate the brakes several times to seat the disc pads in the correct position.
7. Correct the fluid level, install the wheels, lower the vehicle and tighten the wheel lug bolts.

Front Brake Caliper Assembly

REMOVAL AND INSTALLATION

1. Loosen the wheels, raise the front of the vehicle, and support it safely. Remove the wheels.
2. Remove the flexible line from the caliper and plug the line port.
3. Remove the two caliper retaining bolts and remove the caliper from the support.
4. To install the caliper assembly, reverse the removal procedure. Torque the two caliper retaining bolts to 37 to 45 ft/lbs.
5. Refer to Brake System Bleeding to bleed the hydraulic system.

OVERHAUL

1. Refer to Caliper Removal and Installation for the caliper removal procedure.
2. Remove the piston rubber bellows.
3. Apply air pressure to the piston through the brake fluid inlet port and force the piston from its bore.

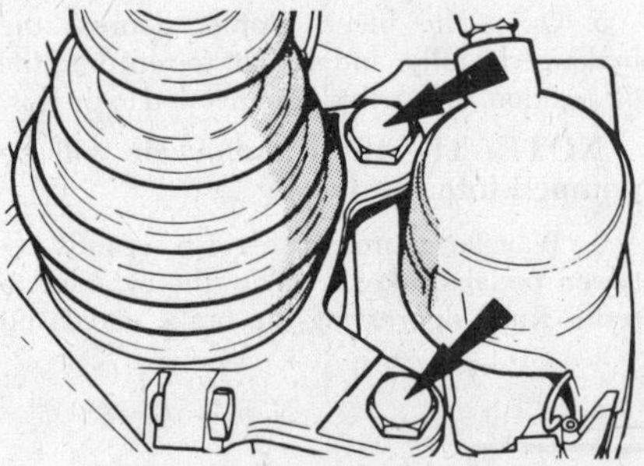

Caliper retaining bolt location

CAUTION

Do not allow your fingers to be caught between the piston and caliper body when air pressure is applied.

4. Remove the piston seal from its annular groove in the piston housing.
5. Clean the piston and caliper housing in approved cleaners; alcohol, methylated spirits or brake fluid.

CAUTION

Do not use gasoline or other petroleum based liquids.

6. Assemble the piston seal in its groove in the piston housing and lubricate with brake fluid.
7. Lubricate the piston with brake fluid and push it into the bore as far as possible.

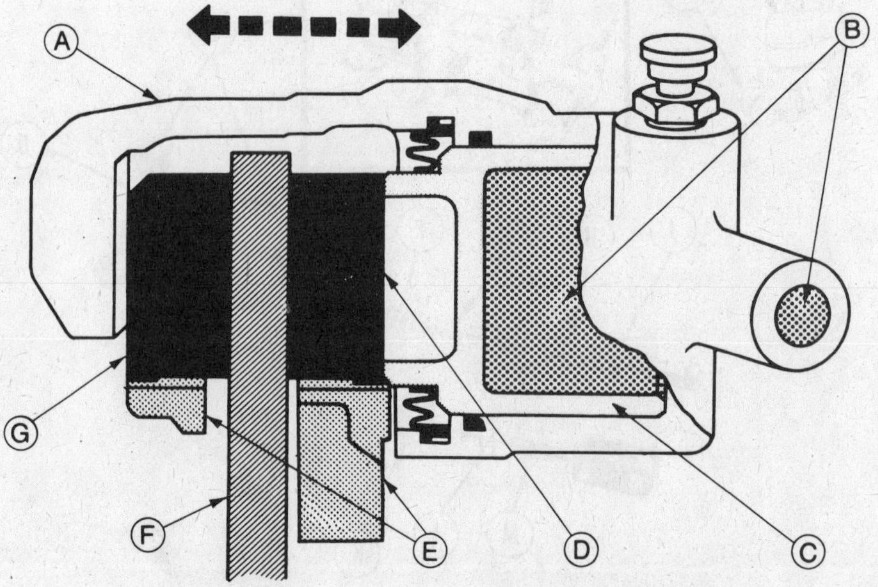

A—Piston housing
B—Brake fluid
C—Piston
D—Inner brake pad
E—Pad housing (anchor bracket)
F—Brake disc
G—Outer brake pad

Cross section of caliper brake assembly

8. Install the rubber bellows between the piston housing and piston.
9. Reinstall the caliper. Bleed the hydraulic system.

Disc

REMOVAL AND INSTALLATION

The disc is retained by the wheel lug bolts and a single retaining screw.

To remove the disc, remove the wheel, caliper assembly, the retaining screw, and lift the disc from the hub.

To install the disc, reverse the removal procedure.

NOTE: Do not allow the weight of the caliper to hang from the flexible brake hose. Support the caliper with wire.

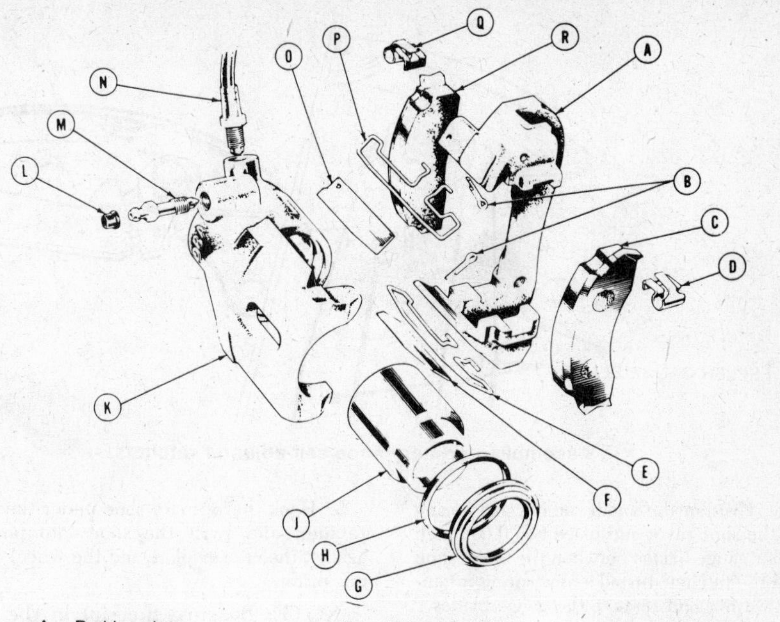

A—Pad housing
B—Retaining pins
C—Brake pad
D—Anti-rattle clip
E—Caliper tension spring
F—Key
G—Rubber bellows
H—Piston seal
J—Piston
K—Caliper housing
L—Dust cap
M—Bleed screw
N—Fluid hose
O—Key
P—Tension spring
Q—Anti-rattle clip
R—Brake pad

Exploded view of front disc brake assembly

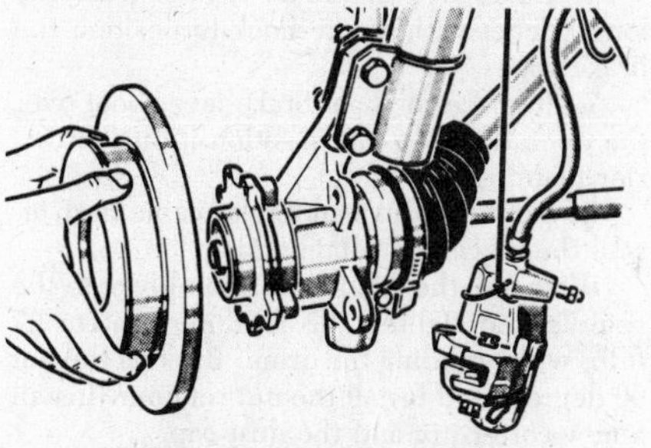

Disc removal from hub

Rear Brake Shoes

REMOVAL

1. Loosen the wheel lug bolts, raise the rear of the vehicle, and support it safely. Remove the wheels.
2. Fully release the handbrake and disconnect the cable from the lever at the rear wheel, by removing the spring clip and clevis pin. Remove the rubber dust cover from the brake carrier plate.
3. Remove the hub/drum assembly from the spindle by removing the retaining cotter pin and spindle nut.
4. Remove the brake shoe hold down spring from the primary shoe.

NOTE: The primary shoe has the self-adjusting mechanism mounted to the inside of the shoe.

5. Twist the shoe outward from the carrier plate and inward toward the spindle. Remove the shoe by detaching the shoe return springs.
6. Remove the secondary shoe hold down spring and slide the lower end of the spacer strut out of the slot in the carrier plate.
7. Twist the shoe upward and remove the handbrake operating lever and shoe as an assembly.
8. Separate the secondary shoe from the handbrake spacer strut by twisting and removing the spring.

INSTALLATION

Primary Shoe Assembly

NOTE: Replacement shoes may have the self-adjuster mechanism previously installed. If not, follow the following assembly procedure.

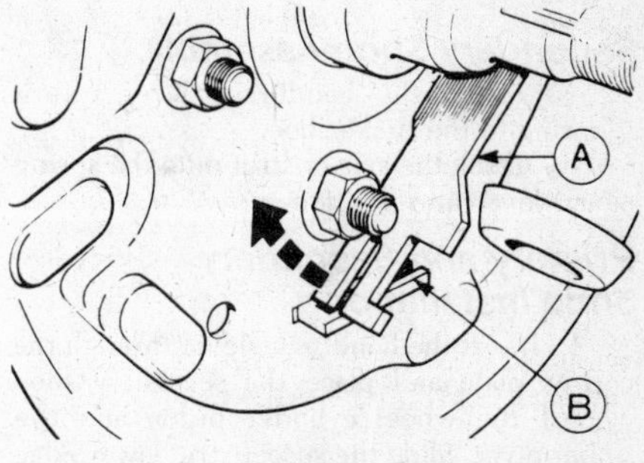

A—Spacer strut
B—Slot

Removing spacer strut from carrier plate

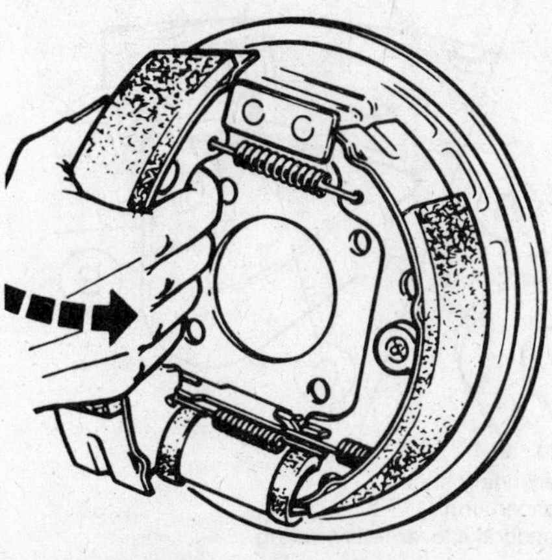

Removing primary shoe

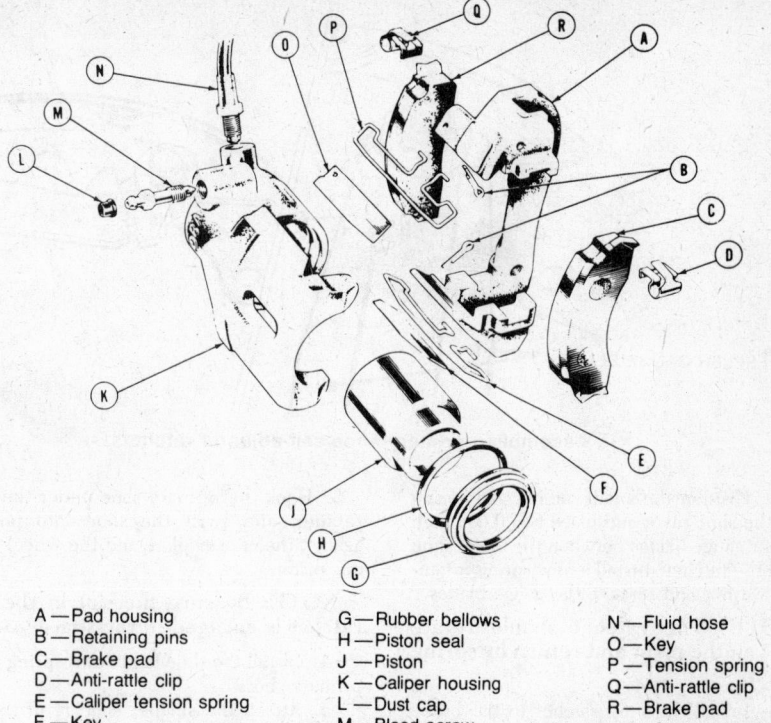

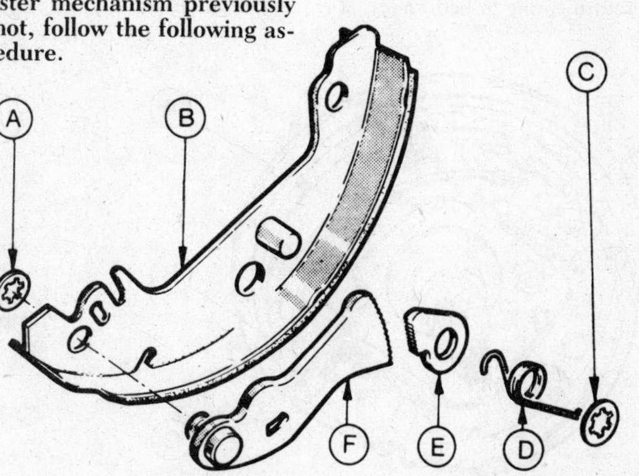

A—Spring washer
B—Primary shoe
C—Spring washer
D—Spring
E—Short ratchet
F—Long ratchet

Exploded view of primary shoe and self-adjusting mechanism

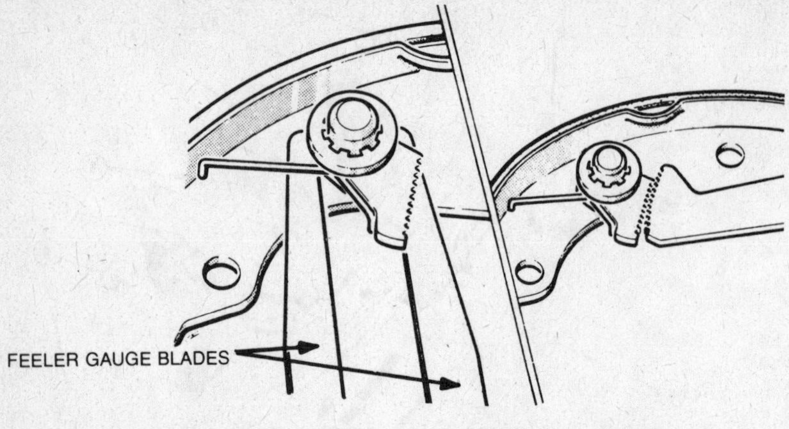

Assembling primary shoe self-adjuster ratchets

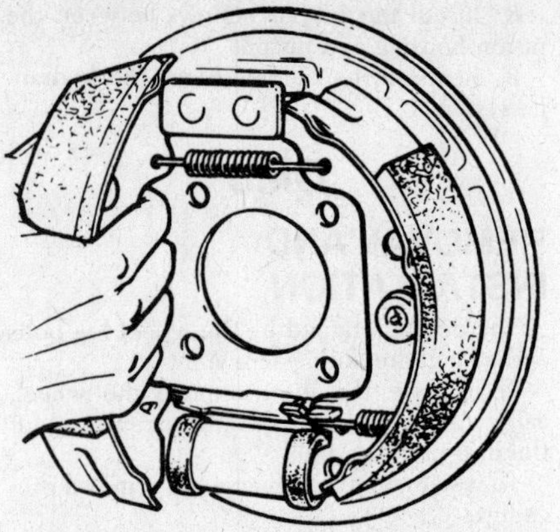

Installation of primary shoe to carrier plate

a. Position the small ratchet and spring on the shoe pivot and place two 0.008 inch feeler gauge blades between the brake shoe and the ratchet. Install a new spring retaining washer and remove the gauge blades.

NOTE: The ratchet should rotate freely on the pivot and return by spring tension.

b. Install the long ratchet to the brake shoe and install a new spring clip.

c. Position the two ratchets together with the long ratchet closer to the shoe web.

Secondary Shoe Assembly

a. Install the handbrake lever return spring to the brake shoe.

b. Hook the spacer strut onto the spring and lever into position

Primary and Secondary Shoe Installation

1. Insert the handbrake lever through the carrier plate and place the secondary shoe against the wheel cylinder piston and the upper pivot. Slide the spacer strut lower edge into the slot in the carrier plate and install the shoe hold down spring.
2. Position the primary shoe at a 90 degree angle to the carrier plate and connect the stronger shoe return spring to both shoes, at the pivot end.
3. Hook the primary shoe under the pivot retainer and twist the shoe into position against the carrier plate and the wheel cylinder piston.

NOTE: Be sure the slot in the long ratchet is engaged in the spacer strut.

4. Install the shoe hold down spring to the primary shoe.
5. Attach the smaller shoe return spring to the two shoes at the wheel cylinder end with the use of brake spring pliers or equivalent tool.

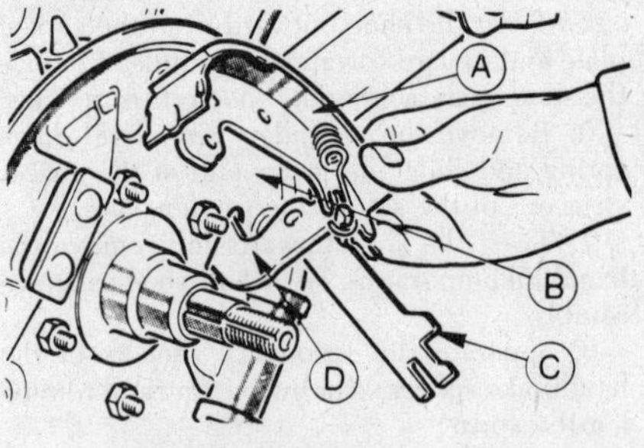

A—Secondary shoe
B—Carrier plate
C—Spacer strut
D—Handbrake operating lever

Removing hand brake lever and secondary shoe assembly

6. Disengage the small ratchet from the long ratchet with a wire hook to position the brake shoes.
7. Replace the handbrake lever boot over the operating arm and position it on the carrier plate.
8. Connect the handbrake cable and install the clevis pin retaining clip.
9. Install the drum/hub assembly onto the spindle and tighten the retaining nut to 27 ft/lbs while rotating the drum. Back off the nut 90 degrees and install the nut retainer. Install a new cotter pin and the dust cap.
10. Adjust the brakes by depressing the brake pedal several times to set self-adjusters.
11. Mount the wheels, lower the vehicle to the floor, and tighten the wheel lug bolts.
12. Road test to check brake operation.

Rear Wheel Cylinder

REMOVAL AND INSTALLATION

1. Remove the rear brake shoes.
2. Disconnect the brake line and plug to avoid fluid leakage.
3. Remove the two capscrews holding the wheel cylinder to the carrier plate and remove the cylinder.
4. Installation is the reverse of removal.
5. Bleed the brake system.

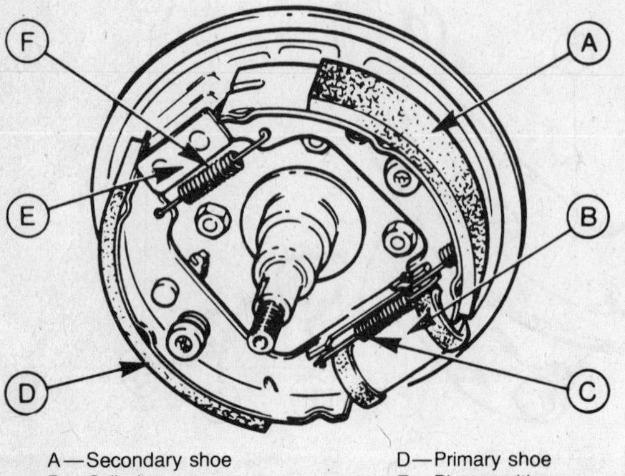

A—Secondary shoe
B—Cylinder
C—Spring—weaker
D—Primary shoe
E—Pivot position
F—Spring—stronger

Location of stronger and weaker springs

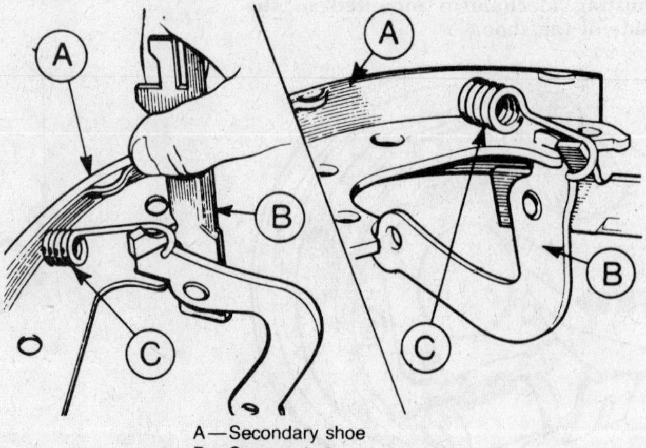

A—Secondary shoe
B—Spacer strut
C—Handbrake lever return spring

Assembling secondary shoe components

Rear Wheel Bearings

ADJUSTMENT

1. Tighten the retaining nut to 27 ft/lbs torque while rotating the wheel.
2. Back off the retaining nut 90 degrees and install the nut retainer, new cotter pin, and the dust cap.

Parking Brake

The parking brake is comprised of a floor mounted lever assembly, a primary or forward cable, left and right cables connected to an equalizer bracket assembly and to the rear wheel handbrake levers. Adjustment is made at the rear of the primary cable with an adjustment nut.

ADJUSTMENT

1. Raise the vehicle and support it safely.
2. Loosen the adjuster locknut and rotate the cable adjuster to put slack in the cable.
3. Tighten the cable until all slack is removed and the handbrake levers just begin to move off the back stops of the carrier plates.
4. Move the adjuster three complete turns and secure the locknut.

NOTE: After the adjustment is complete, the machined groove in the primary cable threaded shaft must not protrude past the locknut.

5. Be sure the rear brakes do not drag. Lower the vehicle to the floor.

CHASSIS ELECTRICAL

Heater Assembly

REMOVAL

1. Disconnect the battery ground cable.
2. Drain the cooling system and remove the heater hoses from the core tubes.
3. Remove the cover plate for the core tubes from the firewall. Plug the tubes to avoid leakage.
4. Remove the four screws holding the right and left lower dash trim panels.
5. Remove the ash tray and bracket.
6. Remove the two vent hoses from the heater assembly adapter.
7. Remove the heater assembly to instrument panel bracket and the two retaining nuts holding the heater assembly to the top cowl panel.
8. Pull the heater assembly rearward until the core tubes clear the firewall opening.
9. Disconnect the blower motor wires and remove the heater assembly, complete with the control panel, to the right and out of the vehicle.

INSTALLATION

1. Position the heater assembly into the

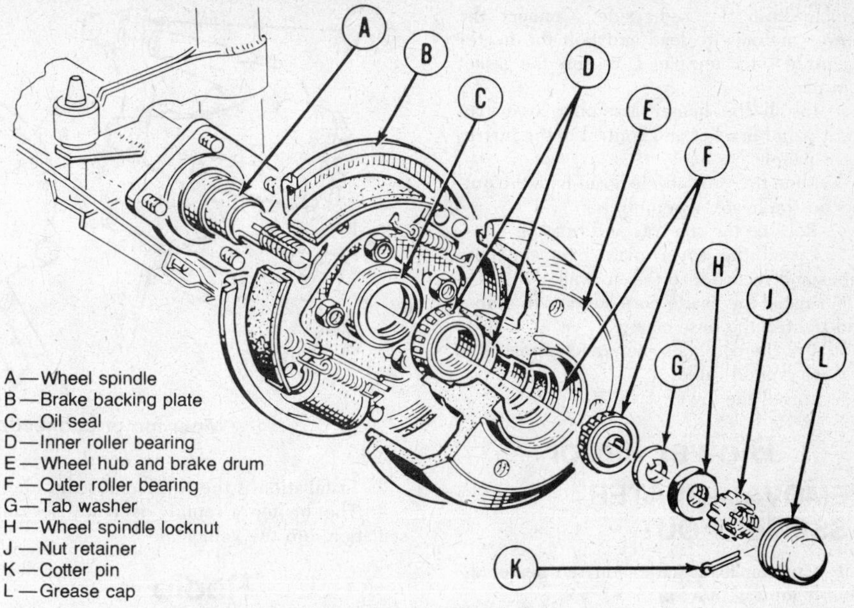

A—Wheel spindle
B—Brake backing plate
C—Oil seal
D—Inner roller bearing
E—Wheel hub and brake drum
F—Outer roller bearing
G—Tab washer
H—Wheel spindle locknut
J—Nut retainer
K—Cotter pin
L—Grease cap

Exploded view of rear wheel bearing assembly

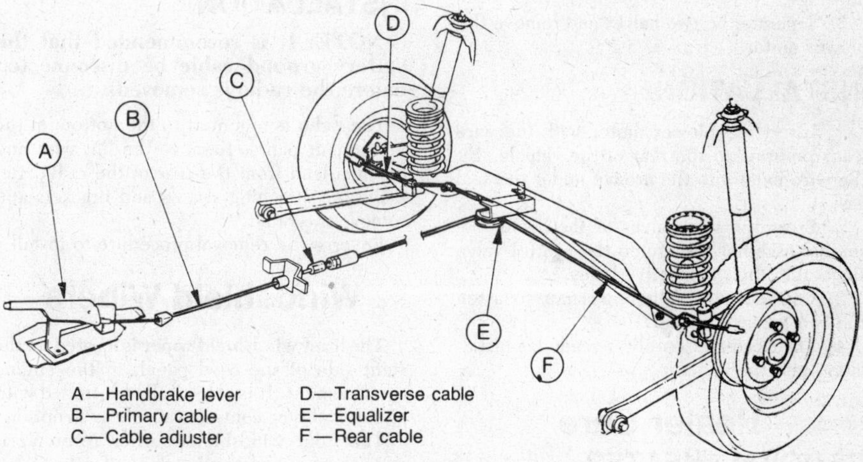

A—Handbrake lever
B—Primary cable
C—Cable adjuster
D—Transverse cable
E—Equalizer
F—Rear cable

Exploded view of hand brake components

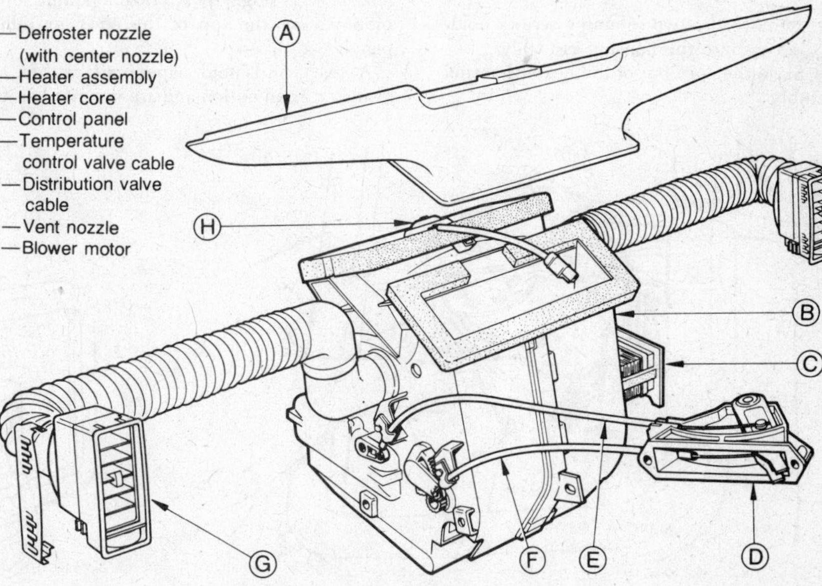

A—Defroster nozzle (with center nozzle)
B—Heater assembly
C—Heater core
D—Control panel
E—Temperature control valve cable
F—Distribution valve cable
G—Vent nozzle
H—Blower motor

Heater-defroster assembly with controls

vehicle from the right side. Connect the blower motor wire lead and bolt the heater assembly to the top panel. Be sure the gasket is in place.

2. Install the heater assembly to instrument panel bracket and control to the instrument panel.
3. Slide the vent nozzle hoses onto the outlets on the heater assembly.
4. Replace the ash tray and bracket.
5. Install the cover plate over the core tubes and secure it to the firewall.
6. Install the heater core hoses to the tubes and tighten the hose clamps.
7. Fill the cooling system and connect the battery ground cable.
8. Install the lower dash trim panels.

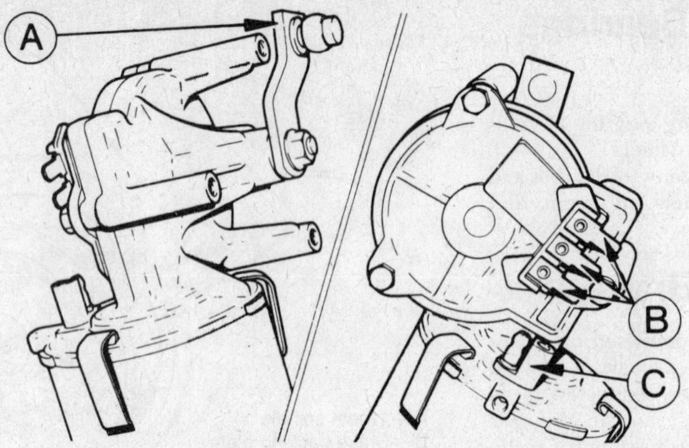

Wiper motor connections for linkage and wiring

Blower Motor

REMOVAL–HEATER ASSEMBLY OUT

1. Cut the foam gasket on the heater assembly joint with a knife.
2. Remove the two retaining clamps from the motor mounting and separate the two housings.
3. Separate the two halves and remove the blower motor.

INSTALLATION

1. Insert the blower motor with the wire leads pointing to the rear of the vehicle. Fit the wire loom into the groove under the seal gasket.
2. Press the two halves of the heater assembly together and guide the control valve shafts into their respective holes.
3. Use additional retaining clamps to fasten the two halves together.
4. The heater assembly is ready for installation into the vehicle.

Heater Core

REMOVAL–HEATER ASSEMBLY OUT

1. Remove the two retaining screws holding the core into the housing assembly.
2. Slide the core out of the heater housing assembly.
3. Installation is the reverse of removal.
4. The heater assembly is ready for installation into the vehicle.

Radio

REMOVAL AND INSTALLATION

NOTE: It is recommended that the battery ground cable be disconnected before the radio is removed.

The radio is mounted to the bottom of the instrument panel. Remove the hot wire and antenna lead from the rear of the radio. Remove the attaching screws and brackets and remove the radio.

Reverse the removal procedure to install.

Windshield Wipers

The front windshield wiper is located on the right side of the cowl panel, in the engine compartment. It is electrically controlled with an interval type control available as an option.

The front windshield washer reservoir is near the front of the left inner fender panel and is powered by an electric pump. The nozzle is a single post, dual opening unit, mounted on the top of the cowl air intake panel.

A rear windshield wiper and washer are available as an option and are mounted on the rear liftgate. The rear washer reservoir is on the left rear floor panel.

Front Wiper Motor

REMOVAL

1. Disconnect the battery ground cable.
2. Disconnect the two multi-plugs from the wiper motor
3. Remove the three mounting bolts and pull the wiper motor and bracket away from the cowl panel so that the wiper linkage is accessible.
4. Disconnect the wiper linkage from the wiper operating arm and remove the wiper motor from the vehicle.

INSTALLATION

1. Position the wiper motor and bracket to the cowl panel and install the wiper linkage to the motor operating arm.
2. Apply the sealer to the mating surfaces of the mounting bracket and the cowl panel.
3. Install the retaining bolts and tighten the motor bracket securely to the cowl panel.
4. Connect the two multi-plugs to the wiper motor and connect the battery ground cable.

Front Wiper Linkage

To service the wiper linkage, the hood lock

Blower motor retainer clip location

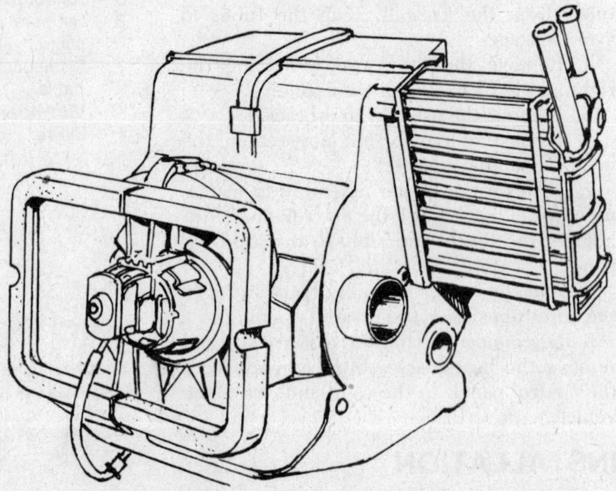
Heater core location in the heater assembly

mounting plate must be removed. The linkage is removed or replaced through the opening.

Wiper Arms

To remove or replace the wiper arms on the pivot shaft assemblies, lift the rear cover of the arm upward to expose the nut and washer used to retain the wiper arm to the pivot shaft.

Before installing the wiper arm, make sure the wiper motor is in the park position.

Instrument Cluster

REMOVAL AND INSTALLATION

1. Remove two retaining screws from the lower instrument panel cover and remove the cover, if any.
2. Grasp the speedometer cable lock and press in on the grooved section to disconnect the cable from the rear of the instrument cluster.
3. Remove the cluster bezel by pulling outward on the bezel opening sides.
4. Remove the instrument cluster retaining screws and move the cluster toward the steering wheel.
5. Disconnect the wiring connectors from the rear of the cluster and remove the cluster.
6. Installation is the reverse of removal.

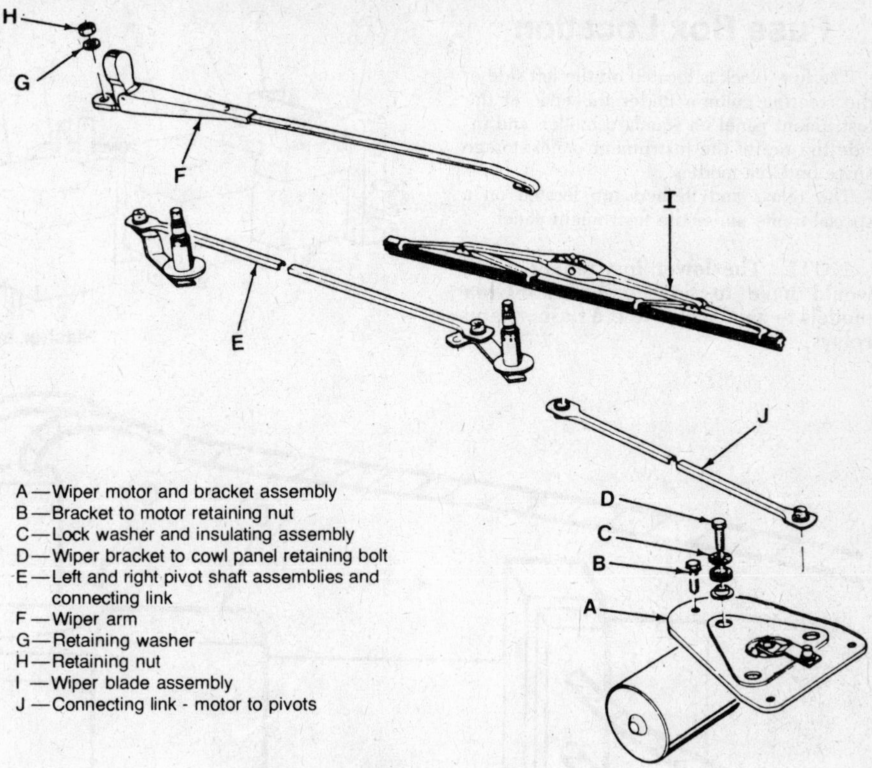

A—Wiper motor and bracket assembly
B—Bracket to motor retaining nut
C—Lock washer and insulating assembly
D—Wiper bracket to cowl panel retaining bolt
E—Left and right pivot shaft assemblies and connecting link
F—Wiper arm
G—Retaining washer
H—Retaining nut
I—Wiper blade assembly
J—Connecting link - motor to pivots

Exploded view of wiper components

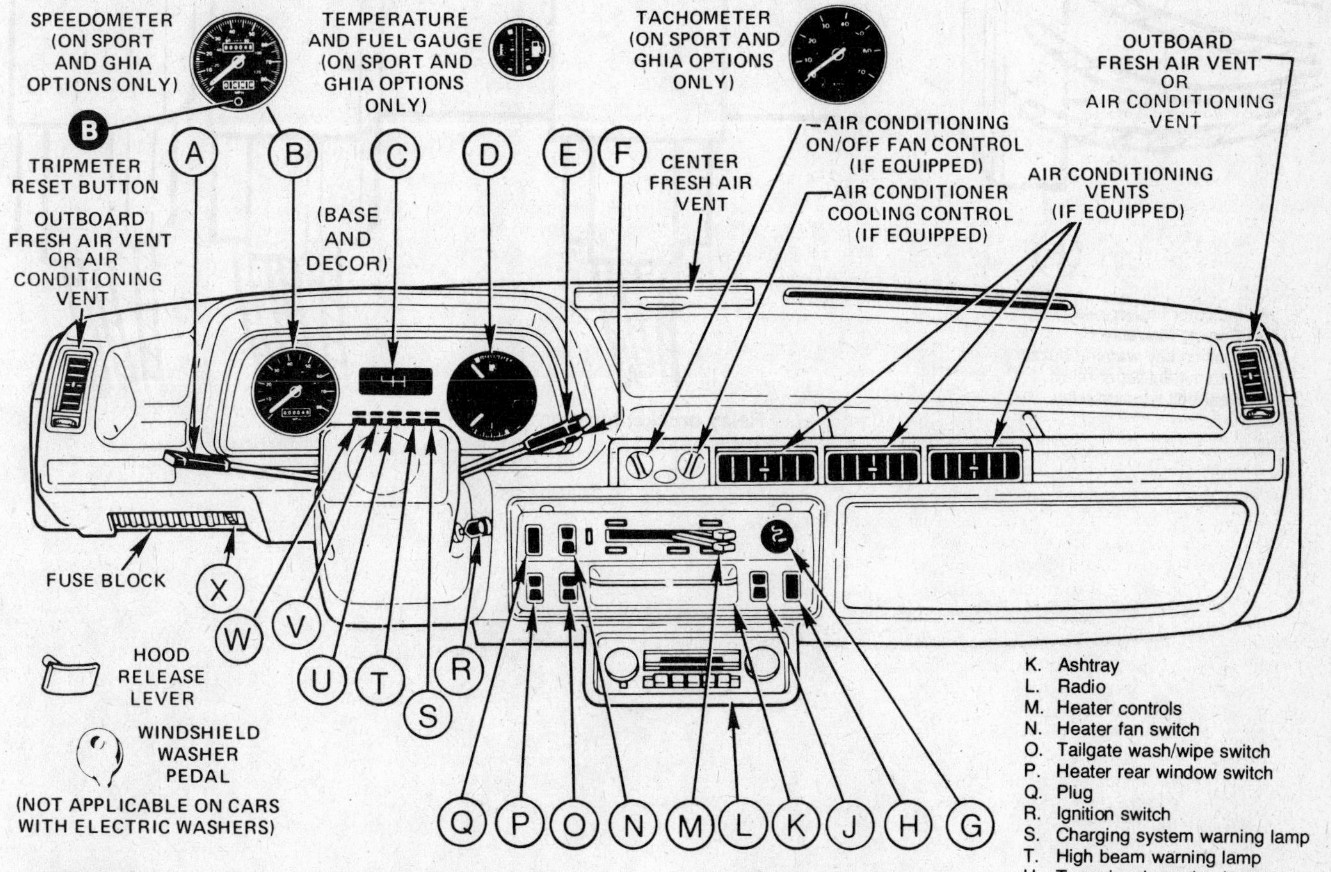

A. Multifunction lever
B. Speedometer
C. Shift pattern
D. Fuel temperature gauges
E. Headlamp lever
F. Windshield wash-wipe lever
G. Cigarette lighter
H. Seat belt warning lamp
J. Hazard flasher switch
K. Ashtray
L. Radio
M. Heater controls
N. Heater fan switch
O. Tailgate wash/wipe switch
P. Heater rear window switch
Q. Plug
R. Ignition switch
S. Charging system warning lamp
T. High beam warning lamp
U. Turn signal warning lamp
V. Parking brake warning lamp
W. Oil pressure brake warning lamp
X. Rheostat instrument illumination switch

Fiesta instrument panel, Sport and Ghia options

Fuse Box Location

The fuse block is located on the left side of the steering column under the edge of the instrument panel on standard models and inside the top of the instrument panel storage space on Ghia models.

The relays and flashers are located on a special frame under the instrument panel.

NOTE: The lower instrument panel would have to be removed on Ghia models to gain access to the flashers and relays.

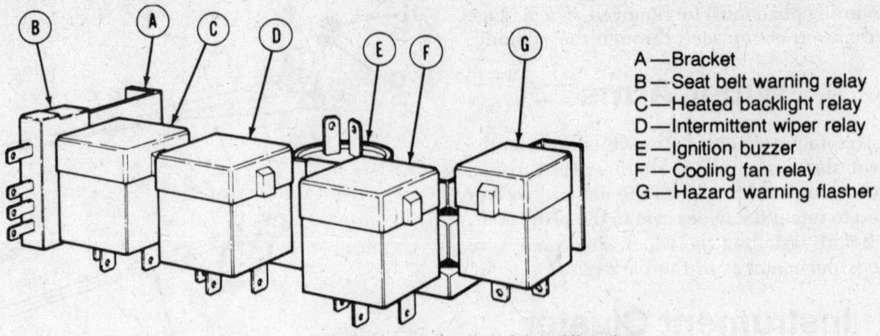

Flasher and relay identification

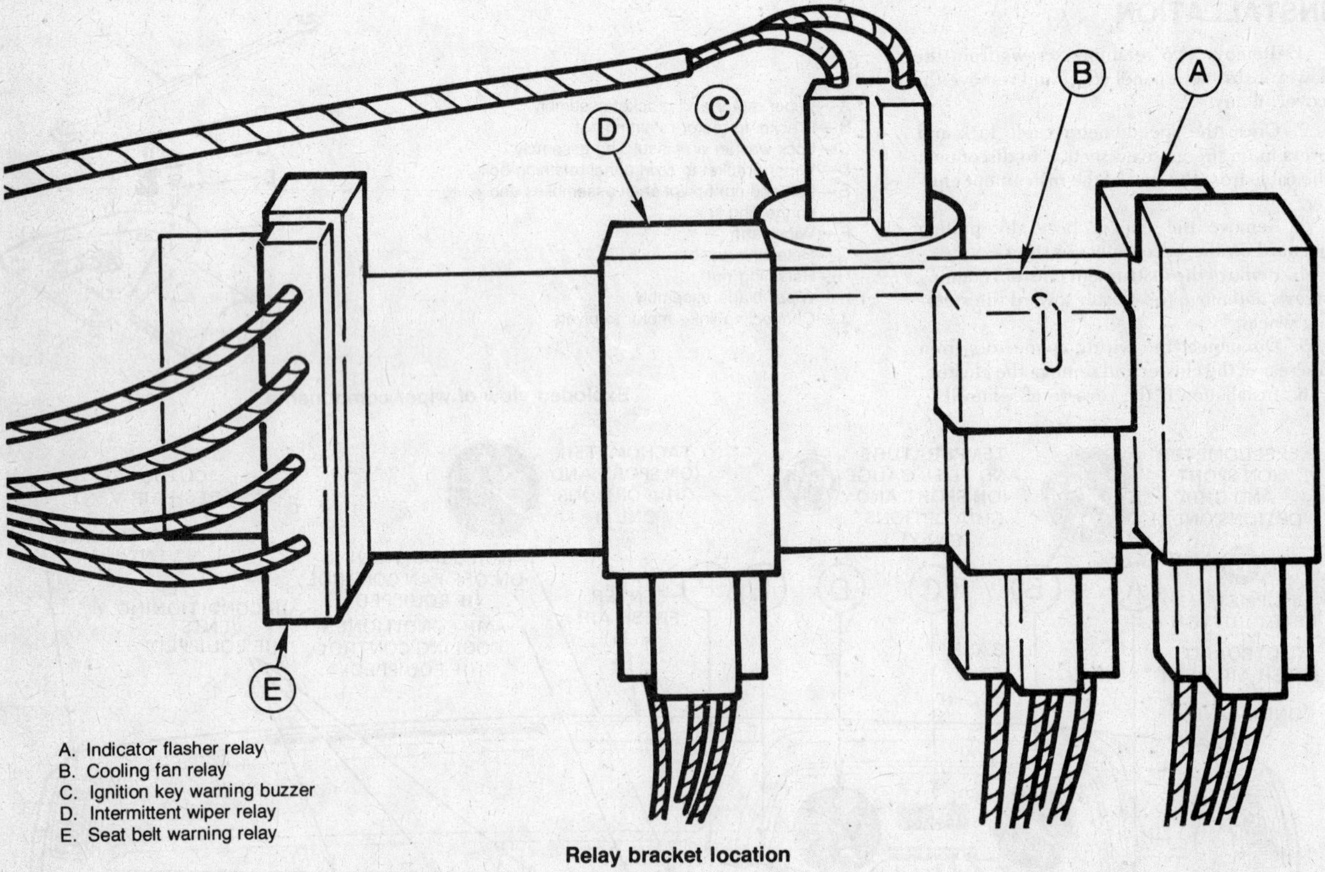

A. Indicator flasher relay
B. Cooling fan relay
C. Ignition key warning buzzer
D. Intermittent wiper relay
E. Seat belt warning relay

Relay bracket location

SPECIFICATIONS

INDEX

BEFORE SERVICING, SEE THE SAFETY NOTICE ON THE CONTENTS PAGE

SERIAL NUMBER IDENTIFICATION

Chassis Number Identification

Honda vehicle identification numbers are mounted on the top edge of the instrument panel and are visible from the outside. In addition, there is a Vehicle/Engine Identification plate under the hood on the hood mounting bracket.

Engine Number Identification

The engine serial number is stamped into the clutch casing. The first three digits indicate engine model identification. The remaining numbers refer to production sequence. This same number is also stamped onto the Vehicle/Engine Identification plate mounted on the hood bracket.

Serial number identification

Transmission Number Identification

The transmission serial number is stamped on the top of the transmission/clutch case.

SERIAL NUMBER IDENTIFICATION CHART

Year	Model	VIN (Chassis Number)	Engine Number
1975	Civic	3300001–4000000	EB2-2000001–2025158
	Civic CVCC	1000001–2000000	ED1-1000001–1999999
	Civic CVCC Wagon	1000001–2000000	ED2-1000001–1999999
1976	Civic	4000001–5000000	EB2-2025159–2999999
	Civic CVCC	2000001–3000000	ED3-2000001–2499999
	Civic CVCC ①	2000001–3000000	ED3-2500001–2999999
	Accord	1000001–2000000	EF1-1000001–2000000
1977	Civic	5000001-6000000	EB2-3000001–4000000
	Civic CVCC KL	3000001–4000000	EB3-3000001–3499999
	Civic CVCC KA	3000001–4000000	ED3-3500001–3899999
	Civic CVCC KH	3000001–4000000	ED3-3900001–4000000
	Accord KL	2000001–3000000	EF1-2000001–2499999
	Accord KA	2000001–3000000	EF1-2500001–2899999
	Accord KH	2000001–3000000	EF1-2900001–3000000
1978	Civic	6000001–7000000	EB3-1000001–1500000
	Civic CVCC KL	4000001–5000000	ED3-4000001–4499999
	Civic CVCC KA	4000001–5000000	ED3-4500001–4899999
	Civic CVCC KH	4000001–5000000	ED3-4900001–5000000
	Accord KL	3000001–4000000	EF1-3000001–3499999
	Accord KA	3000001–4000000	EF1-3500001–3899999
	Accord KH	3000001–4000000	EF1-3900001–4000000
1979	Civic	7000001–8000000	EB3-1500001–2000000
	Civic CVCC KL	5000001–6000000	ED3-5000001–5499999
	Civic CVCC KA	5000001–6000000	ED3-5500001–5899999
	Civic CVCC KH	5000001–6000000	ED3-5900001–6000000
	Accord KL	4000001–5000000	EF1-4000001–4499999
	Accord KA	4000001–5000000	EF1-4500001–4899999
	Accord KH	4000001–5000000	EF1-4900001–5000000
1980-81		N.A.	N.A.

NOTE: Beginning 1976, Civic CVCC Wagons have engine serial numbers prefixed ED4. KL, KH and KA designations still apply.

① 5 speed/49 States

KL: California

KH: High Altitude

KA: 49 States

GENERAL ENGINE SPECIFICATIONS

Year	Model	Engine Displacement (cc)	Carburetor Type	Horsepower @ rpm	Bore x Stroke (in.)	Compression Ratio	Torque @ rpm (ft. lbs.)
1975-79	Civic Exc. CVCC	1237	Hitachi 2 bbl	N.A.	2.83 x 2.99	8.1:1	N.A.
1975	CVCC	1487	Keihin 3bbl	53 @ 5000	2.91 x 3.41	8.1:1	68 @ 3000
1976-81	CVCC	1487	Keihin 3 bbl	63 @ 5000	2.91 x 3.41	7.9:1	77 @ 3000
1976-78	CVCC	1600	Keihin 3 bbl	68 @ 5000	2.91 x 3.66	8.0:1	85 @ 3000
1979-81	CVCC	1751	Keihin 3 bbl	72 @ 4500	3.03 x 3.70	8.0:1 ①	94 @ 3000
1980-81	CVCC	1335	Keihin 3 bbl	N.A.	2.83 x 3.23	7.9:1	N.A.

① 1981 Prelude: 8.9:1 in Calif.
N.A. Not available

TUNE-UP SPECIFICATIONS

When analyzing compression test results, look for uniformity among cylinders, rather than specific pressures.

Year	Model	Engine Displacement (cc)	Original Equipment Spark Plugs Type	Original Equipment Spark Plugs Gap (in.)	Distributor Point Dwell (deg)	Distributor Point Gap (in.)	Basic Ignition Timing (deg) MT	Basic Ignition Timing (deg) AT	Intake Valve Fully Opens (deg)	Fuel Pump Pressure (psi)	Idle Speed (rpm) MT	Idle Speed (rpm) AT	Valve Clearance (in.) Intake (cold)	Valve Clearance (in.) Auxiliary (cold)	Valve Clearance (in.) Exhaust (cold)
1975-76	Civic	1237	BP6ES or W20EP	0.028-0.032	49-55	0.018-0.022	7B ⑧	7B ⑧	10A	2.56 ④	750-850 ⑤	700-800	0.004-0.006	—	0.004-0.006
1977	Civic	1237	BP6ES or W20EP	0.028-0.032	49-55	0.018-0.022	TDC ⑧	TDC ⑧	10A	2.56	700-800 ④	700-800 ⑤	0.004-0.006	—	0.004-0.006
1978-79	Civic	1237	BP6ES or W20EP	0.028-0.032	49-55	0.018-0.022	2B ⑧	2B ⑧	10A	2.56	650-750 ④	650-750 ⑤	0.004-0.006	—	0.004-0.006
1975	Civic CVCC	1487	BP6ES or W20ES ②	0.028-0.032	49-55	0.018-0.022	TDC ⑨	3A ⑨	10A	1.85-2.56	800-900 ④	700-800 ⑤	0.005-0.007	0.005-0.007	0.005-0.007
1976	Civic CVCC	1487	B-6ES or W20ES W20ES ②	0.028-0.032	49-55	0.018-0.022	2B ⑥ ⑨	2B ⑦ ⑨	10A	1.85-2.56	800-900 ④	700-800 ⑤	0.005-0.007	0.005-0.007	0.005-0.007
1977	Civic CVCC	1487	B6EB or W20ES-L	0.028-0.032	49-55	0.018-0.022	6B ⑩	6B ⑩⑦	10A	1.85-2.56	750-850 ④	650-750 ⑤	0.005-0.007	0.005-0.007	0.005-0.007
1978-79	Civic CVCC	1487	B6EB or W20ES-L	0.028-0.032	49-55	0.018-0.022	6B ⑩	6B ⑩	10A	1.85-2.56	650-750 ④	600-700 ⑤	0.005-0.007	0.005-0.007	0.007-0.009
1976-77	Accord CVCC	1600	B6ES or W20ES ① ②	0.028-0.032	49-55	0.018-0.022	2B ⑨	TDC ⑨	10A	1.85-2.56	750-850 ④	630-730 ⑤	0.005-0.007	0.005-0.007	0.005-0.007
1978	Accord	1600	B6EB or W20ES-L	0.028-0.032	49-55	0.018-0.022	6B ⑨ ⑩	6B ⑨ ⑩	10A	2.13-2.84	750-850 ④	650-750 ⑤	0.005-0.007	0.005-0.007	0.007-0.009
1979	Accord	1751	B7EB	0.028-0.032	Electronic		6B ⑨ ⑫	4B ⑬ ⑪	10A	2.13-2.84	650-750 ④	650-750 ⑤	0.005-0.007	0.005-0.007	0.010-0.012

TUNE-UP SPECIFICATIONS

When analyzing compression test results, look for uniformity among cylinders, rather than specific pressures.

Year	Model	Engine Displacement (cc)	Original Equipment Spark Plugs Type	Original Equipment Spark Plugs Gap (in.)	Distributor Point Dwell (deg)	Distributor Point Gap (in.)	Basic Ignition Timing (deg.) MT	Basic Ignition Timing (deg.) AT	Intake Valve Fully Opens (deg)	Fuel Pump Pressure (psi)	Idle Speed (rpm) MT	Idle Speed (rpm) AT	Valve Clearance (in.) Intake (cold)	Valve Clearance (in.) Auxiliary (cold)	Valve Clearance (in.) Exhaust (cold)
1980-81	Civic	1487	B7EB-11	0.42	Electronic		15B (14)	TDC (15)	—	2.5	700-800	700-800	.005-0.007	.005-.007	.007-0.009
	Civic	1335	W20ES-L11	0.42	Electronic		2B	TDC	10A	2.5	700-800	700-800	0.005-0.007	0.005-0.007	0.007-0.009
	Accord	1751	B7EB	0.30	Electronic		4B	TDC	—	2.5	750-850	700-800	.005-.007	.005-.007	.010-.012
	Prelude	1751	B7EB	0.30	Electronic		TDC	TDC	—	2.5	750-850	700-800	.005-.007	.005-.007	.010-.012

NOTE: The underhood specifications sticker often reflects tune-up specification changes made in production. Sticker figures must be used if they disagree with those in this chart.

(1) For continuous highway use over 70 mph, use cooler NGK B-7ES, Nippon Denso W-22ES or equivalent
(2) For continuous low-speed use under 30 mph, use hotter NKG B-5ES, Nippon Denso W-16ES or equivalent
(4) In neutral, with headlights on
(5) In drive range, with headlights on
(6) 5-speed Sedan (Hatchback) from engine number 2500001-up—6B
(7) Station wagon—TDC
(8) Aim timing light at red notch on crankshaft pulley with distributor vacuum hose(s) connected at specified idle speed
(9) Aim timing light at red mark (yellow mark, 1978-79 Accord M/T) on flywheel or torque converter drive plate distributor vacuum hose connected at specified idle speed
(10) California (KL) and High Altitude (KH) models: 2B
(11) Aim light at blue mark (49 states models)
(12) California (KL) and High Altitude (KH) models: TDC (white mark)
(13) California (KL) and High Altitude (KH) models: 2 ATDC (black mark)
(14) 49 States Wagon 10B
(15) California and High Altitude TDC

TDC—Top Dead Center
B—Before top dead center
A—After top dead center
—Not applicable
N.A. Not available

FIRING ORDERS

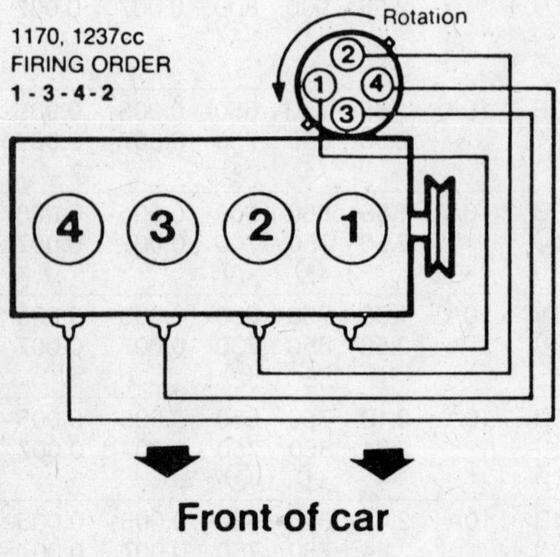

Non-CVCC firing order

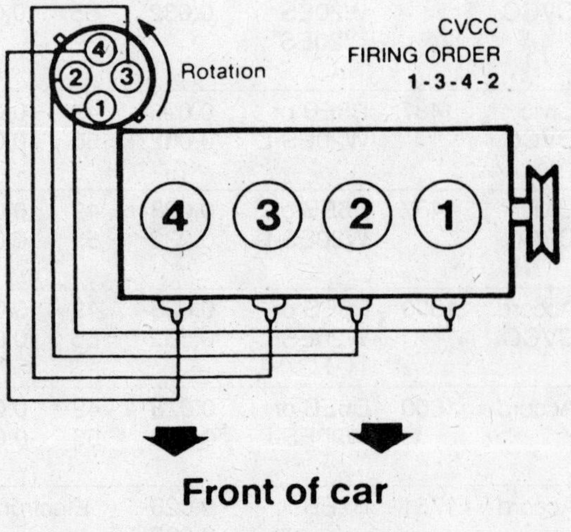

CVCC firing order

VALVE SPECIFICATIONS

Year	Engine Displacement (cc)	Seat Angle (deg)	Face Angle (deg)	Spring Installed Height (in.)	Stem to Guide Clearance (in.) Intake	Stem to Guide Clearance (in.) Exhaust	Stem to Guide Clearance (in.) Auxiliary	Stem Diameter (in.) Intake	Stem Diameter (in.) Exhaust	Stem Diameter (in.) Auxiliary
1975-79	1237	45	45	Inner — 1.6535 Outer — 1.5728 ①	0.0004-0.0016 ②	0.0020-0.0031-	—	0.2591-0.2594	0.2579-0.2583	—
1975-78	1487 CVCC	45	45	Inner — 1.358 Outer — 1.437 Auxiliary — 0.906 ④	0.0004-0.0016	0.0020-0.0031	0.0008-0.0020	0.2592-0.2596	0.2580-0.2584	0.2162-0.2166
1976-78	1600 CVCC	45	45	①	0.0008-0.0020	0.0020-0.0032	0.0008-0.0020	0.2591-0.2594	0.2579-0.2583	0.2157-0.2161
1979-81	1335, 1487 CVCC	45	45	Intake inner — 1.401 Intake outer — 1.488 Exhaust inner — 1.358 Exhaust outer — 1.437 Auxiliary — 0.906	0.0004-0.0016	0.0020-0.0031	0.0008-0.0021	0.2592-0.2596	0.2580-0.2584	0.2162-0.2166
1979-81	1751 CVCC	45	45	Intake inner — 1.000 Intake outer — 1.094 Exhaust inner — 1.031 Exhaust outer — 1.109 Auxiliary — 0.875	0.0008-0.0020	0.0024-0.0035	0.0009-0.0023	0.2748-0.2753	0.2732-0.2736	0.2587-0.2593

① Intake Inner — 1.6654
Outer — 1.6649
Exhaust Inner — 1.9882
Outer — 2.1181
Auxiliary (CVCC) — 1.1457
② 1978-79: 0.0008-0.0020
③ Spring free length — 1237, 1600 CVCC
④ 1978 Intake Inner — 1.401
Outer — 1.488
⑤ 1980-81 1335 cc — .2154-.2160

CAPACITIES

Year	Model	Engine Displacement (cc)	Engine Crankcase (qts) ②	TRANSMISSION (PTS) Manual 4-sp	Manual 5-sp	Auto. ③	Gasoline Tank (gals)	Cooling System (qts)
1975-78	Civic	1237	3.8	5.2	—	5.2	10.6	4.2
	Civic CVCC	1487	3.8	5.2	5.2	5.2	10.6 ①	4.2
	Accord	1600	3.8	5.2	5.2	5.2	13.2	4.2
1979	Civic	1237	3.8	5.2	—	5.2	10.6	4.8
	Civic	1487	3.8	5.2	5.6	5.2	10.6 ①	4.8
	Accord	1751	3.8	5.2	5.2	5.2	13.2	6.4
	Prelude	1751	3.8	5.2	5.2	5.2	13.2	6.0
1980-81	Civic	all	3.8	4.8	5.2	5.2	10.8	5.2
	Accord & Prelude	1751	3.8	5.0	5.0	5.2	13.2	6.4

① Sta. Wgn.: 11.0
② Includes filter
③ Does not include torque converter. Total capacity from dry is 8.8 pts.

CRANKSHAFT AND CONNECTING ROD SPECIFICATIONS

All measurements given in in.

Year	Engine Displacement (cc)	CRANKSHAFT Main Brg Journal Dia	Main Brg Oil Clearance	Shaft End-Play	Thrust on No.	CONNECTING ROD Journal Dia	Oil Clearance	Side Clearance
1975-79	1237	1.9685-1.9673-	0.0009-0.0017	0.0039-0.0138	3	1.5736-1.5480	0.0008-0.0015	0.0079- ④ 0.0177
1975-81	1335, 1487, 1600, 1751	1.9687-1.9697	0.0010- ① 0.0021	0.0039- ③ 0.0138	3	1.6525- ② 1.6535	0.0008-0.0015	0.0059-0.0118

① 1335, 1751 —.009-.0017
② 1335 —1.5739-1.5748
③ 1335, 1751 —.004-.014
④ 1975-76: 0.0059-0.0118

PISTON AND RING SPECIFICATIONS

All measurements are given in inches

Year	Engine Displacement (cc)	Piston Clearance	RING GAP Top Compression	Bottom Compression	Oil Control	RING SIDE CLEARANCE Top Compression	Bottom Compression	Oil Control
1975-79	1237	0.0012-0.0039	0.0098-0.0157	0.0098-0.0157	0.0118-0.0394	0.0008-0.0018	0.0008-0.0018	Snug
1975-78	1487 CVCC, 1600	0.0012-0.0039	0.0079-0.0157	0.0079-0.0157	0.0079-0.0354 ①	0.0008-0.0018	0.0008-0.0018	Snug
1979-81	1335, 1487 CVCC	0.0012-0.0060	0.0079-0.0157	0.0079-0.0157	0.0079-0.0354	0.0008-0.0018	0.0008-0.0018	Snug
	1751 CVCC	0.0008-0.0028	0.0059-0.0138	0.0059-0.0138	0.0118-0.0354	0.0008-0.0018	0.0008-0.0018	Snug

① 1600 engine oil control ring gap —0.0118-0.0354

TORQUE SPECIFICATIONS

All readings are given in ft. lbs.

Year	Engine Displacement (cc)	Cylinder Head Bolts	Main Bearing Bolts	Rod Bearing Bolts	Crankshaft Pulley Bolts	Flywheel to Crankshaft Bolts	MANIFOLD In	MANIFOLD Ex	Spark Plugs	Oil Pan Drain Bolt
1975-79	1237	30-35 ① 37-42 ②	27-31	18-21	34-38	34-38	13-17	13-17 ③	9-12	29-36
1975-78	1487 CVCC, 1600	40-47	30-35	18-21	34-38	34-38	15-17	15-17	11-18	29-36
1979-80	1335, 1487	33	29	21	61	51	18	18	15	33
1979-80	1751	43	48	23	61	51	18	18	15	33

① To engine number EB 1-1019949
② From engine number EB 1-1019950
③ 1975-76 models w/air —22-33 ft. lbs.

TORQUE SEQUENCE

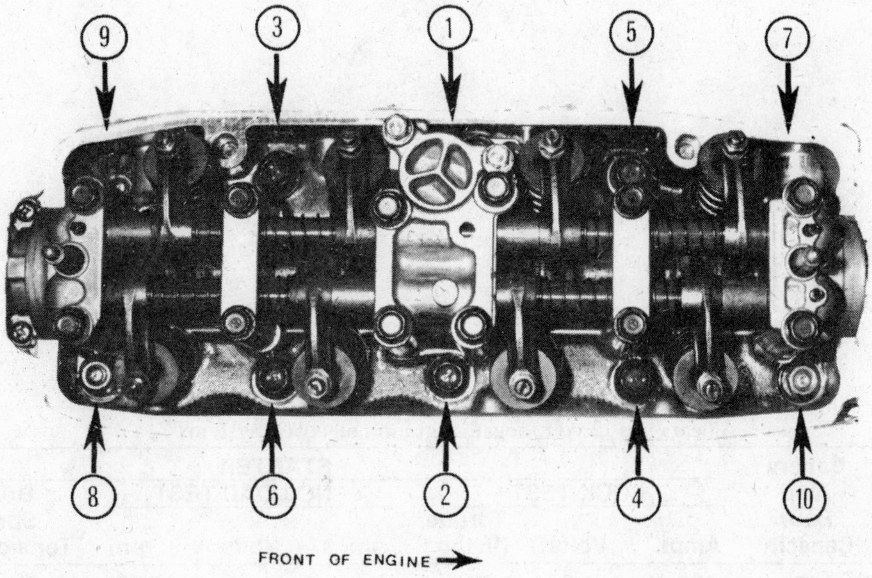

BRAKE SPECIFICATIONS

All measurements given are (in.) unless noted

Year	Model	Lug Nut Torque (ft. lbs.)	BRAKE DISC Minimum Thickness	BRAKE DISC Maximum Run-Out	BRAKE DRUM Inner Diameter	BRAKE DRUM Max. Machine O/S	MINIMUM LINING THICKNESS Front	MINIMUM LINING THICKNESS Rear
1975-81	Civic Sedan, Hatchback	51-65	0.354	0.006	7.087	7.126	0.063 ③	0.079
1975-81	Civic Wagon	51-65	0.449 ①	0.006	7.874	7.913 ②	0.300	0.118 ④
1976-81	Accord, Prelude	51-65	0.433	0.006	7.087	7.126	0.039	0.079

① 0.437 —1977
② 7.93 —1977 and later
③ 0.24 —1977 and later
④ 0.08 —1977 and later

ALTERNATOR AND REGULATOR SPECIFICATIONS

	ALTERNATOR				REGULATOR: FIELD RELAY				REGULATOR: REGULATOR		
Year	Engine Displacement (cc)	Part No. or Manufacturer	Field Current @ 12V (amps)	Output (amps) @ 5,000 rpm	Part No. or Manufacturer	Yoke Gap (in.)	Point Gap (in.)	Volts to Close	Yoke Gap (in.)	Point Gap (in.)	Volts @ 5,000 rpm
1975-81	1237	Hitachi	2.5	40 ① 35 ②	Hitachi	0.008-0.018	0.0016-0.0472	4.5-5.8	0.008-0.024	0.010-0.018	13.5-14.5
1975-81	1487 CVCC	Nippon Denso	2.5	35 ③ 45 ④	Nippon Denso	N.A.	0.016-0.047	4.5-5.8	0.020	0.016-0.020	13.5-14.5
1976-78	1600 CVCC	Nippon Denso	2.5	50	Nippon Denso	N.A.	0.016-0.047	4.5-5.8	0.020	0.016-0.047	13.5-14.5
1980-81	1335 CVCC	Nippon Denso	2.5	45	Nippon Denso	0.008-0.018	0.02-0.05	N.A.	0.02	0.02-0.05	13.5-14.5
1979-81	1751 CVCC	Nippon Denso	2.5	50	Nippon Denso	0.008-0.024	0.016-0.047	N.A.	0.020	0.016-0.047	13.5-14.5

① From no. 1011759
② Up to no. 1011158
③ Without A/C
④ With A/C
N.A. Not applicable

BATTERY AND STARTER SPECIFICATIONS

All cars use 12 volt, negative ground electrical systems

			STARTER: LOCK TEST			STARTER: NO LOAD TEST				
Year	Model (cc)	Battery Amp Hour Capacity	Amps	Volts	Torque (ft. lbs.)	Amps	Volts	rpm	Brush Spring Tension (oz.)	Min. Brush Length (in.)
1975-77	(1237)	45	380 or less	4.9	5.4	less than 70	12	7000 or more	56-57	0.16
1978-79	(1237)	45	380 (max.)	5.5	6.15	70 (max.)	11	6000	56-57	0.16
1980-81	CVCC (1335)	47	230	8.0	4.7	90 ②	11.5 ①	3000 ③	N.A.	0.39
1975-81	CVCC (1487)	47	160	9.6	N.A.	less than 80	11.5	N.A.	N.A.	0.39
1976-78	CVCC (1600)	47	300 (max.)	2.5	5.0	90 (max.)	11.5	3000	53-67	0.35
1979-81	CVCC (1751)	47	400 (max.)	2.4	7.9	90 (max.)	11.5	3500	N.A.	0.55

① Cal. Nippon Denso; Hitachi 11.0
② Cal. Nippon Denso; Hitachi 70
③ Cal. Nippon Denso 5000; Hitachi 6000
N.A. Not available

WHEEL ALIGNMENT SPECIFICATIONS

Year	Model	CASTER Range (deg)	CASTER Preferred Setting (deg)	CAMBER Range (deg)	CAMBER Preferred Setting (deg)	Toe-Out (in.)	Steering Axis Inclination (deg)
1975-81	Civic—all exc. Station Wagon	1¼P-2¼ ①	1¾P ②	0-1P	½P	0.04	8.9 ③
1975	Civic Station Wagon	1½P-2½P	2P	0-1P	½P	0.04	9.3
1976-81	Civic Station Wagon	½P-1½P	1P ④	0-1P	½P	0.04	9.3
1976-77	Accord	1⅓P-2⅓P	1⅚P	⅙P-1⅙P	⅔P	0.04	12.2
1978	Accord	1P-3P	2P	0-1P	½P	0.04	12.2
1979-81	Accord, Prelude	—	1½P	—	0	0	12.8

① 1-2P —1977
0-1P —1978-79
② 1½ —1977
½P —1978-79
③ 9.3 —1977-79
④ ½P —1978-79
P —Positive

TUNE-UP PROCEDURES

Spark Plugs

REMOVAL

1. Place a piece of masking tape around each spark plug wire and number it according to its corresponding cylinder.
2. Pull the wires from the spark plugs, grasping the wire by the end of the rubber boot and twisting off.

NOTE: Avoid spark plug removal while the engine is hot. Since the cylinder head spark plug threads are aluminum, the spark plug becomes tight due to the different coefficients of heat expansion. If a plug is too tight to be removed even while the engine is cold, apply a solvent around the plug followed with an application of oil once the solvent has penetrated the threads. Do this only when the engine is cold.

3. Loosen each spark plug with a 13/16 in. spark plug socket. When the plug has been loosened a few turns, stop to clean any material from around the spark plug holes. Compressed air is preferred; however, if air is not available, simply use a rag to clean the area.

NOTE: In no case should foreign matter be allowed to enter the cylinders. Severe damage could result.

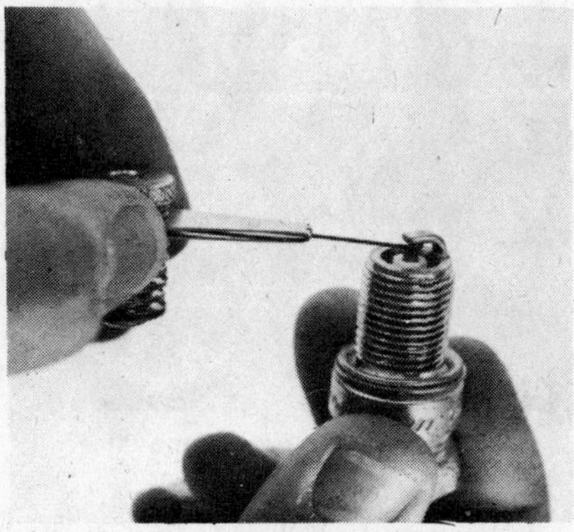

Using a round wire gauge to check spark plug gap

4. Finish unscrewing the plugs and remove them from the engine.

INSPECTION AND CLEANING

Before attempting to clean and re-gap plugs, be sure that the electrode ends aren't worn or damaged and that the insulators (the white porcelain covering) are not cracked. Replace the plug if this condition exists.

Clean reusable plugs with a plug cleaner or a wire brush. The plug gap should be checked and readjusted, if necessary, by bending the ground (side) electrode with a spark plug gapping tool.

NOTE: Do not use a flat gauge to check plug gap; an incorrect reading will result. Use a wire gauge only.

INSTALLATION

1. Lightly oil the spark plug threads and hand tighten them into the engine.
2. Tighten the plugs securely with a spark plug wrench (about 10 ft/lbs of torque).

CAUTION

Do not overtighten because of the aluminum threads.

3. Reconnect the wires to the plugs, making sure that each is securely fitted.

Breaker Points and Condenser

1979 Accords and all 1980 and later models have electronic ignition, eliminating the breaker points and condenser. No routine maintenance is required.

NOTE: There are two rules that should always be followed when adjusting or replacing points. The points and condenser are a matched set; never replace one without replacing the other. If you change the point gap (or dwell) of the engine, you also change the ignition timing. Therefore, if you adjust the points, you must also adjust the timing.

INSPECTION

1. Disconnect the high-tension wire from the coil.
2. Unfasten the two retaining clips to remove the distributor cap.

3. Remove the rotor from the distributor shaft by pulling it straight up. Examine the condition of the rotor; if it is cracked or the metallic tip is excessively burned, replace it.

4. Pry the breaker points open with a screwdriver and examine the condition of the contact points. If the points are excessively worn, burned, or pitted they should be replaced.

NOTE: Contact points which have been used for several thousand miles will have a gray, rough surface, but this is not necessarily an indication that they are malfunctioning. The roughness between the points matches so that a large contact area is maintained.

5. If the points are in good condition, polish them with a point file. If the points are to be filed, they should be removed from the distributor to keep the grit from falling into it.

NOTE: Do not use emery cloth or sandpaper as they may leave particles on the points which could cause them to arc.

After polishing the points, refer to the section following the breaker point replacement procedures for proper adjustment. If the points need replacing, refer to the following procedure.

REMOVAL AND INSTALLATION

1. Remove the small nut from the terminal screw located in the side of the distributor housing and remove the nut, screw, condenser wire, and primary wire from the terminal. Remove the terminal from the slot in the distributor housing.

2. Remove the screw(s) which attaches the condenser to the outside of the distributor housing (most models), or to the breaker plate inside the distributor (CVCC Hondamatic models), and remove the condenser.

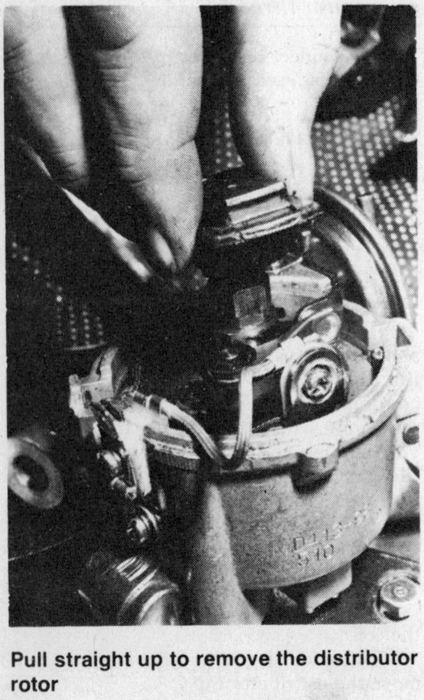

Pull straight up to remove the distributor rotor

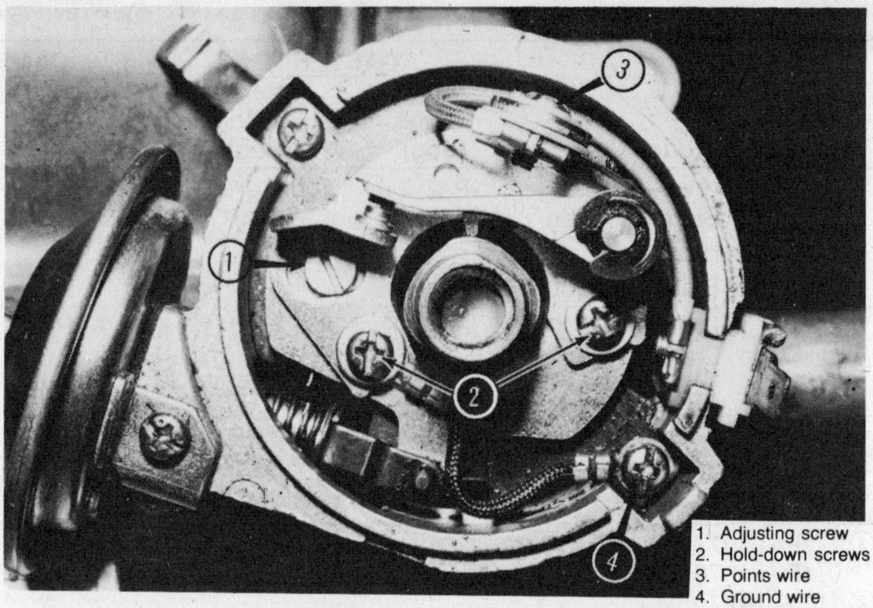

Internal components of distributor

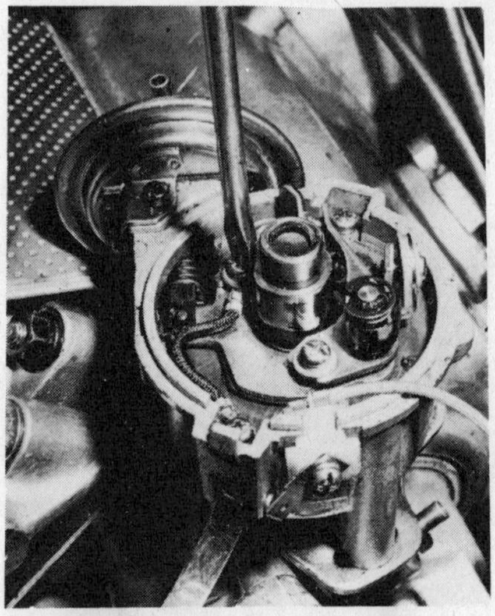

Point set screw removal

3. Unscrew the Phillips head screw which holds the ground wire to the breaker point assembly and lift the end of the ground wire out of the way.

4. Remove the two Phillips head screws which attach the point assembly to the breaker plate and remove the point assembly.

NOTE: You should use a magnetic or locking screwdriver. Trying to locate one of these tiny screws after you've dropped it can be an excruciating affair.

5. Wipe all dirt and grease from the distributor plate and cam with a lint-free cloth. Apply a small amount of heat resistant lubricant to the distributor cam. Although the lube is supplied with most breaker point kits, you can buy it at any auto parts store if necessary.

6. Properly position the new points on the breaker plate of the distributor and secure with the two point screws. Attach the ground wire, with its screw, to the breaker plate assembly. Screw the condenser to its proper position on the distributor housing, or breaker plate.

7. Fit the terminal back into its notch in the distributor housing and attach the condenser and primary wires to the terminal screw and fasten with the nut. Adjust the gap using the following procedure.

ADJUSTMENT

With a Feeler Gauge

1. Rotate the crankshaft pulley until the point gap is at its greatest (where the rubbing block is on the high point of the cam lobe). This can be accomplished by using either a remote starter switch or by rotating the crankshaft pulley by hand.

2. At this position, insert the proper sized feeler gauge between the points. A slight drag

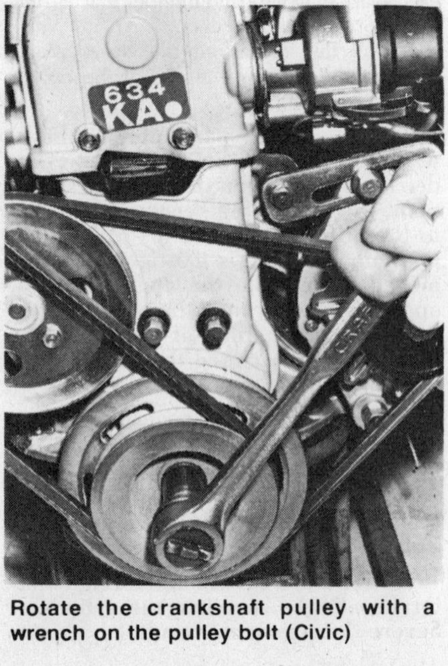

Rotate the crankshaft pulley with a wrench on the pulley bolt (Civic)

Adjust the point gap with a flat feeler gauge

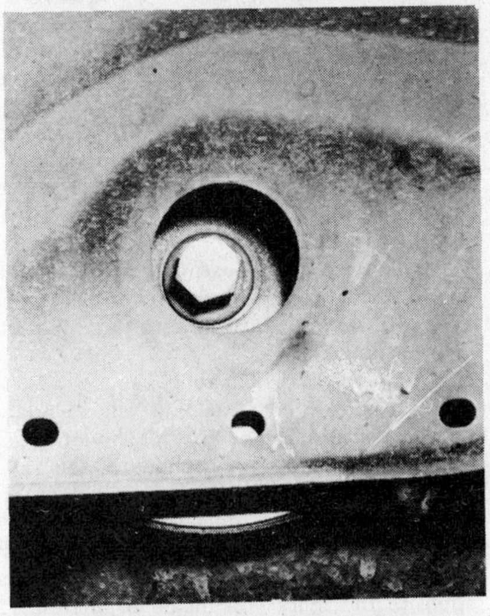

Crankshaft pulley bolt access window on left front fender—CVCC models

should be felt. Point gap should be 0.018-0.022 in.

3. If no drag is felt, or if the feeler gauge cannot be inserted, loosen, but do not remove the two breaker point set screws.

4. Adjust the points as follows:

Insert a screwdriver through the hole in the breaker point assembly and into the notch provided on the breaker plate. Twist the screwdriver to open or close the points. When the correct gap has been obtained, retighten the point set screws.

5. Recheck the point gap to be sure that it did not change when the breaker point attaching screws were tightened.

6. Align the rotor with the distributor shaft and push the rotor onto the shaft until it is fully seated.

7. Reinstall the distributor cap and the coil high-tension wire.

With a Dwell Meter

Connect a dwell/tachometer, in accordance with its manufacturer's instructions, between the distributor primary lead and a ground.

With the engine warmed up and running at the specified idle speed (see the tune-up chart), take a dwell reading.

If the point dwell is not within specifications, shut the engine off and adjust the point gap, as outlined above.

NOTE: Increasing the point gap decreases the dwell angle and vice versa.

Install the dust cover, rotor, and cap. Check the dwell reading again and adjust it, as required.

Ignition Timing

Honda recommends that the ignition timing be checked at 15,000 mile intervals. Also, the timing should always be adjusted after installing new points or adjusting the dwell angle. On all non-CVCC engines, the timing marks are located on the crankshaft pulley, with a pointer on the timing belt cover; all visible from the driver's side of the engine compartment. On all CVCC engines, the timing marks are located on the flywheel (manual transmission) or torque converter drive plate (automatic transmission), with a pointer on the rear of the cylinder block; all visible from the front right-side of the engine compartment after removing a special rubber access plug in the timing mark window. In all cases, the timing is checked with the engine warmed to operating temperature (176° F), idling in Neutral (manual trans.) or 2nd gear (Hondamatic), and with all vacuum hoses *connected.*

1. Stop the engine, and hook up a tachometer according to the manufacturer's instructions.

NOTE: On some models you will have to pull back the rubber ignition coil cover to reveal the terminals.

2. Hook up a timing light to the engine according to the manufacturer's instructions.

3. Make sure that all wires are clear of the cooling fan and hot exhaust manifolds. Start the engine. Check that the idle speed is set to specifications with the transmission in Neutral (manual transmission) or 2nd gear (Hondamatic). If not, adjust as outlined later. At any engine speed other than the specified idle speed, the distributor advance or retard mechanisms will actuate, leading to an erroneous timing adjustment.

CAUTION

Make sure that the parking brake is firmly applied and the front wheels blocked to prevent the car from rolling forward when the automatic transmission is engaged.

4. Point the timing light at the timing marks. On non-CVCC cars, align the pointer with the "F" or red notch on the crankshaft pulley. On CVCC cars, align the pointer with the red notch on the flywheel or torque converter drive plate (except on cars where the timing specifications is TDC in which case the "T" or white notch is used).

NOTE: Different colors are used in different years; see the footnotes below the "Tune-up Specifications" Chart for details.

5. If necessary, adjust the timing by loosening the larger distributor hold-down (clamp) bolt and slowly rotate the distributor in the required direction while observing the timing marks.

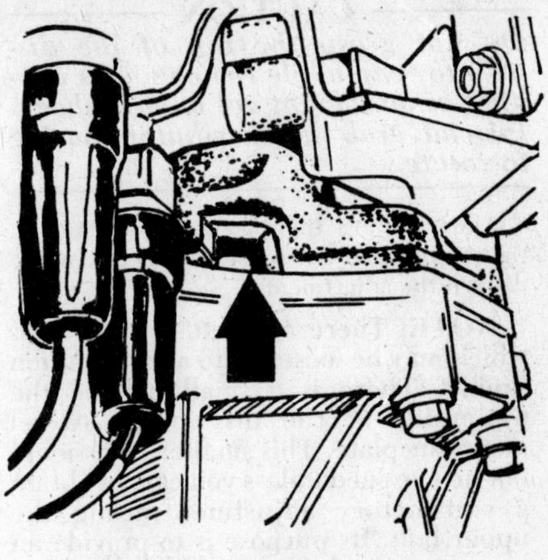

CVCC timing mark window

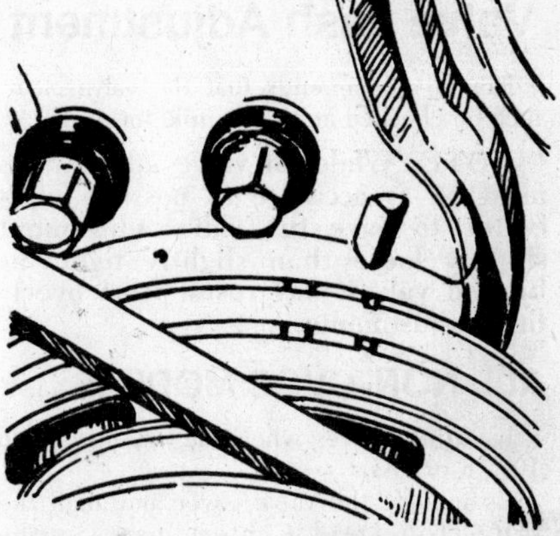

Non-CVCC timing marks. The white notch is TDC

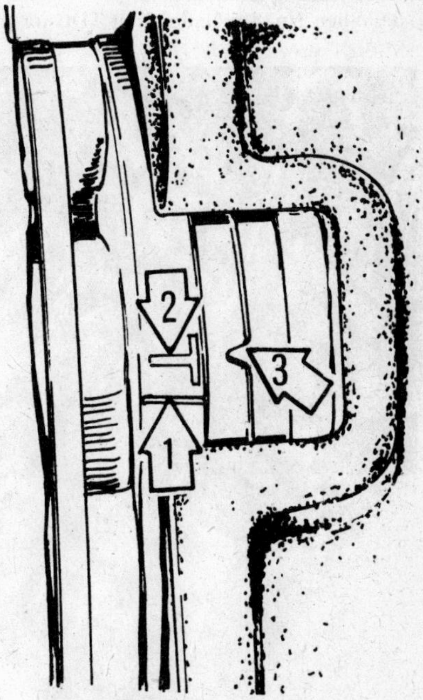

1. Ignition timing mark (red notch)
2. TDC mark
3. Timing pointer

CVCC timing marks

CAUTION

Do not grasp the top of the distributor cap while the engine is running as you might get a nasty shock. Instead, grab the distributor housing to rotate.

After making the necessary adjustment, tighten the hold-down bolt, taking care not to disturb the adjustment.

NOTE: There are actually two bolts which may be loosened to adjust ignition timing. There is a small bolt on the underside of the distributor swivel mounting plate. This smaller bolt should not be loosened unless you cannot obtain a satisfactory adjustment using the upper bolt. Its purpose is to provide an extra range of adjustment, such as in cases where the distributor was removed and then installed one tooth off.

Valve Lash Adjustment

Honda recommends that the valve clearance be checked at 15,000 mile intervals.

NOTE: While all valve adjustments must be as accurate as possible, it is better to have the valve adjustment slightly loose than slightly tight, as burned valves may result from overly tight adjustments.

ALL NON-CVCC MODELS

1. Adjust valves when the engine is cold (100° F or less).
2. Remove the valve cover and align the TDC (Top Dead Center) mark on the crankshaft pulley with the index mark on the timing belt cover. The TDC notch is the one immediately following the red 5° BTDC notch used for setting ignition timing.
3. When No. 1 cylinder is at TDC on the compression stroke, check and adjust the following valves (numbered from the crankshaft pulley end of the engine):

Intake—Nos. 1 and 2 cylinders
Exhaust—Nos. 1 and 3 cylinders

Adjust the valves as follows:

a. Check valve clearance with a flat feeler gauge between the tip of the rocker arm and the top of the valve. There should be a slight drag on the feeler gauge;
b. If there is no drag or if the gauge cannot be inserted, loosen the valve adjusting screw locknut;
c. Turn the adjusting screw with a screwdriver to obtain the proper clearance;
d. Hold the adjusting screw and tighten the locknut;
e. Recheck the clearance.

4. Then rotate the crankshaft 360° and adjust:

Intake—Nos. 3 and 4 cylinders
Exhaust—Nos. 2 and 4 cylinders

Valve adjustment—all models

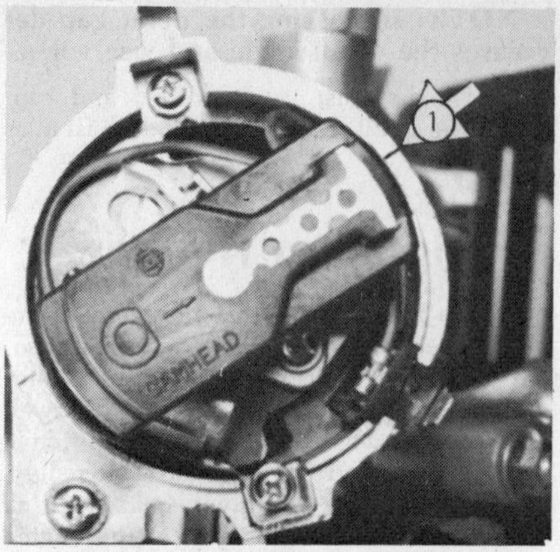

Distributor rotor at TDC (#1 cylinder)

CVCC MODELS

1. Make sure that the engine is cold (cylinder head temperature below 100° F).

Valve adjustment—CVCC auxiliary valve

2. Remove the valve cover. From the front of the engine, take a look at the forward face of the camshaft timing belt gear. When No. 1 cylinder is at Top Dead Center (TDC), the keyway for the woodruff key retaining the timing gear to the camshaft will be facing up. On 1976 and later models the word "UP" will be at the top of the gear. You can doublecheck this by distributor rotor position. Take some chalk or crayon and mark where the No. 1 spark plug wire goes into the distributor cap on the distributor body. Then, remove the cap and check that the rotor points toward that mark.
3. With the No. 1 cylinder at TDC, you can adjust the following valves (numbered from the crankshaft pulley end of the engine):

Intake—Nos. 1 and 2 cylinders
Auxiliary Intake—Nos. 1 and 2 cylinders
Exhaust—Nos. 1 and 3 cylinders

Adjust the valve as follows:

a. Check valve clearance with a flat feeler gauge between the tip of the rocker arm and the top of the valve. There should be a slight drag on the feeler gauge;
b. If there is no drag or if the gauge cannot be inserted loosen the valve adjusting screw locknut;
c. Turn the adjusting screw with a screwdriver to obtain the proper clearance;
d. Hold the adjusting screw and tighten the locknut;
e. Recheck the clearance.

4. To adjust the remaining valves, rotate the crankshaft to the No. 4 cylinder TDC position. To get the No. 4 cylinder to the TDC position, rotate the crankshaft 360 degrees. This will correspond to an 180 degree movement of the distributor rotor and camshaft timing gear. The rotor will now be pointing opposite the mark you made for the No. 1 cylinder. The camshaft timing gear keyway or "UP" mark will now be at the bottom (6 o'clock position). At this position, you may adjust the remaining valves:

Intake—Nos. 3 and 4 cylinders
Auxiliary Intake—Nos. 3 and 4 cylinders
Exhaust—Nos. 2 and 4 cylinders

Carburetor

IDLE SPEED AND MIXTURE ADJUSTMENT

NOTE: All carburetor adjustments must be made with the engine fully warmed up to operating temperature (176° F.)

Non-CVCC

1. The idle speed is adjusted with the headlights on and the radiator cooling fan off. To make sure that the cooling fan stays off while you are making your adjustments, disconnect the fan leads.

NOTE: Do not leave the cooling fan leads disconnected for any longer than necessary, as the engine may overheat.

Manual transmission cars are adjusted with the transmission in Neutral. On Hondamatic cars, the idle adjustments are made with the car in gear "1." As a safety precaution, firmly apply the parking brake and block the front wheels.

2. Remove the plastic limiter cap from the idle mixture screw. Hook up a tachometer to the engine with the positive lead connected to the distributor side (terminal) of the coil and the negative lead to a good ground. On 1976 models, disconnect the breather hose from the valve cover.
3. Start the engine and adjust first the mixture screw (turn counterclockwise to richen), and then the idle speed screw for the best quality idle at 870 rpm (Hondamatic in gear).
4. Then, lean out the idle mixture (turn mixture screw clockwise), until the idle speed drops to the correct idle speed, according to the Tune-Up Specifications chart or the emission control decal in the engine compartment.
5. Replace the limiter cap, connect the cooling fan, and disconnect the tachometer.

CVCC with Kelhin 3-bbl

1. The idle speed is adjusted with the headlights on and the radiator cooling fan on. With the engine warmed to operating temperature and idling, the cooling fan should come on. But, if it doesn't, you can load the engine's electrical system (for purposes of adjusting the idle speed), by turning the high-speed heater blower on instead. Do not have both the cooling fan and heater blower operating simultaneously, as this will load the engine too much and lower the idle speed abnormally. Manual transmission cars are adjusted with the transmission in Neutral. On Hondamatic cars, the idle adjustments are made with the car in gear "2" (that's right, Hi-gear). As a safety precaution, apply the parking brake and block the front wheels.
2. Remove the plastic cap from the idle mixture screw. Hook up a tachometer to the engine with the positive lead connected to the distributor side (terminal) of the coil and the negative lead to a good ground.
3. Start the engine and rotate the idle mixture screw counterclockwise (rich), until the highest rpm is achieved. Then, adjust the idle speed screw to 910 rpm (manual transmission), or 810 rpm (Hondamatic in Second gear) for the Civic. Adjust the idle to 880 rpm (manual) or 730 rpm (automatic) for the Accord and Prelude.
4. Finally, lean out the idle mixture (turn mixture screw in clockwise), until the idle speed drops to the correct idle speed, according to the Tune-Up Specifications chart or the emission control decal in the engine compartment.
5. Replace the limiter cap and disconnect the tachometer.

1. Idle speed screw
2. Idle mixture screw

Idle speed and mixture screws—Keihin 3 bbl carburetor

ENGINE ELECTRICAL

Distributor

REMOVAL AND INSTALLATION

1. Disconnect the high tension and primary lead wires that run from the distributor to the coil.
2. Unsnap the two distributor cap retaining clamps and remove the distributor cap. Position it out of the way.
3. Using chalk or paint, carefully mark the position of the distributor rotor in relation to the distributor housing, and mark the relation of the distributor housing to the engine block. When this is done, you should have a line on the distributor housing directly in line with the tip of the rotor, and another line on the engine block directly in line with the mark on the distributor housing.

NOTE: This aligning procedure is very important because the distributor must be reinstalled in the exact location from which it was removed, if correct ignition timing is to be maintained.

4. Note the position of the vacuum line(s) on the vacuum diaphragm with masking tape and then disconnect the lines from the vacuum unit.
5. Remove the bolt which attaches the distributor to the engine block or distributor extension housing (CVCC), and remove the distributor from the engine.

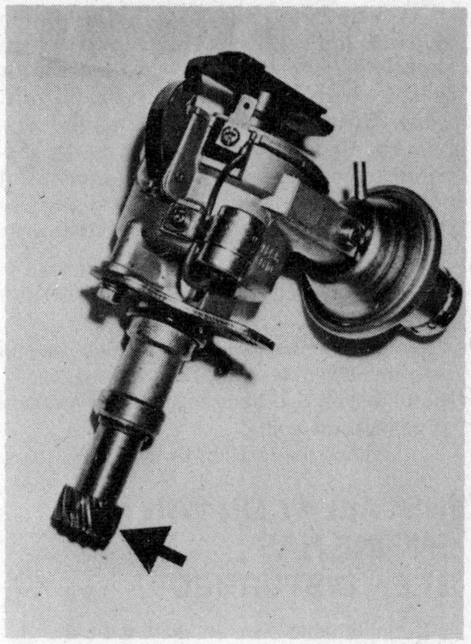

Distributor—arrow points to the helical drive gear

CAUTION

Do not disturb the engine while the distributor is removed. If you attempt to start the engine with the distributor removed, you will have to retime the engine.

6. To install, place the rotor on the distributor shaft and align the tip of the rotor with the line that you made on the distributor housing.
7. With the rotor and housing aligned, insert the distributor into the engine while aligning the mark on the housing with the mark on the block, or extension housing (CVCC).

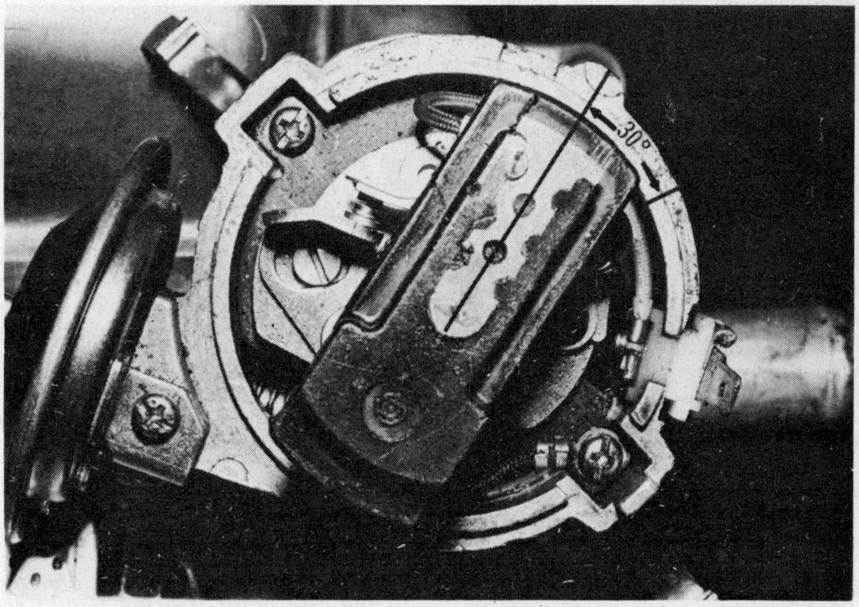

Distributor rotation will be approximately 30° on removal and installation

NOTE: Since the distributor pinion gear has helical teeth, the rotor will turn slightly as the gear on the distributor meshes with the gear on the camshaft. Allow for this when installing the distributor by aligning the mark on the distributor with the mark on the block, but positioning the tip of the rotor slightly to the side of the mark on the distributor.

8. When the distributor is fully seated in the engine, install and tighten the distributor retaining bolt.
9. Align and install the distributor cap and snap the retaining clamps into place.
10. Install the high-tension and primary wires onto the coil.
11. Check the ignition timing.

INSTALLATION WHEN ENGINE HAS BEEN DISTURBED

If the engine was cranked with the distributor removed it will be necessary to retime the engine. If you have installed the distributor incorrectly and the engine will not start, remove the distributor from the engine and start from scratch.

1. Install the distributor with No. 1 cylinder at the top dead center position on the compression stroke (the "TDC" mark on the crankshaft pulley or flywheel aligned with the index mark on the timing belt cover or crankcase and both intake and exhaust valves closed).
2. Line up the metal end of the rotor head with the protrusion on the distributor housing.
3. Carefully insert the distributor into the cylinder head opening with the attaching plate bolt slot aligned with the distributor mounting hole in the cylinder head. Then secure the plate at the center of the adjusting slot. The rotor head must face No. 1 cylinder.

NOTE: Since the distributor pinion gear has helical teeth, the rotor will turn slightly as the gear on the distributor meshes with the gear on the camshaft. Allow for this when installing the distributor by positioning the tip of the rotor to the side of the protrusion.

4. Inspect and adjust the point gap and ignition timing.

Alternator

PRECAUTIONS

1. Observe the proper polarity of the battery connections by making sure that the positive (+) and negative (−) terminal connections are not reversed. Misconnection will allow current to flow in the reverse direction, resulting in damaged diodes and an overheated wire harness.
2. Never ground or short out any alternator or alternator regulator terminals.
3. Never operate the alternator with any of its or the battery's leads disconnected.
4. Always remove the battery or disconnect its output lead while charging it.
5. Always disconnect the ground cable when replacing any electrical components.
6. Never subject the alternator to excessive heat or dampness if the engine is being steam-cleaned.
7. Never use arc-welding equipment with the alternator connected.

REMOVAL AND INSTALLATION

1. Disconnect the negative (−) battery terminal.
2. Label and unplug the wires from the plugs on the rear of the alternator.
3. Loosen and remove the two alternator mounting bolts and remove the V-belt and alternator assembly.
4. To install, reverse the removal procedure. Adjust the alternator belt tension according to the "Belt Tension Adjustment" section below.

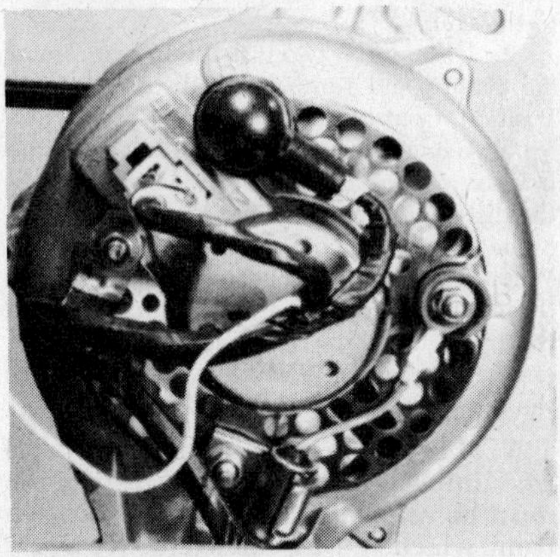

CVCC alternator wiring connections—others similar

BELT TENSION ADJUSTMENT

The initial inspection and adjustment to the alternator drive belt should be performed after the first 3,000 miles or if the alternator has been moved for any reason. Afterwards, you should inspect the belt tension every 12,000 miles. Before adjusting, inspect the belt to see that it is not cracked or worn. Be sure that its surfaces are free of grease and oil.

1. Push down on the belt halfway between pulleys with a force of about 24 lbs. The belt should deflect 0.47-0.67 in. (12-17 mm).
2. If the belt tension requires adjustment, loosen the adjusting link bolt and move the alternator with a pry bar positioned against the front of the alternator housing.

CAUTION
Do not apply pressure to any other part of the alternator.

3. After obtaining the proper tension, tighten the adjusting link bolt.

CAUTION
Do not overtighten the belt; damage to the alternator bearings could result.

Check belt tension midway between pulleys

Voltage Regulator

REMOVAL AND INSTALLATION

The regulator is inside the engine compartment, attached to the right fender wall just above the battery.

1. Disconnect the negative (−) terminal from the battery.
2. Remove the regulator terminal lead wires.

NOTE: You should label these wires to avoid confusion during installation.

3. Unscrew the two regulator retaining bolts and remove the regulator from the car.
4. To install, reverse the removal procedure.

Starter

REMOVAL AND INSTALLATION

1. Disconnect the ground cable at the battery negative (−) terminal, and the starter motor cable at the positive terminal.
2. Disconnect the starter motor cable at the motor.
3. Remove the starter motor by loosening the two attaching bolts. On CVCC models, the bolts attach from opposing ends of the starter.
4. Reverse the removal procedure to install the motor. Be sure to tighten the attaching bolts to 29-36 ft/lbs and make sure that all wires are securely connected.

Starter Drive Replacement

All Non-CVCC Civics, and California and High Altitude CVCC Civics

1. Remove the solenoid by loosening and removing the attaching bolts.

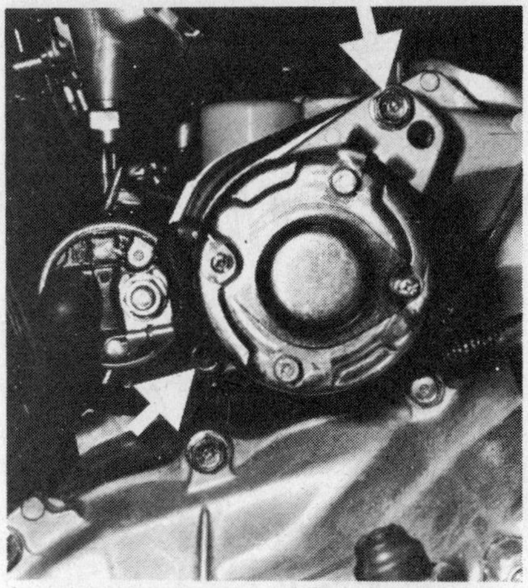

Mounting bolts—non-CVCC starter

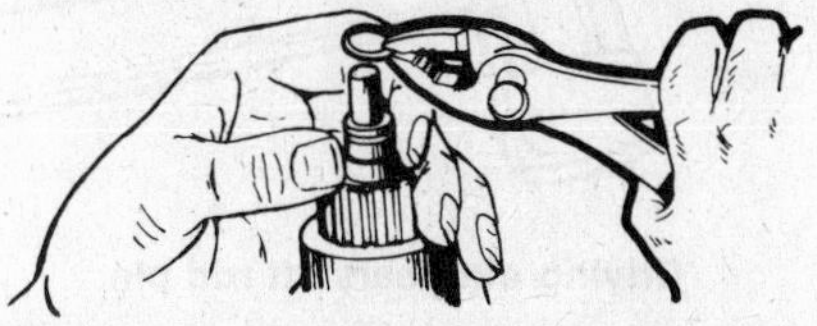

Removing pinion gear from armature

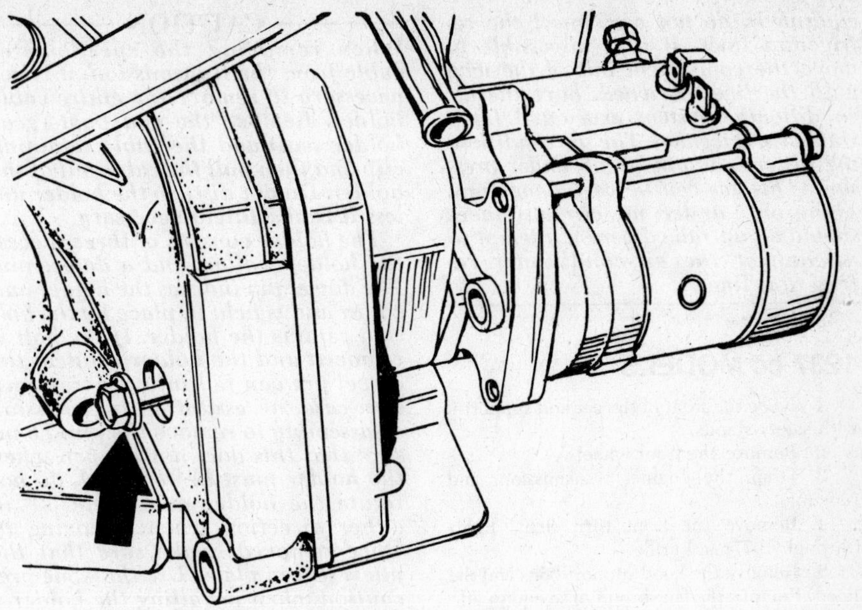

Rear mounting bolt—CVCC starter

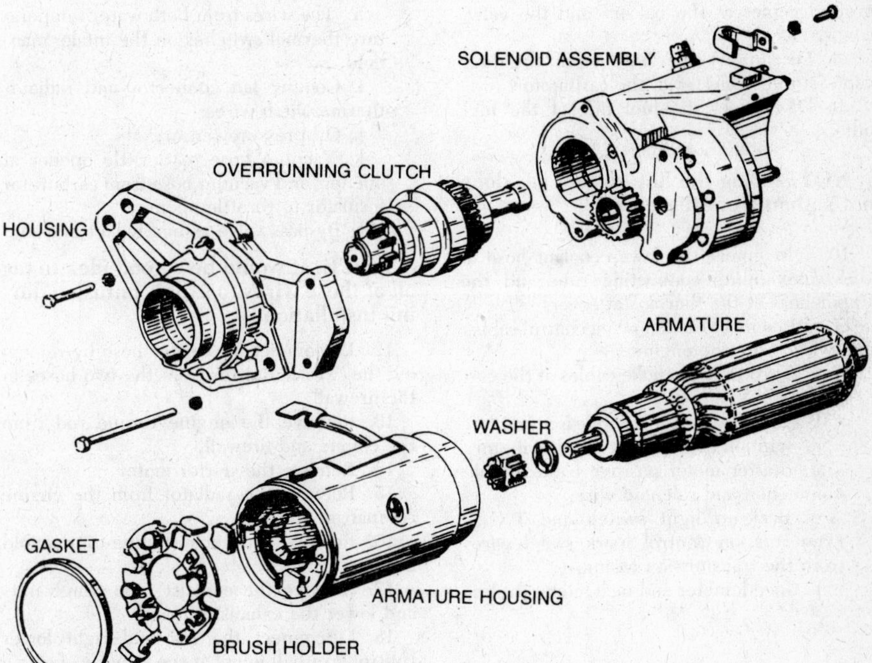

Exploded view of CVCC starter

2. Remove the two brush holder plate retaining screws from the rear cover. Also pry off the rear dust cover along with the clip and thrust washer(s).

3. Remove the two through bolts from the rear cover and lightly tap the rear cover with a mallet to remove it.

4. Remove the four carbon brushes from the brush holder and remove the brush holder.

5. Separate the yoke from the case. The yoke is provided with a hole for positioning, into which the gear case lock pin is inserted.

6. Pull the yoke assembly from the gear case, being sure to carefully detach the shift lever from the pinion.

7. Remove the armature unit from the yoke casing and the field coil.

8. To remove the pinion gear from the armature, first set the armature on end with the pinion end facing upward and pull the clutch stop collar downward toward the pinion. Then remove the pinion stop clip and pull the pinion stop and gears from the armature shaft as a unit.

9. To assemble and install the starter motor, reverse the disassembly and removal procedures. Be sure to install new clips, and be careful of the installation direction of the shift lever.

Reduction Gear Type

A reduction gear starter is used on the Prelude Accord and the 49 States CVCC Civics.

1. Remove the solenoid end cover. Pull out the solenoid. There is a spring on the shaft and a steel ball at the end of the shaft.

2. Remove the through bolts retaining the end frame to the motor and solenoid housing.

3. Remove the end frame. The overrunning clutch assembly complete with drive gear can be removed. The idler and motor pinion gears can be removed separately. The idler gear retains five steel roller bearings.

4. The clutch assembly is held together by a circlip. Push down on the gear against the spring inside the clutch assembly and remove the circlip with a circlip expander. Slide the stopper ring, gear, spring, and washer out of the clutch assembly.

5. Assembly is the reverse. The stopper ring is installed with the smaller end with the lip towards the clutch. Be sure that the steel ball is in place at the end of the solenoid shaft. Grease all sliding surfaces of the solenoid before reassembly.

ENGINE MECHANICAL

Engine Removal and Installation

CAUTION

If any repair operation requires the removal of a component of the air conditioning system (on vehicles so equipped), do not disconnect the refrigerant lines. If it is impossible to move the component out of the way with the lines attached, have the air conditioning system evacuated by a trained serviceman. The air conditioning system contains freon under pressure. This gas can be very dangerous. Therefore, under no circumstances should an untrained person attempt to disconnect the air-conditioner refrigerant lines.

1237 cc MODELS

1. Raise the front of the car and support it with safety stands.
2. Remove the front wheels.
3. Drain the engine, transmission, and radiator.
4. Remove the front turn signal lights (through 1977) and grille.
5. Remove the hood support bolts and the hood. Remove the fan shroud, if so equipped.
6. Remove the air cleaner case, and air intake pipe at the air cleaner.
7. Disconnect the battery and engine ground cables at the battery and the valve cover.
8. Disconnect the hose from the fuel vapor storage canister at the carburetor.
9. Disconnect the fuel line at the fuel pump.

NOTE: Plug the line so that gas does not siphon from the tank.

10. Disconnect the lower coolant hose at the water pump connecting tube and the upper hose at the thermostat cover.
11. Disconnect the following control cables and wires from the engine:
    a. Throttle and choke cables at the carburetor;
    b. Clutch cable at the release arm;
    c. Ignition coil wires at the distributor;
    d. Starter motor positive battery cable connection and solenoid wire;
    e. Back-up light switch and T.C.S. (Transmission Control Spark) switch wires from the transmission casing;
    f. Speedometer and tachometer cables;

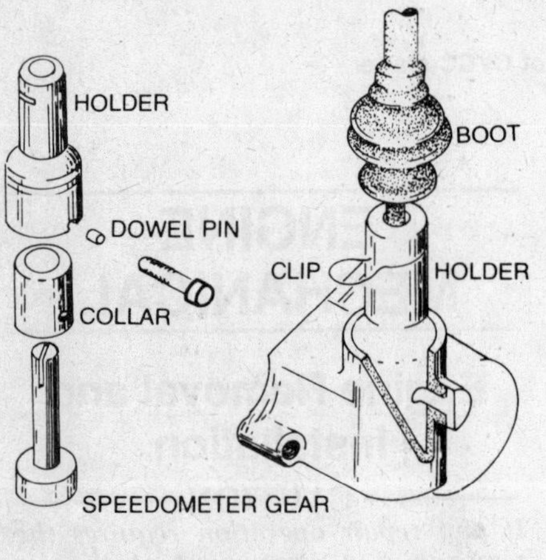

Speedometer cable removal

CAUTION

When removing the speedometer cable from the transmission, it is not necessary to remove the entire cable holder. Remove the end boot (gear holder seal) and the cable retaining clip and then pull the cable out of the holder. Do not disturb the holder unless it is absolutely necessary.

The holder consists of three pieces: the holder, collar, and a dowel pin. The dowel pin indexes the holder and collar and is held in place by the bolt that retains the holder. If the bolt is removed and the holder rotated, the dowel pin can fall into the transmission case, necessitating transmission disassembly to remove the pin. To insure that this does not happen when the holder must be removed, do not rotate the holder more than 30° in either direction when removing it. Once removed, make sure that the pin is still in place. Use the same precaution when installing the holder.

    g. Alternator wire and wire harness connector;
    h. The wires from both water temperature thermal switches on the intake manifold;
    i. Cooling fan connector and radiator thermoswitch wires;
    j. Oil pressure sensor;
    k. Vacuum hose to throttle opener at opener, and vacuum hose from carburetor insulator to throttle opener;
    l. By-pass valve assembly and bracket.

NOTE: It would be a good idea to tag all of these wires to avoid confusion during installation.

12. Disconnect the heater hose by removing the "H" connector from the two hoses in the firewall.
13. Remove the engine torque rod from the engine and firewall.
14. Remove the starter motor.
15. Remove the radiator from the engine compartment.
16. Remove the exhaust pipe-to-manifold clamp.
17. Remove the exhaust pipe flange nuts and lower the exhaust pipe.
18. Disconnect the left and right lower control arm ball joints at the knuckle, using a ball joint remover (or special tool 07941-6340000).
19. Hold the brake disc and pull the right and left drive shafts out of the differential case.

20a. Manual transmission only: Drive out the gearshift rod pin (8 mm) with a drift and disconnect the rod at the transmission case.

NOTE: Do not disconnect the shift lever end of the gearshift rod and extension.

20b. Hondamatic only: Disconnect shift cable at console and cooler line at transmission.

21. Disconnect the gearshift extension at the engine (man. trans. only).
22. Screw in two engine hanger bolts in the torque rod belt hole and the bolt hole just to the left of the distributor. Then, engage the lifting chain hooks to the hanger bolts and lift the engine just enough to take the load off the engine mounts.

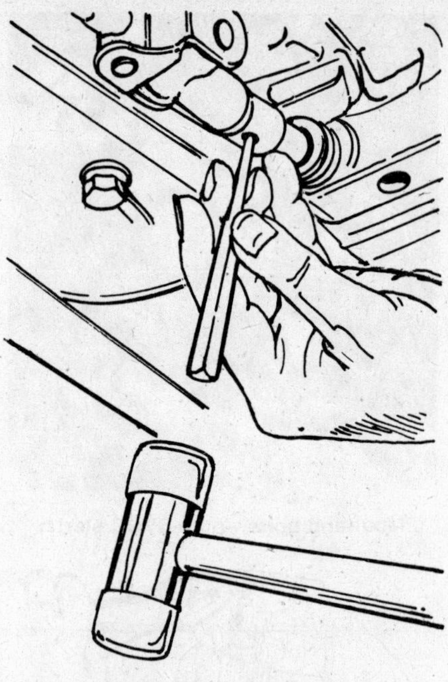
Driving out gearshift rod pin

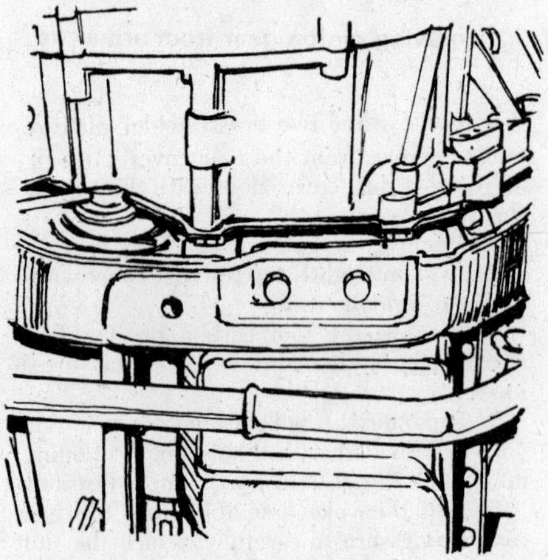
Center mount nuts

23. After being sure that the engine is properly supported, remove the two center mount bracket nuts.
24. Remove the left engine mount.
25. Lift the engine out slowly, taking care not to allow the engine to damage other parts of the car.
26. To install, reverse the removal procedure. Pay special attention to the following points:
    a. Lower the engine into position and install the left mount. Do not attach mounting bolts at this time.
    b. Align the center mount studs with the beam and tighten the nuts and washer several turns (just enough to support the beam).
    c. Lower the engine so it rests on the lower mount. Torque the lower mount nuts to 7-12 ft/lbs;

d. Use a new shift rod pin;

e. After installing the driveshafts, attempt to move the inner joint housing in and out of the differential housing. If it moves easily, the driveshaft end clips should be replaced;

f. Make sure that the control cables and wires are connected properly;

g. When connecting the heater hoses, the upper hose goes to the water pump connecting pipe and the lower hose to the intake manifold;

h. Refill the engine, transmission, and radiator with their respective fluids to the proper levels;

i. On Hondamatic cars, check shift cable adjustment.

1487 cc CIVIC CVCC

1. Raise the front of the car and support it with jackstands. On models through 1979, remove both front wheels.

2. Disconnect the battery and on 1980 models, remove the battery, hold-down equipment, tray and mount.

3. Remove the headlight rim attaching screws and the rims.

4. Open the hood. Disconnect both parking light connectors; remove the parking light retaining bolts and backing plate and remove the parking lights, through 1977 only.

5. Remove the lower grill molding and remove the six grille retaining bolts and the grille.

6. Disconnect the windshield washer hose and remove it from the underside of the hood.

7. Remove the upper torque (engine locating) arm.

8. Disconnect the vacuum hose at the power brake booster, thermosensors "A" and "B" at their wiring connectors, and the coolant temperature gauge sending unit wire.

9. Drain the radiator. After all coolant has drained, install the drain bolt finger tight.

10. Disconnect all four coolant hoses. Disconnect cooling fan motor connector and the temperature sensor. Remove the radiator hose to the overflow tank.

11. On Hondamatic cars only, remove both ATF cooler line bolts.

NOTE: Save the washers from the cooler line banjo connectors and replace if damaged.

12. Remove the radiator.

13. Label and disconnect the starter motor wires. Remove the two starters mounting bolts (one from each end of the starter), and remove the starter.

14. Label and disconnect the spark plug wires at the plug. Remove the distributor cap and scribe the position of the rotor on the side of the distributor housing. Remove the top distributor swivel bolt and remove the distributor (the rotor will rotate 30° because the drive gear is beveled).

15. On manual transmission cars, remove the C-clip retaining the clutch cable at the firewall. Then, remove the end of the clutch cable from the clutch release arm and bracket. First, pull up on the cable, and then push it out to release it from the bracket. Remove the end from the release arm.

16. Disconnect the back-up light switch wires. Disconnect the control valve vacuum hose, the air intake hose, and the preheat air intake hose. Disconnect the air bleed valve hose from the air cleaner. Label and disconnect all remaining vacuum hoses from the underside of the air cleaner. Remove the air cleaner.

17. Label and disconnect all remaining emission control vacuum hoses from the engine. Disconnect the emission box wiring connector and remove the black emission box from the firewall.

18. Remove the engine mount heat shield.

19. Disconnect the engine-to-body ground strap at the valve cover.

20. Disconnect the alternator wiring connector and oil pressure sensor leads.

21. Disconnect the vacuum hose from the start control and electrical leads to both cut-off solenoid leads.

22. Disconnect the vacuum hose from the charcoal canister and both fuel lines to the carburetor. Mark the adjustment and disconnect the choke and throttle cables at the carburetor.

23. On Hondamatic cars only, remove the center console and disconnect the gear selector control cable at the console. This may be accomplished after removing the retaining clip and pin.

24. Drain the transmission oil.

CAUTION

On cars with air conditioning, be sure to use the following procedure.

a. Disconnect the heater hose with the heater valve cable attached.

b. Remove the compressor belt cover, then loosen the adjusting nut.

c. Loosen the belt on the compressor hose bracket at the radiator.

d. Remove the compressor mounting bolt then lift the compressor out of the bracket with the hoses attached and wire it up to the firewall.

NOTE: The system does not have to be discharged.

e. Remove the compressor bracket (5 bolts).

25. Remove the fender well shield under the right fender, exposing the speedometer drive cable. Remove the set screw securing the speedometer drive holder. Then, slowly pull the cable assembly out of the transmission, taking care not to drop the pin or drive gear. Finally, remove the pin, collar, and drive gear from the cable assembly.

26. Disconnect the front suspension stabilizer bar from its mounts on both sides. Also, remove the bolt retaining the lower control arm to the subframe on both sides.

27. Remove the forward mounting nut on the radius rod on both sides. Then, pry the constant velocity joint out about ½ in. and pull the stub axle out of the transmission case. Repeat for other side.

28. Remove the six retaining bolts and remove the center beam.

29. On manual transmission cars only, drive out the pin retaining the shift linkage.

30. Disconnect the lower torque arm from the transmission.

31. On Hondamatic cars only, remove the bolt retaining the control cable stay at the transmission. Loosen the two U-bolt nuts and pull the cable out of its housing.

32. Disconnect the exhaust pipe at the manifold. Disconnect the retaining clamp also.

33. Remove the rear engine mount nut.

34. Attach a chain pulley hoist to the engine. Honda recommends using the threaded bolt holes at the extreme right and left ends of the cylinder head (with special hardened bolts) as lifting points, as opposed to wrapping a chain around the entire block and risk damaging some components such as the carburetor, etc.

35. Raise the engine enough to place a slight tension on the chain. Remove the nut retaining the front engine mount. Then, remove the three bolts retaining the front mount. While lifting the engine, remove the mount.

36. Remove the three retaining bolts and push the left engine support into its shock mount bracket to the limit of its travel.

37. Slowly raise the engine out of the vehicle.

ACCORD 1600 AND ACCORD AND PRELUDE 1751

1. Disconnect the negative battery terminal.

2. Drain the radiator of coolant, and drain the engine and transmission oil.

3. Jack up the front of the car and remove the front wheels. Be sure to support the car with safety stands.

4. Remove the air cleaner.

5. Remove the following wires and hoses:

a. The coil wire and the ignition primary wire from the distributor.

b. The engine subharness and the starter wires. (Mark the wires before removal to ease installation).

c. The vacuum tube from the brake booster.

d. On Hondamatic models, remove the ATF cooler hose from the transmission.

e. The engine ground cable.

f. Alternator wiring harness.

g. Carburetor solenoid valve connector.

h. Carburetor fuel line.

6. Remove the choke and throttle cables.

7. Remove the radiator and heater hoses.

8. Remove the emission control "black box."

9. Remove the clutch slave cylinder with the hydraulic line attached.

10. Remove the speedometer cable. Pull the wire clip from the housing, and remove the cable from the housing. Do not, under any circumstances, remove the housing from the transmission.

11. Attach an engine hoist to the engine block, and raise the engine just enough to remove the slack from the chain.

12. Disconnect the right and left lower ball joints, and the tie rod ends. You will need a ball joint remover tool for this operation. An alternative method is to leave the ball joints connected, and remove the lower control arm inner bolts, and the radius rods from the lower control arms.

13. Remove the driveshafts from the

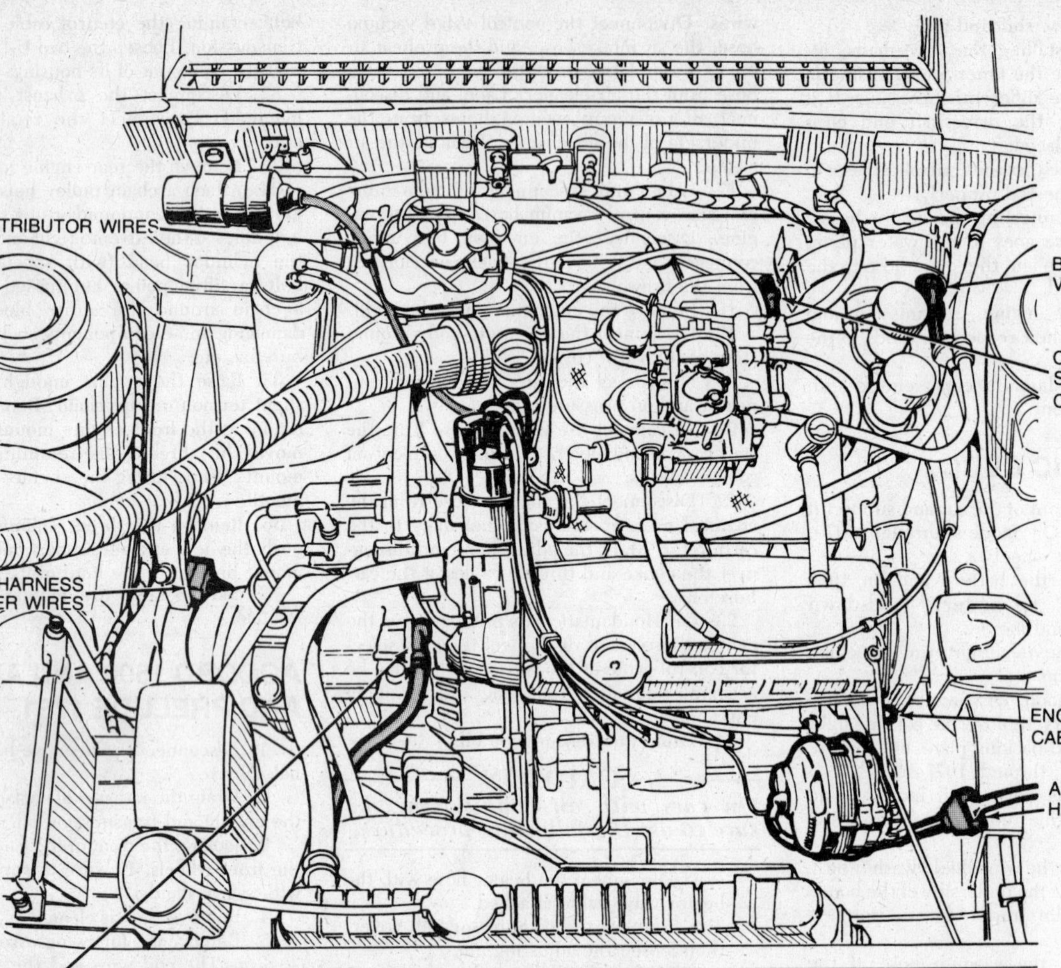

Accord component removal points

transmission by prying the snap-ring off the groove in the end of the shaft. Then, pull the shaft out by holding the knuckle.

14. Remove the center engine mount.
15. Remove the shift rod positioner from the transmission case.
16. Drive out the pin from the shift rod using a small pin driver.
17. On Hondamatics, remove the control cable.
18. Disconnect the exhaust pipe.
19. Remove the three engine support bolts and push the left engine support into the shock mount bracket.
20. Remove the front and rear engine mounts.
21. Raise the engine carefully and remove it from the car.

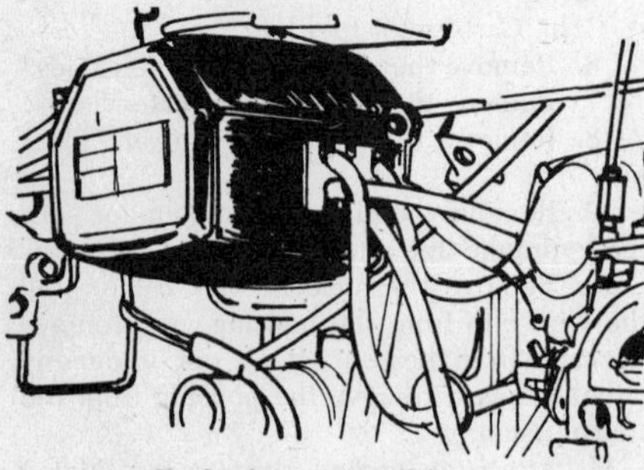

Emission control box

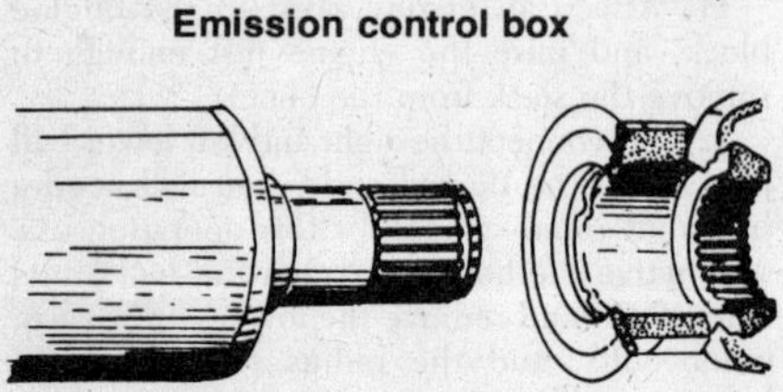

Accord driveshaft removal

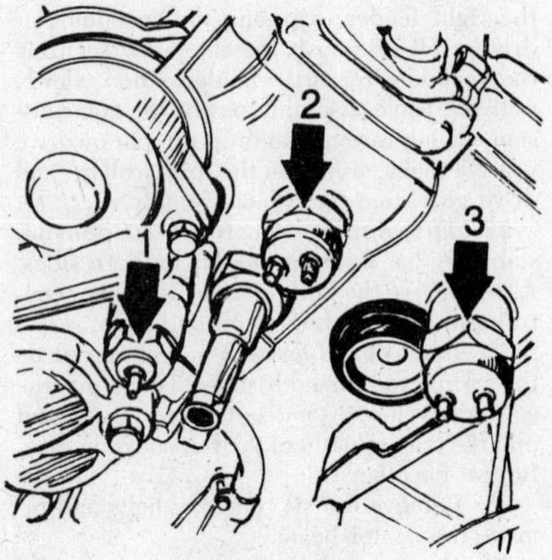

1. Temperature
2. Thermosensor A
3. Thermosensor B

CVCC sending unit locations

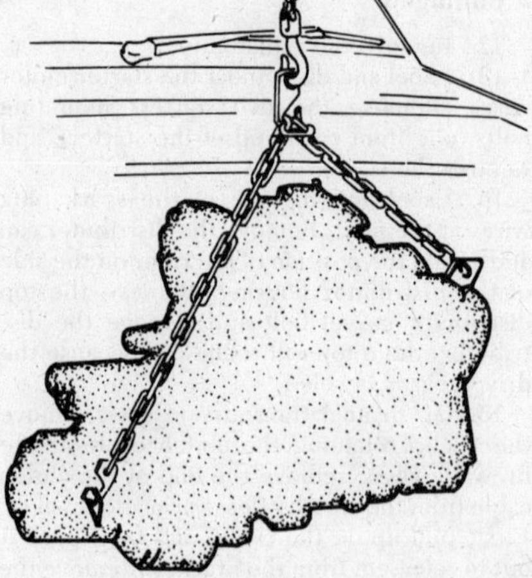

Accord engine removal

22. Install the engine in the reverse order of removal, making the following checks:

a. Make sure that the clip at the end of the driveshaft seats in the groove in the differential. ***Failure to do so may lead to the wheels falling off.***

b. Bleed the air from the cooling system.

c. Adjust the throttle and choke cable tension.

d. Check the clutch for the correct free play.

e. Make sure that the transmission shifts properly.

Cylinder Head

REMOVAL AND INSTALLATION

NOTE: You will need a 12 point socket to remove and install the head bolts on the CVCC engine.

Removal Precautions

1. To prevent warping, the cylinder head should be removed when the engine is cold.

2. Remove oil, scale or carbon deposits accumulated from each part. When decarbonizing take care not to score or scratch the mating surfaces.

3. After washing the oil holes or orifices in each part, make sure they are not restricted by blowing out with compressed air.

4. If parts will not be reinstalled im-

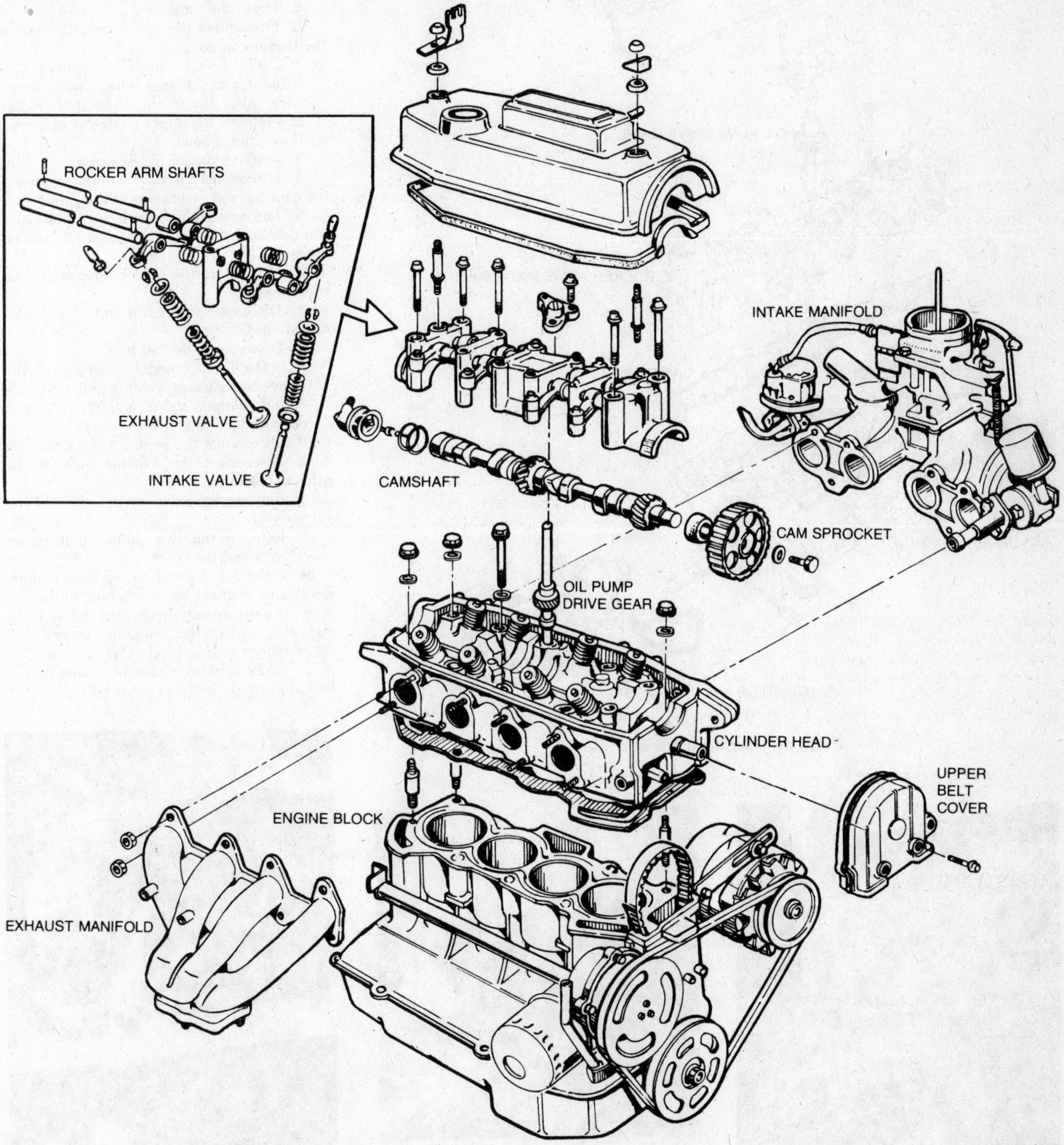

Exploded view of 1170 and 1237 cc engine

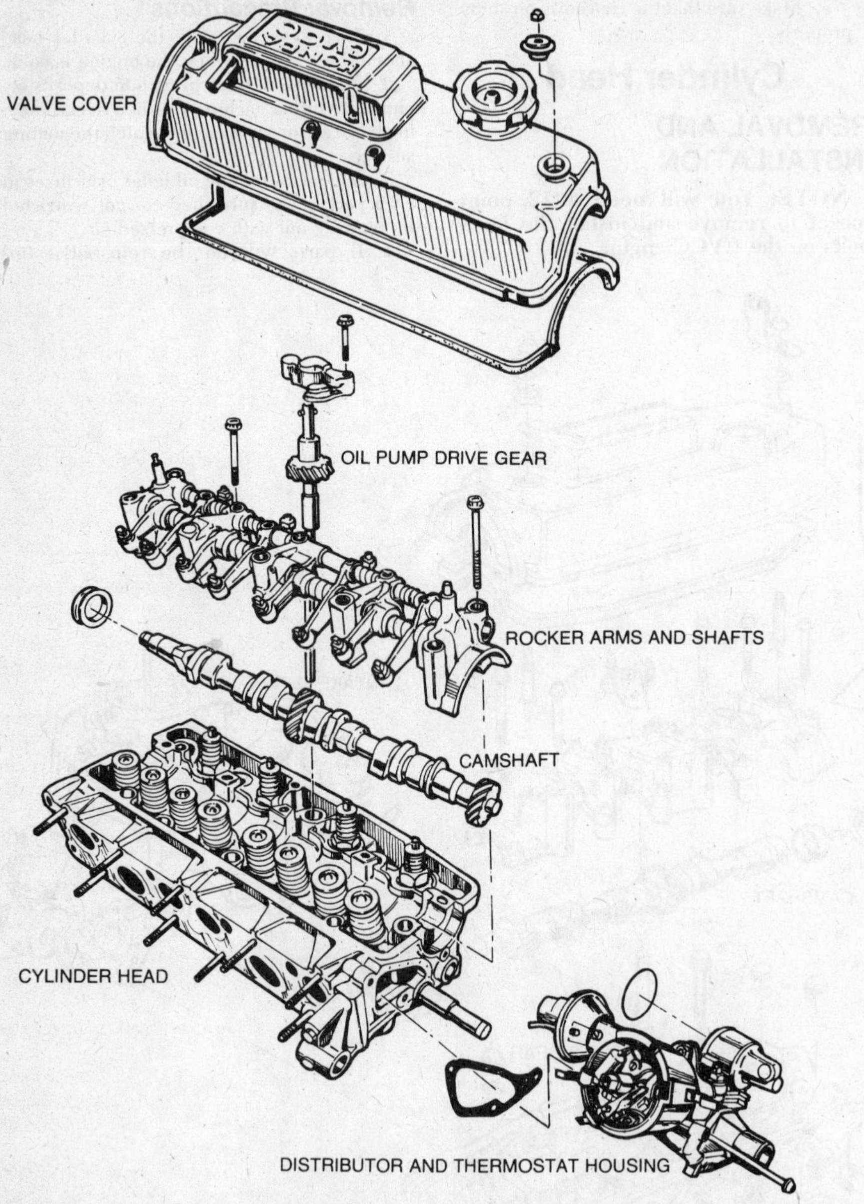

CVCC cylinder head components

mediately after washing, spray parts with a rust preventive to protect from corrosion.

All Except Accord and Prelude 1751 cc

NOTE: If the engine has already been removed from the car, begin with Step 12 in the following procedure.

1. Remove the turn signals, grille, and hood (Civic through 1977 only). Disconnect the negative battery cable.
2. Drain the radiator.
3. Disconnect the upper radiator hose at the thermostat cover.
   a. On CVCC models, remove distributor cap, ignition wires and primary wire. Also, loosen the alternator bracket and remove the upper mounting bolt from the cylinder head.
4. Remove the air cleaner case.
5. Disconnect the tube running between the canister and carburetor at the canister.
6. Disconnect the throttle and choke control cables. Label and disconnect all vacuum hoses.
7. Disconnect the heater hose at the intake manifold.
8. Disconnect the wires from both thermoswitches.
9. Disconnect the fuel line.
   a. On CVCC models, disconnect the temperature gauge sending unit wire, idle cut-off solenoid valve, and primary/main cut-off solenoid valve.
10. Disconnect the engine torque rod.
11. Disconnect the exhaust pipe at the exhaust manifold.
12. Remove the valve cover bolts and the valve cover.
13. Remove the two timing belt upper cover bolts and the cover.
14. Bring No. 1 piston to top dead center. Do this by aligning the notch next to the red notch you use for setting ignition timing, with the index mark on the timing belt cover (1237 cc) or rear of engine block (CVCC).
15. Loosen, but do not remove, the timing belt adjustment bolt and pivot bolt.

Timing belt pivot and adjustment bolts

Remove the non-CVCC camshaft sprocket with the woodruff key facing up

Hidden bolt next to the oil pump gear

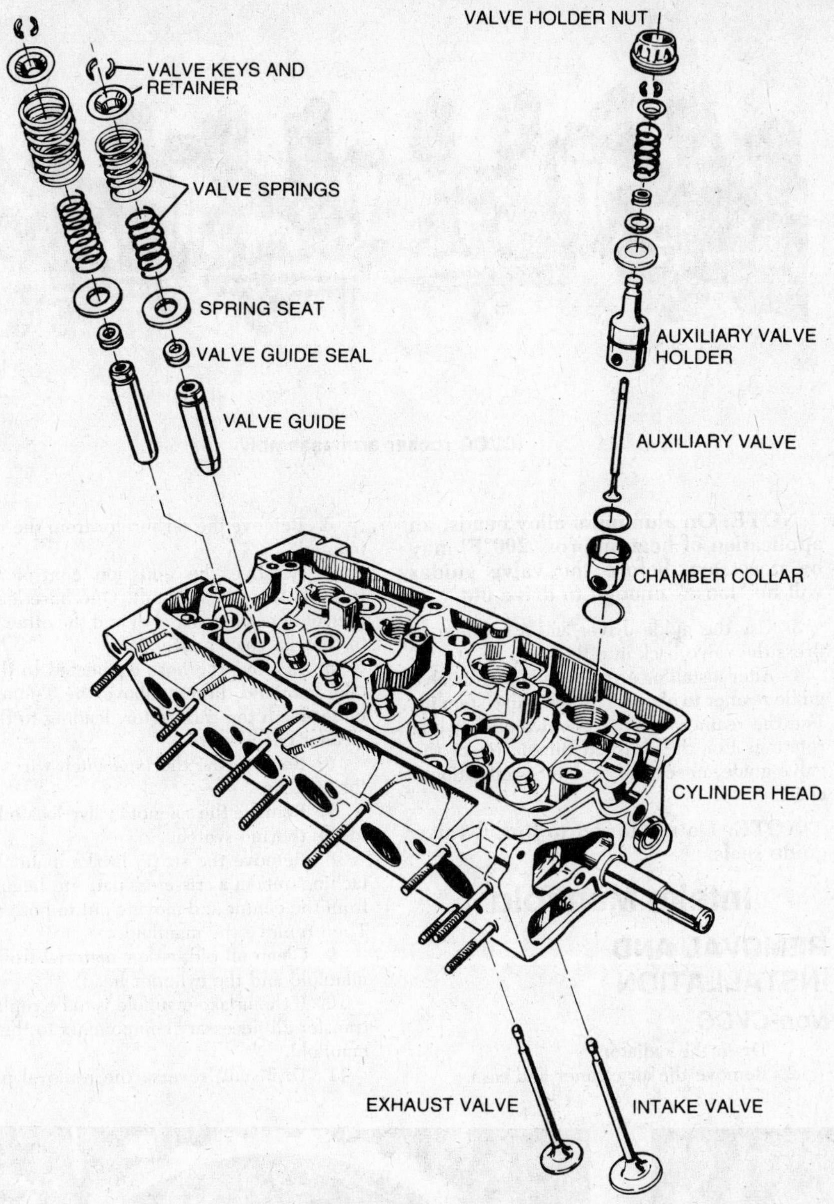

CVCC cylinder head and valve train

16. On 1237 cc models only, remove the camshaft pulley bolt. Do not let the woodruff key fall inside the timing cover. Remove the pulley with a pulley remover (or special tool 07935-6110000).

CAUTION

Use care when handling the timing belt. Do not use sharp instruments to remove the belt. Do not get oil or grease on the belt. Do not bend or twist the belt more than 90°.

17. On 1237 cc models only, remove the fuel pump and distributor.
18. On 1237 cc models only, remove the oil pump gear holder and remove the pump gear and shaft.
19. Loosen and remove the cylinder head bolts in the *reverse* order given in the head bolt tightening sequence diagram. The number one bolt is hidden underneath the oil pump.
20. Remove the cylinder head with the carburetor and manifolds attached.
21. Remove the intake and exhaust manifolds from the cylinder heads.

NOTE: After removing the cylinder head, cover the engine with a clean cloth to prevent materials from getting into the cylinders.

22. To install, reverse the removal procedure, being sure to pay attention to the following points:
    a. Be sure that No. 1 cylinder is at top dead center before positioning the cylinder head in place;
    b. Use a new head gasket and make sure the head, engine block, and gasket are clean.
    c. The cylinder head aligning dowel pins should be in their proper place in the block before installing the cylinder head;
    d. Tighten the head bolts in three progressive steps to the proper torque according to the diagram;
    e. After the head bolts have been tightened, install the woodruff key and camshaft pulley (if removed), and tighten the pulley bolt according to specification. On the non-CVCC engine, align the marks on the camshaft pulley so they are parallel with the top of the head and the woodruff key is facing up; on the CVCC engine, the word "UP" should be facing upward and the mark on the cam sprocket should be aligned with the arrow on the cylinder head;
    f. After installing the pulley (if removed), install the timing belt. Be careful not to disturb the timing position already set when installing the belt.

Accord and Prelude 1751 cc

CAUTION

Cylinder head temperature must be below 100°F.

1. Disconnect the battery ground cable.
2. Drain the cooling system.
3. Remove the air cleaner, tagging all hoses for installation.
4. Disconnect the wires from the thermosenser temperature gauge sending unit, idle cut-off solenoid valve, primary/main cut-off solenoid valve, and the automatic choke.
5. Disconnect the fuel lines and throttle cable from the carburetor.
6. Tag all emission hoses going to the carburetor then remove them and the carburetor.
7. Disconnect all wires and hoses from the distributor, tagging them for installation, and remove the distributor.
8. Remove all coolant hoses from the head.
9. Disconnect the hot air ducts and head pipe from the head. Loosen the exhaust manifold-to-engine bracket bolts to ease assembly.
10. On cars without A/C, remove the bolt holding the alternator bracket to the head. Loosen the adjustment bolt.
11. On cars with A/C, remove the alternator and bracket from the car.
12. Disconnect the brake booster vacuum hose at the one-way valve.
13. Remove the valve cover and timing bolt upper cover.
14. Loosen the timing belt pivot and adjust bolts and slide the belt off the pulley.
15. Remove the oil pump gear cover and pull the oil pump shaft out of the head.
16. Remove the heat bolt in sequence working from the ends, across the head, toward the center. This is the reverse of the tightening sequence.
17. Carefully lift the head from the block.
18. Thoroughly clean the mating surfaces to the head and block.
19. Always use a new gasket.
20. Install the head in reverse order of the removal procedure. Make sure the head dowel pins are aligned. Make sure that the UP mark on the timing belt pulley is at the top. Torque the cylinder head bolts in three equal steps to 43 ft/lbs.

Camshaft and Rocker Shafts

REMOVAL AND INSTALLATION

NOTE: To facilitate installation, make sure that No. 1 piston is at Top Dead Center before removal of camshaft.

1. Follow the "Cylinder Head" removal procedure before attempting to remove the camshaft.
2. Loosen the camshaft and rocker arm shaft holder bolts in a crisscross pattern, beginning on the outside holder.
3. Remove the rocker arms, shafts, and holders as an assembly.
4. Lift out the camshaft and right head seal (or tachometer body if equipped).
5. To install, reverse the removal procedure, being sure to install the holder bolts in the reverse order of removal.

NOTE: Back off valve adjusting screws before installing rockers. Then adjust valves as outlined earlier.

Valves and Valve Guides

REMOVAL AND INSTALLATION

All Models

1. Using a valve spring compressor, remove the valve keepers, retainers, springs, and seats. Then remove the valves.
2. Remove the valve guides with a hammer and a valve guide driver. Drive the guides out from the combustion chamber side.

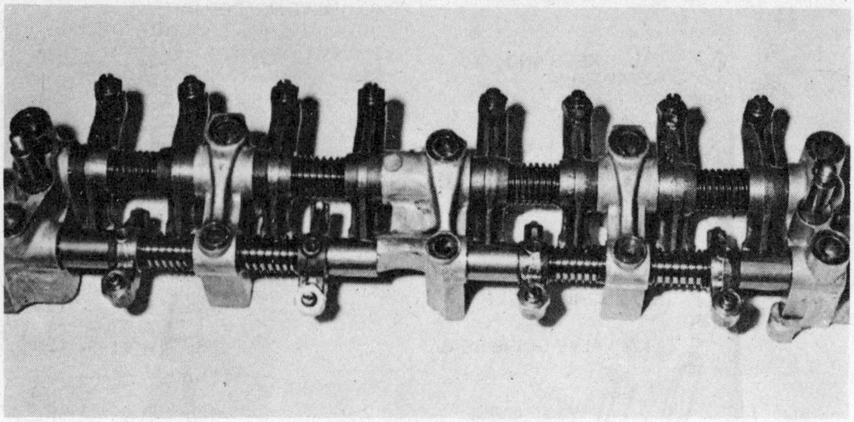

CVCC rocker arm assembly

NOTE: On aluminum alloy heads, an application of heat (approx. 200°F) may be necessary before the valve guides will be "loose" enough to drive out.

3. Use the guide driver and a hammer to press the valve back into the head.
4. After installing a valve guide, use a valve guide reamer to obtain a proper valve stem fit. Use the reamer with an in-out motion while rotating. For the finished dimension of the valve guide, check the "Valve Specifications" chart.

NOTE: Do not forget to install valve guide seals.

Intake Manifold

REMOVAL AND INSTALLATION

Non-CVCC

1. Drain the radiator.
2. Remove the air cleaner and case.
3. Remove the carburetor from the intake manifold.
4. Remove the emission control hoses from the manifold T-Joint. One hose leads to the condensation chamber and the other leads to the charcoal canister.
5. Remove the hose connected to the intake manifold directly above the T-joint and underneath the carburetor, leading to the air cleaner check valve.
6. Remove the thermo-switch wires from the switches.
7. Remove the solenoid valve located next to the thermo-switch.
8. Remove the six (6) intake manifold attaching nuts in a crisscross pattern, beginning from the center and moving out to both ends. Then remove the manifold.
9. Clean all old gasket material from the manifold and the cylinder head.
10. If the intake manifold is to be replaced, transfer all necessary components to the new manifold.
11. To install, reverse the removal proce-

On CVCC engines, when the camshaft sprocket is in the correct position, the word "UP" will be facing up, and the small arrow will point to the sprocket mark. The marks are slightly off in this photograph.

On non-CVCC engines, align the marks on the cam sprocket with the top of the cylinder head.

dure, being sure to observe the following points:

a. Apply a water-resistant sealer to the new intake manifold gasket before positioning it in place;

b. Be sure all hoses are properly connected;

c. Tighten the manifold attaching nuts in the reverse order of removal.

Exhaust Manifold

REMOVAL AND INSTALLATION

Non-CVCC

CAUTION

Do not perform this operation on a warm or hot engine.

1. Remove the front grille.
2. Remove the three (3) exhaust pipe-to-manifold nuts and disconnect the exhaust pipe at the manifold.

a. Disconnect the air injection tubes from the exhaust manifold and remove the air injection manifold.

3. Remove the hot air cover, held by two bolts, from the exhaust manifold.
4. Remove the eight (8) manifold attaching nuts in a crisscross pattern starting from the center, and remove the manifold.
5. To install, reverse the removal procedure. Be sure to use new gaskets and be sure to tighten the manifold bolts in the reverse order of removal to the proper tightening torque.

Intake and Exhaust Manifold

REMOVAL AND INSTALLATION

CVCC Models

1. Drain the radiator. Disconnect manifold coolant hoses.

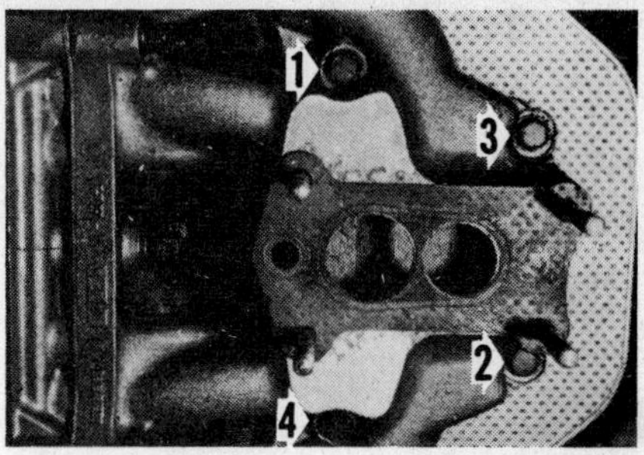

When installing the CVCC combination manifold, tighten the four bolts after the manifolds have been installed to avoid cracking the manifold ears.

2. Remove the air cleaner assembly.
3. Label and disconnect all emission control vacuum hoses and electrical leads.
4. Disconnect the fuel lines, throttle, and choke linkage.
5. Remove the carburetor from the intake manifold.
6. Remove the upper heat shield. Loosen, but do not remove the four bolts retaining the intake manifold to the exhaust manifold.
7. Disconnect the exhaust pipe from the exhaust manifold.
8. Remove the nine nuts retaining the intake and exhaust manifolds to the cylinder head. The two manifolds are removed as a unit.
9. Reverse the above procedure to install, using new gaskets. The thick washers used beneath the cylinder head-to-manifold retaining nuts must be installed with the dished (concave), side toward the engine. Readjust the choke and throttle linkage and bleed the cooling system.

CVCC rocker arm assembly removal

CVCC cylinder head components

Timing Gear Cover

REMOVAL AND INSTALLATION

1. Align the crankshaft pulley (1237 cc), or flywheel pointer (CVCC), at Top Dead Center (TDC).
2. Remove the two bolts which hold the timing belt upper cover and remove the cover.
3. Loosen the alternator and air pump (if so equipped), and remove the pulley belt(s).
4. Remove the three water pump pulley bolts and the water pump pulley.
5. Remove the crankshaft pulley attaching bolt. Use a two-jawed puller to remove the crankshaft pulley.

NOTE: The crankshaft bolt cannot be reused. It must be replaced whenever removed.

6. Remove the timing gear cover retaining bolts and the timing gear cover.
7. To install, reverse the removal procedure. Make sure that the timing guide plates, pulleys and front oil seal are properly installed on the crankshaft and before replacing the cover.

Timing Belt and Tensioner

REMOVAL AND INSTALLATION

1. Turn the crankshaft pulley until it is at Top Dead Center of the compression stroke. This can be determined by observing the valves (all closed) or by feeling for pressure in the sparkplug hole (with your thumb or a compression gauge) as the engine is turned.

2. Remove the pulley belt, water pump pulley, crankshaft pulley, and timing gear cover. Mark the direction of timing belt rotation.

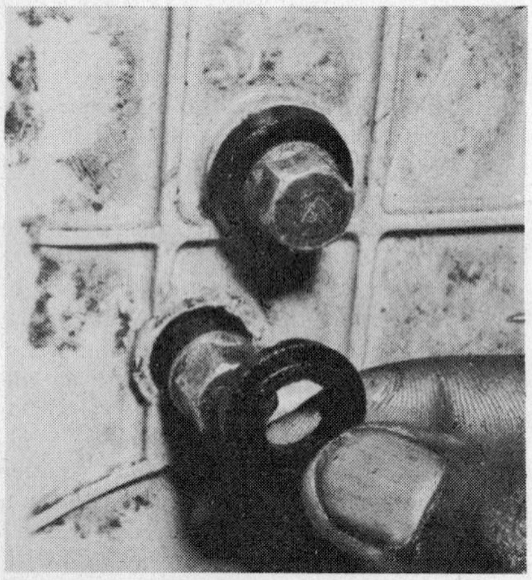

Remove the washers behind the tensioner and adjuster bolts to allow removal of the cover without removing the bolts.

3. Loosen, *but do not remove*, the tensioner adjusting bolt and pivot bolt.

4. Slide the timing belt off the camshaft timing sprocket and the crankshaft pulley sprocket and remove it from the engine.

5. To remove the camshaft timing sprocket, first remove the center bolt and then remove the sprocket with a pulley remover or a brass hammer. This can be accomplished by simply removing the timing belt upper cover, loosening the tensioner bolts, and sliding the timing belt off to expose the sprocket for removal.

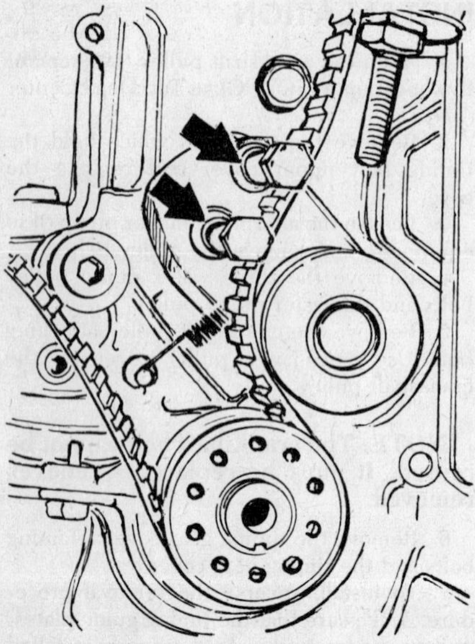

Belt adjustment (lower) and pivot (upper) bolts

NOTE: If you remove the timing sprocket with the timing belt cover in place, be sure not to let the woodruff key fall inside the timing cover when removing the sprocket from the camshaft.

Inspect the timing belt. Replace if over 10,000 miles old, if oil soaked (find source of oil leak also), or if worn on leading edges of belt teeth.

6. To install, reverse the removal procedure. Be sure to install the crankshaft and camshaft timing sprockets in the top dead center position. (See "Cylinder Head Removal" for further details.) On the non-CVCC engine, align the marks on the camshaft timing gear so they are parallel with the top of the cylinder head and the Woodruff key is facing up.

When installing the timing belt, do not allow oil to come in contact with the belt. Oil will cause the rubber to swell. Be careful not to bend or twist the belt unnecessarily, since it is made of fiberglass; nor should you use tools having sharp edges when installing or removing the belt. Be sure to install the belt with the arrow facing in the same direction it was facing during removal.

After installing the timing belt, adjust the belt tension by first rotating the crankshaft counterclockwise ¼ turn. Then, retighten the adjusting bolt and finally the tensioner pivot bolt.

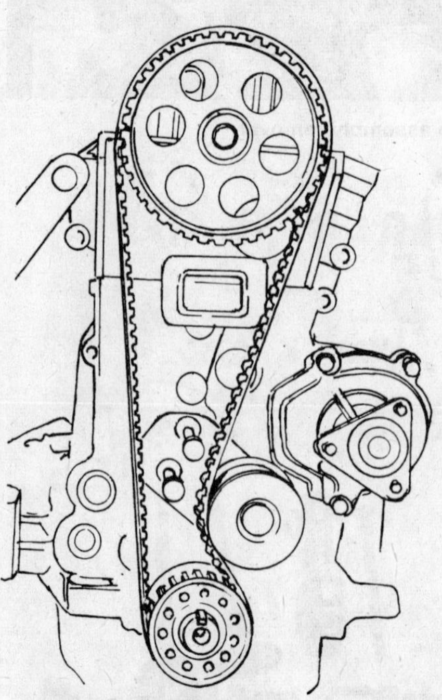

Non CVCC engine timing bolt installation. The crankshaft key is straight up and the cam sprocket marks are parallel with the cylinder head

CAUTION

Do not remove the adjusting or pivot bolts, only loosen them. When adjusting, do not use any force other than the adjuster spring. If the belt is too tight, it will result in a shortened belt life.

Pistons and Connecting Rods

REMOVAL AND INSTALLATION

For removal with the engine out of the car, begin with Step 8.

1. Remove the turn signals (Civic through 1977), grille, and engine hood.
2. Drain the radiator.
3. Drain the engine oil.
4. Raise the front of the car and support it with safety stands.
5. Attach a chain to the clutch cable bracket on the transmission case and raise just enough to take the load off the center mount.

NOTE: Do not remove the left engine mount.

6. Remove the center beam and engine lower mount.
7. Remove the cylinder head (see "Cylinder Head Removal and Installation").
8. Loosen the oil pan bolts and remove the oil pan and flywheel dust shield. Loosen the oil pan bolts in a criss-cross pattern beginning with the outside bolt.

To remove the oil pan, lightly tap the corners of the oil pan with a mallet. It is not necessary to remove the gasket unless it is damaged.

CAUTION

Do not pry the oil pan off with the tip of a screwdriver.

9. Remove the oil passage block and the oil pump assembly.

CAUTION

As soon as the oil passage block bolts are loosened, the oil in the oil line may flow out.

NOTE: Before removing the pistons, check the top of the cylinder bore for carbon build-up or a ridge. Remove the carbon or use a ridge-reamer to remove the ridge before removing the pistons.

10. Working from the underside of the car, remove the connecting rod bearing caps. Using the wooden handle of a hammer, push the pistons and connecting rods out of the cylinders.

NOTE: Bearing caps, bearings, and pistons should be marked to indicate their location for reassembly.

11. When removing the piston rings, be sure not to apply excessive force as the rings are made of cast iron and can be easily broken.

NOTE: A hydraulic press is necessary for removing the piston pin.

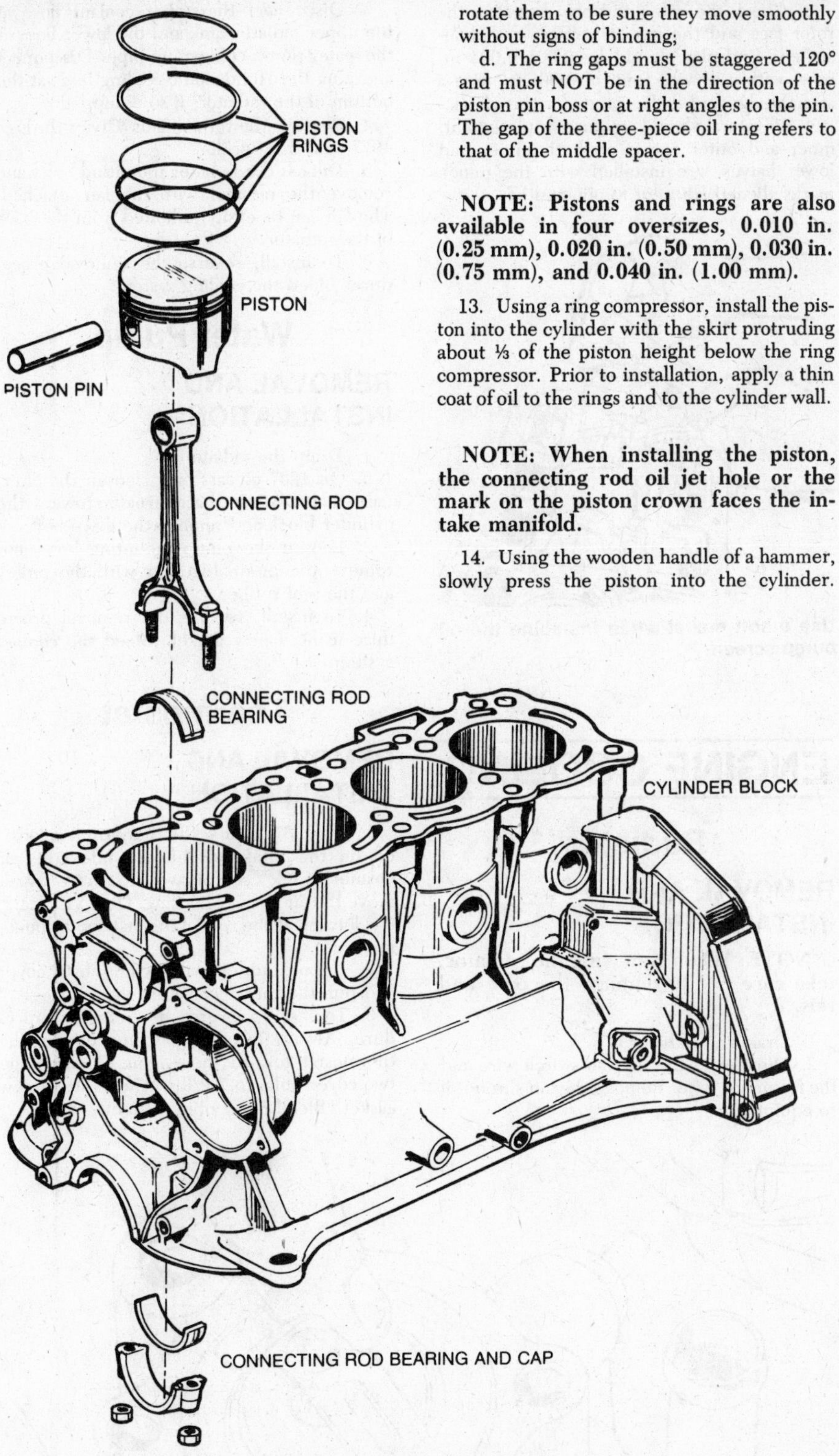

CVCC engine block and piston

12. Observe the following points when installing the piston rings:

a. When installing the three-piece oil ring, first place the spacer and then the rails in position. The spacer and rail gaps must be staggered 0.787-1.181 in. (2-3 cm);

b. Install the second and top rings on the piston with their markings facing upward;

c. After installing all rings on the piston, rotate them to be sure they move smoothly without signs of binding;

d. The ring gaps must be staggered 120° and must NOT be in the direction of the piston pin boss or at right angles to the pin. The gap of the three-piece oil ring refers to that of the middle spacer.

NOTE: Pistons and rings are also available in four oversizes, 0.010 in. (0.25 mm), 0.020 in. (0.50 mm), 0.030 in. (0.75 mm), and 0.040 in. (1.00 mm).

13. Using a ring compressor, install the piston into the cylinder with the skirt protruding about ⅓ of the piston height below the ring compressor. Prior to installation, apply a thin coat of oil to the rings and to the cylinder wall.

NOTE: When installing the piston, the connecting rod oil jet hole or the mark on the piston crown faces the intake manifold.

14. Using the wooden handle of a hammer, slowly press the piston into the cylinder. Guide the connecting rod so it does not damage the crankshaft journals.

15. Reassemble the remaining components in the reverse order of removal. Install the connecting rod bearing caps so that the recess in the cap and the recess in the rod are on the same side. After tightening the cap bolts, move the rod back and forth on the journal to check for binding.

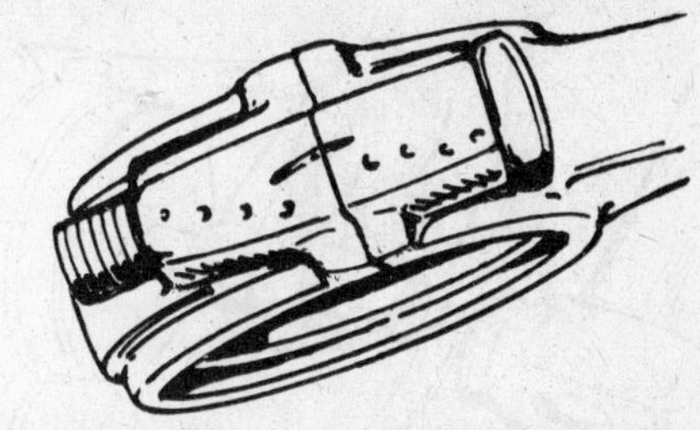

Mark the pistons and rods if they are not marked from the factory

ENGINE LUBRICATION

Oil Pan

REMOVAL AND INSTALLATION

1. Drain the engine oil.
2. Raise the front of the car and support it with safety stands.
3. Attach a chain to the clutch cable bracket (Civic) or slave cylinder (Accord) on the transmission case and raise just enough to take the load off the center mount.

NOTE: Do not remove the left engine mount.

4. Remove the center beam and engine lower mount.
5. Loosen the oil bolts and remove the oil pan flywheel dust shield.

NOTE: Loosen the bolts in a criss-cross pattern beginning with the outside bolt. To remove the oil pan, lightly tap the corners of the oil pan with a mallet. It is not necessary to remove the gasket unless it is damaged.

6. To install, reverse the removal procedure. Apply a coat of sealant to the entire mating surface of the cylinder block, except the crankshaft oil seal, before fitting the oil pan. Tighten the bolts in a circular sequence, beginning in the center and working out towards the ends.

Rear Main Oil Seal

REPLACEMENT

The rear oil seal is installed in the rear main bearing cap. Replacement of the seal requires the removal of the transmission, flywheel and clutch housing, as well as the oil pan. Refer to the appropriate sections for the removal and installation of the above components. Both the front and rear main seal are installed after the crankshaft bearing caps have been torqued, if the crankshaft has been removed. Special drivers must be used.

Oil Pump

REMOVAL AND INSTALLATION

To remove the oil pump, follow the proce-

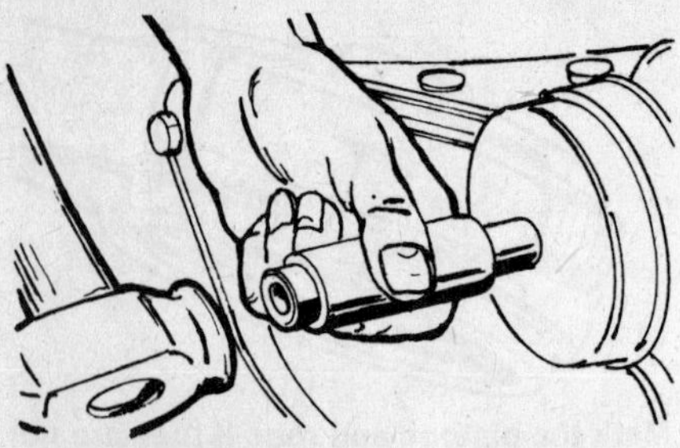

Driving in the rear main seal

Oil pump retaining bolt under screen

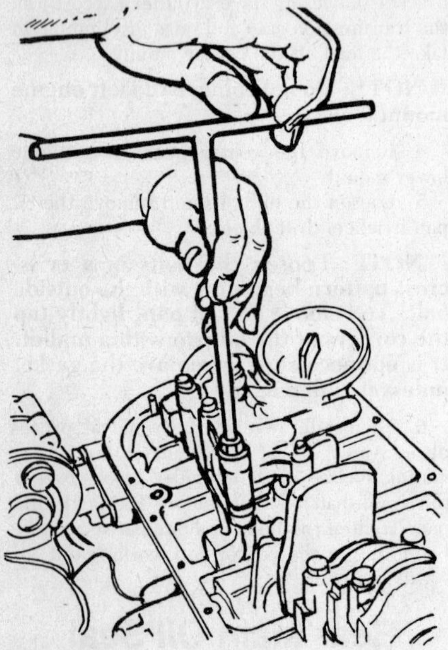

Oil pump removal; there is a bolt under the screen

dure given for oil pan removal and installation. After the oil pan has been dropped, simply unbolt the oil passage block and oil pump assembly from the engine. Remove the oil pump screen to find the last bolt. When installing the pump, tighten the bolts to no more than 8 ft/lbs.

OIL PUMP OVERHAUL

1. Check the rotor radial clearance on both the upper and lower rotors. Clearance is 0.006-0.008 in.
2. Check body-to-rotor clearance on both rotors. Clearance is 0.004-0.007 new, with 0.008 in. as the service limit.
3. Check the rotor end-play between the rotor face and the gasket surface, gasket installed. End-play should be 0.001-0.004 in. new, with a service limit of 0.006 in. Use a straightedge and feeler gauge for this check.
4. If rotors should require replacement, inner and outer rotors on both upper and lower halves, are installed with the punch marks aligned adjacent to one another.

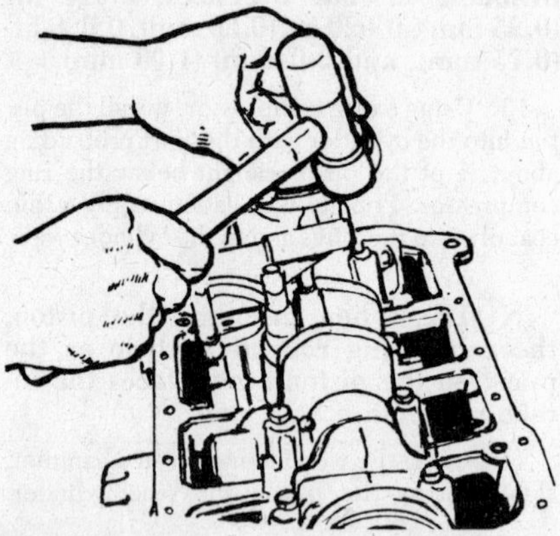

Use a soft mallet when installing the oil pump screen

ENGINE COOLING

Radiator

REMOVAL AND INSTALLATION

NOTE: When removing the radiator, take care not to damage the core and fins.

1. Drain the radiator.
2. Disconnect the thermo-switch wire and the fan motor wire. Remove the fan shroud, if so equipped.
3. Disconnect the upper coolant hose at the upper radiator tank and the lower hose at the water pump connecting pipe. Disconnect and plug the Hondamatic cooling lines at the bottom of the radiator, if so equipped.
4. Remove the turn signals (Civics through 1977) and front grille.
5. Detach the radiator mounting bolts and remove the radiator with the fan attached. The fan can be easily unbolted from the back of the radiator.
6. To install, reverse the removal procedure. Bleed the cooling system.

Water Pump

REMOVAL AND INSTALLATION

1. Drain the radiator.
2. On 1237 cc cars only, loosen the alternator bolts. Move the alternator toward the cylinder block and remove the drive belt.
3. Loosen the pump mounting bolts and remove the pump together with the pulley and the seal rubber.
4. To install, reverse the removal procedure using a new gasket. Bleed the cooling system.

Thermostat

REMOVAL AND INSTALLATION

1. On 1237 cc cars, the thermostat is located on the intake manifold, under the air cleaner nozzle, so you will first have to remove the air cleaner housing. On CVCC cars, it is located at the rear of the distributor housing.
2. Unbolt and remove the thermostat cover and pull the thermostat from the housing.
3. To install, reverse the removal procedure. Always install the spring end of the thermostat toward the engine. Tighten the two cover bolts to 7 ft/lbs. Always use a new gasket. Bleed the cooling system.

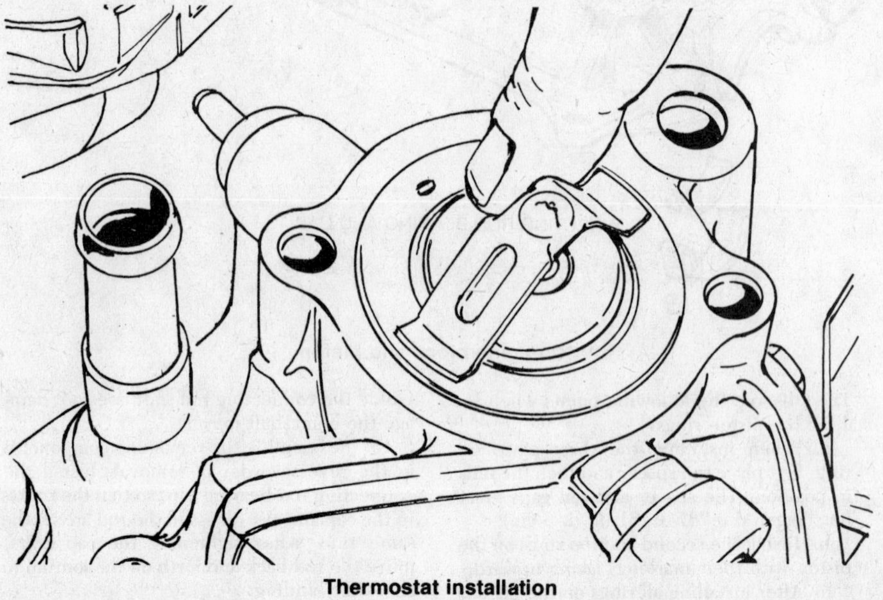

Thermostat installation

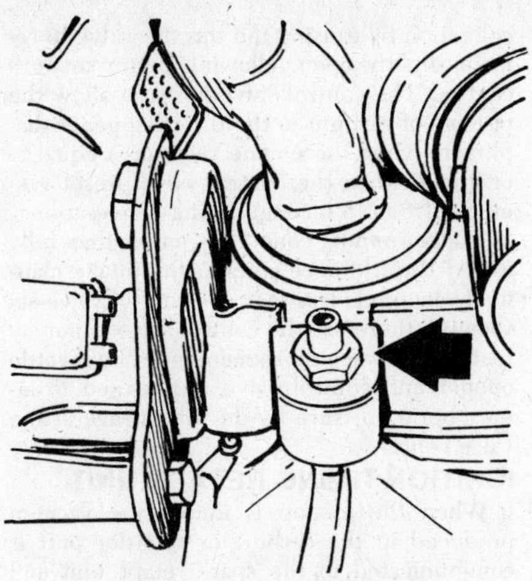

Cooling system bleed bolt

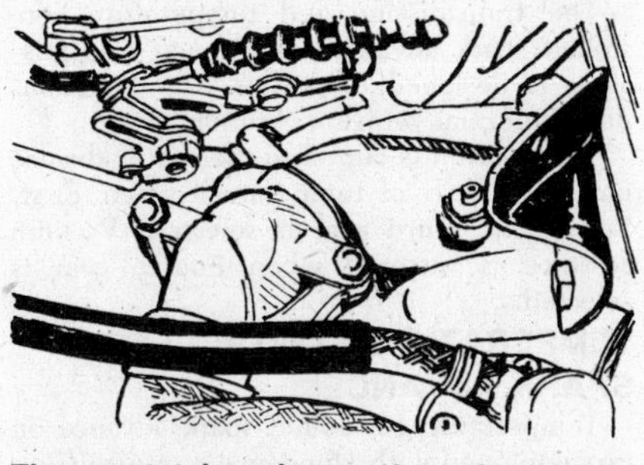

Thermostat housing and coolant bleed bolt, non-CVCC

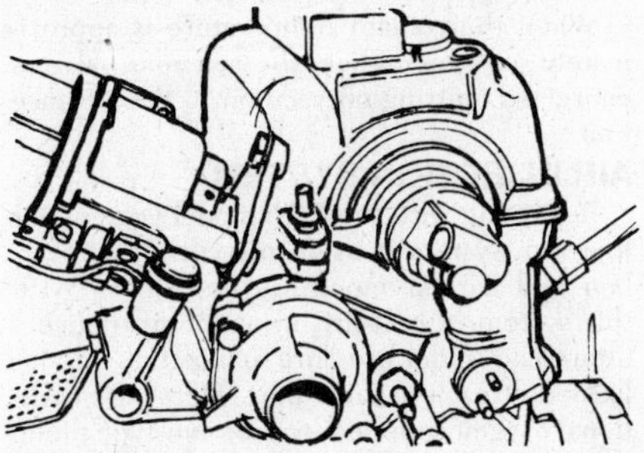

Thermostat housing and coolant bleed bolt, CVCC

EMISSION CONTROLS

Emission controls fall into three basic systems: Crankcase Emission Control System, Exhaust Emission Control System and Evaporative Emission Control System.

Crankcase Emission Control System

All engines are equipped with a "Dual Return System" to prevent crankcase vapor emissions. Blow-by gas is returned to the combustion chamber through the intake manifold and carburetor air cleaner. When the throttle is partially opened, blow-by gas is returned to the intake manifold through breather tubes leading into the tee orifice located on the outside of the intake manifold. When the throttle is opened wide and vacuum in the air cleaner rises, blow-by gas is returned to the intake manifold through an additional passage in the air cleaner case.

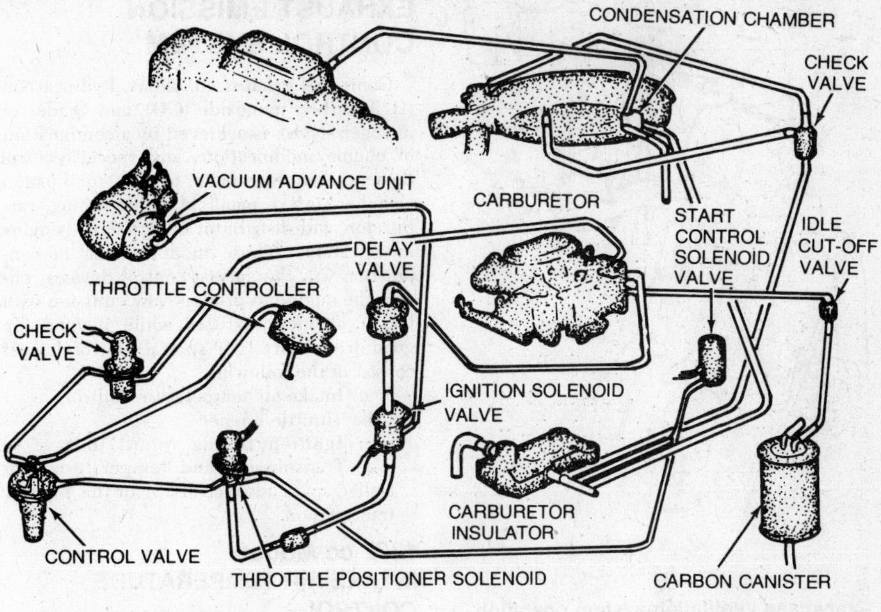

Emission controls system schematic—Accord with manual transmission

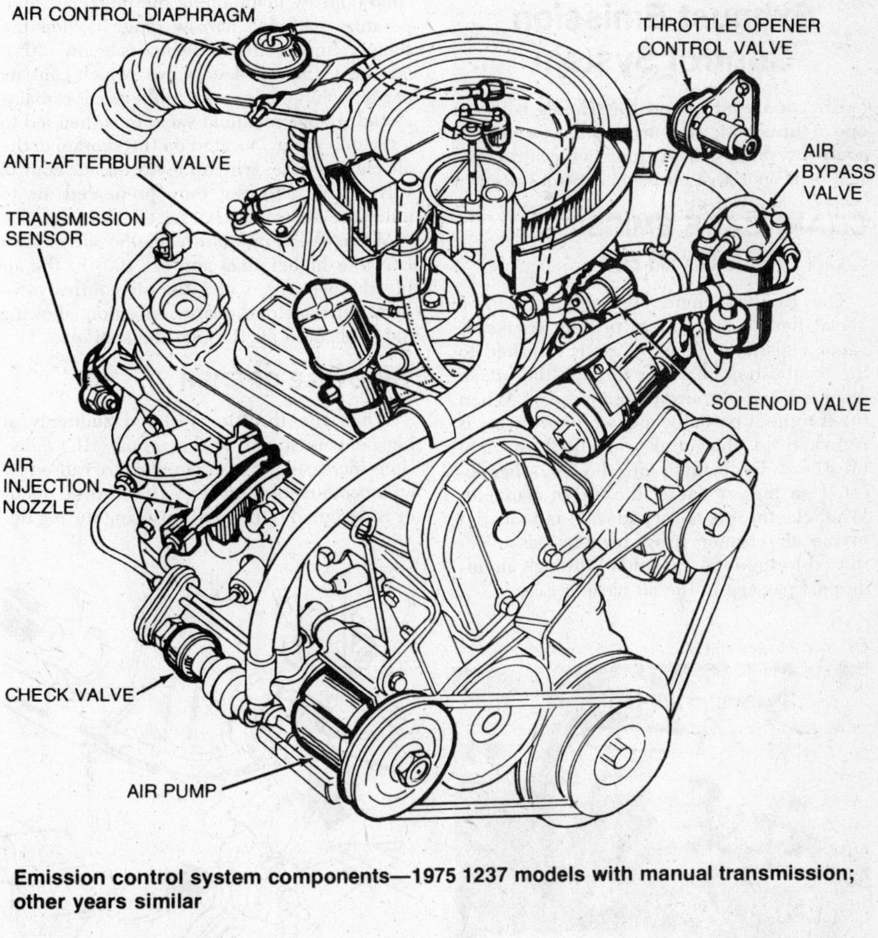

Emission control system components—1975 1237 models with manual transmission; other years similar

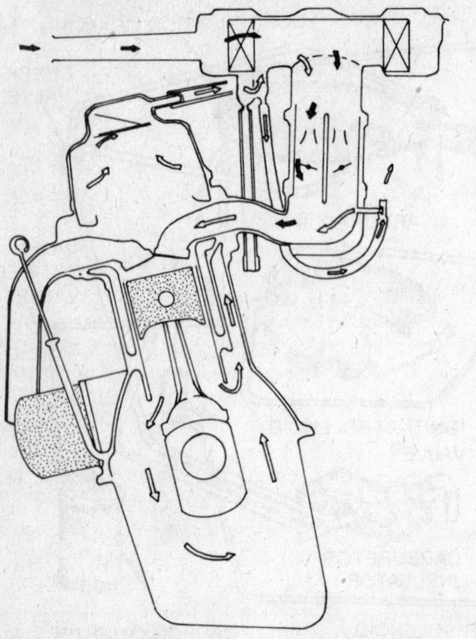

Crankcase ventilation system operation, 1170 and 1237 cc engines—CVCC similar

Exhaust Emission Control System

Emission controls on the Honda fall into one of three basic systems: crankcase emission control system, exhaust emission control system or evaporative emission control system.

CRANKCASE EMISSION CONTROL SYSTEM

The Honda's engine is equipped with a "Dual Return System" to prevent crankcase vapor emissions. Blow-by gas is returned to the combustion chamber through the intake manifold and carburetor air cleaner. When the throttle is partially opened, blow-by gas is returned to the intake manifold through breather tubes leading into the tee orifice located on the outside of the intake manifold. When the throttle is opened wide and vacuum in the air cleaner rises, blow-by gas is returned to the intake manifold through an additional passage in the air cleaner case.

1975 and later CVCC PCV system orifice location

EXHAUST EMISSION CONTROL SYSTEM

Control of exhaust emissions, hydrocarbon (HC), carbon monoxide (CO), and Oxides of nitrogen (NO_x), is achieved by a combination of engine modifications and special control devices. Improvements to the combustion chamber, intake manifold, valve timing, carburetor, and distributor comprise the engine modifications. These modifications, in conjunction wih the special control devices, enable the engine to produce low emission with leaner air-fuel mixtures while maintaining good driveability. The special control devices consist of the following:

a. Intake air temperature control;
b. Throttle opener;
c. Ignition timing retard unit
d. Transmission and temperature controlled spark advance (TCS) for the 4-speed transmission.

1237 cc Models

INTAKE AIR TEMPERATURE CONTROL

Intake air temperature control is designed to provide the most uniform carburetion possible under various ambient air temperature conditions by maintaining the intake air temperature within a narrow range. When the temperature in the air cleaner is below 100° F (approx.), the air bleed valve, which consists of a bimetallic strip and a rubber seal, remains closed. Intake manifold vacuum is then led to a vacuum motor, located on the snorkel of the air cleaner case, which moves the air control valve door, allowing only preheated air to enter the air cleaner.

When the temperature in the air cleaner becomes higher than approx. 100° F, the air bleed valve opens and the air control valve door returns to the open position allowing only unheated air through the snorkel.

THROTTLE OPENER

When the throttle is closed suddenly at high engine speed, hydrocarbon (HC) emissions increase due to engine misfire caused by an incombustible mixture. The throttle opener is designed to prevent misfiring during deceleration by causing the throttle valve to remain slightly open, allowing better mixture control. The control valve is set to allow the passage of vacuum to the throttle opener diaphragm when the engine vacuum is equal to or greater than the control valve preset vacuum (21.6±1.6 in. Hg) during acceleration.

Under running conditions, other than fully closed throttle deceleration, the intake manifold vacuum is less than the control valve set vacuum; therefore the control valve is not actuated. The vacuum remaining in the throttle opener and control valve is returned to atmospheric pressure by the air passage at the valve center.

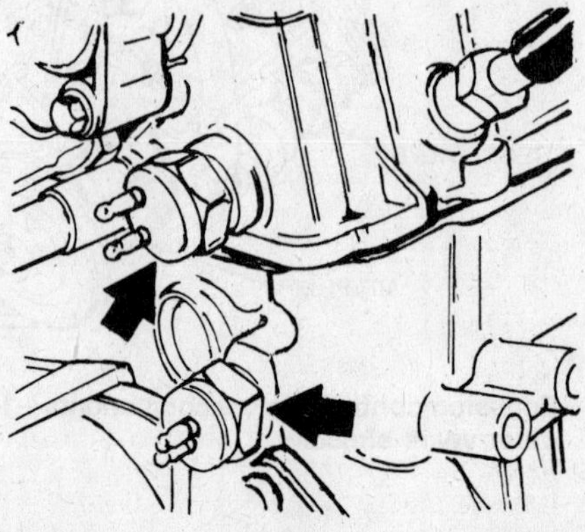

Thermosensors: upper energizes a solenoid, giving vacuum advance (engine cold); lower is used when the engine is warm (1977 and earlier)

IGNITION TIMING RETARD UNIT

When the engine is idling, the vacuum produced in the carburetor retarder port is communicated to the spark retard unit and the ignition timing, at idle, is retarded.

TCS SYSTEM

The transmission and temperature controlled spark advance for 4-speed transmissions is designed to reduce NO_x emissions during normal vehicle operation.

The vacuum is cut off to the spark advance unit regardless of temperature when First, Second, or Third gear is selected. Vacuum advance is restored when Fourth gear is selected.

TEMPERATURE CONTROLLED SPARK ADVANCE

Temperature controlled spark advance on cars equipped with Hondamatic transmission is designed to reduce NO_x emissions by disconnecting the vacuum to the spark advance unit during normal vehicle operation.

When the coolant temperature is approximately 120° or higher, the solenoid valve is energized, cutting off vacuum to the advance unit.

AIR INJECTION SYSTEM

Beginning with the 1975 model year, an air injection system is used to control hydrocarbon and carbon monoxide emissions. With this system, a belt-driven air pump delivers filtered air under pressure to injection nozzles located at each exhaust port. Here, the additional oxygen supplied by the vane-type pump reacts with any uncombusted fuel mixture, promoting an afterburning effect in the hot exhaust manifold. To prevent a reverse flow in the air injection manifold when exhaust gas pressure exceeds air supply pressure, a non-return check valve is used. To prevent exhaust afterburning or backfiring during deceleration, an anti-afterburn valve delivers air to the intake manifold instead. When manifold vacuum rises above the preset vacuum of the air control valve and/or below that of the air by-pass valve, air pump air is returned to the air cleaner.

1487, 1600, 1751 cc Models

INTAKE AIR TEMPERATURE CONTROL

Same as 1237 cc models.

THROTTLE CONTROLS

This system controls the closing of the throttle during periods of gear shifting, deceleration, or anytime the gas pedal is released. In preventing the sudden closing of the throttle during these conditions, an overly rich mixture is prevented which controls excessive emissions of hydrocarbons and carbon monoxide. This system has two main parts; a dashpot system and a throttle positioner system. The dashpot diaphragm and solenoid valve act to dampen or slow down the throttle return time to 1-4 seconds. The throttle positioner part consists of a speed sensor, a solenoid valve, a control valve and an opener diaphragm which will keep the throttle open and predetermined minimum amount any time the gas pedal is released when the car is traveling 15 mph or faster, and closes it when the car slows to 10 mph.

IGNITION TIMING CONTROLS

This system uses a coolant temperature sensor to switch distributor vacuum ignition timing controls on or off to reduce hydrocarbon and oxides of nitrogen emissions. The coolant switch is calibrated at 149°F for 1487 and 1600 cc engines and 167°F for 1751 cc engines.

HOT START CONTROL

This system is designed to prevent an over-rich mixture condition in the intake manifold due to vaporization of residual fuel when starting a hot engine. This reduces hydrocarbon and carbon monoxide emissions.

Start control solenoid valve

ANTI-AFTERBURN VALVE

1979-80 1751 cc engines have an anti-afterburn valve. This unit is used only on models with manual transmission. The valve lets fresh air into the intake manifold when it senses sudden increases in manifold vacuum. The valve responds only to sudden increases in vacuum and the amount of time it stays open is determined by an internal diaphragm which is acted on by the vacuum level.

CVCC ENGINE MODIFICATIONS

By far, the most important part of the CVCC engine emission control system is the Compound Vortex Controlled Combustion (CVCC) cylinder head itself. Each cylinder has three valves: a conventional intake and conventional exhaust valve, and a smaller auxiliary intake valve. There are actually *two* combustion chambers per cylinder: a pre-combustion or auxiliary chamber, and the main chamber. During the intake stroke, an extremely lean mixture is drawn into the main combustion chamber. Simultaneously, a very rich mixture is drawn into the smaller pre-combustion chamber via the auxiliary intake valve. The spark plug, located in the precombustion chamber, easily ignites the rich pre-mixture, and this combustion spreads out into the main combustion chamber where the lean mixture is ignited. Due to the fact that the volume of the auxiliary chamber is much smaller than the main chamber, the overall mixture is very lean (about 18 parts air to one part fuel). The result is low hydrocarbon emissions due to the slow, stable combustion of the lean mixture in the main chamber; low carbon monoxide emissions due to the excess oxygen available; and low oxides of nitrogen emissions due to the lowered peak combustion temperatures. An added benefit of burning the lean mixture is the excellent gas mileage.

EVAPORATIVE EMISSION CONTROL SYSTEM

This system prevents gasoline vapors from escaping into the atmosphere from the fuel tank and carburetor and consists of the components listed in the illustration.

Fuel vapor is stored in the expansion chamber, in the fuel tank, and in the vapor line up to the one-way valve. When the vapor pressure becomes higher than the set pressure of the one-way valve, the valve opens and allows vapor into the charcoal canister. While the engine is stopped or idling, the idle cut-off valve in the canister is closed and the vapor is absorbed by the charcoal.

At partially opened throttle, the idle cut-off valve is opened by manifold vacuum. The vapor that was stored in the charcoal canister and in the vapor line is purged into the intake manifold. Any excessive pressure or vacuum which might build up in the fuel tank is relieved by the two-way valve in the filler cap.

MAINTENANCE AND SERVICE

Components Pertaining To Emission Controls

The proper control of exhaust emissions depends not only on the primary components of the emission controls mentioned above, but also on such related areas as ignition timing, spark plugs, valve clearance, engine oil, cooling system, etc. Before tackling the primary emission controls, you should determine if the related components are functioning properly, and correct any deficiencies.

Crankcase Emission Control System

1. Squeeze the lower end of the drain tube and drain any oil or water which may have collected.
2. Make sure that the intake manifold T-joint is clear by passing the shank end of a No. 65 (0.035 in. dia.) drill through both ends (orifices) of the joint.
3. Check for any loose, disconnected, or deteriorated tubes and replace if necessary.

Exhaust Emission Control System

INTAKE AIR TEMPERATURE CONTROL SYSTEM (ENGINE COLD)

1. Inspect for loose, disconnected, or deteriorated vacuum hoses and replace as necessary.
2. Remove the air cleaner cover and element.
3. With the transmission in Neutral and the blue distributor disconnected, engage the starter motor for approximately two (2) seconds. Manifold vacuum to the vacuum motor should completely raise the air control valve door. Once opened, the valve door should stay open unless there is a leak in the system.
4. If the valve door does not open, check the intake manifold port by passing a No. 78 (0.016 in. dia.) drill or compressed air through the orifice in the manifold.
5. If the valve door still does not open, proceed to the following steps:
   a. Vacuum Motor Test—Disconnect the vacuum line from the vacuum motor inlet pipe. Fully open the air control valve door, block the vacuum motor inlet pipe, then release the door. If the door does not remain open, the vacuum motor is defective. Replace as necessary and repeat Steps 1-3;
   b. Air Bleed Valve Test—Unblock the inlet pipe and make sure that the valve door fully closes without sticking or binding. Reconnect the vacuum line to the vacuum motor inlet pipe. Connect a vacuum source (e.g. hand vacuum pump) to the manifold vacuum line (disconnect at the intake manifold fixed orifice) and draw enough vacuum to fully open the valve door. If the valve door closes with the manifold vacuum line plugged (by the vacuum pump), then vacuum is leaking through the air bleed valve. Replace as necessary and repeat Steps 1-3;

CAUTION

Never force the air bleed valve (bi-metal strip) on or off its valve seat. The bi-metal strip and the valve seat may be damaged.

   c. Check Valve Test—Again draw a vacuum (at the manifold vacuum line) until the valve door opens. Unplug the line by disconnecting the pump from the manifold vacuum line. If the valve door closes, vacuum is leaking past the check valve. Replace as necessary and repeat Steps 1-3.
6. After completing the above steps, replace the air cleaner element and cover and fit a vacuum gauge into the line leading to the vacuum motor.
7. Start the engine and raise the idle to 1500-2000 rpm. As the engine warms, the vacuum gauge reading should drop to zero.

NOTE: Allow sufficient time for the engine to reach normal operating temperature—when the cooling fan cycles on and off.

If the reading does not drop to zero before the engine reaches normal operating temperature, the air bleed valve is defective and must be replaced. Repeat Step 3 as a final check.

TEMPERATURE AND TRANSMISSION CONTROLLED SPARK ADVANCE (ENGINE COLD)—ALL MODELS

1. Check for loose, disconnected, or deteriorated vacuum hoses and replace as necessary.
2. Check the coolant temperature sensor switch for proper operation with an ohmmeter or 12V light. The switch should normally be open (no continuity across the switch terminals) when the coolant temperature is below approximately 120° F (engine cold). If the switch is closed (continuity across the terminals), replace the switch and repeat the check.
3. On manual transmission models, check the transmission sensor switch. The switch should be open (no continuity across the connections) when Fourth gear is selected, and closed (continuity across the connections) in all other gear positions. Replace if necessary and repeat the check.
4. Remove the spark control vacuum tube, leading between the spark advance/retard unit and the solenoid valve, and connect.

Evaporative Emission Control System (Engine at Normal Operating Temperature)

CHARCOAL CANISTER

1. Check for loose, disconnected, or deteriorated vacuum hoses and replace where necessary.
2. Pull the free end of the purge air guide tube out of the body frame and plug it securely.
3. Disconnect the fuel vapor line from the charcoal canister and connect a vacuum gauge to the charcoal canister vapor inlet according to the diagram.
4. Start the engine and allow it to idle. Since the vacuum port in the carburetor is closed off at idle, the vacuum gauge should register no vacuum. If vacuum is available, replace the charcoal canister and recheck for no vacuum. A vacuum reading indicates that the charcoal canister idle cut-off valve is broken or stuck.
5. Open the throttle to 2000 rpm and make sure that the charcoal canister idle cutoff valve is opening by watching the vacuum.
   a. Disconnect the vacuum signal line and connect the vacuum gauge to the carburetor T-joint orifice formerly occupied by the signal line. The vacuum reading at 2000 rpm should be greater than 3 in. Hg. If vacuum is now available (with the throttle open), replace the charcoal canister and repeat Steps 4 & 5. If vacuum is still not available, or is below 3 in. Hg proceed to the next step;
   b. If vacuum is less than 3 in. Hg (with the throttle open), the carburetor vacuum port or T-joint might be plugged. Clear the passages with compressed air. If vacuum is now available, repeat Steps 4 & 5. If vacuum is not available, or below 3 in. Hg, the carburetor vacuum port is blocked. Repair or replace as necessary and repeat Steps 4 & 5. If vacuum is *still* not available, proceed to the next step;
   c. Plug the solenoid valve vacuum line (the other line to the carburetor T-joint) and recheck for vacuum. If vacuum is now available, the leak is in the advance/retard solenoid valve. Repair or replace as necessary and repeat Steps 4 & 5.

FUEL SYSTEM

1237 cc models use a two-barrel downdraft Hitachi carburetor. Fuel pressure is provided by a camshaft-driven mechanical fuel pump. A replaceable fuel filter is located in the engine compartment in-line between the fuel pump and carburetor.

On the CVCC Civic and Accord a Keihin three-barrel carburetor is used. On this carburetor, the primary and secondary venturis deliver a lean air/fuel mixture to the main combustion chamber. Simultaneously, the third or auxiliary venturi which has a completely separate fuel metering circuit, delivers a small (in volume) but very rich air/fuel mixture to the precombustion chamber. Fuel pressure is provided by an electric fuel pump which is actuated when the ignition switch is turned to the "on" position. The electric pump is located under the rear seat beneath a special access plate on Civic sedan and hatchback models, and located under the rear of the car adjacent to the fuel tank on station wagon models and the Accord. A replaceable in-line fuel filter located on the inlet side of the electric fuel pump is used on all CVCC models.

Fuel Filter

REPLACEMENT

CAUTION

Before disconnecting any fuel lines, be sure to open the gas tank filler cap to relieve any pressure in the system. If this is not done, you may run the risk of being squirted with gasoline.

All models use a disposable-type fuel filter which cannot be disassembled for cleaning. The filter is replaced after the first 15,000 miles, and every 30,000 miles thereafter.

On Civics with the 1237 cc engine, the filter is located in the engine compartment, inline between the fuel pump and carburetor. Replacement is a simple matter of pinching the lines closed, loosening the hose clamps and discarding the old filter.

On all CVCC Sedan models, the filter is located beneath a special access cover under the rear seat on the driver's side. The rear seat can be removed after removing the bolt at the rear center of the cushion and then pivoting the seat forward from the rear. Then, remove the four screws retaining the access cover to the floor and remove the cover. The filter, together with the electric fuel pump, are located in the recess. Pinch the lines shut, loosen the hose clamps and remove the filter.

On all Wagons and Accord models, the filter is located under the car, in front of the spare tire, together with the electrical fuel pump. To replace the fuel filter, you must raise the rear of the car, support it with jackstands, and clamp off the fuel lines leading to and from the filter. Then, loosen the hose clamps and, taking note of which hose is the inlet and which is the outlet, remove the filter. Some replacement filters have an arrow embossed or printed on the filter body, in which case you want to install the new filter with the arrow pointing in the direction of fuel flow. After installing the new filter, remember to unclamp the fuel lines. Check for leaks.

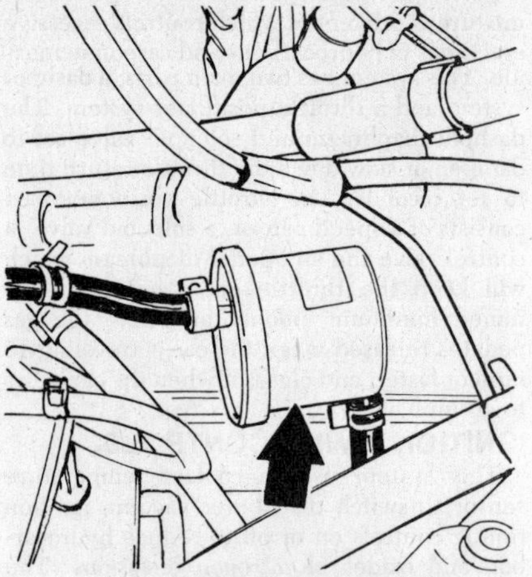

Fuel filter (non-CVCC Civic)

1. Fuel pump
2. Filter

Fuel filter, CVCC sedan

Mechanical Fuel Pump

REMOVAL AND INSTALLATION

All Except CVCC

The fuel pump in the Civic is located in back of the engine, underneath the air cleaner snorkle.

1. Remove the air cleaner and cover assembly.
2. Remove the inlet and outlet fuel lines at the pump.
3. Loosen the pump nuts and remove the pump.

NOTE: Do not disassemble the pump. Disassembly may cause fuel or oil leakage. If the pump is defective, replace it as an assembly.

Checking fuel pump pressure

4. To install the fuel pump, reverse the removal procedure.

Inspection

1. Check the following items:
   a. Looseness of the pump connector.
   b. Looseness of the upper and lower body and cover screws.
   c. Looseness of the rocker arm pin.
   d. Contamination or clogging of the air hole.
   e. Improper operation of the pump.
2. Check to see if there are signs of oil or fuel around the air hole. If so, the diaphragm is damaged and you must replace the pump.
3. To inspect the pump for operation, first disconnect the fuel line at the carburetor. Connect a fuel pressure gauge to the delivery side of the pump. Start the engine and measure the pump delivery pressure.
4. After measuring, stop the engine and check to see if the gauge drops suddenly. If the gauge drops suddenly and/or the delivery pressure is incorrect, check for a fuel or oil leak from the diaphragm or from the valves.
5. To test for volume, disconnect the fuel line from the carburetor and insert it into a one quart container. Crank the engine for 64 seconds at 600 rpm, or 40 seconds at 3000 rpm. The bottle should be half full (1 pint).

Mechanical fuel pump; arrow indicates air hole

MECHANICAL FUEL PUMP PERFORMANCE SPECIFICATIONS

Engine rpm	Delivery Pressure (lb/in²)	Vacuum (in. Hg.)	Displacement (in.³/minute)
600	2.56	17.72	27
3,000	2.56	7.87-11.81	43
6,000	2.56	7.87-11.81	46

Electrical Fuel Pump

REMOVAL AND INSTALLATION

CVCC Models

1. Remove the gas filler cap to relieve any excess pressure in the system.
2. Obtain a pair of clothes pins or other suitable clamps to pinch shut the fuel lines to the pump.
3. Disconnect the negative battery cable.
4. Locate the fuel pump. On Civic sedan and hatchback models, you will first have to remove the rear seat by removing the bolt at the rear center of the bottom cushion and pivoting the seat forward from the rear. The pump and filter are located on the driver's side of the rear seat floor section beneath an access plate retained by four Phillips head screws.

On station wagon models and the Accord, you will probably have to raise the rear of the car, or park it with two wheels up on a curb to obtain access. In all cases, make sure, if you are crawling under the car, that the car is securely supported. *Do not venture beneath the car when it is supported only by the tire changing jack.*

5. Pinch the inlet and outlet fuel lines shut. Loosen the hose clamps. On station wagon and Accord models, remove the filter mounting clip on the left hand side of the bracket.
6. Disconnect the positive lead wire and ground wire from the pump at their quick disconnect.
7. Remove the two fuel pump retaining bolts, taking care not to lose the two spacers and bolt collars.
8. Remove the fuel lines and fuel pump.
9. Reverse the above procedure to intstall. The pump cannot be disassembled and must be replaced if defective. Operating fuel pump pressure is 2-3 psi.

Carburetor

OVERHAUL

Efficient carburetion depends greatly on careful cleaning and inspection during overhaul since dirt, gum, water, or varnish in or on the carburetor parts are often responsible for poor performance.

Overhaul your carburetor in a clean, dust-free area. Carefully disassemble the carburetor, referring often to the exploded views. Keep all similar and lookalike parts segregated during disassembly and cleaning to avoid accidental interchange during assembly. Make a note of all jet sizes.

When the carburetor is disassembled, wash all parts (except diaphragms, electric choke units, pump plunger, and any other plastic, leather, fiber, or rubber parts) in clean carburetor solvent. Do not leave parts in the solvent any longer than is necessary to sufficiently loosen the deposits. Excessive cleaning may remove the special finish from the float bowl and choke valve bodies, leaving these parts unfit for service. Rinse all parts in clean solvent and blow them dry with compressed air or allow them to air dry. Wipe clean all cork, plastic, leather, and fiber parts with a clean, lint-free cloth.

Blow out all passages and jets with compressed air and be sure that there are no restrictions or blockages. Never use wire or similar tools to clean jets, fuel passages, or air bleeds. Clean all jets and valves separately to avoid accidental interchange.

Check all parts for wear or damage. If wear or damage is found, replace the defective parts. Especially check the following:

1. Check the float needle and seat for wear. If wear is found, replace the complete assembly.
2. Check the float hinge pin for wear and the float(s) for dents or distortion. Replace the float if fuel has leaked into it.
3. Check the throttle and choke shaft bores for wear or an out-of-round condition. Damage or wear to the throttle arm, shaft, or shaft bore will often require replacement of the throttle body. These parts require a close tolerance of fit; wear may allow air leakage, which could affect starting and idling.

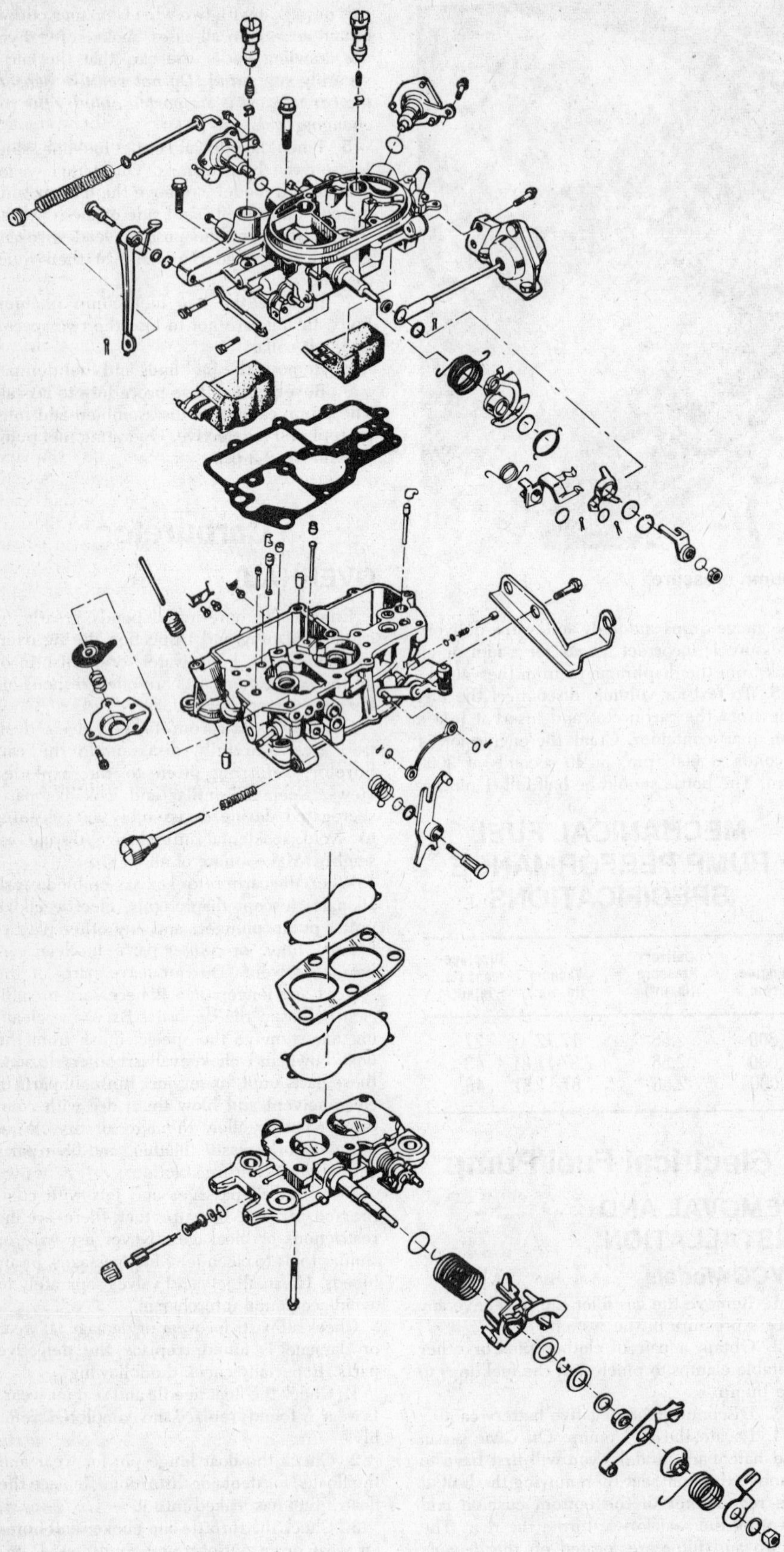

Exploded view of the Keihin 3 bbl used on CVCC engines

NOTE: Throttle shafts and bushings are not included in overhaul kits. They can be purchased separately.

4. Inspect the idle mixture adjusting needles for burrs or grooves. Any such condition requires replacement of the needle, since you will not be able to obtain a satisfactory idle.
5. Test the accelerator pump check valves. They should pass air one way but not the other. Test for proper seating by blowing and sucking on the valve. Replace the valve if necessary. If the valve is satisfactory, wash the valve again to remove breath moisture.
6. Check the bowl cover for warped surfaces with a straightedge.
7. Closely inspect the valves and seats for wear and damage, replacing as necessary.
8. After the carburetor is assembled, check the choke valve for freedom of operation.

Carburetor overhaul kits are recommended for each overhaul. These kits contain all gaskets and new parts to replace those that deteriorate most rapidly. Failure to replace all parts supplied with the kit (especially gaskets) can result in poor performance later.

After cleaning and checking all components, reassemble the carburetor, using new parts and referring to the exploded view. When reassembling, make sure that all screws and jets are tight in their seats, but do not overtighten, as the tips will be distorted. Tighten all screws gradually, in rotation. Do not tighten needle valves into their seats; uneven jetting will result. Always use new gaskets. Be sure to adjust the float level when reassembling.

REMOVAL AND INSTALLATION

1. Disconnect and label the following:
   a. Hot air tube.
   b. Vacuum hose between the oneway valve and the manifold—at the manifold.
   c. Breather chamber (on air cleaner case) to intake manifold at the breather chamber.
   d. Hose from the air cleaner case to the valve cover.
   e. Hose from the carbon canister to the carburetor—at the carburetor.
   f. Throttle opener hose—at the throttle opener.
2. Disconnect the fuel line at the carburetor. Plug the end of the fuel line to prevent dust entry.
3. Disconnect the choke and throttle control cables.
4. Disconnect the fuel shut-off solenoid wires.
5. Remove the carburetor retaining bolts and the carburetor. Leave the insulator on the manifold.

NOTE: After removing the carburetor, cover the intake manifold parts to keep out foreign materials.

THROTTLE LINKAGE ADJUSTMENT

1237 cc Models

1. Check the gas pedal free-play (the amount of free movement before the throttle cable starts to pull the throttle valve). Adjust

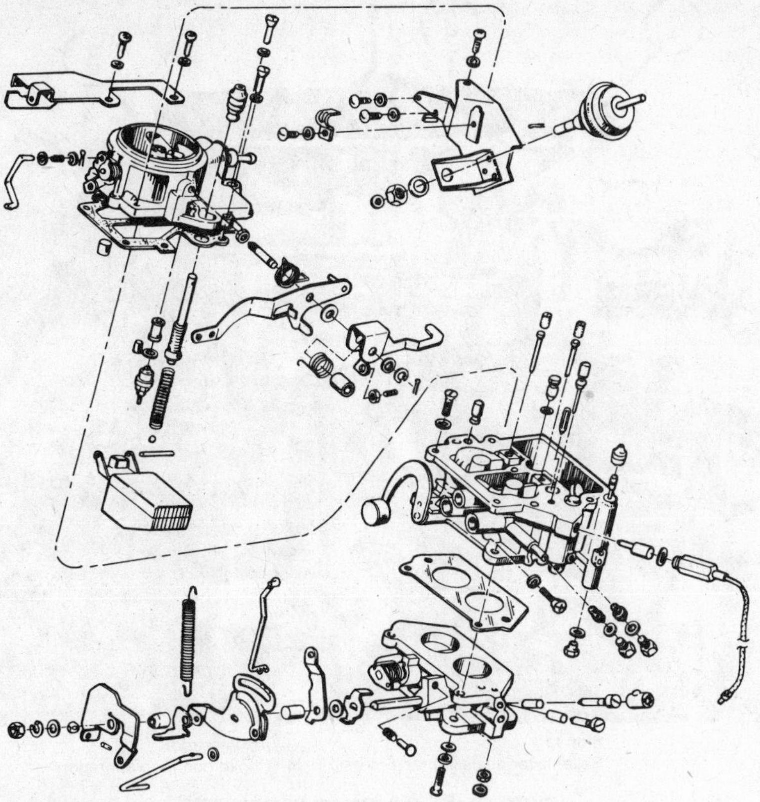

Exploded view of the Hitachi 2 bbl used on non-CVCC engines

CVCC throttle cable adjusting location

the free-play at the throttle cable adjusting nut (near the carburetor) so the pedal has 0.04-0.12 in. (1.0-3.0 mm) freeplay.

2. Make sure that when the accelerator pedal is fully depressed, the primary and secondary throttle valves are opened fully (contact the stops). If the secondary valve does not open fully, adjust by bending the secondary throttle valve connecting rod.

1487, 1600 and 1751 cc CVCC Models

1. Remove the air cleaner assembly to provide access.

2. Check that the cable free-play (deflection) is 0.16-0.40 in. This is measured right before the cable enters the throttle shaft bellcrank.

3. If deflection is not to specifications, rotate the cable adjusting nuts in the required direction.

4. As a final check, have a friend press the gas pedal all the way to the floor, while you look down inside the throttle bore checking that the throttle plates reach the wide open throttle (WOT) vertical position.

5. Install the air cleaner.

FLOAT AND FUEL LEVEL ADJUSTMENT

1237 cc Models

1. Check the float level by looking at the sight glass on the right of the carburetor. Fuel level should align with the dot on the sight glass. If the level is above or below the dot, the carburetor must be disassembled and the float level set.

NOTE: Try to check float level with the dot at eye level.

2. Remove the carburetor from the engine and disconnect the air horn assembly from the carburetor body.

NOTE: When removing the air horn, do not drop the float pin.

3. Invert the air horn and raise the float.

4. Measure the distance between the float tang and the needle valve stem. The distance should be 0.051-0.067 in. (1.3-17 mm). Adjust by bending the float stop tang.

5. For 1977 and later models, remove and invert the air horn until the float arm just touches the needle valve, or there is about 0.1 mm (0.004 in.) clearance between them. Measure the distance between the bottom of the air horn (gasket installed) and the center of the bottom of the float. The distance should measure 36.4 mm (1.39-1.47 in.). Adjust by turning the needle valve seat. Be careful not to allow the valve seat to protrude from the seat attaching boss, which would allow the valve to fall. If this is the case, bend the float arm slightly until the proper clearance can be obtained.

6. When the carburetor is installed, recheck the float level by looking into the carburetor float sight glass. Fuel level should be within the range of the dot on the glass.

1487, 1600 and 1751 cc CVCC Models

Due to the rather unconventional manner in which the Keihin 3-bbl carburetor float level is checked and adjusted, this is one job best left to the dealer, or someone with Honda tool No. 07501-6570000 (which is a special float level gauge/fuel catch tray/drain bottle assembly not generally available to the public). This carburetor is adjusted while mounted on a running engine. After the auxiliary and the primary/secondary main jet covers are removed, the special float gauge apparatus is installed over the jet apertures. With the engine running, the float level is checked against a red index line on the gauge. If adjustment proves necessary, there are adjusting screws provided for both the auxiliary and the primary/secondary circuits atop the carburetor.

FAST IDLE ADJUSTMENT

During cold engine starting and the engine warm-up period, a specially enriched fuel mixture is required. If the engine fails to run properly or if the engine over-revs with the choke knob pulled out in cold weather, the fast idle system should be checked and adjusted. This is accomplished with the carburetor installed.

1237 cc Models

1975-76

1. Open the primary throttle plate and insert an 0.8 mm (0.032 in.), diameter drill bit between the plate and the bore.

2. With the throttle plate opened 0.8 mm, bend the reference tab so that it is midway between the two scribed lines on the throttle control lever.

1977-81

1. With the engine running at normal operating temperature, pull the choke knob all the way out.

2. The engine speed should increase to 1400-2200 rpm. The arm of the choke lever should align with the boss on the carburetor.

3. Adjust by bending the link lever.

1487 and 1600 cc CVCC Models

1. Run the engine until it reaches normal operating temperature.

2. Place the choke control knob in its second detent position (two clicks out from the dash). With the choke knob in this position, run the engine for 30 seconds and check that the fast idle speed is 3000 rpm plus or minus 500 rpm.

3. To adjust on all models except 1978 and later Accords, bend the slot in the fast idle adjusting link. Narrow the slot to lower the

CVCC fast idle adjusting location

1. Stop tab
2. Relief lever adjusting tang
3. Actuator rod
4. Choke opener diaphragm

CVCC choke adjustment components

fast idle, and widen the slot to increase. Make all adjustments in small increments.

4. On 1978 and later Accords, adjust the fast idle by means of the fast idle adjusting screw, located on the throttle arm below the choke housing.

1751 cc Models

1. Run the engine to normal operating temperature.
2. Connect a tachometer according to the manufacturer's specifications.
3. Disconnect and plug the hose from the fast idle unloader.
4. Shut the engine off, hold the choke valve closed, and open and close the throttle to engage the fast idle cam.
5. Start the engine, run it for one minute. Fast idle speed should be 2300 to 3300 rpm for manual transmission models and 2200 to 3200 rpm for automatic transmission models.
6. Adjust the idle by turning the fast idle screw.

CHOKE ADJUSTMENT

1237 cc Models

The choke valve should be fully open when the choke knob is pushed in, and fully closed with the choke knob pulled out. The choke valve is held in the fully closed position by spring action. Pull the choke knob to the fully closed position and open and close the choke valve by rotating the choke valve shaft. The movement should be free and unrestricted.

If adjustment is required, adjust the cable length by loosening the cable clamp bolt.

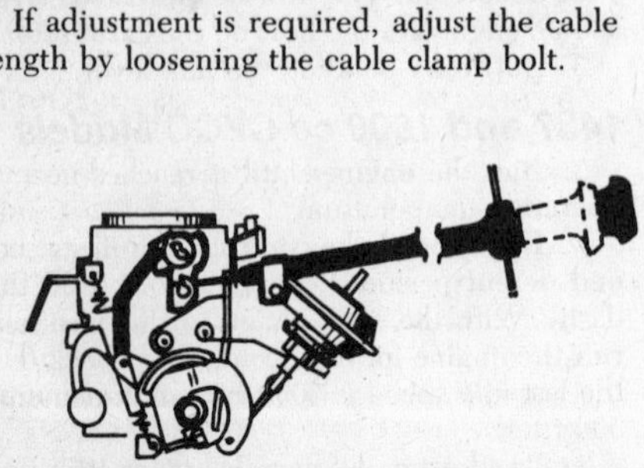

Choke adjustment—1170, 1237 cc models

PRECISION ADJUSTMENT

1. Using a wire gauge, check the primary throttle valve opening (dimension G1) when the choke valve is fully closed. The opening should be 0.050-0.066 in (1.28-1.68 mm).
2. If the opening is out of specification, adjust it by bending the choke rod. After installing, make sure that the highest fast idle speed is 2500-2800 rpm while the engine is warm.

NOTE: When adjusting the fast idle speed, be sure the throttle adjusting screw does not contact the stop.

1487, 1600 cc CVCC Models

1. Push the choke actuator rod towards the diaphragm, so it does not contact the choke valve linkage.
2. Pull the choke knob out to the first detent (click) position from the dash. With the knob in this position, check the distance between the choke butterfly valve and the venturi opening with a 3/16 in. drill (shank end).
3. Adjust as necessary by bending the relief lever adjusting tang with needle nose pliers.
4. Now, pull out the choke knob to its second detent position from the dash. Again, make sure the choke actuator rod does not contact the choke valve linkage.
5. With the choke knob in this position, check that the clearance between the butterfly valve and venturi opening is ⅛ in. using the shank end of a ⅛ in. drill.
6. Adjust as necessary by bending the stop tab for the choke butterfly linkage.

1751 cc Models

The choke plate should close to less than 3 mm (⅛ in.) clearance when the engine is cold (ignition on) on models with the automatic choke.

1. Remove the choke cover (3 screws) and check free movement of the linkage. Repair or replace as necessary.
2. Install the choke cover and adjust so that the index marks on the cover and thermostat body align. If the choke still does not close properly, replace the cover and retest.

CHOKE CABLE ADJUSTMENT

1975-76 1237 cc Models

NOTE: Perform the adjustment only after the throttle plate opening has been set.

1. Make sure that the choke cable is correctly adjusted.
   a. With the choke knob in, the choke butterfly should be completely open;
   b. Slowly pull out the choke knob and check for slack in the cable. Remove any excessive free-play and recheck for full open when the knob is pushed in.
2. Check the link rod adjustment by pulling the choke knob out to the first detent. The two scribed lines on the throttle control lever should line up on either side of the reference tab. If not, adjust by bending the choke link rod.

1977 and Later 1237 cc Models

Turn the adjusting nut until there is zero clearance between the choke lever and stay plate. The choke should be fully closed when the knob is pulled all the way out, and fully

1. Choke butterfly valve
2. Adjusting nut
3. Locknut

CVCC choke cable adjustment

opened when the knob is pushed all the way in.

All 1487 cc CVCC Civics; 1600 cc CVCC Accords through 1977

1. Remove the air cleaner assembly.
2. Push the choke knob all the way in at the dash. Check that the choke butterfly valve (choke plate) is fully open (vertical).
3. Next, have a friend pull out the choke knob while you observe the action of the butterfly valve. When the choke knob is pulled out to the second detent position, the butterfly valve should just close. Then, when the choke knob is pulled all the way out, the butterfly valve should remain in the closed position.
4. To adjust, loosen the choke cable locknut and rotate the adjusting nut so that with the choke knob pushed flush against the dash (open position), the butterfly valve just rests against its positioning stop tab. Tighten the locknut.
5. If the choke butterfly valve is notchy in operation, or if it does not close properly, check the butterfly valve and shaft for binding. Check also the operation of the return spring.

THROTTLE VALVE OPERATION

1237 cc Models through 1976

1. Check to see if the throttle valve opens fully when the throttle lever is moved to the fully open position. See if the valve closes fully when the lever is released.
2. Measure the clearance between the primary throttle valve and the chamber wall where the connecting rod begins to open the secondary throttle valve. The clearance should be 0.221-0.237 in. (5.63-6.03 mm).
3. If the clearance is out of specification, adjust by bending the connecting rod.

NOTE: After adjusting, operate the throttle lever and check for any sign of binding.

ACCELERATOR PUMP ADJUSTMENT

1237 cc Models

Check the pump for smooth operation. See if fuel squirts out of the pump nozzle by operating the pump lever or the throttle lever. When the pump is operated slowly, fuel must squirt out until the pump comes to the end of its travel. If the pump is defective, check for clogging or a defective piston. Adjust the pump by either respositioning the end of the connecting rod arm in the pump lever, or the arm itself.

1487 and 1600 cc CVCC Models

1. Remove the air cleaner assembly.
2. Check that the distance between the tang at the end of the accelerator pump lever and the lever stop at the edge of the throttle body is 11.0-13.3 (0.43-0.53 in.) through 1977, or 14.5-15.1 mm (0.57-0.6 in.) 1978 and later. This corresponds to effective pump lever travel.
3. To adjust, bend the pump lever tang in the required direction.
4. Install the air cleaner.

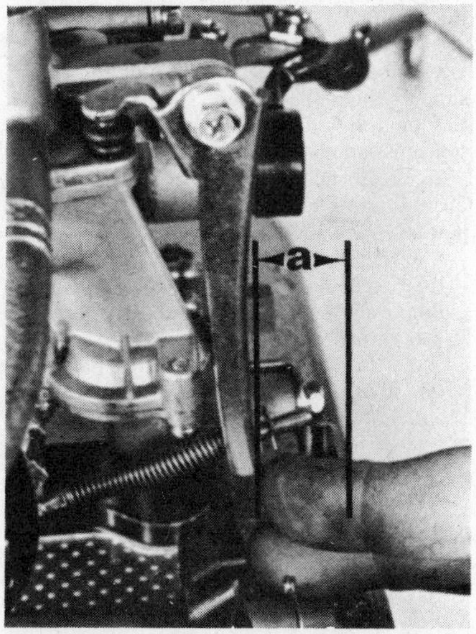

CVCC accelerator pump adjustment; "a" is 0.57–0.60 in.

1751 cc Models

1. Remove the air cleaner.
2. Make sure that the pump shaft is moving freely throughout the pump stroke.
3. Check that the pump lever is in contact with the pump shaft.
4. Measure between the bottom end of the pump lever and the lever stop tang. The gap should be $^{9}/_{16}$ to $^{19}/_{32}$ inch. If not, bend the tang to adjust.

Fuel Tank

REMOVAL AND INSTALLATION

1. Drain the tank by loosening the tank drain bolt.

NOTE: Catch the fuel in a clean, safe container.

2. Disconnect the fuel tubes, filler neck connecting tube and the clear viny tube.

NOTE: Disconnect the fuel tubes by removing the clips, taking care not to damage the tubes.

3. Disconnect the fuel meter unit wire at its connection.
4. Remove the fuel tank by removing its attaching bolts.
5. To install, reverse the removal procedure. Be sure that all tubes and fuel lines are securely fastened by the clips.

MANUAL TRANSAXLE

Removal and Installation

FOUR- AND FIVE-SPEED EXCEPT PRELUDE

1. Disconnect the battery ground cable at the battery and the transmission case. Unlock the steering column; place the transmission in neutral.
2. Drain the transmission.
3. Raise the front of the car and support it with safety stands.
4. Remove the front wheels.
5. Remove the starter motor positive battery cable and the solenoid wire. Then remove the starter.
6. Disconnect the following cables and wires:
   a. Clutch cable at the release arm (Civics);
   b. Back-up light switch wires;
   c. TCS (Transmission Controlled Spark) switch wires;

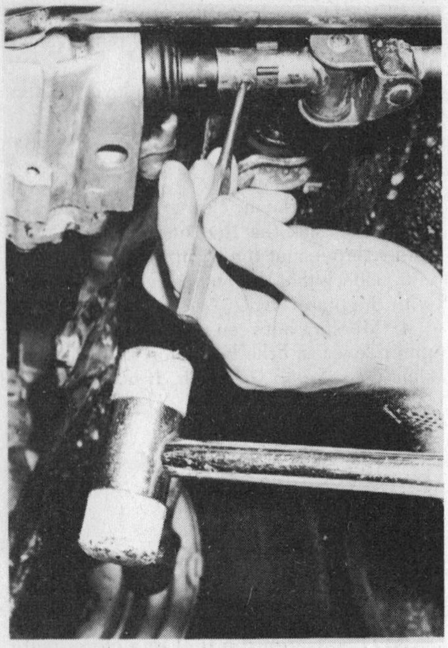

Driving out gearshift rod pin

Engine center mount nuts

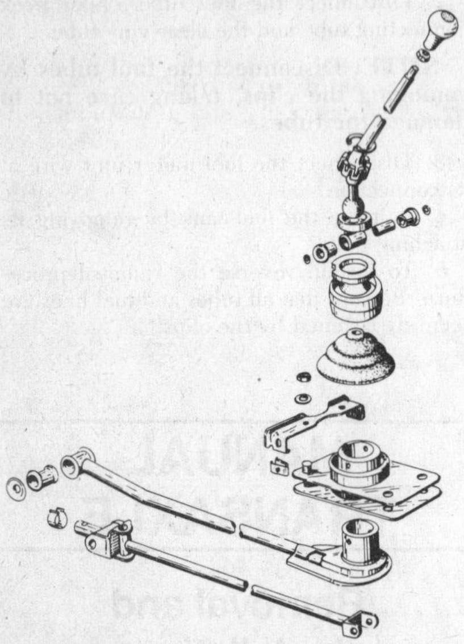

Exploded view of the gearshift mechanism

d. Speedometer cable;

e. Hydraulic hose at slave cylinder (Accord).

CAUTION

When removing the speedometer cable from the transmission, it is not necessary to remove the entire cable holder. Remove the end boot (gear holder seal), the cable retaining clip and then pull the cable out of the holder. In no way should you disturb the holder, unless it is absolutely necessary. For further details, see the Engine Removal section.

7. Disconnect the left and right lower ball joints at the knuckle, using a ball joint remover.

8. Pull on the brake disc and remove the left and right driveshafts from the differential case.

9. Drive out the gearshift rod pin (8 mm) with a drift and disconnect the rod at the transmission case.

10. Disconnect the gearshift extension at the clutch housing.

11. Screw in the engine hanger bolts (see the "Engine Removal" section) to the engine torque rod bolt hole and to the hole just to the left of the distributor. Hook a chain onto the bolts and lift the engine just enough to take the load off the engine mounts.

12. After making sure that the engine is properly supported, remove the two center beam-to-lower engine mount nuts. Next, remove the center beam, followed by the lower engine mount.

13. Reinstall the center beam (without mount) and lower the engine until it rests on the beam.

14. Place a jack under the transmission and loosen the 4 attaching bolts. Using the jack to support the transmission, slide it away from the engine and lower the jack until the transmission clears the car.

15. To install, reverse the removal procedure. Be sure to pay attention to the following points:

a. Tighten all mounting nuts and bolts to their specified torque (see the "Engine Removal" section);

b. Use a new shift rod pin;

c. After installing the driveshafts, attempt to move the inner joint housing in and out of the differential housing. If it moves easily, the driveshaft end clips should be replaced;

d. Make sure that the control cables and wires are properly connected;

e. Be sure the transmission is refilled to the proper level.

PRELUDE

1. Disconnect the battery ground.

2. Unlock the steering and place the transmission in neutral.

3. Disconnect the following wires in the engine compartment:

a. battery positive cable
b. black/white wire from the solenoid
c. temperature gauge sending unit wire
d. ignition timing thermosensor wire
e. backup light switch
f. distributor wiring

4. Unclip and remove the speedometer cable at the transmission. Do not disassemble the speedometer gear holder!

5. Remove the clutch slave cylinder with the hydraulic line attached.

6. Remove the side and top starter mounting bolts.

7. Raise and support the car.

8. Drain the transmission.

9. Remove the splash shields from the underside.

10. Remove the stabilizer bar.

11. Disconnect the left and right lower ball joints and tie rod ends, using a ball joint remover.

12. Turn the right steering knuckle out as far as it will go. Place a heavy screwdriver against the inboard CV joint, pry the right axle out of the transmission about ½ inch. This will force the spring clip out of the groove inside the differential gear splines. Pull it out the rest of the way. Repeat this procedure on the other side.

13. Disconnect the shift lever torque rod from the clutch housing.

14. Remove the bolt from the shift rod clevis.

15. Raise the transmission jack securely against the transmission to take up the weight.

16. Remove the engine torque rods and brackets.

17. Remove the remaining starter mounting bolts and take out the starter.

18. Remove the remaining transmission mounting bolts and the upper bolt from the engine damper bracket.

19. Start backing the transmission away

from the engine and remove the two lower damper bolts.

20. Pull the transmission clear of the engine and lower the jack.

21. To ease installation, fabricate two 14 mm diameter dowel pins and install them in the clutch housing.

22. Raise the transmission and slide it onto the dowels. Slide the transmission into position aligning the mainshaft splines with the clutch plate.

23. Attach the damper lower bolts when the positioning allows. Tighten both bolts until the clutch housing is seated against the block.

24. Install two lower mounting bolts and torque them to 33 ft/lb.

25. Install the front and rear torque rod brackets. Torque the front torque rod bolts to 54 ft/lb, the front bracket bolts to 33 ft/lb, the rear torque rod bolts to 54 ft/lb and the rear bracket bolts to 47 ft/lb.

26. Remove the transmission jack.

27. Install the starter and torque the mounting bolts to 33 ft/lb.

28. Turn the right steering knuckle out far enough to fit the end into the transmission. Use new 26 mm spring clips on both axles. Repeat procedure for the other side.

CAUTION

Make sure that the axles bottom fully so that you feel the spring clip engage the differential.

29. Install the lower ball joints. Torque the nuts to 32 ft/lb.

30. Install the tie rods. Torque the nuts to 32 ft/lb.

31. Connect the shift linkage.

32. Connect the shift lever torque rod to the clutch housing and torque the bolt to 7 ft/lb.

33. Install the stabilizer bar.

34. Install the lower shields.

35. Install the front wheels and torque the lugs to 108 ft/lb.

36. Install the remaining starter bolts and torque to 33 ft/lb.

37. Install the clutch slave cylinder.

38. Install the speedometer cable using a new O-ring coated with clean engine oil.

39. Connect all engine compartment wiring.

40. Fill the transmission with SAE 10W-40 engine oil.

Halfshaft (Driveshaft) Removal and Installation

The front driveshaft assembly consists of a sub-axle shaft and a driveshaft with two universal joints.

A constant velocity ball joint is used for both universal joints, which are factory-packed with special grease and enclosed in sealed rubber boots. The outer joint cannot be disassembled except for removal of the boot.

1. Remove the hubcap from the front wheel and then remove the center cap.

2. Pull out the 4 mm cotter pin and loosen, but do not remove, the spindle nut.

3. Raise the front of the car and support it with safety stands.

4. Remove the wheel lug nuts and then the wheel.

5. Remove the spindle nut.

6. Drain the transmission.

7. Remove the lower arm ball joints at the knuckle by using a ball joint remover.

8. To remove the driveshaft, hold the knuckle and pull it toward you. Then slide the driveshaft out of the knuckle. Pry the CV joint out about ½ in. Pull the inboard joint side of the driveshaft out of the differential case.

9. To install, reverse the removal procedure. If either the inboard or outboard joint boot bands have been removed for inspection or disassembly of the joint (only the inboard joint can be disassembled), be sure to repack the joint with a sufficient amount of bearing grease.

CAUTION

Make sure the CV joint sub-axle bottoms so that the spring clip may hold the sub-axle securely in the transmission.

SHIFT LINKAGE ADJUSTMENT

The Honda shift linkage is non-adjustable. However, if the linkage is binding, or if there is excessive play, check the linkage bushings and pivot points. Lubricate with light oil, or replace worn bushings as necessary.

CLUTCH

All models use a single dry disc with a diaphragm spring type pressure plate. The Civic clutch is cable operated. However, on the Accord, a hydraulic master and slave cylinder system is used.

Clutch Removal and Installation

1. Follow Steps 1 through 14 of the transaxle removal procedure, previously given. Matchmark the flywheel and clutch for reassembly.

2. Hold the flywheel ring gear with a tool made for the purpose, remove the retaining bolts and remove the pressure plate and clutch disc.

NOTE: Loosen the retaining bolts two turns at a time in a circular pattern. Removing one bolt while the rest are tight may warp the diaphragm spring.

3. The flywheel can now be removed, if it needs repairing or replacing. Inspect it for scoring and wear, and reface or replace as necessary. Installation torque is 35 ft/lbs. Tighten in a criss-cross pattern.

4. To separate the pressure plate from the diaphragm spring, remove the 4 retracting clips.

5. To remove the release, or throwout bearing, first straighten the locking tab and

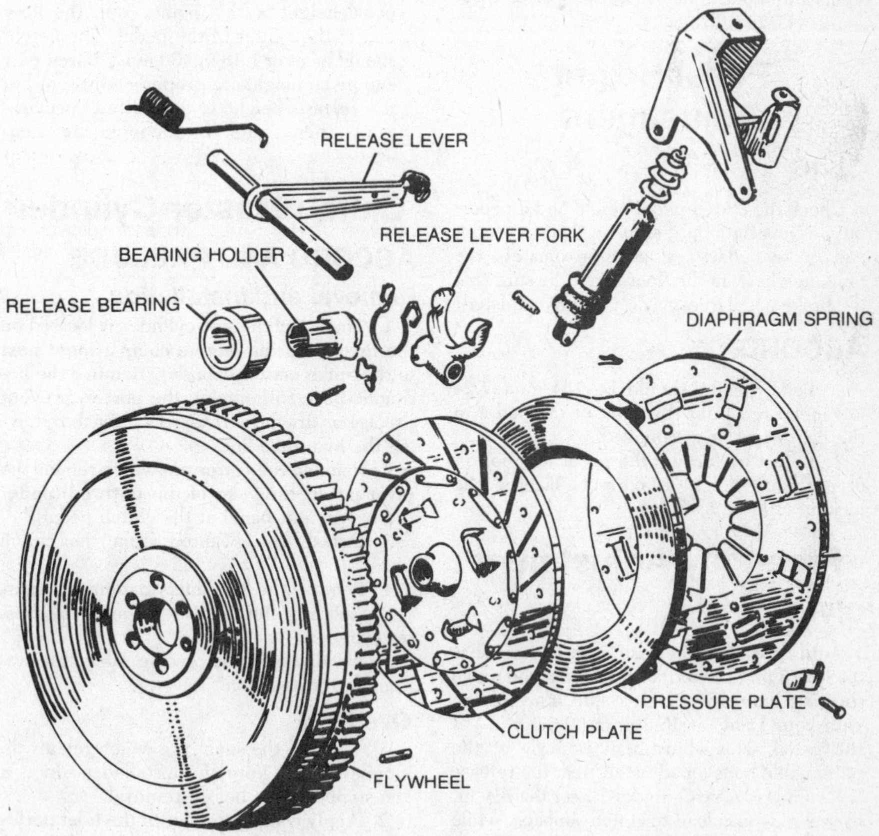

Civic CVCC clutch, flywheel, and related parts

remove the 8 mm bolt, followed by the release shaft and release arm with the bearing attached.

NOTE: It is recommended that the release bearing be removed after the release arm has been removed from the casing. Trying to remove or install the bearing with the release arm in the case will damage the retaining clip.

6. If a new release bearing is to be installed, separate the bearing from the holder, using a bearing drift.
7. To assemble and install the clutch, reverse the removal procedure. Be sure to pay attention to the following points:
   a. Make sure that the flywheel and the end of the crankshaft are clean before assembling;
   b. When installing the pressure plate, align the mark on the outer edge of the flywheel with the alignment mark on the pressure plate. Failure to align these marks will result in imbalance;
   c. When tightening the pressure plate bolts, use a pilot shaft to center the friction disc. The pilot shaft can be bought at any large auto supply store or fabricated from a wooden dowel. After centering the disc, tighten the bolts two turns at a time, in a criss-cross pattern to avoid warping the diaphragm springs; tighten to 7 ft/lbs;
   d. When installing the release shaft and arm, place a lock tab washer under the retaining bolt;
   e. When installing the transmission, make sure that the mainshaft is properly aligned with the disc spline and the aligning pins are in place, before tightening the case bolts (17-22 ft/lbs).

Pedal Height Adjustment

CIVIC

Check the clutch pedal height and if necessary, adjust the upper stop, so that the clutch and brake pedals rest at approximately the same height from the floor. First, be sure that the brake pedal free-play is properly adjusted.

ACCORD

1. Pedal height should be 184 mm (7.24 in.) measured from the front of the pedal to the floorboard (mat removed).
2. Adjust by turning the pedal stop bolt in or out until height is correct. Tighten the locknut after adjustment.

Free-Play Adjustment

CIVIC

Adjust the clutch release lever so that it has 0.12-0.16 in. (3-4 mm) of play when you move the clutch release lever at the transmission with your hand, or 15-20 mm (0.6-0.8 in.) at the pedal. This adjustment is made at the outer cable housing adjuster, near the release lever on non-CVCC models. Less than ⅛ in. of free-play may lead to clutch slippage, while more than ⅛ in. clearance may cause difficult shifting.

CAUTION

Make sure that the upper and lower adjusting nuts are tightened after adjustments.

On CVCC models, the free-play adjustment is made on the cable at the firewall. Remove the C-clip and then rotate the threaded control cable housing until there is 0.12-0.16 in. free-play at the release lever.

ACCORD

1. Free-play should measure 2.0-2.6 mm (0.08-0.1 in.) at the clutch release fork.
2. Adjust by loosening the locknut on the slave cylinder pushrod. Turn the pushrod in or out to adjust. Standard adjustment is made by turning the pushrod in until all play is removed, then backing out the pushrod 1¾-2 turns to achieve specified free-play. Tighten the locknut after adjustment.

Pedal Release Height

CIVIC

You will probably need two people to perform this measurement; one to start and run the car, and the other to observe and measure.

To check the pedal release height:
   a. Raise the front wheels off the ground and support the car with safety stands:
   b. Place the transmission in Fourth gear;
   c. Depress the clutch pedal and start the engine;
   d. Release the clutch pedal until the front wheels begin to turn and measure the pedal height at this point, from the floor mat to the center of the pedal. The height should be over 1.18 in. (30 mm). If free-play and pedal height are properly adjusted, but the release height is not within specifications, then clutch components are damaged.

Clutch Master Cylinder

ACCORD AND PRELUDE

Removal and Installation

1. The clutch master cylinder is located on the firewall in the engine compartment next to the brake master cylinder. Remove the hydraulic line. Either plug the port to prevent leakage or drain the reservoir prior to removing the hydraulic line.
2. Remove the cotter pin which retains the pivot pin in the yoke of the pushrod (under the instrument panel at the clutch pedal).
3. Detach the pushrod from the clutch pedal.
4. Remove the two bolts retaining the master cylinder to the firewall. Remove the master cylinder.
5. Installation is the reverse. Bleed the system after installation.

Overhaul

1. Remove the snap ring which retains the stopper plate. Note the installed position of the stopper plate before removal.
2. Apply compressed air to the inlet port to remove the piston assembly. Note the order of all components.
3. Check the cylinder bore for corrosion or wear. Light scores or scratches can be removed with crocus cloth or a brake cylinder hone. The cylinder should be replaced if heavily worn.
4. Replace the piston and spring with new ones. Reassemble in correct order. Coat the inside of the cylinder and the piston with clean brake fluid before installation.
5. Install the cylinder and bleed the system.

Clutch Slave Cylinder

ACCORD AND PRELUDE

Removal and Installation

1. The slave cylinder is retained by two bolts. Disconnect and plug the hydraulic line at the slave cylinder and remove the two mounting bolts. Remove the return spring and remove the slave cylinder.
2. Installation is the reverse. Bleed the system after installation.

Overhaul

1. Apply compressed air to the inlet port to remove the piston and seal.
2. Inspect the cylinder bore for pitting, corrosion, or wear. Replace the cylinder if worn.
3. Coat the parts with clean brake fluid and reassemble.

Accord slave cylinder locknut and adjusting nut

Clutch Hydraulic System Bleeding—Accord

The hydraulic system must be bled whenever the system has been leaking or dismantled. The bleed screw is located on the slave cylinder.

1. Remove the bleed screw dust cap.
2. Attach a clear hose to the bleed screw. Immerse the other end of the hose in a clear jar half filled with brake fluid.
e. Fill the clutch master cylinder with fresh brake fluid.
4. Open the bleed screw slightly and have an assistant slowly depress the clutch pedal. Close the bleed screw when the pedal reaches

the end of its travel. Allow the clutch pedal to return slowly.

5. Repeat Steps 3 and 4 until all air bubbles are expelled from the system.

6. Discard the brake fluid in the jar. Replace the dust cap. Refill the master cylinder.

AUTOMATIC TRANSAXLE

Hondamatic

REMOVAL AND INSTALLATION

Civic and Accord

The automatic transmission is removed in the same basic manner as the manual transmission (refer to Manual Transmission Removal and Installation). The following exceptions should be noted during automatic transmission removal and installation.

1. Remove the center console and control rod pin.
2. Remove the front floor center mat and control cable bracket nuts.
3. Jack and support the front of the car.
4. Remove the two selector lever bracket nuts at front side.
5. Loosen the bolts securing the control cable holder and support beam and disconnect the control cable.
6. Disconnect the transmission cooler lines at the transmission.
7. Remove the transmission together with the engine. Remove the engine mounts and torque converter case cover.
8. Remove the starter motor and separate the transmission from the engine.
9. Installation of the automatic transmission is the reverse of removal. Close attention should be paid to the following points.
10. Be sure that the stator hub is correctly located and moves smoothly. The stator shaft can be used for this purpose.
11. Align the stator, stator shaft, main shaft and torque converter turbine serrations.
12. After installation of the engine-transmission unit in car, make all required adjustments.

SHIFT LEVER

Inspection

1. Pull up fully on the parking brake lever and run the engine at idle speed, while depressing the brake pedal.

CAUTION

Be sure to check continually for car movement.

2. By moving the shift selector lever slowly forward and backward from the "N" position, make sure that the distance between the "N" and the points where the D clutch is engaged for the "2" and "R" positions are the same. The D clutch engaging point is just before the slight response is felt. The reverse gears will make a noise when the clutch engages. If the distances are not the same, then adjustment is necessary.

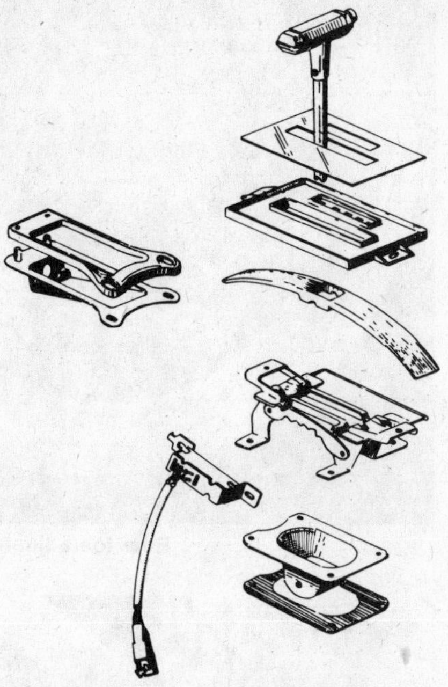

Exploded view of Hondamatic gearshift mechanism

Adjustment

1. Remove the center console retaining screws, and pull away the console to expose the shift control cable and turnbuckle.
2. Adjust the length of the control cable by turning the turnbuckle, located at the front bottom of the shift lever assembly. After adjustment, the cable and turnbuckle should twist toward the left (driver's) side of the car when shifted toward the "R" position and toward the right-side when shifted into the "2" position. The hole in the cable end should be perfectly aligned with the holes in the selector lever bracket (pin removed).

REAR SUSPENSION

All Civic sedan and hatchback models and the Accord and Prelude utilize an independent MacPherson strut arrangement for each

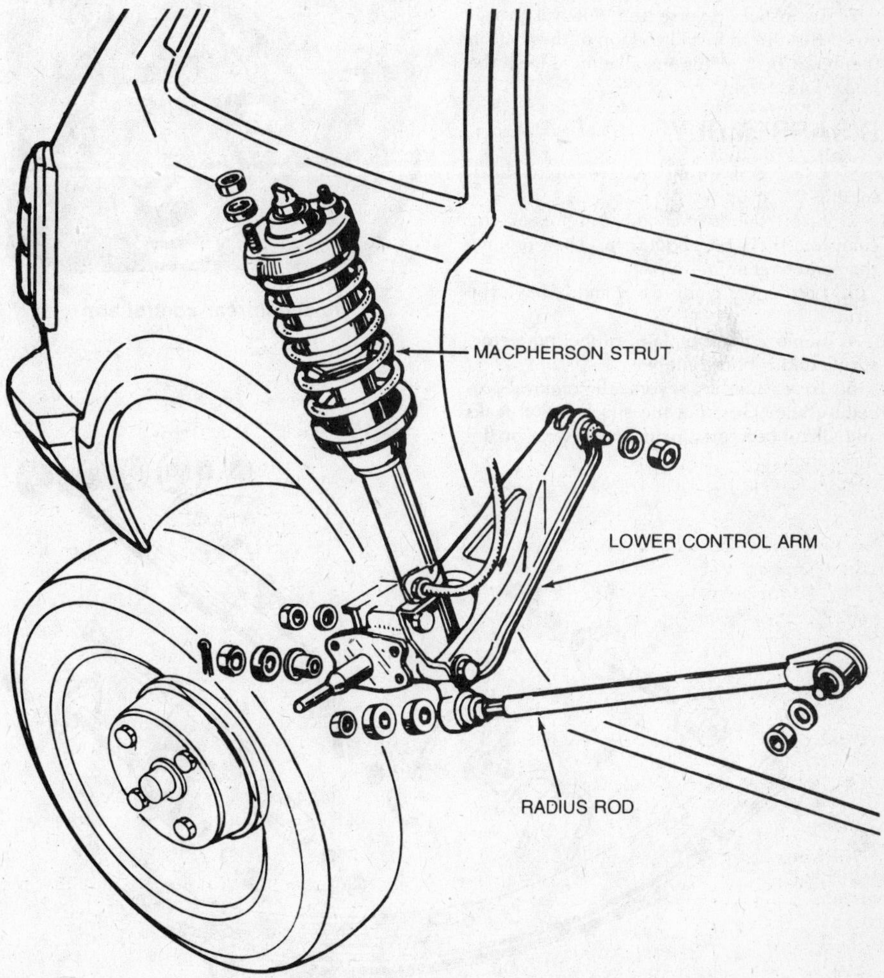

Civic sedan and hatchback rear suspension

rear wheel. Each suspension unit consists of a combined coil spring/shock absorber strut, a lower control arm, and a radius rod. The Accord and Prelude have adjustable rear suspension.

Station wagon models use a more conventional leaf spring rear suspension with a solid rear axle. The springs are three-leaf, semi-elliptic types located longitudinally with a pair of telescopic shock absorbers to control rebound. The solid axle and leaf springs allow for a greater load carrying capacity for the wagon.

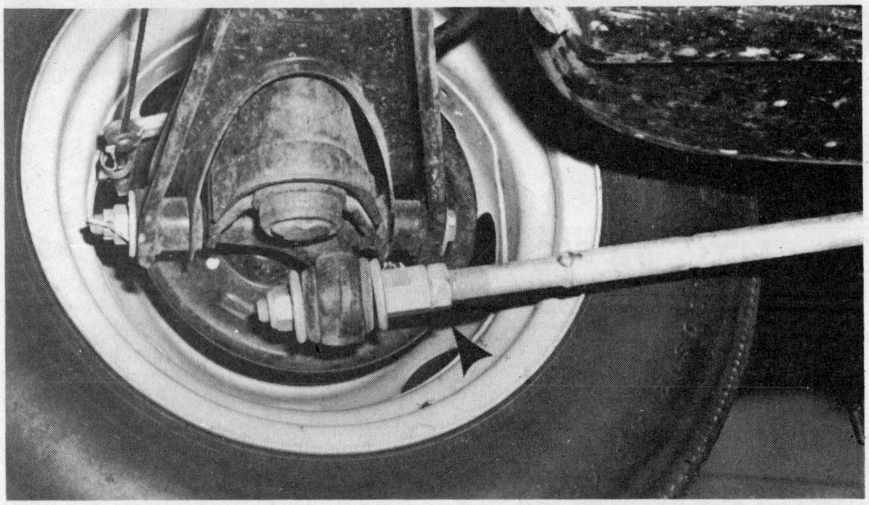

Rear toe adjustment location—Civic

Strut Assembly

REMOVAL AND INSTALLATION

1. Raise the rear of the car and support it with safety stands.
2. Remove the rear wheel.
3. Disconnect the brake line at the shock absorber. Remove the retaining clip and separate the brake hose from the shock absorber.
4. Disconnect the parking brake cable at the backing plate lever.
5. Remove the lower strut retaining bolt or pinch bolt and hub carrier pivot bolt. To remove the pivot bolt, you first have to remove the castle nut and its cotter pin.
6. Remove the two upper strut retaining nuts and remove the strut from the car.
7. To install, reverse the removal procedure. Be sure to install the top of the strut in the body first. After installation, bleed the brake lines.

DISASSEMBLY

1. Use a coil spring compressor to disassemble the strut.
2. Insert the strut in the compressor and compress the strut about 2 in. Then remove the center retaining nut.
3. Loosen the compressor and remove the strut.
4. Remove the top plate, rubber protector, spring and rubber bumper.
5. To reassemble, reverse the removal procedure after checking the shock for oil leaks and all rubber parts for damage, wear or deterioration.

Civic sedan rear control arm

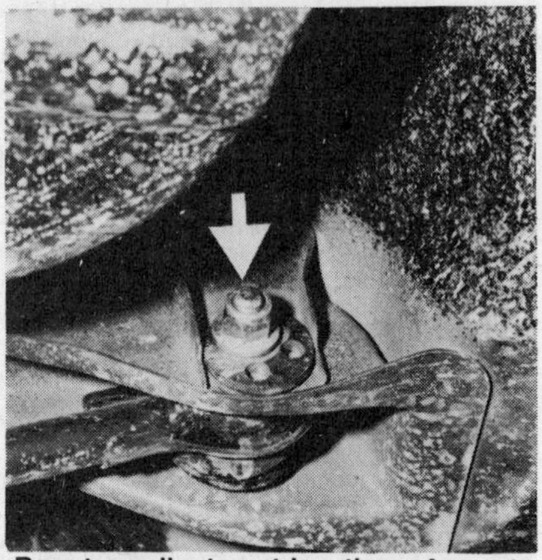

Rear toe adjustment location—Accord

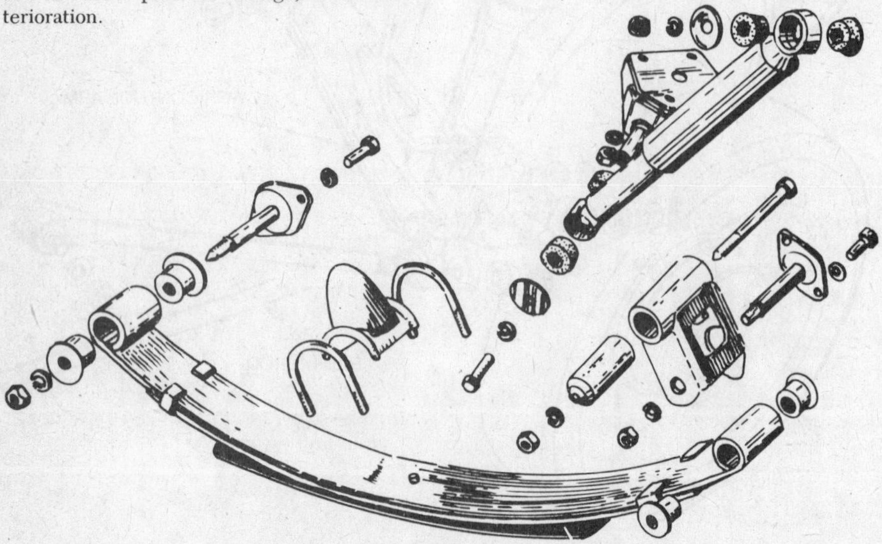

Exploded view of station wagon rear suspension

Rear Control Arm

REMOVAL AND INSTALLATION

1. Remove the control arm outboard and inboard pivot bolts.
2. Pull the inboard side of the arm down until it clears the body.
3. Slide the arm towards the center of the car until it is free of the hub carrier.
4. To install, reverse the removal procedure. Be sure to check the bushings at each end of the control arm and the control arm for damage and wear.

Rear Wheel Alignment

Caster and camber are fixed as on the front suspension. However, toe-out is adjustable by means of an eccentric adjusting bolt at the forward anchor of the radius rod.

Leaf Spring

REMOVAL AND INSTALLATION

Station Wagon Only

1. Raise the rear of the car and support it on stands placed on the frame. Remove the wheels.

2. Remove the shock absorber lower mounting bolt.
3. Remove the nuts from the U-bolt and remove the U-bolts, bump rubber, and clamp bracket.
4. Unbolt the front and rear spring shackle bolts, remove the bolts, and remove the spring.
5. To install, first position the spring on the axle and install the front and rear shackle bolts. Apply a soapy water solution to the bushings to ease installation. Do not tighten the shackle nuts yet.
6. Install the U-bolts, spring clamp bracket and bump rubber loosely on the axle and spring.
7. Install the wheels and lower the car. Tighten the front and rear shackle bolts to 33 ft/lbs. Also tighten the U-bolt nuts to 33 ft/lbs, after the shackle bolts have been tightened.
8. Install the shock absorber to the lower mount. Tighten to 33 ft/lbs.

Shock Absorbers

REMOVAL AND INSTALLATION

Station Wagon Only

1. It is not necessary to jack the car or remove the wheels unless you require working clearance. Unbolt the upper mounting nut and lower bolt and remove the shock absorber. Note the position of the washers and lock washers upon removal.
2. Installation is the reverse. Be sure the washers and lock washers are installed correctly. Tighten the upper mount to 44 ft/lbs and the lower mount to 33 ft/lbs.

FRONT SUSPENSION

All models use a MacPherson strut type front suspension. Each steering knuckle is suspended by a lower control arm at the bottom and a combined coil spring/shock absorber unit at the top. A front stabilizer bar, mounted between each lower control arm and the body, doubles as a locating rod for the suspension. Caster and camber are not adjustable and are fixed by the location of the strut assemblies in their respective sheet metal towers.

Front Strut Assembly

INSPECTION

1. Check for wear or damage to bushings and needle bearings.
2. Check for oil leaks from the struts.
3. Check all rubber parts for wear or damage.
4. Bounce the car to check shock absorber effectiveness. The car should continue to bounce for no more than two cycles.

REMOVAL AND INSTALLATION

1. Raise the front of the car and support it with safety stands. Remove the front wheels.
2. Disconnect the brake pipe at the strut and remove the brake hose retaining clip.
3. Loosen the bolt on the knuckle that retains the lower end of the shock absorber.

Strut lower retaining (pinch) bolt

Push down firmly while tapping it with a hammer until the knuckle is free of the strut.

4. Remove the three nuts retaining the upper end of the strut and remove the strut from the car.
5. To install, reverse the removal procedure. Be sure to properly match the mating surface of the strut and the knuckle notch. Tighten the knuckle bolt to 40 ft/lbs (43-51 ft/lbs—Accord).

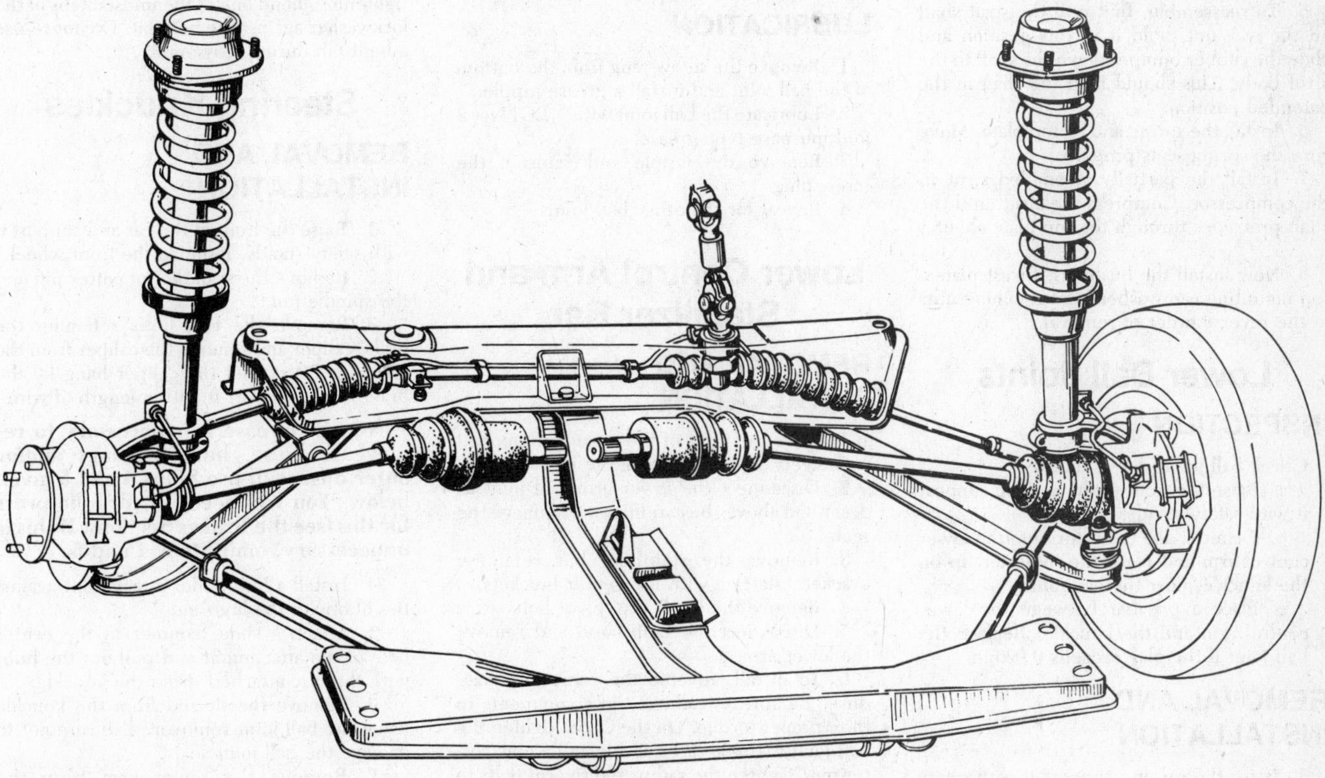

Front suspension and steering gear

Strut upper mounting nuts

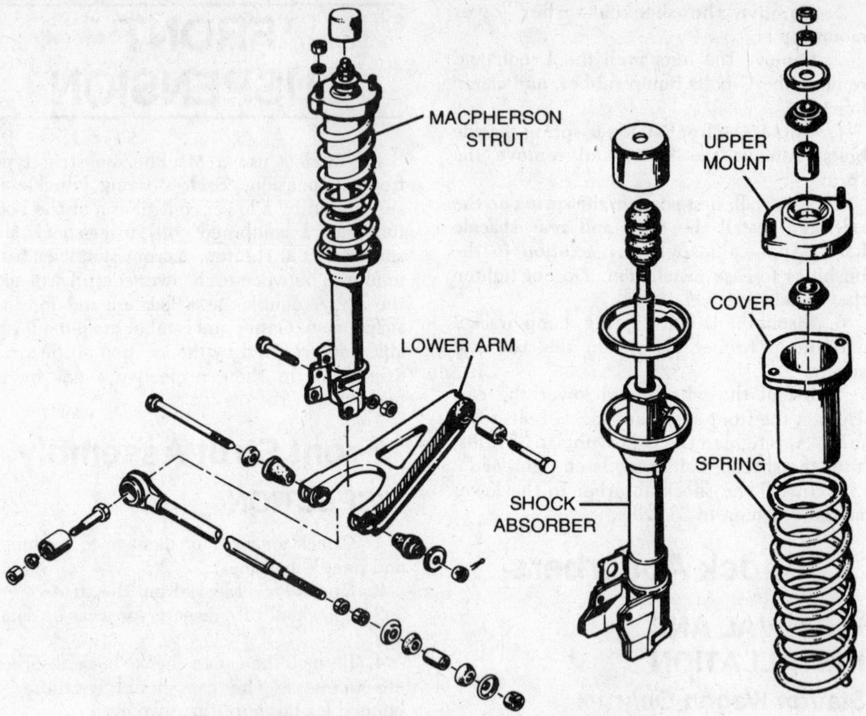

Exploded view of lower control arm assembly

DISASSEMBLY

1. Disassemble the strut according to the procedure given in the rear strut disassembly section.
2. Remove the rubber cover and remove the center retaining nuts.
3. Slowly release the compressor and remove the spring.
4. Remove the upper mounting cap, washers, thrust plates, bearings and bushings.

NOTE: Before discarding any parts, check a parts list to determine which parts are available as replacements.

5. To reassemble, first pull the strut shaft all the way out, hold it in this position and slide the rubber bumper down the shaft to the strut body. This should hold the shaft in the extended position.
6. Install the spring and its top plate. Make sure the spring seats properly.
7. Install the partially assembled strut in the compressor. Compress the strut until the shaft protrudes through the top plate about 1 in.
8. Now install the bushings, thrust plates, top mounting cap washers and retaining nuts in the reverse order of removal.

Lower Ball Joints

INSPECTION

Check ball joint play as follows:

a. Raise the front of the car and support it with safety stands.

b. Clamp a dial indicator onto the lower control arm and place the indicator tip on the knuckle, near the ball joint;

c. Place a pry bar between the lower control arm and the knuckle. Replace the ball joint if the play exceeds 0.020 in.

REMOVAL AND INSTALLATION

1. Raise the car and support it with safety stands.
2. Remove the front wheel.
3. Pull out the cotter pin holding the ball joint castle nut and remove the nut.
4. Remove the ball joint from the knuckle using a ball joint remover.
5. To install, reverse the removal procedure. Tighten the ball joint nut to 29-35 ft/lbs of torque and install a new cotter pin. Be sure to grease the ball joint.

LUBRICATION

1. Remove the screw plug from the bottom of the ball joint and install a grease nipple.
2. Lubricate the ball joint with NLGI No. 2 multipurpose type grease.
3. Remove the nipple and reinstall the screw plug.
4. Repeat for the other ball joint.

Lower Control Arm and Stabilizer Bar

REMOVAL AND INSTALLATION

1. Raise the front of the car and support it with safety stands. Remove the front wheels.
2. Disconnect the lower arm ball joint as described above. Be careful not to damage the seal.
3. Remove the stabilizer bar retaining brackets, starting with the center brackets.
4. Remove the lower arm pivot bolt.
5. Disconnect the radius rod and remove the lower arm.
6. To install, reverse the removal procedure. Be sure to tighten the components to their proper torque. On the Civic, tighten the ball joint to 29-35 ft/lbs and install a new cotter pin. Tighten the radius rod to arm bolts to 25-36 ft/lbs, and the stabilizer bar to radius rod bracket bolts to 5-9 ft/lbs. Tighten the lower arm pivot bolts to 25-36 ft/lbs.

On the Accord, tighten the ball joint nut to 29-35 ft/lbs and install a new cotter pin. Tighten the radius rod to arm bolts to 36-43 ft/lbs and the stabilizer bar to rod bracket bolts to 14-18 ft/lbs. Raise the lower arm with a jack to simulate body weight before tightening the arm pivot bolt to 25-36 ft/lbs. After tightening, bend one of the unused tabs of the lockwasher against the bolt flat. Do not re-use a bent tab during reassembly.

Steering Knuckles

REMOVAL AND INSTALLATION

1. Raise the front of the car and support it with safety stands. Remove the front wheel.
2. Remove the spindle nut cotter pin and the spindle nut.
3. Remove the two bolts retaining the brake caliper and remove the caliper from the knuckle. Do not let the caliper hang by the brake hose, support it with a length of wire.

NOTE: In case it is necessary to remove the disc, hub, bearings and/or outer dust seal, use Steps 4 and 5 given below. You will need a hydraulic press for this (see the Brakes Section). If this is unnecessary, omit Steps 4 and 5.

4. Install a hub puller attachment against the hub with the lug nuts.
5. Attach a slide hammer in the center hole of the attachment and pull out the hub, with the disc attached, from the knuckle.
6. Remove the tie-rod from the knuckle using the ball joint remover. Use care not to damage the ball joint seals.
7. Remove the lower arm from the knuckle using the ball joint remover.

8. Loosen the lockbolt which retains the strut in the knuckle. Tap the top of the knuckle with a hammer and slide it off the shock.

9. Remove the knuckle and hub, if still attached, by sliding the driveshaft out of the hub.

10. To install, reverse the removal procedure. If the hub was removed, refer to Brake Disc Removal, for procedures with the hydraulic press. Be sure to visually check the knuckle for visible signs of wear or damage and to check the condition of the inner bearing dust seals.

TORQUE SPECIFICATIONS

Part(s)	Torque (ft/lbs)
Lower ball joint retaining nut	
Civic	22-29
Accord and Prelude	33
Lower control arm-to-body mount bolts	
Civic	25-36
Accord and Prelude	40
Front radius rod-to-knuckle bolt	40
Rear radius rod-to-carrier bolt	40-54
Rear radius rod-to-body bolt	40
Front stabilizer mount bolts	5-9
Strut center nut (front and rear)	40-50
Strut to body retaining bolts (front and rear)	16
Front strut-to-knuckle retaining bolt	36-43
Rear strut-to-carrier mount bolts	26-35
Rear strut-to-control arm bolt	36-47

Front End Alignment

CASTER AND CAMBER ADJUSTMENT

Caster and camber cannot be adjusted on any Honda. If caster, camber or kingpin angle is incorrect or front end parts are damaged or worn, they must be replaced.

TOE-OUT ADJUSTMENT

Toe is the difference of the distance between the forward extremes of the front tires and the distance between the rearward extremes of the front tires. On Hondas, the fronts of the tires are further apart than the rear to counteract the pulling-together effect of front wheel drive.

Toe-out can be adjusted on all Hondas by loosening the locknuts at each end of the tie-rods. To increase toe-out, turn the right tie-rod in the direction of forward wheel rotation and turn the left tie-rod in the opposite direction. Turn both tie-rods an equal amount until toe-out becomes 0.039 in. (1 mm).

STEERING

Steering Wheel

REMOVAL AND INSTALLATION

1. Remove the steering wheel pad by lifting it off.

2. Remove the steering wheel retaining nut. Gently hit the backside of each of the steering wheel spokes with equal force from the palms of your hands.

CAUTION

Avoid hitting the wheel or the shaft with excessive force. Damage to the shaft could result.

3. Installation is the reverse of the removal procedure. Be sure to tighten the steering wheel nut to 22-33 ft/lbs.

Turn Signal Switch

REMOVAL AND INSTALLATION

1. Remove the steering wheel.

2. Disconnect the column wiring harness and coupler.

3. Remove the four attaching bolts (remove the upper two bolts first), holding the steering column to the instrument panel and lower the column.

CAUTION

Be careful not to damage the steering column or shaft.

4. Remove the upper and lower column covers.

5. Loosen the screw on the turn signal switch cam nut and lightly tap its head to permit the cam nut to loosen. Then remove the turn signal switch assembly and the steering shaft upper bushing.

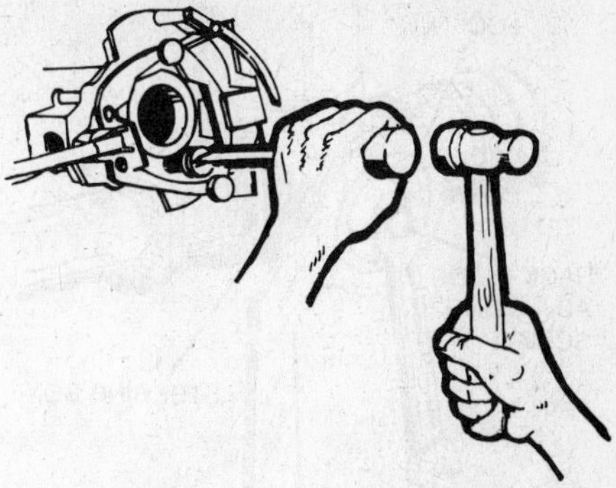

Loosening the turn signal cam nut screw

6. To assemble and install, reverse the above procedure. When installing the turn signal switch assembly, engage the locating tab on the switch with the notch in the steering column. The steering shaft upper bushing should be installed with the flat side facing the upper side of the column. The alignment notch for the turn signal switch will be centered on the flat side of the bushing.

NOTE: If the cam nut has been removed, be sure to install it with the small end up.

Ignition Switch

REMOVAL AND INSTALLATION

1. Remove the steering shaft hanger retaining bolts and lower the steering shaft from the instrument panel to expose the ignition switch.

2. Remove the steering column housing upper and lower covers.

3. Disconnect the ignition switch wiring at the couplers.

4. The ignition switch assembly is held onto the column by two shear bolts. Remove these bolts, using a drill, to separate and remove the ignition switch.

5. To install, reverse the removal procedure. You will have to replace the shear bolts with new ones.

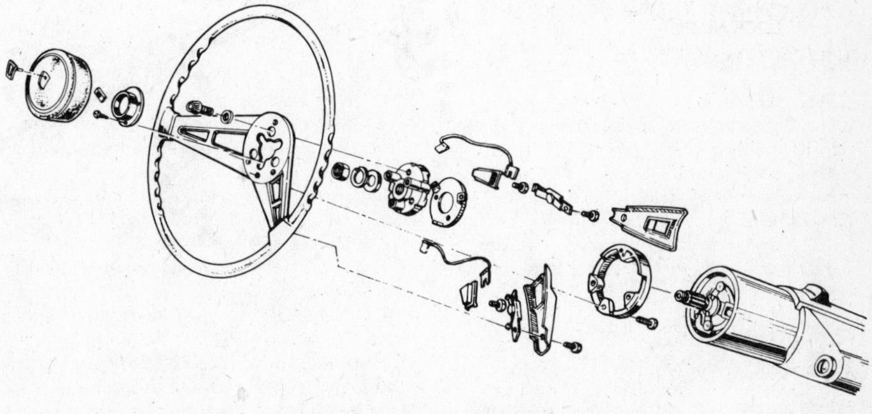

Exploded view of steering wheel and related parts

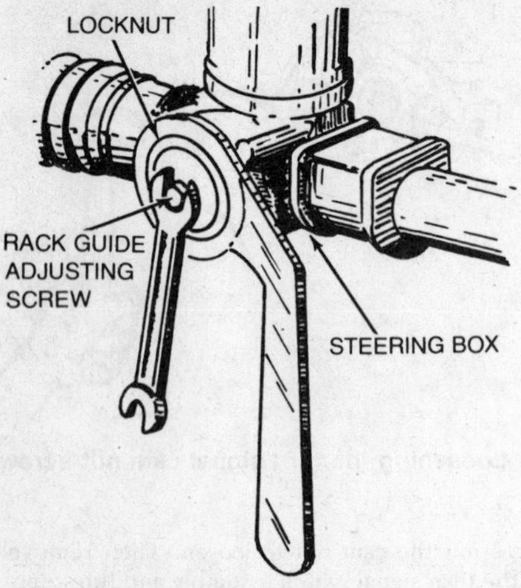

Steering box adjustment

Steering Gear

TESTING

1. Remove the dust seal bellows retaining bands and slide the dust seals off the left and right side of the gearbox housing.
2. Turn the front wheels full left and, using your hand, attempt to move the steering rack in an up-down direction.
3. Repeat with the wheel turned full right.
4. If any movement is felt, the steering gearbox must be adjusted.

ADJUSTMENT

1. Make sure that the rack is well lubricated.
2. Loosen the rack guide adjusting locknut.
3. Tighten the adjusting screw just to the point where the front wheels cannot be turned by hand.
4. Back off the adjusting screw 45 degrees and hold it in that position while adjusting the locknut.
5. Recheck the play, and then move the wheels lock-to-lock, to make sure that the rack moves freely.
6. Check the steering force by first raising the front wheels and then placing them in a straight-ahead position. Turn the steering wheel with a spring scale to check the steering force. Steering force should be no more than 3.3 lbs.

REMOVAL AND INSTALLATION

1. Jack and support the front of the car.
2. Remove the front wheels.
3. Raise the engine off the mounts.
4. Remove the tie rod ends from the knuckles with a ball joint remover.
5. Disconnect the exhaust pipe at the manifold.
6. On models with manual transmission, disconnect the gear shift rod and extension at the engine, and remove the center beam.
7. On models with Hondamatic, remove the center engine mount and the transmission splash guard. Disconnect the control cable from the transmission.
8. On Accords with power steering, use flare nut wrenches (12 mm, 14 mm, and 17 mm) to disconnect the hydraulic lines from the steering gear box. Plug the lines upon removal.
9. Position the steering wheel fully to the left. Remove the steering U-joint from the pinion shaft.
10. Remove the steering gear box retaining bolts.
11. Move the left tie rod upward and lower the rack until the pinion clears the body. Rotate the rack until the pinion is facing down. Move the rack to the right side of car until the left tie rod can be lowered out the bottom. Remove the rack through the bottom of the subframe.
12. Install in the reverse order of removal.

Tie-Rods

REMOVAL AND INSTALLATION

1. Raise the front of the car and support it with safety stands. Remove the front wheels.
2. Use a ball joint remover to remove the tie-rod from the knuckle.

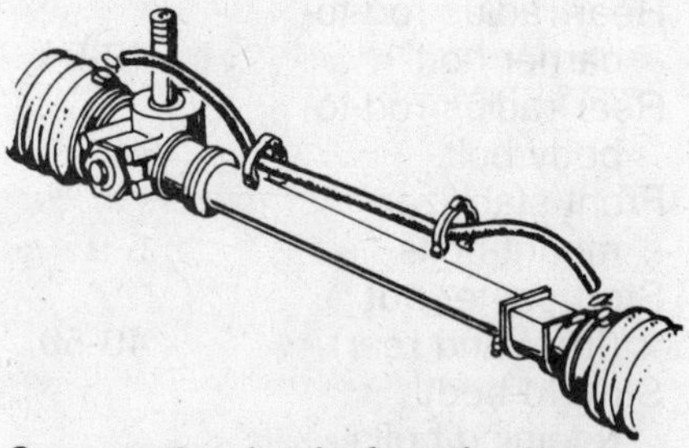

Separate the air tube from the dust boot

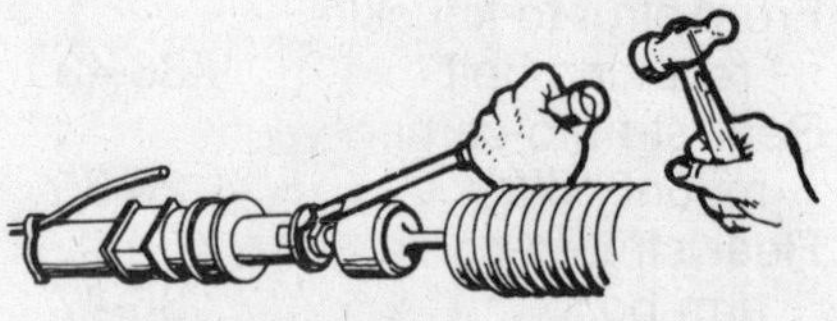

Tie–rod lockwasher removal

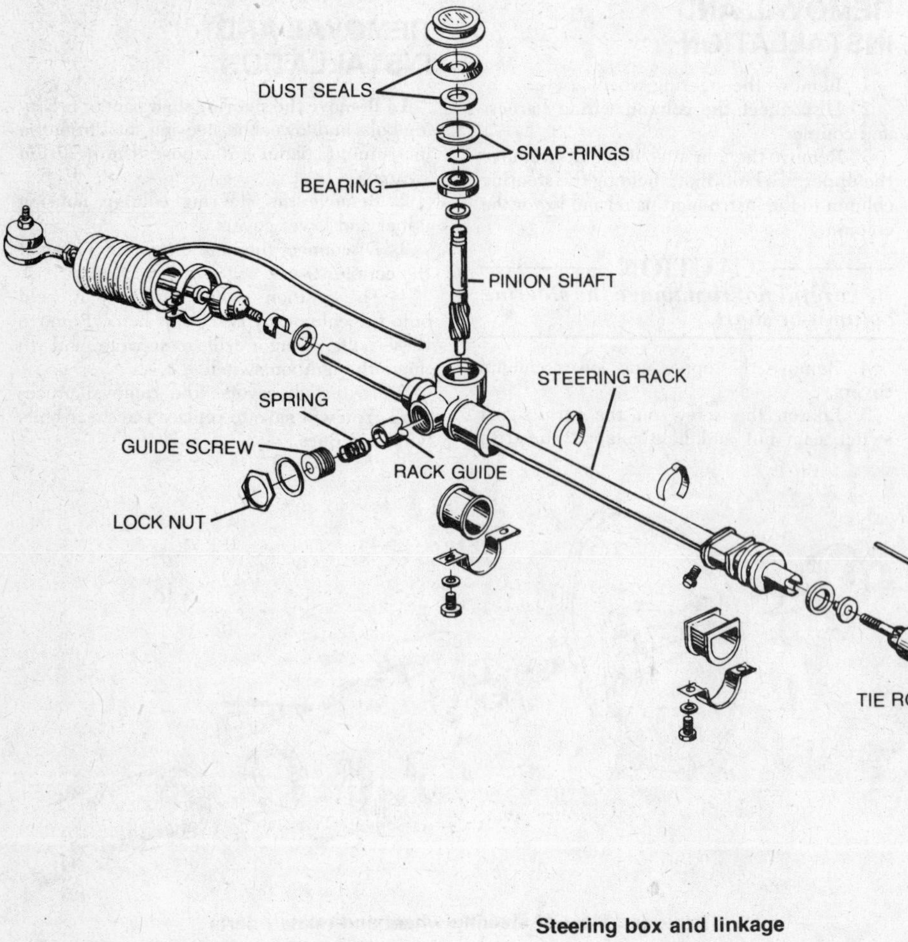
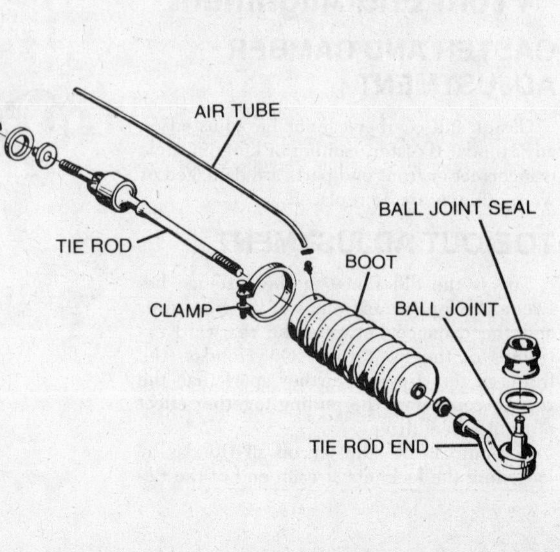

Steering box and linkage

3. Disconnect the air tube at the dust seal joint. Remove the tie-rod dust seal bellows clamps and move the rubber bellows on the tie-rod rack joints.

4. Straighten the tie-rod lockwasher tabs at the tie-rod-to-rack joint and remove the tie-rod by turning it with a wrench.

5. To install, reverse the removal procedure. Always use a new tie-rod lockwasher during reassembly. Fit the locating lugs into the slots on the rack and bend the outer edge of the washer over the flat part of the rod, after the tie-rod nut has been properly tightened.

Power Steering Pump

REMOVAL AND INSTALLATION

1. Drain the fluid from the system: Disconnect the cooler return hose from the reservoir and place the end in a large container. Start the engine and allow it to run at fast idle. Turn the steering wheel from lock to lock several times, until fluid stops running from the hose. Shut off the engine and discard the fluid. Reattach the hose.

2. Disconnect the inlet and outlet hoses at the pump.

3. Remove the drive belt.

4. Remove the bolts and remove the pump.

5. To install, install the pump on its mounts, install the belt, adjust belt tension, and install the fluid hoses.

6. Fill the reservoir with fresh fluid, to the full mark. Use only genuine Honda power steering fluid; ATF or other brands of fluid will damage the system.

7. Start the engine and allow to fast idle. Turn the steering wheel from side to side several times, lightly contacting the stops. This will bleed the system of air. Check the reservoir level and add fluid if necessary.

BELT ADJUSTMENT

1. Loosen the bolt on the adjuster arm.

2. Move the pump toward or away from the engine, until the belt can be depressed approximately $^{9}/_{16}$ in. at the midpoint between the two pulleys under moderate thumb pressure. If the tension adjustment is being made on a new belt, the deflection should only be about $^{7}/_{16}$ in., to allow for the initial stretching of the belt.

There is a raised bump on the top of the adjusting arm. If the belt has stretched to the point where the adjustment bolt is at or beyond the bump, the belt should be replaced.

3. Tighten the bolt and recheck the adjustment.

STEERING TORQUE SPECIFICATIONS
Ft/Lbs

Tie-rod end locknut	29.0-35.0
Tie-rod ball joint nut	29.0-35.0
Bask guide locknut	29.0-36.0
Steering wheel retaining nut(s)	22.0-33.0

BRAKE SYSTEM

Honda uses a dual hydraulic system, with the brakes connected diagonally. In other words, the right front and left rear brakes are on the same hydraulic line and the left front and right rear are on the other line. This has the added advantage of front disc emergency braking, should either of the hydraulic systems fail. The diagonal rear brake serves to counteract the sway from single front disc braking.

A leading/trailing drum brake is used for the rear brakes, with disc brakes for the front. All Hondas are equipped with a brake warning light, which is activated when a defect in the brake system occurs.

Adjustments

BRAKE PEDAL FREE-PLAY

Free-play is the distance the pedal travels from the stop (brake light switch) until the pushrod contacts the vacuum booster, which actuates the master cylinder.

To check free-play, first measure the distance (with the carpet removed) from the floor to the brake pedal. Then push down the pedal until contact is felt and again measure the distance from the floor to the brake pedal. The difference between the two measurements is the pedal free-play. The specified free-play is 0.04-0.20 in. Free-play adjustment is made by loosening the locknut on the brake light switch and rotating the switch body until the specified clearance is obtained.

FRONT DISC BRAKES

The front discs are inherently self adjusting. No adjustments are either necessary or possible.

REAR DRUM BRAKES

1. Block the front wheels, release the parking brake and raise the rear of the car, supporting it with safety stands.

2. Depress the brake pedal two or three times and release.

3. The adjuster is located on the inboard side, underneath the control arm. Turn the adjuster clockwise until the wheel no longer turns.

4. Back off the adjuster two (2) clicks and turn the wheel to see if the brake shoes are dragging. If they are dragging, back off the adjuster one more click.

Master Cylinder

REMOVAL AND INSTALLATION

CAUTION

Before removing the master cylinder, cover the body surfaces with fender covers and rags to prevent damage to painted surfaces by brake fluid.

1. Disconnect and plug the brake lines at the master cylinder.

2. Remove the master cylinder-to-vacuum

Drum brake adjustment location

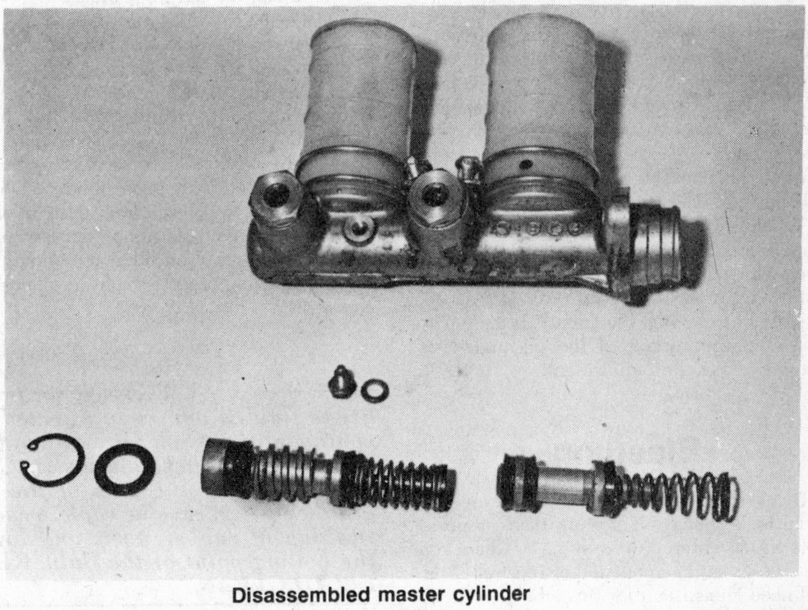

Disassembled master cylinder

booster attaching bolts and remove the master cylinder from the car.

3. To install, reverse the removal procedure. Before operating the car, you must bleed the brake system (see below).

DISASSEMBLY AND OVERHAUL

1. Remove the fluid reservoir caps and floats, and drain the reservoirs.
2. Loosen the retaining clamps and remove the reservoirs.
3. Remove the primary piston stop bolt.
4. Remove the piston retaining clip and washer, and remove the primary piston.
5. Wrap a rag around the end of the master cylinder, so that it blocks the bore. Hold your finger over the stop bolt hole and direct a small amount of compressed air into the primary outlet. This should slide the primary piston to the end of the master cylinder bore, so that it can be removed.
6. Remove the two union caps, washers, check valves and springs.
7. For overhaul, check the following:
   a. Clogged orifices in the pistons and cylinder;
   b. Damage to the reservoir attaching surface;
   c. Damage to the check valves;
   d. Wear or damage to the piston cups;
   e. The clearance between the master cylinder bore and the pistons. The clearance should be 0.0008-0.0039 in.
8. Assembly of the master cylinder is the reverse of the disassembly procedures. Be sure to check the following:
   a. The check valve and piston cups should be replaced when the master cylinder is assembled, regardless of their condition.
   b. Apply a thin coat of brake fluid to the pistons before installing. When installing the pistons, push in while rotating to prevent damage to the piston cups;
   c. Tighten the union cap and stop bolts.
9. Before the master cylinder is installed on the vacuum booster, the push-rod clearance must be checked. This can be done with any standard master cylinder piston to vacuum booster pushrod clearance gauge. This is an "H" shaped gauge which is first installed over the piston end of the master cylinder. The threaded gauge of the tool is then screwed down until it contacts the master cylinder piston. The gauge is then placed over the vacuum booster pushrod. Clearance should be 0.1-0.6 mm (0.004-0.023 in.) measured with a flat feeler gauge. If incorrect, the booster pushrod length can be adjusted. Be careful not to scratch the surface of the pushrod. Coat the surface of the pushrod with silicone grease after adjustment.

Bleeding

The system must be bled whenever the pedal feels spongy, indicating that compressible air has entered the system, or whenever the system has been opened or repaired. You will need an assistant for this job.

CAUTION

Never re-use brake fluid which has been bled from the system.

1. The order for bleeding is left front, right rear, right front, and left rear.
2. Clean the bleeder screw at each wheel.
3. Fill the master cylinder with fresh DOT 3 brake fluid.

NOTE: Brake fluid absorbs moisture from the air. Do not leave the fluid container or master cylinder uncovered any longer than necessary. Do not drip fluid on painted surfaces—it eats paint.

Check the fluid level often when bleeding, and refill the reservoir as necessary.

4. Attach a length of clear vinyl tubing to the bleeder screw on the brake. Insert the other end of the tube into a clear jar half full of brake fluid.
5. Have your helper pump the pedal several times, then apply steady pressure.
6. Open the bleeder screw slightly and allow the fluid to run through the tube. Then close the screw before, or just as, the pedal reaches the end of its travel. Have your assistant slowly release the pedal. Repeat the process until no air bubbles appear in the expelled fluid.

NOTE: If the pedal is depressed too rapidly, small air bubbles will form in the fluid.

7. Repeat this process at each wheel. Do not move the car until a firm pedal is obtained. Discard the fluid bled from the system.

When it is necessary to flush the brake hydraulic system because of parts replacement or fluid contamination, the following procedure should be observed:

1. Loosen the wheel cylinder bleeder screw. Drain the brake fluid by pumping the brake pedal. Pump the pedal until all of the old fluid has been pumped out and replaced by new fluid.
2. The flushing procedure should be performed in the following sequence:
   a. Bleed the left front brake;
   b. Bleed the right rear brake;
   c. Bleed the right front brake;
   d. Bleed the left rear brake.
3. Bleed the back of the master cylinder before the front, through the two bleed valves. Fasten one end of a plastic tube onto the bleed valve and immerse the other end in a clear jar filled with brake fluid. When air bubbles cease to emerge from the end of the tubing, the bleeding is completed. Be sure to keep the fluid reservoir filled at all times during the bleeding process so air does not enter the system.

CAUTION

Brake fluid is adversely affected by contamination from dirt, automotive petroleum products and water. Contaminants can plug part of the hydraulic system, causing rapid wear or swelling of rubber parts and lower the boiling point of the fluid. KEEP FLUID CLEAN.

Vacuum Booster

INSPECTION

A preliminary check of the vacuum booster can be made as follows:

a. Depress the brake pedal several times using normal pressure. Make sure that the pedal height does not vary;
b. Hold the pedal in the depressed position and start the engine. The pedal should drop slightly;
c. Hold the pedal in the above position and stop the engine. The pedal should stay in the depressed position for approximately 30 seconds.
d. If the pedal does not drop when the engine is started or rises after the engine is stopped, the booster is not functioning properly.

REMOVAL AND INSTALLATION

1. Disconnect the vacuum hose at the booster.
2. Disconnect and plug the brake lines at the master cylinder.
3. Remove the brake pedal-to-booster link pin and the four nuts retaining the booster. The pushrod and nuts are located inside the car under the instrument panel.
4. Remove the booster with the master cylinder attached.
5. To install, reverse the removal procedure. Check the vacuum booster pushrod-to-master cylinder piston clearance as outlined in the master cylinder removal procedure. Don't forget to bleed the brake system before operating the car.

FRONT DISC BRAKES

Disc Brake Pads

1975-78 Models

1. After removing the wheel, remove the pad retaining clip which is fitted in the holes of the pad retaining pins.
2. Remove the two retaining pins and fitting springs with pliers. When removing them, care must be taken to prevent the springs from flying apart.
3. The front brake pad can be removed, together with the shim, after removing the springs and pins. If the pads are difficult to remove, open the bleeder valve and move the caliper in the direction of the piston. The pads will become loose and can be easily removed.

NOTE: After the pads are removed, the brake pedal must not be touched.

The disc pads should be replaced when approximately 0.08 in. lining thickness remains (thickness of lining material only).

To provide space for installing the pad, loosen the bleed valve and push the inner piston back into the cylinder. Also push back

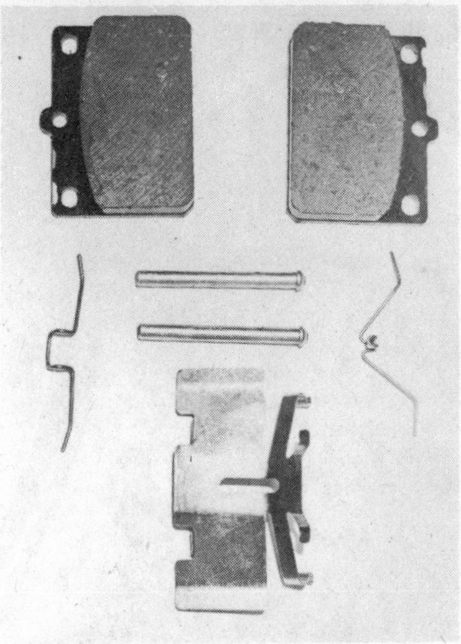

Disc brake pads, springs, and pins

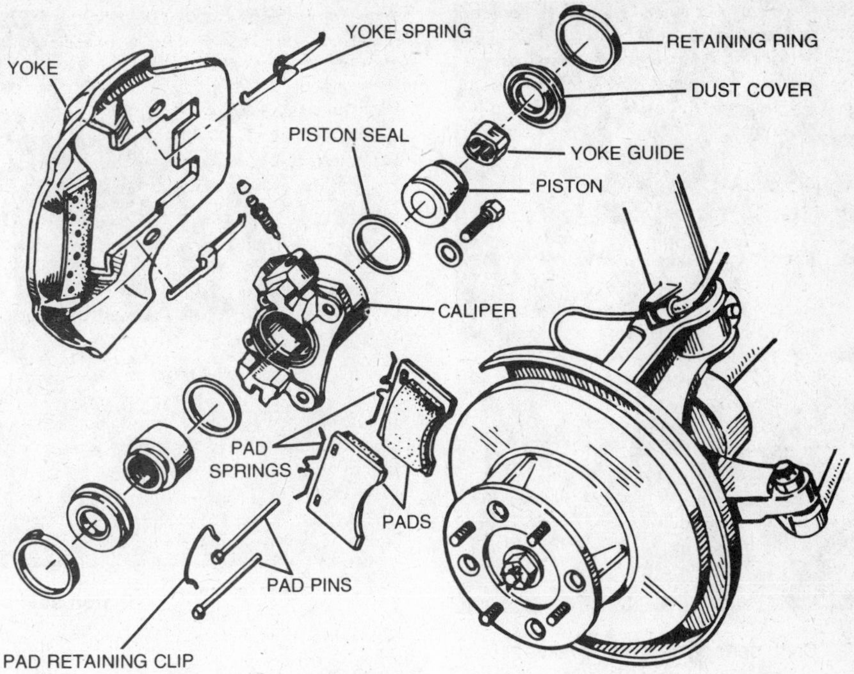

Exploded view of Civic sedan and hatchback disc brakes

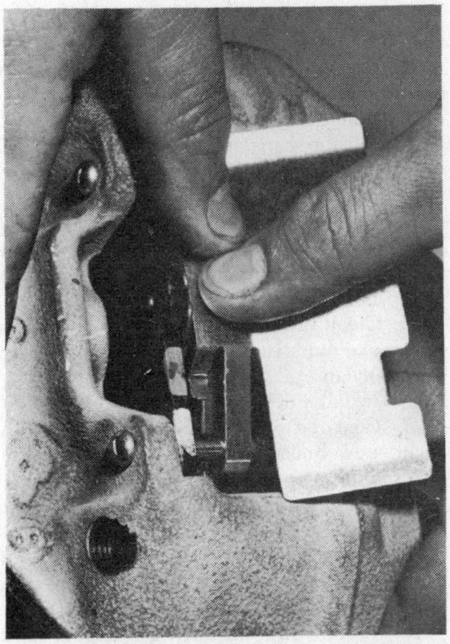

Pad retaining clip removal

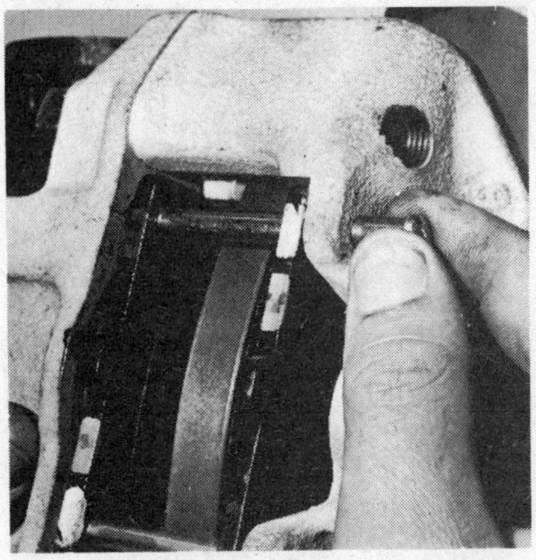

Pad retaining pin removal

the outer piston by applying pressure to the caliper. After providing space for the pads, close the bleed valve and insert the pad. Insert a shim behind each pad with the arrow on the shim pointing up. Incorrect installation of the shims can cause squealing brakes.

1979-81 Models

1. Raise and support the car. Remove the wheels.
2. Remove the lower caliper support pin and pivot the caliper up and away from the rotor.
3. Remove the pads, shim and anti-rattle spring. Clean all points where the shoes and shim touch the caliper and mount. Apply a thin film of silicone grease to the cleaned areas.
4. Place the anti-rattle springs in position.
5. Install the pads with the shim against the outside shoe.
6. Loosen the bleed screw slightly and push in the caliper piston to allow mounting of the caliper over the rotor. Tighten the bleed screw.
7. Pivot the caliper down over the rotor and install the lower support pin. Tighten the pin to 13 ft/lb.

Disc Brake Calipers

REMOVAL AND INSTALLATION

All Civics

1. Raise the front of the car and support it with safety stands. Remove the front wheels.
2. Loosen the brake line at the wheel cylinder.
3. The caliper housing is mounted to the knuckle with two bolts located behind the cylinder. Remove these bolts and the caliper. On the station wagon, be sure you are not removing the bridge bolts which hold the caliper halves together.

To install, reverse the removal procedure. Be sure to inspect all parts before installing and bleed the brake system before operating the car.

Accord and Prelude

1. Remove the brake pads as outlined above.
2. Remove the lower anti-rattle clip, and disconnect the brake hose.
3. Remove the two bolts retaining the caliper mounting support to the knuckle and lift off.

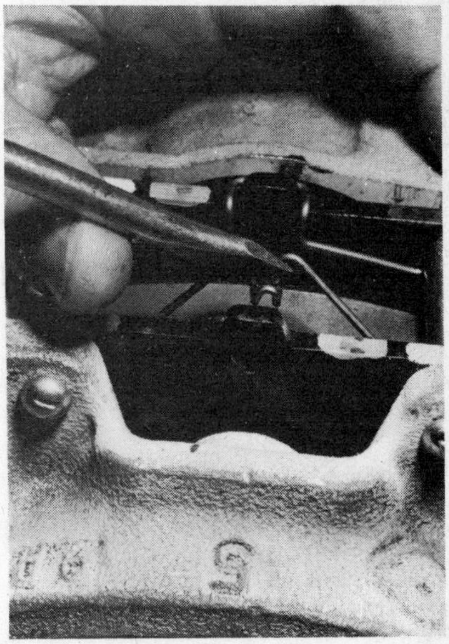

Pad retaining pin spring removal

Civic sedan front disc brakes

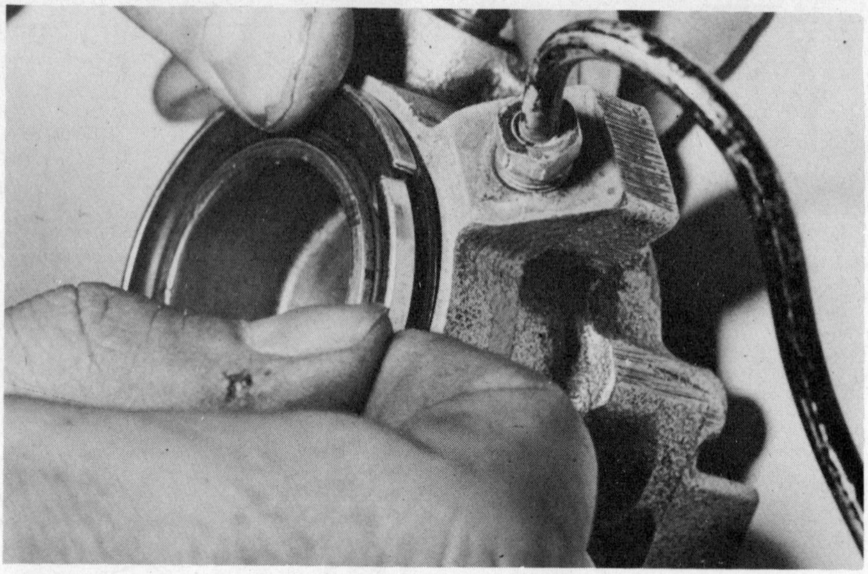

Piston seal snap ring installation

4. Reverse the above to install. Bleed the brakes.

INSPECTION AND OVERHAUL

All Civics Except Station Wagon

NOTE: Wash all parts in brake fluid. Do not use cleaning solvent or gasoline.

1. Remove the inner and outer pad springs and pin clips. Then remove the pins and pads.

NOTE: The springs are different, so note the location and method of installation before removing.

2. Push the yoke toward the rear (inboard side) of the cylinder, until it is free to separate the yoke from the cylinder. You may have to tap lightly with a plastic hammer (where the mounting bolts are located) to remove the cylinder. Exercise extreme care to avoid damaging the cylinder body. If only the cylinder body moves, without the outer piston, a gentle tap on the piston should loosen it.
3. To dismantle the cylinder, first remove the retaining rings at both ends of the cylinder with a screwdriver, being careful not to damage the rubber boot.
4. Both pistons can be removed from the cylinder body either by pushing through one end with a wooden rod or by blowing compressed air into the cylinder inlet port.

NOTE: If the wheel cylinder pistons are removed for any reason, the piston seals must be replaced.

5. Remove the piston seals, installed on the inside of the cylinder at both ends, with a screwdriver.
6. Inspect the caliper operation. If the lining wear differs greatly between the inner and outer pads, the caliper may be unable to move properly due to rust and dirt on the sliding surfaces. Clean the sliding part of the caliper and apply brake grease.

NOTE: All brake parts are critical items. If there is any question as to the serviceability of any brake part—replace it.

7. Check the piston-to-cylinder clearance. The specified clearance is 0.0008-0.0005 in. Also check the pistons and cylinder bore for scuffing and scratching.
8. Check the dust covers, retaining rings, nylon retainers and all other parts for wear or damage.
9. To reassemble the caliper, reverse the removal procedure. Lubricate all sliding surfaces with high temperature silicone grease. Lubricate internal parts with clean brake fluid. After reassembly, measure the force necessary to slide the caliper from the neutral position with a spring scale. The specified force is 55 lbs. Bleed the brake system.

Civic Station Wagon

1. Remove the caliper.
2. Remove the bridge bolts which hold the caliper halves together.
3. Separate the caliper halves.
4. The rubber bushing, wiper seal, and retainer should be inspected for wear and replaced if necessary.
5. Remove the piston snap ring. Remove the dust seal with a pointed piece of wood or plastic to avoid scratching the piston or bore. Discard the seal.
6. Apply low air pressure to the fluid inlet to remove the piston. Remove the O-ring with the wood or plastic tool. Discard the O-ring.
7. Inspect the piston and caliper bore for scoring or roughness. Replace if scratched or scored.
8. Lubricate the bore, piston, new O-ring, and new seal with clean brake fluid and install into the caliper. Install the snap ring.
9. Lubricate the sliding surfaces with high temperature silicone grease. Assemble in reverse of removal. Torque the bridge bolts to 63 ft/lbs. The aluminum washers on each side of the brake hose caliper fitting should be replaced.

Accord and Prelude

1. Remove the brake pads and caliper as outlined above.
2. Remove the snap-ring and piston boot from the caliper piston body.
3. Apply pressure through the brake hose hole and carefully force out the piston.
4. Using a screwdriver (or preferably a blunt plastic or wooden instrument) pry out the piston seal. Be sure not to scratch the piston bore.
5. Clean the piston and caliper bore with new brake fluid. Inspect for corrosion, scoring or other damage.
6. Install a new piston seal.
7. Coat the piston and caliper bore with clean, new brake fluid and press the piston into the bore by hand.
8. Install the piston boot and fit the snap-ring.
9. Wire brush the sliding surfaces of the caliper piston body and caliper mounting support.
10. Install the mounting support and torque the two bolts to 58-66 ft/lbs.
11. Connect the brake hose using new washers. Tighten to 7-10 ft/lbs.
12. Install the brake pads as outlined above.
13. Bleed the brakes and road-test.

Brake Disc

REMOVAL AND INSTALLATION

NOTE: The following procedure for brake disc removal necessitates the use of a hydraulic press. You will have to go to a machine or auto shop equipped with a press. Do not attempt this procedure without a press.

1. Raise the front of the car and support it with safety stands. Remove the front wheels.
2. Remove the center spindle nuts.
3. Remove the caliper assembly. Do not let

the caliper assembly hang by the brake hose.

4. Use a slide hammer with a hub puller attachment or a conventional hub puller, to extract the hub with the disc attached.

5. Remove the four bolts and separate the hub and disc.

6. Remove the knuckle from the car.

7. Remove the wheel bearings from the knuckle (see below).

NOTE: If, for any reason, the hub is removed, the front wheel bearings must be replaced.

8. To install the disc, you have to use a hydraulic press for both the bearings and the hub. After installing the bearings (see below), install the front hub. Position the hub with the knuckle underneath on the base and press it down through the base.

INSPECTION

1. The brake disc develops circular scores after long usage when there is frequent braking. Excessive scoring not only causes a squealing brake, but also shortens the service life of the brake pads. However, light scoring of the disc surface, not exceeding 0.015 in. in depth, will result from normal use and is not detrimental to brake operation.

NOTE: Differences in the left and right disc surfaces can result in uneven braking.

2. Disc run-out is the movement of the disc from side-to-side. Place a dial indicator in the middle of the pad wear area and turn the disc, while checking the indicator. If disc run-out exceeds 0.006 in., replace the disc.

3. Disc parallelism is the measurement of variations in disc thickness at several locations on the disc circumference. To measure parallelism, place a mark on the disc and measure the disc thickness with a micrometer. Repeat this measurement at eight (8) equal increments on the circumference of the disc. If the measurements vary more than 0.0028 in., replace the disc.

NOTE: Only the outer portion of the disc can be checked while installed on the car. If the installed parallelism check is within specifications, but you have reason to suspect that parallelism is the problem, remove the disc and repeat the check using the center of pad wear for a checking point.

Front Wheel Bearings

REMOVAL AND INSTALLATION

NOTE: The following procedure for wheel bearing removal and installation necessitates the use of a hydraulic press. You will have to go to a machine or auto shop equipped with a press. Do not attempt this procedure without a press.

1. Raise the front of the car and support it with safety stands. Remove the front wheel.

2. Remove the caliper assembly from the brake disc and separate the tie-rod ball joint and lower ball joint from the knuckle.

3. Loosen the lockbolt which retains the front strut in the knuckle. Tap the top of the knuckle with a hammer and slide it off the shock. Remove the knuckle and hub by sliding the driveshaft out of the hub.

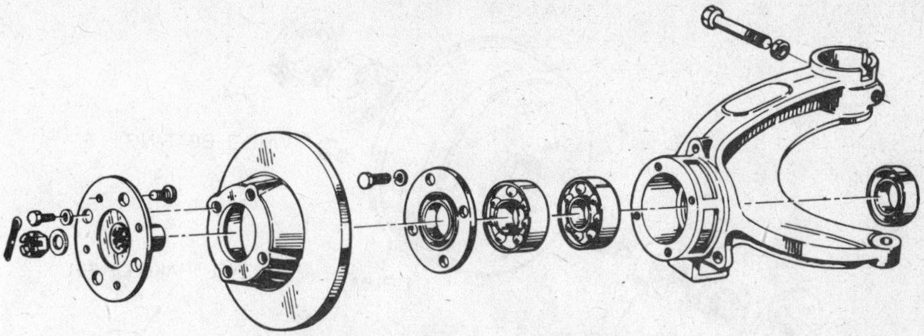

Civic disc, hub, and hub carrier

4. Remove the wheel bearing dust cover on the inboard side of the knuckle.

5. Remove the four bolts which hold the brake disc onto the hub. Remove the splashguard by removing the three retaining screws.

6. Remove the outer bearing retainer .

7. Remove the wheel bearings by supporting the knuckle in a hydraulic press, using two support plates. Make sure that the plates do not overlap the outer bearing race. Now use a proper sized driver and handle to remove the bearings.

NOTE: Whenever the wheel bearings are removed, always replace with a new set of bearings and outer dust seal.

8. Pack each bearing with grease before installing (see below).

9. To install the bearings, press them into the knuckle using the same support plates as above, plus the installing base. Use the same driver and handle you used to remove the bearing.

NOTE: The front wheel bearings are the angular contact type. It is important that they be installed with the manufacturer's markings facing inward (towards each other).

10. Use the press to install the front hub (see above).

11. The rest of installation is the reverse of the removal procedure.

CLEANING AND REPACKING

1. Clean all old grease from the driveshaft spindles on the car.

2. Remove all old grease from the hub and knuckle and thoroughly dry and wipe clean all components.

3. When fitting new bearings, you must pack them with wheel bearing grease. To do this, place a glob of grease in your left palm, then, holding one of the bearings in your right hand, drag the face of the bearing heavily through the grease. This must be done to work as much grease as possible through the ball bearings and the cage. Turn the bearing and continue to pull it through the grease, until the grease is thoroughly packed between the bearing balls and the cage, all around the bearings. Repeat this operation until all of the bearings are packed with grease.

4. Pack the inside of the rotor and knuckle hub with a moderate amount of grease. Do not overload the hub with grease.

5. Apply a small amount of grease to the spindle and to the lip of the inner seal before installing.

6. To install the bearings, check the above procedures.

CHECKING AND ADJUSTING

The front wheel bearings should be inspected and repacked (or replaced) every 30,000 miles. To check the wheel bearings for any play, jack up each wheel and shake it to check the bearings for any play. If any play is felt, tighten the castellated spindle nut to the specified torque (87-130 ft/lbs) and reinspect. If play is still present, replace the bearing.

NOTE: Overtightening the spindle nuts will cause excessive bearing friction and will result in rough wheel rotation and eventual bearing failure.

REAR DRUM BRAKES

Brake Drums

REMOVAL AND INSTALLATION

1. Raise the rear of the car and support it with safety stands. Remove the rear wheels. Make sure that the parking brake is *off*.

Cotter pin removal—Civic rear wheel

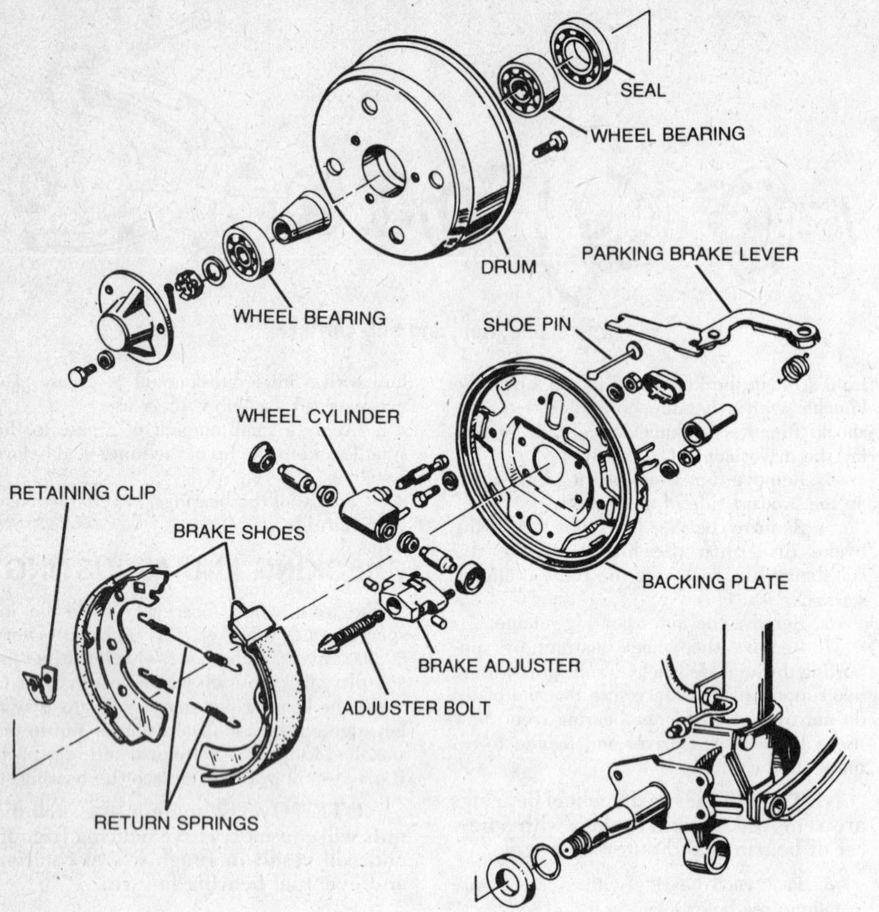

Exploded view of sedan rear drum brakes

2. Remove the bearing cap and the castle nut.
3. Back off the adjuster three or four clicks. Pull off the rear brake drum. If the drum is difficult to remove, use a brake drum puller, or a front hub puller and slide hammer.
4. To install, reverse the removal procedures.

Removing the rear drum with a slide hammer

INSPECTION

Check the drum for cracks and the inner surface of the shoe for excessive wear and damage. The inner diameter (I.D.) of the drum should be no more than specifications, nor should the drum be more than 0.004 in. out-of-round.

Brake Shoes

REMOVAL AND INSTALLATION

1. Remove the brake drum.
2. Remove the tension pin clips and the two brake return springs. Then remove the shoes. If you are installing new shoes, back off the adjusters.

CAUTION

The upper and lower brake shoe return springs on the Civic sedan and hatchback and Accord are different and should not be interchanged. The upper spring is designed so that the spring coils are located on the outboard side of the shoe, while the lower spring is designed so that its coils are located on the inboard side of the shoe with the crossbar facing downward. Station wagons use two upper springs, which fit on the outside of the shoes, and one lower spring, which fits on the inside of the shoes.

3. To install, reverse the removal procedure. Be sure to check the brake lining thickness before assembly. If the thickness is less than specifications, replace the lining.

Wheel Cylinders

REMOVAL AND INSTALLATION

1. Remove the brake drum and shoes.

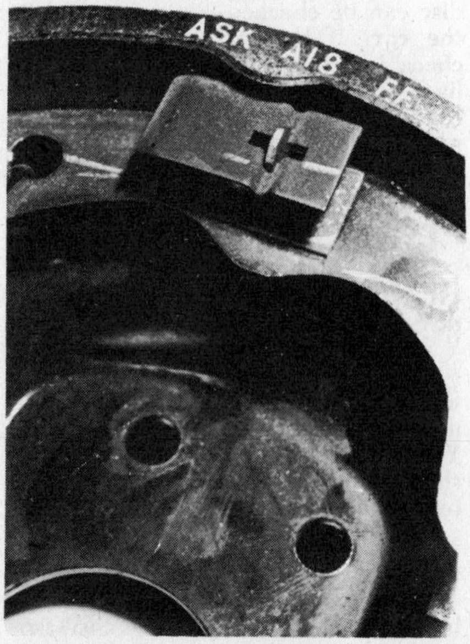

Drum brake shoe retaining clip

Rear brake shoes—Civic sedan

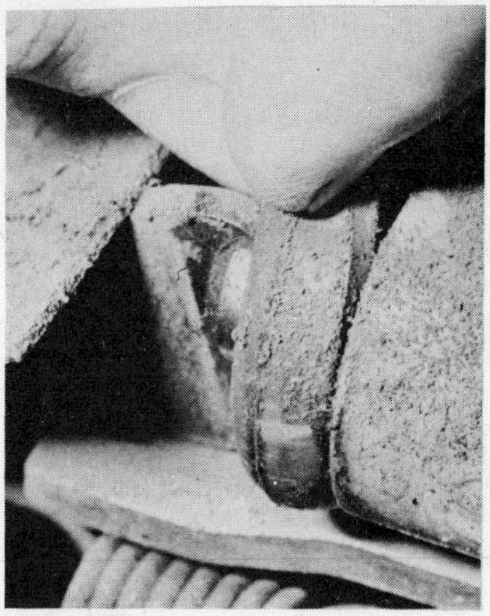

Checking behind seals for wheel cylinder leakage

2. Disconnect the parking brake cable and brake lines at the backing plate. Be sure to have a drip pan to catch the brake fluid.

3. Remove the two wheel cylinders retaining nuts on the inboard side of the backing plate and remove the wheel cylinder.

4. To install, reverse the removal procedure. When assembling, apply a thin coat of grease to the grooves of the wheel cylinder piston and the sliding surfaces of the backing plate. Bleed the brakes.

OVERHAUL

Remove the wheel cylinder dust seals from the grooves to permit the removal of the cylinder pistons.

Wash all parts in fresh brake fluid and check the cylinder bore and pistons for scratches and other damage, replacing where necessary. Check the clearance between the piston and the cylinder bore, by taking the difference between the piston diameter and the bore diameter. The specified clearance is 0.0008-0.004 in.

When assembling the wheel cylinder, apply a coat of brake fluid to the pistons, piston cups and cylinder walls.

Disassembled drum brake wheel cylinder

Handbrake

CABLE REMOVAL AND INSTALLATION

1. Remove the adjusting nut from the equalizer mounted on the rear axle and separate the cable from the equalizer.

2. Set the parking brake lever to a fully released position and remove the cotter pin from the side of the brake lever.

3. After removing the cotter pin, pull out the pin which connects the cable and the lever.

4. Detach the cable from the guides at the front and right side of the fuel tank and remove the cable.

5. To install, reverse the removal procedure, making sure that grease is applied to the cable and the guides.

ADJUSTMENT

Inspect the following items:

a. Check the ratchet for wear;

b. Check the cables for wear or damage and the cable guide and equalizer for looseness;

c. Check the equalizer cable where it contracts the equalizer and apply grease if necessary;

d. Check the rear brake adjustment.

The rear wheels should be locked when the handbrake lever is pulled 1 to 5 notches on the ratchet. Adjustment is made by turning the nut located at the equalizer, between the lower control arms.

Rear Wheel Bearings

ADJUSTMENT

Rear wheel bearings are not adjustable on the Civic models. Tighten the castle nut to 83 ft/lbs and install a new cotter pin whenever removed.

To adjust the bearings on an Accord:

1. Tighten the castle nut to 18 ft/lbs.
2. Rotate the drum a few times.
3. Back off the castle nut about 100°.
4. Tighten the castle nut to 1.1-3.6 ft/lbs.
5. Install the lock nut with its slots as close as possible to the spindle hole. Tighten the castle nut/lock nut just enough to align the slots and the hole, and install a new cotter pin.

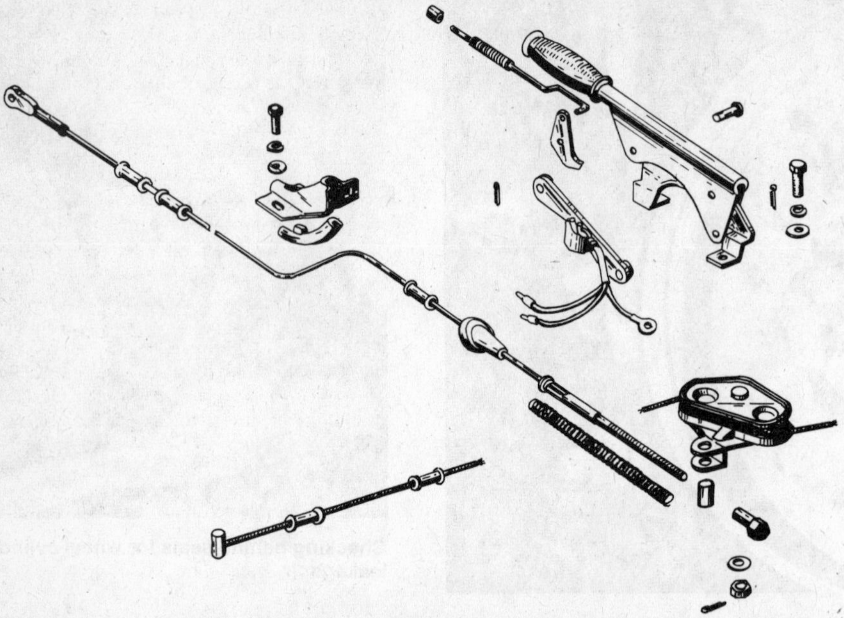

Exploded view of parking brake components

Parking brake equalizer assembly

CHASSIS ELECTRICAL

Heater

REMOVAL AND INSTALLATION

NOTE: These procedures do not apply to cars equipped with air conditioning. On cars equipped with air conditioning, heater removal may differ from the procedures listed below. Only a trained air conditioning specialist should tamper with A/C equipped units. Air conditioning units contain pressurized Freon which can be extremely dangerous (e.g. burns and/or blindness) to the untrained.

Civic

1. Drain the radiator.
2. Disconnect the right and left defroster hoses.
3. Disconnect the inlet and outlet water hoses at the heater assembly.

NOTE: There will be a coolant leakage when disconnecting the hoses. Catch the coolant in a container to prevent damage to the interior.

4. Disconnect the following items:
   a. Fre-Rec control cable;
   b. Temperature control rod;
   c. Room/Def. control cable;
   d. Fan motor switch connector;
   e. Upper attaching bolts;
   f. Lower attaching bolts;
   g. Lower bracket.
5. Remove the heater assembly through the passenger side.
6. To install the heater assembly, reverse the removal procedure. Pay attention to the following points:
   a. When installing the heater assembly, do not forget to connect the right side of the upper bracket;
   b. Connect the inlet and outlet water hoses SECURELY;

NOTE: The inlet hose is a straight type, and the outlet hose is an L-type.

   c. Install the defroster nozzles in the correct position;
   d. Connect the control cables securely. Operate the control valve and lever to check for proper operation;
   e. Be sure to bleed the cooling system.

Accord

NOTE: To remove the heater core, it is necessary to first remove the entire instrument panel and heater assemblies.

1. Drain the cooling system.
2. Remove the steering column lower trim cover.
3. Remove the two nuts and two bolts retaining the column to the firewall support.
4. Remove the instrument wire harnesses from cabin wire harness couplers.
5. Reach behind the instrument cluster and disconnect the speedometer cable and four wiring harness connectors at rear of cluster. Pry out the lock tabs to disconnect.
6. Disconnect radio lead and antenna wire.
7. Remove the heater fan switch knob, heater lever knobs and heater control bezel. Remove heater control center panel. Disconnect cigarette lighter and blower motor leads.
8. Disconnect clock leads.
9. Remove the seven sheet metal screws retaining the instrument panel to the firewall. There are two at each end of the dash (adjacent to windshield pillar), two beneath the radio and one adjacent to the clock.
10. Pull out the instrument panel and support. Check for any wires still connected.
11. Inside the engine compartment, disconnect the two heater hoses at the firewall. Remove the nut retaining the heater unit to the firewall.
12. Disconnect the three heater control cables from the heater unit. Disconnect the cable clip from the heater valve.
13. Remove the heater unit lower mounting bolt and the right and left upper mounting bolts. Separate the blower hose from the heater.
14. Lay some towels underneath to catch residual coolant leakage. Remove the heater unit.
15. To service the heater core, separate the heater housing halves.
16. Reverse the above to install. Bleed the cooling system using the bleed bolt located near the ignition distributor.

Prelude

1. Remove the blower by removing the instrument panel side cover.
2. Remove the glove box and the three blower mounting bolts.
3. Remove the blower from the heater case.
4. Drain the coolant.

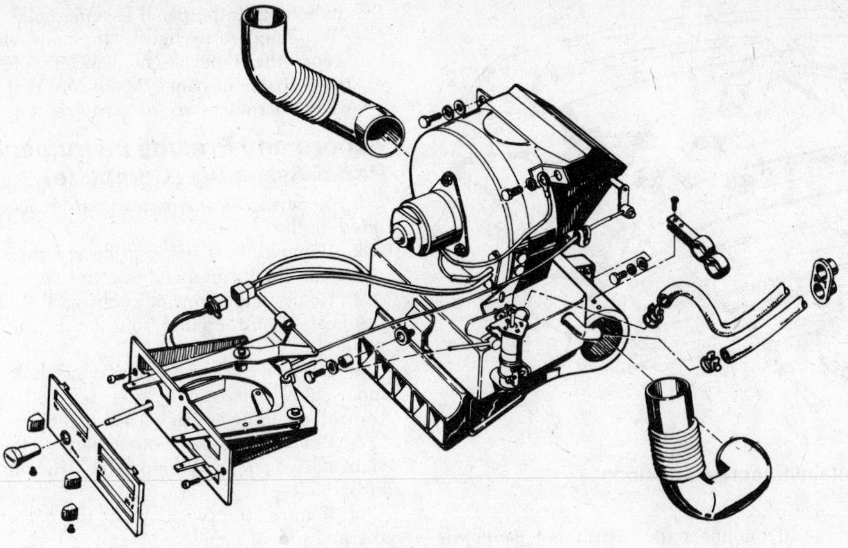

Civic heater components

5. Remove the lower dash panel.

6. Place a drain pan under the case and disconnect both heater hoses at the core tubes.

7. Remove the heater lower mount nut on the firewall.

8. Disconnect the cable at the water valve.

9. Remove the control cables from the heater case.

10. Remove the upper mount bolts and remove the heater.

Blower Motor

REMOVAL AND INSTALLATION

Accord and Prelude

1. Remove the three lower retaining screws for the glovebox. Then, push down and remove the glovebox. Remove the three screws for the glovebox ceiling and remove the ceiling.

2. Disconnect the fresh air control cable from the blower housing. Disconnect the blower leads.

3. Remove the three bolts retaining the blower housing to the firewall. Separate the heater duct hose from the blower housing, and remove the blower housing.

4. To service the blower motor, separate the blower housing halves.

5. Reverse the above to install.

Radio

REMOVAL AND INSTALLATION

CAUTION

Never operate the radio without a speaker; severe damage to the output transistors will result. If the speaker must be replaced, use a speaker of the correct impedance (ohms) or else the output transistors will be damaged and require replacement.

Civic

1. Remove the screw which holds the rear radio bracket to the back tray underneath the instrument panel. Then remove the wing nut which holds the radio to the bracket and remove the bracket.

2. Remove the control knobs, hex nuts, and trim plate from the radio control shafts.

3. Disconnect the antenna and speaker leads, the bullet type radio fuse, and the white lead connected directly over the radio opening.

4. Drop the radio out, bottom first, through the package tray.

5. To install, reverse the removal procedure. When inserting the radio through the package tray, be sure the bottom side is up and the control shafts are facing toward the engine. Otherwise, you will not be able to position the radio properly through its opening.

Accord and Prelude

1. Remove the center lower trim panel beneath the radio. Then remove the three radio lower bracket retaining screws.

2. Pull off the radio knobs and remove the radio shaft nuts.

3. Remove the heater fan switch knob, the heater lever knobs, the heater control bezel, and the heater control center trim panel. Disconnect the cigarette lighter leads.

4. Pull out the radio from the front, and disconnect the power, speaker, and antenna leads.

5. Reverse the above to install.

Windshield Wipers

REMOVAL AND INSTALLATION

Motor and Linkage

The wiper motor on all models is connected to the engine compartment wall, below the front windshield.

1. Remove the negative (−) cable from the battery.

2. Disconnect the motor leads at the connector.

3. Remove the motor water seal cover clamp, and the seal, from the motor.

4. Remove the special nut which holds the wiper arms to the pivot shafts and remove the arms.

5. Remove the left and right pivot nuts and push the pivots down.

6. Remove the three wiper motor mounting bolts and remove the wiper/linkage assembly from the engine compartment.

7. Pull out the motor arm cotter pin and separate the linkage from the motor.

8. Remove the three bracket bolts ro remove the motor from its mounting bracket.

9. To install, reverse the removal procedure. Be sure to inspect the linkage and pivots for wear and looseness. When installing the motor, be sure it is in the "automatic stop" position.

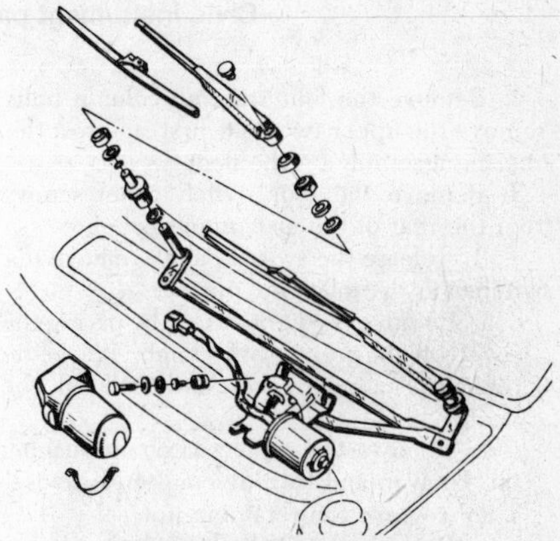

Windshield wiper assembly

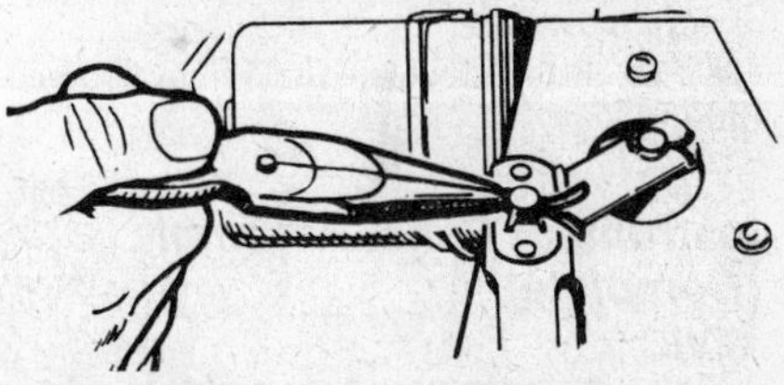

Removing the cotter pin from the motor arm linkage

Instrument Cluster

REMOVAL AND INSTALLATION

Meter Case Assembly

1. Remove the three meter case mounting wing nuts from the rear of the instrument panel.

2. Disconnect the speedometer and tachometer drive cables at the engine.

3. Pull the meter case away from the panel. Disconnect the meter wires at the connectors.

NOTE: Be sure to label the wires to avoid confusion during reassembly.

4. Disconnect the speedometer and tachometer cables at the meter case and remove the case from the car.

5. To install, reverse the removal procedure.

Switch Panel

1. Loosen the four steering wheel column cover screws and remove the upper and lower covers.

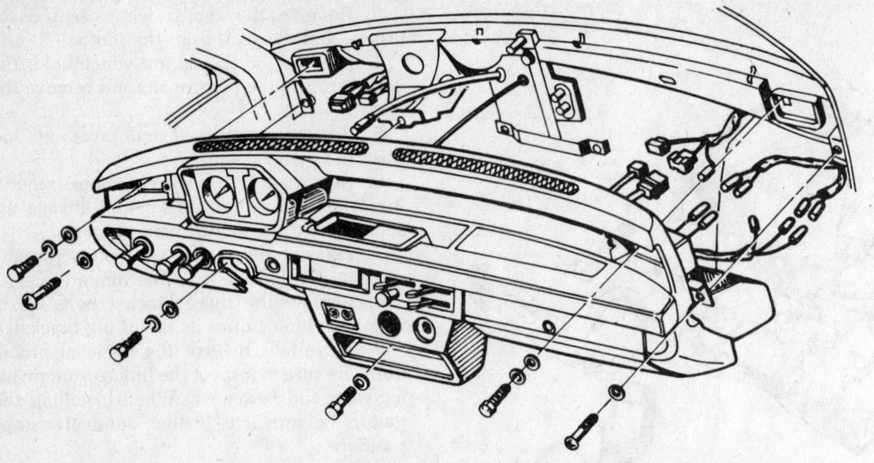

Civic instrument panel retaining screw locations

2. Remove the four steering column bolts (remove the upper two bolts first) and rest the steering assembly on the floor.
3. Remove the four switch panel screws from the rear of the instrument panel.
4. To release the switch panel, remove the switches in the following manner:
   a. Remove the light switch by prying the cover off the front of the knob. Pinch the retaining tabs together and pull off the knob;
   b. Remove the wiper switch by pushing the knob in and turning counterclockwise. Then remove the retaining nut;
   c. Remove the choke knob by loosening the set screw. Then remove the retaining nut.
5. To install, reverse the removal procedure.

Instrument Panel Assembly (Complete)

CIVIC

1. Loosen the four steering wheel column cover screws and remove the upper and lower covers.
2. Remove the four steering column bolts (remove the upper two bolts first) and rest the steering assembly on the floor.
3. Remove the screw on the outside edge of each fresh air vent and pry off the vents with a screwdriver.

Civic fusible link location—Accord similar

4. Disconnect the instrument panel wiring harness from their cabin harnesses by removing the connectors and couplers.
5. Disconnect the speedometer and tachometer cables at the engine.
6. Disconnect the choke cable at the panel.
7. Remove the following switches:
   a. Remove the light switch by prying the cover off the front of the knob. Pinch the retaining tabs together and pull off the knob;
   b. Remove the wiper switch by pushing the knob in and turning counterclockwise. Then remove the retaining nut;
   c. Remove the choke knob by loosening the set screw. Then remove the retaining nut.
8. Disconnect the three heater control cables.
9. Remove the heater fan motor wire connector.
10. Remove the six bolts which attach the panel.
11. Pull the panel out slightly and disconnect the speedometer and tachometer cables at the instruments. Then remove the instrument panel.
12. To install, reverse the removal procedure. Pay attention to the following points:
   a. First, connect the speedometer and tachometer cables to the instruments. Then install the panel in place with the center pin in the panel locating hole;
   b. Temporarily tighten the bolts which secure the upper, right, and left sides of the instrument panel. Make sure that the wiring harnesses are properly routed.

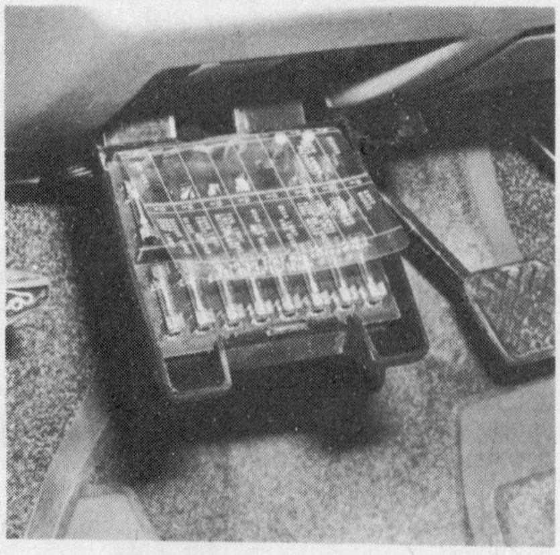

Accord fuse box location

Accord and Prelude Instrument Panel Assembly (Complete)

1. Remove the instrument cluster as outlined earlier.
2. Remove the speaker grille and then remove the clock panel and take out the clock.
3. Remove the control knobs and remove the heater control panel from the instrument panel.
4. Remove the three screws which hold the inner panel. The center panel and the heater control assembly are tightened together.
5. Remove the instrument panel left and right side covers, and remove the two bolts on either side.
6. Remove the two bolts in the center of the instrument panel.
7. Remove the bolt behind the clock panel.
8. You should now be able to remove the instrument panel.
9. Installation is the reverse of removal. Remember the following points:
   a. Avoid bending the heater lever when installing the dashboard. Make sure the heater levers move freely without binding.
   b. Make sure the instrument wiring harnesses aren't pinched.

Fuses and Fusible Links

All models are equipped with a 45 amp (Civic) or 55 amp (Accord) fusible link connected between the starter relay and the main wiring harness of the car, located next to the battery.

The Civic fuse box is located below the glove compartment, on the right bulkhead. It contains 8 fuses, some of which are rated at 10 amps and others at 15 amps. The rating and function of each fuse is posted inside the fuse box cap for quick reference.

The Accord fuse box is a flip down affair, located under the left side of the instrument panel. There are 10 fuses (11 with air conditioning), some rated at 10 amps and others at 15 amps. The rating and function of each fuse is posted inside the fuse box.

Civic fuse box location

SPECIFICATIONS

INDEX

BEFORE SERVICING, SEE THE SAFETY NOTICE ON THE CONTENTS PAGE

INTRODUCTION

Toyo Kogyo Co., Ltd., Mazda's parent company, began manufacturing products over fifty years ago. By 1930 they were producing motorcycles under the Mazda name.

Their first three-wheeled trucks appeared in 1931. The first prototype automobile was built in 1940, but it was not until 1960 that the first Mazda R-360 coupe was sold.

In the interim, Toyo Kogyo produced light three-wheeled trucks, reaching, in 1957, a peak annual production of 20,000 units.

Shortly after automobile production began in 1960, Toyo Kogyo obtained a license from NSU-Wankel to develop and produce the rotary engine.

The first prototype car powered by this engine, the Mazda 110S—a two passenger sports car—appeared in 1963.

In 1970, Toyo Kogyo began exporting its Mazda cars (both rotary engined and conventional) to the United States. At first they were available only in the Pacific Northwest, but they have rapidly expanded their market to include all of the U.S.

SERIAL NUMBER IDENTIFICATION

Vehicle

The serial number is on a plate located on the driver's side windshield pillar and is visible through the glass.

A vehicle identification number (VIN) plate, bearing the serial number and other data, is attached to the cowl.

Engine

The engine number is located on a plate which is attached to the engine housing, just behind the distributor or on a machined pad at the right front side of the engine block.

The engine number consists of an identification number followed by a six-digit production number.

GENERAL ENGINE SPECIFICATIONS—ROTARY

Model	Engine Displacement cu. in. (cc)	Carburetor Type	Net Horsepower @ rpm	Net Torque @ rpm	Rotor Displacement (cu. in.)	Compression Ratio	Oil Pressure @ rpm (psi)
RX-3SP	70 (1146)	4-bbl	95 @ 6000	100 @ 4000	35	9.4:1	71.1 @ 3000
RX-7	70 (1146)	4-bbl	100 @ 6000	105 @ 4000	35	9.4:1	71.1 @ 3000
RX-3	70 (1146)	4-bbl	90 @ 6000	96 @ 4000	35	9.4:1	71.1 @ 3000
RX-4 Cosmo	80 (1308)	4-bbl	110 @ 6000	120 @ 4000	40	9.2:1	71.1 @ 3000

GENERAL ENGINE SPECIFICATIONS—PISTON ENGINE

Year	Model	Engine Displacement cu. in. (cc)	Carb Type	Net Horsepower (@ rpm)	Net Torque @ rpm (ft. lbs.)	Bore x Stroke (in.)	Compression Ratio	Oil Pressure (@ rpm)
1975-78	808	96.8 (1586)	2V	70 @ 5000	82 @ 3400	3.07 x 3.27	8.6:1	50-64 @ 3000
1976-78	808	77.6 (1272)	2V	52 @ 5000	64 @ 3000	2.87 x 2.99	9.2:1	50-64 @ 3000
1979-81	626	120.2 (1970)	2V	75 @ 4500	105 @ 2500	3.15 x 3.86	8.6:1	50-64 @ 3000
1977-78	GLC	77.6 (1272)	2V	52 @ 5000	64 @ 3000	2.87 x 2.99	9.2:1	50-64 @ 3000
1979-80	GLC	86.4 (1415)	2V	77 @ 4300	109 @ 2400	3.03 x 2.99	9.0:1	50-64 @ 3000
1981	GLC	90.9 (1490)	2V	68 @ 5000	82 @ 3000	3.03 x 3.15	9.0:1	43-64 @ 3000

TUNE-UP SPECIFICATIONS—ROTARY ENGINE

When analyzing compression test results, look for uniformity among cylinders, rather than specific pressures

Year	Engine Displacement (cu. in.)	Spark Plugs Type	Spark Plugs Gap (in.)	Distributors Point Dwell (deg)	Distributors Point Gap (in.)	Ignition Timing (deg) Leading Normal	Ignition Timing (deg) Leading Retarded	Ignition Timing (deg) Trailing Normal	Idle Speed (rpm) MT	Idle Speed (rpm) AT
1975	70, 80	N80B	0.024-0.028	58 ± 3	.018	TDC	20A	15A	800-850	750-800 ①
1976	70	RN278B	0.039-0.043	58 ± 3 ②	.018	TDC	15A	20A	700-750	700-750 ①
1976	80	RN278B	0.039-0.043	58 ± 3 ②	.018	5A	20A	20A	700-750	700-750 ①

TUNE-UP SPECIFICATIONS—ROTARY ENGINE

When analyzing compression test results, look for uniformity among cylinders, rather than specific pressures

Year	Engine Displacement (cu. in.)	SPARK PLUGS Type	SPARK PLUGS Gap (in.)	DISTRIBUTORS Point Dwell (deg)	DISTRIBUTORS Point Gap (in.)	IGNITION TIMING (deg) LEADING Normal	IGNITION TIMING (deg) LEADING Retarded	IGNITION TIMING (deg) Trailing Normal	IDLE SPEED (rpm) MT	IDLE SPEED (rpm) AT
1977	70, 80	RN278B	0.039-0.043	58 ± 3	.018	5A	—	25A	725-775	725-775 ①
1978	70 ③	RN278B	0.039-0.043	58 ± 3	.018	0	—	20A	725-775	725-775 ①
1978	80	RN278B	0.039-0.043	58 ± 3	.018	5A	—	25A	725-775	725-775 ①
1979	70	RN280B ①	0.039-0.043	58 ± 3	.018	0	—	20A	725-775	725-775 ①
1980-81	70	RN280B ①	0.039-0.043	Electronic		0	—	20A	725-775	725-775 ①

NOTE: The underhood specifications sticker often reflects tune-up specification changes made in production. Sticker figures must be used if they disagree with those in this chart.

① Transmission in Drive
② Leading retarded dwell angle is 53 ± 3
③ Used in RX-3SP only

TDC—Top dead center
A—After top dead center
B—Before top dead center

MT—Manual transmission
AT—Automatic transmission
deg—degrees

TUNE-UP SPECIFICATIONS—PISTON ENGINE

When analyzing compression test results, look for uniformity among cylinders, rather than specific pressures

Year	Engine Displacement (cu. in.)	SPARK PLUGS Type	SPARK PLUGS Gap (in.)	DISTRIBUTOR Point Dwell (deg)	DISTRIBUTOR Point Gap (in.)	IGNITION TIMING (deg) MT	IGNITION TIMING (deg) AT	Intake Valve Opens (deg)	Fuel Pump Pressure (psi)	Idle Speed (rpm)	VALVE CLEARANCE (in.) In	VALVE CLEARANCE (in.) Ex
1975	96.8	BP6ES	.031	49-55	.020	5B	5B	13	2.8-3.6	800 850 ①	.012	.012
1976-78	96.8	BP6ES	.031	49-55	.020	5B ②	5B ②	13	2.8-3.6	800-850 ③	.012	.012
	77.6	BP6ES	.031	49-55	.020	7B ④	11B	13	2.84-3.84	700-750 ⑤	.010	.012
1979	86.4	BP5ES BPR5ES	.031	49-55	.020	7B ⑥	7B ⑦	15	2.8-3.8	700-750 ⑨⑩	.010	.012
	120.2	BP5ES BPR5ES	.031	—	—	8B	8B	10	2.8-3.6	650-700	.012	.012
1980	86.4	BP5ES BPR5ES	.031	—	—	5B	5B	15	2.8-3.8	700-750 ⑨	.010	.012
	120.2	BP5ES BPR5ES	.031	—	—	5B ⑧	5B ⑧	10	2.8-3.6	650-700	.012	.012
1981	90.9	BP5ES	.031	—	—	8B	8B	16	850 ⑪	N.A.	N.A.	

NOTE: The underhood specifications sticker often reflects tune-up specification changes made in production. Sticker figures must be used if they disagree with those in this chart.

① In Neutral
② California: 8B
③ Automatic: 650-700 in Drive
④ California: 11B
⑤ Automatic: 600-650 in Drive
⑥ California: 5B
Canada: 8A
⑦ California: 5B
Canada: 8B
⑧ Canada: 8B
⑨ Federal:
Automatic: 600-650
⑩ Canada:
Manual: 800-850
Automatic: 700-750
⑪ Automatic 750 in Drive
N.A. Information not available

FIRING ORDERS

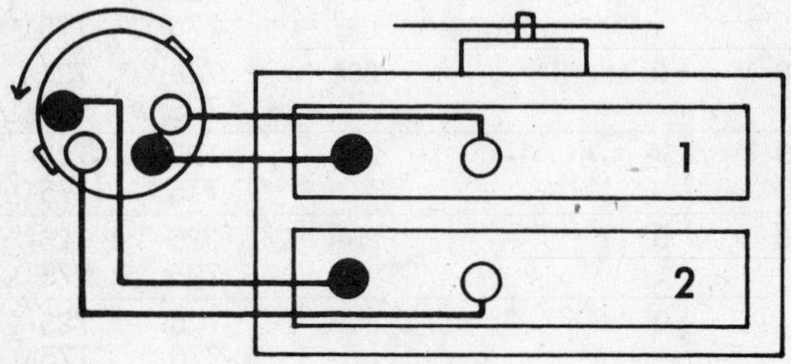

1975 and later

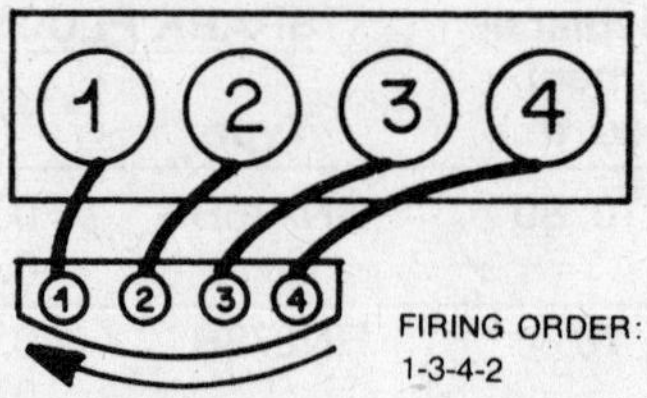

1977–78 1600 cc engine, 1979–80 1415 and 1970 cc engine

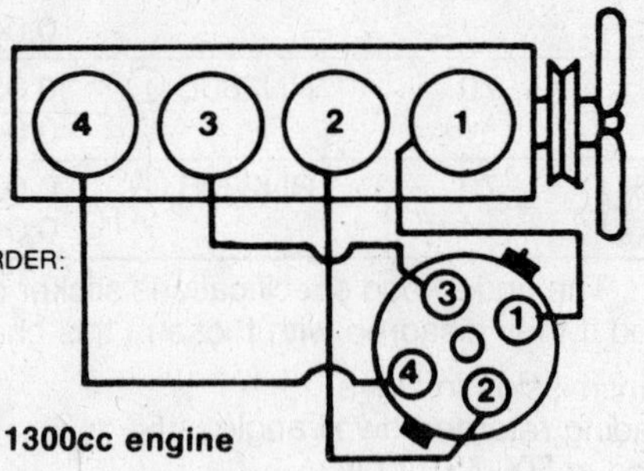

1977–78 1300cc engine

CAPACITIES

Year	Model	Engine Displacement cu. in. (cc)	Engine Crankcase (qts) With Filter	Engine Crankcase (qts) Without Filter	Transmission (pts) Manual 4-spd	Transmission (pts) Manual 5-spd	Transmission (pts) Automatic	Drive Axle (pts)	Gasoline Tank (gals)	Cooling System (qts)
1975	RX-3	70/1146	—	4.8	3.6	—	13.2	3.0	15.6 (1)	10.2
	RX-4	80/1308	6.8	5.3	3.6	—	13.2	2.8	17.2 (3)	10.0
1975	808	96.8/1586	—	3.8	3.2	—	11.6	3.0	11.9 (2)	7.9
1976	RX-3	70/1146	5.5	4.4	3.6	4.6	13.2	3.0	15.6 (5)	9.8
	RX-4	80/1308	—	3.8	3.2	4.6	13.2	2.8	16.9 (4)	10.0
1976-78	808 (1600)	96.8/1586	3.8	—	3.2	3.6	11.6	3.0	11.9 (2)	7.9
	808 (1300)	77.6/1272	3.2	—	2.8	—	—	2.2	11.7 (2)	5.8
1977-78	RX-4, RX-3SP	80/1308	6.8	5.3	3.6	4.6	13.2	2.8	16.9 (4)	10.0
	Cosmo	80/1308	6.8	5.3	—	3.6	13.2	2.6	17.2	10.0
	GLC	77.6/1272 (6)	—	3.2	2.8	3.6	12.0	1.6	10.0	6.8
1979-80	GLC	1415	—	3.2	2.8	3.6	12.0	2.2	10.6 (7)	5.8
1979-81	626	1970	—	4.1	3.0	3.6	13.2	2.6	14.5	7.9
1979	RX-7	70/1146	5.5	4.4	3.6	3.6	13.2	2.6	14.5	7.6
1980-81	RX-7	70/1146	5.5	4.4	3.6	3.6	13.2	2.6	14.5	10.0
1981	GLC	90.9/1490	—	3.9	6.8	6.8	11.6	—	11.1	6.3

(1) Station wagon: 14.3
(2) Station wagon: 10.4
(3) Station wagon: 17.7
(4) Station wagon: 17.4
(5) Station wagon: 14.3
(6) Also available with 60.1 cu. in./985 cc engine: same oil capacity
(7) Station wagon: 11.9

ECCENTRIC SHAFT SPECIFICATIONS—ROTARY

All measurements are given in inches

Model	Journal Diameter: Main Bearing	Journal Diameter: Rotor Bearing	Oil Clearance: Main Bearing	Oil Clearance: Rotor Bearing	Eccentric Shaft End-Play: Normal	Eccentric Shaft End-Play: Limit	Min. Shaft Run-Out
All	1.6929	2.9134	0.0016-0.0028	0.0016-0.0031	0.0016-0.0028	0.0035	0.0008

CRANKSHAFT AND CONNECTING ROD SPECIFICATIONS—PISTON ENGINE

All measurements are given in inches

Year	Engine Displacement cu. in. (cc)	Crankshaft: Main Brg. Journal Dia.	Crankshaft: Main Brg. Oil Clearance	Crankshaft: Shaft End-Play	Crankshaft: Thrust on No.	Connecting Rod: Journal Dia.	Connecting Rod: Oil Clearance	Connecting Rod: Side Clearance
1972-78	96.8 (1586)	2.4804	0.001-0.002	0.003-0.009	5	2.0866	0.001-0.003	0.004-0.008
1976-78	77.6 (1272)	2.4804	0.0012-0.0024	0.003-0.009	5	1.7717	0.0011-0.0029	0.004-0.008
1979-80	86.4 (1415)	1.9685	0.0009-0.0017	0.004-0.006	5	1.5748	0.0009-0.0019	0.004-0.008
1979-81	120.2 (1970)	2.4804	0.0012-0.0020	0.003-0.009	5	2.0866	0.001-0.003	0.004-0.008
1981	90.9 (1490)	Information not available at press time						

ROTOR AND HOUSING SPECIFICATIONS—ROTARY ENGINE

All measurements are given in inches

Model	Rotor: Side Clearance	Rotor: Standard Protrusion of Land	Rotor: Limit of Protrusion of Land	Housings: Front and Rear: Distortion Limit	Housings: Front and Rear: Wear Limit	Housings: Rotor: Width	Housings: Rotor: Distortion Limit	Housings: Intermediate: Distortion Limit	Housings: Intermediate: Wear Limit
RX-3, RX-3SP	0.0051-0.0067	0.004-0.006	0.003	0.002	0.004	2.7539	0.002	0.002	0.004
RX-7	0.0047-0.0071-	—	—	0.0016	0.0039	2.7559	0.0024	0.0016	0.0039
RX-4, Cosmo	0.0039-0.0083	—	—	0.0016	0.0039	3.150	0.0024	0.0016	0.0039

SEAL CLEARANCES—ROTARY ENGINE

All measurements are given in inches

Model	Apex Seals to Side Housing: Normal	Apex Seals to Side Housing: Limit	Apex Seals to Rotor Groove: Normal	Apex Seals to Rotor Groove: Limit	Corner Seal to Rotor Groove: Normal	Corner Seal to Rotor Groove: Limit	Side Seal to Rotor Groove: Normal	Side Seal to Rotor Groove: Limit	Side Seal to Corner Seal: Normal	Side Seal to Corner Seal: Limit
RX-3, RX-3SP	0.0020-0.0028 ①	0.0039	0.0014-0.0029	0.0039	0.0008-0.0019	0.0031	0.0016-0.0028	0.0039	0.002-0.006	0.016
RX-4, Cosmo	0.0051-0.0067	0.0118	0.0020-0.0035	0.006	0.0008-0.0019	0.0031	0.0016-0.0028	0.0040	0.0020-0.0059	0.0157
RX-7	0.0051-0.0075	—	0.0020-0.0035	0.0059	—	—	0.0012-0.0031	0.0039	0.0020-0.0059	0.0157

① Arctic Specifications—0.0004-0.0020

SEAL SPECIFICATIONS—ROTARY ENGINE

All measurements are given in inches

Model	APEX SEAL		Corner Seal	SIDE SEAL		OIL SEAL CONTACT WIDTH OF LIP	
	Normal Height	Height Limit	Width (OD)	Thickness	Height	Normal	Limit
RX-3, RX-3SP	0.03937	0.03150	0.2756	0.0394	0.1378	0.008	0.031
RX-4, Cosmo	0.33500	0.27600	0.4331	0.0394	0.1378	0.008	0.031
RX-7	0.3347	0.2756	0.4331	0.0394	0.1378	0.0197	—

PISTON AND RING SPECIFICATIONS

All measurements are given in inches

Year	Engine Displacement cu. in. (cc)	Piston Clearance	RING SIDE CLEARANCE			RING GAP		
			Top Compression	Bottom Compression	Oil Control	Top Compression	Bottom Compression	Oil Control
1975-79	96.8 (1586)	0.0022-0.0028	0.0014-0.0028	0.0012-0.0025	0.008-0.016	0.008-0.016	0.008-0.016	0.008-0.016
1976-78	77.6 (1272)	0.0021-0.0026	0.0014-0.0028	0.0012-0.0025	0.008-0.016	0.008-0.016	0.008-0.016	0.008-0.016
1979-80	86.4 (1415)	0.0021-0.0026	0.008-0.016	0.008-0.016	0.012-0.035	0.0012-0.0025	0.0012-0.0025	0.008-0.016
1979-81	120.2 (1970)	0.0014-0.0030	0.008-0.016	0.008-0.016	0.012-0.035	0.0012-0.0028	0.0012-0.0025	0.008-0.016
1981	90.9 (1490)	N.A.	N.A.	N.A.	N.A.	N.A.	N.A.	N.A.

N.A. Not available

VALVE SPECIFICATIONS—PISTON ENGINE

Year	Engine Displacement cu. in. (cc)	Seat Angle (deg)	Face Angle (deg)	Spring Test Pressure (lbs. @ in.)	Spring Installed Height (in.)	STEM-TO-GUIDE CLEARANCE (in.)		STEM Diameter (in.)	
						Intake	Exhaust	Intake	Exhaust
1975-77	96.8 (1586)	45	45	①	②	0.0007-0.0021	0.0007-0.0023	0.3150	0.3150
1976-78	77.6 (1272)	45	45	③	④	0.0007-0.0021	0.0007-0.0023	0.3150	0.3150
1977-78	109.6 (1796)	45	45	⑤	②	0.0007-0.0021	0.0007-0.0023	0.3150	0.3150
1979-80	86.4 (1415)	45	45	⑥	④	0.0007-0.0021	0.0007-0.0021	0.3150	0.3150
1979-81	120.2 (1970)	45	45	⑦	②	0.0007-0.0021	0.0007-0.0021	0.3150	0.3150
1981	90.9 (1490)	45	45	N.A.	N.A.	N.A.	N.A.	N.A.	N.A.

① Outer: 31.4 @ 1.339
Inner: 20.9 @ 1.260
② Outer: 1.339
Inner: 1.260
③ Outer: 43.7 @ 1.319
Inner: 20.9 @ 1.260
④ Outer: 1.319
Inner: 1.260
⑤ Outer: 31.4 @ 1.339
Inner: 20.9 @ 1.260
⑥ Outer: 36.6 @ 1.319
Inner: 17.9 @ 1.260
⑦ Outer: 31.4 @ 1.339
Inner: 17.9 @ 1.260
N.A. Not available

TORQUE SPECIFICATIONS—ROTARY ENGINE

All figures in ft. lbs.

Engine Displacement cu. in. (cc)	Front Cover	Bearing Housing	Rear Stationary Gear	Eccentric Shaft Pulley Bolt	Flywheel to Eccentric Shaft Nut	MANIFOLDS Intake	MANIFOLDS Exhaust	Oil Pan	Tension Bolts
70 (1146)	15	15	15	45	325	15	30 ②	7	20 ③
80 (1308)	—	—	—	54-69 ①	289-362	15	32-43	5-7	23-27

① 1977-78 —72-87 ② RX-7: 35 ③ RX-7: 25

TORQUE SPECIFICATIONS—ROTARY ENGINE

All figures in ft. lbs.

Year	Engine Displacement (cc)	Cylinder Head Bolts (cold)	Rod Bearing Bolts	Main Bearing Bolts	Crankshaft Pulley Bolt	Flywheel to Crankshaft Bolts	MANIFOLDS Intake	MANIFOLDS Exhaust
1975-78	1600	56-60	36-40	61-65	101-108	112-118	14-19	16-21
1976	1300	56-60	36-40	61-65	101-108	112-118	14-19	16-21
1977-78	1300	47-51	29-33	43-47	80-87	60-65	14-19	12-17
1979-80	1415	47-51	22-25	43-47	80-87	60-65	14-19	12-17
1979-81	1970	59-64	29-33	61-65	101-108	112-118	14-19	16-21
1981	1490	56-60	36-40	61-65	101-110	115-122	14-19	14-19

TORQUE SEQUENCES

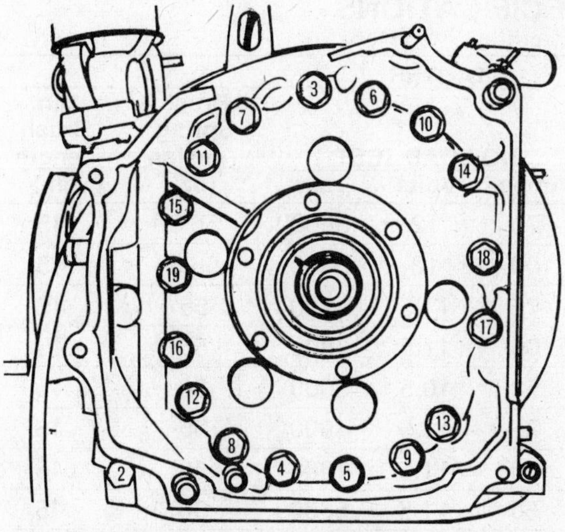

Tension bolt loosening sequence, 1975 and later

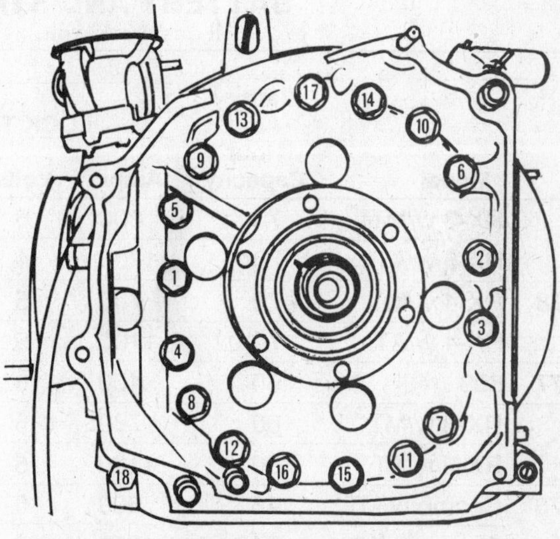

Tension bolt tightening sequence, 1975 and later

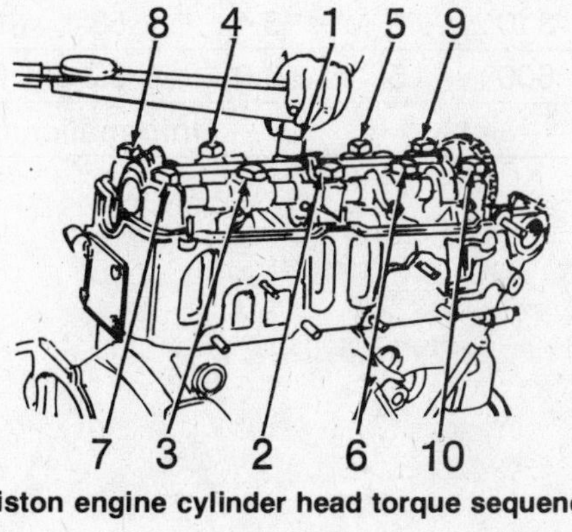

Piston engine cylinder head torque sequence

BRAKE SPECIFICATIONS

All measurements given are in. unless noted

Model	Lug Nut Torque (ft. lbs.)	Master Cylinder Bore	BRAKE DISC Minimum Thickness	BRAKE DISC Maximum Run-Out	BRAKE DRUM Diameter	BRAKE DRUM Max. Machine O/S	BRAKE DRUM Max. Wear Limit	MINIMUM LINING THICKNESS Front	MINIMUM LINING THICKNESS Rear
RX-3	65	0.875	0.394	0.003	7.874	7.90	7.9135	0.276	0.039
RX-4	65-72	0.875	0.433	0.004	9.0	9.025	9.0395	0.276	0.039
808	65-72	0.8125	0.394	0.004	7.874	7.90	7.9135	0.256	0.039
Cosmo	65-72	0.875	0.6693 ①	0.0024 ②	—	—	—	0.276	0.276
GLC	65-72 ④	13/16	0.4724	0.0024	7.874	③	7.9135	0.276	0.039
626	65-80	7/8	0.4724	0.004	7.874	③	7.9135	0.256	0.039
RX-7	65-80	0.8125	0.6693	0.0039	7.8741	③	7.9135	0.236	0.039

NOTE: Minimum lining thickness is as recommended by the manufacturer. Due to variations in state inspection regulations, the minimum allowable thickness may be different than recommended by the manufacturer.

① Rear: 0.354
② Rear: 0.004
③ No machining maximum given—remove minimum amount which smooths surface, then ensure drum inner diameter meets specification
④ 65-80—1979-80

BATTERY AND STARTER SPECIFICATIONS

All cars use 12 volt, negative ground electrical systems

Year	Model	Battery Amp Hour Capacity	STARTER LOCK TEST Amps	LOCK TEST Volts	LOCK TEST Torque (ft. lbs.)	NO LOAD TEST Amps	NO LOAD TEST Volts	NO LOAD TEST rpm	Brush Spring Tension (oz)	Min. Brush Length (in.)
1975	RX-3 w/MT	70	600	6	19.5	70	12	3600	56.3	.45
	RX-3 w/AT	70	1200	4	19.5	100	12	5400	56.3	.45
1975-78	RX-4 w/MT	70	780	5	7.96	75	11.5	4900	56	.45
	RX-4 w/AT	70 ①	1100	5	17.36	100	11.5	7800	56	.45
1975-77	808	60	400	6	6.7	53	10.5	5000	56	.45
1976	RX-3 w/MT	60	780	5	8.0	75	11.5	4900	56	.45
	RX-3 w/AT	60	1100	5	17.4	100	11.5	7800	56	.45
1977-78	Cosmo w/MT	45	600	5	6.9	50	11.5	5600	56	.45
	Cosmo w/AT	70	1050	5	15.9	100	11.5	6600	56	.45
1977-80	GLC	45 ②	310	5	5.4	53	11.5	6800	56	.45
1979-81	626	45	310	5	5.4	53	11.5	6800	56	.45
1979-81	RX-7	55	600	5	6.9	50	11.5	5600	56	.45
1981	GLC	45 ③	Information not available							

① 60 amp w/MT
② 1977 Canada: 45 amp
Exc Calif.: 60 amp
Calif.: 35 amp
1978 Calif.: 35 amp
1979-80 Calif.: 33 amp
③ Calif.: 35
MT—Manual transmission
AT—Automatic transmission

ALTERNATOR AND REGULATOR SPECIFICATIONS

		ALTERNATOR		REGULATOR						
				FIELD RELAY			REGULATOR			
Year	Model	Field Current @ 14 v	Output (amps)	Air Gap (in.)	Point Gap (in.)	Back Gap (in.)	Air Gap (in.)	Point Gap (in.)	Back Gap (in.)	Volts @ 75°
1975-76	RX-3, RX-4	—	56	0.035-0.055	0.028-0.043	0.028-0.059	0.028-0.051	0.012-0.018	0.028-0.059	14-15
1975-78	808	—	40	0.035-0.055	0.028-0.043	0.028-0.059	0.028-0.051	0.012-0.018	0.028-0.059	14-15
1977-78	All Rotary	—	63	0.035-0.055	0.028-0.043	0.028-0.049	0.028-0.051	0.012-0.018	0.028-0.059	14
1977-80	GLC	—	30	0.039-0.059	0.020-0.035	0.028-0.059	0.028-0.051	0.012-0.018	0.028-0.059	14-15
1979-81	RX-7	—	40	0.035-0.055	0.028-0.043	0.028-0.059	0.028-0.051	0.012-0.018	0.028-0.059	14-15
1981	GLC	—	50	Information Not Available						

WHEEL ALIGNMENT SPECIFICATIONS

		CAMBER		CASTER			
Year	Model	Range (deg)	Preferred Setting (deg)	Range (deg)	Preferred Setting (deg)	Toe-In (in.)	Steering Axis Inclination (deg)
1975	RX-3	1P-2P	$1\frac{1}{2}$P	$\frac{1}{2}$N-$1\frac{1}{2}$P	$\frac{1}{2}$P	0-0.24	$8\frac{7}{10}$P
	RX-4	$1\frac{1}{2}$P-$2\frac{1}{2}$P	2P	0-2P	1P	0-0.24	$9\frac{1}{2}$P
	808	$\frac{2}{3}$P-$2\frac{1}{6}$P	$1\frac{1}{3}$P	$\frac{1}{2}$N-$1\frac{1}{2}$P	$\frac{1}{2}$P	0-0.24	$8\frac{3}{4}$P
1976	808 (1600)	①	②	3 -2P	$\frac{1}{2}$P	0-0.24	$8\frac{1}{2}$P
1976-77	808 (1300)	④	⑤	$\frac{1}{2}$N-$1\frac{1}{2}$P	$\frac{1}{2}$P	0-0.24	$8\frac{2}{3}$P
1976-78	RX-3, RX-3SP	③	⑥	$\frac{1}{2}$N-$1\frac{1}{2}$P	$\frac{1}{2}$P	0-0.24	$8\frac{2}{3}$P
	RX-4	1P-2P	$1\frac{1}{2}$P	⑦	⑧	0-0.24	$9\frac{2}{3}$P ⑨
1977	Cosmo	$1\frac{1}{2}$P-3P ⑩	$2\frac{1}{4}$P ⑪	0-2P	1P	0-0.24	$9\frac{3}{4}$P
1977-78	808 (1600)	⑫	⑬	⑭	⑮	0-0.24	⑯
	GLC	—	$\frac{2}{3}$P	$\frac{5}{8}$P-$2\frac{1}{3}$P	$1\frac{35}{60}$	0-0.24	$8\frac{1}{2}$P
1978	Cosmo	0P-2P	1P	$1\frac{1}{2}$P-3P ⑰	$2\frac{1}{4}$ ⑱	0-0.24	$9\frac{3}{4}$P
1979-80	GLC	15′-1°15′ ⑲	45′ ⑳	15′-2°25′ ㉑	1°45′ ㉒	0-0.24	8°45′
1979-81	626	45′-1°45′	1°15′	㉓	㉔	0-0.24	10°40′
1979-81	RX-7	40′P-1°40′P	1°10′	㉕	㉖	0-0.24	10°44′
1981	GLC	—	50′P	—	1°25′P	0.12 out-0.12 in	12°20′

① Sedan: $\frac{5}{6}$P-$2\frac{1}{3}$P
coupe: 1P-$2\frac{1}{2}$P
wagon: 1P-$2\frac{1}{3}$P
② Sedan: $1\frac{1}{2}$P
coupe: $1\frac{5}{6}$P
wagon: $1\frac{2}{3}$P
③ Sedan & wagon: $\frac{5}{6}$N-$1\frac{1}{5}$P
coupe: $1\frac{1}{12}$P-2P
④ Sedan: $\frac{2}{3}$P-$2\frac{1}{6}$P
coupe wagon: 1P-$2\frac{1}{3}$P
⑤ Sedan: $1\frac{1}{3}$P
coupe wagon: $1\frac{2}{3}$P
⑥ Sedan & wagon: $1\frac{2}{3}$P
coupe: $1\frac{1}{2}$P
⑦ Sedan & hardtop: 0-2P
wagon: $\frac{1}{3}$P-$1\frac{1}{3}$P
⑧ Sedan & hardtop: 1P
wagon: $\frac{1}{2}$P
⑨ Wagon: $9\frac{1}{3}$P
⑩ Manual: 1P-2P
⑪ Manual: $1\frac{1}{2}$P
⑫ Sedan & wagon: 1P-$2\frac{1}{2}$P
coupe: $1\frac{1}{3}$P-$2\frac{5}{6}$P
⑬ Sedan & wagon: $1\frac{5}{6}$P
coupe: $2\frac{1}{12}$P
⑭ Sedan & coupe: $\frac{1}{12}$P-$2\frac{1}{2}$P
wagon: $\frac{1}{4}$P-$2\frac{1}{4}$P
⑮ Sedan & coupe: $1\frac{1}{12}$P
wagon: $1\frac{1}{4}$P
⑯ Sedan & coupe: $8\frac{5}{12}$P
wagon: $8\frac{1}{4}$P
⑰ Manual: $1\frac{5}{60}$-$2\frac{35}{60}$
⑱ Manual: $1\frac{5}{8}$
⑲ Station wagon: 30′-1°30′
⑳ Station wagon: 1°
㉑ Station wagon: 1°-2°30′
㉒ Station wagon: 1°45′
㉓ Right side: 2°55′-4°25′
Left side: 2°25′-3°55′
㉔ Right side: 3°45′
Left side: 3°10′
㉕ Right side: 4°P-5°P
Left side: 3°30′P-4°30′P
㉖ Right side: 4°30′P
Left side: 4°P

TUNE-UP PROCEDURES

Compression

ROTARY ENGINE

Because of the unusual shape of the combustion chamber, the lack of valves and because there are three chambers for each rotor, a normal gauge is useless for the measurement of rotary engine compression.

Mazda makes a special recording compression tester which produces a separate graph for each of the three chambers.

This is an expensive piece of equipment and not one that most mechanics are likely to have. If low compression is suspected, check with your local Mazda dealer.

PISTON ENGINE

The compression is checked in the conventional manner.

Compression pressures are considered normal if lowest reading is within 75% of the highest.

Breaker Points and Condenser

ALL MODELS

1975-78 Mazda RX-3 and RX-4 models are equipped with two distributors. One distributor operates the leading set of plugs and the other the trailing set.

There are 2 condensers. The smaller of the two is for radio suppression and need be replaced only if a clicking sound is heard through the radio. Both are externally mounted.

The distributor points and condensers are changed in the conventional manner.

An electronic ignition system is used on the 1978 and later GLC (except California). Starting in 1980 all models use electronic ignition. The system consists of the distributor, control assembly and ignition coil.

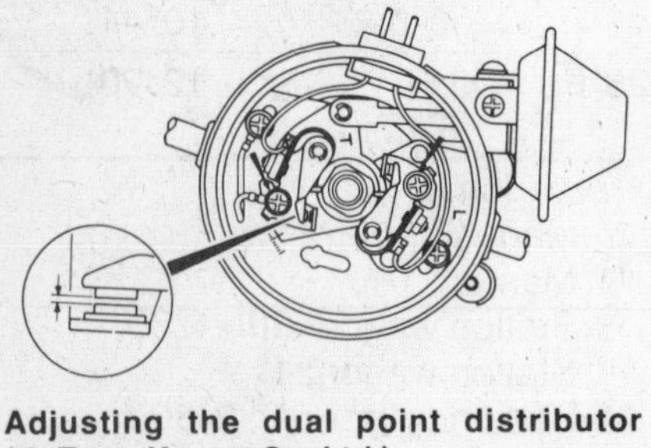

Adjusting the dual point distributor (© Toyo Kogyo Co. Ltd.)

The pick-up coil gap can be measured by using a brass or plastic feeler gauge of .012 in. thickness and measuring the gap between the pick-up coil and one of the rotating pole pieces on the distributor shaft. If adjustment is needed, loosen the two adjusting screws and slide the pick-up coil towards or away from the rotating pole piece until the gap is correct. Tighten the adjusting screws.

Electronic Ignition

ROTARY ENGINE

1. Spark plugs—rotary engine type with 3 electrodes
2. Distributor—breakerless type
   a. Signal rotor—timing teeth
   b. Vacuum and centrifugal advance—standard
   c. Pick-up coils—1 leading and 1 trailing; generates the signals to the igniter (control unit)

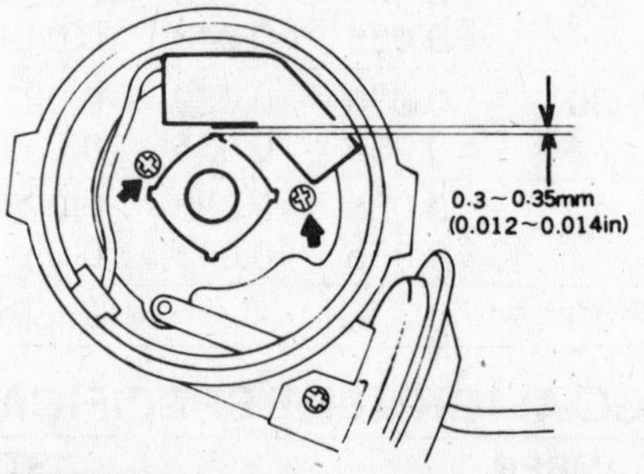

Checking the air gap in the electronic ignition distributor (© Toyo Kogyo Co. Ltd.)

3. Igniter—receives signals from the pick-up coils and switches the primary ignition current off and on
4. Ignition Coils—1 leading and 1 trailing coil; not to be exchanged with standard ignition coils

PISTON ENGINES

In 1979 the 626 and GLC models were equipped with electronic ignition. Unlike the rotary engines the piston engines have a single coil ignition system. As of 1980, all Mazda vehicles sold in the USA, were equipped with electronic ignition.

Ignition Timing

ROTARY ENGINE TIMING MARKS

1975 ROTARY

The vacuum line should be plugged. Connect the timing light to lower (leading) plug of the front rotor housing.

1. If the trailing timing is not within specification, adjust the trailing and leading timing as follows:
2. Adjust the trailing timing to specification by rotating the distributor body.
3. Check the leading timing again and record how much it differs from specification.
4. Remove the distributor cap and rotor.
5. Loosen the breaker base setscrews (the ones directly opposite each other near the outside of the distributor body) and turn the distributor base plate until the correct leading plug timing is obtained again.
6. Recheck the timing.

1976 ROTARY ENGINES

1. Run the engine at normal operating temperature.

1976—1586 cc (Except Calif.) (© Toyo Kogyo Co. Ltd.)

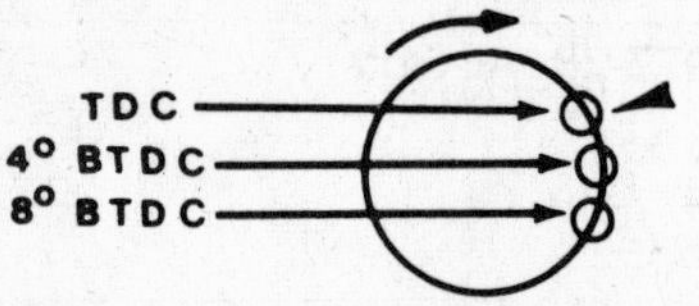

1976—1586 cc (Calif.) (© Toyo Kogyo Co. Ltd.)

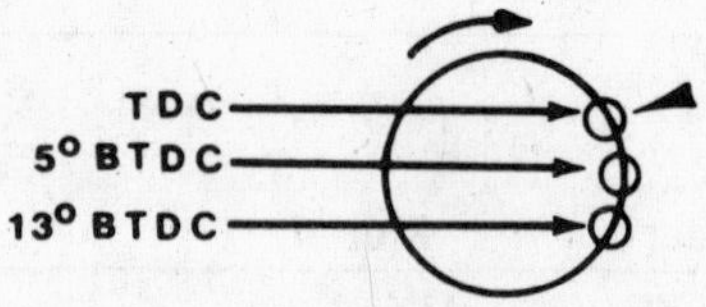

1977 and later 1586 cc, exc Calif.

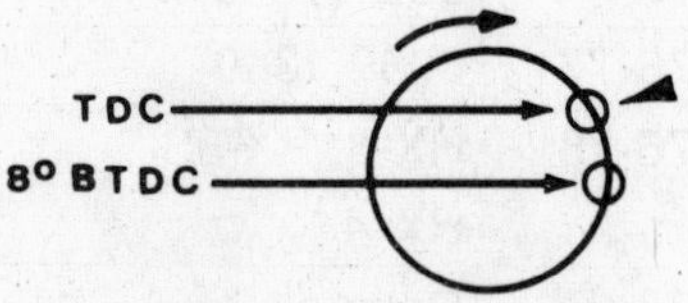

1977 and later 1586 cc, Calif.

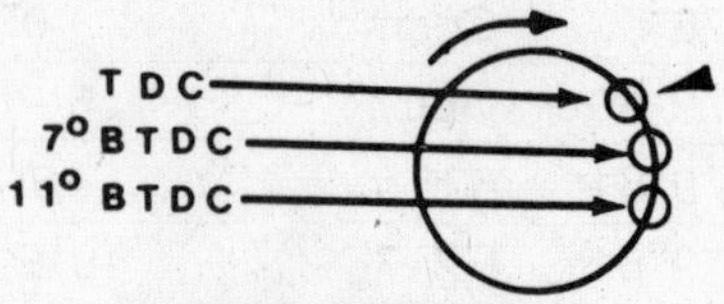

1976 and later 1272 cc

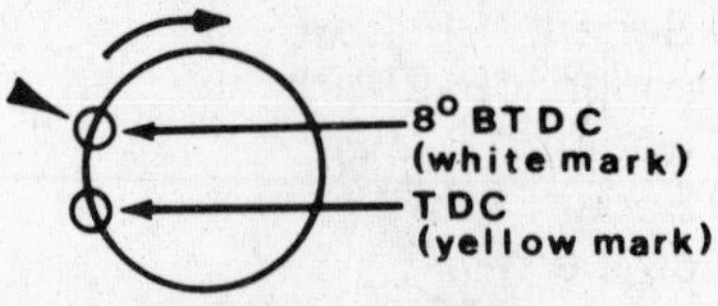

1977 and later 1796 cc

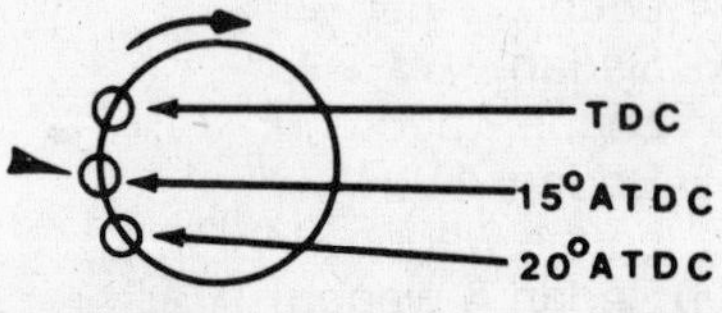

1975-76—1146 cc, 1975—1308 cc (© Toyo Kogyo Co. Ltd.)

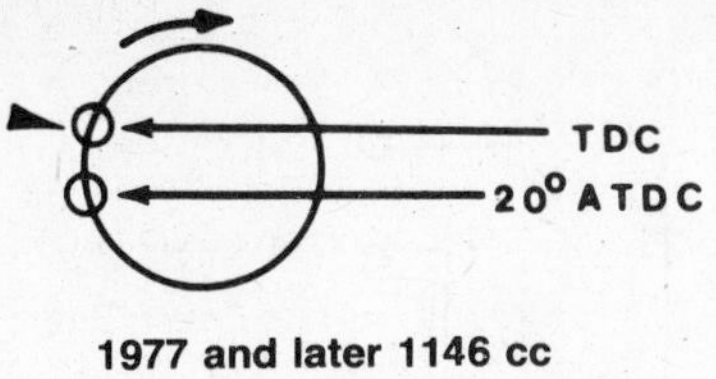

1977 and later 1146 cc

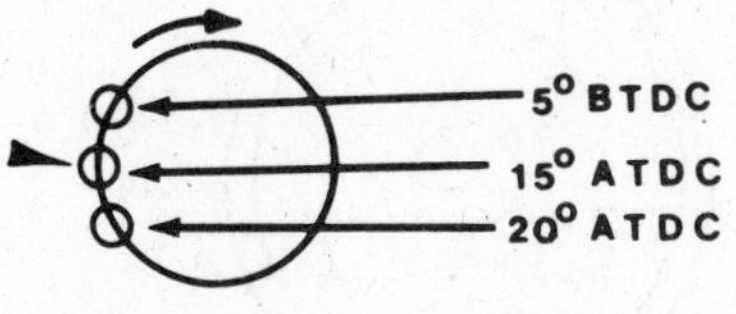

1976—1308 cc (© Toyo Kogyo Co. Ltd.)

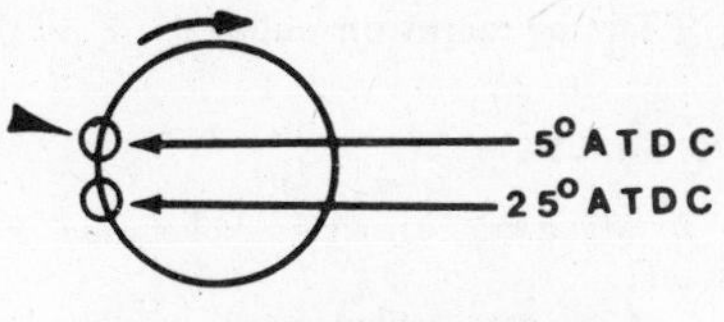

1977 and later 1308 cc

2. Connect a tachometer.
3. Connect a timing light to the leading sparkplug of the front rotor housing.
4. Run engine at idle speed.
5. If the timing is not correct, rotate the distributor housing until the timing mark on the pulley aligns with the indicator pin.
6. Recheck the leading timing.
7. Connect the timing light to the trailing spark plug of the front rotor housing.
8. Check the trailing timing.
9. If the trailing timing is not correct, note the amount of error and stop the engine.
10. Remove the distributor cap and rotor.
11. Disconnect the primary wire from the leading retard point set.
12. Remove the breaker base plate and external lever for leading set.
13. Slightly loosen the breaker base set screws of the trailing side and turn the base plate as required. Install the leading breaker base assembly, rotor and cap.
14. Check the trailing and leading timing. If they are not correct, repeat the above steps.
15. Leave timing light connected to trailing plug of the front rotor housing.
16. Connect a jumper between both terminals in the coupler of the primary lead wires.
17. Check the leading retard timing. Adjust by moving the external adjusting lever.

1977 AND LATER ROTARY ENGINE

1. Have the engine at normal operating temperature.
2. Connect a timing light to the leading spark plug wire and a tachometer to the engine.
3. Operate the engine at the specified idle speed. On automatic transmission equipped vehicles, place the selector in DRIVE and block the wheels.
4. Check the timing on the crankshaft pulley and if the leading timing is not correct, loosen the distributor body locknut and rotate the distributor housing to correct the timing. Tighten the locknut and recheck the timing.
5. Install the timing light on the trailing spark plug and check the trailing timing.
6. If the trailing timing is not correct, loosen the vacuum unit for the trailing points and move the unit in or out until the correct timing is obtained.
7. Tighten the trailing vacuum unit and recheck the trailing timing.

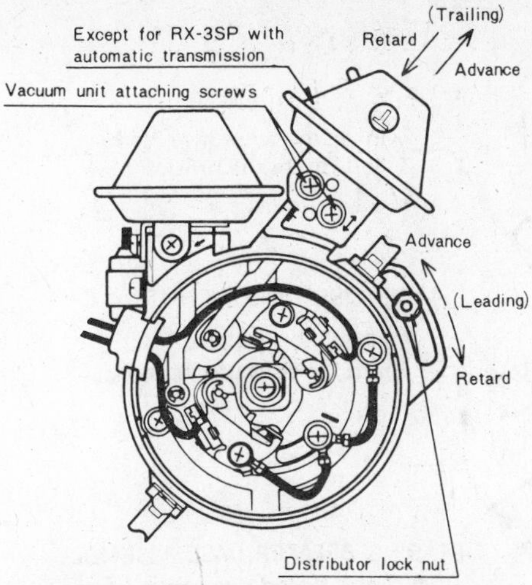

Trailing timing adjustment for 1978-79 rotary engines (© Toyo Kogyo Co. Ltd.)

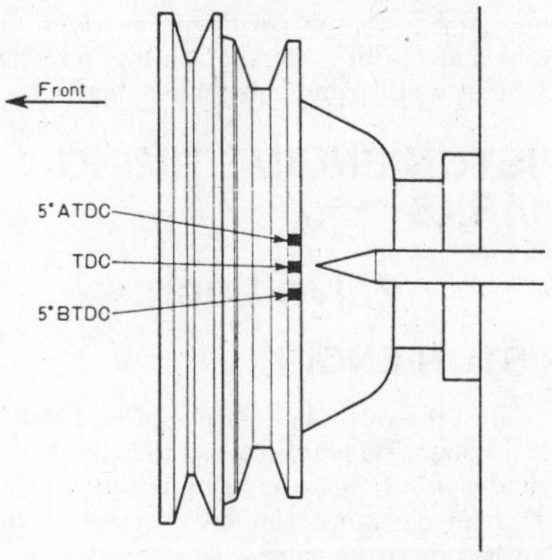

Ignition timing marks: typical of those found on piston engine (© Toyo Kogyo Co. Ltd.)

Alternate Dwell and Timing Method for Rotary Engines with Standard Type Ignition

An alternate method can be used to set the dwell and timing while the engine is running. By connecting the high tension wires directly from the ignition coils to the leading spark plugs, the engine can be run at idle with the distributor cap and rotor removed. When adjusting the dwell and timing, follow the basic procedures.

1. Check the dwell angle and set it to the specification.

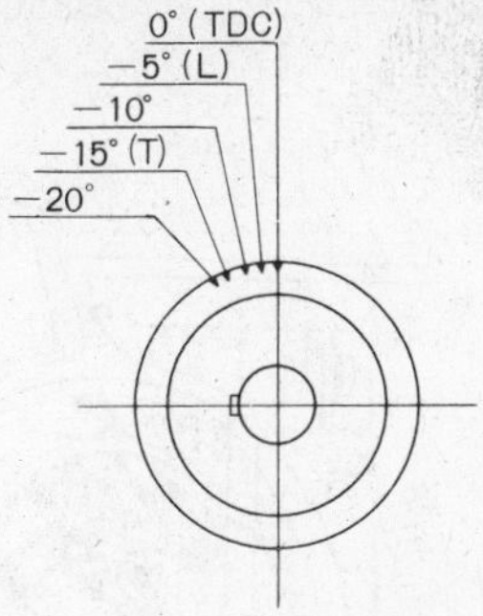

Ignition timing marks 1975 Rotary

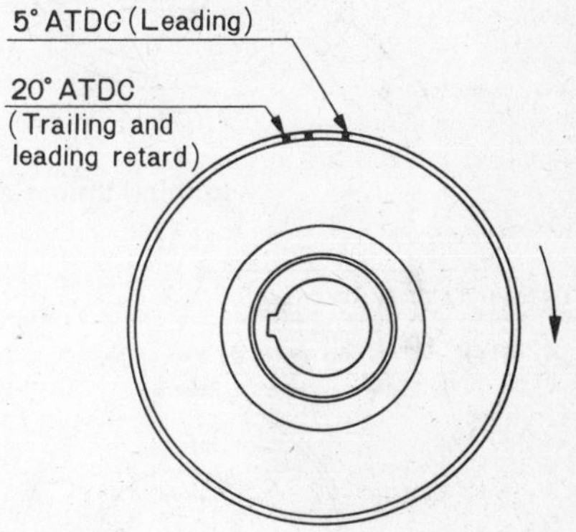

Timing marks, 1976 RX-4 (© Toyo Kogyo Co. Ltd.)

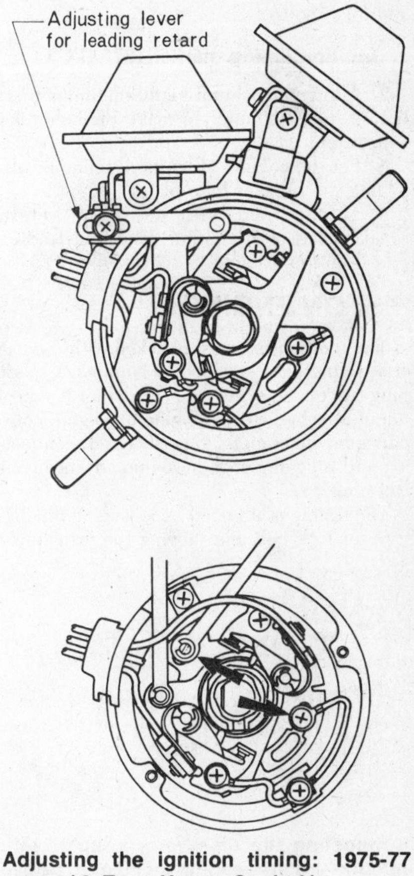

Adjusting the ignition timing: 1975-77 rotary (© Toyo Kogyo Co. Ltd.)

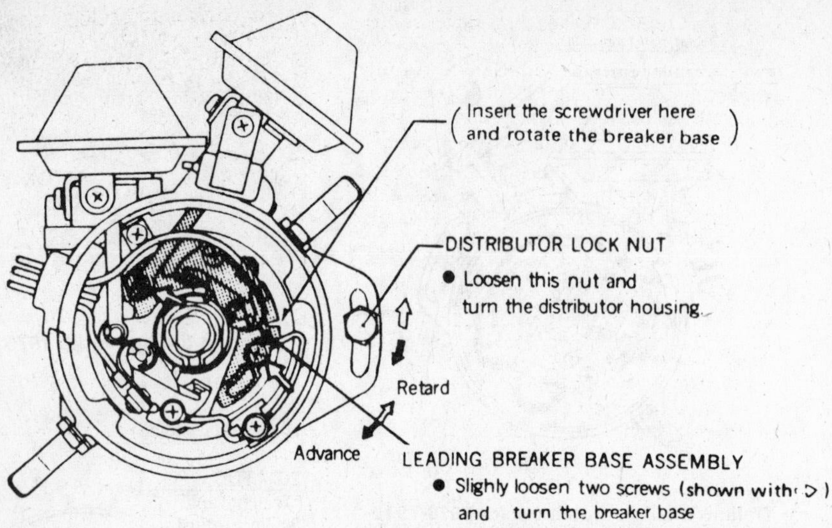

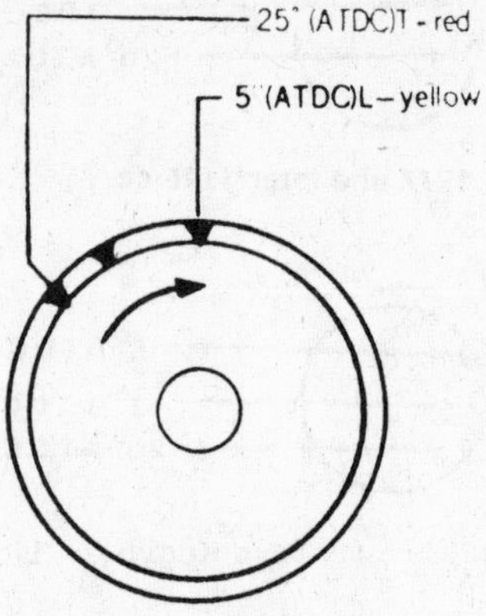

(Timing marks on pulley)

Ignition timing adjustment: 1977-79 RX-4 and Cosmo (© Toyo Kogyo Co. Ltd.)

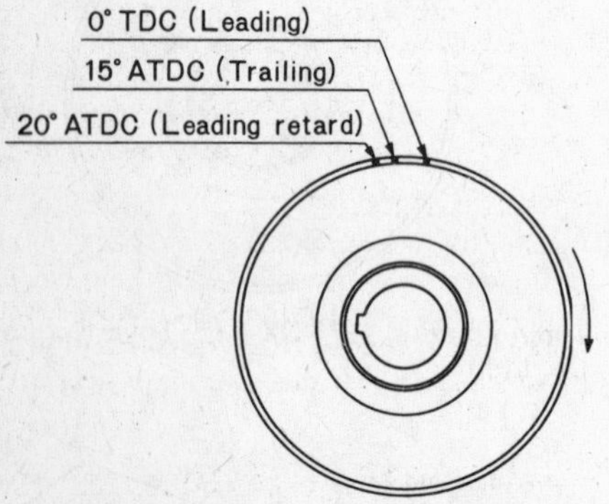

Ignition timing marks, 1976 RX-3

2. Adjust the column I ignition timing first. Rotate the distributor to make the column I adjustment.

3. Set the column II ignition timing by adjusting the breaker base plate.

4. If equipped with a leading retard breaker plate or distributor, adjust the leading retard ignition timing.

PISTON ENGINE

The ignition timing is checked with the use of a timing light attached to Number 1 spark plug wire. Refer to the Emission Control Label attached to the engine or engine compartment sheet metal to verify the disconnecting and plugging of the vacuum advance control hose.

The timing is adjusted by loosening the distributor lock bolt and moving the distributor body to align the proper degree mark on the crankshaft pulley to the timing pointer. Tighten the distributor body lock bolt.

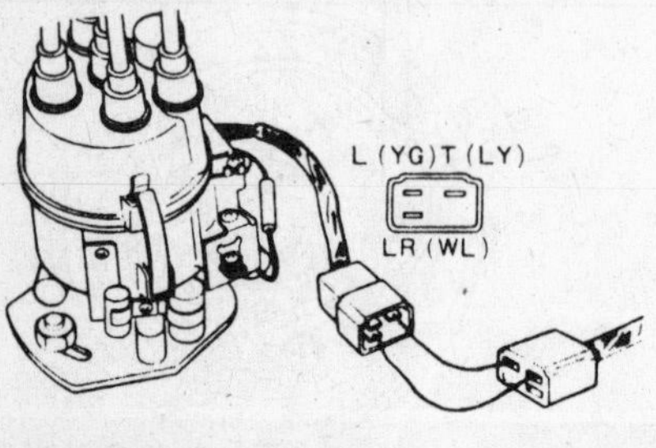

Connecting the distributor coupler with jumper—rotary engine (© Toyo Kogyo Co. Ltd.)

PISTON ENGINE TIMING MARKS

Valve Lash

PISTON ENGINE

Adjust the valves in the firing order 1-3-4-2.

1. Rotate the crankshaft so that the No. 1 cylinder (front) is in the firing position.

2. The clearance can be checked at the camshaft or at the valve.

3. If the valve clearance is incorrect, loosen the adjusting screw locknut and adjust the clearance.

4. Rotate the crankshaft (in the normal direction of rotation), adjusting the valves for each cylinder at TDC of the compression stroke.

Carburetor

NOTE: For further carburetor adjustments see the "Fuel System."

IDLE SPEED AND MIXTURE

Piston Engine

1. Thoroughly warm the engine.

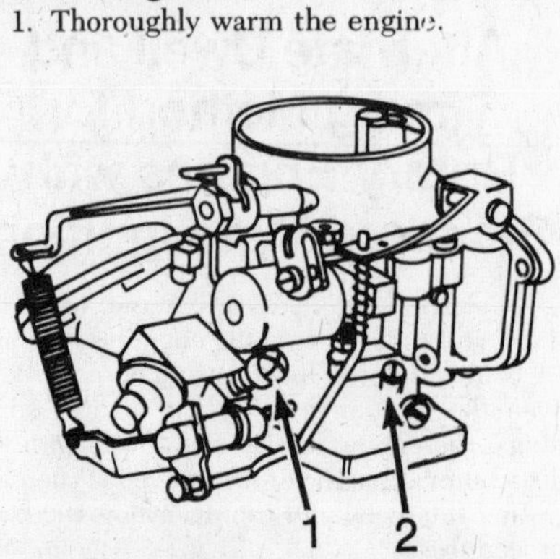

Idle speed (1) and mixture (2) screws —piston engine

2. Make sure that the choke valve is fully open.

3. Connect a tachometer.

4. Adjust the idle speed screw to specifications.

5. The mixture should be checked by a CO meter. The carbon monoxide percentage at idle should be 0.1%-2.0%.

6. Disconnect the tachometer.

Idle and Throttle Screw Adjustment

If for some reason the idle and throttle screws need adjustment, use the following procedure.

HC/CO Analyzer

1. Adjust the throttle angle opening to specifications. Make the adjustment from the fully closed position.

2. Adjust the idle speed.

3. Using the gas analyzer, check the HC (hydrocarbon) and CO (carbon monoxide) readings. If the HC is less than 200 ppm (parts per million) and the CO is between 0.1-2.0%, no further adjustment is needed.

4. If the HC and CO are not within specifications, adjust the CO reading to as close to 0.1% as possible, keeping the HC reading below 200 ppm. Use the idle fuel screw to make this adjustment.

5. Recheck the idle speed.

1975 Rotary

Idle speed changes with air temperature. It is suggested by Mazda that the idle adjustment be made indoors with a floor fan blowing through the radiator to assist in cooling. Whenever operating an engine indoors, make certain that provision is made for removal of exhaust gases. Idle speed should be adjusted with the engine at normal operating temperature, all accessories off and fuel tank cap removed.

1. Connect a tachometer.

2. Set idle speed.

3. Check the float level.

4. Using a reliable CO meter, check the CO density at idle.

5. If density is not within 0.1%-2.0%, adjust the idle mixture with the mixture screw.

6. Adjust the CO density to 0%, then turn the adjusting screw counterclockwise until the density is 0.5%.

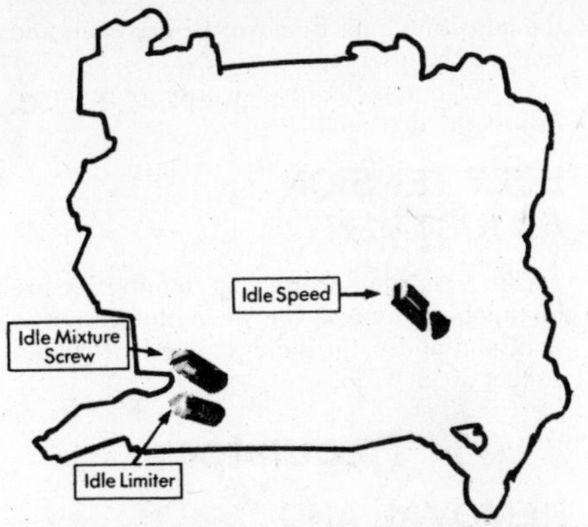

Idle adjustments—rotary engine (© Toyo Kogyo Co. Ltd.)

7. Turn the screw clockwise until the density reaches 0.1%. Then turn screw an additional one quarter turn.
8. Check idle speed and reset if necessary.

1976-80 Rotary

As with 1975 models, the idle speed should be set indoors. See the starting paragraph under 1975 Rotary.

1. Disconnect the idle compensator tube at the air cleaner.
2. Run the engine at normal operating temperature and make sure that the choke is wide open.
3. Check the float level.
4. Connect an exhaust gas analyzer and tachometer.
5. With engine at idle, check the CO density.
6. Adjust the idle speed to specification with the idle adjusting screw.
7. Turn the mixture adjusting screw clockwise until the engine lopes severely.
8. Turn the screw slowly counterclockwise until the CO density reaches 0.1%, then turn it an additional one quarter turn in the same direction.

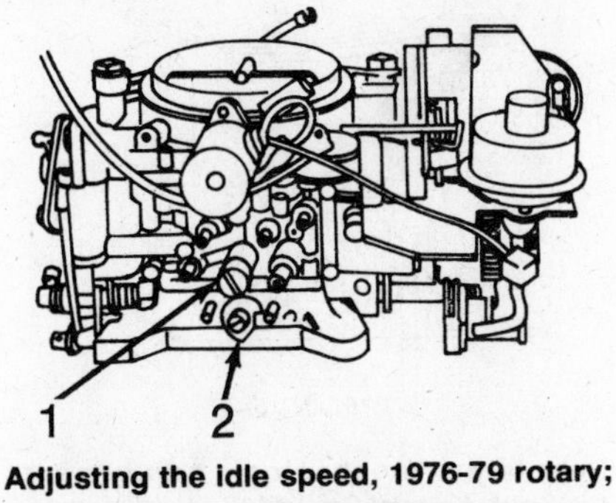

Adjusting the idle speed, 1976-79 rotary; (1) air adjust screw, (2) mixture screw

1981 Rotary

When adjusting the idle speed and mixture on the 1981 rotary engines, take the following steps.

1. Start with a cold engine.
2. Set the parking brake and block the wheels.
3. Remove the fuel filler cap.
4. Switch off all accessories.
5. Disconnect the vacuum line at the idle compensator in the air cleaner and plug the line.
6. Check the dash pot rod and the air conditioner throttle opener. Make certain these devices are not stopping the throttle linkage from returning to a fully seated idle stop position.
7. Connect a tachometer to the negative terminal of the leading coil and a good ground. The leading coil is the rear coil on the driver's side fender well.
8. Bring the engine up to operating temperature.
9. Set vehicles equipped with automatic transmissions in the drive selector position. Adjust the idle stop screw to obtain 750 rpm in drive. Adjust manual transmission equipped vehicles to 750 rpm in neutral.
10. Adjust the idle mixture by removing the mixture screw limiter cap. Richen the idle mixture to obtain the highest rpm before it starts to drop. Reset the idle speed to specification. Repeat these procedures until both the highest rpm and the idle speed are correct. Install a replacement limiter cap on the idle mixture screw.

ENGINE ELECTRICAL

Distributor

REMOVAL AND INSTALLATION

Rotary Engine–1975 and Later

NOTE: Both the distributors and the front housing are marked with a "T" or an "L"; insert the distributor which has the same letter as the housing, into its proper socket.

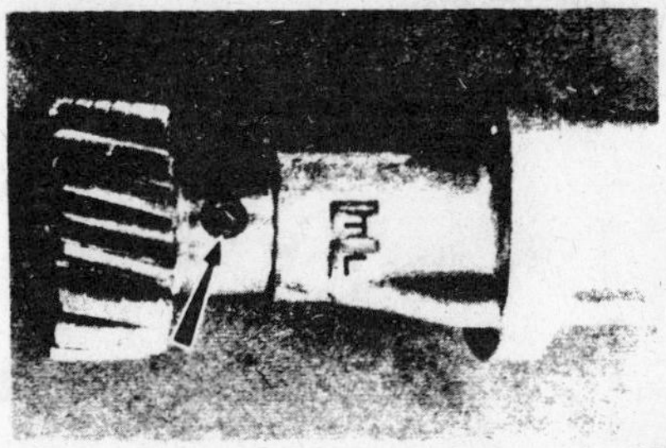

Align the distributor identification marks prior to installation (© Toyo Kogyo Co. Ltd.)

NOTE: TDC cannot be found by feeling for compression at the Number one spark plug hole, as in a conventional piston engine.

The distributor is removed in the conventional manner.

To install the distributor, turn the eccentric shaft until the TDC mark on the drive pulley align with the indicator pin on the front cover. Align the matchmarks on the distributor housing and drive gear.

Install the distributor so that the distributor lockbolt is located in the center of the slot.

Piston Engine

The distributor is removed and installed in the conventional manner. If the engine is cranked while the distributor is removed, set the engine to TDC on No. 1 cylinder and align the matchmarks on the distributor gear and body.

Alternator

REMOVAL AND INSTALLATION

Disconnect all of the leads. Remove the alternator adjusting link bolt. Do not remove

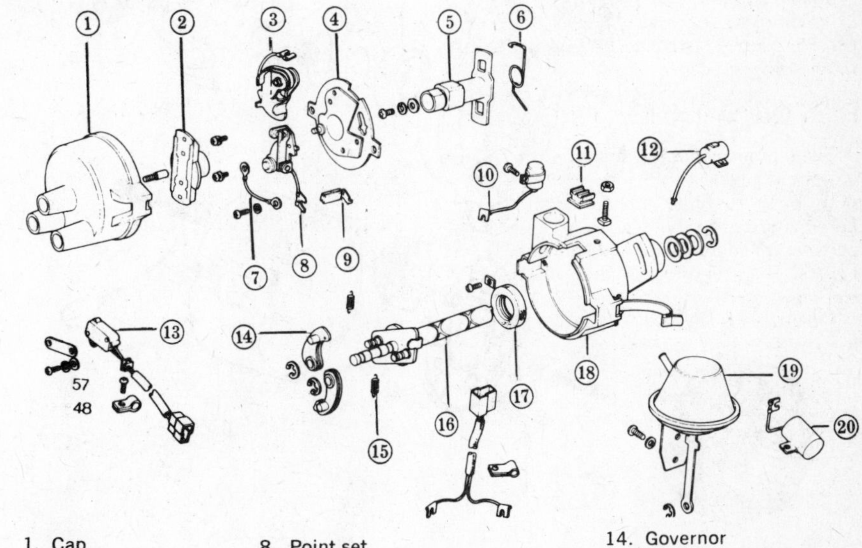

1. Cap
2. Rotor
3. Point set
4. Breaker plate
5. Cam
6. Spring
7. Ground wire
8. Point set
9. Felt
10. Ignition condenser
11. Terminal
12. Radio supression condenser
13. Vacuum switch—trailing distributor only
14. Governor
15. Governor spring
16. Shaft
17. Oil seal
18. Distributor housing
19. Vacuum advance unit
20. Ignition condenser

Distributor components (© Toyo Kogyo Co. Ltd.)

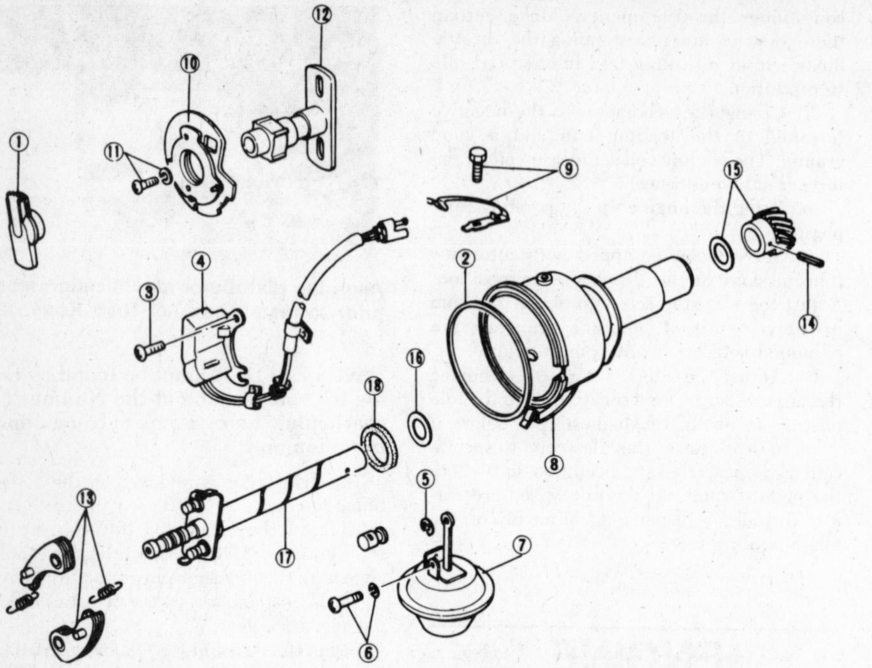

1. Rotor
2. Rubber seal
3. Screw
4. Pick-up coil
5. Clip
6. Screw and washer
7. Vacuum advance unit
8. Cap retaining clip
9. Cap retaining clip and screw
10. Pick-up coil plate
11. Screw and washer
12. Cam
13. Advance weights and springs
14. Retaining pin
15. Drive gear and washer
16. Thrust washer
17. Shaft
18. Oil seal

Exploded view of electronic ignition distributor (© Toyo Kogyo Co. Ltd.)

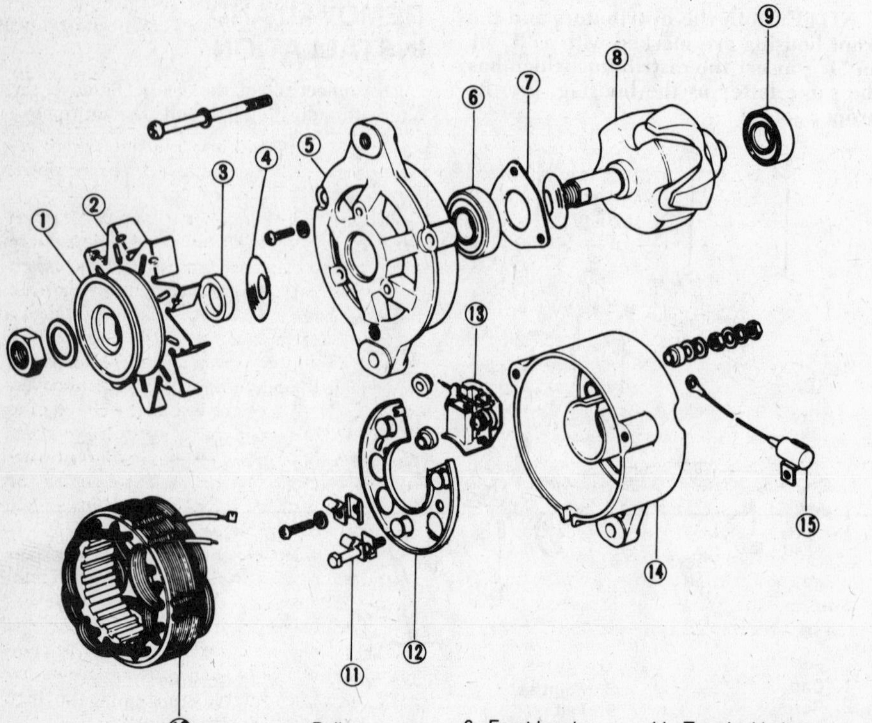

1. Pulley
2. Fan
3. Spacer
4. Slinger
5. Front housing
6. Front bearing
7. Bearing retainer
8. Rotor
9. Rear bearing
10. Stator
11. Terminal bolt
12. Diode plate (rectifiers)
13. Brush holder
14. Rear housing
15. Condenser

Exploded view of typical alternator (© Toyo Kogyo Co. Ltd.)

the adjusting link. Remove the drivebelt and remove the alternator.

Installation is the reverse order of removal. Adjust the drivebelt.

BELT TENSION ADJUSTMENT

Check tension by applying thumb pressure to the belt, midway between the eccentric shaft and alternator pulleys. The belt should deflect about ½ in.

Regulator

REMOVAL AND INSTALLATION

Externally Mounted

Disconnect the wiring and remove the regulator mounting screws. Remove the regulator.

Installation is the reverse of removal.

VOLTAGE ADJUSTMENTS

Models With Ammeters Only

1. Remove the cover.
2. Check the air gap, the point gap, and the back gap with a feeler gauge.
3. Adjust the gaps by bending the stationary contact bracket.
4. Connect a voltmeter between the "A" and "E" terminal of the regulator.
5. Run the engine at 2000 rpm. The voltmeter reading should be 13.5-14.5 V.
6. Stop the engine.
7. Bend the upper plate *down* to decrease the voltage setting or *up* to increase the setting, as required.
8. If the regulator cannot be brought within specifications, replace it.

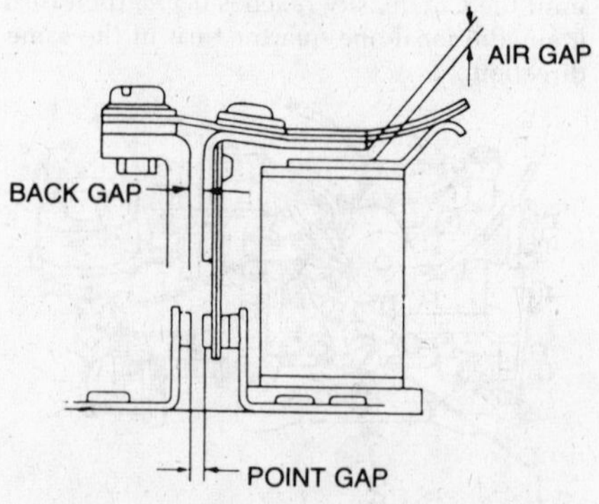

Regulator mechanical adjustments (© Toyo Kogyo Co. Ltd.)

REGULATOR TEST

Models With Warning Light

Constant Voltage Relay

1. Use an almost fully charged battery and connect a voltmeter between the "A" and "E" terminals of the regulator.
2. Run the engine at 2000 rpm and read the voltmeter. It should read from 14-15 volts.
3. If not, adjust the voltage relay.

Pilot Lamp Relay

1. Using a voltmeter and variable resistor, construct a circuit as shown.

2. Light the pilot lamp.
3. Gradually increase voltage.
4. Read the voltage between the "N" and "E" terminals of the regulator. If the voltage is 3.7-5.7 volts, it is operating properly.
5. Decrease the voltage. Note the point on the voltmeter where the light will light again. If the reading is less than 3.5 volts, the unit is working properly.

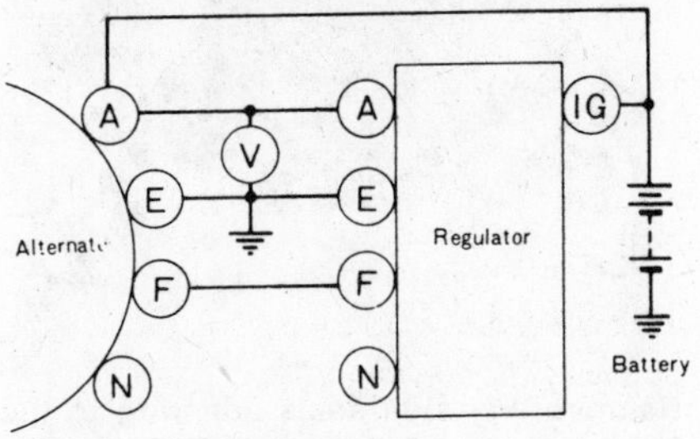

Testing the voltage regulator (© Toyo Kogyo Co. Ltd.)

Constant Voltage Relay
Air gap 0.028-0.043 in.
Point gap 0.012-0.016 in.
Back gap 0.028-0.043 in.
Pilot Lamp Relay
Air gap 0.035-0.047 in.
Point gap 0.028-0.043 in.
Back gap 0.028-0.043 in.

Internally Mounted

Late model alternators have the voltage regulator mounted within the unit as part of the brush holder assembly. No adjustments can be made to the regulator assembly and the alternator must be removed and disassembled to replace the voltage regulator.

Starter

REMOVAL AND INSTALLATION

Rotary Engine

The starter is removed in the conventional manner. If the car is equipped with the lower mounted starter, remove the gravel shield from underneath the engine.

Installation is the reverse of the above steps.

REMOVAL AND INSTALLATION

Piston Engine

The air cleaner/air intake tube must be removed. Remove the starter out below the emission system hoses.

STARTER DRIVE REPLACEMENT

Unless disassembly of the starter is desired, do not remove the thru-bolts.

1. Remove the solenoid.
2. Remove the plunger from the drive engagement fork.
3. Remove the nuts from the thru-bolts.
4. Remove the drive housing.
5. Remove the engagement fork, spring and spring seat.

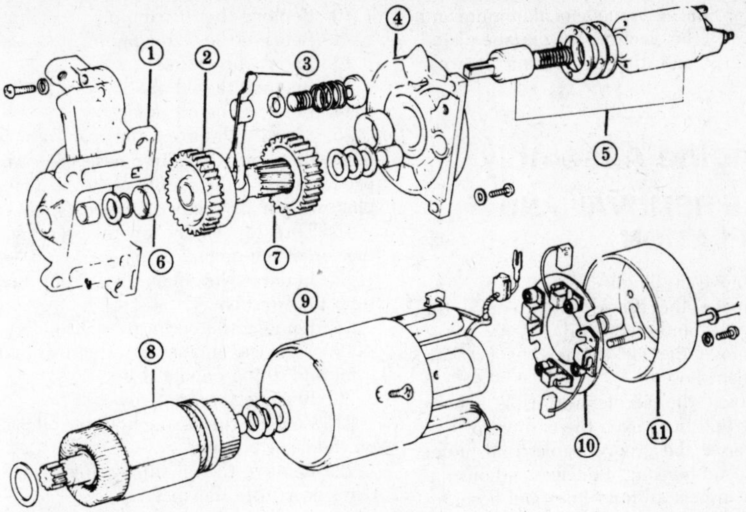

1. Front housing
2. Overruning clutch
3. Engagement fork
4. Center frame
5. Solenoid
6. Stop
7. Idler gear
8. Armature
9. Field coil
10. Brush holder
11. End frame

Starter components (© Toyo Kogyo Co. Ltd.)

6. Withdraw the over-running clutch from the armature shaft.

Assembly is the reverse order of disassembly. Check the clearance between the pinion and the stop collar with the solenoid closed. It should be 0.001-0.006 in.

ENGINE MECHANICAL ROTARY ENGINE

NOTE: Because of the unique design of the Mazda rotary engine, some procedures require the use of special factory tools. The text notes where these tools are necessary. If the tools are not available, the job should not be undertaken.

Design

The Mazda rotary engine replaces conventional pistons with three-cornered rotors which have rounded sides. The rotors are mounted on a shaft which has eccentrics rather than crank throws.

The chamber which the rotor travels in is roughly oval-shaped, but with the sides of the oval bowed in slightly. The technical name for this shape is a two-lobe epitrochoid.

As the rotor travels its path in the chamber, it performs the same four functions as the piston in a traditional piston engine.

1. Intake
2. Compression
3. Ignition
4. Exhaust

But all four functions in a rotary engine are happening concurrently, rather than in four separate stages.

Ignition of the compressed fuel/air mixture occurs each time a side of the rotor passes the spark plugs. Since the rotor has three sides, there are three complete power impulses for each complete revolution of the rotor.

As it moves, the rotor exerts pressure on the cam of the eccentric shaft, causing the shaft to turn.

Because there are three power pulses for every revolution of the rotor, the eccentric shaft must make three complete revolutions for every one of the rotor. To maintain this ratio, the rotor has an internal gear that meshes with a fixed gear in a three-to-one ration. If it were not for this gear arrangement, the rotor would spin freely and timing would be lost.

The Mazda rotary engine has two rotors mounted 60 degrees out of phase. This produces six power impulses for each complete revolution of both rotors and two power impulses for each revolution of the eccentric shaft.

Because of the number of power impulses for each revolution of the rotor, and because all four functions are concurrent, the rotary engine is able to produce a much greater amount of power for its size and weight than a comparable reciprocating piston engine.

Instead of using valves to control the intake and exhaust operations, the rotor uncovers and covers ports on the wall of the chamber as it turns. Thus, a complex valve train is unnecessary. The resulting elimination of parts further reduces the size and weight of the engine, as well as eliminating a major source of mechanical problems.

Spring-loaded carbon seals are used to prevent loss of compression around the rotor apexes and cast iron seals are used to prevent loss of compression around the side faces of the rotor. These seals are equivalent to compression rings on a conventional piston but must be more durable because of the high rotor rpm to which they are exposed.

Oil is controlled by means of circular seals mounted in two grooves on the side face of the rotor. These oil seals function to keep oil out of the crankcase, in a similar manner to the oil control ring on a piston.

The rotor housing is made of aluminum and the surfaces of the chamber are chrome plated for durability and the prevention of wear damage.

Engine Assembly

ENGINE REMOVAL AND INSTALLATION

1. Remove the hood.
2. Remove the gravel shield; drain the cooling system and engine oil.
3. Remove the air cleaner, its bracket, and attendant hoses.
4. Detach the accelerator cable, choke cable, and fuel lines from the carburetor.
5. Remove the ground cable from under the thermostat housing. Replace the housing.
6. Disconnect all fluid lines and hoses.
7. Disconnect all electrical lines and leads.
8. Remove the fan shroud.
9. Remove the fan clutch.

NOTE: Keep the fan clutch in an upright position, so that its fluid does not leak out.

10. Detach the heater hoses.
11. Tie the clutch cylinder up out of the way.
12. Remove the exhaust pipe thermal reactor.
13. Unbolt the clutch housing to the engine.
14. Support the transmission.
15. Unbolt the engine mounts.
16. Connect a hoist.
17. Pull the engine forward until it clears the transmission input shaft. Lift the engine straight up and out of the car.
18. Remove the heat stove from the exhaust manifold.
19. Installation is the reverse of removal.

OVERHAUL

Disassembly

1975 AND LATER

NOTE: Because of the design of the rotary engine, it is not practical to attempt component removal and installation. It is best to disassemble and assemble the entire engine, or, go as far as necessary with the disassembly procedure. Refer to the specification charts for measurements of the components.

1. Mount the engine on a stand.
2. Remove the oil hose support bracket from the front housing.
3. Disconnect the vacuum hoses, air hoses and remove the decel valve.
4. Remove the air pump and drive belt. Remove the air pump adjusting bar.
5. Remove the alternator and drive belt.
6. Disconnect the metering oil pump connecting rod, oil tubes and vacuum sensing tube from the carburetor.
7. Remove the carburetor and intake manifold as an assembly.
8. Remove the gasket and two rubber rings.
9. Remove the thermal reactor and gaskets.
10. Remove the distributor.
11. Remove the water pump.
12. Invert the engine.
13. Remove the oil pan.
14. Remove the oil pump.
15. Identify the front and rear rotor housings with a felt tip pen. These are common parts and must be identified to be reassembled in their respective locations.
16. Turn the engine on the stand so that the top of the engine is up.
17. Remove the engine mounting bracket from the front cover.
18. Remove the eccentric shaft pulley.
19. Turn the engine on a stand so that the front end of the engine is up.
20. Remove the front cover.
21. Remove the O-ring from the oil passage on the front housing.
22. Remove the oil slinger and distributor drive gear from the shaft.

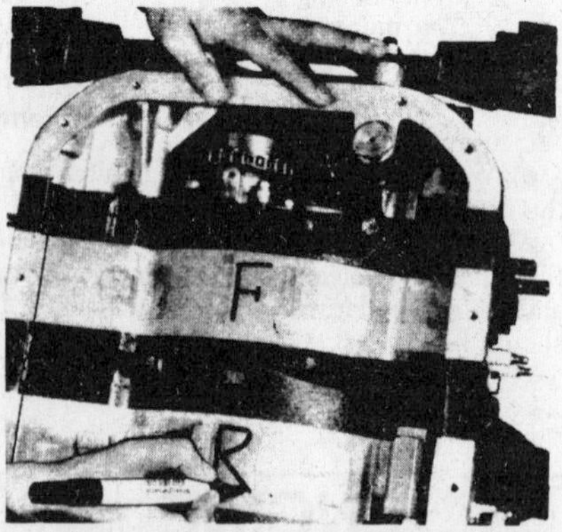

Mark the front and rear rotor housings to prevent confusion during assembly (© Toyo Kogyo Co. Ltd.)

23. Unbolt and remove the chain adjuster.
24. Remove the locknut and washer from the oil pump driven sprocket.
25. Slide the oil pump drive sprocket and driven sprocket together with the drive chain off the eccentric shaft and oil pump simultaneously.
26. Remove the keys from the eccentric and oil pump shafts.
27. Slide the balance weight, thrust washer and needle bearing from the shaft.
28. Unbolt the bearing housing and slide the bearing housing, needle bearing, spacer and thrust plate off the shaft.
29. Turn the engine on the stand so that the top of the engine is up.
30. If equipped with a manual transmission, remove the clutch pressure plate and clutch disc. Remove the flywheel with a puller.
31. If equipped with an automatic transmission, remove the drive plate. Remove the counterweight.
32. Working at the rear of the engine, loosen the tension bolts.

NOTE: Do not loosen the tension bolts one at a time. Loosen the bolts evenly in small stages to prevent distortion. Mark tension bolts to replace in original holes during reassembly.

33. Lift the rear housing off the shaft.

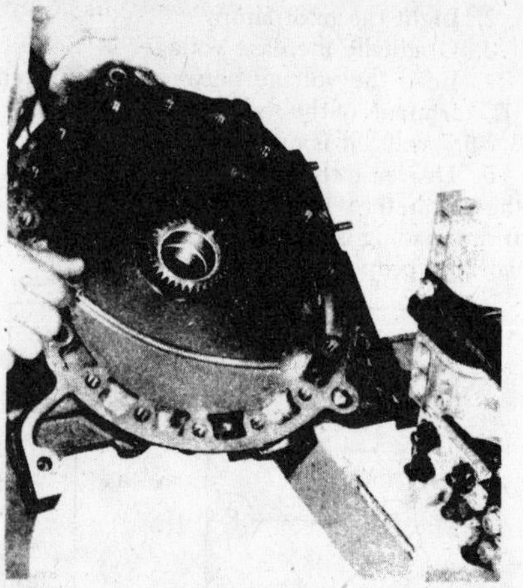

Remove any side seals adhering to the front housing surfaces (© Toyo Kogyo Co. Ltd.)

34. Remove any seals that are stuck to the rotor sliding surface of the rear housing and reinstall them in their original locations.
35. Remove all the corner seals, corner seal springs, side seal and side seal springs from the rear side of the rotor. Mazda has a special tray which holds all the seals and keeps them segregated to prevent mistakes during reassembly. Each seal groove is marked to prevent confusion.
36. Remove the two rubber seals and two O-rings from the rear rotor housing.
37. Remove the dowels from the rear rotor housing.
38. Lift the rear rotor housing away from the rear rotor, being very careful not to drop the apex seals on the rear rotor.
39. Remove each apex seal, side piece and spring from the rear rotor and segregate them.
40. Remove the rear rotor from the eccentric shaft and place it upside down on a clean rag.
41. Remove each seal and spring from the other side of the rotor and segregate these.
42. If some of the seals fall off the rotor, be careful not to change the original position of each seal.
43. Identify the rear rotor with a felt tip pen.

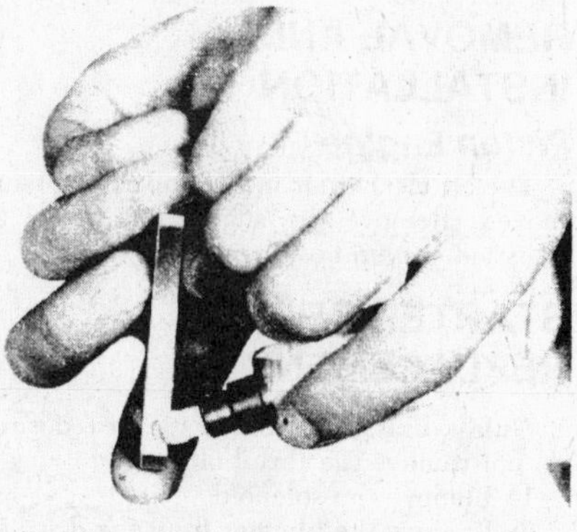

Use a felt-tipped pen to mark the bottom of each apex seal (© Toyo Kogyo Co. Ltd.)

44. Remove the oil seals and the springs. Do not exert heavy pressure at only one place on the seal, since it could be deformed. Replace the O-rings in the oil seal when the engine is overhauled.

45. Hold the intermediate housing down and remove the dowels from it.

46. Lift off the intermediate housing being careful not to damage the eccentric shaft. It should be removed by sliding it beyond the rear rotor journal on thd eccentric shaft while holding the intermediate housing up and, at the same time, pushing the eccentric shaft up.

47. Lift out the eccentric shaft.

48. Repeat the above procedures to remove the front rotor housing and front rotor.

Inspection and Replacement

FRONT, INTERMEDIATE AND REAR HOUSINGS

1. Check the housing for signs of gas or water leakage.

2. Remove the carbon deposits from the front housing with extra fine emery cloth.

3. Remove any of the old sealer which is adhering to the housing, using a brush or a cloth soaked in Ke-tone.

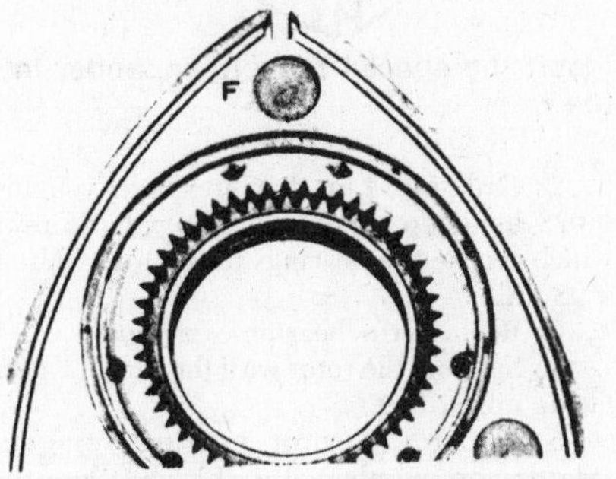

The front rotor is marked with an "F" on its internal gear side; The rear rotor is marked with an "R" in a similar manner. (© Toyo Kogyo Co. Ltd.)

4. Check for distortion by placing a straightedge on the surface of the housing. Measure the clearance between the straightedge and the housing with a feeler gauge. If the clearance is greater than 0.002 in. at any point, replace the housing.

5. Use a dial indicator to check for wear on the rotor contact surfaces of the housing. If the wear is greater than 0.004 in., replace the housing.

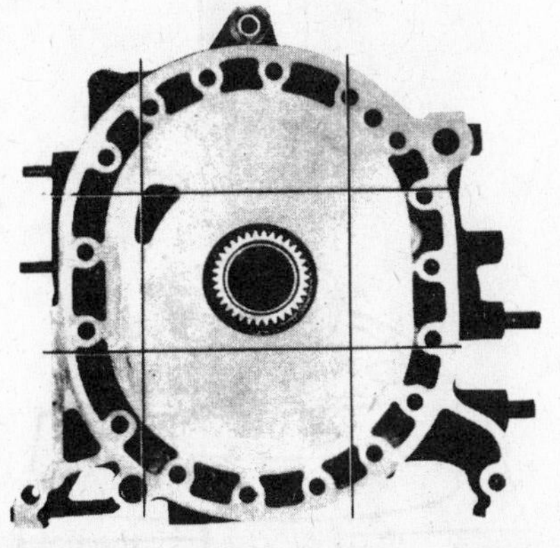

Measure the housing distortion along the axes indicated (© Toyo Kogyo Co. Ltd.)

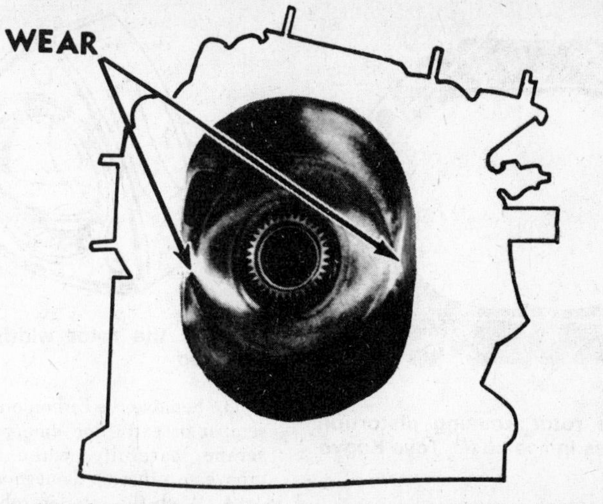

Most of the front and rear housing wear occurs at the end of the minor axis as shown. (© Toyo Kogyo Co. Ltd.)

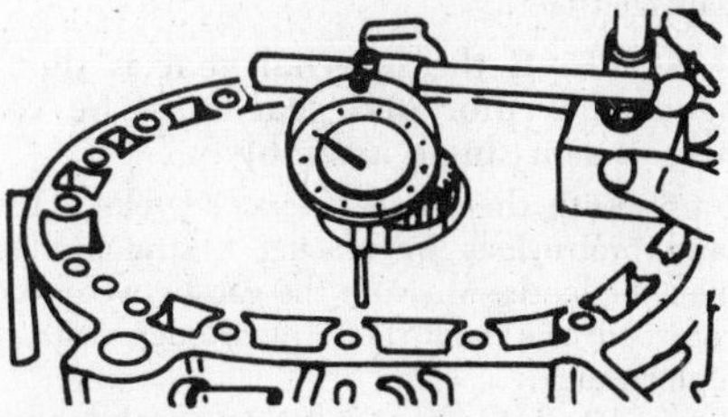

Measuring housing wear with a dial indicator

NOTE: The wear at either end of the minor axis is greater than at any other point on the housing. However, this is normal and should be no cause for concern.

FRONT STATIONARY GEAR AND MAIN BEARING

1. Examine the teeth of the stationary gear for wear or damage.

2. Be sure that the main bearing shows no signs of excessive wear, scoring, or flaking.

3. Check the main bearing-to-eccentric journal clearance by measuring the journal with a vernier caliper and the bearing with a pair of inside calipers.

MAIN BEARING REPLACEMENT

1. Unfasten the securing bolts, if used. Drive the stationary gear and main bearing assembly out of the housing with a brass drift.

2. Press the main bearing out of the stationary gear.

3. Press a new main bearing into the stationary gear so that it is in the same position that the old bearing was.

4. Align the slot in the stationary gear flange with the dowel pin in the housing and press the gear into place. Install the securing bolts, if required.

NOTE: To aid in stationary gear and main bearing removal and installation, Mazda manufactures a special tool, part number 49 0813 235.

REAR STATIONARY GEAR AND MAIN BEARING

Inspect the rear stationary gear and main bearing in a similar manner to the front. In addition, examine the O-ring, which is located

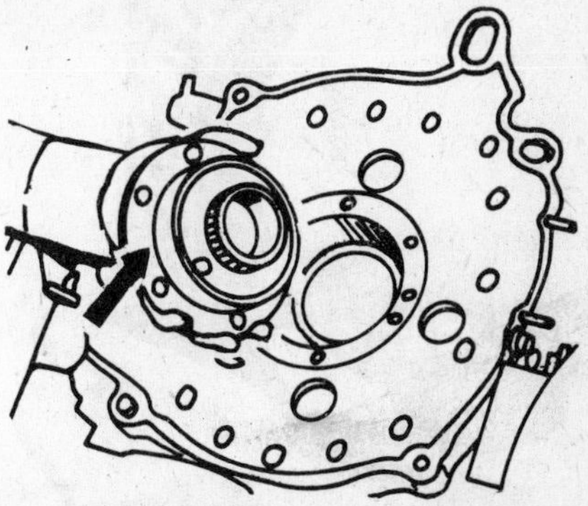

Position the O-ring in the groove on the stationary gear (arrow)

in the stationary gear, for signs of wear or damage. Replace the O-ring, if necessary.

To replace the stationary gear, use the following procedure.

1. Remove the rear stationary gear securing bolts.

2. Drive the stationary gear out of the rear housing with a brass drift.

3. Apply a light coating of grease to a new O-ring and fit it into the groove on the stationary gear.

4. Apply sealer to the flange of the stationary gear.

5. Install the stationary gear on the housing so that the slot on its flange aligns with the pin on the rear housing.

CAUTION

Use care not to damage the O-ring during installation.

6. Tighten the stationary gear bolts evenly, and in several stages, to 15 ft-lbs.

ROTOR HOUSINGS

1. Examine the inner margin of both housings for signs of gas or water leakage.

2. Wipe the inner surface of each housing with a clean cloth to remove the carbon deposits.

NOTE: If the carbon deposits are stubborn, soak the cloth in a solution of Ke-tone. Do not scrape or sand the chrome plated surfaces of the rotor chamber.

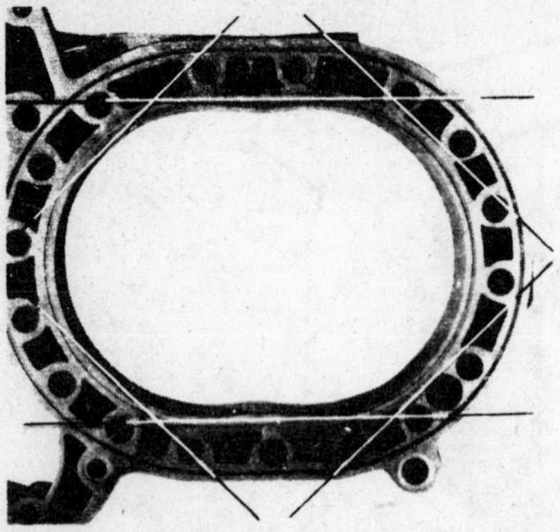

Measure the rotor housing distortion along the axes indicated (© Toyo Kogyo Co. Ltd.)

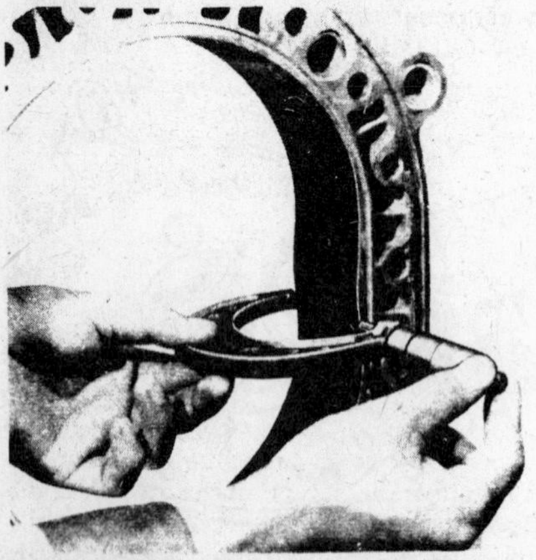

Check the rotor housing width at eight points near the trochoid surface (© Toyo Kogyo Co. Ltd.)

3. Clean all of the rust deposits out of the cooling passages of each rotor housing.
4. Remove the old sealer with a cloth soaked in Ke-tone.
5. Examine the chromium plated inner surfaces for scoring, flaking, or other signs of damage. If any are present, the housing must be replaced.
6. Check the rotor housings for distortion by placing a straightedge on the axes.
7. If distortion exceeds 0.002 in., replace the rotor housing.
8. Check the widths of both rotor housings, at a minimum of eight points near the trochoid surfaces of each housing, using a vernier caliper.

If the difference between the maximum and minimum values obtained is greater than 0.0031 in. (RX-3) or 0.0024 in. (RX-4, RX-7), replace the housing. A housing in this condition will be prone to gas and coolant leakage.

ROTORS

1. Check the rotor for signs of blow-by around the side and corner seal areas.
2. The color of the carbon deposits on the rotor should be brown, just as in a piston engine.

NOTE: Usually the carbon deposits on the leading side of the rotor are brown, while those on the trailing side tend toward black, as viewed from the direction of rotation.

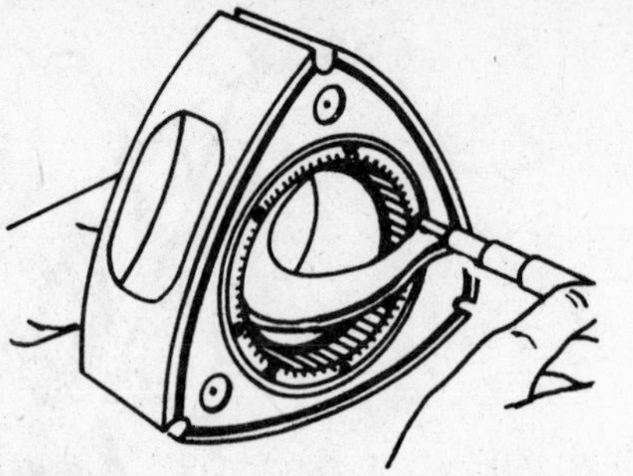

Measure the rotor width at the point indicated

3. Remove the carbon on the rotor with a scraper or extra fine emery paper. Use the scraper carefully, when doing the seal grooves, so that no damage is done to them.
4. Wash the rotor in solvent and blow it dry with compressed air.
5. Examine the internal gear for cracks or damaged teeth.

NOTE: If the internal gear is damaged, the rotor and gear must be replaced as a single assembly.

6. With the oil seal removed, check the land protrusions by placing a straightedge over the lands. Measure the gap between the rotor surface and the straightedge with a feeler gauge.
7. Check the gaps between the housings and the rotor on both of its sides.
   a. Measure the rotor width with a vernier caliper.
   b. Compare the rotor width against the width of the rotor housing which was measured above.
   c. Replace the rotor, if the difference between the two measurements is not within 0.0051-0.0067 in.
8. Check the rotor bearing for flaking, wearing, or scoring and proceed as indicated in the next section, if any of these are present.

The rotors are classified into five lettered grades, according to their weight. A letter between A and E is stamped on the internal gear side of the rotor. If it becomes necessary to replace a rotor, use one marked with a "C" because this is the standard replacement rotor, and it can be used in most balancing combinations.

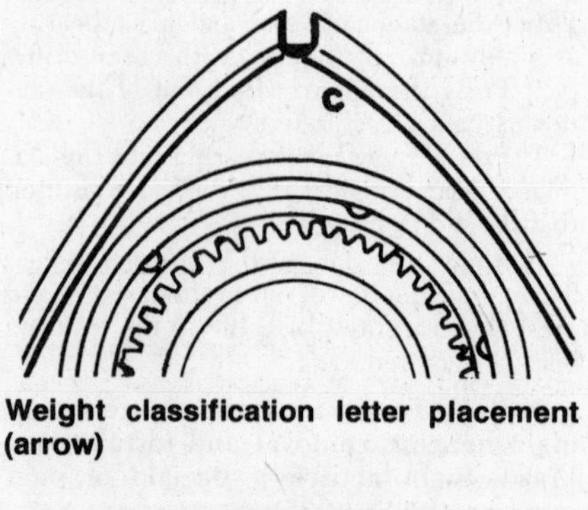

Weight classification letter placement (arrow)

Rotor Bearing Replacement

CAUTION

The use of the special service tools, as indicated in the text, is mandatory, if damage to the rotor is to be avoided.

Check the clearance between the rotor bearing and the rotor journal on the eccentric shaft. Measure the inner diameter of the rotor bearing and the outer diameter of the journal; The wear limit is 0.0039 in.; replace the bearing if it exceeds this.

1. Install the bearing expander (Mazda part number 49 0813 245) in the rotor bearing. If the expander is not used, bearing deformation will result when the holes are drilled.

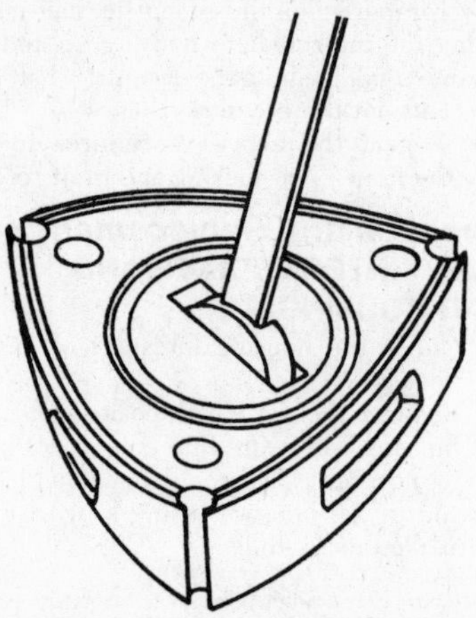

Insert the special bearing expander into the rotor

2. Drill a 0.14 in. diameter hole, roughly 0.028 in. deep, into each of the lockscrews which secure the bearings to the rotor. Use a #28 drill.
3. Remove the bearing expander.
4. Support the rotor with the internal gear facing upward.
5. Using the rotor bearing remover (Mazda part number 49 0813 240), less the adaptor ring, press the bearing out of the rotor.

CAUTION

Be extremely careful not to damage the internal gear. It cannot be replaced separately from the rotor.

6. If the bore in which the bearing is installed is damaged, dress it with emery paper and blow it clean with compressed air.
7. With the rotor internal gear facing upward, press-fit a new bearing into the bore. Use the bearing replacer with the adaptor screws removed.

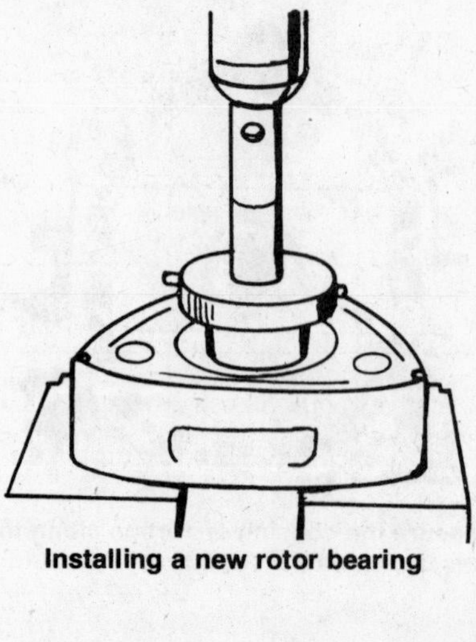

Installing a new rotor bearing

NOTE: Be sure that the oil hole in the bearing is aligned with the hole in the apex side of the rotor. Once the bearing is installed, it should be flush with the rotor boss.

8. Insert the rotor bearing expander into the new bearing, as in Step 1.
9. Drill 0.14 in. holes, about 0.28 in. deep, within 0.28 in. of the original lockscrew holes (either to the left or right of them) with a #28 drill. The center of the holes must be 0.02 in. from the rotor bore.

NOTE: The new holes should all be in the same direction from the original holes; e.g., if the first hole is drilled to the left of the original hole, drill the remaining holes to the left of the other lockscrew holes.

10. Thread the holes with an M4, P-0.70 mm metric tap.
11. Install the bearing lockscrews and stake them with a punch so that they cannot work loose.
12. Wash the rotor and blow it dry with compressed air.

OIL SEAL INSPECTION

NOTE: Inspect the oil seal while it is mounted in the rotor.

1. Examine the oil seal.
2. If the width of the oil seal lip is greater than 0.031 in., replace the oil seal.
3. If the protrusion of the oil seal is greater than 0.020 in., replace the seal.

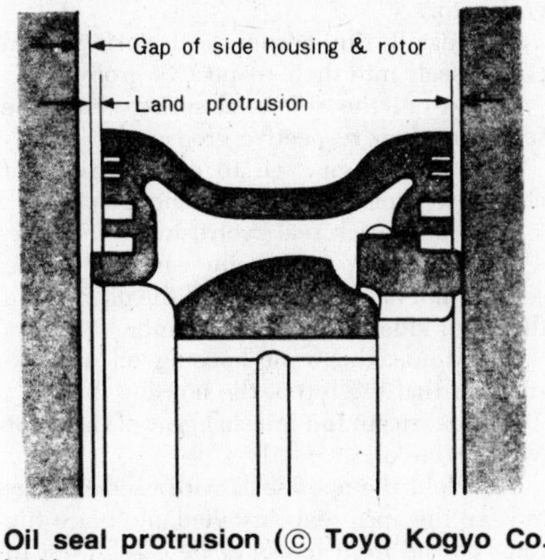

Oil seal protrusion (© Toyo Kogyo Co. Ltd.)

OIL SEAL REPLACEMENT

NOTE: Replace the rubber O-ring in the oil seal as a normal part of engine overhaul.

1. Pry the seal out by inserting a screwdriver into the slots on the rotor.

CAUTION

Be careful not to deform the lip of the oil seal if it is to be reinstalled.

2. Fit both of the oil seal springs into their respective grooves so that their ends are facing upward and their gaps are opposite each other on the rotor.
3. Insert a new O-ring into each of the oil seals.

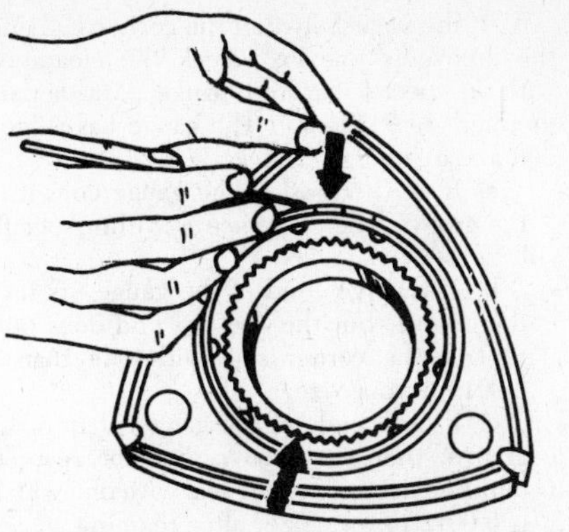

Position the oil seal spring gaps at arrows

NOTE: Before installing the O-rings into the oil seals, fit each of the seals into its proper groove on the rotor. Check to see that all of the seals move smoothly and freely.

4. Coat the oil seal groove and the oil seal with engine oil.
5. Gently press the oil seal into the groove with your fingers. Be careful not to distort the seal.

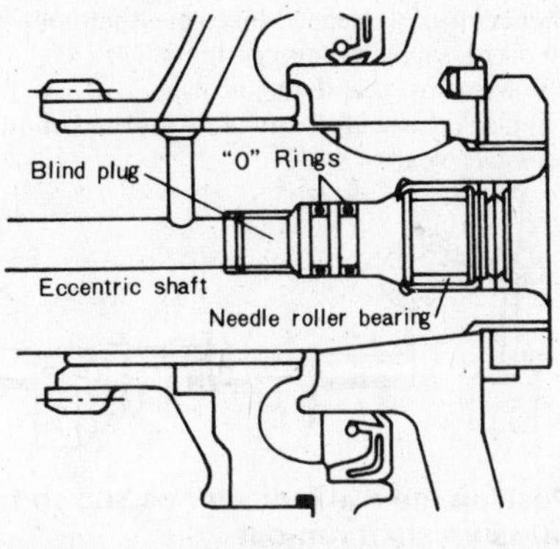

Eccentric shaft blind plug assembly (© Toyo Kogyo Co. Ltd.)

NOTE: Be sure that the white mark is on the bottom side of each seal when it is installed.

6. Repeat the installation procedure for the oil seals on both sides of each rotor.

APEX SEALS

CAUTION

Although the apex seals are extremely durable when in service, they are easily broken when they are being handled. Be careful never to drop them.

1. Remove the carbon deposits from the apex seals and their springs. Do not use emery cloth on the seals as it will damage their finish.
2. Wash the seals and the springs in cleaning solution.
3. Check the apex seals for cracks.
4. Test the seal springs for weakness.
5. Use a micrometer to check the seal height. Refer to specifications chart.
6. With a feeler gauge, check the side clearance between the apex seal and the

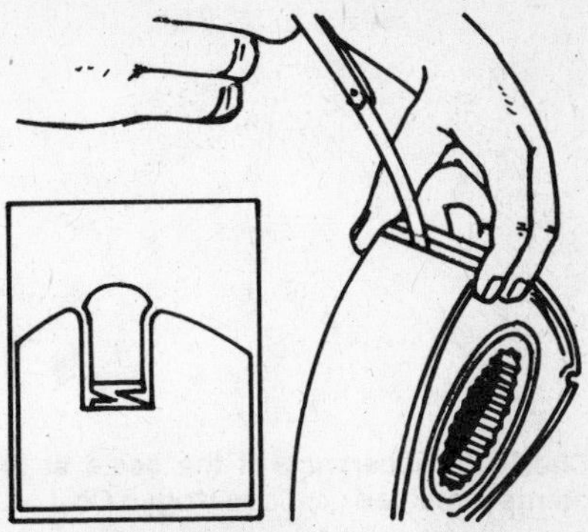

Check the gap between the apex seal and groove with a feeler gauge

Apex seal-to-side housing gap (© Toyo Kogyo Co. Ltd.)

groove in the rotor. Insert the gauge until its tip contacts the bottom of the groove. If the gap is greater than 0.005 in., replace the seal.
7. Check the gap between the apex seals and the side housing in the following manner:
   a. Use a vernier caliper to measure the length of each apex seal.
   b. Compare this measurement to the *minimum* figure obtained when the rotor housing width was being measured.
   c. If the seal is too long, sand the ends of the seal with emery cloth until the proper length is reached.

CAUTION

Do not use the emery cloth on the faces of the seal.

SIDE SEALS

1. Remove the carbon deposits from the side seals and their springs.
2. Check the side seals for cracks.
3. Check the clearance between the side seals and their grooves with a feeler gauge. Replace any side seals with a clearance of more than 0.0039 in.
4. Check the clearance between the side seals and the corner seals with both installed in the rotor.
   a. Insert a feeler gauge between the end of the side seal and the corner seal.

NOTE: Insert the gauge against the direction of the rotor's rotation.

   b. Replace the side seal if the clearance is greater than 0.016 in.
5. If the side seal is replaced, adjust the clearance between it and the corner seal as follows:
   a. File the side seal on its reverse side,

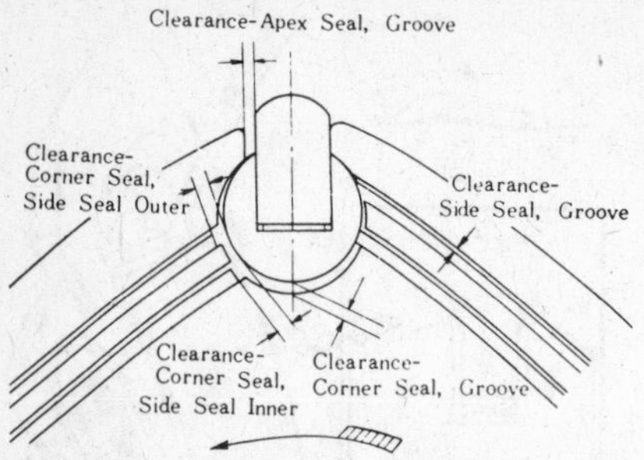

Check the clearance of the seals at the points indicated (© Toyo Kogyo Co. Ltd.)

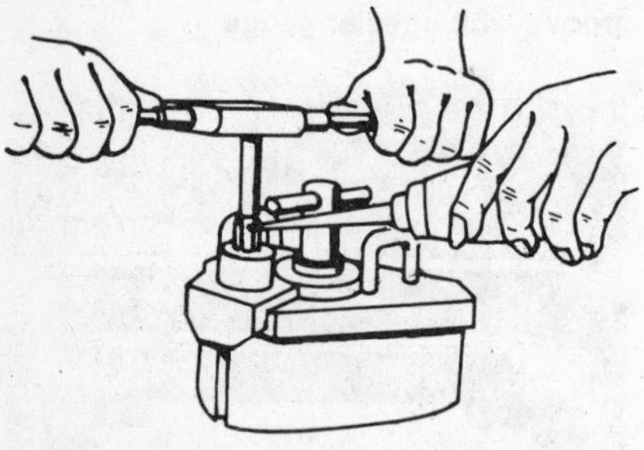

Reaming the corner seal groove

in the same rotational direction of the rotor, along the outline made by the corner seal.

b. The clearance obtained should be 0.002-0.006 in. If it exceeds this, the performance of the seals will deteriorate.

CAUTION

There are four different types of side seals, depending upon location. Do not mix the seals up and be sure to use the proper type of seal for replacement.

CORNER SEALS

1. Clean the carbon deposits.
2. Examine each of the seals.
3. Measure the clearance between the corner seal and its groove. The clearance should be 0.008-0.0019 in. The wear limit of the gap is 0.0031 in.

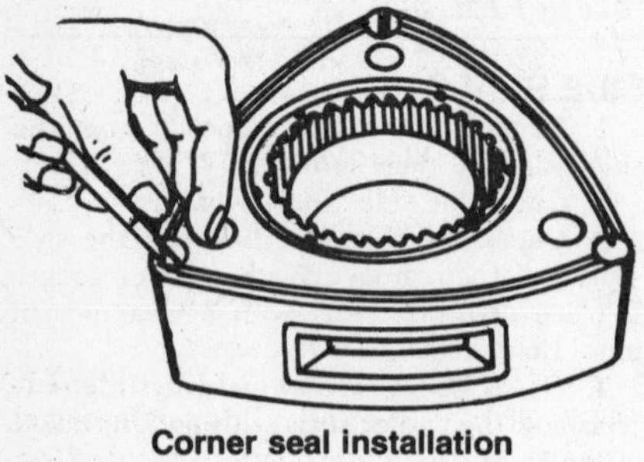

Corner seal installation

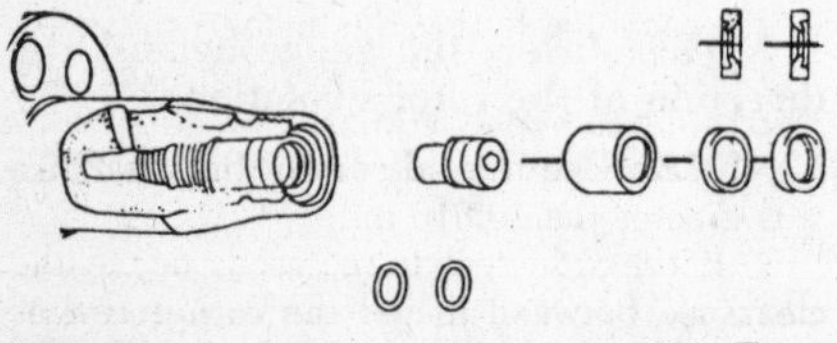

Needle bearing components (© Toyo Kogyo Co. Ltd.)

4. If the wear between the corner seal and the groove is uneven, check the clearance with the special "bar limit gauge" (Mazda part number, 49 0839 165). The gauge has a "go" end and a "no go" end.

a. If neither end of the gauge goes into the groove, the clearance is within specifications.

b. If the "go" end of the gauge fits into the groove, but the "no go" end does not, replace the corner seal with one that is 0.0012 in. oversize.

c. If both ends of the gauge fit into the groove, then the groove must be reamed out. Replace the corner seal with one which is 0.0072 in. oversize, after reaming.

NOTE: Take the measurement of the groove in the direction of maximum wear, i.e., that of rotation.

SEAL SPRINGS

Check the seal springs for damage or weakness. Be exceptionally careful when checking the spring areas which contact either the rotor or the seal.

ECCENTRIC SHAFT

1. Wash the eccentric shaft in solvent and blow the oil passages dry with compressed air.
2. Check the shaft for wear, cracks, or other signs of damage. Make sure that none of the oil passages are clogged.
3. Measure the shaft journals.

Replace the shaft if any of its journals shows excessive wear.

Position the dial indicator as shown to measure shaft run-out

4. Check eccentric shaft runout. Rotate the shaft slowly and note the dial indicator reading. If runout is more than specifications, replace the eccentric shaft.
5. Check the blind plug at the end of the shaft. If it is loose or leaking, remove it with an Allen wrench and replace the O-ring.
6. Check the operation of the needle roller bearing for smoothness by inserting a mainshaft into the bearing and rotating it. Examine the bearing for signs of wear or damage.
7. Replace the bearings, if necessary, with the special bearing replacer (Mazda part numbers 49 0823 073 and 49 0823 072).

ASSEMBLY

1975 AND LATER

1. Place the rotor on a rubber pad or cloth.
2. Install the oil seal rings in their respective grooves in the rotors with the edge of the spring in the stopper hole. The oil seal springs are painted cream or blue in color. The cream colored springs must be installed on the front faces of both rotors. The blue colored springs must be installed on the rear faces of both rotors. When installing each oil seal spring,

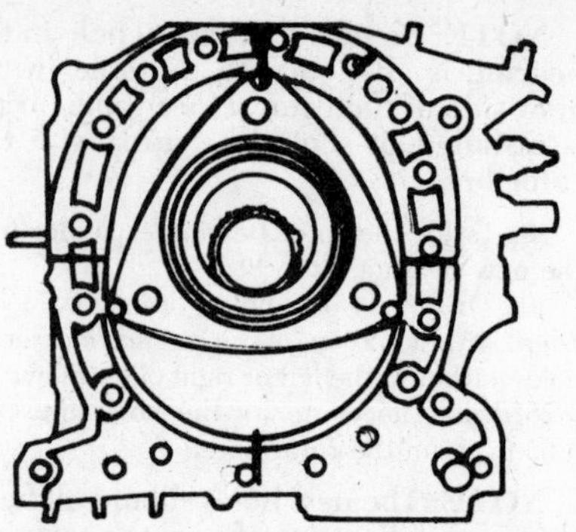

The rear rotor must be positioned as shown during engine assembly

the painted side (square side) of the spring must face upward (toward the oil seal).

3. Install a new O-ring in each groove. Place each oil seal in the groove so that the square edge of the spring fits in the stopper hole of the oil seal. Push the head of the oil seal slowly with the fingers, being careful that the seal is not deformed. Be sure that the oil seal moves smoothly in the groove before installing the O-ring.
4. Lubricate each oil seal and groove with engine oil and check the movement of the seal. It should move freely when the head of the seal is pressed.
5. Check the oil seal protrusion and install the seals on the other side of each rotor.
6. Install the apex seals without springs and side pieces into their respective grooves so that each side piece positions on the side of each rotor.
7. Install the corner seal springs and corner seals into their respective grooves.
8. Install the side seal springs and side seals into their respective grooves.
9. Apply engine oil to each spring and check each spring for smooth movement.
10. Check each seal protrusion.
11. Invert the rotor being careful that the seals do not fall out, and install the oil seals on the other side in the same manner.
12. Mount the front housing on a workstand so that the top of the housing is up.
13. Lubricate the internal gear of the rotor with engine oil.
14. Hold the apex seals with used O-rings to keep the apex seals installed and place the rotor on the front housing. Be careful not to drop the seals. Turn the front housing so that the sliding surface faces upward.
15. Mesh the internal and stationary gears so that one of the rotor apexes is at any one of the four places shown and remove the old O-ring which is holding the apex seals in position.
16. Lubricate the front rotor journal of the eccentric shaft with engine oil and lubricate the eccentric shaft main journal.
17. Insert the eccentric shaft. Be careful that you do not damage the rotor bearing and main bearing.
18. Apply sealing agent to the front side of the front rotor housing.
19. Apply a light coat of petroleum jelly onto new O-rings and rubber seals (to prevent them from coming off) and install the O-rings and rubber seals on the front side of the rotor housing.

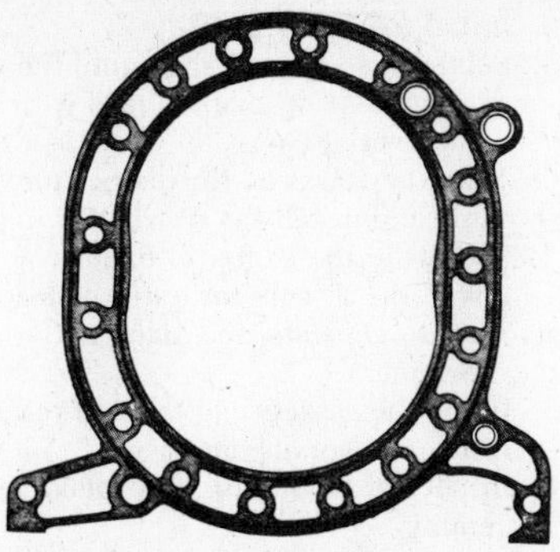

Apply sealer to the grey shadowed areas of the rotor housing (© Toyo Kogyo Co. Ltd.)

NOTE: The inner rubber seal is of the square type. The wider white line of the rubber seal should face the combustion chamber and the seam of the rubber seal should be positioned as shown. Do not stretch the rubber seal.

20. If the engine is being overhauled, install the seal protector to only the inner rubber seal to improve durability.
21. Invert the front rotor housing, being careful not to let the rubber seals and O-rings fall from their grooves, and mount it on the front housing.
22. Lubricate the dowels with engine oil and insert them through the front rotor housing holes and into the front housing.
23. Apply sealer to the front side of the rotor housing.
24. Install new O-rings and rubber seals on the front rotor housing in the same manner as for the other side.
25. Insert each apex spring seal, making sure that the seal is installed in the proper direction.
26. Install each side piece in its original position and be sure that the springs seat on the side piece.
27. Lubricate the side pieces with engine oil. Make sure that the front rotor housing is free of foreign matter and lubricate the sliding surface of the front housing with engine oil.
28. Turn the front housing assembly with the rotor, so that the top of the housing is up. Pull the eccentric shaft about 1 in.
29. Position the eccentric portion of the eccentric shaft diagonally, to the upper right.
30. Install the intermediate housing over the eccentric shaft onto the front rotor housing. Turn the engine so that the rear of the engine is up.
31. Install the rear rotor and rear rotor housing following the same steps as for the front rotor and the front housing.

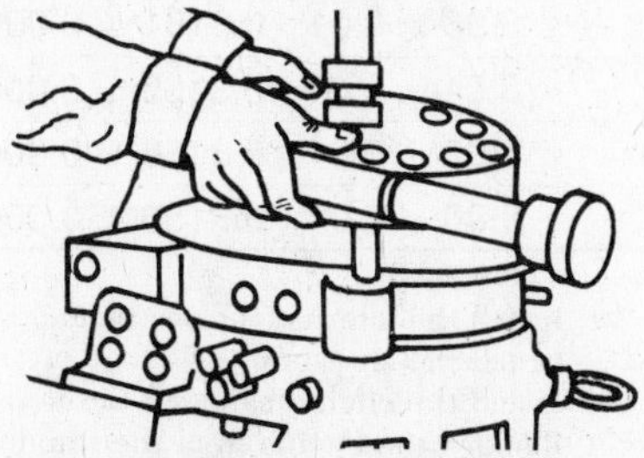

Intermediate housing installation

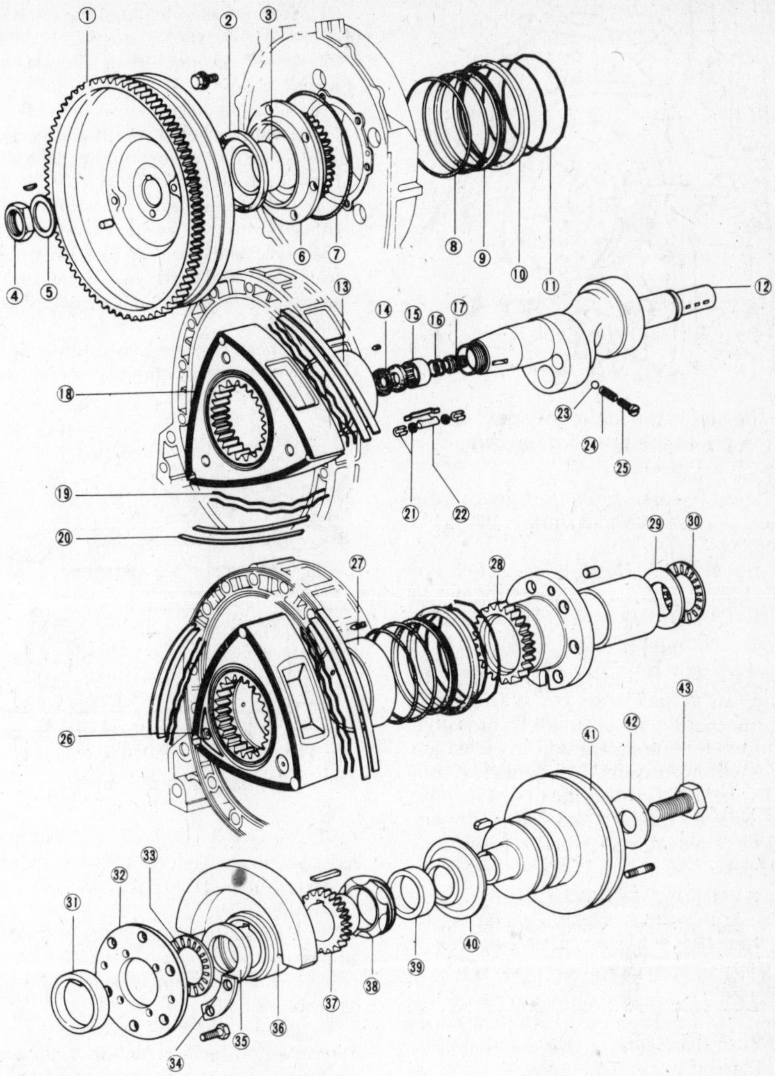

1. Flywheel
2. Oil seal
3. Main bearing
4. Locknut
5. Washer
6. Rear stationary gear
7. O-ring
8. Oil seal O-ring
9. Oil seal
10. Oil seal
11. Oil seal spring
12. Eccentric shaft
13. Rotor bearing
14. Grease seal
15. Needle bearing
16. O-ring
17. Blind plug
18. Front rotor
19. Side seal spring
20. Side seal
21. Corner seal and spring
22. Apex seal and spring
23. Ball
24. Spring
25. Oil nozzle
26. Rear rotor
27. Rotor bearing
28. Front stationary gear
29. Thrust washer
30. Thrust bearing
31. Spacer
32. Bearing housing
33. Needle bearing
34. Washer
35. Thrust plate
36. Balance weight
37. Oil pump drive sprocket
38. Distributor drive gear
39. Spacer
40. Oil slinger
41. Eccentric shaft pulley
42. Washer
43. Pulley bolt

Rotor and eccentric shaft components (© Toyo Kogyo Co. Ltd.)

32. Turn the engine so that the rear of the engine is up.
33. Lubricate the stationary gear and main bearing.
34. Install the rear housing onto the rear rotor housing. If necessary, turn the rear rotor slightly to mesh the rear housing stationary gear with the rear rotor internal gear.
35. Install a new washer on each tension bolt, and lubricate each bolt with engine oil.
36. Install the tension bolts and tighten them evenly, in several stages following the sequence shown. The specified torque is 23-27 ft/lbs.

NOTE: Be sure bolts are installed in their original positions. Longer bolts are used in later engines and are not interchangeable.

37. After tightening the bolts, turn the eccentric shaft to be sure that the shaft and rotors turn smoothly and easily.
38. Lubricate the oil seal in the rear housing.
39. On vehicles with manual transmission, install the flywheel on the rear of the eccentric shaft so that the keyway of the flywheel fits the key on the shaft.

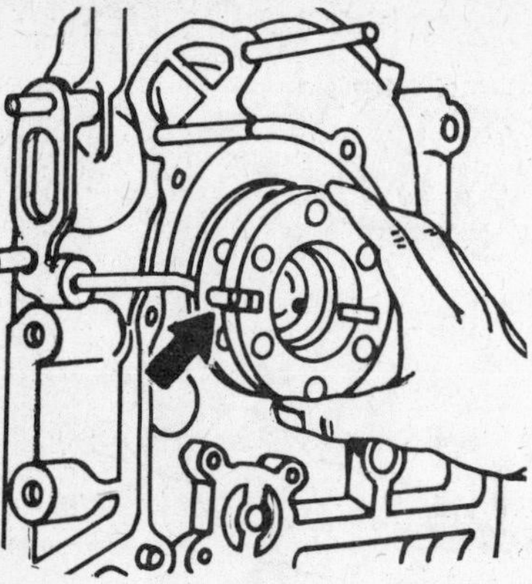

Align the slot in the stationary gear flange with the pin in the housing (arrow)

40. Apply sealer to both sides of the flywheel lockwasher and install the lockwasher.
41. Install the flywheel locknut. Hold the flywheel SECURELY and tighten the nut to THREE HUNDRED AND FIFTY FT/LBS (350 ft/lbs) of torque.

NOTE: 350 ft/lbs is a great deal of torque. In actual practice, it is practically impossible to accurately measure that much torque on the nut. At least a 3 ft. bar will be required to generate sufficient torque. Tighten it as tight as possible, with no longer than 3 ft. of leverage. Be sure the engine is held SECURELY.

42. On vehicles with automatic transmission, install the key, counterweight, lockwasher and nut. Tighten the nut to 350 ft. lbs. SEE STEP 41 AND THE NOTE FOLLOWING STEP 41. Install the drive plate on the counterweight and tighten the attaching nuts.
43. Turn the engine so that the front faces up.
44. Install the thrust plate with the tapered face down, and install the needle bearing on the eccentric shaft. Lubricate with engine oil.
45. Install the bearing housing on the front housing. Tighten the bolts and bend up the lockwasher tabs.

The spacer should be installed so that the center of the needle bearing comes to the center of the eccentric shaft and the spacer should be seated on the thrust plate.

46. Install the needle bearing on the shaft and lubricate it with engine oil.
47. Install the balancer and thrust washer on the eccentric shaft.
48. Install the oil pump drive chain over both of the sprockets. Install the sprocket and chain assembly over the eccentric shaft and oil pump shafts simultaneously. Install the key on the eccentric shaft.

NOTE: Be sure that both of the sprockets are engaged with the chain before installing them over the shafts.

49. Install the distributor drive gear onto the eccentric shaft with the "F" mark on the gear facing the front of the engine. Slide the spacer and oil slinger onto the eccentric shaft.
50. Align the keyway and install the eccentric shaft pulley. Tighten the pulley bolt to 60 ft/lbs.
51. Turn the engine top of the engine faces up.
52. Check eccentric shaft end-play in the following manner:
    a. Attach a dial indicator to the flywheel. Move the flywheel forward and backward.
    b. Note the reading on the dial indicator; it should be 0.0016-0.0028 in.
    c. If the end-play is not within specifications, adjust it by replacing the front spacer. Spacers come in four sizes, ranging from 0.3150-0.3181 in. If necessary, a spacer can be ground on a surface plate with emery paper.
    d. Check the end-play again and, if it is now within specifications, proceed with the next step.

Installing oil pump

53. Remove the pulley fron the front of the eccentric shaft. Tighten the oil pump drive sprocket nut and bend the locktabs on the lockwasher.
54. Fit a new O-ring over the front cover oil passage.
55. Install the chain tensioner and tighten its securing bolts.
56. Position the front cover gasket and the front cover on the front housing, then secure the front cover with its attachment bolts.
57. Install the eccentric shaft pulley again. Tighten its bolt to 60 ft/lbs.
58. Turn the engine so that the bottom faces up.
59. Cut off the excess gasket on the front cover along the mounting surface of the oil pan.
60. Install the oil strainer gasket and strainer on the front housing and tighten the attaching bolts.
61. Apply sealer to the joint surfaces of each housing.
62. Install the oil pan.
63. Turn the engine so that the top is up.

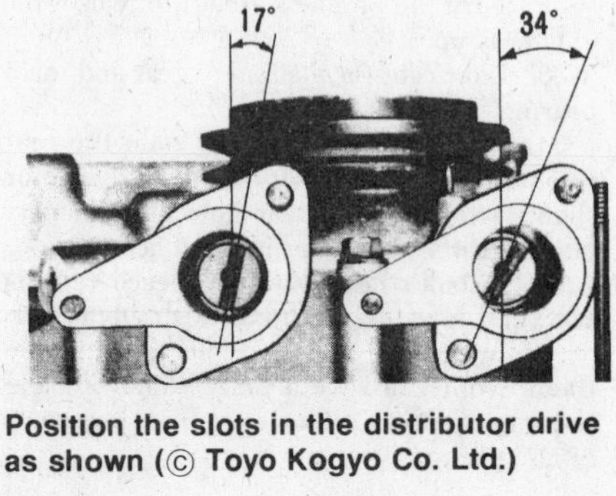

Position the slots in the distributor drive as shown (© Toyo Kogyo Co. Ltd.)

64. Install the water pump.
65. Rotate the eccentric shaft until the yellow mark (leading side mark) aligns with the pointer on the front cover.
66. Align the marks on the distributor gear and housing and install the distributor so that the lockbolt is in the center of the slot.
67. Rotate the distributor until the leading points start to separate and tighten the distributor locknut.
68. Install the gaskets and thermal reactor.
69. Install the hot air duct.
70. Install the carburetor and intake manifold assembly.
71. Connect the oil tubes, vacuum tube and metering oil pump connecting rod to the carburetor.

Use a dial indicator attached to the flywheel to measure eccentric shaft end-play

72. Install the decel valve and connect the vacuum lines, air hoses and wires.
73. Install the alternator bracket, alternator and bolt and check the clearance. If the clearance is more than 0.006 in., adjust the clearance using a shim. Shims are available in three sizes: 0.0059 in., 0.0118 in., and 0.0197 in.

ECCENTRIC SHAFT SPACER THICKNESS CHART

Marking	Thickness mm	Thickness in.
X	8.08 ± 0.01	0.3181 ± 0.0004
Y	8.04 ± 0.01	0.3165 ± 0.0004
V	8.02 ± 0.01	0.3158 ± 0.0004
Z	8.00 ± 0.01	0.3150 ± 0.0004

74. Install the alternator drive belt.
75. Install the air pump.
76. Install the engine hanger bracket.
77. Remove the engine from the stand.
78. Install the engine in the vehicle.

Intake Manifold

REMOVAL AND INSTALLATION

To remove the intake manifold and carburetor assembly with the engine remaining in the automobile, proceed in the follwoing manner:

1. Perform Steps 2-7 "Engine Removal and Installation". Do not remove the engine. Do not drain the engine oil; merely remove the metering oil pump hose from the carburetor.
2. Perform Steps 1-4 of "Engine Disassembly".

Install the intake manifold and carburetor assembly in the reverse order of removal.

Thermal Reactor

REMOVAL AND INSTALLATION

CAUTION

The thermal reactor operates at extremely high temperatures. Allow the engine to cool completely before attempting to remove it.

To remove the thermal reactor, which replaces the exhaust manifold:

NOTE: The bottom nut is difficult to reach. Mazda makes a special wrench (part number 49 213 001) to remove it. If the wrench is unavailable, a flexible drive metric socket wrench may be substituted.

1. Remove the air cleaner.
2. Unbolt and remove the air injection pump.
3. Remove the intake manifold complete with carburetor.
4. Remove the heat stove from the thermal reactor.
5. Unfasten the thermal reactor securing nuts, including those on the exhaust pipe flange.
6. Remove the thermal reactor.
7. Installation is the reverse of removal.

ENGINE LUBRICATION—ROTARY

A conventional oil pump, which is chain driven, circulates oil through the rotary engine. A full-flow filter is mounted on the top of the rear housing and an oil cooler is used to reduce the temperature of the engine oil.

An unusual feature of the rotary engine lubrication system is a metering oil pump which injects oil into the float chamber of the carburetor. Once there, it is mixed with the fuel which is to be burned, thus providing extra lubrication for the seals. The metering oil pump is designed to work only when the engine is working under a load.

Oil Pan

REMOVAL AND INSTALLATION

The oil pan is easily removed after removing the gravel shield.

Installation is the reverse of removal.

Oil Pump

REMOVAL AND INSTALLATION

Oil pump removal and installation is contained in the engine overhaul section above. Perform only those steps needed to remove the oil pump.

Checking Clearances

1. Separate the halves of the oil pump.
2. The clearance between the lobes of the rotors should be 0.0004-0.0035 in. Replace both of the rotors if the clearance exceeds 0.006 in.

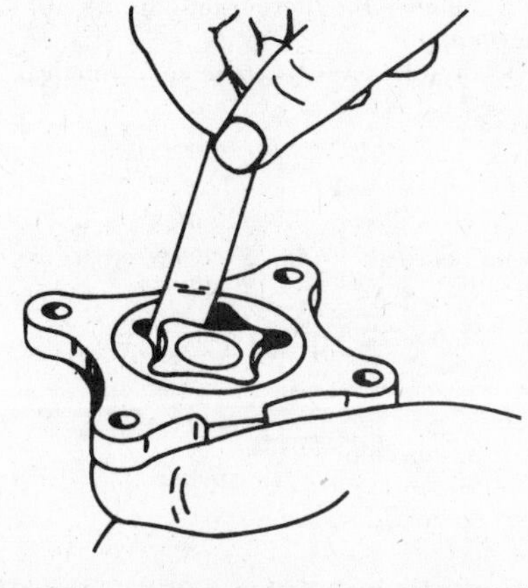

Measure the clearance between the rotors with a feeler gauge

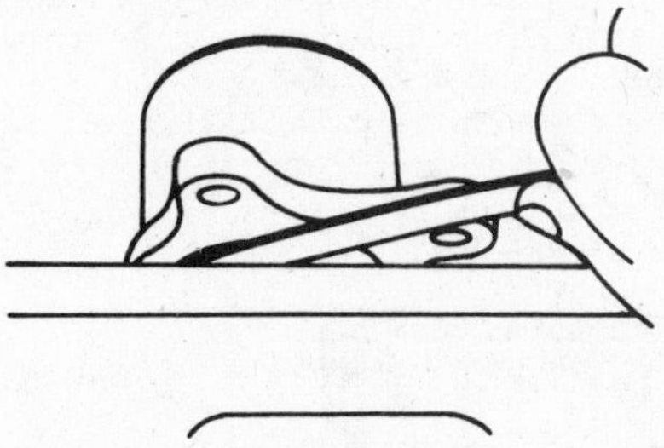

Measure the gap between the straightedge and the housing

3. The clearance between the outer rotor and the housing should be 0.008-0.010 in. If the clearance is greater than 0.012 in., replace both of the rotors.
4. Place a straightedge across the pump housing. Measure the gap between the straightedge and the housing with a feeler gauge. The gap should be 0.001-0.005 in. If the gap exceeds 0.012 in., replace the rotors or the pump housing.

Metering Oil Pump

OPERATION

A metering oil pump, mounted on the top of the engine, is used to provide additional lubrication to the engine when it is operating under a load. The pump provides oil to the carburetor, where it is mixed in the float chamber to be burned.

The metering pump is a plunger type and is controlled by throttle opening. A cam arrangement, connected to the carburetor throttle lever, operates a plunger. The plunger, in turn, acts on a differential plunger, the stroke of which determines the amount of oil flow.

When the throttle opening is small, the amount of the plunger stroke is small; as the throttle opening increases, so does the amount of the plunger stroke.

TESTING

1. At the carburetor, disconnect the oil lines which run from the metering oil pump to the carburetor.
2. Use a container which has a scale calibrated in cubic centimeters (cc) on its side to catch the pump discharge from the oil lines.
3. Run the engine at 2,000 r.p.m. for six minutes.
4. At the end of this time, 2.4-2.9 cc should be collected in the container. If not, adjust the pump.

ADJUSTMENTS

Rotate the adjusting screw on the metering oil pump to obtain the proper oil flow. Clockwise rotation of the screw *increases* the flow; counterclockwise rotation *decreases* the oil flow.

Arrow (right) indicates the metering oil pump adjusting screw. The 3 arrows (left) indicate the connecting rod adjusting holes

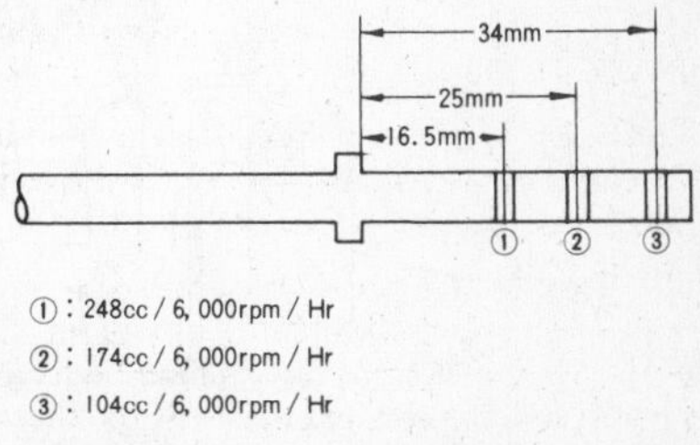

①: 248cc / 6, 000rpm / Hr
②: 174cc / 6, 000rpm / Hr
③: 104cc / 6, 000rpm / Hr

Connecting rod adjusting holes
(© Toyo Kogyo Co. Ltd.)

If necessary, the oil discharge rate may be further adjusted by changing the position of the cam in the pump connecting rod. The shorter the rod throw, the more oil will be pumped. Adjust the throw by means of the three holes provided.

Oil Cooler

REMOVAL AND INSTALLATION

The oil cooler is easily removed after removing the gravel shield and disconnecting the lines. Unbolt the cooler from the radiator.

Installation is the reverse of removal.

ENGINE COOLING—ROTARY

Radiator

REMOVAL AND INSTALLATION

1. Drain the engine coolant.
2. Remove the shroud.
3. Remove the upper, lower, and expansion tank hoses.
4. Remove the oil cooler.
5. Withdraw the radiator.
6. Install in the reverse order of removal.

Water Pump

REMOVAL AND INSTALLATION

1. Drain the engine coolant.
2. Remove the air cleaner.
3. Loosen, but do not remove, the water pump pulley bolts.
4. Remove the alternator drivebelt.
5. Remove the water pump pulley.
6. Remove the pump.
7. Separate the pump body from the casing.
8. Installation is the reverse of removal.

Thermostat

REMOVAL AND INSTALLATION

CAUTION

The thermostat is equipped with a plunger which covers and uncovers a by-pass hole at its bottom. Because of this unusual construction, only the specified Mazda thermostat should be used for replacement. A standard thermostat will cause the engine to overheat.

1. Drain the engine coolant.
2. Remove the thermostat housing and the thermostat.
3. Installation is the reverse of removal.

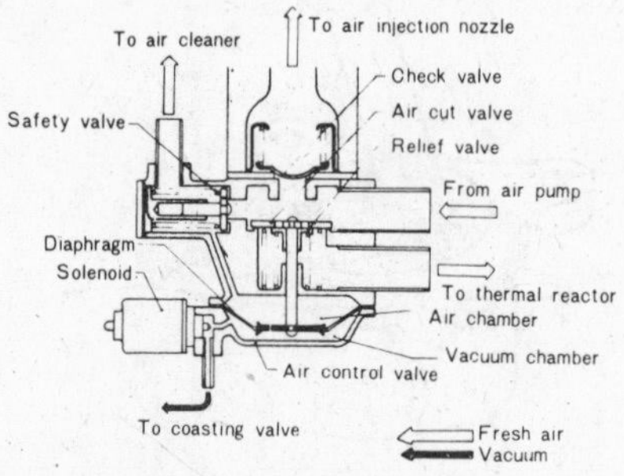

Thermostat installation and by-pass circuit (© Toyo Kogyo Co. Ltd.)

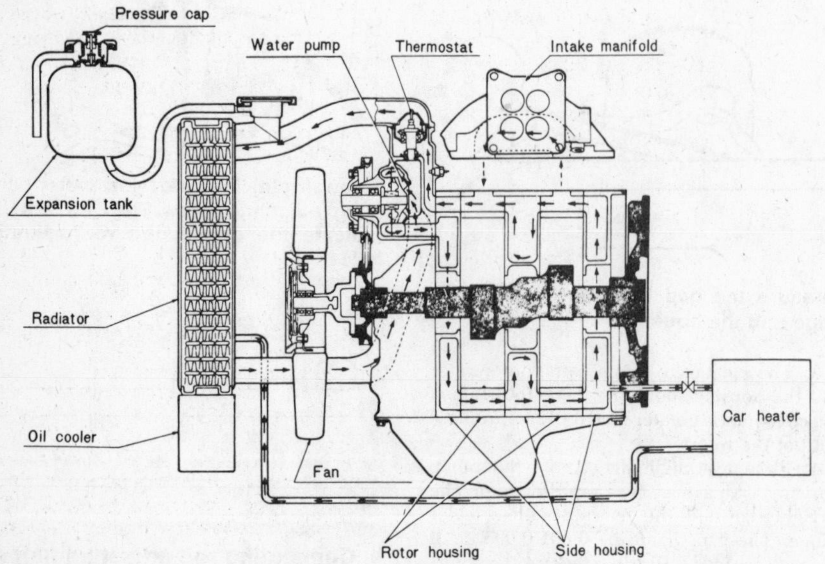

Cooling system (© Toyo Kogyo Co. Ltd.)

ENGINE MECHANICAL PISTON ENGINE

The Mazda piston engines are four cylinder, chain driven single overhead camshaft operating double rocker arm assemblies. The engines are water cooled and lubricated by a chain driven oil pump. Five main bearings support the crankshaft. Varied displacement engines are used in the Mazda models.

1. 96.8 cu. in.—1586 cc
2. 77.6 cu. in.—1272 cc
3. 120.2 cu. in.—1970 cc
4. 86.4 cu. in.—1415 cc
5. 90.9 cu. in.—1490 cc

The varied engines are constructed basically the same, but with many external differences, such as distributor and fuel pump locations, carburetor usages and Emission Control components. Many differences exist internally and the manufacturer sources must be consulted before any attempt is made to interchange internal parts.

Engine Assembly

REMOVAL AND INSTALLATION

Rear Wheel Drive

The engine is removed separately, leaving the transmission in place.

1. Remove the hood.
2. Remove the engine splash shield.
3. Drain the coolant.
4. Drain the engine oil.
5. Disconnect all electrical wires and leads. Remove battery.
6. Disconnect all fluid lines and hoses.
7. Remove the air cleaner.
8. Unbolt and remove the radiator and cowling.
9. Disconnect the throttle cable from the carburetor and remove the throttle linkage from the rocker cover.
10. Disconnect the choke cable.
11. Remove the starter.
12. Disconnect the exhaust pipe.
13. Remove the clutch cover plate. Support the transmission.
14. Unbolt the right and left engine mounts.
15. Attach a lifting sling to the engine and pull the engine forward until it clears the clutch shaft.
16. Lift the engine from the vehicle.
17. Installation is the reverse of removal.

1981 GLC–Front Wheel Drive

The engine/transaxle assembly is removed from under the vehicle as a unit. The assembly is attached to the body by four rubber engine mounts, two bolted between the engine and the crossmember at the bottom, and the other two bolted between the engine and the body at the left and right side at the top, to stabilize the engine while operating.

NOTE: The 1981 GLC is a front wheel drive vehicle with the engine-transaxle positioned transversely in the front of the body.

No standard procedure has been developed for the removal and installation of the engine/transaxle assembly at time of printing, but the assembly can be removed and installed by a repairman, skilled in R & R procedures for front wheel drive vehicles, by adapting the various procedures needed. A general removal and installation procedure is outlined with precautions noted as required.

1. Lift the vehicle as required and support safely. Drain the coolant, oils and disconnect the battery from the electrical system.
2. Disconnect all electrical wiring and connections, fuel lines, coolant hoses and control linkages from the engine and transaxle. Mark the wiring for ease of reconnection.
3. Remove the front wheels and disconnect the lower ball joints from the steering knuckles.
4. Pull the driveshafts from the differential gears.

NOTE: A circlip is positioned on the driveshaft ends and engages in a groove, machined in the differential side gears. The driveshafts may have to be forced from the differential housing to release the clip from the groove.

CAUTION

Do not allow the driveshafts to drop. Damage may occur to the ball and socket joints and to the rubber boots. Wire the shafts to the vehicle body when released from the differential.

5. Position a lifting device under the engine/transaxle assembly crossmember and remove the Numbers 3 and 4 engine mounts from the engine compartment, or disconnect.
6. Unbolt the crossmember and lower the engine/transaxle assembly from the vehicle.
7. The installation of the engine/ transaxle assembly is in the reverse of the removal procedure.
8. When installing the assembly in place and before tightening the crossmember bolts, attach the Numbers 3 and 4 mounts loosely. Tighten the crossmember bolts and then the Numbers 3 and 4 attaching bolts.

CAUTION

Be sure the rubber mounts are not twisted or distorted and not in contact with the body.

9. To properly install the driveshafts in the differential side gears, position the open end of the circlip in the up position, and with the driveshaft in a horizontal position, push the driveshafts into the side gears. To be sure the circlip engages the groove, a sound may be heard or attempt to pull the driveshaft from the differential. Reconnect the ball joints at the lower arms.
10. Complete the assembly, connecting all lines, wires and hoses. Fill the coolant and oil reservoirs to their proper levels.

Cylinder Head

REMOVAL AND INSTALLATION

Be sure that the cylinder head is cold before removal. This will prevent warpage. Do not remove the cam gear from the timing chain. The relationship between the chain and gear teeth should not be distrubed.

1. Drain the cooling system.
2. Remove the air cleaner.
3. Disconnect all applicable electrical wires and leads.
4. Rotate the crankshaft to put the No. 1 cylinder at TDC on the compression stroke.
5. Remove the distributor.
6. Remove the rocker arm cover.
7. Raise and support the vehicle. Disconnect the exhaust pipe from the manifold.
8. Remove the accelerator linkage.
9. Remove the nut, washer and the distributor gear from the camshaft.
10. Remove the nut, washer and camshaft gear.
11. Remove the cylinder head bolts and cylinder head-to-front cover bolt.
12. Remove the rocker arm assembly.
13. Remove the camshaft from the camshaft gear.
14. Lift off the cylinder head.
15. Installation is the reverse of removal. Adjust the chain tension, and valves.

Valve Guide

REMOVAL AND INSTALLATION

Consult the "Engine Rebuilding" section for general procedures that will apply.

Rocker Shafts

REMOVAL AND INSTALLATION

This operation should only be performed on a cold engine; the bolts which hold the rocker shafts in place also hold the cylinder head to the block.

1. Disconnect the choke cable.
2. If equipped, disconnect the air by-pass valve cable.
3. Remove the rocker cover.
4. Remove the rocker arm shaft attaching bolts.
5. Installation is the reverse of removal. Install the rocker arm assemblies on the cylinder head. Temporarily tighten the cylinder head bolts to specifications and offset each rocker arm support 0.04 in. from the valve stem center.

Intake Manifold

REMOVAL AND INSTALLATION

1. Drain the cooling system.
2. Remove the air cleaner.
3. Remove the accelerator linkage.
4. Disconnect the choke cable and fuel line.
5. Disconnect the PCV valve hose.
6. Disconnect the heater return hose and by-pass hose.
7. Remove the intake manifold-to-cylinder head attaching nuts.
8. Remove the manifold and carburetor as an assembly.
9. Installation is the reverse of removal.

Exhaust Manifold

REMOVAL AND INSTALLATION

1. Remove the two attaching nuts from the exhaust pipe at the manifold.
2. Remove the retaining nuts and remove the manifold.
3. Installation is the reverse of removal.

Front Cover

REMOVAL AND INSTALLATION

1. Drain the cooling system.
2. Remove the radiator.
3. Remove the accessory drive belts.
4. Remove the crankshaft pulley and the water pump.
5. Remove the cylinder head-to-front cover bolt.
6. Remove the engine skid plate.
7. Disconnect the emission line from the oil pan. Drain the oil.
8. Remove the oil pan.
9. Remove the alternator and bracket and lay the alternator aside.
10. Remove the steel tube from the front of the engine.
11. Unbolt and remove the front cover.
12. Installation is the reverse of removal.

Front Cover Oil Seal

REMOVAL AND INSTALLATION

The front cover oil seal can be removed and a new one installed without removing the front cover.

1. Drain the cooling system.
2. Remove the radiator.
3. Remove the drive belt(s).
4. Remove the crankshaft pulley.
5. Pry the front oil seal from the front cover.
6. Installation is the reverse of removal.

Timing Chain and Tensioner

REMOVAL AND INSTALLATION

Remove the cylinder head and front cover. It is not necessary that the intake and exhaust manifolds be removed from the head. When installing be sure valve timing is as illustrated. Move the cam gear to obtain exact alignment.

1. Remove the oil pump and chain.
2. Remove the timing chain tensioner.

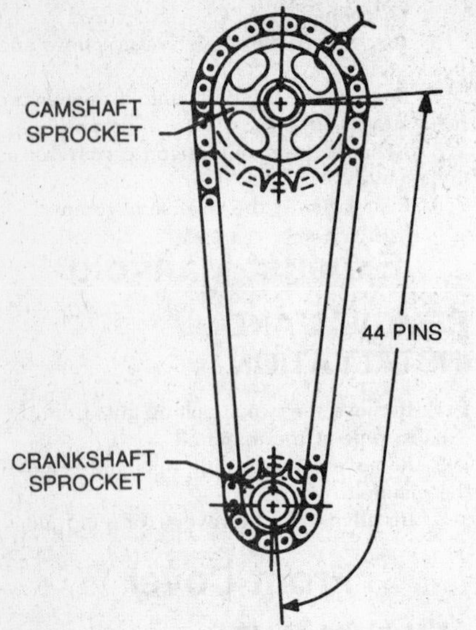

Installing timing chain, 1796 cc piston engine

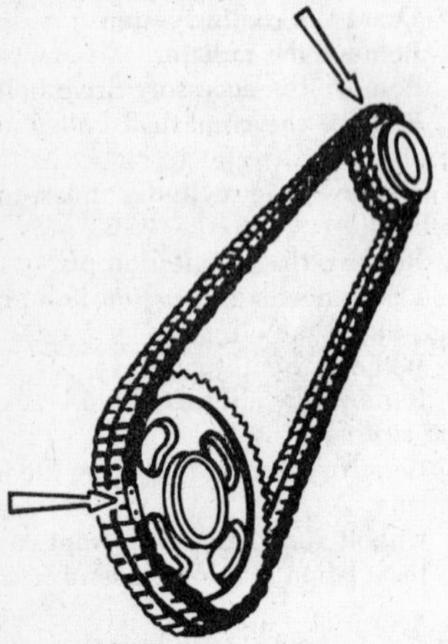

Align the bright links and the marks, 1586 cc piston engine

3. Loosen the timing chain guide strip screws.
4. Remove the oil slinger.
5. Remove the oil pump gear and chain as an assembly.
6. Remove the timing chain, crankshaft gear and camshaft gears from the engine.

To install the timing chain, timing gears and tensioner:

7. Position the crankshaft gear in the timing chain.
8. Position the oil pump chain and gear on the crankshaft and oil pump. Check the oil pump drive chain slack. It should be 0.15 in. Adjusting shims (between the oil pump body and cylinder block) are available in thickness of 0.006 in.
9. Install the oil slinger.
10. Install the oil pump washer and nut. Bend the washer over the nut.
11. Install the timing chain tensioner. Fully compress the snubber spring and wedge a screwdriver into the tensioner release mechanism. Without removing the screwdriver, install the tensioner.
12. Further installation is the reverse of removal.

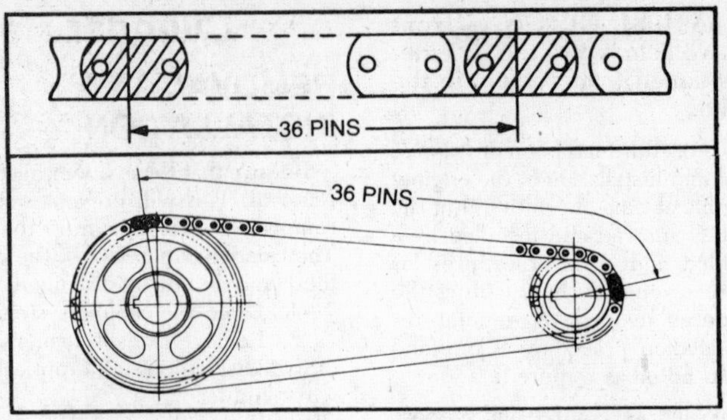

Installing timing chain, 1272 cc piston engine (© Toyo Kogyo Co. Ltd.)

Timing Chain Tensioner

REMOVAL, INSTALLATION AND ADJUSTMENT

Front Cover Installed

1. Remove the water pump. (Early engines).
2. Remove the tensioner cover.
3. Remove the attaching bolts from the tensioner. Remove the tensioner.

To install the tensioner:

4. Fully compress the snubber spring. Insert a screwdriver into the tensioner release mechanism.
5. Without removing the screwdriver, insert the tensioner and align the bolt holes. Install and torque the bolts.
6. Adjust the chain tension as follows:
   a. Remove the two blind plugs and aluminum washers from the front cover.
   b. Loosen the guide strip attaching screws.
   c. Press the top of the chain guide strip through the adjusting hole in the cylinder head.
   d. Tighten the guide strip attaching screws.
   e. Remove the screwdriver from the tensioner and let the snubber take up the slack in the chain.
   f. Install the blind plugs and aluminum washers.
   g. Install the tensioner cover and gasket.
   h. Install a new gasket and water pump, if removed. Install the crankshaft pulley and drive belt and adjust the tension. Check the cooling system level.

Camshaft

REMOVAL AND INSTALLATION

Perform this operation on a cold engine only. Do not remove the camshaft gear from the timing chain. Be sure that the gear teeth and chain relationship is not disturbed. Wire the chain and cam gear to a place so that they will not fall into the front cover.

1. Remove the water pump if necessary.
2. Rotate the crankshaft to place the No. 1 cylinder on TDC of the compression stroke.
3. Remove the distributor.
4. Remove the valve cover.
5. Release the tension on the timing chain.
6. Remove the cylinder head bolts.
7. Remove the rocker arm assembly.
8. Remove the nut, washer and distributor gear from the camshaft.
9. Remove the nut and washer holding the camshaft gear.
10. Remove the camshaft.
11. Installation is the reverse of removal. End-play should be 0.001-0.007 in.

Pistons and Connecting Rods Positioning

REMOVAL AND INSTALLATION

Refer to the "Engine Rebuilding" section for general engine service.

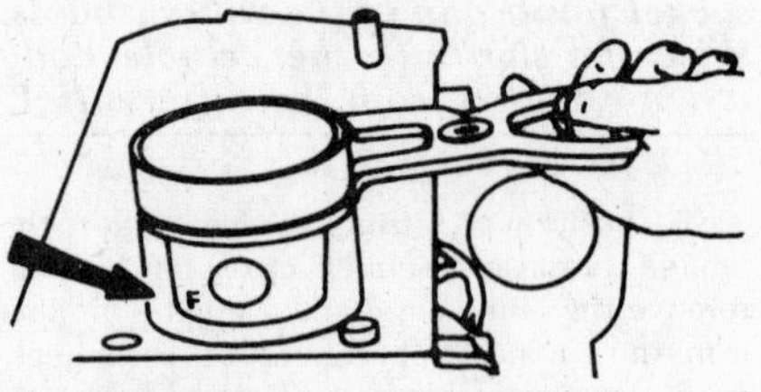

The "F" marks (arrow) face the front of the engine

ENGINE LUBRICATION—PISTON ENGINE

Oil Pan

REMOVAL AND INSTALLATION

Remove the clutch release cylinder and let the cylinder hang. Remove the engine rear brace attaching bolts and loosen the bolts on the left-side. Disconnect the emission line from the oil pan.

Remove the oil pan and rest it on the crossmember. Remove the oil pump pickup tube. Remove the oil pan.

Installation is the reverse of removal.

Rear Main Oil Seal

REPLACEMENT

If the rear main oil seal is being replaced independently of any other parts, it can be done with the engine in place. If the rear main oil seal and the rear main bearing are being replaced, together, the engine must be removed.

1. Remove the transmission.
2. Remove the clutch disc, pressure plate and flywheel.
3. Punch two holes in the crankshaft rear oil seal. They should be punched on opposite sides of the crankshaft, just above the bearing cap-to-cylinder block split line.
4. Install a sheet metal screw in each hole. Pry against both screws at the same time to remove the oil seal.
5. Clean the oil recess in the cylinder block and bearing cap. Clean the oil seal surface on the crankshaft.
6. Coat the oil seal surfaces with oil. Coat the oil surface and the seal surface on the crankshaft with Lubriplate. Install the new oil seal and make sure that it is not cocked. Be sure that the seal surface was not damaged.
7. Install the flywheel. Coat the threads of the flywheel attaching bolts with oil-resistant sealer.
8. Install the clutch, pressure plate and transmission.

Oil Pump

CHECKING OIL PUMP

1. Measure the clearance between the lobes of the rotors. If the clearance exceeds 0.010 in., replace both rotors.
2. Check the clearance between the outer rotor and the pump body. Clearance should be 0.006-0.010 in. If it exceeds 0.012 in., replace the pump.
3. Place a straight-edge across the pump body and measure the clearance between the rotor and the straight-edge. Place a straight-edge across the pump cover and measure the clearance between the straight-edge and the cover. The combined clearances is the rotor end-play. If it is 0.006 in. or more, correct it by grinding the cover. End-play should be 0.002-0.004 in.

REMOVAL AND INSTALLATION

Remove the oil pan. Remove the oil pump gear attaching nut. Remove the bolts attaching the oil pump to the block. Loosen the gear on the pump. Remove the oil pump and gear.

Installation is the reverse of removal.

ENGINE COOLING—PISTON ENGINE

Radiator

REMOVAL AND INSTALLATION

1. Drain the cooling system.
2. Remove the fan shroud.
3. Remove the fan. On California models, remove the fan clutch.
4. Unbolt and remove the radiator.
5. Installation is the reverse of removal.

Water Pump

REMOVAL AND INSTALLATION

All, Except 1981 GLC

1. Drain the cooling system.
2. Remove the lower hose.
3. Remove the radiator where required.
4. Remove the drive belts.
5. Remove the fan and pulley. Remove the crankshaft pulley.
6. Unbolt and remove the water pump.
7. Installation is the reverse of removal.

1981 GLC

The water pump is bolted to the radiator side of the engine block and is driven by a v-belt from the crankshaft. A thermostatically controlled electric fan is used for the radiator cooling.

1. To remove and install the pump, disconnect the lower radiator hose and the heater return pipe from the pump body.
2. Remove the pump body attaching bolts and remove the pump from the engine block. Clean the old gasket from the mating surfaces.
3. To install, use a new gasket and bolt the pump body to the engine block.
4. Attach the lower radiator hose and the heater return pipe to the pump body. Fill the system with coolant. Install the drive belt and adjust. Start the engine and check for leakage.

NOTE: Heater return pipe uses a rubber O-ring to seal pipe to water pump.

Thermostat

REMOVAL AND INSTALLATION

Drain enough coolant to bring the coolant level down below the thermostat housing. The thermostat housing is located on the left front side of the cylinder block. Disconnect the temperature sending unit wire.

EMISSION CONTROLS

The Emission Control System is separated into three different categories.

1. Crankcase emission control system
2. Evaporative emission control system
3. Engine exhaust gas emission control system

The three sub-systems vary in application on the vehicle models, depending upon the areas in which the vehicle is to be operated, such as Federal, California, High Altitude or Canada. The engine/ transmission applications will vary the requirements needed to comply with the Federal or State regulations.

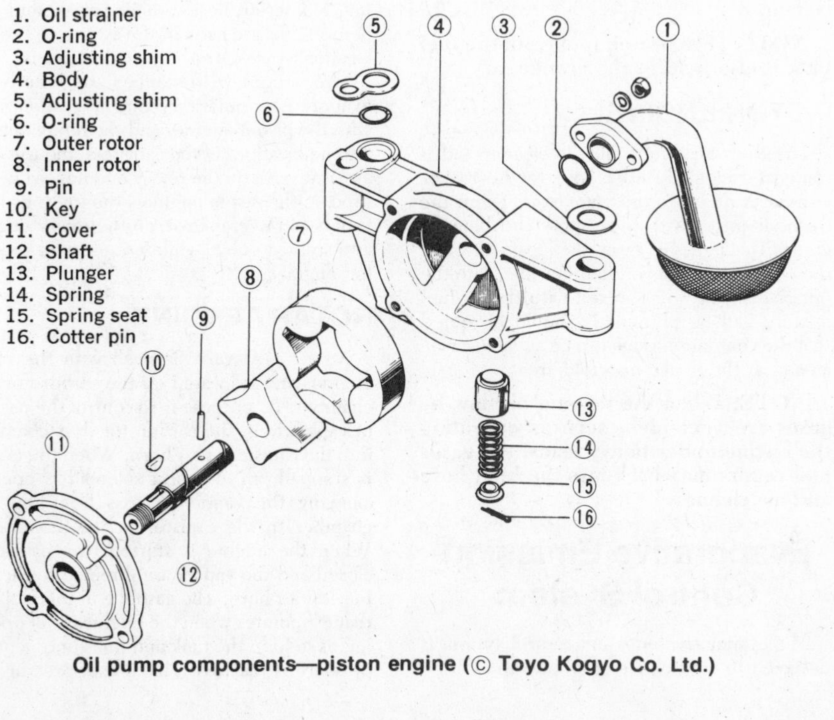

Oil pump components—piston engine (© Toyo Kogyo Co. Ltd.)

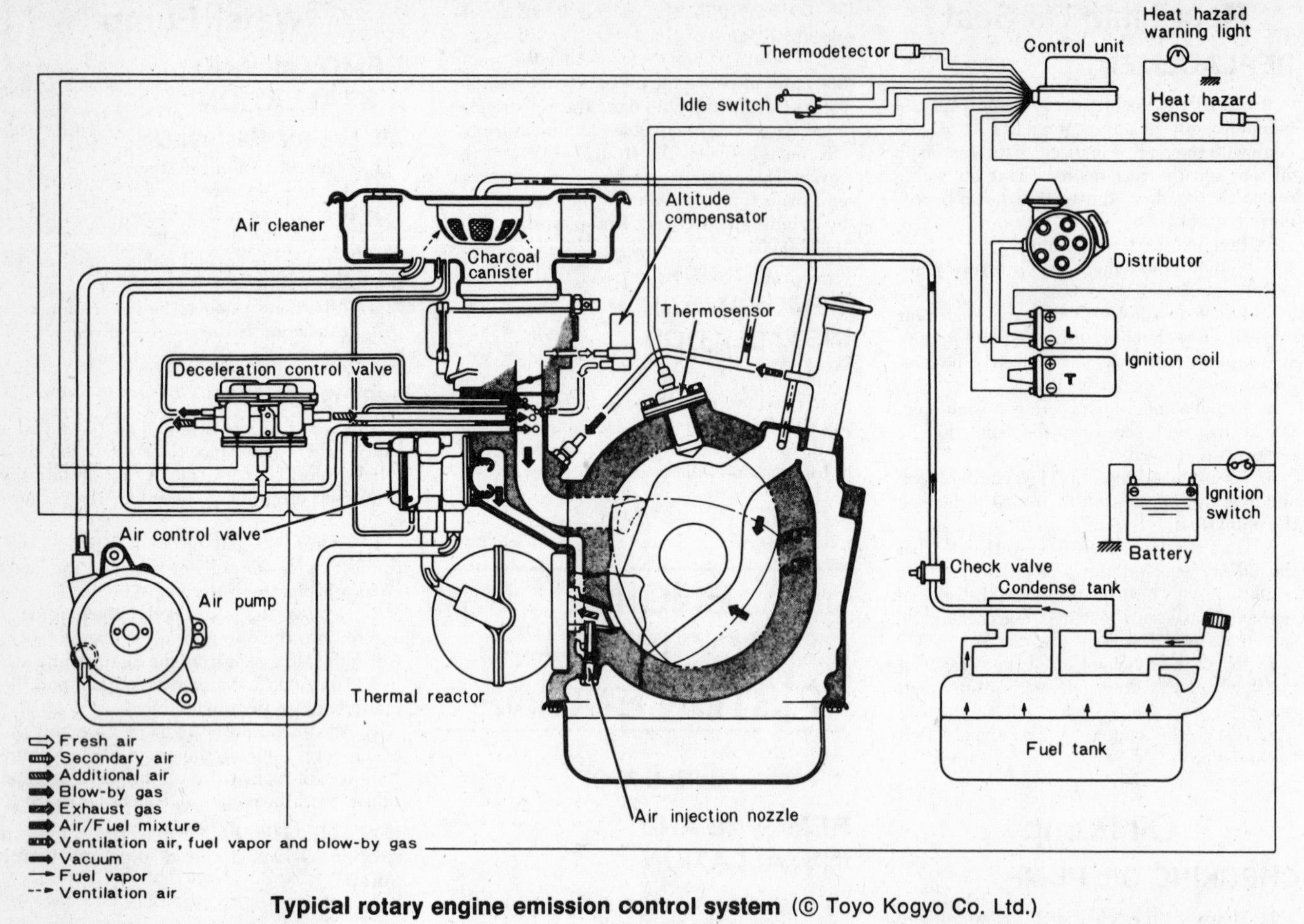

Typical rotary engine emission control system (© Toyo Kogyo Co. Ltd.)

Crankcase Emission Control System

The crankcase emission control system is a closed system, maintaining a specific ventilation in the crankcase and positively prevents vapors from being emitted to the atmosphere by being recirculated to the combustion chamber for burning with the air/fuel mixture.

ROTARY ENGINE

The fresh air enters the air cleaner and is routed through the inlet hose and into the engine air space. The fresh air then mixes with the blow-by gases and any other vapors in the engine air space. The blow-by gases then pass through the outlet hose and ventilation valve, to be routed to the intake manifold and to be mixed with the air/fuel mixture and be burned.

NOTE: Evaporated fuel from the fuel tank is also held in the crankcase.

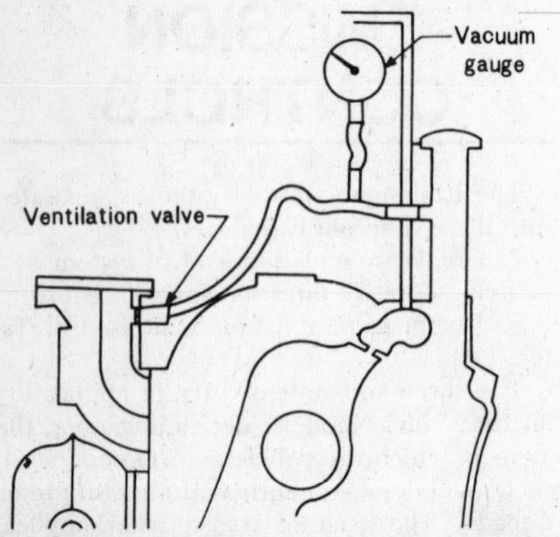

Testing the PCV valve (© Toyo Kogyo Co. Ltd.)

PISTON ENGINE

The fresh air enters the air cleaner and is routed through the inlet hose to the rocker arm cover and into the crankcase. There the fresh air mixes with the vapors and blow-by gases. The blow-by gases then pass through the outlet hose and ventilation valve, into the intake manifold to be mixed with the air/fuel mixture and be burned. It should be noted that the ventilation valve can be at valve cover area or at the intake manifold area.

NOTE: When the volume of blow-by gases are very high, such as operating the engine under heavy loads, the gases and vapors may back into the inlet hose and air cleaner.

Evaporative Emission Control System

The evaporative emission control system is designed to control the gasoline vapors from the carburetor and fuel tank areas, from entering the atmosphere. The vapors are stored in a canister containing activated carbon (charcoal) while the engine is stopped and are drawn into the intake manifold to be burned with the air/fuel mixture, when the engine is operating. Numerous hoses, check valves, and condense tanks are used in the systems. Size and locations vary with the vehicle models.

The major differences between the evaporative emission control system used with the piston engines and the rotary engines are the locations of the canisters, the use of an air vent valve on the rotary engines, while not used on the piston engines, the routing of fuel vapors to the crankcase on the rotary engines as a storage point, while not used on the piston engines.

ROTARY ENGINE

An air vent valve is used with the rotary engines and is located on the carburetor float chamber. Its purpose is to control the passage of vapors from the carburetor float chamber, into the canister or air horn. When the engine is stopped, an electrical solenoid is opened, allowing the vapors to pass from the float chamber to the canister in the air cleaner. When the engine is started, the passage is closed and the vapors are directed to the carburetor air horn. The gasoline in the fuel tank that evaporates when the engine is not operating, is held in the tank and lines until a preset pressure is reached. This preset pressure operates the check valve in the ventilation and check valve assembly, allowing the excess gasoline vapors to be routed to the crankcase and to the canister, where it is held until the engine is started and then burned with the air/fuel mixture.

A check and cut valve is used in the vapor line and has three functions. When the pressure in the fuel tank becomes high, the check valve opens to the atmosphere and release the excess pressure. When the negative pressure in the tank becomes high, the check valve again opens and allows atmosphere pressure to enter and equalize the inner and outer pressures. The third function of the valve is to prevent fuel from flowing out, should the vehicle overturn.

PISTON ENGINES

The system for the piston engines consists of either condensing tanks or spaces for the fuel vapors to be collected and be condensed back into fuel and returned to the fuel tank. The vapors that are not condensed are routed through a check valve and into a canister containing activated charcoal which absorbs the vapors. When the engine is started, the vapors are drawn into the intake manifold, mixed with the air/fuel mixture and burned. The check valve is used to prevent negative pressure in the tank and to open at a specific point to allow atmosphere pressure to flow into the tank. When positive pressures build up in the tank and the canister and lines can accept no more vapors, the check valve will open at a specific pressure and allow a controlled release of the pressure from the tank to avoid tank damage.

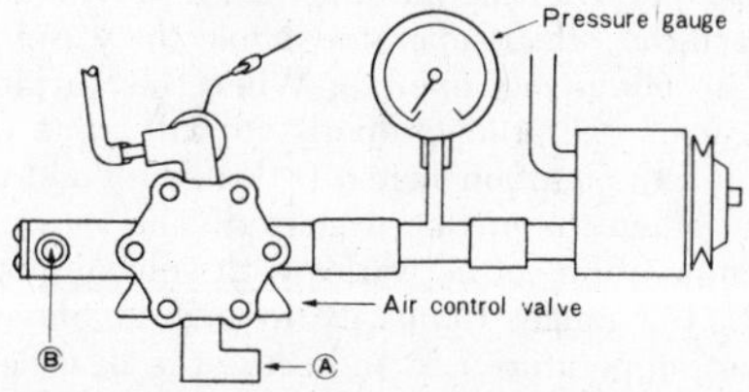

Testing the air control valve (© Toyo Kogyo Co. Ltd.)

Engine Exhaust Emission Control System

AIR INJECTION AND THERMAL REACTOR SYSTEM

Rotary Engines

This system is designed to direct fresh air (secondary air) into the hot exhaust gases, just released from the combustion chambers and into the thermal reactor, through the exhaust ports. The purpose of the addition of fresh air to the exhaust is to completely burn the HC and CO contained in the exhaust gases. The fresh air is supplied by an air pump, driven by the engine. The air is directed through lines and a check valve, to the thermal reactor. The thermal reactor is a chamber to maintain the temperature of hot gases as high as possible to facilitate reaction between the hot gases and the fresh or secondary air. The check valve also performs the function of preventing the exhaust gases from backflowing into the air pump and causing damage.

The check valve or air control valve, contains three valves. A Number one relief valve, a Number two relief valve and an anti-afterburn valve. The Numbers one and two relief valves control the air from the air pump according to engine needs, determined by engine speed and load.

NUMBER ONE RELIEF VALVE OPERATION

Excessive high heat can cause the thermal reactor to deteriorate rapidly, because of the high temperatures, needed to burn the unburned elements in the exhaust gases. The function of the Number one relief valve is to aid in the cooling of the outer jacket of the thermal reactor when air pressure in the system becomes higher than specified. The operation of the Number one relief valve is the same for vehicles, so equipped.

NUMBER TWO RELIEF VALVE OPERATION FEDERAL AND CANADA

The number two relief valve is closed when the engine rpm is below 1500. When the engine speed is increased to over 1500 rpm, the relief valve is opened by intake manifold vacuum, controlled by the engine load. As the relief valve is opened, the air from the air pump is directed to the air cleaner, rather than to the thermal reactor.

CALIFORNIA

The relief valve remains closed under the following conditions.

1. When the engine is below 1500 rpm.
2. When the choke knob is fully pulled.
3. When accelerating in any gears except 4th and 5th within 130 seconds after engine starting with the choke used.
4. When accelerating in any gears except 4th and 5th, after the 130 seconds, with the engine rpm below 3000.

Under any other conditions than those listed above, the valve opens and releases part of the air from the air pump into the air cleaner, accordingly to the vacuum signal to the valve, which is controlled by the load applied to the engine. The result is a balanced air-exhaust gas mixture required for the reburning of the exhaust gases in the thermal reactor.

AIR INJECTION SYSTEM DIAGNOSIS CHART

Problem	Cause	Cure
1. Noisy drive belt	1a. Loose belt 1b. Seized pump	1a. Tighten belt 1b. Replace
2. Noisy pump	2a. Leaking hose 2b. Loose hose 2c. Hose contacting other parts 2d. Air control or check valve failure 2e. Pump mounting loose 2g. Defective pump	2a. Trace and fix leak 2b. Tighten hose clamp 2c. Reposition hose 2d. Replace 2e. Tighten securing bolts 2g. Replace
3. No air supply	3a. Loose belt 3b. Leak in hose or at fitting 3c. Defective air control valve 3d. Defective check valve 3e. Defective pump	3a. Tighten belt 3b. Trace and fix leak 3c. Replace 3d. Replace 3e. Replace
4. Exhaust backfire	4a. Vacuum or air leaks 4b. Defective air control valve 4c. Sticking choke 4d. Choke setting rich	4a. Trace and fix leak 4b. Replace 4c. Service choke 4d. Adjust choke

SPLIT-AIR SYSTEM (1981)

Rotary Engines

A new system, using the air injection principle and major components, eliminates the thermal reactor, but uses two catalytic converters in its place. A reactive exhaust manifold is bolted to the engine and acts as a chamber to combust the unburned Hydrocarbons (HC) and Carbon Monoxide (CO) by the addition of fresh or secondary air. The exhaust gases then pass through the first of the two catalysts, a monolith type, and then through the second, which is a two bed, pellet type. The air pump is driven by the engine with the air flow controlled by an air control valve, which directs the fresh air to either the exhaust port, the pellet catalyst or to the engine air cleaner assembly, as required by the engine speed and/or load.

During the operation of the engine at low speeds, when the HC and the CO pollutants are produced in larger amounts, the air is directed to the engine exhaust port to begin the oxidization of the HC and CO in the exhaust port and to continue in the 1st and 2nd catalytic converters.

With the engine operating at mid-range speeds, the air control valve directs the fresh air to the pellet or second converter. The air from the air pump is injected through a nozzle located between the two pellet beds and stopped from entering the exhaust port manifold. The front pellet bed acts as a three way catalyst, primarily taking care of the oxides of nitrogen (NO_x), while the rear bed with the split air continues to oxidize HC and CO pollutants.

The function of the 1st or monolith catalyst, consisting of a small capacity platinum and rhodium base three-way catalyst, is as a back-up unit, for the reactive exhaust manifold to oxidize the increased amounts of HC and CO pollutants. It is also used to heat up the exhaust gases, shorten the warm-up time of the pellet catalyst so that it will reach full operating capacity in a shorter period of time.

Low inherent NO_x emissions are experienced with the rotary engine. With this air injected system used, there is no need for the exhaust gas recirculation (EGR) valve, normally used to control the NO_x.

Piston Engines

The air injection system is used to inject fresh or secondary air into the exhaust manifold for the purpose of reburning the unburned elements in the exhaust gases. The system consists of the air pump, air injection manifold, air injection nozzles, (one for each cylinder), port liners, air control valve, control unit and heat hazard sensor.

Certain vehicles do not use the control unit or the sensors, but rely upon the vacuum signal from the engine intake manifold to the control valve, to direct the fresh or secondary air to the injection nozzles or to the air cleaner assembly. A second type of air injection system is used. This system does not use the air pump, but relies upon the pulse of the exhaust gases to draw fresh air into the exhaust manifold through a one-way reed valve.

AIR INJECTION SYSTEM WITH CONTROL UNIT

The air pump is supplied fresh air from the air cleaner and directs the air, under pressure, to the air control valve. The control valve has two valves, Number one relief valve which controls the exhausting of the compressed air to the atmosphere when the engine speed is over 4000 rpm or when the floor temperature reaches 302° F. The Number two relief valve controls the injection of fresh or secondary air into the exhaust manifold by the intake manifold vacuum signals, dependent upon the speed and the load of the engine.

The electric control switch (engine speed switch) sends the electrical signal to the solenoid valve of the air control valve to release the fresh or secondary air and to prevent heat damage to the exhaust system when the engine speed is over 4000 rpm. The heat hazard switch sends an electrical signal to the solenoid valve of the air control valve, to release the fresh or secondary air to the atmosphere to prevent heat damage to the floor when the floor temperature reaches 302° F from the exhaust system burning of the unburned elements in the exhaust gases.

Two check valves are used. The check valve on the injection pipes is used to prevent the backflow of exhaust gases into the air pump, while the check valve for the Number one relief valve controls the intake manifold vacuum to the Number one relief valve of the air control valve, accordingly to the engine load and speed.

AIR INJECTION AND CATALYTIC CONVERTER SYSTEM

Reed Valve Operation

This system inducts fresh or secondary air into hot gases, flowing into the exhaust system from the cylinder head exhaust ports, for the purpose of reburning the unburned elements of the exhaust gases. A catalytic converter is used to convert the hydrocarbons (HC) and the carbon monoxide (CO), contained in the exhaust gases, into harmless water (H_2O) and carbon dioxide (CO_2).

The system consists of a reed valve, air distribution manifold, air injection nozzles, air silencer and catalytic converter.

The reed valve is operated by the exhaust gas pulsations to induct the fresh or secondary air into the exhaust ports from the air cleaner assembly. A silencer is used in the air cleaner to insulate the noise of the reed valve during its operation. The air manifold divides and distributes the inducted air to the injection nozzles, one for each cylinder, and placed to direct the injected fresh air into the hot gases discharged from the cylinder head exhaust ports. As the exhaust gases are directed through the exhaust system, the gases enter the catalytic converter. The inducted air continues the combustion of the unburned elements in the exhaust gases and the catalytic converter converts the remaining hydrocarbons (HC) and carbon monoxide (CO) into harmless water (H_2O) and carbon dioxide (CO_2).

Air Pump Operation

The operation of the air injection and catalytic converter system, using an air pump is virtually the same as the air injected system, with the exception of the addition of a catalytic converter to the exhaust system. The air pump is used in place of the reed valve to inject a more positive force of fresh air into the exhaust gases. The electric control box may or may not be used in this type of system, along with the floor heat hazard warning system.

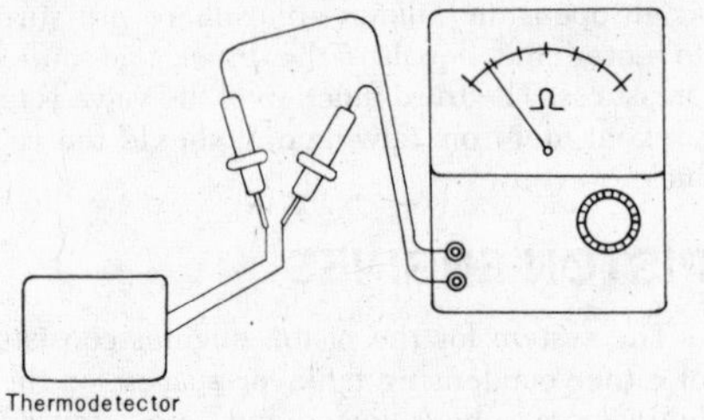

Testing the thermodetector (© Toyo Kogyo Co. Ltd.)

HEAT HAZARD WARNING SYSTEM

The heat hazard warning system is used to prevent potential heat hazard to the vehicle due to the excessive heat radiated from the exhaust system and the catalytic converter. A test system for the warning light is provided to warn the vehicle operator should the warning lamp circuit not operate. When the warning lamp is operating properly, it will come on when the ignition switch is turned on and go out when the engine is started. The warning temperature setting varies with vehicle models, but ranges from 212° to 302° F. Should the temperature rise and cause the heat hazard warning system to operate, the fresh or secondary air is directed from the exhaust system to deny the exhaust gases the fresh air to continue the combustion of the unburned elements in the exhaust system and the catalytic converter, which in turn, lowers the heat from the exhaust system.

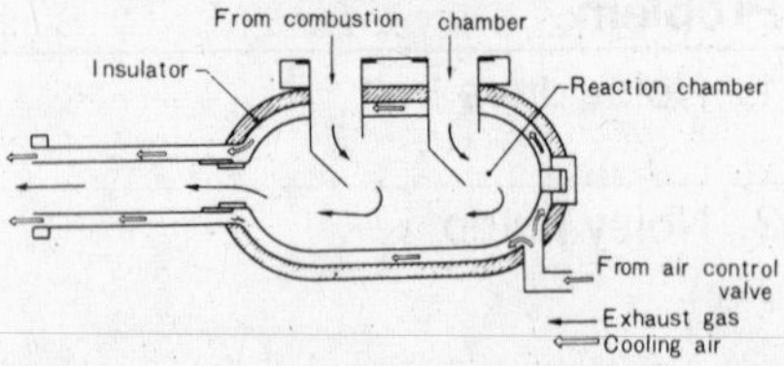

Thermal reactor cooling circuit (© Toyo Kogyo Co. Ltd.)

Catalytic Converters

Various catalytic converter configurations are used from the monolithic (block type) to the pellet type, each containing, but not limited to, platinum, palladium and rhodium as the catalyst. The construction of the various converters differ, depending upon the vehicle model usage, but the main purposes of the units are to reduce the oxides of nitrogens (NO_x) and to oxidize the hydrocarbons (HC) and carbon monoxide (CO) into harmless water (H_2O) and carbon dioxide (CO_2).

CATALYTIC CONVERTER PRECAUTIONS

1. Unleaded fuel must be used to avoid contaminating the converter catalyst.
2. Do not park the vehicle over inflammable materials.
3. Do not operate the engine with the spark plug wires disconnected.
4. Do not coast the vehicle with the ignition switch turned off and the engine internal parts rotating.
5. Avoid driving with the choke control knob (manual) pulled out with the engine warmed up.

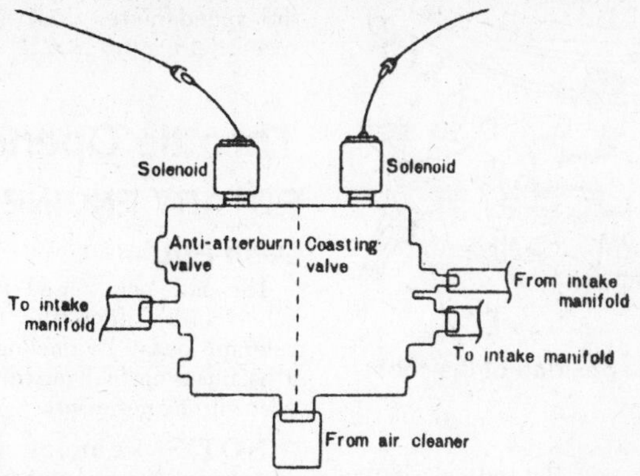

Combination anti-afterburn and coasting valve connections (© Toyo Kogyo Co. Ltd.)

Deceleration Control System

ROTARY ENGINES

The deceleration control system is designed to maintain a balanced air/fuel mixture and to prevent excessive afterburn in the exhaust system. The system uses a deceleration control valve, idle switch and control unit. The deceleration control valve contains two valves; one, the anti-afterburn valve which prevents the fuel detonation and two, the coasting valve which compensates for the insufficient air/fuel mixtures. Both valves will allow fresh air to enter the intake manifold to prevent the exhaust afterburn, when the ignition switch is turned off. At the beginning of sudden deceleration, rich air/fuel mixture is present in the intake manifold and is supplied to the cylinders. This excessively rich mixture does not completely burn in the combustion chambers and when this unburned rich mixture is discharged into the exhaust manifold and the injected fresh air is mixed with it, an undesirable combustion type explosion occurs in the exhaust system. To prevent this occurance in the exhaust system, the anti-afterburn valve permits fresh air to enter the intake manifold upon sudden increase of the manifold vacuum and the fresh air mixes with the over-rich mixture of air and fuel, reducing the mixture to a combustible mixture so that it can be burned normally in the engine combustion chambers.

The system consists of the following.

1. Anti-afterburn valve–allows fresh air to enter the intake manifold.
2. Coasting valve–allows fresh air to enter the intake manifold.
3. Solenoids–when energized, close the air passages for the anti-afterburn and coasting valves air chambers.
4. Idle switch–detects decelerating conditions and cuts the electric current from the ignition switch to the coasting valve, through the control unit.
5. Control unit–detects the operational mode condition and sends the signals to the solenoids.

The afterburn and coasting valves operate under the following conditions.

1. Immediately after the ignition switch is turned off. When the ignition switch is turned off, the solenoids for the two valves are turned off, which allows the air chambers to open. Atmospheric pressure acts on the diaphragms to open the valves. As a result, fresh air is allowed to enter the intake manifold for a brief period of time.

NOTE: On California and Federal models with automatic transmissions, the coasting valve is closed and cannot operate.

2. Immediately after deceleration–anti-afterburn valve. Immediately after deceleration, the anti-afterburn valve is opened by a difference of pressures between the air chamber and the vacuum chamber. The solenoid on the valve is not off, but is turned on by the ignition switch being in the "ON" position. As the intake manifold pressure is increased, the diaphragm is pulled down and the valve is opened to supply fresh air to the intake manifold, momentarily. The metering orifice controls the time of valve operation (open) as the vacum equalizes through the top of the diaphragm.
3. Immediately after deceleration–coasting valve. During deceleration over 1150 rpm of engine speed, the coasting valve is opened by the difference of pressure between the atmospheric pressure in the air chamber and the vacuum pressure in the vacuum chamber. The electrical signals from the idle switch and the control unit are not sent to the coasting valve solenoid, which allows the air passage to be opened to the air chamber of the coasting valve diaphragm. As a result, the coasting valve is opened by the pressure difference between the air chamber and the vacuum chamber, which in turn, allows air to enter the intake manifold.

When the engine speed decreases below 1150 rpm during the deceleration, the electrical signals from the idle switch and the control unit are sent to the solenoid on the coasting valve, closing the air passage and not allowing fresh air to enter the intake manifold.

Shutter Valve (1981)

To eliminate misfirings and the accompanying emissions of raw hydrocarbons (HC), which is a common characteristic of the early rotary engines, a shutter valve is installed in the primary intake passage for the rear rotor chamber and is closed by vacuum during deceleration and diverts the total air/fuel mixture through a bypass port and into the front rotor chamber. The front chamber continues to run with sufficient air/fuel mixture to eliminate engine misfiring. To avoid an abnormally high manifold vacuum from the rear chamber, a coasting valve, linked to the shutter valve, is opened as the shutter valve closes, allowing fresh air to enter the rear chamber and reducing the vacuum.

PISTON ENGINES

The deceleration control system used on the piston engines are designed to balance the air/fuel mixture during deceleration. The system utilizes an anti-afterburn valve to prevent afterburning of the rich mixture in the exhaust system and coasting richer valve to compensate for lean (insufficient) air/fuel mixtures in automatic equipped vehicles.

At the beginning of sudden deceleration, the engine air/fuel mixture is extremely rich and will not burn completely in the combustion chamber. This overrich mixture is discharged into the exhaust system and when mixed with the fresh air supplied by the air injection system, abnormal combustion and explosions occur within the exhaust system. To prevent this condition, the anti-afterburn valve allows fresh air to be routed to the intake manifold, diluting the overly rich mixture and allowing the mixture to be burned properly in the combustion chambers before entering the exhaust system.

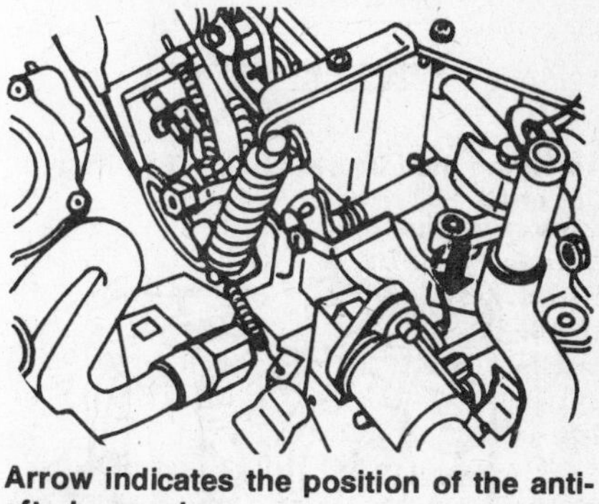

Arrow indicates the position of the anti-afterburn valve

Coasting Richer Valve (Automatic Transmission Equipped Only)

The coasting richer valve is attached to the carburetor and begins to operate during the deceleration and after the anti-afterburn valve has started its operation. The air/fuel mixture

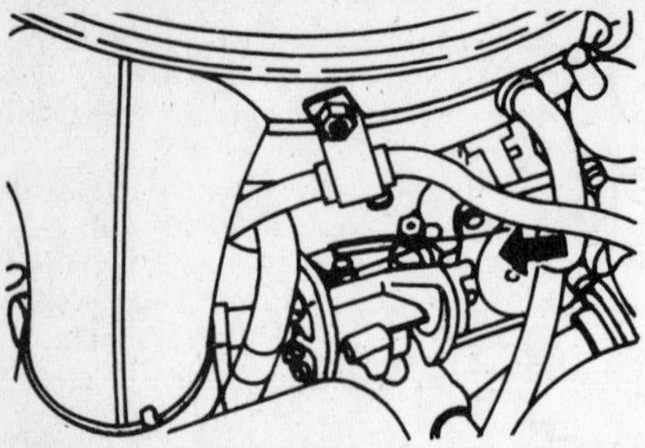

Arrow indicates the position of the coasting valve

is extremely rich before the anti-afterburn valve operates, and after the valve has opened its passage and allowed fresh air to enter the manifold, the mixture becomes too lean. Should this occur, the mixture would not complete its combustion to burn the elements from the exhaust gases and the mixture being too lean, the air injected into the exhaust manifold would be of no value. To avoid this condition, a coasting richer valve, attached to the carburetor, opens and allows fuel passage to the secondary stage of the carburetor to supply an additional amount of fuel, to prevent the mixture from becoming too lean, so that the complete combustion of the mixture can take place in the combustion chambers and the emissions of hydrocarbons (HC) and carbon monoxide (CO) are reduced.

The operation of the coasting richer valve is controlled by the accelerator switch and the vehicle speed switch, and operates only for a duration while both switches are in the circuit for the coasting richer valve. The accelerator switch is mounted on the accelerator linkage and depressing the accelerator pedal opens the circuit. The speed switch is mounted on the speedometer and operates when the speed is 16 ± 1.5 m.p.h. and over.

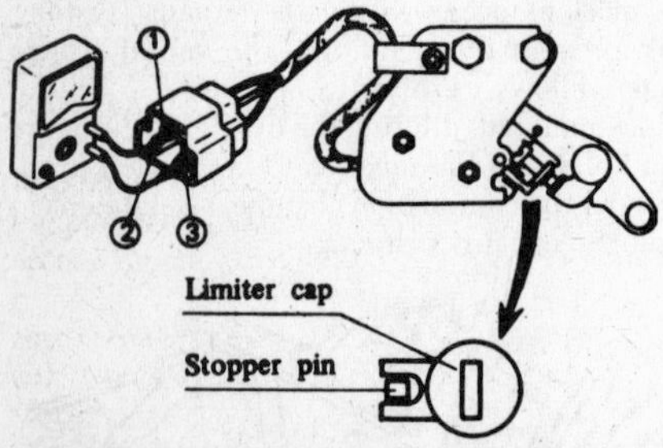

Adjusting the idle switch (© Toyo Kogyo Co. Ltd.)

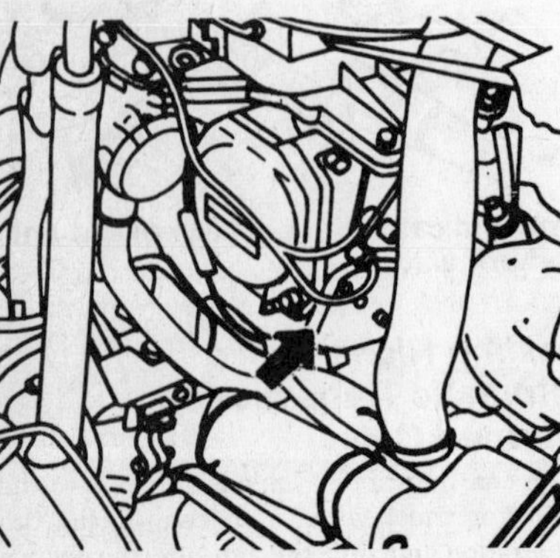

Idle switch position

Throttle Opener System

ROTARY ENGINE

Dash Pot

The dash pot is used to slow the throttle valve return upon the release of the accelerator pedal. By slowing the throttle valve, a balanced air/fuel mixture is maintained to prevent engine misfire.

NOTE: Vehicles with automatic transmissions are not equipped with the dash pot or coasting valve, although an anti-afterburn valve is used.

Coasting Valve

The coasting valve allows additional air to enter the intake manifold to prevent misfiring during the deceleration of the engine at speeds over 1150 rpm.

PISTON ENGINES

The throttle opener system is in operation during the deceleration of the engine at times of high engine vacuum, sensed by a vacuum control valve to open a passage so that engine vacuum can react on the servo-diaphragm to open the primary throttle valve slightly, to provide the additional richness to the lean air/fuel mixture. The diaphragm return spring of the vacuum control valve is set to start operating when the intake manifold vacuum exceeds 22.4 in. Hg. Under this vacuum setting, the throttle opener system does not operate, therefore controlling the system only on deceleration. An altitude corrector (bellows) in the vacuum control valve prevents varied responses due to the differences in atmospheric pressure at the different levels of altitude, by adjusting the diaphragm return spring to the proper tension.

NOTE: Canadian vehicles equipped with the throttle opener system operates above 22.0 in. Hg and does not have the altitude correction bellows included in the vacuum control valve.

Dash Pot

The dash pot is used to maintain a balanced air/fuel mixture during gearshifting to prevent excessive hydrocarbons (HC), to accumulate during the deceleration of the engine when

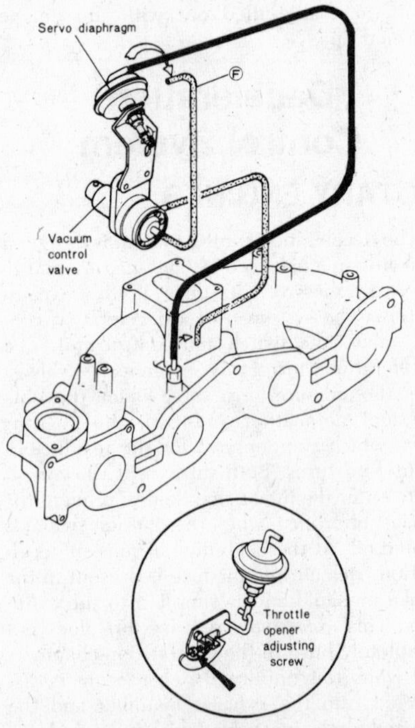

GLC servo diaphragm check; "F" is the vacuum sensing tube. If the idle speed increases to 1400 rpm, the system is ok. (© Toyo Kogyo Co. Ltd.)

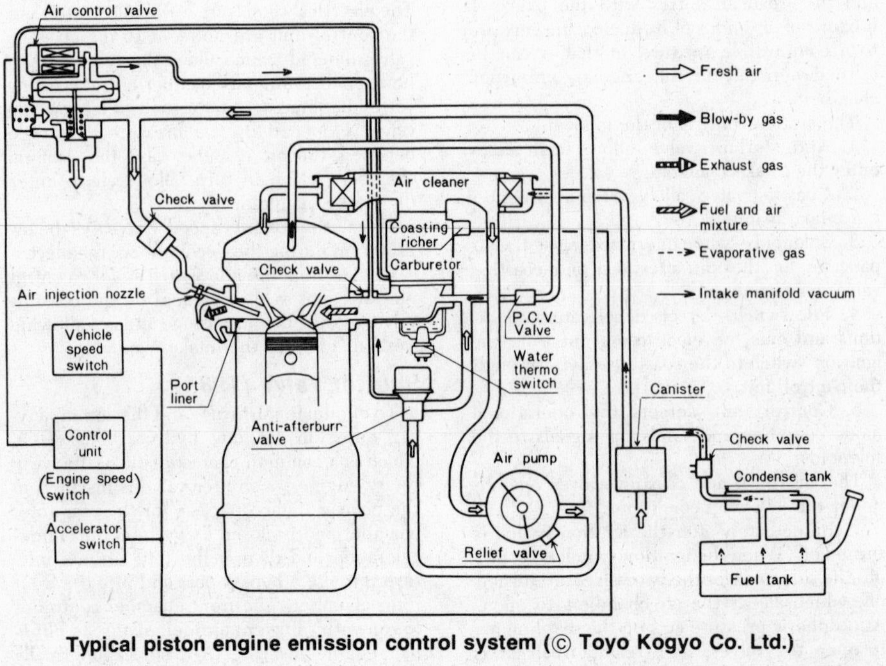

Typical piston engine emission control system (© Toyo Kogyo Co. Ltd.)

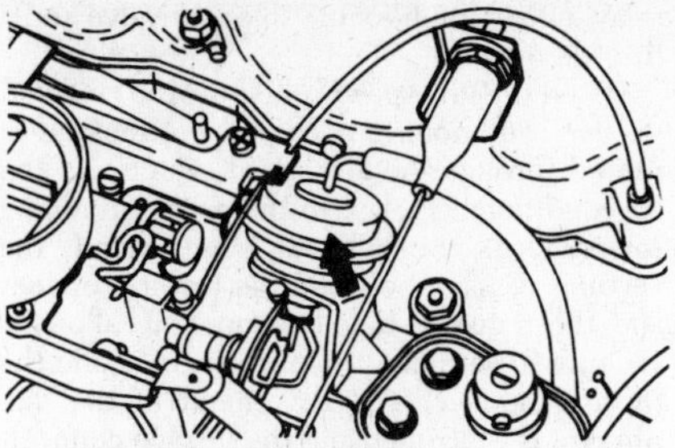

Servo diaphragm

the accelerator is released, to allow the throttle valve to gradually return to normal idle.

A combination of spring pressure and air pressure is used to operate the dash pot. A metered orifice with a check valve connects the two chambers of the dash pot diaphragm with a spring operated assist against the diaphragm and stem during acceleration, to move the stem towards the throttle lever of the carburetor. When the throttle lever is released by the release of the accelerator pedal and the tension of the throttle return spring overcomes the diaphragm return spring pressure, the stem and diaphragm is moved into the dash pot. The metered air orifice connecting the two chambers in the dash pot diaphragm, controls the rate of movement of the stem. The duration of the rod movement of 0.18 inch with a 2.4 lb. load on the stem, is 0.8 seconds, approximately.

Exhaust Gas Recirculation (EGR) System

The increase of exhaust temperatures also increase the emissions of oxides of nitrogen (NOx) from the exhaust gases. The EGR system is used to dilute the air/fuel mixture in the intake manifold with a small percentage of exhaust gas. The exhaust gas does not burn, but absorbs some of the combustion heat to lower the emissions of NOx.

The EGR system consists of the EGR control valve, three way solenoid valve and water temperature switch. The EGR valve is a cone type valve and meters the exhaust gases into the intake manifold in response to the varying vacuum signals of the engine. The three way solenoid valve closes the vacuum line leading to the EGR valve when the coolant temperature is lower than approximately 131° F to provide good driveability of the vehicle when cold. The system operates only on acceleration.

Federal Models With Automatic Transmission

The EGR relay is controlled by the water temperature switch. When the temperature of the coolant is higher than 140° F, the relay is allowed to be turned on.

California Models With Automatic Transmission

The EGR relay is controlled by the water temperature switch and control unit so that the relay turns on to close the circuit from the number one vacuum switch to the EGR solenoid, when the engine coolant temperature is more than 140° F or after 130 seconds from starting the engine with the choke knob pulled out.

EGR Warning System

This system is used to alert the operator to either perform or have performed, the EGR maintenance service on the system. A warning lamp on the dashboard will illuminate every 12,500 miles of operation.

To reset the EGR maintenance interval detector, located under the left side of the dash panel, simply reverse the connector to the detector terminals.

PISTON ENGINES

The EGR system used on the piston engines consists of the EGR valve, three way solenoid valve and a coolant temperature switch. The EGR control valve is used to modulate the exhaust gas flow into the intake manifold in response to the varying vacuum signal of the intake manifold when the vehicle is in the acceleration mode. The system is not in operation when the coolant temperature is less than 131° F. When the coolant temperature is lower than 131° F, the three-way solenoid valve is energized to close the vacuum passage between the three-way valve and the EGR valve. When the coolant temperature is over 131° F, the three-way switch is de-energized and the passage from the three-way solenoid valve to the EGR valve is opened so that vacuum from the carburetor acts on the EGR valve diaphragm to open the EGR valve stem, to allow the exhaust gas to enter the intake manifold.

NOTE: At engine idle and full throttle, the exhaust gas is not mixed with the air/fuel mixture, so that full power and a smooth idle can be obtained.

A vacuum amplifier is used on certain vehicles used in the state of California. The purpose of the vacuum amplifier is to increase or amplify the weak vacuum signal from the carburetor venturi and to give a more positive vacuum signal to the EGR valve.

Automatic Choke Release System

ROTARY ENGINE

Type 1

The automatic choke release system controls the opening and the closing of the choke valve in the air horn of the carburetor, to provide the correct air/fuel mixture at the time of engine start-up. The choke valve is operated manually to restrict the air flow through the carburetor and remains closed while the engine is cranking. As soon as the engine has started, the choke valve opens slightly to allow more air to enter the air horn so as to correct the air/fuel mixture. The choke valve is opened slightly by a vacuum diaphragm and the force of a bi-metal spring. The tension of the bi-metal spring is weakened by the electrical circuit flowing through the choke switch to the choke heater, when the choke lever is pulled.

It should be noted that when the engine is being cranked the intake manifold vacuum is so low that the vacuum diaphragm does not operate. When the engine starts a high intake manifold vacuum is created and is routed to the vacuum diaphragm to open the choke valve in a preset manner. As the carburetor heater for the choke bi-metal spring is heated, the choke valve is gradually opened. This prevents an overly rich mixture during start-ups or while driving with the choke knob pulled out.

Type 2
Federal

To avoid excessively high temperatures in the thermal reactor from an overly rich air/fuel mixture during the engine warm-up period, the manually operated choke control pull rod is held in place by an electrical magnet, when the coolant temperature is below a specified degree and is released automatically when the coolant temperature rises above the specified degree, governed by a coolant temperature switch.

The choke operation is basically the same as the choke mechanism used on many piston engines, but with wiring differences. The type two rotary engine choke magnet is grounded through the choke switch case or from a case connector lead to ground, while the piston engine choke magnet is grounded through the coolant temperature switch.

California

To more closely control the automatically returned choke valve to the vertical position, to avoid excessive high temperatures to be developed in the thermal reactor due to an overly rich air/fuel mixture, in addition to the controls of the federal vehicle choke assembly, the following components are required in the state of California.

1. The full choke magnet switch which controls the electric current to the choke magnet according to the Number two vacuum switch operation.
2. Number two vacuum switch which stops the electric current to the full choke switch.
3. Number two delay valve which controls the Number two vacuum switch operating time.

With the choke knob control pulled half way out, the operation is the same as the Federal choke operation. With the control knob pulled all the way out and the ignition switch turned on, the electric current flows to the choke magnet and holds the control rod in the full closed position. After approximately 30 seconds from engine starting, the vacuum switch cuts or stops the current between the ignition switch and the choke magnet, according to the intake manifold vacuum and the choke knob is forcibly returned to the "OFF" position.

PISTON ENGINES

To avoid having the choke valve on for a long period of time and causing an overly rich air/fuel mixture, the choke control pull rod is held in place by an electrical magnet, wired in series with a coolant temperature switch, with the electrical current controlled by the ignition switch. The choke control pull rod can be controlled manually by the vehicle operator, when the magnet is in use.

With the coolant temperature below 131° F, the coolant switch is on and current is allowed to move from the ignition switch, to the magnet and to the temperature switch, energizing the magnet and holding the choke control pull rod in the "ON" position, as set by the operator. As the coolant temperature rises over 131° F the coolant temperature switch contacts open and the flow of electrical current is interrupted, causing the magnetic field to collapse and release the choke control pull rod. Internal linkage forces the rod to move to the "OFF" position and allows the choke valve to open, thereby allowing more air to enter the carburetor and preventing the air/ fuel mixture from becoming too rich.

Intake Air Temperature Control System

ROTARY ENGINES

This system is designed to keep the temperature of the air drawn into the carburetor as even as possible, regardless of the ambient temperature.

When the temperature of the intake air is more than 45 ± 43° F, the bimetal strip connected to the air duct valve begins to operate. It closes the cold air intake from the engine compartment area and opens the hot air intake from the thermal reactor area.

When the temperature is more than 115 ± 45° F, the bimetal strip connected to the air duct valve again begins to operate. The hot air duct from the thermal reactor is closed and the duct from the engine compartment is opened to allow the colder air to enter the air cleaner assembly and carburetor.

PISTON ENGINES

Both a thermostat type and a vacuum operated type flapper valve arrangement is used on the piston engine carburetors to control the temperature of the induction air.

The vacuum operated valve has a metered amount of vacuum to operate the flapper valve when cold and a thermostatic valve to overcome the metered vacuum pressure to open the flapper valve when warm.

The fully thermostatic valve operated flapper valve is controlled by the temperature of the inducted air flowing through the intake tube, to either close or open the air ducts.

Fuel Enrichment System

ROTARY ENGINES

Richer Solenoid

This system is used in two different modes of operation, depending upon the area and the transmission equipment. The richer solenoid is used on Federal and California vehicles, equipped with manual transmissions. The purpose of the system is to supply additional fuel to the intake manifold to prevent engine misfire during the deceleration mode, with engine speeds greater than 1150 rpm. This additional fuel maintains a balanced air/fuel mixture during the deceleration.

During the deceleration over 1150 rpm, the electric signal from the control unit is sent to the richer solenoid through the idle switch, causing the richer solenoid to open and supply the additional fuel to the intake manifold.

As the engine speed decreases to below 1150 rpm during the deceleration, the electrical signal is stopped by the low speed switch in the control unit, and the additional fuel is cut off from entering the intake manifold.

Power Valve Solenoid

This system is used on Federal vehicles using automatic transmissions and on the California vehicles using both manual and automatic transmissions. The power valve solenoid for the California vehicles differs in its function and operation, from that used on the Federal and Canada vehicles. The solenoid appearance is the same, but the timing of the opening and closing of the valve differs.

CALIFORNIA

The power valve solenoid closes the vacuum passage to the power valve so that the additional fuel can be supplied from the power valve to the intake manifold at the following times.

1. When accelerating in any gear except 4th and 5th at any engine speed of 1150 to 3000 rpm.
2. When accelerating over 4600 rpm and when the engine is 1150 to 4600 rpm within 130 seconds from the initial engine starting with the choke used.

FEDERAL AND CANADA

The power valve closes the vacuum passage leading to the power valve during acceleration so that the additional fuel is supplied by the power valve to the intake manifold.

Idle Compensation System

ROTARY ENGINES

The need to stabilize the engine idle under various operating conditions are required and an idle compensator and throttle opener are used.

Idle Compensator

The idle compensator is used to supply a small amount of air into the intake manifold under extremely hot conditions, through an opening of a bimetal valve, located in the carburetor air cleaner, with the air routed to the intake manifold by a tube or hose. The compensator valve opens when the inlet air temperature reaches and exceeds 149 ± 8° F.

Throttle Opener

The throttle opener system is used to improve the idle stability of an engine in an air condition equipped vehicle, with the air conditioning turned on and the engine speed under 1150 rpm.

The system consists of a control unit, housing a low speed switch, an air conditioning relay, an air conditioning solenoid valve and a throttle opener.

When the idle speed is below 1150 rpm and the air conditioning is turned on, current is routed through the low speed switch and the air conditioning relay, to the air conditioning solenoid. As the solenoid is energized, the vacuum passage between the throttle opener and the intake manifold is opened, allowing vacuum to act upon the diaphragm inside the throttle opener. The movement of the diaphragm is controlled and the linkage connecting the diaphragm stem to the throttle valve is moved, causing the primary throttle valve to open slightly more than at idle, causing an increase in the engine rpm and preventing stalling out of the engine.

Kickdown Control System

ROTARY ENGINE

The purpose of the kickdown system is to increase the engine speed when the choke knob is pulled out, by having the automatic transmission in a reduction gear.

When the choke valve is pulled out, the choke switch allows electrical current to flow to the kickdown relay and operates the kickdown valve in the transmission. When the choke knob is released, the transmission is allowed to up-shift into the higher gear ratios.

NOTE: This system is related to the shifting operation of the transmission and not to any other emission control system or device.

Ignition Control System

ROTARY ENGINES

California Models

The ignition control system is used to warm-up the thermal reactor quickly by controlling the operation of the leading and trailing ignition systems.

The methods of ignition controls are as follows.

1. The leading spark plug ignition only (normal or retarded modes).
2. Both leading or trailing spark plug ignition.

The system consists of the following.

1. Trailing ignition relay–controls the trailing ignition circuit.
2. Retard relay–selects the flow of electrical current sent from the leading or trailing coil when the choke knob is pulled out. Usually the leading coil will be connected to the trailing contact points and the trailing coil will be disconnected from the circuit.
3. Idle, choke and overdrive switch–detects the specific conditions such as, deceleration, cold starting or cruising in overdrive. Each electrical signal is sent to the control unit separately.
4. Vacuum control valve–closes the vacuum sensing tube to the trailing vacuum diaphragm, so that under a cold condition, no vacuum advance will occur at the trailing contact points.

5. Control unit–sends the electrical signal to the trailing ignition relay and retard relay.

Retarded Leading Ignition

The following conditions must occur simultaneously to retard the leading ignition timing. When this happens, there is no trailing ignition.

1. During 130 seconds after the engine starting, with the choke knob pulled out, except during engine deceleration (choke switch and timer are "ON" and idle switch is "OFF".
2. Engine speed is over 1150 rpm and under 4600 rpm.

NOTE: If the choke knob is pushed back in during the 130 seconds, the engine idle speed should be over 1150 and under 4000 rpm.

Normal Leading Ignition California Models with Automatic Transmissions

To have normal leading ignition, the following conditions must occur simultaneously.

1. Engine speed is over 1150 and under 2500 rpm, except while in a deceleration condition.
2. The time span should be more than 130 seconds when the choke knob is pulled out (timer "OFF").

California Models with Manual Transmission

To have normal leading ignition, the following conditions must occur simultaneously.

1. Engine speed over 1150 and under 3000 rpm, except while in a deceleration mode.
2. The time span should be more than 130 seconds when the choke knob is pulled out (timer "OFF").

Both Leading and Trailing Spark Plug Ignition

The leading and trailing spark plugs will ignite when the trailing ignition relay is "ON", the retard relay is deactivated and the following conditions are occurring.

1. When the engine speed is lower than 1150 rpm and the timer is "OFF".
2. During deceleration.
3. When the engine speed is more than 3000 rpm (manual transmission) or 2500 rpm (automatic transmission) after 130 seconds from starting with the choke knob pulled out or in cases of starting without the choke.
4. During operation of the engine while the transmission is in overdrive gear (5th–manual transmission).
5. When starting the engine with the choke knob pulled out during the 130 seconds and the engine speed is over 4600 rpm.

NOTE: Should the choke knob be pushed back in within the 130 seconds, the engine speed will be altered to 4000 rpm.

PISTON ENGINES

Federal With Electronic Ignition and Manual Transmission

The ignition control system retards or advances the ignition timing as required, with the engine operating under certain conditions. The system consists of a top switch, accelerator switch and the transistorized ignition system. The timing advances normally when the accelerator and top switches are in the "OFF" position and retards when the switches are in the "ON" position.

The accelerator switch is "ON" when the accelerator pedal is depressed to ¾ of its travel, while the top switch is on when the transmission is in the 1st, 2nd, 3rd or reverse gear positions.

Federal and Canada With Dual Point Distributors

The system consists of a dual point distributor, containing a retard and an advance (normal) set of ignition points, a vehicle speed switch (Federal) or a water temperature switch (Canada) to control the retard or advanced sets of ignition points during the operation.

The operating conditions are as follows.

1. The advanced set of ignition points operate when the vehicle speed is higher than 42 mph (Federal) or when the coolant temperature is more than 112-140° F (Canada).
2. The retard set of ignition points operate when the vehicle speed is lower than 42 mph (Federal) or when the coolant temperature is lower than 122-140° F (Canada).

FUEL SYSTEM

Electric Fuel Pump

The electric fuel pump is located in the luggage compartment of the coupes and sedans. On station wagons, it is located behind the left-hand trim panel in the luggage compartment.

REMOVAL AND INSTALLATION

Sedans and Coupes

1. Remove the rear inside trim panel.

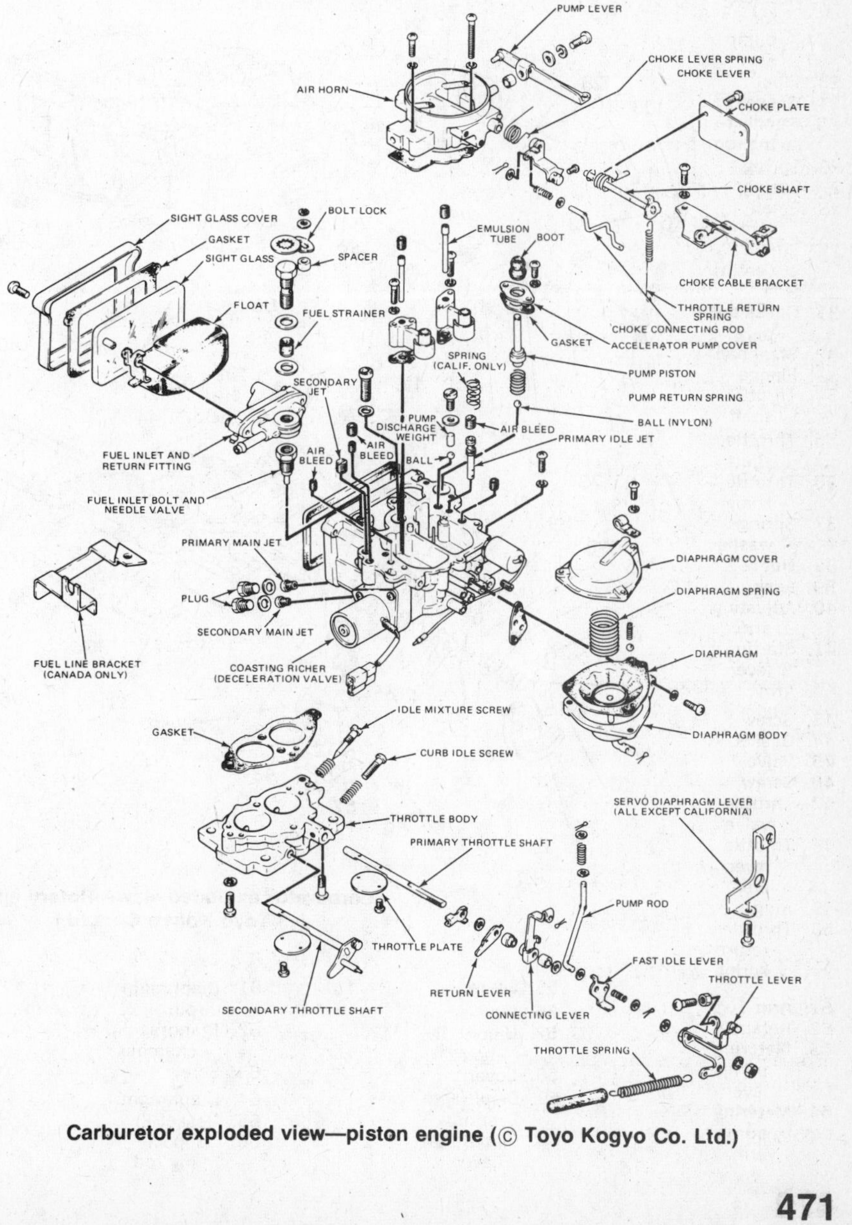

Carburetor exploded view—piston engine (© Toyo Kogyo Co. Ltd.)

1. Air horn
2. Choke valve lever
3. Clip
4. Choke lever shaft
5. Screw
6. Setscrew
7. Spring
8. Choke valve
9. Connector
10. Connecting rod
11. Spring
12. Fuel return valve
13. Hanger
14. Screw
15. Ring
16. Bolt
17. Carburetor body
18. Bolt
19. Diaphragm cover
20. Screw
21. Diaphragm
22. Accelerator pump arm
23. Float
24. Gasket
25. Connecting rod
26. Spring
27. Spring
28. Small venturi
29. Small venturi
30. Bolt
31. Check ball plug
32. Steel ball
33. Flange
34. Throttle shaft
35. Throttle shaft
36. Throttle lever
37. Spring washer
38. Nut
39. Lock
40. Adjusting arm
41. Starting lever
42. Arm
43. Screw
44. Gasket
45. Valve
46. Screw
47. Throttle valve
48. Throttle lever link
49. Ring
50. Throttle return spring
51. Arm
52. Retainer
53. Metering pump lever
54. Metering pump arm
55. Screw
56. Pin
57. Union bolt
58. Cover
59. Diaphragm spring
60. Diaphragm lever
61. Diaphragm pin
62. Diaphragm chamber
63. Screw
64. Diaphragm
65. Gasket
66. Connecting rod
67. Pin
68. Ring
69. Washer
70. Diaphragm stop ring
71. Diaphragm stop ring
72. Screw
73. Level gauge screw
74. Gasket
75. Gasket
76. Stop ring
77. Float pin
78. Needle valve seat
79. Gasket
80. Collar
81. Throttle adjusting screw
82. Idle adjusting screw
83. Spring
84. Main jet
85. Main jet
86. Gasket
87. Plug
88. Gasket
89. Air bleed
90. Air bleed
91. Slow jet
92. Step jet
93. Air bleed screw
94. Air bleed step
95. Cover
96. Diaphragm
97. Spring
98. Gasket
99. Washer
100. Shim
101. Jet
102. Bleed plug
103. Retainer
104. Pin
105. Screw
106. Gasket
107. Plug
108. Gasket
109. Gasket
110. Bolt
111. Nut
113. Cover
114. Gasket
115. Sight glass
116. Gasket
117. Filter
118. Accelerator nozzle
119. Gasket
120. Plug
121. Cover
122. Coasting valve bracket
123. Clip
124. Screw
125. Spring
126. Screw
127. Spring
128. Shim
129. Throttle positioner
130. Nut
131. Rod
132. Collar
133. Shim
134. Collar
135. Arm
136. Plate
137. Retaining spring
138. Lever
139. Setscrew
140. Ring

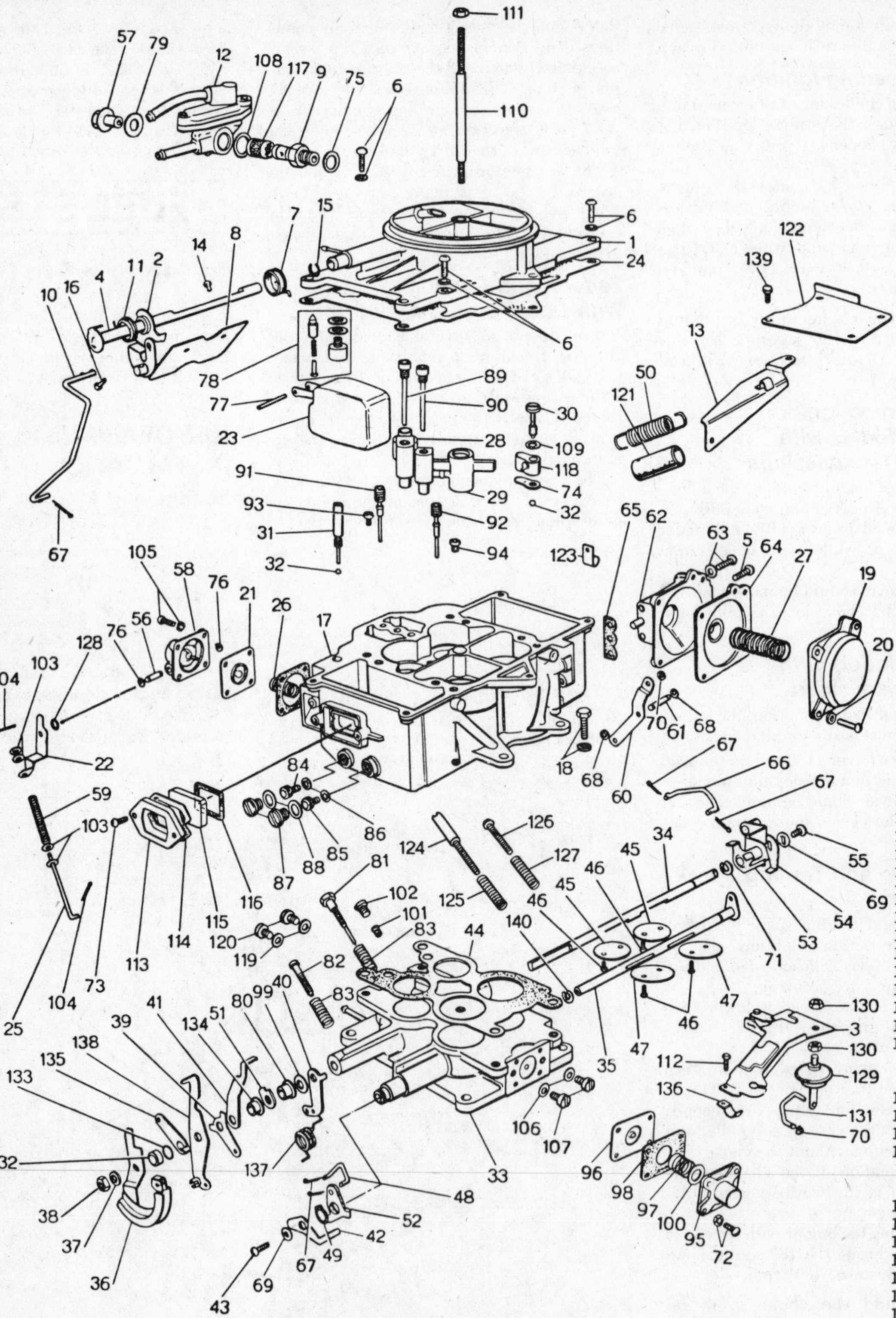

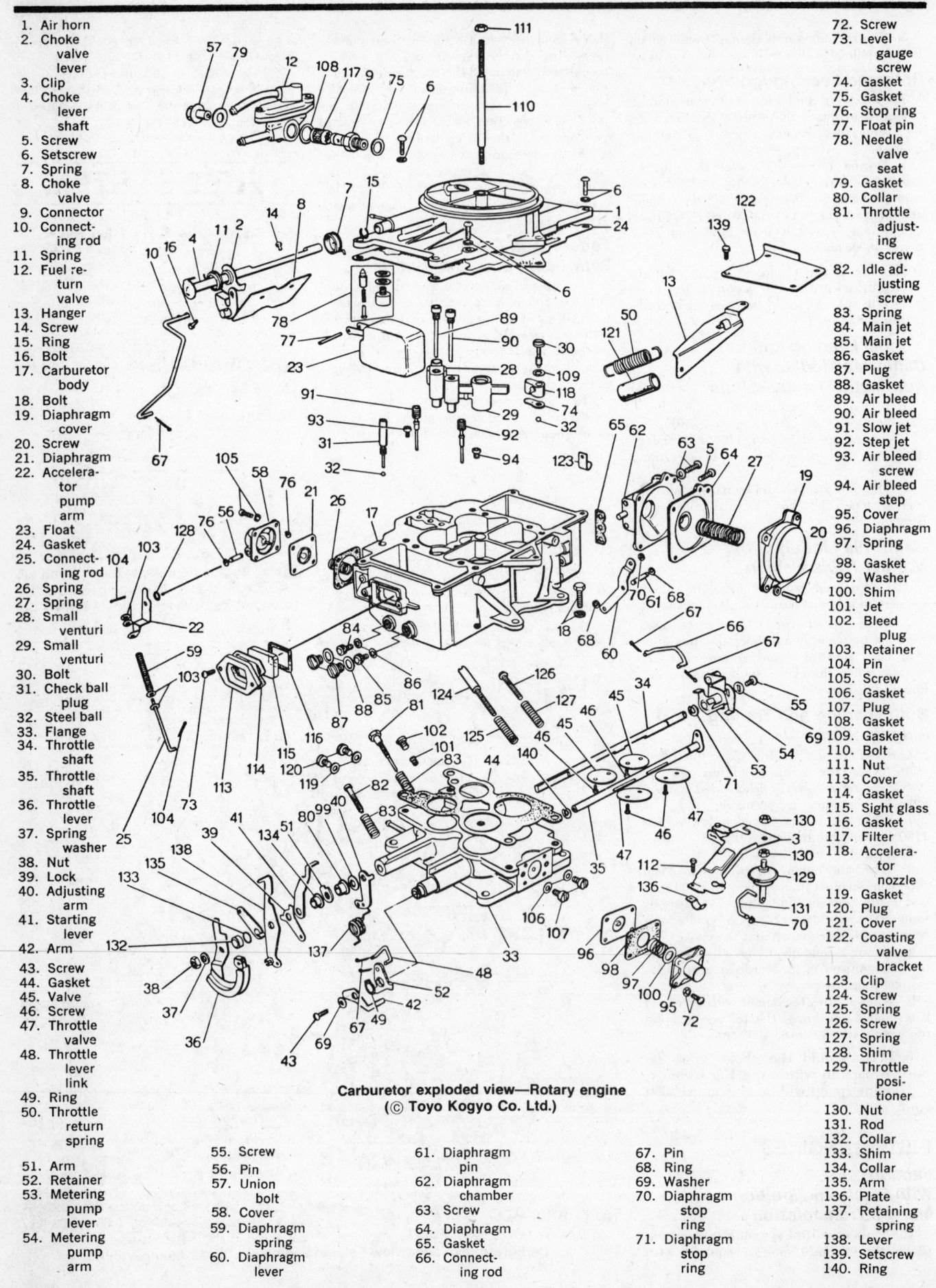

Carburetor exploded view—Rotary engine
(© Toyo Kogyo Co. Ltd.)

2. Disconnect the wiring and the fuel lines.
3. Remove the pump.
4. Installation is the reverse of removal.

Station Wagon

1. Remove the left-hand cargo compartment trim panel.
2. Disconnect the wiring and fuel lines.
3. Remove the pump.
4. Installation is the reverse of removal.

Mechanical Fuel Pump (GLC Models)

The mechanical fuel pump is mounted on the right front side of the engine block.

NOTE: The 1981 GLC fuel pump is mounted at the front top of the engine.

REMOVAL AND INSTALLATION

1. Slide the two fuel line clips from the pump inlet and outlet hoses. Remove the hoses.
2. Remove the fuel pump mounting bolts and remove the pump, gasket and spacer.
3. The installation is the reverse of the removal procedure.

Carburetor

REMOVAL AND INSTALLATION

Rotary Engine

1. Remove the air cleaner.
2. Detach the choke and accelerator cables.
3. Disconnect the fuel and vacuum lines.
4. Remove the oil line.
5. Remove all electrical wiring from carburetor.
6. Remove the carburetor.
7. Installation is the reverse of removal.

Piston Engine

1. Remove the air cleaner and duct.
2. Disconnect the accelerator shaft.
3. Disconnect the fuel supply and fuel return lines.
4. Disconnect the leads from the throttle solenoid and deceleration valve at the quick-disconnects.
5. Disconnect the throttle return spring.
6. Disconnect the choke cable.
7. Remove the carburetor.
8. Installation is the reverse of removal.

ACCELERATOR LINKAGE ADJUSTMENT

1975 808

Remove the air cleaner and depress the accelerator fully. The carburetor throttle valves should be wide open. If not, check for proper installation, binding or wear.

RX-4, Cosmo, RX-3, RX-3SP, RX-7 and 1976-79 808

1. Check the pedal position. The accelerator pedal should be lower than the brake pedal by 2.3 in.-rotary pickup, 1.0 in.-808, 2.2 in.-Cosmo, 1.6 in.-RX-3, RX-4 and GLC, 1.7 ± 0.2 in. RX-7.
2. If necessary, adjust the nut on the linkage above the pedal to obtain the proper height.
3. Check the free-play of the cable at the carburetor. It should be 0.04-0.12 in. If not, adjust by turning the clevis nut.

FLOAT AND FUEL LEVEL ADJUSTMENTS

RX-3 and RX-3SP

1. Bend the float stop to adjust the fuel amount through the needle valve. Distance between lowest part of the float and lower air horn face should be 2.1-2.2 in.
2. Invert the air horn (float seat lip contacting needle valve).
3. The distance between float and the surface of the air horn gasket should be 0.47 in.
4. Bend the float seat lip in order to adjust the float setting.

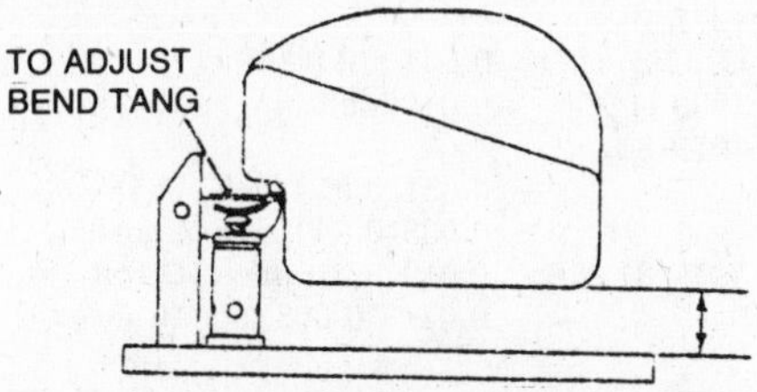

Float level adjustment, float bowl inverted and gasket installed (© Toyo Kogyo Co. Ltd.)

1975 and Later RX-4 and Cosmo

1. With the engine running, check the fuel level in the sight glass, using a mirror.
2. If the fuel levels are not within the specified marks on the sight glass, remove the air horn with the floats.
3. Invert the air horn and let the float hang so that it just contacts the needle valve.
4. Measure the clearance between the float and the air horn gasket, which should be 0.100 in. for 1975 and later models. Bend the float seat lip to adjust the clearance if necessary.

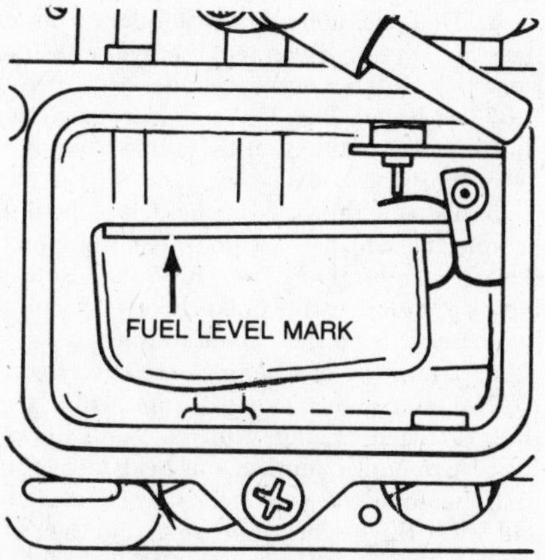

Fuel level mark on sight glass: piston engine

808 (1300), GLC

1. Remove the carburetor air horn assembly.
2. Invert the air horn and allow the float to hang so that the needle valve contacts the seat.
3. Measure the clearance between the float and the air horn **without** the air horn gasket in place.
4. The clearance should be 0.433 inches.
5. Adjust by bending the float seat lip.
6. Reassemble and recheck idle.

808 (1600)

1. With the engine running, observe the fuel level in the fuel bowl sight glass.
2. If the adjustment is necessary, stop the engine and remove the carburetor assembly.
3. Remove the fuel bowl sight glass and invert the carburetor.
4. Measure the clearance between the float and the top of the bowl (now inverted).
5. The clearance should be 0.236 inches.
6. Adjust the float by bending the float seat lip.

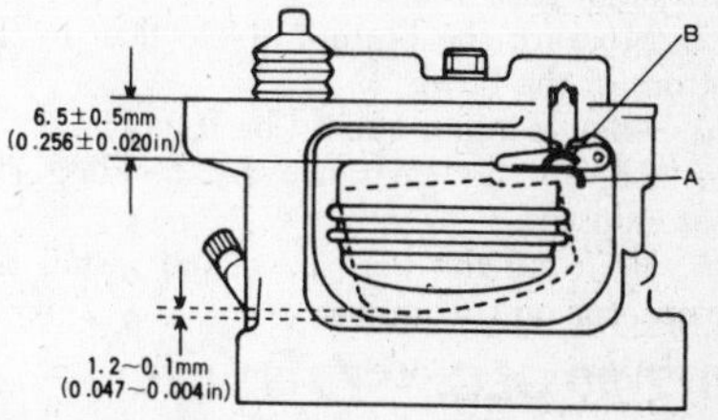

Piston engine float adjustment: bend tab "A" to adjust float drop and bend tab "B" to adjust float level (© Toyo Kogyo Co. Ltd.)

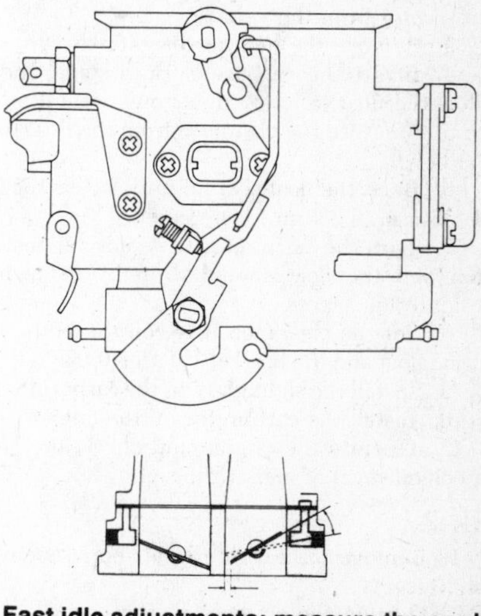

Fast idle adjustments: measure the angle "A" and clearance "B" (© Toyo Kogyo Co. Ltd.)

RX-7

1. Remove the carburetor air horn assembly.
2. Invert the air horn to a position with the float facing upward. The air horn gasket surface must be level. Place the air horn on a carburetor work stand, if available, in order to insure a level position.
3. The distance between the float and the air horn gasket should be 0.63 ± 0.02 in., measured at the toe of the float.
4. Install the air horn assembly.

FLOAT DROP

1975 and Later RX-4, Cosmo and RX-3, RX-3SP

1. Remove the air horn with the floats and allow the floats to hang free.
2. Measure the clearance between the bottom of the float and the air horn gasket. The clearance should be 2.05 in. (2.13 RX-3).
3. If not, adjust the distance by bending the float stop.

808 (1300), GLC

1. With the air horn inverted, lift the float and measure the clearance between the float seat lip and the needle valve.
2. The clearance should be 0.051 to 0.067 inch.
3. Adjust the clearance by bending the float stopper.

808 (1600)

1. Have the carburetor upright and the fuel bowl sight glass removed.
2. Measure the bottom of the float to the bottom of the bowl.
3. The clearance should be 0.047 inch.
4. Adjust the clearance by bending the float stopper.
5. Reinstall the float bowl and install the carburetor on the engine.

1977-80 GLC, 1979-81 626 w/1970 cc Engine

1. With engine running, check fuel level in the fuel bowl sight glass.
2. When the fuel level is not at the specified level on the sight glass, remove the carburetor from the vehicle.
3. Remove the fuel bowl sight glass.
4. Invert the carburetor on a stand and allow the float to lower by its own weight.
5. Measure the clearance from the float to the bowl.
6. Bend the float seat lip until a clearance of 8.5 mm (0.335 in.) is obtained.
7. Turn the carburetor to its normal position and the float should drop by its own weight.
8. Set the clearance between the bottom of the float and the bowl at 1.0 mm (0.039 in.).
9. Install the sight glass on the carburetor.
10. Install the carburetor on the engine.
11. Operate the engine and check for the specified level of fuel at the sight glass.

RX-7

1. Remove the carburetor air horn assembly.
2. Position the air horn in the normal installed position. The air horn gasket surface should be level.
3. The float should be in a fully dropped position. Measure the distance between the lowest part of the float and the air horn gasket.
4. The measured distance should be 2.0 ± 0.02 in. If the distance is not correct, bend the tab on the float to obtain the correct distance.
5. Install the air horn.

FAST IDLE ADJUSTMENT

1. Remove the carburetor from the engine.
2. With the choke valve fully closed, adjust the clearance between the primary throttle valve and the wall of the throttle bore by bending the connecting rod between the choke valve and the throttle valve to the following specifications:

808 (1300)	0.052 inch
808 (1600), RX-3, RX-3 SP	MT-0.079 ± 0.008 inch AT-0.079 ± 0.008 inch (Calif. AT 0.087 ± 0.008 inch)
1975-76 RX-4	0.073 ± 0.006 inch
1977-78 RX-4	0.043 ± 0.004 inch (Calif. 0.056 ± 0.056 ± 0.004 inch)
1976-77 Cosmo	0.041 ± 0.004 inch (Calif. 0.054 ± 0.004 inch)
1978 Cosmo	0.043 ± 0.004 inch (Calif. 0.056 ± 0.004 inch)
1977-79 GLC	0.054 ± 0.006 inch
1980 GLC	0.043 inch
1979-81 RX-7	0.051-0.059 inch (U.S.A.) 0.035-0.040 inch (Canada)
1979-81 626	0.019-0.026 inch (U.S.A.) 0.041 + 0.008 − 0.006 inch (Canada)

MANUAL TRANSMISSION

REMOVAL AND INSTALLATION

4 or 5-Speed

1. Remove the console over the shift lever.
2. Remove the floor mat.
3. Remove shift lever.
4. Tie the clutch release cylinder up out of the way. Do not disconnect the hydraulic line from the clutch release cylinder. On RX-4, RX-7 and Rotary Pick-Up models, remove the starter motor and loosen the 3 upper engine-to-transmission bolts.
5. Detach the back-up light switch multiconnector which is located near the clutch release cylinder. On RX-4s, RX-7s and Rotary Pick-Up, remove the brake booster vacuum line bracket from the clutch housing.
6. Drain the oil. Remove the driveshaft.
7. Detach the exhaust pipe from the thermal reactor flange. On RX-4 and Rotary Pick-Up models, remove the heat insulators first. Remove the converter cover, brackets and lower the exhaust pipe (rear) and the pellet converter assembly on the RX-7 models.
8. Unfasten the speedometer cable.
9. Remove the starter.
10. Support the transmission.
11. Unbolt the transmission support.
12. Remove the bolts which retain the bell housing.
13. Carefully slide the transmission rearward until the input shaft has cleared the clutch disc.
14. Lower the transmission.
15. Transmission installation is the reverse of removal. Align the clutch plate with an arbor or an old input shaft. Adjust the clutch and shift linkage as detailed elsewhere. Refill the transmission with gear oil.

SHIFT LEVER ADJUSTMENT

The shift lever may be adjusted during transmission installation by means of the adjusting shims on the three bolts between the cover plate and the packing. The force required to move the shift knob should be 4.4-8.8 lbs.

MANUAL TRANSAXLE

REMOVAL AND INSTALLATION

NOTE: No standard procedure has been developed for the removal and installation of the transaxle assembly at the time of publication of this manual. The assembly can be removed and installed by the repairman, skilled in R&R procedures for front wheel drive vehicles, by adapting the various procedures needed to complete the job. A general procedure is outlined with precautions noted as required.

1. Raise the vehicle on a hoist and support it safely. Disconnect the negative battery cable.
2. Disconnect all electrical wiring and connections, control linkages from the transaxle. Mark these units to aid in reassembling.
3. Remove the front wheels. Disconnect the lower ball joints from the steering knuckles. Pull the driveshafts from the differential gears.

NOTE: A circlip is positioned on the driveshaft ends and engages in a groove, machined in the differential side gears. The driveshafts may have to be forced from the differential housing to release the clip from the groove.

CAUTION

Do not allow the driveshafts to drop. Damage may occur to the ball and socket joints and to the rubber boots. Wire the shafts to the vehicle body when released from the differential.

4. Support the engine with a jack. Remove the mounting bolts retaining the transaxle in place. Remove the unit from the vehicle.
5. Installation is the reverse of removal.

CAUTION

Be sure the rubber mounts are not twisted or distorted and not in contact with the body.

6. To properly install the driveshafts in the differential side gears, position the open end of the circlip in the up position, and with the driveshaft in a horizontal position, push the driveshafts into the side gears. To be sure the circlip engages the groove, a sound may be heard or attempt to pull the driveshaft from the differential. Reconnect the ball joints at the lower arms.

CLUTCH AND FLYWHEEL

REMOVAL AND INSTALLATION

The flywheel nut on rotary engine models is tightened to 350 ft/lbs with no more than a 3 foot extension on the wrench.

1. Remove the transmission.
2. Remove the clutch cover.
3. Remove the clutch disc.
4. Remove the flywheel.

From the Clutch Housing:

5. Unhook the return spring from the throwout bearing and remove the bearing.
6. Pull out the release fork until the retaining spring frees itself from the ball stud.
7. Installation is the reverse of removal.

Apply Loctite® (RX-3 only) on the eccentric shaft threads.

Apply sealer to both sides of the flywheel lockwasher and position the lockwasher on the eccentric shaft.

Install the flywheel locknut(s) and tighten it to 350 ft/lbs (Rotary), (112-118 ft/lbs—Piston); then bend the tabs of the lockwasher up around it.

PEDAL HEIGHT ADJUSTMENT

Loosen the locknut on the adjusting bolt. Turn the adjusting bolt until the clearance between the pedal pad and the floormat is 7.5 in. Carefully tighten the locknut.

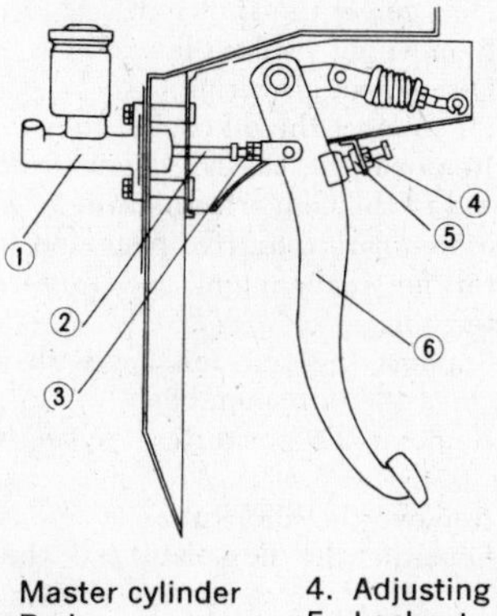

1. Master cylinder
2. Rod
3. Locknut
4. Adjusting bolt
5. Locknut
6. Clutch pedal

Clutch pedal height adjustment (© Toyo Kogyo Co. Ltd.)

1. Clutch disc
2. Bolt
3. Clutch cover and pressure plate assembly
4. Service hole cover
5. Release fork
6. Oil seal

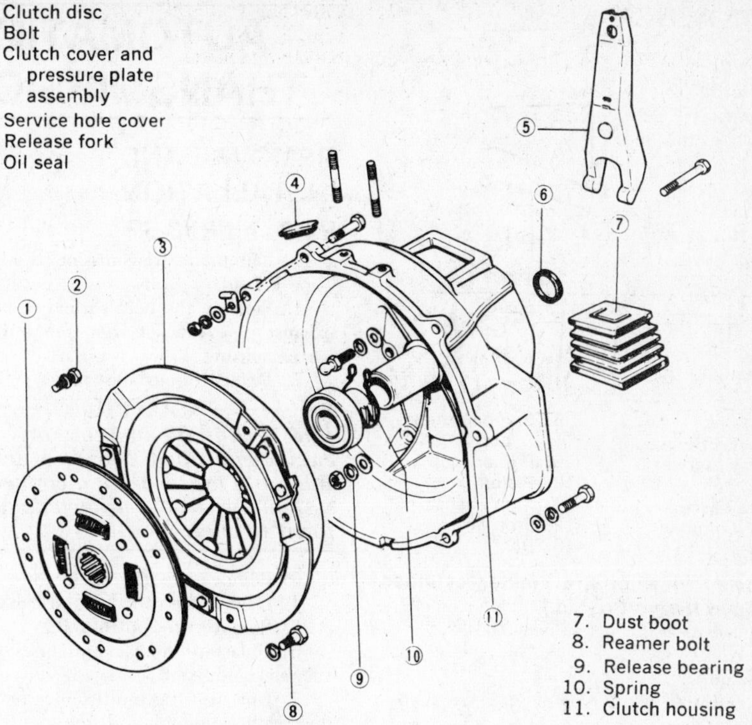

7. Dust boot
8. Reamer bolt
9. Release bearing
10. Spring
11. Clutch housing

Clutch components (© Toyo Kogyo Co. Ltd.)

PEDAL FREE-PLAY ADJUSTMENT

1975 and Later RX-3, RX-4, Cosmo, 1975 and Later 808

The free-play of the clutch pedal before the pushrod contacts the piston in the master cylinder should be 0.02-0.12 in.

To adjust the free-play, loosen the locknut and turn the pushrod until the proper adjustment is obtained. Tighten the locknut after the adjustment is complete.

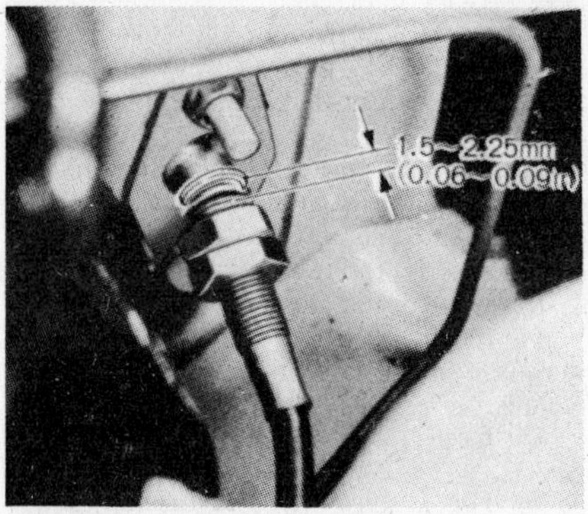

GLC clutch cable adjustment (© Toyo Kogyo Co. Ltd.)

GLC

Loosen the locknut and pull the outer cable away from the engine side of the firewall. Turn the adjusting nut on the cable to obtain a 0.060 to 0.090 inch clearance between the adjusting nut and the firewall. Tighten the locknut. Adjust the 1981 GLC cable to obtain free play of 0.39-0.59 in.

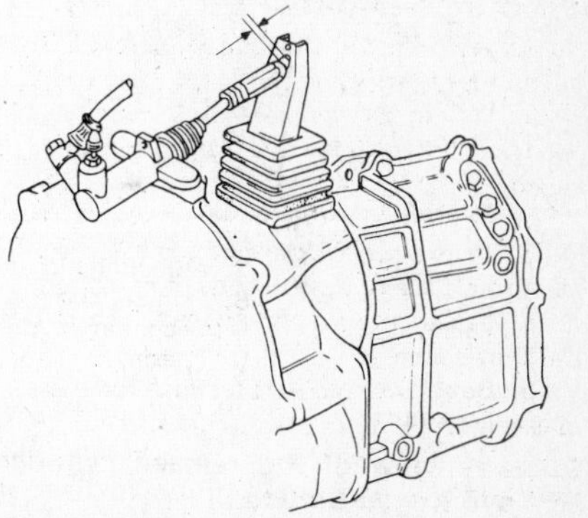

Release fork free-play is measured at arrows (© Toyo Kogyo Co. Ltd.)

1979-81 RX-7 and 626

Loosen the locknut on the clutch master cylinder pushrod. Turn the pushrod to obtain 0.02-0.12 in. free play between the pedal and the pushrod. Tighten the locknut on the pushrod.

Clutch Master Cylinder

REMOVAL AND INSTALLATION

Unfasten the hydraulic line from the master cylinder outlet. Remove the master cylinder.

Installation is the reverse of removal. Bleed the hydraulic system.

Clutch Release Cylinder

REMOVAL AND INSTALLATION

1. Unscrew the hydraulic line.

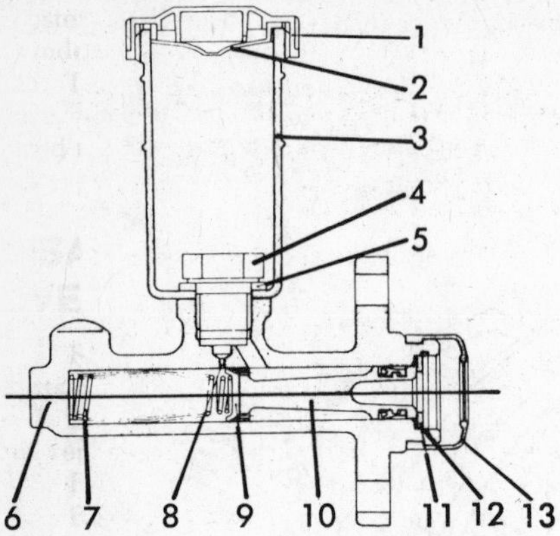

1. Cap
2. Baffle
3. Reservoir
4. Bolt
5. Washer
6. Cylinder
7. Return spring
8. Compensating port
9. Primary cup
10. Piston
11. Stop washer
12. Stop wire
13. Boot

Cutaway view of the master cylinder (© Toyo Kogyo Co. Ltd.)

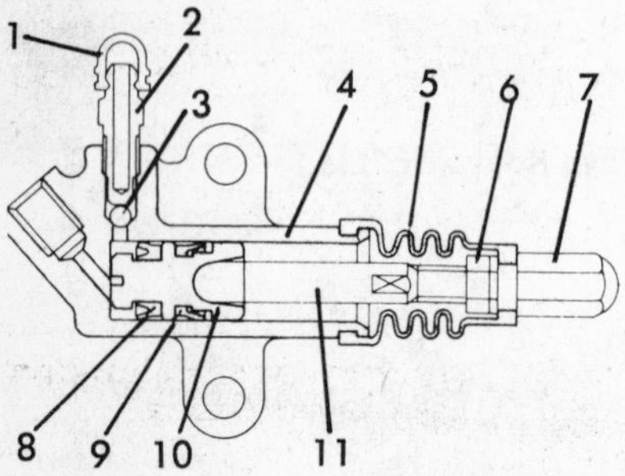

1. Cap
2. Bleeder screw
3. Valve
4. Cylinder
5. Boot
6. Lock nut
7. Adjusting nut
8. Primary cup
9. Secondary cup
10. Piston
11. Push rod

Cutaway view of the release cylinder (© Toyo Kogyo Co. Ltd.)

2. Unhook the release fork return spring from the cylinder.
3. Remove the release cylinder.

Installation is the reverse of removal. Bleed the hydraulic system. Adjust the release fork free-play.

Bleeding the Clutch Hydraulic System

1. Remove the rubber cap from the bleeder screw on the release cylinder.
2. Place a bleeder tube over the end of the bleeder screw.
3. Submerge the other end of the tube in a jar half-filled with hydraulic (brake) fluid.
4. Depress the clutch pedal fully and allow it to return slowly.
5. Keep repeating Step 4, while watching the hydraulic fluid in the jar. As soon as the air bubbles disappear, close the bleeder screw.

NOTE: During the bleeding procedure the reservoir must be kept at least ¾ *full*.

AUTOMATIC TRANSMISSION

REMOVAL AND INSTALLATION

RX-3 and RX3-SP

The automatic transmission is filled with Type F fluid.

1. Remove the heat shroud. Remove the exhaust pipe bracket from the torque converter housing.
2. Detach the exhaust pipe.

CAUTION

The exhaust system on rotary engine-equipped Mazda's gets considerably hotter than a conventional system; be sure to allow enough time for it to cool.

3. Remove the driveshaft.
4. Detach the speedometer cable.
5. Remove the control rod.
6. Unfasten the vacuum lines from the vacuum modulator.
7. Unfasten the multiconnector from the downshift solenoid and the neutral safety switch.

Loosening the torque converter bolts

8. Disconnect the oil cooler lines.
9. Remove the starter.
10. Matchmark the torque converter and the flex-plate.
11. Working through the starter motor mounting hole, remove the four bolts which secure the torque converter to the flex-plate.
12. Support the transmission.
13. Remove the crossmember.
14. Remove the bolts which secure the torque converter housing to the top of the engine.
15. Raise the transmission so that it is level.
16. Use a screwdriver to carefully apply pressure between the torque converter and the flex-plate.
17. Slide the transmission rearward and lower it from the car.

CAUTION

Do not rest the weight of the transmission on the torque converter splines.

Automatic transmission installation is the reverse of removal. There are several points which should be noted, however:

Before installing the transmission, use a dial indicator to measure flex-plate runout. If runout exceeds 0.020 in., the flex-plate must be replaced.

Hand-tighten the four torque converter installation bolts and then lock the flex-plate with a brake. Next, tighten the four bolts evenly, and in several stages, to 29-36 ft-lbs.

Check the fluid level again and road test the car.

RX-4, RX-7 and Cosmo

The transmission is filled with Type F fluid.

1. Remove the converter access hole cover. Lock the flex-plate by holding the drive pulley lockbolt with a wrench.
2. Matchmark the converter and flex-plate. Unfasten the four converter-to-flex-plate securing bolts.
3. Remove the exhaust pipe.
4. Remove the driveshaft.
5. Remove speedometer cable.
6. Remove all vaccuum lines and electrical leads from the transmission.
7. Remove the starter.
8. Remove the bottom cover from the converter housing.
9. Support the transmission and remove the crossmember.
10. Disconnect the oil cooler.
11. Unbolt the converter housing, raise the transmission to a level place and separate it from the flex-plate.
12. Automatic transmission installation is the reverse of removal. There are several points which should be noted, however.

Before installing the transmission, use a dial indicator to measure flex-plate runout. Runout should be around 0.012 in. If runout exceeds 0.020 in., the flex-plate must be replaced.

After completing transmission installation, rotate the eccentric shaft to be sure that there is no interference in the transmission.

808, 1977-80 GLC and 626

Use only Type F transmission fluid.

1. Drain the transmission.
2. Remove the heat insulator.
3. Disconnect the exhaust pipe.
4. Disconnect the driveshaft at the rear axle flange.
5. Remove the driveshaft.
6. Disconnect the speedometer cable.
7. Disconnect the shift rod.
8. Remove all vacuum hoses.
9. Disconnect all wiring.
10. Disconnect the oil cooler lines.
11. Remove the access cover from the lower end of the converter housing.
12. Matchmark the drive plate and torque converter for realignment and remove the converter bolts.
13. Support the transmission with a jack and remove the crossmember.
14. Remove the converter housing-to-engine bolts.
15. Remove the filler tube.
16. Separate the flex-plate and the converter.
17. Remove the transmission and converter as an assembly.
18. To install the transmission, reverse the removal procedure.

SHIFT LINKAGE ADJUSTMENT

1975

1. Unfasten the T-joint on the intermediate lever.
2. Place the range selector lever, which is mounted on the side of the transmission case, in Neutral (N); i.e., so that the slot in the selector shaft is pointing straight up and down.
3. Adjust the console-mounted gear selector lever by turning the T-joint until it indicates Neutral (N).
4. Reconnect the T-joint. Check the gear selector operation in all other ranges and to see that the linkage has no slack.

1976-81
All Models Except RX-7

1. Place the transmission selector lever in Neutral.
2. Disconnect the clevis from the lower end of the selector arm.
3. Move the manual lever to the N position.

NOTE: The N position is the third detent from the back.

4. Loosen the two clevis retaining nuts and adjust the clevis so that it freely enters the lever hole.

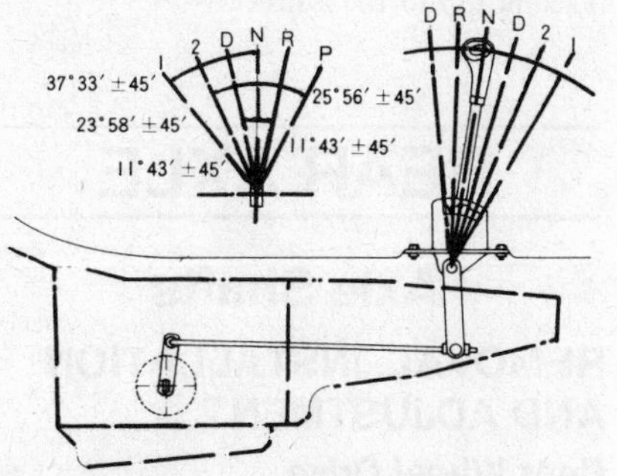

Transmission linkage adjustment (© Toyo Kogyo Co. Ltd.)

5. Tighten the retaining nuts.
6. Connect the clevis to the lever and secure with the spring washer, flat washer and retaining clip.

NEUTRAL SAFETY SWITCH ADJUSTMENT

RX3-SP, RX-3 and RX-7

1. Check the shift linkage.
2. Remove the nut from the gear selector lever and the neutral safety switch attaching bolts.
3. Unfasten the screw underneath the switch body.
4. Place the selector shaft in Neutral by using the gear selector lever.

NOTE: If the linkage is adjusted properly, the slot in the selector shaft should be vertical.

5. Move the switch body so that the screw hole in the case aligns with the hole in the internal rotor.

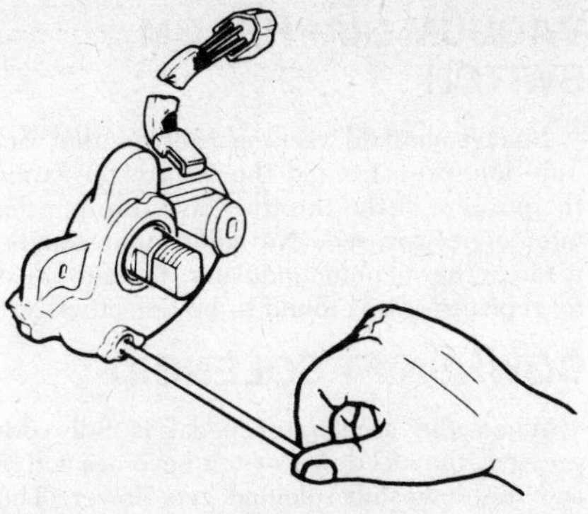

Align the neutral safety switch by inserting a drill through the holes on it. (© Toyo Kogyo Co. Ltd.)

6. Check the alignment by inserting an 0.009 in. diameter pin or a No. 53 drill through the holes.
7. Once the proper alignment is obtained, tighten the switch mounting bolts.
8. If it still is not operating properly, i.e., the car starts in position other than P (Park) or N (Neutral) or the back-up lights come on in gears other than R (Reverse), replace the switch.

RX-4, Cosmo and 626

1. Remove the housing from the shift lever.
2. Adjust the shift lever so that there is 0-0.012 in. clearance between the pin and the guide plate, when the lever is in Neutral.
3. Adjust the neutral safety switch so that the pin hole in the switch body is aligned with the pin hole of the sliding plate when the shift lever is in Neutral.
4. Check the adjustment by trying to start the engine in all gears. It should only start in Park or Neutral.
5. Reinstall the housing on the shift lever.

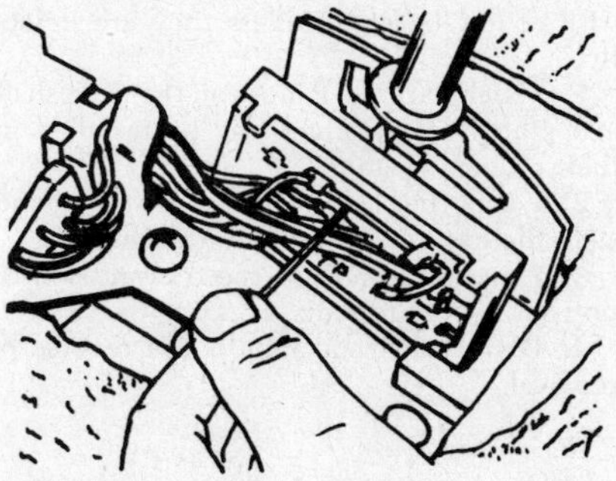

Adjusting the RX-4, Cosmo and Rotary Pickup neutral safety switch

808, 1977-80 GLC

1. Place the manual lever in N. N is the third detent from the back.
2. Remove the manual lever.
3. Loosen the neutral switch attaching bolts and remove the screw from the alignment hole at the bottom of the switch.
4. Rotate the switch so that the hole in the switch aligns with the hole in the internal rotor. The 0.078 in. diameter pin should be inserted while tightening switch.
5. Install the alignment hole screw and manual lever.

KICKDOWN SWITCH AND DOWNSHIFT SOLENOID ADJUSTMENT

1. Check the accelerator linkage for smooth operation.
2. Turn the ignition on but do not start the engine.
3. Depress the accelerator pedal fully to the floor. As the pedal nears the end of its travel, a light "click" should be heard from the downshift solenoid.
4. If the kickdown switch operates too soon, loosen the locknut on the switch shaft. Adjust the shaft so that the accelerator linkage makes contact with it when the pedal is depressed $\frac{7}{8}$-$\frac{15}{16}$ of the way to the floor. Tighten the locknut.
5. If no noise comes from the solenoid at all, then check the wiring for the solenoid and the switch.

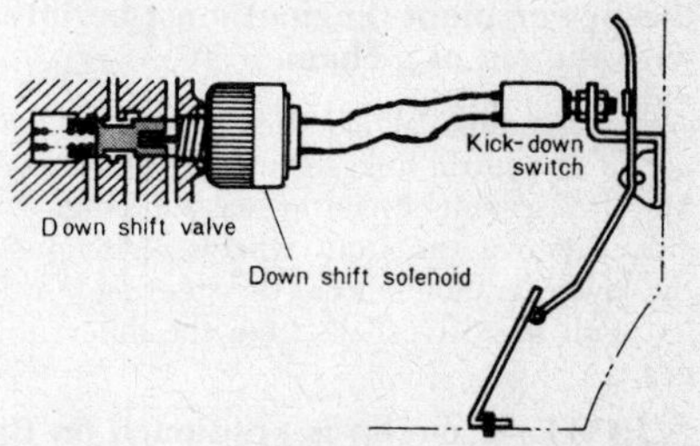

Kickdown switch the downshift solenoid circuit (© Toyo Kogyo Co. Ltd.)

6. If the wiring is in good condition, remove the wire from the solenoid and connect it to a 12V power source. If the solenoid does not click when connected, it is defective and should be replaced.

NOTE: When the solenoid is removed, about two pints of transmission fluid will leak out.

BAND ADJUSTMENT

JATCO Model 3N71B

1. Raise the vehicle and support safely.
2. Drain the transmission fluid and remove the transmission pan.
3. Loosen the locknut and torque the servo adjusting bolt to 9-11 ft/lbs.
4. Back off the servo bolt two full turns and tighten the locknut.
5. Complete the pan assembly and fill with fluid.

JATCO Model R3A

1. Raise the vehicle and support safely.
2. Locate the servo cover and remove from the right side of the transmission case.
3. Loosen locknut and tighten the servo adjusting bolt to 9-11 ft/lbs. torque.
4. Loosen the servo bolt two full turns and tighten the locknut.
5. Install the servo cover and lower vehicle.

AUTOMATIC TRANSAXLE

REMOVAL AND INSTALLATION

NOTE: No standard procedure has been developed for the removal and installation of the transaxle assembly at the time of publication of this manual. The assembly can be removed and installed by the repairman, skilled in R&R procedures for front wheel drive vehicles, by adapting the various procedures needed to complete the job. A general procedure is outlined with precautions noted as required.

1. Raise the vehicle on a hoist and support it safely. Disconnect the negative battery cable.

NOTE: When removing or installing the transaxle assembly the rear end of the power plant (engine) must be lifted with the aid of a chain.

2. Disconnect all electrical wiring and connections, control linkages from the transaxle. Mark these units to aid in reassembling.
3. Remove the front wheels. Disconnect the lower ball joints from the steering knuckles. Pull the driveshafts from the differential gears.

NOTE: A circlip is positioned on the driveshaft ends and engages in a groove, machined in the differential side gears. The driveshafts may have to be forced from the differential housing to release the clip from the groove.

CAUTION

Do not allow the driveshafts to drop. Damage may occur to the ball and socket joints and to the rubber boots. Wire the shafts to the vehicle body when released from the differential.

4. Support the engine with a jack. Remove the mounting bolts retaining the transaxle in place. Remove the unit from the vehicle.
5. Installation is the reverse of removal.

CAUTION

Be sure the rubber mounts are not twisted or distorted and not in contact with the body.

6. To properly install the driveshafts in the differential side gears, position the open end of the circlip in the up position, and with the driveshaft in a horizontal position, push the driveshafts into the side gears. To be sure the circlip engages the groove, a sound may be heard or attempt to pull the driveshaft from the differential. Reconnect the ball joints at the lower arms.

SHIFT LEVER ADJUSTMENT

The shift lever adjustment should be performed by the forward and backward of the shift lever with the shift lever setting at the "P" range.

VACUUM DIAPHRAGM SWITCH

Intake manifold vacuum controls the vacuum line pressure and the diaphragm varies the position of the throttle valve through the interconnecting rod. No adjustment can be made to the vacuum modulator, the unit must be replaced if it is found to be defective.

DOWNSHIFT SOLENOID

When the accelerator pedal is fully depressed, the kickdown switch becomes active and the downshift solenoid gets power. The downshift valve in the control valve is pushed up to kickdown position 3-to-2 and position 2-to-1 at a given speed.

NEUTRAL SAFETY/REVERSE LAMP SWITCH

The switch contacts should operate when the switch plunger is moved into its respective operating positions. The switch operates from closed (starter solenoid on) to the neutral (or "off") position and then to the reverse light ("on" position). The switch plunger must operate smoothly otherwise the gear selector will be affected.

DRIVELINE

Driveshaft and U-Joints

REMOVAL AND INSTALLATION

1977-80 GLC, RX-3, RX-3SP, RX-7 and 808 Models

Do not remove the oil seals from models with center bearing, unless they are defective.

1. Matchmark the flanges on the driveshaft and pinion so that they may be installed in their original position.
2. Lower the back end of the driveshaft and slide the front end out of the transmission.
3. Plug up the hole in the transmission to prevent it from leaking.
4. Driveshaft installation is the reverse of removal.

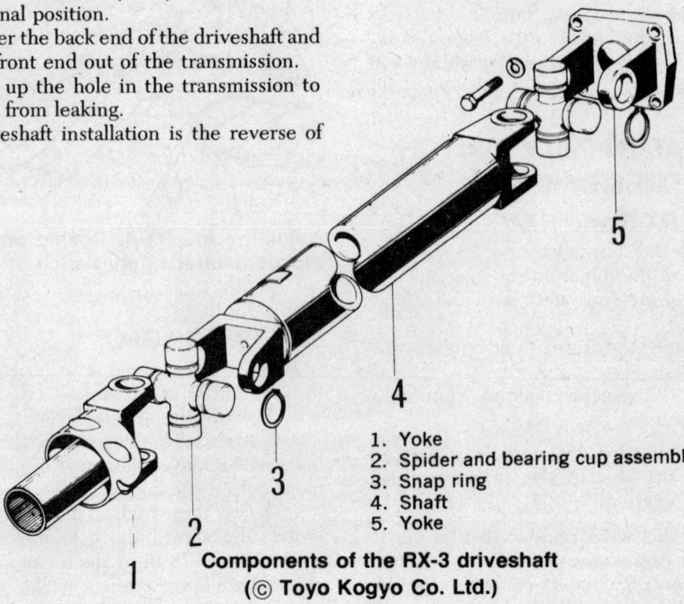

1. Yoke
2. Spider and bearing cup assembly
3. Snap ring
4. Shaft
5. Yoke

Components of the RX-3 driveshaft
(© Toyo Kogyo Co. Ltd.)

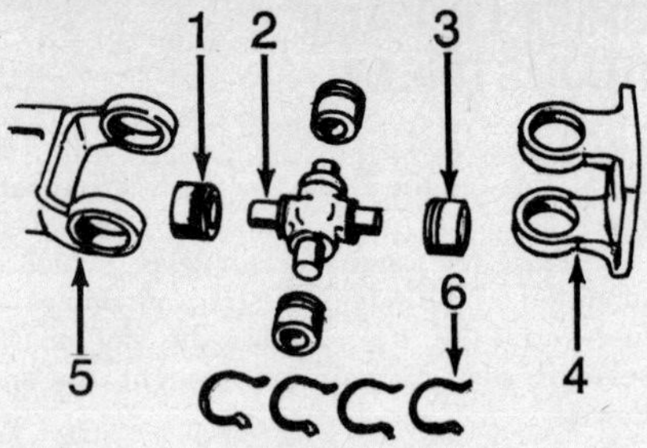

1. Roller bearing (cup)
2. Spider
3. Oil seal
4. Yoke
5. Driveshaft
6. Snap-ring

Components of the U-joint

RX-4, 626 and Cosmo Models

Perform this operation only when the exhaust system is *cold*.

1. Remove the front heat insulator.
2. Remove the nuts which secure the downpipe to the thermal reactor flange.
3. Remove the downpipe from the main muffler flange.
4. Matchmark the pinion and driveshaft flange bolts.
5. Unfasten the center bearing.
6. Remove the driveshaft.
7. Driveshaft installation is the reverse of removal. Tighten the yoke-to-front driveshaft locknut to 116-130 ft/lbs.

REAR AXLE

Axle Shafts

REMOVAL, INSTALLATION AND ADJUSTMENT

Rear Wheel Drive

1. Remove the wheel.
2. Remove the brake shoes.

3. Remove the brake backing plate and the bearing retainer.
4. Withdraw the axle shaft with a puller.
5. Apply grease to the oil seal lips and then insert the oil seal into the axle housing.
6. Check the axle shaft end-play.
 a. Temporarily install the brake backing plate on the axle shaft.
 b. Measure the depth of the bearing seat and then measure the width of the bearing outer race.
 c. The difference between the two measurements is equal to the overall thickness of the adjusting shims required. Shims are available in thicknesses of 0.004 and 0.016 in.

NOTE: The maximum permissible end-play is 0.004 in.

7. Remove the backing plate, apply sealer to the rear axle surfaces and install the backing plate.
8. Install the rear axle shaft, bearing retainer, gasket, and shims. Coat the shims with sealer.
9. Install the brake shoes.

Axle Shaft Bearing and Seal

REPLACEMENT

Rear Wheel Drive

1. Install the retainer and spacer on the shaft.
Position the bearing on the shaft with the sealed side toward the shaft flange. Press it on until the spacer comes in contact with the shoulder of the shaft.
Press the bearing retaining collar onto the shaft until it contacts the bearing inner race.

NOTE: If the bearing retaining collar can be press fitted with a force less than 2.5 tons, replace the collar.

2. Remove the rear axle shaft.
3. Press the axle shaft out of the collar and bearing.

NOTE: If the pressure needed to press out the shaft exceeds 10 tons, grind off part of the bearing retaining collar and cut it with a cold chisel.

4. Remove the bearing retainer.

Differential

REMOVAL AND INSTALLATION

Rear Wheel Drive

1. Drain the lubricant.
2. Remove the driveshaft.
3. Remove both of the axle shafts.
4. Remove the differential carrier.
5. Installation is the reverse of removal.

OVERHAUL

All Mazda differentials are of similar design. Prior to disassembling measure and record, pinion bearing preload, side bearing preload and make a tooth contact pattern check.

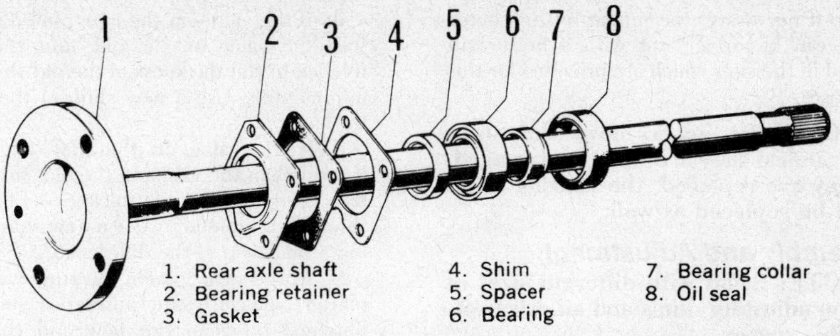

1. Rear axle shaft
2. Bearing retainer
3. Gasket
4. Shim
5. Spacer
6. Bearing
7. Bearing collar
8. Oil seal

Components of the axle shaft assembly (© Toyo Kogyo Co. Ltd.)

Disassembly

1. Mount the carrier on a workstand.
2. Matchmark the carrier, bearing caps, and adjuster.
3. Remove the adjusting nut lockplates.
4. Loosen, but do not remove, the bearing cap securing nuts and then back off on the adjuster, just enough to remove bearing preload.
5. Remove the differential.

CAUTION

Be sure that each bearing outer race remains with its bearing.

6. Remove the differential bearings.
7. Remove the ring gear.
8. Drive the pinion gear shaft lock pin out of the case.
9. Withdraw the pinion gear shaft.
10. Rotate each of the pinion (spider) gears 90° and remove them, complete with thrust washers.
11. Remove the side gears and thrust washers.
12. Remove the pinion nut and pinion.
13. Remove the collar, if so equipped, and the collapsible spacer from the pinion.
14. Press out the rear bearing and remove the adjustable shim. Save the shim for later reference.
15. Withdraw the oil seal and the front bearing from the carrier.

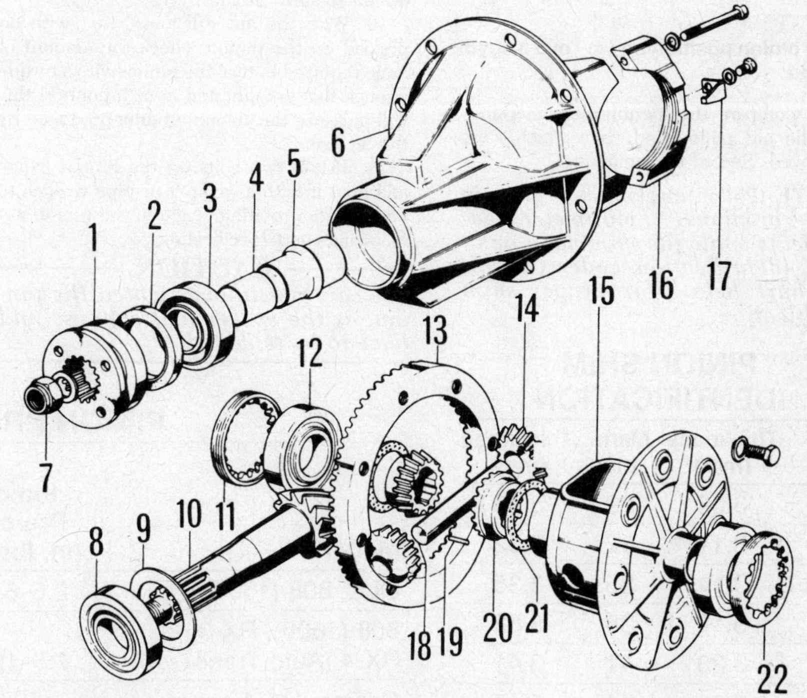

1. Pinion flange
2. Pinion oil seal
3. Pinion front bearing
4. Pinion bearing collar
5. Collapsible pinion bearing spacer
6. Carrier
7. Pinion nut
8. Pinion rear bearing
9. Adjusting washer (Adjusting spacer)
10. Drive pinion
11. Pinion side adjusting nut
12. Side bearing
13. Ring gear
14. Pinion gear
15. Differential gear case
16. Bearing cap
17. Adjusting nut lock
18. Pinion shaft
19. Pinion shaft lock pin
20. Side gear
21. Thrust washer
22. Ring gear side adjusting nut

Differential components (© Toyo Kogyo Co. Ltd.)

16. If necessary, the pinion bearing outer races can be driven out with a brass drift placed in the slots which are provided for this purpose.

NOTE: Do not remove the outer races unless they are worn or damaged. If they are replaced, the bearing cones must be replaced as well.

Assembly and Adjustment

NOTE: Begin with different sizes of pinion adjusting shims and an extra collapsible spacer.

1. If the old pinion/ring gear assembly and rear bearing are being used, replace the shim with a new one of the same size (identification marking) as was removed. Use a new collapsible spacer.

2. If a new pinion/ring gear assembly or rear bearing is being used, determine the correct adjustment shim size:

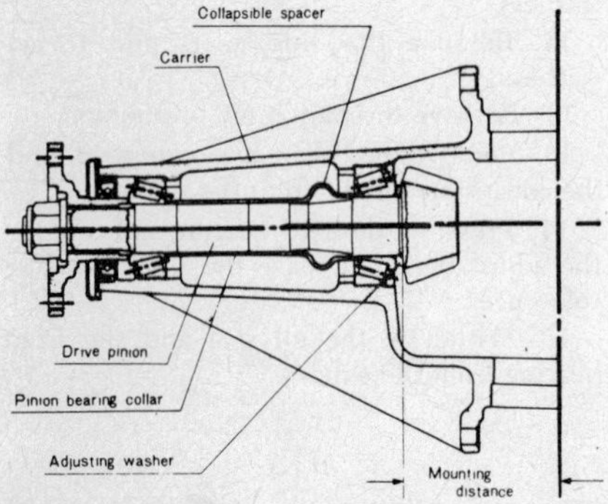

Proper pinion positioning (© Toyo Kogyo Co. Ltd.)

a. Compare the identification markings on the old pinion and shim which were removed. Record their markings.

NOTE: Pinion markings are given in plus *(+) or minus (−) millimeter measurements while the shim has a numbered identification code. Consult the chart below for proper shim identification.*

PINION SHIM IDENTIFICATION

Marking	Thickness (mm)	Marking	Thickness (mm)
08	3.08	29	3.29
11	3.11	32	3.32
14	3.14	35	3.35
17	3.17	38	3.38
20	3.20	41	3.41
23	3.23	44	3.44
26	3.26	47	3.47

b. Compare the identification measurement stamped on the new pinion and note its value.

c. Calculate the difference between the measurements of the new and old pinions by adding or subtracting, as necessary.

d. If the value on the new pinion is *less* than the value on the old, *add* the difference to the thickness of the old shim (in millimeters). Use a new shim of the total thickness.

e. If the value on the new pinion is *greater* than the value on the old, *subtract* the difference from the thickness of the old shim (in millimeters). Use a new shim having a thickness of the difference.

f. If the rear pinion bearing was replaced, measure the difference (in millimeters) between the new and the old bearing. Add or subtract the difference between the two bearings from the size of the adjusting shim.

g. Select the proper size adjusting shim, as determined in the steps above, from one of the following:

3. Position the adjusting shim, and install the rear pinion bearing.

4. If they were removed, install the pinion bearing outer races in the carrier.

5. Place the pinion assembly through the collapsible spacer and into the carrier.

NOTE: Use a new collapsible spacer.

6. Position the front bearing on the pinion. Hold the pinion as far forward as it will go and drive the front bearing on to the pinion until it is fully seated.

7. Coat the lips of the pinion oil seal with grease and fit the seal into the carrier.

8. Tap the pinion flange on.

9. Install the pinion washer and nut but do not tighten the nut.

10. With the nut still loose, i.e., with no preload on the pinion, check the amount of force required to turn the pinion with a torque wrench that is calibrated in inch pounds; this will measure the amount of drag produced by the oil seal.

11. Install two bolts on the pinion flange and hold it with a spanner or pipe wrench to keep it from rotating. Tighten the pinion nut following chart specifications.

CAUTION

Use care not to overtighten the pinion, as the spacer will collapse and have to be replaned.

12. Release the pinion flange and measure the amount of preload obtained using the inch/pound torque wrench.

13. Continue tightening the pinion nut, if necessary, a little at a time. Check the preload after each small amount of tightening, until the final preload figure is reached.

14. Install thrust washers on both of the side gears and install the gears.

15. Install the two pinion (spider) gears into the case, through the opening, so that they are exactly 180° apart.

16. Turn the gears through 90° so that the pinion shaft holes in the case align with the holes in the pinion gears.

17. Insert the pinion gear shaft into the holes in the case and through the holes in the pinion gears.

18. Check the backlash between the side gears and the pinion gears with a dial indicator. The backlash between the gear teeth should be 0-0.004 in. If backlash exceeds 0.008 in., adjust it to specifications by selecting one of the following side gear thrust washers:

THRUST WASHER IDENTIFICATION

Marking	Thickness (in.)
0	0.0787
1	0.0827
2	0.0866

NOTE: Use the same thickness thrust washers for both side gears

NOTE: Use the same thickness thrust washers for both side gears.

19. Install and stake the lockpin onto the pinion shaft.

20. Bolt the ring gear up to the gear case. Lock the bolts in place.

21. Install the gear bearings in the gear case hub and fit each of the outer races into its respective bearing.

PINION PRELOAD TABLE

Model	Pinion Preload (in. lbs.) ①	Pinion Nut Minimum Torque (ft. lbs.)	Pinion Nut Maximum Torque (ft. lbs.)
GLC, 808 (1300) ②	2.6-6.1	87	130
808 (1600), RX-3, RX-4 (Auto Trans)	7.8-12.2	94	130
Cosmo, RX-4 (Manual Trans)	7.8-12.2	101	145
RX-7	7.8-12.2	94	130

NOTE: If specified preload is not obtained with the pinion nut at maximum torque, replace the collapsible spacer. Proper preload cannot be obtained by simply backing off the pinion nut.
① Less oil seal drag
② 1977-80 GLC

22. Place the differential gearset in the carrier.

NOTE: Be sure that the marks used for backlash adjustment, which are stamped on the faces of the ring gear and pinion teeth, are aligned.

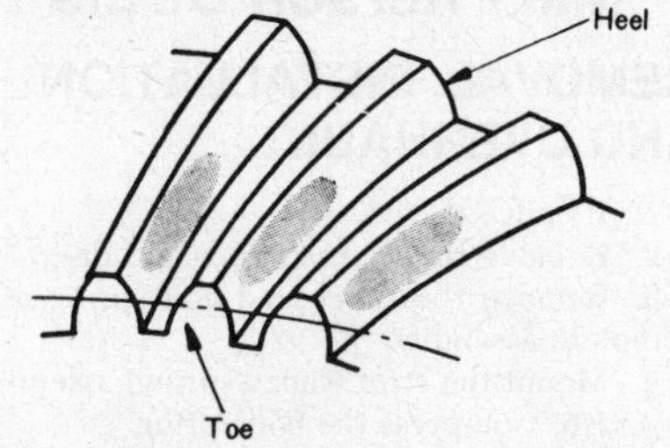

Correct contact pattern (© Toyo Kogyo Co. Ltd.)

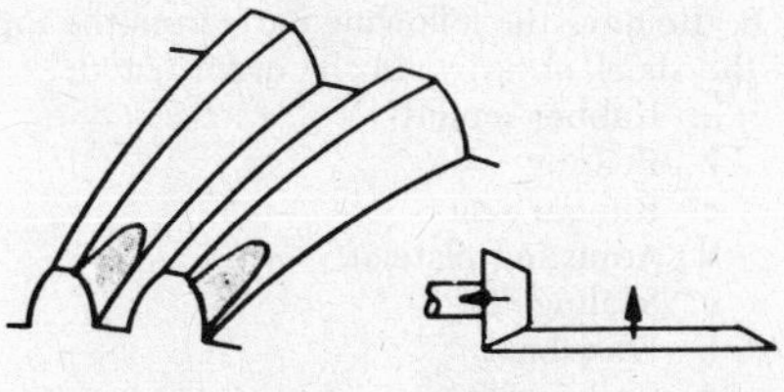
Too much toe contact (© Toyo Kogyo Co. Ltd.)

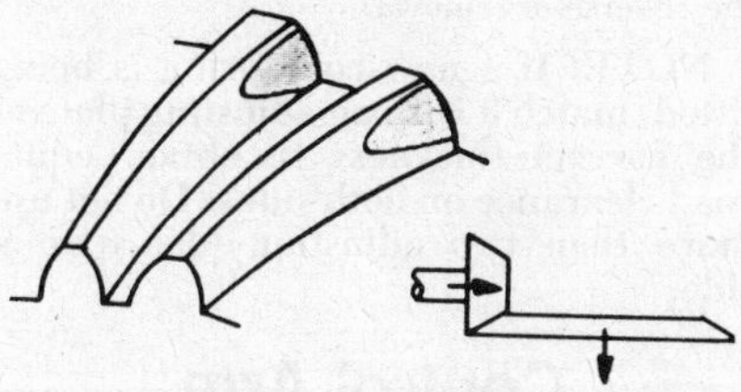
Too much heel contact (© Toyo Kogyo Co. Ltd.)

23. Install the adjusters on their respective sides.
24. Install the bearing cups.
25. Rotate the adjusters until the bearings are properly positioned in their outer races and end-play is eliminated.

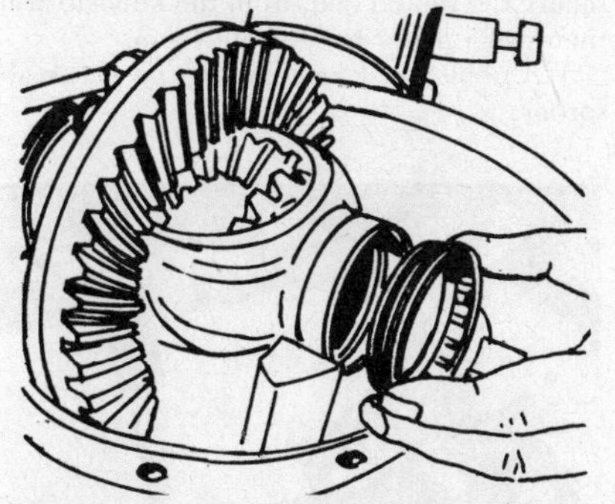
Installing the differential bearing adjuster

26. Finger tighten one of the bearing cap bolts on each bearing.
27. Check the backlash between the pinion and the ring gear teeth:
  a. If backlash is *more* than specified, loosen the adjusting nut on the pinion side one notch and tighten the ring gear adjusting nut one notch.
  b. If the backlash is *less* than specified, loosen the adjusting nut on the ring gear side one notch and tighten the pinion adjusting nut one notch.
  c. Repeat the procedure until the specified backlash of 0.0067-0.0075 in.
28. Tighten the adjusting nut on the differential bearings to obtain proper preload. Proper preload is determined when the distance between the pilot sections of the bearing caps is 7.3033 in. Measure the distance with a vernier caliper.

NOTE: Be careful not to disturb the backlash between the pinion and the ring gear teeth while adjusting the bearing preload.

29. Tighten the bearing cap securing bolts. Install the lockplate on the bearing adjuster.
30. Check the tooth contact pattern. See General Information.
31. Install the carrier.

REAR SUSPENSION

Springs

REMOVAL AND INSTALLATION

RX-3, RX-4 and 808 Models

1. Remove the wheel.
2. Support the rear axle housing.
3. On RX-4 and 808 models, disconnect the lower part of the shock from the spring clamp. On all models, remove the U-bolt seat, rubber pad, plate, and the U-bolt itself.
4. Unfasten the two bolts and the nut that secure the spring pin to the front end of the rear spring.
5. Pry the spring pin out with a large, flat screwdriver inserted between the spring pin and its body bracket.
6. Unfasten the nuts and the bolts which attach the rear shackle to the body.
7. Withdraw the rear spring assembly, complete with its shackle.
8. Remove the shackle assembly from the end of the spring.
9. Pull the rubber bushings out from both ends of the spring.
10. Rear spring installation is the reverse of removal. When installing the rubber bushings, do not lubricate them.

Cosmo

1. Remove the rear wheels.
2. Support the lower arms with a jack.
3. Remove the pivot bolt and nut which secures the rear end of the lower arm to the axle housing.
4. Lower the jack to relieve the spring pressure on the lower arm and remove the spring.
5. If replacing one spring only, a suitable adjusting plate will be necessary to give equal road clearance on each side.
6. Install spring in reverse order of removal, but do not tighten bolts while car is on stands.

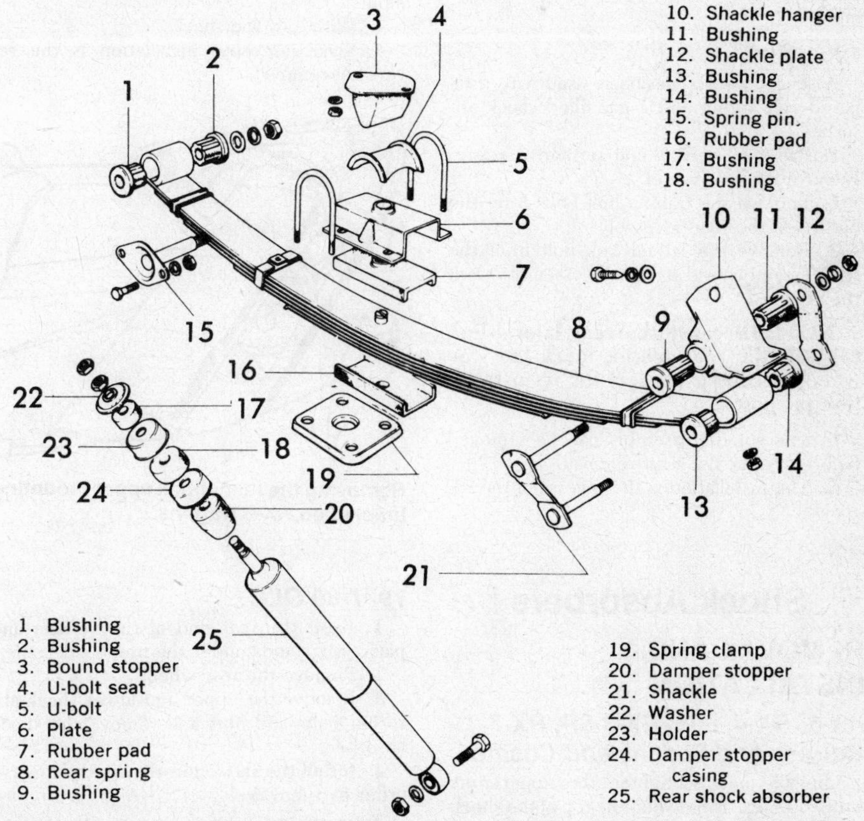

RX-3 sedan and coupe rear suspension—wagon and RX-4 similar (© Toyo Kogyo Co. Ltd.)

1977-80 GLC

1. Raise the rear end of the vehicle and place jack stands under the frame side rails.
2. Remove the rear wheel.
3. Remove the upper and lower shock absorber bolts and nuts and remove the shock absorber.
4. Place a jack under the lower arm to support it.
5. Remove the pivot bolt and nut that secures the rear end of the lower arm to the axle housing.
6. Slowly lower the jack to relieve the spring pressure on the lower arm, then remove the spring.
7. Install the spring in the reverse order of removal.

RX-7

1. Raise the rear of the vehicle and support it safely.
2. Remove the rear wheel.
3. Disconnect the shock absorber lower end and the lower link bolt (just to the front of the lower shock bolt). Remove the rear bolt from the upper link.

NOTE: These trailing control arm links run parallel from the front to rear on the vehicle, with the smaller watt links running side to side on the vehicle.

4. Disconnect the front ends of the stabilizer bar (if equipped).
5. Remove the right and left watt links at the rear axle housing.
6. Carefully lower the rear axle housing and remove the coil spring and the rubber seat.
7. The installation is the reverse of the removal.

1981 GLC

A strut type suspension is used with a tapered coil spring and a gas filled shock absorber.

1. Raise the vehicle and support it safely. Remove the rear wheel.
2. Remove the trailing link bolts from the bottom of the strut assembly.
3. Remove the lateral link bolt from the strut assembly and lower the assembly from the vehicle.

NOTE: Because the rear lateral link controls the rear toe-in, mark the star wheel (eccentric spacer) for re-installation purposes.

4. The spindle assembly can be removed before or after the strut removal.
5. The installation is the reverse of the removal.

Shock Absorbers

REMOVAL AND INSTALLATION

RX-3, RX-4, 808, RX-3 SP, RX-7 Coupes and Sedans and Cosmo

On 808 models, tighten the upper nuts until ¼ in. exists between the top of the shock absorber rod and the top of the top nut.

Remove the trim panel from the rear of the

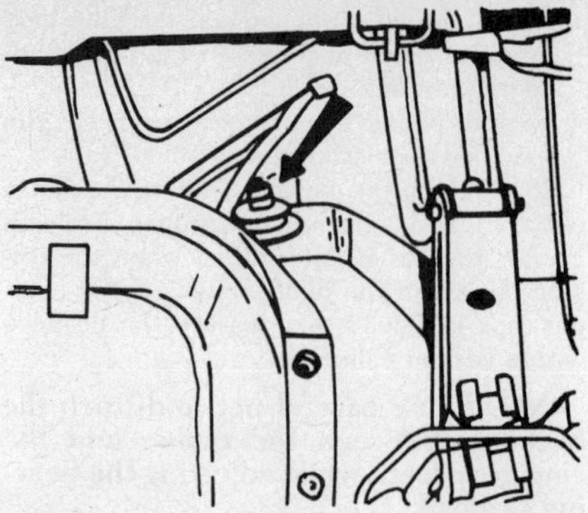

Arrow shows the location of the upper rear shock nut on RX-3 coupes and sedans

luggage compartment. On RX-4 models it will be necessary to remove the rear seat first.

1. Unfasten the nuts, then remove the washers and rubber bushings from the upper shock absorber mounts.
2. Unfasten the nut and bolt which secure the end of the rear shock to the axle housing.
3. Remove the shock.
4. Installation is the reverse of removal.

RX-3, RX-4, 808 Wagons

On 808 models tighten the upper nuts until ¼ in. exists between the bottom of the shock absorber rod and the bottom of the nut.

1. Remove the locknuts, washers, and rubber bushings from the bottom shock absorber mount.
2. Compress the shock. Unfasten the bolts which secure the upper shock absorber mount.
3. Withdraw the shock.
4. Shock absorber installation is the reverse of removal.

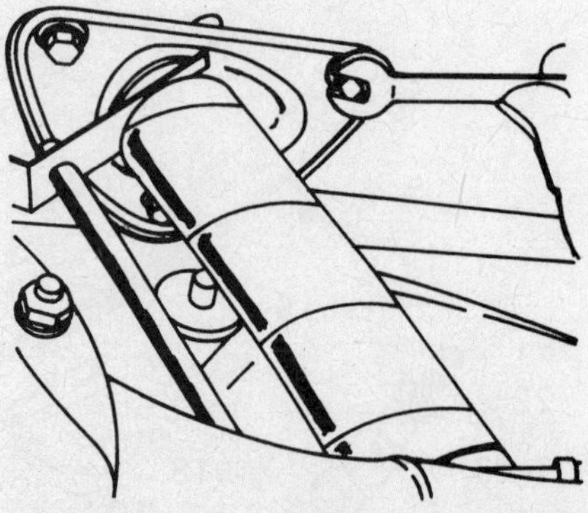

Removing the rear shock upper mounting bracket on RX-3 wagons

1977-80 GLC

1. Raise the rear end of the vehicle and place jack stands under the frame side rails.
2. Remove the rear wheel.
3. Remove the upper and lower shock absorber bolts and nuts and remove the shock absorber.
4. Install the shock absorber in the reverse order of removal.

NOTE: The 1981 GLC shock absorber is part of the strut assembly.

FRONT SUSPENSION

MacPherson Struts

REMOVAL, INSTALLATION AND OVERHAUL

1. Remove the wheel.
2. Remove the brake caliper and disc.
3. Remove the shock and coil spring as a complete assembly.
4. Mount the strut (shock/spring) assembly in a vise. Compress the coil spring.
5. Hold the upper end of the shock piston rod with a pipe wrench and remove the locknut.
6. Remove the following parts from the top of the shock absorber in the order listed:
   a. Rubber mount
   b. Bearing
   c. Rubber seat
   d. Adjusting plate(s)
   e. Sealing ring
   f. Dust boot
   g. Coil spring
   h. Lower seat
7. Installation of the MacPherson strut is the reverse of removal.

NOTE: If a new coil spring is being fitted, match it with an adjusting plate of the correct thickness to obtain equal road clearance on both sides. Do not use more than two adjusting plates on a side.

Control Arm

REMOVAL AND INSTALLATION

Remove the control arm and steering knuckle as an assembly.

1. Remove the wheel.
2. Remove the cotter pin and nut, which secure the tie rod end, from the knuckle arm; then use a puller to separate them.
3. Unbolt the lower end of the shock absorber.

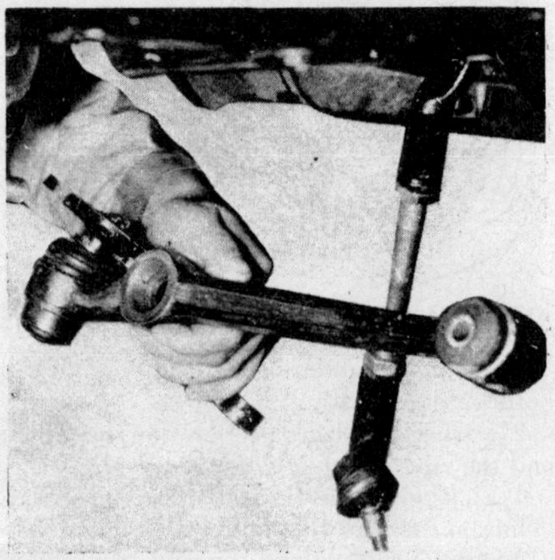

Removing the control arm (© Toyo Kogyo Co. Ltd.)

4. Remove the nut, then withdraw the rubber bushing and washer which secure the stabilizer bar to the control arm.
5. Unfasten the nut and bolt which secure the control arm to the frame member.
6. Push outward on the strut assembly while removing the end of the control arm from the frame member.
7. Remove the control arm and steering knuckle arm as an assembly.
8. Separate the knuckle arm from the control arm with a puller.
9. Installation of the control arm is the reverse of removal.

Ball Joints

INSPECTION

All Exc. GLC

1. Perform steps 1-5 of the control arm removal procedure.
2. Check the ball joint dust boot.
3. Check the amount of pressure required to turn the ball stud, by hooking a pull scale into the tie rod hole in the knuckle arm. Pull the spring scale until the arm just begins to turn; this should require 13-24 ft/lbs–RX-3, 27-40 ft/lbs–1977 and earlier RX-4 and Cosmo, 17.6-30 ft/lbs–808, or 4.4-8.8 ft/lbs–1978-79 Cosmo and RX-4 or 4.6-9.2 ft/lbs–RX-3SP.

If the reading is lower than 14 oz. on the RX-7, replace the ball joint and the suspension arm as a unit.

GLC (1977-80)

1. Check the dust boot for wear.
2. Raise the wheels off the ground and grip the tire at the top and bottom and alternately push and pull to check ball joint end-play. Wear limit is .04 in. If necessary, replace the ball joint and control arm assembly.

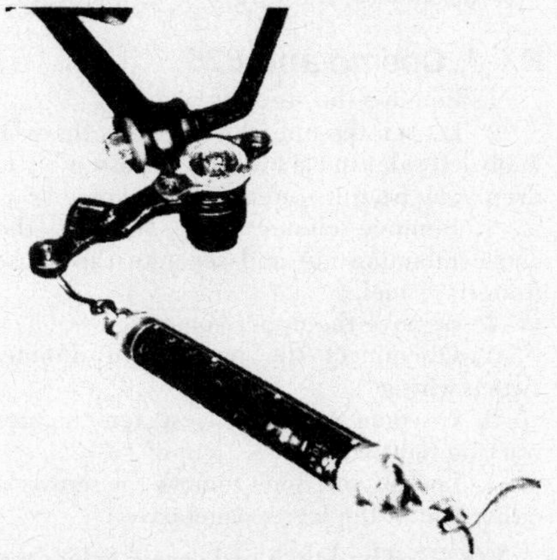

Checking the ball stud rotational torque with a spring scale (© Toyo Kogyo Co. Ltd.)

REMOVAL AND INSTALLATION

All Exc. GLC

Remove the control arm.

1. Remove the set-ring and the dust boot.
2. Press the ball joint out of the control arm.

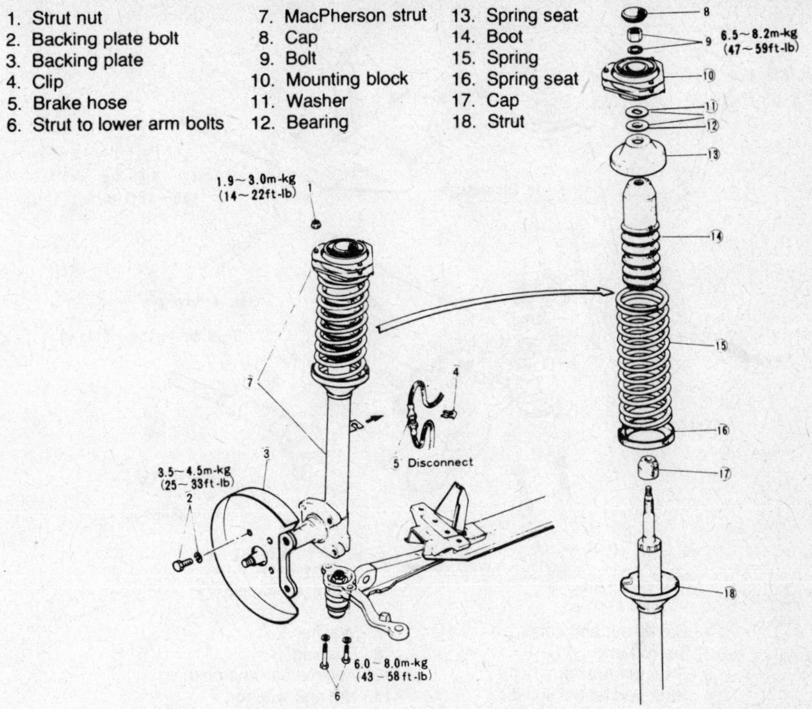

GLC MacPherson strut (© Toyo Kogyo Co. Ltd.)

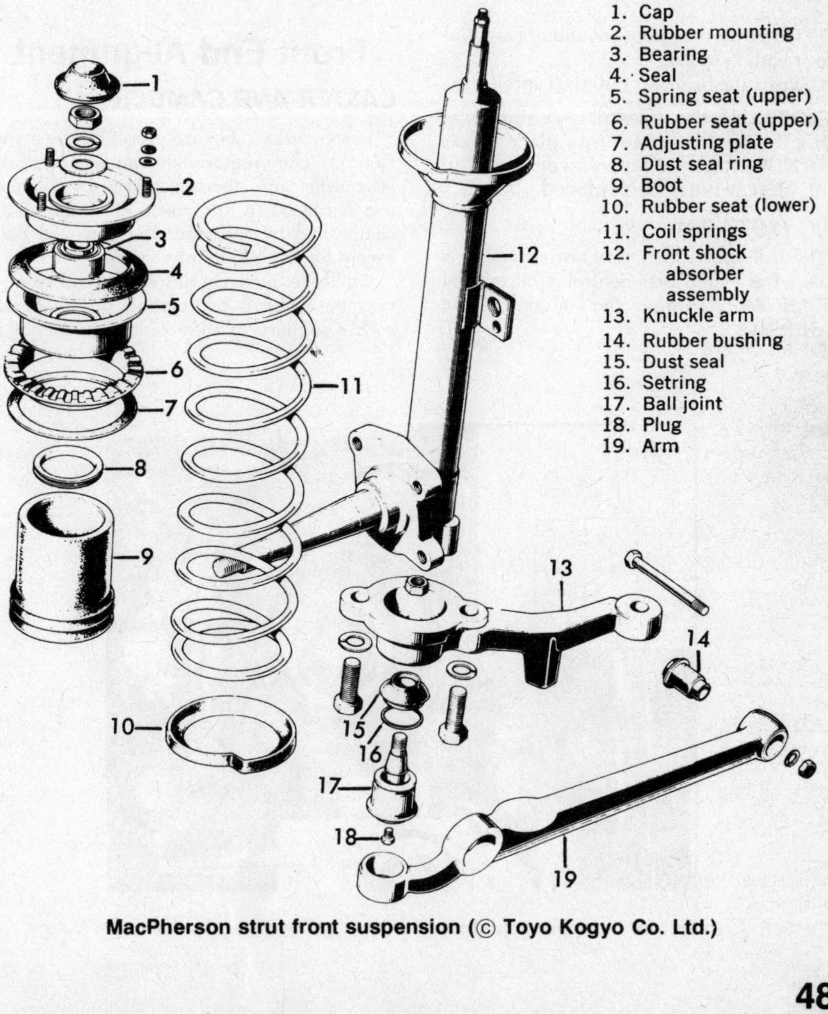

MacPherson strut front suspension (© Toyo Kogyo Co. Ltd.)

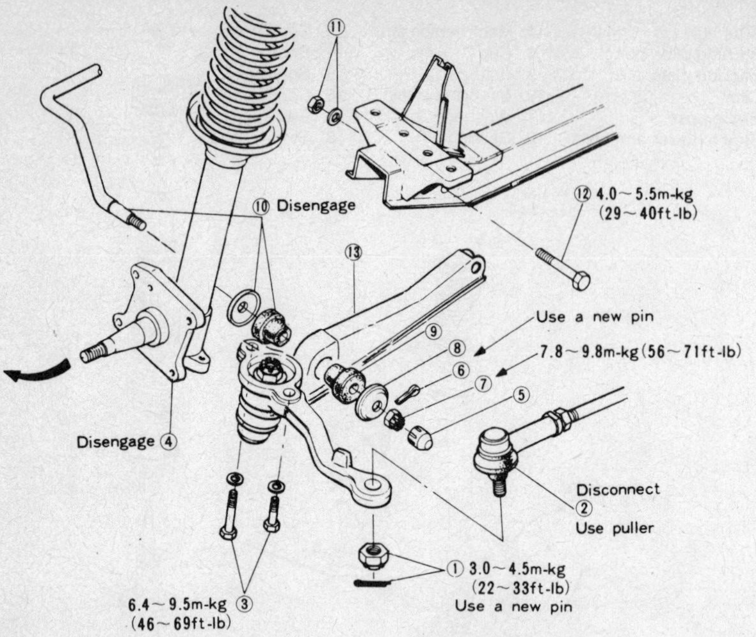

1. Castle nut and cotter pin
2. Tie-rod end
3. Strut to lower arm bolts
4. Strut and wheel spindle
5. Cap nut
6. Cotter pin
7. Castle nut
8. Washer
9. Bushing
10. Anti-roll bar and bushing
11. Nut and washer
12. Suspension arm bolt
13. Suspension arm

GLC MacPherson strut and lower arm components (© Toyo Kogyo Co. Ltd.)

3. Clean the ball joint mounting bore and coat it with kerosene.
4. Press the ball joint into the control arm.

NOTE: If the pressure required to press the new ball joint into place is less than 3,300 lbs., the bore is worn and the control arm must be replaced.

GLC (1977-80)

The ball joint and control arm assembly is replaced as a unit. See Control Arm removal and installation. Torque the ball joint nut to 43-51 ft/lbs

Front End Alignment

CASTER AND CAMBER

Caster and camber are preset by the manufacturer. They require adjustment only if the suspension and steering linkage components are damaged. In this case, adjustment is accomplished by replacing the damaged part, except for the RX-4 and Cosmo.

On these models, the caster and camber may be changed by rotating the shock absorber support. If they can't be brought to within specifications, replace or repair suspension parts as necessary.

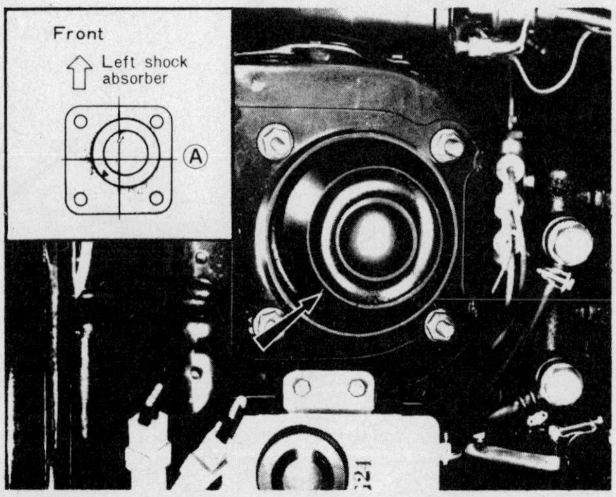

Caster and camber adjustment—RX-4 (© Toyo Kogyo Co. Ltd.)

TOE-IN ADJUSTMENT

To adjust the toe-in, loosen the tie rod locknuts and turn both tie rods an equal amount, until the proper specification is obtained.

STEERING

Steering Wheel

REMOVAL AND INSTALLATION

1. Remove the crash pad/horn button assembly. On four-spoke steering wheels, pull the center cap toward the wheel top.
2. Punch matchmarks on the steering wheel and steering shaft.
3. Remove the wheel.
4. Installation is the reverse of removal.

Combination (Turn Signal) Switch

REPLACEMENT

808, RX-3, RX-3SP and RX-7

1. Remove the steering wheel.
2. Remove the left-hand column shroud.
3. Remove the retaining ring (screw on 808) from the combination (turn signal) switch.
4. Withdraw the switch over the steering column.
5. Installation is the reverse of removal.

RX-4, Cosmo and 626

1. Remove the steering wheel.
2. Loosen the nut which secures the vent knob (left side) and allow the knob assembly to drop away from its mounting bracket.
3. Remove choke knob. Remove the choke retaining nut and separate the choke from the panel.
4. Remove the upper column cover.
5. Disconnect the panel light dimmer switch wiring.
6. Disconnect the exhaust temperature warning light wiring.
7. Loosen, but don't remove the screws at either end of the lower panel cover.

NOTE: The left-hand screw is located in the hole which was covered by the upper column cover and the right-hand screw is above the ashtray opening (ashtray removed).

8. Pull the upper column cover away from the instrument panel.
9. Disconnect the combination switch connector.
10. Remove the retaining ring from the steering column.
11. Unfasten the combination switch retaining screw and remove the switch.
12. Installation is the reverse of removal.

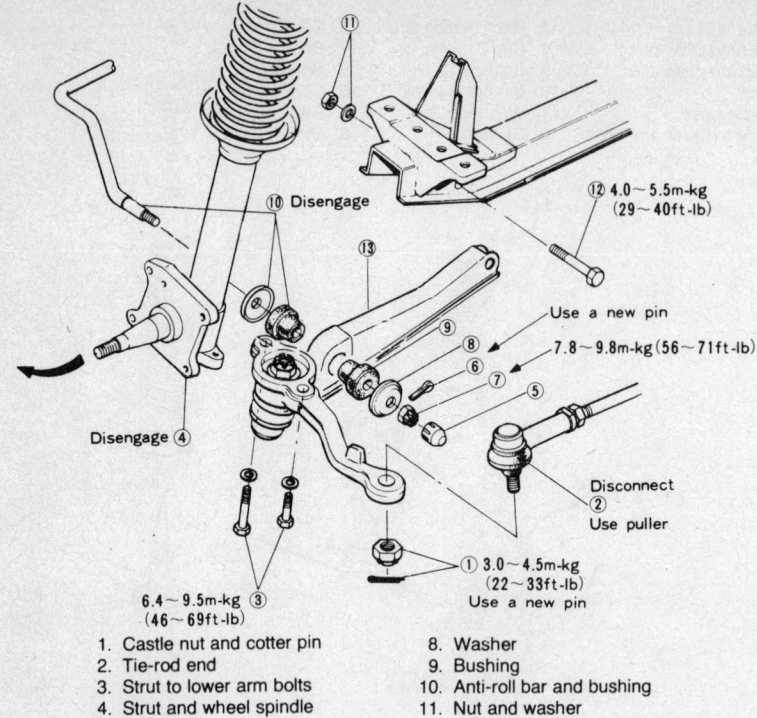

GLC

1. Disconnect the negative battery cable.
2. Remove the horn cap and steering wheel.
3. Remove the steering column covers.
4. Disconnect the wire connectors.
5. Remove the stop ring from the shaft.
6. Remove the attaching screw and remove the combination switch.
7. To install reverse the removal procedure.

Ignition Lock/Switch Assembly

REMOVAL AND INSTALLATION

RX-3, RX-3SP, RX-7 and 808

NOTE: For 808 models, follow procedure for removing combination switch, then skip to Step 5.

1. Remove the light switch knob.
2. Remove the left and right steering column shrouds.
3. Disconnect the multiconnector from the switch assembly.
4. Use a file or a hacksaw to make slots in the switch securing bolts. Remove the bolts with a screwdriver.
5. Withdraw the switch assembly.
6. To install the switch, reverse the removal procedure. After tightening the switch securing bolts, break their heads off, in order to make the switch difficult for a thief to remove.

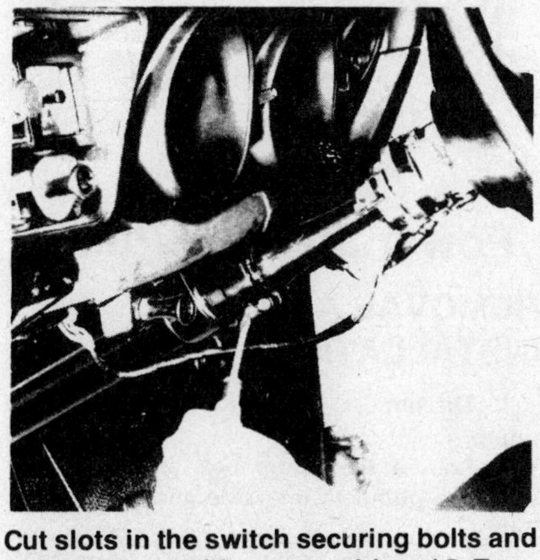

Cut slots in the switch securing bolts and remove them with a screwdriver (© Toyo Kogyo Co. Ltd.)

RX-4, GLC, Cosmo and 626

1. Follow steps under Combination Switch Replacement.
2. Remove the instrument frame brace.
3. Disconnect the switch wires.
4. Remove the switch.
5. Installation is the reverse of removal.

Steering Linkage

REMOVAL AND INSTALLATION

The front wheels should point straight ahead. Align the marks on the pitman arm and the sector shaft to ensure proper steering linkage alignment.

1. Remove the cotter pins and the castellated nuts which secure the ends of the tie rods to the center link and the steering knuckle.
2. Remove the tie rods.
3. Remove the idler arm.
4. Remove the pitman arm. Remove the center link. On RX-4 models, remove steering damper first.
5. Unfasten the nut which secures the pitman arm to the sector shaft and use a puller to separate them.
6. Installation is the reverse of removal.

Idler Arm

REPLACEMENT

All exc. 1977-80 GLC

1. Remove the front wheels.
2. Disconnect the center link from the idler arm.
3. Unbolt the idler arm bracket from the frame.
4. Hold the assembly in a vise and remove the arm from the bracket by turning the arm counterclockwise.
5. Check all parts for wear and replace as necessary.
6. Insert the spring into the bracket and screw the idler arm into the bracket until the distance between the lip edge on the idler arm and the leading edge of the bracket is 0.157-0.236 in.
7. Check the revolving torque of the arm with a spring scale. If the torque is less than 0.2 lb., screw in the arm until the correct reading is obtained. If the torque is greater than 6.6 lb., unscrew the arm until the correct torque is obtained.
8. If the correct torque cannot be obtained, replace the spring.
9. Grease the assembly through a nipple replacing the plug in the end of the bracket.
10. Attach the idler arm and bracket assembly to the frame.
11. Connect the idler arm to the center link.

1977-80 GLC

1. Remove the front wheels.
2. Disconnect the center link from the idler arm by removing the nut and split pin and using a puller.
3. Unbolt the idler arm bracket from the frame.
4. Remove the split pin and nut from the idler arm at the frame bracket and remove the arm from the bracket.
5. To install reverse the removal procedure. Torque the bracket to frame bolt and nut to 32-40 ft/lbs and the center link to idler arm nut to 18-25 ft/lbs.

Pitman Arm

REMOVAL AND INSTALLATION

1. Remove the wheels.
2. Disconnect the center link at the pitman arm.
3. Remove the pitman arm.
4. Install the pitman arm onto the sector shaft, aligning the identification marks. Tighten the nut to 94-123 ft/lbs (1975-76), 108-130 ft/lbs (1977-79 exc GLC), 58-87 ft/lbs (GLC).
5. Connect the center link to the pitman arm.

Tie Rod

REMOVAL AND INSTALLATION

1. Disconnect the tie rod from the center link and knuckle arm. A puller will be necessary.
2. Install the tie rod to the center link and knuckle arm. Tighten the nuts to 22-32 ft/lbs and install new cotter pins.

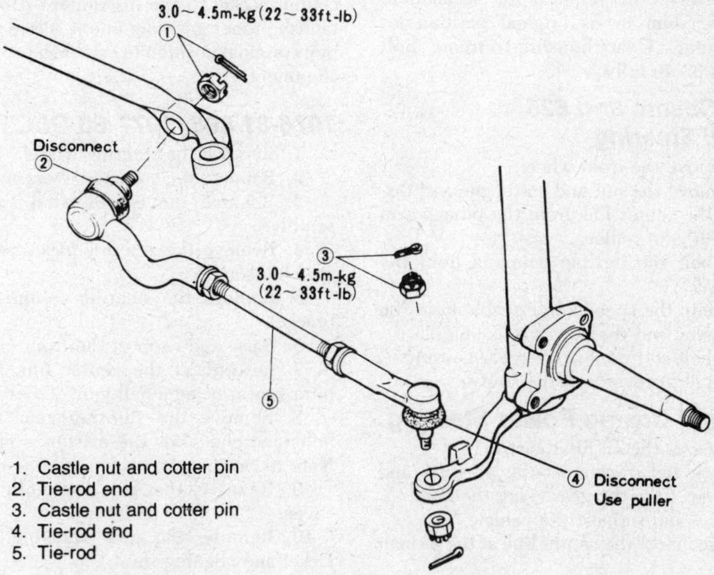

GLC tie-rod removal; other models similar (© Toyo Kogyo Co. Ltd.)

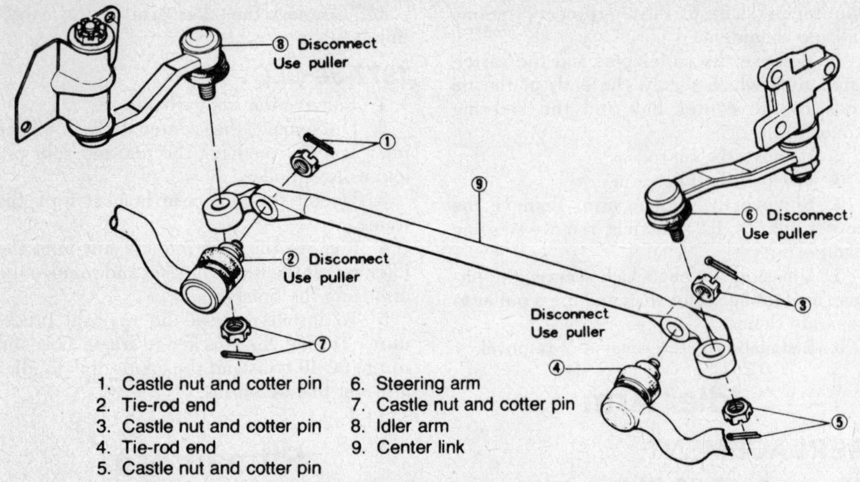

GLC center link removal; other models similar (© Toyo Kogyo Co. Ltd.)

Steering Gear

REMOVAL AND INSTALLATION

RX-3, RX-3SP and RX-7

1. Remove the steering wheel.
2. Remove the column covers.
3. Remove the combination switch assembly.
4. Remove the steering lock and ignition switch assembly.
5. Remove the steering column support bracket.
6. Raise and support the front end.
7. Remove the front wheel.
8. Remove the cotter pin and nut and disconnect the center link from the pitman arm using a ball joint puller.
9. Unbolt the steering gear from the frame, taking note of the presence of any shim for realigning the gear with the shaft.
10. Remove the steering column dust cover and remove the gear housing, column jacket and aligning shim.
11. Reverse the removal for installation. Place the shim in its original position for realignment. Gear housing-to-frame bolt torque is 32-40 ft/lbs.

RX-4, Cosmo and 626 Manual Steering

1. Remove the front wheel.
2. Remove the nut and cotter pin and disconnect the center link from the pitman arm with a ball joint puller.
3. Unbolt the flexible coupling from the worm shaft.
4. Unclip the speedometer cable from the gear housing and the power brake unit.
5. Unbolt and remove the gear housing.
6. Install in reverse of the above.

RX-4 and Cosmo Power Steering

1. Remove the oil filter cartridge.
2. Mark and disconnect the pressure and return lines from the gear. Plug the lines.
3. Raise and support the vehicle.
4. Disconnect the center link at the pitman arm.
5. Remove the gear housing-to-frame bolts.
6. Remove the clamp that holds the flexible coupling to the steering gear and slide the gear off the coupling.
7. Install in reverse of removal. Fill and bleed the system.

1975 808

1. Remove the steering wheel.
2. Remove the column covers.
3. Remove the combination switch.
4. Remove the steering lock and ignition switch.
5. Remove the steering column support bracket.
6. Open the hood and remove the steering column dust cover.
7. Remove the left headlight and horn.
8. Raise and support the vehicle.
9. Remove the front wheel.
10. Disconnect the center link from the pitman arm using a ball joint puller.
11. Unbolt and remove the steering gear housing from the frame, noting the position of any shim for realignment.
12. Reverse the above for installation. Before installing the gear housing, install the column jacket to the instrument panel to establish proper gear alignment. Place the shim in its original position to establish proper shaft alignment.

1976-81 808, 1977-80 GLC

1. Remove the steering wheel.
2. Remove the column covers.
3. Remove the combination switch assembly.
4. Remove the steering lock and ignition switch assembly.
5. Remove the steering column support bracket.
6. Raise and support the front end.
7. Disconnect the center link from the pitman arm using a ball joint puller.
8. Remove the steering gear retaining bolts and check for the existence of a shim. Note its position for realignment.
9. Remove the steering column dust cover.
10. Remove the gear housing, column jacket and aligning shim.
11. Installation is the reverse of removal.
12. Place shim in its original position.

STEERING GEAR ADJUSTMENT

Worm Bearing Preload

1. Remove the gear.
2. Rotate the worm shaft with a torque wrench and check the torque. Rotating torque should be 7.8-13 in/lb for RX-3; 8-10 in/lb for RX-4; 0.44-1.1 lb. For RX-7; 5-11 in/lbs for Cosmo; 8-13 in/lb for 808; 5-7 in/lb for GLC. If not, adjust as follows:
3. Remove the end cover and shims.
4. If the preload was too light, remove shims; if too heavy, add shims.
5. Install the end cover.

Backlash

The sector shaft adjusting screw, located in the cover, raises or lowers the sector shaft to provide proper mesh with the sector gear and rack. Adjust as follows:

1. Turn the wormshaft gently and stop it at the center position.
2. Loosen the locknut and turn the adjusting screw in or out. The standard backlash is 0-0.0039 in.
3. Tighten the adjusting screw.

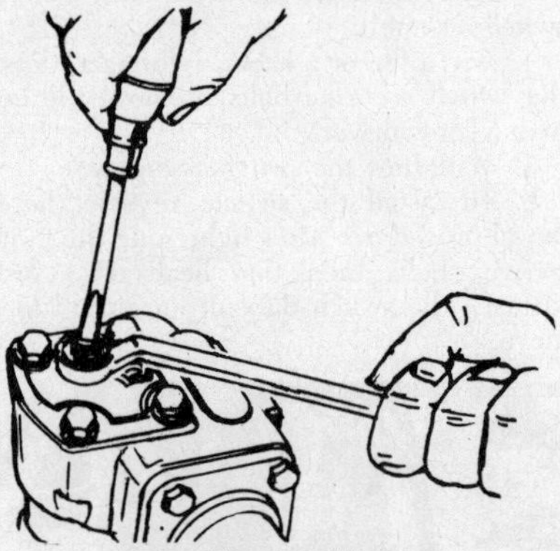

Adjusting backlash

Power Steering Pump

REMOVAL AND INSTALLATION

1. Disconnect the fluid hoses from the pump.
2. Loosen the pump belt adjusting bolt, slide the pump to one side and remove the belt.
3. Support the pump, remove the mounting bolts and lift out the pump.
4. Installation is the reverse of removal. Adjust belt to give a ½ in. deflection at the mid-point of its longest stretch. Fill the reservoir and bleed the system.

BRAKE SYSTEM

Adjustments

REAR DRUM BRAKE

All Exc. 1977-80 GLC

1. Release the parking brake completely.

2. Remove the adjusting hole plugs.
3. Engage the adjuster with a brake spoon. Turn the adjuster in the direction of the arrow stamped on the backing plate until the brake shoes are locked.
4. Pump the brake pedal several times to be sure that the brake shoe contacts the drum evenly.

NOTE: If the wheel turns after you remove your foot from the brake pedal, continue turning the adjuster until the wheel will no longer rotate.

5. Back off on the adjuster, about five notches (2-3 notches–RX-4). The wheel should rotate freely, without dragging.

NOTE: The RX-7 has rear disc brakes as an option. No adjustment is needed.

1977-80 GLC

1. Release the parking brake.
2. Loosen the locknut that secures the anchor pin.
3. Hold the locknut and turn the anchor pin counterclockwise until the wheel is locked. See illustration.

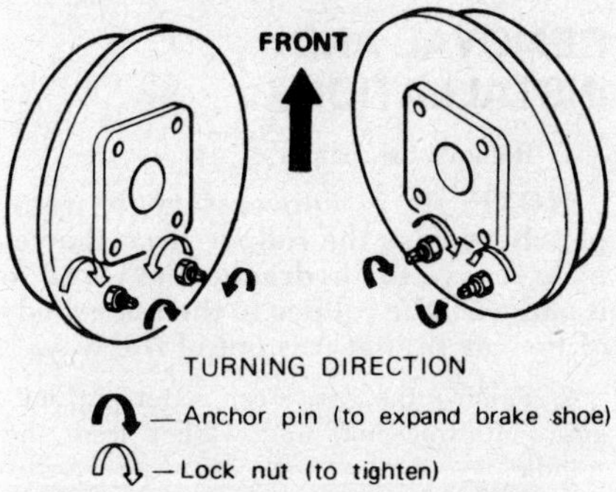

GLC rear brake adjustment (© Toyo Kogyo Co. Ltd.)

4. Then release the anchor pin until the wheel just turns freely.
5. Hold the anchor pin in position and tighten the locknut.
6. Repeat the above adjustment for each brake shoe.

NOTE: 1981 GLC has self-adjusting brakes.

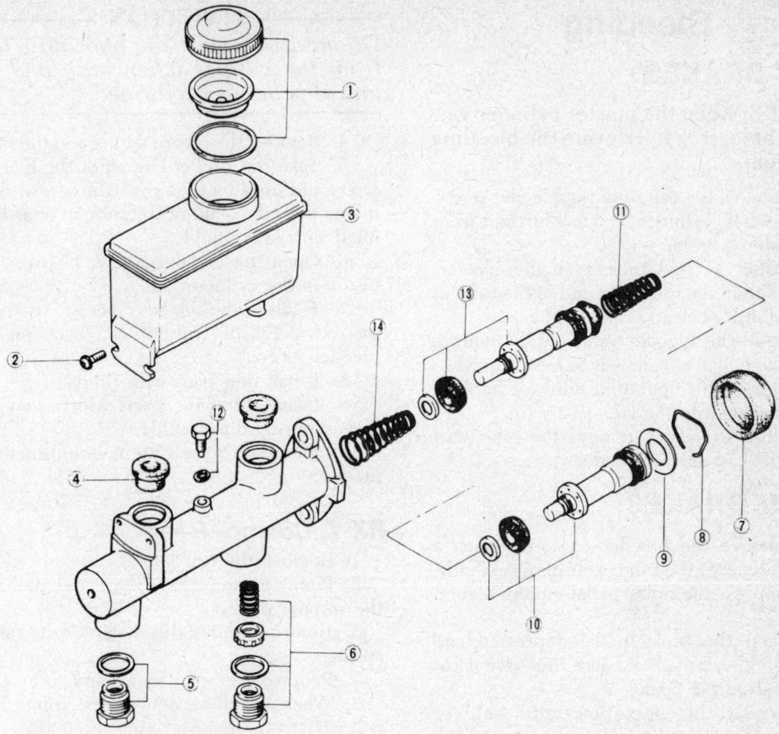

GLC brake master cylinder; others similar (© Toyo Kogyo Co. Ltd.)

Brake Pedal

1. Detach the wiring from the brake light switch terminals.
2. Loosen the locknut on the switch.
3. Turn the switch until the distance between the pedal and the floor is 7.3 in.
4. Tighten the locknut on switch.
5. Loosen the locknut located on the push rod.
6. Rotate the pushrod, until a pedal free travel of 0.2-0.6 in. is obtained.
7. Tighten the pushrod locknut.

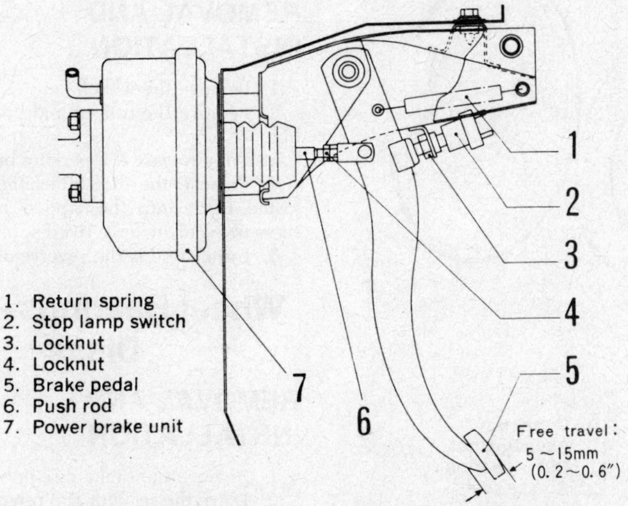

Brake pedal component (© Toyo Kogyo Co. Ltd.)

Master Cylinder

REMOVAL AND INSTALLATION

NOTE: On models which have a fluid reservoir located separately from the master cylinder, remove the lines which run between the two and plug the lines to prevent leakage.

Detach and plug the lines. Unbolt and remove the master cylinder.

Installation is the reverse of removal.

Brake Failure Warning Valve

CENTRALIZING

1. Turn the ignition switch to the ON position.
2. Make sure that the fluid level in the master cylinder is at the ¾ mark.
3. Depress the brake pedal and the piston will center itself causing the light to go off.
4. Turn the switch to OFF and check the fluid level. Check for a firm pedal.

Bleeding

DISC BRAKES

NOTE: Keep the master cylinder reservoir at least ¾ full during the bleeding operation.

1. Remove the cap from the bleeder screw on that wheel cylinder which is furthest from the master cylinder.
2. Install a vinyl tube over the bleeder screw. Submerge the other end of the tube in a jar half-full of clean brake fluid.
3. Open the bleeder valve. Fully depress the brake pedal and allow it to return slowly.
4. Repeat this operation until air bubbles cease flowing into the jar.
5. Close the valve, remove the tube, and install the cap on the bleeder valve.

DRUM BRAKES

1. Remove the bleeder cap and attach a tube. Submerge the tube in clean brake fluid.
2. Depress the brake pedal rapidly several times.
3. Keep the brake pedal depressed and open the bleeder valve. Close the valve without releasing the pedal.
4. Repeat this operation until bubbles cease to appear in the jar.
5. Remove the tube and install the cap on the bleeder valve.

Disc Brake Pads

REMOVAL AND INSTALLATION

All Models–Front

1. Remove the wheel.
2. On all 1975 models, remove the retainer and the locating pins.
3. On 1976-81 models, remove the securing clips, the stop plates, the caliper assembly, and the anti-rattle spring.

CAUTION

Do not disconnect the hydraulic line from the caliper when only pad removal is being performed.

4. Remove the return spring and the pad.
5. Take the rubber cap off of the bleeder screw and install a tube over the screw. Submerge the other end of the tube in a jar half-filled with brake fluid.
6. Open the bleeder screw. Depress the piston in the cylinder.
7. Tighten the bleeder screw. Remove the tube. Fit the rubber cap back on the bleeder screw.
8. Install new pads with shims.
9. Install all of the parts which were removed during disassembly.
10. Bleed the brake system, as outlined below.

RX-7, Cosmo–Rear

1. Remove the rear wheel.
2. Remove the locking clips and pull out the stopper plates.
3. Remove the caliper and anti-rattle spring.
4. Remove the brake shoes and shims.
5. When installing new shoes, some fluid will have to be removed from the master cylinder to allow the new shoes to be positioned. Lightly lubricate the stopper plates.

Disc Brake Calipers

REMOVAL AND INSTALLATION

All Models

1. Remove the disc brake pad.
2. Detach the hydraulic line from the caliper.
3. Unbolt and remove the caliper.
4. Follow the caliper removal procedure in reverse to install. Bleed the system.

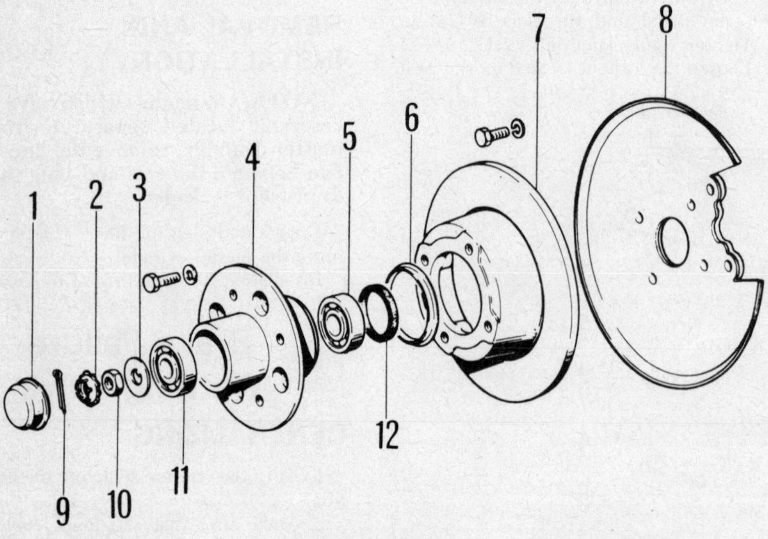

1. Grease cap
2. Nut lock
3. Flat washer
4. Hub
5. Inner bearing
6. Dust ring
7. Brake disc
8. Backing plate
9. Cotter pin
10. Adjusting nut
11. Outer bearing
12. Grease seal

RX-3 front wheel hub assembly—RX-2 similar (© Toyo Kogyo Co. Ltd.)

OVERHAUL

All Models

1. Remove the dust boot retainer and the boot.
2. Apply compressed air through the hydraulic line fitting and remove the piston.

NOTE: If the piston is frozen and cannot be removed from the caliper, tap lightly around it while air pressure is being applied.

3. Withdraw the piston and seal from the caliper bore.
4. If necessary, remove the bleeder screw.
5. Wash all of the parts in clean brake fluid. Dry them off with compressed air.

NOTE: Discard the old piston seal and dust boot. Replace them with new ones.

6. Assemble the caliper in the reverse order of disassembly. Install it on the car and bleed the brake system.

Front Brake Disc

REMOVAL AND INSTALLATION

1. Remove the caliper.

NOTE: It is unnecessary to completely remove the caliper from the vehicle. Leave the hydraulic line wired to it and wire the caliper to the underbody of the car so that it is out of the way.

2. Remove the grease cap cotter pin, nut-lock, adjusting nut, and washer from the spindle.
3. Take the thrust washer and outer bearing off of the hub.
4. Pull the brake disc/wheel hub assembly off of the spindle.
5. Unbolt and separate the brake disc from the hub after matchmarking them for proper installation.
6. Installation of the disc and hub is the reverse of removal. Adjust the bearing.

Rear Brake Disc

REMOVAL AND INSTALLATION

1. Remove the wheel.
2. Remove the caliper and bracket assembly.
3. Fully release the parking brake.
4. Remove the disc attaching screws and install them into the tapped holes. Screw them in evenly to force the disc off the flange.
5. Installation is the reverse of the above.

Wheel Bearings–Front Discs

REMOVAL AND INSTALLATION

1. Remove the brake disc/hub.
2. Drive the seal out and remove the inner bearing.

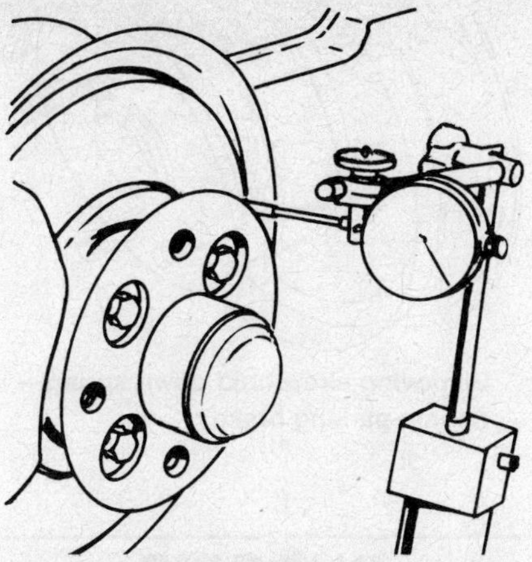

Checking the front brake disc run-out

3. Drive the outer bearing races out.
4. Installation is the reverse of removal. Repack the bearings and the hub cavity with lithium grease. Adjust the bearing.

ADJUSTMENT

NOTE: This operation is performed with the wheel, grease cap, nut lock, and cotter pin removed.

1. To seat the bearings, back off on the adjusting nut three turns and then rotate the hub/disc assembly while tightening the adjusting nut.
2. Back off on the adjusting nut about $^1/_6$ of a turn.
3. Hook a spring scale in one of the bolt holes on the hub.
4. Pull the spring scale squarely, until the hub just begins to rotate. The scale reading should be 0.9-2.2 lbs.–all passenger cars exc. GLC; 0.33-1.32 lbs.–GLC. Tighten the adjusting nut until the proper spring scale reading is obtained.
5. Place the castellated nut lock over the adjusting nut. Align one of the slots on the nut-lock with the hole in the spindle and fit the cotter pin into place.

Front Brake Drum

REMOVAL AND INSTALLATION

1. Remove the wheel.
2. Remove the brake drum attaching screws and install them in the tapped holes in the brake drum.
3. Turn these screws in evenly to force the brake drum away from the wheel hub.

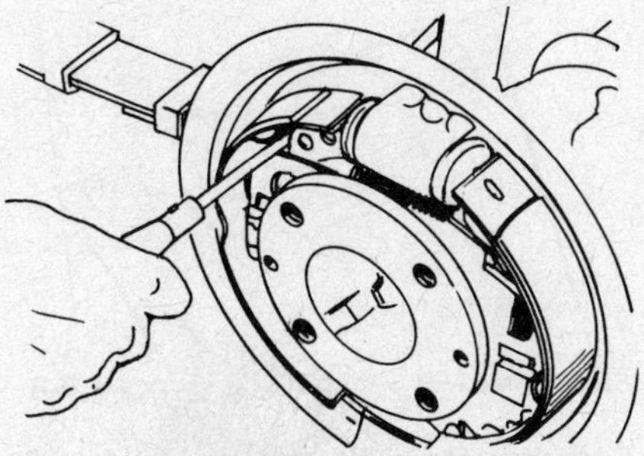

Shoe return spring removal

4. Remove and inspect the brake drum.
5. Installation is the reverse of removal.

Front Brake Shoes

REMOVAL AND INSTALLATION

Brake shoes are installed on the backing plate with the slot in the shoe web toward the wheel cylinder starwheel.

1. Remove the wheel.
2. Remove the brake drum.
3. Remove the brake shoe retracting springs.
4. Remove the shoe retaining spring guide pin and the retaining spring.
5. Remove the brake shoes.
6. Installation is the reverse of removal.

Wheel Cylinder

REMOVAL AND INSTALLATION

1. Remove the wheel.
2. Remove the brake drum and brake shoes.
3. Disconnect and plug the brake line.
4. Remove the stud nuts and bolt attaching the wheel cylinder to the backing plate and remove the wheel cylinder.
5. Installation is the reverse of removal.

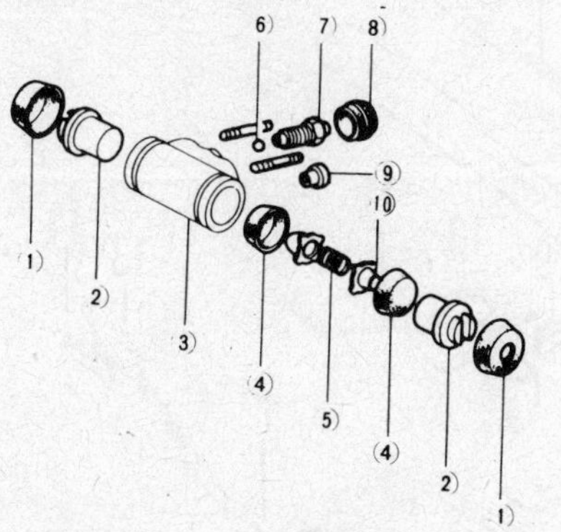

1. Boot
2. Piston
3. Cylinder body
4. Piston cup
5. Return spring
6. Steel ball
7. Bleeder screw
8. Bleeder screw cap
9. Hydraulic line seat
10. Push rod

Rear wheel cylinder components (© Toyo Kogyo Co. Ltd.)

Front Wheel Bearings–Drum Brakes

ADJUSTMENT

Primary Procedure

1. Remove the wheel.
2. Attach a spring scale onto a hub bolt.
3. Pull the spring scale squarely and read the pull as the hub begins to turn. It should be 1.3-2.4 lbs.
4. Adjust the bearings with the spindle until the proper reading is obtained.
5. Align the holes of the adjusting nut and spindle and install a new cotter pin.
6. Install the grease cap, wheel and tire.

Alternate Procedure

If a spring scale is not available, the following procedure can be used.

1. Rotate the hub and tighten the adjusting nut until the hub binds.
2. Back the adjusting nut off $^1/_6$ turn. Be sure that the hub rotates freely with no side-play.
3. Align the holes of the nut and spindle and install a new cotter pin.

REMOVAL, INSTALLATION AND PACKING

1. Remove the wheel.
2. Remove the grease cap from the hub. Remove the cotter pin, nut lock, adjusting nut and flat washer from the spindle.
3. Remove the hub and drum.
4. Remove and discard the old grease retainer. Remove the inner bearing cone and roller from the hub.
5. Clean the grease from the inner and outer bearing cups with solvent and inspect the cups for scratches, pits, or wear.
6. If the cups are worn or damaged, remove them with a drift.
7. Thoroughly clean the inner and outer bearing cones and rollers.
8. If the inner or outer bearing cups were removed, install the new replacement cups in the hub. Be sure that they are seated squarely and properly.
9. Pack the inside of the hub with wheel bearing grease. Add grease to the hub until grease is flush with the inside diameter of both bearing cups.

NOTE: It is important that all the old grease is removed, because the more popular lithium base grease is not compatible with the sodium base grease that was originally installed.

10. Pack the bearing cone and roller with wheel bearing grease.
11. Installing the inner bearing cone and roller in the inner cup.
12. Install the hub and drum.
13. Install the outer bearing cone and roller and the flat washer on the spindle. Install the adjusting nut.
14. Install the wheel.
15. Adjust the wheel bearings.

Rear Brake Drums

REMOVAL AND INSTALLATION

Remove the wheel. Remove the bolts which secure the drum to the rear axle shaft flange. Pull the brake drum off of the flange.

NOTE: If the drum will not come off easily, screw the drum securing bolts into the two tapped holes in the drum. Tighten the bolts evenly in order to force the drum away from the flange.

Installation is the reverse of removal.

Brake Shoes

REMOVAL AND INSTALLATION

1. Remove the brake drum.
2. Remove the return springs.
3. Remove the shoe retaining spring.
4. Remove the primary shoes and the parking brake link.
5. Disengage the parking brake lever from the secondary shoes.
6. Remove the secondary shoe.
7. Installation is the reverse of removal.

Wheel Cylinders

REMOVAL AND INSTALLATION

1. Remove the brake drums and shoes.
2. Disconnect the hydraulic line from the wheel cylinder.
3. Remove the wheel cylinder.

Installation of the wheel cylinder is the reverse of removal. Bleed the hydraulic system and adjust the brake shoes.

Parking Brake

ADJUSTMENT

1. Adjust the rear brake shoes.
2. Adjust the front cable with the nut located at the rear of the parking brake handle. The handle should require 3-7 notches for RX-3, RX-4, GLC and Cosmo models, 3-4 notches for 808, 6-8 notches for RX-7 to apply the parking brake.
3. Operate the parking brake several times; check to see that the rear wheels do not drag when it is fully released.

Parking Brake Shoes

REPLACEMENT

Cosmo Only

1. Remove the brake disc.
2. Remove the brake shoe return springs.
3. Remove the secondary brake shoe retaining spring and guide pin.
4. Remove the brake shoe.
5. Installation is the reverse of removal.

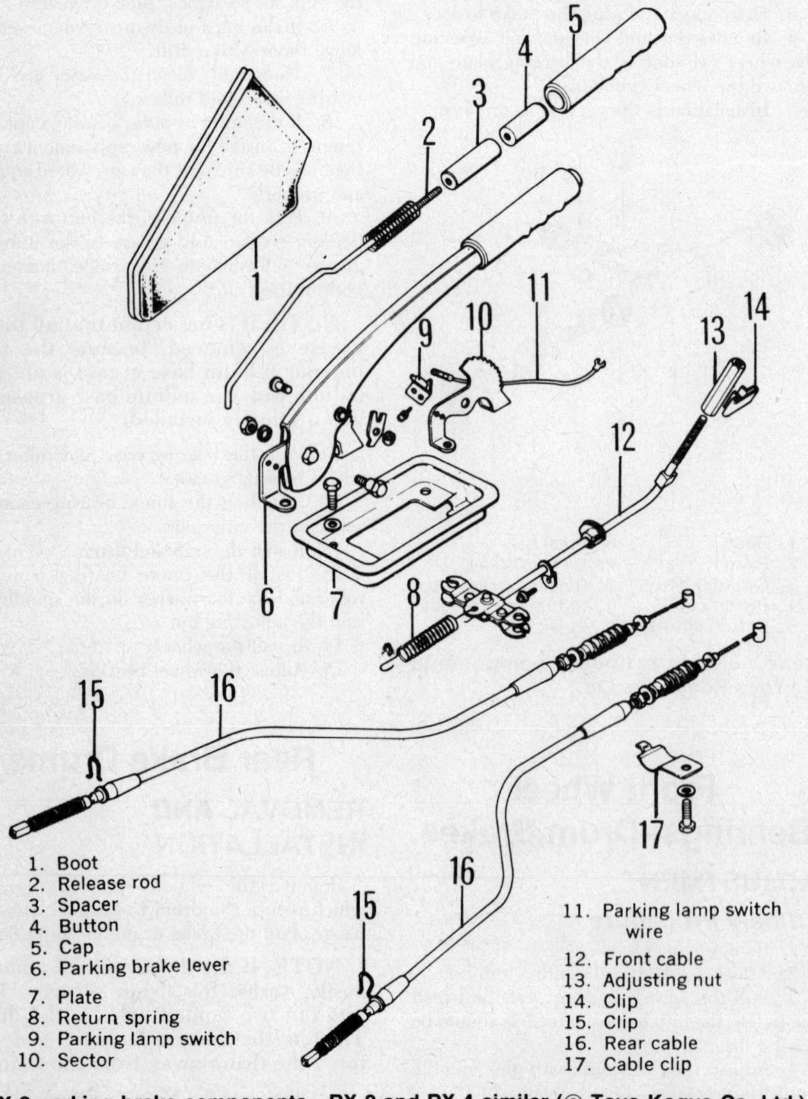

1. Boot
2. Release rod
3. Spacer
4. Button
5. Cap
6. Parking brake lever
7. Plate
8. Return spring
9. Parking lamp switch
10. Sector
11. Parking lamp switch wire
12. Front cable
13. Adjusting nut
14. Clip
15. Clip
16. Rear cable
17. Cable clip

RX-3 parking brake components—RX-2 and RX-4 similar (© Toyo Kogyo Co. Ltd.)

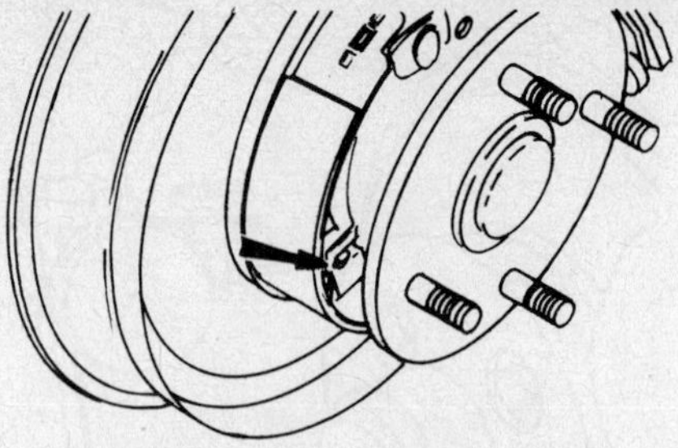

Removing show hold down spring—Cosmo parking brake

CHASSIS ELECTRICAL

Wiper Motor

REPLACEMENT

1. Remove the wiper arms.
2. Remove the cowl plate screws, move the cowl plate up at the front and disconnect the washer hose. Remove the cowl plate.
3. Disconnect the wires from the wiper motor.
4. Unbolt and remove the motor.
5. Installation is the reverse of removal.

Instrument Cluster

REMOVAL AND INSTALLATION

RX-3, RX-3 SP and RX-7 Models

1. Pull the knob off of the steering column-mounted headlight switch. Remove the halves of the steering column shroud.
2. Open the left-hand (driver's side) door, to gain access to the screw located on the side of the instrument cluster.
3. Remove the three retaining screws which are located underneath the instrument cluster.
4. Tip the top of the cluster toward the steering wheel.
5. Disconnect the wiring and the speedometer cable from the back of the instrument cluster.
6. Remove the cluster.
7. Installation is the reverse of removal.

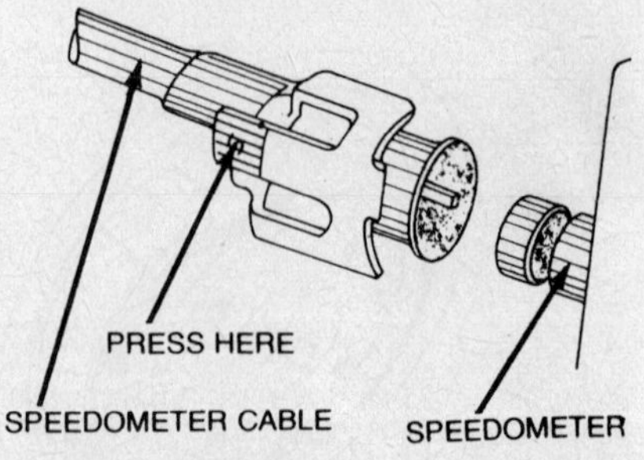

Speedometer cable removal, all models (© Toyo Kogyo Co. Ltd.)

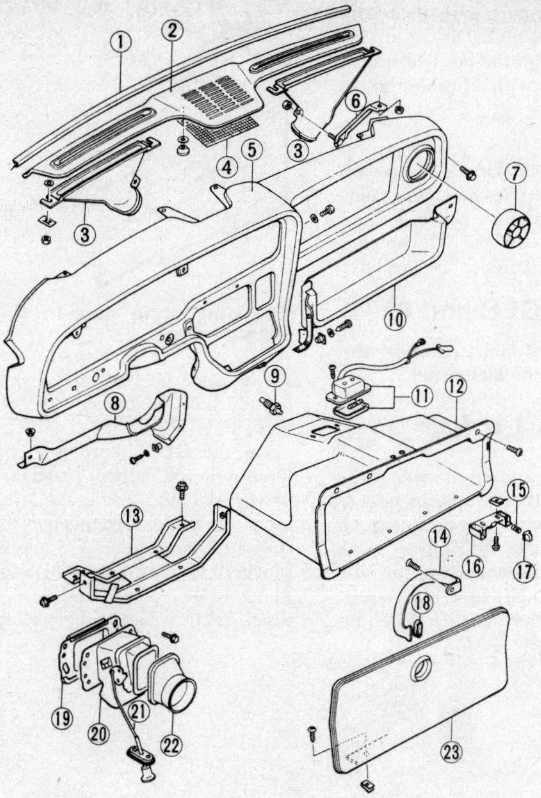

1. Seaming welt
2. Garnish
3. Defroster nozzle
4. Cloth cover
5. Instrument panel pad
6. Defroster nozzle bracket
7. Louver
8. Instrument panel lower
9. Glove box switch
10. Instrument panel lower
11. Glove box lamp
12. Glove tray
13. Instrument panel center bracket
14. Stopper
15. Spring
16. Striker
17. Spring plate
18. Cushion
19. Gasket
20. Ventilator
21. Control wire
22. Duct
23. Glove box lid

Cosmo instrument panel (© Toyo Kogyo Co. Ltd.)

808, RX-4, Cosmo, and 626

1. Remove the steering wheel.
2. Loosen the nut which secures the vent knob (left side) and allow the knob assembly to drop away from its mounting bracket.
3. Remove choke knob. Remove the choke retaining nut and separate the choke from the panel.
4. Remove the upper column cover.
5. Disconnect the panel light dimmer switch wiring.
6. Disconnect the exhaust temperature warning light wiring.
7. Loosen, but don't remove the screws at either end of the lower panel cover.

NOTE: The left-hand screw is located in the hole which was covered by the upper column cover and the right-hand screw is above the ashtray opening (ashtray removed).

8. Pull the upper column cover away from the instrument panel.
9. Remove the instrument cluster surround.
10. Unfasten the instrument cluster wiring harness(es).
11. Disconnect the speedometer cable.
12. Tilt the top of the cluster forward, and lift the cluster out.
13. Installation is the reverse of removal.

GLC (Standard Dash)

1. Disconnect the negative battery cable.
2. Remove the screw above each meter and remove the instrument cluster outside cover.
3. Remove the woodgrain center panel cover by removing the screw from the left side and unclipping the panel from the right side.
4. Remove the instrument panel pad by removing the three screws located under the front edge of the pad.
5. Disconnect the speedometer cable.
6. Remove the three instrument cluster retaining screws and pull the cluster out of the dash.
7. To install reverse the removal procedure.

GLC meter cover retaining screws (© Toyo Kogyo Co. Ltd.)

GLC meter retaining screws (© Toyo Kogyo Co. Ltd.)

GLC (Sport Dash)

1. Disconnect the negative battery cable.
2. Remove the tripmeter knob and the cluster cover retaining screws and clips.
3. Remove the woodgrain center panel cover by removing the screw from the left side and unclipping the panel from the right side.
4. Remove the instrument panel pad by removing the three screws located under the front edge of the pad.
5. Remove the three screws and remove the instrument cluster outward.
6. Disconnect the electrical connectors and the speedometer cable.
7. To install reverse the removal procedure.

Fuse Box Location

RX-3, COSMO

On the RX-3 models, the box is located just above the lower parcel shelf, and uses a back-hinged cover.

The cover has the location, amperage, and the circuit protected by each individual fuse, stamped on it.

The cable running from the positive side of the battery is equipped with a fusible link.

RX-4, 808

The main fuse and secondary fuse block are located next to the battery in the engine compartment. An additional fuse box is located beneath the glove compartment. The amperage of each fuse is printed on the fuse box lids.

RX-3 SP, RX-7, GLC and 626

The main fuse block is mounted under the dash near the driver's side kick panel.

Fusible Links

On all rotary engine cars and the 808, these are located in either one or two boxes next to the battery in the engine compartment. If these links blow, they may be replaced with the specified parts by disconnecting the battery, disconnecting wiring to each link requiring replacement, removing the attaching screws and the link, and installing the new link or links in the reverse of the removal procedure.

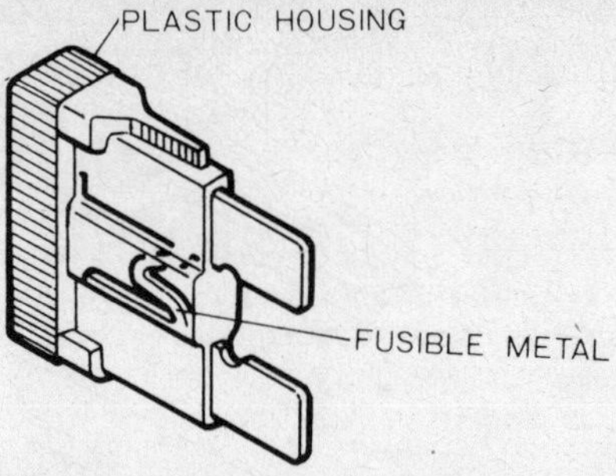

The new style plug-in fuse used on 1980-81 cars

On the GLC, there is a connector block located on the radiator panel on the right side of the radiator inside the engine compartment. Two links connected there are color coded red and green and may simply be unplugged to remove them, and replaced by plugging in replacement parts. Make sure to disconnect the battery before replacing them.

SPECIFICATIONS

INDEX

BEFORE SERVICING, SEE THE SAFETY NOTICE ON THE CONTENTS PAGE

DEVELOPMENT

While the name Mercedes-Benz is familiar to most Americans, few are aware that the founders of Mercedes-Benz share credit for inventing the automobile. Two mechanical engineers, Gottlieb Daimler and Karl Benz, brought their revolutionary machines to life in 1886, 22 years before Henry Ford's Model T.

In addition to pioneering such technical advances as fuel injected engines and the first diesel powered car, Mercedez-Benz has played a prominent role in racing. No other car manufacturer can match Mercedes' record of over 4000 competition victories: a long string stretching back to history's first auto race from Paris to Rouen in 1894. In the pursuit of land speed records, Mercedes-Benz has been equally successful. The legendary Blitzen Benz was the world's fastest automobile from 1911 to 1924; and a 1938 Mercedes-Benz record of 271.5 mph still stands as the highest speed ever recorded on a highway.

In 1968 Mercedes-Benz introduced the "New Generation" of Mercedes-Benz cars. These new sedans, the 220D/8, 220/8, 230/8 and the 250/8, share the same body style and represent a nine year advance in automotive design (the preceding models were first introduced in 1959). The new bodies featured a sharply sloping hood with decreased frontal area, to insure a smoother flow of air over the car, greater glass area and a squared off rear deck. These new features combine to give the cars a look that is clean and simple, and at the same time, classic. The smaller sedans were followed by the 280 series and the 300 series, all the way up to the 300SEL 6.3 in 1970. All bodies share the same basic concept of clean and timeless styling. Such features as independent suspension and four wheel disc brakes are notable safety features of Mercedes-Benz cars.

The 350SLC (450SLC in 1973) marks an important change in the coupe design philosophy of Mercedes-Benz. Previous coupe designs were derived from the contemporary sedan models but the 350 and 450SLC models are based on the 350SL coupe/roadster, resulting in a vehicle which combines sports car performance with luxurious looks and comfort. The 350 and 450SLC replace the coupe and convertible models which were built until 1971. The introduction of the 350 and 450SL and SLC models was followed by the introduction of the 450SE and 450SEL in 1973. These cars share the wedge body design with the newer SL and SLC series. The 450SE and 450SEL use the 4.5 liter DOHC V8 used in the 450SL and 450SLC. The front axle is a modified design taken from the rotary engined test vehicle, the C-111. The 6.9, successor to the 300SEL 6.3 was introduced in 1977, using the 6.9 liter engine and 450SEL body with a hydropneumatic suspension.

In 1975, the 280S was introduced, basically a 450SE/SEL body with the DOHC 6-cylinder engine from the 1973-75 280, 280C. This was followed by the 1977 280SE, 280E and the 240D, 300D and 230 which also share the new wedge body.

The 280 and 280C were introduced in 1973, using the body originally introduced in 1968.

The 240D, introduced in 1974 is basically a larger engine than the 220D. A major improvement in 1975 was the 300D, using the same body as the 220D and 240D, but with a 3 liter, 5 cylinder diesel, followed by the 300CD, the coupe version. 1978 saw the introduction of the 300SD, the first turbocharged, 5-cylinder production diesel, and in 1979, the 300TD, Mercedes first station wagon became available.

In 1981, the 380SL, 380SLC, and 380SEL replaced the 450SL and 450SEL, respectively. These cars are basically a redesigned body with a new 3.8 liter V8 engine.

ENGINE/VEHICLE IDENTIFICATION

Model	Chassis Type	Engine Model	No. of Cyls.	Engine Type	Engine Description (Fuel, Fuel Delivery, Valve Gear, Displacement)	Years
240D	115.117	0M616	4	616.916	Diesel (2404 cc)	1975-76
240D	123.123	0M616	4	616.912	Diesel (2400 cc)	1977-81
300D	115.114	0M617	5	617.910	Diesel (3005 cc)	1975-76
300D	123.130	0M617	5	617.912	Diesel (3005 cc)	1977-81
300CD	123.150	0M617	5	617.912	Diesel (3005 cc)	1978-81
300SD	116.120	0M617	5	617.950	Diesel, Turbocharged (3005 cc)	1978-80
300SD	126.120	0M617	5	617.951	Diesel, Turbocharged (3005 cc)	1981
300TD	123.190	0M617	5	617.912	Diesel (3005 cc)	1979
300TD Turbo	123.193	0M617	5	617.952	Diesel, Turbocharged (3005 cc)	1981
230	115.017	M115	4	115.951	Gas, Carb., OHC (2307 cc)	1974-76
230	123.023	M115	4	115.954	Gas, Carb., OHC (2307 cc)	1977-80
280	114.060	M110	6	110.921	Gas, Carb., DOHC (2746 cc)	1975-76
280C	114.073	M110	6	110.921	Gas, Carb., DOHC (2746 cc)	1975-76
280S	116.020	M110	6	110.922	Gas, Carb., DOHC (2746 cc)	1975-76
280E	123.033	M110	6	110.984	Gas, Fuel Inj., OHC (2778 cc)	1977-81
280CE	123.053	M110	6	110.984	Gas, Fuel Inj., DOHC (2746 cc)	1978-81
280SE	116.024	M110	6	110.985	Gas, Fuel Inj., OHC (2778 cc)	1977-80
380SEL	126.033	M116	8	116.961	Gas, Fuel Inj., OHC (3800 cc)	1981
380SL	107.045	M116	8	116.960	Gas, Fuel Inj., OHC (3800 cc)	1981
380SLC	107.025	M116	8	116.960	Gas, Fuel Inj., OHC (3800 cc)	1981

ENGINE/VEHICLE IDENTIFICATION

Model	Chassis Type	Engine Model	No. of Cyls.	Engine Type	Engine Description (Fuel, Fuel Delivery, Valve Gear, Displacement)	Years
450SE	116.032	M117	8	117.983	Gas, Fuel Inj., OHC (4520 cc)	1975
450SEL	116.033	M117	8	117.983	Gas, Fuel Inc., OHC (4520 cc)	1975
450SL	107.044	M117	8	117.982	Gas, Fuel Inj., OHC (4520 cc)	1975
450SLC	107.044	M117	8	117.982	Gas, Fuel Inj., OHC (4520 cc)	1975
450SE	116.032	M117	8	117.986	Gas, Fuel Inj., OHC (4520 cc)	1976
450SEL	116.033	M117	8	117.986(5)	Gas, Fuel Inj., OHC (4520 cc)	1976-80
450SL	107.044	M117	8	117.985	Gas, Fuel Inj., OHC (4520 cc)	1976-80
450SLC	107.024	M117	8	117.985	Gas, Fuel Inj., OHC (4520 cc)	1976-80
6.9	116.036	M100	8	100.985	Gas, Fuel Inj., OHC (6836 cc)	1978-79

SERIAL NUMBER IDENTIFICATION

1. Certification tag (left door pillar)
2. Identification tag (left window post)
3. Chassis no.
4. Body no. and paintwork no.
5. Engine no.

Location of important information—230, 240D, 280, 280C, 300D models through 1976

1. Catalyst and certification tag (left door pillar)
2. Identification tag (left window post)
3. Chassis no.
4. Body no. and paintwork no.
5. Engine no. on rear engine block
6. Emission control information

Location of important information—450SL, 450SLC, 380SL, 380SLC

1. Certification tag (left door pillar)
2. Identification tag (left window post)
3. Chassis no.
4. Body no. and paintwork no.
5. Engine no.
6. Emission control tag
7. Emission control tag catalyst information

Location of important information—300SD, 300TD

1. Certification tag (left door pillar)
2. Identification tag (left window post)
3. Chassis no.
4. Body no. and paintwork no.
5. Engine no. on engine block, rear
6. Emission control information

Location of important information—1977 and later models except 300SD, 300TD, 450SL, 450SLC, 380SL and 380SLC

Example: Engine Family 80.22.45.30

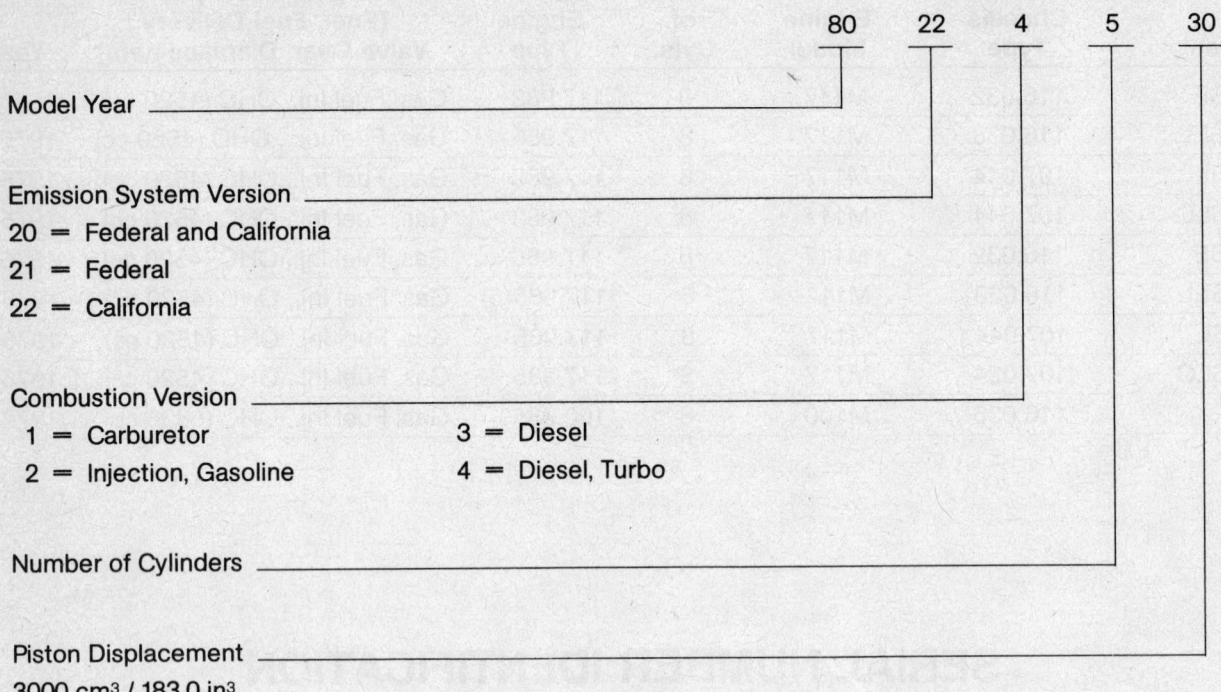

80 22 4 5 30

Model Year — 80

Emission System Version — 22
20 = Federal and California
21 = Federal
22 = California

Combustion Version — 4
1 = Carburetor
2 = Injection, Gasoline
3 = Diesel
4 = Diesel, Turbo

Number of Cylinders — 5

Piston Displacement — 30
3000 cm^3 / 183.0 in^3

The key to 1980 Vehicle Identification is an 8 digit number

Example: Engine Family B MB 3.8 V 6 F B 4

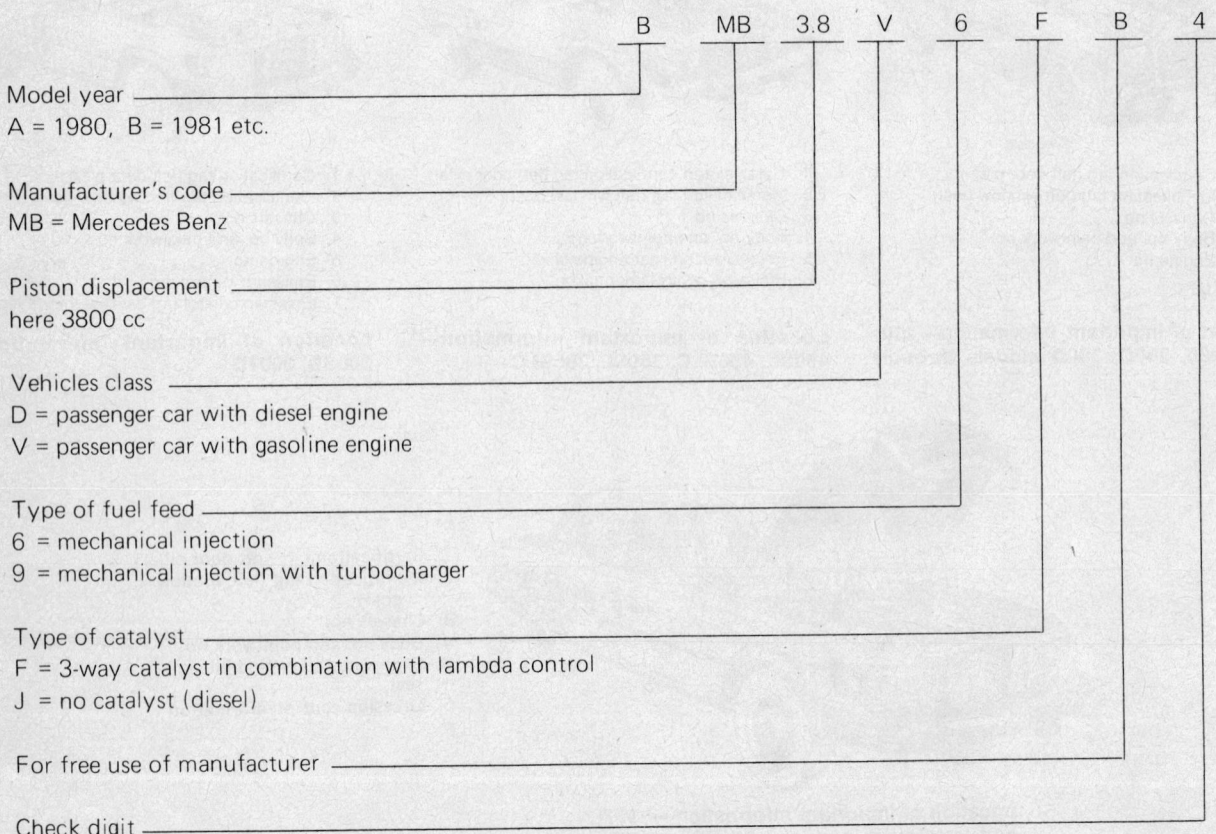

B MB 3.8 V 6 F B 4

Model year — B
A = 1980, B = 1981 etc.

Manufacturer's code — MB
MB = Mercedes Benz

Piston displacement — 3.8
here 3800 cc

Vehicles class — V
D = passenger car with diesel engine
V = passenger car with gasoline engine

Type of fuel feed — 6
6 = mechanical injection
9 = mechanical injection with turbocharger

Type of catalyst — F
F = 3-way catalyst in combination with lambda control
J = no catalyst (diesel)

For free use of manufacturer — B

Check digit — 4

The key to 1981 engine identification is a 10 digit number

TRANSMISSION APPLICATIONS

Model	Automatic Transmission	Manual Transmission
230	W4B 025	—
240D	W4B 025	G-76/18C (4-spd.)
280, 280C	W4B 025	—
280E, 280CE	W4B 025	—
280S, 280SE	W4B 025	—
300D, 300CD, 300TD	W4B 025	—
300TD Turbo (1981)	W4A 040	—
300SD 1978-80	W4B 025	—
300SD 1981	W4A 040	—
380SL, 380SLC, 380SEL	W4A 040	—
450SE, 450SEL, 450SL, 450SLC	W3A 040	—
6.9	W3B 050	—

Transmission Identification

Mercedes-Benz cars for the U.S. market have been equipped with either a 4-speed manual transmission or with a fully automatic 3 or 4-speed unit. Starting 1973, the automatic transmissions were equipped with a torque converter.

Seriat numbers on the manual transmission are located on a pad on the side cover of the transmission (left side).

Automatic transmission serial numbers are located on a metal plate which is attached to the driver's side of the transmission.

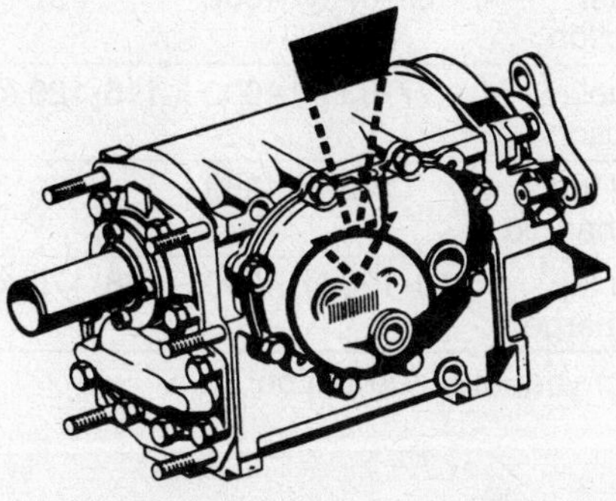

Transmission identification number

SPECIAL LUBRICANTS

Automatic Level Control

Mercedes-Benz recommends that only the following fluids be used in the automatic level control unit:

- Aral 1010 (must be used on 6.9)
- Gasolin 1010
- Shell Tellus T 17
- Shell Aero Fluid 4

GENERAL GASOLINE ENGINE SPECIFICATIONS

Year/Model	Engine Model	Engine Displacement (cc)	Carburetor Type	Horsepower @ rpm (SAE)	Torque @ rpm (ft. lbs.) (SAE)	Bore x Stroke (mm)	Compression Ratio	Firing Order
230	M115	2307	Stromberg 175 CDT	95 @ 4800 ①	128 @ 2500 ②	93.75 x 83.6	8.0:1	1 3 4 2
280S (1975-76)	M110	2746	Solex 4-bbl	120 @ 4800	143 @ 2800	86.00 x 78.80	8.0:1	1 5 3 6 2 4
280, 280C (1975-76)	M110	2746	Solex 4-bbl	120 @ 4800	143 @ 2800	86.00 x 78.80	8.0:1	1 5 3 6 2 4
280E, 280CE (1977-81) 280SE (1977-81)	M110	2746	Fuel Injection	142 @ 5750 ③	149 @ 4600 ④	86.00 x 78.80	8.0:1	1 5 3 6 2 4
1981 380SL 380SLC 380SEL	M116	3839	Fuel Injection	155 @ 4750	196 @ 2750	88.0 x 78.9	8.3:1	1 5 4 8 6 3 7 2
1975-80 450SE 450SEL 450SL 450SLC	M117	4520	Fuel Injection	180 @ 4750	220 @ 3000	92.00 x 85.00	8.0:1	1 5 4 8 6 3 7 2

GENERAL GASOLINE ENGINE SPECIFICATIONS

Year/Model	Engine Model	Engine Displacement (cc)	Carburetor Type	Horsepower @ rpm (SAE)	Torque @ rpm (ft. lbs.) (SAE)	Bore x Stroke (mm)	Com-pression Ratio	Firing Order
6.9	M100	6836	Fuel Injection	250 @ 4000	360 @ 2500	107.0 x 95.0	8.0:1	1 5 4 8 6 3 7 2

NOTE: Horsepower may vary depending on year of application.
① 1975 California—85 @ 4500
② 1975-79 California—122 @ 2500
③ 1977 and later California—137 @ 5750
④ 1977 and later California—142 @ 4600

GENERAL DIESEL ENGINE SPECIFICATIONS

Car Model	Engine Model	Engine Displace. (cc)	Fuel Delivery	Horsepower @ rpm (SAE)	Torque @ rpm (ft. lbs.) (SAE)	Bore x Stroke (mm)	Com-pression Ratio	Firing Order
240D	0M616	2404	Fuel Injection	62-67 @ 4000	97 @ 2400	91.0 x 92.4	21:1	1 3 4 2
300D, 300CD, 300TD	0M617	3005	Fuel Injection	77-83 @ 4000	115-120 @ 2400	91.0 x 92.4	21:1	1 2 4 5 3
300TD Turbo	0M617	3005	Fuel Inj. Turbocharged	120 @ 4350	170 @ 2400	91.0 x 92.4	21:1	1 2 4 5 3
300SD	0M617	3005	Fuel Inj. Turbocharged	110-120 @ 4200	168-170 @ 2400	91.0 x 92.4	21:1	1 2 4 5 3

NOTE: Horsepower may vary depending on year and application.

TUNE-UP SPECIFICATIONS

When analyzing compression test results, look for uniformity among cylinders, rather than specific pressures

Year	Model	SPARK PLUGS Type	SPARK PLUGS Gap (in.)	Distributor Point Dwell (deg)	Ignition Timing (deg)	Intake Valve Opens (deg)	Fuel Pump Pressure (psi) @ Idle	▲ Idle Speed (rpm)	VALVE CLEARANCE* (in.) In (cold)	VALVE CLEARANCE* (in.) Ex (cold)
1975	230	N9Y	0.024	47-53	10B w/vacuum	14B	2-3	800-900	0.004	0.008
	280, 280C, 280S	N9Y	0.024	34-40	7B w/vacuum	7B	3.5-5.0	800-900	0.004	0.010
	450SE, 450SEL	N9Y	0.024	30-34	TDC w/vacuum	②	30 ①	700-800	0.004	0.008
	450SL, 450SLC	N9Y	0.024	30-34	TDC w/vacuum	②	30 ①	700-800	0.004	0.008
1976	230	N9Y	0.024	47-53	10B w/vacuum	14B	2-3	800-900	0.004	0.008
	280, 280C, 280S	N9Y	0.024	34-40	7B w/o vacuum	7B	3.5-5.0	800-900	0.004	0.010
	450SE, 450SEL	N9Y	0.024	Elec.	TDC w/vacuum	③	75-84 ①	700-800	Hyd.	Hyd.
	450SL, 450SLC	N9Y	0.024	Elec.	TDC w/vacuum	③	75-84 ①	700-800	Hyd.	Hyd.

TUNE-UP SPECIFICATIONS

When analyzing compression test results, look for uniformity among cylinders, rather than specific pressures

Year	Model	SPARK PLUGS Type	SPARK PLUGS Gap (in.)	Distributor Point Dwell (deg)	Ignition Timing (deg)	Intake Valve Opens (deg)	Fuel Pump Pressure (psi) @ Idle	▲ Idle Speed (rpm)	VALVE CLEARANCE* (in.) In (cold)	VALVE CLEARANCE* (in.) Ex (cold)
1977	230	N10Y	0.028	46-53	10B w/vacuum	14B	2-3	850	0.004	0.008
	280E	N10Y	0.028	Elec.	TDC w/vacuum	7B	75-84 ①	800	0.004	0.010
	280SE	N10Y	0.028	Elec.	TDC w/vacuum	7B	75-84 ①	800	0.004	0.010
	450SE, 450SEL	N10Y	0.028	Elec.	TDC w/vacuum	③	75-84 ①	750	Hyd.	Hyd.
	450SL, 450SLC	N10Y	0.028	Elec.	TDC w/vacuum	③	75-84 ①	750	Hyd.	Hyd.
1978-79	230	N10Y	0.032	Elec.	10B w/vacuum	14B	2-3	850	0.004	0.008
	280E, 280CE, 280SE	N10Y	0.032	Elec.	TDC w/vacuum	7B	75-84 ①	800	0.004	0.010
	450SEL	N10Y	0.032	Elec.	TDC w/vacuum	③	75-84 ①	750	Hyd.	Hyd.
	450SL, 450SLC	N10Y	0.032	Elec.	TDC w/vacuum	③	75-84 ①	750	Hyd.	Hyd.
	6.9	N10Y	0.032	Elec.	TDC w/vacuum	④	75-84 ①	600	Hyd.	Hyd.
1980	280E, 280CE, 280SE	N10Y	0.032	Elec.	10B	N.A.	⑤	700-800	0.004	0.010
	450SEL	N10Y	0.032	Elec.	5B	N.A.	⑤	600-700	Hyd.	Hyd.
	450SL, 450SLC	N10Y	0.032	Elec.	5B	N.A.	⑤	600-700	Hyd.	Hyd.
1981	280E, 280CE	N10Y	0.032	Elec.	10B	N.A.	⑤	700-800	0.004	0.010
	380SEL	N10Y	0.032	Elec.	5B	N.A.	⑤	500	Hyd.	Hyd.
	380SL 380SLC	N10Y	0.032	Elec.	5B	N.A.	⑤	500	Hyd.	Hyd.

CAUTION: If the specifications listed above differ from those on the tune-up decal in the engine compartment, use those listed on the tune-up decal.

NOTES: 1. On transistor ignitions, only a transistorized dwell meter can be used. Transistor ignitions are recognizable by the "Blue" ignition coil, 2 series resistors and the transistor switchgear.
2. To counteract wear of the fiber contact block, adjust the dwell to the lower end of the range.

① Injection pump pressure
② Right side camshaft—3° BTDC
Left side camshaft—5° BTDC
③ Right side camshaft—4.5° BTDC
Left side camshaft—6.5° BTDC
④ Right side camshaft—12° BTDC
Left side camshaft—10° BTDC
⑤ Approximately 1 quart in 30 seconds
A After Top Dead Center
B Before Top Dead Center
w/vacuum—vacuum advance connected
w/o vacuum—vacuum advance disconnected
* Below 0° F; increase valve clearance by 0.002 in.
— Not Available
▲ In Drive

DIESEL TUNE-UP SPECIFICATIONS

Model	Valve Clearance (cold) ① Intake (in.)	Valve Clearance (cold) ① Exhaust (in.)	Intake Valve Opens (deg)	Injection Pump Setting (deg)	Injection Nozzle Pressure (psi) New	Injection Nozzle Pressure (psi) Used	Idle Speed (rpm) ②	Cranking Compression Pressure (psi)
220D	0.004	0.016	12.5B	24B	1564-1706	1422-1706	750-800	284-327
240D	0.004	0.016	13.5B	24B	1564-1706	1422-1706	750-800	284-327
300D, 300CD, 300TD (5-cylinder)	0.004	0.012	13.5B ④	24B	1635-1750 ③	1422	700-800	284-327
300SD, 300TD Turbo	0.004	0.014	13.5B	24B	1958-2074	1740	650-850	284-327

① In cold weather (below 5° F.), increase valve clearance 0.002 in.
② Manual transmission in Neutral; Automatic in Drive.
③ Difference in opening pressure on injection nozzles should not exceed 71 psi.
④ The injection pump is in start of delivery position when the mark on the pump camshaft is aligned with the mark on the injection pump flange.
B Before Top Dead Center

FIRING ORDERS

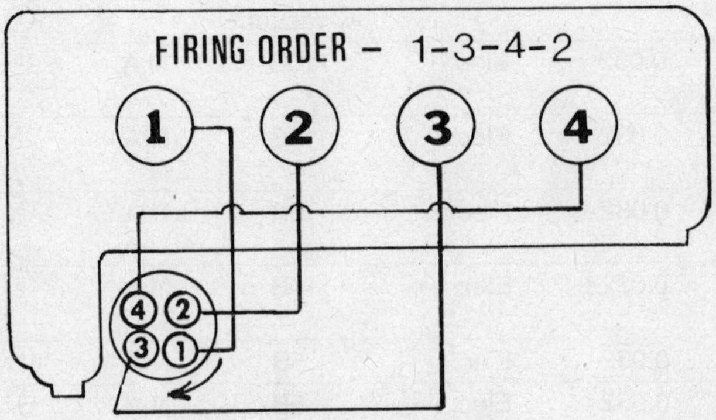

4-cylinder gas engine

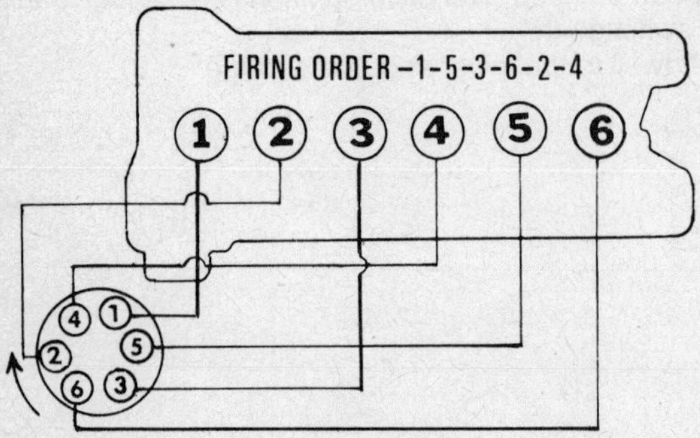

6-cylinder gas engine

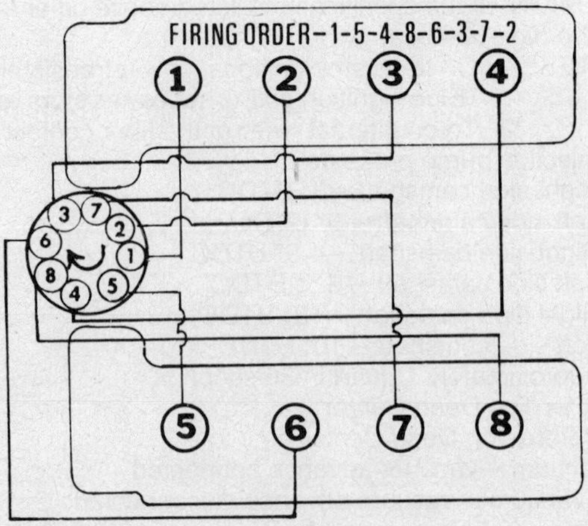

V-8

NOTE: The position of No. 1 tower on the distributor cap may vary. To avoid confusion when replacing wires, always replace wires one at a time. The notch cut into the rim of the distributor body always indicates No. 1 cylinder.

CAPACITIES

Year	Model	Cooling System (qts)	Engine Crankcase (qts) ▲ With Filter	Engine Crankcase (qts) ▲ Without Filter	Transmission (pts) Manual (4-spd)	Transmission (pts) Automatic	Drive Axle (pts)	Steering Gear (pts) Power	Steering Gear (pts) Manual	Level Control (qts)
1974-80	230	10.5	5.8	5.3	—	11.5	②	3.0	5/8	—
1975-76	240D	10.5	6.3	5.3	3.4	11.5	②	3.0	5/8	—
1977-81	240D	10.5	6.3	5.3	3.4	11.5	②	3.0	5/8	—
1975-76	280, 280C	11.5	6.3	5.8	—	12.3	②	3.0	—	—
1977-81	280E, 280CE	11.5	6.3	5.8	—	12.3	2.1	3.0	—	—
1975-76	280S	11.5	6.3	5.8	—	12.3	2.1	3.0	—	—
1977-80	280SE	11.5	6.3	5.8	—	12.3	2.1	3.0	—	—
1975-76	300D	11.7	6.8	5.8	—	11.5	③	3.0	—	—
1977-81	300D, 300CD	⑤	6.8	5.3	—	11.5	③	3.0	—	—
1978-80	300SD, 300TD	12.7 ⑤	6.8	5.3	—	11.5	2.1	3.0	—	6.2 ④
1981	300SD, 300TD Turbo	13.2	8.0	7.5	—	13.0	⑥	2.5	—	—
1981	380SL, 380SLC	13.7	8.5	8.0	—	13.0	2.7	⑦	—	—
1973-80	450SE, 450SEL, 450SL, 450SLC	16.0	8.5	8.0	—	16.5	①	3.0	—	—
1978-79	6.9	16.0	11.5	10.5	—	16.5	2.7	3.0	—	6.2 ④

① 450SL, 450SLC—2.7 pts
450SE, 450SEL—3.0 pts
② See text: 1st version—2.4 pts
2nd version—2.1 pts
③ 1975-76—1st version—2.4 pts
2nd version—2.1 pts } See Text
④ Approximately 1 qt between dipstick maximum and minimum marks
⑤ 300D—11.7 qts; 300SD—13.0 qts.
⑥ 300SD—2.7
300TD—2.1
⑦ 380SEL—2.5
380SL, SLC—3.0
▲ Add approximately ½ quart if equipped with additional oil cooler
— Not Applicable

CRANKSHAFT AND CONNECTING ROD SPECIFICATIONS

All measurements are given in millimeters

Car Model	Engine Displace. (cc)	Engine Model	Crankshaft Main Brg. Journal Dia.	Crankshaft Main Brg. Oil Clearance	Crankshaft Shaft End-Play	Crankshaft Thrust on No.	Connecting Rod Journal Diameter	Connecting Rod Oil Clearance	Connecting Rod Side Clearance
240D	2404	OM616	69.955-69.965	0.045-0.065	0.100-0.240	①	51.955-51.965	0.035-0.055	0.110-0.260
300D, 300CD, 300TD, 300SD	3005	OM617	69.955-69.965	0.045-0.065	0.100-0.240	①	51.955-51.965	0.035-0.055	0.110-0.260
230	2307	M115	69.955-69.965	0.045-0.065	0.100-0.240	①	51.955-51.965	0.035-0.055	0.110-0.260
450SL 450SLC 450SE 450SEL	4520	M117	63.955-63.965	0.035-0.075	0.100-0.240	①	51.955-51.965	0.035-0.065	0.220-0.380

CRANKSHAFT AND CONNECTING ROD SPECIFICATIONS

All measurements are given in millimeters

Car Model	Engine Displace. (cc)	Engine Model	CRANKSHAFT Main Brg. Journal Dia.	Main Brg. Oil Clearance	Shaft End-Play	Thrust on No.	CONNECTING ROD Journal Diameter	Oil Clearance	Side Clearance
280 280C 280S 280E 280CE 280SE	2746	M110	59.96- 59.95	0.03- 0.07	0.10- 0.24	①	47.95- 47.96	0.15- 0.50	0.11- 0.23
6.9	6836	M100	69.945- 69.965	0.045- 0.065	0.100- 0.240	①	54.940- 54.600	0.045- 0.065	0.220- 0.359
380SEL 380SL 380SLC	3839	M116	N.A.	0.045- 0.065	0.100- 0.240	①	—	0.045- 0.065	0.220- 0.359

① Center main on 5 main bearing engines; rear main on 7 main bearing engines; 3rd from front on 300D (5-cylinder)

N.A. Not Available

VALVE TIMING SPECIFICATIONS

Model	Camshaft Code Number	INTAKE VALVE Opens ATDC	Closes ABDC	EXHAUST VALVE Opens BBDC	Closes ATDC
240D	02	13.5	15.5	19	17
300D, 300CD, 300TD, 300SD	00	13.5	15.5	19	17
230	05	14	20	22	12
450SE (1975-76) ③ 450SEL (1975-77) ③ 450SL (1975-77) ③ 450SLC (1975-77) ③	56/57 ③ 54/55 ③	5	21	25	5
450SE, 450SL, 450SEL, 450SLC (1977-80)	00/01	L-6.5 R-4.5	L-18.5 R-16.5	L-23 R-25	L-8 R-10
280, 280C, 280S, 280E, 280SE (1975-80)	67/71	7	21	30	12
6.9	36/37	L-12 R-10	L-25 R-23	L-32 R-34	L-19 R-21
380SL, 380SLC, 380SEL	62/63 L R	24	7.5	4	12.5

① Camshafts with identification number 46, 48, or 52 are for the left bank of cylinders (5-8). Camshafts with identification code number 47, 49 or 53 are for the right bank of cylinders (1-4).

② Code number 30 for exhaust camshaft
Code number 33 for intake camshaft

③ New engine with new timing chain

L Left
R Right
BTDC Before Top Dead Center
ABDC After Bottom Dead Center
BBDC Before Bottom Dead Center

VALVE SPECIFICATIONS

Car Model	Engine Displacement (cc)	Seat Angle (deg)	Spring Test Pressure (mm @ KP)	Spring Installed Height (mm)	STEM DIAMETER (mm)	
					Intake	Exhaust
240D	2404	30 + 15′	38.4 @ 23-26.4	29.9	9.920-9.905	9.918-9.940
300D, 300CD, 300TD, 300SD	3005	30 + 15′	38.4 @ 23-26.4	29.9	9.920-9.905	9.918-9.940
230	2307	45 + 15′	39 @ 36 ①	30.0 ①	8.948-8.970	10.918-10.940
450SL 450SLC 450SE 450SEL	4520	45 + 15′	42 @ 29.5-32.5 ①	30.5 ①	8.955-8.970	10.928-10.950
280 280C 280CE 280S 280E 280SE	2746	45 + 15′	84-92 @ 30.5	N.A.	N.A.	0.431 (thru 1979) 0.353 (1980 and later)
6.9	6834	45 + 15′	44.5 42.3	35.4	8.948-8.970	11.932-11.950
380SL 380SLC 380SEL	3839	N.A.	N.A.	N.A.	8.955-8.970	9.0

① Outer spring—the spring should be installed so that the close coils are in contact with the cylinder head

TORQUE SPECIFICATIONS

All readings in ft. lbs.

Car Model	Engine Model	Cylinder Head Bolts ②	Rod Bearing Bolts	Main Bearing Bolts	Crankshaft Pulley Bolt	Flywheel To Crankshaft Bolts	Cam Sprocket Bolt(s)	Exhaust Manifold Bolts
240D	0M616	65	①	65	151-158	①	18	18-21
300D, 300CD 300TD, 300SD	0M617	65	①	65	195-240	①	18	18-21
230	M115	58	①	58 ③	151-158	①	18	18-21
450SL 450SLC 450SE 450SEL	M117	36	①	④	180-194	①	36	18-21
280 280C 280S 280E 280CE 280SE	M110	58	①	58	206-226	①	58	N.A.

TORQUE SPECIFICATIONS

All readings in ft. lbs.

Car Model	Engine Model	Cylinder Head Bolts ②	Rod Bearing Bolts	Main Bearing Bolts	Crankshaft Pulley Bolt	Flywheel To Crankshaft Bolts	Cam Sprocket Bolt(s)	Exhaust Manifold Bolts
6.9	M100	65	①	⑤	289	①	72	N.A.
380SL 380SEL 380SLC	M116	⑥	30- 37 ①	⑤	289	①	74	N.A.

① See text
② With cold engine; cylinder head bolts should be tightened in at least 3 stages
③ 65 on M115 engines
④ M 10 bolts—37 ft. lbs.
M 12 bolts—72 ft. lbs.
⑤ M 10 bolts—43 ft. lbs.
M 12 bolts—58 ft. lbs.
⑥ Tighten to 22 ft. lbs. then to 45 ft. lbs. in proper sequence. After 10 mins., loosen and tighten again to 45 ft. lbs.
N.A. Not available

TORQUE SEQUENCES

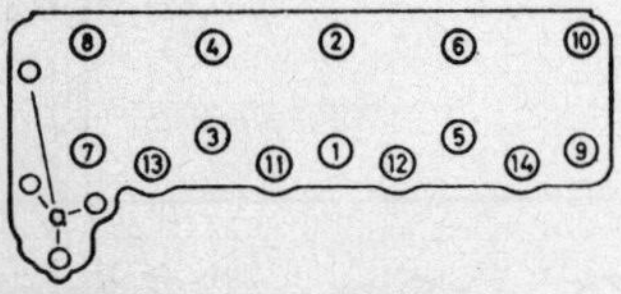

4-cylinder gas engine

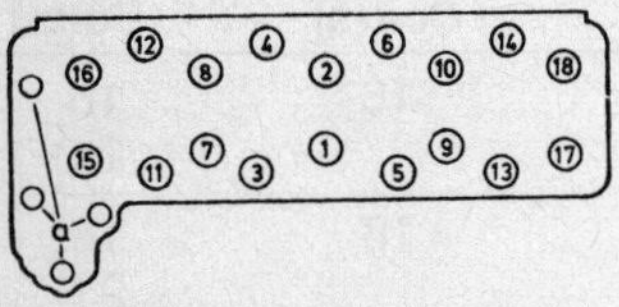

4-cylinder diesel engine

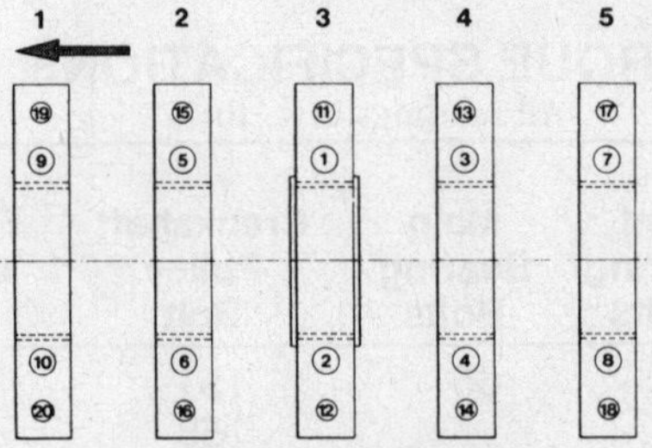

V8 main bearing caps

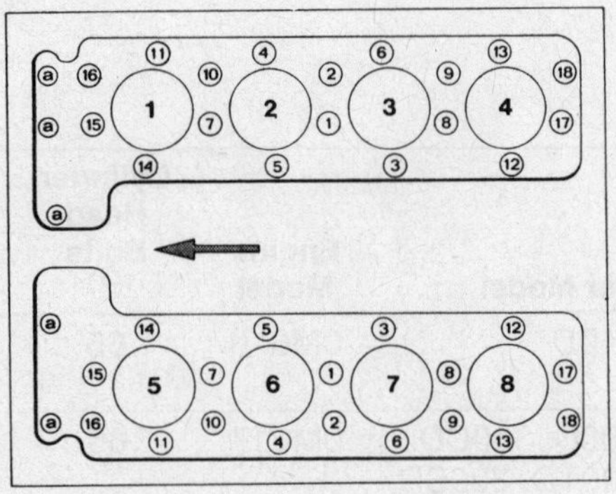

V8 cylinder head

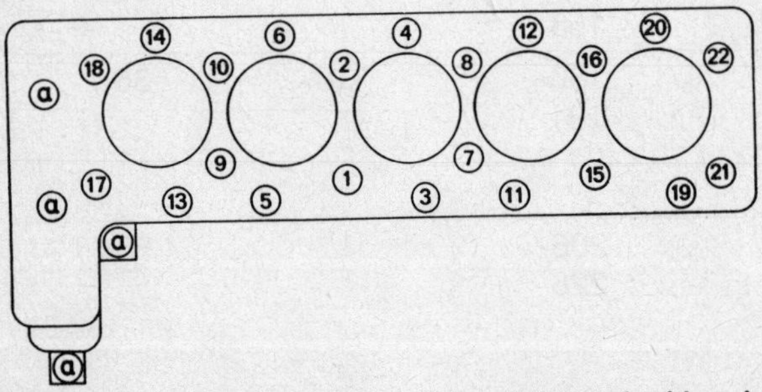

5-cylinder diesel bolts marked "a" are tightened with a hex socket bit

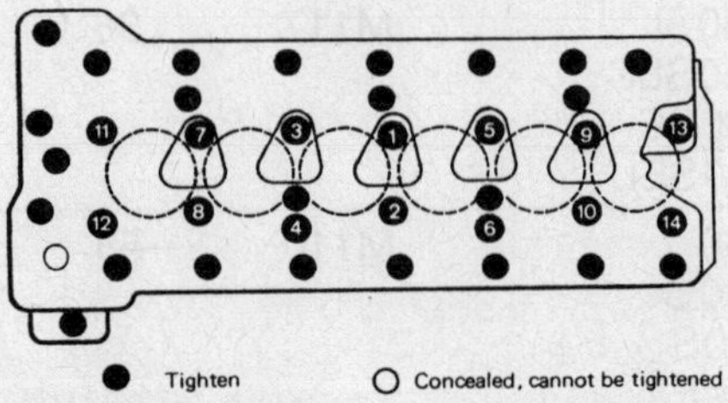

6-cylinder gasoline cylinder head and camshaft housing

BATTERY AND STARTER SPECIFICATIONS

All cars use 12 volt, negative ground electrical systems

Engine Model	Lock Test Amps	Lock Test Volts	Lock Test Torque (ft. lbs.)	No Load Test Amps	No Load Test Volts	No Load Test rpm	Brush Spring Tension (oz)	Min. Brush Length (in.)
All w/Diesel Engine	650-750	9.0	1000-1200	80-95	12	7500-8500	N.A.	N.A.
All w/Gas Engine	290-300	9.0	1600-1800	50-70	12	9000-11000	N.A.	0.5

N.A. Not specified by manufacturer

BRAKE SPECIFICATIONS

All measurements given are in inches unless noted
See following summary of Brake Pad Application

Model	Lug Nut Torque (ft. lbs.)	Master Cylinder Bore	Brake Disc Minimum Thickness	Brake Disc Maximum Run-Out	Brake Drum Diameter	Brake Drum Max. Machine O/S	Brake Drum Max. Wear Limit	Minimum Lining Thickness Front ▲	Minimum Lining Thickness Rear ▲
240D 300D 300CD 300TD 230 280 280C 280E 280CE	75	15/16	0.44	0.0047 (max.)	—	—	—	0.08 ③	0.08 ③
450SL 450SLC	75	15/16	0.36	0.0047 (max.)	—	—	—	0.08 ③	0.08 ③
450SE 450SEL 280S 280SE 300SD 6.9	75	15/16	0.79	0.0047 (max.)	—	—	—	0.08 ③	0.08 ③

NOTE: Minimum lining thickness is as recommended by the manufacturer. Due to variations in state inspection regulations, the minimum allowable thickness may be different than recommended by the manufacturer.

① Caliper w/57 mm piston diameter—0.81 in.
Caliper w/60 mm piston diameter—0.79 in.

② Caliper w/57 mm piston diameter—0.44 in.
Caliper w/60 mm piston diameter—0.42 in.

▲ New thickness of brake lining and backing plate—0.59 in.
New thickness of backing plate—0.20 in.
New thickness of brake lining—0.39 in.

— Not Applicable

SUMMARY OF BRAKE PAD APPLICATION

Model	Arrangement mm/in.	Thickness of Pad mm/in.	Brake Pad Repair Set Part No.	Color Code	Remarks
107 1st version 114.010, 015, 023 115 except 115.114	Front axle Caliper with 57/2.244 dia. piston	15/0.591	001 586 19 42 001 586 31 42	gn-yl-gn-gn gn-gn-gn-gn-bu	—
Without brake pad sensor 107 2nd version 114.060, 073 116 1st version 115.114	Front axle Caliper with 60/2.362 dia. piston	15/0.591	001 586 18 42 001 586 32 42	gn-yl-gn-gn gn-gn-gn-gn-bu	—

SUMMARY OF BRAKE PAD APPLICATION

Model	Arrangement mm/in.	Thickness of Pad mm/in.	Brake Pad Repair Set Part No.	Color Code	Remarks
With brake pad sensor 107 3rd version 116 2nd version 123 1st version	Front axle Caliper with 60/2.362 dia. piston	15/0.591	001 586 33 42 001 586 36 42	gn-yl-gn-gn gn-gn-gn-gn-bu	—
With brake pad sensor 116 123 As of Model Year 1980	Front axle Caliper with 60/2.362 dia. piston	17.5/0.689	002 586 45 42 002 586 46 42	gn-gn-gn-gn-bu gn-yl-gn-gn	These linings must only be combined with the rear axle linings 002 586 47 42 or 002 586 48 42
107 All except 116 1980 models 123	Rear axle Caliper with 38/1.496 dia. piston	15/0.591	000 586 76 42	gn-gn-bu-bu	—
116 As of Model 123 Year 1980	Rear axle Caliper with 38/1.496 dia. piston	15.0/0.610	002 586 47 42 002 586 48 42	gn-gn-bu-gn-bu gn-yl-yl-gn-yl	These linings must only be combined with the front axle linings 002 586 45 42 or 002 586 46 42
123.190 All	Rear axle Caliper with 42/1.654 dia. piston	15/0.591	001 586 64 42	gn-gn-bu-bu-bu	—

gn—green
yl —yellow
bu—blue

WHEEL ALIGNMENT SPECIFICATIONS

Car Model	FRONT WHEELS Camber (deg)	Caster (deg) Power Steering	Toe-In (in.)	REAR WHEELS Camber (deg)	Toe-In (mm)
230 (thru '76) 240D (thru '76) 300D (thru '76)	0°15′+10′ −20′	3°40′±20′	0.08-0.16	See Chart 1	See Chart 2
240D (1977-81) 300D (1977-81) 300CD (1977-81) 300TD (1979-81) 280E (1977-80) 280CE (1977-80) 230 (1977-80)	0°±10′	8°45′±30′	0.08-0.16	See Chart 3	See Chart 4
280 (1975-76) 280C (1975-76)	0°15′+10′ −20′	3°40′±15′	0.04-0.12	See Chart 1	0±2
280S (1975-76)	20′N ①	9°30′-10°30′	0.08-0.16	See Chart 5	See Chart 4
450SL 450SLC	0°+10′ −20′	3°40′±20′	0.04-0.12	See Chart 1	See Chart 2
450SE 450SEL 280SE 300SD (thru '80) 6.9	20′N	9°30′-10°30′	0.08-0.16	See Chart 5	See Chart 4

WHEEL ALIGNMENT SPECIFICATIONS

Car Model	FRONT WHEELS Camber (deg)	FRONT WHEELS Caster (deg) Power Steering	FRONT WHEELS Toe-In (in.)	REAR WHEELS Camber (deg)	REAR WHEELS Toe-In (mm)
380SL 380SLC	$0°^{+10'}_{-20'}$	3°40′ ± 20′	0.04- 0.12	0°10′ to 0°40′ See Chart 6	0-35
380SEL 300SD (1981)	0° ± 10′	9°15′-10°15′	0.13 0.21	See Chart 7	②

① A 0°10′ change in a positive or negative direction yields a 0°10′ change in caster in the corresponding direction

② If trailing arm position is 0-35 mm toe-in .06-.18
35-50 mm toe-in is .08-.19
50-60 mm toe-in is .10-.21

N Negative

WHEEL ALIGNMENT CHART 1

Control Arm Position mm (in.)	Corresponds to Rear Wheel Camber on: 220, 220D, 230, 240D, 300D, 280, 280C	Corresponds to Rear Wheel Camber on: 450SL, 450SLC
+80 (3.17″)	+2°30′ ± 30′	—
+75 (2.98″)	+2°15′ ± 30′	—
+70 (2.78″)	+2° ± 30′	—
+65 (2.58″)	+1°45′ ± 30′	—
+60 (2.38″)	+1°30′ ± 30′	—
+55 (2.18″)	+1°15′ ± 30′	—
+50 (1.99″)	+1° ± 30′	+0°50′ ± 30′
+45 (1.79″)	+0°45′ ± 30′	+0°35′ ± 30′
+40 (1.59″)	+0°30′ ± 30′	+0°20′ ± 30′
+35 (1.39″)	+0°15′ ± 30′	+0°05′ ± 30′
+30 (1.12″)	0° ± 30′	−0°10′ ± 30′

Control Arm Position mm (in.)	Corresponds to Rear Wheel Camber on: 220, 220D, 230, 240D, 300D, 280, 280C	Corresponds to Rear Wheel Camber on: 450SL, 450SLC
+25 (0.99″)	−0°15′ ± 30′	−0°25′ ± 30′
+20 (0.79″)	−0°30′ ± 30′	−0°40′ ± 30′
+15 (0.60″)	−0°45′ ± 30′	−0°55′ ± 30′
+10 (0.40″)	−1° ± 30′	−1°10′ ± 30′
+ 5 (0.20″)	−1°15′ ± 30′	−1°25′ ± 30′
0	−1°30′ ± 30′	−1°40′ ± 30′
− 5 (0.20″)	−1°45′ ± 30′	−1°55′ ± 30′
−10 (0.40″)	−2° ± 30′	−2°10′ ± 30′
−15 (0.60″)	−2°15′ ± 30′	−2°25′ ± 30′
+20 (0.79″)	−2°30′ ± 30′	−2°40′ ± 30′

WHEEL ALIGNMENT CHART 2

1973-76 220, 220D, 230, 240D, 300D

Rear Wheel Control Arm Position mm (in.)	Corresponds to Rear Wheel Toe-In of:
0 to +35 mm (0-1.39″)	1^{+2}_{-1} mm or $0°10'^{+20'}_{-10'}$
+35 to +50 mm (1.39″-1.99″)	1.5^{+2}_{-1} mm or $0°15'^{+20'}_{-10'}$
+50 to +60 mm (1.99″-2.38″)	2^{+2}_{-1} mm or $0°20'^{+20'}_{-10'}$
+60 to +70 mm (2.38″-2.78″)	2.5^{+2}_{-1} mm or $0°25'^{+20'}_{-10'}$
+70 to +80 mm (2.78″-3.17″)	3.0^{+2}_{-1} mm or $0°30'^{+20'}_{-10'}$

WHEEL ALIGNMENT CHART 4

All models except 1974-76 230, 240D, 300D

Rear Wheel Control Arm Position	Corresponds to Rear Wheel Toe-In of:
0 to +35 mm (0 to +1.38″)	$0°10'^{+20'}_{-10'}$ or 1^{+2}_{-1} mm ($0.04''^{+0.08''}_{-0.04''}$)
+35 to +50 mm (+1.38″ to +1.97″)	$0°15'^{+20'}_{-10'}$ or 1.5^{+2}_{-1} mm ($0.06''^{+0.08''}_{-0.04''}$)
+50 to +60 mm (+1.97″ to +2.36″)	$0°20'^{+20'}_{-10'}$ or 2^{+2}_{-1} mm ($0.08''^{+0.08''}_{-0.04''}$)
+60 to +70 mm (+2.36″ to +2.76″)	$0°25'^{+20'}_{-10'}$ or 2.5^{+2}_{-1} mm ($0.10''^{+0.08''}_{-0.04''}$)
+70 to +80 mm (+2.76″ to +3.15″)	$0°30'^{+20'}_{-10'}$ or 3^{+2}_{-1} mm ($0.12''^{+0.08''}_{-0.04''}$)

CHART 3
REAR WHEEL CAMBER

1977-79 230, 240D, 280E, 280CE, 300D, 300CD, 300TD

Semi-trailing Arm Position mm (inches)	Corresponds to Rear Wheel Camber
+70 (+2.76)	+1°45′ ±30′
+65 (+2.56)	+1°30′ ±30′
+60 (+2.36)	+1°15′ ±30′
+55 (+2.17)	+1° ±30′
+50 (+1.97)	+0°45′ ±30′
+45 (+1.77)	+0°30′ ±30′
+40 (+1.58)	+0°15′ ±30′
+35 (+1.37)	0° ±30′
+30 (+1.18)	−0°15′ ±30′
+25 (+0.98)	−0°30′ ±30′
+20 (+0.79)	−0°45′ ±30′
+15 (+0.59)	−1° ±30′
+10 (+0.39)	−1°15′ ±30′
+ 5 (+0.20)	−1°30′ ±30′
0 (0)	−1°45′ ±30′
− 5 (−0.20)	−2° ±30′
−10 (−0.39)	−2°15′ ±30′
−15 (−0.59)	−2°30′ ±30′

CHART 5
REAR WHEEL CAMBER

450SE, 450SEL, 300SD, 280S, 280SE, 6.9

Semi-trailing Arm Position mm (inches)	Corresponds to Rear Wheel Camber
+65 (2.58″)	+1°45′ ±30′
+60 (2.38″)	+1°30′ ±30′
+55 (2.18″)	+1°15′ ±30′
+50 (1.99″)	+1° ±30′
+45 (1.79″)	+0°45′ ±30′
+40 (1.59″)	+0°30′ ±30′
+35 (1.39″)	+0°15′ ±30′
+30 (1.12″)	0° ±30′
+25 (0.99″)	−0°15′ ±30′
+20 (0.79″)	−0°30′ ±30′
+15 (0.60″)	−0°45′ ±30′
+10 (0.40″)	−1° ±30′
+ 5 (0.20″)	−1°15′ ±30′
0	−1°30′ ±30′
− 5 (0.20″)	−1°45′ ±30′
−10 (0.40″)	−2° ±30′
−15 (0.60″)	−2°15′ ±30′
−20 (0.79″)	−2°30′ ±30′

REAR WHEEL ALIGNMENT CHART 6

380SL, 380SLC

Semi-trailing Arm Position mm	Corresponds to Rear Wheel Camber
35	0° ±30′
30	−0°15′ ±30′
25	−0°30′ ±30′
20	−0°45′ ±30′
15	−1° ±30′
10	−1°15′ ±30′
5	−1°30′ ±30′
0	−1°45′ ±30′
− 5	−2° ±30′
−10	−2°15′ ±30′
−15	−2°30′ ±30′
−20	−2°45′ ±30′

WHEEL ALIGNMENT CHART 7

1981 300SD, 380SEL

Semi-trailing Arm Position mm	Corresponds to Rear Wheel Camber
+65	+1°30′±30′
+60	+1°15′±30′
+55	+1° ±30′
+50	+0°45′±30′
+45	+0°30′±30′
+40	+0°15′±30′
+35	0° ±30′
+30	−0°15′±30′
+25	−0°30′±30′
+20	−0°45′±30′
+15	−1° ±30′
+10	−1°15′±30′
+ 5	−1°30′±30′
0	−1°45′±30′
− 5	−2° ±30′
−10	−2°15′±30′
−15	−2°30′±30′
−20	−2°45′±30′

TUNE-UP PROCEDURES

Ignition System Precautions

Mercedes-Benz has determined that some transistorized switching units have been damaged due to improper handling during service and maintenance work. The following precautions should be observed when working with transistorized switching units.

1. Do not shut off a running engine by shorting terminal 15 (terminal 1 or 15 on 1981 6-cylinder engines) of the ignition coil to ground or the transistorized switching unit will be destroyed.
2. Do not steam clean or apply water pressure to transistorized switching units, fuel injection control units, or ignition components, since water may enter these and short them.
3. Do not assume that transistor switching units are defective without checking the plug terminals. The plug terminals are frequently corroded because the rubber boot was not properly seated. In addition, the terminals can become corroded even if the rubber boot is properly seated. Mercedes-Benz recommends that all contacts be cleaned before assuming that a transistorized switching unit is defective.
4. Do not test for spark by holding a spark plug wire at a distance from the plug or pull off a spark plug wire with the engine running.

Spark Plugs

Spark plugs should be checked frequently (approximately 600 miles) depending on use.

NOTE: Spark plugs should be removed and inspected one at a time to avoid confusion. On most models, the plug wires are numbered at the cap and on the wire with small yellow rings.

To gap the spark plugs, remove each one in turn and measure the gap with a round feeler gauge of the appropriate thickness. Prior to removing the plugs, blow dirt away with compressed air. This is especially necessary on 6 cylinder DOHC engines. Insert the round feeler gauge between the center and side electrode. To adjust the gap, bend the side electrode with the tool on the end of the feeler gauge until the specified gap is obtained.

Reinstall and tighten the spark plugs to 18-21 ft/lbs and install the spark plug wires on their respective plugs.

Check the spark plug wires and replace any that are cracked or brittle. Bend the wires into a loop to check for cracks.

Breaker Points and Condenser

NOTE: 1976 V8, 1977 and later 6-cylinder and 1978 and later 4-cylinder engines are equipped with electronic ignition and have no points. Some 6-cylinder engines may be equipped with a flyweight in the distributor rotor to limit maximum rpm. 1981 6-cylinder engines are equipped with a new style electronic ignition identified by a "Danger! High Voltage" plate on the air cleaner.

REPLACEMENT

NOTE: Transistor ignitions prior to 1976 (V8), 1977 (6-cylinder) or 1978 (4-cylinder) can be recognized by the blue ignition coil, 2 series resistors and transistor switchgear.

1. Remove the rubber or plastic cover from the distributor (if equipped).

The condenser attaching screw is located on the outside of the distributor housing

1. Condenser
2. Point set
3. Point set attaching screw
4. Vacuum advance unit
5. Adjusting lugs and notch in breaker plate
6. Point gap (must be on the high point of the distributor cam to measure)
7. Notch in distributor rim indicating no. 1 cylinder

Internal view of breaker point type distributor

2. Release the clips on the side of the distributor cap and remove the cap. Lay it aside.

3. Remove the rotor and dust shield from the distributor shaft. Some distributors have a protective cover installed over the points.

4. Remove the distributor contact holder by removing the screw or screws. Some models also have a snap-ring on the bearing contact lever, which must also be removed. Pry the wire from the connecting terminal or loosen the screw at the terminal and remove the wire from the connecting terminal.

5. Disconnect the condenser wire and remove the condenser from its bracket.

6. Before installing new points, clean the contact surfaces by squeezing them against a clean matchbook cover. This will remove any film or condensate.

7. Lightly coat the slide piece of the contact breaker with high temperature multipurpose grease. It isn't necessary to lubricate the felt pad.

8. Check to be sure that the contacts are parallel and at the same level with each other when closed. Misalignment can be corrected by bending the fixed contact support. Never bend the movable contact support.

9. Install a new condenser and connect the wire.

10. Install a new contact set or sets into the distributor. If equipped, install the protective cover over the points.

11. Install the hold-down screw(s) and/or the snap-rings on the bearing pins of the contact plate.

12. Connect the wire to the terminal and tighten the nut, if necessary.

13. Install the plate and rotor on the shaft.

14. Install the cap.

15. Check the dwell angle and ignition timing. Adjust if necessary.

Dwell Angle

ADJUSTMENT

When setting ignition contact points, it is advisable to observe the following general rules:

1. If the points are used they should not be adjusted using a feeler gauge. The gauge will not give an accurate reading on a pitted surface.

2. Never file the points—this removes their protective coating and results in rapid pitting.

3. When using a feeler gauge to set new points, be certain that the points are fully open. The fiber rubbing block must rest on the highest point of the cam lobe.

4. Always make sure the feeler gauge is free of oil or grease before setting points.

5. Make sure the points are properly aligned and that the feeler gauge is not tilted. If points are misaligned, bend the fixed contact support only, never the movable breaker arm.

A dwell meter virtually eliminates errors in point gap caused by distributor cam lobes being unequally worn, or human error. In any case, point dwell should be checked as soon as possible after setting with a feeler gauge, because it is a far more accurate check of point operation under normal operating conditions.

Because the fiber block wears down gradually in service, it is good practice to set the dwell on the low side of any dwell range (smaller number of degrees) given in specifications. As the block wears, the dwell becomes greater (toward the center of the range) and point life is increased between adjustments.

All Engines Without Electronic Ignition

1. The dwell angle should be measured at idle speed.

2. Raise the hood and connect a dwell meter and tachometer.

3. Start the engine and allow it to reach normal idle speed. Read the dwell angle from the meter on the appropriate scale.

4. If the dwell varies by 5 or more degrees from the specifications, the points should be replaced.

5. If the dwell angle is not according to specifications, remove the distributor cap and adjust the dwell angle. Reduce the point gap if the dwell angle is too small, or increase the contact point gap if the dwell angle is too large.

6. To actually adjust the point gap, loosen the hold-down screw and insert a screwdriver between the lugs on the breaker plate and move the plate to the desired location. Tighten the hold-down screw. On some models the point gap is adjusted with the eccentric screw in the breaker plate.

7. Recheck the dwell angle and adjust the gap again if it is still not satisfactory. Repeat the process until the dwell angle is as specified.

All Engines With Electronic Ignition

It is not possible to adjust the dwell angle on Mercedes-Benz electronic ignitions.

Ignition Timing

ADJUSTMENT

Before setting the ignition timing, be sure that the point gap (dwell angle) is set to the proper specifications since this will influence the timing, while timing will have no influence on the dwell angle.

Before attempting to set the timing, read the "Ignition Timing Specifications" chart carefully and determine at what speed the timing should be set and whether the vacuum should be connected or disconnected.

NOTE: It is a good idea to paint the appropriate timing mark with dayglow or white paint to make it quickly and easily visible.

On engines with transistorized coil ignition, the timing light may or may not work depending on the construction of the light. If in doubt, consult a Mercedes-Benz dealer.

All Gas Engines

The diesel uses no distributor, so requires no ignition timing adjustment.

1. Raise the hood and connect a tachometer.

2. Connect a timing light as specified by the manufacturer.

3. On carbureted 280, 280C and 280S engines, disconnect and plug both vacuum lines.

4. Run the engine at the specified speed and read the firing point on the balancing plate or vibration damper while shining the light on it.

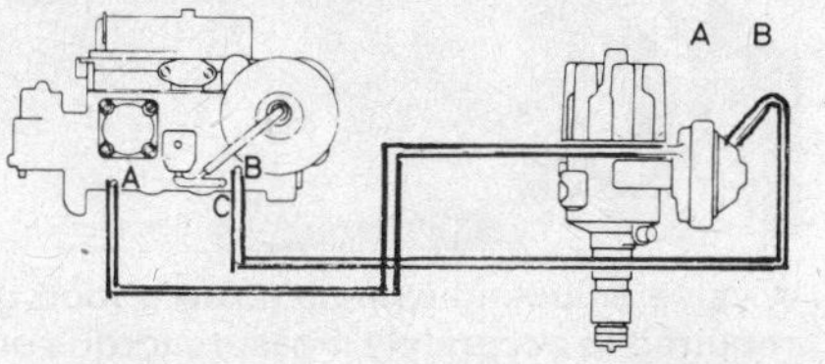

Vacuum connections—280, 280C, 280S (1975-76)

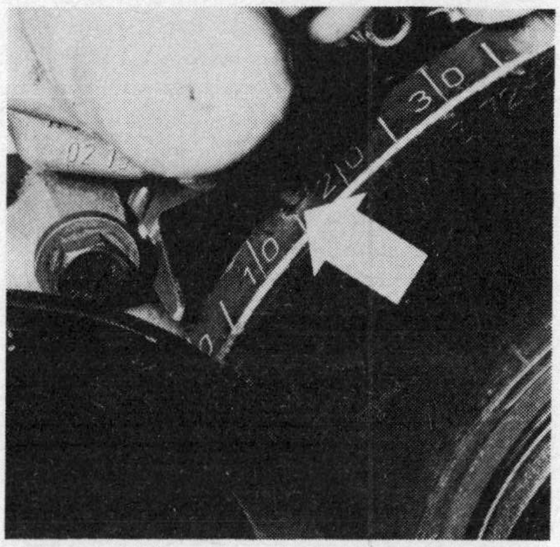

If 2 timing scales are used, the TDC scale is the one with the pin (arrow)

NOTE: The balancer on some engines has 2 timing scales. If in doubt as to which scale to use, rotate the crankshaft (in the direction of rotation only) until the distributor rotor is aligned with the notch on the distributor housing (No. 1 cylinder). In this position, the timing pointer should be at TDC on the proper timing scale.

5. Adjust the ignition timing by loosening the distributor clamp bolt and rotating the distributor. To advance the timing, rotate the distributor in the opposite direction of normal rotation. To retard the timing, rotate the distributor in the direction of normal rotation.

6. Once the timing has been adjusted, recheck the timing once more to be sure that it has not been disturbed.

7. Remove the timing light and tachometer and connect any wires that were removed.

Valve Clearance

ADJUSTMENT

The valve clearance of all gasoline engines can be checked and, if necessary, adjusted when the engine is hot or cold. Consult the valve location illustrations. The valve clearance on intake and exhaust valves is different, but all valves should be set slightly loose, rather than too tight.

4 and 6-Cylinder Gasoline Engines

The valve clearance is measured between the sliding surface of the rocker arm and the heel of the camshaft lobe. The highest point of the camshaft lobe should be at a 90° angle to the sliding surface of the rocker arm.

1. Remove the air vent hose and air cleaner from the valve cover. Remove the spark plugs.

2. Remove the valve cover and gasket.

3. Note the position of the intake and exhaust valves.

4. Rotate the crankshaft, by means of a socket wrench on the crankshaft pulley bolt, until the heel of the camshaft lobe is perpendicular to the sliding surface of the rocker arm.

NOTE: Do not rotate the engine using the camshaft sprocket bolt. The strain will distort the timing chain tensioner rail. Always rotate the engine in the direction of normal rotation only.

5. Some models have holes in the vibration damper plate to assist in crankshaft rotation. In this case, a screwdriver can be used to carefully rotate the crankshaft.

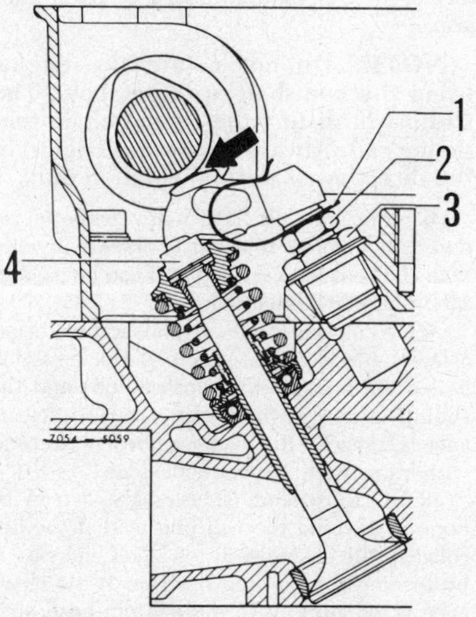

1. Tension spring 3. Threaded bushing
2. Adjusting screw 4. Pressure piece

Check the valve clearance between the sliding surface of the rocker arm and the heel of the camshaft lobe on DOHC—6-cylinder engines

6. To measure the valve clearance, insert a feeler blade of the specified thickness between the heel of the camshaft lobe and the sliding surface of the rocker arm. The clearance is correct if the blade can be inserted and withdrawn with a very slight drag.

7. If adjustment is necessary, it can be done by turning the ball pin head at the hex collar. If the clearance is too small, increase it by turning the ball pin head in. If the clearance is too large, decrease it by turning the ball pin head out. If the adjuster turns too easily or the proper clearance can't be obtained, check the torque of the adjuster.

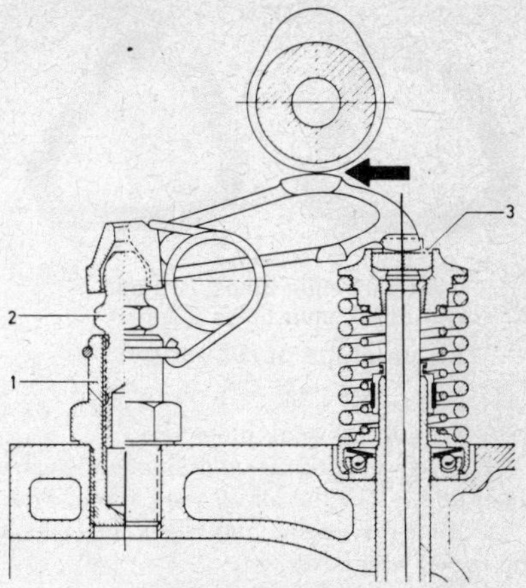

1. Threaded bushing
2. Adjusting screw
3. Pressure piece

Measure the valve clearance between the sliding surface of the rocker arm and the heel of the camshaft lobe on 4-cylinder engines

NOTE: This adjustment is ideally made with a special adapter and a torque wrench. By using it, the torque wrench can be directly aligned with the ball pin head.

8. When the ball pin head is turned, the adjusting torque should be 14-25 ft/lbs. If the torque is less than 14 ft/lbs, the ball pin head will vibrate and the clearance will not remain as set. If the valve clearance is too small, and the ball pin head cannot be screwed in far enough to correct it, a thinner pressure piece should be installed in the spring retainer. To replace the pressure piece, the rocker arm must be removed.

9. After all the valves have been checked and adjusted in the manner described above, install the valve cover. Be sure that the gasket is seated properly. It is best to use a new gasket whenever the valve cover is removed.

NOTE: Two types of triangular rubber gaskets are used on 6-cylinder engines, but only the later type with 3 notches are supplied for service.

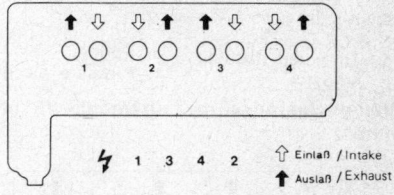

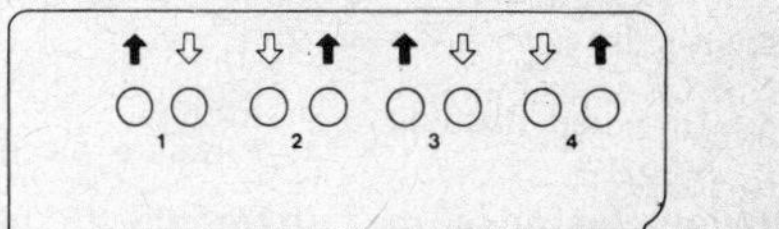

Valve location—4-cylinder engines

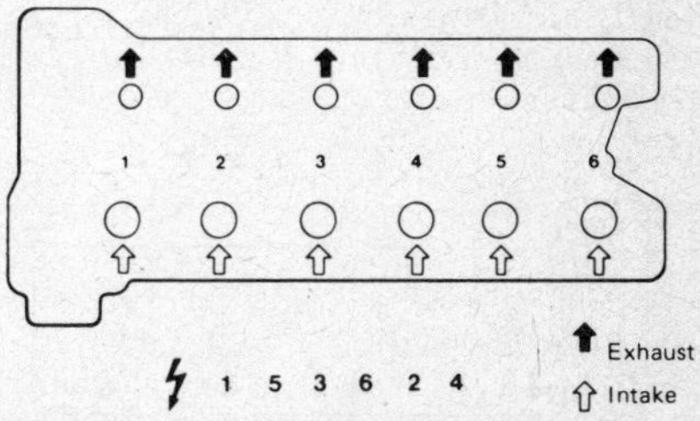

Valve location—DOHC 6-cylinder engine

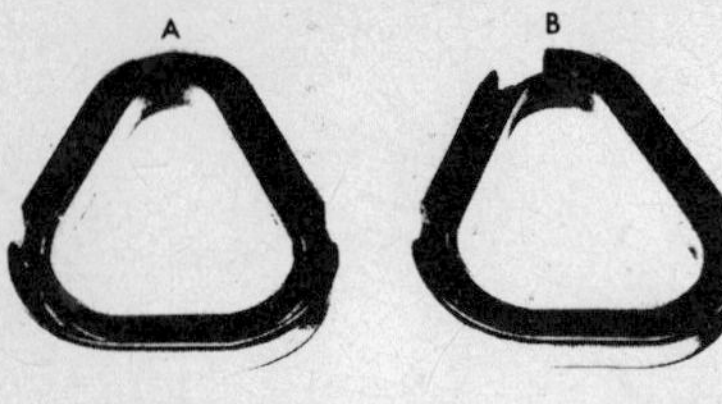

(a)—Spark plug holes 1, 3 and 5
(b)—Spark plug holes 2 and 4

Two versions of rubber gaskets

10. Install the spark plugs.

11. Reconnect the air vent line to the valve cover and install the air cleaner, if removed.

12. Run the engine and check for leaks at the rocker arm cover.

V8 Engines

NOTE: 1976 and later V8 engines use hydraulic valve lifters and require no periodic adjustment.

The valve clearance is measured between the sliding surface of the rocker arm and the heel of the camshaft lobe. The highest point of the camshaft lobe should be at a 90° angle to the sliding surface of the rocker arm.

1. Loosen the venting line and remove the regulating linkage. Remove the valve cover.

2. Disconnect the cable from the ignition coil.

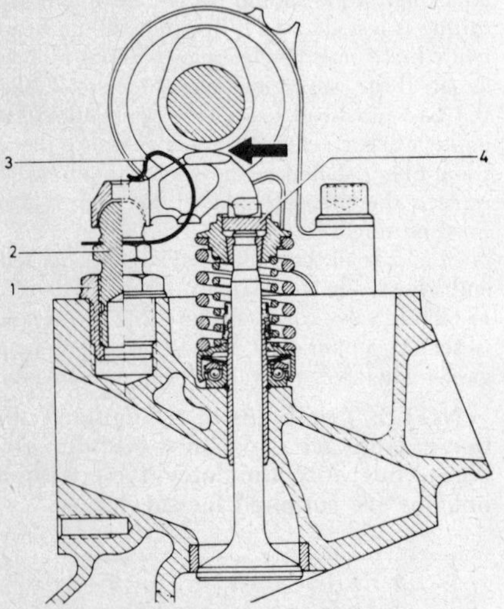

1. Threaded bushing
2. Adjuster
3. Spring
4. Pressure piece

Valve clearance measurement—V8 engines

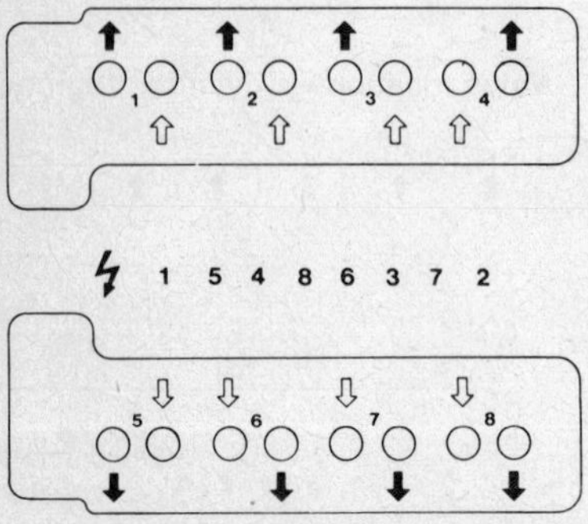

V8 (except 6.9) valve location

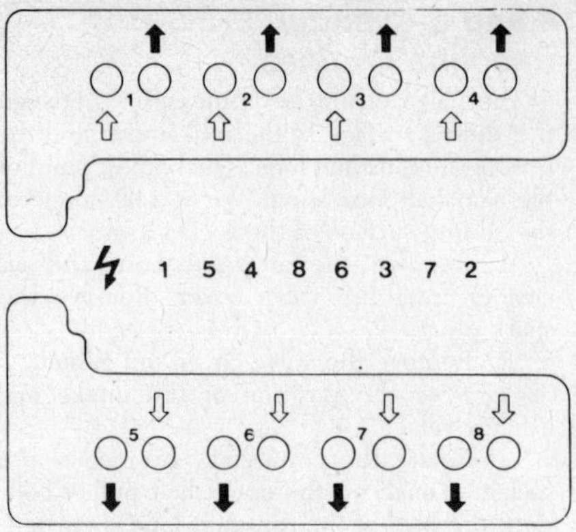

Valve locations—6.9 V8

3. Identify all of the valves, as intake or exhaust.

4. Beginning with No. 1 cylinder, crank the engine with the starter to position the heel of the camshaft approximately over the sliding surface of the rocker arm.

5. Rotate the crankshaft by means of a socket wrench on the crankshaft pulley bolt until the heel of the camshaft lobe is perpendicular to the sliding surface of the rocker arm.

NOTE: Do not rotate the engine using the camshaft sprocket bolt. The strain will distort the timing chain tensioner rail. Always rotate the engine in the direction of normal rotation only.

6. Some models have holes in the vibration damper plate to assist in crankshaft rotation. In this case, a screwdriver can be used to carefully rotate the crankshaft.

7. To measure the valve clearance, insert a feeler blade of the specified thickness between the heel of the camshaft lobe and the sliding surface of the rocker arm. The clearance is correct if the blade can be inserted and withdrawn with a very slight drag.

8. If adjustment is necessary, it can be done by turning the ball pin head at the hex collar. If the clearance is too small, increase it by turning the ball pin head in. If the clearance is too large, turn the ball pin head out.

NOTE: If the adjuster turns very easily, or if the proper clearance can't be obtained, check the torque on the adjuster using a special adapter ("crow's foot").

9. When the ball pin head is turned, the adjusting torque should be 14-29 ft/lbs. If the torque is lower, either the adjusting screw, the threaded bolt, or both will have to be replaced. If the valve clearance is too small, and the ball pin head cannot be screwed in far enough to correct it, a thinner pressure piece should be installed in the spring retainer. To replace the pressure piece, the rocker arm must be removed. (See the Engine Mechanical Section.)

10. Install the regulating linkage, valve cover gasket, and valve cover. Be sure the gasket is seated properly.

11. Connect the cable to the coil and the venting line. Run the engine and check for leaks at the valve cover.

A valve adjusting wrench (crow's foot) is required to accurately measure torque on all models

Diesel Engines

1. Remove the valve cover and note the position of the intake and exhaust valves.

2. Turn the engine with a socket and breaker bar on the crankshaft pulley or by using a remote starter, hooked to the battery (+) terminal and the large, uppermost starter solenoid terminal. Due to the extremely high compression pressures in the diesel engine, it will be considerably easier to use a remote starter. If a remote starter is not available, the engine can be bumped into position with the normal starter.

NOTE: Do not turn the engine backwards or use the camshaft sprocket bolt to rotate the engine.

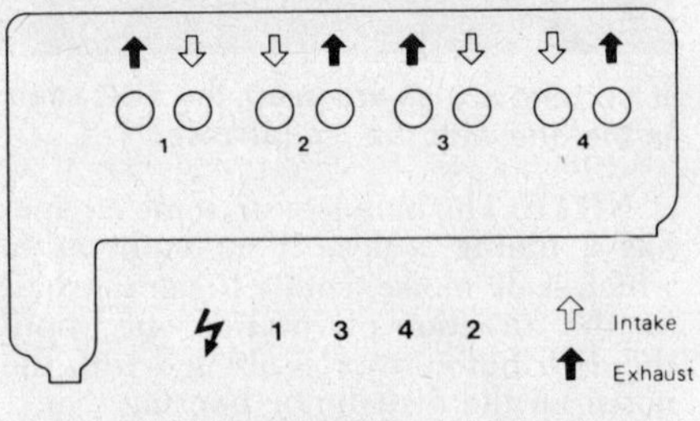

Valve arrangement—4-cylinder diesels

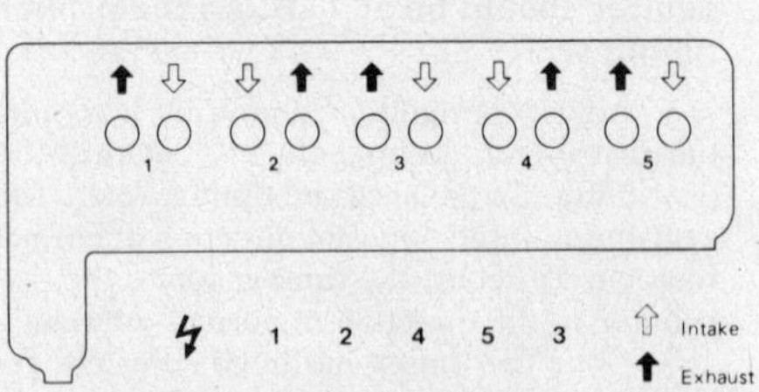

Valve arrangement—5-cylinder diesels

3. Measure the valve clearance when the heel of the camshaft lobe is directly over the sliding surface of the rocker arm. The lobe of the camshaft should be vertical to the surface of the rocker arm. The clearance is correct when the specified feeler gauge can be pulled out with a very slight drag.

4. To adjust the clearance, loosen the cap nut while holding the hex nut. Adjust the valve clearance by turning the hex nut.

5. After adjustment hold the cap nut and lock it in place with the hex nut. Recheck the clearance.

6. Check the gasket and install the rocker arm cover.

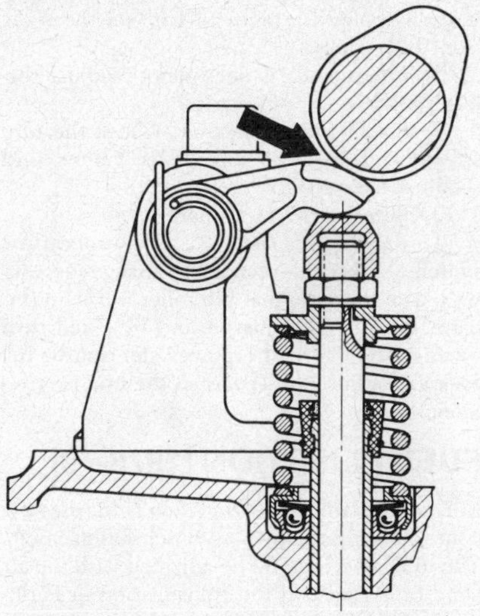

Measure valve clearance on diesel engines at arrow

7. Capnut 14. Holding wrench
8. Locknut 16. Adjusting wrench

Adjusting valve clearance on diesel engine

Idle Speed

CATALYTIC CONVERTER PRECAUTIONS

With the exception of diesels and the 230 (1975-76), all 1975-81 Mercedes-Benz cars are equipped with catalysts. The following points should be adhered to:

1. Use only unleaded gas.
2. Maintain the engine at the specified intervals.
3. Avoid running the engine with an excessively rich mixture. Do not run the engine excessively on fast idle.
4. Prolonged warm-up after a cold start should be avoided.
5. Do not check exhaust emissions over a long period of time without air injection.
6. Do not alter the emission control system in any way.

STROMBERG 175 CDT

1. Turn off the heater and A/C and run the vehicle to normal operating temperature.
2. Check the throttle valve for ease of operation.
3. Connect a tachometer and adjust the idle speed to specifications with the idle speed adjusting screw.
4. See whether the idle speed stop is resting against the throttle valve lever and not against the vacuum governor. Set the vacuum governor back if required.
5. If an exhaust gas analyzer (CO meter) is available, check the exhaust gas for percentage of CO. On 1975-76 models, check CO without air injection. Disconnect and plug the center line from the blue switchover valve. On 1977 models, be sure the wheel for altitude compensation is set correctly.
6. If required, adjust the CO by means of the fuel mixture screw or idle shut-off valve on the 1975 and later 230. Loosen the locknut while simultaneously holding the nozzle screw and turning the fuel shut-off valve. Accelerate a brief instant after each adjustment of the idle speed and fuel control screw, to stabilize the mixture.
7. Check the idle speed again and adjust with the idle speed adjusting screw, if required.
8. Adjust the control linkage as follows:

Run the engine at idle speed. Set the control rod so that it can be attached with no binding.

Idle speed adjusting screw (B), 1975 230

Idle speed adjusting screw (8)—1975-76 230

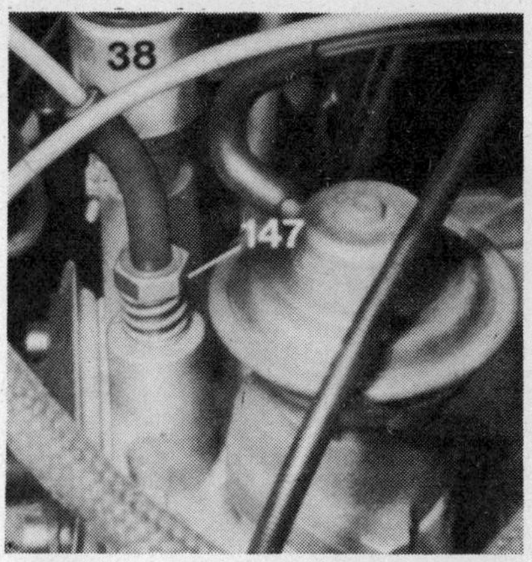

Idle speed adjusting screw (8)—1977 and later 230

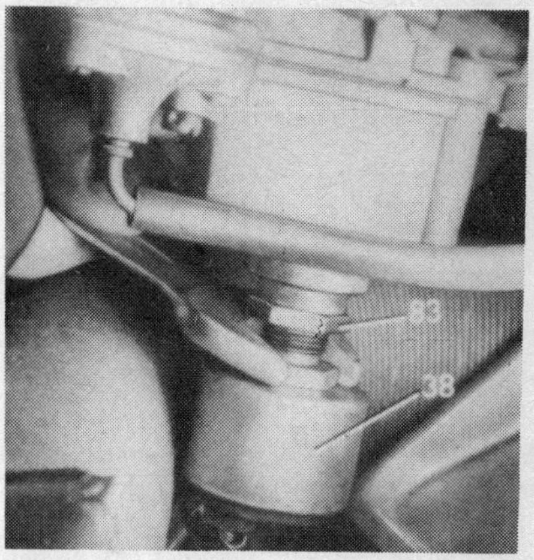

Adjust idle by turning the idle shut-off valve on 1975-76 230

CO adjustment—1977 and later 230

SOLEX 4 A 1

1. The idle speed adjustment on this carburetor is made with the air cleaner installed and the crankcase breather connected. If equipped with cruise control, be sure the cable is connected to the regulating lever without binding.
2. Warm the engine to normal operating temperature. Do not adjust the idle after the engine has been driven very far because the engine will be too hot.

61. Adjusting nut
68. Idling speed adjusting screw
130. Regulating rod

Solex 4A 1 idle speed adjustment

Mixture adjusting screws—carbureted 6-cylinder engines

3. On 1975-76 280, 280C and 280S models with catalytic converter, disconnect the blue/purple vacuum line, to prevent air injection.
4. Check the throttle valve shaft for binding.
5. Adjust the idle speed to specifications with the idle speed adjusting screw. This should be done with a tachometer installed. Be sure that the idle speed stop is on the throttle valve lever and not on the vacuum governor. Loosen the spring of the vacuum governor, if necessary, by altering the setting of the adjusting nut.
6. Check the CO content of the exhaust gas. Follow the manufacturer's directions. If necessary, turn both mixture control screws to the right against the stop. Turn both screws simultaneously to the left until the CO percentage is within specifications. Turning the screws out will give a richer mixture and turning the screws in will give a leaner mixture.
7. Check the idle speed once again until both the idle speed and CO percentage of the exhaust gas are as specified.
8. On 1975-76 280, 280C and 280S, reconnect the blue/purple vacuum line.

ELECTRONIC FUEL INJECTION (V8) 1975

Adjustment should be made with the A/C off and transmission in PARK.

1. Run the engine to normal operating temperature. The idle speed should not be adjusted when the engine is extremely hot. Be sure the cruise control cable is free of tension.
2. Remove the air cleaner.
3. Disconnect the connecting rod from the valve connection and check to be sure that the throttle valve closes completely without binding.
4. Re-attach the connecting rod so that it does not bind.
5. Connect a tachometer and adjust the idle speed to specifications with the idle speed air screw.
6. Check the exhaust gas content with a CO meter. On 1975 models with catalytic converter, disconnect the 63° F temperature switch, located in the right-front of the engine compartment. Connect the switch lead to ground, to prevent air injection. If necessary, adjust the CO content with the adjusting screw on the control unit. Turning the screw clockwise will give a richer mixture while turning the screw counterclockwise will give a leaner mixture.

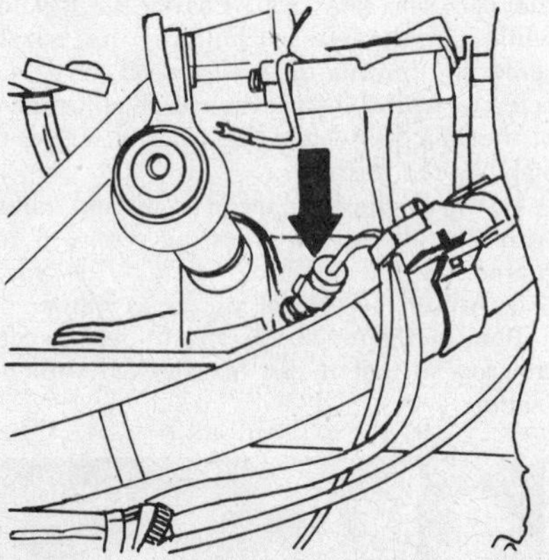

Disconnect the 63° F. temperature switch (arrow) on 1975 V-8 engines

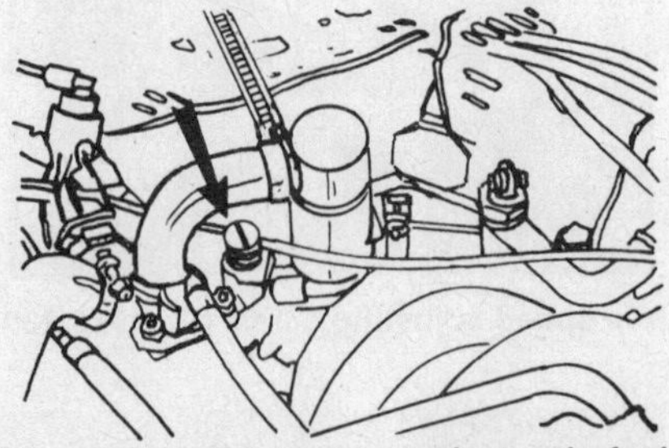

Idle speed adjustment on electronic fuel injection

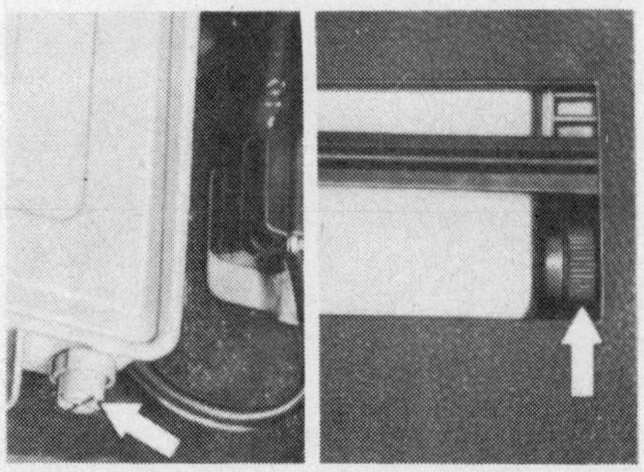

Idle mixture on 1975 V-8's is done at the control box

7. The control unit can be reached after removing the inner lining below the glove box. On other cars, the control unit adjusting screw is behind a piece of trim on the right front kick panel.
8. Check and, if necessary, readjust the idle speed.
9. Install the air cleaner. Check the idle speed and exhaust emissions values and readjust if necessary.
10. Remove the tachometer.
11. Reconnect the 63° F temperature switch. Adjust the regulating linkage (on cars with gate lever) so that the roller is free in the gate. Put the transmission in Drive and turn on the A/C. Turn the power steering to full lock and adjust the speed so the engine runs smoothly.

FUEL INJECTION (1976-79)

The mechanical fuel injection is the air flow controlled type known as Bosch K-Jetronic®. The idle speed should be adjusted with the air conditioner off and the transmission in Park.

1. Connect a tachometer.
2. Be sure the cruise control cable is connected to the regulating lever with no binding or kinking.
3. Run the engine to normal operating temperature.
4. Be sure the throttle valve rests against the idle speed stop.
5. Set the idle speed to specifications with the idle air screw.
6. If possible, check the CO level.

All 1976 engines—Check CO without air injection. Disconnect the blue/purple vacuum line at the blue thermal valve and plug the opening at the thermal valve to stop air injection.

1977-79 models—Disconnect the hose at the exhaust back pressure line and connect

Adjust the idle speed on 1976-79 V-8's at the idle air screw (arrow)

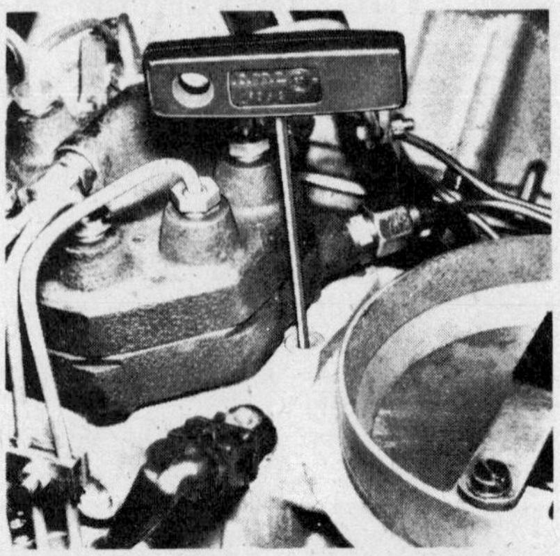

Adjust the CO with a special wrench on 1976 and later V8 fuel injection

the CO tester to the line. On Federal V8 engines, check CO with air injection connected. On all others, disconnect the blue/purple vacuum line from the blue thermal valve and plug the thermo valve to cancel air injection.

7. Adjust the CO value by unscrewing the plug and inserting the special adjusting tool (Allen wrench). Turn the screw in to richen the mixture and out to lean the mixture.

8. Accelerate briefly and check the speed and CO again.

9. Reconnect the vacuum lines and check the CO value again. It should be below the specified value.

10. Adjust the regulating lever so that the roller rests in the gate lever without binding. Put the transmission in Drive and turn on the A/C. Turn the wheels to full lock and adjust the idle speed so the engine runs smoothly.

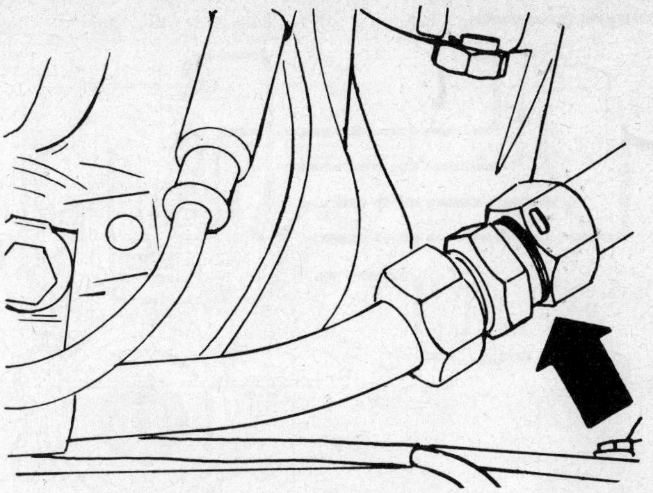

CO tap on 1976 and later V8's

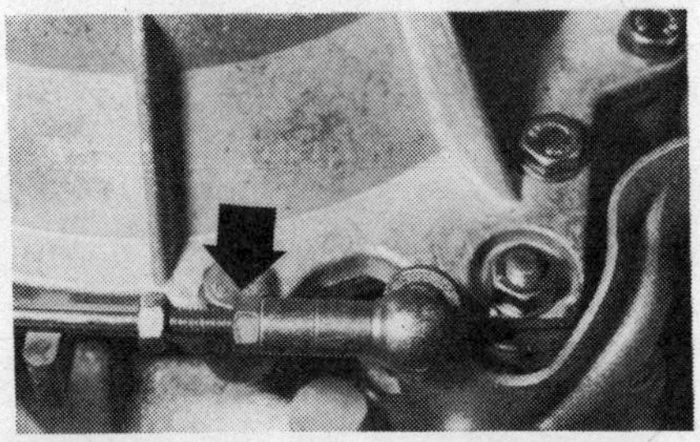

Regulating lever adjustment—1976 and later V8's

1980 6-CYLINDER AND 1980-81 V8

These engines have electronically controlled engine speed. 1981 models use a solenoid to accomplish this.

1. Connect a tachometer and remote oil temperature gauge.

2. Run the engine to approximately 176° F oil temperature.

3. The automatic transmission should be in Park and the A/C off.

4. Be sure the throttle valve lever rests against the idle stop.

5. Adjust the Bowden cable with the adjusting screw so there is no tension against the throttle valve lever.

6. Check idle speed. If necessary, adjust with idle air adjustment screw.

1981 6-CYLINDER

1. Run the engine to normal operating temperature (167°-185° oil temperature) and connect a tachometer.

2. The automatic transmission should be in Park and A/C off.

3. Be sure the throttle valve lever rests against the idle speed stop.

4. Be sure the cruise control actuating rod rests against the idle speed stop. Disconnect the connecting rod and push the lever of the actuating lever clockwise to the idle speed position.

5. Reconnect the connecting rod; make sure that the actuating element is approximately .04 in. from the idle speed stop. Adjust this clearance with the pull rod.

6. Check and adjust the idle speed. Idle speed is adjusted at the idle speed air screw.

DIESEL ENGINES

1975-80 Except 1980 Turbodiesels

Since the diesel engine has no ignition distributor or ignition coil there is no way to connect an external tachometer to measure idle speed. While using the built-in tachometer on the dash is not the most accurate way, the only other possibility is to set the idle speed by ear.

1. On models before 1977, turn the knob on the instrument panel completely clockwise. Turn it again counterclockwise. The travel before the idle speed is raised should not exceed about ½ turn. If required, adjust the travel with the nut.

2. On 1977 and later models, turn the knob on the instrument panel completely clockwise and check the distance between the adjusting ring and the specially shaped spring. It should be approximately .04 in.

3. With the engine stopped, depress the accelerator pedal while turning the idle knob counterclockwise.

4. Start the engine. The idle should be 1000-1100 rpm. Adjust this with the adjusting screw, but do not exceed 1100 rpm.

Adjusting nut for dashboard idle speed knob

Idle speed adjusting screw—1980 and later 6-cylinder

Idle speed adjusting screw—1980 V-8

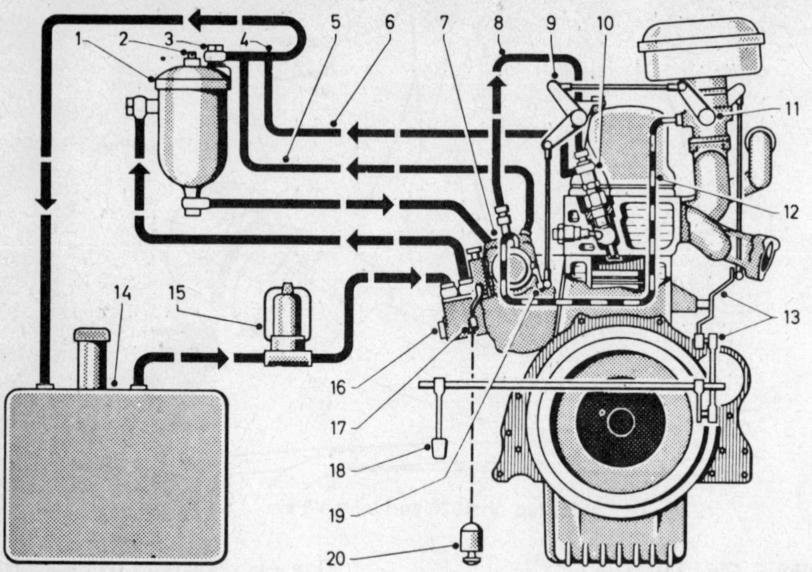

1. Main fuel filter
2. Vent screw
3. Hollow screw with throttle screw
4. Fuel return line
5. Overflow line
6. Injection nozzle leakage line
7. Injection pump
8. Pressure line from injection pump to injection nozzle
9. Angular lever for auxiliary mechanical control
10. Injection nozzle
11. Venturi control unit
12. Vacuum line with throttle screw
13. Linkage and lever for accelerator pedal control
14. Fuel tank
15. Fuel prefilter
16. Fuel feed pump with hand pump
17. Adjusting lever
18. Accelerator pedal
19. Lever for auxiliary mechanical control
20. Heater plug starting switch with starting and stopping cable

Schematic diagram of diesel fuel system

5. On 1977 and later models, be sure the special spring is installed correctly.
6. Run the engine to operating temperature.
7. Turn the idle adjusting knob on the dash fully to the right.
8. Disconnect the regulating rod and adjust the idle speed with the idle speed adjusting screw. 1977 and later models have a locknut on the idle speed adjusting screw.
9. Reconnect the regulating rod.

1980 Turbodiesel and 1981

1. Run the engine to normal operating temperature.
2. On normally aspirated engines, turn the idle speed adjuster on the dash completely to the right.
3. Disconnect the pushrod at the angle lever.
4. Check the idle speed. Adjust by loosening the locknut and adjusting the idle speed screw. Tighten the locknut.

Diesel engine idle speed adjustment (4)—300D and 300CD

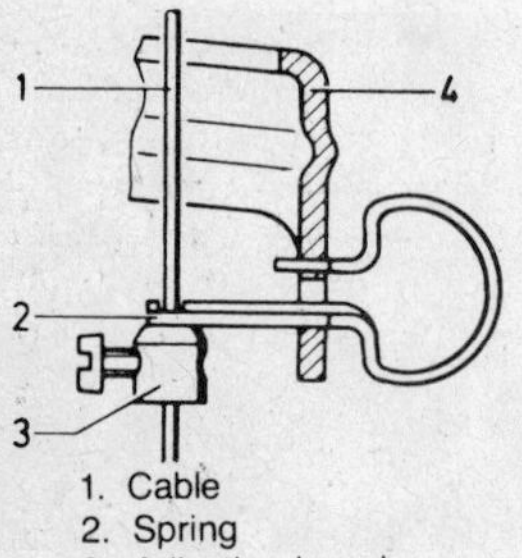

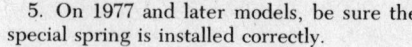

1. Cable
2. Spring
3. Adjusting barrel
4. Lever

Be sure the specially shaped spring is installed as shown

Diesel engine idle speed adjustment—4-cylinder

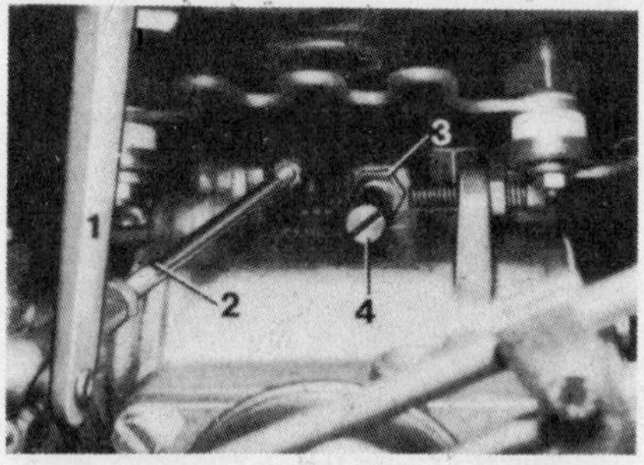

Diesel engine idle speed adjustment—1976 and later

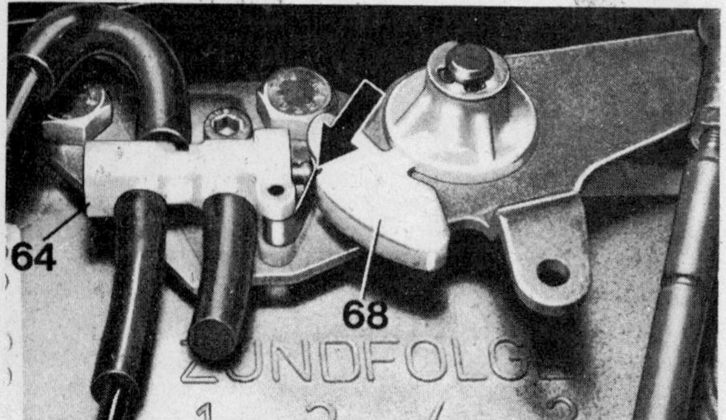

Clearance between cam and actuator on switchover valve 1980-81 except turbo diesel

1. Adjusting screw 2. Bowden cable, cruise control

Bowden cable adjustment—1980-81 diesels

5. On all except 1981 Turbodiesels, adjust the pushrod so that a clearance of approximately .2 in. exists between the cam on the lever and the actuator on the switchover valve. The lever on the fuel injection pump must rest against the idle stop.

6. On all models except the 1981 Turbodiesel, depress the stop lever as far as possible. The cruise control Bowden cable should be free of tension against the angle lever. Use the adjusting screw to alter the tension. Let go of the stop lever. The Bowden cable should now have a slight amount of play.

7. On 1981 Turbodiesels, adjust the pushrod, so that the roller in the guide lever rests free of tension against the end stop.

8. Put the automatic transmission in Drive and turn the steering wheel to full lock. The engine should run smoothly. If not, adjust the idle speed.

CAUTION

If the engine speed is adjusted higher, it will be above the controlled idle speed range of the governor and the engine can increase in speed to the maximum rpm.

ENGINE ELECTRICAL

Distributor

REMOVAL AND INSTALLATION

The removal and installation procedures for all distributors on Mercedes-Benz vehicles are basically similar. However, certain minor differences may exist from model to model.

1. The distributor is usually located on the front of the engine.
2. Remove the dust cover, distributor cap, cable plug connections, and vacuum line.
3. Rotating the engine in the normal direction, crank it around until the distributor rotor points to the mark on the rim of the distributor housing. This indicates No. 1 cylinder.
4. The engine can be cranked with a socket wrench on the balancer bolt or with a screwdriver inserted in the balancer.
5. Matchmark the distributor body and the engine so that the distributor can be returned to its original position. White paint can be used for this purpose.
6. Remove the distributor hold-down bolt and withdraw the distributor from the engine.

NOTE: Do not crank the engine while the distributor is removed.

7. To install the distributor, reverse the removal instructions. Insert the distributor so that the matchmarks on the distributor and engine are aligned.
8. Tighten the clamp bolt and check the dwell angle and ignition timing.

Electronic Ignition

TESTING-ALL EXCEPT 1981 6-CYLINDER

1. Check the screw type plug terminals and the plug wires.
2. With the ignition ON, a primary current of about 8 amps will flow continuously through the system.
3. Check the input voltage at the terminal block. Terminal 15 should show 4.5 volts and terminal 1 should show 0.5-2.0 volts. If the voltage at terminal 1 is excessive, replace the switching unit.

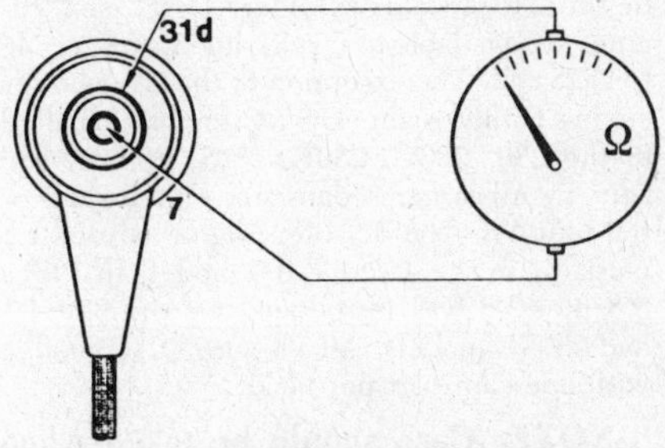

Testing armature resistance—electronic ignition prior to 1980

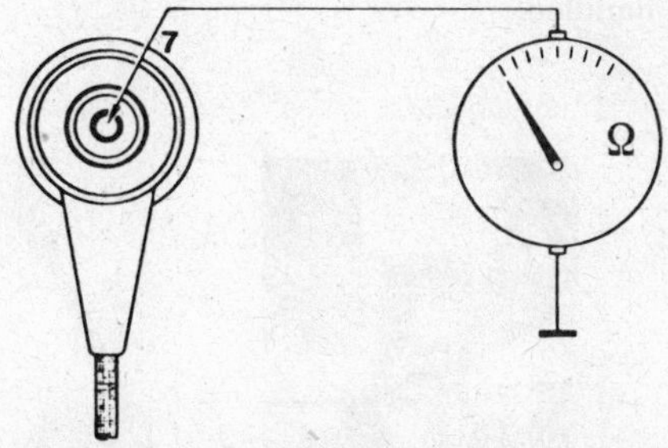

Testing pick-up coil resistance—electronic ignition prior to 1980

4. If there is no spark but terminal 1 voltage is OK, check the armature resistance (terminal 7 and 31 d). Resistance should be 450-750 ohms.
5. Test the pick-up coil resistance. There should be infinite resistance between terminal 7 and ground.
6. Check the armature and pick-up coil for mechanical damage. An air gap should exist between them.
7. Check the dwell angle. Even though it cannot be adjusted, it should be 25-39° at 1400-1500 rpm.
8. If the armature and pick-up coil are functioning, replace the switching unit. If the armature and pick-up coil indicate no damage, replace the switching unit. If the armature or pick-up coil are defective, replace the distributor.

1981 6-CYLINDER

This engine uses a new breakerless transistorized ignition system with no preresistance and no current flow unless the engine is running. The new system consists of ignition coil, distributor, harness and switching unit. Do not replace the coil with a previously used coil. Also, see the ignition system precautions given previously.

TESTING-1981 6-CYLINDER

1. Test the voltage between bushing 5 of the diagnosis plug and ground with the ignition ON. Nominal battery voltage should be indicated. If not, test the voltage via the ignition switch. If voltage is correct, go to Step 2.
2. Test the voltage between bushing 4 and 5 of the diagnosis plug socket. Zero voltage should be indicated. If voltage is more than 0.1 volt, switch off the ignition immediately. Renew the switching unit. Check the pressure relief plug in the ignition coil and the ohmic value of the ignition coil between terminals 1 and 15. If the pressure relief plug has popped out or the resistance is not .7Ω, replace the ignition coil.
3. Test the dwell angle. It should be 7-25°. If more than 25°, replace the switching unit. If no reading or the reading is correct, go to Step 4.
4. Disconnect the green control line from the switching unit and test the resistance between terminals 3 and 7. Resistance should be 500-700 ohms. If the resistance is wrong, pull the green cable from the distributor and see if there are 500-700 ohms present at the connector plugs. If so, replace the green cable. If not, replace the distributor.
5. Remove the green cable from the control unit. There should be 200 kΩ between terminals 3 or 7 and ground. If not, disconnect the green cable from the distributor and test the resistance between any of the plugs and ground. If 200 kΩ are not present, replace the distributor.

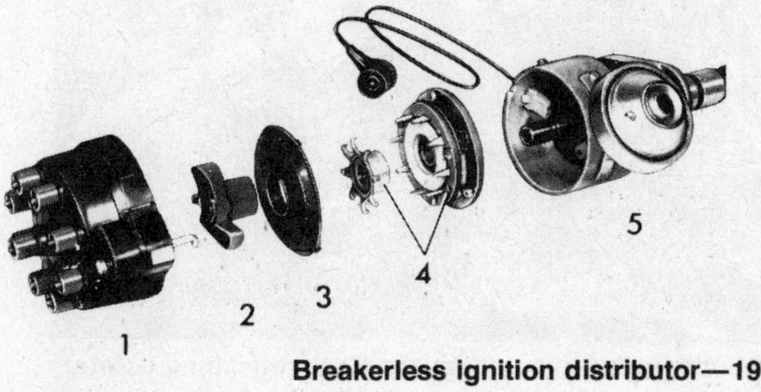

1. Distributor cap
2. Rotor
3. Dust cover
4. Armature and pick-up assembly
5. Distributor housing with pick-up connection

Breakerless ignition distributor—1975-80

Alternator

All Mercedes-Benz cars covered in this book use 12 volt electrical systems with alternators, in conjunction with the transistor or electronic ignition system.

ALTERNATOR PRECAUTIONS

Some precautions that should be taken into consideration when working on this, or any other, AC charging system are as follows:

1. Never switch battery polarity.
2. When installing a battery, always connect the grounded terminal first.
3. Never disconnect the battery while the engine is running.
4. If the molded connector is disconnected from the alternator, do not ground the hot wire.
5. Never run the alternator with the main output cable disconnected.
6. Never electric weld around the car without disconnecting the alternator.
7. Never apply any voltage in excess of battery voltage during testing.
8. Never "jump" a battery for starting purposes with more than 12 volts.

REMOVAL AND INSTALLATION

Viewing the engine from the front, the alternator is located on the left or right-hand side, usually down low. Because of the location, it is sometimes easier to remove the alternator from below the vehicle. The following is a general procedure for all models.

1. Locate the alternator and disconnect and tag all wires.
2. Loosen the adjusting (pivot) bolt or the adjusting mechanism and swing the alternator in toward the engine.
3. Remove the drive belt from the alternator pulley.
4. The alternator can now be removed from its mounting bracket or the bracket and alternator can be removed from the engine.
5. Installation is the reverse of removal.
6. Tighten all of the drive belts that were loosened.

Belt Tension Adjustment

All alternator drive belts should be tensioned to approximately ½ in. deflection under thumb pressure at the middle of the longest span.

Starter

All Mercedes-Benz passenger cars are equipped with 12-volt Bosch electric starters of various rated outputs. The starter is actuated and the pinion engaged by an electric solenoid mounted on top of the starter motor.

When removing the starter, note the exact position of all wires and washers since they should be installed in their original locations. Also, on some models it may be necessary to position the front wheels to the left or right to provide working clearance.

REMOVAL AND INSTALLATION

1. Remove all wires from the starter and tag them for location.
2. Disconnect the battery cable.
3. Unbolt the starter from the bellhousing and remove the ground cable.
4. Remove the starter from underneath the car.
5. Installation is the reverse of removal. Be sure to replace all wires and washers in their original locations.

Battery

The battery is located in the engine compartment and can be easily removed by disconnecting the battery cables and removing the hold-down clamp.

ENGINE MECHANICAL

Mercedes-Benz has used a variety of different engines since 1973. All engines have an overhead valve design, operating the valve through individual rocker arms. The smallest of the engines is the 2307 cc gasoline engine installed in the 230. A 4-cylinder diesel engine of 2404 cc displacement is also available in the 240D/8. Six-cylinder, OHC cam engines are available in displacements from 2746 to 2778 cc's. The exception to the six-cylinder engine family is the DOHC engine installed in the 280, 280C, 280E, 280S, 280SE, and 280CE. All larger sedans use either a 4.5 or 6.9 liter V8. The 6.9 liter engine is used exclusively in the 450SEL 6.9 model. In 1981 a 3.8 liter V8 was introduced for the 380SEL and 380SL models. All V8's are OHC models with one camshaft per head.

NOTE: Care should be taken when working on Mercedes-Benz engines, since there are many aluminum parts which can be damaged if carelessly handled.

ENGINE REMOVAL AND INSTALLATION

NOTE: In all cases, Mercedes-Benz engines and transmissions are removed as a unit.

CAUTION

Air conditioner lines should not be indiscriminately disconnected without taking proper precautions. It is best to swing the compressor out of the way while still connected to its hoses. Never do any welding around the compressor–heat may cause an explosion. Also, the refrigerant, while inert at normal room temperature, breaks down under high temperature into hydrogen fluoride and phosgene (among other products), which are highly poisonous.

230, 240D, 300D, 300CD, 300TD, 300SD

1. First, remove the hood, then drain the cooling system and disconnect the battery. While not strictly necessary, it is better to remove the battery completely to prevent breakage by the engine as it is lifted out.
2. Remove the fan shroud, radiator, and disconnect all heater hoses and oil cooler lines.
3. Remove the air cleaner and all fuel, vacuum and oil hoses (e.g., power steering and power brakes). Plug all openings to keep out dirt.
4. Remove the viscous coupling and fan and, on applicable engines, disconnect the carburetor choke cable.
5. On diesel engines, disconnect the idle control starting cables. On the 300SD, loosen the oil filter cover slightly; siphon off the power steering fluid and disconnect the hoses.
6. On all engines, disconnect the accelerator linkage.
7. Disconnect all ground straps and elec-

Engine removal—6-cylinder gas engine. Inset shows lift attaching points.

trical connections. It is a good idea to tag each wire for easy reassembly.

8. Detach the gearshift linkage and the exhaust pipes from the manifolds.

9. Loosen the steering relay arm and pull it down out of the way, along with the center steering rod and hydraulic steering damper.

10. The hydraulic engine shock absorber should be removed.

11. Remove the hydraulic line from the clutch housing and the oil line connectors from the automatic transmission.

12. Unbolt the clutch slave cylinder from the bellhousing after removing the return spring.

13. Remove the exhaust pipe bracket attached to the transmission and place a wood-padded jack under the bellhousing, or place a cable sling under the oil pan, to support the engine. On the 300SD, disconnect the exhaust pipes at the turbo charger.

14. Mark the position of the rear engine support and unbolt the two outer bolts, then remove the top bolt at the transmission and pull the support out.

15. Disconnect the speedometer cable and the front driveshaft U-joint. Push the driveshaft back and wire it out of the way.

16. Unbolt the engine mounts on both sides and, on four-cylinder engines, the front limit stop.

17. Unbolt the power steering fluid reservoir and swing it out of the way; then, using a chain hoist and cable, lift the engine and transmission upward and outward. An angle of about 45° will allow the car to be pushed backward while the engine is coming up.

18. Reverse the procedure to install, making sure to bleed the hydraulic clutch, power steering, power brakes and fuel system.

V8 Engines

NOTE: Removal of a V8 engine equipped with air conditioning, requires disconnecting the air conditioning system. This should only be done by an air conditioning specialist. Take the car to an air conditioning specialist to have the system discharged prior to engine removal.

1. Remove the hood.
2. Drain the cooling system.
3. Remove the radiator and fan shroud.
4. Remove the cable plug from the temperature switch.
5. Remove the battery, battery frame and air filter.
6. Drain the power steering reservoir and windshield washer reservoir.
7. Disconnect and plug the high pressure and return lines on the power steering pump.
8. Detach the fuel lines from the fuel filter, pressure regulator, and pressure sensor.
9. If equipped, loosen the line to the supply and anti-freeze tanks. On the 6.9, disconnect the lines to the hydro-pneumatic suspension.
10. Disconnect the cables from the ignition coil and transistor ignition switchbox.
11. Disconnect the brake vacuum lines.
12. Detach the cable connections for the following:
    a. venturi control unit
    b. temperature sensor
    c. distributor

1. U-Joint flange
2. Front driveshaft
3. Hex bolt
4. U-Joint plate
5. Wooden block

Supporting the transmission—V8's

    d. temperature switch
    e. cold starting valve
    f. speedometer inductance transmitter (3.8 only)

13. Remove the regulating shaft by pushing it in the direction of the firewall.
14. Disconnect the thrust and pullrods.
15. Disconnect the heater lines.
16. Detach the lines to the oil pressure and temperature gauges.
17. Remove the ground strap from the vehicle.
18. Detach the cables from the alternator, terminal bridge, and battery. Remove the battery.
19. On the 6.9, remove the oil line shield and disconnect the oil lines between the oil pan and oil reservoir.
20. Position a lifting sling on the engine and take up the slack in the chain.
21. Remove the left-hand engine mount and loosen the hex nut on the right-hand mount.
22. Remove the exhaust system. Remove the connecting rod chain on the rear level control valve and loosen the torsion bar slightly. Raise the vehicle slightly at the rear and remove the exhaust system in a rearward direction.
23. Disconnect the handbrake cable.
24. Remove the shield plate from the transmission tunnel.
25. Place a block of wood between the transmission and cross yoke so the engine will not sag, when the rear mount is removed.
26. Loosen the driveshaft intermediate bearing and the driveshaft slide.
27. Support the transmission with a jack.
28. Mark the installation of the crossmember and remove the crossmember. Remove the rear engine carrier with the engine mount.
29. Unbolt the front U-joint flange on the transmission and push it back. Do not loosen the clamp nut on the intermediate bearing. Support the driveshaft.
30. Disconnect the speedometer shaft, shift rod, control pressure rod, regulating linkage (on automatic transmissions), kickdown switch cable, starter lockout switch cable, and the cable for the back-up light switch.
31. Remove the front engine mounting bolt and remove the engine at approximately a 45° angle.
32. Installation is the reverse of removal. Lower the engine until it is behind the front axle carrier. Place a jack under the transmission and tower the engine into its compartment. While lowering the engine, install the right-hand shock mount.

Fill the engine with all required fluids and start the engine. Check for leaks.

280, 280C, 280E, 280CE, 280SE, 280S

1. Scribe alignment marks on the hood hinges and remove the hood. Drain the coolant from the radiator and block.
2. Remove the radiator.
3. Disconnect the lines from the vacuum pump.
4. On vehicles with air conditioning, remove the compressor and place it aside.

CAUTION

Do not remove the refrigerant lines from the compressor. Physical harm could result.

5. Disconnect and tag all electrical connections from the engine.
6. Disconnect all coolant and vacuum lines from the engine.
7. Disconnect and plug the pressure oil lines from the power steering pump, after draining the pump reservoir.
8. Remove the accelerator linkage control rod by pulling off the lockring and pushing the shaft in the direction of the firewall.
9. Loosen and remove the exhaust pipes from the manifold and transmission supports.
10. Disconnect the transmission linkage and all other connections.
11. Loosen the front right (driving direction) shock absorber from the front axle carrier.
12. Remove the left-hand engine shock absorber from the engine mount.
13. Attach a lifting device to the engine and tension the cables.
14. Unbolt the engine and transmission mounts and remove the engine at a 45° angle.
15. Installation is the reverse of removal. Be sure to check all fluids and fill or top up as necessary. Check all adjustments on the engine.

Cylinder Head

REMOVAL AND INSTALLATION

4 and 5-Cylinder Engines

In order to perform a valve job or to inspect cylinder bores for wear, the head must be removed. While this may seem fairly straightforward, some caution must be observed to ensure that valve timing is not disturbed.

1. Drain the radiator and remove all hoses and wires.
2. Remove the camshaft cover and associated throttle linkage, then press out the

spring clamp from the notch in the rocker arm.

3. Push the clamp outward over the ball cap of the rocker, then depress the valve with a large screwdriver and lift the rocker arm out of the ball pin head.

4. Remove the rocker arm supports and the camshaft sprocket nut.

5. On diesels, the rockers and their supports must be removed together.

6. Using a suitable puller, remove the camshaft sprocket, after having first marked the chain, sprocket and cam for ease in assembly.

7. Remove the sprocket and chain and wire it out of the way.

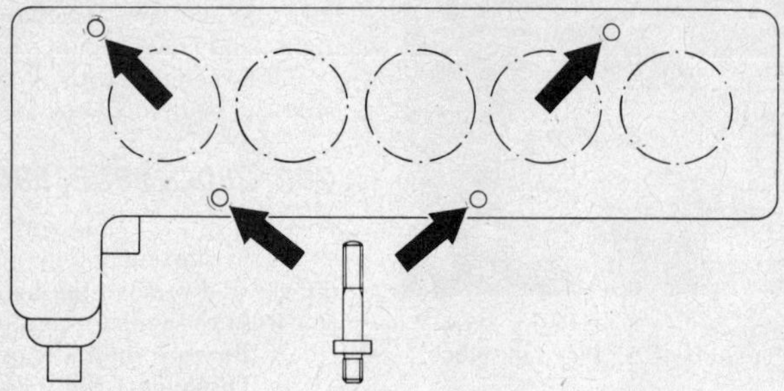

Studs (arrows) on the 5-cylinder engine are for attaching the rocker cover.

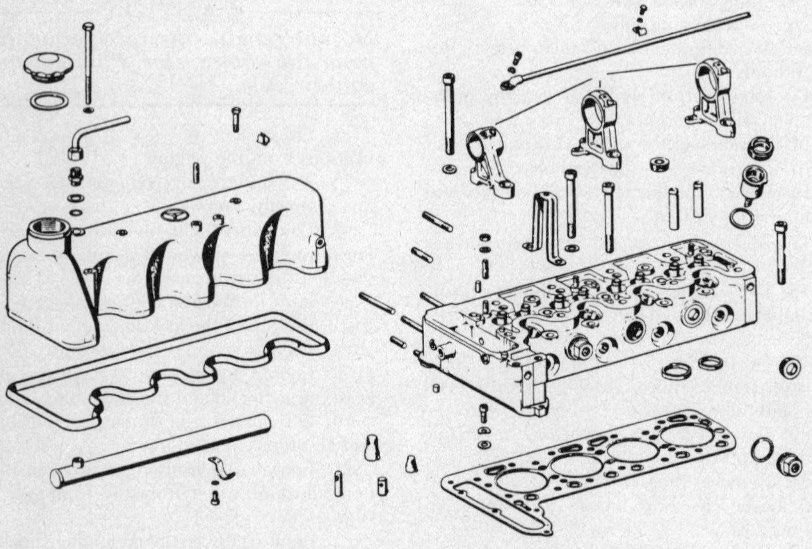

4-cylinder diesel engine cylinder head (5-cylinder is similar)

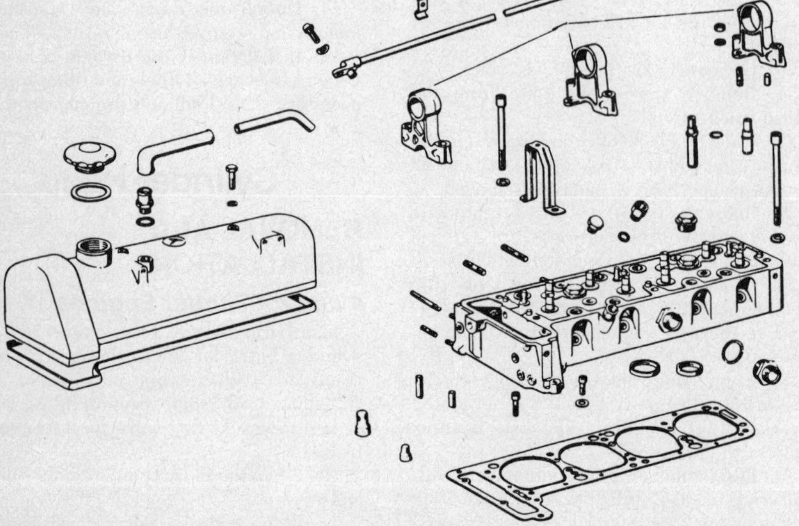

4-cylinder head

CAUTION

Make sure the chain is securely wired so that it will not slide down into the engine.

8. Unbolt the manifolds and exhaust header pipe and push them out of the way.

9. Then loosen the cylinder head hold-down bolts in the reverse order of that shown in torque diagrams for each model. It is good practice to loosen each bolt a little at a time, working around the head, until all are free. This prevents unequal stresses in the metal.

10. Reach into the engine compartment and gradually work the head loose from each end by rocking it. Never, under any circumstances, use a screwdriver between the head and block to pry, as the head will be scarred badly and may be ruined.

11. Installation is the reverse of removal.

V8 Engines

Before removing the cylinder head from a V8, be sure you have the 4 special tools necessary to torque the head bolts; without them it will be impossible. Do not confuse the left and right-hand head gaskets—the left side has 2 attaching holes in the timing chain cover, the right side has only 1 hole.

Cylinder heads on 3.8 and 4.5 liter V8's are not interchangeable.

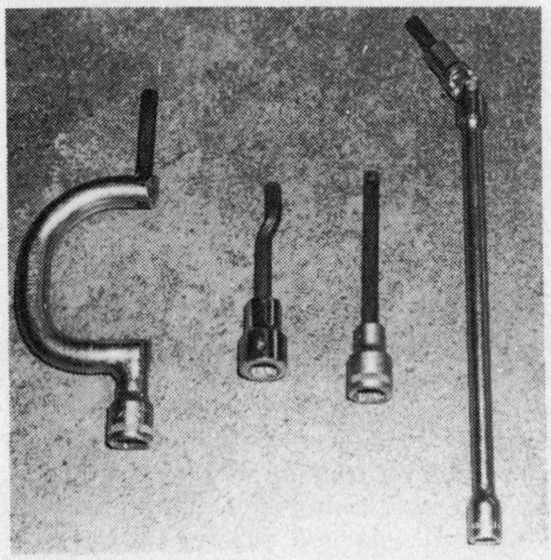

You need these tools to remove or install the V8 cylinder head. Without them it is practically impossible.

NOTE: Cylinder heads can only be removed with the engine cold.

1. Drain the cooling system.
2. Remove the battery.
3. Remove the air cleaner. Remove the fan and fan shroud.
4. Pull the cable plug from the temperature sensor.
5. On the 6.9, to remove the right-hand head, remove the alternator (with bracket), windshield washer reservoir and bracket and automatic transmission dipstick tube.
6. Detach the vacuum hose from the venturi control unit.
7. Remove the following electrical connections:
   a. injection valves
   b. distributor
   c. venturi control unit
   d. temperature sensor and temperature switch

e. starting valve
f. temperature switch for the auxiliary fan.
8. Loosen the ring line on the fuel distributor.
9. Loosen the screws on the injection valves and pressure regulator or mixture regulator. Remove the ring line with the injection valves and pressure regulator.
10. Plug the holes for the injection valves in the cylinder head.
11. Remove the regulating shaft by disconnecting the pull rod and the thrust rod.
12. Remove the ignition cable plug.
13. Loosen the vacuum connection on the intake manifold.
14. Loosen the vacuum connection for the central lock at the transmission.
15. Remove the oil filler tube from the right-hand cylinder head and remove the temperature connector.
16. Remove the oil pressure gauge line from the left-hand cylinder head.
17. Loosen the coolant connection on the intake manifold.
18. Remove the intake manifold. This is not necessary on 3.8 liter V8's although the intake manifold bolts must be removed.
19. Loosen the alternator belt and remove the alternator and mounting bracket.
20. Remove the electrical connections from the distributor and electronic ignition switchgear.
21. Drain some fluid from the power steering reservoir and disconnect and plug the return hose and high pressure supply line.
22. Disconnect the exhaust system. On 3.8 liter V8's, remove the exhaust manifolds.
23. Loosen the right-hand holder for the engine damper.
24. Remove the right-hand chain tensioner.

Be careful removing the cylinder head bolts on a V8. The inner row of cam bolts are the only bolts NOT holding the head on. Note the angle of the bolts.

25. Matchmark the camshaft, camshaft sprocket, and chain. Remove the camshaft sprocket and chain after removing the cylinder head cover. Be sure to hang the chain and sprocket to prevent it from falling into the timing chain case.
26. Remove the upper slide rail. On 3.8 liter V8's, remove the ignition distributor and remove the inner slide rail on the left cylinder head. Remove the rail after the camshaft sprocket.
27. Unscrew the cylinder head bolts. This should be done with a cold engine. Unscrew the bolts in the reverse order of the illustrated torque sequences. Unscrew all the bolts a little at a time and proceed in this manner until all the bolts have been removed. On the 6.9, you'll need to raise the engine to remove No. 12 and 18 bolts on the left-side head. To do this, place the level adjusting switch at "S" (first notch).

NOTE: Cylinder head bolts on 3.8 liter V8's are nickel plated and 10 mm longer than those for previous engines.

28. Remove the cylinder head. Do not pry on the cylinder head.
29. Remove the cylinder head gasket.
30. Clean the cylinder head and cylinder block joint faces.
31. To install, position the cylinder head gasket.
32. Do not confuse the cylinder head gaskets. The left-hand head has two attaching

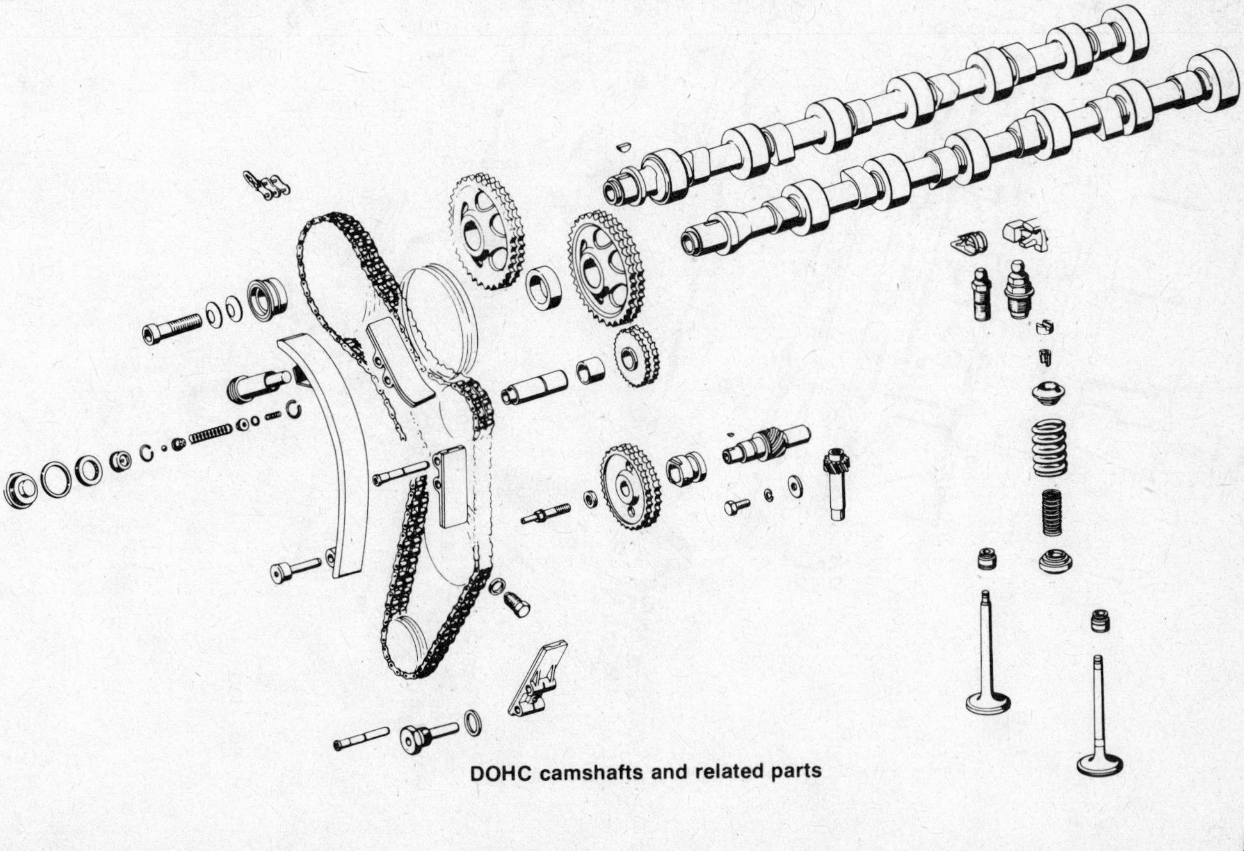

DOHC camshafts and related parts

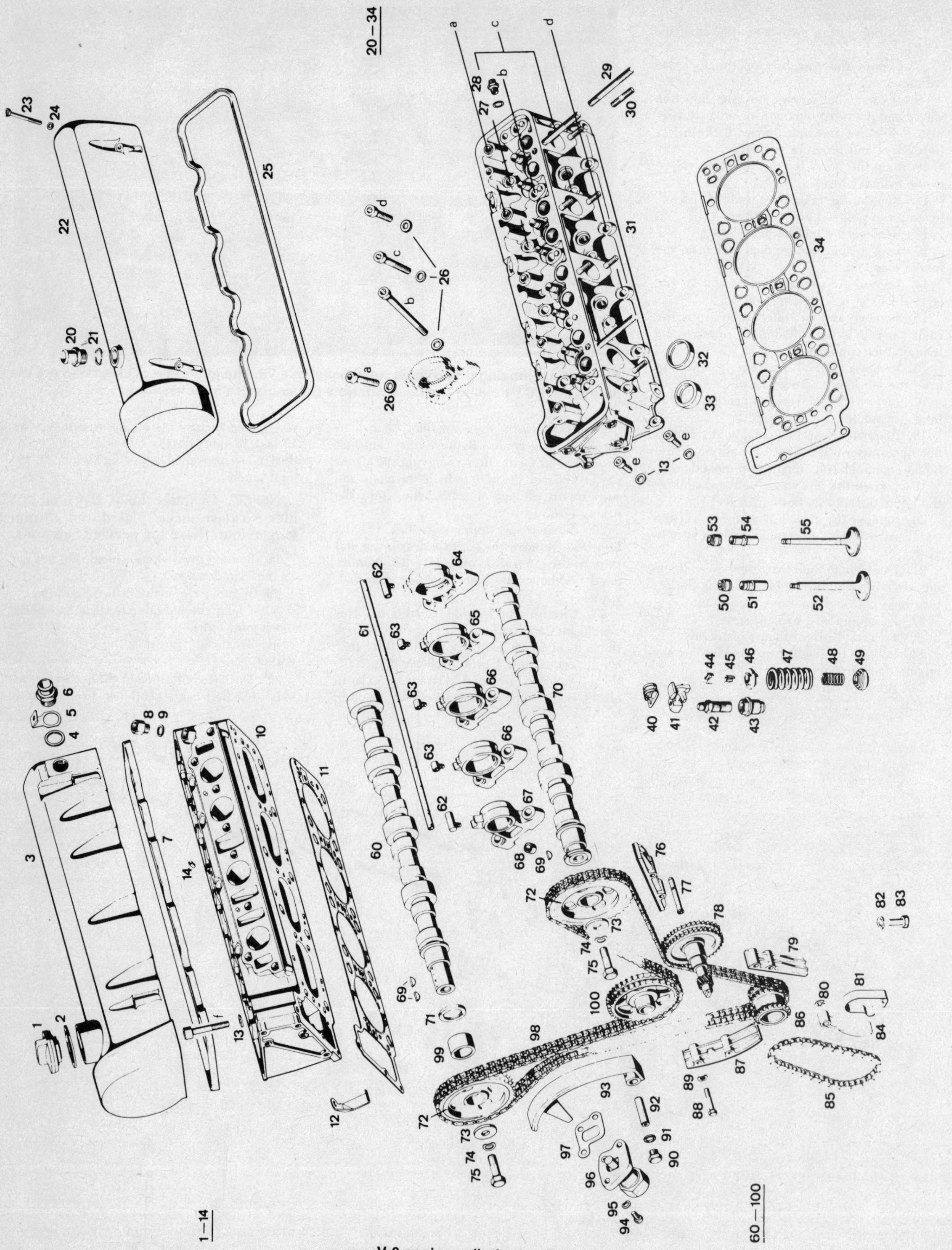

V-8 engine cylinder head

Cylinder head right 1-14

1. Filler plug
2. Sealing ring
3. Cylinder head cover
4. Sealing ring
5. Holder for cable to injection valves
6. Connection
7. Valve cover gasket
8. Connection to temperature sensor
9. Sealing ring
10. Cylinder head
11. Cylinder head gasket
12. Cable holder
13. 5 Washers
14. Hollow dowel pins

Cylinder head left 20-34

20. Connection
21. Sealing ring
22. Cylinder head cover
23. 8 Screws
24. 8 Sealing rings
25. Cylinder head cover gasket
26. 36 Washers
27. Sealing ring
28. Screw connection oil pressure gauge
29. 3 Studs
30. 13 Studs
31. Cylinder head
32. Valve seat ring—intake
33. Valve seat ring—exhaust
34. Cylinder head gasket

Cylinder head bolts

(a)—10 M 10 x 50chrauben)
(camshaft bearing fastening bolts)
(b)—10 M 10 x 155
(c)—18 M 10 x 80
(d)—8 M 10 x 55
(e)—4 M 8 x 30
(f)—1 M 8 x 70

Valve arrangement 40-55

40. Tensioning spring
41. Rocker arm
42. Adjusting screw
43. Threaded bushing
44. Thrust piece
45. Valve cone piece
46. Valve spring retainer
47. Outer valve spring
48. Inner valve spring
49. Rotator
50. Intake valve seal
51. Exhaust valve guide
52. Intake valve
53. Exhaust valve seal
54. Exhaust valve guide
55. Exhaust valve

Engine timing 60-100

60. Camshaft-right
61. Oil pipe (external lubrication) Oil pipe to camshaft bearing
62. Connecting piece
63. Connecting piece
64. Camshaft bearing-flywheel end
65. Camshaft bearing 4
66. Camshaft bearing 2 and 3
67. Camshaft bearing-cranking end
68. 5 Hollow dowel pins
69. Spring washer
70. Camshaft-left
71. Compensating washer
72. Camshaft gear
73. Washer-camshaft gear
74. Spring washer
75. Bolt
76. 3 Slide rails
77. 6 Bearing bolts
78. Drive gear ignition distributor
79. Guide rail
80. Lockwasher
81. Spring—chain tensioner, oil pump
82. Washer
83. Screw
84. Clamp
85. Single roller chain (oil pump drive)
86. Crankshaft gear
87. Slide rail
88. 4 Screws
89. 4 Spring washers
90. Plug
91. Sealing ring
92. Bearing bolt
93. Tensioning lever
94. 2 Bolts
95. 2 Spring washers
96. Chain tensioner
97. Gasket
98. Double roller chain
99. Spacer ring
100. Idler gear

V8 engine cylinder head

holes in the timing chain cover while the right-hand head has three.

33. Install the cylinder head and torque the bolts according to the illustrated torque sequence.

34. Further installation is the reverse of removal. On 3.8 liter V8's, insert the rear cam bearing cylinder head bolt before positioning the cylinder head. Also, install the exhaust manifolds only after the cylinder head bolts have been tightened. The camshaft sprocket should be installed so that the flange faces the camshaft. Check the valve clearance and fill the engine with oil. Top up the power steering tank and bleed the power steering system.

35. Run the engine and check for leaks.

6-Cylinder DOHC Engine

NOTE: Two people are best for this job. The head must be removed STRAIGHT up. The 2 bolts in the chain case are removed with a magnet.

To install use 2 pieces of wood ½ in. x 1½ in. x 9 in. to lay the head on while aligning the bolt holes. The exhaust camshaft gear bolt is 0.2 in. shorter.

1. Completely drain the cooling system.
2. Remove the air filter.
3. Remove the radiator.
4. Remove the rocker arm cover.
5. Remove the battery. Remove the idler pulley and the holding bracket for the compressor.
6. Remove the compressor and bracket and lay it aside without disconnecting any of the lines.

CAUTION

Disconnecting any of the refrigerant lines could result in physical harm.

7. Unbolt the cover from the camshaft housing.
8. Disconnect the heating water line from the carburetor, the vacuum line on the starter housing, and the distributor vacuum line.
9. Disconnect all electrical connections,

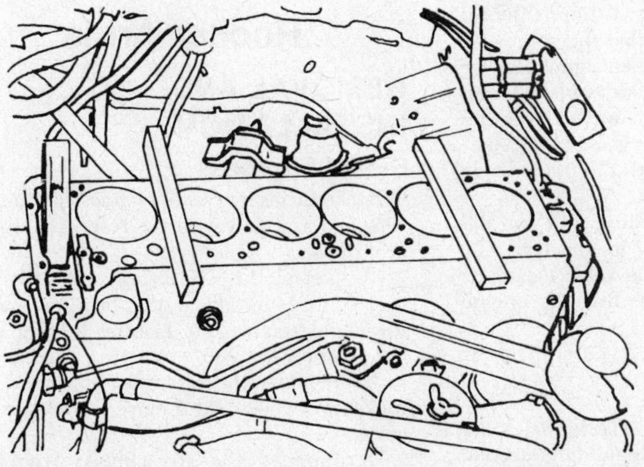

Fabricated tools for installing the cylinder head on DOHC 6-cylinder engines

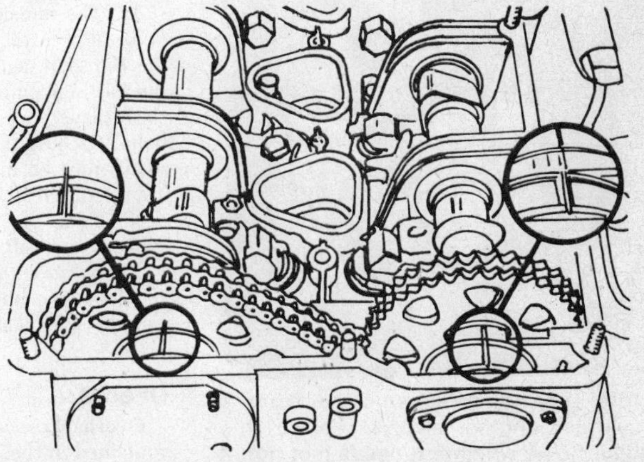

The marks on the camshaft and bearing housing must align on DOHC 6-cylinder engines when the engine is at TDC

water lines, fuel lines, and vacuum lines which are connected to the cylinder head. Tag these for reassembly.

10. Remove the regulating linkage shaft.
11. Remove the EGR line between the exhaust return valve and the exhaust pipe.
12. Disconnect and plug the oil return line at the cylinder head.
13. At the thermostat housing, loosen the hose which passes between the thermostat housing and the water pump. Unscrew the bypass line on the water pump.
14. Loosen the oil dipstick tube from the clamp and bend it slightly sidewards.
15. Unbolt the exhaust pipes from the exhaust manifolds and bracket on the transmission.
16. Force the tension springs out of the rocker arm with a screwdriver.
17. Remove all of the rocker arms.
18. Crank the engine to TDC. This can be done with a socket wrench on the crankshaft pulley bolt. The marks on the camshaft sprockets and bearing housings must be aligned.
19. Hold the camshafts and remove the bolt which holds each camshaft gear to the camshaft.
20. Remove the upper slide rail. Knock out the bearing bolts with a puller.
21. Remove the chain tensioner.
22. Push both camshafts toward the rear and remove the camshafts' sprockets.
23. Remove the spacer sleeves on both camshafts. The sleeves are located in front of the camshaft bearings.
24. Remove the guide wheel by unscrewing the plug and removing the bearing bolt.
25. Lift off the timing chain and suspend the chain from the hood with a piece of wire. Pull out the guide gear.
26. Remove the slide rail in the cylinder head by removing the bearing pin with a puller.
27. Loosen the cylinder head bolts in small increments, using the reverse order of the tightening sequence. This should be done on a cold engine to prevent the possibility of head warpage.

While the head is removed from a 6-cylinder engine, always replace this rubber hose, whether it needs it or not; it is impossible to replace with the cylinder head installed.

Replacing valve guides

28. Pull out the two bolts in the chain case with a magnet. Be careful not to drop the washers.
29. Pull up on the timing chain and force the tensioning rail toward the center of the engine.
30. Lift the cylinder head up in a vertical direction.

NOTE: Mercedes-Benz recommends two people for this job.

31. Remove the cylinder head gasket and clean the joint faces of the block and head.
32. To install, cut two pieces of wood ½ in. x 1½ in. x 9½ in. Lay one piece upright between cylinders 1 and 2; lay the other flat between cylinders 5 and 6.
33. Install the cylinder head in an inclined position so that the timing chain and tensioning rail can be inserted.
34. Lift the cylinder head at the front and remove the front piece of wood toward the exhaust side. Carefully lower the cylinder head until the bolt holes align.
35. Lift the head at the rear so that the board can be removed toward the exhaust side. Carefully lower the cylinder head until all the bolt holes align.
36. Tighten the cylinder head bolts in gradual steps until they are fully tightened. Follow the torque sequence illustrated.
37. Check to be sure that both camshafts rotate freely after the bolts are tight.
38. The remainder of installation is the reverse of removal. Be sure that the spacer for the camshaft gear with the engaging lugs for the vacuum pump drive gear is installed on the exhaust side. Also, the washers for the bolts attaching the camshaft gears to the camshafts must be installed with the domed side against the head of the bolt.
39. Note that the attaching bolt for the exhaust camshaft gear is 0.2 in. shorter.
40. Be sure to adjust the valve clearance and fill the cooling system. Run the engine and check for leaks.

Overhaul

Overhaul procedures for cylinder heads are contained in the "Engine Rebuilding" section of this book. Consult this section for detailed overhaul procedures.

Valve Guides

REMOVAL AND INSTALLATION

See the "Engine Rebuilding" Section also.

1. Remove the cylinder head.
2. Clean the valve guide with a brush, knocking away all loose carbon and oil deposits.
3. Knock out the old valve guide with a drift.
4. Check the bore in the cylinder head and clean up any rough spots. Use a reamer for this purpose. If necessary, the valve guide bore can be reamed for oversize valve guides.
5. Clean the basic bores for the valve guides.
6. Heat the cylinder head in water to approximately 176-194° F.
7. If possible cool the valve guides slightly.
8. Drive the valve guides into the bores with a drift. Coat the bores in the cylinder head with wax prior to installation and be sure that the circlip rests against the cylinder head.
9. Let the head cool and try to knock the valve guide out with light hammer blows and a plastic drift. If the guide can be knocked out, try another guide with a tighter fit.
10. Install the cylinder head.

Rocker Arms

REMOVAL AND INSTALLATION

Diesel Engines

Rocker arms on diesel engines can only be removed as a unit with the respective rocker arm blocks.

1. Detach the connecting rod for the venturi control unit from the bearing bracket lever and remove the bearing bracket from the rocker arm cover.
2. Remove the air vent line from the rocker arm cover and remove the rocker arm cover.
3. Remove the stretchbolts from the rocker arm blocks and remove the blocks with the rocker arms. Turn the crankshaft in each

case so that the camshaft does not put any load on the rocker arms.

NOTE: Turn the crankshaft with a socket wrench on the crankshaft pulley bolt. Do not rotate the engine by turning the camshaft sprocket.

4. Before installing the rocker arms, check the sliding surfaces of the ball cup and rocker arms. Replace any defective parts.
5. To install, assemble the rocker arm blocks and insert new stretchbolts.
6. Tighten the stretchbolts. In each case, position the camshaft so that there is no load on the rocker arms. See the previous NOTE.
7. Check to be sure that the tension clamps have engaged with the notches of the rocker arm blocks.
8. Adjust the valve clearance.
9. Reinstall the rocker arm cover, air vent line, and bearing bracket for the reverse lever. Attach the connecting rod for the venturi control unit to the reversing lever.
10. Make sure that during acceleration, the control cable can move freely without binding.
11. Start the engine and check the rocker arm cover for leaks.

Gasoline Engines

NOTE: 1976 and later V8's use hydraulic valve lifters.

Before removing the rocker arm(s), be sure that they are identified by their position relative to the camshaft lobe. They should be installed in the same place as they were before assembly. Be very careful removing the thrust pieces. They can easily fall into the engine.

1. Remove the rocker arm cover or covers.
2. Force the clamping spring out of the notch in the top of the rocker arm. Slide it in an outward direction across the ball socket of the rocker arm.

NOTE: Turn the engine each time to relieve any load from the rocker arm.

3. On V8 models, the clamping spring must be forced from the adjusting screw with a screwdriver.
4. Force the valve down to remove load from the rocker arm.

NOTE: Don't depress the spring too far. When the piston is up as it should be, the valve will hit the piston. As the spring goes down, the thrust piece will fall off into the engine.

5. Lift the rocker arm from the ball pin and remove the rocker arm.
6. To install the rocker arm(s), force the rocker arm down until the rocker arm and its ball socket can be installed in the top of the ball pin.
7. Install the rocker arms.
8. Slide the clamping spring across the ball socket of the rocker arm until it rests in the notch of the rocker arm.
9. On V8 models, engage the clamping spring into the recess of the adjusting screw.
10. Check and, if necessary, adjust the valve clearance.
11. After completion of the adjustment, check to be sure that the clamping springs are correctly seated.
12. Install the rocker arm cover and connect any hoses or lines that were disconnected.
13. Run the engine and check for leaks at the rocker arm cover.

Hydraulic Valve Lifters

1976 AND LATER V8 ENGINES

Hydraulic valve lifters are used with overhead cams on 1976 and later V8 engines. The rocker arm is always in contact with the cam, reducing noise and eliminating operating clearance.

Checking Base Setting

The base setting is the clearance between the upper edge of the cylindrical part of the plunger and the lower edge of the retaining cap (dimension A) when the cam lobe is vertical.

NOTE: A dial indicator with an extension and a measuring thrust piece (MBNA #100 589 16 63 00, 0.187 in. thick are necessary to perform this adjustment.

1. Turn the cam lobe to a vertical position.
2. Attach a dial indicator and tip extension and insert the extension through the bore in the rocker arm onto the head plunger. Preload the dial indicator by 2 mm and zero the instrument.
3. Depress the valve with a valve spring compressor. The lift on the dial indicator should be 0.028-0.075 in.
4. If the lift is excessive, the base setting can be changed by installing a new thrust piece.
5. Remove the dial indicator.
6. Remove the rocker arm.
7. Remove the thrust piece and insert the measuring disc.
8. Install the rocker arm and repeat Steps 1-3.
9. Select a thrust piece according to the table. If the measured valve was 0-0.002 in. and the 0.2146 in. thrust piece will not give the proper base setting, use the 0.2283 in. thrust piece.

SELECTIVE THRUST PIECES

Measured Value (in.)	Thrust Piece Thickness(s) (in.)
0-0.002	0.2146/0.2283
0.002-0.034	0.2008
0.035-0.066	0.1870
0.067-0.099	0.1732
0.099-0.131	0.1594
above 0.131	0.1457

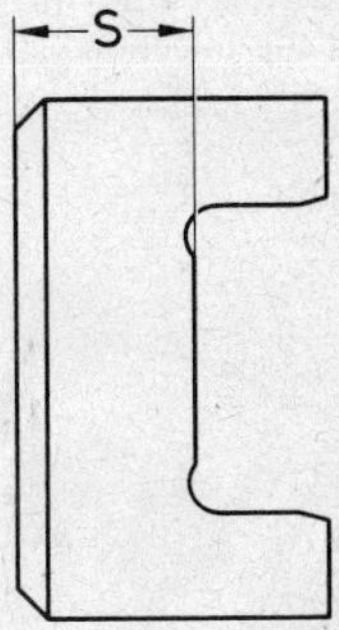

Thrust piece thickness

10. Remove the dial indicator and the rocker arm. Install the selected thrust piece.
11. Reinstall the rocker arm and dial indicator and repeat Steps 1-3.

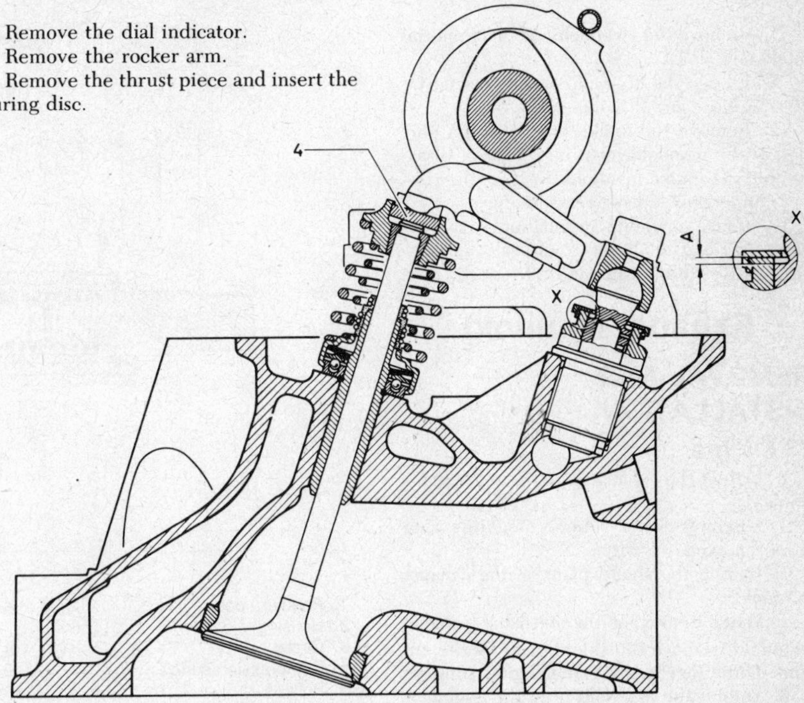

Cutaway view of hydraulic valve lifter

Removal and Installation

Temporarily removed valve lifters must be reinstalled in their original locations. When replacing worn rocker arms, the camshaft must also be replaced. If the rocker arm, or hydraulic lifter is replaced, check the base setting.

Remove the rocker arm and unscrew the valve lifter with a 24 mm socket

Intake Manifold

REMOVAL AND INSTALLATION

V8 Engine

1. Partially drain the coolant.
2. Remove the air cleaner.
3. Disconnect the regulating linkage and remove the longitudinal regulating shaft.
4. Pull off all cable plug connections.
5. Disconnect and plug the fuel lines on the pressure regulator and starting valve.
6. Unscrew the nuts on the injection valves and set the injection valves aside.

Replace the rubber connecting pieces on the intake manifold, anytime the manifold is removed.

7. Remove the 16 attaching bolts from the intake manifold.
8. Loosen the hose clip on the thermostat housing hose and disconnect the hose.
9. Remove the intake manifold. If a portion of the manifold must be replaced, disassemble the intake manifold. Replace the rubber connections during reassembly.
10. Intake manifold installation is the reverse of removal. Replace all seals and gaskets. Adjust the linkage and idle speed.

Exhaust Manifold

REMOVAL AND INSTALLATION

V8 Engine

1. Unbolt the exhaust pipes from the manifolds.
2. Disconnect the rubber mounting ring from the exhaust system.
3. Loosen the shield plate on the exhaust manifold.
4. When removing the left-hand exhaust manifold, remove the shield plate for the engine mount together with the engine damper.
5. Unbolt the manifold from the engine.
6. Pull the manifolds off of the mounting.

15. Valve connection
16. Nut
17. Washer
18. Gasket
19. Idle speed air line
20. Screw connection
21. Sealing ring
22. Upper Intake manifold
23. Holder
24. Hex bolt
25. Connection
26. Sealing ring
27. Gasket
28. Screw connection
29. Sealing ring
30. Screw connection
31. Sealing ring
32. Bottom intake manifold
33. Rubber connecting piece
35. Hex bolt
34. Hex bolt
36. Sealing ring
37. Plug
38. Hose

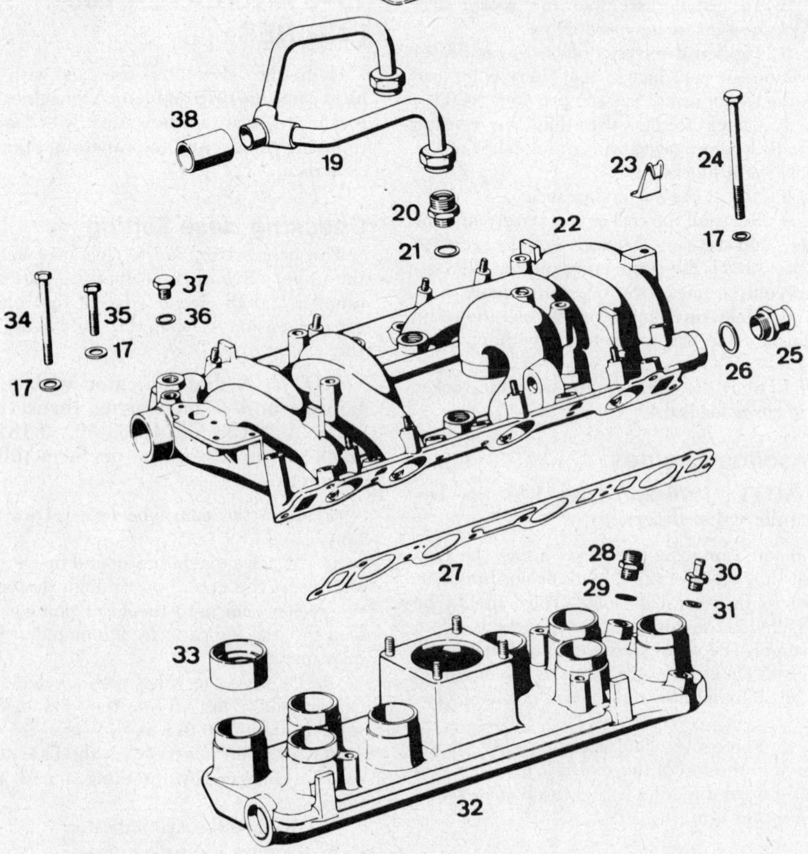

V8 intake manifold

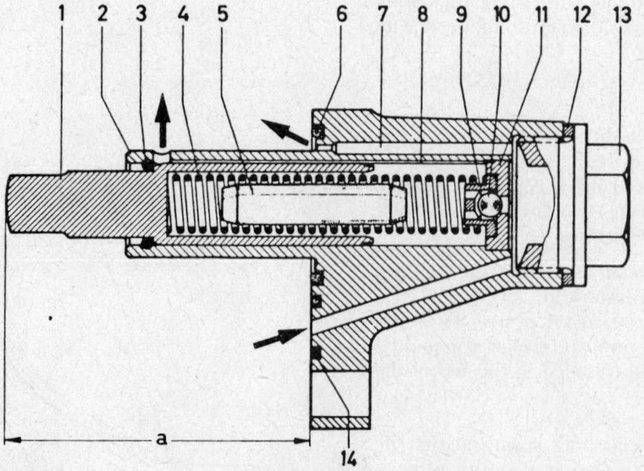

1. Pressure bolt
2. Housing
3. Circlip
4. Compression spring
5. Bolt
6. Sealing ring
7. Return bore
8. Compensating bore
9. Ball cage
10. Ball
11. Ball seat ring
12. Sealing
13. Closing plug
14. Sealing ring

a = 57 mm

Timing chain tensioner

Timing Chain Tensioner

REMOVAL AND INSTALLATION

4 and 5-Cylinder Engines

There are 2 kinds of timing chain tensioners. One uses an O-ring seal and the other a flat gasket. Do not install a flat gasket on a tensioner meant to be used with an O-ring.

Chain tensioners should be replaced as a unit if defective.

1. Drain the coolant. If the car has air conditioning, disconnect the compressor and mounting bracket and lay it aside. Do not disconnect the refrigerant lines.

On diesel engines, drain the coolant from the block.

2. Remove the thermostat housing.
3. Loosen and remove the chain tensioner. Be careful of loose O-ring.
4. Check the O-rings or gasket and replace if necessary.
5. To fill the chain tensioner, place the tensioner (pressure bolt down) in a container of SAE 10 engine oil, at least up to the flat flange. Using a drill press, depress the pressure bolt slowly, about 7-10 times. Be sure this is done slowly and uniformly.
6. Install the chain tensioner. Tighten the bolts evenly.

V8 Engines

The chain tensioner is connected to the engine oil circuit. Bleeding occurs once oil pressure has been established and the tensioner is filling with oil.

Since December of 1974, a venting hole has been installed in the tensioner to prevent oil foaming. If you have a lot of timing chain noise, use this type of tensioner, which is identified by a white paint dot on the cap.

Service procedures for tensioners and rails on the 3.8 liter V8 is the same as for the 4.5 liter V8. Arrangement of parts however, is slightly different.

The inside bolt (arrow) on the V8 chain tensioner can only be reached by inserting a long, straight allen key underneath the exhaust manifold.

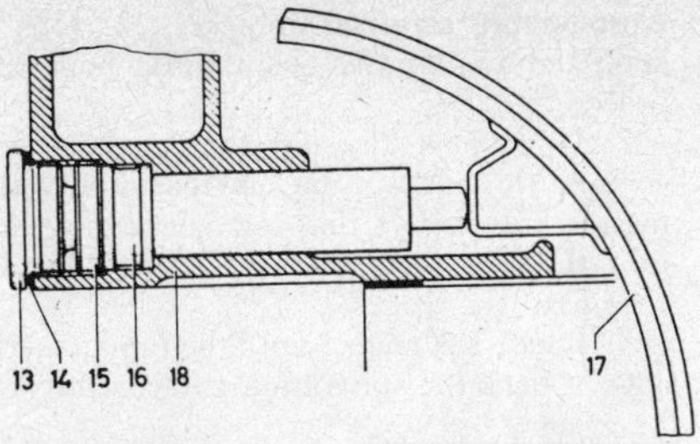

13. Closing plug
14. Sealing ring
15. Threaded ring
16. Chain tensioner
17. Tension rail
18. Cylinder head

6-cylinder timing chain tensioner

Remove the plug with a 17 mm allen key

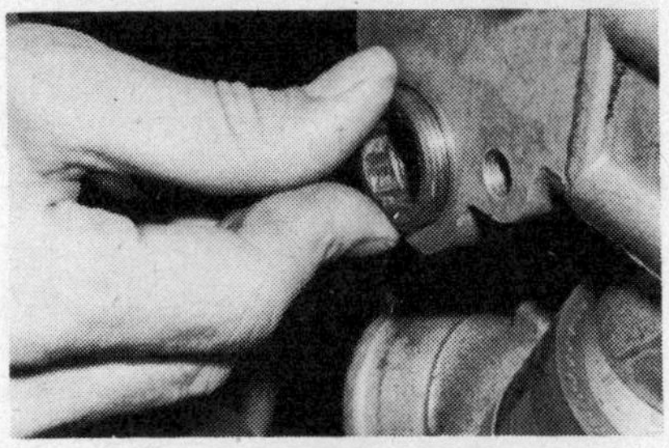

Remove the threaded plug.

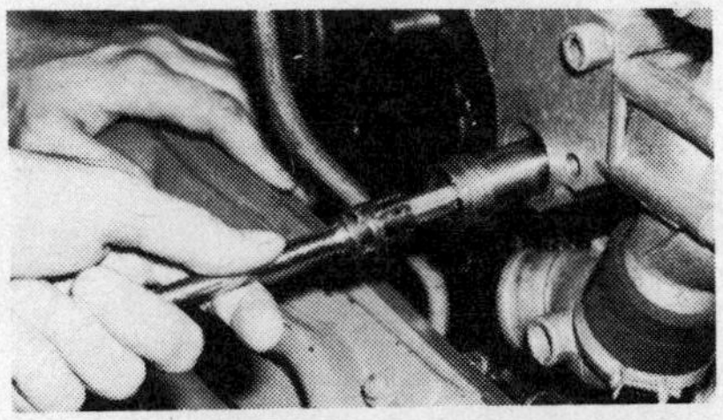

Remove the chain tensioner with a 10 mm allen key

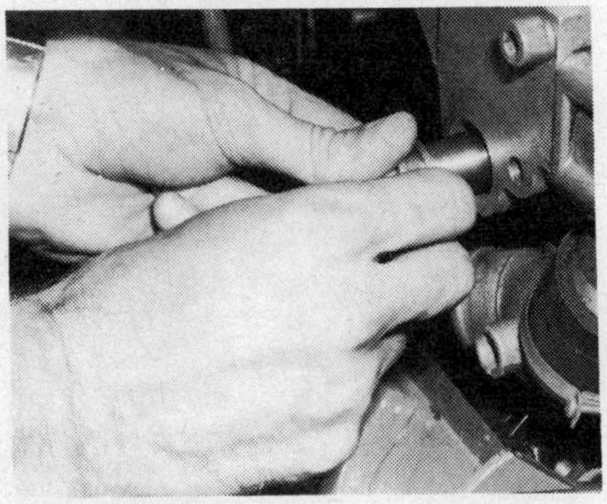

Install the chain tensioner

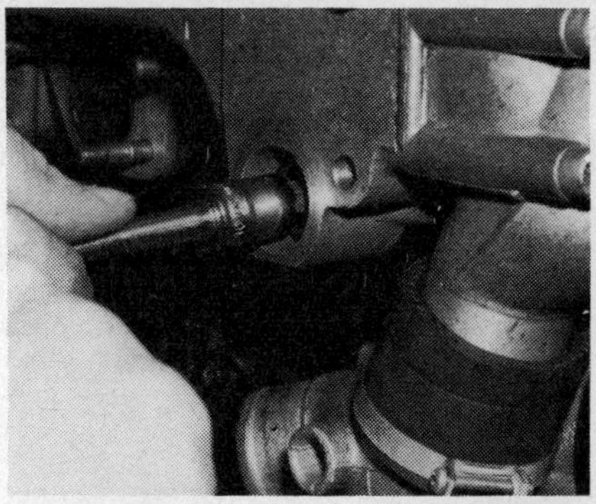

Tighten the tensioner until it "clicks"

1. On California models, disconnect the line from the tensioner.
2. Remove the attaching bolts and remove the tensioner. The inside bolts will probably require a long, straight 6 mm Allen key to bypass the exhaust manifold. It is a tight fit.
3. Place the tensioner vertically in a container of engine oil. Operate the pressure bolt to fill the tensioner. After filling, it should permit compression very slowly under considerable force. If not, replace the tensioner with a new unit.
4. Install the tensioner and tighten the bolts evenly.

6-Cylinder Engines

1. On A/C vehicles, remove the battery. Unbolt the refrigerant compressor and lay it aside. Do not disconnect the refrigerant lines.
2. Remove the plug with a 17 mm Allen key.
3. Tighten the threaded ring and loosen the ball seat ring.
4. Remove the threaded ring.
5. Remove the chain tensioner with a 10 mm Allen key.
6. Be sure the tight side of the chain is tight.
7. Compress the tensioner and install the chain tensioner with a 10 mm Allen key. Do not bump the Allen key or the tensioner will release.
8. Screw in the threaded ring and tighten it to 44 ft/lbs.
9. Tighten the ball seat ring to 18 ft/lbs. The pressure bolt should jump forward with an audible click. If it does not, the assembly must be removed and the installation repeated until it does click.
10. Install the plug.
11. Reinstall the A/C compressor, battery and air cleaner.

Timing Chain

REPLACEMENT

All Models

An endless timing chain is used on production engines, but a split chain with a connecting link is used for service. The endless chain can be separated with a "chain-breaker." Only one master link (connecting link) should be used on a chain.

1. Remove the spark plugs.
2. Remove the valve cover(s).
3. Clamp the chain to the cam gear and cover the opening of the timing chain case

with rags. On 6-cylinder and V8 engines, remove the rocker arms from the right-hand camshaft.

4. Separate the chain with a chain breaker.
5. Attach a new timing chain to the old chain with a master link.
6. Using a socket wrench on the crankshaft, slowly rotate the engine in the direction of normal rotation. Simultaneously, pull the old chain through until the master link is uppermost on the camshaft sprocket. Be sure to keep tension on the chain throughout this procedure.
7. Disconnect the old timing chain and connect the ends of the new chain with the master link. Insert the new connecting link from the rear, so that the lockwashers can be seen from the front.
8. Rotate the engine until the timing marks align. Check the valve timing. Once the new chain is assembled, rotate the engine (by hand) through at least one complete revolution to be sure everything is OK. See valve timing for illustrations.

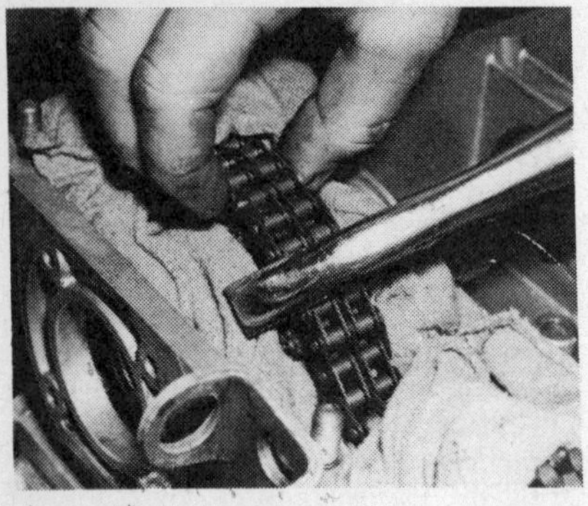

Clamp the chain to the gear and cover the opening with rags

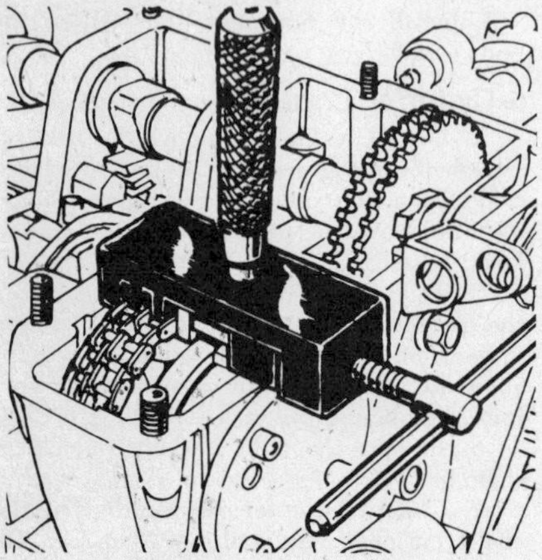

Remove the link with a chain breaker

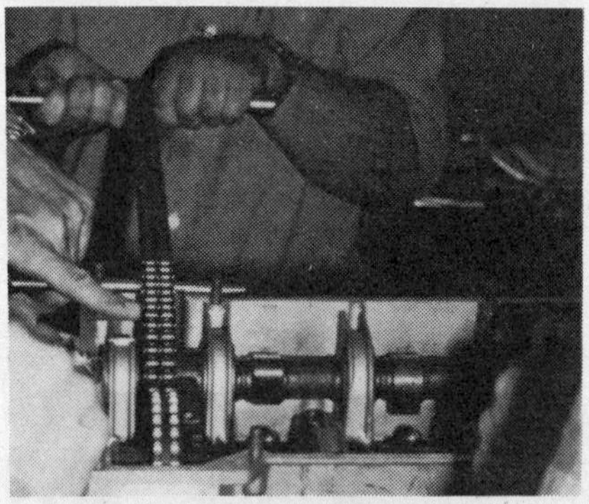

Crank the engine by hand until the new chain has come all the way through the engine. Be sure to keep tension on chain.

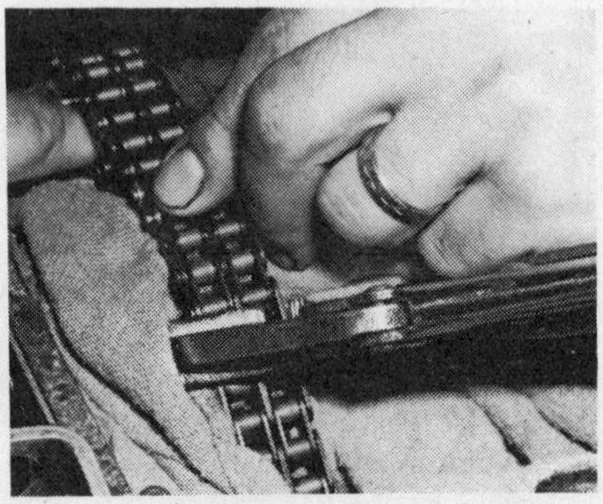

Clamp the chain again, cover the opening and remove the old chain from the master link. Connect both ends of the new chain.

Camshaft

REMOVAL AND INSTALLATION

4 and 5-Cylinder Engines

When the camshaft is replaced, be sure the rocker arms are also replaced.

1. Remove the valve cover.
2. Remove the chain tensioner.
3. Remove the rocker arms.
4. Set the crankshaft at TDC for No. 1 cylinder and be sure that the camshaft timing marks are aligned.
5. Hold the camshaft and loosen the cam gear bolt. Remove the cam gear and wire it securely so that the chain does not loose tension nor slip down into the chain case.
6. Remove the camshaft.
7. Installation is the reverse of removal. Be sure to check that the valve timing marks align when No. 1 cylinder is at TDC. Check the valve clearance.

6-Cylinder Engines

With the engine installed in the car, the camshafts can only be removed together with the camshaft housing. If a new camshaft is installed, be sure to use new rocker arms.

1. Remove the refrigerant compressor but do not disconnect the refrigerant lines.
2. Remove the battery.
3. Remove the vacuum pump from the right-hand cylinder head.
4. Drain the coolant and remove the water hoses.
5. Remove the rocker arm cover.
6. Remove the cover from the front of the camshaft housing.
7. Remove the rocker arm springs.
8. Remove the rocker arms.

Remove the rocker arm springs, rocker arms and thrust pieces.

Remove the vacuum pump and camshaft cover.

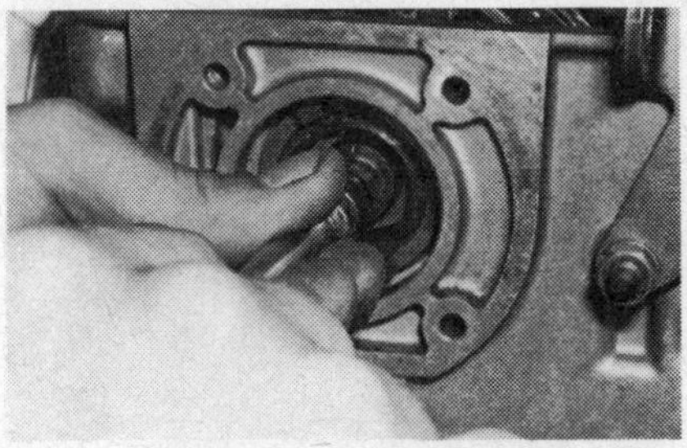

Loosen the camshaft bolts.

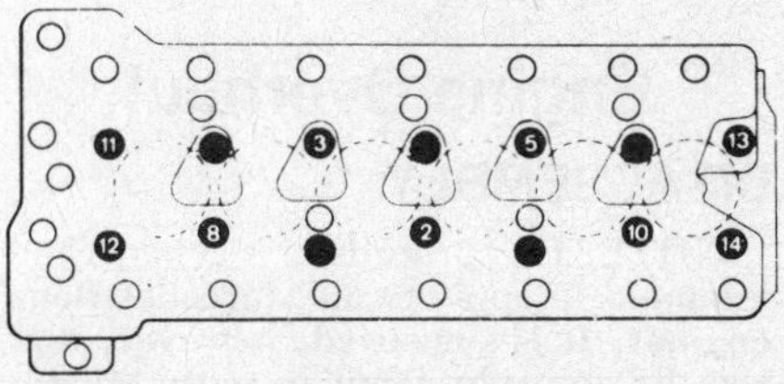

Bolts to be removed during the camshaft housing removal

○ Unscrew M 8 bolts

① Unscrew cylinder head bolts in reverse order

● Do not loosen bolts

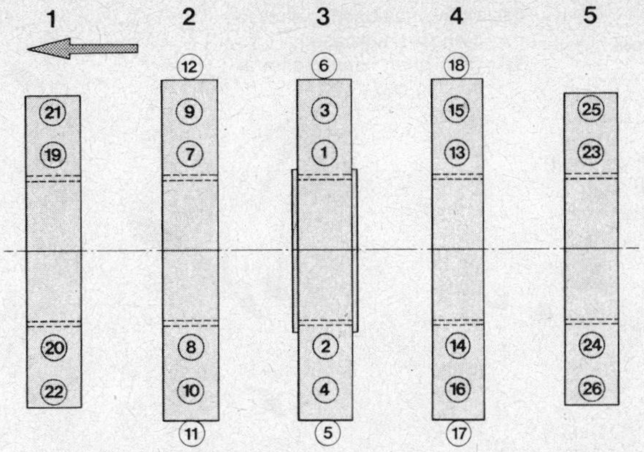

Main bearing cap torque sequence—3.8 liter V-8's

9. Crank the engine around in the normal direction of rotation (using the crankshaft bolt) until No. 1 piston is at TDC, the pointer aligns with the TDC mark on the crankshaft pulley and the camshaft timing marks are aligned.

10. Hold the camshaft(s) and loosen the camshaft bolts.

NOTE: Wire the camshaft gears up so that tension is applied to the chain. The chain must not be allowed to slip off the camshaft or crankshaft gears.

11. Remove the chain tensioner.

12. Remove the slide rail from the camshaft housing. You'll need a small puller for this.

13. Loosen the cover at the right-hand rear side of the camshaft housing and push the right-hand camshaft toward the rear. Remove the camshaft gear.

14. Loosen the camshaft housing retaining bolts. Do not loosen the 5 lower cylinder head bolts or the 2 M8 bolts.

15. Remove the camshaft housing with the camshafts.

16. Remove the rear covers from the camshaft housing.

17. Hold the left-hand camshaft and loosen the attaching bolt.

18. Push the camshaft rearward and remove the camshaft gear. Remove the spacer from the intake camshaft.

19. Remove both camshafts from the housing.

20. Oil the bearings and install the intake camshaft (left-hand) with cam gear and spacer. Use retaining bolt and washer (not springs).

21. Install the exhaust (right-hand) camshaft. Do not install the gear until the housing is installed.

22. Install the rear camshaft covers. Do not tighten the one on the right-hand side.

23. Install the camshaft housing.

24. Lubricate the bolts and tighten them in 3 stages:

- Starting with Bolt #2, tighten to 30 ft/lbs.
- Starting with Bolt #2, tighten to 44 ft/lbs.
- Starting with Bolt #1, tighten to 67 ft/lbs. First, slightly loosen the 5 lower cylinder head bolts.

25. When you are finished torquing the camshaft housing bolts, torque the cylinder head bolts. When all bolts have finally been tightened, the camshafts should rotate easily and freely.

26. Install the righthand camshaft gear. Be sure the cam timing is accurate and the engine is set at TDC on No. 1 cylinder.

CAUTION

Some engines have a scale for BDC as well as one for TDC. The TDC mark is next to the pin in the balancer.

27. Install the timing chain rail.

28. Install the rockers and tension springs. Adjust the valve.

29. Crank the engine by hand and check the valve timing.

30. Tighten the camshaft gear bolts to 59 ft/lbs.

31. Install the chain tensioner.

32. Install the camshaft rear housing covers (if not already done) and the vacuum pump.

33. Install the rocker covers.

V8 Engines

Experience shows that the right-hand camshaft is always the first one to require replacement. When the V8 camshaft is removed, keep the pedestals with the camshaft. In particular, make sure that the 2 left-hand rear cam pedestals are not swapped. The result will be no oil pressure. Always replace the oil gallery pipe with the camshaft.

Using a puller, remove the pins from the slide rails and remove the slide rails.

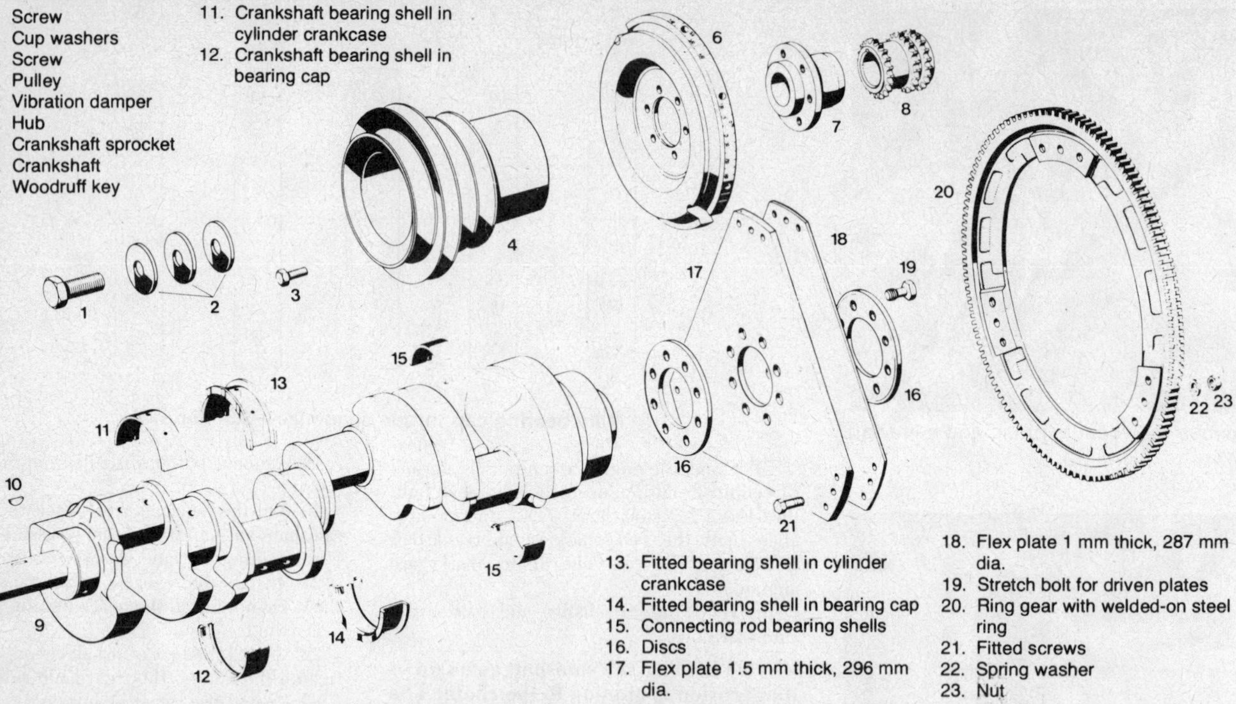

1. Screw
2. Cup washers
3. Screw
4. Pulley
6. Vibration damper
7. Hub
8. Crankshaft sprocket
9. Crankshaft
10. Woodruff key
11. Crankshaft bearing shell in cylinder crankcase
12. Crankshaft bearing shell in bearing cap
13. Fitted bearing shell in cylinder crankcase
14. Fitted bearing shell in bearing cap
15. Connecting rod bearing shells
16. Discs
17. Flex plate 1.5 mm thick, 296 mm dia.
18. Flex plate 1 mm thick, 287 mm dia.
19. Stretch bolt for driven plates
20. Ring gear with welded-on steel ring
21. Fitted screws
22. Spring washer
23. Nut

Exploded view of 3.8 liter V-8 crankshaft and related parts

NOTE: Arrangement of parts on the 3.8 liter V8 is slightly different compared to the 4.5 liter V8. Service procedures are the same.

1. Remove the valve cover.
2. Remove the tensioning springs and rocker arms.
3. Using a wrench on the crankshaft pulley, crank the engine around until No. 1 piston is at TDC on compression. Using some stiff wire, hang the camshaft gear so that the chain will not slip off the gears.
4. Remove the camshaft gear.
5. Unbolt the camshaft, camshaft bearing pedestals and the oil pipe. Note the angle of the bolts holding the cam bearing pedestals to the engine. The inner row of bolts are the only bolts that do not hold the head to the block.
6. Install the bearing pedestals and camshaft. On the left-hand camshaft, the outer bolt on the rear bearing must be inserted prior to installing the bearings or it will not clear the power brake unit. Tighten the bolts from the inside out. When finished tightening, the camshaft should rotate freely.
7. Check the oil pipes for obstructions and replace if necessary.
8. When installing the oil pipes, also check the 3 inner connecting pipes.
9. Install the compensating washer so that the keyway below the notch slides over the Woodruff key of the camshaft.
10. Install the rocker arms and tensioning springs.
11. Adjust the valve clearance and check the valve timing. See valve timing for illustrations.

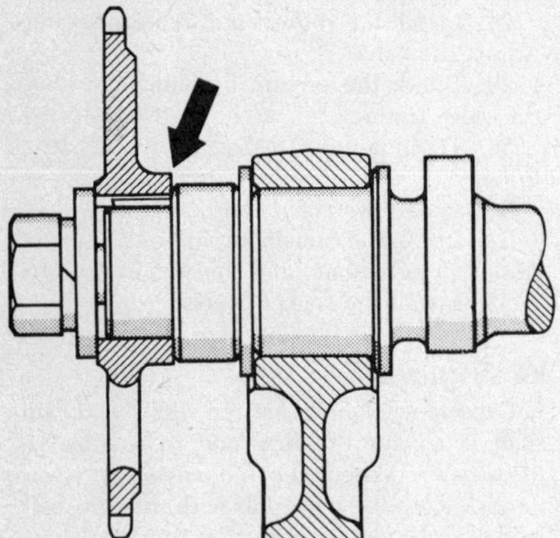

The camshaft flange (arrow) on 3.8 liter V-8's faces rearward

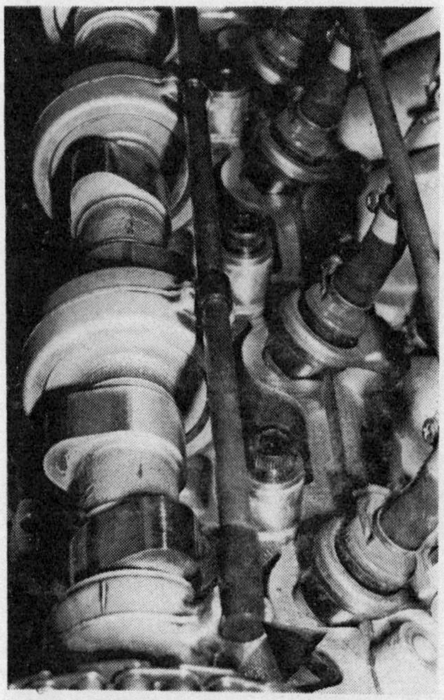

Check the oil pipes (arrow) on a V8 engine.

Engine Overhaul

DISASSEMBLY

NOTE: This procedure is general and intended to apply to all Mercedes-Benz engines. It is suggested, however, that you be entirely familiar with Mercedes-Benz engines and be equipped with the numerous special tools before attempting an engine rebuild. If at all in doubt concerning any procedure, refer the job to a qualified dealer. While this may be more expensive, it will probably produce better results in the end. If you attempt the rebuild yourself, refer often to the "Engine Rebuilding" section, and read the procedure carefully before beginning.

1. Remove the engine and support it on an engine stand or other suitable support.
2. Set the engine at TDC and match-mark the timing chain and timing gear(s). Remove the cylinder head(s) and gasket(s).
3. Remove the oil pan bolts and the pan and, on most models, the lower crankcase section.
4. Remove the oil pump.
5. Matchmark the connecting rod bearing caps to identify the proper cylinder for reassembly. Matchmark the sides of the connecting rod and side of the bearing cap for proper alignment. Pistons should bear an arrow indicating the front. If not, mark the front of the piston with an arrow using a magic marker. Also identify pistons as to cylinder so they may be replaced in their original location.
6. Remove the connecting rod nuts, bearing caps, and lower bearing shells.

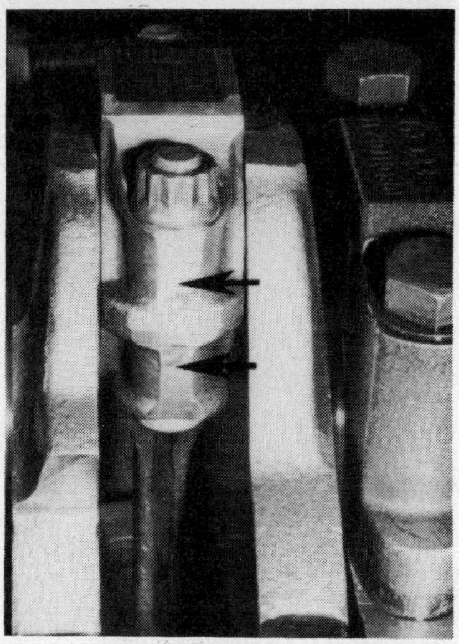

Match mark the connecting rod bearing caps.

7. Place small pieces of plastic tubing on the rod bolts to prevent crankshaft damage.

8. Inspect the crankshaft journals for nicks and roughness and measure diameters.

9. Turn the engine and ream the ridge from the top of the cylinders to remove all carbon deposits.

10. Using a hammer handle or other piece of hardwood, gently tap the pistons and rods out from the bottom.

11. The cylinder bores can be inspected at this time for taper and general wear. See the Engine Rebuilding section.

12. Check the pistons for proper size and inspect the ring grooves. If any rings are cracked, it is almost certain that the grooves are no longer true, because broken rings work up and down. It is best to replace any such worn pistons.

13. The pistons, pins and connecting rods are marked with a color dot assembly code. Only parts having the same color may be used together.

14. If the cylinders are bored, make sure the machinist has the pistons beforehand—cylinder bore sizes are nominal, and the pistons must be individually fitted to the block. Maximum piston weight deviation in any one engine is 4 grams.

15. The flywheel and crankshaft are balanced together as a unit. Matchmark the location of the flywheel relative to the crankshaft, then remove the flywheel. Stretch bolts are used on some newer flywheels and can be identified by their "hourglass" shape. Once used, they should be discarded and replaced at assembly.

16. Remove the water pump, alternator, and fuel pump, if not done previously.

17. Unbolt and remove the vibration damper and crankshaft pulley. On certain models, it is necessary to clamp the vibration damper with C-clamps before removing the bolts. Otherwise, the vibration damper will come apart.

18. Remove the timing chain tensioner and chain cover.

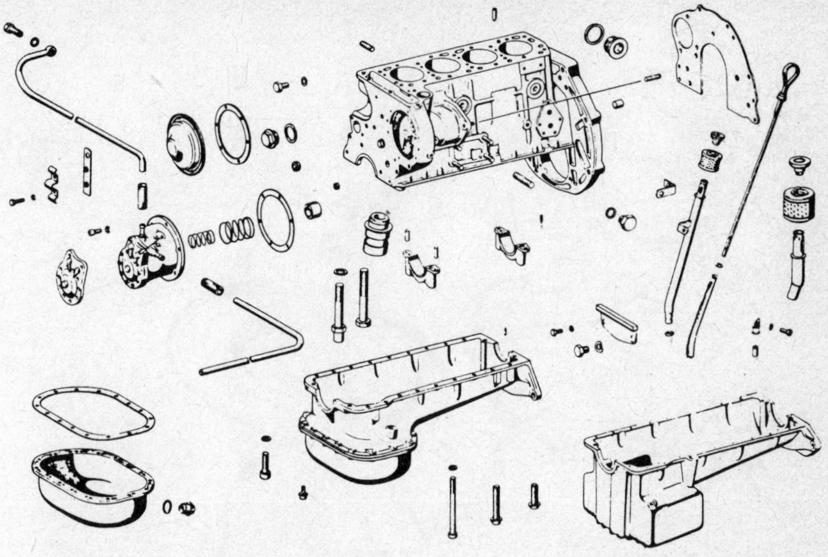

4-cylinder diesel engine cylinder block components (5-cylinder 300D is similar)

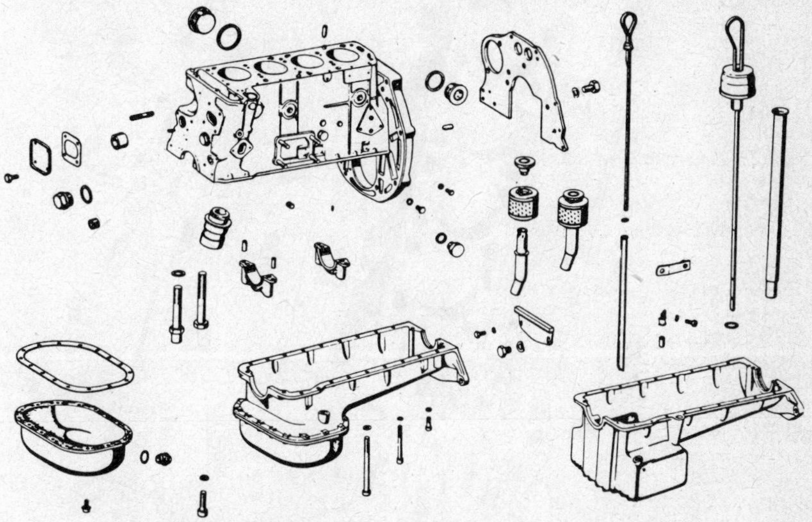

4-cylinder gasoline engine cylinder block components

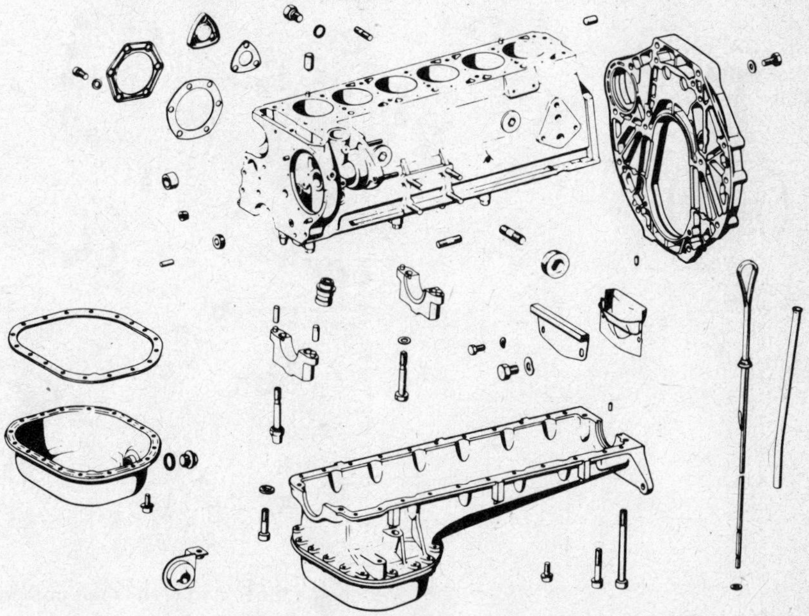

6-cylinder engine block components

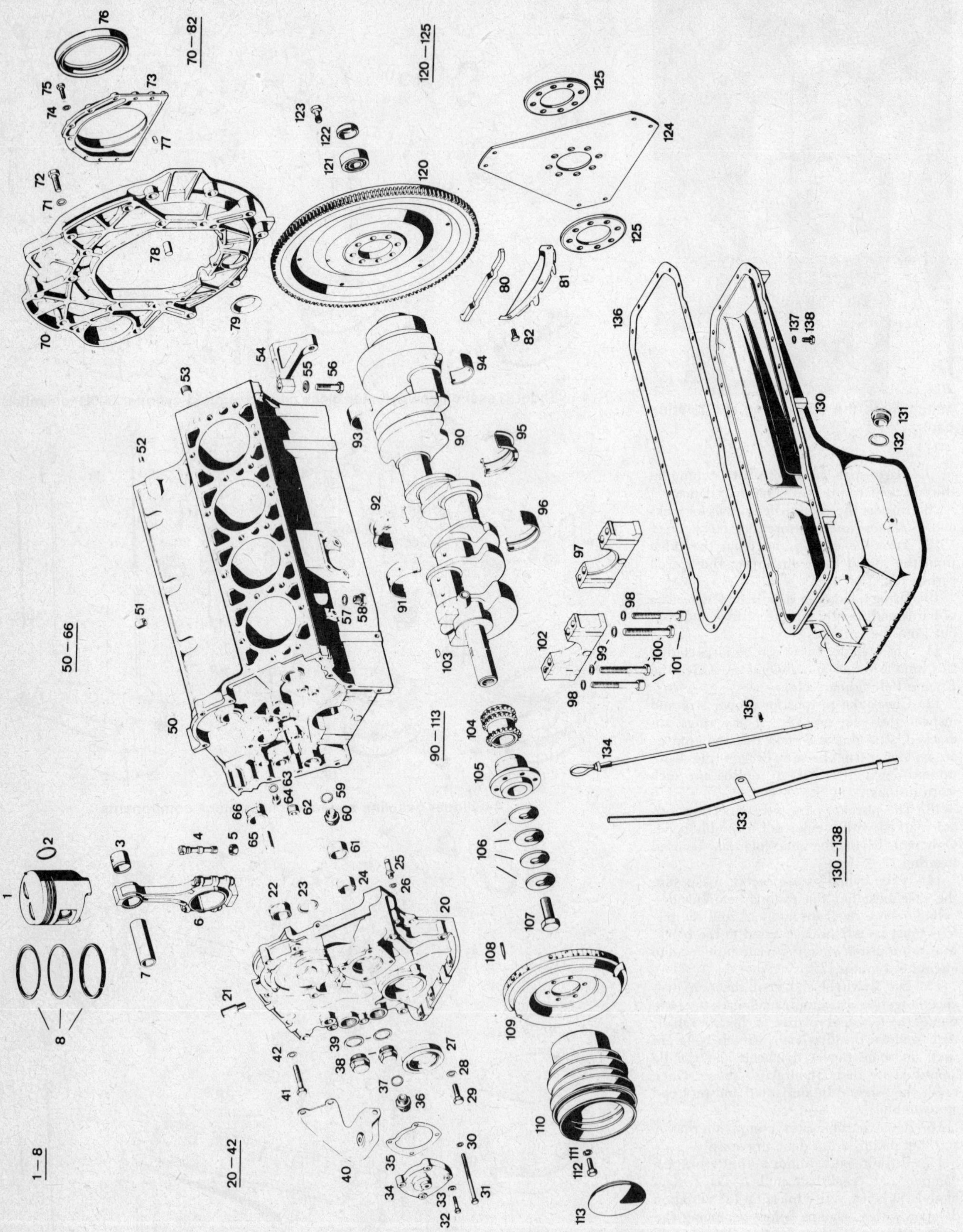

V-8 engine block and crankshaft components

Piston and connecting rod 1-8

1. Piston
2. Circlip
3. Connecting rod bearing
4. Connecting rod bolt
5. Nut
6. Connecting rod
7. Wrist pin
8. Piston rings

Timing housing cover 20-42

20. Timing housing cover
21. Threaded bolts for adjusting lever of ignition distributor
22. Bearing bushing (guidewheel bearing)
23. 2 O-rings
24. Bearing bushing (intermediate gear shaft)
25. Bolt
26. Spring plate
27. Crankshaft sealing ring (front)
28. Washer
29. Screw
30. Washer
31. Screw
32. 4 Screws
33. 4 Washers
34. End cover
35. Gasket
36. Screw connection
37. Sealing ring
38. Plug
39. Sealing ring
40. Holder-engine damper
41. 6 Screws
42. 6 Washers

Cylinder crankcase 50-66

50. Cylinder block
51. 4 Hollow dowel pins
52. 3 Plugs (oil duct)
53. Plug (rear main oil duct)
54. 2 Supporting angle pieces
55. 2 Washers
56. 2 Screws
57. 2 Sealing rings
58. 2 Plugs
59. Sealing ring
60. Screw connection
61. Bearing bushing intermediate gear shaft rear
62. Plug (front main oil duct)
63. Sealing ring
64. Plug
65. 2 Cyl. pins
66. Idler gear bearing

Intermediate flange 70-82

70. Intermediate flange
71. 4 Spring washers
72. 4 Screws
73. Cover (crankcase sealing ring, rear)
74. 8 Washers
75. 3 Screws
76. Crankshaft sealing ring (rear)
77. 2 Cyl. pins
78. 2 Set pins
79. Cover
80. Sealing strip
81. Cover plate
82. 3 Screws

Crankshaft 90-113

90. Crankshaft
91. Main bearing shell (top)
92. Fitted bearing shell (top)
93. Connecting rod bearing shell (top)
94. Connecting rod bearing shell (bottom)
95. Fitted bearing shell (bottom)
96. Main bearing shell (bottom)
97. Crankshaft bearing cap (fitted bearing)
98. 10 Washers
99. 10 Washers
100. 10 Hex bolts
101. 10 Hex socket bolts
102. Crankshaft bearing cap (main bearing)
103. Key
104. Crankshaft gear
105. Vibration damper pulley
106. Plate springs
107. Bolt
108. Indicating needle
109. Vibration damper
110. Pulley
111. 6 Circlips
112. 6 Screws
113. Pulley cover

Flywheel and driven plate 120-125

120. Flywheel
121. Ball bearing 6202
122. Closing ring
123. 8 bolts
124. Driven plate
125. Spacers

Oil pan 130-138

130. Oil pan
131. Oil drain plug
132. Sealing ring
133. Guide tube (oil dipstick)
134. Oil dipstick
135. Stop-ring (oil dipstick)
136. Oil pan gasket
137. 30 washers
138. 30 Screws

V8 engine cylinder block and crankshaft components

Pistons normally are marked with an arrow (a) indicating front and a weight or size marking (b).

Before removing the flywheel, mark its position. It should be returned to its original position

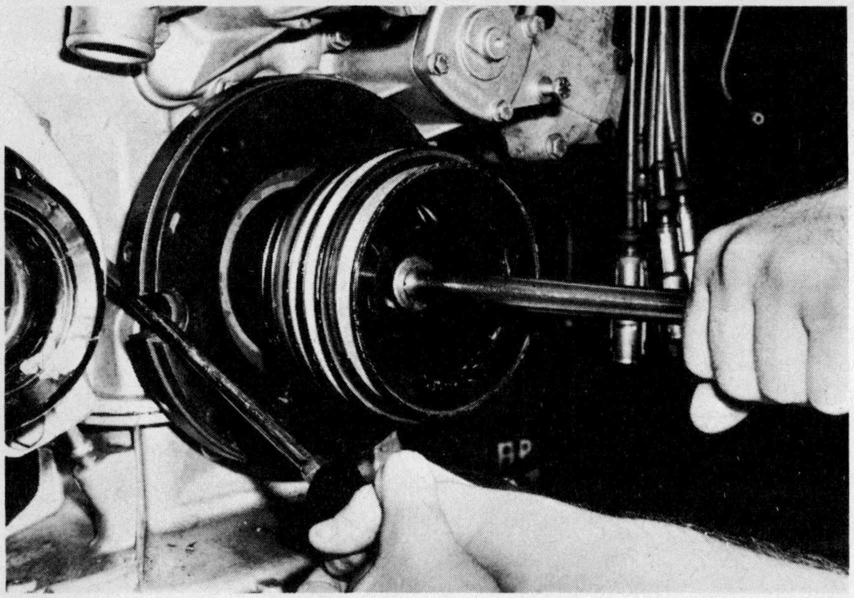

Unbolt and remove the crankshaft pulley (V8 shown,

On V8 models, dress the inside of the vibration damper hub before reinstalling. This will allow you to "feel" the key when installing. On early models, the key extends only 1/3 of the length of the keyway; on later models, ½ the length of the keyway.

19. Matchmark the position of the timing chain on the timing gear of the crankshaft.
20. Matchmark the main bearing caps for number and position in the block. It is important that they are installed in their original positions. Most bearing caps are numbered for position. Remove the bearing caps.
21. Lift the crankshaft out of the block in a forward direction.
22. With the block completely disassembled, inspect the water passages and bearing webs for cracks. If the water passages are plugged with rust, they can be cleaned out by boiling the block at a radiator shop.

CAUTION

Aluminum parts must not be boiled out. They will be eroded by chemicals.

23. Measure piston ring end-gap by sliding a new ring into the bore and measuring. Measure the gap at top, bottom, and midpoint of piston travel and correct by filing or grinding the ring ends.
24. To check bearing clearances, use Plastigage® inserted between the bearing and the crankshaft journal. Blow out all crankshaft oil passages before measuring; torque the bolts to specification. Plastigage® is a thin plastic strip that is crushed by the bearing and cap and spreads out an amount in proportion to clearance. After torquing the bearing cap, remove the cap and compare the width of the Plastigage® with the scale.

NOTE: Do not rotate the crankshaft. Bearing shells of various thicknesses are available, and should be used to correct clearance; it may be necessary to machine the crankshaft journals undersize to obtain the proper oil clearance.

CAUTION

Use of shim stock between bearings and caps to decrease clearance is not a good practice.

25. Check crankshaft end-play using a feeler gauge.
26. When installing new piston rings, ring grooves must be cleaned out, preferably using a special groove cleaner, although a broken ring will work as well. After installing the rings, check ring side clearance.

ASSEMBLY

1. Assemble the engine using all new gaskets and seals and make sure all parts are properly lubricated. Bearing shells and cylinder walls must be lubricated with engine oil before assembly. Make sure no metal chips remain in the cylinder bores or crankcase.

NOTE: 1975 V8s use camshafts coded 56 and 57. These cams have an oil groove in the 5th bearing journal and are not interchangeable with previous designs.

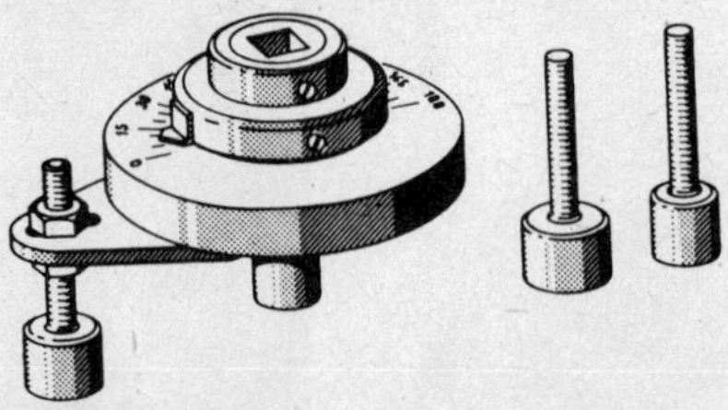

Preferred tools for torqueing by angle rotation. A torque wrench is also needed.

2. To install pistons and rods, turn the engine right side up and insert the rods into the cylinders. Clamp the rings to the piston, with their gaps equally spaced around the circumference, using a piston ring compressor. Gently tap the piston into the bore, using a hammer handle or similar hard wood, making sure the rings clear the edge.
3. Torque the rod and main caps to specification and try to turn the crankshaft by hand. It should turn with moderate resistance, not spin freely or be locked up. Stretchbolts are used for the connecting rods. These bolts are tightened by angle of rotation rather than by use of a torque wrench. Make sure the stretch section diameter is greater than 0.35 in. (−0.003 in.). Remove the bolt from the rod and measure the diameter at the point normally covered by the rod; it should be at least 0.31 in. For reasons of standardization, the angle of rotation for all the screw connections tightened according to angle of rotation has been set to 90° + 10°. Initially the bolts should be torqued to 22-35 ft/lbs, then an additional 90°.
4. Disassemble the oil pump and check the gear backlash. Place a straightedge on the cover and check for warpage. Deep scoring on the cover usually indicates that metal or dirt particles have been circulating through the oil system. Covers can be machined, but it is best to replace them if damaged.
5. Install the oil pump.
6. Install the oil pan and lower crankcase and tighten the bolts evely all around, then turn the engine right side up and install the cylinder head gasket and head. Make sure the gasket surfaces are clean before installation; a small dirt particle could cause gasket failure.

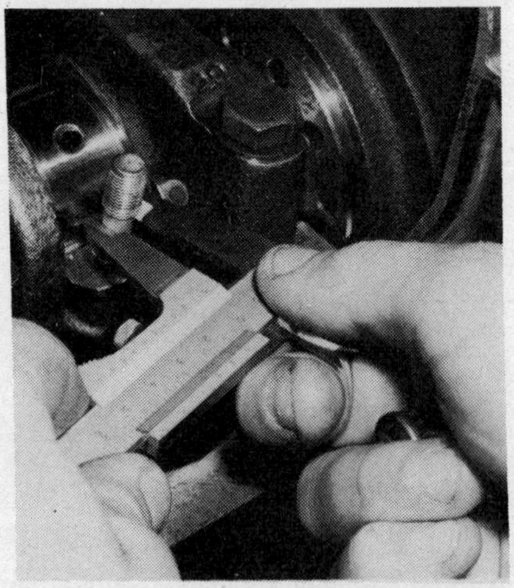

Check the connecting rod bolts

Tighten the cylinder head bolts in sequence, in stages, to insure against distortion. Don't forget the small bolts at the front of the head.

7. Install the engine into the vehicle.

NOTE: It is a good practice to use a good break-in oil after an engine overhaul. Be sure that all fluids have been replaced and perform a general tuneup. Check the valve timing.

Valve Timing

Ideally, this operation should be performed by a dealer who is equipped with the necessary tools and knowledge to do the job properly.

Checking valve timing is too inaccurate at the standard tappet clearance, therefore timing values are given for an assumed tappet clearance of 0.4 mm. The engines are not measured at 0.4 mm but rather at 2 mm.

1. To check the timing, remove the rocker arm cover and spark plugs. Remove the tensioning springs. On the 6-cylinder engine install the testing thrust pieces. Eliminate all valve clearance.
2. Install a degree wheel.

NOTE: If the degree wheel is attached to the camshaft as shown, values read from it must be doubled.

3. A pointer must be made out of a bent section of 3/16 in. brazing rod or coathanger wire, and attached to the engine.
4. With a 22 mm wrench on the crankshaft pulley, turn the engine, in the direction of rotation, until the TDC mark on the vibration damper registers with the pointer and the distributor rotor points to the No. 1 cylinder mark on the housing.

The camshaft timing marks should align at this point.

NOTE: Due to the design of the chain tensioner on V-8 engines, the right side of the chain travels slightly farther than the left side. This means the right-side cam will be almost 7° retarded compared to the left side, and both marks will not simultaneously align.

5. Turn the loosened degree wheel until the pointer lines up with the 0° (OT) mark, then tighten it in this position.

The V8 timing marks on the left-hand cam

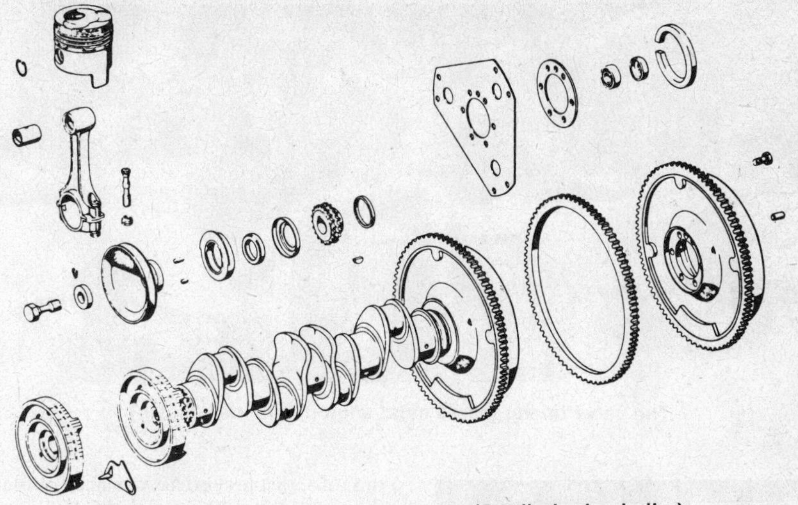

4-cylinder diesel engine components (5-cylinder is similar).

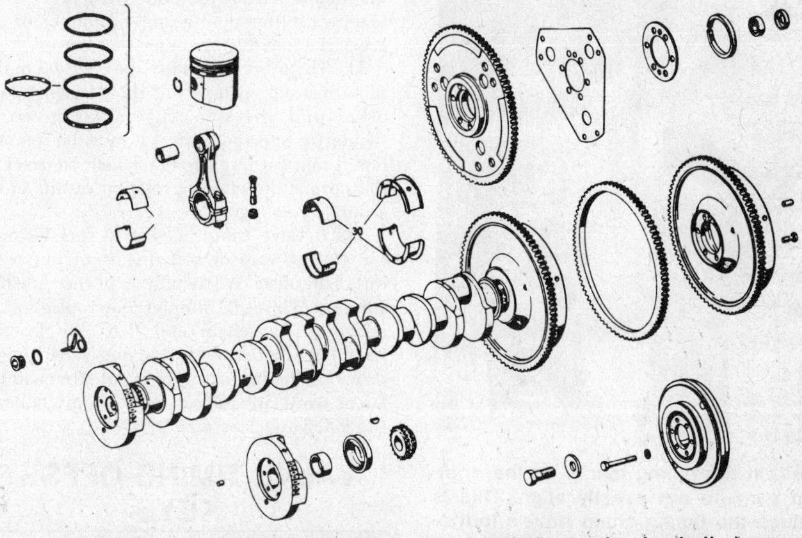

6-cylinder crankshaft and components (4-cylinder engine is similar)

On 6 cylinder engines, always replace the thrust piece (arrow) if the front seal is replaced. If you don't it will almost always leak. If a new thrust piece is not available, at least remove it and turn it around. This provides a new surface for the seal because the seal does not ride on the centerline of the thrust piece.

The valve timing marks must align (6-cylinder shown)

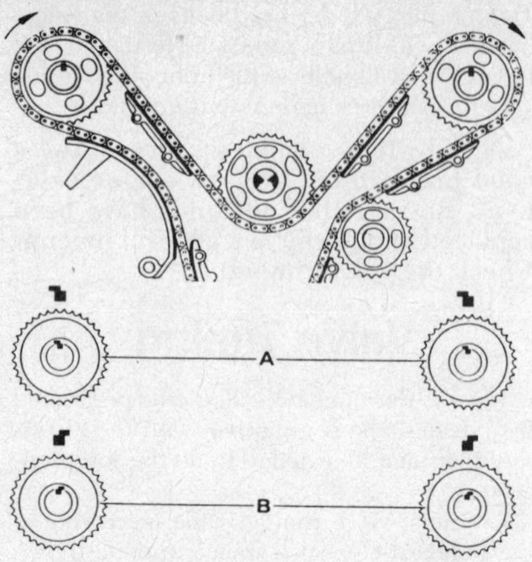

Offset woodruff keys for V8 engine

With installation position "A" opening begins earlier

With installation position "B" opening begins later

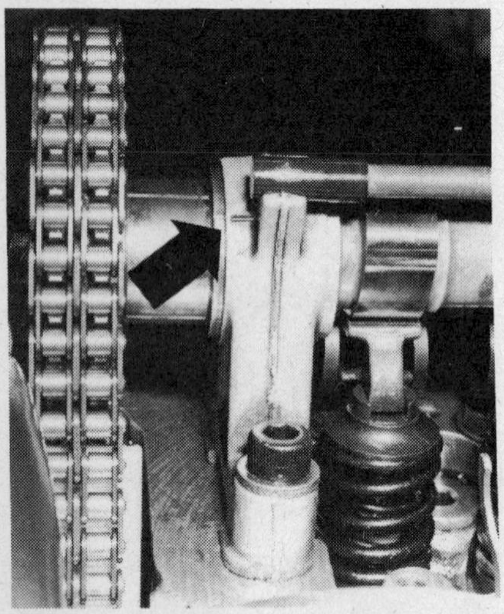

Note that the timing marks on the right-hand cam do not exactly align. This is because the timing chain travels farther on the right side than on the left.

6. Continue turning the crankshaft in the direction of rotation until the camshaft lobe of the associated valve is vertical (e.g., points away from the rocker arm surface). To take up tappet clearance, insert a feeler gauge (thick enough to raise the valve slightly from its seat) between the rocker arm cone and the pressure piece.

7. Attach the indicator to the cylinder head so that the feeler rests against the valve spring retainer of No. 1 cylinder intake valve. Preload the indicator at least 0.008 in. then set to zero, making sure the feeler is exactly perpendicular on the valve spring retainer. It may be necessary to bleed down the chain tensioner at this time to facilitate readings.

8. Turn the crankshaft in the normal direction of rotation, again using a wrench on the crankshaft pulley, until the indicator reads 0.016 in. less than zero reading.

9. Note the reading of the degree wheel at this time, remembering to double the reading if the wheel is mounted to the camshaft sprocket.

10. Again turn the crankshaft until the valve is closing and the indicator again reads 0.016 in. less than zero reading. Make sure, at this time, that preload has remained constant, then note the reading of the degree wheel. The difference between the two degree wheel readings is the timing angle (number of degrees the valve is open) for that valve.

11. The other valves may be checked in the same manner, comparing them against each other and the opening values given in "Tune-Up Specifications." It must be remembered that turning the crankshaft contrary to the normal direction of rotation results in inaccurate readings.

12. If valve timing is not to specification, the easiest way of bringing it in line is to install an offset Woodruff key in the camshaft sprocket. This is far simpler than replacing the entire timing chain and it is the factory-recommended way of changing valve timing provided the timing chain is not stretched too far or worn out. Offset keys are available in the following sizes:

VALVE TIMING OFFSET KEYS

Offset	Part No.	For a Correction at Crankshaft of
2° (0.7)	621 991 04 67	4°
3°20′ (0.9)	621 991 02 67	6½°
4° (1.1)	621 991 01 67	8°
5° (1.3)	621 991 00 67	10°

VALVE TIMING OFFSET KEYS

13. The Woodruff key must be installed with the offset toward the "right", in the normal direction of rotation, to effect advanced valve opening; toward the "left" to retard.

14. Advancing the intake valve opening too much can result in piston and/or valve damage (the valve will hit the piston). To check the clearance between the valve head and the piston, the crankshaft must be positioned at 5° ATDC (on intake stroke). The procedure is essentially the same as for measuring valve timing.

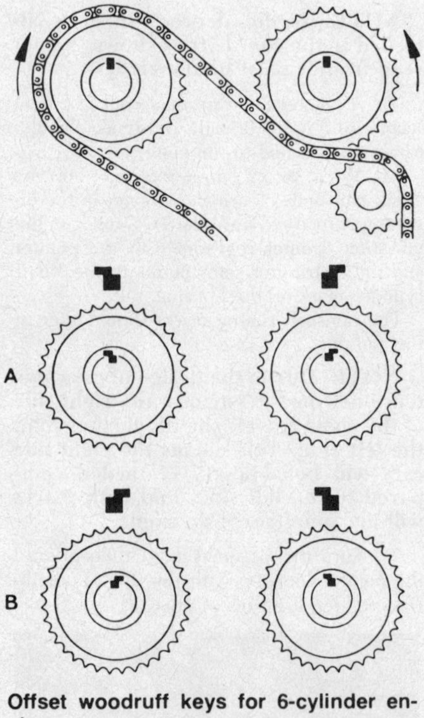

Offset woodruff keys for 6-cylinder engine

15. As before, the dial indicator is set to zero after being preloaded, then the valve is depressed until it touches the top of the piston. As the normal valve head-to-piston clearance is approximately 0.035 in., you can see that the dial indicator must be preloaded at least 0.042 in. so there will be enough movement for the feeler.

If the clearance is much less than 0.035 in., the cylinder head must be removed and checked for carbon deposits. If none exist, the valve seat must be cut deeper into the head. Always set the ignition timing after installing an offset key.

ENGINE COOLING

Mercedes-Benz passenger car engines are all equipped with closed, pressurized, water cooling systems. Care should be exercised when dealing with the cooling system. Always turn the radiator cap to the first notch and allow the pressure to decrease before completely removing the cap.

Radiator

REMOVAL AND INSTALLATION

1. Remove the radiator cap.
2. Unscrew the radiator drain plug and drain the coolant from the radiator. If all of the coolant in the system is to be drained, move the heater controls to WARM and open the drain cocks on the engine block.
3. If the car is equipped with an oil cooler, drain the oil from the cooler.
4. If equipped, loosen the radiator shell.
5. Loosen the hose clips on the top and bottom radiator hoses and remove the hoses from the connections on the radiator.
6. Unscrew and plug the bottom line on the oil cooler.
7. If the car is equipped with an automatic transmission, unscrew and plug the lines on the transmission cooler.
8. Disconnect the right-hand and left-hand rubber loops and pull the radiator up and out of the body. On 450SL and SLC and 280S models, push the retaining springs toward the fenders to remove the radiator from the shell.
9. Inspect and replace any hoses which have become hardened or spongy.
10. Install the radiator shell and radiator (if the shell was removed) from the top and connect the top and bottom hoses to the radiator.
11. Bolt the shell to the radiator.
12. Attach the rubber loops or position the retaining springs, as applicable.
13. Position the hose clips on the top and bottom hoses.
14. Attach the lines to the oil cooler.
15. On cars with automatic transmissions, connect the lines to the transmission cooler.
16. Move the heater levers to the WARM position and slowly add coolant, allowing air to escape.
17. Check the oil level and fill if necessary. Run the engine for about one minute at idle with the filler neck open.
18. Add coolant to the specified level. Install the radiator cap and turn it until it seats in the second notch. Run the engine and check for leaks.

Water Pump

REMOVAL AND INSTALLATION

All Except V8

1. Drain the water from the radiator.
2. Loosen the radiator shell and remove the radiator.
3. Remove the fan with the coupling and set it aside in an upright position.
4. Loosen the belt around the water pump pulley and remove the belt.
5. Remove the bolts from the harmonic balancer and remove the balancer and pulley.
6. Unbolt and remove the water pump.
7. Installation is the reverse of removal. Tighten the belt and fill the cooling system.

V8 Models

NOTE: The water pump on 3.8 liter V8's cannot be used on 4.5 liter V8's.

1. Drain the water from the radiator and block.
2. Remove the air cleaner.
3. Loosen and remove the drive belt.
4. Disconnect the upper water hose from the radiator and thermostat housing.
5. Remove the fan and coupling.
6. On 3.5 engines, remove the bottom water hose from the water pump housing.
7. Remove the hose from the intake (top) connection of the water pump.
8. Set the engine at TDC. Matchmark the distributor and engine and remove the distributor. Crank the engine with a socket wrench on the crankshaft pulley bolt or with a screwdriver inserted in the balancer. Crank in the normal direction of rotation only.
9. Turn the balancer so that the recesses provide access to the mounting bolts. Remove the mounting bolts. Rotate the engine in the normal direction of rotation only.
10. Remove the water pump.
11. Clean the mounting surfaces of the water pump and block.
12. Installation is the reverse of removal. Always use a new gasket. Set the engine at TDC and install the distributor so that the distributor rotor points to the notch on the distributor housing. Fill the cooling system and check and adjust the ignition timing.

Thermostat

REMOVAL AND INSTALLATION

4 and 5-Cylinder Engines

The thermostat housing is a light metal casting attached directly to the cylinder head.

1. Open the radiator cap and depressurize the system.
2. Open the radiator drain cock and partially drain the coolant. Drain enough coolant to bring the coolant level below the level of the thermostat housing.
3. Remove the four bolts on the thermostat housing cover and remove the cover.
4. Note the installation position of the thermostat and remove it.
5. Installation is the reverse of removal. Be sure that the thermostat is positioned with the ball valve at the highest point and that the 4 bolts are tightened evenly against the seal.
6. Refill the cooling system and check for leaks.

V8 Engines

1. Drain the coolant from the radiator and block.
2. Remove the air cleaner.
3. Disconnect the battery and remove the alternator. Usually this need not be done on 450SL, 450SLC, 450SE, 450SEL, 38SL, 380SLC or 380SEL.
4. Unscrew the housing cover on the side of the water pump and remove the thermostat. Note that the thermostat used on 4.5 liter V8 models differs from the one used on other models due to a different positioning of the ball valve.
5. If a new thermostat is to be installed, always install a new sealing ring.
6. Installation is the reverse of removal. Be sure to tighten the screws on the housing cover evenly to prevent leaks. Refill the cooling system and check for leaks.

6-Cylinder Engines

1. Drain the coolant from the radiator.
2. Remove the vacuum pump and put the pump aside.
3. Remove the three bolts on the thermostat housing.
4. Remove the cover and the thermostat.
5. Installation is the reverse of removal. Install the thermostat so that the ball valve is at the highest point. Refill the cooling system.

EMISSION CONTROLS

1975

The 230 (California only) and all other gasoline engines are equipped with catalysts. These models must be operated only with unleaded gasoline.

All of the following tests should be made in the specified sequence with the engine at operating temperature.

As of 1975, the base color of vacuum lines for emission control is white. Lines originating at a vacuum source have only one color stripe. These lines are connected to the center connection of the switchover valve of the same color. Lines terminating at a vacuum operated device have 2 color stripes. Purple is always the second color. The lines are connected to the outer connection of the switchover valve of the same color.

Switchover valve filter caps are color coded as follows:

RED—Valve for ignition advance
GREY—Valve for throttle lift
BROWN—Valve for EGR
BLUE—Valve for air injection

230

Testing the System

77° F. TEMPERATURE SWITCH

1. Disconnect the temperature switch plug and ground the switch. The engine rpm should increase.
2. If not, check the vacuum line connections.
3. Unplug the relay box and connect terminals 7 and 1; an audible click should be heard. If not, replace the relay box.
4. Disconnect and ground the temperature

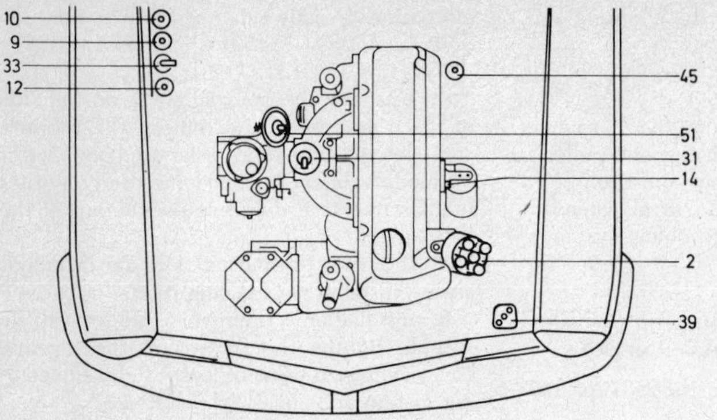

2. Distributor
9. Switchover valve, ignition (red)
10. Switchover valve, throttle lift (grey)
12. Switchover valve, EGR (brown)
14. 77° F temperature switch
31. EGR valve
33. Switchover valve, air injection (blue)
45. Muffler (air filter for noise suppression)
51. Vacuum control, throttle lift

1975-76 230 emission control component location

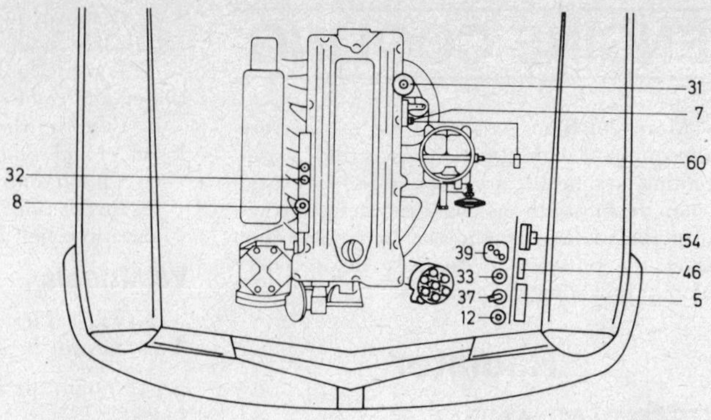

5. Relay box
7. 62° F temperature switch
8. 212° F temperature switch
12. Switchover valve, EGR (brown)
31. EGR valve
32. 149° F temperature switch
33. Switchover valve, air injection (blue)
37. Switchover valve, fuel evaporation control system (green)
39. Charcoal canister
46. Resistor, automatic choke cover
54. Vacuum booster
60. Venturi connection

1975-76 280 and 280C emission control component location

switch. Place your hand over the air pump muffler. A light air flow should be present.

5. If no air flow is present, check the vacuum line connections (see Step 2).

6. Disconnect the plug from the relay box and connect terminals 6 and 7. The blue switchover valve should click. If not, replace the switchover valve. If the valve does click, the relay is defective.

RPM SWITCH

1. Increase engine speed to about 2500 rpm and remove the red/purple vacuum line from the distributor. The engine speed should drop slightly. Below about 2000 rpm, there should be 13 volts at the switch. If there is less than 11 volts, temporarily replace the rpm relay or relay box and repeat the test.

EGR SWITCHOVER VALVE

1. Disconnect the brown vacuum line at the carburetor and brown/purple vacuum line at the carburetor. Blow into the brown vacuum line and simultaneously increase the rpm to about 3600. At idle, air can be blown through the line, while above 3600, no air should pass.

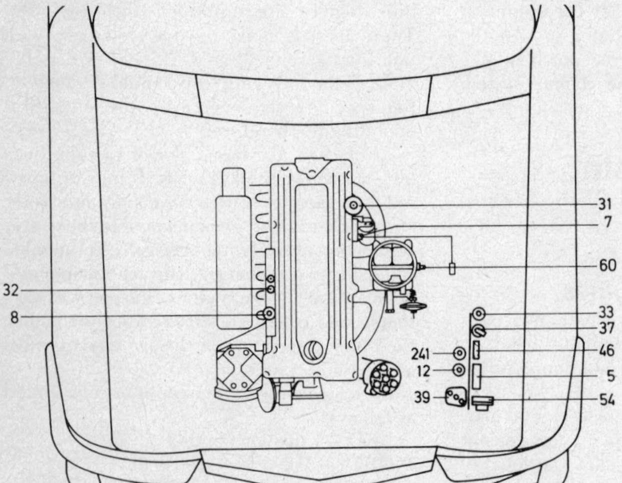

5. Relay box
7. 62° F temperature switch
8. 212° F temperature switch
12. Switchover valve, EGR (brown)
31. EGR valve
32. 149° F temperature switch
33. Switchover valve, air injection (blue)
37. Switchover valve, fuel evaporation control system (green)
39. Charcoal canister
46. Resistor, automatic choke cover
54. Vacuum booster
60. Venturi connection

1975-76 280S emission control component location

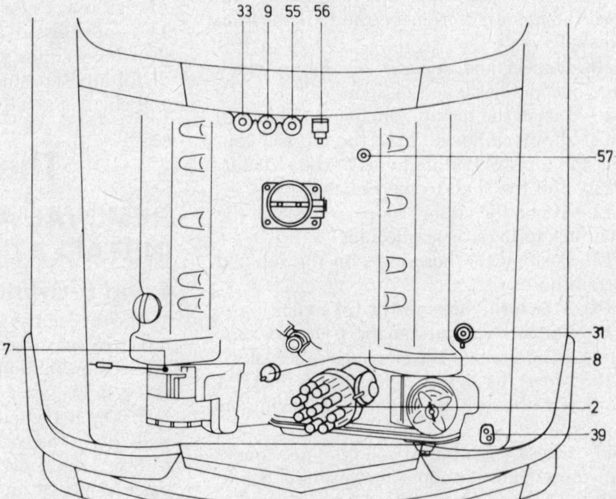

2. Distributor
7. 62° F (17° C) temperature switch
8. 212° F (100° C) temperature switch
9. Switch-over valve, ignition retard (yellow)
31. EGR valve
33. Switch-over valve, air injection (blue)
39. Charcoal canister
55. Switch-over valve, EGR/ ignition advance (red)
56. Vacuum control switch
57. 104° F (40° C) temperature switch

1975 450SE and 450SEL emission control component location

EGR VALVE

1. Connect the EGR valve to intake manifold vacuum. Disconnect the red line at the caburetor and the brown/purple line at the carburetor. Connect both lines together. The engine should run poorly or stall. If not be sure that the valve stem is moving and if not, replace the valve. If the valve works, clean the EGR valve with a 10 mm drill.

VACUUM GOVERNOR

1. Increase the engine speed to about 2500 rpm and release the throttle slowly. At the same time watch the vacuum control on the carburetor. It should pop out about 2000 rpm and retract below 1800 rpm. If not, remove the plug from the relay box and connect terminals 2 and 7. With the ignition ON, the valve should click audibly. If it does, replace the relay box.

280, 280C AND 280C

The system remains basically unchanged except for different color coding of vacuum lines and addition of a catalytic converter in all states.

Testing the System

EGR

1. Remove the brown/purple vacuum line from the EGR valve and turn the ignition ON. Blow air into the line. Place the gear selector in a driving position (not N or P). The line should be closed.

2. Remove the brown vacuum line on the carburetor and the green line on the carburetor. Connect the brown line in place of the green line. Start the engine and place the gear selector in a driving position (not N or P).

3. The engine should run roughly or stall. If not, either the vacuum booster or the EGR valve is at fault.

AIR INJECTION

1. Remove the air injection hose at the air filter (center hose) and run the engine at idle. There should be no air flow present. If air is discharged at idle, replace the diverter valve.

62° F TEMPERATURE SWITCH

1. Disconnect the plug from the switch in the oil filter housing and ground the switch. Air flow in the injection line should cease. If it does not, disconnect the plug from the blue switchover valve and connect a voltmeter. Disconnect and ground the temperature switch. Turn the ignition ON; the voltmeter should read about 12 volts. If no voltage is present, replace the relay box.

AUTOMATIC CHOKE RESISTOR

1. Connect a voltmeter to the resistor outlet (top connection) and to ground. Disconnect the plug of the 62° F temperature switch and connect it to ground. Disconnect the plug of the 149° F temperature switch and turn the ignition ON. With the 62° switch grounded the voltmeter should read about 7-8 volts. If the ground is interrupted, it should read about 12 volts.

2. If the voltage is not as specified, check the relay box. Connect a voltmeter to the input of the resistor (lower connection) and to ground. Ground the plug of the 62° temperature switch and the voltmeter should read about 12 volts. If not, replace the relay box.

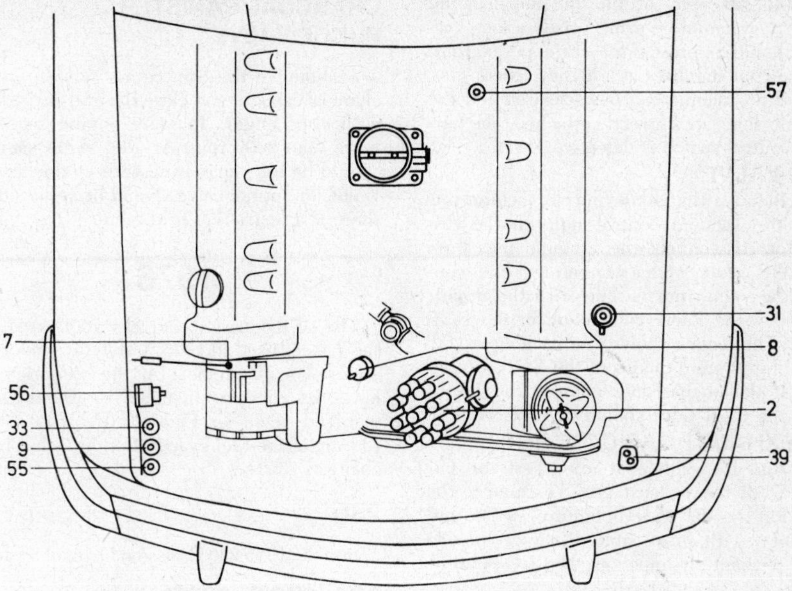

2. Distributor
7. 62° F (17° C) temperature switch
8. 212° F (100° C) temperature switch
9. Switch-over valve, ignition retard (yellow)
31. EGR valve
33. Switch-over valve, air injection (blue)
39. Charcoal canister
55. Switch-over valve, EGR/ ignition advance (red)
56. Vacuum control switch
57. 104° F (40° C) temperature switch

1975 450SL and 450 SLC emission control component location

FLOAT CHAMBER VENT VALVE

1. Connect a vacuum gauge to the green/purple vacuum line to the float chamber vent valve. Start the engine and briefly accelerate. The vacuum should build up and remain constant. With the ignition OFF, the vacuum should drop to zero.

2. If no vacuum is present, connect a voltmeter to the switchover valve. About 13 volts should be present, and the valve should click audibly.

If vacuum does not remain constant, unscrew the float chamber vent valve. With the vacuum line connected run the engine at idle. The valve rod should move. If necessary, replace the valve vacuum diaphragm.

CHARCOAL CANISTER PURGE VALVE

1. Remove the thin center hose from the charcoal canister and close the end of the hose with your finger. Increase engine speed to more than 2000 rpm. At idle, slight vacuum should be felt, increasing with engine speed. If not, the purge valve should be replaced, or there is a restriction in the line.

450SL, SLC AND 450SE, SEL

This system is basically the same as the 1974 system with the addition of a dual diaphragm distributor and catalytic converter.

Testing the System

212° F TEMPERATURE SWITCH

1. Unplug the temperature switch and ground it. The engine rpm should increase and the auxiliary fan should run on the 450SE and 450SEL. If not connect terminals 3 and 4 of the relay box plug. With the ignition ON, the switchover valve should click. If not, replace the relay.

2. Switch ON the air conditioning. The engine rpm should rise slightly. If the engine rpm does not increase, check the air conditioning. If the air conditioning works, replace the relay.

VACUUM CONTROL UNIT

1. Remove the yellow/purple and red/purple vacuum lines from the vacuum control on the distributor. The engine rpm should increase slightly. Connect the yellow/purple vacuum line to the upper connection of the vacuum control unit. The engine speed should increase slightly. If not, replace the vacuum control unit.

EGR SWITCHOVER VALVE

1. Remove the red/purple vacuum line at the EGR valve. Connect a vacuum gauge to the red/purple line and to the red connection of the EGR valve. Run the engine at idle and increase the rpm to 2500. At idle the gauge should show no vacuum. It higher rpm, there should be some vacuum.

2. If not, shut the engine OFF and turn the ignition to ON. Remove the plug from the 104° F temperature switch. The switchover valve should click. If it does not click, replace the switchover valve with a new one and repeat the test. If it still does not click, replace the relay.

EGR VACUUM CONTROL SWITCH

1. Remove the brown/purple vacuum line from the EGR valve. Connect a vacuum gauge to the brown/purple line and to the bottom of the EGR valve. Start the engine and increase

speed to 2500 rpm. At idle, the gauge should show no vacuum. During acceleration, vacuum should be present for a brief period until engine rpm stabilizes at a higher speed.

2. If no vacuum can be measured and the vacuum lines are correctly attached, the vacuum control switch is defective.

EGR VALVE

1. Remove the yellow/purple vacuum line from the vacuum control unit on the distributor. Disconnect the vacuum lines from the EGR valve. With a vacuum test line, connect the yellow/purple line with the upper, and then the lower connection of the EGR valve. The engine should run roughly or stall in both operating phases of the EGR valve.

2. If the engine does not run roughly or stall, the EGR valve should be replaced.

CO EXHAUST GAS CONTENT

1. Run the engine at idle. Test the CO content of the exhaust gas. Disconnect the plug for the 62° F temperature switch and ground it with a test cable. Measure the CO again without air injection. The CO content should change noticeably.

2. If it does not change noticeably, disconnect and ground the 62° temperature switch. The blue switchover valve should click. If it doesn't, replace the switchover valve.

3. If the switchover valve functions, remove the air filter on the diverter valve. Disconnect and ground the 62° temperature switch. Air should exit from the diverter valve. If there is no air flow, replace the diverter valve and repeat the test. Also, check the air pump and air pump drive belt tension.

CHARCOAL CANISTER PURGE VALVE

1. Remove the thin center hose from the charcoal canister and close the end of the hose with your finger. Increase engine speed to more than 2000 rpm. At idle, slight vacuum should be felt, increasing with engine speed. If not, the purge valve should be replaced, or there is a restriction in the line.

1976

The 1976 emission control system is close to the system used in 1975. Catalytic converters are used on all engines, but the 450 series cars have the catalysts installed on the exhaust manifold. Due to Federal regulations, the routing of the fuel evaporation lines has been changed.

230

See the 1975 230 Emission Control System.

280, 280C, 280S

See the 1975 280, 280C and 280S Emission Control System.

450SE, 450SEL, 450SL, 450SLC

These cars with the M117 engine use one emission system for the entire U.S. market, including California.

The base color of the vacuum lines is opaque (white). Lines originating at a vacuum source have only one color stripe; lines terminating at a vacuum source have 2-color stripes. Purple is always the second color.

Thermo vacuum valves are used to control the ignition changeover, EGR and air injection. They are color coded:

Black—104° F valve
Blue—63° F valve

The retard side of the vacuum control unit is only activated when the coolant is below 212° F, during deceleration with the A/C off. The advance side of the vacuum control unit is activated when temperatures at the thermovalve are 104° F or above and the advance is determined by the position of the throttle plate.

The EGR valve works in 2 stages. The first stage (small amount) takes place with coolant temperature above 104° F. There is no EGR with coolant temperature below 86° F.

The second (larger) stage of EGR occurs during acceleration with coolant temperature above 140° F and vacuum less than 7.9 in. Hg. Air injection takes place above 62° F and is cancelled below 50° F (coolant temperatures).

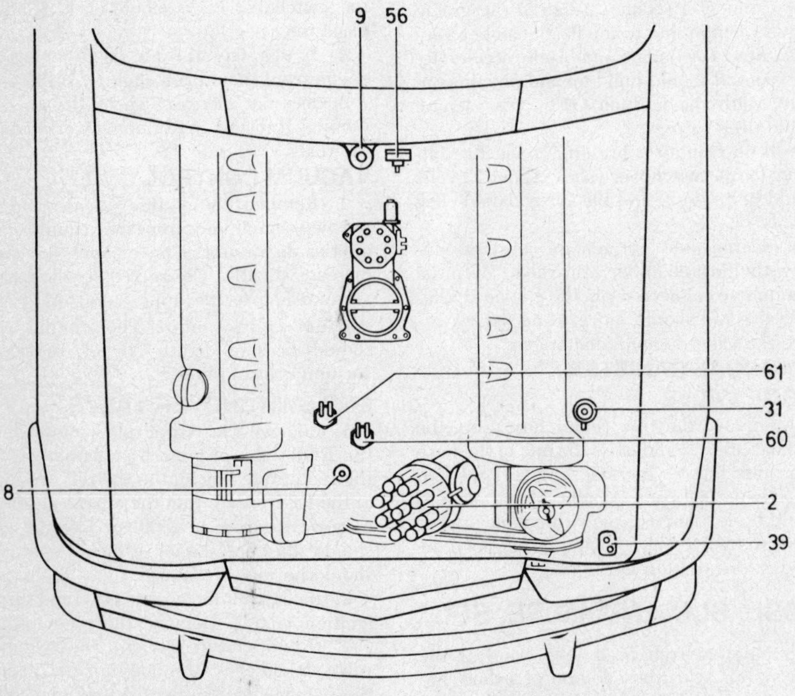

2. Distributor
8. 212° F temperature switch
9. Switch-over valve, ignition retard (yellow)
31. EGR valve
39. Charcoal canister
56. Vacuum control switch
60. 104° F thermo-vacuum valve (black)
61. 63° F thermo-vacuum valve (blue)

1976 450SE, 450SEL, 450SL and 450SLC emission control component location

Testing the System

IGNITION CHANGEOVER SWITCH

Unplug and ground the temperature switch. The engine rpm should increase and the auxiliary fan should operate.

If the engine speed does not increase, check the vacuum lines. The yellow line from the throttle valve housing should go to the center of the yellow switchover valve. The yellow/purple line goes to the outer connection of the switchover valve to the inner chamber of the vacuum unit (retard). Disconnect the plug from the relay and bridge terminals 3 and 4. With the ignition ON, the switchover valve should click. If not, replace the relay. If the switchover valve does not function, replace the valve.

Check the auxiliary fan. Disconnect the relay and bridge terminals 1 and 3. With ignition ON, the fan should run. If not, replace the fan.

Check the relay. Remove the plug and bridge terminals 1 and 3. With the ignition ON, the fan should run. If so, replace the relay.

IGNITION RETARD RELAY

Switch on the A/C. The engine rpm should increase slightly. If not, check that the A/C is operating. If the A/C is operating, replace the relay.

IGNITION ADVANCE

Remove the yellow/purple and red/purple vacuum lines from the distributor. The engine speed should increase slightly. Connect the yellow/purple vacuum line to the upper connection at the vacuum diaphragm. The engine speed should increase.

If not, replace the 2-way vacuum diaphragm.

EGR SWITCHOVER VALVE

Remove the red/purple vacuum line at the EGR valve. Connect a vacuum gauge to the red/purple line and run the engine at idle. Increase speed to 2500 rpm. At idle, the gauge should show no vacuum; at 2500 rpm, vacuum should be present.

If no vacuum is indicated, check the line conections. The red line from the red connection at the throttle valve housing should go to the angular connection of the thermo-vacuum valve. The red/purple line should be attached to the vertical connection at the thermo-vacuum valve, to the red connection of the vacuum control switch and red connection of the EGR valve.

Check the 104° F thermo-vacuum valve. It should open if the surrounding temperature is above 104° F. It should close below 86° F. If the valve is not functioning properly, check the bore of the throttle housing vacuum connection.

VACUUM CONTROL SWITCH

Remove the brown/purple vacuum line from the EGR valve. Connect a vacuum gauge between the line and the bottom of the EGR valve. Increase engine speed to 2500 rpm. At idle vacuum should not be present. During acceleration, vacuum should be present briefly until the rpm stabilizes. If no vacuum is present, check the vacuum lines. The red/purple line should be connected to the red connection at the vacuum control switch, the white line to the center of the vacuum control switch and the red/purple line to the brown control switch connection. If vacuum still is not present, replace the control switch.

EGR VALVE

Disconnect the yellow/purple line from the distributor diaphragm. Disconnect both vacuum lines at the EGR valve. Connect the yellow/purple line with the upper, then the lower connection of the EGR valve. The engine should run rough or stall in both cases. If not, replace the EGR valve.

DIVERTER VALVE

Run the engine at idle. Connect a CO tester. Note the reading. Remove the blue/purple vacuum line from the blue thermovalve and note reading again. It should change noticeably.

If not, check the vacuum lines. The blue line runs to the angular connection on the blue thermo-vacuum valve. The blue/purple line goes to the vertical connection of the same valve.

Check the diverter valve. Remove the muffler on the valve. Disconnect the blue/purple vacuum line at the blue thermovacuum valve. Air should flow from the diverter valve. If there is no air flow, replace the diverter valve. If necessary, check the drive belt tension.

CHARCOAL CANISTER

Remove the thin hose from the charcoal canister. Cover the hose opening with finger or connect vacuum gauge. Slowly increase rpm to 2500. At idle a small amount of vacuum should be present, and vacuum should increase with engine speed.

If no vacuum is present at idle, check the purge line to the intake manifold. Disconnect the charcoal canister hose at the purge valve and clean it by blowing through with compressed air in the direction of the intake manifold. Replace the purge valve if necessary.

If vacuum does not increase at idle, check the vacuum at the purge valve. Disconnect the white vacuum line at the purge valve. Connect a vacuum gauge or close the line with a finger. Increase engine speed. At idle, there should be no vacuum. With increasing engine speed, vacuum should increase. If vacuum is present replace the purge valve. If no vacuum is present, blow through the line towards the throttle valve housing.

1977

The following tests should be performed in the order given with the engine at normal operating temperature.

230

Testing the System

EGR

1. Run the engine at idle speed.
2. Remove the brown vacuum line at the carburetor and the gray vacuum line at the intake manifold. Connect the brown line at the intake manifold.
3. The engine should run roughly or stall. If the rpm does not change, check the vacuum line connections. Check for leaks and blow through the vacuum connection on the carburetor.
4. Check the thermo-vacuum valve (blue plastic portion and "50AB5" stamped in metal housing). Remove the brown/purple vacuum line and race the engine. Vacuum must be present at the open connection when accelerating.
5. Check the EGR valve. Remove the EGR valve. Connect the brown/purple vacuum line to the EGR valve and slowly increase engine rpm. Cover the bores in the intake manifold. The valve stem should lift from its seat; if not replace the EGR valve with a new one.

AIR INJECTION

1. Connect a CO tester to the test connection and remove the vacuum hose from the vertical connection of the thermo-vacuum valve. The air injection thermo-vacuum valve has "50AA" stamped in the metal housing. Plug the connection on the valve. The CO reading should drop noticeably.
2. If the CO does not drop, and vacuum IS indicated, replace the thermo-valve. If the CO does not drop and vacuum is NOT indicated, clean the vacuum line to the intake manifold with compressed air.
3. Check the connection of the vacuum lines.
4. Check the vertical connection of the thermal-vacuum valve for vacuum. If vacuum is present, replace the diverter valve. If no vacuum is present, remove the blue vacuum line from the thermo-vacuum valve and check for vacuum at the line.
5. If the CO still does not decrease, check that the thermo-valve is open; if not, replace the valve.

NOTE: Below approximately 120° F, the valve should be open; above that, it should be closed.

THROTTLE VALVE LIFT

1. Remove the vacuum hose from the vacuum governor on the carburetor. The idle speed should increase. Reconnect the hose. The idle speed should decrease.
2. If the rpm does not increase, check the connection of the hose. Check the hose for leaks.
3. Run the engine at idle. Remove the vacuum line on the carburetor; the idle speed should increase. If not, replace the vacuum governor.

FUEL EVAPORATION CONTROL SYSTEM

1. Remove the solenoid plug from the float chamber vent valve. Reconnect the solenoid; it should click audibly.
2. If the solenoid does not click, turn on

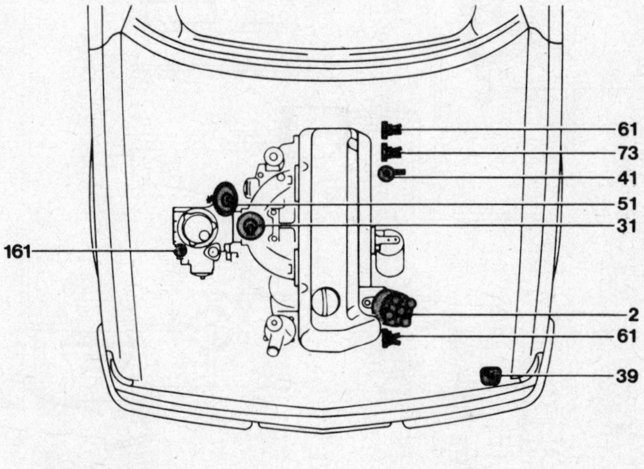

2. Distributor
31. EGR valve
39. Charcoal canister
41. Diverter valve
51. Vacuum governor
61. 62° F thermo-vacuum valve (blue); for EGR, located at front of engine next to distributor
61. 62° F thermo-vacuum valve (blue), for air
73. 122° F thermo-vacuum valve (black with green dot)
161. Float chamber vent valve

1977-79 230 emission control component location

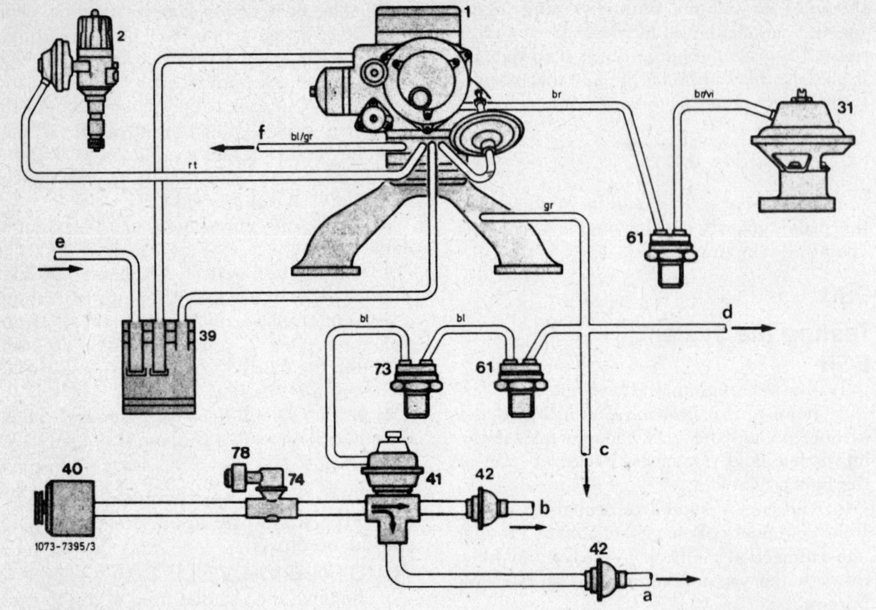

1. Carburetor
2. Distributor
31. EGR valve
39. Charcoal canister
40. Air pump
41. Diverter valve
42. Check valve
61. 62° F thermo-vacuum valve (blue), for EGR, located at front of engine next to distributor
61. 62° F thermo-vacuum valve (blue), for air injection, located at rear of engine
73. Thermo-vacuum valve 50° C/122° F
74. Pressure relief valve
78. Air filter for noise suppression

A To cylinder head
B To catalyst
C Air conditioning
D Central locking system
E Fuel tank ventilation connection
F To air filter

rt = red
gr = gray
bl = blue
br = brown
vi = purple

1977 230 emission control schematic

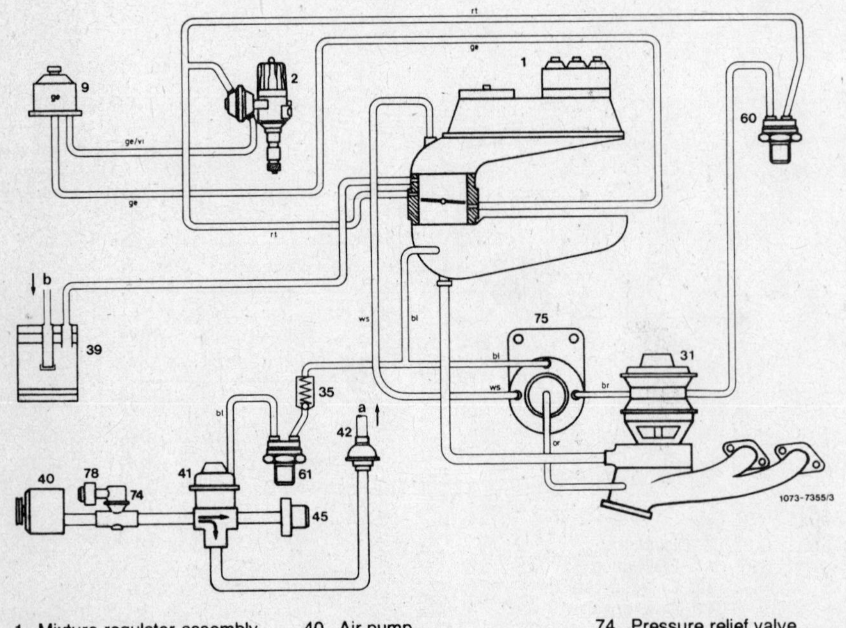

1. Mixture regulator assembly
2. Ignition distributor
9. Ignition switch-over valve
31. EGR valve
35. Check valve
39. Charcoal canister
40. Air pump
41. Diverter valve
42. Check valve
45. Muffler (air filter)
60. 104° F thermo-vacuum valve
61. 62° F thermo-vacuum valve
74. Pressure relief valve
75. Exhaust pressure transducer
78. Muffler (air filter)

A. Air injection line
B. Connection, fuel tank vent

1977 280E, 280SE Federal emission control schematic

the ignition and connect a test lamp to the plug. The test lamp should light with the ignition ON. If not, check the proper fuse. If the lamp still does not light, replace the solenoid.

3. Remove the middle purge hose to the carburetor from the charcoal canister and cover the hose opening with your finger. Slowly increase engine speed to over 2000 rpm. At idle no vacuum should be present. As engine speed increases, vacuum should increase. If no vacuum is present as the engine speed increases, check the connection of the purge hose. Check the hose for leaks and clean it out with compressed air.

4. On 1978-79 models, remove the hose from the purge valve and repeat the test. If vacuum is present, replace the purge valve.

280E AND 280SE (FEDERAL)

Testing the System

The following tests should be performed with the engine at idle speed, at operating temperature and in the order listed.

EGR

1. Remove the brown vacuum line from the EGR valve and slowly increase engine rpm. At about 1200 rpm, the engine should run roughly or stall.

2. If it does not run roughly or stall, check the vacuum line connections. The connections at the exhaust pressure transducer are marked with colored rings and must be connected to the same color code.

3. Disconnect the vacuum line from the vertical connection of the thermo-vacuum valve marked "50AA4" in the metal housing. Run the engine and increase rpm. Vacuum should be present at the connection.

4. Run the engine at idle and disconnect the brown line between the EGR valve and exhaust pressure transducer. Cover the line with your finger; vacuum must be present at idle. If not, replace the exhaust pressure transducer.

5. Run the engine at idle and remove both vacuum lines from the EGR valve. Connect the brown line to the connection on the red/purple line on the EGR valve. The engine should run roughly or stall. If not, replace the EGR valve.

AIR INJECTION

1. Connect a CO tester to the exhaust back pressure line. Remove and plug the vacuum hose from the vertical connection at the thermo-vacuum valve. The CO should increase.

2. If not, check the vacuum line connections. The (large) cap end connection of the check valve must face the intake manifold (Federal only).

3. Remove the blue vacuum line from the thermo-vacuum valve and cover it with your finger. Vacuum must be present at idle; if not, check for leaks and clean the line with compressed air.

4. If vacuum is present, check the thermo-vacuum valve and replace if necessary.

5. Disconnect the blue/purple line from the thermo-vacuum valve marked "50AB5" on the metal housing. Run the engine. Vacuum

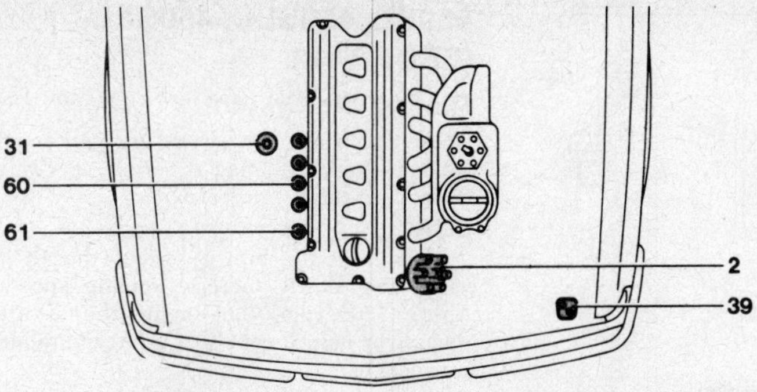

2. Distributor
31. EGR valve
39. Charcoal canister
60. 104° F thermo-vacuum valve
61. 62° F thermo-vacuum valve

1977-79 280E, 280CE, 280SE Federal emission control component location

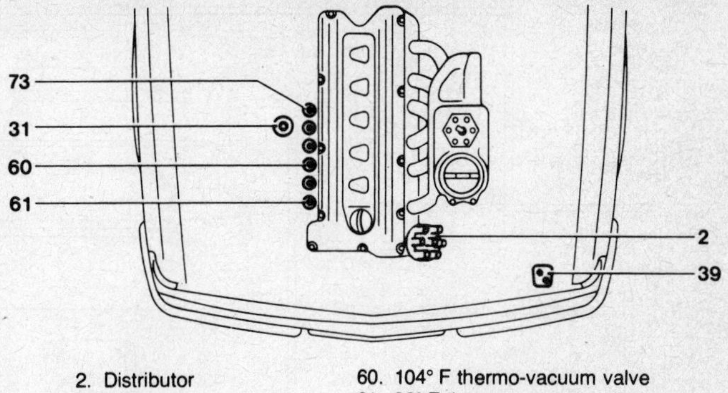

2. Distributor
31. EGR valve
39. Charcoal canister
60. 104° F thermo-vacuum valve
61. 62° F thermo-vacuum valve
73. 122°F thermo-vacuum valve

1977-79 280E, 280CE, 280SE California emission control component location

should be present at the vertical connection. If not, replace the diverter valve.

FUEL EVAPORATION CONTROL SYSTEM

1. Remove the black purge line from the charcoal canister. Cover the opening with your finger and increase rpm to over 2000 rpm. No vacuum should be present at idle and vacuum should increase with engine speed. If not, check the vacuum line connections, check for leaks and clean the line with compressed air.

280E AND 280SE (CALIFORNIA)

Testing the System

EGR

See 280E and 280SE (Federal).

AIR INJECTION

1. Connect a CO tester to the exhaust pressure transducer. Remove the vacuum line from the vertical connection of the 122° F thermo-vacuum valve and connect it to the vertical connection of the 62° F thermo-vacuum valve. The CO should drop.

2. If not, check the vacuum line connections.

3. Run the engine at idle and check for vacuum at the vertical connection of the 62° F thermo-vacuum valve. If vacuum is present, replace the diverter valve.

If no vacuum is present, remove the blue line from the 62° F thermo-vacuum valve and check for vaccum at the valve. If vacuum is present, replace the thermo-vacuum valve. If no vacuum is present, remove the line from the intake manifold and clean it with compressed air.

4. If the CO still does not drop, check the 122° F thermo-vacuum valve. It will have "50AA13" stamped in the metal housing. Above 122° F, the valve is closed and no vacuum should be present at the vertical connection. Below 122° F, vacuum should be present at the vertical connection. If these conditions are not met, replace the valve.

FUEL EVAPORATION CONTROL SYSTEM

See 280E and 280SE (Federal).

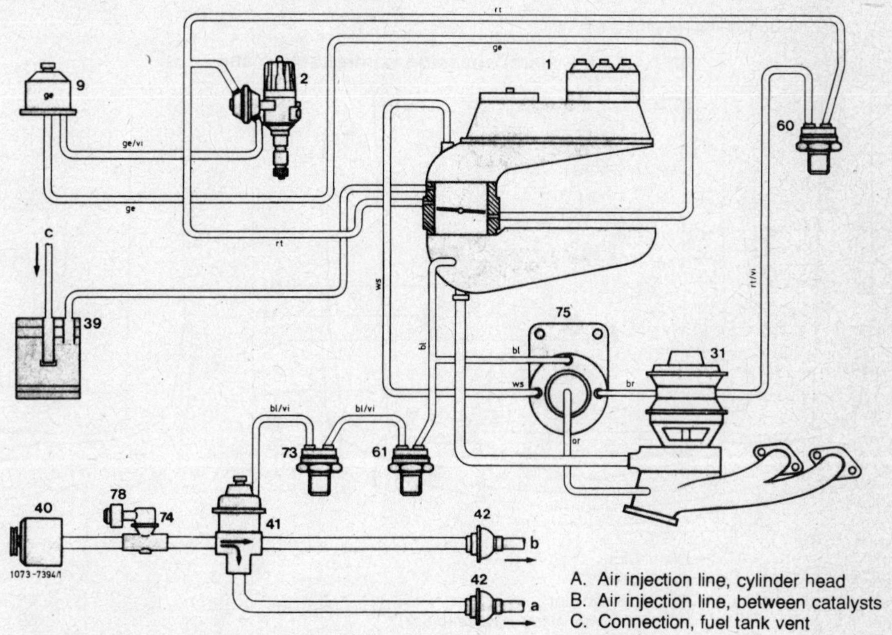

A. Air injection line, cylinder head
B. Air injection line, between catalysts
C. Connection, fuel tank vent

1. Mixture regulator assembly
2. Ignition distributor
9. Switch-over valve, ignition
31. EGR valve
39. Charcoal canister
40. Air pump
41. Diverter valve
42. Check valve
60. 104° F thermo-vacuum valve
61. 62° F thermo-vacuum valve
73. 122° F thermo-vacuum valve
74. Pressure relief valve
75. Exhaust pressure transducer
78. Muffler (air filter)

1977 280E, 280SE California emission control schematic

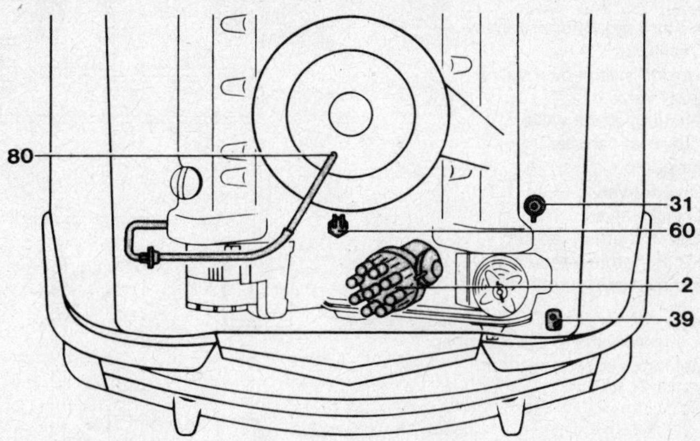

2. Distributor
31. EGR valve
39. Charcoal canister
60. 104° F thermo-vacuum valve (black)
80. Suction hose to aspirator/check valve

1977-79 4.5 V8 Federal emission control location

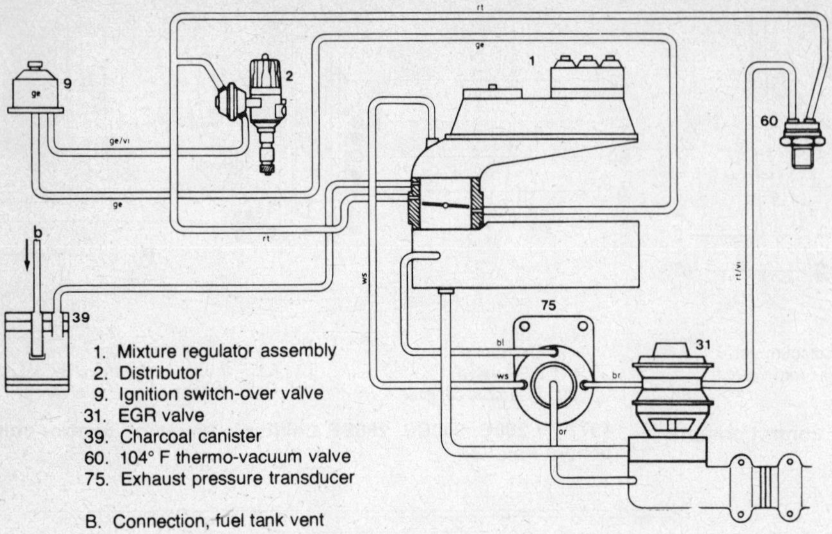

1. Mixture regulator assembly
2. Distributor
9. Ignition switch-over valve
31. EGR valve
39. Charcoal canister
60. 104° F thermo-vacuum valve
75. Exhaust pressure transducer

B. Connection, fuel tank vent

1977 4.5 V8 Federal emission control schematic

450SL, 450SLC, 450SEL (FEDERAL)

Testing the System

The following tests should be performed with the engine running at normal operating temperature in the order given.

EGR

1. Remove the brown line at the EGR valve and slowly increase engine speed. Above 1200 rpm, the engine should run roughly or stall. If not check the vacuum line connections.

2. Check the thermo-vacuum valve with "50AA4" stamped in the metal housing (104° F valve). Remove the red/purple line from the vertical connection, run the engine and accelerate briefly. Vacuum should be present at the vertical connection.

3. Run the engine at idle and remove the brown vacuum line at the EGR valve. If no vacuum is present at idle, replace the exhaust pressure transducer.

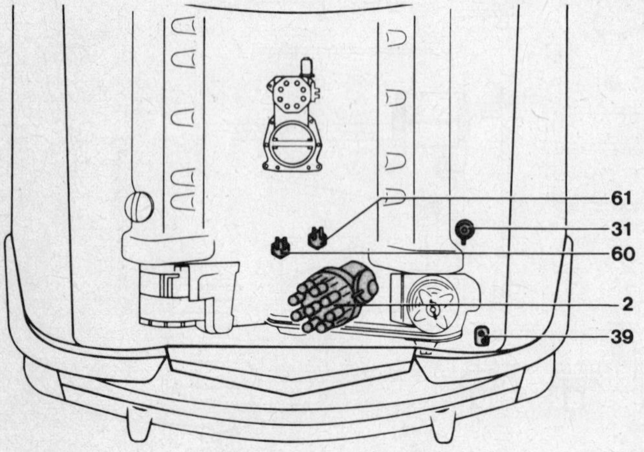

2. Distributor
31. EGR valve
39. Charcoal canister
60. 104° F thermo-vacuum valve (black)
61. 62° F thermo-vacuum valve (blue)

1977-79 V8 California emission control component locations

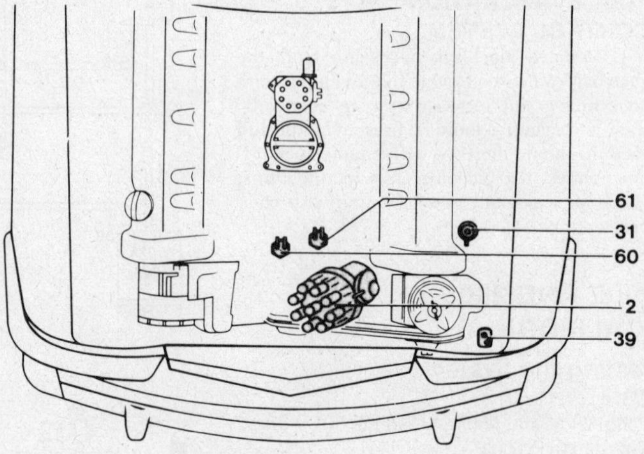

2. Distributor
31. EGR valve
39. Charcoal canister
60. 104° F thermo-vacuum valve
61. 62° F thermo-vacuum valve

1977 6.9 emission control component location

1. Mixture regulator assembly
2. Distributor
9. Ignition switch-over valve
31. EGR valve
35. Vacuum check valve
39. Charcoal canister
40. Air pump
41. Diverter valve
42. Check valve
60. 104° F thermo-vacuum valve
61. 62° F thermo-vacuum valve
75. Exhaust pressure transducer

A. Air injection line to cylinder head
B. Fuel tank vent connection

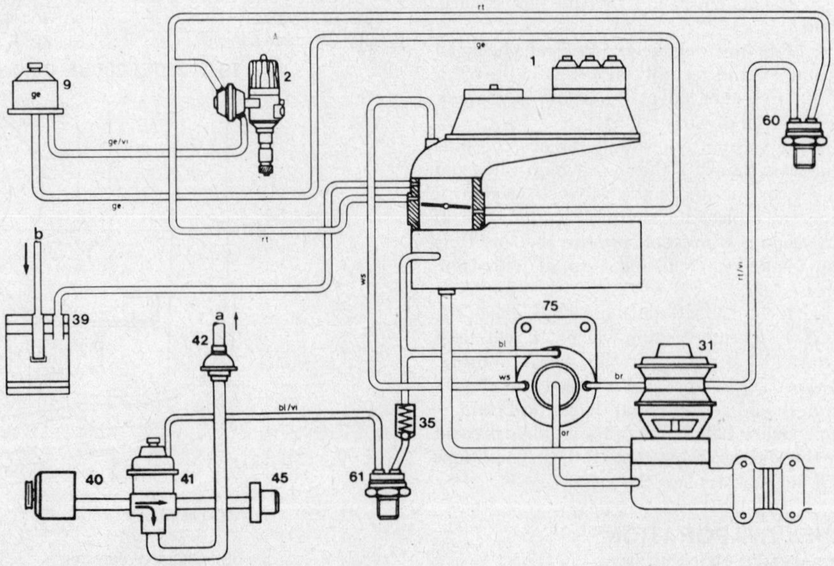

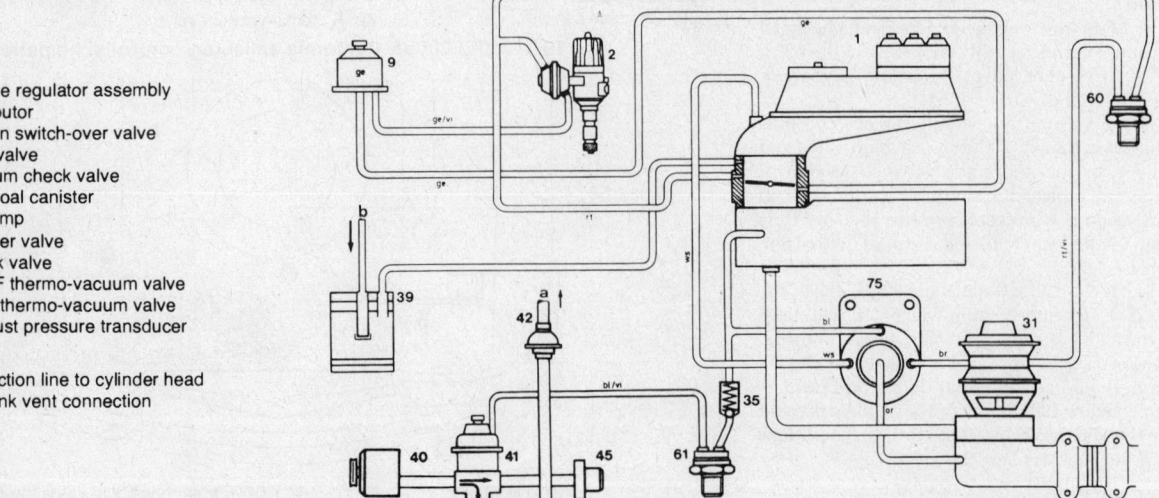

1977 4.5 V8 California emission control schematic

4. Run the engine at idle and remove both lines from the EGR valve. Connect the brown line to the connection for the red/purple line. The engine should run roughly or stall. If not, replace the EGR valve.

AIR INJECTION

1. Remove the suction hose from the aspirator/check valve in the air cleaner and cover with your finger. Vacuum should be present and a suction noise should be audible. If no vacuum is present, replace the aspirator/check valve.

FUEL EVAPORATION CONTROL SYSTEM

See this test under 280E and 280SE (Federal).

450SL, 450SLC, 450SEL (CALIFORNIA) AND 6.9

Testing the System

EGR

See 450SL, 450SLC, 450SEL (Federal).

AIR INJECTION

1. Connect a CO tester to the exhaust gas back pressure line and remove the blue/purple vacuum line from the vertical connection of the 62° F thermo-vacuum valve. Plug the connection. The CO should increase.

2. If not, check the vacuum line connections. The check valve must be installed with the larger (cap) end toward the intake manifold.

3. Remove the vacuum line from the angular connection of the 62° F thermo-vacuum valve and cover the valve with your finger. If no vacuum is present at idle, check the lines for leaks and clean the vacuum pick-up bore with compressed air.

4. If vacuum is present, check the thermo-vacuum valve and replace if necessary.

5. The thermo-vacuum valve can be identified by the "50AB5" stamped in the metal body. Remove the blue/purple vacuum line, run the engine at idle and accelerate briefly. Vacuum should be present at the vertical connection; if not, replace the diverter valve.

FUEL EVAPORATION CONTROL SYSTEM

See this test under 280E and 280SE (Federal).

1978-79

The emission control system for 1978-79 models is very similar in components and operation to the 1977 version.

230

Perform the following tests in the order given with the engine at idle at normal operating temperature.

Testing the System

See the 1977 230 procedures for "Testing the System."

1. Mixture regulator assembly
2. Distributor
5. Purge valve
9. Ignition switch-over valve
31. EGR valve
39. Charcoal canister
60. 104° F thermo-vacuum valve
75. Exhaust pressure transducer
80. Auxiliary air valve
81. Shaped hose

B. Fuel tank vent connection

bl = blue
br = brown
ge = yellow
gr = gray
or = orange
rt = red
vi = purple
ws = white

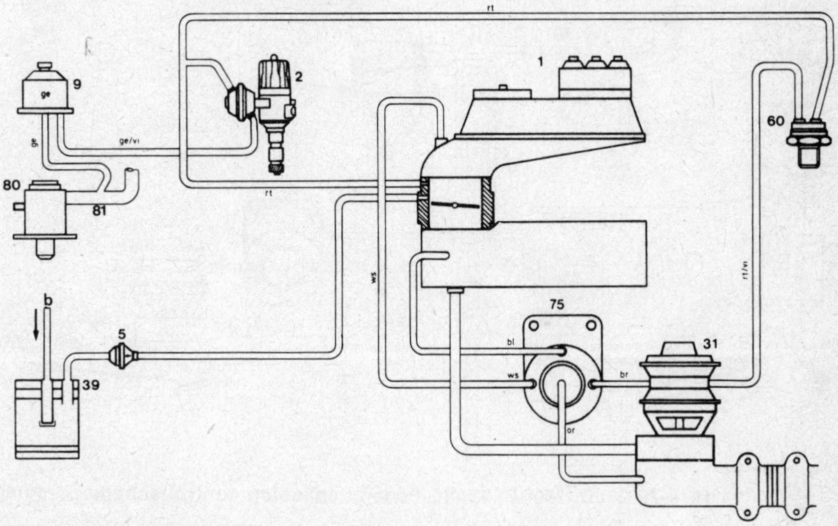

1978-79 4.5 V8 Federal emission control schematic component. Location same as 1977

1. Carburetor
2. Distributor
5. Fuel evaporation control system purge valve
31. EGR valve
39. Charcoal canister
40. Air pump
41. Diverter valve
42. Check valve
61. 62° F thermo-vacuum valve (blue), for EGR, located at front of engine next to distributor
61. 62° F thermo-vacuum valve (blue), for air injection, located at rear of engine
73. 122° F thermo-vacuum valve
74. Pressure relief valve
78. Air filter for noise suppression

A. To cylinder head
B. To catalyst
C. Air conditioning
D. Central locking system
E. Fuel tank ventilation connection
F. To air filter

bl = blue
br = brown
gr = gray
rt = red
vi = purple

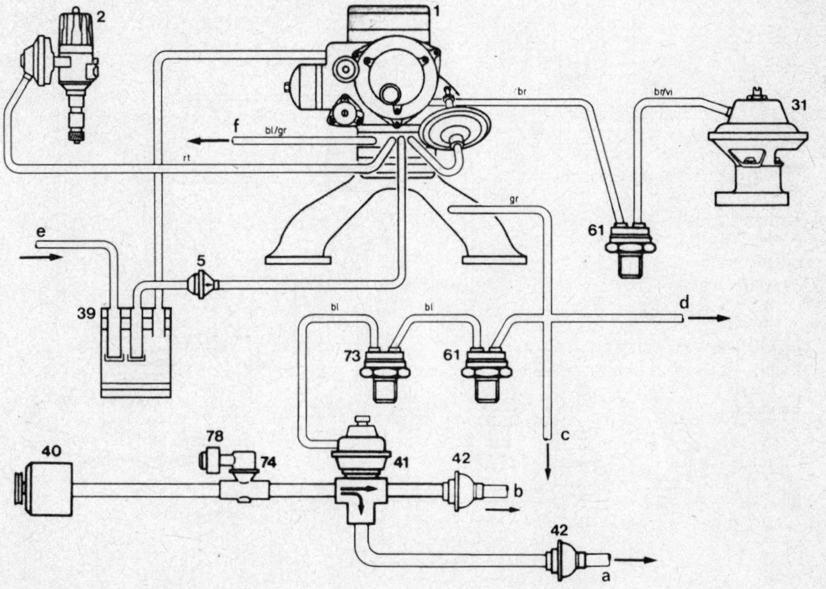

1978-79 230 Emission control schematic component. Location same as 1977

280E, 280CE, 280SE (FEDERAL)

Perform the following tests in the order given with the engine at normal operating temperature and idling.

Testing the System

See the 1977 280E and 280SE (Federal) procedures for "Testing the System."

280E, 280CE, 280SE (CALIFORNIA)

Perform the following tests in the order given with the engine at idle and normal operating temperature.

Testing the System

See the procedures under "Testing the System" for 1977 280E and 280SE California models.

450SL, 450SLC, 450SEL (FEDERAL)

Perform the following tests in the order given with the engine idling at normal operating temperature.

Testing the System

See the procedures for "Testing the System" under 1977 450SL, 450SLC, 450SEL (Federal) models.

450SL, 450SLC, 450SEL (CALIFORNIA) AND 6.9

Perform the following tests in the order given with the engine idling at normal operating temperature.

Testing the System

See the procedures for "Testing the System" under 1977 450SL, 450SLC, 450SEL (California) and 6.9 models.

Catalyst Replacement Warning Indicator

A warning light in the instrument cluster comes on at 37,500 mile intervals, indicating

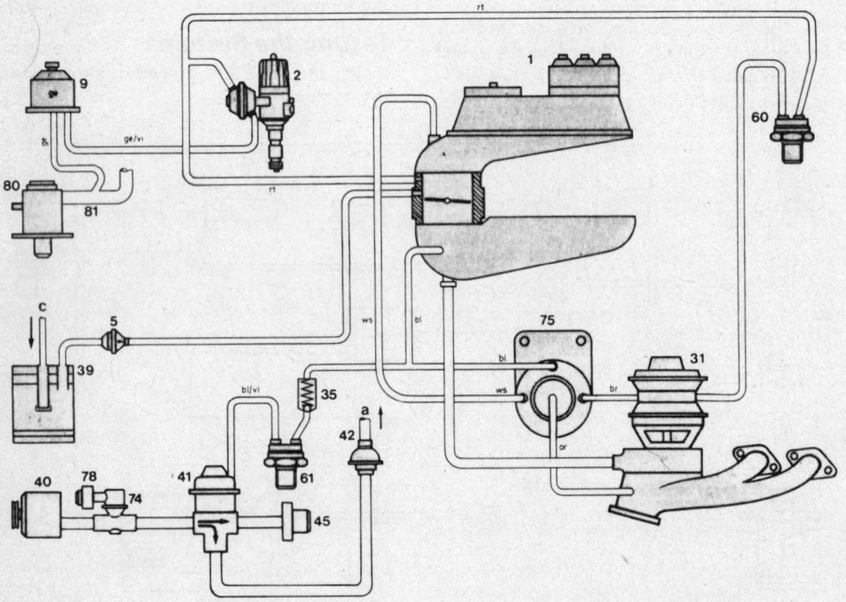

1. Mixture regulator assembly
2. Ignition distributor
5. Purge valve
9. Ignition switch over valve
31. EGR valve
39. Charcoal canister
40. Air pump
41. Diverter valve
42. Check valve
60. 104° F thermo-vacuum valve
61. 62° F thermo-vacuum valve
73. 122° F thermo-vacuum valve
74. Pressure relief valve
75. Exhaust pressure transducer
78. Muffler (air filter)
80. Auxiliary air valve
81. Shaped hose

A. Air injection line, cylinder head
B. Fuel tank vent connection

1978-79 280E, 280CE, 280SE Federal emission control schematic component. Location same as 1977.

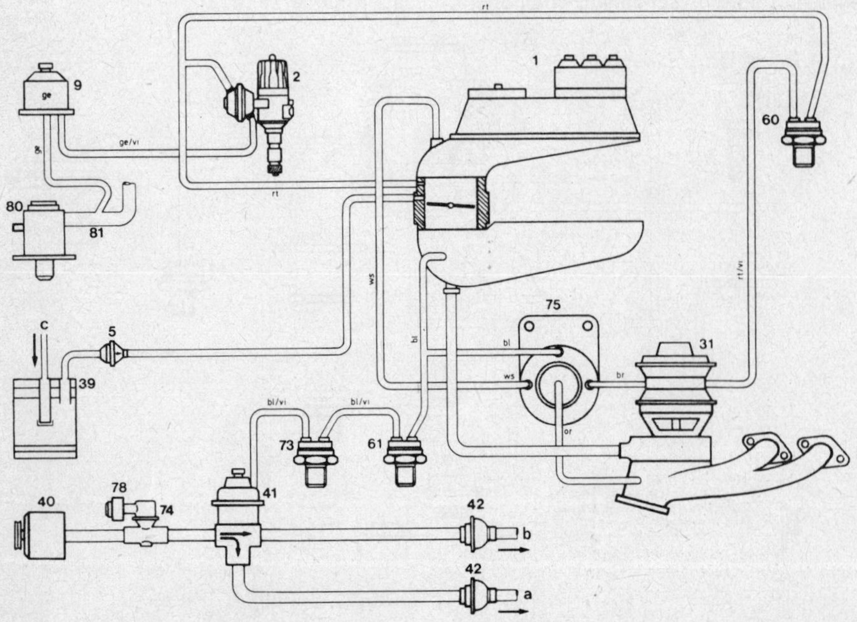

1. Mixture regulator assembly
2. Ignition distributor
5. Purge valve
9. Ignition switch-over valve
31. EGR valve
39. Charcoal canister
40. Air pump
41. Diverter valve
42. Check valve
60. 104° F thermo-vacuum valve
61. 62° F therm74. Pressure relief valve
75. Exhaust pressure transducer
78. Muffler (air filter)
80. Auxiliary air valve
81. Shaped hose

A. Air injection line, cylinder head
B. Air injection line, between catalysts
C. Fuel tank vent connection

bl = blue
br = brown
ge = yellow
gr = gray
or = orange
rt = red
vi = purple
ws = white

1978-79 280E, 280CE, 280SE California emission control schematic component. Location same as 1977

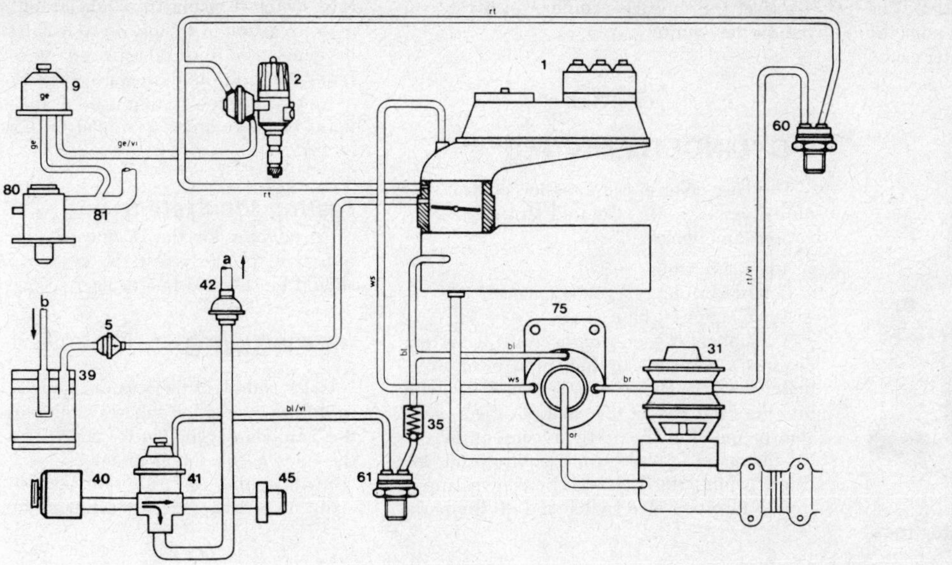

1. Mixture regulator assembly
2. Distributor
5. Purge valve
9. Ignition switch-over valve
31. EGR valve
35. Vacuum check valve
39. Charcoal canister
40. Air pump
41. Diverter valve
42. Check valve
60. 104° F thermo-vacuum valve
61. 62°F thermo-vacuum valve
73. 122°F thermo-vacuum valve
74. Pressure relief valve
75. Exhaust pressure transducer
80. Auxiliary valve
81. Shaped hose

A. Air injection line to cylinder head
B. Fuel tank vent connection

bl = blue
br = brown
ge = yellow
gr = gray
or = orange
rt = red
vi = purple
ws = white

1978-79 V8 Federal emission control schematic component. Location same as 1977

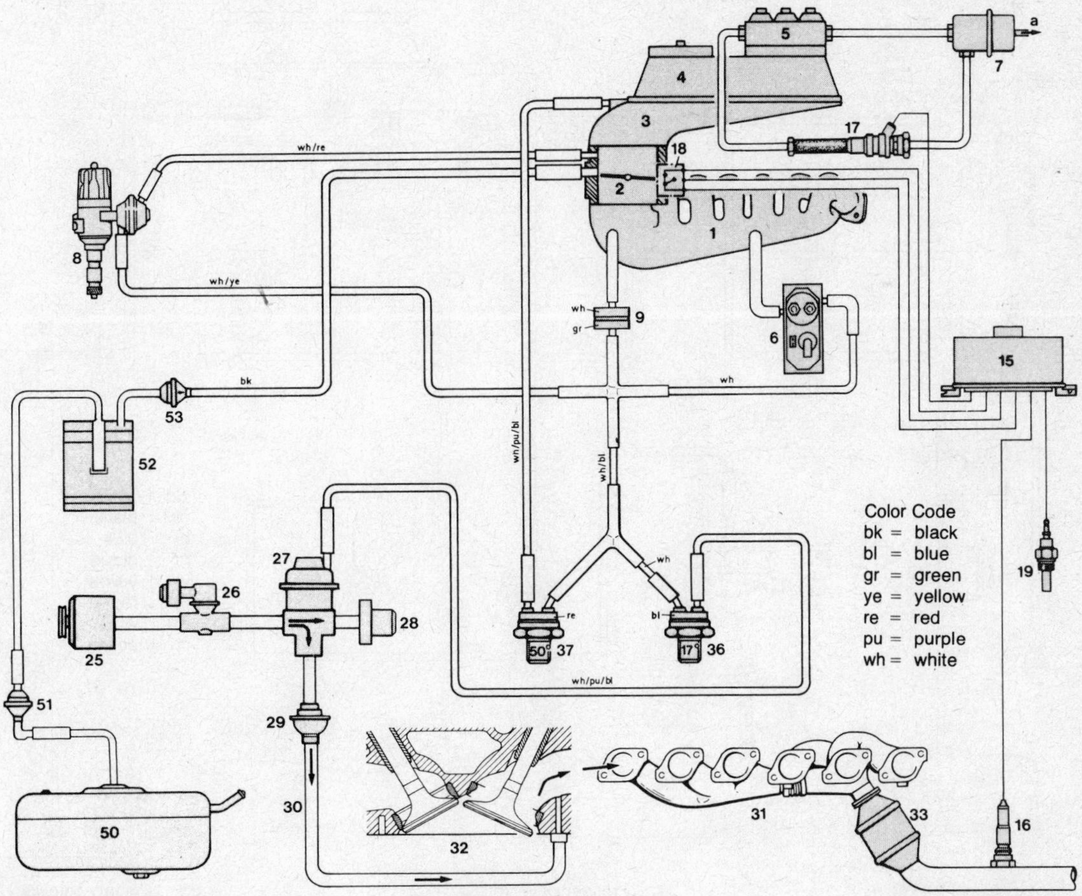

Color Code
bk = black
bl = blue
gr = green
ye = yellow
re = red
pu = purple
wh = white

1. Intake manifold
2. Throttle valve housing
3. Air duct housing
4. Air flow sensor
5. Fuel distributor
6. Warm-up enrichment compensator
7. Pressure damper
8. Ignition distributor
9. Restricting orifice
15. Electronic control unit
16. Oxygen sensor
17. Frequency valve
18. Throttle valve switch
19. Temperature switch, oil 60° F
25. Air pump
26. Pressure relief valve
27. Diverter valve
28. Muffler (air filter)
29. Check valve
30. Air injection line
31. Exhaust manifold
32. Cylinder head
33. Primary catalyst
36. Thermo-vacuum valve 63° F
37. Thermo-vacuum valve 122° F
50. Fuel tank
51. Vent valve
52. Charcoal canister
53. Purge valve
a. Leak-off connection

Emission control schematic—1980 6-cylinder engines

that the catalyst should be replaced. The catalyst mileage counter is located under the dash and is driven by the speedometer cable.

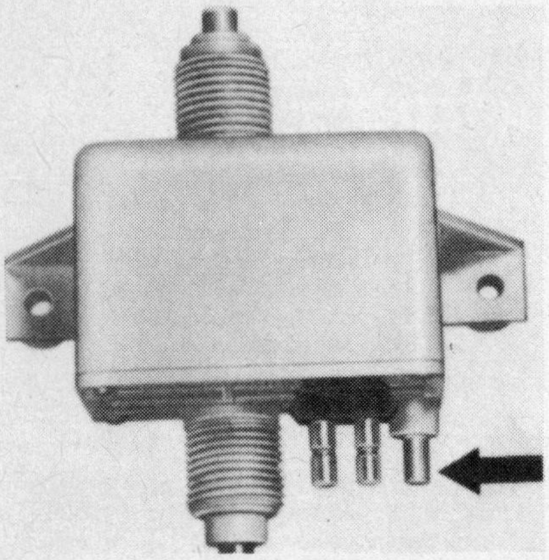

Catalyst elapsed mileage indicator reset button (arrow)

To reset the mileage counter, push the rest pin on the counter.

1980

6-CYLINDER ENGINES

The base color of the emission control vacuum lines is white. Colored stripes identify various functions:

Advanced timing = red
Retarded timing = yellow/purple
Air injection = blue

A Lambda oxygen sensor control system ensures a constant air fuel ratio of approximately 14.5:1. The oxygen sensor is screwed into the front part of the exhaust pipe to constantly monitor the oxygen content of the exhaust gases. An electronic control unit, located behind the kick panel, receives input from a throttle valve switch and oil temperature switch to maintain an ideal fuel mixture in conjunction with the 3-way catalyst. The oxygen sensor must be replaced every 30,000 miles (light on the dash warns driver).

An air injection system is used, the components of which are very similar to those used in 1979.

Testing the System

An adapter for the diagnostic plug is required to properly test the system. Testing should be referred to a dealer.

V8 ENGINES

Color coding of the vacuum lines is identical to the 6-cylinder engines and operation of the Lambda oxygen sensor control system is the same as 6-cylinder engines.

Air injection uses a shut-off valve in a specially shaped hose between the air filter and

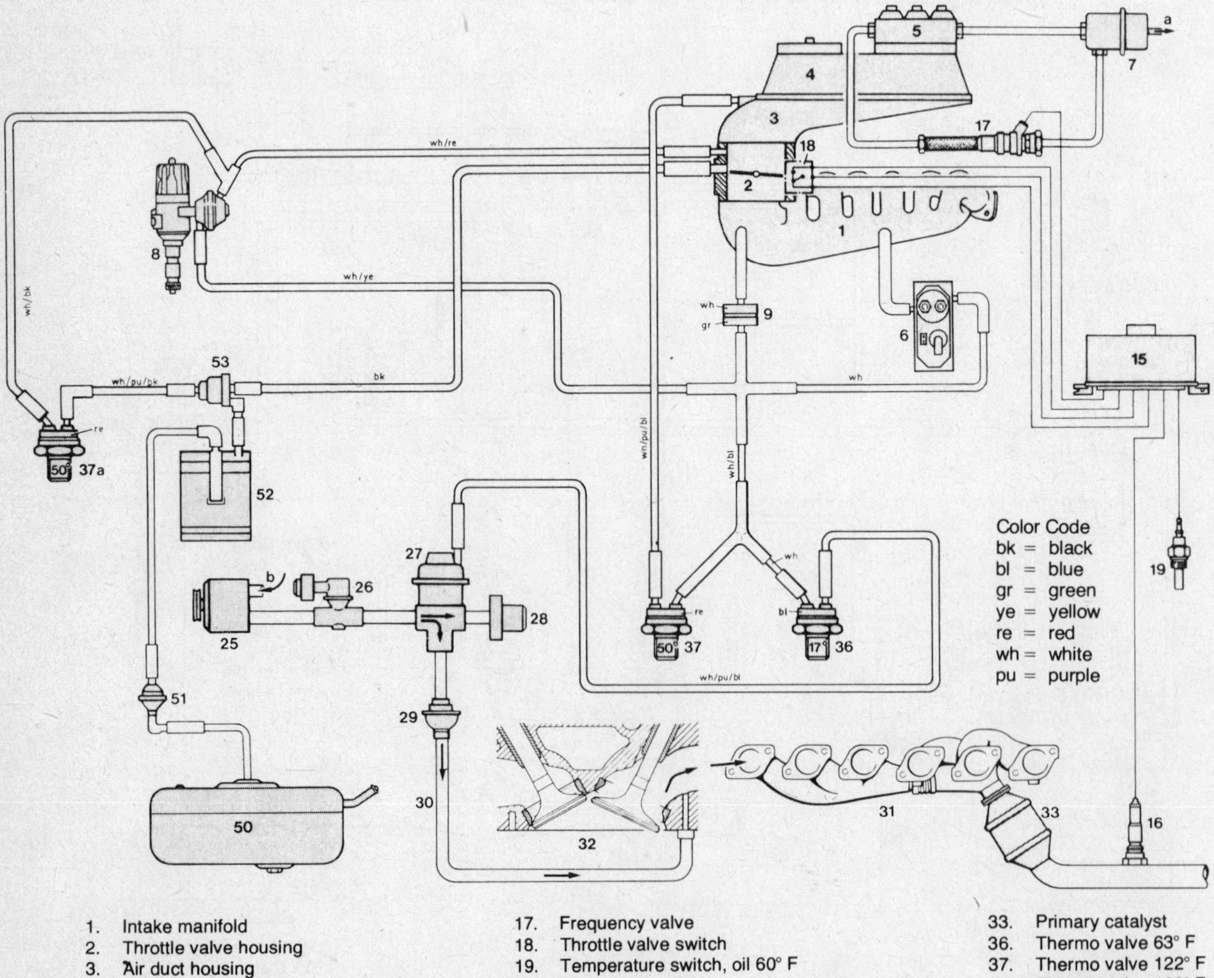

1. Intake manifold
2. Throttle valve housing
3. Air duct housing
4. Air flow sensor
5. Fuel distributor
6. Warm-up compensator
7. Silencer (damper)
8. Ignition distributor
9. Orifice
15. Control unit
16. Oxygen sensor
17. Frequency valve
18. Throttle valve switch
19. Temperature switch, oil 60° F
25. Air pump
26. Pressure relief valve
27. Diverter valve
28. Silencer
29. Check valve
30. Air injection line
31. Exhaust manifold
32. Cylinder head
33. Primary catalyst
36. Thermo valve 63° F
37. Thermo valve 122° F
37a. Thermo valve 122° F
50. Fuel tank
51. Vent valve
52. Charcoal canister
53. Purge valve

a. Leak-off connection
b. from the air cleaner

Emission control schematic—1981 6-cylinder engines

the aspirator valve, which is in the air injection line leading to the cylinder head.

Primary, underfloor and catalyst/muffler combination catalytic converters are used, depending on application.

The fuel evaporation control system is identical to the 1979 system.

Testing the System

An adapter for the diagnostic plug is required to properly test the system. Testing should be referred to a Mercedes-Benz dealer.

1981

6-CYLINDER ENGINES

The emission control system is the same as 1980, with two exceptions. The air pump intake is connected to the clean side of the air cleaner. A rubber scoop inside the air cleaner facilitates air intake. The second change is that the fuel evaporation control purge system is controlled by a thermo valve and is effective only at temperatures above 122° F.

Color coding of the vacuum lines is as follows:

Device	Color of line originating at a vacuum source	Color of line terminating at a vacuum operated device
Ignition advance	red	
Ignition retard	yellow	
Air injection	blue	blue/purple
Fuel evaporation thermo valve	black	black/purple

Lines originating at a vacuum source have only one color stripe; lines terminating at a vacuum operated device have 2 color stripes and purple is always the second color.

Testing the System

An adapter for the diagnostic plug is required to properly test the system. Testing should be referred to a Mercedes-Benz dealer.

V8 ENGINES

Color coding of the vacuum lines is identical to the 6-cylinder engines. Operation of the Lambda oxygen sensor control system is the same as 1980. Only the oxygen sensor itself has been modified for production reasons. The air pump is a maintenance-free vane type pump, similar in operation to the 1980 system. Three-way catalysts have been slightly modified dimensionally, but operate the same as those in 1980. The fuel evaporation control system is the same as 1980, except that the purge system is controlled by a thermo valve that allows purge only at coolant temperatures below approximately 122° F.

Testing the System

An adaptor for the diagnostic plug is required to properly test the system. Testing should be referred to a Mercedes-Benz dealer.

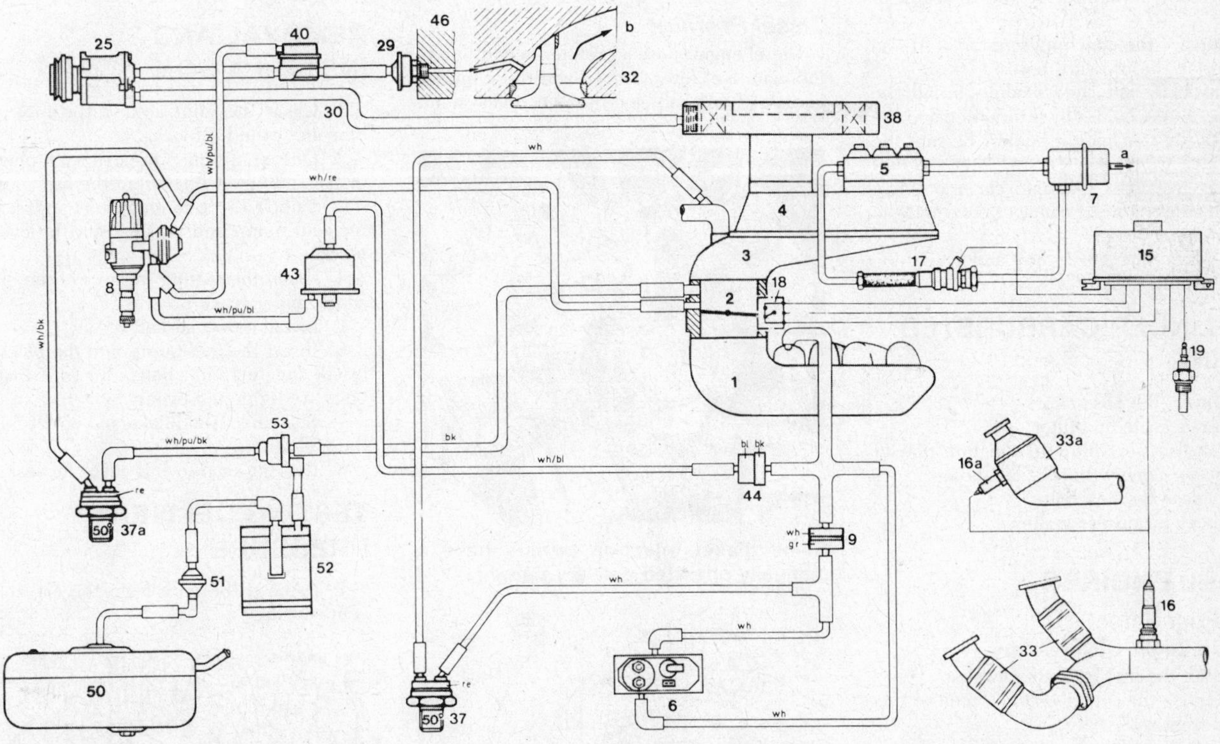

1. Intake manifold
2. Throttle valve housing
3. Air duct housing
4. Air flow sensor
5. Volume distributor
6. Warm-up compensator
7. Pressure damper
8. Ignition distributor
9. Restricting orifice
15. Control unit
16. Oxygen sensor (model 107)
16a. Oxygen sensor (model 126)
17. Frequency valve
18. Throttle valve switch
19. Temperature switch 61° F oil
25. Air pump
29. Check valve (injected air)
30. Intake line
32. Cylinder head
33. Pre-catalyst (model 107)
33a. Pre-catalyst (model 126)
37. Thermo valve 122° F
37a. Thermo valve 122° F
38. Air cleaner
40. Air injection shutoff valve
43. Switchover valve
44. Check valve (vacuum)
46. Timing chain cover
50. Fuel tank
51. Vent valve
52. Charcoal canister
53. Purge valve

a. Leak connection
b. to exhaust manifold

Color Code
bk = black
bl = blue
gr = green
pu = purple
re = red
wh = white

Emission control schematic—1981 3.8 liter V-8 engines

FUEL SYSTEM

Fuel Filter

6-CYLINDER CARBURETED ENGINES

The fuel filter is located in the carburetor housing. Put some rags under the fuel return valve to absorb the inevitable gasoline spillage.

1. Unscrew the fuel return valve and plug it at the carburetor.
2. Remove the fuel filter.
3. Renew the gasket at the seal plug.
4. Install a new filter. Check for leaks.

6-CYLINDER (FUEL INJECTED) AND V8

Two types of filter are used, one on the electronically controlled fuel injection and the other on the CIS fuel injection. Both are located between the rear axle and the fuel tank.

1. Unscrew the cover box.
2. Remove the pressure hoses.
3. Loosen the attaching screws and remove the filter. Remove the connecting plug from the old filter and install it on a new filter using a new gasket.
4. Install a new filter in the direction of flow.
5. Replace the attaching screws.
6. Install the pressure hoses.
7. On 1976 and later models, install the fuel filter in the holder by positioning it in the center of the transparent holder. Be sure the plastic sleeve between the fuel filter and fuel pump is installed. Galvanic corrosion may occur in cases of direct contact between these components.
8. Replace the cover box and check for proper sealing.

4-CYLINDER CARBURETED ENGINE

1. Loosen the hose clips.
2. Remove the fuel filter.
3. Install a new filter in the direction of flow (arrow) along with new fuel hoses.
4. Replace the hose clips.
5. Check for proper sealing.

DIESEL ENGINES

Main Fuel Filter

1975-76 240D, 300D

1. Drain the fuel from the housing.
2. Remove the center bolt and remove the filter housing and filter.
3. Wash the filter housing in clean diesel fuel and install a new filter element.
4. Use a new gasket in the filter cap and reassemble the filter and housing.
5. Bleed the fuel filter. Loosen the bleed bolt on the fuel filter housing and release the manually operated delivery pump. Operate the delivery pump until the fuel emerges free of bubbles at the bleed screw. Close the bleed bolt and operate the pump until the overflow valve on the injection pump opens (a buzzing

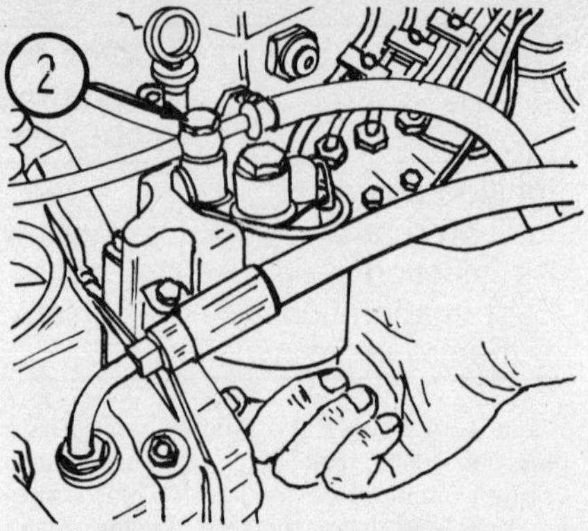

Remove the main diesel fuel filter after removing the center attaching bolt. The bleed screw is (2).

noise will be heard). Close the manual pump before starting the engine. To bleed the injection pump on 4-cylinder diesels, loosen the bleed screw on the injection pump and keep pumping the hand pump until fuel emerges free of bubbles.

1977 AND LATER DIESELS

Loosen the center attaching bolt and remove the filter cartridge downward. Lubricate the new filter gasket with clean diesel fuel and install a new filter cartridge.

To bleed the fuel filter, see Step 5 preceding.

Diesel Prefilter

Diesel engines use a prefilter in addition to the main fuel filter, since even the minutest particle of dirt will clog the injection system.

Some diesel injection pumps have a manually operated delivery pump (1)

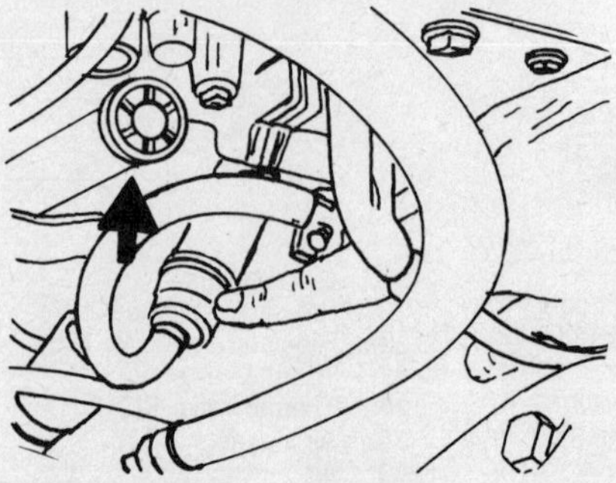

Diesel engines use a pre-filter in addition to the main fuel filter. The arrow indicates the hard operated delivery pump

The prefilter is located in the line just before it enters the injection pump.

To replace it, simply unscrew the clamps on each end and remove the old filter. Install a new filter and bleed the system (see Main Fuel Filter).

Fuel Pump Strainer (Carbureted Engines)

Plunger type fuel pumps on carbureted engines use a strainer located behind the cover.

1. Disconnect and plug the fuel line at the pump.
2. Remove the center screw and remove the cover. A small amount of fuel will run out.
3. Replace the strainer, gasket, screw and aluminum washer, all of which are part of the replacement kit.
4. Replace the cover. There are assembly marks on the cover and fuel pump body.
5. Reconnect the fuel line. Start the engine and check for leaks.

Mechanical Fuel Pump

All Mercedes-Benz carbureted engines use a diaphragm type fuel pump, which is mounted on the side of the block. It is operated by a gear driven eccentric shaft through a rocker arm on the fuel pump.

REMOVAL AND INSTALLATION

1. Clean the joint around the fuel pump base and cylinder block.
2. One at a time, remove and plug the intake and outlet lines from the fuel pump.
3. Unbolt the retaining bolts and remove the fuel pump and gasket from the cylinder block.
4. Clean the mating surfaces of the engine and cylinder block.
5. Install a new gasket.
6. Insert the fuel pump into the block and install the retaining bolts. Be sure that the bolts are tightened evenly.
7. Reconnect the intake and outlet lines to the fuel pump.
8. Run the engine and check for leaks.

TESTING DELIVERY PRESSURE

1. Remove the wire from the coil to prevent starting.

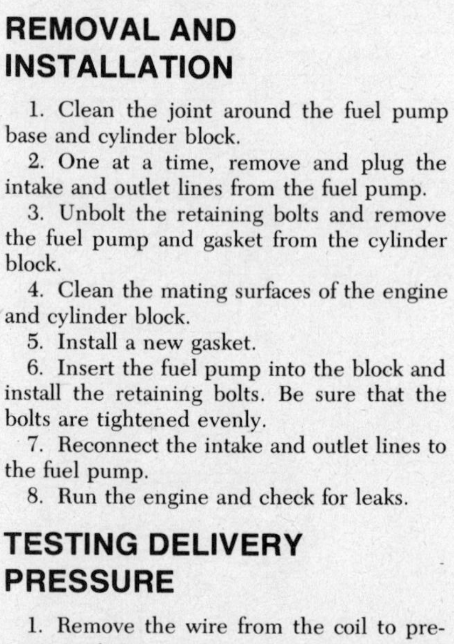

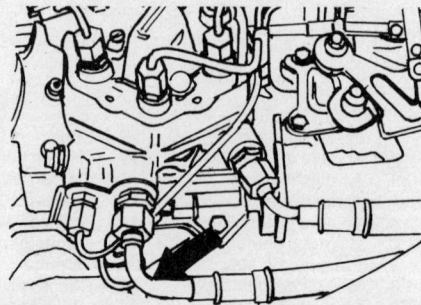

Testing fuel pump pressure, 1976 and later

2. Connect a pressure gauge into the output line of the fuel pump.

3. Crank the engine and read the delivery pressure on the pressure gauge. The pressure should be a constant 1.5-2.5 psi.

4. If the pressure is not within specifications or is erratic, remove the pump for service or for replacement with a new or rebuilt unit. No adjustment is provided.

Electric Fuel Pump

NOTE: Do not confuse the electric fuel pump with the injection pump.

All Mercedes-Benz fuel injected engines are equipped with electric fuel pumps. The electric fuel pump is located underneath the rear floor panel. The fuel return line was also eliminated and a check ball installed in its place. Beginning in 1980, the fuel pump uses a replaceable check valve on the outside of the pump which can be replaced separately.

Two types of fuel pumps have been used. One, the large pump, has been replaced with a new small design which has a bypass system to prevent vapor lock.

REMOVAL AND INSTALLATION

1. Jack the left rear of the car and support it on jack stands. This will provide sufficient working clearance.
2. Remove and plug the intake, outlet and bypass lines from the pump.
3. Disconnect the electrical leads.
4. Unbolt and remove the fuel pump and vibration pads.
5. Install the fuel pump in the reverse order of removal. Be sure that the electrical leads are connected to the proper terminals. The negative wire (brown) is connected to the negative terminal (brown plastic plate) and the positive wire (black/red) is connected to the positive terminal (red plastic plate). If the terminals are reversed, the pump will operate in the reverse direction of normal rotation and will deliver no fuel.

TESTING FUEL PUMP DELIVERY PRESSURE

1975

1. Reduce the pressure in the ring line by pulling the plug on the starting valve. Connect the terminals of the starting valve to the positive and negative terminals of the battery for about 20 seconds. Reconnect the plug to the starting valve.
2. Remove the air filter and connect a pressure gauge at the branch connection of the ring line.
3. Run the engine at idle speed and measure the pressure in the ring line. The pressure should be 28.0-29.5 psi.
4. Stop the engine. The pressure may drop to 25 psi. Wait another five minutes and the pressure may drop to 22 psi. This is normal.
5. The pressure may drop uniformly to 0 psi. This indicates that there is a leak somewhere in the system.

1976 and Later

Remove the fuel return hose from the fuel distributor. Connect a fuel line and hold the end in a measuring cup. Disconnect the plug from the safety switch on the mixture regulator and turn on the ignition for 30 seconds. If the delivery rate is less than 1 liter in 30 seconds, check the voltage at the fuel pump (11.5) and the fuel lines for kinks. Disconnect the leak off line between the fuel accumulator and the suction damper. Check the delivery rate again. If it is low replace the accumulator.

Replace the fuel filter and test again. If still low, replace the fuel pump.

Carburetors

Carburetor Applications

Model	Year	Carburetor
220	1973	1 Stromberg 175 CDT
230	1974-78	
280	1973-76	1 Solex 4A1
280C	1973-76	
280S	1975-76	

REMOVAL AND INSTALLATION

Stromberg 175CDT (1975-78 230)

1. Remove the air cleaner.
2. Remove and plug the fuel lines.

CAUTION

Do not pull off the fuel lines. They should be pried off along with the securing discs.

3. Disconnect the control linkage.
4. Remove the vacuum lines.
5. Disconnect the water hoses for the automatic choke.
6. Disconnect the leads for the automatic choke and fuel shut-off valve.
7. Remove the carburetor retaining nuts and remove the carburetor.
8. Installation is the reverse of removal. Adjust the carburetor. See "Tune-Up".

Solex 4 A 1 (280, 280C and 280S)

1. Remove the air filter.
2. Remove the electric cable from the starter cover and cut-off valves.
3. Remove the vacuum lines.
4. To prevent corrosion from leaked coolant, cover the starter housing with a rag. Release the pressure in the cooling system by cracking the radiator cap until pressure has escaped. Install and tighten the radiator cap. Remove and plug the coolant water hoses from the carburetor.
5. Remove and plug the fuel lines.

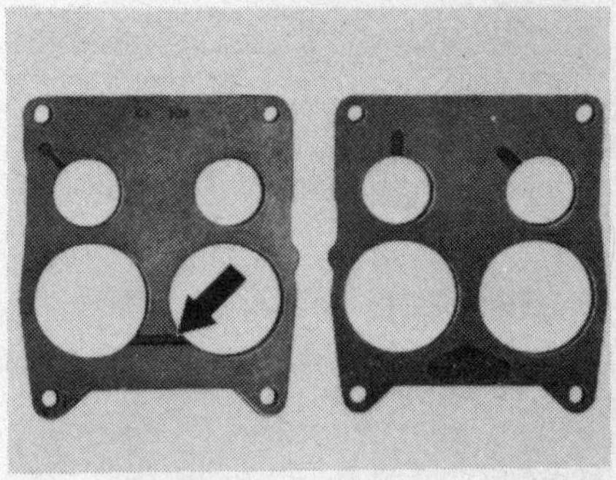

New style gasket on Solex 4A1 beginning 1974. The top is shown on the left and the bottom on the right

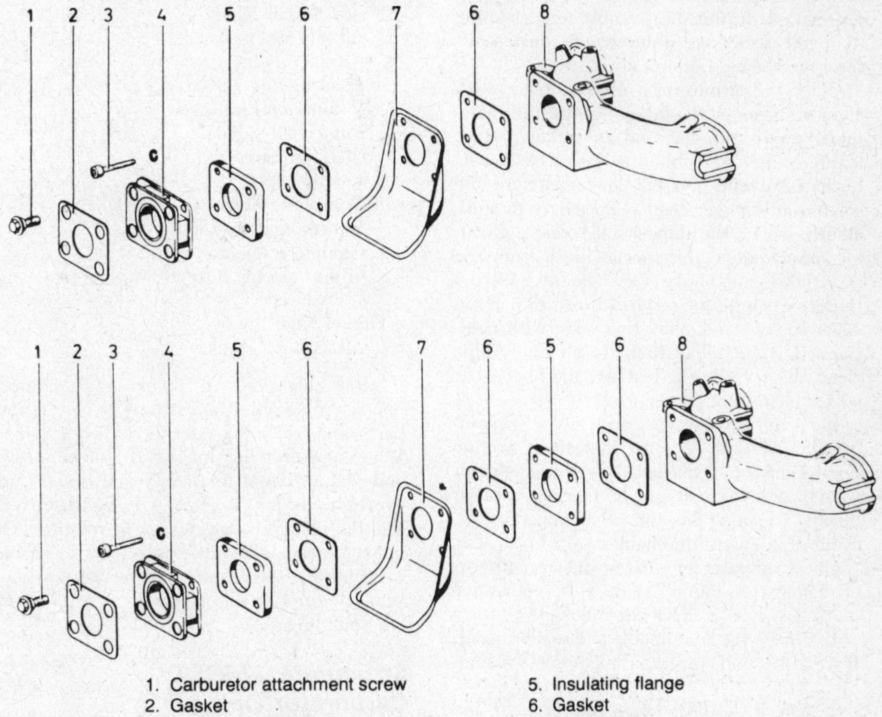

1. Carburetor attachment screw
2. Gasket
3. Rubber flange fastening screw
4. Rubber flange
5. Insulating flange
6. Gasket
7. Shielding plate
8. Intake pipe

Stromberg 175 CDT carburetor gaskets

Install the gasket on a Solex 4A1 carburetor with the mark as shown (lower left corner)

6. Remove the retaining nuts and remove the carburetor from the manifold.

7. Installation is the reverse of removal. Install the insulating flange on the intake manifold as shown. The paper side of the insulating flange must face UP. In 1974, a new style insulating flange was used, which can be installed on previous engines.

8. Install the retaining nuts and tighten evenly, torquing the nuts in a crossing pattern. Torque the nuts to 7-11 ft/lbs.

9. Be sure to adjust the idle speed. See "Tune-Up".

OVERHAUL

Efficient carburetion depends greatly on careful cleaning and inspection during overhaul. Since dirt, gum, water or varnish in or on the carburetor parts are often responsible for poor performance.

Overhaul your carburetor in a clean, dust-free area. Carefully disassemble the carburetor, referring often to the exploded views. Keep all similar and lookalike parts segregated during disassembly and cleaning to avoid accidental interchange during assembly. Make a note of all jet sizes.

When the carburetor is disassembled, wash all parts (except diaphragms, electric choke units, pump plunger, and any other plastic, leather, fiber or rubber parts) in clean carburetor solvent. Do not leave parts in the solvent any longer than is necessary to sufficiently loosen the deposits. Excessive cleaning may remove the special finish from the float bowl and choke valve bodies, leaving these parts unfit for service. Rinse all parts in clean solvent and blow them dry with compressed air or allow them to air dry. Wipe clean all cork, plastic, leather, and fiber parts with a clean, lint-free cloth.

Blow out all passages and jets with compressed air and be sure that there are no restrictions or blockages. Never use wire or similar tools to clean jets, fuel passages, or air bleeds. Clean all jets and valves separately to avoid accidental interchange.

Check all parts for wear or damage. If wear or damage is found, replace the defective parts. Especially check the following:

1. Check the float needle and seat for wear. If wear is found, replace the complete assembly.

2. Check the float hinge pin for wear and the float(s) for dents or distortion. Replace the float if fuel has leaked into it.

3. Check the throttle and choke shaft bores for wear or an out-of-round condition. Damage or wear to the throttle arm, shaft or shaft bore will often require replacement of the throttle body. These parts require a close tolerance of fit; wear may allow air leakage, which could affect starting and idling.

NOTE: Throttle shafts and bushings are not included in overhaul kits. They can be purchased separately.

4. Inspect the idle mixture adjusting needles for burrs or grooves. Any such condition requires replacement of the needle, since you will not be able to obtain a satisfactory idle.

5. Test the accelerator pump check valves. They should pass air one way but not the other. Test for proper seating by blowing and sucking on the valve. Replace the valve if necessary. If the valve is satisfactory, wash the valve again to remove breath moisture.

6. Check the bowl cover for warped surfaces with a straightedge.

7. Closely inspect the valves and seats for wear and damage, replacing as necessary.

8. After the carburetor is assembled, check the choke valve for freedom of operation.

Carburetor overhaul kits are recommended for each overhaul. These kits contain all gaskets and new parts to replace those that deteriorate most rapidly. Failure to replace all parts supplied with the kit (especially gaskets) can result in poor performance later.

Some carburetor manufacturers supply overhaul kits of three basic types: minor repair; major repair; and gasket kits. Basically, they contain the following:

Minor Repair Kits:
- All gaskets
- Float needle valve
- Volume control screw
- All diaphragms
- Spring for the pump diaphragm

Major Repair Kits:
- All jets and gaskets
- All diaphragms
- Float needle valve
- Volume control screw
- Pump ball valve
- Main jet carrier
- Float
- Complete intermediate rod
- Intermediate pump lever
- Complete injector tube
- Some cover hold-down screws and washers

Gasket Kits:
- All gaskets

After cleaning and checking all components, reassemble the carburetor, using new parts and referring to the exploded view. When reassembling, make sure that all screws and jets are tight in their seats, but do not overtighten, as the tips will be distorted. Tighten all screws gradually, in rotation. Do not tighten needle valves into their seats; uneven jetting will result. Always use new gaskets. Be sure to adjust the float level when reassembling.

Stromberg 175CDT Carburetor Only

The preceding information applies to Stromberg carburetors also, but the following, additional suggestions should be followed.

1. Soak the small cork gaskets (jet gland washers) in penetrating oil or hot water for at least a half-hour prior to assembly, or they will invariably split.

2. When the jet is fully assembled, the jet tube should be a close fit without any lateral play, but it should be free to move smoothly. A few drops of oil or polishing of the tube may be necessary to achieve this.

3. If the jet sealing ring washer is made of cork soak it in hot water for a minute or two prior to installation.

4. Adjust the float height.

5. Center the jet so that the piston will fall freely (when raised) and seat with a distinct click. If the jet is not centered properly, it will hang up in the tube.

STROMBERG 175CDT ADJUSTMENTS

Damper Fluid Level

1. Unscrew the top of the damper and check the fluid level.

2. If necessary, top up the reservoir with engine oil, or in cold weather, automatic transmission fluid (ATF). 1975-78 models use only ATF.

3. The fluid level should be to the top edge of the piston ring or on 1975-77 models, to the lower edge of the filler plug threads.

4. Replace the top of the reservoir.

Float Adjustment

1. Remove the carburetor.

2. Remove the float chamber cover and idling speed cut-off valve.

3. Do not loosen the lock screw from the needle, or the needle will have to be recentered.

4. Remove the fuel nozzle and compensating element.

5. Push the float down until the float needle valve ball is fully pushed in.

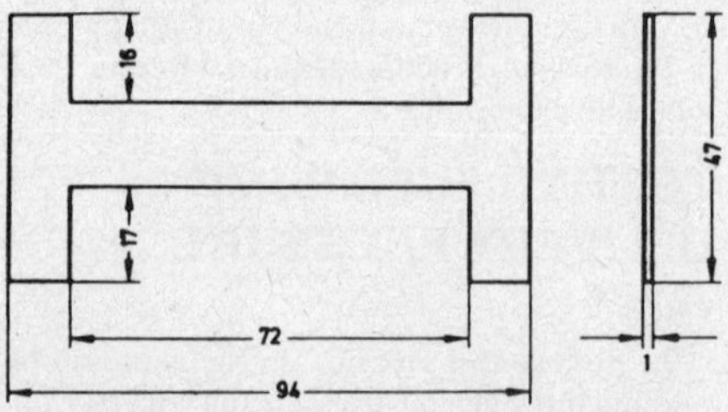

Home-made gauge for measuring Stromberg 175 CDT float level (dimensions in mm)

6. Check the float level with a homemade gauge.

7. To correct the float level, bend the float arm at the tang over the needle valve. The float arm must always remain perpendicular to the needle valve. Also, check the sealing ring under the needle valve for specified thickness (1.5 mm) and replace if necessary.

8. Replace the float chamber cover and install the carburetor.

9. Adjust the idle.

Automatic Choke

1. The idle should be set and the engine should be at normal operating temperature.

1. Carburetor housing
2. Tickler
3. Compression spring
4. Locking spring
5. Gasket
6. Water connection cover
7. Screw
8. Idling speed adjusting screw
9. Spring washer
10. Throttle valve lever
11. Spring washer
12. Actuating lever
13. Lockwasher
14. Nut
15. Gasket for starter housing
16. Starter housing
17. Screw
18. Starter cover
19. Rubber sealing ring
20. Water connection
21. Aluminum sealing ring
22. Screw
23. Insulating seal
24. Screw
25. Screw
26. Connecting rod (compl.)
27. Draw spring
28. Diaphragm for fuel return valve
29. Spring plate
30. Compression spring
31. Valve cover
32. Vacuum hose
33. Countersunk head screw
34. Guide bushing for fuel nozzle (pressed-in)
35. Rubber sealing ring
36. Temperature-controlled compensating element with fuel nozzle
37. Compression spring
38. Idling speed shutoff valve
39. Float needle valve
40. Sealing ring
41. Bracket for float shaft
42. Snap-ring
43. Screw
44. Float shaft
45. Float
46. Air piston
47. Screw
48. Vacuum diaphragm
49. Gasket for float chamber
50. Float chamber
51. Nozzle needle
52. Stud for attaching nozzle needle
53. Compression spring
54. Carburetor cover
55. Screw
56. Washer
57. Cheese head screw
58. Damper for air piston
59. Washer
60. Damper piston
61. Locking spring
62. Capillary pipe
63. Spring clip
64. Rubber sealing ring
65. Closing cover
66. Screw
67. Damper oil filler plug
68. Vacuum box with fastening elements
69. Vacuum hose
70. Screw
71. Snap-ring
72. Washer
73. Grounding cable
74. Rubber closing cap
75. Holding disc
76. Cheese head screw
77. Compression spring
78. Adjusting nut
79. Thrust bolt

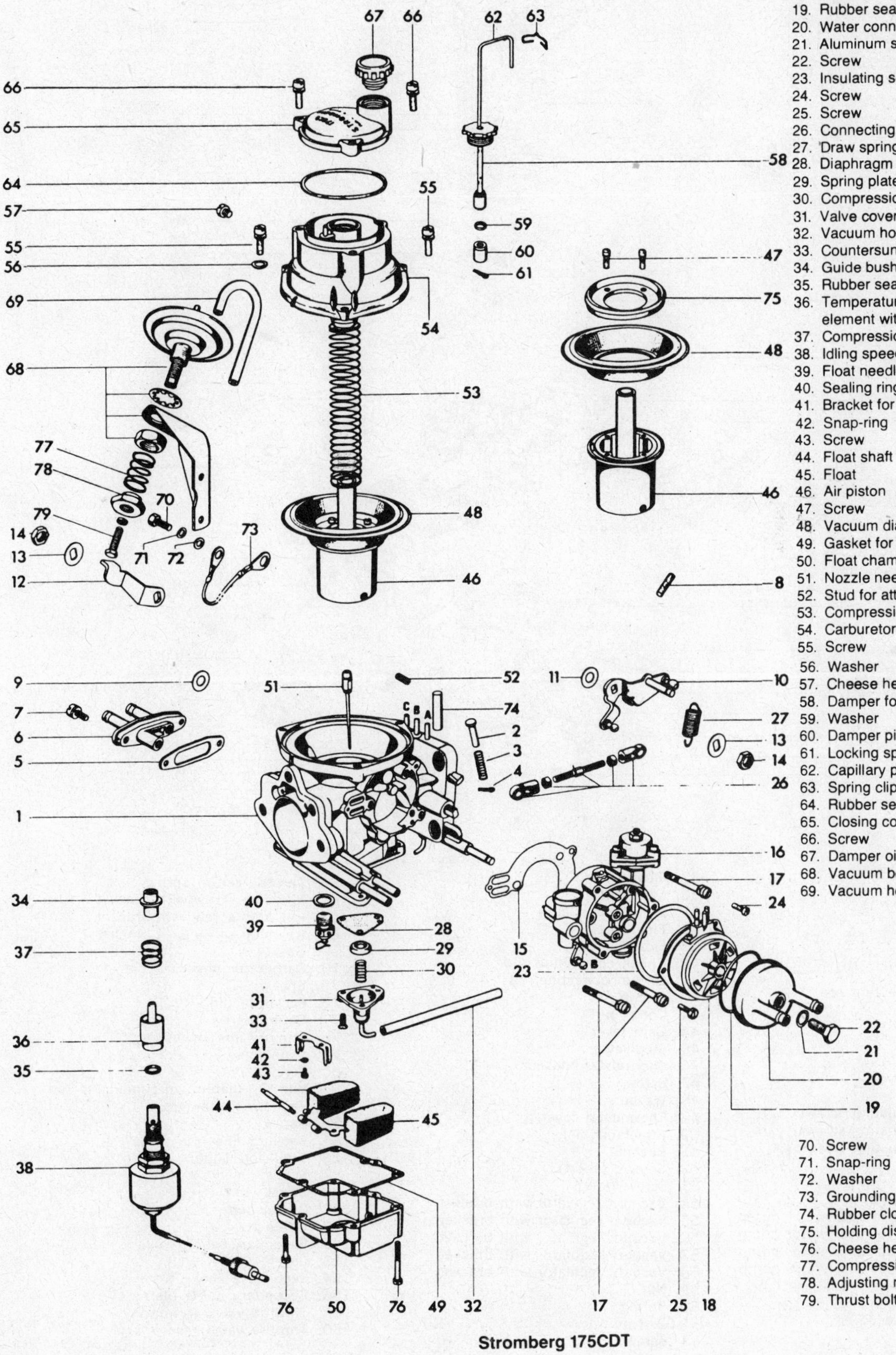

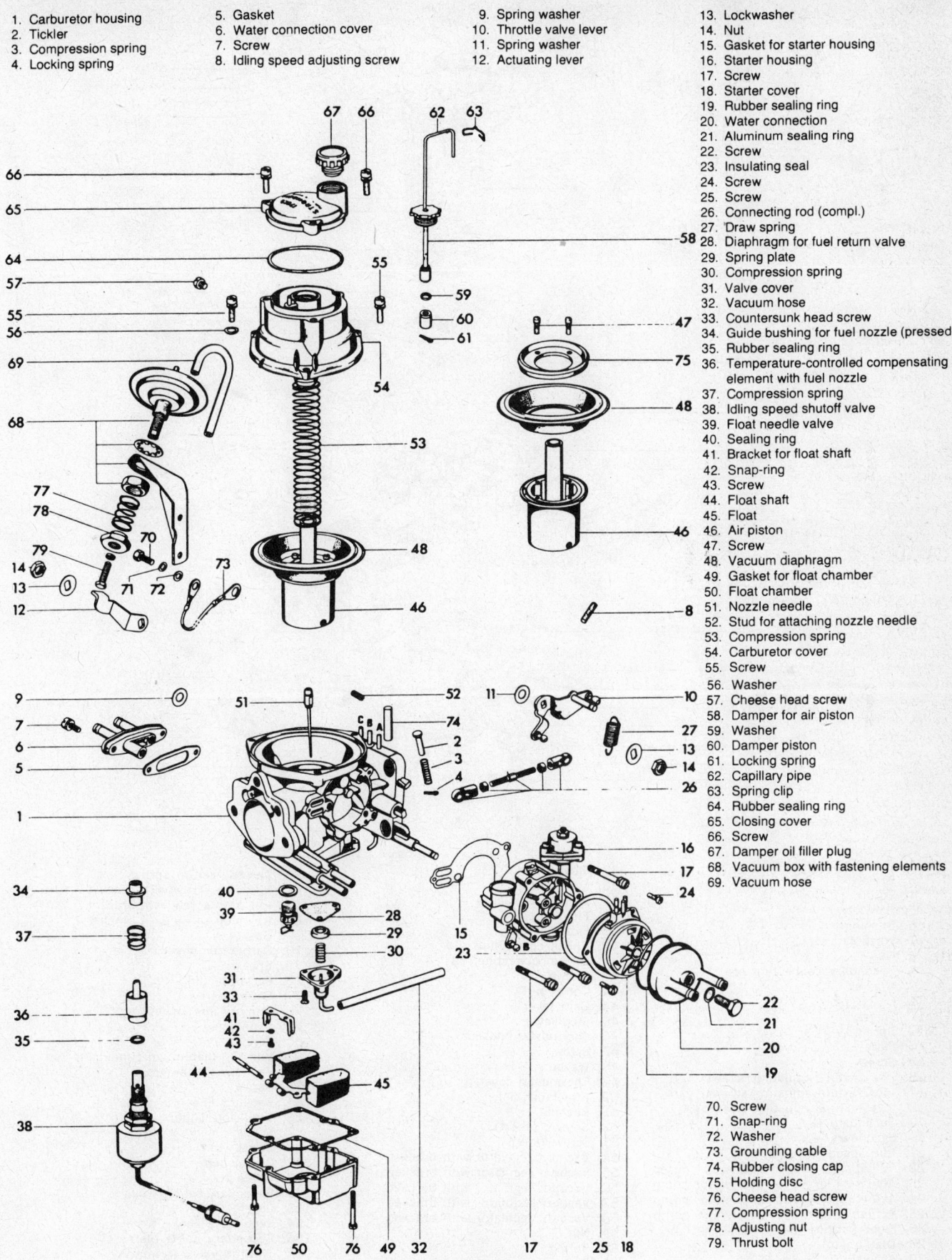

Stromberg 175CDT

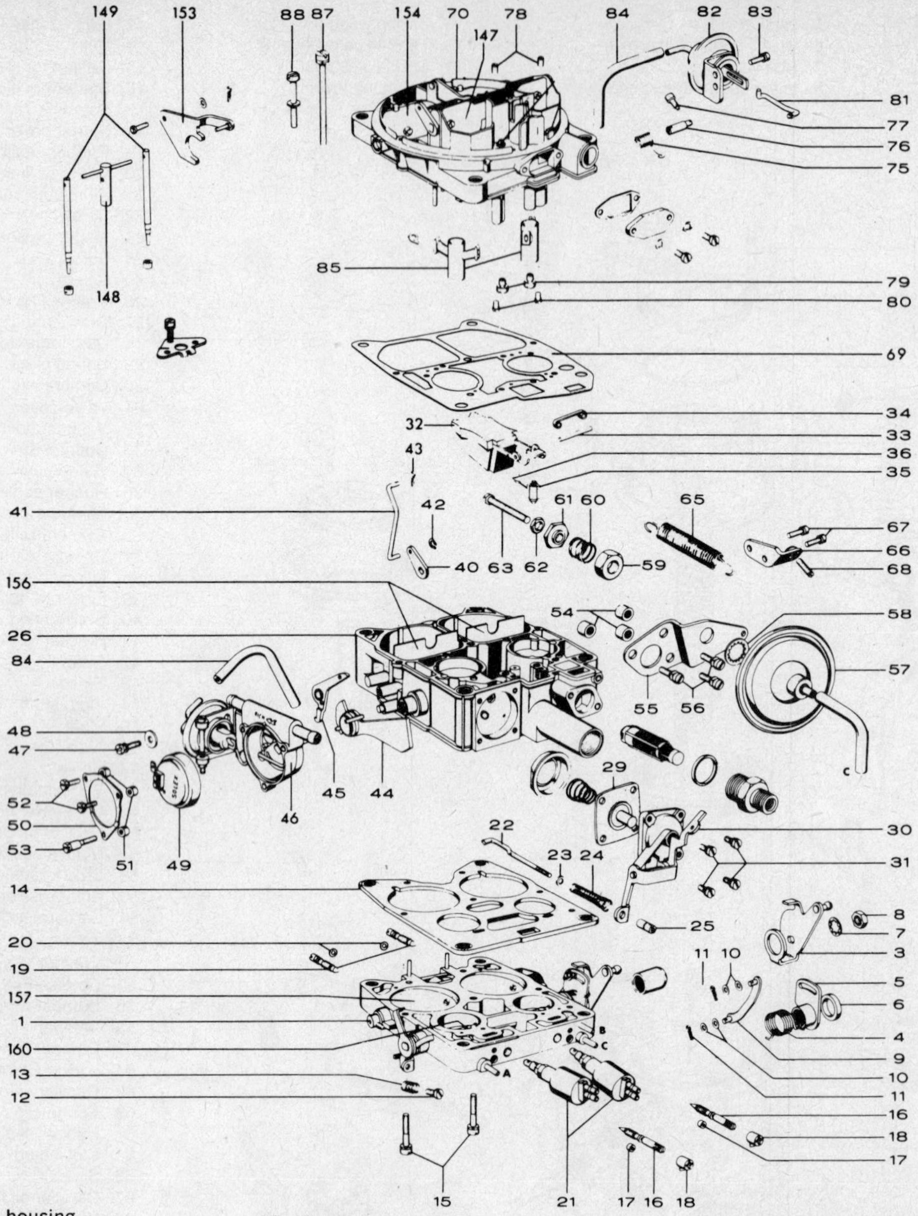

1. Throttle valve housing
3. Bracket
4. Spring
5. Cam lever
6. Bushing
7. Washer
8. Nut
9. Secondary connecting rod
10. Washer
11. Cotter pin
12. Screw
13. Spring
14. Plate
15. Screw
16. Idle mixture adjusting screws
17. Idle mixture adjusting screws
18. Idle mixture adjusting screws
19. Secondary jets
20. Secondary jets
21. Idle speed solenoid
22. Actuating levers for accelerator pump
23. Actuating levers for accelerator pump
24. Actuating levers for accelerator pump
25. Actuating levers for accelerator pump
26. Float housing
29. Diaphragm
30. Accelerator pump cover
31. Screws
32. Float
33. Float shaft
34. Hold-down clamp
35. Float needle
36. Float needle
40. Choke connecting rod
41. Choke connecting rod
42. Circlip
43. Cotter pin
44. Cam lever
45. Step lever
46. Thermostat housing
47. Screw
48. Washer
49. Thermostat cover
50. Attaching plate
51. Bushing
52. Screws (short)
53. Screw (long)
54. Vacuum regulator with bracket
55. Vacuum regulator with bracket
56. Vacuum regulator with bracket
57. Vacuum regulator with bracket
58. Vacuum regulator with bracket
59. Nut
60. Spring
61,62. Nut
63. Screw
65. Throttle return spring
66. Idle stop screw with bracket
67. Idle stop screw with bracket
68. Idle stop screw with bracket
69. Gasket
70. Carburetor cover
75. Spring
76. Eccentric pin
77. Clamp screw
78. Primary idle air jets
79. Main jets
80. Screws
81. Vacuum diaphragm connecting rod
82. Vacuum diaphragm
83. Screw
84. Vacuum line
85. Emulsion Tube
87. Screw
88. Screw
147. Choke plate
148. Guide pin
149. Secondary needle valve
153. Lever
154. Secondary choke plate
156. Secondary baffle plates
157. Throttle valve (primary)
160. Throttle valve (secondary)

Solex 4A1 carburetor

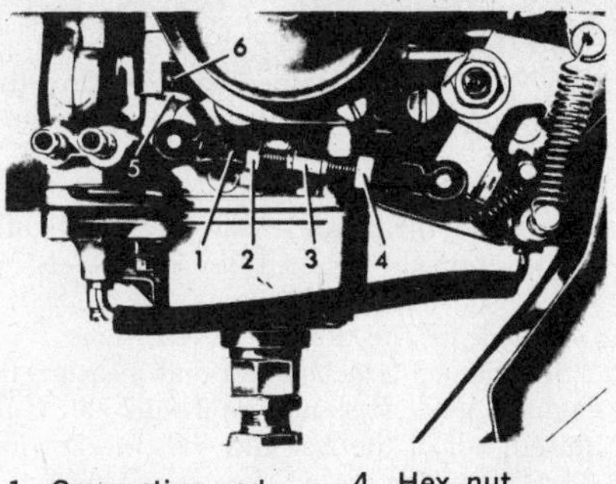

1. Connecting rod
2. Hex nut
3. Threaded bolt
4. Hex nut
5. Actuating lever
6. Venting valve

Stromberg 175CDT automatic choke adjustment

2. On vehicles with air conditioning, remove the air cleaner and air intake.
3. Check the adjustment of the choke cover. The index marks should be aligned.
4. Raise the throttle linkage slightly and insert a screwdriver through the slot of the starter housing on the carburetor. Push the screwdriver against the engaging lever in the direction of the engine. Release the throttle linkage and engaging lever. This will set the engine at fast idle.
5. The fast idle speed should be 3300-3600 rpm. If the speed requires adjustment, loosen both locknuts on the connecting rod and turn the threaded bolt. ½ turn of the bolt will change the engine rpm by about 200-300 rpm. Decreasing the length of the bolt will decrease rpm and increasing the length will increase rpm.

Fast Idle (1975-78 Only)

The fast idle adjustment is done with the cam on the second step.
1. Run the engine to normal operating temperature.
2. With the engine idling, raise the throttle linkage slightly.
3. At the same time, push the engaging lever with a small screwdriver, through the slot of the choke housing in the direction of the engine, against the stop on the pull down diaphragm rod. Do not force it past the stop.
4. Raise the throttle linkage, while holding the engaging lever against the stop.
5. Check the CO and fast idle.

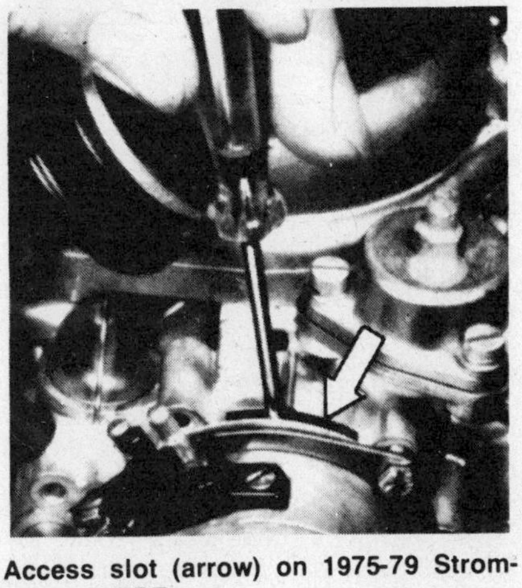

Access slot (arrow) on 1975-79 Stromberg 175CDT

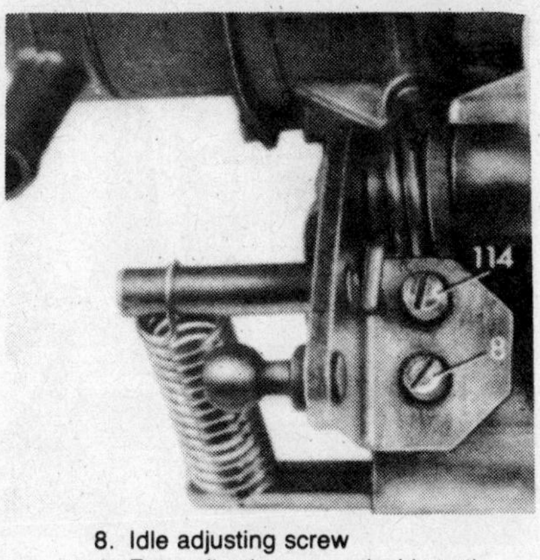

8. Idle adjusting screw
114. Fast adjusting screw (cold start).

Fast idle adjusting screw (114) on 1975-79 Stromberg 175CDT

6. Adjust the fast idle speed with the upper adjusting screw to 1600-1800 rpm.
7. Adjust the CO with the mixture adjusting screw to 5-8%. To check the CO, the center vacuum line for the air injection switchover valve must be disconnected and plugged.

Full Throttle Stop (1975-78 California Only)

1. With the accelerator pedal fully depressed, adjust the full throttle stop screw so that a clearance of .02 in. exists between the throttle valve lever and carburetor housing.

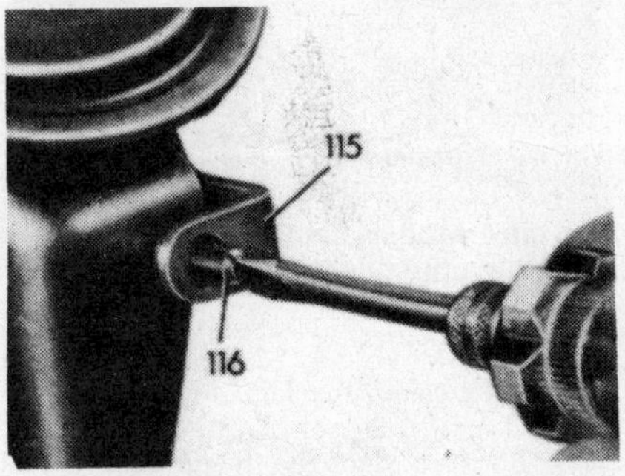

115. Throttle valve lever
116. Full throttle adjusting screw

Full throttle stop adjusting screw

Thermo Air Valve

1. Disconnect the hoses from the thermo air valve and blow into one hose. If the valve is cold, no air can pass through the valve. If the valve is warm (slightly above room temperature) air should pass through the valve.

SOLEX 4A1 ADJUSTMENTS

Fuel Level

1. There is no provision for measuring the fuel level, other than with the special Mercedes-Benz tool. It is a measuring rod which is inserted through the bore of the carburetor cover, and can be purchased from a dealer or fabricated.
2. Run the engine briefly at fast idle and shut off the ignition.
3. Insert the measuring gauge through the bore of the carburetor cover as far as it will go.

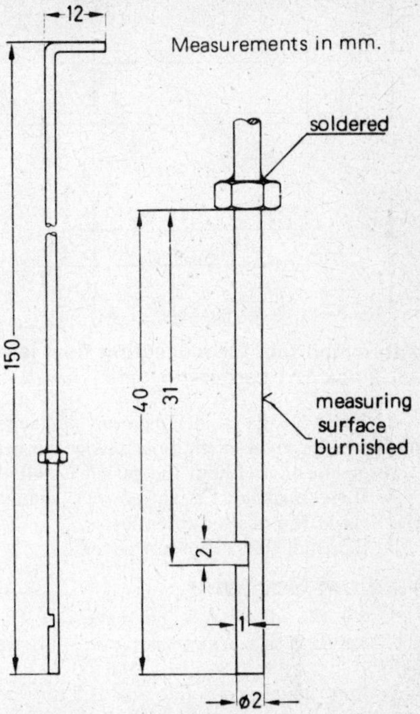

Fabricated tool for measuring fuel level on Solex 4A1 carburetor

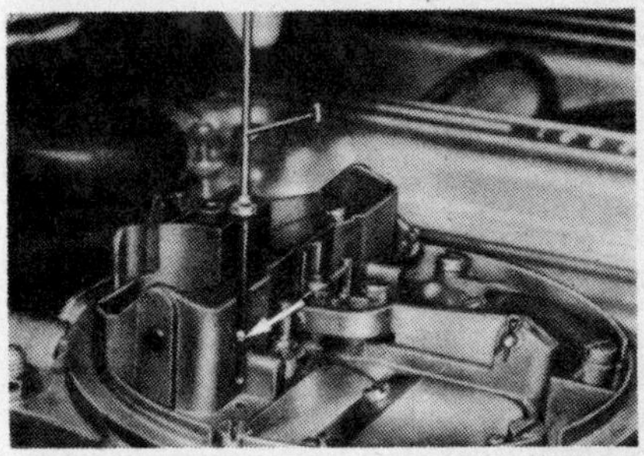

Measuring fuel level on Solex 4A1 carburetor

4. Remove the gauge and read the fuel level. The reading should be within the tolerance range marked on the stick.
5. To adjust the level, remove the carburetor cover and adjust the float by bending it on the hinge.
6. Reinstall the cover and test the level again.

Float Level

1. Remove the carburetor cover. The carburetor does not have to be removed.
2. With the float needle valve installed, push the connecting web of the float arms down until a noticeable stop. Be sure to push at the web. If not, the float shaft will lift from the bottom and result in an incorrect measurement.

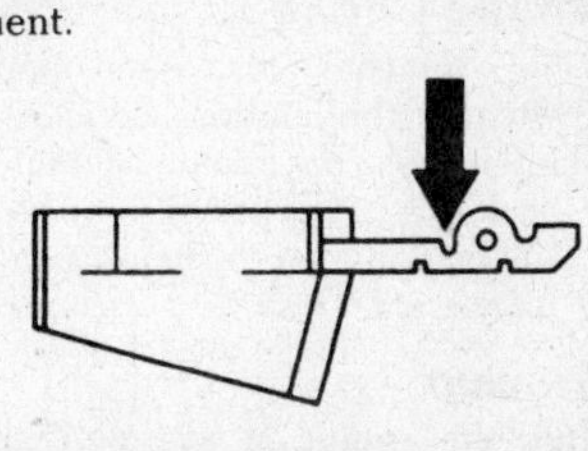

Bend the float at the arrow to adjust the float level on Solex 4A1 carburetor

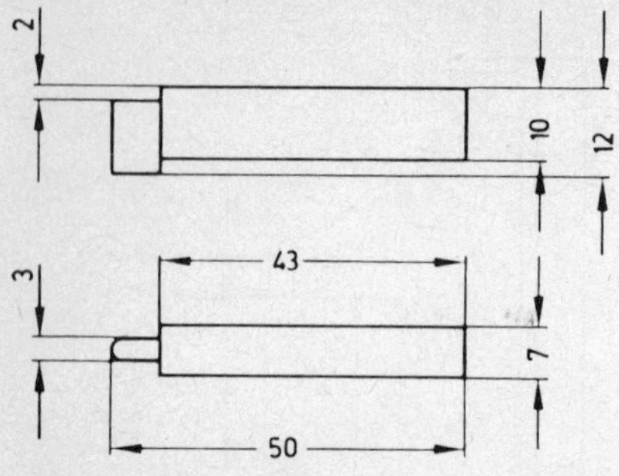

Fabricated tool for measuring float level on Solex 4A1 carburetor

3. Using a T-gauge or a homemade gauge, measure the level of the float below the carburetor housing without the gasket installed.
4. If the float level is not correct, remove the float in the desired direction.
5. Reinstall the carburetor cover.

Vacuum Governor

1. Set the idle speed and make sure that the engine is at normal operating temperature.
2. Run the engine at idle and pull the vacuum hose from the governor.
3. Set the engine speed to approximately 1200-1400 rpm. Loosen the locknut and adjust the rpm with the adjusting screw. Hold the diaphragm rod and turn the adjusting nut.
4. Adjust the compression spring with the transmission in gear.
5. The speed should be 600-700 rpm. If necessary, adjust the compression spring with the adjusting nut.
6. Turn on the air conditioning, and turn the wheels to full lock. The engine should keep running. If it does not, adjust the speed with the adjusting nut again. See Step 3.

3. Throttle valve lever
60. Spring
61. Adjusting nut
62. Counternut
63. Adjuting screw

Vacuum governor adjustment—Solex 4A1

Automatic Choke

1. Check the choke for ease of operation.
2. Switch on the ignition and check to be sure that the choke opens after a minute or so.
3. Check the adjustment on the choke cover. The markings on the housing and cover should be aligned.

Choke Gap

1. Run the engine at idle until the diaphragm in the vacuum unit has been pulled completely against the stop.

Automatic choke adjustment—Solex 4A1. If the choke gap is too large, push the bend apart; if the choke gap is too small, push the bend together

On later models, adjust the choke gap with the adjusting screw (211) located in the housing (210)

2. Then clamp the hose to block all vacuum.
3. Be sure that the diaphragm is still against the stop and slightly raise the throttle valve lever. Position the stepped disc upward against the top stop. Release the throttle valve lever.
4. Push the lever of the bi-metallic spring until the stop is felt. The connecting rod will now be against the stop in the slot of the lever.
5. Measure the choke gap with a drill (0.060 in.-1973-74 Federal; 0.010 in. 1973-74 California; 0.108-0.120 in.-1975-76) between the choke plate and the wall of the air horn.
6. To adjust the gap, remove the coolant hose from the choke housing. Cover the choke housing with a rag and release the pressure in the radiator. Tighten the radiator cap again. Remove the coolant hose and clamp it shut.
7. Hold the connecting rod with a screwdriver. Bend the connecting rod with a second screwdriver. On later models, the adjustment is made by turning the adjusting screw in the choke housing cover in (decrease gap) or out (increase gap).
8. While making the adjustment, be sure that the diaphragm in the vacuum unit is still against its stop.

Fast Idle

1. Adjust the idle speed and be sure that the engine is at normal operating temperature.
2. Run the engine at idle speed.
3. Raise the throttle valve lever slightly and position the stepped disc completely upward against the top stop.
4. Release the throttle valve lever.
5. Connect a tachometer and measure the engine speed. It should be 2400-2600. If required, adjust the fast idle with the fast idle speed adjusting screw.

Solex 4A1 fast idle adjustment

Accelerator Pump

1. Move the throttle valve lever several times. A strong jet of fuel should be forced out of the fuel outlets.
2. If not, remove the accelerator pump cover and check the diaphragm. Blow out the ducts with compressed air.
3. Install the accelerator pump cover.
4. If there still is no fuel from the injection tube, remove the carburetor cover.
5. Actuate the accelerator pump. If fuel emerges from the ball valves, blow out the injection holes in the carburetor cover with compressed air.
6. Install the carburetor cover. Tighten the screws evenly to 11 ft/lbs.

Solex 4A1 accelerator pump adjustment

Fuel Return Valve

1. Pull the fuel return hose from the connection to the return line below the fuel pump.
2. Hold the return hose in a container and check whether a strong fuel jet comes from the line with the automatic transmission in Drive and the air conditioning on.

Fuel Injection

Several types of fuel injection are used on Mercedes-Benz gasoline engine. Due to the sensitive nature of these systems, and the numerous special tools required, it is best to refer any service or adjustment, other than idle speed adjustment, to a qualified Mercedes-Benz service facility.

CAUTION

Even a seemingly minor adjustment, such as idle speed, can necessitate adjustments to other portions of the fuel injection system. Be extremely careful when adjusting the idle. If any difficulty at all is experienced, immediately refer the vehicle to a Mercedes-Benz dealer. Further attempts at adjustment will only upset the balance of an already delicate system.

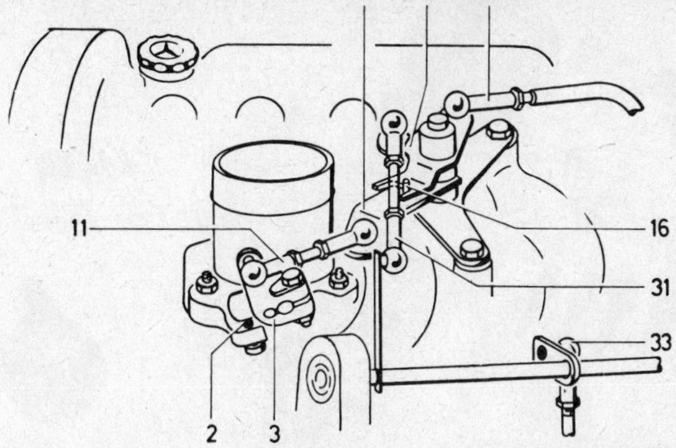

2. Idling speed stop
3. Throttle valve level
11. Connecting rod
13. Control pushrod
14. Regulating lever
15. Regulating lever
16. Stop pin
31. Connecting rod
33. Pushrod

Electronic fuel injection regulating linkage

BOSCH ELECTRONIC FUEL INJECTION–1975 V8 ENGINES

This system is a constant pressure, electronically controlled unit. The "brain" of the system, actually a small computer that senses the determining factors for fuel delivery, is located behind the passenger kick panel on the right-hand side.

A Bosch tester is necessary to accurately test the solid state circuitry and components, but there are a few checks that can be carried out independently of the tester.

Tests

DELIVERY PRESSURE

See "Testing the Fuel Pump Delivery Pressure" under Fuel Pump earlier in this section.

Adjustments

FUEL PRESSURE

The fuel pressure can be adjusted on the regulator with the adjusting screw. Adjust to 28 psi. If a slight turn of the screw shows no change of pressure replace the regulator.

Before replacing the regulator or removing the pressure gauge, reduce the pressure in the ring line by unplugging the starting valve and connecting it to battery voltage for 20 seconds.

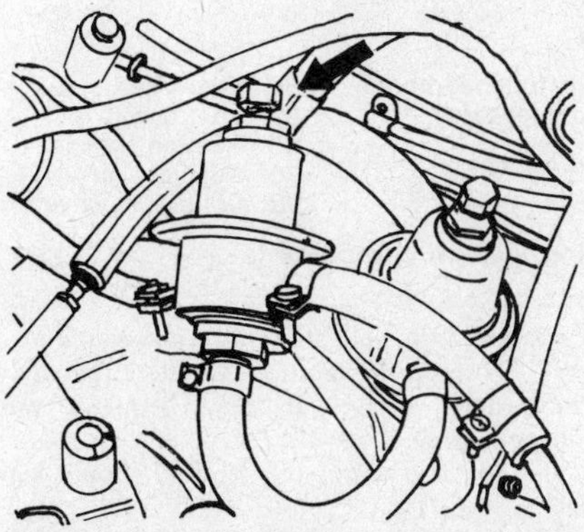

Electronic fuel injection pressure regulator adjusting screw

REGULATING SHAFT

Step on the accelerator pedal up to the kickdown. The regulating lever should rest against the fuel throttle stop of the valve.

Loosen the hex bolt and push the linkage up to the full throttle stop if adjustment is required.

REGULATING LINKAGE

1. Check the linkage for ease of operation.
2. Check that the throttle valve closes completely. Disconnect the regulating rods.
3. Adjust the pushrod to a length of 4 in. from the center of the rubber mount to the center of the ball socket and attach.

On vehicles with manual transmission:

4. Adjust the connecting rod to a length of 3.5 in. (4.1 in. for cars with gate shift lever with bore next to ball head) and attach it.
5. Push the throttle lever against the idle speed stop. Adjust the connecting rod so that the regulating lever rests with the roller against the end stop of the gate shift lever.

On cars with automatic transmission and no gate shift lever:

6. Adjust the connecting rod (31) to 4.2 in. and the connecting rod (11) to 2.7 in. and attach.
7. Push the control rod to the rear against the stop and attach it tension free. During adjustment of the control pushrod, the ball socket must be held next to the ball head.

On cars with automatic transmission and gate shift lever:

8. Adjust the connecting rod to 4.2 in. and attach.
9. Push the throttle valve lever against the idle speed stop. Adjust the connecting rod so that the regulating lever rests with the roller against the end stop of the gate lever. Push the regulating lever to the rear against the stop pin.
10. Push the control pushrod against the stop and connect it tension free. The ball socket must be held next to the ball head.

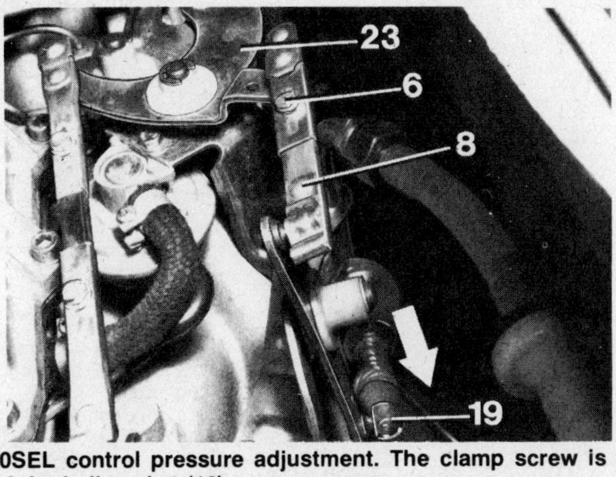

380SEL control pressure adjustment. The clamp screw is (6) and the ball socket (19)

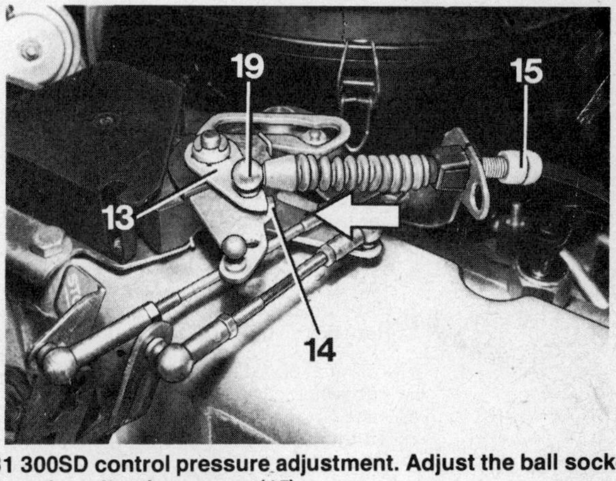

1981 300SD control pressure adjustment. Adjust the ball socket (19) at the adjusting screw (15)

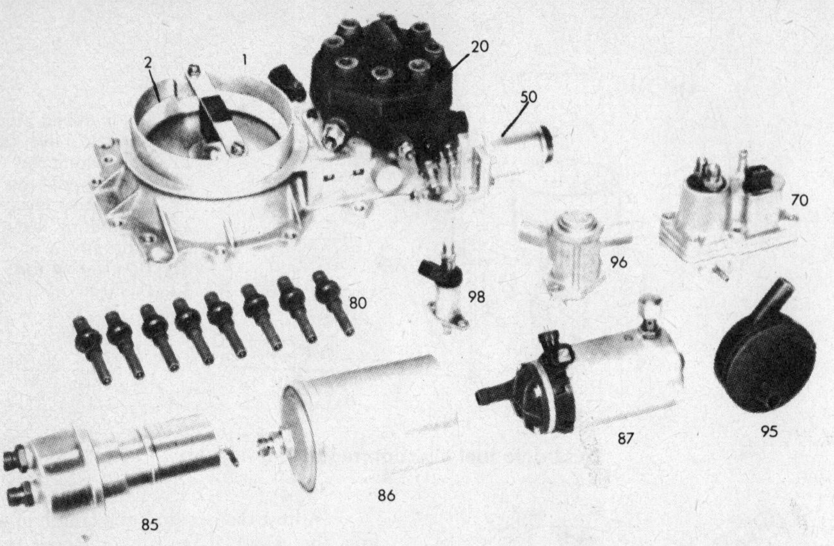

1. Mixture regulator assembly
2. Airflow sensor
20. Fuel distributor
50. Hot-start solenoid
70. Warm-up/full-load enrichment compensator
80. Injection nozzles
85. Fuel accumulator
86. Fuel filter
87. Fuel pump
95. Suction damper
96. Auxiliary air valve
98. Cold-start valve

Air Flow Controlled injection system components

CIS FUEL INJECTION 1976-81

This system replaces the electronic system of earlier years. In contrast to the intermittent type fuel injection, this system measures air volume through and air flow sensor and injects fuel continuously in front of the intake valves, regardless of firing position.

Testing–1976-81

DELIVERY CAPACITY

See "Testing Fuel Pump Output" under Fuel Pump earlier in this section.

COLD START VALVE

1. Disconnect the plugs from the safety switch and mixture control regulator.
2. Remove the cold start valve with fuel line connected.
3. Hold the cold start valve in a container.
4. Turn on the ignition. Connect the valve to battery voltage. It should emit a cone shaped spray.
5. Dry the nozzle off. No fuel should leak out.

HOT START SYSTEM

Perform the test at coolant temperature 104°-122° F.

1. Remove the coil wire.
2. Connect a voltmeter to hot start terminal 3 and ground.
3. Actuate the starter. In approximately 3-4 seconds, the voltmeter should read about 11 volts for 3-4 seconds.
4. If 11 volts are not indicated, check fuse 10. Connect the plug of the 104° F temperature switch and ground and repeat the test. If 11 volts are now indicated, replace the temperature switch. If 11 volts are not indicated, or if the time periods are wrong, replace the hot start relay.

FUEL PUMP SAFETY CIRCUIT

The pump will only run if the starter motor is actuated or if the engine is running.

1. Remove the air filter.
2. Turn on the ignition and briefly depress the sensor plate.
3. Remove the coil wire from the distributor.
4. Connect a voltmeter to the positive fuel pump terminal and ground.
5. Actuate the starter. Voltmeter should indicate 11 volts.
6. If the fuel pump runs only when the sensor plate is depressed or only when the engine is cranked, replace the fuel pump relay. If the pump is already running when the ignition is turned ON, replace the safety switch.

Adjustments–1976-79

CONTROL LINKAGE

1. Check the control linkage for ease of operation.
2. Disconnect the control rod. The throttle valve should rest against the idle stop. Reconnect the control rod.
3. Adjust the control rod so that the roller rests tension free in the gate slot.

FULL THROTTLE STOP

1. With the engine stopped, press the accelerator pedal until it rests against the kickdown switch.
2. The throttle valve lever should rest against the full throttle stop. If necessary, adjust the throttle valve lever.
3. If the full throttle stop is not reached, adjust the control rod (bell crank lever to accelerator pedal) to 4.8 in. (from center to center of ball sockets).
4. Adjust the accelerator pedal linkage if necessary with the fastening screw.

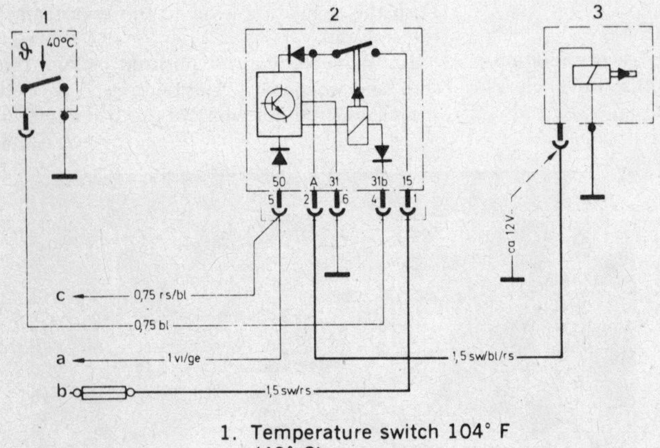

1. Temperature switch 104° F (40° C)
2. Hot-start relay
3. Hot-start solenoid

a. Terminal 50 (starter lock-out switch)
b. Fuse No. 10 (15/54)
c. To thermo-time switch

Hot start wiring schematic

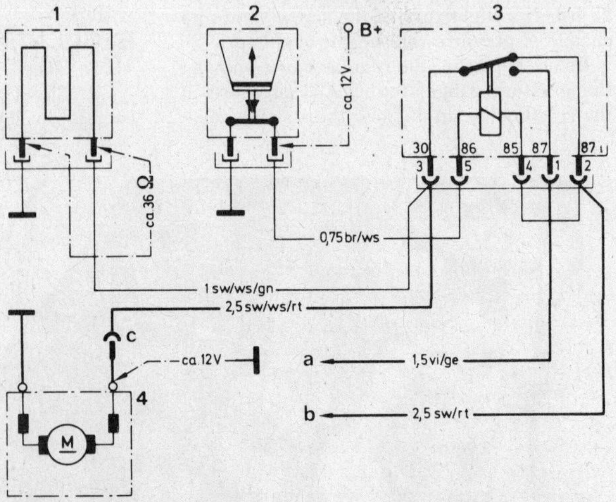

1. Heating coil, warm-up/full-load enrichment compensator
2. Safety switch, sensor plate
3. Relay, fuel pump
4. Fuel pump

a. To terminal 50 (starter)
b. To terminal 15/54 (ignition)
c. To plug connection, tail light harness

Safety circuit wiring schematic

5. Adjust the control pressure rod (at idle) by compressing the adjusting clip, and moving the rod completely to the rear against the stop.

ADJUSTMENTS–1980-81

Throttle Valve Switch

1. Set an ohmmeter to 0-infinity.
2. Check the idle speed stop. Push the throttle valve against the idle speed stop. Connect the ohmmeter across terminals 1 and 2. Rotate the throttle valve switch until the ohmmeter reads 0.
3. Advance the throttle valve slightly. The ohmmeter should read 0-infinite ohms.
4. Check the full throttle stop. Push the throttle valve against the full throttle stop and connect an ohmmeter across terminals 2 and 3. The reading should be 0 ohms.
5. Turn the throttle valve back slightly. A reading of infinite ohms should result.

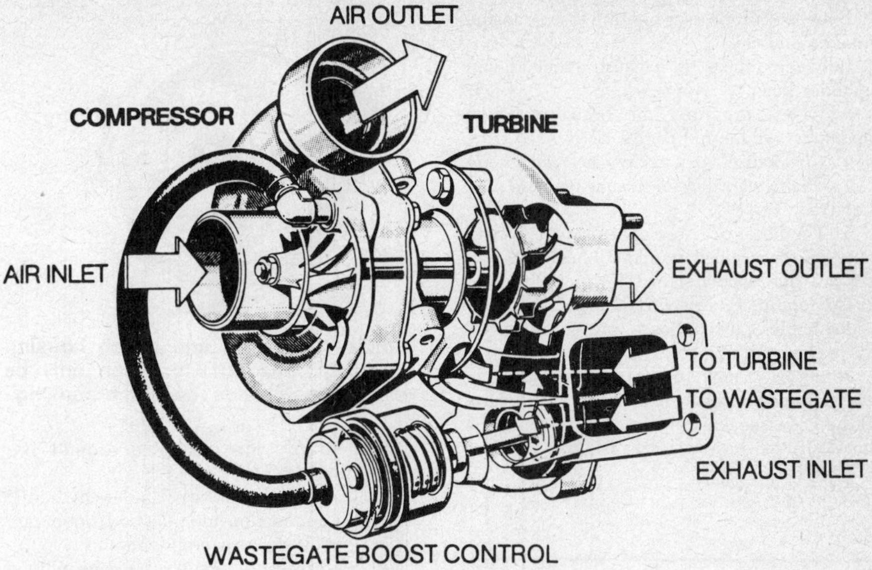

Garret TA0301 turbocharger operation

Turbocharger–300SD and 300TD (1981) Only

NOTE: There is no particular maintenance associated with the turbocharger. It should also be noted that a turbocharger cannot be installed on an engine that was not meant for one, without incuring serious engine damage.

The exhaust gas turbocharger is a Garret Model TA 0301. It uses the aerodynamic energy of the exhaust gases to drive a centrifugal compressor which in turn delivers high pressure air to the cylinders of the diesel engine. The turbine wheel and the compressor wheel are mounted on a common shaft. The turbocharger is mounted between the exhaust manifold and the exhaust pipe. For lubrication and cooling, the turbocharger is connected directly to the engine lubrication system.

A boost pressure control valve (wastegate valve) is attached to the turbine housing to insure that a certain boost pressure is not exceeded. Should the boost pressure control valve malfunction, an engine overload protection system will prevent a failure of the engine.

OPERATION

Turbocharger

The exhaust gases of the engine are routed via the exhaust manifold directly into the turbine housing (6) and to the turbine wheel (7). The velocity of the exhaust gases causes the turbine wheel (7) to turn. This turns the compessor wheel (2) which is directly connected to the turbine wheel via the shaft (5). The turbocharger can obtain a maximum of approximately 100,000 rpm; the fresh air drawn in by the compressor wheel is compressed and delivered to the pistons of the engine.

At idle speed, the engine operates as a naturally aspirated engine. With increasing load and engine rpm, (increasing velocity of the exhaust gases), the turbine wheel (7) accelerates and boost pressure is produced by the compressor wheel (2). The boost pressure is routed via the intake manifold to the individual cylinders.

The exhaust gases produced by the combustion are routed into the turbine housing and from there into the exhaust pipe.

Boost Pressure Control Valve

In order not to exceed the designed boost pressure, a boost pressure control valve (8) is installed on the turbine housing (6). The boost pressure is picked up at the compressor housing (1) and connected to the boost pressure control valve (8) via a connecting hose (9). If the maximum permissible boost pressure is obtained, the boost pressure control valve (8) starts to open the bypass canal (c) for the exhaust gas around the turbine wheel (7). A part of the exhaust gas flows now directly into the exhaust pipe. This keeps the boost pressure constant and prevents it from increasing beyond its designed limits.

REMOVAL AND INSTALLATION

1. Remove the air filter.
2. Disconnect the electrical cable from the temperature switch.
3. Loosen the lower hose clamp on the air duct that connects the air filter with the compressor housing.
4. Remove the vacuum line and crankcase breather pipe.
5. Remove the air filter and air intake duct.
6. Disconnect the oil line at the turbocharger.
7. Remove the air filter mounting bracket.
8. Disconnect the turbocharger at the exhaust flange.
9. Disconnect and remove the pipe bracket on the automatic transmission.
10. Push the exhaust pipe rearward.
11. Remove the mounting bracket at the intermediate flange.
12. Unbolt and remove the turbocharger.
13. Remove the intermediate flange and oil return line at the turbocharger.
14. Installation is the reverse of removal. Before installing the turbocharger, install the oil return line and intermediate flange. Install the flange gasket between the turbocharger and exhaust manifold with the reinforcing bead toward the exhaust manifold.

Use only heat proof nuts and bolts and fill a new turbocharger with ¼ pint of engine oil through the engine oil supply bore before operating.

1. Mounting bracket
2. Intermediate flange
3. Turbocharger

Remove the mounting nuts (arrow) to remove the turbocharger

TROUBLESHOOTING THE TURBOCHARGER

To properly evaluate the turbocharger, the full throttle stop, maximum no-load engine rpm, start of delivery and opening pressure of the injection nozzles must be within specifications.

Complaint: Poor engine performance
Probable cause: Boost pressure too low
Remedy:

1. Clean air filter and check air intake shroud and duct for obstructions.
2. Check turbocharger for leaks at following points:

Between exhaust manifold and turbine housing; tighten nuts.

Between compressor housing discharge and intake manifold.

Between intake or exhaust manifold and cylinder head.

3. Check pressure line between intake manifold and aneroid compensator.

4. Check fuse No. 4 or the black/red wire at the switchover valve for breaks or loose connection.

5. The boost pressure control valve (wastegate) on the turbocharger should close. If not, replace the turbocharger.

Complaint: Engine surges at full load.

Probable cause: Boost pressure control valve does not open.

Remedy: Check the connecting hose between the compressor housing and wastegate. If the hose is leaking or has a kink, replace the hose. If the hose is OK, replace the turbocharger.

MANUAL TRANSMISSION

The 220D and 240D are the only models imported into the U.S. since 1972 that use a manual transmission. A 4-speed, side cover, model G76/18 4-speed is used on all models, with certain minor modifications.

The transmission should only be removed with the engine as a unit, since the transmission-to-bellhousing bolts can only be reached from the inside. Once the engine/transmission unit has been removed from the vehicle, the transmission and bellhousing must be separated from the engine, as follows:

REMOVAL AND INSTALLATION—WITH ENGINE

See the "Engine" section to remove the engine/transmission.

1. After removing the engine/transmission unit, unbolt the bellhousing from the engine. The bolts which hold the transmission to the bellhousing cannot be reached except from inside the bellhousing.
2. Remove the starter from its mounting position and pull the transmission and bellhousing from the engine.
3. The bolts which secure the bellhousing to the transmission are now visible and can be removed to separate the bellhousing and transmission.
4. To install, connect the engine, bellhousing, and transmission, after coating the splines of the mainshaft with grease.
5. Install the starter.
6. Further installation is the reverse of removal.

REMOVAL AND INSTALLATION—WITHOUT THE ENGINE

1. Support the car on jack stands.
2. Disconnect the battery.
3. Disconnect the exhaust pipe and/or muffler to provide clearance around the bellhousing.

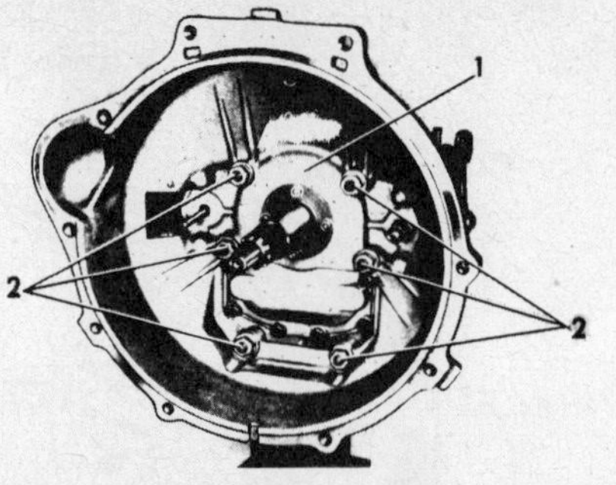

Clutch housing (1) and clutch housing attaching bolts (2) which can only be reached from inside the clutch housing

4. Unhook the slave cylinder hydraulic line at the connection and plug both openings.
5. Unbolt the rear engine mount.
6. Slightly raise the transmission with a jack and remove the lower plate covering the transmission tunnel.
7. Disconnect the speedometer cable from the rear of the transmission.
8. Disconnect the shift rods from the transmission shift levers.
9. Loosen, but do not remove, the intermediate bearing bolts.
10. Matchmark the U-joint and driveshaft coupling and loosen the U-joint.
11. Matchmark the driveshaft flange and adapter. Loosen the 3 driveshaft bolts. Remove 2 of the bolts and pivot the driveshaft around enough to reinstall the 2 bolts. Remove the 3rd bolt and position the driveshaft rearward as far as the center bearing permits. Use a piece of wood to block the driveshaft up in the driveshaft tunnel. Reinstall the 3rd bolt. The adapter plate should remain on the 3-legged transmission flange.
12. Remove the starter.
13. Remove all bolts attaching the transmission to the intermediate flange, but remove the upper 2 bolts last.

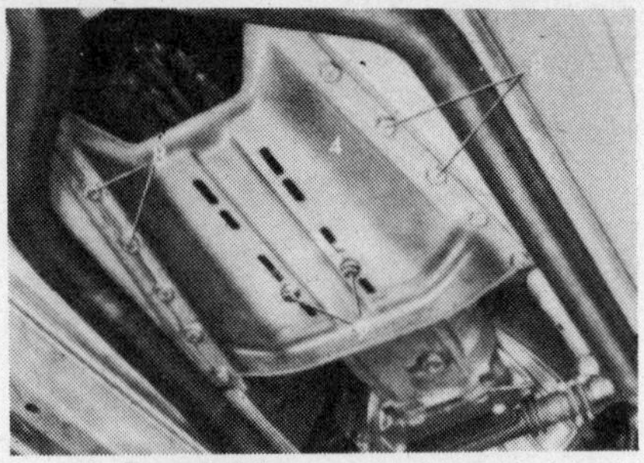

4. Tunnel plate
8. Bolts for tunnel plate
9. Bolts for rear engine rubber mount

Remove the driveshaft tunnel

NOTE: The clutch housing is heavily ribbed. Because of this, most of the bolts can only be reached with a 17 or 19 mm insert and extension.

14. Turn the transmission 45° to the left so that the starter domes on both sides of the clutch housing do not scrape the transmission tunnel.
15. Keep the transmission level and slide it out.
16. The clutch housing bolts can only be reached from inside. Unbolt the housing and remove it.
17. Installation is the reverse of removal.

LINKAGE ADJUSTMENT

The only type of shifter used is a floor mounted type.

CAUTION

On all types of transmissions, never hammer or force a new shift knob on with the shift lever installed, as the plastic bushing connected to the lever will be destroyed and cause hard shifting.

Proper adjustment of the shift linkage is dependent on both the position of the levers

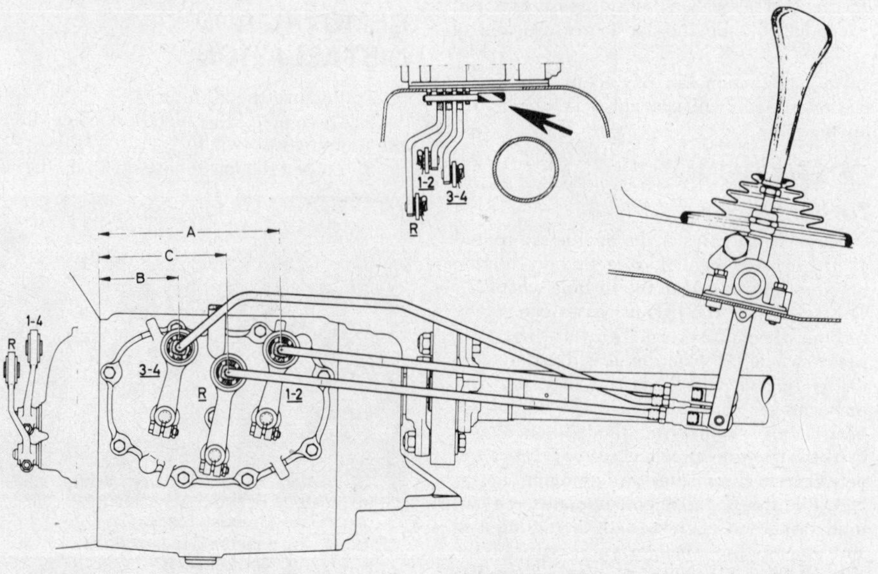

4-speed transmission linkage Arrow at top shows locating pin installed prior to adjustment

at the transmission and the length of the shift rods. The shift levers and bearing block are under the floor tunnel which may have to be removed, from underneath the car.

1. Check the positioning of the shift levers at the transmission (see illustration) and correct by loosening the clamp bolts. The diagram shows the levers in Neutral.

2. Lock the three levers by inserting a 0.2156 in. rod (a No. 3 drill will do or other tool of approximately the same diameter) through the levers and the hole in the bearing block.

3. With the shift levers at the lower steering column locked and the levers at the transmission adjusted, try hooking the shift rods into their respective levers. If they are too long or short, adjust their length by loosening the locknuts and turning the ball socket ends. Remove the locking rod and try shifting through the gears. Very slight further adjustments may clear up any binding.

CLUTCH

REMOVAL AND INSTALLATION

1. To remove the clutch, first remove the transmission and bell housing.

2. Loosen the clutch pressure plate hold-down bolts evenly, 1-1½ turns at a time, until tension is relieved. Never remove one bolt at a time, as damage to the pressure plate is possible.

3. Examine the flywheel surface for blue heat marks, scoring, or cracks. If the flywheel is to be machined, always maçhine both sides.

4. To reinstall, coat the splines with high temperature grease and place the clutch disc against the flywheel, centering it with a clutch pilot shaft. A wooden shaft, available at automotive jobbers, is satisfactory, but an old transmission mainshaft works best.

5. Tighten the pressure plate hold-down bolts evenly 1-1½ turns at a time until tight, then remove the pilot shaft.

CAUTION

Most clutch plates have the flywheel side marked as such (Kupplungsseite). Do not assume that the pressure springs always face the transmission.

CHECKING CLUTCH PLATE WEAR

A spring plate clutch that automatically compensates for wear is used, so no periodic adjustments are required. Apart from the usual slippage which accompanies severe wear of the clutch plate or disc, Mercedes-Benz has a simple tool, which can be purchased from a dealer that measures the amount of wear on the clutch plate. Actually, it is a simple "go-no go" gauge.

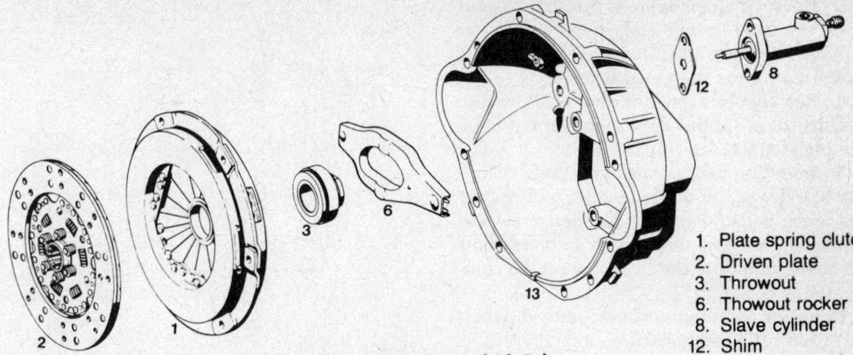

Exploded view of clutch

1. Plate spring clutch
2. Driven plate
3. Throwout
6. Thowout rocker
8. Slave cylinder
12. Shim
13. Clutch housing

1. A plastic shim is installed between the slave cylinder and the bell housing.

2. The shim is provided with two flat grooves running diagonally from bottom to center. When the shim is installed, these grooves appear as slots. Use groove (a) for left-hand drive vehicles and groove (b) for right-hand drive vehicles.

3. The clutch slave cylinder pushrod has two different diameters. The jar width of the test device corresponds to the smaller diameter of the pushrod. If the notches on the test device disappear when the test device is inserted as far as it will go, the clutch plate is still operational.

4. If, however, the notches on the test device remain visible, this is an indication that the clutch plate is worn severely and should be replaced.

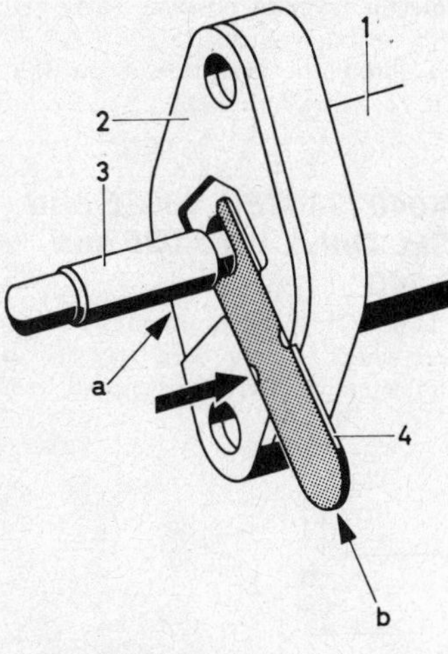

1. Clutch slave cylinder
2. Plastic shim
3. Thrust rod
4. Measuring gauge (Part No. 115 589 07 23 00)

(a)—Direction of measuring on lefthand drive vehicle with steering wheel and center shift, as well as on righthand drive vehicles with center shift

(b)—Direction of measuring on righthand drive vehicles with steering wheel shift

Wear limit has not been reached

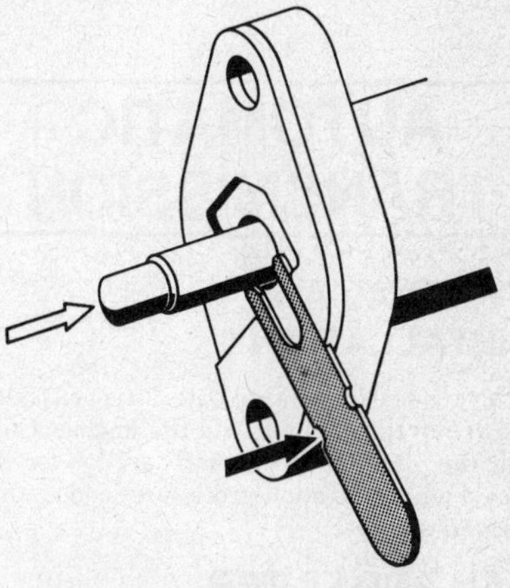

Wear limit has been reached

Clutch Slave Cylinder

REMOVAL AND INSTALLATION

1. Detach and plug the pressure line from the slave cylinder.

2. Remove the attaching screws from the slave cylinder.

3. Remove the slave cylinder, pushrod, and spacer.

4. To install, place the grooved side of the spacer in contact with the housing and hold it in position.

5. Install the slave cylinder and pushrod into the housing. Be sure that the dust cap is properly seated.

6. Install the attaching screws.

7. Connect the pressure line to the slave cylinder.

8. Bleed the slave cylinder.

BLEEDING THE SLAVE CYLINDER

The same principle is used as in bleeding the brakes.

1. Check the brake fluid level in the compensating tank and fill to maximum level.

2. Put a hose on the bleeder screw of the right front caliper and open the bleeder screw.

3. Have a helper depress the brake pedal until the hose is full and there are no air bubbles. Be sure that the bleeder screw is closed each time the pedal is released.

4. Put the free end of the hose on the bleeder screw of the slave cylinder and open the bleeder screw.

5. Keep stepping on the brake pedal. Close the bleeder screw on the caliper and release the brake pedal. Open the bleeder screw and repeat the process until no air bubbles show up at the mouth of the inlet line on the compensating tank.

Between operations, check, and, if necessary, refill the compensating tank.

6. Close the bleeder screws on the caliper and slave cylinder and remove the hose.

7. Check the clutch operation and the fluid level.

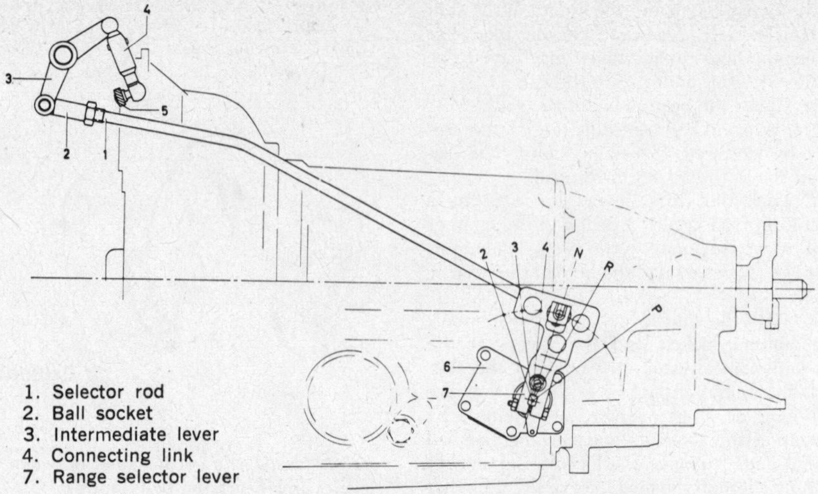

Column mounted selector rod linkage—W3A 040

AUTOMATIC TRANSMISSION

REMOVAL AND INSTALLATION

Mercedes-Benz automatic transmissions are removed as a unit with the engine. Consult the "Engine Mechanical" section for removal and installation procedures concerning a given engine.

PAN AND FILTER REPLACEMENT

1. Drain the transmission of all fluid by loosening the dipstick tube.
2. Remove the transmission pan.
3. Remove the bolt or bolts which retain the filter to the transmission.
4. Remove the filter and replace it with a new one.
5. Install the transmission pan, using a new gasket.
6. Refill the transmission to the proper level with the specified brand of fluid.

Bottom view of automatic transmission showing dipstick tube (1), converter drain plug (2) and pan (3)

SELECTOR ROD LINKAGE ADJUSTMENT

NOTE: Before performing this adjustment on any Mercedes-Benz vehicle, be sure that the vehicle is resting on its wheels. No part of the vehicle may be jacked for this adjustment.

COLUMN MOUNTED LINKAGE

W3A 040

1. Loosen the counternut on the ball socket.
2. Disconnect the selector rod from the shift lever bracket.
3. Set the transmission selector lever and the selector rod in Neutral.
4. Adjust the length of the selector rod until the ball socket aligns with the end of the ball on the intermediate lever.
5. Attach the ball socket to the intermediate lever, making sure that the play in the selector lever in position Three (D) and Four (S) is about equal.
6. Tighten the counternut on the ball socket.

W3A 040 (380SEL, 450SE and 450SEL Only), W4B 025 and W4A 040

1. Loosen the counternut on the rear selector rod while holding both recesses of the front selector rod with an open end wrench.
2. Disconnect the selector rod from the selector lever.
3. Set the selector lever on the transmission and on the column to Neutral.
4. Adjust the selector rod until the bearing pin is aligned with the bearing bushing in the selector lever.
5. Connect the rear selector lever to the selector rod and secure it with the lock. Be sure that the clearance of the selector lever in D and S is equal.
6. Tighten the locknut on the rear selector rod while holding the front selector rod as in Step 1.

Floor Mounted Linkage

NOTE: The vehicle must be standing with the weight normally distributed on all four wheels. No jacks may be used.

1. Disconnect the selector rod from the selector lever.
2. Set the selector lever in Neutral and make sure that there is approximately 1 mm clearance between the selector lever and the N stop of the selector gate.
3. Adjust the length of the selector rod so that it can be attached free of tension.
4. Retighten the counternut.

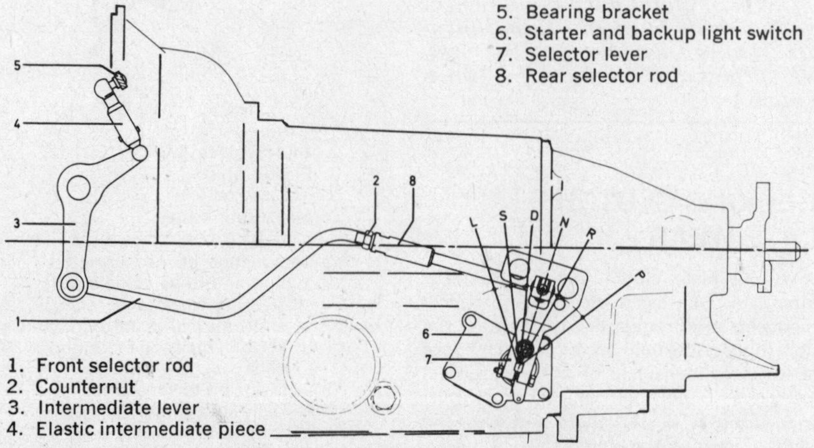

Selector rod linkage on W3A 040 (450SE, SEL only) and W4B 025

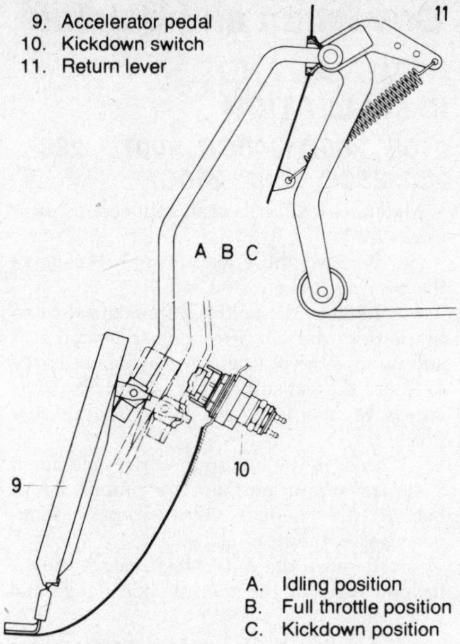

Kickdown switch adjustment

1. Selector range lever
2. Washer
3. Adjusting screw
4. Shaft
5. Locating pin
6. Clamping screw

(a)—Column shift for left-hand and right-hand drive vehicles 220/8, 220 D/8, 230/8, 280 S/8, 280 SE/8 and 300 SEL/8.

(b)—Steering wheel shift for left-hand drive vehicles (220/8, 220 D/8, 230/8, 250/8)

(c)—Steering wheel shift for right-hand drive vehicles (220/8, 220 D/8, 230/8, 250/8)

(d)—Steering wheel shift for left-hand drive vehicles (280S/8, 280 SE/8, 300 SEL/8, 280 SE/3.5 and 300 SEL/3.5)

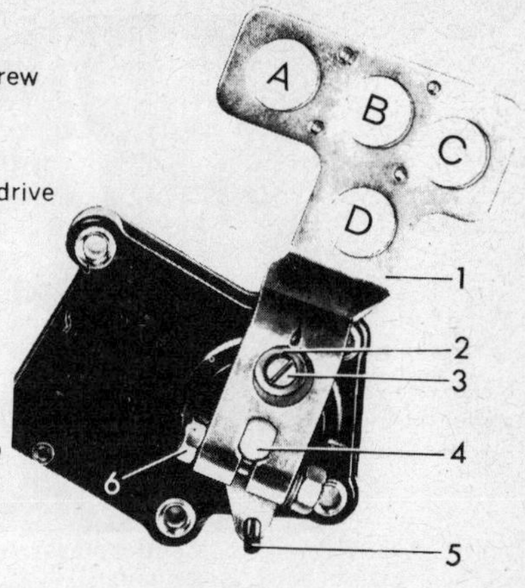

Starter lockout and backup light switch adjustment

STARTER LOCKOUT AND BACK-UP LIGHT SWITCH ADJUSTMENT

1. Disconnect the selector rod and move the selector lever on the transmission to position Neutral.
2. Tighten the clamping screw prior to making adjustments.
3. Loosen the adjusting screw and insert the locating pin through the driver into the locating hole in the shift housing.
4. Tighten the adjusting screw and remove the locating pin.
5. Move the selector lever to position N and connect the selector rod so that there is no tension.
6. Check to be sure that the engine cannot be started in Neutral or Park.

KICKDOWN SWITCH

1. The kickdown position of the solenoid valve is controlled by the accelerator pedal.
2. Push the accelerator pedal against the kickdown limit stop. In this position the throttle lever should rest against the full load stop of the venturi control unit.
3. Adjustments are made by loosening the clamping screw on the return lever on the accelerator pedal shaft and turning the shaft. Tighten the clamping screw again.

CONTROL PRESSURE ROD (1975-81 EXCEPT 1981 300SD, 300TD, 380SL, 380SLC AND 380SEL).

230

1. Remove the vacuum control unit from the carburetor.
2. Disconnect the automatic choke connecting rod so the throttle valve rests against the idle stop.
3. Loosen the screw and turn the levers against each other so the control rod rests against the idle stop.
4. Tighten the screw and depress the accelerator to the kickdown position. The throttle valve must rest against the full throttle stop. If necessary adjust the full throttle stop (see Fuel System).
5. Install the vacuum control unit on the distributor and connect the automatic choke rod.

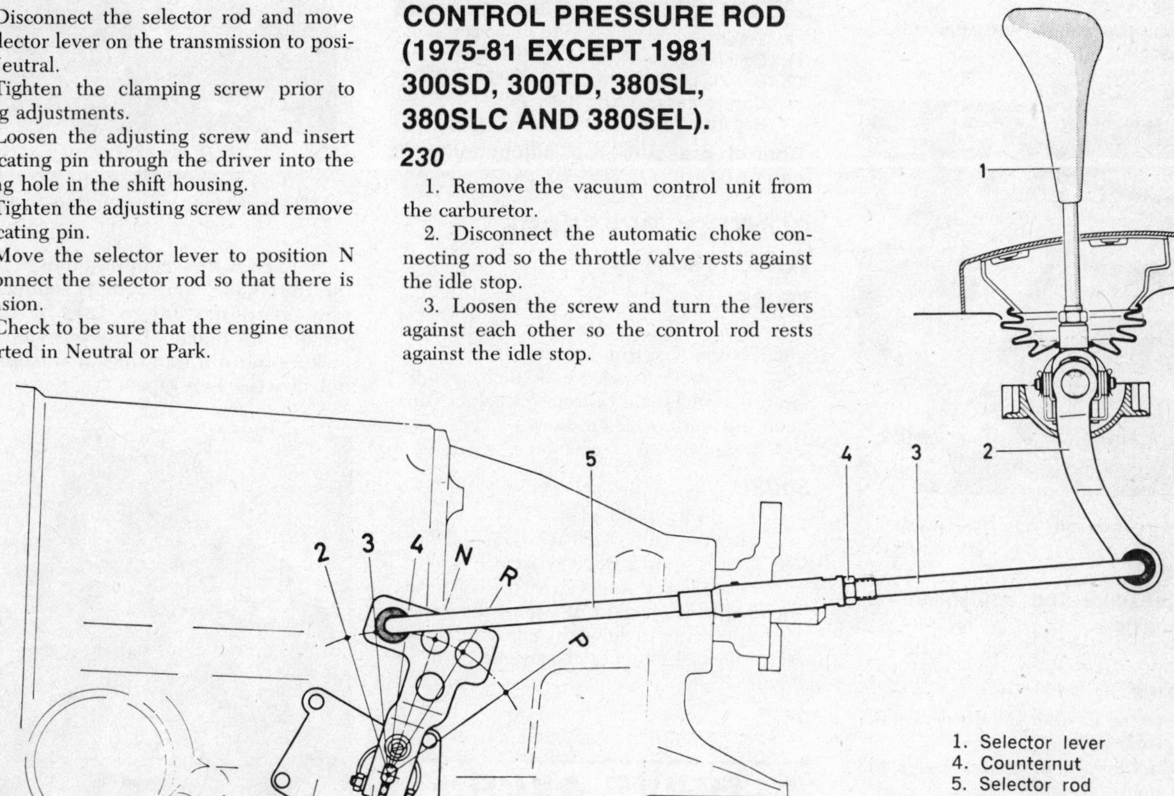

1. Selector lever
4. Counternut
5. Selector rod
6. Gear selector lever

Floor mounted selector rod linkage

1. Control pressure rod
2. Bellcrank
3. Screw
4. Bellcrank

Control pressure rod adjustment—1975-79 230

Diesel Engines

The control pressure rod can only be adjusted with a special gauge available only from Mercedes-Benz dealers.

6-Cylinder Engines

1. Disconnect the control pressure rod.
2. Push the angle lever in the direction of the arrow.
3. Push the control pressure rod rearward against the stop and adjust its length so there is no binding.
4. Tighten the counternut after adjustment.

57. Control pressure rod
58. Ball socket
59. Counternut
120. Angle lever
144. Connecting rod

Control pressure rod adjustment—6-cylinder engine

V8 Engines

1. Remove the air filter and disconnect the control pressure linkage.
2. The throttle valve should rest against the idle speed stop.
3. Push the regulating lever and angle lever to the idle position.
4. Push the control pressure rod completely rearward against the stop and adjust the length of the rod so there is no tension.
5. When checking the rod for length, hold it to the left of the socket, not above to compensate for rotary motion of the linkage.

7. Roller
11. Connecting rod
12. Bearing bracket
13. Control pressure rod
17. Regulating lever
18. Stop pin
19. Gate lever
20. Angle lever
31. Connecting rod

Control pressure rod adjustment—V8 engine

CONTROL PRESSURE WIRE (1981)

380SEL

1. Remove the air cleaner.
2. Loosen the clamping screw.
3. Push the ball socket back, then carefully forward until a slight resistance is felt. At this point, tighten the clamp screw.
4. Install the air cleaner.

300SD

1. Pry off the ball socket.
2. Push the ball socket back, then pull carefully forward until a slight resistance is felt.
3. Hold the ball socket above the ball head. The drag lever should rest against the stop.
4. Adjust the cable at the adjusting screw so that the ball socket can be attached with no strain.

DRIVE AXLE

Mercedes-Benz automobiles use either two or three piece driveshafts to connect the transmission to a hypoid independent rear axle. All models covered in this book use independent rear suspension with open or enclosed driveshafts to the rear wheels.

Driveshaft and U-Joints

REMOVAL AND INSTALLATION

240D, 300D, 300CD, 300TD, 230, 280, 280C, 280E, 280CE

Matchmark all driveshaft connections prior to removal.

1. Remove the equalizer and disconnect the parking brake cables.
2. Remove the bolts which secure the two brackets to the chassis at the front and rear and remove the brackets. It may be necessary to lower the exhaust system slightly to allow access to the left-hand bolts on the rear bracket.
3. Loosen the nut on the driveshaft about 2 turns without pushing the rubber sleeve back (it slides along). On a two-piece shaft, only loosen the front clamp nut.
4. Remove the nuts which secure the attaching plate to the transmission flange and rear axle.

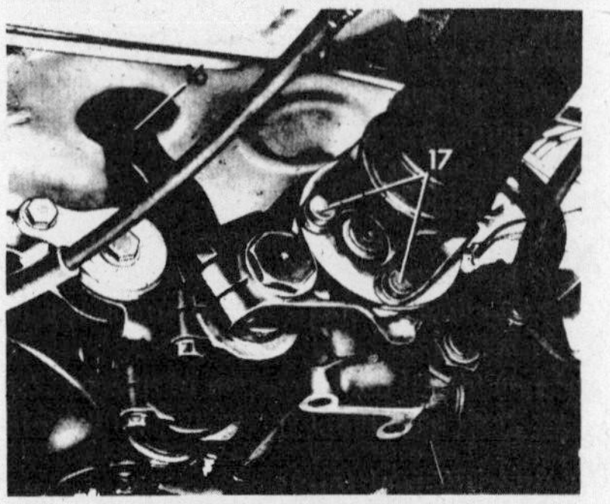

16. Rear axle carrier
17. Cheesehead bolts

Rear driveshaft mounting flange

NOTE: A new coupling flange is used on 1981 280E and 280CE models. The new coupling flange uses a thinner washer in place of the previous self-locking hex nut and thicker washers. Do not mix the two types.

1981 driveshafts use a new design coupling flange with thinner washers

5. Remove the bolts which secure the intermediate bearing(s) to the chassis. Push the

driveshaft together and slightly down, and remove the driveshaft from the vehicle.

NOTE: If possible, do not separate the parts of the driveshaft since each driveshaft is balanced at the factory. If separation is necessary, all parts must be marked and reassembled in the same relative positions to assure that the driveshafts will remain reasonably well balanced.

6. Installation is the reverse of removal.
7. Pack the cavities of the two centering sleeves with special Mercedes-Benz grease.
8. Install the driveshaft and attach the intermediate bearing(s) to the chassis.
9. Rock the car backward and forward several times to be sure that the driveshaft is properly centered without forcing.
10. Prior to tightening the clamp nuts on a three piece driveshaft, be sure that the intermediate shaft does not contact either the front or rear intermediate bearing. The clearance between the intermediate shaft and the bearing should be the same at both ends.

All Other Models

NOTE: Steps 1-3 apply to V8 models. Matchmark all driveshaft connections prior to removal.

1. Fold the torsion bar down after disconnecting the level control linkage (if equipped).
2. Remove the exhaust system.
3. Remove the heat shield from the frame.
4. Support the transmission with a jack and completely remove the rear engine mount crossmember.
5. Without sliding the rubber sleeve back, loosen the clamp nut approximately two turns (the rubber sleeve will slide along).

NOTE: On 3 piece driveshafts, only the front clamp nut need be loosened.

6. Unscrew the U-joint mounting flange from the U-joint plate.

NOTE: The 1981 380SEL uses a new design coupling flange with thinner washers under a new hex nut. The previous design used thicker washers. Do not mix the two types.

7. Bend back the locktabs and remove the bolts that attach the driveshaft to the rear axle pinion yoke.
8. Remove the bolts which attach the intermediate bearing(s) to the frame. Push the driveshaft together slightly and remove it from the vehicle.
9. Try not to separate the driveshafts. If it is absolutely necessary, matchmark all components so that they can be reassembled in the same order.
10. Installation is the reverse of removal. Always use new self-locking nuts. After the driveshaft is installed, rock the car back and forth several times to settle the driveshaft. Make sure that neither intermediate shaft is binding against either intermediate bearing, and that the clearance between the intermediate bearing and the driveshaft is the same at both ends.

Axle Shaft

NOTE: The rubber covered joints are filled with special oil. If they are disassembled for any reason, they must be refilled with special oil.

REMOVAL AND INSTALLATION

Models Without Torque Compensator (Torsion Bar)

NOTE: On the 280, 280C and 280E only axle shafts identified with a yellow paint dot or part No. 107 350 07 10 (left) or part No. 107 350 0810 (right) can be installed.

Most models do not use a torque compensator (torsion bar) which is actually a steel bar used to locate the rear axle under acceleration. In general, only the 450 series sedans and 300SD use a torque compensator, but it is wise to check for one prior to servicing the axle shaft. The illustrations apply to either type.

1. Jack up the rear of the car and remove the wheel and center axle hold-down bolt (in hub).
2. Remove the brake caliper and suspend it from a hook.
3. Drain the differential oil and place a jack under the differential housing.

Most models do not use a torque compensator (arrow)

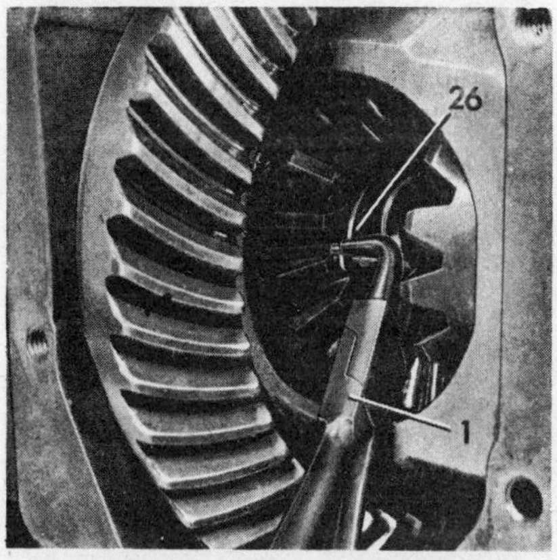

Removing the lock-ring (26) from the axle shaft with pliers (1) or a screwdriver

4. Unbolt the rubber mount from the chassis and the differential housing, then remove the differential housing cover to expose the ring and pinion gears.
5. Press the shaft from the axle flange. If necessary, loosen the shock absorber.
6. Using a screwdriver, remove the axle lock ring inside the differential case.
7. Pull the axle from the housing by pulling the splined end from the side gears, with the spacer.

NOTE: Axle shafts are stamped R and L for right and left units. Always use new lockrings.

Axle shaft markings (r)

8. Installation is the reverse of removal. Fill the rear axle. New radial seal rings are used on 1980 and later models. Lubricate the outside diameter of rubber covered radial sealing rings with hypoid gear lubricant prior to installation.

CAUTION

Check end-play of the lockring in the groove. If necessary, install a thicker lockring or spacer to eliminate all end-play, while still allowing the lockring to rotate. Do not allow the joints in the axle shaft to hang free or the joint bearing may be damaged and leak.

Models with Torque Compensator (Torsion Bar)

1. Drain the oil from the rear axle.
2. Disconnect and plug the brake lines.
3. Loosen the connecting rod and unscrew the torsion bar bearing bracket. Lower the exhaust system slightly and remove the torsion bar.
4. Loosen the shock absorber.
5. Remove the bolt which attaches the rear axle shaft to the rear axle shaft flange.
6. Disconnect the brake cable control. Remove the bracket from the wheel carrier, remove the rubber sleeve, and push back the cover.
7. Force the rear axle shaft out of the flange with a suitable tool.
8. Support the rear axle with a jack.
9. Remove the rubber mount.
10. Clean the axle housing and remove the cover from the housing.

NOTE: The axle shafts are the floating type and can be compressed in the constant velocity joints.

11. Remove the locking ring from the end of the axle shafts which engage the side gears in the differential.
12. Disengage the axle shaft from the side gear and remove the axle shaft together with the spacer.

CAUTION

Do not hang the outer constant velocity joint in a free position (without any support) as the shaft may be damaged and the constant velocity joint housing may leak.

13. Installation is the reverse of removal.
14. If either axle shaft is replaced, be sure that the proper replacement shaft is installed. Axle shafts are marked L and R for left and right.
15. Check the end-play between the lockring on the axle shaft and the side gear. There should be no noticeable end-play, but the lock ring should be able to turn in the groove.
16. Be sure to bleed the brakes and fill the rear axle with the proper quantity and type of lubricant. New radial seal rings are used on 1980 and later models. Lubricate the outside diameter of rubber covered radial seal rings with hypoid gear lubricant prior to installation.

Differential

REMOVAL AND INSTALLATION

All Models

1. Drain the oil from the rear axle.
2. On cars without torque compensation, remove the brake caliper and suspend it on a hook.
3. On cars with torque compensation, disconnect the brake cable control, unbolt the holding bracket on the wheel carrier, remove the rubber sleeve and push the cover back.
4. Remove the bolt from both sides that holds the rear axle shaft to the flange.
5. Press the rear axle shaft out of the flange.
6. If required, loosen the right-hand rear shock absorber and lower it to the stop.
7. Remove the exhaust system, if necessary.
8. On the 450 series and 280S, 280SE, 300SD remove the heat shield.
9. Loosen the clamp nut and remove the intermediate bearing from the floor pan. On 3-piece driveshafts, only remove the front nut.
10. Unbolt the driveshaft and remove it.
11. Support the rear axle housing.
12. Unbolt the rear rubber mount from the frame floor.
13. On the 450 and 380 series and 280S, 280SE, 300SD, lower the jack until the self-locking nuts are accessible.
14. Unbolt the rear axle center housing from the rear axle carrier.
15. On all other models, remove the bolt from the rubber mount on the cover of the rear axle housing. Fold back the rubber mat in the trunk and remove the rubber plugs; unbolt the rear axle center housing from the rear axle carrier.
16. Lower the rear axle center housing and remove it with the axle shaft. Do not allow the axle shafts to hang free, or the seals will be damaged, resulting in leaks.
17. Installation is the reverse of removal. Install new self-locking nuts, adjust the parking brake and fill the rear axle with the correct fluid.

REAR SUSPENSION

Springs

REMOVAL AND INSTALLATION

240D, 230, 280, 280C, 280CE, 300D, 300TD, 300CD, 450SL, 450SLC, 380SL, 380SLC

1. Jack up the rear of the car.
2. Remove the rear shock absorber.
3. With a floor jack, raise the control arm to approximately a horizontal position. Install a spring compressor to aid in this operation.
4. Carefully lower the jack until the control arm contacts the stop on the rear axle support.
5. Remove the spring and spring compressor with great care.

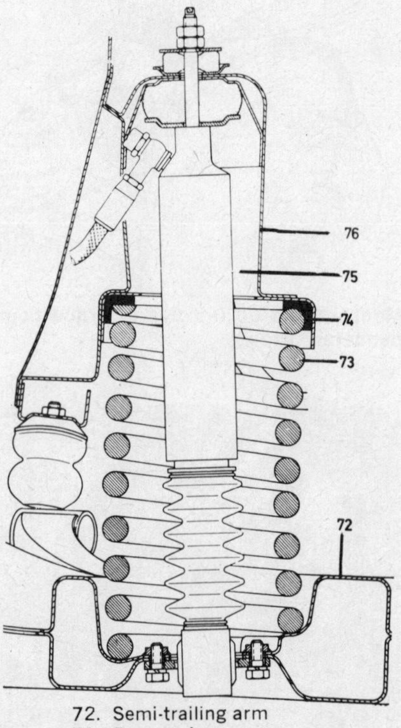

72. Semi-trailing arm
73. Rear spring
74. Rubber mounting
75. Shock absorber or spring strut
76. Dome on frame floor

Rear spring—450SE, 450SEL, 280SE, 300SD, 6.9, 380SEL, 280S, 280SE

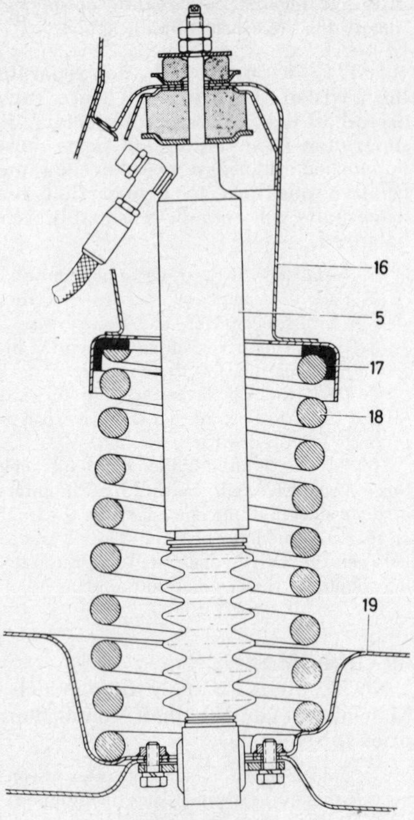

5. Spring strut
16. Dome on frame floor
17. Rubber mount
18. Rear spring
19. Semi-trailing arm

Rear spring—230, 240D, 280, 280C, 280E, 280CE, 300D, 300TD, 300CD, 450SL, 450SLC, 380SL, 380SLC

6. Installation is the reverse of removal. For ease of installation, attach the rubber seats to the springs with masking tape.

280S, 280SE, 300SD, 450SE, 450SEL, 6.9, 380SEL

1. Jack and support the rear of the car and the trailing arm.
2. Remove the rear shock absorber.
3. Be sure that the upper shock absorber attachment is released first.
4. Compress the spring with a spring compressor.
5. Remove the rear spring with the rubber mount.
6. Installation is the reverse of removal. When installing the shock absorber, tighten the lower mount first.

Shock Absorbers

REMOVAL AND INSTALLATION

230, 240D, 280, 280C, 280CE, 280E, 300D, 300CD, 300TD, 450SL, 450SLC, 380SL and 380SLC

1. Jack up the rear of the car and support the control arm.

2. From inside the trunk (sedans), remove the rubber cap, locknut, and hex nut from the upper mount of the shock absorber. On 450SL, 450SLC, 380SL and 380SLC the upper mount of the rear shock absorber is accessible after removing the top, top flap, rear seat, backrest and lining.

3. Unbolt the mounting for the rear shock absorber at the bottom and remove the shock absorber.

4. Installation is the reverse of removal.

280S, 280SE, 300SD, 450SE, 450SEL, 6.9, 380SEL

1. Remove the rear seat and backrest.
2. Remove the cover from the rear wall.
3. Jack and support the car and the trailing arm.
4. Loosen the nuts on the upper mount. Remove the washer and rubber ring.
5. Loosen the lower mount and remove the shock absorber downward.
6. Installation is the reverse of removal. Tighten the upper mounting nut to the end of the threads.

Independent Rear Suspension Adjustments

Suspension adjustments should only be checked when the vehicle is resting on a level surface and is carrying the required fluids (full tank of gas, engine oil, etc.).

CAMBER

All Models

Rear wheel camber is determined by the position of the control arm. The difference in

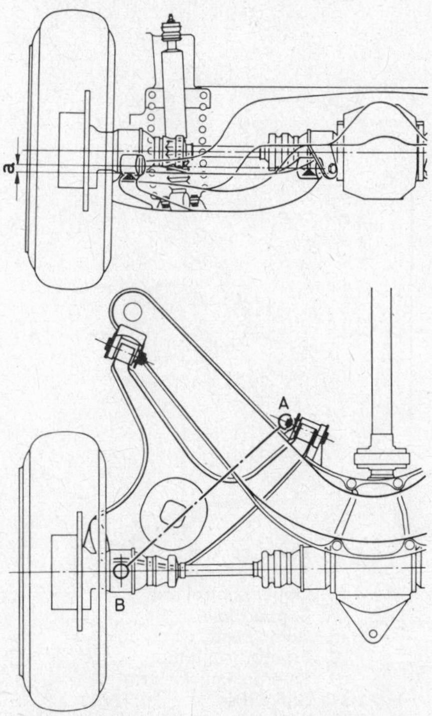

Rear wheel camber measurement—all models except 1974-76 230, 240D, 280, 280C, 300D and all 450SL, 450SLC, 380SL, 380SLC

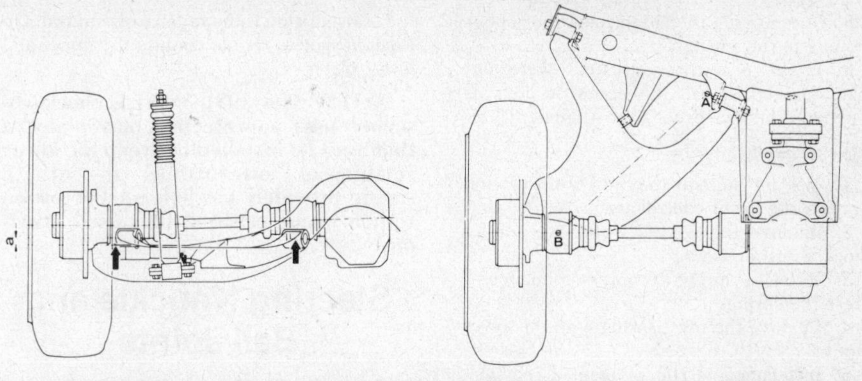

Rear wheel camber measurement on 1974-76 230, 240D, 280, 280C and 300D and all 450, 450SLC, 220D models. Control arm position (difference in height between the axis of the rear control arm mount (A) and the lower edge of the cup on the outer constant velocity joint (B)

height (a) between the axis of the control arm mounting point on the rear axle subframe and lower edge of the cup on the constant velocity joint is directly translated in degrees of camber.

Toe-In

Toe-in, on the rear wheels, is dependent on the camber of the rear wheels.

FRONT SUSPENSION

Springs

REMOVAL AND INSTALLATION

1975-76 230, 240D, 280C, 300D Models and All 450SL, 450SLC

NOTE: Be extremely careful when attempting to remove the front springs as they are compressed and under considerable load.

1. Front axle carrier
3. Lower control arm
4. Upper control arm
10. Front spring
11. Front shock absorber
12. Torsion bar
29. Rubber mounting
31. Rubber mounting for front spring

Front spring removal—1974-76 230, 240D, 280, 280C, 300D models 450SL, 450SLC, 380SL and 380SLC

1. Jack up the front of the car, put up jack stands and remove the front wheels.
2. Remove the front shock absorber and disconnect the sway bar.
3. First punchmark the position of the eccentric adjusters, then loosen the hex bolts.
4. Support the lower control arm with a jack.
5. Then knock out the eccentric pins and gradually lower the arm until spring tension is relieved.
6. The spring can now be removed.

NOTE: Check caster and camber after installing a new spring.

7. Installation is the reverse of removal.

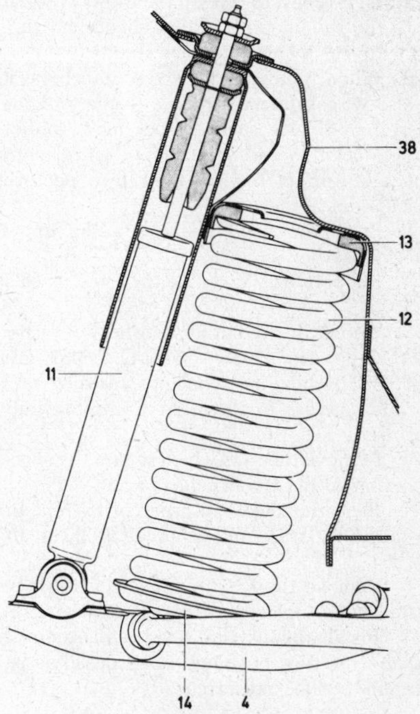

4. Lower control arm
11. Front shock absorber
12. Front spring
13. Rubber mount for front spring
14. Retainer for front spring
38. Front end

Front spring—all models except 1974-76 230, 240D, 280, 280C, 300D and all 450SL, 450SLC, 380SL, 380SLC

8. For ease of installation, tape the rubber mounts to the springs.

9. If the eccentric adjusters were not matchmarked, install the eccentric bolts as illustrated under "Front End Alignment".

All Other Models

1. Jack and support the front of the car and support the lower control arm.
2. Remove the wheel. Unbolt the upper shock absorber mount.
3. Install a spring compressor and compress the spring.
4. Remove the front spring with the lower mount.
5. Installation is the reverse of removal. Tighten the upper shock absorber suspension.

Shock Absorbers

REMOVAL AND INSTALLATION

1975-76 230, 240D, 280, 280C, 300D Models and All 450SL, 450SLC, 380SL, 380SLC

Shock absorbers are normally replaced only if leaking excessively (oil visible on outside cover) or if worn internally to a point where the car no longer rides smoothly and rebounds after hitting a bump. A good general test of shock absorber condition is made by bouncing the front of the car. If the car rebounds more than two or three times it can be assumed that the shock absorbers need replacement.

1. For removal and installation of shock absorbers, it is best to jack up the front of the car until the weight is off of the wheels and support the car securely on jack stands.
2. When removing the shock absorbers, it is also wise to draw a simple diagram of the location of parts such as lockrings, rubber stops, locknuts and steel plates, since many shock absorbers require their own peculiar installation of these parts.
3. Raise the hood and locate the upper shock absorber mount.
4. Support the lower control arm with a jack.
5. Unbolt the mount for the shock absorber at the top. On 450SL, 450SLC, 380SL and 380SLC, remove the coolant expansion tank to allow access to the right front shock absorber.
6. Remove the nuts which secure the shock absorber to the lower control arm.
7. Push the shock absorber piston rod in, install the stirrup, and remove the shock absorber.
8. Remove the stirrup, since this must be installed on replacement shock absorbers.
9. Installation is the reverse of removal. Always use new bushings when installing replacement shock absorbers.

All Other Models

1. Jack and support the car. Support the lower control arm.
2. Loosen the nuts on the upper shock absorber mount. Remove the plate and ring.
3. Place the shock absorber vertical to the lower control arm and remove the lower mounting bolts.
4. Remove the shock absorber.
5. Installation is the reverse of removal. On Bilstein shocks, do not confuse the upper and lower plates.

NOTE: The 1981 380SEL shock absorber uses a protective plastic sleeve that must be installed between the lower retainer and lower rubber ring. Also, a slot is provided for holding the piston rod, in place of the 2 flats used previously.

Steering Knuckle and Ball Joints

CHECKING BALL JOINTS

1. To check the steering knuckles or ball joints, jack up the car, placing a jack directly under the front spring plate. This unloads the front suspension to allow the maximum play to be observed.
2. Late model ball joints need to be replaced only if dried out with plainly visible wear and/or play.

REMOVAL AND INSTALLATION

1975-76 230, 240D, 280, 280C, 300D, and All 450SL, 450SLC, 380SL and 380SLC

1. Jack and support the car. For safety, it's a good idea to install some type of clamp on the front spring. Position jack stands at the ouside front against the lower control arms.
2. Remove the wheel.
3. Remove the steering knuckle arm from the steering knuckle.
4. Remove and suspend the brake caliper.
5. Remove the front wheel hub.
6. Loosen the brake hose holder on the cover plate.
7. Loosen the nut on the guide joint and remove the joint from the steering knuckle.
8. Loosen the nut on the support joint.
9. Swivel the steering knuckle outward and force the ball joint from the lower control arm.
10. Remove the steering knuckle.
11. If necessary, remove the cover plate from the steering knuckle.
12. Installation is the reverse of removal. Use self-locking nuts and adjust the wheel bearings.

All Other Models

1. This should only be done with the front shock absorber installed. If, however, the front shock absorber has been removed, the lower control arm should be supported with a jack and the spring should be clamped with a spring tensioner. In this case, the hex nut on the guide joint should not be loosened without the spring tensioner installed.
2. Jack up the front of the car and support it on jack stands.
3. Remove the wheel.
4. Remove the brake caliper.
5. Unbolt the steering relay lever from the steering knuckle. For safety, install spring clamps on the front springs.

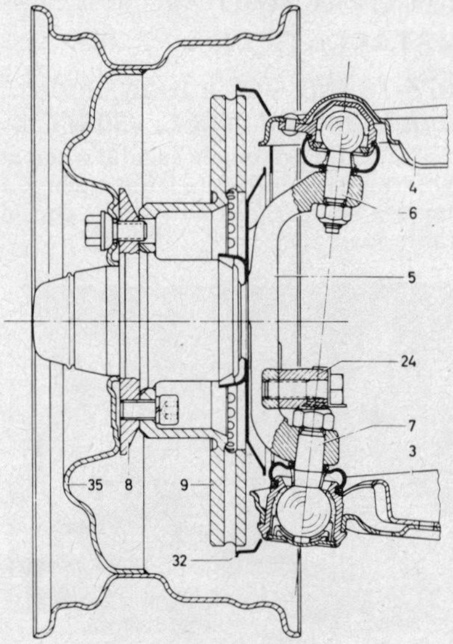

3. Lower control arm
4. Upper control arm
5. Steering knuckle
6. Guide joint
7. Supporting joint
8. Front wheel hub
9. Brake disc
24. Steering knuckle arm
32. Cover plate
35. Wheel

Steering knuckle and ball joints

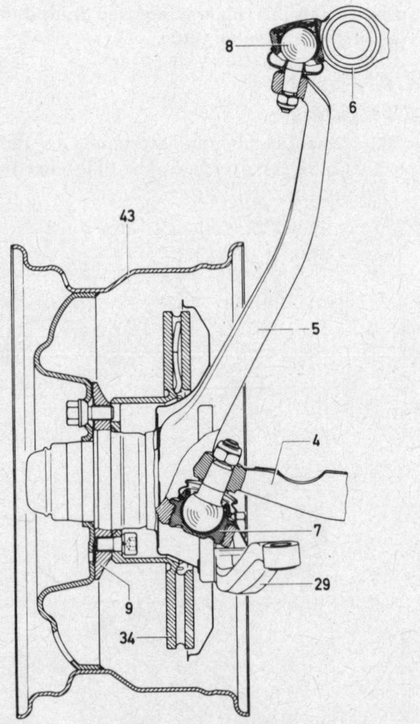

4. Lower control arm
5. Steering knuckle
6. Upper control arm
7. Support joint
8. Guide joint
9. Front wheel hub
29. Steering knuckle arm
34. Brake disc
43. Wheel

Steering knuckle—450SE, 450SEL, 380SEL, 280S, 280SE, and 1977 and later 230, 240D, 300D and 280E

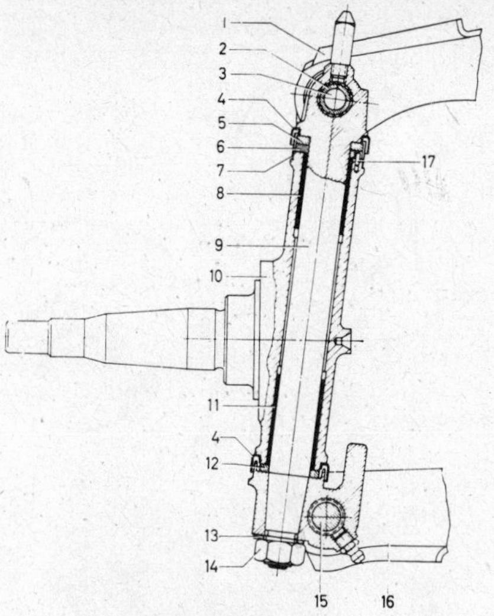

1. Upper control arm
2. Threaded bolt
3. Cam bolt
4. Dust cap
5. Thrust washer (top)
6. Thrust washer (bottom)
7. Dust sleeve
8. Upper bearing bushing
9. Kingpin
10. Steering knuckle
11. Bottom bearing bushing
12. Compensating washer
13. Lockwasher
14. Hex nut
15. Steering knuckle carrier with threaded bolt
16. Lower control arm
17. Pin

Cross-section of steering knuckle and kingpin

6. Remove the hex nuts from the upper and lower ball joints.
7. Remove the ball joints from the steering knuckle with the aid of a puller.
8. Remove the steering knuckle.
9. Installation is the reverse of removal. Be sure that the seats for the pins of the ball joints are free of grease.
10. Bleed the brakes.

Upper Control Arm

REMOVAL AND INSTALLATION

All Models Except 1975-76 230, 240D, 280, 280C, 300D Models and All 450SL, 450SLC, 380SL, 380SLC

1. Jack and support the car. Position jack stands at the outside front against the lower control arms.
2. Remove the wheel.
3. Loosen the nut on the guide joint.
4. Remove the guide joint from the steering knuckle.
5. Secure the steering knuckle with a hook on the upper control arm stop to prevent it from tilting.
6. Loosen the clamp screw and separate the upper control arm from the torsion bar.
7. Loosen the upper control arm bearing at the front and remove the upper control arm.

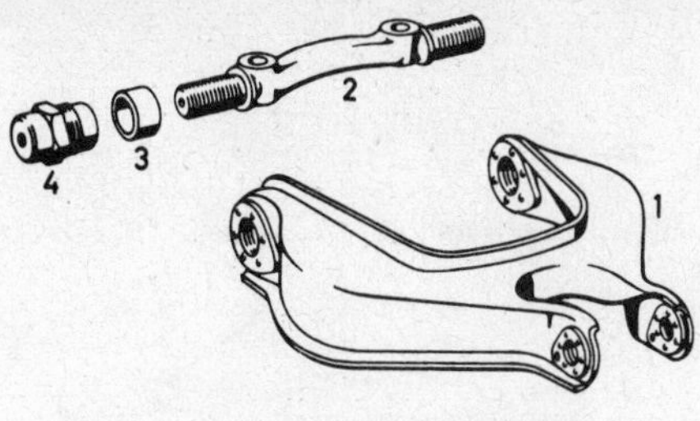

1. Upper control arm
2. Pivot pin
3. Rubber sealing ring
4. Threaded bushing

Upper control arm and pivot shaft

8. Installation is the reverse of removal. Use new self-locking nuts and check the front wheel alignment.

1975-76 230, 240D, 280, 280C, 300D Models and All 450SL, 450SLC, 380SL, 380SLC

1. The front shock absorbers should remain installed. Never loosen the hex nuts of the ball joints with the shock absorber removed, unless a spring clamp is installed.
2. Jack the front of the car and remove the wheel.
3. Support the front end on jack stands.
4. Remove the steering arm from the steering knuckle.
5. Separate the brake line and brake hose from each other and plug the openings.
6. Support the lower control arm and unscrew the nuts from the ball joints.
7. Remove the ball joints from the steering knuckle.
8. Loosen the bolts on the upper control arm and remove the upper control arm.
9. Installation is the reverse of removal.

CAUTION

Mount the front hex bolt from the rear in a forward direction, and the rear hex bolt from the front in a rearward direction.

10. Bleed the brakes.

Lower Control Arm

REMOVAL AND INSTALLATION

All Models Except 1975-76 230, 240D, 280, 280C, 300D and All 450SL, 450SLC, 380SL, 380SLC

The lower control arm is the same as the front axle half. For safety install a spring compressor on the coil spring.

1. Jack and support the front of the car and remove the wheels.
2. Remove the front shock absorber. Loosen the top mount first.
3. Remove the front springs.
4. Separate and plug the brake lines.
5. Remove the track rod from the steering knuckle arm.
6. Matchmark the position of the eccentric bolts on the bearing of the lower control arm in relation to the from crossmember.
7. Remove the shield from the cross yoke.
8. Support the front axle half.
9. Loosen the eccentric bolt on the front and rear bearing of the lower control arm and knock them out.
10. Remove the bolt from the cross yoke bearing.
11. Loosen the screw at the opposite end of the cross yoke bearing.
12. Pull the cross yoke bearing down slightly.
13. Loosen the support of the upper control arm on the torsion bar. Remove the clamp screw from the clamp.
14. Remove the upper control arm bearing on the front end.
15. Remove the front axle half.
16. Installation is the reverse of removal. Tighten the eccentric bolts of the lower control arm bearing with the car resting on the wheels. Bleed the brakes and check the front end alignment.

1975-76 230, 240D, 280, 280C, 300D and All 450SL, 450SLC, 380SL, 380SLC

1. Since the front shock absorber acts as a deflection stop for the front wheels, the lower shock absorber attaching point should not be loosened unless the vehicle is resting on the wheels or unless the lower control arm is supported.
2. Jack up the front of the vehicle and support it on jack stands.
3. Support the lower control arm.
4. Loosen the lower shock absorber attachment.
5. Unscrew the steering arm from the steering knuckle.
6. Separate the brake line and brake hose and plug the openings.
7. Remove the front spring.
8. Unscrew the hex nuts on the ball joints.
9. Remove the lower ball joint and remove the lower control arm.
10. Installation is the reverse of removal. Bleed the brakes and check the front end alignment.

Front End Alignment

Caster and camber are critical to proper handling and tire wear. Neither adjustment should be attempted without the specialized equipment to accurately measure the geometry of the front end.

CASTER/CAMBER ADJUSTMENT

All Models Except 1975-76 230, 240D, 280, 280C, 300D and All 450SL, 450SLC, 380SL, 380SLC

The front axle provides for caster and camber adjustment, but both wheel adjustments can only be made together. Adjustments are made with cam bolts on the lower control arm bearings.

The front bearing cam bolt is used to set caster, while the rear bearing cam bolt is used for camber.

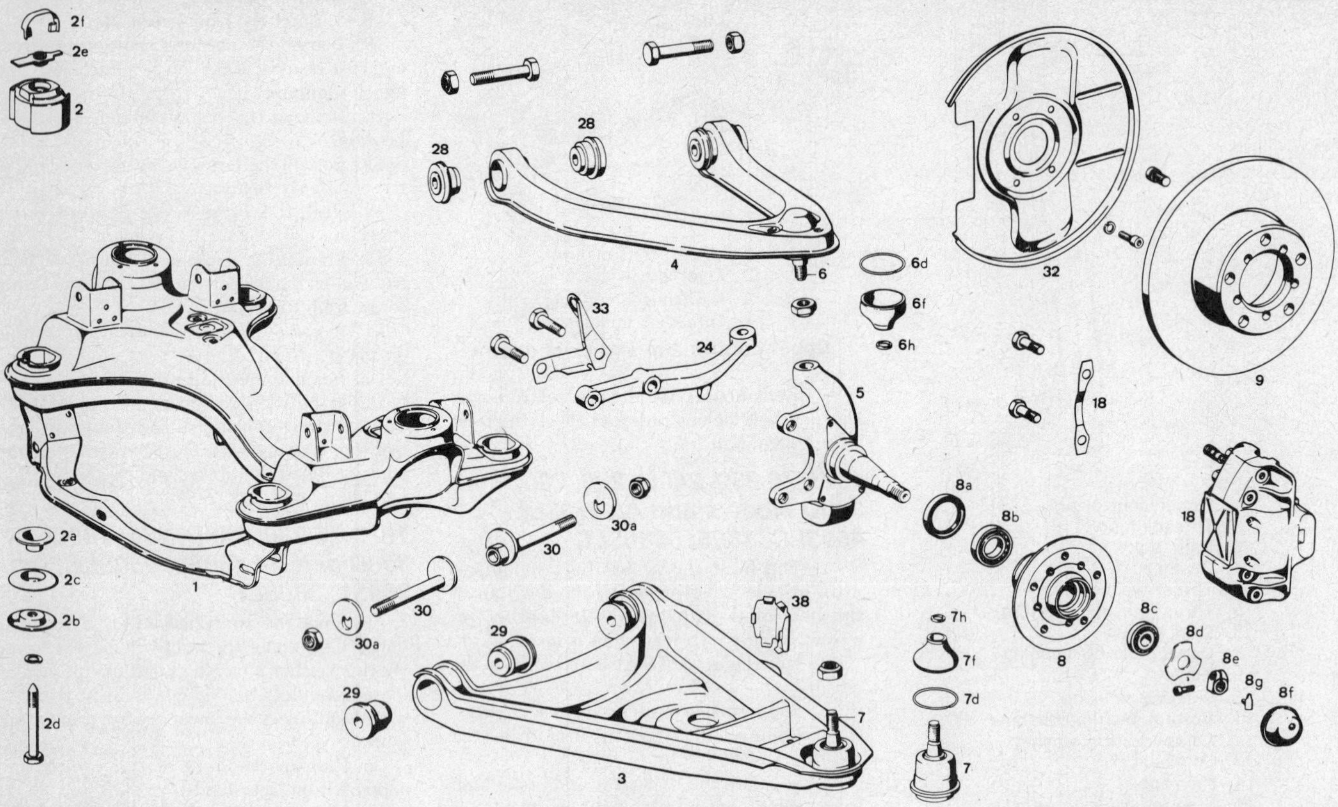

1. Front axle carrier
2. Rubber mount for suspension of front axle
2a. Stop buffer for inward deflection
2b. Stop plate
2c. Stop buffer for outward deflections
2d. Hex. bolt with snap-ring
2e. Fastening nut
2f. Nut holder
3. Lower control arm
4. Upper control arm
5. Steering knuckle
6. Guide joint
6d. Circlip
6f. Sleeve
6h. Clamping ring
7. Supporting joint
7d. Circlip
7f. Sleeve
7h. Clamping ring
8. Front wheel hub
8a. Radial sealing ring
8b. Inside tapered roller bearing
8c. Outside tapered roller bearing
8d. Washer
8e. Clamp nut
8f. Wheel cap
8g. Contact spring
9. Brake disc
18. Brake caliper
18a. Lockwasher
24. Steering knuckle arm
28. Rubber slide bearing
29. Rubber bearing (torsion bearing)
30. Cam bolt
30a. Cam washer
32. Cover plate
33. Holder for brake hose
38. Protective cap for steering lock

Lower control arm and pivot shaft

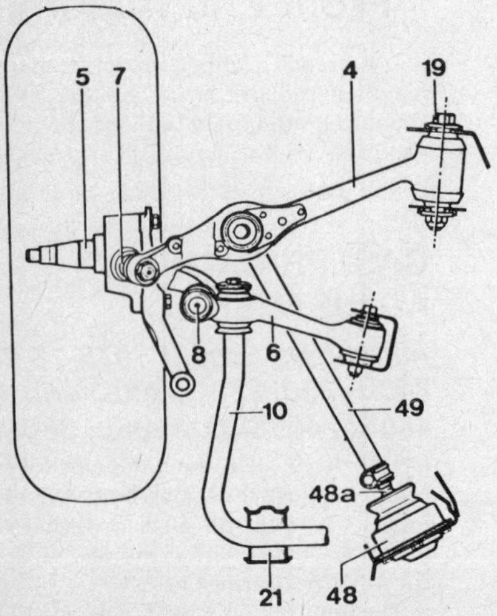

1. Frame side member
2. Frame cross member for front axle
4. Lower control arm
5. Steering knuckle
6. Upper control arm
7. Supporting joint
8. Guide joint
10. Torsion bar
19. Eccentric bolt (camber adjustment)
21. Torsion bar mounting on front end
48. Supporting joint
48a. Ball pin (caster adjustment)
49. Supporting tube

Camber and caster adjustment points on 1977 and later 230, 240D, 280CE, 300D, 300CD and 300TD

1975-76 230, 240D, 280, 280C, 300D and All 450SL, 450SLC, 380SL, 380SLC

Caster and camber are dependent upon each other and cannot be adjusted independently. They can only be adjusted simultaneously.

Caster is adjusted by turning the lower control arm around the front mounting, using the eccentric bolt.

Camber is adjusted by turning the lower control arm about the rear mounting, using the eccentric bolt. Bear in mind that caster will be changed accordingly.

When camber is adjusted in a positive direction, caster is changed in a negative direction, and vice versa. Adjustment of camber by 0° 15′ results in a caster change of approximately 0° 20′. Adjustment of caster by 1° results in a camber change of approximately 0° 7′.

Caster Adjustment
Toe-In Adjustment

Toe-in is the difference of the distance between the front edges of the wheel rims and the rear edges of the wheel rims.

To measure toe-in, the steering should be in the straight ahead position and the marks on the pitman arm and pitman shaft should be aligned.

Toe-in is adjusted by changing the length of the two tie rods or track rods with the wheels in the straight ahead position. Some older models have a hex nut locking arrangement rather than the newer clamp, but adjustment is the same.

NOTE: Install new tie rods so that the left-hand thread points toward the left-hand side of the car.

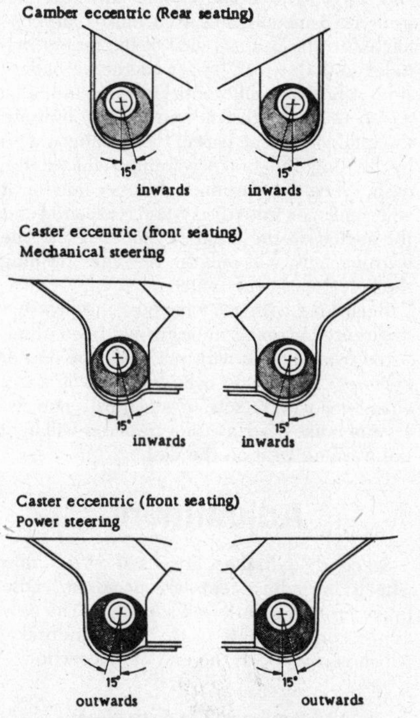

Basic caster and camber settings on 1975-76, 240D, 280, 280C, 300D

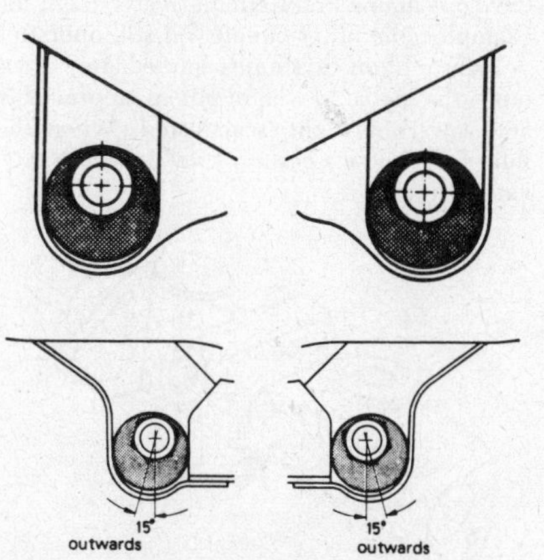

Basic caster and camber setting on 450SL, 450SLC, 380SL and 380SLC

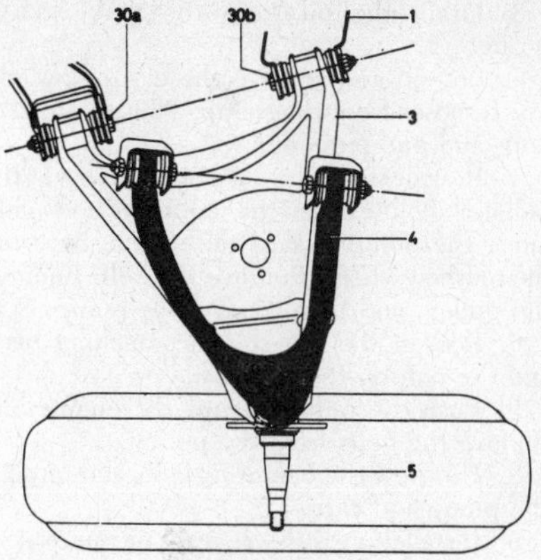

1. Front axle carrier
3. Lower control arm
4. Upper control arm
5. Steering knuckle
30a. Cam bolt front (caster)
30b. Cam bolt rear (camber)

Caster and camber adjustment points on 1975-76 230, 240D, 280, 280C, 300D models and all 450SL and 450SLC models

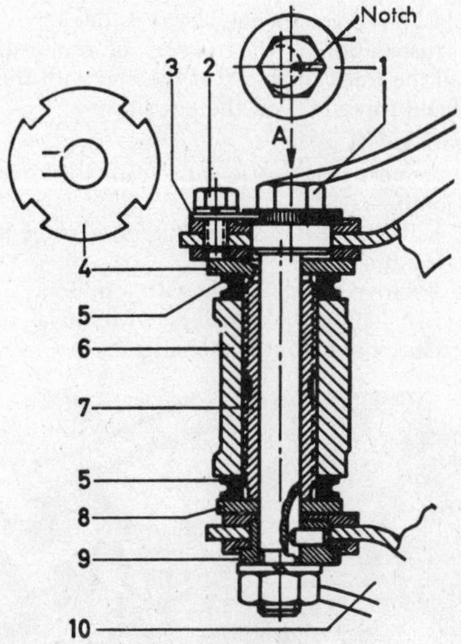

1. Eccentric bolt for camber adjustment
2. Hex screw with lockwasher
3. Locking plate
4. Adjusting washer for caster adjustment
5. Rubber sealing ring
6. Kingpin
7. Threaded bolt
8. Eccentric bushing with drive pin
10. Upper control arm

Caster and camber adjustment points—280 and 300 series (except 280, 280C, 280E, 280S and 280SE 1977 and later and 300D)

STEERING

Steering Wheel

REMOVAL AND INSTALLATION

450SL, 450SLC, 380SL, 380SLC

1. Pry the three-pointed star trademark from the center padding.
2. Unscrew the hex nut from the steering shaft and remove the spring washer and the steering wheel.

NOTE: 1980 and later models use an Allen screw in place of a hex nut. The Allen screw must be renewed if removed.

3. Installation is the reverse of removal. Be sure that the alignment mark on the steering shaft is pointing upward and be sure that the slightly curved spoke of the steering wheel is down.

All Models Except 450SL, 450SLC, 380SL, 380SLC

1. Remove the padded plate. Pull at one corner near the wheel spokes.
2. Unscrew the hex nut from the steering shaft and remove the spring washer and the steering wheel.

NOTE: 1980 and later models use an Allen screw in place of the hex nut. The Allen screw must be replaced if removed.

3. Installation is the reverse of removal. Be sure that the alignment mark on the steering shaft is pointing upward and be sure that the slightly curved spoke of the steering wheel is down.

Power Steering Gear

REMOVAL AND INSTALLATION

1. Suck the oil from the power steering reservoir using a syringe.
2. Detach the high-pressure hose and oil return hose from the steering assembly.
3. Cap both lines to prevent entry of dirt, then remove the clamp screw from the lower part of the coupling flange.
4. Remove the rubber plug from the cover plate and remove the U-joint socket screw. On LS90 power steering units, remove the steering spindle. Pull the steering spindle up only until the coupling is no longer engaged with the worn gear.
5. The tailpipe and left side exhaust pipe may have to be removed for access.
6. Detach the tie rod and center tie rod (or drag link and track rod) from the pitman arm, using pullers or a tie rod splitter.
7. Remove the hex-head bolts that hold the gearbox to the frame, then press the worm shaft stub from the steering coupling and remove the gearbox from underneath the car.
8. To install, first install the pitman arm (if it has been removed) aligning the matchmarks. Tighten the pitman arm nut to 110

ft/lbs and install the cotter pin. Use new self-locking nuts to attach the gear to the frame.

9. Remove the screw plug from the steering box. Turn the wormshaft until the center of the power piston is directly below the bore in the housing. Check dimension (a) which can be altered by changing the position of the pitman arm on its shaft.

10. Center the steering wheel.

11. Press the worm shaft stub into the steering shaft coupling, making sure not to damage the serrations.

NOTE: Install assembly pin as for manual steering.

12. Install and tighten the hex-head screws that hold the gearbox to the chassis, then install and tighten the coupling clamp screw.

13. Install the plug in the gearbox, using a new gasket; attach the tie rods to the pitman arm and make sure that the steering knuckle arms rest against their stops at full left and right lock.

14. Check toe-in and correct if necessary. Remove the dust covers from the fluid lines, then reconnect the high- and low-pressure lines.

15. Fill the reservoir and connect a hose between the bleed screw on the steering and the reservoir.

16. Open the bleed screw and, with engine running, bleed the system and top up.

Power Steering Pump

REMOVAL AND INSTALLATION

Many types of power steering pumps are used on Mercedes-Benz vehicles. Use only the instructions that apply to your vehicle.

1974-76 230, 240D, 300D

1. Remove the wing nut on the reservoir and remove the cover, spring, and damping plate.

2. Suck the fluid from the reservoir with a syringe.

3. Loosen the hose on the pump and plug both pump and hose.

4. On pumps with the reservoir attached, loosen the return hose and plug it.

5. On other types, loosen the connecting hose from the reservoir to the pump.

6. Remove the radiator.

7. Remove the nut from the pulley shaft. On pumps with cylindrical shafts, remove the pulley.

8. On pumps with tapered shafts, pull the pulley from the shaft with a jaw type puller.

9. Unscrew both front mounting bolts.

10. Remove the rear mounting bolt with spacer.

11. Remove the pump from the mounting bracket.

12. On all 4 cylinder models, remove the screws between the pump housing and the bracket. Remove the pump and pulley.

13. Installation, in all cases, is the reverse of removal.

All Models Except 1975-76 230, 240D, 300D

1. Remove the nut from the supply tank.

2. Remove the spring and damping plate.

3. Drain the oil from the tank with a syringe.

4. Loosen and remove the expanding and return hoses from the pump. Plug all connections and pump openings.

5. If necessary for clearance, loosen the radiator shell. Loosen the mounting bolts, and move the pump toward the engine by using the toothed wheel. Remove the belt. Remove the pulley, and then remove the pump.

6. Loosen the nut on the attaching plate and the bolt on the support.

7. Push the pump toward the engine and remove the belts from the pulley.

8. Unscrew the mounting bolts and remove the pump and carrier.

9. Installation is the reverse of removal.

Steering Linkage

ALL MODELS EXCEPT 280SE 4.5, 280SEL 4.5, 300SEL 4.5

Removal and Installation

TRACK ROD

1. Remove the cotter pins and castellated nuts from the track rod joints.

2. Remove the track rod from the steering arms with a puller.

3. Check the track rod ends. The rods use 22 mm ball joints and should be replaced if either ball joint is defective.

4. Check the rubber sleeves. The ball joint should be replaced if the sleeve is defective.

5. Installation is the reverse of removal. Install the track rods so that the end with the left-hand threads is on the left side.

DRAG LINK

1. Remove the castle nuts from the drag link joints.

2. Unbolt the steering damper and force it from the bracket.

3. Remove the drag link with a puller.

4. Installation is the reverse of removal.

5. Check the front wheel alignment.

Bottom view of steering linkage showing track rod and drag link

BRAKES

All Mercedes-Benz cars imported into the U.S. are equipped with 4-wheel disc brakes. The disc brakes are basically similar on all models, though there may be slight differences in design from model to model. The caliper bore sizes, for instance, differ depending upon application. The bore size (in mm) is usually stamped on the outside of the caliper, but occasionally, a code is used. For instance, the 14 on a Teves (ATE) caliper is really a 57 mm bore (obviously, it isn't a 14 mm bore).

Three different manufacturers make calipers for Mercedes-Benz production—Teves (ATE), Bendix or Girling—but calipers of the same manufacturer are installed on the same axle. For service, install calipers of the same manufacturer on the front axle; on the rear axle, calipers of any manufacturer can be installed.

Most models are equipped with brake pad wear indicators to indicate when the pad lining requires replacement. Beginning in 1976, a new design, step-type master cylinder is used which eliminates the need for the vacuum pump previously used on 230, 280, 280C and 280S. The brake circuits are reversed from 1975 models; the front brakes are connected to the primary side of the master cylinder and the rear brakes to the secondary side. A pressure differential warning indicator is also used, which will immediately indicate the total loss of one part of the braking system by lighting the brake warning light on the dash. Once the warning light has come on, it will remain on until the system is repaired and the switch on the master cylinder reset. The warning light will only go out after pushing the reset pin in the switch.

Beginning with 1978 models, the pressure differential warning indicator has been eliminated from models with the step-type master cylinder. The master cylinder reservoir has 2 chambers with 2 sets of electrical contacts. Loss of brake fluid in either reservoir will light the warning light on the dash.

Adjustment

Since disc brakes are used at all four wheels, no adjustments are necessary. Disc brakes are inherently self-adjusting. The only adjustment possible is to the handbrake, which is covered at the end of this section.

Master Cylinder

The dual master cylinder has a safety feature which the single unit lacks—if a leak develops in one brake circuit (rear wheels, for example), the other circuit will still operate.

Failure of one system is immediately obvious—the pedal travel increases appreciably and a warning light is activated. When the fluid falls below a certain level, a switch activates the circuit.

Reset pin (arrow) on master cylinder with pressure warning differential

---

CAUTION

This design was not intended to allow driving the car for any distance with, in effect, a two-wheel brake system. If one brake circuit fails, braking action is correspondingly lower. Front circuit failure is the more serious, however, since the front brakes contribute up to 75% of the braking force required to stop the car.

REMOVAL AND INSTALLATION

1. To remove the master cylinder, first open a bleed screw at one front, and one rear, wheel.
2. Pump the pedal to empty the reservoir completely. Make sure both reservoirs are completely drained.
3. Disconnect the switch connectors using a small screwdriver. Disconnect the brake lines at the master cylinder. Plug the ends with bleed screw caps or the equivalent.
4. Unbolt the master cylinder from the power brake unit and remove. Be careful you do not lose the O-ring in the flange groove of the master cylinder.
5. Installation is the reverse of removal. Be sure to replace the O-ring between the master cylinder and the power brake unit, since this must be absolutely tight. Torque the nuts to 12-15 ft/lbs. Be sure that both chambers are completely filled with brake fluid and bleed the brakes.

OVERHAUL

1. To disassemble, pull the reservoir out of the top of the cylinder.
2. Remove the screw cap, strainer, and splash shield.
3. Unscrew the cover caps and take out the inserts and O-ring.
4. Push the piston inward slightly and remove the stop screws.
5. Remove the piston stop-ring in the same manner, then pull out the piston and other components.
6. The spring must be unscrewed from the piston.
7. Clean all parts in clean brake fluid.
8. Check the housing bore for score marks and rust. Do not hone the cylinder bore. If slight rust marks do not come out with crocus cloth, replace the housing.
9. Assembly is the reverse of disassembly. Before installing the pistons, coat the sleeves of both pistons with brake fluid.

NOTE: Do not force the pistons into the housings. A special tool is available to install the pistons, but if it is not available, install the pistons very carefully with a slight twisting motion. The special assembly tools can be fabricated in the shop from light metal alloy, according to the dimensions given.

BRAKE BLEEDING

Always bleed the brakes after performing any service, or if the pedal seems spongy (soft). The location of the bleed screws can be seen by consulting the illustrations throughout this section. Prior to bleeding each wheel,

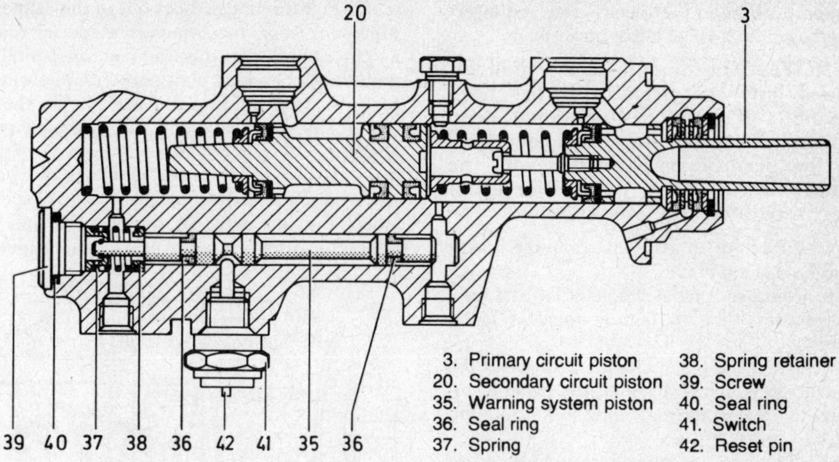

3. Primary circuit piston
20. Secondary circuit piston
35. Warning system piston
36. Seal ring
37. Spring
38. Spring retainer
39. Screw
40. Seal ring
41. Switch
42. Reset pin

Step-type master cylinder used on 1976 and later models

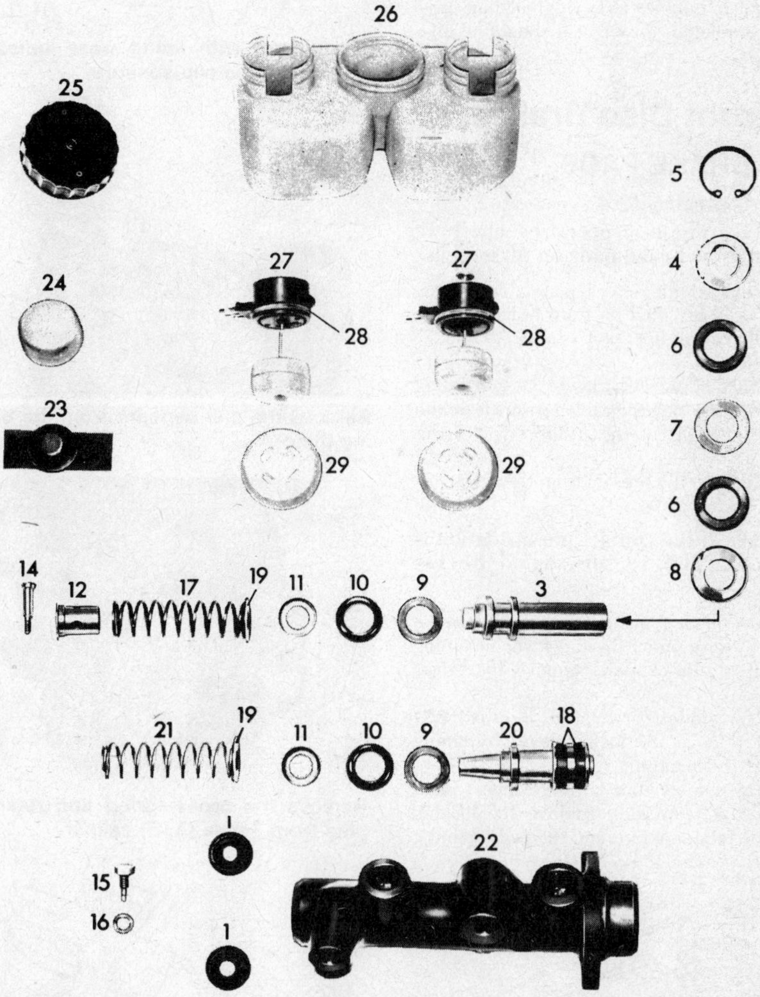

1. Container plug
3. Piston (push rod circuit)
4. Stop washer
5. Lock ring
6. Vacuum seal
7. Intermediate ring
8. Bearing ring
9. Filler
10. Primary sleeve
11. Supporting ring
12. Spring retainer
14. Connecting screw
15. Stop-screw
16. Sealing ring (copper)
17. Compresion spring
18. Ring sleeve
19. Spring plate
20. Intermediate piston
21. Compression spring
22. Housing
23. Splash guard
24. Strainer
25. Closing cover
26. Compensating tank
27. Contact insert
28. O-ring
29. End cover

Exploded view of tandem master cylinder

connect a hose to the bleed screw and insert the hose into a jar of clean brake fluid.

NOTE: On dual master cylinders, bleed only the circuit that has been opened. If both circuits have been opened, first bleed the circuit connected to the pushrod bore starting with the wheel farthest from the master cylinder, then bleed the other circuit.

1. First have an assistant pump the brakes and hold the pedal.
2. Then, starting at the point farthest from the master cylinder, slightly open the bleed screw.
3. When the pedal hits the floor, close the bleed screw before allowing the pedal to return (to prevent air from being sucked into the system).
4. Continue this procedure until no more air bubbles exit from the bleed screw hole, then go to the next wheel. Fluid, which has been bled from the system, is filled with microscopic air bubbles after the bleeding process is completed, therefore it should be discarded.

Front Disc Brakes

DISC BRAKE PADS

Replacement

NOTE: These procedures apply to front or rear brake pads on all models.

1. Remove the cover plate. The cover plate is only installed on front brakes of cars with solid brake discs (not ventilated) and 57 mm calipers.
2. On models with the brake pad lining wear indicator, pull the cable sensors from the plug connections at the inside edge of the caliper.
3. Remove the sensors from the brake lining or backing plate.

NOTE: If the contact pin insulation is worn, the clip sensor should be replaced.

4. On models with Teves (ATE) brake calipers, use a punch to knock the retaining pins out of the caliper. Remove the cross-spring.
5. On models with the Bendix (BX) caliper, remove the locking eyes, retaining pins and pad retaining springs.
6. On models with Girling calipers (usually only at rear axle), remove the locking eyes, the retaining pins and the pad retaining plates.

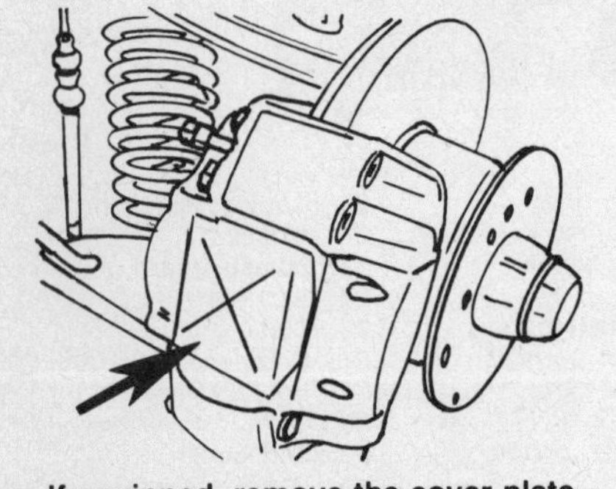

If equipped, remove the cover plate

7. Pull the brake shoes out of the caliper. Mercedes-Benz recommends a special tool, an impact puller for this, but you can carefully grab the pad backing plate ears with pliers or a piece of bent welding rod and wiggle them out. It's best to leave one pad in the caliper always.
8. Use a small brush to clean the pad guides on the inside of the brake caliper. Check the dust boots for cracks or damage. If necessary, remove and overhaul the caliper.

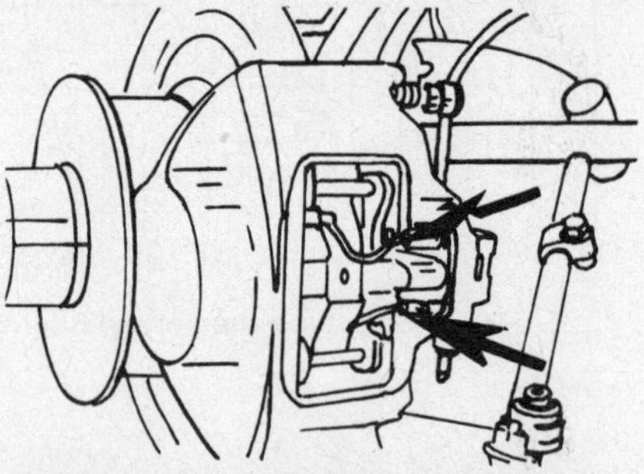

If equipped with lining wear indicator, disconnect the clip sensors

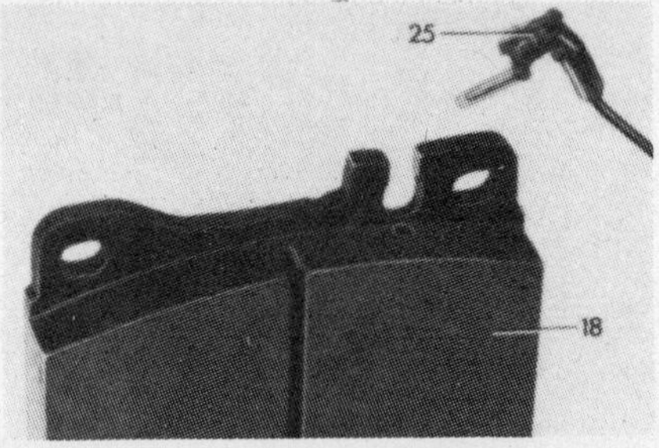

Remove the clip sensors from the backing plate

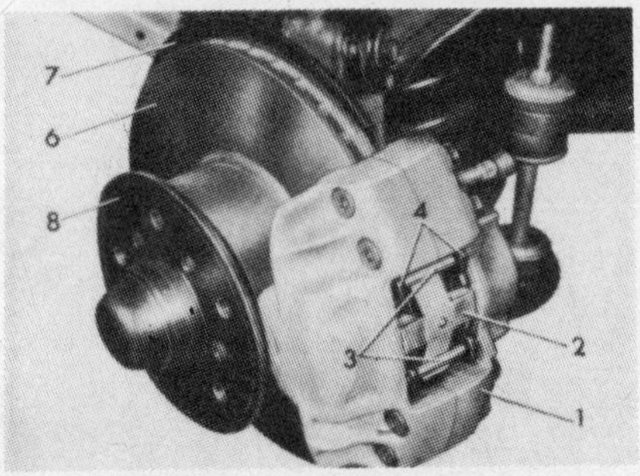

Remove the cross-spring and retaining pins from Teves (ATE) caliper

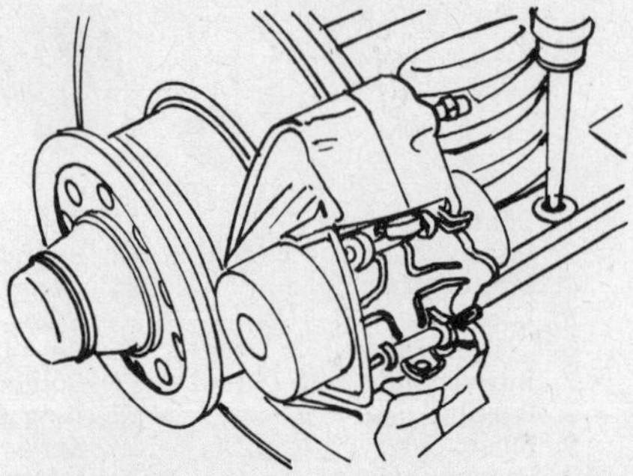

Remove the retaining pins and springs from Bendix (BX)

9. When the pads are removed, the pistons will move forward slightly, due to hydraulic pressure in the system. To install the pads, the pistons must be pushed back slightly. Mercedes-Benz recommends a special tool to do this, but a flat piece of hardwood will do if used carefully. Other tools will increase the chances of damaging the piston or dust boots.

NOTE: It should be relatively easy to push the pistons back.

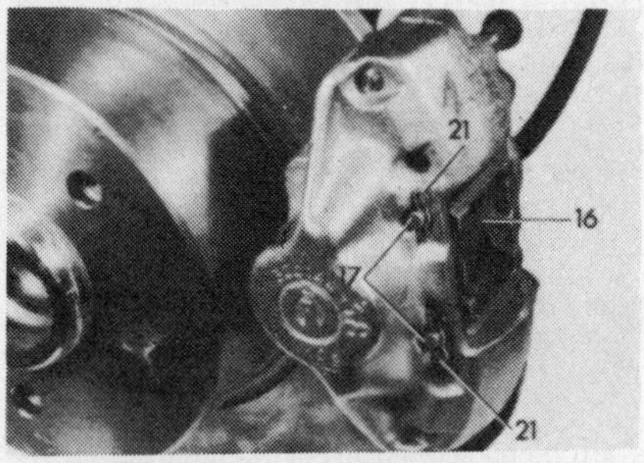

On Girling caliper, remove the retaining pins and plates

Remove the brake pads

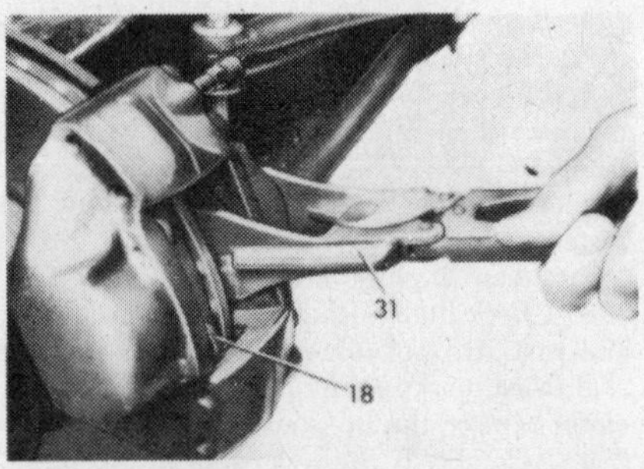

Force the pistons back into the caliper

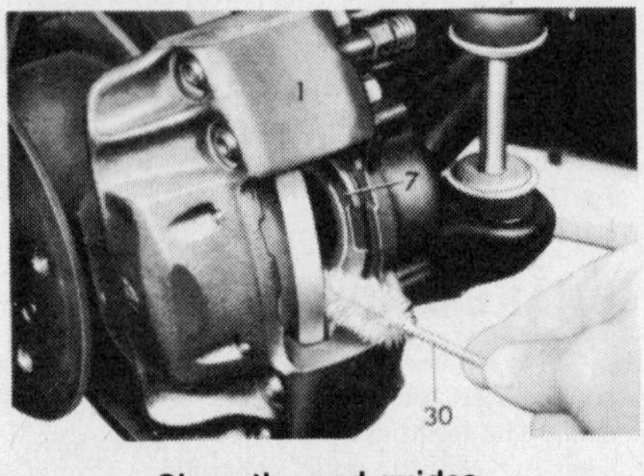

Clean the pad guides

10. Check the thickness of the brake disc. Refer to the brake specifications for tolerances.

11. Check the brake discs for scoring or cracks. Score marks up to 0.02 in. deep can be accepted as normal scoring.

12. Clean the air passages of ventilated discs with a thin piece of wire. Blow out all loose dirt. Do not clean with solvent unless the disc is removed from the car.

13. Clean the rain groove in the backing plate and measure the thickness of the lining. See the Brake Specifications for minimum lining thickness.

14. Apply a heat resistant, long-term lubricant to the backing plate as shown. Install the brake pad.

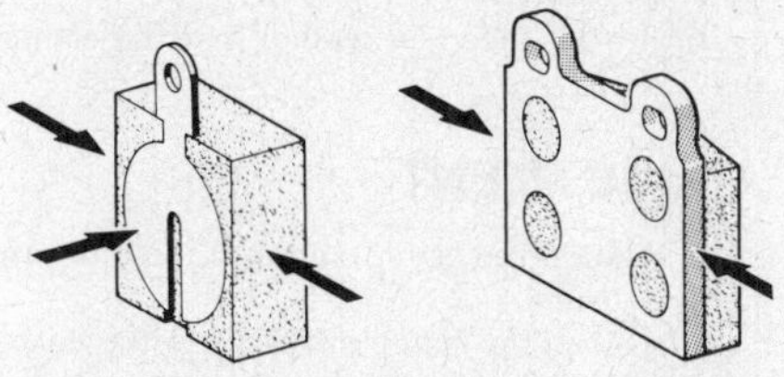

Lubricate the brake pads where shown

15. Depending on the type of caliper, install the cross-spring, retaining plate, retaining pins and locking eyes.

16. On cars with a brake pad wear indicator, connect the sensors into the brake lining and the cable to the plug connection.

17. If equipped, install the cover plate.

18. On vehicles with a pressure differential warning system (1976 and 1977), the warning indicator may light when pads are replaced. To extinguish the light, push the reset pin (42) on the switch (41) after replacing the lining. The switch is located on the outboard side of the master cylinder.

Disc Brake Calipers

REMOVAL AND INSTALLATION

1. Drain brake fluid from the front brake circuit through an open bleeder screw.

2. Disconnect the brake hose from the brake line (or, on some models, disconnect the brake line from the caliper).

3. Immediately plug the lines and openings to prevent loss of fluid.

4. On models where the brake line does not connect directly to the caliper, remove the hose from the caliper.

5. Remove the brake hose from the bracket.

6. Plug the connection at the brake caliper.

7. Unlock the lockwasher and remove the hex mounting bolts.

CAUTION

The caliper mounting bolts should not be removed unless the calipers are at approximately room temperature.

8. Remove the calipers from the steering knuckle. As the caliper is removed, take note

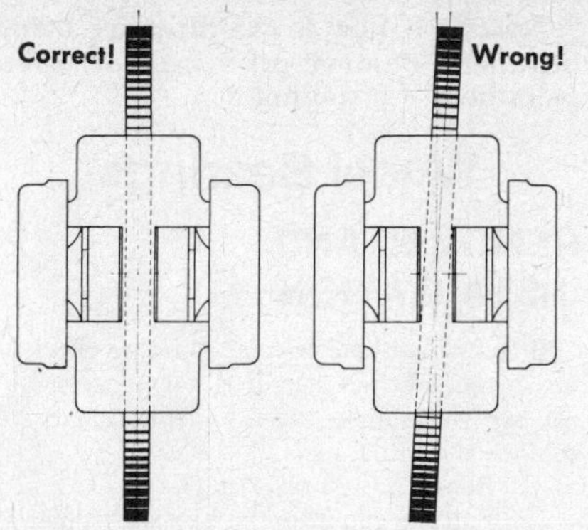

Uneven brake pad wear will result from misaligned calipers and discs

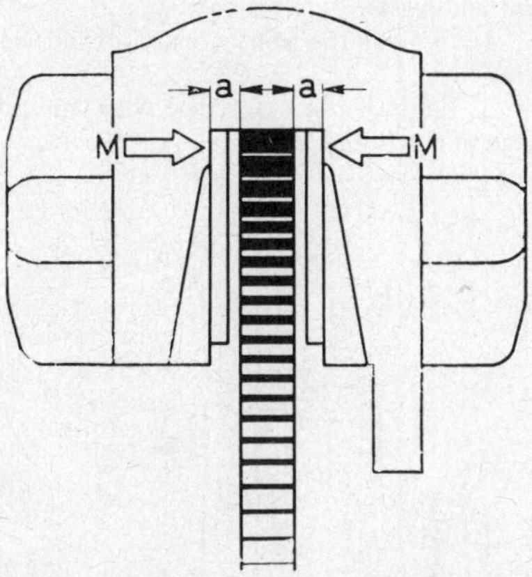

Measure the clearance (a) on each side of the disc at point (M)

of any shim that may be installed and tape these (if any) in their original position.

9. To install, use a new lockplate and attach the brake caliper to the steering knuckle. The proper torque for the mounting bolts is 82 ft/lbs.

It is extremely important that the brake disc be parallel to the caliper. Using a feeler gauge, measure the clearance at the top and bottom of the caliper (between disc and caliper) and on both sides of the disc. The clearance should not vary more than 0.15 mm. If the clearance varies, position the brake caliper by adding or subtracting shims as required. This procedure only applies to models equipped with shims, usually on the rear brake calipers.

10. Insert the brake hose into the bracket, making sure that the grommet is not damaged, or connect the brake line to the calipers. If applicable, connect the brake hose to the brake line. Make sure that the hose is not twisted.

11. On some models a locking disc is attached to the brake line bracket. Install the brake hose into the disc so that the disc or hose does not bind.

12. Turn the steering lock-to-lock to make sure that the brake hose or lines do not bind.

13. Fill the master cylinder and bleed the brake system.

14. Before driving the car, depress the brake pedal lever, several times, to seat the pads.

PISTON SEAL REPLACEMENT (FRONT BRAKE CALIPER)

CAUTION

Do not unbolt the two caliper halves for any reason. Remove the brake caliper for easier service.

1. Remove the friction pads, brake line, and dust cap, then pry the clamp ring from the housing.

2. Using a rubber-backed piece of flat steel, hold one piston in place while blowing the other one out with compressed air (7-8 psi).

3. Remove the piston seals from the cylinder bores and examine the bores. Scored bores necessitate replacement of the entire caliper, since the inner surface is chrome plated and cannot be honed.

4. Clean the bores with crocus cloth only, never emery paper.

5. Install the new seals, coating them with brake fluid beforehand, then install the (front) piston so that the projection points downward. The rear caliper pistons must be installed with the projection facing downward.

NOTE: If the projection is in any other position, the brakes may squeal badly.

6. Install the dust cap, clamp ring and heat shield.

7. The recess in the heat shield must fit the piston projection, but be above the shield lever by about 0.004 in.

NOTE: The heat shields differ from inner and outer pistons.

8. Install the friction pads and the caliper assembly, then bleed the brakes.

Brake Disc

REMOVAL AND INSTALLATION

1. Removal for the various types is similar.

2. On all models, remove the brake caliper. On 1975-76 230, 240D, 300D, 280 and 280C models and on 450SL, 450SLC, 380SL, 380SLC models, the hub and disc can be removed by prying off the dust cap, removing the socket screw and clamp nut and pulling off the wheel hub. Fasten the hub in a vise or holding fixture (be careful not to distort the housing), matchmark the disc and hub, then unbolt the brake disc.

3. On all other models the disc can be unbolted from the hub.

4. Inspect the disc for burning (blue color), cracks and scoring. The disc becomes scored slightly in normal service; therefore, replace it only if the depth of individual scores exceeds 0.020 in.

5. To ensure proper alignment, clean the hub and disc with emery paper to remove all rust and/or burrs, then bolt the disc to the hub.

6. It is a wise precaution to use new lockwashers under the bolts.

7. Install the hub and disc, then check the

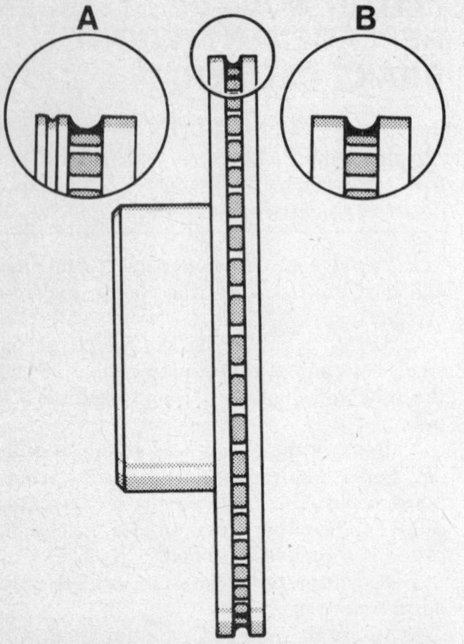

1980 and later brake discs can be identified with a groove (insert A). New rotors are for use with thicker brake pads. Insert B shows earlier rotors without grooves.

disc for runout (wobble), using a dial indicator as illustrated.

8. If runout is excessive, it sometimes helps to remove the disc and reseat it on the hub. Install the caliper assembly and bleed the brakes.

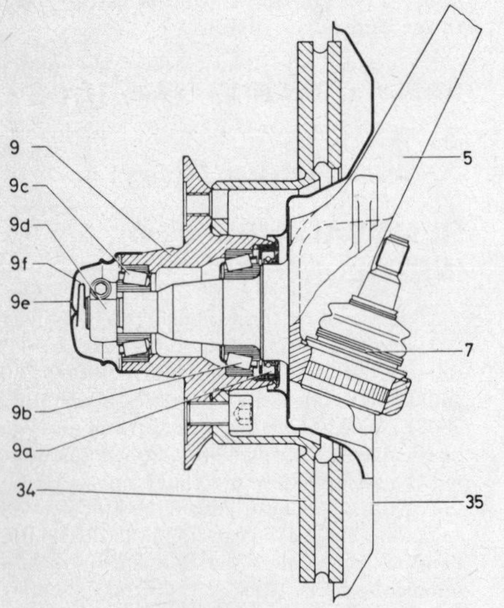

5. Steering knuckle
7. Supporting joint
9. Front wheel hub
9a. Radial sealing ring
9b. Tapered roller bearing, inside
9c. Tapered roller bearing, outside
9d. Clamping nut
9e. Wheel cap
9f. Contact spring
34. Brake disc
35. Cover plate

Wheel bearing cutaway—450SE, 450SEL, 380SEL, 6.9, 300SD, 280S, 280SE and 1977 and later 230, 240D, 280E, 280CE, 300D, 300CD and 300TD

NOTE: If new brake discs are being installed, remove the anti-corrosion paint before installing it.

Wheel Bearings

REMOVAL AND INSTALLATION

If the wheel bearing play is being checked for correct setting only, it is not necessary to remove the caliper. It is only necessary to remove the brake pads.

1. Remove the brake caliper.
2. Pull the cap from the hub with a pair of channel-lock pliers. Remove the radio suppression spring, if equipped.
3. Loosen the socket screw of the clamp nut on the wheel spindle. Remove the clamp nut and washer.
4. Remove the front wheel hub and brake disc.
5. Remove the inner race with the roller cage of the outer bearing.

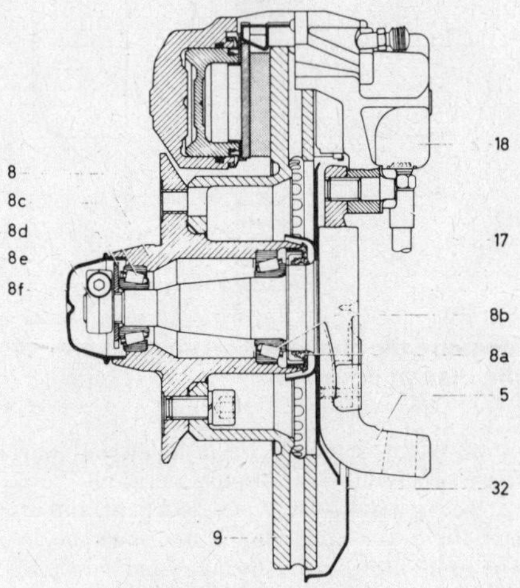

5. Steering knuckle
8. Wheel hub
8a. Radial sealing ring
8b. Tapered roller bearing, outside
8c. Tapered roller bearing, inside
8d. Washer
8e. Clamping nut
8f. Wheel cap
9. Brake disc
17. Brake hose
18. Brake caliper
32. Cover plate

Wheel bearing cutaway—1974-76 230, 240D, 280, 280C, 300D and all 450SL, 450SLC, 380SL, 380SLC models

6. Using a brass or aluminum drift, carefully tap the outer race of the inner bearing until it can be removed with the inner race, bearing cage, and seal.
7. In the same manner, tap the outer race of the bearing out of the hub.
8. Separate the front hub from the brake disc.
9. To assemble, press the outer races into the front wheel hub.
10. Pack the bearing cage with bearing grease and insert the inner race with the bearing into the wheel hub.
11. Coat the sealing ring with sealant and press it into the hub.
12. Pack the front wheel hub with 45-55 grams of wheel bearing grease. The races of the tapered bearing should be well packed and also apply grease to the front faces of the rollers. Pack the front bearings with the specified amount of grease. Too much grease will cause overheating of the lubricant and it may lose its lubricity. Too little grease will not lubricate properly.
13. Coat the contact surface of the sealing ring on the wheel spindle with Molykote® paste.
14. Press the wheel hub onto the wheel spindle.
15. Install the inner race and cage of the outer bearing.
16. Install the steel washer and the clamp nut.

ADJUSTMENT

1. Tighten the clamp nut until the hub can just be turned.
2. Slacken the clamp nut and seat the bearings on the spindle by rapping the spindle sharply with a hammer.
3. Attach a dial indicator, with the pointer indexed, onto the wheel hub.
4. Check the end-play of the hub by pushing and pulling on the flange. The end-play should be approximately 0.0004-0.0008 in.

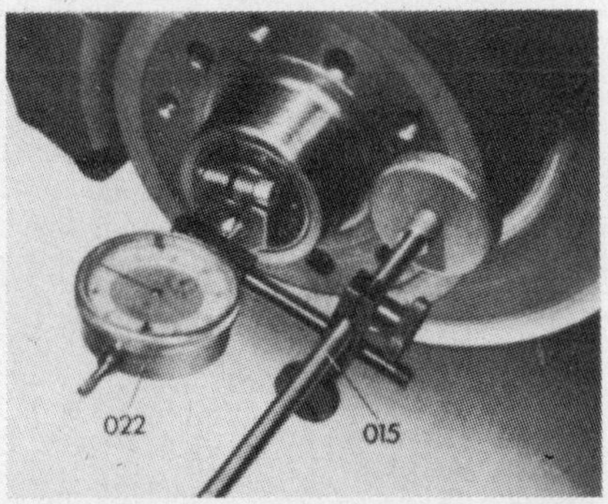

Dial indicator set-up for checking wheel bearing play

5. Make an additional check by rotating the washer between the inner race of the outer bearing and the clamp nut. It should be able to be turned by hand.
6. Check the position of the suppressor pin in the wheel spindle and the contact spring in the dust cap.
7. Pack the dust cap with 20-25 grams of wheel bearing grease and install the cap.
8. Install the brake caliper and bleed the brakes.

Rear Disc Brakes

DISC BRAKE PADS

Removal and Installation

The procedure for removing the rear disc brake pads is the same as for front disc brake pads. Use the instructions given under "Front Disc Brake Pad Removal and Installation", with the accompanying illustrations.

Disc Brake Calipers

REMOVAL AND INSTALLATION

Use the procedure given under "Front Brake Caliper Removal and Installation." Some rear brake calipers have no disc run-out compensating feature. These calipers can only be installed on vehicles where the rear axle shaft is supported on grooved ball bearings. Calipers with a compensating feature may be installed on axles with grooved ball bearings or self-aligning bearings.

OVERHAUL

Rear disc brake caliper overhaul procedures are the same as those given for front disc brake caliper overhaul.

Brake Discs

REMOVAL AND INSTALLATION

1. Remove the brake caliper.
2. Remove the brake disc from the rear axle shaft flange. Jammed brake discs can be loosened from the axle shaft flanges by light taps with a plastic hammer. Be sure that the parking brake is fully released.
3. Installation is the reverse of removal.
4. Inspection procedures are the same as those for front brake discs.

Handbrake

FRONT CABLE

Removal and Installation

230, 240D, 300D, 300CD, 300TD, 280, 280C, 280CE

1. Remove the spring from the equalizer.
2. Back off the adjusting screw completely.
3. Detach the relay lever from the bracket on the frame and from the adjusting shackle.
4. Detach the cable from the relay lever by pulling the cotter pin out of the bolt.
5. Remove the clip from the cable guide. Remove the clips from the chassis.
6. Detach the brake cable from the parking brake link. Remove the clip from the cable guide and detach the brake cable from the parking brake.
7. Pull the cable downward from the chassis.
8. Installation is the reverse of removal.

450SL, 450SLC, 380SL, 380SLC

1. Remove the exhaust system.
2. Disconnect the return spring.
3. Remove the bolts which attach the guide to the intermediate lever.
4. Remove the adjusting screw from the adjusting bracket.
5. Loosen the brake control cables on the intermediate lever and pull the cotter pin from the flange bolt. Remove the flange bolt.
6. Remove the spring clamp from the cable guide and remove the cable control from the bracket.
7. Remove the tunnel cover.
8. Disconnect the brake control from the parking brake and remove the spring clamp from the cable guide. Remove the cable control from the parking brake.
9. Remove the brake control cable out of the frame toward the rear.
10. Installation is the reverse of removal.

280S, 280SE, 300SD, 380SEL, 450SE, 450SEL, 6.9

1. Remove the floor mat.
2. Remove the legroom cover (upper and lower).
3. Remove the air duct.
4. Disconnect the 4 rubber rings and lower and support the exhaust system.
5. Remove the shield above the exhaust pipes.
6. Disconnect the return spring from the bracket.
7. Back off the adjusting screw on the bracket.
8. Disconnect the intermediate lever from the adjusting bracket.
9. Loosen the brake cable controls on the intermediate lever while pulling the cotter pin from the flange bolt. Remove the flange bolt.
10. Remove the spring clip from the cable guide on the floor pan.
11. Disconnect the brake cable control from the parking brake bracket.
12. Remove the spring clip from the cable and remove the cable control from the parking brake.
13. Pull the cable away upward.
14. Installation is the reverse of removal. Adjust the parking brake.

Rear Brake Cable

Removal and Installation

230, 240D, 280, 280C, 280CE, 280E, 300D, 300CD, 300TD

1. Remove the parking brake shoes after removing the wheel.
2. Remove the screws from the wheel support and detach the brake cable.
3. Back off the adjusting screw from the adjusting shackle.
4. Remove the spring clips, detach the cable, and remove the equalizer.
5. Installation is the reverse of removal.

450SL, 450SLC, 380SL, 380SLC

1. Remove the parking brake shoes.
2. Remove the bolt from the wheel carrier and remove the cable.
3. Remove the exhaust system. On some models the exhaust system can be lowered and supported after removing the rubber rings. If equipped, remove the heat shield from above the exhaust pipes.
4. Disconnect the draw spring from the holder.
5. Detach the guide from the intermediate lever.
6. Remove the adjusting screw from the bracket.
7. Disconnect the intermediate lever on the bearing and remove it from the adjusting bracket.
8. Remove the holder, compensating lever, cable control plates, and intermediate lever from the tunnel.
9. Remove the spring clamps and disconnect the cable from the plate.
10. Installation is the reverse of removal.

Adjustment

ALL MODELS

1. If the floor pedal can be depressed more than two notches before actuating the brakes, adjust by jacking up the rear of the car, then removing one lug bolt and adjusting the star wheel with a screwdriver.
2. Move the screwdriver upward on the left (driver's) side, downward on the right (passenger's) side to tighten the shoes.

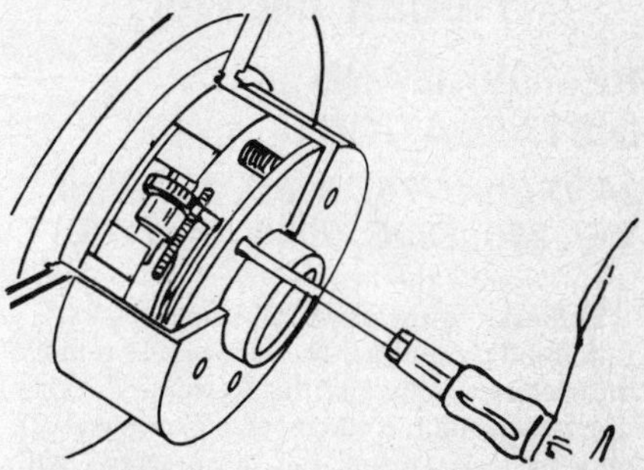

Cut-away view of rear brake shoe adjustment

3. When the wheel is locked, back off about 2-4 clicks.
4. With this type system, the adjusting bolt on the cable relay lever only serves to equalize cable length; therefore, do not attempt to adjust the brakes by turning this bolt.

Parking Brake Shoes

REMOVAL AND INSTALLATION

1. Remove the brake caliper.
2. Remove the brake disc.
3. Disconnect the lower spring with brake pliers.
4. Turn the rear axle shaft flange so that one hole faces the spring. With brake spring removal pliers, disconnect and remove the spring from the cover plate.
5. Remove the spring on the other brake shoe in a similar manner.
6. Pull both brake shoes apart so that they can be removed past the rear axle shaft flange.
7. Disconnect the upper return spring from the brake shoes and remove the adjuster.
8. Force the pin out of the expanding lock and remove the expanding lock from the brake cable.

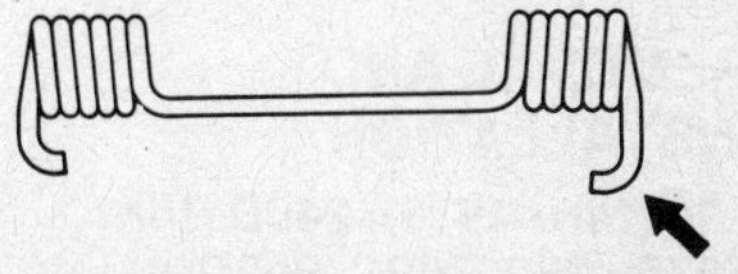

Install the lower parking brake show spring with the small eye to the brake shoes

9. Remove the brake shoes.
10. Installation is the reverse of removal. Coat all bearing and sliding surfaces with Moylkote® prior to installation. Attach the lower spring with the small eye to the brake shoes.
11. Adjust the parking brakes.

CHASSIS ELECTRICAL

Heater Blower

REMOVAL AND INSTALLATION

240D (thru '76), 300D, 230 (thru '76), 280, 280C, 300D (thru '76)

1. Remove the heater box.
2. Back out the three retaining screws.
3. Slightly pull out the blower and remove the electrical plug and the blower.
4. Installation is the reverse of removal. To prevent leaks, install the three screws with three new special washers exactly like those removed.

450SL, 450SLC, 380SL, 380SLC

1. Remove the panel which covers the heater blower.
2. Loosen the blower retaining nuts.
3. Pull the plug from the series resistance that is located on the firewall.
4. Remove the series resistance.
5. Lift the cable and remove the blower.
6. Installation is the reverse of removal. Be sure that the sealing frame is not damaged.

230 (1977 and later), 240D (1977 and later), 280E, 280CE, 300D (1977 and later), 300CD, 300TD, 280S, 280SE, 300SD, 450SE, 450SEL, 6.9, 380SEL

1. Unplug the resistor on the firewall, located just above the automatic transmission and dipstick.
2. Unscrew the resistor.
3. Remove the air intake grille.
4. Remove the glove compartment.
5. Remove the cover under the right-hand instrument panel.
6. Remove the hose between the center air duct and right-hand outlet.
7. Remove the clip and disconnect the wire control from the lever.
8. Unbolt and remove the blower.
9. Installation is the reverse of removal.

Instrument Cluster

REMOVAL AND INSTALLATION

230 (thru 1976), 240D (thru 1976), 280, 280C, 300D (thru 1976)

1. Remove the cover plate from the left side underneath the dashboard.
2. On vehicles with automatic transmission, disconnect the Bowden cable for the gear selector lever, after engaging Park.
3. Remove the bracket holding the handbrake.
4. Unscrew the knurled nut and pull the instrument cluster slightly forward.
5. Disconnect the tachometer drive.
6. Cover the steering column to prevent scratches.
7. If only bulb replacement is desired, this is sufficient. To remove the entire cluster, continue with the remaining steps.

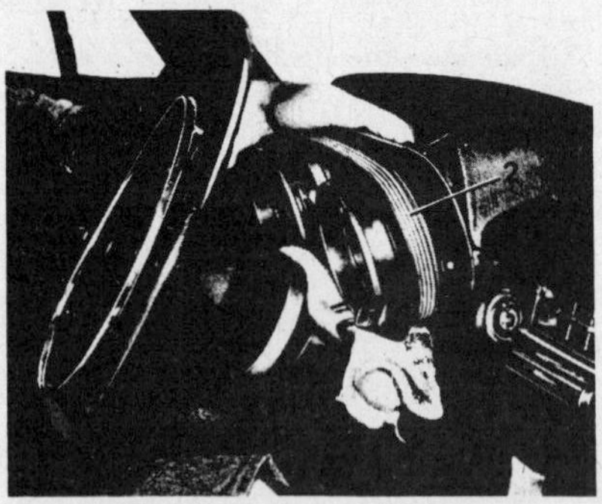

Instrument panel removal showing rubber retaining strip (2)

8. Disconnect the oil pressure line.
9. Remove the electrical plug connections.
10. Release the excess pressure in the cooling system and install the cap afterward.
11. Remove the temperature sensor from the cylinder head and plug the hole.
12. Carefully remove the instrument cluster with the capillary tube and temperature sensor.

CAUTION

Do not bend the capillary tube.

13. Installation is the reverse of removal.

280S, 280SE, 300SD (thru 1980), 450SE, 450SEL, 380SL, 380SLC, 450SL, 450SLC, 6.9

1. Remove the padding from the steering wheel.
2. Remove the steering wheel.
3. The instrument cluster is held in place by a rubber ring which fits into a groove. Remove the ring and pull the instrument cluster slightly forward.

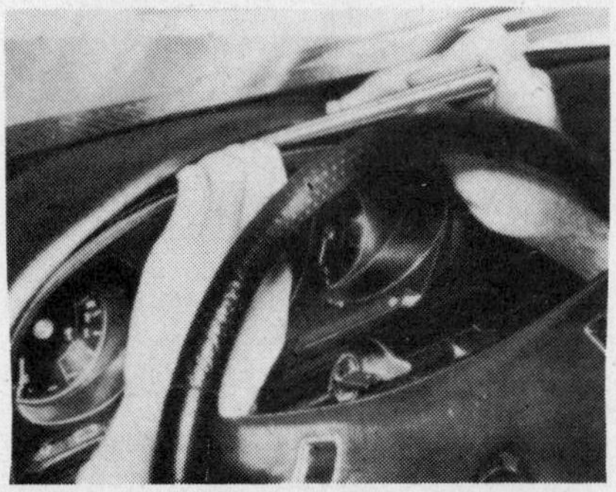

Remove the instrument cluster with a small screwdriver

4. Loosen and disconnect the speedometer shaft, the electrical plug connections, and the oil pressure line.
5. Completely remove the instrument cluster.

CAUTION

Do not bend the oil pressure line.

6. Installation is the reverse of removal. Be sure that the speedometer is not bent excessively or it will vibrate when running.

1977 and Later 230, 240D, 280E, 280CE, 300D, 300CD, 300TD, 1981 and later 300SD, 380SEL

1. Remove the instrument cluster slightly by hand. Don't pull on the edge of the glass.
2. A removal hook can be fabricated and inserted between the instrument cluster and the dashboard.
3. Guide the removal hook up to the right to the recess (arrow) and pull the instrument cluster out.

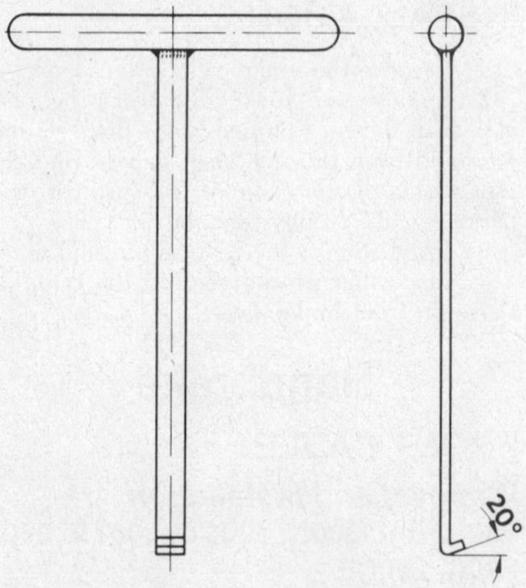

Fabricated tool for removing the instrument cluster

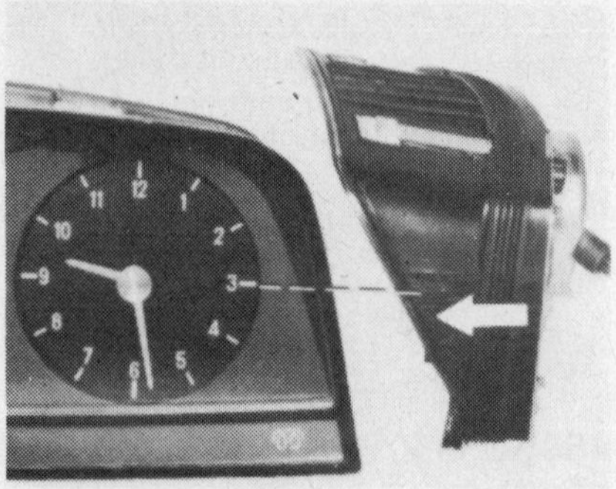

Recess slot in the instrument cluster

NOTE: The 1981 380SEL and 300SD models use 5 clips to hold the instrument cluster in place.

4. Pull it out as far as possible and disconnect the speedometer cable, electrical connections and oil pressure line.
5. To install, reconnect the electrical connections, oil pressure line and speedometer cable. To avoid speedometer cable noise, guide it into the largest radius possible.

6. Push the instrument cluster firmly into the dashboard.

Ignition Switch

REMOVAL AND INSTALLATION

All Models with Ignition Switch in Dashboard

1. Remove the instrument cluster.
2. Remove the right-hand cover plate under the dashboard.
3. Remove the plug connection from the ignition switch.
4. Remove the screws which hold the ignition switch to the rear of the lock cylinder and remove the ignition switch.
5. To install the ignition switch, attach the plug connection, after fastening the switch to the steering lock.
6. Install the instrument cluster.
7. Check the switch for proper function and install the lower cover.

Lock Cylinder (Key Can Be Removed in Position 1)

REMOVAL AND INSTALLATION

1. Turn the key to position 1 and remove the key.
2. Pry the cover sleeve from the lock cylinder with a small screwdriver.
3. Using a bent paper clip, hook onto the cover sleeve and remove the sleeve. Be sure that you do not remove the rosette in the dashboard also.
4. Insert the paper clip between the rosette and the steering lock and push in the lock pin. Remove the lock cylinder slightly with the key.

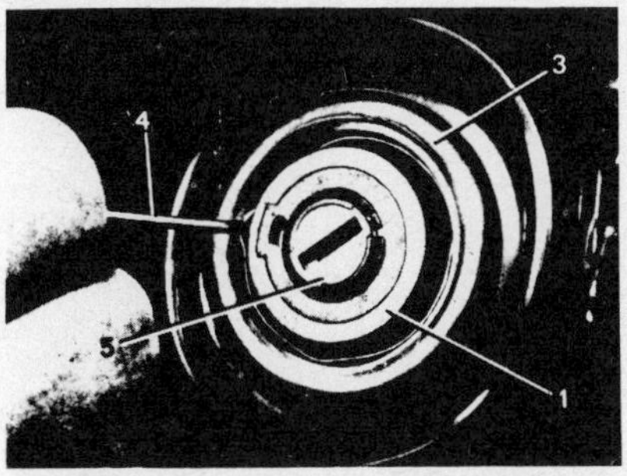

1. Steering lock 3. Rosette 4. Steel wire (paper clip) 5. Locking cylinder

Ignition lock cylinder removal from the instrument panel (both types)

5. Insert the paper clip into the locking hole and pull the lock cylinder completely out.
6. Installation is the reverse of removal. Turn the lock cylinder to position 1 and insert it into the steering lock, making sure that the lock pin engages. Push the cover sleeve into position 1.
7. Make sure that the cylinder operates properly.

Lock Cylinder (Key Cannot Be Removed in Position 1)

REMOVAL AND INSTALLATION

Because of legal requirements, the lock was changed from the previous version, so that the key can only be removed in position ??

1. Turn the key to position 1.
2. Lift the cover sleeve to the edge of the key and turn the key to position 0.
3. Remove the key and cover sleeve.
4. Insert the key into the lock cylinder and turn to position 1 (90° to the right), push in the lock pin and remove the lock cylinder.
5. To install the lock cylinder, turn the lock cylinder to position 1 and insert the lock cylinder, making sure that the locking pin engages.
6. Turn the key to position 0 and remove the key.
7. Place the cover sleeve on the steering lock, insert and turn the key, and push in the cover sleeve at position 1.
8. Check the locking cylinder for proper function.

Steering Lock

REMOVAL AND INSTALLATION

1. Disconnect the ground cable from the battery.
2. Remove the instrument cluster.
3. Remove the plug connection from the ignition switch behind the dashboard.
4. Pull the ignition key to position 1.
5. Loosen the attaching screw for the steering lock.
6. Remove the cover sleeve from the steering lock.
7. On vehicles with the latest version of the steering lock, pull the connection for the warning buzzer.
8. Push in the lock pin with a small punch.
9. Turn the steering lock and remove it from the holder in the column jacket. Be sure that the rosette is not damaged.

CAUTION

The lock pin can only be pushed in when the cylinder is in position 1.

10. To install the steering lock, connect the warning buzzer if so equipped.
11. Place the steering lock in position 1 and insert the lock into the steering column while pushing the lock pin in. Be sure that the lock pin engages.
12. Tighten the attaching clamp screw.
13. Attach the plug connection to the ignition switch.
14. Push the cover sleeve onto the lock in position 1.
15. Install the instrument cluster.
16. Check to be sure that the steering lock works properly.

Seat Belts

Beginning in August of 1973 (1974 models), all Mercedes-Benz cars conformed to the regulation requiring a starter interlock system that prevented starting the engine if the seal belts were not buckled. To eliminate the possibility of defeating the system by permanently buckling the seatbelts, the system required that buckling the belts and starting the car take place in a preset sequence. Each front seat contains a contact switch that closes when the seat is occupied. The buckle on the front seat belts also contains a switch that closes if the belt is unbuckled. 1974 cars can be started by reaching in through the open window and starting the car with the key.

1975 models are equipped with the same basic system, but with an additional over-ride switch, located in the engine compartment. In case the engine cannot be started due to a malfunction in the seat belt warning system, the starter interlock can be bypassed for ONE starting attempt, by pushing the button on the switch with the ignition ON and the transmission in N or P. As soon as the transmission is shifted out of N or P, or the ignition is turned OFF, and the relay in the over-ride switch is opened. To repeat the process, the switch must be depressed again.

DISABLING THE INTERLOCK SYSTEM

As a result of Federal legislation, the starter interlock system used on 1974-75 cars was replaced with a light and buzzer reminder system. The new law, which took effect 12/

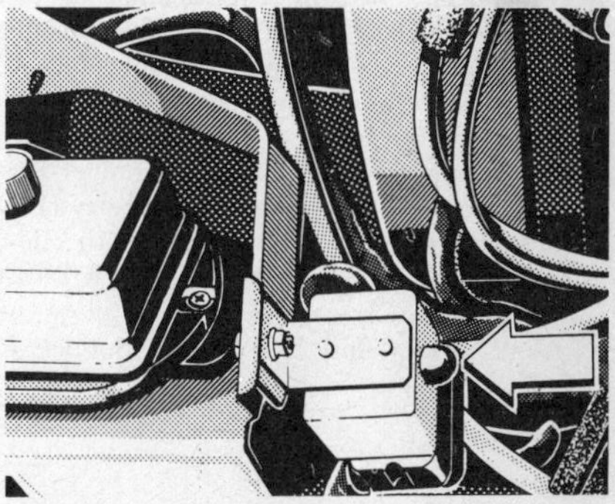

Ignition interlock over-ride switch location—1975 230

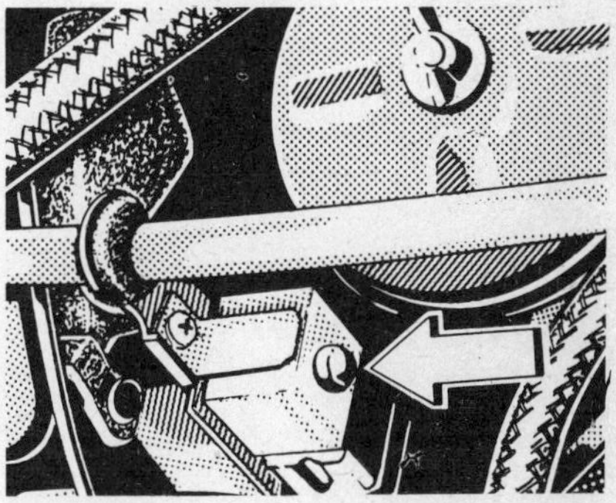

Ignition interlock over-ride switch location—1975 280, 280C

Ignition interlock over-ride switch location—1975 450SL, SLC

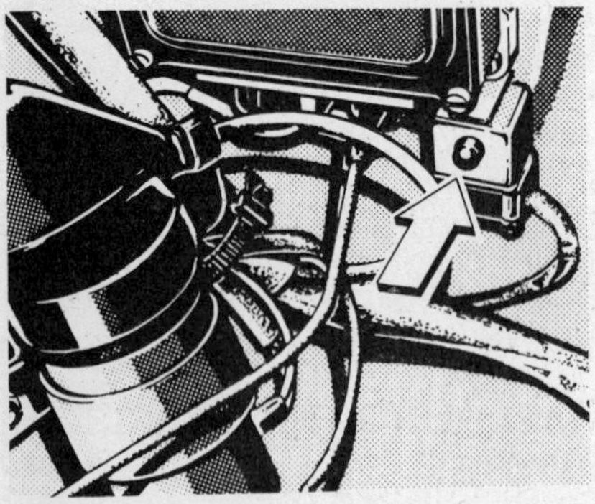

Ignition interlock over-ride switch location—1975 450SE, SEL

26/74, permitted the disconnection of the starter interlock system, (but not the warning light) and Mercedes-Benz does not advocate that this be done.

To bypass the interlock feature on all models so equipped (with or without an over-ride switch), replace the seatbelt logic relay (Part No. 000 545 69 32 or 000 545 68 32) with a new relay (Part No. 001 545 00 32). This will disable the interlock feature, but still allow the warning buzzer and buckle-up sequence to remain in effect.

NOTE: Under no circumstances should the interlock system be bypassed by bridging either the over-ride switch relay or the logic relay, since this could allow the car to be started in gear.

Headlights

REMOVAL AND INSTALLATION

230 (Thru 1976), 280, 280C, 240D (thru 1976)

1. Loosen the screw on the lower portion of the unit.
2. Remove the trim ring together with the lower part of the unit.
3. Push the retaining ring in and, at the same time, turn the ring left to the stop.
4. Remove the ring, sealed beam lamp, and disconnect the plug.
5. Installation is the reverse of removal. If installing a Mercedes-Benz replacement sealed beam, be sure that the number "2" is at the top in the center. Be sure to have the headlights adjusted.

1981 300SD, 380SEL

1. Open the hood and unscrew the 5 plastic knurled nuts.
2. Remove the assembly from the front of the car. Unplug the electrical connector.
3. Remove the headlight attaching screws.
4. Disconnect the electrical connector and remove the headlight.
5. Installation is the reverse of removal.

All Other Models

1. Loosen the attaching screws and remove the cover.
2. Remove the headlight attaching screws and remove the retaining ring and light as a unit.

NOTE: Do not disturb tbe headlight aiming screws.

3. Pull the retaining ring and light slightly forward and disconnect the plug.
4. Remove the headlight and retaining ring.
5. Installation is the reverse of removal. Be sure that the plug and socket on the rear of the light are tight.

Fuses

A listing of the protected equipment and the amperage of the fuse is printed in the lid of the fuse box. Spare fuses and a tool for removing and installing fuses are contained in the vehicle tool kit.

Fuses cannot be repaired—they must be replaced. Always determine the cause of the blown fuse before replacing it with a new one.

FUSE BOX LOCATION

230, 240D, 300D, 300TD, 280, 280C, 280E, 280CE, 300CD

On early models, the fuse box may be found in the kick panel on the driver's side. On later models the fuse box is located in the engine compartment on the driver's side, next to the brake master cylinder. Some models have separate fuse boxes or inline fuses for additional equipment. The radio is usually fused with a separate inline glass fuse behind the radio and the ignition is unfused.

280S, 280SE, 300SD, 450SE, 450SEL, 6.9, 380SEL

The fuse box is located in the engine compartment, on the driver's side, next to the brake master cylinder. Some models may have separate fuse boxes or inline fuses in the engine compartment for additional equipment. The radio is usually fused with a separate inline glass fuse behind the radio and the ignition is unfused. The fuse box also contains various relays.

450SL, 450SLC, 380SL, 380SLC

The fuse box is located in the right-hand (passenger's side) kick panel, behind a cover plate. There may also be separate fuse boxes or inline fuses in the engine compartment for additional equipment. The radio is usually fused with a separate inline glass fuse behind the radio and the ignition is unfused. The kick panel area also contains various relays and switches.

SPECIFICATIONS

INDEX

BEFORE SERVICING, SEE THE SAFETY NOTICE ON THE CONTENTS PAGE

SERIAL NUMBER IDENTIFICATION

The Vehicle Serial Number can be found stamped on a plate located on the inner fender panel of the engine compartment. Late model cars have this plate located on the top of the dashboard, visible through the windshield.

VEHICLE IDENTIFICATION—MIDGET

Serial number prefix codes

The car number prefix comprises a series of letters and numbers, presenting in code the make, the engine type, the body type, the series, and, where applicable, left-hand drive.

1st PREFIX LETTER—Name	2nd PREFIX LETTER—Engine type
G—MG	A

3rd PREFIX LETTER—Body type
N—2-seater Tourer

4th PREFIX—Series of model	5th PREFIX (used to denote car if different to standard right-hand drive)	6th PREFIX (Model Year)—USA and CANADA
6—6th series, MG	L—Left-hand drive U-USA	F—1975 G—1976 H—1977 J—1978

CODE EXAMPLE

G — A N 6 — 25788

- 25788—Serial number
- 6—6th Series
- N—2-seater Tourer
- A—'A' type Engine
- G—MG

VEHICLE IDENTIFICATION—MG

Serial number prefix codes

The car number prefix comprises a series of letters and numbers presenting in code the make, engine type, body type and the series.

1st PREFIX LETTER—NAME	2nd PREFIX LETTER—Engine type	3rd PREFIX LETTER—Body type
G—MG	H	N—2 seater tourer D—Coupe or GT
4th PREFIX	**5th PREFIX**	**6th PREFIX—Model Year**
5—5th series	L—LHD U—USA	G—1976 H—1977 J—1978

CODE EXAMPLE

G — H D 5

- **Serial number**
- 5—5th Series
- D—GT
- H—'B' type Engine
- G—MG

G — H N 5 U G

- **Serial number**
- G—1976
- U—USA
- 5—5th Series
- N—Tourer
- H—'B' type Engine
- G—MG

Engine Number Identification

The engine serial number is located on a plate riveted to the engine block on the distributor side.

ENGINE IDENTIFICATION—MIDGET

Year	Engine Code	No. of Cylinders	Displacement (cc)
1975-80	PE94J	4	1275

ENGINE IDENTIFICATION—MGB

Year	Engine Code	No. of Cylinders	Displacement (cc)
1975-80	18V	4	1798

GENERAL ENGINE SPECIFICATIONS

Model	Year	Engine Code	Displacement (cc)	Carburetor Type	Advertised Horsepower @ rpm	Advertised Torque @ rpm	Bore x Stroke (in.)	Comp. Ratio	Oil Pressure
Midget	1975-80	PE94J	1500	CD4 (1)	50 @ 5000	67 @ 2500	2.90 x 3.44	7.5:1	40-60
MGB	1975-80	18V	1798	CD5 (1)	62.5 @ 4600	88 @ 2500	3.16 x 3.50	8:1	50-80

TUNE-UP SPECIFICATIONS

Model	Year	Engine Code	SPARK PLUGS Orig. Equip.	SPARK PLUGS Gap (in.)	DISTRIBUTOR Dwell (deg)	DISTRIBUTOR Gap (in.)	Timing (deg)	Compression pressure (psi)	VALVES Clearance (in.) Intake	VALVES Clearance (in.) Exhaust	VALVES Intake Opens (deg)	Idle Speed (rpm)	Fuel Pump Pressure (psi)
Midget	1975-76	PE94J	N12Y	0.025	①	①	2A	120	0.010C	0.010C	18B	800	2.5-3.0
	1977-80	PE94J	N12Y	0.025	①	①	10B ③	145	0.010C	0.010C	18B	800	—
MGB	1975-76	18V	N9Y	0.025	①	①	12B ②	160	0.013H	0.013H	16B	850	2.5-3.0
	1977-80	18V	N9Y	0.035	①	①	10B ②	120	0.013H	0.013H	8B	850	—

NOTE: The underhood specifications sticker often reflects tune-up specification changes made in production. Sticker figures should be used if they disagree with this chart.

① Factory installed electronic ignition with fixed dwell. If adjustment is needed, use brass or plastic feeler. Pick-up air gap should be: Midget 0.014-0.016 in., MGB 0.010-0.017 in.

② @ 1500 rpm

B Before top dead center

H Engine hot

C Engine cold

FIRING ORDERS

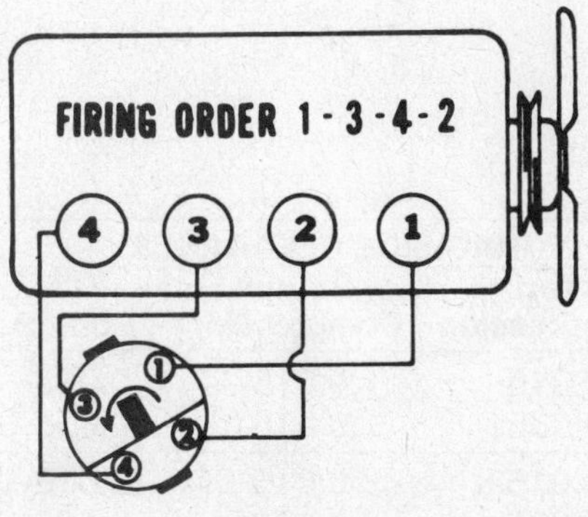

Midget

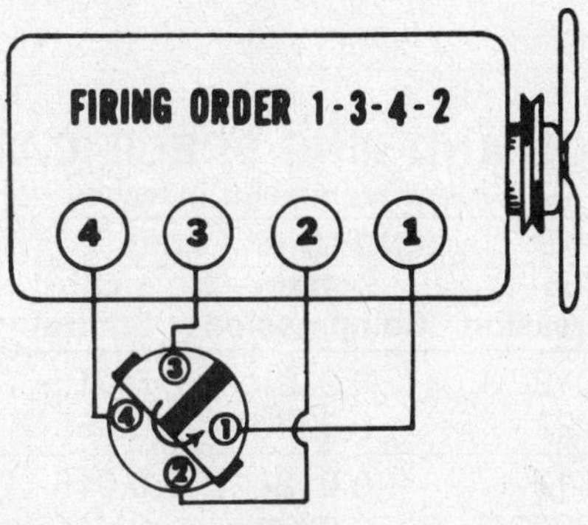

MGB

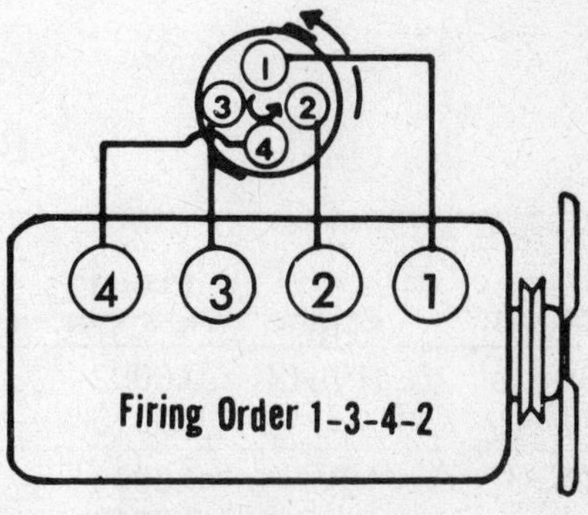

1975-79 (PE94J Engine)

CAPACITIES

Model	Engine	Crankcase (qts.) With Filter	Crankcase (qts.) Without Filter	4-Speed Transmission (pts.)	Drive Axle (pts.)	Fuel Tank (gals.)	Coolant with Heater (qts.)
Midget	PE94J	4.8	4.2	3.0	2.1	7.2	6.3
MGB	18V	4.5	4.5	6.0	2.0	12.0 ①	6.0 ②

① 1978-80—13 gallons
② 1978-80—7¼ quarts

CRANKSHAFT SPECIFICATIONS

		MAIN BEARING JOURNALS (in.)					CONNECTING ROD BEARING JOURNALS (in.)			
		Journal Diameter					Journal Diameter			
Model	Engine	New	Minimum	Oil Clearance	Shaft End-Play	Thrust on No.	New	Minimum	Oil Clearance	Side Clearance
Midget	PE94J	2.3115-2.3120	−0.010	0.0005-0.0025	0.006-0.014	3	1.8750-1.8755	−0.030	0.001-0.003	N.A.
MGB	18V	2.1262-2.1270	−0.040	0.001-0.0027	0.004-0.005	3	1.8759-1.8764	−0.040	0.001-0.0027	0.008-0.012

N.A. Not available

VALVE SPECIFICATIONS

Model	Engine	Face Angle (deg)	Seat Angle (deg)	Valve Spring Free Length (in.) Inner	Valve Spring Free Length (in.) Outer	Spring Pressure (lbs.) ① Intake	Spring Pressure (lbs.) ① Exhaust	Stem Diameter (in.) Intake	Stem Diameter (in.) Exhaust	Stem to Guide Clearance (in.) Intake	Stem to Guide Clearance (in.) Exhaust	Guide Height Above Head (in.)
Midget	PE94J	45.5	44.5	1.52	N.A.	123	123	0.3107-0.3113	0.3100-0.3105	0.0007-0.0023	0.0015-0.0030	.750
MGB	18V	44.5	45.5	1.92	2.141	142	142	0.3429-0.3434	0.3417-0.3422	0.0008-0.0018	0.002-0.003	①

① Intake 0.750, exhaust 0.625
N.A. Not available

PISTON AND RING SPECIFICATIONS

All measurements in inches

			RING GAP			RING SIDE CLEARANCE		
Model	Engine	Piston Clearance	Top Compression	Bottom Compression	Oil Control	Top Compression	Bottom Compression	Oil Control
Midget	PE94J	0.0002-0.0016	0.012-0.022	0.012-0.022	0.015-0.055	0.015-0.035	0.015-0.035	0.016-0.036
MGB	18V	0.0006-0.0012	0.012-0.022	0.012-0.022	0.015-0.045	0.015-0.035	0.015-0.035	0.016-0.036

TORQUE SPECIFICATIONS
(ft. lbs.)

Model	Engine	Cylinder Head Bolts	Main Bearing Bolts	Rod Bearing Bolts	Crankshaft Damper Bolt(s) ①	Flywheel to Crankshaft Bolt(s)	MANIFOLD NUTS Intake	MANIFOLD NUTS Exhaust
Midget	PE94J	50	65	50	70	40	14	14
MGB	18V	45-50	70	35-40	70	40	15	15

① Torque figure given applies to crankshaft pulley on cars not equipped with damper

TORQUE SEQUENCES

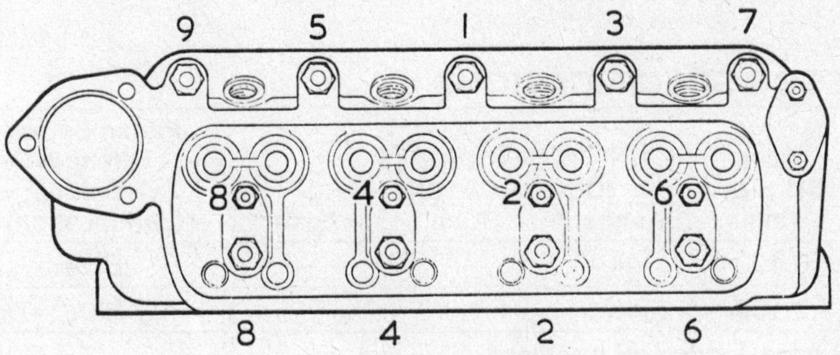

Cylinder head—Midget

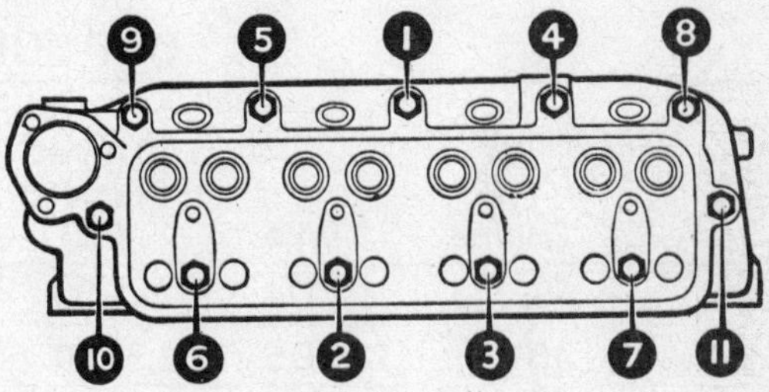

Cylinder head—MGB

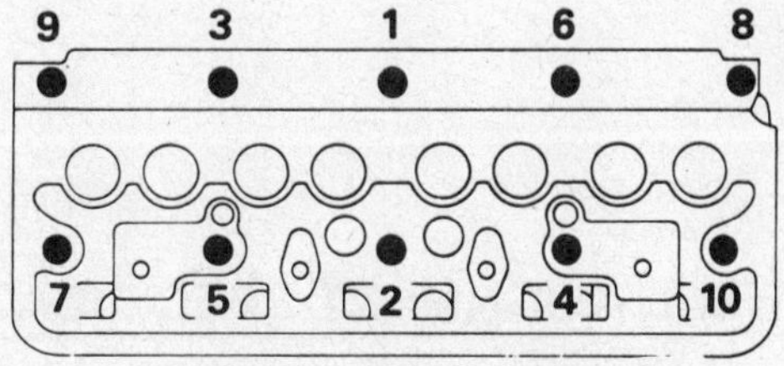

Cylinder head—PE94J engine

ALTERNATOR AND REGULATOR SPECIFICATIONS

Model	Engine	ALTERNATOR (LUCAS) Type	Output Volts	Output Amps	Field Current Draw (amps @ 12V)	Brush Tension (oz.)	REGULATOR (LUCAS) Type	Field Relay Air Gap (in.)	Field Relay Point Gap (in.)	Field Relay Point Close (volts)	Field Relay Air Gap (in.)	Volts @ 125 deg
MGB	18V	18ACR	12-15	34 ②	3	7-10	8TR 11TR	Integral with alternator, transistor type—no adjustment				14.0-14.4 14.0-14.4
Midget	PE94J	16ACR	12-15	34 ①	3	9-13	—	Integral with alternator, transistor type—no adjustment				14.0-14.4

① 34 amps at 6000 alternator rpm (3000 engine rpm) @ 14 volts
② 43 amps at 6000 alternator rpm (3000 engine rpm) @ 14 volts

BATTERY AND STARTER SPECIFICATIONS

All cars use 12 volt, negative ground electrical systems

		BATTERY		STARTER (LUCAS)						Brush Spring Tension
				Lock Test			No Load Test			
Model	Engine	Capacity (amp hrs.)	Type	Amps	Volts	Torque (ft. lbs.)	Amps	Volts	rpm	(oz.)
Midget	PE94J	50 ②	M35J ②	250-375	7	7.0	65	11.5	8000-10000	28
MGB	18V	66	2 M100 ①	463	7	14.4	40	11.5	6000	36

① 1976 and later—Lucas 18ACR
② 1976 and later—Lucas A9/AZ-9 (45 amp hr), A11/AZ-11 (50 amp hr)

CARBURETOR SPECIFICATIONS

			Throat Diameter	Main Jet Size	JET NEEDLE IDENTIFICATION NO. ①			Piston Spring Strength (Color
Model	Engine	Type	(in.)	(in.)	Standard	Rich	Lean	Identification)
Midget	PE94J	CD4	1.50	0.100	44A	—	—	Blue
MGB	18V	CD5	1.50	0.100	45H	—	—	Blue

① Most emission control engines are fitted with spring-loaded jet needles

WHEEL ALIGNMENT SPECIFICATIONS

		CASTER (deg)		CAMBER (deg)		Toe-In	Kingpin Inclination	WHEEL PIVOT RATIO (deg)	
Model	Engine	Range	Ideal	Range	Ideal	(in.)	(deg)	Inner	Outer
Midget	PE94J	—	3P	—	3/4N	1/8	6 3/4	20	19 3/4
MGB	18V	5P-7 1/4P	7P	1/4N-1 1/4P	1P	1/16	8	20	19

P Positive
N Negative

OIL PUMP SPECIFICATIONS

	ENGINE MODELS	
Oil Pump Clearances Locations	PE94J	18V
Inner and outer rotor end-play	0.0004 in. (0.1 mm)	0.005 in. (0.127 mm)
Outer rotor to pump body clearance	0.008 in. (0.2 mm)	0.010 in. (0.254 mm)
Rotor lobe clearance	0.010 in. (0.25 mm)	0.006 in. (0.152 mm)

BRAKE SPECIFICATIONS

All measurements given are in inches unless noted

				BRAKE DISC		BRAKE DRUM			MINIMUM LINING THICKNESS	
Model	Engine	Lug Nut Torque (ft. lbs.)	Master Cylinder Bore	Minimum Thickness	Maximum Run-Out	Diameter	Max. Machine O/S	Max. Wear Limit	Front	Rear
Midget	PE94J	45	3/4	0.29	0.006	7.0	0.015	0.030	1/16	40% ②
MGB	18V	60-65	3/4 ①	.340-.350	0.003 ③	10.0	0.015	0.030	1/16	40% ②

NOTE: Minimum lining thickness is as recommended by the manufacturer. Due to variations in state inspection regulations, the minimum allowable thickness may be different than recommended by the manufacturer.
① 13/16 in. from vehicle number G-HD3/138, 401 (GT only)
② If riveted; 25% if bonded
③ 1978-80—0.006

TUNE-UP PROCEDURES

Spark Plugs

Number each spark plug wire by placing a piece of tape on the wire indicating the cylinder number. Grasp each spark plug wire by the rubber boot on the end of the wire and remove the wire from the plug.

Using a socket and a ratchet remove the spark plugs. Before installing new plugs, gap each plug according to specification in the "Tune-up Specification Chart." Install the new plugs by hand then tighten them snugly with the wrench.

Electronic Distributor

Pick-up air gap–Adjustment

1. Disconnect the battery ground strap.
2. Remove the distributor cap, rotor and antiflash shield.
3. With a brass or plastic feeler gauge, check the gap between the pick-up coil and the reluctor. The gap should be 0.010 to 0.017 inch.
4. If adjustment is required, loosen the screws securing the pick-up coil to the distributor plate. Move the pick-up coil to obtain the proper air gap.
5. Tighten the securing screws and recheck the air gap.
6. Install the anti-flash shield, rotor and distributor cap. Reconnect the battery ground cable.

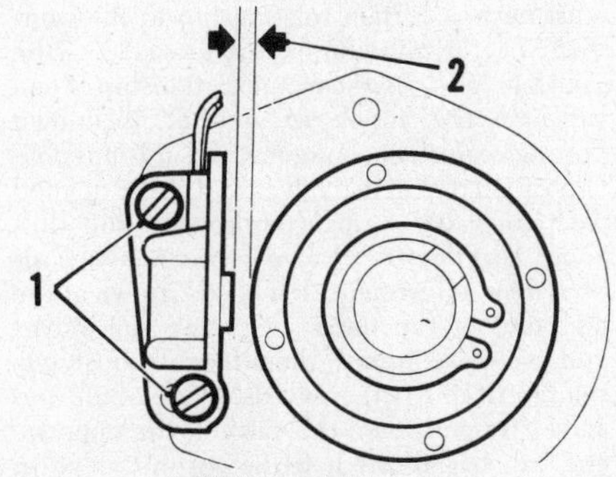

1. Pick-up retaining screws
2. Air gap

Air gap and pickup retaining screw locations

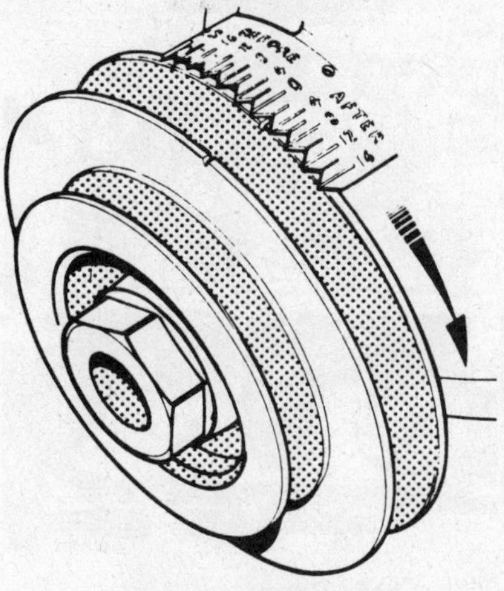

Midget timing marks

Ignition Timing

Dynamic (engine running) timing is done with a timing light. Connect the light as per manufacturer's instructions. Mark the notch in the crankshaft pulley with a bright color that will be easily visible (such as yellow crayon). Disconnect and plug the vacuum advance line from the intake manifold.

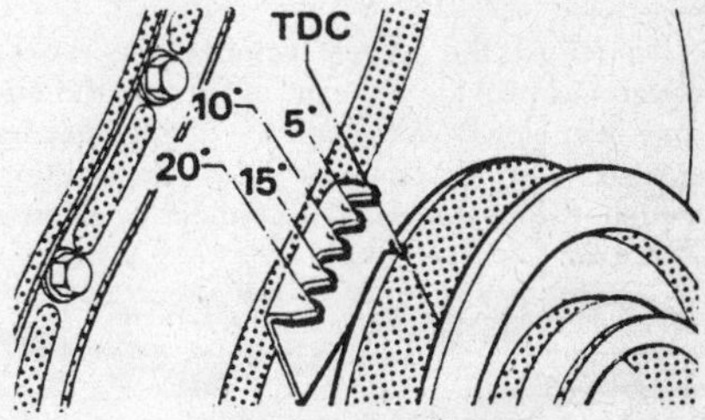

MGB timing marks

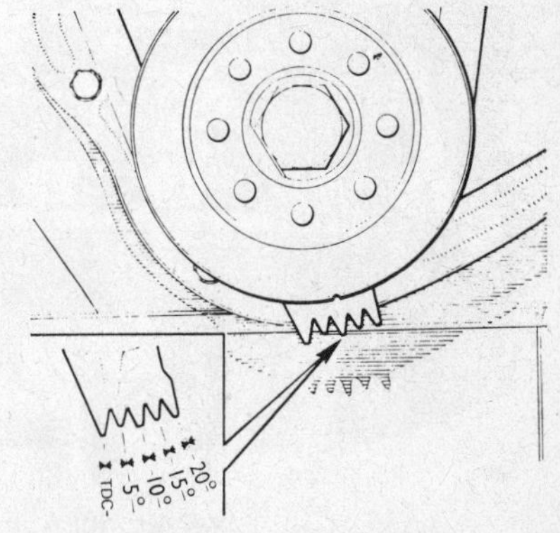

Midget timing marks—Model 12V engine

The engine should be warm and running steadily at the correct rpm when the timing check is made. If the timing is no more than 5 degrees off, correction can usually be made with the vernier adjustment knob on the vacuum advance unit of the distributor. Otherwise, the distributor clamp pinch-bolt will have to be loosened and the distributor rotated to the correct position. Check the timing once again after the pinch-bolt has been tightened, and reconnect the vacuum advance line after final adjustment is made to check operation of the vacuum advance unit.

Valve Adjustment

Valve clearances for the different MG models can be found in "Tune-Up Specifications." Adjustment procedures for all models are the same. Valve adjustment should be carried out at every engine tune-up or whenever excessive valve train noise is noticed. Loose valve clearance will generally only cause a metallic thrashing sound, while over-tight adjustment can cause rough running and burnt valves.

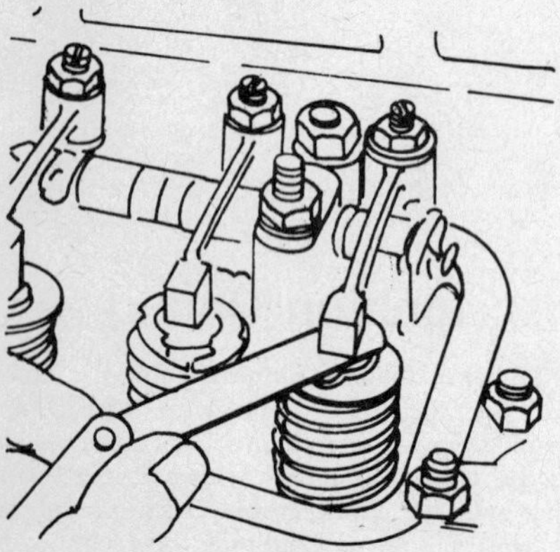

Measuring valve lash

To adjust the valves, remove the rocker cover and provide a means of turning the engine over slowly. Although the engine may be turned over by hand or with the ignition switch, the best method is connecting an auxiliary starter wire to the solenoid. An auxiliary starter wire can be either a two-position switch with one lead connected to the battery cable terminal at the solenoid and the other lead connected to the small gauge wire at the separate solenoid terminal, or simply a short length of wire connected momentarily in the above manner to turn the engine over.

VALVE ADJUSTMENT CHART

With this Valve Open	Adjust this Valve
1	8
2	7
3	6
4	5
5	4
6	3
7	2
8	1

Valve rocker clearance adjusting sequence.

CAUTION

Make sure that the transmission is in Neutral before turning the engine over while outside the vehicle.

In order to adjust an individual valve, it must be in a certain relationship to the camshaft; i.e., it must be on the low side of the camshaft lobe. Because the relationship of one valve to the action of another is known (through camshaft configuration), it is possible to position one of the valves in its fully opened position (valve spring compressed) and thus know that another valve is correctly positioned for adjustment. If a line is drawn at the midpoint of the head separating the valves into two equal groups, then this relationship is symmetrical. In other words, if one of the end valves is open, then the valve at the opposite end can be adjusted; if the second valve in from one end is open, the second valve in from the other end can be adjusted, etc.

Valves No. 4 and 7 Open, Valves No. 5 and 2 Positioned for Adjustment

When a valve is correctly positioned for adjustment, check the clearance between the valve stem and the rocker arm. If clearance is incorrect, loosen the adjusting screw locknut and turn the screw (clockwise to decrease clearance, counterclockwise to increase clearance) until the feeler gauge blade slides in and out with some resistance. To double check adjustment, try inserting the next size thinner and next size thicker feeler blade. If, for example, desired clearance is 0.010 in., the 0.009 in. blade should fit quite easily, while the 0.011 or 0.012 in. blade should be too thick to fit. When correct clearance has been obtained, hold the adjusting screw from turning and tighten the locknut. Recheck clearance in case the adjustment screw turned slightly when the locknut was tightened.

When all valves have been adjusted, reinstall the rocker cover. Make sure that the cover gasket is in good condition or an oil leak will develop. Breather hose connections at the rocker cover (if any) should be tight.

Carburetors

For 1975, the Midget is equipped with a Zenith-Stromberg CD4 unit while the MGB series continues with the HIF type S.U. carburetors. Late 1975 MGB's are equipped with one Zenith-Stromberg CD2 carburetor instead of the twin HIF type. Midgets from 1976 on are equipped with a Zenith-Stromberg 150 CD4. MGBs from 1976 and later are equipped with a Zenith 175 CD5T.

IDLE SPEED AND MIXTURE ADJUSTMENTS

Prior to adjusting the carburetors, the following checks should be made to ensure that accurate adjustment is possible. Start the engine and spray or squirt a safe solvent (e.g., Gumout®) on the carburetor bodies at the

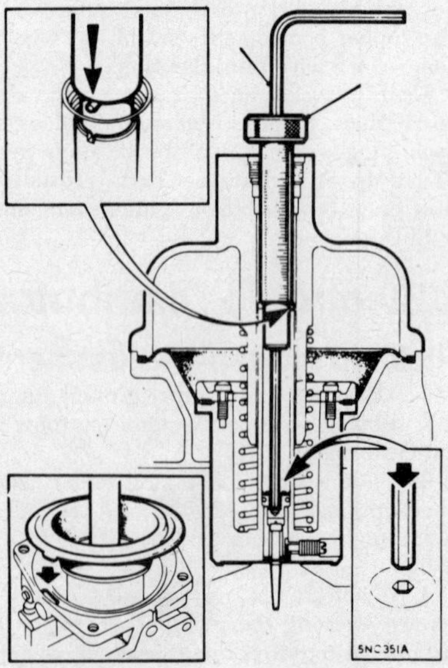

1. Outer tool lug
2. Inner tool lug
3. Outer tool
4. Inner tool bit
5. Engage diaphragm tab

Air/fuel mixture adjusting tool—CD-4 and CD-5 carburetors

throttle shaft pivots. If engine speed changes, an air leak is indicated and adjustment of the carburetors will prove impossible. To alleviate the situation, the carburetors must be rebuilt and the throttle shaft bushings and/or shafts replaced.

Check the carburetor pistons for sticking by lifting them all the way and letting them fall. Their descent should be steady and a metallic click should be heard when they hit bottom. If there is evidence of sticking, remove and clean the pistons in solvent. Do not lubricate any part of the piston except the rod. Check that the piston damper chambers have the proper amount of oil. On carburetors with vented damper caps the level should be ½ in. above the piston rod, and with non-vented caps the level should be ½ in. below the rod.

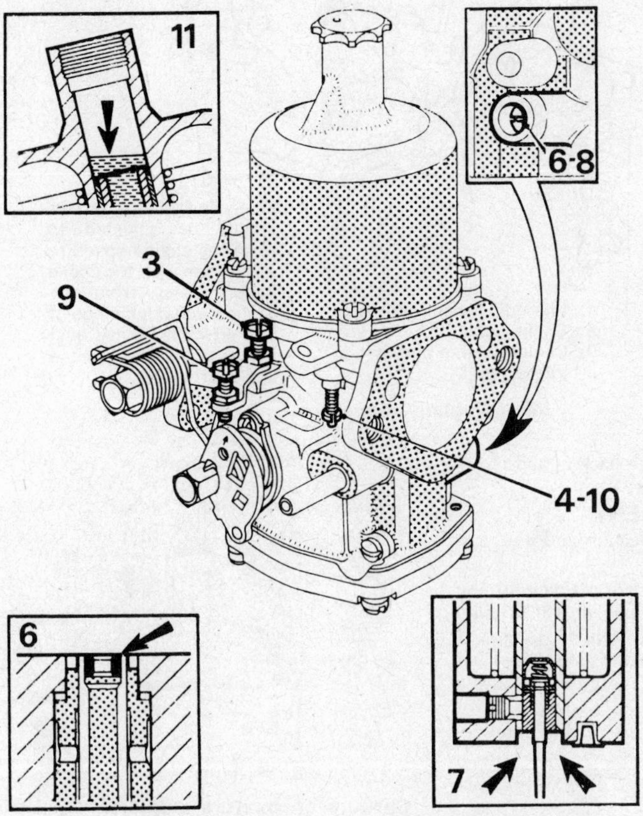

3. Throttle adjusting screw
9. Fast idle adjusting screw
4-10. Lifting pin
11. Reservoir oil level
6-8. Jet adjusting screw
6. Jet adjusting screw, flush with bridge
7. Needle guide

Type HIF carburetor

26. Throttle adjusting screws

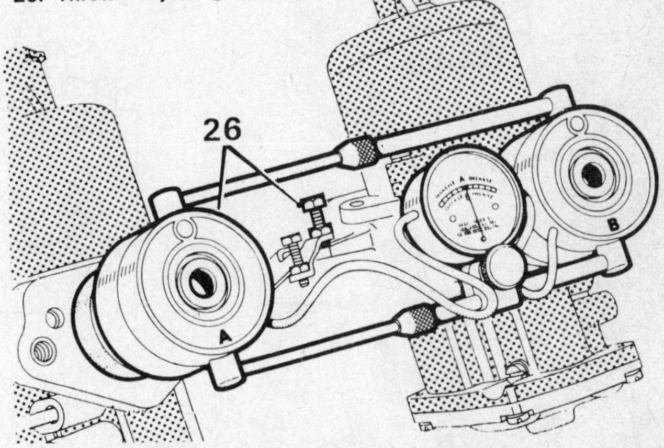

Balance Meter on HIF carburetors

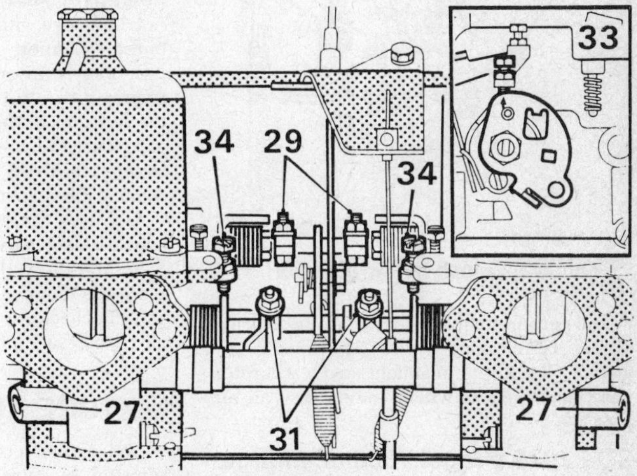

34. Fast idle adjusting screws
29. Throttle interconnection clamping lever
33. Choke
27. Jet adjusting screw
31. Choke interconnection screws

Adjusting screws—HIF carburetor

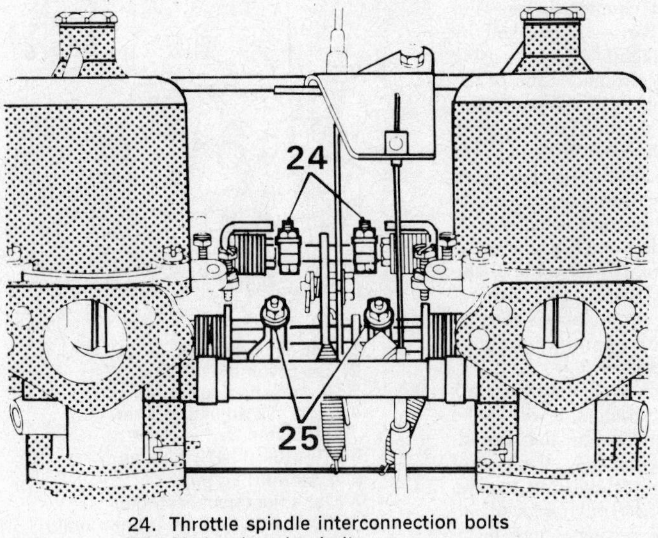

24. Throttle spindle interconnection bolts
25. Choke clamping bolts

HIF carburetor interconnection screws

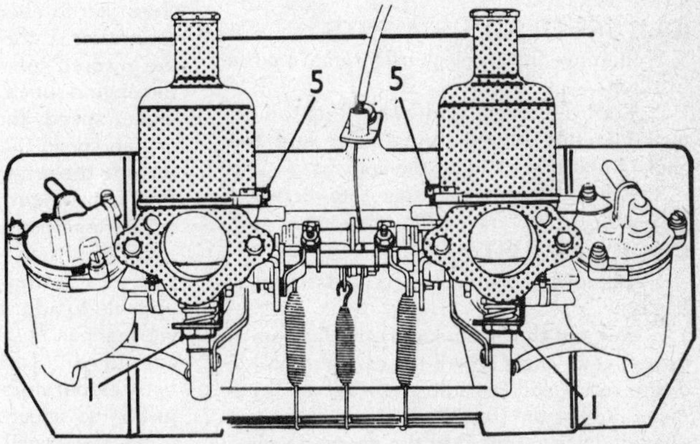

Idle adjusting screw (5), jet adjusting nuts (1)

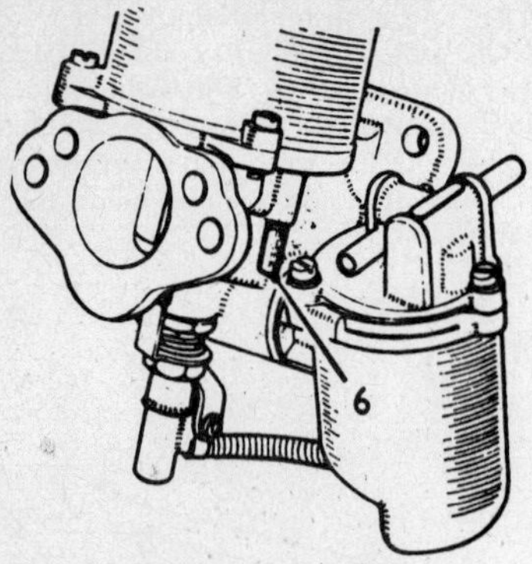

Piston lifting pin (6)

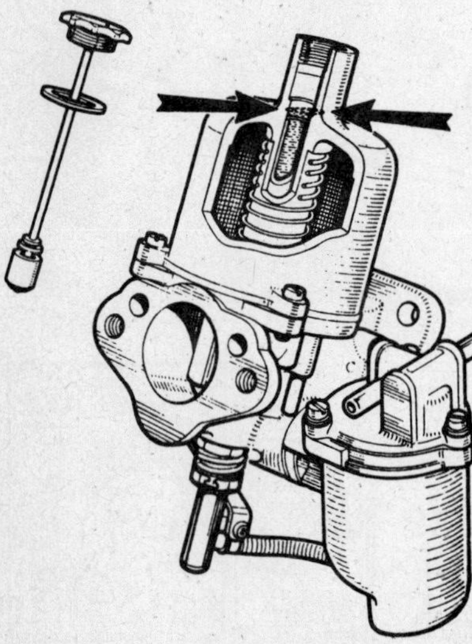

Oil level ½ inch below the tube

The carburetor bodies and throttle linkage should be cleaned before adjustments are made. Check the manifold and carburetor nuts for looseness which could cause an air leak.

CD4 1975 Midget 1500 cc Engine

There are three permissible adjustments on the 150 CD4 carburetor attached to the 1975 Midget. These are idle speed, fast idle and mixture. After these adjustments have been made, it is necessary that an exhaust gas test be made to ensure that the adjustments have not raised the level of pollution permissible for the car.

IDLE SPEED ADJUSTMENTS

1. Remove the air cleaner by removing the two bolts.
2. Start the engine and warm it up to normal operating temperature; make sure the choke knob is pushed all the way in.
3. Adjust the engine speed to between 800-850 rpm by turning the idle screw.

CHOKE ADJUSTMENT

1. Remove the air cleaners and start the engine.
2. Pull out the choke knob until the cam is turned at an angle where the cam pivot cable clamp screw and fast idle screw are in alignment. Adjust the fast idle by turning the fast idle adjusting screw until the engine reaches between 1100-1300 rpm.

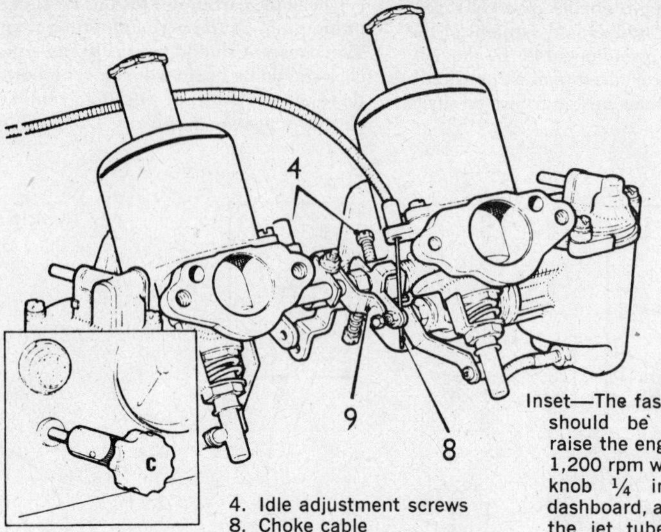

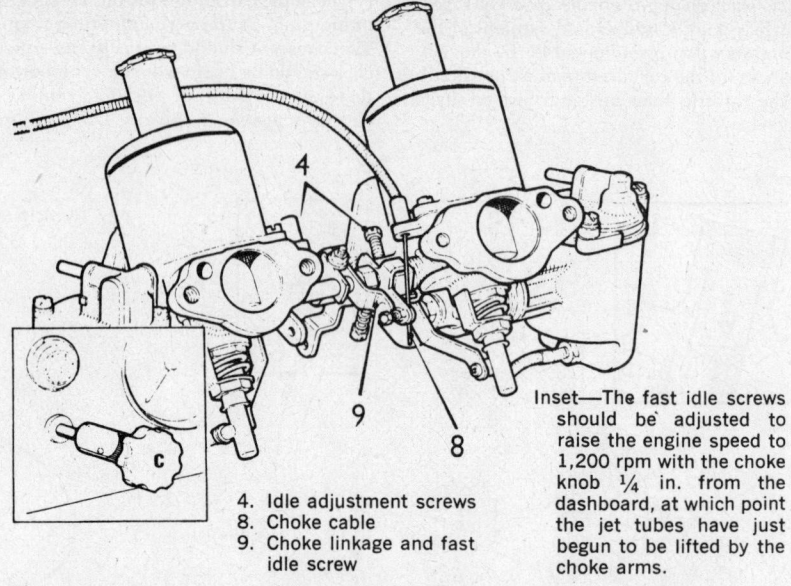

4. Idle adjustment screws
8. Choke cable
9. Choke linkage and fast idle screw

Inset—The fast idle screws should be adjusted to raise the engine speed to 1,200 rpm with the choke knob ¼ in. from the dashboard, at which point the jet tubes have just begun to be lifted by the choke arms.

Idle adjusting points

3. Push the choke knob back in and check the exhaust gas emissions.

MIXTURE ADJUSTMENT

1. Remove the air cleaner and the carburetor damper.
2. Slowly insert an Allen wrench to the proper size into the dashpot until it fits into the hexagon in the needle adjuster plug.
3. Turn the wrench clockwise to richen and counterclockwise to lean the mixture, until a smooth idle is obtained.
4. Check the exhaust gas reading, and readjust if necessary.
5. Add oil to the dashpot if necessary, replace the damper.
6. Recheck the idle speed and replace the air cleaner assembly.

MIXTURE ADJUSTMENT

Non-emission control carburetor mixture is adjusted by turning the jet adjusting nut clockwise to lean and counterclockwise to richen the mixture. Mixture is checked by lifting the piston very slightly (1/32 in.), using the small lifting pin on the underside of the carburetor and listening for a change in engine speed. When you do this, you are effectively disabling that carburetor, which enables you to check the mixture on the other carburetor. If the engine slows and remains at the lowered speed, the mixture is too lean. If the engine speed increases and remains at the higher speed, the mixture is too rich. If the engine speed increases slightly and then returns to the original speed, mixture is correct. If jet adjustment is necessary, turn the adjusting nut one flat, and recheck.

On Emission Control System carburetors with jet adjusting nut restrictors, it will not be possible to adjust the mixture in the proceding manner because of the limited range of adjustment. Turn the jet adjusting nut on both carburetors over the full range of adjustment, selecting the setting where maximum idle speed is consistent with smoothness. Do not remove or reposition the jet

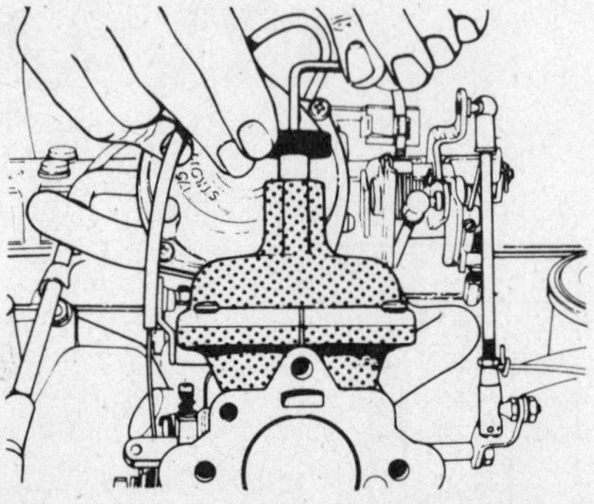

Carburetor mixture adjustment, 1975 Midget

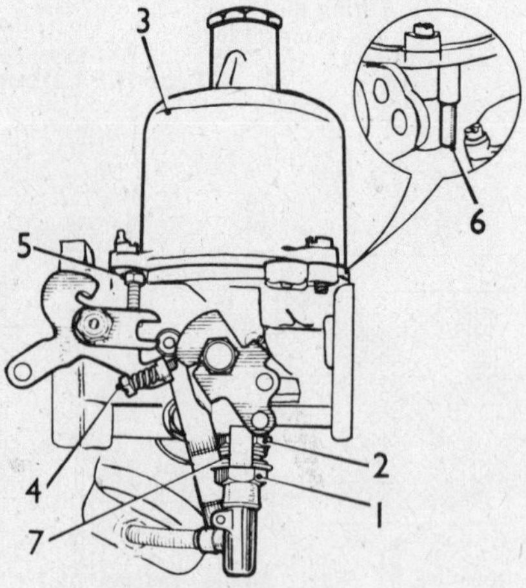

1. Jet adjusting nut
2. Jet assembly locknut
3. Piston-chamber
4. Fast idle adjusting screw (actuated by the choke)
5. Throttle (idle) adjusting screw
6. Piston lifting pin
7. Jet adjustment restrictor (Emission Control System only)

Emission control carburetor adjusting points

adjusting nut restrictors, as the adjusting range permitted is in the range of minimum exhaust emissions.

Altering the mixture strength will have altered the engine speed in either case, and the idle speed will have to be reset. Both of the throttle screws should be turned an equal amount so that carburetor synchronization will not be upset.

CD-2 Late 1975 MGB's

1. Warm the engine to normal operating temperature before attempting to adjust the carburetor.
2. Disconnect the float chamber vent and the air manifold.
3. Set the idle speed to 850 ± 100 rpm with the idle speed screw, and adjust the mixture to give a smooth idle.
4. Reconnect the air manifold and float chamber vent; recheck the idle speed.

NOTE: Run the engine to 2500 rpm to clear out the carburetor before each adjustment.

All 1976 and Later Cars

The only adjustment that can be made on these cars is that for normal idle speed. A carbon-monoxide meter is required for mixture adjustment under all circumstances. You can, however, take the car to a diagnostic center for checking of CO (carbon-monoxide) emissions. If you are experiencing rough idle and poor running at low speeds, a CO reading well off specification would confirm the need for carburetor adjustment or repair by a qualified shop with the proper equipment. See the engine compartment sticker for CO specifications.

Make the idle speed adjustment with the engine hot as after a drive of several miles, using an accurate tachometer. On the Midget, first make sure the fast idle screw is not touching the fast idle cam. On the MGB, first disconnect the air manifold hose at the air pump and plug it, disconnect the float chamber vent pipe at the carburetor, and then run the engine at 2500 rpm for 30 seconds. Then, make the adjustment immediately.

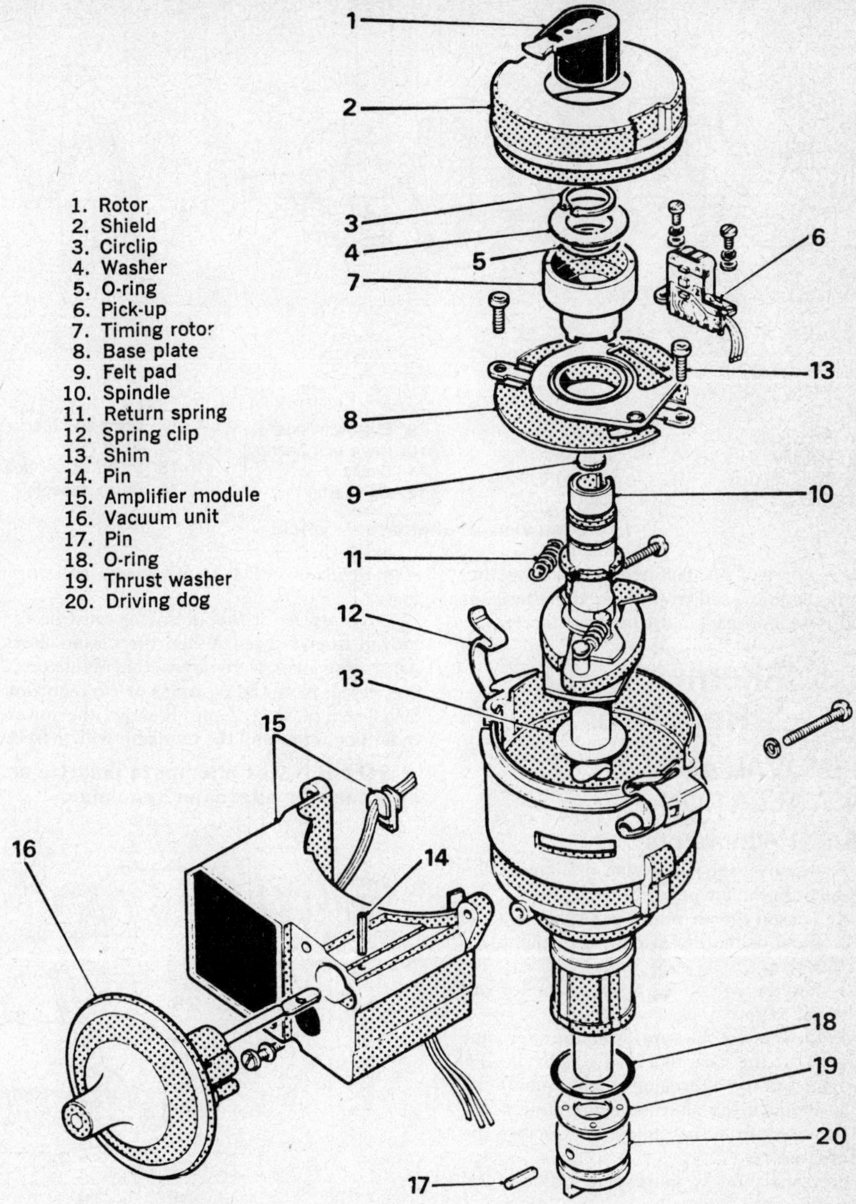

Exploded view of distributor with electronic ignition

ENGINE ELECTRICAL

Distributor

REMOVAL AND INSTALLATION

The distributor can be removed and replaced without disturbing the ignition timing, provided the pinch-bolt on the clamp that positions the distributor is not loosened.

1. Remove the distributor cap and disconnect the low tension lead from the terminal on the distributor.
2. Disconnect the vacuum advance line (if applicable) from the diaphragm unit at the distributor.

NOTE: On Midgets equipped with mechanically driven tachometers it will be necessary to unscrew the tachometer drive from its connection at the rear of the generator.

3. Remove the bolts securing the distributor clamp to the cylinder block and lift the distributor out.
4. To replace the distributor, insert the shaft into the housing until the driving dog rests on the distributor driveshaft.
5. Turn the rotor until the dog is felt to engage in the slot in the driveshaft. Both the driving dog and the slot are offset so that the distributor will not fall into place until it is properly positioned.
6. Turn the distributor body to align the clamp and housing bolt holes and replace the bolts.
7. Replace the distributor cap, the vacuum advance line, the low tension lead from the coil, and reconnect the tachometer drive to the generator (if applicable).

Alternator

ALTERNATOR PRECAUTIONS

1. Do not run the engine with the batteries out of the circuit or any of the charging circuit wires disconnected (except as given in test procedures). All charging circuit electrical connections must be clean and tight, and the drive belt properly adjusted.
2. Correct battery and alternator polarity (negative ground) must be maintained or the

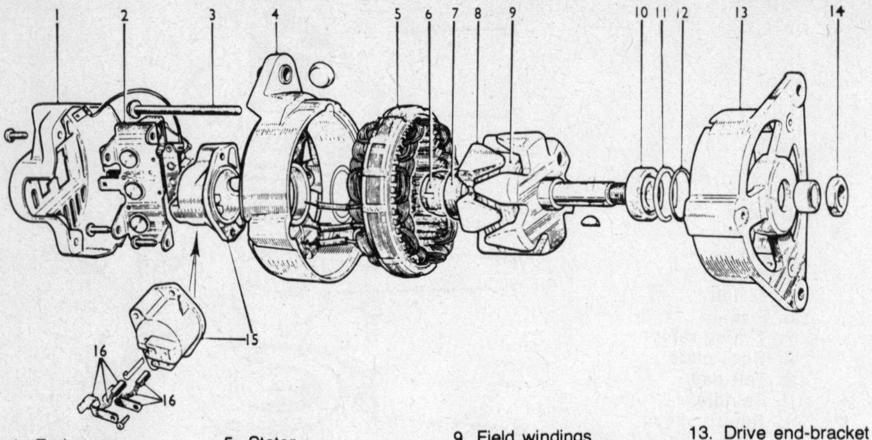

1. End cover
2. Rectifier pack
3. Through-bolt
4. End bracket
5. Stator
6. Slip-rings
7. Slip-ring bearing
8. Rotor
9. Field windings
10. Drive end bearing
11. Circlip
12. Oil sealing ring
13. Drive end-bracket
14. Shaft nut
15. Brush holder box
16. Brush assembly

Exploded view of alternator—typical

alternator will be destroyed. If arc welding equipment is used on the car the alternator and regulator leads must be disconnected.

Alternator and Regulator

REMOVAL AND INSTALLATION

16ACR Alternators

To remove the alternator disconnect the hoses from the air pump outlets.

1. Loosen the air pump mounting bolt.
2. Remove the bolt from the air pump adjusting strut.
3. Slip the belt off the air pump pulley and raise the pump.
4. Disconnect the wires from the alternator (do not let the wire that connects to the B+ terminal on the alternator touch ground).
5. Remove the alternator mounting bolts, slip the belt from the pulley, and remove the alternator.
6. Installation is in reverse order of removal.

8TR, and 11TR Regulators

The 8TR and 11TR regulators are used interchangeably with the 16ACR alternator.

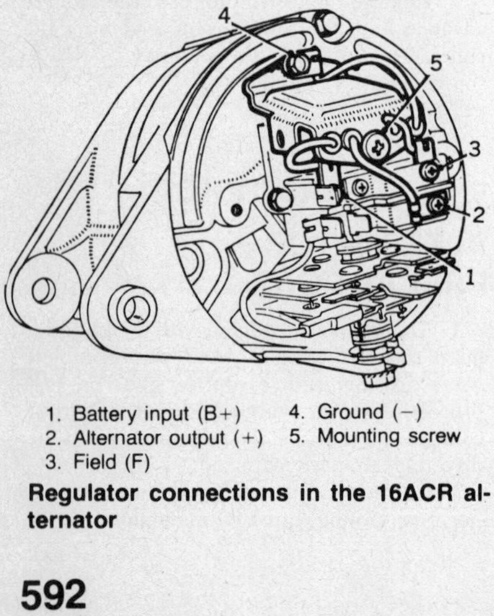

1. Battery input (B+)
2. Alternator output (+)
3. Field (F)
4. Ground (−)
5. Mounting screw

Regulator connections in the 16ACR alternator

The regulator unit is located *inside the alternator.*

1. To replace it the alternator must be removed from the car. When the plastic alternator end-cover is removed the regulator is accessible. Note the positions of the regulator leads and remove them. Remove the lower mounting screw and the regulator will be free.

NOTE: Never attempt to polarize an alternator or alternator regulator.

Starter

REMOVAL AND INSTALLATION

1. Disconnect the battery. Remove the distributor or, if necessary, the fuel pump (MGB and Midget only).
2. On the Midget, remove the skid plate. Remove the top starter bolt.
3. Disconnect and tag the starter wires.
4. Remove the lower starter bolt and remove the starter.
5. Installation is the reverse of removal.

STARTER DRIVE REPLACEMENT

1. Disconnect the cable from the terminal on the solenoid marked "STA".
2. Remove the solenoid attaching nuts.
3. Remove the solenoid from the starter case and disengage it from the drive lever.
4. Remove the brush cover and remove the brushes.
5. Remove the through-bolts from the end bracket.
6. Remove the lever pivot pin from the drive gear.
7. Separate the drive end bracket from the yoke and remove the drive gear engagement lever.
8. Remove the armature and separate the commutator plate from the yoke.

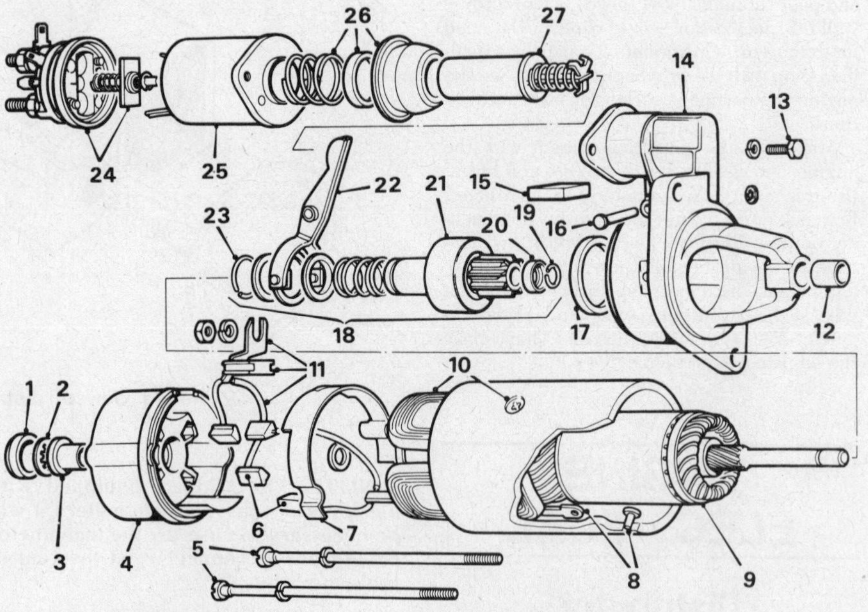

1. Armature end cap
2. Retaining ring
3. Bearing bush
4. Commutator end cover
5. Through-bolts
6. Brushes—field winding
7. Seal
8. Rivet—field winding connection
9. Armature
10. Field winding and pole-shoe screw
11. Brushes—terminal connector
12. Bearing bush
13. Screw and spring washer
14. Drive-end bracket
15. Sealing block
16. Pivot pin—engagement lever
17. Seal—drive end bracket
18. Drive assembly
19. Jump ring
20. Thrust collar
21. Roller clutch and pinion
22. Engagement lever and thrust washers
23. Spring ring
24. Cover and contacts
25. Solenoid unit
26. Spring, seat and dust excluder
27. Plunger and return spring

Exploded view of starter—typical for MGB models

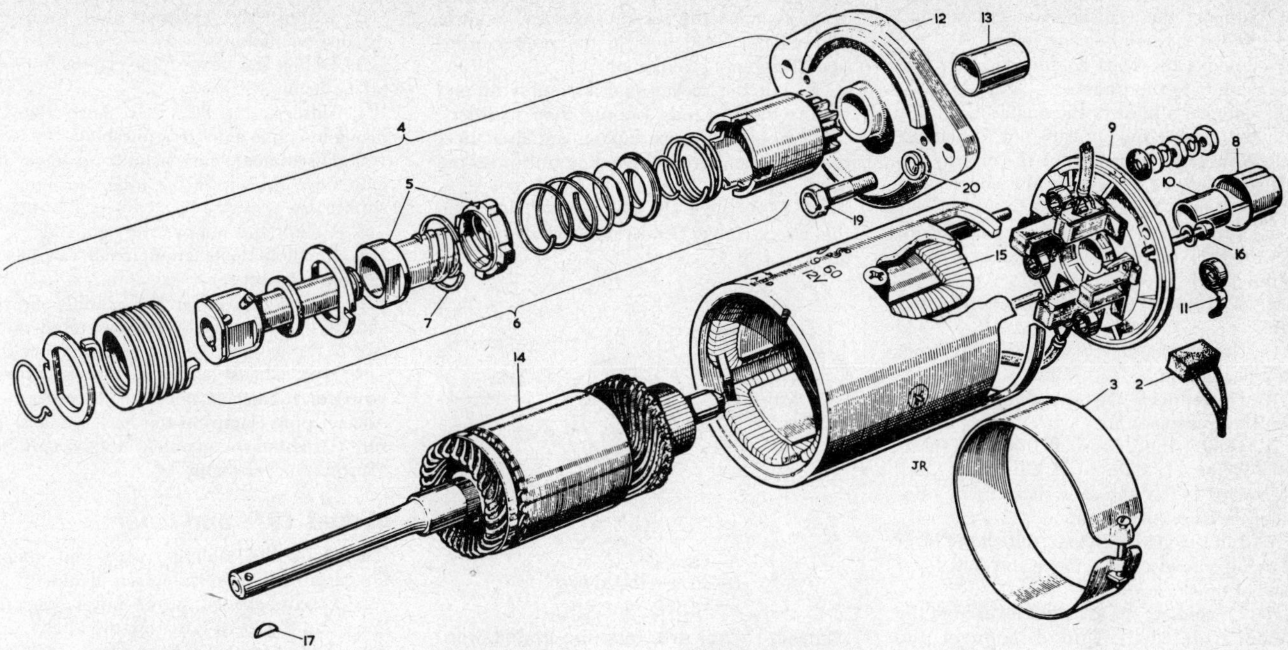

2. Brush
3. Retaining band
4. Drive assembly
5. Clutch assembly
6. Drive assembly components
7. Retaining ring
8. End cap
9. End plate
10. Brushing
11. Brush tension spring
12. Drive end bracket
13. Drive end bushing
14. Armature
15. Field coils
16. End cover bolts
17. Shaft key
19. Starter bolt
20. Washer, spring and screw

Exploded view of starter—typical for Midget models

9. Remove the thrust washers from the shaft.
10. Remove the drive gear. Reverse the procedure to install.

ENGINE MECHANICAL

Engine Removal and Installation

Midget

The engine of the Midget can be removed with or without the transmission. Either way, the preliminary steps are:

1. Drain the crankcase.
2. Disconnect the battery.
3. Remove the hood.
4. Disconnect the radiator and heater hoses and oil cooler lines (late models only), and remove the radiator.
5. Disconnect the choke and throttle cables and tachometer cable.
6. Disconnect the oil pressure gauge pipe from the engine.
7. Disconnect and tag all electrical connections to the engine.
8. Disconnect the high tension wires from the coil and spark plugs, and remove the distributor cap.
9. Unbolt the exhaust header pipe from the manifold and tie the pipe out of the way.
10. Remove the air cleaners and disconnect the fuel line.

At this point, the engine can be removed either with or without the transmission. If it is desired to remove only the engine:

1. Remove the starter motor.
2. Remove the fuel filter bowl (only).
3. Support the transmission with a jack, and remove the bell housing bolts.
4. Connect a hoist to the engine and unbolt the right-side engine mount from the chassis bracket.
5. Disconnect the left-side engine mount from the front engine plate and lift the engine from the vehicle, taking care not to damage the transmission mainshaft.

If it is desired to remove the engine and the transmission as a unit:

1. Drain the transmission oil and disconnect the back-up light switch lead (later models only).
2. Remove the gearshift lever cover, and remove the spring cap, spring and plunger.
3. Unbolt the shift lever retaining plate and lift out the lever.
4. With the carpet turned back, remove the rear transmission mount bolts.
5. From underneath the car, unscrew the speedometer cable from the transmission housing and release the cable support bracket from the bell housing.
6. Unbolt the clutch slave cylinder from the bell housing.
7. Unbolt the driveshaft from the differential flange and slide it out. Be sure to mark the flanges so that the driveshaft can be reinstalled correctly.
8. Connect a hoist to the engine and remove the remaining transmission mounting bolts.
9. Unbolt the right-side engine mount from the chassis bracket and disconnect the left-side mount from the front engine plate.
10. Lift the engine/transmission unit from the vehicle.

Installation of the engine or engine/transmission unit is in reverse order of removal. Be sure to refill the engine, transmission, and radiator.

MGB

The engine of the MGB can be removed with or without the transmission, but it is recommended that the engine/transmission be removed as a unit. This will avoid possible damage to the clutch when separating and installing the transmission.

Either way, the preliminary steps are:

1. Drain the crankcase.
2. Disconnect the battery(s).
3. Remove the hood.
4. Disconnect the oil cooler and pressure gauge lines from the engine.
5. Disconnect the heater and radiator hoses, and unbolt and remove the radiator, radiator shroud, and oil cooler as a unit.
6. Disconnect and tag all electrical connections to the engine.
7. Disconnect the high tension leads from the coil and spark plugs, and remove the distributor cap.
8. Disconnect the choke and throttle cables and the tachometer cable (early models only).
9. Unbolt the exhaust header pipe from the manifold, and disconnect the bell housing bracket.
10. Remove the air cleaners and disconnect the fuel line.

At this point, the engine can be removed either with or without the transmission. If it is desired to remove only the engine:

1. Support the transmission with a jack, and remove the bell housing bolts.
2. Remove the bolts holding the front engine mounts to the frame.
3. Connect a hoist to the engine and lift it from the chassis, taking care not to damage the transmission mainshaft or the oil pan.

If it is desired to remove the engine and transmission as a unit:

1. Drain the transmission oil and disconnect the back-up light switch lead (later models only).
2. Disconnect the overdrive solenoid wire.
3. Unbolt the clutch slave cylinder from the bell housing.
4. Disconnect the speedometer cable from the transmission.
5. Unbolt the driveshaft from the differential flange and slide it out. Be sure to mark the flanges so that the driveshaft can be reinstalled in its original position.
6. Lift the gearshift boot, unbolt the lever retaining screws, and remove the shift lever (manual transmission).
7. Disconnect the gearshift lever from the transmission shaft, and disconnect the downshift cable from the carburetors (automatic transmission).
8. Connect a hoist to the engine and remove the rear crossmember and the transmission mounts, along with the transmission stabilizer rod or bracket.
9. Remove the bolts securing the front engine mounts to the frame.
10. Lift the engine/transmission unit from the vehicle.

Installation of the engine or engine/transmission unit is in reverse order of removal. Be sure to refill the engine, transmission, and radiator.

Cylinder Head

REMOVAL AND INSTALLATION

The cylinder head nuts should be loosened, gradually in the same order as they are tightened, to prevent the head from warping (see "Tightening Sequences"). For the same reason, the head should be removed only when the engine is cold. When the cylinder head nuts and all accessories have been unbolted from the head, it may be necessary to tap each side of the head with a rubber mallet to break the head gasket seal. When the head is free, lift it evenly over the studs. If any water has found its way into the cylinders it should be immediately removed and the cylinder walls coated with oil. If the head is not to be installed for a day or more, it is a good idea to stuff towels into the cylinders to protect them.

The cylinder head removal procedure for all models is as follows:

1. Drain the radiator.
2. Disconnect the radiator and heater hoses from the cylinder head.
3. Remove the heater control valve and unbolt the top radiator bracket.
4. Remove the carburetors and air cleaners, and unbolt the manifolds and pull them back out of the way.
5. Remove the rocker cover and remove the cylinder head nuts in the proper order (see "Tightening Sequences").
6. Lift the rocker shaft assembly off and remove the pushrods, keeping them in order.
7. Remove the spark plugs and disconnect the water temperature sending unit from the head.
8. Disconnect the air supply hose from the check valve (Emission Control models only).

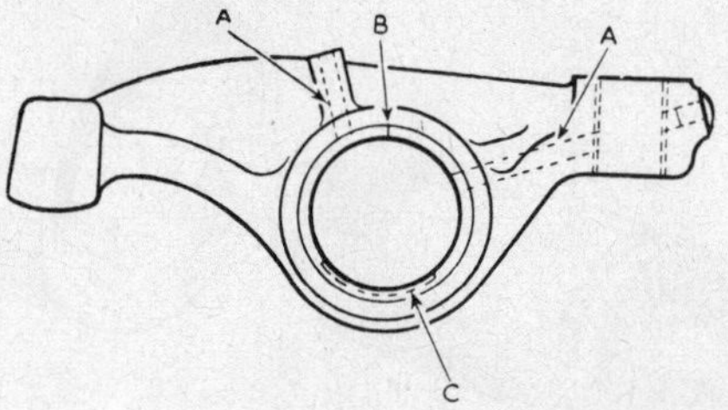

A—Oilways
B—Joint in rocker bush
C—Oil groove

Correct rocker arm bushing installation

9. Unbolt the air pump from its mounting point on the head (Emission Control models only).
10. Lift the head from the cylinder block.

Installation is in reverse order of removal. Thoroughly clean the mating surfaces of the cylinder block and head, and always use a new gasket. The gasket is marked Top and Front to facilitate correct installation. Gasket sealing compound is not necessary, but may be used. Cylinder head nuts should be tightened gradually, in the correct sequence (see "Tightening Sequences"), and to the proper torque value (see "Torque Specifications"). When the head has been tightened the valves must be adjusted (see "Valve Adjustment"). After running the engine for between 200 and 500 miles, the head should be retorqued and the valves readjusted. When retorquing the head, simply back off each nut slightly and retighten to specification, one at a time and in the proper sequence.

OVERHAUL

See "Engine Rebuilding Section."

Rocker Shafts

REMOVAL AND INSTALLATION

See Cylinder Head Removal and Installation.

Intake/Exhaust Manifold

REMOVAL

Midget 1975

1. Remove the carburetors and air cleaners (see "Carburetor Removal and Installation").
2. Unbolt the exhaust pipe from the exhaust manifold.
3. Unbolt the heater pipe clamps from the intake manifold.
4. Unscrew the PCV valve hose from the manifold connection (if applicable).
5. Disconnect the vacuum advance and gulp valve lines from the intake manifold (if applicable).
6. Unbolt and remove the manifolds.
7. Manifold installation in all cases is in reverse order of removal.
8. Thoroughly clean the mating surfaces and use new gaskets. The perforated metal face of the gasket should face the manifold.
9. New exhaust header ring gaskets should be used. It may be necessary to use a new exhaust pipe clamp on the early models. Be sure to tighten the manifold studs evenly (see "Torque Specifications").

Midget 1976 and Later

1. Drain the cooling system and remove the carburetor from the intake manifold.
2. Disconnect all water hoses, vacuum lines, and the EGR line from the intake manifold. Remove the EGR line from the EGR valve. Remove the running-on control valve vacuum pipe adapter.
3. Remove the three nuts, bolts, and washers, and disconnect the exhaust pipe. Remove and discard the gasket.
4. Remove the nut and washer connecting intake and exhaust manifolds. Remove the flame trap bracket and the water return pipe bracket.
5. Remove the six nuts and washers that hold the manifolds onto the cylinder head. Pull the manifolds out slightly from the head, and remove the intake manifold and spacer. Then, remove the exhaust manifold and gasket.
6. In installation, install a new gasket, and then position the exhaust manifold onto the cylinder head studs. Install the two larger clamps and their washers to the two lower studs. Start the two longer nuts onto the two inner, lower studs.
7. Position the intake manifold and spacer onto the exhaust manifold, locate it properly on the cylinder head dowels with the clamps properly positioned, and then push the manifolds into position as an assembly. Reverse the remaining procedures.

MGB 1975

1. Remove the carburetors and air cleaners (see "Carburetor Removal and Installation").
2. Disconnect the distributor vacuum advance line and the gulp valve line (if applicable).
3. Unscrew the PCV valve hose from the intake manifold connection (if applicable).
4. Unbolt the exhaust header pipes from the exhaust manifold.
5. Unbolt and remove the manifolds.
6. Manifold installation in all cases is in reverse order of removal.
7. Thoroughly clean the mating surfaces and use new gaskets. The perforated metal face of the gasket should face the manifold.
8. New exhaust header ring gaskets should be used. Be sure to tighten the manifold studs evenly (see "Torque Specifications").

MGB 1976–77

1. Remove the air cleaner and carburetor.
2. Disconnect the distributor vacuum line, brake booster vacuum line, and running-on control valve at the manifold.
3. Remove the EGR and gulp valves.
4. Remove the hot air duct. Remove the two attaching screws, and remove the heat shield from the water line.
5. Disconnect the exhaust pipe. Remove the six nuts and washers, and remove the two manifolds. Note that the four center nuts use larger washers and hold both intake and exhaust manifolds in position, while the nuts at the ends, using smaller washers hold only the exhaust manifold in place.
6. In installation, use a new gasket, reverse the above procedures, and be sure to torque to specification.

MGB 1978 and Later

1. Drain the cooling system.
2. Remove the air cleaner. Disconnect: the vapor return hose from the carburetor; the heater pipe at the lower radiator hose; the wire at the induction heater.
3. Remove carburetor attaching nuts, and remove the carburetor, intake heater, bracket, and heat shield.
4. Disconnect the brake vacuum hose at the manifold, the running-on control valve hose at the manifold, and the small gulp valve hose at the manifold.
5. Loosen the clamp for the large gulp valve hose, and then remove the bolt which attaches the gulp valve to the intake manifold. Be careful not to lose the copper washers. Pull the gulp valve off the manifold, disconnecting the large hose.
6. Remove the hot air shroud.
7. Jack up the car and remove the bolt which holds the exhaust pipe to the front bracket. Disconnect the exhaust pipe going to the rear of the car from the catalytic converter, retaining the seal.
8. Remove the two bolts, three nuts, and flat washers attaching the manifold to the head, and pull off the manifold and hot air shroud base plate.
9. In installation, use a new manifold gasket and replace other exhaust seals wherever they are damaged. Tighten the connection between exhaust pipe and catalytic converter before connecting the exhaust pipe to the front bracket.

Timing Gear Cover and Oil Seal

REMOVAL AND INSTALLATION

Midget

To remove the timing gear cover:

1. Remove the radiator.
2. Loosen the generator adjustment bolts and remove the fan belt.

NOTE: It is necessary to unbolt the engine mounts and exhaust pipe in order to raise the front of the engine to provide clearance for removal of the pulley.

3. Bend the locktab back and unscrew the crankshaft pulley nut.
4. Carefully pry the pulley from the crankshaft.
5. Unbolt and remove the timing gear cover.

To replace the timing gear cover oil seal:

1. Pry the old seal out of the cover.
2. Lubricate the new seal and install it evenly into the cover in the same position as the old one, taking care not to damage it.
3. If the seal is made of rubber, fill the groove between the seal lips with grease. Felt seals do not need to be lubricated in this manner.
4. Make sure that the oil thrower behind the crankshaft pulley is installed with the face marked F away from the engine.

The cover and pulley are installed together to ensure that the oil seal is centered correctly. To reinstall:

1. Lubricate the hub of the pulley and insert it into the oil seal, turning the pulley in a clockwise direction to avoid damaging the seal.
2. Align the pulley keyway with the crankshaft key and push the pulley (with the cover and cover gasket) onto the crankshaft.
3. Replace the cover bolts and tighten them evenly.
4. Tighten and lock the crankshaft pulley nut.
5. Reinstall the fan belt, and replace and fill the radiator.

MGB through 1977

Timing gear cover removal and installation and oil seal replacement procedures for the MGB are the same as for the Midget, with one exception: on 18GB and later engines, the steering rack must be unbolted from the body and moved forward to provide clearance for removal of the crankshaft pulley. It is not necessary to raise the front of the engine to remove the pulley on the MGB.

MGB 1978 and Later

1. Remove the acoustic insulating board. Remove the radiator.
2. Loosen adjusting and attaching bolts on the air pump and alternator, and remove belts.
3. Remove the crankshaft pulley retaining bolt, and remove the pulley with a wheel puller.
4. Remove the screws and washers, and remove the timing cover.
5. Reverse the procedure to install, using a new gasket and a new lockwasher on the crankshaft pulley.

Timing Gear and Chain

REMOVAL AND INSTALLATION

The camshafts in all MG engines are driven by a chain from the crankshaft. The MGB has an endless, duplex chain and a chain tensioner. Chain tensioner removal and service procedures can be found under "Timing Chain Tensioner Service—MGB."

The crankshaft and camshaft timing gears and the timing chain usually do not require service or replacement unless, due to high mileage or improper lubrication, gear tooth wear is noticeable. If wear is evident, replace all three components. Worn gears or chain stretch as isolated problems almost never occur.

MGB

1. To remove the chain and gears, first remove the timing gear cover (see preceding section). On the MGB, remove the chain tensioner or retract and lock the rubbing block by removing the plug from the tensioner body and turning the adjusting bolt clockwise (see following section).
2. Bend the locktab back and remove the camshaft timing gear nut. The camshaft and crankshaft timing gears may now be removed together with the chain by easing the gears off the shafts simultaneously, using a puller or suitable levers.
3. When replacing the timing chain and gears, set the crankshaft with its keyway at twelve o'clock and the camshaft with its keyway at one o'clock as seen from the front. The washers behind the crankshaft gear are spacers to align the two gears properly.
4. When reassembling, the same number of washers should be installed as were removed *unless* any of the following components have been replaced: crankshaft, crankshaft main bearings and thrust washers, crankshaft timing gear, camshaft, camshaft timing gear, or camshaft locating plate. If any of the above components have been replaced, timing gear alignment can be checked and adjusted by placing a straightedge across the gear sides and adding or subtracting washers to eliminate any gaps between the gear side surfaces and the straightedge (after the gears have been installed).
5. To install the timing gears and chain, assemble the chain onto the gears with the

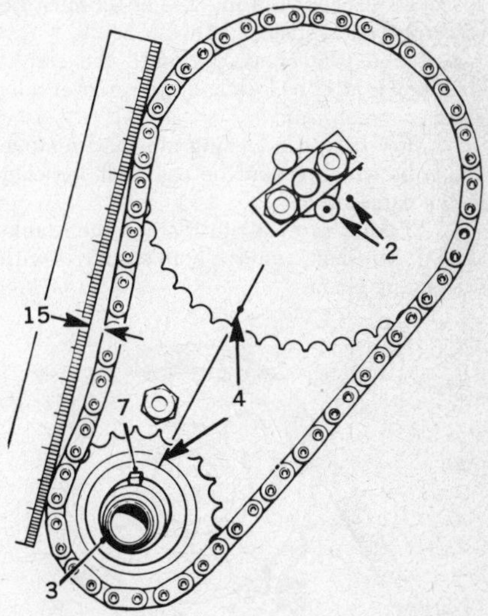

2. Camshaft gear to camshaft mark alignment
3. Crankshaft
4. Crankshaft and camshaft gear markings and alignment
7. Crankshaft keyway
15. Measuring for allowable timing chain free play—0.40 inch or less

Timing gear alignment and timing chain looseness inspection—PE94J engine

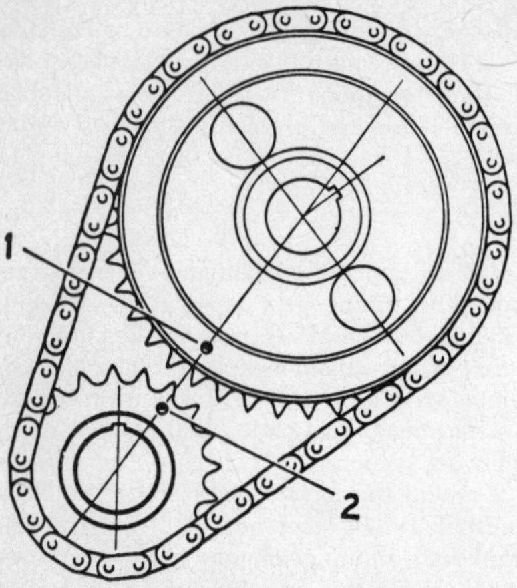

Timing gear marks, MGB

gear marks facing each other so that a line drawn through them would pass through the camshaft and crankshaft axes. Keeping the gears in this position, start the crankshaft gear onto the crankshaft (with the gear keyway and crankshaft key aligned).

6. Install the camshaft gear onto the camshaft, turning the camshaft to align the key with the keyway if necessary.

7. Make a final check of alignment of the timing gears and gear marks, and install the camshaft gear lockwasher and nut. Replace the timing cover.

Midget

1. Remove the timing gear cover as outlined in the applicable "Timing Gear Cover Removal and Installation" procedure.

2. Remove the oil thrower.

3. Check timing chain wear by placing a straightedge along the slack length of chain. If the free-play between the straightedge and the chain at a point midway between the two sprockets exceeds 0.4 in., the chain must be discarded and replaced.

4. Rotate the crankshaft until the crankshaft key is at 12 o'clock and the sprocket dots align.

5. Pry back the locking tabs and remove the bolts which retain the camshaft sprocket to the camshaft.

6. Taking care not to disturb the crankshaft or camshaft, remove both sprockets with the timing chain.

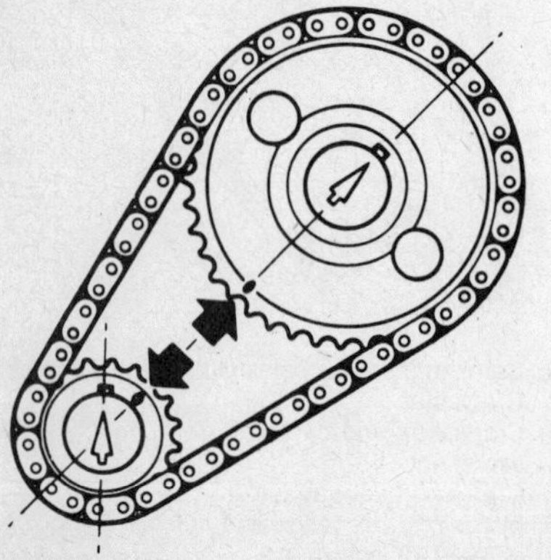

Timing chain gear alignment and shaft keyway location—18V engines

7. To check alignment of the sprockets, remove the crankshaft drive key and temporarily install both sprockets. Place a straightedge across the teeth of both sprockets. Correct any misalignment by placing shims behind the crankshaft sprocket.

8. After checking the alignment, remove the sprockets, install the crankshaft drive key, and place the sprocket and chain assembly into position, aligned dot to dot, and install the camshaft sprocket retaining bolts using a new lockplate.

9. Install the oil thrower.

10. Install the timing gear cover as outlined in the applicable "Timing Gear Cover Removal and Installation" procedure.

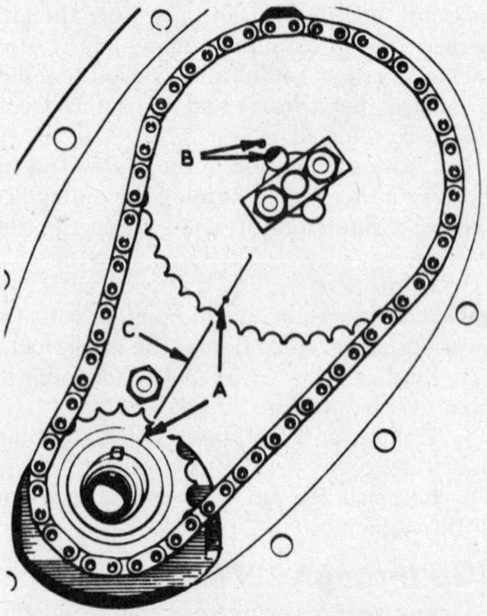

Timing gear marks, Midget

Timing Chain Tensioner

REMOVAL INSTALLATION AND ADJUSTMENT

1. To remove the tensioner (after the timing gear cover has been removed), first unscrew the plug from the tensioner body.

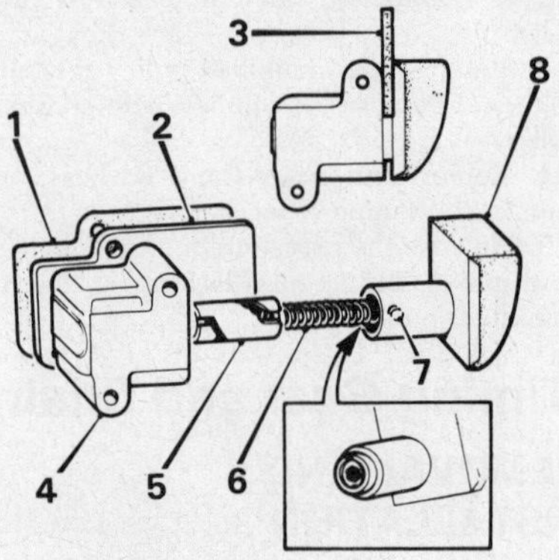

1. Gasket
2. Backplate
3. Spacer to prevent disengagement
4. Tensioner body
5. Inner cylinder
6. Spring
7. Peg
8. Slipper head

Timing chain tensioner—exploded view

Using a ⅛ in. Allen wrench, turn the tension adjusting bolt clockwise until the rubbing block is fully retracted and locked behind the limit peg.

2. Unbolt and remove the tensioner and its backing plate.

3. Withdraw the rubbing block and plunger from the tensioner body, and turn the tension adjusting bolt clockwise until the piston and spring are released.

4. Clean the components in solvent and blow out the oil passages with compressed air.

5. Check the bore of the tensioner body for ovalness. If the diameter of the bore at or near the mouth varies more than 0.003 in., the complete tensioner unit should be replaced. If within the limit given, it is acceptable to replace just the rubbing block.

6. To reassemble the tensioner, insert the spring and piston into the bore and compress the spring.

7. Turn the piston clockwise until the inner end is below the peg. Install the rubbing block plunger into the bore.

CAUTION

Do not attempt to turn the tension adjusting bolt counterclockwise.

8. Bolt the backing plate and tensioner onto the cylinder block and lock the mounting bolts with the locktab.

9. Release the rubbing block for operation by turning the adjusting bolt clockwise until the block contacts the chain under spring pressure.

10. Check the rubbing block for freedom of movement and make sure that it does not bind against the backing plate.

11. Replace and lock the plug in the tensioner body.

Camshaft

REMOVAL

Removal of the camshaft from the Midget or the MGB can be accomplished without removing the engine from the chassis. The following procedure can, however, be used whether the engine is in or out of the car.

1. Drain the crankcase and remove the oil pan from the engine.

2. Remove the rocker cover from the head and unbolt and remove the rocker shaft assembly and pushrods, keeping the pushrods in order.

3. Remove the intake and exhaust manifolds.

4. Remove the lifter covers from the side of the cylinder block.

5. Remove the lifters, and, as with the pushrods, keep them in order.

6. Remove the timing cover and gears.

7. Remove the oil pump.

8. Remove the distributor.

9. Remove the camshaft locating plate.

10. Pull the camshaft from the front of the engine rotating it slowly to assist removal.

NOTE: Removal procedures for individual units such as the oil pump, timing gear cover, etc. can be found under appropriate subheads in the "Engine" section.

INSTALLATION

All Models

Camshaft installation in all cases is in the reverse order of removal. Camshaft bearings, except in cases of insufficient lubrication, almost never need replacement. Clearance can be checked with a feeler gauge. Replacement of bearings requires special pullers and machine tools (for align-boring) and should be left to a machine shop.

Camshaft end-play can be checked before installation by assembling the locating plate and timing gear onto the camshaft and measuring fore and aft play. If it exceeds specification, the locating plate should be replaced.

CAMSHAFT SPECIFICATIONS (IN.)

Model	End Play	Oil Clearance
Midget	0.003-0.007	0.001-0.002
PE94J	0.0045-0.0085	0.0016-0.0036
MGB	0.003-0.007	0.001-0.002

NOTE: Valve lift for the different engine models can be found under VALVE SPECIFICATIONS. Intake valve opening timing (deg. BTDC) can be found under TUNE-UP SPECIFICATIONS.

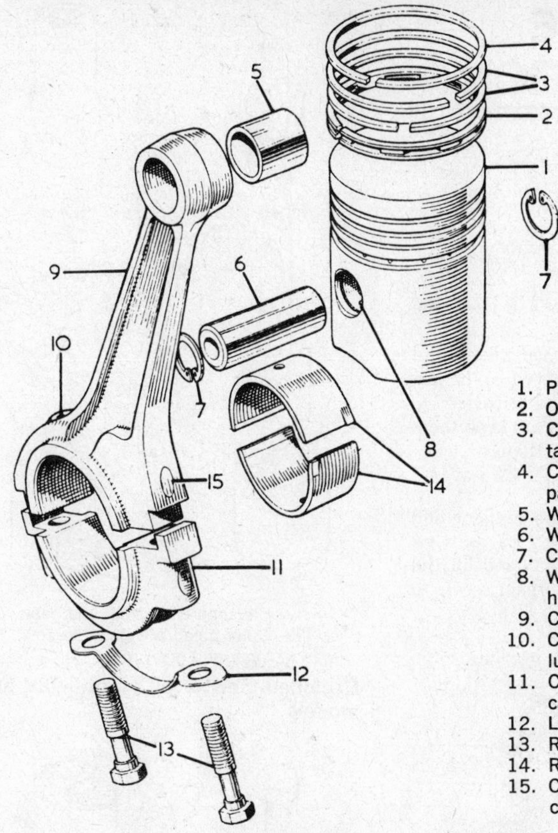

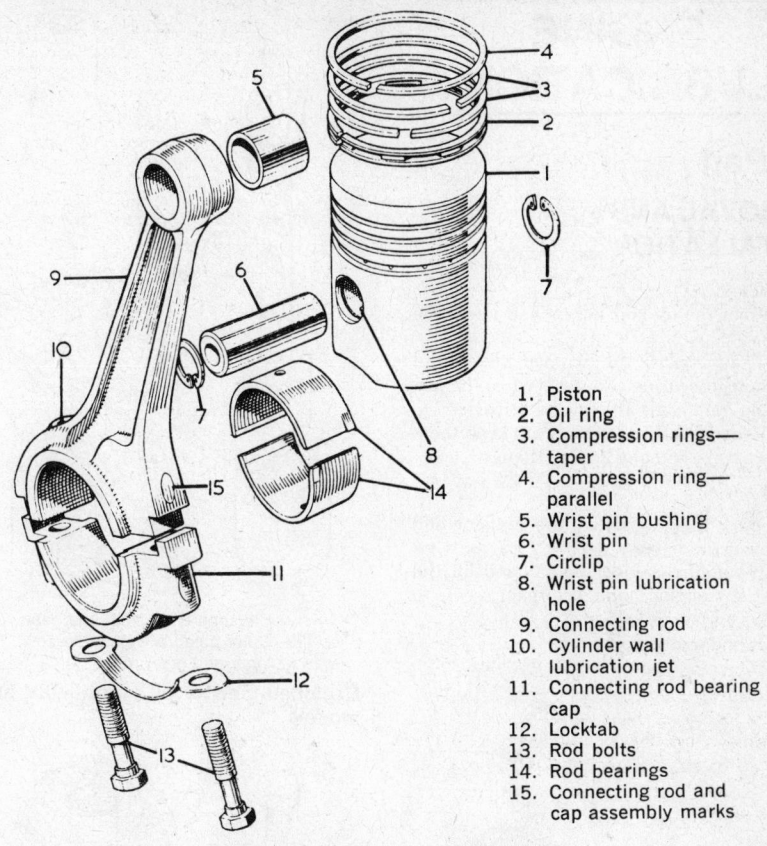

1. Piston
2. Oil ring
3. Compression rings—taper
4. Compression ring—parallel
5. Wrist pin bushing
6. Wrist pin
7. Circlip
8. Wrist pin lubrication hole
9. Connecting rod
10. Cylinder wall lubrication jet
11. Connecting rod bearing cap
12. Locktab
13. Rod bolts
14. Rod bearings
15. Connecting rod and cap assembly marks

Piston and connecting rod, MGB

Pistons and Connecting Rods

NOTE: On engines with floating or press-fit type wrist pins, the pistons are select-fitted to the bores, and the piston crowns and cylinders are marked with identification numbers.

Piston and connecting rod installation position for all models is indicated in the accompanying illustrations. Unmarked pistons must be identified with regard to cylinder and installation position prior to removal so that they may be reinstalled in the same position. Select-fitted pistons are identified by a number enclosed in a diamond stamped on the piston crown and block. Oversize dimensions are stamped on the piston crown, enclosed in some cases in an ellipse.

All later pistons are marked with the word "Front", or a triangular indentation which must face the front of the engine.

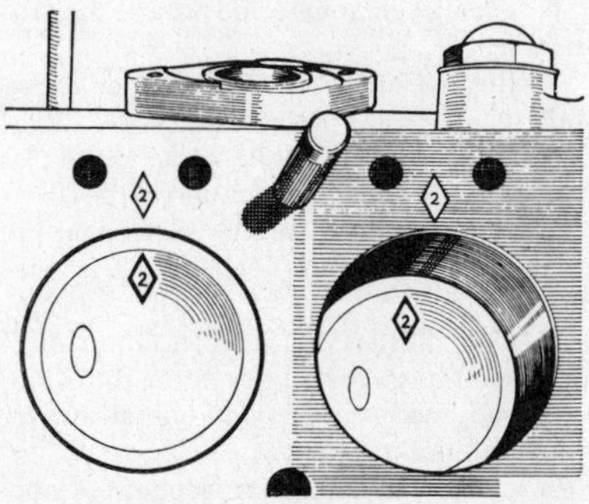

Oversize piston markings

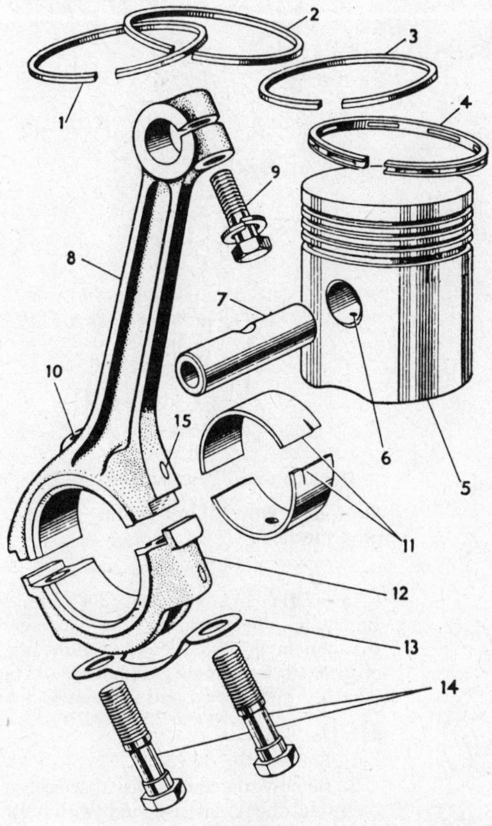

1. Piston ring—parallel
2. Piston ring—taper
3. Piston ring—taper
4. Piston ring—scraper
5. Piston
6. Piston pin lubricating hole
7. Piston pin
8. Connecting rod
9. Clamping screw and washer
10. Cylinder wall lubricating jet
11. Connecting rod bearings
12. Connecting rod cap
13. Lock washer
14. Bolts
15. Connecting rod and cap marking

Piston and connecting rod, Midget

ENGINE LUBRICATION

Oil Pan

REMOVAL AND INSTALLATION

Midget

1. Drain the oil and unbolt and lower the oil pan.
2. Always replace the two pan gaskets and the two main bearing cork seals when the pan has been removed. It may be necessary to soak the cork seals in hot water to keep them from breaking when installing them.

MGB

1. Drain the oil. Drain the radiator and disconnect the hoses.
2. Unbolt the engine mounts and lift the front of the engine enough to gain access to the front oil pan bolts.
3. Unbolt and lower the pan.

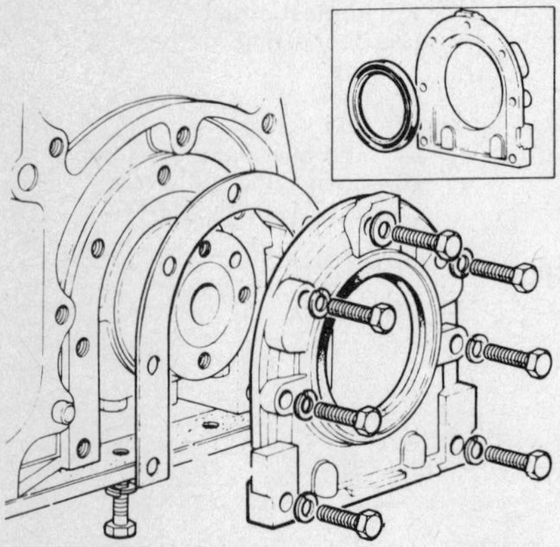

Rear main bearing oil seal components—typical

4. Clean the cylinder block and oil pan mating surfaces and replace the pan gasket to preclude the possibility of an oil leak.

Oil Pump

REMOVAL AND INSTALLATION

Midget

1. Remove the oil pan.
2. Remove the three bolts and withdraw the oil pump assembly.

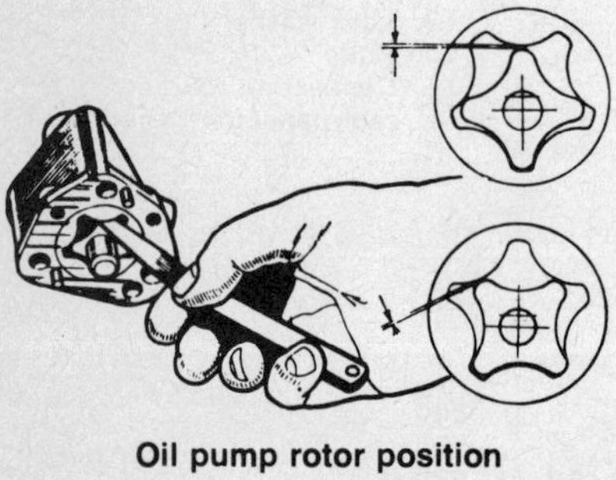

Oil pump rotor position

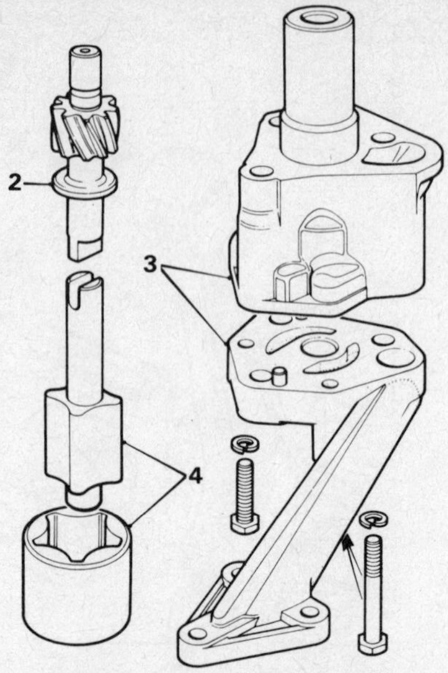

2. Oil pump drive shaft and gear
3. Outer pump body and cover
4. Inner and outer rotors

Exploded view of oil pump—18V engine models

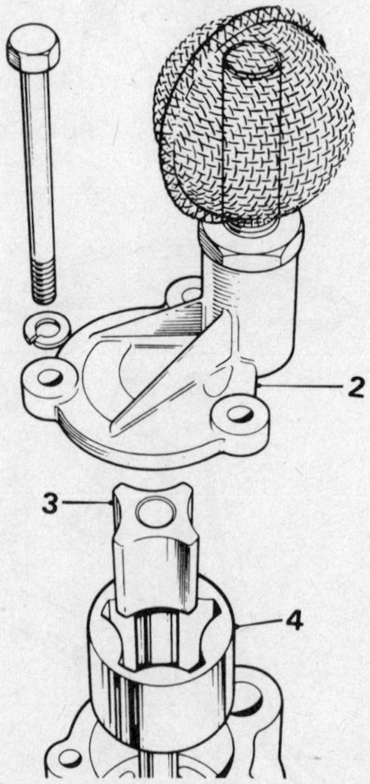

2. Oil pump cover 3. Inner rotor 4. Outer rotor

Exploded view of oil pump—PE94J engine models

Installation is in reverse order of removal. Be careful when installing the paper gasket, that the intake and delivery ports are not obstructed. Use a new gasket if the old one is damaged in any way, and use new locktabs.

MGB

1. Remove the oil pan.
2. Remove the three nuts that secure the pump to the crankcase and withdraw the pump assembly.

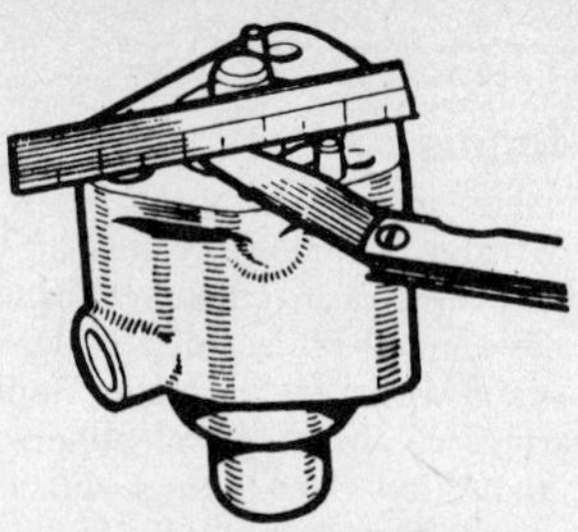

Checking rotor end play

Installation is in reverse order of removal. Use a new gasket when the pump is reinstalled.

OIL PUMP CLEARANCES

Midget

Concentric Engineering pump:

The concentric pump is replaceable as a unit only; parts are not available.

Burman pump:

1. Remove the pump cover and withdraw the rotor and vane assembly. Remove the sleeve from the end of the rotor and remove the vanes.
2. Replace any worn or damaged parts.
3. Coat all parts with motor oil before assembly.

Holbourn-Eaton pump:

4. Remove the pump cover and lift out the inner and outer rotors.
5. Check clearance between the outer rotor and the pump body. If the clearance exceeds 0.010 in., the complete pump assembly should be renewed.

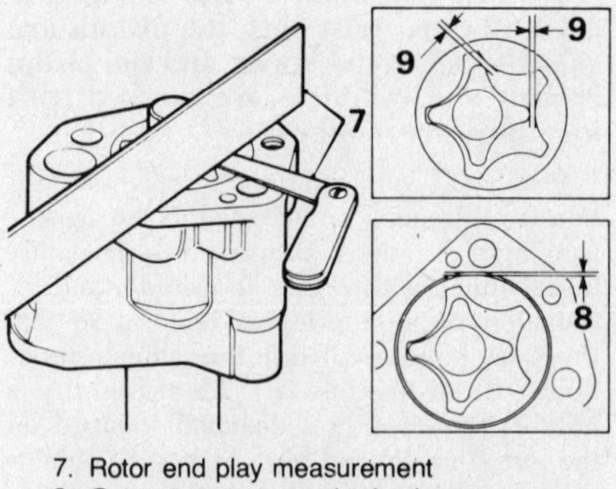

7. Rotor end play measurement
8. Outer rotor to pump body clearance
9. Inner rotor lobe to outer rotor clearance

Measurement position for oil pump component clearances

6. Check clearance between the rotor lobes.
7. Replace the rotors if clearance exceeds 0.006 in.
8. Check the rotor end float. If the clearance exceeds 0.005 in., remove the dowels from the pump body mating surface and mill or lap the surface until clearance is within specification.
9. Coat all parts with fresh motor oil before assembling. Install the outer rotor in the pump body with the beveled end at the drive end of the pump body.
10. Check the pump for freedom of movement after assembly.

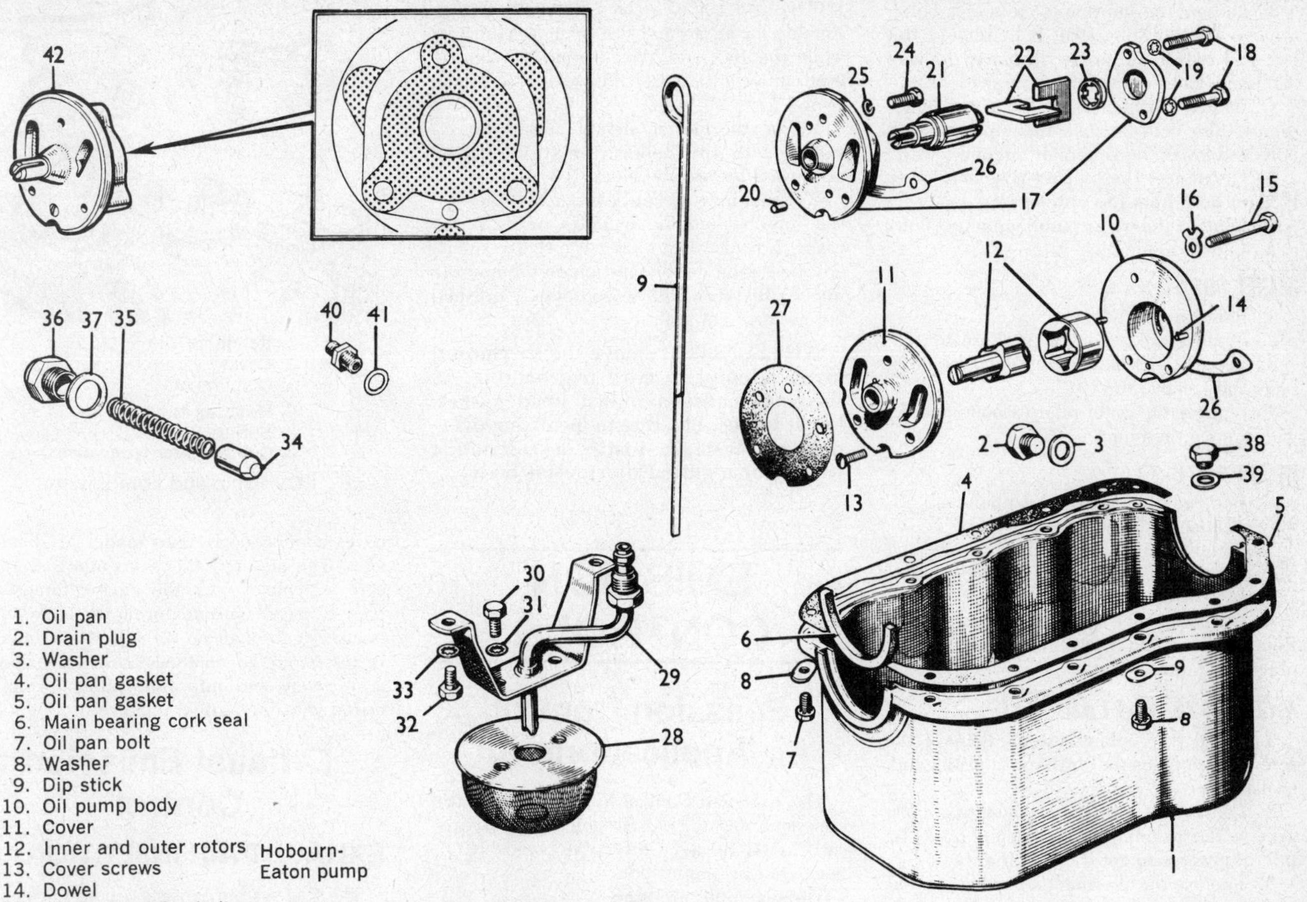

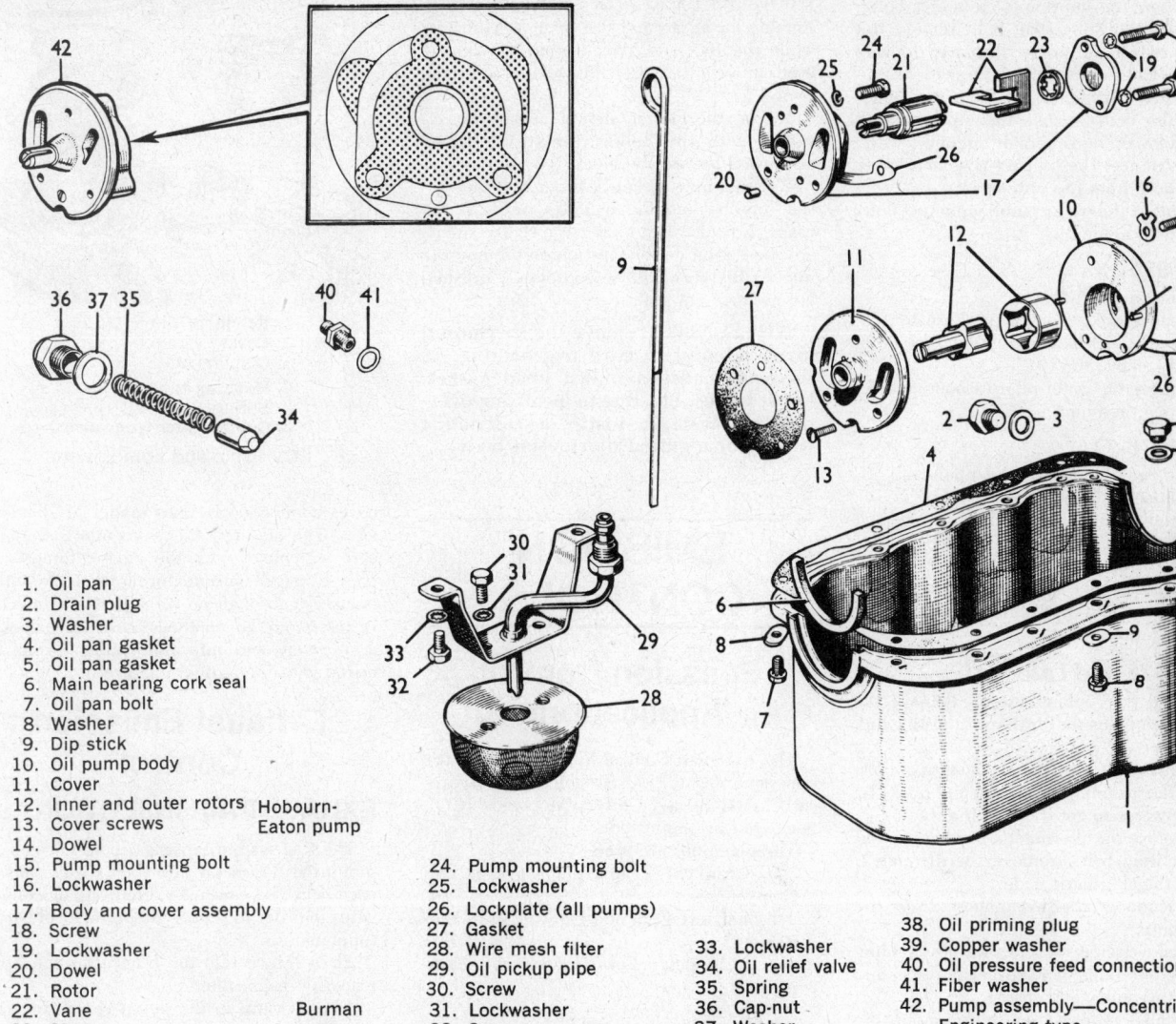

1. Oil pan
2. Drain plug
3. Washer
4. Oil pan gasket
5. Oil pan gasket
6. Main bearing cork seal
7. Oil pan bolt
8. Washer
9. Dip stick
10. Oil pump body
11. Cover
12. Inner and outer rotors
13. Cover screws
14. Dowel
15. Pump mounting bolt
16. Lockwasher

Hobourn-Eaton pump

17. Body and cover assembly
18. Screw
19. Lockwasher
20. Dowel
21. Rotor
22. Vane
23. Sleeve

Burman pump

24. Pump mounting bolt
25. Lockwasher
26. Lockplate (all pumps)
27. Gasket
28. Wire mesh filter
29. Oil pickup pipe
30. Screw
31. Lockwasher
32. Screw
33. Lockwasher
34. Oil relief valve
35. Spring
36. Cap-nut
37. Washer
38. Oil priming plug
39. Copper washer
40. Oil pressure feed connection
41. Fiber washer
42. Pump assembly—Concentric Engineering type

Oil pump

MGB

MGB oil pump service procedures are identical to those of the Hobourn-Eaton pump on the Midget.

Oil Cooler

REMOVAL AND INSTALLATION

On all models equipped with oil coolers, disconnect the oil cooler pipes from the oil filter, cylinder block, and oil cooler connections. Next, remove the oil cooler attaching bolts and remove the cooler. Withdraw the oil cooler pipes from the radiator diaphragm grommets. When replacing, start the line fittings onto the connections by hand to avoid crossing the threads. Tighten the fittings, check the engine idle until the oil pressure is developed, and check the oil lines for leaks. Shut off engine and recheck oil level.

ENGINE COOLING

Radiator

REMOVAL AND INSTALLATION

Midget

1. Drain the cooling system by opening the radiator tap.
2. Remove the radiator grille.
3. Disconnect the upper and lower hoses from the radiator.
4. Remove the nuts securing the top and bottom radiator cowl plates to the body.
5. Disconnect the oil cooler lines on cars so equipped.
6. Remove the radiator retaining bolts and lift the radiator out (complete with shroud, Mk. III).
7. Installation is in reverse order of removal.

MGB

1. Open the radiator tap and drain the coolant.
2. Disconnect the upper and lower radiator hoses.
3. If the car is not equipped with an oil cooler, remove the shroud bolts and remove the radiator and shroud as an assembly.
4. If the car has an oil cooler, loosen the shroud mounting bolts, remove the overflow hose clamp, and remove the radiator-to-shroud bolts. Withdraw the radiator from the shroud.
5. Installation is in reverse order of removal.

Water Pump

REMOVAL

Midget

1. Remove the radiator.
2. Remove the fan retaining bolts and remove the fan.

3. Loosen the air pump mounting bolts, remove the adjusting strut bolt, remove the belt and swivel and pump up out of the way (Emission Control models only).

4. Loosen the generator mounting bolts, remove the belt, remove the top mounting bolts and lower the generator out of the way.

5. Disconnect the by-pass hose and lower radiator hose from the water pump.

6. Remove the water pump mounting bolts and remove the pump.

MGB 1975

1. Remove the radiator.
2. Remove the generator or alternator.
3. Remove the fan and pulley retaining bolts and remove the fan.
4. Remove the water pump mounting bolts and remove the pump.

MGB 1976-77

1. Remove the radiator. Unbolt and remove the fan and drive pulley.
2. Remove the air pump adjusting link screws. Remove the top mounting bolt, nut, and washer from the alternator.
3. Disconnect the water pump lower hose. Remove water pump retaining bolts and remove the pump.

MGB 1978 and Later

1. Drain the cooling system. Remove the screw which holds the air pump adjusting link in place.
2. Loosen the air pump mounting bolt, remove the air pump drive belt and pivot the pump upwards to get it out of the way.
3. Remove the alternator adjusting link nut and mounting bolts, remove the drive belt, and put the alternator aside.
4. Disconnect the lower hose from the water pump.
5. Remove screws and lockwashers holding the drive belt pulley and spacer in place, and remove the pulley and spacer.
6. Remove the water pump mounting bolts. Remove the air pump adjusting link brackets. Remove the water pump.

INSTALLATION

All Models

Installation in all cases is a reversal of removal procedures. Make sure that the mating surface of the cylinder block is cleaned of pieces of the old gasket that may remain. Always use a new gasket, and torque the mounting bolts evenly.

Thermostat

REMOVAL AND INSTALLATION

The thermostat on all MGs is located in the aluminum housing, bolted to the cylinder head, that connects to the upper radiator hose.

1. Replacement involves simply unbolting the housing and lifting out the thermostat.

2. Before unbolting the housing, drain (and save) about half of the coolant from the radiator to prevent loss when the housing is removed. Thermostats of three different opening temperatures are available: 160° F, 180° F, and 190° F. The 180° thermostat is suitable for all around use in most climates, while the 160° and 190° thermostats can be used in very hot or cold weather, respectively.

3. The thermostat should always be installed with the bellows or spring facing downward toward the block.

4. Use a new gasket between the thermostat housing and the cylinder head. If the gasket is made of cork, as some replacements are, be careful not to overtighten the housing nuts or the cork will be completely crushed out and will not seal.

NOTE: Never remove the thermostat in an attempt to cure overheating, as this may cause a blown head gasket, burnt valves, etc. due to localizing overheating. Instead, install a restricting washer or a gutted thermostat body.

EMISSION CONTROLS

Emission Control Applications

The Emission Control Systems reduce the emissions of Oxide of Nitrogen (NO_x), Hydrocarbons (HC), and Carbon Monoxide (CO), generated by combustion.

Three systems are used:

a. Crankcase Emission Control and Components

b. Exhaust Emission Control and Components

c. Evaporative Loss Control and Components

Crankcase Emission Control

The crankcase air is metered through filter canister of the Evaporative Loss Control System. (Restrictor located in the rocker arm cover connection on late model MGB vehicles.) The metered air passes into the crankcase and mixes with the engine fumes and blow-by gases. This mixture is drawn from the crankcase through an oil separator/flame arrestor, mounted on the engine valve rocker arm cover, and into the carburetor to be mixed with the air/fuel mixture.

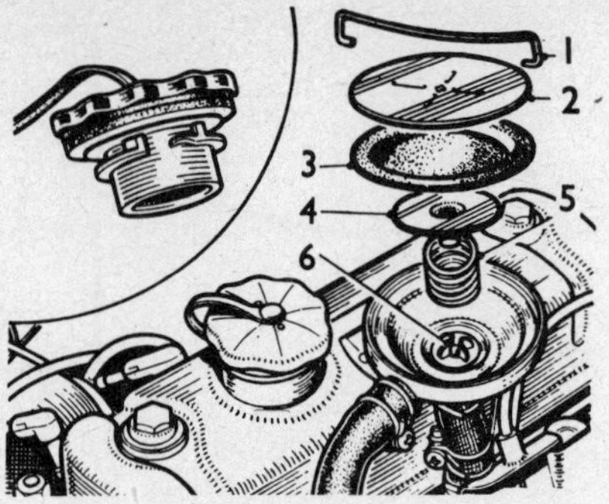

1. Retaining clip
2. Cover
3. Diaphragm
4. Metering valve
5. Spring
6. Guides (later type valves)

PCV valve and components

Exhaust Emission Control

EXHAUST AIR INJECTION

The EAI system consists of a belt driven air pump that forces air into the exhaust port of each cylinder, causing a reburning of exhaust gases in order to reduce the number of harmful emissions.

Air is drawn into the pump through a replaceable paper filter.

A relief valve in the pump vents excessive air pressure, created by high rpm operation, to the atmosphere.

A check valve, located in the pump output line to the injection manifold, protects the pump from exhaust gas backflow.

A gulp valve, located in the pump output line to the intake manifold, leans out the rich

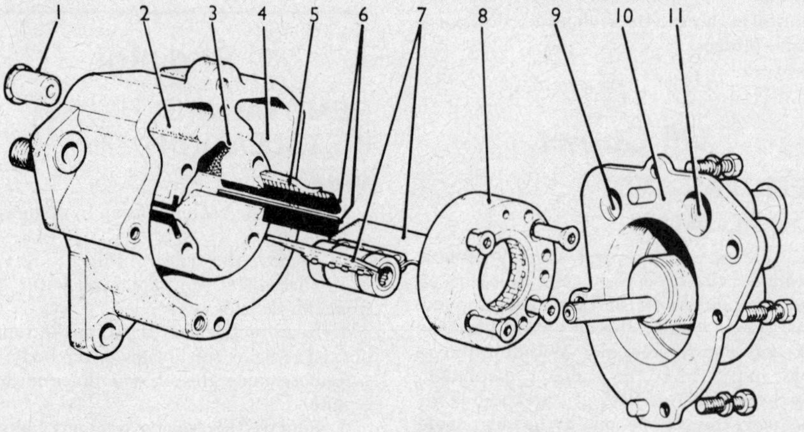

1. Relief valve
2. Intake chamber
3. Rotor
4. Output chamber
5. Spring
6. Carbons
7. Vane assemblies
8. Rotor bearing support plate
9. Output port
10. End-cover
11. Intake port

Air Pump Components

fuel/air mixture that develops when the engine is decelerating (engine overrun). A line between the intake manifold and the gulp valve allows the valve to be activated by changes in manifold vacuum. On some engines a restrictor is located in the output line between the pump and valve to prevent engine surge when the valve is operating.

In addition to the air pump and its attendant equipment, all vehicles with emission control systems are equipped with the distributor and carburetors modified to meet emission standards. These units are covered separately in the "Engine Electrical" and "Fuel System" sections, as well as in the "Specifications" section.

The efficient and trouble-free operation of the emission control system depends to a large extent upon the engine being correctly tuned. Proper tuning specifications given for a particular engine should be strictly adhered to (see "Tune-Up Specifications").

Maintenance

At the time of an engine tune-up (6,000 miles recommended), the entire exhaust air injection system should be inspected. Clean or replace the air pump air filter element. Check the air hoses and connections for any evidence of leaking. (This is very important, because an air leak can cause overheating, resulting in burnt valves, a blown head gasket, etc.) Check the air pump drive belt tension and adjust it if necessary. Properly adjusted, the belt should have a total deflection of ½ inch midway between the pulleys. Adjustment is made by loosening the mounting bolt and adjusting strut bolts, in the same manner as generator adjustment.

Component Testing

1. To check the air pump and relief valve, first make sure that the pump drive belt is properly adjusted and that the air filter is clean.
2. Disconnect and plug the air supply hose to the gulp valve. Disconnect the injection manifold air hose at the check valve, and connect a pressure gauge to the hose.
3. At an engine speed of 1000 rpm (Midget—1200 rpm), the pressure gauge should not read less than 2.75 lb/sq in. If a lower reading is obtained, tape the relief valve shut and repeat the test. If the reading is now satisfactory, replace the relief valve (it can be removed by prying with a screwdriver or with a gear puller).
4. If the reading is still low, replace or overhaul the air pump unit.

NOTE: If the pump is removed for service, do not hold it in a vise. Even a small amount of pressure will distort the pump body.

5. To test the check valve, disconnect the air supply hose from the valve and unscrew it from the injection manifold. Blow through the valve at each connection (do not use compressed air). Air should pass through the valve only from the air supply side (from the air pump) to the manifold connection. If air passes in the opposite direction or not at all, the valve must be replaced.
6. To test the gulp valve, disconnect the valve air supply hose from the air pump connection.

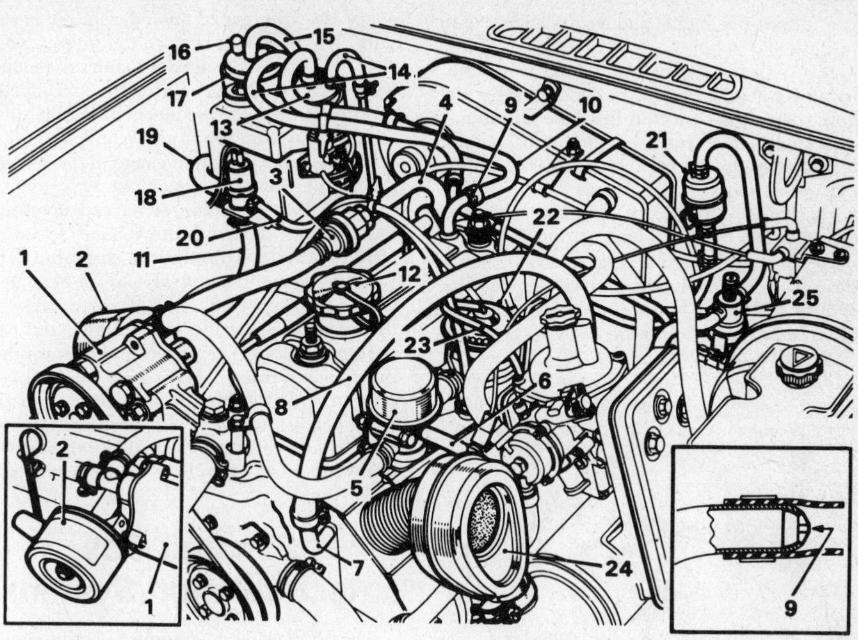

1. Air pump
2. Air pump air cleaner
3. Check valve
4. Air manifold
5. Gulp valve
6. Sensing pipe
7. Oil separator/flame trap
8. Breather pipe
9. Restricted connection
10. Purge line
11. Air vent pipe
12. Sealed oil filter cap
13. Primary charcoal absorption canister
14. Vapour lines
15. Canister inter-connecting pipe
16. Sealing cap
17. Secondary charcoal absorption canister
18. Running-on control valve
19. Running-on control hose
20. Running-on control pipe
21. Fuel filter
22. Exhaust gas recirculation (E.G.R.) valve
23. E.G.R. valve hose
24. Air temperature control valve
25. Fuel cut-off valve

Emission control components—typical—1978 MGB shown

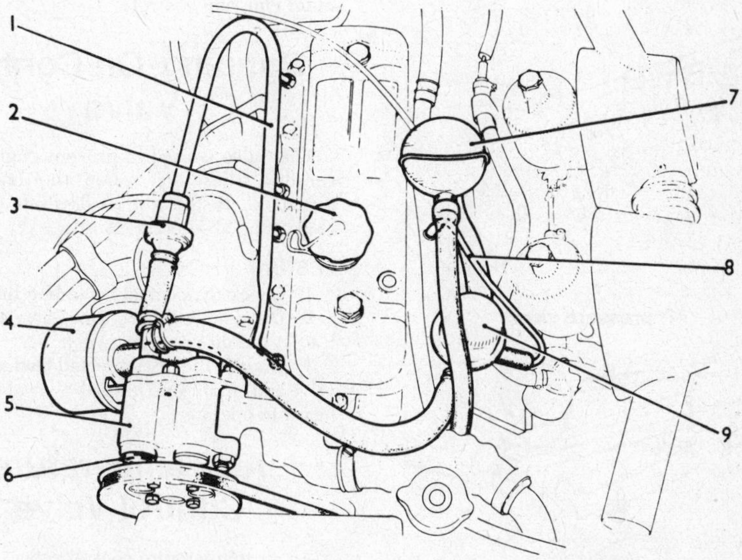

1. Air manifold
2. Oil filler cap
3. Check valve
4. Air pump air filter
5. Air pump
6. Relief valve
7. PCV valve
8. Vacuum sensing line
9. Gulp valve

Air injection system

7. Start the engine and let it idle for a few seconds.

8. With the engine still idling, connect a vacuum gauge to the end of the gulp valve air hose that is disconnected from the air pump. The gauge should read zero for approximately fifteen seconds. If a vacuum is registered, the gulp valve should be replaced.

9. If the valve passes the test, snap the throttle open once and let it spring shut.

10. Repeat this test several times, breaking the connection between the vacuum gauge and the gulp valve hose before each operation of the throttle to return the gauge to zero. In every case the gauge should register a vacuum. If it does not, replace the gulp valve.

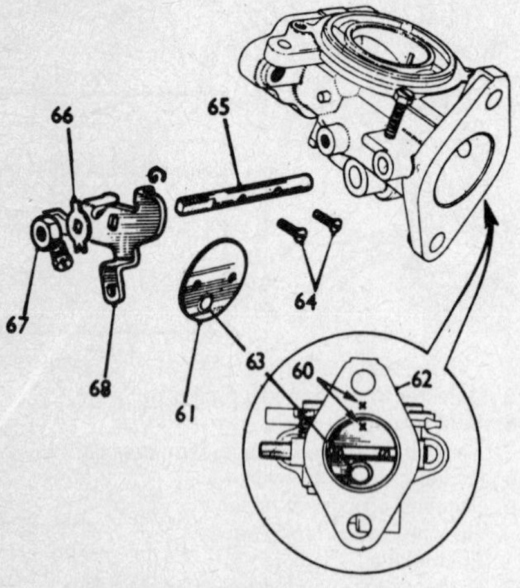

60. Alignment marks (scribed in)
61. Throttle butterfly
62. Carburetor body
63. Intake manifold vacuum limit valve
64. Butterfly retaining screws
65. Throttle shaft
66. Locktab
67. Spindle nut
68. Throttle lever

Throttle butterfly and vacuum limit valve

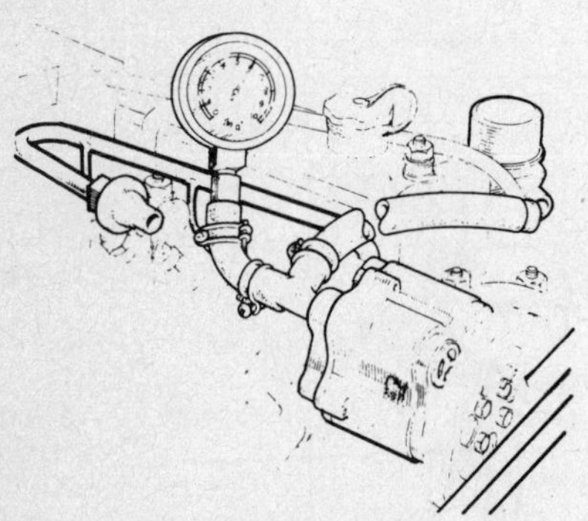

Air pressure check

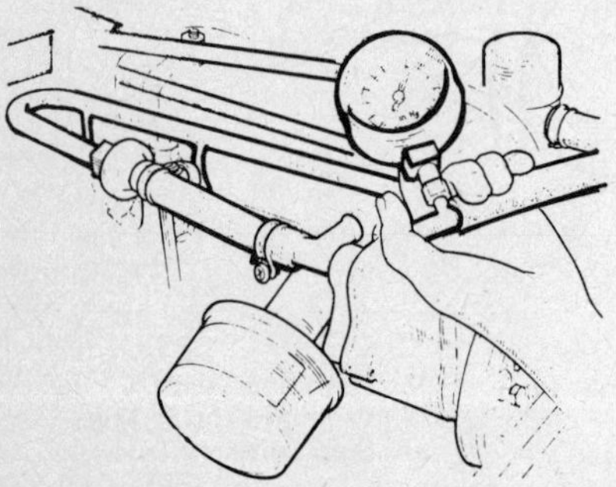

Vacuum gauge connected to gulp valve

11. To check the intake manifold vacuum limit valve (integral with the carburetor throttle butterfly), disconnect the gulp valve sensing line from the intake manifold.

12. Connect a vacuum gauge to the sensing line connection at the manifold.

13. With the engine at normal operating temperature, increase the engine speed to 3000 rpm and let the throttle snap shut. The vacuum gauge reading should immediately rise to between 20.5 and 22.0 in. vacuum. If the reading is outside these limits, the carburetors must be removed and the throttle butterflies replaced. Make sure, in each carburetor, that the butterfly is centered in the bore before the securing screws are tightened. Carburetor removal and tuning procedures can be found in the "Fuel System" section.

Exhaust Gas Recirculation System

The EGR valve is mounted on the engine manifold and controls the introduction of exhaust gas into the intake manifold. A spring-loaded diaphragm, connected to the valve pintle shaft, is controlled by engine vacuum and regulates the amount of exhaust gas to be mixed with the air/fuel mixture and is governed by engine speed.

Maintenance

The only maintenance required is to clean the exhaust ports, or replace a mounting gasket or vacuum control hose. The valve is replaced as a unit.

Modified Carburetor

The carburetors are manufactured to special specifications and are factory tuned to give the best engine performance with the maximum emission control.

Running-On Control Valve

This valve is used to prevent engine overrunning (dieseling) when the ignition is turned off. It stops the air flow into the manifold at the absorption canister.

Testing

1. Check the control valve line fuse.
2. Disconnect the control valve electrical lead at the oil pressure switch.
3. Ground the disconnected lead and if the valve and circuits are normal, the valve will be heard to operate.

Air Temperature Control Valve

An air temperature control valve is used in the carburetor air induction system to direct air, warmed by the exhaust manifold, to the carburetor during the warm-up period and during cold weather. As the engine compartment and the air passing over the valve warms, the valve will automatically move to allow a blend of cool and warm air to enter the carburetor.

Testing

1. The engine and air cleaner should be cold.
2. The valve plate should be resting against the cold air intake and blocking the passage.
3. Run the engine to normal operating temperature.
4. Observe the valve plate action. The plate should move towards the cool air position to allow the cool and hot air to blend.
5. The valve assembly must be replaced as a unit.

Catalytic Converters

Catalytic converters are used on various models to assist in the reduction of exhaust emissions.

Evaporative Loss Control System

The system is designed to collect fuel vapor from the fuel tank and carburetor float chambers. The vapor is stored in the absorption canister while the engine is stopped, and when the engine is restarted it passes through the crankcase ventilation system and into the combustion chambers. Vapors are drawn into the engine directly when the engine is running. An air bleed chamber is located in the fuel tank to prevent overfilling, and a small separation tank, between the fuel tank and absorption canister, prevents liquid fuel from being drawn into the canister.

The only component of the system that needs servicing is the absorption canister. The filter pad should be replaced at 12,000 mile intervals, and the canister unit should be replaced at 50,000 miles. If the canister becomes saturated with fuel, it must be replaced sooner. Do not attempt to clear the canister with compressed air.

1. To remove the canister, disconnect the lines and loosen the clamp screw, and lift it out.
2. To replace the filter pad, unscrew the lower end cap of the canister.
3. Remove the filter, clean the cap, install a new filter, and replace the end cap.
4. To pressure check the fuel system for leaks, first make sure that there is fuel in the tank and that the fuel system is primed.
5. Disconnect the fuel tank ventilation line from the absorption canister.
6. Connect a low scale pressure gauge between the fuel tank ventilation line and a low pressure air supply (such as a tire pump). Pressurize the system to 1 psi. Do not exceed this pressure at any time. The pressure should not fall below ½ psi over a period of ten seconds. If there is evidence of a leak, check all fuel system components and connections beginning with the fuel filler cap. The cap is not vented and should not allow any pressure loss. When the test is completed, remove the fuel filler cap and check that the gauge returns to zero. Reconnect the fuel tank ventilation line to the canister.

NO_x Control System

The regulation of nitrogen oxide (NO_x) emissions is accomplished through slight modifications to engine components, and no special service is necessary. To ensure that the engine is within emission standards, particular attention should be paid to tune-up specifications and procedures.

FUEL EXPANSION

An air chamber is provided within the fuel tank to provide space for fuel expansion during periods of high temperature operation.

FUEL CUT-OFF VALVE

A fuel cut-off valve is fitted in the main fuel line between the fuel filter and the carburetor. Should the vehicle receive an impact or overturn, the valve automatically cuts off the fuel supply to the carburetor. To reset the valve, depress the valve plunger.

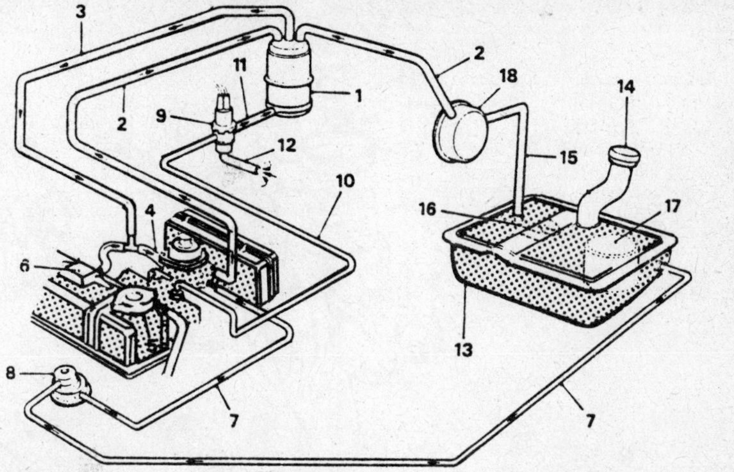

1. Charcoal adsorption canister
2. Vapor lines
3. Purge lines
4. Restricted connection
5. Sealed oil cap
6. Oil flame trap
7. Fuel pipe
8. Fuel pump
9. Break in control valve
10. Running-on control pipe
11. Running-on control hose
12. Air vent pipe
13. Fuel tank
14. Sealed filler cap
15. Vapor line
16. Vapor tube
17. Capacity limiting tank
18. Separation tank

Evaporative loss control system

FUEL SYSTEM

Fuel Pump

REMOVAL AND INSTALLTION

Midget

All Midgets are equipped with an AC mechanical diaphragm type fuel pump on the left side of the engine.

To remove the fuel pump, disconnect fuel inlet and outlet lines.

NOTE: Gasoline will spill on the engine unless precautions are taken.

Unscrew the attaching nuts. The pump will now be free and can be removed.

When installing, make sure that the pump lever (rocker arm) is positioned correctly above its lobe on the cam.

DISASSEMBLY

When removing the diaphragm assembly, turn the assembly 90° counterclockwise before lifting it out of engagement with the link lever. When replacing the inlet and outlet valve assemblies, be sure that the valves are pointed in the proper directions. Fuel pump delivery pressure should be 1½-2½ pounds per square inch (psi).

CAUTION

Be certain that the fuel lines are snug to the pump, but do not overtighten them.

CLEANING

Every 12,000 miles the fuel pump should be serviced. This may be accomplished by:

1. Removing the top bolt and domed cover.
2. Removing the gauze filter and thoroughly washing it in a safe solvent.
3. Cleaning out the sediment in the fuel bowl with a small screwdriver. The preferred method for removing loosened sediment is compressed air. Wipe out the interior of the fuel bowl with a soft, clean rag.

CAUTION

The interior of the fuel bowl must be absolutely free of grease or lint.

4. Renew the cork gasket if it is cracked or brittle. Fuel pump parts are delicate; use caution. When reassembling, be sure that the filter gauze is facing down.

TESTING AND ADJUSTMENT

No adjustments may be made to the fuel pump. Before removing and overhauling the old fuel pump, the following test may be made while the pump is still installed on the engine.

CAUTION

To avoid accidental ignition of fuel during the test, remove the coil high-tension wire from the distributor and the coil.

1. If a fuel pressure gauge is available, connect the gauge to the engine and operate engine until the pressure stops rising. Stop the engine and take the reading. If the reading is within the specifications given in the "Tune-up Specifications" chart, the malfunction is not in the fuel pump. Also check the pressure drop after the engine is stopped. A large pressure drop below the minimum specification indicates leaky valves. If the pump proves to be satisfactory, check the tank and inlet line.
2. If a fuel pressure gauge is not available, disconnect the fuel line at the pump outlet, place a vessel beneath the pump outlet, and crank the engine. A good pump will force the fuel out of the outlet in steady spurts. A worn diaphragm spring may not provide proper pumping action.
3. As a further test, disconnect and plug the fuel line from the tank at the pump, and hold your thumb over the pump inlet. If the pump is functioning properly, a suction should be felt on your thumb. No suction indicates that the pump diaphragm is leaking, or that the diaphragm linkage is worn.
4. Check the crankcase for gasoline. A ruptured diaphragm may leak fuel into the engine.

REMOVAL AND INSTALLATION

MGB

1. Disconnect the electrical supply and ground wires from the pump, and insulate the supply wire against grounding.
2. Disconnect the fuel lines and the breather pipe (later cars) from the pump and cap the fuel lines.
3. Remove the pump bracket bolts and remove the pump.
4. When installing the pump, make sure that the ground wire makes a good connection and that the breather pipe is correctly routed.

TESTING THE FUEL PUMP ON THE VEHICLE

S.U. Electric Pump

S.U. electric fuel pumps maintain a low, constant pressure, thus making fuel delivery more even and easing the load on the temperamental carburetor needle and seat units. When fuel pressure drops below a predetermined level the pump will operate (audible as a series of clicks), and when pressure is built up again it will shut itself off.

1. To check pump operation, disconnect the fuel line at the carburetors and switch the ignition on.

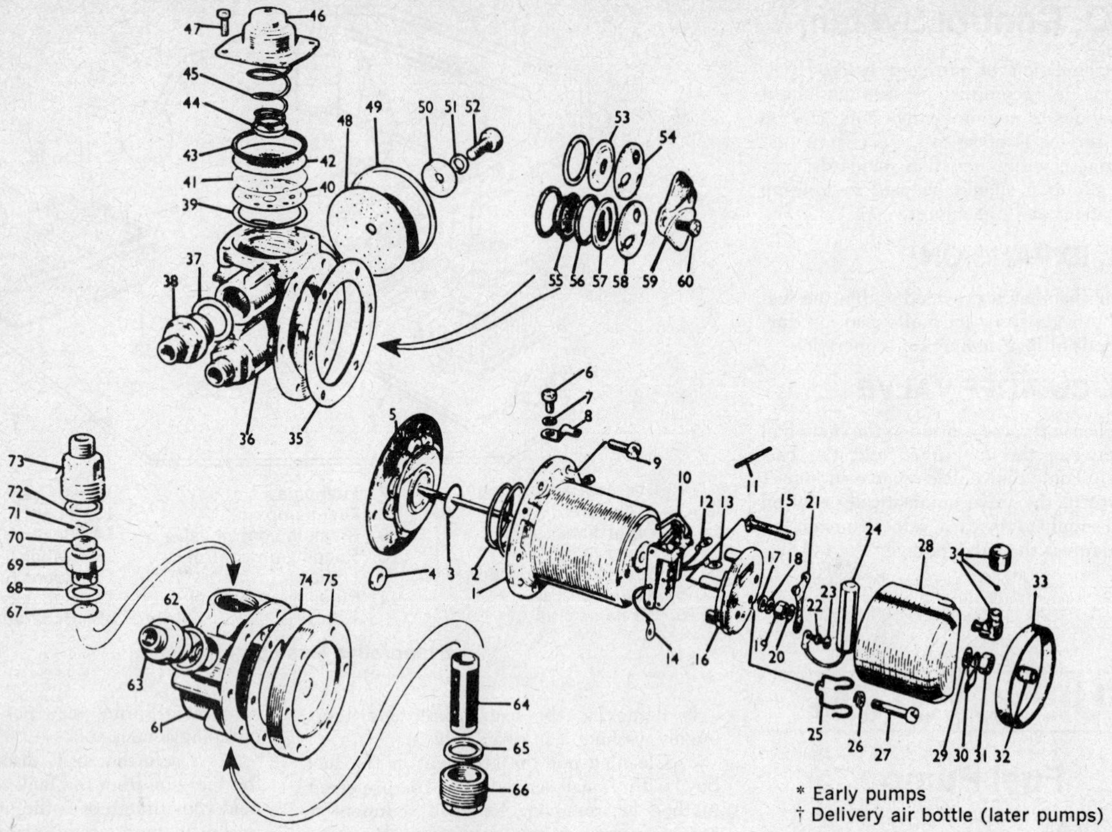

* Early pumps
† Delivery air bottle (later pumps)

1. Coil housing
2. Armature spring
3. Impact washer
4. Armature centralizing roller
5. Diaphragm and spindle assembly
6. Set screw
7. Spring washer
8. Ground connector
9. Set screw
10. Rocker mechanism
11. Rocker pivot pin
12. Terminal tag
13. Terminal tag
14. Ground tag
15. Terminal stud
16. Pedestal
17. Spring washer
18. Lead washer
19. Terminal nut
20. End cover seal washer
21. Contact blade
22. Washer
23. Contact blade screw
24. Condenser
25. Condenser clip
26. Spring washer
27. Pedestal screw
28. End cover
29. Shakeproof washer
30. Lucar connector
31. Nut
32. Insulating sleeve
33. Sealing band
34. Vent valve
35. Gasket

AUF 300 type (36–50):

36. Pump body
37. Fiber washer
38. Outlet connection
39. Sealing washer
*40. Diaphragm plate
41. Plastic diaphragm barrier
*42. Rubber diaphragm
43. Rubber "O" ring
*44. Spring end cap
*45. Diaphragm spring
†46. Delivery flow smoothing device cover
47. Set screw
48. Gasket
49. Inlet air bottle cover
50. Dished washer

AUF 300 type (51–60):

51. Spring washer
52. Set screw
53. Outlet valve
54. Valve cap
55. Filter
56. Sealing washer
57. Inlet valve
58. Valve cap
59. Clamp plate
60. Set screw

61. Pump body
62. Fiber washer
63. Outlet connection
64. Filter
65. Washer
66. Plug

HP type (67–75):

67. Inlet valve
68. Thin fiber washer
69. Outlet valve cage
70. Outlet valve
71. Spring clip
72. Medium fiber washer
73. Outlet connection
74. Gasket
75. Sandwich plate

Electric fuel pump—exploded view

2. The pump should be heard to operate and fuel should flow readily from the line.

If it does not, disconnect the output line at the pump and switch the ignition on again. If the pump now operates, the fuel line to the carburetors is blocked and should be cleared with compressed air. If the pump does not operate, disconnect the fuel intake line from the pump and check for a free flow of gasoline from the tank.

3. The line may be cleared, if necessary, with compressed air by pressurizing the gas tank through the tank filler tube.

CAUTION

Never blow compressed air through the fuel pump; and on vehicles equipped with Evaporative Loss Control systems the fuel lines must never be pressurized unless the absorption canister is disconnected.

If the fuel lines are clear and the pump will not operate, the electrical connections at the pump should be checked.

4. Switch on the ignition and connect a test light between the supply (battery) wire and ground. If it does not light, the pump is not being supplied with electricity. If it does light, check the ground wire continuity by connecting a jumper wire between the ground terminal on the pump and a good chassis ground.

5. If the pump still does not operate, the fault lies in the pump unit itself. Refer to the following section.

SERVICING THE FUEL PUMP

S.U. Electric Pump

If the pump unit is not operating correctly, remove it from the vehicle.

1. Remove the intake and outlet line fittings from the pump body and remove the small fuel filter (if fitted).

2. Examine the ports for any foreign matter that may be lodged inside.

3. Clean the ports, if necessary, and clean and replace the filter and line fittings.

4. Remove the plastic end-cover by removing the electrical terminal retaining nut and the rubber or tape joint seal.

5. Examine the contact points for burning, and check the contact rotor assembly movement. If the end-cover was not sealed properly, the contact and rocker assemblies will have been exposed to water and dirt and should be thoroughly cleaned or replaced.

If the contacts are not badly burnt, they may be smoothed with fine sandpaper and cleaned with a non-oily solvent such as an aerosol-type carburetor cleaner.

6. When adjusting the points, make sure that when the outer rocker is pressed onto the pump housing, the contact blade rests on the narrow rib of the pedestal. The contact blade may be bent slightly if necessary.

7. Proper sealing of the plastic endcover is very important.

8. Check that there are no cracks in it, and, after the cover is installed on the pump, wrap electrical tape around the mating surface of the pump housing and cover.

9. Pump operation should be checked by temporarily connecting the electrical wires and fuel lines to it and switching on the ignition.

10. Allow a few seconds for the pump to prime itself, and check fuel flow at the carburetors.

11. At this point, if the pump is still not operating correctly, the pump unit will have to be replaced. Do not discard the pump, as most MG dealers carry factory rebuilt S.U. fuel pumps instead of new ones (at a considerable savings), and will allow some trade-in on the old unit.

Fuel Filter

On vehicles equipped with the Evaporative Loss Control system an inline filter is located on the fuel feed line to the carburetors. The filter element requires no maintenance, but should be replaced at 12,000 mile intervals.

Carburetors

REMOVAL AND INSTALLATION

1. Remove the air filters.

2. Disconnect the fuel lines and remove the overflow tubes from the float chamber.

3. Disconnect the accelerator and choke cables.

4. Disconnect the vacuum advance line and remove the throttle return springs.

5. Unbolt the carburetor retaining nuts and remove the carburetors, being careful not to bend the throttle linkage.

6. Installation is in reverse order of removal. Make sure that the carburetor and manifold spacer gaskets are in good condition or an air leak will result. The carburetors and linkages will have to be adjusted after reinstallation.

THROTTLE LINKAGE ADJUSTMENT AND CARBURETOR SYNCHRONIZATION

1. Make sure the throttle moves freely.

2. With the accelerator pedal fully depressed, adjust the throttle linkage, if necessary, to open the throttle valve completely.

CHOKE

Manual

1. Remove the air cleaner and start the engine.

2. Pull the choke knob and cable until the fast idle cam is turned to align the fast idle cam pivot cable clamp and the fast idle screw.

3. Adjust the fast idle speed to 1100-1300 rpm.

4. Push the choke knob and cable to the off position and be sure the choke valve is completely open.

5. Reinstall the air cleaner.

Automatic

1. Remove the air cleaner assembly.

2. Be assured that all choke movable parts are free and operate under spring tension.

3. Adjust the gap between the choke and throttle levers to $^3/_{32}$ inch by turning the idle speed screw.

4. Adjust the throttle stop screw to obtain a clearance of 0.025 inch between the end of the fast idle pin and cam. Tighten the locknut.

5. Align the index mark on the choke cover with the aligning mark on the choke body.

6. Install the air cleaner assembly.

FLOAT LEVEL

1. Remove the carburetor from the engine and separate the float chamber from the carburetor body.

2. Invert the float body so that the needle valve is held closed by the weight of the float.

3. Measure the distance between the float chamber face and the highest point on the floats. Adjust the top of the floats to 0.625-0.672 inch from the chamber face.

4. Adjust the floats by bending the float tabs or by installing washers under the needle valve and seat assembly.

5. Reassemble the carburetor.

DECELERATION BY-PASS VALVE

1. Run the engine to normal operating temperature.

2. Disconnect the vacuum line from the distributor and block the end of the pipe.

3. The idle speed should increase to approximately 1300 rpm.

4. If the engine speed increases to 2000-2500 rpm, the valve is floating and an adjustment is needed.

5. Turn the adjusting screw counterclockwise until the engine speed is at 1300 rpm.

6. Increase the engine speed several times and be assured the engine speed returns to 1300 rpm. Adjust as necessary.

7. Turn the adjusting screw ½ final turn to seat the valve correctly and reconnect the vacuum line.

OVERHAUL

Midget

1. Remove the carburetor(s).

2. Remove the damper.

3. Lever out the bottom plug.

4. Drain the carburetor of oil and fuel.

5. Remove the O-ring from its plug.

6. Remove the six screws which secure the float chamber to the body.

7. Remove the float chamber.

8. Remove the float assembly by gently prying the spindle from the clip on each end.

9. Remove the needle valve.

10. Remove the four screws which secure the top cover to the body.

11. Remove the top cover.

12. Remove the spring.

13. Remove the air valve assembly.

14. Remove the four screws which secure the diaphragm and retaining ring to the air valve assembly.

15. Remove the diaphragm and retaining ring.

16. Loosen the set screw in the side of the air valve.

17. Insert tool S353 or an Allen wrench of the proper diameter into the stem of the air valve, turn it counterclockwise approximately two turns, and withdraw the needle and housing by pulling firmly and straight with your fingers.

18. Remove the two screws which secure the starter box to the body.

19. Remove the starter box.

20. Remove the two screws which secure the temperature compensator to the body.

21. Remove the temperature compensator and two rubber washers of different diameters.

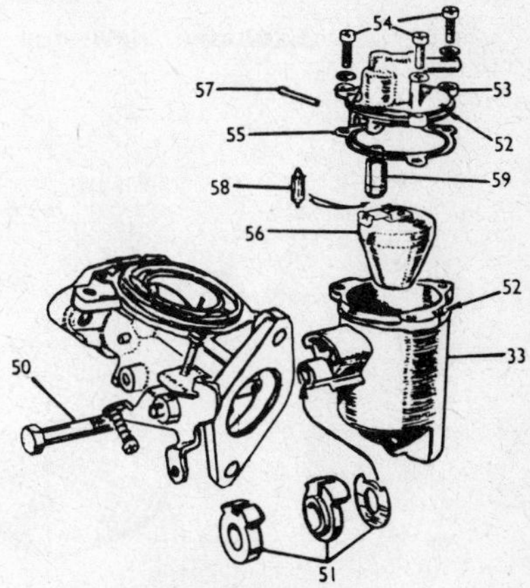

33. Float bowl
50. Mounting bolt
51. Mounting washers
52. Alignment marks—to be scribed in upon removal
53. Float bowl cover
54. Retaining screws
55. Gasket
56. Float
57. Float hinge pin
58. & 59. Needle and seat assembly

Float bowl components

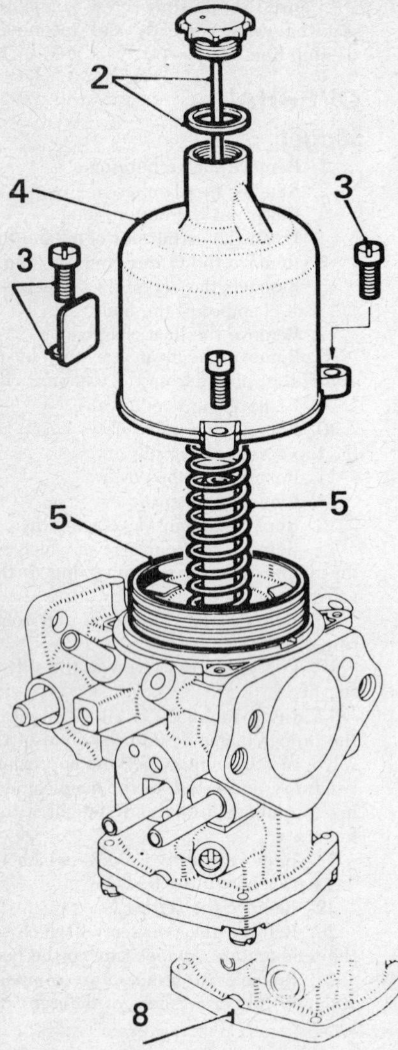

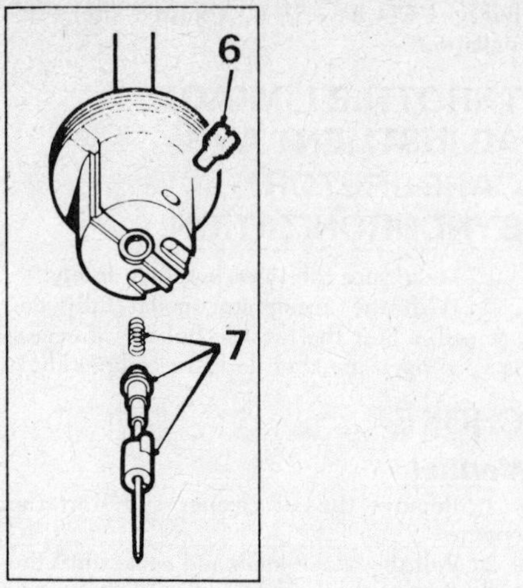

2. Piston damper and washer
4. Suction piston chamber
3. Suction piston chamber screws
5. Carburetor body
6. Jet adjusting screw
7. Needle assembly
8. Bottom cover plate

Exploded view—top section HIF carburetor

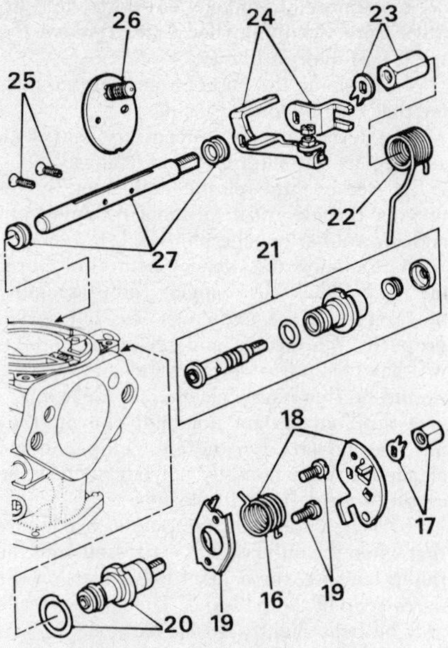

25. Throttle disc screws
26. Throttle disc
24. Throttle and throttle actuating lever
23. Throttle lever nut
27. Throttle spindle
21. Valve spindle assembly
22. Throttle lever return spring
18. Fast idle cam
19. Starter unit cover
16. Fast idle cam lever spring
19. Starter unit screws
17. Cam lever retaining nut

Fast idle and throttle assembly

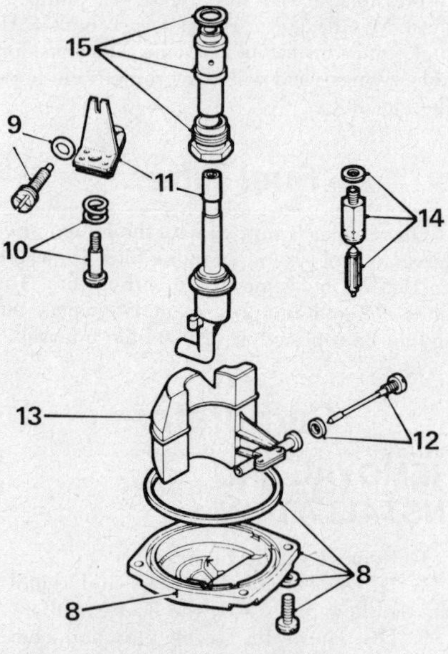

15. Jet bearing assembly
9. Jet adjusting screw and O-ring
9. Jet adjusting assembly with lever
10. Jet adjusting lever retaining screw and spring
14. Needle valve assembly
12. Float pivot spindle
13. Float
8. Bottom cover plate and screws

HIF jet and jet bearing

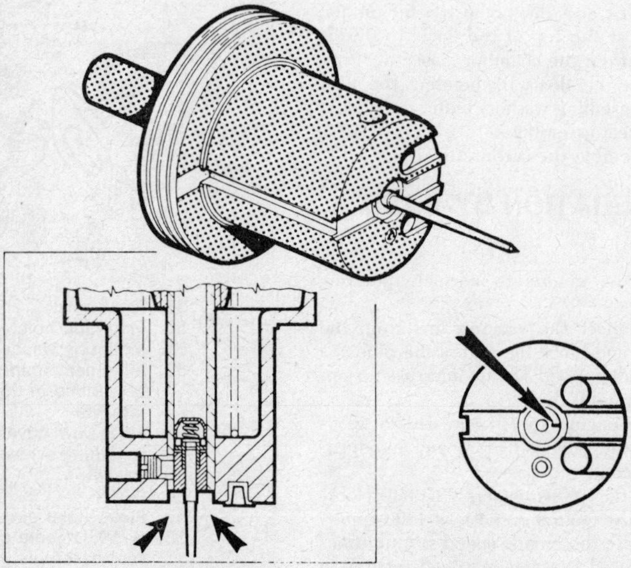

Replacing the needle assembly

22. Remove the three (slotted) screws which secure the by-pass valve to the body.

23. Remove the by-pass valve and gasket.

24. Remove the two screws which secure the butterfly to the spindle.

25. Turn the spindle return spring.

26. Release the spindle return spring.

27. Withdraw the spindle and spring.

28. Remove the spindle seals from the body by hooking them out with a small screwdriver.

29. Wash all components in clean fuel. Allow them to air dry or use compressed air. Place all components on a clean surface. Discard all seals and gaskets. Scrape all old gaskets material from the mating surfaces.

30. Examine the condition of all components for wear, paying special attention to the needle and seat and the air valve and diaphragm which should be replaced unless in exceptionally good condition.

31. Use compressed air to blow through all ports, needle valve, and starter box.

32. Fit the spindle seals to the body, tapping them gently into position, with the metal casing of the seals flush with the body of the carburetor.

33. Insert the spindle, loading and locating the spindle return spring while doing so.

34. Insert the butterfly with the two protruding spots facing outboard and below the spindle. Tighten the screws.

35. Install the starter box and tighten the screws.

36. Install the by-pass valve and gasket and tighten the screws.

37. Install the temperature compensator and tighten the screws.

38. Insert the needle housing assembly into the bottom of the air valve.

39. Install tool S353 or an Allen wrench of the proper diameter, turning it clockwise to engage the threads of the needle valve assembly with the adjusting screw. Then, continue turning until the slot in the needle housing is aligned with the set screw.

40. Tighten the set screw.

NOTE: The set screw does not tighten on the needle housing but locates into the slot. This ensures that during adjustment the needle will remain in its operating position, i.e. biased by a spring in the needle housing toward the air cleaner side of the carburetor.

41. Install the diaphragm, locating the inner tag into the recess in the air valve.

42. Install the diaphragm retaining ring and secure it with four screws.

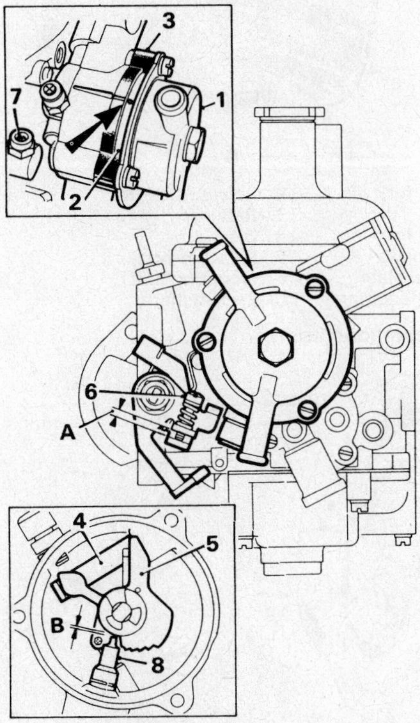

1. Water jacket
2. Heat mass
3. Insulator
4. Rod-vacuum kick piston
A—3/32 in (2.4 mm)
5. Fast idle cam
6. Idle speed screw
7. Throttle stop screw
8. Fast idle pin
B—0.025 in (0.64 mm)

Adjustment of automatic choke and fast idle linkage

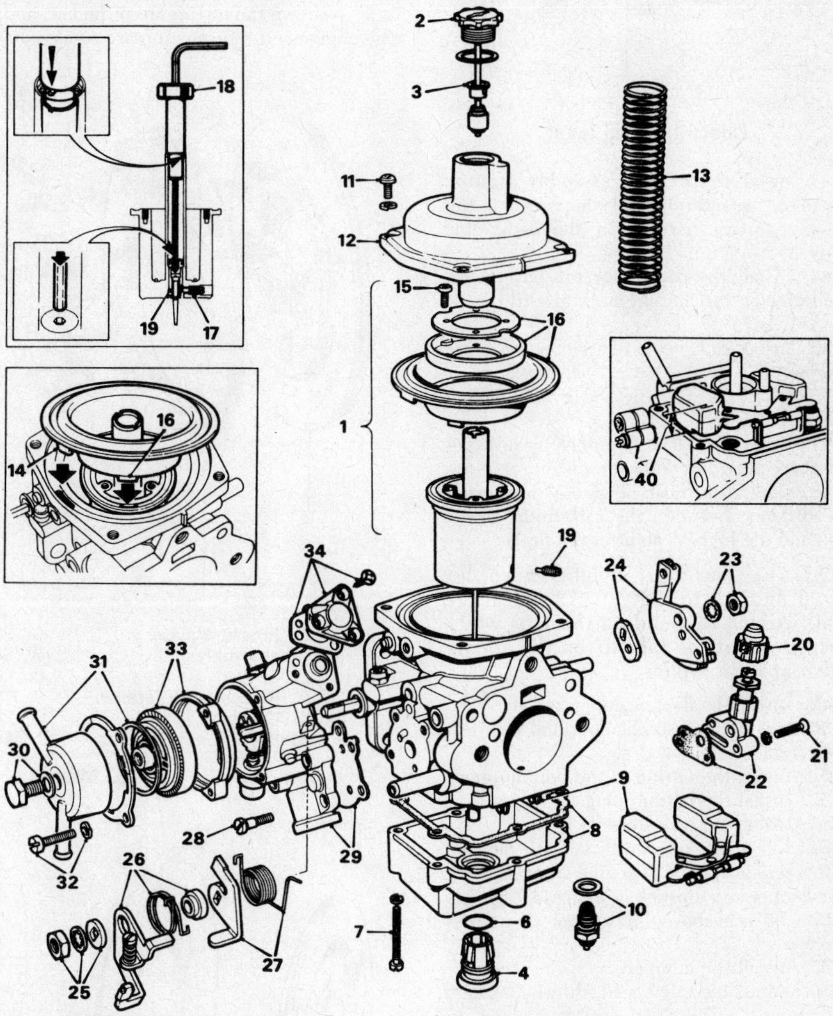

1. Air valve and diaphragm assembly
2. Damper cap
3. Air valve piston
4. Bottom float chamber plug
6. "O" ring
7. Float chamber to body screws (6)
8. Float chamber and gasket
9. Float and float hinge
10. Inlet needle valve and seat with washer
11. Top cover screws (4)
12. Top cover
13. Piston spring
14. Outer locating tab of air valve diaphragm
15. Diaphragm retaining screws
16. Inner locating tab of air valve diaphragm
17. Needle valve retaining screw (grubscrew)
18. Special tool S-353 for idle air/fuel adjustment
19. Needle valve
20. Idle air regulator cover
21. Idle air regulator retaining screw
22. Idle air regulator and gasket
23. Retaining nut and washer
24. Throttle guadrant and locating plate
25. Choke operating lever retaining nut and washer
26. Choke linkage outer lever, bushing and spring
27. Choke inner lever and spring
28. Choke housing retaining screws
29. Choke housing assembly and gasket
30. Choke water jacket retaining screws
31. Choke water jacket and sealing ring
32. Choke cover retaining screws
33. Choke bi-metal spring assembly
34. Vacuum kick piston cover and gasket
40. Float measurement location

Exploded view—CD-5 carburetor. CD-4 similar

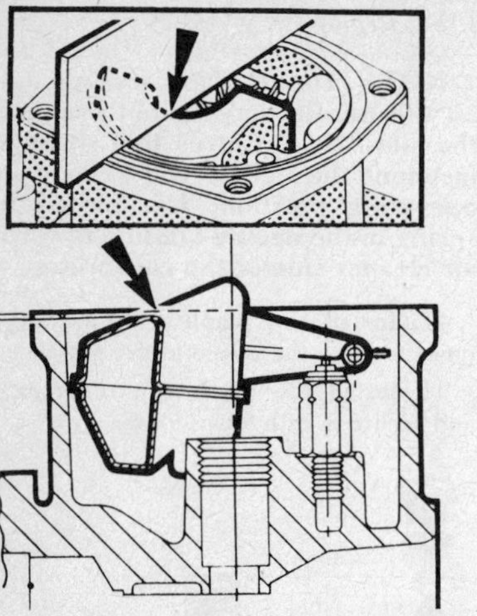

Checking float level

43. Install the air valve assembly, locating the outer tag and rim of the diaphragm in the complementary recesses in the carburetor body.
44. Install the carburetor top cover with the bulge on the housing neck toward the air intake.
45. Install and evenly tighten the top cover screws.
46. Install the needle valve and sealing washers and tighten them.
47. Install the float assembly by levering the pivot pin gently into the piston.
48. Check the float height by measuring the distance between the carburetor gasket face and the highest point of the floats.

NOTE: The float heights must be equal and set to 0.625-0.672 in. (16-17 mm). Adjust by bending the tabs while ensuring that the tab sits on the needle valve at right angles.

49. Install the float chamber gasket.
50. Install the float chamber and secure it with six screws.
51. Install the O-ring to the bottom plug.
52. Install the bottom plug.
53. Install the carburetor(s).
54. Fill the carburetor damper dashpot with a seasonal grade of engine oil until, using the damper as a dipstick, the threaded plug is 0.25 in. (6 mm) above the dashpot when resistance is felt.
55. Install the damper.
56. Adjust the idle speed, throttle linkage, and choke.

MANUAL TRANSMISSION

REMOVAL AND INSTALLATION

On all models the engine and transmission are removed as a unit (see "Engine Removal and Installation"). On the Midget, MGB, the transmission can be unbolted from the engine by simply removing the bell housing bolts.

Installation in all cases is in reverse order of removal. On the Midget, MGB, the clutch disc will have to be centered if the clutch assembly has been removed (see "Clutch Removal and Installation").

CLUTCH

REMOVAL AND INSTALLATION

All Models

1. Remove the engine from the car, and, if the engine and transmission are removed as a unit, separate them. On the Midget, remove the starter motor.
2. Loosen the clutch pressure plate bolts gradually until the spring pressure is released, and remove the pressure plate and disc from the flywheel.
3. Examine the flywheel surface for scoring and signs of overheating. If scored at all, the flywheel should be turned down on a lathe or replaced. If it appears to have been overheated (blue discoloration), the surface should be checked for warpage and turned down if necessary. If disc wear is evident, the pressure plate and release bearing, as well as the disc, should be replaced. The pilot bushing in the end of the crankshaft should be checked for wear and replaced if galled or elongated.

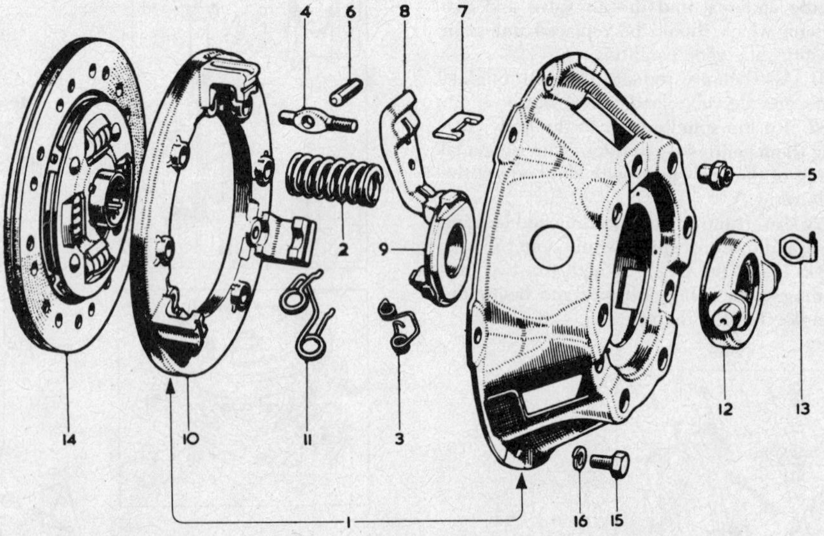

1. Pressure plate assembly
2. Spring
3. Release fork retainer
4. Eyebolt
5. Eyebolt nut
6. Release fork pin
7. Strut
8. Release fork
9. Thrust plate
10. Pressure plate
11. Anti-rattle spring
12. Release bearing
13. Retainer
14. Disc
15. Pressure plate mounting bolt
16. Lockwasher

MG Midget clutch components

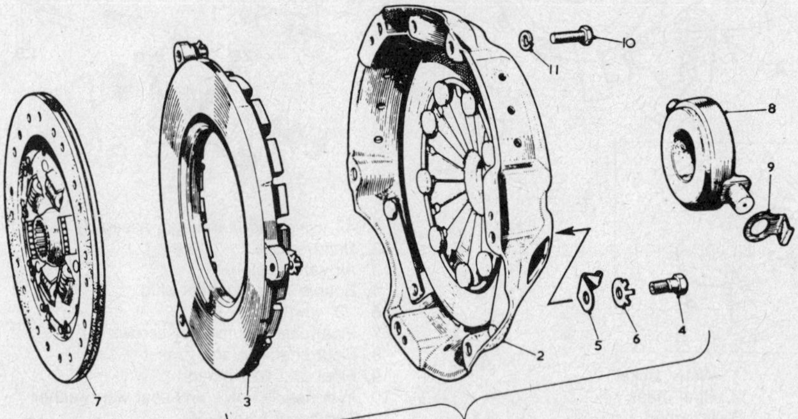

1. Pressure plate assembly
2. Cover with driving struts and springs
3. Pressure plate
4. Strut bolt
5. Clip
6. Locktab
7. Disc
8. Release bearing
9. Bearing retainer clip
10. Pressure plate mounting bolt
11. Lockwasher

MGB clutch components

Lubricate the bushing with a graphite base grease or white grease such as *Molykote*.

4. Upon reinstallation of the disc and pressure plate, the disc must be centered so that the transmission mainshaft will engage the pilot bushing as well as the disc splines. To accomplish this, install the disc and pressure plate on the flywheel with the bolts only finger tight so that the disc can be moved.

5. At this point a dummy transmission mainshaft or clutch aligning tool (available from most tool manufacturers and from MG dealers) should be inserted through the disc hub and into the pilot bushing to hold the disc in position while the pressure plate plate bolts are tightened.

6. Tighten the bolts gradually and evenly, and remove the centering tool. If a new coil type pressure plate is used, be sure to remove the small U-shaped tabs that keep the spring slightly compressed. The tabs are used to prevent distortion of the plate, due to its unloaded condition, during storage and shipping.

7. Bolt the transmission back onto the engine if they were removed as a unit; on Midget, install the starter motor, and reinstall the engine in the chassis.

NOTE: If a clutch centering tool is not available it is possible to center the disc by eye, if it is done very carefully. If trouble is experienced in mating the engine and transmission, the indication is that the disc is not centered properly and it should be rechecked.

ADJUSTMENTS

When the clutch has been replaced, it will be necessary to adjust the release lever stop and the release bearing stop. The lever stop should be adjusted first, and the procedure is as follows:

1. Pull the release lever outward until all free movement is taken up.

2. Using a feeler gauge, check the gap between the lever and the head of the adjustment bolt. The gap should be 0.020 in.

3. If adjustment is necessary, loosen the locknut and turn the adjustment bolt in the required direction until the proper clearance is obtained. Tighten the locknut.

Periodic adjustment of the release lever may be necessary as wear occurs; however, the release bearing stop should need adjustment only when the clutch is replaced. To adjust the bearing stop:

1. Screw the stop and locknut away from the clutch cover housing to the limit of travel.

2. Have a helper fully depress and hold the clutch pedal. Screw the stop in until it contacts the housing.

3. Release the clutch pedal, and turn the stop in a further 0.002-0.005 in. (approximately 30° rotation).

4. Tighten the locknut, and recheck the release lever stop clearance.

Clutch Hydraulic System

ADJUSTMENTS

No adjustments to the master or slave cylinder should be attempted.

MASTER CYLINDER–REMOVAL AND INSTALLATION

Midget and MGB 1975

To remove the clutch master cylinder, remove the screws securing the mounting bracket cover plate and lift the cover off. Disconnect the pushrod from the clutch pedal. Disconnect the hydraulic line from the clutch master cylinder and cap it. Remove the cylinder mounting bolts and lift the cylinder out.

Installation is in reverse order of removal. When the hydraulic line has been reconnected, the clutch hydraulic system must be bled.

MGB 1976-77

1. Remove the cover screws and remove the brake/clutch master cylinder cover.

2. Attach a rubber tube to the bleed screw in the slave cylinder. Bleed the system by opening the bleed screw on full turn and depressing the clutch pedal fully and holding. Then close the bleed screw and release the clutch pedal. Repeat the operation until the system is drained.

3. Remove the cotter pin, washer, and clevis pin from the pushrod, and disconnect the elutch pedal lever.

4. Clean the hydraulic pipe connection, disconnect the pipe, and plug the open fitting in the cylinder.

5. Unscrew the mounting bolts and remove the master cylinder from the mounting bracket.

6. Installation is in reverse order. The longer bolt goes through the mounting bracket where it is braced. Bleed the system.

MGB 1978 and Later

1. Install a bleed line onto the bleed screw on the clutch slave cylinder, and open the bleed screw.

2. Pump the clutch pedal with the master cylinder cap removed to drain fluid out of the master cylinder.

3. Remove the left hand lower dash panel.

4. Remove the access plug from the firewall.

5. Remove the eight screws, and remove the cover plate and seal from the pedal box.

6. Remove the clevis pin which secures the pushrod to the clutch pedal.

7. Loosen the hydraulic line banjo bolt, unscrew the union, and pull the hydraulic line off the master cylinder.

8. Unscrew the mounting bolts and nuts, and remove the master cylinder from the pedal box. Access to one bolt is from inside the car through the access hole in the dash.

9. To install, reverse the removal procedure and bleed the system.

SLAVE CYLINDER–REMOVAL AND INSTALLATION

On all models, to remove the slave cylinder simply disconnect and cap the hydraulic line, disconnect the pushrod from the clutch release lever, and unbolt and remove the cylinder.

Installation is in reverse order of removal. When the hydraulic line has been reconnected, the clutch hydraulic system must be bled.

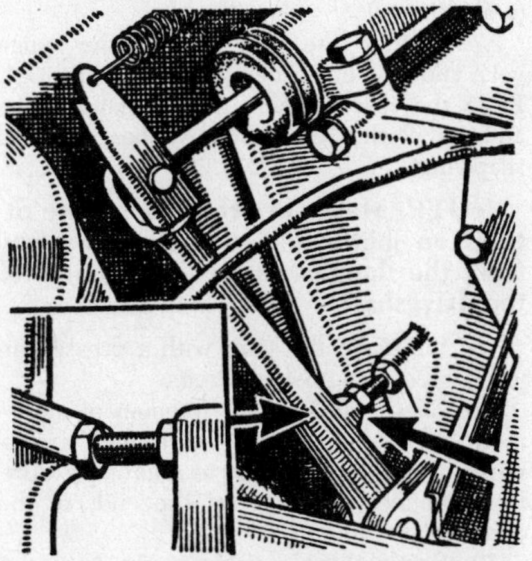

Clutch release lever adjustment

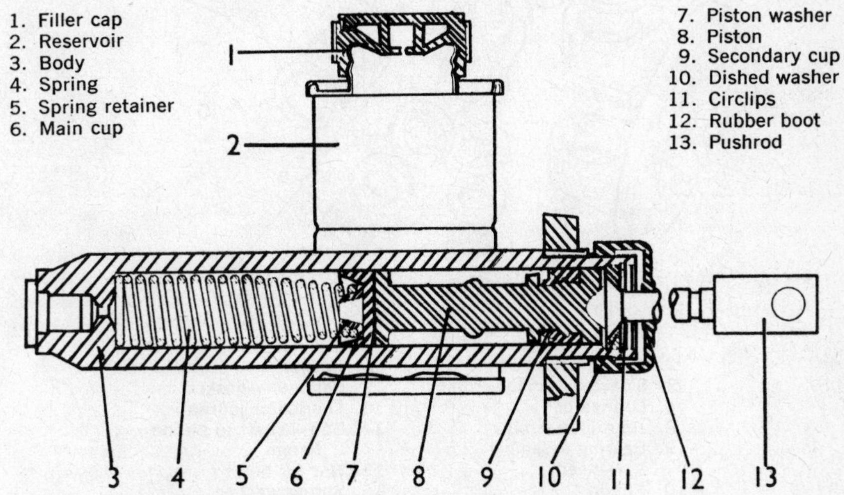

Cross-section—Midget clutch master cylinder

MASTER AND SLAVE CYLINDER REBUILDING

Rebuilding kits are available, and usually contain the rubber seals and metal washers. Pistons and springs are available as individual pieces.

When the piston assembly has been removed from the cylinder, examine the bore. If it is pitted or scored the entire cylinder assembly should be replaced. If bore damage is light it may be honed, but in most cases the repair will not be lasting and the cylinder may begin to leak again after a short time. When honing a cylinder, occasionally dip the hone in clean brake fluid for lubrication.

Whenever a cylinder is disassembled for inspection or rebuilding, the rubber seals should be replaced as a matter of course. Before installing the seals lubricate them thoroughly with brake fluid or the special lubricant that is included in some rebuilding kits. All internal components of the cylinder, especially the bore, must be completely free of dirt and grit or the cylinder may leak or fail to operate properly. When installing the piston and seals into the bore make sure that the seal lips are not turned back as they enter the cylinder. Once the cylinder has been installed on the car the clutch hydraulic system must be bled.

BLEEDING THE CLUTCH HYDRAULIC SYSTEM

The purpose of bleeding the hydraulic system is to expel air that is trapped in the cylinders and lines. Air in the system is what gives the pedal a spongy feel, because air can be compressed while a liquid, for all practical purposes, cannot be. Bleeding is accomplished in the following manner:

1. Fill the master cylinder with brake fluid. (Recheck the fluid level often during bleeding.)
2. Attach a rubber tube to the slave cylinder bleed valve and immerse the other end of the tube in a jar or can containing a small amount of clean brake fluid.
3. Have a helper in the car pump the clutch pedal several times until some resistance can be felt, hold the pedal down, and open the bleed valve about ½ turn.
4. With the bleed valve still open, pump the pedal slowly through its full travel several times. Close the bleed valve and check the pedal for firmness and proper free-play (about 0.5-1.0 in. free-play before the release bearing contacts the pressure plate).
5. If sponginess or excessive free-play indicates that some air is still in the system, it may be necessary to repeat Step 3 until the fluid running from the bleed valve is clear and free of air bubbles.

DRIVE AXLE

Driveshaft

REMOVAL AND INSTALLATION

To remove the driveshaft on the Midget, MGB, mark the U-joint flanges and the transmission and differential flanges (for assembly purposes). Remove the nuts and bolts from the flanges and lower the driveshaft assembly. When reinstalling the driveshaft make sure that the alignment marks on the flanges are positioned correctly.

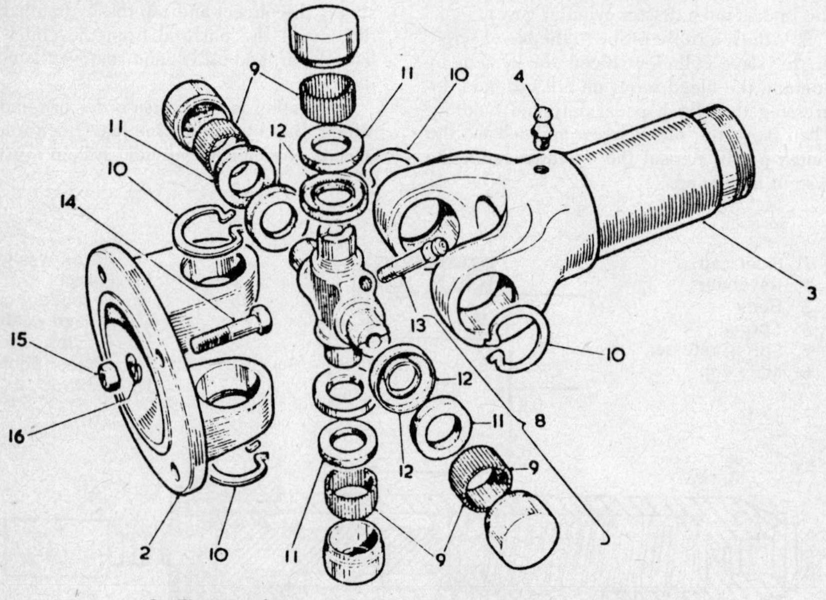

2. Flange yoke
3. Sleeve assembly—yoke
4. Lubricator
8. Journal assembly
9. Bearing assembly —needle
10. Circlip
11. Gasket
12. Retainer—gasket
13. Lubricator journal
14. Bolt—shaft to pinion flange
15. Nut for bolt
16. Spring washer

MG Midget U-joint

Universal Joint

REMOVAL, INSTALLATION AND OVERHAUL

NOTE: If only the rear U-joint is to be replaced, unbolt the differential flange from the driveshaft flange and pull the driveshaft out toward the rear of the car to separate the driveshaft at the spline.

After the driveshaft has been removed and the outside surfaces of the U-joints have been cleaned:

1. Remove all four snap-rings retaining the bearing cups. If the ring does not come out, tap the bearing cup lightly to relieve pressure on the ring.
2. Tap the flange and driveshaft yokes with a hammer until one of the bearings begins to come out. If difficulty is experienced, use a small screwdriver to tap the bearings out from the inside. Repeat this operation until all four bearing cups and their rollers have been removed.
3. Thoroughly clean the flange and driveshaft yokes.

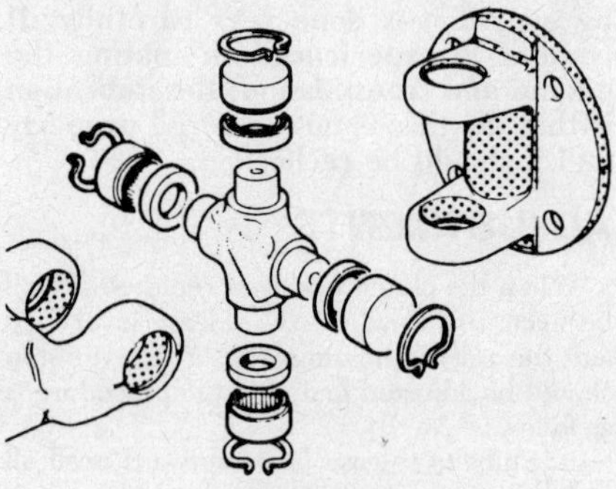

MGB U-joint

4. Fill the reservoir holes in the spider journals with grease (sealed joints without grease fittings).
5. Fill the bearing cups to a depth of ⅛ in. with grease and install the needle rollers in the cups.
6. Install the seals on the spider journals (sealed joints).
7. Position the spider inside the flange yoke and install the bearings and snap-rings. Place the spider inside the driveshaft yoke and install the remaining two bearings and snap-rings.

NOTE: Make sure that the grease fittings on joints so equipped face away from the flanges, toward the center of the driveshaft.

8. Lubricate the joint with a grease gun (early type with grease fitting).
9. Check the joint for freedom of movement. If it binds, tap it lightly with a soft-metal or wooden hammer to relieve pressure from the bearing cups on the ends of the journals.
10. Remove any surplus grease from the joint and replace the driveshaft.

Axle Shaft

REMOVAL AND INSTALLATION

Midget

1. Raise the rear of the vehicle and support it under the springs.
2. Release the parking brake and back off the brake adjusters if the wheel does not spin freely.
3. Remove the brake drum retaining screws and remove the drum.

WIRE WHEELS

1. Remove the nuts which secure the axle hub to the splined wheel hub.
2. Remove this splined wheel hub, and withdraw the axle shaft, gasket, and O-ring.

DISC WHEELS

1. Remove the axle shaft retaining screws and withdraw the axle and gasket.
2. Installation is in reverse order of removal. Always use a new gasket and O-ring (wire wheels). Adjust the brakes if necessary after the wheel have been installed.

MGB Tubetype Axle

The tube-type axle has been used on the MGB since 1967. The tube-type axle is semi-floating, with hypoid ring and pinion gearset. The axle shafts and the pinion oil seal can be removed with the drive axle in place.

NOTE: The GT uses stronger springs which should not be used on the convertible except in axle pairs.

AXLE SHAFT AND PINION OIL SEAL REMOVAL

1. Raise the rear of the car and remove the wheel.
2. Back off the brake adjuster if the brake drum will not spin freely, and remove the drum.
3. Remove the cotter pin and unscrew the axle shaft nut. Remove the wheel hub.
4. Disconnect the parking brake cable and hydraulic line, and remove the backing plate. Plug the hydraulic line.
5. Remove the oil seal collar, bearing cap, and oil seal from the axle shaft.
6. Attach a slide hammer to the hub and remove it. Remove the axle shaft.
7. Installation is the reverse of removal. The oil seal should be replaced at this time; also the brakes should be bled and adjusted after the drums have been installed.

Differential

REMOVAL AND INSTALLATION

MGB/MGB-GT

The removal of the differential unit requires a special tool to stretch the axle case and even with this tool it is very easy to permanently damage the case while using the tool. For these reasons, removal and installation of the differential should be left to an MG dealer.

Midget

1. Drain the drive axle.
2. Remove the axle shafts as previously described.
3. Mark the flanges and disconnect the driveshaft from the differential.
4. Remove the nuts securing the differential assembly to the drive axle and withdraw the complete assembly.
5. Installation is in reverse order of removal. Always use a new gasket, and make sure that the differential and drive axle mating surfaces are clean.

DISASSEMBLY

1. Mark and remove the housing caps, and withdraw the differential cage.
2. Remove the bearings and shims from the cage.
3. Bend back the locktabs, remove the ring gear bolts, and remove the ring gear.
4. Drive out the dowel pin which locates the pinion shaft. The pin is ⅛ in. in diameter, and it must be driven out from the ring gear side of the differential cage.
5. Remove the pinions and thrust washers. Remove the pinion nut, drive flange, and end-cover.
6. Drive the pinion shaft toward the rear

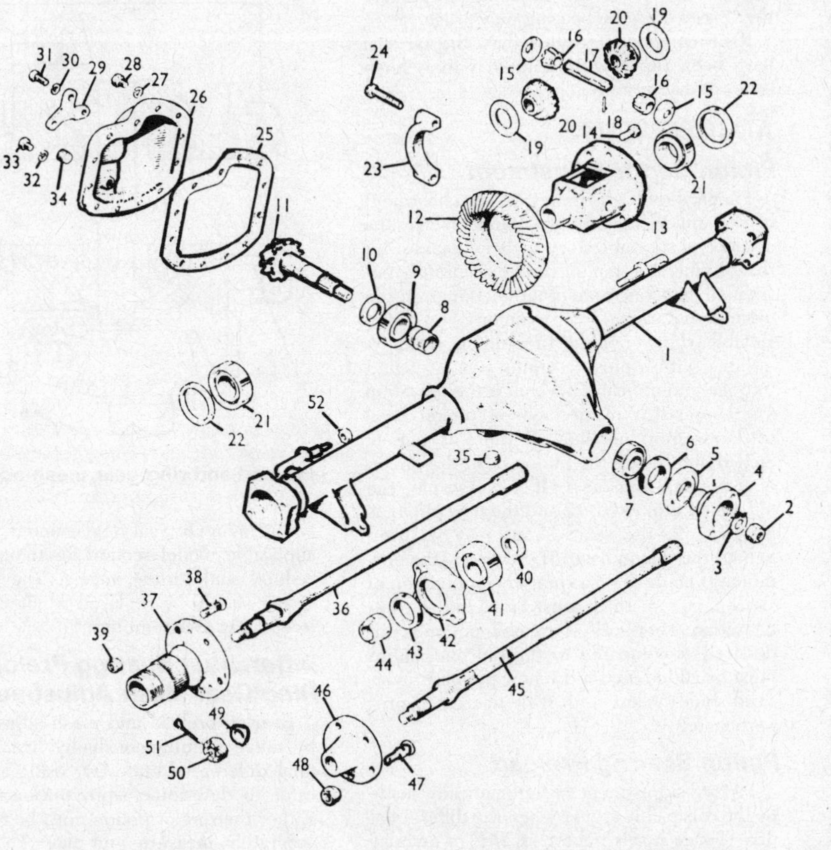

1. Case assembly
2. Nut
3. Plain washer
4. Universal joint flange
5. Dust cover
6. Oil seal
7. Outer pinion bearing
8. Bearing spacer
9. Inner pinion bearing
10. Pinion thrust washer
11. Pinion
12. Ring gear
13. Differential cage
14. Bolt
15. Thrust washer
16. Differential pinions
17. Pinion pin
18. Roll pin
19. Thrust washer
20. Differential wheels
21. Differential bearing
22. Spacers
23. Bearing cap
24. Bolt
25. Joint washer
26. Axle case cover
27. Spring washer
28. Set-screws
29. Compensating lever bracket
30. Spring washer
31. Set-screw
32. Spring washer
33. Set-screw
34. Filler and level plug
35. Drain plug
36. Axle shaft
37. Driving flange
38. Stud
39. Nut
40. Bearing spacer
41. Bearing
42. Bearing hub cap
43. Oil seal
44. Oil seal collar
45. Axle shaft
46. Driving flange
47. Wheel stud
48. Wheel nut
49. Axle shaft collar
50. Axle shaft nut
51. Cotter pin

Wire wheels only (37–39)

Disc wheels only (46–48)

Rear axle components—MGB

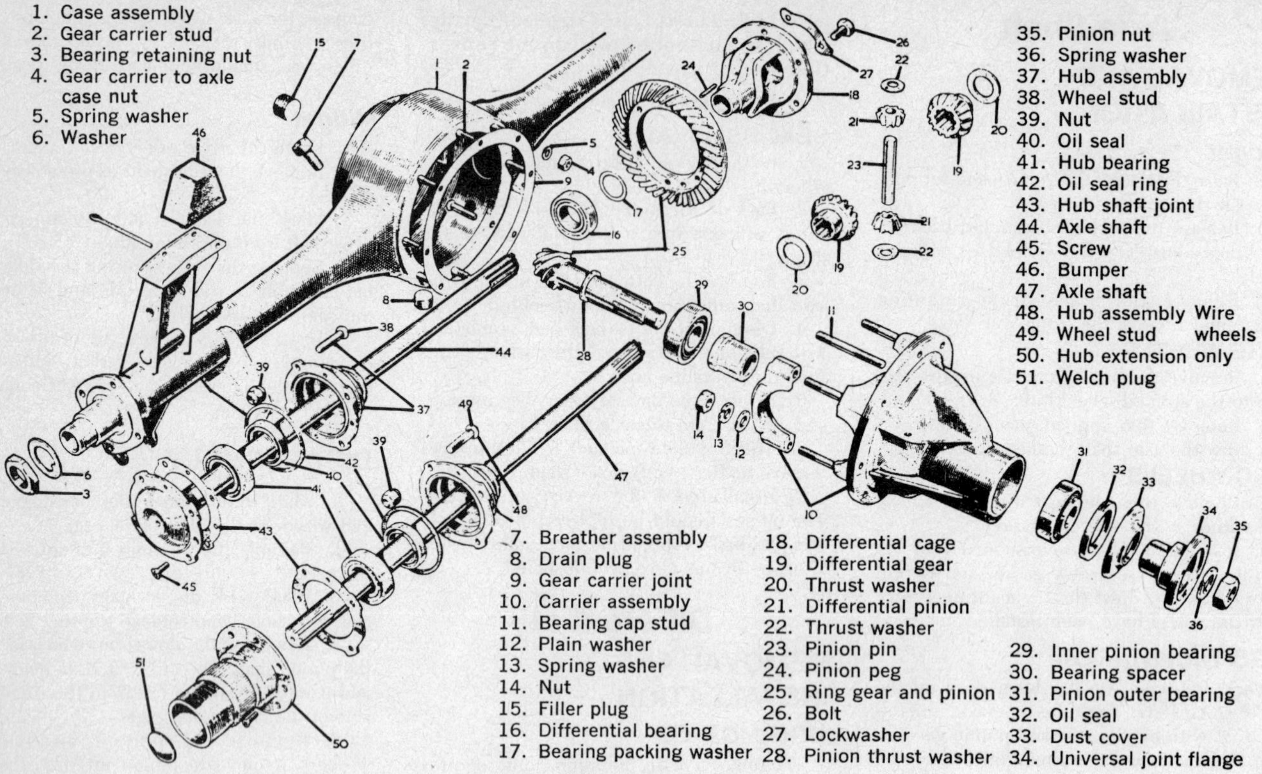

1. Case assembly
2. Gear carrier stud
3. Bearing retaining nut
4. Gear carrier to axle case nut
5. Spring washer
6. Washer
7. Breather assembly
8. Drain plug
9. Gear carrier joint
10. Carrier assembly
11. Bearing cap stud
12. Plain washer
13. Spring washer
14. Nut
15. Filler plug
16. Differential bearing
17. Bearing packing washer
18. Differential cage
19. Differential gear
20. Thrust washer
21. Differential pinion
22. Thrust washer
23. Pinion pin
24. Pinion peg
25. Ring gear and pinion
26. Bolt
27. Lockwasher
28. Pinion thrust washer
29. Inner pinion bearing
30. Bearing spacer
31. Pinion outer bearing
32. Oil seal
33. Dust cover
34. Universal joint flange
35. Pinion nut
36. Spring washer
37. Hub assembly
38. Wheel stud
39. Nut
40. Oil seal
41. Hub bearing
42. Oil seal ring
43. Hub shaft joint
44. Axle shaft
45. Screw
46. Bumper
47. Axle shaft
48. Hub assembly — Wire wheels only
49. Wheel stud — Wire wheels only
50. Hub extension — Wire wheels only
51. Welch plug

Rear axle components—Midget

through the carrier. It will carry with it the inner race and rollers of the rear bearing.

7. Remove the inner race of the front bearing and the oil seal.

8. Remove the bearing outer races using a puller.

9. Slide off the pinion sleeve and shims.

10. Remove the rear bearing inner race, the spacer, and the bearing outer race.

ASSEMBLY

If no components other than the oil seal have been replaced, assembly is in reverse order of disassembly. Note that the thrust face of the differential bearings are marked with the word THRUST.

If any gears or bearings have been replaced see "Differential Gear Adjustment."

OVERHAUL

Midget

1. Mark and remove the housing caps, and withdraw the differential cage.

2. Remove the bearings and shims from the cage.

3. Bend back the locktabs, remove the ring gear bolts, and remove the ring gear.

4. Drive out the dowel pin which locates the pinion shaft. The pin is ⅛ in. in diameter, and it must be driven out from the ring gear side of the differential cage.

5. Remove the pinions and thrust washers. Remove the pinion nut, drive flange, and end-cover.

6. Drive the pinion shaft toward the rear through the carrier. It will carry with it the inner race and rollers of the rear bearing.

7. Remove the inner race of the front bearing and oil seal.

8. Remove the bearing outer races using a puller.

9. Slide off the pinion sleeve and shims.

10. Remove the rear bearing inner race, the spacer, and the bearing outer race.

If no components other than the oil seal have been replaced, assembly is in reverse order of disassembly.

ADJUSTMENTS

Pinion Depth Adjustment

Pinion depth adjustment is an adjustment of the pinion mounting distance D. In the absence of special factory tools for measuring this distance the pinion can be accurately positioned by taking note of the markings on the original and replacement pinions and using suitable shims behind the pinion head. A number with a plus or minus sign is etched into the pinion head C, which is the deviation (in thousandths of an inch) of pinion head thickness from nominal. If there is not an etched number on the pinion head the pinion is of nominal thickness. If, for example, the old pinion is marked −2 and the new pinion is marked −2, the same shims may be used behind the pinion head. If, however, the new pinion is marked −5 a shim or combination of shims 0.003 in. thick must be added as compensation. Therefore, if the new pinion is undersized as compared to the old one, shims must be added, and if the new pinion is oversized shim thickness must be decreased proportionately.

Pinion Bearing Preload

Preload adjustment is automatically made by the collapsible spacer when the differential drive flange nut is tightened. *It is of extreme importance that the nut is not overtightened.*

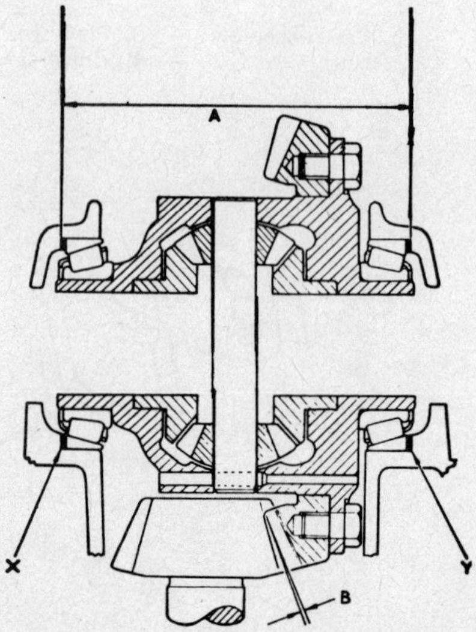

Preload and ring gear mesh adjustment

See "Pinion Oil Seal Replacement" under the applicable model section for tightening procedures and torque values. The collapsible spacer should be replaced whenever the differential is disassembled.

Differential Bearing Preload and Ring Gear Mesh Adjustment

Bearing preload and mesh adjustment can be made simultaneously by first measuring total differential end-play, using a dial indicator to determine shim thickness needed. Either the ring or pinion must be removed to accurately measure end-play. To this measurement must be added 0.004 in., which is

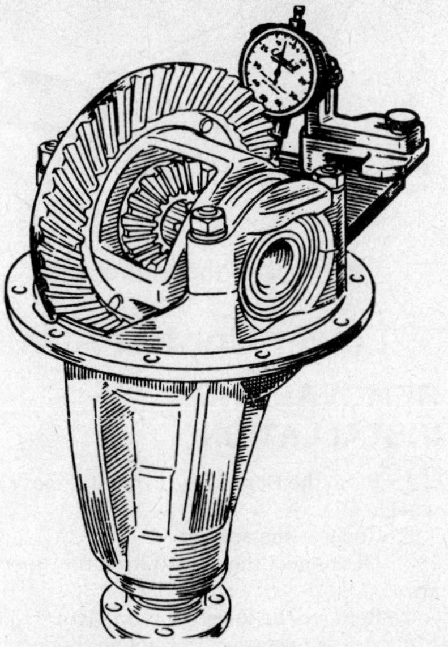

Checking ring gear backlash

the amount of pinch needed to properly preload the bearings (all models).

1. With both gears in position, shift the differential assembly to one side so that the gap at Y is reduced to zero, and measure ring gear backlash with a dial indicator.

2. From the measurement obtained, subtract the correct backlash figure, which is etched into the rear face of the ring gear. This will give the shim thickness required at Y. Subtract this figure from A +0.004 in., and the remainder will be shim thickness required.

If the above calculations have been done correctly, backlash should be within specification and the ring gear should be meshing properly with the pinion gear.

3. Gear mesh can be checked by painting the ring gear teeth with red lead or machinist's blue dye and rotating the gear to obtain a mesh pattern. If correction is necessary do not alter the total number of shims (total thickness), but increase or decrease thickness as needed.

REAR SUSPENSION

Springs

REMOVAL AND INSTALLATION

Midget

1. Raise and support the car.
2. Remove the wheels.
3. From inside the car remove the bolts which secure the spring anchor bracket to the body.
4. From beneath the car remove the two front bracket bolts.
5. Remove the four U-bolt nuts and the shock absorber anchor plate.
6. Remove the rear shackle nuts, pins, and plates, and remove the spring.
7. Installation is in reverse order of removal. The axle limit strap may be removed to facilitate U-bolt installation. Tighten the spring bolt fully after the car is lowered and the spring is loaded.

MGB

1. Remove the wheel adjacent to the spring that is to be removed.
2. Raise and support the body and support the axle with a hydraulic jack to enable the axle to be lowered to relieve tension in the spring.
3. Disconnect the shock absorber link from its bracket and the rebound strap from the rebound spindle.
4. Remove the nuts and spring washers from the eyebolt and shackle plate pins and take off the outer shackle plate.
5. Using a small screwdriver, tap each shackle plate pin alternately until the plate and pins are free of the spring and mounting bracket.
6. Remove the eyebolt from the front of the spring.

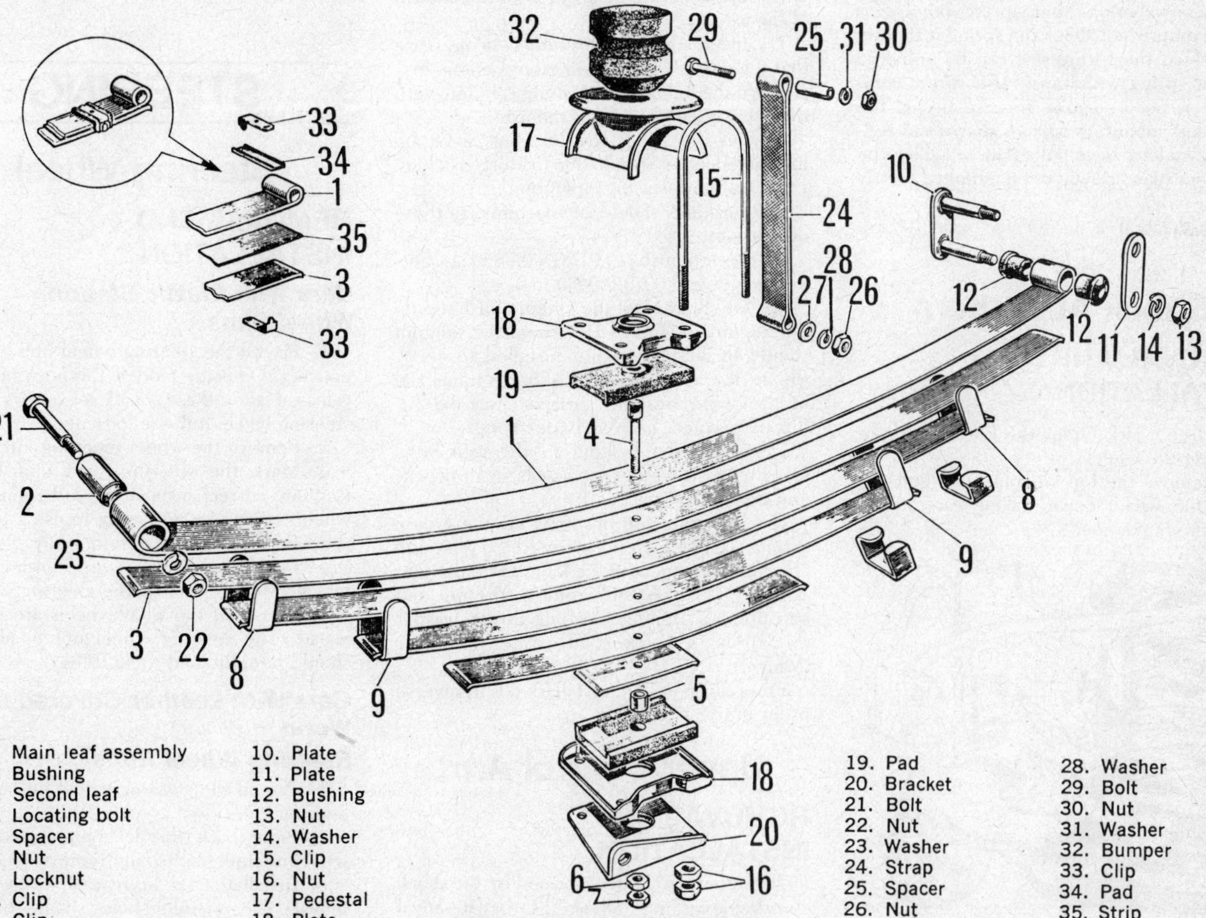

1. Main leaf assembly
2. Bushing
3. Second leaf
4. Locating bolt
5. Spacer
6. Nut
7. Locknut
8. Clip
9. Clip
10. Plate
11. Plate
12. Bushing
13. Nut
14. Washer
15. Clip
16. Nut
17. Pedestal
18. Plate
19. Pad
20. Bracket
21. Bolt
22. Nut
23. Washer
24. Strap
25. Spacer
26. Nut
27. Washer
28. Washer
29. Bolt
30. Nut
31. Washer
32. Bumper
33. Clip
34. Pad
35. Strip

Rear suspension components

7. Remove the locknuts and nuts from the two U-bolts. Remove the shock absorber bracket, locating plate, and pad which will fall from the under side of the spring.
8. Remove the spring, the upper locating plate pad, pedestal, and U-bolts.
9. Installation is the reverse of removal.

Shock Absorber

REMOVAL AND INSTALLATION

1. To remove a rear shock absorber simply disconnect the connecting link arm from the shock lever and unbolt the unit. Shock absorbers should be replaced in axle sets (pairs).
2. If a new shock absorber appears to operate erratically, allow the hydraulic fluid a few minutes to become deaerated.

FRONT SUSPENSION

Springs

REMOVAL AND INSTALLATION

1. Removal of a front spring requires a spring compressor. Once the spring is slightly compressed the spring seat can be unbolted and the spring withdrawn. If a spring compressor is not available, remove two of the spring seat mounting bolts as shown and substitute two long slave bolts that will allow the spring to expand slowly when unbolted evenly (Midget only).
2. Installation is in reverse order or removal.

Shock Absorbers

REMOVAL AND INSTALLATION

1. Place a jack under the lower wishbone and raise the wheel.
2. Remove the top kingpin pivot bolt and swing the wheel down, taking care not to strain the brake line.

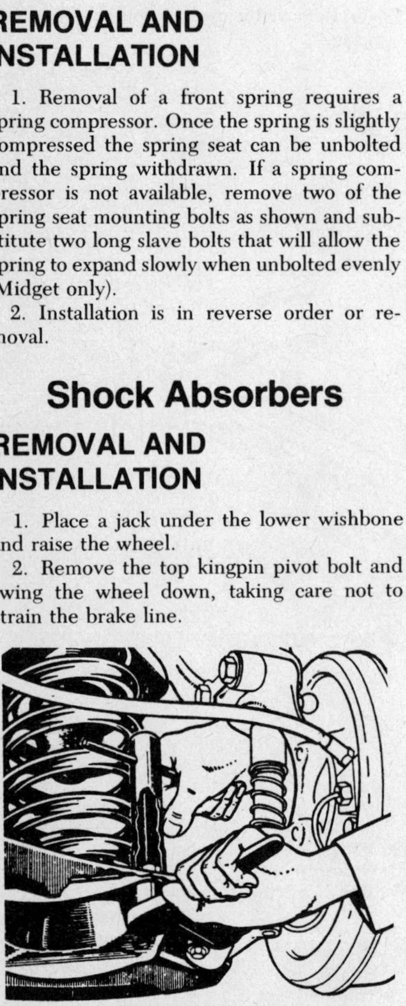

Spring removal

NOTE: The clamp bolt must be removed before the pivot bolt can be withdrawn.

3. Unbolt and remove the shock absorber unit.
4. Installation is in reverse order of removal.

Kingpin

REMOVAL AND INSTALLATION

1. Place a jack under the lower wishbone and raise and remove the wheel.
2. Disconnect the tie rod from the steering arm.
3. Unbolt the brake caliper and support it clear of the hub.
4. Remove the hub and brake disc.
5. Remove the top kingpin pivot bolt and swing the stub axle down.
6. On the Midget, remove the nut from the lower pivot locating pin and drive the pin completely out. Unscrew the pivot end plug (core plug on later models) and unscrew the pivot using a screwdriver.
7. On the MGB, unscrew the nut from the lower pivot bolt and remove the bolt.
8. Withdraw the stub axle and kingpin assembly from the lower control arm.
9. Unscrew the nut from the top of the stub axle and kingpin assembly and remove the kingpin, washers, and seals.
10. Press the bushings out from the bottom of the axle.
11. Install the new bushings, taking care that the open end of the oil groove enters first and that the hole in the bushing is in line with the lubrication channel in the axle.
12. On the MGB the bushings must be line-bored after installation. (Most machine shops can perform this operation).

The bushings should be machined to these dimensions:

MGB—top bushing: 0.7815-0.7820 in.; bottom bushing: 0.9075-0.9080 in.

13. On the Midget the kingpin bushings do not require reaming. However, the kingpin should be lubricated and installed to check the fit. If it takes excessive effort to rotate the kingpin, the bushing surfaces may be refinished using a brake cylinder hone.
14. Install the kingpin in the axle body along with the washers and seals, as removed, and tighten the nut.
15. Lubricate the bushings via the grease fittings using a high pressure grease gun, and check the resistance of the kingpin to rotation. If it is excessively stiff, remove the nut and substitute a thinner floating thrust washer (MGB) or a thicker adjustment washer (Midget).

From this point on, installation is in reverse order of removal.

Upper Control Arm

REMOVAL AND INSTALLATION

The upper wishbone is formed by the shock absorber lever. See "Shock Absorber Removal and Installation."

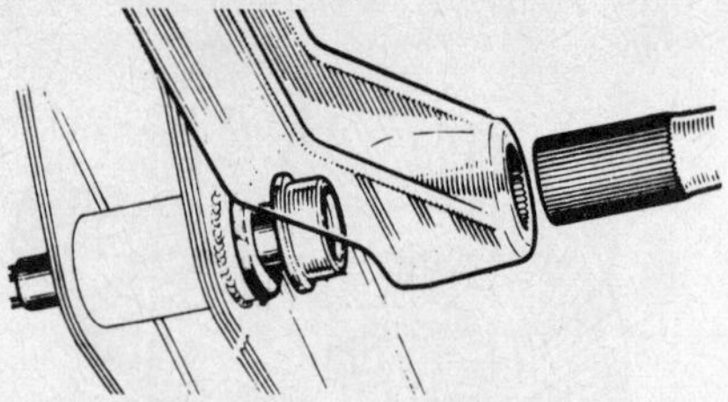

Rear half of the control arm

Lower Control Arm

REMOVAL AND INSTALLATION

1. Raise the front of the car and remove the wheel.
2. Remove the spring.
3. Disconnect the tie rod from the steering arm.
4. Remove the lower kingpin pivot. On the Midget it is necessary to remove the locating pin and pivot bolt end cap before the pivot can be unscrewed.
5. Swivel the stub axle and hub assembly up slightly and support it.
6. Unbolt the wishbone pivot bracket and remove the wishbone.

Adjustments

Front suspension geometry is preset and nonadjustable.

STEERING

Steering Wheel

REMOVAL AND INSTALLATION

Cars With Plastic Steering Wheel Rims

1. Pry off the steering wheel hub emblem housing. On some models the horn button is released after three small set-screws in the steering wheel hub are loosened.
2. Remove the wheel retaining nut.
3. Mark the steering shaft and hub to facilitate correct installation and remove the wheel. It may be necessary to use a puller if the wheel does not come off easily.
4. Installation is in reverse order of removal. Make sure that the steering wheel is centered when the front wheels are straight ahead. The steering wheel nut in all cases should be tightened to 40 ft/lbs.

Cars With Leather Covered or Wood Steering Wheel Rims

1. Pry off the steering wheel hub emblem housing.
2. Bend back the locktabs, remove the wheel retaining bolts, and remove the wheel.
3. Installation is in reverse order of removal. The retaining bolts should be tightened to 12-17 ft/lbs.

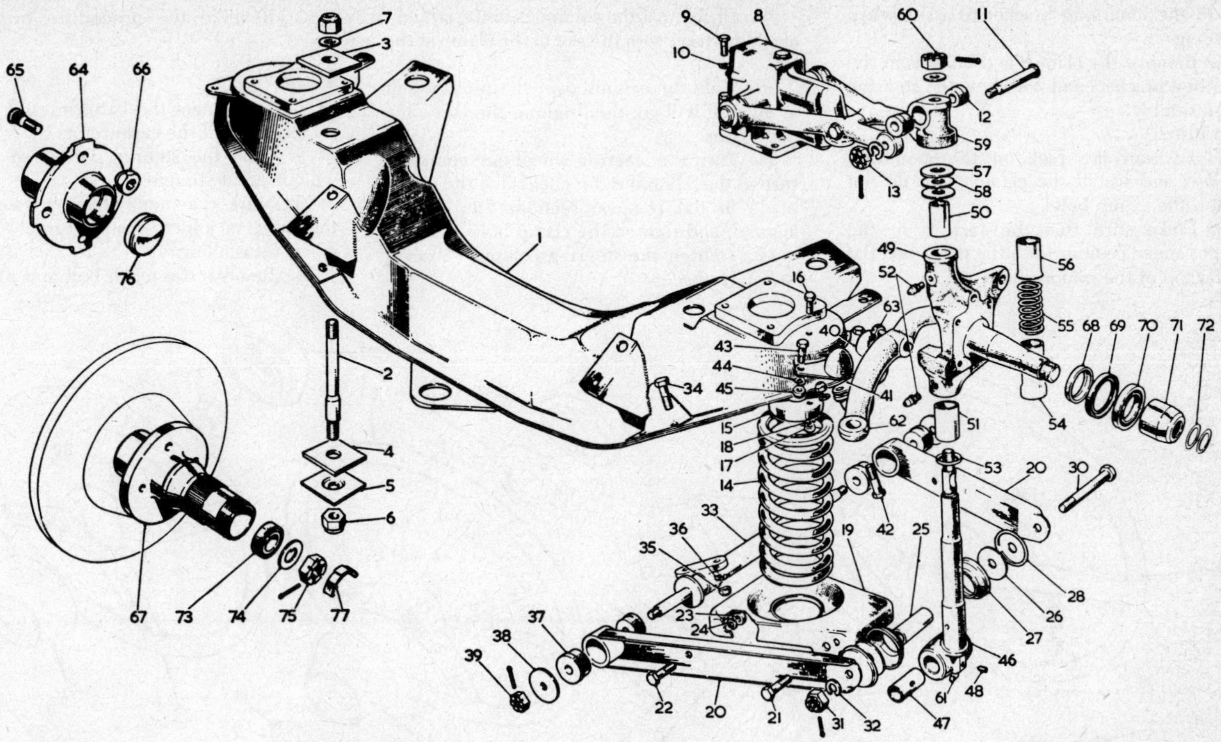

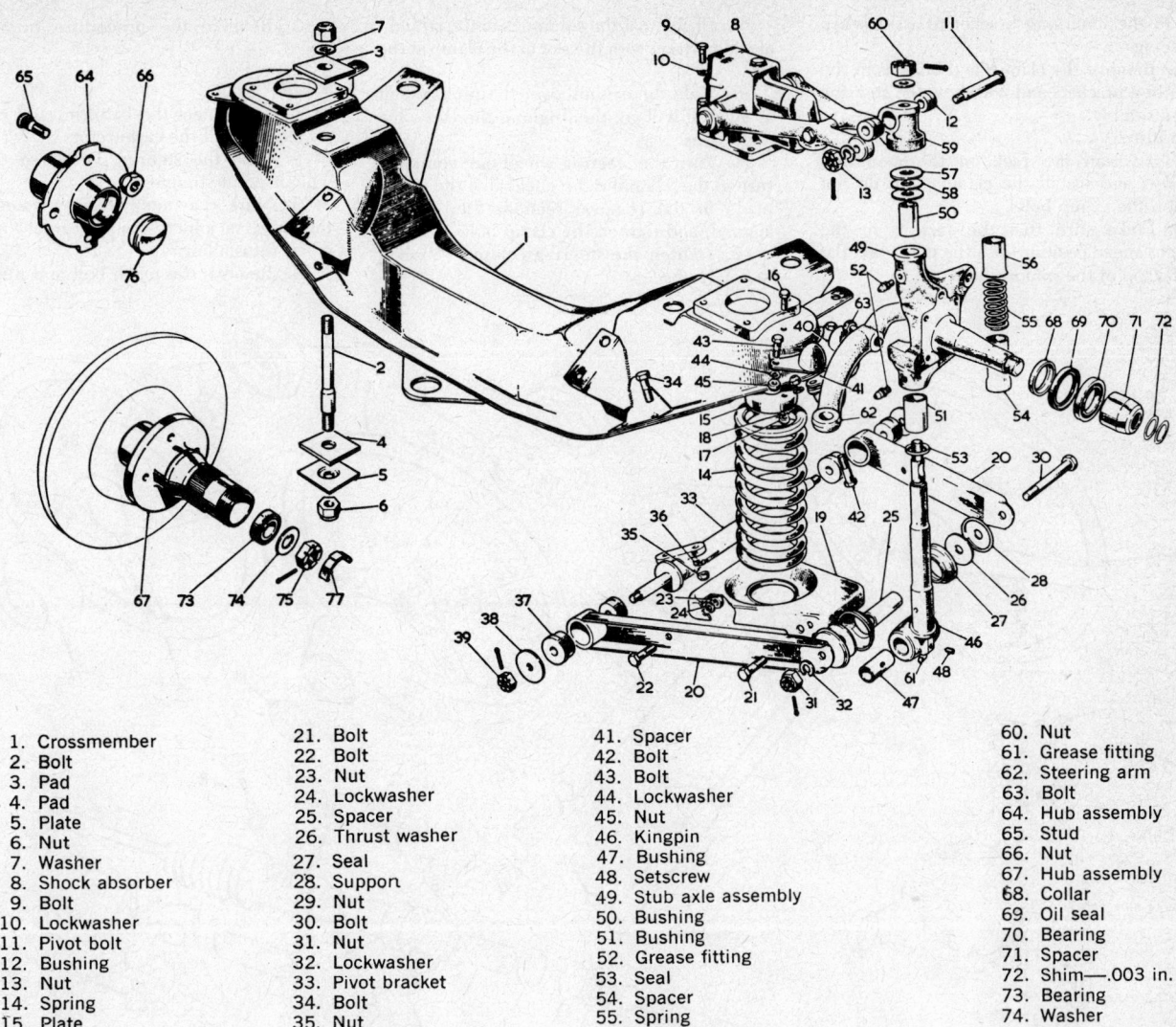

1. Crossmember
2. Bolt
3. Pad
4. Pad
5. Plate
6. Nut
7. Washer
8. Shock absorber
9. Bolt
10. Lockwasher
11. Pivot bolt
12. Bushing
13. Nut
14. Spring
15. Plate
16. Bolt
17. Nut
18. Lockwasher
19. Spring pan assembly
20. Wishbone assembly
21. Bolt
22. Bolt
23. Nut
24. Lockwasher
25. Spacer
26. Thrust washer
27. Seal
28. Suppon
29. Nut
30. Bolt
31. Nut
32. Lockwasher
33. Pivot bracket
34. Bolt
35. Nut
36. Lockwasher
37. Bushing
38. Washer
39. Nut
40. Buffer
41. Spacer
42. Bolt
43. Bolt
44. Lockwasher
45. Nut
46. Kingpin
47. Bushing
48. Setscrew
49. Stub axle assembly
50. Bushing
51. Bushing
52. Grease fitting
53. Seal
54. Spacer
55. Spring
56. Spacer
57. Thrust washer
58. Floating thrust washer—.052 to .057 in.
59. Trunnion—suspension link.
60. Nut
61. Grease fitting
62. Steering arm
63. Bolt
64. Hub assembly
65. Stud
66. Nut
67. Hub assembly
68. Collar
69. Oil seal
70. Bearing
71. Spacer
72. Shim—.003 in.
73. Bearing
74. Washer
75. Nut
76. Grease cap
77. Collar

MGB front suspension

Turn Signal Switch

Midget and MGB through 1977

Unfasten the screws that hold the halves of the steering column shroud together. Remove both halves, except on the late MGB models, on which it is necessary only to remove the left (turn signal side) of the shroud.

Disconnect the snap connector (underneath the instrument panel) and remove the screws that mount the switch. Withdraw the switch assembly.

Installation is the reverse of removal.

MGB 1978 and Later

1. Loosen the three bolts which hold the steering column in place at the firewall.

NOTE: In the next step, the bolts holding the column to the underside of the dash must be removed. Column alignment is obtained through use of various numbers of washers used on these bolts. When removing the bolts, do not allow bolts and washers to be separated, or, alternatively, count and record the number of washers attached to each bolt. If washers are not replaced in original position, column misalignment and steering problems will result.

2. Support the column and remove column-to-dash mounting bolts.
3. Unscrew the bolts holding the havles of the column cover together. Remove the attaching screw for the left-hand cowl and remove the cowl. Remove the indicator/wiper switch.
4. Installation is the reverse of removal, but make sure steering column-to-dash bolts are shimmed as discussed in the note above and torqued to 15 ft/lbs.

Steering Gear

REMOVAL AND INSTALLATION

Midget

1. Remove the radiator and turn the steering wheel to the straight ahead position with the slot of the column clamp uppermost. Remove the wheels.
2. Remove the nuts from the tie rod assemblies and detach the tie rod assemblies from the steering levers.
3. Remove the steering column "U" bolt and the three toe plate bolts.
4. Loosen the three steering column upper retaining bolts and pull the column back enough to disengage the sleeve from the pinion.
5. Mark the steering rack housing in rela-

tion to the mounting bracket to assist when replacing.

6. Remove the clamps and bolts from the mounting brackets and withdraw the steering rack assembly.

To install:

7. Position the rack on the mounting brackets and install the clamps, but do not tighten the clamp bolts.

8. Make sure that the rack is in the straight ahead position with the pinch bolt flat on the top of the pinion shaft.

9. Check that the column is in the straight ahead position with the slot of the clamp at the top.

10. Slide the column over the pinion shaft as far as it will go; then tighten the three toe plate bolts.

11. Turn the steering wheel one complete turn to the left and right; check that the marks made in the removal section, Step 5, are aligned, and tighten the clamp bolts.

12. Tighten the steering column "U" bolt to 9-12 ft/lbs.

13. Reverse the procedure in Steps 1 and 2.

MGB

1. Disconnect the batteries and take the air cleaners off the carburetors.

2. Turn the steering wheel so that the wheels point straight ahead.

3. Mark the inner steering column and the universal joint to ensure correct alignment when reinstalling.

4. Remove the pinch bolt and nut secur-

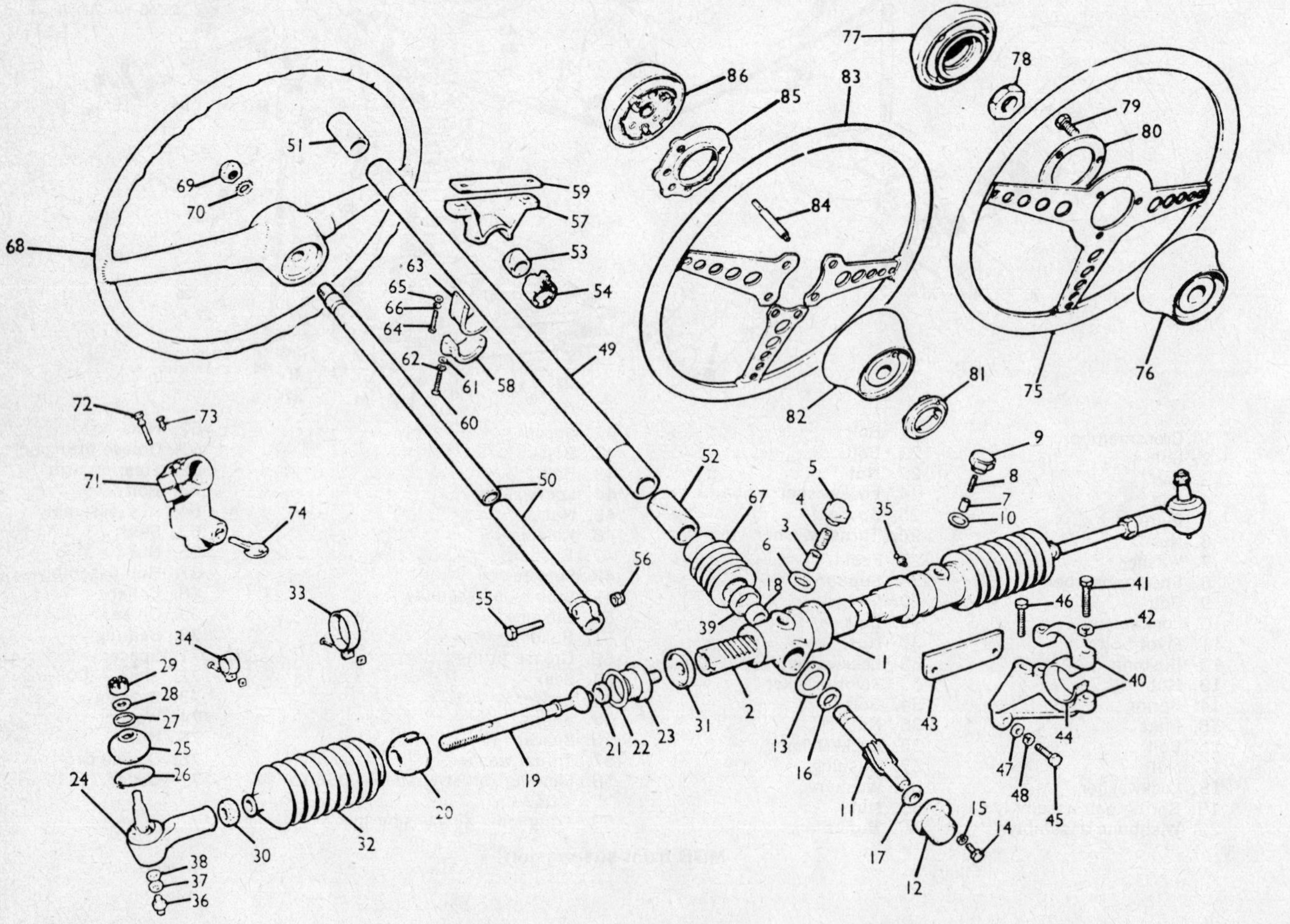

1. Rack housing
2. Rack
3. Damper pad
4. Damper pad spring
5. Damper pad housing
6. Shim
7. Secondary damper pad
8. Secondary damper spring
9. Secondary damper housing
10. Housing washer
11. Pinion
12. Pinion tail bearing
13. Shim
14. Setscrew
15. Spring washer
16. Pinion thrust washer (top)
17. Pinion thrust washer (bottom)
18. Pinion seal
19. Tie-rod
20. Ball housing (female)
21. Ball seat
22. Shim
23. Ball housing (male)
24. Ball socket assembly
25. Boot
26. Clip
27. Ring
28. Plain washer
29. Nut
30. Locknut
31. Lock washer
32. Seal
33. Clip (inner)
34. Clip (outer)
35. Lubricator
36. Lubricator
37. Dished washer
38. Fiber washer
39. Retainer
40. Bracket and cap assembly
41. Setscrew
42. Spring washer
43. Seating
44. Packing
45. Setscrew
46. Setscrew
47. Plain washer
48. Spring washer
49. Outer column
50. Inner column tube
51. Felt bearing (top)
52. Felt bearing (bottom)
53. Felt bearing (bottom)
54. Clip
55. Bolt
56. Nut
57. Bracket
58. Bracket cap
59. Shim
60. Setscrew
61. Plain washer
62. Spring washer
63. Seating
64. Setscrew
65. Plain washer
66. Spring washer
67. Draught excluder
68. Steering wheel
69. Nut
70. Lockwasher
71. Steering column lock
72. Shear bolt
73. Locating screw
74. Lock key
75. Steering wheel
76. Steering wheel nut
77. Badge — Midget Mk. III (GAN5)
78. Nut
79. Set screw
80. Locking ring
81. Slip-ring
82. Steering wheel boss
83. Steering wheel — From car number Midget Mk. III (GAN5) 89515
84. Horn contact
85. Lock-ring
86. Horn push

Steering gear components—Midget

ing the universal joint to the steering column.

5. Disconnect the multi-connector block; disconnect the wiring from the ignition switch.

6. Remove the bolts retaining the steering column upper and lower support clamp brackets; note the location, quantity, and thickness of the packing washers between the column upper fixing flanges and the body brackets. Remove the washers.

NOTE If the packing washers are mislaid or their installed positions not recorded, the steering must be aligned when the column is refitted.

7. Remove the steering column complete with outer tube, steering wheel, direction indicator and ignition/steering lock switch.

Installation is the reverse of removal but note the following:

8. Check that the steering rack is in the straight ahead position.

9. Check that the steering column is in the straight ahead position.

10. Note that in Steps 1 and 4-8, the outer

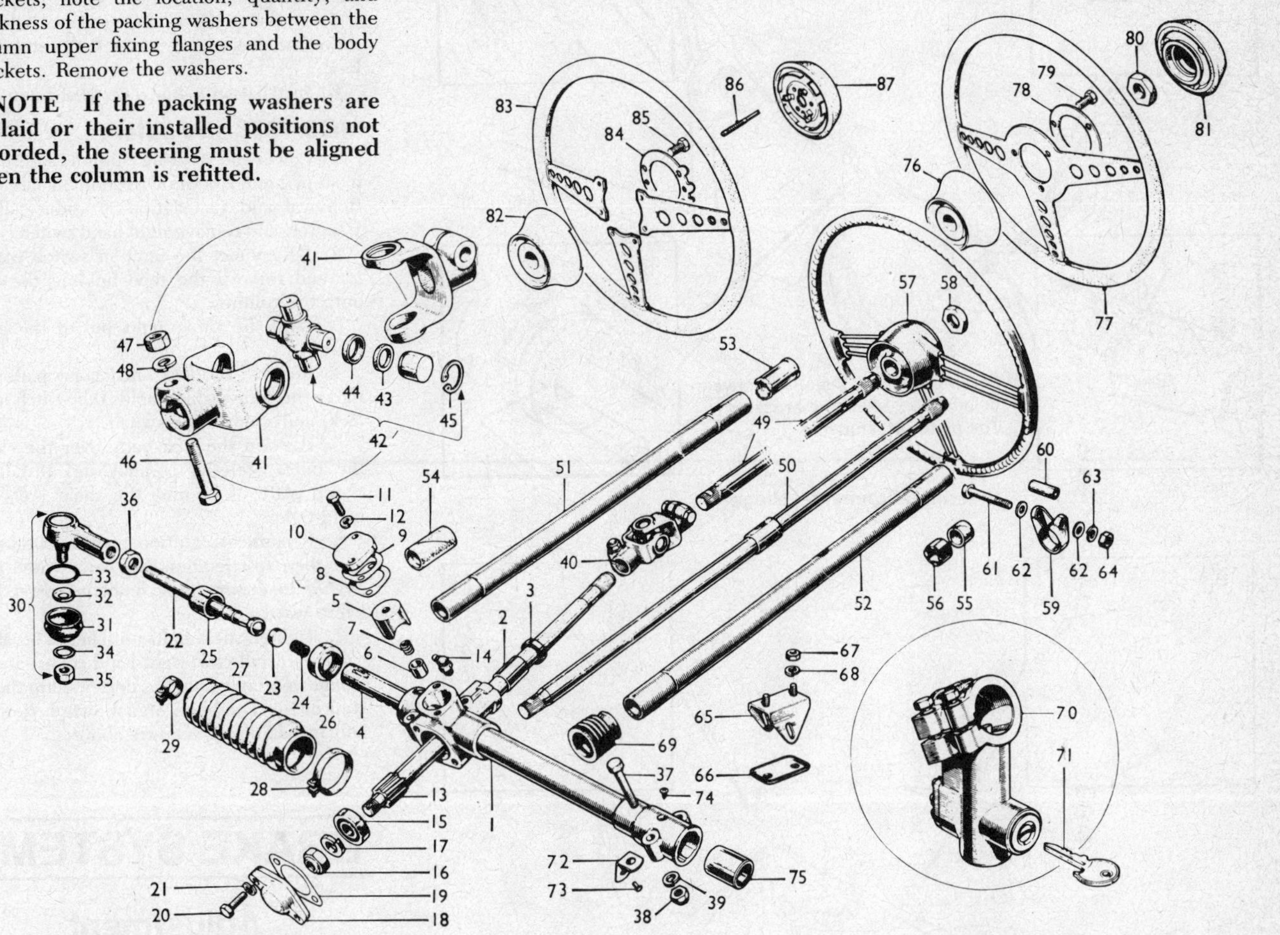

1. Housing assembly
2. Bushing
3. Seal
4. Rack
5. Yoke
6. Damper
7. Spring
8. Shim
9. Gasket
10. Cover plate
11. Bolt
12. Lockwasher
13. Pinion
14. Grease fitting
15. Pinion bearing
16. Nut
17. Lockwasher
18. End cover
19. Gasket
20. Bolt
21. Lockwasher
22. Tie-rod
23. Ball seat
24. Thrust spring
25. Housing
26. Locknut
27. Seal
28. Clip
29. Clip
30. Socket assembly
31. Boot
32. Retainer
33. Spring
34. Washer
35. Nut
36. Locknut
37. Bolt
38. Nut
39. Lockwasher
40. Steering column U-joint
41. Yoke
42. Journal assembly
43. Seal
44. Retainer
45. Circlip
46. Bolt
47. Nut
48. Lockwasher
49. Column assembly—inner
50. Column assembly—inner—R.H.D.
51. Coumn tube
52. Column tube—R.H.D.
53. Bearing
54. Bearing
55. Bushing (felt)
56. Clip
57. Steering wheel
58. Nut
59. Clamp
60. Spacer
61. Bolt
62. Washer
63. Lockwasher
64. Nut
65. Bracket
66. Plate
67. Nut
68. Lockwasher
69. Boot
70. Lock assembly—steering and ignition
71. Key
72. Shim
73. Rivet
74. Bushing locating screw
75. Bushing
76. Wheel hub
77. Steering wheel
78. Ring
79. Bolt
80. Nut
81. Emblem housing
82. Wheel hub
83. Steering wheel
84. Ring
85. Bolt
86. Horn push contact
87. Horn push

When steering lock is fitted. 1970 and later cars.

MGB steering components

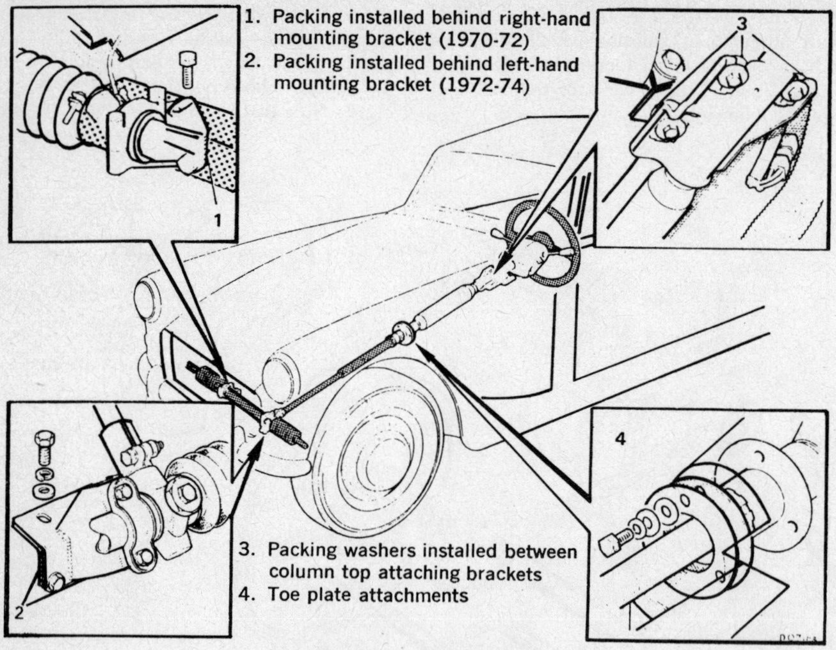

Steering alignment—Midget

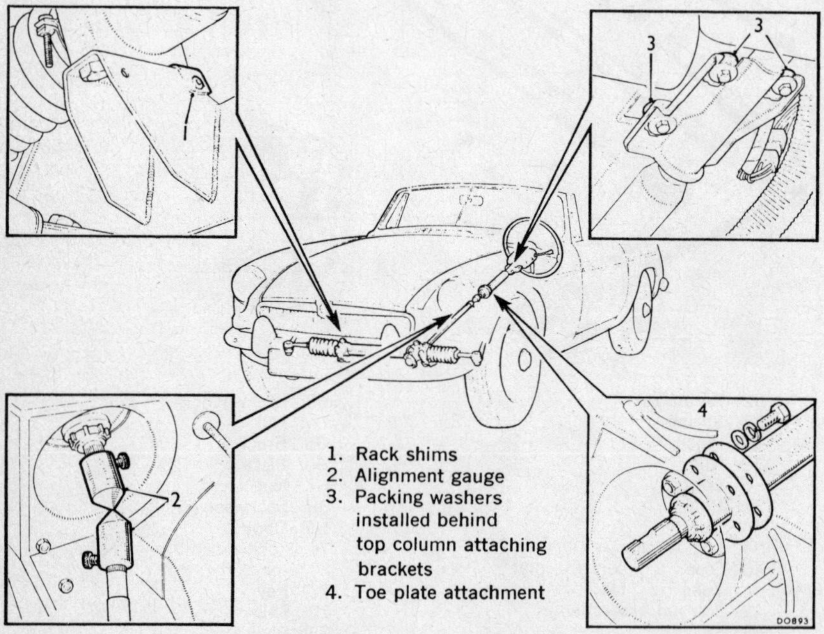

Steering alignment—MGB

tube is installed to the steering column with the gaitered end towards the floor board. In Step 3, ensure that the marks align when installing the inner column to the universal joint.

To align the steering column:

11. Remove the three bolts from the steering column retaining plate near the firewall.

12. Install the rack assembly with the shims that were originally removed and check, by pushing and pulling, that the column slides reasonably freely over the steering rack pinion shaft. If the column is stiff, shims may be added or removed from behind the rack or the steering column support bracket.

ADJUSTMENTS

No adjustments are possible.

Steering/Ignition Lock Switch

REMOVAL AND INSTALLATION

Midget and MGB through 1977

1. Remove the steering column, along with the steering wheel and center hub.
2. Remove the combined turn signal-high beam switch.
3. Remove the turn signal lever from the inner column.
4. Loosen the top lock bracket and slide it off the steering column, turn the key to the unlocked position.
5. Drill out the retaining shear bolts, remove the positioning screw, and remove the lock.
6. Installation is the reverse of removal.

MGB 1978 and Later

1. Lower the steering column as described in steps 1 and 2 of the Direction Signal Switch Removal and Installation procedure above. Unscrew and remove right hand switch cover.
2. Disconnect the ignition switch connector and remove the tape holding the cable onto the column.
3. Drill the shear bolts out of the clamp plate.
4. Remove the lock and clamp plate. Remove the screw which holds the switch in the lock, and remove the switch.
5. Position the lock body over the slot in the outer steering column and install the clamp plate, tightening the shear bolts *only* hand-tight.
6. Reconnect ignition switch connector, and then test ignition lock and switch *thoroughly* to ensure they function correctly in every way.
7. Tighten shear bolts until heads break off.
8. Reinstall cowl right-hand cover, and reinstall steering column as described in the last step of the Direction Signal Switch Removal and Installation procedure above.

BRAKE SYSTEMS

Adjustment

While turning wheel, rotate adjuster clockwise until shoes lock the drum, then turn back slightly until wheel rotates freely.

Master Cylinder

REMOVAL AND INSTALLATION

Midget

1. Disconnect H.T. wire from ignition coil. Disconnect white/blue lead from the connector.
2. Remove the four cover plate mounting screws, and remove the plate and coil.
3. Remove cotter pin, and washer, and disconnect linkage at clevis pin.
4. Unscrew all hydraulic connections and plug master cylinder and pipe connections.
5. Unbolt the master cylinder from the pedal box, being careful to retain all bolts, nuts, and washers.
6. Install in reverse order, and completely bleed the system.

MGB 1975

1. Remove the cover of the master cylinder and drain the fluid.

2. Cap and plug the brake and clutch fluid lines.
3. Remove the cotter pin from the pushrod and disconnect the pedal lever.
4. Disconnect the clutch and brake return springs; remove the lower left dash panel.
5. Remove the pedal box retaining screws.
6. Remove the nut holding the pedal pivot bolt, remove the bolt and center spacer and then replace the bolt.
7. Remove the six pedal box retaining screws and remove the box complete with master cylinders.
8. Remove the two master cylinder retaining bolts and remove the master cylinder.
9. Installation is the reverse of removal, remember to bleed the systems after installing.

MGB 1976 and Later

1. Siphon the fluid from the reservoir or pump the fluid out the front brake bleed screw by opening the front brake bleed and pumping the brake pedal.
2. Disconnect warning light wiring.
3. Disconnect the secondary feed pipe, which enters the cylinder at an angle from below on the left side.
4. Disconnect the primary lines, which enter the cylinder on the left side horizontally. Plug both secondary lines and both secondary cylinder ports.
5. Remove the two nuts and lockwashers, and remove the master cylinder from the brake booster.
6. Reverse the removal procedure to install and bleed the system.

OVERHAUL

Rebuilding kits are available, and usually contain the check valve, rubber seals, and metal washers. Pistons and springs are available as individual pieces.

When the piston assembly has been removed from the cylinder, examine the bore. If it is pitted or scored the entire cylinder assembly should be replaced. If bore damage is light, it may be honed; but in most cases the repair will not be lasting and the cylinder may begin to leak again after a short time. When honing a cylinder, occasionally dip the hone in clean brake fluid for lubrication.

Whenever a cylinder is disassembled for inspection or rebuilding, the rubber seals should be replaced as a matter of course. Before installing the seals lubricate them thoroughly with brake fluid or the special lubricant that is included in some rebuilding kits. All internal components of the cylinder, especially the bore, must be completely free of dirt and grit or the cylinder may leak or fail to operate properly. When installing the piston and seals into the bore, make sure that the seal lips are not turned back as they enter the cylinder. Once the cylinder has been installed on the car the brakes must be bled.

Brake Bleeding

There are two methods of accomplishing this. The quickest and easiest of the two is pressure bleeding, but special pressure equipment is needed to externally pressurize the hydraulic system. The other, more commonly used method is gravity bleeding.

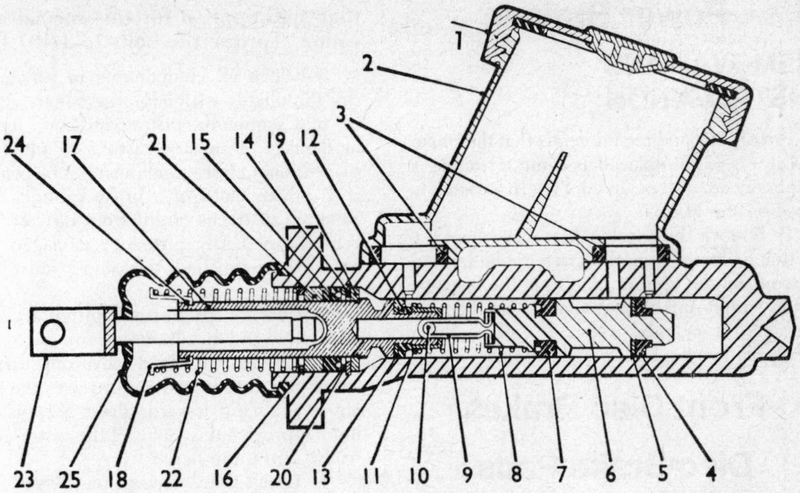

1. Filler cap
2. Plastic reservoir
3. Reservoir seals
4. Main cup
5. Piston washer
6. Piston
7. Main cup
8. Spring
9. Piston link
10. Pin
11. Pin retainer
12. Main cup
13. Pinion washer
14. Circlip
15. Cup
16. Circlip
17. Piston
18. Spring retainer
19. Stop washer
20. Washer
21. Spacer
22. Spring
23. Pushrod
24. Retainer ring

Cross-section of the dual master cylinder

NOTE: Only brake fluid conforming to SAE specification J1703 should be used.

GRAVITY BLEEDING PROCEDURE

1. Clean the bleed valve at each wheel.
2. Attach a small rubber hose to the bleed valve on one of the rear wheel cylinders and place the other end in a container of brake fluid.
3. Top up the master cylinder with brake fluid (check often during bleeding).
4. Open the bleed valve about one-quarter turn, have assistant press the brake pedal to the floor and slowly release it. Continue until no more air bubbles are forced from the cylinder on application of the brake pedal.
5. Repeat for each of the remaining wheel cylinders, beginning with the other rear wheel.

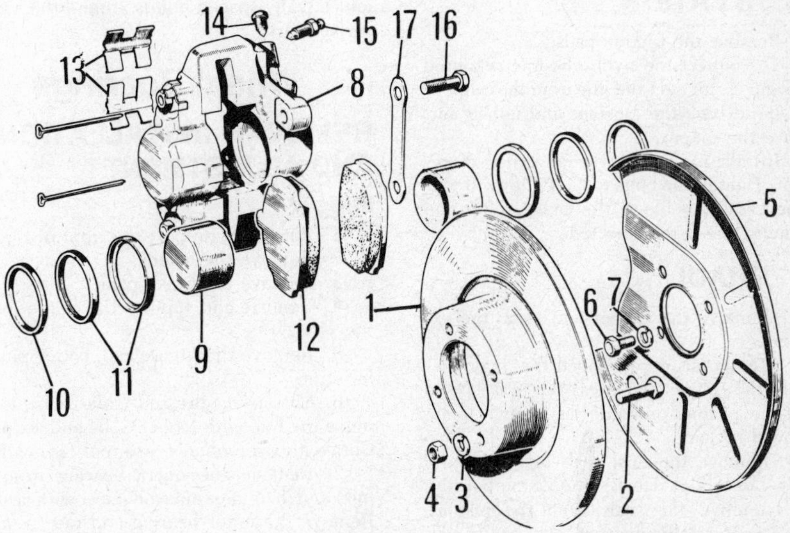

1. Disc
2. Bolt
3. Lockwasher
4. Nut
5. Dust cover
6. Bolt
7. Lockwasher
8. Caliper
9. Piston
10. Piston seal
11. Dust seal and retainer
12. Pad
13. Retaining springs
14. Plug
15. Bleed valve
16. Bolt
17. Locktab

Disc brake components, MGB

Power Brakes

REMOVAL AND INSTALLATION

British Leyland recommends that the brake booster is to be replaced as a unit if trouble is experienced. A Lockheed Type 6 booster is used on the MGB.

To remove the booster, first disconnect the hydraulic line(s) from the master cylinder and disconnect the vacuum line from the booster. Then simply unbolt and remove the booster and master cylinder as an assembly. Upon reinstallation the brakes must be bled.

Front Disc Brakes

Disc Brake Pads

REMOVAL AND INSTALLATION

1. Raise the front of the car and remove the wheel.
2. Remove the two cotter pins that locate the pad retaining spring(s).
3. Remove the retaining spring and pull the pads and anti-squeal shims from the caliper.
4. Installation is in reverse order of removal. It may be necessary to push the pistons back into the caliper so that the new pads will fit. Be careful not to mar the disc in doing so. Install the anti-squeal shims in their original positions or they will not function properly. Pads should never be allowed to wear to a thickness of less than $^{1}/_{16}$ in. Replace pads in axle sets (two pair).

Disc Brake Calipers

REMOVAL AND INSTALLATION

1. Remove the friction pads.
2. Disconnect the hydraulic line retaining plate and disconnect the line from the caliper.
3. Bend back the locktabs and unbolt and remove the caliper.
4. Installation is in reverse order of removal. Tighten the bolts to 40-45 ft/lbs. It will be necessary to bleed the brakes after the hydraulic line is reconnected.

OVERHAUL

1. Remove the caliper and clean the exterior.
2. Temporarily reconnect the hydraulic line to the caliper and press the brake pedal until the pistons protrude far enough to be removed by hand.
3. Remove the dust seals and retainers, taking care not to damage the piston bores.
4. Remove the seals from the pistons using a non-metallic instrument.

NOTE: It is not normally necessary to separate the caliper halves. If the separation is necessary the fluid transfer hole seal, bridge bolts, and bolt locktabs must be replaced with new parts. Only use bolts obtained from an MG dealer that are supplied for this special application. Torque the bolts to 34-37 ft/lbs.

5. Clean all components in solvent and dry thoroughly with compressed air.
6. Examine the pistons and bores for wear or damage. Damaged pistons should be replaced. Slight bore roughness can be removed with crocus cloth or a brake cylinder hone. Remove all traces of grit from the bore after refinishing. Badly pitted or damaged bores cannot be refinished; the caliper must be replaced.
7. Coat the pistons and piston seals with brake fluid and install the seals on the pistons.
8. Loosen the bleed valve one turn and install the pistons in the bores with the piston cut-away facing inward. Press the piston in until approximately ⅜ in. of the piston is protruding from the bore.
9. Install the dust seals on the pistons.
10. Install the caliper(s) and bleed the brakes.

Brake Disc

REMOVAL AND INSTALLATION

1. Remove the caliper.
2. Remove the grease cap and cotter pin, and remove the hub retaining nut. Withdraw the hub assembly.
3. Unbolt and remove the disc from the hub.
4. Installation is in reverse order of removal.

Any disc that is badly scored should be replaced. Light scoring is not detrimental to the operation of the brakes, but friction pad life will be reduced. Runout is measured at the outer edge of the disc friction surface with a dial indicator or runout gage. Parallelism refers to variations in the thickness of the disc. The disc should be measured for parallelism at four equally spaced points around the friction surface.

Wheel Bearings

REMOVAL, INSTALLATION AND ADJUSTMENT

Midget

1. Raise and support the front of the car.
2. Remove the wheel.
3. Remove the brake pads.
4. Remove and support the caliper out of the way.
5. Remove the grease cap, cotter pin and hub nut.
6. Cars using pressed (solid) wheels, remove the hub with tool 18G304 and adapters. Cars with wire wheels, use tool 18G1032.
7. Remove the outer bearing from the hub and hammer out the race with a drift. Remove the inner bearing and race in a like manner.
8. Pack the new bearings with grease so that the grease protrudes from the bearings.
9. Drive the races into place and install the bearings and grease seal.
10. Pack the hub recess with grease and install the hub on the spindle.
11. Tighten the hub bolt to 46 ft/lbs and align the cotter pin hole by tightening, if necessary, the nut.
12. Assemble remaining parts in reverse of removal.

MGB

1. Raise and support the front of the car.
2. Remove and support the caliper out of the way.
3. Remove the grease cap, cotter pin and nut.
4. On cars with solid wheels, remove the hub with tool 18G304 and adapters. On cars with wire wheels, use tool 18G363.
5. From the hub, remove the bearing retaining washer, outer bearing, shims, spacer, inner bearing, oil seal collar and oil seal.
6. If necessary, the races may be hammered out with a drift.
7. Install new races, if necessary.
8. Pack each bearing with grease until it squeezes out.
9. Fill the cavity between the bearing and the oil seal with grease and lightly grease the spacer.
10. Assemble hub parts, minus the shims, and install hub on spindle.
11. Install the retaining washer and nut and tighten the nut until the bearings bind.
12. Remove the nut and hub and pull the outer race.
13. Install enough shims to produce excessive end-play, install the parts and hub and check the end-play with a dial gauge. Reduce the number of shims to give an end-play of 0.0020.004".
14. When desired end-play is attained, tighten the nut to 40-70 ft/lbs, aligning the cotter pin hole.
15. Install a new cotter pin. Install remaining parts.

Drum Brake Shoes

REMOVAL AND INSTALLATION

Brake shoes should always be replaced in axle sets. Replace reveted shoe assemblies or linings when they have less than 40% of original thickness left at the thinnest point, and bonded shoe assemblies or linings when they have less than 25% of original thickness left at the thinnest point. Examine the linings for signs of cracking and oil or brake fluid contamination.

With the drum off, examine the wheel cylinders for leakage. Check the brake springs for stretching and clean the backing plate after the shoes have been removed. Lightly lubricate the brake shoe contact points on the backing plate before installing the new shoes. Adjust the brakes after installation.

Brake Drums

REMOVAL AND INSTALLATION

1. Raise the car and remove the wheel.
2. Back off the brake adjuster if the drum will not spin freely.

1. Backing plate
2. Bolt
3. Nut
4. Lockwasher
5. Shoe assembly
6. Spring
7. Spring
8. Shoe retaining pin
9. Brake-shoe retaining spring
10. Retainer washer
11. Adjuster assembly
12. Tappet
13. Wedge spindle
14. Nut
15. Washer
16. Wheel cylinder assembly
17. Piston
18. Piston seal
19. Piston boot
20. Wheel cylinder retaining clip
21. Bleed valve
22. Parking brake lever
23. Parking brake lever boot
24. Brake drum
25. Drum retaining screw
26. Drum retaining nut (wire wheels)

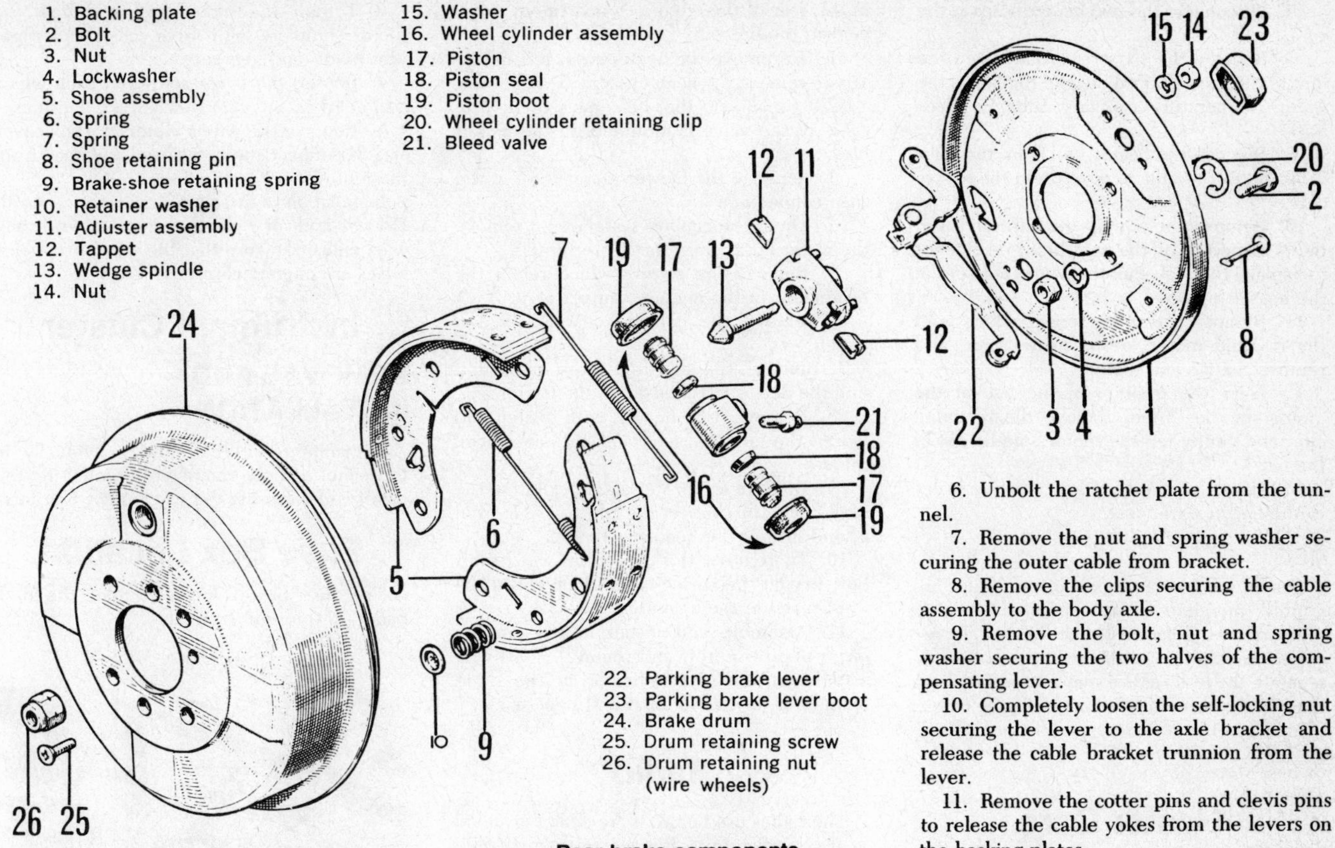

Rear brake components

3. Remove the drum retaining screws or nuts and pull the drum off the hub.
4. Installation is in reverse order of removal. Adjust the brakes when the drum has been replaced on the hub.

Wheel Cylinders

Ideally, wheel cylinder assemblies should be replaced when they begin to leak. However, seal kits are available and a rebuilt cylinder should function well if it has been rebuilt carefully. Use the illustrations at the beginning of the brake section for disassembly and assembly, and refer to "Master Cylinder Rebuilding" for inspection and rebuilding notes. It is possible to rebuild a wheel cylinder without removing it from the backing plate. In any case, cleanliness is of extreme importance. Adjust and bleed the brakes after the drum has been reinstalled.

Parking Brake

CABLE

Adjustment

Adjustment can be made at the brake balance lever where the main parking brake cable splits into separate cables for each rear wheel, underneath the car near the axle. Adjust the cable so that the brake is fully applied when the lever is pulled up four or five notches. Some cars have grease fittings on the cables and balance lever pivot, and these points must be lubricated regularly to prevent brake drag.

Removal and Installation

Midget

1. Raise and support the rear of the car at the axle.
2. Disconnect the battery ground.
3. Remove the driver's seat.
4. Unbolt the handbrake lever from the mounting plate.
5. Remove the warning switch wires.
6. Unbolt the mounting plate from the tunnel and rotate it 180°.
7. Pull the handbrake lever away from the tunnel and remove the cotter pin and clevis.
8. Remove and separate the handbrake lever and mounting plate.
9. Remove the cotter pin, washer and clevis pin from the equalizer lever.
10. Free the cable rear adjustment nut and slide it along the cable.
11. Remove the threaded sleeve and cable from the equalizer.
12. Remove the cable front locknut and remove the cable from the front bracket and tunnel.
13. Installation is the reverse of removal. Use new cotter pins.

MGB

1. Raise and support the car.
2. Remove the adjusting nut and remove the cable end from the lower end of the lever.
3. Remove the nut securing the lever to the spindle and remove the spring washer, forked lever and plain washer. Remove the lever.
4. Remove the right side seat.
5. Disconnect the brake switch wiring.
6. Unbolt the ratchet plate from the tunnel.
7. Remove the nut and spring washer securing the outer cable from bracket.
8. Remove the clips securing the cable assembly to the body axle.
9. Remove the bolt, nut and spring washer securing the two halves of the compensating lever.
10. Completely loosen the self-locking nut securing the lever to the axle bracket and release the cable bracket trunnion from the lever.
11. Remove the cotter pins and clevis pins to release the cable yokes from the levers on the backing plates.
12. Replacement is the reverse of removal.

CHASSIS ELECTRICAL

Heater Blower

REMOVAL AND INSTALLATION

Midget 1975

The heater blower is adjacent to the heater box, on the right-hand side of the engine compartment. To remove the blower, loosen both hose clamps retaining ducts to the unit, and pull off the ducts. Disconnect the ground and hot leads, remove the sheet metal mounting screws, and remove the blower.

Install in the reverse order of removal.

Midget 1976 and Later

1. Remove the battery. Remove the battery tray.
2. Disconnect the bottom radiator hose to drain the cooling system.
3. Disconnect fan motor wires at the connectors.
4. Disconnect the control cable by removing the bolt holding it to the air intake tube. Loosen the bolt on the air intake flap lever and pull the inner cable out of the clamp on the lever.
5. Pull the air intake hose off the tube on the heating unit.

6. Disconnect the two heater hoses at the core.

7. Remove the six screws that fasten the unit to the firewall. Pull the clip that holds the water temperature capillary tube in place aside.

8. Remove the heater unit from the car.

9. Turn the unit so as to drain the heater core.

10. Remove the five spring clips and pull the heater cover off the unit, being careful not to damage the seal. Pull the heater core out of the heater unit.

11. Remove the three screws which hold the fan and motor to the heater unit, and remove the fan and motor.

12. Note the position of the fan on the motor spindle. Then, remove the retaining clip, and gently tap the motor spindle out of the fan.

13. Install in reverse order, applying sealer to the heater cover seal.

MGB

The heater blower is part of the heater assembly, mounted in the rear of the engine compartment, adjacent to the firewall. To remove the blower, disconnect the batteries, separate the leads at the snap connectors, and remove the three blower mounting bolts.

Install in the reverse order of removal.

Heater Core

REMOVAL AND INSTALLATION

Midget 1975

The heater core is located in the heater box, mounted directly in front of the battery in the engine compartment. To remove the core, it is necessary to drain the cooling system and proceed as follows:

1. Disconnect the battery cables, and the heater valve control cable. Remove the screws which retain the heater box to the tray.

2. Separate the water hoses and the blower duct from the heater box. Disconnect the air hose from the heater air intake tube.

3. Lift the heater box out of the car as a unit.

4. The heater core may be removed from the heater box by removing the retaining sheet and metal screws.

5. Install in the reverse order of removal.

6. Bleed the system, if necessary, by removing the return hose from its connector, and extending it with an additional piece of hose, so that water may be returned to the radiator filler.

7. Plug the open connection, and run the engine until water flow into the radiator is free of bubbles.

8. Reconnect the hose as quickly as possible.

Midget 1976 and Later

Follow steps 1-10 of the blower removal and installation procedure.

MGB

The heater core is located in the heater box, in the rear of the engine compartment, adjacent to the firewall.

1. To remove the heater core, it is necessary to remove the heater assembly as follows:

2. Disconnect the heater valve control cable (if the valve is mounted on the heater box).

3. Separate the blower motor leads at the snap connectors.

4. Drain the cooling system, and remove the water hoses from the heater unit.

5. Remove the screws which retain the heater box in the engine compartment.

6. Remove the center console (speaker panel).

7. Remove the defroster hose plate and pull the defroster tubes out of the heater box.

8. Remove the heater trim panel and loosen the clip which retains the air control cable.

9. Remove the heater air control from the dash panel, disconnect the control cable from it, and lift out the heater assembly.

10. To remove the core from the heater box, pry off the spring clips which retain the front panel to the assembly.

11. Assemble and install in the reverse order of disassembly and removal. Following installation, bleed the heater in the same manner as described for the Midget.

Radio

The radios used in MGs are dealer installed or aftermarket units. It is therefore impossible to give specific procedures for these radios. The following information applies generally to all radios installed in MGs.

Care should be exercised during installation to prevent reversing the ground and power leads. Reversal of the leads will result in serious damage to the radio. The power lead may be identified by an in-line fuse holder. The ground lead is not fused.

Should the speaker require replacement, it must be replaced with one of the same impedance. A speaker of the proper impedance must also be used during initial radio installation (consult the radio manual). Failure to observe proper impedance can result in rapid transistor failure. When installing a second speaker, it is also necessary to maintain impedance at the proper level by using a fader control or altering the entire system to maintain the specified load.

CAUTION

Never operate a radio without load (no speaker), or with the speaker leads shorted together. This will result in transistor failure.

Windshield Wiper Motor

REMOVAL AND INSTALLATION

1. Disconnect the electrical wires from the wiper motor.

2. Remove the wiper arms and wiper arm pivot nuts.

3. Unbolt the motor and withdraw the motor complete with drive cables and wiper arm pivots and gearboxes.

4. Loosen the cover screws in each wiper arm gearbox and remove the rack housings.

5. Remove the wiper motor gearbox cover and disconnect the cross-head and rack from the motor.

Installation is in reverse order of removal. Do not kink or bind the drive cable in any way, and make sure that the wiper arm gearboxes are aligned correctly.

Instrument Cluster

REMOVAL AND INSTALLATION

Instruments are mounted individually in the panel and are removed by unbolting the panel and releasing the instrument brackets.

Fuse Box Location

The fuse box is located under the dash panel on the right-hand side.

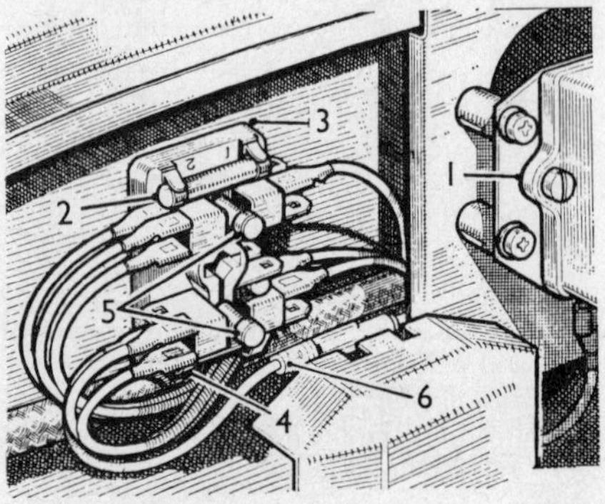

1. Regulator.
2. AUX. IGN. fuse (35-amp.).
3. Fuse block.
4. AUX. fuse (35-amp.).
5. Spare fuses.
6. Line fuse—heated back-light light (GT)

Regulator and fuse block, MGB

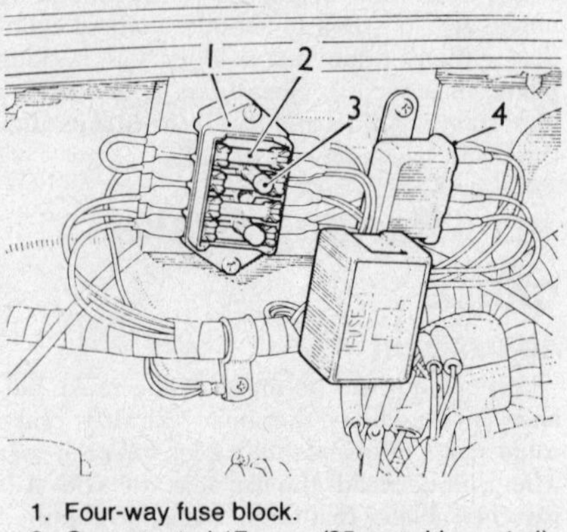

1. Four-way fuse block.
2. Current rated 17-amp. (35-amp. blow rated) fuses.
3. Spare fuses.
4. Starter solenoid.

Lucas type 7FJ fuse block, Midget

SPECIFICATIONS

INDEX

BEFORE SERVICING, SEE THE SAFETY NOTICE ON THE CONTENTS PAGE

INTRODUCTION

Chosen as a replacement for the Opel Manta (German produced), the Japanese Isuzu sports a 4-cylinder, single-over-head-cam engine displacing 1817 cc (110.8 cu. in.). This is the same engine as used in Chevrolet's series 5 "Luv."

Originally planned as an Oldsmobile product, Buick picked-up the model after Olds opted for a smaller Starfire instead of the, then, Isuzu "Gemini."

The Isuzu sports a 4-speed manual transmission, or an extra cost 3-speed Turbo Hydra-Matic, installed in a conventional, front-engine, rear-drive power train. A 5-speed manual became available in 1977. The engine is slightly smaller than the 1975 Manta (1817 cc to 1897 cc) and develops only one less horsepower.

SERIAL NUMBER IDENTIFICATION

Vehicle

The vehicle identification number is carried on an embossed plate attached to the top, left end of the instrument panel as seen from the driver's seat.

You can further understand your vehicle's identification number by referring to the Vehicle Identification Number Breakdown shown.

Engine

The engine serial number (different from the vehicle identification) is pressure-stamped on the top, right front corner of the engine block.

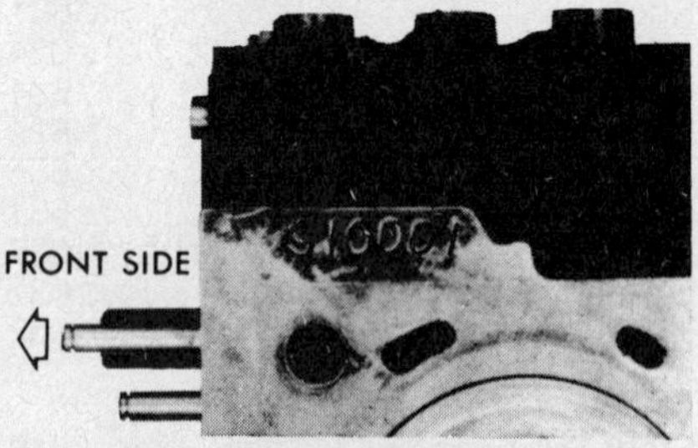

Engine serial number location

Transmissions

The Isuzu is equipped with either a 4-speed or 5-speed manual transmission, or optional 3-speed Turbo Hydra-Matic unit. The manual transmissions are conventionally designed fully synchronized units.

The Isuzu 200 automatic transmission is fully automatic and only requires foot pressure on the accelerator pedal to activate it. There is a three-element torque converter, a compound planetary gear set, multiple-disc clutches, a roller clutch and a band providing the elements required to drive the automobile.

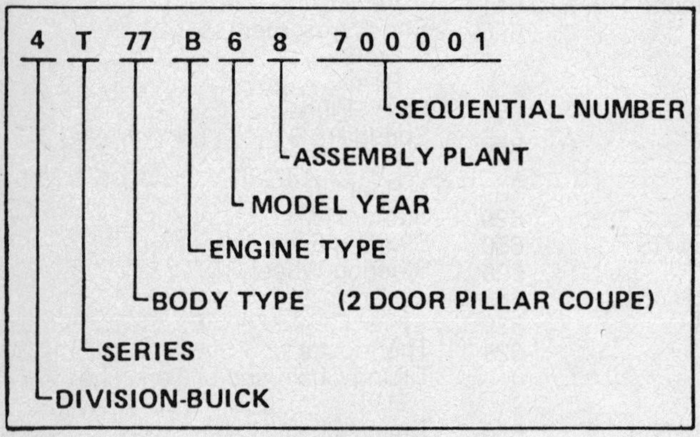

Vehicle identification breakdown

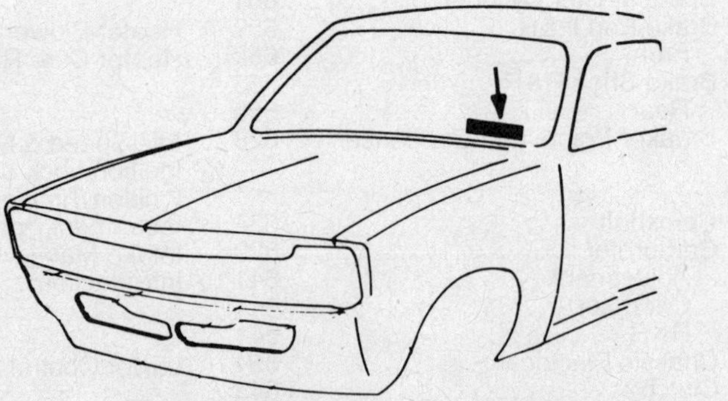

Vehicle identification number location

GENERAL ENGINE SPECIFICATIONS

Year	Engine Displacement (cu. in.)	Carburetor Type	Horsepower (@ rpm)	Torque @ rpm (ft. lbs.)	Bore x Stroke (in.)	Compression Ratio	Oil Pressure @ rpm (psi)
1976-79	110.8	Nikki 2V ①	80 @ 4800	95 @ 3000	3.31 x 3.23	8.5:1	56.88 @ 1400

① 1977-79 Nippon Co. Kikaki Co. Ltd.—2V

TUNE-UP SPECIFICATIONS

When analyzing compression test results, look for uniformity among cylinders, rather than specific pressures

Year	Engine Displacement (cu. in.)	Spark Plugs Type	Spark Plugs Gap (in.)	Distributor Point Dwell (deg)	Distributor Point Gap (in.)	Ignition Timing (deg) MT	Ignition Timing (deg) AT	Intake Valve Opens (deg)	Fuel Pump Pressure (psi)	Idle Speed (rpm)	Valve Clear (in.) (cold) In	Valve Clear (in.) (cold) Ex
1976-79	110.8	NGK-BPR6ES ①	0.030	52	0.018	6B	6B	21	3.3	700	0.006	0.010

NOTE: The underhood specifications sticker often reflects tune-up specification changes made in production. Sticker figures must be used if they disagree with this chart.
① AC-R44XLS
B Before top dead center

FIRING ORDER

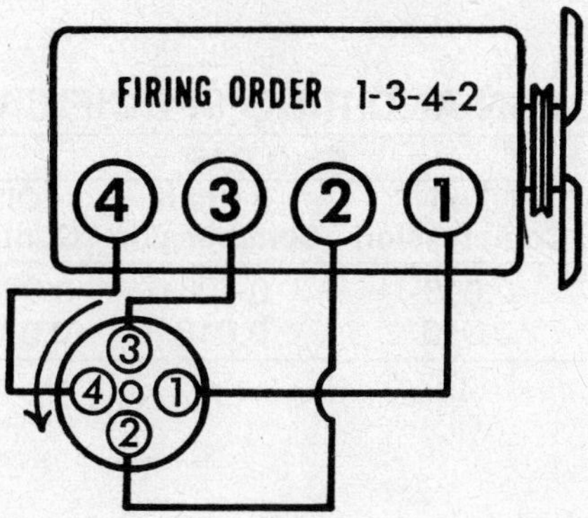

CAPACITIES

Year	Model	Engine Displacement (cu. in.)	Engine Crankcase (qts) With Filter	Engine Crankcase (qts) Without Filter	Transmission (pts) Manual 4-spd	Transmission (pts) Manual 5-spd	Transmission (pts) Automatic	Drive Axle (pts)	Gasoline Tank (gals)	Cooling System (qts) W/ AC	Cooling System (qts) W/O AC
1976-79	All	110.8	4.7	5.7	2.3	3.3	10½ ①	2½	13.7	6½ ②	6½ ②

① 1978-79—13 pts
② 1978-79—6.8

CRANKSHAFT AND CONNECTING ROD SPECIFICATIONS

All measurements are given in inches

Year	Engine Displacement (cu. in.)	Crankshaft Main Brg. Journal Dia.	Crankshaft Main Brg. Oil Clearance	Crankshaft Shaft End-Play	Crankshaft Thrust on No.	Connecting Rod Journal Diameter	Connecting Rod Oil Clearance	Connecting Rod Side Clearance
1976-79	110.8	2.205	0.0008-0.0025	0.0024-0.0094	3	1.929 ①	0.0007-0.0030	0.008-0.016

① 1977-79—1.926-1.927

VALVE SPECIFICATIONS

Year	Engine Displacement (cu. in.)	Seat Angle (deg)	Face Angle (deg)	Spring Test Pressure (lbs. @ in.)	Spring Installed Height (in.)	STEM TO GUIDE CLEARANCE (in.)		STEM DIAMETER (in.)	
						Intake	Exhaust	Intake	Exhaust
1976-79	11.8	45 ①	45	outer-34.5 @ 1.614 inner-20 @ 1.516	outer-1.61 inner-1.51	0.009-0.0022	0.0015-0.0031	0.315	0.315

① Because of the aluminum head and valve seat inserts, cut the valve seat with 15, 45 or 75 degree cutters. Use the minimum necessary to remove dents or damage, leaving the contact width inside the 0.0472-0.063 range.

PISTON AND RING SPECIFICATIONS

Year	Engine Displacement (cu. in.)	Piston Clearance	RING GAP			RING SIDE CLEARANCE		
			Top Compression	Bottom Compression	Oil Control	Top Compression	Bottom Compression	Oil Control
1976-79	110.8	0.001-0.0026	0.008-0.016	0.008-0.016	0.008-0.035	0.0010-0.0024	0.0010-0.0024	0.0008

ALTERNATOR AND REGULATOR SPECIFICATIONS

Year	Model	ALTERNATOR			REGULATOR						
						FIELD RELAY			REGULATOR		
		Part No. or Manufacturer	Field Current @ 12v	Output (amps)	Part No. or Manufacturer	Air Gap (in.)	Point Gap (in.)	Volts to Close	Air Gap (in.)	Point Gap (in.)	Volts @ 75°
1976	All	Hitachi	—	40	—	0.12	.030	4.9	.012	.015	14
1977-79	All	Nippon-Denso	—	40	Nippon-Denso	—	—	—	—	—	13.8-14.8

TORQUE SPECIFICATIONS

All readings in ft. lbs.

Year	Engine Displacement (cu. in.)	Cylinder Head Bolts	Rod Bearing Bolts	Main Bearing Bolts	Crankshaft Pulley Bolt	Flywheel to Crankshaft Bolts	MANIFOLDS	
							Intake	Exhaust
1976-79	110.8	72 ①	33	72	87	60	17	17

① Initially install the bolts, according to pattern, to 61 ft. lbs. Then torque to 72 ft. lbs.

TORQUE SEQUENCE

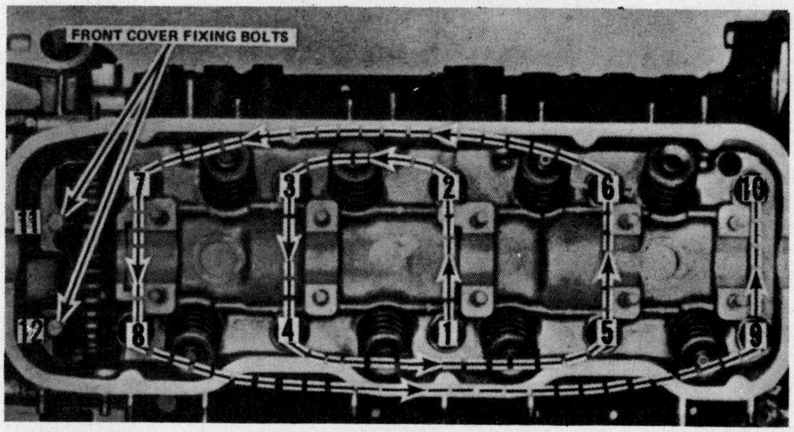

Cylinder head torque sequence

BATTERY AND STARTER SPECIFICATIONS

All cars use 12 volt, negative ground electrical systems

Year	Model	Battery Amp Hour Capacity	STARTER: Lock Test Amps	Lock Test Volts	Lock Test Torque (ft. lbs.)	No Load Test Amps	No Load Test Volts	No Load Test rpm	Brush Spring Tension (oz)	Min. Brush Length (in.)
1976-79	All	50	280-320	6 min.	N.A.	30-50	10.6	7300-8500	56	0.472

N.A. Not available

BRAKE SPECIFICATIONS

All measurements given are in. unless noted

Year	Model	Lug Nut Torque (ft. lbs.)	Master Cylinder Bore	Brake Disc Minimum Thickness	Brake Disc Maximum Run-Out	Brake Drum Diameter	Brake Drum Max. Machine O/S	Brake Drum Max. Wear Limit	Minimum Lining Thickness Front	Minimum Lining Thickness Rear
1976-79	All	30	0.875	.339	.006	8.98	9.04	9.06	.067	.040

WHEEL ALIGNMENT SPECIFICATIONS

Year	Model	Caster Range (deg)	Caster Preferred Setting (deg)	Camber Range (deg)	Camber Preferred Setting (deg)	Toe-In (in.)
1976-79	All	4P-6P	5P	½N-½P	0	⅛

TUNE-UP PROCEDURES

The Isuzu automobile comes equipped with a tune-up label in the engine compartment. This label has information developed during production. Should the information in any way disagree with the specifications given here, follow the label.

Spark Plugs

REMOVAL AND INSTALLATION

Before removing the spark plug leads, number the towers on the distributor cap with tape. Grasp each spark plug boot and pull it straight out. Check the condition of the rubber boot and replace if necessary. Install a rubber-lined spark plug socket on the plug's hex and remove it. If removal is difficult, loosen the plug only slightly and drip some light oil onto the threads. Allow the oil to penetrate and then unscrew the spark plug to prevent damaging the threads in the cylinder head. Be sure to keep the socket straight to avoid breaking the ceramic insulator. Inspect the plugs using the "Troubleshooting" section illustrations and then clean or discard them according to their condition. Recommended spark plug gap is given in the "Tune-up Specifications Chart." Use a spark plug wire gauge for checking the gap. The wire should pass through the electrodes with just a slight drag. Using the electrode bending tool on the end of the gauge, bend the side electrode to adjust the gap. Never attempt to adjust the center electrode. Lightly oil the threads of the replacement plug and install it hand-tight. The spark plugs should be tightened to a torque of 18-21 ft/lbs. Install the ignition wire boots firmly on the spark plugs.

Breaker Points and Condenser

REMOVAL AND INSTALLATION

Release the two clamps on either side of the distributor with a screwdriver.

After the cap is removed there will be a black bakelite piece with a brass "T" on one end. This is the rotor. Pull it straight up to remove. Under that will be a dustproof cover. Lift it out to expose the points.

Remove the two retaining screws and disconnect the wire leads and take out the point set. Examine them. If they are pitted, corroded, the contacts black or excessively worn, replace them. Check the tension on the breaker arm. If this seems loose it also indicates replacement. A slightly gray coating is alright, just take a small file (point file) and remove it. Check that the points meet squarely. If not, gently bend the fixed point mount.

The condenser is located just behind the vacuum control assembly and is removed by loosening the screw holding it to the distributor and disconnecting its lead wire (note

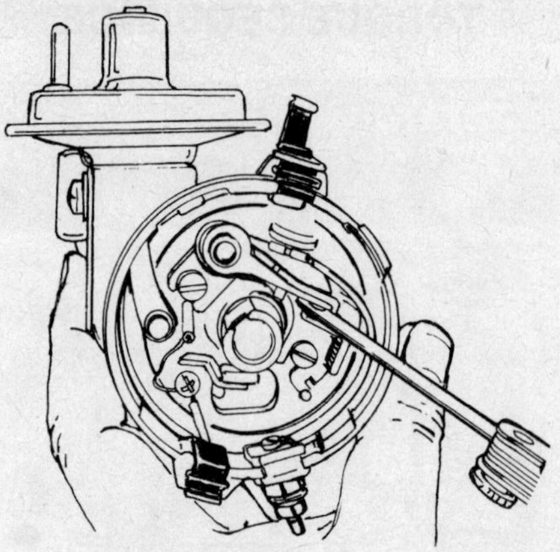

Measuring point gap with a feeler gauge

the order of removal of the insulators and washers).

To reassemble, reverse the procedure. Put the point set in the distributor and loosely tighten retaining screws. Plug the lead wire into the terminal assembly. Turn the crankshaft pulley (spark plugs removed) until the heel of the point set rubbing block is in contact with a high point on the cam lobe.

Using flat feeler gauges and a screwdriver, adjust the point gap to 0.018 inch and tighten the retaining screws all the way. Install the dust shield, rotor and the distributor cap.

Dwell Angle

Dwell angle is the number of degrees of distributor rotation when the points are closed. Setting the angle requires the use of a dwell meter. Timing must be checked after setting dwell, because a change of 1° in dwell angle causes a 2° change in ignition timing.

ADJUSTMENT

1. Connect the dwell meter according to the manufacturer's instructions.
2. Remove the high tension lead from the coil to the distributor. Crank the engine (turn the ignition key to "Start") and observe the dwell meter reading.
3. If the reading is incorrect, remove the distributor cap, rotor, and dust shield, and adjust the points. Reducing the point gap increases dwell, and vice versa.
4. After making adjustments, reconnect the high tension lead and check the dwell with the engine running. A variation of more than 3 degrees as engine speed is increased to 2500 rpm indicates worn distributor parts (shaft, bushings, or breaker plate).

Ignition Timing

ADJUSTMENT

The timing marks are located at the front of the crankshaft pulley and consist of a graduated degree scale attached to the engine block and a notch in the crankshaft pulley.

1. Set the dwell angle as outlined.
2. Locate the timing marks on the pulley and the front of the engine. Clean off the marks. Using chalk or white paint, color the proper degree number on the timing scale and the timing notch in the pulley to make them more visible. The proper degree setting can be found in the "Tune-up Specifications" chart or on the emission control decal in the engine compartment.
3. Connect a tachometer to the engine.
4. Connect a timing light to the engine according to the manufacturer's instructions. The engine is timed from the Number one spark plug (closest to the front of the car).
5. Disconnect the vacuum hose to the distributor at the distributor, and plug it with a pencil, a golf tee, or the like.
6. Check that all wires are clear of the fan and pulleys, and start the engine.
7. Adjust the idle to the correct setting.
8. Aim the timing light at the marks. If the marks are aligned under the flashes from the light, the timing is correct; shut off the engine. Loosen the distributor lockbolt (at the base of the distributor shaft) just enough to enable the distributor to be turned.
10. Start the engine. Aim the light at the timing marks. Slowly turn the distributor until the marks are aligned. Turning the distributor in the direction of rotor rotation will retard the spark (move it towards zero), and vice versa.
11. When the marks are aligned, tighten the distributor lockbolt, and recheck the timing. Shut off the engine, disconnect the equipment, and reconnect the vacuum hose.

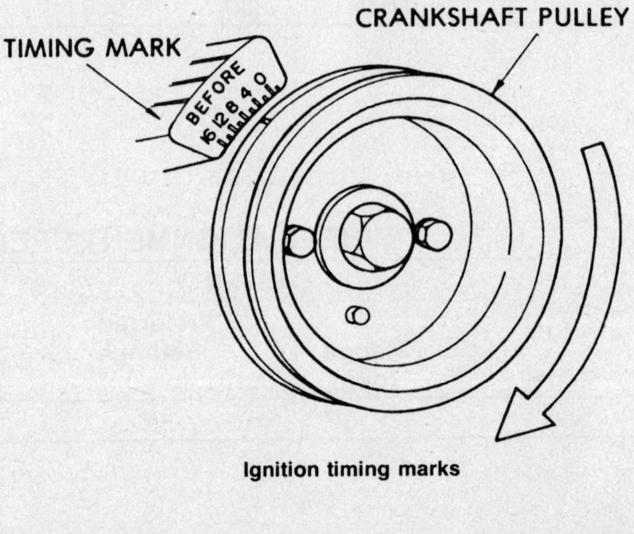

Ignition timing marks

Valve Lash

The valves in the Isuzu are driven by a single, overhead camshaft, acting directly on the rocker arms.

ADJUSTMENT

Valve adjustment should be carried out at every tune-up or whenever excessive valve noise is noticed. The engine must be dead cold.

1. Remove and tag the various hoses from the air cleaner, then unbolt and remove it.
2. Disconnect the accelerator cable from the carburetor, and remove and tag the various wires and hoses crossing the valve cover. Remove the valve cover.
3. Remove the spark plugs. Use a wrench on the crankshaft pulley bolt to rotate the crankshaft until the notch in the pulley is aligned with the "O" mark on the timing scale. This places the engine at TDC.
4. Before adjusting the valves, be sure all of the rocker shaft bracket nuts are tightened to 16 ft/lbs.
5. Half of the valves will be compressed, half will be free. Adjust the free valves to the correct clearance, as specified in the "Tune-up Specifications" chart. Use a flat feeler gauge to measure the clearance. Note that the clearances are different for intake and exhaust valves. The intake valves are on the carburetor side of the engine, the exhaust valves are on the other.

Adjustment is made by loosening the locknut above the valve on the rocker arm, then loosening or tightening the adjuster with a screwdriver. If correctly done, there will be a slight drag on the flat feeler gauge as it is pulled through. Hold the adjuster with the screwdriver and tighten the locknut. Recheck the adjustment.

6. Rotate the crankshaft one complete turn, aligning the pulley notch with the "O" mark again. The other set of valves will now be free. Adjust them in the same manner.
7. After all adjustments are made, replace the valve cover, using a new gasket and sealer. Replace the carburetor linkage, the various emission and vacuum hoses, the spark plugs and wires, and the air cleaner.

Number of Cylinders	1		2		3		4	
Valve Arrangement	Exh.	In.	In.	Exh.	Exh.	In.	In.	Exh.
When piston in No. 1 cylinder is held at T.D.C.	0	0	0		0			
When piston in No. 4 cylinder is held at T.D.C.				0		0	0	0

Valve adjusting sequence

CARBURETOR

The engine is equipped with a Nikki, down-draft, 2-barrel carburetor. The primary venturi operates at relatively low speed and load. The secondary side opens when engine load and speed are increased. The unit is equipped with an electric automatic choke for easier starting at low temperatures.

IDLE SPEED AND MIXTURE

As with all adjustments made with the engine running, set the parking brake, block the drive wheels and put the transmission in Neutral. Warm the engine to operating temperature, check to make sure the choke is open, turn off the air conditioner (if installed), install the air cleaner and disconnect the distributor and idle compensator vacuum line and plug them.

1. Turn the idle mixture adjusting screw all the way in and back it out three (3) turns.

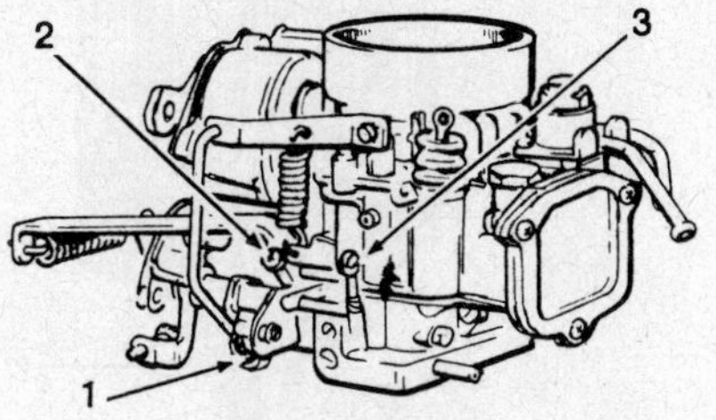

1. Fast idle screw
2. Idle speed screw
3. Idle mixture screw

Carburetor adjustments

2. Adjust the throttle adjusting screw to 900 rpm.
3. Go back to the idle mixture screw and turn it in and out, until reaching a point where the idle is the highest. Reset the throttle adjusting screw to 900 rpm.
4. Turn the idle mixture adjusting screw clockwise (lean) until down to 850 rpm. Then turn the screw ½ turn clockwise (rich).
5. Reset the throttle adjusting screw to 900 rpm.
6. Reconnect the vacuum lines.

NOTE: If equipped with air conditioning, add the following steps.

7. Turn the air conditioning on to maximum and set the blower on high. Open the throttle about ⅓ and allow it to close (this opens the speed-up solenoid).
8. Set idle to 900 rpm with the speed-up controller adjusting screw.

ENGINE ELECTRICAL

Distributor

REMOVAL AND INSTALLATION

1. Remove the distributor cap.
2. Disconnect the vacuum hose.
3. Scribe matchmarks on the distributor body and the engine block.
4. Scribe another mark on the distributor body to indicate the position of the rotor.
5. Disconnect the primary wires.
6. Remove the distributor clamp bolt and clamp and remove the distributor.

NOTE: Do not rotate the engine with the distributor removed, if possible.

7. To install, if the engine was cranked while the distributor was removed, turn the crankshaft until the No. 1 cylinder is at the top of the compression stroke. This can be determined by feeling compression with your thumb through the spark plug hole. The crankshaft pulley notch should be aligned with the "O" mark on the timing scale. Slide the distributor into the engine with the rotor aligned with the No. 1 firing position, until the shaft engages the oil pump slot.
8. If the engine has not been cranked, slide the distributor into place, aligning the matchmarks made during removal.
9. Install the hold-down clamp and bolt, but do not tighten. Install the cap and wires. Set the timing and tighten the clamp. Reconnect the vaccum line.

Alternator

PRECAUTIONS

When making connections always insure against mistakenly reversing the polarity (hooking a "+" wire to a "−" pole) this will cause a short and burn out the diodes.

Do not connect the alternator "B" terminal to a ground. This terminal is connected to the battery and will cause it to short, burning out the wires.

Whenever charging the battery, always remove the negative cable. Not doing so can burn out the diodes due to the pulse voltage of the charger.

Keep the alternator dry.

REMOVAL AND INSTALLATION

1. Disconnect the negative cable from the battery.
2. Remove the stone shield and two lower attaching bolts.
3. Remove the horn and disconnect all wiring from the alternator.

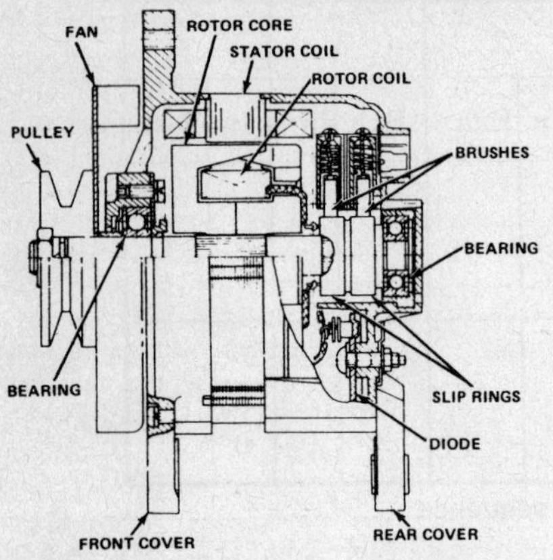

Cross section of alternator—typical

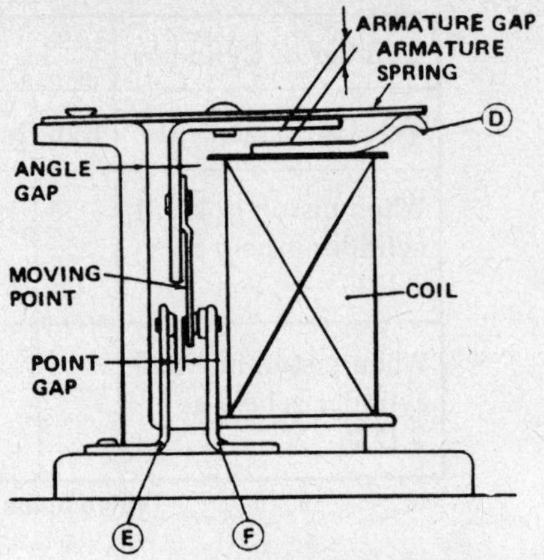

Voltage regulator adjustment

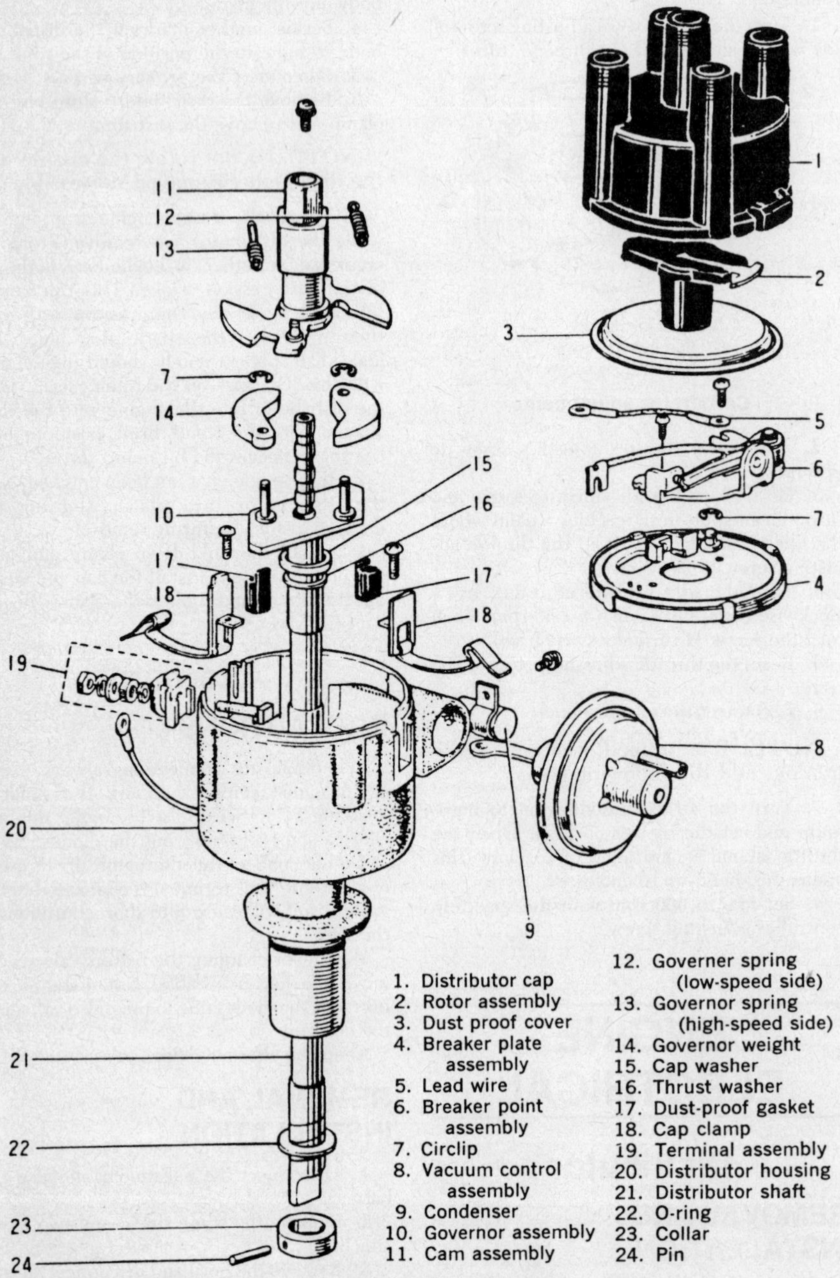

1. Distributor cap
2. Rotor assembly
3. Dust proof cover
4. Breaker plate assembly
5. Lead wire
6. Breaker point assembly
7. Circlip
8. Vacuum control assembly
9. Condenser
10. Governor assembly
11. Cam assembly
12. Governer spring (low-speed side)
13. Governor spring (high-speed side)
14. Governor weight
15. Cap washer
16. Thrust washer
17. Dust-proof gasket
18. Cap clamp
19. Terminal assembly
20. Distributor housing
21. Distributor shaft
22. O-ring
23. Collar
24. Pin

Exploded view of distributor

4. Remove the top bolt and take off the belt, the adjusting bracket and bolt. Remove the alternator.

5. Installation is the reverse. Adjust the belt tension after installation.

BELT TENSION ADJUSTMENT

Loosen all attaching bolts and, using your hand or a lever, apply enough pressure to the alternator housing to give the belt about ½ in. play halfway along its length.

Regulator

The voltage regulator is a separate unit and not attached to the alternator. The unit actually contains two parts: the voltage regulator and a voltage relay.

REMOVAL AND INSTALLATION

You will find the voltage regulator protective box behind the windshield washer tank. Removing the two sheet metal screws holding it to the inside of the fender-well will allow you to remove it. Unplug the unit from the harness. Installation is just the reverse.

AIR GAP VOLTAGE ADJUSTMENT

Connect a voltmeter between the condenser lead and the ground with all electrical loads disconnected including the blower relay connector.

Start the engine and increase engine speed gradually. The voltage should climb with the rpms up to 1400-1850 rpm. A normal condition is indicated when the voltage is between 13.5 and 14.5 volts.

If the voltage is too high, bend core arm "D" down. If too low, bend the arm up.

If bending the core arm does not correct the voltage difference, go on to a point gap adjustment.

Disconnect the battery ground cable and depress the armature until the moving point contacts "E" side point. Bend point arm "E" to get a gap of 0.012 or more.

Release the pressure and by bending point arm "F" set a distance of 0.012-0.018. After the adjustments are made, recheck the voltage. Repeat, if necessary.

Starter

REMOVAL AND INSTALLATION

Without air conditioning, the entire starter removal process may be done through the engine compartment. With air conditioning, you will have to jack the car and, using U-joint and extensions, reach from beneath over the crossmember and behind the solenoid to remove the starter-to-flywheel-housing nut and washer.

1. Disconnect the negative cable from the battery and the wiring to the solenoid.

2. Remove the starter-to-flywheel-housing top retaining nut and washer and the lower

retaining bolt. This will allow you to lift the starter forward, to clear the stud, and remove it from the engine compartment.

3. Reverse Steps 1 and 2 for installation.

STARTER DRIVE

Removal and Installation

1. Remove solenoid.
2. Pry off dust cover, remove snap ring and washer.
3. Remove the two through bolts.
4. Remove the cover assembly.
5. Separate the yoke and gear case.
6. Remove the armature shift lever.
7. Remove drive assembly snap-ring and retainer.
8. Slide drive assembly from shaft.
9. Assembly is the reverse.

NOTE: When installing armature, set shift lever on lever guide of pinion assembly. Do not turn armature after installation as shift lever may come off guide.

1. Armature assembly
2. Snap ring
3. Thrust washer
4. Thrust washer
5. Retainer
6. Snap ring
7. Yoke assembly
8. Field coil assembly
9. Screw
10. Brush (+)
11. Rear cover assembly
12. Rear cover bushing
13. Pinion assembly
14. Gear case assembly
15. Gear case bushing
16. Brush holder assembly
17. Brush (−)
18. Brush spring

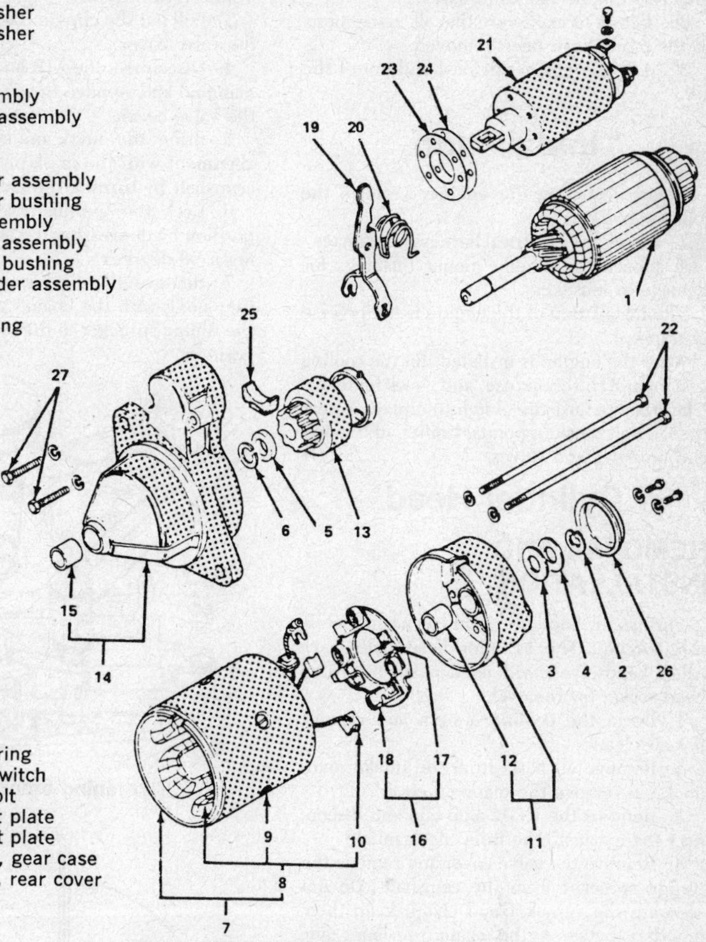

19. Shift lever
20. Torsion spring
21. Magnetic switch
22. Through-bolt
23. Adjustment plate
24. Adjustment plate
25. Dust cover, gear case
26. Dust cover, rear cover
27. Bolt

Exploded view of starter

ENGINE MECHANICAL

Removal and Installation

There are several basic precautions you must take if you plan on removing the engine and transmission.

1. Handle all aluminum alloy parts with extreme care. They are easily damaged.
2. Keep the nut and bolt combinations in separate locations to prevent mixing them. They vary in design and composition, depending on their position and use.
3. Remove and install the engine and transmission as a unit.

Removal

1. Remove the battery cables.
2. Outline the position of the mounting hinges on the hood and remove it.

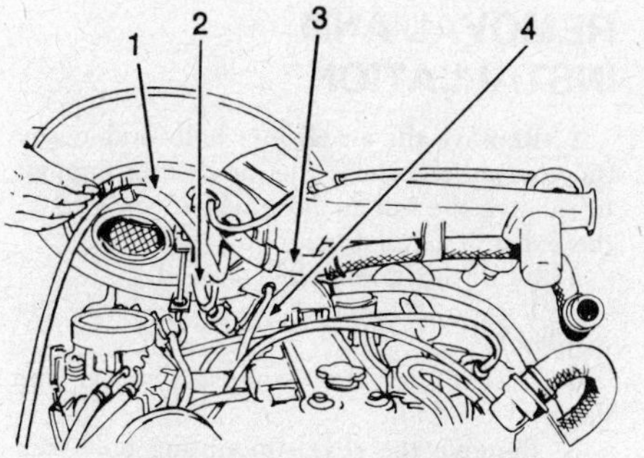

1. CCS-to-hot idle compensator hose
2. PCV hose
3. AIR hose
4. CCS-to-thermosensor hose

Air cleaner hose connections

3. Remove the engine under-cover and drain the cooling system by opening the drains on the radiator and block.
4. Drain the oil from the crankcase.
5. Disconnect all hoses connected to the air cleaner and remove the air cleaner.
6. Disconnect the CCS hose and remove the manifold cover.
7. Unplug the alternator wiring.
8. Disconnect the exhaust pipe from the manifold.
9. Free the clutch control cable by turning the adjusting unit.
10. Disconnect the heater hoses from the engine, and the heater.
11. Remove the cable from the water petcock and remove the petcock and hose.
12. Attach the engine lift brackets to the exhaust manifold stud bolts.
13. Disconnect the ground cable from the frame.
14. Remove fuel hoses from the carburetor.
15. Disconnect all ignition wires.
16. Remove the vacuum hose from the rear part of the intake manifold.
17. Remove the accelerator cable and all wiring from the carburetor.
18. Disconnect the starter motor connections.
19. Disconnect the thermo-unit, and oil pressure switch.
20. Unplug the back-up light switch and top/third switch (neutral switch wiring for California models) at the rear part of the engine.
21. Remove the ECS hose from the oil pan.
22. Remove the engine mounting nut and stopper plate.
23. Install engine lift brackets using one intake manifold stud bolt and one engine hanger mounting stud.
24. Raise the engine slightly and remove the left side engine mounting stopper plate.
25. Remove the top and lower water hoses from the outlet pipe and radiator, respectively.
26. Remove the nuts holding the radiator and remove it by pulling upwards.
27. From inside the car, remove the bolts holding the gearshift lever and remove the unit.
28. Remove the parking brake return spring.
29. Unbolt the driveshaft at the axle flange and remove it from the vehicle.
30. Remove the clutch cable heat protector.
31. Remove the clutch return spring.
32. Disconnect the clutch cable from the lever and engine torque rod.
33. Remove the exhaust pipe bracket from the transmission.
34. Remove the speedometer cable.

35. Slightly lift the engine and remove the four rear engine mounting bolts.
36. Check to make sure that all connections to the frame have been removed.
37. Lift the engine forward and out of the car.

Installation

Before installing the engine, perform the following steps:
1. Check the electrical harness for damage.
2. Check the engine mount bushings for damage or looseness.

The installation of the engine is the reverse of removal.

After the engine is installed, fill the cooling system and the crankcase, and check for leaks. Check and adjust the clutch free-play. Adjust the fan belt tension, points, timing, idle speed and mixture, and valves.

Cylinder Head

REMOVAL AND INSTALLATION

Perform this operation only on a completely cold engine. The cylinder head bolts have Allen heads; you will need a special Allen head socket for removal.
1. Drain the cooling system and remove the air cleaner.
2. Remove all parts from the intake manifold and remove the manifold cover.
3. Remove the EGR pipe clip and disconnect the exhaust pipe from the manifold.
4. Remove the valve cover and remove the timing sprocket from the camshaft. Do not separate the sprocket and chain; keep them together between the chain tensioner and guide.
5. Disconnect the AIR hoses from the check valve and air pump. Remove the air bypass valve bracket and valve.
6. Remove the two bolts from the cylinder head to the front cover and remove the head bolts. Remove the cylinder head complete with intake and exhaust manifolds.

To reinstall the cylinder head, reverse the removal procedures.

NOTE: Make sure to wipe the faces of the cylinder head and block absolutely clean. Apply a thin coat of sealer around the cam chain opening before installing the new head gasket; be careful not to drip any sealer into the block. Apply engine oil to the threaded portions of the head bolts.

When installing, tighten the head bolts evenly to 61 ft/lbs. Again, do it in sequence.

After the installation is complete, check the valve timing.

OVERHAUL

See Engine Rebuilding Section.

Rocker Shafts

REMOVAL AND INSTALLATION

1. Remove the air cleaner.
2. Disconnect the accelerator control cable from the carburetor.
3. Pull out the clips and ignition wires from the valve cover.
4. Disconnect the AIR hose from the intake manifold and remove the PCV hose. Remove the valve cover.
5. Bring the mark on the camshaft into alignment with the mark on the No. 1 rocker arm shaft by turning the crankshaft.
6. Lock the automatic chain adjuster in position by depressing the slide pin and rotating it 90 degrees.
7. Remove the timing sprocket from the cam along with the chain. Make sure to hold the timing sprocket to the chain, keeping it in position.

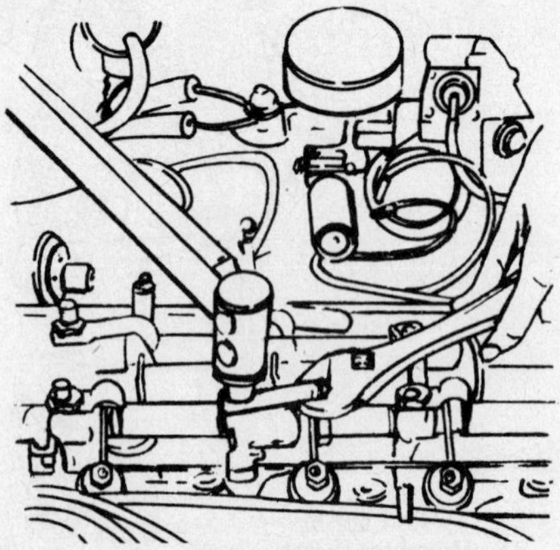

Tightening bracket nuts

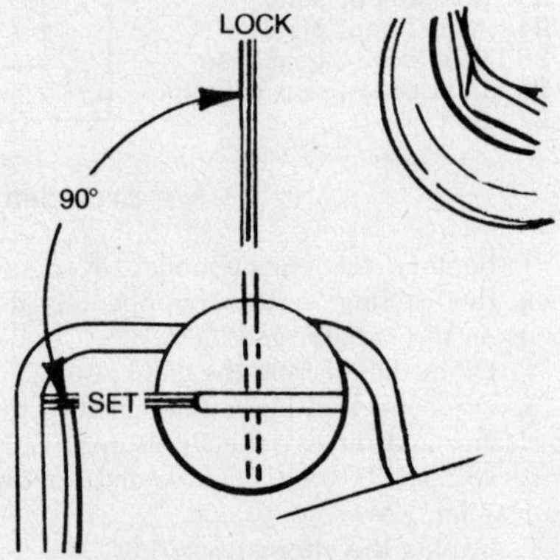

Locking the chain adjuster

8. Loosen the nuts holding the rocker arm shaft a little at a time. Loosen them in sequence, starting on the outside. Remove the nuts and rocker assembly.

To install:
1. Apply a good amount of new oil to the cam and bearing faces before attempting installation. Do the same with the rocker arms and shaft.
2. Align the rocker arm shaft brackets with the stud bolts on the head.

NOTE: Make sure the punch mark at the end of the rocker shaft is pointed upward.

3. Make sure the mark on the cam and the mark on the No. 1 rocker shaft align.
4. Snug-down the rocker arm shaft nuts evenly and then tighten them fully to 16 ft/lbs. Hold the rocker arm springs with an adjustable wrench.

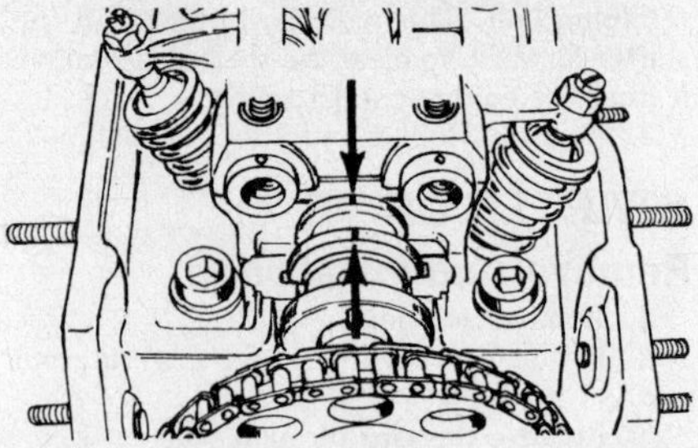

Aligning marks for camshaft installation

5. Install the timing sprocket by aligning the dowel pin hold and tighten to 58 ft/lbs.
6. Apply liquid gasket to the arched portion of the plugs and install them.
7. Set the automatic chain adjuster by turning the slide pin back 90 degrees (counterclockwise).

NOTE: After chain adjuster is set, check for proper chain tension.

8. Adjust the valve clearances and reinstall the remaining parts by reversing their removal.

Intake Manifold

REMOVAL AND INSTALLATION

1. Drain the cooling system completely. Any coolant remaining will flow into the cylinders when the manifold is removed.
2. Remove and tag the various hoses from the air cleaner, then unbolt and remove it.
3. Remove the coolant hose from the outlet pipe at the front of the manifold, and the two heater hoses from the rear of the manifold.
4. Disconnect the fuel line, accelerator cable, vacuum hose, and choke and solenoid wiring at the carburetor.
5. Disconnect the vacuum hose from the manifold.
6. Disconnect the EGR pipe.
7. Remove the eight intake manifold bolts and the bolt for the coolant hose clip and remove the manifold.
8. Installation is the reverse of removal. Use a new gasket. Tighten the manifold bolts in a circular pattern from the center outwards in two stages.

Exhaust Manifold

REMOVAL AND INSTALLATION

1. Remove the air cleaner bolts and loosen the clamp bolt. Raise the air cleaner enough to remove the hot air hose which connects to the exhaust manifold shroud.
2. Remove the manifold shroud.
3. Disconnect the EGR pipe from the manifold.
4. Disconnect the exhaust pipe at the flange.
5. Remove the seven mounting bolts and the exhaust manifold.
6. Installation is the reverse. Use new gaskets and tighten the mounting bolts evenly, working in a pattern from the center outwards.

Crankshaft Pulley and Front Cover

The Isuzu is equipped with a chain-driven over-head cam. The chain is located behind the engine front cover.

REMOVAL AND INSTALLATION

1. Remove the fan and belts. Drain the cooling system and remove the hoses from the water pump.
2. Remove the oil pan and remove the crankshaft pulley bolt from under the engine. Remove the pulley together with pulley boss.
3. Remove the oil filter and the distributor. Remove the oil pump pickup tube from the oil pump.
4. Remove the nine cover bolts and pull off the cover, together with the water and oil pumps.

To install:

1. Install a new gasket on the cylinder block.
2. Turn the punch-marked side of the oil pump drive gear to the filter side of the engine. Align the center of the dowel pin with the alignment mark on the oil pump case.
3. Bring pistons No. 1 and 4 to top dead center by aligning the "O" timing mark with the pulley keyway.
4. Attach the front cover by engaging the pinion gear with the oil pump drive gear.
5. Make sure that the punch mark on the drive gear is turned to the rear, as seen through the gap between the front cover and block.

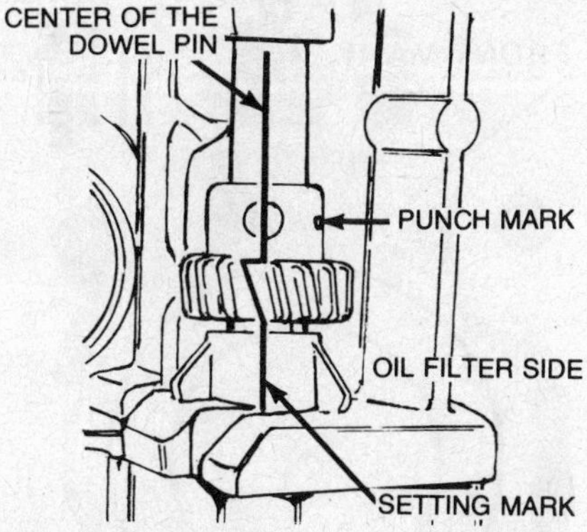

Oil pump alignment for installation of front cover

Punch mark in correct position

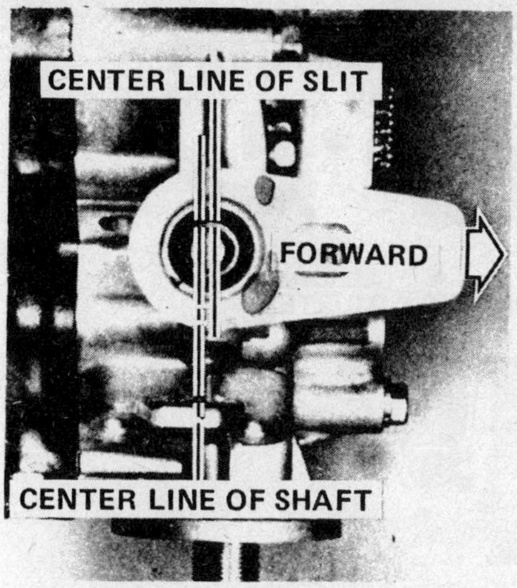

Shaft in correct position

6. Check that the slit at the end of the oil pump shaft is parallel with the front face of the block and that it is offset forward.
7. After checking for the exact settings, secure the front cover assembly.

FRONT COVER OIL SEAL REPLACEMENT

1. Remove the fan, belts and crank pulley.
2. Pry off the old oil seal.
3. Fill the gap between the lips of the new seal with grease and install the seal to the front cover, using an installer or other suitable tool.
4. Apply oil to the oil seal fitting face of the crank pulley and install, tightening the pulley bolt to 87 ft/lbs.

Timing Chain and Tensioner

REMOVAL

1. Remove front cover.
2. Pull out the crankshaft pinion gear and remove the chain with the camshaft timing sprocket.
3. Remove the two chain guide bolts and remove the guide.

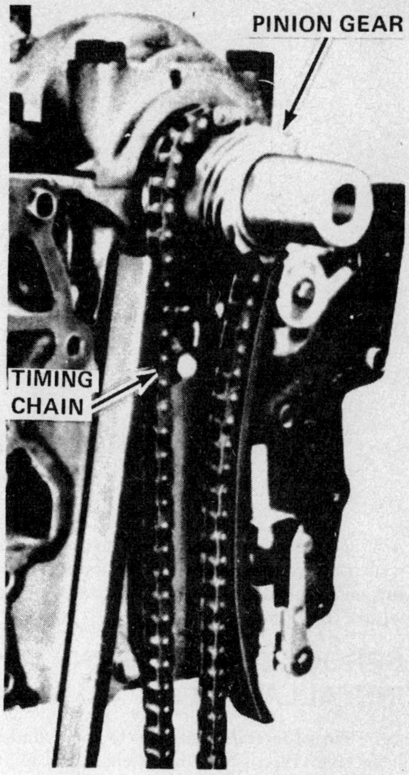

Crankshaft gear and timing chain

4. Remove the snap rings from both the chain adjuster and tensioner and remove.

INSTALLATION

1. Install the guide by aligning the groove in the guide with the cutaway portion of the oil jet.

NOTE: Check that the oil port in the jet is free of restrictions. The oil jet should be installed so the oil port is pointed in toward the crankshaft.

2. Assemble the chain tensioner to the set pin and secure it with a snap ring.
3. Assemble the automatic adjuster locking plate with the curved arm as shown in the illustration.

NOTE: If these parts are not properly assembled, the chain tensioner will not contact the curved arm smoothly.

Chain guide position

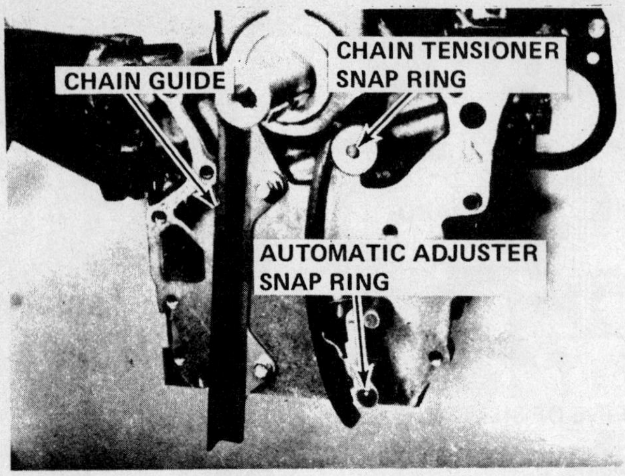

Chain tensioner and adjuster

4. Connect the automatic adjuster slide pin with the pivot pin so that the slide pin head is turned toward the cylinder head side. Secure with a snap ring.

SPROCKET AND CHAIN INSTALLATION

1. Turn the crankshaft key to the cylinder head side. Install the timing chain and align the mark plate on the chain with the aligning mark on the crankshaft sprocket as follows:
   a. The side of the chain with the plate must be on the front side of the engine.
   b. The part of the chain with the most links between the mark plates, must be positioned toward the chain guide side.
2. Install the camshaft sprocket so the aligning mark side is on the front side of the engine. Match the aligning mark (triangle) with the mark plate.
3. Install the pinion gear to the crankshaft so the groove faces the front cover. Reassemble the front cover, belts and fan.

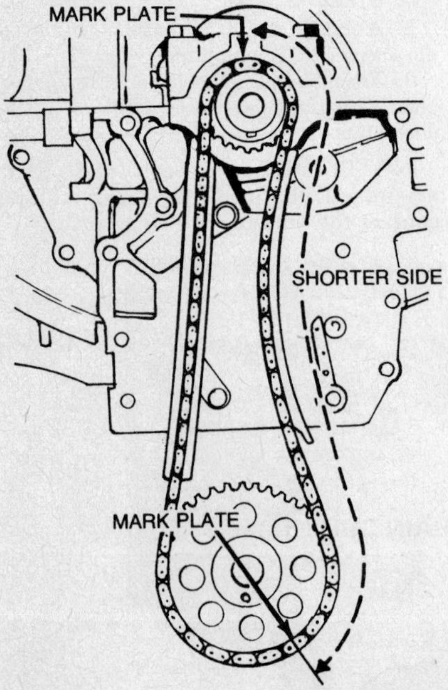

Sprocket and chain installation

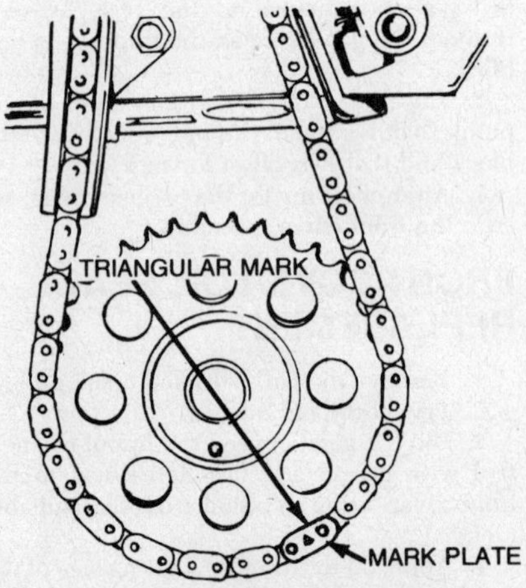

Timing sprocket installation

Camshaft

REMOVAL

1. Remove the air cleaner.
2. Disconnect the accelerator control cable.
3. Remove all wires and hoses connected to the valve cover.
4. Disconnect the AIR vacuum hose from the intake manifold.
5. Disconnect the PCV hose, take out the four bolts and remove the valve cover.
6. Turn the crankshaft so that the mark on the camshaft aligns with the mark on the No. 1 rocker arm shaft.
7. Lock the automatic chain adjuster by depressing the slide pin downward and turning it clockwise 90°.
8. Remove the timing sprocket and chain. Keep the timing chain in position on the sprocket.
9. Loosen the rocker arm bracket bolts a little at a time, starting with the outer ones, and remove the rocker arm assemblies.

INSTALLATION

1. Thoroughly coat all parts with clean engine oil before assembly.
2. Position camshaft on head.
3. Install rocker arm assemblies. Check that the punch mark at the end of the shaft is turned upward.
4. Bring the camshaft mark into alignment with the mark on the No. 1 rocker bracket by turning the camshaft.
5. Tighten rocker shaft bolts evenly to 16 ft/lbs. Hold the rocker arm springs with an adjustable wrench to prevent them from turning.
6. Align the dowel pin hole and install the timing sprocket and chain on the camshaft. Torque bolt to 58 ft/lbs.
7. Apply sealer to the arched portion of the plug and install it in the front of the head.
8. Set the timing chain adjuster by turning the slide pin 90° counterclockwise.
9. Check valve adjustment.
10. Install remaining parts in reverse order of removal.

Pistons and Connecting Rods

REMOVAL AND INSTALLATION

See the "Engine Rebuilding" section. Upon installation, the piston mark should face forward, the cylinder number mark on the face of the connecting rods should be turned toward the starter side of the block, and the numbers on the rods and rod bearing caps should align.

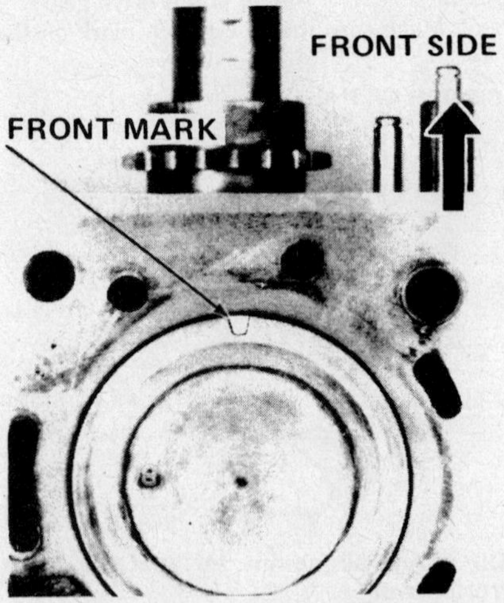

Position of correctly installed piston

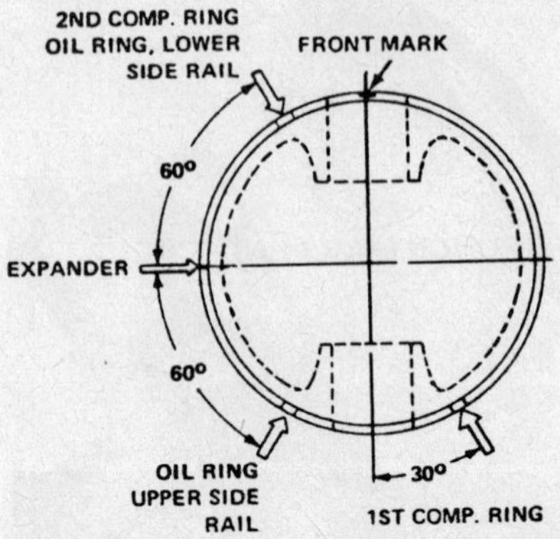

Position of piston rings

ENGINE LUBRICATION

Oil Pan

REMOVAL

1. Remove the oil pressure switch from the block.

NOTE: If you have an oil pressure gauge, remove the pressure unit and switch, together with the adapter.

2. Remove the 14 bolts and six nuts in the pan edge and remove. This will expose the two dust cover bolts. Remove them and drop the undercover.

INSTALLATION

1. Apply a thin coating of liquid gasket (RTV type) to the areas shown in the illustration.
2. Align the gasket with the bolt holes and install the pan. Tighten the bolts and nuts evenly to 3.6 ft/lbs. Check the edge of the gasket to see it is set correctly.

Rear Main Oil Seal

REPLACEMENT

1. Remove the clutch pressure plate assembly.
2. Flatten the flywheel bolt lockplates and remove the flywheel.
3. using a screwdriver, pry off the oil seal from the retainer.
4. Fill the gap between the lips of the new seal with grease and apply engine oil to the seal fitting face of the crank. Apply a thin coat of oil to the fitting face of the seal, and install the new seal with a setting tool.

NOTE: After installation, check that the flanged part of the seal is properly seated on the retainer.

5. Install the remaining parts in reverse of removal and, using new lock plates, tighten the flywheel bolts to 69 ft/lbs.

Oil Pump

REMOVAL

1. Remove the rocker cover.
2. Remove the distributor.
3. Remove the oil pan.
4. Remove the oil pickup tube.
5. Remove the oil pump mounting bolts and remove the pump from the front cover.
6. To install: Align the camshaft mark with the No. 1 rocker arm shaft bracket mark. Align the crankshaft pulley timing notch with the "O" mark on the timing scale.
7. Install the driven rotor, aligning its mark next to that of the drive rotor.
8. Install the pump assembly: engage the pump drive gear with the pinion gear on the crankshaft. The alignment mark on the drive gear must be turned rearward and away from the crankshaft by approximately 20° (clockwise).
9. Check installation: the mark on the oil pump drive gear must be turned to the rear

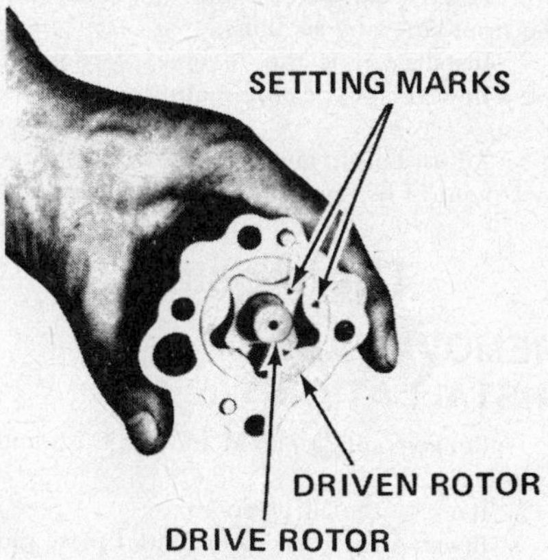

Driven and drive rotor marks aligned

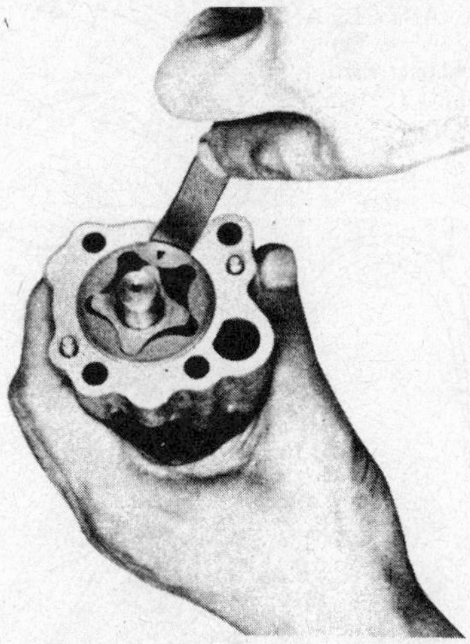

Checking outer rotor-to-case clearance

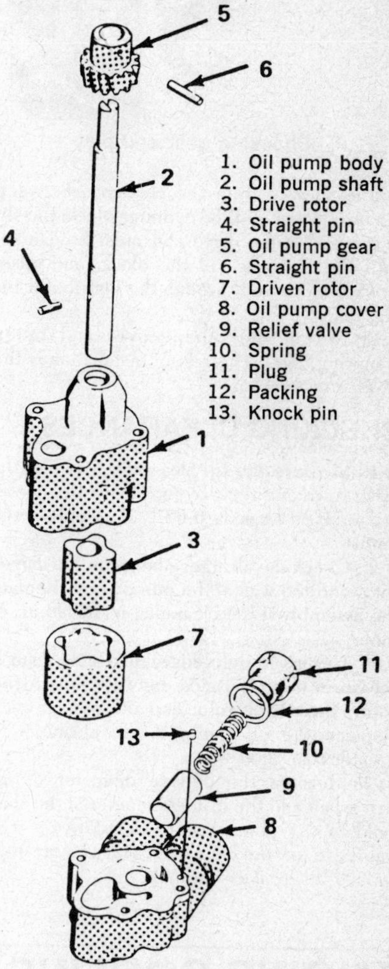

Exploded view of oil pump

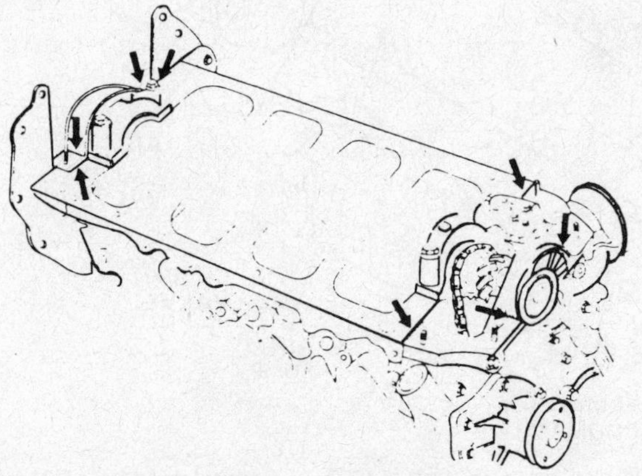

Liquid gasket application points

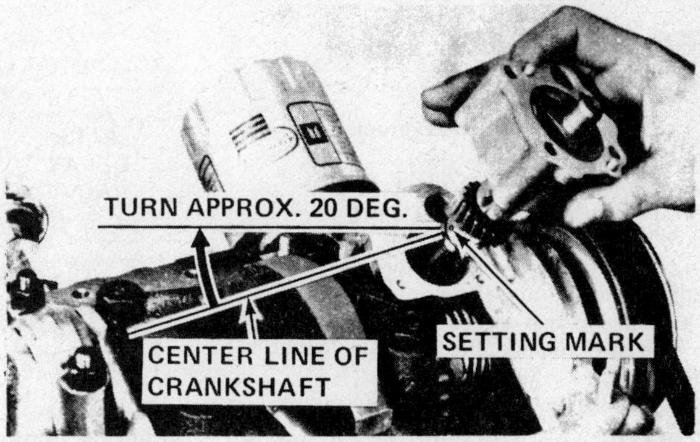

Installing oil pump

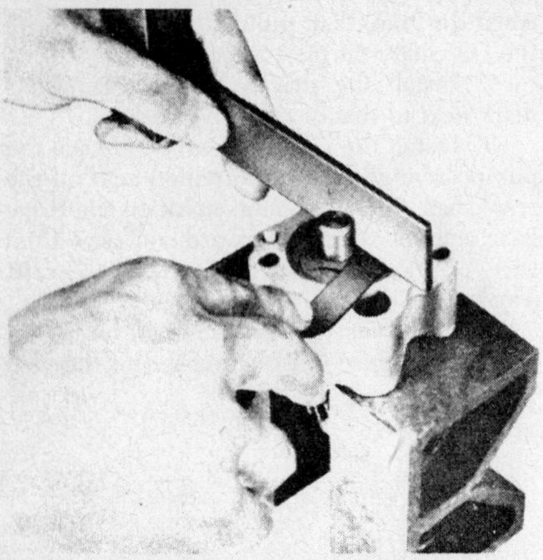

Checking gear end play

side as viewed from the clearance between the front cover and the cylinder block; the slit at the end of the driveshaft must be parallel with the front face of the block, and offset forward as viewed through the distributor fitting hole.

10. Install the pump cover and pump mounting bolts. The rest of installation is the reverse of removal.

CHECKING CLEARANCES

1. Measure the tip clearance between the drive rotor and the driven rotor with a feeler gauge. If it exceeds 0.0079 in., replace the unit.
2. Check the clearance between the driven rotor and the wall of the pump body. Replace the assembly if the clearance is 0.0098 in. or more.
3. Using a straight-edge and a feeler gauge, measure the clearance between the drive rotor, the driven rotor and the pump cover. Replace the oil pump if the clearance is greater than 0.0079 in.
4. Measure the outside diameter of the driveshaft and the inside diameter of the shaft hold in the pump cover. Compare the two values to get the clearance. If it is more than 0.0098 in., replace the unit.

ENGINE COOLING

Radiator

REMOVAL AND INSTALLATION

1. Disconnect the battery ground cable at the battery.
2. Remove the splash shield (4 bolts).
3. Drain the radiator and loosen and remove the top and bottom hoses. Remove and plug the transmission cooler lines if equipped with automatic transmission.
4. Remove two nuts and lift the radiator straight up to remove. Be careful not to hit the fan.
5. Installation is the reverse procedure.

NOTE: To fill cooling system, use a 50% water to antifreeze solution.

Water Pump

REMOVAL AND INSTALLATION

1. Disconnect battery ground cable.
2. Remove the splash shield (4 bolts).
3. Drain the cooling system and remove the fan (4 nuts).
4. Remove air pump and generator bolts and both drive belts.
5. Remove the fan pulley.
6. Remove the water pump. It is secured to the front cover by six bolts.
7. Installation is the reverse of removal; use a new gasket. Be sure mating surfaces are clean.
8. Adjust belt to give a ½″ deflection at the mid-point of its longest straight stretch.

Thermostat

REMOVAL AND INSTALLATION

1. Remove splash shield and drain cooling system.
2. Remove the air cleaner.
3. Remove the thermostat outlet pipe and water hose and remove the thermostat from the intake manifold.
4. Installation is the reverse procedure; use a light coating of gasket sealer on the outlet pipe gasket before installation.

EMISSION CONTROLS

Positive Crankcase Ventilation

The positive crankcase ventilation system (PCV) forces blow-by gases, generated in the crankcase, back into the intake manifold to the engine for burning.

It is a closed-type system with a baffle plate to remove oil particles from the gases and a regulating orifice to control the amount of suction needed to draw the gases off.

SERVICE

Clean all hoses, inside and out, and blow away any dirt with compressed air. Check the

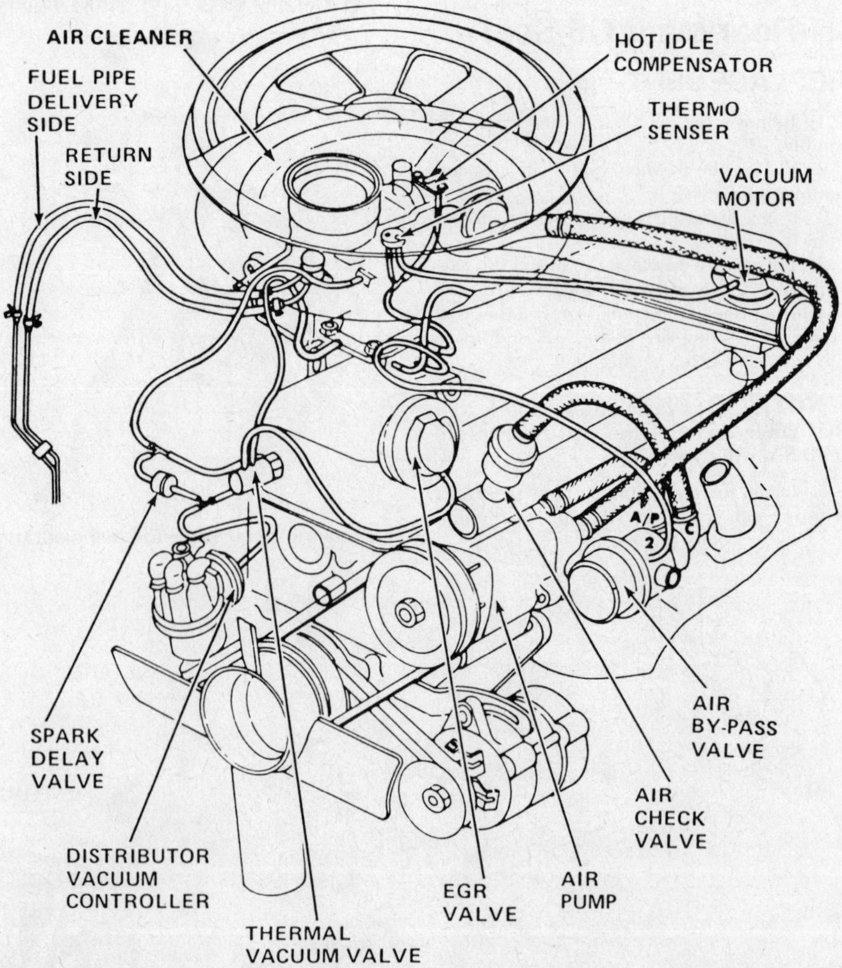

Emission control components and hose routing—1977-79 Federal models with automatic transmission

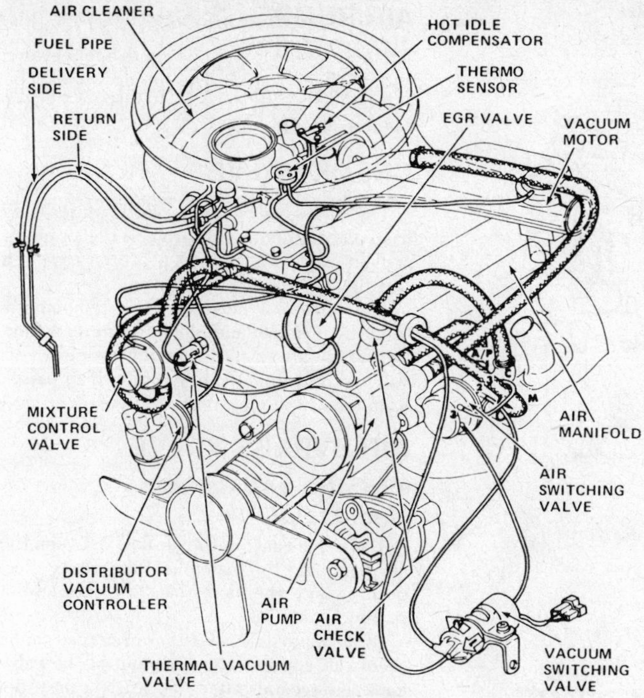

Emission control components and hose routing—1977-79 California and High Altitude models

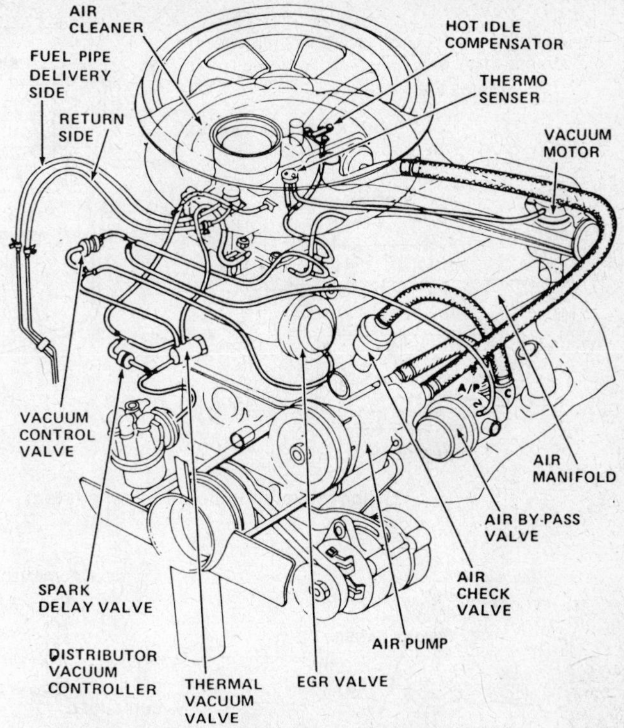

Emission control components and hose routing—1977-79 Federal models with manual transmission

hoses for cracks, fatigue and swelling. Replace if necessary.

Evaporative Emissions Control System

The evaporative emission control system takes gasoline vapors from the fuel tank into the crankcase for mixture with blow-by gases and burning. The system consists of a vapor separator tank, check and relief valves and the tubes connecting these parts.

SERVICE

Remove check valve and inspect for leaks by blowing air into the ports.

a. When air is forced from the tank side, the valve should allow air to pass into the pan side, but not allow it into the air cleaner side.

b. If air is applied to the pan side it should be restricted.

c. If applied from the air cleaner side, air should pass into the fuel tank side, but not into the crankcase side.

Check rubber hoses for cracks or fatigue and the separator tank for fuel leaks, distortion or dents. Replace parts as necessary.

Exhaust Emission Control

The Air Injector Reactor (AIR) system is designed to pressurize outside air and inject it through a series of nozzles to a location near the exhaust valves. Because of the temperature of the gases leaving the exhaust chambers, the added air causes a reignition and further burning of any unused portions of fuel remaining.

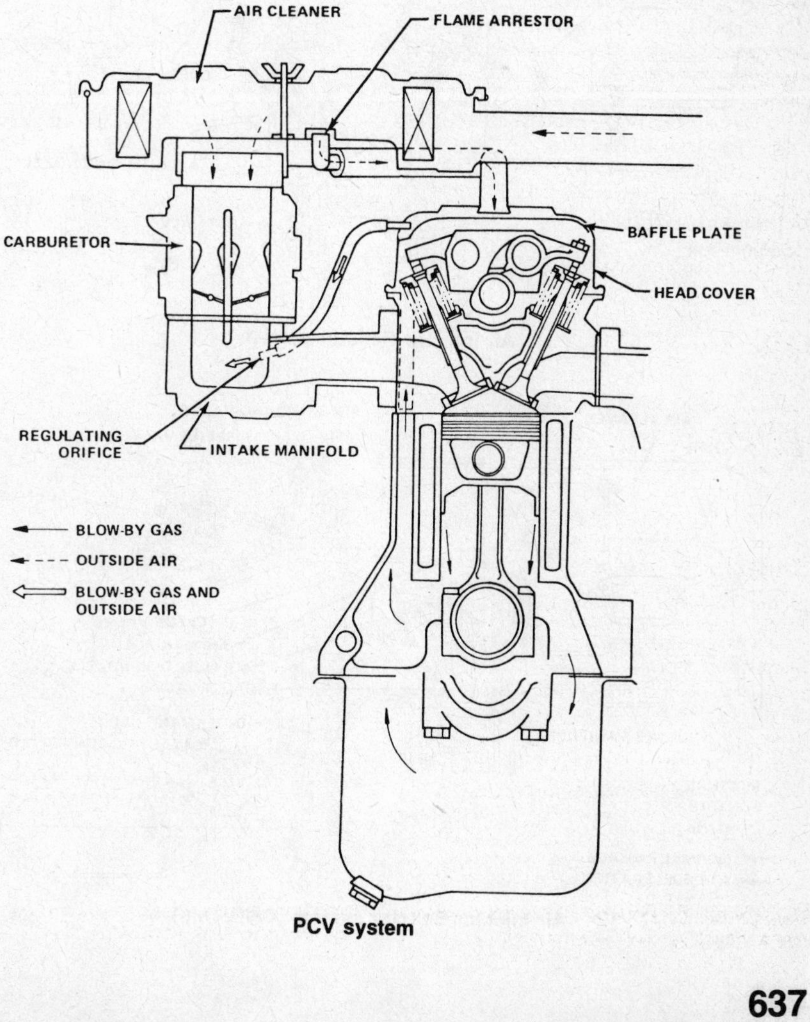

PCV system

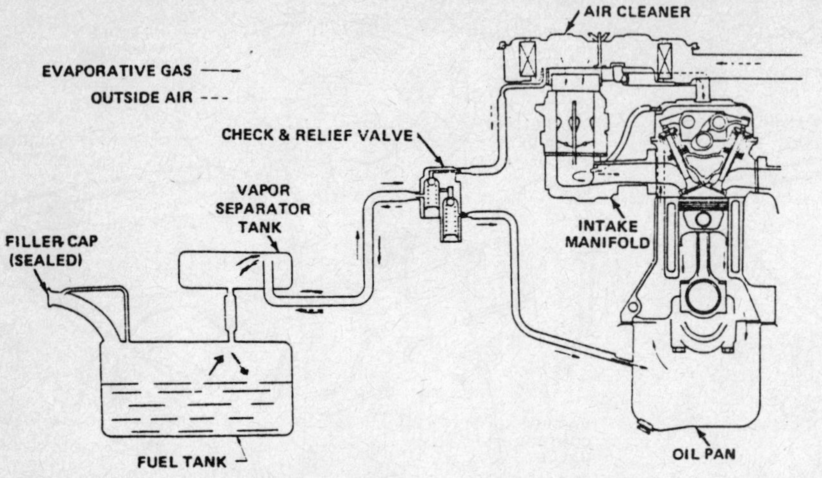

Evaporative emission control system

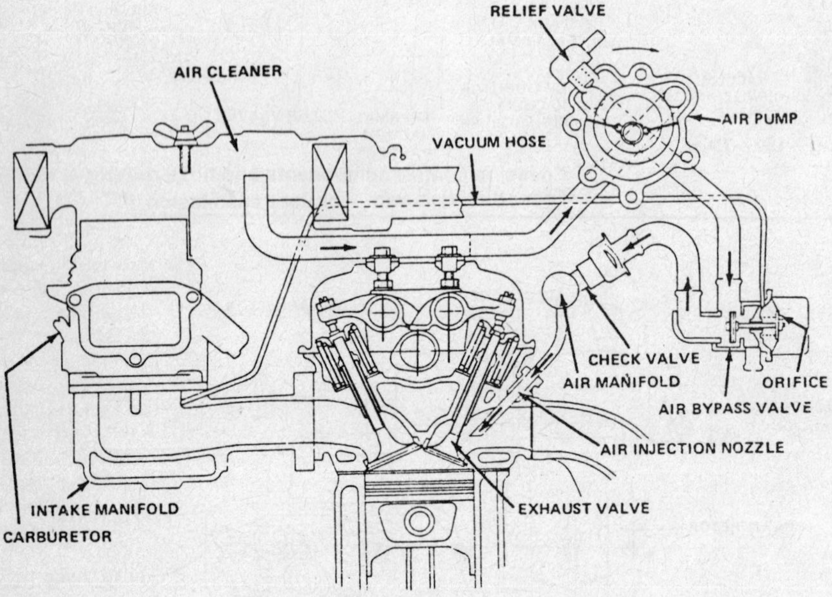

Air Injector Reactor system

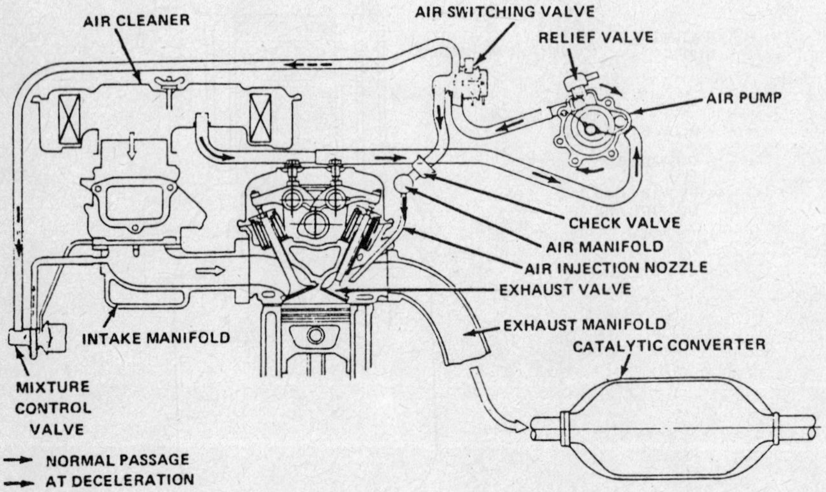

Air Injector Reactor system (California)

AIR PUMP

The air pump is equipped with a relief valve and a check valve. The pump should be checked for excess noise and replaced if found to be malfunctioning.

CHECK VALVE

The check valve allows air to enter only from one direction. This protects the air pump and hoses if a belt breaks or in the case of a backfire.

The valve may be checked by removing it from the manifold and blowing air into it from the air pump side. If working properly, air will pass only from the pump side. If air passes from anywhere else, replace valve.

AIR BYPASS VALVE

49 States and Canada Models Only

This valve controls the air flow between the air pump and the manifold. It prevents afterburning and, therefore, backfires, because of rich fuel mixtures.

If the air bypass valve is working normally, excess air continues to blow out of the valve for a few seconds after the accelerator is depressed and released. If air should continue to escape for five seconds or more, replace the valve.

MIXTURE CONTROL VALVE

California Models Only

To prevent afterburning during deceleration, the mixture control valve supplies air into the intake manifold to prevent too rich a mixture when the throttle is closed suddenly.

Disconnect the hose between the valve and the manifold. As in the case with the bypass, if air continues to escape from the unit for more than five seconds, replace it.

MANIFOLD AND NOZZLE INSPECTION

With the engine running at 2000 rpm check around the manifold for air leaks. If air is leaking from the nozzle fixing sleeves, tighten them.

Inspect all hoses, clamps and clips for cracks and fatigue. Make sure the hoses do not contact any other parts.

Exhaust Emission Control

EXHAUST GAS RECIRCULATION SYSTEM

In this system, exhaust gas is drawn into the intake manifold through a pipe from the exhaust manifold and through an EGR valve. The EGR valve vacuum diaphragm chamber is connected to a timed signal port in the carburetor flange through a thermal vacuum valve. This valve, connected in series between the vacuum port in the carburetor and the EGR valve, senses coolant temperature.

EGR Valve Inspection

1. Apply an outside vacuum source to the vacuum supply tube at the top of the diaphragm. The diaphragm should move fully to the up position at about 8" vacuum.

Thermal Vacuum Valve Inspection

Place the thermo sensing portion into hot water (118-126° F) and check the valve by blowing through it. If air does not pass through, replace the valve.

EGR Valve Replacement

1. Disconnect hose from valve.
2. Disconnect pipe from valve.
3. Unbolt and remove valve from manifold.

Thermal Vacuum Valve Replacement

1. Disconnect hoses.
2. Unscrew valve from water gallery.

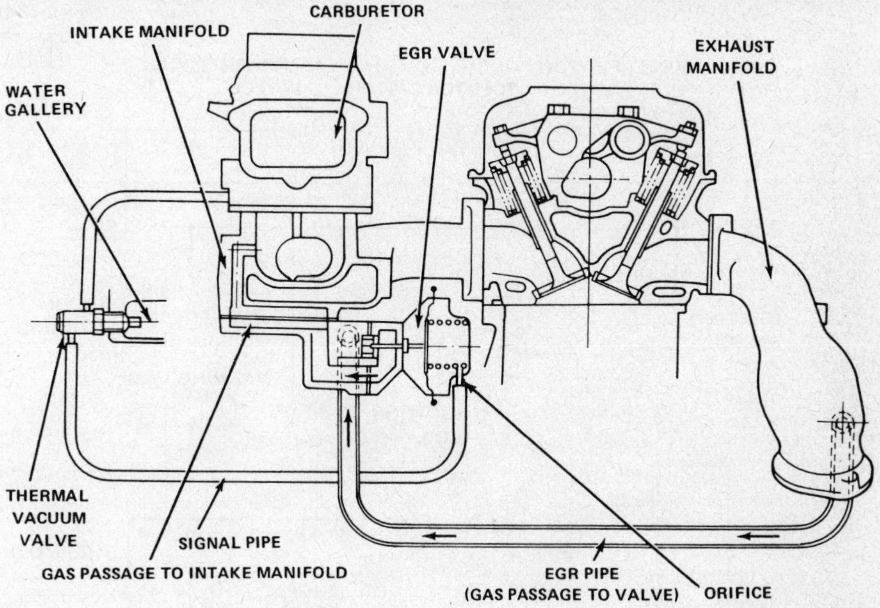

Typical EGR system, all models

CONTROLLED COMBUSTION SYSTEM

This system consists, principally, of a thermo sensor, vacuum motor, hot air control valve and hot idle compensator. The components are mounted on and in the air cleaner body and snorkel. The system channels warm air (from around the exhaust manifold) to the carburetor when the engine is cold. As the engine warms, the air cleaner door closes, admitting cooler air into the carburetor. When the engine is off, the spring holds the vacuum motor door closed across the heat stove passage from the manifold. When started cold, the thermo sensor allows maximum vacuum to the vacuum motor causing the door to open completely, closing off the outside air supply. Heavy acceleration will cause a drop in vacuum and the admission of cold air. As engine temperature builds past 100° F the door will begin to close over the heat stove passage. At 111° F, the door should be completely closed. During heat buildup, excessive fuel vapors will enter the intake manifold. To prevent rough idle and increased emissions, the air cleaner is equipped with a hot idle compensator. The compensator opens to feed cold air into the manifold to temporarily lean out the mixture.

Inspection

Little maintenance is necessary other than checking and cleaning, if necessary, the viscous type air filter element. This should be done every 30,000 miles.

COASTING RICHER SYSTEM

This system allows for enrichment of the fuel mixture during engine coasting. It consists of a solenoid valve coupled with one of the following equipment groups:

Non-California manual transmission—accelerator switch, clutch switch, transmission 4th/3rd gear switch.

California manual transmission—accelerator switch, clutch switch, transmission neutral switch, engine speed sensor.

California automatic transmission—accelerator switch, inhibitor switch, engine speed sensor. The system is not used on non/California automatic transmission models.

When all the switches in a system are on, the solenoid valve and magnet on the secondary side of the carburetor become energized and cause the valve to open. Fuel is drawn out of the float bowl and is metered through the coasting jet and mixed with air through the coasting bleed. The mixture is supplied, through the coasting valve into the secondary part of the throttle valve.

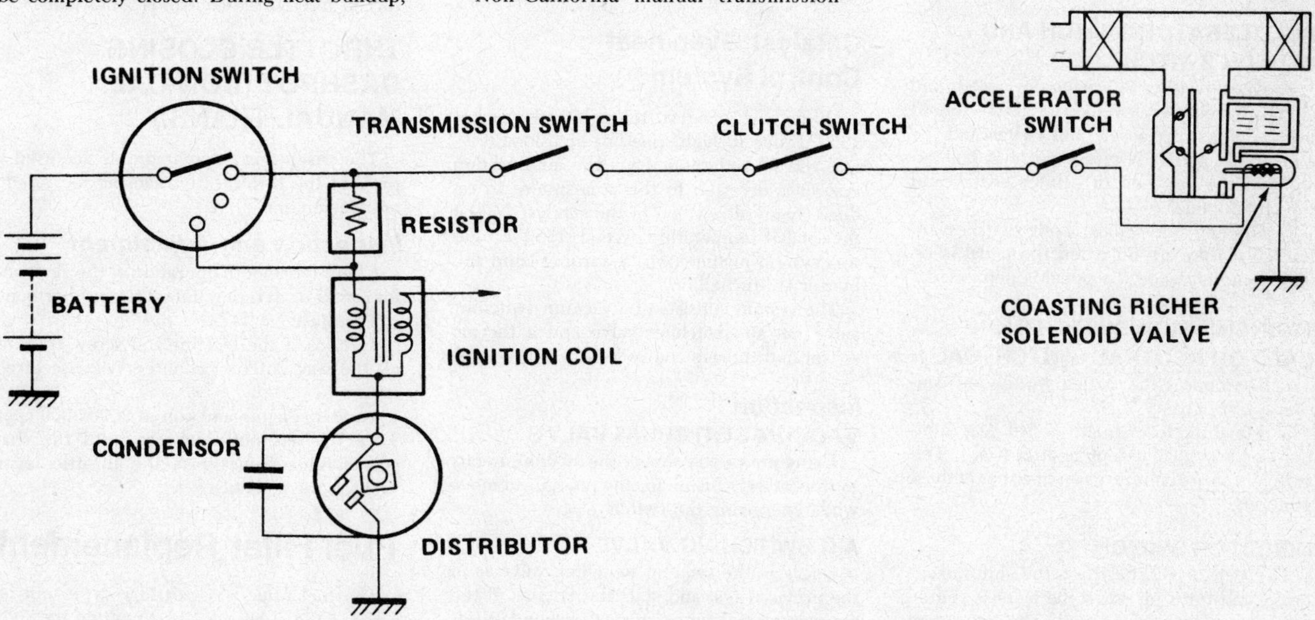

Coasting Richer System electrical circuits—Federal models

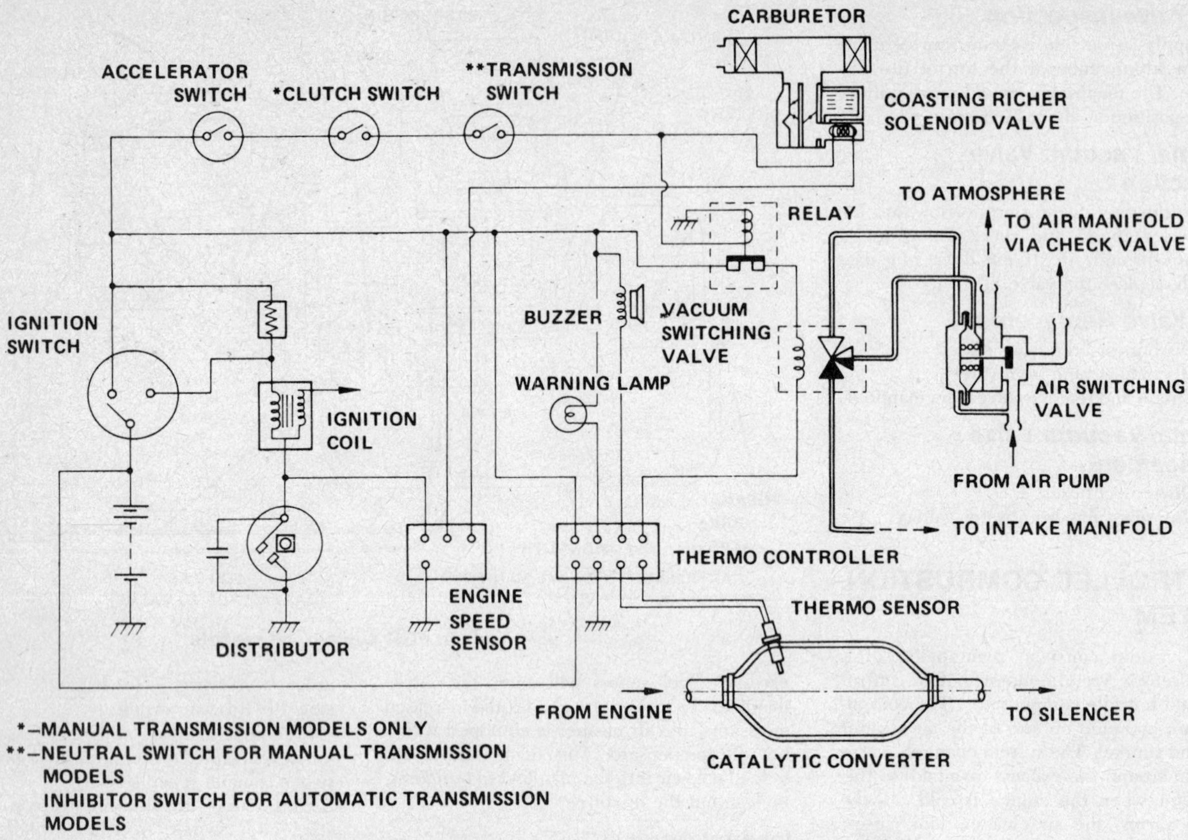

Coasting Richer System electrical circuits—California models

Inspection

ENGINE SPEED SENSOR

Disconnect the speed sensor wiring and, using jumpers, connect terminals B BR and BY to each other. Start the engine and check for continuity among the terminals. Continuity should exist at engine speeds over 1500-1700 rpm.

ACCELERATOR SWITCH AND CLUTCH SWITCH

1. Check setting of accelerator switch and clutch switch. A clearance of 0.04" should exist between the accelerator switch and the accelerator pedal. A clearance of 0.02-0.04" should exist between the clutch switch and the clutch pedal.
2. Operate the pedals. Both switches are normal if they are on when the pedal is released and off when the pedal is depressed.

TRANSMISSION SWITCH (NON-CAL.) OR NEUTRAL SWITCH (CAL.)

1. Disconnect the switch wiring and connect a test light.
2. Move the lever to 4th or 3rd gear (non-Cal.) or any gear except neutral (Cal.). The switch is normal if it turns on in either of these positions.

INHIBITOR SWITCH

The switch is installed on the shift linkage lever, and turns on when the lever is shifted into Drive, Low, or Second. The switch can be checked with a test lamp.

Catalytic Converter System

All 1976 and later California models use an oxidizing catalytic converter, installed in the exhaust system to control the emission of hydrocarbons and carbon monoxide through chemical reaction

Catalyst Over-heat Control System

When the catalyst temperature reaches 1350° F due to high speed or high load driving, the secondary air from the air injection system is diverted to the atmosphere to reduce chemical reaction in the catalyst. When the catalyst temperature exceeds 1850° F, due to a system malfunction, a warning lamp and buzzer are turned on.

The system consists of a vacuum switching valve, an air switching valve and a thermo sensor and thermo controller.

Inspection

VACUUM SWITCHING VALVE

Using jumpers, connect the switch directly to the battery. Listen for the plunger to move while energizing the switch.

AIR SWITCHING VALVE

Energize the vacuum switching valve as in the previous test and start the engine. If the air switching valve is normal, secondary air will blow from the air switching valve.

THERMO SENSOR

Run the engine at idle for a few minutes, then disconnect the switch wiring. Check for continuity across the terminals of the switch. If no continuity exists, replace the switch.

THERMO CONTROLLER

If the converter warning light and buzzer operate for a few seconds when the key is turned to ON, the controller is normal.

THROTTLE CLOSING DASHPOT (NON-CAL. MANUAL TRANS.)

The dashpot is a diaphragm device used to prevent the throttle from closing too rapidly on deceleration.

Inspection and Adjustment

Check for smooth operation of the shaft and for cracks or deterioration of the rubber boot.

To adjust:

1. Loosen the locknut and screw the unit all the way out in a counterclockwise direction.
2. Start engine and run at 2600-3000 rpm. Turn the dashpot clockwise until the shaft comes into contact with the throttle lever. Tighten the locknut.

Fuel Filter Replacement

The fuel filter is a cartridge type unit located in the engine compartment on the right inner fender. The filter should be replaced every 15,000 miles of operation. Disconnect the inlet and outlet fuel lines from the filter and replace it with a new one.

Electric Fuel Pump

The fuel pump is located near the bottom of the fuel tank. It is a motor-driven, centrifugal type.

REMOVAL AND INSTALLATION

1. Disconnect the fuel return hose from pipe and drain.
2. Remove the fuel tank and fuel pipe covers.

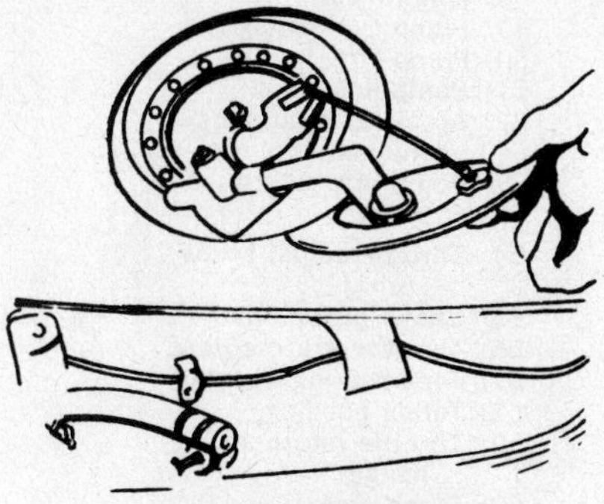

Removing fuel pump

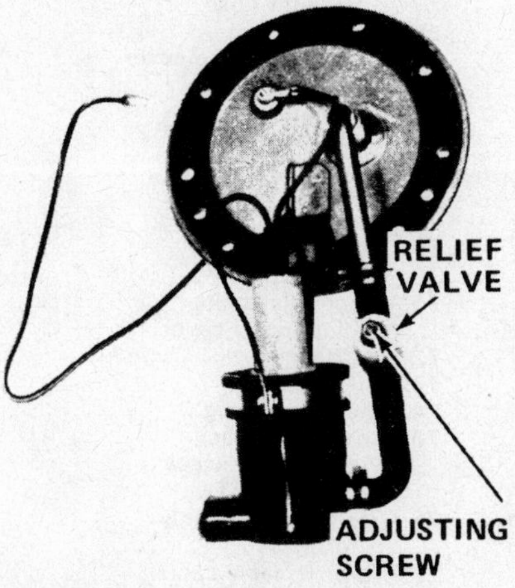

Fuel pump relief valve and adjusting screw

3. Disconnect the fuel hose and the pump wiring. Remove the attaching screws (9) and take out the assembly.
4. Installation is the reverse of removal.

ADJUSTMENTS

Repair or adjustments are not possible. Replace if defective.

TESTING

NOTE: Do not run pump when disconnected from fuel supply.

To test for pressure of delivery, you should:
1. Disconnect main fuel line at the carburetor and connect a fuel pump tester with a three-way connector.

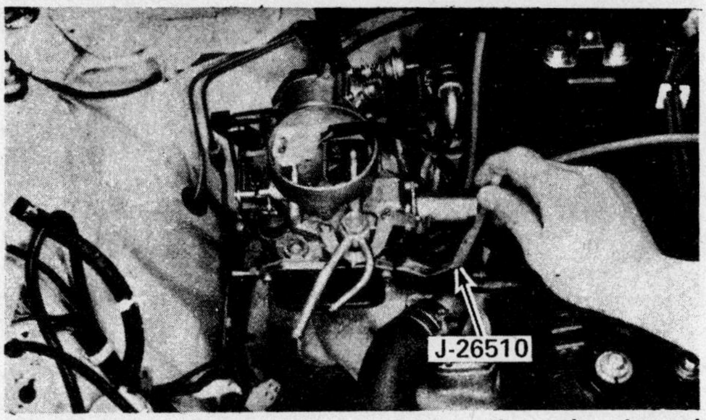

An angled wrench is necessary to remove the carburetor nuts

2. Start the engine and read the tester.
3. Fuel pump pressure should be 3.3 psi. If it deviates from this, remove the pump and adjust the relief valve.
   a. Loosen the locknut and turn the screw clockwise to increase the pressure and counterclockwise to decrease.

Carburetor

REMOVAL AND INSTALLATION

1. Remove the air cleaner and CCS hose from carburetor.
2. Disconnect the fuel lines at both the main and return side joints and disconnect the vacuum advance and EGR vacuum hoses.
3. Disconnect the accelerator cable from the throttle lever and disconnect the automatic choke and solenoid valve wiring at connector. Remove the clip from the water outlet pipe.
4. Remove the carburetor mounting nuts and remove the carburetor. A special angled wrench will be necessary for this.
5. Installation is the reverse of removal.

NOTE: After installation, check for leaks and check that the accelerator cable is within specifications. Adjust engine idle after warm up.

OVERHAUL

Efficient carburetion depends greatly on careful cleaning and inspection during overhaul, since dirt, gum, varnish, water in or on the carburetor parts are mainly responsible for poor performance.

Carburetor overhaul should be performed in a clean, dust-free area. Carefully disassemble the carburetor, keeping look-alike parts segregated. Note all jet sizes.

Once the carburetor is disassembled, wash all parts (except diaphragms, electric choke units, pump plunger and any other plastic, leather or fiber parts) in clean carburetor solvent. Do not leave the parts in solvent any longer than necessary to sufficiently loosen the deposits. Excessive cleaning may remove the special finish from the float bowl and choke valve bodies, leaving them unfit for service. Rinse all parts in clean solvent and blow dry with compressed air. Wipe all plastic, leather or fiber parts with a clean, lint-free cloth.

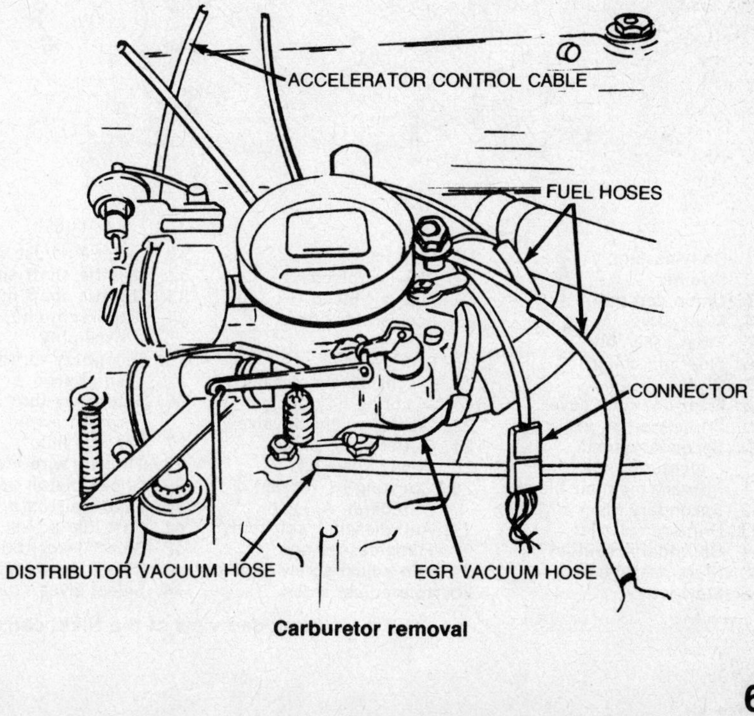

Carburetor removal

Blow out all passages and jets with compressed air and be sure there are no restrictions or blockages. Never use wire to clean jets, fuel passages or air bleeds.

Check all parts for wear or damage. If wear or damage is found, replace the complete assembly. Especially check the following:

1. Check the float and needle seat for wear. If any is found, replace the assembly.
2. Check the float hinge pin for wear and the floats for distortion or dents. Replace the float if fuel has leaked into it.
3. Check the throttle and choke shaft bores for out-of-round. Damage or wear to the throttle arm, shaft or shaft bore will often require replacement of the throttle body. These parts require close tolerances and air leaking here can cause poor starting and idling.
4. Inspect the idle mixture adjusting needles for burrs or grooves. Burrs or grooves will usually require replacement of the needles since a satisfactory idle cannot be obtained.
5. Test the accelerator pump check valves. They should pass air one way but not the other. Test for proper seating by blowing and sucking on the valve. If the valve is satisfactory, wash the valve again to remove breath moisture.
6. Check the bowl cover for warping, with a straightedge.
7. Closely inspect the valves and seats for wear or damage, replacing as necessary.
8. After the carburetor is assembled, check the choke valve for freedom of operation.

Carburetor overhaul kits are recommended

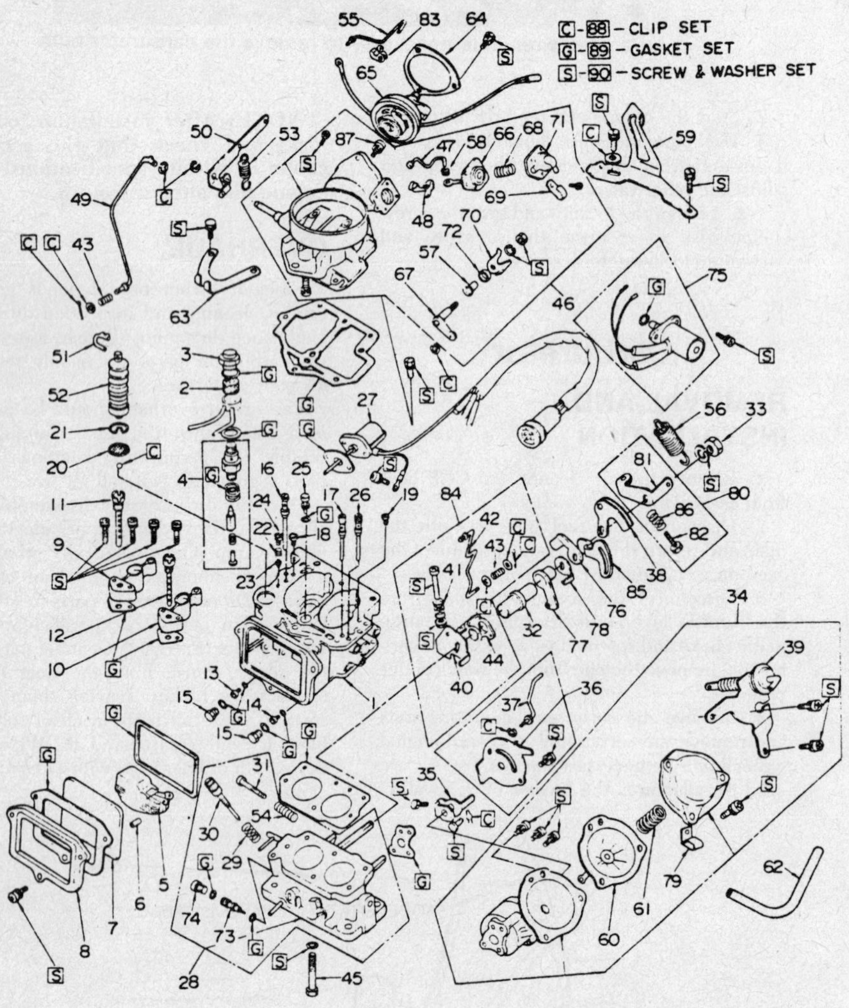

1. Body assembly
2. Strainer
3. Union cap nut
4. Float valve
5. Float assembly
6. Float pin collar
7. Glass
8. Float chamber cover
9. Primary small venturi
10. Secondary small venturi
11. Primary main air bleed
12. Secondary main air bleed
13. Primary main jet
14. Secondary main jet
15. Main passage plug
16. Slow jet
17. Step jet
18. Slow air bleed
19. Step air bleed
20. Accelerator pump strainer
21. Strainer clip
22. Discharge check valve spring
23. Discharge check valve
24. Outlet valve plug
25. Power valve jet
26. Coasting jet (except federal, A/T)
27. Anti-dieseling solenoid
28. Flange assembly
29. Idle adjust screw spring
30. Idle adjust screw
31. Throttle adjust screw
32. Throttle shaft sleeve
33. Throttle shaft nut
34. Diaphragm chamber assembly
35. Secondary throttle shaft arm
36. Secondary throttle return arm
37. Throttle link
38. Throttle wire lever
39. Choke piston assembly
40. Choke piston arm
41. Fast idle adjust spring
42. Select lever rod
43. Select lever rod spring
44. Select lever
45. Bolt
46. Air horn assembly
47. Choke diaphragm rod
48. Link holder
49. Pump connecting rod
50. Pump arm
51. Pump link
52. Accelerator pump plunger
53. Pump arm return spring
54. Throttle adjust screw spring
55. Choke piston link
56. Throttle return spring
57. Tape bearing bushing
58. Teflon bushing
59. Throttle return spring hanger
60. Diaphragm
61. Diaphragm spring
62. Automatic choke vacuum hose
63. Clamp
64. Thermostat case cover
65. Thermostat case
66. Automatic choke diaphragm
67. Select arm lever
68. Automatic choke diaphragm spring
69. Lead wire clip
70. Select arm
71. Automatic choke diaphragm cover
72. Washer
73. Idle nozzle
74. Idle nozzle plug
75. Coasting richer solenoid (except federal, A/T)
76. Dash pot arm (only for M/T)
77. Throttle valve cable lever (only for A/T)
78. Throttle valve cable stopper (only for A/T)
79. Lead wire clip
80. Fast idle lever assembly
81. Fast idle lever
82. Speed up controller adjusting screw
83. Link holder
84. Throttle adjust arm assembly
85. Primary throttle arm
86. Speed up controller adjusting spring
87. Screw & washer
88. Clip set
89. Gasket set
90. Screw & washer set

NOTE:
A/T ...... Automatic Transmission Models
M/T ...... Manual Transmission Models

Exploded view of the Nikki carburetor

for each overhaul. These kits contain all gaskets and new parts to replace those that deteriorate most rapidly. Failure to replace all parts supplied with the kit (especially gaskets) can result in poor performance later.

After cleaning and checking all components, reassemble the carburetor using new parts and using the exploded views if necessary. Make sure that all screws and jets are tight in their seats, but do not overtighten, or the tips will be distorted. Do not tighten needle valves into their seats or uneven jetting will result. Always use new gaskets and adjust the float.

FUEL LEVEL

Fuel level can be seen through an access window on the float bowl. The fuel should always be at the level mark, whether the engine is running or not.

Level adjustment is made with copper gaskets at the float valve seat. Adding gaskets raises the level, and vice versa.

FAST IDLE ADJUSTMENT

1. Disconnect and plug the vacuum advance hose at the distributor and EGR hose at the EGR valve.
2. Remove the air cleaner.
3. Open the throttle halfway and close the choke valve, release the throttle, and release the choke.
4. Connect a tachometer to the engine. Start the engine without moving the throttle. Set the fast idle with the fast idle screw to 3000 rpm for automatic transmission or 3200 rpm for manual transmission.

AUTOMATIC CHOKE ADJUSTMENT

1. Align the mark on the choke cover with the mark on the choke case, then tighten the three retaining screws.
2. With the bimetal lever held against the stopper, check that the choke piston stroke is within range of 3/16-7/32". If not, adjust by bending the piston link.

CHOKE UNLOADER ADJUSTMENT

1. Open throttle valve fully while holding down on choke valve.
2. Choke valve should be forced open part way.
3. Using a wire or drill gauge, measure the distance between the air horn wall and the lower edge of the choke valve. The gap should be 0.215". If not, remove the choke heater coil cover and bend the unloader tang to obtain the correct setting.

MANUAL TRANSMISSION

REMOVAL

1. Disconnect the battery negative cable.
2. From inside the car, remove the shift lever assembly.
3. Loosen the clutch cable adjusting nuts at the left side of the engine compartment.
4. Remove the upper starter bolt and disconnect the wiring. Raise and support the car.
5. Remove the driveshaft and disconnect the speedometer cable.
6. Remove the clutch cable heat shield and cable. Remove the lower starter bolt and remove the unit.
7. Disconnect the exhaust pipe from the manifold and remove the flywheel inspection cover.
8. Remove the transmission rear support mounting bolt. Supporting the transmission under the case, remove the rear support from the frame.
9. Lower the transmission, leaving it about four inches lower than mounted.
10. Disconnect the backup light and CRS switch wires.
11. Remove the transmission housing-to-engine block bolts and move the unit straight back and lower away from the car.

INSTALLATION

Lubricate drive gear shaft with light coating of grease and reverse steps 1 through 11 of the removal procedure. Adjust the clutch and fill transmission with SAE 30 engine oil.

CLUTCH

REMOVAL AND INSTALLATION

1. Remove the transmission.
2. Loosen the clutch pressure plate bolts gradually until all pressure is released and slip the pressure plate and disc from the flywheel.
3. Check over the surface of the flywheel for scoring and signs of overheating. If scored, the flywheel should be resurfaced or replaced. If overheating is indicated, check for warpage and reface as needed.
4. If disc wear is indicated, the pressure plate, release bearing and disc should be replaced.
5. To install you must be sure that the disc is centered so the transmission mainshaft will engage the pilot bushing as well as the disc splines. A dummy mainshaft or a clutch aligning tool should be inserted through the disc hub and into the pilot bushing while tightening pressure plate bolts.
6. Tighten the bolts gradually and evenly and reassemble the transmission to the engine.

FREE-PLAY ADJUSTMENT

1. Loosen the lock and adjusting nuts on the clutch cable.
2. Pull the cable toward the front of the car to take up the slack and turn the adjusting nut until the clutch pedal free travel is approximately ⅝ inch. Tighten the locknut.

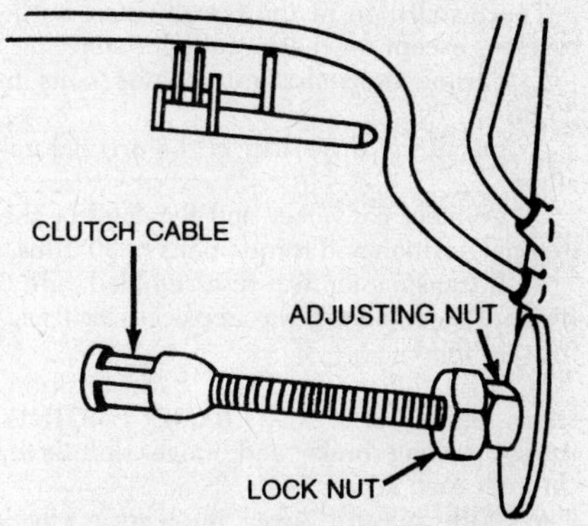

Clutch cable adjusting and lock nuts

AUTOMATIC TRANSMISSION

REMOVAL AND INSTALLATION

1. Disconnect the negative battery cable.
2. Disconnect the throttle valve cable at right side of carburetor.
3. Disconnect the exhaust pipe from the manifold.
4. Disconnect the wiring and remove the starter.
5. Remove the flywheel inspection cover, converter bolts and mark for reassembly in the same position.

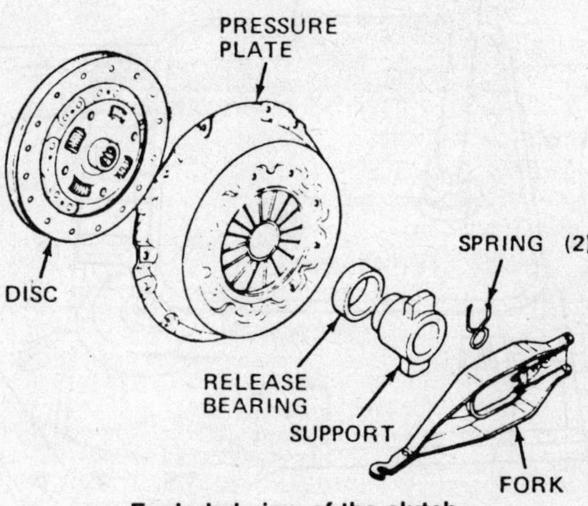

Exploded view of the clutch

6. Mark the driveshaft and flange, and remove the driveshaft.

7. Remove the rear transmission mount pad bolts.

8. Raise the transmission and remove the crossmember support and mount.

9. Lower the transmission still holding its weight at the lowest position.

10. Disconnect the shift linkage and speedometer cable, as well as the throttle valve cable and cooler lines.

11. Remove the transmission-to-engine bolts and filler pipe and move the transmission back and lower away from the car. You must use a holding tool to hold the converter in place.

The installation of the transmission is the reverse, except for these reminder steps:

1. Torque transmission-to-engine bolts to 35 ft/lbs.

2. Install the driveshaft in the original position.

3. Connect converter and flywheel in the original position and torque bolts to 30 ft/lbs.

4. If transmission was disassembled, add 6 pints (9 if converter was replaced) of transmission fluid.

5. With shift lever in the "Park" position, start engine. DO NOT RACE ENGINE. Apply parking brake and move shift lever through each gear.

6. With selector lever in "Park", check fluid level. Make sure the engine is running.

7. Add additional fluid to bring level to between the two small dimples below the "add" mark on the dipstick. This is the correct reading for room temperature.

PAN REMOVAL AND INSTALLATION

1. Remove the bolts around the outside edge of transmission oil pan. Discard gasket.

2. Installation is the reverse of removal and all bolts should be tightened to 12 ft/lbs.

FLUID CHANGE AND FILTER SERVICE

1. Remove oil pan and discard gasket.

2. Remove the oil screen and discard the surrounding gasket.

3. Clean the screen in clean transmission fluid and blow dry with compressed air.

4. Assembly is the reverse of removal. Make sure all gaskets seat firmly. Hold the gaskets in place by using a light coating of petroleum jelly. Torque all bolts (screen and pan) to 12 ft/lbs.

NEUTRAL SAFETY SWITCH

The neutral safety switch (located on top of transmission) prevents the engine from starting in any position other than Park or Neutral. Should the engine start in any other gear, check the connection and replace if there is a malfunction. There is no adjustment on this unit.

SHIFT LINKAGE ADJUSTMENT

1. Remove lever from transmission manual shaft and put the transmission in Neutral.

2. Place the shift indicator in Neutral and loosen the locking nut. Adjust lever until it lines up with the manual shaft.

3. Install the lever on the manual shaft and tighten the locking nut. Recheck shift patterns.

THROTTLE LINKAGE ADJUSTMENT

1. Loosen cable adjusting nuts on right side of carburetor.

2. Move the carburetor lever to wide open and adjust the cable until a play of approximately 0.040 is reached above the adjusting nuts. Tighten the nuts.

DRIVE AXLE

Driveshaft and U-Joints

REMOVAL AND INSTALLATION

1. Raise the rear of the car and support on jackstands. Disconnect the parking brake return spring from rod.

2. Mark mating parts for reassembly and remove bolts and nuts.

3. Push the driveshaft slightly forward to clear the rear attachment and lower rear joint slightly; pull toward the back at the same time. Remove the thrust spring from the front of the driveshaft.

4. Install a plug in the transmission extension housing to prevent the loss of oil.

NOTE: Do not replace fasteners with an inferior grade. They must be replaced with one of the same part number or an equivalent. Torque values must be followed to assure proper retention of the parts.

To install the driveshaft:

1. Remove the plug from the rear of the transmission.

2. Slide the thrust spring onto the transmission output shaft and slide the driveshaft through the oil seal. Make sure not to damage the rear seal.

3. Align the pinion flange with the locating marks and install bolts and lock plates. Tighten bolts to 18 ft/lbs. Connect the parking brake spring to the rod.

U-JOINT OVERHAUL

1. Remove the driveshaft.

2. Remove the snap rings (4) on each assembly and tap on flange with hammer until one of the bearing caps starts to come out. Remove this cap with pliers. Remove the remaining caps in a similar fashion.

3. After removing the bearing caps, bearings and spider, thoroughly clean the flange and yoke.

4. Fill the holes in the journals with grease and put about ⅛ in. of grease in the bearing caps.

5. If reusing old joint, put the needle bearings into the caps and, putting the spider inside the flange, slip the caps into the yoke. Caps may be pressed into position with a strong vise. Take care not to lose any needle bearings. Install the snap rings.

Axle Shafts

REMOVAL AND INSTALLATION

1. Raise and support the rear of the car.

2. Remove the wheel and brake drum.

3. Unscrew the rear axle shaft retaining plate and, using an axle shaft puller, coupled with a slide hammer, on flange, remove the shaft.

To install the shafts:

1. Coat shaft splines with hypoid gear lubricant and insert into housing.

2. Using a mallet, drive the shaft completely in and install the lock washers and nuts. Torque to 28 ft/lbs.

3. Install the brake drum and wheel and lower the car.

BEARING AND SEAL REPLACEMENT

1. Remove axle shaft.

2. Remove the bearing retaining ring by cutting with a cold chisel.

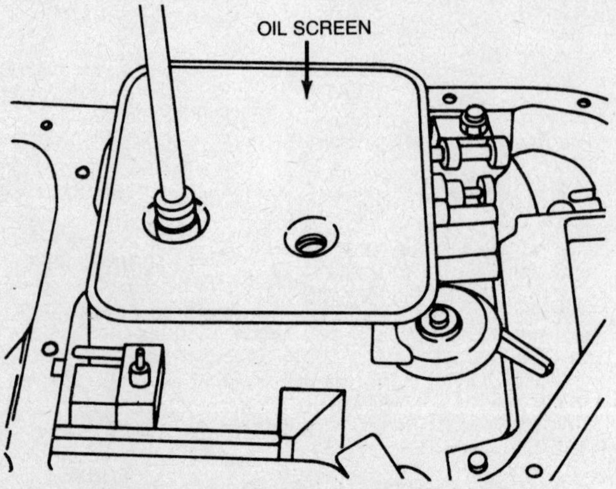

Removing the automatic transmission filter

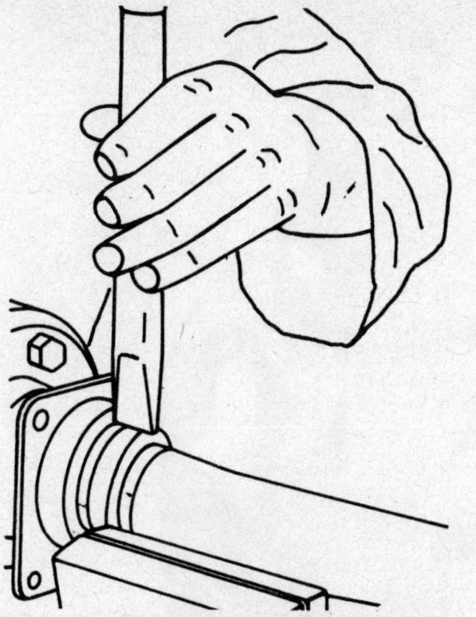

Removing axle bearing and retaining ring

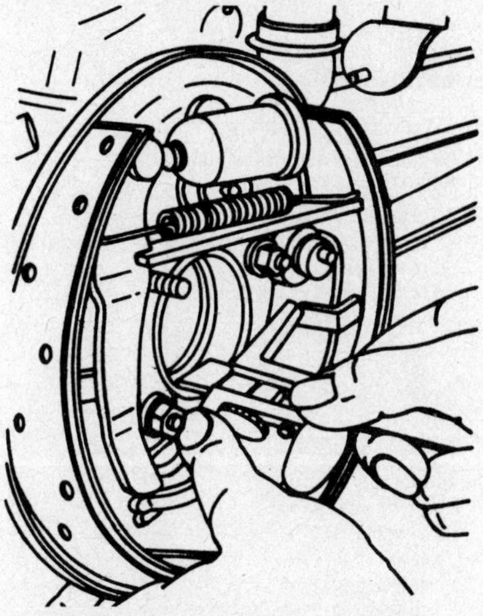

Measuring for axle bearing depth

3. Press off the bearing.

To check for end-play, measure the depth of the rear axle bearing seal with the backing plate and gaskets in place.

Next, measure the width of the bearing outer race. The difference between the two measurements indicates the required thickness of the shims.

The maximum permissible end-play is 0.002 in. If necessary to reduce it, add 0.004 in. shims behind the bearing as necessary. A slight crush fit is desirable.

After shim depth has been determined, install the grease-coated bearing in place. Reinstall the axle, the wheels and lower the car.

Differential

REMOVAL AND INSTALLATION

1. Raise and support the car.
2. Remove differential cover bolts and let lubricant drain into container.
3. Disconnect left end of track rod and wire it to left shock absorber.
4. Remove both rear wheels and brake drums. Remove the dust shield and backing plates and unscrew the axle shaft retaining plates.
5. Pull the axle shafts; be careful not to damage oil seals. Remove the differential cover and discard gasket.
6. Using a dial indicator, check and record the ring gear backlash.
7. Mark side bearing caps with a punch for reassembly to the original position, and remove.
8. Using two wooden handles, pry the differential case assembly from the housing. Be careful not to drop or confuse the bearing outer races.

To install the differential to the carrier:

1. Position the differential and outer races in the carrier. Use a soft faced hammer to drive the case into the carrier until the side bearing outer races bottom in their bores. Install the bearing caps to their original position as marked and torque the bolts to 35 ft/lbs.
2. Rotate the case assembly several times to seat the bearings and check the backlash with a dial indicator and preload by using a torque wrench on a ring gear bolt. Torque should be 25 inch lbs. for new bearings and 15 inch lbs. for used. If not correct, it will be necessary to reshim the side bearings.
3. Install the torque tube assembly and insert the axle shafts.

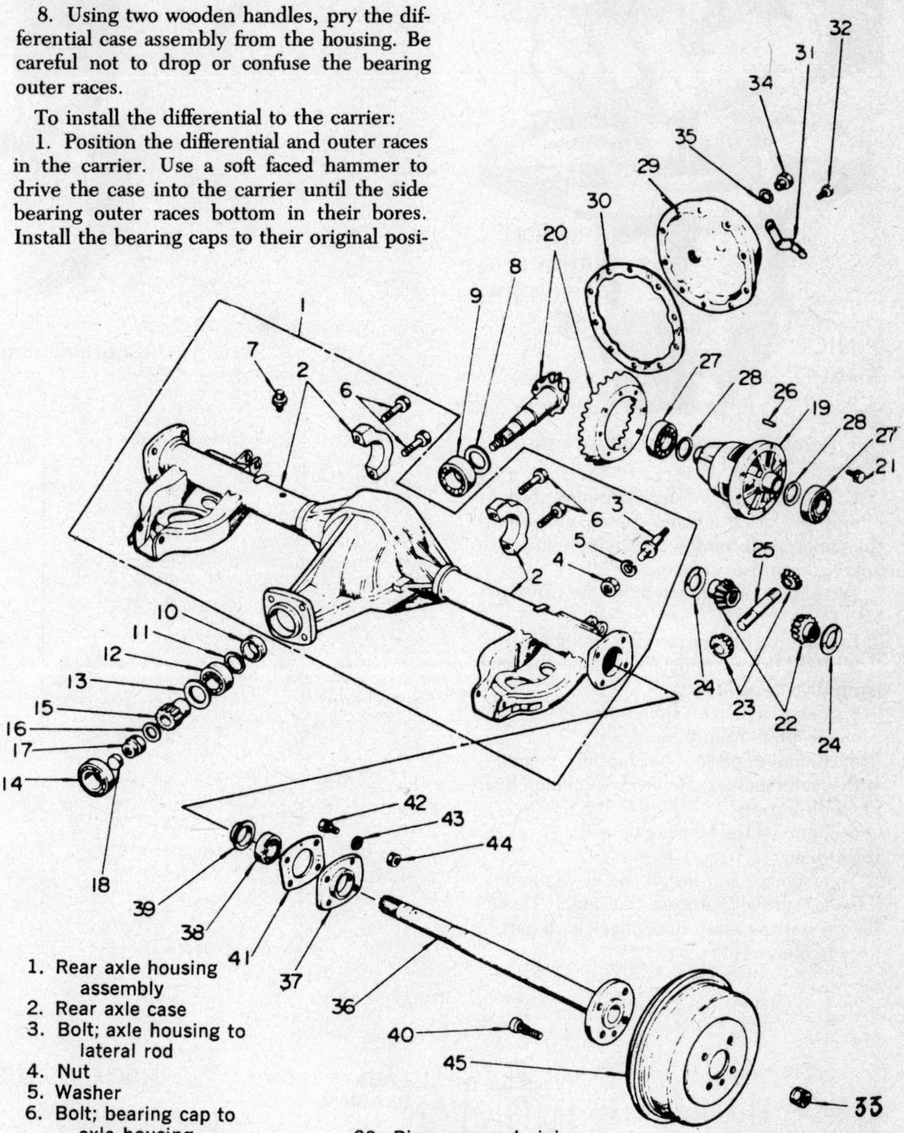

1. Rear axle housing assembly
2. Rear axle case
3. Bolt; axle housing to lateral rod
4. Nut
5. Washer
6. Bolt; bearing cap to axle housing
7. Rear axle breather assembly
8. Pinion bearing shim
9. Pinion bearing (inner)
10. Collapsible distance spacer
11. Shim; distance piece
12. Pinion bearing (outer)
13. Oil thrower
14. Sliding sleeve oil seal
15. Barrel spline sleeve
16. Final pinion washer
17. Pinion nut
18. Pressure cap
19. Differential case
20. Ring gear and pinion
21. Ring gear setting bolt
22. Side gears
23. Pinion gears
24. Side gear thrust washer
25. Differential pinion pin
26. Lock pin
27. Side bearing
28. Side gear shim
29. Rear axle housing rear cover
30. Rear axle housing gasket
31. Brake pipe union bracket
32. Union bracket bolt
33. Wheel nut
34. Oil filler plug
35. Oil filler gasket
36. Rear axle shaft
37. Axle shaft bearing retainer
38. Axle shaft bearing
39. Axle shaft sleeve
40. Wheel pin
41. Axle shaft shim
42. Bolt; brake to axle case
43. Spring washer
44. Nut
45. Rear brake drum

Exploded view of the rear axle

OVERHAUL

1. Remove the differential case from the carrier and remove the side bearings.
2. Remove the differential case-to-ring gear bolts and tap off the case using a soft hammer.

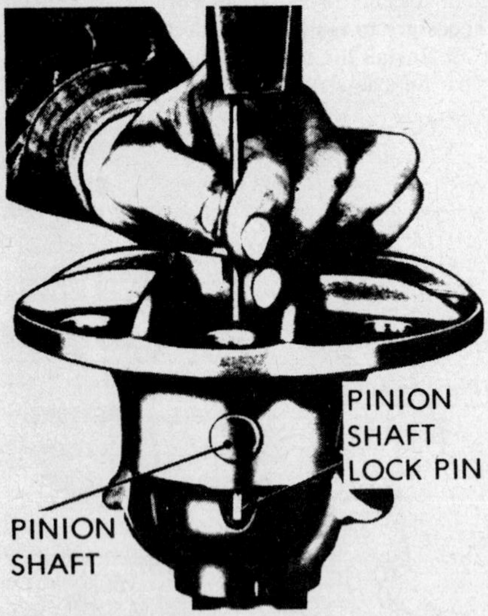

Removing pinion shaft lock pin

3. Remove the differential pinion shaft retaining pin using a ⅛ in. punch and remove the pinion shaft, pinion gears, differential side gears and thrust washers.

To remove and disassemble the drive pinion:

1. Remove the torque tube assembly.
2. Hold barrel spline and remove the bearing preload nut.
3. Using a barrel spline sleeve remover remove spline from pinion.
4. Remove pinion by tapping rearward with a soft hammer. Remove the pinion bearing with a press.
5. Remove the bearing outer races using a brass drift.

To assemble and install the drive pinion:

Make sure all parts are thoroughly cleaned before starting assembly. Check each part for imperfections.

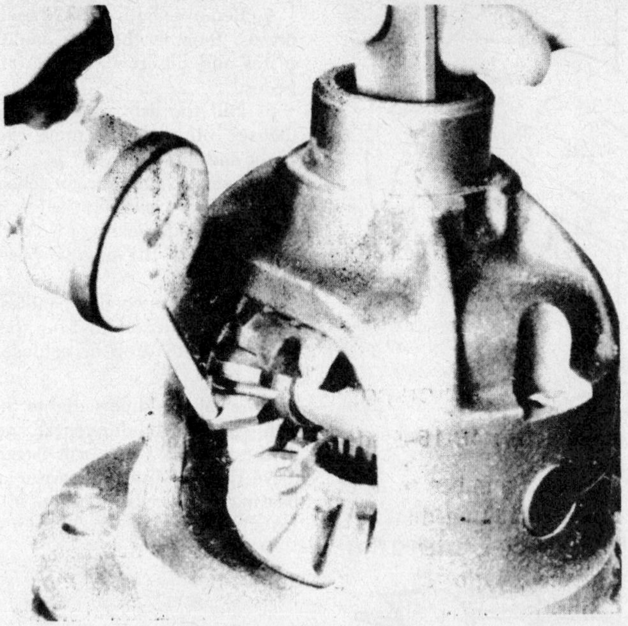

Checking ring gear backlash

PINION DEPTH CODE NUMBER	ALTER SHIM THICKNESS AS DETERMINED BY DIAL INDICATOR AS FOLLOWS:
+20	SUBTRACT 0.20 MM (0.0079 IN.)
+18	" 0.18 MM (0.0071 IN.)
+16	" 0.16 MM (0.0063 IN.)
+14	" 0.14 MM (0.0055 IN.)
+12	" 0.12 MM (0.0047 IN.)
+10	" 0.10 MM (0.0039 IN.)
+ 8	" 0.08 MM (0.0032 IN.)
+ 6	" 0.06 MM (0.0024 IN.)
+ 4	" 0.04 MM (0.0016 IN.)
+ 2	" 0.02 MM (0.0008 IN.)
0	USE DIAL INDICATOR READING
- 2	ADD 0.02 MM (0.0008 IN.)
- 4	" 0.04 MM (0.0016 IN.)
- 6	" 0.06 MM (0.0024 IN.)
- 8	" 0.08 MM (0.0032 IN.)
-10	" 0.10 MM (0.0039 IN.)
-12	" 0.12 MM (0.0047 IN.)
-14	" 0.14 MM (0.0055 IN.)
-16	" 0.16 MM (0.0063 IN.)
-18	" 0.18 MM (0.0071 IN.)
-20	" 0.20 MM (0.0079 IN.)

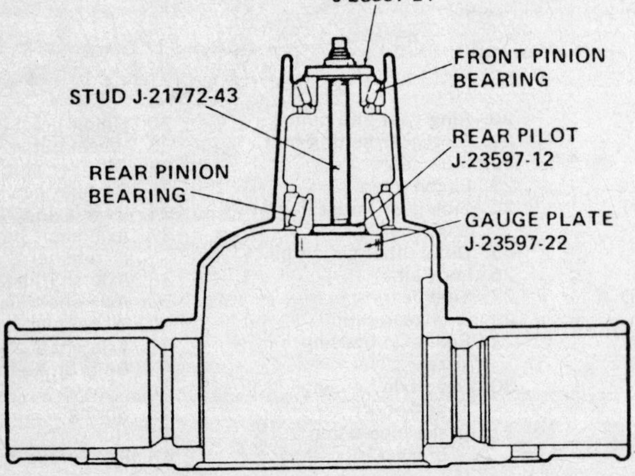

Gauge plate set-up for determining pinion depth

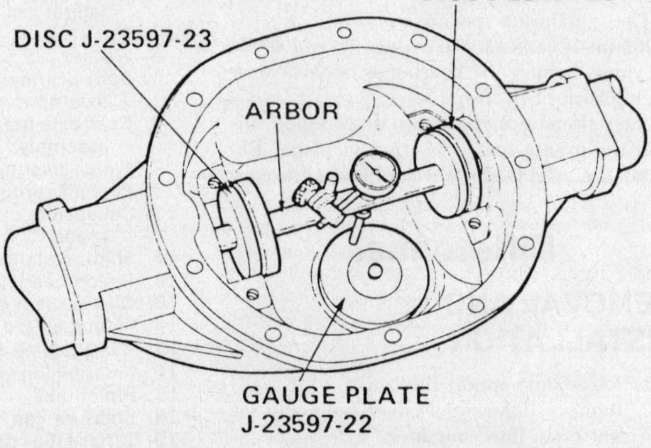

Dial gauge set-up to measure pinion depth

1. Install front pinion bearing outer race using an installer and driver handle.
2. Install the rear pinion bearing outer race using an installer and driver handle.

This next procedure requires a special tool called a gauge plate to determine the correct pinion depth setting.

3. Make sure all gauge parts are clean, lubricate the new front and rear bearings and position them in their races.
4. Thread the stud into gauge plate and install on the rear pinion inner race. Put the pilot on front pinion bearing.
5. Install the nut on the stud and hold the stud stationary with a wrench and tighten the nut with a torque wrench until there is a reading of 20 in/lbs.
6. Clean differential side bearing support bores. Make sure there are no burrs.
7. Install the discs on the gauge shaft.
8. Position the gauge shaft in the carrier so the dial rod is centered on the gauging area of the gauge block and the discs are fully seated in the bearing bores. Install the bearing caps and torque to 35 ft/lbs.
9. Set the dial to "O" and contact the indicator pad with the button on the shaft. Push the dial down until the needle goes about ¾ the way around the dial. Lock in position and reset.
10. Rotate the gauge shaft back and forth until the dial reaches its greatest point of deflection. At this point, set the dial to "O" and repeat to verify.
11. Rotate the shaft until the dial rod does not touch the block. Record the reading.

NOTE: Example: if the dial reading showed .003, this would indicate a shim thickness of .003.

Use this procedure to select the proper shim.

12. Examine the head of the drive pinion. The depth code is stamped by chemical ink. The number indicates the change necessary in the mounting distance. A "Plus" number indicates the need for greater mounting distance (decrease shim thickness) and a "−" indicates th need for smaller (increase shim thickness).

If there is no code the pinion is "nominal."

13. IF the figure is plus, convert it from millimeters to inches and subtract from Step 11. If the figure is minus, convert and add tc 11. Use the chart to determine the proper variation to use to compensate.
14. Place the shim on the drive pinion and install the pinion bearing.

To set or check the bearing preload:

1. Lubricate pinion bearings and assemble the drive pinion, collapsible spacer, front pinion bearing, oil deflector plate and barrel spline sleeve in the carrier.
2. Pull the spline sleeve through the pinion far enough to engage the pinion nut.
3. Install the nut, and, holding the spline barrel, tighten the preload nut until 9 in/lbs are required to rotate the pinion on new bearings. A spring scale should be used to determine preload. For used bearings, the setting is 6 in/lbs.
4. Install a new oil seal that has been soaked in differential lubricant.

To assemble the differential case:

1. Install the side gears and thrust washers. Put them into the case.

Pinion depth code

2. Lubricate and install pinion gears 180 degrees apart and rotate the gears as an assembly until the pinion gear bores are aligned with the shaft bores in the case.
3. Install the pinion shaft and use a dial indicator to measure the amount of backlash between the gears. One gear must be held stationary while making this check. If backlash is greater than .003 in., make the adjustments with thrust washers. Increasing thickness will decrease backlash and decreasing thickness will increase backlash.
4. Intall the lock pin into the pinion shaft and caulk to prevent loosening. Install the ring gear after making sure there are no burrs or dirt. Tighten bolt to 47 ft/lbs.
5. Check the lateral runout of the ring gear. Maximum allowable is .033 in. If the runout is greater, make sure there are no burrs holding the gear in a cocked position and that the bolts are evenly torqued.

Check for side bearing preload and backlash:

1. Install side bearings. Make sure to support the opposite side of the case on the pilot to prevent bearing damage.
2. Put the case assembly into the carrier, less the side bearing shims. Using two sets of feeler gauges, insert enough feeler thickness to remove all end-play. Make sure the feelers are pushed to the bottom of the bearing bores.
3. Mount a dial gauge, as illustrated, at right angles to a tooth on the ring gear. Adjust feeler thickness from side to side until ring gear backlash is .005 in. to .007 in.
4. Remove the feeler gauges and determine the amount of thickness needed. Add .002 in. to each shim pack for side bearing preload.
5. Remove the case assembly and both side bearings and install shim packs with respective side bearing.
6. Put the case assembly and races into the carrier. Use a soft-faced hammer to drive it in until the side bearing races bottom in their bores. Install the side bearing caps in their original location and torque the bolts to 35 ft/lbs.
7. Rotate the case several times to seat the bearings and check the backlash and preload using a torque wrench on a ring gear bolt. The torque required to turn the case should be 25 in/lbs for new bearings and 15 in/lbs for used. If torque is not correct, it will be necessary to reshim the side bearings.
8. Install the torque tube assembly and put in the axle shafts.

REAR SUSPENSION

Springs

REMOVAL AND INSTALLATION

1. Raise the car and remove the wheels.
2. Raise the axle with another jack.
3. Disconnect the lower end of the shock absorbers.
4. Lower the jack holding the axle until the spring can be removed by hand.

Installation is the reverse. Torque the shock nut to 29 ft/lbs, and the lug nuts to 50 ft/lbs.

Shock Absorbers

REMOVAL AND INSTALLATION

1. Raise the car and remove the wheel.
2. Disconnect the lower end of absorber from the axle.
3. Remove the fuel tank cover from inside the trunk and disconnect the upper end of the shock.

Installation is the reverse procedure. Torque shock-to-axle nut to 29 ft/lbs and lug nuts to 50 ft/lbs.

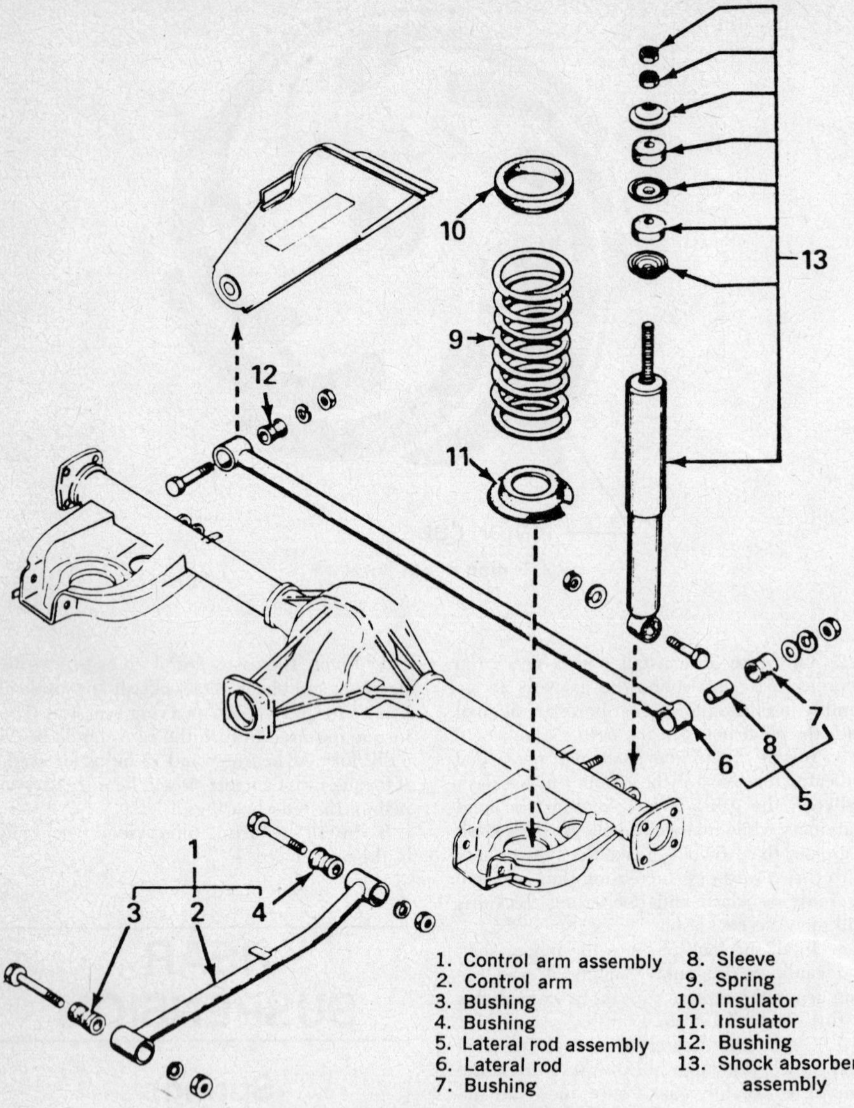

1. Control arm assembly
2. Control arm
3. Bushing
4. Bushing
5. Lateral rod assembly
6. Lateral rod
7. Bushing
8. Sleeve
9. Spring
10. Insulator
11. Insulator
12. Bushing
13. Shock absorber assembly

Exploded view of rear suspension

FRONT SUSPENSION

Springs

REMOVAL AND INSTALLATION

1. Raise the car and remove the wheel.
2. Remove the tie rod cotter key and castle nut. Disconnect the tie rod end from the steering knuckle.
3. Remove the lower shock bolt and collapse the shock. Remove the stabilizer bar bolt and grommet assembly from lower control arm.
4. Remove the upper brake caliper bolt and slide hose clip back ½ in.
5. Compress spring with a reliable spring compressor. Raise the lower control arm until level and support it with a jackstand.
6. Loosen the lower ball joint castle nut until the top of the nut is flush with the top of the ball joint. Disconnect the lower ball joint from the steering knuckle. A ball joint remover is necessary.
7. Remove the hub assembly and steering knuckle from lower ball joint and support it out of the way with a piece of wire.
8. Remove the support from under the control arm and loosen the compressor while prying the control arm down.

To install the spring:

1. Seat the spring between the lower control arm and crossmember. Compress it until the control arm can be moved to a level position.
2. Replace the support under the control arm and remove the compressor.
3. Attach the hub assembly and steering knuckle to the joint and torque castle nut to 72 ft/lbs.
4. Attach the upper ball joint to steering knuckle and torque to 40 ft/lbs.
5. Install the stabilizer bar bolt and grommet to the lower control arm and tighten the nut to the end of the threads on the bolt.
6. Install the lower shock bolt and torque to 29 ft/lbs. Slide the hose clip in place and install the upper caliper bolt. Torque to 36 ft/lbs.
7. Attach the tie rod end to the steering knuckle and torque castle nut to 29 ft/lbs. Put in a NEW cotter pin.
8. Install the wheels and torque lug nuts to 50 ft/lbs.

Shock Absorbers

REMOVAL AND INSTALLATION

1. Raise the car and remove the wheel.
2. Disconnect the shock from the upper control arm.
3. From inside the engine compartment, remove the shock nuts and take out the shock.

To install:

1. Install the shock absorber.
2. Install grommets and washers and tighten thicker nut to the end of the threads and install locknut.
3. Connect shock to upper control arm and torque to 29 ft/lbs. Replace wheel and torque lug nuts to 50 ft/lbs.

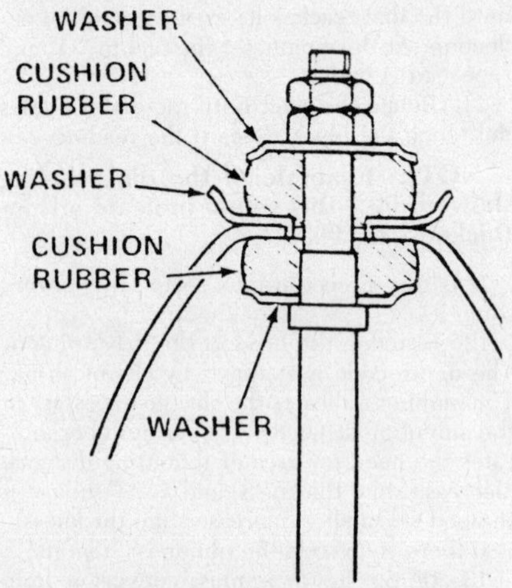

Front shock absorber installation

Upper Ball Joint

REMOVAL AND INSTALLATION

To remove the upper ball joint:

1. Raise the car and remove wheel.
2. Remove the upper caliper bolt and slide hose clip back ½ in. Remove the lower shock absorber bolt and compress shock absorber.
3. Raise the lower control arm until level and support it with a jackstand. Loosen the upper ball joint castle nut until the top of the nut is flush with the top of the ball joint. Disconnect the ball joint from the steering knuckle with a ball joint remover.
4. Remove the two bolts holding the ball joint to the control arm.
5. Installation is the reverse procedure. Torque control arm bolts to 29 ft/lbs and the upper castle nut to 40 ft/lbs.

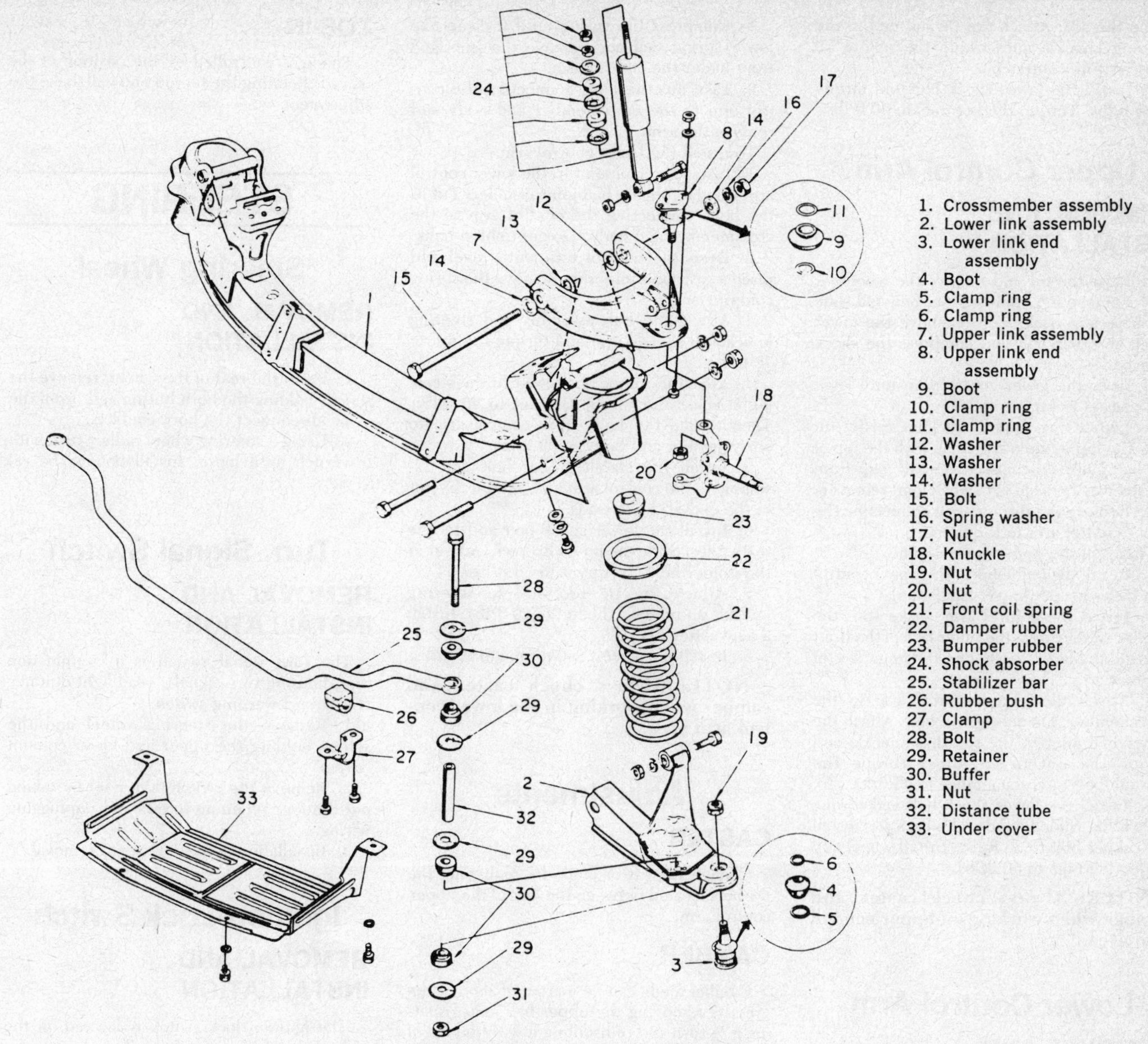

Exploded view of front suspension

6. The shock absorber should be torqued to 29 ft/lbs and the upper brake caliper bolt to 36 ft/lbs. Torque the lug nuts to 50 ft/lbs.

Lower Ball Joint

REMOVAL AND INSTALLATION

1. Raise the car and remove wheel.
2. Remove tie rod cotter pin and castle nut. Disconnect the tie rod end from the steering knuckle and remove the stabilizer bar bolt from the lower control arm.
3. Remove the upper caliper bolt and slip hose clip back ½ in. Remove the lower shock absorber bolt and compress the shock absorber.
4. Put the spring compressor over the upper control arm and let it hang. Place a support under the lower control arm and loosen lower ball joint castle nut until the top of the nut is flush with the top of the ball joint.
5. Disconnect the ball joint from the steering knuckle with a ball joint remover. Remove the hub assembly and steering knuckle from the ball joint and tie them to the side with wire.
6. Put the spring compressor between the first exposed coil of the spring, tighten and remove the jackstand from under the control arm.
7. Remove the lower ball joint from the control arm.

To install the ball joint:

1. Install the new ball joint using a reliable ball joint installer. DO NOT STRIKE the ball joint bottom during installation.
2. Place the jackstand under the lower control arm and remove the compressor. Attach the hub and steering knuckle and torque nut to 72 ft/lbs.
3. Slide the hose clip back and install the upper caliper bolt. Tighten to 36 ft/lbs.
4. Install the stabilizer bar bolt and grommet to control arm. Tighten the nut to the end

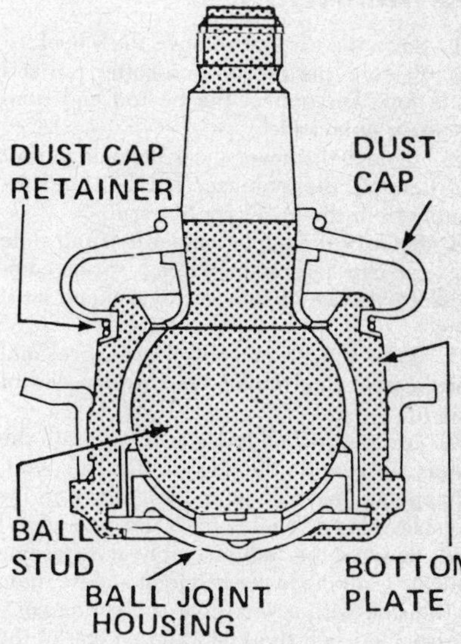

Lower ball joint

of the threads. Attach the tie rod end to the steering knuckle and torque the nut to 29 ft/lbs. Put in a cotter pin.

5. Install the lower shock bolt and torque to 29 ft/lbs. Torque the lug nuts to 50 ft/lbs.

Upper Control Arm

REMOVAL AND INSTALLATION

1. Raise the car and remove the wheel.
2. Remove the upper caliper bolt and slide the hose clip back ½ in. Remove the lower shock absorber bolt and compress the shock absorber.
3. Raise the lower control arm until level and place a jackstand under it.
4. Loosen the upper ball joint castle nut until the top of the nut is flush with the top of the ball joint. Disconnect the ball joint from the steering knuckle with a ball joint remover.
5. Remove the through bolt connecting the upper control arm to the frame.

To install the upper control arm:

1. Install the ball joint to the upper control arm (refer to Ball Joint Installation).
2. Install the control arm; make sure the smaller washer is on the inner face of the front arm and the larger washer on the inner face of the rear arm.
3. Attach the upper control arm to the crossmember. Do not tighten bolt. Attach the upper ball joint to the steering knuckle and torque the nut to 40 ft/lbs. Torque the through bolt-to-crossmember to 43 ft/lts.
4. Install the lower shock bolt and torque to 29 ft/lbs. Slide the hose clip back and install the caliper bolt to 36 ft/lbs. Install wheel and torque lug nuts to 50 ft/lbs.

NOTE: Always check caster and camber when working on upper control arm area.

Lower Control Arm

REMOVAL AND INSTALLATION

1. Raise the car and remove the wheel.
2. Remove the tie rod end cotter pin and castle nut. Disconnect the tie rod end from the steering knuckle.
3. Remove the lower shock bolt and push it up. Remove the stabilizer bar bolt and assembly from the lower control arm.
4. Remove the upper caliper bolt and slide the hose clip back ½ in. Place a spring compressor over the upper control arm and let it hang.
5. Raise the lower control arm level and place a jack stand under the extreme end of the arm.
6. Loosen the ball joint castle nut until the nut is flush with the top of the ball joint. Disconnect the ball joint from the steering knuckle using a reliable ball joint remover.
7. Remove the hub assembly and steering knuckle from the lower ball joint and tie them to the side with a wire. Put the spring compressor between the first exposed coil of the spring.
8. Compress the spring until it clears the lower spring seat and remove the jackstand from under the control arm.
9. Take out the bolts connecting the control arm to the crossmember and body and remove the arm.

To install the lower control arm:

1. Install the ball joint to the lower control arm using a reliable ball joint installer. Put in the bolts connecting the control arm to the crossmember and body. Do not tighten bolts.
2. Raise the control arm until level and place a jackstand under it. Remove the spring compressor.
3. Attach the hub assembly and steering knuckle to control arm and torque the nut to 72 ft/lbs.
4. Attach the upper ball joint to the steering knuckle and torque the nut to 40 ft/lbs. Then torque the bolts from control arm to crossmember and body to 43 ft/lbs.
5. Install the stabilizer bar bolt and assembly to the control arm and tighten the nut to the end of the threads.
6. Install the lower shock bolt and torque to 29 ft/lbs. Slide the hose clip back and put in the caliper bolt. Torque it to 36 ft/lbs.
7. Attach the tie rod end to steering knuckle and torque the nut to 29 ft/lbs. Install a new cotter pin.
8. Install the wheels and torque to 50 ft/lbs.

NOTE: Always check caster and camber when working in the lower control arm area.

Adjustments

CASTER

Change the caster angle by realigning the washers located between the legs of the upper control arm.

CAMBER

Camber angle can be increased about 1 degree by removing the upper ball joint, rotating it ½ turn and reinstalling it with the flat of the upper flange on the inboard side of the control arm.

TOE-IN

Toe-in is controlled by the position of the tie rod. Rotating the tie rod end will make the adjustment.

STEERING

Steering Wheel

REMOVAL AND INSTALLATION

1. From the rear of the wheel, remove the screws holding the horn button and, from the front, disconnect the horn contacts.
2. Using a steering wheel puller, turn with a wrench until loose. Installation is the reverse.

Turn Signal Switch

REMOVAL AND INSTALLATION

The turn signal switch is a combination unit, housing turn signals, head light dimmer and hazard warning switch.

1. Remove the steering wheel and the screws holding the upper and lower column covers.
2. Remove the switch (left side) by taking out the four retaining screws and unplugging wiring.
3. Installation is the reverse of removal.

Ignition Lock Switch

REMOVAL AND INSTALLATION

The ignition lock switch is located on the right side of the steering column, near the windshield wiper switch.

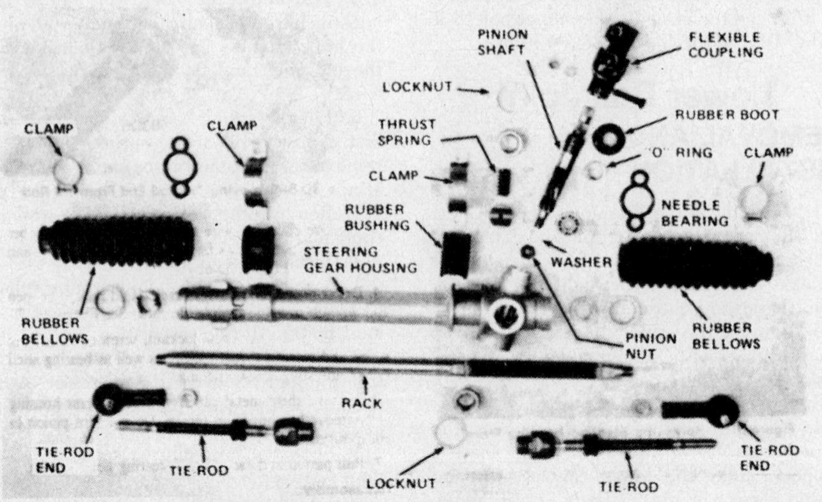

Exploded view of steering gear

1. Remove steering wheel and column covers.
2. Remove the snap ring and the three bolts holding the switch to the column. Unplug the wiring.
3. Installation is the reverse of removal.

Steering Gear

ADJUSTMENT

1. Set the wheels straight ahead, with the steering wheel centered.
2. Loosen the locknut around the adjusting screw in the steering gear housing and turn the screw in until resistance is felt.
3. Back out the screw ⅛ to ¼ of a turn and tighten the locknut to 49 ft/lbs.

BRAKES

Adjustment

Both front and rear brakes are self-adjusting.

MASTER CYLINDER

Removal and Installation

1. Disconnect the front and rear outlet pipes from the master cylinder.
2. Remove the nuts holding the master to the brake booster and support bracket.
3. Remove the bolts holding the fluid reservoir bracket and take out the master cylinder assembly complete with reservior.

NOTE: Be careful not to drip brake fluid on painted surfaces.

To install the master cylinder:

1. Place the unit, together with the fluid reservoir (with rubber hoses) in line with the reservoir bracket and bolt it on.
2. Install the nuts holding the master cylinder to the brake booster and support bracket.
3. Connect the front and rear brake pipes.
4. Torque the master-to-brake booster bolt to 10 ft/lbs. Tighten the brake pipes to 12 ft/lbs. Bleed the brake system.

Overhaul

1. Remove the master cylinder.
2. Pour the fluid out of the reservoir.
3. Place the master cylinder in a vise and remove the pipe connectors. Remove the check valves, springs and retainers.
4. Push in the primary piston with a screwdriver and remove the secondary piston stop bolt and snap-ring.
5. Remove the primary and secondary piston assemblies from the cylinder.
6. Clean the parts with brake fluid. *Do not* use any other type of solvent. Dry with compressed air.
7. Using a good caliper measure the cylinder bore diameter and outside diameter of the primary and secondary pistons. Compare the two to determine the clearance. Replace the master cylinder assembly if clearance is beyond 0.0006 in.

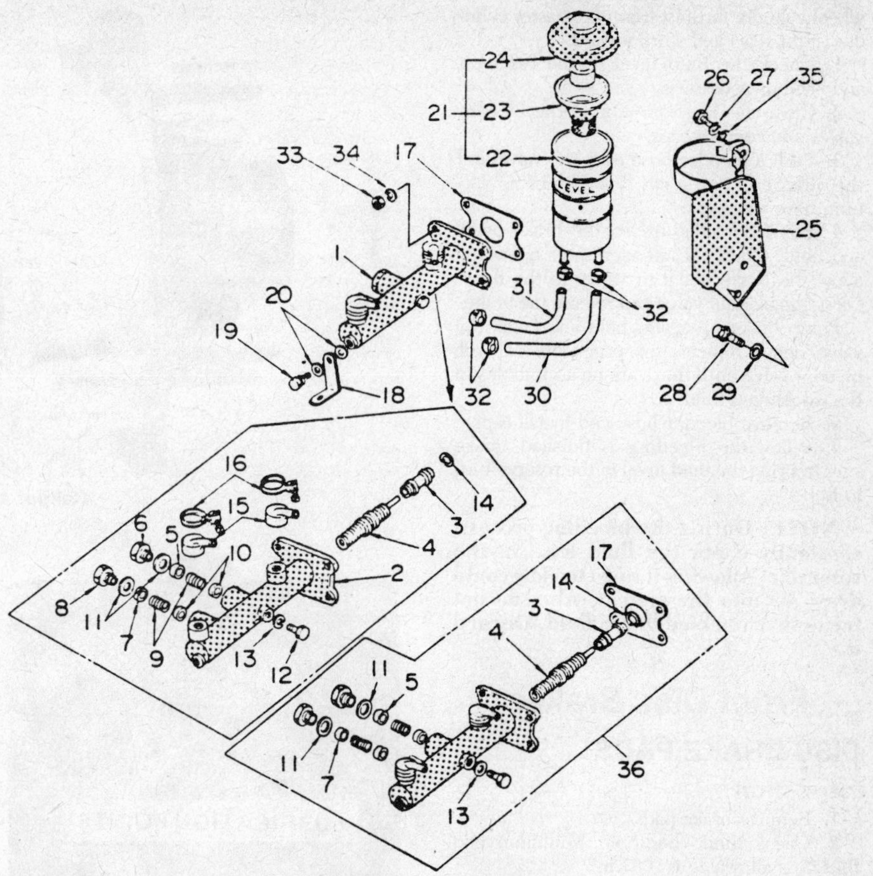

1. Tandem master cylinder assembly
2. Cylinder body
3. Primary piston assembly
4. Secondary piston assembly
5. Primary check valve
6. Connector
7. Secondary piston assembly
8. Connector
9. Check valve spring
10. Check valve spring retainer
11. Gasket
12. Stopper bolt
13. Gasket
14. Snap ring
15. Connector
16. Clip
17. Gasket
18. Bracket
19. Bolt
20. Washer
21. Fluid reservoir assembly
22. Body
23. Filter
24. Cover
25. Bracket
26. Screw
27. Washer
28. Bolt
29. Washer
30. Rubber hose, front
31. Rubber hose, rear
32. Clip
33. Nut
34. Washer
35. Washer
36. Tandem master cylinder repair kit

Exploded view of master cylinder

8. Check the master cylinder inner wall for damage. Replace if necessary. Check the pistons for wear or damage. Replace if necessary.
9. Always replace the piston cups as their condition affects the performance of the system. Piston must also be replaced if damaged. They are not repairable.
10. Check the front and rear check valves for poor contact or damage. Check the fluid reservoir and rubber hoses for damage, cracking or bulging. Check the snap-rings and gaskets for fatigue and replace if necessary.

To Assemble:

1. Check for dirt in the cylinder bore, or any parts going into it. Lubricate the brake parts with clean brake fluid.
2. Assemble the retainer, spring, check valve, gasket and pipe connector to the cylinder body and semi-tighten the connector. The check valve in the front has a center hole. Install the one without the hole in the rear.
3. Clamp the cylinder body in a soft-jawed vise and tighten the connector to 87 ft/lbs. Install the secondary piston assembly.
4. Install the primary piston assembly and secure with snap-ring. Note the direction of setting when assembling. Do not force the piston as damage to the cups may result.
5. Press the primary piston all the way in with a screwdriver and hold. Install the secondary piston stop bolt with gasket on the cylinder body. Tighten the bolt to 14 ft/lbs.
6. Install the master cylinder.

Brake System Indicator Light

The brake system light is connected in parallel with the parking brake switch. The sending unit is located on the master cylinder and cannot be adjusted. Any malfunction of the unit requires replacement.

Bleeding

The engine *must be running* during the bleeding operation, to prevent damage to the brake booster pushrod seal; therefore, perform this operation only in a well-venilated area. Begin the bleeding operation with the wheel cylinder farthest from the master cylinder (right rear) and work towards it.

1. Check the fluid level in the reservoir and refill as necessary.
2. Clean all dirt from around the bleeder valves and remove caps.
3. Push a bleeder hose over the valve and the other end into a jar. A length of ⅛" vacuum hose will work.
4. Pump up pressure on the brake pedal and hold. Crack the bleeder valve open and allow the brake pedal to travel to the floor. Close the bleeder valve and release the brake.

Pump brake up again, hold and crack the valve open. Repeat this procedure at each bleeder valve until there are no air bubbles in the discharged fluid.

5. Remove bleeder hose and install caps.
6. When the bleeding is finished, make sure to bring the fluid level in the reservoir up to full.

NOTE: During the bleeding process, constantly check the fluid level in the reservoir. Allowing it to go too low could draw air into the system. Also, do not try to save the bled brake fluid. Discard it.

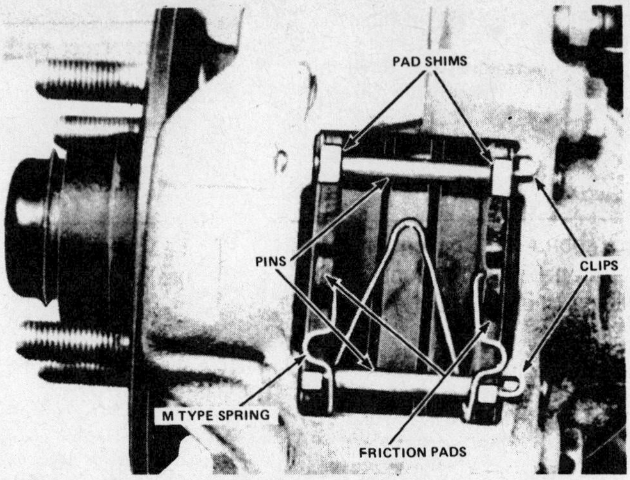

Caliper and brake pad

Front Disc Brakes

DISC BRAKE PADS

Inspection

1. Remove brake pads.
2. Check their condition. Minimum pad thickness allowable is .067 in.

Removal and Installation

1. Raise and support the front of the car, and remove the wheels.
2. Remove clips, pins, "M" type spring, pad shims and friction pads.

Pad lubrication points

3. Remove any dirt from friction pad recess and visually inspect piston seals for leakage.
4. Apply grease (included in pad repair kit) to the small areas on the pad.
5. Push the pistons into bores and while holding, open bleeder valves slightly to keep from overflowing the reservoir. Tighten valve when pistons bottom.
6. Put anti-rattle shims on brake pads with arrows pointing forward. Install caliper.
7. Install the "M" type spring, pins and clips. Install the wheels and lower the car.

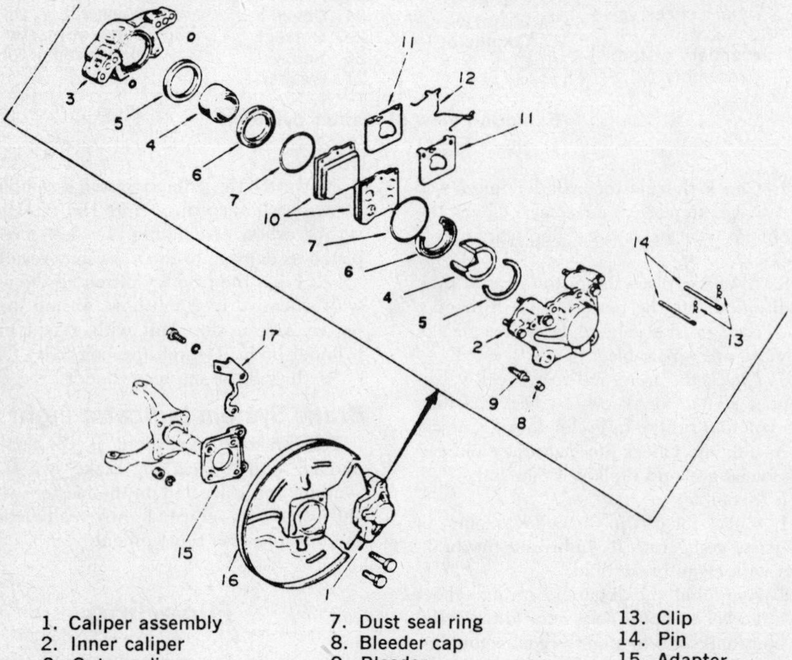

1. Caliper assembly
2. Inner caliper
3. Outer caliper
4. Piston
5. Piston seal
6. Dust seal
7. Dust seal ring
8. Bleeder cap
9. Bleeder
10. Pad assembly
11. Pad shim
12. M type spring
13. Clip
14. Pin
15. Adapter
16. Dust cover
17. Bracket

Exploded view of front disc brake

DISC BRAKE CALIPERS

Removal and Installation

1. Raise front of car, support, and remove wheel.
2. Disconnect the brake pipe from hose and cap or tape ends to protect from dirt.
3. Remove the caliper bolts and remove the caliper.
4. Installation is the reverse. Torque the caliper bolts to 36.2 ft/lbs and the brake flare nut to 11.6 ft/lbs.

Overhaul

1. Remove caliper and brake pads.
2. Remove the dust seal ring and take out dust seals from each piston.
3. Install clamp on mounting half of caliper and remove rim half piston by applying compressed air at the brake line connection.
4. Install the clamp on the rim half to remove the mounting half piston.
5. Remove fluid seals from annular grooves in caliper piston bores.

NOTE: The caliper is integral in design and cannot be taken apart. If fluid is leaking from a joint, replace the entire unit. NEVER disturb any of the bridge bolts.

To reassemble the caliper:

1. Apply grease compatible with the seals to the seal and cylinder wall. Insert new piston.
2. Carefully install the piston in the bottom of the bore using only finger pressure to avoid scratching.

3. Install the dust seal and seal ring. Insert pads as outlined in the Disc Brake Pads section.

4. Put the caliper on the disc and knuckle assembly and connect the brake hose to the pipe. Bleed the brakes.

BRAKE DISC

Removal and Installation

1. Raise the front of the car and support. Remove the wheel.
2. Remove the caliper and support it with a wire attached to the upper control arm.
3. Remove the hub and disc assembly by removing castle nut and bearing.
4. Clamp hub and disc in a vise using protective pads and remove retaining bolts.
5. Installation is the reverse of removal. Torque hub retaining bolts and caliper attaching bolts to 36 ft/lbs.

Inspection

Check the condition of the disc for scoring and wear. Minimum allowable thickness is 0.339 in. If disc warpage is .006 or more, the disc must be refaced.

WHEEL BEARINGS

Adjustment

1. Remove grease cap, cotter pin and castle nut.
2. Torque castle nut to 21 ft/lbs while turning the wheel forward. This allows the bearing to seat.
3. Back off the castle nut ¼ turn. If slot and cotter pin hole are staggered, back off farther. Never tighten the nut to align the slot and hole. Install a new cotter pin. A properly adjusted wheel bearing has a slight amount of end-play and a loose nut when adjusted this way.

Rear Drum Brakes

BRAKE DRUMS

Inspection

1. Jack up the rear of the car, support, and remove the wheels.
2. Tap the outside of the drum lightly with a hammer and pull the brake drum straight off. Tap the outside edge of the drum on the ground to knock out any loose dirt. Never blow out drum or brake part with compressed air. Asbestos particles cause cancer when inhaled. Clean the drum in solvent.
3. Look the inside of the drum over for scoring or evidence of heat. Keep your fingers off the contact surface as much as possible.
4. The original diameter for the drum is 8.980 inches and the maximum machined diameter is 9.040 inches.

Should the drum have an inside diameter of 9.060 inches, it must be discarded and replaced. If the drum is out of round by .003 or more, the drum should be turned.

Installation

Check the linings for any oil or grease. Align the holes in the drum with the adjustment holes in the axle flange and gently push the drum onto the wheel lugs. Install the wheel and torque lug nuts to 50 ft/lbs.

BRAKE SHOES

Removal and Installation

1. Raise the rear of the car, support, and remove the wheels and drums.

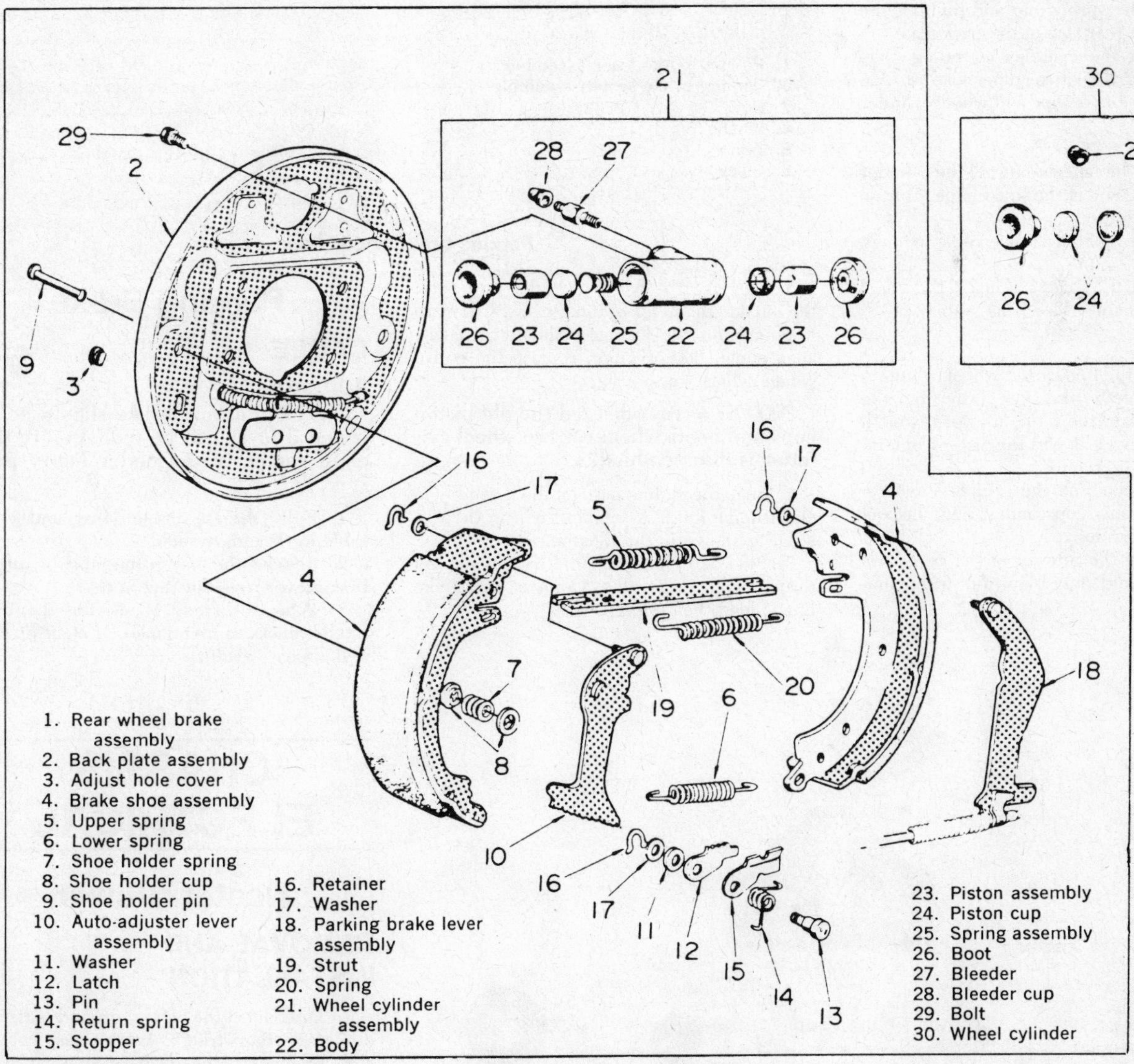

Exploded view of rear brakes

2. Remove the return springs, shoe holding pins, cups and springs.
3. Move the adjuster lever in the direction of expansion and disconnect the strut. Remove the primary shoe.
4. Disconnect the parking brake cable from the lever and remove the secondary shoe.

At this point, look over the shoes for wear or contamination with grease or oil.

Should the brakes show 0.040 or less, they must be replaced.

To install:

NOTE: When installing the brakes, make sure not to scratch the wheel cylinder boots.

1. Install the secondary shoe and the parking brake cable to the lever.
2. Install the primary shoe, the strut and the automatic adjusting lever.
3. Install the return springs, shoe holding pins, cups and springs.
4. Install the wheel and drum assembly.

WHEEL CYLINDERS

Removal and Installation

1. Remove brake shoes.
2. Pry on the spring cup and pull out the cable from the rear face of the back plate.
3. Take out the cylinder mounting bolts and disconnect the brake pipe. Cap or tape the ends of the brake pipe and wheel cylinder to keep out dirt.

To install:

1. Remove the tape and install the cylinder assembly and connect the brake pipe. Torque the bolts to 7 ft/lbs.
2. Install the parking brake cable through the back plate.
3. Assemble the shoes and install the wheel and drum assembly. Bleed the system.

Overhaul

1. Remove the brakes and wheel cylinder.
2. Pry (carefully) the boot away from the cylinder bore and see if the interior is wet. If it is, it indicates a leak past the pistons and the cylinder must be rebuilt.
3. Pry the boots off the cylinders and remove the pistons, cups and spring. Inspect the cylinders carefully.
4. Wash out the interior of the bore with clean brake fluid and blow out with compressed air.

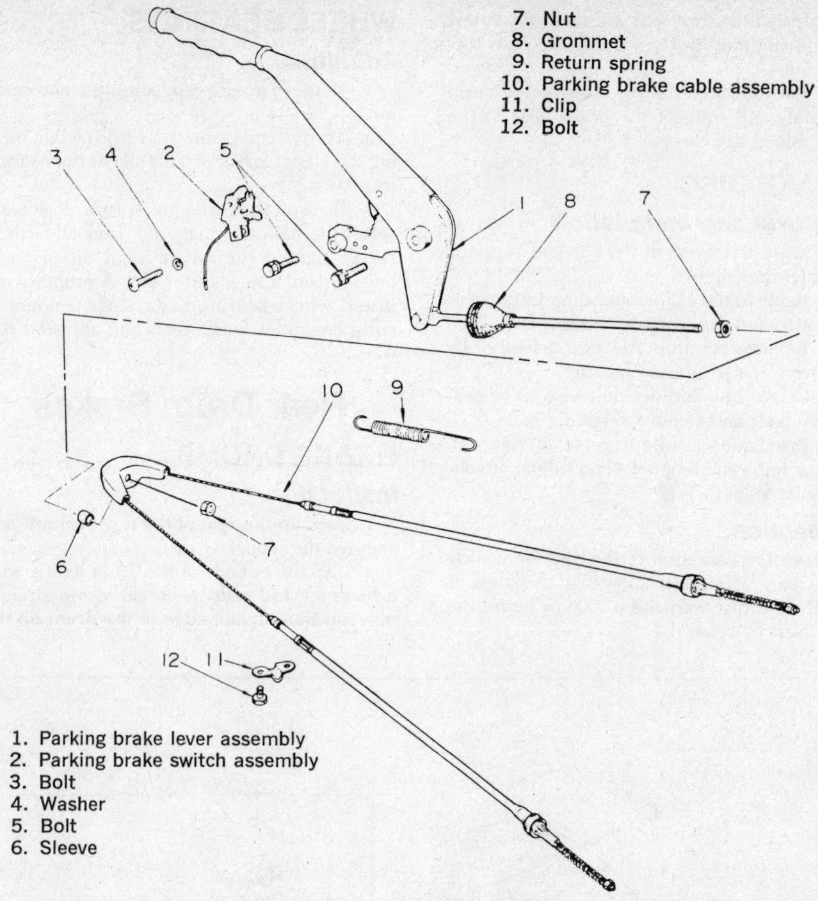

Parking brake and linkage

5. Measure the wheel cylinder bore, and the outside diameter of the pistons. Compare to determine the clearance. Should the clearance equal .006 or more, replace the entire wheel cylinder assembly.

NOTE: Always discard the old piston cups and boots whenever the wheel cylinder is disassembled.

1. Soak the sliding parts of the assembly in clean brake fluid. Assemble them in the cylinder as shown in the illustration.
2. Put the cylinder on the back plate and torque bolts to 7 ft/lbs. Connect the brake line. Bleed the system.

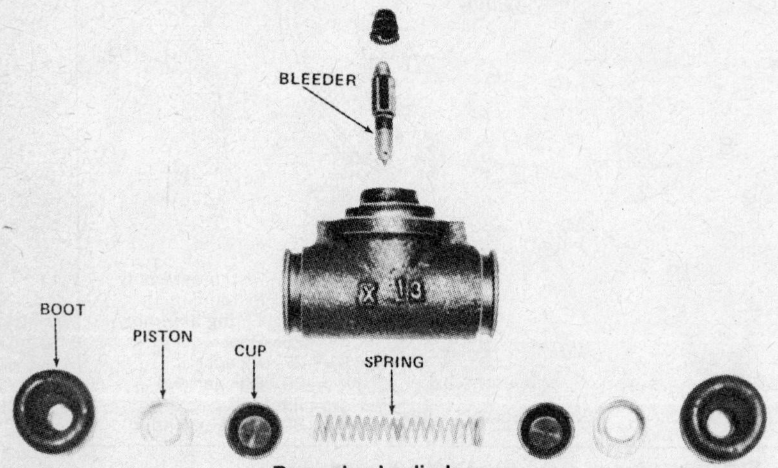

Rear wheel cylinder

Parking Brake

CABLE

Adjustment

NOTE: Parking brake should be adjusted if lever can be pulled more than eight ratchet clicks under heavy pressure.

1. Fully release brake lever and check cable for free movement.
2. Remove the play in the cable by turning brake lever rod adjusting nut.
3. Whe adjusted, check for the eight ratchet clicks as mentioned. If eight or more still appear, readjust.

CHASSIS ELECTRICAL

Heater Blower

REMOVAL AND INSTALLATION

1. Disconnect the battery ground cable and disconnect the wiring at the blower.
2. Remove the heater hose coupling at the cowl.

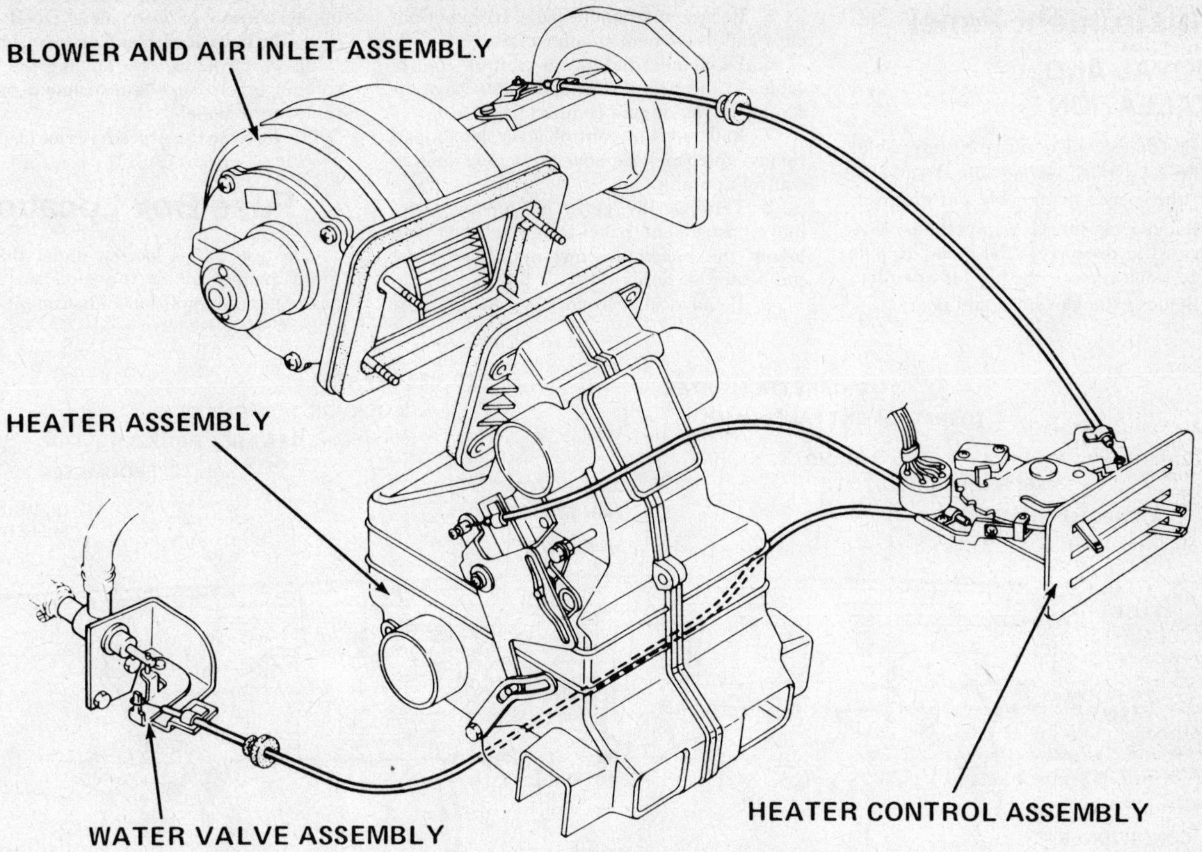

Exploded view of heater and blower assembly

3. Remove the screws and pull out the blower motor and squirrel cage.
4. Remove the clip holding the cage to the motor and remove cage.
5. To install, reverse removal procedures.

Heater Core

REMOVAL AND INSTALLATION

1. Disconnect battery ground cable and drain the radiator.
2. Disconnect heater hoses at connections and plug core tubes to stop spilling.
3. Remove blower case cover and disconnect air door cable. Disconnect the temperature cable at the water valve.
4. Remove the steering wheel and the instrument cluster. Disconnect the wiring for gauges, remove console retaining screws, untie shift lever leather and remove.
5. Remove heater control and radio face plate. Remove the radio and glove box.
6. Disconnect selector cable from driver's side of heater unit. Carefully pull temperature and fresh air cables through cowling and remove control panel.
7. Remove instrument panel assembly.
8. Remove the bolt from the heater unit located at the rear, bottom. Remove four nuts holding unit and blower together and remove heater.
9. Separate heater unit case halves and remove core.
10. Installation is the reverse procedure.

Radio

REMOVAL AND INSTALLATION

Disconnect negative battery cable.

1. Remove ash tray and tray support. Remove radio knobs by pulling off.
2. Remove the radio shaft nuts and trim panel.
3. Remove retainer screws from under dash.
4. Disconnect electrical connectors and lead-in cable and take the radio out through the back of the dash.
5. To install, reverse removal procedures.

Windshield Wiper Motor

REMOVAL AND INSTALLATION

1. Disconnect negative battery cable.
2. Remove nut, washer and crank arm from under the instrument panel.
3. Disconnect wiring at connector.
4. Remove the rubber boot, three screws and the motor assembly.
5. Installation is the reverse of removal.

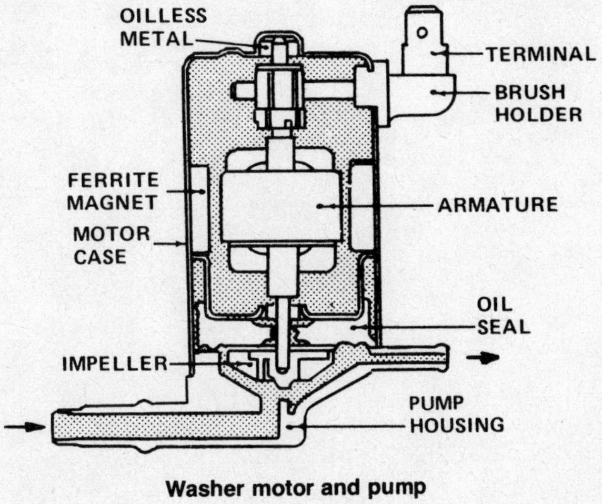

Washer motor and pump

Instrument Panel

REMOVAL AND INSTALLATION

1. Disconnect the negative battery cable.
2. Remove the steering wheel and disconnect the speedometer cable and wing nut.
3. Remove cluster screws, rotate the cluster outward to disconnect the 6 and 12 pole connectors and remove the cluster assembly.
4. Remove the glove box and door.
5. Release instrument panel harness from clips and disconnect at connectors.
6. Disconnect the heater control, control cables at the heater unit and water valve assembly in the engine compartment.
7. Pull out the control lever knobs and remove the panel. Remove the screws and the control assembly.
8. Through the glove box opening, remove instrument panel-to-bracket bolt and loosen the bracket-to-cowl nut. Disconnect the heater air hoses.
9. Remove the three nuts holding the upper portion of instrument panel and remove the bolts at each end of the inside panel.
10. Remove the nuts holding the steering column bracket to the instrument panel and remove the panel.
11. Reverse the procedures for installation.

Fuse Box Location

The fuse box is located under the instrument panel, along the side wall of the passenger's side of the compartment.

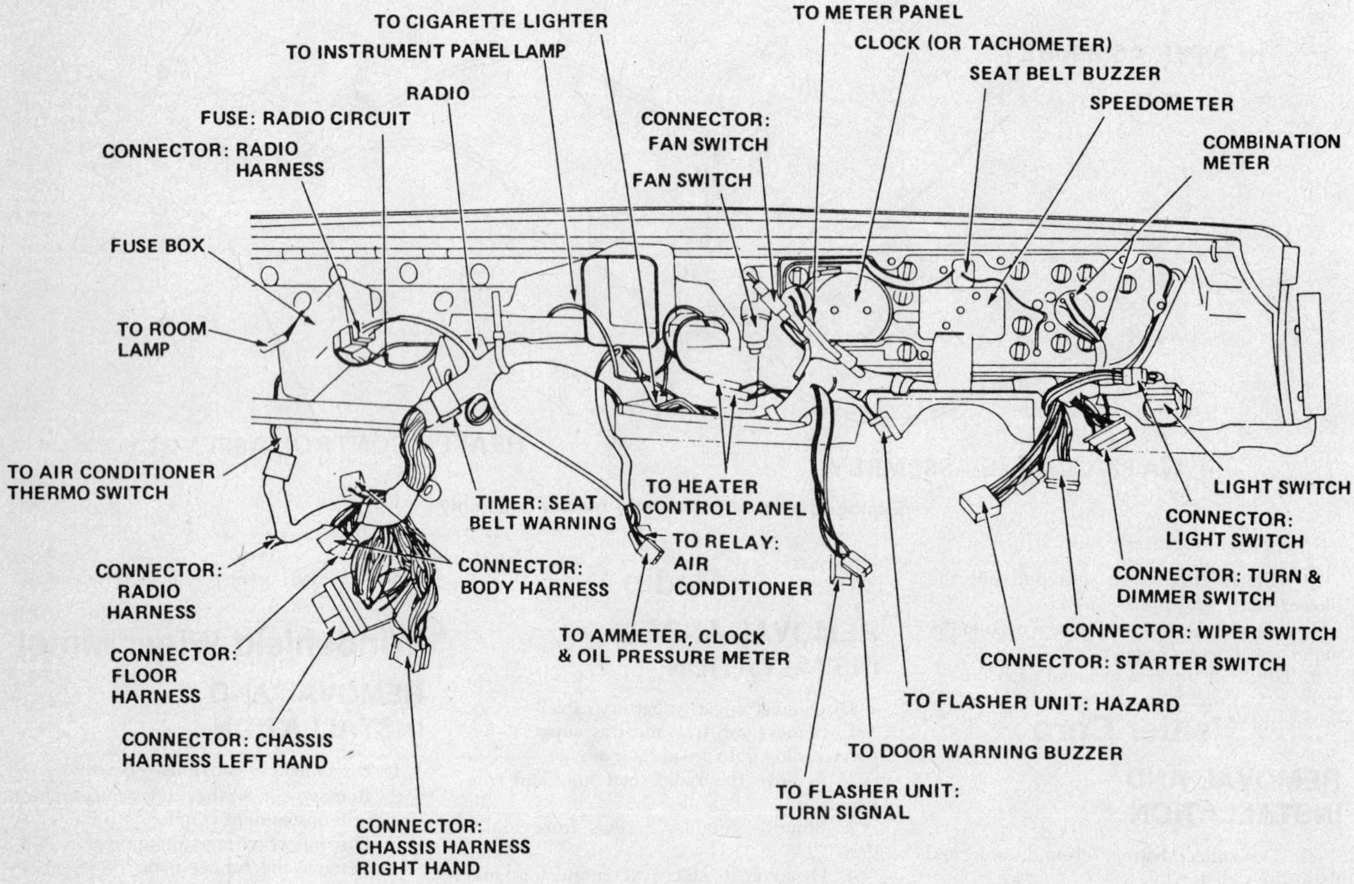

Connections to the rear of the instrument panel

SPECIFICATIONS

INDEX

BEFORE SERVICING, SEE THE SAFETY NOTICE ON THE CONTENTS PAGE

INTRODUCTION

Peugeot Motor Company built its first vehicle in 1889, a steam powered three wheeler. Peugeot later acquired the patent rights for the Daimler engines and began production of their first gasoline powered vehicles. Although Peugeot sold automobiles in one hundred and five countries throughout the world, none were imported to the United States until 1958. At that time, the 403 model was introduced, followed by the 404 model. The models 504 and 304 (front wheel drive) replaced the 404 model in 1970, with the 304 model being discontinued after the 1971 model year. The 604 model was introduced in 1977, with the 505 model replacing the 504 model during the 1980 model year. Four cylinder engines were and are used in the 403, 404, 304, 504 and 505 models, while the 604 is powered by a V6 engine. Diesel engines are available for the 504 and 505 models.

SERIAL NUMBER IDENTIFICATION

Vehicles

504, 505 MODELS

The vehicle serial number is stamped on the left hand engine mounting lug. The same number is stamped on the right front fender well. The manufacturer's identification plate is located on the right fender well.

604 MODELS

The serial number is stamped on the right front fender well and the manufacturer's plate is located on the right front fender well.

Engine

The engine number is stamped on the camshaft tunnel of the engine. The number consists of a letter followed by 5 digits, and a final identification letter. The identification letter codes are as follows.

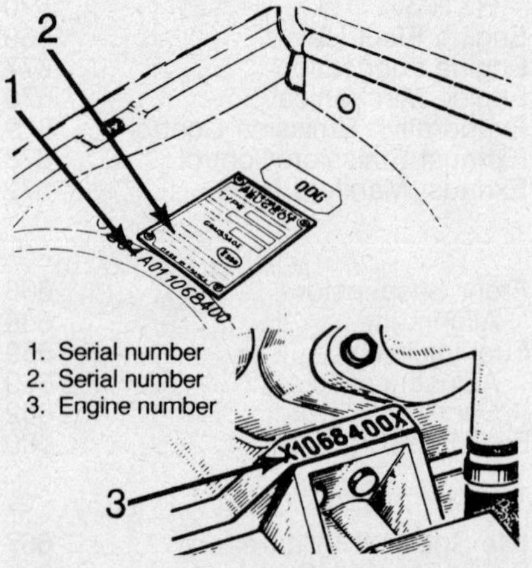

The 504 and 505 serial number is located on the right fender well. The engine number is located on the camshaft tunnel

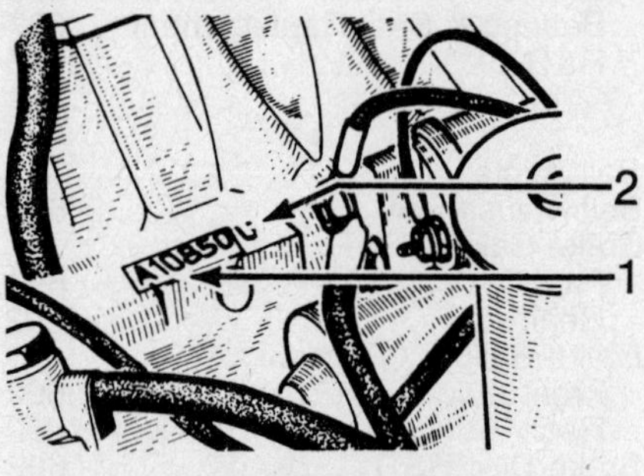

The last digit of the 504 and 505 engine number is a letter code that is keyed to the engine type

ENGINE IDENTIFICATION CODES

Model	Code	Engine cu. in. (cc)	Carburetor	Transmission
504	U, UA, UB	XN1 120.3 (1971)	Two-1bbl ①	BA7 Manual
	X, XA, XB	XN1 120.3 (1971)	Two-1bbl ①	ZF Automatic
505	N.A.	XN6 120.3 (1971)	Fuel Injected	BVM Manual ZF Automatic
604	9	112 165 (2664)	One-1bbl One-2bbl	BA10 Manual ZF Automatic
	N.A.	151 174 (2849)	One-1bbl One-2bbl	BA10 Manual ZF Automatic

① Some 504 models in the US will have One-2bbl carburetor
N.A. Not Available

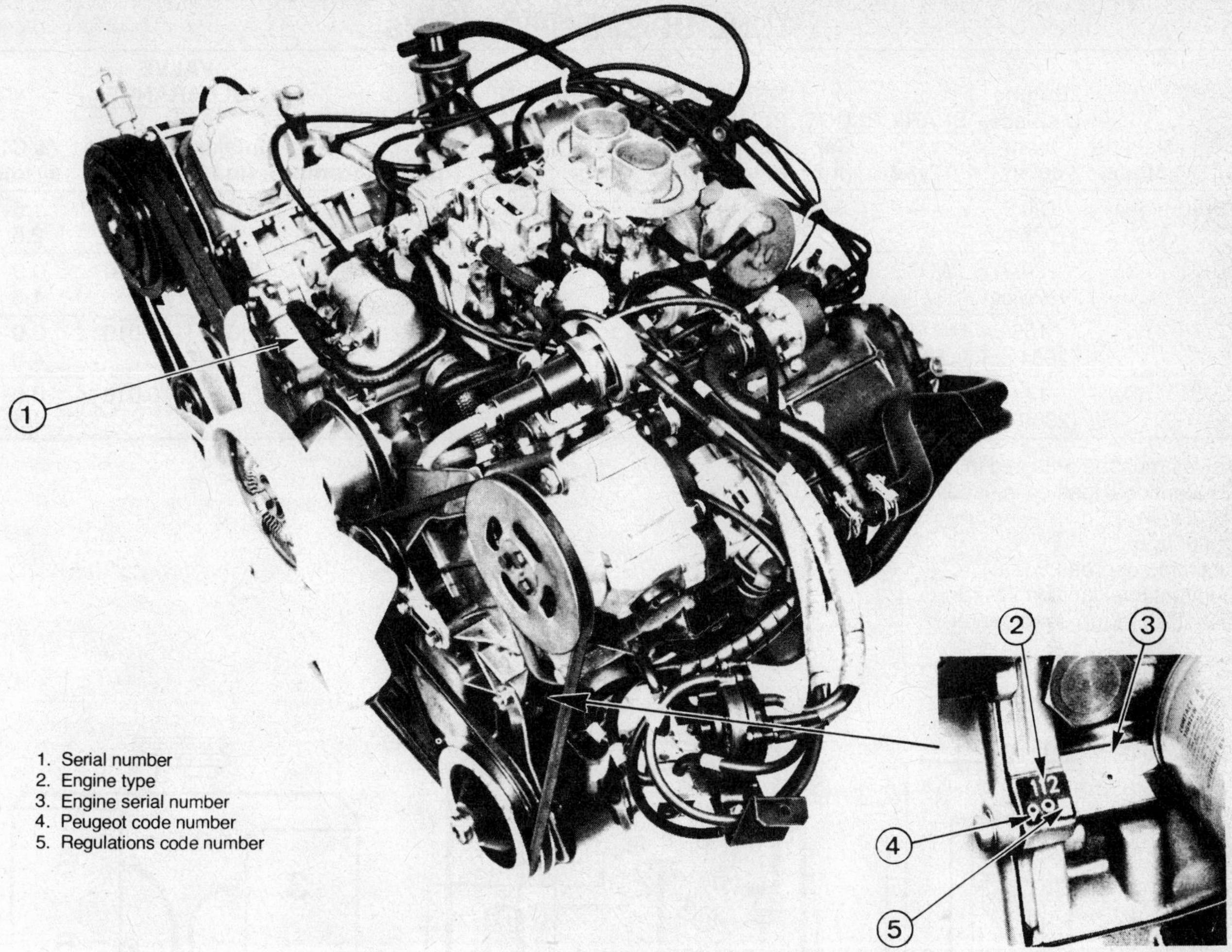

1. Serial number
2. Engine type
3. Engine serial number
4. Peugeot code number
5. Regulations code number

The location of model 604 engine and vehicle serial numbers

GENERAL ENGINE SPECIFICATIONS

Year	Vehicle Model	Engine Displacement cu. in.	Carburetor Type	SAE Horsepower @ rpm	SAE Torque @ rpm (ft. lbs.)	Bore x Stroke (in.)	Compression Ratio	Oil Pressure (psi)
1975-80	504	120.3 (1971 cc)	Twin-1 barrel	87 @ 5500	119 @ 3000	3.46 x 3.19	7.6:1	27-50
1980-81	505	120.3 (1971 cc)	K Jetronic Fuel injec.	96 @ 4900	116 @ 3300	3.46 x 3.19	8.4:1	27
1977-78	604	165 (2664 cc)	1-1 barrel 1-2 barrel	133 @ 5750	150 @ 3500	3.47 x 2.87	8.2:1	28
1979-81	604	174 (2849 cc)	1-1 barrel 1-2 barrel	133 @ 5250	161 @ 3000	3.58 x 2.87	8.2:1	28

TUNE-UP SPECIFICATIONS

Year	Vehicle Model	Engine Displacement cu. in.	Spark Plugs Type	Spark Plugs Gap (in.)	Distributor Point Dwell (deg)	Distributor Point Gap (in.)	Ignition Timing ④ MT (deg)	Ignition Timing ④ AT (deg)	Idle Speed MT (rpm)	Idle Speed AT (rpm)	Valve Clearance ① Intake (in.)	Valve Clearance ① Exhaust (in.)	% CO @ Idle
1975-80	504	120.3 (1976 cc)	44XL	.024	55-59	0.016	5	5	800-850	800-850	0.006	0.012	1.5-2.5
1980-81	505	120.3 (1976 cc)	WR7DS	.024	Electronic		8 ③	8 ③	900-950	900-950	0.004	0.010	0.5-1.5
1977-78	604	165 (2664 cc)	42.5LTS BN9Y	.024	Electronic ② ⑤		10	10	900-950	900-950	0.004	0.010	3.0-4.5
1979-81	604	174 (2889 cc)	42.5LTS BN9Y	.024	Electronic ② ⑤		10	10	900-950	900-950	0.004	0.010	3.0-4.5

① Valves must be adjusted in proper sequence
② Conventional ignition is used in Canada (.016 in gap or 76° dwell)
③ At 900 rpm
④ All timing degrees BTDC
⑤ Conventional ignition 72-80°
BTDC Before top dead center

FIRING ORDERS

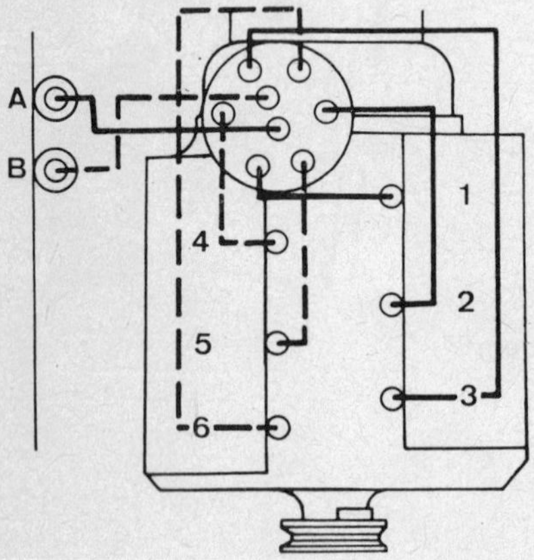

V6 engine firing order, conventional ignition

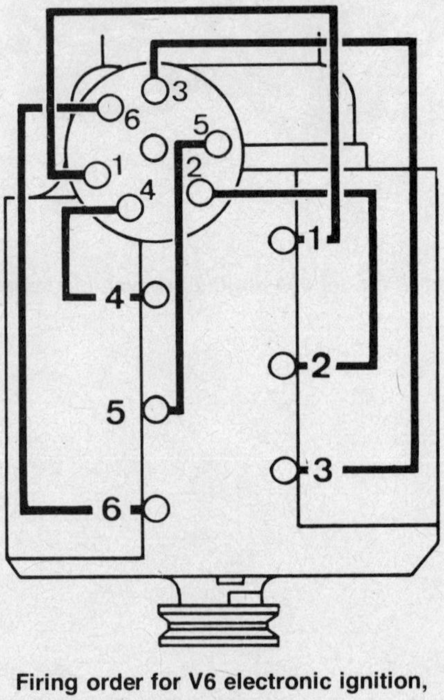

Firing order for V6 electronic ignition, (1-6-3-5-2-4), Bosch®

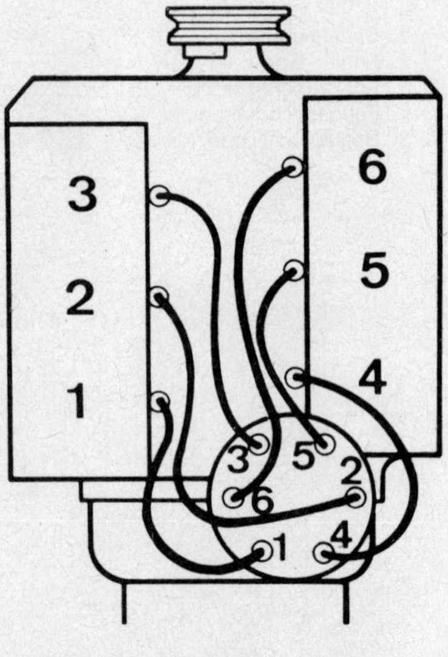

Firing order for Schlumberger® V6 electronic ignition

CAPACITIES

Year	Vehicle Model	Engine Crankcase (qts) With filter	Transmission (qts) Man	Transmission (qts) Auto	Drive Axle (qts)	Gasoline Tank (gals)	Cooling System (qts)
1975-80	504 Sedan	4.3	1.0	1.8	1.4	14.8	8.5
	504 SW	4.3	1.0	1.8	1.4	15.8	8.5
1980-81	505 Sedan	4.3	1.7	5.5	1.6	17.4	7.5
1977-81	604 Sedan	6.3	1.4	1.6	1.6	18.5	11.0

CRANKSHAFT AND CONNECTING ROD SPECIFICATIONS

All measurements in inches

		CRANKSHAFT				CONNECTING ROD		
Year/ Model	Engine Number	Engine Displacement cu. in.	Main Bearing Journal Dia.	Main Bearing Oil Clearance	Crankshaft End-Play	Journal Diameter	Oil Clear	Side Clear
1975-80 504	XN1	120.3	①	N.A.	0.0031-0.0079	1.9679-1.9685	N.A.	N.A.
1980-81 505	XN6	120.3	①	N.A.	0.0031-0.0079	1.9679-1.9685	N.A.	N.A.
1977-81 604	112	165	2.7576-2.7583	N.A.	0.0028-0.0106	2.0578-2.0585	N.A.	N.A.
	—	174						

① Rear journal 2.1616-2.1646
Rear interm. 2.2102-2.2073
Center 2.2509-2.2515
Front interm. 2.3050-2.3060
Front journal 2.3386-2.3392
N.A. Not available

MODEL 504 ALTERNATOR SPECIFICATIONS

Manufacturer	Type	Output @ 14V	Alternator Output rpm	Rotor Resistance In Ohms @ 68°F (20°C)
Ducellier	7529	20A	3000	7.0
	7575	30A	3000	5.5
Paris Rhone	A12M8	30A	3500	7.0
	A13M3	20A	3000	7.0
	A13R95	30A	3000	5.5
	A13R120	48A	3500	4.6
	A13R144	45A	3500	5.5
	A13R151	32A	3000	5.5
	A13R152	45A	3500	5.5
	A13R157	32A	3000	5.5
	A13R171	45A	3500	5.5
	A13R178	45A	3500	5.5
	A13R185	45A	3500	5.5
Sev	71229002	35A	4000	5.5
	71229302	35A	4000	5.5
Femsa	ALG12-7	35A	4000	5.5

TORQUE SPECIFICATIONS

All readings in ft. lbs.

Year	Vehicle Model	Cylinder Head Bolts	Rod Bearing Bolts	Main Bearing Bolts	Crankshaft Pulley Bolt	Flywheel to Crankshaft Bolts
1975-80	504	①	29	55	123.5	49
1980-81	505	①	29	55	123.5	49
1977-81	604	②	34	N.A.	119.0	31.5

① Torque the head bolts in sequence to 36.0 ft. lbs. (51.4 Nm). Loosen the head bolts and retorque to 15 ft. lbs. (20.3 Nm). Match-mark the bolt head to the cylinder head and tighten ¼ of a turn more on the head bolts (90 degrees).

② Torque the head bolts in sequence to 43.2 ft. lbs. (58.8 Nm). Fully loosen the head bolts and then retorque them in sequence to 14.4 ft. lbs. (19.6 Nm). Match-mark the head bolts to the cylinder head and tighten ¼ of a turn more on the head bolts (90 degrees).

N.A. Not available

TORQUE SEQUENCES

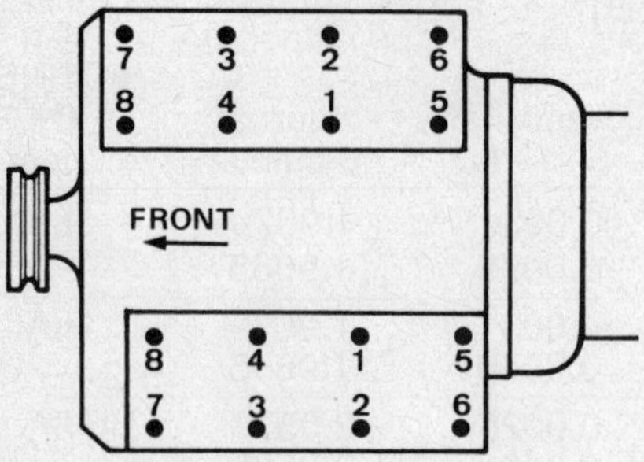

V6 cylinder head torque sequence

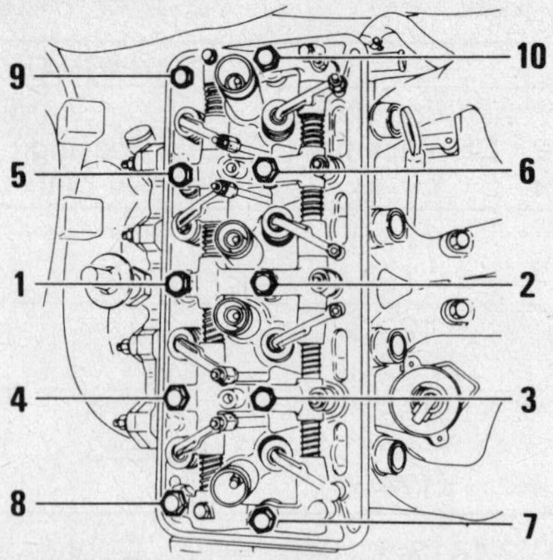

504 and 505 cylinder head torque sequence

BATTERY AND STARTER SPECIFICATIONS

12 volt negative ground

Year	Vehicle Model	Battery Amp Hr Rating	Starter Draw (amps)	Lock Test Torque (ft. lbs.)	No Load Test (volts)
1975-80	504	45	225	N.A.	10.6
1980-81	505	60	N.A.	N.A.	N.A.
1977-81	604	45	440	10.8 ①	N.A.

① Paris-Rhone R 450 amp starter lock test = 11.5 ft. lbs.
N.A. Not available

BRAKE SPECIFICATIONS

All measurements in inches

Year	Vehicle Model	Lug Nut Torque (ft. lbs.)	Master Cyl. Bore (in.)	FRONT DISC Minimum Thickness	FRONT DISC Maximum Run-Out	REAR DISC ③ Minimum Thickness	REAR DISC ③ Maximum Run-Out	MINIMUM LINING THICKNESS Front	MINIMUM LINING THICKNESS Rear
1975-80	504	43.5	①	0.43	0.0028	0.42 ②	0.0028	0.10	0.10
1975-81	604	61.2	0.86	N.A.	N.A.	N.A.	N.A.	0.10	0.10
1980-81	505	43.5	N.A.	0.43	0.0028	0.42	0.0028	0.10	0.10

① There are seven different type master cylinders on 504 models. The bore could be 0.824 in. or 0.76 in. depending on the type master cylinder in the vehicle.
② Some earlier type rear discs have minimum thickness of 0.34 in. (Girling type AH12MK1)
③ Models equipped with rear drum brakes have a maximum drum oversize of 11.3 in. except Saloon L models which have a maximum oversize of 10.3 inches.
N.A. Not available

WHEEL ALIGNMENT SPECIFICATIONS

Year	Model	CASTER Range (deg)	CASTER Pref. Setting (deg)	CAMBER Range (deg)	CAMBER Pref. Setting (deg)	Toe-In (in.)	King Pin Inclination (deg)
1975-80	504	2°40′±30′	2°40′	0°38′±30′	0°38′	1/32-5/32 ②	8°54′±30′
1975-81	604 ①	3°30′±30′	3°30′	0°30′±45′	0°30′	1/32-5/32 ②	10° ±30′
1980-81	505	3°30′±30′	3°30′	0°42′±45′	0°42′	1/32-5/32 ②	9°05′±30′

① Rear wheels Camber Range 1° to 2°
Pref. 1°30′
Toe-in Range 1/32 to 5/32 inch
Pref. 5/64 inch

② Preferred setting is 5/64 inch

TUNE-UP PROCEDURES

Breaker Points and Condenser

Early USA 504 models and all 604 Canadian models are equipped with conventional ignition.

1. Remove the distributor cap, and inspect it for carbon tracks and cracks. Check for excessive wear of the rotor contacts.
2. Remove and inspect the rotor.
3. Check the points for burning, pitting, excess wear and alignment.
4. Lightly lubricate the rubbing block and pivot point. Install the points and condenser.
5. Set the point gap to specifications and replace the rotor and cap. Check the dwell.

DWELL ANGLE

504 Models (4 Cylinder)

1. Remove the distributor cap and connect the dwell meter.
2. Set the point gap at 0.016 inch.
3. Crank the engine and adjust the dwell to 55-59°.
4. Install the rotor and cap. Check the dwell again with the engine running at idle speed.

604 Models (V6)

The 604 models with conventional ignition (Canada) have dual points and dual coils. These distributors are equipped with a three lobe cam. With the three lobe cam and the rotor arrangement on this distributor, each set of points fires only three cylinders. For this reason, the dwell specification on each individual set of points is larger than the normal V6 dwell specification. Another feature of this system is that the distributor cap, has unevenly spaced contacts in it. This unusual arrangement seems complicated; however, it is not hard to service.

1. Remove the distributor cap and set the gap on each individual set of points to 0.016 inch.
2. Install the rotor and cap and start the engine. The dwell on each separate point set should be 70-82°.

Electronic Ignition

Electronic ignition is used on all 504, USA 50 states, starting with serial number 3021045 and Canadian serial number 3000052. In the United States, 604 models use electronic ignition. All 505 models use the electronic ignition.

Electronic ignition uses transistorized switching triggered by magnetic pulse signals to eliminate breaker points.

MAJOR COMPONENTS

1. Magnetic pulse generator
   a. Polarity wheel (reluctor): Timer teeth

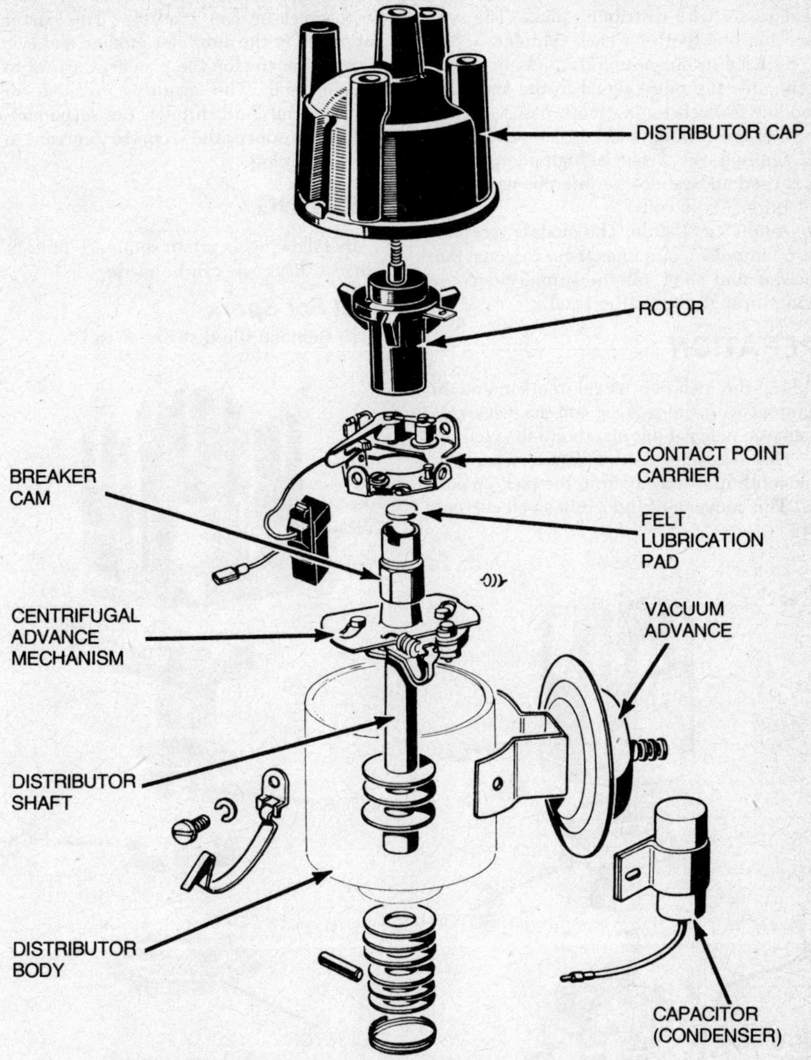

Exploded view of the 504 conventional ignition distributor

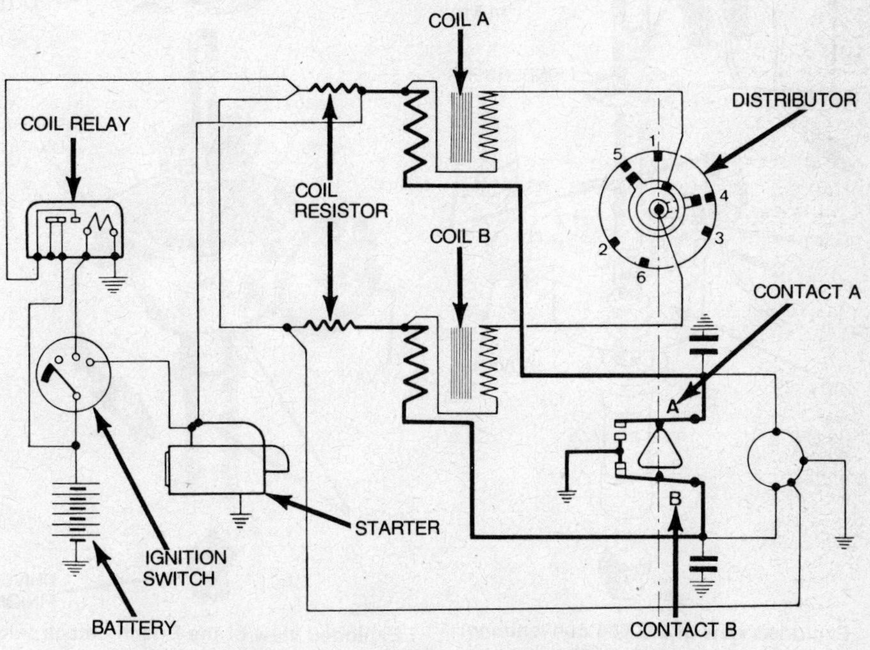

Wiring diagram of the 604 conventional ignition distributor

that rotate with distributor shaft. The system has one tooth for each cylinder.

b. Electro-magnet coil (pick-up coil): generates the pulse signal to the amplifier module as each timing tooth passes by the core of the pick-up coil.

2. Ignition coil: A special high energy type coil is used and cannot be interchanged with conventional type coils.

3. Amplifier Module: The module receives pick-up impulses, amplifies them to signal the transistor and shuts off the primary current flowing through the ignition coil.

OPERATION

When the polarity wheel teeth come in alignment with the pick-up coil magnet core, a magnetic field is built up around the pick-up coil. This magnetic field collapses when the timer tooth moves away from the pick-up coil core. This movement induces a small current in the pick-up coil windings. This current is amplified in the amplifier module and triggers a transistor to stop the primary current to the ignition coil. The resulting collapse of the primary coil field through the secondary coil windings induces the secondary current to fire the spark plug.

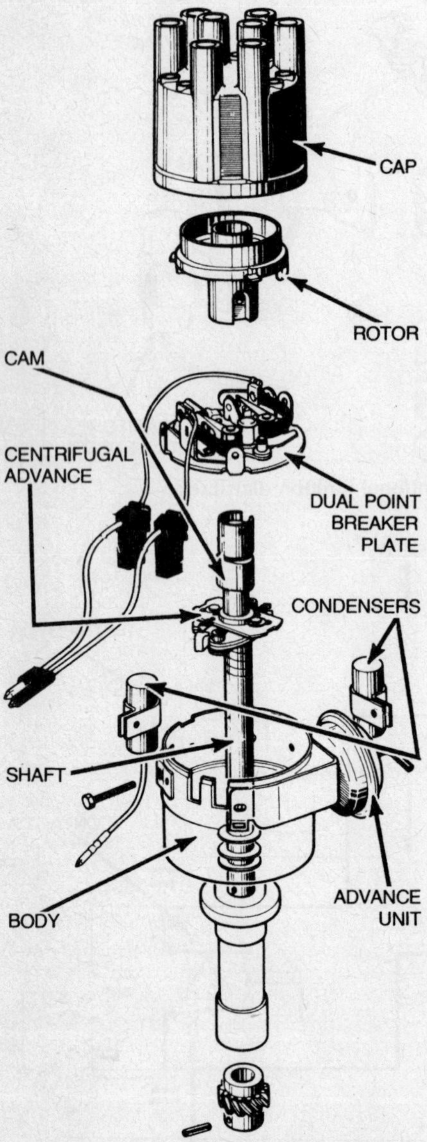

Exploded view of the 604 conventional ignition distributor

TESTING

By following a certain sequence of tests the correct diagnosis can be made.

Test For Spark

1. Remove the distributor cap.

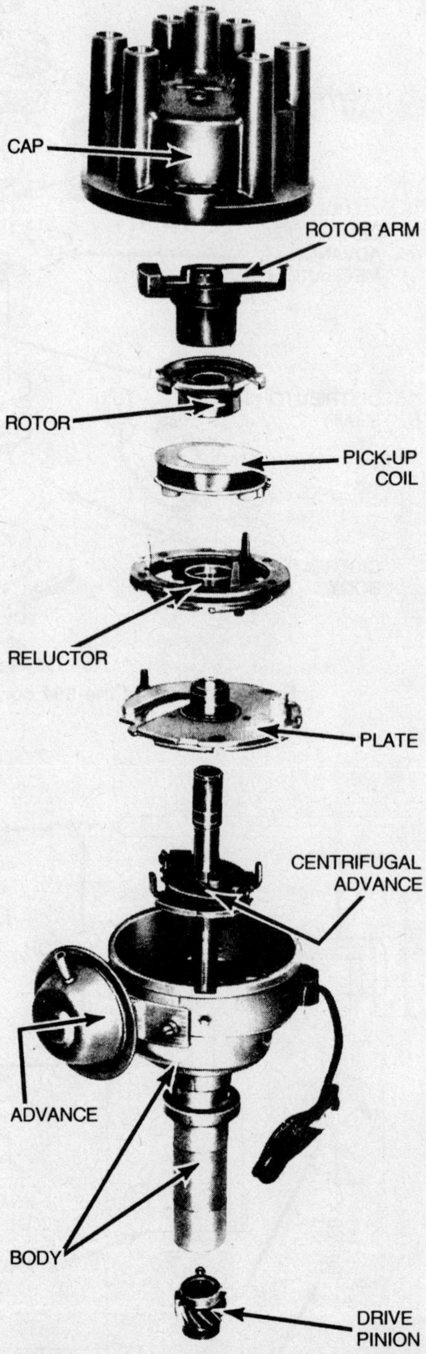

Exploded view of the Bosch® electronic ignition distributor used on 604 models

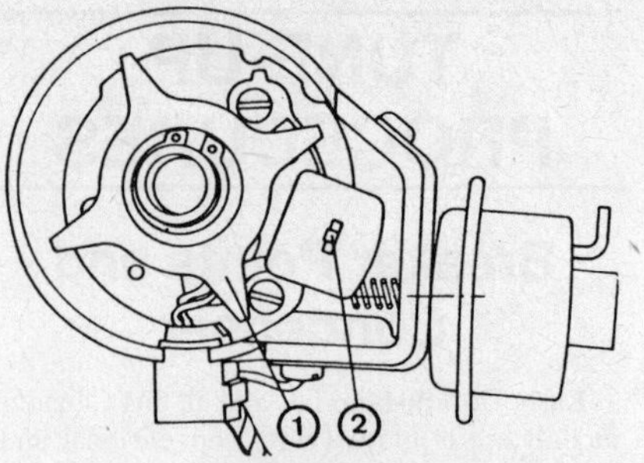

1. Reluctor tooth
2. Pick-up core

To test for spark, position the timing teeth on either side of the pick-up core

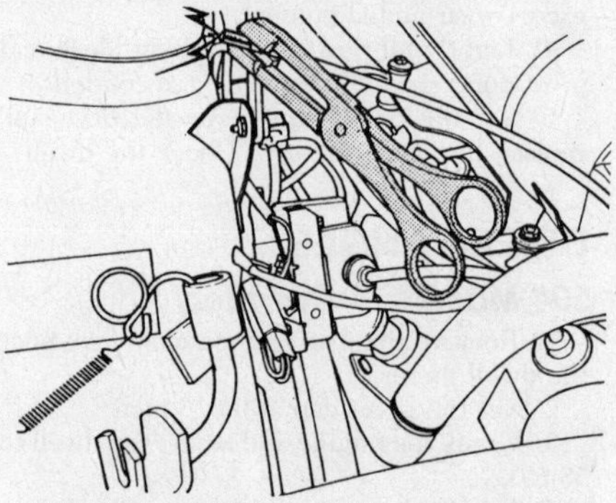

Position the high tension lead from the coil, ½ in. from ground, to test for spark

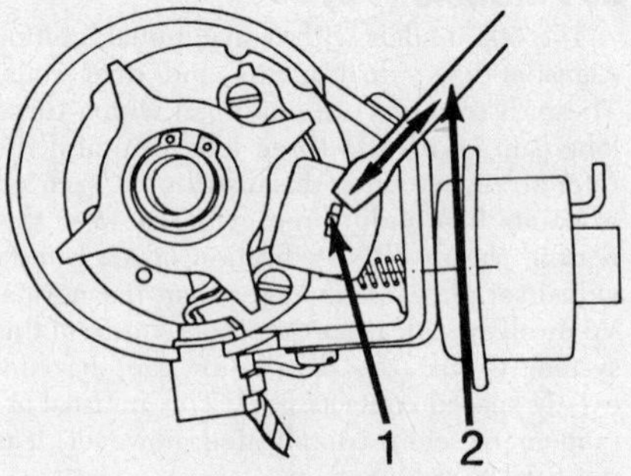

1. Pick-up core
2. Screwdriver

Pass a screwdriver over the pick-up core and a spark should occur

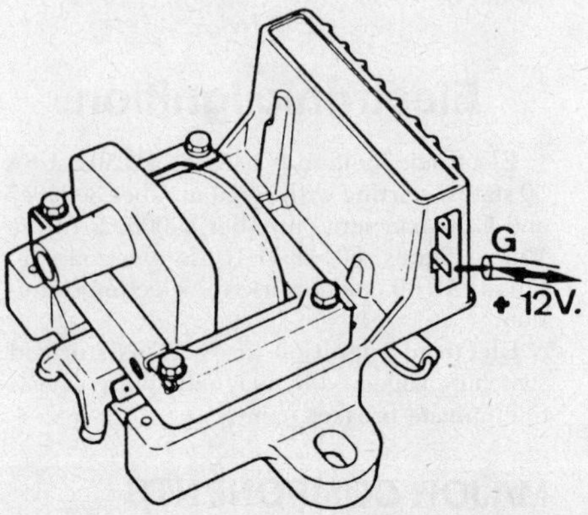

Check for voltage at the electronic control module

2. Position the polarity wheel (reluctor) so that two teeth are on either side of the pick-up core (teeth not aligned with the core).
3. Remove the high tension lead from the distributor cap.
4. Turn the ignition key on.
5. Position the high tension lead ½ inch away from ground.

NOTE: Choose a ground point as far away from the coil and module as possible.

6. Pass a screwdriver over the pick-up coil core. A spark should occur with each pass of the screwdriver.
7. If there is no spark:
   a. Check the primary voltage at the ignition coil
   b. Check the pick-up coil
   c. Test the ignition coil
   d. Test the amplifier module

Primary Voltage Test at the Ignition Coil

1. Connect a test lamp from the coil positive terminal to ground. If the test lamp lights, continue with the electronic ignition test procedures. If the test lamp does not light, check for a primary ignition wiring problem or faulty ignition switch.

Test the Pick-Up Coil

1. Turn the ignition off and disconnect the pick-up coil connector from the module.
2. Attach an ohmmeter between the pick-up coil terminals.
3. Check the pick-up coil resistance for 900-1100 ohms.
4. Remove the vacuum line from the vacuum advance unit and attach an outside vacuum source to the advance unit.
5. While observing the ohmmeter, apply slowly and steadily, up to 20 inches of vacuum to the advance unit.

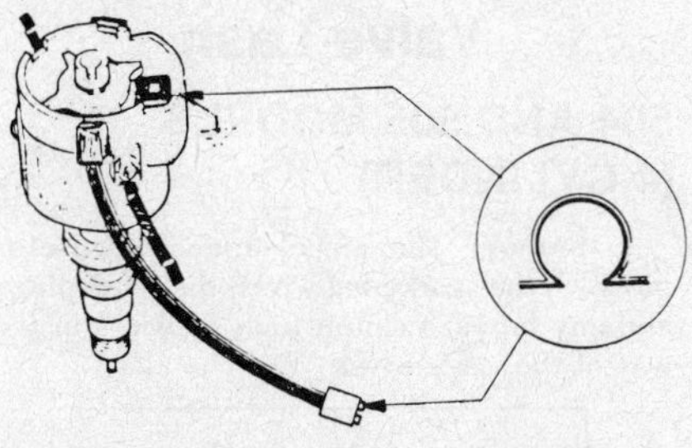

Check the pick-up coil for insulation to ground

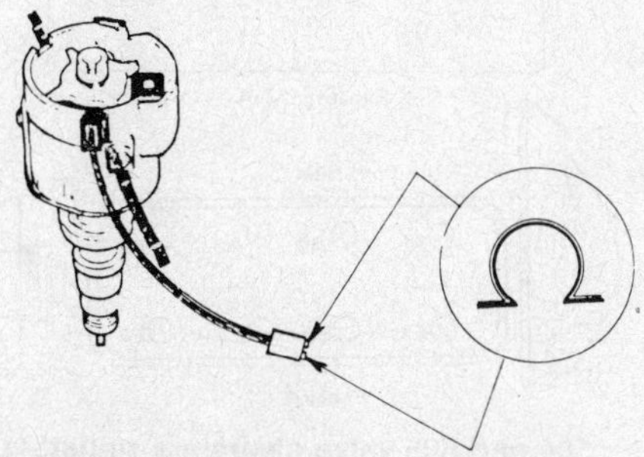

Check the pick-up coil for resistance

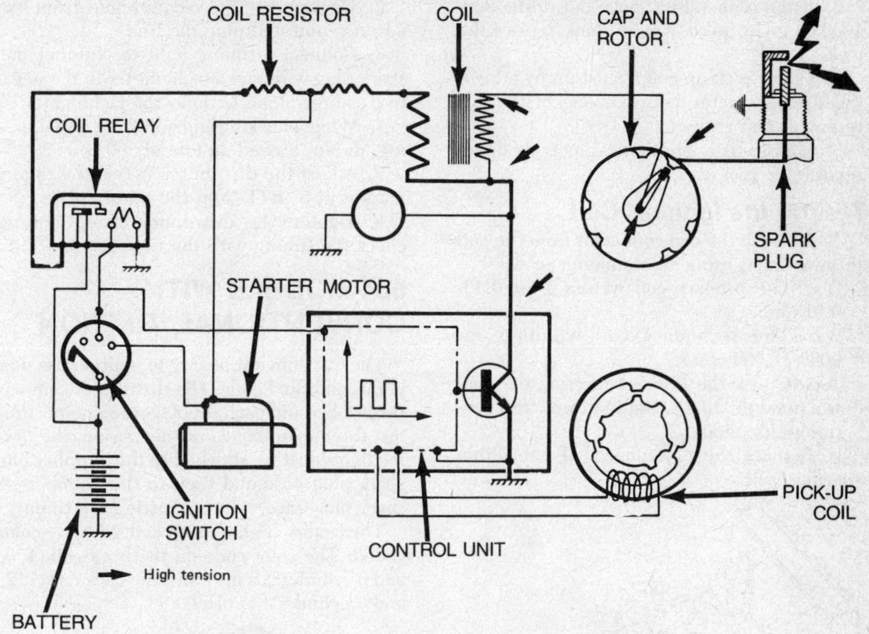

Model 604, Bosch®, electronic ignition wiring diagram

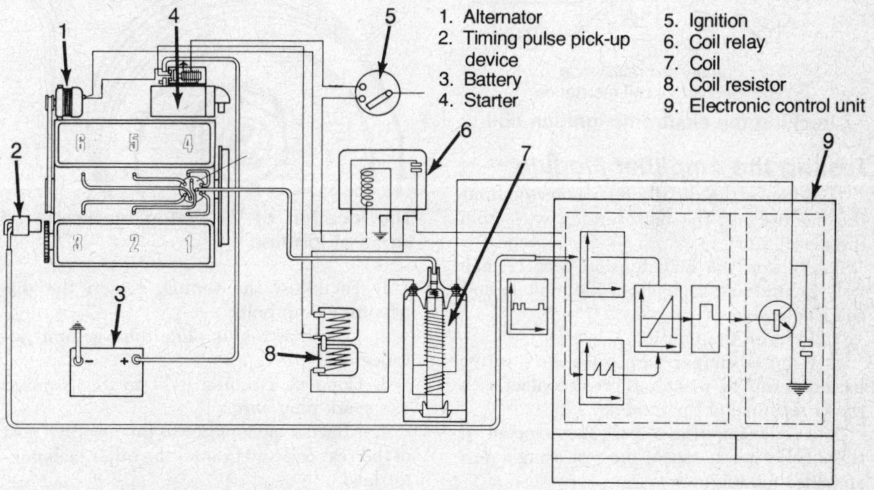

Wiring diagram of Schlumberger® electronic iginition used on 604 models

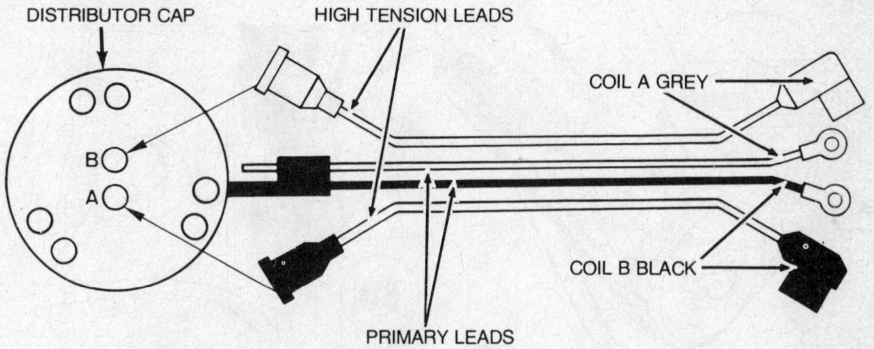

Color codes on the distributor-to-coil high tension wires

6. If the ohm values move out of the 900-1100 range by more than 50 ohms, replace the pick-up coil.
7. Check pick-up coil insulation by attaching the ohmmeter between one of the coil terminals and ground.
8. If a less than infinite reading is obtained, replace the pick-up coil.

Testing the Ignition Coil

1. Remove the coil connector from the coil terminals and using an ohmmeter, check:
   a. The primary coil windings for 0.48-0.61 ohms.
   b. The secondary coil windings for 9000-11,000 ohms.
   c. Check the leads connecting the control module to the ignition coil for continuity (0) ohms.
2. Replace the ignition coil if not within specifications.

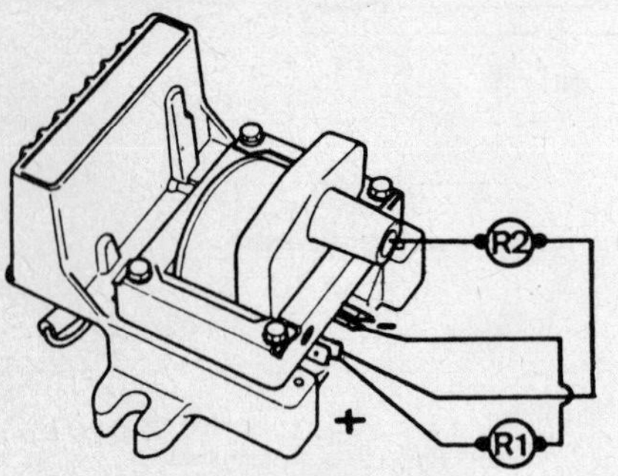

R1. Primary coil resistance
R2. Secondary coil resistance

Checking the electronic ignition coil

Testing the Amplifier Module

1. Remove the distributor connector from the module and the high tension wire from the distributor cap.
2. Position the high tension wire ½ inch from ground and as far from the module and coil as possible.
3. Turn on the ignition.
4. Using a jumper wire from the positive battery terminal, make and break contact with the G terminal of the module.
5. At each impulse, a spark should occur. If there is no spark, repeat the test using a new amplifier module.

Ignition Timing

504 AND 505 MODELS

1. Loosen the distributor clamp bolt.
2. Disconnect the vacuum line from the advance unit and plug the line.
3. Connect a timing light to Number one spark plug wire and a tachometer to the negative coil terminal. Ground the tachometer.
4. While checking and adjusting initial timing, do not exceed an idle of 850 rpm.
5. Adjust the distributor so that the timing mark is at 5° BTDC on the timing plate.
6. Tighten the distributor clamp and recheck the timing with the timing light.

604 MODELS WITH CONVENTIONAL IGNITION

The 604 conventional type ignition has dual points and dual coils. The distributor cam has three lobes and each set of ignition points fires just three cylinders. For this reason, the timing light must be attached to the Number one spark plug wire and then to the Number six spark plug wire, when adjusting the timing.

The factory high tension coil leads are color coded. The color code on the front coil (4, 5, and 6 cylinders) is grey and the back coil (1, 2, and 3 cylinders) is black.

The location of V6 timing marks on all types of ignition

1. To adjust the timing, loosen the distributor clamp bolt.
2. Disconnect and plug the vacuum advance line.
3. Connect a timing light to the Number one spark plug wire.
4. Attach a tachometer to the negative post of the rear coil and ground the other tachometer lead.
5. Check the timing on Number one cylinder and adjust it to 10° BTDC. To adjust the Number one cylinder timing; rotate the distributor.
6. Check the timing on Number six spark plug wire and adjust it to 10° BTDC. To adjust the Number six cylinder timing; turn the screw located on the outside of the distributor body.

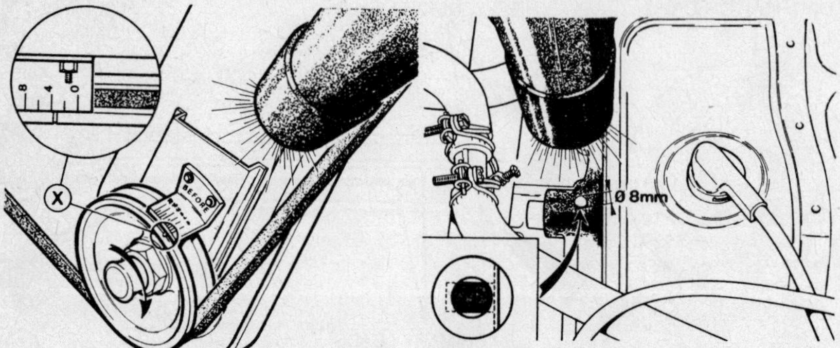

Model 504 timing marks and timing hole

604 MODELS WITH SCHLUMBERGER® ELECTRONIC IGNITION

1. Remove the vacuum advance line and plug it.
2. Attach a tachometer to the negative coil post and ground the other tachometer lead.
3. Connect a timing light to Number one spark plug wire.
4. Start the engine and idle it at a maximum of 950 rpm.
5. If the timing is out of specifications, loosen the timing sensor (at the front of the left cylinder head) and rotate the sensor counterclockwise to increase advance and clockwise to decrease advance.
6. Tighten the sensor and recheck the timing.

604 MODELS WITH BOSCH® ELECTRONIC IGNITION

1. Remove the vacuum advance line and plug it.
2. Attach the timing light to Number six spark plug wire. Connect a tachometer to the negative coil post and ground.
3. Start the engine and idle it a maximum of 900 rpm.
4. Set the timing to a specification of 12° BTDC. If the timing is out of specification adjust it by rotating the distributor until the timing light shows the pulley mark lining up with 12° BTDC on the timing plate.
5. Stop the engine, reconnect the vacuum advance hose and remove the tachometer and timing light.
6. If necessary adjust the idle speed to 900 rpm.

Valve Lash

504 AND 505 MODELS (4 CYLINDER)

1. Remove the air cleaner (carburetor models), the spark plug wires, the spark plugs and any hoses, vacuum lines or wires in the way of the valve cover.

Set fully open	to adjust	
E_1	A_3	E_4
E_3	A_4	E_2
E_4	A_2	E_1
E_2	A_1	E_3

E = Exhaust – A = Inlet

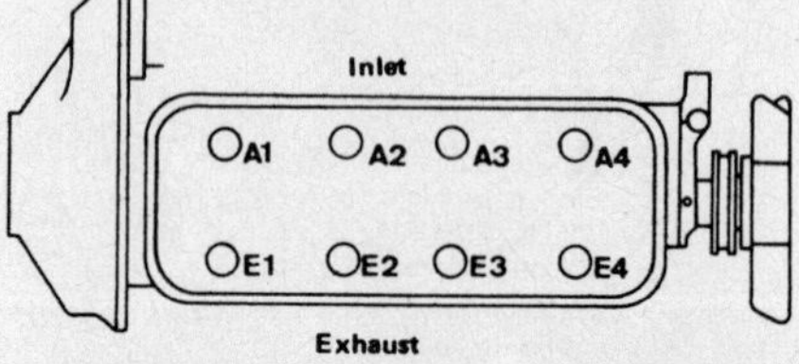

504 and 505 valve clearance adjusting sequence

2. Always adjust the valve clearances with the engine cold (6 hrs. minimum cooling time).

3. Check and adjust the clearances in the specified sequence.

4. Loosen the locknut and turn the adjuster at the rocker arm to obtain the specified clearance. Tighten the locknut and recheck the valve clearance.

5. Install the valve cover and vacuum hoses.

604 MODELS

1. Using a remote starter switch, bring the Number one piston up to TDC of the compression stroke.

2. Remove the distributor cap. The rotor

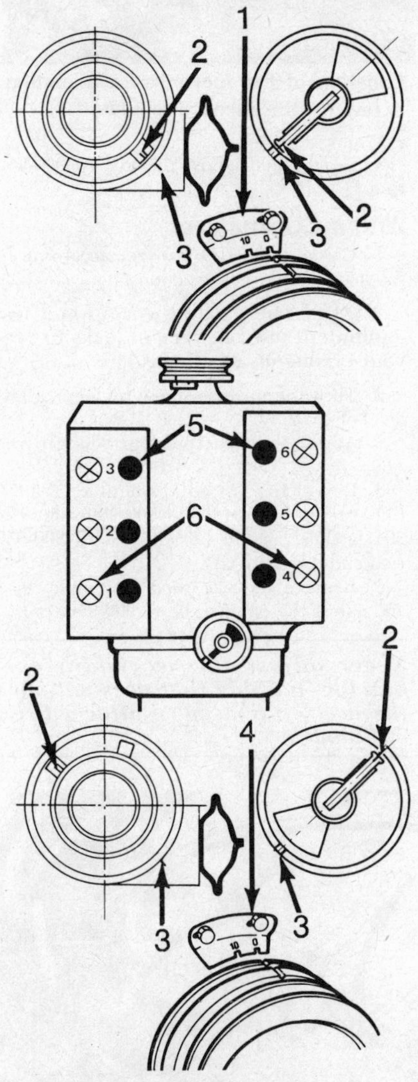

1. Position of the rotor with #1 cylinder on TDC of the compression stroke
2. Mark on rotor
3. Mark on distributor
4. Position of the rotor with #1 cylinder on the end of the exhaust stroke and the beginning of the intake stroke
5. Intake valve
6. Exhaust valve

Valve lash sequence for V6 engines

VALVE CLEARANCES SPECIFICATIONS

Model	Engine (cc)	Inlet	Exhaust
504	1796	0.006″ (0.15 mm)	0.012″ (0.30 mm)
505	1796	0.004″ (0.10 mm)	0.010″ (0.25 mm)
604	2664 & 2889	0.004″ (0.10 mm)	0.010″ (0.25 mm)

N° 1 Piston on TDC	Rocker Arms To Be Adjusted	
Firing stroke	A1 ①	E1 ②
	A2 ①	E3 ②
	A4 ①	E6 ②
End of exhaust Commencement of inlet stroke	A3 ①	E2 ②
	A5 ①	E4 ①
	A6 ①	E5 ②

① inlet: 0.10 mm ② exhaust: 0.25 mm

arm should be directly in line with the marks on the distributor case.

3. The notch of the belt pulley should be aligned with the "O" notch on the timing plate.

4. With the Number one piston at this position adjust Number 1, 2, and 4 intake valves and Number 1, 3, and 6 exhaust valves.

5. Using a remote starter switch, bring the Number one piston up to the end of the exhaust stroke and the beginning of the intake stroke.

6. Check for the rotor arm to be pointing 180° opposite of the markings on the distributor case.

7. The notch of the belt pulley should be aligned with the "O" notch on the timing plate.

8. With Number one piston at this position, adjust Number 3, 5, and 6 intake valves. Then adjust Number 2, 4, and 6 exhaust valves.

9. Install the valve covers, distributor cap and vacuum lines.

Carburetors

IDLE SPEED AND MIXTURE

General

1. Select Park or Neutral on a manual transmission.

2. Set the parking brake.

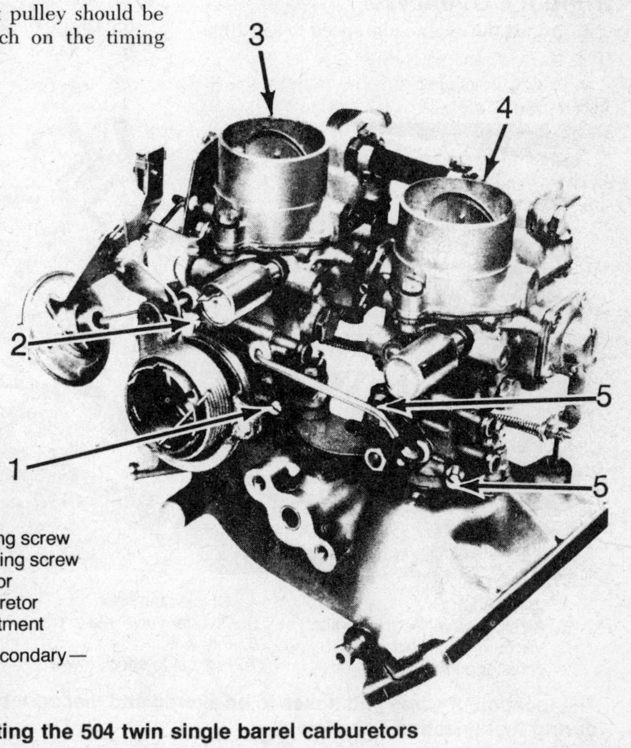

1. Richness adjusting screw
2. Idle speed adjusting screw
3. Primary carburetor
4. Secondary carburetor
5. Secondary adjustment

Do not adjust secondary—preset at factory

Adjusting the 504 twin single barrel carburetors

1. Primary carburetor
2. Secondary carburetor
3. Idle speed screw
4. Idle mixture screw

Adjusting the 604 carburetors

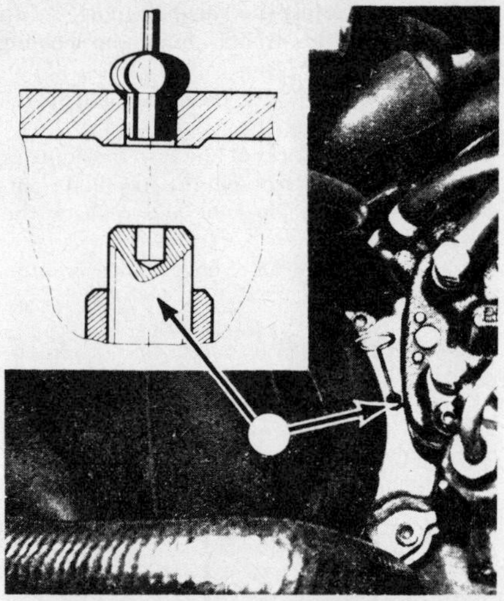

Location of the fuel mixture adjusting screw on the mixture regulator

3. Turn off the air conditioning and all electrical accessories.

4. Route the pressure from the air injector pump, away from the manifolds by connecting a jumper wire across the electro-valve control switch terminals.

Without CO Analyzer

1. Adjust the engine idle speed to 950-1000 rpm.

2. Adjust the idle mixture screw to obtain the highest rpm.

3. Adjust the idle speed back to 950-1000 rpm.

4. Repeat these procedures until the 950-1000 rpm is obtained as the highest idle mixture rpm.

5. Adjust the idle speed to 900-950 rpm.

6. Remove the jumper wire from the electro-valve and adjust the idle to 900-950 rpm.

With a CO Analyzer

1. Connect the CO analyzer according to the manufacturers instructions.

NOTE: The exhaust system and test equipment must be free of leaks to prevent erroneous readings.

2. Turn the mixture screw to obtain a CO level of 1.5-2.5%.

3. Adjust the idle speed to 900-950 rpm again.

4. Repeat the procedures until a 1.5-2.5% CO reading is obtained at 900-950 rpm. The 604 models, should be adjusted to 800-850 rpm and 3.0-4.0% CO.

5. Remove the electro-valve jumper wire and adjust the engine idle to 900-950 rpm.

CAUTION

Never adjust the secondary carburetor (the side that does not have the deceleration valve attached) on 504 models.

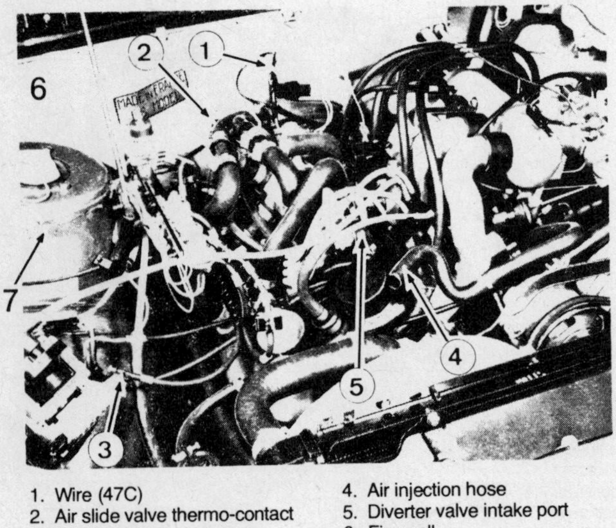

1. Wire (47C)
2. Air slide valve thermo-contact
3. Vacuum supply hose to canister purge valve
4. Air injection hose
5. Diverter valve intake port
6. Fire wall
7. Right side shock tower

The location of wires and hoses to be altered and disconnected during fuel injection adjustment

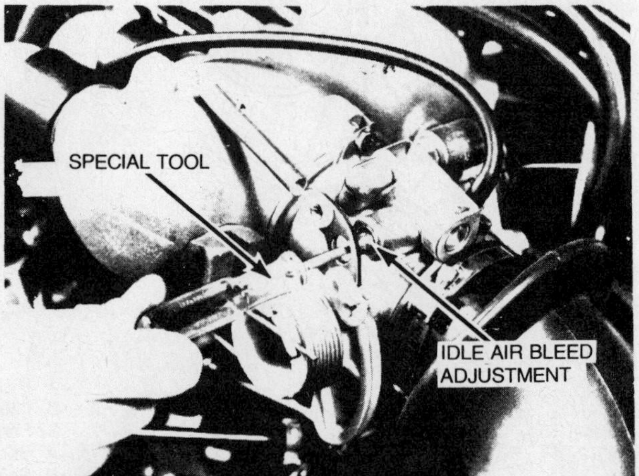

Adjusting the idle speed on Peugeot K-Jetronic® fuel injection system

NOTE: During adjustments if the engine idles for more than three minutes at a time, increase the engine speed to 2000 rpm for one minute to clear the engine of a rich idle mixture.

Fuel Injection 505 Models

IDLE SPEED AND MIXTURE

Several Peugeot special tools or their equivalent will be needed to adjust the idle speed and fuel mixture on Peugeot K-Jetronic® fuel injection. The tools are: a mixture adjusting tool, an idle speed adjusting tool and a CO sampling connecting tube.

In addition, a good tachometer and an infra-red HC/CO analyzer will be needed.

1. Connect the tachometer and using the idle adjustment tool, adjust the air bleed to obtain an idle speed of 900-950 rpm.
2. Disconnect the wire 47c from the air slide valve thermo-contact and connect it to ground number five (5) on the shock tower.
3. Disconnect and plug the vacuum supply hose at the canister purge valve.
4. Remove the air injection hose at the intake port of the diverter valve and plug it with a 0.9 in. (23 mm) plug.
5. Attach the CO sampling tube to the front of the catalytic converter. Connect the CO analyzer.
6. Locate the CO mixture regulator and remove the access plug to the CO mixture screw.
7. Start the engine and set the idle at 900 rpm.
8. Using the CO mixture adjusting tool or equivalent, adjust the CO reading to 0.5-1.5%.

NOTE: Do not push down on the adjusting tool as it will change the CO reading.

9. Repeat the procedure until both the idle and the CO % are correct.
10. Install the mixture plug.
11. Connect the wire 47c to the thermo-contact, the vacuum hose to the canister purge valve, the air injection hose on the diverter valve and remove the sampling tube from the catalytic converter. Install the cap nut on the converter tap.

ENGINE ELECTRICAL

Distributor

REMOVAL AND INSTALLATION

1. Remove the common intake manifold on 505 models only.
2. Bring the number one piston to TDC of the compression stroke. Match mark the position of the rotor to the distributor body.

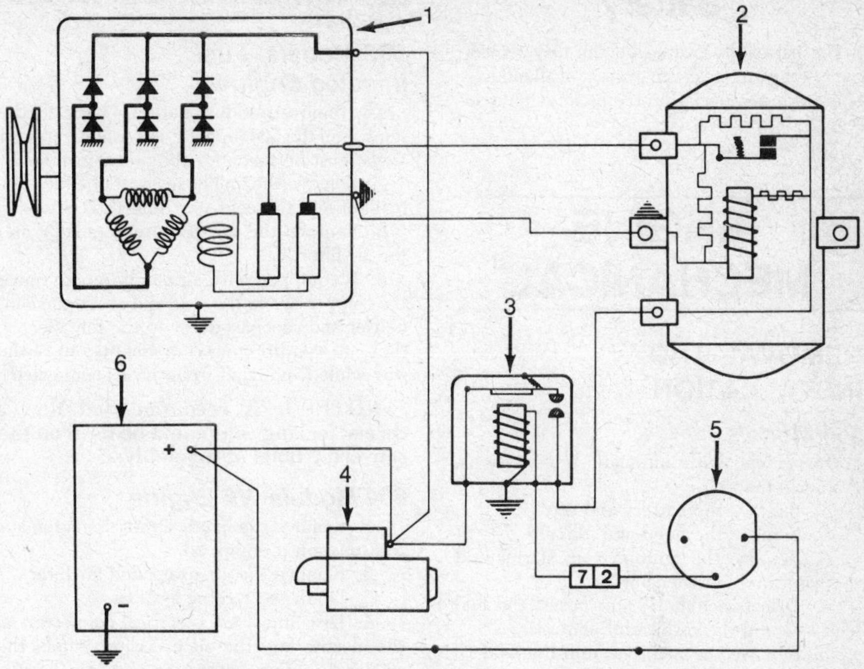

Typical starter and charging circuit

3. Remove the distributor bolt and lift out the distributor. Do not rotate engine crankshaft.
4. Install the distributor in the same position it was when it was removed.
5. Install the common intake manifold on the 505 models.
6. Check and adjust the timing.

Alternator

REMOVAL AND INSTALLATION

1. Disconnect the battery ground cable.
2. Remove the wire leads from the alternator.
3. Remove the adjusting strap bolt.
4. Remove the mounting bolt and the alternator.
5. Installation is the reverse of removal.

Regulator

ADJUSTMENT

The regulator should be set to produce between 13.6 and 14.8 volts at 3000 rpm. There is a switch on the regulator that can be set to heavy or light electrical load. Position number one (1) is for high electrical load and position number two (2) is for light electrical load.

Starter

REMOVAL AND INSTALLATION

The starter is removed in the conventional manner. Disconnect the battery ground cable and all starter connections. Unbolt and remove the starter. Installation is the reverse of removal.

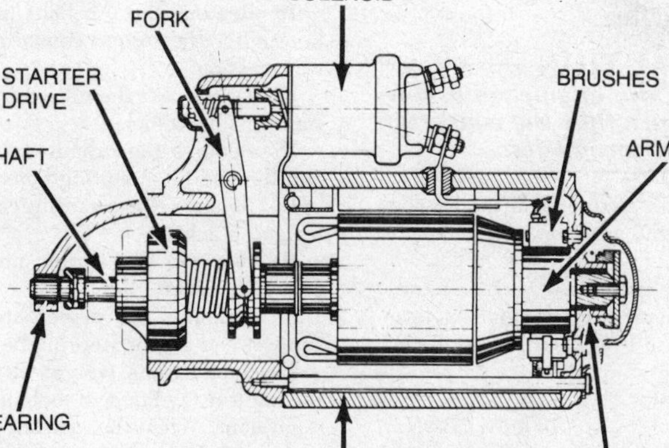

Cross section of a typical starter motor

Battery

The battery is located on the driver's side front of the engine compartment of all models. There are no special problems to gaining access to the battery.

ENGINE MECHANICAL

REMOVAL AND INSTALLATION

504 Models

On vehicles with automatic transmissions, drain the fluid.

1. Remove the battery and tray.
2. Remove the hood and radiator.
3. Remove the ignition coil, starter and the windshield washer bottle.
4. Disconnect the heater hoses, the fuel feed line and the carburetor controls.
5. Remove the main vacuum line and all electrical wires that interfere with the engine removal.
6. Remove the air filter and the air filter bracket.
7. Turn the steering wheel to the left and lower steering rack housing.
8. Remove the exhaust pipe from the exhaust manifold.
9. Remove the flywheel protector plates and the clutch housing bolts.
10. Using Peugeot tool 8 0102X engine hoist or equivalent, attach the hoist hooks in the holes marked "404", and raise the engine until its under a slight load.
11. Remove the four bolts securing the engine mountings to the crossmember.

CAUTION

Make sure that the front left brake line is tight against the crossmember.

12. Raise the engine until the gearbox touches the tunnel.
13. Using Peugeot tool 80125 X gearbox support bar or equivalent, support the gearbox.
14. On automatic transmissions, remove the torque converter-to-flywheel bolts and disengage the converter.

CAUTION

Never remove the engine with converter. Make sure that the converter stays with the transmission.

15. Separate the engine from the gearbox without altering the position of the engine hoist.
16. Installation is the reverse of removal. Torque the automatic transmission converter bolts to 16 ft/lbs (22.1 Nm). Other installation torques are:

Clutch housing-to-engine	40 ft/lbs (53.9Nm)
Starter bolts	14.5 ft/lbs (19.6Nm)
Crossmember	7.2 ft/lbs (9.8Nm)

17. Refill the automatic transmission and check the engine oil level before starting the engine.

505 Models–Fuel Injected Engines

The removal and installation is basically the same as in the 504 models. The following extra steps must be taken for the fuel injection.

1. Remove the fuel hoses from the fuel distributor and the cold start injector.
2. Remove the air mixture regulator and the air filter.
3. If equipped with air conditioning, move the compressor to the side and move the condenser and receiver-dryer to the left. Secure these air conditioning components out of the way while leaving all freon hoses connected.

NOTE: It is recommended that a thread locking compound be used on the converter bolts at assembly.

604 Models–V6 Engine

1. Remove the hood. Drain the automatic transmission if equipped.
2. Remove the air mixer and air filter.
3. Drain the cooling system.
4. Disconnect the electrical connectors at the electric fan, the oil pressure switch, the air conditioning compressor and the thermostat.
5. Remove the electric fan.
6. Remove the radiator supports and battery on air conditioned cars.
7. Remove the top and bottom radiator hoses and transmission cooler lines if equipped.
8. Separate the condenser and receiver dryer from the radiator.
9. Remove the fan shroud and the radiator.
10. Remove the air conditioning compressor and set it on the right fender, leaving the freon lines attached.
11. Disconnect the battery ground cable, the temperature sending unit, the vacuum line to the brake booster and the fuel pump lines.
12. Remove the carburetor controls and the primary and secondary coil leads.
13. On air conditioned vehicles, disconnect the electro-valve wire and the lead to the carburetor idle cut out switch.
14. Remove the heater hoses and plug the ends.
15. Disconnect the starter and alternator harness connectors.
16. Remove the top bolts from the clutch housing or the torque converter if automatic transmission.
17. Disconnect the filler tube on automatic transmission vehicles.
18. Remove the exhaust pipe clamp bolts and the engine mounting bolts.
19. Remove the exhaust pipes, heat deflector and brackets.
20. Remove the starter and the clutch/converter cover.
21. Remove the power steering pump, support and power steering belt.
22. Support the weight of the engine on the hoist, using Peugeot tool number 80135 or equivalent. When the gearbox makes contact with the transmission tunnel, then lower it .04 in. (1 cm).
23. Remove the power steering pump and set it to one side without disconnecting the lines.
24. Retract the front seats and remove the inner securing bolts.
25. Raise and safely support vehicle. Using the threaded rods supplied with Peugeot tool number 8.1511, install the tool (drive shaft support bar) under the floor of the vehicle. Use the threaded rods in the seat bolt holes under the floor.
26. Remove the upper flex coupling bolt from the steering shaft.
27. Temporarily install the two rear main crossmember bolts in place.
28. Remove the front crossmember securing bolts and loosen the rear crossmember bolts enough to lower the crossmember ⅛ in. (3 mm).
29. On automatic transmissions remove the torque converter-to-ring gear bolts.
30. Remove the two lower clutch housing or torque converter housing bolts.
31. Move the engine forward in order to separate from transmission. Hold the torque converter in place on automatic transmission equipped vehicles.
32. Installation is the reverse of removal except for the following adjustments.
33. Adjust the automatic transmission kick down cable. Set the accelerator pedal stop at 2 inches (51 mm). Place a 0.3 inch (7 mm) spacer between the stop and the accelerator pedal.
34. Hold the carburetor control quadrant in the fully open position. Unclip the linkage return springs. Secure the accelerator cable in place, pull on the cable lightly to tension it, but do not compress the compensator spring. The accelerator cable goes through a hole in the quadrant and is secured ⅔ of the way around the quadrant at the accelerator holding tab.
35. Clip the kickdown cable into the control quadrant. Put tension on the kickdown cable by pulling on it lightly.
36. Set the cable stop into the cable bracket and tighten the nuts on both sides of the bracket.
37. One nut will tighten against the lug. Adjust the other nut to obtain 0.04 inches (1 mm) clearance between the nut and the bracket.
38. Remove the spacer at the accelerator pedal and check for proper carburetor operation.
39. When the engine is hot, the clearance on the accelerator cable should be 0.08 in. (2 mm).

Use the following torque specifications when installing the 604 V6 engine:

Flywheel to starter ring	34.2 ft/lbs (46.6 Nm)
Crossmember to frame	30.6 ft/lbs (41.6 Nm)
Steering column clamp	10.8 ft/lbs (14.7 Nm)
Gearbox to engine	28.8 ft/lbs (39.2 Nm)
Compressor mounting	12.6 ft/lbs (17.2 Nm)
Compressor pulley	9.0 ft/lbs (12.3 Nm)

Cylinder Head

REMOVAL AND INSTALLATION

504 Models (Carburetor Engines)

1. Drain the coolant from the block.

2. Remove the air cleaner, carburetor, ignition distributor, spark plugs, upper radiator hose and water pump belt.
3. Remove the spark plug tube seals and cups.
4. Separate the exhaust pipe from the manifold.
5. Remove the head bolts and install the cylinder head guide pins.
6. Remove the rocker shaft assembly and pushrods.
7. Remove the guide pin from the front end of the engine.
8. Pivot the head to separate it from the block and lift off the head. Remove the gasket and second cylinder head guide.
9. Lock the cylinder liners with the Peugeot tool 8.0104D or equivalent retaining screws.
10. Installation is the reverse of removal.
11. Torque the head bolts in sequence to 36 ft/lbs (49 Nm). Loosen the head bolts, and retorque to 15 ft/lbs (20.3 Nm). Then match mark the bolt head to the cylinder head. Then tighten exactly 90° (¼ turn) more. Do this to all head bolts, in sequence.

505 Models (Fuel Injected)

1. Drain the cooling system and remove the Lambda® sensor (if equipped) from the exhaust header pipe.
2. Remove the header pipe from the exhaust manifold connector.
3. Remove the mounting brackets from the intake/exhaust manifold.
4. Disconnect the battery ground cable.
5. Separate the intake manifold.
6. Remove the distributor cap.
7. On fuel injected vehicles, remove the fuel injectors. Remove the diagnostic plug bracket.
8. Remove and tag the following electrical wires:
   a. Primary ignition at the coil.
   b. Secondary ignition at the coil.
   c. Temperature sending unit at the engine.
   d. Thermo-time switch at the engine.
   e. Thermocontact sender unit in the heater hose.
   f. Temperature sending units at the water pump.
   g. Spark plug wires at the spark plugs.
9. Remove and tag the following air and vacuum hoses:
   a. All injection pump hoses and the auxiliary air device.
   b. Two vacuum hoses on the fuel distributor.
   c. Vacuum hoses at the three vacuum regulators on the fender well (manifold side of engine). All other vacuum lines on the manifold side.
10. Remove the upper radiator hose and the water pump ends of the lower radiator hose and heater hose.
11. Remove the power steering pump reservoir bracket from the head.
12. Remove the radiator fan shroud.
13. Remove the fan blades. Remove only the 3 nuts that are lined up with the recesses in the fan hub.
14. Remove the water pump belt.
15. Remove the vacuum hoses, electrical wire and coolant hoses from the air slide valve. Remove the air slide valve bracket.
16. Remove the remaining air injection hoses and the air injection assembly.
17. Remove the rocker arm oil feed pipe (sometimes referred to as "banjo fittings").
18. Remove the valve cover, declutchable fan brush holder and spark plug tube sealing rings.
19. Remove the rocker arm assembly, pushrods and cylinder head bolts.
20. Using Peugeot tools number 0.0149 or equivalent, break the cylinder head loose.
21. Install Peugeot tools 8.0132A1Z or equivalent retainers to keep the cylinder sleeves from moving in the engine block.
22. Installation of the head is the reverse of removal. Follow the specified torque sequence on head bolts and torque the bolts to 36 ft/lbs (49 Nm). Loosen the head bolts, and retorque to 15 ft/lbs (20.3 Nm). Then match mark the head bolt to the cylinder head. Then tighten exactly 90° (¼ turn) more. Do this to all head bolts, in sequence. Torque the rocker arm nuts to 10.9 ft/lbs (14.7 Nm).
23. Adjust the valve clearances.

604 Models (V6)

1. Drain the cooling system.
2. Remove the hood, air mixer chamber casing, air filter and battery.
3. Remove the intake manifold.
4. Remove the plate fitted under the intake manifold.
5. Remove the clips between the cylinder head and the water pump.
6. When removing the head from under the power brake booster, the engine crossmember must be lowered.
7. The accessories on the head opposite the brake booster do not have to be removed.
8. Remove all hoses and vacuum lines.
9. On the left hand cylinder head:
   a. Remove the fuel pump leaving the line connected.
   b. Remove the hot air duct.
   c. Loosen the positive battery lead and remove the negative battery lead.
10. On the right hand cylinder head:
   a. Remove the distributor and the front ignition coil.
   b. Remove the automatic transmission fill tube if equipped.
11. Remove the front exhaust silencer mounting bracket.
12. Remove the exhaust pipe from the exhaust manifold.
13. On the left side, remove the bolt from the steering flex coupling upper end.
14. Using Peugeot tool 8.1511C or equivalent; lower the crossmember 0.12 inch or (3 mm).
15. Remove the rocker arm cover and camshaft rear cover plate.
16. Remove the camshaft sprocket bolt access plug from both heads.
17. Position both sprockets with the drive studs (timing marks) at the top.
18. Hold the crankshaft from turning with a 35 mm box wrench. Loosen the camshaft sprocket with Peugeot tool ST 10 or equivalent Allen type socket wrench tool.
19. Place the Peugeot tool 8.0134M or equivalent camshaft sprocket supports on the timing gear casing. Secure the support fingers tight with two bolts. Torque the bolts to 10.8 ft/lbs (14.7 Nm).
20. Unscrew 8 bolts on each cylinder head and remove all but the two bolts under the power brake booster. Raise the two bolts as far as they will go and secure them with a rubber band.
21. Loosen the camshaft thrust flange bolt and remove the thrust flange.
22. Remove the camshaft. Make sure the cams do not foul the rocker arm pads while unscrewing the sprocket bolt.
23. On the left hand cylinder, lift the rocker arm to clear the camshaft.
24. Remove the timing gear case-to-cylinder head bolts from both the left and right heads.
25. Insert the two levers, Peugeot tool 0.0149 into two head bolts holes. Break the cylinder head loose by prying on the levers.
26. Remove the rocker arm assembly.
27. Clean the head gasket surface and retain the cylinder liners with special retainers, Peugeot tool 8.0132A or equivalent.
28. Remove the cylinder head locating dowels using Peugeot tool 8.0134L (extractor) or equivalent.
29. Install the Peugeot temporary camshaft bearing tools 8.0134N or equivalent on both heads.
30. Shims may be required under the bearing bracket, on the head surface.
31. Installation is the reverse of removal.

CAUTION

Do not release the timing chain tension or disturb the chain position while removing and installing heads.

32. Torque the camshaft flange bolts to 9.4 ft/lbs (12.7 Nm). Torque the camshaft sprocket bolts to 54.0 ft/lbs (73.5 Nm).
33. Torque the head in sequence and to 36 ft/lbs (49 Nm). Loosen the head bolts, and retorque to 15 ft/lbs (20.3 Nm). Then match mark the head bolt to the cylinder head. Then tighten exactly 90° (¼ turn) more. Do this to all head bolts, in sequence.
34. Adjust the valve clearances.
35. Install the rocker covers and follow the reverse of procedures one through thirteen for completing the re-installation. Install coolant and check the system by running the engine.

Rocker Arms and Shafts

REMOVAL AND INSTALLATION

504 and 505 Models

1. Remove the rocker arm cover.
2. Remove the five rocker stand nuts and ten head bolts. Lift off the rocker shaft.
3. Install in the reverse order of removal. Torque the head bolts in sequence to 36 ft/lbs (12.7 Nm). Loosen the head bolts, and retorque to 15 ft/lbs (20.3 Nm). Then match mark the head bolt to cylinder head. Then tighten exactly 90° (¼ turn) more. Do this to all head bolts, in sequence.
4. Adjust the valve clearances.

CAUTION

With the head bolts removed, the cylinder head can be broken loose from the block. Do not jar the cylinder head or rotate the crankshaft.

604 Models

1. Remove the air filter, heated air inlet, battery ground cable and rocker arm covers.
2. Remove the rocker shaft retaining bolts from the left rear and right front support bosses.
3. Remove all head bolts from both banks. The two left rear head bolts under the brake booster may be hard to remove. If necessary, move the engine slightly so they will clear the brake booster.

CAUTION

With the head bolts removed, the cylinder head can be broken loose from the block. Do not jar the cylinder head or rotate the crankshaft.

4. Installation is the reverse of removal.
5. Torque the head bolts in sequence to 36 ft/lbs (12.7 Nm). Loosen the head bolts, and retorque to 15 ft/lbs (20.3 Nm). Then match mark the head bolt to cylinder head. Then tighten exactly 90° (¼ turn) more. Do this to all head bolts, in sequence.

Intake Manifold

REMOVAL AND INSTALLATION

504 Models

1. Remove the air intake tubing and any wires or vacuum lines in the way of manifold removal.
2. Remove the air cleaner and carburetor.
3. Remove the intake manifold bolts. Lift out the manifold.

505 Models

1. Remove the air intake boot and electrical and vacuum connections from the throttle plate housing.
2. Remove the intake manifold mounting brackets and slide the intake manifold back and out.

604 Models

1. Drain the cooling system.
2. Remove the air mixer casing and intake tube.
3. Remove the air filter and disconnect the negative battery cable.
4. Remove the intake manifold.
5. Installation is the reverse of removal.

Exhaust Manifold

REMOVAL AND INSTALLATION

505 Models

1. Remove the Lambda® sensor wire and the three nuts holding the header pipe to the exhaust manifold.
2. Remove the exhaust manifold retaining nuts and lift out the manifold.
3. Installation is the reverse of removal.

604 Models–V6

1. Remove the right and left side exhaust pipes from the manifolds.
2. Remove six manifold-to-head bolts on the right and left sides of the engine.
3. Lift out the manifolds.
4. Installation is the reverse of removal.

Timing Chain Cover

REMOVAL AND INSTALLATION

504 and 505 Models

1. Drain the coolant.
2. Remove the radiator, fan belt, spark plugs and the crankshaft pulley.

NOTE: To hold the crankshaft from turning in manual transmission equipped vehicles, apply the handbrake and engage 4th gear. On vehicles with automatic transmissions, remove the torque converter cover and hold the flywheel.

3. Remove the timing housing.
4. Installation is the reverse of removal.

604 Models

1. Drain the engine oil.
2. Disconnect the negative battery cable.
3. Remove the air filter and the air mixer casing and the hot air duct.
4. Drain the cooling system.
5. Remove the radiator struts, radiator hoses and separate the fan casing from the radiator.
6. Remove the fan and the fan casing.
7. Remove the power steering belt and the alternator belt.
8. Remove the power steering pump and hang it to the fender well with wire.
9. Remove the clutch or converter housing cover plate.
10. Use Peugeot tool 8.01234 or equivalent to lock the flywheel in place.
11. Remove the crankshaft pulley.
12. Remove the power steering pump bracket, the hot air duct and the rocker arm covers.
13. Remove the timing gear casing bolts and lift the timing gear casing from the engine.
14. Installation is the reverse of removal. Torque the crankshaft pulley nut to 123 ft/lbs (166 Nm).

Timing Chain Cover Oil Seal Replacement

504 MODELS

The 504 (XN1 engine) uses an oil slinger on the front end of the crankshaft. This means that some leakage can occur when parking on steep grades. There is no oil seal to be replaced.

505 AND 604 MODELS

1. Remove the crankshaft pulley and the oil seal.
2. Install the seal and the woodruff key.
3. Install the crankshaft pulley. Torque the nut to 123 ft/lbs (166 Nm).

Timing Chain and Tensioner (Valve Timing)

REMOVAL AND INSTALLATION

504 and 505 Models

1. Remove the timing chain cover.
2. Loosen the tensioner spring.

RENOLD® TENSIONER

a. Remove the tensioner adjuster plug.
b. Using a .12 inch (3 mm) Allen wrench, turn the adjuster key clockwise to release the tension on the timing chain.

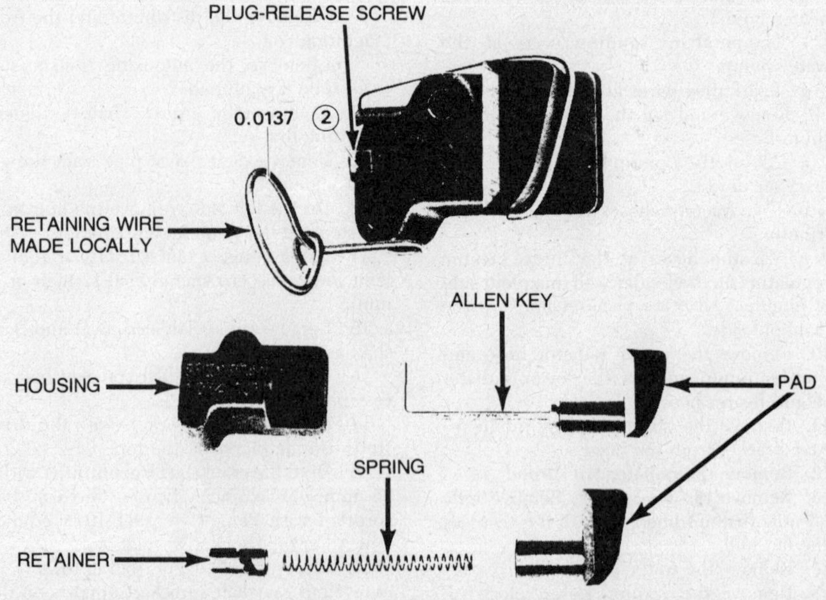

Reynholds® timing chain tensioner used in some 504 models

SEDIS® TENSIONER

a. Turn the rachet clockwise with a screwdriver to release the tension on the timing chain.

3. Remove the tensioner and tension plate.
4. Remove the filter from the block.
5. Before removing the timing chain, position the crankshaft Woodruff key slot to the left and the two white timing chain links to the right, while facing the front of the engine. An imaginary line through the Woodruff key slot and the middle of the two white links should be parallel to the leading edge of the oil pan.

CAUTION

If either the crankshaft or camshaft are rotated with the timing chain removed, valve damage might occur. Never rotate the crankshaft and always position the crankshaft as described in Step 5 before rotating the camshaft, when the timing chain is removed.

6. Take the tensioner apart and clean it.

CAUTION

On the Sedis® tensioner, do not remove the rachet screw (tension adjusting screw). Once removed it is impossible to put it back.

7. Without altering the position of the crankshaft, install the Woodruff key and the sprocket.
8. Keep the two white timing chain links at the camshaft sprocket mark and the one white link at the crankshaft sprocket mark with the centers of the crankshaft and camshaft, forming a straight line through the white chain links and the reference marks on the sprockets.
9. Install the new tab washers on the camshaft sprocket and torque the camshaft sprocket bolts to 16 ft/lbs (20 Nm).
10. Lock the bolts by bending the tabs around the bolt heads.
11. Install the filter.
12. Using Peugeot tool 0.0137 or equivalent to hold the tensioner together, install the tensioner.
13. On the Renold® tensioner, load the tensioner by turning the Allen key clockwise. Install a new tab washer and install the plug. Bend the tab to lock the plug.
14. Remove the retaining tool.

CAUTION

Never assist the tensioner action.

15. Load the Sedis® tensioner by turning the screw clockwise.

NOTE: The Sedis® and Renold® tensioners are interchangeable as a unit.

16. Install the thrust washer if needed and the oil thrower cup.

NOTE: The 505 uses an oil seal. Always install a new seal during reassembly.

17. Use a new housing gasket and center the timing housing with Peugeot tool 0.0128 or equivalent.

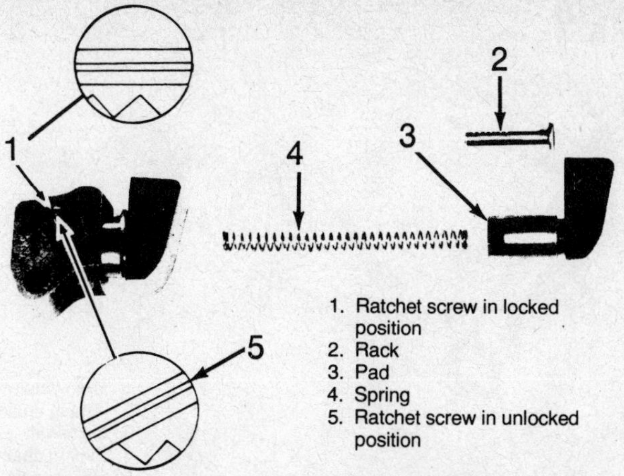

1. Ratchet screw in locked position
2. Rack
3. Pad
4. Spring
5. Ratchet screw in unlocked position

Sedis timing chain tensioner used in some 504 models

18. Install the Woodruff key and the crankshaft pulley. Torque the pulley nut to 123 ft/lbs (166 Nm).
19. Bend the tab around the nut.
20. Install remaining components in the reverse order of removal.
21. Fill the engine with oil and the radiator with coolant.
22. Check the timing.

604 Models–V6

TIMING CHAIN

1. Remove the timing chain cover.
2. Check the timing chain tensioner projection. If the projection is greater than 0.38 in. (9.5 mm) replace the timing chains.
3. Rotate both the tensioner adjusters counterclockwise to release the timing chain tension.
4. Remove the oil pump drive chain and sprockets. Also remove the oil pump crankshaft spacer and Woodruff key.
5. Remove the oil pump.
6. Bring the number one piston up to TDC on the compression stroke and mark the position of the crankshaft sprocket reference line. Also, mark the position of both of the camshaft sprocket reference lines.
7. Secure the crankshaft from rotating by installing Peugeot tool 8.013H or equivalent on the flywheel.
8. Remove the camshaft sprocket bolts.
9. Remove the right hand camshaft sprocket and timing chain and then the left side camshaft sprocket and timing chain.
10. Remove both tensioners and the small oil filter in the block behind each tensioner.
11. Install the left bank chain and sprocket along with the crankshaft sprocket and Woodruff key. The camshaft sprocket reference mark should be centered between the two white marks on the timing chain. The crankshaft sprocket reference should be directly in line with the single white mark on the timing chain. This means that there is no slack in the lower half of the chain and all of the slack is on the upper side (tensioner side). The match marks should be exactly where they were marked before the chain was removed.
12. Install the right bank chain and camshaft sprocket. Position the camshaft sprocket reference mark between the two white marks on the timing chain. The single white mark on the chain should be directly opposite the crankshaft sprocket reference mark. This means that all of the slack is on the tensioner side of the timing chain. The match marks should be exactly where they were marked before the timing chain was removed.
13. Install the tensioners and filters. Torque the tensioner bolts to 5.5 ft/lbs (7.8 Nm).
14. Place the two chains under tension by turning the tensioner adjusters clockwise.

CAUTION

Never attempt to assist the tensioning action of the tensioners.

15. Install the spacer, Woodruff key and sprocket for the oil pump chain drive.
16. Install the oil pump, using new lock washers on the four bolts. Torque the oil pump bolts to 9 ft/lbs (13 Nm).
17. Place the chain over both sprockets and install the three sprocket to oil pump bolts. Use new lock washers on the bolts and torque them to 4.0 ft/lbs (5.9 Nm).
18. Install new timing chain cover gaskets and secure the cover with twenty five bolts. Torque the bolts to 9 ft/lbs (13 Nm).
19. Lubricate and install a new crankshaft pulley seal. Use Peugeot special tool 8.0134 or equivalent and tap the seal in with a mallet.
20. Install the crankshaft pulley and bolt. Coat the bolt threads with a medium duty locking compound. Torque the bolts to 123 ft/lbs (166 Nm).
21. Reinstall all components removed during the removal procedure of the timing chain cover.
22. Install engine oil and coolant.
23. Remove the special tool holding flywheel in place and install the clutch or converter housing cover plate.

VALVE TIMING

If the timing is not marked while the piston of the Number one cylinder is on the compression stroke or the marks are lost, then use the following valve timing procedure.

1. Rotate the crankshaft clockwise so that the Woodruff key slot is straight up in a vertical position.
2. On the left hand cylinder head, place the camshaft so that the rocker arms on

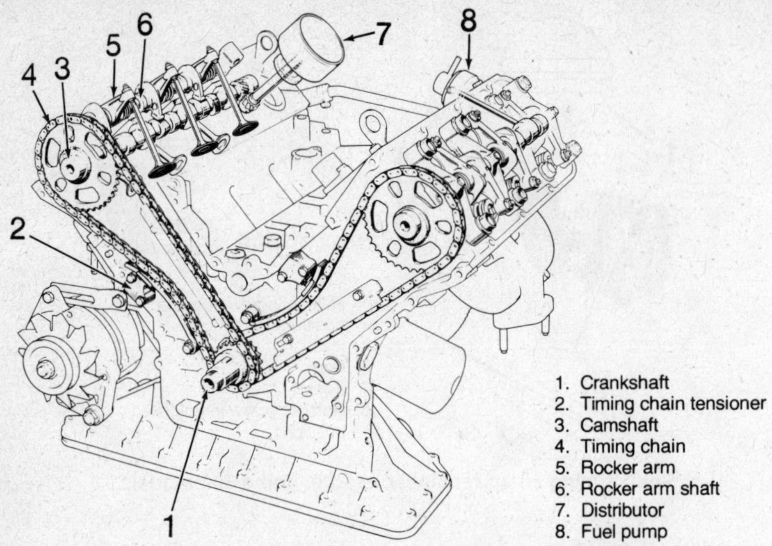

Cutaway view of the 604 engine timing and valve train

Number one cylinder are in balance. The camshaft slot will be aligned with the edge of the camshaft thrust flange. The slot and sprocket reference mark will be in a vertical position with head installed on the block.

3. Rotate the crankshaft clockwise until the crankshaft Woodruff key slot is aimed at the center line of the left bank camshaft.

4. Install the timing chain over the left camshaft sprocket with the reference mark centered between the two white marks on the timing chain.

5. Install the timing chain over the crankshaft sprocket with the reference mark lined up with the single white mark on the timing chain.

6. Fasten the camshaft sprocket with the sprocket bolt and torque the bolt to 51 ft/lbs (73 Nm).

7. Rotate the right side camshaft to a position where the Number four cylinder rocker arms are balanced. The slot in the camshaft will be pointing to an imaginary line through the center of the camshaft and parallel to the lower surface of the head.

8. Turn the crankshaft clockwise until the crankshaft sprocket reference mark lines up with the center of the lowest oil pump bolt hole.

9. Install the timing chain over the right side camshaft sprocket with the reference mark between the two white marks on the timing chain.

10. Install the timing chain on the outer crankshaft sprocket with the single white mark on the chain lined up with the reference mark on the crankshaft sprocket.

11. Install the bolt and the camshaft sprocket on the camshaft and torque the bolt to 51 ft/lbs (73 Nm).

12. Install the timing chain tensioners and filters. Torque the tensioner bolts to 5.5 ft/lbs (7.8 Nm).

13. Place the timing chains under tension by turning the tensioner adjusters clockwise.

CAUTION

Never attempt to assist the tensioning action of the tensioners.

14. Install the timing gear cover, using new gaskets.

15. Install a new timing cover oil seal.

16. Install the crankshaft pulley and install the bolt to a torque of 123 ft/lbs (166 Nm).

17. Install the power steering pump brackets and the power steering pump.

18. Install the rocker arm covers and the hot air duct.

19. Install the power steering and water pump belts.

20. Install the fan casing and fan.

21. Install the radiator hoses and radiator struts.

22. Install the engine coolant and engine oil.

23. Install the air mixer, hot air duct and air filter. Connect the negative battery cable.

Camshaft

REMOVAL AND INSTALLATION

504 and 505 Models

1. Drain the engine oil, the coolant and disconnect the battery ground cable.

2. Remove the air cleaner assembly, spark plugs, distributor, carburetor, rocker arm cover, fan belt, radiator and various wire and hose connections.

NOTE: On 505 fuel injected vehicles, remove the Lambda® sensor wire at the exhaust pipe, fuel injectors at the intake manifold, all electrical wires, air hoses, water hoses, power steering, thermoslide valve connections, air induction hoses and rocker arm oil feed line.

3. Remove the spark plug tubes from the head and the exhaust pipe from the exhaust manifold.

4. Remove the head bolts and install Peugeot head guide tools 8.0115Y or equivalent.

5. Remove the rocker shaft and the push rods.

6. Remove the front head guide and pivot the head on the back head guide to break it loose from the block and lift off the head.

7. Lock the cylinder liners with special retainer tools, Peugeot number 8.0104D or equivalent.

8. Remove the valve lifters (cam followers).

9. Remove the crankshaft pulley nut.

NOTE: On vehicles with manual transmissions, apply the parking brake and engage 4th gear to hold the crankshaft from rotating while removing the crankshaft pulley and camshaft sprocket. To remove the crankshaft pulley and camshaft sprocket on automatic transmission vehicles, remove the converter cover and use a flywheel tool to hold the engine.

10. Remove the timing chain cover.

11. If the engine is equipped with a Renold® tensioner, remove the plug and turn the adjuster clockwise with an Allen wrench to release the timing chain tension.

12. If the engine is equipped with a Sedis® tensioner, turn the rachet adjuster counterclockwise with a screwdriver to release the timing chain tension.

13. Remove the chain tensioner and the filter behind it.

14. Remove the camshaft sprocket, crankshaft sprocket, Woodruff key and the timing chain.

15. Remove the camshaft thrust flange and withdraw the camshaft.

16. Installation is the reverse of removal.

17. Install a new filter behind the tensioner and use Peugeot special tool 0.0137 or equivalent to hold the tensioner together while installing it.

604 Models

1. Drain the engine oil and engine coolant.

2. Disconnect the ground cable from the battery.

3. Remove the air filter, the air mixer casing and the hot air duct.

4. Remove the radiator struts, disconnect the hoses and separate the fan casing from the radiator.

5. Remove the fan and the fan casing.

6. Remove the power steering belt and the alternator drive belt.

7. Remove the power steering pump and hang it to the side, without removing the hoses.

8. Remove the clutch/converter housing cover plate.

9. Install the flywheel locking tool Peugeot number 0.0134C or equivalent.

10. Remove the crankshaft pulley.

11. Remove the hot air duct from the exhaust manifold and the rocker arm covers.

12. Remove the power steering pump support bracket.

13. Remove the timing chain cover.

14. Remove both oil pump drive sprockets, the oil pump chain, the spacer and the Woodruff key.

15. Remove the oil pump.

16. Release the two tensioners.

17. Match mark the camshaft drive sprockets to the head.

18. Remove the right camshaft sprocket and timing chain and then remove the left camshaft sprocket and timing chain.
19. Remove both chain tensioners and the filters behind them.
20. Remove the camshaft sprocket and Woodruff key.
21. Remove the right and the left side rocker arm assemblies. Mark the rocker arms right and left for reinstallation.
22. Remove the camshaft thrust flange from the front of the head, the bearing cover plate and gasket.
23. Remove the camshaft from the rear of the head.
24. Installation is the reverse of removal.

NOTE: The left hand camshaft has the fuel pump cam on it and the right hand camshaft has the distributor drive pinion on it.

25. Torque the rear cover plates to 4.3 ft/lbs (5.8 Nm).
26. Torque the thrust flange bolts to 9.4 ft/lbs (12.7 Nm).

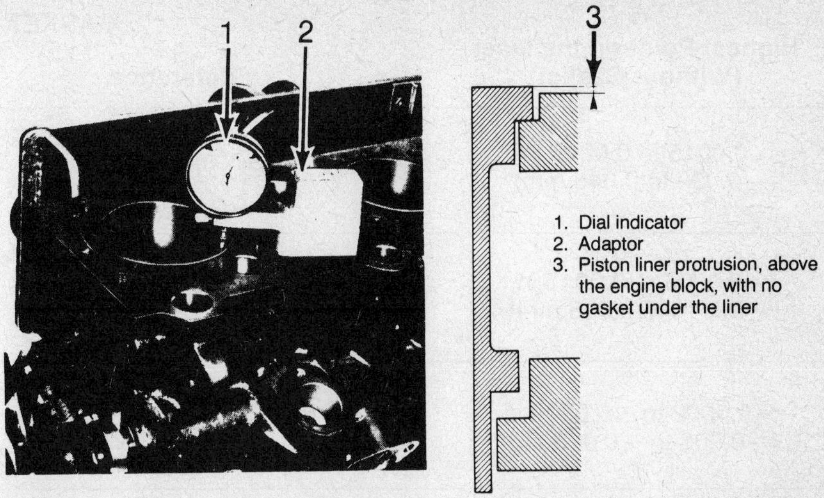

Checking the liner protrusion above the block on 504 models, 505 models are similar

Pistons and Connecting Rods

REMOVAL AND INSTALLATION

504 and 505 Models

1. Remove the cylinder head.
2. Remove the lifters, the distributor support and the distributor driveshaft.
3. Remove the oil pan and oil pump.
4. Mark the pistons and rods with Number one through four, rear to front. Number one cylinder is at the clutch end of the engine.
5. Remove the end caps from the connecting rods. Push the piston and liner assembly from the block. Keep the end caps with the proper piston and liner as it is removed.
6. Set the liners in position in the block without the seals and check them for distortion with a flat surface and a dial indicator.
7. Take a dial indicator reading at four points around the liner. The difference between the four measurements should be less than 0.0028 in. (0.07 mm).

NOTE: The 505 procedure is the same except that the protrusion specification is 0.0055 in. (0.14 mm) and the maximum difference between liners is 0.0016 in. (0.04 mm).

NOTE: The distance being measured is the amount of protrusion of the cylinder liners above the cylinder block.

8. Select the proper size liner seal by subtracting the measured distance with no seal from the maximum allowable liner protrusion. Pick the seal size nearest to and not exceeding the subtracted difference.
9. Install the liners in the same positions as match marked before removal.

PISTON AND LINER MATCHING CHART ②

Mark On Piston	Matching Mark On The Liner ①
A	1 mark
B	2 marks
C	3 marks

① Machined lines mark the upper edge of the liner.
② Piston ring gap and clearance specifications are not given. It is recommended by the manufacturer that pistons, rings and liners be replaced as complete new set for all cylinders.

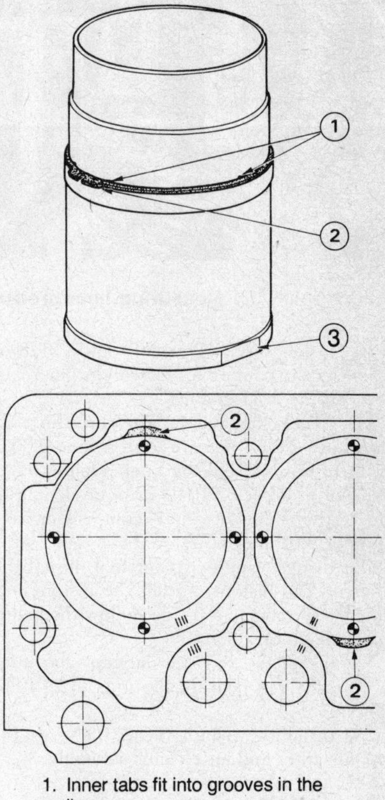

1. Inner tabs fit into grooves in the liner
2. Reference tab position at right angle to the flat spot
3. Flat spot

Installing piston liner seals, with the tab in the proper position in the 504 and 505 models

604 MODEL SELECTIVE CYLINDER LINER SEALS

Color	Thickness
Blue	0.0034 in. (0.087 mm)
White	0.0040 in. (0.102 mm)
Red	0.0048 in. (0.122 mm)
Yellow	0.0058 in. (0.147 mm)

Highest Point on the Liner (Without Gasket)	GASKET TO BE FITTED Reference	Thickness
0.0015 to 0.0018 in. (0.039 to 0.045 mm)	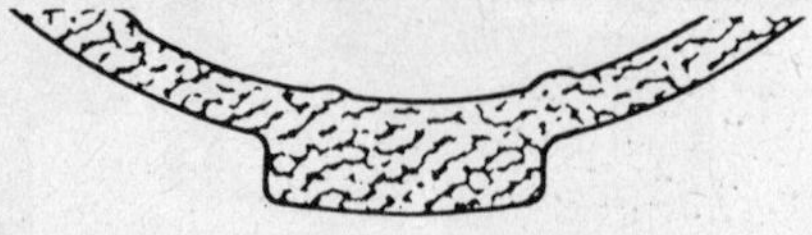	0.0028 to 0.0041 in. (0.070 to 0.105 mm)
0.0007 to 0.0015 in. (0.019 to 0.038 mm)	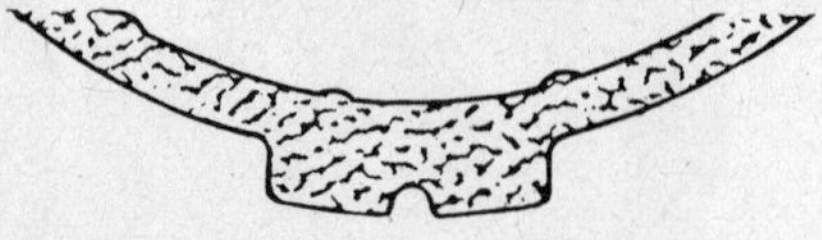	0.0033 to 0.0047 in. (0.085 to 0.120 mm)
−0.0002 to +0.0007 in. (−0.006 to +0.018 mm)	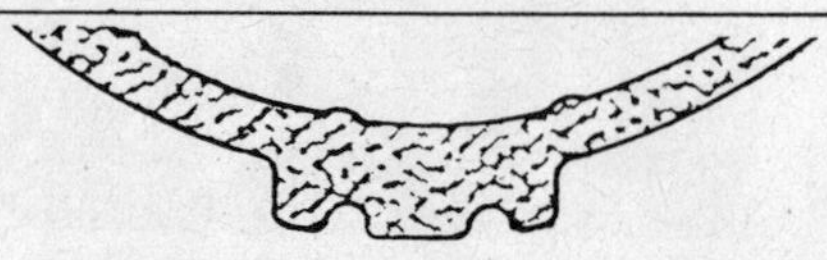	0.0041 to 0.0055 in. (0.105 to 0.140 mm)
−0.0037 to −0.0003 in. (−0.095 to −0.007 mm)	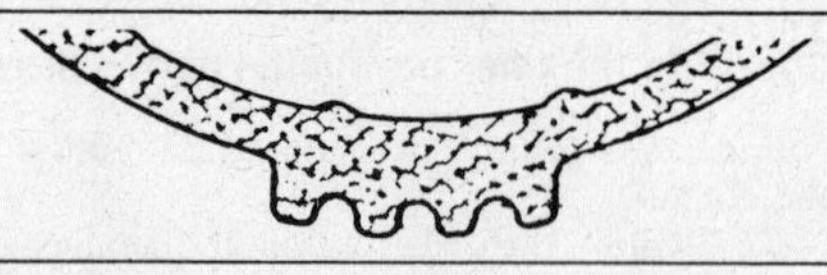	0.0051 to 0.0065 in. (0.130 to 0.165 mm)

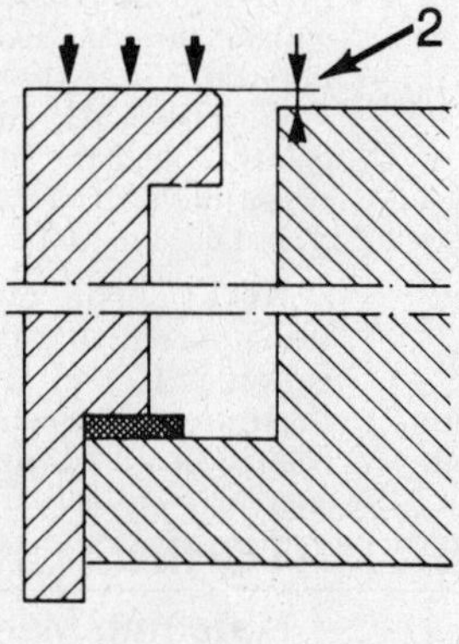

1. Liner compressing tool
2. Piston liner protrusion

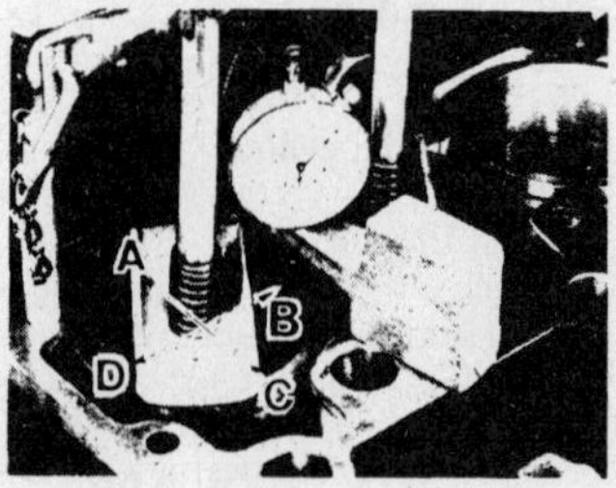

Measuring liner protrusion with the gasket installed on 504 models with compressed type liners

10. Install special Peugeot tools 8.0128 or equivalent to compress the cylinder liner gaskets, on the XN1 engines.

11. Check the dial indicator readings on each liner and if they are from zero to 0.0055 in. (0.14 mm), install the liner retainer bolts, Peugeot number 8.0104D or equivalent. Remove the Peugeot liner compressor tool number 8.0128 or equivalent.

12. Using a ring expander tool, install the rings on the pistons. Install the pistons into the liners from the top side, follow the match marks made on removal.

13. Install the rod bearing caps and nuts. Torque the rod bearing cap nuts to 29 ft/lbs (39 Nm).

14. Install the cylinder head, the wires, the vacuum lines and air cleaner assembly.

604 Models

1. Remove the air cleaner, wires, vacuum lines and the cylinder heads.

2. Use Peugeot tool 8.0134N and M or equivalents on both head surfaces to secure the camshaft sprockets. Shims are available in selective thicknesses to install under the camshaft sprocket holding tools. The shims may be needed to ensure the tightness of the timing chains while working on the pistons.

CAUTION

If slack is allowed in the timing chains or the special tools are not available the timing chains will have to be removed and the valve timing reset.

3. Use the special tools, cylinder liner retainers, Peugeot number 8.0132A or equivalent, to secure the cylinder liners in the block.

4. Remove the lower oil pan, the oil strainer, the anti-emulsion baffle, the sump securing bolts, the main bearing securing nuts and remove the oil sump.

5. Remove the connecting rod cap nuts.

6. Matchmark the cylinder liners to the block and the connecting rod caps to the connecting rods. Normally, the pistons have arrows on them to mark the direction of installation. If the pistons have the arrows, note the direction before removal and reinstall in the same direction. If no arrows are on the pistons, mark them with a felt tip pen for future reference.

7. Remove the pistons, piston rods and cylinder liners at the same time. Keep matching parts together.

8. If the liner is distorted beyond specification, install a new liner set.

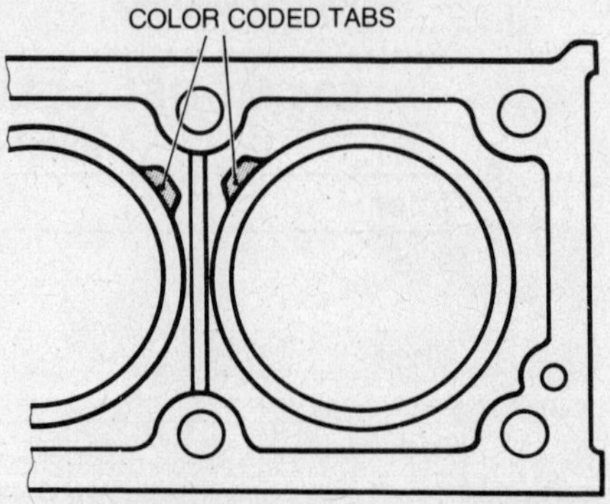

Correct position of the tabs on the 604 model piston liners, when correctly installed

NOTE: Pistons, rings, and liners are available in sets only. This helps retain engine balance.

9. The piston liners must project above the cylinder block gasket face between 0.0064 in. (0.16 mm) and 0.0092 in. (0.23 mm).
10. Cylinder liner seals are to be installed between the liner and the lower flange of the block.
11. Cylinder liner seals are available in the following thicknesses:
12. Measure the cylinder liner projection above the engine block with no seal under it. Subtract this measurement from 0.0092 in. (0.23 mm) and select a seal that will provide a maximum cylinder liner projection of 0.0092 in. (0.23 mm), or as close to it as possible without exceeding the maximum. For example:

Maximum allowable projection	0.0092 in.
Largest measurement—no seal	0.0040 in.
Difference to be taken up by the selected seal	0.0052 in.

The seal selected will be red 0.0488 in. (0.122 mm).
13. Install the seals with their color code facing the top of the engine.
14. Install the liners and seals in a position so that the color tabs are visible and will not be squeezed under the adjacent liner.
15. Check the final liner projection above the block for each cylinder liner. Mark the position of the liners on the straight edge of the block.
16. Install a piston ring tool around the piston crown and compress the rings. Oil the liner and install the piston. Match the marks on the liner and the piston.
17. When installing pistons and liners, always match the letter on the piston crown to the number of machine marks on the liner.
18. Install the piston and liner assemblies into the block.
19. Install the rod bearings and rod caps. Torque the rod bearing cap nuts to 34 ft/lbs (46 Nm).
20. Install the cylinder heads and all related wires, vacuum lines and the air cleaner assembly.

ENGINE LUBRICATION

Oil Pan

REMOVAL AND INSTALLATION

504 and 505 Models

The Peugeot four cylinder engines have a separate oil sump pan on the bottom of the crankcase pan.

1. To remove the oil sump, drain the oil, remove the retaining bolts and the sump pan.
2. To remove the entire crankcase pan, the engine will have to be raised for working clearances.
3. Installation is the reverse of removal.

604 Models

The 6 cylinder engines have a front lower oil sump that is removable with the engine in the vehicle. If the entire crankcase must be removed, the engine must be removed from the vehicle.

NOTE: If the entire crankcase must be removed, refer to the engine removal and installation section of the Peugeot Procedures in this book.

1. Drain the engine oil.
2. Remove the sump pan bolts and take off the sump pan.
3. Clean off the gasket surfaces and install a new gasket.
4. Install the sump pan and torque the bolts to 9.4 ft/lbs (12.7 Nm).
5. Torque the drain plug to 27 ft/lbs (36 Nm).
6. Fill the engine with 6.3 quarts (6.0 liters) of engine oil.

Rear Main Oil Seal

REMOVAL AND INSTALLATION

504 and 505 Models

Seals are not used on the rear of the crankshaft. An oil slinger arrangement is used to direct the oil back into the reservoir. The crankshaft may need new thrust washers, if end play is excessive. Side seals are used on the rear main bearing cap.

1. Check the end float of the crankshaft. The end float (end-play) must be between 0.003 in. (0.08 mm) and 0.008 in. (0.20 mm).
2. If there is too much end float (end-play), oversize thrust washers are available in thicknesses of: 0.096 in. (2.4 mm), 0.098 in. (2.45 mm), and 0.10 in. (2.5 mm).
3. Install the new rear bearing cap side seals and torque the bearing cap bolts to 55 ft/lbs (73.5 Nm).

604 Models

The transmission and the flywheel must be removed on 604 models in order to work on the rear main seal. See Transmission Removal and Installation in this section of this book, for procedures.

1. Check the crankshaft end play for between 0.0028 in. (0.07 mm) and 0.0108 in. (0.27 mm).
2. If needed, install oversized thrust washers selected from available sizes of: 0.092 in. (2.3 mm), 0.096 in. (2.4 mm), 0.098 in. (2.45 mm) and 0.10 in. (2.5 mm).
3. Remove the seal and fit a new seal by hand.
4. Install the flywheel and transmission.

Oil Pump

REMOVAL AND INSTALLATION

504 and 505 Models

1. Drain the oil.
2. Remove the oil sump and oil pump. Do not lose the two oil pump locating dowels.
3. Install a new O-ring on the bottom of the oil pump.
4. Be certain that the locating dowels are in place.
5. Be certain that the oil pump drive blade engages the oil pump drive rod.
6. Torque the bolts to 7 ft/lbs (9.8 Nm).
7. Use a new gasket and install the oil sump.
8. Torque the sump bolts to 7 ft/lbs (9.8 Nm).
9. Install the drain plug and fill the engine with oil.

CAUTION

Oil sumps made of either pressed steel or aluminum which do not have an oil return passage, must not be installed on XM engines with a rear main bearing cap which incorporates an oil return hole.

CAUTION

A special oil pan gasket of rubber/asbestos must be used on USA models with a metal alloy sump.

604 Models

1. Drain the engine oil and remove the timing chain cover.
2. Remove the oil pump drive sprockets, drive chain and Woodruff key.
3. Remove the oil pump.
4. Installation is the reverse of removal.
5. Torque the oil pump sprocket bolts to 4 ft/lbs (5.0 Nm).
6. Torque the oil pump bolts to 9 ft/lbs (12.7 Nm).

ENGINE COOLING

Radiator

REMOVAL AND INSTALLATION

504 and 505 Models

1. Drain the coolant.
2. Remove the fan shroud retaining bolts.
3. Remove the upper and lower radiator hose.
4. Remove the lower radiator bolts.
5. Remove the radiator.
6. Installation is the reverse of removal.

604 Models

1. Drain the cooling system.
2. On air conditioned vehicles:
   a. Remove the electric fan lead,
   b. Remove the oil pressure switch wires,
   c. Remove the compressor wire,
   d. Remove the temperature sending wire,
   e. Remove the three electric fan bolts,
   f. Remove the radiator stays,
   g. Remove the battery.
3. Remove the overflow hose from the left side of the radiator.
4. Remove the top and the bottom radiator hoses.
5. On vehicles with an automatic transmission, remove the transmission cooler lines.

6. On air conditioned vehicles, disconnect the condenser receiver/dryer assembly from the radiator.
7. Remove the fan cowl and the radiator.
8. Installation is the reverse of removal.
9. Refill the cooling system.

Water Pump

REMOVAL AND INSTALLATION

504 and 505 Models

1. Drain the coolant.
2. Remove the top radiator hose and the heater hose from the water pump.
3. Remove the fan belt.
4. Remove the water pump bolts and remove the water pump.
5. Clean the gasket surfaces.
6. Replace the gasket and install the pump in the reverse order or removal.
7. Install coolant in the engine.

604 Models

1. Drain the cooling system.
2. Remove the air mixer casing and duct, the hot air duct and the air filter.
3. Remove the intake manifold and the insulating plate under the manifold.
4. Remove the water pump belt and the alternator drive belt.
5. Separate the fan casing from the radiator.
6. Remove the heater and radiator hoses at the water pump.
7. Remove the wire lead from the temperature sending unit.
8. Loosen the hose clamps on the two rubber hoses at the heads.
9. Remove the bolts securing the water casings to the block.
10. Remove the two heater hoses from the back of the water pump.
11. Remove the water pump bolts.
12. Remove the water pump and casing as an assembly.
13. Installation is the reverse of removal.

NOTE: Install new O-rings where the casing fits to the block.

14. Torque the water casing bolts to 9.4 ft/lbs (12.7 Nm).
15. Torque the water pump bolts to 14.6 ft/lbs (17.2 Nm).

Radiator Fan

REMOVAL AND INSTALLATION

504 Models

1. Remove the water pump.
2. Using a pulley holder tool mounted in a vise, remove the pump hub nut.
3. Tap on the end of the shaft to disengage the pump body from the pulley. Remove the Woodruff key from the slot in the shaft.
4. Installation is the reverse of removal.
5. Torque the pump hub nut to 25 ft/lbs (34.2 Nm).

505 and 604 Models

1. Remove the fan casing from the radiator.
2. Remove the four fan-to-thermostatic fan clutch bolts.
3. Lift off the fan.
4. Installation is the reverse of removal.

Belt Tension Adjustment

Peugeot recommends that all of their belts be adjusted by measuring reference marks on the belts, except on the model 505 air pump-alternator belt. On the 505 air pump-alternator belt the adjustment is made by loosening the idler pulley bolts and torqueing idler bracket nut to 58.0 ft/lbs (78.4 Nm).

504, 505 AND 604 MODELS (ALL OTHER BELTS)

1. Loosen the belt adjusting bracket bolts.
2. With no tension on it, mark two reference lines on the belt, 4 inches (100 mm) apart.
3. Stretch the belt when tightening it so that the reference marks will be 4.12 inches (103 mm) apart.

EMISSION CONTROLS

The Peugeot emission controls are composed of three major systems: crankcase emissions control, evaporative emissions control and exhaust emissions control.

Differences may occur between California and Federal vehicles. Therefore, the emission control information label on the vehicle should be consulted before repairs are made.

Crankcase Emission Control System

The system is considered a closed system with the crankcase breathing from the air cleaner air intake. The PCV valve vents measured amounts of crankcase gases and vapors into the intake manifold to be burned with the air/fuel mixture.

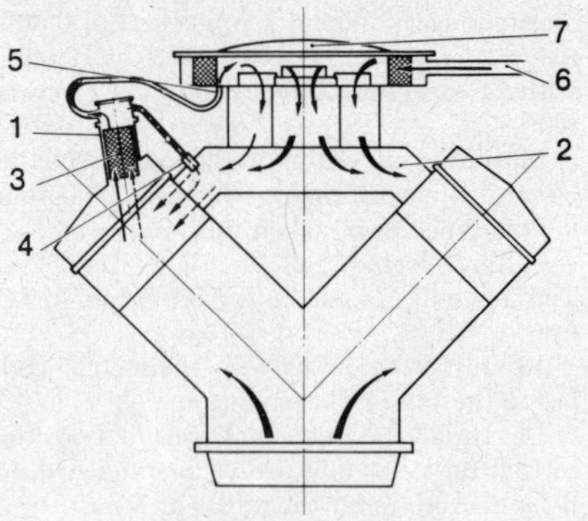

1. PCV recirculating tube
2. Intake manifold
3. Filter
4. Calibrated jet
5. Calibrated hole in air cleaner
6. Air intake
7. Air cleaner assembly

604 crankcase emission system

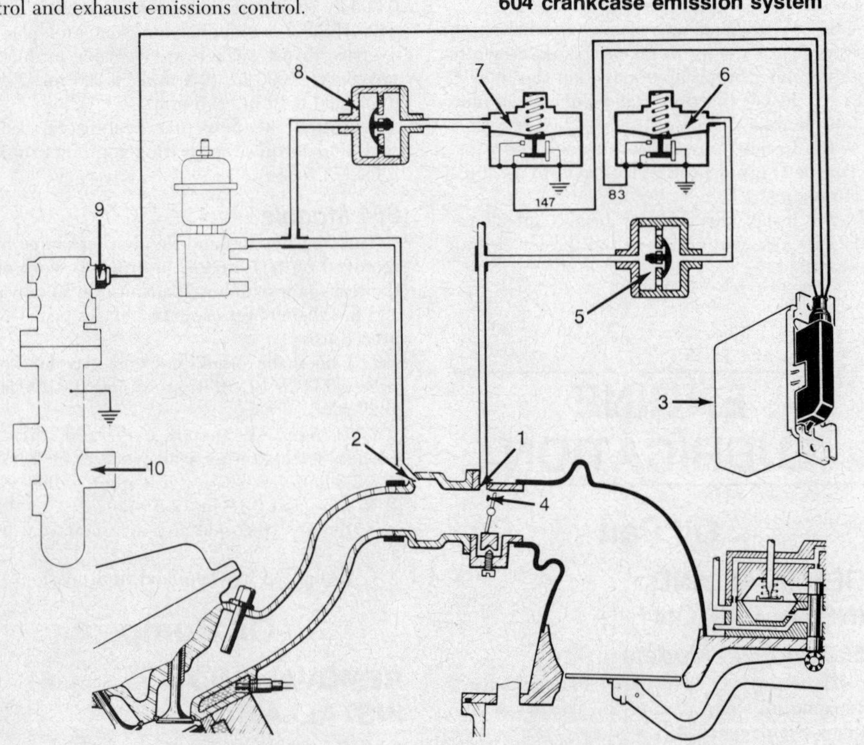

1. Vacuum port
2. Vacuum port
3. Electronic control unit
4. Throttle plate
5. Delay valve
6. Delay valve
7. Vacuum switch
8. Vacuum switch
9. Thermo-contact wire
10. Air slide valve

Model 505 emission control components located in the engine compartment

Evaporative Emission Control System

In order to control the evaporation of fuel into the atmosphere from the fuel tank and the carburetor when the engine is shut off, both are vented into a charcoal canister. A calibrated valve in the fuel tank line meters the flow of vapors into the charcoal canister to an amount that the canister can handle. The station wagons have an additional vapor-liquid separator located near the fuel tank. When the engine is started, the system pulls the vapors out of the charcoal canister and into the intake manifold, thereby purging the canister of fuel vapors.

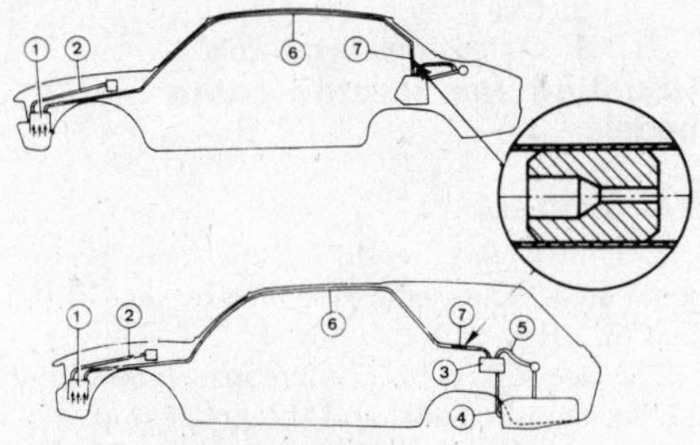

1. Charcoal canister
2. Canister to carburetor vapor hose
3. Vapor-liquid separator (wagon only)
4. Separator return hose (wagon only)
5. Filler neck to separator hose (wagon only)
6. Fuel tank to canister hose
7. Calibrated jet

Evaporative emission system all models

Exhaust Emission Control Systems

AIR INJECTION

The air injection system adds oxygen into the exhaust manifold, allowing unburned hydrocarbons (HC) in the hot exhaust gases to be burned more completely. The system consists of a belt driven rotary vane air pump, a diverter valve, and an electro-valve, an intake manifold injection valve and non-return valves.

Air Pump

Some precautions should be taken when working on the air pump.

1. Do not operate the engine with the pump removed or drive belt disconnected.

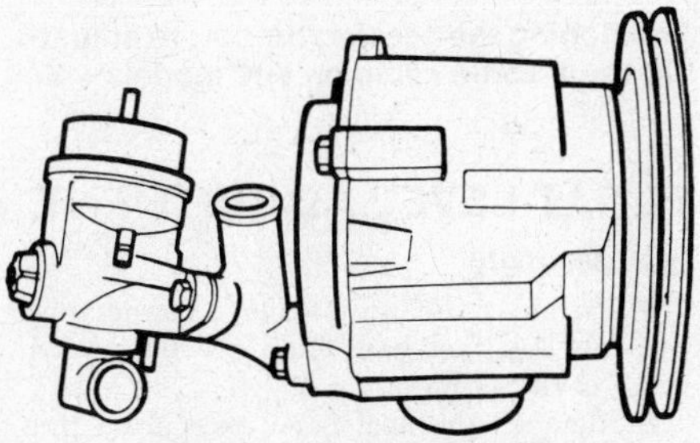

504 air injection pump

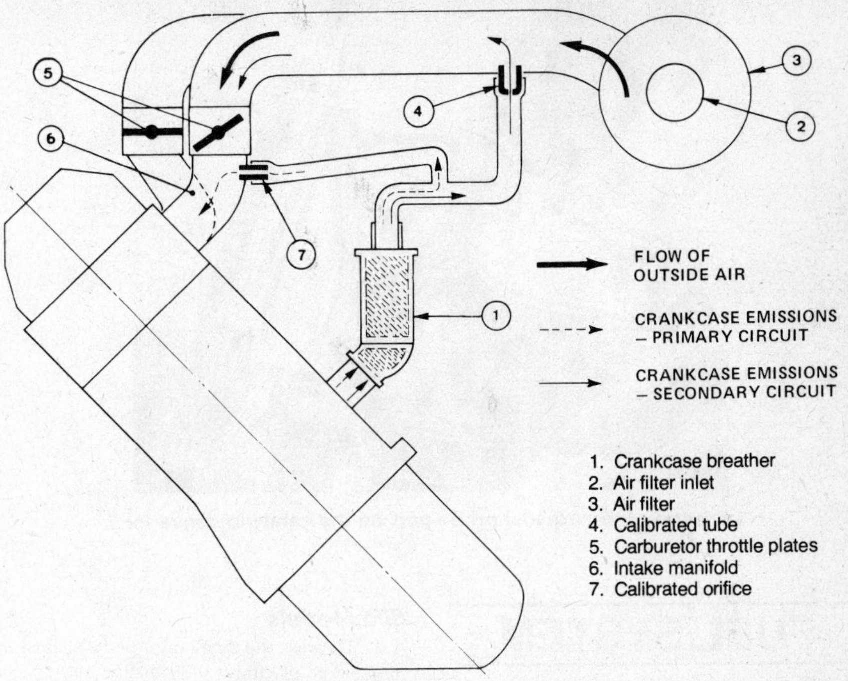

1. Crankcase breather
2. Air filter inlet
3. Air filter
4. Calibrated tube
5. Carburetor throttle plates
6. Intake manifold
7. Calibrated orifice

504 and 505 crankcase emission system

2. Do not lubricate the pump.
3. If the filter is contaminated, replace it. Do not attempt to clean it.
4. When adjusting the drive belt, never pry on the pump body.
5. Never clamp the pump body in a vise.
6. The internal parts of the air pump are not serviceable. Replace the pump as an assembly.
7. The following external parts may be replaced on the pump: drive pulley, filter and pressure relief valve.
8. Do not hand rotate the pulley on a new pump and never rotate the pulley in the direction opposite to the normal direction.

EGR VALVE

In order to reduce the nitrogen oxide (NO_x) in the exhaust, a controlled amount of exhaust gas is recirculated into the intake manifold. The main component of the system is the valve, which opens between the exhaust and intake manifolds. The valve opening is controlled by vacuum, according to engine conditions, by a vacuum control electro-valve and a vacuum amplifier. California engines have an additional vacuum switch.

ELECTRO-VALVE

During engine start up and warm up, the electro-valve stops the flow of vacuum to the EGR valve, to prevent the EGR valve from opening when the choke is operating.

VACUUM AMPLIFIER

This valve controls the amount of vacuum to the EGR valve according to engine conditions.

VACUUM SWITCH

This switch reacts to close the EGR valve during high intake manifold vacuum situa-

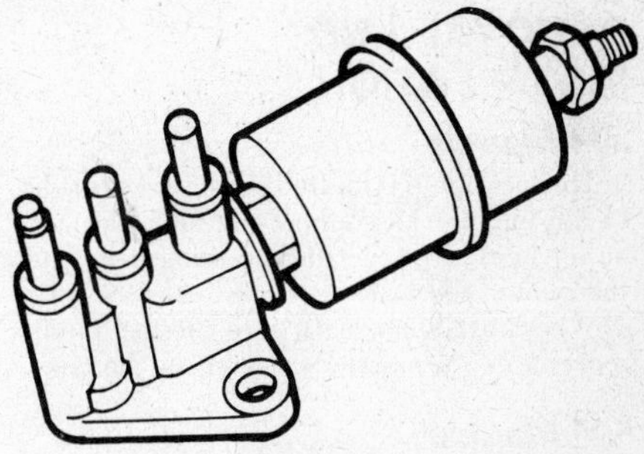

504 deceleration valve

tions. The valve is only used on California vehicles.

CATALYTIC CONVERTER

The catalytic converter reduces hydrocarbons (HC) and carbon monoxide (CO) by converting them to carbon dioxide and water.

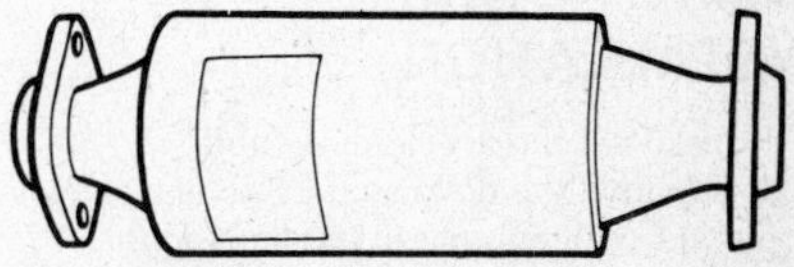

504 catalytic converter

Lambda® Sensor

The 505 fuel injected models use the Lambda® oxygen sensor system to check the exhaust gases for unburned hydro-carbons. The sensor sends signals from the exhaust pipe to the control unit. Under certain conditions, the signals will cause the control unit to alter the fuel ratio to bring it into specifications. If the engine has not reached operating temperature the signals will be overridden and the enrichment system will operate.

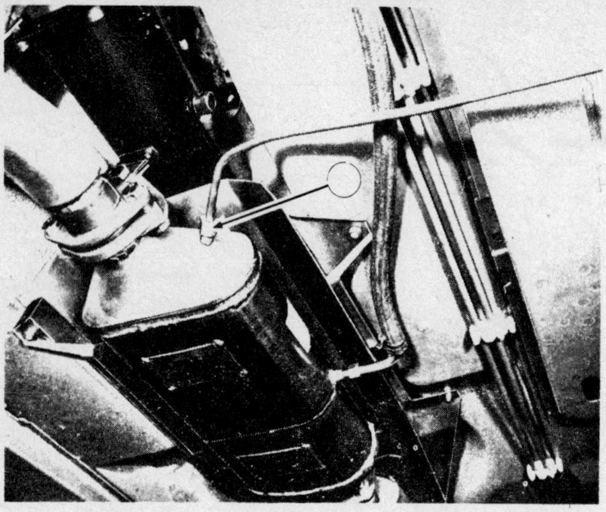

Location of the exhaust probe port on the catalytic converter

FUEL SYSTEM

Fuel Pump

REMOVAL AND INSTALLATION

504 Models

The fuel pump is located on the drivers side of the engine. Disconnect the fuel inlet and outlet lines. Remove the attaching bolts and the pump.

When installing, make sure the fuel pump rocker arm is positioned correctly on the cam.

604 Models

The fuel pump is located on the driver's side of the engine. Disconnect the fuel inlet and outlet lines. Remove the attaching bolts and the pump.

When installing, make sure the pump arm is positioned correctly on the cam.

Carburetors

REMOVAL AND INSTALLATION

1. Remove the accelerator cable.
2. Remove the downshift cable on vehicles equipped with automatic transmissions.
3. Remove all fuel and vacuum lines.
4. Remove the carburetor mounting bolts and lift off the carburetor.
5. Installation is the reverse of removal.
6. Adjust the accelerator linkage to free play of 0.08 in. (2 mm).

THROTTLE LINKAGE ADJUSTMENT

504 Models

Adjust the throttle linkage to 0.08 in. (2 mm) of clearance, with the engine warm.

505 Models

1. Depress the accelerator pedal against its stop, after placing a 0.20 in. (5 mm) spacer between the pedal and the stop.
2. Connect the accelerator cable to the throttle drum of the carburetor.
3. Rotate the carburetor drum to full throttle position.
4. Exert a light pull on the throttle cable housing stop, to place the cable and control under a slight load.
5. Install the retaining clip on the cable housing in a way that will leave a 0.02 in. (.5 mm) clearance between the clip and the cable support bracket.

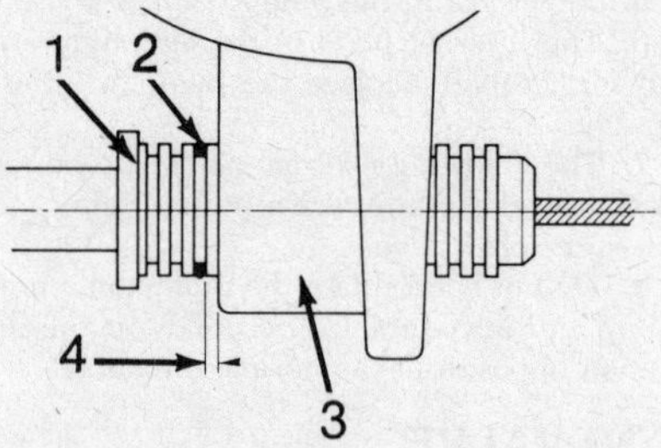

1. Throttle cable
2. Snap ring
3. Common intake manifold
4. 0.08 in. (2 mm)

Adjusting the throttle cable on 505 models

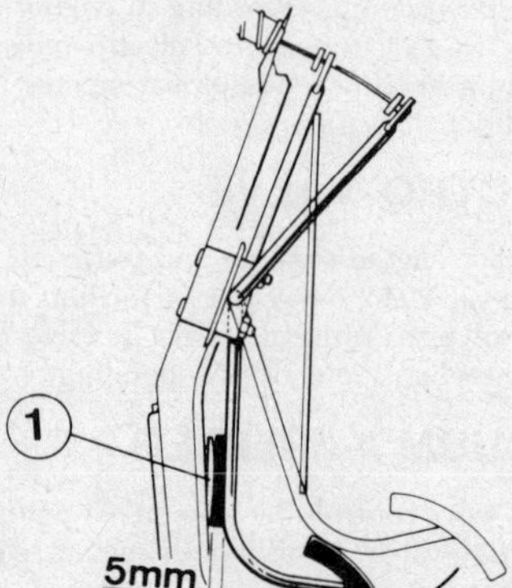

Positioning the accelerator in order to adjust the throttle cable on 505 models

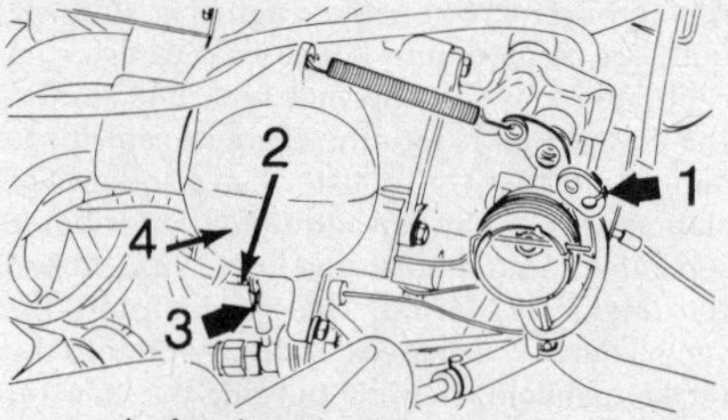

1. Accelerator cable
2. Accelerator cable housing stop
3. Clip
4. Common intake manifold

Adjusting the throttle cable on 505 models

604 Models

1. Check the height of the accelerator pedal stop. The pedal stop height should be 2.04 in. (51 mm).
2. Place a 0.28 in. (7 mm) spacer between the accelerator pedal and the pedal stop.
3. Hold the accelerator pedal and the spacer in a fully depressed position.
4. Remove the two linkage return springs.
5. Hold the carburetor control quadrant in the fully open position.
6. Secure the accelerator cable in place on the control quadrant, pulling on the cable just enough to tension it. Do not compress the compensator spring on the cable when tensioning it.
7. Install the two linkage return springs.
8. Remove the spacer from under the accelerator pedal.
9. When the engine is hot, the clearance on the accelerator cable to holding bracket should be 0.08 in. (2 mm).

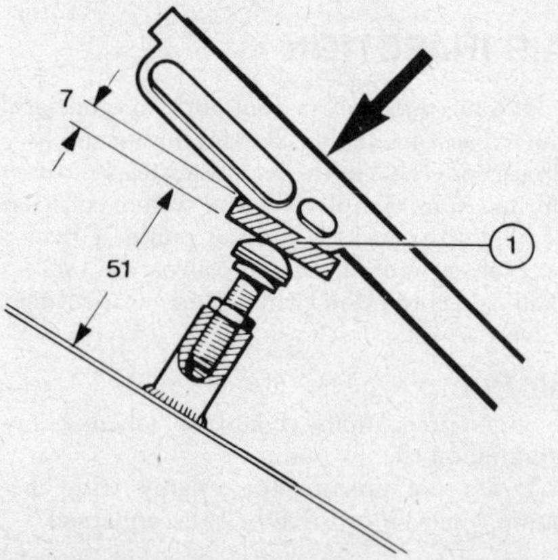

Positioning the accelerator before adjusting the throttle cable on 604 models

FLOAT LEVEL ADJUSTMENT

504 Models

1. Remove the air cleaner, connecting linkages and fuel lines from the float bowl cover of the carburetor.
2. Remove the float bowl cover from the carburetor.

3. With the needle valve completely closed, check the float level, by measuring the distance from the float bowl cover mating surface to the small diameter of the float.

4. If the float level does not measure 1.4 in. (35.5 mm) adjust it by bending the pivot arm on the float.

604 Models

1. Remove the air cleaner, linkages and fuel line.

2. Remove the float chamber cover.

3. Drain the fuel and clean out the float chamber.

4. Hold the float chamber cover in a vertical position with the fuel inlet pointing up.

5. With float chamber gasket in position, check the float level from the mating surface of the cover to the bottom of the float.

6. If the float level does not check to 1.6 in. (40 mm), adjust the float level by bending the tab on the float.

7. Invert the air horn so that the float is at its lowest point. Check the float for 0.5 in. (12.5 mm) of drop. Adjust by bending the float drop tab.

AUTOMATIC CHOKE ADJUSTMENT

504 Models

1. Pull out the manual choke control.

2. Push in the vacuum pull-off rod to obtain the initial choke opening.

3. Measure the opening between the venturi and the choke butterfly at the notch in the lower end of the butterfly.

4. If the gap is not between 0.08 in. (2 mm) and 0.12 in. (3 mm), adjust by bending the tab on the linkage.

604 Models

1. Start the engine and bring it up to operating temperature.

CAUTION

Make sure the gearshift is in Neutral or Park and the handbrake is set.

2. Always check the idle speed and mixture for correct setting before adjusting the choke.

3. Remove the air and choke housing cover plate.

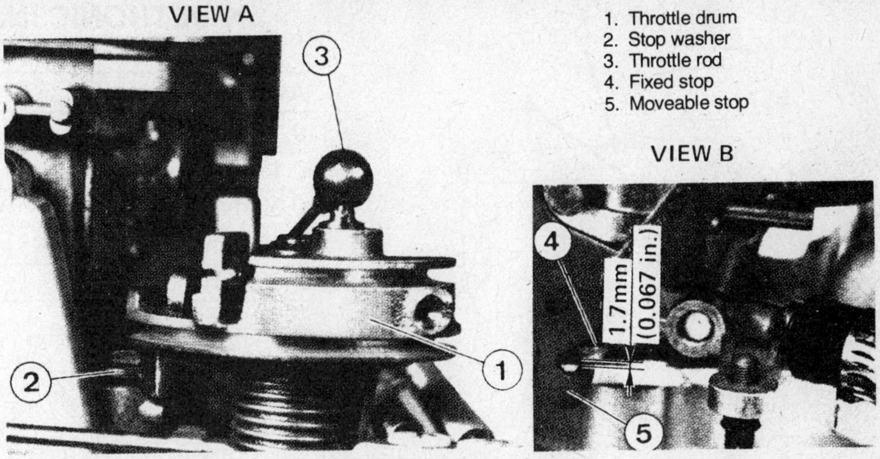

604 throttle linkage adjustment

Adjusting the throttle cable at the retaining bracket on 504 and 604 models

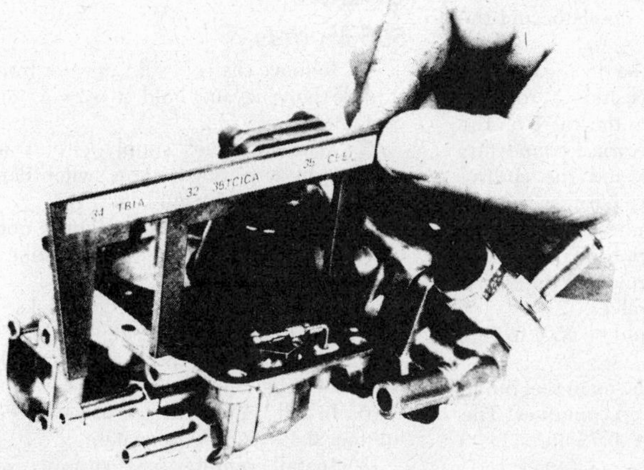

Checking the float level on 34TBIA Solex® carburetors used on 604 models

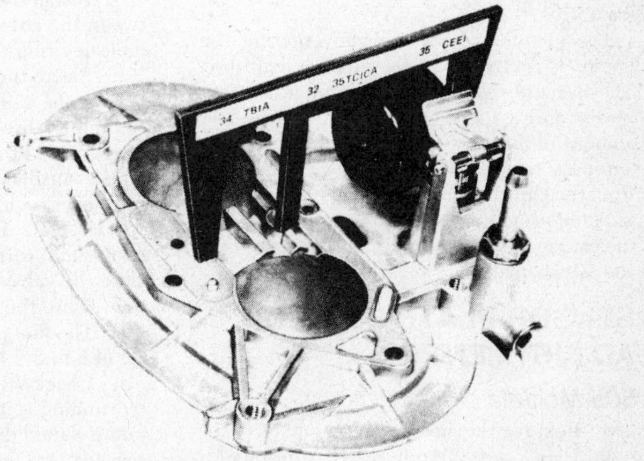

Checking the float level the 35CEEI Venturi injection carburetor used on 604 models

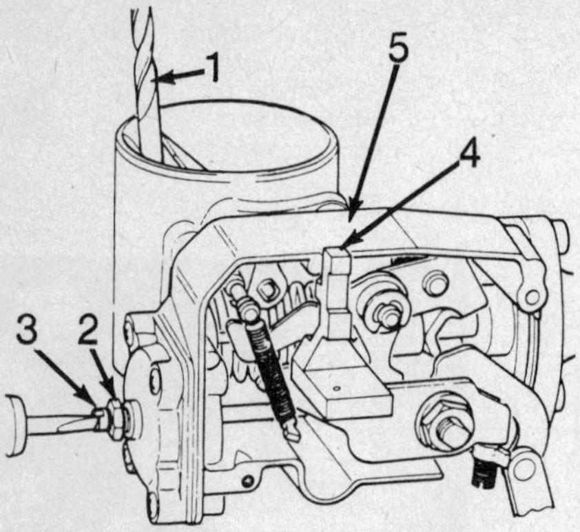

1. 0.295 in. (7 mm) drill or gauge rod
2. Locknut
3. Adjusting screw
4. Choke gauge tool (8.0143)
5. Choke housing

604 choke adjustment

4. Install the Peugeot choke gauge tool 8.0143 or equivalent to engage the choke mechanism pivoting roller onto the tool. Rock the tool back and forth slightly until it contacts the choke housing.

5. Increase the engine speed to obtain the total choke opening after start (COAS). The pull-off opening should be 0.295 in. (7.5 mm) from the choke plate to the wall of the choke bore.

6. If the choke plate clearance is incorrect, loosen the adjusting locknut and turn the screw to obtain the proper clearance. Tighten the locknut.

7. Remove the gauge tool.

8. Install the choke housing cover and the air cleaner assembly.

Fuel Injection

GENERAL OPERATING PRINCIPLES

505 Models

The fuel is supplied by two fuel pumps. A priming pump located in the fuel tank supplies 2.1 psi (0.15 bar)—6.4 psi (0.45 bar) of fuel pressure to the main feed pump. The main feed pump supplies the fuel distributor under a pressure of approximately 71.0 psi (5 bar).

The amount of air and fuel entering the engine is controlled by the mixture regulator. The mixture regulator consists of an air flow sensor and a fuel metering distributor. The amount of air drawn into the engine is measured by the sensor plate installed upstream from the throttle plate. The fuel metering distributor provides fuel evenly to the injectors in relation to the amount of air measured by the sensor plate.

SENSOR PLATE POSITION ADJUSTMENT

505 Models

1. Remove the air cleaner assembly.

2. Using a 0.004 in. (0.10 mm) feeler gauge, check the clearance around the sensor plate at four opposite points around the plate.

K-JETRONIC INJECTION PRESSURE REGULATOR SHIM CHART

Available Shims	Difference Of Pressure
0.10 mm	2.18 psi (0.15 bar)
0.15 mm	3.34 psi (0.23 bar)
0.30 mm	6.53 psi (0.45 bar)
0.40 mm	8.7 psi (0.60 bar)
0.50 mm	10.88 psi (0.75 bar)

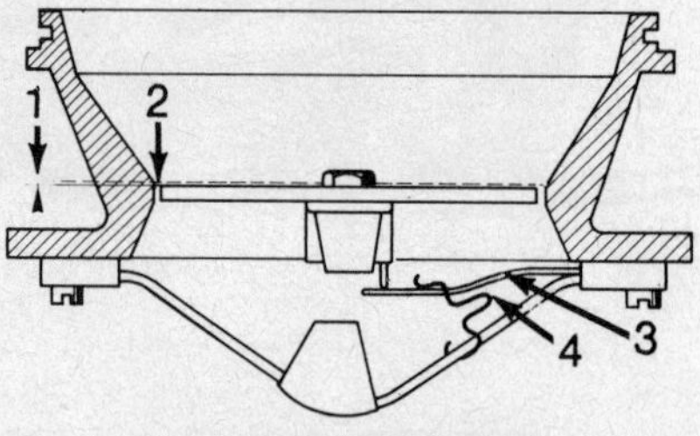

1. 0.020 in. (0.5 mm) gap
2. Upper edge of the narrow part of the venturi
3. Blade
4. Spring

Setting the sensor plate gap on fuel injected models

3. If necessary, loosen the bolt in the center of the sensor plate and center the plate. Torque the bolt to 3.6 ft/lbs (4.9 Nm).

CAUTION

Do not scratch the venturi or the plate.

4. Check the distance from the sensor plate to the upper edge of the narrowest part of the venturi.

5. If this measurement is not correct, bend the spring holding the fuel distributor blade.

NOTE: The sensor plate must be installed face up. The upper face will be marked with 5 punch marks or the word "top" will appear on it.

CONTROL PRESSURE TEST

505 Models

1. Install the testing apparatus in series between the control pressure regulator and the fuel metering distributor.

2. Bleed the air from the test gauge by placing the gauge in a low position in relation to the fuel distributor. Open the valve on the gauge line. Remove the electrical connectors at the auxiliary air device and the control pressure regulator. Using harness switch special tool, Peugeot number 8.0141P, or equivalent, turn the fuel supply on. Open and close the valve every 10 seconds, 5 times in a row. Close the test gauge valve.

3. The fuel pressure should be 65.4 to 75.4 psi (4.5 to 5.2 bar).

4. Check the volume of the main fuel pump by running it into a measured container. The pump should deliver 1.6 pts. (0.75 liters) in 30 seconds.

5. If the supply pressure is low, check the main fuel pump return hose.

6. Check the pressure from the pressure regulator, in the fuel distributor.

7. If the pressure regulator line does not have 68.2 to 70.4 psi (4.7 to 4.9 bar), increase the shims in the pressure regulator.

8. If the regulator pressure is too high, first check for a pinched hose or kinked pipe; then reduce the shims in the regulator and replace any worn O-rings in the regulator.

THERMO-TIME SWITCH CHECK

505 Models

The thermo-time switch limits the time that the cold start injector remains open in direct relationship to engine temperature.

1. Remove the thermo-time switch.

2. Install special test harness Peugeot number 8.0141BH or equivalent, on the thermo-time switch.

3. Connect a test light in series with the black test lead and the positive battery terminal.

4. Connect a jumper wire between the thermo-time switch body and the negative battery terminal.

5. Place the temperature sensing end of the thermo-time switch and a thermometer in a water container.

6. When the water temperature is below 86° F (30° C), the test lamp should light.

7. Heat the water slowly and note the temperature at which the test lamp goes out.

8. If the lamp does not come on at below 86° F (30° C) or does not go out between 86° F. to 104° F (30° C to 40° C), replace the thermo-time switch.

COLD START INJECTOR CHECK

505 Models

1. Remove the cold start injector from the throttle housing and hold it over a suitable container.

2. Place the fuel supply circuit under pressure by activating harness switch Peugeot number 8.0141P or equivalent.

3. The cold start injector should not leak more than the maximum allowable one drop of fuel per minute.

4. If the cold start injector leaks more than one drop per minute, replace it.

5. Always check the cold start injector while the engine is cold.

6. Install remote starter harness, Peugot number 0.1203ZB or equivalent.

7. Install remote fuel supply switch, Peugeot number 8.0141P or equivalent and activate the fuel supply system.

8. Activate the starter motor using the remote switch.

9. The injector should atomize, with an angle of spray across an 80° span. The spray should last from 2 to 5 seconds.

10. If the cold start injector does not atomize, use the test harness to supply current to the cold start injector. This replaces the normal wiring from the thermo-time switch to the cold start injector.

11. If the cold start injector does not spray with the new wiring, replace the injector.

12. If the cold start injector sprays with the new wiring, then check the power supply at the blue wire to the cold start valve and the brown wire to the thermo-time switch.

13. If the blue and the brown wire have current present, check the thermo-time valve.

AUXILIARY AIR DEVICE CHECK

505 Models

NOTE: Perform the tests on a cold engine.

1. Locate the auxiliary air device behind throttle housing on the common intake manifold. Remove the wire connector from the auxiliary air device.

2. Start the engine and note the idle speed.

3. Pinch the hose between the auxiliary air device and the intake manifold. The idle speed should drop.

4. Install the electrical connector on the auxiliary air device and warm up the engine. Pinch the hose again and the idle speed should stay constant.

5. If either of these tests have failed, replace the auxiliary air device.

Injector

REMOVAL AND INSTALLATION

1. Remove the fuel line from the injector.

2. Pull the injector out of the rubber seal.

CAUTION

Do not pull on the fuel line when removing the injector. Pull directly on the injector body.

3. Always use a new rubber seal when reinstalling an injector.

NOTE: Moisten the new rubber seal with fuel before installing the injector.

4. Press in the injector until it is fully seated.

Testing

1. Use injector test stand, Peugeot number 8.0141A and adaptors 8.0141B, 8.0141C and 8.0141H or equivalents.

2. Close the test stand valve.

3. Install adaptors 8.0141B and 8.0141C or equivalents on the test stand.

4. Install test adaptor 8.0141H or equivalent on the injector and install the assembly onto the test stand. Do not tighten the assembly.

5. Before tightening the nut on the test stand pipe, activate the tester several times to bleed the pipe.

6. Tighten the nut on the pipe to adaptor fitting.

7. Activate the tester several times until the injector is bled.

8. Open the test stand valve one turn.

9. Pump the test stand lever one stroke every two seconds until the injector sprays.

10. The injector opening pressure should be from 43.6 to 59.5 psi (3 to 4.1 bar).

11. If the opening pressure is not within specifications, replace the injector.

NOTE: The injectors can be replaced individually.

12. Loosen the test stand valve and increase the pressure to 7.0 lbs (0.5 bar) below the opening injector pressure. Maintain this pressure for 15 seconds. No leakage should occur. If an injector leaks, replace it.

13. During spray testing, the injector should make a groaning noise and have a spray span of 35°. If an injector is not operating properly, replace it.

Fuel Filter

REMOVAL AND INSTALLATION

1. Remove the negative cable from the battery.

2. Remove the fuel filter mounting screw.

3. Remove the fuel filter from its mounting.

4. Loosen the fuel lines to relieve the pressure, then remove the fuel lines. Remove the filter.

5. Install new sealing rings on the filter fittings and torque the inlet and outlet nuts to 24.5 ft/lbs (32.3 Nm). Torque the outlet banjo bolt to 18.0 ft/lbs (23.8 Nm.)

MANUAL TRANSMISSION

REMOVAL AND INSTALLATION

504 and 505 Models

1. Disconnect the negative battery cable.

2. Drain the gear oil.

3. Remove the ignition coil, the upper radiator mounting and both bolts from the lower radiator mounting on the front crossmember.

NOTE: Draining the cooling system will not be necessary.

4. Remove the starter motor and starter motor dust cover plate.

5. Remove the air cleaner.

6. Remove the nuts securing the exhaust pipe to the exhaust manifold.

7. Remove the nut on the hanger holding the exhaust pipe at the front silencer.

8. Remove the hanger on the exhaust pipe near the rear end of the transmission extension housing.

9. Remove the rear tail pipe hanger.

10. Turn the steering wheel to a clockwise position, so that the front exhaust pipe can be disengaged.

11. Allow the exhaust system to rest on the rear crossmember.

12. Remove the heat dissipation plate.

13. Install the gearbox support tool, Peugeot number 8.0125 or equivalent. Line the slot in the bolt adaptor with the notch in the forward flange of the clutch housing.

14. If the special gearbox support tool is not available, use a jack stand to support the clutch housing.

15. Using an 8 mm Allen type socket, remove the three bolts from the differential to gearbox connecting tube (at the gearbox). Loosen the fourth bolt with an 8 mm shouldered Allen key.

16. Remove the two differential to crossmember Allen bolts.

17. Separate the connecting tube and the driveshaft from the gearbox. Install the driveshaft holding plate, Peugeot number 8.0403S or equivalent.

18. Remove the clutch slave cylinder without disconnecting the hydraulic line.

19. Remove the shift lever and shift rods.

20. Remove the back-up light switch leads, gearbox ground strap and speedometer cable.

21. Remove the lower steering shaft pinch clamp bolt, (remove 2 steering knuckle bolts on 505 models).

22. Remove the steering gear housing bolts.

23. Lower the steering gear housing without removing any more bolts.

24. Remove the clutch housing cover plates.

25. Remove the clutch housing support, Peugeot number 8.0125 or the jack stand.

26. Remove the three allen bolts holding the clutch housing to the engine.

27. Install the engine hoisting brackets on the engine.

28. Using an engine crane type lift or equivalent, lift the engine to rotate it on its rubber mounting blocks in order to remove the gearbox from the engine.

29. Install a block of wood between the radiator and the hoisting bracket to avoid damage to the radiator hoses.

30. Rotate the gearbox a quarter turn counterclockwise and remove the gearbox by pulling it back.

31. Remove the clutch release ball bearing.

32. Installation is the reverse of removal.

33. Torque the bolts as follows:

Connecting tube to gearbox	43.5 ft/lbs (58.8 Nm)
Gearbox drain plug	20.0 ft/lbs (22.0 Nm)
Starter motor bolts	14.5 ft/lbs (19.6 Nm)

NOTE: Use grease on the release bearing guide and the engine driveshaft before installing them.

34. Adjust the gear shift linkage and check the clutch pedal for proper operation.

604 Models

On the 604 models, the engine and transmission must be removed as a unit.

1. Drain the gearbox oil.

2. Remove the hood, the air mixer housing and the air filter.
3. Drain the cooling system.
4. Remove the radiator support struts and the battery.
5. Disconnect the radiator hoses at the radiator.
6. Remove the radiator and the fan casing.
7. Remove the ground cable at the engine, the temperature sending unit, the power brake booster vacuum hose and the fuel pump hoses.
8. Remove the carburetor controls, primary coil leads and high tension coil-to-distributor wire.
9. Remove and plug the heater hoses.
10. Remove the starter and alternator harness connections.
11. Remove the exhaust pipe-to-manifold flange bolts and separate the pipe from the manifold.
12. Remove the engine mounting bolts.
13. Remove the exhaust mounting brackets at the silencers, the center exhaust mounting and the heat baffle.
14. Remove the clutch housing lower cover plate.
15. Remove the starter harness retaining clip.
16. Remove the power steering pump and the power steering belt.
17. Raise the engine with engine lift tool Peugeot number 8.0135Z or equivalent, until the gearbox contacts the floor tunnel. Lower the engine until the gearbox clears the tunnel by 0.4 in. (10.16 mm).
18. Push back the front seats and remove the front seat securing bolts.
19. Install studs Peugeot number 8.1511B or equivalent, under the vehicle in the seat bolts holes.
20. Install flat washers and nuts on the studs on the inside of the vehicle. Tighten the nuts.
21. Install the driveshaft support tool Peugeot number 8.1511A or equivalent and adjust the support tool to contact the driveshaft tube.
22. Remove the bolt from the steering shaft pinch clamp at the flexible coupling flange.
23. Remove the two rear main crossmember bolts and replace them with longer bolts, Peugeot number 8.1511C or equivalent.
24. Remove the two front crossmember bolts and lower the longer bolts so that the crossmember drops 1.2 in. (30.5 mm).
25. Remove the clutch cylinder snap-ring and push the cylinder back 0.12 in. (3 mm).
26. Remove the clutch cylinder bolts and wire the cylinder to the side of the vehicle.
27. Remove the back-up light switch leads, the gearshift control and the speedometer drive fitting.
28. Remove the driveshaft tube-to-gearbox bolts.
29. Separate the driveshaft and driveshaft tube from the gearbox and install the driveshaft retaining plate Peugeot number 8.0403SZ or equivalent on the driveshaft.
30. Remove the engine and gearbox together by tilting them up in the front and raising the assembly out of the vehicle.

CAUTION

Do not damage the power steering hoses.

31. Lower the assembly onto an engine stand.
32. Remove the clutch housing cover plate, the starter casing and the clutch housing-to-engine bolts.
33. Separate the gearbox from the engine.
34. Installation is the reverse of removal.
35. Follow these torque specifications:

Clutch housing to engine	12.6 ft/lbs (17.1 Nm)
Driveshaft tube to gearbox	39.6 ft/lbs (53.9 Nm)
Steering shaft pinch-clamp	12.8 ft/lbs (17.1 Nm)

NOTE: The clearance between the steering wheel and the steering column casing should be 0.08 in. (2 mm).

For manual transmission overhaul procedures refer to the Unit Overhaul section.

CLUTCH

REMOVAL AND INSTALLATION

504 Models

1. Remove the transmission. Refer to the transmission Removal and Installation procedures.
2. Matchmark the clutch assembly in relation to the flywheel, if the unit is to be re-used.
3. Remove the clutch assembly retaining bolts and separate the assembly from the flywheel.
4. Check the bearing surface of the disc on the flywheel. If needed, remove the flywheel and true up the surface on a lathe. Always take the same cut from the disc surface and the bolt attaching surface in order to maintain the same clutch diaphragm tension and height.
5. Place the clutch disc correctly with the flexible hub facing the gearbox. Center the disc on the flywheel using a centering tool.
6. Align the matchmarks (on a re-installed unit), and install the clutch assembly to the flywheel with the attaching bolts. Torque the bolts to 10 ft/lbs (15 Nm).
7. Re-install the transmission and complete the assembly.

604 Models

1. Remove the engine and transmission as a unit before separating the transmission.
2. Remove the clutch housing cover plate.
3. Remove the two starter-to-clutch housing bolts. Remove the four clutch housing-to-engine bolts.
4. Matchmark the clutch assembly in relation to the flywheel, (if the unit is to be re-used).
5. Remove the clutch assembly retaining bolts and separate the assembly from the flywheel.
6. Check the bearing surface of the disc on the flywheel. If needed, remove the flywheel and true up the surface on a lathe. Always take the same cut from the disc surface and the bolt attaching surface in order to maintain the same clutch diaphragm tension and height.

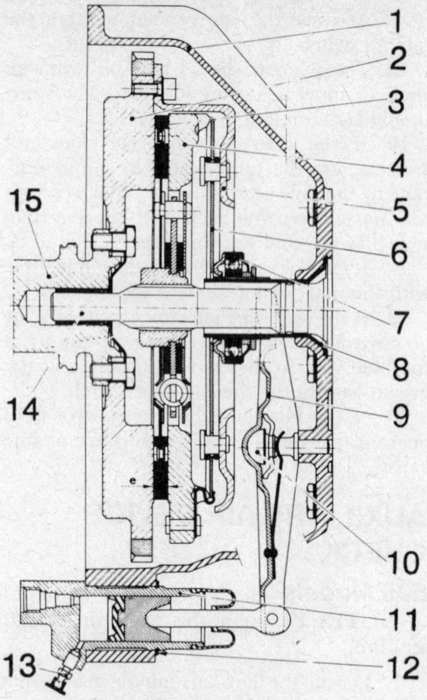

1. Clutch housing
2. Flywheel
3. Clutch disc
4. Clutch pressure plate
5. Cover
6. Diaphragm
7. Guided thrust bearing
8. Bushing
9. Clutch fork
10. Pivot
11. Release cylinder
12. Release cylinder housing
13. Bleed screw
14. Driveshaft
15. Crankshaft

Cross section of the 504 clutch assembly

7. Place the clutch disc correctly with the flexible hub facing the gearbox. Center the disc on the flywheel using a centering tool.
8. Align the matchmarks (on a re-installed unit), and install the clutch assembly to the flywheel with the attaching bolts. Torque the bolts to 15 ft/lbs (20 Nm).
9. Install the gearbox on the engine and torque the bolts to 12 ft/lbs (17 Nm).
10. Install the engine and transmission assembly into the vehicle.

Clutch Slave Cylinder

REMOVAL AND INSTALLATION

1. Remove the hydraulic line and plug it.
2. Remove the cylinder.
3. Install the cylinder and the hydraulic line.
4. Fill the clutch master cylinder reservoir and bleed the system.

BLEED THE SYSTEM

Peugeot recommends using a pressure bleeder tank to bleed the clutch slave cylinder. However, if a pressure tank is not available, the system can be bled manually by depressing the clutch and opening the bleeder screw momentarily, to allow air to escape.

1. Attach a pressure bleeding tank to the bleed screw on the slave cylinder.
2. Adjust the pressure to approximately 25 psi.
3. Open the bleed screw one full turn.
4. Check the rise of fluid in the reservoir.
5. Stop the bleeding when the level in the reservoir is correct.
6. Check the hydraulic control operation.

NOTE: Use Lockheed® 55 or equivalent fluid.

AUTOMATIC TRANSMISSION

REMOVAL AND INSTALLATION

504 and 505 Models

1. Remove the exhaust hanger at the intermediate exhaust pipe, the middle exhaust hanger and the exhaust hanger near the front end of the differential.
2. Remove the two differential side mounting bolts.
3. Place the driveshaft connecting tube on the rear crossmember.
4. Remove the two steering shaft flange bolts on 505 models.
   a. Conventional Steering Gearbox
   Remove the two steering box bolts and lower the steering gearbox without disconnecting the steering links.
   b. Power Steering Gearbox
   Replace the rear bolts on the front crossmember with Peugeot tool number 8.1511C or equivalent and remove the two forward crossmember bolts. Lower the crossmember 2.0 in. (50.8 mm) by turning the special tool bolts.
5. Remove the steering shaft pinch clamp bolt on 504 models and the steering gear housing bolts. Lower the steering, without disconnecting the steering linkage.
6. Drain the transmission fluid.
7. Remove the oil cooler lines at the transmission and plug them.
8. Remove the two starter-to-torque converter housing bolts.
9. Remove the transmission fill tube.
10. Remove the passenger side converter housing cover plate.
11. Remove the sensor plate cover and the sensor from the front driver's side of the transmission converter housing on 505 models, if so equipped.

NOTE: Take care not to alter the adjustment of the sensor.

12. Remove the converter-to-flexplate bolts and lock the ring gear with Peugeot tool number 8.0144B, 8.0110J or equivalents.
13. Secure the torque converter with Peugeot tool number 8.0135A or equivalent.
14. Place a transmission jack under the transmission and raise the jack to support the weight of the transmission.
15. Remove the four driveshaft connecting tube-to-extension housing bolts. Separate the connecting tube and driveshaft from the extension housing.
16. Install Peugeot tool 8.0403SZ or equivalent, driveshaft retaining plate on the driveshaft.
17. Remove the gearshift linkage, transmission wiring harness and speedometer drive fitting.
18. Drop the transmission as far down as it will go by lowering the transmission jack. Remove the converter/flexplate bolts.
19. Install engine lifting bracket, Peugeot number 8.0102X or equivalent.
20. Move the engine as far as it will go with the engine mounts still in place, to clear the transmission under the floor tunnel.
21. Remove the torque converter housing-to-engine bolts and separate the converter from the flexplate.
22. Lower the transmission on the transmission jack.
23. Installation is the reverse of removal.
24. Use the following torque specifications:

Starter	18.0 ft/lbs (24.5 Nm)
Torque converter	39.6 ft/lbs (53.9 Nm)
Flywheel	21.6 ft/lbs (29.4 Nm)
Driveshaft tube	39.6 ft/lbs (53.9 Nm)
505 steering coupling	12.6 ft/lbs (17.1 Nm)
504 steering pinch bolt	12.6 ft/lbs (17.1 Nm)

604 Models

1. Remove the hood.
2. Remove the air filter and assembly.
3. Drain the cooling system.
4. Remove the radiator hoses and upper radiator struts.
5. Remove the battery, the fan motor wires and the transmission cooler lines.
6. Remove the radiator and the fan casing.
7. Remove the ground cable at the engine and the temperature sending unit.
8. Remove the brake booster vacuum hose and the fuel pump lines.
9. Remove the carburetor controls and the primary coil leads. Remove the high tension coil wire.
10. Remove the heater hoses and plug the ends.
11. Remove the starter and alternator harness connectors.
12. Remove the exhaust pipe-to-exhaust manifold bolts and the engine mounting bolts.
13. Remove the front and center exhaust hangers.
14. Remove the heat baffle.
15. Remove the lower torque converter housing cover plate.
16. Remove the starter harness retainer clip.
17. Remove the power assisted steering pump and power steering belt.
18. Secure the power steering pump assembly to the fender well.
19. Lift the engine with a hoist until the transmission makes contact with the tunnel, then lower it approximately 0.4 in. (10.16 mm).
20. Push back the front seats and remove the seat securing bolts.
21. Raise the vehicle. Install threaded rods, Peugeot number 8.1511B or equivalent, into the seat bolts holes.
22. Lower the vehicle. Install flat washers and nuts on the ends of the threaded rods and tighten them.
23. Install the driveshaft support tool, Peugeot number 8.1511 or equivalent, onto threaded rods. Adjust the tool to support the driveshaft tube.
24. Remove the bolt from the pinch clamp on the steering shaft.
25. Remove the two rear main crossmember bolts and install tool, Peugeot number 8.1511C or equivalent. Remove the two front main crossmember bolts. Lower the main crossmember 1.2 in. (30.5 mm), by turning the special bolts.
26. Remove the cooler lines and the electrical connector at the transmission.
27. Remove the driveshaft tube-to-extension housing bolts.
28. Separate the driveshaft and driveshaft tube from the extension housing.
29. Install the driveshaft retaining plate tool, Peugeot number 8.0403SZ or equivalent, onto the driveshaft.
30. Move the back of the engine/transmission assembly out of the vehicle.

CAUTION

Do not damage the power steering hoses or the transmission cooler lines.

31. Separate the transmission from the engine. Leave the converter with the transmission. Installation is the reverse of removal.
32. Use the following torque specifications during reassembly and installation.

Driveshaft tube	43.5 ft/lbs (58.8 Nm)
Starter motor	14.5 ft/lbs (19.6 Nm)
Converter to ring gear	34.7 ft/lbs (46.6 Nm)
Converter housing	28.8 ft/lbs (39.2 Nm)
Steering flange	10.8 ft/lbs (14.9 Nm)

33. Adjust the kickdown cable.
34. Fill the transmission with fluid.

NEUTRAL SAFETY SWITCH ADJUSTMENT

ZF Transmissions

Two types of neutral start switches are used on the ZF automatic transmissions.

TYPE 1

The type 1 switch is attached to the side of the transmission case and is operated by a connecting rod attached to the transmission manual lever. The adjustment of the switch must be checked after the manual linkage has been adjusted.

1. Locate the selector lever in the Neutral position.
2. Loosen the switch retaining screw and the switch lever nut. Adjust the switch so that the engine will start only in the Neutral or Park positions.
3. Tighten the switch retaining screw and the lever nut.

TYPE 2

The type 2 switch is located with the selector lever assembly and cannot be adjusted. To replace the switch assembly, the console assembly must be removed. Remove the shift lever assembly from the floor. Remove the switch retaining screw and install the new switch. The switch pins must be engaged in the holes in the shift gate.

GM Transmission

1. Place the gear shift selector lever in Neutral.
2. Loosen the retaining nuts on the switch retaining bracket.
3. Align the mark on the switch body with the mark on the pivot housing.

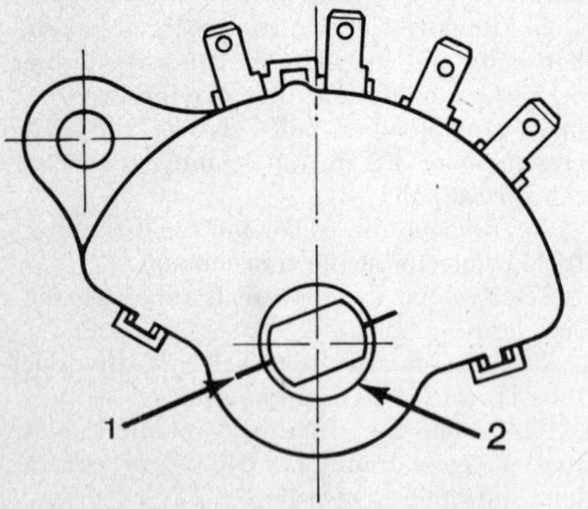

1. Mark on the switch body
2. Pivot housing

Adjusting alignment marks on the GM transmission neutral safety switch

4. Tighten the retaining nuts.
5. Check for starting in Neutral and Park. Check for not starting in Reverse, 3, 2, and 1. In the reverse position, the back-up lights should operate.

SHIFT LINKAGE AND ADJUSTMENT

All Automatic Transmissions

1. Disconnect the rod at the transmission lever.
2. Set the gear shift selector lever in the Neutral position.
3. Set the transmission lever in Neutral. The position is provided by the ball lock inside the transmission.

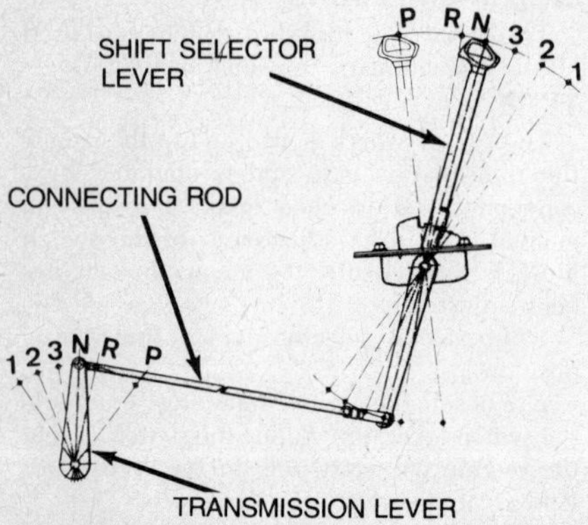

Adjusting the shift linkage on automatic transmissions for all models

4. If the rod will not fit into the transmission lever without moving the lever, adjust the rod length so that it will fit into the transmission lever.
5. Install the rod on the transmission lever.

BAND ADJUSTMENT

ZF Transmissions

The ZF Transmissions have no bands.

GM Transmissions

The GM Transmissions have no external band adjustment. The servo apply pins are available in different lengths. Selecting the proper length pin is equivalent to adjusting the bands. This can only be done with the transmission disassembled.

DRIVE AXLES

Driveshaft (Enclosed Type)

REMOVAL AND INSTALLATION

504 and 505 Models

1. Remove the exhaust system from the exhaust manifold and remove all exhaust hangers. Let the system rest on the front and rear crossmembers.
2. Remove the heat dissipation plate.
3. Remove the two differential bolts. Let the rear part of the driveshaft tube rest on the rear crossmember.
4. Place a jack under the left side crossmember support.
5. Remove the rear seat cushion. Loosen all three left side crossmember nuts. Raise the tab lock and remove the plastic plug from the guide hole. Screw the threaded end of the guide rod, Peugeot number 8.0906K1 or equivalent, through the guide hole and into the crossmember. Insert a pin into the guide rod.
6. Remove the crossmember securing nuts.
7. Lower the jack until the pin rests on the floor. Repeat these operations on the right hand crossmember support.
8. Remove the driveshaft tube from the differential.
9. Move the differential back and support it on a wooden block.
10. Remove the small spring from the end of the driveshaft.

NOTE: If the vehicle is to be moved from one work area to another, secure the differential to the rear crossmember with two Peugeot number 204 cylinder head bolts or equivalent.

11. Remove the driveshaft tube at the transmission.
12. Install driveshaft holding plate, Peugeot tool number 8.0403S or equivalent.
13. Lower the exhaust pipe at the front end.
14. Angle the driveshaft and driveshaft tube and remove them toward the front of the vehicle.
15. Installation is the reverse of removal.
16. Use the following torque specifications:

Driveshaft tube bolts	43.5 ft/lbs (58.8 Nm)
Differential attaching bolts	27.0 ft/lbs (36.8 Nm)

17. Install the rear seat cushion and lubricate the driveshaft center bearing.

604 Models

1. Remove the console shifter trim.
2. Pull back the bellows and remove the two shift lever bolts.
3. Remove the heat baffle and the center exhaust pipe hanger.
4. From under the vehicle, remove the front gearshift lever nut.
5. Using a jack stand or other safe method, take the weight off the extension housing of the transmission.
6. Remove the four driveshaft tube-to-extension housing bolts.
7. Remove the four driveshaft tube-to-differential bolts.
8. Remove the driveshaft and driveshaft tube toward the rear of the vehicle.
9. Install the driveshaft and tube onto the differential and transmission. Torque the bolts to 43.2 ft/lbs (58.8 Nm).
10. Install the front nut on the shift lever, from under the vehicle.
11. Set the exhaust baffles over the muffler.
12. Install the exhaust pipe hangers on the exhaust pipe.
13. Bolt on the heat baffles.
14. Install the two gear shift lever bolts, the bellows and the trim.

OVERHAUL

The tube and/or the shaft will have to be replaced if either is out of balance or damaged.

Axleshafts

REMOVAL AND INSTALLATION

All Models

1. Raise the rear of the vehicle and place jack stands under the suspension arms.
2. Remove the wheel and install holding tool, Peugeot number 8.0521 A or equivalent, on the hub.
3. Loosen the hub nut without removing it and remove the holding tool.
4. Remove the brake thrust spring, pad returning fork and brake pads.
5. Loosen the brake line retaining clamp on the rear control arm.
6. Remove the caliper and hang it on the body without distorting the brake line.
7. Remove the hub-to-disc retaining screw. Mark the location of the retaining screw on the disc.
8. Remove the disc.
9. Remove the bolts holding the spindle hub to the suspension arm.
10. Install special bolts, Peugeot numbers

8.0521 B1 and B2 or equivalents, into the back of the hub assembly. Install the thrust plate, Peugeot number 8.0521 B3 or equivalent, onto the hub.

11. To remove the hub assembly, alternately tighten bolts B1 and B2 against plate B3.
12. Remove the disc brake backing plate, if equipped.
13. Remove the hub nut washer.
14. Remove the final driveshaft from the hub knuckle. Use an arbor press, if necessary.
15. Installation is the reverse of removal.

CAUTION

Use a new final driveshaft nut on every re-installation. Stake the new nut to hold it.

16. Use the following torque specifications:

Brake pad holding fork	31.0 ft/lbs (40.9 Nm)
Final driveshaft nut	181.0 ft/lbs (245 Nm)
Wheel lug nuts	43.5 ft/lbs (58.8 Nm)

NOTE: The station wagon has axle housings attached to the differential and the axle shafts are enclosed.

Rear Wheel Bearings

REMOVAL AND INSTALLATION

All Models

1. Remove the final drive axleshaft from the vehicle.
2. Separate the hub and knuckle assembly from the final drive axleshaft. Use an arbor press if necessary.
3. Clamp the hub assembly in a soft jawed vise.
4. Remove the hub assembly nut.
5. Press the hub from the knuckle assembly.
6. Press out the bearing assembly from the knuckle.
7. Turn the knuckle over in the vise and remove the outer oil seal.
8. Install a new outer oil seal.
9. Install a new inner oil seal.
10. Press in a new bearing assembly.
11. Install the knuckle nut and torque it to 181 ft/lbs (245 Nm).
12. Install the hub onto the knuckle assembly.
13. Install the final drive axleshaft into the hub and knuckle assembly.

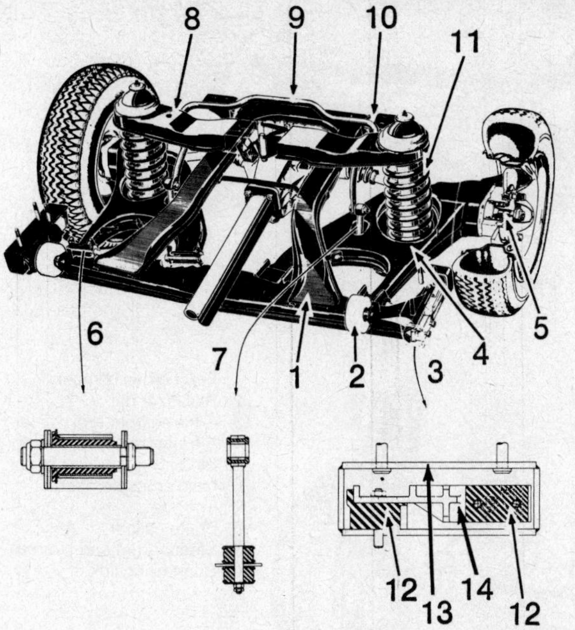

1. Rear crossmember
2. Vibration damper
3. Lower crossmember mounting
4. Trailing suspension arm
5. Hub spindle
6. Trailing arm bushing
7. Stabilizer bar link
8. Upper suspension crossmember
9. Stabilizer bar
10. Upper crossmember mounting
11. Shock absorber and suspension spring
12. Rubber blocks
13. Housing
14. Inner support

604 rear suspension

14. Complete the installation on the vehicle.
15. Torque the final drive axleshaft nut to 181 ft/lbs (245 Nm).

CAUTION

Use a new final drive axleshaft nut on every re-installation. Stake the new nut to hold it.

Differential

REMOVAL AND INSTALLATION

All Models

1. Remove one of the final drive axleshafts, either left or right.

9. Use the following torque specifications:

Driveshaft connect tube	43.5 ft/lbs (58.8 Nm)
Knuckle to rear control arm	29.0 ft/lbs (39.2 Nm)
Brake caliper	31.0 ft/lbs (41.7 Nm)
Brake pad retainer	13.0 ft/lbs (17.2 Nm)
Wheel lug nuts	43.5 ft/lbs (58.8 Nm)

10. Refill the differential with GP 90 weight gear oil.

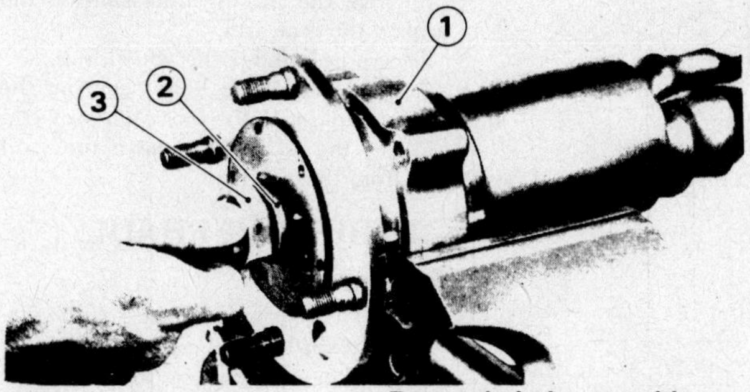

1. Rear axle knuckle assembly
2. Rear axle retaining washer
3. Rear axle retaining nut

Rear axle hub assembly

REAR SUSPENSION

Shock Absorbers

REMOVAL AND INSTALLATION

All Models

1. If a frame contact lift is used, support the control arms before removing the shock absorber bolts.
2. Open the trunk lid and use an open end wrench to hold the shock while removing the shock nut from the shock bolt.
3. Remove the rubber washer and the sheet metal cup from the upper shock bolt.
4. Remove the lower shock bolt from the control arm.
5. Remove the shock by pulling it through the hole in the control arm.
6. Always replace the rubber washer, upper sheet metal cup and upper self locking nut, every time the shock is installed.
7. Fully extend the shock absorber rod and install the thrust cup, rod protector, centering cup, rubber washer and nylon spacer.
8. Use new lockwashers and install the lower shock bolt on the control arm.
9. Place the new rubber washer and metal cup on the shock and secure it with a new locknut.

Rear Control Arm and Coil Springs

REMOVAL AND INSTALLATION

All Models

1. Remove the final driveshafts from both sides.

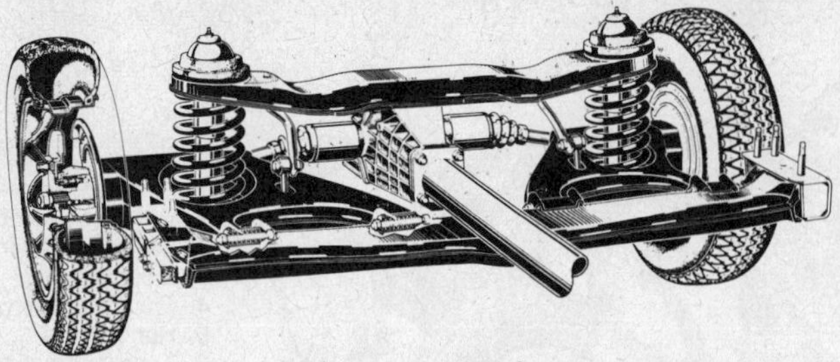

504 rear suspension

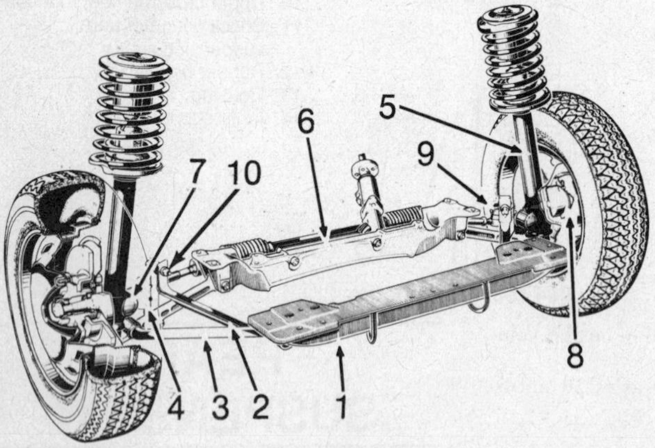

504 and 505 front suspension

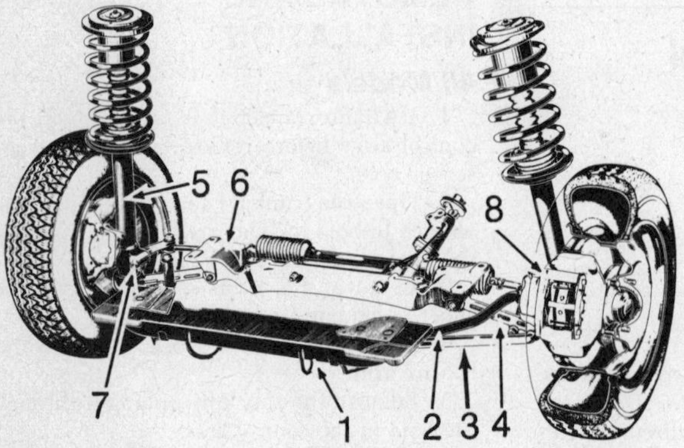

604 front suspension

MacPherson strut and steering knuckle assembly removed from vehicle

2. Support the rear control arms and remove the rear shocks.
3. Remove the stabilizer bar links at the control arms.
4. Slowly lower the rear control arms to release the tension on the coil springs. Remove the coil springs.
5. Remove the four control arm-to-crossmember bolts and lower out the control arms.
6. Installation is the reverse of removal.

FRONT SUSPENSION

The front suspension is of the MacPherson strut type.

MacPherson Strut

REMOVAL AND INSTALLATION

All Models

1. Raise the vehicle and support both sides of the front crossmember.
2. Remove the front wheel.
3. Remove the brake caliper and suspend it from the frame.
4. Remove the steering rod end from the knuckle.

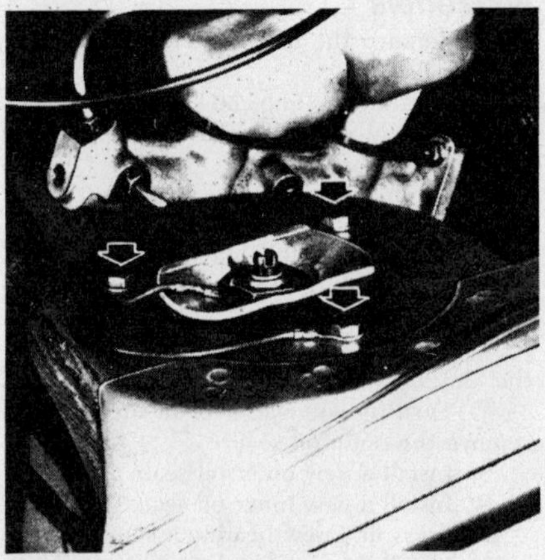

Three strut retaining bolts on the inner fender well, shock tower

5. Remove the connecting link from the rear bar of the triangular suspension arm.
6. Remove the strut from the knuckle.
7. Remove the locking nut securing the front arm to the rear arm.
8. Place a jack under the wheel hub.
9. Remove the three bolts securing the upper spring holder to the inner fender well.
10. Lower the jack and remove the strut assembly from the vehicle.

STRUT OVERHAUL

All Models

1. Use a strut spring compressor to compress the strut spring.
2. Use Peugeot special socket, Peugeot number 8.0906M or equivalent to hold the

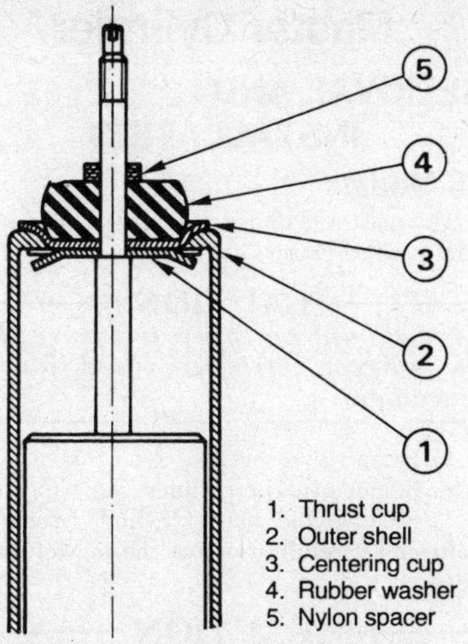

Breakdown of upper shock parts

strut rod while removing the upper strut rod nut.

3. Loosen the spring compressor until the spring is fully extended.

4. Remove the strut spring compressor, the upper spring cup and the spring.

5. Remove the strut rod absorber rubber boot.

6. Use tool Peugeot number 8.0906G (special socket) or equivalent to remove the strut absorber holding nut.

7. Pull the rod and piston slowly from the strut assembly.

NOTE: Fast removal of the rod and piston will spray the oil.

8. Remove the support cup, rod seal, thrust washer, upper spring and O-ring seal from the bushing.

9. Using two suitable prying tools, pry the rebound block from the strut assembly.

10. Remove the shock absorber cylinder and the compensator valve.

11. Always use the following new parts on the shock absorber:
   a. Compensator valve assembly
   b. Bushing O-ring seal
   c. Rod seal
   d. Rubber boot
   e. Strut rod locking nut.

12. Always use the following new parts on the upper support:
   a. Lower rubber seal
   b. Needle bearing (could be re-used if undamaged)
   c. Needle bearing seal ring.

13. Grease the threads and upper assembly body. Install the rebound block.

14. Install the compensator valve and absorber cylinder by tapping gently with a plastic mallet.

15. Place the cylinder in the shock absorber body.

16. Fill the strut body with shock fluid.

17. Install the rod and piston mechanism carefully into the body.

18. Make sure the installed position of the upper bushing is 0.12 in. (3 mm) into the top of the absorber body.

19. Lubricate the bushing O-ring and install it.

20. Install the small spring and thrust washer on the strut rod.

21. Lubricate a new strut rod seal and install it in the upper cup.

22. Install the absorber holding nut and torque it to 58.0 ft/lbs (78.4 Nm). A special socket will be needed to turn the shock absorber holding nut.

23. Pull the strut rod to the fully extended position and secure it.

24. Install the rubber boot on the strut rod and a new seal on the rebound block thrust ring.

25. Assemble the upper strut spring holder, thrust plate, needle bearing, bearing oil seal, bearing thrust plate and shim.

26. Install the strut spring, spring cup and spring holder into the spring compressor tool.

27. Install the spring assembly onto the strut and compress the strut spring until the safety cup and a new locknut can be installed on the strut rod. Torque the nut to 33.0 ft/lbs (44.1 Nm).

28. Remove the spring compressor and rod clamp tool.

29. Install the rubber boot over the absorber holding nut.

Wheel Alignment

All Models

TOE-IN

Toe-in is set by loosening the nuts on the tie rod ends (steering rod). Rotate them in or out as necessary. Toe-in can be set with the tie rod connected.

One full turn of the tie rod equals 0.12 in. (3 mm) difference in the toe-in.

Front Wheel Bearing Adjustment

Torque the hub nut to 28.0 ft/lbs (39.0 Nm), then loosen the nut and re-torque it to 7.0 ft/lbs (9.8 Nm). Lock the hub nut in place.

STEERING

Steering Wheel

REMOVAL AND INSTALLATION

All Models

1. Remove the negative battery cable.
2. Place the wheels in a straight ahead position.
3. Remove the horn cover pad and horn contact assembly.
4. Remove the steering wheel nut.
5. Matchmark the steering wheel and the steering shaft.
6. Use a steering wheel puller tool to remove the steering wheel.
7. Installation is the reverse of removal.

Combination Switch

The horn and turn signal switches are combined as a unit.

REMOVAL AND INSTALLATION

All Models

1. Remove the steering wheel.
2. Remove the horn assembly and column cover.
3. Disconnect all wiring to the switch.
4. Remove the switch.
5. Installation is the reverse of removal.

Ignition Switch

REMOVAL AND INSTALLATION

All Models

The steering wheel does not have to be removed.

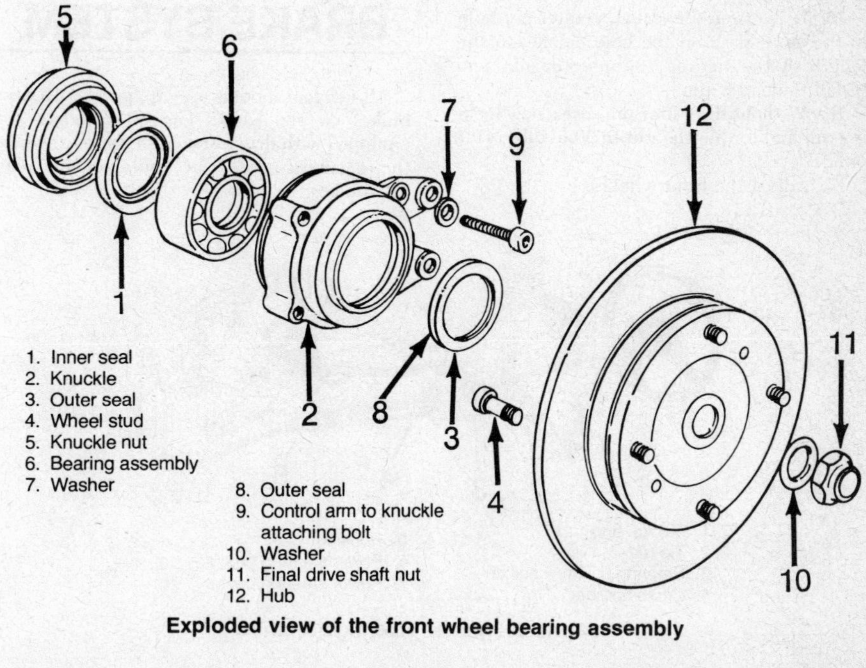

Exploded view of the front wheel bearing assembly

1. Remove the negative battery cable.
2. Remove the steering column and ignition switch cover to expose the ignition switch.
3. Remove the wiring from the switch connections.
4. Remove the switch to column attaching bolts and remove the switch. Installation is the reverse of the removal procedure.

Manual Steering Gear

REMOVAL AND INSTALLATION

All Models

1. Remove the tie rod ends from the steering arm knuckles.
2. Remove the steering gear bolts and the lower shaft flange bolt.
3. Insert a 0.24 in. (6 mm) diameter punch in the flange bolt hole.
4. Disengage the gearbox by rocking it with the punch. Remove the gearbox assembly.
5. When installing, position the steering wheel bars vertically.
6. Place the passenger side front wheel in a straight ahead position.
7. Place the drivers side wheel to a turned-in position.
8. Center the rack in relation to the rack housing.
9. Temporarily connect the tie rod end on the passenger side.
10. Rotate the flange ¼ turn to align the flange collar with the splined end of the steering shaft.
11. Rock the flange slightly to install it on the splined shaft.
12. Install the steering gear to crossmember bolts. Torque the bolts to 22.7 ft/lbs (31.8 Nm).
13. Install the bolt and a new locknut on the flange-to-column collar. Torque the nut to 10.8 ft/lbs (14.7 Nm).
14. Install the tie rod ends on the steering arm knuckles.
15. If the tie rod end has a cotter pin hole in the stud, position the hole parallel to the length of the tie rod, tighten the nut and install the cotter pin.
16. Without the cotter pin, use a new locking nut and torque the nut to 30.6 ft/lbs (41.7 Nm).
17. Adjust the front wheel toe-in.

Power Steering Gear

REMOVAL AND INSTALLATION

All Models

The removal and installation of the power type gearbox is basically the same procedure as the manual type gearbox. The system must be drained of hydraulic fluid and the hydraulic lines disconnected from the pump.

Power Steering Pump

REMOVAL AND INSTALLATION

All Models

1. Remove the high pressure hose and drain the system. Move steering wheel back and forth to insure complete drainage. Do not start engine.
2. Remove the belt adjusting nut, remove the belt and the pump attaching bolts.
3. Remove the pump.
4. Installation is the reverse of removal.

BELT ADJUSTMENT

All Models

1. Make two marks on the belt to be installed 4 in. (100 mm) apart.
2. On a used belt tighten the belt so that the marks are 4.06 in. (101.5 mm) apart.
3. On a new belt, tighten the belt so that the marks are 4.1 in. (102. 5 mm) apart.

SYSTEM BLEEDING

All Models

The power steering system is automatically bled by turning the steering gear to its full stop in both directions, several times.

BRAKE SYSTEM

All Peugeot models are equipped with disc brakes on the front. The 504 models are equipped with drum brakes on the rear, while the remaining models are equipped with rear disc brakes.

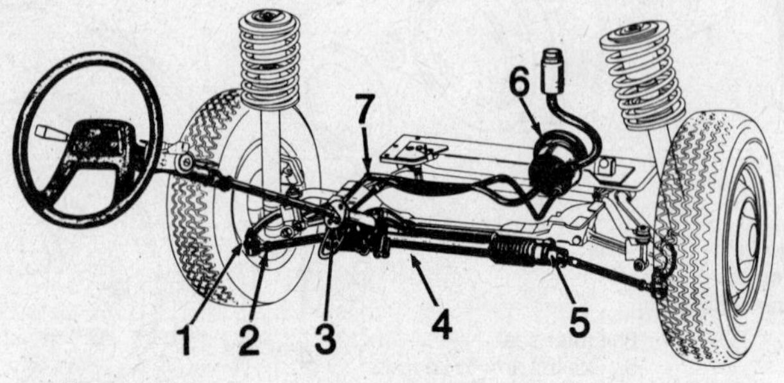

1. Tie rod end
2. Tie rod
3. Steering column knuckle
4. Crossmember
5. Housing
6. Power steering pump
7. Power steering hoses

504 and 505 power steering assembly

Master Cylinder

REMOVAL AND INSTALLATION

All Models

The master cylinder may have a single or a dual type reservoir.

CAUTION

Care should be taken to insure that the correct parts are used for replacement.

1. Drain the reservoir.
2. Remove the brake lines.
3. Remove the master cylinder retaining bolts and carefully remove the master cylinder.

CAUTION

Do not pull the thrust rod from the booster unit.

4. Installation is the reverse of removal.

SYSTEM BLEEDING

All models have disc brakes in the front. Certain models have drum brakes and some models have disc brakes on the rear.

Drum or Disc Brakes On Rear (System Not Drained)

NOTE: The vehicle must be at rest on the wheels.

1. Check the fluid level in the reservoir.
2. Release the handbrake.
3. Press firmly on the brake pedal.
4. While holding firmly on the brake pedal, loosen and retighten each bleed screw to release air trapped in the system.
5. Release the brake pedal slowly and repeat the operation at each wheel until the fluid is free of air bubbles.

Disc Brakes On Rear (System Was Drained)

1. Remove the pads at the wheel where the system lost fluid.
2. Use Peugeot special tool number 8.0803 or equivalent, to allow the caliper piston to be fully extended without coming out.
3. Bleed the caliper at each wheel.
4. Install the brake pads. Repeat the bleeding of the system until all the air bubbles are gone.
5. Check the brakes with the engine running and road test the vehicle.

Power Brake Unit

REMOVAL AND INSTALLATION

All Models

Remove the brake pedal linkage. Drain the brake fluid. Remove the brake lines from the master cylinder and remove the bolts at the firewall. Remove the power brake unit.

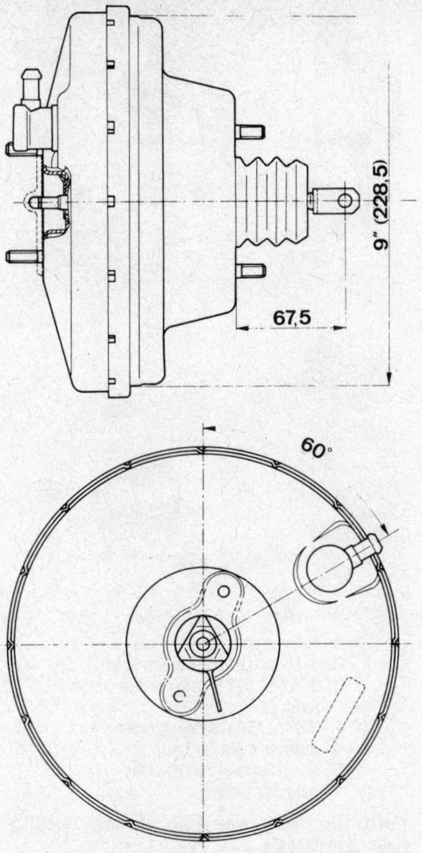

505 power brake booster, Teves® (9")

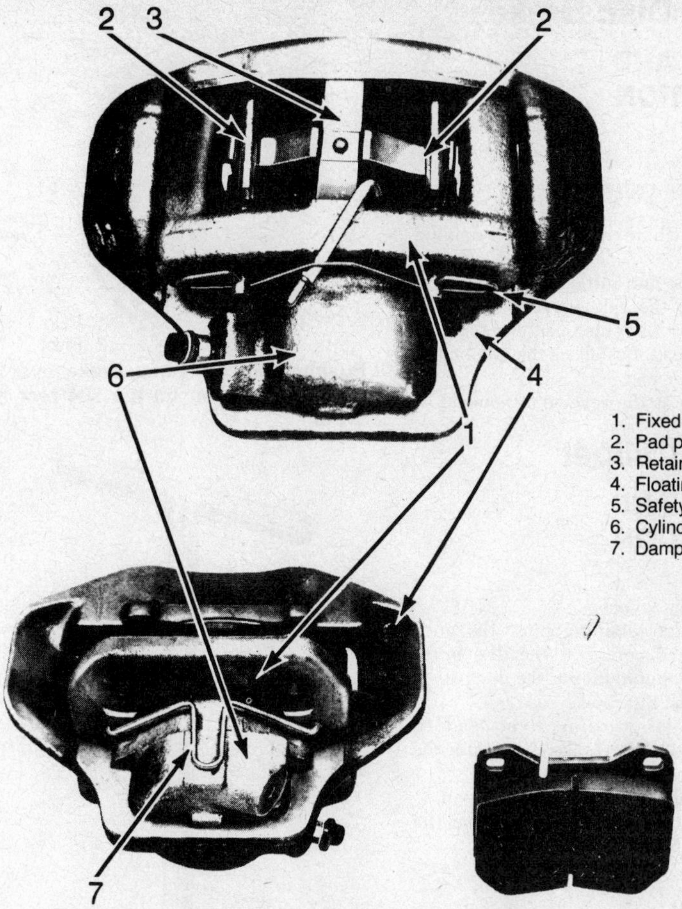

1. Fixed support
2. Pad pins
3. Retaining spring
4. Floating caliper
5. Safety clip
6. Cylinder
7. Damper spring

505 front brakes, Teves® SR54

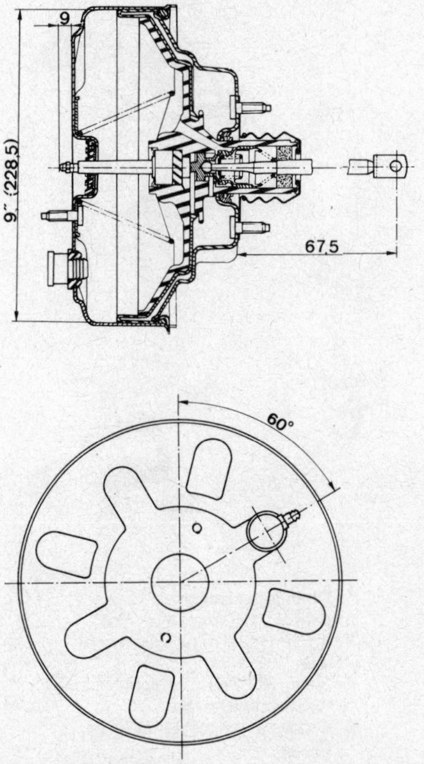

505 power brake booster, DBA® type 225 K

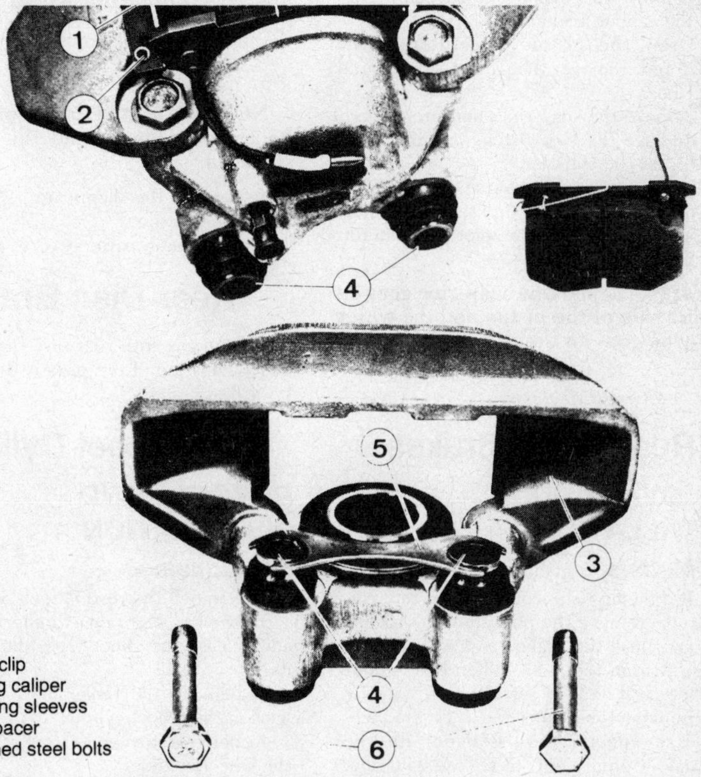

1. Key
2. Safety clip
3. Floating caliper
4. Retaining sleeves
5. Stop spacer
6. Hardened steel bolts

505 front brakes, DBA®, series IV

Front Disc Brakes

REMOVAL AND INSTALLATION

All Models

1. Remove the wheel.
2. Remove the pad wear indicator wire if equipped.
3. Use a punch to remove the retaining pins.
4. Remove the anti-rattle spring.
5. Push back the caliper to uncover the retaining boss on the outer pad and then remove the outer pad. Push back the caliper and remove the inner pad.
6. Installation is the reverse of removal.

Caliper

REMOVAL AND INSTALLATION

All Models

1. Remove the wheels.
2. Remove the retaining pins, the anti-rattle springs and compress the disc brake piston to allow room to lift out the disc pads.
3. Remove the disc brake pads.
4. Remove the warning light lead (if equipped) and the flex (brake) hose from the caliper. Remove the caliper.
5. Installation is the reverse of removal.
6. Use new lock washers and torque the caliper bolts to 50.5 ft/lbs (68.6 Nm).
7. Bleed the system.

OVERHAUL

All Models

1. Remove the caliper bleed screw and drain the caliper assembly.
2. Draw the piston forward from the caliper and remove the thrust spring and caliper body.
3. Remove the snap-rings and protectors.
4. Remove the two pistons and the nylon spacer from the cylinder.
5. Installation is the reverse of removal.
6. Coat all new pistons and seals with brake fluid or approved lubricant before installation.
7. Bleed the brakes.

NOTE: The narrow snap-ring goes on the disc side of the piston and the wider snap-ring goes on the caliper side of the piston.

Rear Drum Brakes

REMOVAL AND INSTALLATION

504 Models

1. If difficulty is encountered in removing the drum, remove the plug from the backing plate and push the brake lever with a tool to release it from the stud. When this is done, the shoes will be fully retracted.
2. Remove the drum.
3. Use special tool Peugeot number 8.0803W or equivalent, to release hold down springs.

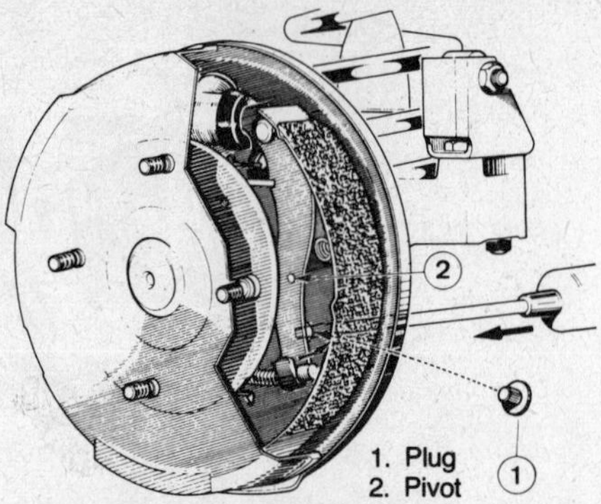

1. Plug
2. Pivot

Pushing the emergency brake lever to release the tension on the 504 rear brake drum

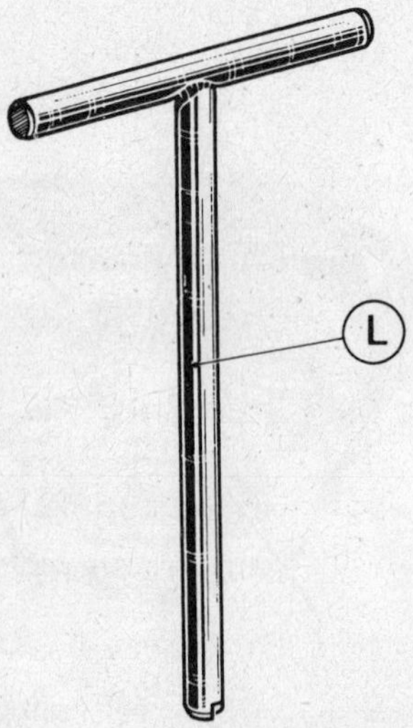

Special 504 drum brake hold down spring tool

NOTE: The hold down springs should be replaced each time the brakes are replaced.

4. Remove the shoe return spring and disassemble the shoes.
5. Installation is the reverse of removal.

Rear Disc Brakes

For models with rear disc brakes, removal and installation of the pads is the same as for front disc brakes.

Rear Wheel Cylinders

REMOVAL AND INSTALLATION

504 Models

1. Remove the road wheels and drums.
2. Remove the brake lining return spring and release the shoes from the wheel cylinder.
3. Remove the brake fluid line from the back of the wheel cylinder.
4. Remove the wheel cylinder bolts and the wheel cylinder.
5. Installation is the reverse of removal.

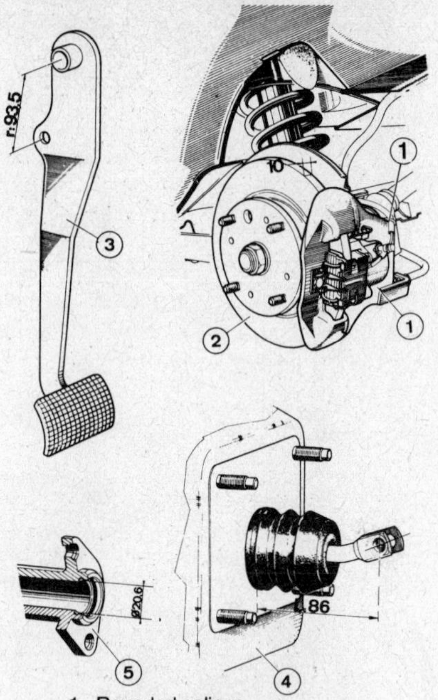

1. Rounded caliper
2. 0.10 in. (10 mm) thick disc
3. 3.70 in. (93.5 mm) brake pedal axis
4. 3.4 in. (86.0 mm) curved master cylinder rod
5. no groove in the master cylinder flange

Early type 504 rear disc brakes, Girling® type AH12MK1

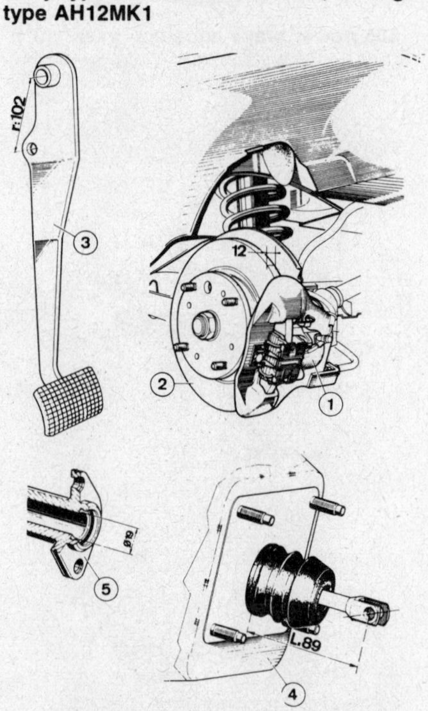

1. Chamfered caliper
2. 0.48 in. (12.0 mm) thick disc
3. 4.1 in. (102.0 mm) brake pedal axis
4. 3.6 in. (89.0 mm) straight master cylinder rod
5. Groove in the master cylinder flange

Later style 504 rear disc brakes, Girling® type AH12MK111

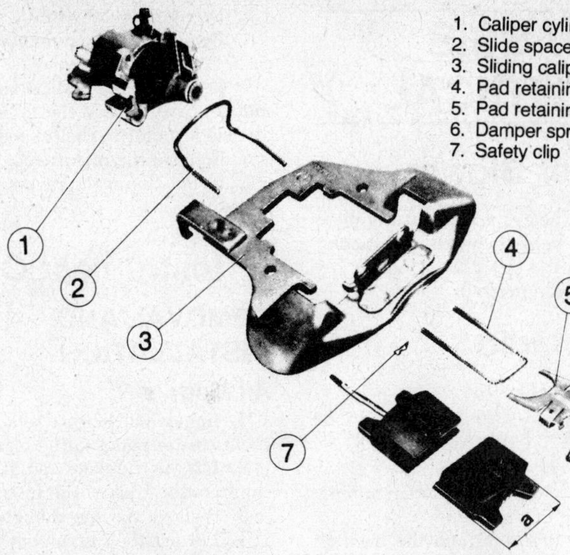

1. Caliper cylinder body
2. Slide spacer
3. Sliding caliper
4. Pad retaining fork
5. Pad retaining spring
6. Damper spring
7. Safety clip

505 rear brakes, Girling® M12AHMK1V

Parking Brake Adjustment

FLOOR MOUNTED LEVER

All Models

1. Raise the vehicle and remove the rear wheels.
2. Loosen the cable adjusting nuts so that no tension exists on the cable.
3. If the vehicle is equipped with drum brakes adjust them.
4. Apply the parking brake four clicks and adjust the cable.
5. Release the handbrake and make sure the rotors or drums can rotate freely.
6. Install the wheels and lower the vehicle.

Brake Compensator

All models have a brake compensator near the rear axle. The purpose of the compensator is to adjust the brake fluid pressure from the front to the rear wheels, when the vehicle load is shifted to the front wheels, such as when stopping the vehicle.

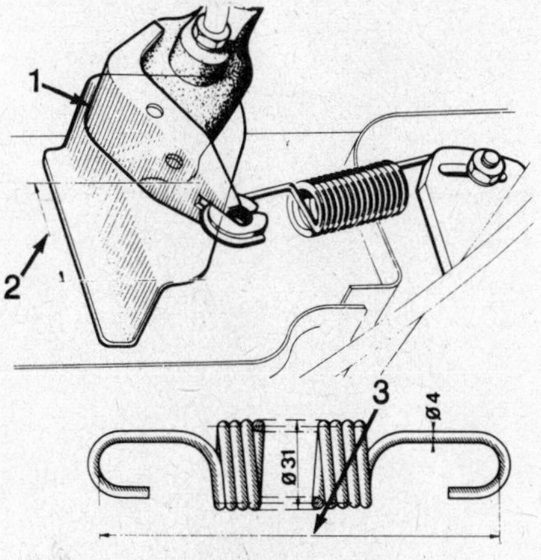

1. Bracket
2. 1.8 in. (45 mm)
3. 5.7 in. (143 mm)

Early 504 type brake compensators are mounted high on the bracket and have a 5.7 in. (143 mm) spring

ADJUSTMENT

504 Models

1. Position the vehicle on a level ramp (wheels supported).
2. Measure the distance from the compensator arm to the spring bracket.

CAUTION

There are two different type compensators. An early type with a spring 5.7 in. (143.0 mm) long and no color to the spring, a later type with a spring 6.0 in. (149.0 mm) long and a blue flash on the spring.

3. Check and adjust the early type to 0.068 in. (1.7 mm).
4. Check and adjust the later type to 0.108 in. (2.7 mm).
5. Loosen the spring bracket nut.
6. Adjust the spring bracket to obtain the specified distance. The spring should be tight, but have no tension on it.
7. Tighten the spring bracket nut.

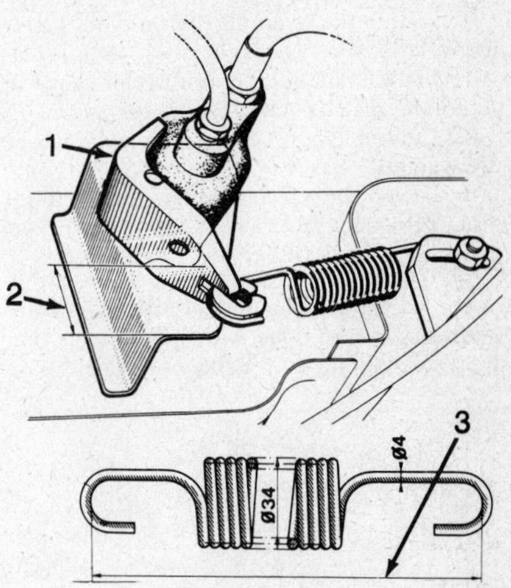

1. Bracket
2. 1.0 in. (25 mm)
3. 6.0 in. (149 mm)

Later type 504 brake compensators are mounted low on the bracket and have a 6.0 in. (149 mm) spring

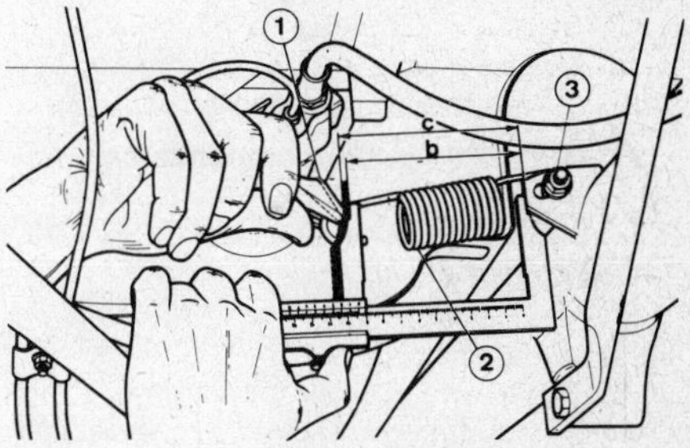

1. Compensator arm
2. Compensator spring
3. Adjusting nut

Adjusting the 504 spring type brake compensator

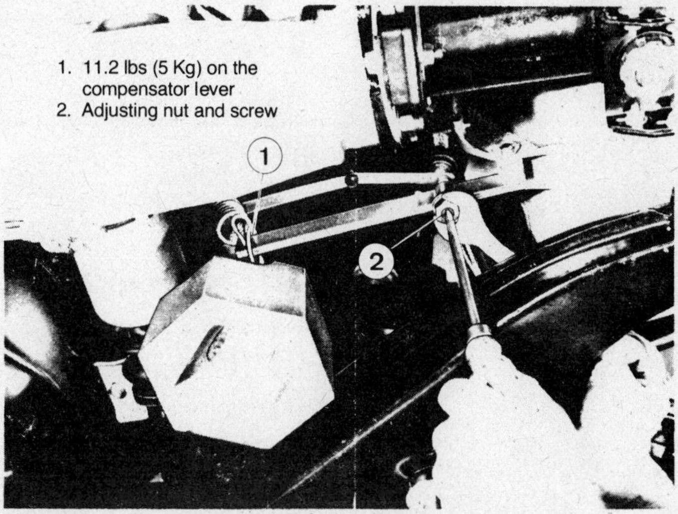

1. 11.2 lbs (5 Kg) on the compensator lever
2. Adjusting nut and screw

Adjusting the 505 brake compensator

505 Models

1. Hook an 11.0 lb (5 Kg) weight on the notch in the compensator lever.
2. Push the compensator piston all the way in.
3. Loosen the retaining nut on the adjuster screw.
4. Use a 0.032 in. (0.8 mm) feeler gauge to adjust the piston-to-arm clearance.
5. Tighten the retaining nut and remove the weight.
6. Lower the vehicle and road test it for proper braking.

604 Models

The adjustment for model 604 brake compensators can be done with special tools that are available only to a Peugeot dealer.

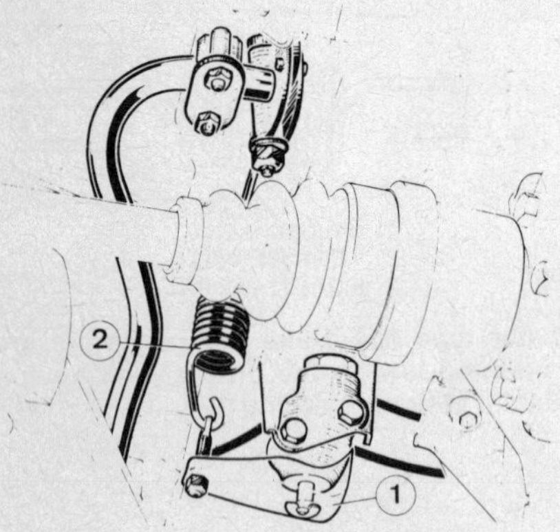

1. Compensator arm
2. Compensator spring

Model 604 brake compensator

CHASSIS ELECTRICAL

Heater Blower

The Model 504 heater and air conditioner blower is located behind the console under the dash. The 505 and 604 blower motors are on the passenger side firewall.

Radio

REMOVAL AND INSTALLATION

1. Remove the console cover.
2. Remove the radio knobs and retaining nuts from the front of the radio.
3. Remove any brackets from the back of the radio and detach the power lead, antenna lead and speaker wires.
4. Installation is the reverse of removal.

Windshield Wiper/Washer Motor

REMOVAL AND INSTALLATION

All Models

1. Disconnect the battery ground cable.
2. Remove the air grill from the area under and in front of the windshield.
3. Disconnect the wires to the motor.
4. Remove the instrument cluster from the dash.
5. Reach into the dash area and remove the spindle drive nut and the three nuts securing the wiper motor to the firewall.
6. Remove the motor from the grill area.
7. Installation is the reverse of the removal procedure.

Instrument Cluster

REMOVAL AND INSTALLATION

All Models

1. Remove all screws retaining the instrument cluster panel to the main dash.
2. Lift the panel out and disconnect all wiring from the back of the instrument cluster.
3. Remove the speedometer cable.
4. Lift out the instrument panel.
5. Installation is the reverse of removal.

Fuse Box Location

504 AND 604 MODELS

The fuse box is located under the driver's side of the dash, to the left of the steering column.

505 MODELS

The fuse box is located on the top of the left inner front fender.

SPECIFICATIONS

INDEX

BEFORE SERVICING, SEE THE SAFETY NOTICE ON THE CONTENTS PAGE

INTRODUCTION

The name Porsche and the term sports car have always been synonymous. The current 911 and 914 series have continued the Porsche tradition of performance and reliability. Myriad competition victories in endurance racing, such as the 24 Hours of Le Mans and The Targa Florio and in Sports Car Club of America production class racing have kept the marque in the vanguard of the high-performance car ranks. Remarkably, Porsche cars have been in production for only thirty-one years, which is difficult to comprehend in view of the legendary reputation and the legion of enthusiasts that the car has attracted. The first Porsches were built in Gmund, Austria, since, at that time, Professor Porsche was denied entrance to Germany. The factory was eventually moved to its present location near Stuttgart, Germany. Porsche has since grown into a multimillion dollar concern, but the painstaking attention to detail, inherited from the small group of men who produced the first cars, was not lost in the transition from workshop to large factory.

SERIAL NUMBER IDENTIFICATION

Chassis

The chassis number on all models is located on the driver's side windshield post and is visible from the outside of the car. The chassis number on 911 and 912E models is also found in the luggage compartment under the rug and on the identification plate near the front hood lock catch. The 914 chassis number is stamped on the right front wheel well and on the identification plate on the right headlight housing inside the luggage compartment.

The 911 and 912E series chassis identification number breaks down in the following manner:

911 SERIES

Serial Number Example—
911-6-2-1-0001

Series Type	911, 911S or or 930 (Turbo)
Model Year	5=1975
	6=1976
	7=1977
	8=1978
	9=1979
	0=1980
	1=1981
Engine Type	1=T
	2=E or 2.7S
	3=S
	4=Carrera
	8=Turbo
Body Type	0=Coupe
	1=Targa

Four Digit Serial Number—Sequential.

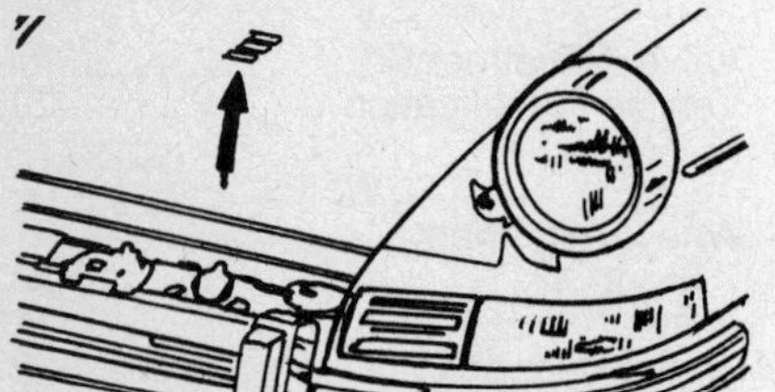

911 chassis serial number location

912 SERIES

Serial Number Example—
912-6-0-0-0001

Vehicle Type	912=Model
Model Year	6=1976
Motor	0=912E/2 ltr.
Body	0=Coupe

Serial Number 0001-9999 (Sequential)

The 914 series chassis identification number is broken down as follows:

914 SERIES

47.5-29-00001

Series Type	47=914 series
Model Year	5=1975
	6=1976

Factory Number 29
Five digit sequential serial number—00001-99999

Engine

The engine number for the 911 model is located on the right side of the crankcase adjacent to the blower. The 1.7 liter, 914 engine number is stamped on the upper right of the crankcase, below the air intake runners. The 2.0 liter, 914 engine number is stamped on the upper part of the crankcase between the oil filler and the blower housing.

The 912E engine number is stamped in the crankcase on the left side near mount for the air pump.

911 engine numbers are divided as follows:

911 SERIES

Engine Number Example—
6-3-6-0001

Engine Type Engine	6=cylinder
Model	1=T—Japan—3.01 ltr.
	2=E—USA—3.01 ltr.
	3=S—Rest of World—3.01 ltr.
	4=Carrera
	5=Calif.—3.01 ltr.
	8=Turbo—3.31 ltr.
Model Year	5=1975
	6=1976
	7=1977
	8=1978
	9=1979
	0=1980
	1=1981

Four digit sequential number—0001

914 and 912E engine numbers are divided as follows:

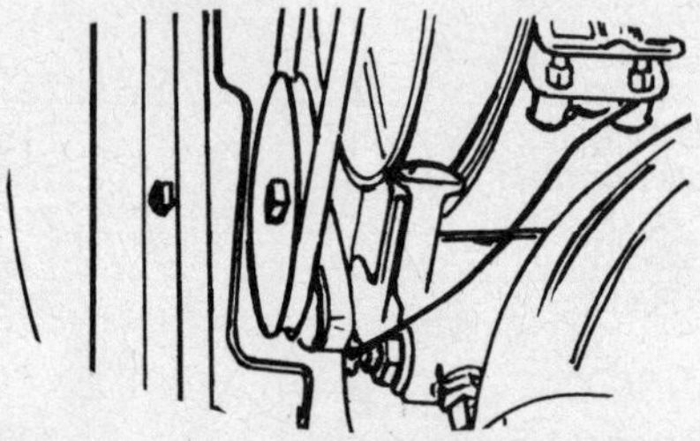

911 identification plate location

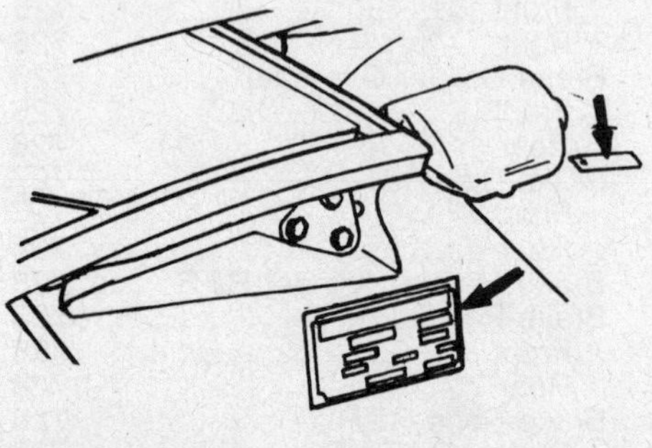

914 identification plate location (bottom) and chassis serial number location (top)

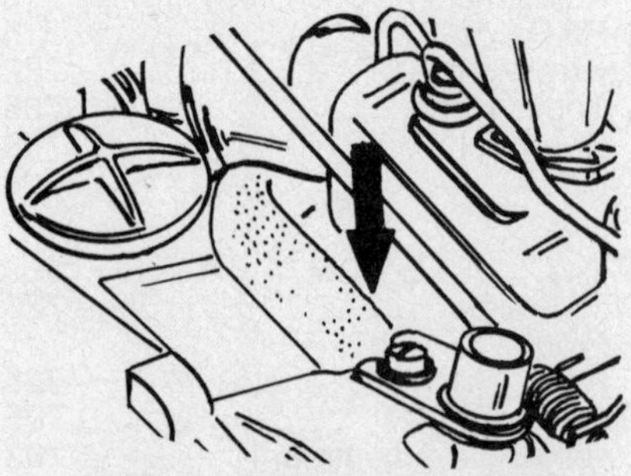

914 2.0 liter engine serial number

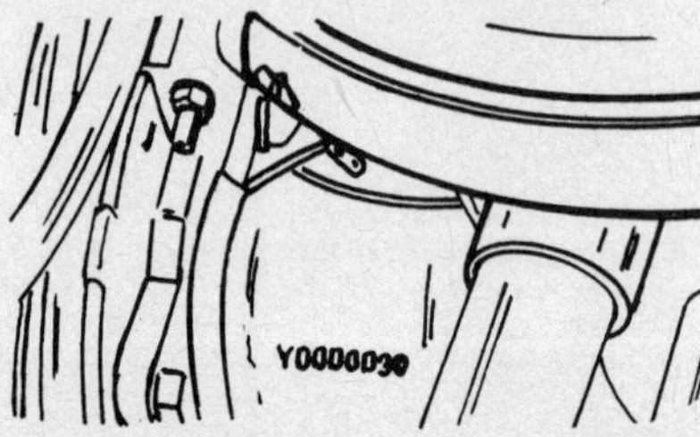

914 1.7 liter engine serial number

914 SERIES

Engine Number Example—
GA-0-000-001

Engine Type
W = 1.7 liter 4 cyl.
EA = 1.7 liter 4 cyl.
EB = 1.7 liter 4 cyl.
GA = 2.0 liter 4 cyl.
EC = 1.8 liter 4 cyl.

Seven digit sequential engine number

NOTE: Small "a" after engine reference letter(s) indicate engine usage in USA except California. Small "b" after engine reference letter(s) indicate engine usage in California.

912E MODEL

One engine was used in this model, a four cylinder, two liter unit. The identification is included in the chassis VIN number.

GENERAL ENGINE SPECIFICATIONS

Year	Model	ENGINE DISPLACEMENT cc	(cu. in.)	Carburetor Type	Horsepower @ rpm (SAE)	Torque @ rpm (SAE)	Bore x Stroke (in.)	Compression Ratio
1975	911S/Carrera	2687	(164)	Fuel inj.	157 @ 5800	166 @ 4000	3.54 x 2.77	8.5:1
	914 (1.8)	1795	(109.5)	Fuel inj.	72.5 @ 4900	89 @ 4000	3.66 x 2.60	7.3:1
	914 (2.0)	1971	(120.3)	Fuel inj.	84 @ 4900	97 @ 4000	3.70 x 2.79	7.6:1
1976	911S	2687	(164)	Fuel inj.	157 @ 5800 ①	166 @ 4000	3.54 x 2.77	8.5:1
	930 Turbo.	2994	(183)	Fuel inj.	234 @ 5500	245 @ 4000	3.74 x 2.77	6.5:1
	912E	1971	(120.3)	Fuel inj.	86 @ 4900	98 @ 4000	3.70 x 2.79	7.6:1
	914 (1.8)	1795	(109.5)	Fuel inj.	72.5 @ 4900	89 @ 4000	3.66 x 2.60	7.3:1
	914 (2.0)	1971	(120.3)	Fuel inj.	84 @ 4900	97 @ 4000	3.70 x 2.79	7.6:1
1977	911S	2687	(164)	Fuel inj.	157 @ 5800	168 @ 4000	3.54 x 2.77	8.5:1
	930 Turbo.	2994	(183)	Fuel inj.	234 @ 5500	245 @ 4000	3.70 x 2.77	6.5:1
1978-81	911, 911SE	2994	(182.7)	Fuel inj.	172 @ 5500	175 @ 4200	3.74 x 2.77	8.5:1
	930 Turbo.	3299	(201.3)	Fuel inj.	261 @ 5500	291 @ 4000	3.82 x 2.93	7.0:1

NOTE: The underhood specifications sticker often reflects tune-up specification changes made in production. Sticker information must be used if it disagrees with the information in this chart.
① California: 152 @ 5800

TUNE-UP SPECIFICATIONS

Year	Model	Engine Displacement cc (cu. in.)	SPARK PLUGS Type ②	SPARK PLUGS Gap (in.)	DISTRIBUTOR Point Dwell (deg)	DISTRIBUTOR Point Gap (in.)	IGNITION TIMING (deg) Basic	IGNITION TIMING (deg) Dynamic @ rpm	Intake Valve Opens (deg)	Com-pres. Press. (psi)	Idle Speed (rpm)	VALVE CLEARANCE (in.) In	VALVE CLEARANCE (in.) Ex
1975	911S/ Carrera	2687 (164)	W235-P21	0.022	38 ± 3	0.016	5A	—	6A	①	850-950	0.004	0.004
	914 1.8	1795 (109.5)	W175-T2	0.028	47 ± 3	0.016	7½B	—	12B	①	850-950	0.006	0.006
	914 2.0	1971 (120.3)	W175-T2	0.028	47 ± 3	0.016	—	27B @ 3500	12B	①	850-950	0.006	0.008
1976	911S	2687 (164)	W235-P21	0.022	38 ± 3 ②	0.016	5A	—	6A	①	850-950	0.004	0.004
	Turbo (930)	2994 (183)	W280-P21	0.024	Electronic		7A	29B @ 4000	3A	①	950-1050	0.004	0.004
	912E	1971 (120.3)	W175-M3	0.028	47 ± 3	0.016	—	27B @ 3500	12B	①	925	0.006	0.008

TUNE-UP SPECIFICATIONS

Year	Model	Engine Displacement cc (cu. in.)	Spark Plugs Type ②	Spark Plugs Gap (in.)	Distributor Point Dwell (deg)	Distributor Point Gap (in.)	Ignition Timing (deg) Basic	Ignition Timing (deg) Dynamic @ rpm	Intake Valve Opens (deg)	Compres. Press. (psi)	Idle Speed (rpm)	Valve Clearance (in.) In	Valve Clearance (in.) Ex
1976	914 1.8	1795 (102.5)	W175-M3	0.028	47 ± 3	0.016	7½B	—	12B	①	850-950	0.006	0.006
	914 2.0	1971 (120.3)	W175-M3	0.028	47 ± 3	0.016	—	27B @ 3500	12B	①	850-950	0.006	0.008
1977	911S	2687 (164)	W235-P21	0.024	38 ± 3 ②	0.016	TDC ③	—	6A	①	900-1000	0.004	0.004
	Turbo (930)	2994 (183)	W280-P21	0.024	Electronic		7A	29B @ 4000	3A	①	950-1050	0.004	0.004
1978-81	911SC	2687 (164)	W235-P21	0.024	Electronic		TDC @ 950 ⑤	—	6A ④	①	900-1000	0.004	0.004
1978-79	Turbo (930)	2994 (183)	W280-P21	0.024	Electronic		7 ± 2° ATDC @ 950	—	1B ④	①	900-1000	0.004	0.004

① All cylinders should be within 22 psi of the highest reading. Compression test to be performed with engine warmer than 140° F
② Bosch spark plugs
② With Bosch distributor, 37° ± 3° with Marelli distributor
③ California: 15ATDC
④ With valve clearance of 1 mm (.0394 in.)
⑤ California 1978-79 15 ± 2° ATDC @ 1000
B Before top dead center
A After top dead center

FIRING ORDERS

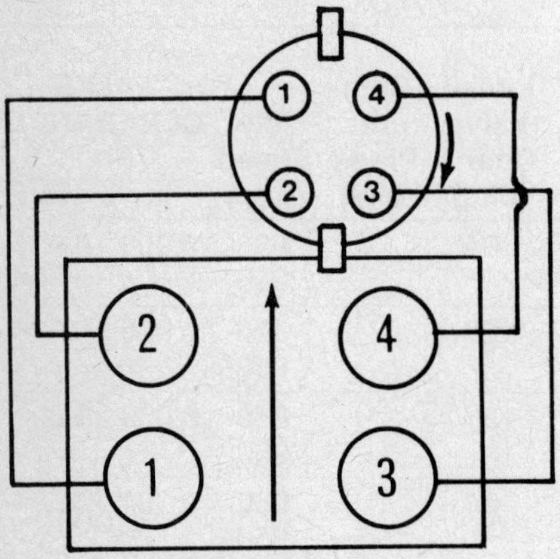

914 series firing order

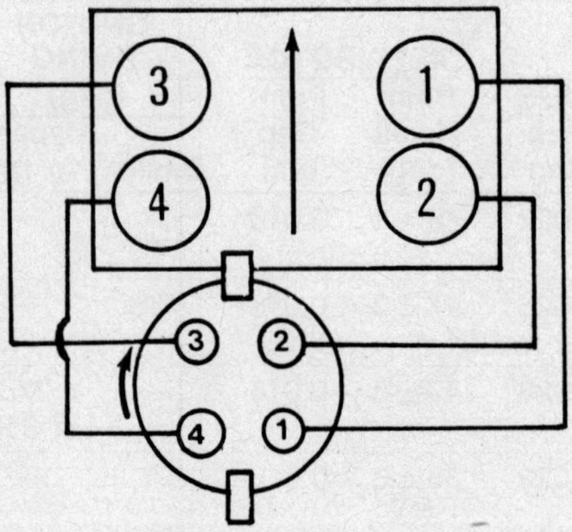

1976 912E Series firing order

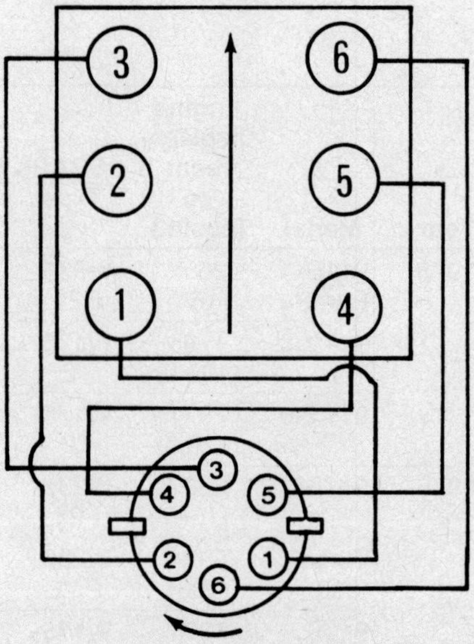

911 series firing order

CAPACITIES

Year	Model	Engine Displacement cc (cu. in.)	Engine Crankcase (qts)	Transaxle (qts)	Gasoline Tank ① (gals)
1975	911S/Carrera	2687 (164)	11.6 ⑤⑧	3.17	21.13
	914	All	3.7 ④	2.6	16.4
1976	911S	2687 (164)	11.6 ⑤⑥	3.17	21.13
	Turbo (930)	2994 (183)	13	3.91	21.13 ③
	912E	1971 (120.3)	3.7 ④	3.17	21.13
	914	All	3.7 ④	2.6	16.4
1977	911S	2687 (164)	13 ⑦	3.17	21.13 ③
	Turbo (930)	2994 (183)	13	3.91	21.13 ③
1978-81	911SC	2994 (182.7)	②	3.2	21 ③
	Turbo (930)	3299 (20.13)	②	4.0	21 ③

① Including 1.6 gal reserve
② Initial filling including oil cooler is 13.7 qts 10.6 qts for refill
③ 1976-79 911 series—2.1 reserve
1976-79 Turbo series—2.0 reserve
④ With filter, 3.2 qts refill without filter
⑤ Total capacity with Sportomatic is 13.6 qts; however, only 10.4 qts are added when refilling
⑥ Total capacity of 14.2 qts with optional oil cooler. Capacity with oil cooler and Sportomatic is 16.9 qts. Normal refill for all models is 10.4 qts.
⑦ 15 qts with Sportomatic

CRANKSHAFT AND CONNECTING ROD SPECIFICATIONS

All measurements in inches

Model	ENGINE DISPLACEMENT cc	(cu. in.)	CRANKSHAFT Main Brg. Journal Dia. ①	Main Brg. Oil Clearance	Shaft End-Play	Thrust on No.	CONNECTING ROD Journal Diameter ①	Oil Clearance	Side Clearance
911, Turbo (930)	All		2.2429-2.2437	0.0004-0.0028	0.0004-0.0077	1	2.0461-2.0468	0.0012-0.0035	0.0079-0.0158
914	1679 1795	(102.5) (109.5)	2.3615-2.3623	0.0197-0.0039	0.0028-0.0051	1	1.5742-1.5748	0.0008-0.0028	0.0039-0.0158
914, 912E	1971 1991	(120.3) (121.5)	2.3615-2.3623	0.0197-0.0039	0.0028-0.0051	1	1.9678-1.9683	0.0008-0.0028	0.0039-0.0158

① Undersize bearings available in 0.0098, 0.0197, 0.0295 inch sizes

VALVE SPECIFICATIONS

Model	Engine Displacement cc (cu. in.)	Face Angle (deg)	Spring Test Pressure (lbs. @ in.)	Spring Installed Height (mm)	Stem to Guide Clearance (mm) Intake	Exhaust	Stem Diameter (mm) Intake	Exhaust
911, 911SE	All	45	176.4 @ 1.21 ①	35 ③	0.030-0.057	0.050-0.077 ④	8.97	8.95
914/912E	All	45 ②	168-186 @ 1.14	30	0.45	0.45	7.94	8.91

① Intake; 165.3 @ 1.25 for exhaust
② 30° for intake valves on 1.7 and 1.8 engines
③ 35.5 mm for exhaust
④ 38.6 mm for exhaust (911SE)

PISTON AND RING SPECIFICATIONS

All measurements in inches

Model	Engine Displacement cc	(cu. in.)	Piston Clearance	Ring Gap Top Compression	Bottom Compression	Oil Control	Ring Side Clearance Top Compression	Bottom Compression	Oil Control
911	2341	(142.8)	0.0008-0.002	0.004-0.008	0.004-0.008	0.0158-0.055	0.0028-0.004	0.002-0.003	0.0008-0.002
911	2687	(164)	0.0008-0.002	0.0039-0.0079	0.0059-0.0018	0.0158-0.055	0.0028-0.004	0.0015-0.0029	0.0008-0.002
911, 911SC, Turbo (930)	2994	(182.7)	0.006	0.004-0.008	0.004-0.008	0.006-0.012	0.003-0.004	0.002-0.003	0.001-0.002
Turbo (930)	3299	(201.3)	0.006	0.004-0.008	0.004-0.008	0.006-0.012	0.003-0.004	0.002-0.003	0.001-0.002
912E, 914/6	1971	(120.3)	0.0008-0.002	0.014-0.022	0.014-0.022	0.010-0.016	0.0015-0.0028	0.0015-0.0028	0.0008-0.020
914/6	1991	(121.5)	0.0022-0.0029	0.0118-0.0177	0.0118-0.0177	0.0098-0.0157	①	①	①
914/4	1679	(102.5)	0.0016-0.0024	0.0138-0.0216	0.0118-0.0138	0.0098-0.0157	0.0024-0.0035	0.0016-0.0028	0.0008-0.0020
914/4	1795	(109.5)	0.0023	0.014-0.021	0.012-0.022	0.016	0.0023-0.0035	0.0016-0.0027	0.0008-0.0019

	Mahle pistons	Schmidt pistons
① Top compression	0.0032-0.0043	0.0028-0.0039
Bottom compression	0.0020-0.0032	0.0016-0.0028
Oil ring	0.0012-0.0024	0.0008-0.0020

TORQUE SPECIFICATIONS

All readings in ft. lbs.

Model	Engine Displacement cc (cu. in.)	Cylinder Head Bolts	Rod Bearing Bolts	Main Bearing Bolts	Crankshaft Pulley Bolt	Flywheel To Crankshaft Bolts
914/912E	All	23	24	24	43	80
911, Turbo (930)	All	24	36	25	58	109

TORQUE SEQUENCE

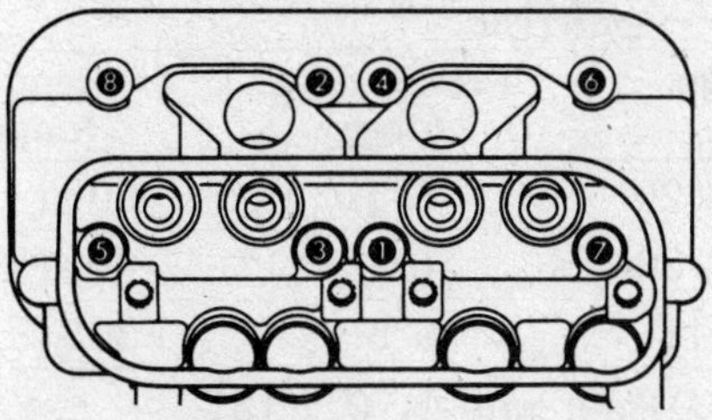

Four cylinder engine cylinder head torque sequence

BATTERY AND STARTER SPECIFICATIONS

All cars use 12 volt, negative ground electrical systems

		STARTER							
		LOCK TEST			NO LOAD TEST				
Model	Battery Amp Hour Capacity	Amps	Volts	Torque (ft. lbs.)	Amps	Volts	rpm	Brush Spring Tension (oz)	Min. Brush Length (in.)
911/912E	(2) 36	160-200	9	1100-1400	33-50	11.5	6400-7900	42.3	0.5
914	45	170-205	9	900-1300	35-45	12	7400-9100	42	N.A.

ALTERNATOR AND REGULATOR SPECIFICATIONS

	ALTERNATOR		REGULATOR						
				FIELD RELAY			REGULATOR		
Model	Part No. or Manufacturer	Output (amps.)	Part No. or Manufacturer	Air Gap (in.)	Point Gap (in.)	Volts to Close	Air Gap (in.)	Point Gap (in.)	Volts @ 75°
911/912E	Bosch	55	Bosch	Not adjustable					13.5-14.5
914	Bosch	50	Bosch	Not adjustable					13.5-14.5

BRAKE SPECIFICATIONS

All measurements given are in inches unless noted

				BRAKE DISC		BRAKE DRUM			MINIMUM LINING THICKNESS	
Year	Model	Lug Nut Torque (ft. lbs.)	Master Cylinder Bore	Minimum Thickness	Maximum Run-Out	Diameter	Max. Machine O/S	Max. Wear Limit	Front	Rear
1975-81	911/912E ①	94	0.75	③	0.008	—	—	—	0.08	0.08
1975-77	914	94	0.687	0.35 ②	0.008	—	—	—	0.08	0.08

NOTE: Minimum lining thickness is as recommended by the manufacturer. Due to variations in state inspection regulations, the minimum allowable thickness may be different than recommended by the manufacturer.

① Solid discs on 912E; ventilated on all 911 models

② Wear limit—0.335 in.

③ 912E (front)—0.45 in.
912E (rear)—0.37 in. (wear limit) 0.35 in.
911 (front/rear)—0.725 (refinish limit) or 0.70 (wear limit) (in.)

—Not applicable; 4 wheel disc brakes used on all models

WHEEL ALIGNMENT

		CASTER		CAMBER		
Year	Model	Range (deg)	Pref Setting (deg)	Range (deg)	Pref Setting (deg)	Toe-In (deg)
1975-77	911/912E	5°50′-6°20′	6°5′	−50′-(+)10′	0° ①	0° ②
1975-77	914	5°30′-6°30′	6°	−40′-(+)20′	0° ③	+20′±10′ ④
1977-81	911, 911SC	6°5′±15′	6°5′	+30′-(±)10′	+30′	0° ⑤

① Rear wheels: −1±10′
② Rear wheels: 0°±20′
③ Rear wheels: −30′±20′
④ Rear wheels: 0°±15′
⑤ Rear wheels: +10′±10′

TUNE-UP

Spark Plugs

In addition to performing their basic function of igniting the air-fuel mixture, spark plugs can also serve as very useful diagnostic tools. Once removed, compare your spark plugs with the samples in the "Troubleshooting" section. Typical plug conditions are illustrated along with their causes and remedies. Plugs which exhibit only normal wear and deposits can be cleaned, gapped, and reinstalled.

Before removing the spark plug leads, number the towers on the distributor cap with tape. Grasp each spark plug boot and pull it straight out. Check the condition of the rubber boot and/or shroud seals and replace them if necessary. Install the spark plug socket on the plug's hex and remove it. If removal is difficult, loosen the plug only slightly and drip some light oil onto the threads. Allow the oil to penetrate and then unscrew the spark plug. Proceeding this way will prevent damaging the threads in the cylinder head. Be sure to keep the socket straight to avoid breaking the ceramic insulator. Most spark plug sockets are lined with rubber for this reason. Inspect the plugs using the "Troubleshooting" section illustrations and then clean or discard them according to their condition. Recommended spark plug gap is given in the "Tune-Up Specifications Chart." Use a spark plug wire gauge for checking the gap. The wire should pass through the electrodes with just a slight drag. Using the electrode bending tool on the end of the gauge, bend the side electrode to adjust the gap. Never attempt to adjust the center electrode. Lightly oil the threads of the replacement plug and install it hand-tight. The spark plugs in all engines should be tightened to a torque of 18-21 ft/lbs. Install the ignition wire boots firmly on the spark plugs. On the 914 models, be sure that the cooling shroud seals are snug or cooling efficiency will be lost.

Breaker Points and Condenser

Snap the two retaining clips off the distributor cap. Remove the cap and examine it for cracks, deterioration, or carbon tracks. Replace the cap, is necessary, by transferring one wire at a time from the old cap to the new one. Some 911 models have a dust cover which must be removed to service the points. Examine the rotor for corrosion or wear and replace it if necessary.

NOTE: Marelli rotors are retained by a screw.

Check the points for pitting and burning. Slight imperfections on the contact surface may be filed off with a point file (fine emery

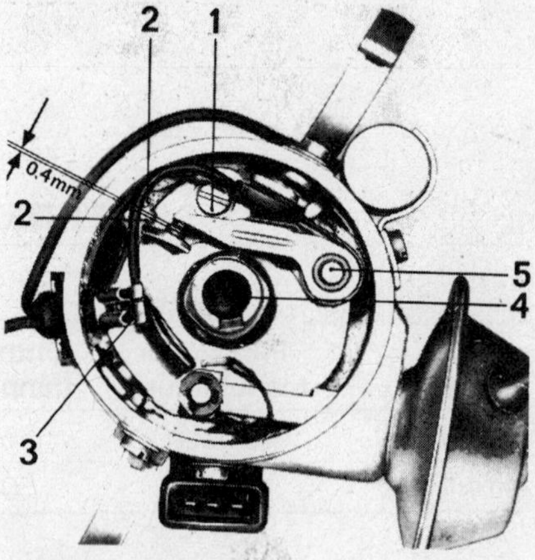

1. Retaining screw
2. Breaker plate
3. Primary connection
4. Distributor shaft felt
5. Breaker arm pivot (place a few drops of oil on 4 and 5)

914 distributor

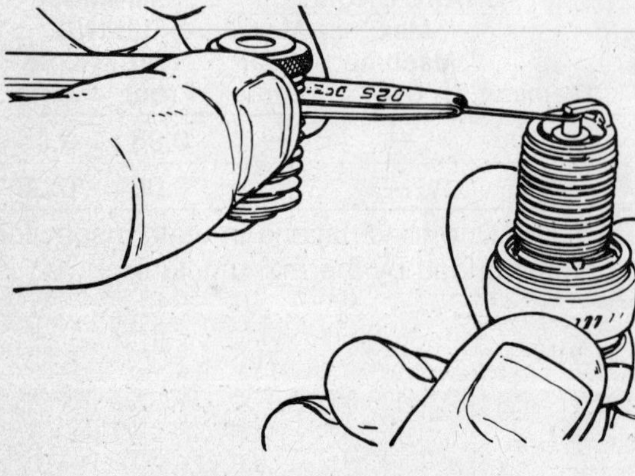

Checking the spark plug gap

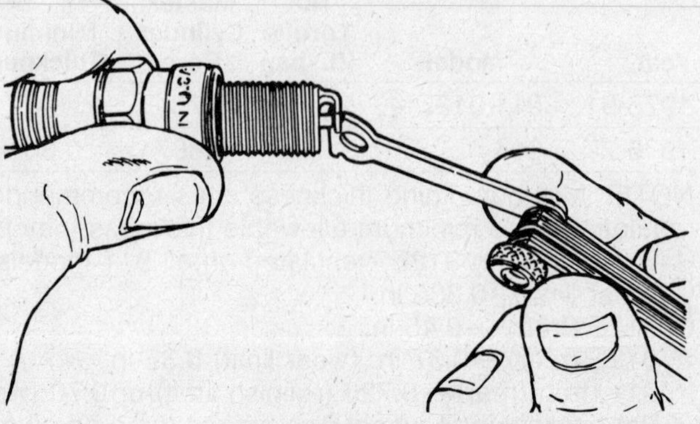

Bending the side electrode

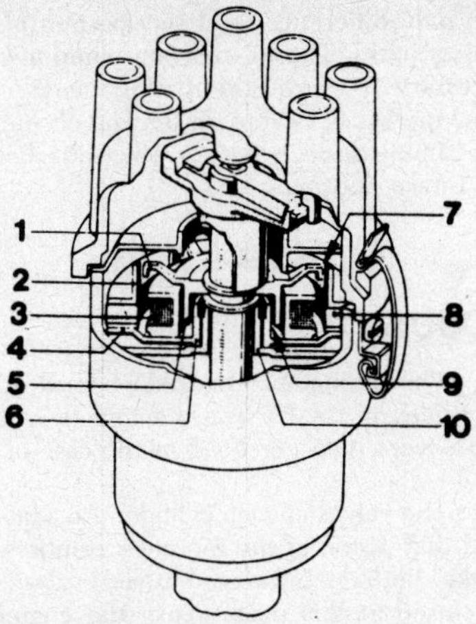

1. Rotor
2. Stator
3. Transmitter coil
4. Stator plate
5. Rotor bushing
6. Stator bushing
7. Outer clearance
8. Magnet
9. Inner clearance
10. Carrier plate and bushing (fixed)

Internal view of electronic distributor

paper will also do), but it is usually wise to replace the breaker point set when tuning. Replace the cap, if necessary, by transferring point set. All Porsches are equpped with externally mounted condensers mounted on the body of the distributor. To replace the condenser, disconnect its lead from the distributor primary terminal and unscrew it from the mounting on the body. Reverse the removal procedure to install a replacement condenser.

BREAKER POINT REMOVAL AND INSTALLATION

911

NOTE: Porsche recommends removing the distributor to replace the breaker points on these models. The problem is one of access and working space. Some mechanics find they are able to remove the points with the distributor in the car; however it is much easier to do it out of the car. Follow the directions in the "Engine Electrical" section to remove the distributor and then remove the points as outlined below.

The Turbo is equipped with pointless, electronic ignition and requires only distributor cap and wire condition checks.

1. Undo the retaining screw(s), if so equipped, and remove the rotor.
2. Remove the breaker point retaining screw(s), disconnect the primary lead from the terminal, and lift out the breaker point set.

NOTE: When removing the points in the car, it is best to use a magnetic screwdriver to prevent dropping the screws.

3. Install the replacement point set, but leave the adjustment screw hand-tight.
4. Turn the engine until the rubbing block

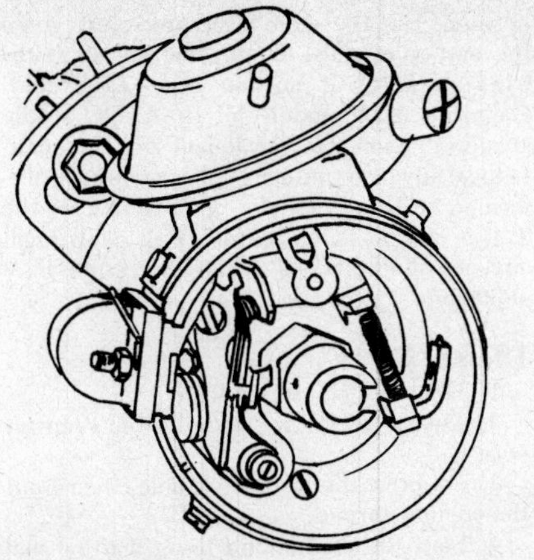

911 distributor showing breaker point retaining screws

of the breaker arm rests on the highest point of a cam lobe.

5. Insert a 0.016 in. feeler gauge between the two contact points. The gauge should pull through the points with just a slight drag.
6. When the gap is adjusted, tighten the retaining screw. Lightly lubricate the cam with silicone grease.
7. Install the rotor.
8. Install the distributor cap. Check the dwell angle and ignition timing as outlined in the following sections.

914 and 912E

The 914, in addition to resistor spark plugs, is equipped with a resistor rotor. The rotor may be checked with an ohmmeter. If a resistance greater than 10k ohms is indicated, the rotor should be replaced.

1. Remove the breaker point retaining screw.
2. Unclip the wire lead and remove the point set.
3. Install the replacement point set, tightening the retaining screw only hand-tight.
4. Turn the engine (with a remote starter switch or by having an assistant "bump" the starter) until the rubbing block of the point set is on the high point of a cam lobe.
5. Using 0.016 in. feeler gauge, adjust the point gap and then tighten the retaining screw.
6. Place a few drops of engine oil on the pivot bearing of the breaker arm and the felt in the center of the distrubutor shaft.
7. Install the rotor and distributor cap.
8. Check the dwell angle and ignition timing as outlined in the following sections.

Dwell Angle

The dwell angle or cam angle is the number of degrees that the distributor cam rotates while the points are closed. There is an inverse relationship between dwell angle and point gap. Increasing the point gap will decrease the dwell angle and vice versa. Checking the dwell angle with a meter is a far more accurate method of measuring point opening than the feeler gauge method.

After setting the point gap to specification with a feeler gauge, check the dwell angle with a meter. Hook-up the dwell meter according to the maker's instruction sheet. The

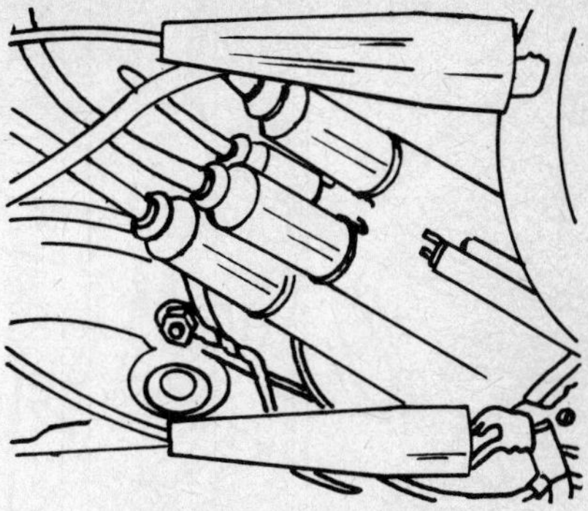

1. Ground connection
2. Primary connection

911 dwell meter hook-up

negative lead is grounded and the positive lead connected to the primary wire (terminal No. 1 on 911 models) that runs from the coil to the distributor. Start the engine, let it idle and reach operating temperature, and observe the dwell. The reading should fall within the allowable range. If it does not, the gap will have to be reset or the breaker points will have to be replaced.

Ignition Timing

CAUTION

When performing this or any other adjustment with the engine running, be very careful of the fan belt and pulley.

Ignition timing should always be checked as part of any tune-up. Timing is checked after the points have been adjusted or replaced. A stroboscopic timing light is a necessity for timing any Porsche and, in addition, a static 12 V timing light is necessary for the 911 and the 914.

1975–79 911

These models are equipped with a vacuum retard unit which retards the ignition to 5° ATDC at idle. Ignition timing is checked both

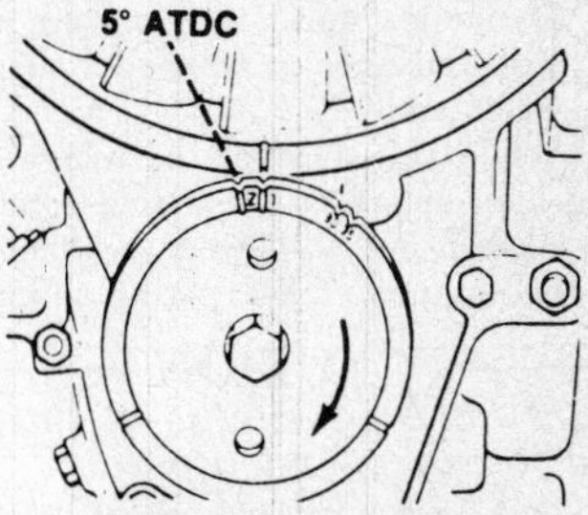

1975-76 series timing mark

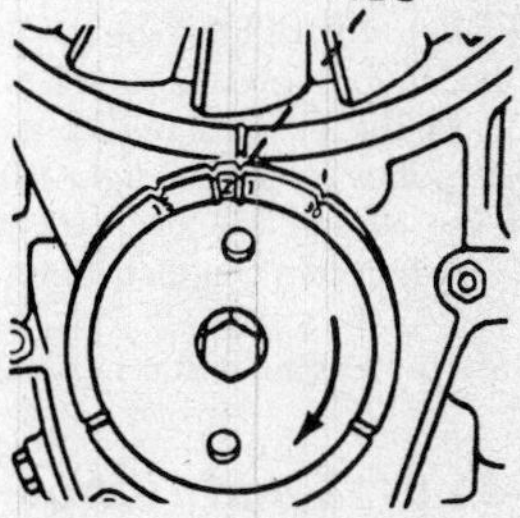

1977 and later 911 series timing marks

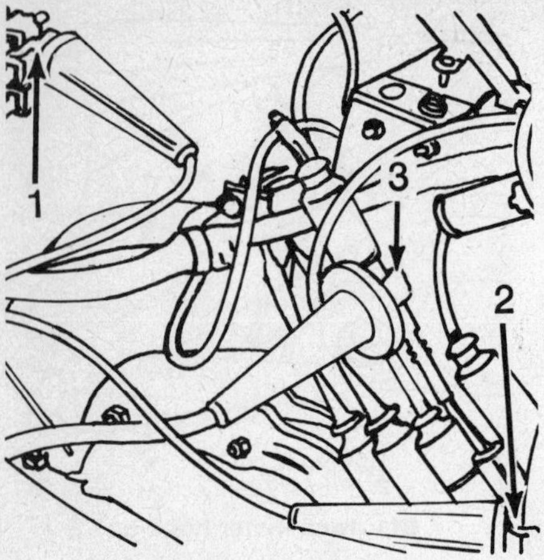

1. Positive connection
2. Ground connection
3. No. 1 terminal

911 timing light hook-up

at idle and at 6000 rpm with a stroboscopic timing light. Leave the vacuum hose on. The crankshaft pulley has a TDC notch ("Z1"), a 5° ATDC notch directly to the left of the "Z1" notch, a 30° BTDC notch, and a 35° notch. The 1973-75 911 distributor has a slotted mounting flange on its base. The retaining nut is loosened and the distributor swivels on the mounting stud to make timing changes.

1. Start the engine and allow it to reach normal operating temperature.
2. Stop the engine and attach a timing light to No. 1 spark plug according to the manufacturer's instructions.
3. Restart the engine. Make sure that the idle speed is according to specifications and that the vacuum advance hose is connected.
4. When the timing light flashes, the 5° ATDC notch in the pulley should be aligned with the reference notch in the blower housing.
5. If the notches do not align, loosen the retaining nut and slowly rotate the distributor as necessary until they line up. Ignition timing is now correct at idle.
6. Dynamic timing is checked at this point. Total advance at 6000 rpm should be between 32° and 38°
7. While you stand at the rear with the timing light aimed at the timing notches on the crankshaft pulley, have an assistant accelerate the engine to 6000 rpm for an instant.

CAUTION

Do not hold the engine at this high speed for an extended period.

8. The pulley has a 30° and 35° notch, so 32-38° would start to the right of the 30° notch and end just to the right of the 35° notch. The blower housing reference notch should be aligned with the desired timing area on the crankshaft pulley when the light flashes.
9. If the timing is incorrect, loosen the nut and slowly rotate the distributor to adjust it.
10. Stop the engine and remove the timing light.

1977–81 911S and Turbo

Ignition timing is done with the vacuum hose on. Use the same basic procedure given the earlier models. Timing for the 49 states 911S is TDC at normal idle (Z1 notch). California 911S models get 15° ATDC at idle speed (15° notch to the left of Z1). The centrifugal advance timing check is no longer performed on these models. Basic timing for the Turbo is 7° ATDC at idle. Full centrifugal advance should be 29° BTDC and come in at 4000 rpm.

1975–76 914

1. Hook up the timing light.
2. Disconnect the distributor vacuum hose(s).
3. Unscrew the inspection hole cover from the cooling shroud.
4. Start the engine and bring it to normal operating temperature.
5. Advance should be 7.5° BTDC at idle speed on 1.8 engine models.

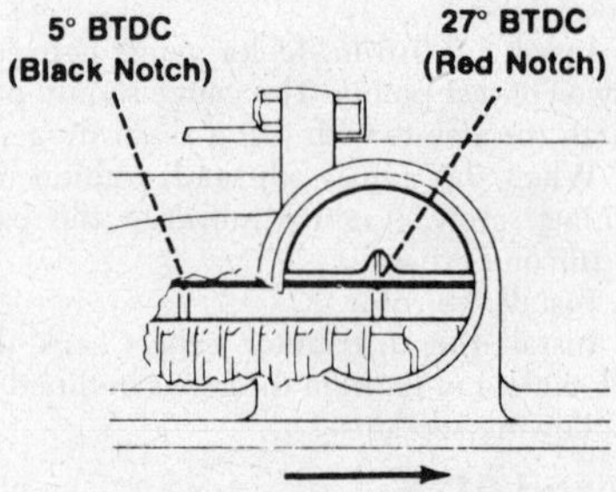

1975 1971 cc engine timing marks

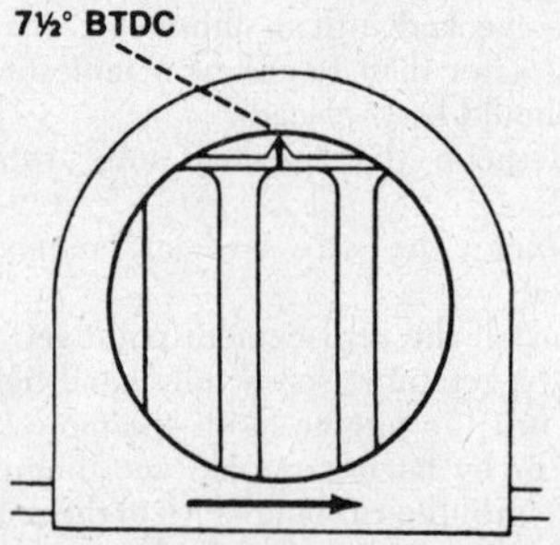

1975-76 914 series timing marks

6. On 2.0 models, accelerate the engine to 3500 rpm. Timing should be at 27° BTDC (red notch aligned with V-shaped notch in blower housing).
7. If the timing is off specifications, loosen the distributor until it is correct.
8. Shut the engine off and connect the vacuum hose(s).

1976 912E

The engine is essentially the same as the 2.0 liter engine used in the 914. Timing is checked in the same manner as the 2.0 914.

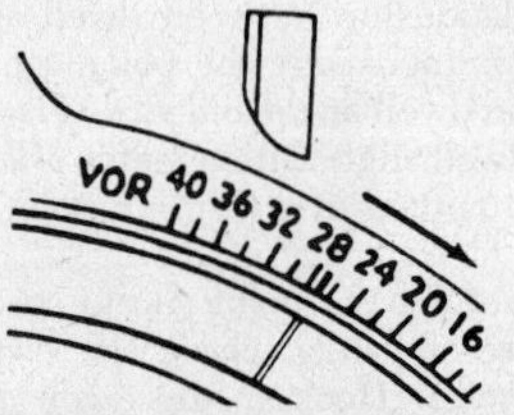

1976 912E Series timing marks

The only difference is in the location of the timing marks. The air injection pump made it necessary to move the timing marks. The TDC marker is located on the fanbelt pulley. The timing scale is on a bracket attached to the intake housing.

Valve Lash

ADJUSTMENT

1. The engine must be cold when adjusting the valves on any Porsche. Remove the rocker arm covers, two per head in the case of the 911.
2. The valves of each cylinder are adjusted with that piston at the top of its compression stroke. Both the intake and exhaust valves will be closed at this point. Turn the engine to align the TDC mark ("Z1" for the 911 and the black notch on 914 models) with the reference mark.
3. Using a feeler gauge (thickness equal to a figure given in the "Valve Clearance" column of the "Tune-Up Specifications Chart"), check the clearance between the valve stem and the rocker arm. The feeler gauge should just slip through: if it has to be forced the clearance will be incorrect.

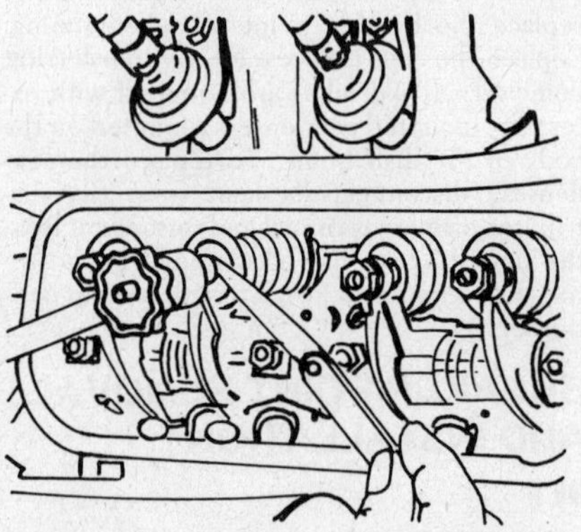

914 valve clearance adjustment (special adjusting tool shown)

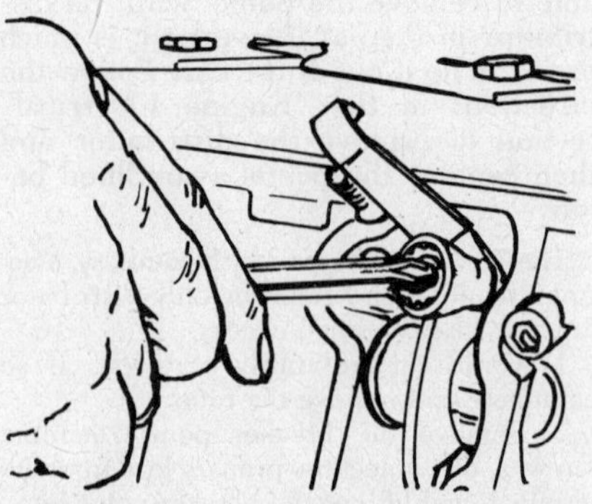

911 and 914/6 valve clearance adjustment

4. If the clearance is not within specifications, loosen the locknut with a box wrench and, using a screwdriver, turn the rocker arm adjusting screw while holding the locknut. A tool to simplify this procedure is available

from automotive suppliers. It has a screwdriver bit which can be turned while the locknut is held with a socket.

5. Tighten the locknut while holding the adjusting screw. Recheck the valve clearance to ensure that it wasn't changed when the locknut was tightened. Repeat this procedure on the other valve of No. 1 cylinder.

6. Proceed to adjust the valves of the remaining cylinders in an order of 1-2-3-4 for four-cylinder engines or 1-6-2-4-3-5 for six-cylinder engines. The piston of the cylinder on which the valves are being adjusted must be at TDC. Turn the engine until both valves of the cylinder being adjusted are closed. Six-cylinder engines have TDC marks for each cylinder on the crankshaft pulley. Adjust the valves in the same manner as No. 1 cylinder.

7. Install the rocker arm or camshaft housing covers with new gaskets. Start the engine and check for leaks.

Fuel Injection

IDLE SPEED

911

The idle speed adjustment on the CIS system used on all later models is done with the bypass screw on the throttle valve housing. The engine should be at normal operating temperature.

1975-76 2.0

1. Remove the air filter and connect a tachometer to the engine.

2. Start the engine and set the idle speed to specifications. Turning the adjustment screw clockwise increases the idle speed. Turning the screw counterclockwise decreases the idle speed.

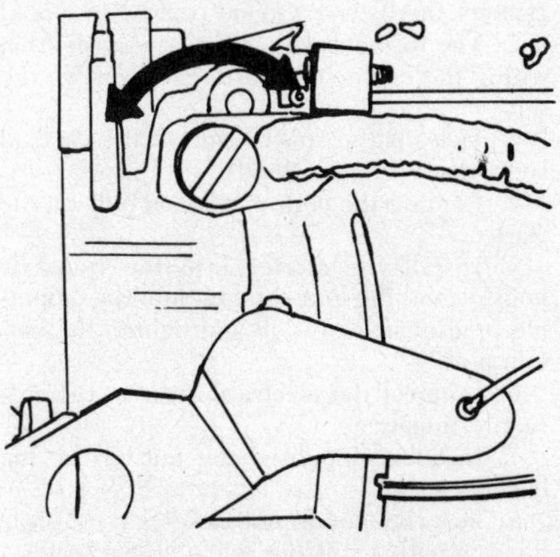

914 idle speed screw

1975-76 914 1.8 and 1976 912E

1. Make sure all hoses are tight. Connect a tachometer to the engine.

2. Start the engine and bring it to normal operating temperature.

3. The idle speed adjustment screw is located on the throttle housing. Do not touch the idle mixture screw which is covered with a plastic plug.

ENGINE ELECTRICAL

Distributor

REMOVAL AND INSTALLATION

911

1. Remove the heated air intake duct.

2. Unsnap and remove the distributor cap. Position it out of the way.

3. Mark the direction in which the rotor is pointing on the body of the distributor.

NOTE: Some models have a scribe mark indicating the correct rotor positioning for No. 1 cylinder. On these models it will be more convenient to turn the engine so that the rotor points to this mark before removing the distributor.

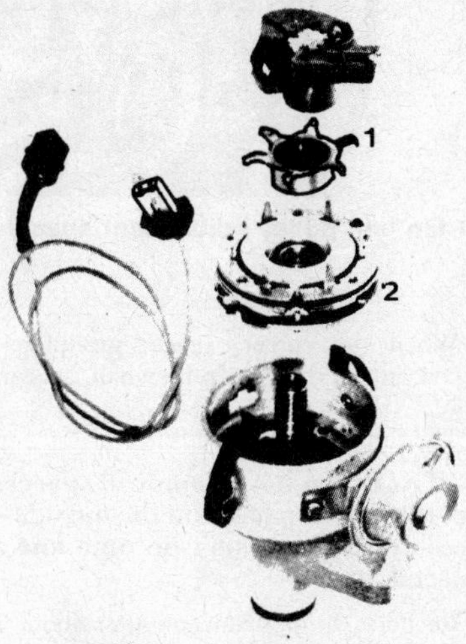

1. Rotor
2. Stator

Electronic distributor disassembled in major components

4. Detach the distributor leads. Remove the vacuum line.

5. Loosen and remove the retaining nut from the base of the distributor. Pull the distributor straight out of the engine. Check and, if necessary, replace the sealing ring on the distributor housing.

6. Insert the distributor into the engine. Turn the rotor back and forth to engage the distributor and crankshaft gears. If the engine has been turned while the distributor was out, bring No. 1 cylinder to TDC as described before under "Ignition Timing."

7. Adjust the static and dynamic timing.

914 and 912E

1. Remove the air cleaner.

2. Loosen the clamp on the right-hand heater hose and pull it from the heater. Position the hose out of the way.

3. Screw the inspection hole cover out of the cooling shroud.

4. Turn the engine until the black notch in the crankshaft pulley aligns with v-shaped notch in the blower housing.

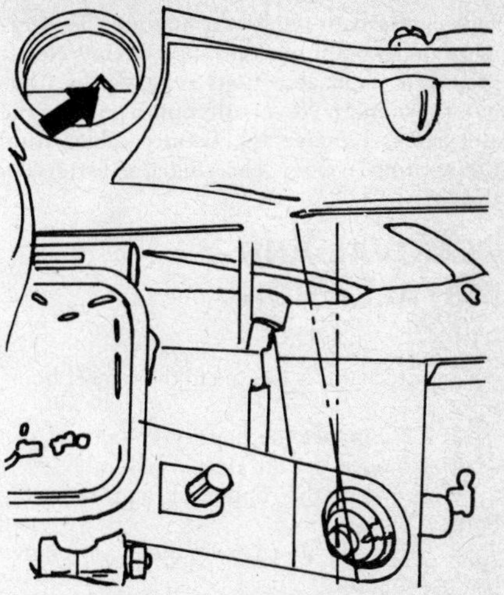

914 distributor drive gear positioning

5. Remove the distributor cap and check that the rotor is, indeed, pointing towards the No. 1 cylinder position.

6. Detach the two electrical leads and vacuum hoses from the distributor.

7. Loosen the retaining nut on the base of the distributor and pull it out of the engine.

To install the distributor with the engine undisturbed.

8. Ensure that the spring is in place in the center bore of the drive gear. A length of wire may be used to install the spring if it has been removed.

9. Insert the distributor, making sure that the dog on the distributor engages the slot in the drive gear. Turning the rotor a few times will ease installation.

10. Push the distributor in firmly. Tighten the clamp nut.

11. Install the distributor leads and vacuum hoses. Install the distributor cap.

12. Check the ignition timing. Install the inspection cover, heater hose, and air cleaner.

Install the distributor in the following manner if the engine has been disturbed:

13. Turn the engine to bring No. 1 cylinder up to TDC. At this point, the black notch in the crankshaft pulley should be aligned with the V-shaped notch in the blower housing and the slot in the distributor drive gear should be at approximately a 12° angle to the engine centerline. The slot should be pointing toward the rear retaining screw of the air filter support and the smaller side of the gear should be facing the center of the engine.

14. Install the distributor using steps 8 through 12.

Alternator

ALTERNATOR PRECAUTIONS

A few precautions should be observed when servicing an electrical system that uses an alternator. Failure to do so can result in serious damage to the charging system. The negative terminal(s) of the battery(ies) is (are) always grounded. Always connect the correct battery terminals when attaching a battery charger or replacing a battery. Never operate the alternator on an open, uncontrolled circuit. Never ground or short across any regulator or alternator terminals. Never attempt to polarize the alternator. Remove the battery cables from the terminals when charging the battery in the car.

REMOVAL AND INSTALLATION

911

The alternator is located in the blower housing.

1. Disconnect the battery ground straps.
2. Remove the air cleaner assembly.
3. Remove the upper shroud retaining bolts.
4. Hold the alternator pulley and remove the pulley nut.
5. Remove the drive belt.

911 alternator pulley nut removal

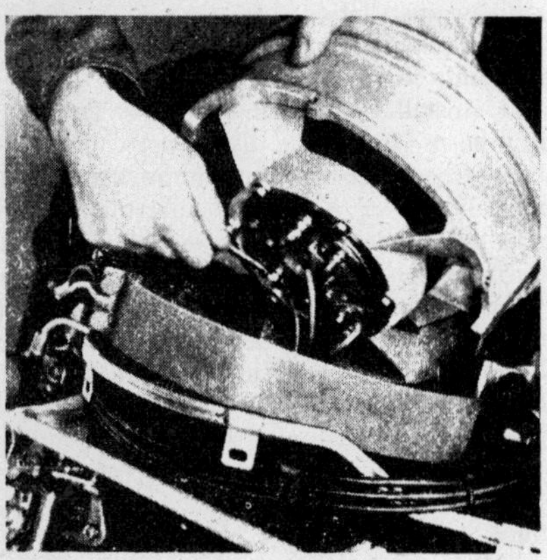

911 alternator removal

6. Remove the blower housing strap retaining bolts.
7. Pull the blower housing/alternator towards the rear until there is enough clearance to disconnect the wiring.
8. Remove the alternator.
9. Install the alternator in a reverse order of the removal. Be sure that the blower housing is seated on the dowel in the crankcase.
10. Tighten the pulley nut to 29 ft/lbs.

912E, 914

Remove the alternator cover plate and the surrounding sheet metal to expose the alternator for removal and installation.

BELT TENSION ADJUSTMENT

911

A correctly tensioned belt can be deflected ½-¾ in. by light hand pressure. If the tension is not within specifications; follow the steps below to adjust or replace the belt.

1. Remove the pulley nut as outlined above in "Alternator Removal and Installation."
2. Remove the outside half of the pulley.
3. Remove the adjustment spacers to increase belt tension. Add spacers to decrease belt tension.

911 fan belt pulley adjustment spacers

4. When the correct spacer grouping is achieved, install the belt, pulley half, spacers, and nut.
5. Tighten the nut to 29 ft/lbs.

NOTE: If you have removed spacers, install the extra spacers on the outside of the pulley so they won't become lost or misplaced.

6. Recheck the belt tension after about 60 miles of driving.

914, 912E

A correctly tensioned belt will be able to be deflected approximately ½ in. by light hand pressure. If the tension is not within specification, follow the steps below to adjust or replace the belt.

1. Remove the small cover plate from the alternator cover.
2. Loosen the socket screw and slide the alternator left or right as necessary.
3. Tighten the screw and replace the cover.

Regulator

REMOVAL AND INSTALLATION

911, 912E and 914

1. Disconnect the ground cable from the battery.
2. Disconnect the wiring from the regulator.
3. Remove the mounting screws and remove the regulator.
4. Install the regulator. Do not overtighten the screws. An alternator system requires no polarization.

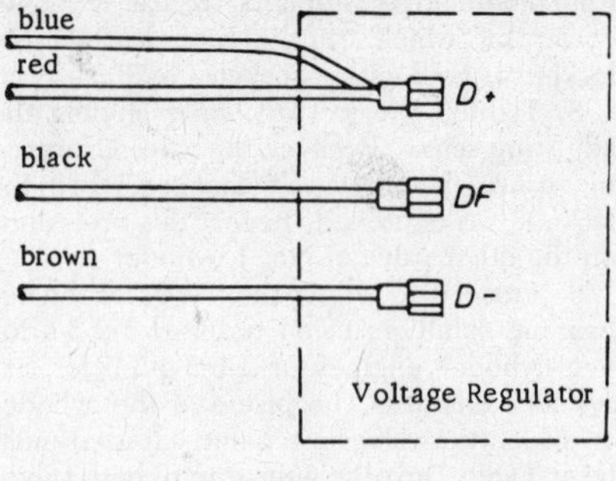

911 voltage regulator wiring schematic

Starter

REMOVAL AND INSTALLATION

911

1. Disconnect the battery(ies) ground strap(s).
2. Jack up the rear of the car and support it with jack stands.
3. Note their locations (tag to be sure) and then remove the starter electrical connections.
4. Loosen the retaining bolts, support the starter, remove the bolts, and then pull out the starter.
5. Install the starter using a reverse order of the removal procedure. Ensure that the terminal connections are correctly installed and tight.
6. Lower the car and connect the battery(ies) ground strap(s).

914 and 912E

1. Open the engine compartment lid. Disconnect the battery ground cable.
2. The top retaining bolt is accessible from within the engine compartment. Remove the nut.
3. Jack up the starter side of the car and support it with jack stands.
4. Remove the bottom bolt and pull out the starter.
5. Install the starter into the transaxle housing and the long top bolt into the mounting bracket hole. Install and tighten the bottom bolt.
6. Connect the electrical leads to the correct terminals.
7. Install and tighten the nut on the top bolt.
8. Seal the mounting bracket and transaxle housing with a suitable self-adhesive sealer.
9. Lower the car and connect the battery cable.

OVERRUN CLUTCH AND DRIVE

Replacement

1. Remove the starter.
2. Press clutch operating shaft by turning slightly.
3. Pull both off shaft by turning slightly.
4. Hold armature in vise and push pinion and sleeve on shaft until detent locks.

Battery

The 911 batteries are located in the front luggage compartment. One battery is located in each fender well behind the headlights. The 914 battery is located in the engine compartment 1975-81 911 and 1976 912E models are equipped with a single battery located in the luggage compartment.

ENGINE MECHANICAL

Engine Removal and Installation

All Porsche engines are removed and installed with the transaxle attached. The recommended method for removal is to raise the rear of the car high enough for working clearance and then support it on jack stands. A hydraulic transmission/differential jack or service jack of at least 800 lbs. capacity is required for lowering the engine/transaxle and raising it back into the chassis. Have an assistant steady the engine/transaxle during removal. Strap the engine to the jack so that it doesn't slide off. Proceed slowly and carefully as the engine/transaxle combination is both heavy and delicate.

911 and 912E

1. Disconnect the battery. Drain the engine and transaxle oil.
2. Open the engine compartment lid and detach the hot air ducts from the air gates and exhaust manifold heat exchangers.
3. Detach the two heater control cables.
4. Remove the hot air ducts from the the T-union between the air cleaners and then remove the T-union from the blower housing.
5. Remove the tops of the air cleaners.
6. Tag for installation and then remove the electrical cables from the generator and blower housing.
7. Tag for installation and remove the wires from the coil.
8. Remove the connections from the oil temperature and pressure sending units.
9. Remove the fuel line from the fuel pump and detach its clip from the engine shield.
10. Remove the Allen bolts retaining the axle shaft flange to the transaxle. Free the axle shaft from the transaxle and drop them out of the way.
11. Remove the starter electrical leads.
12. Disconnect the clutch cable from the control lever.
13. Remove the ground strap.
14. Detach the back-up light lead.
15. Disconnect the throttle linkage from the cross-shaft at the transaxle.
16. Remove the cover in the center of the rear floor.
17. Detach the rubber shift lever cover from the flange on the body and pull it forward on the control lever.

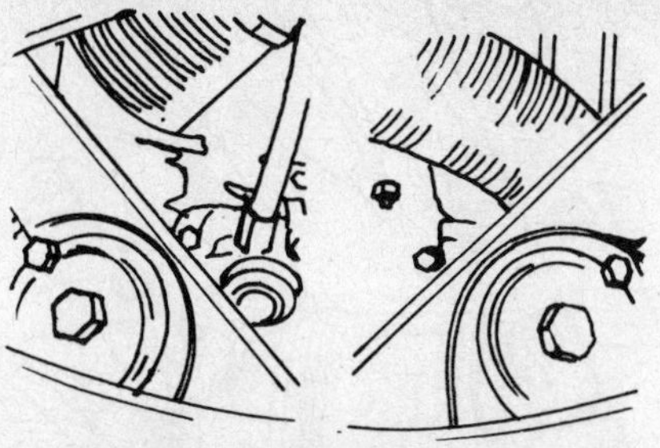

911 and 912 rear engine-to-body mounts

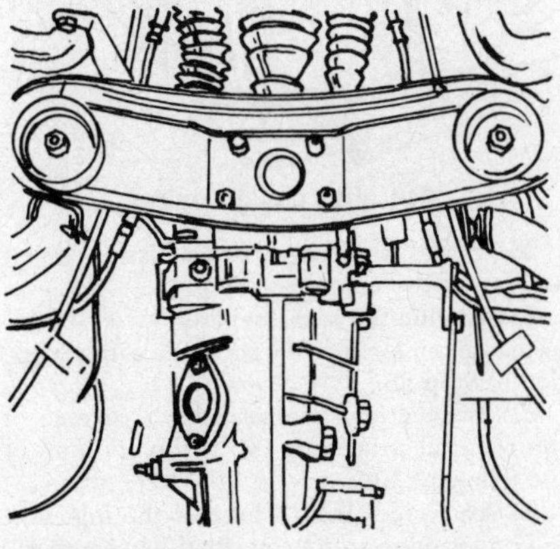

911 and 912 transaxle crossmember mounting

18. Remove the safety wire from the square-headed from the joint. Loosen the screw and slide the shift rod off its base.
19. Position the jack, including the flat support plate, under the engine/transaxle. The jack should be under the point of balance of the powertrain.
20. Riase the jack a slight amount.
21. Remove the body mounting bolts on either side of the engine compartment.
22. Remove the body mounting bolts from the short transaxle crossmember. The engine is removed with this crossmember attached.
23. Very carefully lower the engine, while your assistants help balance it.
24. Roll the engine/transaxle out from under the car.

Follow Steps 25 through 30 for engine and transaxle separation.

Remove the starter. Release the throw-out fork tension by disconnecting the return spring if one is used.

After releasing throwout bearing tension it

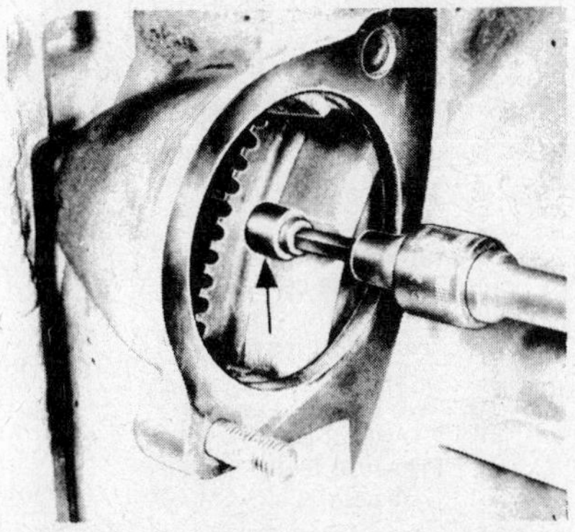

Releasing throwout bearing tension

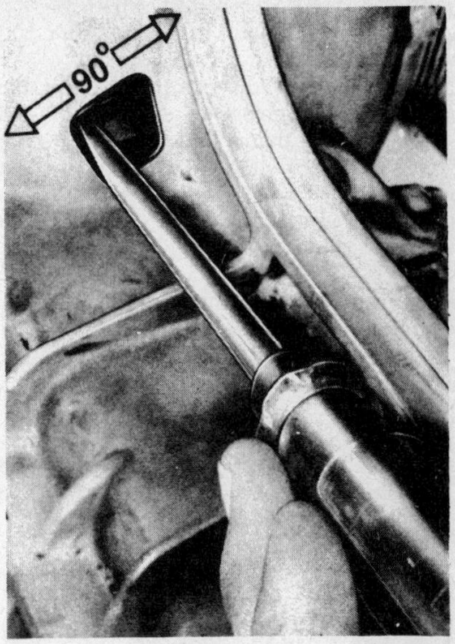

Sliding the fork past the throwout bearing

is necessary to slide the throwout fork past the bearing. To do this, insert a screwdriver in the opening in the transaxle and turn the bearing 90°. Slide the fork past the bearing. The transaxle may now be separated from the engine.

25. Remove the engine-to-transaxle bolts and nuts. Carefully pull the transaxle away from the engine. Be sure that the full weight of the transaxle is supported, so as not to damage the pilot bushing, throwout bearing, clutch disc, or pressure plate.
26. Whichever component you are repairing, rebuilding, or replacing may now be moved to a suitable workbench, dolly, or engine stand.
27. Before reinstalling the transaxle, fill the pilot bushing in the gland nut with a small amount of graphite grease (no more than 3 cc, or $^1/_{10}$ oz.).
28. Lightly grease the transmission input shaft splines, starter shaft bushing, and the starter and flywheel gear teeth.
29. Carefully attach the transaxle to the engine. Remember the transmission input shaft will be passing through the throwout bearing, pressure plate, clutch disc, and pilot bushing, so give it ample support during the attachment procedure.

NOTE: If the clutch disc splines and the input shaft splines don't line up, as they so often won't, have an assistant turn the crankshaft pulley until they do.

30. Push the transaxle home so that the mounting flanges are flush. Align the bottom holes and install the bolts. Install the top bolts, and then tighten all of the retaining bolts evenly.
31. The engine/transaxle is installed by following the removal Steps in reverse order.
32. After the engine is installed, check the clutch adjustment as described in below.
33. Refill the engine and transaxle with the correct lubricant. Lower the car.
34. Start the engine and check for leaks.

914

1. Scribe the hinge positioning, and then remove the engine compartment lid.

2. Disconnect the battery cables.
3. Remove the air cleaner and attendant hoses.
4. Tag each of the eleven cables for the fuel injection (for correct reinstallation) and then disconnect them. Tape the cables to the engine compartment sides so that they are out of harm's way.
5. Disconnect the throttle cable and push it through the front engine firewall.
6. Open the fuel line retaining clip: Disconnect and plug the fuel lines near the pressure regulator.
7. Remove the top retaining nut for the starter (accessible from the engine compartment).
8. Jack up the car and support it safely with stands.
9. Remove the muffler shrouding. Drain the engine and transaxle.
10. Remove the lower heater components.
11. Detach the dust cover and then unscrew the shift rod retainer.
12. Remove the protective cover, unscrew the retaining nuts, and remove the rear shift rod.
13. Remove the heater box, hoses, and control cables.
14. Loosen the cable pulley adjusting nut and retaining nut. Bend the retaining bracket and pull the clutch cable towards the front.
15. Loosen the speedometer cable and pull it forward.
16. Remove the starter. Detach the ground strap from underbody.
17. Detach the axle driveshafts from the transaxle as described below. Wire the driveshafts out of the way.
18. Position the jack and plate under the engine/transaxle and raise it slightly.
19. Unscrew the four transaxle support retaining nuts. Remove the two Allen bolts on the front engine mount.

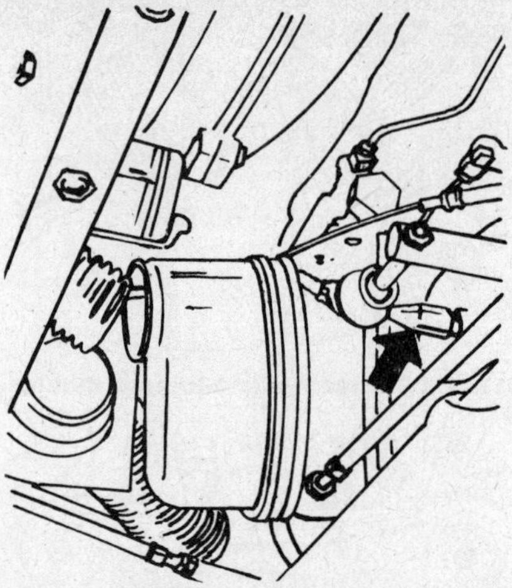

914 shift rod container

20. Lower the engine/transmission down and out of the car.
21. Engine/transaxle separation is similar to that given for the 912 and 911, with exception of Step 25.
22. Installation is essentially a reverse of the removal procedure, with the addition of the following Steps.
23. Be especially careful that the injection valve fuel lines aren't squashed when repositioning the engine. The parking brake cables go above the engine mount.
24. Torque the engine mount Allen bolts to 22 ft/lbs. The transmission mount nuts are tightened to 15 ft/lbs. Tighten the axle driveshaft bolts to 33 ft/lbs.
25. Adjust the clutch as described later.
26. Adjust the throttle cable.
27. Refill the engine and transaxle with lubricant.
28. Lower the car. Start the engine and check for leaks.

Cylinder Head

For removal and installation, see the engine Disassembly and Assembly Section.

Rocker Shafts

REMOVAL AND INSTALLATION

911

Each rocker arm has an individual shaft on this single overhead camshaft engine. One or all of the shafts and rocker arms may be removed with the engine in the chassis.

1. Remove the camshaft housing cover nuts and spring washers. Remove the covers.
2. Scribe the rocker arms being removed so that they can be returned to the same position.
3. Unscrew the Allen bolt in the rocker shaft. Push the shaft out of its bore and remove it along with the rocker arm.

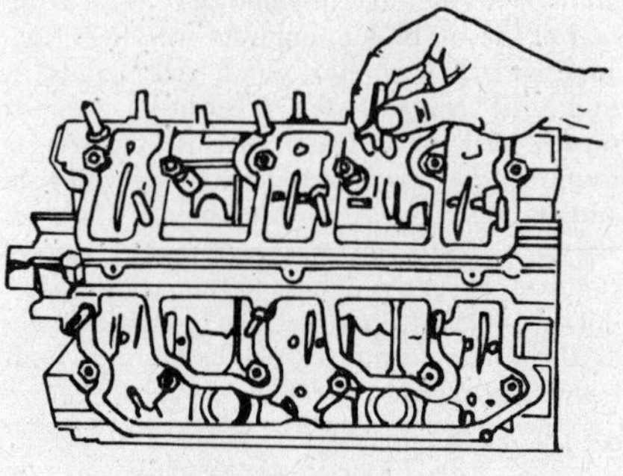

911 rocker arm removal

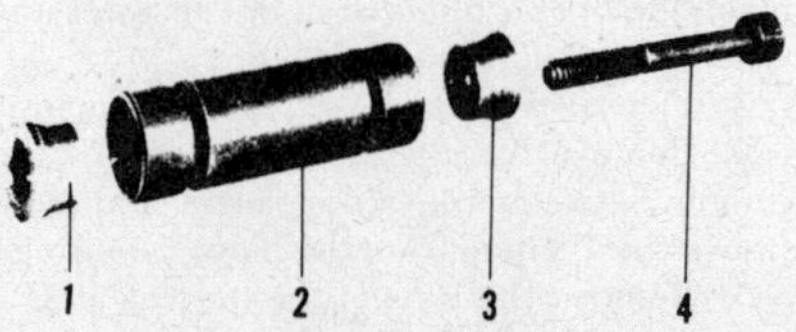

1. Allen nut cone
2. Shaft
3. Bushing cone
4. Allen bolt

911 rocker arm shaft assembly

NOTE: If the rocker is under pressure, you won't be able to push the shaft out. Turn the crankshaft until the rocker rests on the heel of the cam lobe.

4. Check the rocker arm and shaft for excessive wear or damage. Replace any suspect piece.

NOTE: End rockers are installed with the Allen screw heads facing towards cylinders No. 2 and 5 respectively.

5. Place the rocker arm on its shaft.
6. The rocker arm shaft should be centered in its bore so that each groove is recessed 0.059 in (1.15 mm).
   a. Insert a 0.06 in. feeler gauge in the groove on one side of the shaft. Push the

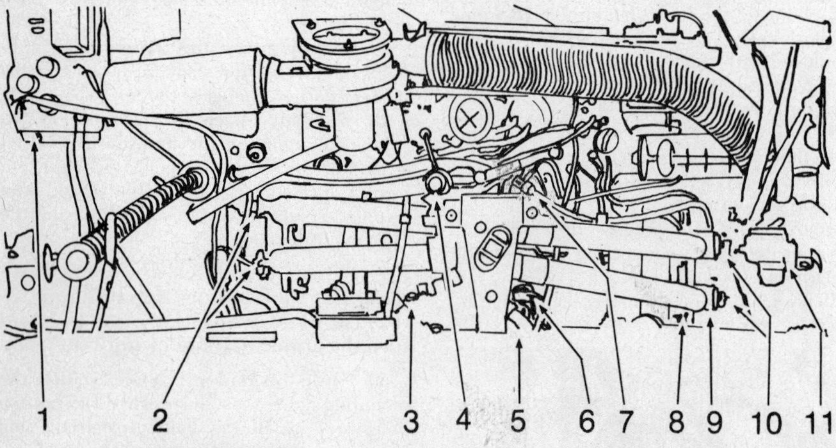

1. Voltage supply relay 4-pole
2. Two injection valves left 2-pole
3. One throttle valve switch 4-pole
4. Temperature feeler 1-pole
5. Mass connections 3-pole
6. Cold starting valve 2-pole
7. Thermal switch 1-pole
8. Ignition distributor release contact 3-pole
9. Temperature feeler 1-pole
10. Two injection valves right 2-pole
11. Pressure feeler 4-pole

914 fuel injection connections

shaft in until the feeler gauge is held tight against the edge.

b. Carefully remove the gauge and push the shaft in approximately 0.06 in. more, using the feeler gauge to judge the distance.

7. Tighten the Allen bolt to 156 in/lbs.
8. Install the camshaft cover.

914 and 912E

Each cylinder head mounts two rocker assemblies, each one consisting of a shaft and two rocker arms. Each shaft is mounted in two bearings which are positioned on studs and retained by nuts. The rocker arm shaft assemblies can be removed with the engine in the car.

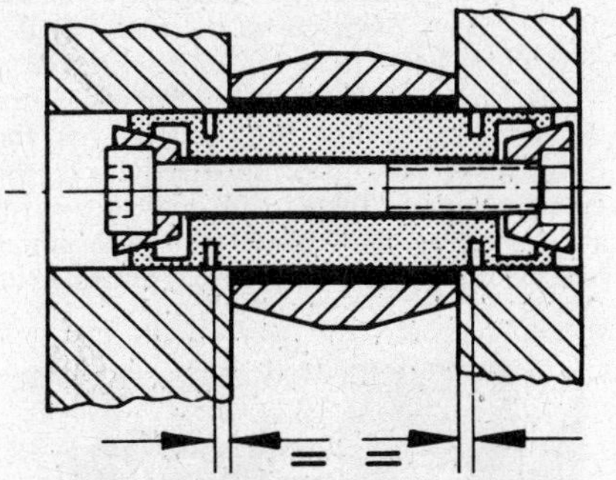

Correct rocker arm shaft positioning

1. Remove the rocker arm cover.
2. Unscrew the retaining nuts and lift the rocker arm assemblies off the cylinder head.
3. When installing the rocker arm assemblies, the open slots of the bearings must face down.
4. With the rocker assemblies mounted on the head, tighten the retaining nuts to 120 in/lbs.

Exhaust Pipe and Muffler

REMOVAL AND INSTALLATION

911 and 912E

1. Remove the flange nuts and bolts.
2. Loosen the retaining clamps and detach the muffler from its support.
3. Position the muffler on its support and then fit the clamps.
4. Install new gaskets between the muffler and exhaust manifold/heat exchanger.
5. Install and alternately tighten the flange nuts and bolts.

To remove only the exhaust pipe:

1. Remove the two tailpipe-to-muffler retaining bolts.
2. Pull the tailpipe out of the muffler.
3. Install the tailpipe using two new gasket rings. Tighten the two retaining bolts.

To remove the tailpipe and muffler:

1. Remove the three flange nuts on each side.
2. Pry the muffler loose and remove it.
3. Use new flange gaskets when installing the muffler. Tighten the six flange retaining nuts alternately.

Exhaust Manifold/Heat Exchanger

REMOVAL AND INSTALLATION

911, 912E and 914

1. Remove the muffler as previously outlined. Detach and remove the connecting hose from the heat exchanger to the heater valve chamber.
2. Detach the heater hose from the heat exchanger.
3. Remove the three sunken bolts from the bottom of the heat exchanger.
4. Remove the six cylinder head-to-heat exchanger nuts using a universal socket set-up.

NOTE: For 914 models, skip Steps 3 and 4 and loosen the four retaining clamps.

5. Remove the heat exchanger.
6. Examine the heat exchanger for damaged flanges or cracks. Replace it, if necessary.
7. Install the heat exchanger in a reverse order of the removal procedure. Use new flange gaskets and tighten the retaining nuts and bolts alternately.

Engine Disassembly and Assembly

Further component removal and installation requires engine removal and disassembly. Follow the steps of engine disassembly and then assembly for the part being replaced. A general engine rebuilding section is included at the end of the book.

911

Follow the disassembly procedure for four cylinder Porsche engines up to the rocker carriers and the cylinder heads. Further disassembly of the 911 engine is as follows:

Removal of the cylinder heads on the 911 involves removing the overhead camshafts. All three cylinder heads on each bank can be removed as a unit complete with the camshaft and rockers or each cylinder head can be removed individually. For access to the cylinder heads and valves, the camshaft housing must be disassembled and removed.

Rockers. Scribe a mark on the rockers for later installation. Remove the 5 mm Allen retaining screws in the rocker shafts, holding the cone-nut that is released on the other end of the shaft. Push out the shafts and lift away the rockers. *Position the camshaft so that the cam lobe does not press against the rocker being removed.*

Camshaft. Remove the timing chain cover at each camshaft. Unbolt the chain tensioner and the intermediate wheel, using tools P 202 and P 203. Withdraw the dowel pin from the camshaft wheel with tool P212. Remove the sliding wedges and withdraw the wheel and flange. Take the key from the camshaft, unscrew the three sealing ring screws, and remove the sealing ring together with the O-ring and the gasket. Withdraw the camshaft toward the rear. Note that both camshafts turn in the same direction and therefore require that the cam lobes be positioned differently.

Cam housing. Unscrew the hex nuts and the three Allen screws to lift off the camshaft housing. Each housing fits either cylinder bank.

Cylinder head. Loosen the cylinder head securing nuts (using tool P 119) and remove the cylinder head. Cylinders are numbered

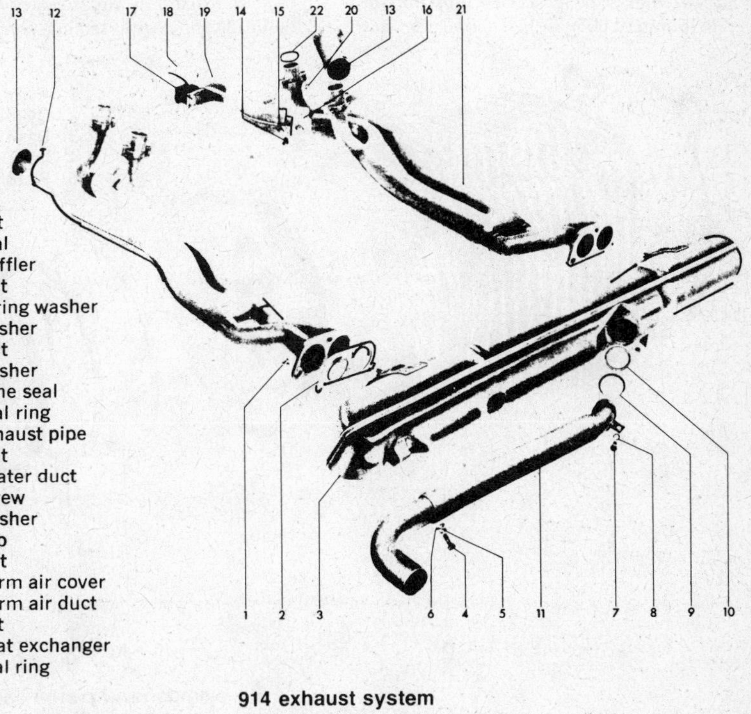

1. Nut
2. Seal
3. Muffler
4. Bolt
5. Spring washer
6. Washer
7. Bolt
8. Washer
9. Cone seal
10. Seal ring
11. Exhaust pipe
12. Bolt
13. Heater duct
14. Screw
15. Washer
16. Clip
17. Bolt
18. Warm air cover
19. Warm air duct
20. Nut
21. Heat exchanger
22. Seal ring

914 exhaust system

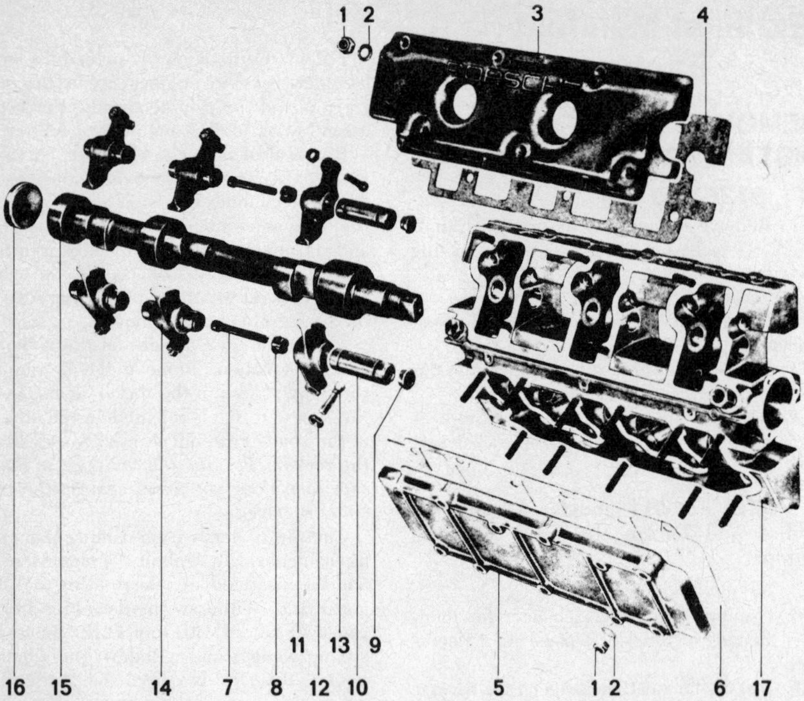

1. Nut
2. Aluminum washer
3. Cover
4. Gasket
5. Cover
6. Gasket
7. Bolt
8. Bushing
9. Nut
10. Rocker arm shaft
11. Rocker arm
12. Nut
13. Adjusting screw
14. Rocker arm assembly
15. Camshaft
16. Cover
17. Housing

Six cylinder camshaft housing assembly

from the crankshaft pulley on the left bank as 1, 2 and 3 (left when facing the front of the car), and on the right bank as 4, 5 and 6.

The upper and lower sealing surfaces of the cylinder head (between the head and the camshaft and between the head and the cylinder) should not be machined. Permitted distortion at the cylinder seating surface must not exceed 0.15 mm (0.0059 in.). Examine the mating surfaces to ensure that they are in good condition.

When installing the cylinder heads, use new cylinder head gaskets with the perforations set toward the cylinder. Carefully position each head, insert the washers and tighten the hex nuts lightly.

The camshaft housing is sealed to the cylinder heads only with sealing compound. Assemble the camshaft housing and oil return pipes on the cylinder heads, but only hand-tighten.

The Porsche factory workshop manual suggests that at this point in reassembly, the cylinder head be torqued down first and then the camshaft housing. Some mechanics prefer to torque the camshaft housing first for more accurate tensioning. Either way, the camshaft must be checked frequently for free turning. If tightening one side binds the crankshaft, tightening the opposite side must free it again. If not, the housing must be loosened and tightening steps must be made in a different sequence.

Tighten the cylinder head to 21.6-23.8 ft/lbs (3.0-3.3 mkg). Tighten the camshaft housing to 15.9-18.1 ft/lbs (2.2-2.5 mkg).

From this point, further disassembly of the 911 engine is the same as the four cylinder procedure. Valve timing is outlined below.

Valve timing adjustment for the 911. Turn the crankshaft until the mark Z1 on the crankshaft pulley lines up exactly with the crankcase joint. Taking care that the valves and pistons do not collide with each other, turn both camshafts (tool P 202) to bring the

Removing the camshaft housing and cylinder heads as a unit

1. Head gasket
2. Cylinder
3. Base seal
4. Lock ring
5. Piston pin
6. Piston
7. Top compression ring
8. Bottom compression ring
9. Oil control ring

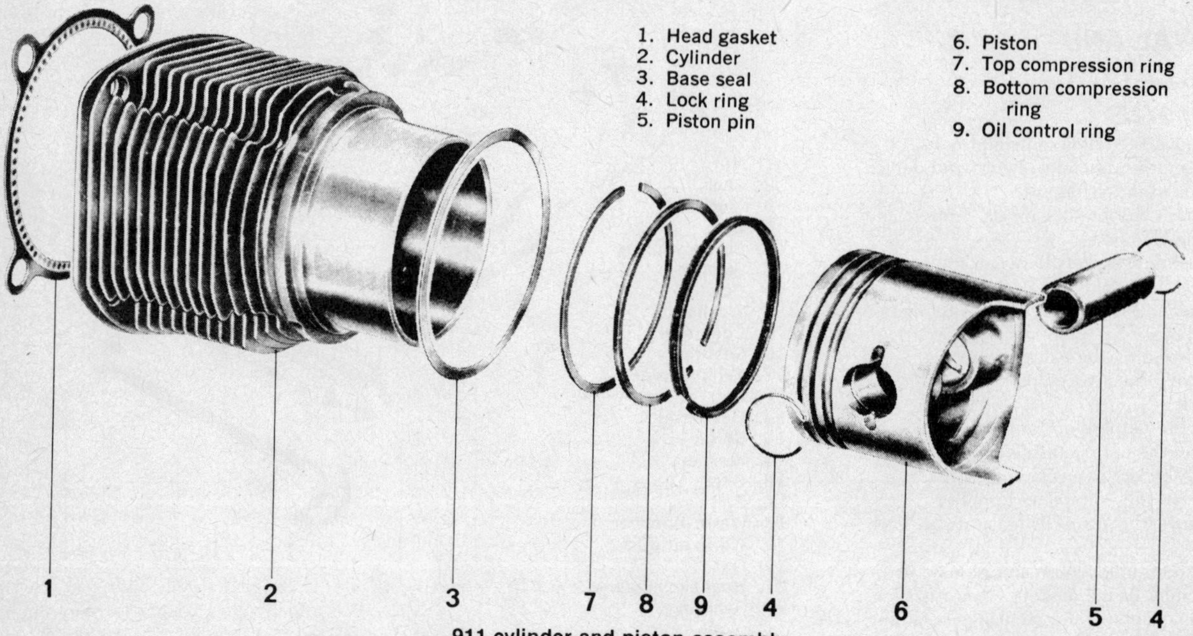

911 cylinder and piston assembly

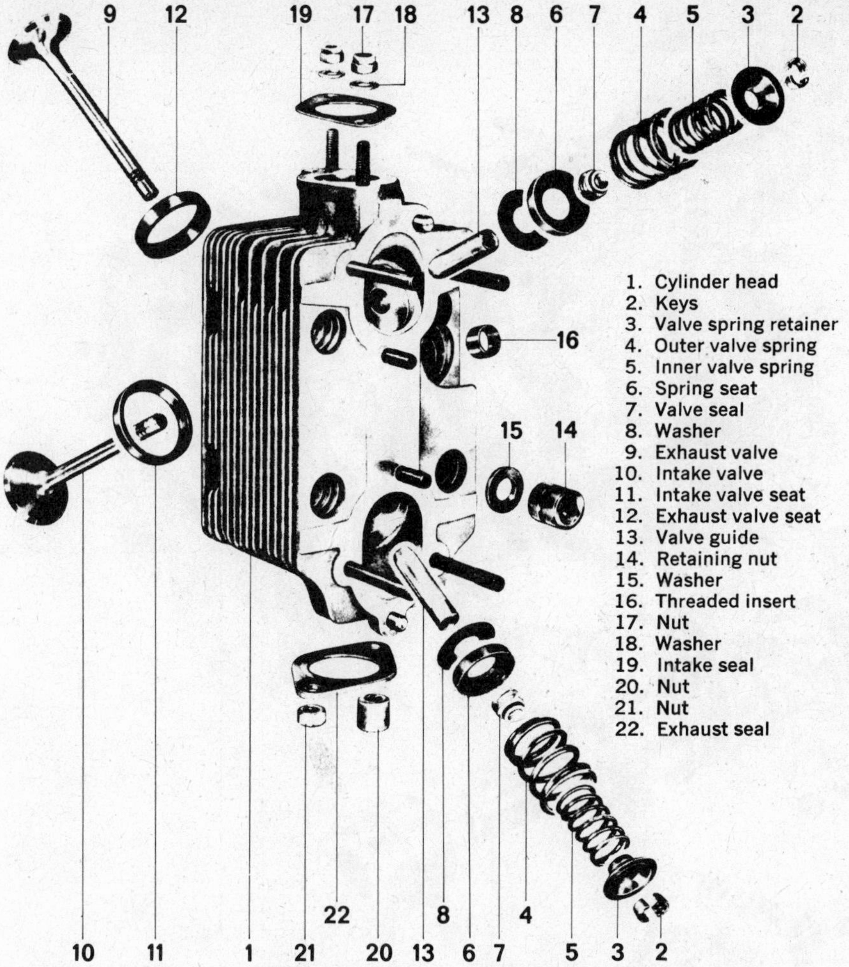

911 cylinder head components

Six cylinder valve timing position

Four cylinder engine timing marks

punch marks, stamped on the face of the camshafts, exactly above the shaft vertical center. Back off a little if the slightest resistance is felt during the turn. Then turn the free shaft to bring the valves and pistons into proper harmony before continuing with the first shaft.

With the crankshaft timing marks aligned and the camshaft punch marks exactly on the top, the engine is timed at the firing point in cylinder No. 1 with overlapping in cylinder No. 4. Find which hole in the camshaft sprocket lines up with a corresponding hole in the sprocket flange and insert the aligning dowel pin.

Slip on the washer and tighten the retaining nut to 101 ft/lbs (14.7 mkg).

Adjust cylinder No. 1 intake valve clearance to 0.10 mm (0.004 in.) and attach a dial gauge. The gauge sensor must be positioned exactly on the edge of the valve spring retaining collar. Adjust the gauge to a preload of 10 mm (0.39 in.) to provide for sensor travel when the cam lobe depresses the valve. Depress the chain tensioner with a screwdriver to tighten the chain (on the side to be measured) and turn the crankshaft one complete turn until the timing marks are aligned again. The dial gauge should read between 4.2 and 4.6 mm (0.165-0.181 in.). A preferred range is 4.25 to 4.45 mm.

If the gauge shows a lower or higher reading, the camshaft has to be readjusted as follows:

1. Remove the sprocket retaining nut, spring washer and aligning dowel pin.
2. Make sure that the crankshaft pulley mark is still aligned with the crankcase joint.
3. Depress the tensioner to tighten the chain and turn the camshaft until the dial gauge indicates 4.4 to 4.45 mm (0.173-0.175 in.).
4. Find the hole in the camshaft sprocket which lines up with the sprocket flange and insert the dowel pin. Replace the spring washer and nut and tighten.
5. Turn the crankshaft two complete turns to the right and read the dial gauge. If the specified value is still not obtained, repeat the steps above.

When the valves overlap in cylinder No. 1, cylinder No. 4 is at firing point (TDC). Repeat the procedure for cylinder No. 4 valve timing adjustment.

914 AND 912E

Mount the engine on a stand. Drain the engine oil and remove the muffler and heat exchanger. Remove the rear engine cover plate. Remove the intake distributor and intake pipe with the injection valves (on fuel injection engines). Remove the ignition distributor and the front engine cover plate. Remove the cooling blower impeller. Remove the cooling blower housing with the alternator attached. Remove the engine mount. Remove the front and rear cylinder jackets with the warm air guides. Remove the oil cooler, oil filter and oil pump. Remove the rocker arm shafts with the protective tubes, pushrods and tappets. Remove the cylinder heads, cylinders and pistons. Remove the clutch and flywheel. Disassemble the crankcase, being careful not to score any of the mating surfaces by trying to pry the halves apart. Remove the camshaft and crankshaft with the connecting rods.

Assembly is the reverse of disassembly, noting the following procedures. Check the riveting of the camshaft gear and the camshaft. Check the camshaft for out-of-true using V-blocks. The maximum allowable wear is 0.0016 in. Check the end-play of the guide bearing which should be 0.0016-0.0051 in. The oil holes in the crankshaft bearing journals and bearings should have no sharp edges. Carefully remove any metallic foreign substances. Install the crankshaft and connecting rods. Install the camshaft and gear so that the tooth marked with a 0 is located between the two teeth of the crankshaft gear which are identified with a punch mark. Coat the mating surfaces of the housing halves with a thin coat of sealing compound. Be sure that no sealing compound enters the oil ducts. Assemble the crankcase halves and lightly tighten the screw for the oil intake pipe. Screw on the sealing nuts with the sealing ring on the outside and tighten to the specified torque. Rotate the crankshaft to ensure free rotation. Grease the needle bearing in the flywheel with a small amount of multipurpose grease. Moisten the felt ring with engine oil, wiping off any excess. Install the flywheel and adjust the axial play of the crankshaft. Measure the axial play by installing the flywheel with two spacing washers

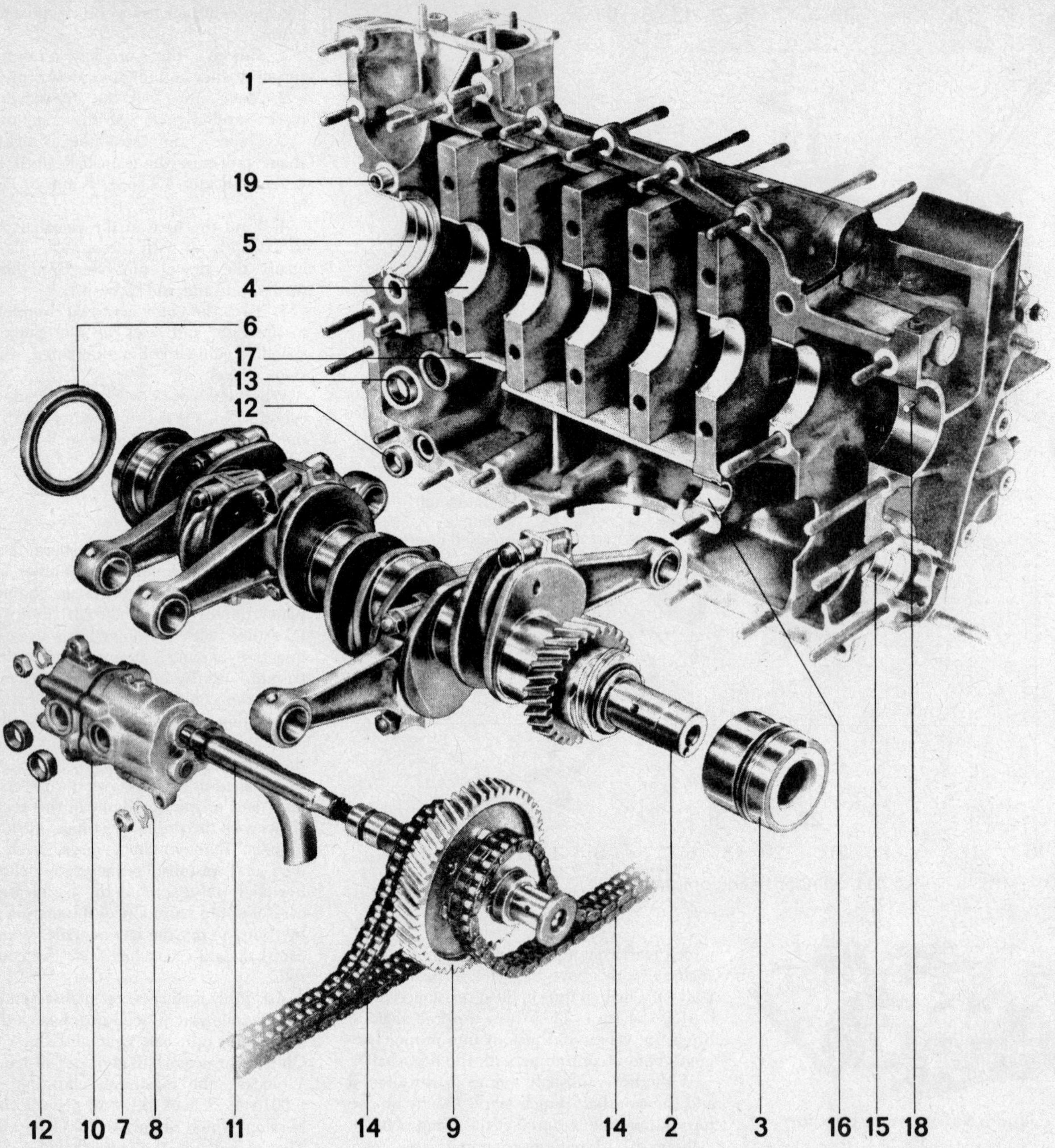

1. Crankcase half
2. Crankshaft assembly
3. No. 8 bearing
4. Bearing shell
5. Thrust bearing shell
6. Seal
7. Nut
8. Lock washer
9. Intermediate shaft
10. Oil pump assembly
11. Connecting shaft
12. Seal
13. Seal
14. Camshaft chain
15. Intermediate shaft thrust bearing
16. Intermediate shaft bearing
17. Oil strainer
18. pin
19. bushing

Six cylinder crankcase assembly

but without the sealing rings. Using a dial gauge, measure the play by rotating the flywheel. The thickness of the third spacer can be computed by subtracting 0.0039 in. from the measured result. Remove the flywheel and install the sealing ring, felt ring, and three spacers. Three spacers must always be installed for the required thickness. Spacers are available in the following sizes: 0.0094, 0.0118, 0.0126, 0.0134, 0.0142 and 0.0150 in. Each spacer is marked for proper identification. The axial play of the crankshaft, measured with the engine assembled and the flywheel screwed on, should be 0.0028-0.0051 in. Clean the contact surface of the clutch disc and flywheel. Check the splining of the input shaft and coat lightly with molybdenum disulphide powder, applied with a brush. The clutch disc should slide easily. Check the throwout bearing. Do not wash in any solvent but wipe it clean. Replace bearings which are contaminated or noisy. Grease the guide bushing lightly with molybdenum disulphide paste. Center the clutch disc and clutch on

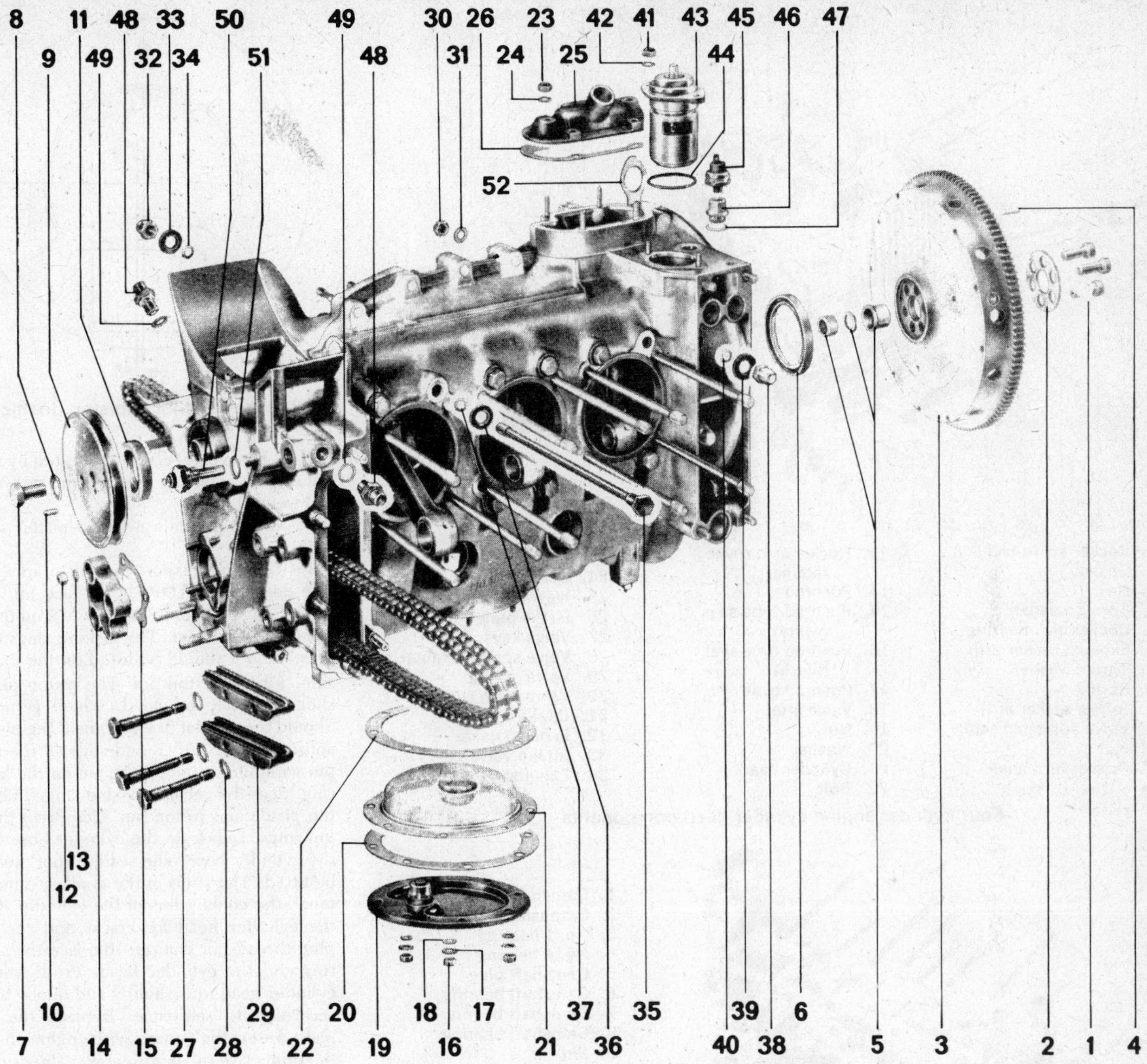

1. Bolt
2. Washer
3. Flywheel
4. Pin
5. Bushing
6. Seal
7. Bolt
8. Spring washer
9. Pulley
10. Pin
11. Seal
12. Nut
13. Washer
14. Cover
15. Seal
16. Nut
17. Spring washer
18. Washer
19. Cover
20. Seal
21. Oil strainer
22. seal
23. Nut
24. Washer
25. Breather cover
26. Seal
27. Slide rail bolt
28. Seal
29. Slide rail
30. Nut
31. Washer
32. Nut
33. Washer
34. Seal
35. Crankcase bolt
36. Washer
37. Seal
38. Nut
39. Washer
40. Seal
41. Nut
42. Spring washer
43. Thermostat
44. Seal
45. Oil pressure switch

Six cylinder crankcase assembly

the flywheel using an input shaft. When a new clutch is installed, the balancing marks should be 180° apart. A white paint stripe on the outside edge of the flywheel indicates the heavy end, and a white paint stripe indicates the heavy end of the clutch. Tighten the bolts to 14.5 ft/lbs. Clean all pistons and check for wear. Check the marking of the pistons according to the following designations:

A.—The letter next to the arrow is the index of the spare parts number.

B.—The punched in arrow indicates that the piston must be installed with the arrow facing the flywheel.

C.—The color dot (blue, pink or green) indicates the paired size of the piston.

D.—A statement of weight class (+ or −) is punched in or printed.

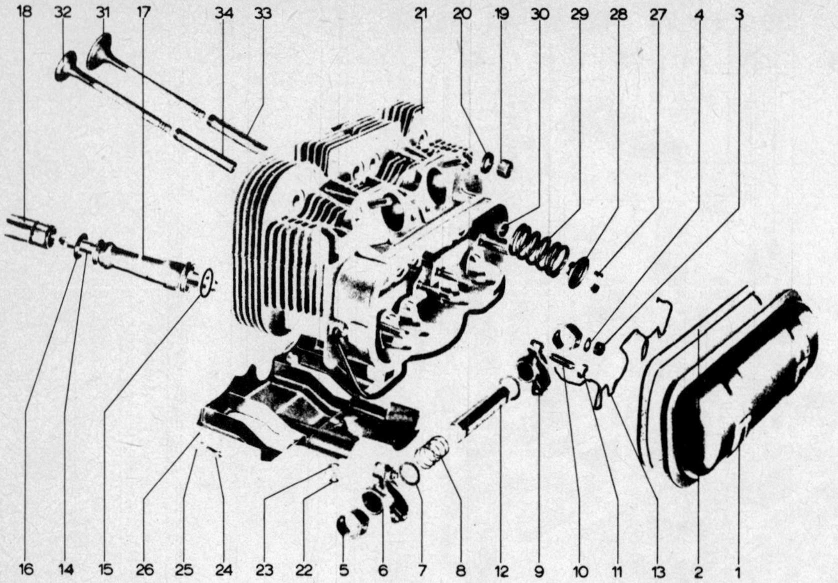

1. Rocker arm cover
2. Gasket
3. Nut
4. Spring washer
5. Rocker arm bearing
6. Exhaust rocker arm
7. Thrust washer
8. Spring
9. Intake rocker arm
10. Valve adjusting screw
11. Nut
12. Rocker arm shaft
13. Rocker arm cover retainer
14. Pushrod
15. Pushrod tube seal (white)
16. Pushrod tube seal (black)
17. Pushrod tube
18. Valve lifter
19. Nut
20. Washer
21. Cylinder head
22. Bolt
23. Washer
24. Bolt
25. Washer
26. Baffle plate
27. Valve keys
28. Valve spring retainer
29. Valve spring
30. Valve stem seal
31. Intake valve
32. Exhaust valve
33. Intake valve guide
34. Exhaust valve guide

Four cylinder engine cylinder head components

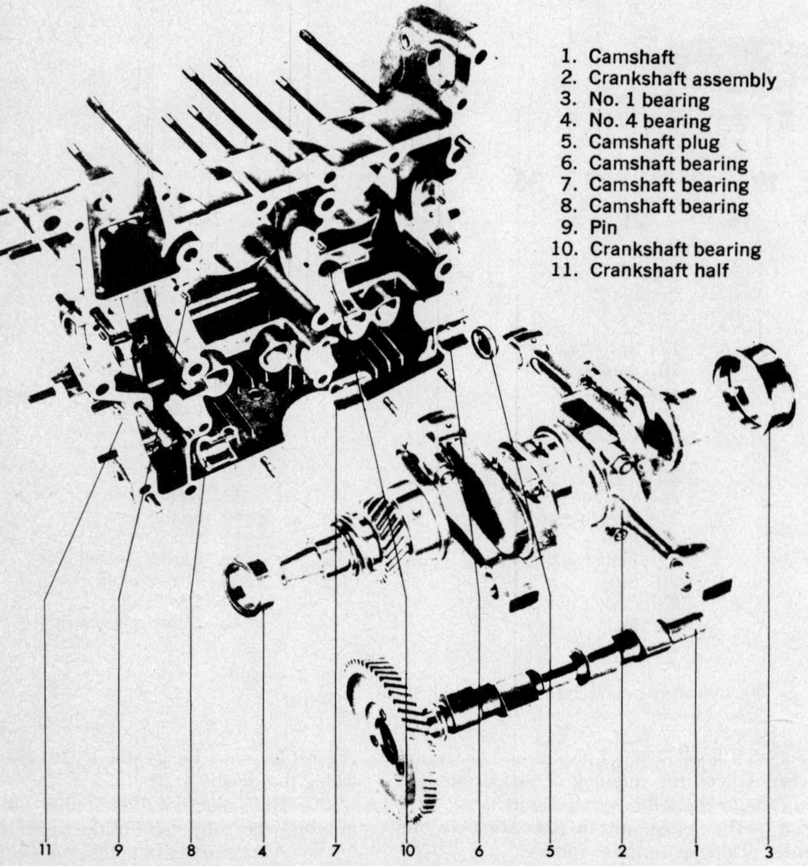

1. Camshaft
2. Crankshaft assembly
3. No. 1 bearing
4. No. 4 bearing
5. Camshaft plug
6. Camshaft bearing
7. Camshaft bearing
8. Camshaft bearing
9. Pin
10. Crankshaft bearing
11. Crankshaft half

Four cylinder engine crankcase and crankshaft assembly

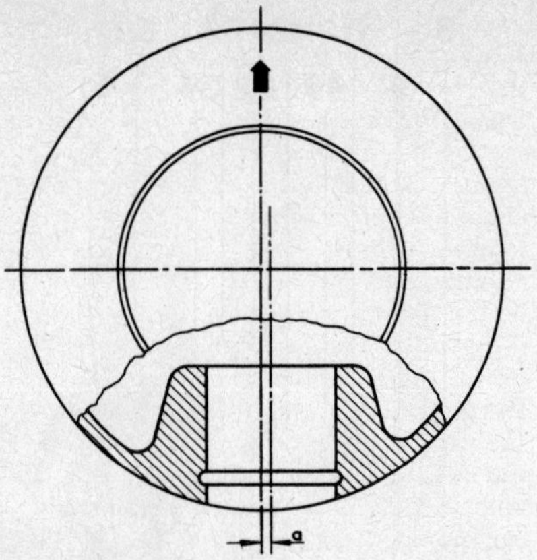

Four cylinder engine piston positioning

E.—The weight class is indicated by a color dot (brown equals (−) weight and grey equals (+) weight).

F.—Number indicates the piston size in mm.

Fit the compression and oil scraper rings. The designation TOP should face up. Insert the locking rings of pistons 1 and 2 on the side facing the flywheel. The locking rings of pistons 3 and 4 should be fitted on the impeller side. Fit the piston pin. The piston pin may slide in easily by hand, which is normal. Should the pin not fit easily, heat the piston to approximately 176° F and slide in the piston pin without bottoming the pin on the locking ring. Seat the second locking ring. Lubricate the piston and piston pin. Compress the piston rings. Lubricate the cylinder bore and fit the cylinder bore. The sealing ring must also be fitted. The studs of the crankcase may not touch the cooling fins of the cylinder. Check the cylinder head for cracks and the spark plug threads for damage. Replace the sealing ring and the cylinder head. Pre-tighten the cylinder head nuts slightly and finally tighten according to sequence. Replace the baffle plate. Insert the tappets with engine oil. Slide the protective tubes with new sealing rings up to the stop, taking care not to damage the sealing rings. Slide the bearing pieces on the rocker arm shafts so that the slots face downward and the broken edges outward when settling on the studs. The clip which secures the protective tubes should enter the slots of the bearing pieces and rest against the bottom edges of the protective tubes. Lubricate the gear wheel and driveshaft and insert into the oil pump housing. Install the oil pump cover with the lubricated rubber sealing ring. Check the gear wheels for proper running. Install the oil pump, with a new seal, into the crankcase. The journal of the driveshaft should be in alignment with the slot in the camshaft gear. Center the oil pump by two crankshaft revolutions and tighten the nuts. Clean the sealing surface on the flange for the oil filter. Lubricate the rubber seal slightly and screw the filter in until the filter is seated. Tighten the oil filter. Replace the oil cooler after checking for leaks and tightening all welded seats. Replace the front and rear cylinder jackets and warm air guides. Replace the engine mount. Replace the cooling blower housing with the alternator and adjust the V-belt tension. Replace the cooling blower impeller and the front engine cover plate. Replace the ignition distributor. Bring cylinder No. 1 to the firing point. The black notch should be in alignment with the reference mark. The center offset slot in the head of the ignition distributor driveshaft should be at an angle of approximately 12° in relation to the longitudinal axis of the engine. Turn the distributor rotor to the mark for cylinder No. 1 on the distributor housing. Insert the ignition distributor. Replace the oil filler neck with the oil vent. Replace the intake distributor with the intake pipes and injection valves. Mount the rear engine cover plate. Replace the exhaust muffler and heat exchanger. Fill the engine with oil and replace the engine in the car. Adjust the ignition timing.

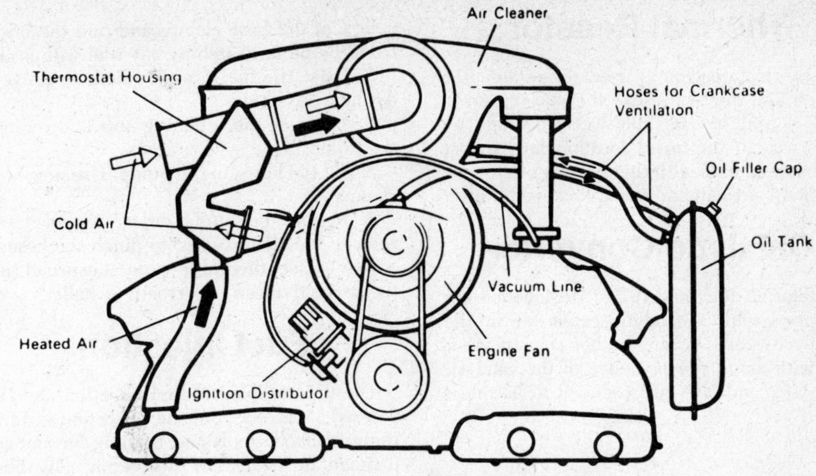

911 crankcase ventilation schematic

EMISSION CONTROLS

Crankcase Ventilation System

All models are equipped with a crankcase ventilation systems. The purpose of the crankcase ventilation system is two-fold. It keeps harmful vapors from escaping into the atmosphere and prevents the buildup of pressures within the crankcase which could cause oil leaks.

The 911 system carries vapors from the crankcase to the oil tank and then to the air cleaner. The crankcase emissions are then burned along with the air/fuel mixture. The ventilation system on 914 models supplies fresh air from the air cleaner to the rocker arm covers, where it mixes with crankcase vapors and continues through the pushrod tubes and into the crankcase. The mixture of fresh air and crankcase vapors is then released through the oil breather and a regulator valve into the intake air distributor to be burned with the air/fuel mixture. The only maintenance required on the crankcase ventilation system is a periodic check. At every tune-up, examine the hoses for clogging or deterioration. Clean or replace the hoses as required.

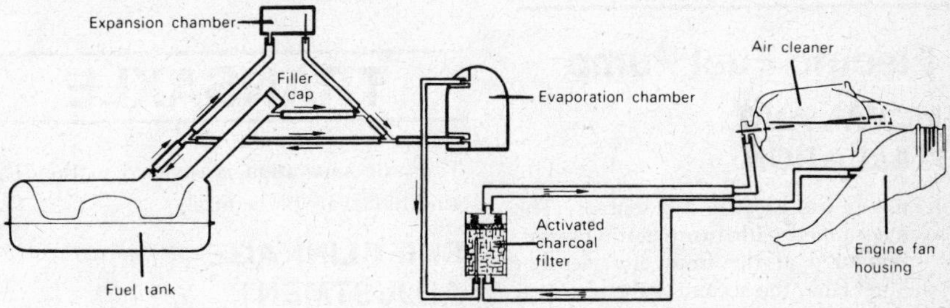

911 evaporative emission control system

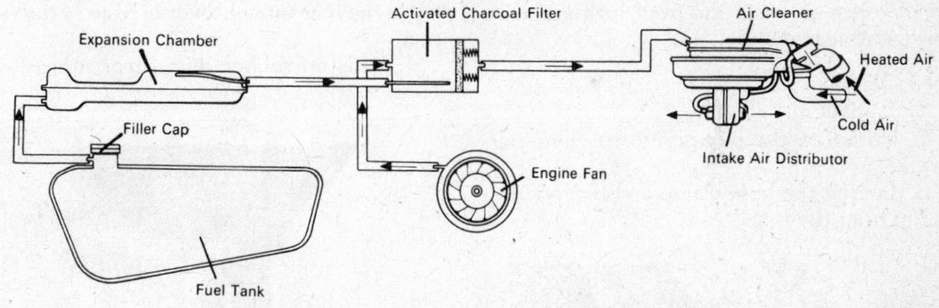

914 evaporative emission control system

Evaporative Emission Control System

The systems used on the 911, 912E and 914 are basically similar and consist of an expansion chamber evaporation chamber, and an activated charcoal filter. Fuel vapors which reach the filter deposit hydrocarbons on the surface of the charcoal element. The engine fan forces fresh air into the charcoal filter when the engine is running. The air purges the filter and the hydrocarbons are sent into the air cleaner where they become part of the air/fuel mixture and are burned.

Maintenance on this system consists of checking the condition of the various connecting lines and the charcoal filter at 10,000 mile intervals. The charcoal filter, which is located in the front luggage compartment on all models, should be replaced at 50,000 mile intervals.

Dual Diaphragm Distributors

The purpose of the dual diaphragm distributor is to improve exhaust emissions during idling. The distributor has a vacuum retard diaphragm, in addition to a vacuum advance diaphragm.

TESTING

All Models

1. Connect a timing light to the engine. Check the ignition timing.

2. Remove the retard hose from the distributor and plug it. Increase the engine speed. The ignition timing should advance. If it doesn't, then the vacuum unit is faulty and must be replaced.

Air Injection System

All 1975 914, 912E models and some 911 models are equipped with this system. A belt driven air pump supplies air to the exhaust ports. Injection of air at this point causes combustion of unburned hydrocarbons in the exhaust manifold rather than allowing them to escape into the atmosphere.

Exhaust Gas Recirculation

California 914 models, all 912E models and some 911 models are equipped with EGR. This system directs a portion of the exhaust gases back into the intake where they combine with the incoming mixture. This diluting of the mixture lowers peak combustion temperatures and reduces NO_x.

Thermal Reactor

A thermal reactor is used on certain 911 models and the 912E. The thermal reactor is used to reduce HC and CO emissions by supplying an improved location for exhaust combustion. 911s with the thermal reactor are equipped with an additional heater blower.

Catalytic Converter

California delivered 1975-76 914 models are equipped with a catalytic converter in the exhaust system. When the hot exhaust gases mix with air in the presence of the catalyst, HC, CO, and NO_x are reduced to harmless gases.

FUEL SYSTEM

Electric Fuel Pump

REMOVAL AND INSTALLATION

All models use electric fuel pumps. The Turbo is equipped with two electric pumps. One is mounted at the front crossmember near the fuel tank, the second at the rear near the engine. All 911 and 912E model fuel pumps are located at the front near the tank. The 1975-76 fuel pump is located behind a small access panel in the front luggage compartment near the fuel tank.

911, 912E

1. Remove the cap nuts.
2. Withdraw the pump with its mounting bracket.
3. Loosen the hose clamp and remove the pump from the bracket.

911 fuel pump removal

4. Loosen the hose clamps and remove the three fuel lines from the pump.
5. Install the pump using a reverse of the removal procedure. Coat both electrical terminals with grease and make sure that the rubber boot is firmly seated.

914

1. Pinch the fuel hoses to prevent spillage and remove the cable plug.
2. Cut the hose clamps and pull the hoses from the pump, catching any fuel with a rag.
3. Raise the fuel pressure hose to prevent draining any fuel.
4. Unscrew the retaining nuts and remove the pump.
5. Fit the hoses to the pump. Use new hose clamps.
6. Mount the pump on its supports and remove the clamps used to pinch the hoses.
7. Replace the cable plug, ensuring that the protective cap is correctly installed.

Fuel Injection

The 911 mechanical fuel injection and the 914 and 912E electronic fuel injection systems require special tools and training for any adjustment or repair. For this reason, only those having access to these tools and possessing this training should work on these systems.

TRANSAXLE

Transaxle separation is covered in the "Engine Removal" procedure.

SHIFT LINKAGE ADJUSTMENT

911, 912E

1. Position the shift lever in Neutral. Remove the rear tunnel cover in front of the rear seat.
2. Pull the rubber dust cover forward on the shift rod.

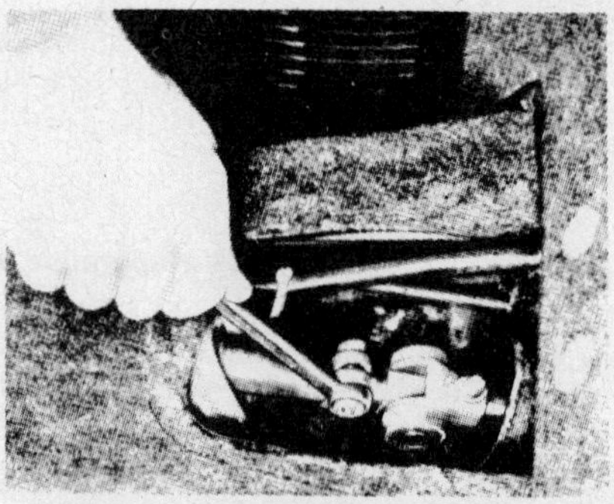

911 and 912 linkage adjustment

3. Loosen the clamp bolt on the shift rod.
4. Move the transmission selector shaft all the way to its left stop, keeping it in Neutral.
5. With the transmission still in Neutral, move the gearshift rod to the right to its stop.
6. Tighten the clamp bolt to 18 ft/lbs.
7. Test the shift lever. Play should be the same in all gears in all directions.

1975-76 914

1. Loosen the shift linkage retaining bolt on the shift mount.
2. Place the shift lever in Neutral and to the right (toward the Fourth and Fifth gear side).
3. Remove the rear tunnel cover in the passenger compartment.
4. Rotate the shift rod clockwise (facing toward the front of the car).
5. Tighten the mounting screw hand-tight.
6. Shift lever travel must be the same for Second, Third, Fourth, and Fifth gears. Make sure that First and Reverse are easily engaged.
7. Finally tighten the mounting bolt to 18 ft/lbs.

CLUTCH

REMOVAL AND INSTALLATION

All Models

Each Porsche covered in this section is equipped with single dry disc clutch and diaphragm pressure plate. Clutch actuation is controlled by a cable.

1. Separate the engine/transaxle.
2. Gradually loosen the pressure plate bolts one or two turns at a time in a criss-cross pattern to prevent distortion.
3. Remove the pressure plate and clutch disc.
4. Check the clutch disc for uneven or excessive lining wear. Examine the pressure plate for cracking, scorching, or scoring. Replace any questionable components.
5. On 912 and 911 models, fill the pilot bearing with about 2 cc of grease.

Clutch disc centering

6. Install the clutch disc and pressure plate. Use a pilot shaft or an old transaxle input shaft to keep the disc centered.
7. Gradually tighten the pressure plate-to-flywheel bolts in a criss-cross pattern. Torque the bolts to 25 ft/lbs on the 912 models. Tighten the bolts on the 914 to 15 ft/lbs. On 911S, tighten the bolts to 18 ft/lbs.
8. Install the throwout bearing.
9. Install the transaxle on the engine.

FREE PLAY ADJUSTMENT

1975-76 911 and 912E

This adjustment is made at the throwout arm on the transaxle. Free-play should be between ¾ in. and 1 in.

1. Jack up the rear of the car and support it on stands.
2. On older models, loosen the locknut on the clevis and turn the adjusting nut as necessary to obtain the correct free-play.

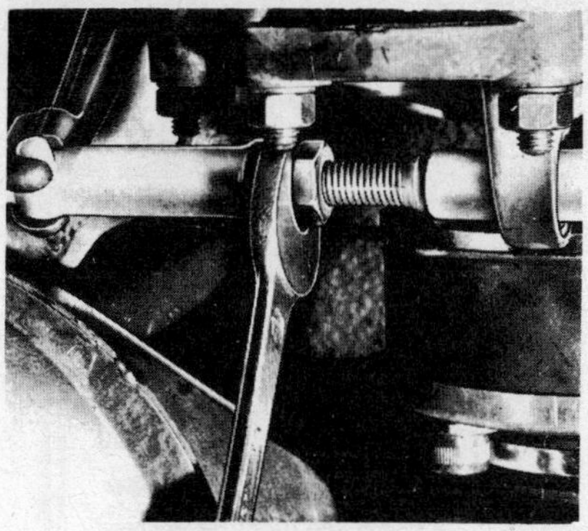

Free-play adjustment

3. A threaded cable extension is provided on later models. While holding the flats on the cable end to prevent it from turning, screw the self-locking nut in or out for the correct free-play.

1977-81 911S and Turbo

These models are equipped with an auxiliary spring to reduce pedal effort. Free-play is no longer checked at the pedal. Play is checked by measuring the distance between the adjusting belt and the positioning lever. The distance should be 1 mm (0.04 in.).

1. Release the cable.
2. Adjust clutch play to 1.2 mm (0.047 in.).
3. Tighten the cable at the holder until play is reduced to 1 mm. (0.04 in.).
4. Adjust the stop on the pedal floor plate so that the release travel is 25 mm (0.984 in.) for the S or 27 mm (1.063 in.) when the clutch pedal is depressed.

914

1. Raise the rear of the car and support it on jackstands.
2. Hold the threaded cable end with pliers and turn the self-locking adjustment nut in or out until the free-play is ½ in. to ¾ in.

PEDAL TRAVEL ADJUSTMENT

1. Pull the front carpeting back.
2. Loosen the two retaining bolts on the pedal stop.
3. Move the pedal up or down until reverse can be engaged with only a slight amount of gear clash.
4. Tighten the pedal stop bolts.
5. Double check the adjustment by shifting into reverse several times. Reinstall the floor carpeting.

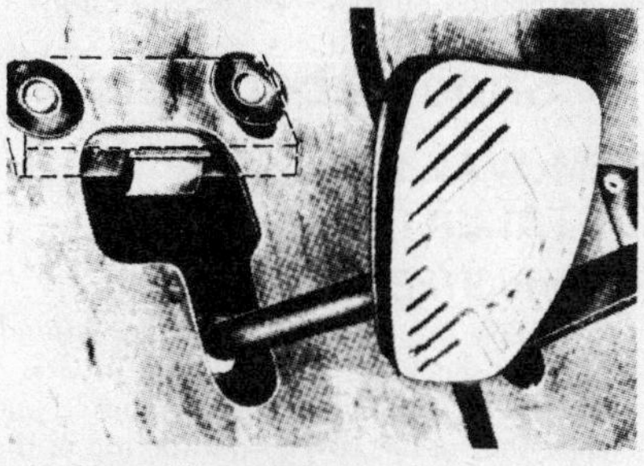

911 and 912 pedal travel adjustment

DRIVE AXLES

Axle Driveshaft

REMOVAL AND INSTALLATION

911 and 912E

1. Jack up the rear of the car and support it on stands.
2. Remove the wheels. Remove the brake caliper and disc.
3. Raise the trailing arm with a hydraulic jack.
4. Remove the lower shock absorber mounting.
5. Install a fixture similar to Porsche tool P36b to hold the hub.

Hub nut removal (Porsche tool P36b shown)

6. Remove the cotter pin and using a long ratchet handle extension, remove the hub nut.
7. Remove the Allen bolts at the axle driveshaft/transaxle flange.
8. Use a flat chisel to pry the flanges apart.

CAUTION

Don't damage the flanges when separating them.

9. Check the axle driveshaft joints for excessive play and replace them if necessary.
10. Use a new gasket on the transaxle flange. Ensure that the flanges are clean and free from burrs.
11. Pack the joints with a moly grease.
12. Install the axle driveshaft using a reverse of the removal procedure.
13. Tighten the flange bolts to 60 ft/lbs. The hollow side of the lock washer should face the spacer slate.
14. Using a long extension handle wrench, tighten the castellated nut to 217-253 ft/lbs and install a new cotter pin.

NOTE: Be prepared to apply considerable force on this nut.

15. Tighten the shock absorber bolt to 54 ft/lbs.
16. Install the brake caliper and disc.
17. Install the wheels and lower the car.

Disconnecting inner driveshaft joint at transaxle

914

1. Raise the rear of the car and support it on jackstands.
2. Remove the wheels.
3. Remove the brake caliper and disc as described in the brake section.
4. Using a ratchet handle with a long extension (a pipe will provide more leverage), remove the castellated hub nut.
5. Remove the heat exchangers.
6. Unscrew the Allen bolts at the transaxle/driveshaft flange.
7. Using a chisel or flat-edged screwdriver, pry the flanges apart and separate the driveshaft.
8. Pull the driveshaft from the hub and down out of the case. Be careful not to damage the flange surfaces.
9. Clean the flanges and install a new gasket.
10. Install the axle driveshaft and tighten the flange bolts to 31 ft/lbs. Use new lock washers and install them so that their hollow ends are against the spacer plate.
11. Tighten the hub nut to 217-253 ft/lbs, using a long extension on the wrench handle and plenty of muscle.
12. Install the brake disc and caliper
13. Install the wheels and lower the car.

REAR SUSPENSION

All models covered in this section have independent rear suspension. The 911 and

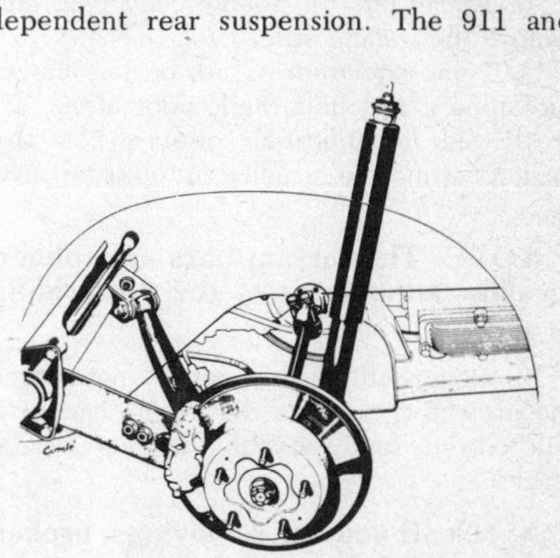

911 and 912 rear suspension

912E rear suspension is a semi-trailing arm design. Springing is provided by transverse torsion bars located forward of each trailing arm. Telescopic shock absorbers at each wheel provide dampening. A rear stabilizer bar is standard equipment on the 911S Turbo and Carrera and optional on the other two 911 models.

The 914 is also equipped with trailing arms, but they are one piece arms as opposed to the two piece arms on the 911. Telescopic strut/shocks with concentric coil springs support the weight of the car. A rear stabilizer bar is optionally available on later models.

Torsion Bars

REMOVAL AND INSTALLATION

911 and 912E

1. Jack up the rear of the car and support it safely with stands.
2. Remove the wheel on the side where the torsion bar is being removed.
3. Fabricate a fixture similar to the one shown. The fixture is necessary to hold the trailing arm while it is raised and lowered. The special Porsche tool for this purpose is number P 289.
4. Using a hydraulic jack under the holding fixture, raise the trailing arm.
5. Remove the lower shock absorber bolt.
6. Remove the trailing arm retaining bolts. Remove the toe and camber adjusting bolts.

Raising the trailing arm

7. Remove the four retaining bolts from the trailing arm cover. Withdraw the spacer.
8. Using two screwdrivers, pry off the trailing arm cover.
9. Remove the holding fixture.
10. Knock out the round body plug and remove the trailing arm.
11. Paint a reference mark on the torsion bar support, matching the location of the "L" or "R" side identification letter, so that the torsion bar may be installed in the same position.

NOTE: The torsion bars are splined to allow adjustment of the rear riding height.

12. Remove the torsion bar. Do not scratch the protective paint on the torsion bar, or it will corrode and possibly develop fatigue cracks.

NOTE: If you are removing a broken torsion bar, the inner end can be knocked from its seat by removing the opposite torsion bar and tapping through with a steel rod. Torsion bars are not interchangeable from side-to-side and are marked "L" and "R" for identification.

13. Check the torsion bar splines for damage and replace it if necessary. If any corrosion is present on the bar, replace it.
14. Coat the torsion bar lightly with a multi-purpose grease. Carefully grease the splines.
15. Apply glycerine or another rubber preservative to the torsion bar support.
16. Install the torsion bar, matching the "L" or "R" with the paint mark you made before removal.

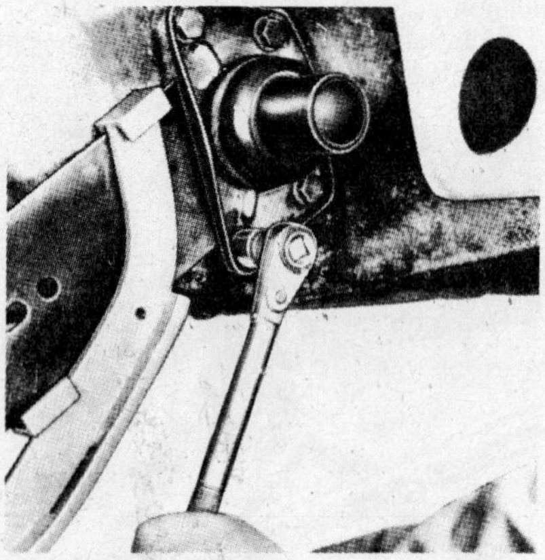

Installing the trailing arm cover

17. Install the trailing arm cover into position and start the three accessible bolts.
18. Raise the trailing arm into place with the holding fixture (or special tool P 289) until the spacer and the fourth bolt can be installed.
19. Assemble the remaining components in a reverse order of their removal.
20. Tighten the trailing arm cover bolts to 34 ft/lbs. Tighten the trailing arm retaining bolts to 65 ft/lbs.
21. Tighten the camber adjusting bolt to 43 ft/lbs and the toe-in adjusting bolt to 36 ft/lbs. Tighten the shock absorber bolt to 45 ft/lbs.
22. Adjust the rear wheel camber and toe-in.

Spring Strut

REMOVAL AND INSTALLATION

914

1. Jack up the rear of the car and support it safely with stands.
2. Support the wheel on the side where the spring strut is being removed.
3. Loosen and remove the bottom through-bolt and nut from the trailing arm.
4. Loosen and remove the nut at the top of the strut. Hold the strut shaft whle loosening the nut.
5. Remove the strut by pulling it down and out of the car.
6. When reinstalling the strut, use a nut at the top. Install the bottom nut and bolt.
7. Tighten the top nut to 36-43 ft/lbs. Torque the bottom bolt to 72-87 ft/lbs.

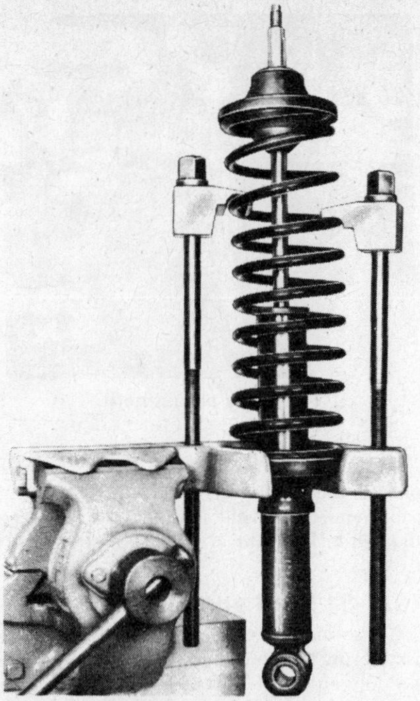

Compressing the coil spring

DISASSEMBLY

914

1. Remove the strut as outlined above.
2. Install the strut in a vise. Grip at the bottom spring retainer.
3. Install a compressor on the coil spring.
4. Alternately tighten the compressor bolts to hold the spring.

CAUTION

Be sure that the lips of the compressor are gripping the coils firmly.

5. Remove the two threaded bushings and remove the top spring retainer.
6. Gradually release the spring compressor. When the spring tension is fully released, remove the spring, bushing, and washer.
7. Using a drift, drive the cap off the shock absorber.
8. Remove the bottom spring retainer by pulling over the top of the shock absorber.
9. Check the shock absorber for correct action by pushing and pulling on the rod. If there is any sloppiness present, replace the shock absorber.
10. Slight oil leakage is within tolerance, but if the shock is leaking badly replace it.
11. Reassembly is basically a reverse of the disassembly Steps. The threaded bushing on the top should be tightened to 11-14 ft/lbs.

Shock Absorbers

REMOVAL AND INSTALLATION

911 and 912E

1. Leave the car standing on the ground, so that the shock absorber is not tensioned.
2. Open the engine compartment lid and remove the rubber cover from the top of the shock absorber.

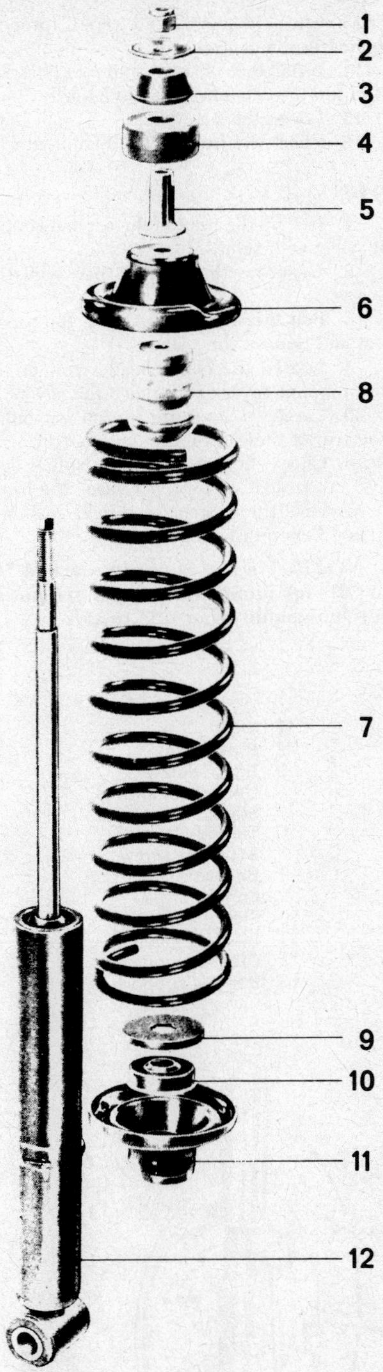

1. Nut
2. Washer
3. Bushing
4. Bushing
5. Threaded bushing
6. Top spring retainer
7. Coil spring
8. Bumper
9. Stop washer
10. Cap
11. Bottom spring retainer
12. Shock absorber

Strut components

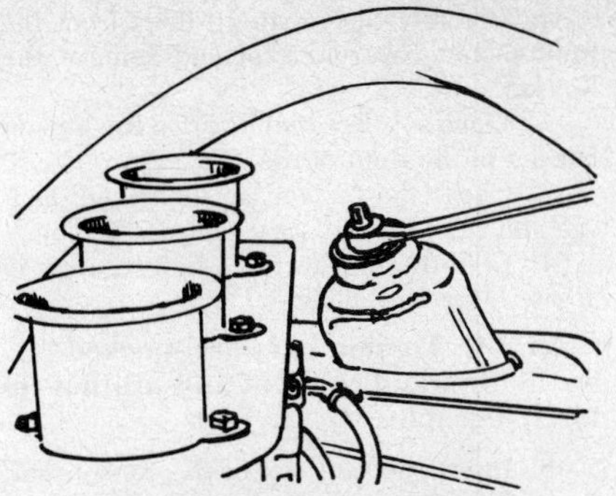

Top shock absorber mounting

Bottom shock absorber mounting

3. Hold the shock absorber shaft and remove the nut.
4. On the bottom, remove the retaining nut and bolt.
5. Remove the shock absorber.
6. If the shock exhibits excessive free travel or is leaking, replace it.
7. Install the shock up through the body and screw the nut on hand-tight.
8. Align the shock absorber eye with the hole in the trailing arm and install the nut and bolt.
9. Tighten the top nut and install the rubber cover.
10. Tighten the bottom retaining bolt to 54 ft/lbs.

Stabilizer

REMOVAL AND INSTALLATION

911 and 912E

1. Jack the rear of the car and safely support it with stands.
2. Using a large screwdriver, pry the upper eyes of the stabilizer bar off the studs in the trailing arm.
3. Remove the body mounting brackets.
4. Remove the stabilizer.
5. Check the rubber bushings for wear or damage and, if necessary, replace them.
6. Install the stabilizer bar using a reverse of the removal steps.

Adjustments

CAMBER ADJUSTMENT

911 and 912E

The rearmost of the two Allen bolts on the trailing arm provides camber adjustment. Tighten the bolt to 43 ft/lbs after the camber is adjusted to specifications.

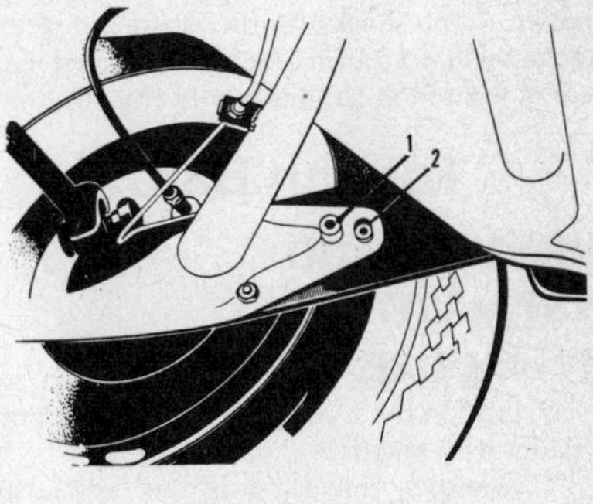

1. Camber
2. Toe-in

911 and 912 rear wheel alignment adjustment points

914

Camber is adjusted by removal or insertion of shims under the trailing arm bearing plate. Scribe the plate's position, so the toe-in setting isn't lost, and then remove the center bolt and loosen the two end bolts. Each 1 mm shim results in a 10′ change in camber. Tighten the bolts to 18 ft/lbs after the correct camber is reached.

TOE-IN ADJUSTMENT

911 and 912E

The front Allen bolt on the trailing arm adjusts the toe-in. Tighten the bolt to 36 ft/lbs after toe-in is adjusted to specification.

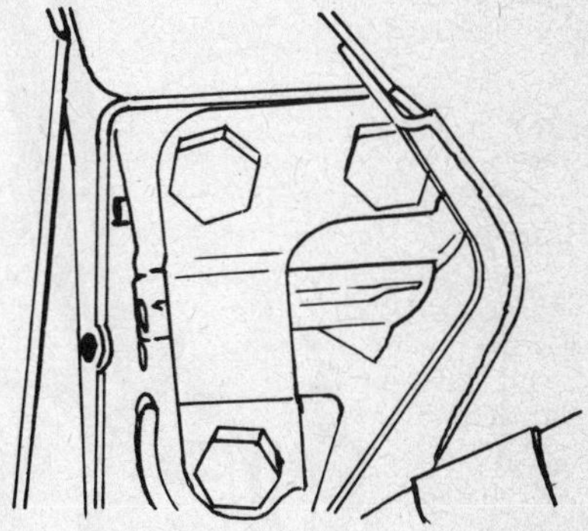

914 rear wheel alignment adjustment point

914

Loosen all three bolts on the trailing arm bearing plate and push the arm forward or backward as necessary to correct the toe-in. Tighten the bolts to 18 ft/lbs when the adjustment is complete.

FRONT SUSPENSION

Front suspension is similar in design on all models; but parts are not interchangeable from one type to the other. Springing is provided by a longitudinal torsion bar at each wheel. A triangular lower arm links the torsion bar to the shock absorber strut and steering knuckle. A permanently lubricated ball joint is located at the bottom of the strut.

Torsion Bars

REMOVAL AND INSTALLATION

911 and 912E

1. Jack up the front of the car and support it safely with stands.
2. Remove the torsion bar adjusting screw.
3. Take the adjusting lever off the torsion bar and withdraw the seal.
4. Unscrew the retaining bolts from the front mount cover bracket and remove the bracket.
5. Using a drift, carefully drive the torsion bar out of the front of the arm.
6. Check the torsion bar for spline damage and rust. If necessary, replace the bar.
7. Give the torsion bar a light coating of grease before installing it.

NOTE: Torsion bars are marked "L" or "R" to identify them and are not interchangeable.

8. Insert the end cap of the torsion bar, protruding side out, into the control arm. Drive the torsion bar into position with a drift. Carefully.
9. Tighten the retaining bolts on the front mount to 34 ft/lbs.
10. Slide the seal onto the torsion bar from the open side of the crossmember.
11. Using a tire iron, or other suitable lever, pry the control arm down as far as possible. While holding the control arm, slide the adjusting lever onto the splines of the torsion bar. There should only be a slight amount of clearance at the lever adjusting point.
12. Grease the adjusting screw threads with a moly grease and hand tighten the screw.
13. Check that the end cap is properly seated in the control arm.
14. Install the rubber mount cover bracket. Tighten the retaining bolts to 34 ft/lbs.
15. Lower the car.
16. Check the front wheel alignment.

914

1. Jack up the front of the car and support it safely with stands.
2. Unscrew the torsion bar adjusting screw.
3. Pull the adjusting lever off the torsion bar and remove the seal.
4. Loosen the cheesehead screw for the front mount cover and remove the cover.
5. Carefully drive the torsion bar out of the rear of the control arm with a drift.
6. Check the torsion bar for spline damage and rust. If necessary, replace the bar.
7. Give the torsion bar a light coating of grease before installing it.

NOTE: Torsion bars are marked "L" or "R" for identification and are not interchangeable from side-to-side.

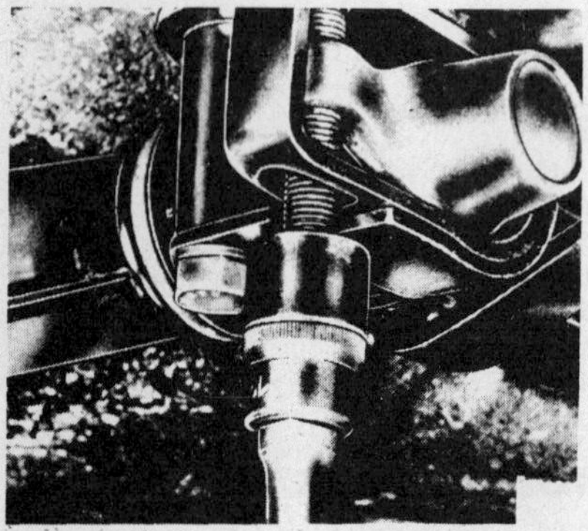

Loosening torsion bar adjusting screw

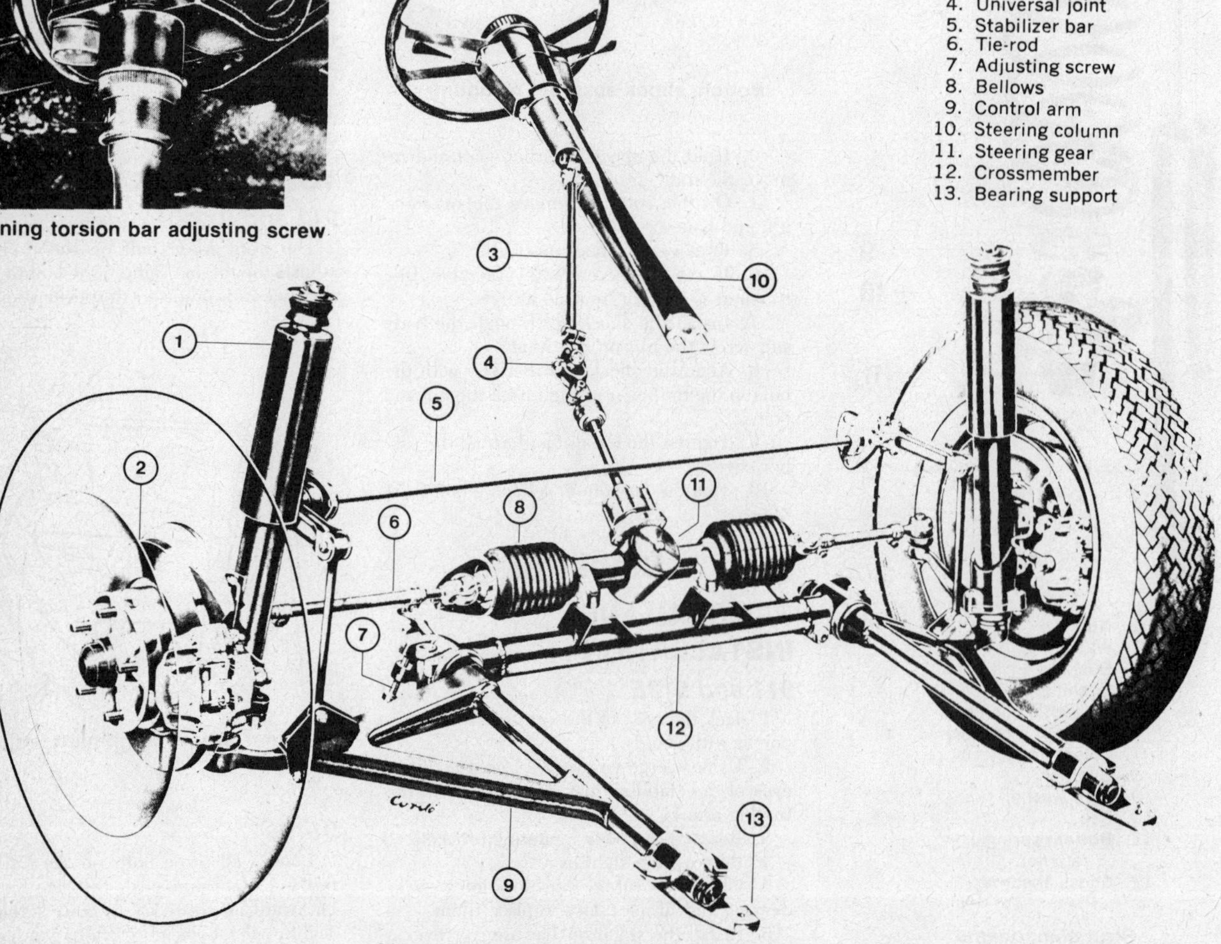

911 and 912 front suspension and steering

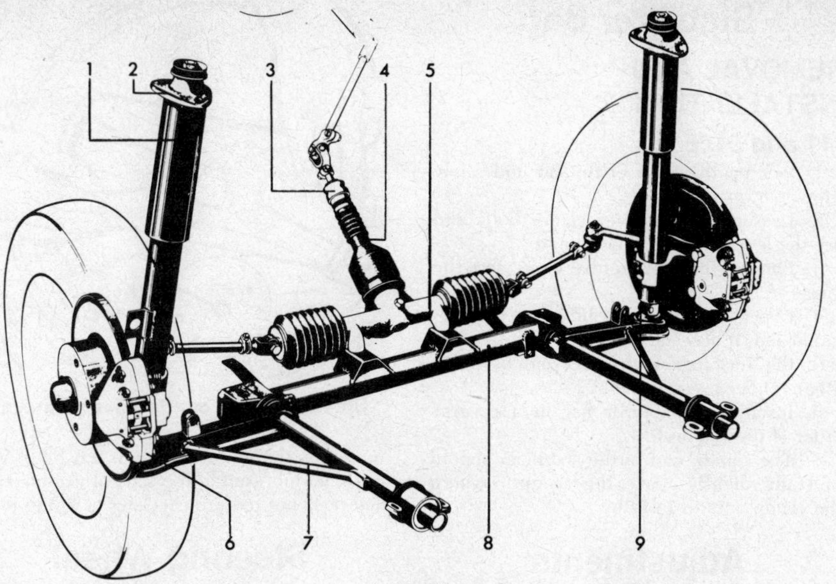

1. Strut
2. Strut support bracket
3. Steering shaft
4. Dust boot
5. Steering gear
6. Brake caliper
7. Control arm
8. Crossmember
9. Ball joint

914 front wheel suspension and steering

8. Slide the seal onto the torsion bar.
9. Using a tire iron, or other suitable lever, pry the control arm down as far as possible against the stop in the shock absorber strut. Push the adjusting lever onto the torsion bar as closely as possible against the stop.
10. Grease the adjusting screw threads and then install it hand-tight.
11. Make sure that the cover in the control arm is correctly seated. Improper assembly of the adjusting lever may force the torsion bar out of the control arm splines at the front.
12. Screw on the front mount cover.
13. Lower the car.
14. Check the front wheel alignment.

Shock Absorbers

REMOVAL AND INSTALLATION

911 and 912E

1. Jack up the front of the car and support it safely on stands. Remove the wheels.
2. Remove the brake line from the clip on the suspension strut. A small amount of brake fluid will run out of the line, plug it so that dirt cannot enter the system.
3. Unscrew the retaining bolts and remove the caliper.
4. Using a soft mallet, tap the hub cap to loosen it.
5. Pry the hub cap off with a screwdriver.
6. Loosen the Allen screw in the wheel bearing clamp. Unscrew the clamp nut and remove the nut and washer.
7. Remove the wheel hub along with the brake disc and wheel bearing.
8. Remove the backing plate retaining bolts and remove the plate.
9. Withdraw the cotter pin from the castellated nut on the steering tie rod end and remove the nut. Using a suitable puller, remove the tie rod joint from the strut.
10. Remove the control arm-to-strut ball joint retaining bolt and pull the ball joint out of the strut by pulling down on the lower control arm.

NOTE: The torsion bar adjusting screw will have to be loosened and the adjusting arm removed.

11. Remove the keeper for the nut on the top of the strut. Unscrew the nut and remove it, the keeper plate, and washer.
12. Remove the strut from the bottom. It will be necessary to loosen and pull the side of the luggage compartment out for clearance.
13. Check the shock absorber strut for excessive free travel and leaking. Replace the shock absorber if it is at all suspect.
14. Install the strut in a reverse order of the removal.
15. Tighten the top nut to 58 ft/lbs. Use a new keeper plate and ensure that the peg on the plate is pointing up.
16. Tighten the ball joint bolt to 47 ft/lbs.

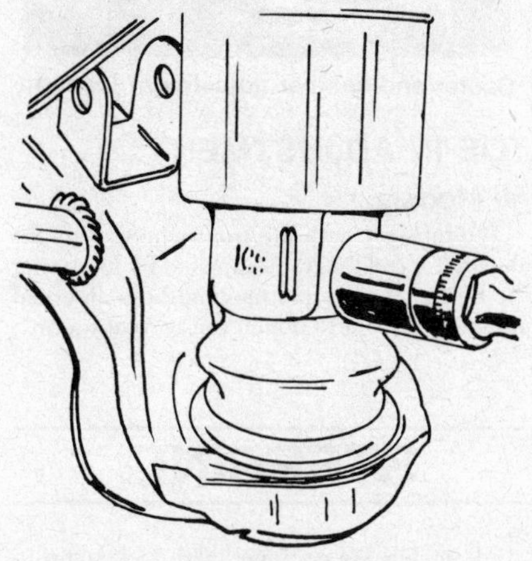

Loosening ball joint retaining bolt

NOTE: Remember to install the washer between the ball joint seal and strut.

17. Install the torsion bar adjusting lever as described in "Torsion Bar Removal and Installation."
18. Tighten the tie rod nut to 33 ft/lbs and install a new cotter pin.
19. Torque the backing plate bolts to 18 ft/lbs.
20. Install and adjust the wheel bearings as outlined in the "Brake" section.
21. Tighten the caliper retaining bolts to 50 ft/lbs.
22. Bleed the hydraulic system as outlined in the "Brake" section.
23. Install the wheels and lower the car.
24. Check the wheel alignment.

914

1. Jack up the front of the car and support it safely with stands. Remove the wheels.
2. Remove the brake line from its retainer on the shock absorber strut.
3. Remove the retaining bolts and detach the caliper.
4. Carefully pry the hub cap off.
5. Loosen the screw in the wheel bearing clamp nut. Unscrew the clamp nut and remove the washer.
6. Remove the brake disc and the wheel bearings.
7. Remove the retaining bolt and remove the splash shield.
8. Remove the cotter pin and nut and remove the tie rod joint from the strut with a suitable puller.
9. Loosen the torsion bar adjusting screw and remove the adjusting lever.
10. Loosen the ball joint retaining bolt on the strut. Pull the control arm down to free the strut from the ball joint.

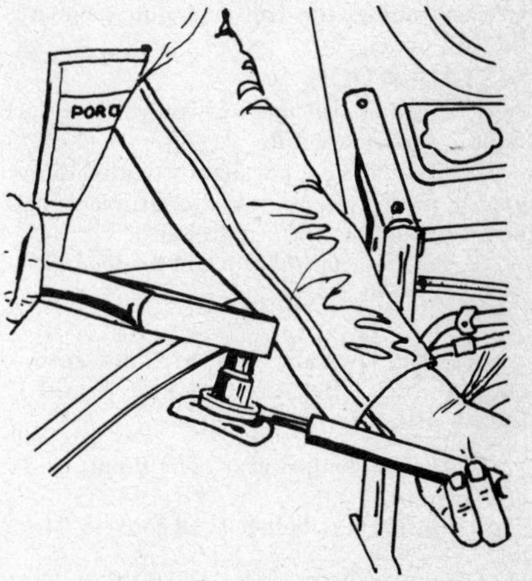

Top mounting nut removal

11. Open the front luggage compartment lid. Remove the strut retaining nut, lock washer, and tab washer.
12. Pull the strut down and out of the car.
13. Check the shock absorber strut for excessive free travel and leaking and replace it, if necessary.
14. Installation of the strut is essentially a reverse order of the removal. Remember to install the washer on the ball joint before attaching the strut.

15. Tighten the top nut to 58 ft/lbs. Use a new lock washer and ensure that its tab points up. Torque the ball joint bolt in the strut to 47 ft/lbs.

16. Reinstall the torsion bar adjusting lever as outlined in "Torsion Bar Removal and Installation."

17. Tighten the tie rod end nut to 33 ft/lbs and install a new cotter pin. Torque the three splash shield bolts to 18 ft/lbs.

18. Install and adjust the wheel bearings as described in the "Brake" section.

19. Install new lock washers on the caliper retaining bolts. Tighten both bolts to 51 ft/lbs.

20. Bleed the brake system.

21. Install the wheels and lower the car.

22. Check the wheel alignment.

CONTROL ARM AND BALL JOINT

914

REMOVAL

1. Remove torsion bar adjusting screw and pull adjusting lever from torsion bar. Remove seal.

2. Loosen ball joint hex bolt, push control arm downward and pull ball joint from shock absorber strut.

3. Remove control arm and auxiliary carrier hex bolt.

4. Unbolt and remove front control arm bearing protective cap.

5. Remove control arm bearing bolts.

6. Push control arm together with torsion bar out of auxiliary carrier and remove.

NOTE: If both control arms are to be removed, first remove one arm and tighten the control arm and carrier hex bolt so that the carrier is supported.

7. Clamp the control arm in a softjawed vise and unlock the ball joint nut, removing the ball joint.

INSTALLATION

1. Position ball joint in control arm and tighten nut to 108 ft/lbs.

2. Coat torsion bar lightly with lithium grease, paying attention to the serrations, and insert torsion bar into control arm.

3. Position control arm and torsion in carrier.

NOTE: Torsion bars are not interchangeable. They are marked R and L for identification.

4. Torque control arm bolts (front) to 34 ft/lbs.

5. Torque hex bolt for ball joint to 34 ft/lbs.

6. Slide seal across torsion bar and push control arm, with shock absorber connected, down against stop in strut. Slide the adjusting lever as closely as possible against the stop of the auxiliary carrier for the adjusting screw on the torsion bar.

7. Grease the threads of the adjusting screw with molybdenum di-sulfide grease and slightly tighten the adjusting screw.

8. Check the closing cover in the control arm for a good seal.

9. Attach the control arm protective cap.

10. Check front end height.

Stabilizer Bar

REMOVAL AND INSTALLATION

911 and 912E

1. Jack up the front of the car and safely support it on stands.

2. Loosen the stabilizer clamp bolts and pry the lever ends off their mounts.

3. Remove the stabilizer bar along with the levers.

4. Check the rubber bushings for deterioration and, if necessary, replace them. Lubricate the bushings with glycerine or some other rubber preservative.

5. Install the stabilizer bar in a reverse order of the removal.

6. The square end of the stabilizer should protrude slightly above the clamp. Tighten the clamp nuts to 18 ft/lbs.

Adjustments

CAMBER ADJUSTMENT

All Models

Camber is adjusted at the top of the strut. Pull back the luggage compartment rug to expose the three mounting bolts. Scrape the undercoating from the bolts and plates. Scribe the positions of the two plates under the bolts. Loosen the bolts and move the strut in or out as necessary to correct the camber angle.

CASTER ADJUSTMENT

All Models

Caster is adjusted in the same manner as camber, except that the strut is moved forward or backward to change the caster angle.

Caster and camber adjustment location

TOE-IN ADJUSTMENT

All Models

Toe-in is set with the front wheels straight ahead. Tie rod length is adjusted by loosening the tie rod clamps and moving them an equal amount in or out to obtain the correct toe-in.

STEERING

All models are equipped with rack and pinion type steering gear. No maintenance is required on the steering system. It is filled with a special lubricant at the time of manufacture and does not require checking or filling.

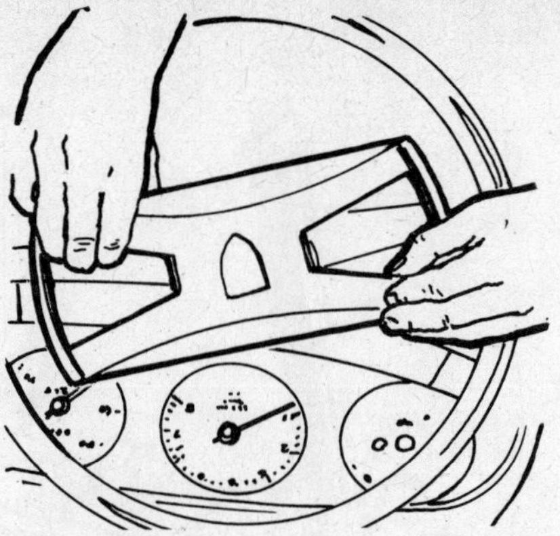

Steering wheel center cover removal

Steering Wheel

REMOVAL AND INSTALLATION

1. Disconnect the battery(ies). Place the wheels in a straight ahead position.

2. Twist the center cover to the left and remove it.

3. Remove the horn contact pin.

4. Remove the steering wheel nut.

5. Mark the steering wheel and the shaft so that it can be reinstalled in the same position.

6. Remove the steering wheel. Catch the bearing support ring and spring.

7. Install the spring and bearing support ring on the wheel hub.

8. Lightly grease the horn contact ring.

9. Install the wheel. Make sure that you align the match marks made before removal.

10. Tighten the steering wheel nut to 58 ft/lbs on 911 models and 36-43 ft/lbs on 914s.

11. Twist the center cover back on to the right to snap it into place.

Turn Signal/Headlight Flasher Switch

REMOVAL AND INSTALLATION

911 and 912E

The combination turn signal, headlight dimmer, and flasher switch is located in the steering column housing. The wiper/washer switch removal and installation procedure is identical.

1. Remove the steering wheel as outlined above.

2. Reach under the instrument panel and disconnect all wiring to the switch.

3. Remove the two horn contact ring screws, disconnect the wire, and remove the ring.

4. Remove the two upper housing retaining nuts. Pull the entire assembly off the column, leading the switch wires through the hole in the housing.

5. Remove the three retaining screws and remove the switch.

6. Reverse the removal steps to reinstall the switch.

914

Both the turn signal/headlight dimmer and wiper/washer switches are located within the steering column cover halves.

1. Remove the steering wheel as previously outlined.
2. Unscrew and remove the horn contact ring.
3. Remove the screw retaining the horn ground wire and remove the wire.
4. Remove the retaining screw from the top and bottom covers. Detach the covers.
5. Remove the switch attaching screws and remove the switch.
6. Installation is a reverse of the removal procedure. Make sure that the turn singal switch is in Neutral, or the cancelling cams will be damaged.

Ignition Switch/ Steering Lock

REMOVAL AND INSTALLATION

911 and 912E

1. Remove the ignition switch cover.
2. Drill out the two shear bolts which retain the switch.
3. Remove the steering lock and spacer.
4. Disconnect the electrical wiring and remove the switch.
5. Place the steering lock into position.
6. Insert the protective plate.
7. Install and evenly tighten the new shear bolts until their heads break off.

Steering Gear

REMOVAL AND INSTALLATION

911 and 912E

1. Remove the front luggage compartment carpeting. Jack up the front of the car and support it safely with stands.
2. Remove the auxiliary heater duct from the steering post and position it to one side.
3. Open the access door and the intermediate steering shaft cover by prying the spring clips off with a screwdriver.
4. Remove the three heater fuel pump retaining bolts and position the pump to one side.

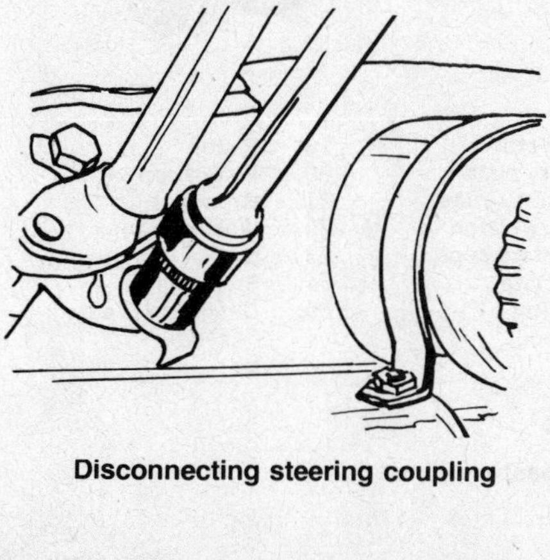

Disconnecting steering coupling

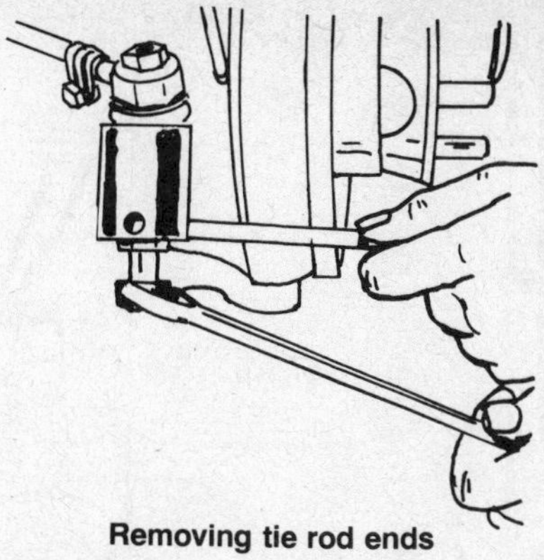

Removing tie rod ends

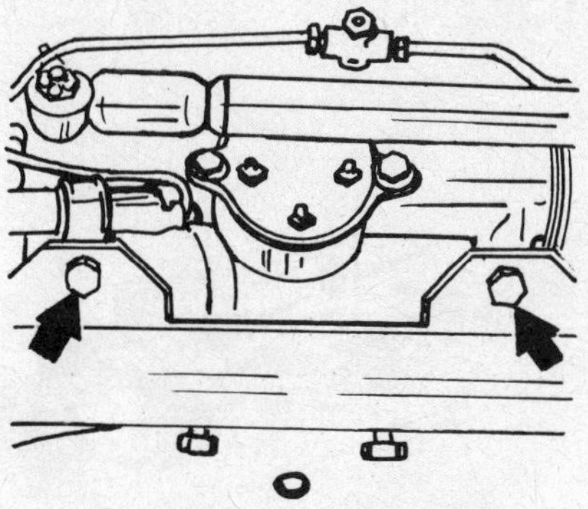

Rack and pinion retaining bolts

5. Remove the cotter pin from the lower universal joint bolt and loosen the castellated nut. Pull the universal joint off the steering shaft.
6. Remove the Allen bolts from the steering shaft bushing bracket. Remove the bracket and pull the bushing and dust cover.
7. Loosen and remove the steering coupling bolts.
8. Remove the retaining bolts and remove the bottom shield.
9. Remove the cotter pins and nuts, and then pull the tie rod ends out of the suspension struts with a suitable puller.
10. Remove the two rack and pinion housing retaining bolts.
11. Remove the right side crossmember brace.
12. Pull the steering assembly out the right side of the car.
13. Remove the retaining bolts from the tie rod yokes.
14. Installation is the reverse of the removal procedure.
15. Tighten the yoke bolts to 34 ft/lbs.
16. Make sure that the crossmember brace mounts without binding. Tighten the nuts to 47 ft/lbs and the bolts to 34 ft/lbs.
17. Install the steering housing bolts with new lockwashers and tighten to 34 ft/lbs.
18. Tighten the tie rod end nuts to 33 ft/lbs and install new cotter pins.
19. Tighten the steering bushing bracket Allen bolts to 18 ft/lbs.
20. Install new washers on the steering coupling bolts and tighten them to 18 ft/lbs.
21. Lower the car.

914

1. Raise the front of the car and support it safely on stands.
2. Remove the nut and bolt from the bottom universal joint.
3. Remove the cotter pins and castellated nuts from the tie rod ends. Using a suitable puller, remove the tie rod ends from the struts.
4. Remove the front shield.
5. Loosen the crossmember retaining bolts for the steering gear.
6. Loosen the torsion bar adjusting screws.
7. Remove the adjusting levers and seals from the torsion bars.
8. Remove the crossmember and control arm retaining bolts and remove the crossmember.
9. Remove the steering gear and tie rods.
10. Detach the tie rods from the steering gear by removing the yoke bolts.
11. Installation is essentially a reverse of the removal procedure. Reinstall the torsion bar adjusting levers as described in "Torsion Bar Removal and Installation."
12. The tie rod yoke bolts are tightened to 34 ft/lbs, the steering housing mounting bolts to 34 ft/lbs, and the crossmember mounting bolts to 65 ft/lbs.
13. Torque the tie rod end nuts to 33 ft/lbs. Tighten the steering coupling bolts and universal shaft nut to 18 ft/lbs.

BRAKE SYSTEM

All models are equipped with four wheel disc brakes. Fixed, two-piston calipers are utilized on each system. The discs on the 914 and 912E are solid. 911s are equipped with internally vented discs at each wheel. Disc brakes on all of these models are self-adjusting and require no periodic adjustment.

Each car has a tandem master cylinder, remote reservoir (mounted in the front luggage compartment for convenience), and separate hydraulic circuits for the front and rear brakes. The 914 rear circuit includes a pressure regulator which maintains maximum rear brake pressure at a predetermined level to prevent rear wheel lockup under hard braking. The 1977-81 911S and Turbo models are equipped with power brakes. A vacuum booster is mounted in tandem with the master cylinder. It is located under the luggage compartment carpet.

Master Cylinder

REMOVAL AND INSTALLATION

1. Pull the accelerator back and out of its pushrod. Pull back the driver's side carpeting.
2. Unscrew the floorboard retainer(s) under the brake and clutch pedals.
3. Remove the master cylinder dust cover.
4. Jack the front of the car up and support it with stands.
5. Siphon the brake fluid out of the reservoir. Discard the fluid, don't save it for reuse.
6. Unbolt the front splash shield.
7. Remove the brake lines from the mas-

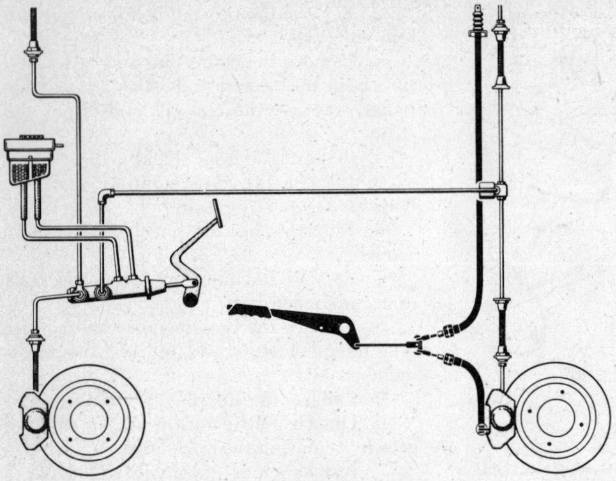

914 brake system

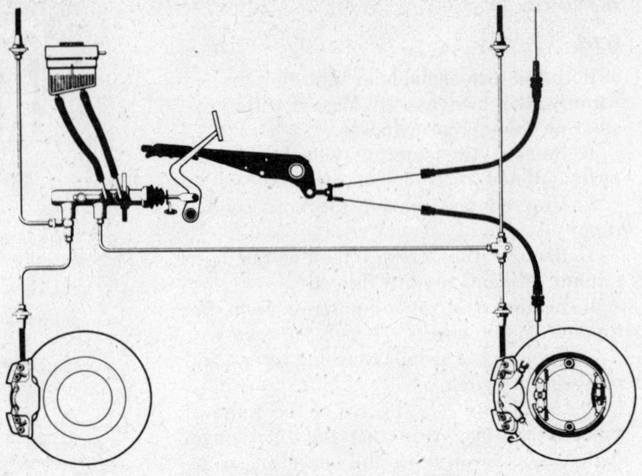

911 and 912 brake system

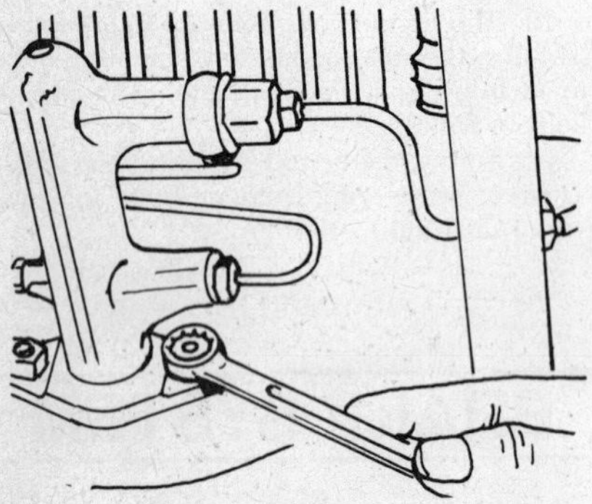

Master cylinder removal

ter cylinder. Disconnect the brake failure warning light sending unit wire.

8. Remove the two master cylinder mounting nuts.

9. Disconnect the reservoir lines and remove the master cylinder.

10. Before installing the master cylinder, apply body sealer around the mounting flange.

11. Install the cylinder, making sure that the piston pushrod is correctly positioned. Torque the mounting nuts to 18 ft/lbs.

12. The piston pushrod should have 0.04 in (1 mm) clearance between it and the piston. Loosen the piston rod nut and turn the rod to adjust the clearance.

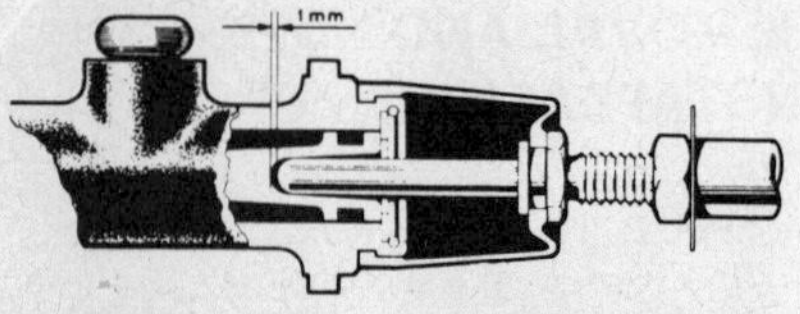

Correct piston pushrod clearance

13. Refill the system with new brake fluid. Bleed the brakes as outlined below.

14. Tighten the splash shield bolts to 34 ft/lbs (larger bolt) and 18 ft/lbs (smaller bolt).

15. Test the brake failure warning light.

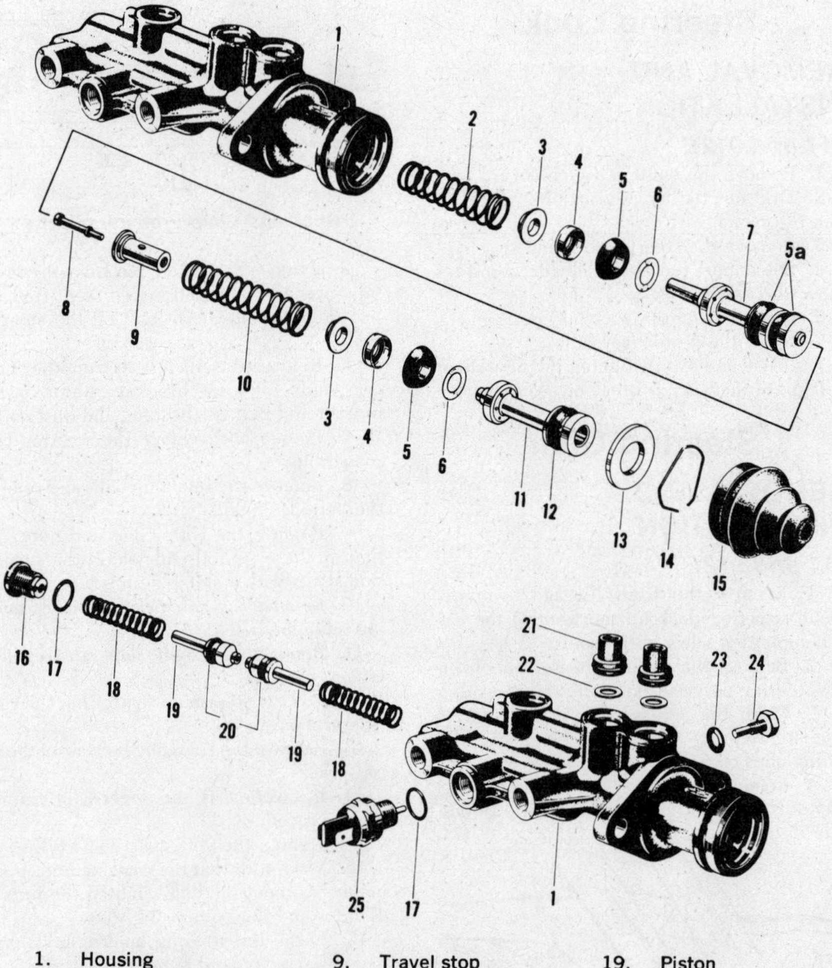

1. Housing
2. Secondary piston return spring
3. Spring seat
4. Supporting washer
5. Primary cup
5(a) Primary collar or separating collar
6. Filler disc
7. Secondary piston
8. Stroke limiting bolt
9. Travel stop
10. Primary piston return spring
11. Primary piston
12. Secondary cup
13. Stop plate
14. Lock ring
15. Dust boot
16. Bolt
17. O-ring
18. Spring
19. Piston
20. Piston cup
21. Grommet
22. Washer
23. Gasket
24. Stop bolt
25. Circuit failure sender

Exploded view of master cylinder

a. Switch on the ignition. The handbrake warning light will go on. If it doesn't, replace the bulb.

b. Start the engine. While you depress the brake pedal, have an assistant open a bleeder valve on one of the wheels to simulate a brake failure. The light should go on.

c. When your assistant closes the valve, the light should go out.

d. Repeat the test on the other brake circuit.

If the light fails to light during one of the tests, check the circuit failure sender which screws into the master cylinder.

OVERHAUL

1. Mount the master cylinder in a vise. Use cloths to protect the cylinder from the vise jaws.
2. Using a small screwdriver, carefully pry out the lock ring in the end of the master cylinder.
3. Remove the stop plate and the complete primary piston assembly.
4. Unscrew the secondary piston stop bolt and blow the piston out with compressed air.
5. Remove the spring, spring seat, and the support washer.
6. Carefully clamp the primary piston in a vise. Slightly compress the spring and screw out the stroke limiting bolt.
7. Remove the primary piston stop sleeve, stop-bolt, spring, spring seat, and support washer.
8. Replace the used parts with those supplied in the overhaul kit.
9. Clean all metal parts in denatured alcohol and dry them with compressed air.
10. Check every part you are reusing. Pay close attention to the cylinder bores. If there is any scoring or rust, replace the master cylinder.
11. Lightly coat the bores and cups with brake fluid. Assemble the cylinder components in the sequence shown in the illustration.
12. Insert the secondary piston into the cylinder, along with the filler disc, primary cup, supporting washer, spring seat, and the spring.

NOTE: The large coil of the spring must face the bottom of the housing.

13. Using a plastic rod or other nonmetallic tool, push the secondary piston into the housing until the stop-bolt and washer can be screwed in and tightened (7-9 ft/lbs).

NOTE: Check the stop-bolt seating. It must be ahead of the secondary piston and the piston must move freely to the bottom of the housing.

14. Assemble the filler disc, primary cup, and supporting washer onto the primary piston. Fasten the spring, spring seat, and stop sleeve to the piston with the stroke limiting bolt.
15. Assemble the remaining master cylinder components in a reverse order of disassembly. Ensure that the lock ring is fully seated and that the piston cups are properly positioned.
16. Torque the cap bolt and brake failure warning sending unit to 11 ft/lbs.

PRESSURE REGULATOR VALVE

REMOVAL AND INSTALLATION

914

1. Have an assistant slightly depress the brake pedal to prevent the fluid in the reservoir from running out.
2. Disconnect the brake lines at the brake pressure regulator.
3. Remove the retaining bolts and remove the valve.
4. Install the regulator valve.
5. Bleed the brakes.

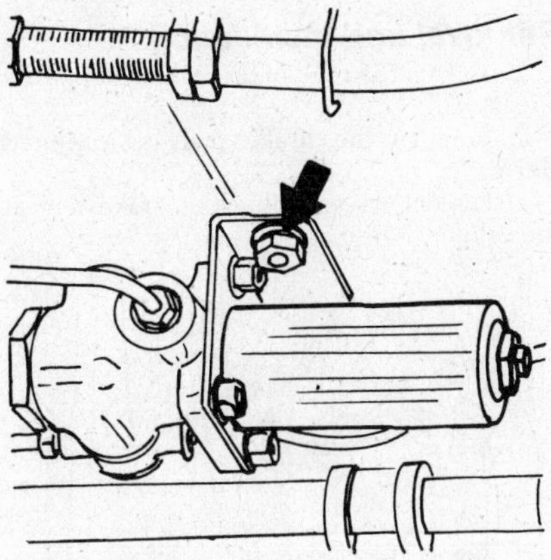

914 brake pressure regulator

CHECKING AND ADJUSTMENT

914

The brake pressure regulator is not repairable and must be replaced if defective. To check if the valve is operating, have an assistant depress the brake pedal while you hold your hand on the valve. When your assistant releases the brake pedal, you should feel a slight knock in the regulator. High pressure gauges are required to thoroughly check and adjust the valve. If you suspect the valve, replace it.

BLEEDING

Anytime a brake line has been disconnected, the hydraulic system should be bled. The brakes should also be bled when the pedal travel becomes unusually long ("soft pedal") or the car pulls to one side during braking. You will require one assistant to bleed the brakes. The proper bleeding sequence for 911 and 912E models is: left rear wheel (outer bleeder valve and then the inner), right rear wheel (outer bleeder valve and then the inner), right front wheel, and then left front wheel. 914 models use the following sequence: right rear, left rear, left front, and then right front.

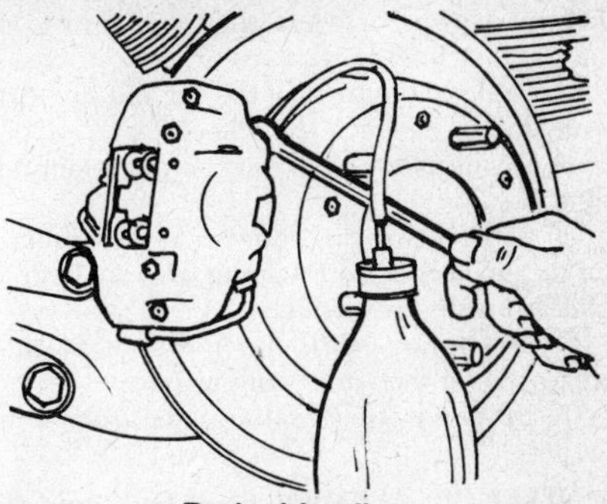

Brake bleeding

NOTE: If the system has been drained, first refill it with fresh brake fluid. Following the above sequence, open each bleeder valve ½ to ¾ of a turn and pump the brake pedal until fluid runs out of the valve. Proceed with the bleeding as outlined below.

1. Remove the bleeder valve dust cover and install a rubber bleeder hose.
2. Insert the other end of the hose into a container about ⅓ full of brake fluid.
3. Have your assistant pump the brake pedal several times until the pedal pressure increases.
4. Hold the pedal under pressure and then start to open the bleeder valve about ½ to ¾ of a turn. At this point, have your assistant depress the pedal all the way and then quickly close the valve. The helper should allow the pedal to return slowly.

NOTE: Keep a close check on the brake fluid in the reservoir and top it up as necessary throughout the bleeding process.

5. Keep repeating this procedure until no more air bubbles can be seen coming from the hose in the brake fluid.
6. Remove the bleeder hose and install the dust cover.
7. Continue the bleeding at each wheel in sequence.

Front Disc Brakes

BRAKE DISC PADS

Removal and Installation

Brake pads should be replaced when there is no visible clearance between the pads and

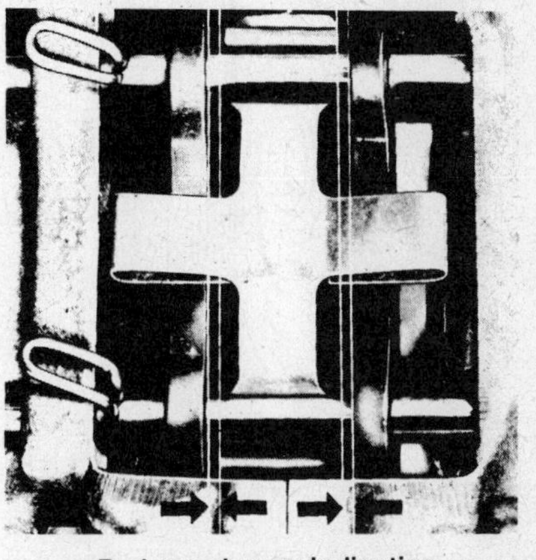

Brake pad wear indication

the cross-spring or when they are worn to a thickness of 0.08 in. (2 mm) or less.

1. Jack up the front of the car and support it on stands. Remove the wheels.
2. Using pliers, pull out the pin retaining clips.
3. While pressing down on the cross-spring, push the pad retaining pins out with a drift or small screwdriver.
4. Reference mark the positions of the brake pads if they are being reused.
5. Remove the brake pads from the caliper.

NOTE: Porsche has a special tool for this purpose, P 86, but using a small drift or punch you can pry the pad out of the caliper until it can be gripped by pliers and removed.

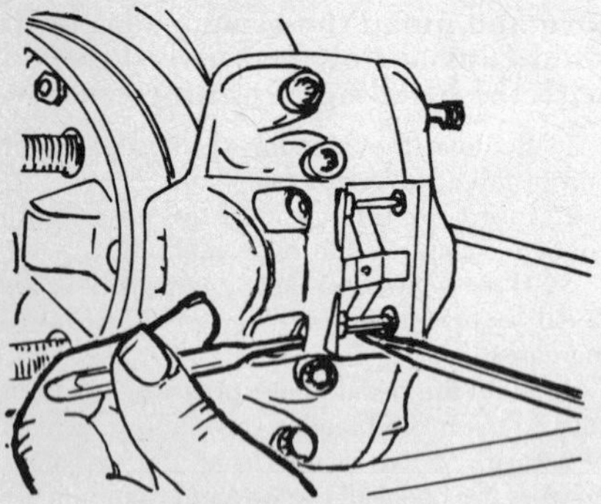

Retaining pin removal

6. Siphon out half of the brake fluid in the reservoir to prevent it from overflowing when the pistons are pushed in and new thicker pads are inserted.
7. Using a flat, smooth piece of hardwood, push the pistons back into the caliper. Do this carefully so that you don't damage either the piston or the brake disc.
8. Clean the brake pad slots in the caliper with alcohol. On 914 models, remove the piston anti-rotation plate. Blow out any foreign matter dislodged by the cleaning.
9. Examine the piston boots for damage or deterioration. Any questionable parts should be replaced.
10. Dress any ridges on the disc edge with crocus cloth.

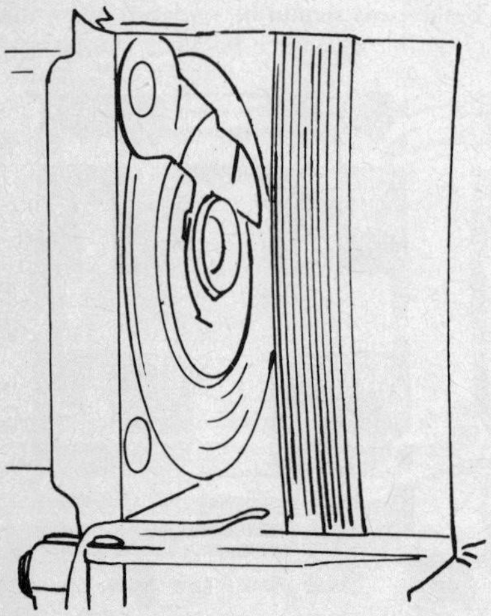

914 piston anti-rotation plate positioning

11. On 914 models, install the antirotation plate onto the piston.
12. Install the brake pads into the caliper. Pads must be free in their slots, there should be no binding.

NOTE: Replace used pads in the side of the caliper from which they were removed. When installing new pads, always replace the pads on the opposite wheel at the same time.

13. Position a new cross-spring in the caliper, and then carefully tap the pad retaining pins into place with a small hammer. Install the pin clips. If the clips are rusty, replace them.
14. New brake pads must be run-in for approximately 100 miles. During this period, try not to apply the brakes extremely hard. Use them moderately and gradually during break-in.

BRAKE CALIPERS

Removal and Installation

1. Jack up the front of the car and support it on stands.
2. Remove the brake pads as outlined above.
3. Disconnect and plug the brake line at the caliper.

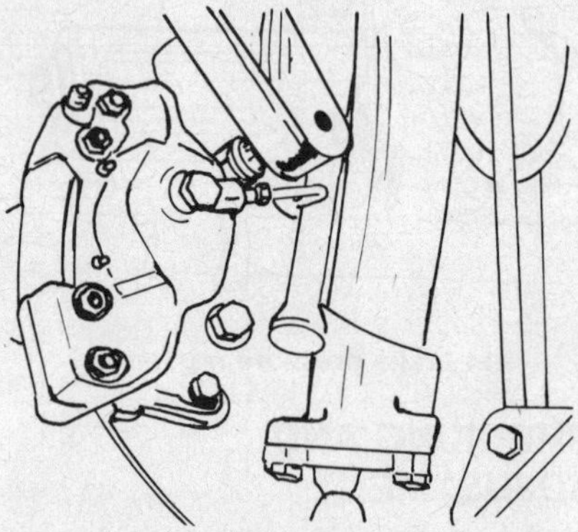

Removing caliper pin retaining bolts

4. Remove the retaining bolts and remove the caliper.
5. Install the caliper using a reverse of the removal procedure. Tighten the two retaining bolts to 50 ft/lbs.
6. Bleed the brakes.

Overhaul

1. Remove the caliper from the car.
2. Screw out the bleeder valve and apply air pressure to clean out any brake fluid.
3. Mount the caliper in a soft-jawed vise or place cloths over the jaws to protect the caliper.

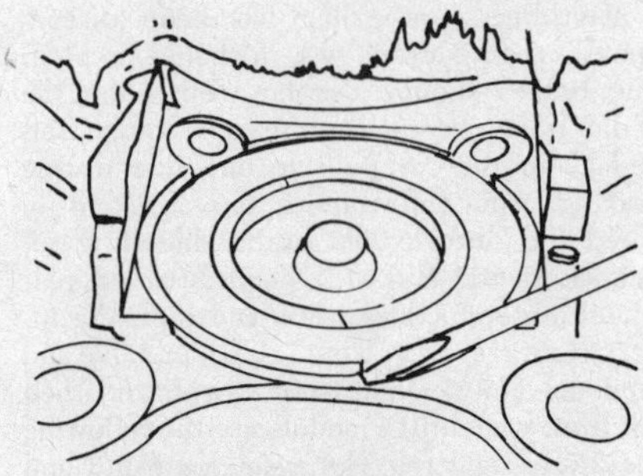

Removing piston retaining bolts

4. Remove the anti-rotation plate on 914 models.

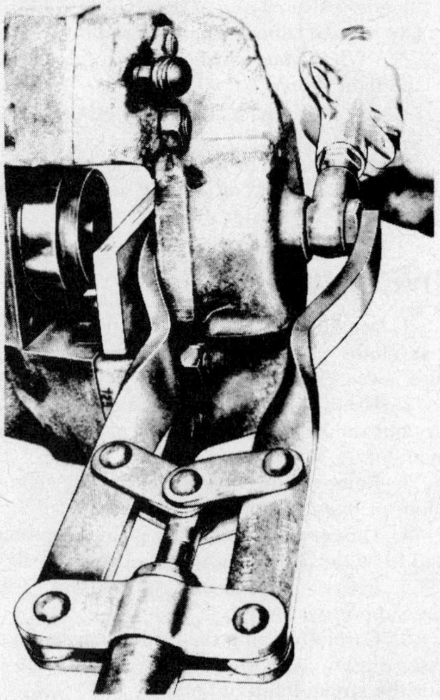

Forcing the piston out of the caliper

5. Using a screwdriver, pry out the retaining ring and remove the boot from one piston.
6. Depress the other piston with a C-clamp and a flat piece of wood or metal. This setup will do the same job as Porsche tool P83.
7. Insert another flat piece of wood or metal in the caliper to protect the piston which is being removed. Apply an initial air pressure of 30 psi to the bleeder valve to force the piston from its bore in the caliper.

CAUTION

Keep your hands away from the inside of the caliper. Air pressure of 147 psi produces an equivalent pressure of 550 lbs.

8. When the piston pops out of the caliper, remove the rubber seal with a wood or plastic pin to avoid damaging the seal groove.
9. Clean all metal parts with denatured alcohol. Never use any mineral based solvents such as gasoline, kerosene, acetone, or the like. These solvents deteriorate rubber parts. Inspect the pistons and bores. They must be free of scoring and pitting. Replace the caliper if there is any damage.
10. Discard all rubber parts. Caliper rebuilding kits include new boots and seals which should be used as the caliper is reassembled.
11. Lightly coat the cylinder bore, piston, seals with a brake cylinder assembly paste.
12. Install the piston seal in the cylinder groove. Install the piston into its bore.
13. Fabricate a 20° piston alignment gauge, similar to the one in the illustration, from heavy cardboard. Using the gauge, position

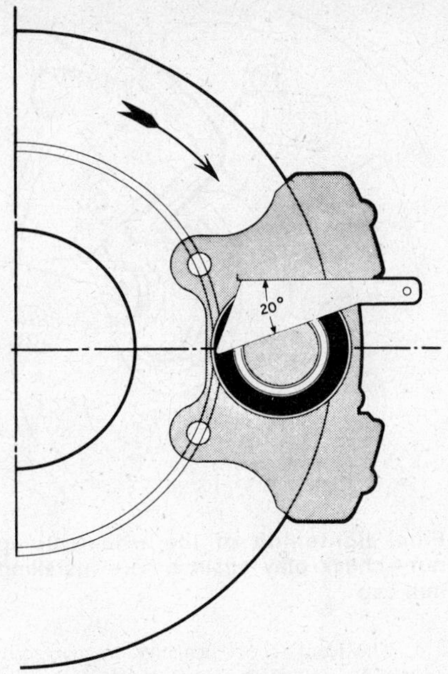

Piston alignment gauge

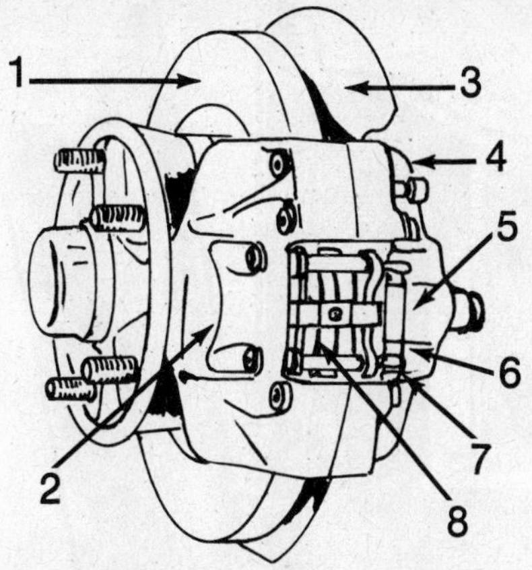

1. Brake disc
2. Caliper cover
3. Disc shroud
4. Caliper base housing
5. Brake pad segment
6. Cross-spring
7. Pin retainer
8. Retaining pin

912 and 911 front disc brake components

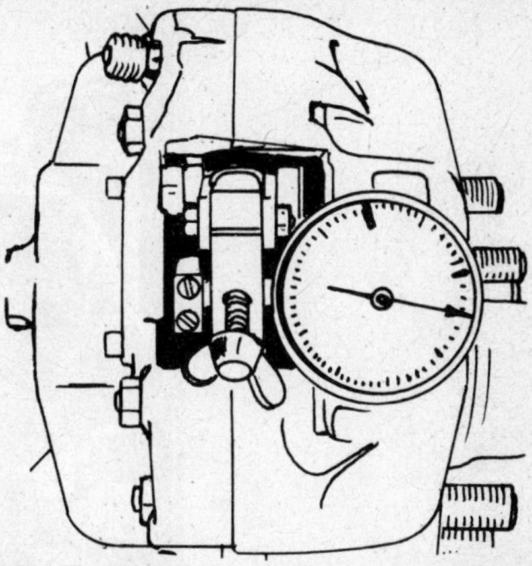

Dial indicator set-up for determining lateral disc run-out

the step-down on the piston so that it faces the direction of brake disc rotation.

14. Wipe off any excess assembly paste on the piston and install the boot and retaining ring. Install the anti-rotation plate on 914 models.

15. Repeat the above operation on the second piston. Overhaul is complete at this point, unless the caliper half O-rings are leaking. In this case, the caliper must be split.

NOTE: Light alloy calipers on some 911S models are one piece and cannot be disassembled. Do not remove the caliper side cover on these models.

16. Remove the four caliper assembly bolts.

17. Remove the caliper cover housing. Remove the spacer plate on vented disc models.

18. Install two fresh O-rings in the fluid passages. Replace the assembly bolts and nuts. The outside bolts are shorter.

19. Align the halves and place the caliper in a soft-jawed vise. On 914 models, tighten the bolts to 7 ft/lbs in the sequence shown. 911 models use the same tightening sequence, but are first torqued to 12.5 ft/lbs and then final torqued to 25 ft/lbs (6.5 and 13 ft/lbs for rear calipers).

BRAKE DISC

Removal and Installation

911 AND 912E

1. Jack up the front of the car and place it on stands. Remove the wheels.

2. Remove the brake caliper as outlined above.

3. Using two screwdrivers, pry off the hub cap.

4. Loosen the screw in the hub clamp nut. Unscrew the clamp nut and thrust washer.

5. Grip the disc with both hands and give it a sharp pull to remove it. A stud-born disc should be removed with a puller. Never strike the disc with a hammer.

6. Match mark the hub and disc, if the disc is being reused, and separate them.

7. The disc is installed in a reverse order of removal. Install the disc-to-hub bolts from the inside out and tighten the nuts to 17 ft/lbs.

8. Install the disc/hub assembly on the spindle. Install the thrust washer and clamp nut.

9. Install the brake caliper.

10. Adjust the wheel bearings as outlined below.

11. Bleed the brakes.

914

1. Jack up the front of the car and support it safely on stands. Remove the wheels.

2. Remove the brake caliper as described above.

3. Pry off the hub cap.

4. Loosen the screw in the hub clamp nut and unscrew the clamp nut.

5. Pull off the brake disc along with the inner and outer wheel bearings.

6. Installation is the reverse of removal.

7. Adjust the wheel bearings as outlined below.

8. Bleed the hydraulic system.

INSPECTION AND CHECKING

Brake discs may be checked for lateral runout while installed on the car. This check will require a dial indicator gauge and stand to mount it on the caliper. Porsche has a special tool for this purpose which mounts the dial indicator in the brake pad slots of the caliper, but a dial indicator can also be mounted on the shaft of a C-clamp attached to the outside of the caliper.

1. Adjust the front wheel bearings.

2. Mount the dial indicator using either of the above methods. The feeler should touch the disc about ½ in. below the outer edge.

3. Rotate the disc and observe the gauge. Lateral runout (wobble) must not exceed 0.008 in. (0.2 mm). A disc which exceeds this specification must be replaced or refinished.

4. Brake discs which have excessive lateral runout, sharp ridges, or scoring can be refinished. Final grinding must be done on both sides of the disc to prevent squeaking and vibrating. Discs which have only light grooves and are otherwise acceptable can be used without refinishing.

NOTE: Ventilated brake discs (911) are balanced by special clips inserted into the vent fins of the disc. Do not remove the clips or the original balance will be lost.

Wheel Bearings

REMOVAL AND INSTALLATION

911 and 912E

NOTE: The inner bearing, seal, and outer bearing may be removed and lubricated once the hub/disc assembly is off the car. If after cleaning, the bearings are noticeably worn or damaged they should be replaced along with their races. If the bearings are satisfactory, skip the race removal steps.

1. Remove the brake disc/hub assembly.

2. Match mark the hub and disc for correct reassembly, remove the five assembly bolts, and separate the hub and disc.

3. Pry the inner seal out of the hub. Remove the inner bearing and outer bearing.

4. Wash the bearings in solvent and blow them dry. Examine the bearings for pitting, scoring, or other damage. Replace the bearing and race as a unit if there is any question as to their condition.

5. Heat the wheel hub to 250°-300° F.

6. Press the inner bearing race out of the hub on a press table, using suitable spacers to prevent damaging the hub.

7. Press out the outer bearing race, using suitable spacers and a support fabricated from the accompanying drawing.

8. Press a new inner bearing race into the hub and then press in a new outer bearing race.

9. Pack the bearings with a lithium multipurpose grease.

10. Align the match marks and install the hub on the disc. Insert the assembly bolts from the inside out and tighten them to 17 ft/lbs.

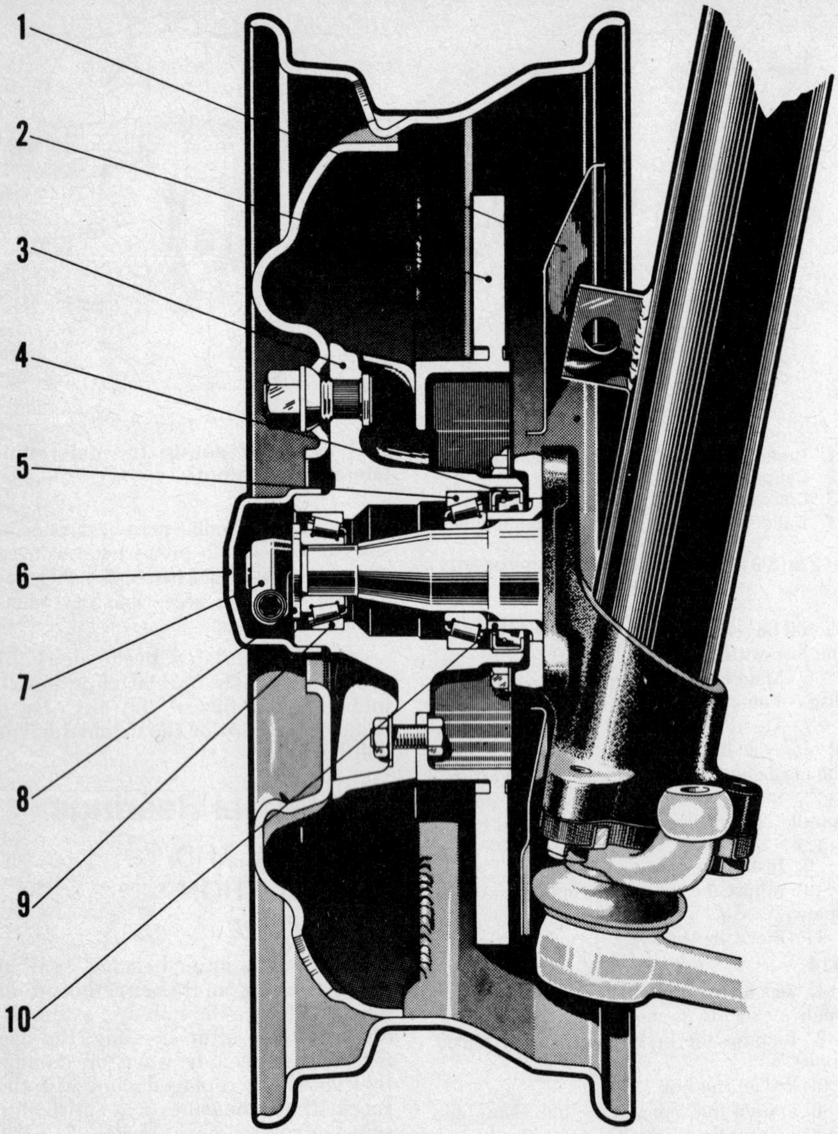

1. Cover shroud
2. Brake disc
3. Front wheel hub
4. Seal
5. Tapered roller bearing
6. Grease cap
7. Clamping nut
8. Washer
9. Tapered roller bearing
10. Distance ring

Cross-section of 911 and 912 brake disc/hub assembly

11. Lightly coat the spindle with grease. Fill the hub with about 2 oz of grease. Lubricate and install the bearings.
12. Grease the sealing edges of a new inner oil seal and carefully tap it into place. The oil seal must be flush with the hub.
13. Install the hub/disc assembly on the car.
14. Adjust the wheel bearings.

914

Wheel bearing procedures are similar to those for the above models, except that the hub and disc are one piece and the bearing races can be driven out with a brass or copper drift.

ADJUSTMENT

Check and adjust the front wheel bearings after the car has not been run for a few hours. The bearings will be cold then.

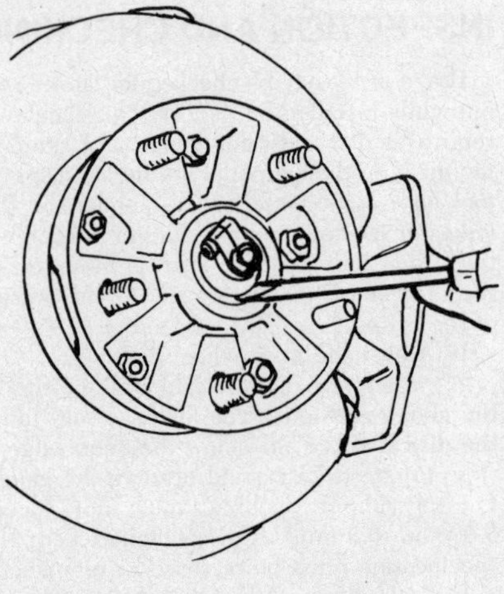

Checking wheel bearing play

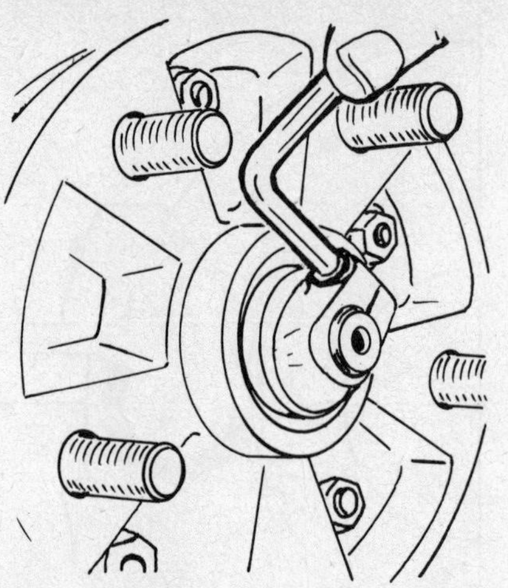

Final tightening of the wheel clamp nut—check play again before installing hub cap

1. The front wheel bearings are correctly adjusted when the thrust washer can be moved slightly sideways under light pressure from a screwdriver, but no bearing play is evident when the wheel hub is shaken axially.
2. Jack up the front of the car, support it on stands, and remove the wheels. Turn the hub several times to seat the bearings.
3. Pry the hub cap off with a screwdriver and perform the check described in Step 1.

NOTE: Don't press the screwdriver against the hub. Hold it lightly in your hand so you get a better feel.

4. If the bearings require an adjustment, loosen the allen screw and turn the clamp nut in or out as necessary.
5. Tighten the clamp nut allen screw to 11 ft/lbs without altering the adjusted position of the clamp nut.
6. Double check the adjustment and readjust, if necessary.
7. Give the clamp nut and thrust washer a light coating of lithium grease. Tap the hub cap into place with a plastic or rubber mallet.
8. Install the wheels and lower the car.

Rear Disc Brakes

DISC BRAKE PADS

Removal and Installation

911 AND 912E

Brake pad removal and installation is identical to that for front pads.

914

Removal of the rear brake pads is the same as that for the front pads. Installation, however, differs due to the automatic adjuster mechanism necessary for the handbrake.

1. Using two flat pieces of hardwood, or Porsche tool P 83, lightly pre-load the pistons. Unless you have four hands, an assistant becomes just about a necessity at this point.
2. Have your assistant remove the cover screw on the outside of the caliper. Loosen the locknut and insert a 4 mm allen key into the adjusting screw.
3. Set the piston back by turning the allen

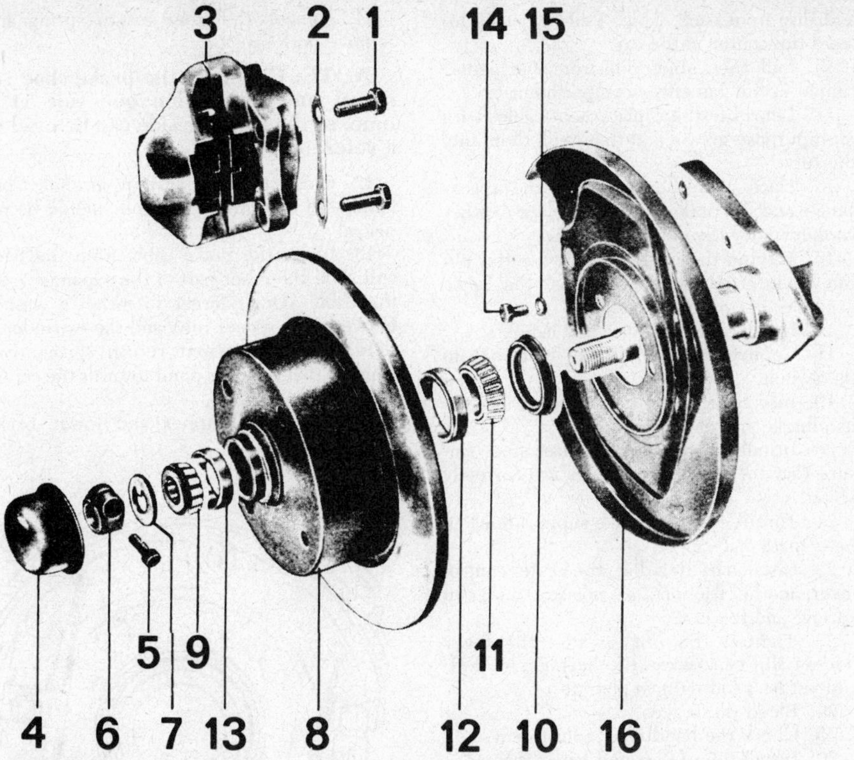

1. Bolt
2. Lockplate
3. Caliper
4. Hub cap
5. Bolt
6. Clamp nut
7. Hose washer
8. Disc
9. Outer bearing
10. Seal
11. Inner bearing
12. Inner bearing race
13. Outer bearing race
14. Bolt
15. Lock washer
16. Rear shroud

Exploded view of 914 brake disc/hub assembly

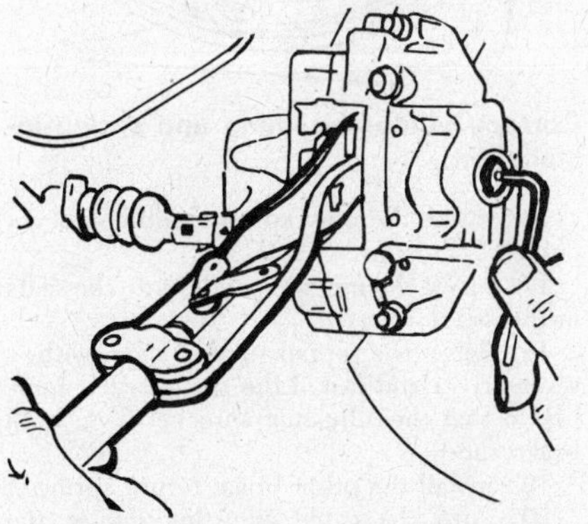

Setting the outer piston back (special tool shown)

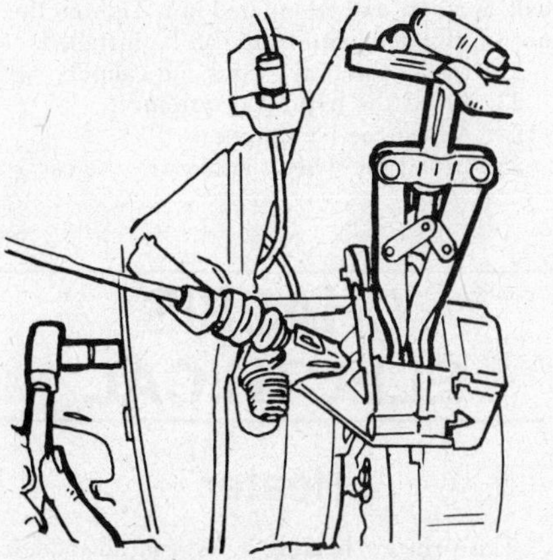

Setting inner piston back

key clockwise, all the while maintaining tension on the pistons with the flat boards.

4. Remove the cover bolt on the inside caliper half. Insert a 4 mm allen socket (an extension handle will be necessary) through the trailing arm access hole. Set the piston back by turning the adjusting screw counterclockwise, again maintaining constant pressure on the piston with the flat board.
5. Install the brake pads with retaining pins, but without the cross-spring.
6. Insert a 0.08 in. (0.2 mm) feeler gauge between the pad and the disc. Adjust the pistons for that much clearance by turning the allen screws on both sides as necessary.
7. Remove the retaining pins and install them again with the cross-spring. Install the pin clips.
8. Install the wheel and lower the car.

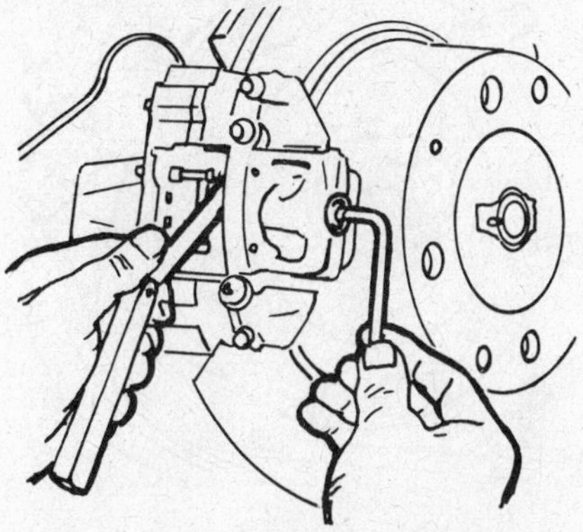

Adjusting pad and disc clearance

DISC BRAKE CALIPER

Removal and Installation

911 AND 912E

Remove the shields from the rear of the brake and then use the same procedure as the front calipers. Tighten the caliper retaining bolts to 44 ft/lbs and the shield bolts to 18 ft/lbs.

914

Disconnect the handbrake cables and then proceed as outlined in the front caliper section.

Overhaul

Overhaul is exactly the same as the front calipers, except that the 914 rear calipers should not be split as there is a possibility of damaging the automatic adjuster. If the O-ring seals are leaking, replace the caliper.

BRAKE DISCS

Removal and Installation

1. Remove the rear shroud on 911 models. Detach the handbrake cables on 914 models.
2. Remove the brake caliper.
3. Remove both countersunk screws from the disc and pull it off the car.
4. Installation is the reverse of the removal procedure.

Inspection and Checking

The rear brake disc procedure is similar to that for the front, except that the disc must be fastened to the hub. Install the wheel nuts on 911 models and tighten them in a criss-cross pattern to 72 ft/lbs. On 914 models, install the wheel bolts and tighten them to 80 ft/lbs.

Handbrake

The 911 and 912E models are equipped with a separate handbrake system. The center, pull-up lever mechanically operates a pair of brake shoes inside each rear disc, which act as drums through a pot-shaped center section.

The 914 handbrake mechanically applies the rear service brakes. The rear calipers are equipped with automatic adjusting mechanisms.

CABLE

Adjustment

911 AND 912E

1. Jack up the rear of the car and support it on stands. Remove the wheels.
2. Release the handbrake lever.
3. Push the brake pads away from the disc so that it can be turned by hand.
4. Loosen the cable adjusting nuts to release tension.
5. Insert a screwdriver into the disc access hole and rotate the handbrake star wheel until the disc can no longer be turned by hand.
6. Repeat this operation on the other side.
7. Readjust the cable nuts to take up the slack.
8. Pull up the center tunnel cover and handbrake lever boot at the rear. By looking through the two inspection holes, see if the cable equalizer is exactly perpendicular to the car's centerline.
9. If the equalizer positioning is off, cor-

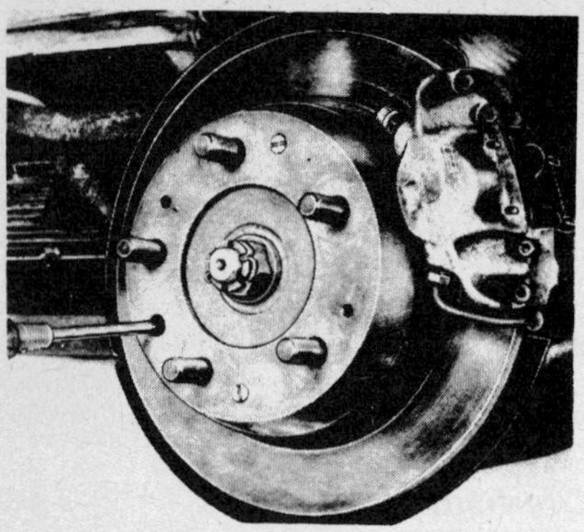

Adjusting the handbrake

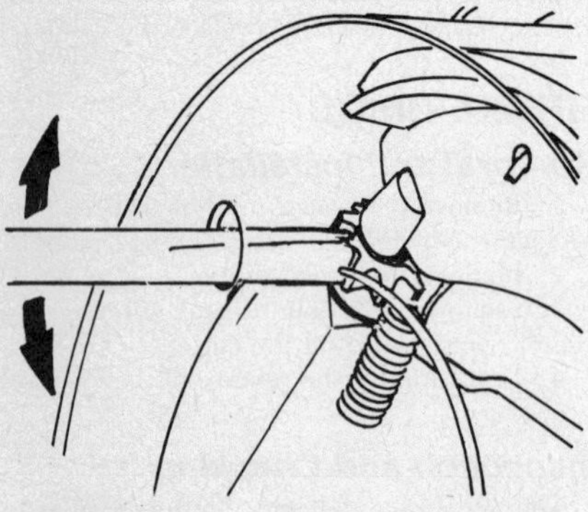

Hand brake star wheel adjustment

rect it by loosening or tightening the cable adjusting nuts. Tighten the locknuts after the adjustment is correct.

10. Back off each brake star wheel by four or five teeth until the disc can be turned by hand.

11. Check the handbrake lever clearance. There should be a slight clearance at the lever. The handbrake should be set when the lever is pulled up.

12. After completing the handbrake adjustment, depress the brake pedal several times to reposition the rear caliper pistons. Check the fluid level in the reservoir and top it up, if necessary.

Removal and Installation

1. Jack up the rear of the car and support it on stands. Remove the wheels.
2. Remove the center tunnel cover and handbrake lever boot.
3. Remove the heater control knob.
4. Undo the handbrake support housing bolts.
5. Unscrew the heater control lever nut. Remove the cup spring, discs, and the lever.
6. Slightly raise the handbrake support housing. Snap off the retaining clip and pull out the cable equalizing stud.
7. Disconnect the handbrake light switch wire.
8. Remove the handbrake support housing.
9. Detach the cables from the cable equalizer.
10. Remove the rear brake calipers.
11. Remove the rear brake discs and spacer rings.
12. Remove the cotter pin, castellated nut, and disc from each cable. Pull the cable toward the center of the car.
13. Pull the cables out from the center tunnel in the passenger compartment.
14. Lubricate the replacement cables with multipurpose grease and then feed them into the tube.
15. Place a washer between the spacer sleeve and the brake expander. Place another washer under the castellated nut.
16. Tighten the nut until a new cotter pin can be inserted. Make sure that the brake expander is correctly seated.
17. Install the brake disc and calipers.
18. Connect the handbrake light wire to the switch.
19. Insert the heater control lever into the handbrake support housing.
20. Install and clip the equalizer stud. Ensure that the handbrake cables are correctly seated.
21. Torque the handbrake support housing bolts to 18 ft/lbs.
22. Install a friction disc, the heater control lever, another friction disc, pressure disc, cup spring, and the nut.
23. Tighten the nut so that the lever doesn't slip back when the heater is on full, and yet isn't too tight to operate.
24. Bleed the brakes.
25. Check the handbrake adjustment.
26. Install the wheels and lower the car.

BRAKE SHOES

Removal and Installation

911 and 912E

1. Jack up the rear of the car and support it on stands. Remove the wheels.
2. Remove the brake calipers.
3. Detach the brake discs.
4. Remove the cotter pin, castellated nut, and washer from the brake cable.
5. Pull the cable out toward the center of the car.
6. Remove the expander and spring.
7. Depress the upper spring and twist the holddown cup to remove it and the spring.
8. Pull the brake shoe outward and remove the pin through the rear.
9. Using a screwdriver, raise the upper brake shoe and remove the star wheel assembly. Unhook the spring.
10. Repeat steps 7 and 8 for the bottom shoe.

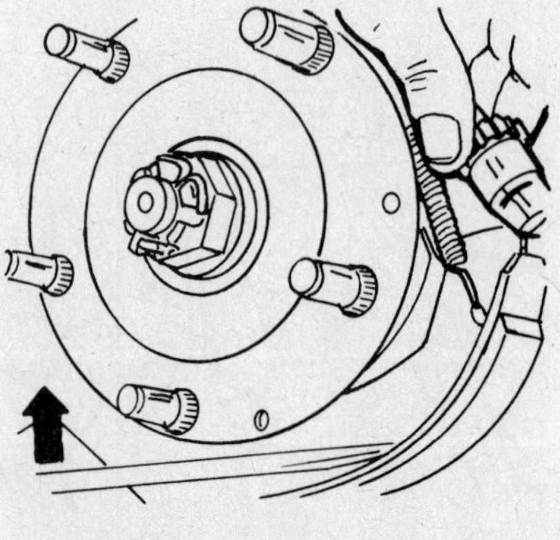

Star wheel assembly removal

11. Unhook the front return spring and remove both shoes.

NOTE: Complete the brake shoe removal and installation one side at a time, so the opposite side can be used as a reference.

12. Clean all metal parts in alcohol. Contaminated or worn brake shoes should be replaced.
13. Insert the brake cable from the back and slide the inner part of the expander onto the cable. Don't forget to install a washer between the spacer tube and the expander.
14. Install the front return spring (two coils) so that the coils point towards the center of the axle.
15. Install the upper and lower brake shoes.

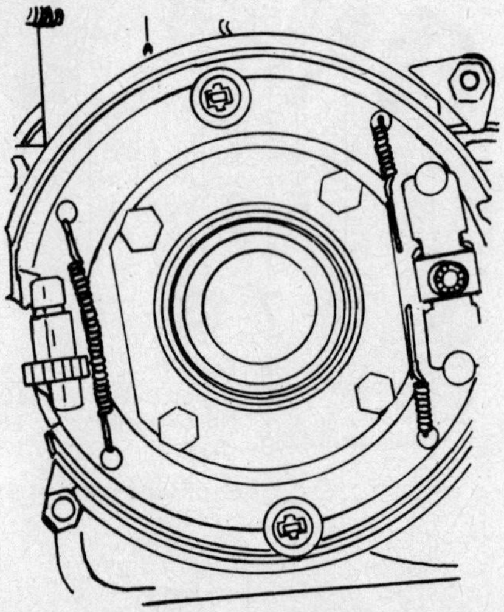

Correct handbrake lining and spring installation

16. Install the pins, springs, and holddown cups.
17. Insert the inner expander into the seats in the brake shoes.
18. Raise the upper brake shoe with a screwdriver and install the star wheel assembly so that the adjusting sprocket is on both brake shoes.
19. Install the other brake return spring.
20. Turn the cable adjusting nut in the tube all the way back.
21. Install the spring, second expander half, washer, and castellated nut. Tighten the nut until a new cotter pin can be installed.
22. Install the brake discs and calipers.
23. Bleed the hydraulic system.
24. Adjust the handbrake.
25. Install the wheels and lower the car.

CHASSIS ELECTRICAL

Heater

The primary heating system in all models uses fresh air drawn in by the engine cooling fan, directs it to heat exchangers around the exhaust pipes, through a muffler, and distributes warm air into the passenger compartment via a system of ducts. A variable speed blower, located in the front luggage compartment on all models, speeds the circulation of heated and/or fresh air. 914 models are equipped with a blower motor in the engine compartment. An auxiliary, gasfired heater is an option on 911 models.

Blower

REMOVAL AND INSTALLATION

911 and 912E

1. Disconnect the batter cables.
2. Remove the front luggage compartment carpeting.
3. Open the blower compartment lid. Remove the steering shaft cover.
4. Disconnect the electrical wiring.
5. Loosen the hose clamps and disconnect the hoses from the blower.
6. Pull the blower off the air intake stack and remove it from the car.
7. Install the blower on the intake stack. Make sure that the sealing ring is correctly seated.
8. Fasten the hoses on the blower and tighten the hose clamps.
9. Connect the electrical wiring.
10. Install the steering shaft cover and close the blower compartment lid.
11. Cement the carpeting to the right front side panel.
12. Connect the battery cables.

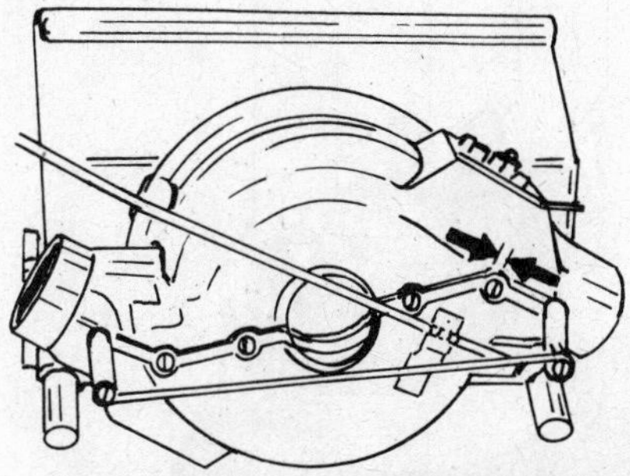

Correct blower cable installation

914

1. Remove the front luggage compartment lid.
2. Remove the fuel tank.
3. Unscrew the mounting bolt on each end of the fresh air intake box.
4. Loosen the hose clamps on the two air hoses and pull them from the blower.
5. Squeeze the corbin clamps on the two water drain hoses and pull them from the fresh air box.
6. Loosen the cable clamp nut and detach the cable from the blower by pushing the retaining clip off. Be careful not to bend the cable.
7. Disconnect the electrical wiring.
8. Remove the fresh air box and blower as an assembly.
9. Unscrew the attaching bolts and separate the fresh air box and blower.
10. Install the blower in the fresh air box.
11. Install the cable on the blower. The cable casing should protrude from the retaining clip by about ¼ in.
12. Install the fresh air box/blower assembly in a reverse manner of removal. Adjust the cable, if necessary.

Auxiliary Heater

The 911 auxiliary heater assembly is mounted in the front luggage compartment in the place of the standard blower.

REMOVAL AND INSTALLATION

1. Jack up the front of the car and support it on stands.
2. Disconnect the batter cables.
3. Remove the luggage compartment lid.
4. Open the heater compartment lid.
5. Loosen the clamp on the hot air hose and pull the hose off the heater unit.
6. Remove the three mixture pump retaining bolts and remove them from the bracket.
7. Disconnect the fuel lines and wiring from the pump.
8. Working under the car, loosen the front muffler clamp. Disconnect the exhaust pipe and bend it down and out of the way.
9. Remove the muffler clamp and slide the white collar onto the heater unit.
10. Disconnect all wiring to the heater and carefully lift it out of the car.
11. Installation is the reverse of the removal procedure. Ensure that the wiring is correctly reinstalled.

Windshield Wiper Motor and Linkage

REMOVAL AND INSTALLATION

911 and 912E

The windshield wiper motor and linkage are located in front of the instrument panel.

1. Pull back the front luggage compartment carpeting. Disconnect the battery cables.
2. Remove the retaining clip and air duct. Remove the fresh air box.
3. Disconnect the blower motor wires.
4. Remove the wiper arms. Remove the rubber bushings under the arms and unscrew the shaft retaining nuts.
5. Pull the motor and linkage down as a unit. Separate the motor and linkage.
6. Installation is the reverse of the removal procedure.

914

The windshield wiper motor and linkage are mounted on a common frame.

1. Disconnect the battery.
2. Unscrew the retaining nut on each wiper arm.
3. Remove the rubber bearing cap.
4. Unscrew the retaining nut and remove the washers and seals.
5. Remove the fuel tank.
6. Remove the evaporative emission charcoal canister.
7. Remove the fresh air box and blower as previously described.
8. Remove the anti-vibration bearing retaining nut from under the instrument panel. Make sure that the bearing isn't twisted.
9. Pull the windshield wiper assembly down and out.
10. Disconnect the electrical wires.
11. To separate the motor and linkage:
    a. Remove the wiper motor shaft nut and washer.
    b. Using a puller, remove the linkage drive crank from the motor shaft.
    c. Remove the three retaining bolts and remove the motor.
12. To install the motor onto the linkage:
    a. The motor must be in the park position. Ground the motor and connect terminals 53 and 53a to a positive battery wire.
    b. Run the motor for a few seconds and then disconnect terminal 53. The motor will be parked.
    c. Position the drive crank parallel to the drive rod.
    d. Attach the motor with a washer and nut. Install the three retaining bolts.

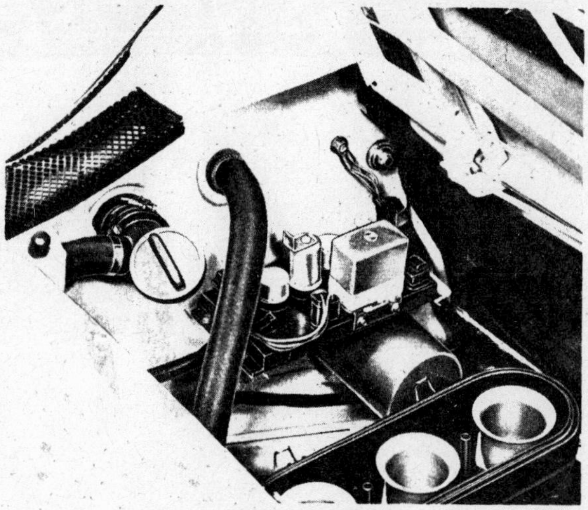

914 and 914/6 relay location

13. Connect the electrical wiring.
14. Install the wiper arms in a reverse order of removal. Ensure that they are in the parked position.
15. Install the fresh air box/blower assembly.
16. Connect the battery.

911 Rear Window Wiper

1. Pull the wiper arm from the rear window.
2. Open the engine comparment lid.
3. Disconnect the wiper motor electrical wiring.
4. Disconnect the wiper arm linkage at the bellcrank.
5. Remove the three wiper motor bracket bolts and remove the motor/linkage assembly.
6. Install the wiper motor/linkage assembly in a reverse order of removal.
7. Adjust the linkage at the bellcrank for correct wiper operation.

Instrument Panel

REMOVAL AND INSTALLATION

911 and 912E

The gauges are mounted in individual rubber rings.

911 and 912 instrument removal

1. Pry the gauge out until you can grip it firmly, and then pull it out of the instrument panel.
2. Disconnect the wiring and/or cable and remove the gauge.
3. Connect the wiring or cable and position the gauge in its opening.
4. Align the gauge and then push it into place.

914

1. Disconnect the battery.
2. Remove the steering wheel as outlined in the "Steering" section.
3. Remove the four Phillips retaining screws.
4. Disconnect the speedometer cable and the trip odometer cable.
5. Pull the instrument panel out.
6. Individual gauges are retained by rubber rings. Push the gauge out towards the front to remove it.
7. Be sure that the wires are correctly reinstalled on the gauge.
8. Install the instrument panel in a reverse order of removal.

Fuse Box Location

The 911 and 912E fuse box is located in the left front of the luggage compartment. The 914 fuse box is located under the instrument panel to the left of the steering column.

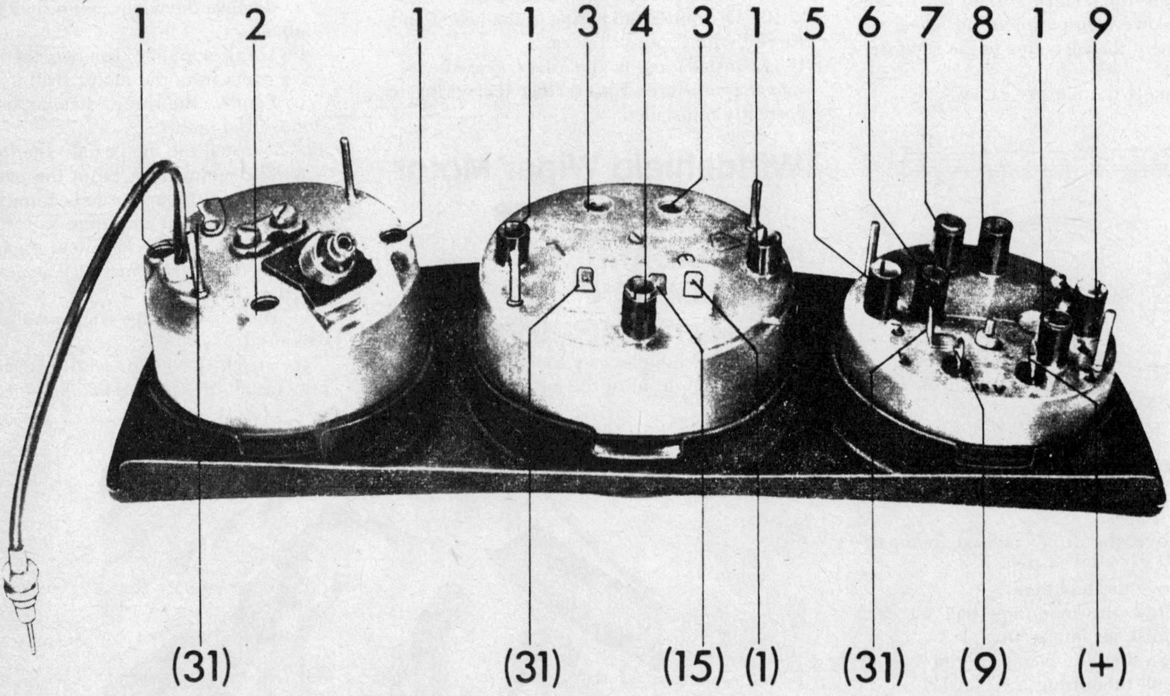

1. Instrument lights
2. Side marker indicating light (green)
3. Turn signal indicating light (green)
4. High beam indicating light (blue)
5. Charging control light (red)
6. Warning light, fuel reserve (red)
7. Oil temperature warning light (red); 914/6 only
8. Hand brake warning light (red)
9. Oil pressure indicating light (green)

The numbers in parenthesis are terminal designations

914 and 914/6 instrument panel connections

SPECIFICATIONS

INDEX

BEFORE SERVICING, SEE THE SAFETY NOTICE ON THE CONTENTS PAGE

INTRODUCTION

The Porsche 924 was introduced during the 1976 model year, with the Porsche 928 introduced during the 1978 model year, in the United States.

The Porsche 924 is powered by a four cylinder, overhead cam, inline, water cooled engine, while the Porsche 928 is powered by an aluminum block, water cooled V8 engine.

Both engines are front mounted and are connected to the rear mounted transaxle assembly by a rigid driveshaft tube.

Only one model, a two door sport coupe, is available in either series.

SERIAL NUMBER IDENTIFICATION

Vehicle

The chassis serial number is located on the left windshield post and can be viewed from the outside. The vehicle identification plate is in the engine compartment near the battery.

Engine

The engine serial number is stamped on the left of the crankcase near the clutch housing.

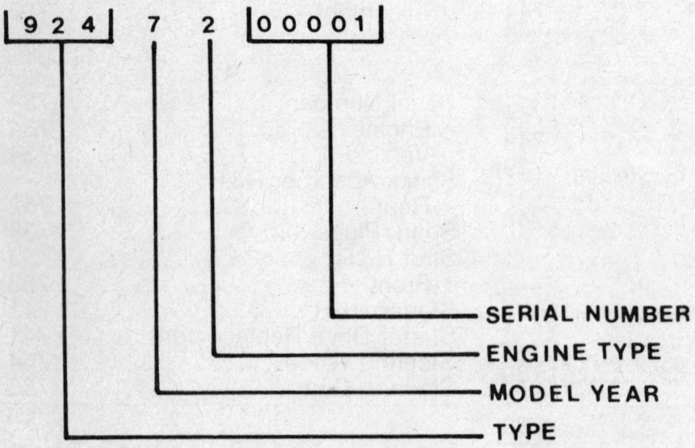

924 Serial number

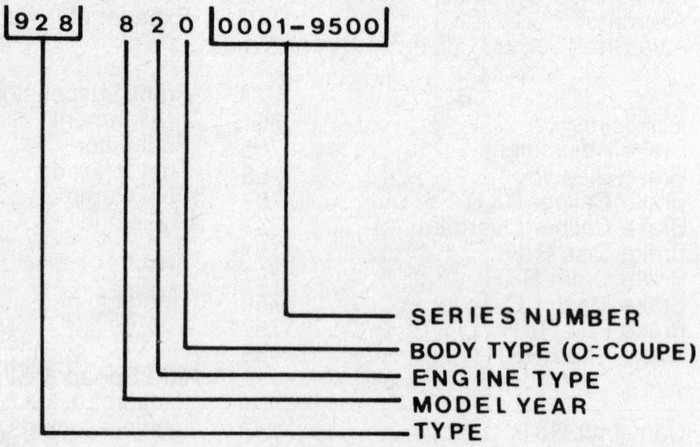

928 Serial number

GENERAL ENGINE SPECIFICATIONS

Year	Model	ENGINE DISPLACEMENT cc	ENGINE DISPLACEMENT (cu. in.)	Carburetor	Horsepower @ rpm (SAE)	Torque @ rpm (SAE)	Bore x Stroke (in.)	Compression Ratio	Oil Pressure @ rpm (psi)
1976-77	924	1984	(121)	Fuel inj.	95.4 @ 5500	109.2 @ 3000	3.41 x 3.32	8.0:1	71-100 @ 5000
1978-81	924	1984	(121)	Fuel inj.	110 @ 5750	111.3 @ 3500	3.41 x 3.32	8.5:1	71-100 @ 5000
1979-81	924 Turbo.	1984	(121)	Fuel inj.	143 @ 5500	147 @ 3000	3.41 x 3.32	7.5:1	N.A.
1978-81	928	4474	(273)	Fuel inj.	219 @ 5250	245 @ 3600	3.74 x 3.11	8.5:1	70 @ 5500

N.A. Not available at time of publication

TUNE-UP SPECIFICATIONS

Year	Model	ENGINE DISPLACEMENT cc	ENGINE DISPLACEMENT (cu. in.)	SPARK PLUGS Type	SPARK PLUGS Gap (in.)	Ignition Timing ①② (rpm)	Intake Valve Opens (deg)	Idle Speed (rpm)	VALVE CLEARANCE (cold) (in.) Intake	VALVE CLEARANCE (cold) (in.) Exhaust
1976-81	924	1984	(121)	W200-T30	.028-.032	10°ATDC @ 925	5°BTDC	850-1000	.004	.016
1979-81	924 Turbo.	1984	(121)	WR7DS	.024	20°BTDC @ 2000	—	900-1000	.004	.004

TUNE-UP SPECIFICATIONS

		ENGINE DISPLACEMENT		SPARK PLUGS			Intake		VALVE CLEARANCE (cold) (in.)	
Year	Model	cc	(cu. in.)	Type	Gap (in.)	Ignition Timing ① ② (rpm)	Intake Valve Opens (deg)	Idle Speed (rpm)	Intake	Exhaust
1978-79	928	4474	(273)	W145-T30	.028-.032	31°BTDC @ 3000	8°ATDC ③	800	Hyd.	Hyd.
1980-81	928	4474	(273)	WR8DS	.028	23°BTDC @ 3000	8°ATDC	700-800	Hyd.	Hyd.

NOTE: The underhood specifications sticker often reflects tune-up changes made in production. Sticker figures must be used if they disagree with the figures in this chart.
① With .039 in. valve clearance
② With vacuum hose disconnected
③ .0393 in., zero valve clearance

FIRING ORDERS

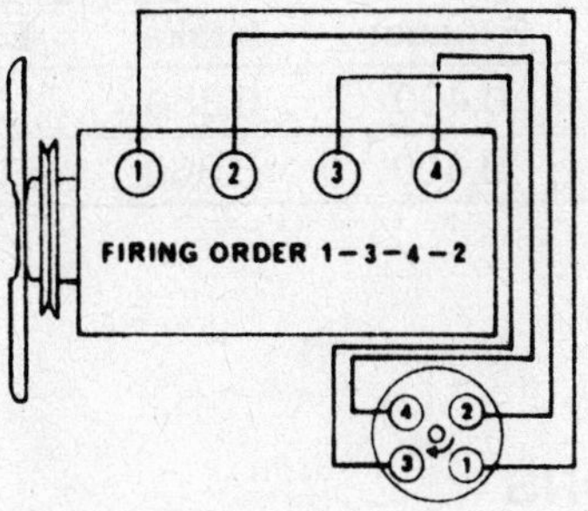

924

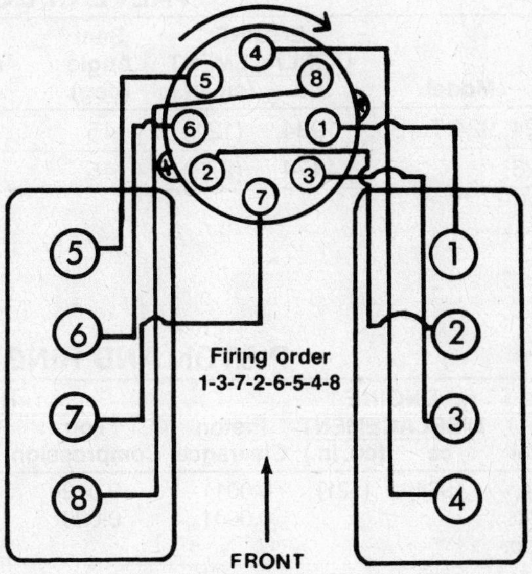

928

CRANKSHAFT AND CONNECTING ROD SPECIFICATIONS
(All measurements given in inches)

			CRANKSHAFT				CONNECTING ROD		
Year	Model	Engine Displacement (cu. in.)	Main Brg. Journal Diameter	Main Brg. Oil Clearance	Shaft End-Play	Thrust on No.	Journal Diameter	Oil Clearance	Side Clearance
1976-81	924	(121)	2.4	0.0020-0.0040	0.0040	3	1.9	0.0008-0.0032	0.0040-0.0092
1979-81	924 Turbo.	(121)	2.5	0.0008-0.0030	0.0040	3	1.89-1.97	0.0008-0.0030	0.0020-0.0120
1978-81	928	(273)	2.8	0.0008-0.0039	0.0044-0.0124	3	2.08	0.0008-0.0028	—

CAPACITIES

Year	Model	ENGINE DISPLACEMENT cc	(cu. in.)	ENGINE CRANKCASE (qts.) With Filter	Without Filter	TRANSAXLE (qts.) Manual	Auto.	Gasoline Tank (gal.)	Cooling System (qts.)
1976-81	924	1984	(121)	5.3	4.75	2.75 ①	3.17 ②	16.4	8.11
1979-81	924 Turbo.	1984	(121)	5.8	—	—	5.5	18.6	—
1978-81	928	4474	(273)	7.9	6.4	4.0 ③	—	22.7	16.2

① SAE 80 or 80W gear oil
② At oil change ATF Dexron®, differential 1.06 qt. SAE 90 gear oil
③ Mid-1978 model year—change manual gear oil usage to Dexron® ATF

VALVE SPECIFICATIONS

Year	Model	ENGINE DISPLACEMENT cc	(cu. in.)	Seat Angle (deg)	Face Angle (deg)	STEM-TO-GUIDE CLEARANCE Intake	Exhaust	STEM DIAMETER Intake	Exhaust
1976-81	924, 924 Turbo.	1984	(121)	45	45¼	0.100	0.400	0.360	0.360
1978-81	928	4474	(273)	45	45	0.100	0.400	0.360	0.360

PISTON AND RING SPECIFICATIONS

Year	Model	ENGINE DISPLACEMENT cc	(cu. in.)	Piston Clearance	RING GAP Top Compression	Bottom Compression	Oil Control	RING SIDE CLEARANCE Top Compression	Bottom Compression	Oil Control
1976-81	924, 924 Turbo.	1984	(121)	0.0011-0.0031	0.012-0.020	0.012-0.020	0.012-0.020	0.0016-0.0028	0.0016-0.0028	0.0016-0.0028
1978-81	928	4474	(273)	0.014	0.012-0.020	0.012-0.020	0.012-0.020	0.0020-0.0030	0.0020-0.0030	0.0020-0.0030

TORQUE SPECIFICATIONS

Year	Model	ENGINE DISPLACEMENT cc	(cu. in.)	Cylinder Head Bolts	Rod Bearing Bolts	Main Bearing Bolts	Crankshaft Pulley Bolt	Flywheel to Crankshaft Bolts	MANIFOLD Intake	Exhaust
1976-81	924	1984	(121)	56 ①	34-42	58 ②	181	65	15	15
1979-81	924 Turbo.	1984	(121)	72	47	58 ②	181	65	15	15
1978-81	928	4474	(273)	58 ③	42	29 ④	181	69	N.A.	N.A.

① 63 ft. lbs. warm
② Allen head bolts on cap #5 are torqued to 47 ft. lbs.
③ Torqued in four steps: 14 ft. lbs., 36 ft. lbs., 61 ft. lbs., and after 30 minutes loosen the head bolts ¼ turn and retorque them to 58 ft. lbs.
④ Torqued in two steps: 14 ft. lbs., 29 ft. lbs.
N.A. Not available

TORQUE SEQUENCES

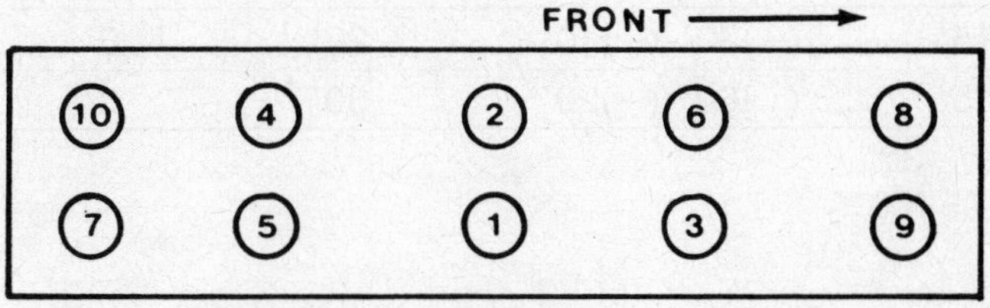

924

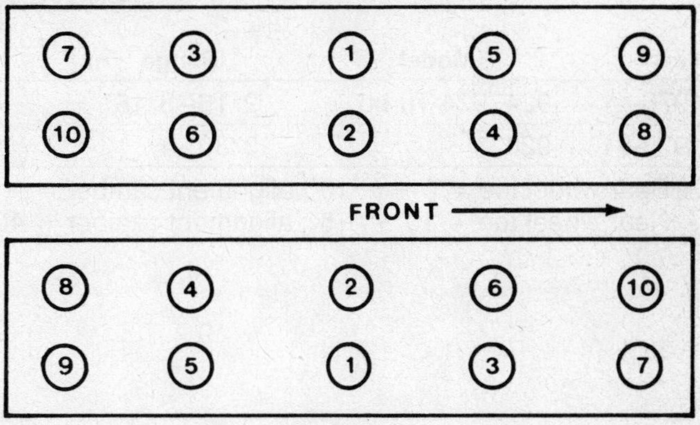

928

ALTERNATOR AND REGULATOR SPECIFICATIONS

Year	Model	ALTERNATOR Manufacturer	ALTERNATOR Output (amps)	REGULATOR Manufacturer	FIELD RELAY Air Gap (in.)	FIELD RELAY Point Gap (in.)	FIELD RELAY Volts to Close	REGULATOR Air Gap (in.)	REGULATOR Point Gap (in.)	REGULATOR Volts @ 75 degrees
1976-81	924	Bosch	75	Bosch	—Sealed unit not adjustable—					13.5-14.5
1979-81	924 Turbo.	Bosch	68	Bosch	—Sealed unit not adjustable—					13.5-14.5
1978-81	928	Bosch	90	Bosch	—Sealed unit not adjustable—					13.5-14.5

BATTERY AND STARTER SPECIFICATIONS

All cars use 12 volt, negative ground electrical systems

Model	Year	Battery Amp Hour Capacity	STARTER Lock Test Amps	Lock Test Volts	Lock Test Torque (ft/lbs)	No Load Test Amps	No Load Test Volts	No Load Test RPM	Brush Spring Tension (oz)	Min. Brush Length (in.)
924	1976-81	63	250-300	7	N.A.	N.A.	N.A.	N.A.	N.A.	0.47
928	1978-81	88	N.A.	N.A.	N.A.	N.A.	N.A.	N.A.	N.A.	N.A.

BRAKE SPECIFICATIONS

Year	Model	Lug Nut Torque (ft. lbs.)	Master Cylinder Bore	BRAKE DISC Minimum Thickness	BRAKE DISC Maximum Run-Out	BRAKE DRUM Diameter	BRAKE DRUM Maximum Machine (O/S)	BRAKE DRUM Maximum Wear Limit	MINIMUM LINING THICKNESS Front	MINIMUM LINING THICKNESS Rear
1976-81	924	80 ①	0.81	0.41	N.A.	9.06	0.30	N.A.	0.07	0.09
1979-81	924 Turbo.	80 ①	0.83	0.48	N.A.	9.20	0.30	N.A.	0.07	0.09
1978-81	928	80 ①	0.95	0.72	N.A.	N.A.	N.A.	N.A.	0.08	0.08

① Alloy wheel 94 ft. lbs. torque
N.A. Not available

WHEEL ALIGNMENT SPECIFICATIONS

Year	Model	Caster Range	Caster Preferred Setting	Camber Range	Camber Preferred Setting	Toe-In
1976-81	924, 924 Turbo. ①	2°15′-3°15′	2°45′	(−)30′-(+)10′	−20′	0°
1978-81	928 ②	3°30′-4°	3°45′	(−)60′-(+)20′	−30′	0°

① Rear wheel toe = 0°+/−10′; alignment camber = −1°+/−30′
② Rear wheel toe = 10′+/−5′; alignment camber = 40′+/−108

TUNE-UP PROCEDURES

Spark Plugs

Spark plugs are located on the passenger side of the engine and are removed with a standard 13/16 in. spark plug socket. Spark plug tightening torque is 22 ft/lbs (3 mkg).

Ignition

CAUTION

The engine should be turned off or the battery cable disconnected when ignition system parts are replaced or engine test equipment is connected to the ignition system, because of the dangerous current that can be present in the primary and secondary circuits. Personal injury could occur.

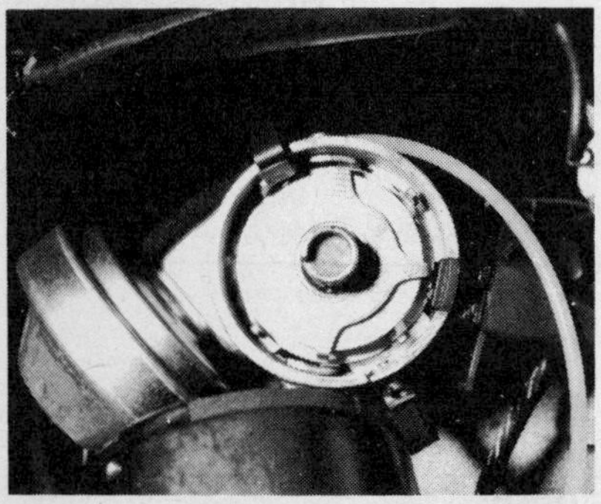

Electronic ignition reluctor and sensor—model 924

The ignition is fully electronic, using no breaker points. A control unit is located at the front of the engine compartment. The coil and two ballast resistors are located on the firewall on the 924 and on the left front of the engine compartment on the 928. Tune-up maintenance is limited to checking the ignition wires, distributor cap and rotor condition, and rotor resistance (5000 ohms). The distributor cap is retained by two snap clips. When replacing the cap, be sure to reinstall the shield over the cap.

ATTENTION. HAUTE TENSION
Danger de mort en cas de travaux
sur l' allumage et compte-tours.
BOSCH

The CD ignition control unit. Never touch this unit or any other ignition terminals with the ignition on, because of the danger of a high voltage shock.

Ignition Timing

924

The timing light is attached in the usual way. The timing marks are not on the crankshaft pulley, but on the flywheel, visible through a small access hole in the clutch housing. Loosen the distributor holddown bolt, if adjustment is necessary. Basic timing at idle should be 10° ATDC with vacuum hoses(s) left connected.

928

The timing marks are located on the crankshaft pulley and are colored for identification. (TDC and 31° BTDC).

If timing adjustment is necessary, loosen the distributor holddown bolt and move the

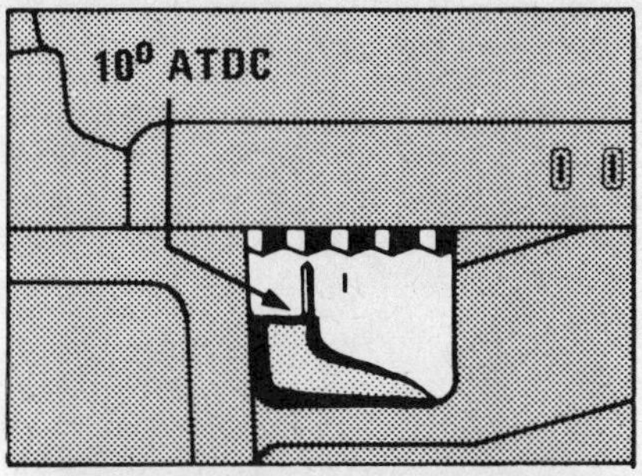

10° mark should be aligned with timing window ledge in the clutch housing opening—model 924

distributor body as required. Retighten the hold-down bolt when the adjustment is completed.

The vacuum hose should be disconnected from the vacuum retard unit during the adjustment.

Valve Lash

924

CAUTION

When turning the engine for valve adjustment, do not turn it with the camshaft pulley. Use the crankshaft pulley or bump the starter. The timing belt can be damaged by turning the camshaft pulley.

Adjustment is made by means of a wedge type adjustment screw which is flat on one side. The flat side rides directly on the valve stem. Five different diameter adjustment screws are available to compensate for wear. Adjustment is made by inserting an Allen wrench through the hole in the cam follower. Adjustment is made in full turns. If more than several turns are necessary to correct the clearance, the adjustment screw will probably have to be replaced with the next larger size. Always start with the smallest adjustment screws (white) after a valve job.

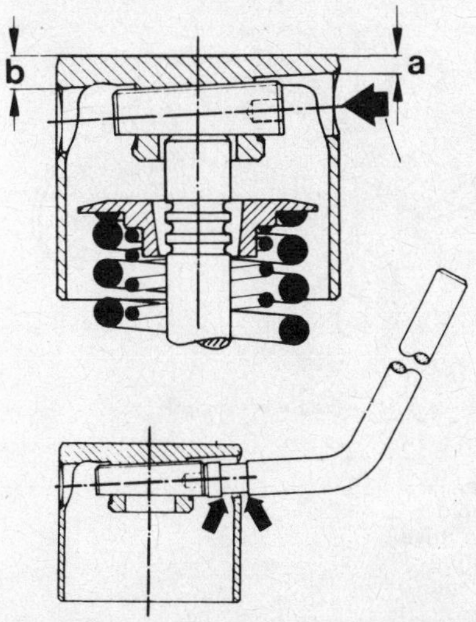

Valve adjustment is made by turning the wedge type screw one full turn at a time—model 924

NOTE: One turn of the screw changes the valve clearance 0.002 in.

1. Remove the camshaft cover.
2. Turn the crankshaft pulley until No. 1 cylinder is at TDC of the compression stroke (both cam lobes pointing up).
3. Insert the correct feeler gauge between the cam follower and the camshaft heel.
4. If adjustment is necessary, insert an Allen wrench and turn the adjustment screw until clearance is correct.
5. Proceed to adjust valve clearance for each cylinder in the same way.

NOTE: Early engine models had paint colors as identifying marks on the adjusting screws. Later engine models use notches, ground on the screw end, opposite the adjusting tool hole, as the identity marks. The higher number of notches indicates the increased thickness of the adjusting screw.

Valve adjusting screw identification #2
White—6.6 mm—Replaced by "no notch" screw
Blue—6.9 mm—Replaced by "one notch" screw
Red—7.2 mm—Replaced by "two notch" screw
No color—new—"three notch screw"
Yellow—7.5 mm—Replaced by "four notch" screw

928

The overhead cams operate bucket-type hydraulic valve lifters, located directly over the valve stems and therefore, no valve adjustment is necessary.

Fuel Injection

The 924 and 928 use CIS fuel injection. The system operates in the same way as the system used on 911s.

924

Idle Speed

Idle speed is adjusted at the bypass screw located on the throttle housing. Turn the screw in or out as necessary to obtain an idle speed of 900-1000 rpm.

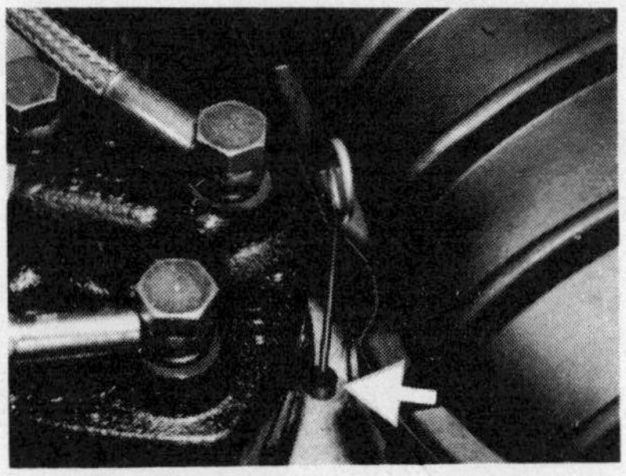

Idle speed screw location—model 924

Idle Mixture

Idle mixture can be adjusted with the CO adjuster located between the fuel distributor and the sensor plate. Remove the plug for access. Special tool P377 is needed for this adjustment. On 49 state cars, HC/CO readings are taken with the air pump disconnected. On California cars, take the sample before the converter.

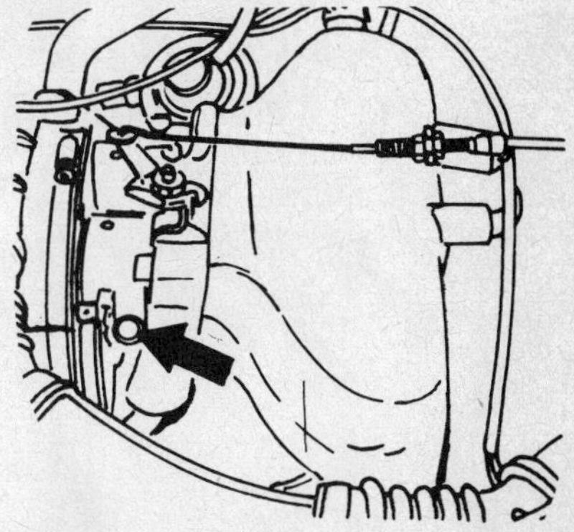

CO adjuster is located under the indicated plug—model 924

928

1. Remove the right air intake hose and the air cleaner upper section to gain access to the diverter valve.
2. Remove and plug the diverter valve hose. Attach a calibrated CO meter to the exhaust.
3. Install air intake hose and the upper air cleaner section.
4. Using an oil temperature gauge, operate the engine until temperature reading of 176 to 194 degrees is obtained.
5. Adjust the idle speed control screw until 800 ± 50 rpm is reached.
6. If necessary, adjust the mixture with the use of a special tool, inserted in the funnel-shaped opening of the mixture control unit, and into the head of the spring loaded driver.

NOTE: It is necessary to press downward approximately ⅝ inch to engage the spring loaded drive in the mixture control screw.

7. Make the necessary adjustments while conforming to the following procedures;
   a. Always make the CO level adjustment from lean to rich.
   b. Turn the mixture screw clockwise for richer or counterclockwise for leaner mixture.
   c. Refer to engine emission label for CO level specification.
8. Remove the plug from the diverter hose and connect the hose to the diverter valve.

ENGINE ELECTRICAL

Distributor

REMOVAL AND INSTALLATION

1. Remove the distributor cap and place it out of the way. Turn the engine so that the rotor points to No. 1 in the cap and the timing marks on the flywheel, or crankshaft pulley align.

Distributor holddown bolt, 924

The alternator on the 924 (white arrow) is buried under the passenger side of the engine. The scoop (black arrow) and air hose keep the alternator cool.

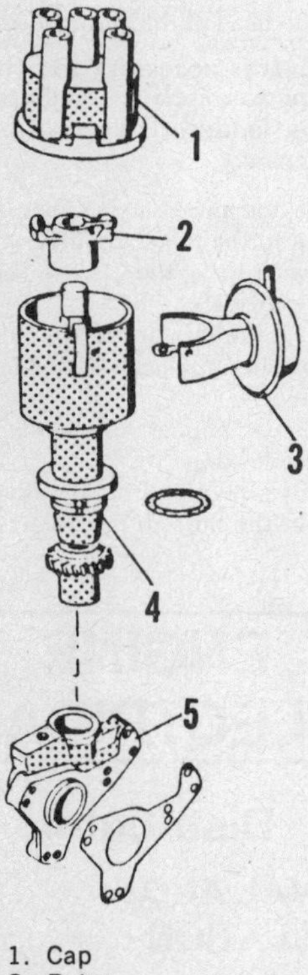

1. Cap
2. Rotor
3. Vacuum advance unit
4. Distributor
5. Mounting housing

Exploded view of distributor—model 924

2. Disconnect the primary wire at the distributor. Matchmark the distributor base and the distributor mount housing.
3. Loosen the holddown bolt and remove the distributor clamp.
4. Pull the distributor from the engine.
5. Installation is the reverse of removal. Use a new distributor base gasket. Check the ignition timing after installation.

Alternator

REMOVAL AND INSTALLATION

924

The alternator and voltage regulator are combined in one housing. No voltage adjustment can be made with this unit. The regulator can be replaced without removing and disassembling the alternator, just unbolt it from the rear.

1. Disconnect the battery cables.
2. Remove the cooling shroud and scoop from the alternator. The scoop is retained by a snap clip.
3. Remove the oil filter.
4. Disconnect the multi-connector from the rear of the alternator.
5. Loosen and remove the two Allen head retaining bolts.

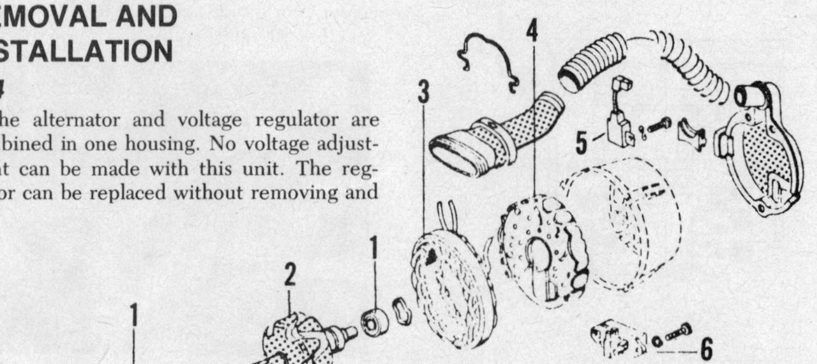

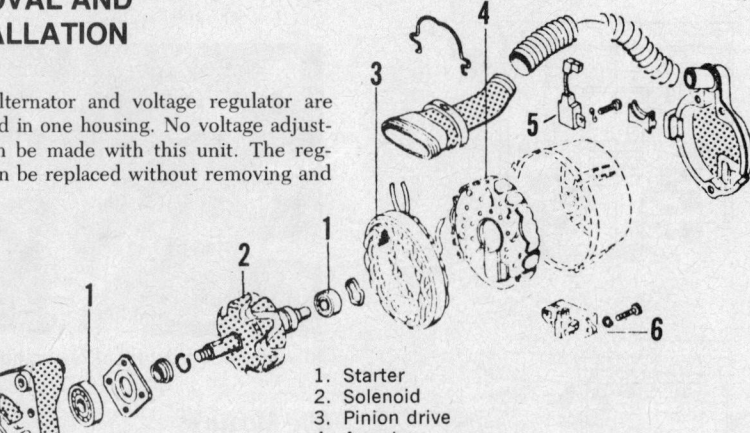

1. Starter
2. Solenoid
3. Pinion drive
4. Armature
5. Field coil
6. Brush

Exploded view of alternator—model 924

6. Remove the fan belt. Remove the alternator.

7. Installation is the reverse of removal. Properly tension the fan belt. Deflection of the belt midway between the pulleys should be about ⅜ in.

928

The voltage regulator is bolted to the rear of the alternator. Remove the alternator before attempting to remove the voltage regulator.

The alternator is removed from the bottom of the vehicle.

1. Remove the battery ground cable.
2. Raise the vehicle and support safely.
3. Remove the engine splash shield and the alternator cooling vent cover and tube.
4. Loosen the belt tension lock bolt, move the alternator inward and remove the belt from the pulley.
5. Remove the wire connections from the rear of the alternator.
6. Remove the alternator pivot bolt and remove the alternator from the engine.
7. Installation is the reverse of removal.

Starter

REMOVAL AND INSTALLATION

1. Disconnect the battery ground cable.
2. Jack up the right front of the car and support it with a stand.
3. Disconnect the two small wires from the starter solenoid. One wire connects to the ignition coil and the second to the ignition switch through the wiring harness.
4. Disconnect the large cable, which is the positive battery cable, from the solenoid.
5. Remove the two starter retaining bolts.
6. Pull the starter straight out and to the front, then drop it out of the car.
7. Installation is the reverse of removal.

OVERHAUL

Use the following procedure to replace brushes or starter drive.

1. Remove the solenoid.
2. Remove the end bearing cap.
3. Loosen both of the long housing screws.
4. Remove the lockwasher and spacer washers.
5. Remove the long housing screws and remove the end cover.
6. Pull the two field coil brushes out of the brush housing.
7. Remove the brush housing assembly.
8. Loosen the nut on the solenoid housing, remove the sealing disc, and remove the solenoid operating lever.
9. Loosen the large screws on the side of the starter body and remove the field coil along with the brushes.

NOTE: If the brushes require replacement, the field coil and brushes and/or the brush housing and its brushes must be replaced as a unit. Turn the armature if it is out-of-round, scored, or grooved.

10. If the starter drive is being replaced, push the stop-ring down and remove the circlip on the end of the shaft. Remove the stop-ring and remove the drive.
11. Assembly of the starter is the reverse of disassembly. Use a gear puller to install the stop-ring in its groove. Use a new circlip on the shaft.

SOELNOID REPLACEMENT

1. Remove the starter.
2. Remove the nut which secures the connector strip on the end of the solenoid.
3. Take out the two retaining screws on the mounting bracket and withdraw the solenoid after it has been unhooked from the operating lever.
4. Installation is the reverse of removal. In order to facilitate engagement of the lever, the pinion should be pulled as far as possible when inserting the solenoid.

ENGINE MECHANICAL

The 924 engine is based on an Audi cylinder block. It is a watercooled, inline four with a belt driven overhead cam. The engine is inclined 40° to the right.

A V8 engine with an overhead cam mounted on each head and driven by a toothed belt from the crankshaft, is used in the 928 models.

The two piece engine block and cylinder heads are of cast aluminum. The cylinder walls are impregnated with a silicone compound, making cylinder liners unnecessary.

Engine Removal and Installation

924

1. Disconnect the battery cables. Raise the car and support it on jack stands.
2. Support the engine. Use an overhead hoist. If using a jack under the engine be careful not to damage the aluminum oil pan. Use a wooden block between the jack and pan.
3. Remove the splash panel. Remove the windshield washer tank and bracket and place it behind the right headlight.
4. Disconnect the clutch cable. Remove the bottom clutch adjustment locknut and detach the cable from the lever.
5. Remove the access plate from the bottom of the clutch housing.
6. Have an assistant turn the engine with the crankshaft pulley. Remove the pressure plate bolts gradually until all pressure is released.
7. Remove the exhaust pipe flange bolts.
8. Remove the bracket at the rear of the transaxle.
9. Remove the entire exhaust system.
10. Remove the back up light switch from the transaxle.
11. Disconnect the axle driveshafts at the transaxle and let them hang down out of the way.

NOTE: If the car is going to be moved around with the engine out of the car, wire the driveshafts up so that they don't become damaged.

12. Remove the clutch housing-to-engine bolts.
13. Place a wooden block under the front tunnel reinforcement to support the transaxle tube.
14. Remove the transaxle mounting bolts and slide the transaxle toward the rear.
15. Remove the air cleaner. Disconnect the brake booster vacuum line.
16. Disconnect and plug the fuel line.
17. Disconnect the accelerator cable.
18. Drain the cooling system.
19. Disconnect the radiator hoses. Remove the electric cooling fan.
20. Remove the hood. Detach the air conditioning compressor and place it out of the way. Do not disconnect the lines.
21. Remove the radiator and expansion tank. Disconnect the heater hoses from the engine.
22. Disconnect the starter wiring.
23. Attach the engine lift chains to the hoist points on the engine. Disconnect the steering at the rack universal joint.
24. Disconnect the two side mounts on the

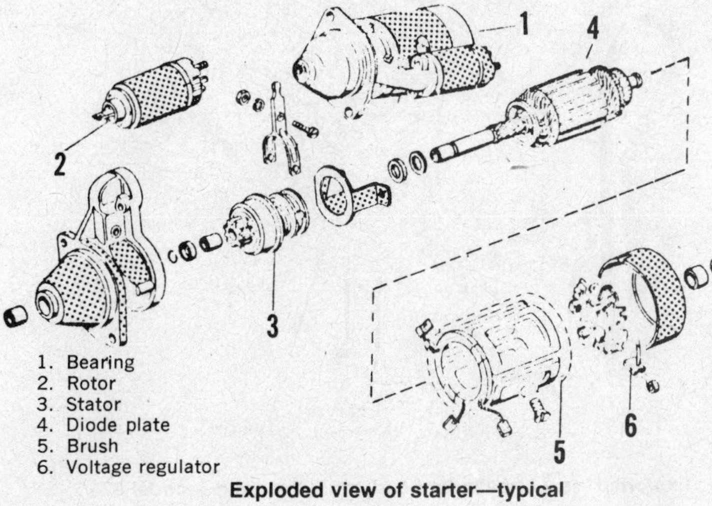

Exploded view of starter—typical

engine block. Remove the left side mount from the car.

25. Lift the engine from the car.

26. Installation is basically the reverse of removal. Tighten the pressure plate bolts to 24 ft/lbs, the clutch housing bolts to 60 ft/lbs (12 mm bolt), 36 ft/lbs (10 mm bolt) and 20 ft/lbs (8 mm bolt).

928

1. Disconnect the battery ground cable.
2. Remove the engine compartment cross brace.

NOTE: The vehicle must be on its wheels when the cross brace is removed or replaced.

3. Disconnect wiring and hoses to the under side of the hood, loosen hood bolts and supports, and remove the hood.
4. Remove the air intake hoses and the air cleaner assembly.
5. Raise the vehicle and support safely.
6. Remove the bottom splash pan and drain the coolant from the radiator.
7. Drain the engine block of coolant by removing the drain plugs on the right and left sides of the crankcase.
8. Drain the engine oil.
9. Remove the lower body brace.
10. Disconnect the exhaust pipes at the exhaust manifolds and the right and left side heat shields.
11. Disconnect the body ground cable from the engine.
12. Remove the clutch slave cylinder at the clutch housing. Do not disconnect the hydraulic line.
13. Disconnect the starter wires and remove the starter along with the clutch housing cover.
14. Disconnect the clutch release lever at the ball pin by depressing the release lever in the direction of the clutch.
15. Remove the starter wires from the clamps on the steering crossmember.
16. Remove the bolts from the clamping sleeve on the driveshaft and slide the sleeve rearward.
17. Unscrew the throwout bearing sleeve mounting bolts and push the sleeve towards the clutch.
18. Disconnect the left and right engine shock absorber at the control arms and remove with the right and left upper shock mounts.
19. On vehicles with air conditioning:
    a. Disconnect the temperature switch wires on the radiator.
    b. Disconnect the power lead to the compressor.
    c. Loosen the compressor, remove the belt and remove the compressor from the mounting brackets. Do not remove the hoses.
    d. Suspend the compressor from the frame with a wire.
20. Remove the air pump filter housing and disconnect the alternator cooling hose.
21. Remove the lower fan shroud from the radiator, remove the cooling hoses and the oil cooler line from the radiator bottom.
22. By lifting the engine one side at a time, remove the engine mounts and carefully set the engine on the front crossmember.
23. Remove the clutch housing to engine bolts and lower the vehicle to the floor.
24. Remove the upper coolant hose and the vent from the radiator and thermostat housing.
25. Remove the upper oil cooler line from the upper part of the radiator.
26. Loosen the top mountings of the radiator and remove the assembly carefully.
27. Remove the heater hoses and electrical connections from the engine.
28. Remove the electronic control unit and loosen the ignition coil and set aside.
29. Disconnect the feed and return fuel lines.
30. Disconnect the lines at the power steering pump.
31. Disconnect the vacuum line to the power brake cylinder at the manifold.
32. Disconnect the accelerator cable by removing the holder and clamp.

NOTE: On air conditioned vehicles, cover the condenser with a wood board to prevent damage during the engine removal.

33. Attach a lifting cable to lifting device and to the engine.
34. Raise the assembly slightly and remove the engine block-to-clutch housing upper mounting bolts.
35. Pull the engine forward and remove the short driveshaft with the guide tube.
36. Lift the engine carefully from the engine compartment.
37. Installation is the reverse of removal.

Cylinder Head

REMOVAL AND INSTALLATION

924

1. Disconnect the battery cables.
2. Drain the cooling system.
3. Remove the air cleaner.
4. Disconnect the radiator and heater hoses.
5. Disconnect all electrical wires from the cylinder head.
6. Detach the spark plug wires. Remove the distributor.
7. Disconnect the exhaust manifold from the exhaust pipe.
8. Disconnect the EGR line. Remove the exhaust manifold.
9. Remove the fuel injection lines from the cylinder head.
10. Remove the throttle valve housing and intake manifold as a unit.

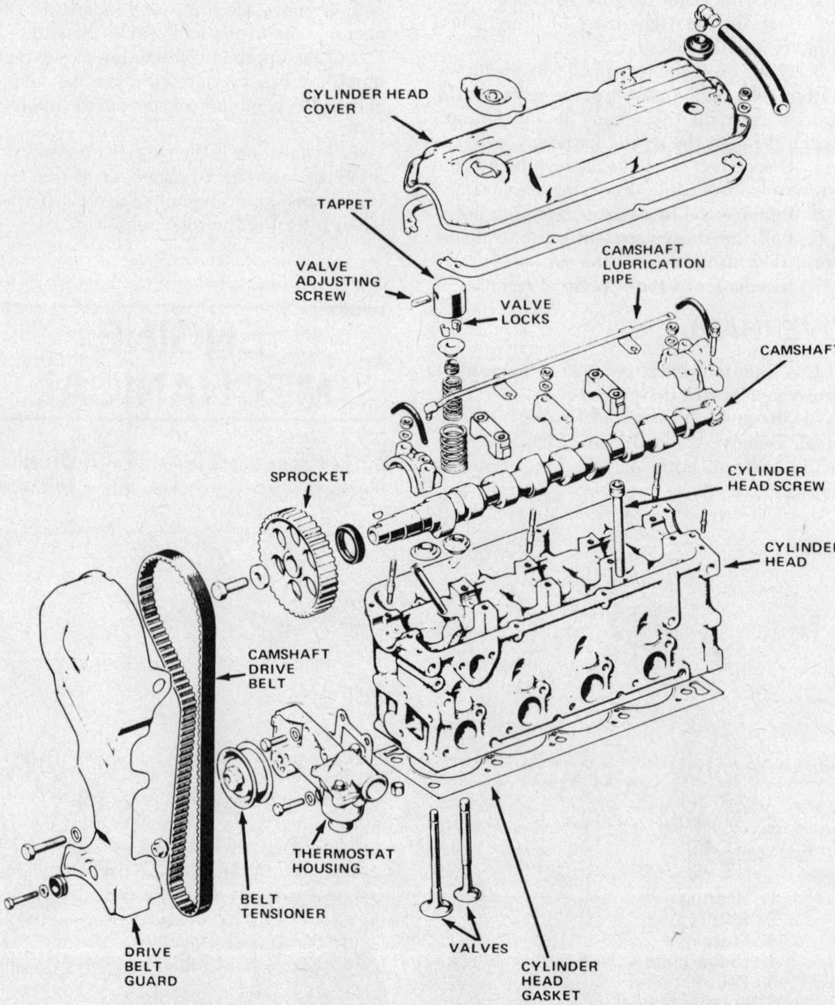

Exploded view of cylinder head and valve train—model 924

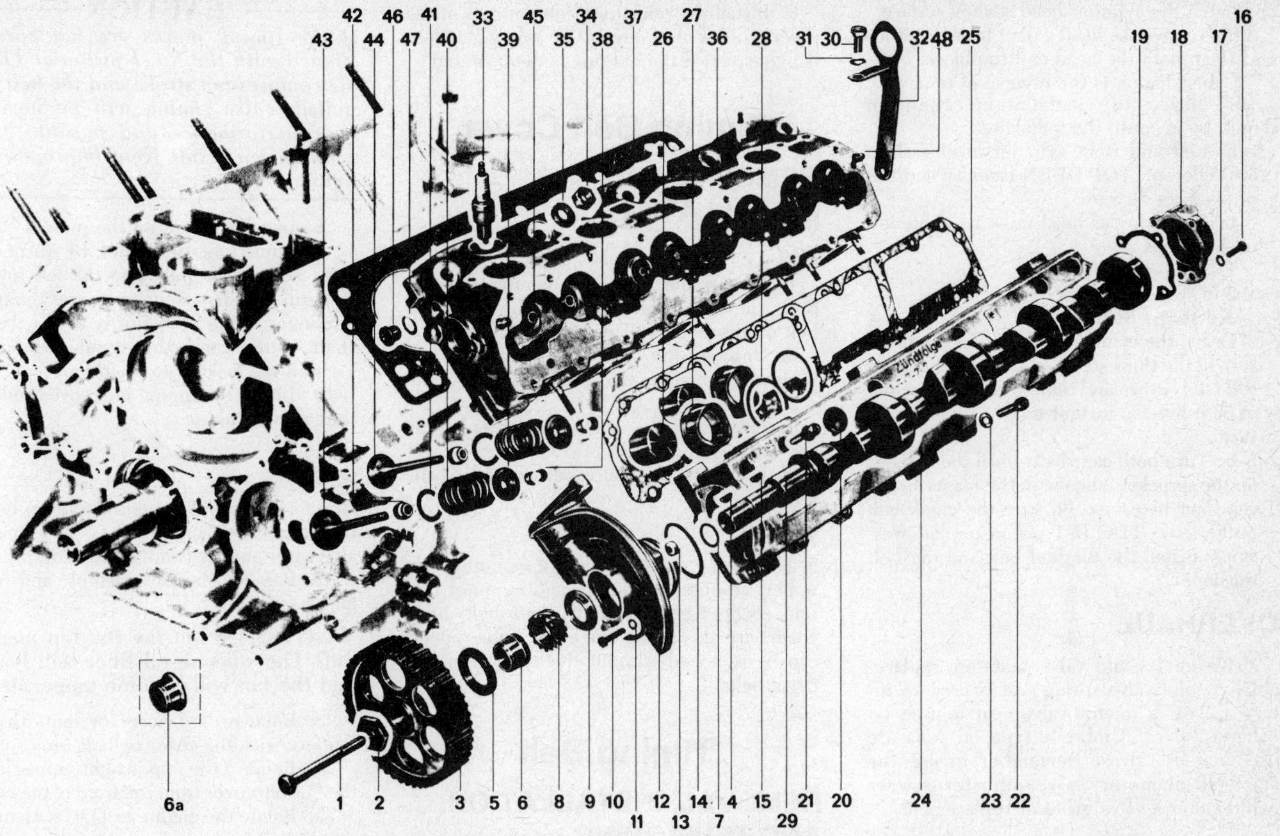

Exploded view of cylinder head and cam housing assemblies—model 928

1. Bolt	13. Seal	26. Hydraulic valve lifter	39. Spring retainer
2. Washer	14. O-ring	27. Lifter sleeve	40. Valve spring
3. Camshaft sprocket	15. Woodruff key	28. Gasket	41. Shim
4. Woodruff key	16. Bolt	29. Left camshaft	42. Valve stem seal
5. Camshaft oil seal	17. Washer	30. Bolt	43. Intake valve
6. Spacer	18. End cover	31. Washer	44. Exhaust valve
6a. Spacer	19. Gasket	32. Lifting eye	45. Valve guide
7. O-ring	20. Plug	33. Spark plug	46. Plug
8. Distributor drive gear	21. Bolt with washers	34. Nut	47. Seal
9. Spacer	22. Bolt	35. Washer	48. Dowel pin
10. Bolt	23. Washer	36. Cylinder head	
11. Washer	24. Camshaft housing	37. Left gasket	
12. Bearing carrier	25. Gasket	38. Valve keeper	

11. Disconnect the air pump lines on models so equipped.

12. Remove the timing belt cover. Loosen the tensioner and remove the belt.

13. Loosen and remove the cylinder head bolts according to the sequence and remove the bolts.

14. Carefully lift off the cylinder head.

15. Installation is the reverse of removal. Be sure to correctly position the new cylinder head gasket. Align the timing marks and install the timing belt and properly tension it. This procedure is under Timing Belt. Tighten the cylinder head bolts to 58 ft/lbs in the sequence shown.

NOTE: Cylinder head bolts should be retorqued after 600 miles. Loosen the bolts ¼ turn and then tighten to 65 ft/lbs.

928

NOTE: The cylinder heads can be removed with the engine in the vehicle.

1. Drain the cooling system; both radiator and engine block.

CAUTION

Because of the use of aluminum, do not allow the anti-freeze coolant mixture to enter the cylinders. Severe engine damage could result after engine start-up.

2. Remove the upper timing belt cover assembly.

3. Remove the upper coolant hoses and heater hoses from the thermostat housing area.

4. Remove the air intake tube and the air cleaner assembly.

5. Remove all connecting linkages, wires and hoses from the intake manifold and injector system.

6. Rotate the engine to bring the crankshaft pulley mark to TDC, and, if working with the left cylinder head, mark and remove the distributor assembly.

7. Remove the intake manifold and injector system from the cylinder head and engine block.

8. From the lower right side of the engine block, loosen the timing belt tensioner bolt and remove the timing belt from the sprockets.

NOTE: Accessory drive belts may have to be either loosened or removed.

9. Remove the rubber plugs from the upper portion of the camshaft housing and remove the Allen head screws from the holes.

10. Remove the exposed Allen head screws from the lower portion of the camshaft housing and remove the housing from the cylinder head.

NOTE: The camshaft housing must be removed and replaced as an assembly.

11. Remove the exhaust manifold from the cylinder head. Remove the inner right and left belt housing, as necessary.

12. Remove the cylinder head nuts and washers by starting from the center and alternating toward each end.

13. Remove the cylinder head from the engine block studs, being careful not to mark

or scratch the cylinder head sealing surface.

14. Remove the head gasket from the studs and clean both the head and the block.

15. Installation is the reverse of removal.

16. During the installation, attention should be given to the following:

a. Left and right cylinder head gaskets are different. TOP/OBEN faces up and the arrow faces forward.

b. The cylinder head must be tightened in four steps.

1st step—14 ft/lbs.
2nd step—36 ft/lbs.
3rd step—61 ft/lbs.

Leave the cylinder head under the pressure of the third step for 30 minutes, loosen the nuts ¼ turn and tighten to a final torque of 58 ft/lbs. No further tightening is necessary.

c. Turn both camshafts until the notches on the sprockets align with the marks on the camshaft housings. Be sure the crankshaft pulley is at TDC (#1 piston on compression). Install the toothed belt and the belt tensioner.

OVERHAUL

Valve guides and valve seats are replaceable. A solid valve spring seat is used on intake valves, a rotator valve seat is used on exhaust valves. Umbrella type oil seals are used on all valves. Remember to use the smallest diameter valve adjuster screws (white) after a valve grind or replacement.

Intake Manifold

REMOVAL AND INSTALLATION

1. Remove the air cleaner.
2. Disconnect the accelerator cable.
3. Disconnect the EGR connections.
4. Detach all electrical leads.
5. Disconnect the auxiliary air regulator hose.
6. Remove all vacuum hoses attached to the intake manifold.
7. Remove the eight retaining nuts and remove the throttle valve housing and intake manifold as a unit.
8. Installation is the reverse of removal. Tighten the nuts to 15 ft/lbs.

Exhaust Manifold

REMOVAL AND INSTALLATION

1. Disconnect the EGR line from the manifold.
2. On models so equipped, remove the air pump connections.
3. Disconnect the exhaust pipe(s) from the manifold(s).
4. Remove the retaining nuts and remove the manifold(s)
5. Clean the cylinder head(s) and manifold mating surfaces.
6. Using new gaskets (there are four), install the exhaust manifold(s).
7. Tighten the nuts to 15 ft/lbs. Work from the inside out.
8. Install the remaining components in the reverse order of removal. Use a new manifold flange gasket if the old one is deteriorated.

Timing Belt Cover

REMOVAL AND INSTALLATION

924

1. Loosen the alternator mounting bolts, pivot the alternator over, and slip the drive belt off the pulleys.
2. Unscrew the cover retaining bolts and remove the cover. Keep the washers and spacers together.
3. Reposition the spacers and then install the washers and bolts.
4. Install the alternator belt and adjust the tension.

928

The timing cover consists of an outer right upper, an outer left upper and an outer bottom cover. Left and right inner belt guide covers are also used. The outer upper covers can be removed without the removal of the drive belts.

Timing Belt

REMOVAL, INSTALLATION AND TENSIONING

924

1. Remove the timing belt cover.
2. While holding the large hex on the tensioner pulley, loosen the pulley locknut.
3. Release the tensioner from the timing belt.
4. Slide the belt off the two toothed pulleys and remove it.
5. Using the large center bolt on the crankshaft pulley, turn the engine until the No. 1 cylinder is at TDC of the compression stroke. At this point, both valves will be closed and the timing marks at the flywheel will be aligned.
6. Check that the timing dot on the rear face of the camshaft pulley is aligned with the camshaft cover as shown in the illustration. If not, turn the pulley so that it does.
7. Check that the V-notch in the crankshaft pulley aligns with the adjusting lug on the oil pump housing as shown. If they don't align, turn the crankshaft until they do.

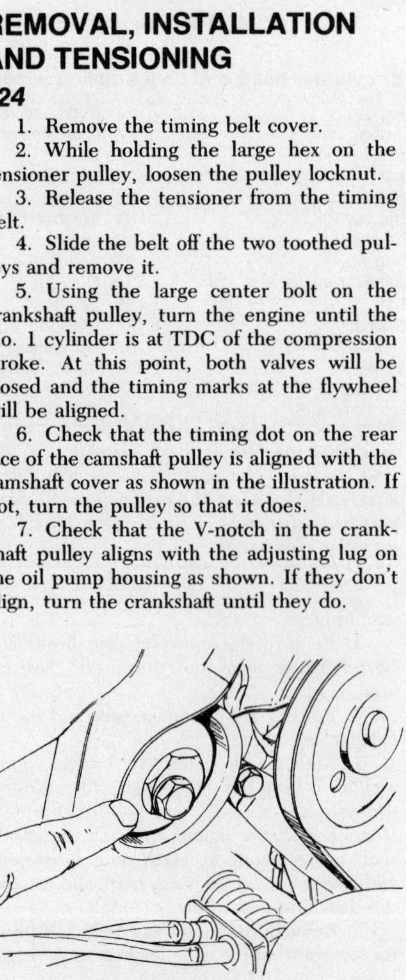

924 timing belt tension

CAUTION

If the timing marks are not correctly aligned with the No. 1 piston at TDC of the compression stroke and the belt is installed, valve timing will be incorrect. Poor performance and possible engine damage can result from improper valve timing.

8. Install the belt on the pulleys.
9. Adjust the tensioner by turning the large hex on the pulley to the left until the belt can be twisted 90° with the thumb and forefinger at the midpoint between the camshaft pulley and the crankshaft pulley. Tighten the locknut to 30 ft/lbs.
10. Install the timing belt cover and check the ignition timing.

928

1. Loosen and remove the drive belts for the proper steering pump, fan and air pump, alternator and air conditioning compressor.
2. Remove the fan assembly and bracket for clearance.

NOTE: Do not lay the fan assembly flat. The silicone oil filler will leak out and the fan will become inoperative.

3. Remove any hoses or lines that may intefere with the cover or belt removal.
4. Remove the upper right, upper left and the bottom cover from the front of the engine.
5. Rotate the engine to TDC with number one piston on the compression stroke and the distributor rotor pointing to number one cylinder spark plug wire terminal of distributor cap.
6. Loosen the belt tensioner bolt and remove the belt from the sprockets.
7. Align the camshaft notches with the marks on the cam housings and install a new toothed belt, being sure the crankshaft marks remain aligned at TDC.

NOTE: The water pump pulley is turned by the back of the toothed belt.

8. Tighten the belt tensioner bolt until the belt can be twisted only 90° between the tension roller and the right camshaft sprocket.
9. Install the covers, hoses or lines, fan and bracket assembly, and the drive belts. Adjust the drive belts to have a deflection of ½ inch between pulleys.
10. Check and adjust the ignition timing as necessary.

Timing Pulleys

REMOVAL AND INSTALLATION

The camshaft and crankshaft pulleys are located by keys on their respective shafts and each is retained by a bolt. To remove either or both of the pulleys, first remove the timing belt cover and belt and then use the following procedure.

NOTE: When removing the crankshaft pulley on the 924, don't remove the four bolts which retain the outer belt pulley to the timing belt pulley.

1. Remove the center bolt.
2. Gently pry the pulley off the shaft. If the pulley is stubborn, use a gear puller. Don't hammer on the pulley.
3. Remove the pulley and the key.
4. Install the pulley in the reverse order of removal.
5. Tighten the center bolt on the crankshaft pulley to 58 ft/lbs. Tighten the camshaft pulley retaining bolt to 15 ft/lbs.
6. Install the timing belt, check valve timing, .tension belt, and install the cover.

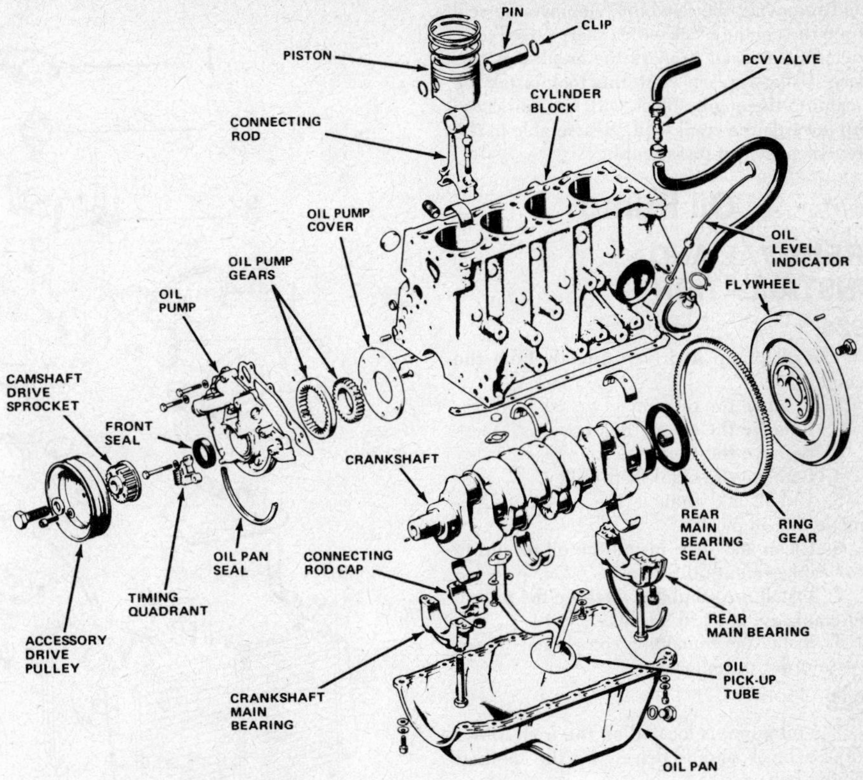

Exploded view of the 924 cylinder block, oil pan, and oil pump

Camshaft

REMOVAL AND INSTALLATION

924

1. Remove the timing belt.
2. Remove the camshaft sprocket.
3. Remove the air cleaner.
4. Remove the camshaft cover.
5. Remove the distributor and mounting housing.
6. Remove the oil injection tube and then reinstall the retaining nuts hand tight.
7. Unscrew and remove the nos. 1, 3 and 5 bearing caps (No. 1 is at the front of the engine).
8. Unscrew the Nos. 2 and 4 bearing caps, diagonally and in increments.
9. Lift the camshaft out of the cylinder head.
10. Lubricate the camshaft journals and lobes with assembly lube or gear oil before installing it in the cylinder head. Bolts are tightened to 8 ft/lbs and nuts to 20 ft/lbs.
11. Tighten bearing caps Nos. 2 and 4 carefully in a diagonal pattern.
12. Install bearing caps Nos. 1, 3 and 5.
13. Install the oil injection tube. You will have to loosen the nuts on Nos. 2 and 4 again.
14. Install the camshaft cover using new gaskets and seals.
15. Install the camshaft pulley and the timing belt.
16. Check the valve clearance.

928

Refer to the cylinder head removal and installation section for the removal of the cam housings as a unit.

1. Remove the hydraulic lifters, lifter sleeves and gaskets from the cam housing.
2. Remove the rear housing end plate and gasket.
3. Remove the timing belt gear, the front bearing carrier on the right head and the distributor and bearing carrier on the left cam housing.
4. Pull the camshaft to the rear and out of the cam housing.
5. The distributor gear and spacer can be removed from the camshaft at this time.
6. Installation is the reverse of removal.

NOTE: The front camshaft seals can be replaced while the front bearing carriers are off the cam housings or when the timing sprocket is removed from the camshaft.

ENGINE LUBRICATION

The 924 full pressure lubrication system consists of a wet sump, crankshaft driven oil pump, oil temperature gauge with sender in the oil pan, and a disposable type oil filter on the passenger side of the block.

The 928 oil sump lower section is divided into four chambers to maintain a constant oil supply for the suction pipe during periods of high speed driving and sharp turns. A thermostatically controlled oil cooler is located in the radiator and the oil pump is mounted on the front of the engine and is driven by the toothed belt. The oil filler tube and oil level sending unit are threaded into the top of the oil pan front. A full pressure lubrication system is used.

Oil Pan

REMOVAL AND INSTALLATION

924

1. Drain the oil. Remove the engine splash shield.
2. Disconnect the temperature sending unit wire.
3. Disconnect the side engine mounts and raise the engine for pan removal clearance.
4. Remove the pan retaining bolts and lower the pan from the car.
5. Install the pan using the reverse of the removal procedure. Use new gaskets and seals.

928

1. Raise the vehicle and support safely.
2. Remove the bottom protective engine plate.
3. Drain the engine oil and unscrew the oil fill pipe from the pan. Disconnect the oil level indicator wire.
4. Remove the oil pan retaining bolts and maneuver the oil pan downward so that the oil pump suction tube is not twisted or damaged.
5. Using a new gasket, install the oil pan in the reverse order of removal.

Rear Main Seal

REPLACEMENT

924

The rear main oil seal is located in the back of the cylinder block and so replacement involves disconnecting the torque tube and pulling the transaxle back, removing the clutch housing, and then removing the flywheel.

1. Carefully pry the seal out with a screwdriver.
2. Lightly oil the replacement seal with engine oil and carefully tap it into place. Do not damage the seal or score the flywheel.
3. Install the flywheel, clutch housing and torque tube and transaxle. Tighten the flywheel-to-crankshaft bolts to 65 ft/lbs.

928

The rear main oil seal can be replaced by separating the clutch housing from the engine and removing the flywheel. Remove the seal from the engine block with a sharp edged tool, being careful not to mark the crankshaft surface. Using a special centering tool, install the seal into the engine block with the lubricated lip towards the crankshaft. Reassemble in the reverse order of disassembly.

Oil Pump

REMOVAL AND INSTALLATION

924

The oil pump is driven directly from the crankshaft.

1. Remove the oil pan.
2. Remove the timing belt cover.
3. Remove the timing belt.
4. Remove the crankshaft pulley.
5. Unbolt and remove the oil pump. Remove the oil pickup.
6. Clean and then install the oil pickup to the replacement oil pump.
7. Install the oil pump. Tighten the pump-to-crankcase bolts to 8 ft/lbs.
8. Install the remaining components in reverse order of removal.

928

The oil pump is located on the front of the engine block and is driven by the toothed timing belt.

1. Remove the toothed timing belt. (Refer to the timing belt removal and installation section).
2. Remove the oil pump sprocket and the oil pump retaining bolts.
3. Remove the oil pump from the engine block.
4. Installation is the reverse of removal. Install a new O-ring seal on the pump body.

NOTE: An oil pump shaft seal is used and can be replaced after removal of the sprocket and woodruff key.

ENGINE COOLING

The 924 cooling system consists of a radiator, belt driven water pump, expansion tank, electric thermostatically controlled fan, and a conventional thermostat.

The 928 cooling system includes a radiator, belt driven water pump located on the upper front of the engine block, thermostat and a temperature controlled fan assembly. An expansion tank and coolant level sending unit is located in the right rear of the engine compartment.

Radiator

REMOVAL AND INSTALLATION

1. Drain the cooling system.
2. Remove the fan and radiator shroud.
3. Remove the radiator hoses.
4. Disconnect the expansion tank (924) and move it out of the way.

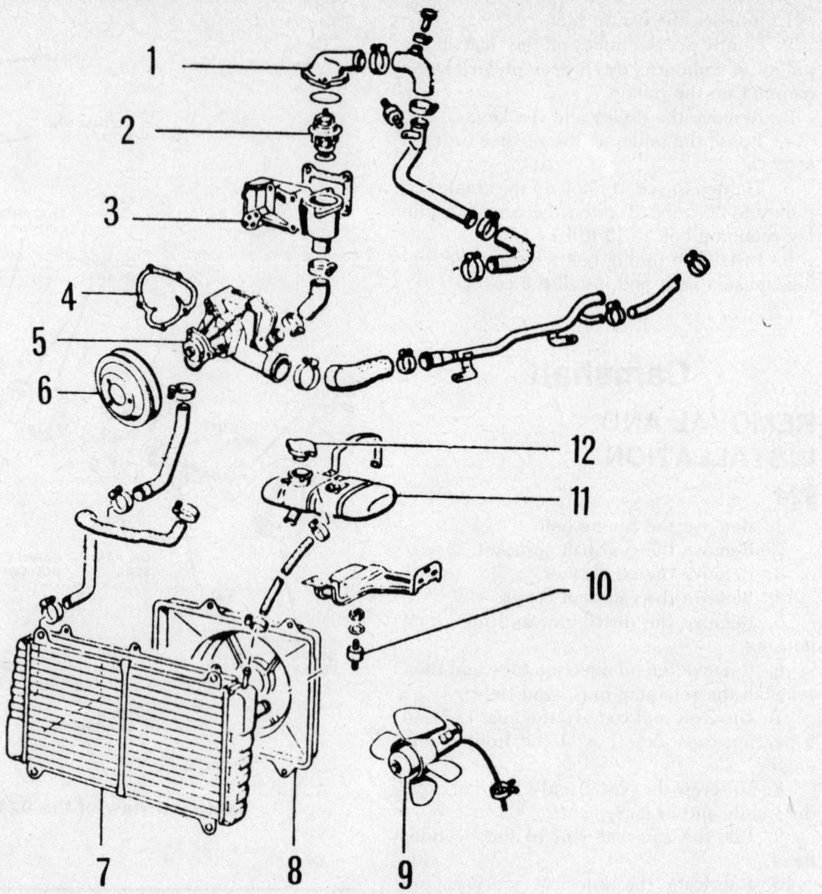

1. Coolant neck
2. Thermostat
3. Lower thermostat housing
4. Gasket
5. Water pump
6. Pulley
7. Radiator
8. Fan shroud
9. Fan
10. Bolt
11. Expansion tank
12. Cap

Exploded view of the 924 cooling system

5. Unbolt the radiator and remove it.
6. Installation is the reverse of removal. Refill the cooling system as follows: set the heater on the hot position, remove the vent plug on the radiator hose, fill the cooling system, start the engine and run it for one minute at fast idle, replace the vent plug where no more air bubbles appear at the plug opening.

Water Pump

REMOVAL AND INSTALLATION

924

1. Drain the cooling system.
2. Remove the timing belt cover.
3. Remove the fan belt.
4. Disconnect the radiator hoses from the pump.
5. Unbolt and remove the water pump.
6. Clean the crankcase and pump mating surfaces.
7. Install the water pump using a new gasket.
8. Install the remaining components in the reverse order of removal. Refill the cooling system. See "Radiator Removal and Installation."

928

1. Drain the cooling system.
2. Rotate the engine to TDC, with the Number one piston on the firing stroke and the distributor rotor pointing to Number one terminal of the distributor cap.
3. Remove the upper right and left timing belt covers and remove the fan and bracket.

NOTE: Maintain upright position of the fan assembly so that the silicone fluid does not drain out.

4. Loosen and remove the toothed belt from the water pump pulley. (Refer to the timing belt removal and installation section).
5. Remove the bolts and water pump from the engine block.
6. Using a new gasket, install the water pump in the reverse order of removal.

Thermostat

The thermostat is located in the upper radiator hose neck on the engine.

1. Drain the cooling system.
2. Don't disconnect the radiator hose, unbolt the neck and lift out the thermostat.
3. Clean the mating surfaces and install the

new thermostat (spring down) using a new gasket.

4. Refill the cooling system. See "Radiator Removal and Installation."

EMISSION CONTROLS

Positive Crankcase Ventilation

The 924 uses a conventional crankcase ventilation system. A PCV valve, located on the driver's side of the engine, meters blow-by gases into the air intake.

The 928 crankcase ventilation system utilizes an oil separator, which is also used as an oil filler tube. The crankcase fumes are routed through the separator pipe, where the liquid oil can settle and flow back into the crankcase. The fumes continue through a hose to the lower section of the air cleaner, where a flame arrestor is located. A coolant preheat line is placed along a portion of the vent hose to warm the crankcase fumes before entering the air cleaner.

SERVICE

The PCV valve should be replaced at the recommended intervals. Check hoses for plugging and cracking and replace where necessary.

Exhaust Gas Recirculation

All models are equipped with this system which lowers NOx emissions. Metered amounts of cooling exhaust gases are added to the air/fuel mixture. The recirculated gas lowers the peak flame temperature during combustion to cut the output of oxides of nitrogen. Exhaust gas from the exhaust pipe passes through a filter where it is cleaned. The vacuum operated EGR valve controls the amount of exhaust gas which enters the intake.

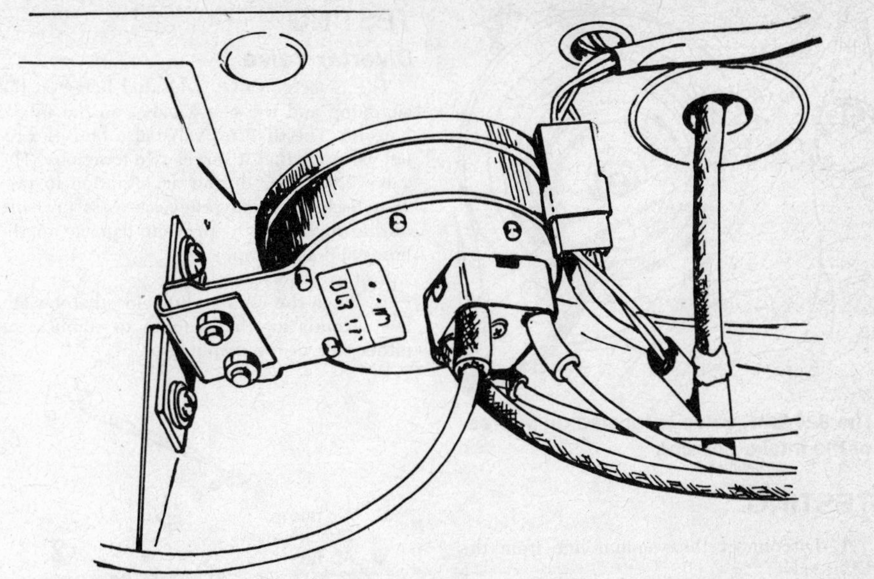

The EGR vacuum amplifier is located on the right side inner fender panel—model 924

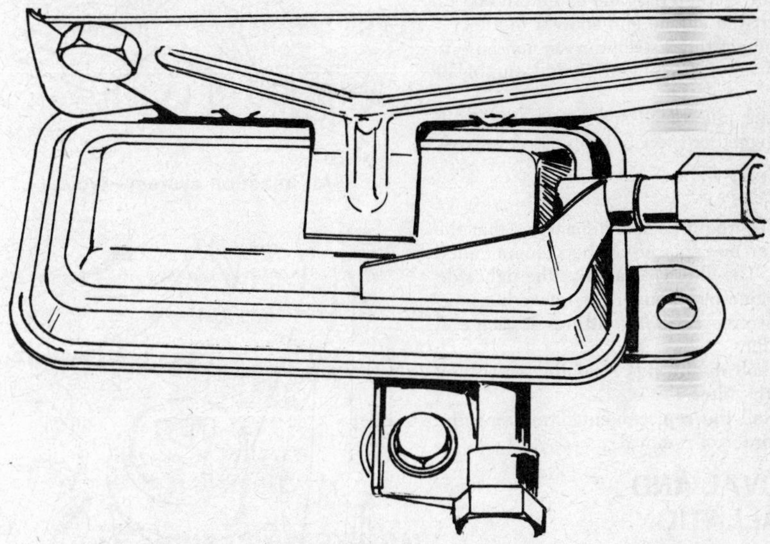

The 924 EGR filter is located on the driver's side of the engine

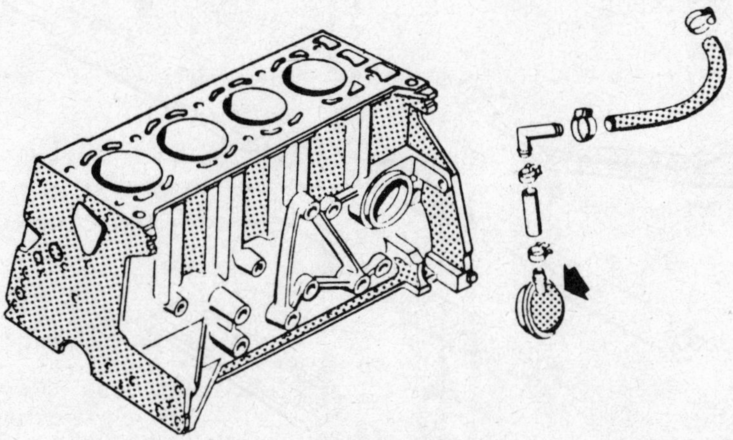

924 PCV location

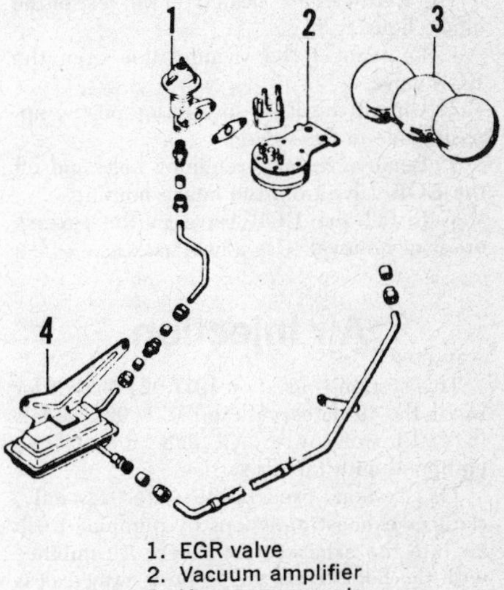

1. EGR valve
2. Vacuum amplifier
3. Vacuum reservoir
4. EGR filter

EGR system—typical

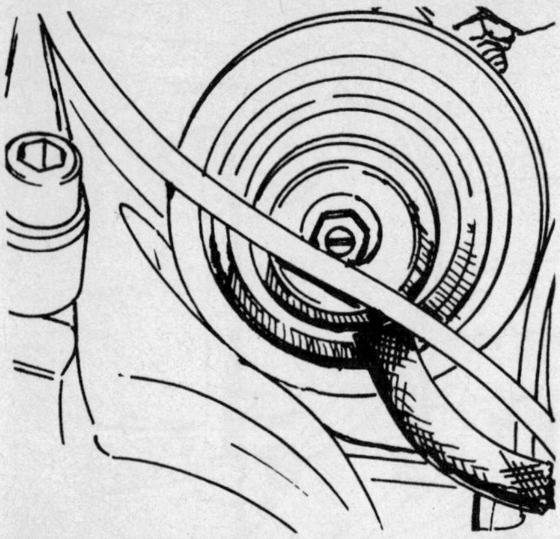

The 924 EGR valve is located on the rear of the intake housing

TESTING

1. Disconnect the vacuum line from the EGR valve.
2. Disconnect the vacuum hose from the distributor vacuum unit and extend the hose.
3. Start the engine and allow it to idle.
4. Connect the distributor vacuum hose to the EGR valve. The engine should stumble or stall.
5. If the idle speed stays even, the EGR line is clogged or the EGR valve is defective.

SERVICE

The only required maintenance is that the EGR filter be replaced at the recommended intervals. The filter is located on the right side of the engine block under the intake housing.

1. Disconnect the line fittings at each end of the filter.
2. Unbolt the bracket retaining screws and remove the filter.
3. Install the replacement filter using the reverse order of removal.

REMOVAL AND INSTALLATION

EGR Valve

The EGR valve is located on the rear of the intake housing.

1. Disconnect the vacuum line from the EGR valve.
2. Unbolt the EGR line fitting on the opposite side of the valve.
3. Remove the two retaining bolts and lift the EGR valve from the intake housing.
4. Install the EGR valve in the reverse order of removal. Use a new gasket.

Air Injection

This system is used on 1977 924 models for use in the 49 states and the 1977½ 924 models in California only. All 928 models are equipped with the air system.

This system, used on 49 state 924s only, reduces exhaust emissions by pumping fresh air into the exhaust port. There it combines with the hot exhaust gas to burn away excess hydrocarbons and reduce carbon monoxide. The system consists of a belt driven pump, air filter, diverter valve and check valve.

TESTING

Diverter Valve

The diverter valve is located between the air pump and the check valve on the intake housing. The diverter valve also houses a relief valve, so that it serves two functions. The valve diverts air during deceleration to prevent backfiring and relieves excess pressure during high rpm to prevent damage to the hoses and air pump.

To test the valve:

1. Pinch the vacuum line closed and wait a few seconds for the vacuum to stabilize on either side of the diaphragm.

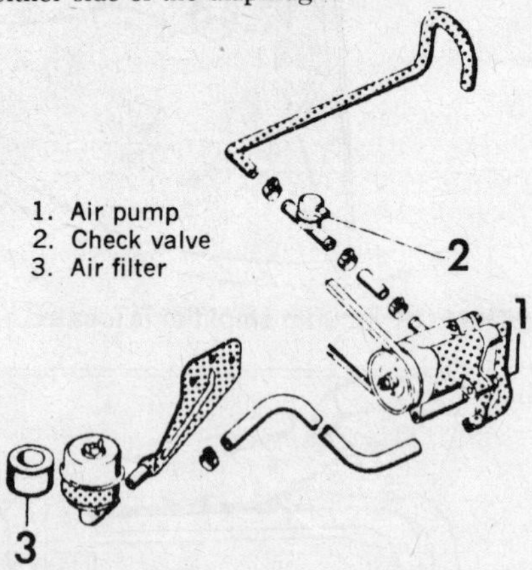

Air injection system—typical

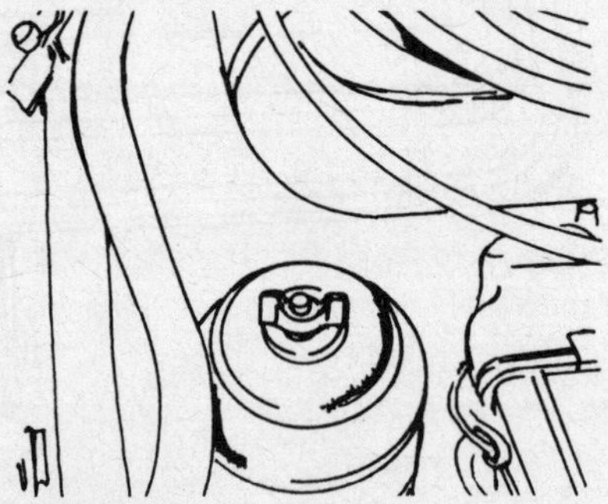

The 924 injection filter is under the expansion tank

2. When you release the line, the sudden surge of vacuum will make the valve work. If it's operating properly, you should be able to hear it open and exhaust air.

Check Valve

The check valve is located on the intake housing. It keeps hot exhaust gases from flowing back into the pump and hoses and destroying them.

To test the valve:

1. With the engine off and cool enough so that there is no danger of being burned, disconnect the hose and use mouth pressure to blow through it.
2. You should be able to easily blow through the valve towards the intake housing, but the valves should seal tightly when you suck back. Replace the valve if it doesn't seal.

Air Pump

1. Disconnect a hose at the diverter valve.
2. With the engine idling, check the flow of air by feeling at the hose with your hand.
3. Increase the engine speed to about 1500 rpm and again check the air flow. If it increases as the engine is accelerated, the pump output is sufficient.
4. Inspect the filter element in the air cleaner for blockage and replace it if necessary before assuming the pump to be deficient.

Catalytic Converter

Catalytic converters were used on the 1977 924 models for California only, but were made standard on all 1977½ and later 924 and 928 models. This device contains noble metals which act as catalysts to cause a reaction to convert hydrocarbons and carbon monoxide into harmless water and carbon dioxide. Service on the converter consists of replacing it when it malfunctions.

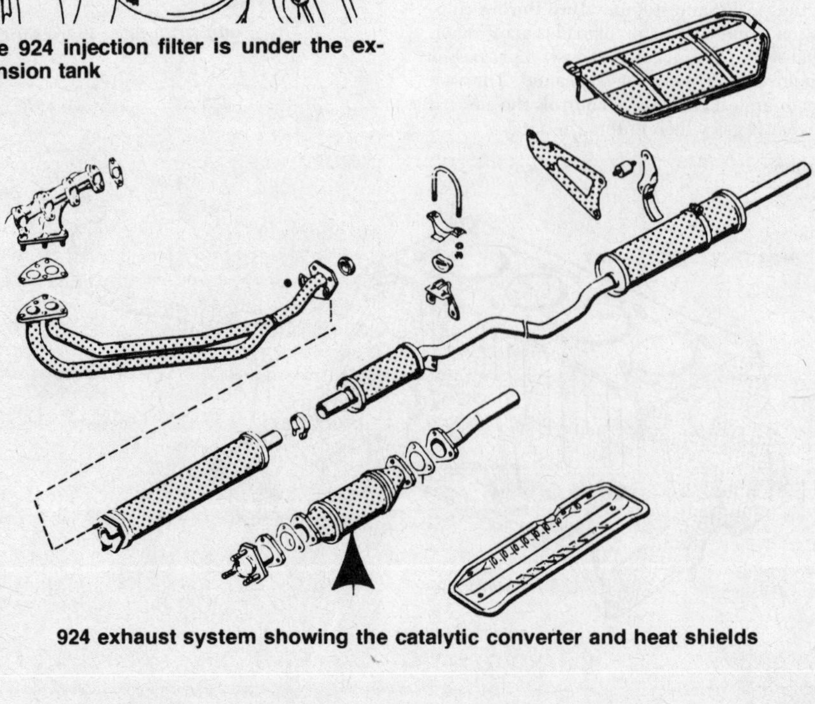

924 exhaust system showing the catalytic converter and heat shields

Evaporative Emission Control System

This system prevents the escape of raw fuel vapors into the atmosphere. The system consists of a charcoal canister and an expansion chamber. Vapors from the fuel tank are trapped in the canister. When the engine is running, fresh air is drawn in through the charcoal filter. The fresh air cleans the canister and routes the unburned hydrocarbons through the air cleaner to be burned during combustion. The fuel tank is vented to an expansion chamber which prevents fuel vapors from entering the atmosphere.

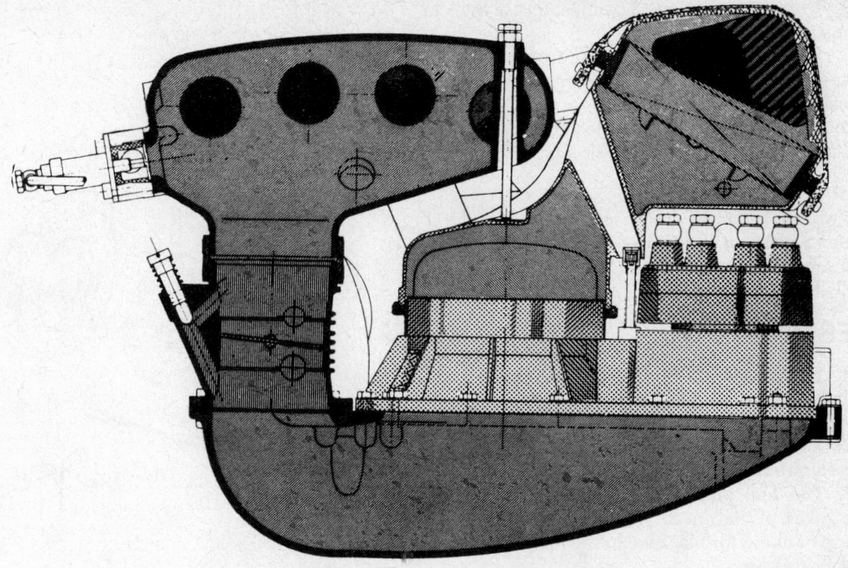

Fuel injection system—model 928

FUEL SYSTEM

All models are equipped with a Bosch continuous flow fuel injection system.

Fuel Filter

REPLACEMENT

924

The fuel filter is located in the fuel line on the driver's side of the engine compartment.

1. Place a shop rag under the filter.
2. Using a line wrench, unscrew both line connections from the filter.
3. Remove the filter.
4. Install the replacement filter in the line and tighten both fittings.

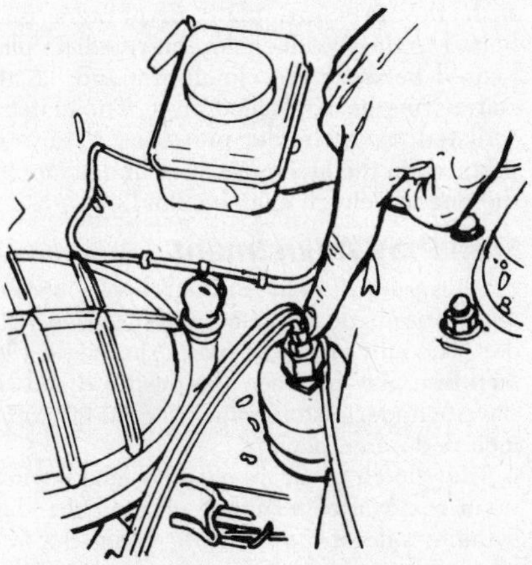

Fuel filter location—model 924

928

The fuel filter and fuel accumulator are located behind a cover, in front of the right rear wheel well.

Electric Fuel Pump

REMOVAL AND INSTALLATION

924

The fuel pump is located near the fuel tank behind the right rear wheel.

1. Disconnect the battery ground cable.

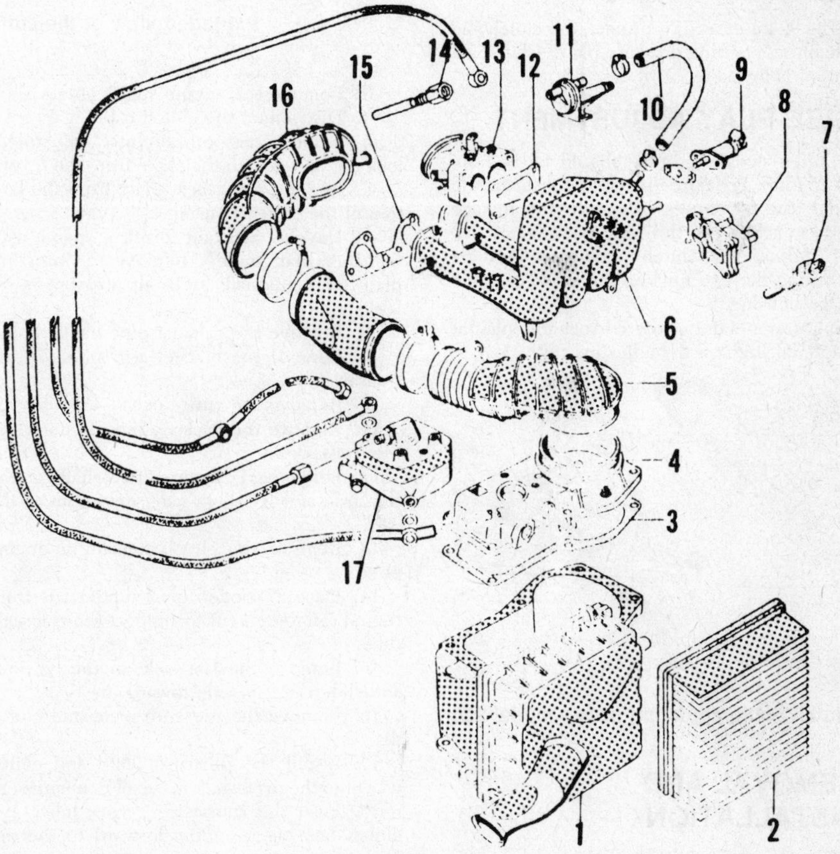

1. Air cleaner
2. Filter
3. Gasket
4. Air flow sensor
5. Air intake elbow
6. Air intake manifold
7. Thermo time switch
8. Warm-up regulator
9. Cold start valve
10. Vacuum hose
11. Auxiliary air regulator
12. Gasket
13. Throttle valve housing
14. Injector
15. Gasket
16. Air intake elbow
17. Fuel distributor

Fuel injection system—model 924

2. Unplug the electrical connections at the pump.
3. Disconnect the fuel lines.
4. Unscrew the retaining clamp and remove the pump.
5. Install the new pump. Clean the electrical connections to ensure continuity.

928

Two fuel pumps are used, one located under a plate on the rear of the fuel tank and the second mounted in the right rear wheel well, behind the wheel.

TESTING

1. Disconnect the fuel line from the fuel distributor to fuel pump and hold it in a container.
2. Switch the ignition on and disconnect the electrical plug at the air sensor.
3. The fuel pump should deliver at least one quart of fuel in 40 seconds. Replace the pump or check for blockage in the fuel lines, if fuel flow is less.

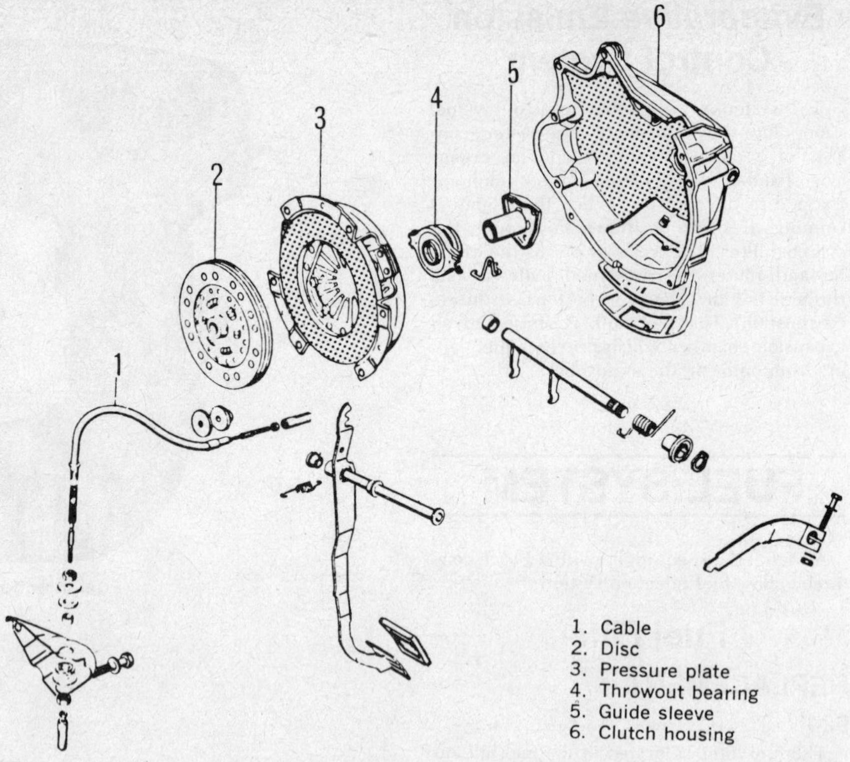

1. Cable
2. Disc
3. Pressure plate
4. Throwout bearing
5. Guide sleeve
6. Clutch housing

Exploded view of the clutch and linkage—model 924

CLUTCH

924

The 924 uses a conventional, dry clutch and a diaphragm spring pressure plate. Clutch actuation is by cable.

FREE-PLAY ADJUSTMENT

Clutch pedal free-play should be ¾-1 in. (20-25 mm). Pedal free-play is the distance the pedal can be depressed before the linkage starts to act on the throwout bearing.

1. Adjust the clutch pedal free-play by loosening the two nuts on the cable near the intake housing.
2. After obtaining the correct free-play at the pedal, tighten the adjusting nuts.

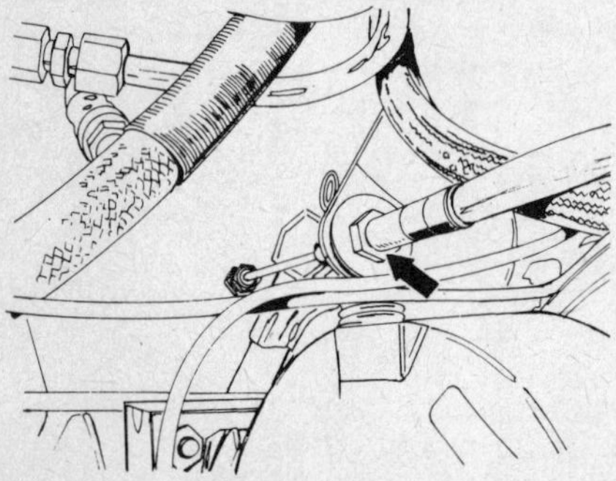

Clutch cable adjusting nuts—model 924

REMOVAL AND INSTALLATION

To gain access to the clutch disc and pressure plate assembly the transaxle, torque tube and clutch housing must be dismounted and pulled back out of the way.

1. Disconnect the battery ground cable. Raise the car and support it on jack stands.
2. Support the engine with an overhead hoist or a jack and cradle under the engine.
3. Remove the engine splash shield.
4. Disconnect the clutch cable.
5. Remove the bottom clutch adjustment lock nut and detach the cable from the lever.
6. Remove the access plate from the bottom of the clutch housing.
7. Have an assistant turn the engine with the crankshaft pulley. Remove the pressure plate bolts gradually until all pressure is released.
8. Remove the exhaust pipe flange bolts.
9. Remove the bracket at the rear of the transaxle.
10. Remove the entire exhaust system.
11. Remove the back-up light switch from the transaxle.
12. Disconnect the axle driveshafts at the transaxle and let them hang down out of the way.
13. Remove the clutch housing-to-engine bolts.
14. Place a wooden block under the front tunnel reinforcement to support the transaxle tube.
15. Remove the transaxle mounting bolts and slide the transaxle toward the rear.
16. Remove the pressure plate and clutch disc.
17. Install the pressure plate and clutch disc onto the driveshaft in the clutch housing.
18. Push the transaxle, torque tube, and clutch housing assembly forward to the engine.
19. Install the clutch housing-to-engine bolts. Tighten the 12 mm bolts to 60 ft/lbs, the 10 mm bolts to 36 ft/lbs and the 8 mm bolts to 20 ft/lbs.
20. Tighten the pressure plate-to-flywheel bolts to 24 ft/lbs in a gradual diagonal pattern.
21. Install the remaining components in the reverse order of removal. Adjust the clutch.

928

The 928 models use two dry clutch plates with the pressure plate diaphragm plate bolted to the flywheel. An intermediate plate is used between the clutch disc and has the starter ring gear installed on it. The clutch is actuated by hydraulic pressure. A separate partition in the brake master cylinder supplies the needed clutch cylinder fluid.

Free Play Adjustment

Clutch adjustment is not necessary because of the automatic adjustment of the slave cylinder. The only clearance check should be a 3/32 inch free play between the push rod and the slave cylinder piston, which should give a 3/16 inch pedal free play.

The clutch wear limit is reached when, upon removal of a rubber plug on the slave cylinder side of the clutch housing, the front edge of the release lever can be seen.

Removal and Installation

1. Disconnect the battery ground strap.
2. Raise the vehicle and support safely.
3. Remove the lower body brace.
4. Remove the clutch slave cylinder and keep hydraulic lines attached.
5. Remove the starter and clutch housing cover as a unit and attach to the stabilizer bar with a wire.
6. Remove the coupling screws and push the coupler rearward on the driveshaft.
7. Remove the release bearing sleeve bolts and move the sleeve towards the flywheel.
8. Matchmark the clutch components and loosen all pressure plate mounting bolts

evenly until all the pressure is removed from the plate.

9. Remove the mounting bolts and press down on the release lever (towards the flywheel) and disconnect the release lever at the ball stud.

10. Push the complete clutch assembly rearward and move the assembly downward and out of the clutch housing.

NOTE: The clutch assembly consists of the pressure plate, front and rear clutch discs, release lever, release bearing sleeve and short driveshaft.

NOTE: The clutch discs are different.
a. The clutch disc with the rigid center is installed between the flywheel and the intermediate plate.
b. The clutch disc with the spring center is installed between the intermediate plate and the pressure plate.

CAUTION

To prevent clutch drag, move the three stop brackets towards the pressure plate until a gap of 0.0275 to 0.0394 inch exists between the intermediate plate and the stop bracket.

TRANSAXLE

924

The 924 4-speed transmission and differential are mounted in a single transaxle housing at the rear of the car. An automatic transaxle is optional.

REMOVAL AND INSTALLATION

Remove the transaxle as outlined in Clutch Removal and Installation. Disconnect the torque tube from the transaxle for servicing.

928

The 928 five speed standard transmission and differential are mounted as a combined transaxle unit at the rear of the car.

An automatic transmission is available as an option and is mounted as a combined transaxle unit.

REMOVAL AND INSTALLATION

1. Remove the nuts from the spring struts bolts, extending into the trunk compartment.
2. Remove the battery and loosen the rear wheels.
3. Place the transmission in fifth gear.
4. Raise the vehicle and remove the rubber plug from underneath the front of the transmission. Looking into the hole, position the coupling bolt head between the drive and input shafts, so that it can be removed.

NOTE: During removal of the bolt, do not allow the shaft to turn and jam the socket or bolt in the transmission housing.

5. Place the transmission in Neutral, remove the rear wheels and remove the brake calipers, wire them to the frame.
6. Remove the exhaust system from the catalytic converter rearward.
7. Remove the exhaust heat shield and the battery box.
8. Disconnect the back-up light switch wires and loosen the pulse transmitter for the speedometer. Remove the wires from the clip.
9. Move the dust cover from the shift rod coupling and remove the locking set screw. Remove the shift rod from the main rod.
10. Disconnect the axle shafts at the transmission end. Suspend the axles from the crossmember.
11. Disconnect the stablizer bar at the lower control arm.
12. With the use of a strap, chain or heavy wire, support the transaxle assembly from the stablizer bar.
13. Remove the transmission-to-rear axle crossmember bolts and the bolts between the rear axle crossmember and frame.
14. Mark the position of the rear axle crossmember and place a jack under member. Remove the bolts and tilt the rear axle so that the spring struts and control arms do not twist. Support the rear axle in the tilted position to keep the weight off the lower control arm link pins.
15. Place jack under the transmission assembly and remove the bolts between the driveshaft tube and the transmission. Remove the holding strap, pull the unit rearward and lower.
16. Installation is the reverse of removal.

Axle Driveshafts

Power is transferred to the rear wheels by independent axle driveshafts. These are similar to the ones used on the VW Type 2. Each shaft has a constant velocity joint at either end.

REMOVAL AND INSTALLATION

1. Jack the rear of the car up and support it on jack stands.
2. Remove the six star bolts on the inside joint at the transaxle.
3. Remove the six star bolts at the stub axle. Use a wide, flat bladed prybar to pry the flanges apart.
4. Drop the axle driveshaft down and out of the 924. On the 928, remove the axle from the upper left side of the hub assembly.
5. Pack the constant velocity joints with grease before installation.
6. Installation is the reverse of removal. Tighten the bolts to 30 ft/lbs.

REAR SUSPENSION

924

Rear suspension is by lateral torsion bars, trailing arms and conventional shock absorbers.

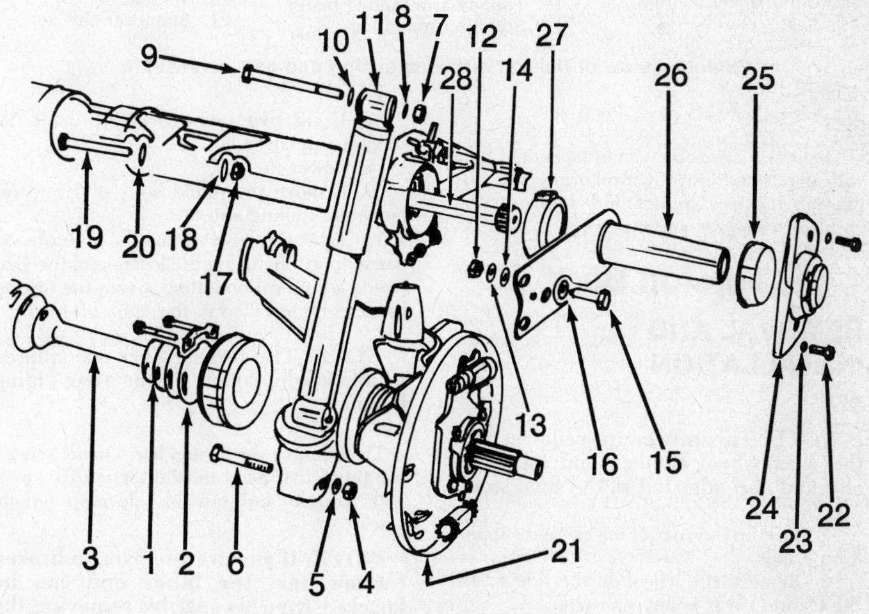

1. Allen head bolt
2. Plate
3. Axle shaft
4. Nut
5. Lockwasher
6. Bolt
7. Nut
8. Lockwasher
9. Bolt
10. Washer
11. Shock absorber
12. Nut
13. Washer
14. Plain washer
15. Bolt
16. Plain washer
17. Nut, self-locking
18. Plain washer
19. Bolt
20. Plain washer
21. Trailing arm
22. Bolt
23. Lockwasher
24. Cover
25. Rubber mount, outer
26. Torsion plate
27. Rubber mount, inner
28. Torsion bar

Exploded view of rear suspension assembly—model 924

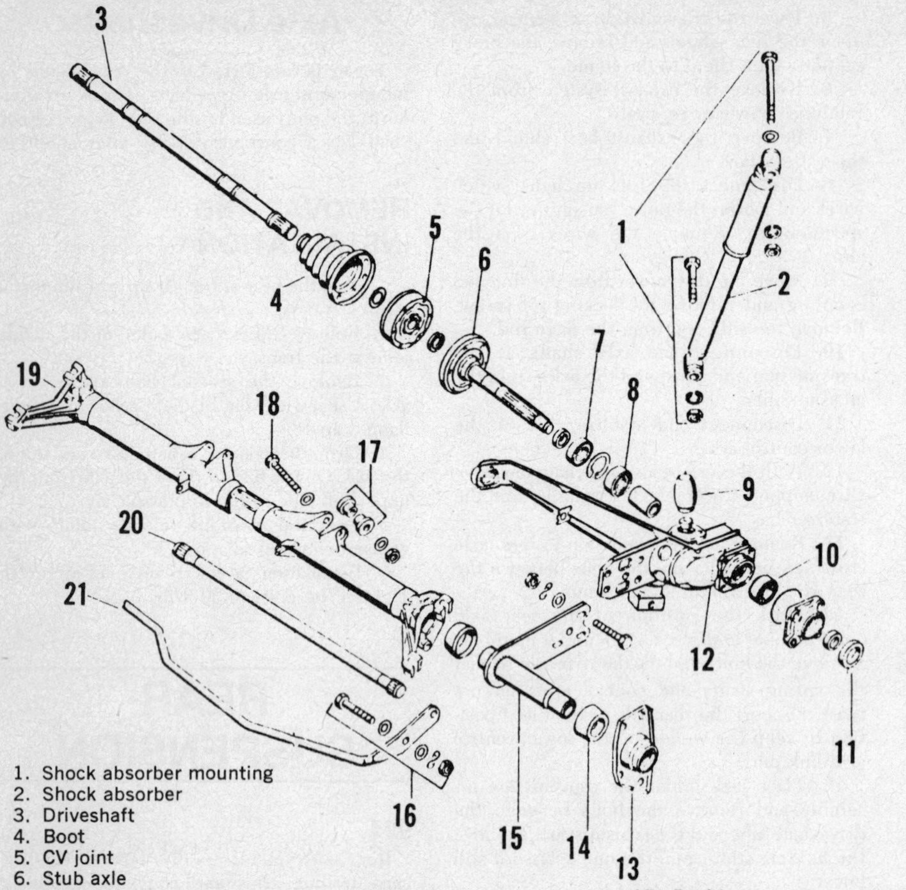

1. Shock absorber mounting
2. Shock absorber
3. Driveshaft
4. Boot
5. CV joint
6. Stub axle
7. Seal
8. Inner wheel bearing
9. Bumper
10. Outer wheel bearing
11. Seal
12. Control arm
13. Torsion bar cover
14. Bearing
15. Trailing arm (spring plate)
16. Stabilizer mounting
17. Bushings
18. Bolt
19. Torsion bar housing
20. Torsion bar
21. Stabilizer bar

Exploded view of the 924 rear suspension and axle driveshaft

928

The rear suspension is an independent type with upper and lower control arms. The suspension has coil springs and double action shock absorbers as one unit.

Torsion Bars

REMOVAL AND INSTALLATION

924

NOTE: This procedure requires that the rear wheel camber and toe-in be checked and adjusted as the final step.

1. Jack up the rear of the car and support it on stands.
2. Remove the wheel on the side where the torsion bar is being removed.
3. Using a hydraulic jack and a block of wood with a slot cut in it, raise the trailing arm.
4. Remove the lower shock absorber bolt.
5. Remove the trailing arm retaining bolts. Remove the toe and camber adjusting bolts.
6. Remove the four retaining bolts from the trailing arm cover.
7. Using two screwdrivers, pry off the trailing arm cover.
8. Lower the jack.
9. Remove the round body plug and remove the trailing arm.
10. Paint a reference mark on the torsion bar support, matching the location of the L or R side identification letter, so that the torsion bar may be installed in the same position.

NOTE: The torsion bars are splined to allow adjustment of the rear riding height.

11. Remove the torsion bar. Do not scratch the protective paint on the torsion bar, or it will corrode and possibly develop fatigue cracks.

NOTE: If you are removing a broken torsion bar, the inner end can be knocked from its seat by removing the opposite torsion bar and tapping it through with a steel bar. Torsion bars are not interchangeable from side to side and are marked L and R for identification.

12. Check the torsion bar splines for damage and replace the bar if necessary. If there is any corrosion on the bar, replace it.
13. Coat the torsion bar lightly with grease. Carefully grease the splines.
14. Apply glycerine or another rubber preservative to the torsion bar support.
15. Install the torsion bar, matching the L or R with the paint mark you made before removal.
16. Install the trailing arm cover into position and start the three accessible bolts.
17. Raise the trailing arm into place with a jack and wooden block until the spacer and the fourth bolt can be installed.
18. Assemble the remaining components in the reverse order of their removal.
19. Tighten the trailing arm cover bolts to 25 ft/lbs. Tighten the shock absorber bolt to 50 ft/lbs.
20. Adjust rear wheel camber and toe-in.

Upper Control Arm

REMOVAL AND INSTALLATION

928

1. Raise the vehicle and support it safely. Remove the rear wheels and support the lower arm assembly with a jack.
2. Loosen and remove the inner and outer bolts from the upper arm ends.
3. Remove the upper arm from the rear crossmember and from the rear flexible mount.

NOTE: The bushings are replaceable.

Installation is the reverse of removal.

Lower Control Arm

REMOVAL AND INSTALLATION

928

1. Raise the vehicle and support safely. Remove the rear wheels.
2. Support the hub assembly and the spring strut with a jack.
3. Remove the outer pivot pin nuts and washers. Disconnect the stabilizer bar link.
4. Remove the inner pivot bolts from the arm and pull the front pivot pin from the hub assembly and the spring strut.

NOTE: The bushings are replaceable.

5. Installation is the reverse of removal.

Shock Absorbers

REMOVAL AND INSTALLATION

924

1. Raise the car on a drive-on hoist or support the wheels on stands for this procedure.
2. Remove the bottom retaining bolt and nut.
3. Remove the top bolt.
4. Remove the shock absorber.
5. Install the replacement shock in the reverse order of removal. Tighten the retaining bolts to 50 ft/lbs.

928

1. Remove the locking nuts from the spring strut, located within the trunk area.
2. Raise the vehicle, support safely and remove the wheel.
3. Remove the front nut on the outer pivot pin rod and remove the pivot rod from the rubber bushings.
4. Disconnect the stablizer bar link from the lower control arm.
5. Remove the spring strut from the vehicle.
6. Installation is the reverse of removal.

NOTE: The spring can be removed from the shock unit with the use of a spring clamping tool. An adjusting nut and sleeve is used to control the vehicle rear height.

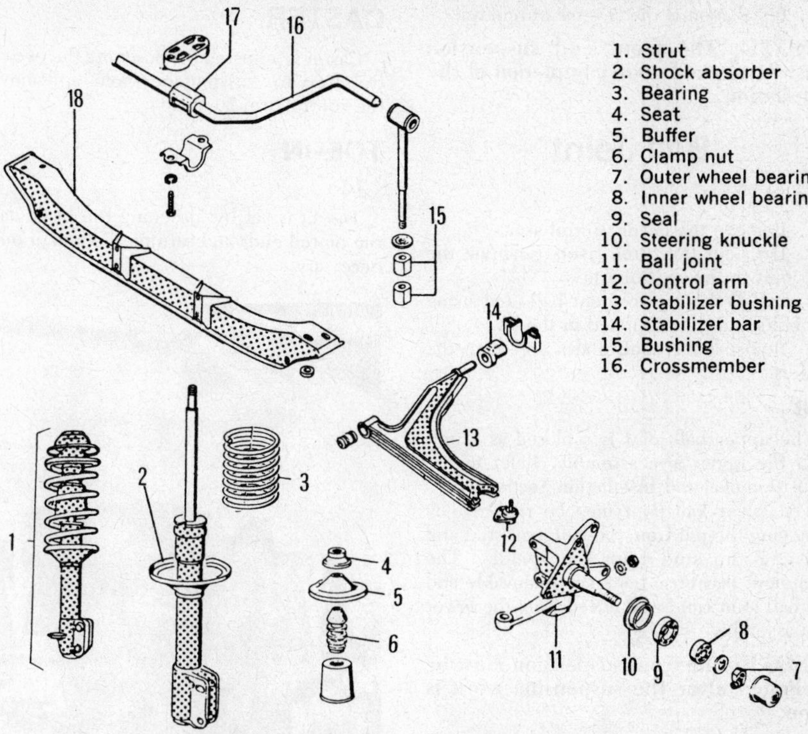

1. Strut
2. Shock absorber
3. Bearing
4. Seat
5. Buffer
6. Clamp nut
7. Outer wheel bearing
8. Inner wheel bearing
9. Seal
10. Steering knuckle
11. Ball joint
12. Control arm
13. Stabilizer bushing
14. Stabilizer bar
15. Bushing
16. Crossmember

Exploded view of the 924 front suspension

Wheel Alignment Adjustments

CAMBER

Rear wheel camber is adjusted by changing the trailing arm spring plate setting. To increase positive camber, loosen the spring plate-to-trailing arm bolts (with the wheels on the ground). To increase negative camber, do so with car on hoist. Tighten bolts after adjustment.

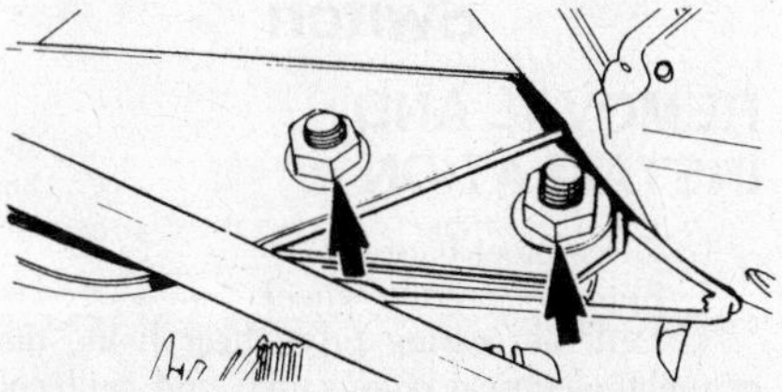

Rear wheel alignment is adjusted on the 924 at the trailing arm-to-spring bolts

TOE-IN

Rear wheel toe-in is adjusted by moving the control arm in the slots of the spring plates.

FRONT SUSPENSION

924

The 924 front suspension is a MacPherson strut design. The strut consists of the strut housing, a shock absorber insert in the housing, and a concentric coil spring. The steering knuckle is bolted to the strut assembly. A lower control arm locates the strut at the bottom. A ball joint is riveted to the control arm and bolted to the steering knuckle.

928

The 928 front suspension is an independent type with upper and lower control arms, coil springs mounted on the shock absorbers and upper and lower ball joints. Provisions for front end alignment are provided by eccentrics located at the bottom of the lower ball joint mounting plate.

Strut

REMOVAL AND INSTALLATION

924

1. Jack up the front of the car and support it on stands.
2. Remove the brake line from the bracket on the strut.
3. Remove the two through bolts that retain the strut to the steering knuckle.
4. Remove the four retaining nuts from the inner fender in the engine compartment.
5. Pry the lower control arm down and remove the strut from the car.
6. To replace either the spring or shock absorber, place the strut in a spring compressor and remove the large retaining nut at the top.
7. Installation is the reverse of removal. Front wheel alignment must be reset after a strut is removed.

928

1. Remove the self-locking nuts on the upper strut mount, located on the inner fender panel.
2. Remove the front wheel. Remove the flange locknut and press the upper ball joint from the spindle carrier.
3. Remove the inner pivot shaft nuts from the upper control arm.
4. Remove the shock absorber mounting bolts and remove the shock and upper arm as an assembly.

Lower Control Arm

REMOVAL AND INSTALLATION

924

1. Jack up the front of the car and support it on stands.
2. Remove the through-bolt at the front that retains the control arm to the suspension crossmember.
3. Detach the stabilizer bar from the control arm.
4. Remove the two bolts that retain the control arm bracket at the rear.
5. Remove the ball joint pinch bolt at the steering knuckle.
6. Pry the control arm down and remove it from the car.
7. Installation is the reverse of removal. Caster must be reset after the control arm has been removed.

928

1. Raise the vehicle and remove the wheel.
2. Mark the alignment eccentrics on the lower arm for approximate installation location, if the ball joint is to be removed.
3. Remove the strut bottom link bracket and stabilizer link bolt.
4. Remove the lower ball joint stud nut and press the stud from the spindle. Move the spindle and upper arm upward and block it to gain working clearance.
5. Remove the bolts from the tie-down bracket and control arm bracket. Lower the control arm from the vehicle.
6. The lower ball joint can be replaced, if necessary, while the lower arm is out of the vehicle.

7. Installation is the reverse of removal.

NOTE: The front end suspension must be aligned upon completion of the installation.

Ball Joint

924

1. Remove the lower control arm.
2. Drill out the three rivets retaining the ball joint to the control arm.
3. Install the replacement ball joint using the bolts and nuts supplied in the kit.
4. Reinstall the control arm and align the wheels.

928

The upper ball joint is replaced as a unit with the upper arm assembly. Refer to the Strut Removal and Installation Section.

The lower ball joint may be replaced by removing the nut from the ball joint stud and pressing the stud from the spindle. The alignment eccentric bolts are removable and the ball joint can be removed from the lower arm assembly.

NOTE: The front suspension must be realigned after the suspension work is done.

CAMBER

924

Camber is adjusted at the upper strut-to-steering knuckle retaining bolt.

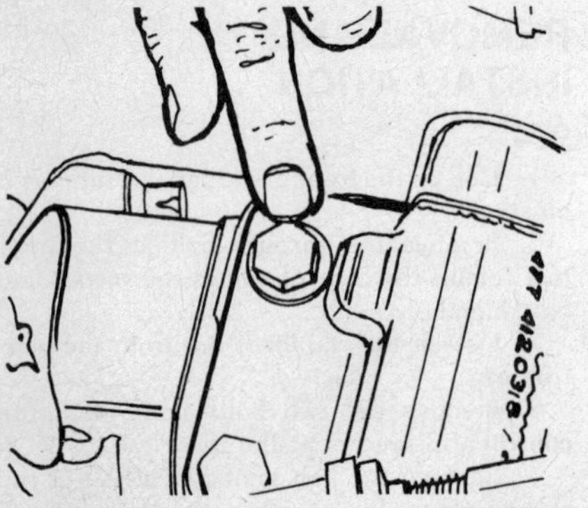

Camber is adjusted at the upper strut eccentric—model 924

928

Camber is adjusted by turning the cam bolts on the inner arm bushings.

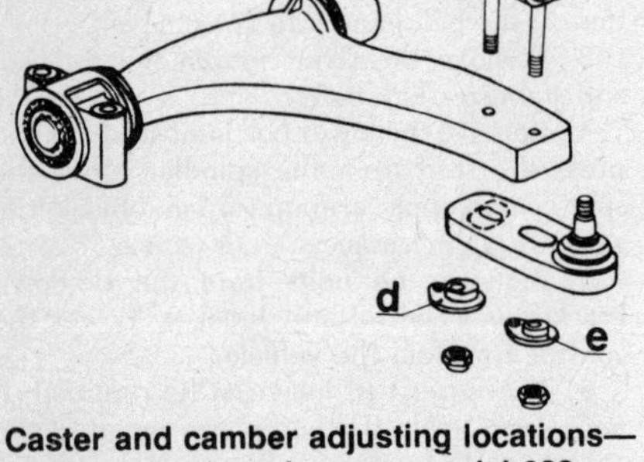

Caster and camber adjusting locations—front lower control arms—model 928

CASTER

Caster is adjusted by loosening the two control arms to crossmember bolts and moving the control arm laterally.

TOE-IN

924

Toe-in is set by loosening the locknuts on the tie rod ends and turning them in or out as necessary.

Adjust caster at the lower control arm mounting—model 924

928

Toe-in adjustments are made by turning cam bolts, located at the front of the rear control arms.

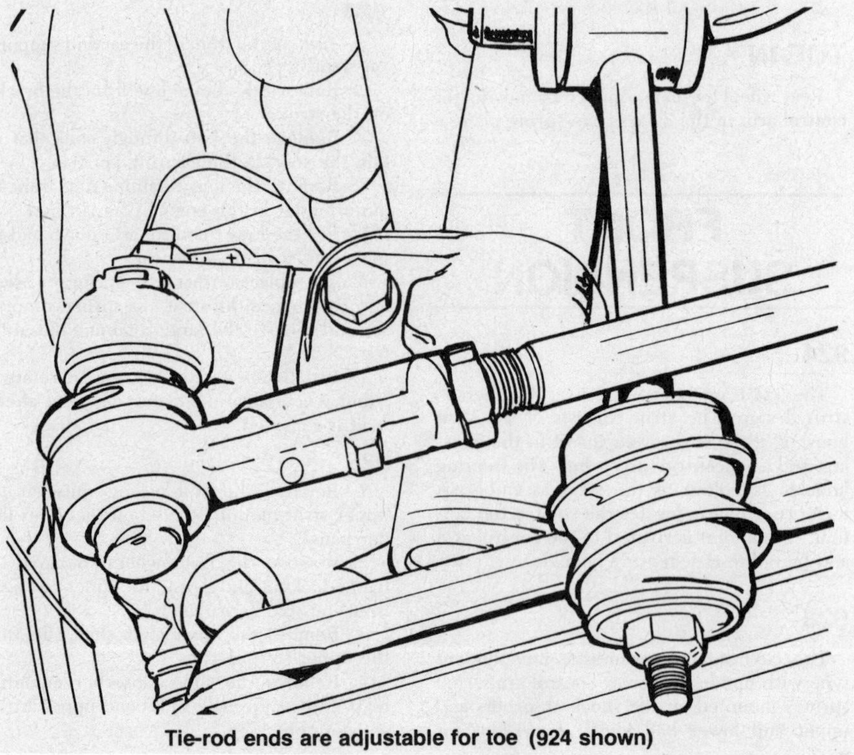

Tie-rod ends are adjustable for toe (924 shown)

STEERING

Steering Wheel

REMOVAL AND INSTALLATION

1. Remove horn pad.
2. Remove retaining nut and washer.
3. Using a steering wheel puller, remove the wheel.
4. Installation is the reverse of above. Make sure the wheels are straight ahead and steering wheel is centered. Torque steering wheel nut to 33 ft/lbs.

Turn Signal Switch

REMOVAL AND INSTALLATION

1. Remove steering wheel.
2. Disconnect electrical connector at switch.
3. Remove four screws holding switch.
4. To install, reverse the above.

Ignition Lock and Switch

REMOVAL AND INSTALLATION

1. Disconnect battery.
2. Remove steering wheel.
3. Drill out casing tube shear bolts, disconnect electrical connectors, and pull column and casing out of car.

4. Remove the casing from steering column.
5. Remove pinch bolt holding switch housing to column.
6. Remove retaining screw and pull ignition switch from rear of casing.
7. Depress lock cylinder retainer with an ice pick or similar tool and remove lock cylinder.
8. Installation is the reverse of removal.

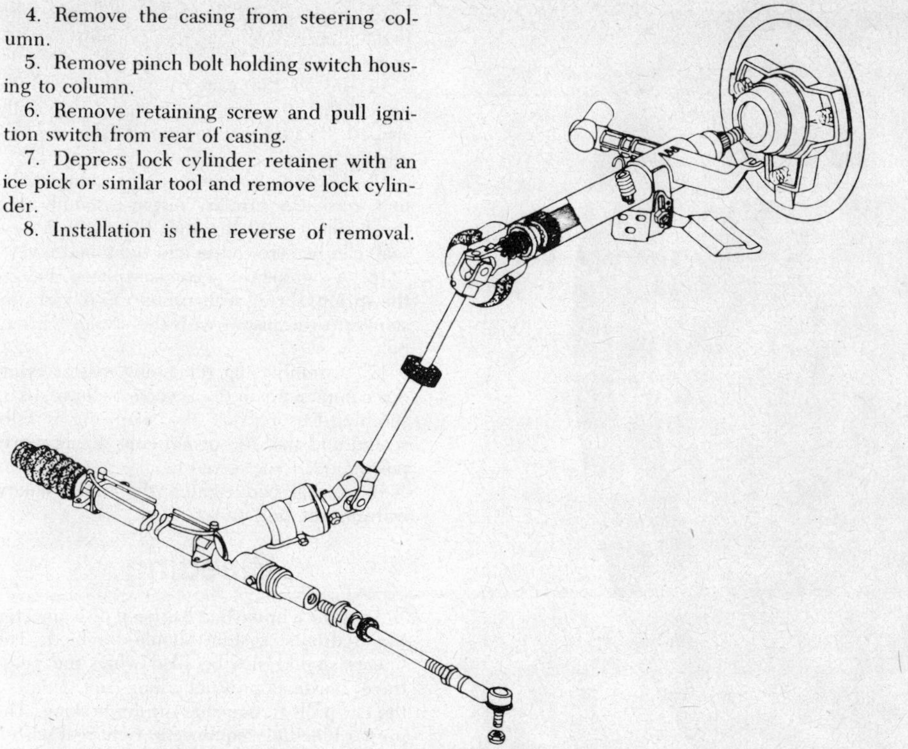

Steering column and steering gear assembly—model 928

Make sure the wheels are straight ahead and steering wheel is centered when installing. Torque steering wheel nut to 33 ft/lbs. Torque shear bolts to 23 ft/lbs.

Steering Gear

REMOVAL AND INSTALLATION

1. Remove bolt connecting gear box to steering column driveshaft.
2. Press out tie rod ends.
3. Remove steering gear and tie rods from car.
4. Remove tie rods from steering gear.
5. To install, reverse the above. Center steering gear with VW tool 9116 or its equivalent. Be sure that both tie rod lengths are equal (68-68.5 mm). Tighten tie rod counter nuts to 29 ft/lbs and gear box to driveshaft bolt to 23 ft/lbs.

STEERING GEAR ADJUSTMENT

1. Tighten adjusting screw (on front of gear box) until it just touches the washer.
2. Hold adjusting screw tightly and tighten locknut.

BRAKES

The 924 is equipped with power assisted front disc brakes and drum rear brakes.

The 928 uses disc brakes on both front and rear wheels with the hydraulic circuit split diagonally, so that braking stability is maintained if one brake circuit fails.

The parking brake is mechanically operated to expand dual drum shoes on the rear wheel rotors.

A brake sensor is used to indicate pad wear on the four wheel assemblies.

ADJUSTMENT

The front disc brakes require no adjustment, as disc brakes automatically adjust themselves to compensate for pad wear. The rear drum brakes must be periodically adjusted, or whenever free travel is one third or more of the total pedal travel.

1. Raise the rear of the car.
2. Block the front wheels and release the parking brake. Step on the brake pedal hard to center the linings.
3. Remove the rubber plugs from the rear of the backing plate on each wheel.
4. Insert a brake adjusting tool or wide-blade screwdriver and turn the adjuster wheel until the brakes drag as you turn the tire/wheel.
5. Turn the adjuster in the opposite direction until you just pass the point of drag.
6. Repeat on the other wheel.
7. Lower the car and road-test. Readjust, if necessary.

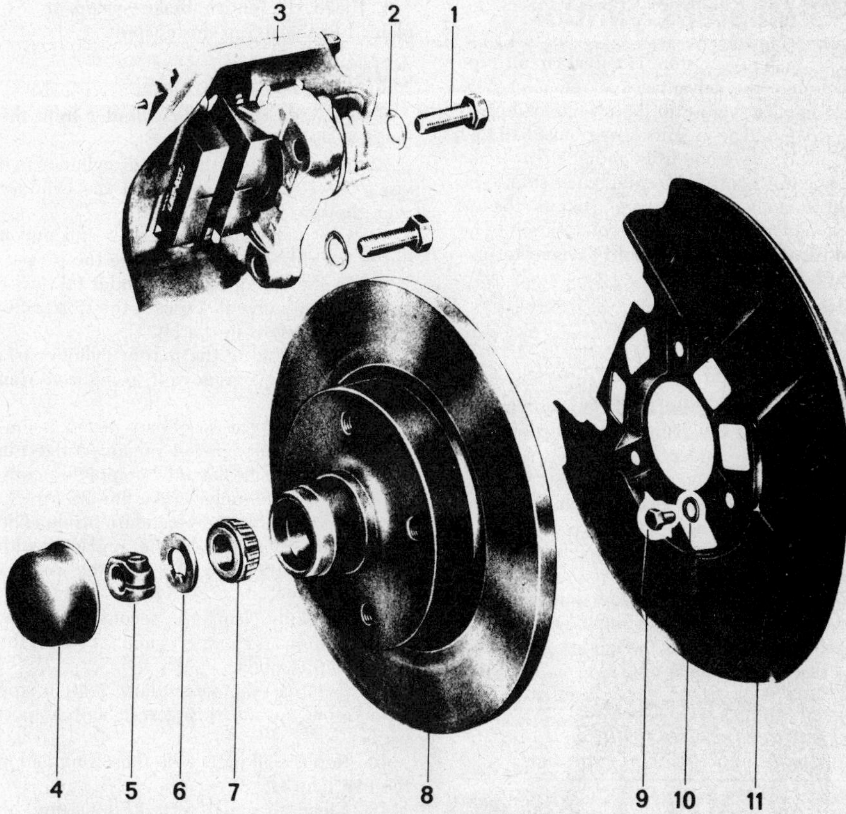

1. Hex nut
2. Washer
3. Floating caliper
4. Hub cap
5. Clamping nut with Allen head bolt
6. Thrust washer
7. Wheel bearing, outer
8. Brake disc
9. Bolt
10. Washer
11. Guard

Front disc brake assembly—model 924

924 rear brake adjusters are behind the rubber plugs

Master Cylinder

The hydraulic system is a dual circuit type which has the advantage of retaining 50% braking effectiveness in the event of failure in one system. The circuits are arranged so that you always have one front and one rear brake for a more controlled emergency stop. The right front and left rear are one circuit; the left front and right rear the second circuit. The booster uses intake manifold vacuum to provide pedal assist.

REMOVAL AND INSTALLATION

1. To prevent brake fluid from spilling out and damaging the paint, place a protective cover over the fender.
2. Disconnect the plug and brake lines.
3. Disconnect the electrical plug from the sending unit for the brake failure switch.
4. Remove the two master cylinder mounting nuts.
5. Lift the master cylinder and reservoir out of the engine compartment being careful not to spill any fluid on the fender. Empty out and discard the brake fluid.

CAUTION

Do not depress the brake pedal while the master cylinder is removed.

6. Position the master cylinder and reservoir assembly onto the studs for the booster and install the washers and nuts. Tighten the nuts to no more than 10 ft/lbs.
7. Remove the plugs and connect the brake lines.
8. Bleed the entire brake system as explained further on in this chapter.

OVERHAUL

1. Remove the master cylinder from the booster.
2. Firmly mount the master cylinder in a vise. Use clean rags to protect the cylinder from the vise jaws.
3. Grasp the plastic reservoir and pull it out of the rubber plugs. Remove the plugs.
4. In the center of the cylinder there is a stop screw; remove it. Discard the stop screw seal, a new one is in the kit.
5. At the end of the master cylinder is a snap-ring (circlip); remove it, using snap-ring pliers.
6. Shake out the secondary piston assembly. If the primary piston remains lodged in the bore, it can be forced by applying compressed air to the open brake line fitting.
7. Disassemble the secondary piston. The two secondary rings will be replaced with those in the rebuilding kit. Save the washers and spacers.
8. Carefully clamp the secondary piston, slightly compress the spring and screw out the stroke limiting bolt.
9. Remove the secondary piston stop sleeve bolt, spring, spring seat, and support washer.
10. Replace all parts with those supplied in the overhaul kit.
11. Clean all metal parts in denatured alcohol and dry them with compressed air.
12. Check every part you are reusing. Pay close attention to the cylinder bores. If there is any scoring or rust, have the master cylinder honed or replace it.
13. Lightly coat the bores and cups with brake fluid. Assemble the cylinder components.
14. Install the primary piston assembly; notice that the primary spring is conically shaped. Be sure that you aren't using the secondary spring.
15. Using a plastic rod or other nonmetallic tool, push the primary piston assembly into the housing until the stop bolt (with a new seal) can be screwed in and tightened.
16. Assemble the secondary piston. Fasten the spring, spring seat, primary cup, and stop sleeve to the piston with the stroke limiting bolt.
17. Assemble the remaining master cylinder components in the reverse order of disassembly. Ensure that the snap-ring is fully seated and that the piston cups are properly positioned.
18. Install and tighten the brake failure warning sending unit.

Bleeding

Anytime a brake line has been disconnected the hydraulic system should be bled. The brakes should also be bled when the pedal travel becomes unusually long (soft pedal) or the car pulls to one side during braking. The proper bleeding sequence is: right rear wheel, left rear wheel, right front caliper, and left front caliper. You'll need a helper to pump the brake pedal while you open the bleeder valves.

NOTE: If the system has been drained, first refill it with fresh brake fluid. Following the above sequence, open each bleeder valve by ½ to ¾ of a turn and pump the brake pedal until fluid runs out of the valve. Proceed with the bleeding as outlined below.

1. Remove the bleeder valve dust cover and install a rubber bleeder hose.
2. Insert the other end of the hose into a container about ⅓ full of brake fluid.
3. Have your assistant pump the brake pedal several times until the pedal pressure increases.
4. Hold the pedal under pressure and then start to open the bleeder valve about ½ to ¾ of a turn. At this point, have your assistant depress the pedal all the way and then quickly close the valve. The helper should allow the pedal to return slowly.

NOTE: Keep a close check on the brake fluid in the reservoir and top it up as necessary throughout the bleeding process.

5. Keep repeating this procedure until no more air bubbles can be seen coming from the hose in the brake fluid.
6. Remove the bleeder hose and install the dust cover.
7. Continue the bleeding at each wheel in sequence.

Front and Rear Disc Brakes

All models use single piston, floating caliper disc brakes. In this design, the single piston forces one pad against the rotating brake disc. Counter pressure forces against the floating frame and the frame then pushes the second pad into the disc. The advantages of the floating caliper are, better heat dissipation, simpler repairs, fewer leaks, and less sensitivity to variance in disc thickness and parallelism.

NOTE: The rear disc brake system on the 928 is identical to the front system.

BRAKE PADS

Removal and Installation

924

Brake pads should be replaced when there is no visible clearance between the pads and the cross-spring or when they are worn to a thickness of 0.08 in.

1. Jack up the front of the car and support it on stands. Remove the wheels.
2. Pry the clip out of both retaining pins.
3. While pressing down on the cross-spring, push the pad retaining pins out with a drift or small screwdriver.
4. Reference mark positions of the brake pads if they are being reused.
5. Remove the cross-spring from the caliper.
6. Remove the inner brake pad. A special tool is available for this purpose, but by using a small drift or punch you can pry the pad out of the caliper until it can be gripped by a pair of pliers and removed.
7. The outer brake pad is positioned in a notch. Use a flat, smooth piece of hardwood or metal to press the floating caliper frame and piston cylinder outward.

Drive the front disc brake retaining pins on the 924 out in the direction shown. Use new pins on installation.

8. Grip the outer pad and remove it. Press the piston back into the cylinder with the flat piece of wood or metal.
9. Siphon out about half of the brake fluid in the reservoir to prevent if from overflowing when the piston is pushed in and new thicker pads are inserted.
10. Check that the piston is at the proper 20° angle. Make a gauge out of stiff cardboard.
11. Install the brake pads into the caliper.

NOTE: Replace used pads in the side of the caliper from which they were removed. When installing new pads always replace the pads on the opposite wheel at the same time.

12. Position the cross-spring in the caliper and then carefully tap the pad retaining pins into place with a small hammer. Install the pin clip.

928

1. Raise the vehicle, support safely and remove the wheels.
2. Remove the brake pad wear sensor indicator from the pad backing plate.
3. Remove the spring lock from the retaining pins and remove the retaining pins.
4. Remove the inner brake pad with the use of a hook type tool.
5. Remove the outer brake pad.

NOTE: The caliper frame will have to be moved until the brake pad protrudes from the pin on the caliper frame.

CAUTION

Withdraw a small amount of brake fluid from the brake cylinder reservoir to avoid overflowing upon movement of the piston.

6. The rear brake pads are removed in the same manner.
7. Installation is the reverse of removal.

CALIPERS

Removal and Installation

1. Jack up the front of the car and support it on stands.
2. Remove the brake pads as previously outlined.
3. If you are removing the caliper for overhaul, disconnect and plug the brake line at the caliper. If not, do not remove the hose—hang it by a wire.
4. Remove the two caliper-to-strut retaining bolts and remove the caliper.
5. Install the caliper using the reverse of the removal procedure. Tighten the two retaining bolts to 43 ft/lbs.
6. Bleed the brakes.

Overhaul

1. Remove the caliper as outlined above.
2. Mount the caliper in a soft-jawed vise or place cloths over the jaws to protect the caliper.
3. Pry the fixed mounting frame off the floating frame.
4. Separate the caliper cylinder from the floating frame by prying it and the guide spring off the frame. Use a brass drift to lightly tap on the cylinder and place a piece of wood under the piston to protect it.
5. Using pliers remove the piston clamp ring. Remove and discard the rubber dust cover; a new one is supplied with the rebuilding kit.
6. Remove the piston from the cylinder. If it is stubborn, remove the bleeder screw and blow it out with compressed air.

CAUTION

Hold the piston over a block of wood when doing this as the piston will fly out with considerable force.

7. When the piston pops out of the caliper, remove the rubber seal with a wood or plastic pin to avoid damaging the seal groove.
8. Clean all metal parts in denatured alcohol. Never use a mineral based solvent such as gasoline, kerosene, acetone or the like. These solvents deteriorate rubber parts. Inspect the pistons and their bores. They must be free of scoring and pitting. Replace the cylinder if there is any damage.
9. Discard all rubber parts. The caliper rebuilding kit includes new boots and seals which should be used as the caliper is reassembled.
10. Lightly coat the cylinder bore, piston, and seal with brake assembly paste or fresh brake fluid.
11. Using a vise, install the piston into the cylinder.
12. Position the guide spring in the groove of the brake cylinder and, using a brass drift, install the cylinder on the floating frame.
13. Place the mounting frame in the guide spring and slip it onto the floating frame. The fixed frame has two grooves which position it over the raised ribs of the floating frame.
14. Install pads, caliper, and bleed the brakes.

BRAKE DISC REPLACEMENT

1. Remove caliper and suspend from a suspension member by means of a wire.
2. Remove the dust cap and loosen and remove adjusting clamp.
3. Pull the disc and hub assembly from the spindle, taking care not to drop the outer wheel bearing.
4. When installing, turn wheel while tightening adjusting clamp. Proper adjustment is achieved when flat washer can be just moved by finger pressure on a screwdriver.

WHEEL BEARING ADJUSTMENT

See procedures under Brake Disc Replacement.

Rear Drum Brakes

BRAKE DRUMS

Removal and Installation

NOTE: The axle nut is tightened to 220-290 ft/lbs torque.

1. With the wheels still on the ground, remove the cotter pin from the slotted nut on the rear axle and remove the nut from the axle.

CAUTION

Make sure the emergency brake is now released.

2. Jack up the car and remove the wheel and tire.
3. The brake drum is splined to the rear axle and the drum should slip off the axle. However, the drum sometimes rusts on the splines and it is necessary to remove the drum using a puller.
4. Before installing the drum, lubricate the splines. Install the drum on the axle and

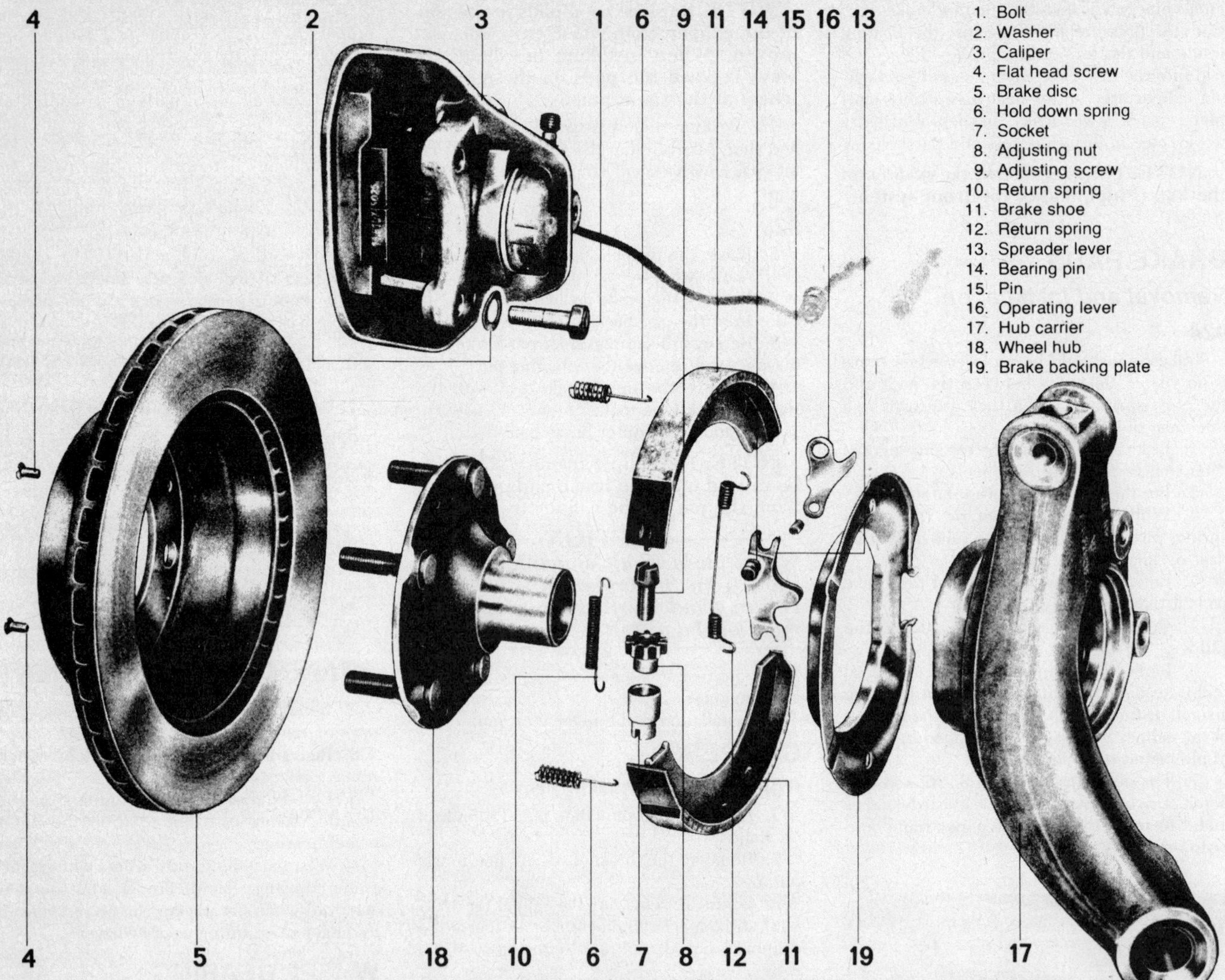

Exploded view of rear brake assembly—model 928

tighten the nut on the axle to 220-290 ft/lbs. Line up a slot in the nut with a hole in the axle and insert a cotter pin. Never loosen the nut to align the slot and hole.

BRAKE SHOES

Removal and Installation

1. Remove the brake drum.
2. Remove both shoe retaining springs.
3. Disconnect the lower return spring.
4. Disconnect the handbrake cable from the lever attached to the rear shoe.
5. Remove the upper return spring and clip.
6. Remove the brake shoes and connecting link.
7. Remove the emergency brake lever from the rear shoe.
8. Lubricate the adjusting screws and the star wheel against the head of the adjusting screw.
9. Reverse Steps 1-7 to install the shoes.
10. Adjust the brakes.

WHEEL CYLINDERS

Removal and Installation

Remove the brake drum and brake shoes. Disconnect the brake line from the cylinder and remove the bolts which secure the cylinder to the backing plate. Remove the cylinder from the vehicle.

Overhaul

1. Remove the wheel cylinder.
2. Remove the brake adjusters and remove the rubber boot from each end.

NOTE: The Type 2 cylinder has only one rubber boot, piston, and cup. The rebuilding procedures are the same.

3. Push in on one of the pistons to force out the opposite piston and rubber cup.
4. Wash the pistons and cylinder in clean brake fluid or alcohol.
5. Inspect the cylinder bore for signs of pitting, scoring, and excessive wear. If it is badly scored or pitted, the whole cylinder should be replaced. It is possible to remove the glaze and light scores with crocus cloth on a brake cylinder hose. Before rebuilding the cylinder, make sure the bleeder screw is free. If the bleeder is rusted shut or broken off, replace the entire cylinder.
6. Dip the new pistons and rubber cups in brake fluid. Place the spring in the bore and insert the rubber cups into the bore against the spring. The concave side of the rubber cup should face inward.
7. Place the pistons in the bore and install the rubber boot.
8. Install the cylinder and bleed the brakes after the shoes and drum are in place. Make sure that the brakes are adjusted.

Rear Disc Brakes

Follow the procedures for front disc brakes.

Parking Brake

CABLE

924

ADJUSTMENT

1. Raise the rear wheels and support on stands. Adjust the brakes.
2. Remove the parking brake handle boot.
3. Pull the lever up two teeth.
4. Tighten the adjusting nut until both wheels can just barely be turned by hand.

928

1. Raise the vehicle and remove the rear wheels.
2. Release the parking brake lever and move the disc brake pads so that the rotor can be easily moved.

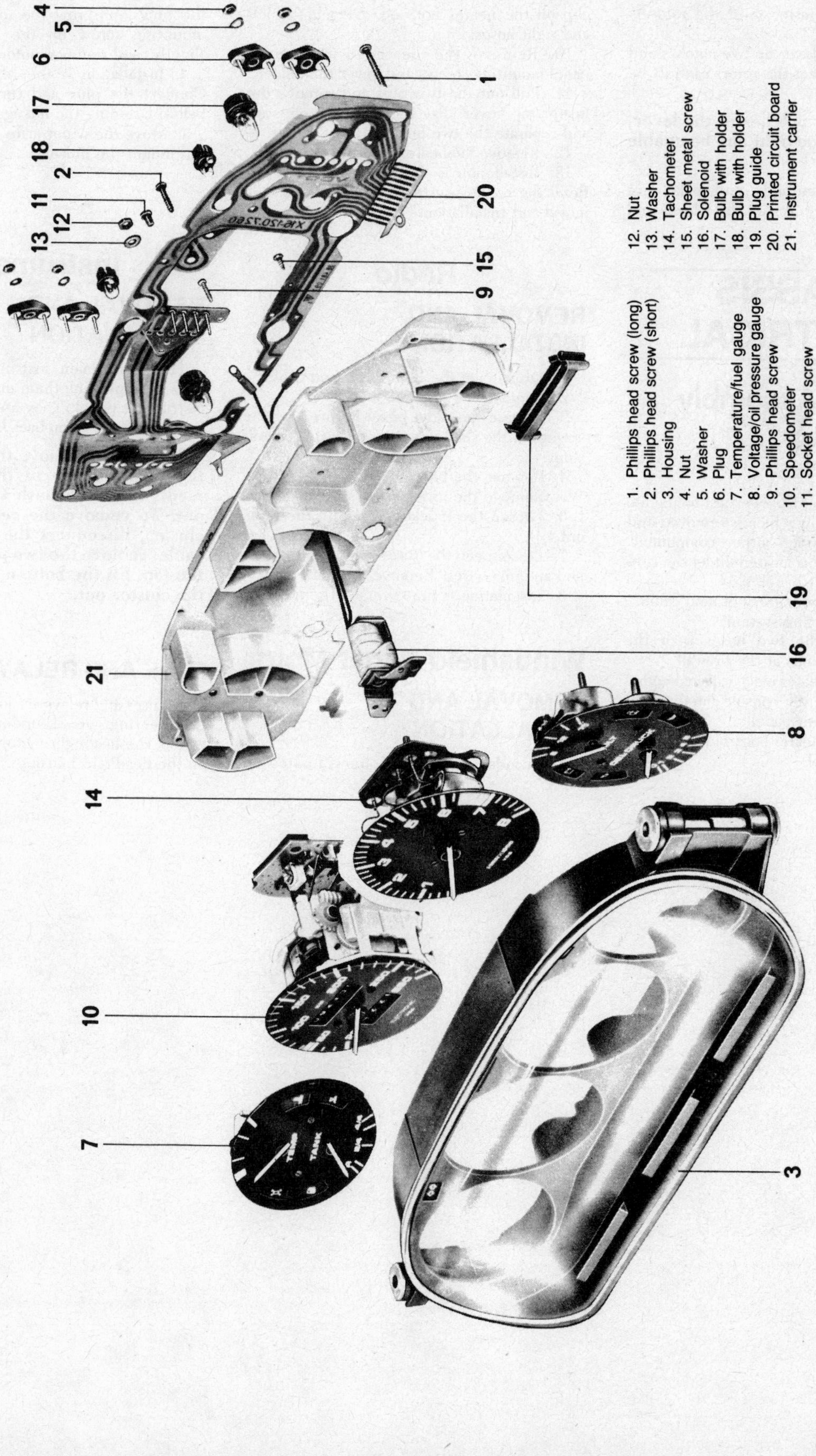

1. Phillips head screw (long)
2. Phillips head screw (short)
3. Housing
4. Nut
5. Washer
6. Plug
7. Temperature/fuel gauge
8. Voltage/oil pressure gauge
9. Phillips head screw
10. Speedometer
11. Socket head screw
12. Nut
13. Washer
14. Tachometer
15. Sheet metal screw
16. Solenoid
17. Bulb with holder
18. Bulb with holder
19. Plug guide
20. Printed circuit board
21. Instrument carrier

Typical dashboard layout

3. Loosen the cable adjusting nuts so that no tension exists on the cable.
4. Insert a screwdriver through the hole in the brake rotor and turn the brake adjuster until the rotor cannot be moved.
5. Loosen the adjuster until the rotor is free to turn.
6. Pull the brake lever up two notches and adjust the cable so that the rotors can just be turned.

NOTE: At four notches of the lever, the rotors should be tight and be unable to turn.

7. Release the handbrake and make sure the rotors turn freely. Install the wheels and lower the vehicle.

CHASSIS ELECTRICAL

Heater Assembly

REMOVAL AND INSTALLATION

The heater core and blower are contained in the heater assembly which is removed and disassembled to service either component. The heater assembly is located under the center of the instrument panel.

1. Disconnect the battery ground cable.
2. Drain the cooling system.
3. Disconnect the two hoses from the heater core connections at the firewall.
4. Unplug the heater electrical connector.
5. Detach the center console and the right side of the instrument panel.
6. Remove the heater control knobs from the instrument panel.
7. Remove the two retaining screws and remove the controls from the instrument panel.
8. Disconnect the heater control cables.
9. Using a screwdriver, pry the retaining clip off the heater housing. Detach the left and right hoses.
10. Remove the heater-to-instrument panel mounting screws and lower the heater.
11. Pull out the two pins and remove the heater top cover. Pry the retaining clips off and separate the two heater halves.
12. Remove the heater core and/or blower.
13. Installation is the reverse of removal. Refill the cooling system. See "Radiator Removal and Installation."

Radio

REMOVAL AND INSTALLATION

1. Disconnect the battery ground cable.
2. Remove the radio knobs.
3. Release the radio bezel by pressing the springs in the shaft openings outward to their stops.
4. Remove the bezel.
5. Remove the nuts on the shafts.
6. Loosen the brackets and pull the radio out.
7. Disconnect the fuse, ground, speaker, and antenna wires. Remove the radio.
8. Installation is the reverse of removal.

Windshield Wiper Motor

REMOVAL AND INSTALLATION

The windshield wiper motor is located on the driver's side of the cowl under a plastic cover.

1. Remove the cover.
2. Disconnect the battery ground cable.
3. Unscrew the wiper linkage, disconnect the plugs, unscrew the motor, remove the mounting screw on the frame, lift frame slightly, and remove motor.
4. Installation is the reverse of removal. Connect the plug and turn on the ignition before fastening the linkage.
5. Move the wiper arms to the off position and mount the linkage.

Instruments

REMOVAL AND INSTALLATION

The three main instruments can be removed by pushing them out from behind the instrument panel. They are mounted in rubber rings. Push them back into place to install.

NOTE: To remove the speedometer, first remove one of the other instruments and then push the speedometer out. To remove the center instrument cluster, disconnect the battery ground cable, remove the two phillips screws at the top, lift the bottom slightly and pull the cluster out.

FUSE AND RELAY BOX

All fuses and relays are located to the left of the steering wheel under the instrument panel. The headlight motor relays are located on the headlight housings.

SPECIFICATIONS

INDEX

BEFORE SERVICING, SEE THE SAFETY NOTICE ON THE CONTENTS PAGE

INTRODUCTION

The French automaker, Renault, has been manufacturing transportation vehicles of many types for over three-quarters of a century. These vehicles have included passenger cars, buses, trucks, street sweepers, military and farm equipment, and even snowmobiles. Renault has been established in the United States since about 1906, when the company sold its first buses, trucks and street sweepers.

Louis Renault invented the first shaft drive in 1898, which eliminated the troublesome chain and belt drive systems used previously. It goes without saying that the shaft drive was accepted and adopted by nearly every automobile manufacturer. Renault has always been a progressive company, willing to deviate from engineering norms if the outcome of a given project will improve a certain vehicle in the areas of efficiency, economy or comfort.

The theme of passenger cars built by this manufacturer has ranged from utter simplicity to comfortable sophistication. If the phrase "racing improves the breed" is valid, a Renault automobile should be able to handle any given situation.

The most popular Renault passenger cars have been equipped with a front mounted engine/front wheel drive drivetrain configuration, which Renault has claimed to pioneer.

Renault and American Motors Corporation (AMC) combined their engineering efforts to develop the Renault 18i, which was introduced in the beginning of the 1981 model year. Also, AMC has recently begun marketing Renault vehicles through the AMC dealer network.

SERIAL NUMBER IDENTIFICATION

Engine Number and Identification

LE CAR

The engine registration plate is located at the rear of the engine block above the clutch housing. The engine type number for 1979 and earlier models is 810-28; the engine number for 1980 and later models is 847-25. Both engines are of the same basic design, though the bore, stroke, compression and camshaft profiles differ between engines.

GORDINI

The engine registration plate is located on the left side of the engine, either above the oil filter or behind the water pump on the engine block. The Gordini model has used the 843-13 engine since 1975.

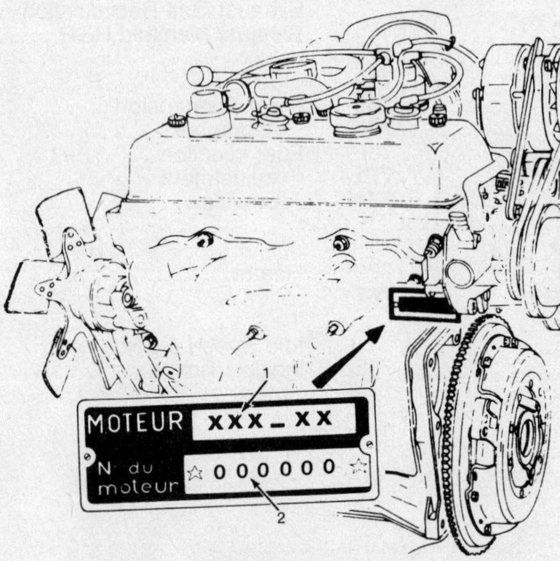

1. Engine type number
2. Engine fabrication number

Engine identification plate—Gordini and 18i

Vehicle Identification Plate

1979 AND EARLIER LE CAR–MODEL R1228

These vehicles use two identification plates: one diamond shaped and one oval shaped, both of which are located in the engine compartment.

1980 AND LATER LE CAR–MODEL R1229

These vehicles use one rectangular plate located on the fender apron.

1975-79 GORDINI–MODEL R1326

See 1979 and earlier Le Car.

18i–MODELS R1348 & R1358

A vehicle identification plate is found on the upper left corner of the instrument panel visible through the windshield. A VIN number plate is found on the driver's door center pillar, and an oval manufacturer's plate is found on the right front inner fender liner.

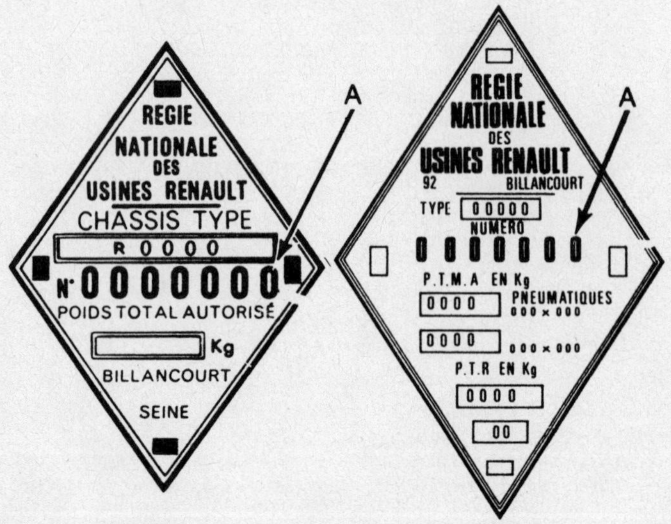

Diamond identification plate

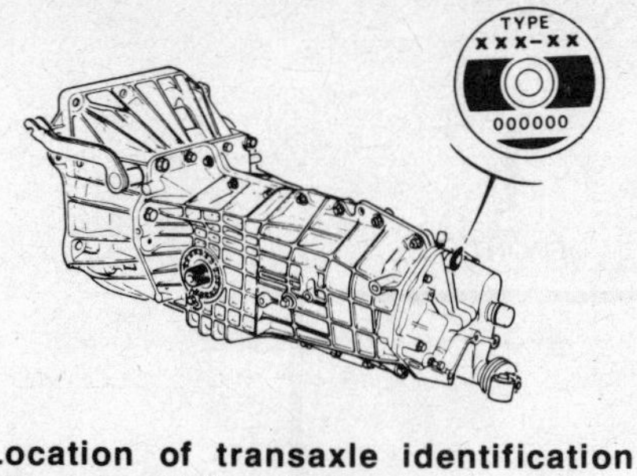

Location of transaxle identification plate—Gordini and 18i

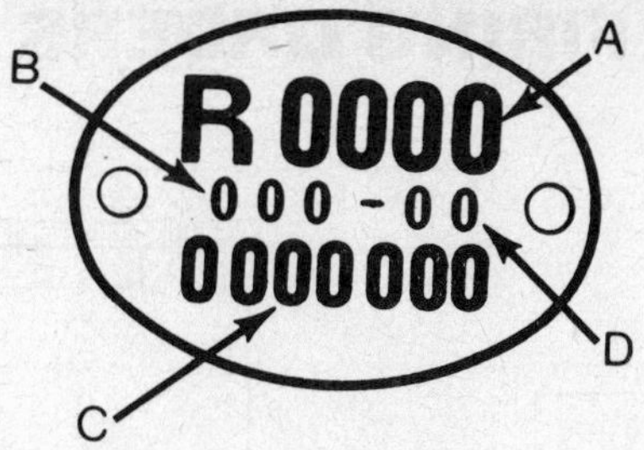

GORDINI

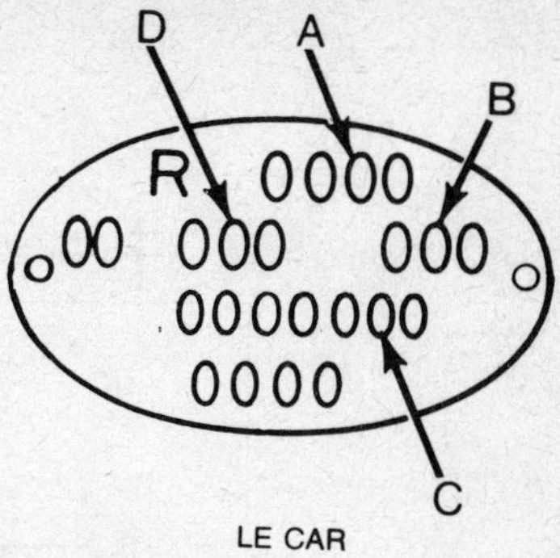

LE CAR

A. Vehicle type
B. Equipment number
C. Manufacturing number
D. Version number

Oval identification plate

GENERAL ENGINE SPECIFICATIONS

Year	Model	Engine Displacement (cu. in.)	Horsepower @ rpm (SAE)	Torque @ rpm (ft. lbs.)	Bore x Stroke (inches)	Firing Order
1975-79	Gordini	100.5	95 @ 6250	90 @ 3500	3.110 x 3.307	1-3-4-2
1976-79	Le Car	78.7	60 @ 6000	70 @ 3500	2.874 x 3.031	1-3-4-2
1980-81	Le Car	85.2	N/A	N/A	2.992 x 3.031	1-3-4-2
1981	18i	100.5	82 @ 5500	N/A	3.110 x 3.307	1-3-4-2

N/A Not available

TUNE-UP SPECIFICATIONS

Year	Model	Engine Displacement (cu. in.)	Spark Plugs Type ①	Spark Plugs Gap (in.)	Distributor Point Dwell (deg)	Ignition Timing ⑤	Idle Speed (rpm)	Valve Clearance (cold) (in.) Intake	Valve Clearance (cold) (in.) Exhaust
1975-79	Gordini	100.5	W5D ④	.025-.028	57 ③	12°BTDC ⑥	850 ⑥	.010	.012
1976-79	Le Car	78.7	W7B ②	.025-.028	57 ③	TDC	850	.006	.008
1980-81	Le Car	85.2	WR9DS	.025-.028	Electronic	3° ± 2° BTDC	750	.006	.008
1981	18i	100.5	WR7DS	.022-.026	Electronic	10°BTDC	⑦	.008	.010

① Listings for spark plugs are Bosch, although no brand name is recommended in particular.
② 1977-79 Federal uses W8B spark plug.
③ Some 1979 models may be equipped with electronic ignition.
④ 1977 uses W7D spark plug.
⑤ Check the timing with the vacuum advance disconnected.
⑥ 1977 and later: ignition timing—TDC; idle speed—900 rpm.
⑦ Manual trans.—850 rpm, Auto. trans.—650 rpm (in "Drive").

FIRING ORDERS

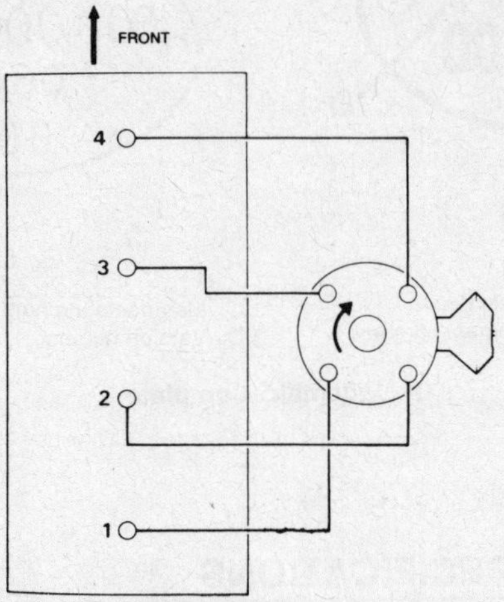

Spark plug wiring diagram—Gordini and 18i

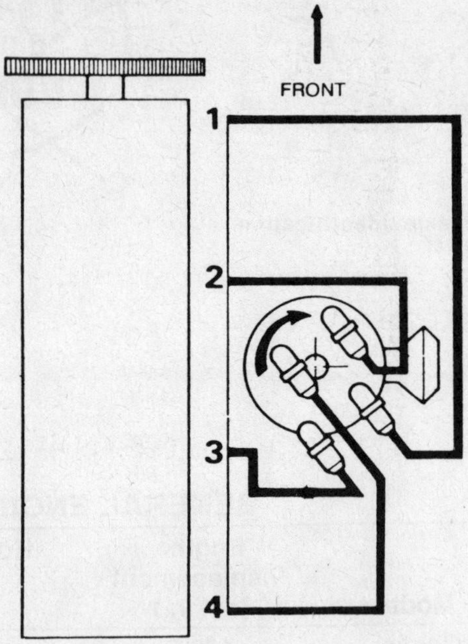

Spark plug wiring diagram —Le Car

CRANKSHAFT AND CONNECTING ROD SPECIFICATIONS

All measurments in inches

Year	Model	Engine Displacement (cu. in.)	CRANKSHAFT Main brg. Journal dia.	Main brg. Oil clearance	Shaft End-Play	CONNECTING ROD Journal Diameter	Oil Clearance	Side Clear.
1976-79	Le Car	78.7	2.157	0.0004-0.0014	0.002-0.009	1.731	0.0010-0.0026	0.012-0.023
1980-81	Le Car	85.2	2.158	0.0004-0.0014	0.002-0.009	1.732	0.0010-0.0026	0.012-0.023
1975-79	Gordini	100.5	2.158	0.0006-0.0015	0.002-0.009	1.890	N/A	N/A
1981	18i	100.5	2.158	0.0006-0.0015	0.002-0.009	1.890	N/A	N/A

N/A Not available

VALVE SPECIFICATIONS

Year	Model	Engine Displacement (cu. in.)	Seat Angle (deg)	Face Angle (deg)	STEM TO GUIDE CLEARANCE (in.) Intake	Exhaust	STEM DIAMETER (in.) Intake	Exhaust
1976-79	Le Car	78.5	45°	45°	0.006	0.006	0.276	0.276
1980-81	Le Car	85.2	45°	45°	0.006	0.006	0.276	0.276
1975-79	Gordini	100.5	45°	45°	0.006	0.006	0.315	0.315
1981	18i	100.5	45°	45°	N/A	N/A	0.315	0.315

N/A Not available

TORQUE SPECIFICATIONS

All readings in ft. lbs.

Year	Model	Engine Displacement (cu. in.)	Cylinder Head Bolts	Rod Bearing Bolts	Main Bearing Bolts	Crankshaft Pulley Bolt	Flywheel to Crankshaft Bolts	MANIFOLD Intake	MANIFOLD Exhaust
1976-79	Le Car	78.7	40	35	50	N/A	40	10	10
1980-81	Le Car	85.2	45	35	50	N/A	40	10	10
1975-79	Gordini	100.5	55-60	30	45	N/A	35	25	25
1981	18i	100.5	55-60	30	45	N/A	35	25	25

N/A Not available

TORQUE SEQUENCES

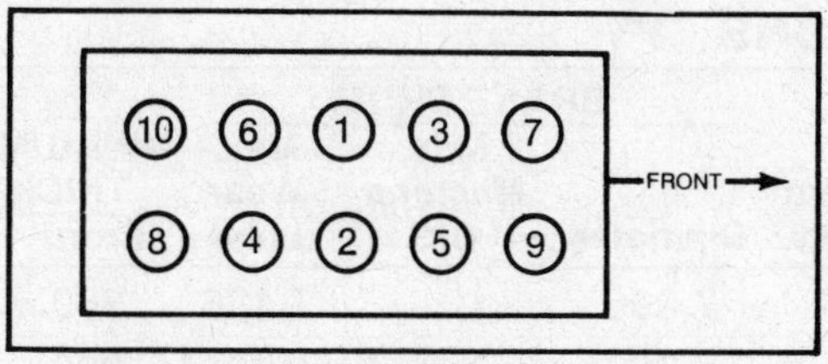

Cylinder head bolt torque sequence—Gordini and 18i

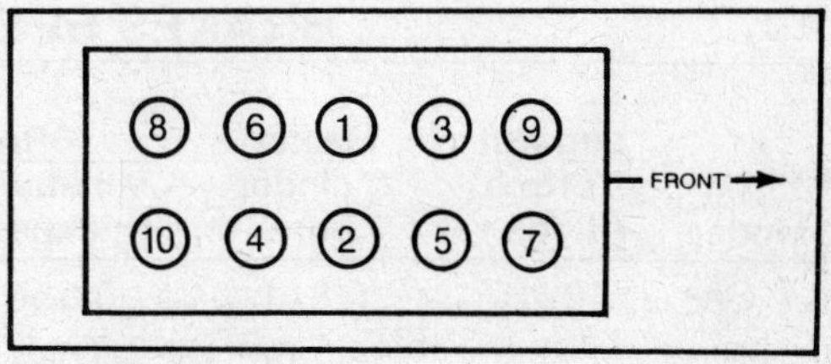

Cylinder head bolt torque sequence—Le Car

ALTERNATOR AND REGULATOR SPECIFICATIONS

ALTERNATOR Part No.	ALTERNATOR Output (amps.)	REGULATOR Part No.	REGULATOR Volts
A13R154	50 ①	AYB218	13.4-14.4
A13R243	50 ①	Integral	13.5-15.0

① Air conditioning—60 amp

BATTERY AND STARTER SPECIFICATIONS

12 volt negative ground

Starter Part No.	Battery Amps	STARTER LOCK TEST Amps	STARTER LOCK TEST Volt	STARTER LOCK TEST Torque (ft. lbs.)	STARTER Min. Brush Length (in.)
D8E121	45	400	N/A	9	5/16
D10E54	45	400	N/A	13	N/A

N/A Not available

CAPACITIES

Year	Model	Engine Displacement (cu. in.)	Crankcase With Filter (qts.)	TRANSMISSION (pts.) Manual	TRANSMISSION (pts.) Automatic	Gasoline Tank (gals.)	Cooling System (qts.)
1975-79	Gordini	100.5	4.5	4.0	6.6	12.5	8.0
1976-81	Le Car	All	3.5	4.0	6.6	10.0	6.5
1981	18i	100.5	4.5	4.0 ①	②	14.0	8.0

① Both the four and five-speed transmissions have the same capacity.
② Oil change—2⅔ quarts
Converter—2 quarts
Transmission total (excluding converter)—5¼ quarts

BRAKES SPECIFICATIONS

Year	Model	Lug Nut Torque (ft. lbs.)	Master Cylinder Bore	BRAKE DISC Minimum Thickness	BRAKE DISC Maximum Run-Out	BRAKE DRUM Diameter	BRAKE DRUM Max. Machine O/S	BRAKE DRUM Max. Wear Limit	MINIMUM LINING THICKNESS Front	MINIMUM LINING THICKNESS Rear
1976-81	Le Car	40-45	0.811	0.354	0.008	7.096	①	7.136	.280	N/A
1975-79	Gordini	45-60	0.748	0.354	0.008	9.000	①	9.035	.280	N/A
1981	18i	45-60	0.748	0.354	0.007	8.996	①	9.035	.276	N/A

① The manufacturer does not recommend machining of the brake drums
N/A Not available

WHEEL ALIGNMENT

Year	Model	CASTER Range (deg)	CASTER Pref. Setting (deg)	CAMBER Range (deg)	CAMBER Pref. Setting (deg)	Toe Setting (inches)
1976-77	Le Car	+12 to +13	+12	—	+1°30′	+0.047″ to +.188″
1978-79 ③	Le Car	+12 to +13	+12	0 to 1	1/2	+0.093″ to +.188″
1979-81 ③	Le Car	—	+6	—	+1°30′	−3/63″ to −3/16″
1975-78 ①	Gordini	—	+4	—	+1°30′	+0.093″ to +.188″
1979	Gordini	—	+4	—	+1°30′	−3/64″ to −5/32″
1981	18i	②	②	0 ± 30′	0	0 to +1/16″

① 1977 Gordini GTL: toe setting—+0.047″ to +0.156″
② w/power steering: +1°30′ to +3°
w/manual steering: 0°30′ to +2°
③ Some early 1979 models may be equipped with the 12° caster suspension. The 6° caster suspension (late 1979) is identified by steering arms with adjustment provisions at the ball socket end of the steering arm. See the test for further information.

TUNE-UP

The Renault Le Car used a conventional point/condenser ignition system in vehicles made prior to September 1979, at which point the current transistorized breakerless ignition system began production. The 18i also uses electronic ignition.

The electronic (transistorized breakerless) ignition uses an "impulse generator" which consists of a rotating trigger plate with one arm per cylinder, magnetic impulse senders and an impulse sender coil. Two impulse senders are used, the main impulse sender and the secondary impulse sender. At times when the engine oil temperature is below 60° F (15° C), and oil temperature switch triggers a relay which activates the secondary impulse sender, the secondary impulse sender then advances the spark 3° (6° flywheel). Dwell in the electronic ignition distributor cannot be adjusted, although the trigger plate gap and the ignition timing are adjustable.

The Renault Gordini has used a conventional point/condenser ignition system until the model was discontinued in 1979. A somewhat unique feature of this distributor is that the dwell is externally adjustable.

Breaker Points and Condenser

REMOVAL AND INSTALLATION

Le Car

1. Release the two spring steel clamps which retain the distributor cap and move the cap aside (with the plug wires connected).
2. Remove the rotor and disconnect the wiring at the point set.
3. Loosen the condenser bracket mounting screw and remove the condenser.
4. Remove the point set. Installation is the reverse of the removal procedure. Adjust the dwell after the new points have been installed.

Gordini

(Vehicles equipped with only a vacuum advance system)

1. Remove the distributor cap—leave the plug wires connected.
2. Loosen the dwell adjustment nut and the two screws adjacent to the dwell adjustment nut on the outside of the distributor body.
3. Remove the plug next to the distributor body wiring connector and extract the retaining lug.
4. Remove the dwell adjustment rod and spring to gain access to the fixed contact point retaining screw.
5. Remove the fixed contact point retaining screw.
6. Remove the fixed contact point.
7. Disconnect the wiring at the movable contact point.
8. Remove the breaker plate stud-to-contact stud clip and remove the movable contact point. Assembly is the reverse of the removal procedure.

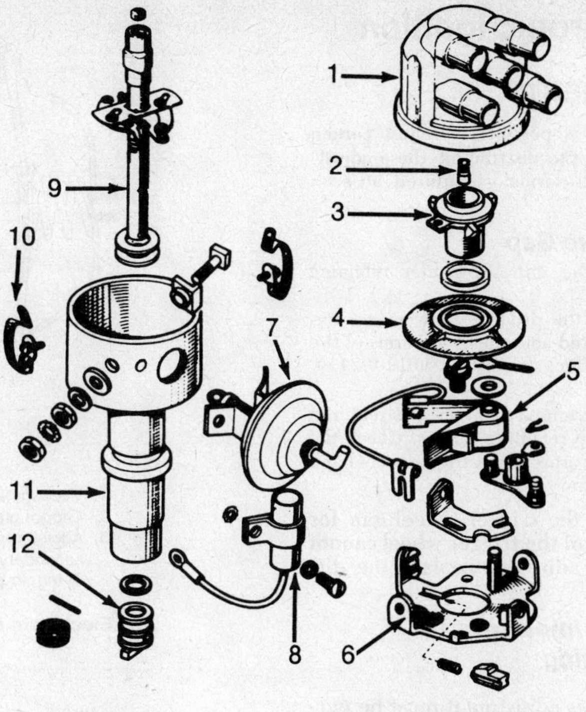

1. Distributor cap
2. Contact
3. Rotor
4. Dust cover
5. Point set
6. Breaker plate
7. Vacuum advance unit
8. Condenser
9. Mainshaft
10. Cap retaining clip
11. Body
12. Drive flange

Point-type distributor exploded view—Le Car

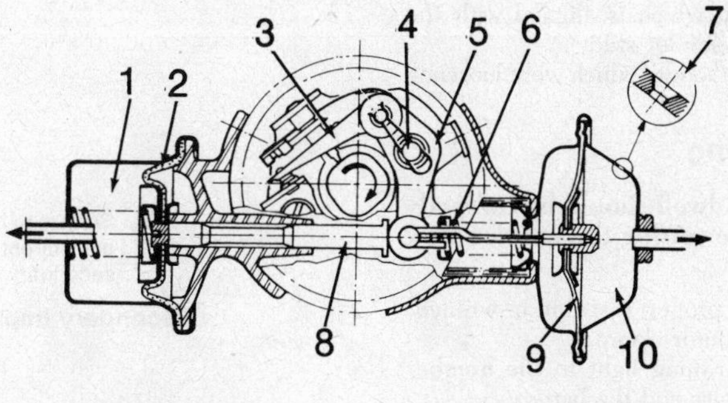

1. Retard capsule
2. Retard diaphragm
3. Point set
4. Pivot
5. Lever
6. Advance spring
7. Atmospheric vent
8. Spindle
9. Advance diaphragm
10. Advance capsule

Advance/retard point-type ignition—Gordini

NOTE: When servicing later models equipped with the vacuum advance/retard system, eliminate previous steps two through four.

Dwell Angle—Point Type Ignition

ADJUSTMENT

1. Connect a dwell meter to the engine, start the engine, and read the dwell meter.
2. Set the dwell to specifications: On Le Car models, turn off the engine and manually move the contact point set. On the Gordini without the advance/retard system, rotate the dwell adjustment nut on the outside of the distributor housing (engine running). On the Gordini with the advance/retard system, turn off the engine, remove the distributor cap and change the position of the points manually to alter the dwell.

Electronic Ignition

ADJUSTMENTS

Although it is possible to adjust certain components of the distributor, these adjustments are not normally required at each tune-up.

Trigger Plate Gap

1. Loosen the impulse sender retaining screws slightly.
2. Measure the distance between an impulse sender stud and one of the arms of the trigger plate. The gap must be 0.012-0.24 in. (0.3-0.6 mm).
3. Move the impulse sender(s) as required and tighten the retaining screws. Check the gap for all four arms of the trigger wheel and adjust as necessary.

NOTE: If the trigger wheel gap for certain arms of the trigger wheel cannot be correctly adjusted, replace the distributor.

Secondary Impulse Sender Timing

NOTE: This adjustment must be performed after every trigger plate gap adjustment.

1. Loosen the screws (A) as illustrated in the accompanying diagram.
2. Align one arm of the trigger plate with the primary impulse sender stud (B).
3. Move the secondary impulse sender so that the center of the secondary impulse sender stud (C) is located opposite the edge of the trigger plate arm which is aligned with the primary impulse sender stud.
4. Tighten the screws which were loosened in Step one.

Ignition Timing

NOTE: The dwell should be correctly adjusted before setting the ignition timing.

1. Using the proper distributor wrench, loosen the distributor clamp.
2. Connect a timing light to the number one spark plug wire and the battery.
3. Disconnect the vacuum line to the distributor vacuum advance.
4. Start the engine and allow the engine to idle.
5. Rotate the distributor to align the clutch housing mark (number one for Le Car as illustrated) with the timing mark on the flywheel. Note that number two in the Le Car illustration denotes advanced timing of four degrees.
6. Tighten the distributor hold-down clamp and recheck the timing setting.

Valve Clearance

ADJUSTMENT

1. Connect a remote starting switch into the starting circuit to bypass the ignition switch circuit.
2. Following the proper valve adjusting sequence, loosen the jamnuts and turn the adjusters as necessary.

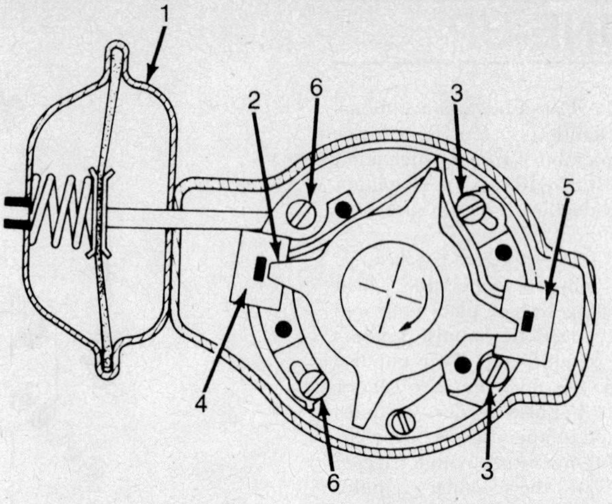

1. Vacuum advance capsule
2. Trigger plate
3. Adjustment screws for the secondary impulse sender-to-trigger plate clearance
4. Main impulse sender
5. Secondary impulse sender
6. Adjustment screws for the main impulse sender-to-trigger plate clearance

Electronic ignition parts identification—Le Car and 18i

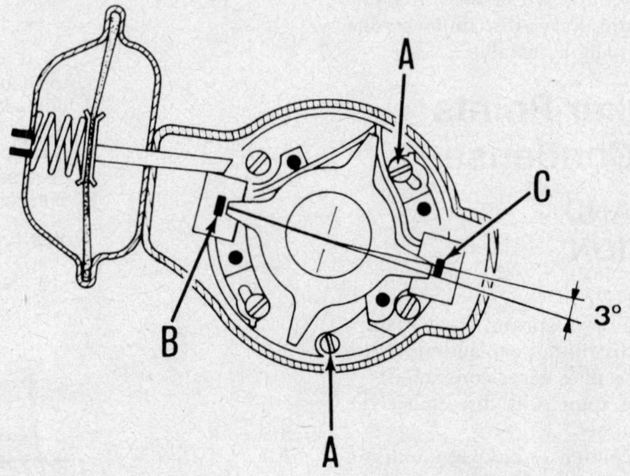

A. Screws to be loosened for adjustment of the secondary impulse sender
B. Primary impulse sender stud
C. Secondary impulse sender stud

Secondary impulse sender timing adjustment—Le Car and 18i

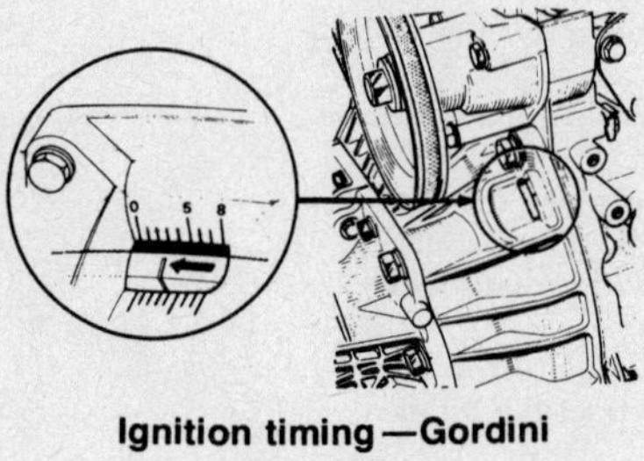

Ignition timing—Gordini

Exh. valve fully open on cyl. no.	Adj. int. valve on cyl. no.	Adj. exh. valve on cyl. no.
1	3	4
3	4	2
4	2	1
2	1	3

Valve adjustment sequence—Le Car

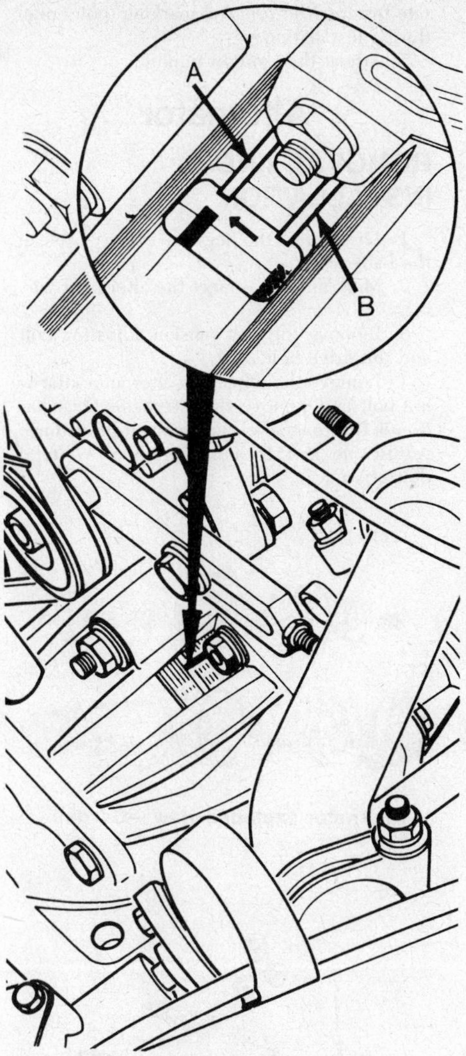

A. Top dead center
B. 4 degrees advanced

Ignition timing—Le Car

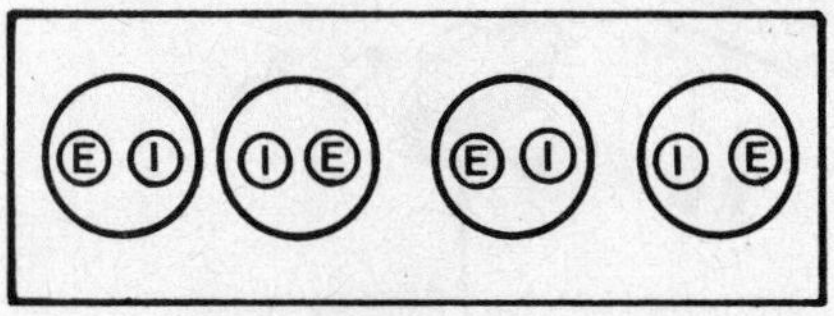

Valve arrangement—Le Car

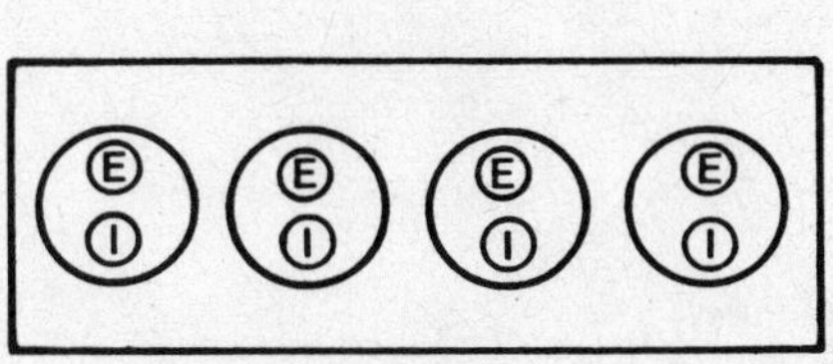

DISTRIBUTOR SIDE OF ENGINE

Valve arrangement—Gordini and 18i

VALVE ADJUSTING SEQUENCE—GORDINI AND 18i

Valve Position	Cylinder Number			
Exhaust valve fully open on	1	2	3	4
Adjust exhaust valve on	4	3	2	1
Intake valve fully open on	1	2	3	4
Adjust intake valve on	4	3	2	1

Carburetor

IDLE SPEED AND MIXTURE ADJUSTMENT

NOTE: 1977 California models and all 1978-81 models must be adjusted with the use of a CO meter to obtain the correct emissions reading and idle speed. It is advised that these procedures be performed only be a qualified service person. Previous models may be adjusted by the lean drop method.

Without a CO Meter (1977 and Earlier Except California)

1. Clamp off the air injection hose between the divertor valve and the engine, using the appropriate special tool.

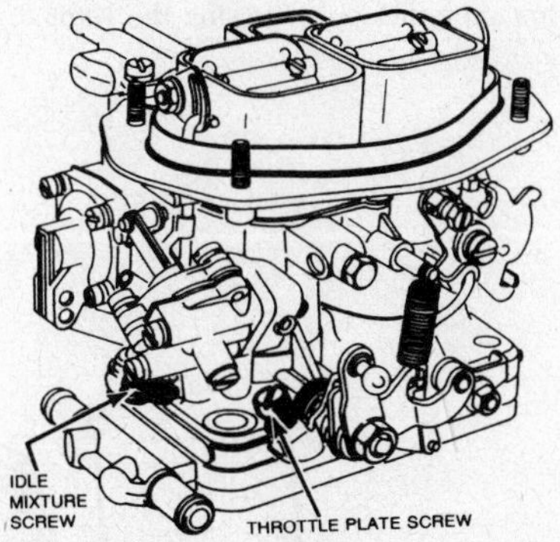

Carburetor adjustment screws—Le Car

2. Turn the throttle plate screw so that the engine speed is 775 rpm.
3. Turn the idle mixture screw to obtain the highest possible idle speed.
4. Lower the engine speed 20-25 rpm by turning the idle mixture screw clockwise. Remove the air injection hose block-off clamp and check the idle speed which should be 850 ± 50 rpm. If the idle speed is incorrect, turn the throttle plate screw to adjust.

With a CO Meter

1. Clamp off the air injection hose between the divertor valve and the engine using the appropriate special tool.
2. Turn the throttle plate screw so that the engine speed is 775 rpm.
3. Turn the idle mixture screw to obtain the following readings:

1976-79	2.5% + .5% −2%
1980 Federal	2.0% + .5% −2%

4. Remove the air injection hose block-off clamp and recheck the idle speed. Idle speeds should read as follows:

1976	800 ± 50 rpm
1977	850 ± 50 rpm
1978	800 ± 50 rpm
1979	850 ± 50 rpm
1980	750 ± 50 rpm
1981	850 ± 50 rpm MT
	650 ± 50 rpm AT

5. Repeat Steps two through four if necessary.

With a Vacuum Gauge (1980 California)

1. Tee a vacuum gauge into the line which runs from the vacuum solenoid regulator to the carburetor. The amount of vacuum applied to the carburetor actuators will be measured.
2. Adjust the fuel metering screw to obtain an idle speed of 750 ± 50 rpm.
3. Adjust the mixture screw to obtain a vacuum reading of 1.5 ± 1.2 Hg.
4. Readjust the fuel metering screw to correct the idle speed.

NOTE: To obtain the correct idle speed, only the fuel metering screw should be adjusted.

Fuel Injection—L-Jetronic

IDLE SPEED AND MIXTURE ADJUSTMENT

With a CO Meter

1. Bring the engine to normal operating temperature.
2. Clamp off the air injection hose between the divertor valve and the engine using the appropriate special tool.
3. Rotate the throttle plate housing screw as necessary to obtain an idle speed of 800 rpm.
4. Turn the airflow meter bypass screw until a CO meter reading of 2 ± 1% is obtained.
5. Remove the air injection hose block-off clamp and readjust the idle speed to specifications with screw.

Without a CO Meter

1. Bring the engine to normal operating temperature.
2. Clamp off the air injection hose between the divertor valve and the engine using the appropriate special tool.
3. Turn the flowmeter bypass screw completely inward.

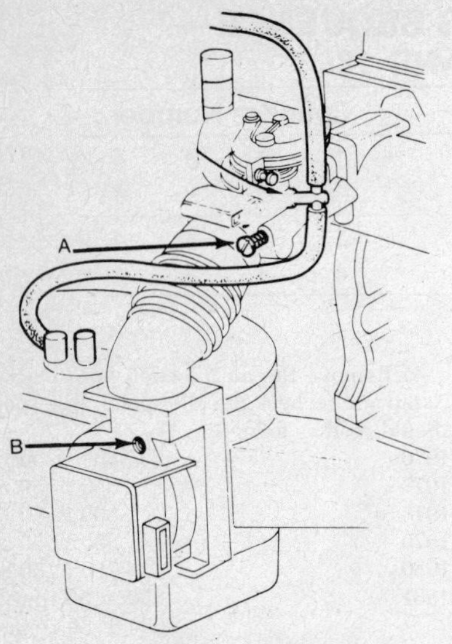

A. Throttle plate housing screw
B. Airflow meter bypass screw

Idle speed and mixture adjustment—Gordini fuel injection

4. Turn the throttle housing screw as necessary to obtain an idle speed of 850 rpm.
5. Turn the flowmeter bypass screw outward slowly to lower the idle speed to 800 rpm.
6. Remove the air injection hose block-off clamp and set the idle speed to specifications with the throttle housing screw.

ENGINE ELECTRICAL

Distributor

REMOVAL AND INSTALLATION

1. Rotate the engine in order to position the Number one cylinder at top dead center. Remove the distributor cap.
2. Mark the relationship between the distributor body and the engine, and the firing point of the rotor and the distributor body (point one).
3. Remove the hold-down clamp and remove the distributor. Mark the position of the rotor on the distributor body after removal (point two).
4. Installation is the reverse of the removal procedure. Do not turn the engine while the distributor is removed. Position the rotor at the mark made during Step three (point two). The distributor drive (camshaft) and driven gears are helical cut, causing the rotor to rotate towards the removal marking (point one) during installation.
5. Adjust the ignition timing.

Alternator

REMOVAL AND INSTALLATION

1. Disconnect the negative battery cable at the battery.
2. Mark and disconnect the alternator wiring.
3. Remove the belt tension adjusting bolt and the drive belt.
4. Remove the remaining alternator attaching bolt and remove the alternator. Installation is the reverse of the removal procedure. Adjust the belt to a maximum of ½″ total deflection.

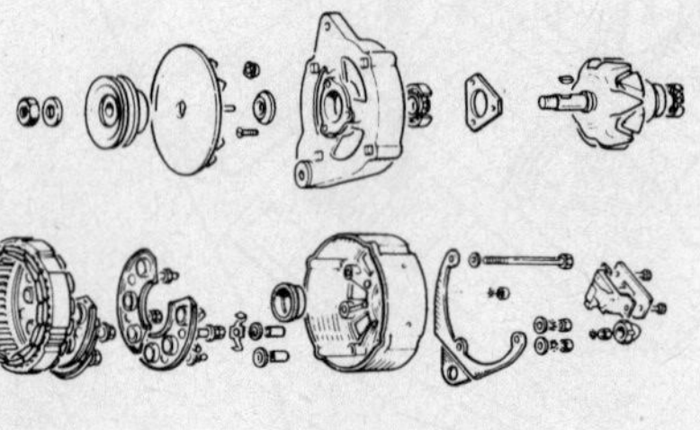

Alternator exploded view—Gordini

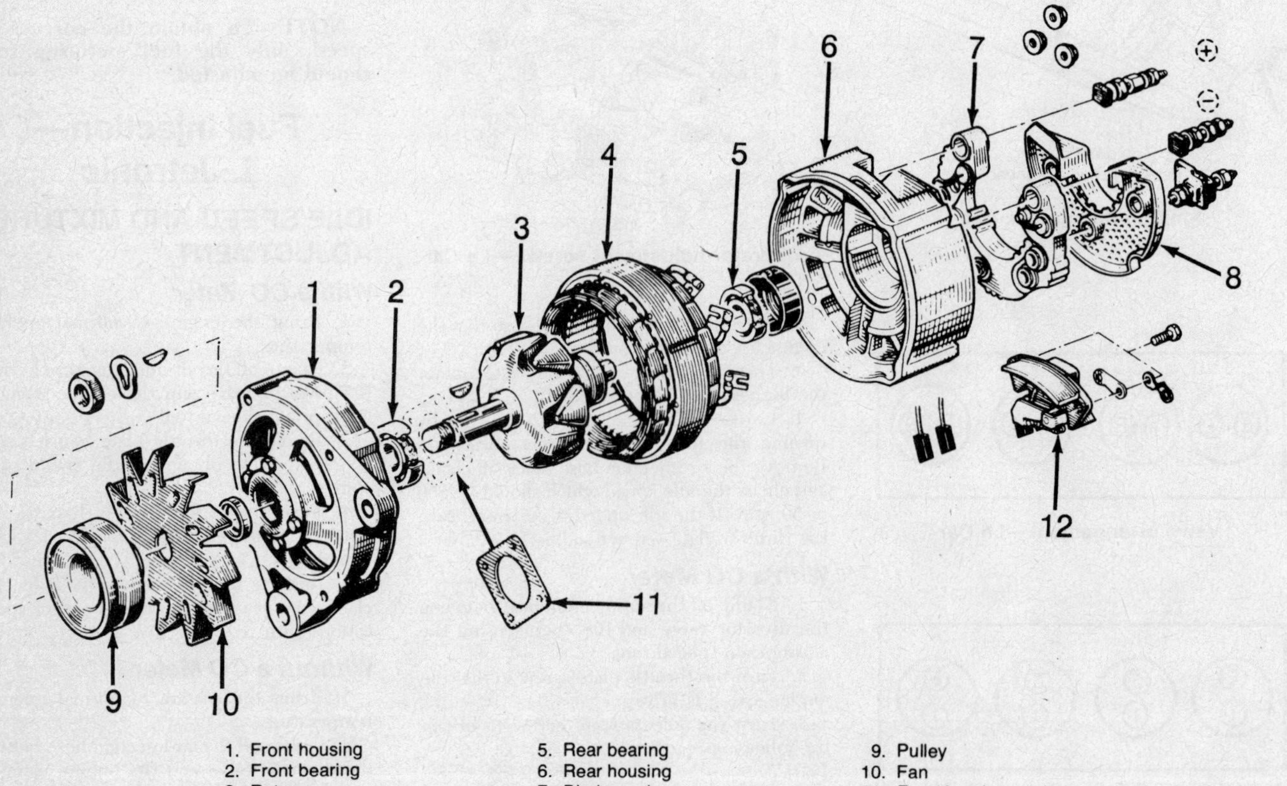

1. Front housing
2. Front bearing
3. Rotor
4. Stator
5. Rear bearing
6. Rear housing
7. Diode carrier
8. Shield
9. Pulley
10. Fan
11. Front bearing retainer
12. Brush holder

Alternator exploded view—Le Car

Starter

REMOVAL AND INSTALLATION

Le Car

1. Remove the air cleaner assembly.
2. Drain the cooling system, disconnect the hoses and linkage.
3. Disconnect the negative battery cable.
4. Remove the flange coupling at the exhaust manifold and remove the manifold.
5. Disconnect the positive battery cable at the starter.
6. Disconnect the starter solenoid feed line.
7. Remove the starter attaching bolts and remove the starter. Installation is the reverse of the removal procedure.

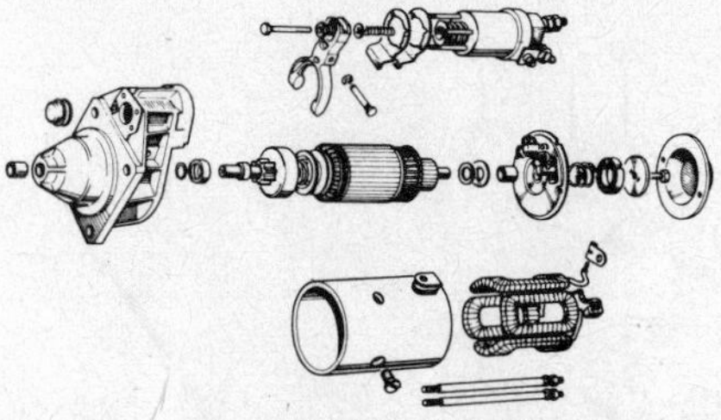

Starter—typical

Gordini and I8i

1. Disconnect the negative battery cable.
2. Disconnect the positive battery cable at the starter.
3. Disconnect the ignition switch-to-solenoid feed wire.
4. Remove the starter heat shield fasteners.
5. Remove the starter retaining bolts, slide the starter towards the rear, then sideways and remove the starter. Installation is the reverse of the removal procedure.

ENGINE MECHANICAL

Engine Removal and Installation

Le Car

1. Disconnect and remove the battery.
2. Drain the cooling system.
3. Drain the lubricating fluids from both the engine and the transaxle.
4. Remove the following items:
   a. Grille
   b. Hood
   c. Inner fender support braces (2)
5. Disconnect all wiring, water and vacuum hoses, and cables. Mark for identification during reconnection.
6. Loosen the windshield washer bottle and place it on its side.
7. Remove the transaxle cover.
8. Remove the air filter support rod.
9. Disconnect the exhaust pipe at the manifold flange.
10. Remove the radiator assembly.
11. Remove the flex coupling bolts from the steering shaft.
12. Remove the front wheels and the brake calipers—do not disconnect the brake lines.
13. Disconnect the steering arms at the end of the rack.
14. Disconnect the upper ball joints and tilt the spindles outward.
15. Mark the steering box shims to identify the right and left sides, and remove the steering box.
16. Remove the air injection filter, pump, and pump bracket.
17. Remove the two top transaxle bolts and position a lifting hook (Renault tool # Mot. 498 or its equivalent) onto the transaxle. Install two 1⅜″ long bolts in place of the transaxle bolts to secure the lifting tool to the transaxle.

NOTE: The tool securing bolts must be 1⅜″ long to distribute the lifting stress over a sufficient number of threads.

18. Remove the engine mount bolts and the right side reinforcement bolts.
19. Remove the transmission shift rod support bolts.
20. Free the clutch cable from the clutch fork and push the sleeve retainer back from the support tab.
21. Attach a suitable engine hoist to the lifting tool.
22. Remove the front transaxle mount.
23. Push the transaxle side-to-side and free the driveshaft ends from the transaxle.
24. Remove the engine/transaxle assembly.
25. Installation is the reverse of the removal procedure. Take note of the following:
   a. Lightly lubricate the clutch shaft and driveshaft splines.
   b. When reinstalling the driveshafts, pay special attention so as not to damage the oil seal lips for the differential adjusting ring nut.
   c. Be sure to reinstall the rubber bushing between the flex coupling and the intermediate shaft flange.
   d. After the tie rod inner pins have been reinstalled, make sure that they are positioned horizontally (applicable to 1979 and earlier Le Car).
   e. Adjust the clutch, accelerator cable and the choke cable.

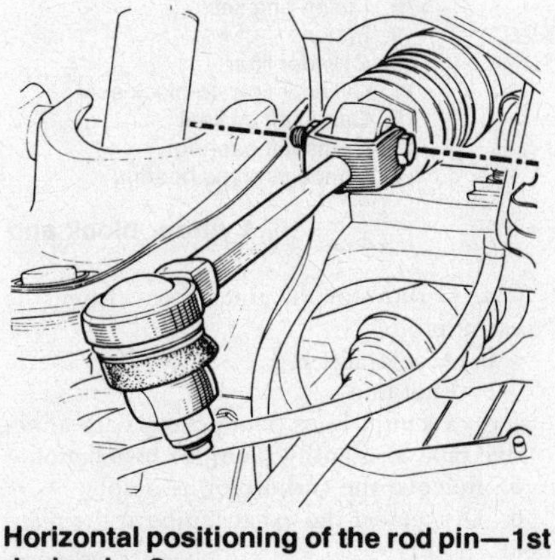

Horizontal positioning of the rod pin—1st design Le Car

Gordini

NOTE: The following procedure outlines the removal of the engine without the transaxle.

1. Disconnect the battery.
2. Drain the cooling system.
3. Disconnect all wiring, water and vacuum hoses, and cables. Mark these items for identification during reconnection.
4. Remove the following items:
   a. Hood
   b. Air cleaner
   c. Radiator
   d. Starter
   e. Camshaft drive belt and pulley
5. Remove the upper transaxle-to-engine bolts.
6. Disconnect the exhaust pipe at the manifold and drop the pipe down from the transaxle crossmember.
7. Remove the following items:
   a. Crankshaft drive pulley
   b. Cooling fan and pulley
   c. Protective clutch cover
8. Attach hoisting slings to each side of the engine and attach an engine hoist to the slings.
9. Jack the hoist upward a small amount to relieve the engine weight from the engine mounts.
10. Remove the engine mounting bolts.
11. Securely support the transaxle.
12. Remove the lower transaxle-to-engine bolts.
13. Pull the engine forward and remove the engine from the vehicle.
14. Installation is the reverse of the removal procedure. Take note of the following:
   a. Lightly lubricate the clutch shaft.
   b. When installing the crankshaft pulley, use a mild grade of Loctite on the pulley retaining bolt.

Cylinder Head

REMOVAL AND INSTALLATION

Le Car

1. Disconnect the battery cables at the battery.
2. Drain the cooling system.
3. Remove the air cleaner assembly.
4. Disconnect all wiring, water and vacuum hoses, and cables. Mark for identification during reconnection.
5. Remove the air injection pump drive belt.
6. Disconnect the exhaust pipe at the manifold.
7. Remove the valve cover.
8. Remove all of the cylinder head bolts except the bolt next to the distributor, which should be loosened slightly.
9. Tap lightly on the ends of the cylinder head with a soft-faced (preferably plastic) hammer to break the cylinder head loose from the block. Remove the remaining cylinder head bolt.
10. Mark and remove the pushrods. Remove the cylinder head.

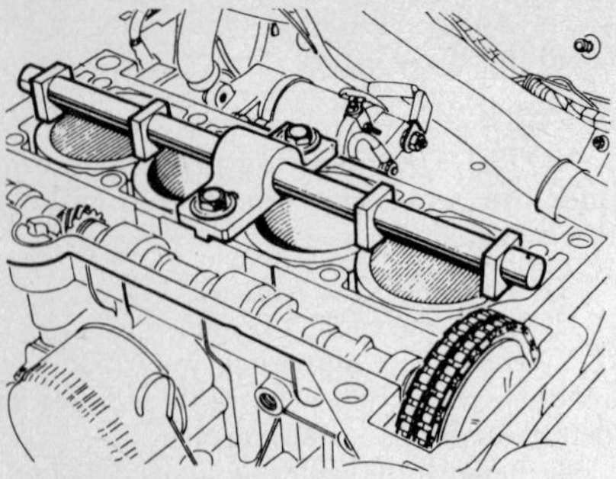

Retention of the cylinder liners after head removal—typical

NOTE: Turn the cylinder head on the block to break it loose from the cylinder liners (rotating motion) before lifting the head; if this is not done, the lower liner seals may break.

11. Installation is the reverse of the removal procedure.

NOTE: The cylinder liners must be securely retained to avoid breaking the cylinder liner-to-block seals.

Gordini and 18i

1. Disconnect the battery cables at the battery.
2. Drain the cooling system.
3. Remove the air cleaner assembly.
4. Remove the following items:
   a. Distributor
   b. Alternator (w/drive belt)
   c. Water pump drive belt
   d. Valve cover
5. Disconnect the exhaust pipe at the manifold and remove the manifold.
6. Remove the rocker shaft.
7. Mark and remove the pushrods.
8. Remove all of the cylinder head bolts except the bolt next to the distributor, which should be loosened slightly.
9. Tap lightly on the ends of the cylinder head with a soft-faced (preferably plastic) hammer to break the cylinder head loose from the block.
10. Remove the remaining cylinder head bolt and remove the cylinder head.

NOTE: Turn the cylinder head on the block to break it loose from the cylinder liners (rotating motion) before lifting the head; if this is not done, the lower liner seals may break.

11. Installation is the reverse of the removal procedure.

NOTE: The cylinder liners must be securely retained to avoid breaking the cylinder liner-to-block seals.

Intake/Exhaust Manifold

REMOVAL AND INSTALLATION

Le Car

1. Disconnect the battery cables at the battery.
2. Remove the air cleaner intake hose.
3. Drain the cooling system.
4. Remove the following items:

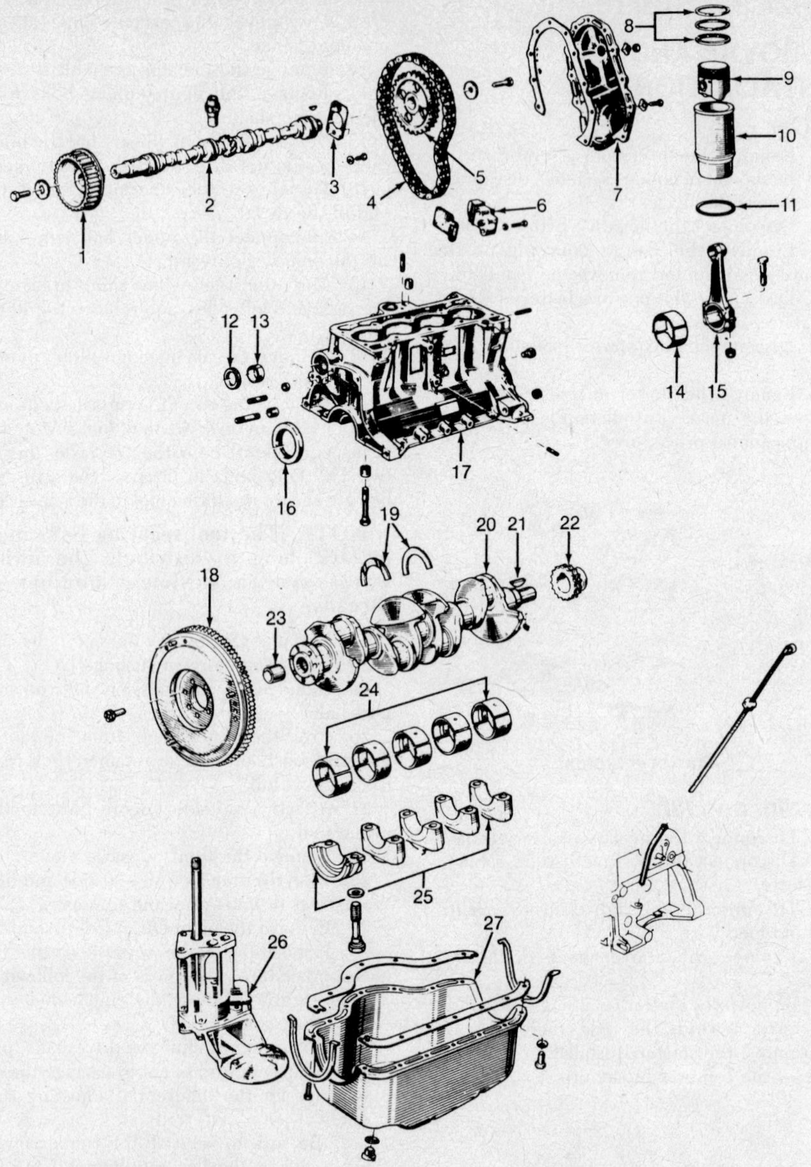

1. Camshaft pulley
2. Camshaft
3. Camshaft flange
4. Timing chain
5. Camshaft sprocket
6. Timing chain tensioner
7. Timing cover
8. Piston ring set
9. Piston
10. Cylinder liner
11. Cylinder liner-to-block seal
12. Camshaft oil seal
13. Camshaft bearing
14. Connecting rod bearing
15. Connecting rod
16. Crankshaft oil seal
17. Cylinder block
18. Flywheel
19. Crankshaft thrust bearings
20. Crankshaft
21. Crankshaft key
22. Crankshaft sprocket
23. Pilot bearing
24. Main bearings
25. Main caps
26. Oil pump
27. Oil pan

Cyinder block and components—Le Car

   a. Carburetor heating hoses from the carburetor
   b. Accelerator rod
   c. Fuel line
   d. Vacuum lines (mark them with adhesive tape to identify them for installation)
5. Remove the carburetor assembly.
6. Disconnect the exhaust pipe at the manifold.
7. Remove the manifold-to-cylinder head fasteners and remove the manifold along with the starter heat shield.

NOTE: If the manifold is excessively difficult to remove, disconnect the left engine mount and tilt the engine slightly to the right to provide extra clearance for manifold removal.

8. Installation is the reverse of the removal procedure.

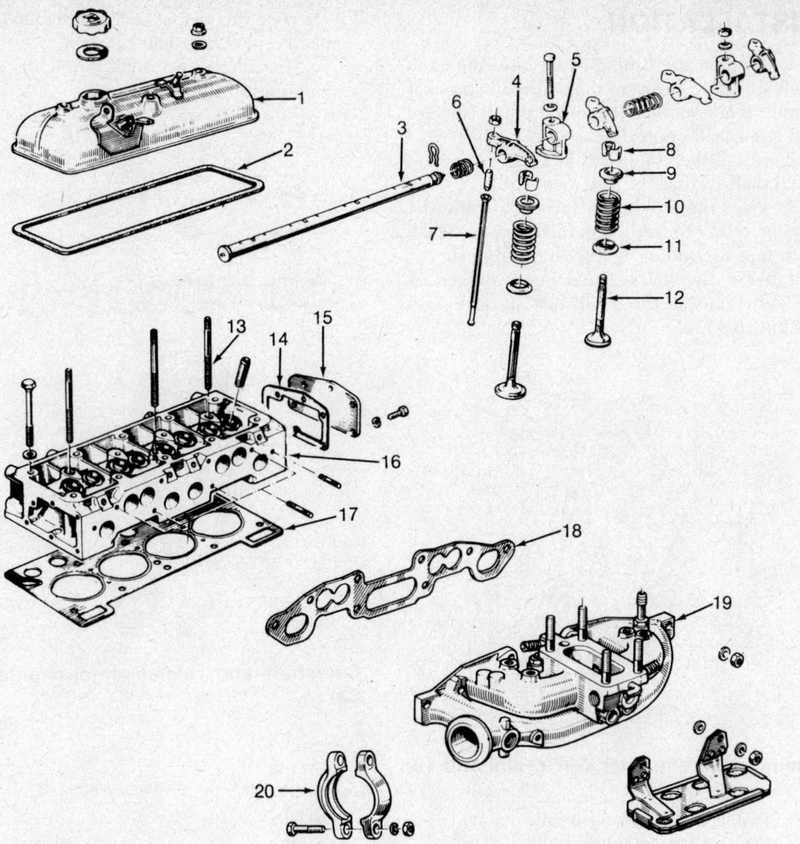

1. Rocker arm cover
2. Rocker arm cover gasket
3. Rocker arm shaft
4. Rocker arm
5. Rocker arm shaft pedestal
6. Rocker arm adjuster
7. Pushrod
8. Valve locks
9. Valve spring retainers
10. Valve springs
11. Valve spring seats
12. Valves
13. Cylinder head studs
14. End plate gasket
15. End plate
16. Cylinder head
17. Cylinder head gasket
18. Manifold-to-head gasket
19. Intake/exhaust manifolds
20. Exhaust manifold-to-exhaust pipe connector

Cylinder head and manifolds—Le Car

Timing Chain and Related Components

DISASSEMBLY: TIMING COVER, TIMING CHAIN TENSIONER, TIMING COVER GASKET AND SEAL

Le Car

1. Remove the engine/transaxle assembly from the vehicle according to the engine removal and installation procedure in the beginning of this section.
2. Remove the timing cover and clean all of the gasket surfaces.
3. If the timing chain is to be replaced, secure the shoe of the tensioner (component that actually contacts the chain) to the body of the tensioner with a piece of wire.
4. Remove the chain tensioner assembly.

NOTE: If the timing chain tensioner must be serviced, refer to the next section.

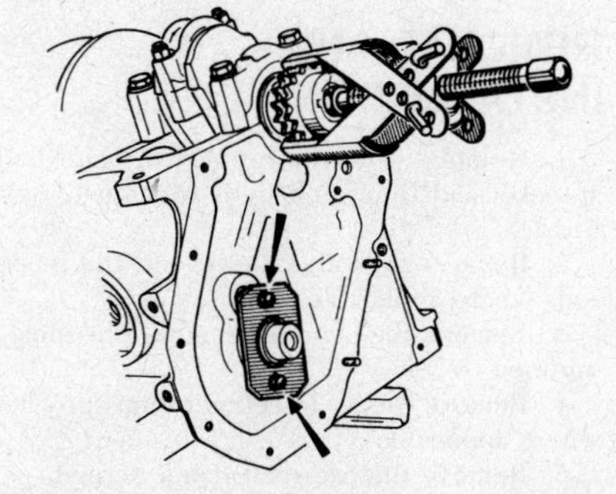

Removing the crankshaft sprocket and location of the camshaft flange (retaining) screws—Le Car

5. Remove the camshaft sprocket bolt and install a suitable puller. Tighten the puller to draw the camshaft sprocket and chain off of the camshaft.
6. If the crankshaft gear is to be replaced, draw the gear off of the crankshaft with a suitable puller.

ASSEMBLY

1. Press the crankshaft sprocket onto the crankshaft using a suitable tool.
2. Temporarily install the camshaft sprocket (marking facing outward) without the timing chain and align the timing marks.

CAUTION

Do not rotate either the camshaft or the crankshaft once the timing marks are aligned.

3. Remove the camshaft sprocket.
4. Position the timing chain onto the camshaft sprocket and reinstall the camshaft sprocket/timing chain assembly, making sure that the timing marks are aligned properly.
5. Install the camshaft sprocket retaining bolt and torque the bolt to 20 ft/lbs.
6. Install the timing chain tensioner.
7. Using a new gasket and cover-to-oil pan seal, install the timing cover.
8. Install the engine/transaxle assembly according to the engine removal and installation procedure in the beginning of this section.

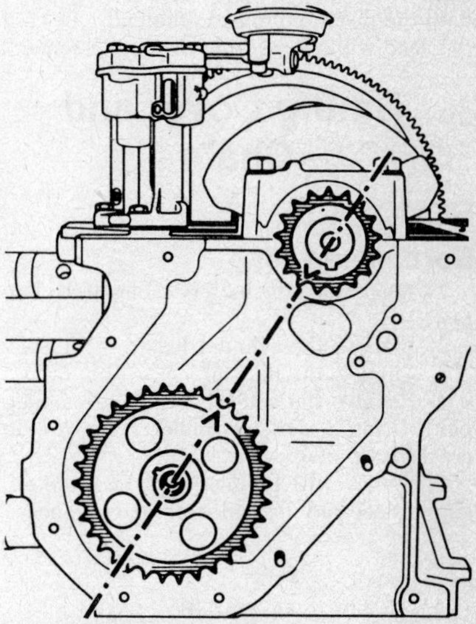

Aligning the timing marks—Le Car

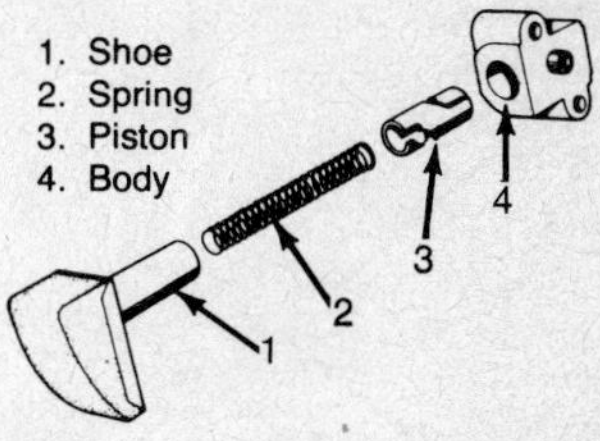

1. Shoe
2. Spring
3. Piston
4. Body

Timing chain tensioner exploded view—Le Car

Timing Chain Tensioner

The timing chain tensioner is an automatic wear take-up mechanism which eliminates the necessity of manual timing chain adjustments.

DISASSEMBLY

Le Car

1. Release the wire which was installed

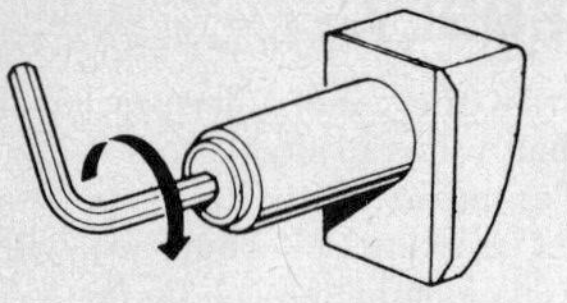

Locking the chain tensioner—Le Car

around the tensioner shoe and body in step three of "Timing Chain and Related Components—Disassembly".

2. Separate the tensioner shoe from the tensioner body.

3. Inspect the shoe, spring, piston and tensioner body for damage.

ASSEMBLY

1. Lock the piston into the shoe using a 3 mm Allen wrench.

2. Insert the shoe into the body and place a 2 mm thick shim between the shoe and the body to prevent inadvertent take-up.

3. Install the tensioner and the timing chain.

4. Remove the shim and press on the shoe until the piston bottoms in the body. Release the shoe without assisting the spring action.

Timing Cover and Chain

REMOVAL

Gordini and 18i

1. Disconnect the battery cables at the battery.

2. Remove the cylinder head.

3. Remove the radiator.

4. Remove the crankshaft pulley retaining bolt. Using a suitable puller, remove the crankshaft pulley.

5. Remove the timing cover; raise the engine if necessary to gain working clearance.

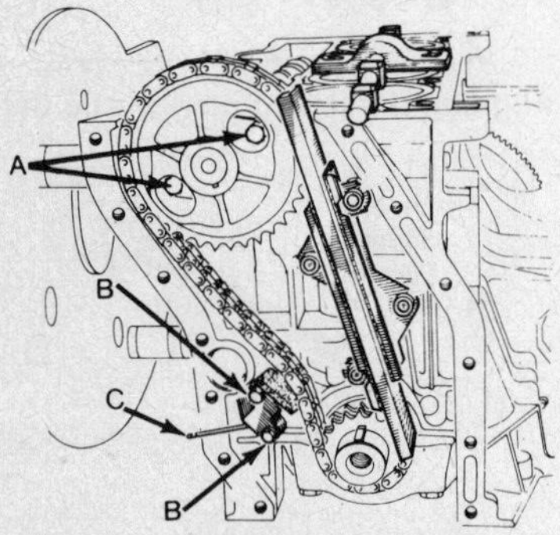

A. Camshaft flange bolts
B. Chain tensioner bolts
C. Unlocking the chain tensioner

Timing chain—Gordini and 18i

6. Remove the timing chain guide shoes and chain tensioner.

7. Remove the two camshaft retaining bolts.

8. Using a suitable puller, remove the crankshaft sprocket and key along with the timing chain.

INSTALLATION

1. Position the timing chain onto the camshaft sprocket. Position the camshaft sprocket timing mark so that the mark points toward the crankshaft centerline.

2. Install the crankshaft key and rotate the crankshaft so that the key faces up.

3. Place the crankshaft sprocket inside the timing chain to simulate installation. Make sure that the timing marks align properly.

4. After the marks have been aligned as necessary, install the crankshaft sprocket and timing chain.

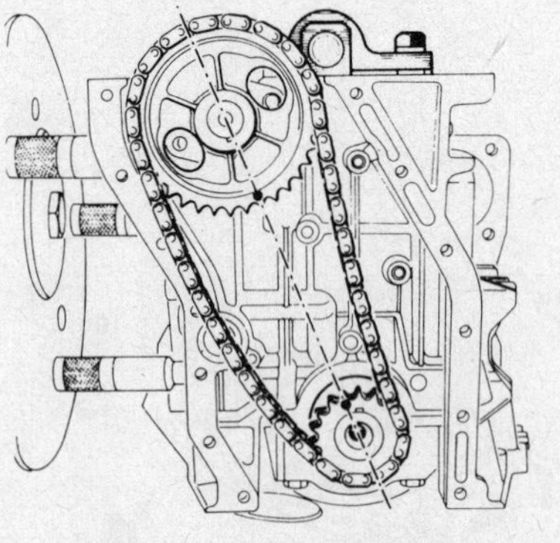

Timing mark alignment—Gordini and 18i

5. Install the following items:
   a. Camshaft retaining bolts
   b. Timing chain tensioner
   c. Timing chain guide shoes—push the chain guides against Renault gauge Mot. 420 (or its equivalent) and tighten the guide bolts.
   d. Timing cover, using a new gasket and seal
   e. Radiator
   f. Crankshaft pulley
   g. Cylinder head
6. Reconnect the battery cable.

Camshaft

REMOVAL AND INSTALLATION

1. Remove the timing cover, camshaft sprocket and timing chain as previously outlined.

2. Remove the valve cover (and the pushrods where applicable).

3. Remove the cylinder head as previously outlined.

4. Remove the air injection pump sprocket where applicable.

5. Remove the camshaft flange screws.

6. Temporarily reinstall the camshaft sprocket (to assist in removal as a handle) and carefully withdraw the camshaft from the engine.

7. Remove the camshaft oil seal.

8. Installation is the reverse of the removal procedure. Take note of the following:
   a. On Le Car models, check the clearance between the camshaft and the flange with a feeler gauge. The clearance should be between 0.002-0.005 in. If the clearance is excessive, the flange should be replaced.
   b. Use the proper seal installation tool to install a new camshaft oil seal.
   c. Install the camshaft from the timing chain end of the engine.

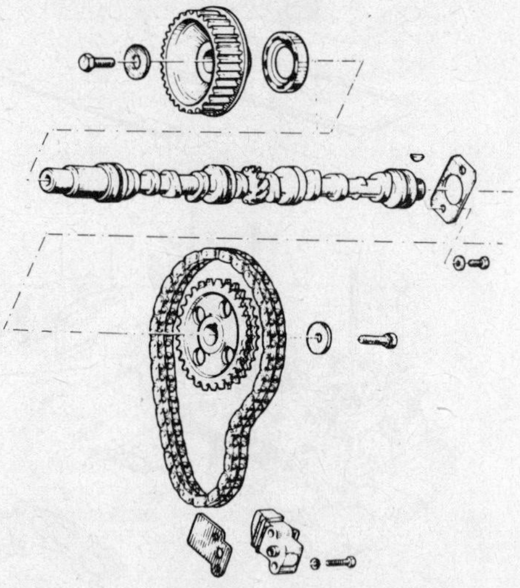

Camshaft and related components—Le Car

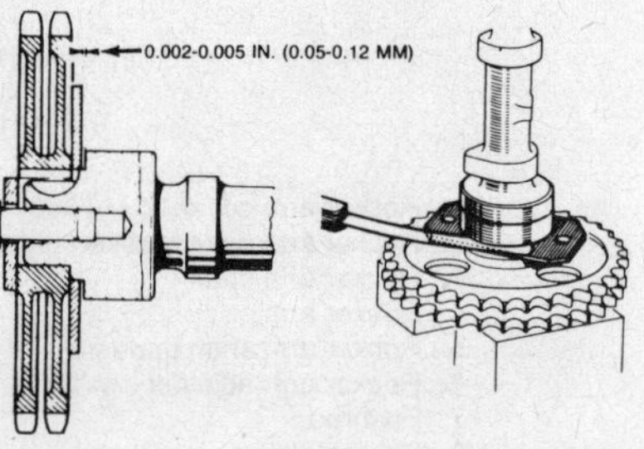

Checking the camshaft flange clearance—Le Car

EMISSION CONTROLS

Most vehicles are equipped with the following systems:

Air Injection

A belt-driven pump delivers fresh, compressed air to the exhaust ports of the engine. The presence of oxygen will lengthen the combustion process, which reduces the amount of unburned gases in the exhaust. A relief valve and a divertor valve control the amount of air delivered to the exhaust ports. Depending upon whether the engine is accelerating/cruising or decelerating, the divertor valve either delivers the air to the exhaust ports, or closes off the air passage to the exhaust ports, respectively. A check valve is provided in the system which will prevent damage to the air injection pump should the engine backfire.

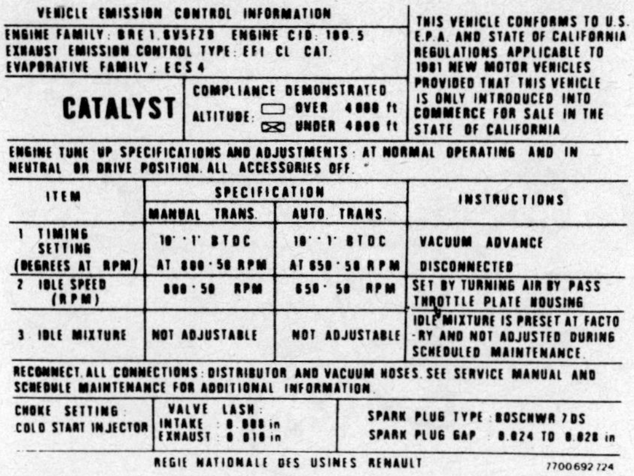
VEHICLE EMISSION CONTROL INFORMATION

ENGINE FAMILY: BRE1.6V5FZ9 ENGINE CID: 100.5
EXHAUST EMISSION CONTROL TYPE: EFI CL CAT.
EVAPORATIVE FAMILY: ECS4

CATALYST

COMPLIANCE DEMONSTRATED
ALTITUDE: ☐ OVER 4000 ft ☒ UNDER 4000 ft

THIS VEHICLE CONFORMS TO U.S. E.P.A. AND STATE OF CALIFORNIA REGULATIONS APPLICABLE TO 1981 NEW MOTOR VEHICLES PROVIDED THAT THIS VEHICLE IS ONLY INTRODUCED INTO COMMERCE FOR SALE IN THE STATE OF CALIFORNIA

ENGINE TUNE UP SPECIFICATIONS AND ADJUSTMENTS: AT NORMAL OPERATING AND IN NEUTRAL OR DRIVE POSITION. ALL ACCESSORIES OFF.

ITEM	SPECIFICATION		INSTRUCTIONS
	MANUAL TRANS.	AUTO. TRANS.	
1 TIMING SETTING (DEGREES AT RPM)	10° · 1° BTDC AT 800 · 50 RPM	10° · 1° BTDC AT 650 · 50 RPM	VACUUM ADVANCE DISCONNECTED
2 IDLE SPEED (RPM)	800 · 50 RPM	650 · 50 RPM	SET BY TURNING AIR BY PASS THROTTLE PLATE HOUSING
3 IDLE MIXTURE	NOT ADJUSTABLE	NOT ADJUSTABLE	IDLE MIXTURE IS PRESET AT FACTO-RY AND NOT ADJUSTED DURING SCHEDULED MAINTENANCE.

RECONNECT ALL CONNECTIONS: DISTRIBUTOR AND VACUUM HOSES. SEE SERVICE MANUAL AND SCHEDULE MAINTENANCE FOR ADDITIONAL INFORMATION.

CHOKE SETTING: COLD START INJECTOR	VALVE LASH: INTAKE: 0.008 in EXHAUST: 0.010 in	SPARK PLUG TYPE: BOSCHWR 7DS SPARK PLUG GAP: 0.024 TO 0.028 in

REGIE NATIONALE DES USINES RENAULT 7700692724

Emission control label—typical (18i shown)

ENGINE FAMILY BRE1 . 6V5 FZ9

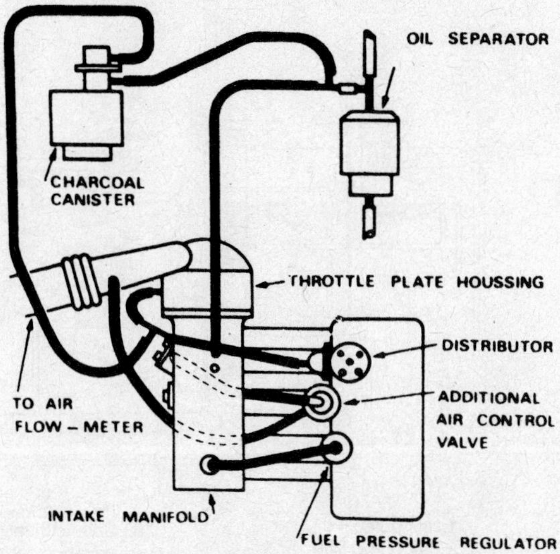

Vacuum line diagram—typical (18i shown)

Accelerated Idle System

This system is intended to reduce the amount of hydrocarbon emissions during deceleration. The primary throttle plate is opened slightly during deceleration, between speeds of 15-20 miles per hour.

Evaporative Emission Control System

The main component is a cannister containing charcoal and a filter. When the engine is off, gasoline vapor settles in the charcoal instead of being vented to the atmosphere. When the engine is started, intake manifold vacuum pulls fresh air in from beneath the charcoal (filtered) and carries the unburned gases to the intake manifold to be burned in the combustion chambers. The vacuum will continue to draw a small amount of vapor from the tank (through a calibrated orifice) even while the engine is running. The process will cycle in this manner, beginning at the time the engine is turned off.

Ignition Timing Advance Control System

A contact switch which works in conjunction with the choke cable (on Le Car models) closes and activates a solenoid which admits full vacuum to the distributor vacuum advance unit for improved emissions and driveability when the choke valve is closed. Some models use a coolant temperature sensing switch to activate the solenoid.

Three-way catalytic converter—typical (18i shown)

Oxygen sensor—typical (18i shown)

Carburetor Air Intake Pre-Heating System

A thermostatically controlled air cleaner mixes heated and ambient incoming air to the carburetor, thereby improving fuel vaporization which assists in improving emissions and driveability during cold engine operation.

P.C.V. (Positive Crankcase Ventilation) System

Crankcase vapors are routed to the induction system to be burned in the combustion chambers instead of merely being vented to the atmosphere.

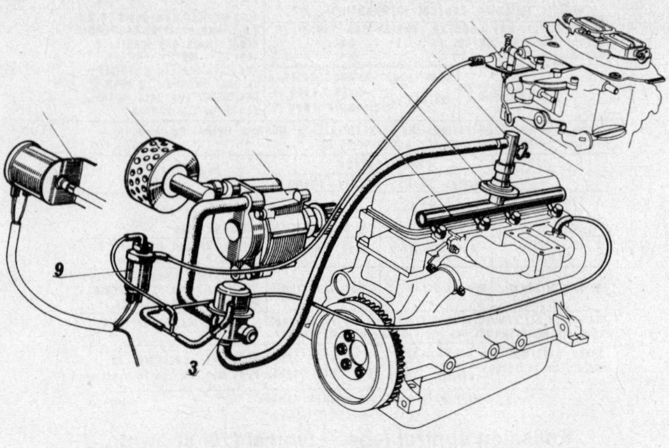

Air injection reactor system (A.I.R.)—typical (Le Car shown)

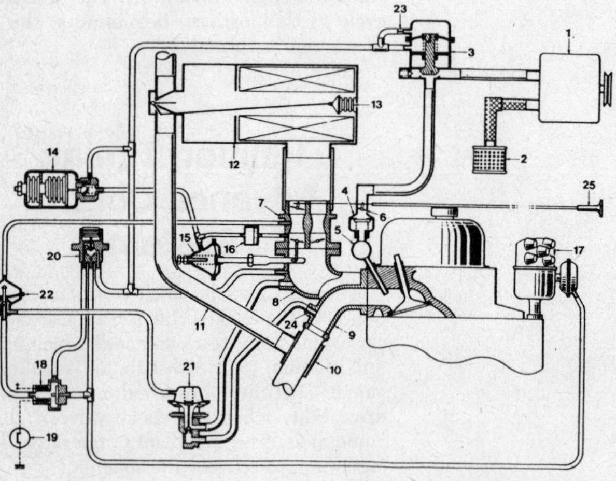

1. Air pump
2. Air pump filter
3. Relief and divertor valve assembly
4. Check valve
5. Air injection manifold
6. Air shut-off valve
7. Carburetor
8. Intake manifold
9. Exhaust manifold
10. Air filter pre-heated air take-off
11. Air filter pre-heated air intake duct
12. Air filter
13. Thermovalve activating sensor
14. Vacuum actuated valve
15. Throttle plate opener
16. Idle delay valve
17. Distributor
18. Solenoid valve
19. Transmission switch (contacts closed in 4th gear)
20. Thermovalve
21. EGR valve
22. Vacuum amplifier
23. Calibrated orifice
24. Calibrated orifice
25. Choke knob

Emission control diagram—1976 and 1977 Federal Le Car

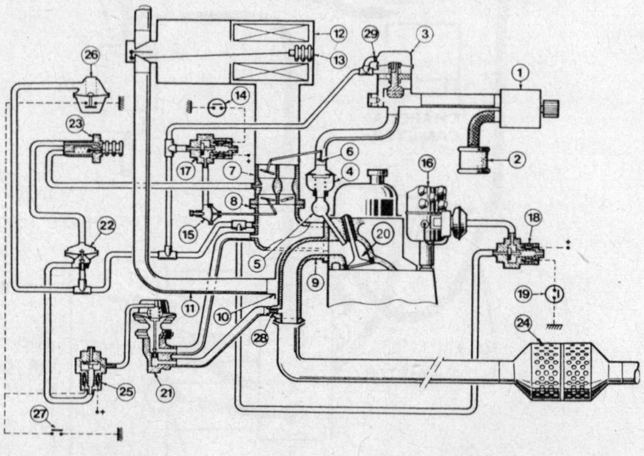

1. Air pump
2. Air pump filter
3. Relief and divertor valve assembly
4. Check valve
5. Air injection manifold
6. Air shut-off valve
7. Carburetor
8. Intake manifold
9. Exhaust manifold
10. Air filter pre-heated air take-off
11. Air filter pre-heated air intake duct
12. Air filter
13. Thermovalve activating sensor
14. Electronic governor
15. Throttle plate opener
16. Distributor
17. Solenoid valve
18. Solenoid valve for vacuum advance capsule
19. Choke plate switch
20. Exhaust valve
21. EGR valve
22. Vacuum amplifier
23. Coolant temperature switch (opens channel at 130° F./45° C.)
24. Catalytic convertor
25. EGR solenoid
26. Vacuum controlled switch (closes as vacuum exceeds 10″ or 254 mm hg.)
27. Transmission switch (contacts closed in 4th gear)
28. Calibrated orifice
29. Calibrated orifice

Emission control diagram—1976 California Le Car

Catalytic Converter

The catalytic converter chemically alters the exhaust gases before the gases reach the atmosphere. A "two-way" catalyst uses either pellets or screens coated with platinum and palladium. The chemical content of the precious metals oxidizes (neutralizes) controlled amounts of carbon monoxide and hydrocarbons. A "three-way" catalyst uses platinum, palladium, and rhodium, which acts on oxides of nitrogen emissions. Some "three-way" convertors also are ported to accept fresh air (from an injection pump) which further reduces oxides of nitrogen emissions.

E.G.R. (Exhaust Gas Recirculation) System

The E.G.R. valve admits varying amounts of exhaust gases into the combustion chambers, thereby diluting the incoming air/fuel mixture to reduce oxides of nitrogen. The introduction of "pre-burned" gases into the combustion chambers also lowers combustion chamber temperature. If detonation is a problem, check the E.G.R. system for proper operation.

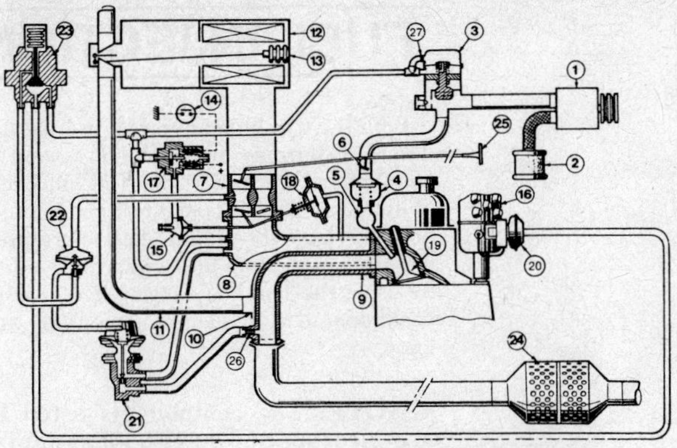

1. Air pump
2. Air pump filter
3. Relief and divertor valve assembly
4. Check valve
5. Air injection manifold
6. Air shut-off valve
7. Carburetor
8. Intake manifold
9. Exhaust manifold
10. Air filter pre-heated air take-off
11. Air filter pre-heated air intake duct
12. Air filter
13. Thermovalve activating sensor
14. Electronic governor
15. Throttle plate opener
16. Distributor
17. Fast idle solenoid valve
18. Vacuum operated throttle plate plunger
19. Exhaust valve
20. Vacuum advance unit
21. EGR valve
22. Vacuum switch
23. Thermovalve
24. Catalytic convertor
25. Choke knob
26. Calibrated orifice
27. Calibrated orifice

Emission control diagram—1977 California Le Car

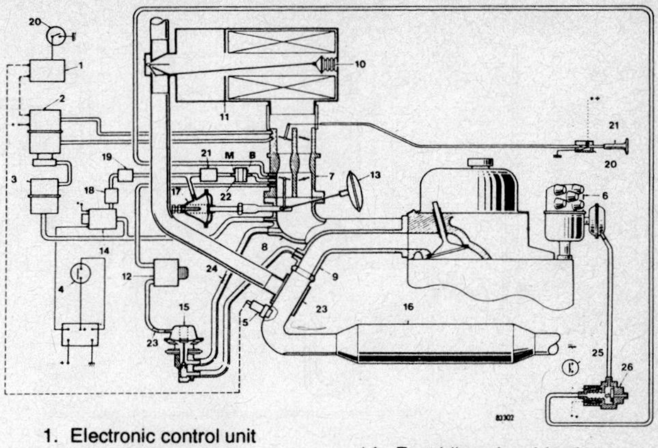

1. Electronic control unit
2. Vacuum solenoid regulator
3. Vacuum tank (fuel control system)
4. Magnetic pick-up
5. Oxygen sensor
6. Distributor
7. Carburetor
8. Intake manifold
9. Exhaust manifold
10. Thermovalve activating sensor
11. Thermostatic air cleaner
12. Coolant temperature switch
13. Dashpot
14. Fast idle solenoid valve
15. EGR valve
16. Catalytic converter
17. Throttle plate opener
18. Vacuum regulator
19. Check valve
20. Choke control switch
21. Vacuum reservoir (fast idle system)
22. Delay valve
23. Calibrated orifice
24. Calibrated orifice
25. Oil thermoswitch
26. Vacuum advance solenoid valve
27. White side of delay valve

Emission control diagram—1980 California Le Car

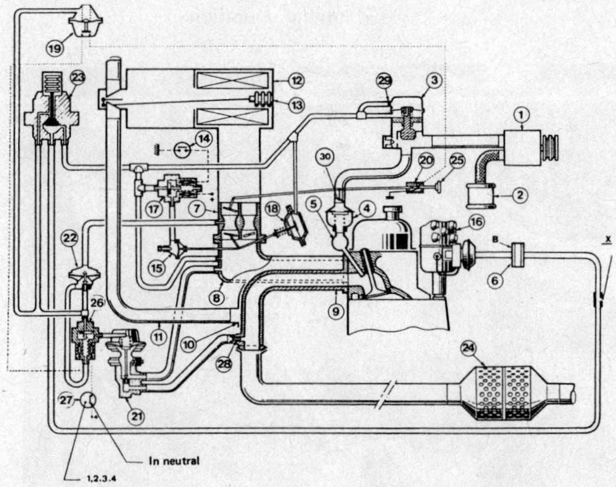

1. Air pump
2. Air pump filter
3. Relief and divertor valve assembly
4. Check valve
5. Air injection manifold
6. Delay valve
7. Carburetor
8. Intake manifold
9. Exhaust manifold
10. Air filter pre-heated air take-off
11. Air filter pre-heated air intake duct
12. Thermostatic air cleaner
13. Thermovalve activating sensor
14. Electronic tachometer switch
15. Throttle plate opener
16. Distributor
17. Throttle plate opening solenoid
18. Throttle plate plunger
19. Electro-vacuum switch
20. Choke control switch
21. EGR valve
22. Vacuum amplifier
23. Thermovalve
24. Catalytic converter
25. Choke knob
26. Solenoid valve
27. Transmission switch
28. Calibrated orifice
29. Calibrated orifice
30. Air shut-off valve

B. Blue side of delay valve
X. Calibrated orifice

Emission control diagram—1979 California Le Car

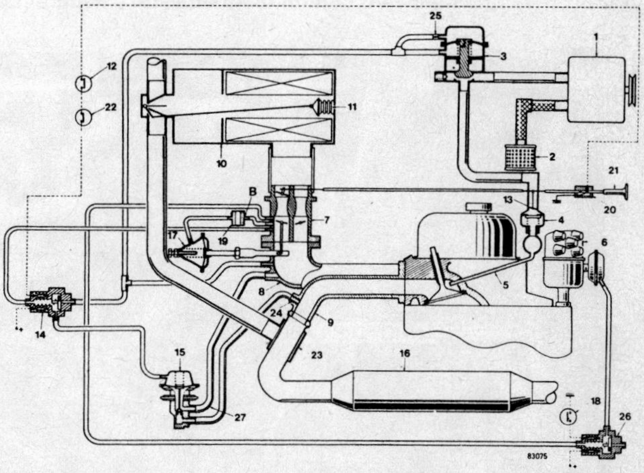

1. Air pump
2. Air pump filter
3. Relief and divertor valve assembly
4. Check valve
5. Air injection manifold
6. Distributor
7. Carburetor
8. Intake manifold
9. Exhaust manifold
10. Thermostatic air cleaner
11. Thermovalve activating sensor
12. Coolant temperature switch
13. Air shut-off valve
14. EGR solenoid valve
15. EGR valve
16. Catalytic converter
17. Throttle plate opener
18. Oil thermoswitch
19. Delay valve
20. Choke control switch
21. Choke control cable
22. Transmission switch
23. Air intake system pre-heated air stove
24. Calibrated orifice
25. Calibrated orifice
26. Solenoid valve (vacuum advance)
27. Calibrated orifice

B. White side of vacuum delay valve

Emission control diagram—1980 Federal Le Car

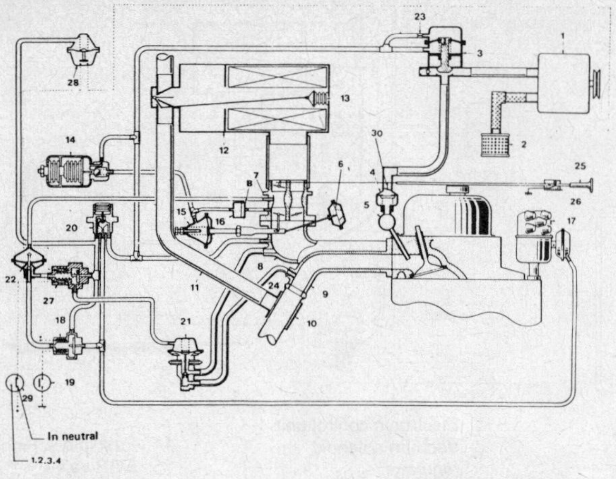

1. Air pump
2. Air pump filter
3. Relief and divertor valve assembly
4. Check valve
5. Air injection manifold
6. Dashpot
7. Carburetor
8. Intake manifold
9. Exhaust manifold
10. Air filter pre-heated air take-off
11. Air filter pre-heated air intake duct
12. Thermostatic air cleaner
13. Thermovalve activating sensor
14. Deceleration valve
15. Throttle plate opener
16. Idle delay valve
17. Distributor
18. Solenoid valve
19. 4th gear switch
20. Thermovalve
21. EGR valve
22. Vacuum amplifier
23. Calibrated orifice
24. Calibrated orifice
25. Choke knob
26. Choke control switch
27. Solenoid valve
28. Electro-vacuum switch
29. Transmission switch
30. Air shut-off valve

B. White side of delay valve

Emission control diagram—1979 Federal Le Car

FUEL INJECTION

Both the Gordini and the 18i use the Bosch design "L-Jetronic" fuel injection system. The two systems are nearly identical but because of emission standards at the time of production, the later 18i system offers more precise metering of the fuel under varying conditions by using the Lambda oxygen sensor system. Basic operation of the components is as follows:

NOTE: The components listed here are incorporated in the 18i system and are numbered accordingly.

1. *Control Unit*—Receives data from the engine sensors and varies the injection valve opening time accordingly.
2. *Injection Valve*—Atomizes and injects fuel in front of the intake valve according to the input from the control unit.
3. *Air Flow Meter*—Measures the amount and the velocity of the incoming (intake) air and sends data to the control unit to compensate accordingly.
4. *Temperature Sensor II*—Sends engine temperature information to the control unit.
5. *Thermo-Time Switch*—The thermo-time switch controls the operation of the cold start valve through sensing of the engine temperature.
6. *Cold Start Valve*—Injects extra fuel to the intake tract to richen the mixture during cold engine operation.

18i—fuel injection

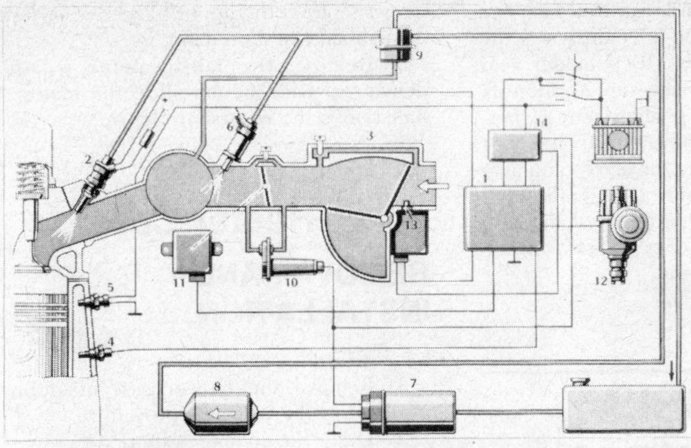

1. Control unit
2. Injection valve
3. Air flow meter
4. Temperature sensor II
5. Thermo-time switch
6. Cold start valve
7. Fuel pump
8. Fuel filter
9. Pressure regulator
10. Auxiliary air valve
11. Throttle switch
12. Ignition distributor
13. Temperature sensor I
14. Relay set

L-Jetronic fuel injection system—18i

Air flow meter—18i fuel injection

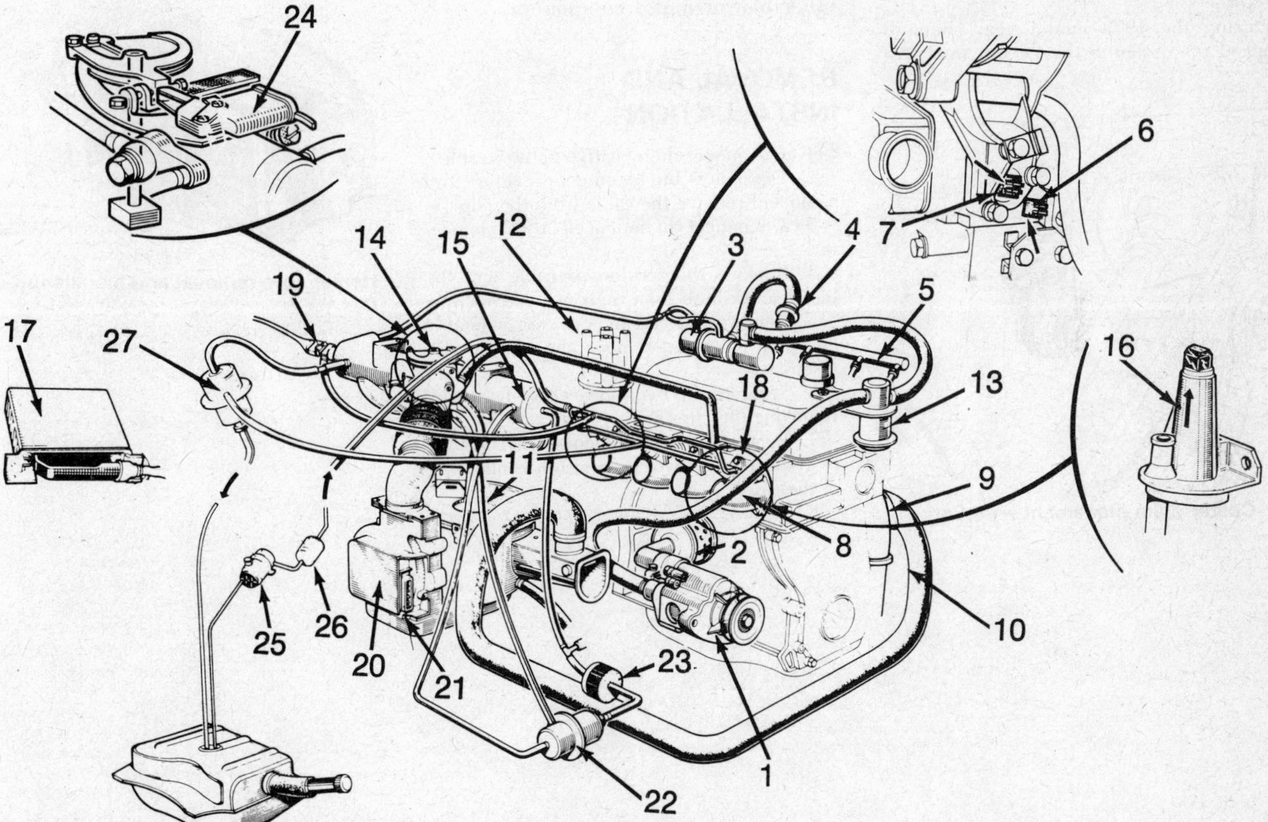

1. Air pump
2. Air pump filter
3. Divertor valve
4. Check valve
5. Air injection manifold
6. Coolant temperature sensor
7. Cold start coolant temperature time switch
8. Intake manifold
9. Pre-heated air intake stove
10. Pre-heated air intake duct
11. Thermostatic air cleaner
12. Ignition distributor
13. Relief valve
14. Throttle
15. Air manifold
16. Auxiliary air control valve
17. Computer unit
18. Fuel injector (injection valve)
19. Cold start fuel injector
20. Air flow meter
21. Air flow meter pick-up
22. Deceleration valve
23. Deceleration circuit delay valve
24. Throttle plate switch
25. Fuel pump
26. Fuel filter
27. Fuel pressure regulator

L-Jetronic fuel injection system—Gordini

7. *Fuel Pump*—Pressurizes fuel from the tank and supplies this fuel to the engine.
8. *Fuel Filter*—Self explanatory.
9. *Pressure Regulator*—Self explanatory.
10. *Auxiliary Air Valve*—Supplies extra air to the engine during warm-up.
11. *Throttle Valve Switch*—Sends throttle position information to the control unit.
12. *Ignition Distributor*—Sends engine speed and timing information to the control unit.
13. *Temperature Sensor I*—Sends air intake temperature information to the control unit.
14. *Relay Set*—Controls the power at the fuel pump and the control unit.

The injection system requires special tools and training for any adjustment or repair other than idle speed.

FRONT SUSPENSION

Le Car

During the 1979 model year, Renault changed the design of the Le Car front suspension. The early design is referred to as the 12° caster suspension, the later design is the 6° caster suspension. The 1979 model year includes both designs; make sure to identify the suspension before an alignment is performed. Suspension components are *not interchangeable* between the early and late designs, unless the front axle (complete), steering box and steering arms are changed to the desired design. Service parts are available for both suspension designs.

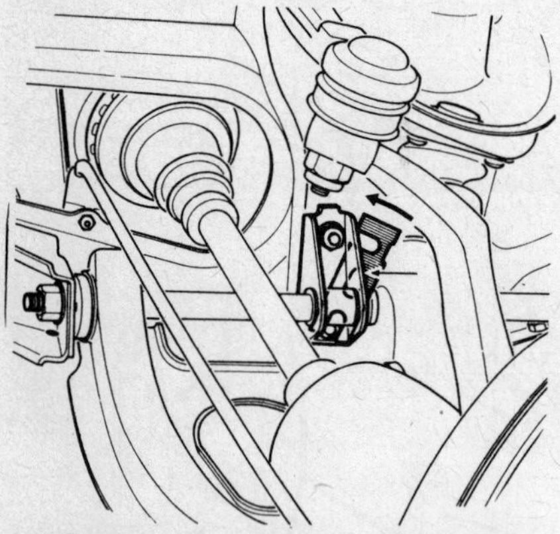

Caster shim placement—Le Car

CHASSIS ELECTRICAL

Heater Blower—Le Car

NOTE: The motor brushes are the only blower motor components that are serviceable. The blower motor assembly must be replaced if a fault exists in any other blower motor component.

REMOVAL AND INSTALLATION

1. Disconnect the negative battery cable.
2. Disconnect the blend door lever control cable and remove the cable from the clip.
3. Disconnect the motor electrical connector.
4. Remove the accelerator cable and the bleed screw hose from their respective clips.
5. Remove the two blower case assembly fastening bolts and remove the blower case assembly.
6. Separate the two blower case halves by removing the clips.
7. Remove the blend door support panel by removing the two clips on the air inlet side of the case.
8. Remove the blower motor retaining screws (3) from the upper blower case. Retain the rubber vibration dampers.
9. Remove the fan-to-motor retaining sleeve and take the fan off of the motor. Installation is the reverse of the removal procedure.

Heater Core

REMOVAL AND INSTALLATION

Le Car

1. Remove the blower case assembly as outlined in the previous procedure.
2. Drain the cooling system.
3. Remove the bottom heater hose, the heater control valve, and the bleed screw hose.
4. Remove the heater core mounting bolts and withdraw the heater core. Installation is the reverse of the removal procedure.

Heater core removal and installation—Le Car

SPECIFICATIONS

INDEX

BEFORE SERVICING, SEE THE SAFETY NOTICE ON THE CONTENTS PAGE

INTRODUCTION

The SAAB 99, a new and entirely different design from earlier SAAB models, was made available to the public after extensive development. A newly designed, aerodynamic sedan body, and an in-line, overhead cam four cylinder engine, designed by Ricardo Engineering in England are used. In 1978, a turbocharged version of this engine was added as an option in the 99 series. 1979 and later 99 and 900 models offer the turbocharger as an option.

In 1979, the 900 series was added to the SAAB vehicle line. This vehicle uses the same driveline as the SAAB 99 series. It is available with either automatic or manual transmission.

SERIAL NUMBER IDENTIFICATION

Vehicle

The vehicle serial number is located in two places on all SAAB models: the serial number is stamped on a plate at the lower left hand corner of the windshield, and the serial number is punched in the car body under the left side of the rear seat cushion.

Engine

On the 1985 cc engine the number is stamped on a plate which is secured to the upper portion of the engine directly forward of the fuel injection unit.

A B

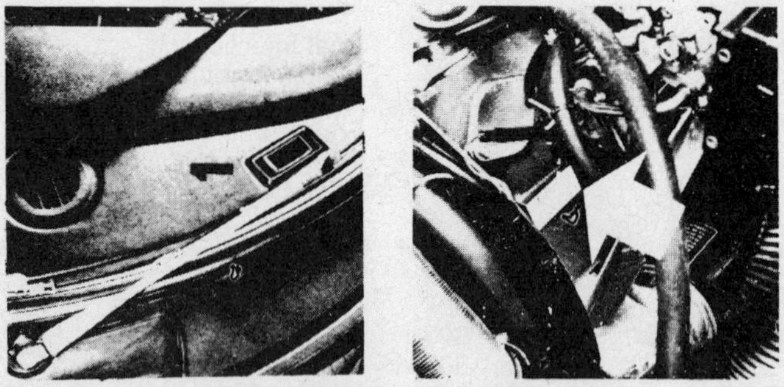

Vehicle identification number location—Saab 99 (A)
Engine identification number location—Saab 900 (B)

GENERAL ENGINE SPECIFICATIONS

Year	Engine Displacement cc (cu. in.) [liters]	Fuel Delivery Type	Horsepower @ rpm	Torque @ rpm	Bore X Stroke (in.)	Compression Ratio	Maximum Oil Pressure (psi)
1975-81	1985 (121.0) [2.0]	Bosch Fuel injection	②	③	3.543 x 3.071	①	Dual rotor type 57-71

① See Emission Control Equipment Chart under Emission Control
② 115 @ 5500—Federal
110 @ 5500—California
118 @ 5500—Canada
135 @ 5500—Turbo
③ 123 @ 3500—Federal and Canada
119 @ 3500—California

TUNE-UP SPECIFICATIONS

Year	Engine Displace-ment cc	SPARK PLUGS Type	SPARK PLUGS Gap	DISTRIBUTOR Point Dwell (deg)	DISTRIBUTOR Reluctor Gap (in.)	Basic Ignition Timing (deg)	Intake Valve Opens (deg)	Fuel Pump Pressure psi	Idle Speed rpm	VALVE CLEARANCE Intake	VALVE CLEARANCE Exhaust
1975-81	1985	NGK BP6ES ③	0.024-0.028	Electronic	0.016	②	10 BTDC ⑤	①	875	0.008-0.010	0.016-0.018 ④

NOTE: If these specifications differ from those on the engine compartment stickers, use the sticker specifications.

① Fuel injected engines (all models): Fuel line pressure before the control pressure regulator is 66.9-69.7 (setting valve), and 48.5-54.0 psi (warm engine) after the control pressure regulator (located in fuel distributor).
② 1975-76 Federal—14° BTDC @ 800 rpm
1975-76 California—12° BTDC @ 800 rpm
1975-81—20° @ 2000 rpm
1975-81 Canada, manual transmission—20° BTDC @ 2000 rpm
1975-81 Canada, automatic transmission—23° BTDC @ 2000 rpm
③ Turbo—NGK-BP7ES
④ Turbo—.018-.020
⑤ Turbo—12° BTDC

FIRING ORDER

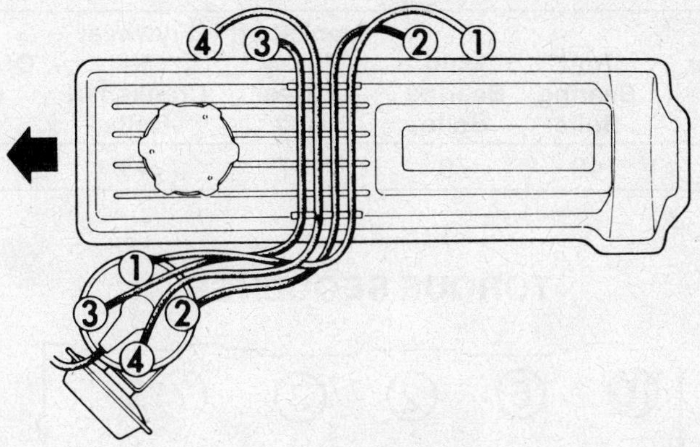

Firing order and ignition cable positioning—1985 cc engine

CAPACITIES

Year	Engine Displacement (cc)	Engine Crankcase (qts.) With Filter	Engine Crankcase (qts.) Without Filter	Transmission (pts.) Manual	Transmission (pts.) Automatic	Drive Axle (pts.)	Fuel Tank (gals.)	Cooling System (qts.) w/o AC
1975-81	1985	3.7	3.2	4.4 ①	17	1.3	14.5	8.5 ②

① 5.3—5 speed trans. & 4 speed w/o dipstick
② 10.5—900 series vehicles

VALVE SPECIFICATIONS

Year	Engine Displacement (cc)	Seat Angle (deg)	Valve Face Angle (deg)	Spring Test Pressure (lbs. @ in.)	Installed Spring Height (in.)	Stem to Guide Clearance (in.) Intake	Stem to Guide Clearance (in.) Exhaust	Stem Diameter (mm) Intake	Stem Diameter (mm) Exhaust
1975-81	1985	45	44.5	178-198 @ 1.16	1.56	0.020 ①	0.020 ①	7.960-7.975	7.955-7.980

① Maximum clearance measured with valve face pulled 3 mm (0.12 in.) from valve seat

CRANKSHAFT AND CONNECTING ROD SPECIFICATIONS

Year	Engine Displacement (cc)	Crankshaft Main Bearing Journal Diameter (mm)	Crankshaft Main Bearing Oil Clearance (in.)	Crankshaft Shaft End-Play (mm)	Crankshaft Thrust on No.	Connecting Rod Journal Diameter (mm)	Connecting Rod Oil Clearance (in.)
1975-81	1985	57.981-58.000	0.0008-0.0025	0.08-0.28	3	51.981-52.00	0.0010-0.0025

PISTON AND RING SPECIFICATIONS

Year	Engine Displacement (cc)	Piston Diameter (mm)	Ring Gap (mm) Top Compression	Ring Gap (mm) Bottom Compression	Ring Gap (mm) Oil Control	Ring Side Clearance (in groove) (mm) Top Compression	Ring Side Clearance (in groove) (mm) Bottom Compression
1975-81	1985	89.980-89.986	0.35-0.55	0.30-0.45	0.38-1.4	0.050-0.082	0.040-0.072

TORQUE SPECIFICATIONS
(ft. lbs.)

Year	Engine Displacement (cc)	Cylinder Head Bolts	Rod Bearing Bolts	Main Bearing Bolts	Crankshaft Pulley or Gear Bolt	Flywheel to Crankshaft Bolts	Camshaft Gear Bolt	Intake Manifold	Exhaust Manifold
1975-81	1985	69	40	79	137	43	14	13	18 ①

① 1976 and later—14

TORQUE SEQUENCE

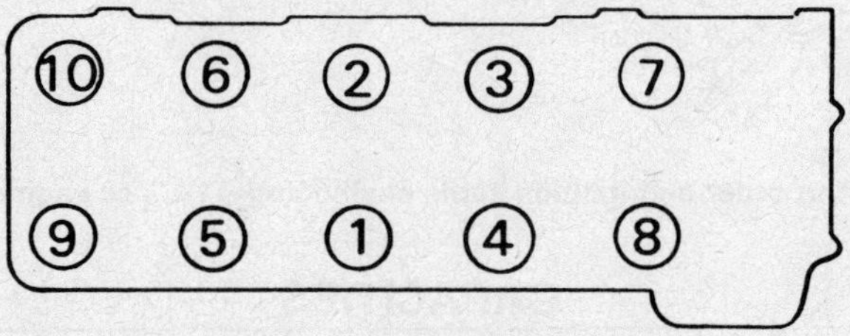

Cylinder head bolt torque sequence—1985 cc engine

ALTERNATOR AND REGULATOR SPECIFICATIONS

Year	Engine Displacement (cc)	Model	Rated Voltage (volts @ rpm)	ALTERNATOR Maximum Continuous Load (amps. @ rpm)	ALTERNATOR Minimum Brush Length (in.)	ALTERNATOR Brush Spring Pressure (oz.)	Regulating Voltage
1975-80	1985	99	14 @ 2000	55 @ 5000	0.34	10.5-14	13.5-14.2
1975-81	1985	900	14 @ 2000	55 @ 5000	—	—	—
1975-81	1985	900	14 @ 2100	65 @ 5000	—	—	—
1975-81	1985	900	14 @ —	70 @ 5000	—	—	—

BATTERY AND STARTER SPECIFICATIONS

Year	Engine Displacement (cc)	BATTERY Ampere Hour Capacity	BATTERY Volts	BATTERY Terminal Ground	STARTER LOAD TEST Amps.	STARTER LOAD TEST Volts	STARTER LOAD TEST @ rpm	STARTER NO LOAD TEST Amps.	STARTER NO LOAD TEST Volts	STARTER NO LOAD TEST @ rpm	Brush Spring Tension (oz.)
1975-81	1985	60	12	Neg.	205-235	9	1000-1300	35-55	11.5	6500-8500	41-46

BRAKE SPECIFICATIONS

Year	Wheel Lug Nut Torque (ft. lbs.)	Master Cylinder Bore	BRAKE DISC Minimum Thickness	BRAKE DISC Maximum Axial Run-Out
1975-81	65-80	7/8	0.461 Front 0.374 Rear	0.004

WHEEL ALIGNMENT

Year	Caster	Camber	Toe-In (in.) ①	King Pin Angle	Wheel Angle During Turns (deg) Inner Wheel	Outer Wheel
1975-81	1° ± ½° ②	½° ± ½°	.08 ± .04″	11½° ± 1°	20¾° ± ½° ③	20°

① Measured at the rims
② 2° ± ½°—vehicles equipped with power steering
③ 20½° ± 1°—SAAB 99 series

TUNE UP

All vehicles that are sold in the United States are equipped with a breakerless ignition system with an electromagnetic pulse generator in the distributor and an electronic control unit which performs the task of the conventional point system.

Ignition Timing

Ignition timing is set in the conventional manner, using the marks that are located on the flywheel.

However, the engine is also equipped for checking the timing using an ignition service instrument.

The equipment in the vehicle comprises a pin in the engine flywheel and a service socket in the clutch cover. The ignition service instrument is connected to the clutch cover by means of a special connector and to the plug lead No. 1 cylinder by means of a terminal. The ignition service instrument is also connected to the ignition service socket at the fuse box and by means of an impulse transmitter at the plug lead for No. 1 cylinder.

NOTE: The SAAB ignition service instrument consists of a tachometer, cam angle meter, stroboscope lamp and switch for operating the starter.

Valve Lash

1. Remove the valve cover.
2. Using an appropriate special tool (Saab #8392185 or its equivalent), rotate the crankshaft as necessary to position the high point of the camshaft lobe 180° away from the valve depressor face (base circle of the cam lobe must contact the valve depressor) on the valve which the clearance is to be checked.

NOTE: The special crankshaft turning wrench fits the center screw of the crankshaft belt pulley at the dash panel.

3. Try the maximum and minimum clearances with a feeler gauge. The minimum feeler should slip in, but the maximum feeler should not.
4. Measure and record the clearance of all the valves in the same manner. Adjust the clearance of any valves that do not lie within the following limits.

Intake valves: 0.008-0.010 inch
Exhaust valves (except turbo.): 0.016-0.018 inch
Exhaust valves (turbo.): 0.018-0.020 inch

5. To adjust the valves, remove the camshaft, tappets and adjusting pallets (shims) of any valves that need to be adjusted.

NOTE: See the proper procedure for camshaft removal and installation which is located in this section of this manual.

6. Using a micrometer, measure and record the thickness of the pallet (shim). This thickness plus the valve clearance adds up to the total distance between the valve and the cam.
7. The choice of the adjusting pallet (shim) is determined by the measured total distance between the valve depressor (tappet) and the cam, less the specified valve clearance for an intake or exhaust valve as the case may be.
8. Insert the new adjusting pallet (shim) and the valve depressor (tappet) and reinstall the camshaft.
9. Repeat the measurement procedure to insure that the clearances are correct.
10. Install the valve cover using a new valve cover gasket.

Fuel Injection

IDLE SPEED AND MIXTURE

1. Run the engine until it reaches operating temperature.
2. Adjust the idle speed to 875 ± 50 rpms.
3. If the vehicle is not equipped with a catalytic converter, remove the pulse-air hose and plug the air intake to the non-return valves. On 1979 vehicles sold in the United States and Canada, remove the large bore hose from the charcoal canister. Connect the CO meter sensor to the exhaust pipe.
4. On 1979 vehicles equipped with a catalytic converter, remove the large bore hose at the charcoal canister. Connect the CO

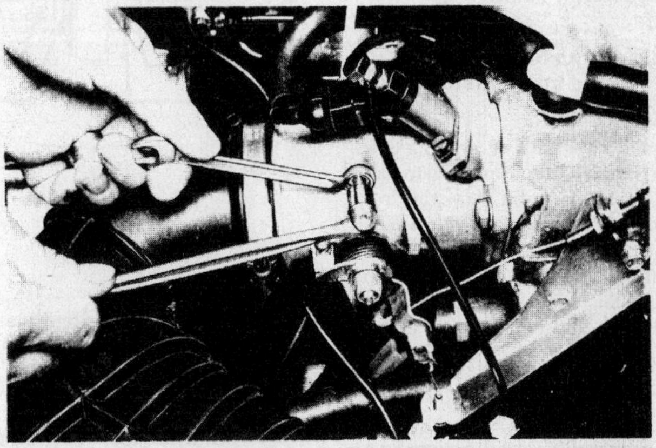

Adjusting the idle speed

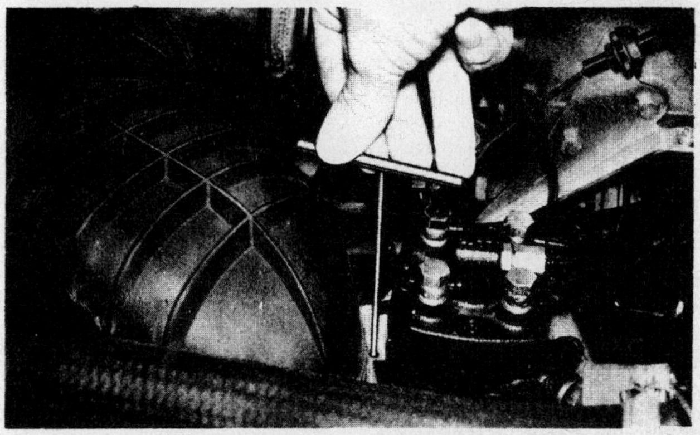

Adjusting the CO value

CO METER SETTING

1978 vehicles without catalytic converters	1.25±.75%
1979 vehicles without catalytic converters	.75±.25%
1979 vehicles with catalytic converters	.75+.25% −.5% ①
1980 and later vehicles with catalytic converters	1.0±.25% ②
Vehicles sold in Canada except Turbo.	1.5±.5%

① Sensor disconnected after catalytic converter
② Sensor disconnected before catalytic converter

meter sensor to the exhaust pipe. Remove the oxygen sensor wire.

5. On 1980 and later vehicles equipped with a catalytic converter, remove and plug the front exhaust pipe and connect the CO meter sensor to the pipe with the aid of a connecting piece. Remove the oxygen sensor wire.

6. Read and adjust the idle speed and CO value as required. Before each reading, increase the engine speed and allow it to return to idle. Wait 30 seconds before taking the next CO reading.

7. Adjust the idle speed by turning the idle adjusting screw on the throttle valve housing.

8. Adjust the CO by turning the adjusting screw located on the fuel distributor (clockwise = richer mixture; counterclockwise = leaner mixture).

NOTE: These adjustments effect each other, therefore the adjustments should be carried out in steps.

9. On 1980 and later catalyst equipped vehicles: Connect the oxygen sensor wire and remove the CO meter probe from the front exhaust pipe connection. Install the plug in the front exhaust pipe. Insert the probe at the rear of the tailpipe. The CO meter reading should be less than .4% with the engine at idle, and the engine and converter at normal operating temperature.

ENGINE ELECTRICAL

Distributor

REMOVAL AND INSTALLATION

1. Release the distributor cap hold-down clips, and lift the cap off of the distributor and out of the way. On some models, it may be necessary to remove the cap from the vehicle completely due to space limitations.

2. Disconnect the low voltage wire from the ignition coil. Pull off the vacuum hose.

3. Crank the engine until the flywheel marking is at the ignition position on No. 1 cylinder.

4. Remove the distributor retaining screw and remove the distributor from the engine.

5. Installation is the reverse of removal.

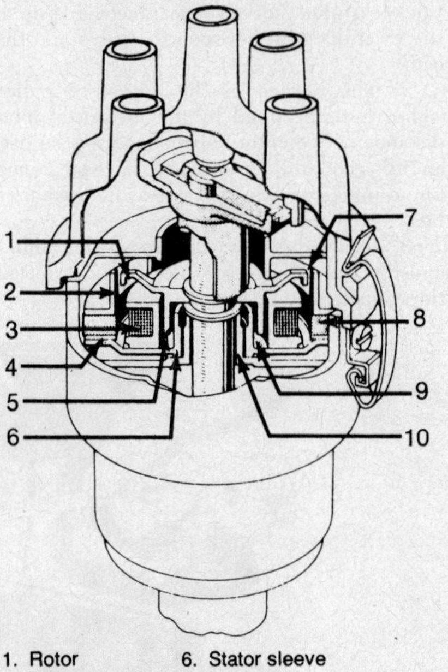

1. Rotor
2. Stator
3. Induction coil
4. Stator plate
5. Rotor sleeve
6. Stator sleeve
7. Outer gap
8. Magnet
9. Inner gap
10. Retaining plate and sleeve

Distributor—exploded view

Alternator

REMOVAL AND INSTALLATION

1. Disconnect the negative battery cable.
2. Remove the alternator wiring connections, retaining screw and the adjusting screw.
3. Remove the alternator belt.
4. Remove the alternator from the vehicle.
5. Installation is the reverse of removal.

BELT TENSION ADJUSTMENT

Adjust the alternator belt tension so that the belt can be depressed about ½ inch at the mid-point of its longest straight run.

Regulator

REMOVAL AND INSTALLATION

NOTE: On 900 series, the voltage regulator is incorporated into the back of the alternator.

1. Disconnect the negative battery cable.
2. Remove the voltage regulator connecting wires.
3. Remove the hold-down screws and remove the unit from the vehicle.
4. Installation is the reverse of removal.

Starter

REMOVAL AND INSTALLATION

All Except Turbo

1. Disconnect the battery. On the 99 series, disconnect the pre-heater hose.
2. Remove the flywheel cover. Remove the gearbox dipstick if the vehicle is equipped with manual transmission.
3. Remove the starter motor heat shield and the rear mounting bolts.
4. Disconnect the starter motor wires. Remove the front mounting bolts.
5. Carefully remove the starter from the vehicle.
6. Installation is the reverse of removal.

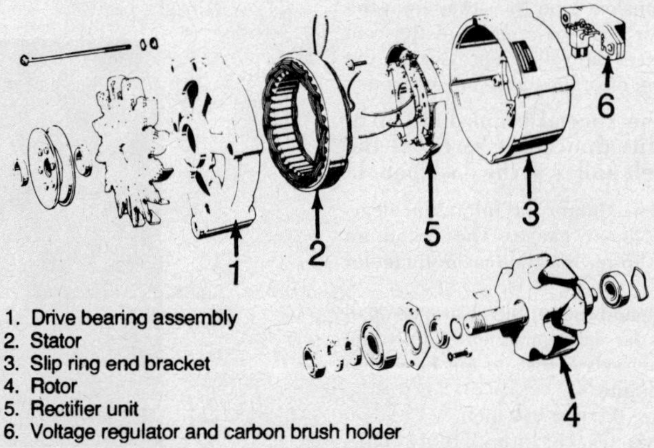

1. Drive bearing assembly
2. Stator
3. Slip ring end bracket
4. Rotor
5. Rectifier unit
6. Voltage regulator and carbon brush holder

Alternator—exploded view (900 series)

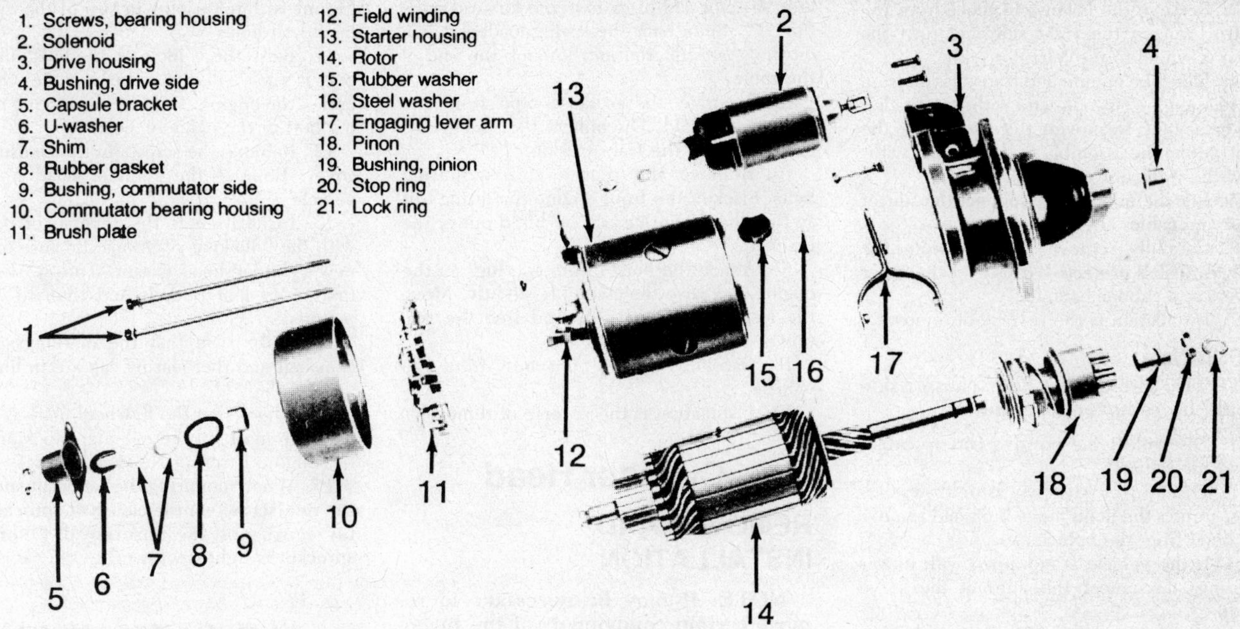

Starter—exploded view

Turbo

1. Disconnect the battery. On the 99 series, remove the battery and the battery tray.
2. Remove the turbocharger suction pipe, pre-heater hose and the flywheel cover.
3. On the 900 series, remove the gearbox dipstick (manual transmission only). Remove the bracket and bolts between the turbocharger and the gearbox.
4. Disconnect the starter motor wires. On the 99 series, remove the front starter mounting bolts.
5. Loosen the oil return pipe on the turbocharger enough to allow it to be bent outwards somewhat. On the 99 series, remove the oil return pipe.
6. Remove the starter motor heat shield and the rear mounting bolts.
7. On the 900 series, remove the front starter mounting bolts.
8. Carefully remove the starter from the vehicle.
9. To install, reverse the removal procedure. Be careful to fit a new gasket on the oil return pipe connecting flange on the turbocharger.

ENGINE MECHANICAL

Engine

REMOVAL AND INSTALLATION

99 Series

NOTE: The engine and transmission should be removed from the vehicle as a unit.

1. Remove the hood.
2. Disconnect the battery cables. Remove the battery.
3. Remove the servo cylinder vacuum hose from the inlet manifold and remove the rubber bellows from between the air flow sensor and the inlet manifold.
4. Remove the connections on the fuel distributor and detach the lines. Disconnect the electrical connection on the air flow sensor.
5. On vehicles sold in California, detach the EGR system vacuum hoses from the venturi tap at the air cleaner and from the EGR valve at the throttle valve housing. Remove the clamps at the rubber bellows.
6. Remove the air cleaner and the mixture control unit.
7. Remove the cable connections from the ignition coil, temperature transmitter, radiator fan, thermostat contact, headlights and the switch on the transmission (automatic transmission only).
8. Disconnect the cables from the injection system at the warm-up regulator, auxiliary air valve, cold start valve and the thermo-time switch.
9. Detach the throttle control cable from the bracket on the throttle valve housing.
10. Detach the hoses at the connections to the thermostat housing, radiator, inlet manifold and water pump.
11. Remove the grille. Remove the hood lock operating cable from its position at the dash panel and wheel housing. Remove the two front sheet metal screws and nuts, and the four sheet metal screws holding the headlights to the body. Remove the complete front assembly by lifting forward and upward.
12. If the vehicle is equipped with manual transmission, on 1975 cars, remove the slave cylinder and hang it up in a convenient place. On 1976 and later vehicles, disconnect the clutch hose from the slave cylinder. Plug the hose and the hole in the slave cylinder.
13. If the vehicle is equipped with automatic transmission, remove the protective cover from the exhaust manifold.
14. Disconnect the exhaust pipe at the exhaust manifold.
15. Disconnect the ground cable from the transmission. On some vehicles it may be necessary to remove the alternator, depending on the type of engine lifting crane that is being used for the removal procedure.
16. On California vehicles, remove the air pump.
17. Raise the vehicle on a hoist and support it safely.
18. If the vehicle is equipped with manual transmission, put the gear lever in Neutral. Tap out the front taper pin from the gear shift rod joint and pull the rubber bellows free of the groove in the gear selector rod. Separate the gear selector rod from the gear selector joint.

NOTE: The rubber bellows has been discontinued (1977) and need not be installed in older vehicles when repair is being made.

19. If the vehicle is equipped with automatic transmission, remove the gear selector cable retaining screw from the transmission and position the gear selector lever in "P".

NOTE: On early models, detach the spring which holds the cable to the gear selector by inserting a pliers in the end of the spring. Rotate it slightly and then pull out the cable. On later models, push back the spring-loaded sleeve on the gear selector lever and release the end of the cable.

20. Remove the speedometer cable from the transmission. Remove the engine brackets.
21. Remove the large clips from around the rubber bellows on the inner universal joints.
22. Install the engine lifting hoist to the two engine lifting lugs.

23. Remove the lower end piece from the control arm on the right side and turn the steering wheel to the left.

24. Raise the engine and transmission from the rear engine cushions and withdraw the left universal joint, by moving the assembly to the right. Move the assembly to the left and withdraw the right universal joint.

25. Lift the unit and disconnect the starter wires and cables.

26. Carefully remove the unit from the vehicle. Install protective caps over the inner drivers and rubber bellows.

27. Installation is the reverse of removal.

900 Series

NOTE: The engine and transmission should be removed as a unit.

1. Disconnect the positive battery cable. Drain the radiator.

2. Disconnect the windshield washer hose, unbolt the hood hinge links and remove the hood from the vehicle.

3. If the vehicle is equipped with power steering, disconnect the lines at the servo pump.

4. Disconnect the positive battery lead at the starter. Remove the radiator hoses. Remove the engine ground wire. Disconnect the temperature transmitter cable. Remove the coil.

5. Disconnect the cable harness from the clutch cover. If the vehicle is equipped with manual transmission, disconnect the hydraulic line from the clutch slave cylinder and plug the lines.

6. Disconnect the CI system electrical connections from the warm-up regulator, thero-time switch cold start valve and the auxiliary air valve. On catalytic converter equipped vehicles, also disconnect the oxygen sensor and the throttle switch cables.

7. Disconnect the oil pressure transmitter cable. Loosen the fuel line connections at the fuel distributor. Remove the air filter along with the mixture control unit.

8. Disconnect the throttle cable. Disconnect the hose at the expansion tank. Disconnect the heater hoses at the heater. Disconnect the brake vacuum hose.

9. Remove the clips and remove the bellows from the inner drivers.

10. Place the spacer (Saab tool No. 83-93-209) or equivalent between the upper control arm underside and the car body.

NOTE: Insert the tool from the engine compartment side. The spacer makes the front suspension unloaded when the vehicle is raised.

11. Lift the front end of the vehicle and support it safely.

12. Remove the lower end piece from the control arm. Pull out the steering knuckle assembly and support the end piece against the control arm outer end.

13. If the vehicle is equipped with manual transmission put the gear lever in Neutral. Remove the nut and tap out the taper pin in the gear shift rod joint. Separate the joint from the gear shift rod.

14. If the vehicle is equipped with automatic transmission, remove the retaining screw from the gear selector cable at the transmission. Withdraw the cable with the gear selector rod in its extreme forward position "P". Slide back the spring-loaded sleeve on the gear shift rod and unhook the end of the cable.

15. Separate the exhaust pipe from the exhaust manifold. Disconnect the speedometer cable from the transmission.

16. Remove the rear engine mounting bolts. Slacken the front engine mounting nut so that the mounting can be lifted out of the bracket.

17. Attach the hoist to the two lugs on the engine and raise the assembly slightly. Move the assembly to one side and free the two universal joints.

18. Carefully remove the unit from the vehicle.

19. Installation is the reverse of removal.

Cylinder Head

REMOVAL AND INSTALLATION

NOTE: It may be necessary to remove certain components of the turbocharging system on vehicles so equipped. Turbocharger removal and installaton procedures are outlined following the Engine Repair Section.

1. Disconnect the battery cables. Drain the radiator.

2. Remove the rubber bellows from between the air flow sensor and the throttle valve housing and disconnect the throttle cable from the throttle valve housing.

3. Disconnect the cable from the temperature transmitter. Remove the vacuum hose of the power brake booster from the intake manifold.

4. Disconnect the fuel lines from the fuel distributor to the injection valves. Tape the ends of the lines to prevent dirt from entering the system. Remove the bracket from the throttle valve housing mounting.

5. Remove the hose clamps at the connections to the thermostat housing, water pump and intake manifold.

6. Unbolt the exhaust pipe from the exhaust manifold.

7. Remove the distributor cap and the ignition wires. Remove the valve cover.

8. Remove the camshaft sprocket as follows: On 1975 vehicles, screw an M8 nut on to the threaded center stud of the camshaft sprocket and clamp the center stud against the mounting plate provided for this purpose. On 1976 and later vehicles, bolt the mounting plate to the center of the camshaft sprocket, using one of the camshaft sprocket retaining screws.

NOTE: Tighten the nut (screw) securely to immobilize the center stud. Otherwise the chain tensioner will tighten the chain and lock in a new position so that the sprocket cannot be refitted. The chain tensioner cannot be reset without lifting the engine out of the car.

9. Remove the retaining screws from the camshaft sprocket. Separate the wheel from the camshaft plate until it hangs free in the mounting plate by the center stud.

10. Remove the cylinder head bolts. Mount two guide pins in two of the cylinder head bolt holes.

11. Raise the vehicle on the hoist and support it safely. Place a support under the rear end of the engine. Remove the engine mounting bolt in the cylinder head.

12. Remove the screws in the transmission cover. Remove the cylinder head from the vehicle.

13. Installation is the reverse of removal with the following additions: Be sure to use a new cylinder head gasket. Torque the bolts first to 44 foot pounds and then to 70 foot pounds.

14. Make sure that the markings on the camshaft and the bearing cap are in line with one another.

15. Check that the flywheel mark is in line with the mark on the cylinder block and that the engine is set on No. 1 cylinder.

16. When mounting the camshaft sprocket, the nut (screw) on the camshaft sprocket center must not be unscrewed before the sprocket is tightly screwed to the camshaft.

Intake Manifold

REMOVAL AND INSTALLATION

NOTE: It may be necessary to remove certain components of the turbocharging system on vehicles so equipped. Turbocharger removal and installation procedures are outlined following the Engine Repair Section.

1. Disconnect all hoses, wires and connectors that would inhibit the intake manifold from being removed.

NOTE: It may be necessary to remove the distributor cap and the ignition wires to gain clearance.

2. Remove the throttle valve housing.

3. Remove the manifold bolts and remove the manifold from the vehicle together with the engine lifting lug.

4. Installation is the reverse of removal.

Exhaust Manifold

REMOVAL AND INSTALLATION

NOTE: It may be necessary to remove certain components of the turbocharging system on vehicles so equipped. Turbocharger removal and installation procedures are outlined following the Engine Repair Section.

1. Disconnect all necessary hoses, wires and connectors that would inhibit the exhaust manifold from being removed.

2. Unbolt the exhaust pipe at the connecting flange.

3. If the vehicle is equipped with a heat shield, remove it.

4. Remove the manifold bolts and remove the exhaust manifold from the vehicle.

5. Installation is the reverse of removal.

Timing Chain

REMOVAL AND INSTALLATION

NOTE: In order to accomplish the following procedure the engine will have to be removed from the vehicle.

1. Remove the engine from the vehicle.
2. Remove the cylinder head. See the proper procedure in this section of the repair manual.
3. Remove the belt pulley bolt and the pulley, using the necessary puller.
4. Remove the timing chain cover. Remove the timing chain tensioner.
5. Remove the chain guides and the mounting plate with the camshaft sprocket and the timing chain.
6. Remove the crankshaft sprocket using a suitable gear puller, if necessary.
7. Remove the idler shaft sprocket, if it is going to be replaced.
8. Installation is the reverse of removal. Note the following.
9. If it was removed, install the idler shaft. The marking (the bulge in the hold on the idler shaft chainwheel) should line up with the small hole in the keeper plate.
10. Assemble the camshaft sprocket and mounting plate if they have been disassembled. Fit the chain over the camshaft sprocket. Lower the timing chain and mounting plate past the camshaft flange until the center stud of the sprocket is lined up with the camshaft.
11. Rotate the camshaft sprocket until the screw holes match the threaded holes in the camshaft flange.
12. Install the timing chain over the other sprockets so that it hangs straight from the camshaft to the crankshaft.

NOTE: The shaft settings must not be altered.

13. Guide the center stud of the camshaft sprocket into the camshaft. Install the retaining bolts.
14. Mount the curved chain guide plate together with the mounting plate (the chain guide plate nearest the block) with its mounting bolts and stretch the chain as required.
15. Check the camshaft-crankshaft-idler shaft setting.
16. Install the timing chain tensioner.

NOTE: Different versions of the chain tensioner exist and the assembly procedures are different.

Reynholds Version

Before installation, remove the tensioner neck. Tension the spring, by turning the ratchet sleeve (actuated by the spring) clockwise and at the same time pushing it until it locks in its innermost position. Fit the tensioner neck and a spacer piece, so that the tensioner neck will not bottom in the chain tensioner housing and release the self-adjuster.

Jwis Version

Place the lock washer with the spiral rod in the chain tensioner housing. Install the spring with the small diameter against the lock washer. Fit the tensioner neck into the housing by simultaneously pressing and turning it into its inner position. The tensioner neck must be held depressed while the chain tensioner is being fitted, right until the chain has been tensioned.

Timing chain tensioner (Reynholds)

17. Mount the chain tensioner with the guide plate on the engine block.
18. Press the curved chain guide against the chain to stretch it and push the tensioner neck against the spacer piece. Remove the spacer piece while the chain is kept tensioned. Then adjust to leave a clearance of 0.02″ between the housing and the tensioner neck.

Tighten the chain guides.

19. Rotate the crankshaft one full turn in its normal sense and check the chain tension. The movement of the tensioner neck from its butted position must be at least 0.02″ and not more than 0.06″.
20. Remove the bolt from the camshaft sprocket center. Install the timing chain cover using a new gasket.

TIMING CHAIN OIL SEAL

The timing chain oil seal can be removed without removing the engine from the vehicle.

1. Disconnect the negative battery cable. Remove the alternator belt. If the vehicle is equipped with power steering or air conditioning, remove the required belts.
2. Remove the clutch cover (torque converter cover) and lock the crankshaft using Saab tool #83-92-987 or equivalent by locking the tool to the ring gear.
3. From beneath the vehicle, remove the pulley retaining bolt using Saab tool #83-92-961 or equivalent. Remove the pulley from the vehicle.
4. Pull off the old seal ring using a suitable tool.
5. Installation is the reverse of removal. Torque the retaining bolt to 137 foot pounds.

CHECKING TIMING CHAIN TENSION

In order to prevent damage caused by the chain tensioner running out too far, the position of the chain tensioner can be checked with the engine mounted in the car.

1. Remove the valve cover.
2. Insert a steel ruler down against the rubber neck on the chain tensioner and measure the distance to the level of the cylinder head cover.
3. The distance should be more than 11.8″. If the distance is less than 11.8″, the engine should be removed as soon as possible for correction. For completely tight chain tensioners (newly adjusted chains), the distance should be about 12.3″.

Camshaft

REMOVAL AND INSTALLATION

1. Remove the valve cover.
2. Remove the camshaft sprocket as follows. On 1975 vehicles, screw an M8 nut on to the threaded center stud of the camshaft sprocket and clamp the center stud against the mounting plate provided for this purpose. On 1976 and later vehicles, bolt the mounting plate to the center of the camshaft sprocket using one of the camshaft sprocket retaining screws.

NOTE: Tighten the nut (screw) securely to immobilize the center stud. Otherwise the chain tensioner will tighten the chain and lock in a new position so that the sprocket cannot be refitted. The chain tensioner cannot be reset without lifting the engine out of the car.

3. Undo the retaining screws from the camshaft sprocket. Separate the wheel from the camshaft plate until it hangs free in the mounting plate by the center stud.
4. Remove the camshaft bearing caps.
5. Remove the camshaft from the vehicle.
6. Installation is the reverse of removal with the following notations.
7. Make sure that the markings on the camshaft and the bearing caps are in line with one another.
8. Check that the flywheel mark is in line with the mark on the No. 1 cylinder block and that the ignition is set on No. 1 cylinder.
9. The screw on the camshaft sprocket center must not be unscrewed before the sprocket is tightly screwed to the camshaft.

Pistons and Connecting Rods

REMOVAL AND INSTALLATION

1. Remove the engine from the vehicle and separate the unit from the transmission.

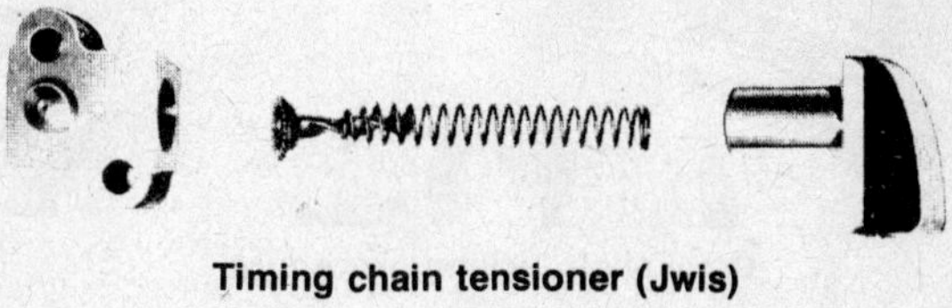

Timing chain tensioner (Jwis)

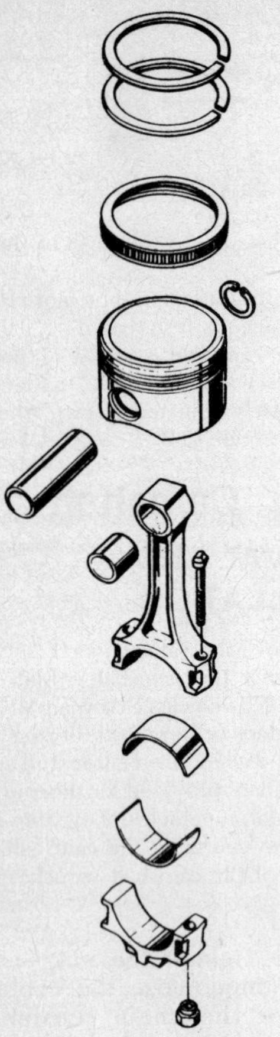

Piston assembly

2. Inspect the connecting rods to make sure that all rods have been numbered correctly.
3. Remove the ring ridge at the top of the cylinder bore, if present, to avoid ring and piston damage, upon removal of the pistons.
4. Loosen the connecting rod cap bolts and lightly tap the caps to loosen. Remove the caps and push the connecting rod and piston assembly upward and out of the cylinder bore.
5. Upon installation of the piston rings, place the lower compression ring with the side marked "TOP" uppermost.
6. Rotate the compression rings so that the gaps in alternate rings will be at 180 degrees to each other, positioned alternately over the two ends of the piston pins.
7. Make sure that the spring gaps of the top and bottom rings in the three-piece scraper ring are staggered.

NOTE: Oil the piston rings before assembly.

8. Continue the installation in the reverse of the removal procedure.

ENGINE LUBRICATION

Rear Main Oil Seal

REMOVAL AND INSTALLATION

This seal is otherwise known as the crankshaft seal at the flywheel end. The seal can be changed with the engine in the vehicle, but the clutch and flywheel must first be removed.

1. Remove the clutch and the flywheel from the vehicle.
2. Remove the old seal ring using the proper tool.
3. Install the new seal with the spring ring turned inwards toward the crankshaft using the proper seal installation tool.
4. Continue the installation in the reverse order of the removal.

Oil Pump

REMOVAL AND INSTALLATION

1. Remove the four retaining screws from the oil pump body.
2. Remove the oil pump and the sealing ring between the pump and the intermediate plate from the vehicle.
3. Installation is the reverse of removal.

CHECKING CLEARANCES

1. Remove the screws holding the pump cover and the pump housing together and separate the two.
2. Remove the rotors and the O-ring from the pump housing.

Crankshaft locking procedure

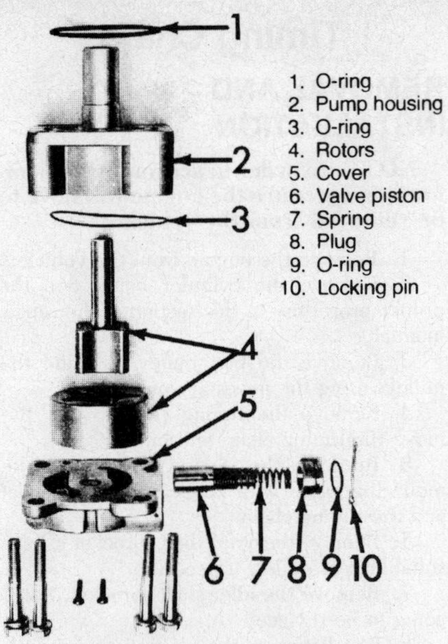

Oil pump—exploded view

3. Remove the pressure reducing valve located in the cover by pulling out the locking pin and then removing the plug, the O-ring, the spring and the valve piston.
4. Check the axial clearance of the inner and outer rotors to the rotor housing with a rule and feeler gauge. The clearance should be 0.00197-0.00354".
5. If the clearance must be adjusted, grind the sealing surface of the housing or the sides of the rotor with fine emery cloth on a flat surface.
6. Check the evenness to the cover with a ruler. All deformities, scratches and pits should be removed by grinding.
7. Assemble the pump in the reverse order of the removal.

NOTE: The chamfered edge of the outer rotor faces inwards in the pump housing (toward the driveshaft).

ENGINE COOLING

Radiator

REMOVAL AND INSTALLATION

99 Series

1. Drain the radiator.
2. Remove the hose clamps at the radiator and disconnect the hoses.
3. Disconnect the wiring terminals for the radiator fan and the thermoswitch.
4. Remove the grill. Remove the hood lock operating cable from its fastenings at the dash panel and wheel housing.
5. Remove the two front sheet retaining screws and nuts, and the four screws holding the headlights to the body.
6. Remove the front sheet metal complete with the radiator assembly, lifting forward and upward.

7. Installation is the reverse of removal.

900 Series

1. Drain the radiator.
2. Remove the hose clamps on the radiator hoses and disconnect the hoses from the radiator.
3. Disconnect the leads to the radiator fan and the auxiliary fan, if equipped.
4. Disconnect the lead to the thermal switch. Remove the ignition coil.
5. Remove the two bolts in the upper radiator support, and lift the radiator out of the vehicle, pulling the top of the radiator slightly backwards.
6. Installation is the reverse of removal.

Water Pump

REMOVAL AND INSTALLATION

NOTE: The water pump is available in three different types which require different removal and installation procedures. Types one and two are used on the 99 series from 1975 through 1977, type three is used on all Saabs from 1977. Type 1: Impeller retained by means of a bolt (cylindrical fitting on the shaft). Type 2: Impeller retained by a nut (conical fitting on the shaft). Type 3: Impeller pressed on the shaft. The thread on the end of the shaft is only provided for dismantling purposes. No nut is required.

1. Drain the radiator. Remove the battery ground cable. Disconnect the intake manifold.
2. Remove the alternator and the alternator bracket.
3. On 99 series vehicles, unbolt both rear engine mounts. Place a jack under the rear of the engine and raise the engine high enough to remove the upper bolt holding the alternator bracket to the transmission cover. Slacken the lower retaining screw and turn the bracket so that it is as far from the engine as possible.
4. Remove the retaining bolts from the water pump cover and remove the cover.

NOTE: Tapping-out hammers or equivalent must not be used during the removal or installation process on types two and three water pumps.

Type 1

1. Remove the center bolt from the impeller. Hold the impeller with a pair of pliers and unscrew it clockwise (left-handed thread). Save the washer.
2. Using the tapping-out hammer with adapter Saab tool #83-92-136 or equivalent on the water pump shaft, carefully withdraw the pump unit.

NOTE: The bearing housing may be left behind in the cylinder block. If so, extract the bearing housing with a tapping-out hammer fitted with a nut and flat washer, external diameter 1.0″.

Type 2

1. Position Saab tool #83-92-441 or equivalent over the water pump. Install the two bolts without tightening. Turn the tool counterclockwise so that the peg on the tool engages the fins of the impeller. Tighten the two bolts.
2. Loosen the impeller center nut (left-handed thread). Remove the water pump using Saab tool #83-92-649 or 83-92-490 or equivalent.

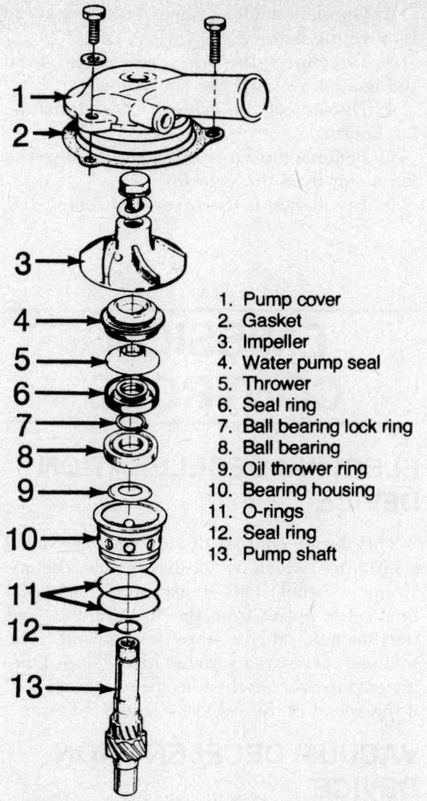

Water pump—exploded view (type 1)

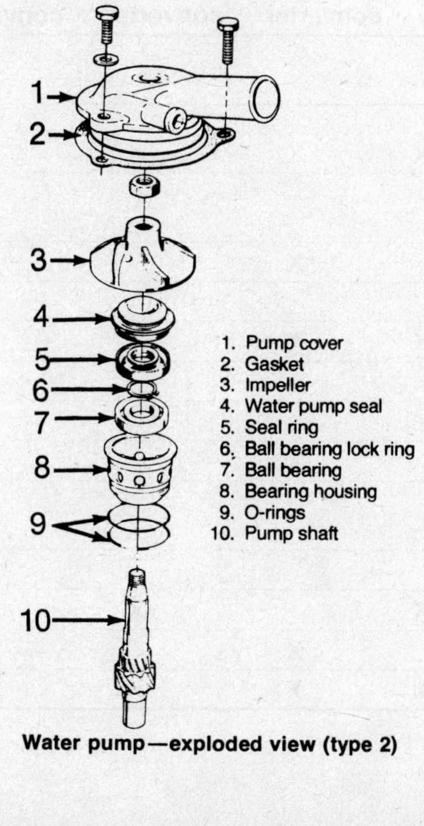

Water pump—exploded view (type 2)

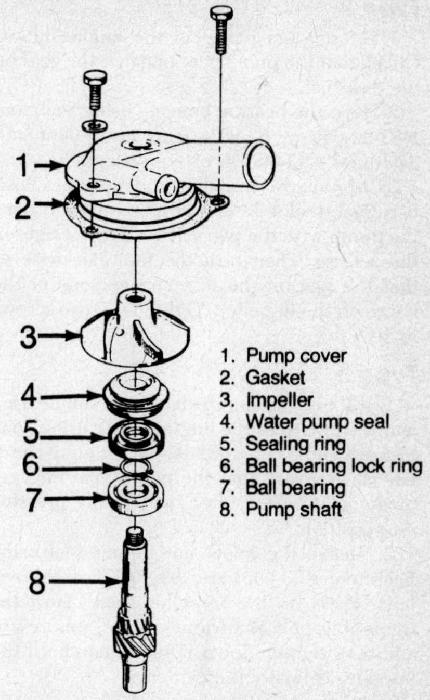

Water pump—exploded view (type 3)

NOTE The bearing housing may be left behind in the cylinder block. If so, extract the bearing housing by means of a tapping-out hammer fitted with a nut and flat washer with an external diameter of 1.0″.

Type 3

Remove the water pump using Saab tool #83-92-649 or 83-92-490 or equivalent. The tool fits into the threaded end of the shaft.

NOTE: With regard to all three types of water pump removal, if the impeller is not immobilized while the center bolt is unscrewed, the gear teeth on the pump shaft and idler shaft are liable to be damaged. Up to and including model 1976 (Types 1 and 2), the pump bearing and seals are mounted in a separate bearing housing, which in turn is mounted in the engine block. From model 1977 (Type 3), the pump bearing and seals are mounted directly in the engine block. On most 1975-76 models, the bottom end of the pump shaft is seated in a bush. In later engines, the shaft end is seated directly in the engine block.

INSTALLATION

Installation is the reverse of removal with the exception of the following notations.

Type 1

1. Mount the pump in the engine block. Check that the pump gear engages the gear on the idler shaft.
2. Seat the bearing housing using Saab tool #83-90-536 or equivalent. Make certain that the flange on the bearing housing butts against the plane of the engine block.
3. Install the impeller with the washer and bolt. Torque the bolt to 18 ft/lbs.

Type 2

1. Mount the pump in the engine block. Check that the pump gear engages the gear on the jackshaft.
2. Seat the bearing housing using Saab tool #83-92-649 or 83-92-490 or equivalent and Saab tool #83-90-536 or equivalent.
3. Mount the impeller and the nut. Position Saab tool #83-92-441 or equivalent over the pump with the two screws. Do not tighten the screws. Then turn the tool clockwise so that the peg on the tool engages one of the wings on the impeller. Tighten the two screws to 10.8 ft/lbs.

Type 3

1. Mount the pump shaft with the bearing and the circlip in the engine block using Saab tool #83-90-551 and 82-92-490 or equivalent. Check to insure that the pump gear engages to the gear on the idler shaft before pressing into position.
2. Install the lower and upper seal using Saab tool #83-0551 and 83-90-536 or equivalent. Press on the impeller shaft. Turn the tightening bolt ¼ turn at a time, unscrew it and then tighten down ¼ turn again until the impeller is finally in position.

RADIATOR FAN

REMOVAL AND INSTALLATION

1. Disconnect the negative battery cable.
2. On some models, it may be necessary to remove the battery.
3. Disconnect the wires and cables from the ignition coil and the fan motor.
4. Disconnect the cable harness from the fan housing.
5. Remove the fan housing and remove the fan motor from the vehicle.
6. Installation is the reverse of removal.

EMISSION CONTROLS

ELECTRIC DECELERATION DEVICE

This device consists of an electronic speed transmitter which is located below the instrument panel. This transmitter is actuated by electric pulses from the speedometer and the solenoid at the throttle housing. The solenoid serves as a variable idling stop. During engine overrun the idle speed is increased if the speed of the vehicle exceeds 10 mph.

VACUUM DECELERATION DEVICE

This system consists of a vacuum controlled spring-loaded valve cone which is actuated by the vacuum in the intake manifold.

DASHPOT DECELERATION DEVICE

This device is installed on the throttle housing and acts to mechanically dampen the throttle valve when it shuts. The retardation time can be altered by loosening the locknut and screwing it in away from the throttle stop, which causes shorter deceleration time or toward the throttle stop, which causes longer deceleration time.

DELAY VALVE

A delay valve is mounted in the vacuum passage between the throttle valve housing and the vacuum control unit of the distributor. The valve delays the formation of a vacuum by around 6 seconds. The ignition advance is therefore also delayed during acceleration and the emission of nitric oxide (NO_X) is reduced.

The white end of the delay valve should be towards the vacuum control unit of the distributor. It is also important that the valve is fitted with the shorter hose running between the valve and the vacuum control unit of the distributor.

When the suction line is to be disconnected (e.g. in conjunction with checking of ignition timing), always disconnect the hose at the throttle housing. Otherwise there will be a

EMISSION CONTROL EQUIPMENT

System	1975-76 Federal	Calif.	1977 w/o catalytic converter	1977-79 with catalytic converter	1978-79 w/o catalytic converter	1980 and Later with catalytic converter	Turbo. 1979	Turbo. 1980 and Later
Deceleration device electric							X	
Deceleration device vacuum	X	X	X	X	X			
Deceleration device dashpot						X		X
Delay valve			X		X			
EGR on-off	X ①							
EGR proportional		X	X					
EGR two port					X			
Air injection		X						
Pulse air			X		X			
Oxygen sensor & catalytic converter				X		X	X	X
Compression 7.2:1							X	X
Compression 8.7:1	X	X		X				
Compression 9.25:1			X		X	X		
ELCD system	X	X	X	X	X	X	X	X

① Automatic transmission only

risk of dirt entering and clogging the delay valve.

ON-OFF EGR

When this type of EGR valve opens, a small quantity of exhaust gases flows via the metering orifice from the exhaust manifold, through the EGR crosspipe and the EGR valve to the inlet manifold. The EGR valve is controlled by means of a vacuum from the throttle valve housing. The vacuum hole is located relative to the throttle valve so that a vacuum signal is obtained when the engine speed is about 1.900 rev/min. or somewhat higher. Even during conditions of small loads, a sufficiently strong vacuum is obtained to open the valve completely. At full throttle and slightly below, the vacuum is so weak that the valve does not open.

The PVS valve senses the temperature of the coolant and cuts out the vacuum at temperatures lower than approximately 100° F (38° C) which means that improved driveability is obtained immediately after starting with a cold engine.

PROPORTIONAL EGR

The EGR valve is controlled by means of a vacuum regulator. When the valve opens, a small quantity of the exhaust gases is recirculated through the EGR crosspipe and the EGR valve to the inlet manifold. When the induction air passes through the venturi, a venturi signal which is proportional to the total air flow is obtained. The signal is transmitted to the EGR vacuum amplifier which amplifies the signal 14 times by means of the manifold vacuum reservoir.

The manifold vacuum reservoir is connected to the amplifier. The amplified signal then goes via the vacuum signal switch and the PVS valve to the EGR valve. The vacuum signal switch cuts out the EGR signal at engine speed below 2.500 ±500 rev/min. This has been arranged by means of a hole drilled through the throttle valve housing. (During the running-in of the engine, the cut-off speed can be somewhat lower). The PVS valve senses the temperature of the coolant and cuts off the EGR signal at temperatures lower than approx. 100° F, which results in improved driveability immediately after cold engine starting. At wide open throttle, the vacuum in the manifold reservoir disappears after a few seconds and the EGR valve closes.

TWO-PORT EGR

In the two-port EGR system, the opening of the EGR valve is regulated by two adjacent vacuum ports in the throttle valve housing, a holding valve, a release valve and a PVS valve. When the EGR valve opens, a small proportion of the exhaust gases are recirculated to the inlet manifold.

As the throttle valve is opened slightly and the valve passes the two vacuum ports, a gradual increase in the vacuum is obtained and, consequently, a gradual opening of the EGR valve.

When the throttle valve is opened wide and the vacuum in the ports diminishes, the earlier vacuum at the EGR valve is maintained for about six seconds by means of the holding valve.

When the throttle valve is closed, the EGR valve must also be closed to prevent rough idling of the engine. A release valve is fitted for this purpose and the valve is regulated by an additional port located inside the throttle valve housing. Thus, the vacuum maintained by the holding valve is released.

When the temperature of the engine is below approx. 104° F (40° C), the PVS valve shuts off the vacuum between the throttle valve and the EGR valve to improve the running of the engine during the warming-up period.

AIR INJECTION SYSTEM

The function of the air injection system is to create afterburning in the exhaust pipes and the exhaust manifold. The air pump is driven by a belt from the crankshaft pulley. The air is drawn into the pump via a labyrinth seal at the pulley and is pumped out to the air hose and the distributor pipe. A relief valve opens if the pressure in the distributor becomes too great.

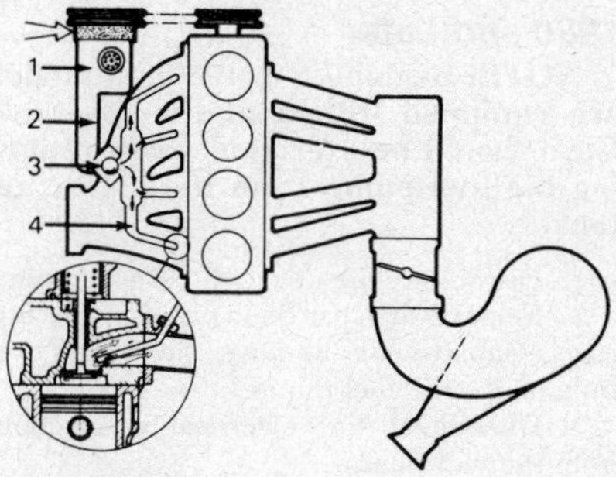

1. Air pump
2. Air inlet hose
3. Check valve
4. Air distribution pipe with injection tubes

Air injection system

The function of the check valve is to prevent exhaust gases from entering the air pump if the belt should break. The air distribution pipe connects the check valve with the four injection tubes. The ends of injection tubes are located at the hottest part of the exhaust passage in order to achieve a maximum afterburning effect.

The pump noise is partly absorbed by the labyrinth seal and partly by a small silencer located above the relief valve. In addition insulation is glued to the dash panel behind the pump.

PULSE AIR SYSTEM

Federal cars are equipped with a pulse air system. In common with the air injection system, the purpose of the pulse air system is to supply air to the exhaust gases from the engine to bring about continued oxidation of the hydrocarbons and carbon monoxide in the exhaust system.

The system is composed of two check valves which are connected to the exhaust manifold by means of dual inlet pipes. The pipes open into the exhaust valves where the exhaust gases are hot, which is important to achieving efficient oxidation in the exhaust system.

The check valves are grouped so that one goes to No. 1 and No. 4 cylinders, and the other to No. 2 and No. 3 cylinders. Air is

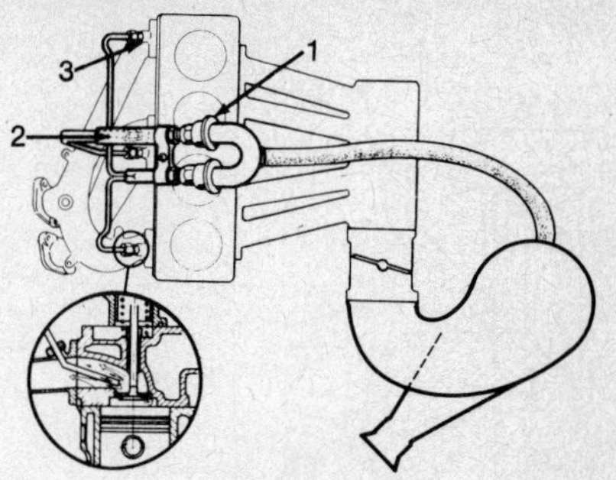

1. Check valves
2. Distribution pipes
3. Inlet pipes

Pulse air system

supplied to the valves by means of a hose from the air cleaner.

The function of the pulse air system is based on the vacuums occurring in the exhaust system during the pulses. For a brief moment immediately prior to the closing of the exhaust valve (at the start of the suction stroke), a vacuum is produced in the exhaust manifold whereupon the check valve opens and a small amount of air is drawn into the exhaust manifold.

Inspection Service

Remove the hose between the air cleaner and the check valve and check that it is free from dents or cracks. Run the engine at idling speed and check that air is drawn through the check valves. Suction should be felt with the thumbs placed over the openings.

CATALYTIC CONVERTER

The converter is located in the exhaust system between the engine and the muffler. The unit is composed of a ceramic material insert of honeycomb design. The walls of the converter are coated with catalytic material made of platinum and rhodium.

EVAPORATIVE LOSS CONTROL DEVICE (ELCD)

The ELCD device is a charcoal filter, which absorbs the vapor from the fuel tank. The charcoal canister is placed in the engine compartment. It is connected to the vent hose of the fuel tank and with a hose to the air cleaner. When the engine is running, fresh air is drawn through the charcoal filter and to the engine inlet system. The filter will then be cleaned of vapors. The vehicles are equipped with a roll-over valve. The valve is connected to the ventilation hose between the filler tube and the charcoal canister. In the event of the car rolling over or ending up on its side, a pendulum will actuate the valve which will shut off the ventilation hose thereby preventing the escape of fuel.

OXYGEN-SENSOR REGULATED CI-SYSTEM

Some vehicles are equipped with a special continuous injection system combined with an electronic control system which is regulated by an oxygen sensor that is located in the exhaust manifold. These vehicles are also equipped with a three-way catalytic converter

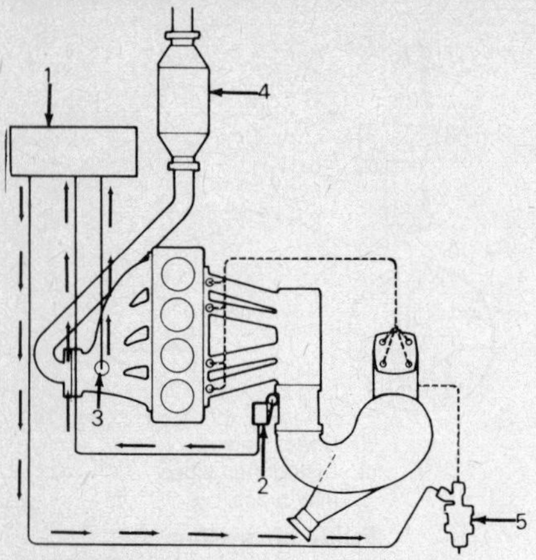

1. Control unit
2. Throttle valve switch, full-load enrichment
3. Oxygen sensor
4. Catalytic converter
5. Modulating valve

Oxygen-sensor regulated CI system

which is located between the exhaust manifold and the muffler in the exhaust system. The sensor-regulated injection system ensures that the air/fuel mixture is continually kept within the required limits for vehicle operation.

FUEL SYSTEM

Fuel Pump

REMOVAL AND INSTALLATION

1975-79

1. Disconnect the negative battery cable.
2. On all vehicles except SAAB 900 series and the 99 Combi Coupe, roll back the carpet in the trunk.
3. On the 900 series and the 99 Combi Coupe, remove the rear floor cover and the floor panel in the luggage compartment.
4. Remove the circular cover plate on top of the pump mounting.
5. Remove the rubber cover from the fuel pump, if equipped. Disconnect the electric terminals at the fuel pump.
6. Disconnect the fuel line from the fuel pump.

NOTE: Hold the fuel pump with an open-end spanner wrench when loosening the connection.

7. Using the proper tool, turn the fuel pump mounting counterclockwise to the nearest groove to unlock the bayonet socket.
8. Lift the fuel pump out carefully. Save the O-ring for installation.

NOTE: The fuel pump can only be removed in one position, as one of the bayonet tongues is wider than the others.

9. Installation is the reverse of removal.

1980 and Later

NOTE: Beginning in 1980, all models are equipped with a plastic gas tank. Care should be exercised when removing the fuel pump from the plastic gas tank.

1. Disconnect the negative battery cable.
2. Remove the rear floor panel in the luggage compartment. Remove the valve cover from above the fuel pump.
3. Disconnect the electrical connections from the fuel pump.
4. Disconnect the fuel pipes from the pump.

NOTE: Use an open-ended spanner wrench to hold the pump steady while loosening the connections.

5. Remove the fuel pump mounting clamp. Lift the fuel pump from the vehicle.
6. Installation is the reverse order of removal.

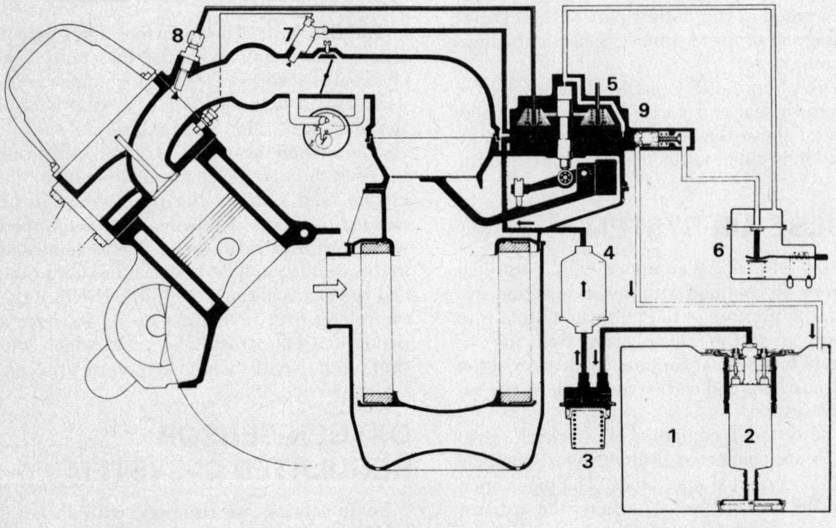

1. Fuel tank
2. Fuel pump
3. Fuel accumulator
4. Fuel filter
5. Fuel distributor
6. Warm-up regulator
7. Cold start valve
8. Injection valves
9. Line pressure regulator

Fuel injection system

Fuel Injection

All Saab vehicles sold in the U.S. are equipped with a Bosch CI (continuous injection) injection system.

An electric fuel pump which is mounted inside the gas tank provides fuel at a constant pressure to the mixture control unit. The latter consists of an air flow sensor which measures the flow of air to the engine and which acts mechanically on the fuel distributor. The fuel distributor provides the injection valves with the correct amount of fuel. The fuel is injected continuously into the intake manifold immediately upstream of the inlet valve. 900 series vehicles sold in California and High Altitude states are equipped with a special CI system which is composed of an electronic control unit that is regulated by an oxygen sensor located in the exhaust manifold.

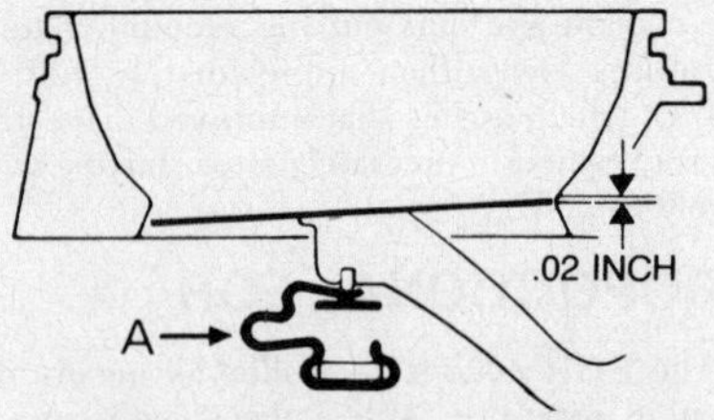

Sensor plate position adjustment

SENSOR PLATE POSITION ADJUSTMENT

1. Turn the ignition switch off.
2. The top of the sensor plate should be level with the bottom edge of the air venturi. This is the highest position for the sensor plate.
3. The position should be checked in line with the lever. A position slightly beneath the lower edge of the venturi is acceptable (.02 in./.5 mm max.)
4. Adjust as required by bending the loop (A) on the wire underneath the sensor plate. The air flow sensor must be removed to accomplish this procedure.

AUXILIARY AIR REGULATOR CHECK

NOTE: The engine must be cold to complete this procedure.

1. Disconnect the terminal on the air flow sensor.
2. Switch on the ignition. The opening should completely close after about five minutes.
3. If the air valve does not close, check the power supply. If there is no fault here, the auxiliary air valve should be replaced.

FUEL PUMP DELIVERY CHECK

Voltage Check

1. Remove the round cover plate from the top of the fuel pump.
2. Measure the voltage between the positive and negative terminals when the fuel pump is operating.
3. The lowest permissible voltage is 11.5 volts.

Capacity Check

NOTE: Be sure that the fuel filter is not clogged and that the battery is fully charged.

1. Disconnect the return fuel pipe from the fuel distributor.
2. Connect the test pipe to the fuel distributor and place the other end in a suitable container.
3. On vehicles with the safety switch on the air flow sensor, remove the switch connector from the air flow sensor.
4. On vehicles with the fuel pump relay and the pulse sensor, remove the pump relay. Connect a jumper lead between terminals 15 and 87 on 99 series and terminals 30 and 87 on 900 series vehicles.
5. Switch on the ignition and allow the pump to run for 30 seconds. Measure the quantity of fuel. The proper specification should be 750 cm^3/30 sec. for fuel pump no. 0-580-254-994 and 900 cm^3/30 sec. for fuel pump no. 0-580-254-978.

THERMO-TIME SWITCH CHECK

When the engine temperature is below 113° F current is allowed to flow for a short period of time (depending upon temperature) while the starter is running.

Check that the switch closes when the engine is started by connecting a test lamp in series across the contacts of the cold state valve plug.

NOTE: It is not possible to make a more accurate check of the thermo-time switch. If doubt exists replace the switch.

COLD-START VALVE CHECK

1. Remove the cold start valve plug and unscrew the latter from the throttle valve housing. Allow the fuel line to remain connected.
2. Connect a wired plug to the cold start valve and connect the wires to the main beam terminal and body of one of the headlights.
3. Switch on the ignition and disconnect the electrical connection to the air flow sensor. The fuel pump is now running. Place the cold start valve in a container and have an assistant switch the headlights to main beam for a short period (30 seconds max.). Fuel should spray out of the valve during this period.
4. Dry the valve nozzle and let the fuel pump run for another minute. No fuel should pass through the valve during this time.
5. Correct as required.

Cold start valve

CONTROL PRESSURE TEST–ENGINE COLD

NOTE: The engine should cool overnight before this test is carried out to ensure that the engine is at ambient temperature. The engine must not be run before this test.

1. Open the valve. Disconnect the plug at the warm-up regulator. Turn on the ignition.
2. Compare the pressure gauge reading with the recommended pressure (18-25 psi at 68 degreees).
3. If the values differ, replace the warm-up regulator.

INJECTOR TESTING

1. Remove the rubber bellows from the air flow sensor.
2. Remove the injection valves from the intake manifold. Place the valves in a suitable container.

NOTE: The fuel lines should be left connected.

3. Turn on the ignition and remove the safety circuit plug from the air flow sensor. On 1977 and later 99 series vehicles, connect a jumper lead between terminals 15 and 87 in the relay holder. This will enable the fuel pump to operate.
4. For fuel atomization, lift the lever in the air flow sensor and check the spray pattern that is being emitted at the injection valves. If atomization is poor, correct as necessary.
5. For valve tightness, turn off the ignition to obtain the rest pressure. Wipe the area dry around the injection nozzles. Lift the lever and check for leakage. It should not take less than 15 seconds for a drop to form. Correct as required.

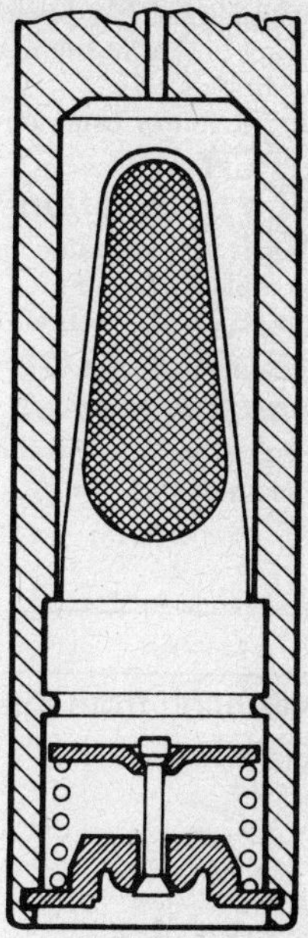

Injection valve

FUEL DISTRIBUTOR

Removal and Installation

1. Clean and remove fuel lines at distributor.
2. Remove retaining bolts and carefully lift out distributor. Take care not to drop control piston.

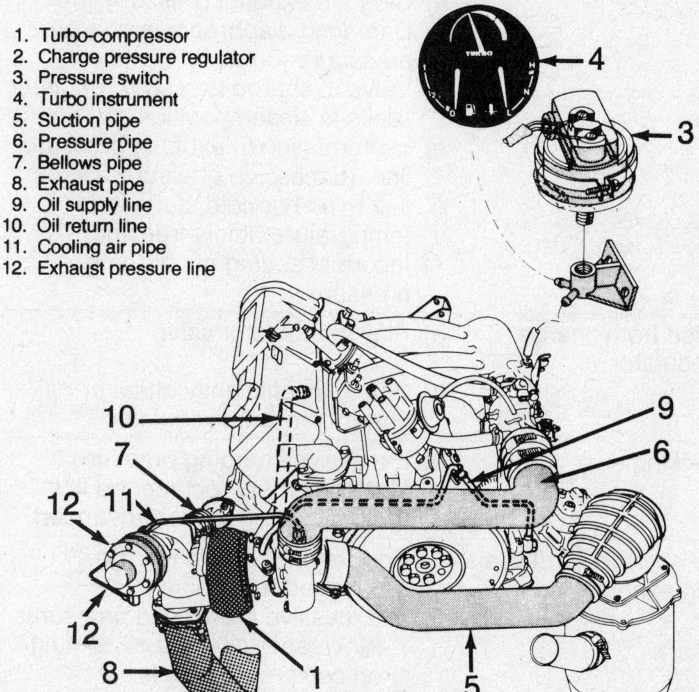

Turbocharging system

3. If control plunger has been removed, moisten with fuel before installing and insert small shoulder first.

4. Reinstall distributor using new O-rings.

FUEL FILTER

Removal and Installation

The fuel filter is bolted in-line and must be uncoupled for replacement. Filter is installed with arrows pointing in direction of flow.

FUEL ACCUMULATOR

Removal and Installation

1. Clean the area around the fuel accumulator connections.

2. Disconnect the connections and remove the fuel accumulator from the vehicle.

3. Installation is the reverse of removal.

Turbocharger

Turbocharging is achieved by means of a turbo-compressor which utilizes the exhaust gases from the engine to drive the turbine. The exhaust gases are routed to an exhaust gas turbine, causing the wheel to rotate. The turbine wheel is mounted on the same shaft as a compressor impeller which rotates at the same speed. The compressor is located in the induction system where it effects an increase in the charging pressure in the combustion chamber.

The Saab Turbo has been designed to start operating at relatively low engine speeds, in order to provide increased torque at engine speeds typical of normal driving conditions.

TURBO UNIT

Removal and Installation

1. Remove the charge pressure regulator and block off the exhaust pipe.

2. Disconnect the hose between the compressor and the throttle housing.

TROUBLE DIAGNOSIS

Problem	Cause	Solution
Noise or vibration from the turbo compressor	a) Poor lubrication of the turbo shaft bearing	a) Check the oil pressure and flow to the turbo. If the fault should persist after remedial action (permanent bearing damage) exchange the turbo compressor
	b) Leakage in the induction or exhaust system	b) Tighten leaking connections and replace defective seals and gaskets
	c) Unbalanced turbo shaft owing to damage	c) Exchange the turbo compressor
Insufficient charging pressure	a) Leakage between the compressor and cylinder head or between the cylinder head and turbine	a) Tighten leaking connections and replace defective seals and gaskets
	b) Incorrect setting of charging pressure	b) Adjust the charge pressure regulator
	c) Valve in charge pressure regulator sticks in open position	c) Overhaul the charge pressure regulator
	d) Partially clogged exhaust system	d) Clean or replace exhaust system
	e) Clogged air cleaner	e) Change cartridge
	f) Binding turbo shaft	f) Exchange turbo compressor
Excessive charging pressure	a) Leakage at exhaust pressure line connections	a) Tighten; if necessary, replace nipples
	b) Clogged exhaust pressure line	b) Remove and clean
	c) Damaged diaphragm in charge pressure regulator	c) Replace diaphragm
	d) Valve in charge pressure regulator sticks in closed position	d) Overhaul the charge pressure regulator
	e) Ice formation in exhaust pressure line. (Excessive pressure occurs 1-2 min after cold start when temperature below freezing)	e) Avoid heavy loading of engine immediately after cold starting
	f) Incorrect setting of charging pressure	f) Adjust charge pressure regulator
Metallic noise from charge pressure regulator	a) Play in regulator valve	a) Overhaul the charge pressure regulator
	b) Spring insufficiently offset in charge pressure regulator	b) Adjust position of spring (replace as necessary)
Engine knocking	a) Excessive charging pressure	a) Adjust charging pressure
	b) Unsuitable fuel (octane too low)	b) Change fuel
	c) Ignition setting too far advanced	c) Adjust timing
Oil leakage at turbo shaft seals (oil fumes in exhaust)	a) Poor return flow from turbo: Clogged return line; Excessive crankcase pressure; Air cleaner clogged oil coating on compressor seals	a) Check: Return line; Crankcase ventilation; Change air cleaner
	b) Turbo unit seals damaged	b) Exchange turbo compressor

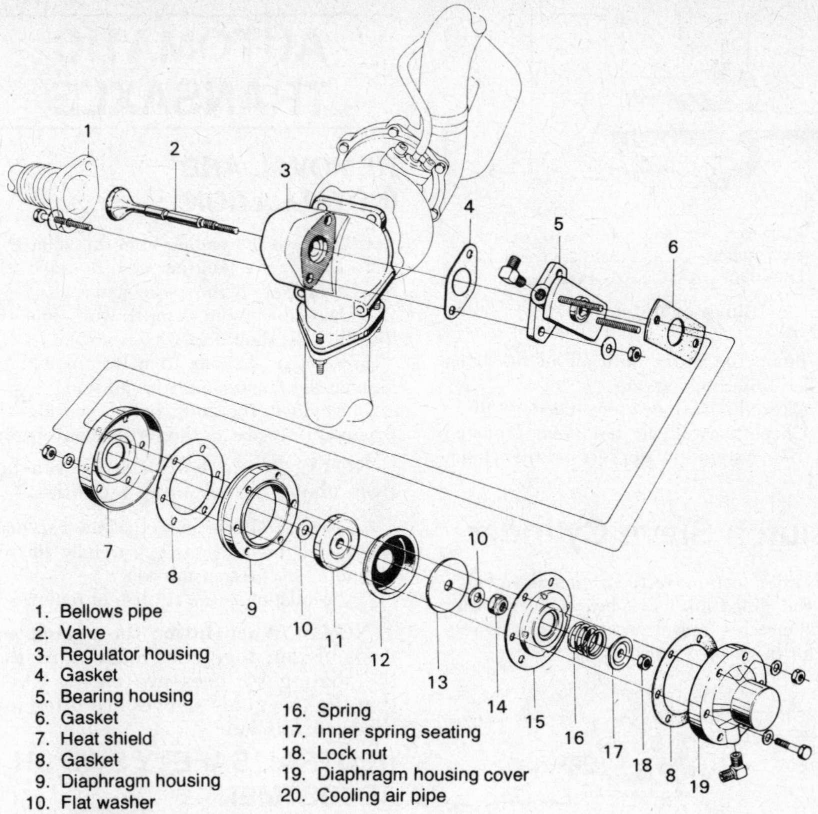

1. Bellows pipe
2. Valve
3. Regulator housing
4. Gasket
5. Bearing housing
6. Gasket
7. Heat shield
8. Gasket
9. Diaphragm housing
10. Flat washer
11. Inner diaphragm washer
12. Diaphragm
13. Outer diaphragm washer
14. Diaphragm nut
15. Inner spring seating (Model 1979 six holes, model 1980 four holes)
16. Spring
17. Inner spring seating
18. Lock nut
19. Diaphragm housing cover
20. Cooling air pipe

Charge pressure regulator—exploded view

3. Disconnect the oil supply line and the oil return line at the turbo unit.
4. Remove the retaining bolts securing the turbo to the exhaust manifold. Remove the turbo unit from the vehicle. Plug the holes in the turbo unit to prevent dirt from entering.
5. Installation is the reverse of removal with the following exceptions.
6. Fill the lubricating inflow of the turbo unit with engine oil before connecting the oil return line at the turbo.
7. Crank the engine for about 30 seconds with terminal 15 on the ignition coil disconnected. This will fill the lubricating system of the turbo before the engine is started.

Pressure plate and related components

MANUAL TRANSAXLE

REMOVAL AND INSTALLATION

1. Remove the engine from the vehicle.
2. Drain the engine oil. Remove the clutch cover. Remove the starter.
3. Withdraw the clutch shaft using a tapping-out tool or equivalent.
4. On 1975 vehicles, remove the three screws of the release bearing guide sleeve. Back off the adjusting screw and disconnect the clutch lever.
5. On 1976 and later vehicles, remove the three bolts for the slave cylinder.
6. Remove the screws in the mating flanges of the engine and transmission.
7. Carefully separate the engine from the transmission. At the same time, remove the release bearing guide sleeve.
8. Installation is the reverse of removal.

NOTE: When fitting the engine and transmission together, make sure that the mating surfaces are clean. Check that the two guide sleeves are fitted in the transmission. Install a new gasket on the transmission flange.

OVERHAUL

For transmission overhaul procedures, refer to the Unit Repair Section.

CLUTCH

REMOVAL AND INSTALLATION

99 Series

1. Drain the radiator. Remove the hood. Disconnect the negative battery cable.
2. Disconnect the cable harness from the fan housing. Disconnect the cables to the ignition coil, oil pressure switch, temperature transmitter, headlamp wiper motor and the fan thermal switch on the radiator.
3. Disconnect the hoses from the radiator. Remove the grille. Remove the radiator assembly.
4. Remove the clutch cover bolts, then remove the clutch cover.
5. Mount spacer (Saab part #8390023) between the clutch cover and the diaphragm spring. When installing the spacer, make sure that the clutch pedal is fully depressed.

NOTE: A different clutch housing was used on some 1976 vehicles, therefore a special spacer (Saab part #8790826) must be used to remove the housing. This spacer is deeper than the standard spacer.

6. On 1975 vehicles, remove the spring at the slave cylinder. Slacken the clutch adjustment by backing off the adjusting screw. Remove and lower the clutch lever.
7. Remove the retaining clip (lock-ring on 1975-77 vehicles) and the seal cap from the clutch shaft. Remove the plastic propeller (O-ring on 1975-77 vehicles) from the clutch shaft.
8. Remove the clutch shaft using a tapping-out hammer or equivalent.
9. Remove the retaining bolts that secure the slave cylinder (guide sleeve) to the primary gear housing.
10. Remove the clutch retaining screws, the clutch, clutch disc, slave cylinder (guide sleeve) and the release bearing. It is not necessary to disconnect the hydraulic hose on the slave cylinder (guide sleeve).

NOTE: On 1976 and later vehicles, be sure that the diaphragm spring does not damage the slave cylinder.

11. Installation is the reverse of removal.

900 Series

1. Remove the clutch housing cover.
2. Install the spacer (Saab part #8390023) between the clutch fork and the diaphragm spring. Keep the clutch pedal depressed when the ring is being installed.
3. Unhook the spring clip and remove the cover located in front of the clutch shaft. Remove the clutch shaft plastic propeller.
4. Remove the clutch shaft by means of an M8 bolt installed in the shaft end and Saab tool no. 83-93-175. Withdraw the shaft as far as possible.

5. Remove the clutch slave cylinder retaining bolts.

6. Remove the clutch retaining bolts and remove the clutch, clutch disc and the slave cylinder complete with the clutch release bearing.

NOTE: Make sure that the slave cylinder sleeve is not damaged by the clutch during the removal procedure.

7. Installation is the reverse of removal.

PEDAL FREE-PLAY ADJUSTMENT—1975

The clutch play is regulated by an adjusting screw that threads into the transmission case and acts as the fulcrum of the clutch lever. The gap is increased when the screw is backed off. The gap should be checked at the outer end of the clutch lever. The specification should be .12±.02 inch.

Clutch Master Cylinder

REMOVAL AND INSTALLATION

1. Remove the clamp holding the pipe from the cylinder at the body and remove the pipe at the cylinder.

2. Remove the left-hand screen under the instrument panel.

3. Remove the pin holding the push rod to the clutch pedal.

4. Remove the bolts inside the dash panel. Remove the clutch cylinder from inside the engine compartment.

5. Remove the hose from the fluid container and hang it out of the way so that the fluid does not come out.

6. Installation is the reverse of removal.

BLEEDING

1. Connect a hose to the slave cylinder bleeder valve. Place the other end of the hose in a suitable jar partially filled with brake fluid.

2. Fill the master cylinder with brake fluid.

3. Open the bleeder valve on the slave cylinder a half turn.

4. Place a cooling system tester gauge over the opening of the master cylinder.

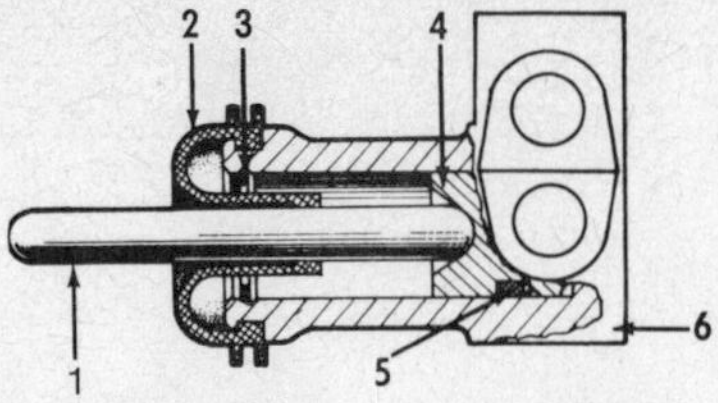

1. Push rod
2. Sealing cap
3. Lock ring
4. Piston
5. Piston seal
6. Housing

Slave cylinder—1975

5. Pump the tester until all air has been expelled from the system.

6. Close the slave cylinder bleeder valve.

7. Check that all air has been removed from the system by depressing the clutch pedal.

Clutch Slave Cylinder

In order to remove the clutch slave cylinder, the clutch must first be removed. Refer to the clutch removal procedure in this section for the proper information.

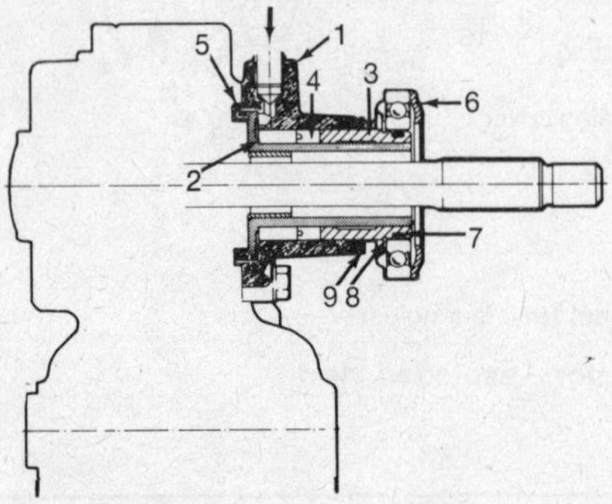

1. Slave cylinder housing
2. Sleeve
3. Piston
4. Lip seal
5. O-ring
6. Release bearing
7. O-ring
8. Lock ring
9. Lock ring

Slave cylinder—1976 and later

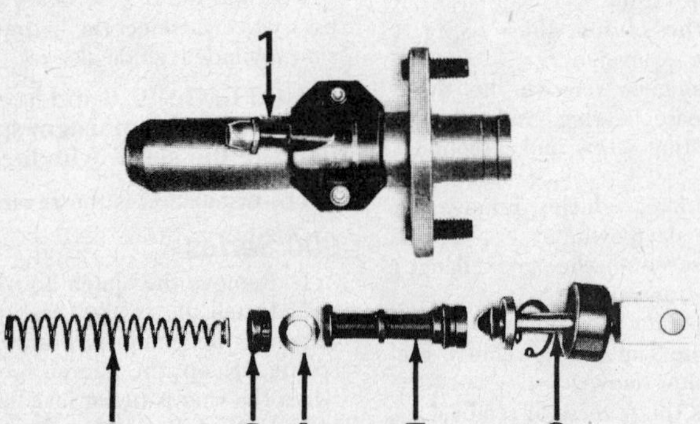

1. Housing
2. Spring with seat
3. Sealing
4. Washer
5. Piston and rear seal
6. Push rod assembly

Clutch master cylinder—exploded view

AUTOMATIC TRANSAXLE

REMOVAL AND INSTALLATION

1. Remove the engine from the vehicle.

2. Drain the engine oil. Remove the flywheel cover. Remove the starter.

3. Disconnect the throttle wire from the throttle valve housing.

4. Remove all bolts from the mating surfaces of the engine and transmission.

5. Remove the four bolts securing the flywheel ring gear to the torque converter.

NOTE: These bolts can be reached from above the oil pump mounting.

6. Turn the flywheel so that the two plate angles will be horizontal. Carefully lift the engine off of the transmission.

7. Installation is the reverse of removal.

NOTE: When fitting the engine and transmission together, make sure that the mating surfaces are clean. Check that the two guide sleeves are fitted into the transmission.

NEUTRAL SAFETY SWITCH ADJUSTMENT

1. Disconnect the wires from the switch.

NOTE: The wide terminals are for back-up lights and the narrow ones are for the starter motor.

2. Loosen the locknut using an 11/16 inch crows foot and unscrew the switch two turns.

3. With the selector in Drive, connect a test light between the narrow terminals. The light should light up.

4. Screw in the switch until the light goes out. Mark that position on both the transmission and the switch.

5. Move the test lamp, the wide terminals and screw switch in until the light goes out again. Count the number between the two lights going out.

6. Turn the switch to a point halfway between the two lights out points.

7. Secure the locknut to 4 to 6 ft/lbs torque.

NOTE: If the safety switch is locked too tight, it may be damaged.

SHIFT LINKAGE

Checking

1. Move the selector lever to "N". Check the clearance from the selector lever pin to the neutral detent.

2. Move the selector lever to "D". Check the clearance from the selector lever pin to the drive detent. The clearance at the "N" and the "D" position should be equal. If they are not equal adjust the cable.

3. Check for proper selector lever pin position in the "P", "R", "2" and "1" ranges.

Adjusting

1. Remove the gear selector lever cover.

2. Slack off the gear selector lever housing nuts with tool no. 839123 or equivalent.

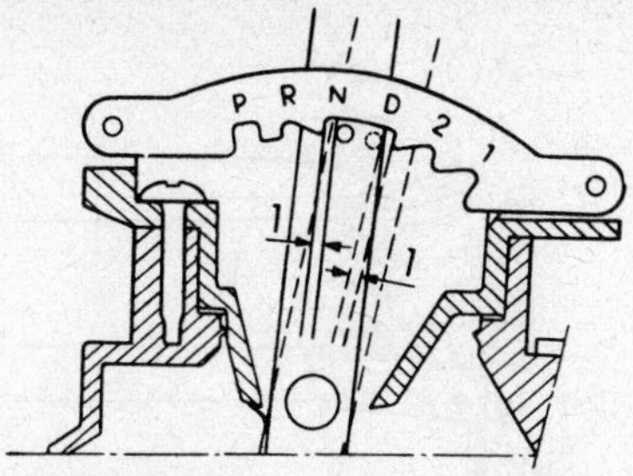

Manual linkage clearance, equal in "N" and "D"

3. Lift the gear selector lever housing and turn it so that the adjustment nuts of the cable will be reachable.
4. Adjust the cable longer or shorter to bring the "N" and "D" clearance into equality.
5. Assemble the gear selector housing and check the clearance in "N" and "D".
6. A fine setting of the selector cable can be accomplished by adding or removing shims at the transmission case end of the cable. A maximum of three shims may be used.

BAND ADJUSTMENT

Front Band

1. Place tool no. 879007 or equivalent, ¼ inch thickness gauge between the adjusting screw and the piston.
2. Loosen the lock nut.
3. Tighten the adjusting screw to 10 inch pounds of torque and tighten the lock nut.

NOTE: On transmissions with self-adjusting mechanism, check the gap between the self-adjusting spring and the lever. It should be 1.5 to 2.0 thread flights.

Rear Band

The rear band adjusting screw is located outside the transmission case on the driver's side.

1. Loosen the lock nut a few turns.
2. Tighten the adjusting screw to 10 ft/lbs and then back off ¾ turn.
3. Hold the adjusting screw and torque the lock nut to 30 to 40 ft/lbs.

DRIVE AXLES

Driveshaft

REMOVAL AND INSTALLATION

NOTE: The entire front axle assembly must be removed in order to remove the driveshaft from the vehicle.

1. On 900 series vehicles, remove the upper bolt of the shock absorber before jacking up the vehicle.
2. Raise the vehicle on a hoist and support it safely. Remove the wheel.
3. Remove the brake housing and hang it on the wheel housing to avoid damage to the brake hose. Remove the brake disc and parking brake assembly with the cable.

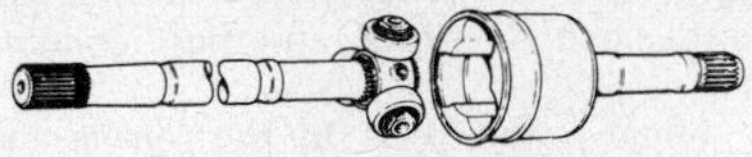

Inner universal joint

4. Remove the large clamp from the rubber bellows on the inner universal joint.

NOTE: To separate the inner universal joint, install the cover (Saab part # 7323736) in the rubber bellows to stop the needle bearings from falling out and to keep dirt from entering. Install the protective cap (Saab part # 7838469) on the inner driver.

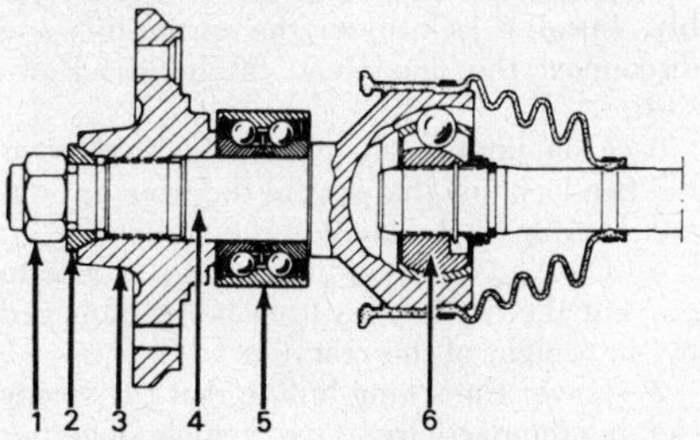

1. Lock nut
2. Washer
3. Wheel hub
4. Outer drive shaft
5. Bearing with seals
6. Outer drive shaft joint

Outer universal joint

5. Disconnect the tie rod from the steering arm using the proper tool. Remove the nut on the upper ball joint. Remove the bolts from the lower control arm bracket.
6. Remove the driveshaft through the wheel housing and remove the entire front axle assembly.
7. If the differential bearing cap is to be removed, remove the retaining bolts and remove the cap and the inner driver using the proper removal tools.
8. Installation is the reverse of removal.

OVERHAUL

1. Mount the steering knuckle housing in a press and press out the outer driveshaft.
2. Remove the intermediate driveshaft from the outer universal joint by loosening the rubber bellows on the outer universal joint and sliding it along the shaft.
3. Mount the shaft in a press and press together the two conical washers so that the circlip inside the hub can move in its groove.
4. Open the circlip using a pliers to remove the pressure.
5. Withdraw the intermediate shaft from the hub together with the spherical shaped washer, the two conical washers and the shaft locking ring. The circlip on the hub remains in the groove.
6. Installation is the reverse of removal.

REAR AXLE

REMOVAL AND INSTALLATION

1. Jack up the rear of the vehicle and support it safely.

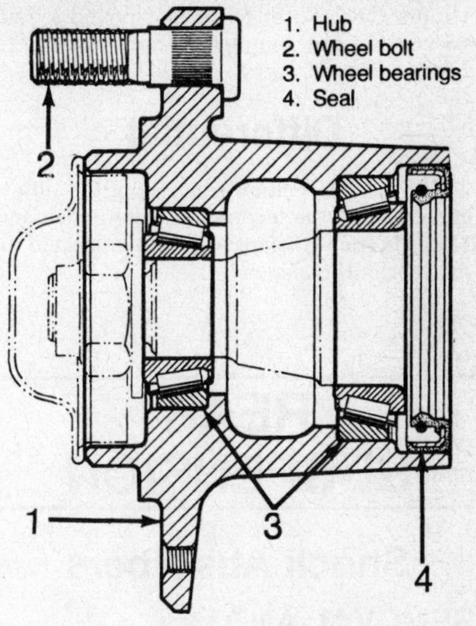

Rear wheel hub—typical

2. Disconnect the brake hoses in front of the rear axle. Disconnect the lower shock absorber bolts and the cross bar.
3. Place a jack under the rear axle. Lower the axle and remove the rear springs.
4. Remove the bolts of the spring link rear bushings and lift away the rear axle assembly.
5. Installation is the reverse of removal. Bleed the hydraulic brake system.

NOTE: The rubber bearings must be mounted in such a way that no strain occurs when the weight of the vehicle is supported by the wheels. They must be drawn tight only when the vehicle is standing empty on its four wheels.

Rear Wheel Bearings

REMOVAL AND INSTALLATION

NOTE: Each rear wheel hub has two tapered roller bearings. From 1975 until 1978, these two bearings were the same size. Beginning with the 1979 models, the inner bearing has a larger diameter than the outer bearing.

1. Raise the vehicle on a hoist and support it safely.

NOTE: Do not place the jack under the rear axle, as this is likely to deform the axle.

2. Remove the wheel. Remove the brake housing and the brake disc. Support the brake housing to avoid damage to the brake pipe.
3. Remove the dust cap. Remove the locknut and the washer. Pull off the hub. If necessary, use a suitable puller.
4. Break out the seal ring with a suitable tool (it cannot be removed intact). Remove the inner rings of both bearings.
5. Place a suitable drift in the milled recesses of the hub and drive out the outer bearing rings.

NOTE: It is advisable to place a wooden board under the hub to avoid deforming the end faces.

6. Installation is the reverse of removal.

Torque the locknut to 36 foot pounds, than slacken the nut completely and torque it to 2.9 foot pounds.

Differential

For the information concerning the differential refer to the sections on Differentials and Manual Transmissions which are located in the rear of this manual.

REAR SUSPENSION

Shock Absorbers

REMOVAL AND INSTALLATION

1975–Oil Filled

1. Raise the vehicle on a hoist and support it safely.
2. Remove the wheel.
3. Remove the shock absorber by removing the retaining bolts from each end of the shock assembly.
4. Installation is the reverse of removal.

1976 and Later–Pneumatic Shock

NOTE: Pneumatic shock absorbers are gas filled which can cause injury if not handled properly. In order to avoid the risk of injury the shock absorbers should be emptied of the gas before being scrapped. This is accomplished by drilling a 2 mm hole in the pressure chamber 10-15 mm from the edge of the shock housing.

1. Raise the vehicle on a hoist and support it safely.
2. Place an additional jack stand under the rear axle to prevent it from dropping and stretching the brake lines.
3. Insert a jack at the rear of the spring-link. Remove the shock absorber retaining nuts.
4. Remove the bolts in the spring-link mounting on the rear axle.
5. Using the jack, lower the spring-link so that the shock absorber can be removed from the vehicle.
6. Installation is the reverse of removal.

Springs

REMOVAL AND INSTALLATION

1. Raise the vehicle on a hoist and support it safely.
2. Remove the hub cap, tire wheel assembly. Install a jack under the spring-link and disconnect the lower end of the shock absorber.
3. From underneath of the vehicle, remove the two locknuts that secure the front spring-link bearing to the body of the vehicle.
4. Place a jack stand under the rear axle to prevent the brake lines from being damaged by the weight of the rear axle.
5. Lower the spring-link so that the spring can be removed from the vehicle together with the upper spring support and the rubber spacer at the lower spring seating which is retained by the spring tension.
6. Installation is the reverse of removal.

FRONT SUSPENSION

Shock Absorbers

Some vehicles are equipped with pneumatic shocks.

NOTE: Pneumatic shock absorbers are gas-filled which can cause injury if not handled properly. In order to avoid the risk of injury, the shock absorbers should be emptied of the gas before being scrapped. This is accomplished by drilling a 2 mm hole in the pressure chamber 10-15 mm from the edge of the shock housing.

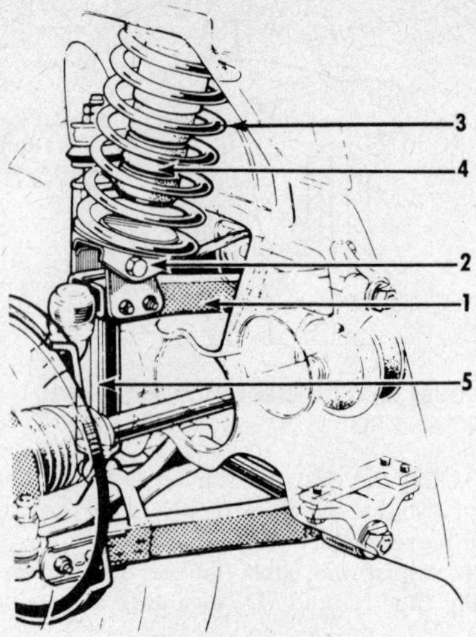

1. Upper control arm
2. Lower spring support
3. Coil spring
4. Rubber buffer
5. Shock absorber

Front suspension

REMOVAL AND INSTALLATION

1. On 900 series vehicles, remove the upper shock absorber nut before raising the vehicle.
2. Raise the vehicle and support it safely. Remove the wheels.
3. Remove the shock absorber retaining bolts and remove the shock from the vehicle. Save all washers and rubber parts.
4. Installation is the reverse of removal.

Ball Joints

REMOVAL AND INSTALLATION

1. Raise the vehicle and support it safely. Remove the wheel.
2. Remove the brake housing and hang it out of the way so that the brake hose will not be damaged.
3. Remove the nut that holds the ball joint ball bolt in the steering knuckle housing. Remove the bolt using the proper removal tool.
4. Remove the ball joint from the control arm assembly.
5. Installation is the reverse of removal.

Springs

REMOVAL AND INSTALLATION

1. On 900 series remove the upper shock absorber nuts before raising the vehicle.
2. Raise the vehicle on a hoist and support it safely. Remove the wheel.
3. Install a spring compression tool or equivalent, engaging the upper shanks di-

1. Rear axle
2. End piece
3. Stub axle
4. Spring links
5. Rear links
6. Cross bar
7. Spring seat
8. Coil spring
9. Spring insulator
10. Rubber buffer
11. Stop
12. Shock absorber

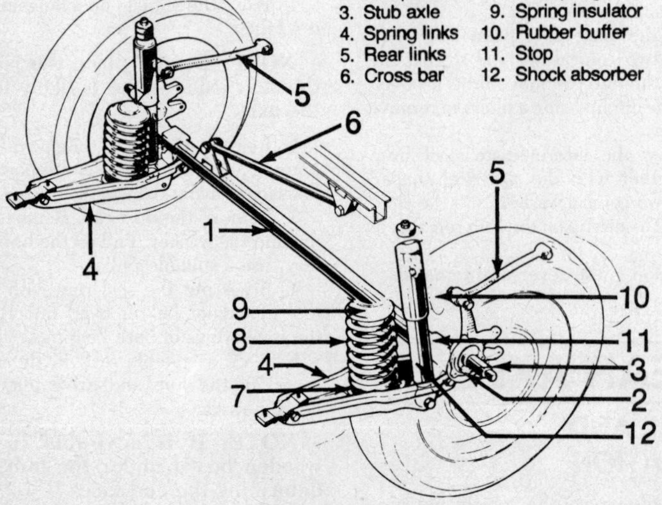

Rear suspension

rectly in the spring at the second free turn from the top of the lower shanks around the spring cups.

NOTE: These are located on the last turn of the spring with the color-coded cup right beside the end of the coil.

4. Compress the spring at the top end. If the upper spring attachment or the steel cone is left behind in the wheel housing, remove it.
5. Remove the spring and the steel cone from the vehicle.
6. Installation is the reverse of removal.

Upper Control Arm

REMOVAL AND INSTALLATION

NOTE: To remove the left upper control arm, the engine must first be removed from the vehicle. See the engine removal procedure in this section of this manual.

1. Raise the vehicle on a hoist and support it safely.
2. Remove the wheel. Remove the shock absorber. Compress the coil spring, using a spring compression tool.

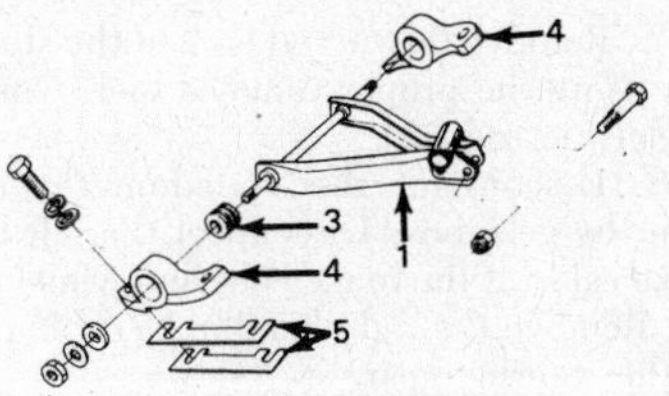

1. Upper control arm
3. Rubber bushing
4. Bearing
5. Spacers

Upper control arm assembly

3. Back-off and remove the two bolts attaching the upper ball joint and lower spring seat to the upper control arm.
4. Remove the bolts from both upper control arm bearing brackets.
5. Remove the coil spring from the vehicle.
6. Remove the control arm and bearings from the vehicle.

NOTE: Save the spacers under the bearings and record the number of spacers used under each bearing.

7. Remove both of the bearing nuts. Now the bearings and bushings can be removed from the control arm.
8. Installation is the reverse of removal.

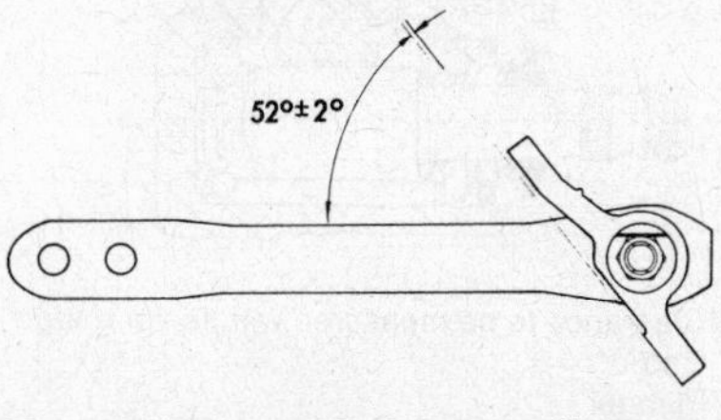

Checking the angle between the upper control arm and bearing

NOTE: When mounting the bearings to the control arm, the angle between the control arm and the bearing should be 52±2° when both nuts are tightened.

Lower Control Arm

REMOVAL AND INSTALLATION

1. Raise the vehicle on the hoist and support it safely. Remove the wheel.
2. Disconnect the lower end of the shock absorber.
3. Back-off and remove the two bolts that attach the ball joint to the control arm.
4. Remove the lower control arm attaching bolts from under the engine compartment floor.

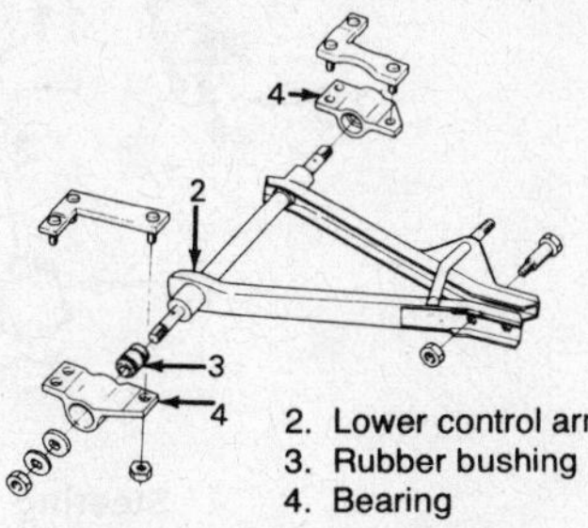

2. Lower control arm
3. Rubber bushing
4. Bearing

Lower control arm assembly

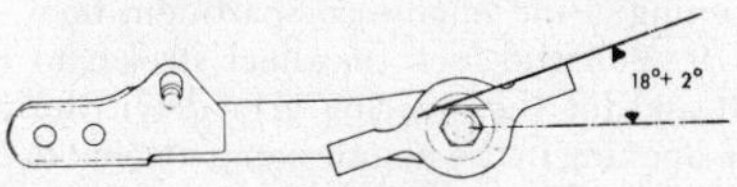

Checking the angle between the lower control arm and bearing

5. Remove the control arm and its attaching brackets from the vehicle.
6. Remove the control arm bearing nuts and remove the bearings from the control arm.
7. Installation is the reverse of removal.

NOTE: When mounting the bearings to the control arm, the angle between the control arm and the bearing should be 18±2° when both nuts are tightened.

Front End Alignment

TOE-IN

1. Roll the car straight forward on a level floor and stop it without using the brakes. It must not be moved backward after this.

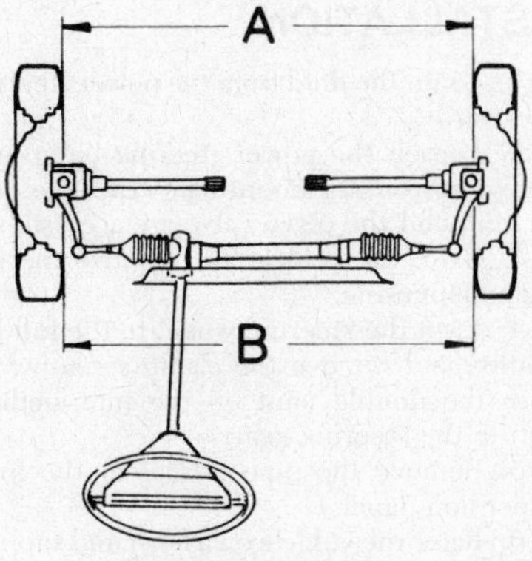

Toe-in adjustment

2. Take a reading of measurement A with the toe-in gauge between the front wheel rims level with the axles. Mark the measurement points with chalk. Roll the car forward until the chalk marks are level with but behind the axles, and take a reading of B. Any necessary adjustment is made by altering the length of the tie rod.
3. Remove the nut on the outer end of the tie rod and the outer clip on the steering gear rubber bellows.
4. Use a suitable pair of grippers to twist the tie rod right or left; adjust until the toe-in is right. Hold the bellows during the twisting.

CASTER

The caster is the angle by which the steering knuckle axis departs from the vertical when viewed from the side and the measurement is generally expressed in degrees. If the caster needs adjusting, spacers are inserted under the bearing brackets of the upper control arms.

To increase the caster, transfer spacers from the front bracket to the rear bracket. To reduce the caster, transfer spacers from the rear bracket to the front bracket. In either case, the total spacer thickness removed from one bracket must be added to the other one.

CAMBER

Camber is the angle by which the centerlines of the wheels lean from the vertical. The camber is positive (+) if the wheels lean outward, and negative (−) if they lean inward.

The camber, and with it the "king pin" angle, can be adjusted with spacers placed under the two bearing brackets of the upper control arms. The desired result can thus be obtained by increasing or reducing the number of spacers used. To increase or reduce camber, use the same number of spacers under both brackets.

Front Wheel Bearings

REMOVAL AND INSTALLATION

NOTE: The entire front axle assembly must be removed from the vehicle when removing the wheel bearings.

1. On 900 series vehicles, remove the upper bolt of the shock absorber before jacking up the vehicle.
2. Raise the vehicle on a hoist and support it safely. Remove the wheel.
3. Remove the brake housing and hang it by the wheel housing to avoid damage to the brake hose. Remove the brake disc and parking brake assembly with the cable.
4. Remove the large clamp from the rubber bellows on the inner universal joint.

NOTE: To separate the inner universal joint, install the cover (Saab part #7323736) in the rubber bellows to stop the needle bearings from falling out and to keep dirt from entering. Install the protective cap (Saab part #7838469) on the inner driver.

5. Disconnect the tie rod from the steering arm using the proper tool. Remove the nut on the upper ball joint. Remove the bolts from the lower control arm bracket.
6. Remove the driveshaft through the wheel housing and remove the entire front axle assembly.
7. Place the steering knuckle housing in a press and press out the driveshaft.
8. Remove the lock-ring and press out the bearing using a suitable drift.
9. Installation is the reverse of removal.

STEERING

Steering Wheel

REMOVAL AND INSTALLATION

1. Disconnect the negative battery cable.
2. On early models, remove the bottom cover of the steering wheel bearing.
3. Remove the steering wheel safety pad. Remove the horn contact. Remove the steering wheel holding nut and washer.
4. Remove the steering wheel using the proper steering wheel removal tool.
5. Installation is the reverse of removal.

Combination Switch

REMOVAL AND INSTALLATION

1. Disconnect the negative battery cable.
2. Remove the steering wheel.
3. Remove the cover beneath the bearing support.
4. Remove the combination switch retaining bolts and electrical connections.
5. Remove the switch from the vehicle.
6. Installation is the reverse of removal.

Manual Steering Gear

REMOVAL AND INSTALLATION

1. Remove the left screen under the instrument panel and loosen the rubber bellows at the body lead-through for the steering gear intermediate shaft.
2. Raise the vehicle and remove the bolt holding the joint to the steering gear pinion.
3. Loosen the steering column tube from the body and separate the steering column joint from the pinion.

NOTE: Hang up the steering column so that the wiring harness is not damaged.

4. Remove the front wheels from the vehicle.
5. Remove the tie rod ends at the steering arms with the proper removal tool.
6. Remove the two steering gear clamps.
7. Move the rack to the right as far as possible.
8. Lift the steering gear to the right so

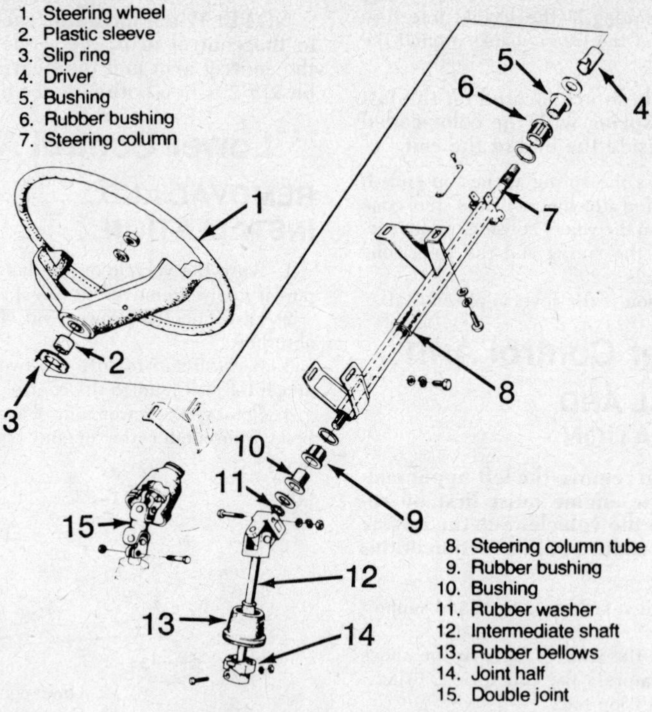

Steering column assembly—typical

that the tie rod can be bent down in the opening of the engine compartment floor.
9. Pull the rack (maximal stroke) to the left and lift the steering gear down through the opening in the engine compartment floor.
10. Installation is the reverse of removal.

ADJUSTMENT

Radial Play

1. Fit the plunger without the spring and screw on the cap without the gasket by hand until it butts against the plunger. Do not use a wrench, as you will damage the cap.
2. Measure the clearance between the cap and the housing with a feeler gauge.
3. Add 0.002-0.006" to the measured clearance to allow for the play to be left between the plunger and cap after assembly. Measure the thickness of the gasket and shims with a micrometer. Shims are available in thicknesses of 0.005", 0.0075", 0.010", 0.015" and 0.020".

Power Steering Gear

REMOVAL AND INSTALLATION

1. Drain the fluid from the power steering reservoir.
2. Loosen the power steering pump and remove it from its mounting so that the double joint and the servo valve are accessible.
3. Raise the vehicle and remove the left engine mounting.
4. Turn the steering wheel to the full left position and remove the clamp screw which holds the double joint on the intermediate shaft to the steering gear.
5. Remove the pipe clamps at the front suspension panel.
6. Raise the vehicle on a hoist and support it safely. Remove the wheels.
7. Remove the tie rod ends at the steering arm using the proper removal tool. Unscrew the left tie rod end.
8. Disconnect the speedometer cable from the gear box. Disconnect the left handbrake cable at the brake yoke and wheel housing. Remove the right handbrake cable clamp on the steering gear.
9. Remove the steering gear mountings from the body. On the left side, remove the two retaining bolts and remove the intermediate piece. On the right side, remove the yoke and the intermediate piece.
10. Disconnect the hoses from the servo valve.
11. Release the intermediate shaft by pulling the steering gear downward and slightly to the right.
12. Move the steering gear to the right until the left tie rod can be bent down through the opening in the body. At the same time, twist the valve housing backwards.
13. Remove the steering gear from the vehicle by guiding it down and to the left.
14. Installation is the reverse of removal.

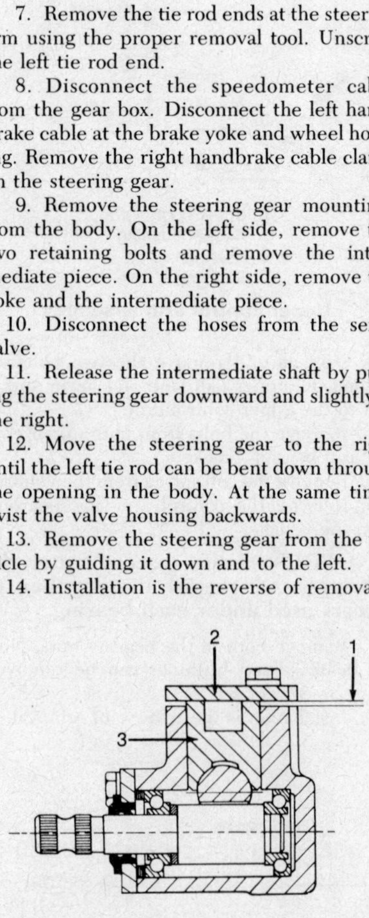

1. Clearance to be measured with feeler gauge
2. Cap
3. Plunger

Radial-play adjustment

ADJUSTMENT

Radial Play

1. Screw in the adjusting screw all the way until the resistance of the twisting steering gear is felt.
2. Back off the adjusting screw 1/12 turn.
3. Check that the steering gear can be turned from lock to lock in both directions without jamming.
4. Tighten the lock nut with a torque of 50-60 ft/lbs.

Power Steering Pump

REMOVAL AND INSTALLATION

1. Drain the fluid from the power steering pump.
2. Drain the coolant from the drain cock on the engine block and disconnect the hose from between the expansion tank and the water pump.
3. Disconnect the power steering pump hoses.

NOTE: Grip the hexagonal nipple on the pump when removing the delivery line.

4. Unbolt the pump unit from the bracket and the engine mounting. Lift off the power steering belt and remove the pump unit complete with its mounting.
5. Installation is the reverse of removal.

BELT ADJUSTMENT

Tighten the belt so that when pressure is applied to the belt at a given point the distance between both belt pulleys is 5-10 mm.

SYSTEM BLEEDING

1. Fill the power steering pump with the proper fluid.
2. Start the engine and top-off the level of fluid to .4 inch above the bottom of the filter.
3. Turn the steering wheel from left to right several times to expel air from the system.
4. Refill the pump as needed.

Steering Linkage

REMOVAL AND INSTALLATION

Tie Rod Ends

1. Raise the vehicle on the hoist and support it safely.
2. Remove the wheel. Remove the nut.
3. Disconnect the ball bolt from the steering arm using the proper removal tool.

NOTE: Do not knock the ball bolt out, as this could cause damage to the ball bolt and other related parts.

4. Back off the nut that locks the end assembly to the tie rod.
5. Unscrew the end assembly from the tie rod.
6. Installation is the reverse of removal. Check and adjust the toe-in as required.

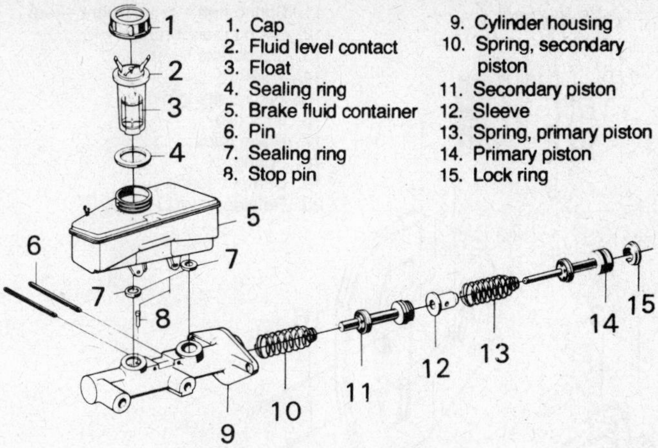

Master cylinder—typical

BRAKE SYSTEM

Master Cylinder

REMOVAL AND INSTALLATION

1. Disconnect the electrical connection to the brake warning switch.
2. Disconnect the hose from the clutch master cylinder to the fluid reservoir. Insert a plastic stopper in the nipple of the reservoir.
3. Disconnect the brake lines to the master cylinder.
4. Remove the nuts that hold the master cylinder to the power brake booster. Remove the master cylinder from the vehicle.
5. Installation is the reverse of removal. Bleed the system as required.

SYSTEM BLEEDING

1. Make sure that the master cylinder is full and kept at least ¾ full throughout the entire bleeding process.
2. Install a rubber hose over the bleeder valve nipple.
3. Place the other end of the bleeder hose into a clear container of brake fluid.
4. Open the wheel cylinder bleeder valve counterclockwise about ¾ of a turn. Have an assistant depress the brake pedal. Just before the brake pedal reaches the end of its travel, close the bleeder valve and allow the brake pedal to return slowly to the released position. Repeat this operation until the brake fluid being expelled is free from air bubbles, then close the bleeder valve tightly.
5. Bleeding sequence is as follows:
   a. Left rear wheel.
   b. Right front wheel.
   c. Right rear wheel.
   d. Left front wheel.

Vacuum Booster

REMOVAL AND INSTALLATION

1. Remove the upper circlip on the brake pedal push rod.
2. Remove the two electrical connections on the brake light switch.
3. Remove the vacuum hose from the non-return valve which is located on the vacuum booster.
4. Disconnect the brake lines and the electrical connections for the brake warning switch from the master cylinder. Disconnect the line to the clutch master cylinder from the fluid reservoir. Insert stoppers in the lines to prevent loss of the brake fluid.
5. Remove the vacuum booster together with the master cylinder and the bracket.

NOTE: The bracket is mounted on the dash panel with four bolts. Three of these bolts are accessible from underneath in the passenger compartment after removal of the screen section and parts of the dash panel insulation felt below the instrument panel. The fourth nut is accessible from the engine compartment by the bracket.

6. Separate the master cylinder and the bracket from the vacuum booster.
7. Installation is the reverse of removal. Bleed the system as required.

Front Disc Brakes

REMOVAL AND INSTALLATION

1. Raise the vehicle on a hoist and support it safely. Remove the wheels.
2. Rotate the brake disc so that one of the recesses in the edge of the disc is in line with the brake pads.
3. Remove the damper spring, pin retaining clip and the U-pin.
4. Remove the disc brake pads.
5. Installation is the reverse of removal. Adjust the handbrake cable as required.

Front Caliper

REMOVAL AND INSTALLATION

1. Raise the vehicle on the hoist and support it safely. Remove the wheels.
2. Remove the disc brake pads.

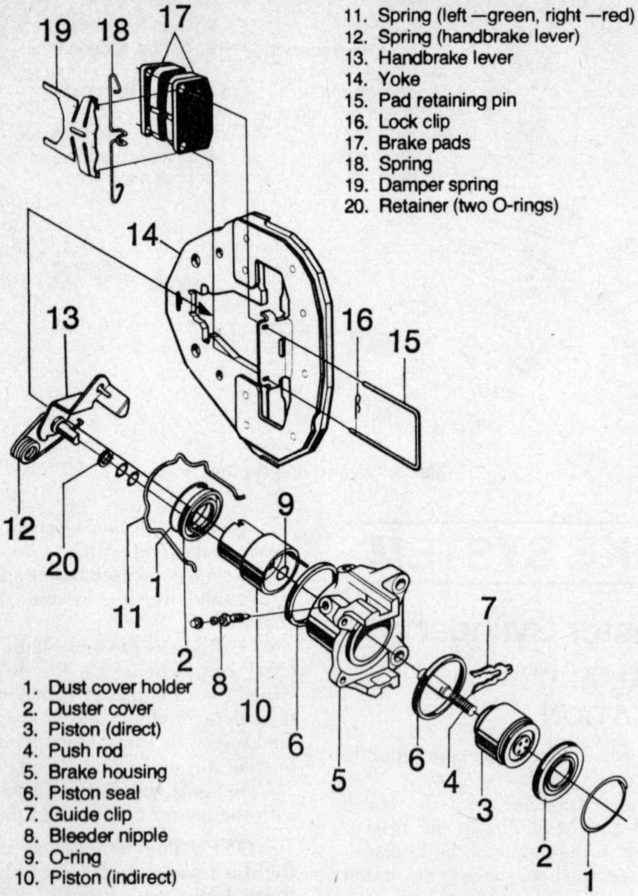

1. Dust cover holder
2. Duster cover
3. Piston (direct)
4. Push rod
5. Brake housing
6. Piston seal
7. Guide clip
8. Bleeder nipple
9. O-ring
10. Piston (indirect)
11. Spring (left—green, right—red)
12. Spring (handbrake lever)
13. Handbrake lever
14. Yoke
15. Pad retaining pin
16. Lock clip
17. Brake pads
18. Spring
19. Damper spring
20. Retainer (two O-rings)

Front brake assembly—exploded view (Girling type)

3. Disconnect the handbrake cable from the caliper assembly.
4. Remove the brake lines from the caliper assembly at the hose connection.
5. Remove the two bolts that hold the caliper assembly to the steering knuckle housing.
6. Remove the caliper assembly from the vehicle.
7. Installation is the reverse of removal. Adjust the handbrake as required.

OVERHAUL

1. Remove the return spring on the handbrake lever. Remove the yoke from the caliper assembly. Remove the spring and the handbrake lever.
2. Remove the dust cover retaining ring and the dust cover. Force out the indirect piston using compressed air.
3. Press the push rod so that the direct piston is separated from the cylinder.
4. Remove the O-rings and the seal rings from the piston and the cylinder bore.

NOTE: The O-ring retainer in the handbrake lever should only be removed if it is damaged.

5. Assembly is the reverse of disassembly.

NOTE: Check the clearance between the sliding surfaces of the yokes and the caliper assembly. Greater play can result in vibration and noises when braking.

Rear Disc Brakes

REMOVAL AND INSTALLATION

1. Raise the vehicle on a hoist and support it safely. Remove the wheels.

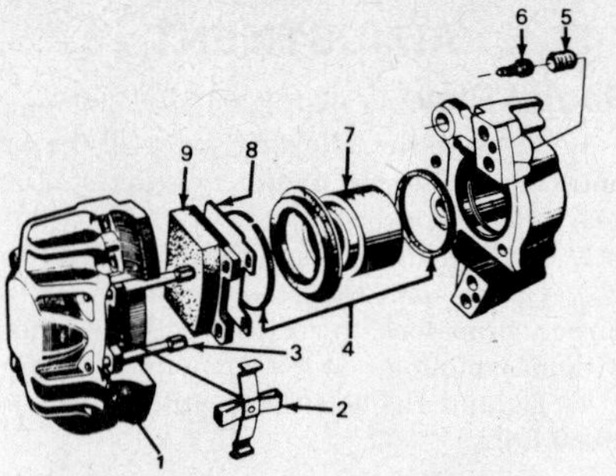

1. Brake housing
2. Damper spring
3. Lock pin
4. Piston seal
5. Rubber cap
6. Bleeder nipple
7. Piston
8. Twist stop
9. Brake pad

Rear brake assembly—exploded view (ATE type)

2. Rotate the brake disc so that one of the recesses in the edge of the disc is in line with the brake pads.
3. Remove the damper spring, pin retaining clip and the U-pin (Girling). Remove the cover plate, locking pins and the spring (ATE).
4. Remove the disc brake pads.
5. Installation is the reverse of removal. Adjust the handbrake cable as required on the Girling system.

Rear Caliper

REMOVAL AND INSTALLATION

1. Raise the vehicle on the hoist and support it safely. Remove the wheels.
2. Remove the disc brake pads.
3. Disconnect the brake lines at the caliper assembly.
4. Remove the bolts that hold the caliper assembly to the rear axle.
5. Remove the caliper assembly from the vehicle.
6. Installation is the reverse of removal.

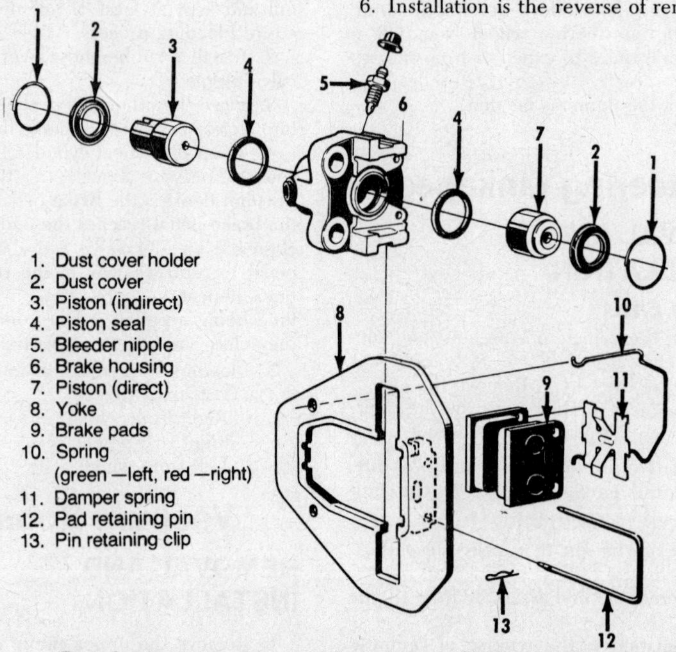

1. Dust cover holder
2. Dust cover
3. Piston (indirect)
4. Piston seal
5. Bleeder nipple
6. Brake housing
7. Piston (direct)
8. Yoke
9. Brake pads
10. Spring (green—left, red—right)
11. Damper spring
12. Pad retaining pin
13. Pin retaining clip

Rear brake assembly—exploded view (Girling type)

OVERHAUL

Girling

1. Remove the yoke from the caliper assembly by lifting it toward the bleeder screw. Remove the yoke spring.
2. Remove the retaining ring and the dust cover. Remove the indirect piston using compressed air.
3. Push out the direct piston. Remove the piston seals from the cylinder bore.
4. Assembly is the reverse of disassembly.

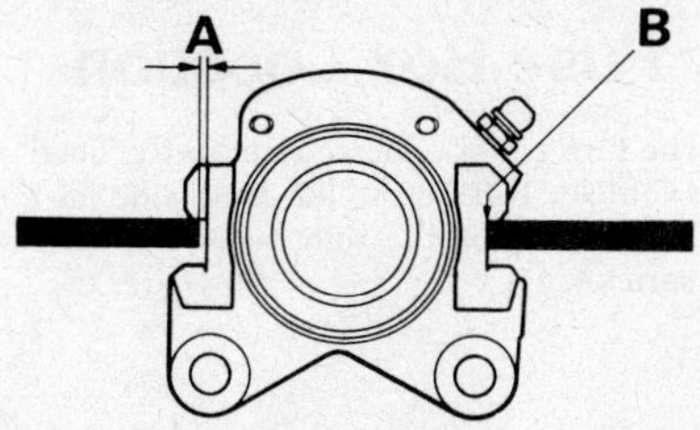

Brake housing clearance—front wheel (Girling type) A—.006-.012 inch; B—no clearance

NOTE: Check the clearance between the sliding surfaces of the yoke and the caliper assembly. Greater clearance than that specified can cause vibrations and noise when braking.

ATE

1. Secure a clamp to one of the pistons and press out the other piston using compressed air blown through the brake line connection.
2. Carefully remove the seal from the cylinder.

NOTE: Take care not to damage the sealing groove and the cylinder bore.

3. After the first seal and piston have been reinstalled, remove the other piston from the assembly. The removal method for both pistons is the same.

NOTE: The two sections of the caliper assembly should never be separated.

Parking Brake

ADJUSTMENT

Check the adjustment of the handbrake cable. Check the distance between the hand-

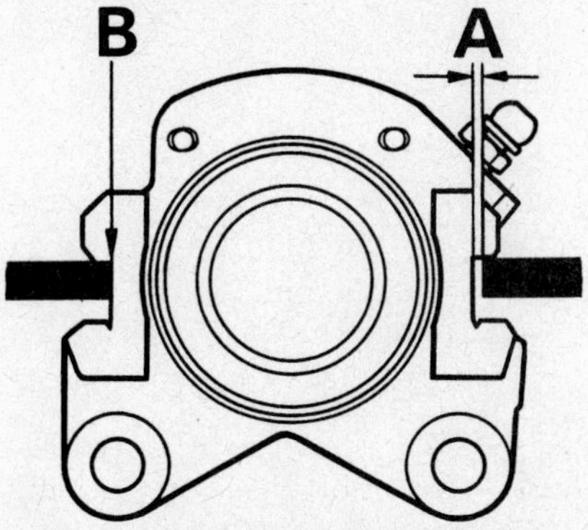

Brake housing clearance—rear wheel (Girling type) A—.006-.012 inch; B—no clearance

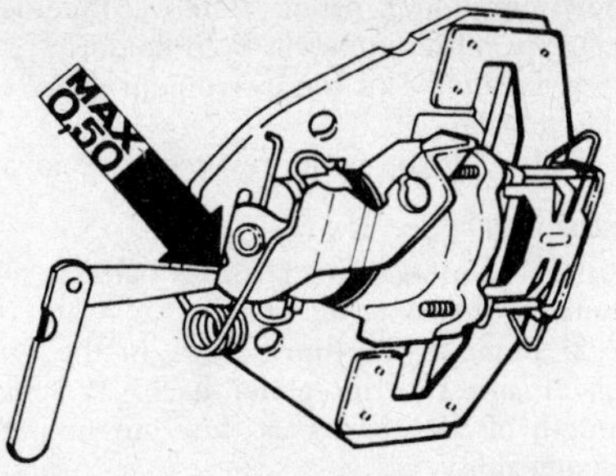

Parking brake adjustment procedure

brake lever and the yoke: the clearance should be a maximum 0.019 in. (0.50 mm) and should be equal on both sides. Adjust as necessary using the adjustment nut on the handbrake lever.

Note that the cables cross over, therefore the right-hand adjustment nut should be used to adjust the left-hand brake mechanism and vice versa.

CHASSIS ELECTRICAL

Heater Blower Motor

REMOVAL AND INSTALLATION

99 Series

1. Remove the windshield wiper motor assembly.
2. Disconnect the blower motor cables.
3. Remove the three blower motor retaining screws and pull the motor along with the impeller out of the housing carefully.
4. Separate the motor from the impeller at the rubber coupling. Remove the motor first, then the impeller.
5. Remove the plate with the fan bearing on the opposite side of the fan casing.
6. Installation is the reverse of removal.

Heater Core

REMOVAL AND INSTALLATION

99 Series

1. Drain the radiator. Remove the alternator and radiator fan relay.
2. Remove the front part of the fan casing. Unscrew the heater core retaining plate.
3. Remove the water valve cap, remove the control wire and the water valve retaining screws.
4. Loosen the hose clamps on the heater core and the water valve. Disconnect the hoses.
5. Disconnect the thermostat coil from the heater core and remove the water valve with its coil.
6. Remove the heater core from the thermostat housing.
7. Installation is the reverse of removal.

Radio

The radios used in Saab vehicles are dealer-installed or aftermarket units. It is therefore impossible to give specific procedures for removal and installation of these units. Care should be exercised when servicing a vehicle that has a radio problem.

Windshield Wiper Motor

REMOVAL AND INSTALLATION

99 Series

1. Remove the wiper arms from the wiper spindles.
2. Remove the nut that holds the steel tube to the wiper motor.
3. Release the wiper motor and remove the motor and the flexible cable. (Pull the cable out of the tube.)
4. Installation is the reverse of removal.

900 Series

1. Remove the wiper arms from the vehicle. Remove the rubber grommets.

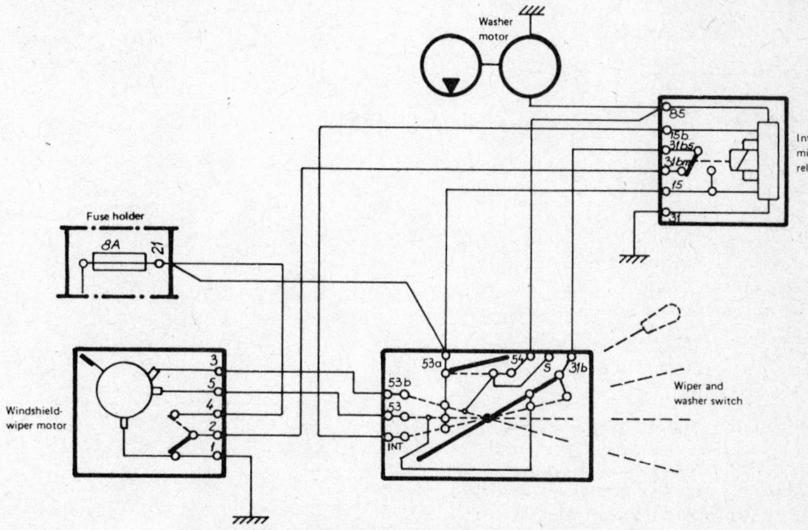

Windshield wiper/washer diagram—(900 series)

2. Remove the four screws and disconnect the lead. Remove the wiper unit from the vehicle.
3. Separate the wiper motor from the wiper assembly.
4. Installation is the reverse of removal.

Instrument Cluster

REMOVAL AND INSTALLATION

99 Series

1. Disconnect the negative battery cable. Remove the safety padding.
2. Remove the four screws that secure the panel.
3. Disconnect the speedometer wire and the electric wiring to the clock and combination instrument panel. Remove the instrument panel illumination bulb holder.
4. Carefully lift the instrument panel from the vehicle.
5. Installation is the reverse of removal.

900 Series

1. Disconnect the positive battery cable. Remove the steering wheel.
2. Remove the four screws in the switch panel and tilt the panel back. Watch the length of the screws as they are not interchangeable.
3. Remove the left speaker/defroster grille. Pull apart the instrument panel connectors. Disconnect the speedometer cable.
4. Remove the instrument panel retaining screws. Carefully remove the unit from the vehicle.
5. Installation is the reverse of removal.

Ignition Switch

REMOVAL AND INSTALLATION

1. Disconnect the negative battery cable.
2. Remove the center console.
3. Disconnect the electrical connections from the switch.
4. Remove the assembly from the vehicle.
5. Installation is the reverse of removal.

Fuse Box Location

The fuse panel is located under the hood of the vehicle. It is on the left-hand side for the 900 series and on the right hand side for the 99 series.

SPECIFICATIONS

INDEX

BEFORE SERVICING, SEE THE SAFETY NOTICE ON THE CONTENTS PAGE

INTRODUCTION

Subaru vehicles are made by Fuji Heavy Industries, Ltd., of Japan. There is a full range of body styles, with coupe, sedan, wagon, and pickup-style models. Notable features include four-wheel independent suspension, a horizontally opposed flat four watercooled engine, front-wheel drive, and a parking brake operating on the front wheels. Automatic, four, and five-speed manual transmissions are available.

Three four-wheel drive models are available, the 2 door hatchback (1980), the station wagon and the pickup-style BRAT (Bi-drive-Recreational-All-Terrain vehicle). These are normally front-wheel drive vehicles, with a rear-wheel drive system that can be engaged as necessary.

A 1400 cc engine was used through 1976 and a 1600 cc version starting 1976. The 1800 cc engine was introduced in 1980. All engines have emission systems designed to allow the use of regular leaded fuel through 1979 with the exception of the 1979 California cars which require unleaded fuel. 1980 cars, with or without a catalytic converter require unleaded fuel.

SERIAL NUMBER IDENTIFICATION

The Vehicle Identification Number is stamped on a tab located on the top of the dashboard on the driver's side, visible through the windshield. The Vehicle Identification Plate is on the bulkhead in the engine compartment. The engine number is stamped on the crankcase, behind the distributor.

VEHICLE IDENTIFICATION

Year	Model	Body Type	Transmission Type		Serial Number		
1975	1400 DL	2-dr sedan	4-speed	A22L	923001	to	924000
			automatic	A22L	102001	and	after
		4-dr sedan	4-speed	A22L	819001	to	819500
			automatic	A22L	602001	and	after
		2-dr coupe	4-speed	A22L	726001	and	after
			5-speed	A22L	402001	to	404000
			automatic	A22L	202001	and	after
		station wagon	4-speed	A62L	725001	to	735500
			automatic	A62L	602001	and	after
	1400 GF	hardtop	4-speed	A22L	020001	and	after
			5-speed	A22L	002001	and	after
			automatic	A22L	302001	and	after
	1400 4WD	station wagon	4-wheel drive	A64L	802001	and	after
1976	1400 STD	2-dr sedan	4-speed	A22L	924001	and	after
	1400 DL	2-dr sedan	4-speed	A22L	924001	and	after
		4-dr sedan	4-speed	A22L	819501	and	after
		2-dr coupe	5-speed	A22L	404001	and	after
		station wagon	4-speed	A62L	735501	and	after
	1400 GF	hardtop	5-speed	A22L	005001	and	after
	1400 4WD	station wagon	4-wheel drive	A64L	806001	and	after
	1600 DL	2-dr sedan	automatic	A26L	106001	to	730000
		4-dr sedan	automatic	A26L	605001	to	610000
		station wagon	automatic	A66L	604001	to	609000
	1600 GF	hardtop	automatic	A26L	305001	to	309000
1977	1600 STD	2-dr sedan	4-speed	A26L	205001	to	209000
	1600 DL	2-dr sedan	4-speed	A26L	405001	to	409000
			automatic	A26L	730001	to	732000
		4-dr sedan	4-speed	A26L	505001	to	507000
			automatic	A26L	610001	to	612000
		2-dr coupe	5-speed	A26L	905001	to	909000
		station wagon	4-speed	A66L	705001	to	710000
			automatic	A66L	609001	to	612000
	1600 GF	hardtop	5-speed	A26L	805001	to	808000
			automatic	A26L	309001	to	310000
	1600 4WD	station wagon	4-wheel drive	A67L	002001	to	010000

VEHICLE IDENTIFICATION

Year	Model	Body Type	Transmission Type		Serial Number		
1978	1600 STD	2-dr sedan	4-speed	A26L	209001	to	215000
	1600 DL	2-dr sedan	4-speed	A26L	409001	to	419000
			automatic	A26L	732001	to	739000
		4-dr sedan	4-speed	A26L	507001	to	511000
			5-speed	A26L	662001	to	670000
			automatic	A26L	612001	to	618500
		2-dr coupe	5-speed	A26L	909001	to	915500
		station wagon	4-speed	A66L	710001	to	716500
			5-speed	A66L	302001	to	313000
			automatic	A66L	612001	to	619000
	1600 GF	hardtop	5-speed	A26L	808001	to	816500
			automatic	A26L	310001	to	314500
	1600 4WD	station wagon	4-wheel drive	A67L	010001	to	047000
1979	1600 STD	2-dr sedan	4-speed	A26L	215001	and	after
	1600 DL	2-dr sedan	4-speed	A26L	419001	and	after
			automatic	A26L	739001	and	after
		4-dr sedan	4-speed	A26L	511001	and	after
			5-speed	A26L	670001	and	after
			automatic	A26L	618501	and	after
		2-dr coupe	5-speed	A26L	915501	and	after
		station wagon	4-speed	A66L	716501	and	after
			5-speed	A66L	313001	and	after
			automatic	A66L	619001	and	after
			4-wheel drive	A67L	047000	and	after
		BRAT (M.P.V.)	4-wheel drive	A69L	026001	and	after
	1600 FE	2-dr coupe	5-speed	A26L	670001	and	after
	1600 GF	hardtop	5-speed	A26L	816501	and	after
			automatic	A26L	314501	and	after
	1600 GL	station wagon	4-wheel drive	A67L	502001	and	after
		BRAT (M.P.V.)	4-wheel drive	A69L	502001	and	after
1980	1600 STD	2 dr-sedan	4-speed	AF21FAG	002001	and	after
		2-dr sedan with converter	4-speed	AF21FAG	802001	and	after
		2-dr sedan	4-wheel drive	AF31FAG	702001	and	after
	1600 DL	hardtop	5-speed	AW21FAG	502001	and	after
		hardtop with converter	5-speed	AW21FAG	402001	and	after
		2 dr-sedan	5-speed	AF21FAG	202001	and	after
		2-dr sedan with converter	5-speed	AF21FAG	402001	and	after
		2-dr sedan	4-wheel drive	AF31FAG	702001	and	after
		4-dr sedan	4-speed	AB21FAG	002001	and	after
		4-dr sedan with converter	4-speed	AB21FAG	802001	and	after
		station wagon	4-speed	AM21AG	002001	and	after
		station wagon	4-wheel drive	AM31FAG	702001	and	after
		BRAT (M.P.V.)	4-wheel drive	A69L	041001	and	after
	1600 GL	4-dr sedan	4-wheel drive	AB21FAG	202001	and	after
		station wagon	5-speed	AM21FAG	202001	and	after
		station wagon	4-wheel drive	AM31FAG	702001	and	after
		BRAT (M.P.V.)	4-wheel drive	A69L	515001	and	after
	1600 GLF	hardtop	5-speed	AW21FAG	202001	and	after
	1800 DL	2-dr sedan	automatic	AF41FAG	502001	and	after

VEHICLE IDENTIFICATION

Year	Model	Body Type	Transmission Type		Serial Number		
	1800 GL	4-dr sedan	automatic	AB41FAG	502001	and	after
		station wagon	automatic	AM41FAG	502001	and	after
	1800 GLF	hardtop	automatic	AW41FAG	502001	and	after

ENGINE CODES

Year	Displacement (cm^3/cu. in.)	Transmission Type	Code
1975	1361/83.2	4-speed	EA63AF5, F6*
		5-speed	EA63AP3, P4*
		4-wheel drive	EA63EF2, F3*
		automatic	EA63AT5
1976	1361/83.2	4-speed	EA63AFA, FB*
		5-speed	EA63AP5, P6*
		4-wheel drive	EA63EF4, F5*
	1590/97	automatic	EA71AT, T2*
1977	1590/97	4-speed	EA71AF, F3, F2*
		5-speed	EA71AP, P3, P2*
		4-wheel drive	EA71EF, F3, F2*
		automatic	EA71AT4, T6, T5*
1978	1590/97	4-speed	EA71AA, AH, AK, AC*
		5-speed	EA71GA, GH, GK, GC*
		4-wheel drive	EA71WA, WH, WK, WC*
		automatic	EA71TA, TH, TK, TC*
1979	1595/97	4-speed	E71AA2, AK2, AC2*
		5-speed	E71AA2, AK2, AC2*
		5-speed (FE)	E71GA2A, GK2A
		4-wheel drive	E71WA2, WK2, WC2*
		automatic	E71TA2, TK2, TC2*
1980	1595/97	4-speed	E71AA3, GA3A, GK3A, AC3*
		5-speed	E71AA3, GA3A, GK3A, AK3, E71AC3*
		4-wheel drive	E71WA3, WA4, WK3, WK4, E71WC3, WC4*
	1800/109	automatic	E81TA, TK, TC*

* California vehicles only

GENERAL ENGINE SPECIFICATIONS

Year	Type	Displacement cu. in. (cc)	Carburetor	Horsepower @ rpm (SAE)	Torque @ rpm (SAE)	Bore and Stroke (in.)	Comp. Ratio	Normal Oil Pressure (psi)
1975	4 cylinder horizontally opposed	83.2 (1400)	2 bbl	58 @ 5200 ①	68 @ 2400 ②	3.35 x 2.36	9.0:1	36-57
1976	4 cylinder horizontally opposed	83.2 (1400)	2 bbl	58 @ 5200 ①	68 @ 2400 ②	3.35 x 2.36	8.5:1	36-57
	4 cylinder horizontally opposed	97 (1600)	2 bbl	67 @ 5200 ③	81 @ 2400 ④	3.62 x 2.36	8.5:1	36-57

GENERAL ENGINE SPECIFICATONS

Year	Type	Displacement cu. in. (cc)	Carburetor	Horsepower @rpm (SAE)	Torque @rpm (SAE)	Bore and Stroke (in.)	Comp. Ratio	Normal Oil Pressure (psi)
1977-81	4 cylinder horizontally opposed	97 (1600)	2 bbl	67 @ 5200	81 @ 2400	3.62 x 2.36	8.5:1	36-57
1980-81	4 cylinder horizontally opposed	109 (1800)	2 bbl	72 @ 4800	92 @ 2400	3.62 x 2.64	8.7:1	50-57

① 4WD: 56 @ 5200
② 4WD: 67 @ 2400
③ 4WD: 65 @ 5200
④ 4WD: 80 @ 2400

TUNE-UP SPECIFICATIONS

When analyzing compression test results, look for uniformity among cylinders, rather than specific pressures

Year	Engine Displacement (cu. in.)	SPARK PLUGS* Type	SPARK PLUGS* Gap (in.)	DISTRIBUTOR Point Dwell (deg)	DISTRIBUTOR Point Gap (in.)	Ignition Timing (deg)	Intake Valve Opens (deg)	Fuel Pump Pressure (psi)	Idle Speed (rpm)	VALVE CLEARANCE (in.) In	VALVE CLEARANCE (in.) Ex
1975	EA63 (1400)	BP6ES	.030	49-55	0.020	8B @ 800(M) 8B @ 900(A)	24B	1.8-2.6	800M 900A	0.012	0.014
1976	EA63 (1400)	BP6ES	.032	49-55	0.018	8B @ 900	24B	1.8-2.6	900	0.011	0.015
	EA71 (1600)	BP6ES	.032	49-55	0.018	8B @ 900	24B	1.8-2.6	900	0.011	0.015
1977-79	EA71 (1600)	BP6ES	.032	49-55 ②	0.018 ②	8B @ 850	24B	2.6	850 ①	0.010	0.014
1980-81	(1600)	BP6ES	.032	Electronic		8B @ 850	24B	2.6	850 ①	0.009	0.013
	(1800)	BP6ES	.032	Electronic		8B @ 850	24B	2.6	850 ①	0.009	0.013

NOTE: The underhood specifications sticker often reflects tune-up specification changes made in production. Sticker figures must be used if they disagree with those in this chart.
① California 900
② California—Electronic ignition
* OEM spark plugs or NGK.
B —Before top dead center
M—Manual transmission
A —Automatic transmission

FIRING ORDER

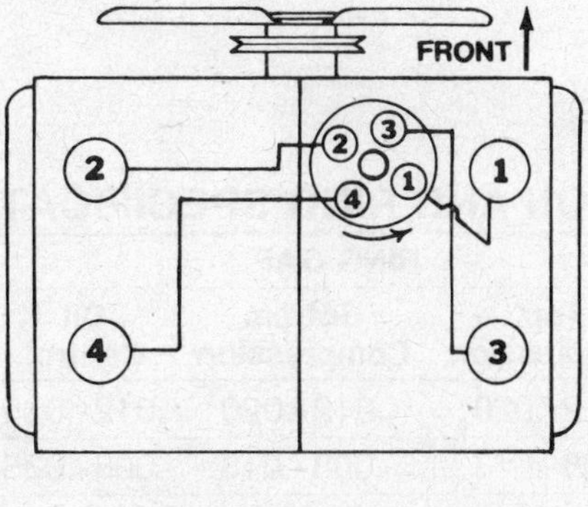

Firing order is 1-3-2-4

CRANKSHAFT AND CONNECTING ROD SPECIFICATIONS

All measurements are given in inches

Year	Engine	CRANKSHAFT Main Brg. Journal Dia.	CRANKSHAFT Main Brg. Oil Clearance	CRANKSHAFT Shaft End-Play	CRANKSHAFT Thrust On. No.	CONNECTING ROD Journal Diameter	CONNECTING ROD Oil Clearance	CONNECTING ROD Side Clearance
1975	1400	1.9688-1.9692	0.001-0.002	0.0019-0.0054	2	1.7715-1.7720	0.001-0.003	0.0028-0.0118
1976	1400, 1600	1.9667-1.9673 ①	0.0004-0.0020 ②	0.0016-0.0054	2	1.7715-1.7720	0.0012-0.0029	0.0028-0.0130
1977-81	1600	1.9667-1.9673 ①	0.0004-0.0016 ③	0.0016-0.0054	2	1.7715-1.7720	0.0008-0.0028	0.0028-0.0130
1980-81	1800	2.1636-2.1642	0.0004-0.0012 ④	0.0016-0.0054	2	1.7715-1.7720	0.0008-0.0028	0.0028-0.0130

① Center: 1.9673-1.9677 inch
② Center: 0.0000-0.0014 inch
③ 1977-79 center: 0-0.0018
1980-81: 0.0004-0.0014 with the center: 0.0004-0.0010
④ Center: 0.0004-0.0010

VALVE SPECIFICATIONS

Year	Engine Year	Seat Angle (deg)	Face Angle (deg)	Spring Test Pressure (lbs.) Inner	Spring Test Pressure (lbs.) Outer	Spring Compressed Height (in.) Inner	Spring Compressed Height (in.) Outer	Stem-to-Guide Clearance (in.) ▲ Intake	Stem-to-Guide Clearance (in.) ▲ Exhaust	Stem Diameter (in.) Intake	Stem Diameter (in.) Exhaust
1975-76	1400	45	45	40-47 @ 1.16	91-105 @ 1.25	1.01	1.16	.0014-.0026	.0020-.0032	.3130-.3136	.3124-.3130
1976	1600	45	45	39-45 @ 1.16	88-101 @ 1.25	1.16	1.25	.0014-.0026	.0020-.0032	.3130-.3136	.3124-.3130
1977-79	1600	45	45	43-50 @ 1.10	91-105 @ 1.22	1.008	1.16	.0015-.0026	.0016-.0028	.3130-.3136	.3128-.3134
1980-81	1600	45	45	42-48 @ 1.22	112-127 @ 1.201	—	1.20	.0014-.0026	.0016-.0028	.3130-.3136	.3128-.3134
1980-81	1800	45	45	42-48 @ 1.22	112-127 @ 1.201	—	1.20	.0014-.0026	.0016-.0028	.3130-.3136	.3128-.3134

▲ Valve guides are removable

PISTON AND RING SPECIFICATIONS

Year	Engine	Piston Clearance	Ring Gap Top Compression	Ring Gap Bottom Compression	Ring Gap Oil Control	Ring Side Clearance Top Compression	Ring Side Clearance Bottom Compression	Ring Side Clearance Oil Control
1975-79	1400, 1600	.001-.002	.012-.020	.012-.020	.012-.035	.001-.003	.001-.003	None
1980-81	1600	.001-.002	.008-.013	.008-.013	.008-.035	.001-.003	.001-.003	None
1980-81	1800	.001-.002	.008-.013	.008-.013	.008-.035	.001-.003	.001-.003	None

TORQUE SPECIFICATIONS

All readings in ft. lbs.

Year	Engine	Cylinder Head Bolts	Rod Bearing Bolts	Crankcase Halves	Crankshaft Pulley Bolt	Flywheel To Crankshaft Bolt	MANIFOLD Intake	MANIFOLD Exhaust
1975-81	1400, 1600, 1800	37-43 ① ②	29-31	10 mm bolts 29-35 8 mm bolts 17-19 6 mm bolts 3-4	39-42	30-33	13-16	12-15

① 1975-78; 1600 cc (1st step) 14 ft. lbs.
(2nd step) 25-29 ft. lbs.
(3rd step) 37-43 ft. lbs.

② 1979-81; 1600 cc 1980-81; 1800 cc (1st step) 22 ft. lbs.
(2nd step) 43 ft. lbs.
(3rd step) 47 ft. lbs.

TORQUE SEQUENCES

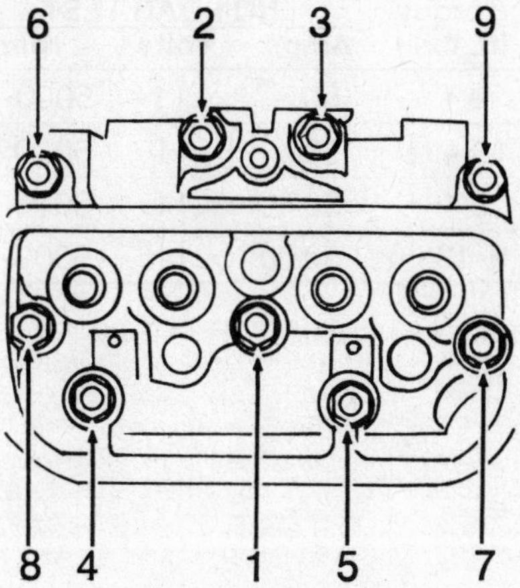

Cylinder head, 1975

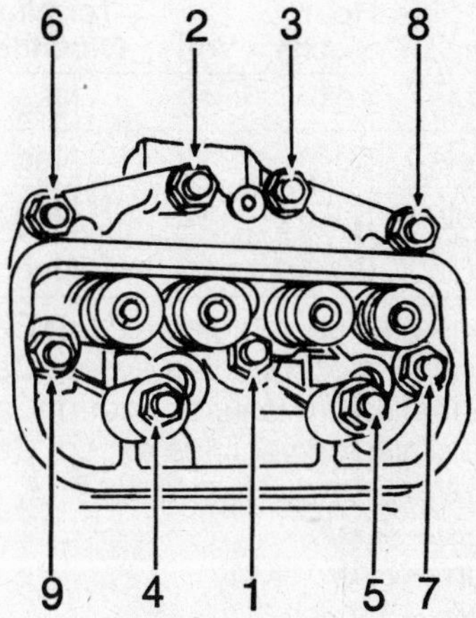

Cylinder head, 1976-79

CAPACITIES

Year	Model	Engine Displacement cu. in. (cc)	Engine Crankcase (qts.) With Filter	Engine Crankcase (qts.) Without Filter	Transmission (pts.) Manual 4-spd	Transmission (pts.) Manual 5-spd	Transmission (pts.) Automatic▲	4WD• Transaxle (pts)	Gasoline Tank (gals)	Cooling System (qts) W/ AC	Cooling System (qts) W/O AC
1975	1400 series	1400	3.8	3.5	5.2	5.8	12.5	2.5	13.2 ③	—	6.5
1976	1400 series	1400	3.8	3.5	5.2	5.8	—	2.5	13.2 ③	—	6.5
1976	1600 series	1600	3.8	3.5	—	—	12.5	—	13.2 ③	—	6.3
1977-79	1600 series	1600	3.8	3.5	5.2	5.8	12.5	2.5	13.2 ③	—	6.3
1980-81	1600 series 1800 series	1600 1800	3.8 ④	3.5	5.8	5.8	12.5	2.5	13.2 ③	—	11.2

① Station Wagon—9.5 gal.
② Station Wagon—11.8 gal.
③ Station Wagon—11.9 gal.
④ Automatic trans—4.3 qts.
• Rear differential capacity is 1.7 pts.
▲ Final gear box capacity is 2.5 pts.
— Not Applicable

ALTERNATOR AND REGULATOR SPECIFICATIONS

			REGULATOR							
			CHARGE RELAY				VOLTAGE REGULATOR			
Year	Model	Alternator Output (amps) @ 12 Volts	Yoke Gap (in.)	Core Gap (in.)	Point Gap (in.)	Volts to Open	Yoke Gap (in.)	Core Gap (in.)	Point Gap (in.)	Volts @ 1200 & 75°
1975-76	all models	50	.035	.032-.039	.016-.024	8-10	.035	.024-.039	.012-.016	14.0
1977-79	all models	50	.035	.032-.039	.016-.024	8-10	.035	.024-.039	.014-.018	14.0
1980-81	all models	50 ①	.035	.032-.039	.016-.024	8-10	.035	.024-.039	.014-.018	14.0

① 1980 station wagon 4WD GL: 55A

BATTERY AND STARTER SPECIFICATIONS

		BATTERY			LOCK TEST			NO LOAD TEST			
Year	Model	Amp-Hour Capacity	Volts	Terminal Grounded	Amps	Volts	Torque (ft. lbs.)	Amps	Volts	rpm	Brush Spring Tension (oz.)
1975	all models	50	12	Neg	470	7.7	9.4	50	11	5000	35-54
1976	all models	50	12	Neg	700 ①	7.7 ②	9.4 ③	50	11	5000	35-54
1977-79	all models	50	12	Neg	600	7.7 ②	9.4 ③	50 ④	11	5000	37-47.6
1980-81	all models	60 ⑤	12	Neg	600 ⑥	7.7 ⑦	9-13 ⑧	50 ⑨	11	5000 ⑩	37-47.6

① Automatic transmission vehicles except California—600
② Automatic transmission vehicles except California—7.0
③ Automatic transmission vehicles except California—13.0
④ Automatic transmission vehicles except California—60
⑤ Optional—65A
⑥ Gear reduction—400A
⑦ Gear reduction—2.4V
⑧ Gear reduction—8 ft. lbs.
⑨ Gear reduction—90A
⑩ Gear reduction—4100 rpm

BRAKE SPECIFICATIONS

All measurements given are (in.) unless noted

				BRAKE DISC		BRAKE DRUM			MINIMUM LINING THICKNESS	
Year	Model	Lug Nut Torque (ft. lbs.)	Master Cylinder Bore	Minimum Thickness	Maximum Run-Out	Diameter	Maximum Machine O/S	Maximum Wear Limit	Front	Rear
1975	DL Sedan & Wagon	40-54	.75	—	—	9.01-F 7.09-R	9.08-F 7.17-R	9.08-F 7.17-R	.04-P .06-S	.06
	GL & GF Coupe	40-54	.75	.33	.006	7.09	7.17	7.17	.06	.06
1976-79	All Models	58-72	.75	.33	.006	7.09	7.17	7.17	.06	.06
1980-81	All Models	58-72	.8125	.394	.0039	7.09	7.17	7.17	.295 ①	.06

NOTE: Minimum lining thickness is as recommended by the manufacturer. Because of variations in state inspection regulations, the minimum allowable thickness may be different than recommended by the manufacturer.

① Includes back metal
F—Front
R—Rear
P—Primary
S—Secondary

REAR END ALIGNMENT

Year	Model	Body Type	Ride* Height (in.)	Camber (deg)	Toe-In (in.)	Tracking (in.) ▲
1975-76	DL, GL, GF	Sedan, Coupe, H.T.	11.3-11.9	¼P-1½P	.04-.20	−.12-+.12
	DL	Wagon	12.2-12.8	1P-2P	.08-.24	−.12-+.12
	4WD	Wagon	14.2-14.8	1½P-2¼P	.08-.24	0-+.16
1977-79	DL, GL, GF	Sedan, Coupe, H.T.	11.2-12.0	¼N-1P	.04-.20	−.12-+.12
	DL	Wagon	12.2-13.0	¼P-2P	.08-.24	−.12-+.12
	4WD	Wagon	13.6-14.4	½P-2P	.08-.24	0-+.16
1980-81	exc. 4WD	Sedan, H.T.	10.2-11.0	¾N-¾P	—	−.20-+.20
	exc. 4WD	Station Wagon	11.0-11.8	¾N-¾P	—	−.20-+.20
	4WD	Sedan	12.6-13.4	¾N-¾P	—	−.20-+.20
	4WD	exc. Sedan	13.1-13.9	⅓N-1P	—	−.20-+.20

* Measured from outer center of torsion bar
▲ Measured with one passenger aboard

WHEEL ALIGNMENT

Year	Model	CASTER ① Range (deg)	CASTER ① Pref. Setting (deg)	CAMBER ① Range (deg)	CAMBER ① Pref. Setting (deg)	Toe-In (in.)
1975-76	Sedan, Coupe, H.T.	0-1½P	¾P	1P-2P	1½P	.08-0.32
	Station Wagon	0-1½P	¾P	1P-2P	1½P	.08-0.32
	4WD	0-1½P	¾P	2P-3P	2½P	.24-0.47
1977-79	Sedan, Coupe, H.T.	1½N-5N	3¼N	¾P-2¼P	1½P	.08-0.32
	Station Wagon	1N-½P	¼N	1P-2½P	1P	.08-0.32
	4WD	1½N-5N	3¼N	1½P-3P	2¼P	.24-0.47
1980-81	Sedan and H.T.	1⅙N-⅓P	—	¾P-2¼P	—	.08-0.31
	Station Wagon	⅚N-⅔P	—	1P-2½P	—	.08-0.31
	Sedan 4WD	1¼N-¼P	—	1⅚P-3⅓P	—	.24-0.47
	4WD	1⅓N-1/12P	—	1⅚P-3⅓P	—	.24-0.47

① Not adjustable—MacPherson Strut

TUNE-UP PROCEDURES

Spark Plugs

NOTE: Number the spark plug wires before removing them.

1. Using a spark plug wrench, remove all of the spark plugs.
2. Check them for damage or wear and clean or replace them.
3. Set the gap between the two electrodes, using a spark plug gap gauge.
4. Install the spark plugs in the engine, tightening to 13-17 ft/lbs.

Breaker Points and Condenser

1. To replace the points, remove the hold-down screws, the ground lead and the condenser lead.
2. Lift out the point assembly and insert the new assembly.

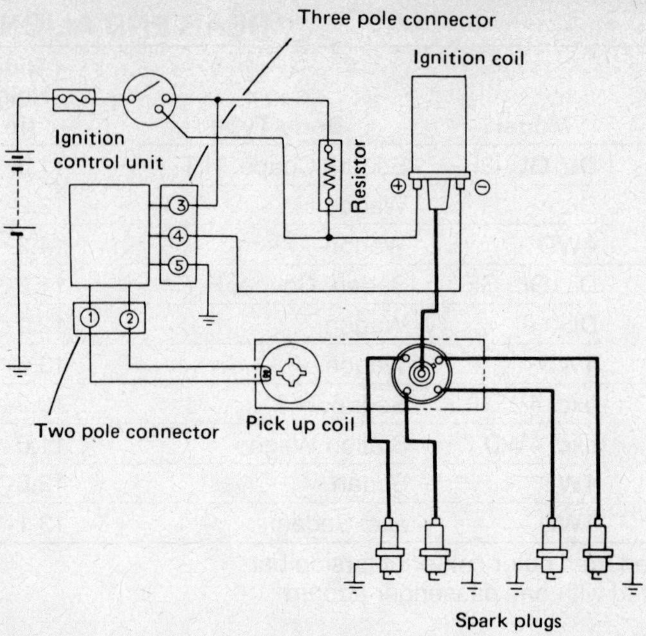

Ignition circuit using breakerless type distributor—California models only, 1977 and later

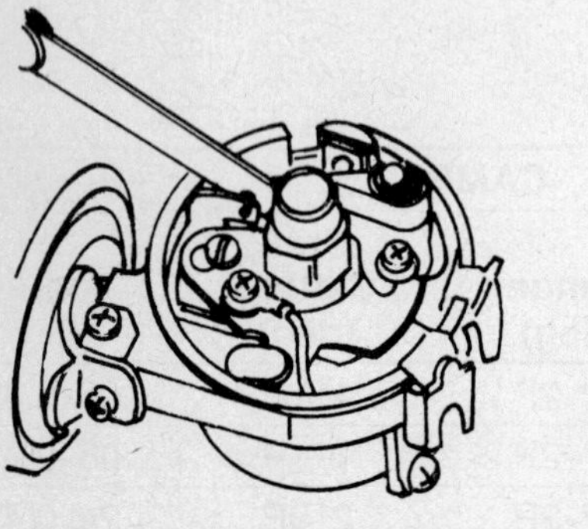

Checking the breaker point gap

NOTE: Always replace the condenser when replacing the points.

3. Install the hold-down screws and the leads in their proper positions. Do not tighten the attaching screws, just leave them snug so the point gap can be adjusted.
4. Adjust the gap by placing the proper size feeler gauge between the contacts and turning the adjusting eccentric with a screwdriver.
5. The breaker point arm must be on a high point of the cam. Turn the eccentric screw until there is a slight drag when the gauge is drawn through the gap.
6. Lubricate the cam surface with cam lube.
7. Replace the distributor cap, making sure that the spark plug wires are installed tightly in the top of the cap.

Dwell Angle

1. Hook up a dwell meter according to the manufacturer's instructions. Start the engine and read the dwell on the meter. If the dwell is correct, then shut off the engine and remove the dwell meter.
2. If the dwell must be adjusted, shut off the engine, remove the distributor cap and adjust the point gap.
3. Open the points to decrease the dwell, close them to increase the dwell.
4. Replace the cap and start the engine. Check the dwell. If it is correct, shut off the engine and remove the dwell meter. If the dwell is not correct, repeat the above steps.

Breakerless Distributor

1977 through 1979, California engines and all 1980 engines have a breakerless distributor. The centrifugal advance, vacuum advance, and retard units are the same as with the conventional distributor.

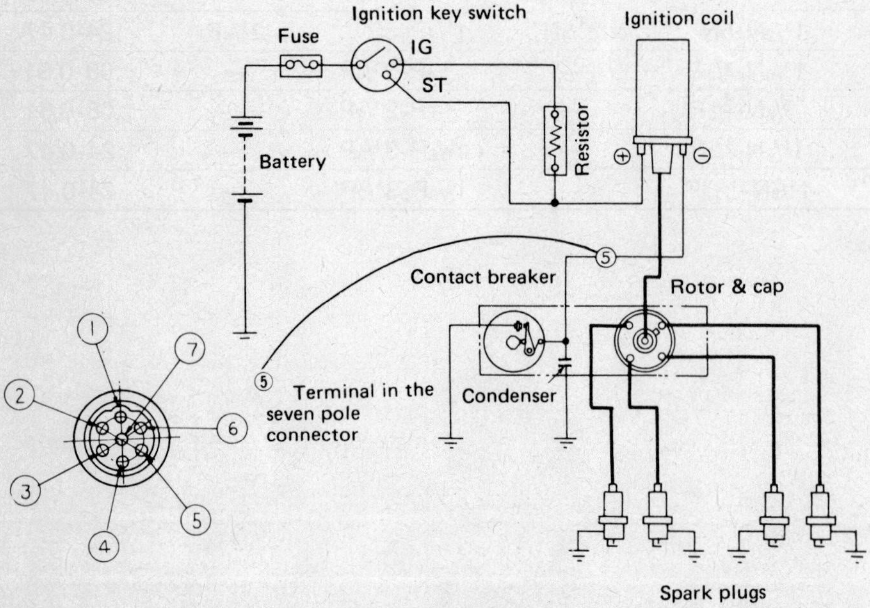

Ignition circuit using breaker points—49 states, high altitude and 1975-76 California

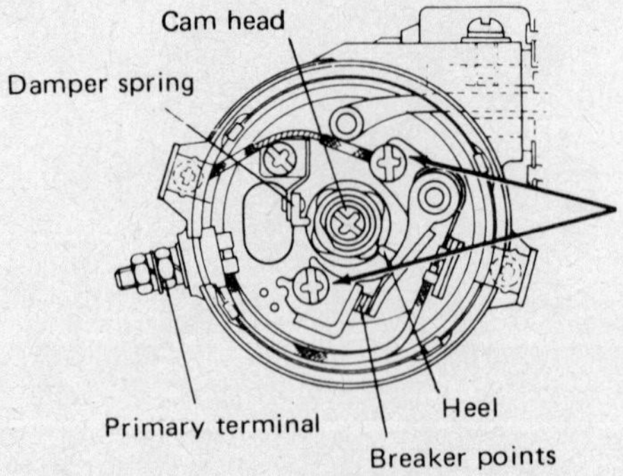

Components of distributor plate—typical

The air gap between the reluctor and pick-up coil is adjustable; it should be 1977 through 1979 California manual transmission vehicles and 1980 and later except 4WD vehicles; .008-.016: 1977 through 1979 California automatic transmission vehicles and 1980 4WD vehicles; .012-.016. The ignition timing should be checked if the air gap is changed.

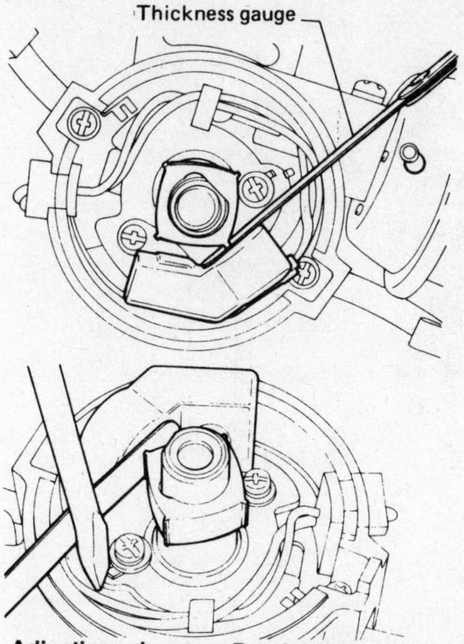

Adjusting air gap—Breakerless distributor

Ignition Timing

The ignition timing marks are located on the edge of the flywheel, graduated in 2° increments from 0° to 16°. The marks are visible through a port in the flywheel housing, just behind the dipstick. There is usually a plastic cap in the opening. Set the timing with the engine at normal operating temperature.

NOTE: If your vehicle is equipped with electronic ignition, an inductive timing light is recommended because it is not susceptible to crossfiring or false triggering due to the greater voltage.

1. After cleaning the timing marks, hook a timing light to the positive battery terminal and the number one spark plug. Disconnect and plug the distributor vacuum retard line.
2. Start the engine and aim the timing light at the timing marks on the flywheel.

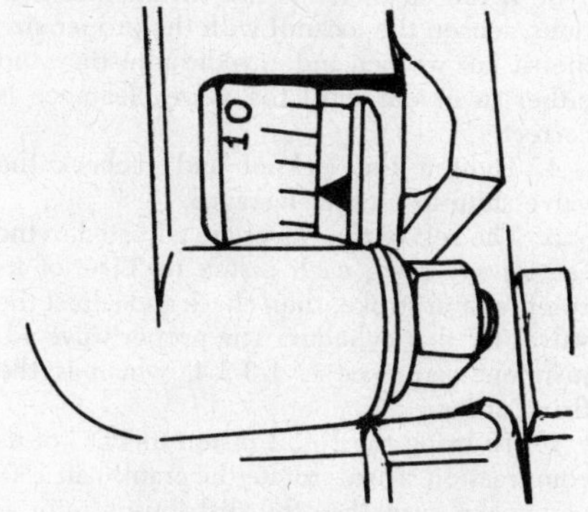

Ignition timing marks

3. Adjust the ignition timing by loosening the bolt on the distributor retaining plate, and rotating the distributor clockwise to advance or counterclockwise to retard the timing.

Valve Lash

Valve Lash Adjustment

Before adjusting the valves, make sure the cylinder head nuts/bolts are torqued (tightened) to the proper specifications. To torque the head and intake manifold nuts/bolts, use the following procedure.

1. Make sure the engine is cold.
2. Remove the valve covers from both sides of the engine.
3. Loosen the three bolts holding the intake manifold on the right (#1-#3) side cylinder head (as viewed from the driver's seat). These bolts should be loosened no more than 60 degrees. Do not loosen the left side (#2-#4) intake manifold bolts.
4. Refer to the "Tightening Sequence Chart" for the correct pattern to use while checking and retorquing the cylinder head.

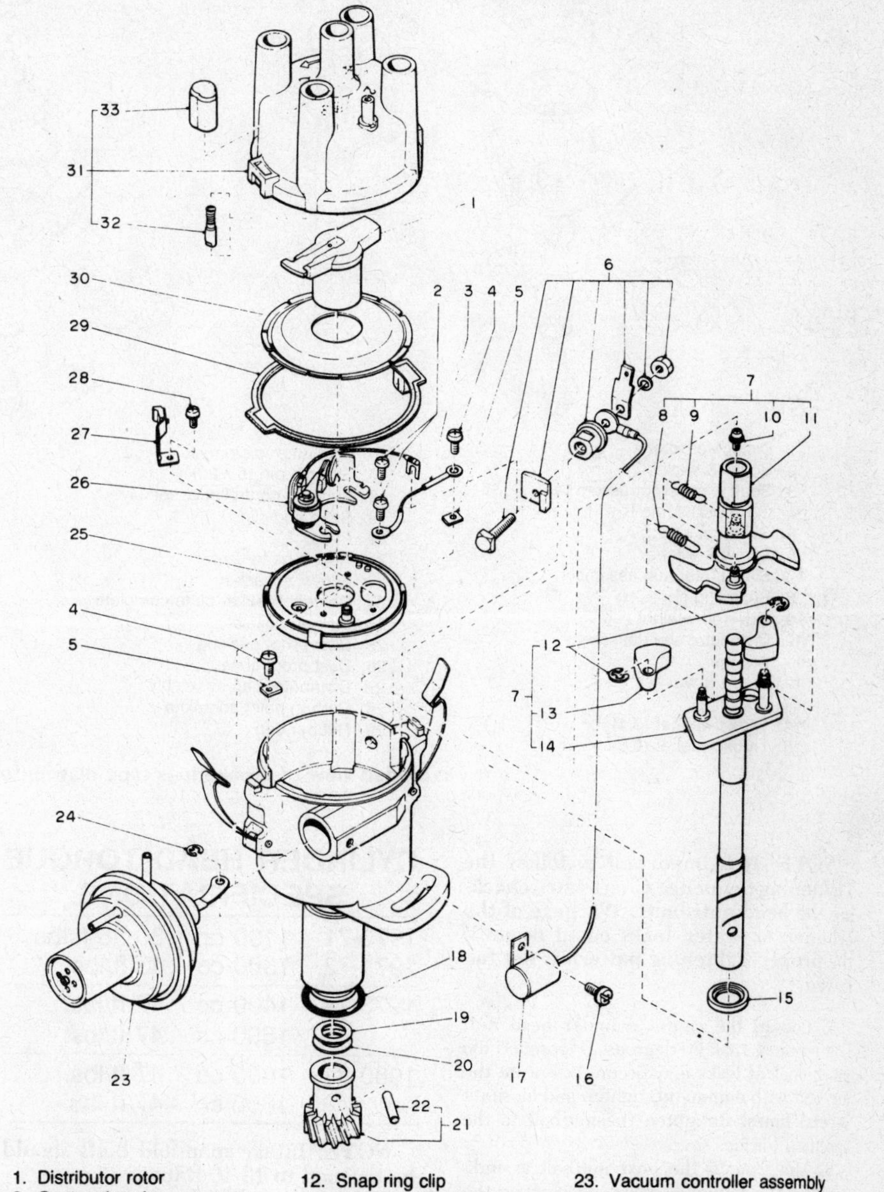

1. Distributor rotor
2. Contact breaker set screw
3. Distributor earth wire
4. Round head screw
5. Plate
6. Terminal set
7. Shaft and governor assembly
8. Governor spring B
9. Governor spring A
10. Screw & washer
11. Distributor cam assembly
12. Snap ring clip
13. Governor weight
14. Distributor shaft assembly
15. Washer
16. Screw & washer
17. Distributor condenser
18. "O" ring
19. Thrust washer (0.1)
20. Thrust washer (0.3)
21. Distributor pinion set
22. Straight pin (5 x 20)
23. Vacuum controller assembly
24. Snap ring clip
25. Contact breaker plate complete
26. Contact breaker set
27. Damper spring
28. Screw & washer
29. Dust proof packing
30. Dust proof
31. Distributor cap assembly
32. Carbon point complete
33. Rubber cap

Exploded view of conventional type distributor

1) For MT

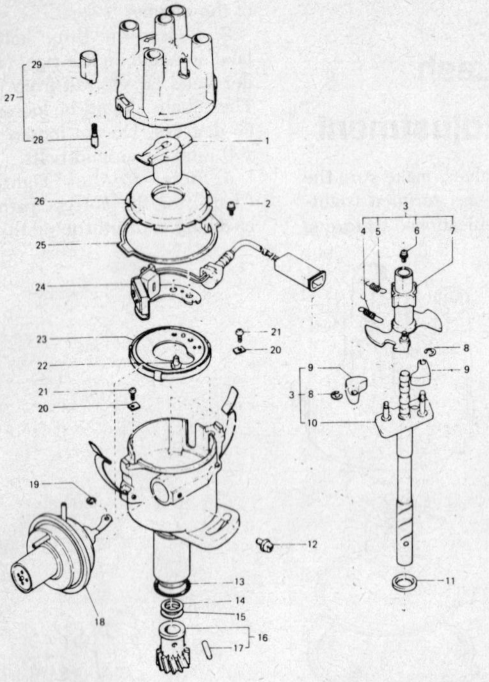

2) For AT

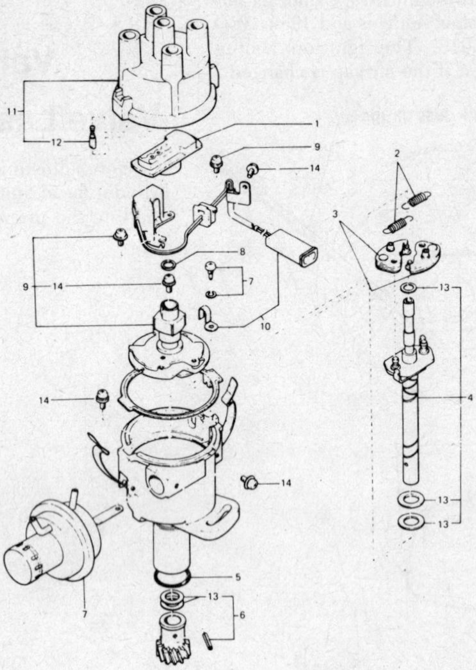

1. Distributor rotor
2. Screw & washer
3. Shaft & governor assembly
4. Governor spring B
5. Governor spring A
6. Screw & washer
7. Signal rotor sub assembly
8. Snap ring clip
9. Governor weight
10. Distributor shaft assembly
11. Washer
12. Screw & washer
13. "O" ring
14. Thrust washer (0.1)
15. Thrust washer (0.3)
16. Distributor pinion set
17. Straight pin (5 x 20)
18. Vacuum controller assembly
19. Snap ring clip
20. Plate
21. Round head screw
22. Screw & washer
23. Contact breaker plate complete
24. Pick-up coil set
25. Dust proof packing
26. Dust proof cover
27. Distributor cap assembly
28. Carbon point complete
29. Rubber cap

1. Rotor
2. Governor spring set
3. Weight
4. Shaft & governor assembly
5. "O" ring
6. Point set
7. Vacuum controller assembly
8. Dust proof packing
9. Contact breaker plate complete
10. Pick up coil set
11. Cap
12. Carbon point
13. Thrust washer
14. Screw kit

Exploded view of breakerless type distributor

NOTE: It is important to follow the Tightening Sequence Chart when checking the head nuts/bolts. Warpage of the cylinder or water leaks could occur if the proper tightening pattern is not followed.

5. Loosen the center cylinder head nut/bolt no more than 60 degrees. If loosened too much coolant leaks may occur. Lubricate the nut/bolt with engine oil, tighten and loosen it several times. Retighten the nut/bolt to the specified torque.

6. Move on to the next nut/bolt as indicated on the sequence chart and perform the same steps as before, proceed until all of the nuts/bolts have been tightened.

7. Go back to number one nut/bolt and recheck the torque, tighten if necessary. Recheck the rest of the nuts/bolts following the specified order.

8. After rechecking all the head nuts/ bolts ...ten the intake manifold bolts on the right ...#1-#3) cylinder head.
...ust the valve lash.

CYLINDER HEAD TORQUE SPECIFICATIONS

1970-71	1100 cc	30-35 ft/lbs.
1971-72	1300 cc	43 ft/lbs.
1973-79	1400 cc	47 ft/lbs.
	1600 cc	47 ft/lbs.
1980-81	1600 cc	47 ft/lbs.
	1800 cc	47 ft/lbs.

NOTE: Intake manifold bolts should be torqued to 13-16 ft/lbs.

TO ADJUST VALVE LASH;

1. Rotate the engine so that the No. 1 piston is at top dead center (TDC) of its compression stroke. To determine TDC, remove the distributor cap and the plastic flywheel housing dust cover. The No. 1 piston is at top dead center when the distributor rotor is pointing to No. 1 spark plug lead terminal (as though the distributor cap were in place) and the "O" mark on the flywheel is opposite the pointer on the housing.

2. Check the clearance of both the intake and exhaust valves of the No. 1 cylinder by inserting a feeler gauge between each valve stem and rocker arm. See the "Tune-Up Specifications" chart for the proper stem-to-rocker arm clearance.

3. If the clearance is not within specifications, loosen the locknut with the proper size metric box wrench and turn the adjusting stud either in or out until the valve clearance is correct.

4. Tighten the locknut and recheck the valve stem-to-rocker clearance.

5. The rest of the valves are adjusted in the same way; bring each piston to TDC of its compression stroke, then check and adjust the valves for that cylinder. The proper valve adjustment sequence is 1-3-2-4, which is the firing order.

6. To bring the No. 3 piston to TDC of its compression stroke, rotate the crankshaft 180° and make sure that the distributor rotor is pointing to the No. 3 spark plug terminal.

Rotate the crankshaft 180° after each valve adjustment before going on to the next adjustment.

7. When the valve adjustment is complete, install the distributor cap, the valve covers, and the dust cover on the flywheel housing port.

Carburetor

IDLE SPEED AND MIXTURE ADJUSTMENT

1. Run the engine and allow it to reach normal operating temperature.
2. Stop the engine and connect a tachometer in accordance with the manufacturer's instructions.
3. Disconnect and plug the hose that runs to the distributor vacuum retard unit.
4. Remove the air cleaner by disconnecting the emission control system hoses from it, unfastening the wing nut, and removing the screws which secure it to its mounting brackets.

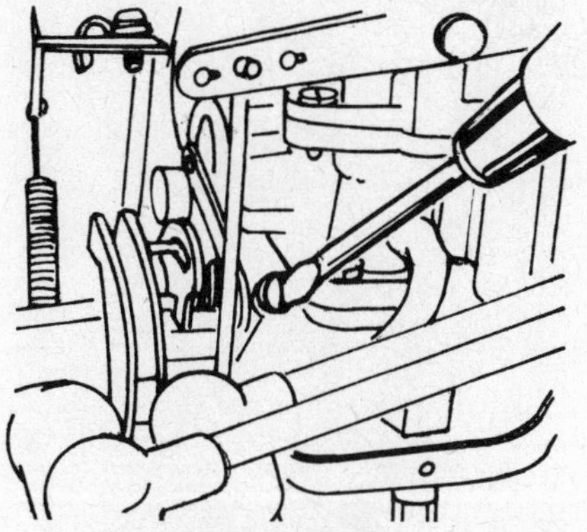

Throttle adjustment

5. Check proper idle speed in "Tune-Up Specifications" chart and adjust to that setting by turning the throttle adjusting screw.
6. Continue adjusting the idle, this time by means of the throttle adjusting screw and the idle mixture adjusting screw, until a reading of 50 rpm above the proper idle setting is attained.

NOTE: The idle mixture adjusting screw should have a plastic limiter cap on it; all adjustments must be made within the range of this cap or exhaust emissions will be increased. Do not remove the cap.

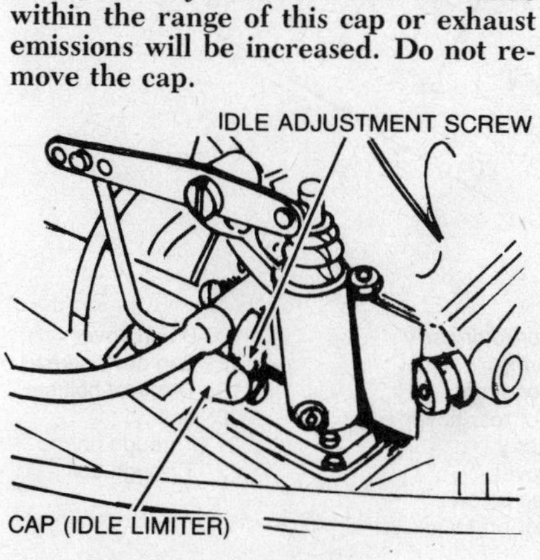

Idle mixture adjustment

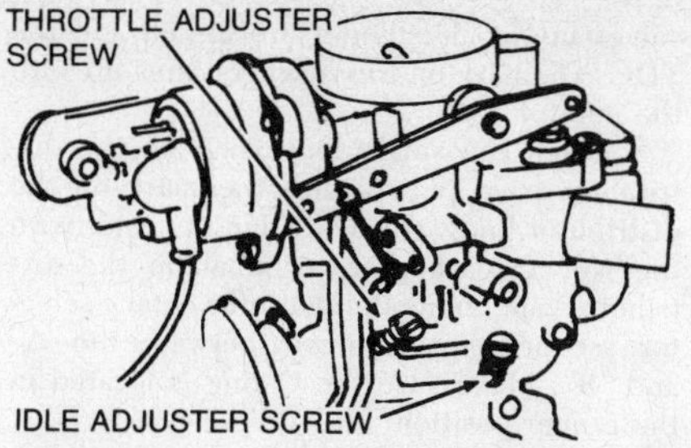

Throttle adjuster and idle adjuster screw locations

7. Then, turn the idle mixture adjusting screw *clockwise* until the idle speed drops to the figure given in the "Tune-Up Specifications" chart.

NOTE: Following this procedure should keep the carbon monoxide (CO) emission level within pollution law standards. However, it is a good idea to have the CO level checked by a qualified garage with an exhaust analyzer whenever a tune-up is performed.

8. Disconnect the tachometer. Reconnect the hoses to the air injection manifold (if equipped). Install the air cleaner.

ENGINE ELECTRICAL

Distributor

REMOVAL AND INSTALLATION

1. Remove the air cleaner assembly, taking note of the hose locations.
2. On models equipped with conventional ignition system, disconnect the primary wire at the coil. On models equipped with breakerless ignition, disconnect the distributor wiring connector from the vehicle wiring harness.
3. Note the positions of the vacuum line(s) on the distributor diaphragm, disconnect the

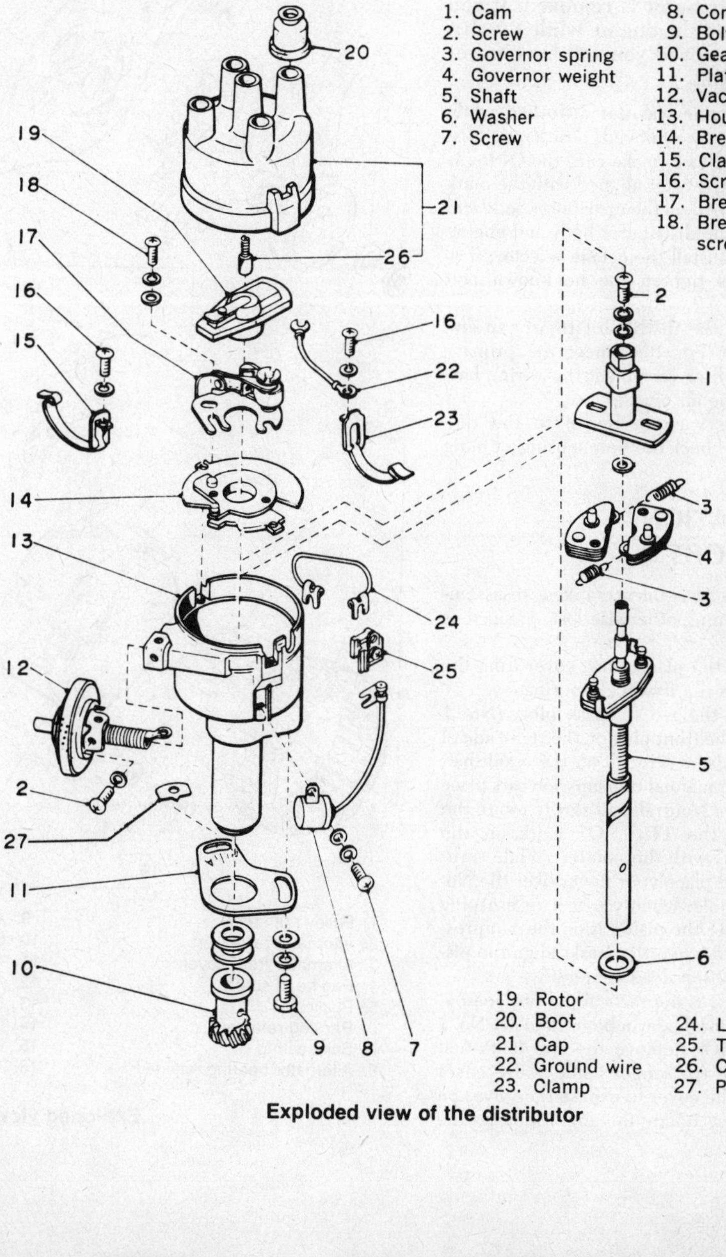

1. Cam
2. Screw
3. Governor spring
4. Governor weight
5. Shaft
6. Washer
7. Screw
8. Condenser
9. Bolt
10. Gear
11. Plate
12. Vacuum unit
13. Housing
14. Breaker plate
15. Clamp
16. Screw
17. Breaker points
18. Breaker point set screw
19. Rotor
20. Boot
21. Cap
22. Ground wire
23. Clamp
24. Lead wire
25. Terminal
26. Carbon brush
27. Pointer

Exploded view of the distributor

lines at the diaphragm. Unsnap the two distributor cap retaining clamps and remove the cap. Position the cap and ignition wires to one side.

NOTE: If it is necessary to remove the ignition wires from the cap to get enough room to remove the distributor, make sure to label each wire and the cap for easy and accurate reinstallation.

4. Use chalk or paint to carefully mark the position of the distributor rotor in relationship to the distributor housing and mark the position of the distributor housing in relationship to the engine block. When this is done, you should have a line on the distributor housing directly in line with the tip of the rotor and another line on the engine block directly in line with the mark on the distributor housing. This is very important because the distributor must be reinstalled in the exact same position from which it was removed, if correct ignition timing is to be maintained.

5. Remove the distributor hold-down bolt.

6. Remove the distributor from the engine, taking care not to damage or lose the O-ring.

NOTE: Do not disturb the engine while the distributor is removed. If you crank or rotate the engine while the distributor is removed you will have to retime the engine.

7. If the engine was not disturbed while the distributor was removed, position the distributor in the block (make sure the O-ring is in place) have the rotor aligned with the mark previously scribed on the distributor body and the marks on the distributor body and engine in alignment. Install the octane selector, if so equipped, and tighten the hold-down bolt finger tight.

8. Reinstall the distributor rotor, cap and wires, if removed. Reconnect the primary wire to the coil or reconnect the wiring harness. Install the air cleaner.

9. Plug the vacuum line(s) to the distributor and recheck the timing using a timing light.

INSTALLATION–TIMING LOST

If the engine has been cranked, disassembled or the timing otherwise lost, proceed as follows.

1. Remove the plastic dust cover from the timing port on the flywheel housing.

2. Remove the No. 1 spark plug. (No. 1 spark plug is the front plug on the right side of the engine). Use a wrench on the crankshaft pulley bolt (on manual transmission cars place transmission in Neutral) and slowly rotate the engine until the TDC "O" mark on the flywheel aligns with the pointer. While turning the engine place your finger over the No. 1 spark plug hole, when you feel air escaping past your finger the piston is on the compression stroke and when the marks align the piston is at TDC (top dead center).

2a. If Step 2 is impractical, for any reason, the following method can be used to get No. 1 piston on TDC. Remove the two bolts that hold the right (passenger's side) valve cover and remove the cover to expose the valves on No. 1 cylinder. Rotate the engine so that the valves in No. 1 cylinder are closed and the TDC "O" mark on the flywheel lines up with the pointer.

3. Align the small depression on the distributor drive pinion with the mark on the distributor body; this will align the rotor with the No. 1 spark plug terminal on the distributor cap. On models with the octane selector, set the pointer midway between the "A" and "R". Make sure the O-ring is located in the proper position.

4. Align the matchmarks you have made on the distributor body with those on the engine block and install the distributor in the engine. Make sure the drive is engaged. Install the hold-down bolt fingertight. Time the engine with a timing light.

Alternator

ALTERNATOR PRECAUTIONS

1. Pay particular attention to the polarity connections of the battery when connecting the battery cables. Make sure that you connect the correct cable to the corresponding terminal.

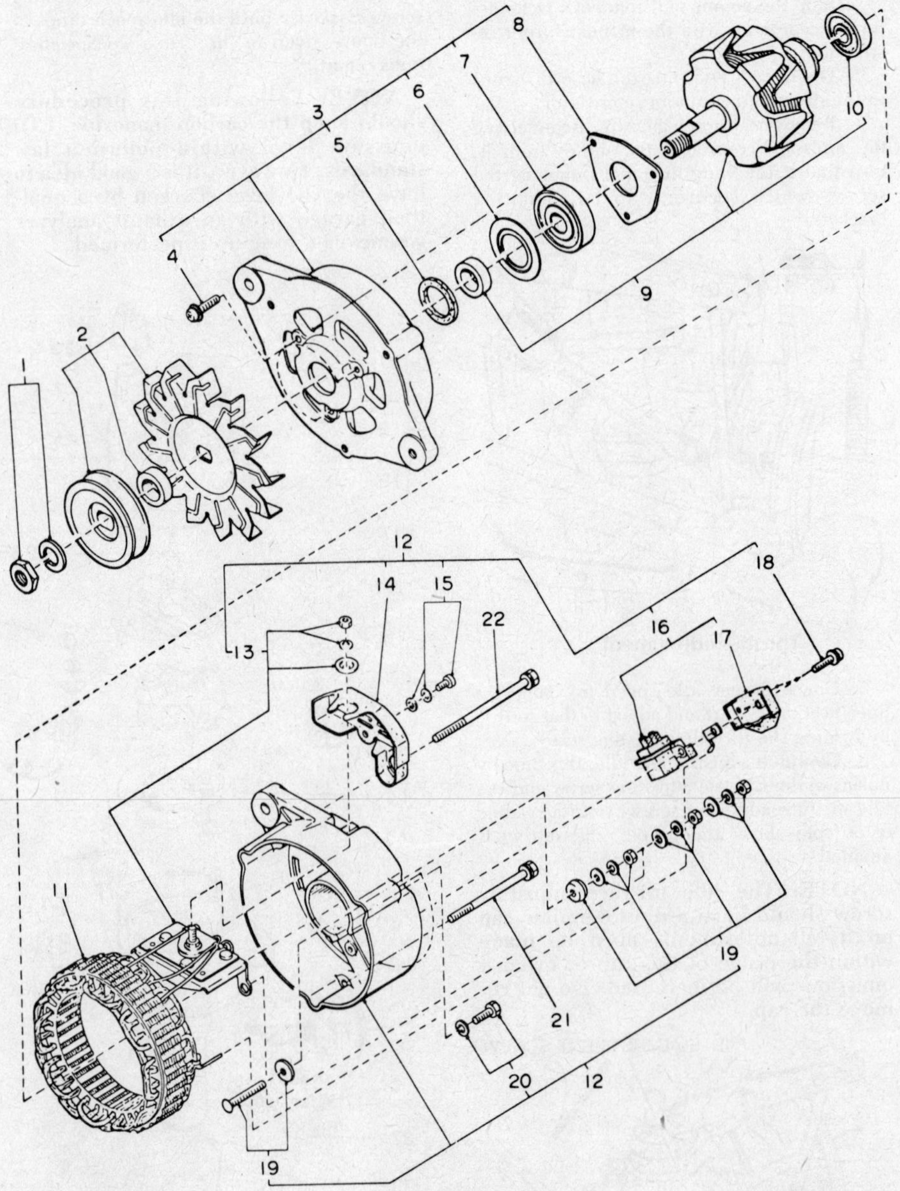

1. Pulley nut set
2. Alternator pulley set
3. Alternator front cover
4. Pan head screw
5. Packing
6. Packing retainer
7. Ball bearing
8. Alternator bearing retainer
9. Alternator rotor ass'y
10. Ball bearing
11. Alternator stator ass'y
12. Alternator rear cover ass'y
13. Diode ass'y
14. Diode cover
15. Pan head screw
16. Alternator brush ass'y
17. Brush cover
18. Pan head screw
19. Terminal bolt set
20. Bolt
21. Through bolt
22. Through bolt

Exploded view of alternator—typical

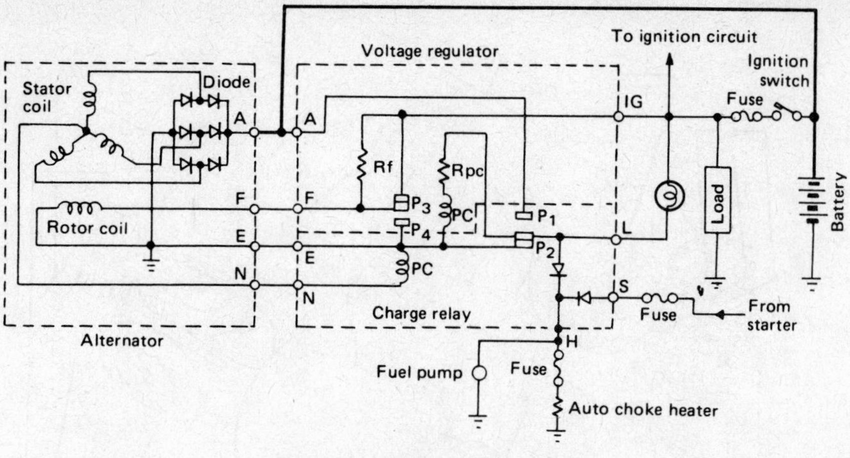

Diagram of charging system

2. If a jumper battery is used to start the vehicle, make sure that the cables leading from the jumper battery are matched with the terminals on the battery being jumped, positive to positive and negative to negative.

3. When testing or adjusting the alternator, install a condenser between the alternator output terminal and the ground. This is to prevent the diode from becoming damaged by a spark which occurs due to testing equipment with a defective connection.

4. Do not operate the alternator with the output terminals disconnected. The diode would be damaged by the high voltage generated.

5. When recharging the battery by a quick charge or any other charging apparatus, disconnect the alternator output terminal before hooking up the charging leads.

6. When installing a battery, always connect the grounded terminal last.

7. Never disconnect the battery while the engine is running.

8. Never electric weld on the car without disconnecting the alternator.

9. Never apply any voltage in excess of the battery voltage during testing.

10. Never jump a battery for starting purposes with more than the battery voltage.

REMOVAL AND INSTALLATION

1. To remove the alternator from the vehicle, first disconnect the negative battery terminal.

2. Disconnect the wiring to the alternator.

3. Remove the alternator attaching bolts and nuts.

4. Remove the drive belt and take out the alternator.

5. Install in the reverse order of removal.

BELT TENSION ADJUSTMENT

1. To adjust the belt tension, first loosen the adjusting bolt on the right of the alternator (looking from the rear).

2. Lift up on the alternator to increase the tension on the belt. When it takes moderate thumb pressure to move the longest span of belt ½ in., the tension adjustment is correct.

3. Tighten the adjusting bolt so that the alternator will not move in the adjusting bracket.

Regulator

REMOVAL AND INSTALLATION

1. Disconnect the cable from the negative (−) battery terminal.

2. Disconnect the multi-wire connector and automatic choke lead (1975 and later models) from the regulator.

3. Remove the two regulator mounting screws and remove the regulator from the fender panel.

Installation is the reverse of the removal procedures.

VOLTAGE ADJUSTMENTS—ON THE CAR

This test should be made after the engine compartment and the regulator have had a chance to cool down. The test should never be done on a "hot engine".

1. Make sure all electrical equipment on the car is turned off or disconnected.

2. Using an ammeter rated at 10 amps, a 30-volt voltmeter, and a resistor rated at .25 ohms, connect up a test circuit as shown in the illustration.

3. BEFORE STARTING THE ENGINE, connect a jumper wire from the far terminal of the .25 ohm resister to the negative (−) terminal of the ammeter. See illustration. After the engine is started, disconnect the jumper but be sure to reconnect it each time the engine is restarted.

4. Start the engine and gradually increase the speed from idle to about 2000 rpm. 2000 engine rpm is equal to about 1200 alternator rpm.

5. The voltage reading shown should compare with that on the spec chart, allowing for the temperature around the regulator.

NOTE: The ammeter reading should be below 5 amps. Recharge or substitute the battery with a charged one if the reading is not below 5 amps.

6. If the voltage is not within the specified range, adjust as follows;

a. Remove the screws and take off the regulator cover. Loosen the locknut and turn the adjusting screw until the voltage falls within specifications.

b. If the voltage cannot be brought within specs, proceed with a mechanical adjustment.

c. If the voltage is now within the required specs: shut off the engine, remove the test equipment, replace the regulator cover and reconnect any electrical system components or accessories you disconnected at the beginning of the test.

VOLTAGE ADJUSTMENTS–OFF THE CAR

Charge Relay Adjustment

NOTE: The opening voltage of the charge relay is 8-10 volts at alternator terminal "A". However, the coil on the charge relay operates at half of this voltage (i.e., 4-5 volts).

1. Remove the regulator from the car.

2. Hook up the test circuit illustrated with a car battery, 0-150 ohm rheostat, voltmeter, heavy-duty switch, and a test light.

3. Close the switch with the rheostat set at 150 ohms (maximum).

4. Gradually decrease the resistance.

5. When the test light goes out, the voltmeter should read 4-5 volts.

6. If the light doesn't go out at the specified setting, remove the regulator cover and make the following adjustments. Loosen the locknut

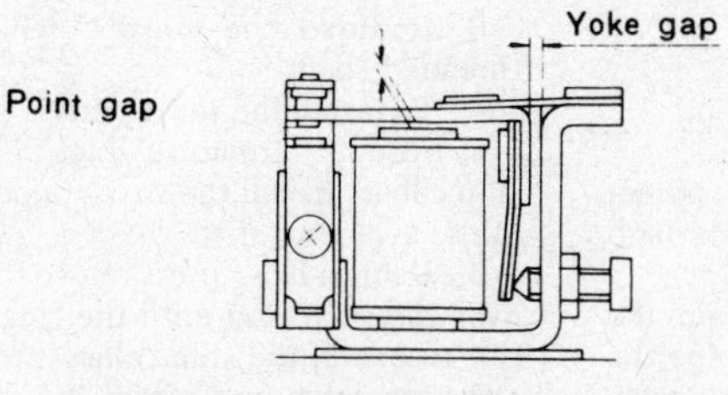

Adjustment points of voltage regulator

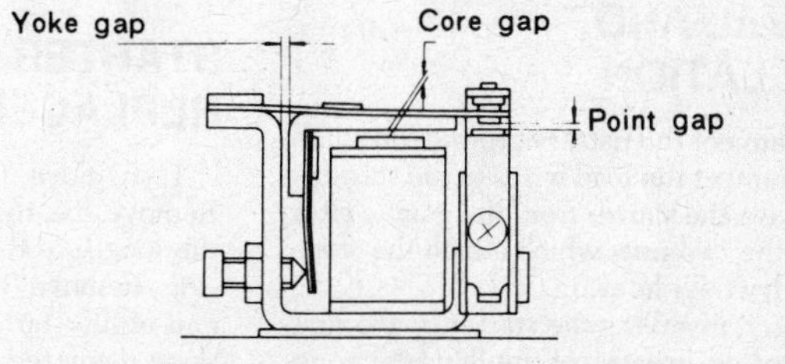

Adjustment points of charge relay

on the charge relay, and turn the adjusting screw until the voltage is within specifications. Tighten the locknut.

7. If the charge relay voltage cannot be brought within specifications, perform the "Mechanical Adjustments" outlined next.

8. If the charge relay is working properly, put the cover on the regulator and install it in the car.

Mechanical Adjustments

CAUTION

All mechanical adjustments must be performed with the regulator removed from the car to prevent battery and charging system damage.

1. Remove the voltage regulator from the car and remove the regulator cover.

2. Inspect both sets of points. If they are rough or dirty, polish them with #500 or #600 emery paper.

NOTE: If the points are so badly damaged that polishing them doesn't help, replace the regulator.

3. Measure and adjust the gaps of both the voltage regulator and the charge relay in the same manner. Use the specifications given in the "Alternator and Regulator Specifications" chart. Adjust both sets of gaps in the following sequence:

NOTE: It is not necessary to adjust the yoke gap.

a. Core gap—measure the clearances for both the regulator and charge relay between their armatures and coil cores. Adjust each, as necessary, by loosening the 4 mm screw which secures the contact set to the yoke and moving the set up or down. Tighten the screw.

b. Point gap—measure the distances between the points for both the voltage regulator and charge relay. Adjust each, as necessary, by loosening the 3 mm screw which secures the upper contact and moving the contact up or down. Tighten the screw.

4. Reinstall the regulator in the car and test its operation as outlined above. If the voltage still cannot be brought within specifications, replace the regulator. If the voltage is still incorrect, the fault probably lies in the alternator.

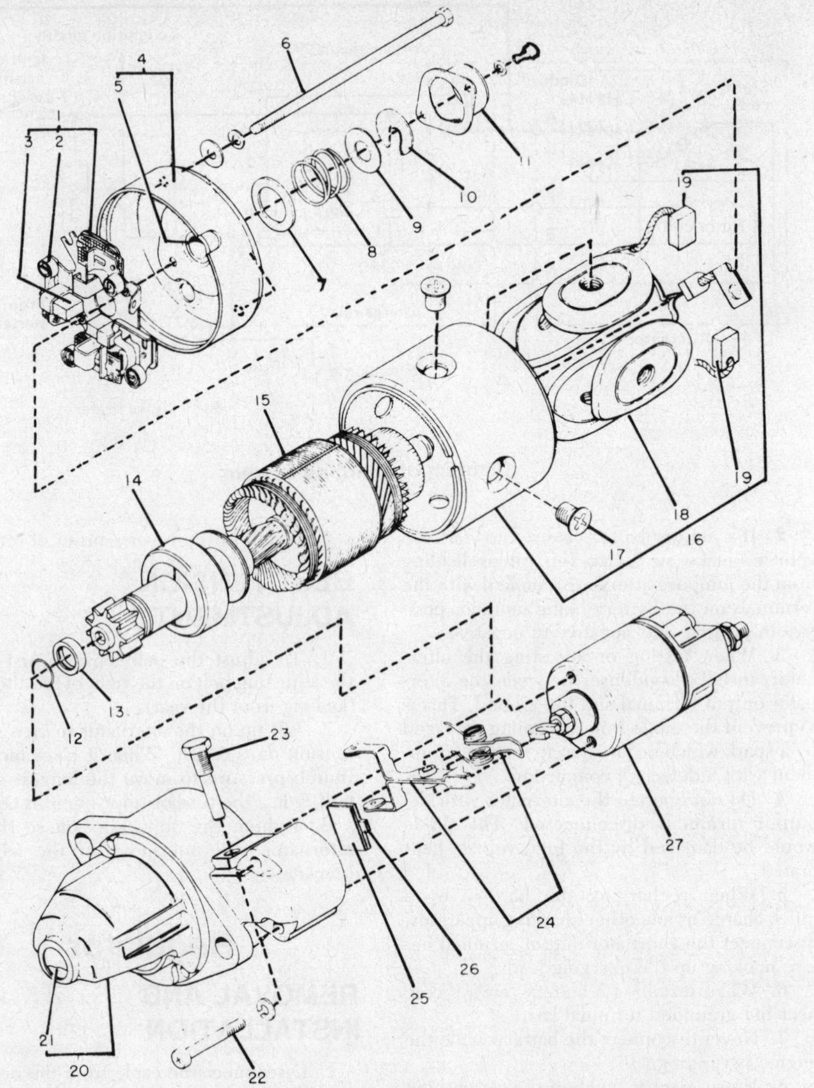

1. Brush holder plate assembly
2. Spring type brush holder
3. Brush
4. Commutator frame assembly
5. Bushing
6. Thru-bolt
7. Rubber parts
8. Spring
9. Washer
10. Lock plate
11. End frame cap
12. Snap ring
13. Pinion stop collar
14. Over running clutch assembly
15. Armature assembly
16. Yoke assembly
17. Pole core screw
18. Field coil assembly
19. Brush
20. Housing assembly
21. Housing bushing
22. Screw
23. Lever set bolt
24. Drive lever assembly
25. Plate
26. Rubber parts
27. Magnet switch assembly

An exploded view of the starter

Starter

REMOVAL AND INSTALLATION

1. Disconnect the battery ground terminal.
2. Disconnect the lead wires to the starter.
3. Remove the starter from the engine after removing the two nuts which attach the starter to the flywheel housing.
4. When reinstalling the starter, make sure that the mating surfaces of the flywheel housing and the starter fit flush against each other.
5. Install the starter in the reverse order of removal.

STARTER DRIVE REPLACEMENT

1. Remove the starter from the engine. Remove the two thru-bolts that run through the length of the starter housing.

2. Remove the pinion housing from the end of the starter. Using a length of pipe the same diameter as the armature shaft, tap the pinion stop collar down toward the starter drive so that it is off the snap-ring. Use a pair of snap-ring pliers to remove the snap-ring from the armature shaft.

3. Remove the starter drive from the threaded shaft.

4. To install the starter drive, slip the drive unit over the armature shaft and install the stop collar. Install the snap-ring in the groove of the armature shaft.

5. Using a hand press, move the stop collar over the snap-ring until the ring is seated in the groove of the stop collar.

6. Assemble and install the starter in the reverse order of disassembly and removal.

ENGINE MECHANICAL

Engine Removal and Installation

NOTE: On these models, the engine is removed separately from the transaxle.

1. Open the hood as far as possible and secure it with the stay.
2. Disconnect the ground cable from the negative (−) battery terminal.
3. Remove the 8 mm bolt which secures the ground cable at the intake manifold and disconnect the cable. It is unnecessary to remove the cable fully; leave it routed along the side of the body.

Engine/transaxle assembly with standard transmission—typical

Engine/transaxle assembly with automatic transmission—typical

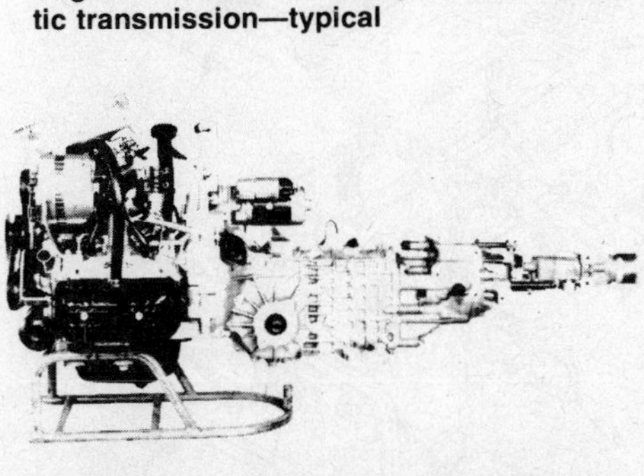

Engine/transaxle assembly with 4WD extension on standard transmission—typical

4. Remove the spare tire from the engine compartment.
5. Remove the emission control system hoses from the air cleaner. Remove the air cleaner brackets, remove the wing nut, and lift the air cleaner assembly off the carburetor.
6. Place a suitable container under the fuel line union to catch the gasoline. Disconnect the hoses at the union by removing the clip and pulling the hose off. Drain the engine oil.
7. Drain the coolant and disconnect the radiator hoses.
   a. Place a clean container, large enough to hold the contents of the cooling system, beneath the radiator drain plug so that the coolant may be reused.
   b. Loosen the drain plug on the radiator and turn it so that its slot faces downward.
   c. Disconnect both of the hoses at the radiator, leaving them connected to the engine.
   d. Disconnect the heater hoses from the pipe at the side of the engine.
   e. On automatic transmission models, disconnect the oil cooler inlet and outlet hoses at the radiator.
8. Disconnect the following electrical wiring.
   a. Alternator multi-connector
   b. Oil pressure sender connection
   c. Three engine cooling fan connectors
   d. Temperature sender connection
   e. Primary distributor lead
   f. Secondary ignition leads (ignition side)
   g. Starter wiring harness
   h. Anti-dieseling solenoid lead
   i. Automatic choke lead (1975 and later)
   j. EGR vacuum solenoid (1975 and later—Calif.)
   k. EGR coolant temperature switch (1975 and later—Calif.)
   l. On automatic transmission models, disconnect the neutral safety switch harness and downshift solenoid harness.
9. Loosen the two radiator securing bolts, remove the ground lead from the upper side of the radiator, and lift the radiator out.

NOTE: On 4WD models, remove the engine fan from the pulley.

10. Remove the horizontal damper in the following order.
    a. Remove the front nut from the damper.
    b. Remove the nut on the body bracket and withdraw the damper.
    c. Pull the damper rearward away from the engine lifting hook. Be careful not to lose any of the damper parts.
11. Remove the starter assembly, as outlined above under "Engine Electrical".
12. Disconnect the following cables, hoses and linkages.
    a. Loosen, but don't remove, the screw in the carburetor throttle lever. Remove the outer end of the accelerator cable and withdraw it.
    b. Remove vacuum hose and purge hose from vapor canister (1977 and later models).
    c. On standard transmission models, remove the clutch return spring from the release lever and intake manifold, and remove the clutch cable from the lever.
    d. On automatic transmission models, disconnect the vacuum hose attached to the transmission.
    e. Disconnect the vacuum hose from the power brake unit (if so equipped).
13. On 4WD models, remove the under guard by unscrewing the 8 mm attaching bolts.
14. Remove the Y-shaped exhaust pipe. (Be careful not to lose the insulators and gaskets.)
    a. Loosen the clamp fastening the air intake hose to the air stove on the exhaust pipe, and remove the hose.
    b. Remove the air stove and remove the four nuts attaching the exhaust pipe to the cylinder heads.
    c. Remove the two bolts and nuts connecting the exhaust pipe to the pre-muffler.
    d. While supporting the exhaust pipe by hand, remove the two bolts attaching the exhaust pipe to the transmission bracket. Lower the exhaust pipe.

NOTE: As the exhaust pipe is heavy, it is a good idea to have help supporting and lowering it.

15. On automatic transmission models, remove the torque converter bolts.
    a. Remove the timing hole cover from the torque converter housing.
    b. Remove the four bolts connecting the torque converter to the drive plate through the timing hole.

NOTE: Be careful that the bolts do not fall into the torque converter housing.

16. Set up a chain hoist on the engine, with hooks at the front and rear engine hangers. Adjust the hoist so that the weight of the engine is supported, but do not raise the engine.

NOTE: The purpose of supporting the engine at this point is to prevent the unstable movement of the engine and protect the people working underneath the vehicle.

17. Position a suitable jack under the transaxle to support its weight when the engine is removed.
18. Remove the four nuts (four each on top and bottom) connecting the engine and transmission.
19. Remove the nuts holding the front engine mounts (rubber) to the crossmember.

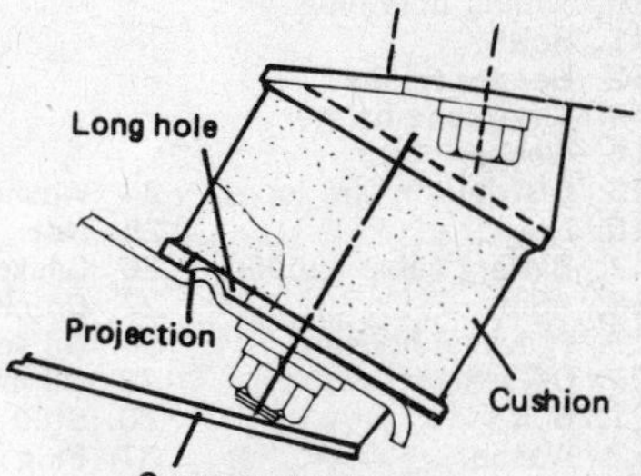

Engine mount alignment

20. Before going on to the next step, be sure that all of the above steps have been completed.

21. Using the hoist, raise the engine slightly (about 1"). Keeping it level, move the engine forward, off the transaxle input shaft.

CAUTION

Do not raise the engine more than one inch prior to removing it from the input shaft or damage may occur to the driveshaft double offset joints. On standard transmission models, be sure that the input shaft does not interfere with the clutch spring assembly. On automatic transmission models, leave the torque converter on the transaxle input shaft.

22. Hoist the engine carefully until it is completely out of the car, and place it on a suitable stand or workbench.

Engine installation is performed in the reverse order of removal. However, be sure to observe the following.

1. Use the following torque specifications when installing the engine.

Transmission to engine: 34-40 ft/lbs

Torque converter to drive plate: 17-20 ft/lbs

Engine mount to cross member: 14-24 ft/lbs

Horizontal damper nut: 7-10 ft/lbs

Exhaust pipe to engine:

12-14 ft/lbs (pre-1977 models)

19-22 ft/lbs (1977 and later models)

Exhaust pipe to pre-muffler: 31-38 ft/lbs

Radiator mounting bolt: 6-10 ft/lbs

2. Use care not to damage the input shaft splines or the clutch spring while lowering the engine in place.

3. When installing the exhaust pipe, always use new gaskets.

4. Perform the following adjustment to the horizontal damper:

a. Tighten the body bracket nut.

b. Turn the front nut until the clearance between the front washer and rubber cushion is zero.

c. Insert the bushing and tighten the front nut to specifications (Step 1).

5. Make all of the clutch and accelerator linkage adjustments, as detailed elsewhere in the book.

6. Replenish the engine oil and coolant supplies.

Cylinder Head

REMOVAL AND INSTALLATION

The engine must be removed from the vehicle to remove the cylinder heads. Although it is physically possible (on some models) to remove the cylinder heads with the engine installed, head gasket failure will result upon installation, due to misalignment of the cylinders. The cylinder heads should be removed with the engine cold to prevent warpage.

1. Remove the engine from the vehicle.

2. Unbolt and remove the intake manifold together with the carburetor and the various pollution control devices. (The pipe attached to the exhaust manifold port in the cylinder head should have been removed before the engine was taken out.) On 1977 and later models, remove the EGR pipe from the intake manifold and cylinder head.

NOTE: Move or disconnect any engine wiring that might impair intake manifold removal.

3. Remove the spark plugs.

4. Disconnect the crankcase ventilation hose(s) and remove the valve covers.

5. Loosen the alternator adjusting bolts, and unbolt the alternator bracket from the cylinder head.

6. Remove the air injection distributor tubes from the cylinder heads by unscrewing the fittings.

7. Loosen the valve rocker locknuts and adjusting screws. Loosen the rocker shaft mounting nuts, and remove the rocker arm assembly and pushrods.

NOTE: If the pushrods are to be reused, keep them in order so that they are installed in the original positions.

8. Gradually loosen the head bolts or nuts in the reverse of the tightening sequence, and remove the cylinder heads and pushrods.

9. Install the heads in the reverse order of removal.

The cylinder heads must be installed with the cylinders vertical, to avoid misalignment, and to permit the head gasket to crush evenly around the cylinder. Prior to installation of the heads, cylinder liner projection must be

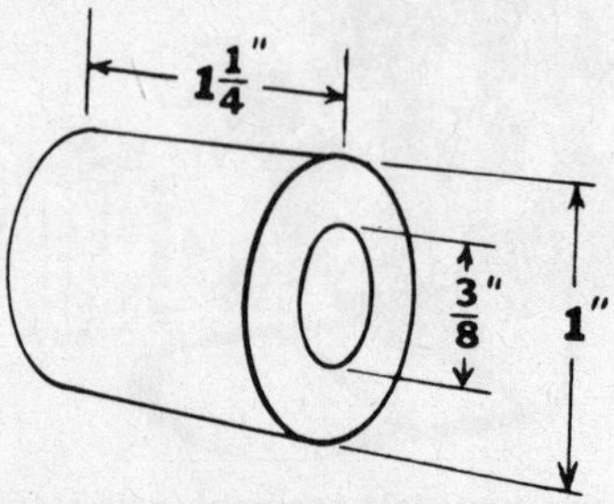

Cylinder head installation spacer

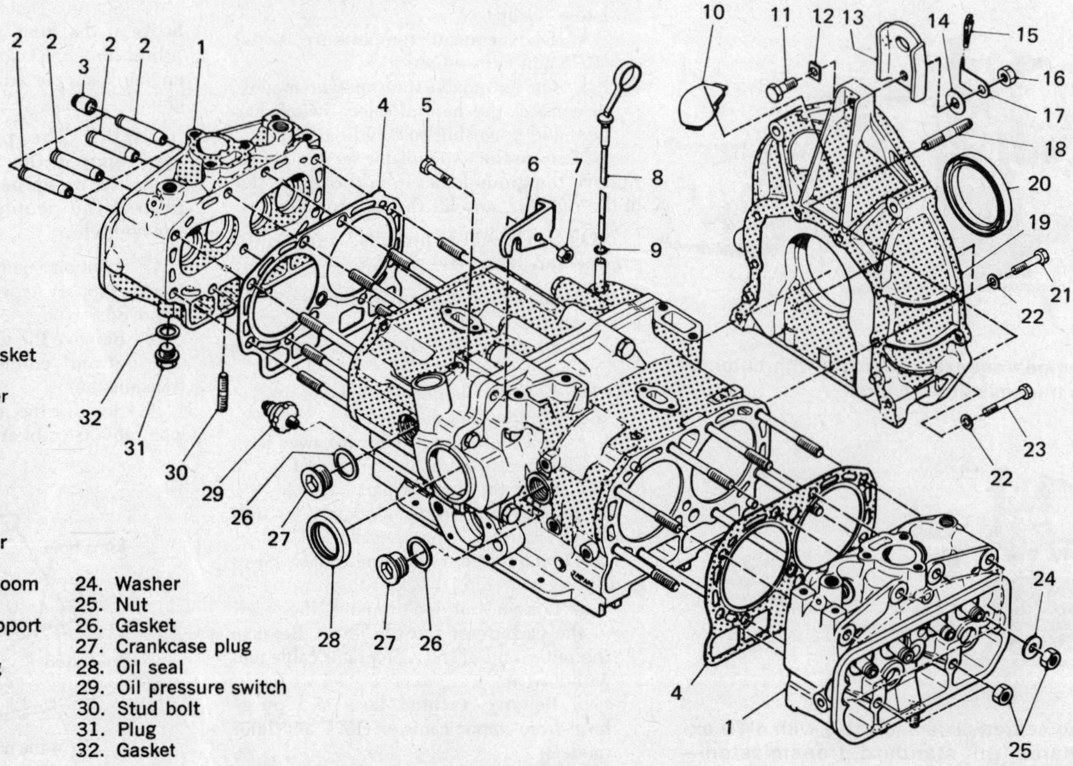

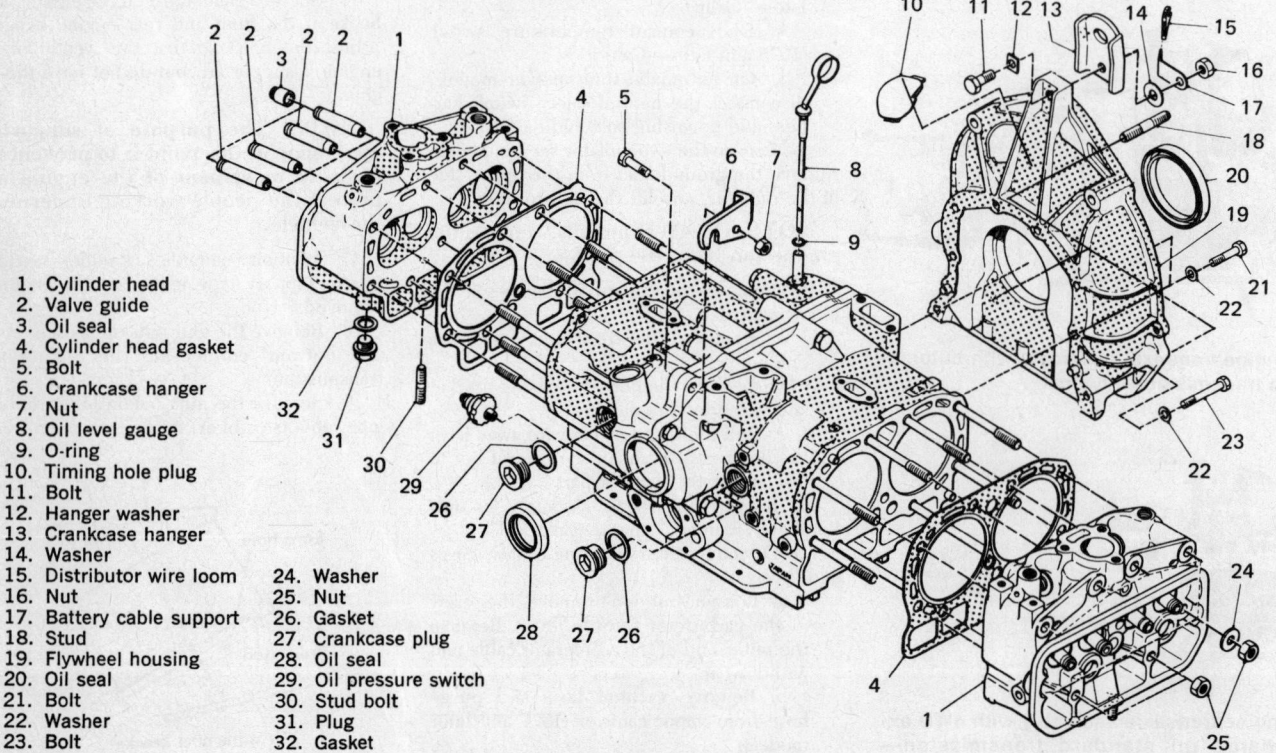

1. Cylinder head
2. Valve guide
3. Oil seal
4. Cylinder head gasket
5. Bolt
6. Crankcase hanger
7. Nut
8. Oil level gauge
9. O-ring
10. Timing hole plug
11. Bolt
12. Hanger washer
13. Crankcase hanger
14. Washer
15. Distributor wire loom
16. Nut
17. Battery cable support
18. Stud
19. Flywheel housing
20. Oil seal
21. Bolt
22. Washer
23. Bolt
24. Washer
25. Nut
26. Gasket
27. Crankcase plug
28. Oil seal
29. Oil pressure switch
30. Stud bolt
31. Plug
32. Gasket

Cylinder heads, flywheel housing (typical)

checked on the 1400 engine. It must be 0.003-0.004 in. Liner projection is adjusted by varying the size of the liner gaskets.

NOTE: Liner projection must be checked whenever a 1400 engine head gasket has failed.

Torque in the specified sequence, in stages, using a spacer in place of the rocker shaft support. After the head is torqued to specifications, remove the rocker shaft bolts (or nuts) and the spacers, and install the rocker shafts.

SERVICE

Using a straightedge, check the cylinder heads for warpage. Should warpage exceed 0.002 in., the cylinder head must be resurfaced (grinding limit 0.016 in.). Should the valve sink exceed approximately 0.040 in., the seats must be replaced. The valve guides are pressed in, and should be replaced if clearance exceeds specifications. The intake valve guide should extend 0.71 and the exhaust 0.91 in. from the spring seat.

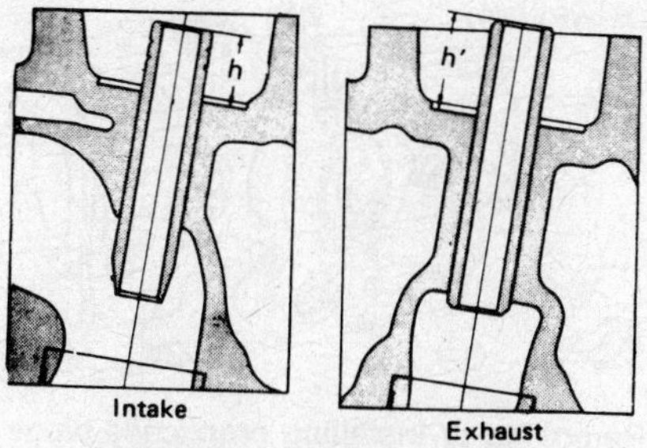

Valve guide installed height

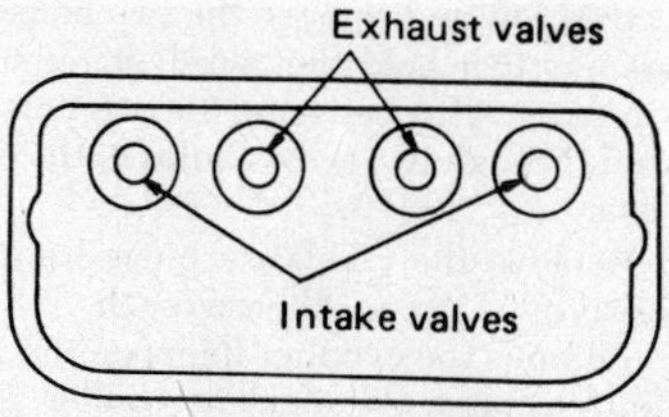

Valve arrangement in cylinder head

Rocker Shafts

With the engine removed from the vehicle, remove the rocker arm covers and gaskets from the cylinder heads. Unscrew the nuts which hold the rocker arm assemblies to the cylinder heads and lift the rocker arm assemblies from the engine. Identify the pushrods so they can be replaced in their original positions. Install in the reverse order of removal.

Intake Manifold

REMOVAL AND INSTALLATION

1975

1. Remove the air cleaner assembly.
2. Disconnect the air distributor connector.
3. Disconnect the radiator hose from the thermostat case cover.

1. Screw
2. Spring washer
3. Accelerator cable clamp
4. Bolt
5. Spring washer
6. Accelerator cable bracket
7. Washer
8. Thermostat cover
9. Thermostat cover gasket
10. Thermostat
11. Hose clamp
12. Water bypass hose
13. Water bypass connector
14. Gasket
15. Water bypass connector
16. Bolt
17. Bolt
18. Intake manifold gasket
19. Intake manifold
20. Stud
21. Plug
22. Temperature sending unit
23. Carburetor gasket
24. Spring washer
25. Nut

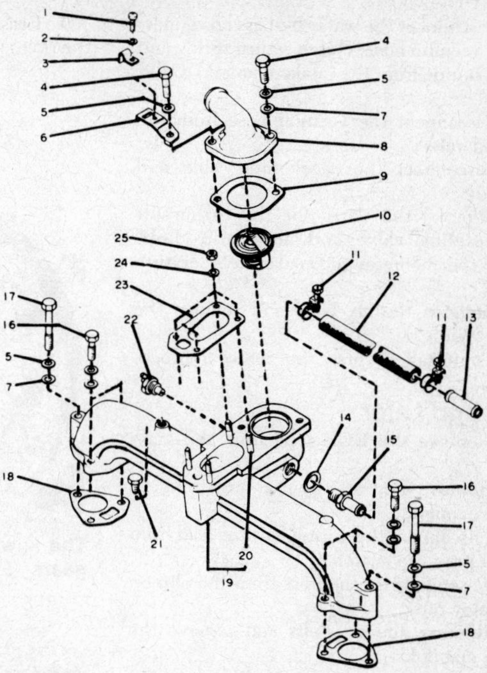

Exploded view of a 1400 intake manifold

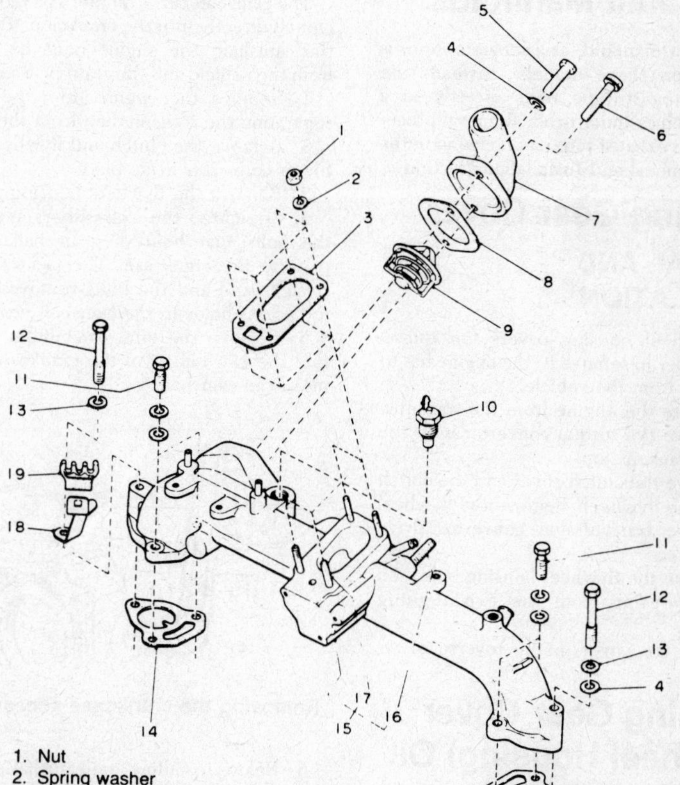

1. Nut
2. Spring washer
3. Carburetor gasket
4. Washer
5. Bolt (8 x 26 x 23)
6. Bolt
7. Thermostat case cover
8. Thermostat case cover gasket
9. Thermostat
10. Thermometer
11. Bolt
12. Bolt
13. Spring washer
14. Intake manifold gasket
15. Intake manifold
16. Stud bolt (8 x 36 x 12)
17. Stud bolt
18. Spark plug cord stay 2
19. Spark plug cord supporter

Exploded view of intake manifold—typical

4. Disconnect the water by-pass hose, master Vac vacuum hose, clutch return spring and the EGR pipe from the intake manifold (Calif. models).
5. Disconnect the vacuum hose from the solenoid valve.
6. Disconnect the accelerator cable and fuel hose.
7. Remove the wires for the carburetor anti-dieseling valve and automatic choke heater, thermometer and coolant temperature switch.
8. Remove the six bolts and remove the intake manifold.
9. To install reverse the removal procedure.

1976 and Later

1. Remove the EGR pipe from the manifold.
2. Remove the water by-pass hose from the intake manifold.
3. Disconnect the wiring harness lead from the oil pressure switch.
4. Disengage the harness from the clip on the water pipe.
5. Remove the six bolts and remove the intake manifold.
6. To install reverse the removal procedure.

Exhaust Manifolds

An exhaust manifold, as a separate item, is not found on these models. Instead, the Y-shaped exhaust pipe bolts directly to a flange on each cylinder head. Removal procedures for this exhaust pipe can be found in the "Engine Removal and Installation" section.

Timing Gear Cover

REMOVAL AND INSTALLATION

The flywheel housing covers the timing gears. In order to remove it, the engine has to be removed from the vehicle.
1. Separate the engine from the transmission. Remove the torque converter with the automatic transmission.
2. Remove the clutch cover and the clutch disc from the flywheel. Remove the flywheel or automatic transmission converter drive plate.
3. Remove the flywheel housing bolts and work the housing from the two aligning dowels.
4. Install the cover in the reverse of removal.

Timing Gear Cover (Flywheel Housing) Oil Seal Replacement

The housing cover oil seal is pressed in.
1. Remove the engine from the vehicle, separating the transmission from the engine.
2. Remove the flywheel and clutch assembly or converter drive plate from the engine.
3. Remove the housing from the engine and remove the oil seal from the housing.
4. Install the new oil seal, pressing it into place.

5. Reassemble the engine and install it in the reverse order of disassembly and removal.

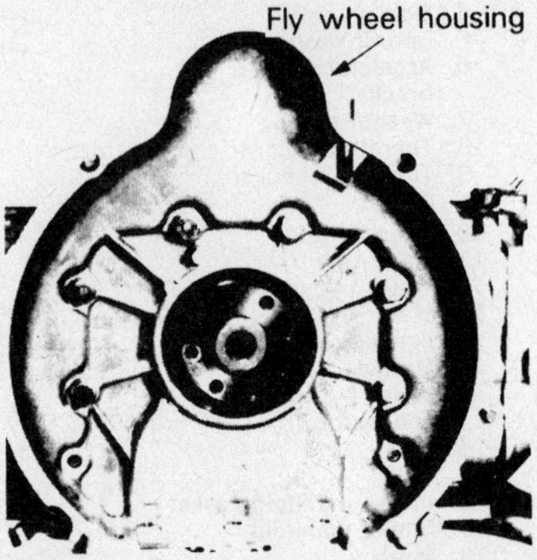

The flywheel housing covers the timing gears

Camshaft

REMOVAL AND INSTALLATION

The camshaft turns on journals that are machined directly into the crankcase. To remove the camshaft, the engine must be removed from the vehicle and the crankcase separated.
1. Remove the engine from the vehicle, separating the transmission from the engine.
2. Remove the clutch and flywheel assembly or converter drive plate.
3. Remove the flywheel housing.
4. Straighten the lockwashers and remove the bolts that hold the camshaft retaining plate to the crankcase. The lockwashers are straightened and the bolts removed through the access holes in the camshaft gear.
5. Remove the intake manifold and separate the two halves of the crankcase and remove the camshaft.

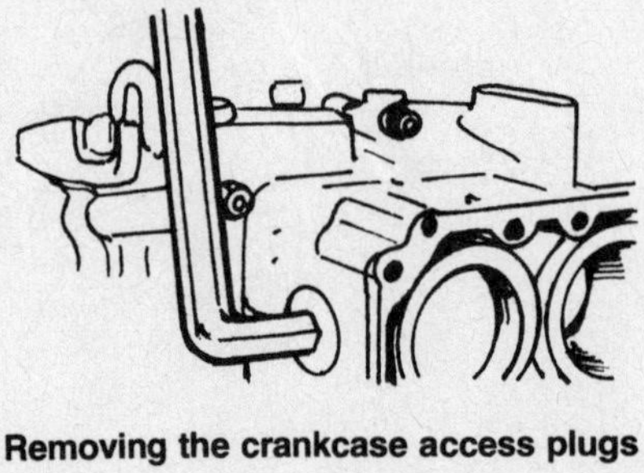

Removing the crankcase access plugs

6. Before installing the camshaft, measure the end-play of the camshaft, using a feeler gauge. The end-play should be 0.012 in. or less. Install the camshaft in the reverse order of removal.
7. Assemble the engine and reinstall it in the vehicle in the reverse order of disassembly and removal.

NOTE: One of the bolt holes in the crankshaft gear has a larger chamber than the others.

Position the crankshaft so that the punch mark on the cam gear tooth can be seen through this bolt hole.

This should position the woodruff key slot of the camshaft at an 11:30 o'clock position, and the crankshaft woodruff key slot at 7 o'clock.

Pistons and Connecting Rods

REMOVAL AND INSTALLATION

To remove the pistons and connecting rods, it is necessary that the engine be removed from the vehicle.

Only the 1400 engine has removeable cylinder liners.
1. Separate the engine and the transmission.
2. Remove the intake manifold, oil pan, flywheel and clutch assembly, flywheel housing, cylinder heads and gaskets.

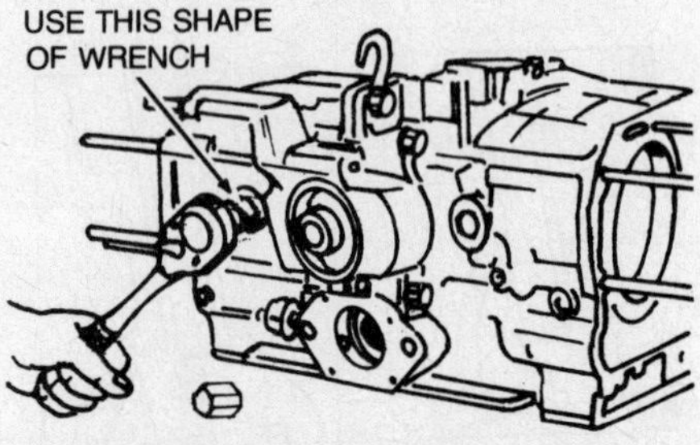

Removing or installing crankcase plugs

3. Unscrew and remove the two bolts and lockwashers that hold the camshaft retaining plate in place. The bolts and lockwashers are removed through two access holes in the camshaft gear.
4. Remove the crankcase plugs from the crankcase by using an Allen wrench.
5. Remove the cylinder liners on the 1400 engine by using a cylinder liner puller.
6. Remove the cylinder liner gaskets, keeping the cylinder liners and the gaskets of each cylinder together. The flanges of the liner should be marked so that they can be reinstalled in the correct positions.
7. Remove the circlips that hold the wrist pins in the pistons by inserting the piston circlip pliers through the crankcase plug holes.

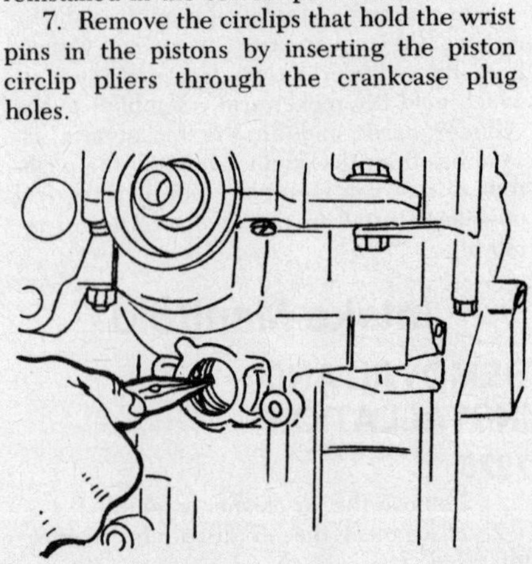

Removing or installing piston pin circlip through crankcase holes

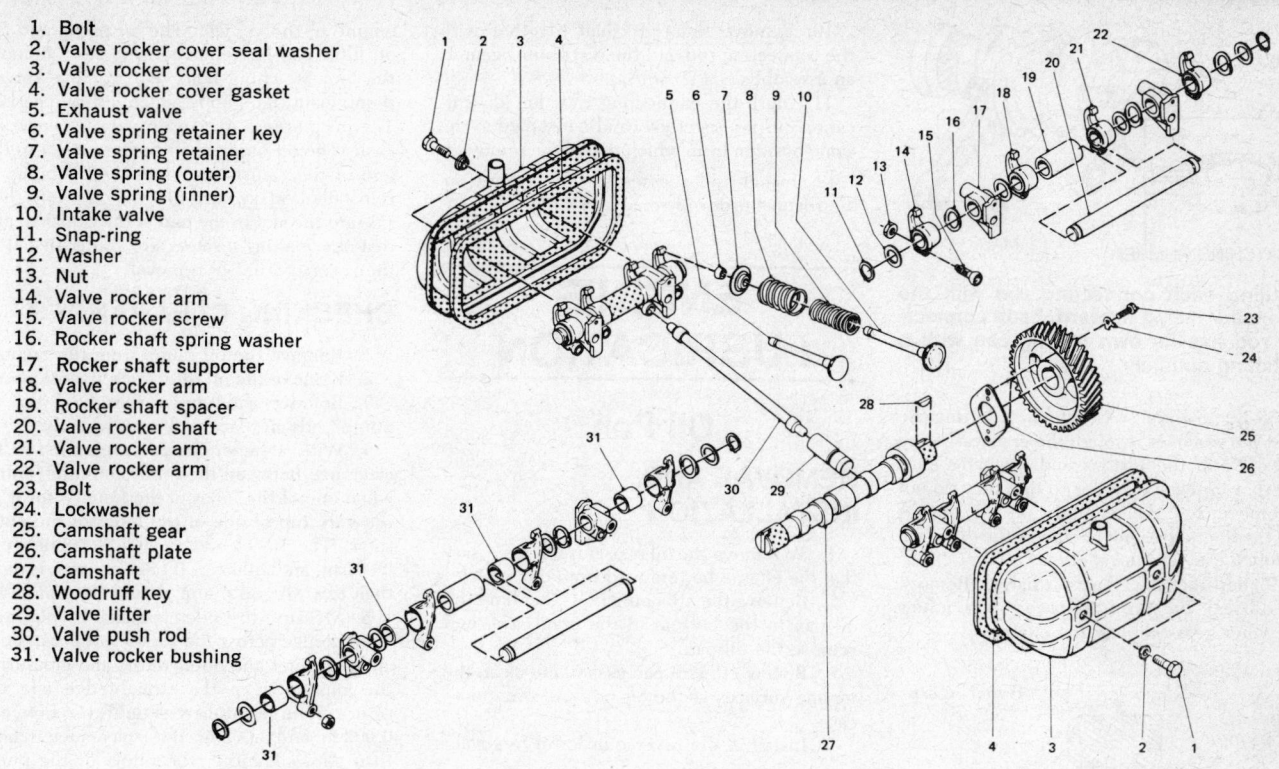

1. Bolt
2. Valve rocker cover seal washer
3. Valve rocker cover
4. Valve rocker cover gasket
5. Exhaust valve
6. Valve spring retainer key
7. Valve spring retainer
8. Valve spring (outer)
9. Valve spring (inner)
10. Intake valve
11. Snap-ring
12. Washer
13. Nut
14. Valve rocker arm
15. Valve rocker screw
16. Rocker shaft spring washer
17. Rocker shaft supporter
18. Valve rocker arm
19. Rocker shaft spacer
20. Valve rocker shaft
21. Valve rocker arm
22. Valve rocker arm
23. Bolt
24. Lockwasher
25. Camshaft gear
26. Camshaft plate
27. Camshaft
28. Woodruff key
29. Valve lifter
30. Valve push rod
31. Valve rocker bushing

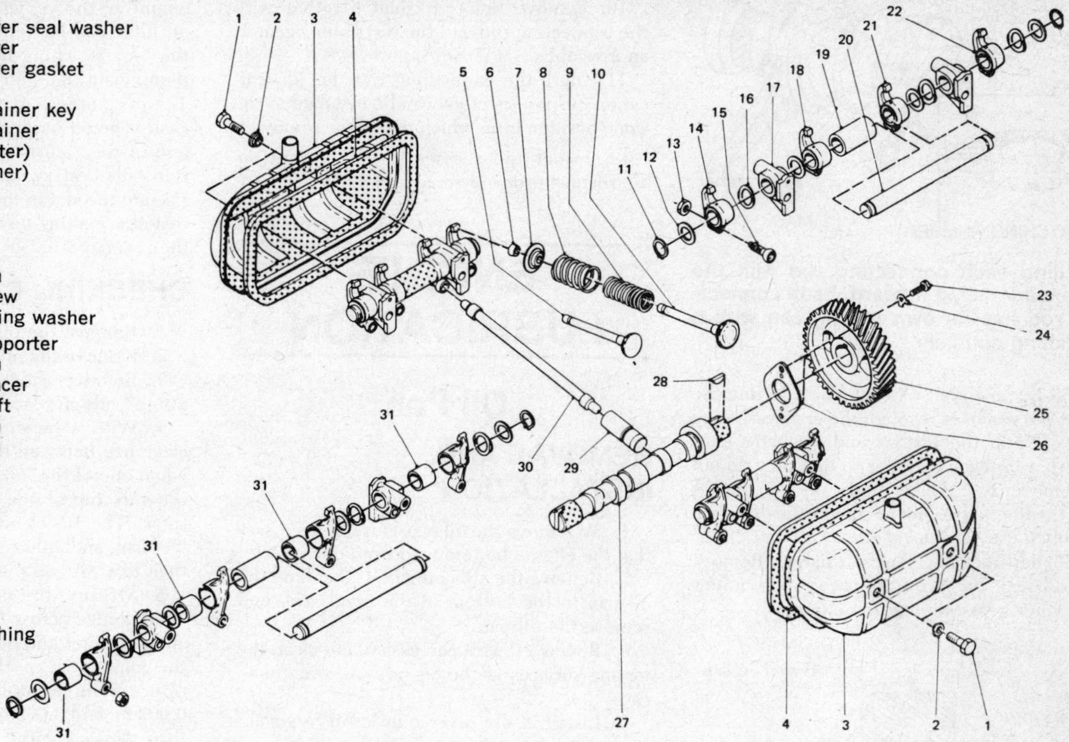

Camshaft and rocker arm assembly (typical)

1. Bolt
2. Washer
3. Crankshaft pulley
4. Drive belt
5. Distributor drive gear
6. Woodruff key
7. Crankshaft
8. Woodruff key
9. Needle bearing
10. Oil seal
11. Crankshaft gear
12. Flywheel (MT)
13. Starter ring gear
14. Bolt
15. Bolt
16. Drive plate (AT)
17. Connecting rod
18. Nut
19. Connecting rod bolt
20. Connecting rod bearing
21. Piston rings
22. Piston
23. Piston pin
24. Circlip

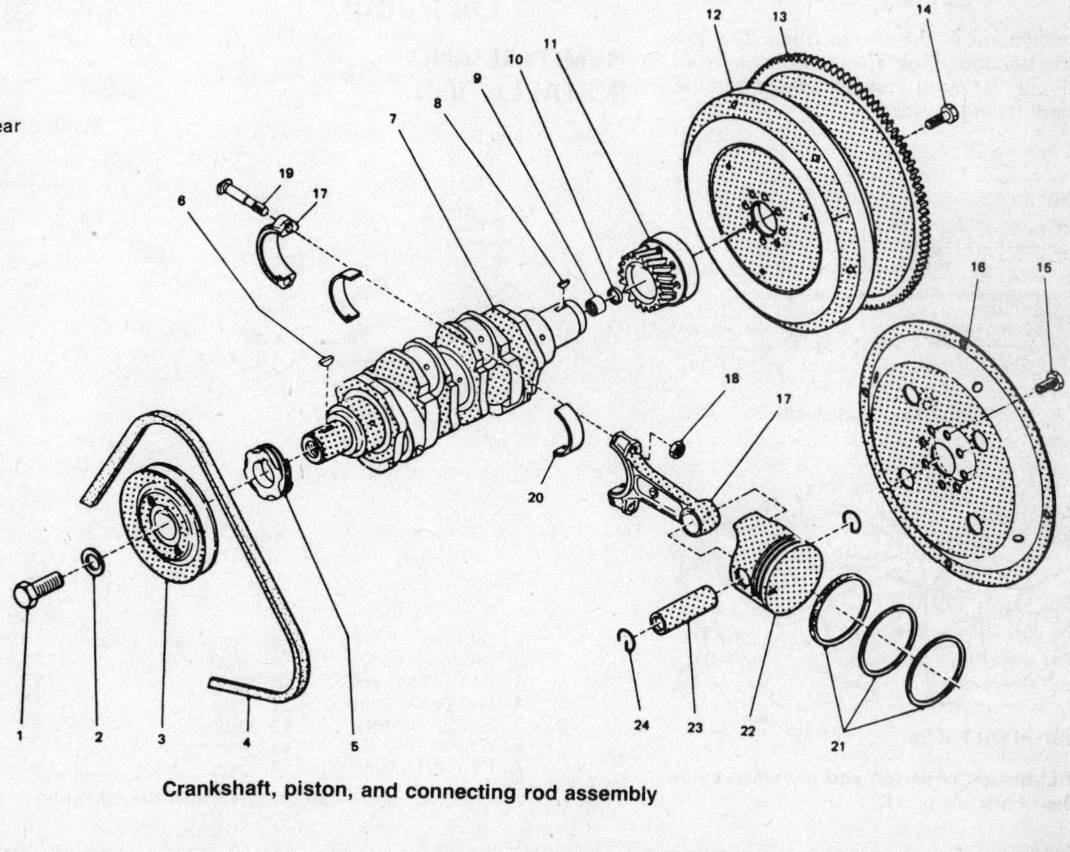

Crankshaft, piston, and connecting rod assembly

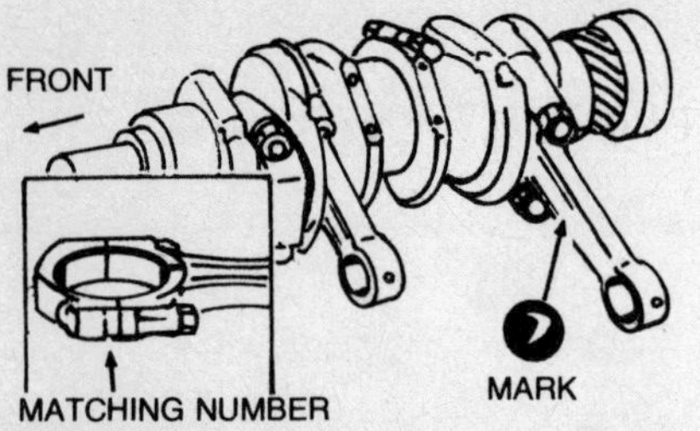

Position each connecting rod with the side mark facing forward. Each connecting rod has its own mating cap with a matching number

8. Remove the wrist pins by inserting the wrist pin remover through the crankcase plug holes. Keep the pistons and the wrist pins together for each cylinder so that they do not become mixed. Make marks on the pistons and the liners so as not to change the direction in which they are installed.

9. Separate the crankcase halves. Remove the oil seal. Be sure to replace it with a new one when reassembling the engine.

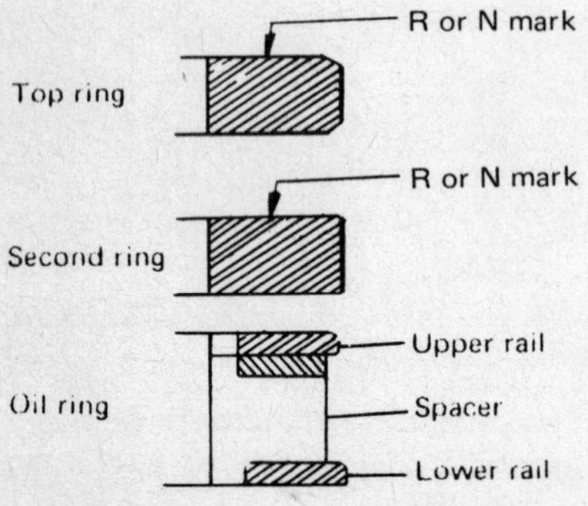

Installation of the piston rings. The top and second rings are provided with an "R" or "N" mark. Install the rings with the mark facing upward.

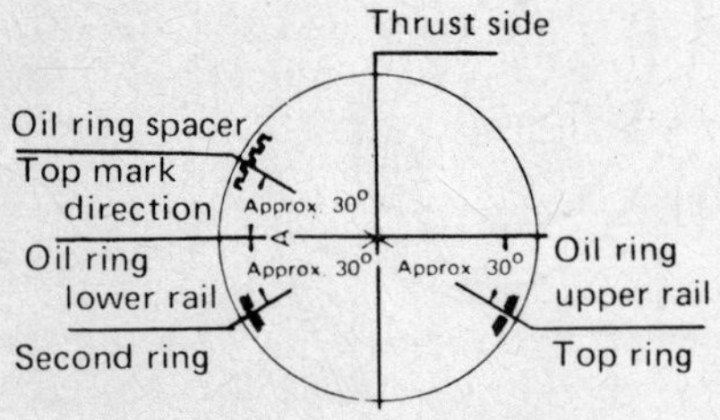

Piston ring gap position

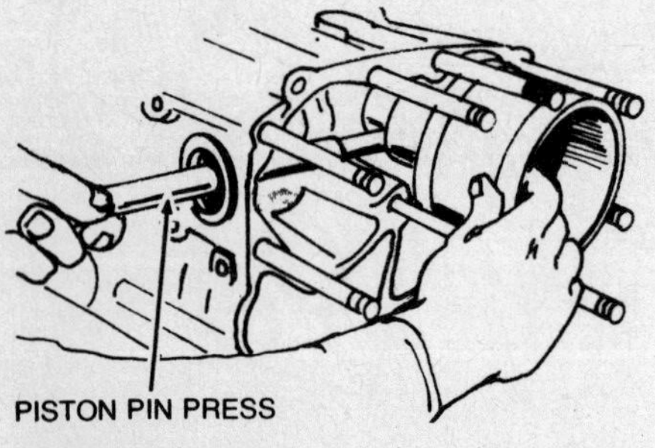

Installation of piston and pin when cylinder liners are used

10. Remove the crankshaft together with the connecting rod and the distributor gear as an assembly.

11. Mark the connecting rods for identification purposes so they can be installed in the same position from which they were removed.

12. Install and reassemble the engine in the reverse order of removal.

ENGINE LUBRICATION

Oil Pan

REMOVAL AND INSTALLATION

1. To remove the oil pan, it is not necessary that the engine be removed from the vehicle.
2. Remove the attaching bolts that hold the oil pan to the bottom of the crankcase, and remove the oil pan.
3. Remove the oil pan gasket and clean the mating surfaces of the oil pan and the crankcase.
4. Install in the reverse order of removal.

REAR MAIN OIL SEAL REPLACEMENT

The rear main oil seal is located in the flywheel housing (timing gear cover). See "Timing Gear Cover Removal and Installation" for the rear main oil seal replacement procedures.

Oil Pump

REMOVAL AND INSTALLATION

The oil pump can be removed with the engine in the vehicle. The oil pump and the oil filter can be removed as a unit. Remove the four attaching bolts, and remove the oil pump from the engine along with the gasket. The oil pump is driven directly by the camshaft. The oil pump shaft fits into a slot in the end of the camshaft. When the oil pump is reinstalled, make sure that the oil pump shaft fits into the slot in the end of the camshaft and that the mating surfaces are flush. Install in the reverse order of removal.

CHECKING CLEARANCES

1. Remove the oil pump from the engine.
2. Remove the oil filter from the oil pump.
3. Remove the screws that hold the oil pump body in place and remove body.
4. With a feeler gauge, measure the tip clearance between the inner and outer rotor, when one of the lobes of the inner rotor is on the very top of one of the lobes of the outer rotor. The tip clearance should be between 0.001 in. and 0.005 in. If the clearance is more than this, the oil pump should be replaced.
5. Measure the side clearance by placing a straightedge across the top of the pump body and the inner and outer rotors and measuring the gap between the straightedge and the rotors. The clearance should be between 0.002 in. and 0.005 in. If the clearance is more than allowed, either the rotors or the pump housing must be replaced.

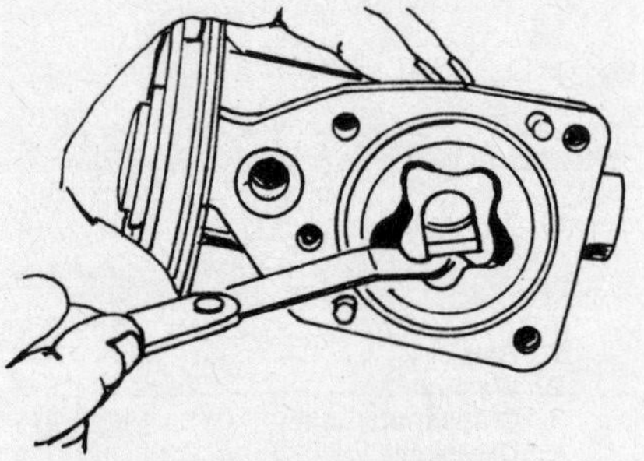

Measuring the tip clearance

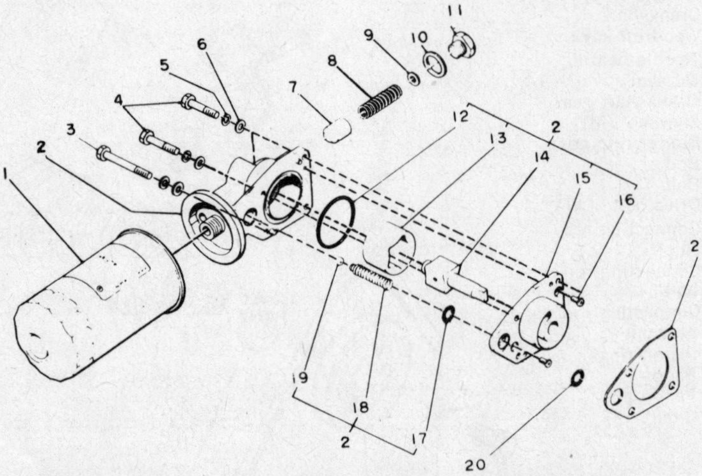

1. Oil filter
2. Oil pump body
3. Bolt (6X54 mm)
4. Bolt (6X32 mm)
5. Spring washer
6. Washer
7. Oil relief valve
8. Relief valve spring
9. Washer (6 mm)
10. Washer
11. Plug
12. O ring
13. Rotor
14. Gear
15. Oil pump holder
16. Screw
17. O ring
18. Bypass valve spring
19. Ball
20. O ring
21. Gasket

Exploded view of the oil pump

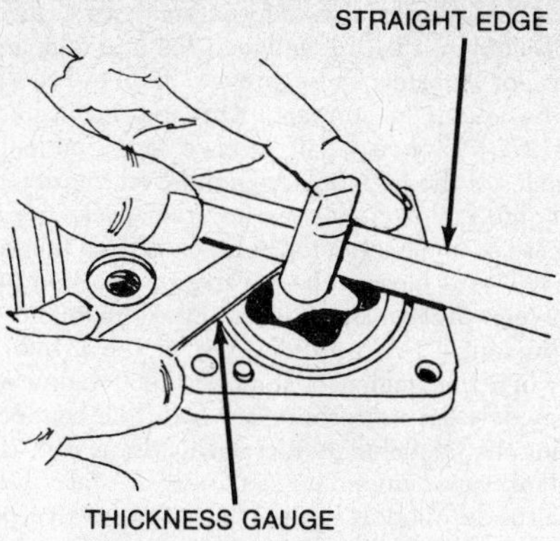

Measuring the side clearance

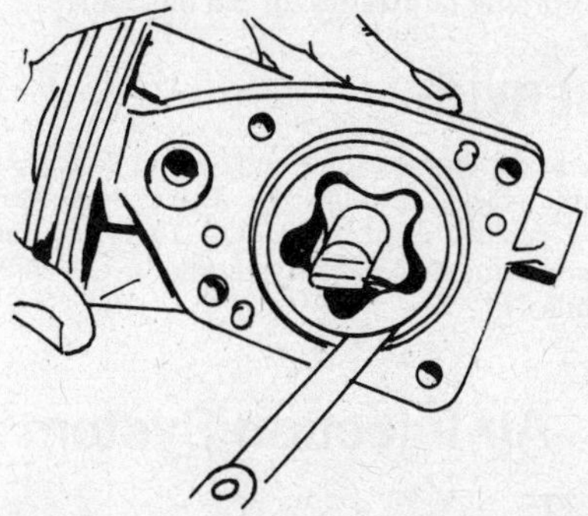
Measuring the clearance between the outside rotor and the pump body

6. Measure the radial clearance between the outer rotor and the pump housing with a feeler guage. The clearance should be between 0.006 in. and 0.008 in.

ENGINE COOLING

Radiators

REMOVAL AND INSTALLATION

1. Drain the cooling system by removing the drain plug in the bottom of the radiator. After loosening the drain plug, remove the radiator cap, which will allow the coolant to drain faster.
2. Loosen the hose clamps and remove the inlet (upper) and outlet (lower) hoses from the radiator.
3. Remove the two radiator mounting bolts.
4. Before removing the radiator from the vehicle, disconnect the wiring harness of the following items: thermostat and thermoswitch wiring, oil pressure switch wiring, fan motor wiring, and secondary terminal of the distributor.
5. Remove the fan and motor assembly from the radiator by removing the four bolts which hold the assembly to the radiator. 4WD models also have an engine driven fan.
6. Install the radiator in the reverse order of removal.

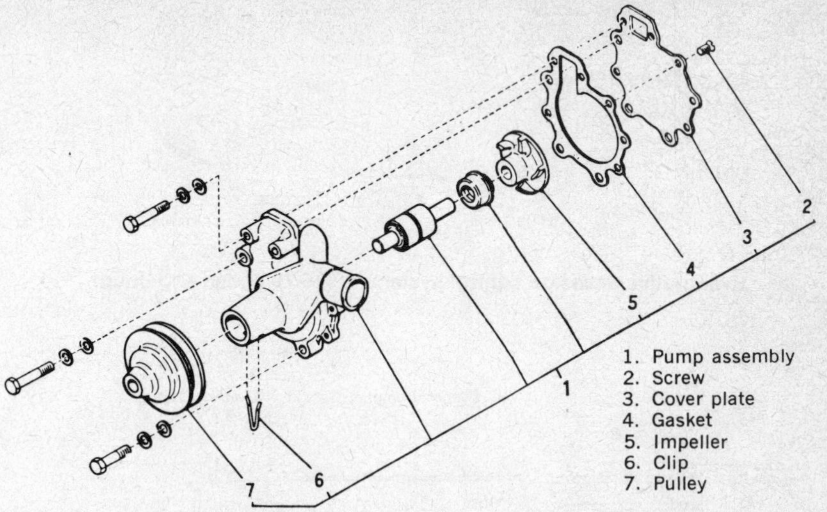

Exploded view of the water pump

Water Pump

REMOVAL AND INSTALLATION

A centrifugal water pump, mounted on the front of the engine, is utilized. To remove, drain the coolant, and remove the radiator hose from the pump. Remove the drive belt, unbolt and lift out the pump.

Install in the reverse order of removal.

Thermostat

REMOVAL AND INSTALLATION

A wax pellet type thermostat is used. It is removed by removing the air cleaner assembly and the thermostat cover, which is adjacent to the carburetor.

Install in the reverse order of removal.

NOTE: It is essential to the proper operation of the cooling system that the thermostat be installed in the proper direction.

EMISSION CONTROLS

Crankcase Emission Control System

EA63 Engines and EA71 Engines Through 1978

The closed crankcase ventilation system used on these engines is a closed system consisting of a sealed oil filler cap, hoses and an oil separator integral with the air cleaner. Blow-by gases from the crankcase are routed to the air cleaner via the two hoses, where they are pulled into the carburetor and burned with the air/fuel mixture.

The oil, which is trapped by the oil separator in the air cleaner, returns through the crankcase ventilation system hoses to the valve covers, where it is mixed with the oil used to lubricate the valve train.

EA71 and EA81 Engines 1979 and Later

These engines use a sealed crankcase emission system, which prevents blow-by gases from being emitted from the air. The system consists of a sealed oil filler cap, valve covers with an emission outlet and a fresh air inlet, connecting hoses, a PCV (positive crankcase ventilation) valve and an air cleaner.

Strong intake vacuum at part throttle suck blow-by gases from the crankcase, through a connecting hose (from #2 and #4 valve cover) and into the intake manifold via the PCV valve. However, at wide open throttle, the increase in volume of blow-by and the decrease in manifold vacuum make the flow through the PCV valve inadequate. Under

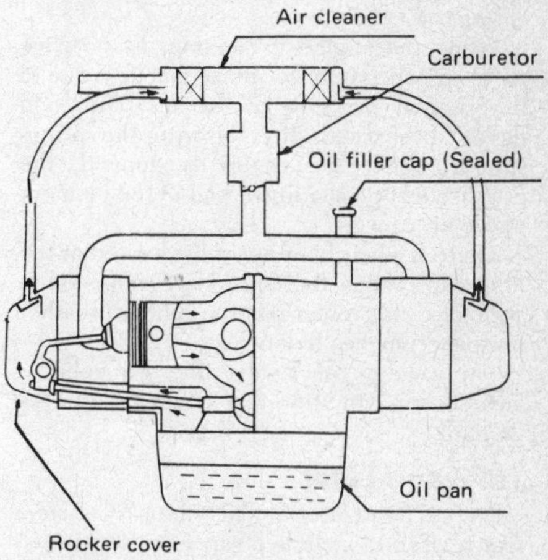

Diagram of the crankcase emission control system

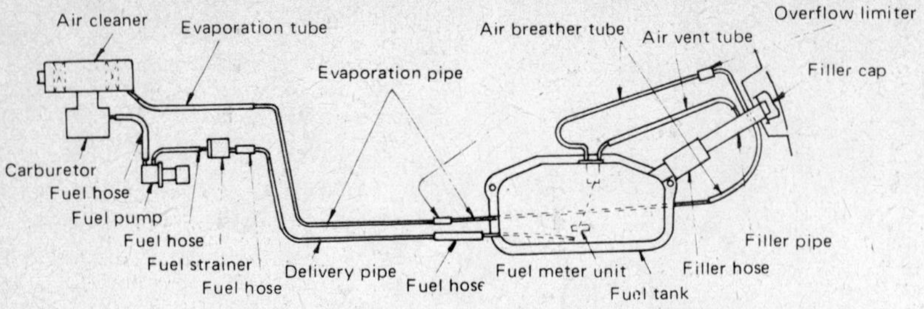

Evaporative emission control system—1975-79 sedan and coupe

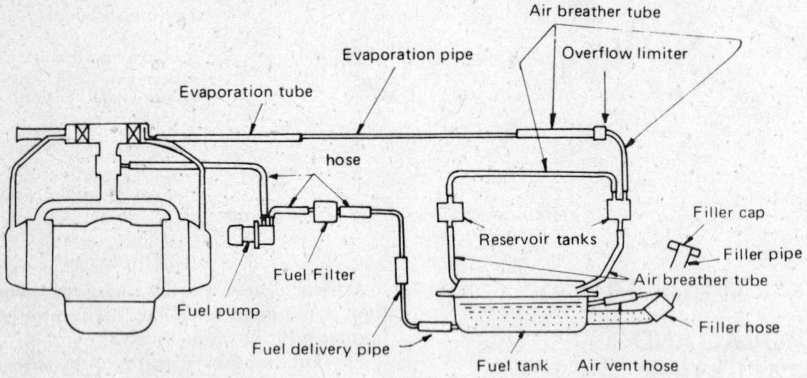

Evaporative emission control system—1975-79 wagons

these conditions excess vapors are drawn into the air cleaner (via a connecting hose from #1 and #3 valve cover) and pass through the carburetor into the engine.

Evaporative Emission Control System

1975-76

Evaporative gas from the fuel tank is not discharged into the atmosphere but conducted to the air cleaner unit and then burned in the combustion chamber. No absorbent is used.

The system consists of a sealed fuel tank and filler cap, two reservoir tanks on the station wagon, an air breather valve or a restriction, breather hoses, breather pipe and the air cleaner.

While the engine is running, evaporative gas is absorbed into the intake manifold due to the suction pressure of the manifold, and never discharged directly into the atmosphere. While the engine is stopped, the gases collect on the inner wall of the element of the air cleaner.

There is an air breather valve located at the filler cap. When the flap (door) is opened, a spring exerts pressure on the rubber breather hose and pinches it shut.

The vacuum relief valve filler cap relieves any vacuum condition that might arise in the gas tank.

1977 and Later

On 1977 and later models, the EEC system was revised to include a vapor canister which collects the fuel vapor before it reaches the carburetor. Once in the canister, the fuel vapor is absorbed on a supply of activated charcoal particles. These particles hold the vapor until the engine idle speed increases to a point where the carburetor vacuum is sufficient to open the purge valve on the canister. With the valve open the fuel vapor is sucked out of the charcoal particles and into the intake manifold; fresh air is drawn through a filter at the bottom of the canister to displace the escaping fuel vapor.

The system also incorporates two orifices located on the line between the fuel tank and vapor canister; these prevent fuel spillage in the event of impact. On station wagons (1977-79), two small reserve tanks on both sides of the fuel tank are employed to prevent liquid fuel from flowing into the air cleaner in case of an abrupt stop, etc. California models (1977-79) have a check valve on the line between the canister and the intake manifold to prevent a build-up of vapor in the manifold when the engine is stopped. 1980 California models have a carburetor vapor line connecting the float chamber and canister, as well as a tank vapor line. The (1977-79) 49 state (high altitude) models employ a two-way valve between the fuel tank and canister. It functions to control the flow of fuel vapor to the canister according to pressure in the fuel tank.

SERVICE

Keep all of the lines in good repair and free from cracks and blockage. The system should be relatively air tight. On 1977 and later models replace the canister filter every 25,000 miles.

Air Injection System

1975

A belt-driven air pump is used to supply air, under pressure, to air distribution manifolds which have openings at each exhaust port. Injection of air at this point causes combustion of the unburned hydrocarbons in the exhaust manifolds. An anti-backfire valve controls the flow of air from the pump to prevent backfiring resulting from an overly rich mixture under deceleration.

Check valves prevent hot exhaust gas back-

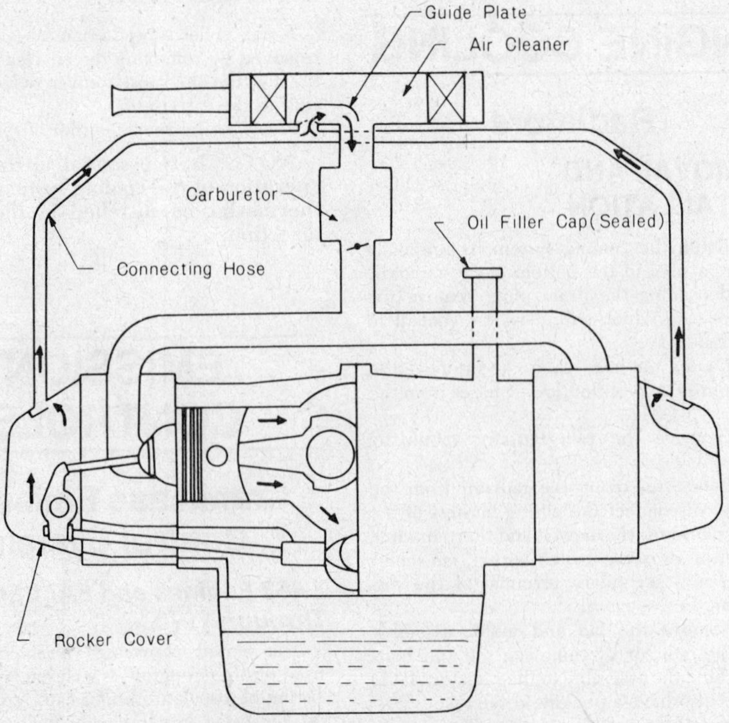

Routing of crankcase emissions

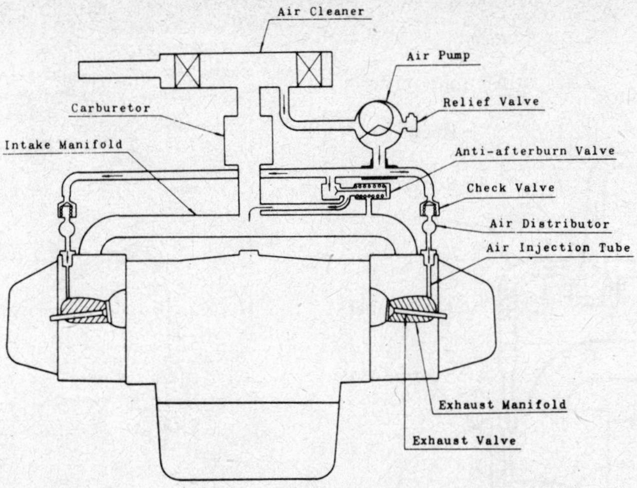

Air injection system

flow into the pump and hoses in case of pump or anti-backfire valve failure.

The air pump has a relief valve to discharge excess pressure at high engine speed.

REMOVAL AND INSTALLATION

Air Pump

1. Disconnect the air hoses from the pump.
2. Loosen the bolt on the adjusting link and remove the drive belt.
3. Remove the mounting bolts and the pump.

Installation is the reverse of removal. Adjust the drive belt tension after installation. Belt deflection should be ⅜ in. with 22 lbs. pressure.

Anti-Backfire Valve

1. Detach the air hoses from the valve.
2. Remove the valve securing bolt.
3. Remove the valve.

Installation is the reverse of removal.

Check Valves

1. Detach the intake hoses from the valves.
2. Use an open-end wrench to remove the valve from its mounting. Save the aluminum gasket.

Installation is the reverse of removal.

Relief Valve

1. Remove the air pump from the car.
2. Support the pump so that it cannot rotate.

CAUTION

Never clamp the pump in a vise, the aluminum case will be distorted.

3. Use a puller to remove the relief valve from the top of the pump.
4. Position the new relief valve over the opening in the pump.

NOTE: The air outlet should be pointing toward the left.

5. Gently tap the relief valve into place using a block of wood and a hammer.
6. Install the pump on the engine.

Air Injection Manifold

1. Remove the check valve.
2. Loosen the air injection manifold attachment nuts and remove the manifold.

TESTING

Air Pump

CAUTION

Do not hammer, pry, or bend the pump housing while tightening the drive belt or testing the pump.

BELT TENSION AND AIR LEAKS

1. Before proceeding with the tests, check the pump drive belt tension.
2. Turn the pump by hand. If it has seized, the belt will slip, making a noise. Disregard any chirping, squealing, or rolling sounds from inside the pump; these are normal when it is turned by hand.
3. Check the hoses and connections for leaks. Hissing or a blast of air is indicative of a leak. Soapy water, applied lightly around the area in question, is a good method for detecting leaks.

AIR OUTPUT

1. Disconnect the air supply hose at the antibackfire valve.
2. Connect a pressure gauge, using an adapter, to the air supply hose.

NOTE: If there are two hoses, plug the second one.

3. With the engine at normal operating temperature, increase the idle speed and watch the gauge.
4. The air flow from the pump should be steady and fall between 1½ and 6 psi. If it is unsteady or falls below this, the pump is defective and must be replaced.

PUMP NOISE DIAGNOSIS

The air pump is normally noisy, as engine speed increases, the noise of the pump will rise in pitch. The rolling sound the pump bearings make is normal. But if this sound becomes objectionable at certain speeds, the pump is defective and will have to be replaced.

A continual hissing sound from the air pump pressure relief valve at idle, indicates a defective valve. Replace the relief valve.

If the pump rear bearing fails, a continual knocking sound will be heard.

Anti-Backfire Valve

1. Detach the air supply hose which runs between the pump and the gulp valve.
2. Connect a tachometer and run the engine to 1,500-2,000 rpm.
3. Allow the throttle to snap closed. This should produce a loud sucking sound from the valve.
4. Repeat this operation several times. If there is no sound, the valve is not working, or the vacuum connections are loose.

Check Valve Test

1. Before starting the test, check all of the hoses and connections for leaks.
2. Detach the air supply hose from the check valve.
3. Insert a probe into the check valve and depress the plate. Release it; the plate should return to its original position against the valve seat. If binding is evident, replace the valve.
4. With the engine running at normal operating temperature, gradually increase its speed to 1,500 rpm. Check for exhaust gas leakage. If there is any replace the valve assembly.

Air Suction System

1976 and Later

The air suction system is very similar to the air injection system, except it does not use an air pump.

To operate, the system utilizes the vacuum created by exhaust gas pulsation and normal intake manifold vacuum. Each exhaust port is connected to the air suction valve by air suction manifolds. When a vacuum is created in the exhaust ports a reed in the suction valve opens allowing fresh air to be sucked through the air cleaner and silencer (pre-1980 models) or the secondary air cleaner (1980 models) and into the exhaust ports. When there is pressure rather than vacuum in the exhaust ports, the reed in the air suction valve closes, preventing the flow of exhaust gases.

The fresh air sucked through the air suction valve is used for oxidation of HC and CO in the exhaust passages and partly for combustion in the cylinders.

MAINTENANCE

1. Check the air suction hose and manifolds for cracks, damage, looseness or leakage.
2. Check the reed valve for cracks or abnormal projections. Check the rubber seat for cracks.

SERVICE

1. Check clearance between the reed valve and the rubber seat.
2. If the clearance is more than 0.079 in., disassemble the reed valve and clean in solvent.
3. If the clearance is still more than 0.079 in. after cleaning, replace the reed valve.
4. The end height of the reed valve stopper is 0.217 to 0.256 in.

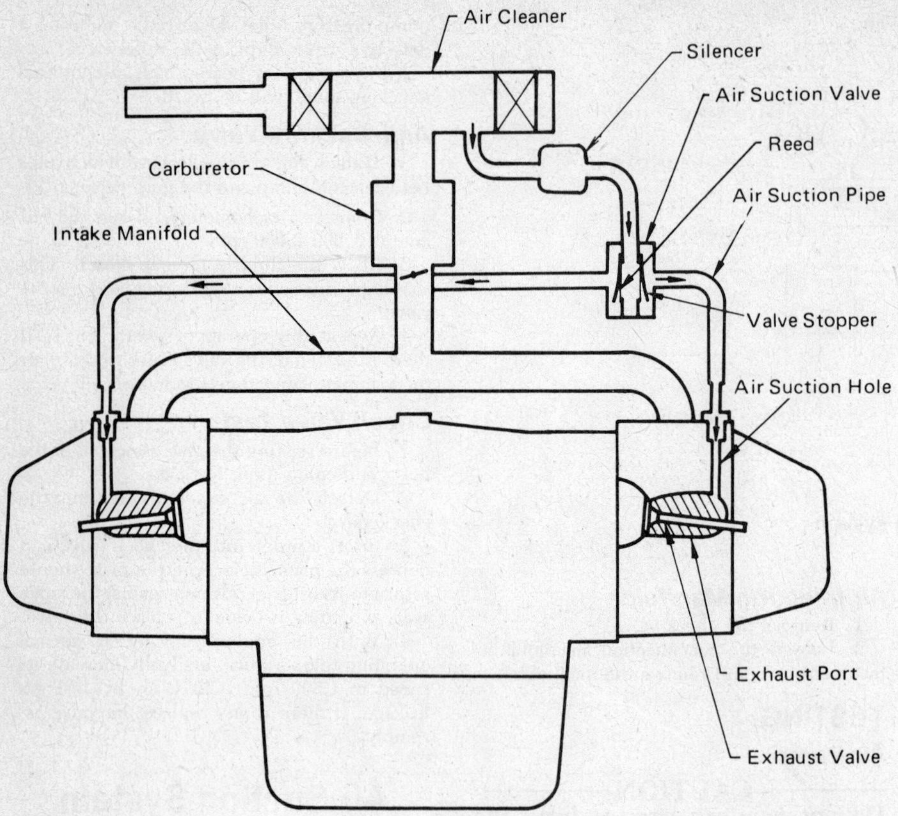

Air suction system

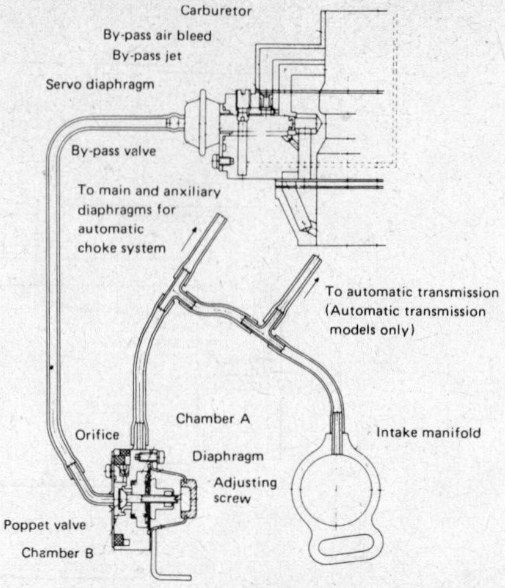

Sectional view—coasting by-pass system

Port Liner–1980 and Later

On models except the federal Hatchback STD, DL, Sedan DL and Hardtop DL an exhaust port liner made from stainless steel plate is built into the cylinder head as one unit.

The port liner has a built in air layer which decreases heat transfer to the cylinder head while keeping the exhaust port at a higher temperature. This insulation of the exhaust port helps oxidation of residual HC and CO with the help of the remaining air in the exhaust gases.

Anti-Afterburning Valve–1980

The anti-afterburning valve prevents afterburning that occurs on cold starts. Below about 50 degrees centigrade the temperature valve has an open passage connecting the afterburning valve with the intake manifold via a vacuum line. The vacuum line remains opened and the afterburning valve in operation until the coolant temperature becomes hot enough to shut off the vacuum and override the afterburning system.

Coasting Bypass System

To control the HC emissions while the vehicle is in the coasting or decelerating mode, a controlled amount of air/fuel mixture is channelled through the coasting bypass passage in the carburetor.

The high engine vacuum reacts on a bypass valve diaphragm, opening a vacuum passage to the servo valve on the carburetor, which in turn opens a metered passage from the carburetor air horn to the section of the throttle bore below the secondary throttle plate.

As engine vacuum drops on acceleration, the bypass valve closes the passage to the servo valve and the carburetor returns to its normal function.

MAINTENANCE

1. Inspect the vacuum hoses for leaks.
2. Test the bypass valve and servo valve diaphragms with a vacuum test pump.

SERVICE

1. Connect a vacuum gauge to the disconnected servo vacuum line.
2. Increase the engine speed to between 3,000 and 4,000 rpm, without load, and immediately release the throttle valve.
3. When a fizzing noise is heard from the bypass valve, read the vacuum measurement.
   a. If the fizzing noise cannot be heard, turn the adjusting screw of the bypass valve (control valve) clockwise until it can be heard.
   b. If the fizzing noise can be heard at idle constantly, turn the adjusting screw counterclockwise until it disappears.
4. Refer to the chart and set the vacuum to specifications by rotating the adjusting screw of the bypass valve.

Engine Modification System

The principle of this system is not only to obtain correct air/fuel mixture while the vehicle is decelerating, but also to promote complete combustion by retarding the ignition timing, thus reducing the amount of emissions released into the atmosphere.

While the vehicle is decelerating, the primary throttle valve is closed, causing a high vacuum in the intake manifold. This vacuum is conducted through a vacuum control valve and on to the carburetor where a by-pass jet is opened and extra mixture is allowed to enter the venturi below the throttle plates. This enriches the mixture and promotes cleaner combustion.

The vacuum is also routed to the distributor vacuum retard unit.

There is an anti-dieseling solenoid mounted opposite the float bowl on the carburetor. This switch prevents the engine from dieseling

Altitude	49 States and High Altitude	California
0 to 2,000 ft.	20.9 ± 0.39 in. hg	18.9 ± 0.39 in. hg
2,000 to 4,000 ft.	19.3 ± 0.39 in. hg ①	17.3 ± 0.39 in. hg ①
Above 4,000 ft.	17.7 ± 0.39 in. hg ②	15.7 ± 0.39 in. hg ②

① Turn adjusting screw ¼ turn counterclockwise after vacuum is set to specifications
② Turn adjusting screw ¾ turn counterclockwise after vacuum is set to specifications

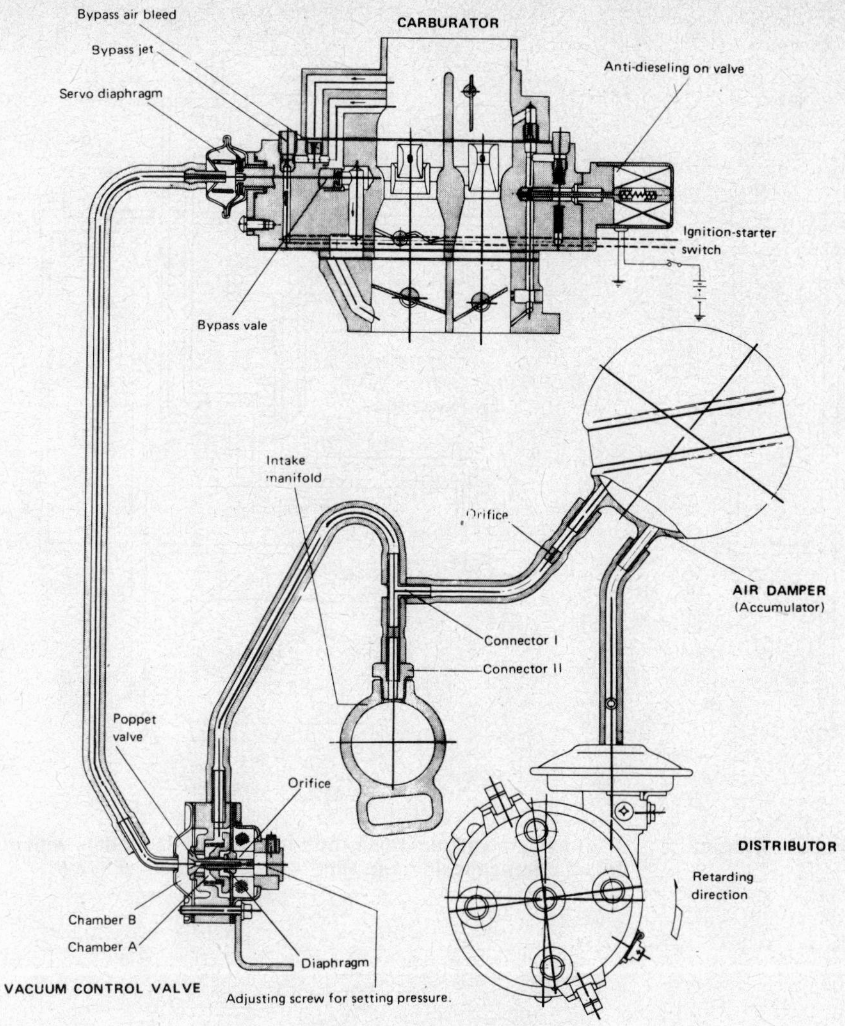

Engine modification system

when the ignition switch is turned off. When the ignition switch is turned off, an electromagnet in the switch is also cut off. A spring inside the housing forces a plunger into position, blocking the fuel passages leading to the opening below the throttle plates. When the ignition switch is turned on, it energizes the electromagnet in the switch and pulls the plunger out of the fuel passage, allowing fuel to reach the opening below the throttle plates.

Electrically Assisted Automatic Choke

The vacuum automatic choke uses a choke cap containing a heating element to speed up choke valve opening and reduce CO emissions during warm-up. The heating element gets its power from a special tap on the voltage regulator, when the ignition is on and the engine running.

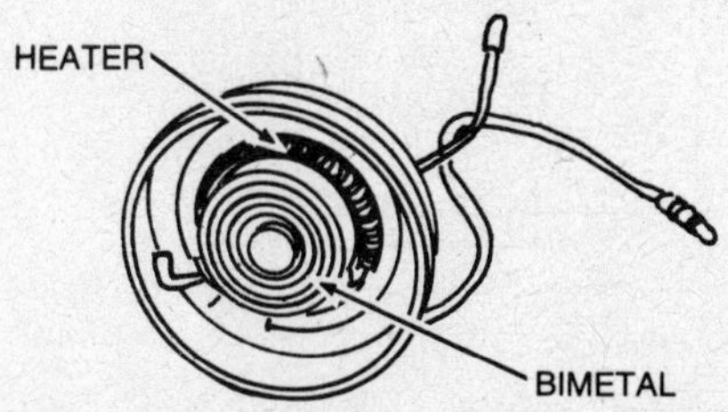

Choke cap with bi-metal spring and heating element

TESTING

1. Disconnect the choke lead from the voltage regulator.
2. Connect an ohmmeter between the lead that you just disconnected and a good ground. The ohmmeter should read about 9 ohms.
3. Replace the choke cap if the reading shows an opened (no resistance) or shorted (infinite resistance) heating coil.

Carburetor Dashpot

ADJUSTMENT

1. Be sure that the throttle valve is in the idle (closed) position.
2. The dashpot stem should be able to move about 0.16 in. beyond the throttle lever's idle position.
3. If the stem does not move the correct distance, adjust the dashpot, by loosening its locknut and rotating the dashpot until the correct amount of movement is obtained.
4. Tighten the locknut and recheck dashpot stem movement.

Exhaust Gas Recirculation (EGR) System

An exhaust gas recirculation (EGR) system is used on 1975-76 California models and all 1977 and later models to reduce NO_x (oxides of nitrogen) emissions by lowering peak flame temperature during combustion. A small portion of the exhaust gases are routed into the intake manifold via a vacuum-operated EGR control valve.

TESTING

EGR System

1. Start the engine and allow it to reach normal operating temperature.
2. Increase the engine speed to 3000-3500 rpm (no load). The valve shaft should move upward.

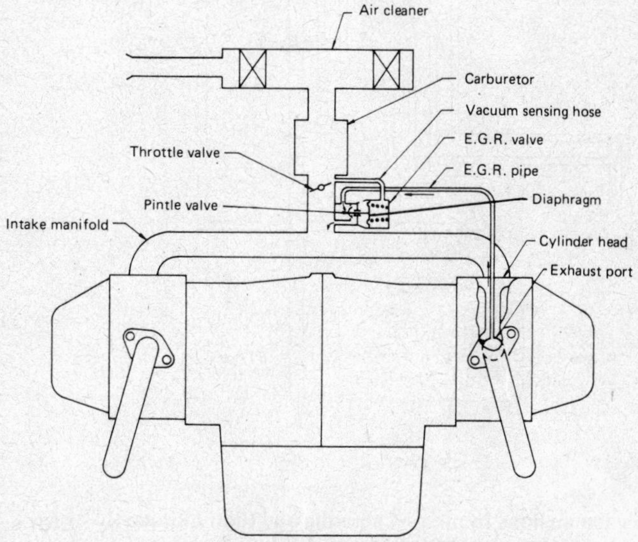

Exhaust gas recirculation system

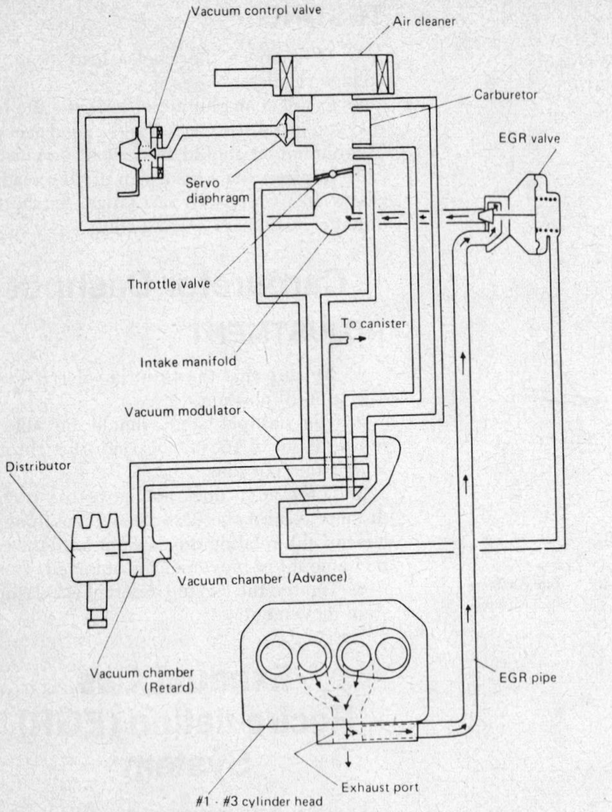

EGR system vacuum hose routing—49 state models with automatic transmission and 4WD

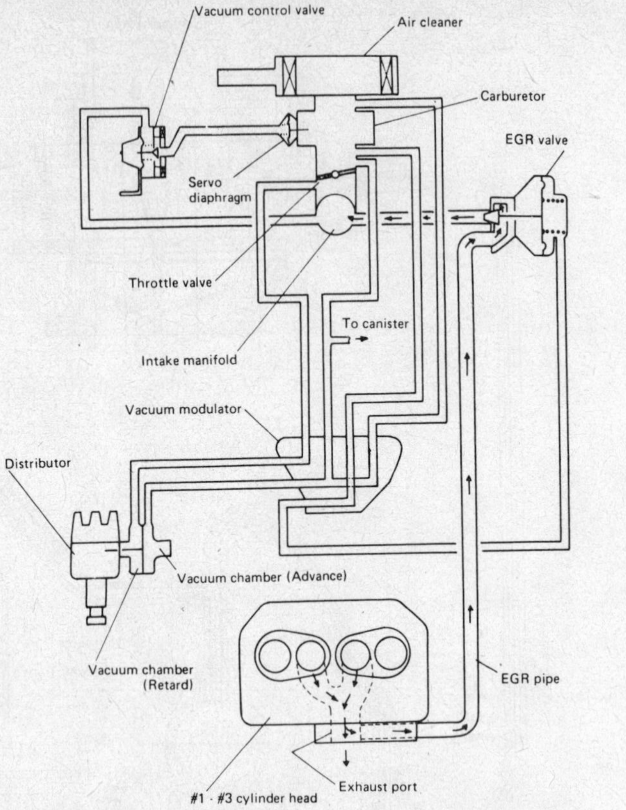

EGR system vacuum hose routing—California models with automatic transmission and High Altitude models with 4WD

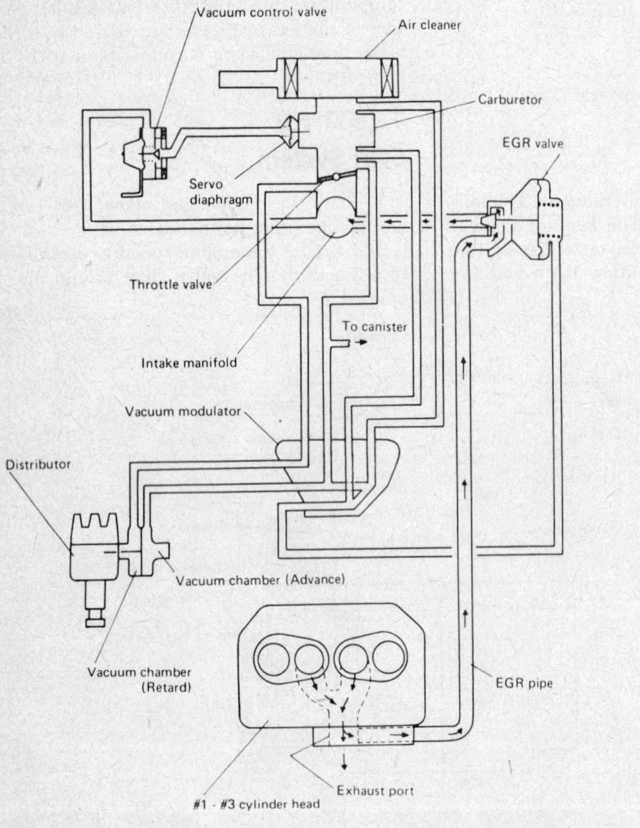

EGR system vacuum hose routing—California and High Altitude models except automatic transmission and 4WD

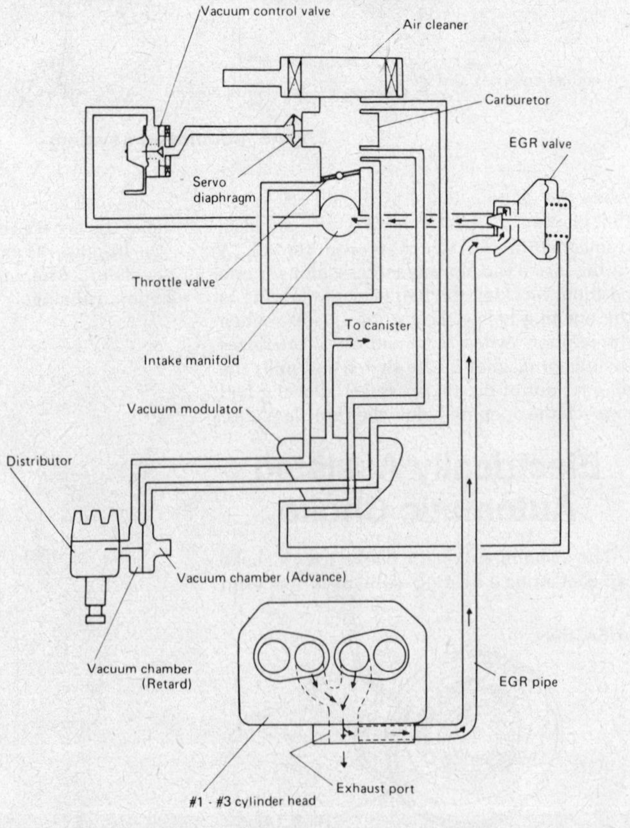

EGR system vacuum hose routing—High Altitude models with automatic transmission

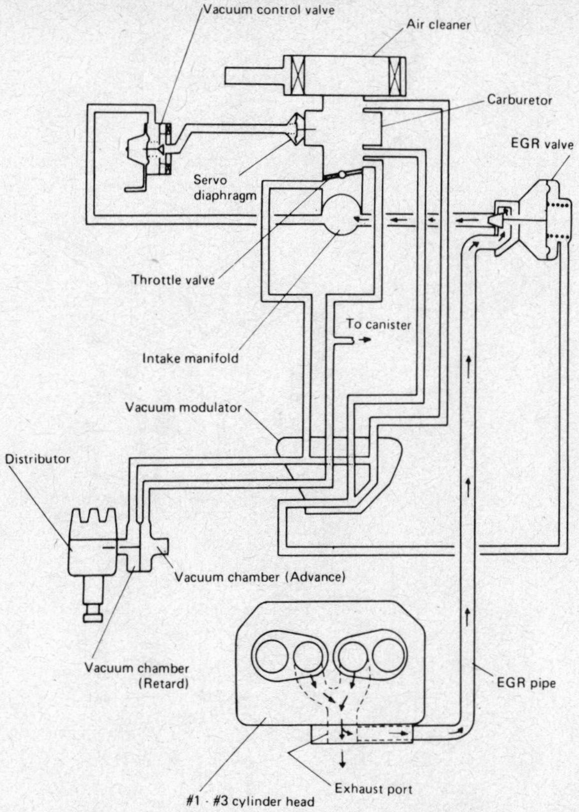

EGR system vacuum hose routing—49 state models except automatic transmission and 4WD models

3. Decrease the engine speed to idle, the valve shaft should go down.

4. If the valve shaft fails to raise in Step 2, check the vacuum lines, connections, and the carburetor throttle vacuum port. Replace any clogged or damaged hoses, and clean the throttle port if it is clogged.

5. Connect the EGR valve vacuum hose directly to the throttle port on the carburetor. Speed the engine up and return it to idle as in Step 2 and 3. If the valve works, the fault lies in the vacuum solenoid valve or the temperature switch.

6. If the EGR valve doesn't work, perform the following EGR valve checks:

a. Remove the EGR valve from the intake manifold.

b. Plug the vacuum inlet on the top of the valve diaphragm.

c. Depress and release the pintle (valve plunger) several times.

d. The pintle should remain depressed as long as the vacuum inlet is plugged. If it doesn't, the diaphragm is leaking and the valve assembly must be replaced.

e. If the valve stem appears to be stuck, clean the pintle with a wire brush or spark plug cleaning machine.

f. Install the valve and retest it.

Vacuum Solenoid Valve and Coolant Temperature Switch

1. Disconnect the vacuum solenoid leads.
2. Connect the solenoid directly to a 12-volt power source. The solenoid should click.
3. If the solenoid is working properly and everything else in the system is in proper operating order, replace the coolant temperature switch.

Hot Air Control System

The hot air control system consists of the air cleaner, the air stove on the exhaust pipe and the air intake hose connecting the air cleaner and air stove. The air cleaner is equipped with an air control valve which maintains the temperature of the air being drawn into the carburetor at 100°-127° F to reduce HC emission when the underhood temperature is below 100° F. Thissystemshould be inspected every 12,000 miles.

TEMPERATURE SENSOR

Removal and Installation

1. Using pliers, flatten the clip securing the vacuum hose to the sensor vacuum pipe.
2. Disconnect the hose from the sensor.
3. Remove the clip from the sensor vacuum pipe and remove the sensor body from the air cleaner.

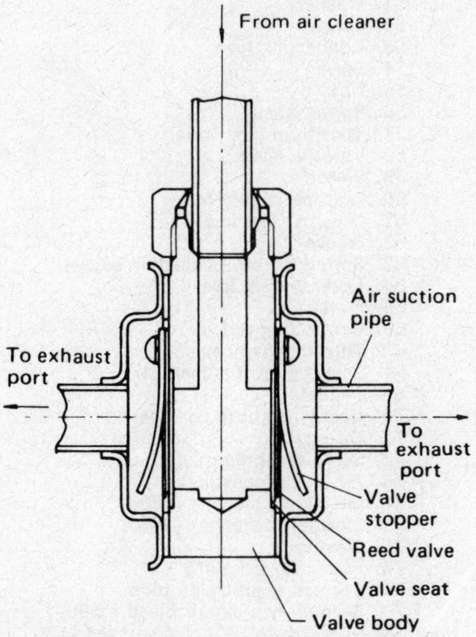

Cross section of reed valve assembly

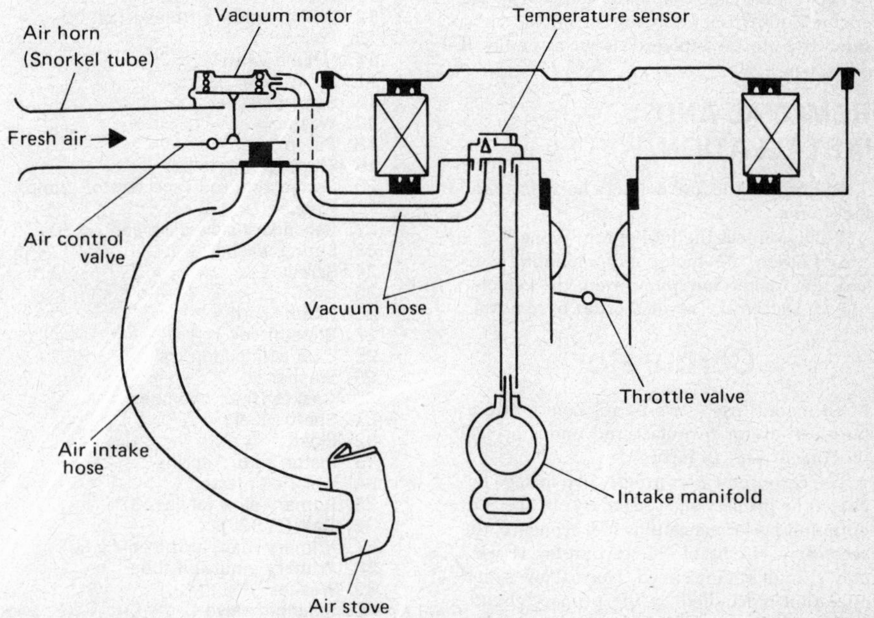

Hot air control system

NOTE: The gasket is glued to the air cleaner and should not be removed.

4. To install reverse the removal procedure.

VACUUM MOTOR

Removal and Installation

1. Remove the screws securing the vacuum motor to the air cleaner.
2. Disconnect the valve shaft, attached to the vacuum motor diaphragm, at the air control valve, and remove the vacuum motor from the air cleaner.
3. To install reverse the removal procedure.

FUEL SYSTEM

Fuel Filter

REPLACEMENT

All Subarus use a cartridge fuel filter, located in the fuel pump-to-carburetor fuel line. The filter is the disposable type which cannot be cleaned.

To replace the filter cartridge:

1. Loosen, but do not remove, the nuts which secure the two hose clamps located at either end of the filter.
2. Work the hoses off the filter necks.
3. Snap the filter out of its mounting bracket, if so equipped.
4. Throw the old filter away.

NOTE: When removing the old filter, be careful not to allow any to drip onto hot engine components. Installation is the reverse of removal. Be sure that the hose clamps are tightened securely.

Fuel Pump

The electric fuel pump is located in the engine compartment, mounted on the right side. It is to be replaced as an assembly if defective.

REMOVAL AND INSTALLATION

1. Remove the fuel delivery hoses from the fuel pump.
2. Disconnect the fuel pump wiring.
3. Loosen the fuel pump mounting nuts and remove the fuel pump from the vehicle.
4. Install in the reverse order of removal.

Carburetor

All models use a two-barrel Zenith-Stromberg carburetor manufactured under license by Hitachi Ltd. in Japan.

The carburetor uses progressive linkage between the primary and secondary circuits. For optimum performance plus fuel economy, the secondary circuit of the carburetor is used only at high engine speed. Normal low speed operation is handled by the primary circuit. 1975 and later models have an automatic choke.

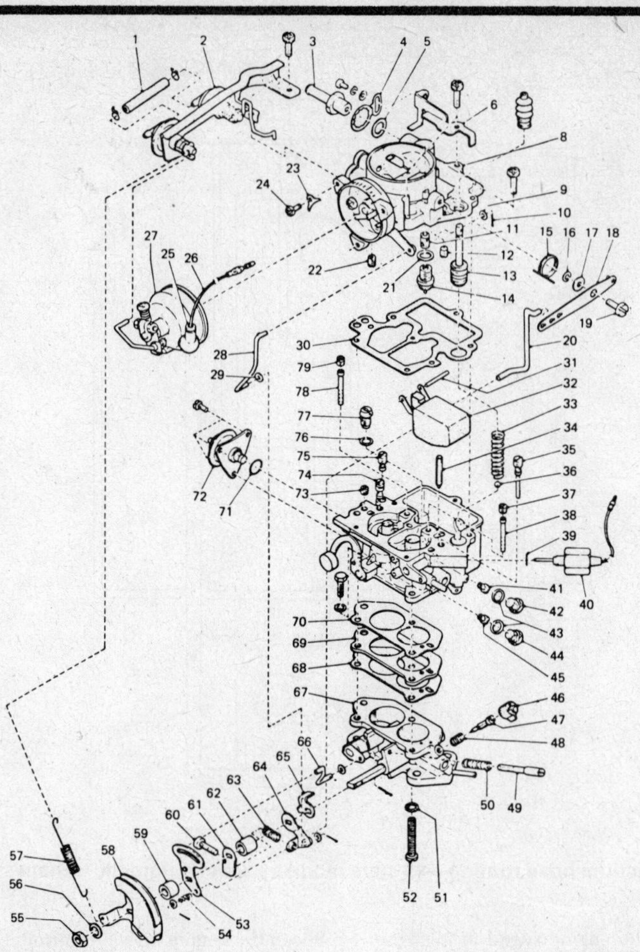

1. Vacuum hose
2. Vacuum diaphragm assembly
3. Nipple (fuel inlet)
4. Stopper
5. Washer
6. Nipple guide
7. Pump cover
8. Choke chamber
9. Washer
10. Cotter pin
11. Filter
12. Primary slow air bleed (#200)
13. Piston
14. Needle valve
15. Pump lever spring
16. Spring washer
17. Washer
18. Pump lever
19. Shaft (pump lever)
20. Connecting rod (accelerator pump)
21. Washer
22. Secondary slow air bleed (#70)
23. Spring washer
24. Screw
25. Boot
26. Heater cord
27. Bimetal cover
28. Cam connecting rod
29. Washer
30. Gasket (float chamber)
31. Shaft (float)
32. Float
33. Piston return spring
34. Weight (injector)
35. Primary slow jet (#43)
36. Ball (5/32")
37. Primary main air bleed (#60)
38. Primary emulsion tube
39. Washer
40. Solenoid valve
41. Primary main jet (#95, #93)
42. Drain plug (primary)
43. Washer
44. Drain plug (secondary)
45. Secondary main jet (#155)
46. Idle limiter cap
47. Idle adjust screw
48. Spring (idle adjust screw)
49. Throttle adjusting screw
50. Spring (throttle adjusting screw)
51. Washer
52. Screw
53. Connecting lever
54. Spring
55. Nut
56. Spring washer
57. Throttle return spring
58. Throttle lever
59. Sleeve
60. Fast idle adjust screw
61. Lever A (fast idle)
62. Sleeve
63. Spring (throttle adjusting screw)
64. Lever B (fast idle)
65. Plate
66. Connecting rod
67. Throttle chamber
68. Gasket (throttle chamber)
69. Insulator
70. Gasket (throttle chamber)
71. O-ring
72. Servo diaphragm
73. Air bleed (coasting)
74. Secondary slow jet (#60)
75. Slow jet (coasting) (#50)
76. Washer
77. Power valve (#45)
78. Secondary emulsion tube
79. Secondary main air bleed (#90)

Exploded view of the 1975-77 GL and DL carburetor with automatic choke

REMOVAL AND INSTALLATION

1. Remove the air cleaner emission control system hoses, mounting bracket screws, wing nut, and lift the air cleaner assembly off the carburetor.
2. Disconnect the fuel lines from the carburetor.
3. Unfasten the vacuum hoses from the servo diaphragm, automatic choke diaphragms, distributor, and the EGR port (if so equipped).
4. Disconnect the anti-dieseling switch and automatic choke heater electrical leads.
5. Remove the accelerator cable from the throttle lever.
6. Unfasten the 4 nuts which secure the carburetor and take it off the intake manifold. Cover the hole in the intake manifold, to prevent anything from falling in.

Installation is the reverse of removal.

OVERHAUL

Generally, when a carburetor requires major service, a rebuilt one is purchased on an exchange basis, or a kit may be bought for overhauling the carburetor.

The kit contains the necessary parts and some form of instructions for carburetor rebuilding. The instructions may vary between a simple exploded view and detailed step-by-step rebuilding instructions. Unless you are familiar with carburetor overhaul, the latter should be used.

There are some general overhaul procedures which should always be observed.

Efficient carburetion depends greatly on careful cleaning and inspection during overhaul since dirt, gum, water, or varnish in or on the carburetor parts are often responsible for poor performance.

Overhaul the carburetor in a clean, dust-free area. Carefully disassemble the carburetor, referring often to the exploded views. Keep all similar and lookalike parts segregated during disassembly and cleaning to avoid accidental interchange during assembly. Make a note of all jet sizes.

When the carburetor is disassembled, wash all parts (except diaphragms, electric choke units, pump plunger, and any other plastic, leather, fiber, or rubber parts) in clean carburetor solvent. Do not leave parts in the solvent any longer than is necessary to sufficiently loosen the deposits. Excessive cleaning may remove the special finish from the float bowl and choke valve bodies, leaving these parts unfit for service. Rinse all parts in clean solvent and blow them dry with compressed air or allow them to air dry. Wipe clean all cork, plastic, leather, and fiber parts with a clean, lint-free cloth.

Blow out all passages and jets with compressed air and be sure that there are no restrictions or blockages. Never use wire or similar tools to clean jets, fuel passages, or air bleeds. Clean all jets and valves separately to avoid accidental interchange.

Check all parts for wear or damage. If wear or damage is found, replace the defective parts. Especially check the following:

1. Check the float needle and seat for wear. If wear is found, replace the complete assembly.
2. Check the float hinge pin for wear and the float(s) for dents or distortion. Replace the float if fuel has leaked into it.
3. Check the throttle and choke shaft bores for wear or an out-of-round condition. Damage or wear to the throttle arm, shaft, or shaft bore will often require replacement of the throttle body. Those parts require a close tolerance of fit; wear may allow air leakage, which could affect starting and idling.

NOTE: Throttle shafts and bushings are usually not included in overhaul kits. They can be purchased separately.

4. Inspect the idle mixture adjusting needles for burrs or grooves. Any such condition requires replacement of the needle, since you will not be able to obtain a satisfactory idle.
5. Test the accelerator pump check valves. They should pass air one way but not the other. Test for proper seating by blowing and sucking on the valve. Replace the valve if necessary. If the valve is satisfactory, wash the valve again to remove breath moisture.
6. Check the bowl cover for warped surfaces with a straightedge.
7. Closely inspect the valves and seats for wear and damage, replacing as necessary.
8. After the carburetor is assembled, check the choke valve for freedom of operation.

Carburetor overhaul kits are recommended for each overhaul. These kits contain all gaskets and new parts to replace those that deteriorate most rapidly. Failure to replace all parts supplied with the kit (especially gaskets) can result in poor performance later.

After cleaning and checking all components, reassemble the carburetor, using new parts and referring to the exploded view. When reassembling, make sure that all screws and jets are tight in their seats, but do not overtighten, as the tips will be distorted. Tighten all screws gradually, in rotation. Do not tighten needle valves into their seats; uneven jetting will result. Always use new gaskets. Be sure to adjust the float level when reassembling.

PRIMARY/SECONDARY THROTTLE LINKAGE ADJUSTMENT

1. With the carburetor removed from the engine, operate the linkage so that the connecting rod contacts the groove on the end of the secondary actuating lever.
2. Measure the clearance between the lower end of the primary throttle valve and its bore. It should be about 0.24 in. for all models.
3. Adjust the clearance by bending the connecting rod.
4. Check that the linkage operates smoothly.

FLOAT AND FUEL LEVEL ADJUSTMENT

On models with a sight glass on the carburetor float bowl, the fuel should be level (within 1/16 in.) with the dot on the glass when the engine is running.

The float level may be adjusted with the carburetor installed on the engine:

1. Disconnect the accelerator pump actuating rod from the pump lever.
2. Remove the throttle return spring.
3. Disconnect the choke cable from the

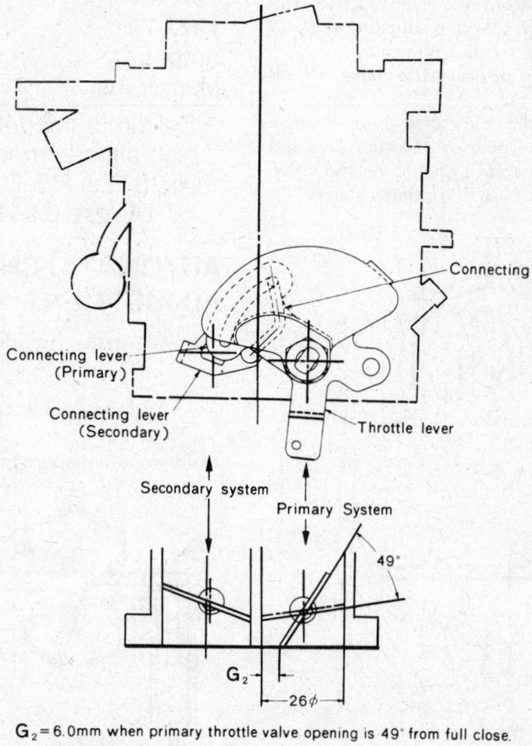

G_2=6.0mm when primary throttle valve opening is 49° from full close. (EA63A)

Throttle linkage adjustment

choke lever, and remove it from the spring hanger.

4. Remove the spring hanger, the choke bellcrank, and the remaining air horn retaining screws.

5. Lift the air horn slightly, disconnect the choke connecting rod, and remove the air horn.

6. Invert the air horn (float up), and measure the distance between the surface of the air horn and the float.

7. Bend the float arm until the clearance is approximately 0.41 in.

8. Invert the air horn to its installed position and measure the distance between the float arm and the needle valve stem. This dimension should be 0.050-0.065 in., and is adjusted by bending the float stops.

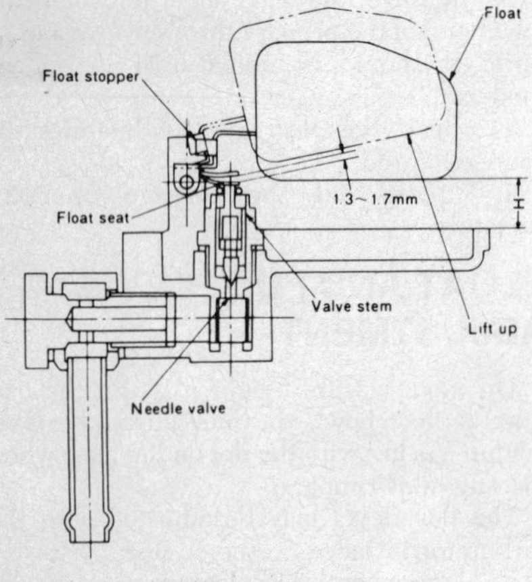

Float adjustment

FAST IDLE ADJUSTMENT

1. With the carburetor removed from the engine, set the fast idle cam adjusting lever on the fourth step of the fast idle cam.

2. Check to be sure that the choke valve is fully closed.

3. Measure the clearance between the lower edge of the primary throttle valve and its bore. The clearance should be the valve specified in the "Fast Idle" chart, above.

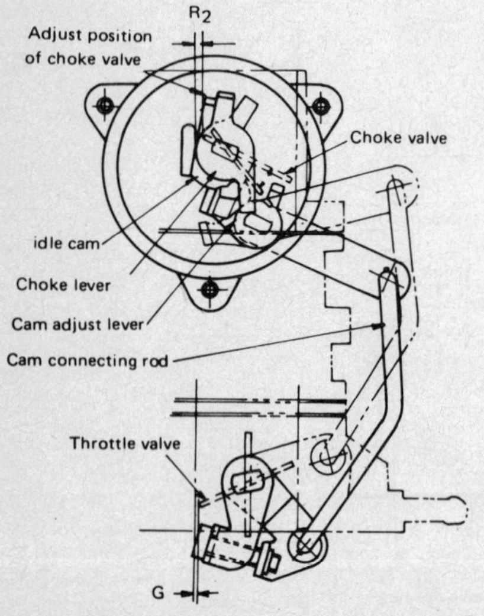

Fast idle adjustment on the 1975-77 carburetor. "G" is the angle to be measured

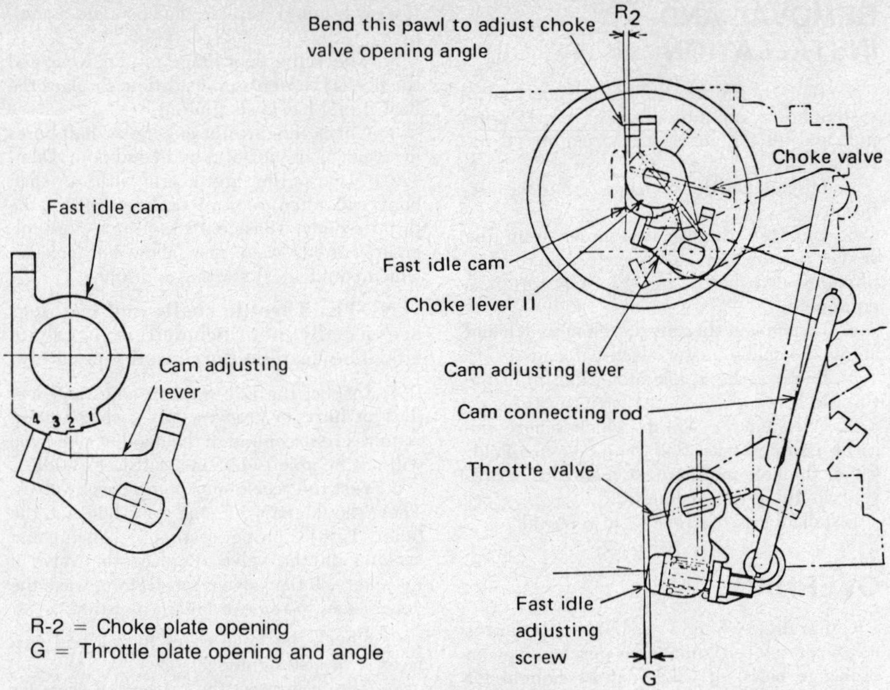

Fast idle adjustment

4. If the clearance is incorrect, turn the fast idle adjusting screw to bring it within specifications. Turning the screw *in* increases the throttle clearance and vice versa.

Model	Primary Throttle-to-Bore Clearance
1975	0.039 in.
1976	0.056 in.
1977-79	0.047 in.①
Auto. trans.	0.060 in.
Man. trans.	0.050 in.②

①California models and 49 state high altitude models—0.060 in.
②HB-STD, HB-DL, SD-DL, and HT-DL use 0.041 in.

AUTOMATIC CHOKE ADJUSTMENT

1. Adjust the fast idle as detailed above, and perform the adjustments which follow, in the sequence given.

2. Pull the main choke diaphragm lever as far as it will go to the left and measure the clearance between the upper end of the choke valve and its bore with a wire gauge. The clearance should be 0.046-0.055 in. Adjust, as necessary, by bending the diaphragm-to-choke connecting rod.

3. Apply 8-9 in. Hg of vacuum to the main diaphragm, it should operate the choke valve. If it does not, replace the diaphragm with a new one.

4. Place the fast idle cam adjusting lever on the *third* step of the fast idle cam. Measure the clearance between the upper end of the choke valve and its bore. The clearance should be 0.063-0.074 in. for 1975-76 cars; 0.026-0.037 in. for 1977-80 cars. Carefully bend (turn) the fast idle cam to obtain the correct clearance, as necessary. To obtain the clearance, bend the cam clockwise; to decrease it, bend the cam counterclockwise.

5. Loosen the 3 choke cap securing screws, and match the line on it up with the longest

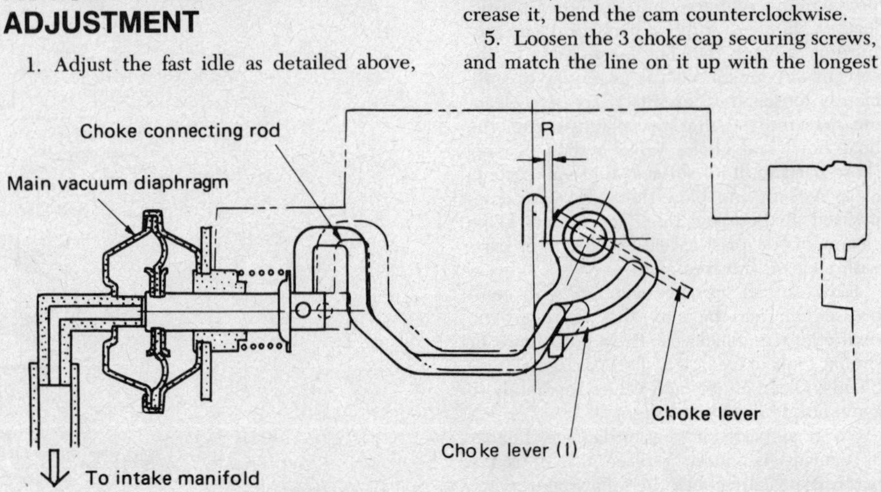

Choke plate opening clearance (R)

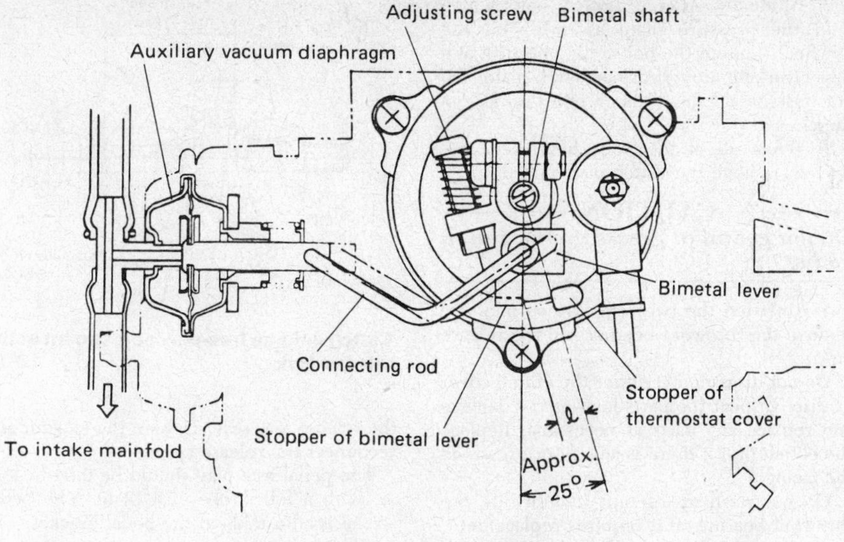

Bi-metal compensation adjustment

line on the choke coil housing. Tighten the retaining screws.

CAUTION

Do not loosen the screw which secures the choke lever.

6. Fit the tang on the bimetal lever, which is connected to the auxiliary diaphragm, against the stop in the choke coil housing. Pull the setting piston of the auxiliary diaphragm back and, with the piston in this position, tighten the compensator adjusting screw so that it contacts the tang on the bimetal lever; the gap should be 0.197 in. on 1975-76 cars, and 0.34 in. on 1977-80 cars.

7. Apply vacuum from an outside source to the auxiliary diaphragm. It should take 9.5-11.8 in. Hg of vacuum to operate the diaphragm on 1975-76 cars; and 6.9-9.2 in. Hg of vacuum in 1977-80 cars. To adjust the vacuum setting, bend the diaphragm rod. Vacuum is reduced when the rod is bent to shorten it and increased when the rod is bent to lengthen it.

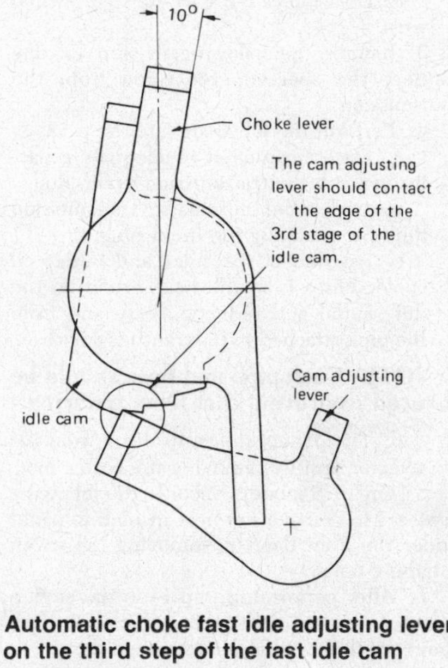

Automatic choke fast idle adjusting lever on the third step of the fast idle cam

NOTE: When the setting piston is released, there should be no clearance between the tang on the bimetal lever and the stop on the coil housing. If they don't contact, the bimetal lever has been bent too much.

MANUAL TRANSMISSION

REMOVAL AND INSTALLATION

If it is necessary to remove the transaxle it must be removed as an assembly with the engine. Be sure to read this entire procedure before proceeding.

1. Perform the engine removal procedure for these models as outlined in "Engine Removal and Installation." Include the additional steps outlined below at the appropriate point in the engine removal procedure, where indicated. *Do not perform Steps 15 through 22 of the engine removal procedure.*
2. Include the following in Step 8.
   a. Disconnect the back-up light switch wire.
   b. On 4WD models, disconnect the drive selector switch wire.
3. Include the following in Step 12: disconnect the speedometer cable from the transmission.
4. On 4WD models, perform the following after Step 13: remove the drive selector lever and gear shift lever.
   a. Pull up the boots on the drive selector lever and gear shift lever (inside the car).
   b. Remove the through bolts and nuts and pull the drive selector lever and gear shift lever out of their brackets.
   c. Remove the brackets from the transmission case.
5. On all models except 4WD, perform the following after Step 12. Disconnect the gear shift system.
   a. Remove the 8 mm through bolt connecting the stay to the engine mounting bracket (rear).
   b. Remove the 8 mm through bolt connecting the rod to the joint. Leave the rubber cushion attaching nut intact, and the rod and stay hanging.

NOTE: On 1975 models, it is necessary to remove the gear shift rod by knocking out the spring pin.

6. On 1975 models, include the following in Step 14. Remove the heat insulating panel under the front floor by removing the seven retaining bolts.
7. After performing Step 14 in the engine removal section raise the vehicle on jackstands, if this has not already been done. 4WD models must be on four stands, all other models need only two in front.

NOTE: Reference to engine removal procedure is not necessary after this point, except to check that all the steps have been completed.

8. On 4WD models, disconnect the propeller shaft from the transmission as follows.
   a. Drain the gear oil by removing the drain plug from the transmission.
   b. Remove the four bolts joining the driveshaft to the companion flange of the rear differential, and pull the propeller shaft out of the transmission to the rear.
   c. Cover the opening at the rear end of the transmission to prevent oil from flowing out.
9. On 4WD models, disengage the handbrake cable from the rear crossmember and from the transverse link by loosening the clamp bolts.
10. Drive the spring pins out of the axle shafts with a small rod and hammer.
11. Separate the transverse links from the front crossmember by removing the through bolts at the inner ends of the transverse links.
12. Remove the nuts retaining the front engine mounts (rubber) on the front crossmember.
13. Set up a chain hoist on the engine, with hooks at the front and rear engine hangers. Adjust the hoist so that the weight of the engine is supported, but do not raise the engine.

NOTE: The purpose of supporting the engine at this point is to prevent the unstable movement of the engine and to protect the people working underneath the vehicle.

14. On 4WD models, remove the stabilizer mounting brackets on the leading rods.
15. Remove the nuts retaining the rear engine mount (rubber) on the crossmember.
16. On 4WD models, remove the rear crossmember, as follows.
   a. Support the transmission with a jack to prevent the transmission from coming down when the crossmember is removed.
   b. Remove the leading rod attaching nuts at the rear crossmember.
   c. Remove the bolts attaching the crossmember to the vehicle body.

17. Before going on to the next step, be sure that all of the above steps have been completed.
18. Remove the engine/transaxle assembly by carefully hoisting out of the vehicle. Be careful not to damage the brake pipes.
19. Place the entire assembly on a suitable stand or workbench.

Installation is the reverse of removal. Consult the engine installation notes in the Engine Removal and Installation section as well as the following precautions before working.

NOTE: If the front suspension was disassembled (e.g., 4WD models), reassemble as follows.

a. Connect the leading rod to the crossmember as shown below.
b. Position the two rear stabilizer bushings so that their outer surfaces are lined up with the paint marks on the stabilizer.

20. Use new self-locking nuts for the leading rods and transverse link bolts.

NOTE: These nuts must be tightened with the wheels on the ground under a no load condition.

21. When connecting axle shafts to the transmission use new spring pins.

CAUTION

After connecting the axle shafts to the transmission, do not raise the engine/transaxle assembly more than one inch measured at the axle shaft inner end.

22. Check the wheel alignment and adjust if necessary.
23. Observe the following torque specifications in addition to those given in the Engine Removal and Installation section, where applicable:

TORQUE SPECIFICATIONS

(ft/lbs)

	1975-80
Transverse link to front crossmember	50
Stabilizer to leading rod and rear crossmember	15
Rear crossmember to vehicle body	60
Front crossmember to vehicle body	40
Front engine mount to crossmember	20
Rear engine mount to crossmember	20
Propeller shaft to rear differential (4WD)	15

CLUTCH

1. To remove the clutch, the engine must be removed from the vehicle.
2. Gradually unscrew the six bolts which hold the pressure plate assembly on the flywheel. Loosen the bolts only one turn at a time, working around the pressure plate. Do not unscrew all the bolts on one side at one time.
3. When all of the bolts have been removed, remove the clutch plate and disc.

CAUTION

Do not get oil or grease on the clutch facing.

4. Unfasten the two retaining springs and remove the throwout bearing and the release fork.

Do not disassemble either the clutch cover or disc. Inspect the parts for wear or damage and replace any parts as necessary. Replace the clutch disc if there is any oil or grease on the facing.

Do not wash or attempt to lubricate the throwout bearing. If it requires replacement, the bearing may be pressed out and a new one pressed into the holder.

Installation is as follows:

1. Fit the release fork boot on the front of the transmission housing. Install the release fork.
2. Insert the throwout bearing assembly and secure it with the two springs. Coat the inside diameter of the bearing holder and the fork-to-holder contact points with grease.
3. Insert a pilot shaft through the clutch cover and disc, then insert the end of the pilot into the needle bearing.
4. Gradually tighten the pressure plate retaining bolts one turn at a time, working around the cover, to 7-9 ft/lbs.

NOTE: When installing the clutch pressure plate assembly, make sure that the O marks on the flywheel and the clutch pressure plate assembly are at least 190° apart. This is for purposes of balance. Also, make sure that the clutch disc is installed properly, noting the FRONT and REAR markings.

5. After installation, adjust the pedal free-play and height.

Clutch Cable

REMOVAL AND INSTALLATION

The clutch cable is connected to the clutch pedal at one end and to the clutch release lever on the other end.

The cable conduit is retained by a bolt and clamp on the clutch pedal bracket and by a clip type clamp on a bracket mounted on the flywheel housing.

To replace the cable assembly, disconnect both the cable and conduit and remove the assembly from under the vehicle.

Install the replacement cable assembly and secure both the cable and conduit.

ADJUSTMENT

Remove the clutch release fork return spring, loosen the cable locknut, and adjust the spherical nut so that there is 0.142 to 0.181 in. play between the spherical nut and the release fork seat. Tighten the locknut and reconnect the release spring.

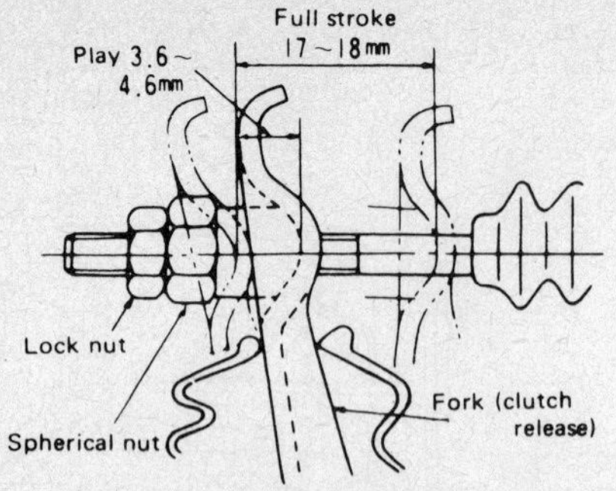

Clutch linkage free-play adjustment at the release fork

The pedal free-play should be 0.94 to 1.18 in. with a full stroke of 5.12 in. The pedal stroke is adjustable at the pedal bracket.

AUTOMATIC TRANSMISSION

REMOVAL AND INSTALLATION

If it is necessary to remove the transaxle it must be removed as an assembly with the engine. Be sure to read this entire procedure before proceeding.

1. Perform the engine removal procedure for these models as outlined in "Engine Removal and Installation." Include the additional steps outlined below at the appropriate point in the engine removal procedure, where indicated. *Do not perform steps 15 through 22 of the engine removal procedure.*
2. Include the following in step 8.
   a. Disconnect the back-up light switch wire.
3. Include the following in step 12: disconnect the speedometer cable from the transmission.
4. Perform the following after step 12.
   a. Place a container of adequate capacity beneath the transmission drain plug.
   b. Drain the automatic transmission fluid by removing the drain plug.
   c. Disconnect the inlet and outlet oil cooler hoses from the hose fitting on the differential and reduction case and from the pipe attached to the transmission case.

NOTE: Each pipe and hose should be covered to prevent dirt from entering.

   d. Disconnect the control rod from the selector arm by removing the cotter pin.
5. On 1975 models, include the following in step 14. Remove the heat insulating panel under the front floor by removing the seven retaining bolts.
6. After performing step 14 in the engine removal section raise the vehicle on jack stands, if this has not already been done.

NOTE: Reference to engine removal procedure is not necessary after this point, except to check that all the steps have been completed.

7. Drive the spring pins out of the axle shafts with a small rod and hammer.
8. Separate the transverse links from the front crossmember by removing the through bolts at the inner ends of the transverse links.
9. Remove the nuts retaining the front engine mounts (rubber) on the front crossmember.
10. Set up a chain hoist on the engine, with hooks at the front and rear engine hangers. Adjust the hoist so that the weight of the engine is supported, but do not raise the engine.

NOTE: The purpose of supporting the engine at this point is to prevent the unstable movement of the engine and to protect the people working underneath the vehicle.

11. Remove the nuts retaining the rear engine mount (rubber) on the crossmember.
12. Before going on to the next step, be sure that all of the above steps have been completed.
13. Remove the engine/transaxle assembly by carefully hoisting out of the vehicle. Be careful no to damage the brake pipes.
14. Place the entire assembly on a suitable stand or workbench.

Installation is the reverse of removal. Consult the engine installation notes in the Engine Removal and Installation section, as well as the following precautions before working.

15. Use new self-locking nuts for the leading rods and transverse link bolts.

NOTE: These nuts must be tightened with the wheels on the ground under a no load condition.

16. When connecting axle shafts to the transmission use new spring pins.

CAUTION

After connecting the axle shafts to the transmission, do not raise the engine/transaxle assembly more than one inch measured at the axle shaft inner end.

17. Check the wheel alignment and adjust if necessary.

Second Gear Band Adjustment

1. Hold the adjusting screw above the pan on the left side of the transmission.
2. Loosen the locknut.
3. Tighten the adjusting screw to 104-129 in/lbs (78 in/lbs for 1977-80) and back off two complete turns.
4. Tighten the locknut, while holding the screw.

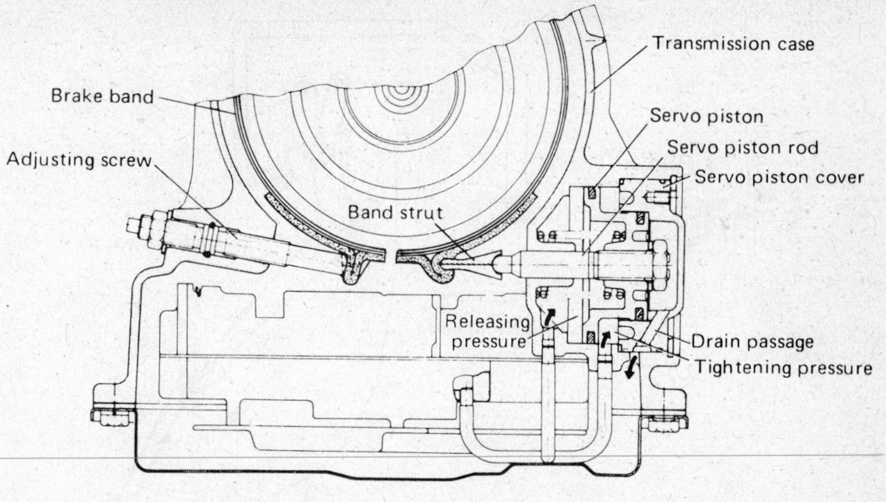

Second gear band adjustment mechanism

Neutral Safety Switch Adjustment

This switch is mounted on the transmission shift lever shaft, bolted to the transmission. It also operates the backup lights.

1. Remove the shift lever shaft nut.
2. Remove the shift lever from the shaft.
3. Make sure that the slot in the shaft is vertical (Neutral position).
4. Remove the switch mounting bolts, but leave the switch in place.
5. Remove the setscrew from the lower face of the switch.
6. Insert a 0.059 in. drill bit through the setscrew hole. Turn the switch slightly so that the bit passes through into the back part of the switch.
7. Bolt the switch down.
8. Remove the bit and replace the setscrew.
9. Replace the lever and tighten the shaft nut.
10. Check that the engine can start only in Park or Neutral, and that the backup lights go on in Reverse.

Shift Linkage Adjustment

1. Loosen the clamp nuts on the shifting rod at the bottom of the shift lever on the transmission.
2. Put the selector lever in Neutral and hold it forward against the detent.
3. Check that the transmission shift lever is in the Neutral position (pull it all the way back into Park and push it forward two position).
4. Tighten the clamp nuts.

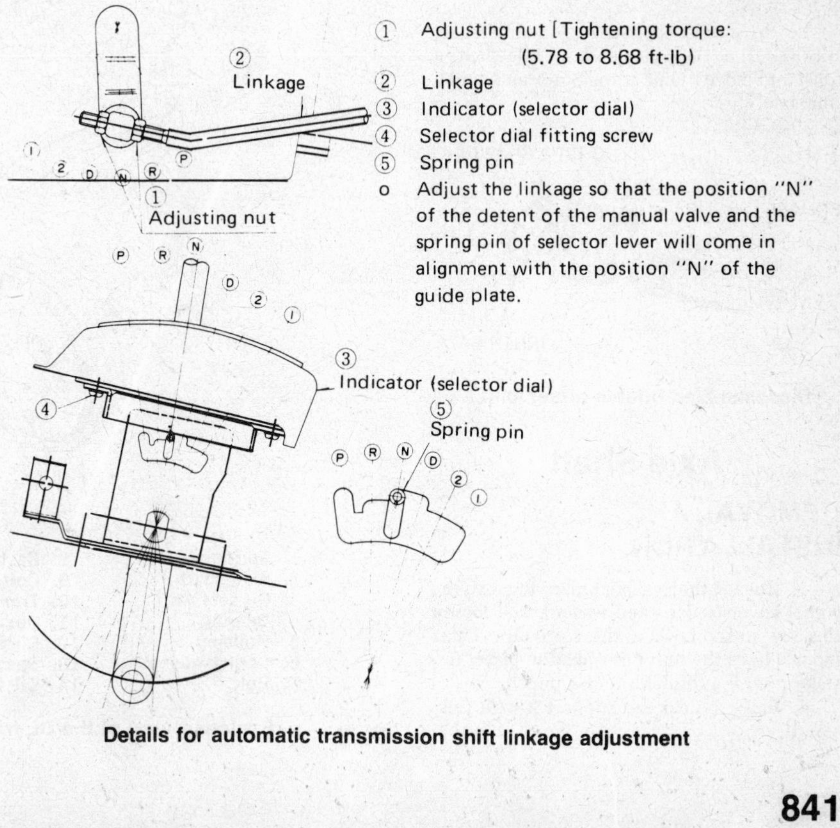

Details for automatic transmission shift linkage adjustment

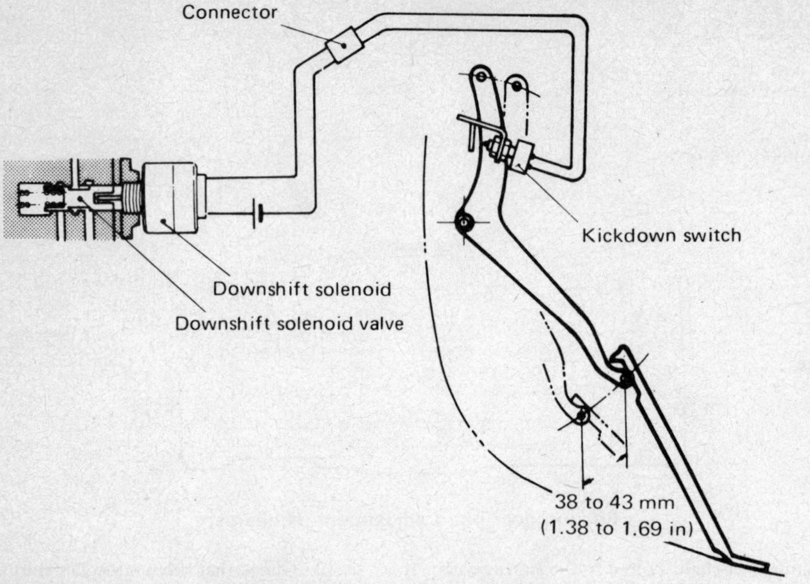

Automatic transmission kickdown system

Kickdown Solenoid

An audible click should be heard from the solenoid on the right side of the transmission, when the accelerator pedal is pushed down all the way with the engine off and the ignition switch on. The switch is operated by the upper part of the accelerator lever inside the car. The position of the switch can be varied to give quicker or slower kickdown response.

DRIVE AXLE

The drive axle consists of a double-offset joint (DOJ) at the inner end, an axle shaft, a constant velocity joint at the outer end, and a stub axle.

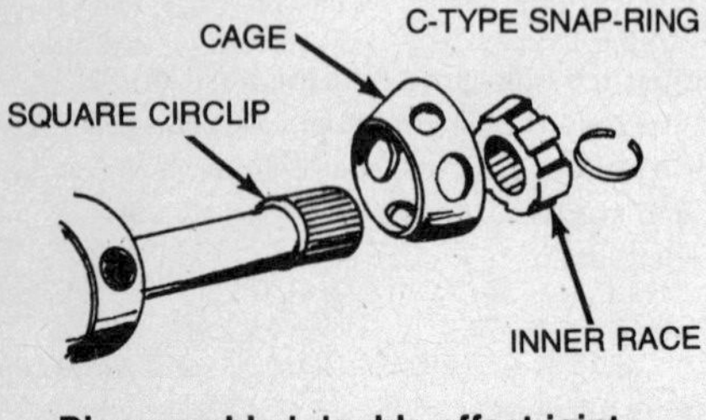

Disassembled double-offset joint

Axle Shaft

REMOVAL AND INSTALLATION

1. Engage the parking brake. Remove the wheel cover (sedans and wagon), and loosen the lug nuts. Loosen the hub nut. Later models have the hub nut staked in place; unstake it with a thin chisel or a punch.
2. Raise the car and support it with jackstands.
3. Remove the lug nuts, wheel and tire. Remove the hub nut.
4. Remove the drum brake or disc brake assembly.
5. On drum brakes, remove the 4 backing plate installing bolts and wire the backing plate to the suspension without disconnecting the hydraulic line.
6. Drive out the spring (roll) pin, which fastens the double-offset joint end of the axle shaft to the driveshaft, by lightly tapping with a hammer. Throw the old pin away; do not reuse it.
7. Remove the self-locking nuts which attach the ends of the control arm to the stabilizer bar and the crossmember inner pivot.
8. Separate the control arm from the crossmember pivot by prying it rearward with a suitable lever.
9. To disconnect the control arm from the stabilizer bar, swing the link forward.
10. Pull the axle shaft out of the driveshaft (double-offset joint side) by pushing outward on the front suspension assembly.
11. Pull the other end of the drive axle out of the housing, while holding the shaft so that it doesn't drop.

Installation is as follows:

1. Thread a metric bolt which is long enough to fit through the axle housing, into the end of the stub axle.
2. Fit the bolt through the axle housing, using care not to damage the oil seal, splines, or bearing. Draw the drive axle assembly into place by grasping the end of the bolt with a puller.

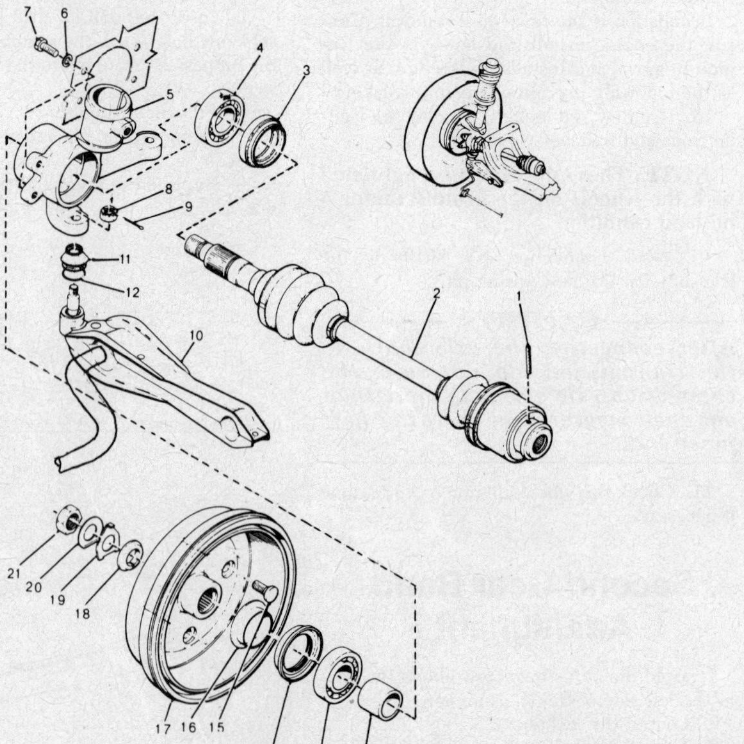

1. Spring pin
2. Axle shaft
3. Oil seal (in.)
4. Bearing
5. Housing
6. Spring washer
7. Bolt
8. Castle nut
9. Cotter pin
10. Transverse link
11. Dust seal (Ball joint)
12. Circlip
13. Spacer
14. Oil seal (out)
15. Hub bolt
16. Sleeve
17. Brake drum
18. Center piece
19. Lock washer
20. Lock plate
21. Nut

Exploded view of the DL front axle assembly (drum brakes)

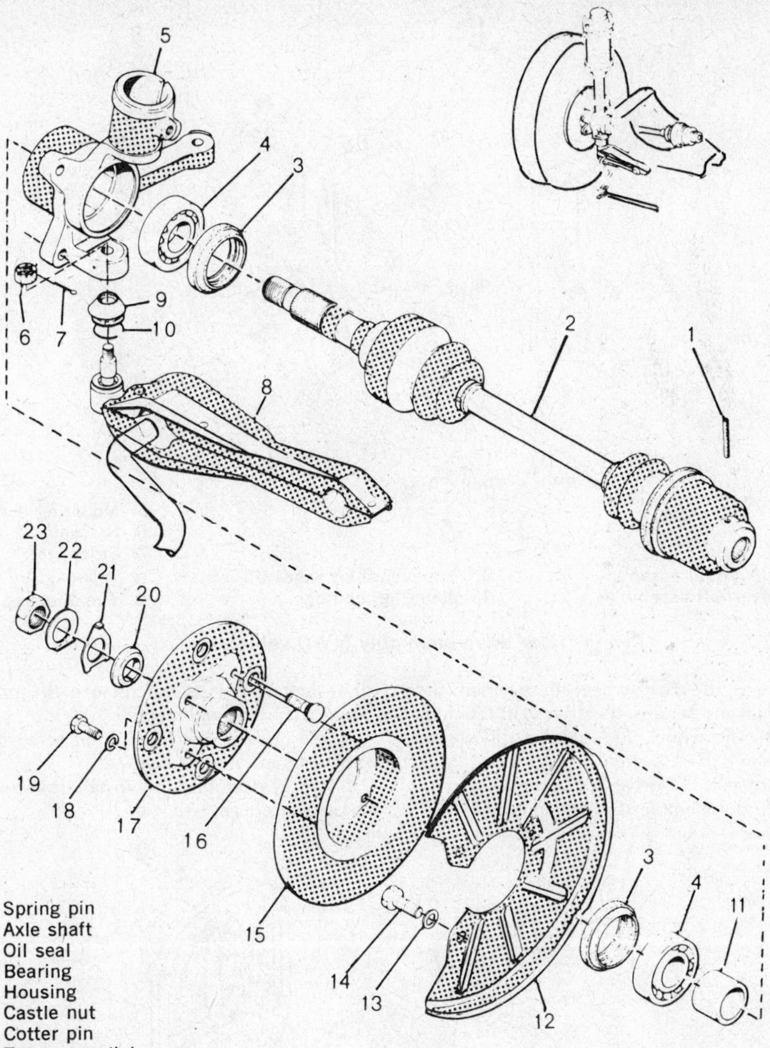

1. Spring pin
2. Axle shaft
3. Oil seal
4. Bearing
5. Housing
6. Castle nut
7. Cotter pin
8. Transverse link
9. Dust seal (Ball joint)
10. Circlip
11. Spacer
12. Disc cover
13. Spring washer
14. Bolt
15. Disc
16. Hub bolt
17. Disc hub
18. Spring washer
19. Bolt
20. Center piece
21. Lock washer
22. Lock plate
23. Nut

Exploded view of the GL front axle assembly (disc brakes)

3. On disc brakes, install the brake disc and hub.

4. On drum brakes, do the following:
   a. Secure the backing plate with its 4 bolts. Tighten the bolts to 22-37 ft/lbs.
   b. Install the brake drum assembly.

5. Install the hub nut:
   a. On 1975 and later models, install the spacer, conical spring washer and the hub nut. Tighten the nut to 160-180 ft/lbs (174 ft/lbs preferred). Secure the hub nut to the axle shaft by using a punch to stake the flange on the nut to the groove in the end of the axle shaft.

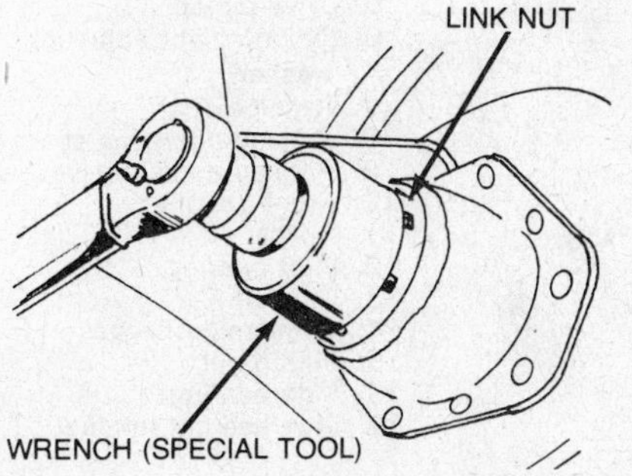

Removing the link nut using special tool

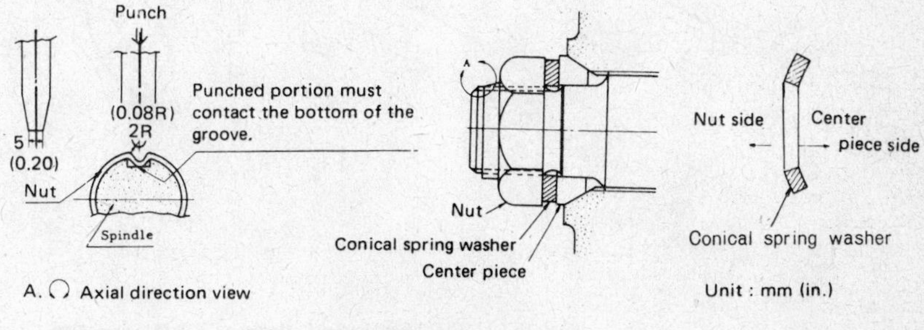

Installing the axle nut

6. Connect the double-offset joint side of the axle shaft to the driveshaft and secure them with a new spring pin.

7. Fit the washer and bushing over the end of the stabilizer bar and then connect the transverse link to the end of the stabilizer.

Install the remaining washer and bushing and temporarily secure them with a new self-locking nut.

8. Install the control arm to the cross-member pivot. Temporarily secure them with another new self-locking nut.

9. On disc brakes, install the dust cover, caliper, and parking brake cable.

10. Install the wheel and remove the jack-stands.

11. Tighten the new self-locking nuts used at each end of the transverse link to 72-87 ft/lbs with the car resting on its wheels.

U-JOINT OVERHAUL

1. Remove the bands from the boots at both the constant velocity and double-offset joints, and slide the boots away from the joints.
2. Pry the circlip out of the double-offset joint, and slide the outer race of the joint off the shaft.
3. Remove the balls from the cage, rotate the cage slightly, and slide the cage inward on the axle shaft.
4. Using snap-ring pliers, remove the outer snap-ring which retains the inner race to the shaft.
5. Slide the inner race, cage, and boot off the axle shaft.

NOTE: Exercise care to avoid damaging the boot on the inner snap-ring.

6. Pull back the constant velocity joint boot and pivot the stub axle around the joint far enough to expose a ball.
7. Remove the exposed ball, and continue this procedure until all balls are removed, at which time the outer race (stub axle) may be removed from the axle shaft.
8. Remove the retaining snap-ring, and slide the inner race off the shaft.
9. Inspect the parts of both joints for wear, damage, or corrosion, and replace if necessary. Examine the axle shaft for bending or distortion, and replace if evident. Should the boots be dried out, cracked, or distorted, they must be replaced.
10. Install the constant velocity joint inner race on the axle shaft, and retain with a snap-ring.
11. Assemble the joint in the opposite order of disassembly.

12. Slide the double-offset joint cage onto the shaft, with the counterbore toward the end of the shaft.

13. Install the inner race on the shaft, and install the retaining snap-ring.

14. Position the cage over the inner race, and fill the cage pockets with grease.

15. Insert the balls into the cage.

16. Fill the well in the outer race with approximately 1 oz. grease, and slide the outer race onto the axle shaft.

17. Install the retaining circlip, and add 1 oz. more grease to the interior of the joint. Fill the boot with approximately 1 oz. grease, and slide it into position over the double-offset joint.

18. Fill the constant velocity joint boot with 3 oz. grease, and install the boot over the joint.

19. Band the boots on both joints tightly enough that they cannot be turned by hand.

NOTE: Use only grease specified for use in constant velocity joints.

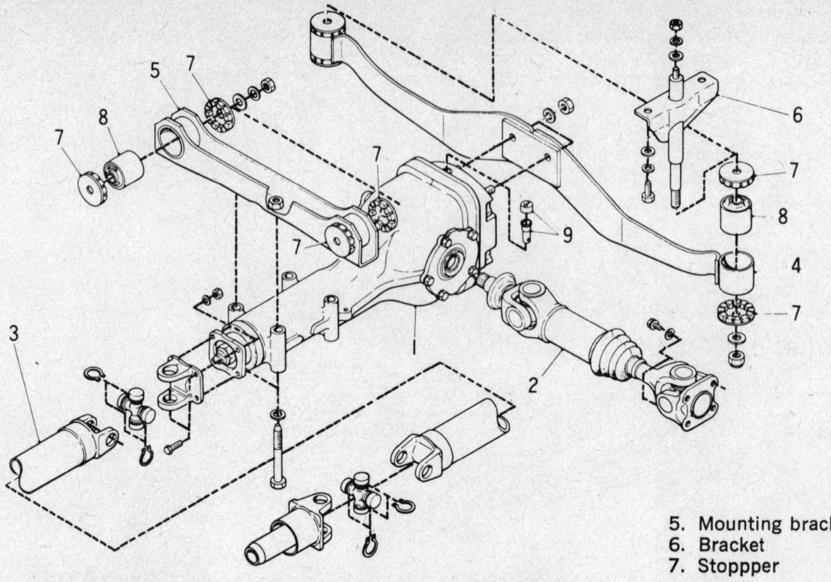

1. Differential assembly
2. Driveshaft assembly
3. Propeller shaft assembly
4. Mounting member
5. Mounting bracket
6. Bracket
7. Stoppper
8. Bushing
9. Breather cap

Rear drive assembly (4WD vehicles)

Rear Axle Shaft (Four Wheel Drive)

REMOVAL AND INSTALLATION

1. Jack up the rear of the body and support with jack stands.

2. Turn the rear wheel to position the driveshaft and remove the driveshaft retaining bolts on the wheel side and the differential gear side.

3. Remove the driveshaft assembly.

4. To disassemble the ball spline hold the driveshaft in a vise and remove the rubber band, snap ring and stopper.

5. To disassemble the U-joint remove the snap ring and needle bearing.

6. To reassemble and install reverse the above procedure.

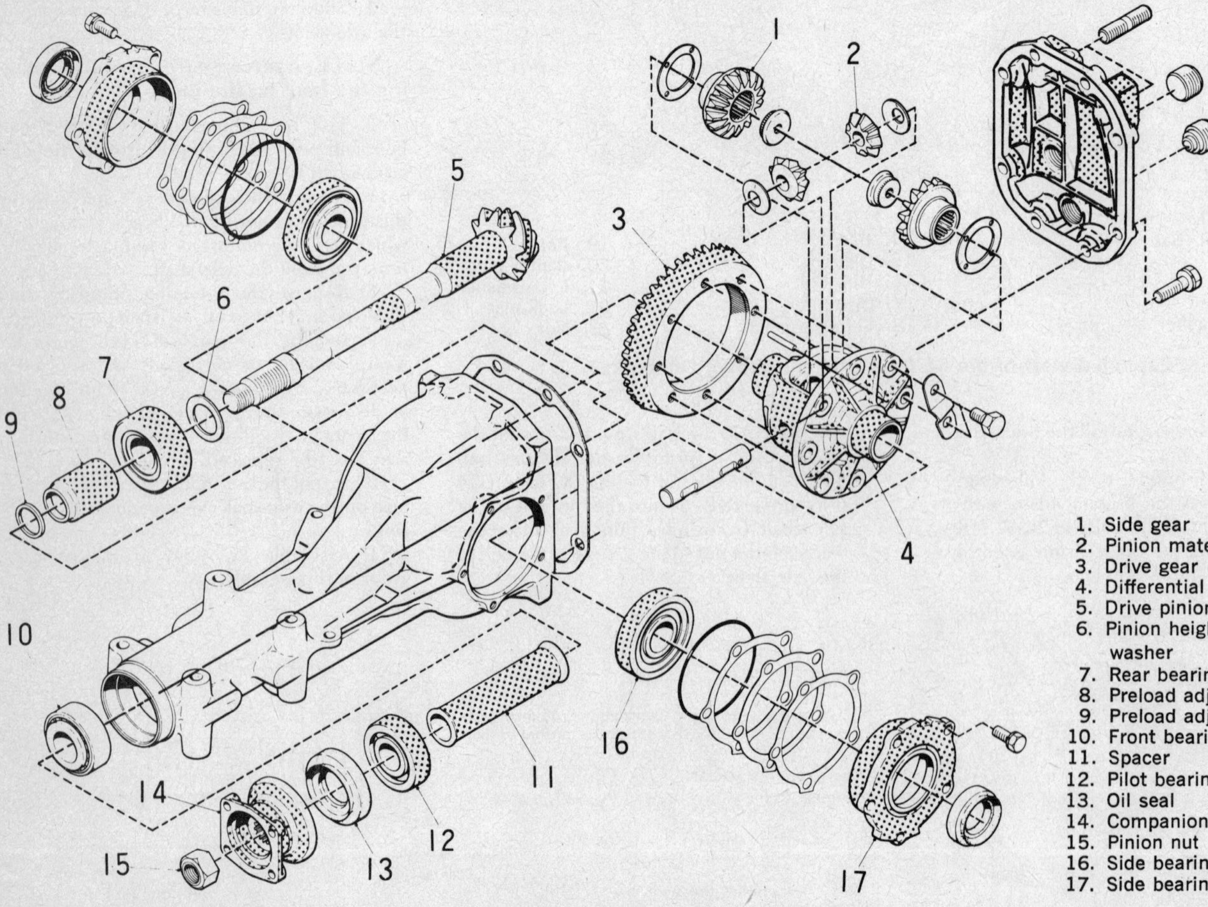

1. Side gear
2. Pinion mate gear
3. Drive gear
4. Differential case
5. Drive pinion
6. Pinion height adjusting washer
7. Rear bearing
8. Preload adjusting spacer
9. Preload adjusting washer
10. Front bearing
11. Spacer
12. Pilot bearing
13. Oil seal
14. Companion flange
15. Pinion nut
16. Side bearing
17. Side bearing retainer

Exploded view of 4WD rear differential

7. Selective snap rings are used to obtain a clearance of 0.0008 inch between the bearing cap and driveshaft yoke.

8. Snap ring thicknesses are as follow:
0.0587 in.
0.0598 in.
0.0610 in.
0.0622 in.
0.0457 in.
0.0646 in.
0.0657 in.

Driveshaft (Four Wheel Drive)

REMOVAL AND INSTALLATION

1. Drain the transmission oil.
2. Jack up the rear of the body, and support with jack stands.
3. Remove the bolts connecting the driveshaft yoke to the rear differential companion flange.
4. Gently pull the driveshaft rearward to remove.
5. To install reverse the removal procedure.

OVERHAUL

Selective snap rings are used to provide proper clearance of the bearing cap to yoke. The clearance should be 0.0008 inch and the opposing snap rings must be of the same thickness.

SELECTIVE SNAP RINGS

Thickness	Paint Color
0.0787 in.	White
0.0795 in.	Yellow
0.0803 in.	Red
0.0811 in.	Green
0.0819 in.	Blue
0.0827 in.	Light Brown
0.0835 in.	No paint
0.0843 in.	Pink

Rear Axle Spindle, Bearing and Seals (Four Wheel Drive)

REMOVAL AND INSTALLATION

1. Jack up the car and remove the wheel.
2. Loosen the axle nut.
3. Disconnect the axle shaft from the rear axle companion flange.
4. Remove the nut retaining the companion flange to the spindle and remove the companion flange.
5. Pull the brake drum and spindle to the outer side, and take the outer oil seal off with the spindle.
6. Remove the axle nut from the spindle, disconnect the brake drum and pull out the outer oil seal.

1. Snap-ring
2. Stopper
3. Ball
4. Ball spacer
5. Rubber boot
6. Boot band
7. Yoke
8. Bolt
9. Spring washer
10. Snap-ring
11. Stopper
12. Sleeve yoke
13. Plug
14. O-ring
15. Snap-ring
16. Spider
17. Bearing race
18. Oil seal
19. Snap-ring
20. Dust cover (oil seal)
21. Bolt
22. Spring washer
23. Washer
24. O-ring
25. Side yoke

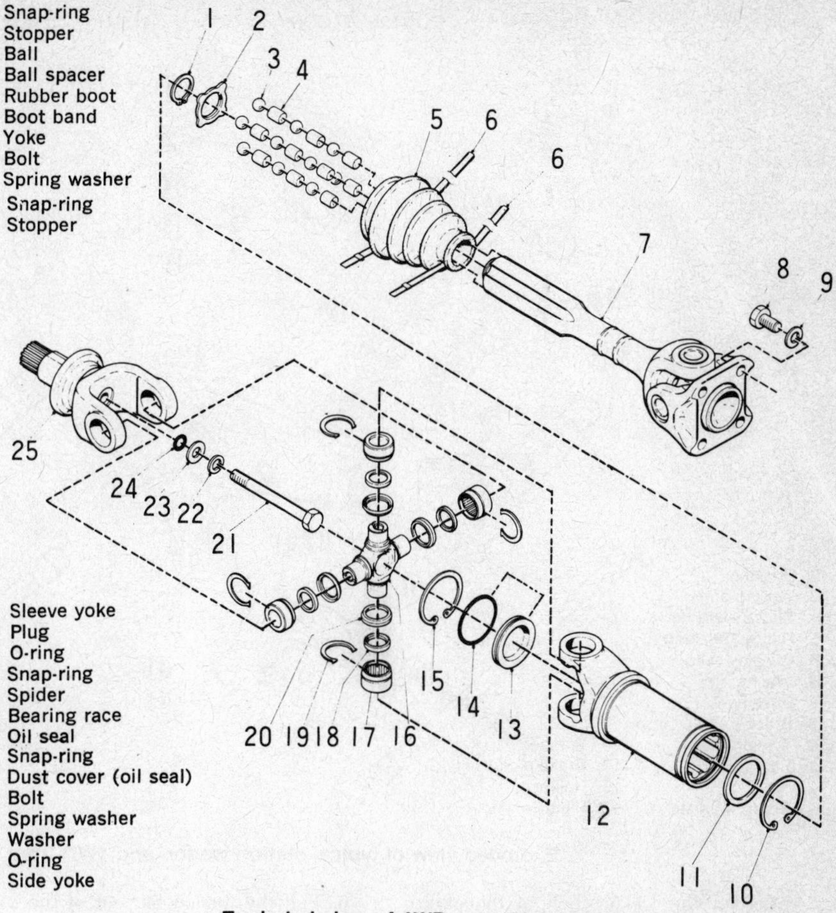

Exploded view of 4WD rear axle shaft

7. Unlock the link nut and remove the nut with a wrench (special tool).
8. Remove the inner seal.
9. New seals may be pressed into place at this time or if the bearing is to be replaced proceed as follows.
10. Dismount the rear suspension including the rear brake back plate.
11. Use a press and remove the bearing.
12. When replacing the inner and outer seals place the inner and outer side of the housing on a V-block and press the seals into place.
13. Hold the trailing arm in a vise and lightly tighten the link nut in the housing with the special wrench. Torque the nut to 130-166 ft/lbs.
14. Lock the link nut.
15. Install the rear trailing arm to the body.
16. Fit the back plate (22-35 ft/lbs) and connect the brake pipe (11-14 ft/lbs).
17. Temporarily fit the brake drum to the spindle.
18. Bleed brake system.
19. Position the companion flange to the spindle inner end and tighten the locknut to 145-181 ft/lbs.

NOTE: When tightening, apply the foot brake to produce reaction force.

20. Make sure the bearing rotates smoothly and stake the locknut.
21. Fit the center piece, conical spring washer and retaining nut onto the axle shaft and tighten the retaining nut to 174 ft/lbs.

NOTE: Punch the flange portion of the retaining nut toward the groove of the axle after tightening.

22. Connect the axle shaft and companion flange and tighten the retaining nuts to 29-36 ft/lbs.
23. Install the spindle and wheel assembly. Tighten the wheel nuts to 58-72 ft/lbs.

REAR SUSPENSION

Semi-trailing arms mounted to torque tubes, which act on an internal torsion bar are used. Shock absorbers are mounted to the trailing arm, close to the stub axle.

Torsion Bars

REMOVAL AND INSTALLATION

1. Raise the vehicle and remove the rear wheels.
2. Remove the shock absorber from the trailing arm and the brake tube from the brake hose.
3. Remove the inner bushing retaining bolts.

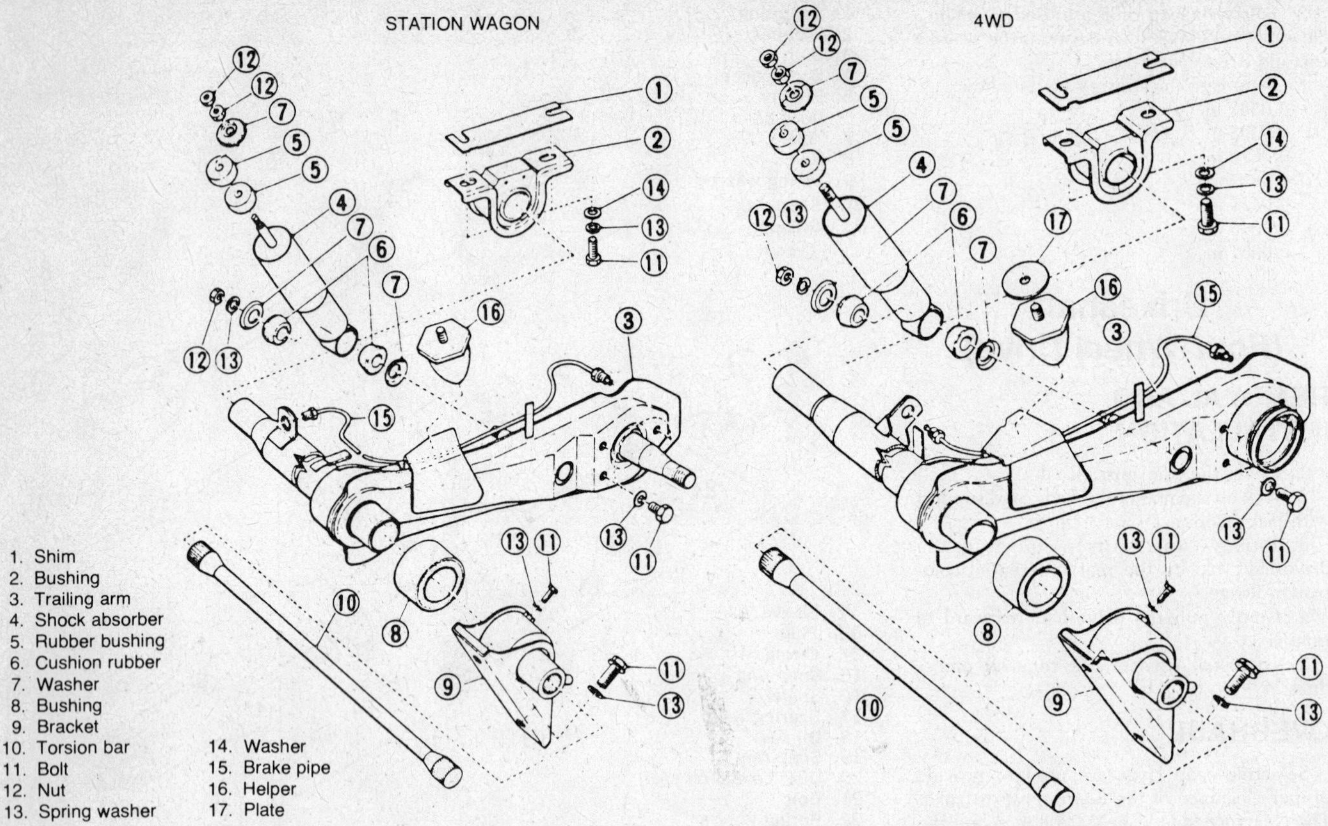

Exploded view of typical station wagon and 4WD front suspension through 1979

4. Loosen the locking bolt of the outer bracket and remove the rear suspension from the body.

5. Pull the outer bracket out of the outer bushing after removing the locking bolt.

6. Pull the torsion bar out of the trailing arm.

7. The inner and outer bushings can be replaced by using a press.

NOTE: The torsion bars are marked L and R and are to be installed on the proper side. Premature breakage of the bars can result if they are installed on the wrong side.

CAUTION

When inserting the torsion bar, align the marks on the end of the torsion bar to that of the outer bracket and inner bushing.

8. Adjust the ride height and rear wheel alignment prior to tightening the inner bushing retaining bolts.

9. Tighten the outer bushing retaining bolts when the vehicle is on the floor and unloaded.

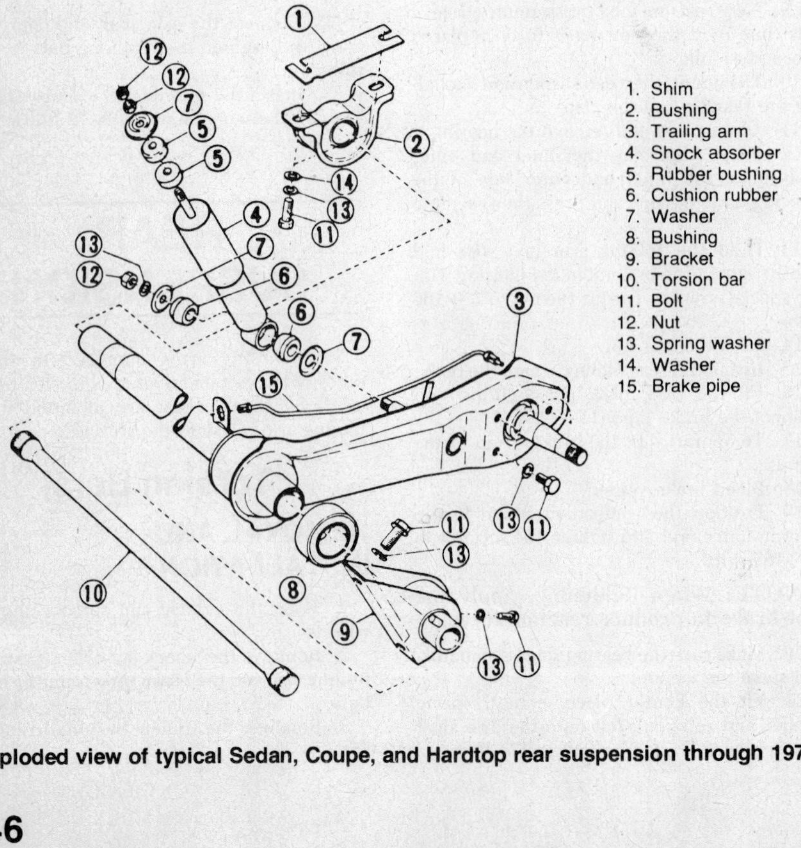

Exploded view of typical Sedan, Coupe, and Hardtop rear suspension through 1979

Shock Absorbers

REMOVAL AND INSTALLATION

1. Remove the wheel cover and loosen the lug nuts. Raise the rear of the car and support it with jackstands, after setting the parking brake and blocking the front wheels.

2. Remove the lug nuts and the rear wheels.

3. Loosen the two upper shock absorber mounting nuts. Remove the washer and the bushing, being sure to note their correct assembly sequence for installation.

4. Unfasten the nut on the trailing arm pin and remove the shock absorber. Note the installing positions of the washers.

Installation is the reverse of removal. Do not fully tighten the upper mounting nuts until the lower shock nut has been installed with the washer and the pin shoulder contacting each other. Tighten the upper nuts to 22-32 ft/lbs. Adjust the ride height bolt.

Rear End Alignment

Camber–Thru 1979

Rear wheel camber is adjusted by changing the number of shims mounted between the inner torsion bar bushing assembly and the body. Each shim corresponds to ¼° of change. Adding shims decreases the camber; removing shims increases it.

Toe-In–Thru 1979

Rear wheel toe-in is changed by loosening the inner torsion bar bushing assembly bolts and sliding the bushing assembly forward or backward. Forward movement decreases toe-in and backward movement increases it. Tighten the bolts after completing the adjustment.

Ride Height

Vehicle height can be adjusted by turning the outer and inner end of the torsion bar by the same number of serration teeth in the opposite direction to the arrow mark on the outer end surface of the torsion bar.

Turning the torsion bar in the direction of the arrow lowers the vehicle height, and changes the height 0.20 in. per tooth shifted.

The torsion bar must be removed from the inner and outer brackets to make the adjustment. 1980 4-wheel drive vehicles have a unique adjusting device that will alter the ride height (in addition to adjusting the torsion bars). See the following procedure.

ADJUSTMENT OF REAR ROAD CLEARANCE

1980 and Later 4 Wheel Drive Vehicles

1. Measure the height of the vehicle from the lowest point of the rear axle crossmember to the ground. On 4WD sedans, it should be 12.60 to 13.39 in. On Wagons, it should be 13.19 to 13.98 in.
2. To adjust the rear height remove the access cover from the service hole in the vehicle floor above the rear axle. Turn the adjusting bolt, clockwise to increase the height; counter clockwise to lower it.

FRONT SUSPENSION

MacPherson Strut Assembly

REMOVAL AND INSTALLATION

NOTE: Use this procedure to remove the entire suspension assembly. If only shock and/or spring removal are desired, use the procedure given under "Shock Absorbers".

1. Raise and support the vehicle. Remove the battery cable from the negative terminal of the battery.
2. Remove the hub caps, loosen the lug nuts, jack up the vehicle until the tire clears the ground and remove the lug nuts and the wheel/tire assembly. Place the jackstands under the vehicle and remove the jack. Perform this operation on the opposite side if the suspension is to be removed from both sides of the vehicle.
3. Remove the handbrake cable bracket and the handbrake cable hanger from the transverse link and the tie rod end. Remove the handbrake cable end.
4. Remove the axle nut, lockplate,

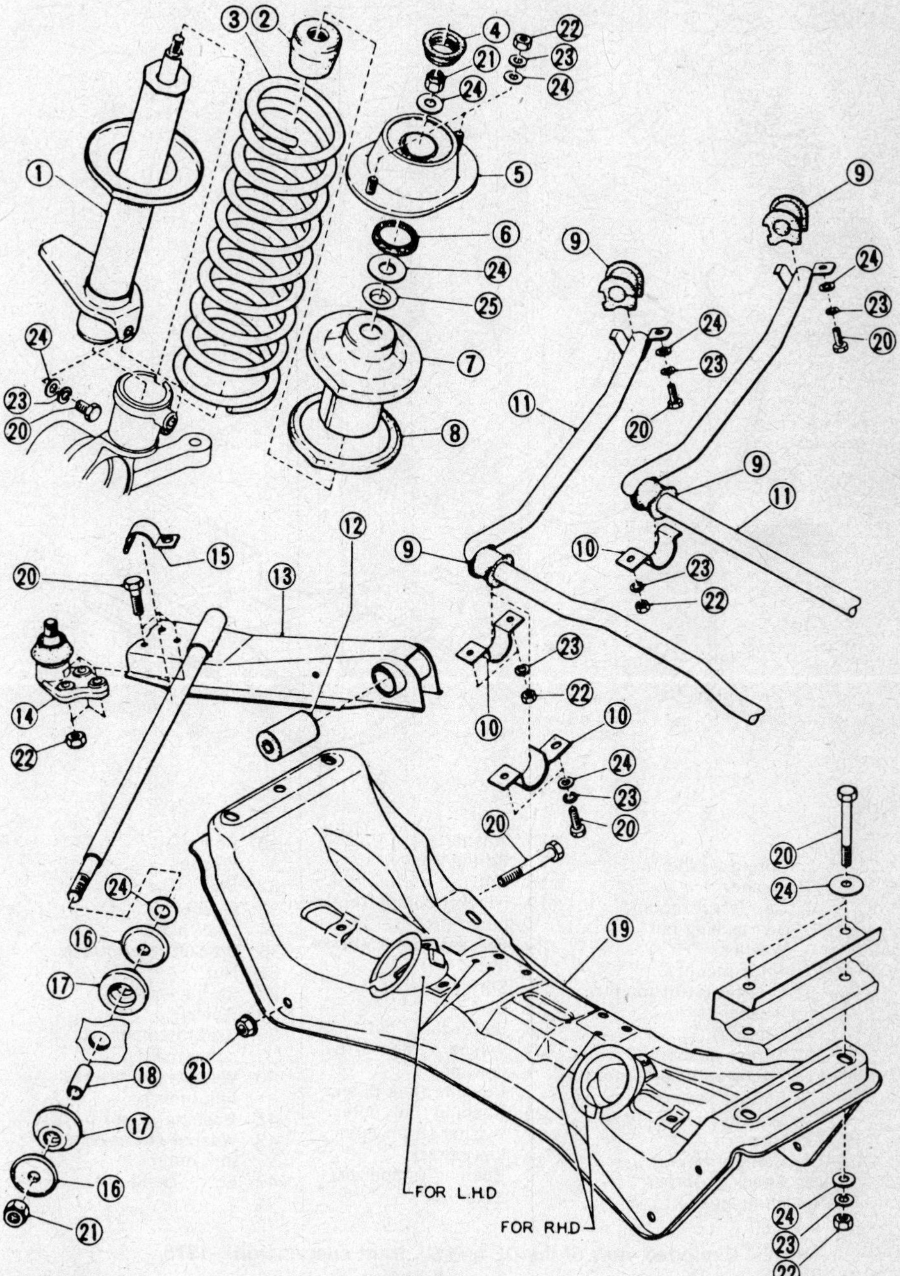

1. Damper strut
2. Helper
3. Coil spring
4. Cap
5. Strut mount
6. Oil seal
7. Spring seat
8. Rubber seat
9. Stabilizer bushing
10. Bracket
11. Stabilizer
12. Rubber bushing
13. Transverse link
14. Ball joint
15. Bracket
16. Plate
17. Bushing
18. Pipe
19. Cross member
20. Bolt
21. Self lock nut
22. Nut
23. Spring washer
24. Washer
25. Thrust washer

Exploded view of front suspension—1977-79

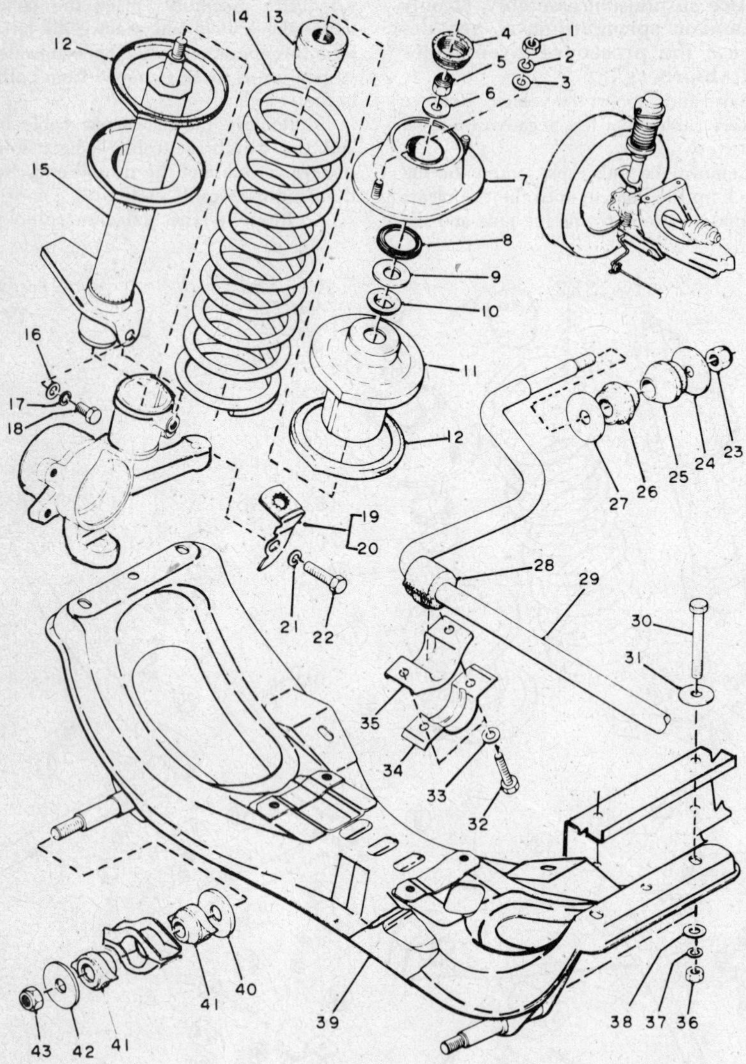

1. Nut
2. Spring washer
3. Washer
4. Cap (strut mount)
5. Self locking nut
6. Washer
7. Strut mount
8. Oil seal (strut mount)
9. Washer (thrust bearing)
10. Thrust washer
11. Spring retainer (upper)
12. Rubber seat (coil spring)
13. Helper
14. Coil spring
15. Shock absorber complete
16. Washer
17. Spring washer
18. Bolt
19. Bracket compl. (brake hose: RH)
20. Bracket compl. (brake hose: LH)
21. Spring washer
22. Bolt
23. Self locking nut
24. Washer (transverse link inner)
25. Bushing (link outer)
26. Bushing (link outer)
27. Washer (transverse link outer)
28. Bushing (stabilizer)
29. Stabilizer
30. Bolt
31. Washer
32. Bolt (10 x 40)
33. Washer
34. Lock plate
35. Bracket (stabilizer)
36. Nut
37. Spring washer
38. Washer
39. Crossmember compl. (F)
40. Washer (transverse link inner)
41. Bushing (inner pivot)
42. Washer (transverse link outer)
43. Self locking nut

Exploded view of the DL and GL front suspension—1975

washer, and center piece and remove the front brake drums by using a puller.

5. Disconnect the brake hoses from the brake fluid pipes.

6. Remove the backing plates with the brake assemblies attached.

7. With front disc brakes, remove the handbrake cable end from the caliper lever. Remove the outer cable clip from the cable-end support bracket at the caliper. Remove the handbrake cable bracket from the housing mount by loosening the nuts.

8. Drive out the spring pins of the double offset joint by using a drift pin and a hammer. The double offset side of the axle is the side closest to the transaxle.

9. Remove the lower control arm by loosening the self-locking nut which holds it to the inner pivot shaft of the crossmember. Loosen and remove the nuts which clamp the control arm to the stabilizer. Remove the stabilizer rearward from the crossmember by using a lever and pulling the control arm out from the end of the stabilizer.

10. Remove the cotter pin from the castle nut and remove the nuts and ball stud from the knuckle arm of the tie rod end ball joint housing. Take care not to bend the housing.

11. Remove the nuts which hold the strut mount to the body (suspension assembly upper mounting nut-top of the shock absorber tower).

12. Pull the double offset joint out of the driveshaft and then remove the suspension assembly from the body.

Install the suspension assembly in the reverse order of removal.

Shock Absorbers

REMOVAL AND INSTALLATION

NOTE: Use this procedure if only shock absorber (strut) or spring removal is desired.

1. Remove the wheel cover and loosen the lug nuts.
2. Raise the front of the car and support it on jackstands.
3. Remove the lug nuts and wheels.
4. Unfasten the bolts which secure the bottom of the strut assembly to the axle housing.
5. Remove the bolts which attach the strut bracket to the axle housing.
6. Detach the end of the tie rod from the axle housing in order to prevent ball joint damage.
7. Remove the strut from the housing, gradually and carefully, by lowering the housing.
8. Unfasten the nuts which attach the upper end of the strut assembly to the wheel arch.
9. Remove the strut (shock and spring) from the body.
10. Use a coil spring compressor to compress the coil spring until it can move freely.
11. Use a large open-end wrench to keep the upper spring seat from turning, while unfastening the shock nut.
12. Remove the components from the top of the shock, being careful to note their order, and remove the compressed spring.

Test the operation of the shock absorber by placing it in an upright position; push and pull on the shock, if it presents little resistance or binds, replace it with a new shock.

Examine the shock for leaks, a bent mounting stud, or other signs of wear or damage.

Installation is the reverse of removal. Be sure to assemble the components on the top of the shock in the correct order. Lubricate the oil seal lips and the thrust washers with a light coating of grease. Tighten the shock absorber-to-mount self-locking nut to 43-54 ft/lbs.

Ball Joints

REMOVAL AND INSTALLATION

1975 and Later

1. Jack up the front of the car and remove the wheel.
2. Disconnect the ball stud from the housing by removing the cotter pin and castle nut.
3. Remove the bolt attaching the ball nut to the transverse link and remove the ball joint.
4. To install reverse the removal procedure. Torque the castle nut to 35-40 ft/lbs, ball joint to transverse link nut to 80-94 ft/lbs.

Lower Control Arm

REMOVAL AND INSTALLATION

These models have only one control arm. To remove and install it, proceed as follows:

1. Remove the wheel cover and loosen the lug nuts.
2. Jack up the car and support it with jackstands. Block the rear wheels.
3. Remove the lug nuts and the wheel.
4. Remove the parking brake cable clamp from the control arm by unfastening its nut.
5. Unfasten the self-locking nut which attaches the control arm to the crossmember. Be sure to note the installation sequence of the washers.
6. Unfasten the self-locking nut which secures the stabilizer bar to the control arm. Again, note the installation sequence of the washers.
7. Pry the control arm off the crossmember.
8. Push the control arm forward and detach it from the end of the stabilizer bar.
9. Remove the cotter pin from the castellated nut. Unfasten the nut and remove the ball joint from the axle housing with a puller.
10. Remove the control arm from under the car.

Installation is the reverse of removal. Do not grease the upper ball joint stud which fits into the axle housing. Tighten the castellated nut to 30-40 ft/lbs. Use new self-locking nuts on the crossmember and stabilizer bar mounts. Tighten the new self-locking nuts to 73-87 ft/lbs with the vehicle resting on the wheels.

Front End Alignment

CASTER AND CAMBER

Caster and camber are not adjustable on these models. If either of these specifications is not within the factory recommended range, this would indicate bent or damaged parts that must be replaced.

TOE-IN

Toe-in is adjusted by loosening the locknuts on the tie rods, and turning the tie rods.

NOTE: Before performing the toe-in adjustment, be sure that the steering gear is centered by aligning the marks on it, and that the wheels are straight-ahead.

Tighten the locknuts after the toe-in adjustment is completed.

STEERING

Steering Wheel

REMOVAL AND INSTALLATION

1. Disconnect the negative battery cable.
2. Unfasten the horn lead from the wiring harness beneath the instrument panel.
3. Working from behind the steering wheel, remove the horn assembly retaining screws.
4. Lift the crash pad assembly off the front of the wheel.
5. Matchmark the steering wheel and the column for installation.
6. Remove the steering wheel retaining nut and pull the wheel from the column with a puller.

Installation is the reverse of removal. Index the matchmarks and tighten the retaining nut to 20-29 ft/lbs.

CAUTION

Do not hammer on the steering wheel or the steering column; damage to the collapsible column could result.

Turn Signal Switch

REMOVAL AND INSTALLATION

1. Remove the steering wheel.

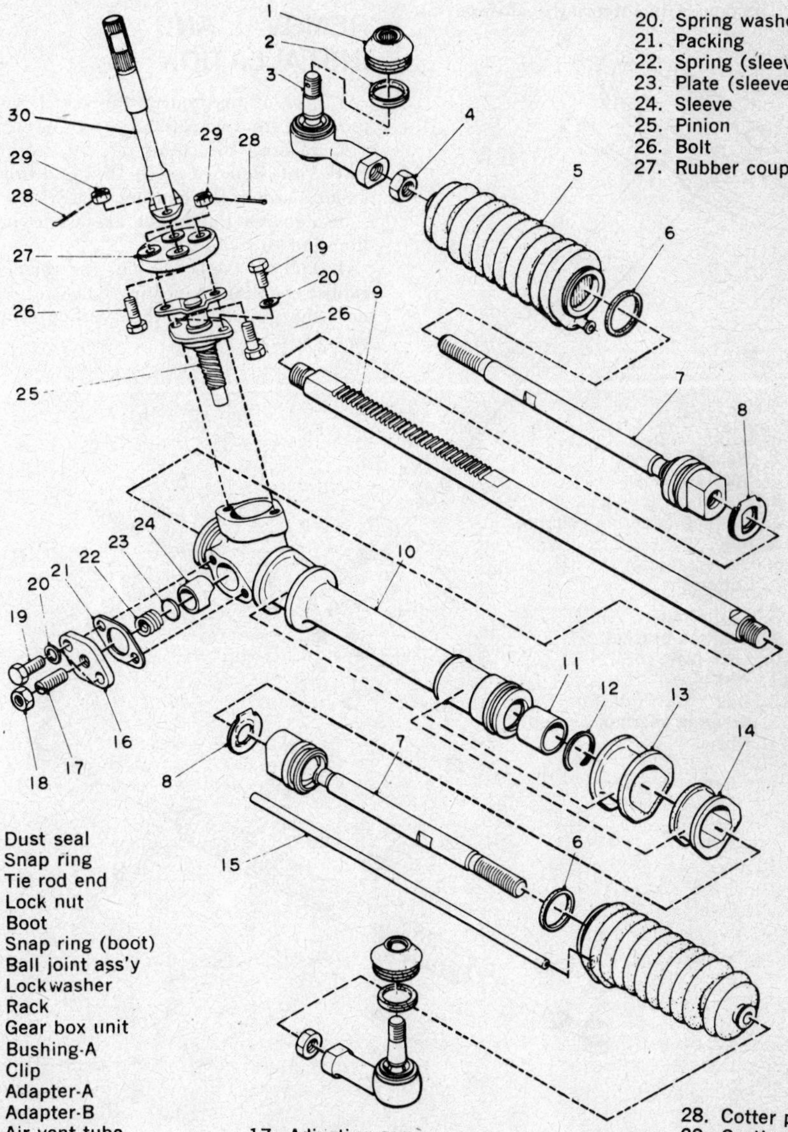

1. Dust seal
2. Snap ring
3. Tie rod end
4. Lock nut
5. Boot
6. Snap ring (boot)
7. Ball joint ass'y
8. Lockwasher
9. Rack
10. Gear box unit
11. Bushing-A
12. Clip
13. Adapter-A
14. Adapter-B
15. Air vent tube
16. Cap (steering gear box)
17. Adjusting screw
18. Lock nut
19. Bolt
20. Spring washer
21. Packing
22. Spring (sleeve)
23. Plate (sleeve)
24. Sleeve
25. Pinion
26. Bolt
27. Rubber coupling
28. Cotter pin
29. Castle nut
30. Torque rod

Exploded view of the steering gear

2. Separate the steering column wiring connectors underneath the instrument panel.

3. Remove the turn signal switch securing screws and unscrew the hazard warning switch knob.

4. Remove the contact plate, cancelling cam, and switch assembly from the steering column housing.

Installation is the reverse of removal.

Ignition Switch

REMOVAL AND INSTALLATION

The ignition switch is mounted to the steering column using shear bolts. These bolts are constructed so that the head is sheared off when the bolt is tightened. For this reason removal of the ignition switch is rather complicated.

1. Remove the steering wheel as outlined above.

2. Disconnect the steering shaft from the universal joint (located near the steering gear box) by loosening the locking bolt.

3. Remove the steering shaft installing bolt from the instrument panel.

4. Pull the steering shaft assembly from the hole in the floor board and remove the assembly from the car.

5. Loosen the screws holding the column cover to the steering column and hazard knob, and pull the steering shaft out of the column cover.

6. Drill into the shaft of the shear bolts and extract them with an E-Z Out®. Remove the switch.

Installation is the reverse of removal. Be sure to use new shear bolts to install the ignition switch.

Manual Steering Gear

All Subaru models are equipped with rack and pinion steering. No maintenance is required.

REMOVAL AND INSTALLATION

1. Jack up the front of the vehicle and remove the front wheels.

2. Remove the cotter pin and loosen the castle nut. Remove the tie rod end from the knuckle arm of the housing.

3. Remove the handbrake cable hanger from the tie rod.

4. Pull out the cotter pins and remove the rubber coupling connecting bolts and disconnect the pinion with the gearbox from the steering shaft.

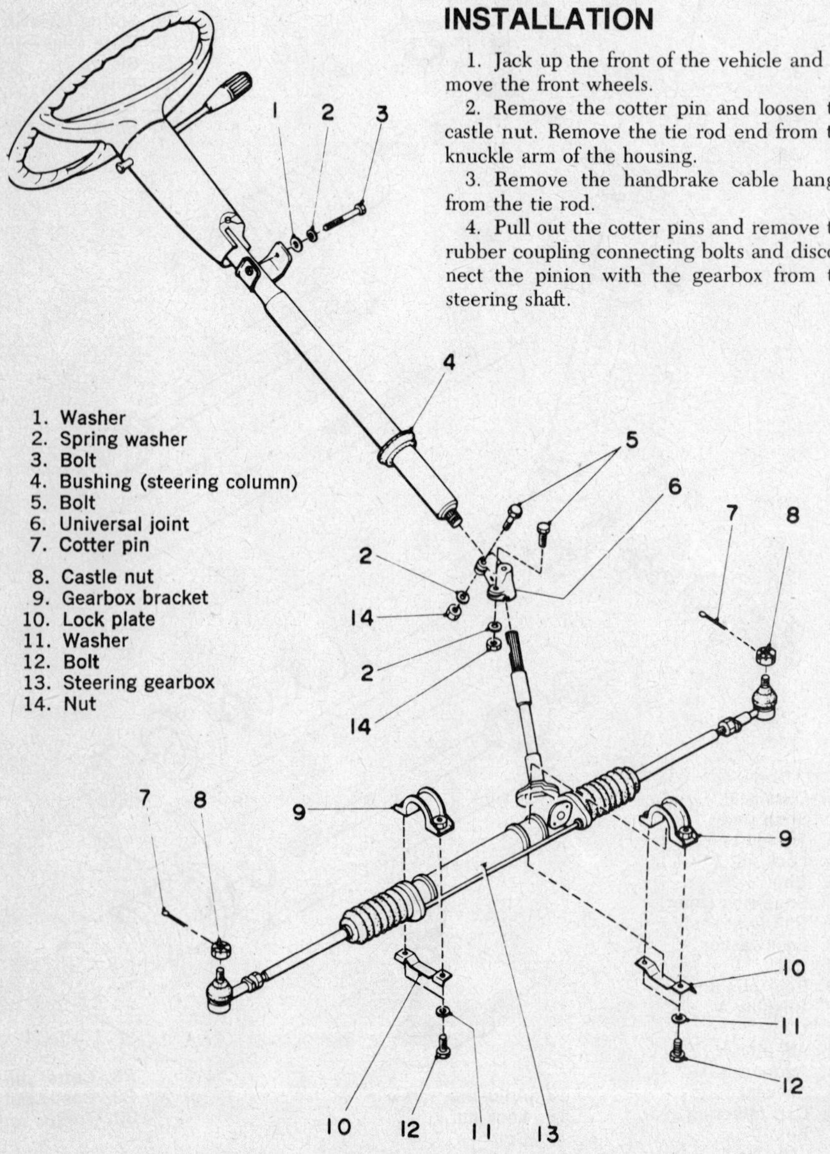

DL, GL, GF steering system

5. Straighten the lockplate and remove the bolts which hold the gearbox bracket to the crossmember.

6. On DL, GF, and GL models, loosen the front engine mounting bolts and lift up the engine by about 0.2 in. to avoid touching the gearbox with the engine. Remove the gearbox from the vehicle.

NOTE: On 4WD models remove the fan protector on top of the radiator and remove the pitching stopper before lifting the engine.

Installation is the reverse of removal. Tighten the rack and pinion assembly securing bolts to 33-40 ft/lbs. Tighten the rubber coupling castellated nut to 4-5 ft/lbs. Tighten the tie rod end castellated nuts to 18-22 ft/lbs. Adjust the toe-in after completing installation.

NOTE: Check the collapsible steering shaft for straightness or looseness and always replace with a new one if found damaged.

ADJUSTMENT

Tighten the backlash adjuster fully to bottom, back off the screw ⅛ turn, and lock the locknut. A clearance of 0.006 inch is provided between the screw tip and the sleeve plate.

BRAKES

Adjustment

The front drum brakes are self-adjusting and seldom, if ever, require manual adjustment. For this reason, prior to manual adjustment, ensure that the self-adjuster is functioning, and that brake linings are not excessively worn. To adjust the front brakes. remove the rubber inspection plug, insert a tool through the hole, and turn the star wheel to adjust the brakes. Pushing the handle of the tool will reduce shoe-to-drum clearance. Front disc brakes have no provision for manual adjustment.

The rear brakes are adjusted by turning a bolt at the bottom of the backing plate. Turn the wedge clockwise to lock the brake, and back off 180°. Secure the bolt with its locknut.

Master Cylinder

REMOVAL AND INSTALLATION

CAUTION

Avoid spilling brake fluid on painted surfaces.

1. Remove the brake line from the master cylinder.

2. Remove the nuts which connect the master cylinder to the pedal bracket or power booster.

3. Pull the master cylinder assembly forward and out.

4. Install in the reverse order of removal.

NOTE: Do not use the old brake fluid drained from the master cylinder. Always refill with new fluid.

OVERHAUL

1. Remove the master cylinder from the car.
2. Remove the reservoir caps and filters and drain the brake fluid. Discard this fluid.
3. Pry the piston stopper snap-ring from the open end of the master cylinder with a screwdriver.
4. Remove the stopper screw and washer from the side or bottom of the master cylinder and then remove the primary and secondary piston assemblies from the master cylinder bore.
5. Remove the caps on the underside of the master cylinder to gain access to the check valves for cleaning.

NOTE: Do not disassemble the brake fluid level gauge, if equipped.

6. Discard all used rubber parts and gaskets. These parts should be replaced with the new components included in the rebuilding kit.

NOTE: Do not remove the master cylinder reservoir tanks unless they are leaking. If they are removed for any reason, they must be replaced with new ones.

7. Clean all the parts in clean brake fluid. Do not use mineral oil or alcohol for cleaning.
8. Check the cylinder bore and piston for wear, scoring, corrosion, or any other damage. The piston and cylinder bore can be dressed with crocus cloth soaked in brake fluid. Move the crocus cloth around the cylinder bore, not in and out. Do the same to the piston, if necessary. Wash both the cylinder bore and the piston with clean brake fluid.
9. Assemble the master cylinder in the reverse order of disassembly. Soak all of the components in clean brake fluid before assembling them.
10. Clamp the master cylinder in a vise by one of its flanges. Fill the reservoirs with fresh fluid and pump the piston with a screwdriver until fluid squirts from the outlet ports. Install the master cylinder and bleed the system.

Drum Brakes

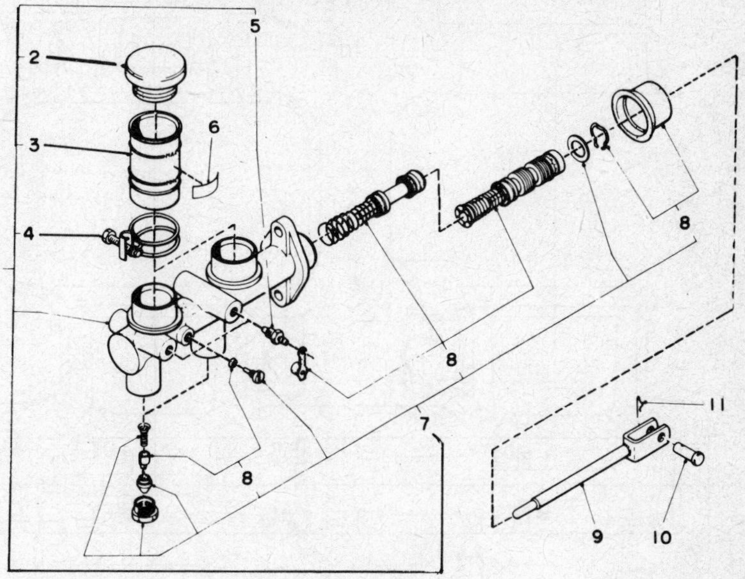

Disc Brakes

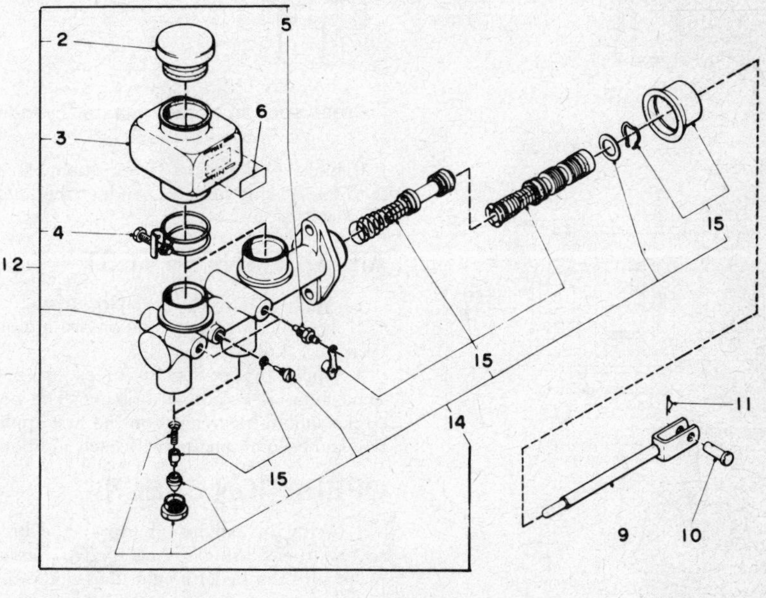

1. Master cylinder ass'y
2. Cap complete (reservoir)
3. Brake fluid reservoir (master cylinder)
4. Reservoir band (master cylinder)
5. Breeder screw
6. Lavel (brake oil tank)
7. Master cylinder repair kit (B)
8. Master cylinder repair kit (A)
9. Push rod
10. Head pin
11. Cotter pin (master cylinder)
12. Master cylinder ass'y
13. Brake fluid reservoir
14. Master cylinder repair kit (B)
15. Master cylinder repair kit (A)

Exploded view of the master cylinders

Bleeding

1. Before beginning to bleed the air from the brake lines, check the pedal play and the level of the brake fluid in the master cylinder. Fill the master cylinder with brake fluid.
2. Begin bleeding the brake lines at the wheel farthest away from the master cylinder.
3. During the bleeding process, fill the reservoir with brake fluid and keep it full during the process.
4. Remove the bleeder screw cap and wipe away any dirt. Then attach the end of a bleeder tube to the bleeder screw end.
5. Insert the other end of the bleeder tube in a glass receptacle containing clean brake fluid.
6. Loosen the bleeder screw and have the person assisting you slowly depress the brake pedal.
7. Continue to depress the pedal until no air bubbles are observed.
8. When there are no more bubbles, tighten the bleeder screw (with the pedal depressed), and then release the pedal.
9. Remove the bleeder tube from the bleeder screw, replace the cap, and go to the next wheel.
10. After bleeding air at all four wheels, check the level of the brake fluid in the master cylinder reservoir and add fluid to the level line. Do not reuse old brake fluid.

Power Brake Booster

The power brake booster uses engine manifold vacuum against a diaphragm to assist in the application of the brakes. The vacuum is regulated to be proportional to the pressure placed on the pedal.

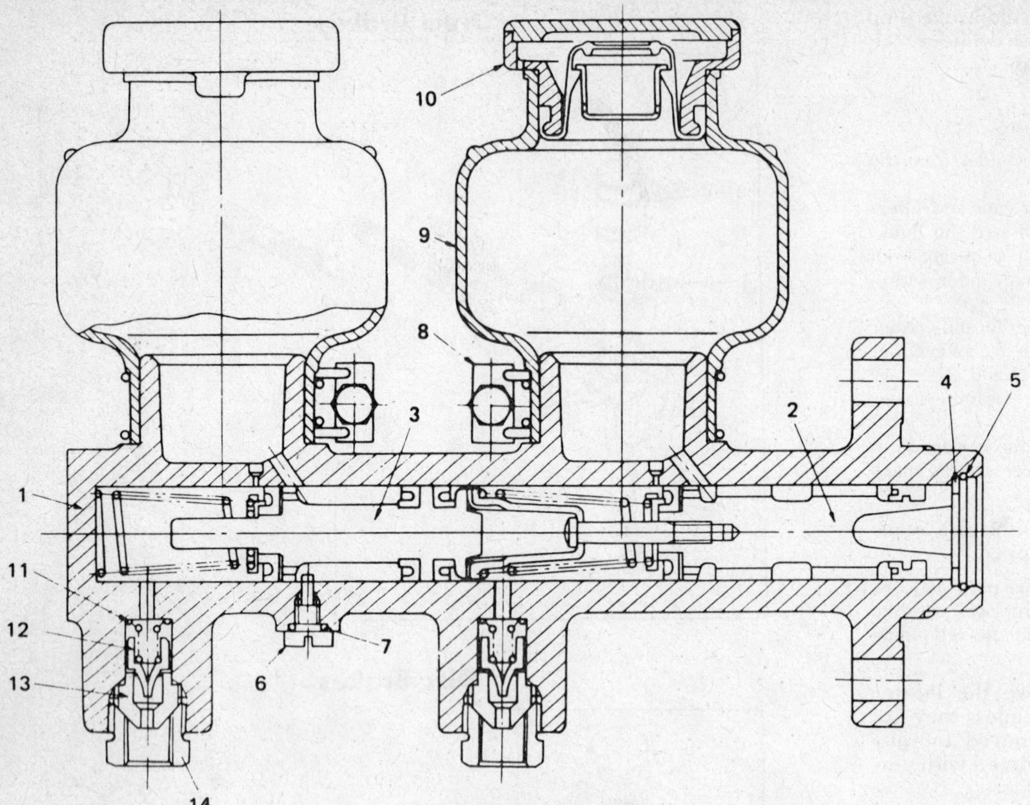

1. Cylinder
2. Primary piston ass'y
3. Secondary piston ass'y
4. Washer (piston stop)
5. Ring (piston stop)
6. Stopper
7. Gasket
8. Band (reservoir)
9. Brake fluid (reservoir)
10. Cap (reservoir)
11. Check valve spring
12. Check valve
13. Tube seat
14. Check valve cap

Cross section of dual master cylinder

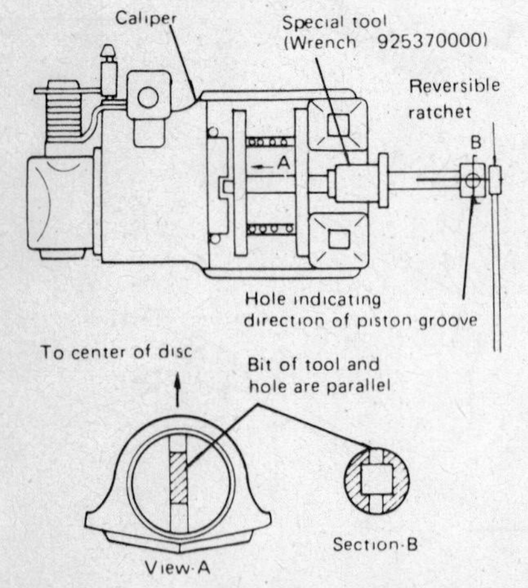

Special tool to seat the piston in the caliper

If brake performance is questionable and the booster unit suspect, conduct the following tests.

AIR TIGHTNESS TEST

1. Apply handbrake and start engine.
2. Run the engine for one or two minutes, then turn it off.
3. Apply brakes several times using the same force as in normal braking. The pedal stroke should be greatest on the first application and become smaller with each additional.

OPERATION CHECK

1. With the engine off. Apply the brakes several times using normal pedal pressure, make sure the pedal height does not vary on each stroke.
2. With the brakes applied, start the engine.
3. When the engine starts the brake pedal should move slightly toward the floor. If no change in the pedal height occurs the power brake unit could be faulty.

INSPECTION

Inspect the vacuum hose and check valve periodically, the hose for cracking or brittleness; the check valve (engine running and brakes applied) for air leaks. Replace hose or valve if necessary. Sometimes a stuck check valve can act like a bad power booster, if this is suspected replace the check valve.

Rebuilding a power brake booster or doing a complete pressure test requires special gauges and tools. It is just not practical for the car owner to attempt servicing the unit except to remove and replace it.

REMOVAL AND INSTALLATION

1. Disconnect the pushrod from the brake pedal by pulling the cotter pin out and removing the pivot pin.
2. Loosen the master cylinder nuts and disconnect the vacuum hose from the (vacuum booster).
3. Remove the bracket nuts from the passenger compartment side.
4. Remove the master cylinder nut, and remove the booster.
5. Installation is the reverse of removal. Make sure that the arrow marking on the check valve is facing toward the engine. Check for fluid leakage after the master cylinder has been installed and the brake pedal is fully depressed for 10 seconds, three or four times.

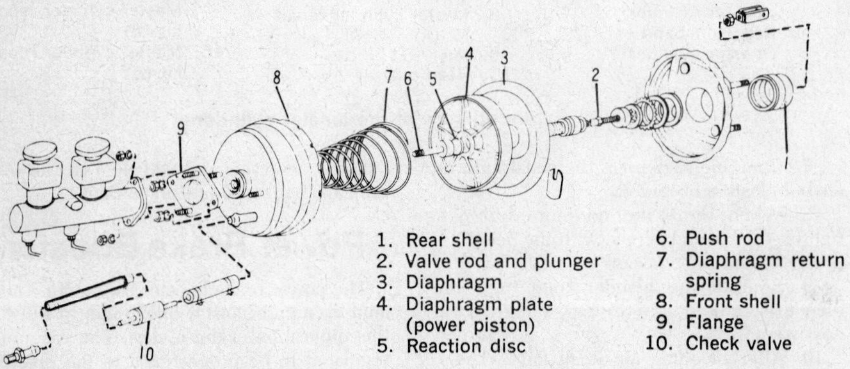

1. Rear shell
2. Valve rod and plunger
3. Diaphragm
4. Diaphragm plate (power piston)
5. Reaction disc
6. Push rod
7. Diaphragm return spring
8. Front shell
9. Flange
10. Check valve

Exploded view of the power brake booster

Front Disc Brakes

Disc Brake Pads

Removal and Installation

1975-79

1. Jack up the front of the vehicle and support it with jack stands. Remove the wheel and tire.
2. Remove the handbrake cable by removing the outer cable clip.
3. Remove the four pins from the caliper.
4. Fit the tip of a screwdriver on the guide and tap lightly to drive it out. When one is removed, the other one can be easily removed.

NOTE: It is not necessary to remove the brake pipe.

Remove the caliper by firmly holding the caliper body and pulling the lower part out while pushing the upper part in.

5. Remove the pad.
6. Check the pads for wear and replace them if the thickness is less than 0.060 in. Replace all four brake pads.
7. Check the disc for wear or damage. Have it resurfaced if it is excessively worn or grooved. The standard thickness is 0.39 in. Do not remove more than 0.06 in. of metal during resurfacing. The disc must be replaced when the thickness is less than 0.33 in.
8. Installation can be done in the reverse order of removal.

NOTE: (1975) Before installing the brake pads, seat the piston in the caliper by pushing it into its cylinder with a screwdriver.
(1976-79) A special tool is needed to push the piston into the caliper by turning it clockwise.

1980 and Later

1. Block the rear wheels. Jack up and support the front of the car with jackstands. Remove the wheel and tire. Release the handbrake and disconnect the cable from the caliper lever.
2. Release the hand brake and disconnect the cable from the caliper lever.
3. Remove the 6 mm lock pin bolt, (lower front of the caliper). Loosen and remove the lock pin.
4. The caliper will now pivot on its support. Swing the caliper from the support and remove the pads.
5. Check the pads for wear—the usable thickness including the backing should be no less than 7.5 mm. Some states require more usable thickness. If the pads show wear, replace them in sets only.
6. Before installing the new brake pads, turn the caliper piston clockwise into the caliper body and align the notches.

CAUTION

Do not force the piston into the caliper body. The piston is mounted on a threaded spindle which will bend.

7. Installation is the reverse of removal.

DISC BRAKE CALIPERS

Removal and Installation

The calipers are removed part of the disc brake pad removal procedure.

BRAKE DISC

Removal and Installation

1. Jack up the vehicle and remove the front wheel, handbrake cable, guides, and caliper as in the brake pad removal and installation procedure.
2. Remove the two bolts that hold the caliper bracket to the housing and remove the bracket from the housing.
3. Pull the disc out of the axle shaft with a puller.
4. Remove the four bolts that hold the disc to the hub.
5. Installation is the reverse of removal.

Inspection

See "Disc Brake Pad Removal and Installation."

WHEEL BEARINGS

Removal and Installation, Packing

1. Jack up the vehicle and remove the front tire and wheel.

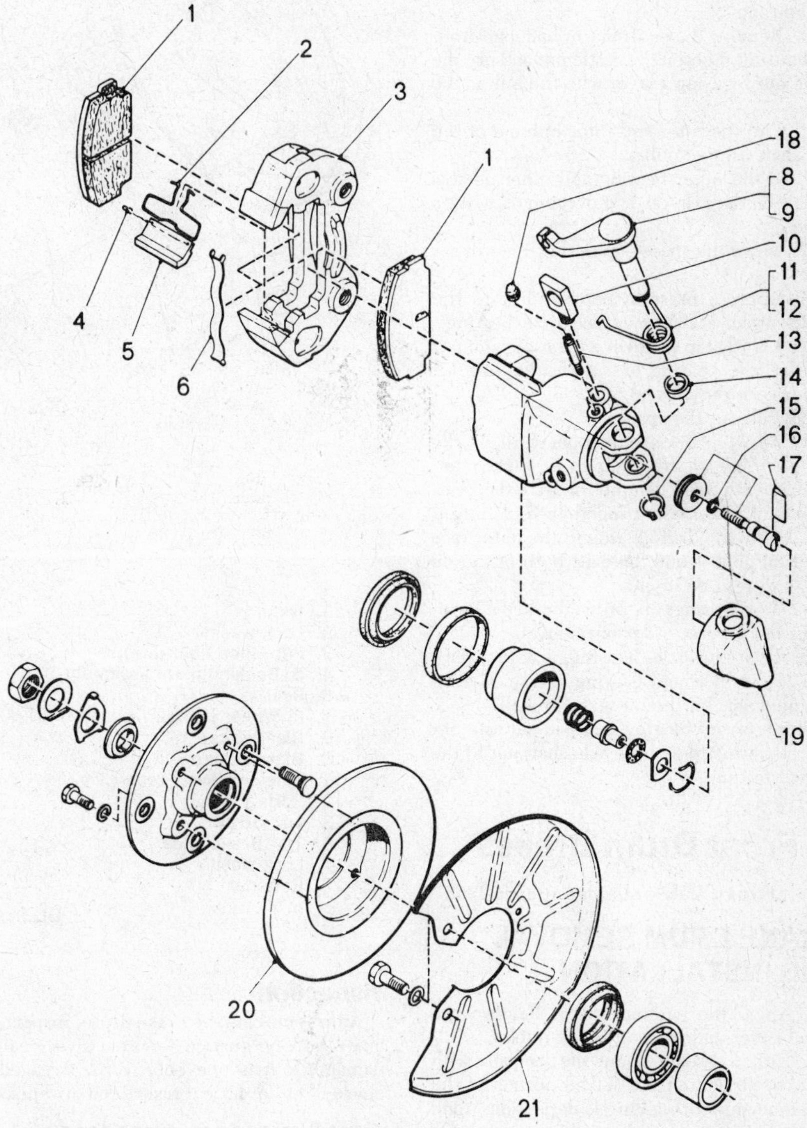

1. Pad (disc brake F)
2. Spring (caliper)
3. Bracket (mounting)
4. Pin (caliper)
5. Stopper (plug)
6. Spring (pad)
7. Body caliper ass'y
8. Lever & spindle ass'y (LH)
9. Lever & spindle ass'y (RH)
10. Bracket (hand brake)
11. Spring (hand brake lever return LH)
12. Spring (hand brake lever return RH)
13. Bleeder screw (wheel cylinder)
14. Bushing (hand brake)
15. Retaining spring
16. Spindle ass'y
17. Connecting link
18. Cap (air bleeder)
19. Cap (lever)
20. Brake disc (F)
21. Cover (disc)

Exploded view of the disc brake assembly

2. Remove the handbrake cable from the lever of the caliper body and disconnect the brake line from the caliper.

3. Remove the stopper (plug) from the caliper bracket.

4. Remove the caliper bracket (mounting) from the disc hub by loosening the two bolts which hold it to the backing plate.

5. Remove the bolts which connect the suspension strut to the housing.

6. Remove the hand brake hanger on the tie rod end. Remove the cable bracket from the housing.

7. Remove the tie rod ball joint from the housing knuckle by using a puller.

8. Carefully pull the housing downward and out to separate the suspension strut from the housing.

9. Remove the control arm ball joint from the housing. Loosen the castle nut and pry the castle nut by using a lever with the hub as the base.

10. Pull the rotor and rotor hub out of the axle shaft using a puller.

11. If the inner bearing and inner oil seal are left on the axle shaft, pull them off using a puller.

12. Move the spacer up or down with your finger.

13. Apply a brass or copper drift to the inside surface of the inner race of the bearing.

14. Lightly tap the drift with a soft hammer to drive the bearing out of the housing together with the oil seal.

15. Pull out the spacer.

16. Apply a brass or copper drift to the inside surface of the outer race. Lightly tap the drift with a soft hammer to drive the bearing out of the housing together with the oil seal. Apply the drift all around the outer race while tapping it out. Discard both of the oil seals and replace them.

17. The bearings are pressed into the housing in the reverse order of removal.

18. Pack the axle housing inside surface with ½ oz. of wheel bearing grease. Grease the inner lips on the oil seals, as well.

There is no bearing preload adjustment other than tightening the axle shaft nut to the correct torque.

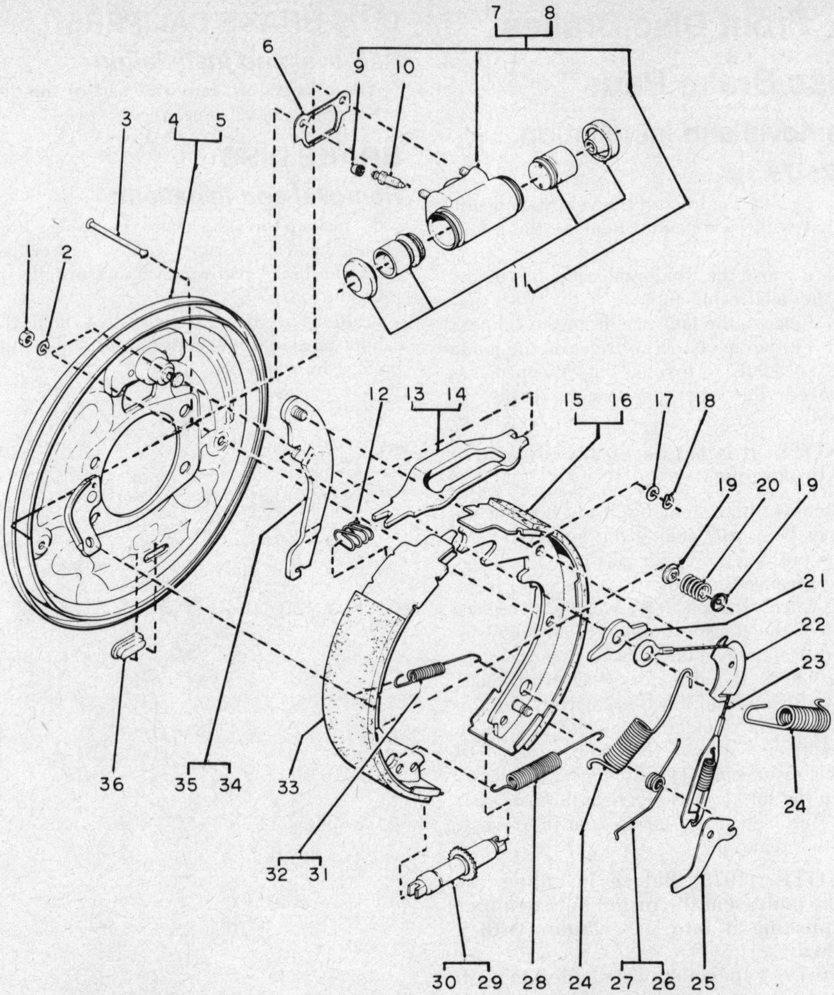

1. Nut
2. Lock washer
3. Pin (shoe hold down)
4, 5. Backing plate assembly
6. Seal
7, 8. Wheel cylinder assembly
9. Bleeder cap
10. Bleeder screw
11. Wheel cylinder repair kit
12. Spring (strut)
13, 14. Strut
15, 16. Brake shoe
17. Lock washer
18. Retainer
19. Cup
20. Spring (shoe hold down)
21. Stopper
22. Cable guide
23. Cable assembly
24. Spring (shoe return, upper)
25. Lever (auto adjuster)
26. 27. Spring (auto adjuster)
28. Spring (shoe return lower)
29. 30. Auto adjuster assembly
31. 32. Spring
33. Brake shoe
34. 35. Lever assembly
36. Cover

DL front drum brakes

Front Drum Brakes

Front drum brakes were last used in 1975.

BRAKE DRUM REMOVAL AND INSTALLATION

1. Apply the parking brake. Remove the wheel cover and loosen the lug nuts.

2. Either straighten out the locktabs with pliers or straighten the staked portion of the axle shaft nut with a chisel, depending upon the year. Loosen, but do not remove the axle shaft nut.

3. Jack up the front of the car and support it with jack stands.

4. Remove the lug nuts and the wheel.

5. Unfasten the axle shaft nut, and release the parking brake.

6. Remove the brake drum with a puller.

Installation is the reverse of removal. Install the axle nut and torque to 170 ft/lbs for 1975. Secure the nut by staking it.

Inspection

After removing the brake drum, inspect the inner braking surface for excessive wear or damage. If it is unevenly worn, streaked or cracked, either have it resurfaced or replaced.

BRAKE SHOE REMOVAL AND INSTALLATION

1. Jack up the vehicle, then remove the wheel and tire and the brake drum.

2. Remove the automatic adjuster spring with a screwdriver and then remove the automatic adjuster lever.

3. Remove the lower shoe return spring and the automatic adjuster.

4. Remove the hand brake cable end from the handbrake lever. Remove the clamp nut with a box wrench. Remove the washer and pull the handbrake cable out.

5. Remove the upper shoe return springs from the anchor pin with a brake tool and remove the automatic adjuster.

6. Remove the shoe set springs with the brake tool and free the brake shoes.

7. Install in the reverse order of removal.

Inspect the shoes for wear rust, or damage. Replace both linings if the thickness is below service limits.

Replace both linings on the other side as well, to prevent uneven braking.

On installation, the shoe-to-drum clearance should be 0.004-0.010 in. Check this by measuring the outside diameter of the installed shoes and comparing against the inside diameter of the drum. Use the adjuster to obtain the correct clearance.

WHEEL CYLINDER REMOVAL AND INSTALLATION

1. Remove the brake drum and the brake shoes from the backing plate.
2. Remove the wheel cylinder from the backing plate by unscrewing the attaching bolts.
3. Remove the rubber boots from both ends of the wheel cylinder and push out the inner pistons and spring together with the rubber cups.
4. Inspect the inside of the wheel cylinder bore. If it is worn or scratched in any way, it should be honed with a wheel cylinder hone or a piece of crocus cloth until the scratches are removed.
5. Replace the rubber cups with new ones. The internal replacement parts are usually supplied in a wheel cylinder rebuilding kit.
6. Reassemble the wheel cylinder and replace it on the backing plate in the reverse order of removal.
7. After reinstalling the brake line and the brake assembly, together with the brake drum, bleed the brake system.

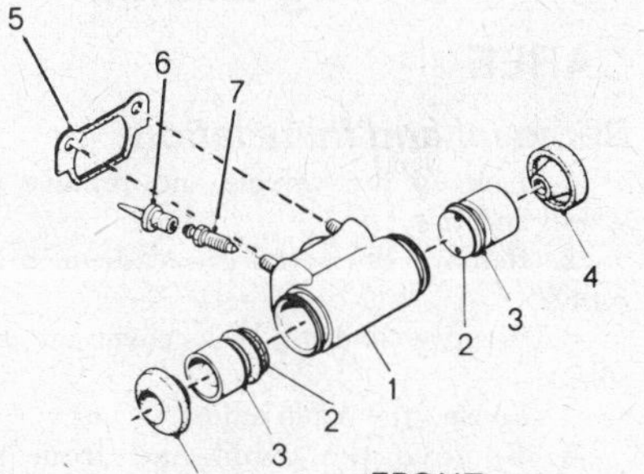

1. Wheel cylinder body
2. Cup
3. Piston
4. Boot
5. Seal (wheel cylinder)
6. Bleeder cap
7. Bleeder screw

Exploded view of the front wheel cylinders

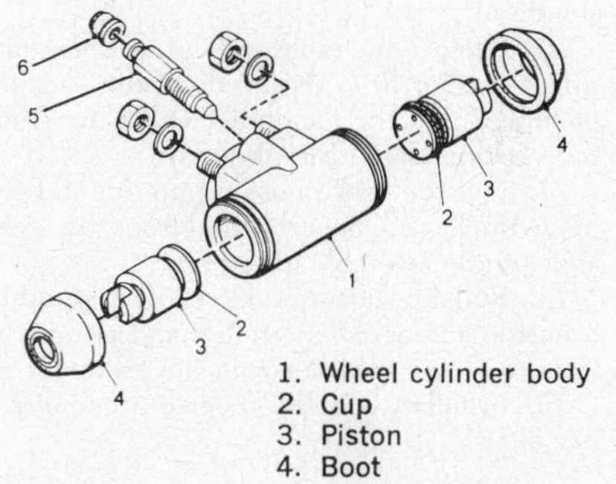

1. Wheel cylinder body
2. Cup
3. Piston
4. Boot
5. Bleeder screw
6. Bleeder cap

Exploded view of the rear wheel cylinders

WHEEL BEARING REMOVAL AND INSTALLATION

1. In order to remove the wheel bearings, the steering knuckle has to be removed from the vehicle.
2. Jack up the vehicle and remove the front wheel and tire.
3. Remove the lock plates and nuts which connect the brake drum to the axle shaft assembly spindle. Removal of the lock plates will be easier if the hand brake is applied.
4. Pull the brake drum off the splines by using a gear puller.
5. Remove the backing plate with the brake assembly by removing the four attaching bolts.
6. Remove the bolts which connect the suspension strut to the housing.
7. Remove the tie rod ball joint from the housing knuckle by using a puller.

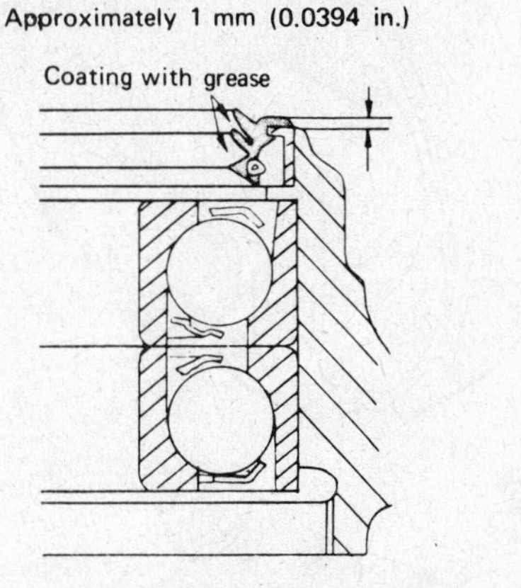

Installation of the outer oil seal

8. Carefully pull the housing downward to separate the suspension strut from the housing.
9. Remove the control arm ball joint from the housing. Install a spacer between the housing and the castle nut and loosen the castle nut.
10. Use a puller to remove the housing from the axle shaft.
11. Move the spacer either up or down using your finger.
12. Insert a brass or copper drift in the inside surface of the inner race of the bearing and lightly tap on the drift with a hammer to drive the bearing out of the housing together with the oil seal.
13. Remove the spacer from the housing.
14. Use the drift to remove the outer race from the housing.
15. The bearings are pressed into the housing.

Pack the axle housing inside surface with wheel bearing grease. Grease the innner lips of the oil seals, as well.

Install the steering knuckle and brake assembly.

There is no bearing preload adjustment, other than tightening the axle shaft nut to the proper specifications.

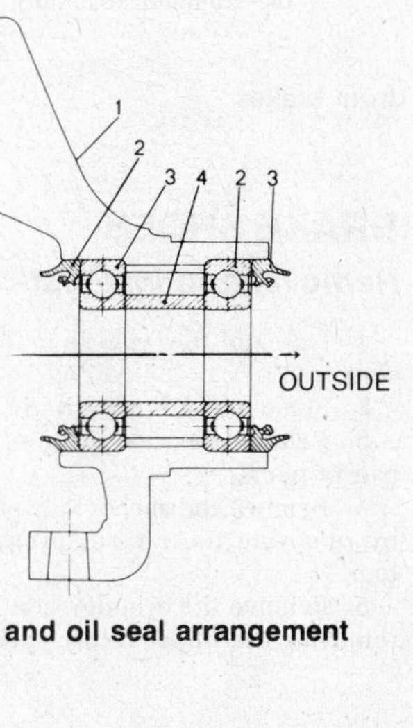

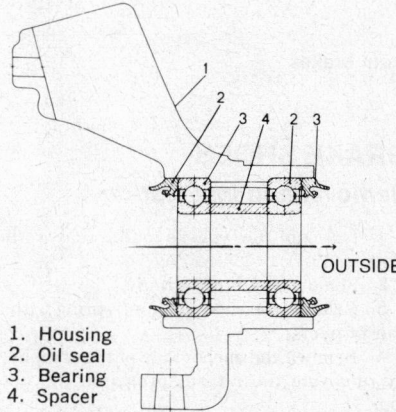

1. Housing
2. Oil seal
3. Bearing
4. Spacer

Bearing and oil seal arrangement

Rear Drum Brakes

BRAKE DRUM REMOVAL AND INSTALLATION

All Except 4WD

1. Jack up the vehicle and remove the wheel and tire. Support it with jack stands and block the front wheels.
2. Remove the 3 cap installing bolts, spring washers, cap and bearing retaining plate.
3. Remove the cotter pin or straighten out the lockwasher, and loosen the castle nut taking care not to damage the bearing seal.
4. Remove the brake drum with a puller.

CAUTION

Do not depress the brake pedal with the brake drum removed.

Installation is performed in the reverse order of removal. Perform the bearing preload adjustment detailed below. Tighten the 3 bearing cap securing plate bolts to 1.7-4.2 ft/lbs.

4WD Models

1. Jack up the vehicle and remove the wheel and tire. Support it with jack stands and block the front wheels.
2. Straighten the staked portion of the axle shaft nut.
3. Apply the footbrake and remove the axle shaft nut.
4. Disconnect the rear axle shaft from the rear axle companion flange.
5. Apply the footbrake and remove the nut retaining the companion flange to the spindle. Remove the companion flange.

NOTE: The nut must be loosened without unstaking because the use of a chisel or similar tool may damage the spline thread.

6. Remove the brake drum and spindle by pulling outward. The outer oil seal can be taken off with the spindle.

Installation is the reverse of removal. Torque the companion flange retaining nut to 145-180 ft/lbs, the axle shaft nut to 175 ft/lbs, and the companion flange bolts to 35 ft/lbs.

Inspection

After removing the brake drum, inspect the inner braking surface for excessive wear or damage. If it is unevenly worn, streaked, or cracked, have it resurfaced or replaced.

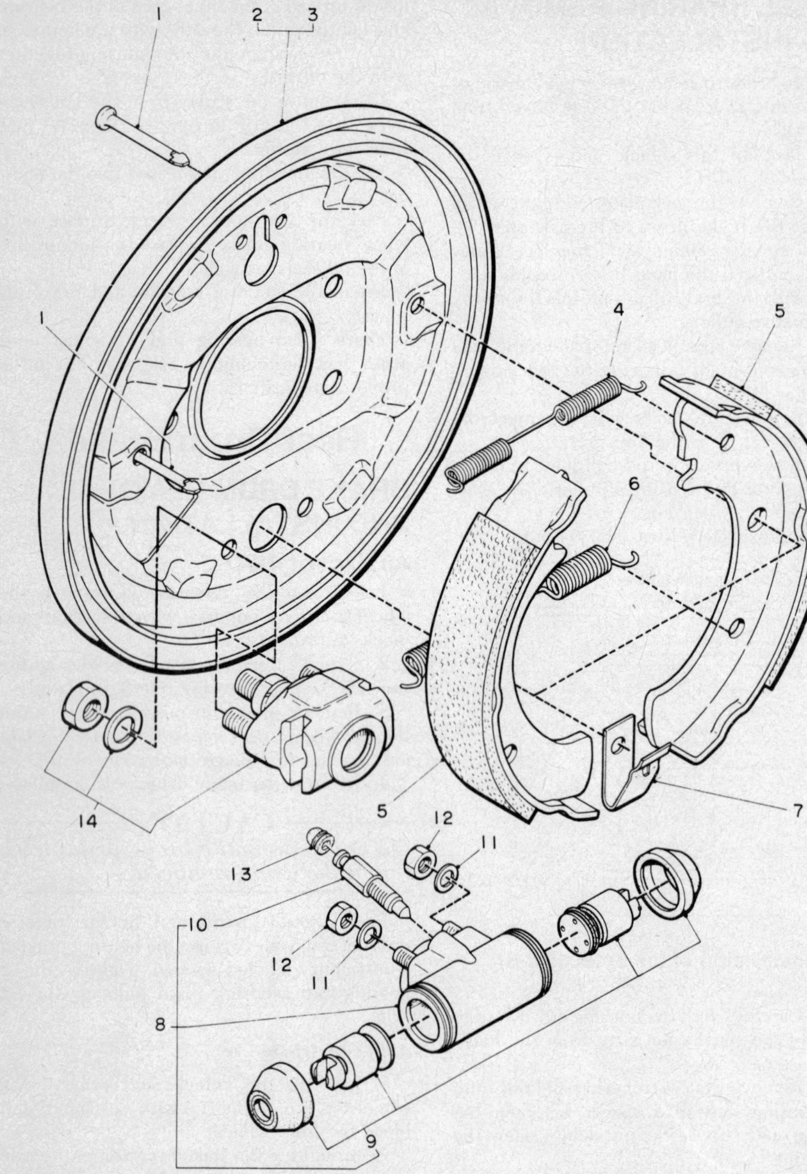

1. Pin (shoe hold down)
2, 3. Backing plate assembly
4. Spring (upper, shoe return)
5. Brake shoe
6. Spring (shoe return, lower)
7. Spring (shoe hold down)
8. Wheel cylinder assembly
9. Wheel cylinder repair kit
10. Bleeder
11. Lock washer
12. Nut
13. Cap
14. Adjuster assembly

DL and GL rear drum brakes

Bearing Preload Adjustment 1975 and Later

1. Tighten the rear bearing adjusting nut enough to seat the bearing. The bearing is seated properly when the brake drum has no side-play but still rotates freely. Do not overtighten.
2. Back off on the nut ⅛ turn.
3. Check the nut starting torque with a torque wrench; it should be 6-9 ft/lbs. Be careful not to tighten the nut.
4. Complete installation in the reverse order of removal.

BRAKE SHOES

Removal and Installation

1. Jack up the vehicle and remove the wheels.
2. Remove the brake drums.
3. Remove the shoe retaining spring with a pair of pliers.
4. Remove the anchor side of the shoe first by removing the return springs on the bottom.
5. Remove the cylinder side of the shoe by removing the upper return springs.
6. Remove the brake shoes from the backing plate.
7. Measure the lining thickness. Replace the linings if they are below the minimum service thickness limits.

Replace the leading and trailing shoes on both sides at the same time. Replacement of the shoes one side or one shoe at a time, will cause uneven braking.

Installation is as follows:

1. Assemble the shoes and the return springs. The upper spring (wheel cylinder side) is thin; the lower spring (anchor side) is thick.
2. Apply brake grease to the backing plate where the brake shoes make contact.
3. Install the shoe and spring assembly to the wheel cylinder first and then to the anchor. Secure the shoes with their retaining springs.

CAUTION

Do not allow grease to get on the surface of the lining.

4. Install the drum and adjust the brakes.

WHEEL CYLINDERS

See the Front Drum Brakes section for removal, installation, and rebuilding of the wheel cylinders.

Parking Brake

CABLE

Removal and Installation

1. Jack up the vehicle and remove the wheel and tire.
2. Remove the brake drum (drum brake type).
3. Remove the hand brake cover and console.
4. Loosen the cable adjusting nut.
5. Remove the cable end from the equalizer.
6. Remove the cable end tightening clip.
7. Remove the service hole cover on the tunnel.
8. Remove the cable clamp from the crossmember.
9. Remove the cable installing bracket from the control arm.
10. Remove the handbrake cable hanger from the tie rod end.
11. Remove the handbrake cable end from the handbrake lever by removing the secondary shoe.
12. Remove the cable end nut, washer, and spring washer from the inside of the backing plate and pull the handbrake cable out from the backing plate (drum brakes).
13. Pull the brake hose clamp out and remove the handbrake cable end from the lever and spindle assembly (disc brakes).
14. Pull the handbrake cable assembly from the engine compartment and remove it from the body together with the grommet.
15. Installation is the reverse order of removal.

Adjustment

The brake should be fully engaged when the lever is pulled up 6-7 notches.

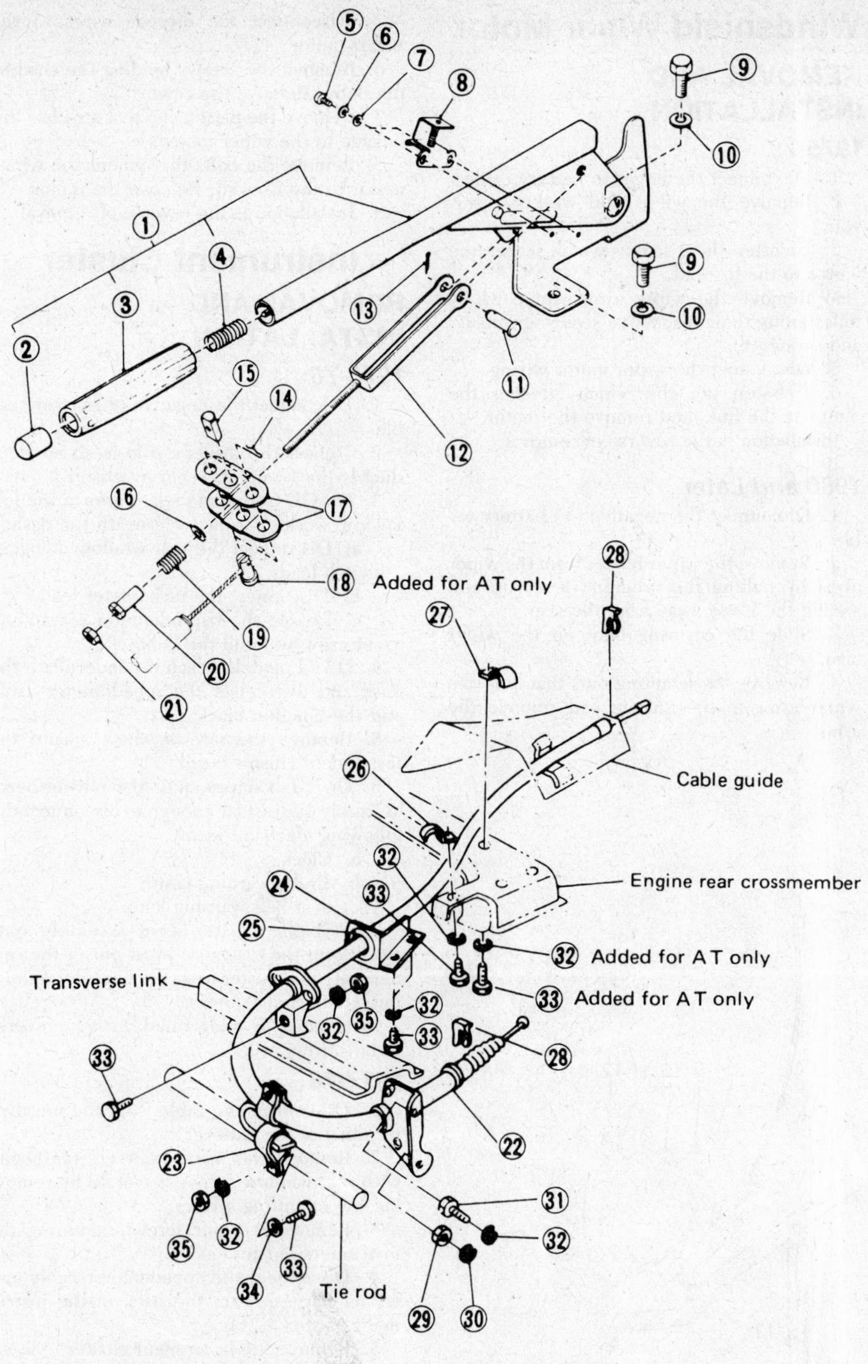

1. Hand brake lever assembly
2. Hand brake lever button
3. Hand brake lever grip
4. Hand brake lever spring
5. Pan head screw
6. Spring washer
7. Washer
8. Hand brake switch
9. Bolt
10. Spring washer
11. Clevis pin
12. Hand brake rod assembly
13. Cotter pin
14. Hand brake cable clip
15. Hand brake pin
16. Washer
17. Equalizer
18. Hand brake pin
19. Hand brake spring
20. Hand brake adjuster
21. Nut
22. Hand brake cable assembly
23. Clamp B
24. Bracket (Side frame)
25. Grommet
26. Clamp (rear crossmember)
27. Clamp (rear crossmember, added for AT only)
28. Hand brake cable clip
29. Nut
30. Spring washer
31. Bolt (6 mm)
32. Spring washer
33. Bolt (6 mm)
34. Washer
35. Nut (6 mm)

Exploded view of typical parking brake

Adjust the cable by loosening the locknut and turning the cable adjusting nut.

CHASSIS ELECTRICAL

Heater Unit

REMOVAL AND INSTALLATION

1975–79

The heater unit contains the core and blower. The entire assembly must be removed from the car before either the blower or core can be serviced. To remove the heater unit:

1. Disconnect the ground cable from the battery.
2. Remove the console, luggage shelf, meter and visor assembly, and center ventilation grill.
3. Drain the coolant and disconnect the two heater hoses in the engine compartment.
4. Disconnect the heater control cable, fan motor harness, and the control rod connecting the air flow fan switch control lever on the instrument panel to the heater unit, on the right side.

Remove the two mounting bolts and remove the heater unit.

5. To install reverse the removal procedure.
6. To reconnect the control rod push up the link provided at the side of the heater unit to its full stroke, set the air/fan switch control lever to vent and then connect the rod to the link.
7. To reconnect the heater control cable set the temperature control lever to cold, the heater control lever on the heater unit to off then connect the cock cable.

1980 and Later

The heater unit contains the core and blower. The entire assembly must be removed from the car before either the blower or core can be serviced. To remove the heater unit, use the following procedure.

1. Disconnect the ground cable (−) from the negative terminal of the battery.
2. Drain the engine coolant through the radiator drain plug.
3. Disconnect the heater hoses in the engine compartment.
4. Remove the rubber grommet the heater hoses run through on the kick panel inside the car. The location is slightly above and to the right of the accelerator pedal.
5. Remove the radio box or console.
6. Remove the instrument panel.
7. Disconnect the heater control cables and fan motor harness.
8. Disconnect the duct between the heater unit and blower assembly. Remove the right and left defroster nozzles.
9. Remove the two mounting bolts at the top sides of the heater unit.
10. Lift up and out on the heater unit.
11. Installation is the reverse of removal.

Radio

REMOVAL AND INSTALLATION

1975 and Later

1. Disconnect the negative battery cable.
2. Use a phillips screwdriver with a short shank to remove the screws holding the speaker grille down. Remove the grille.
3. Disconnect the speaker lead from the radio connector.
4. Remove the instrument cluster bezel screws at the radio end.
5. Unfasten its screws and lift out the console.
6. Pull the knob off the fresh air lever, unfasten the two securing screws at either end, and remove the center outlet grille.
7. Pull both knobs off the radio shafts.
8. Remove the ash tray. Pull the knobs off the heater controls.
9. Remove the nuts from the radio control shafts.
10. Unfasten the screws which secure the radio surround panel. Remove the panel.
11. Unfasten the radio bracket screws.
12. Disconnect the radio leads and pull the radio out of the dash.

Installation is the reverse of removal.

Windshield Wiper Motor

REMOVAL AND INSTALLATION

1975-79

1. Disconnect the negative battery cable.
2. Remove the windshield washer reservoir.
3. Unfasten the 3 screws which secure the motor to the firewall.
4. Remove the wiper arms and cowl by unfastening their respective securing nuts (2) and screws (6).
5. Disconnect the wiper motor wiring.
6. Unfasten the clip which attaches the motor to the link, and remove the motor.

Installation is the reverse of removal.

1980 and Later

1. Disconnect the negative (−) battery cable.
2. Remove the wiper blades from the wiper arms by pulling the retaining lever up and sliding the blade away from the arm.
3. Slide the covering boot up the wiper arm.
4. Remove the retaining nuts that hold the wiper arms to the linkage and remove the arms.
5. Disconnect the electric wires to the wiper motor.
6. Remove the screws holding the cowl to the body. Remove the cowl.
7. Remove the plastic clip that attaches the linkage to the wiper motor.
8. Remove the bolts that mount the wiper motor to the firewall. Remove the motor.
9. Installation is the reverse of removal.

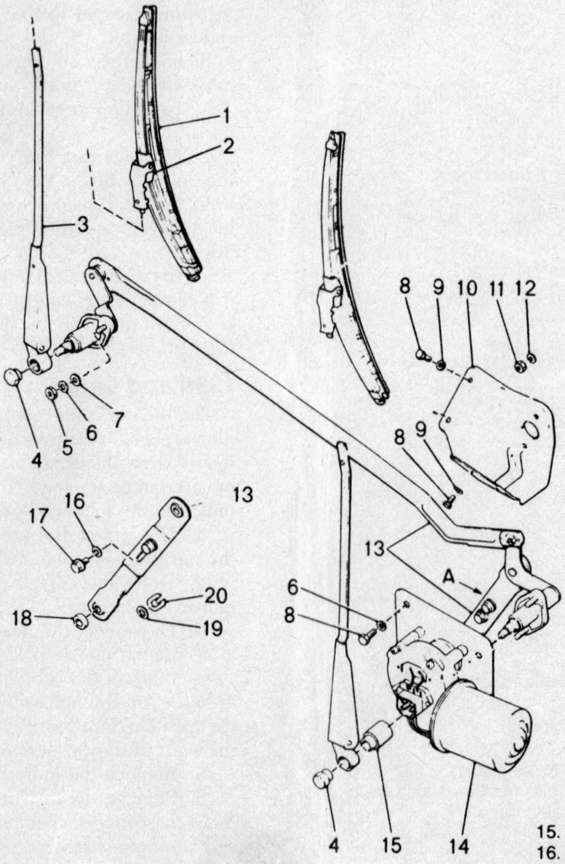

1. Wiper blade
2. Clip
3. Wiper arm
4. Special nut
5. Nut
6. Spring washer
7. Washer
8. Bolt
9. Spring washer
10. Bracket
11. Nut
12. Spring washer
13. Link assembly
14. Wiper motor
15. Cap
16. Spring washer
17. Flange bolt
18. Packing
19. Washer
20. Clip

A—Link adjuster

Exploded view of wiper assembly—typical

Instrument Cluster

REMOVAL AND INSTALLATION

1975-76

1. Disconnect the negative (−) battery cable.
2. Detach the driver's side fresh air vent duct by loosening its securing clamp.
3. On GL Coupe models, perform the following, working from underneath the dash:
   a. Disconnect the rear window defogger switch leads.
   b. Disconnect the tachometer lead.
   c. Loosen the trip odometer reset knob setscrew and pull the knob off.
4. On all models, reach up underneath the dash and disconnect the speedometer cable and the junction block.
5. Remove the screws which secure the instrument cluster bezel.
6. On GL Coupes, pull the cluster/bezel assembly out just far enough to disconnect the following electrical leads:
   a. Clock
   b. Brake warning lamp
   c. Seat belt warning lamp
7. Pull the cluster/bezel assembly out, away from the dash and lift it out of the car. Separate the cluster from the bezel by removing its attaching screws.

Installation is performed in the reverse order of removal.

1977-78

1. Disconnect the cable from the negative terminal of the battery.
2. Remove the instrument cluster bezel, with rear window defogger switch, by removing the mounting screws.
3. Remove the four screws mounting the instrument cluster.
4. Disconnect the speedometer cable and wiring harness from the back of the instrument cluster.
5. Remove the instrument cluster.

Installation is the reverse of removal.

1979 and Later

1. Disconnect the negative battery cable.
2. Remove the bolts securing the steering column and pull it down.
3. Disconnect the electrical wiring connectors then remove the screws securing the meter visor and remove the visor.
4. On the GL and GLF models remove the center ventilator control lever by pulling it.
5. On the station wagon 4WD GL, remove the passing lamp switch.
6. Remove the screws securing the combination meter then pull the meter out far enough to disconnect the speedometer cable and electrical connectors from behind and remove the combination meter.
7. Installation is the reverse of removal.

SPECIFICATIONS

INDEX

BEFORE SERVICING, SEE THE SAFETY NOTICE ON THE CONTENTS PAGE

INTRODUCTION

In 1933, the Toyoda Automatic Loom Works started an automobile division. Several models, mostly experimental, were produced between 1935 and 1937. Automobile production started on a large scale in 1937 when the Toyota Motor Co. Ltd. was founded. The name for the automobile company was changed from the family name, Toyoda, to Toyota, because a numerologist suggested that this would be a more auspicious name to use for this endeavor. It must have been; by 1947, Toyota had produced 100,000 vehicles. Today Toyota is Japan's largest producer of motor vehicles and ranks third largest in world production.

It was not until the late 1950s, that Toyota began importing cars, to the United States. Public reception of the "Toyopet" was cool. The car was heavy and underpowered by U.S. standards. Several other models were imported, including the almost indestructible Land Cruiser. It was not until 1965, however, with the introduction of the Corona sedan, that Toyota enjoyed a real success on the U.S. market. Since that time, Toyota sales have risen at a steady rate, to make the Toyota the largest-selling import in the U.S.

SERIAL NUMBER IDENTIFICATION

Vehicle

All models have the vehicle identification number (VIN) stamped on a plate which is attached to the left side of the instrument panel. This plate is visible through the windshield.

The serial number consists of a series identification number followed by a six-digit production number.

Vehicle Identification Engine

The engine serial number consists of an engine series identification number, followed by a six-digit production number.

The location of this serial number varies from one engine type to another. Serial numbers may be found in the following locations:

1200 cc (3K-C)

The serial number on the 3K-C engine is stamped on the right side of the engine, below the spark plugs.

1600 cc (2T-C)

The serial number is stamped on the left side of this engine, behind the dipstick.

2200 cc (20R)

The serial number is stamped on the left side of the engine, behind the alternator.

2600 cc (4M)

The serial number is stamped on the right side of the cylinder block, below the oil filter.

VEHICLE IDENTIFICATION

Year	Model Type	Series Identification Number
1975-79	Corolla 1600	
	Sedan	TE31L
	Hardtop	TE37L
	Station Wagon	TE38LV
	Sport Coupe	TE51
	Lift Back	TE51
1977-79	Corolla 1200	KE30L
1980-81	Corolla	TE72
1980-81	Corolla Tercel	AL-10, AL-12
1975-77	Corona 2200	
	Sedan	RT105L
	Hardtop	RT115L
	Station Wagon	RT119L
1978-81	Corona	RT134
1975-76	Mark II 2600	
	Sedan	MX13L
	Hardtop	MX23L
	Station Wagon	MX29L
1975-77	Celica 2200	
	Hardtop	RA22L
1978-81	Celica	RA42
1980-81	Celica Supra	MA46
1978-79	Cressida	MX41L
1980-81	Cressida	
	Sedan	MX32
	Station Wagon	MX36

ENGINE IDENTIFICATION

Year	Model	Engine Displacement cu. in.	(cc)	Number of Cylinders	Type	Engine Series Identification
1977-79	Corolla 1200	71.2	(1166)	4	OHV	3K-C
1975-79	Corolla 1600	96.9	(1588)	4	OHV	2T-C
1980-81	Tercel 1500	88.6	(1452)	4	OHV	1A-C, 3A, 3AC
1980-81	Corolla 1800	108.0	(1800)	4	OHV	3T-C
1975-80	Corona 2200	133.6	(2189)	4	OHC	20R
1981	Corona 2400	144.4	(2367)	4	OHC	22R
1975-76	Mark II 2600	156.4	(2563)	6	OHC	4M
1975-80	Celica 2200	133.6	(2189)	4	OHC	20R
1981	Celica 2400	144.4	(2367)	4	OHC	22R
1979½-80	Supra 2600	156.4	(2563)	6	OHC	4M-E
1981	Supra 2800	168.4	(2759)	6	OHC	5M-E
1978-79	Cressida 2600	156.4	(2563)	6	OHC	4M
1980	Cressida 2600	156.4	(2563)	6	OHC	4M-E
1981	Cressida 2800	168.4	(2759)	6	OHC	5M-E

OHV Overhead valve
OHC Overhead cam

GENERAL ENGINE SPECIFICATIONS

Year	Engine Type	Engine Displacement cu. in.	(cc)	Carburetor Type	Horsepower @ rpm ①	Torque @ rpm (ft. lbs.) ①	Bore x Stroke (in.)	Compression Ratio
1975-77	2T-C	96.9	(1588)	2-bbl	75 @ 5800	83 @ 3800	3.35 x 2.76	9.0:1
	20R	133.6	(2189)	2-bbl	96 @ 4800	120 @ 2800	3.48 x 3.50	8.4:1
	4M	151.4	(2563)	2-bbl	108 @ 5000	130 @ 2800	3.15 x 3.35	8.5:1
	3K-C	71.8	(1166)	2-bbl	65 @ 6000	67 @ 3800	2.95 x 2.60	9.0:1
1978-79	4M	156.4	(2563)	2-bbl	108 @ 5000	134 @ 2800	3.15 x 3.35	8.5:1
	2T-C	96.9	(1588)	2-bbl	75 @ 5400	85 @ 2800	3.35 x 2.76	9.0:1
	3K-C	71.8	(1166)	2-bbl	58 @ 5800	63 @ 3800	2.95 x 2.60	9.0:1
	20R	133.6	(2189)	2-bbl	95 @ 4800	122 @ 2400	3.48 x 3.50	8.4:1
1980-81	1A-C	88.6	(1452)	2-bbl	60 @ 4800	72 @ 2800	3.05 x 3.03	8.7:1
	3A	88.6	(1452)	2-bbl	60 @ 4800	72 @ 2800	3.05 x 3.03	8.7:1
	3T-C	108.0	(1800)	2-bbl	75 @ 5000 ②	95 @ 2600 ②	3.35 x 3.07	9.0:1
1980	4M-E	156.4	(2563)	EFI	110 @ 4800	136 @ 2400	3.15 x 3.35	8.5:1
1980	20R	133.6	(2189)	2-bbl	90 @ 4800	122 @ 2400	3.48 x 3.50	8.4:1
1981	3A-C	88.6	(1452)	2-bbl	62 @ 4800	75 @ 2800	3.05 x 3.03	9.0:1
1981	22-R	144.4	(2367)	2-bbl	96 @ 4800	129 @ 2800	3.62 x 3.50	9.0:1
1981	5M-E	168.4	(2759)	EFI	116 @ 4800	145 @ 3600	3.27 x 3.35	8.8:1

① Horsepower and torque ratings are given in SAE net figures
② Calif.: 73 hp @ 5000 rpm; 90 ft. lbs. @ 2600 rpm
EFI Electronic fuel injection

TUNE-UP SPECIFICATIONS

Year	Engine Type	Spark Plugs Type (ND)	Spark Plugs Gap (in.)	Distributor Point Dwell (deg)	Distributor Point Gap (in.)	Ignition Timing (deg) ⑤ MT	Ignition Timing (deg) ⑤ AT	Compression Press.	Fuel Pump Press.	Idle Speed (rpm) MT	Idle Speed (rpm) AT	Valve Clearance (in.) (hot) Intake	Valve Clearance (in.) (hot) Exhaust
1975-77	2T-C	W16EP	0.030	52 ③	0.018	10B ⑦	10B ⑦	171	2.8-4.3 ⑧	850	850	0.008	0.013
	20R	W16EP	0.030	52	0.018 ⑨	8B	8B	156	2.2-4.2	850	850	0.008	0.012
	4M ①	W16EP	0.030	41	0.018	10B	10B	156	4.2-5.4	800	750	0.007	0.010
	4M ②	W16EP	0.030	41	0.018	5B	5B	156	4.2-5.4	800	750	0.007	0.010
	3K-C	W20EP	0.031	52	0.018	5B	—	156	2.8-4.3	750	—	0.008	0.012
1978-79	3K-C	BPR5EA-L	0.031	Electronic		8B	8B	156	3.0-4.5	750	750	0.008	0.012
	2T-C	BP5EA-L	0.031	Electronic		10B ⑩	10B ⑩	171	3.0-4.5	850	850	0.008	0.013
	4M	BPR5EA-L	0.031	Electronic		10B ⑩	10B ⑩	156	4.2-5.4	750	750	0.011	0.014
	20R	BP5EA-L ⑪	0.031	Electronic		8B	8B	156	2.2-4.2	800	850	0.008	0.012
1980-81	1A-C	BP6EK-A	0.039	Electronic ④		5B	—	177	—	650	800	0.008	0.012
	3A	BPR5EA-L	0.031	52	0.018	5B	—	177	—	650	800	0.008	0.012
	3T-C	BPR5EA ⑪	0.043	Electronic ④		10B	10B	163	—	850 ⑥	850 ⑥	0.008	0.013
	4M-E (EFI)	BPR5EA-L	0.031	Electronic ④		12B	12B	156	3.3-3.8	800	800	0.011	0.014
	20R	BP5EA-L	0.031	Electronic ④		8B	8B	156	2.2-4.3	800 ⑫	850	0.008	0.012

NOTE: If the information given in this chart disagrees with the information on the emission control specification decal, use the specifications on the decal.

① Except California
② California only
③ Dual points —main 57°, sub. 52°
④ Air gap 0.008-0.016 inch
⑤ With vacuum advance disconnected
⑥ M/T without power steering —700 rpm
A/T without power steering —750 rpm
⑦ Dual points —main 12B, sub. 19-25B (degrees)
⑧ Electric pump (California) —2.4 to 3.8 psi
⑨ California model Celica GT equipped with transistorized ignition
⑩ California —8B
⑪ Celica —BPR5EA-L
⑫ Four-speed manual —700 rpm

M/T Manual transmission
A/T Automatic transmission
TDC Top dead center
B Before top dead center
A After top dead center

FIRING ORDERS

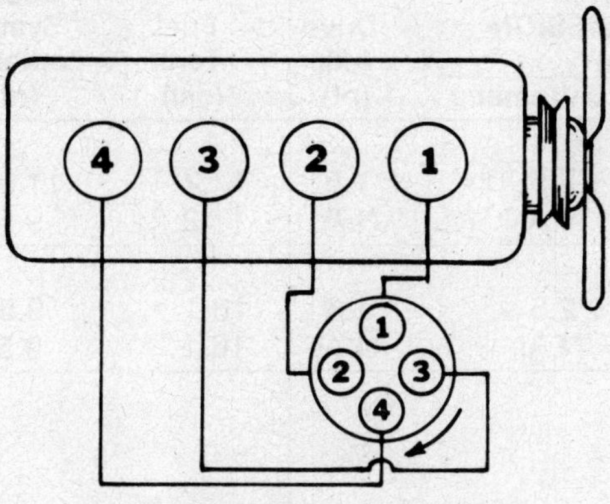

Four cylinder engines—except 20R

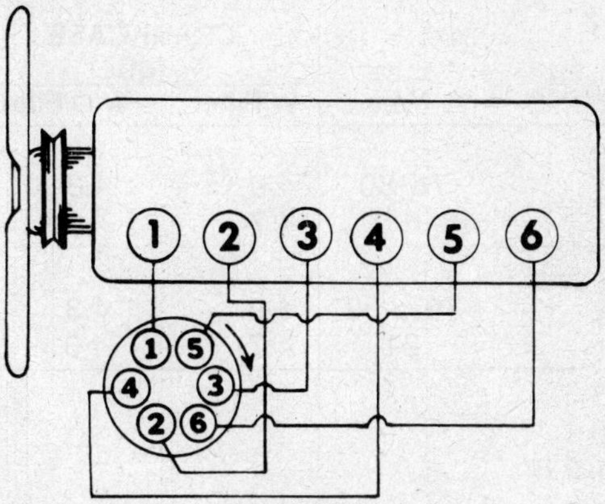

4M engine

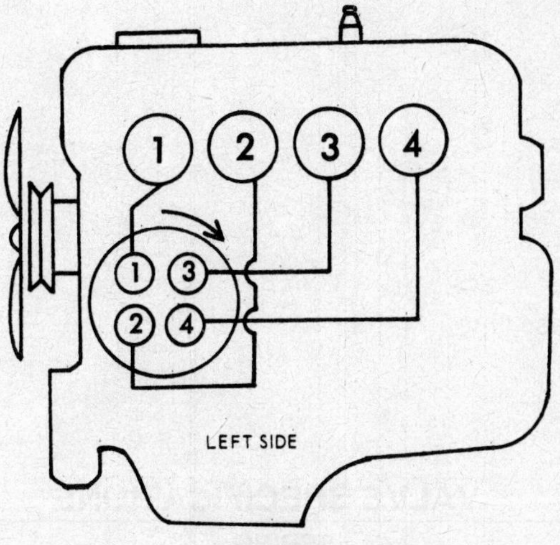

20R engine

CAPACITIES

Model	Year	CRANKCASE (qt) W/Filter	CRANKCASE (qt) W/O Filter	TRANSMISSION (qt) Manual	TRANSMISSION (qt) Automatic	Drive Axle (pt)	Fuel Tank (gal)	Cooling System w/heater (qt)
Corolla								
1200	76-79	3.7	2.9	①	—	2.2	12.0	5.1
1600	75-79	4.6	3.7	1.6	2.5	1.2	13.2	8.8
1800	80-81	4.0	3.5	1.8	2.5	1.1	13.2	8.5
Tercel								
1500	80-81	3.7	3.4	3.4	2.3	2.0	11.9	5.4
Corona								
2200	75-80	4.8	4.1	2.9 ②	2.3 ③	⑤	14.5 ④	7.4 ⑥
2400	81	4.8	4.1	2.9 ②	2.3 ③	N.A.	16.1	8.5
Celica								
2200	75-80	4.9	4.0	2.9 ②	2.3 ③	⑤	13.0 ⑦	8.5 ⑧
2400	81	5.5	4.6	N.A.	N.A.	N.A.	16.1	9.5
Mark II								
2000	1975	5.6	4.6	1.8	3.0	2.6	15.9 ⑨	11.4
2600	75-76	6.2	5.2	2.9	3.0	2.6	15.9 ⑨	12.3

CAPACITIES

Model	Year	CRANKCASE (qt) W/Filter	CRANKCASE (qt) W/O Filter	TRANSMISSION (qt) Manual	TRANSMISSION (qt) Automatic	Drive Axle (pt)	Fuel Tank (gal)	Cooling System w/heater (qt)
Cressida								
2600	78-80	4.9 ⑩	4.3 ⑩	—	2.5 ⑪	1.5	17.2 ⑫	11.6
2800	81	4.7	4.0	—	N.A.	N.A.	17.2 ⑫	9.5
Supra								
2600	79½-80	4.9	4.3	2.8	2.5	1.6	16.1	9.5
2800	81	4.7	4.0	N.A.	N.A.	N.A.	16.1	9.5

① 4 sp: 1.8
5 sp: 2.6
② 5 speed: 2.8
③ 78-80: 2.5
④ 1978-79: 15.5; 1980: 16.1
⑤ Unitized type: 1.3
Banjo type: 1.4
⑥ 79-80: 8.5
⑦ 77: 14.5; 78-79: 15.5; 80: 16.1
⑧ 1978-80: 8.9
⑨ Sta. wag.: 14.5
⑩ 1978: 5.7, 4.7
⑪ 1978: 2.3
⑫ Sta. wag.: 16.2
N.A. Information not available at press time

VALVE SPECIFICATIONS

Engine Type	Seat Angle (deg)	Face Angle (deg)	Spring Test Pressure (lbs) Inner	Spring Test Pressure (lbs) Outer	Spring Installed Height (in.) Inner	Spring Installed Height (in.) Outer	Stem to Guide Clearance (in.) Intake	Stem to Guide Clearance (in.) Exhaust	Stem Diameter (in.) Intake	Stem Diameter (in.) Exhaust
3K-C	45	44.5	—	70.1	—	1.512	0.0010-0.0020 ③	0.0020-0.0030 ④	0.3140 ⑤	0.3140 ⑥
2T-C	45	44.5	—	58.4 ⑤	—	1.484	0.0012-0.0020	0.0012-0.0024	0.3140	0.3140
20R	45	44.5	—	60.0 ⑥	—	1.594	0.0006-0.0024	0.0012-0.0026	0.3141	0.3140
4M	45	44.5	25.7 ⑦	63.1 ①	1.504	1.642 ②	0.0006-0.0018	0.0010-0.0024	0.3146	0.3140
1A-C, 3A	45	44.5	—	52.0	—	1.520	0.0010-0.0024	0.0012-0.0026	0.2747	0.2745
4M-E	45	44.5	15.6	41.6	1.49	1.63	0.0010-0.0024	0.0014-0.0028	0.3141	0.3137
3T-C	45	44.5	—	57.9	—	1.484	0.0010-0.0024	0.0012-0.0026	0.3139	0.3139

① Exhaust valve spring test pressure: inner—24.6 lbs; outer—59.4 lbs; 1978-79 intake and exhaust: 41.9
② Exhaust valve installed height: inner—1.520 in.; outer—1.657 in.
③ 1978 and later: 0.0012-0.0026
④ 1978 and later: 0.0014-0.0028
⑤ 1978 and later: 57.9
⑥ 1978 and later: 55.1
⑦ 1978 and later: 15.5

CRANKSHAFT AND CONNECTING ROD SPECIFICATIONS

All measurements in inches

Engine Type	Crankshaft: Main Brg. Journal Dia.	Crankshaft: Main Brg. Oil Clearance	Crankshaft: Shaft End-Play	Crankshaft: Thrust on No.	Connecting Rod: Journal Diameter	Connecting Rod: Oil Clearance	Connecting Rod: Side Clearance
3K-C	1.9675-1.9685	0.0005-0.0015	0.0020-0.0090 ①	3	1.6525-1.6535	0.0006-0.0015 ②	0.0040-0.0080 ③
2-TC	2.2827-2.2834	0.0012-0.0024 ②	0.0030-0.0070 ④	3	1.8889-1.8897	0.0008-0.0020	0.0063-0.0102
20R	2.3614-2.3622	0.0010-0.0022	0.0008-0.0079 ⑤	3	2.0862-2.0866	0.0010-0.0022	0.0063-0.0102
4M	2.3617-2.3627	0.0012-0.0021	0.0020-0.0100	4	2.0463-2.0472	0.0008-0.0021	0.0020-0.0100 ⑥
1A-C, 3A	1.8892-1.8898	0.0005-0.0019	0.0008-0.0073	3	1.5742-1.5748	0.0008-0.0020	0.0059-0.0098
4M-E	2.3617-2.3627	0.0013-0.0023	0.002-0.010	4	2.0463-2.0472	0.0008-0.0021	0.0063-0.0117
3T-C	2.2825-2.2835	0.0009-0.0019	0.0008-0.0087	3	1.8889-1.8897	0.0009-0.0019	0.0063-0.0012

① 1978 and later: 0.0016-0.0087
② 1978 and later: 0.0009-0.0019
③ 1978 and later: 0.0043-0.0084
④ 1978 and later: 0.0010-0.0090
⑤ 1978 and later: 0.0010-0.0080
⑥ 1978 and later: 0.0063-0.0117

PISTON AND RING SPECIFICATIONS

All measurements in inches

Engine Type	Piston Clearance	Ring Gap: Top Compression	Ring Gap: Bottom Compression	Ring Gap: Oil Control	Ring Side Clearance: Top Compression	Ring Side Clearance: Bottom Compression	Ring Side Clearance: Oil Control
3K-C	0.0010-0.0020	0.0006-0.0014 ①	0.0006-0.0014 ①	0.0006-0.0014 ②	0.0011-0.0027	0.0007-0.0023 ③	0.0006-0.0023
2T-C	0.0024-0.0031	0.0008-0.0016 ④	0.0004-0.0012 ⑤	0.0004-0.0012 ⑥	0.0008-0.0024	0.0008-0.0024 ⑦	0.0008-0.0024 ⑧
20R	0.0012-0.0020	0.0004-0.0012	0.0004-0.0012	Snug	0.0008	0.0008	Snug
4M	0.0010-0.0020 ⑨	0.0006-0.0014 ⑩	0.0006-0.0014 ⑪	0.0008-0.0020	0.0012-0.0028 ⑬	0.0008-0.0024 ⑫	Snug
1A-C, 3A	0.0039-0.0047	0.0079-0.0157	0.0059-0.0138	0.0039-0.0236	0.0016-0.0031	0.0012-0.0028	N.A.
4M-E	0.0020-0.0028	0.0039-0.0110	0.0039-0.0110	0.0079-0.0200	0.0012-0.0028	0.0008-0.0024	N.A.
3T-C	0.0020-0.0028	0.0039-0.0098	0.0059-0.0118	0.0079-0.0276	0.0008-0.0024	0.0006-0.0022	N.A.

① 1978 and later: 0.004-0.011 inch
② 1978 and later: 0.008-0.035 inch
③ 1978 and later: 0.001-0.003 inch
④ 1978 and later: 0.006-0.011 inch
⑤ 1978 and later: 0.008-0.013 inch
⑥ 1978 and later: 0.008-0.028 inch
⑦ 1978 and later: 0.0006-0.0022 inch
⑧ 1978-79: 0.008-0.035
⑨ 1978-79: 0.0020-0.0030 inch
⑩ 1978-79: 0.0039-0.0110 inch
⑪ 1978-79: 0.0059-0.0110 inch
⑫ 1978-79: 0.0008-0.0035 inch
⑬ 1978-79: 0.001-0.003
N.A. Not available

TORQUE SPECIFICATIONS

All readings in ft. lbs.

Engine Type	Cylinder Head Bolts	Rod Bearing Bolts	Main Bearing Bolts	Crankshaft Pulley Bolt	Flywheel to Crankshaft Bolts	MANIFOLD	
						Intake	Exhaust
3K-C	39.0-47.7	28.9-37.6	39.0-47.7	29-43 (11)	39-48	14-22 (1)	
2T-C	52.0-63.5 (12)	28.9-36.1	52.0-63.5	28.9-43.3 (8)	41.9-47.7 (9)	7.2-11.6 (13)	7.2-11.6 (14)
8R-C	75-85	42-48	72-80	43-51	42-49	20-25 (1)	
18R-C	72-82	39-48	69-83	43-51	51-58	30-35 (1)	
2M	(2)	25-30	72-79	43-51	41-46 (3)	22-29 (4)	18-25 (5)
4M	55-61 (6)	30-36	72-78	69-76 (10) (17)	41-46 (7) (18)	17-21 (4)	12-17 (5) (19)
20R	52-64	39-48	69-83	80-94 (15)	62-68 (16)	11-15	29-36
1A-C, 3A	40-47	26-32	40-47	55-61	55-61	15-21	15-21
3T-C	62-68	29-36	53-63	47-61	42-47	14-18	22-32
4M-E	55-61 (6)	31-34	72-78	98-119	51-57	10-15	13-16

(1) Intake and exhaust manifolds combined
(2) 8 mm bolts: 11-14 ft. lbs.
13 mm bolts: 54-61 ft. lbs.
(3) Flex-plate (automatic): 14-22 ft. lbs.
(4) Intake manifold stud bolt: 14-18 ft. lbs.
(5) Exhaust manifold stud bolt: 6-7 ft. lbs.
(6) 8 mm bolts: 7-12 ft. lbs.
(7) 10 mm bolts: 54-61 ft. lbs.
(8) 1975: 43-51 ft. lbs.; 1976: 116-145 ft. lbs.
(9) 1975-76: 58-64 ft. lbs.
(10) 1975-76: 51-58 ft. lbs.
(11) 1977: 32.5-39.8
(12) 1977-79: 61.5-68.7
(13) 1978-79: 14-18
(14) 1978-79: 22-32
(15) 1978-79: 102-130
(16) 1978-79: 73-79
(17) 1978-79: 98-119
(18) 1978-79: 51-57
(19) 1978-79: 10-15

TORQUE SEQUENCES

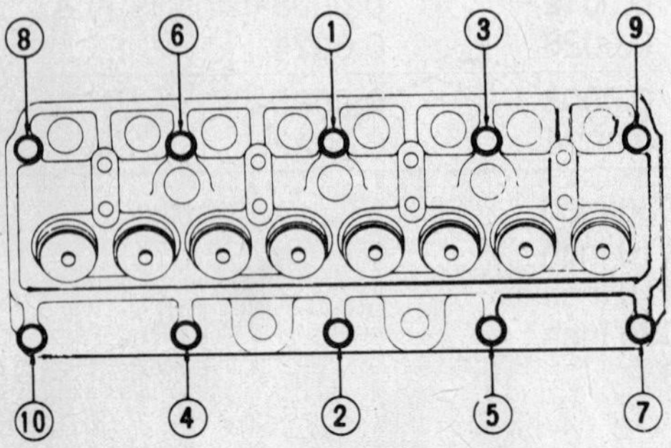

3K-C installation

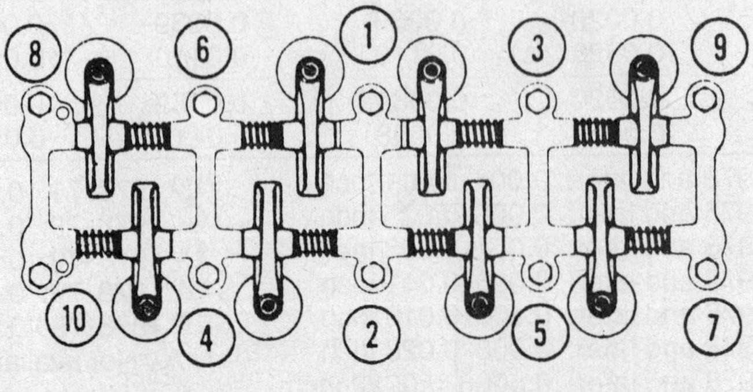

20R cylinder head installation sequence

TORQUE SEQUENCES

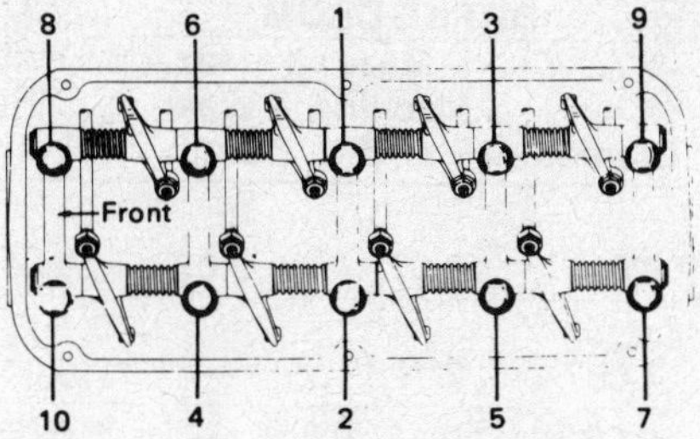

2T-C installation

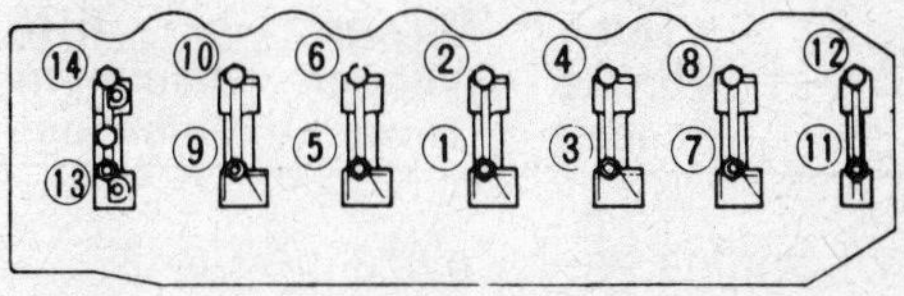

4M installation

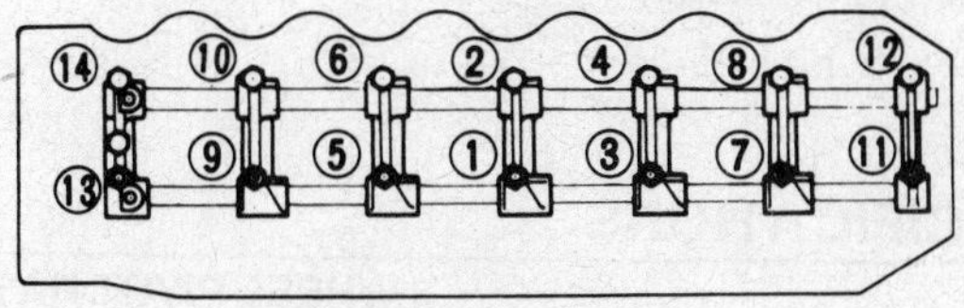

4M installation

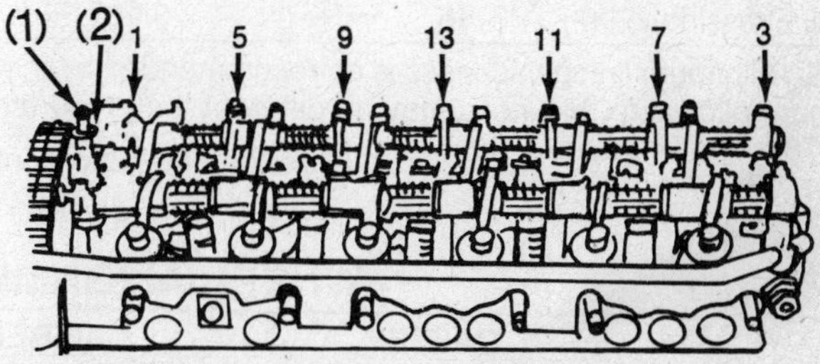

4M removal: first remove the union belt (1) and the union (2)

ALTERNATOR AND REGULATOR SPECIFICATIONS

	ALTERNATOR		REGULATOR						
				FIELD RELAY			REGULATOR		
Engine Type	Manufacturer	Output (amps)	Manufacturer	Contact Spring Deflection (in.)	Point Gap (in.)	Volts to Close	Air Gap (in.)	Point Gap (in.)	Volts
3K-C	Nippon Denso	25 ①	Nippon Denso	0.008-0.024	0.016-0.047	4.5-5.8	0.012	0.010-0.018	13.8-14.8 ②
2TC, 20R ⑤	Nippon Denso	40 ③	Nippon Denso	0.008-0.024	0.016-0.047 ④	4.5-5.8	0.012	0.010-0.018	13.8-14.8 ②
3T-C	Nippon Denso	50	Nippon Denso	Not adjustable					13.4-14.8 ⑦
4M	Nippon Denso	55	Nippon Denso	0.008-0.024	0.016-0.047	4.5-5.8	0.012	0.008-0.024	13.8-14.8
4M-E	Nippon Denso	55	Nippon Denso	Not adjustable					14.0-14.7 ⑥
1A-C & 3A	Nippon Denso	30, 40, 50 & 55	Nippon Denso	Not adjustable					13.8-14.8 ⑦

① 1976-79: 50 and 55
② W/55 amp alt.: 14.0-14.7
③ Optional: 55
④ 1975-79: 0.0118-0.0177
⑤ 1980 has non-adjustable regulator
⑥ 1980: 14.3-14.9
⑦ W/55 amp: 14.0-14.7

BRAKE SPECIFICATIONS

All measurements given are in. unless noted

			BRAKE DISC		BRAKE DRUM			MINIMUM LINING THICKNESS	
Model	Lug Nut Torque (ft. lbs.)	Master Cylinder Bore	Minimum Thickness	Maximum Run-Out	Diameter	Max. Machine O/S	Max. Wear Limit	Front	Rear
Corolla									
1200	65-86	0.626	0.35	0.006	8.0	8.05	8.14	0.25	0.04
1600	65-86	0.813	0.35	0.006	9.08	9.07	9.16	0.25	0.04
1800	66-86	—	0.453	0.0059	9.0	9.079	—	0.04	0.04
Celica (1975-78)	65-86	0.813	0.35 ①	0.006	9.08	9.15	9.23	0.25	0.04
Celica 2200 (1979-81)	66-86	0.813	0.450	0.0059	9.0	9.079	—	0.04	0.04

BRAKE SPECIFICATIONS

All measurements given are in. unless noted

Model	Lug Nut Torque (ft. lbs.)	Master Cylinder Bore	Brake Disc: Minimum Thickness	Brake Disc: Maximum Run-Out	Brake Drum: Diameter	Brake Drum: Max. Machine O/S	Brake Drum: Max. Wear Limit	Minimum Lining Thickness: Front	Minimum Lining Thickness: Rear
Corona 2000/2200 (1975-79)	65-86	0.876	0.45	0.006	9.0	9.07	9.09	0.04	0.04
Tercel D1-AC, 3A (1980-81)	65-86	—	0.354	0.059	7.087	7.126	—	0.04	0.04
Supra, Cressida 2600	66-86	—	0.453 ②	0.0059	9.08 ③	9.15 ③	—	0.04	0.04

NOTE: Minimum lining thickness is as recommended by the manufacturer. Due to variations in state inspection regulations, the minimum allowable thickness may be different than recommended by the manufacturer.

① 1978: 0.45; Fastback 0.49
② Rear: 0.354
③ Cressida only, Supra info. not available at press time

WHEEL ALIGNMENT SPECIFICATIONS

Model	Caster: Range (deg)	Caster: Pref Setting (deg)	Camber: Range (deg)	Camber: Pref Setting (deg)	Toe-In (in.)	Steering Axis Inclination	Wheel Pivot Ratio (deg): Inner Wheel	Wheel Pivot Ratio (deg): Outer Wheel
Corolla 1200	1½P-2⅓	—	½P-1½P	½P	0.04-0.20 ⑤	7½P-8½P	38½-41½ ⑥	30-36 ⑦
1600 (1975)	1½P-2P ①	1¾P	½P-1½P	½P	0.04-0.20	7½P-8½P	38½-41½ ②	27½-33½
(1976-79)	1¼P-1½P	2P	½P-1½P	1P	0.08-0.16 ③	7¼P-8¼P	37-39 ⑥	29¼-33¼ ⑦
1800 exc. sta. wgn.	1°16′P-2°16′P	1°46′P	33′P-1°33′P	1°3′P	0-.08 ⑧	7°55′P-8°55′P	38-40	29-33
1800 sta. wgn.	1°4′P-2°4′P	1°34′P	35′P-1°35′P	1°5′P	0-.08 ⑧	7°50′P-8°50′P	38-40	29-33
Tercel	1°40′P-2°40′P	2°10′P	0-1°P	30′P	0.04-0.12	10°50′P-11°50′P	34-36	33
Celica (1975-76)	½P-1½P	1P	0-1½P	1P	0.20-0.28	7½P	37-39	30-34
Celica (1977)	1¼P-2¾P	1¾P	½P-1½P	1P	0-0.08	7¼P-8¼P	36-38	28¼-32¼
GT (1976-77)	1¼P-2½P	2P	¼P-1¼P	1P	0.04-0.12	7P-8P	36-38	28-32
ST (1976)	½N-1½P	1P	½N-1½P	1P	0.04-0.12 0	7P-8P	36-38	28-32
Celica (1978)	1⅓P-2⅓P	1⅔P	25′P-1°25′P	55′P	④	7½P	38	31
(1979)	1°15′P-2°15′P	1°45′P	35′P-1°35′P	1°5′P	0-0.08	6°55′P-7°55′P	36-38	28-32
(1980-81)	1°10′P-2°10′P	1°40′P	25′P-1°25′P	55′P	0-0.08 ④	7°5′P-8°5′P	36°10′-38°10′	28°15′-32°15′
Corona (1975)	½P-1½P	1P	0-1P	½P	0.06-0.12	7P	—	—
(1976)	½P-1½P	1P	0-1P	½P	0.04-0.12	7P	36½-38½	31
(1977)	⅓-1⅓P	1P	0-1P	½P	0.04-0.12	7P	36½-38½	31
(1978-79)	⅓P-1⅓P	⅘P	1/12P-1⅙P	⅗P	0.04-0.12	7P	37½	31
(1980)	1°15′P-2°15′P	1°45′P	30′P-1°30′P	1°P	0-0.08	7°20′P-8°20′P	36-38	28-32
Cressida	44′P-1°44′P	1°14′P	20′P-1°20′P	50′P	0.08-0.16 out	7°10′P-8°10′P	35-39	32
Mark 11/6 (1975)	0-1P	½P	½P-1½P	1P	0.16-0.24	7P	36½	32½
Mark 11/6 (1976)	1½P-2½P	2P	½P-1½P	1P	0.16-0.24	7P	36½-38½	31-32
Supra	1°15′P-2°15′P	1°45′P	20′P-1°20′P	50′P	0.04 out-0.04 in	7°10′P-8°10′P	35°5′-37°5′	28°20′-32°20′

① 1975 Wagon: ¾P-1½P
② 1975 inner: 37-39 deg
③ 1976-77 (radial): 0-0.08 in.
④ Man. Steering: 0-0.08
Pwr. Steering: 0.12-0.20
⑤ 1978-79 w/bias ply: 0.079″
w/radial ply: 0.039″
⑥ 1978-79: 37-39
⑦ 1978-79: 29-33
⑧ w/bias tires: 0.12 ± 0.04
P Positive
N Negative

TUNE-UP PROCEDURES

NOTE: The procedures outlined below are the specific procedures for Toyota vehicles; general tune-up procedures may be found in the section at the end of this book.

Spark Plugs

Check, clean, and adjust the spark plugs every 6000 miles. Replace them every 12,000 miles. 1980 and later vehicles require plug changes at 15,000 miles.

Clean any foreign material from around the spark plugs before removing them. Use the spark plug wrench supplied in the tool kit.

Clean any plugs which appear to be dirty and file their electrodes flat. Adjust the gap to the figure given in the "Tune-up Specifications" chart, above, using a wire feeler gauge.

NOTE: Do not use a flat gauge; an inaccurate reading will result.

Inspect the spark plug hole threads for rust and, if necessary, use a 14 mm plug tap to clean them.

Examine the condition of the spark plugs and check them against the diagnosis guide at the end of the book.

Lightly oil the threads and torque the plugs to 11-14 ft/lbs. Use caution when tightening the plugs, as most Toyota models use aluminum heads.

Breaker Points and Condenser

Loosen the clips which attach the distributor cap to the distributor body and lift the cap straight up. Leave the leads connected to the cap. Remove the rotor and dust cover.

Clean the distributor cap and rotor with alcohol. Inspect them for cracks and other signs of wear or damage. Polish the points with a point file.

NOTE: Do not use emery cloth or sandpaper; these may leave particles on the points, causing them to arc.

If the points are badly pitted or worn, replace them as follows:

1. Unfasten the point lead connector.
2. Remove the point retaining clip and remove the point hold-down screw.
3. Remove the point set.
4. Installation is the reverse of removal.

After replacing the points, or as routine maintenance, adjust the points to the specifications given in the tune-up chart at the beginning of this section as follows:

1. Rotate the engine by hand or by using a remote starter switch, so that the rubbing block is on the high point of the cam lobe.
2. Insert a 0.018 in. feeler gauge between the points; a slight drag should be felt.
3. If no drag is felt or if the feeler gauge cannot be inserted at all, loosen, but do not remove, the point hold-down screw.
4. Insert a screwdriver into the adjustment

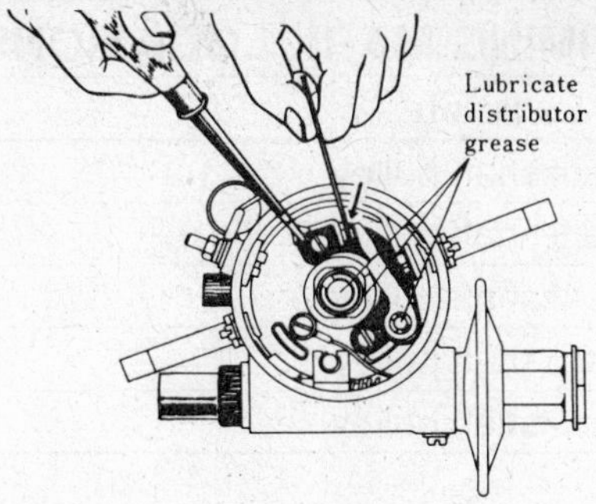

Adjusting breaker point gap

slot. Rotate the screwdriver until the proper point gap is attained. The point gap is increased by rotating the screwdriver counterclockwise and decreased by rotating it clockwise.

5. Tighten the point hold-down screw. Lubricate the cam lobes, breaker arm, rubbing block, arm pivot, and distributor shaft with special high-temperature distributor grease.

Check the operation of the centrifugal advance mechanism by moving the rotor clockwise. Release the rotor; it should return to its original position. If it does not, check it for binding.

Check the vacuum advance unit by removing the cap and pressing in on the octane selector. Release the octane selector. It should snap back to its original position. Check for binding if it fails to do so.

Replace the condenser if it is suspect or as routine maintenance during the point replacement operation, in the following manner:

1. Remove the nut and washer from the condenser lead terminal.
2. Remove the condenser mounting screw and withdraw the condenser.
3. Installation is the reverse of removal.

NOTE: The condenser is mounted on the outside of the distributor body on all models.

Install the dust cover, rotor, and the distributor cap on the distributor. Adjust the dwell and timing, as outlined below.

Dwell Angle

Connect a dwell/tachometer, in accordance with its manufacturer's instructions, between the distributor primary lead and a ground.

CAUTION

On models with electronic ignition, hook the dwell meter or tachometer to the negative (−) side of the coil, not to the distributor primary lead; damage to the ignition control unit will result.

With the engine warmed up and running at the specified idle speed (see the tune-up chart), take a dwell reading.

If the point dwell is not within specifications, shut the engine off and adjust the point gap, as outlined above.

NOTE: Increasing the point gap decreases the dwell angle and vice versa.

Install the dust cover, rotor, and cap. Check the dwell reading again.

Electronic Ignition

Most 1975-77 and all 1978 and later models are equipped with fully transistorized electronic ignition except Tercel with the 2A and 3A engines. These two engines have breaker type ignitions. The system uses an ignition signal generating system in place of the breaker points. It consists of a rotor, a magnetic element and a pickup coil all mounted inside the distributor. The system needs no routine maintenance. Repair is limited to replacement of defective parts. Service should be left to a qualified service person.

Ignition Timing

EXCEPT DUAL POINT SYSTEMS

1. Warm up the engine. Connect a tachometer and check the engine idle speed to see that it is within specifications. Adjust it as outlined below if it is not.

FULLY TRANSISTORIZED IGNITION SPECIFICATIONS

Primary coil resistance	1.35-1.65 ohms
Secondary coil resistance	12,800-15,2000 ohms
External resistor	1.3-1.7 ohms
Positive coil to ground	Infinity ①
Air gap	0.008-0.016 in.
Pick-up coil resistance	130-190 ohms
Signal generator volts peak at 1500 rpm	4.5 volts
Vacuum advance at 15 in.	10°
Mechanical advance at 3000 rpm	10.1°

① Do not apply voltage to an ohmeter

TIMING MARK LOCATIONS

Engine Type	Location	Type of Mark
3K-C and 2T-C	Crankshaft pulley	Notch and number scale
20R	Crankshaft pulley	Pointer and painted slot
4M and 4M-E	Crankshaft pulley	Slot and number scale
1A-C and 3A	Crankshaft pulley	Slot and number scale
3T-C	Crankshaft pulley	Slot and number scale

CAUTION

On models with electronic ignition, hook the dwell meter or tachometer to the negative (−) side of the coil, not to the distributor primary lead; damage to the ignition control unit will result.

If the timing mark is difficult to see, use chalk or a dab of paint to make it more visible.

2. Connect a timing light to the engine, as outlined in the instructions supplied by the manufacturer of the light.
3. Disconnect the vacuum line from the distributor vacuum unit and plug the line.
4. Allow the engine to run at the specified idle speed with the gear shift in Neutral for cars with manual transmissions, and in Drive (D) for cars with automatic transmissions.

CAUTION

Be sure that the parking brake is firmly set and that the wheels are chocked.

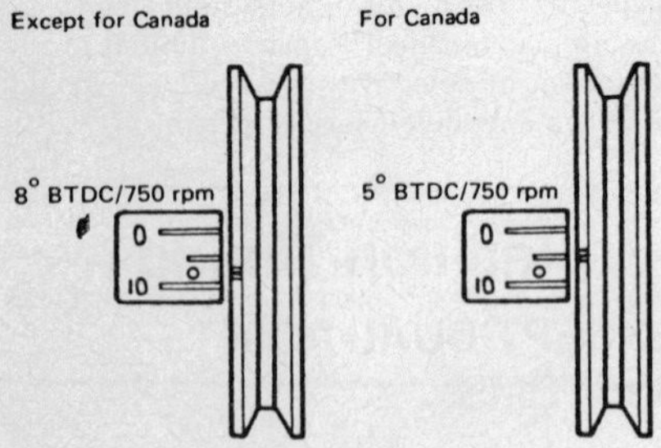

3K-C engine timing marks

Timing Marks

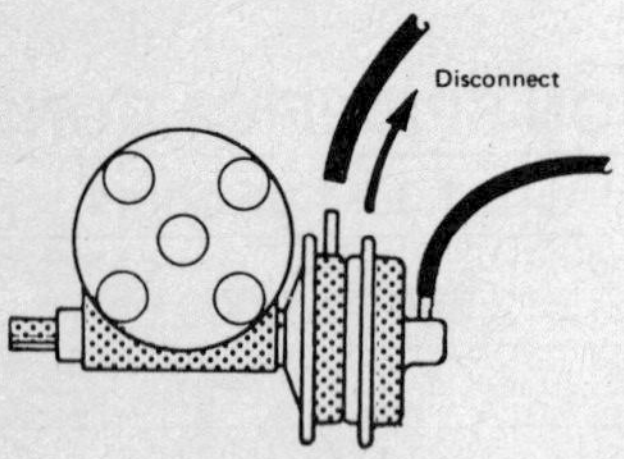

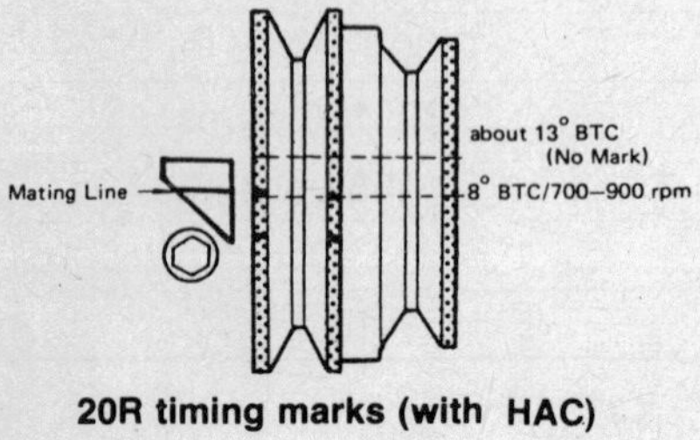

20R timing marks (with HAC)

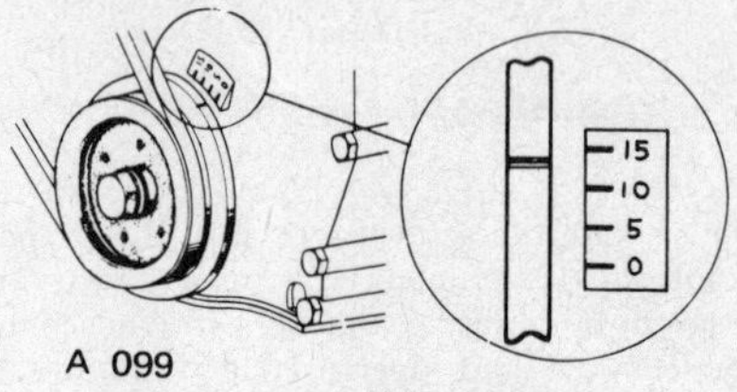

4M

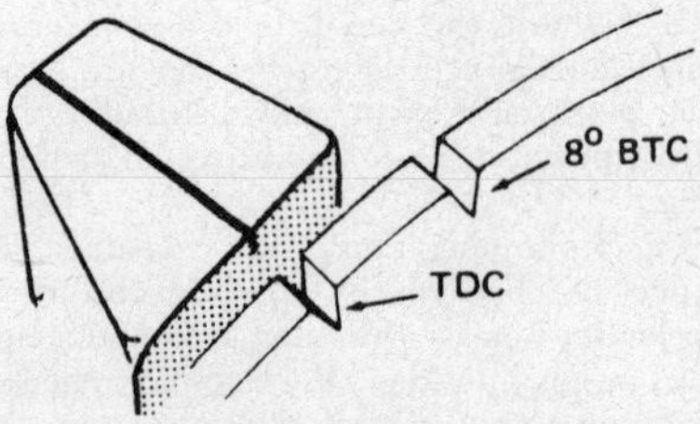

20R engine timing marks

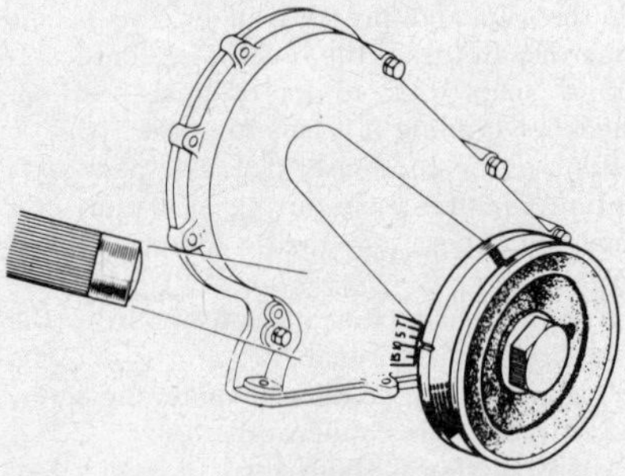

2T-C

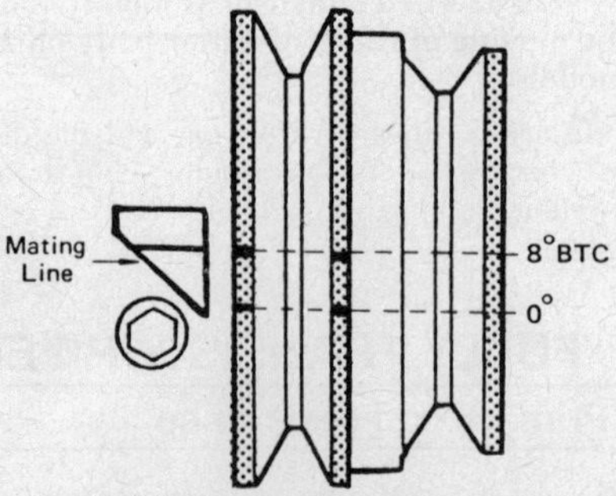

20R timing marks (w/o HAC)

5. Point the timing light at the timing marks indicated in the chart below. With the engine at idle, timing should be at the specification given in the tune-up chart at the beginning of this section. If it is not, loosen the pinch bolt at the base and rotate the distributor to advance or retard the timing, as required.
6. Stop the engine and tighten the pinch bolt. Start the engine and recheck the timing.
7. Stop the engine and disconnect the timing light and the tachometer. Connect the vacuum line to the vacuum advance unit.

DUAL POINT DISTRIBUTOR

A dual point distributor is offered as an option on some Corolla models, sold outside of California, starting in 1975.

To adjust the dual point system, proceed as follows:

1. Adjust the timing for the main set of points as outlined in the "Single Point" section above.
2. Use a jumper wire to ground the terminal on the thermoswitch connector after removing the connector from the thermoswitch. The thermoswitch is threaded into the intake manifold and is connected to the dual point system relay. Be careful not to confuse it with any of the emission control system switches which are connected to the computer.
3. Check the timing with a light as described above, the timing should be 22° before top dead center (BTDC).
4. If the timing is off, connect a dwell meter to the *negative* side of the coil, and adjust the sub-points so that the dwell angle is 52°. The sub-points are adjusted in the same manner as the main points.
5. Remove the test equipment, and reconnect the thermoswitch.

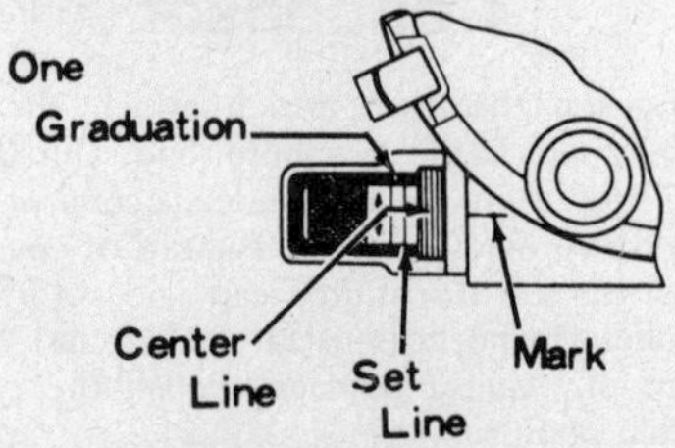

Octane selector

Octane Selector

The octane selector is used as a fine adjustment to match the vehicle's ignition timing to the grade of gasoline being used. It is located near the distributor vacuum unit, beneath a plastic dust cover. Normally the octane selector should not require adjustment, however, if necessary, adjustment is as follows:

1. Align the setting line with the threaded end of the housing and then align the center line with the setting mark on the housing.
2. Drive the car to the speed specified on the chart below, in high gear, on a level road.
3. Depress the accelerator pedal all the way to the floor. A slight "pinging" sound should be heard. As the car accelerates, the sound should gradually go away.
4. If the pinging sound is loud or if it fails to disappear as the vehicle speed increases, retard the timing by turning the knurled knob toward "R" (Retard).

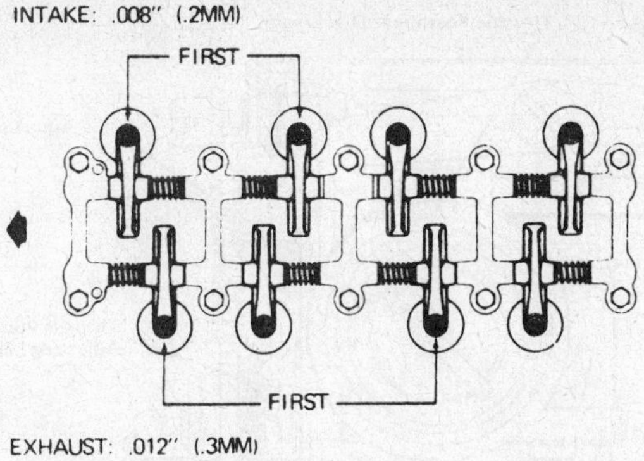

Adjust this set of valves first on the 20R engine

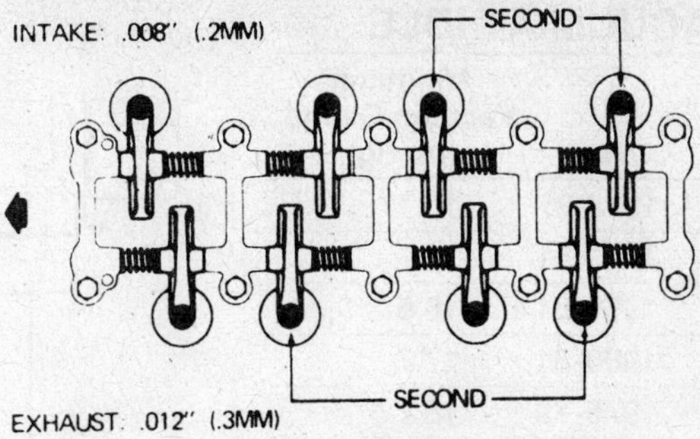

Turn the crankshaft one full turn and then adjust this set of valves on the 20R engine

5. If there is no pinging sound at all, advance the timing by turning the knob toward "A" (Advance).

6. When the adjustment is completed, replace the plastic dust cover.

NOTE: One graduation of the octane selector is equal to about ten degrees of crankshaft angle.

OCTANE SELECTOR TEST SPEEDS

Engine Type	Test Speed (mph)
3K-C	19-21
2T-C, 20R	16-22
4M	25

Valve Lash

3K-C and 2T-C Engines

1. Start the engine and allow it to reach normal operating temperature (165-185° F).

2. Stop the engine. Remove the air cleaner assembly, its hoses, and its bracket. Remove any other hoses, cables, etc. attached to the valve cover. Remove the valve cover.

3. On 3K-C engines tighten the cylinder head bolts, in the proper sequence to the following values:

3K-C—35-48 ft/lbs.

4. Next, on the 3K-C engines, tighten the valve rocker support bolts to 13-17 ft/lbs.

CAUTION

Tighten all of the above bolts in the proper sequence and in three stages.

5. Install a suitable oil tray on the 3K-C engine, to prevent hot engine oil from being splashed out.

NOTE: The tray may be ordered from a dealer or fabricated from sheet metal. (See illustration.)

6. Start the engine. Check the clearance between the rocker arm and the valve stem with a feeler gauge, for each valve. The clearance specifications are given in the tune-up chart at the beginning of this section.

7. If the valves require adjustment, loosen the locknut and turn the adjustment screw to obtain the proper clearance.

8. Tighten the locknut. Check the valve clearance to be sure that it was not disturbed when the locknut was tightened.

9. When the valve inspection and adjustment are completed, replace the valve cover and all of the other components which were removed.

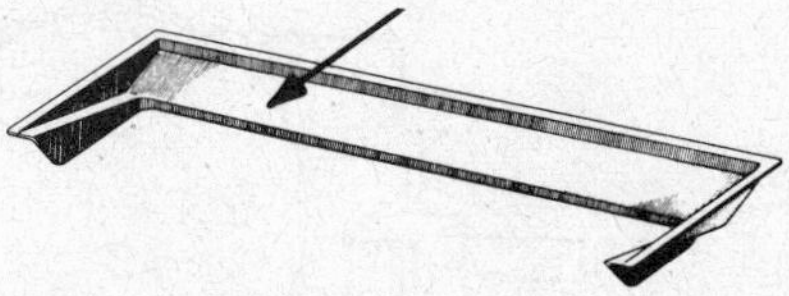

Special oil splash tray for 3K-C engine

20R Engine

1. Start the engine and allow it to reach normal operating temperature (above 180° F).

2. Stop the engine. Remove the air cleaner assembly, its hoses, and bracket. Remove any other cables, hoses, wires, etc., which are attached to the valve cover. Remove the valve cover.

3. Set the No. 1 cylinder at top dead center (TDC) of its compression stroke, with the TDC notch aligned with the pointer.

4. Measure the clearance between the valve stem and the rocker arm with a feeler gauge for the valves shown in the first illustration. See the tune-up chart for the correct clearance.

5. To adjust the valve clearance, loosen the locknut and turn the adjusting screw until the proper clearance is obtained. Tighten the locknut and check the clearance again.

6. Crank the engine *one* revolution (360°) and perform Steps 4 and 5 for the set of valves shown in the second illustration.

7. Install the spark plug in the No. 1 cylinder and reconnect the coil lead. Install the valve cover, air cleaner assembly and any other components that were removed.

4M Engine

1. Allow the engine to reach normal operating temperature. Stop the engine.

2. Remove the air cleaner assembly, air cleaner bracket, spark plug cable guides, and any other components attached to the valve cover. Remove the valve cover.

3. Crank the engine until the Number one cylinder is at TDC of its compression stroke. To determine this, remove the spark plug from the Number one cylinder and place a screwdriver over the spark plug hole. Crank the engine until pressure is felt against the screwdriver and the slot in the crankshaft pulley aligns with the "O" (TDC) on the timing scale.

4. Check and adjust the clearance of the intake valves on 1, 2 and 4 cylinders and of the exhaust valves on 1, 3 and 5 cylinders.

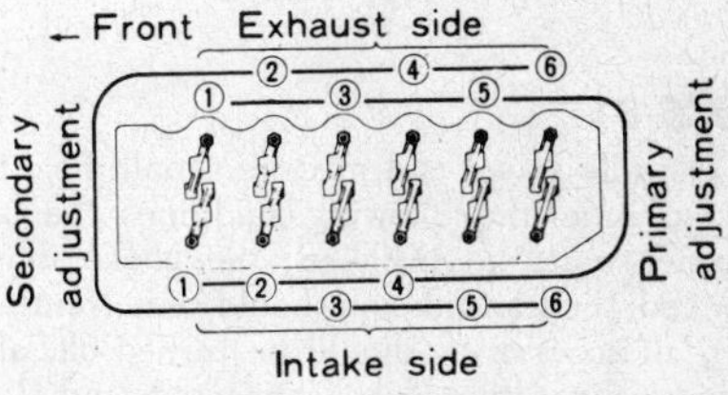

4M valve adjustment sequence

5. Measure the clearance between the valve stem and the adjusting screw with a feeler gauge of the proper size. (See the specification chart at the beginning of this section.)

6. If the valves require adjustment, loosen the locknut and turn the adjusting screw until the proper clearance is obtained. Tighten the locknut. Check the clearance again.

7. Crank the engine one revolution (360°) and repeat Steps 5 and 6 for the remaining valves.

8. Install the cylinder head cover, spark plug cable guides, air cleaner bracket, air cleaner assembly and any other components removed. Replace the Number one spark plug as well.

1A-C, 2A, 3A

1. Run the engine to normal operating temperature.

2. Stop the engine. Remove the air cleaner and any other components that are in the way.

3. Check the clearance between the rocker arm and the valve stem. This measurement is listed in the tune-up chart.

4. If the clearance is not correct loosen the nut and turn the adjusting screw to the correct gap.

NOTE: For this measurement you will need a set of feeler gauges.

5. Once you have the proper clearance tighten the nut, and at the same time hold onto the adjusting screw. This is accomplished by using a box type wrench and a screwdriver.

6. Reinstall the valve cover.

NOTE: Make sure that you install a new valve cover gasket.

VACUUM AT IDLE

Engine	Year	Minimum Vacuum Gauge (in. Hg)
3K-C	1975-77	15.7
1AC-3A	1980-81	17.7
20R	1975-81	16.5
3T-C	1980-81	17.7
2T-C	1975-79	15.7
4M	1975-79	16.3 MT 13.8 AT
4M-E	1980-81	16.9

AT Automatic transmission
MT Manual transmission

Carburetor

NOTE: See "Fuel System," above, for other carburetor adjustments.

1975-81

The idle speed and mixture should be adjusted under the following conditions: the air cleaner must be installed, the choke fully opened, the transmission should be in Neutral (N), all accessories should be turned off, all vacuum lines should be connected, and the ignition timing should be set to specification.

1. Start the engine and allow it to reach normal operating temperature (180° F).
2. Check the float setting; the fuel level should be just about even with the spot on the sight glass. If the fuel level is too high or low, adjust the float level. (See the float adjustment procedure, below.)
3. Connect a tachometer in accordance with its manufacturer's instructions. However, connect the tachometer positive (+) lead to the coil Negative (−) terminal. Do NOT hook it up to the distributor side; damage to the transistorized ignition could result.
4. Turn the idle speed adjusting screw to obtain one of the following initial idle speeds:
   3K-C, 2T-C—930 rpm
   20R—900 rpm
   4M—820 rpm
   1A-C, 2A-3A—750 rpm

NOTE: The idle mixture screw is preset on 1980 vehicles. No adjustment is necessary.

5. Turn the idle mixture adjusting screw to increase the idle speed as much as is possible.
6. Next, turn the idle speed screw to again obtain the same idle speed figure given in Step 4.
7. If possible, turn the idle mixture screw to increase the idle speed again.
8. Keep repeating Steps 6 and 7 until the idle mixture adjusting screw will no longer increase the idle speed above the figure specified in Step 4.
9. Slowly turn the idle mixture screw *clockwise*, until the idle speed specified in the "Tune-up Specifications" chart is reached. (This makes the mixture leaner.)
10. Disconnect the tachometer.

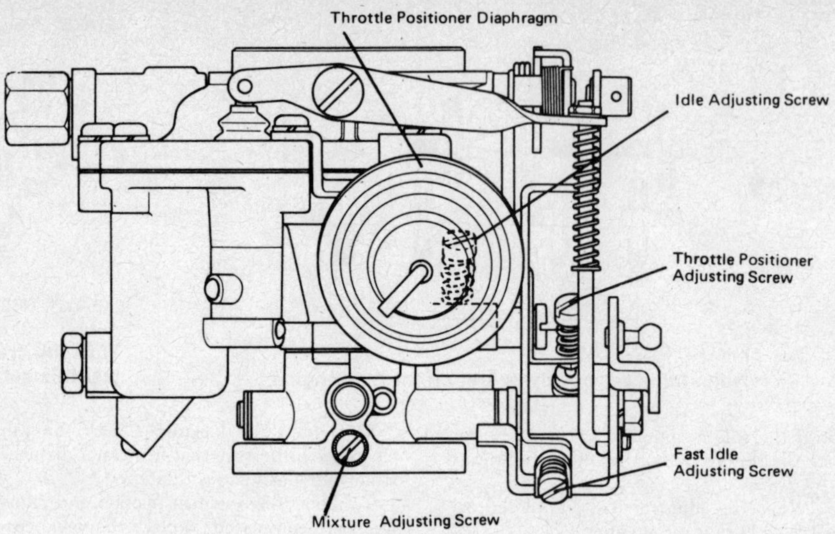

3K-C

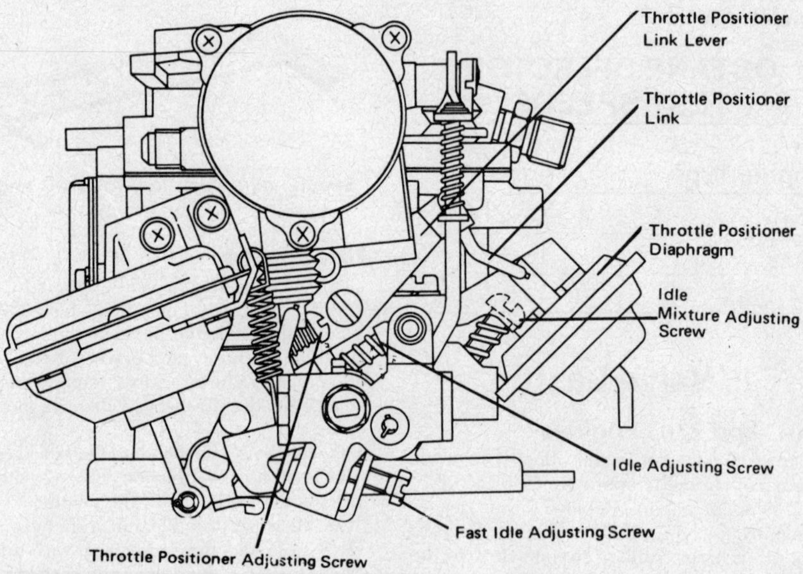

2T-C

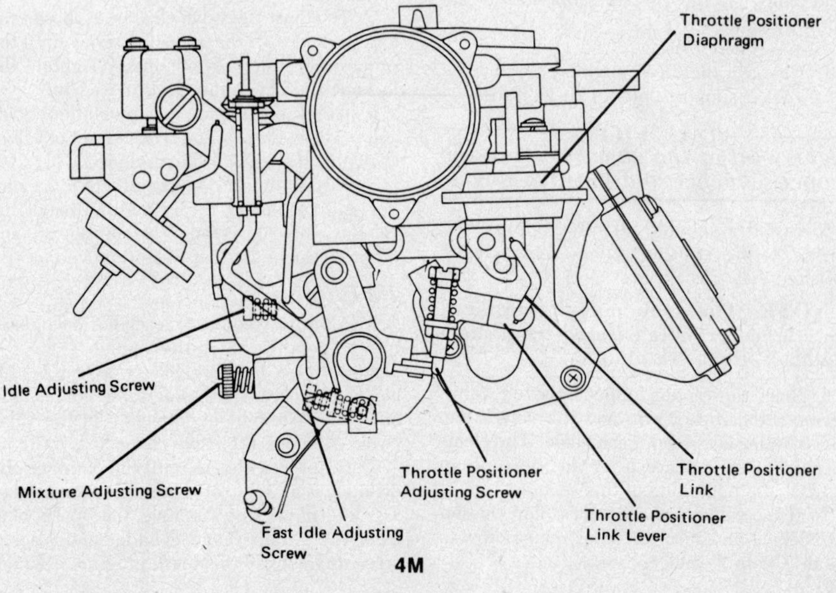

4M

ENGINE ELECTRICAL

Distributor

REMOVAL

1. Unfasten the cables from the spark plugs, after marking the wiring order. Remove the high tension cable from the coil.
2. Remove the primary wire and the vacuum line from the distributor. Remove the distributor cap.
3. Match-mark the distributor housing and the engine block; mark the rotor position in the distributor as well. This will aid in correct positioning of the distributor during installation.
4. Remove the clamp from the distributor. Withdraw the distributor from the block.

NOTE: It is easier to install the distributor if the engine timing is not disturbed while it is removed. If the timing has been lost, see "Installation—Timing Disturbed" below.

INSTALLATION-TIMING NOT DISTURBED

1. Insert the distributor in the block and align the matchmarks made during removal.
2. Engage the distributor drive with the oil pump driveshaft.
3. Install the distributor clamp, cap, high tension wire, primary wire, and vacuum line.
4. Install the wires on the spark plugs.
5. Start the engine. Check the timing and adjust the octane selector.

INSTALLATION-TIMING DISTURBED

If the engine has been cranked, dismantled, or the timing otherwise lost, proceed as follows:

1. Determine top dead center (TDC) of the Number one (No. 1) cylinder's compression stroke by removing the spark plug from the No. 1 cylinder and placing a finger or a compression gauge over the spark plug hole.

Crank the engine until compression pressure starts to build up. Continue cranking the engine until the timing marks indicate TDC (or 0°).

2. Next, align the timing marks to the specifications given in the "Ignition Timing" column of the tune-up chart at the beginning of the Toyota section.
3. Temporarily install the rotor in the distributor shaft so that the rotor is pointing toward the Number one terminal in the distributor cap. The points should just be about to open.
4. Use a small screwdriver to align the slot on the distributor drive (oil pump driveshaft) with the key on the bottom of the distributor shaft.
5. Install the distributor in the block by rotating it slightly (no more than one gear tooth in either direction) until the driven gear meshes with the drive.

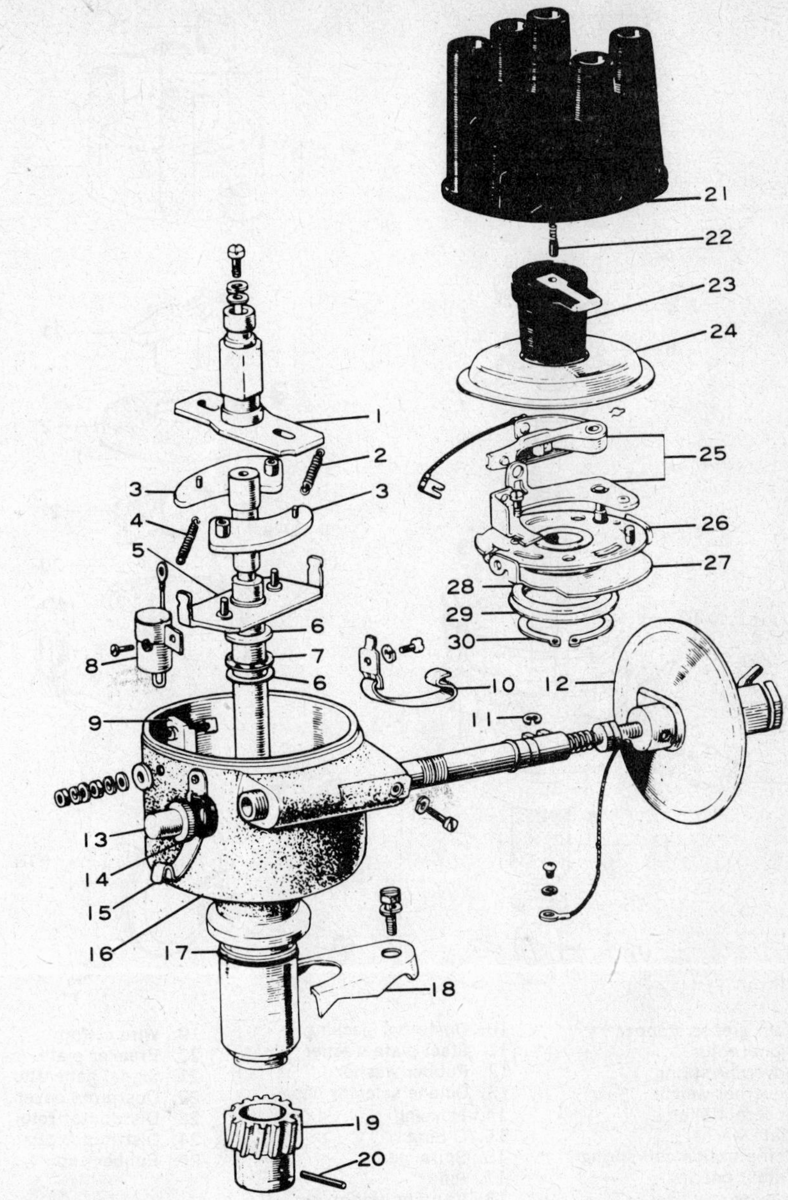

1. Cam
2. Governor spring
3. Governor weight
4. Governor spring
5. Distributor shaft
6. Metal washer
7. Bakelite washer
8. Condenser
9. Insulator
10. Cap spring clip
11. Snap ring
12. Vacuum advance unit
13. Octane selector assembly
14. Rubber washer
15. Cap spring clip
16. Distributor housing
17. O-ring
18. Distributor clamp
19. Spiral gear
20. Pin
21. Distributor cap
22. Spring
23. Rotor
24. Dust cover
25. Breaker point assembly
26. Movable plate
27. Stationary plate
28. Adjusting washer
29. Wave washer
30. Snap ring

Distributor components

NOTE: Oil the distributor spiral gear and the oil pump driveshaft end before distributor installation.

6. Rotate the distributor, once it is installed, so that the points are just about to open. Temporarily tighten the pinch bolt.
7. Remove the rotor and install the dust cover. Replace the rotor and the distributor cap.
8. Install the primary wire and the vacuum line.
9. Install the No. 1 cylinder spark plug. Connect the cables to the spark plugs in the proper order by using the marks made during removal. Install the high tension wire on the coil.
10. Start the engine. Adjust the ignition timing and the octane selector, as outlined above.

ELECTRONIC DISTRIBUTOR

Setting the points (in this case an air gap) is accomplished almost the same as in a conventional system.

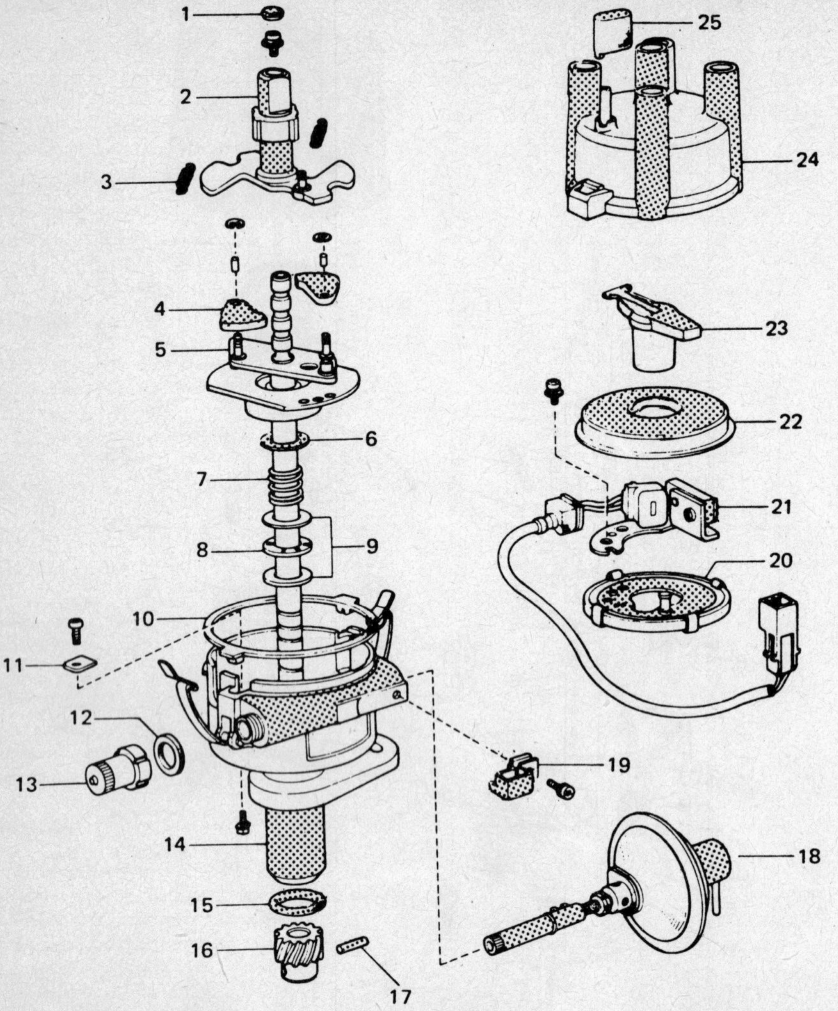

1. Cam grease stopper
2. Signal rotor
3. Governor spring
4. Governor weight
5. Governor shaft
6. Plate washer
7. Compression coil spring
8. Thrust bearing
9. Washer
10. Dustproof packing
11. Steel plate washer
12. Rubber washer
13. Octane selector cap
14. Housing
15. O-Ring
16. Spiral gear
17. Pin
18. Vacuum diaphragm
19. Wire clamp
20. Breaker plate
21. Signal generator
22. Dustproof cover
23. Distributor rotor
24. Distributor cap
25. Rubber cap

Exploded view of the Celica GT (Calif.) transistorized distributor

The air gap should be set using a brass or plastic feeler gauge and *extreme* care must be taken to eliminate the possibility of mixing wiring.

Set the air gap to 0.008-0.016 in.

Alternator

ALTERNATOR PRECAUTIONS

1. Always observe proper polarity of the battery connections; be especially careful when jump-starting the car.
2. Never ground or short out any alternator or alternator regulator terminals.
3. Never operate the alternator with any of its or the battery's leads disconnected.
4. Always remove the battery or disconnect its output lead while charging it.
5. Always disconnect the ground cable when replacing any electrical components.
6. Never subject the alternator to excessive heat or dampness if the engine is being steam-cleaned.
7. Never use arc-welding equipment with the alternator connected.

REMOVAL AND INSTALLATION

NOTE: On some models the alternator is mounted very low on the engine. On these models it may be necessary to remove the gravel shield and work from underneath the car in order to gain access to the alternator.

1. Unfasten the starter-to-battery cable at the battery end.
2. Remove the air cleaner, if necessary, to gain access to the alternator.
3. Unfasten the bolts which attach the adjusting link to the alternator. Remove the alternator drive belt.
4. Unfasten and tag the alternator wiring connection.
5. Remove the alternator attaching bolt and then withdraw the alternator from its bracket.
6. Installation is the reverse order of removal. After installing the alternator, adjust the belt tension.

BELT TENSION ADJUSTMENT

Inspection and adjustment to the alternator drive belt should be performed every 3,000 miles or if the alternator has been removed.

1. Inspect the drive belt to see that it is not cracked or worn. Be sure that its surfaces are free of grease or oil.
2. Push down on the belt halfway between the fan and the alternator pulleys, (or crankshaft pulley) with thumb pressure. Belt deflection should be ⅜-½ in.
3. If the belt tension requires adjustment, loosen the adjusting link bolt and move the alternator until the proper belt tension is obtained.

CAUTION

Do not overtighten the belt; damage to the alternator bearings could result.

4. Tighten the adjusting link bolt.

Regulator

REMOVAL AND INSTALLATION

1. Disconnect the battery-to-starter cable at the battery end.
2. Disconnect the wiring harness connector from the regulator.
3. Remove the regulator securing bolts. Remove the regulator, complete with its condenser.
4. Installation is the reverse order of removal.

VOLTAGE ADJUSTMENT

1. Connect a voltmeter to the battery terminals.
2. Start the engine and gradually increase its speed to about 1500 rpm.
3. At this speed, the voltage reading should fall within the range specified in the chart above.
4. If the voltage does not fall within the specifications, remove the cover from the regulator and adjust it by bending the adjusting arm.
5. Repeat Steps 2 and 3; if the voltage cannot be brought to specifications, proceed with the mechanical adjustments, outlined below.

MECHANICAL ADJUSTMENTS

NOTE: Perform the preceding voltage adjustment before beginning the mechanical adjustments.

Field Relay

1. Remove the cover from the regulator assembly.

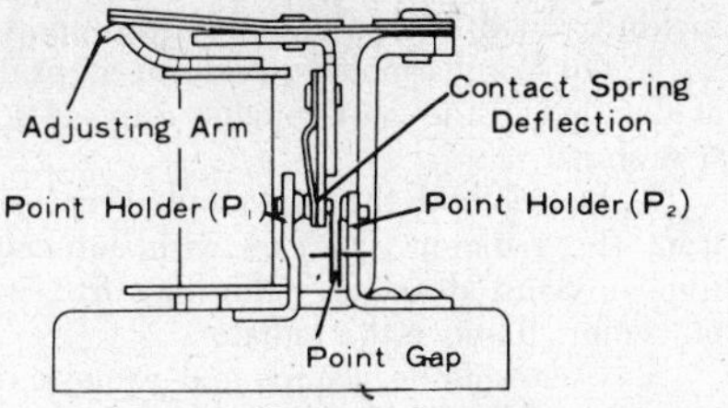

Field relay components

2. Use a feeler gauge to check the amount that the contact spring is deflected while the armature is being depressed.

3. If the measurement is not within specifications (see the chart above), adjust the regulator by bending point holder P (See illustration).

4. Check the point gap with a feeler gauge against the specifications in the chart.

5. Adjust the point gap, as required, by bending the point holder P (See illustration).

6. Clean off the points with emery cloth if they are dirty and wash them with solvent.

Voltage Regulator

1. Use a feeler gauge to measure the air (armature) gap. If it is not within the specifications (see chart), adjust it by bending the *low*-speed point holder. (See illustration.)

2. Check the point gap with a feeler gauge. If it is not within specifications, adjust it by bending the *high*-speed point holder. (See illustration.) Clean the points with emery cloth and wash them off with solvent.

3. Check the amount of contact spring deflection while depressing the armature. The specification should be the same as that for the

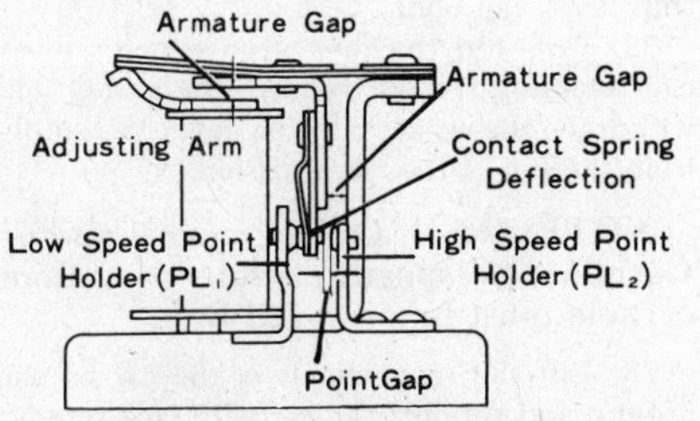

Voltage regulator components

contact spring on the field relay. If the amount of deflection is not within specification, replace, do not adjust, the voltage regulator.

Go back and perform the steps outlined under "Voltage Adjustment," above. If the voltage cannot be brought within specifications, replace the voltage regulator. If the voltage still fails to come within specifications after regulator replacement, the alternator is probably defective and should be replaced.

NOTE: On all vehicles with the "IC" type regulator there are no adjustments necessary. If found to be defective, it must be replaced.

STARTER

REMOVAL AND INSTALLATION

1. Disconnect the cable which runs from the starter to the battery, at the battery end.

2. Remove the air cleaner assembly, if necessary, to gain access to the starter.

NOTE: On some models with automatic transmissions, it may be necessary to disconnect the throttle linkage connecting rod.

3. On Corolla 1200 models, perform the following:

a. Disconnect the manual choke cable and the accelerator cable from the carburetor.

b. Unbolt the front exhaust pipe flange from the manifold and then remove the complete manifold assembly. (See the appropriate section below for details.)

4. Disconnect all of the wiring at the starter.

5. Remove the starter toward the front of the car.

6. Installation is in the reverse order of removal.

STARTER DRIVE REPLACEMENT

1. Disconnect wiring and remove starter from engine.

2. Remove solenoid from starter.

3. Remove through bolts and take off end plate.

4. Slide armature shaft far enough out to disengage clutch forks.

5. Remove retaining clip and washer from shaft.

6. Slide starter drive assembly from shaft.

7. Install in reverse of removal. Always use a new retaining clip.

STARTER SOLENOID AND BRUSH REPLACEMENT

Direct Drive Starter

NOTE: The starter must be removed from the car in order to perform this operation.

1. Remove the field coil lead from the solenoid terminal.

2. Unfasten the solenoid retaining screws. Remove the solenoid by tilting it upward and withdrawing it.

3. Remove the end frame bearing cover screws and remove the cover.

4. Remove the thru-bolts. Remove the commutator end-frame.

5. Withdraw the brushes from their holder if they are to be replaced.

6. Check the brush length against the specification in the "Battery and Starter Specifications" chart, above. Replace the brushes with new ones if required.

7. Dress the new brushes with emery cloth so that they will make proper contact.

8. Use a spring scale to check the brush spring tension against the specification in the chart. Replace the springs if they do not meet specification.

Assembly is the reverse of disassembly. Pack the end bearing cover with multipurpose grease before installing it.

Gear Reduction Type

NOTE: The starter must be removed from the car, in order to perform this operation.

1. Disconnect the solenoid lead.

2. Loosen the two bolts on the starter housing and separate the field frame from the solenoid. Remove the O-ring and felt dust seal.

3. Remove the two screws and separate the starter drive from the solenoid.

4. Withdraw the clutch and gears. Remove the ball from the clutch shaft bore or solenoid.

5. Remove the brushes from the holder.

6. Measure brush length and compare it to the specification given in the "Battery and Starter Specifications" chart. Replace the brushes if they are too short.

7. Check the gears for wear or damage. Replace as required.

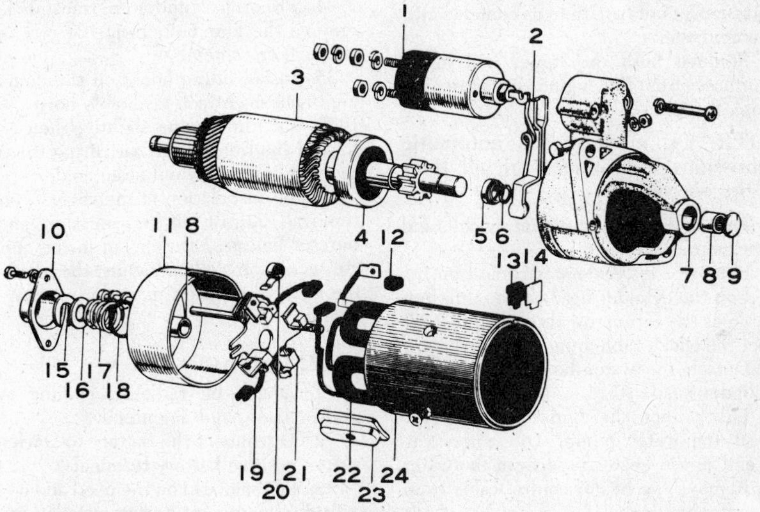

1. Solenoid
2. Engagement lever
3. Armature
4. Overrunning clutch
5. Clutch stop
6. Snap ring
7. Drive housing
8. Bushing
9. Bearing cover
10. Bearing cover
11. Commutator end frame
12. Rubber bushing
13. Rubber grommet
14. Plate
15. Lock plate
16. Washer
17. Brake spring
18. Gasket
19. Brush
20. Brush spring
21. Brush holder
22. Field coil
23. Pole shoes
24. Field yoke

Direct-drive starter components

Assembly is the reverse of disassembly. Lubricate all bearings and gears with high temperature grease. Grease the ball before inserting in the clutch shaft bore. Align the tab on the brush holder with the notch on the field frame. Check the positive (+) brush leads to see that they aren't grounded. Align the mark on the solenoid with the bolt anchors on the field frame.

ENGINE MECHANICAL

Engine

REMOVAL AND INSTALLATION

CAUTION

Be sure that the car is supported securely, during engine removal.

3K-C ENGINE

1. Drain the entire cooling system.
2. Unfasten the cable which runs from the battery to the starter at the battery terminal.
3. Scribe marks on the hood and hinges to aid in hood alignment during assembly. Remove the hood.
4. Unfasten the headlight bezel retaining screws and remove the bezels. Remove the five radiator grille attachment screws and remove the grille.
5. Remove the hood lock assembly after detaching the release cable.
6. Unfasten the nuts from the horn retainers and disconnect the wiring. Remove the horn assembly.
7. Remove the air cleaner from its bracket after unfastening the hoses from it.
8. Remove the windshield washer tank from its bracket but first drain its contents into a clean container.
9. Remove both the upper and lower radiator hoses from the engine after loosening the hose clamps.

NOTE: On models with automatic transmissions, disconnect the oil lines from the oil cooler.

10. Detach the radiator mounting bolts and remove the radiator.
11. Remove the accelerator cable from its support on the cylinder head cover. Unfasten the cable at the carburetor throttle arm. Disconnect the choke cable from the carburetor.
12. Detach the water hose retainer from the cylinder head.
13. Disconnect the bypass and heater hoses at the water pump. Disconnect the other end of the heater hose from the water valve. Remove the heater control cable from the water valve.
14. Disconnect the wiring harness multiconnectors.
15. Detach the downpipe from the exhaust manifold.
16. Detach the wires from the water temperature and oil pressure sending units.
17. Remove the nut from the front left-hand engine mount.
18. Remove the fuel line from the fuel pump.
19. Detach the battery ground cable from the cylinder block.
20. Remove the nut from the front right-hand engine mount.
21. Remove the clip and detach the cable from the clutch release lever.
22. Remove the primary and high-tension wires from the coil.
23. Detach the back-up light switch wire at its connector on the right side of the extension housing.

The following steps apply to Corolla models with manual transmissions:

24. Remove the carpet from the transmission tunnel. Remove the boots from the shift lever.
25. Remove the snap-ring from the gear-shift selector lever base. Withdraw the selector lever assembly.

The following steps apply to Corolla models with automatic transmissions:

26. Disconnect the accelerator linkage torque rod at the carburetor.
27. Disconnect the throttle linkage connecting rod from the bellcrank lever.
28. Drain the oil from the transmission oil pan.
29. Detach the transmission gear selector shift rod from the control shaft.

The following steps apply to Corollas with both manual and automatic transmissions:

30. Raise the rear wheels of the car. Support the car with jack stands.
31. Disconnect the driveshaft from the transmission.

NOTE: Drain the oil from the manual transmission, first, to prevent it from leaking out.

32. Detach the exhaust pipe support bracket from the extension housing.
33. Remove the insulator bolt from the rear engine mount.
34. Place a jack under the transmission and remove the four bolts from the rear (engine support) crossmember.
35. Install lifting hooks on the engine lifting brackets. Attach a suitable hoist.
36. Lift the engine slightly; then move it toward the front of the car. Bring the engine the rest of the way out at an angle.

Engine installation is the reverse order of removal. Adjust all transmission and carburetor linkages, as detailed in the appropriate section. Install and adjust the hood. Refill the engine, radiator, and transmission to capacity.

2T-C Engine

1. Drain the radiator, cooling system, transmission, and engine oil.
2. Disconnect the battery-to-starter cable at the positive battery terminal.
3. Scribe marks on the hood and its hinges to aid in alignment during installation.
4. Remove the hood supports from the body. Remove the hood.

NOTE: Do not remove the supports from the hood.

5. On Carina models, remove the headlight bezels. Disconnect the hood release cable then remove the grille, lower grille molding, hood lock base, and base support.
6. On Corolla models, perform Steps 4-6 as detailed in the 3K-C engine removal section above.
7. Detach both the upper and lower hoses from the radiator. On cars with automatic transmissions, disconnect the lines from the oil cooler. Remove the radiator.
8. Unfasten the clamps and remove the heater and bypass hoses from the engine. Remove the heater control cable from the water valve.
9. Remove the wiring from the coolant temperature and oil pressure sending units.
10. Remove the air cleaner from its bracket, complete with its attendant hoses.
11. Unfasten the accelerator torque rod from the carburetor. On models equipped with automatic transmissions, remove the transmission linkage as well.
12. Remove the emission control system hoses and wiring, as necessary.
13. Remove the clutch hydraulic line support bracket.
14. Unfasten the high-tension and primary wires from the coil.
15. Mark the spark plug cables and remove them from the distributor.
16. Detach the right-hand front engine mount.
17. Remove the fuel line at the pump.
18. Detach the downpipe from the exhaust manifold.
19. Detach the left-hand front engine mount.
20. Disconnect all of the wiring harness multiconnectors.
21. On cars equipped with manual transmissions, remove the shift lever boot and the shift lever cap boot.
22. Unfasten the four gear selector lever cap retaining screws, remove the gasket and withdraw the gear selector lever assembly from the top of the transmission.

NOTE: On all Carina models and on Corolla five-speed models, the floor console must be removed first.

23. Lift the rear wheels of the car off the ground and support the car with jack stands.
24. On cars equipped with automatic transmissions, disconnect the gear selector control rod.
25. Detach the exhaust pipe support bracket.
26. Disconnect the driveshaft from the rear of the transmission.
27. Unfasten the speedometer cable from the transmission. Disconnect the wiring from the back-up light switch and the neutral safety switch (automatic only).
28. Detach the clutch release cylinder assembly, complete with hydraulic lines. Do not disconnect the lines.
29. Unbolt the rear support member mounting insulators.
30. Support the transmission and detach the rear support member retaining bolts. Withdraw the support member from under the car.
31. Install lifting hooks on the engine lifting brackets. Attach a suitable hoist to the engine.
32. Remove the jack from under the transmission.

33. Raise the engine and move it toward the front of the car. Use care to avoid damaging the components which remain on the car.

34. Support the engine on a workstand. Install the engine in the reverse order of removal. Adjust all of the linkages as detailed in the appropriate section. Install the hood and adjust it. Replenish the fluid levels in the engine, radiator, and transmission.

20R Engines

1. Perform Steps 1-4 of the 2T-C engine removal procedure.
2. Remove the headlight bezel and the radiator grille.
3. Remove the fan shroud, the hood lock base and the base support.
4. Perform Steps 7-20 of the 2T-C engine removal procedure.

Perform the following steps on models with manual transmissions:

5. Remove the center console if so equipped.
6. Remove the shift lever boot(s).
7. Unfasten the four shift lever cap retaining screws. Remove the cap and withdraw the shift lever assembly.

Perform the following steps on models equipped with automatic transmissions:

8. Remove the transmission selector linkage:
   a. On models equipped with a floor-mounted selector, disconnect the control rod from the transmission.
   b. On column-mounted gear selector models, remove the shifter rod.
9. Disconnect the neutral safety switch wiring connector.

Perform the following steps on all models:

10. Raise the rear of the vehicle with jacks and support it on jack stands.
11. Remove the retaining screws and remove the parking brake equalizer support bracket. Disconnect the cable which runs between the lever and the equalizer.
12. Remove the speedometer cable from the transmission. Disconnect the back-up light wiring.
13. Detach the driveshaft from the rear of the transmission.

NOTE: If oil runs out of the transmission, an old U-joint yoke sleeve makes an excellent plug.

14. Perform Steps 28-34 of the 2T-C engine removal procedure.

Installation of the engine is the reverse order of removal. Refer to the appropriate chapters for transmission and carburetor adjustments. Refill the engine oil, coolant, and transmission oil to the proper levels.

4M Engines

1. Disconnect the battery cables and remove the battery.
2. Scribe aligning marks on the hood and hinges to aid in their assembly. Remove the hood.
3. Remove the fan shroud and drain the cooling system.
4. Disconnect both the upper and lower radiator hoses. Disconnect and plug the oil lines from the oil cooler on cars with automatic transmissions.
5. Detach the hose which runs to the thermal expansion tank at the tank. Remove the expansion tank from its mounting bracket.
6. Remove the radiator.
7. Disconnect the heater and bypass hoses from the engine.
8. Disconnect the oil pressure light sender wiring, the alternator multiconnector, and the back-up light switch wiring.
9. Disconnect the power brake unit vacuum lines.
10. Disconnect the engine oil cooler hoses at the oil filter, if so equipped.
11. Disconnect the power steering fluid cooler hose, if so equipped.
12. Remove the air cleaner assembly from its bracket, complete with hoses.
13. Detach the emission control system wires and hoses, as required.
14. Unfasten the distributor primary wire and the high tension wire from the coil.
15. Disconnect the wiring from the starter and temperature gauges sender.
16. Remove the fuel line from the fuel pump.
17. Disconnect the heater control cable from the water valve. Unfasten the heater control vacuum hose.
18. Remove the accelerator linkage from the carburetor.
19. Detach the clutch hydraulic line from its master cylinder connections (manual transmission only). Install a cap on the master cylinder fitting to keep the hydraulic fluid from running out.
20. Detach the pressure-feed lines from the steering gear housing on models equipped with power steering.
21. Raise both the front and the rear of the car with jacks. Support the car with jack stands.
22. Detach the exhaust pipe from the downpipe and remove the exhaust pipe hangers.
23. Disconnect the speedometer cable from the right side of the transmission.

The following steps apply to models with manual transmission only:

24. On 1973-74 models:
    a. Remove the center console securing screws, the gearshift knob, the gearshift boot, and then unfasten the console wiring multiconnector. Lift the console over the gearshift lever.
    b. Remove the four screws which attach the shift lever retainer to the shift tower and withdraw the shift lever assembly.

The following steps apply to models with automatic transmissions:

25. On models equipped with a floor-mounted gear selector, unfasten the connecting rod swivel nut and detach the control rod from the gear selector lever.
26. On models equipped with a column-mounted gear selector:
    a. Disconnect the control rod and cross shaft.
    b. Remove both of the throttle link connecting rods.
27. Disconnect the parking brake lever rod, return spring, intermediate rod, and the cable from the equalizer.
28. Disconnect the driveshaft from the end of the transmission.

NOTE: If oil runs out from the transmission, an old U-joint yoke makes a good plug.

29. Remove the left-hand gravel shield and then the front engine mounts.
30. Support the transmission with a jack.
31. Remove the rear engine mounts and the rear crossmember.
32. Attach a hoist to the engine and lift it up and forward, so that it clears the car.

Installation is in the reverse order of removal. Adjust the transmission and carburetor linkages, as detailed in the appropriate sections. Bleed the clutch as outlined below. Install the hood and adjust it. Replenish the fluid levels.

1A-C, 2A and 3A

1. Disconnect the negative battery terminal.
2. Remove the hood.
3. Remove the air cleaner and all necessary lines attached to it.
4. Drain the radiator.
5. Cover both driveshaft boots with a shop towel.
6. Remove the solenoid valve connector, water temperature switch connector, and the electric fan connector.
7. Remove the exhaust support plate bolts, and the exhaust pipe.
8. Remove the top radiator support.
9. Remove the top and bottom radiator hoses and remove the radiator with the fan.

NOTE: On cars equipped with automatic transmissions remove the cooling lines before removing the radiator.

10. Remove the windshield washer tank.
11. Remove the heater hoses and the lines to the fuel pump.

NOTE: Plug the gas line to prevent gas from leaking out.

12. Remove the accelerator cable, choke cable, and the ground strap.
13. Remove the brake booster vacuum line.
14. Remove the coil wire and unplug the alternator.
15. Remove the clutch release cable.
16. Remove the wires on the starter.
17. Remove the temperature sending and oil pressure switch connectors.
18. Remove the battery ground strap from the block.
19. Jack up your vehicle and support it with jack stands.
20. Remove the engine mounting bolts and the engine shock absorbers.
21. Support the differential with a jack.
22. Remove the transaxle mounting bolts.

NOTE: It is probably easier to remove these bolts from underneath the car.

23. Remove the engine.
24. Tie the bell housing to the cowl to keep support on the transaxle.

NOTE: The grill may be removed if necessary to give better leverage when removing the engine.

25. Installation is the reverse of removal. Adjust all linkages as covered in the appro-

priate section. Refill all fluids to the proper levels. Tighten the transaxle bolts 37-57 ft/lbs.

On cars with automatic transmissions, the following procedures are necessary.

1. Remove the starter.
2. Remove the cooling lines from the transmission.
3. Support the transmission with a jack.
4. Remove the transaxle mounting bolts.
5. Remove the torque converter bolts (4).

NOTE: In order to turn the converter, place a wrench on the crankshaft pulley and turn it until you see a bolt appear in the area where the starter was.

6. While the engine is suspended from your hoist, pull it forward about 2 inches.
7. Insert a pry bar in this opening and gently separate the torque converter from the engine.
8. Installation is the reverse of removal.

The following are necessary before the cylinder head can be installed. Confirm that the converter contact surface is 1.02 inches from the housing. Install a guide bolt in one of the mounting bolt holes. Remove the engine mounting insulator (left side) and the mounting bracket (right side). To secure the transaxle to the engine temporarily install the top two mounting bolts. This will facilitate easier engine installation.

Cylinder Head

CAUTION

Do not perform this operation on a warm engine. Remove the head bolts in the sequence and in several steps. Loosen the head bolts evenly, not one at a time. Keep the pushrods in their original order. Do not attempt to slide the cylinder head off of the block, as it is located with dowel pins. Lift the head straight up and off the block.

REMOVAL AND INSTALLATION

3K-C

1. Disconnect the battery and drain the cooling system.
2. Remove the air cleaner assembly from its bracket, complete with its attendant hoses.
3. Disconnect the hoses from the air injection system or the vacuum switching valve lines.
4. Detach the accelerator cable from its support on the cylinder head cover and also from the carburetor throttle arm.
5. Remove the choke cable and fuel lines from the carburetor.
6. Remove the water hose bracket from the cylinder head cover.
7. Unfasten the water hose clamps and remove the hoses from the water pump and the water valve. Detach the heater temperature control cable from the water valve.
8. Disconnect the PCV line from the cylinder head cover.
9. Unbolt and remove the valve cover.
10. Remove the valve rocker support securing bolts and nuts. Lift out the valve rocker assembly.

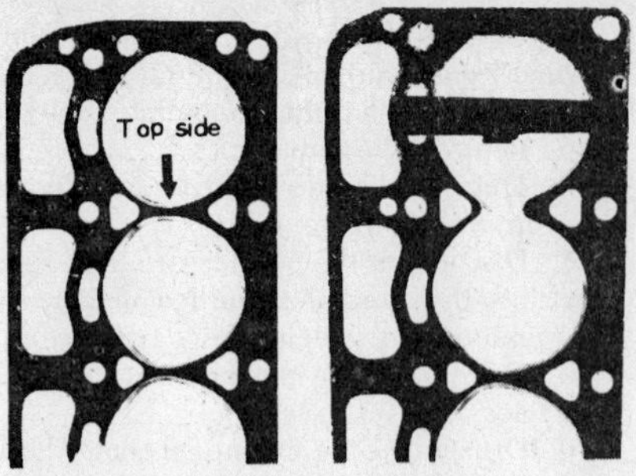

Indentification of the top side of the 3K-C head gasket

11. Withdraw the pushrods from their bores.
12. Unfasten the hose clamps and remove the upper radiator hose from the water outlet.
13. Remove the wires from the spark plugs.
14. Disconnect the wiring and the fluid line from the windshield washer assembly. Remove the assembly.

NOTE: Use a clean container to catch the fluid from the windshield washer reservoir when disconnecting its fluid line.

15. Unfasten the exhaust pipe flange from the exhaust manifold.
16. Remove the head assembly retaining bolts and remove the head from the engine.
17. Place the cylinder head on *wooden* blocks to prevent damage to it.

Installation is essentially the reverse order of removal. Clean both the cylinder head and block gasket mounting surfaces. Always use a new head gasket.

NOTE: Be sure that the top side of the gasket is facing upward. (See illustration.)

When installing the head on the block, be sure to tighten the bolts in the sequence shown (see "Torque Sequences"), in several stages, to the specified torque.

The valve rocker assembly nuts and bolts should be tightened to 13-16 ft/lbs.

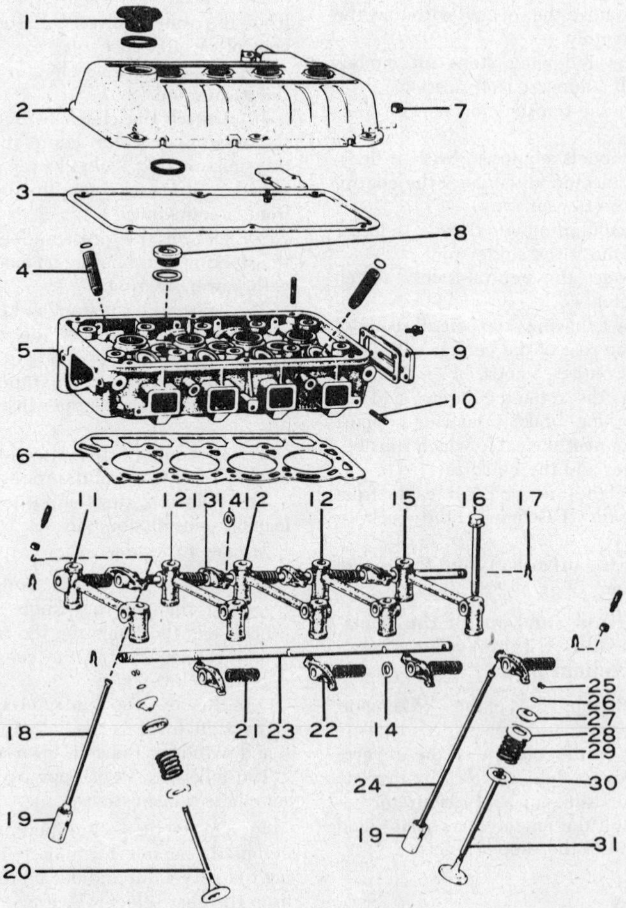

1. Oil filler cap
2. Valve cover
3. Valve cover gasket
4. Valve guide (intake)
5. Cylinder head
6. Cylinder head gasket
7. Nut
8. Screw plug
9. Cylinder head rear cover
10. Stud
11. Valve rocker support
12. Valve rocker support
13. Valve rocker arm
14. Washer
15. Valve rocker support
16. Bolt
17. Retainer spring
18. Pushrod
19. Valve lifter
20. Intake valve
21. Compression spring
22. Valve rocker arm
23. Valve rocker shaft
24. Pushrod
25. Lock spring
26. O-ring
27. Valve spring retainer
28. Oil splash shield
29. Compression spring
30. Plate washer
31. Exhaust valve

2T-C cylinder head components

NOTE: The valve clearance should be adjusted to specification with each piston at top dead center (TDC) of its compression stroke.

2T-C Engine

1. Perform Steps 1-2 of 3K-C head removal procedure.
2. Disconnect the vacuum lines which run from the vacuum switching valve to the various emission control devices mounted on the cylinder head.
3. Disconnect the mixture control valve hose which runs to the intake manifold and remove the valve from its mounting bracket.
4. Perform Step 7 of the K-C and 3K-C head removal procedure.
5. Detach the water temperature sender wiring.
6. Remove the choke stove pipe and its intake pipe.
7. Remove the PCV hose from the intake manifold.
8. Disconnect the fuel and vacuum lines from the carburetor.
9. Remove the clutch hydraulic line bracket from the cylinder head.
10. Raise the car and support it with jack stands. Unfasten the exhaust pipe clamp. Remove the exhaust manifold from the cylinder head. (See below.)
11. Remove the valve cover.
12. Remove the cylinder head bolts in the sequence illustrated under "Torque Sequences."
13. Perform Steps 10-11 of the 3K-C cylinder head removal procedure.
14. Remove the cylinder head, complete with the intake manifold.
15. Separate the intake manifold from the cylinder head.

Install the cylinder head in the following order:

1. Clean the gasket mounting surfaces of the cylinder head and the block completely.

NOTE: Remove oil from the cylinder head bolt holes if present.

2. Place a *new* gasket on the block and install the head assembly.
3. Install the pushrods and the valve rocker assembly.
4. Tighten the cylinder head bolts *evenly*, in stages, as illustrated in the "Torque Sequence" diagrams. See the "Torque Specifications" chart above, for the proper tightening torque.
5. Install the intake manifold, using a new gasket and tighten it to specifications.
6. The rest of the installation procedure is the reverse of removal. Adjust the valve clearances.

20R Engine

1. Disconnect the battery.
2. Remove the three exhaust pipe flange nuts and separate the pipe from the manifold.
3. Drain the cooling system (both radiator and block). Save the coolant to be reused.
4. Remove the air cleaner, complete with hoses, from the carburetor.

NOTE: Cover the carburetor with a clean rag so that nothing can fall into it.

5. Mark all vacuum hoses to aid installation, and disconnect them. Remove all linkages, fuel lines, etc. from the carburetor, cylinder head, and manifolds. Remove the wire supports.
6. Mark the spark plug leads and disconnect them from the plugs.
7. Matchmark the distributor housing and block. Disconnect the primary lead and remove the distributor. Installation will be easier if you leave the cap leads in place.
8. Remove the valve cover.
9. Remove the rubber camshaft seals. Use a 19 mm wrench to remove cam sprocket bolt. Slide the distributor drive gear off of the cam and wire the cam sprocket in place.
10. Remove the timing chain cover 14 mm bolt at the front of the head. This must be done before the head bolts are removed.
11. Remove the cylinder head bolts in the order shown under "Torque Sequences." Improper removal could cause head damage.
12. Using pry bars applied evenly at the front and the rear of the valve rocker assembly, pry the assembly off of its mounting dowels.
13. Lift the head off of its dowels. Do NOT pry it off. Support the head on a workbench.
14. Drain the engine oil from the crankcase *after* the head has been removed, because the oil will become contaminated with coolant while the head is being removed.

Installation is in the following order:

1. Apply liquid sealer to the front corners of the block and install the head gasket.
2. Lower the head over the locating dowels. Do not attempt to slide it into place.
3. Rotate the camshaft so that the sprocket aligning pin is at the top. Remove the wire and hold the cam sprocket. Manually rotate the engine so that the sprocket hole is also at the top. Wire the sprocket in place again.
4. Install the rocker arm assembly over its positioning dowels.
5. Tighten the cylinder head bolts evenly, in three stages, and in order to 52-63 ft/lbs.
6. Install the timing chain cover bolt and tighten it to 7-11 ft/lbs.
7. Remove the wire and install the sprocket over the camshaft dowel. If the chain won't allow the sprocket to reach, rotate the crankshaft bolt to 51-65 ft/lbs.
8. Install the distributor drive gear and tighten the crankshaft bolt to 51-65 ft/lbs.
9. Set the No. 1 piston at TDC of its compression stroke and adjust the valves.
10. After completing valve adjustment, rotate the crankshaft one turn, so that 8°-BTDC mark on the pulley aligns with the pointer.
11. Install the distributor, as outlined above.
12. Install the spark plugs and leads.
13. Make sure that the oil drain plug is installed. Fill the engine with oil after installing the rubber cam seals. Pour the oil over the distributor drive gear and the valve rockers.
14. Install the rocker cover and tighten the bolts to 8-11 ft/lbs.
15. Connect all the vacuum hoses and electrical leads that were removed during disassembly. Install the spark plug lead supports. Fill the cooling system. Install the air cleaner.
16. Tighten the exhaust pipe to manifold flange bolts to 25-33 ft/lbs.
17. Reconnect the battery. Start the engine and allow it to reach normal operating temperature. Check and adjust the timing and valve clearance. Adjust the idle speed and mixture. Road test the vehicle.

4M Engines

1. Perform Steps 1-4 and 6-8 of the 3K-C cylinder head removal procedure. Skip Step 5.

NOTE: On fuel injected engines it is necessary to remove the air intake chamber and the intake manifold before the head can be removed.

2. Remove the fuel and vacuum lines from the carburetor. Remove the carburetor.
3. Remove the spark plug wires from their supports on the cylinder head cover and from the spark plugs themselves.
4. Remove the distributor assembly.
5. Take off the automatic choke stove hoses.
6. Remove the exhaust manifold and the oil pressure light sender.
7. Remove the intake manifold assembly.
8. Unfasten the retaining bolts and remove the valve cover assembly.

NOTE: Place a cloth over the timing gear to prevent anything from falling into the timing gear cover.

9. Remove the valve rocker shaft assembly retaining bolts in the sequence illustrated. Loosen the bolts in two or three stages. Remove the rocker shaft assembly.
10. Remove the timing chain tensioner.

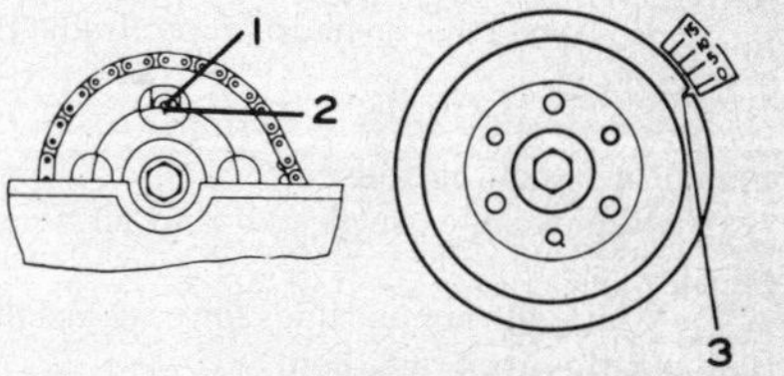

1. Valve timing mark (5/32 in. hole)
2. V-notch—camshaft flange
3. V-notch—crankshaft pulley

Alignment of the timing marks on the crankshaft and camshaft for the 4M engine

11. Straighten out the lockplate and unfasten the timing gear retaining bolt (left-hand thread). Withdraw the timing gear from the camshaft.
12. Perform Steps 12-14 of the 18R-C cylinder head removal procedure.

Installation is performed in the following order:

1. Perform Steps 1-10 of the 18-R-C cylinder head installation procedure.

NOTE: Apply liquid sealer around each cylinder block oil hole but be careful not to get any in the hole itself. Also, apply sealer to the timing chain cover and cylinder block.

2. Align the V-notch on the camshaft with the $^5/_{32}$ in. hole on the No. 1 camshaft bearing.

NOTE: Be sure that the V-notch is also aligned with the mark on the timing chain cover.

3. Install the camshaft timing gear, with the chain, on the end of the camshaft. Align the pin on the camshaft flange with the hole in the gear.

4. Install the timing gear bolt and lockplate. Fasten the bolt with the lockplate.

NOTE: The bolt has a left-hand thread. Tighten it to 47-54 ft/lbs.

5. Install the chain tensioner, complete with shim. Tighten it to 22-29 ft/lbs.

6. Turn the crankshaft two complete revolutions while checking to see that valve timing is correct. If at the end of the two revolutions, the timing marks do not align, repeat Steps 2-4.

7. Apply pressure to the chain tensioner arm. If its movement is less than $^3/_{16}$ in., add additional shims.

8. Install the valve rocker assembly and tighten the bolts to 22-29 ft/lbs, in the sequence illustrated, and in three or four stages.

NOTE: The stud bolt should only be tightened to 11-14 ft/lbs.

9. Install the union on the No. 1 rocker support and the No. 1 camshaft bearing cap. Tighten the union bolts to 6-9 ft/lbs.

10. Adjust the valve clearance, as outlined above, to the following *cold* specifications:
Intake—0.006 in.
Exhaust—0.008 in.

11. The rest of the installation procedure is the reverse of removal.

1A-C, 2A and 3A

1. Disconnect the negative battery terminal.
2. Remove the exhaust pipe from the manifold.
3. Drain the cooling system. Save the coolant as it can be reused.
4. Remove the air cleaner and all necessary hoses.
5. Mark all vacuum lines for easy installation and then remove them.
6. Remove all linkage from the carburetor, fuel lines, etc. from the head and manifold.
7. Remove the fuel pump.

NOTE: Before removing the carburetor cover it with a clean rag to prevent dirt from entering it.

8. Remove the carburetor.
9. Remove the manifold.
10. Remove the valve cover.
11. Note the position of the spark plug wires and remove them.
12. Remove the spark plugs.
13. Set the engine on No. 1 cylinder—top dead center. This is accomplished by removing the No. 1 spark plug, placing your finger over the hole and then turning the crankshaft pulley until you feel pressure exerted against your finger.

CAUTION

Do not put your finger into the spark plug hole.

14. Remove the crankshaft pulley with an appropriate puller.
15. Remove the water pump pulley.
16. Remove the top and bottom timing chain cover.
17. Matchmark the camshaft pulley and timing belt for reassembly.
18. Loosen the belt tensioner.
19. Remove the water pump.
20. Remove the timing belt. Do not bend, twist, or turn the belt inside out.

NOTE: Check the belt for wear, cracks, or glazing. Once the belt is removed it is a good idea to replace it with a new one even though it is not necessary.

21. Remove the rocker arm bolts and remove the rocker arms.
22. Remove the camshaft pulley by holding the camshaft with a pair of channel lock pliers and removing the belt in the pulley end of the shaft.

NOTE: Do not hold the cam on the lobes, as damage will result.

23. Remove the camshaft seal.
24. Remove the camshaft bearing caps and set them down in the order they appear on the engine.
25. Remove the camshaft.
26. Loosen the head bolts in the proper order to prevent warping of the head.
27. Lift the head directly up. Do not attempt to slide it off.
28. Installation is the reverse of removal.

NOTE: When replacing the head always use a new gasket. Also replace the camshaft seal, making sure to grease the lip before installation.

The following torques are needed for installation: cam bearing caps 8-10 ft/ lbs, cam sprocket 29-39 ft/lbs, crankshaft pulley 55-61 ft/lbs, manifold bolts 15-21 ft/lbs, rocker arm bolts 17-19 ft/lbs, timing gear idler bolt 22-32 ft/lbs, belt tension 0.24-0.28 in. Adjust the valves to the proper clearances.

OVERHAUL

NOTE: General cylinder head overhaul procedures are given in the "Engine Rebuilding" section. The operations which differs greatly from those at the end of the book are detailed below.

Valve Guide Replacement–4M, 1A-C, 2A, 3A and 3K-C Engines

1. Heat the cylinder head to 176-212° F, evenly, before beginning the replacement procedure.

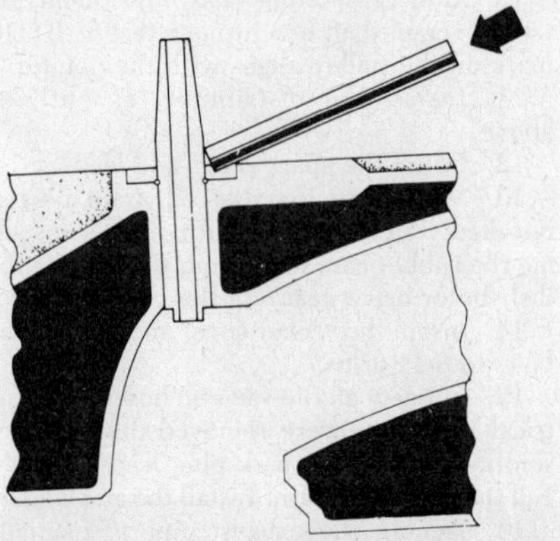

Use a brass drift to break off the valve guide

2. Use a brass rod to break the valve guide off above its snap-ring. (See illustration).
3. Drive out the valve guide, toward the combustion chamber. Use a tool fabricated as described in "Engine Rebuilding" at the end of this book.
4. Install a snap-ring on the new valve guide. Apply liquid sealer. Drive in the valve guide until the snap-ring contacts the head. Use the tool described above.
5. Measure the guide bore; if the stem-to-guide clearance is below specification, ream it out, using a valve guide reamer.

Rocker Arm Shafts

REMOVAL AND INSTALLATION

3K-C Engines

1. Remove air cleaner.
2. Remove PCV valve.
3. Remove spark plug wires.
4. Remove valve cover.
5. Loosen rocker shaft bolts, alternating front to rear.
6. Remove shaft assembly and oil tube.
7. Install in reverse of removal. Torque bolts in alternating, front to rear sequence, to 14-16 ft/lbs. Torque oil pipe bolts to 14 ft/lbs. Check valve clearance.

4M Engine

1. Remove the air cleaner assembly.
2. Remove the choke stove outlet and inlet hose.
3. Remove the valve cover.
4. Remove the two front clamp bolts.
5. Loosen the rocker arm shaft bolts in a rotating order starting at the ends and working toward the center.
6. Remove bolts and lift off rocker shaft assemblies.
7. Install in reverse of removal. Tighten rocker shaft bolts, in a rotating order from the center to the ends, to 25 ft/lbs. Torque the front end clamp bolts to 9 ft/lbs. Check valve clearance.

2T-C Engine

1. Remove the air cleaner.
2. Remove the PCV valve.
3. Remove the spark plug wires.
4. Disconnect the fuel inlet from the carburetor.
5. Remove the valve cover.

NOTE: The cylinder head bolts also serve as the rocker arm shaft bolts. Remove these a little at a time in circular rotation from the ends toward the center.

6. Lift off the shaft assemblies.
7. Install the reverse of removal. Install and tighten the cylinder head bolts in a circular rotation from the center toward the ends. Torque to 63 ft/lbs. Check valve clearance.

20R Engine

1. Remove the air cleaner.
2. Disconnect all hoses and linkage clipped to the valve cover.
3. Remove the spark plug wires.
4. Remove the carburetor.

5. Remove the valve cover.
6. Remove the distributor.
7. Set the No. 1 piston at TDC of the compression stroke.
8. Paint mating marks on the timing chain and sprocket, and drive gear.
9. Remove the distributor drive gear, leaving the chain and sprocket in position.
10. Remove the one 14 mm chain cover bolt in the front of the head. This must be done before the head bolts, which also serve as rocker shaft bolts, are removed.
11. Remove the head bolts in a diagonal pattern. Start at the front carburetor side. This must be done to prevent head warpage.
12. Remove the shaft assemblies from the head. It may be necessary to use a pry bar to evenly lift the assemblies from the dowels.
13. Install in reverse of removal. Torque the head bolts in a diagonal pattern, starting at the center. Tighten in three equal stages to 64 ft/lbs. Torque the chain cover bolt to 12 ft/lbs. Torque drive gear bolt to 65 ft/lbs.

1A-C, 2A and 3A

1. Disconnect the negative battery terminal.
2. Remove the air cleaner and all necessary hoses.
3. Remove all the linkage from the carburetor.
4. Remove the valve cover and gasket.
5. Remove the rocker arm bolts.
6. Installation is the reverse of removal.

NOTE: Remember to install a new valve cover gasket before replacing the valve cover.

7. Tighten the rocker arm bolt 17-19 ft/lbs.

Intake Manifold

REMOVAL AND INSTALLATION

2T-C Engine

1. Drain the cooling system.
2. Remove the air cleaner assembly, complete with hoses, from its bracket.
3. Remove the choke stove hoses, fuel lines, and vacuum lines from the carburetor. Unfasten the emission control system hoses and the accelerator linkage from it.
4. Unfasten the four nuts which secure the carburetor to the manifold and remove the carburetor.
5. Remove the mixture control valve line from its intake manifold fitting (1973-74).
6. Disconnect the PCV hose.
7. Disconnect the water bypass hose from the intake manifold.
8. Unbolt and remove the manifold.

Installation is performed in the reverse order of removal. Remember to use *new* gaskets. Tighten the intake manifold bolts to specifications.

NOTE: Tighten the bolts, in several stages, working from the inside out.

20R Engine

1. Disconnect the battery.
2. Drain the cooling system.
3. Remove the air cleaner, complete with hoses, from the carburetor.

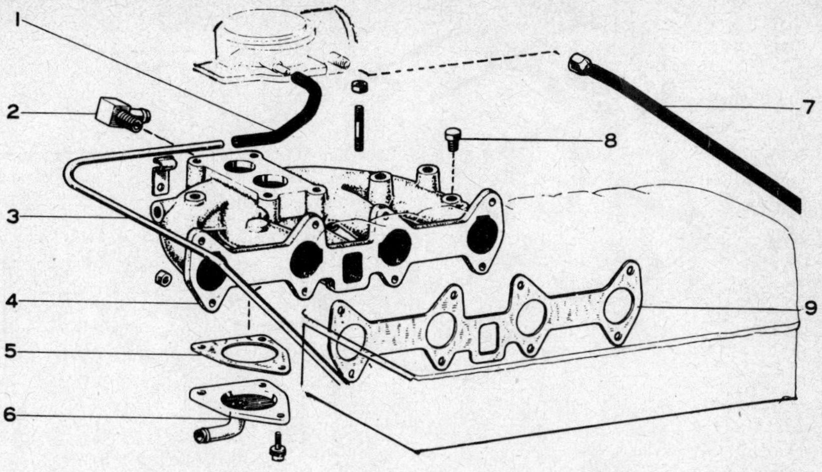

1. Choke stove intake hose
2. Elbow
3. Choke stove intake
4. Intake manifold
5. Gasket
6. Water by-pass outlet
7. Choke stove outlet
8. Plug
9. Intake manifold gasket

2T-C intake manifold

4. Disconnect the vacuum lines from the EGR valve and carburetor. Mark them first, to aid in installation.
5. Remove the fuel lines, electrical leads, accelerator linkage, and water hose from the carburetor.
6. Remove the water by-pass hose from the manifold.
7. Unbolt and remove the intake manifold, complete with carburetor and EGR valve.
8. Cover the cylinder head ports with clean rags to keep anything from falling into the cylinder head or block.

Installation is the reverse of removal. Replace the gasket with a new one. Torque the mounting bolts to specifications. Tighten the bolts in several stages working from the inside bolts outward. Refill the cooling system.

4M Engines

1. Drain the cooling system.
2. Remove the air cleaner assembly, complete with hoses, from its mounting bracket.
3. Remove the distributor cap.
4. Remove the upper radiator hose from the elbow.
5. Remove the wiring from the temperature gauge sending unit.
6. Remove the following from the carburetor: fuel lines; vacuum line; choke stove hoses; emission control system hoses; accelerator torque rod; and automatic transmission linkage (if so equipped).
7. Remove the emission control system lines and wiring from the manifold when equipped with a vacuum switching valve.

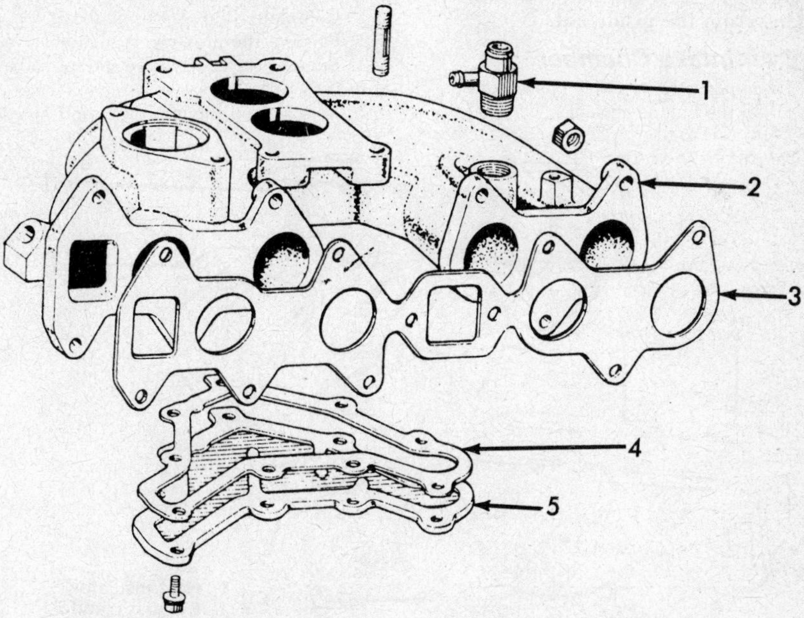

1. Vacuum hose fitting
2. Intake manifold
3. Gasket (to head)
4. Gasket (bottom)
5. Bottom cover

20R intake manifold

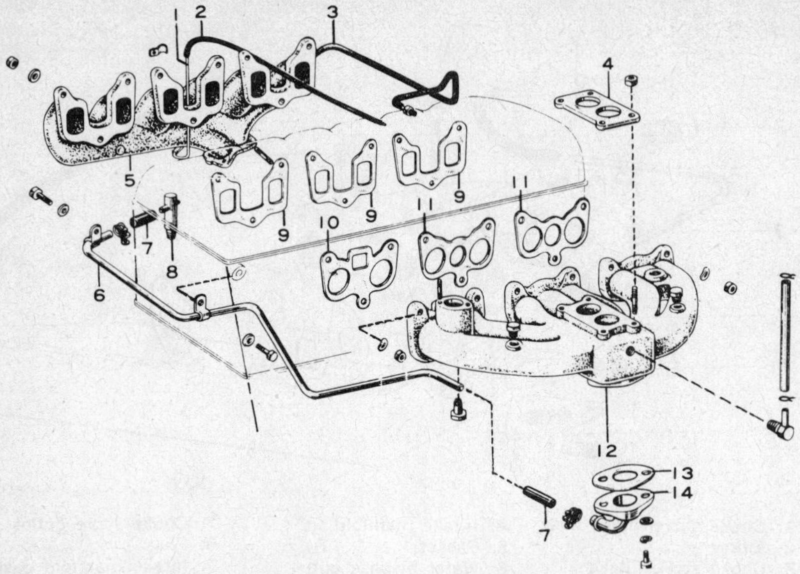

1. Automatic choke stove intake pipe
2. Automatic choke stove intake hose
3. Automatic choke stove outlet pipe
4. Carburetor heat insulator
5. Exhaust manifold
6. Water by-pass line
7. Water by-pass hose
8. Water hose joint
9. Exhaust manifold gasket
10. Intake manifold gasket (1)
11. Intake manifold gasket (2)
12. Intake manifold
13. Gasket
14. Water by-pass outlet

4M intake and exhaust manifolds

Remove the EGR pipe from the intake manifold.

8. Remove the water bypass hose from the manifold.

9. Unbolt and remove the manifold, complete with the carburetor.

Installation is in the reverse order of removal. Remember to replace the gaskets with new ones. Torque the mounting bolts to specifications.

NOTE: Tighten the bolts, in stages, working from the inside out.

4M-E Air Intake Chamber

1. Disconnect the negative battery cable.
2. Drain the engine coolant.
3. Remove all necessary vacuum hoses and other hardware.

NOTE: Remember to mark each line and connector with a number to facilitate proper placement of the lines upon reinstallation.

4. Remove the intake chamber.
5. Installation is the reverse of removal.

4M-E Intake Manifold

1. Complete Steps 1-4 from above.
2. Remove the pressure regulator valve.
3. Remove the heater hose and top radiator hose.
4. Remove the vacuum pipes and hoses.
5. Remove the distributor cap.
6. Remove the manifold and gasket.
7. Installation is the reverse of removal.

NOTE: Always install a new manifold gasket.

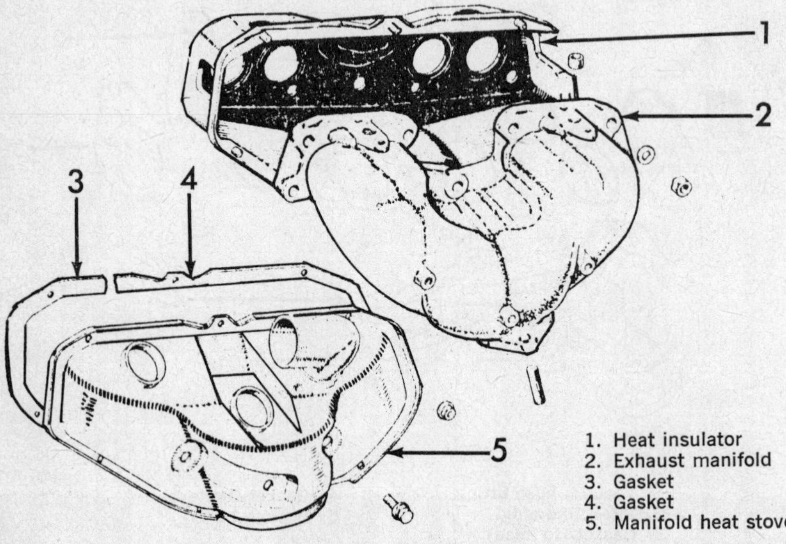

1. Heat insulator
2. Exhaust manifold
3. Gasket
4. Gasket
5. Manifold heat stove

20R exhaust manifold

Exhaust Manifold

REMOVAL AND INSTALLATION

CAUTION

Do not perform this operation on a warm or hot engine.

2T-C Engine

1. Detach the manifold heat stove intake pipe.
2. Unfasten the nut on the stove outlet pipe union.
3. Remove the wiring from the emission control system thermosensor.
4. Unfasten the U-bolt from the downpipe bracket.
5. Unfasten the downpipe flange from the manifold.
6. In order to remove the manifold, unfasten the manifold retaining bolts.

CAUTION

Remove the bolts in two or three stages, working from the inside out.

Installation of the manifold is performed in the reverse order of removal. Remember to use a *new* gasket.

20R Engine

1. Remove the three exhaust pipe flange bolts and disconnect the exhaust pipe from the manifold.
2. Disconnect the spark plug leads.
3. Matchmark the distributor rotor, housing and the engine block. Remove the distributor.
4. Remove the air cleaner tube from the heat stove. Remove the outer part of the heat stove.
5. Remove the manifold (14 mm nuts), complete with air injection tubes and the inner portion of the heat stove.
6. Separate the inner portion of the heat stove from the manifold.

Installation is the reverse of removal. Tighten the retaining nuts to 29-36 ft/lbs working from the inside out. Install the distributor and set the timing. Tighten the exhaust pipe flange nuts to 25-32 ft/lbs.

4M Engine

1. Raise the front and the rear of the car and support it with jack stands.
2. Remove the right-hand gravel shield from beneath the engine.
3. Remove the downpipe support bracket.
4. Unfasten the bolts from the flange and detach the downpipe from the manifold.
5. Remove the automatic choke and air cleaner stove hoses from the exhaust manifold. Remove the EGR valve, if so equipped.
6. Remove, or move aside, any of the air injection system components which may be in the way when removing the manifold.
7. In order to remove the manifold, unfasten the manifold retaining bolts.

CAUTION

Remove and tighten the bolts in two or three stages, starting from the inside, working out.

Installation is performed in the reverse order of removal. Always use a new gasket. Tighten the retaining bolts to specifications in two or three stages.

Combination Manifold

REMOVAL AND INSTALLATION

CAUTION

Do not perform this procedure on a warm engine.

3K-C Engines

1. Remove the air cleaner assembly, complete with hoses.
2. Disconnect the accelerator and choke linkages from the carburetor, as well as the fuel and vacuum lines.
3. Remove, or move aisde, any of the emission control system components which are in the way.
4. On F engines, disconnect the oil filter lines and remove the oil filter assembly from the intake manifold. Unfasten the solenoid valve wire from the ignition coil terminal. Remove the EGR pipes from the exhaust gas cooler, if so equipped.
5. Unfasten the retaining bolts and remove the carburetor from the manifold.
6. Loosen the manifold retaining nuts, working from the inside out, in two or three stages.
7. Remove the intake/exhaust manifold assembly from the cylinder head as a complete unit.

Installation is performed in the reverse order of removal. Always use *new* gaskets. Tighten the bolts, working from the inside out.

NOTE: Tighten the bolts in two or three stages.

1A-C, 2A, and 3A

1. Disconnect the negative battery terminal.
2. Remove the air cleaner and all necessary hoses.
3. Remove all the carburetor linkages.
4. Remove the carburetor.

NOTE: Cover the carburetor with a clean towel to prevent dirt from entering it.

5. Remove the exhaust manifold pipe.
6. Remove the exhaust manifold.
7. Installation is the reverse of removal. Tighten the manifold bolts to 15-21 ft/lbs.

Timing Gear Cover

REMOVAL AND INSTALLATION

3K-C and 2T-C Engines

1. Drain the cooling system and the crankcase.
2. Disconnect the battery.
3. Remove the air cleaner assembly, complete with hoses, from its bracket.
4. Remove the hood latch as well as its brace and support.
5. Remove the headlight bezels and grille assembly.
6. Unfasten the upper and lower radiator hose clamps and remove both of the hoses from the engine.
7. Unfasten the radiator securing bolts and remove the radiator.

NOTE: Take off the shroud first, if so equipped.

8. Loosen the drive belt adjusting link and remove the drive belt. Unfasten the alternator multiconnector, withdraw the retaining bolts, and remove the alternator.
9. Perform Step 8 to the air injection pump, if so equipped. Disconnect the hoses from the pump before removing it.
10. Remove the fan and water pump as an assembly.
11. Unfasten the crankshaft pulley retaining bolt. Remove the crankshaft pulley with a gear puller.
12. Remove the gravel shield from underneath the engine.
13. The following steps apply to the 3K-C engine only:
    a. Remove the nuts and washers from both the right and left front engine mounts.
    b. Detach the exhaust pipe flange from the exhaust manifold.
    c. Slightly raise the front of the engine.
14. On 2T-C engines, remove the right-hand brace plate.
15. Remove the front oil pan bolts, to gain access to the bottom of the timing chain cover.

NOTE: It may be necessary to insert a thin knife between the pan and the gasket in order to break the pan loose. Use care not to damage the gasket.

Installation is basically the reverse order of removal. There are, however, several points to remember:

1. Apply sealer to the two front corners of the 2T-C engine's oil pan gasket.
2. Tighten the crankshaft pulley to specifications.
3. Adjust the drive belts.

20R and 4M Engines

1. Perform the cylinder head removal procedure as detailed in the appropriate section.
2. Remove the radiator.
3. Remove the alternator.
4. On engines equipped with air pumps, unfasten the adjusting link bolts and the drive belt. Remove the hoses from the pump; remove the pump and bracket from the engine.

NOTE: If the car is equipped with power steering see below for its pump removal procedure.

5. Remove the fan and water pump as a complete assembly.

CAUTION

To prevent the fluid from running out from the fan coupling, do not tip the assembly over on its side.

6. Unfasten the crankshaft pulley securing bolts and remove the pulley with a gear puller.

CAUTION

Do not remove the 10 mm bolt from its hole, if installed, as it is used for balancing.

7. Loosen the bolts which secure the front of the oil pan, after draining the engine oil. Lower the front of the oil pan.
8. Remove the bolts which secure the timing chain cover. Withdraw the cover.

Installation is performed in the reverse order of removal. Apply sealer to the gaskets for both the timing chain cover and the oil pan.

NOTE: The 4M engine uses two gaskets on the timing chain cover.

Tighten the timing chain cover bolts to the specifications below:

18R-C engines:
All bolts—11-15 ft/lbs.
20R engines:
All bolts—8-11 ft/lbs.
4M engines:
8 mm bolts—7-12 ft/lbs.
10 mm bolts—14-22 ft/lbs.

1A-C, 2A and 3A

1. Disconnect the negative battery terminal.
2. Remove all the drive belts.
3. Bring the engine to the top dead center timing position. See the cylinder head removal section.
4. Remove the crankshaft pulley with a suitable puller.
5. Remove the water pump pulley.
6. Remove the upper and lower timing case covers.
7. Installation is the reverse of removal.

Tighten the timing belt cover to 61-99 in/lbs.

TIMING CHAIN COVER OIL SEAL REPLACEMENT

All Engines (Except 1A-C, 2A and 3A)

1. Remove the timing chain cover, as detailed in the appropriate section above.
2. Inspect the oil seal for signs of wear, leakage, or damage.
3. If worn, pry the old oil seal out, using a large flat-bladed screwdriver. Remove it toward the *front* of the cover.

NOTE: Once the oil seal has been removed, it must be replaced.

4. Use a socket, pipe, or block of wood and a hammer to drive the oil seal into place. Work from the *front* of the cover.

CAUTION

Be extremely careful not to damage the seal.

5. Install the timing chain cover as outlined above.

Timing Chain and Tensioner

REMOVAL AND INSTALLATION

1A-C, 2A and 3A

1. Remove the crankshaft and water pump pulleys.
2. Remove the top and bottom timing covers.
3. Remove the belt tensioner.
4. Matchmark the belt and camshaft gear for easy reinstallation.
5. Remove the timing belt.

NOTE: Do not bend, twist, or turn the belt inside out. Do not allow grease or water to come in contact with it.

6. Check for damaged teeth, cracks, or excessive wear. If the belt shows any of the problems it should be replaced.
7. Installation is the reverse of removal.

The following torque specifications are needed: crankshaft pulley 55-61 ft/lbs, camshaft pulley 29-39 ft/lbs, timing belt tension 0.24-0.28 in.

3K-C Engine

1. Remove the timing chain cover.
2. Unbolt and remove the chain tensioner.
3. Remove the camshaft chain sprocket and then the chain itself.
4. Check the timing chain for wear, cracks, or loose links.
5. Secure one end of the chain to a fixed hook and pull on the other end with a spring scale. When the scale indicates 11 lbs, the chains should be no longer than 10.7 in. Replace the chain if it exceeds this specification.

Installation is in the following order:

1. Install the crankshaft chain sprocket. Align the sprocket O-mark with the straight pin on the crankshaft, as illustrated.
2. Fit the timing chain on the crankshaft sprocket.
3. Align the mating marks on the timing chain with the O-marks on both sprockets, as illustrated.
4. Align the camshaft sprocket O-mark with the one on the crankshaft.
5. Tighten the camshaft timing sprocket securing bolt to 16-22 ft/lbs.
6. Install the chain tensioner assembly and chain vibration damper. Tighten their bolts to 4-6 ft/lbs.
7. Install the timing chain cover as detailed above.

2T-C Engine

1. Perform Steps 1-3 of the 3K-C timing chain removal procedure.
2. Perform Steps 4-5 of the 3K-C timing chain removal procedure (chain inspection). The chain should stretch no more than 11.47 in. at 11 lbs. on the spring scale.

Installation is performed in the following order:

1. Rotate the crankshaft so its key points straight up.

NOTE: The No. 1 and No. 4 pistons should be at TDC.

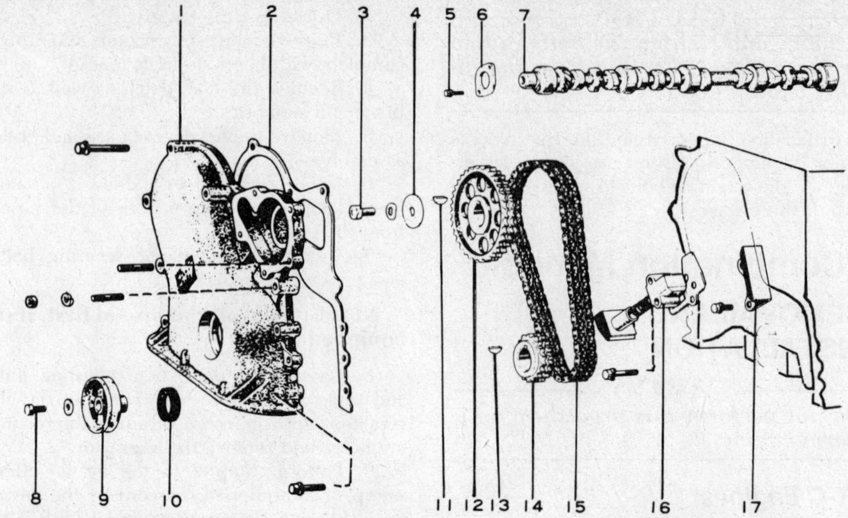

1. Timing chain cover
2. Timing chain cover gasket
3. Bolt
4. Plate washer
5. Bolt
6. Plate
7. Camshaft
8. Bolt
9. Crankshaft pulley
10. Front oil seal
11. Woodruff key
12. Camshaft sprocket
13. Woodruff key
14. Crankshaft sprocket
15. Timing chain
16. Chain tensioner
17. Chain vibration damper

Timing chain covers, timing chain and camshaft—2T-C engine

2. Rotate the camshaft so its key is aligned with the timing mark on the thrust plate.
3. Install the chain on the camshaft and crankshaft timing sprockets so the marks on the timing chain align with the "Toyota" trademarks on each of the sprockets.

NOTE: The above step is performed with the sprockets off the engine.

4. Being careful to keep all the parts in proper alignment, install the timing chain/sprocket assembly to the engine. When assembled, the marks should align as in the illustration.

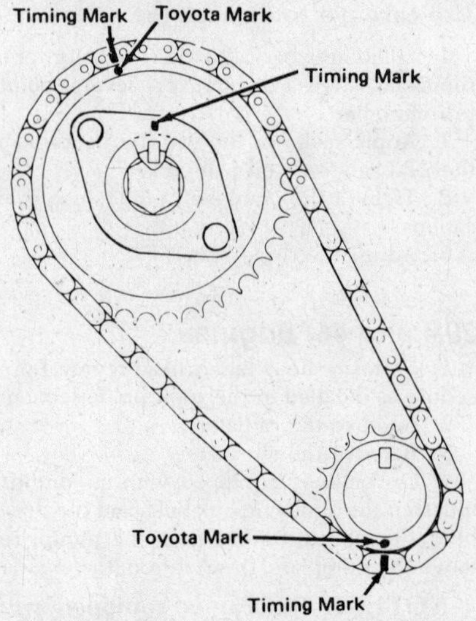

Proper alignment of the marks on 2T-C timing chain and sprocket

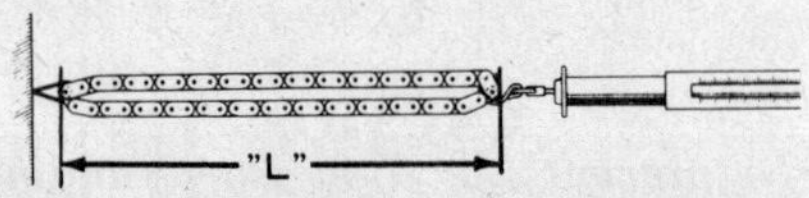

Measure timing chain stretch along "L" on the 3K-C and 2T-C engines

5. Torque the camshaft timing gear bolt to 50-79 ft/lbs.
6. Fill the chain tensioner with engine oil and install it. Install the chain damper.
7. Install the timing chain cover as outlined above.

20R Engine

1. Remove the cylinder head and timing chain cover as outlined above.
2. Separate the chain from the damper, and remove the chain, complete with the camshaft sprocket.
3. Remove the crankshaft sprocket and the oil pump drive with a puller.
4. Inspect the chain for wear or damage. Replace it, if necessary.
5. Inspect the chain tensioner for wear. If it measures less than 0.43 in., replace it.
6. Check the dampers for wear. If they are below specification replace them:

Upper damper—0.20 in.
Lower damper—0.18 in.

Installation is performed in the following order:

1. Rotate the crankshaft until its key is at TDC. Slide the sprocket in place over the key.
2. Place the chain over the sprocket so that its *single* bright link aligns with the mark on the crank sprocket.

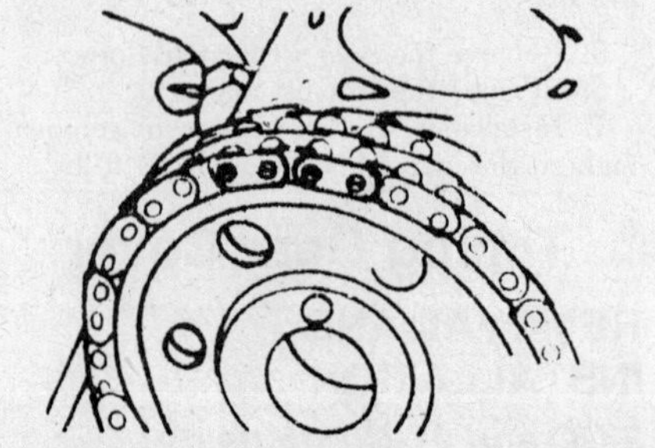

Align the timing marks between the two bright links of the chain—20R engine

3. Install the cam sprocket so that the timing mark falls between the *two* bright links on the chain.

4. Fit the oil pump drive spline over the crankshaft key.

5. Install the timing cover gasket on the front of the block.

6. Rotate the camshaft sprocket counterclockwise to remove the slack from the chain.

7. Install the timing chain cover and cylinder head, as outlined above.

4M Engines

1. Remove the cylinder head and timing chain cover, as outlined above.
2. Remove the chain tensioner assembly (arm and gear).
3. Unfasten the bolts which retain the chain damper and damper guide and withdraw the damper and guide.
4. Remove the oil slinger from the crankshaft.
5. Withdraw the timing chain.
6. Inspect the chain for wear or damage. Replace it if necessary.

Installation is performed in the following manner:

1. Position the no. 1 cylinder at TDC.
2. Position the crankshaft sprocket O-mark downward, facing the oil pan.
3. Align the "Toyota" trademarks on the sprockets as illustrated.
4. Fit the tensioner gear assembly on the block.

NOTE: Its dowel pin should be positioned 1.5 in. from the surface of the block.

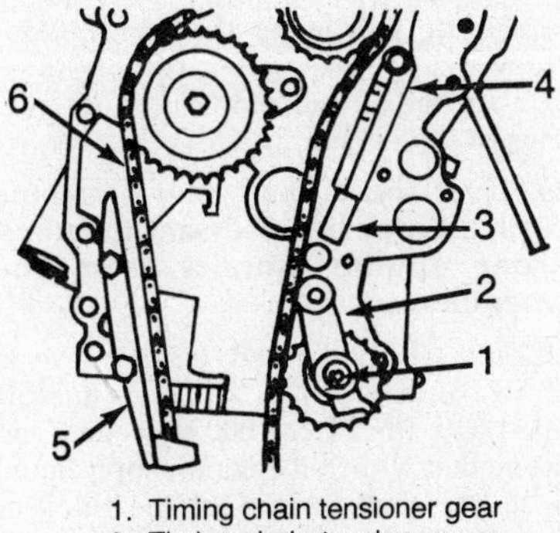

1. Timing chain tensioner gear
2. Timing chain tensioner arm
3. Damper guide
4. Vibration damper
5. Vibration damper
6. Crankshaft oil slinger

Removing the timing chain from the 4M timing marks

5. Install the chain over the two gears while maintaining tension.
6. Install both of the vibration dampers and the damper guide.
7. Fit the oil slinger to the crankshaft.
8. Tie the chain to the upper vibration damper, to keep it from falling into the chain cover, once the cover is installed.
9. Install the timing chain cover, as detailed above.
10. Perform the cylinder head installation procedure as detailed above.

NOTE: If proper valve timing cannot be obtained, it is possible to adjust it by placing the camshaft slotted pin in the

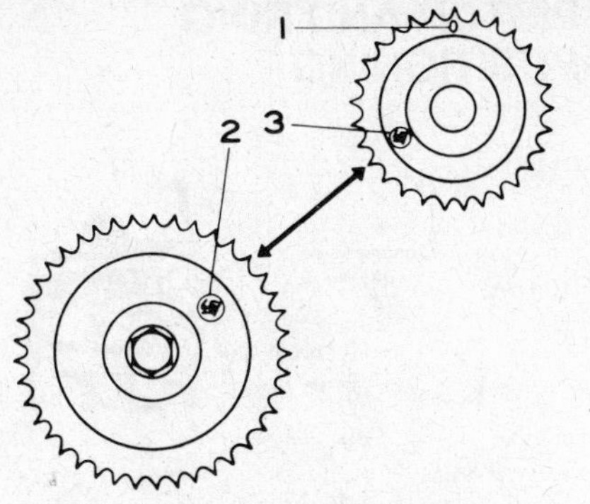

1. Crankshaft sprocket O-mark
2. Camshaft sprocket "Toyota" mark
3. Crankshaft sprocket "Toyota" mark

Proper alignment of the 4M timing marks

second or third hole on the camshaft timing gear, as required. If the timing is out by more than 15°, replace the chain and both of the sprockets.

Timing Gears

REMOVAL AND INSTALLATION

1A-C, 2A and 3A

1. Remove the air cleaner.
2. Remove the throttle linkage.
3. Remove the valve cover.
4. Remove the crankshaft and water pump pulleys.
5. Remove the top and bottom timing belt cover.
6. Remove the belt tensioner.
7. Matchmark the belt and camshaft gear for easy reinstallation.
8. Remove the timing belt.
9. Remove the bolt from the camshaft gear and remove the gear.

NOTE: In order to remove this gear use a pair of channelock pliers to hold the cam from turning. Do not hold the cam by the lobes as damage may result.

10. Installation is the reverse of removal.

Camshaft

REMOVAL AND INSTALLATION

3K-C Engines

1. Perform the timing chain cover and timing chain removal procedure, above.
2. Perform Steps 1-11 of the 3K-C engine cylinder head removal procedure.

NOTE: It is unnecessary to remove the cylinder head.

3. Unfasten the spark plug wires and remove the spark plugs.
4. Remove the valve lifters in sequence.

NOTE: Keep the valve lifters in their proper sequence so that they go back into their original bores.

5. If you have not already done so, disconnect the vacuum line and the primary wire from the distributor, loosen its clamping bolt, and remove it.

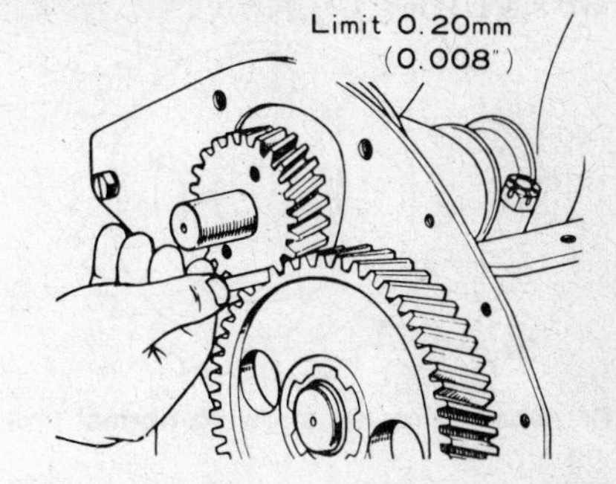

Checking timing gear backlash with a feeler gauge

6. Detach the fuel lines from the fuel pump and remove the pump.
7. Remove the bolts which secure the camshaft thrust plate and then remove the thrust plate, itself.
8. Carefully remove the camshaft from the cylinder block.

CAUTION

Use care not to damage the camshaft lobes, journals, or bearings.

Installation of the camshaft is performed in the reverse order of removal. Coat the camshaft bearings and journals lightly with engine oil. The camshaft thrust plate attaching bolt should be tightened to 4-6 ft/lbs.

2T-C Engine

1. Perform the cylinder head, timing chain cover, and timing chain removal procedures.
2. Unfasten the primary wire and vacuum lines from the distributor. Loosen its clamping bolt and withdraw it from the engine block.
3. Unfasten the lines from the fuel pump and remove the pump.
4. Remove the gear shifter shaft lever.
5. Use a jack to *lightly* support the transmission.
6. Remove the engine rear supporting crossmember.

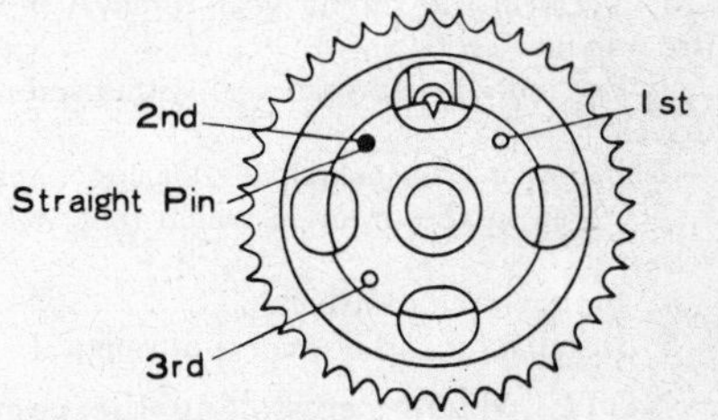

Camshaft sprocket installation—valve timing retarded 3–9°

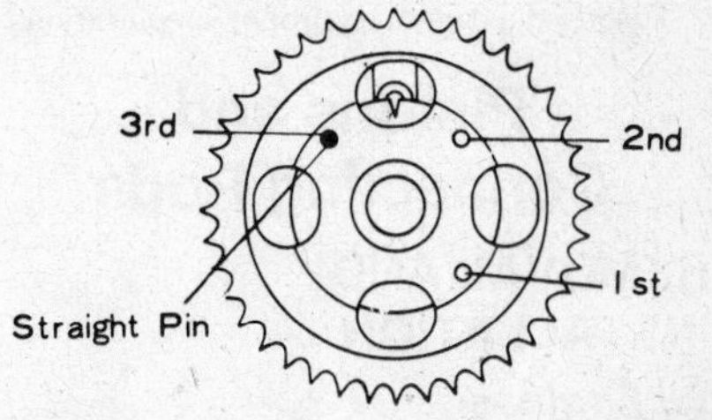

Camshaft sprocket installation—valve timing retarded 9-15°

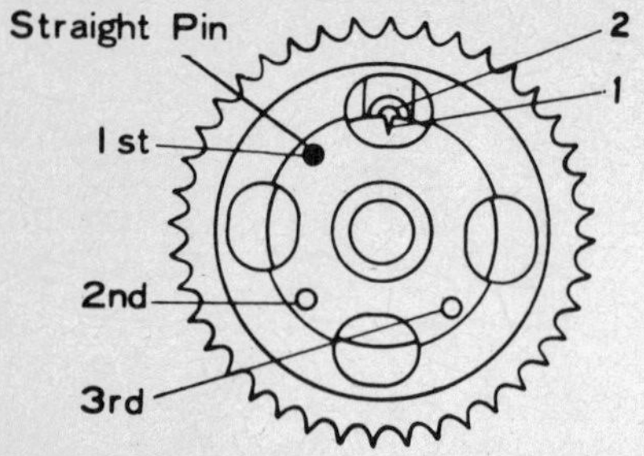

Camshaft sprocket showing normal timing

7. Carefully lower the jack from beneath the transmission.
8. Unbolt and remove the camshaft thrust plate.
9. Ease out the camshaft, being careful not to damage the camshaft lobes or bearings.

Installation is performed in the reverse order of removal. Lubricate the camshaft journals and bearings lightly with engine oil prior to camshaft installation. Tighten the camshaft thrust plate attaching bolts to 7-11 ft/lbs.

20R and 4M Engines

All of these engines utilize a chain-driven overhead camshaft (OHC). Therefore, the procedure for removing the camshaft is given as part of the cylinder head removal procedure. Consult the appropriate section, above, for details.

NOTE: It will not be necessary to completely remove the cylinder head in order to remove the camshaft. Therefore, proceed only as far as is necessary, to remove the camshaft, with the cylinder head removal procedure.

2F Engine

The procedure for removing the camshaft is given as part of the timing gear removal procedure, above; the timing gear is press-fit onto the camshaft and cannot be removed separately from it.

1A-C, 2A and 3A

1. Perform the timing gear removal from the previous section.
2. Pry out the camshaft seal with a screwdriver.
3. Remove the camshaft bearing caps. Keep them in the order in which they were removed.
4. Remove the camshaft.
5. Installation is the reverse of removal.

NOTE: When reinstalling the camshaft seal place some multipurpose grease on the lip of the seal before installation.

Torque the cam to its proper specifications.

Pistons and Connecting Rods

REMOVAL AND INSTALLATION

All Engines

See the procedure in the "Engine Rebuilding Section".

PISTON AND RING POSITIONING

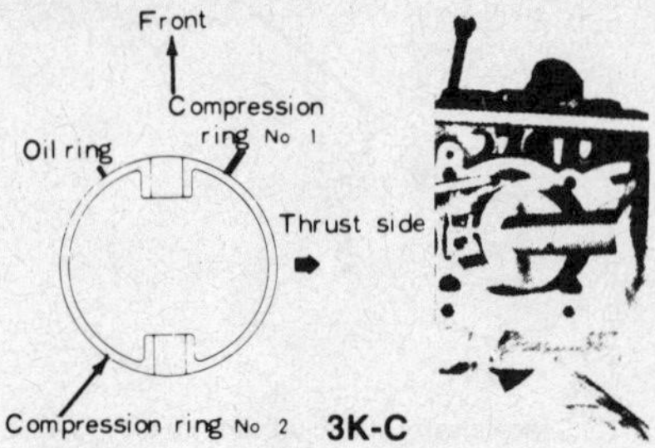

3K-C

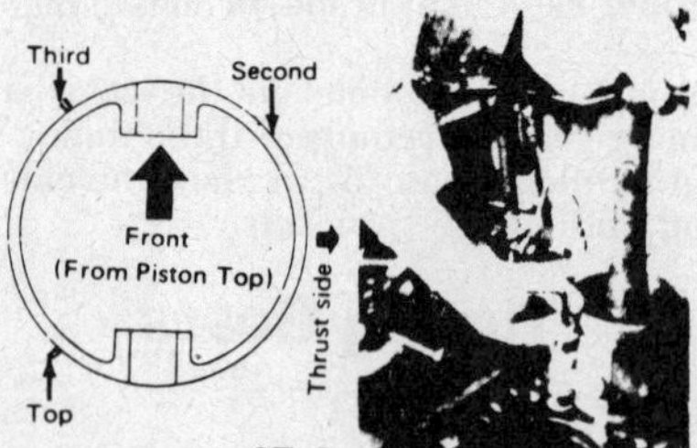

2T-C

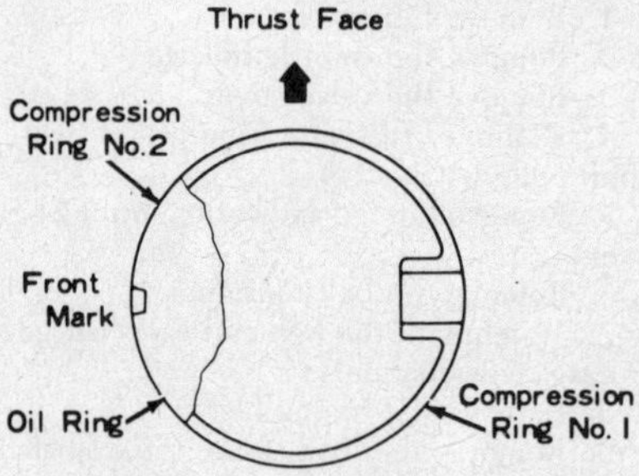

Ring installation on the 20R, 18R-C and 4M engines. The 4M has no front mark

PISTON AND CONNECTING ROD POSITIONING

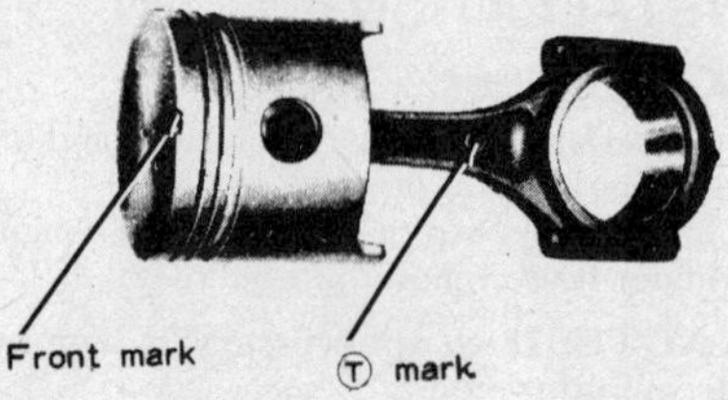

3KC and 2TC

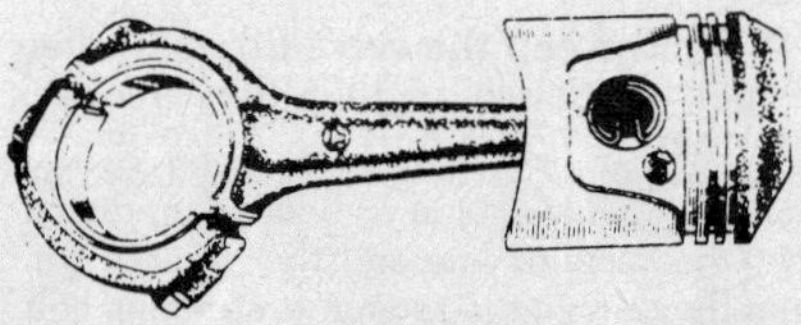

4M

ENGINE LUBRICATION

Oil Pan

REMOVAL AND INSTALLATION

Corolla and 1975-81 Corona

1. Open the engine compartment hood.
2. Raise the front end of the car and support it with jack stands.
3. Remove the splash shield from underneath the engine.
4. Place a jack under the transmission to support it.
5. Unfasten the bolts which secure the engine rear supporting crossmember to the chassis.

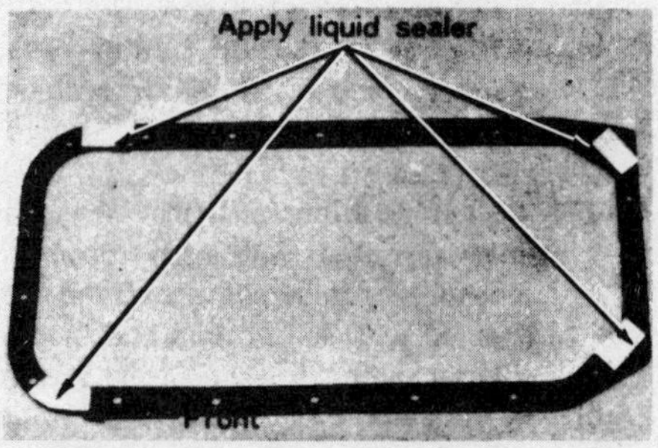

Apply sealer to the 20R and 2TC oil pan gasket as shown

6. Raise the jack under the transmission, *slightly*.
7. Unbolt the oil pan and work it out from underneath the engine.

NOTE: If the oil pan does not come out easily, it may be necessary to unbolt the rear engine mounts from the crossmember.

Installation is performed in the reverse order of removal. On Corolla models equipped with the 2T-C (1600 cc) engine and Corona models with 20R engines, apply liquid sealer to the four corners of the oil pan. Tighten the oil pan securing bolts to the following specifications:

3K-C engine:
2-3 ft/lbs
2T-C engine:
4-6 ft/lbs
18R-C engine:
3-5 ft/lbs
20R engine:
3.0-6.0 ft/lbs
1AC-2A-3A
31-47 in/lbs

Carina, Cressida, Corona Mark II, Celica

1. Drain the oil.
2. Raise the front end of the car with jacks and support it with jack stands.

CAUTION

Be sure that the car is supported securely. Remember, you will be working underneath it.

OIL PUMP CLEARANCE SPECIFICATIONS

All measurements are given in inches unless noted

Engine	Tip Clearance (Driven)	Side Clearance	Body Clearance	Relief Valve Spring Installed Length
3K-C	0.0016-0.0063	0.0012-0.0035	0.004-0.006	1.45
2T-C	0.0016-0.0063	0.0012-0.0035	0.004-0.006	1.45
4M	0.016	0.0012-0.0035	0.0012-0.0024	1.89
20R	0.0059-0.0083	0.0012-0.0035	0.0035-0.0059	—
1A-C, 3A	0.0023-0.0122 ①	0.0014-0.0033	0.0039-0.0075	—
4ME	—	0.0012-0.0035	0.0012-0.0024	②
3T-C	0.0016-0.0063	0.0012-0.0035	0.0039-0.0063	—

① Drive—0.0040-0.0100 inch
② 1980-81 opening pressure 71-85 psi

3. Detach the steering relay rod and the tie rods from the idler arm, pitman arm, and steering knuckles, as detailed below.
4. Remove the engine stiffening plates.
5. Remove the splash shields from underneath the engine.
6. Support the front of the engine with a jack and remove the front engine mount attaching bolts.
7. Raise the front of the engine *slightly* with the jack.
8. Unbolt and withdraw the oil pan.

Installation is performed in the reverse order of removal. Apply liquid sealer to the four corners of the oil pan gasket used on 2T-C engines. Torque the oil pan securing bolts to the following specifications:

2T-C engines:
4-6 ft/lbs.
18R-C engines:
3-5 ft/lbs.
4M engines:
4-6 ft/lbs.

Tercel

1. Disconnect the negative battery terminal.
2. Jack up the vehicle and support it with jack stands.
3. Drain the oil.
4. Remove the sway bar and any other necessary steering linkage parts.
5. Disconnect the exhaust pipe from the manifold.
6. Jack up the engine enough to take the weight off it.
7. Remove the engine mounts and engine shock absorber.
8. Continue to jack up the engine enough to remove the pan.
9. Remove the pan bolts and remove the pan.
10. Installation is the reverse of removal.

Always use a new pan gasket when reinstalling the pan.

Rear Main Oil Seal

REPLACEMENT

All Engines

NOTE: On the 1A-C, 2A, 3A engines, they must be removed before this procedure can be attempted.

1. Remove the transmission.
2. Remove the clutch cover assembly and flywheel.
3. Remove the oil seal retaining plate, complete with the oil seal.
4. Use a screwdriver to pry the old seal from the retaining plate. Be careful not to damage the plate.
5. Install the new seal, carefully, by using a block of wood to drift it into place.

CAUTION

Do not damage the seal; a leak will result.

6. Lubricate the lips of the seal with multipurpose grease.

Installation is the reverse of removal.

Oil Pump

REMOVAL AND INSTALLATION

All engines (Except 20R)

1. Remove the oil pan, as outlined in the appropriate section above.
2. On passenger cars and pick-up trucks, unbolt the oil pump securing bolts and remove it as an assembly.
3. On Land Cruisers:
   a. Remove the oil strainer and unfasten the union nuts on the oil pump pipe.
   b. Remove the lock wire and the oil pump retaining bolts and pipe from the engine.

Installation is the reverse of removal.

20R Engine

1. Remove the oil pan.
2. Remove the three bolts which secure the oil strainer.
3. Remove the drive belts, the pulley bolt, and the crankshaft pulley.
4. Unfasten the bolts which secure the oil pump housing and remove the pump assembly.
5. Remove the oil pump drive spline and the rubber O-ring.

Installation is the reverse of removal. Apply sealer to the top oil pump housing bolt. Use a new oil strainer gasket.

CHECKING CLEARANCE

Wash the pump thoroughly and allow to air dry. Check for shiny spots which indicate wear and scuffling. Check backlash of gears and measure free length of relief valve spring, then check play between gears and housing, gears and pump cover and between gears themselves. See specification chart for tolerances.

ENGINE COOLING

Radiator

REMOVAL AND INSTALLATION

All Models

1. Drain the cooling system.
2. Unfasten the clamps and remove the radiator upper and lower hoses. If equipped with an automatic transmission, remove the oil cooler lines.
3. Detach the hood lock cable and remove

the hood lock from the radiator upper support.

NOTE: It may be necessary to remove the grille in order to gain access to the hood lock/radiator support assembly.

4. Remove the fan shroud, if so equipped.
5. On models equipped with the closed cooling system, disconnect the hose from the thermal expansion tank and remove the tank from its bracket.
6. Unbolt and remove the radiator upper support.
7. Unfasten the bolts and remove the radiator.

Installation is performed in the reverse order of removal. Remember to check the transmission fluid level on cars with automatic transmissions.

Fill the radiator to the specified level.

Water Pump

REMOVAL AND INSTALLATION

All Engines Except 1A-C, 2A and 3A

1. Drain the cooling system.
2. Unfasten the fan shroud securing bolts and remove the fan shroud, if so equipped.
3. Loosen the alternator adjusting link bolt and remove the drive belt.
4. Repeat Step 3 for the air pump, air conditioning compressor, or power steering pump drive belts, if so equipped.
5. Detach the bypass and radiator hoses from the water pump.
6. Unfasten the water pump retaining bolts and remove the water pump and fan assembly, using care not to damage the radiator with the fan.

CAUTION

If the fan is equipped with a fluid coupling, do not tip the fan/pump assembly on its side, as the fluid will run out.

Installation is the reverse of removal. Always use a new gasket between the pump body and its mounting. Check for leaks after installation is completed.

1A-C, 2A and 3A only

1. Drain the radiator. Save the coolant as it can be reused.
2. Loosen all necessary drive belts.
3. Remove the top timing belt cover.
4. Remove the bottom radiator hose from the water pump.
5. Remove the pump bolts and remove the pump.

NOTE: Always use a new gasket when replacing the pump.

6. Installation is the reverse of removal.

Thermostat

REMOVAL AND INSTALLATION

All Engines

1. Drain the cooling system.
2. Unfasten the clamp and remove the upper radiator hose from the water outlet elbow.
3. Unbolt and remove the water outlet (thermostat housing).
4. Withdraw the thermostat.

Installation is performed in the reverse order of removal procedure. Use a new gasket on the water outlet.

CAUTION

Be sure that the thermostat is installed with the spring pointing down.

EMISSION CONTROLS

Positive Crankcase Ventilation (PCV) System

A positive crankcase ventilation (PCV) system is used on all Toyotas sold in the United States. Blow-by gases are routed from the crankcase to the carburetor, where they are combined with the fuel/air mixture and burned during combustion.

A (PCV) valve is used in the line to prevent the gases in the crankcase from being ignited in case of a backfire. The amount of blow-by gases entering the mixture is also regulated by the PCV valve, which is spring-loaded and has a variable orifice.

The valve is either mounted on the valve cover or in the line which runs from the intake manifold to the crankcase.

REMOVAL AND INSTALLATION

Remove the PCV valve from the cylinder head cover on 3K-C and 1A-C-2A-3A engines. Remove the hose from the valve.

On the remainder of the engines, remove the valve from the manifold-to-crankcase hose.

Installation is the reverse of removal.

TESTING

Check the PCV system hoses and connections, to see that there are no leaks; then replace or tighten, as necessary.

To check the valve, remove it and blow through both of its ends. When blowing from the side which goes toward the intake manifold, very little air should pass through it. When blowing from the crankcase (valve cover) side, air should pass through freely.

Replace the valve with a new one, if the valve fails to function as outlined.

NOTE: Do not attempt to clean or adjust the valve; replace it with a new one.

Air Injection System

A belt-driven air pump supplies air to an injection manifold which has nozzles in each exhaust port. Injection of air at this point causes combustion of unburned hydrocarbons in the exhaust manifold rather than allowing them to escape into the atmosphere. An antibackfire valve controls the flow of air from the pump to prevent backfiring which results from an overly rich mixture under closed throttle conditions.

A check valve prevents hot exhaust gas backflow into the pump and hoses, in case of a pump failure, or when the antibackfire valve is working.

In addition newer engines have an air switching valve. On engines without catalytic converters, the ASV is used to stop air injection under a constant heavy engine load.

On engines with catalytic converters the ASV is used to protect the catalyst from overheating, by blocking the air necessary for the reaction.

On all engines, except the 2F, the relief valve is built into the ASV.

REMOVAL AND INSTALLATION

Air Pump

1. Disconnect the air hoses from the pump.
2. Loosen the bolt on the adjusting link and remove the drive belt.
3. Remove the pump.

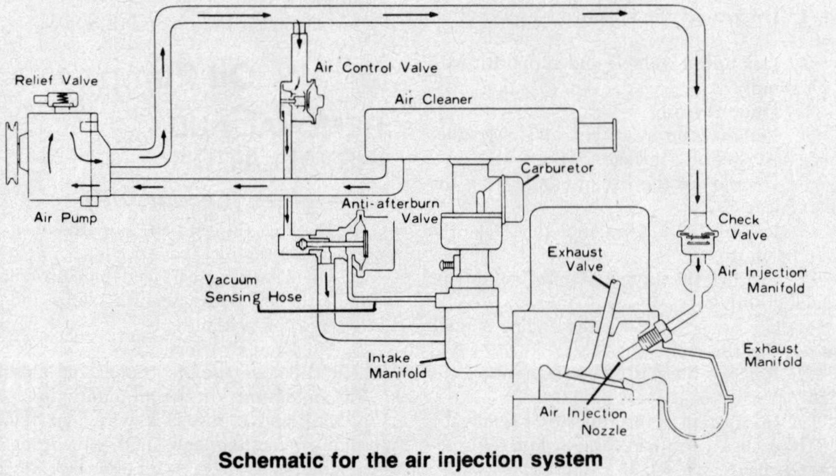

Schematic for the air injection system

CAUTION

Do not pry on the pump housing; it may be distorted.

Installation is in the reverse order of removal. Adjust the drive belt tension to ½-¾ in. under thumb pressure.

Antibackfire Valve and Air Switching Valve

1. Detach the air hoses from the valve.
2. Remove the valve securing bolt.
3. Withdraw the valve.

Installation is performed in the reverse order of removal.

Check Valve

1. Detach the intake hose from the valve.
2. Use an open-end wrench to remove the valve from its mounting.

Installation is the reverse of removal.

Relief Valve

1. Remove the air pump from the car.
2. Support the pump so that it cannot rotate.

CAUTION

Never clamp the pump in a vise; the aluminum case will be distorted.

Removing the relief valve from the air pump

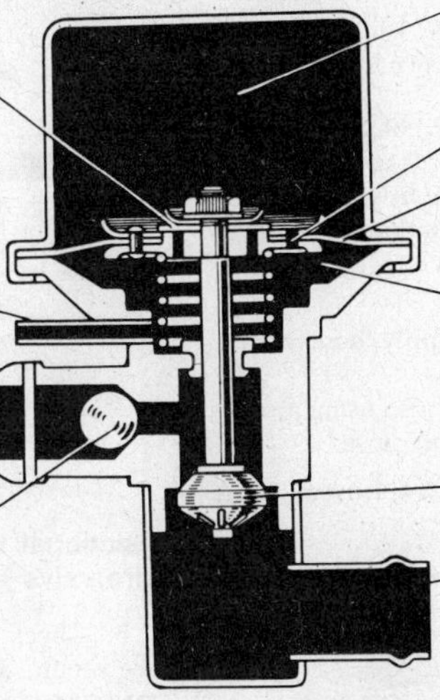

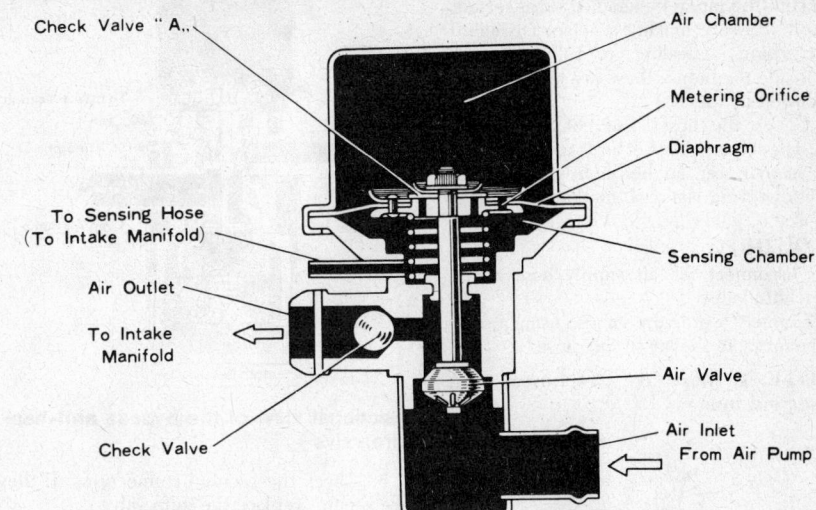

Sectional view of the gulp-type anti-backfire valve

3. Use a jaw-type puller to remove the relief valve from the top of the pump.
4. Position the new relief valve over the opening in the pump.

NOTE: The air outlet should be pointing toward the left.

5. Gently tap the relief valve home, using a block of wood and a hammer.
6. Install the pump on the engine, as outlined above.

Air Injection Manifold

1. Remove the check valve, as outlined above.
2. Loosen the air injection manifold attachment nuts and withdraw the manifold.

NOTE: On 20R and 4M engines, it will first be necessary to remove the exhaust manifold.

Installation is in the reverse of removal.

Air Injection Nozzles

1. Remove the air injection manifold as outlined above.
2. Remove the cylinder head, as detailed in the appropriate section, above.
3. Place a new nozzle on the cylinder head.
4. Install the air injection manifold over it.
5. Install the cylinder head on the engine block.

TESTING

Air Pump

CAUTION

Do not hammer, pry, or bend the pump housing while tightening the drive belt or testing the pump.

BELT TENSION AND AIR LEAKS

1. Before proceeding with the tests, check the pump drive belt tension to see if it is within specifications.

AIR INJECTION SYSTEM DIAGNOSIS CHART

Problem	Cause	Cure
Noisy drive belt	a) Loose belt b) Seized pump	a) Tighten belt b) Replace
Noisy pump	a) Leaking hose b) Loose hose c) Hose contacting other parts d) Diverter or check valve failure e) Pump mounting loose f) Defective pump	a) Trace and fix leak b) Tighten hose clamp c) Reposition hose d) Replace e) Tighten securing bolts f) Replace
No air supply	a) Loose belt b) Leak in hose or at fitting c) Defective anti-backfire valve d) Defective check valve e) Defective pump	a) Tighten belt b) Trace and fix leak c) Replace d) Replace e) Replace
Exhaust backfire	a) Vacuum or air leaks b) Defective anti-backfire valve c) Sticking choke d) Choke setting rich	a) Trace and fix leak b) Replace c) Service choke d) Adjust choke

2. Turn the pump by hand. If it has seized, the belt will slip, making a noise. Disregard any chirping, squealing, or rolling sounds from inside the pump; these are normal when it is turned by hand.

3. Check the hoses and connections for leaks. Hissing or a blast of air is indicative of a leak. Soapy water, applied lightly around the area in question, is a good method for detecting leaks.

AIR OUTPUT

1. Disconnect the air supply hose at the anitbackfire valve.

2. Connect a pressure gauge, using a suitable adaptor, to the air supply hose.

NOTE: If there are two hoses, plug the second one.

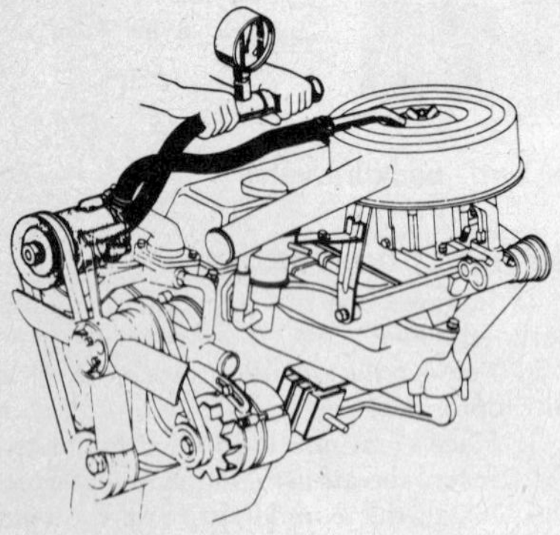

Checking the air pump output

3. With the engine at normal operating temperature, increase the idle speed to 1000-1500 rpm (1950 rpm-2T-C) and watch the vacuum gauge.

4. The air flow from the pump should be steady and fall between 2 and 6 psi. If it is unsteady or falls below this, the pump is defective and must be replaced.

PUMP NOISE DIAGNOSIS

The air pump is normally noisy; as engine speed increases, the noise of the pump will rise in pitch. The rolling sound the pump bearings make is normal. But if this sound becomes objectionable at certain speeds, the pump is defective and will have to be replaced.

A continual hissing sound from the air pump pressure relief valve at idle, indicates a defective valve. Replace the relief valve.

If the pump rear bearing fails, a continual knocking sound will be heard.

Antibackfire Valve Tests

There are two different types of antibackfire valve used with air injection systems. A bypass valve is used on all engines, while 1974 F engines for California use a gulp type of antibackfire valve. Test procedures for both types are given below.

GULP VALVE

1. Detach the air supply hose which runs between the pump and the gulp valve.

2. Connect a tachometer and run the engine to 1500-2000 rpm.

3. Allow the throttle to snap closed. This should produce a loud sucking sound from the gulp valve.

4. Repeat this operation several times. If no sound is present, the valve is not working or else the vacuum connections are loose.

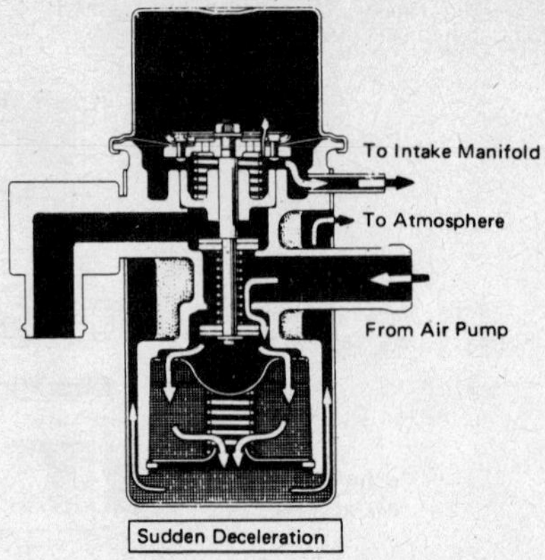

Sectional view of the bypass anti-backfire valve

5. Check the vacuum connections. If they are secure, replace the gulp valve.

BYPASS VALVE

1. Detach the hose, which runs from the bypass valve to the check valve, at the bypass valve hose connection.

2. Connect a tachometer to the engine. With the engine running at normal idle speed, check to see that air if flowing from the bypass valve hose connection.

3. Speed up the engine so it is running at 1500-2000 rpm. Allow the throttle to snap shut. The flow of air from the bypass valve at the check valve hose connection should stop momentarily and air should then flow from the exhaust port on the valve body or the silencer assembly.

4. Repeat Step 3 several times. If the flow of air is not diverted into the atmosphere from the valve exhaust port or if it fails to stop flowing from the hose connection, check the vacuum lines and connections. If these are tight, the valve is defective and requires replacement.

5. A leaking diaphragm will cause the air to flow out both the hose connection and the exhaust port at the same time. If this happens, replace the valve.

Air Switching Valve (ASV) Tests

1975-81 2T-C AND 20R ENGINES

1. Start the engine and allow it to reach normal operating temperature.

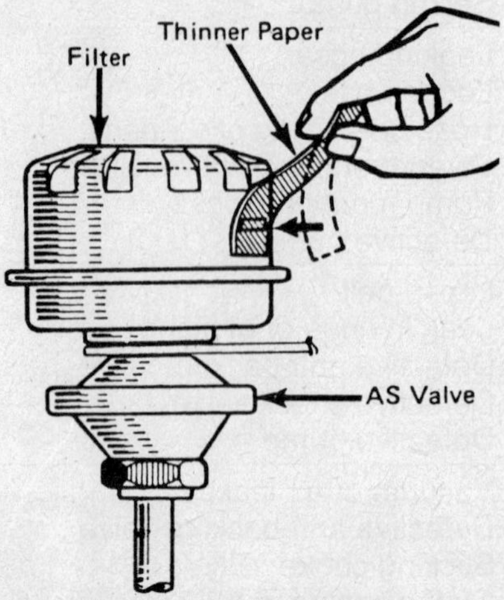

3K-C air suction valve test

2. At curb idle, the air from the bypass valve should be discharged through the hose which runs to the ASV.

3. When the vacuum line to the ASV is disconnected, the air from the bypass valve should be diverted out through the ASV-to-air cleaner hose. Reconnect the vacuum line.

4. Disconnect the ASV-to-check valve hose and connect a pressure gauge to it.

5. Increase the engine speed. The relief valve should open when the pressure gauge registers 2.7-6.5 psi.

6. If the ASV fails any of the above tests, replace it. Reconnect all hoses.

1975-81 4M Engines

1. Start the engine and allow it to reach normal operating temperature.

2. At curb idle, air from the pump should be discharged through the hose which runs to the check valve.

3. Race the engine and allow the throttle valve to snap shut. The air from the pump should be discharged into the air cleaner.

4. Disconnect the ASV-to-check valve hose and connect a pressure gauge to it.

5. Increase the engine speed gradually. The relief valve should open when the gauge registers 3.7-7.7 psi. Reconnect the check valve hose.

6. Unfasten the wiring connector and the hoses from the solenoid valve, which is attached to the ASV. Air should pass through the solenoid valve when either the top or bottom port is blown into.

7. Connect a 12V power source to the terminals on the valve. No air should flow through the valve when either port is blown into.

8. If the solenoid valve or the ASV fail any of the above tests, replace either or both of them, as necessary.

Vacuum Delay Valve Test

1975-81 2T-C AND 20R ENGINES

The vacuum delay valve is located in the line which runs from the intake manifold to either the vacuum surge tank (20R) or to the ASV (2T-C). To check it, proceed as follows:

1. Remove the vacuum delay valve from the vacuum line. Be sure to note which end points toward the intake manifold.

2. When air is blown in from the ASV (surge tank) side, it should pass through the valve freely.

3. When air is blown in from the intake manifold side, a resistance should be felt.

4. Replace the valve if it fails either of the above tests.

5. Install the valve in the vacuum line, being careful not to install it backwards.

Check Valve Test

1. Before starting the test, check all of the hoses and connections for leaks.

2. Detach the air supply hose from the check valve.

3. Insert a suitable probe into the check valve and depress the plate. Release it; the plate should return to its original position against the valve seat. If binding is evident, replace the valve.

4. With the engine running at normal operating temperature, gradually increase its speed to 1500 rpm. Check for exhaust gas

leakage. If any is present, replace the valve assembly.

NOTE: Vibration and flutter of the check valve at idle speed is a normal condition and does not mean that the valve should be replaced.

Air Suction System

The Air Suction System, available on the 3K-C and 2T-C engines brings fresh, filtered air into the exhaust ports to promote better buring of hydrocarbons. It also supplies the air necessary for the oxidizing reaction in the catalytic converter.

There are no adjustments on the system and, should it malfunction, the unit must be replaced as a whole.

To check the system, look over all lines for cracks or damage. If checks indicate no problems, start the engine and put a thin sheet of paper over the inlet port of the filter. If it is drawn to the opening, the unit is operating. If not, remove the filter and test the valve opening the same way. Replace the filter, if necessary.

If there is still no indication of a draw, the valve itself is malfunctioning and must be replaced.

Evaporative Emission Control System

To prevent hydrocarbon emissions from entering the atmosphere, Toyota vehicles use evaporative emission control (EEC) systems. All models use a "charcoal canister" storage system.

The charcoal canister storage system stores fuel vapors in a canister filled with activated charcoal. All models use a vacuum switching valve to purge the system. The air filter is an integral part of the charcoal canister.

REMOVAL AND INSTALLATION

Removal and installation of the various evaporative emission control system components consists of disconnecting hoses, loosening securing screws, and removing the part which is to be replaced from its mounting bracket. Installation is the reverse of removal.

NOTE: When replacing any EEC system hoses, always use hoses that are fuel-resistant or are marked "EVAP."

TESTING

EEC System Troubleshooting

There are several things which may be checked if a malfunction of the evaporative emission control system is suspected.

1. Leaks may be traced by using a hydrocarbon tester. Run the test probe along the lines and connections. The meter will indicate the presence of a leak by a high hydrocarbon (HC) reading. This method is much more accurate than visual inspection which would only indicate the presence of leaks large enough to pass liquid.

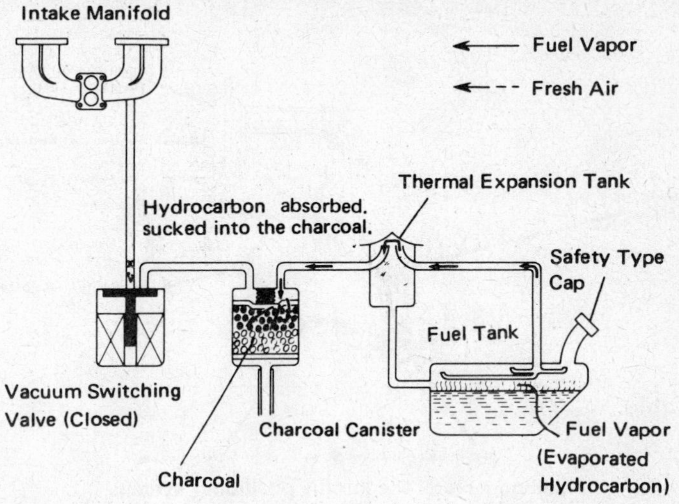

Schematic for charcoal storage system w/thermal expansion tank

2. Leaks may be caused by any of the following:
   a. Defective or worn hoses;
   b. Disconnected or pinched hoses;
   c. Improperly routed hoses;
   d. A defective filler cap or safety valve (sealed cap system).

NOTE: If it becomes necessary to replace any of the hoses used in the evaporative emission control system, use only hoses which are fuel-resistant or are marked "EVAP."

3. If the fuel tank, storage case, or thermal expansion tank collapse, it may be the fault of clogged or pinched vent lines, a defective vapor separator, or a plugged or incorrect filler cap.
4. To test the filler cap (if it is the safety valve type), clean it and place it against your mouth. Blow into the relief valve housing. If the cap passes pressure with light blowing or if it fails to release with hard blowing, it is defective and must be replaced.

NOTE: Use the proper cap for the type of system used; either a sealed cap or safety valve cap, as required.

Purge Control Valve–1975-81

California models equipped with the 4M six-cylinder engine have a canister-mounted purge control valve, starting with 1974 models.

The purge control valve is connected to a carburetor port, which is located above the throttle control valve. When the engine is stopped or idling, there is no vacuum signal at the purge control valve so that it remains closed. When the throttle valve opens, the carburetor port is uncovered and a vacuum signal is sent to the purge control valve, which opens and allows the vapors stored in the canister to be pulled into the carburetor.

Check purge control valve operation in the following manner:

1. Note the routing of the vacuum lines and remove the charcoal canister from the car.
2. Place your finger over the purge control valve opening, which is located at the center of the canister on its top side.
3. Gently blow through the vapor intake (the other opening on the top of the canister). No resistance should be felt.
4. Uncover the purge control valve opening and blow through it. No air should be felt coming from the vapor intake or the fresh air intake (located on the bottom of the canister).
5. If the purge control valve fails either of the tests in Steps 3 or 4, replace the canister assembly. If the valve is OK, then install the canister in the car.
6. If the purge control valve still doesn't appear to be working properly when installed in the car, check for damaged vacuum lines or a clogged carburetor port.

Check Valve

Rough idling when the gas tank is full is probably caused by a defective check valve. To test it, proceed as follows:

1. Run the engine at idle.
2. Clamp the hose between the vacuum switching valve or carburetor (4M-Calif) and the charcoal canister.
3. If the engine idle becomes smooth, replace the check valve.

Throttle Positioner

On Toyotas with an engine modification system, a throttle positioner is included to reduce exhaust emissions during deceleration. The positioner prevents the throttle from closing completely. Vacuum is reduced under the throttle valve which, in turn, acts on the retard chamber of the distributor vacuum unit (if so equipped). This compensates for the loss of engine braking caused by the partially open throttle.

Once the vehicle drops below a predetermined speed, the vacuum switching valve provides vacuum to the throttle positioner diaphragm; the throttle positioner retracts allowing the throttle valve to close completely. The distributor also is returned to normal operation.

ADJUSTMENT

1. Start the engine and allow it to reach normal operating temperature.

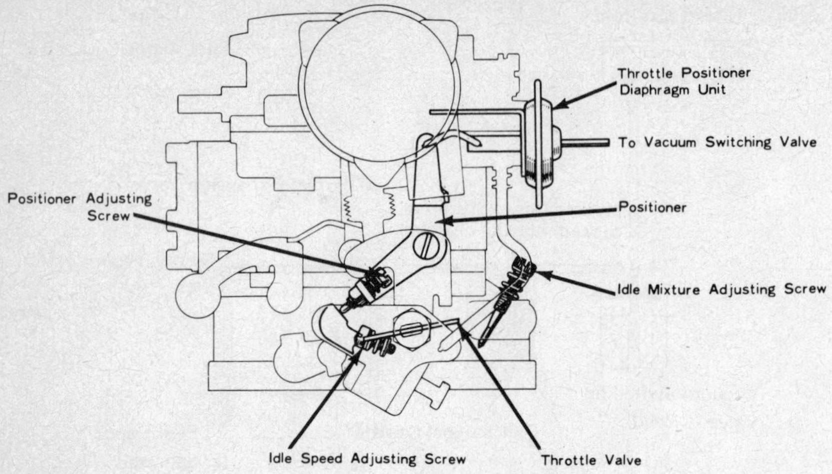

Components of the throttle positioner system

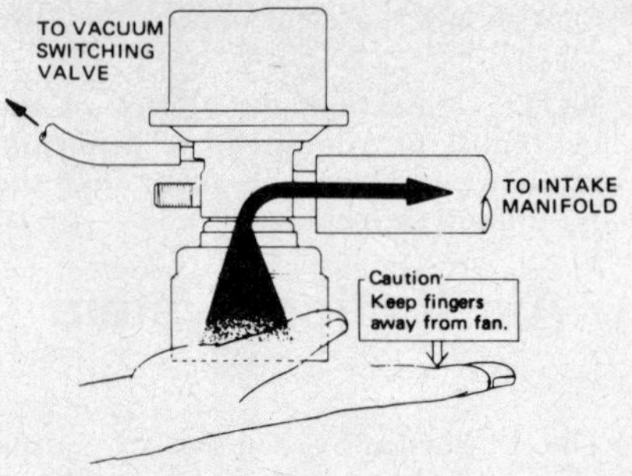

Checking the mixture control valve

2. Adjust the idle speed.

NOTE: Leave the tachometer connected after completing the idle adjustments, as it will be needed in Step 5, below.

3. Detach the vacuum line from the positioner diaphragm unit and plug the line.
4. Accelerate the engine slightly to set the throttle positioner.
5. Check the engine speed with a tachometer when the throttle positioner is set.
6. If necessary, adjust the engine speed, with the throttle positioner adjusting screw, to the specifications.
7. Connect the vacuum hose to the positioner diaphragm.
8. The throttle lever should be freed from the positioner as soon as the vacuum hose is connected. Engine idle should return to normal.
9. If the throttle positioner fails to function properly, check its linkage, and vacuum diaphragm. If there are no defects in either of these, the fault probably lies in the vacuum switching valve or the speed marker unit.

NOTE: Due to the complexity of these two components they require special test equipment.

MIXTURE CONTROL SYSTEM

The mixture control valve, used on all 1978 and later engines (except 4M-E), aids in combustion of unburned fuel during periods of deceleration. The mixture control valve is operated by the vacuum switching valve during periods of deceleration to admit additional fresh air into the intake manifold. The extra air allows more complete combustion of the fuel, thus reducing hydrocarbon emissions.

REMOVAL AND INSTALLATION

1. Remove the vacuuum switching valve line from the mixture control valve.
2. Remove the intake manifold hose from the valve.
3. Remove the valve from its engine mounting.

Installation is the reverse order of removal.

TESTING

1. Start the engine and allow it to idle (warmed up).
2. Place your hand over the air intake at the bottom of the valve.

CAUTION

Keep your fingers clear of the engine fan.

3. Increase the engine speed and then release the throttle.
4. Suction should be felt at the air intake only while the engine is decelerating. Once the engine has returned to idle, no suction should be felt.

If the above test indicates a malfunction, proceed with the next step; if not, the mixture control valve is functioning properly and requires no further attention.

5. Disconnect the vacuum line from the mixture control valve. If suction can be felt underneath the valve with the engine at idle, the valve seat is defective and must be replaced.
6. Reconnect the vacuum line to the valve. Disconnect the other end of the line from the vacuum switching valve and place it in your mouth.
7. With the engine idling, suck on the end of the vacuum line to duplicate the action of the vacuum switching valve.
8. Suction at the valve air intake should only be felt for an instant. If air cannot be drawn into the valve at all, or if it is continually drawn in, replace the mixture control valve.

If the mixture control valve is functioning properly, and all of the hose and connections are in good working order, the vacuum switching valve is probably at fault.

NOTE: Because the vacuum switching valve and related components are complex, special equipment is required to test them.

THROTTLE POSITIONER SETTINGS

(rpm)

Year	Engine	Engine rpm (Positioner Set)
1975-77 ①	2T-C	1500 MT 1400 AT ①
	20R	1400 MT 1050 AT
	4M	1200 AT
	3K-C	1500 (Canada)
1978-80	2T-C	1400 MT 1200 AT
	3T-C	1600 MT 1300 AT ②
	20R	1050
	4M	950
	4M-E	—
	1A-C, 3A	N.A.

① 1977: 1200
② Calif.: 1400
AT Automatic transmission
MT Manual transmission

VACUUM LIMITER SYSTEM

4M-E 1980-81

This system allows fresh air to enter the air intake chamber upon sudden deceleration to reduce hydrocarbons and carbon dioxide emissions.

REMOVAL AND INSTALLATION

1. Remove the two vacuum lines.
2. Remove the intake chamber line.
3. Remove the valve from its mounting.
4. Installation is the reverse of removal.

TESTING

1. Disconnect the air inlet hose of the vacuum limiter from the air connector and plug the air connector port.
2. Start the engine.
3. Close the inlet of the vacuum limiter with your finger.
4. Increase the speed of the engine and then release the throttle.
5. When the throttle valve is opened and closed you should momentarily feel vacuum. If not the vacuum limiter is defective and must be replaced.

Auxiliary System

An auxiliary enrichment system, which Toyota calls an "Auxiliary System", is used on all models, starting in 1975.

When the engine is cold, an auxiliary enrichment circuit in the carburetor is operated to squirt extra fuel into the acceleration circuit in order to prevent the mixture from becoming too lean.

TESTS

1. Check for clogged, pinched, disconnected, or misrouted vacuum lines.
2. With the engine cold (below 75° F), remove the top of the air cleaner, and allow the engine to idle.
3. Disconnect the vacuum line from the carburetor AAP unit. Gasoline should squirt out the accelerator pump jet.

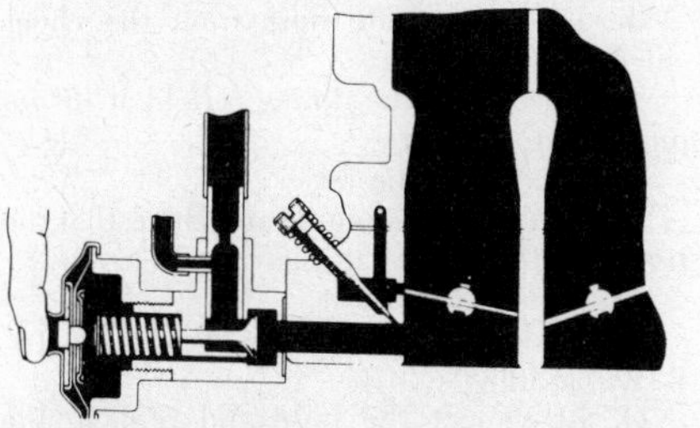

Testing the diaphragm on the auxiliary slow system

4. If gas doesn't squirt out of the jet, check for vacuum at the AAP vacuum line with the engine idling. If there is no vacuum and the hoses are in good shape, the thermostatic vacuum valve is defective and must be replaced.
5. If the gas doesn't squirt out and vacuum is present at the vacuum line in Step 4, the AAP unit is defective and must be replaced.
6. Repeat Step 3 with the engine at normal operating temperature. If gasoline squirts out of the pump jet, the thermostatic vacuum valve is defective and must be replaced.
7. Reconnect all of the vacuum lines and install the top on the air cleaner.

CHOKE RETURN SYSTEM

Because of the chance of seriously damaging the catalytic converter by operating the automobile with the choke out for long periods of time, the 3K-C engine is equipped with an automatic manual choke return system.

Utilizing a holding coil, a holding plate and a return spring, the system generates a magnetic force when the coolant temperature is below 104° F, holding the choke plate open.

However, when the coolant exceeds 104° F, the thermo switch opens, cutting off the current flow and allows the return spring to pull the choke plate open.

Most problems in this system will be electrical. Should the system malfunction, check for continuity in all circuits and replace the part not operating.

CHOKE OPENER SYSTEM

If a cold engine is driven soon after starting, the automatic choke system will close the choke plate, resulting in high levels of emissions. To combat that situation 1975-77 California and high Altitude 2T-C engine and all 1978-81 engines are equipped with a system that forcibly holds the choke plate open.

When the coolant is below 140° F the thermo wax in the TVSV closes the valve and prohibits any vacuum from acting on the choke diaphragm. This keeps the choke open. Above 140° F the wax expands, opening the valve, and allows the choke plate to operate normally. Should the system malfunction, replace the TVSV.

FAST IDLE CAM BREAKER

After warm up this system forcibly releases the fast idle cam which lowers the engine speed.

Testing

1. Use a 3-way connector to connect a vacuum gauge to the fast idle cam breaker.
2. Use enough vacuum line to bring the gauge into the vehicle and set it on the drivers seat.
3. Perform a road test observing the speedometer and vacuum gauge.

NOTE: With the coolant temperature below (122° F) check that the gauge reads zero regardless of engine speed.

4. Warm the engine and check that the vacuum gauge indicates high vacuum below 7 mph.
5. Check that the vacuum gauge indicates lower vacuum than the vacuum indicated in Step 4 at 16 mph.
6. Disconnect the vacuum gauge and reconnect the hose to its proper location.
7. Stop the engine.
8. Disconnect the hose from the fast idle cam breaker.
9. Set the fast idle cam.
10. While holding the throttle valve slightly open, pull up the fast idle cam and then release the throttle.
11. Start the engine, but do not touch the accelerator.
12. Reconnect the hose and check that the fast idle cam is released and the engine rpm is lowered.

NOTE: If the above tests a positive, this procedure is complete. If not, inspect the breaker diaphragm, TVSV valve, speed sensor or VSV.

HOT IDLE COMPENSATION VALVE

This system allows the air controlled by the HIC valve to enter the intake manifold to maintain proper air fuel mixture during high temperatures at idle.

Testing

1. Close the pipe to the intake manifold with your finger.
2. Blow air into the open end. The passage should be closed at temperatures below 86° F.
3. Heat the valve in hot water.

CAUTION

Do not allow water to get in the valve.

4. Blow air into the valve again. As the temperature nears 104° F the passage should open.
5. A small amount of air should flow through the valve when the temperature of the valve is 104° F to 158° F.
6. A large amount of air should flow through the valve when the temperature is above 176° F.
7. If air does not flow through the valve replace it.

SECONDARY SLOW CIRCUIT FUEL CUT SYSTEM

This system cuts off part of the fuel in the secondary slow circuit of the carburetor to prevent dieseling.

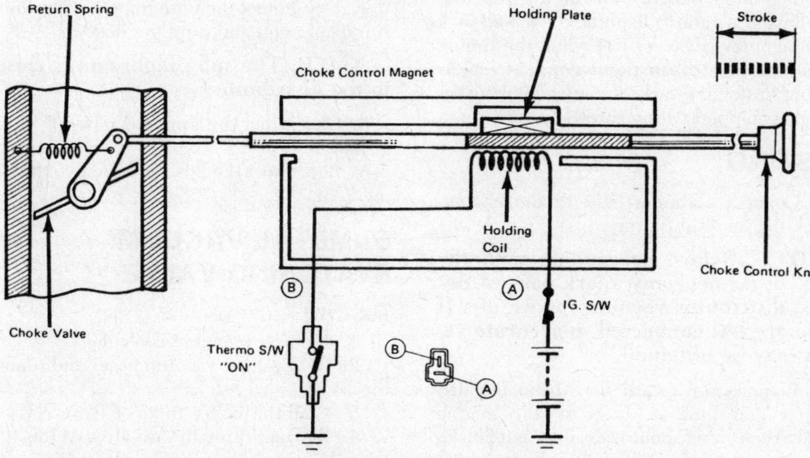

3K-C choke return system

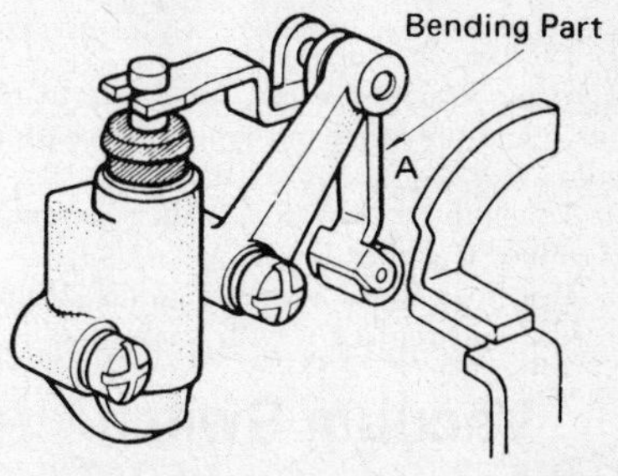

Secondary fuel valve adjustment

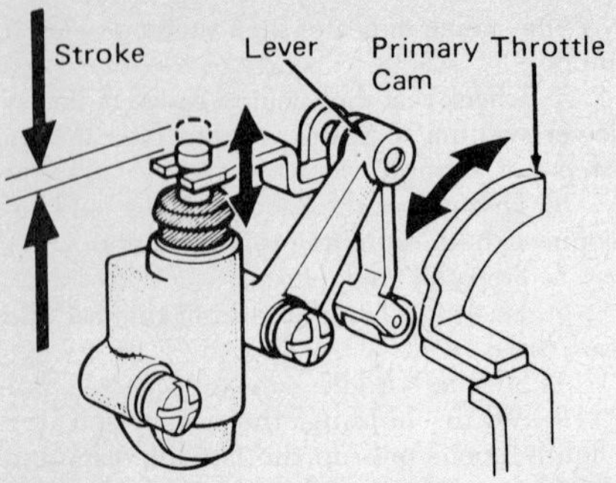

Secondary slow circuit fuel cut system stroke

Testing

1. Completely open and close the throttle valve.
2. Measure the stroke of the valve. (0.059-0.0079 in.)
3. If necessary adjust the stroke.

NOTE: The stroke should be set to the above specifications before the secondary throttle valve opens.

Deceleration Fuel Cut System

This system cuts off part of the fuel in the slow circuit of the carburetor to prevent overheating and afterburning in the exhaust system.

TESTING

1. Start the engine.
2. Check that the engine runs normally.
3. Pinch the vacuum hose to the vacuum switch.
4. Gradually increase the engine speed to 2500 rpm. Check that the engine misfires between 2000-2500 rpm.

CAUTION

Perform this procedure quickly to prevent overheating of the catalytic converter.

5. Release the pinched hose and see that the engine returns to normal operation.
6. Unplug the solenoid valve until the engine misfires or stalls.
7. Stop the engine and reconnect the wire.

NOTE: If the above tests are positive the procedure is complete. If not, inspect the solenoid valve and vacuum switch.

Fuel Solenoid

1. Remove the solenoid.
2. Using two test wires, hook one to the positive and the other to the negative battery terminals.
3. Touch these two wires to the solenoid to determines if it clicks.
4. If it does click, it is operational. If not, discard it and replace it with a new one.

Vacuum Switch

1. Use a ohmmeter to check the continuity between the switch and the terminal body.
2. Start the engine.
3. Check that there is no continuity between the switch and the terminal body. If there is replace the switch.

HIGH ALTITUDE COMPENSATION SYSTEM

For all engines to be sold in areas over 4000 ft. in altitude, a system has been installed to automatically lean out the fuel mixture by supplying additional air. This also results in lower emissions.

Low atmospheric pressure allows the bellows in the system to expand and close a port, allowing more air to enter from different sources.

In the 2T-C and 20R engines, this also results in a timing advance to improve driveability.

All parts in this system must be replaced. The only adjustment available is in the timing.

HOT AIR INTAKE–ALL ENGINES

In order to keep the temperature of the air drawn into the carburetor as constant as possible, all engines are equipped with a Hot Air Intake System (HAI).

In all engines, the system depends on a thermo valve to control the temperature.

At normal temperatures the air is drawn through the inlet in the air filter. When the temperature drops, the valve switches position, opening the way for air to be drawn from around the exhaust manifold.

When inspecting, check all hoses for poor connections or damage and visually check the air control valve in the air duct.

NOTE: When checking valve movement, do not push too strongly on the control face.

Should there be a malfunction, replace the part involved.

Dual-Diaphragm Distributor

Some Toyota models are equipped with a dual-diaphragm distributor unit. This distributor has a retard diaphragm, as well as a diaphragm for advance. Retarding the timing helps to reduce exhaust emissions, as well as making up for the lack of engine braking on models equipped with a throttle positioner.

TESTING

1. Connect a timing light to the engine. Check the ignition timing.

NOTE: Before proceeding with the tests, disconnect any spark control devices, distributor vacuum valves, etc. If these are left connected, inaccurate results may be obtained.

2. Remove the retard hose from the distributor and plug it. Increase the engine speed. The timing should advance. If it fails to do so, then the vacuum unit is faulty and must be replaced.
3. Check the timing with the engine at normal idle speed. Unplug the retard hose and connect it to the vacuum unit. The timing should instantly be retarded from 4 to 10 degrees. If this does not occur, the retard diaphragm has a leak and the vacuum unit must be replaced.

COLD ADVANCE SYSTEM

This system is designed to improve cold engine performance and fuel economy at idle.

Testing

1. Hook up your timing light to the engine.
2. Start the engine.
3. With the coolant temperature below 86° F disconnect the top hose of the BVSV (bi-metal vacuum switching valve) and plug it.
4. Check that the timing is 18° BTDC at idle.
5. Disconnect the hose from the check valve (black side).
6. Check that the timing is held at 18° for one minute or more.
7. Reconnect the hoses.
8. Warm up the engine and check that the timing is 18° BTDC at idle.
9. Repeat Step 3.
10. Check that the timing is now 10° BTDC at idle.
11. Reconnect the hose and remove the timing light.

NOTE: If the above tests are positive, your test is complete. If not inspect the check valve, BVSV or the distributor vacuum advance.

IDLE ADVANCE SYSTEM W/O COLD ADVANCE

This system is designed to improve fuel economy at idle. The ignition system advances the ignition timing only while the engine is idling. The distributor is equipped with two diaphragms that have different vacuum advance characteristics.

Testing

1. Hook up your timing light to the engine.
2. Start the engine.
3. Check that the ignition timing is about 18° BTDC at idle.
4. Disconnect the hose from the distributor sub diaphragm and plug the hose.

NOTE: The sub diaphragm is closest to the distributor.

5. Check that the timing is now 10° BTDC at idle.
6. Reconnect the hose and remove the timing light.

BI-METAL VACUUM SWITCHING VALVE

Testing

1. Drain the engine coolant.
2. Remove the vacuum hoses and remove the BVSV.
3. Cool the BVSV to 86° F.
4. Blow air through the valve. At this time the valve should be closed and not allow air to pass.

5. Heat the valve to 111° F. The valve should open and allow air to pass through.
6. Repeat Step 4.
7. If the valve is inoperative it must be replaced.
8. Apply a liquid sealer to the threads and replace the valve.
9. Reconnect the vacuum lines.
10. Refill the coolant.

DISTRIBUTOR VACUUM ADVANCE TEST

1. Remove the distributor cap and rotor.
2. Check that the advance moves when vacuum is applied to it.

NOTE: If the vacuum advance is not operating, it must be replaced.

3. Reinstall the rotor and distributor cap.

Spark Control System

Starting in 1975, non-California Corolla models have a spark delay valve (SDV) in the distributor vacuum line. In 1978-81 all California 2T-C engines, all non-California 20R engines, and all 3K-C and 4M engines are equipped with the spark control system. The valve has a small orifice in it, which slows down the vacuum flow to the vacuum advance unit on the distributor. By delaying the vacuum to the distributor, a reduction in HC and CO emissions is possible.

When the coolant temperature is below 95° F-140° F (1975-77) or 86° F (1978-81 2T-C) or 122° F (4M), 104° F (20R) or 95° F (1978-81 3K-C), a coolant temperature operated vacuum control valve is opened, allowing the distributor to receive undelayed, ported vacuum through a separate vacuum line. Above 95° F-140° F this line is blocked, and all ported vacuum must go through the spark delay valve.

SPARK CONTROL VALVE OPERATING TEMPERATURES

	Degrees F
Closed	
1975-77 non-Cal. Corolla	95
1978-81 3K-C	95
1978-81 4M	122
1978-81 20R	104
1978-81 2T-C	86
Open	
1975-77 non-Cal	140
1978-81 3K-C	120
1978-81 4M	147
1978-81 20R	129
1978-81 2T-C	111

TESTING

1. Allow the engine to cool, so that the coolant temperature is below that required. See the chart.
2. Disconnect the vacuum line which runs from the coolant temperature operated vacuum valve to the vacuum advance unit at the advance unit end. Connect the vacuum gauge to this line.
3. Start the engine. Increase the engine speed; the gauge should indicate a vacuum.
4. Allow the engine to warm-up to normal operating temperature. Increase the engine speed; this time the vacuum gauge should read zero.
5. Replace the coolant temperature operated vacuum valve, if it fails either of these tests. Disconnect the vacuum gauge and reconnect the vacuum lines.
6. Remove the spark delay valve from the vacuum line, noting which side faces the distributor.
7. Connect a hand-operated vacuum pump which has a built-in vacuum gauge to the carburetor side of the spark delay valve.
8. Connect a vacuum gauge to the distributor side of the valve.
9. Operate the hand pump to create a vacuum. The vacuum gauge on the distributor side should show a hesitation before registering.
10. The gauge reading on the pump side should drop slightly, taking several seconds for it to balance with the reading on the other gauge.
11. If Steps 9 and 10 are negative, replace the spark delay valve.
12. Remove the vacuum gauge from the distributor side of the valve. Cover the distributor side of the valve with your finger and operate the pump to create a vacuum of 15 in. Hg.
13. The reading on the pump gauge should remain steady. If the gauge reading drops, replace the valve.
14. Remove your finger; the reading on the gauge should drop slowly. If the reading goes to zero rapidly, replace the valve.

Engine Modifications System

Toyota uses an assortment of engine modifications to regulate exhaust emissions. Most of these devices fall into the category of engine vacuum controls. There are three principal components used on the engine modifications system, as well as a number of smaller parts. The three major components are: a speed sensor; a computer (speed marker); and a vacuum switching valve.

The vacuum switching valve and computer circuit operates most of the emission control components. Depending upon year and engine usage, the vacuum switching valve and computer may operate the purge control for the evaporative emission control system; the transmission controlled spark (TCS) or speed controlled spark (SCS); the dual-diaphragm distributor; and the throttle positioner systems.

The functions of the evaporative emission control system, the throttle positioner, and the dual-diaphragm distributor are described in detail in the sections above. However, a word is necessary about the functions of the TCS and SCS systems before discussing the operation of the vacuum switching valve/computer circuit.

The major difference between the transmission controlled spark and speed controlled spark systems is in the manner in which systems operation is determined.

Below a predetermined speed, or any gear other than fourth, the vacuum advance unit on the distributor is rendered inoperative or, on F engines, timing is retarded. By changing the distributor advance curve in this manner, it is possible to reduce emissions of oxides of nitrogen (NOx).

NOTE: Some engines are equipped with a thermo-sensor so that the TDS or SCS system only operates when the coolant temperature is 140°-212° F.

Aside from determining the conditions outlined above, the vacuum switching valve computer circuit operates other devices in the emission control system.

The computer acts as a speed marker; at certain speeds it sends a signal to the vacuum switching valve which acts as a gate, opening and closing the emission control system vacuum circuits.

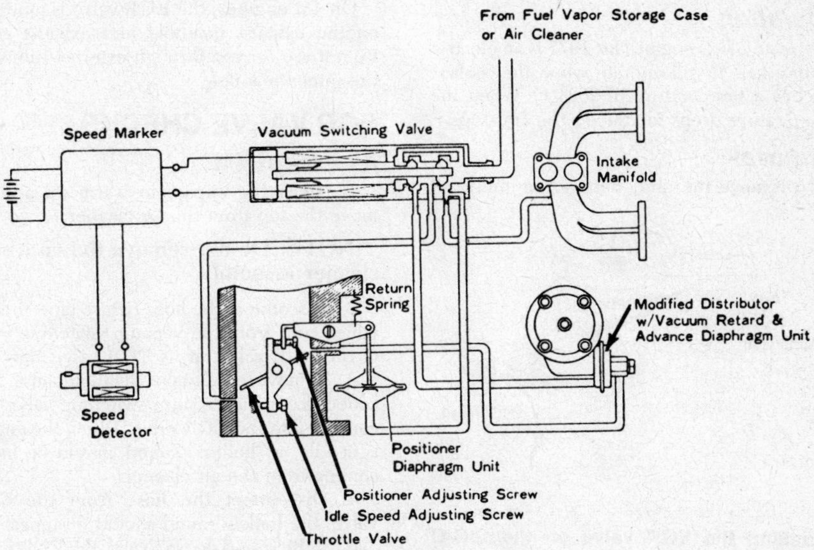

Engine modification system

SYSTEM CHECKS

Due to the complexity of the components involved, about the only engine modification system checks which can be made without the use of special test equipment, are the following:

1. Examine the vacuum lines to see that they are not clogged, pinched, or loose.
2. Check the electrical connections for tightness and corrosion.
3. Be sure that the vacuum sources for the vacuum switching valve are not plugged.
4. On models equipped with speed controlled spark, a broken speedometer cable could also render the system inoperative.
5. Test the thermo-sensor in the following manner:
   a. Remove the lead from its center terminal.
   b. Touch one test prod of an ohmmeter to the sensor housing.
   c. Connect the other test prod in series with a 10 ohm resistor to the center terminal of the sensor.
   d. If the engine temperature is between about 140°-212° F (or 113°-217° F on 1974 California F engines), the meter should show no conductivity.
   e. If the engine is above or below these temperatures, the meter should show conductivity.
   f. Replace the thermo-sensor if it isn't working properly.
6. If everything else is in good working order, the fault probably lies in the vacuum switching valve or the computer (speed marker). About the only way to test these, without using special equipment, is by substitution of new units.

NOTE: A faulty vacuum switching valve or computer could cause more than one of the emission control systems to fail. Therefore, if several systems are out, these two units (and the speedometer cable) would be the first things to check.

ELECTRIC COOLING FAN–3K-C

Operation

New to 3K-C engines for 1977 is an electric cooling fan. It will operate when the coolant reaches a temperature of 203° F. When the temperature drops to 190° F, the fan stops.

Removal

To remove the unit, unplug the multiconnector, remove the fan and loosen the three attaching bolts.

Installation is the reverse of removal.

Inspection

Turning on the ignition switch will cause a "click" in the fan relay. This indicates both switch and relay are operating.

For a low temperature check, unplug the thermo switch. The fan should start. To test for high temperature, allow the engine to idle to fan operating temperature.

Exhaust Gas Recirculation (EGR)

In 1975 EGR was used in all US engines, except the 2T-C engine used in the Corolla. In 1977, the Corolla 2T-C received the system as well.

In all cases, the EGR valve is controlled by the same computer and vacuum switching valve which is used to operate other emission control system components.

On 18R-C and F engines, the EGR valve is operated by vacuum supplied from a port above the throttle blades and fed through the vacuum switching valve.

On 4M engines, vacuum from the carburetor vacuum advance port flows through the vacuum switching valve to an EGR vacuum control valve. The vacuum from the advance port opens the vacuum control valve which then allows venturi vacuum to act on the chamber *above* the EGR valve diaphragm, causing the EGR valve to open. When exhaust gas recirculation is not required, the vacuum switching valve stops sending the advance port vacuum signal to the EGR vacuum control valve which closes, sending intake manifold vacuum to the chamber *below* the EGR valve diaphragm. This closes the EGR valve, blocking the flow of exhaust gases to the intake manifold.

On all engines there are several conditions, determined by the computer and vacuum switching valve, which permit exhaust gas recirculation to take place:

1. Vehicle speed
2. Engine coolant temperature

On 4M engines, the EGR valve is mounted on the exhaust manifold and exhaust gases from it are carried through external tubing to the intake manifold.

EGR VALVE CHECKS

All Except 4M

1. Allow the engine to warm up and remove the top from the air cleaner.

NOTE: Do not remove the entire air cleaner assembly.

2. Disconnect the hose (white tape coded), which runs from the vacuum switching valve to the EGR valve, at its EGR valve end.
3. Remove the intake manifold hose (red coded) from the vacuum switching valve and connect it to the EGR valve. When the engine is at idle, a "hollow" sound should be heard coming from the air cleaner.
4. Disconnect the hose from the EGR valve; the hollow sound should disappear.
5. If the sound doesn't vary, the EGR valve is defective and must be replaced.

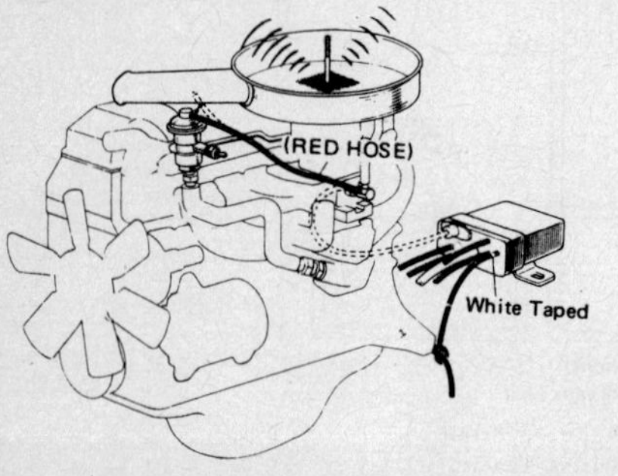

Checking the EGR valve on the 18R-C engine—20R similar

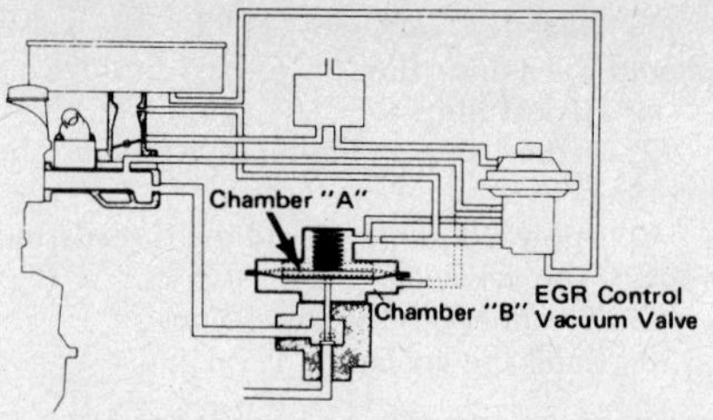

Checking the EGR valve on the 4M engine

6. Reconnect the vacuum hoses as they were originally found. Install the top on the air cleaner.

4M Engine

1. Warm up the engine and allow it to idle.
2. Disconnect the vacuum sensing line from the *upper* vacuum chamber of the EGR valve.
3. Disconnect the sensing line from the *lower* chamber of the EGR valve.
4. Now, take the hose which was disconnected from the *lower* chamber and connect it to the upper EGR valve chamber.

NOTE: Leave the lower chamber vented to the atmosphere.

5. The engine idle should become rough or the engine should stall with the hoses connected in this manner. If the engine runs normally, check the EGR vacuum control valve (see below). If the vacuum control valve is in good working order, then replace the EGR valve.
6. Reconnect the vacuum sensing lines as they were originally found.

EGR VACUUM CONTROL VALVE

1. Connect the EGR vacuum control valve hoses up, so that carburetor advance port vacuum operates directly on its diaphragm (top hose connection).
2. Disconnect the two hoses from the EGR vacuum control valve which run to the upper and lower diaphragm chambers of the EGR valve.
3. Take two vacuum gauges and connect one to each of the ports from which you removed a hose in Step 2.
4. Race the engine; the vacuum gauges should indicate the following:

   Upper chamber port—Venturi vacuum
   Lower chamber port—Atmospheric pressure
5. Disconnect the sensing hose from the carburetor advance port.
6. The vacuum gauges should now show the following:

   Upper chamber port—Atmospheric pressure
   Lower chamber port—Intake manifold vacuum

NOTE: The atmospheric pressure reading should be nearly equal to that obtained in Step 4.

7. Replace the EGR vacuum control valve if the readings on the vacuum gauges are incorrect.
8. Hook up the vacuum lines as they were originally found.

SYSTEM CHECKS

If, after having completed the above tests, the EGR system still doesn't work right and everything else checks out OK, the fault probably lies in the computer or the vacuum switching valve systems. Proceed with the tests outlined under "System Checks" in the Engine Modification Section above.

NOTE: A good indication that the fault doesn't lie in the EGR system, but rather in the vacuum supply system, would be if several emission control systems were not working properly.

CATALYTIC CONVERTERS

Starting in 1975 all Toyota passenger cars sold in California and all Mark IIs sold in the U.S. are equipped with catalytic converters. In 1977, all Toyota vehicles sold in this country were equipped with converters. The converters are used to oxidize hydrocarbons (HC) and carbon monoxide (CO). The converters are necessary because of the stricter emission level standards for the 1975 models.

The catalysts are made of noble metals (platinum and palladium) which are bonded to individual pellets. These catalysts cause the HC and CO to break down into water and carbon dioxide (CO_2) without taking part in the reaction; hence, a catalyst life of 50,000 miles may be expected under normal conditions.

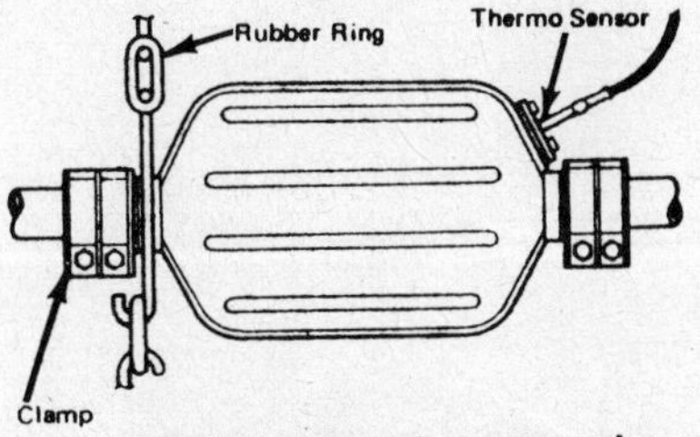

Catalytic converter removal

On the 4M-E engines, there are two catalytic converters. The first one is designed to reduce the NOx to dinitrogen. The second one operates the same as the vehicles equipped with only one converter.

An air pump is used to supply air to the exhaust system to aid in the reaction. A thermosensor, inserted into the converter, shuts off the air supply if the catalyst temperature becomes excessive.

The same sensor circuit also causes a dash warning light labled "EXH TEMP" to come on when the catalyst temperature gets too high.

NOTE: It is normal for the light to come on temporarily if the car is being driven downhill for long periods of time (such as descending a mountain).

The light will come on and stay on if the air injection system is malfunctioning or if the engine is misfiring.

Precautions:

1. Use only unleaded fuel.
2. Avoid prolonged idling; the engine should run no longer than 20 minutes at curb idle, nor longer than 10 minutes at fast idle.
3. Reduce the fast idle speed, by quickly depressing and releasing the accelerator pedal, as soon as the coolant temperature reaches 120° F.
4. Do not disconnect any spark plug leads while the engine is running.
5. Make engine compression checks as quickly as possible.
6. Do not dispose of the catalyst in a place where anything coated with grease, gas, or oil is present; spontaneous combustion could result.

CATALYST TESTING

At the present time there is no known way to reliably test catalytic converter operation in the field. The only reliable test is a 12 hour and 40 minute "soak test" (CVS) which must be done in a laboratory.

An infrared HC/CO tester is not sensitive enough to measure the higher tailpipe emissions from a partially-failed converter. Thus, a bad converter may allow enough HC and CO emissions to escape, so that the car is not in compliance with Federal (or state) standards, but still will not cause the needle on the HC/CO tester to move off zero.

A *completely* failed converter should cause the tester to show a slight reading. As a result, it should be possible to spot one of these in the shop.

As long as the driver of the car avoids severe overheating or use of leaded fuels and the car has less than 50,000 miles on it, it is safe to assume that the converter is working.

WARNING LIGHT CHECKS

NOTE: The warning light comes on while the engine is being cranked, to test its operation, just like any of the other warning lights.

1. If the warning light comes on and stays on, check the components of the air injection system, as outlined above. If these are not defective, check the ignition system for faulty leads, plugs, points, or control box.
2. If no problems can be found in Step 1, check the wiring for the light for shorts or opened circuits.
3. If nothing else can be found wrong in Steps 1 and 2 above, check the operation of the emission control system computer, either by substitution of a new unit, or by taking it to a service facility which has Toyota's special emission control system checker.

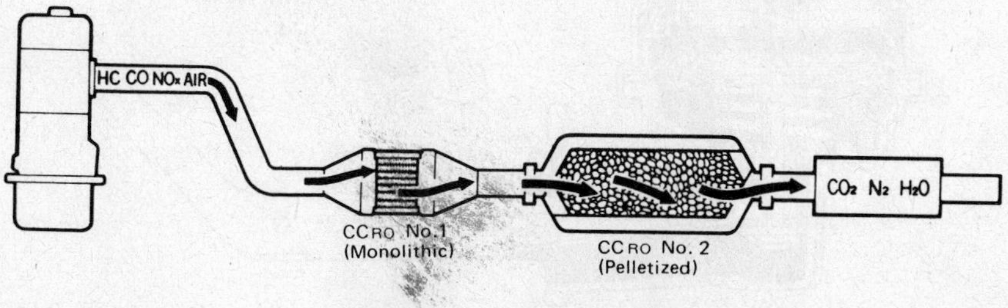

Catalytic converter system, 4 M-E

CONVERTER REMOVAL AND INSTALLATION

CAUTION

Do not perform the operation on a hot (or even warm) engine. Catalyst temperatures may go as high as 1700° F, so that any contact with the catalyst could cause severe burns.

1. Disconnect the lead from the converter thermosensor.
2. Remove the wiring shield.
3. Unfasten the pipe clamp securing bolts at either end of the converter. Remove the clamps.
4. Push the tailpipe rearward and remove the converter, complete with thermosensor.
5. Carry the converter with the thermosensor upward to prevent the catalyst from falling out.
6. Unfasten the screws and withdraw the thermosensor and gasket.

Installation is performed in the following order:

1. Place a new gasket on the thermosensor. Push the thermosensor into the converter and secure it with its two bolts. Be careful not to drop the thermosensor.

NOTE: Service replacement converters are provided with a plastic thermosensor guide. Slide the sensor into the guide to install it. Do not remove the guide.

2. Install new gaskets on the converter mounting flanges.
3. Secure the converter with its mounting clamps.
4. If the converter is attached to the body with rubber O-rings, install the O-rings over the body and converter mounting hooks.
5. Install the wire protector and connect the lead to the thermosensor.

FUEL SYSTEM

Fuel Filter

REPLACEMENT

All engines employ a disposable, inline filter; when dirty, or at recommended intervals, remove from line and replace.

Mechanical Fuel Pump

All 1A-C, 2A and 3A engines use a mechanical type fuel pump. It is located on the right rear of the cylinder head. The 1980 20R engine also uses a mechanical type fuel pump. It

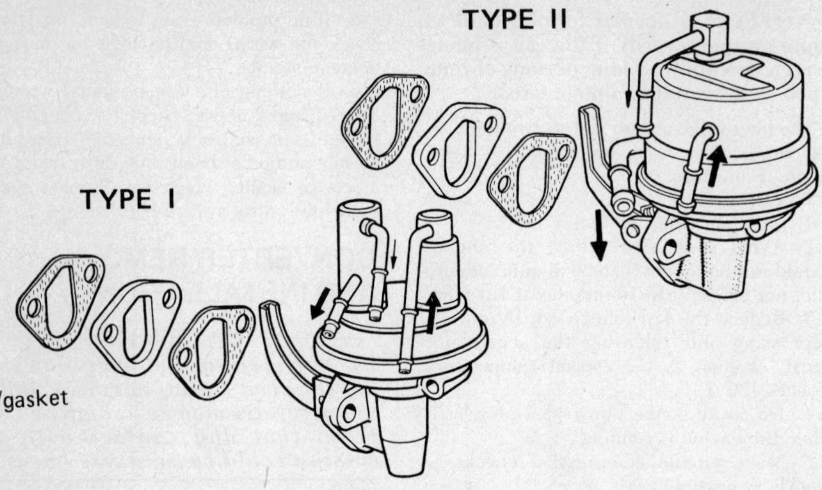

20R fuel pumps

is located on the right front of the cylinder head. There are two types of fuel pumps used on the 1A-C, 2A and 3A engines. There are also two types used on the 20R.

REMOVAL AND INSTALLATION

1. Disconnect the fuel lines to the pump.
2. Remove the bolts which hold the pump to the cylinder head.
3. Remove the pump assembly.

Installation is the reverse of removal. Always use a new gasket when installing a fuel pump.

TESTING

1. Remove the line which runs from the fuel pump to the carburetor.
2. Attach a pressure gauge to the outlet side of the pump.
3. Run the engine and check the pressure.
4. Check the pressure against the specifications.
5. If the pressure is below the specifications replace the pump.
6. Reconnect the carburetor line.

Electric Fuel Pump

From 1975 to 1980, all models used an electric fuel pump.

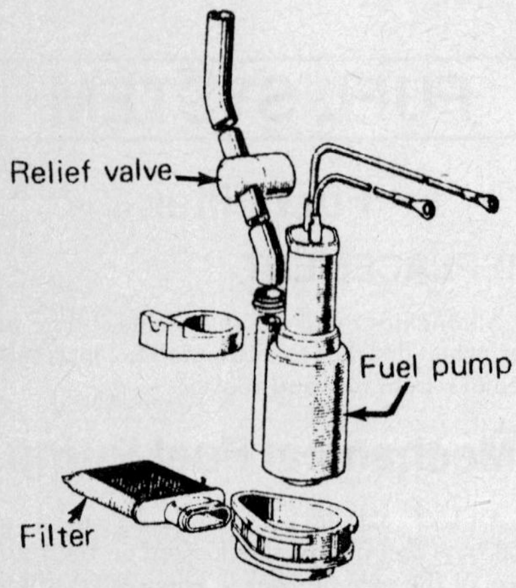

Electric fuel pump

The fuel pump is located inside the gas tank. It is serviced as a unit; if it breaks, replace it.

REMOVAL AND INSTALLATION

1. Disconnect the negative (−) cable from the battery.
2. a. On sedans and hardtops, remove the trim panel from inside the trunk.
   b. On station wagons, raise the rear of the vehicle, in order to gain access to the pump.
   c. On pick-ups remove the fuel tank.
3. Remove the screws which secure the pump access plate to the tank. Withdraw the plate, gasket, and pump assembly.
4. Disconnect the leads and hoses from the pump.

Installation is performed in the reverse order of removal. Use a gasket on the pump access plate.

TESTING

CAUTION

Do not operate the fuel pump unless it is immersed in gasoline and connected to its resistor.

1. Disconnect the lead from the oil pressure warning light sender.
2. Unfasten the line from the outlet side of the fuel filter.
3. Connect a pressure gauge to the filter outlet with a length of rubber hose.
4. Turn the ignition switch to the "ON" position, but do not start the engine.
5. Check the pressure gauge reading against the figure given in the "Tune-Up Specifications" chart above.
6. Check for a clogged filter or pinched lines if the pressure is not up to specification.

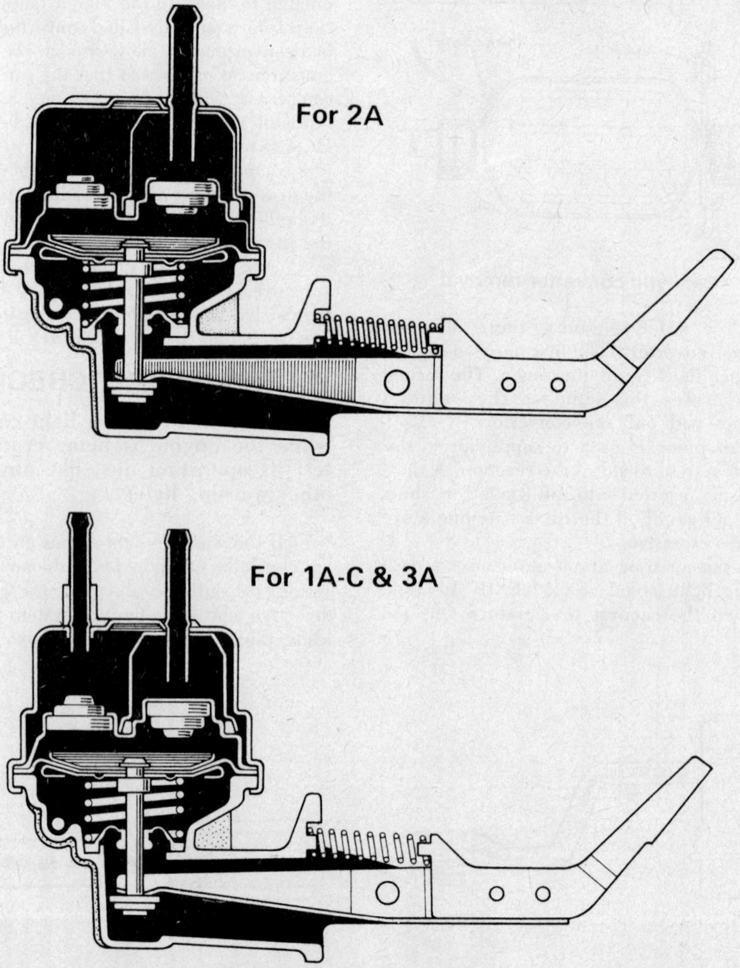

1A-C, 2A, 3A, fuel pumps

7. If there is nothing wrong with the filter or lines, replace the fuel pump.

8. Turn the ignition off and reconnect the fuel line to the filter. Connect the lead to the oil pressure sender.

Fuel Return Cut Valve

The fuel return cut valve controls the amount of fuel returned to the gas tank according to engine load. This prevents percolation when the engine is hot and the load light.

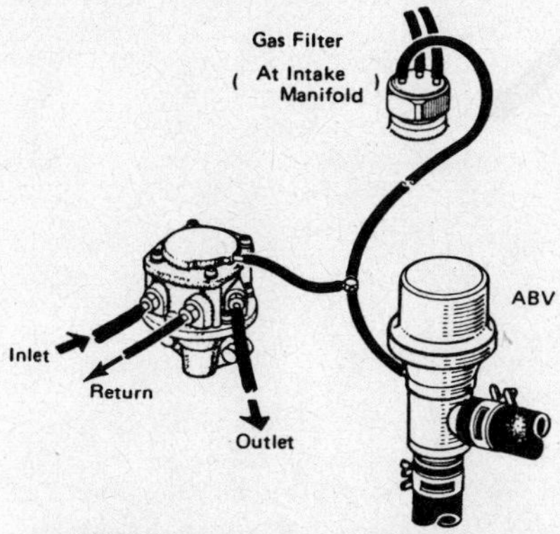

2T-C fuel return cut-off valve

INSPECTION

Attach a long tube to the return pipe of the valve. Put a container under it to catch the fuel. With the engine at idle, fuel should go into the container.

Pinch-off the vacuum line. If valve is operating correctly, the fuel flow should stop.

Fuel Cut-Off Valve

In case of an accident, a fuel cut-off valve was added to all systems in 1976. The valve, installed between the fuel filter and the carburetor, consists of two check balls that clog the fuel line if the automobile is in other than the normal wheels down position.

Combined with a check on the carburetor and specially designed fuel lines, the fuel cut-off system almost eliminates the chance of spilled fuel during an accident.

Carburetors

The carburetors used on Toyota models are conventional two-barrel, down-draft types similar to domestic carburetors.

The main circuits are: *primary,* for normal operational requirements; *secondary,* to supply high-speed fuel needs; *float,* to supply fuel to the primary and secondary circuits; *accelerator,* to supply fuel for quick and safe acceleration; *choke,* for reliable starting in cold weather; and *power valve,* for fuel economy. Although slight differences in appearance may be noted, these carburetors are basically alike. Of course, different jets and settings are demanded by the different engines to which they are fitted.

REMOVAL AND INSTALLATION

1. Remove the air cleaner housing, disconnect all air hoses from the air cleaner base, and disconnect the battery ground cable.

NOTE: On 20R engines, drain the coolant to prevent it from running into the intake manifold when the carburetor is removed.

2. Disconnect the fuel line, choke pipe, and distributor vacuum line. On 20R engines disconnect the choke coolant hose.

3. Remove the accelerator linkage. (With an automatic transmission, also remove the throttle rod to the transmission.)

NOTE: On Land Cruisers disconnect the magnetic valve wire from the coil terminal, if equipped.

4. Remove the four nuts that secure the carburetor to the manifold and lift off the carburetor and gasket.

5. Cover the open manifold with a clean rag to prevent small objects from dropping into the engine.

Installation is performed in the reverse order of removal. After the engine is warmed up, check for fuel leaks and float level settings.

OVERHAUL

Efficient carburetion depends greatly on careful cleaning and inspection during overhaul since dirt, gum, water or varnish in or on the carburetor parts are often responsible for poor performance.

Overhaul your carburetor in a clean, dust-

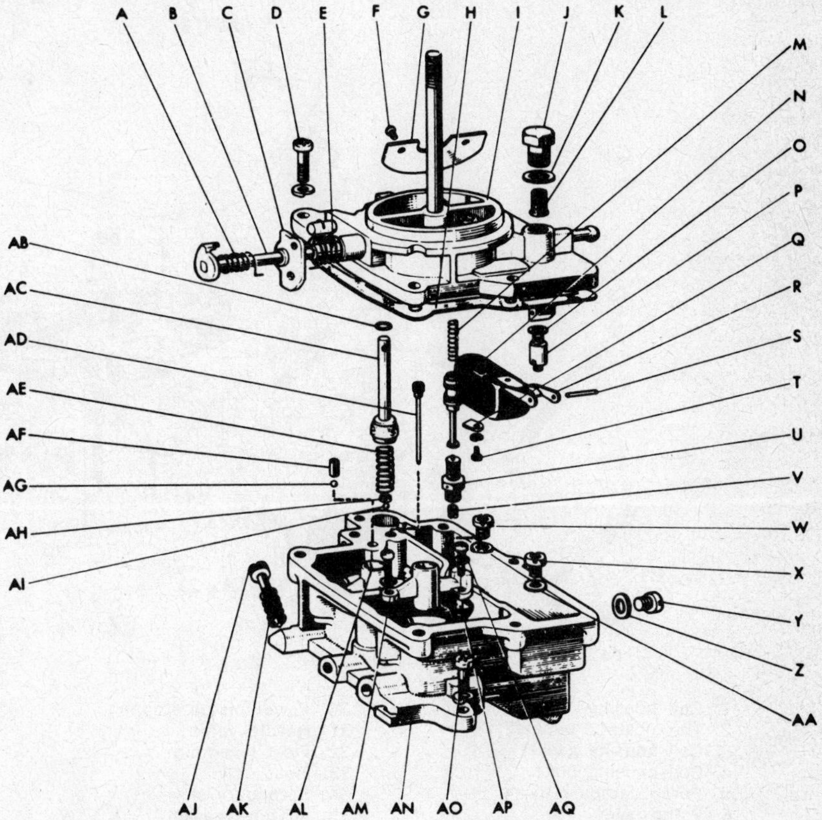

(a)—Choke valve relief spring
(b)—Choke shaft
(c)—Choke lever
(d)—Screw
(e)—Choke return spring
(f)—Screw
(g)—Choke valve
(h)—Air horn gasket
(i)—Air horn
(j)—Main passage plug
(k)—Inlet strainer gasket
(l)—Strainer
(m)—Power piston spring
(n)—Power piston
(o)—Needle valve seat gasket
(p)—Needle valve
(q)—Power piston stopper
(r)—Float
(s)—Float lever pin
(t)—Screw
(u)—Power valve
(v)—Power jet
(w)—Primary main jet
(x)—Secondary main jet
(y)—Drain plug
(z)—Gasket
(aa)—Main jet gasket
(ab)—O-ring
(ac)—Pump plunger
(ad)—Slow jet
(ae)—Pump damping spring
(af)—Pump discharge weight
(ag)—Check ball
(ah)—Check ball retainer
(ai)—Check ball
(aj)—Throttle adjusting screw
(ak)—Spring
(al)—Primary small venturi
(am)—Secondary small venturi
(an)—Main body
(ao)—Screw
(ap)—Venturi No. 1 gasket
(aq)—Screw

3K-C

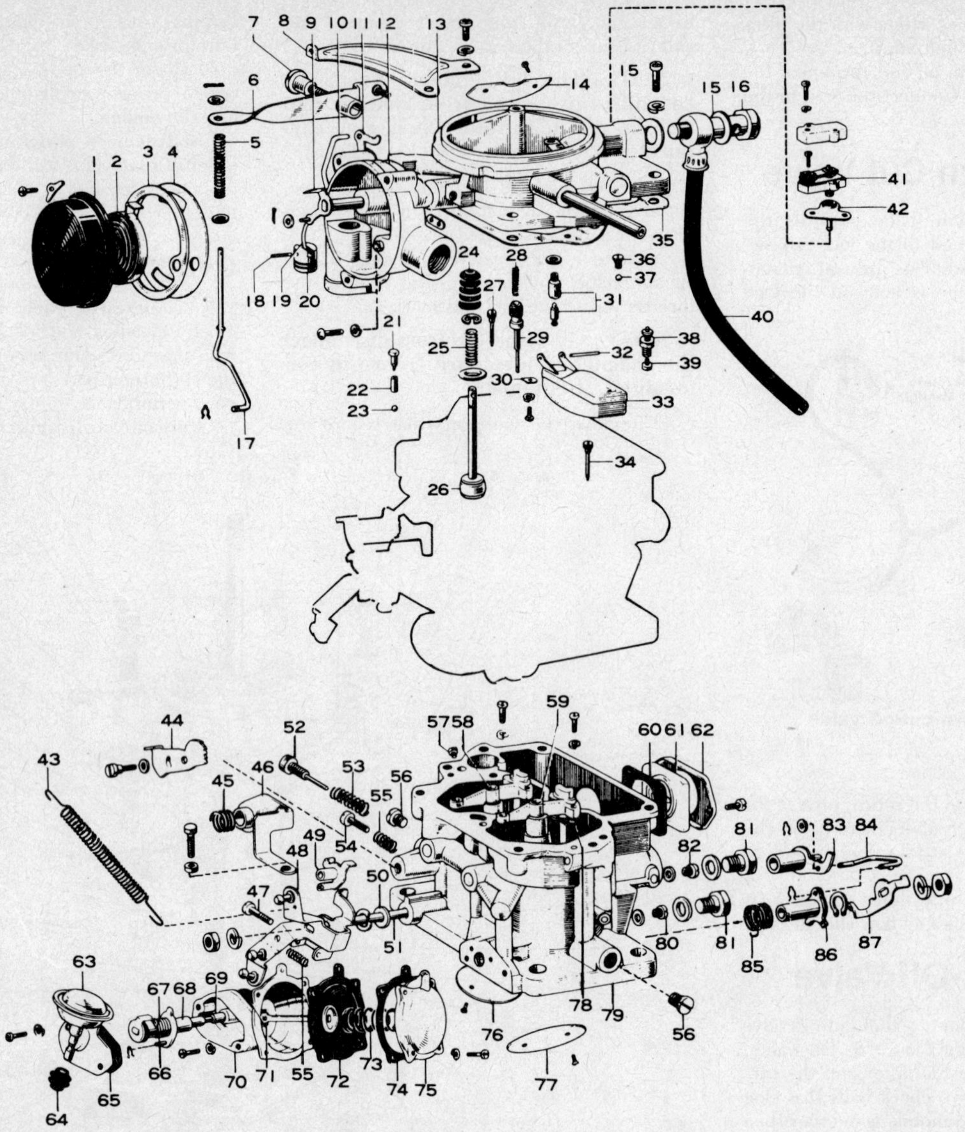

1. Coil housing
2. Thermostatic bimetal coil
3. Coil housing gasket
4. Coil housing plate
5. Pump damping spring
6. Pump lever
7. Pump lever set screw
8. Back spring support
9. Choke shaft
10. Choke lever link
11. Fast idle cam lever
12. Thermostat case
13. Air horn
14. Choke valve
15. Union fitting gasket
16. Union fitting
17. Pump connecting link
18. Piston pin
19. Piston connector
20. Vacuum piston
21. Discharge weight stop
22. Pump discharge weight
23. Steel ball
24. Boot
25. Plunger return spring
26. Pump plunger
27. Primary slow jet
28. Power piston spring
29. Power piston
30. Power piston stopper
31. Needle valve
32. Float lever pin
33. Float
34. Secondary slow jet
35. Air horn gasket
36. Nut plug
37. Steel ball
38. Power valve
39. Power jet
40. Fuel hose
41. Thermostatic valve
42. Bracket
43. Primary throttle return spring
44. Fast idle cam
45. Lever return spring
46. Dash pot lever
47. Fast idle adjusting screw
48. Primary throttle lever
49. Fast idle adjusting lever
50. Throttle valve adjusting shim
51. Primary throttle shaft
52. Idle mixture adjusting screw
53. Adjusting screw spring
54. Idle speed adjusting screw
55. Adjusting screw spring
56. Nut plug
57. Pump jet plug
58. Primary small venturi
59. Secondary small venturi
60. Level gauge gasket
61. Level gauge glass
62. Level gauge clamp
63. Dash pot
64. Boot
65. Diaphragm housing cap gasket
66. Diaphragm relief lever
67. Diaphragm relief spring
68. Collar
69. Secondary throttle shaft
70. Diaphragm housing
71. Diaphragm housing gasket
72. Diaphragm rod
73. Diaphragm spring
74. Diaphragm cap gasket
75. Diaphragm housing cap
76. Primary throttle valve
77. Secondary throttle valve
78. Venturi gasket
79. Carburetor body
80. Secondary main jet
81. Main passage plug
82. Primary main jet
83. First kick lever
84. Throttle shaft link
85. Secondary throttle return spring
86. Second kick lever
87. Second kick arm

4M

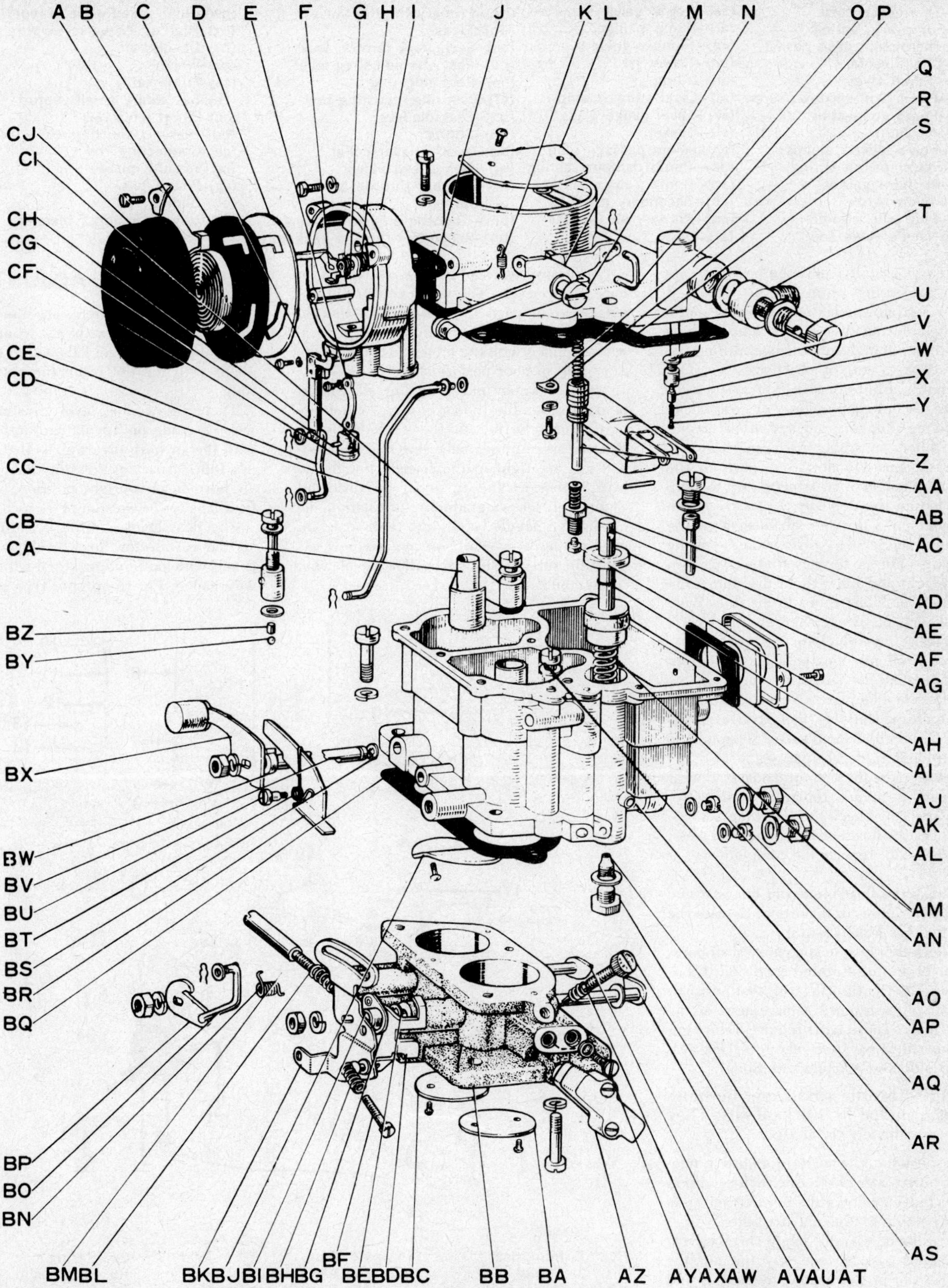

(a)—Thermostat bimetal
(b)—Coil housing gasket
(c)—Fast idle cam follower
(d)—Coil housing plate
(e)—Piston connector
(f)—Choke shaft
(g)—Fast idle cam
(h)—Fast idle cam spring
(w)—Needle valve
(x)—Needle valve spring
(y)—Needle valve push pin
(z)—Float
(aa)—Power piston
(ab)—Slow circuit plug
(ac)—Float lever pin
(ad)—Slow jet
(as)—Discharge check valve
(at)—Main passage plug
(au)—Idle adjusting screw
(av)—Primary throttle shaft
(aw)—Secondary throttle shaft
(ax)—Spring
(ay)—Main passage plug
(az)—Thermostatic valve
(bo)-Throttle shaft link
(bp)-Secondary throttle lever
(bq)-Gasket
(br)-High speed valve stop lever
(bs)-Retaining ring
(bt)-High speed valve stop lever spring
(bu)-Stop lever securing screw
(bv)-High speed valve shaft

2T-C and 18R-C

(i)—Thermostat case
(k—Pump arm spring
(j)—Thermostat case gasket
(l)—Choke valve
(m)—Pump lever
(n)—Pump arm securing screw
(o)—Pump connecting link
(p)—Air horn
(q)—Power piston stopper
(r)—Power piston spring
(s)—Air horn gasket
(t)—Union nipple
(u)—Plug with strainer
(v)—Needle valve seat
(ae)—Power valve
(af)—Pump plunger
(ag)—Plunger guide
(ah)—Power jet
(ai)—O-ring
(aj)—Level gauge clamp
(ak)—Level gauge glass
(al)—Gasket
(am)—Main passage plug
(an)—Pump damping spring
(ao)—Primary main jet
(ap)—Secondary main jet
(aq)—Primary air bleeder
(ar)—Body
(ba)–Primary throttle valve
(bb)–Flange
(bc)–Secondary throttle valve
(bd)–Fast idle adjusting lever
(be)–Retaining ring
(bf)–Fast idle adjusting bolt
(bg)–Fast idle lever
(bh)–Spring
(bi)–Throttle lever collar
(bj)–High speed valve
(bk)–Primary throttle arm
(bl)–Spring
(bm)–Thoottle adjusting screw
(bn)–Secondary throttle back spring
(bw)–High speed valve stopper
(bx)–High speed valve weight
(by)–Check ball
(bz)–Weight
(ca)–Pump jet
(cb)–Secondary small venturi
(cc)–Pump jet screw
(cd)–Pump connecting rod
(ce)–Connecting rod
(cf)–Vacuum piston
(cg)–Piston pin
(ch)–Sliding rod
(ci)–Primary main air bleeder
(cj)–Coil housing

free area. Carefully disassemble the carburetor, referring often to the exploded views. Keep all similar and lookalike parts segregated during disassembly and cleaning to avoid accidental interchange during assembly. Make a note of all jet sizes.

When the carburetor is disassembled, wash all parts (except diaphragms, electric choke units, pump plunger, and any other plastic, leather, fiber, or rubber parts) in clean carburetor solvent. Do not leave parts in the solvent any longer than is necessary to sufficiently loosen the deposits. Excessive cleaning may remove the special finish from the float bowl and choke valve bodies, leaving these parts unfit for service. Rinse all parts in clean solvent and blow them dry with compressed air or allow them to air dry. Wipe clean all cork, plastic, leather, and fiber parts with a clean, lint-free cloth.

Blow out all passages and jets with compressed air and be sure that there are no restrictions or blockages. Never use wire or similar tools to clean jets, fuel passages, or air bleeds. Clean all jets and valves separately to avoid accidental interchange.

Check all parts for wear or damage. If wear or damage is found, replace the defective parts. Especially check the following:

1. Check the float needle and seat for wear. If wear is found, replace the complete assembly.

2. Check the float hinge pin for wear and the float(s) for dents or distortion. Replace the float if fuel has leaked into it.

3. Check the throttle and choke shaft bores for wear or an out-of-round condition. Damage or wear to the throttle arm, shaft, or shaft bore will often require replacement of the throttle body. These parts require a close tolerance of fit; wear may allow air leakage, which could affect starting and idling.

NOTE: Throttle shafts and bushings are not included in overhaul kits. They can be purchased separately.

4. Inspect the idle mixture adjusting needles for burrs or grooves. Any such condition requires replacement of the needle, since you will not be able to obtain a satisfactory idle.

5. Test the accelerator pump check valves. They should pass air one way but not the other. Test for proper seating by blowing and sucking on the valve. Replace the valve if necessary. If the valve is satisfactory, wash the valve again to remove breath moisture.

6. Check the bowl cover for warped surfaces with a straightedge.

7. Closely inspect the valves and seats for wear and damage, replacing as necessary.

8. After the carburetor is assembled, check the choke valve for freedom of operation.

Carburetor overhaul kits are recommended for each overhaul. These kits contain all gaskets and new parts to replace those that deteriorate most rapidly. Failure to replace all parts supplied with the kit (especially gaskets) can result in poor performance later.

After cleaning and checking all components, reassemble the carburetor, using new parts and referring to the exploded view. When reassembling, make sure that all screws and jets are tight in their seats, but do not overtighten, as the tips will be distorted. Tighten all screws gradually, in rotation. Do not tighten needle valves into their seats; uneven jetting will result. Always use new gaskets. Be sure to adjust the float level when reassembling.

FLOAT LEVEL ADJUSTMENT

Float level adjustments are unnecessary on models equipped with a carburetor sight glass, if the fuel level falls within the lines or aligns with the dot when the engine is running.

There are two float level adjustments which may be made on Toyota carburetors. One is with the air horn inverted, so that the float is in a fully *raised* position; the other is with the air horn in an upright position, so that the float falls to the bottom of its travel.

The float level is either measured with a special carburetor float level gauge, which comes with a rebuilding kit, or with a standard wire gauge. For the proper type of gauge, as

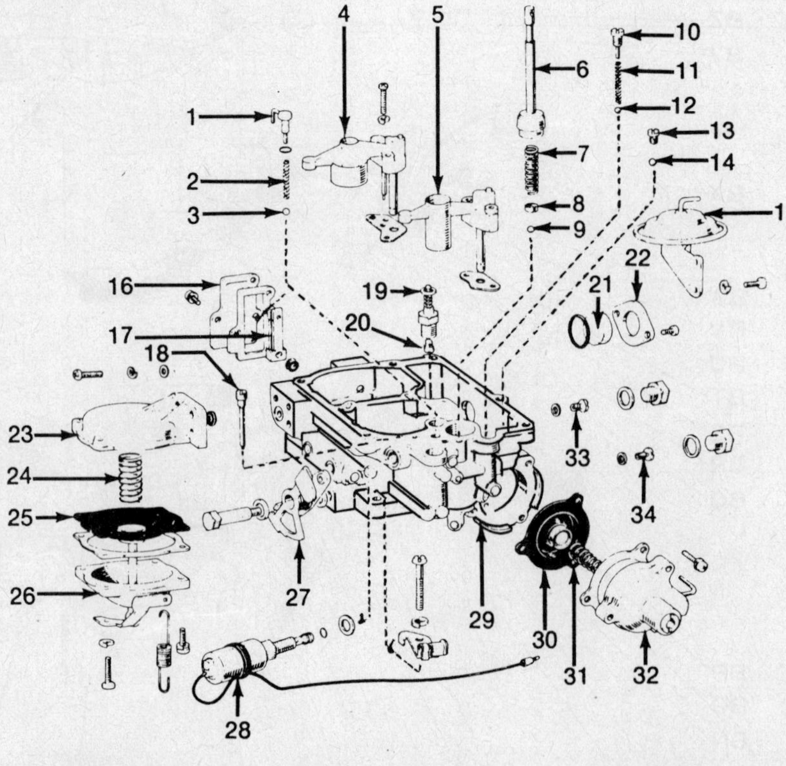

1. Pump jet
2. Spring
3. Outlet check ball
4. Secondary venturi
5. Primary venturi
6. Pump plunger
7. Spring
8. Ball retainer
9. Inlet check ball
10. Plug
11. Spring
12. AAP outlet check ball
13. Plug
14. AAP inlet check ball
15. Throttle positioner
16. Thermostatic valve cover
17. Thermostatic valve
18. Primary slow jet
19. Power valve
20. Power jet
21. Sight glass
22. Glass retainer
23. Diaphragm housing cap
24. Spring
25. Diaphragm
26. Housing
27. Fast idle cam
28. Solenoid valve
29. Carburetor body
30. Diaphragm
31. Spring
32. AAP housing
33. Secondary main jet
34. Primary main jet

Main body assembly—20R

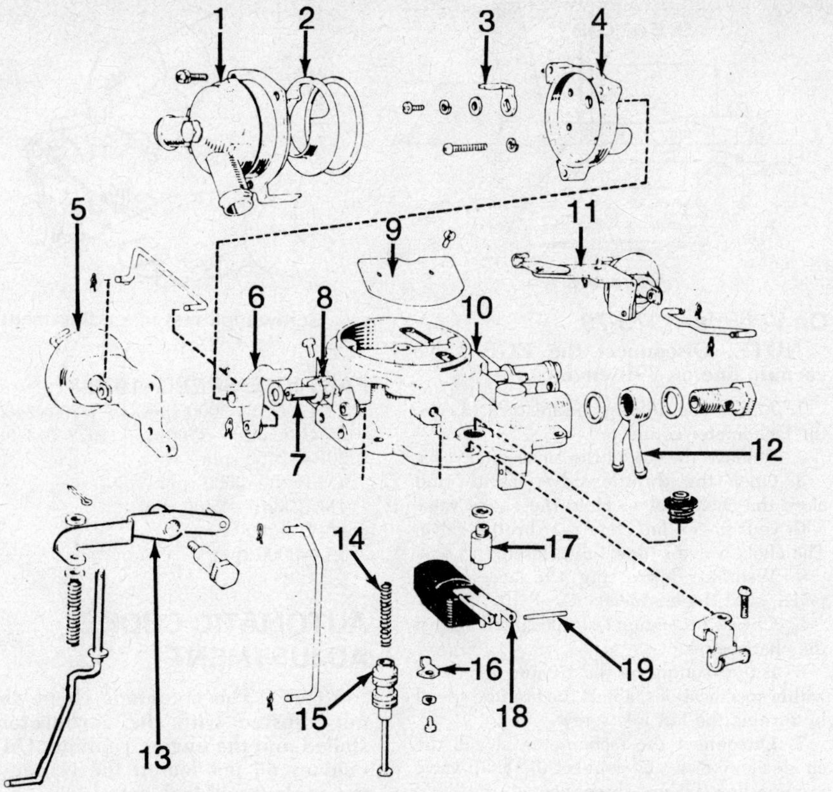

1. Choke coil water housing
2. Choke housing plate
3. Choke lever
4. Choke housing body
5. Choke breaker
6. Relief lever
7. Choke shaft
8. Connecting lever
9. Choke valve
10. Air horn
11. Choke opener
12. Union
13. Pump arm
14. Spring
15. Power piston
16. Piston retainer
17. Needle valve set
18. Float
19. Float pivot pin

Air horn assembly—20R

well as the points to be measured, see the chart at the end of this section.

NOTE: Gap specifications are also given so that a float level gauge may be fabricated. Several different gauges are illustrated.

Adjust the float level by bending the tabs on the float levers, either upper or lower, as required.

FAST IDLE ADJUSTMENT

Off Vehicle–All Years

The fast idle adjustment is performed with the choke valve fully *closed,* except on the 2T-C and 18R-C engines which should have the choke valve fully *opened*.

Adjust the gap between the throttle valve edge and bore to the specifications, where given, in the chart below. Use a wire gauge to determine the gap.

MEASURING THE FLOAT LEVEL

To adjust the float level, bend the upper tab (1) or the lower tab (2)

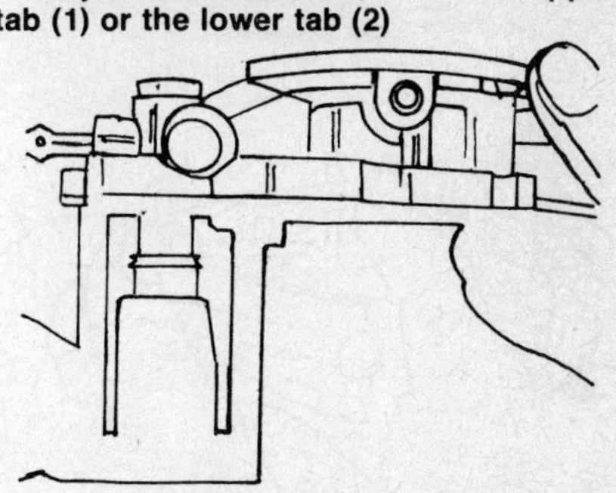

3KC lowered

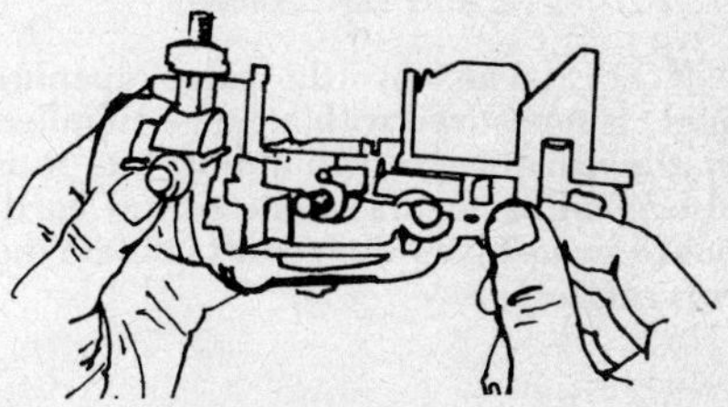

2TC and 18RC lowered

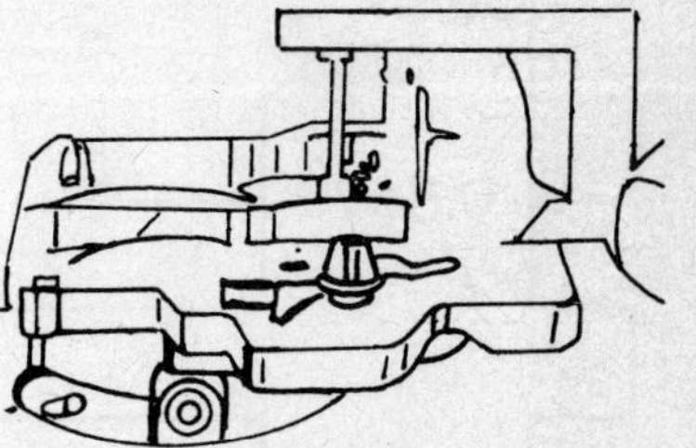

3KC raised

The chart below also gives the proper primary throttle valve opening angle, where necessary, and the proper means of fast idle adjustment.

FLOAT LEVEL ADJUSTMENTS

Engine		Gauge Type	Float Raised, Measure Distance Between	Gap (in.)	Gauge Type	Float Lowered, Measure Distance Between	Gap (in.)
3K-C		Special	Float end and air horn	0.260 ④	Special	Lowest point of float and upper side of gauge	1.89 ③
2T-C, 3T-C ⑨		Block	Float tip and air horn	0.200 ⑤	Wire	Needle valve bushing pin and float lip	0.047
1A-C & 3A ⑧		Special	Float tip and air horn	0.0158	Special	Needle valve plunger and float tip	0.047
20R	1978-80	Special	Float end and air horn	0.197 ⑥	Special	Needle valve bushing pin and float tab	0.039
	1975-77	Special	Float end and air horn	0.370 ①	Special	Float end and air horn	0.910 ②

① 1975-76: 0.394
② 1975-76: 0.039
③ 1976-77: float lip gap 0.035
1978-79: float lip gap 0.024
④ 1978-79: 0.30
⑤ 1978-79: 0.256
⑥ 1978-79: 0.276
⑦ 1980-81: 20R check to middle of sight glass
⑧ 1980-81: 1A-C93A check to middle of sight glass
⑨ 1980-81: 3T-C check to level of dot in sight glass
⑩ 4M-E: Use electronic fuel injection checker to center line on lean-rich scale

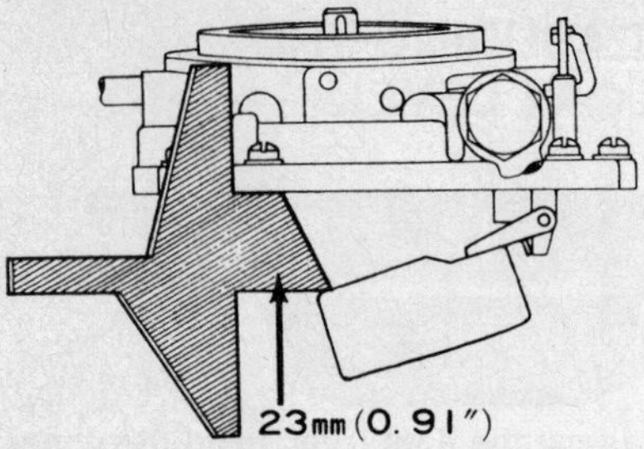

4M lowered

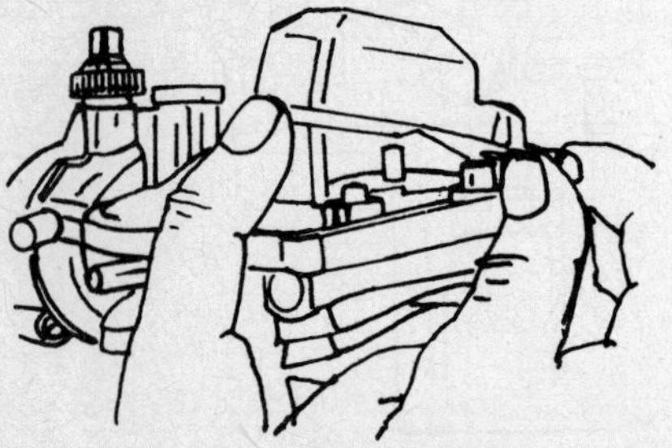

2TC and 18RC raised

NOTE: The throttle valve opening angle is measured with a gauge supplied in the carburetor rebuilding kit. It is also possible to make one out of cardboard by using a protractor to obtain the correct angle.

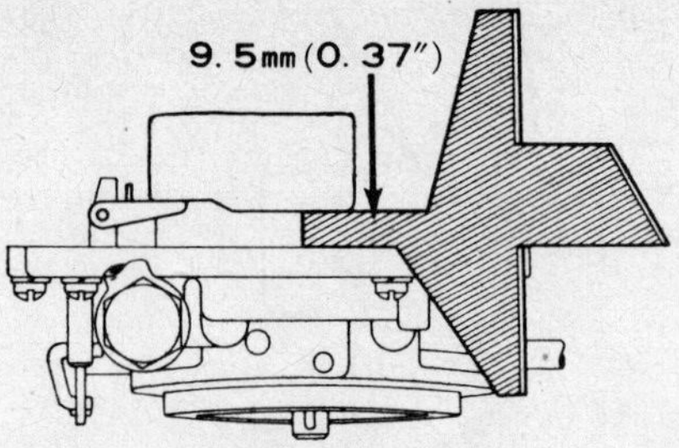

4M raised

On Vehicle—1975-79

NOTE: Disconnect the EGR valve vacuum line on 20R engines.

1. Adjust the idle speed/mixture. Leave the tachometer connected.
2. Remove the top of the air cleaner.
3. Open the throttle valve slightly and close the choke valve. Hold the choke valve with your finger and close the throttle valve. The choke valve is now fully closed.
4. Without depressing the accelerator pedal, start the engine.
5. Check the engine fast idle speed against the chart below.
6. If the reading on the tachometer is not within specifications, adjust the fast idle speed by turning the fast idle screw.
7. Disconnect the tachometer, install the air cleaner cover, and connect the EGR valve vacuum line if it was disconnected.

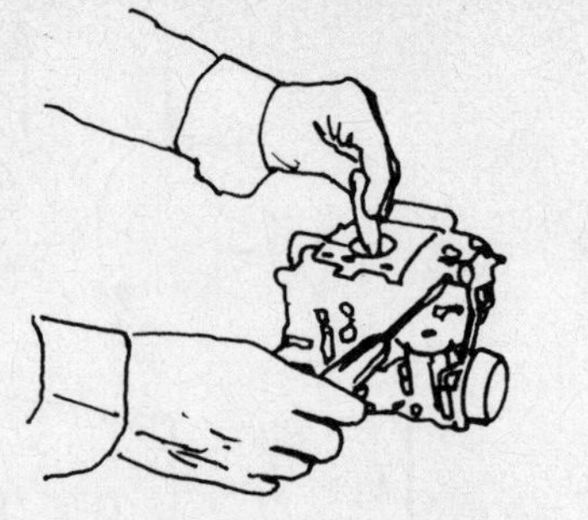

Screw type fast idle adjustment

FAST IDLE SPEED—1975-81

2T-C (US)—3000 rpm (1977-79—3400)
2T-C (Calif.)—2700 rpm (1977-79—3000)
20R—2400 rpm
4M (US)—2600 rpm
4M (Calif.)—2400 rpm
1A-C—3600 rpm
3A—3000 rpm

AUTOMATIC CHOKE ADJUSTMENT

NOTE: The automatic choke should be adjusted with the carburetor installed and the engine running. On 20R engines do not loosen the center bolt; the coolant will leak out.

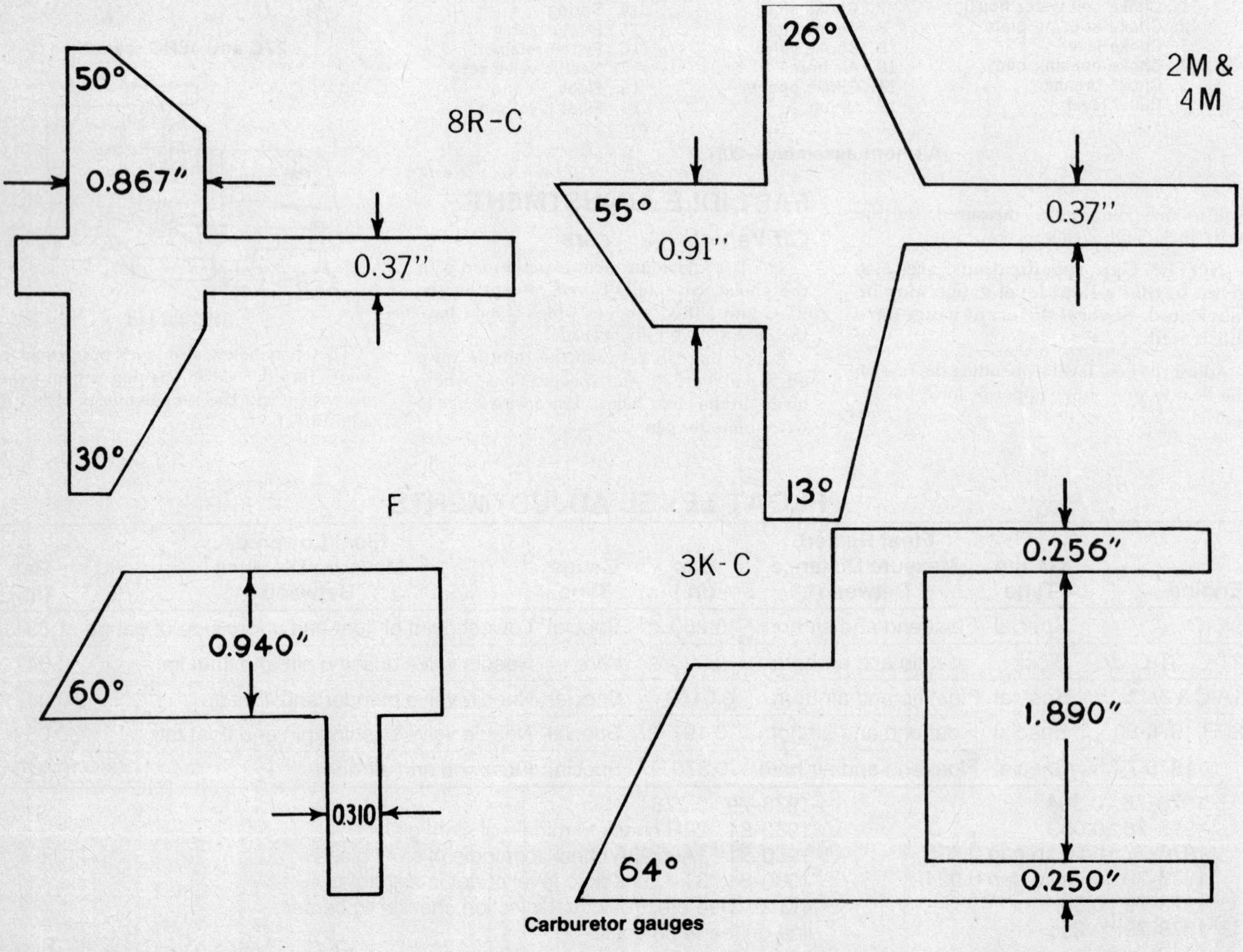

Carburetor gauges

FAST IDLE ADJUSTMENT

Engine	Throttle Valve to Bore Clearance (in.)	Primary Throttle Angle (deg)	To Adjust Fast Idle
3K-C	0.040 ①	9 ②	Bend the fast idle lever
2T-C	0.032 ③	7	Turn the fast idle adjusting screw
3T-C	0.032	—	Turn the fast idle adjusting screw ⑤
20R	0.047	24	Turn the fast idle screw
4M ⑥	—	16—from closed ④	Turn the fast idle adjusting screw
1A-C	—	22	3600 rpm (E.G.R. off)
3A (MT)	—	24	4000 rpm
3A All & 2A (AT)	—	21	3000 rpm

① 0.051 in 1976; 0.056 in 1977; 0.037 in 1978-79
② 20° open
③ 1976-79: 0.043
④ 1977-79: 9°
⑤ Federal & Canada wo/PS—3000 rpm
w/PS—2800 rpm
California wo/PS—2800 rpm
w/PS—2600 rpm
⑥ E.F.I.—Electronic fuel injection
—Not available

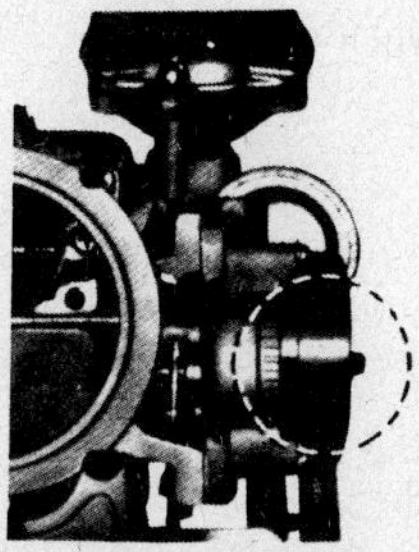

Align the marks on the choke housing

1. Check to see that the choke valve will close from fully opened when the coil housing is turned counterclockwise (2M and 4M engines—clockwise).
2. Align the mark on the coil housing with the center line on the thermostat case. In this position, the choke valve should be fully closed when the ambient temperature is 77° F.
3. If necessary, adjust the mixture by turning the coil housing. If the misture is too *rich,* rotate the housing *clockwise;* if too *lean,* rotate the housing *counterclockwise.* On models equipped with the 4M engine, rotate the housing in exactly the reverse direction of the above.

NOTE: Each graduation on the thermostat case is equivalent to 9° F.

MANUAL CHOKE ADJUSTMENT

1. Close the choke by turning the choke shaft lever.
2. Check the 1st throttle valve opening angle with the tool supplied in the rebuild kit (21 A/T, 24 M/T).
3. Adjust by turning the fast idle adjusting screw.

CHOKE BREAK ADJUSTMENT

20R Engine

1. Push the rod which comes out of the upper (choke break) diaphragm so that the choke valve opens.
2. Measure the choke valve opening angle. It should be 40° (38° 1976-79).
3. Adjust the angle, if necessary, by bending the relief lever link.

CHOKE UNLOADER ADJUSTMENT

Engine	CHOKE VALVE ANGLE (deg) — Throttle Valve Fully Closed (deg)	From Closed to Fully Open (deg)	Throttle Valve Open (Total) (deg)	Bend to Adjust
1975				
2T-C, 3K-C	20	27	47	Fast idle cam follower or choke shaft lip
20R	30	—	50	Fast idle lever
4M	20	15	35	Fast idle lever
1976-80				
3K-C	9	20	90	Fast idle cam follower or choke shaft tab
2T-C	7	38	90	Fast idle lever, follower or choke shaft tab
20R	—	50	90	Fast idle lever, follower or choke shaft tab
3T-C	20	—	47	Fast idle lever
4M	20	15	90	Fast idle lever
1A-C, 3A	20	—	47	Fast idle lever

—Not available

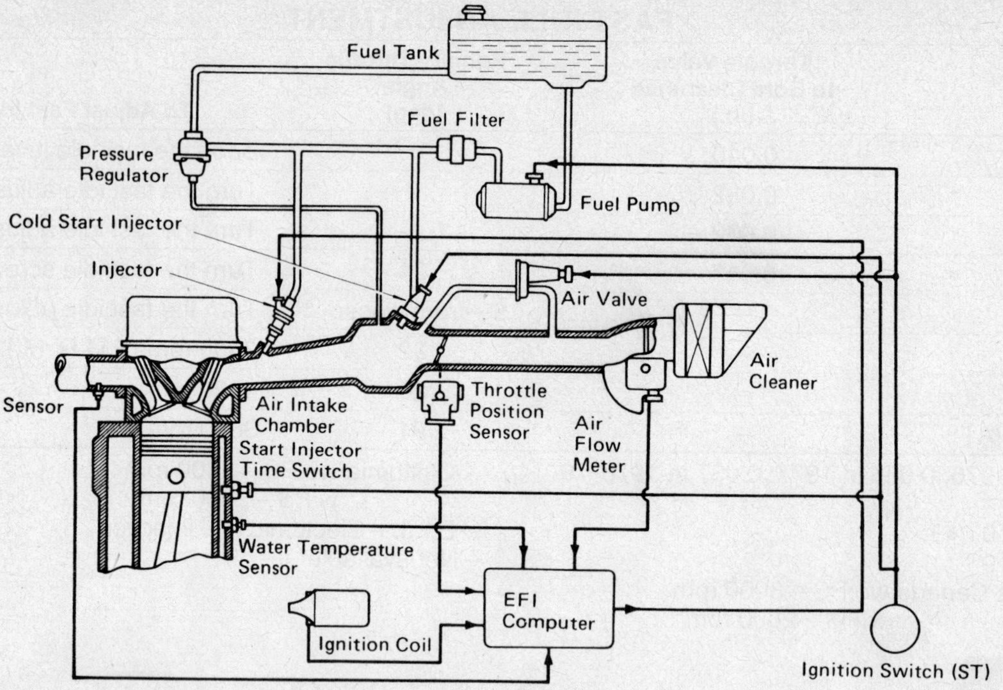

Electronic fuel injection system

INITIAL IDLE MIXTURE SCREW ADJUSTMENT

When assembling the carburetor, turn the idle mixture screw the number of turns specified below. After the carburetor is installed, perform the appropriate idle speed/mixture adjustment as outlined above.

3K-C engine—2 turns from seating
20R engine—1¾ turns from fully closed
4M engines—1½ turns out
1A-C—2¼ turns
3A—2¾ turns

CAUTION

Seat the idle mixture screw lightly; overtightening will damage its tip.

UNLOADER ADJUSTMENT

Make the unloader adjustment with the primary valve fully opened. The total angle of choke valve opening, in the chart, is measured with either a special gauge, supplied in the carburetor rebuilding kit, or a gauge of the proper angle fabricated from cardboard.

Electronic Fuel Injection

The Electronic Fuel Injection (EFI) system used on Toyotas has three basic systems.

FUEL SYSTEM

An electronic fuel pump supplies sufficient fuel, under constant pressure, to the injectors. These injectors meter the fuel into the intake manifold in accordance with signals from the EFI computer. Each injector injects, at the same time, one half of the fuel required for ideal combustion with each engine revolution.

AIR INDUCTION SYSTEM

This system provides sufficient air for proper engine operation. It consists of the air cleaner, air flow meter, air valve, and air intake chamber. These are also controlled by the computer.

EFI COMPUTER

The most important part of the system is the EFI computer. It receives signals indicating a change in operating conditions such as: Air intake volume, air intake temperature, coolant temperature, engine load, acceleration/deceleration, exhaust oxygen content. These signals help the computer determine the injection duration necessary for an optimum air-fuel ratio.

MANUAL TRANSMISSION

REMOVAL AND INSTALLATION

Corolla and Carina

Working from inside of the car, perform the following:

1. Place the gear selector in Neutral. Remove the center console, if so equipped.
2. Remove the trim boot at the base of the shift lever and the boot underneath it on the shift tower.
3. On Corolla 1200 models only:
   a. Unfasten the snap-ring from the base of the shift lever.
   b. Withdraw the conical spring and the shift lever itself.
4. On Corolla 1600 and Carina models only:
   a. Remove the four shift lever plate retaining screws.
   b. Remove the shift lever assembly.
   c. Remove the gasket.

NOTE: Cover the hole with a clean cloth to prevent anything from falling into the transmission case.

Working from inside of the car, perform the following:

5. Drain the cooling system and disconnect the cable from the positive side of the battery.
6. Remove the radiator hoses.
7. On Corolla 1200 models only:
   a. Disconnect the backup lamp switch connector.
   b. Remove the engine fan.
8. On Corolla 1600 and Carina models only:
   a. Remove the air cleaner, complete with hoses.
   b. Unfasten the accelerator torque rod at the carburetor.
   c. Remove the clutch hydraulic line support bracket.
   d. Remove the starter assembly from the left side of the engine.

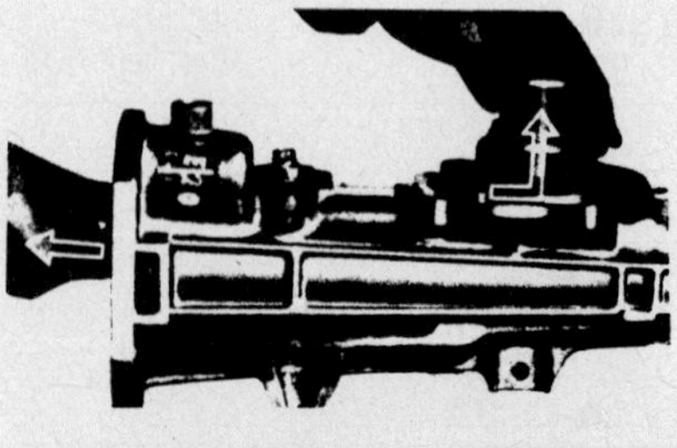

Corolla shift lever retainer removal

e. Remove the upper left-hand clutch housing bolt, from the flat at the top of the clutch housing.

9. Drain the transmission oil.

10. Detach the exhaust pipe from the manifold and remove the exhaust pipe support bracket.

11. Remove the driveshaft.

NOTE: It will be necessary to plug the opening in the end of the transmission with an old yoke or, if none is available, cover it with a plastic bag secured by a rubber band.

12. Unfasten the speedometer cable from the right side of the transmission.

13. On Corolla 1600 and Carina models, only:

a. Remove the clutch release cylinder assembly from the transmission and tie it aside, so that it is out of the way.

b. Unplug the back-up lamp switch connector.

14. Support the front of the transmission with a jack.

15. Unbolt the engine rear mounts. Remove the rear crossmember.

16. Remove the jack from under the transmission.

17. On Corolla 1600 and Carina models, unbolt the clutch housing from the engine and withdraw the transmission assembly.

NOTE: Remove the brace, if so equipped.

18. Perform the following on Corolla 1200 models, before removing the transmission:

a. Remove the cotter pin from the clutch release linkage.

b. Remove the clutch release cable.

c. Remove the stiffener plate, if so equipped.

d. Unbolt the clutch housing from the engine by removing the bolts in the order illustrated.

Installation is the reverse of removal, but observe the following.

Apply a light coating of multipurpose grease to the input shaft end, input shaft spline, clutch release bearing, and driveshaft end. On Corolla 1200 models, apply multipurpose grease to the ball on the end of the gearshift lever assembly; and to the clutch release cable end.

On Corolla 1200 models, install the clutch housing-to-engine bolts in two or three stages, and in the order shown.

After installation:

1. Fill the transmission and cooling system.
2. Adjust the clutch as detailed below.
3. Check to see that the back-up lamps function when Reverse is selected.

1975-81 Corona (4- and 5-Speed)

1. Disconnect the negative battery cable and then the positive battery-to-starter cable, complete with fusible link.

2. Drain the coolant from the radiator into a suitable clean container for re-use. Unfasten the upper radiator hose.

3. Detach the accelerator rod and link at the firewall side.

4. Raise both ends of the car and support them with jack stands.

5. Working underneath the car, remove the exhaust pipe clamp and clutch release cylinder (Don't disconnect its hydraulic line; set the cylinder out of the way). Next, disconnect the back-up light switch lead and speedometer cable.

6. Remove the driveshaft from the transmission, after matchmarking it and the companion flange for assembly.

NOTE: To prevent oil from draining out of the transmission, install a spare U-joint or if none is available, cover the opening with a plastic bag secured with a rubber band.

7. Place a block of wood on the lift pad of a jack to protect the transmission, and support the transmission with it.

8. Cover the back end of the valve cover with cloths, remove the rear crossmember (See "Engine Removal"), and lower the jack.

9. Unfasten the bolts which secure the shift lever, and remove the shift lever.

10. Remove the starter motor from the clutch housing.

11. Remove the bolts which secure the clutch housing to the engine block.

12. Move the transmission and jack rearward, until the input shaft has cleared the clutch cover. Remove the transmission from underneath the car.

Installation is the reverse of removal. Be sure to apply a thin coating of grease to the input shaft splines. The clutch housing-to-cylinder block bolts should be tightened to 37-58 ft/lbs. Adjust the clutch and fill the transmission with API GL-4 SAE 90 gear oil. Grease the shift lever spring seat and shift lever tip. Use the matchmarks to install the driveshaft.

Celica, Cressida, Mark II

Perform the removal procedures as outlined for the Corolla 1600 and Carina. In addition, perform the following:

1. Remove the accelerator connecting rod from the linkage.

2. With the car jacked up and supported:

a. Remove the left-hand, rear stone shield before removing the clutch release cylinder.

b. Remove the flywheel housing lower cover and its braces.

Installation is the reverse of removal.

NOTE: Use a clutch guide tool, during installation, to locate the clutch disc.

Tercel

1. Disconnect the negative battery cable.

2. Drain the coolant from the radiator tank and remove the top radiator hose.

3. Remove the air cleaner intake duct.

4. Remove the intermediate steering shaft.

5. Drain the gear oil from the transmission.

NOTE: Remove all three drain plugs.

6. Remove the exhaust pipe.

7. Remove the No. 1 gear shift rod and shift lever housing rod.

8. Remove the speedometer cable and back up light switch connector.

9. Remove the rear engine support crossmember.

NOTE: Support the transaxle with a jack and a block of wood.

10. Remove the nine transmission bolts.

11. Install 4 bolts on the transaxle side to an equal depth.

12. Separate the transmission by tightening the bolts a little at a time on the transmission side.

13. Remove the transmission.

14. Installation is the reverse of removal. Tighten the transmission bolts 8-11 ft/lbs. Fill the transmission with 6.5 pints of gear oil.

Floor Shifter Adjustment

All Toyota models equipped with a floor shifter have internally-mounted shift linkages. On older models, the linkage is contained in the side cover which is bolted on the transmission case. Newer cars have the shift linkage mounted in the top of the transmission case itself.

No external adjustment is needed or possible.

CLUTCH

The clutch is a single-plate, dry disc type. Later models use a diaphragm-spring pressure plate. Clutch release bearings are sealed ball bearing units which need no lubrication and should never be washed in any kind of solvent. All clutches, except those on the 1975 Corolla 1200 series and the Tercel are hydraulically operated.

REMOVAL AND INSTALLATION

CAUTION

Do not allow grease or oil to get on any of the disc, pressure plate, or flywheel surfaces.

1. Remove the transmission from the car as detailed above.

2. Remove the clutch cover and disc from the bellhousing.

3. Unfasten the release fork bearing clips. Withdraw the release bearing hub, complete with the release bearing.

4. Remove the tension spring from the clutch linkage.

5. Remove the release fork and support.

6. Punch matchmarks on the clutch cover and the pressure plate so the pressure plate can be returned to its original position during installation.

7. Slowly unfasten the screws which attach the retracting springs.

NOTE: If the screws are released too fast, the clutch assembly will fly apart, causing possible injury or loss of parts.

8. Separate the pressure plate from the clutch cover/spring assembly.

Inspect the parts for wear or deterioration. Replace parts as required.

Installation is performed in the reverse order of removal. Several points should be noted, however:

1. Be sure to align the matchmarks on the clutch cover and pressure plate which were made during disassembly.
2. Apply a thin coating of multipurpose grease to the release bearing hub and release fork contact points. Also, pack the groove inside the clutch hub with multipurpose grease.
3. Center the clutch disc by using a clutch pilot tool or an old input shaft. Insert the pilot into the end of the input shaft front bearing and bolt the clutch to the flywheel.

NOTE: Bolt the clutch assembly to the flywheel in two or three stages.

4. Adjust the clutch as outlined following.

PEDAL HEIGHT SPECIFICATIONS

Model/Year	Height (in.)	Measure Between
Corolla 1200 1975-77	2.2 ①	Pedal pad and floor mat
Corolla 1200 1978-81	6.7	Pedal pad and floor mat
Tercel 1980-81	6.65	Pedal pad and floor mat
Corolla 1600 1975-81	6.5	Pedal pad and floor mat
Corona 1975-81	6.5-6.9	Pedal pad and floor mat
Mark II/6 (all)	6.2-6.6	Pedal pad and asphalt seat
Celica		
1975-77	6.3	Pedal pad and floor mat
1978-79	6.67	
1980	6.48-4.87	
Celica Supra 1980-81	6.48-6.87	Pedal and floor mat
Cressida 1975-81	6.1-6.5	From floor mat
Station Wagon (all)	9.6	Pedal pad and firewall

① Pedal depressed

Tercel

In order to replace the clutch, the engine must be removed. See the engine removal section.

1. After the engine has been removed tie the bell housing to the cowl.
2. Place matchmarks on the clutch cover and flywheel.
3. Remove the clutch cover.

NOTE: Loosen each bolt gradually to prevent distortion of the cover.

4. Remove the disc.
5. Installation is the reverse of removal.

NOTE: Do not allow grease to get on the disc lining, flywheel, or cover. When reinstalling the clutch be sure to use a spline alignment tool or an old input shaft to properly align the clutch. Tighten the cover bolts 11-15 ft/lbs.

FREE-PLAY ADJUSTMENT

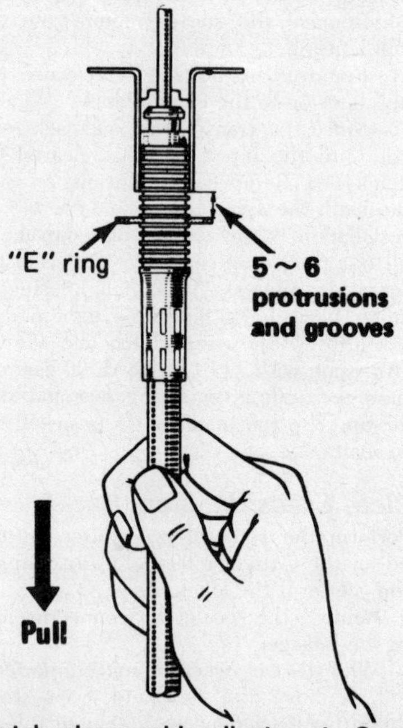

Clutch release cable adjustment—Corolla 1200

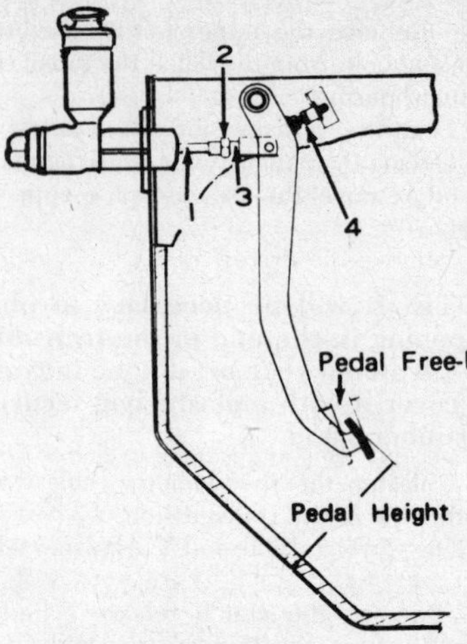

1. Master cylinder push rod
2. Push rod locknut
3. Clevis
4. Pedal stop (bolt)

Clutch pedal adjustments

1975 Corolla 1200

1. Pull on the clutch release cable at the clutch support flange until a resistance is felt when the release bearing contacts the clutch diaphragm spring.
2. Holding the cable in this position, measure the distance between the E-ring and the end of the wire support flange. The distance should be 5-6 threads.
3. If adjustment is required, change the position of the E-ring.
4. After completing the adjustment, check the clutch pedal free-play which should be 0.8-1.4 in. after the pedal is depressed several times.

All Except 75 Corolla 1200

1. Adjust the clearance between the master cylinder piston and the pushrod to the specifications given in the chart below. Loosen the pushrod locknut and rotate the pushrod while depressing the clutch pedal lightly with your finger.
2. Tighten the locknut when finished the adjustment.
3. Adjust the release cylinder free-play by

CLUTCH PEDAL FREE-PLAY ADJUSTMENTS

Model	Master Cylinder piston to pushrod clearance (in.)	Release cylinder to release fork free-play (in.)	Pedal free-play (in.)
Corolla 1200	0.02	1.00-1.40	1.00-1.80 ①
1600	0.02	0.08-0.14 ②	0.79-1.58
1800	Not adj.	Not adj.	0.51-0.91
Corona 1975-77	Not adj.	0.08-0.12 ⑨	0.04-0.28
Corona 1978-80	Not adj.	Not adj.	0.51-0.91
Mark II/6	0.02-0.12	0.08-0.12	1.20-1.80
Celica 1975-77	0.04-0.12	0.08-0.14 ②	1.00-1.75
Celica 2200 1978-81	Not adj.	Not adj.	0.51-0.91
Supra 2600	Not adj.	Not adj.	0.20-0.59

① 1978-79: 0.8-1.4 ② 1978-79: Not adjustable

loosening the release cylinder pushrod locknut and rotating the pushrod until the specification in the chart is obtained.

4. Measure the clutch pedal free-play after performing the above adjustments. If it fails to fall within specifications, repeat Steps 1-3 until it does.

Tercel

The Tercel needs no clutch adjustment as it has the self adjusting type.

Clutch Master Cylinder

REMOVAL AND INSTALLATION

CAUTION

Do not spill fluid on the painted surfaces of the vehicle.

1. Remove the clevis pin.
2. Detach the hydraulic line from the tube.
3. Unfasten the bolts which secure the master cylinder to the firewall. Withdraw the assembly.

Installation is performed in the reverse order of removal. Bleed the system as detailed below. Adjust the clutch pedal height and free-play.

Overhaul

1. Remove master cylinder.
2. Remove the reservoir.
3. Disengage the snap-ring and take out the pushrod and piston.
4. Inspect all parts for pitting and wear and replace as necessary.
5. Apply a grease compatible with rubber to the piston seals.
6. Install the pushrod and piston and secure with a snap-ring and washer.
7. Install the reservoir. Torque to 22 ft/lbs.
8. Install master cylinder.
9. Bleed the system.

Clutch Release Cylinder

REMOVAL AND INSTALLATION

1. Plug the master cylinder cap to prevent fluid leakage.
2. Raise the front of the vehicle and support it with jack stands.
3. Remove the gravel shield, if necessary, to gain access to the release cylinder.
4. Unfasten the clutch fork return spring at the fork.
5. Detach the hydraulic line from the release cylinder.
6. Screw the release cylinder pushrod in.
7. Loosen and remove the securing nuts from the release cylinder. Remove the cylinder.

Installation is performed in the reverse order of removal. Adjust the release fork-to-release cylinder free-play and bleed the hydraulic system, after installation is completed.

OVERHAUL

1. Remove the release cylinder.
2. Remove the pushrod, boot, piston and cup.
3. Inspect all parts for pitting and wear. Replace as necessary.
4. Coat piston seal and cup with a grease compatible with rubber.
5. Install all parts.
6. Install cylinder.
7. Bleed the system.

AUTOMATIC TRANSMISSION

All Celica, Corona and Corolla models use a three-speed transmission made by Aisin-Warner (A-40). All other models use a three-speed Toyoglide.

This section covers routine service, basic adjustments, and transmission removal.

REMOVAL AND INSTALLATION

Tercel

1. Disconnect the negative battery cable.
2. Drain the coolant from the radiator tank and remove the top hose.
3. Remove the air cleaner inlet duct.
4. Remove the intermediate steering shaft.
5. Drain the fluid from the transmission.
6. Remove the exhaust pipe.
7. Remove the shift lever rod.
8. Remove the speedometer cable, back-up light connector and any throttle linkage.
9. Remove the cooling lines from the transmission.
10. Support the transaxle with a jack.
11. Remove the rear crossmember.
12. Separate the transmission from the transaxle.
13. Remove the transmission.
14. Installation is the reverse of removal.

3-Speed Toyoglide

1. Disconnect the battery.
2. Remove the air cleaner and disconnect the accelerator torque link or the cable.
3. Disconnect the throttle link rod at the carburetor side, then disconnect the backup light wiring at the firewall (on early models).
4. Jack up the car and support it on stands, then drain the transmission. (Use a clean receptacle so that the fluid can be checked for color, smell and foreign matter.)
5. Disconnect all shift linkage.
6. On early models, remove the cross shaft from the frame.
7. Disconnect the throttle link rod at the transmission side and remove the speedometer cable, cooler lines and parking brake equalizer bracket.
8. Loosen the exhaust flange nuts and remove the exhaust pipe clamp and bracket.
9. Remove the drive shaft and the rear mounting bracket, then lower the rear end of the transmission carefully.
10. Unbolt the torque converter from the drive plate. Support the engine with a suitable jack stand and remove the seven bolts that hold the transmission to the engine.

Reverse the order of the removal procedures with the following precautions.

1. Install the drive plate and ring gear, tighten the attaching bolts to 37-43 ft/lbs.
2. After assembling the torque converter to the transmission, check the clearance, it should be about 0.59 in.
3. Before installing the transmission, install the oil pump locator pin on the torque converter to facilitate installation.
4. While rotating the crankshaft, tighten the converter attaching bolts, a little at a time.
5. After installing the throttle connecting second rod, make sure the throttle valve lever indicator aligns with the mark on the transmission with the carburetor throttle valve fully opened. If required, adjust the rod.
6. To install the transmission control rod correctly, move the transmission lever to N (Neutral), and the selector lever to Neutral. Fill the transmission with automatic transmission fluid (Type F only), then start the engine. Run the engine at idle speed and apply the brakes while moving the selector lever through all positions, then return it to Neutral.
7. After warming the engine, move the selector lever through all positions, then back to Neutral, and check the fluid level. Fill as necessary.
8. Adjust the engine idle to 550-650 rpm with the selector lever at Drive. Road test the vehicle.
9. With the selector lever at 2 or Drive, check the point at which the transmission shifts. Check for shock, noise and slipping with the selector lever in all positions. Check for leaks from the transmission.

3-Speed A-40

To remove and install the transmission, proceed in the following manner:

1. Perform Steps 1 through 3 of the three-speed Toyoglide removal procedure.
2. Remove the upper starter mounting nuts using a socket wrench with a long extension.
3. Raise the car and support it securely with jack stands. Drain the transmission.
4. Remove the lower starter mounting bolt and lay the starter along side of the engine. Don't let it hang by the wires.
5. Unbolt the parking brake equalizer support.
6. Matchmark the driveshaft and the companion flange, to ensure correct installation. Remove the bolts securing the driveshaft to the companion flange.
7. Slide the driveshaft straight back and out of the transmission. Use a spare U-joint yoke or tie a plastic bag over the end of the transmission to keep any fluid from dripping out.
8. Remove the bolts from the cross-shaft body bracket, the cotter pin from the manual lever, and the cross-shaft socket from the transmission.
9. Remove the exhaust pipe bracket from the torque converter bell housing.
10. Disconnect the oil cooler lines from the transmission and remove the line bracket from the bell housing.
11. Disconnect the speedometer cable from the transmission.
12. Unbolt both support braces from the bell housing.

13. Use a transmission jack to raise the transmission slightly.

14. Unbolt the rear crossmember and lower the transmission about 3 in.

15. Pry the two rubber torque converter access plugs out of their holes at the back of the engine.

16. Remove the six torque converter mounting bolts through the access hole. Rotate the engine with the crankshaft pulley.

17. Cut the head off a bolt to make a guide pin for the torque converter. Install the pin on the converter.

18. Remove the converter bell housing-to-engine bolts.

19. Push on the end of the guide pin in order to remove the converter with the transmission. Remove the transmission rearward and then bring it out from under the car.

CAUTION

Don't catch the throttle cable during removal.

Installation is the reverse of removal. Be sure to note the following, however:

1. Install the two long bolts on the upper converter housing and tighten them to 36-58 ft/lbs.
2. Tighten the converter-to-flex-plate bolts finger-tight, and then tighten them with a torque wrench to 11-16 ft/lbs.
3. When installing the speedometer cable, make sure that the felt dust protector and washer are on the cable end.
4. Tighten the cooling line and exhaust pipe bracket mounting bolts to 37-58 ft/lbs. Tighten the cooling lines to 14-22 ft/lbs.
5. Align the matchmarks made on the driveshaft and the companion flange during removal. Tighten the driveshaft mounting bolts to 11-16 ft/lbs.
6. Be sure to install the oil pan drain plug. Tighten it to 11-14 ft/lbs.
7. Adjust the throttle cable.
8. Fill the transmission to the proper capacity. Use only type "F" (ATF) fluid. Start the engine, run the selector through all gear ranges and place it in Park (P). Check the level on the dipstick and add type F fluid, as necessary.
9. Road test the car and check for leaks.

PAN REMOVAL

1. Remove the plug and drain the fluid from the transmission.
2. Unfasten the pan securing bolts.
3. Remove the pan.

Installation is the reverse of removal. Torque the pan securing bolts to 4-6 ft/lbs. Refill the transmission with fluid.

LOW SERVO AND BAND ADJUSTMENT

FRONT BAND ADJUSTMENT

3 Speed

1. Remove the pan as outlined above.
2. Pry the band engagement lever toward the band with a screwdriver.
3. The gap between the end of the piston rod and the engagement bolt should be 0.138 in.

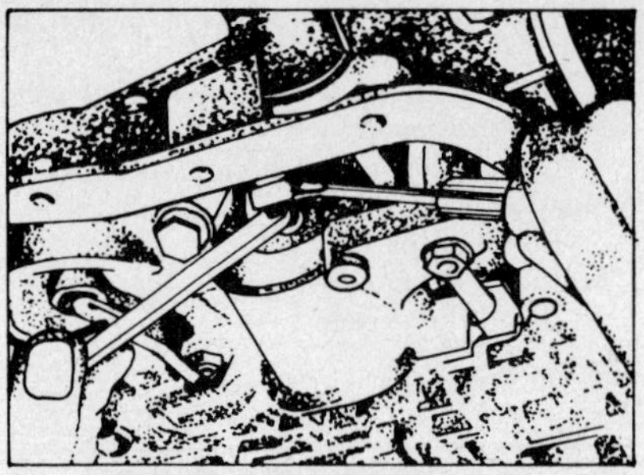

Adjusting the three-speed Toyoglide front band

4. If the gap does not meet the specification, adjust it by turning the engagement bolt.
5. Install the pan and refill the transmission as outlined above.

REAR BAND ADJUSTMENT

3 Speed

The rear band adjusting bolt is located on the outside of the case, so it is not necessary to remove the pan in order the adjust the band.

1. Loosen the adjusting bolt locknut and fully screw in the adjusting bolt.
2. Loosen the adjusting bolt one turn.
3. Tighten the locknut while holding the bolt so that it cannot turn.

BAND ADJUSTMENTS

3-Speed A-40

The A-40 transmission has no bands, and therefore no band adjustments are possible. The only external adjustments are throttle and shift linkages.

NEUTRAL SAFETY SWITCH ADJUSTMENT

Corolla

The neutral safety switch used on Corolla models is not adjustable. If it malfunctions, it must be replaced. To do so, proceed in the following manner:

1. Remove the center console.
2. Unfasten and remove the three screws which secure the transmission selector assembly.
3. Disconnect the neutral safety switch multiconnector.
4. Slightly lift the transmission selector assembly and remove the two neutral safety switch attaching screws.
5. Withdraw the switch.

Installation is the reverse of removal. Position the selector lever in Neutral and install the switch so that installation marks align with each other.

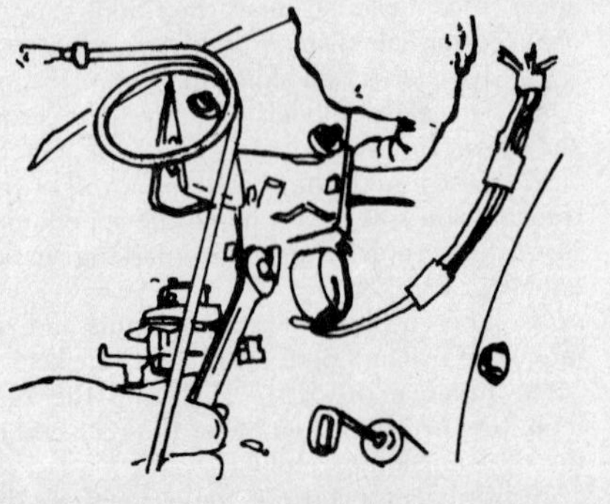

Adjusting the neutral safety switch on models with the three speed Toyoglide and a column-mounted shift

3 Speed–Column Selector

The neutral safety switch/reverse lamp switch on the Toyoglide transmission with a column-mounted selector is located under the hood on the shift linkage. If the switch is not functioning properly, adjust as follows:

1. Loosen the switch securing bolt.
2. Move the switch so that its arm just contacts the control shaft lever when the gear selector is in Drive position.

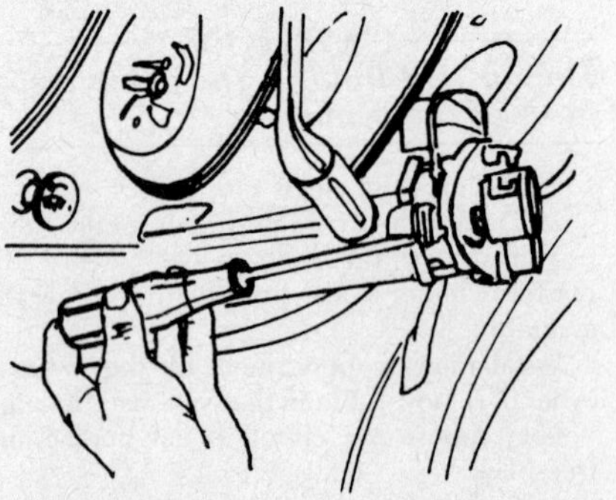

Adjusting the column shift indicator drive cord

3. Tighten the switch securing bolt.
4. Check the operation of the switch; the car should start only in Park or Neutral and the back-up lamps should come on only when Reverse is selected.
5. If the switch cannot be adjusted so that it functions properly, replace it. Perform the adjustment as outlined.

3 Speed–Console Shift

Models with a console-mounted selector have the neutral safety switch on the linkage located beneath the console. To adjust it, proceed in the following manner:

1. Remove the screws which secure the center console.
2. Unfasten the console multiconnector, if so equipped, and completely remove the console.
3. Adjust the switch in the manner outlined in the column selector section, above.
4. Install the console in the reverse order of removal after completion of the switch adjustment.

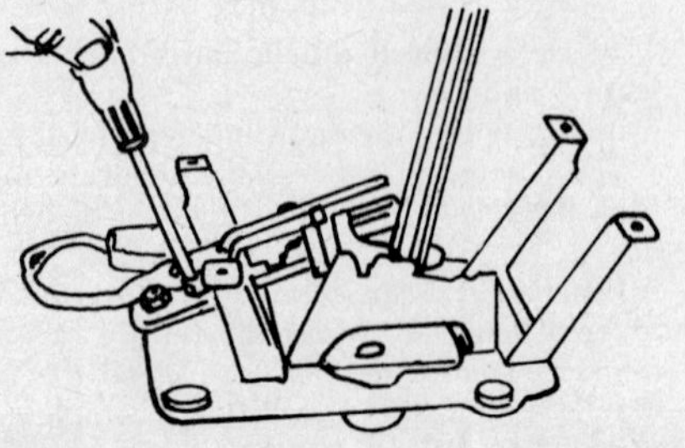

Adjusting the neutral safety switch on models with the three speed Toyoglide and floor mounted shift

SHIFT LINKAGE ADJUSTMENT

Speed Toyoglide

1. Check all of the shift linkage bushings for wear. Replace any worn bushings.
2. Loosen the connecting rod swivel locknut.
3. Move the selector lever and check movement of the pointer in the shift quadrant.
4. When the control shaft is set in the neutral position the quadrant pointer should indicate "N" (Neutral), as well.

Steps 5-7 apply only to cars equipped with column-mounted shift levers.

5. If the pointer does not indicate Neutral, then check the drive cord adjustment.
6. Remove the steering column shroud.
7. Turn the drive cord adjuster with a Phillips screwdriver until the pointer indicates Neutral.

Steps 8-10 apply to both column-mounted and floor-mounted selectors:

8. Position the manual valve lever on the transmission so that it is in the Neutral position.
9. Lock the connecting rod swivel with the locknut so that the pointer, selector, and manual valve lever are all positioned in Neutral.
10. Check the operation of the gear selector by moving it through all ranges.

3-Speed A-40

1. Check the linkage for freedom of movement.
2. Push the manual valve lever toward the front of the car, as far as it will go.
3. Bring the lever back to its third notch (Neutral).
4. Have someone hold the shift lever in Neutral, while you tighten the linkage so that it can't slip.

THROTTLE LINKAGE ADJUSTMENT

3 Speed Toyoglide

1. Loosen the locknut at each end of the linkage adjusting turnbuckle.
2. Detach the throttle linkage connecting rod from the carburetor.
3. Align the pointer on the throttle valve lever with the mark stamped on the transmission case.
4. Rotate the turnbuckle so that the end of the throttle linkage rod and the carburetor throttle lever are aligned.

NOTE: The carburetor throttle valve must be fully opened during this adjustment.

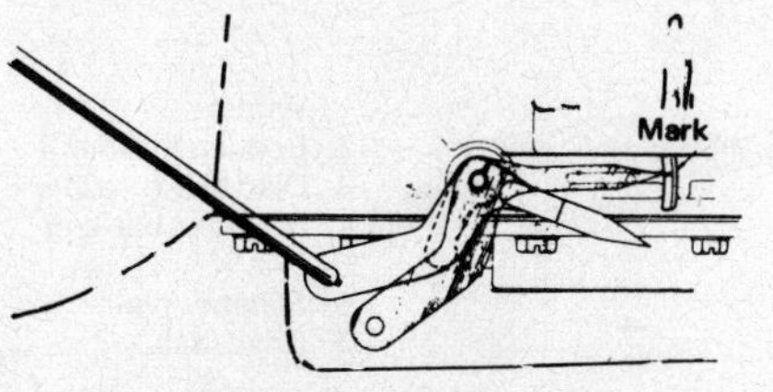

Throttle linkage aligning marks

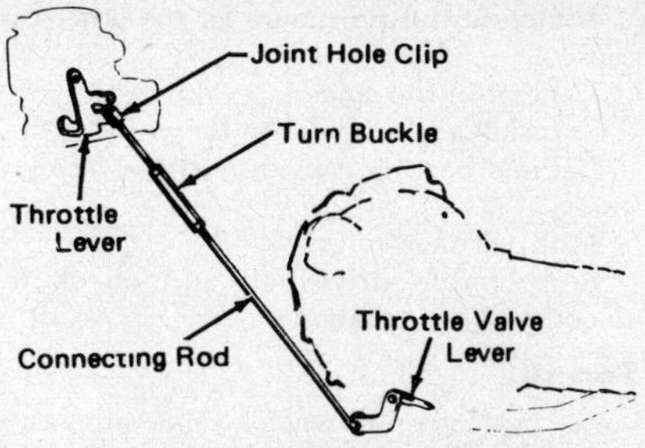

Throttle linkage components

5. Tighten the turnbuckle locknuts and reconnect the throttle rod to the carburetor.
6. Open the throttle valve and check the pointer alignment with the mark on the transmission case.
7. Road-test the car. If the transmission "hunts," i.e., keeps shifting rapidly back and forth between gears at certain speeds or if it fails to downshift properly when going up hills, repeat the throttle linkage adjustment.

3-Speed A-40

1. Remove the air cleaner.
2. Confirm that the accelerator linkage opens the throttle fully. Adjust the link as necessary.
3. Peel the rubber dust book back from the throttle cable.
4. Loosen the adjustment nuts on the throttle cable bracket (rocker cover) just enough to allow cable housing movement.
5. Have someone depress the accelerator pedal fully.
6. Adjust the cable housing so that the distance between its end and the cable stop collar is 2.05 in.
7. Tighten the adjustment nuts. Make sure that the adjustment hasn't changed. Install the dust boot and the air cleaner.

DRIVE AXLE

Driveshaft and U-Joints

REMOVAL AND INSTALLATION

Passenger Cars

1. Raise the rear of the car with jacks and support the rear axle housing with jack stands.
2. Matchmark the driveshaft and companion flange. Unfasten the bolts which attach the driveshaft universal joint yoke flange to the mounting flange on the differential drive pinion.

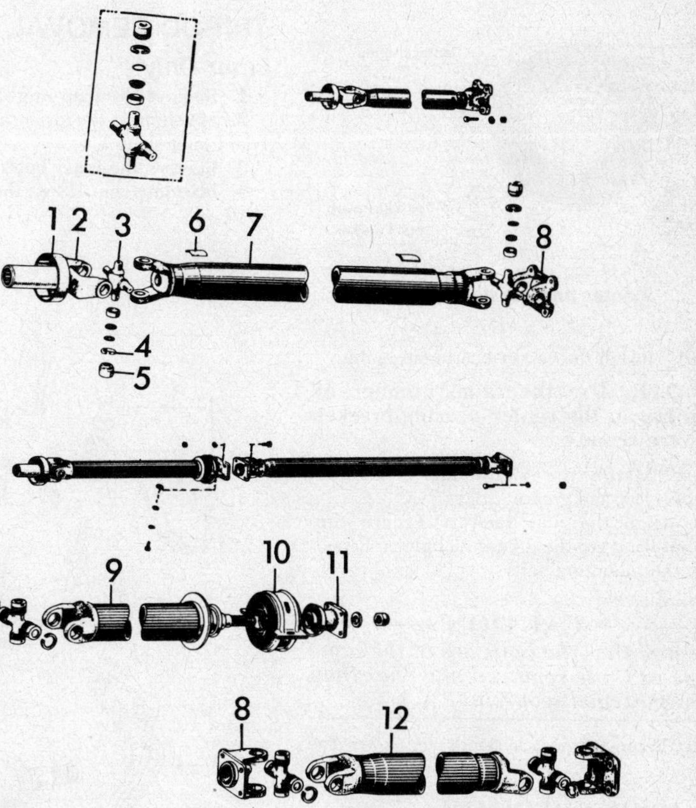

1. Transmission end of driveshaft
2. U-joint yoke and sleeve
3. U-joint spider
4. Snap ring
5. U-joint spider bearing
6. Balancing weight
7. Driveshaft
8. U-joint yoke flange
9. Intermediate driveshaft assembly
10. Center bearing support
11. U-joint flange assembly
12. Driveshaft

Two-piece driveshaft only

Driveshaft components—the upper illustration shows a single piece driveshaft

3. On models equipped with three universal joints, perform the following:
   a. Remove the driveshaft subassembly from the U-joint sleeve yoke.
   b. Remove the center support bearing from its bracket.
4. Remove the driveshaft end from the transmission.
5. Install an old U-joint yoke in the transmission or, if none is available, use a plastic bag secured with a rubber band over the hole to keep the transmission oil from running out.
6. Remove the driveshaft from beneath the vehicle.

Installation is performed in the following order:

1. Apply multipurpose grease on the section of the U-joint sleeve which is to be inserted into the transmission.
2. Insert the driveshaft sleeve into the transmission.

CAUTION

Be careful not to damage any of the seals.

3. For models equipped with three U-joints and center bearings, perform the following:
   a. Adjust the center bearing clearance with no load placed on the driveline components; the top of the rubber center cushion should be 0.04 in. *behind* the center of the elongated bolt hole.

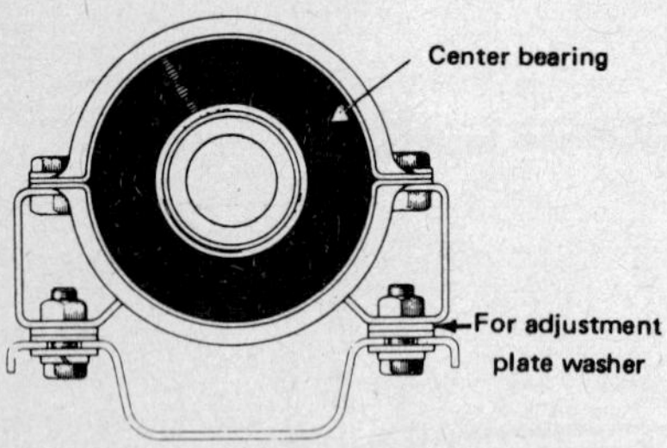

Center bearing adjustment

   b. Install the center bearing assembly.

NOTE: Use the same number of washers on the center bearing bracket as were removed.

   c. Match the arrow marks on the driveshaft and grease fittings.
4. Align the matchmarks. Secure the U-joint flange to the differential pinion flange with the mounting bolts.

CAUTION

Be sure that the bolts are of the same type as those removed and that they are tightened securely.

5. Remove the jack stands and lower the vehicle.

U-JOINT OVERHAUL

1. Mark the flange yoke and shaft for reassembly.
2. Remove the snap-rings and, using a hammer and drift, drive one bearing cap most of the way out. Remove it with pliers.
3. Drive the opposite cap out.
4. Repeat this procedure for the other two caps.
5. Remove the spider.
6. Install a new spider in the yoke.
7. Press bearing caps over spider using a vise.
8. Install snap-rings.
9. Assemble driveshaft and check for smoothness of operation.

Tercel

1. Jack up your vehicle and support it with jack stands.
2. Remove the front wheel.
3. Remove the brake caliper and tie it out of the way.
4. Remove the cotter pin, locknut and adjusting nut, from the hub.
5. Remove the bottom nut from the shock absorber.
6. Pull down on the hub to separate it from the shock.
7. Using a suitable puller pull the axle hub from the driveshaft.
8. Remove the transaxle support bracket.
9. Remove the driveshaft from the transaxle using special tool # 09648-16010 available from your Toyota dealer.

NOTE: Be careful not to damage the rubber boots on the driveshaft.

10. Installation is the reverse of removal.

TRIPOD REMOVAL

Inner Only

1. Remove the snap-ring and boot clamp.
2. Matchmark the driveshaft and the inboard joint shaft.
3. Remove the inner boot.
4. Place matchmarks on the tripod and the shaft.

NOTE: When making these matchmarks be sure to use paint, or chalk. Do not punch mark any of these parts.

6. Drive the tripod off with a drift pin.

NOTE: Do not tap on the roller portion of the tripod.

7. Check for worn or damaged parts.
8. When reinstalling the tripod fill the boot with a lithium base grease.
9. Installation is the reverse of removal.

The manufacturer recommends that the outboard shaft be serviced as a complete unit only.

Tercel

1. Jack up your vehicle and support it with jack stands.
2. Remove the front wheel.
3. Remove the brake caliper and tie it out of the way.
4. Remove the stabilizer bar end.
5. Remove the strut bar end.
6. Remove the tie rod end, with a suitable puller.
7. Support the lower control arm with a jack.
8. Remove the lower control arm bolt.
9. Remove the bolt at the ball joint.
10. Lower the jack and remove the control arm.
11. Remove the bottom shock bolt.
12. Pull the hub from the driveshaft with a suitable puller.
13. Remove the steering knuckle from the shock absorber.
14. Installation is the reverse of removal.

The following torque specifications are needed: bottom shock bolt 40-52 ft/lbs, ball joint bolt 40-52 ft/lbs, stabilizer bar 11-15 ft/lbs, tie rod end 37-50 ft/lbs, lower control arm 51-65 ft/lbs, strut bar 29-39 ft/lbs, brake caliper 33-39 ft/lbs.

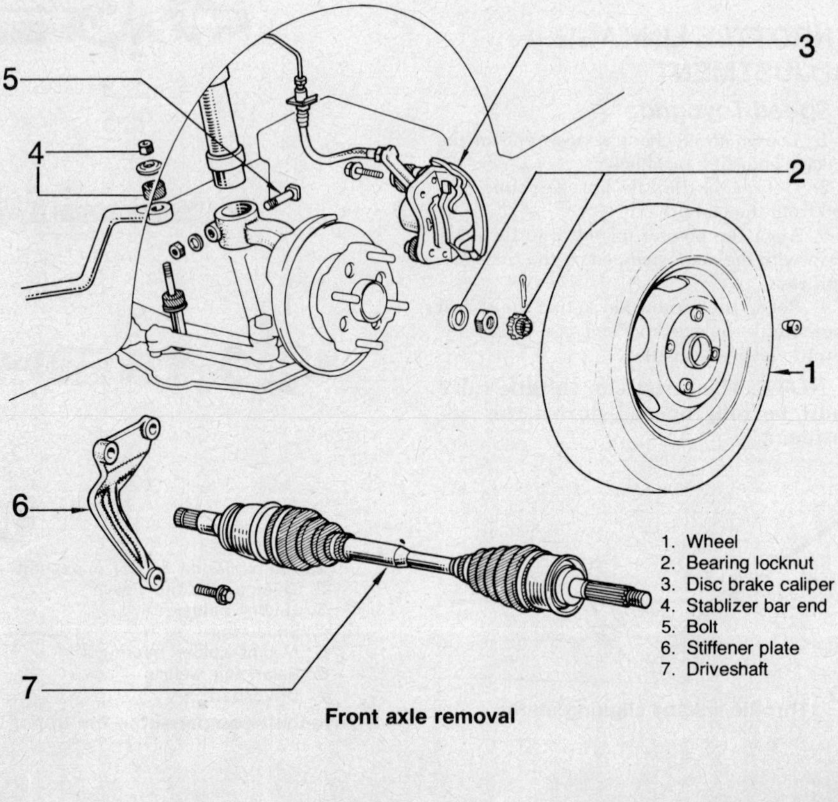

Front axle removal

Axle Shafts

REMOVAL AND INSTALLATION

Passenger Cars

1. Raise the rear of the car and support it securely by using jack stands.
2. Drain the oil from the axle housing.
3. Remove the wheel disc, unfasten the lug nuts, and remove the wheel.
4. Punch matchmarks on the brake drum and the axle shaft to maintain rotational balance.
5. Remove the brake drum and related components, as detailed below.
6. Remove the rear bearing retaining nut.
7. Remove the backing plate attachment nuts through the access holes in the rear axle shaft flange.
8. Use a slide hammer with a suitable adapter to withdraw the axle shaft from its housing.

CAUTION

Use care not to damage the oil seal when removing the axle shaft.

9. Repeat the procedure for the axle shaft on the opposite side.

CAUTION

Be careful not to mix the components of the two sides.

Installation is performed in the reverse order of removal. Coat the lips of the rear housing oil seal with multipurpose grease prior to installation of the rear axle shaft. Torque the bearing retaining nut to the specifications.

NOTE: Always use new nuts, as they are the self-locking type.

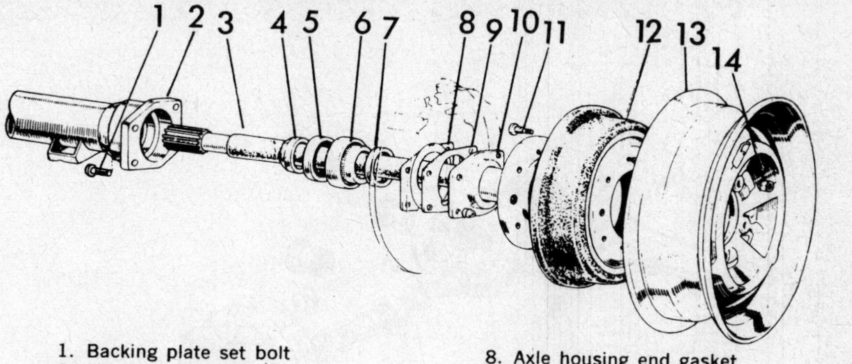

1. Backing plate set bolt
2. Rear axle housing
3. Rear axle shaft
4. Axle bearing inner retainer
5. Oil seal
6. Bearing
7. Spacer
8. Axle housing end gasket
9. Bearing retainer gasket
10. Axle bearing inner retainer
11. Hub bolt
12. Brake drum assembly
13. Wheel
14. Hub nut

Rear axle shaft and related components

AXLE BEARING RETAINING NUT SPECIFICATIONS

Model	Torque range (ft. lbs.)
Corolla 1200	15-22
Corolla 1200/1600	26-38
Carina	26-38
Corona	29-36
Mark II/6	43-52
Tercel	22
Corolla 3T-C	19-23
Celica	19-23
Supra	19-23
Cressida	22

Differential

REMOVAL AND INSTALLATION

NOTE: Rear axle servicing is a complex operation. Repair should not be attempted unless the special tools and knowledge required are readily available.

Rear Carrier–All Models, Except Tercel

1. Remove the axle shafts.
2. Disconnect the driveshaft from the pinion shaft flange.
3. Unfasten the carrier securing nuts and remove the carrier assembly.

Installation is performed in the reverse order of removal. Be sure to apply liquid sealer to both the carrier gasket and the lower carrier securing nuts.

Tercel

1. Disconnect the negative battery terminal.
2. Drain the water from the radiator tank.
3. Remove the top radiator hose from the engine.
4. Remove the clutch cable if so equipped.
5. Remove the starter.

NOTE: On cars equipped with automatic transmissions you must remove the torque converter bolts via the starter inset. Also remember to disconnect the oil cooling lines.

6. Remove the intermediate steering shaft.
7. Remove the bottom bolt on the engine shock absorber.
8. Remove the front driveshafts. See the section relating to this procedure.
9. Remove the exhaust pipe.
10. Remove the shifting linkage.
11. Remove the back-up light connector and the speedometer.

NOTE: On cars with automatic transmissions remove any necessary throttle linkage if so equipped.

12. Drain the oil from the transaxle and the transmission.

NOTE: Remove all three drain plugs on manual transmission cars.

13. Support the rear of the engine with a jack.
14. Remove the rear crossmember.
15. Place a jack under the transaxle.
16. Separate the transmission from the transaxle and remove the transmission.
17. Remove the bellhousing bolts and remove the transaxle.
18. Installation is the reverse of removal.

Because of the many specialized tools required to work on the differential, it is recommended that this work be performed by your dealer or a professional mechanic qualified to handle this type of work.

OVERHAUL

1. Thoroughly wash and rinse the carrier and blow dry with compressed air.
2. Securely clamp the carrier in a vise or suitable stand.
3. Apply a light coating of mechanic's blue to the teeth of the ring gear.
4. Applying a slight drag on the ring gear to avoid backlash, rotate the pinion in a smooth and continuous manner to obtain a good tooth pattern on the ring gear.
5. Next, attach a dial indicator gauge to the carrier base and check the ring gear backlash.
6. Also check ring gear runout at this time. If the tooth pattern obtained is correct, and the backlash and runout are within limits, any gear noise must come from the side gears.
7. With the dial indicator gauge set up on the carrier, check the backlash between the pinion gears and side gears. Excessive backlash usually is due to either worn thrust washers or a worn pinion shaft.
8. Check side gear thrust clearance with a feeler gauge.
9. If everything is within specifications, test the preload on the differential drive pinion nut. Punch mark both pinion and nut in their original positions, then loosen the pinion nut about ½ turn and torque to specifications. If the punch marks line up again (within 60°) the pinion preload was correct.
10. Punch mark both the carrier and the side bearing caps for identification, remove the locknuts and take off the caps.
11. Remove the differential case assembly

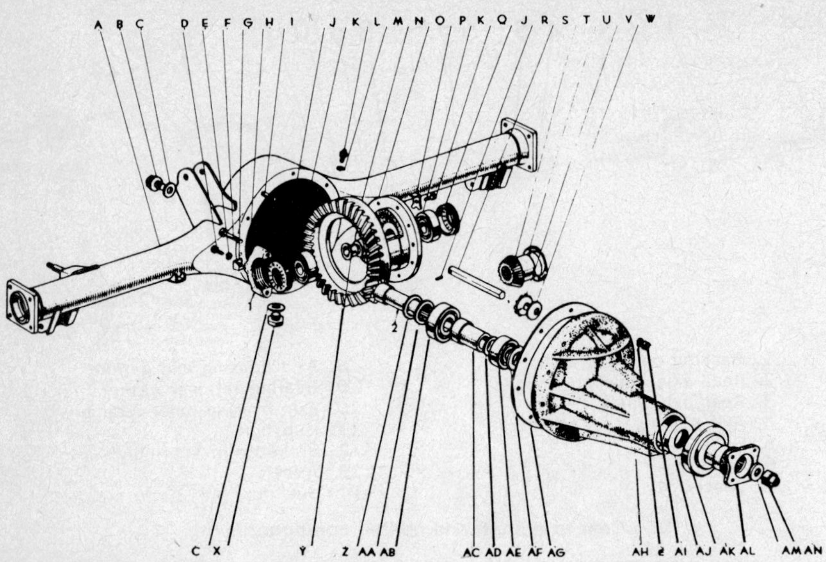

(a)—Housing assembly
(b)—Filler plug
(c)—Gasket
(d)—Bolt
(e)—Lock washer
(f)—Hexagon bolt
(g)—Bearing adjusting nut lock
(h)—Lockwasher
(i)—Stud
(j)—Bearing adjusting nut
(k)—Bearing
(l)—Breather plug
(m)—Lockwasher
(n)—Ring gear and drive pinion 1 and 2
(o)—Case
(p)—Lockplate
(q)—Bolt
(r)—Lockpin
(s)—Pinion shaft
(t)—Side gear
(u)—Thrust washer
(v)—Pinion
(w)—Thrust washer
(x)—Drain plug
(y)—Oil reservoir
(z)—Spacer
(aa)—Shim
(ab)—Bearing
(ac)—Spacer
(ad)—Shim
(ae)—Bearing
(af)—Oil slinger
(ag)—Gasket
(ah)—Carrier
(ai)—Nut
(aj)—Oil seal
(ak)—Dust deflector
(al)—Universal joint flange
(am)—Flat washer
(an)—Nut

Differential components

from the carrier. Do not mix the bearing cups; paint mark them for identification.

12. Remove the differential pinion nut (do not let the pinion drop out), then remove the pinion spacer, yoke and oil seal.

13. With a brass punch, drive out the pinion bearing cups.

NOTE: This should be done only when the bearings are to be replaced.

14. Press or pull off the drive pinion rear bearing. Avoid damaging the flat spacer behind the bearing.

15. Measure the spacer thickness and note the measurement for future use. Remove both side bearings from the differential case and mark them "L" and "R" for identification.

NOTE: Remove side bearings only if they must be replaced.

16. Punch mark the differential case and cover, then remove the cover bolts and the cover (where fitted).

17. Remove the shaft and pinions, the side gears and all thrust washers.

NOTE: Some differential types have four spider pinion gears; punch mark the gears before removal so they can be correctly reinstalled.

Check all bearing cones and cups for wear. Inspect the tooth surfaces of all gears carefully and inspect all thrust washers for wear and signs of slipping in their seats. Check all gear shafts for scoring, wear or distortion. Finally, inspect the case and carrier housing for cracks or other damage. Also check the case for signs of wear at the side gear bores, bearing cap and mounting hubs.

Assembly is performed in the following order:

1. Wash and clean all parts before installation.

2. Lightly oil all bearings and gear shafts, except the ring gear and drive pinion teeth.

3. Place the side gears and the pinion gears, with their thrust washers, into the differential case.

4. Insert the shaft and align the lock pin holes in the case and shaft.

5. Install the case cover in place and install the lock pin (bolt) and tighten the cover bolts to specification; check the play.

6. If the side bearings were removed, install them now. If the ring gear was removed, install it now. Tighten the bolts in symmetrical sequence to avoid distortion and runout.

7. Install the drive pinion bearing cups into the carrier housing, using a suitable installing tool. Make sure the cups are seated solidly.

8. Assemble the drive pinion rear bearing to the drive pinion and insert it into the carrier housing. Install the spacer and front bearing to the drive pinion; install the yoke and tighten the nut to specifications.

CAUTION

The drive pinion oil seal is NOT installed at this point.

9. The drive pinion preload is measured in in/lbs (not ft/lbs). Adjust the preload by changing the length of the bearing spacer (between the front and rear bearings) until the required preload is obtained.

10. Place the previously assembled differential case into position in the bearing hubs and put the caps into position as marked (L and R).

11. Set the case so that there will be the least amount of backlash between the ring gear and pinion (in order to save time adjusting).

12. Install the adjusting nuts (also marked L and R) and take care not to cross-thread them.

13. Finger-tighten the bearing caps until the threads are lined up correctly, then tighten slowly.

14. Back off the right-hand adjusting nut (ring gear teeth side) and screw in the other nut until almost no backlash is felt.

15. Attach a dial indicator gauge so that it reads at right angles to the back of the ring gear, then screw in the right-hand adjusting nut until the gauge indicates that all side play has been eliminated.

16. Tighten the adjusting nut another 1 or 1½ notches (depending on the fit of the lock tabs).

17. Recheck the preload on the drive pinion as before; this time the specifications are different.

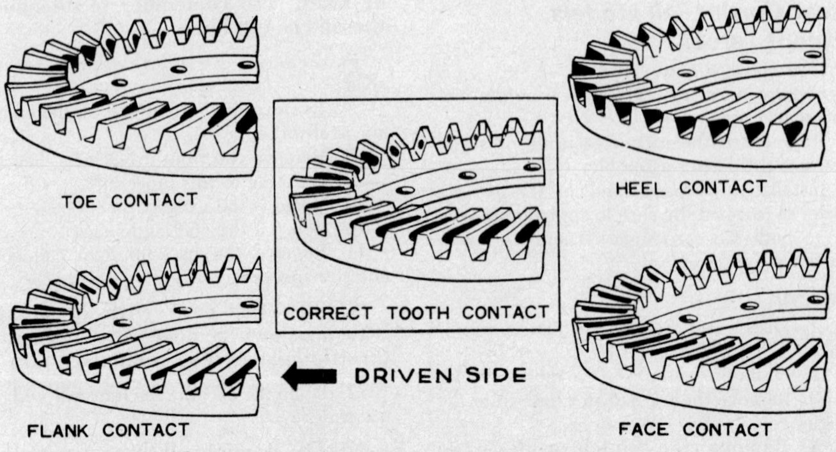

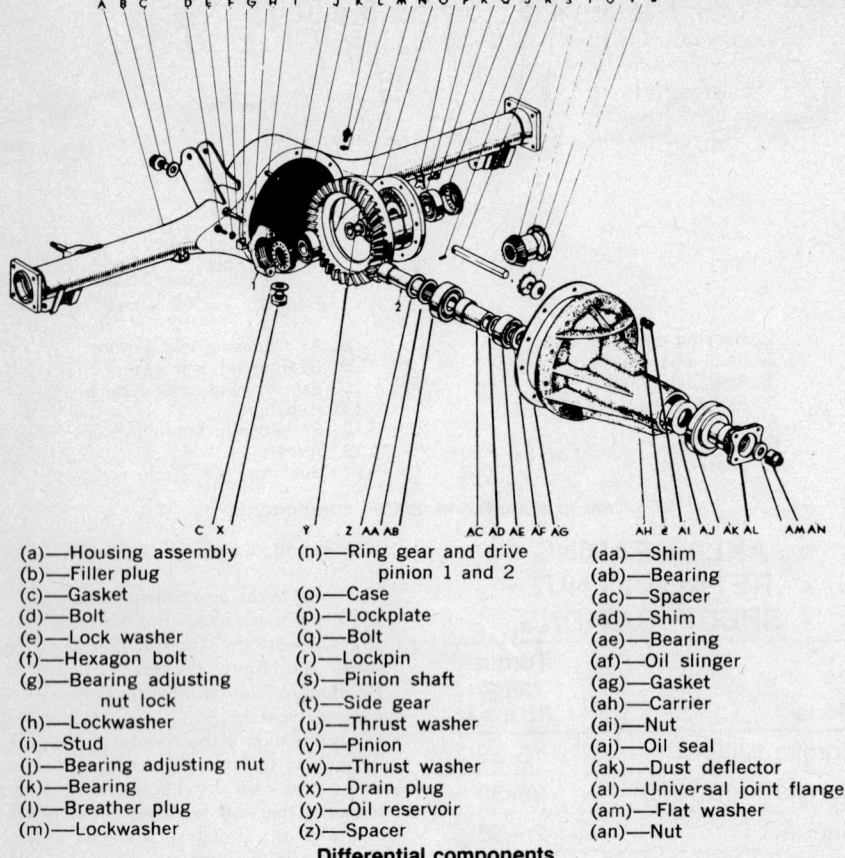

Ring gear tooth contact pattern

DIFFERENTIAL SPECIFICATIONS

Model/Year		Backlash (in.) Ring Gear and Pinion	Backlash (in.) Side Gears	Run-Out (in.) Ring Gear	Torque (ft. lbs.) Side Bearing Cap	Torque (ft. lbs.) Differential Pinion Nut	Pinion Bearing Preload (in. lbs.) New	Pinion Bearing Preload (in. lbs.) Old
Corolla								
	1200	0.0040-0.0060	0.0010-0.0060	0.0028	40-47	65-145	7-12	4-6
	1600 1975-78	0.0040-0.0060	0.0010-0.0060	0.0028	40-47	65-145	7-12	4-6
	1600 1979	0.0051-0.0071	0.0020-0.0080	0.0030	37-50	80-173	8.7-13.9	4.3-69
	1800	0.0051-0.0071	0.0010-0.0079	0.0028	37-50	80-173	8.7-13.9	4.3-6.9
Tercel		0.0039-0.0059	0.0016-0.0094	0.0028	33-39	109-267	4.3-8.7	2.6-4.3
Celica	1975	0.0051-0.0071	0.0030-0.0080	0.0016	36-50	123-145	4-5	2-3
	1976-81	0.0051-0.0071	0.0020-0.0079	0.0028	51-65	80-173	8.7-13.9	4.3-6.9
Corona	1975-77	0.0051-0.0071	0.0020-0.0079	0.0020	50-65	80-160	4-6	1-3
	1978-80	0.0051-0.0071	0.0020-0.0079	0.0028	51-65	80-173	8.7-13.9	4.3-6.9
Supra		0.0051-0.0071	0.0020-0.0079	0.0028	51-65	80-173	16.5-22.6	7.8-11.3
Cressida	1975-77	0.0051-0.0071	0.0020-0.0080	0.0030	51-65	80-173	7-10	2-4
	1978-81	0.0051-0.0071	0.0020-0.0079	0.0028	51-65	80-173	13.8-19.0	6.9-9.5
Mark II		0.0051-0.0071	0.0020-0.0079	0.0030	51-65	80-145	7-10	2-4

18. If too loose, readjust the side bearing preload; if too tight, adjust the ring gear backlash.
19. Install the dial indicator gauge so that it contacts the ring gear teeth at right angles. Adjust the backlash to specifications.
20. If too great, adjust by loosening the bearing cap bolts slightly and screwing the right-hand adjusting nut (ring gear teeth side) out about two notches.
21. Tighten the left-hand adjusting nut the same amount.

NOTE: One notch of the adjusting nut equals about 0.002 in. of backlash.

22. Recheck the backlash, then tighten the bearing cap nuts.
23. Using a dial indicator recheck all run-out dimensions (ring gear back, ring gear outer circumference and differential case).
24. Apply a thin coat of mechanic's blue, red lead or even lipstick to the ring gear teeth. Rotate the gear several times, applying a light drag to the ring gear. Rotate the gear in both directions.
25. Inspect the tooth pattern. There are four basic tooth patterns: heel, toe, flank and face. Most often the tooth pattern obtained will be a combination of two of these patterns and the adjustments must be made accordingly.

Heel contact Move the drive pinion in by increasing the thickness of the spacer (between the pinion head and rear bearing). Readjust backlash by moving the ring gear away from the pinion.

Face contact Adjust same as above.

Toe contact Adjust by moving the drive pinion out by reducing the thickness of the spacer. Readjust backlash.

Flank contact Adjust same as toe contact.

Continue assembling as follows:

26. Remove the drive pinion nut and install the seal into the differential carrier housing, then install the oil slinger, dust shield and yoke and retorque the pinion nut as specified.
27. Install the differential carrier assembly into the axle housing.

REAR SUSPENSION

Springs

REMOVAL AND INSTALLATION

Passenger Cars with Rear Leaf Springs

1. Loosen the rear wheel lug nuts.
2. Raise the rear of the vehicle. Support the frame and rear axle housing with stands.
3. Remove the lug nuts and the wheel.
4. Remove the cotter pin, nut, and washer from the lower end of the shock absorber.
5. Detach the shock absorber from the spring seat pivot pin.
6. Remove the parking brake cable clamp.

NOTE: Remove the parking brake equalizer, if necessary.

7. Unfasten the U-bolt nuts and remove the spring seat assemblies.
8. Adjust the height of the rear axle housing so that the weight of the rear axle is removed from the rear springs.
9. Unfasten the spring shackle retaining nuts. Withdraw the spring shackle inner plate. Carefully pry out the spring shackle with a bar.
10. Remove the spring bracket pin from the front end of the spring hanger and remove the rubber bushings.
11. Remove the spring.

CAUTION

Use care not to damage the hydraulic brake line or the parking brake cable.

Installation is performed in the following order:

1. Install the rubber bushings in the eye of the spring.
2. Align the eye of the spring with the spring hanger bracket and drive the pin through the bracket holes and rubber bushings.

NOTE: Use soapy water as lubricant, if necessary, to aid in pin installation. Never use oil or grease.

3. Finger-tighten the spring hanger nuts and/or bolts.
4. Install the rubber bushings in the spring eye at the opposite end of the spring.
5. Raise the free end of the spring. Install the spring shackle through the bushings and the bracket.
6. Install the shackle inner plate and finger-tighten the retaining nuts.
7. Center the bolt head in the hole which is provided in the spring seat on the axle housing.
8. Fit the U-bolts over the axle housing. Install the lower spring seat.
9. Tighten the U-bolt nuts.

NOTE: Some models have two sets of nuts, while others have a nut and lockwasher.

10. Install the parking brake cable clamp. Install the equalizer, if it was removed.
11. On passenger cars:
    a. Install the shock absorber end at the spring seat. Tighten the nuts.
    b. Install the wheel and lug nuts. Lower the car to the ground.
    c. Bounce the car several times.
    d. Tighten the spring bracket pins and shackles.

Passenger Cars with Coil Spring Rear Suspensions

1. Remove the hubcap and loosen the lug nuts.
2. Jack up the rear axle housing and support the frame with jack stands. Leave the jack in place under the rear axle housing.
3. Remove the lug nuts and wheel.
4. Unfasten the lower shock absorber end.
5. Slowly lower the jack under the rear axle housing until the axle is at the bottom of its travel.
6. Withdraw the coil spring, complete with its insulator.

Inspect the coil spring and insulator for wear, cracks, or weakness; replace either or both, as necessary.

Installation is performed in the reverse order of removal.

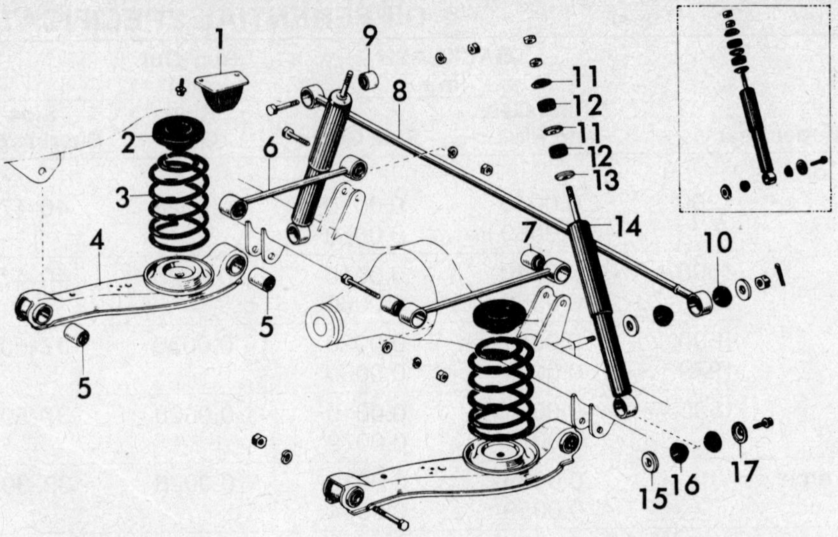

1. Bumper
2. Spring insulator
3. Coil spring
4. Lower control arm
5. Bushing
6. Upper control arm
7. Bushing
8. Bushing
9. Lateral control rod
10. Bushing
11. Retainer
12. Cushion
13. Retainer
14. Shock absorber
15. Washer
16. Bushing
17. Washer

Mark II rear suspension

Rear Shock Absorbers

REMOVAL AND INSTALLATION

1. Jack up the rear end of the vehicle.
2. Support the rear axle housing with jack stands.
3. Unfasten the upper shock absorber retaining nuts and/or bolts from the upper frame member.
4. Depending upon the type of rear springs used, either disconnect the lower end of the shock absorber from the spring seat, or the rear axle housing, by removing its cotter pins, nuts, and/or bolts.
5. Remove the shock absorber.

Inspect the shock for wear, leaks, or other signs of damage. Test it as outlined in the front suspension shock absorber section.

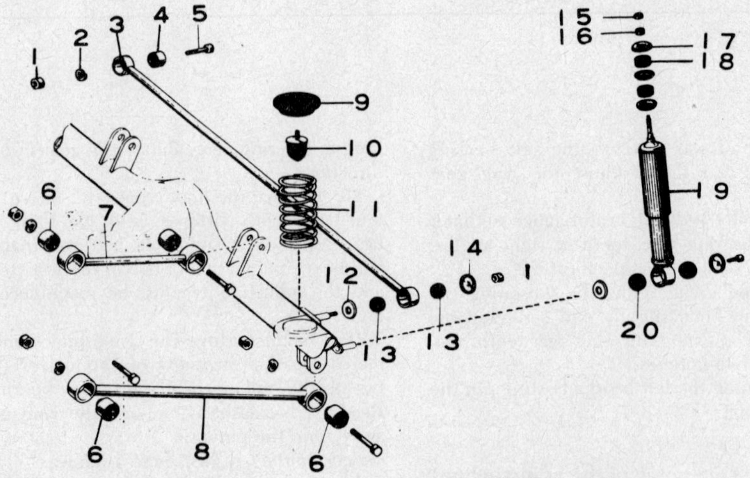

1. Nut
2. Washer
3. Lateral control rod
4. Bushing
5. Bolt
6. Bushing
7. Upper control arm
8. Lower control arm
9. Spring insulator
10. Spring bumper
11. Coil spring
12. Washer
13. Bushing
14. Washer
15. Nut
16. Nut
17. Washer
18. Bushing
19. Shock absorber
20. Bushing

Celica and Carina rear suspension—Crown similar

Installation is performed in the reverse order from removal.

FRONT SUSPENSION

Springs

REMOVAL AND INSTALLATION

Corolla, Carina, Celica and Cressida

1. Remove the hubcap and loosen the lug nuts.
2. Raise the front of the car and support it on the chassis jacking plates provided, with jack stands.

CAUTION
Do not support the weight of the car on the suspension arm; the arm will deform under its weight

3. Unfasten the lug nuts and remove the wheel.
4. Detach the front brake line from its clamp.
5. Remove the brake drum, or the caliper and wire it out of the way.
6. Unfasten the three nuts which secure the upper shock absorber mounting plate to the top of the wheel arch.
7. Remove the two bolts which attach the shock absorber lower end to the steering knuckle lower arm.

NOTE: Press down on the suspension lower arm, in order to remove the shock absorber assembly. This must be done to clear the collars on the steering knuckle arm bolt holes when removing the shock/spring assembly.

8. Fabricate shock absorber/spring assembly mounting stand. Bolt the assembly on the stand and mount the stand on a vise.
9. Use a coil spring compressor to compress the spring until it can be moved freely.
10. Remove the bearing dust cap from the top of the shock absorber assembly.
11. Use a large open-end wrench to keep the upper spring seat from turning and unfasten the 10 mm nut at the top of the shock absorber assembly.

CAUTION
Do not use an impact wrench when loosening the nut.

12. Remove the components from the top of the shock and withdraw the spring in its compressed state.

Check the spring for cracks and weakness. Check the dust seals and spring seats for wear or deterioration. Replace parts, as necessary.

Installation is performed in the reverse order of removal. Be sure to note the following, however:

1. Align the hole in the upper suspension support with the shock absorber piston rod end, so that they fit properly.
2. Always use a *new* nut and nylon washer on the shock absorber piston rod end when securing it to the upper suspension support. Torque the nut to 29-40 ft/lbs.

CAUTION
Do not use an impact wrench to tighten the nut.

3. Coat the suspension support bearing with multipurpose grease prior to installation. Pack the space in the upper support with multipurpose grease, also, after installation.
4. Tighten the suspension support-to-wheel arch bolts to the following specification:
   Corolla—11-16 ft/lbs
   Carina and Celica—14-23 ft/lbs
5. Tighten the shock absorber-to-steering knuckle arm bolts to the following specifications.
   Corolla—50-65 ft/lbs
   Carina and Celica—58-87 ft/lbs
6. Adjust the front wheel bearing preload as outlined below.
7. Bleed the brake system.

Corona

1. Remove the hubcap (if so equipped) and loosen the nuts.
2. Raise the front of the car and support it by using jack stands.
3. Remove the lug nuts and the wheel.
4. Remove the shock absorber as detailed in the appropriate section below. Remove the stabilizer bar from the lower control arm (if so equipped).
5. Install a coil spring compressor and compress the spring until there is no load on it.

NOTE: Place a jack under the lower control arm spring seat, as a safety precaution.

6. Unfasten the lower ball joint retaining bolts and withdraw the ball joint, complete with the steering knuckle, from the lower control arm.
7. Slowly loosen the spring compressor and remove the spring. (Lower the jack).

Inspect the spring, ball joint, and related components for wear or damage. Replace any parts necessary.

Installation is performed in the reverse order of removal.

NOTE: The coil springs are not interchangeable from the right side to the left side.

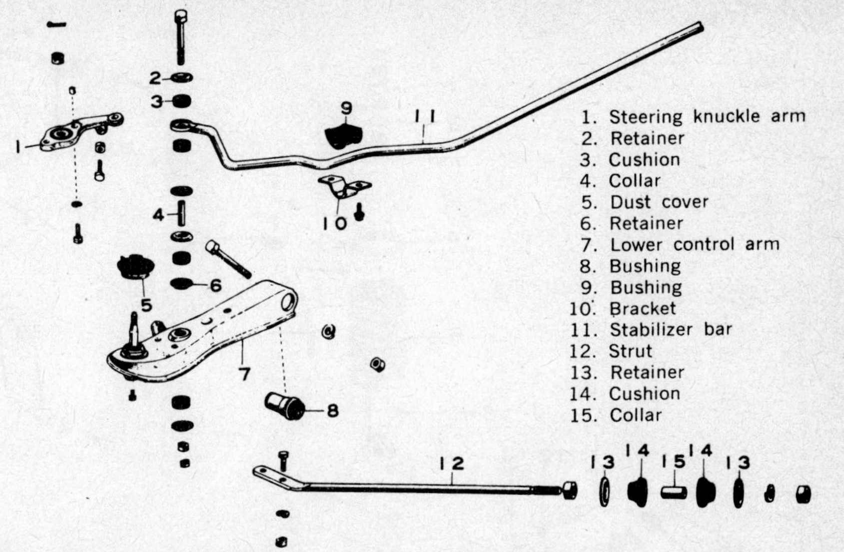

The components of the MacPherson strut front suspension—Corolla, Carina, and Celica

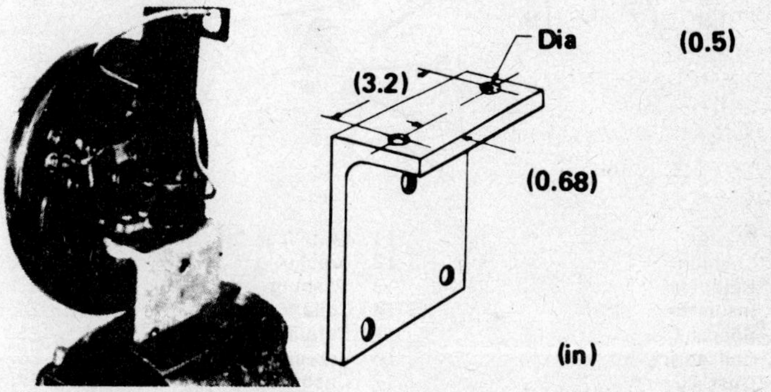

Fabricate the shock absorber bracket and mount it in a vise as shown

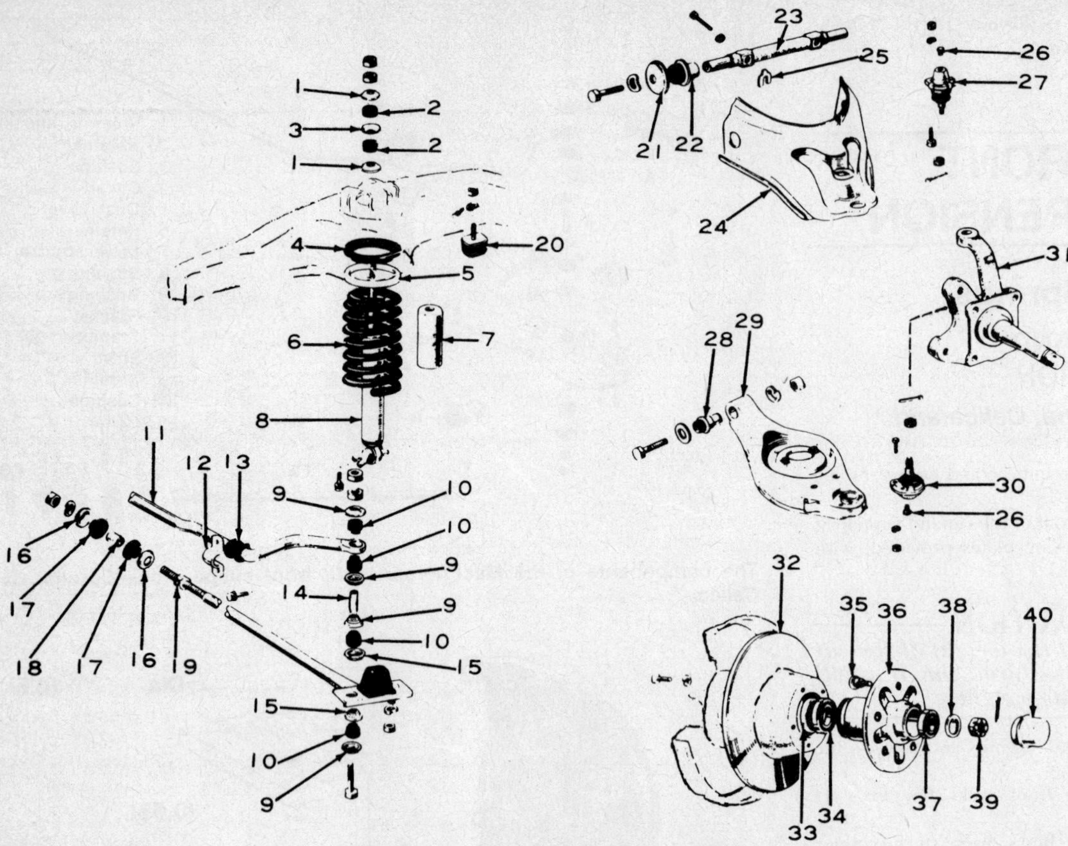

1. Washer
2. Cushion
3. Retainer
4. Insulator
5. Spacer
6. Coil spring
7. Dust cover
8. Shock absorber
9. Retainer
10. Cushion
11. Stabilizer bar
12. Bracket
13. Bushing
14. Collar
15. Retainer
16. Retainer
17. Cushion
18. Collar
19. Strut
20. Bumper
21. Retainer
22. Bushing
23. Shaft
24. Upper control arm
25. Camber adjusting shim
26. Plug
27. Upper ball joint
28. Bushing
29. Lower control arm
30. Lower ball joint
31. Steering knuckle
32. Brake disc
33. Oil seal
34. Roller bearing
35. Hub bolt
36. Axle hub
37. Roller bearing
38. Washer
39. Wheel adjusting nut
40. Hub cap

Mk.II front suspension components

The ball joint/steering knuckle assembly securing bolts should be tightened to the following specifications:

12 mm bolts—58-83 ft/lbs

88 bolts—11-16 ft/lbs

After completing installation of the coil spring, check to see that it is properly seated in the lower suspension arm. Check front end alignment.

Mark II

1. Perform Steps 1-3 of the Corona coil spring removal and installation procedure.
2. Unfasten the stabilizer bar.
3. Measure the distance between the serrated bolt holes on the front side of the torque strut and the attachment nut on the rear side to aid in installation. Remove the strut.
4. Remove the shock absorber.
5. Install the coil spring compressor on the third coil from the bottom. Tighten the compressor until the load is removed from the spring.
6. Remove the lower ball joint with a ball joint puller.
7. Unbolt and remove the lower control arm.
8. Carefully and slowly remove the spring compressor and withdraw the spring.

Specified
Length: 348mm (18.7")

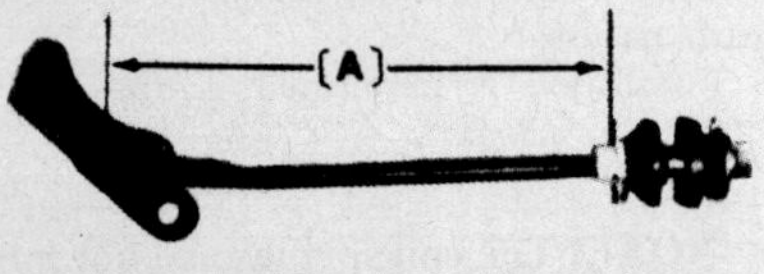

Measure distance A before removing the strut

Inspect the components of the suspension which were removed for signs of wear or damage. Replace parts as required.

Installation is performed in the following order:

1. Install the lower control arm but do not fully tighten the mounting bolts.
2. Compress the spring with the spring compressor and install the spring.

NOTE: Keep the spring compressed after installation.

3. Install the lower ball joint on the steering knuckle and tighten it.
4. Install the strut on the lower control arm and temporarily install the other end on the frame.
   a. The distance between the serrations and the nut should be the same as that measured during removal.
   b. If a new strut is used, check for the proper installation distance.
   c. Carefully install the rear side of the strut to the control arm and tighten the mounting nut to the specifications.
5. Slowly remove the spring compressor from the coil spring.
6. Install the shock absorber.
7. Install the stabilizer bar bracket and the bar.

NOTE: Be sure to assemble the parts of the bracket in the order in which they were removed.

8. Install the wheel, remove the jack stands, and lower the car.
9. Tighten the lower control arm and strut front mount.

NOTE: These parts should be tightened with the equivalent of passenger weight in the car.

10. Check the wheel alignment, after completing installation.

Tercel

1. Jack up your vehicle and support it with jack stands.
2. Remove the front wheel.
3. Remove the brake caliper and tie it out of the way.
4. Remove the stabilizer bar end.
5. Remove the bottom shock bolt.
6. Push down on the steering knuckle to free the bottom of the shock absorber.
7. Remove the top shock bolts.
8. Remove the shock and spring combination.
9. Place the shock portion in a vise, being careful not to crush the shock.

NOTE: You will need special tool #09741-16010 available from your Toyota dealer for the above procedure.

10. Use a spring compressor to compress the spring.

CAUTION

Make sure that the spring compressor is properly secured to the spring when removing it, otherwise serious body harm could result.

11. Remove the upper nut, dust cover, upper seat and insulator.
12. Remove the spring.

NOTE: Do not release the tension on the spring compressor unless you need to replace the spring.

13. Installation is the reverse of removal.

The torque specifications needed are Shock seat bolt 29-39 ft/lbs, Top shock bolts 15-21 ft/lbs, Bottom shock bolt 40-52 ft/lbs, Stabilizer bar 11-15 ft/lbs.

Front Shock Absorber

REMOVAL AND INSTALLATION

Corolla, Carina, and Celica

1. Perform the front coil spring removal procedure as outlined above for the Corolla, Carina, Celica, and Cressida.
2. Remove the wheel hub and brake drum or disc.

Inspect the shock absorber and test it. Inspect the shock absorber and test it. Inspect the other parts of the front suspension system which were removed.

Installation is performed in the reverse order of removal. See the notes at the end of coil spring installation for details.

Corona, Mark II

1. Remove the hubcap and loosen the lug nuts.
2. Raise the front of the car and support it with jack stands.
3. Remove the lug nuts and the wheel.
4. Unfasten the double nuts at the top end of the shock absorber. Remove the cushions and cushion retainers.
5. Remove the two bolts which secure the lower end of the shock absorber to the lower control arm.
6. Remove the shock absorber.

Inspect and test the shock as detailed below.

Installation of the shock is performed in the reverse order of removal. Tighten the securing nuts and bolts to the following specifications:

Upper securing nuts—14-22 ft/lbs
Lower mounting bolts—11-16 ft/lbs

Tercel

Follow the procedure outlined for front spring removal. After you have removed the spring from the shock you can then replace the shock. The reinstallation procedure will be the same as previously detailed.

Lower Ball Joints

INSPECTION

Jack up the lower suspension arm (except Corolla, Carina, Celica and Cressida). Check the front wheel play. Replace the lower ball joint if the play at the wheel rim exceeds 0.1 in. vertical motion or 0.25 in. horizontal motion. Be sure that the dust covers are not torn and that they are securely glued to the ball joints.

CAUTION

Do not jack up the control arm on Corolla, Carina, Celica or Cressida models; damage to the arm will result.

Tercel

1. Jack up the vehicle and place wooden blocks under the front wheels. The block height should be 7.09-7.87 inches.
2. Use jack stands for additional safety.
3. Make sure the front wheels are in a straight forward position.
4. Check the wheels.
5. Lower the jack until there is approximately half a load on the front springs.
6. Move the lower control arm up and down to check that there is no ball joint play.

REMOVAL AND INSTALLATION

NOTE: On models equipped with both upper and lower ball joints—if both ball joints are to be removed, always remove the lower and then the upper ball joint.

Corolla, Carina, Celica, and Cressida

The ball joint and control arm cannot be separated from each other. If one fails, then both must be replaced as an assembly, in the following manner:

1. Perform Steps 1-7 of the Corolla, Carina, Celica and Cressida front coil spring removal procedure. Skip Step 6.
2. Remove the stabilizer bar securing bolts.
3. Unfasten the torque strut mounting bolts.
4. Remove the control arm mounting bolt and detach the arm from the front suspension member.
5. Remove the steering knuckle arm from the control arm with a ball joint puller.

Inspect the suspension components, which were removed for wear or damage. Replace any parts, as required.

Installation is the reverse of removal. Note the following, however:

1. When installing the control arm on the suspension member, tighten the bolts partially at first.
2. Complete the assembly procedure and lower the car to the ground.
3. Bounce the front of the car several times. Allow the suspension to settle, then tighten the lower control arm bolts to 51-65 ft/lbs.

CAUTION

Use only the bolt which was designed to fit the lower control arm. If a replacement is necessary, see an authorized dealer for the proper part.

4. Remember to lubricate the ball joint. Check front-end alignment.

Tercel

1. Jack up your vehicle and support it with jack stands.

CAUTION

Do not jack up your car on the lower control arms.

2. Remove the front wheels.
3. Remove the tie rod end.
4. Remove the stabilizer bar end.
5. Remove the strut bar end.
6. Place a jack under the lower control arm for support.
7. Remove the bolt from the bottom of the steering knuckle.
8. Remove the bolt from the lower control arm.
9. Remove the control arm.

NOTE: The lower ball joint can not be separated from the lower control arm. It must be replaced as a complete unit.

The following torques are required: Bottom steering knuckle nut 40-52 ft/lbs, Stabilizer bar 11-15 ft/lbs. Tie rod end 37-50 ft/lbs, Strut bar 29-39 ft/lbs, Lower control arm 51-65 ft/lbs.

1975-81 Corona

1. Remove the hubcap and loosen the lug nuts.
2. Jack up your vehicle and support it with jack stands.
3. Remove the lug nuts and the wheel.

NOTE: On models with ESP (hardtops) disconnect the wiring harness for the brake wear sensor and remove the wire support from the control arm.

4. Compress the coil spring by placing a jack underneath the control arm and raising it.
5. Remove the cotter pin and the castelated nut from the ball joint.
6. Use a ball joint puller to detach the lower ball joint from the steering knuckle.
7. Wire the steering knuckle out of the way.
8. Remove the bolt and remove the ball joint.

Installation is the reverse of removal. Tighten the stud nut 51-65 ft/lbs.

Mark II

Perform Steps 1-7 of the Mark II coil spring removal procedure. Skip Step 3.

Installation is performed by starting with Step 3 of the Mark II coil spring installation procedure. When Step 3 is completed, go on to Steps 5-10. Lubricate the ball joints and check alignment.

Upper Ball Joint

INSPECTION

Disconnect the ball joint from the steering knuckle and check free-play by hand. Replace the ball joint, if it is noticeably loose.

REMOVAL AND INSTALLATION

NOTE: On models equipped with both upper and lower ball joints—if both are to be removed, always remove the lower one first.

Corona

1. Perform Steps 1-5 of the Corona lower ball joint removal procedure.
2. Suspend the steering knuckle with a wire.
3. Use an open-end wrench to remove the upper ball joint.

Installation is performed in the reverse order from removal. Note the following:

1. Install the upper ball joint dust cover with the escape valve toward the rear.
2. Use sealer on the dust cover before installing it.
3. Tighten the upper ball joint-to-steering knuckle bolt to 40-50 ft/lbs (1975-81).

Mark II

1. Remove the wheel cover and loosen the lug nut.
2. Raise the front of the car and support it with jack stands.
3. Remove the lug nuts and the wheel.
4. Place a jack beneath the lower control arm spring seat. Raise the jack until the spring bumper separates from the frame.
5. Detach the flexible hose from the dust cover.
6. Using a ball joint puller, remove the upper ball joint from the steering knuckle.
7. Use an open-end wrench to remove the ball joint from the upper control arm.

Installation is performed in the reverse order of removal. Tighten the components to the specifications. Lubricate the ball joint. Check front wheel alignment. (See below.) Remember to bleed the air from the flexible hose.

Lower Control Arm

REMOVAL AND INSTALLATION

Corolla, Celica, Carina, Cressida

1. Raise and support front end.
2. Remove wheel.
3. Disconnect the steering knuckle from the control arm.
4. Disconnect the tie rod, stabilizer bar and strut bar from the control arm.
5. Remove the control arm mounting bolts, and remove the arm.
6. Install in reverse of above. Tighten, but do not torque fasteners until car is on ground.
7. Lower car to ground, rock it from side-to-side several times and torque control arm mounting bolts to 51-65 ft/lbs; stabilizer bar to 16 ft/lbs; strut bar to 40 ft/lbs; shock absorber to 65 ft/lbs.

Corona

1. Raise and support the vehicle.
2. Remove the front wheel.
3. Remove the shock absorber and disconnect the stabilizer from the lower arm.
4. Install a spring compressor and fully tighten it.
5. Place a jack under the lower arm seat.
6. Disconnect the lower ball joint from the knuckle and lower the jack.
7. Remove the ball joint from the arm, remove the cam plates and bolts and take off the arm.
8. Install in reverse of above. Tighten all fasteners, but do not torque them to specification until vehicle is on ground.
9. Lower vehicle and rock it from side-to-side several times.
10. With no load in vehicle, torque the lower arm mounting bolts to 94-130 ft/lbs.

Corona and Mark II

1. Remove the stabilizer bar.
2. Measure the length of the strut bar from the bolt hole (front side) to the outer edge of the securing nut at the other end.
3. Remove the shock absorber.
4. Compress the front spring with a spring compressor.

NOTE: It is recommended that the compressor be installed at the third coil from the bottom.

5. Remove the lower ball joint with a puller.
6. Remove the lower arm.
7. Install the lower arm to the frame.
8. Install the ball joint and tighten the nut to 50-65 ft/lbs for the Mark II.
9. Install the strut bar onto the lower arm and temporarily install the front side onto the frame.
10. Set the strut bar to the length noted before removal. If a new lower arm or strut bar is used, the measurement should be 14.16".
11. Torque the strut bar rear end to 50-65 ft/lbs.
12. Remove the spring compressor and install the shock absorber.
13. Install the stabilizer bar.
14. Lower the vehicle and torque the lower arm to 65-80 ft/lbs for the Mark II. Torque the strut bar front end to 44-54 ft/lbs, for the Mark II.

Tercel

See the lower ball joint removal section.

Upper Control Arm

REMOVAL AND INSTALLATION

Corona

1. Remove the upper arm mounting nuts from inside the engine compartment, but do not remove the bolts.
2. Raise the vehicle, support the lower arm and remove the wheel.
3. On vehicles equipped with a ball joint wear sensor, remove the wiring from the clamp on the arm.
4. Remove the upper ball joint.
5. Remove the control arm mounting bolts.
6. Pry out the arm with a pry bar.
7. Install in reverse of removal. Do not tighten fasteners until vehicle is on ground.
8. Lower vehicle and torque the control arm mounting bolts to 95-130 ft/lbs.

Corona and Mark II

1. Raise and support the vehicle at the frame.
2. Remove the flexible hose from the dust cover.
3. Jack up the lower arm and separate the ball jont from the steering knuckle with a ball joint remover.
4. Unbolt and remove the upper arm, taking note of the size and number of aligning shims.
5. Install in reverse of removal. Tighten, but do not torque, the fasteners until the car is on the ground.
6. Lower the car and torque the upper arm mounting bolts to 50-65 ft/lbs for the Mark II; the ball joint nut to 40-54 ft/lbs for the Mark II and 70-96 ft/lbs.

Front-End Alignment

Front-end alignment measurements require the use of special equipment. Before measuring alignment or attempting to adjust it, always check the following points:

1. Be sure that the tires are properly inflated.
2. See that the wheels are properly balanced.
3. Check the ball joints to determine if they are worn or loose.
4. Check front wheel bearing adjustment.
5. Be sure that the car is on a level surface.
6. Check all suspension parts for tightness.

CASTER AND CAMBER ADJUSTMENTS

All models with the MacPherson front suspension can be adjusted for caster only. This is accomplished by adjusting the nuts on the strut bar. There is no adjustment on the camber. These parts must be inspected for

Removing the camber adjusting shims

wear and replaced if the adjustments are not within the specified tolerances.

Measure the caster and camber angles . If they are not within specifications, adjust them by adding or subtracting the shims on the mounting bolts between the upper control arm and the suspension member:

1. To *increase* camber, *remove* shims equally from both of the control shaft mounting bolts. Do the reverse to decrease camber.

2. To *increase* caster, add camber adjusting shims to the *rear* mounting bolt, or remove them from the front mounting bolt. Do the reverse to decrease caster.

NOTE: Caster and camber adjustments should always be performed in a single operation.

1975-81 Corona

Caster and camber angles are measured in the same way and with the same equipment as all the other models above.

However, the method of adjustment is different:

1. Measure the camber and adjust it with the *rear* adjusting cam.

2. Measure the caster and adjust it with the *front* adjusting cam.

3. Check the caster and camber again.

4. Tighten the lower control arm mounting bolts to 94-132 ft/lbs.

NOTE: There should be not more than six graduations difference between the front and rear cams; inspect for damaged suspension parts if there is.

Toe-in Adjustment

Measure the toe-in. Adjust it, if necessary, by loosening the tie rod end clamping bolts and rotating the tie rod adjusting tubes. Tighten the clamping bolts when finished.

NOTE: Both tie rod ends should be the same length. If they are not, perform the adjustment until the toe-in is within specifications and the tie rod ends are equal in length.

STEERING

Steering Wheel

REMOVAL AND INSTALLATION

Three-Spoke

CAUTION

Do not attempt to remove or install the steering wheel by hammering on it. Damage to the energy-absorbing steering column could result.

1. Unfasten the horn and turn signal multiconnector(s) at the base of the steering column shroud.

2. Loosen the trim pad retaining screws from the back side of the steering wheel.

3. Lift the trim pad and horn button assembly(ies) from the wheel.

4. Remove the steering wheel hub retaining nut.

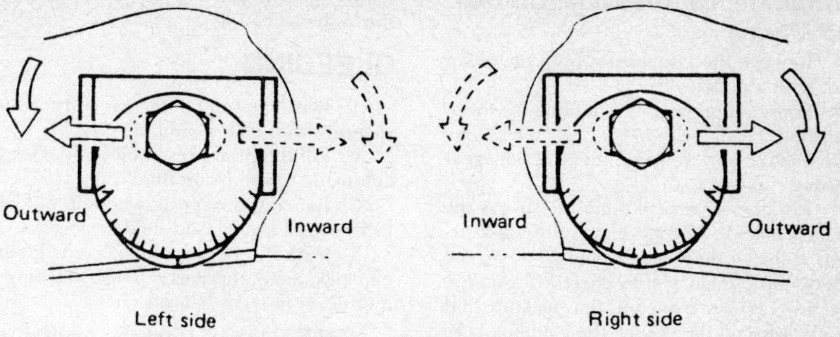

1975 and later front end alignment adjusting cams

5. Scratch matchmarks on the hub and shaft to aid in correct installation.

6. Use a steering wheel puller to remove the steering wheel.

Installation is the reverse of removal. Tighten the wheel retaining nut to 15-22 ft/lbs, except for the Mark II, which should be tightened to 22-29 ft/lbs.

Two-Spoke

The two-spoke steering wheel is removed in the same manner as the three-spoke, except that the trim pad should be pried off with a screwdriver. Remove the pad by lifting it toward the top of the wheel.

Four-Spoke

CAUTION

Do not attempt to remove or install the steering wheel by hammering on it. Damage to the energy absorbing steering column could result.

1. Unfasten the horn and turn signal connectors at the base of the steering column shroud, underneath the instrument panel.

2. Gently pry the center emblem off the front of the steering wheel.

3. Insert a wrench through the hole and remove the steering wheel retaining nut.

4. Scratch matchmarks on the hub and shaft to aid installation.

5. Use a steering wheel puller to remove the steering wheel.

Installation is the reverse of removal. Tighten the steering wheel retaining nut to 15-22 ft/lbs.

TURN SIGNAL SWITCH REPLACEMENT

1. Disconnect the negative (−) battery cable.

2. Remove the steering wheel, as outlined in the appropriate section above.

3. Unfasten the screws which secure the upper and lower steering column shroud halves. On 1975 Corona models, remove the lower instrument panel garnish first.

4. Unfasten the screws which retain the turn signal switch and remove the switch from the column. On 1975-81 Corona and Corolla models, the hazard warning and windshield wiper switches are part of the assembly, and will be removed as well.

Installation is performed in the reverse order of removal.

Ignition Lock/Switch

REMOVAL AND INSTALLATION

1. Disconnect the negative (−) battery cable.

2. Unfasten the ignition switch connector underneath the instrument panel.

3. Remove the screws which secure the upper and lower halves of the steering column cover. Remove the lower instrument panel garnish on 1975-81 Corona models first.

4. Turn the lock cylinder to the "ACC" position with the ignition key.

5. Push the lock cylinder stop in with a small, round object (cotter pin, punch, etc.)

NOTE: On some models it may be necessary to remove the steering wheel and turn signal switch first.

6. Withdraw the lock cylinder from the lock housing while depressing the stop tab.

7. To remove the ignition switch, unfasten its securing screws and withdraw the switch from the lock housing.

Installation is performed in the following order:

1. Align the locking cam with the hole in the ignition switch and insert the switch in the lock housing.

2. Secure the switch with its screw(s).

3. Make sure that both the lock cylinder and the column lock are in the "ACC" position. Slide the cylinder into the lock housing until the stop tab engages the hole in the lock.

4. The rest of installation is performed in the reverse order of removal.

Manual Steering Gear

REMOVAL AND INSTALLATION

Corolla and Corona

1. Remove the bolt attaching the coupling yoke to the steering worm.

2. Disconnect the relay rod from the pitman arm.

3. Remove the steering gear housing down and to the left.

4. Install in reverse of removal. Torque the housing-to-frame bolts to 25-36 ft/lbs; the coupling yoke bolt to 15-20 ft/lbs; the relay rod to 36-50 ft/lbs.

Carina, Celica, Cressida, Corona and Mark II

1. Remove the Pitman arm from the sector shaft with a puller.
2. Loosen the flexible coupling-to-worm-shaft bolt.
3. Unbolt and remove the steering gear housing.
4. Install in reverse of removal. Torque the housing bolts to 37-52 ft/lbs on the Mark 11, 36-41 ft/lbs on the Cressida and 25-36 on the others; the Pitman arm to 36-41 ft/lbs on the Cressida, 80-90 ft/lbs on the pick-up and 72-101 ft/lbs on the others; the coupling yoke bolts to 15-20 ft/lbs.

Tercel

1. Jack up the vehicle and support it with jack stands.
2. Remove both front wheels.
3. Remove the intermediate shaft from the worm gear shaft.
4. Remove both tie rod ends.
5. Remove the lower suspension cross-member.
6. Remove the rack housing bracket mounting bolts and brackets.

NOTE: Be careful not to damage the rubber boots.

7. Remove the steering linkage.
8. Installation is the reverse of removal.

ADJUSTMENTS

Adjustments to the manual steering gear are not necessary during normal service. Adjustments are performed only as part of overhaul.

Power Steering Pump

REMOVAL AND INSTALLATION

1. Remove the fan shroud.
2. Unfasten the nut from the center of the pump pulley.

NOTE: Use the drive belt as a brake to keep the pulley from rotating.

3. Withdraw the drive belt.
4. Remove the pulley and the Woodruff key from the pump shaft.
5. Detach the intake and outlet hoses from the pump reservoir.

NOTE: Tie the hose ends up high so the fluid cannot flow out of them. Drain or plug the pump to prevent fluid leakage.

6. Remove the bolt from the rear mounting brace.
7. Remove the front bracket bolts and withdraw the pump.

Installation is performed in the reverse order of removal. Note the following, however:

1. Tighten the pump pulley mounting bolt to 25-39 ft/lbs.
2. Adjust the pump drive belt tension. The belt should deflect 0.13-0.39 in. under thumb pressure applied midway between the air pump and the power steering pump.
3. Fill the reservoir with "Dexron" automatic transmission fluid. Bleed the air from the system.

BLEEDING

1. Raise the front of the car and support it securely with jack stands.
2. Fill the pump reservoir with "Dexron" automatic transmission fluid.
3. Rotate the steering wheel from lock to lock several times. Add fluid as necessary.
4. With the steering wheel turned fully to one lock, crank the starter while watching the fluid level in the reservoir.

NOTE: Do not start the engine. Operate the starter with a remote starter switch or have an assistant do it from inside of the car. Do not run the starter for prolonged periods.

5. Repeat Step 4 with the steering wheel turned to the opposite lock.
6. Start the engine. With the engine idling, turn the steering wheel from lock to lock two or three times.
7. Lower the front of the car and repeat Step 6.
8. Center the wheel at the midpoint of its travel. Stop the engine.
9. The fluid level should not have risen more than 0.2 in. If it does, repeat Step 7.
10. Check for fluid leakage.

Steering Linkage

REMOVAL AND INSTALLATION

Passenger Cars

1. Raise the front of the vehicle and support it with jack stands.

CAUTION

Be sure that the vehicle is securely supported. Do not support it by the lower control arms.

2. Remove the gravel shields if they prevent access to the steering linkage.
3. Unfasten the nut and, using a puller, disconnect the pitman arm from the sector shaft.
4. Unfasten the idler arm support securing bolts and remove the support from the frame.
5. Detach the tie rod ends with a puller after removing the cotter pins and castellated nuts.

NOTE: On Mark II models, it is necessary to remove the disc brake caliper in order to gain access to the tie rod ends.

6. Remove the steering linkage as an assembly.

Installation is performed in the reverse order of removal. Note the following, however:

1. Tighten the linkage parts to the torque figures given in the chart below.
2. Align the marks on the pitman arm and sector shaft before installing the pitman arm.
3. The self-locking nut used on some models, on the idler arm, may be reused if it cannot be turned by hand when fitted to the bolt.
4. Adjust the toe-in to specifications.
5. Disconnect the end of the steering damper from its bracket on the front cross-member.
6. Remove the center arm attaching nut and use a puller to remove the arm, complete with the damper.
7. Remove the skid plate and then remove the center arm bracket from the frame.

Installation is preformed in the reverse order of removal. Note the following, however:

1. Align the matchmarks, which were made during removal, on the pitman arm and the sector shaft. Tighten the mounting bolt to 120-140 ft/lbs.
2. Lubricate all of the rod ends and damper ends with multipurpose grease.

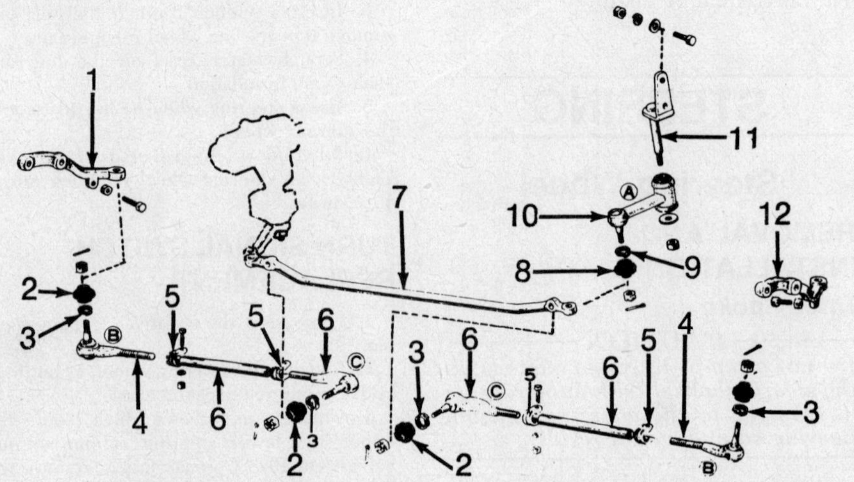

1. Steering knuckle arm—right-hand
2. Dust seal
3. Clip
4. Tie rod end
5. Tie rod end clamp
6. Tie rod adjusting tube
7. Steering relay rod
8. Dust seal
9. Lock ring
10. Steering idler arm
11. Idler arm support
12. Steering knukle arm—left-hand

(a)—Idler arm assembly
(b)—Tie rod end assembly
(c)—Tie rod adjusting tube

Corona steering linkage—other passenger cars similar

3. After the linkage is installed, adjust toe-in to the proper specifications.

BRAKES

Adjustments

REAR DRUM BRAKES

1975 Corolla 1200

These models are equipped with rear drum brakes which require manual adjustment. Perform the adjustment in the following order:

1. Chock the front wheels and fully release the parking brake.
2. Raise the rear of the car and support it with jack stands.
3. Remove the adjusting hole plug from the backing plate.
4. Expand the brake shoes by turning the adjusting wheel with a star-wheel adjuster or a thin-bladed screwdriver.
5. Pump the brake pedal several times, while expanding the shoes, so that the shoe contacts the drum evenly.

NOTE: If the wheel still turns when your foot is removed from the brake pedal, continue expanding the shoes until the wheel locks.

6. Back off on the adjuster, just enough so that the wheel rotates without dragging.
7. After this point is reached, continue backing off for *five* additional notches.

NOTE: On models which have two wheel cylinders at each wheel, adjust each set of brakes separately; never adjust both at once.

8. If the wheel still does not turn freely, back off one or two more notches. If after this, it still drags, check for worn or defective parts.
9. Pump the brake pedal again, and check wheel rotation.
10. Reverse Steps 1-3.

Passenger Cars–Except 1975 Corolla 1200

These models are equipped with self-adjusting rear drum brakes. No adjustment is necessary.

FRONT DRUM BRAKES

1975 Corolla 1200

Perform the adjustment in the same manner as detailed for the rear drum brakes.

FRONT DISC BRAKES

Front disc brakes require no adjustment. Hydraulic pressure maintains the proper brake pad-to-disc contact at all times.

NOTE: Because of this, the brake fluid level should be checked regularly.

Master Cylinder

REMOVAL AND INSTALLATION

CAUTION

Be careful not to spill brake fluid on the painted surfaces of the vehicle; it will damage the paint.

1. Unfasten the hydraulic lines from the master cylinder.

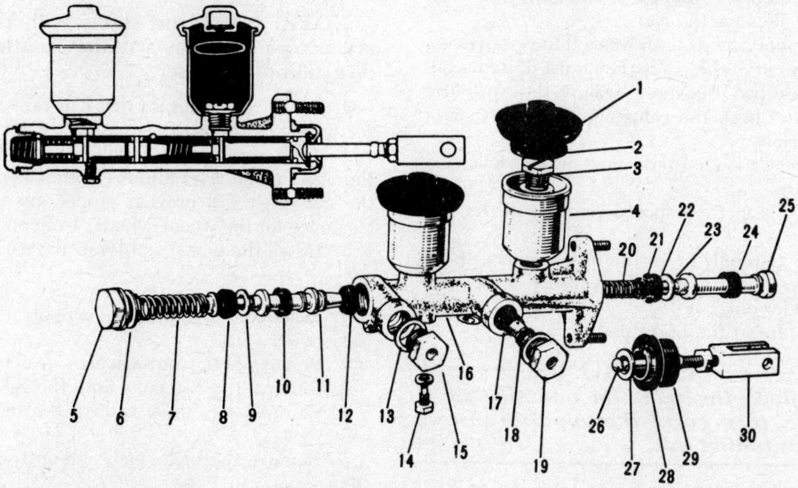

1. Reservoir filler cap
2. Reservoir float
3. Reservoir set bolt
4. Master cylinder reservoir
5. Master cylinder plug
6. Gasket
7. Compression spring
8. Cylinder cup
9. Piston cup spacer
10. Cylinder cup
11. Master cylinder piston No. 2
12. Cylinder cup
13. Gasket
14. Piston stop bolt
15. Valve plug
16. Tandem master cylinder body
17. Compression spring
18. Master cylinder outlet check valve
19. Valve plug
20. Compression
21. Piston return spring retainer
22. Cylinder cup
23. Master cylinder piston cup spacer
24. Cylinder cup
25. Master cylinder piston No. 1
26. Master cylinder pushrod
27. Master cylinder piston stop plate
28. Hole snap-ring
29. Master cylinder boot
30. Master cylinder pusrod clevis

Components of the dual-tandem master cylinder

2. Detach the hydraulic fluid pressure differential switch wiring connectors.
3. Loosen the master cylinder reservoir mounting bolt.
4. Then do one of the following:
   a. On models with manual brakes, remove the master cylinder securing bolts and the clevis pin from the brake pedal. Remove the master cylinder.
   b. On other models with power brakes, unfasten the nuts and remove the master cylinder assembly from the power brake unit.

Installation is performed in the reverse order of removal. Note the following, however:

1. Before tightening the master cylinder mounting nuts or bolts, screw the hydraulic line into the cylinder body, a few turns.
2. After installation is completed, bleed the master cylinder and the brake system.

Overhaul

1. Remove the reservoir caps and floats and unscrew the bolts that hold the reservoir to the main body.
2. Remove warning switches (where fitted), then remove from the rear of the cylinder, in order: boot and snap-ring, stop plate (washer), piston No. 1 with spacer, cylinder cup, spring retainer and spring.
3. Remove the end plug and gasket from the front of the cylinder, then remove the front piston stop bolt from underneath. Pull out the spring and its retainer, piston No. 2, the spacer and the cylinder cup.
4. Remove the two outlet fittings, washers, check valves and springs.
5. Remove the piston cups from their seats on the pistons only if they are to be replaced.

After washing all parts in clean brake fluid, dry with compressed air. Inspect the cylinder bore for wear, scuff marks or nicks. Cylinders may be honed slightly, but the limit is 0.006 in. It is recommended that it be replaced rather than overhauled.

Reverse the sequence of disassembly. Absolute cleanliness is important, and all parts must be coated with clean brake fluid. Bleed the master cylinder and make sure all lines are tightened correctly and do not leak. Use fluid that meets specifications (for standard brakes) and use the special disc brake fluid (DOT-3) for disc brake equipped cars.

Proportioning Valve

A proportioning valve is used on all models to reduce the hydraulic pressure to the rear brakes because of weight transfer during high speed stops. This helps to keep the rear brakes from locking up by improving front to rear brake balance.

REMOVAL AND INSTALLATION

1. Disconnect the brake lines from the valve unions.
2. Remove the valve mounting bolt, if used, and remove the valve.

NOTE: If the proportioning valve is defective, it must be replaced as an assembly; it cannot be rebuilt.

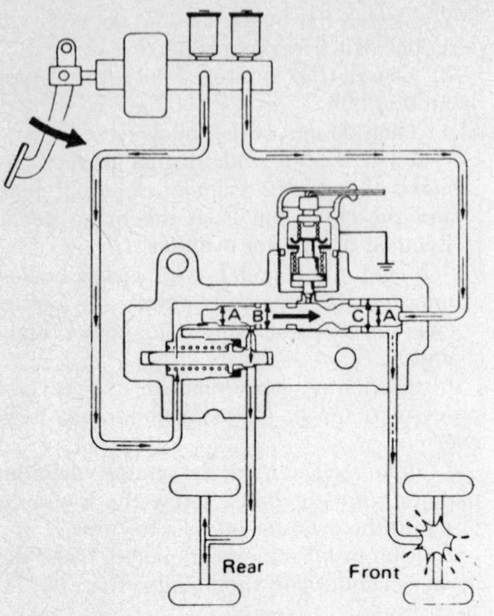

Proportioning bypass valve

Installation is the reverse of removal. Bleed the brake system after it is completed.

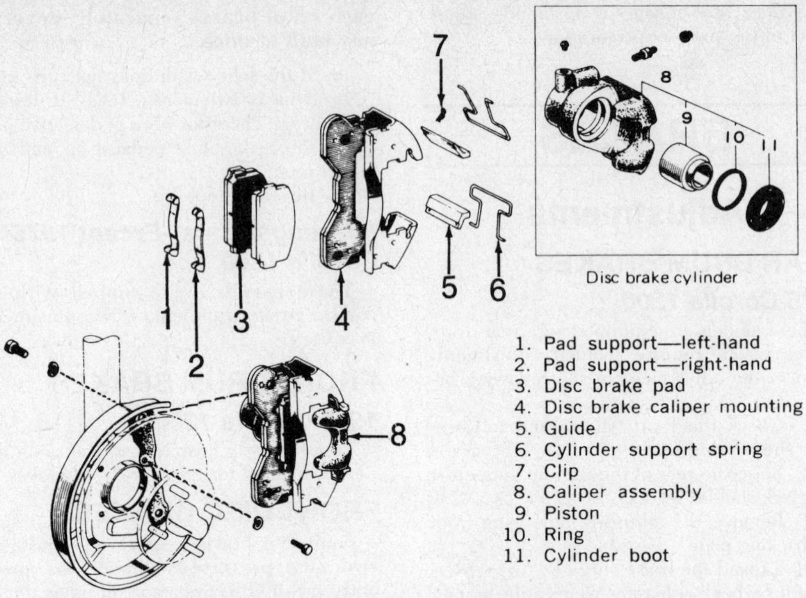

1. Pad support—left-hand
2. Pad support—right-hand
3. Disc brake pad
4. Disc brake caliper mounting
5. Guide
6. Cylinder support spring
7. Clip
8. Caliper assembly
9. Piston
10. Ring
11. Cylinder boot

Corolla, Carina, Corona and Celica disc brake

Bleeding

CAUTION

Do not reuse brake fluid which has been bled from the brake system.

1. Insert a clear vinyl tube into the bleeder plug on the master cylinder or the wheel cylinders.

NOTE: If the master cylinder has been overhauled or if air is present in it, start the bleeding procedure with the master cylinder. Otherwise, (and after bleeding the master cylinder) start with the wheel cylinder which is farthest from the master cylinder.

2. Insert the other end of the tube into a jar which is half filled with brake fluid.
3. Slowly depress the brake pedal (have an assistant do it) and turn the bleeder plug ⅓-½ of a turn at the same time.

NOTE: If the brake pedal is depressed too fast, small air bubbles will form in the brake fluid which will be very difficult to remove.

4. Close the bleeder plug before hydraulic pressure decreases in the cylinder.
5. Repeat this procedure until the air bubbles are removed and then go on to the next wheel cylinder.

CAUTION

Replenish the brake fluid in the master cylinder reservoir, so that it does not run out during bleeding.

Disc Brake Pads

REMOVAL AND INSTALLATION

Corolla, Carina and Celica

1. Remove the hub cap and loosen the lug nuts.
2. Raise the front of the vehicle with a jack and support it with stands on the chassis pads provided.

CAUTION

Do not support Corolla, Carina or Celica models by the lower control arm.

3. Remove the lug nuts and the wheel.
4. Unfasten the four clips which secure the caliper guides and remove.
5. Detach the flexible line from the caliper.

NOTE: Be sure that the master cylinder is closed to prevent brake fluid from leaking out.

6. Remove the caliper assembly.
7. Remove the pads.

Inspect the pads for wear. If the grooves are worn out of the pads, they must be replaced. Check pad thickness against the specifications. Check the caliper guides for wear or deformity.

Installation is performed in the following order:

1. Clean the exposed portions of the piston.
2. Carefully insert the piston in its caliper. If the piston is difficult to install, loosen the bleeder plug.
3. Insert the brake pads.

CAUTION

Replace the pads on one side at a time, to prevent the opposite piston from falling out.

4. Install the caliper assembly, the guides and the clips.
5. Bleed the brake line and lower the vehicle.

Mark II, Cressida and Corona

1. Perform Steps 1-3 of the disc brake pad removal procedure. The "caution" applies to Cressida models.
2. Remove the clips, springs, and the pins (which have the holes).
3. Withdraw the anti-squeal shims and the pads.

NOTE: On Corona and Mark II models with ESP, remove the wiring harness from the steering knuckle bracket. Take out the pad and disconnect it from the wear sensor.

4. Check pad thickness against the specifications.

Install the pads in the following order:

1. Clean the back of the pistons, cylinder boots and the caliper surfaces which contact the brake pads.
2. Fit the pads and anti-squeal shims into the caliper.

NOTE: Install the shims with their arrows pointing toward the rotational direction of the disc.

3. Install the spring so that it presses correctly against the pads.
4. After completing installation, depress the brake pedal several times before lowering the car. This will provide proper operating clearance for the wheel cylinder components.
5. Install the wheel and lower the car.

Tercel

1. Jack up your vehicle and support it with jack stands.
2. Remove both front wheels.
3. Remove the two bolts from the caliper.
4. Remove the caliper and tie it out of the way.
5. Remove the brake pads and anti-squeal shim.
6. Remove some brake fluid from the master cylinder.
7. Use a C-clamp to squeeze the piston back into the caliper.
8. Inspect the pads for wear. The limit is 0.039 in.
9. Install new pads if necessary.

NOTE: Replace pads when lining wear is uneven or only on one side.

10. Refill the master cylinder.
11. Installation is the reverse of removal.

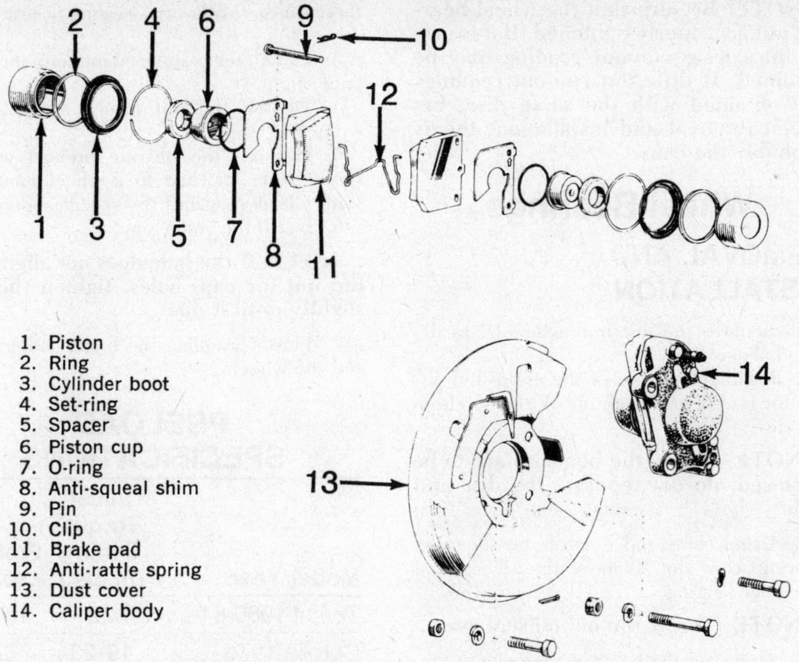

1. Piston
2. Ring
3. Cylinder boot
4. Set-ring
5. Spacer
6. Piston cup
7. O-ring
8. Anti-squeal shim
9. Pin
10. Clip
11. Brake pad
12. Anti-rattle spring
13. Dust cover
14. Caliper body

Caliper components: Mk.II, Cressida, Corona

Disc Brake Calipers

REMOVAL AND INSTALLATION

Corolla, Carina, and Celica

Caliper removal and installation for these models is given as part of the brake pad removal and installation procedure. Consult the appropriate section for details.

Mark II, Corona

CAUTION

Do not unfasten the bridge bolt and separate the caliper halves.

1. Remove the wheel covers and loosen the lug nuts.
2. Raise the front of the car and support it with jack stands.
3. Remove the lug nuts and the wheel.
4. Plug the master cylinder inlet, so that the brake fluid will not run out when the hydraulic line is disconnected.
5. Remove the hydraulic line from the caliper by unfastening the union bolt.

NOTE: On Corona and Mark II models with ESP, remove the wiring harness from the steering knuckle bracket, then remove the pad and separate the pad and wear sensor connection.

6. Remove the lockwire and unfasten the caliper securing bolts. Withdraw the caliper assembly.

NOTE: On all but Cressida, shims are installed between the caliper mounting points and its body to center the caliper over the disc. Count the number of shims at each mounting point. Use care not to mix the shims from the upper and lower mounting points.

Installation is performed in the following order:

1. If the brake disc was not removed or if the caliper was not replaced, use exactly the same number of shims as were removed.

CAUTION

Do not mix the shims from the upper and lower mounting points.

2. If the brake disc was removed or if the caliper was replaced, adjust the number of shims used, so that the caliper assembly is centered over the disc.
3. Tighten the caliper bolts to 67-87 ft/lbs.
4. Install the lockwire on the caliper securing bolts.
5. Connect the hydraulic line to the caliper. Connect the wear sensor to the brake pad and install the wiring harness on the steering knuckle bracket.
6. Bleed the hydraulic system and check for leaks.

OVERHAUL

Corolla, Carina, Celica and Tercel

1. Remove the caliper.
2. Carefully remove the dust boot from around the cylinder bore.
3. Apply compressed air to the brake line union to force the piston out of its bore. Be careful, the piston may come out forcefully.
4. Remove the seal from the piston. Check the piston and cylinder bore for wear and/or corrosion. Replace components as necessary.

Assembly is performed in the following order:

1. Coat all components with clean brake fluid.
2. Install the seal and piston in the cylinder bore, after coating them with the rubber lubricant supplied in the rebuilding kit. Seat the piston in the bore with your fingers.
3. Fit the boot into the groove in the cylinder bore.
4. Install the caliper cylinder assembly.

Mark II, Cressida and Corona

1. Remove the caliper assembly from the car, and separate the pads from the caliper.
2. Remove the snap-ring and the dust boot from both caliper bores.
3. Place block of wood between the pistons and blow them out of their bores by applying compressed air to the brake line union. Use of the wood block is to keep the pistons from striking each other.
4. Withdraw the sealing rings from the caliper bores. Do not mix the pistons; they must be returned to their original bores.

CAUTION

Do not loosen or remove the bridge bolts which secure the halves of the caliper body.

Check the caliper body for cracks and/or distortion. Examine the caliper bores for wear, damage, or corrosion. Replace the guide pins (with holes) if they are bent.

Assembly is performed in the following order:

1. Replace all rubber parts with new ones.
2. Coat the sealing rings and the caliper bore with the rubber grease supplied in the rebuilding kit; do not use any other type of lubricant.
3. Fit the sealing rings into the grooves in the caliper bores.
4. Install the O-rings and spacers (if used) on the pistons and carefully insert each piston into its original bore. Use only finger-pressure to seat the pistons.
5. Install the boots over the bores and secure them with the snap-rings.
6. Install the calipers and the brake pads, then bleed the brake system.

Brake Disc

REMOVAL AND INSTALLATION

1. Remove the brake pads and the caliper.
2. On Corolla, Carina, and Celica models only:
   a. Loosen the bolts which secure the caliper mounting bracket.
   b. Withdraw the bracket, complete with the caliper support plates and springs attached.

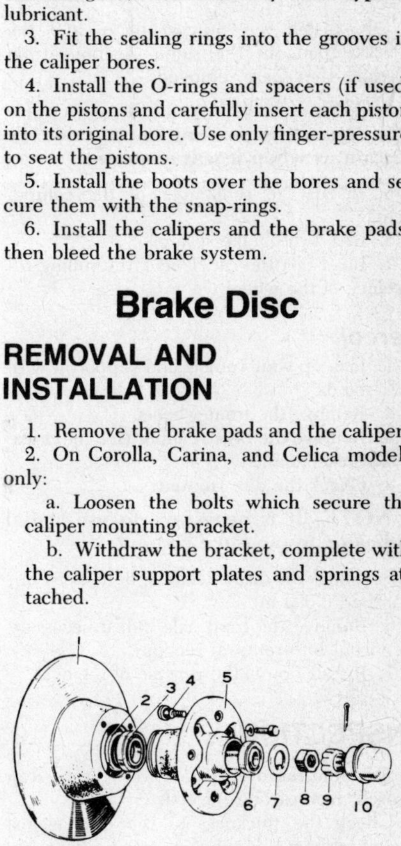

1. Disc
2. Oil seal
3. Tapered roller bearing
4. Hub bolt
5. Hub
6. Tapered roller bearing
7. Washer
8. Nut
9. Adjusting lock cap
10. Grease cap

Brake disc and hub assembly

3. Check the disc run-out, as detailed below, at this point. Make a note of the results for use during installation.
4. Remove the grease cap from the hub. Remove the cotter pin and the castellated nut.
5. Remove the wheel hub with the brake disc attached.

Inspect the disc.

Installation is performed in the following order:

1. Coat the hub oil seal lip with multipurpose grease and install the disc/hub assembly.
2. Adjust the wheel bearing preload, as detailed below.
3. Measure the disc run-out. Check it against the specifications.

NOTE: If the wheel bearing nut is improperly tightened, disc run-out will be affected.

4. On Corolla, Carina and Celica models only:
   a. Install the caliper support, complete with springs. Tighten the securing nuts to the following torque specifications:
   Corolla, Carina and Celica: 20-40 ft/lbs.
   All others: 65-87 ft/lbs.

CAUTION

Be careful not to distort the support springs during installation.

   b. Install the support plates and the brake pads in the same positions from which they were removed.

NOTE: Install the pad support plate with the arrow pointing in the same direction as when it was removed.

5. Install the remainder of the components.
6. Bleed the brake system.
7. Road test the car. Check the rolling resistance of the wheel.

Tercel

1. Jack up your vehicle and support it with jack stands.
2. Remove the front wheels.
3. Remove the brake caliper (see the brake removal section).
4. Check the disc run-out.

NOTE: It is necessary to use a dial indicator to measure run-out.

5. Check the disc thickness, limit 0.354 in., standard 0.394 in.
6. Remove the front axle hub if necessary (see front hub removal section).
7. Installation is the reverse of removal.

INSPECTION

Examine the disc. If it is worn, warped or scored, it must be replaced.

Check the thickness of the disc against specifications. If it is below specifications, replace it. Use a micrometer to measure the thickness. Disc run-out should be measured *before* the disc is removed and again *after* the disc is installed. Use a dial indicator mounted on a stand to determine run-out. If run-out exceeds 0.006 in. (all models), replace the disc.

NOTE: Be sure that the wheel bearing nut is properly tightened. If it is not, an inaccurate run-out reading may be obtained. If different run-out readings are obtained with the same disc, between removal and installation, this is probably the cause.

Wheel Bearings

REMOVAL AND INSTALLATION

1. Remove the disc/hub assembly, as detailed above.
2. If either the disc or the entire hub assembly is to be replaced, unbolt the hub from the disc.

NOTE: If only the bearings are to be replaced, do not separate the disc and hub.

3. Using a brass rod as a drift, tap the inner bearings cone out. Remove the oil seal and the inner bearing.

NOTE: Throw the old oil seal away.

4. Drive out the inner bearing cup.
5. Drive out the outer bearing cup.

Inspect the bearings and the hub for signs of wear or damage. Replace components, as necessary.

Installation is performed in the following order:

1. Install the inner bearing cup and then the outer bearing cup, by driving them into place.

CAUTION

Use care not to cock the bearing cups in the hub.

2. Pack the bearings, hub inner well and grease cap with multipurpose grease.
3. Install the inner bearing into the hub.
4. Carefully install a new oil seal with a soft drift.
5. Install the hub on the spindle. Be sure to install all of the washers and nuts which were removed.
6. Adjust the bearing preload.
7. Install the caliper assembly.

PRELOAD ADJUSTMENT

1. With the front hub/disc assembly installed, tighten the castellated nut to the torque figure specified.
2. Rotate the disc back and forth, two or three times, to allow the bearing to seat properly.
3. Loosen the castellated nut until it is only finger-tight.
4. Tighten the nut firmly, using a box wrench.
5. Measure the bearing preload with a spring scale attached to a wheel mounting stud. Check it against the specifications.
6. Install the cotter pin.

NOTE: If the hole does not align with the nut (or cap) holes, tighten the nut slightly until it does.

7. Finish installing the brake components and the wheel.

Measuring wheel bearing pre-load with a spring scale

PRELOAD SPECIFICATIONS

Model/Year	Initial Torque Setting (ft. lbs.)	Preload (oz.)
Tercel 1980-81	22	13-30
Corolla 1975	19-23	6-13
1976-77	19-23	10-24
1978-80	19-23	11-25
Celica 1975	19-24	10-22
1976-77	19-24	10-24
1978-81	19-26	11-25
Corona 1975-77	19-26	10-22
1978-80	19-26	12-31
Mark II 1975	19-23	10-22
1976	19-23	11-24
Supra	19-23	11-24
Cressida	22	37-56

Brake Drums

REMOVAL AND INSTALLATION

The rear brake drum removal and installation procedure for all models is performed in the same manner as the front brake drum.

NOTE: Release the parking brake before attempting rear drum removal. Do not depress the brake pedal, once the drum has been removed.

Inspection

Inspection for the rear brake drum is performed in the same way as that for the front brake drum (see above).

Brake Shoes

REMOVAL AND INSTALLATION

Corolla, Carina, Celica, Corona (1975-81) and Cressida

1. Remove the drum.
2. Unhook the shoe tension springs from the shoes with the aid of a brake spring removing tool.

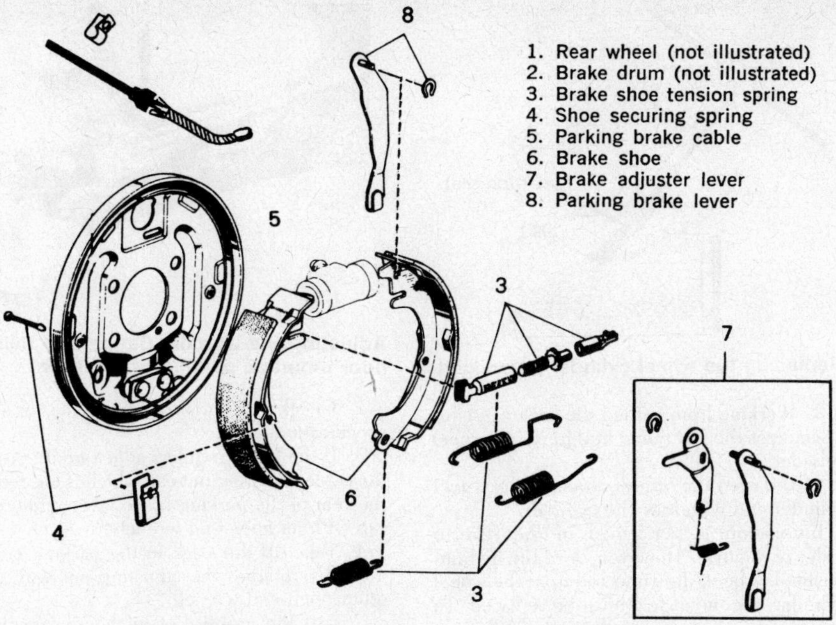

Rear brake shoe removal sequence—all models similar

3. Remove the brake shoe securing springs.
4. Disconnect the parking brake cable at the parking brake shoe lever.
5. Withdraw the shoes, complete with the parking brake shoe lever.
6. Unfasten the C-clip and remove the adjuster assembly from the shoes.

Inspect the shoes for wear and scoring. Replace the linings if their thickness is less than 0.04 in. (0.06 in—Crown).

Check the tension springs to see if they are weak, distorted or rusted.

Inspect the teeth on the automatic adjuster wheel for chipping or other damage.

Installation is performed in the following order:

NOTE: Grease the point of the shoe which slides against the backing plate. Do not get grease on the linings.

1. Attach the parking brake shoe lever and the automatic adjuster lever to the rear of the shoe from which they were removed.
2. Fasten the parking brake cable to the lever on the brake shoe.
3. Install the automatic adjuster and fit the tension spring on the adjuster lever.

NOTE: The tension spring should be installed on the anchor before performing Step 4.

4. Install the securing spring on the *rear* shoe and then install the securing spring on the *front* shoe.
5. Hook one end of the tension spring over the rear shoe, with the tool used during removal; then hook the other end over the front shoe.

CAUTION

Be sure that the wheel cylinder boots are not being pinched by the ends of the shoes.

6. Test the automatic adjuster by operating the parking brake shoe lever.

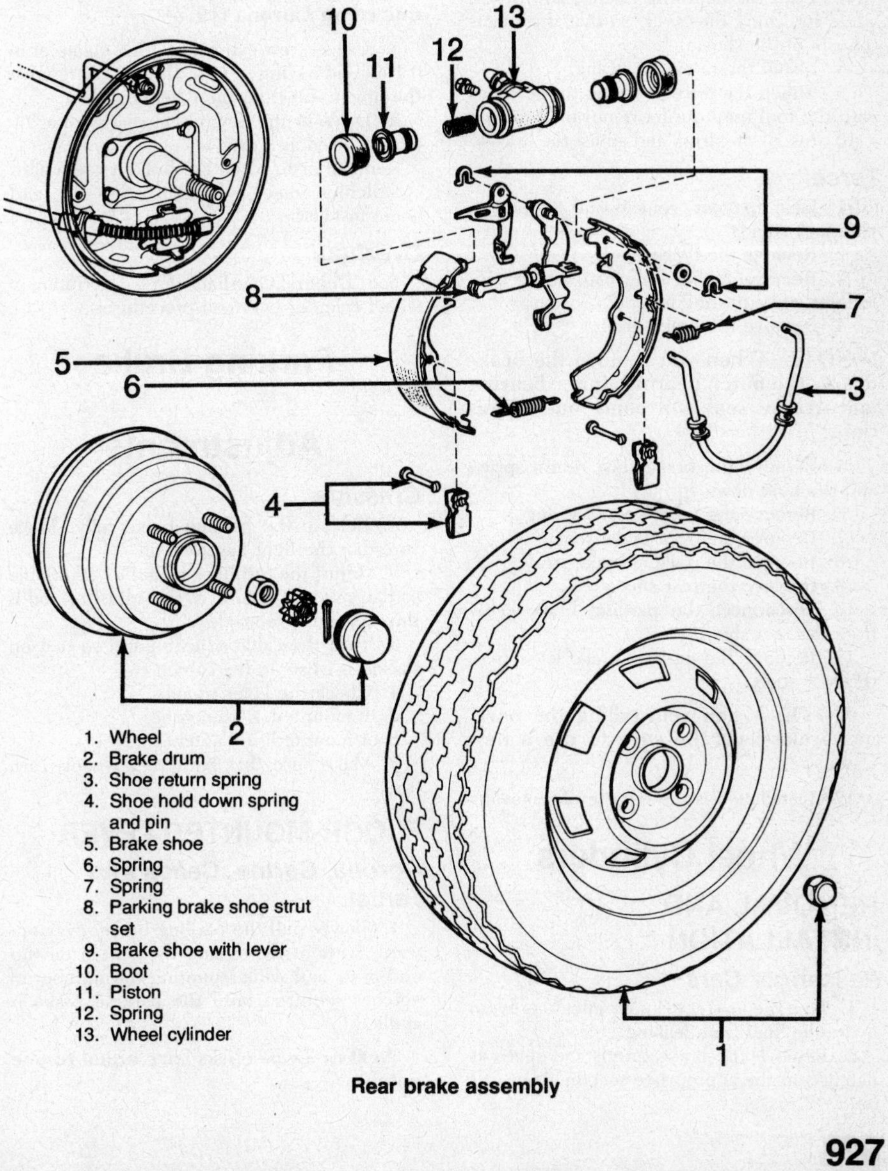

Rear brake assembly

7. Install the brake drum and adjust the brakes.

Corona and Mark II

1. Remove the brake drum.
2. Remove the tension springs from the trailing (rear) shoe with the aid of a brake return spring removal tool.
3. Press down on the brake adjuster ratchet and move the shoe adjusting lever forward, to the center of the drum.
4. Remove the securing spring and remove the leading (front) shoe with the tension spring attached.
5. Disconnect the trailing shoe from the parking brake cable and remove the shoe retaining spring. Withdraw the shoe.

CAUTION

Use care not to get grease on the lining surface.

Inspect all of the parts removed for wear or damage. Check the lining thickness; it should be no less than 0.06 in. If it is less than this have the brakes relined.

Installation is performed in the following order:

1. Install the adjusting lever and ratchet on to the leading shoe. Attach the parking brake cable to the trailing shoe.

NOTE: Use a new retaining clip.

2. Apply non-melting lubricant to the shoe parts which contact other components of the brake.

CAUTION

Do not allow lubricant to get on the surface of the brake lining.

3. Install the parking brake strut on the trailing shoe with its retaining spring (rear brakes only).
4. Attach the parking brake cable to the lever (rear brakes only).
5. Fasten the trailing shoe with its securing spring.
6. Push the adjusting lever toward the center of the brake and install it with the tension spring. Fasten the shoe retaining spring.

NOTE: The longer hook of the tension spring attaches to the leading shoe.

7. Push the adjusting ratchet downward, while returning the lever, so that it contacts the rim of the shoe.
8. Install the retaining spring.
9. Attach the tension spring to the shoes with the tool used during removal.
10. Install the drum and adjust the brakes.

Tercel

1. Jack up your vehicle and support it with jack stands.
2. Remove the rear wheel.
3. Remove the bearing cap, cotter pin, locknut and adjusting nut.
4. Remove the brake drum.

NOTE: When you remove the brake drum, the outer bearing, inner bearing and grease seal will come out at this time.

5. Remove the brake shoe return spring and the hold down springs.
6. Remove the lower return spring.
7. Remove the front brake shoe.
8. Remove the parking brake strut.
9. Remove the rear shoe.
10. Disconnect the parking brake cable from the rear shoe.
11. Remove the parking brake lever from the rear shoe.

NOTE: When reinstalling the parking brake lever be sure to use a new C-washer.

12. Installation is the reverse of removal.

Wheel Cylinders

REMOVAL AND INSTALLATION

Passenger Cars

1. Plug the master cylinder inlet to prevent hydraulic fluid from leaking.
2. Remove the brake drums and shoes as detailed in the appropriate section above.

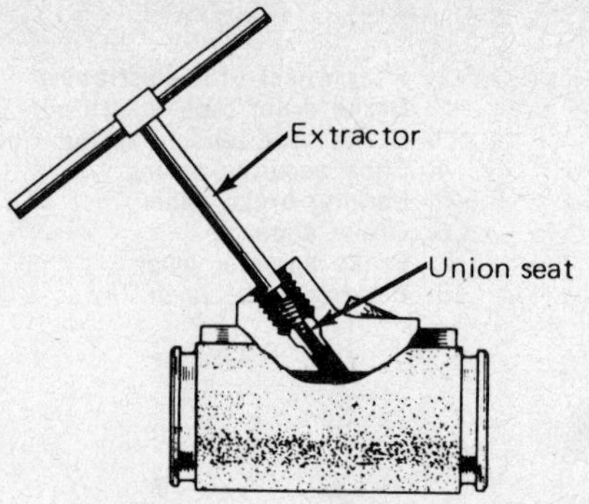

Replacing the wheel cylinder union seat

3. Working from behind the backing plate, disconnect the hydraulic line from the wheel cylinder.
4. Unfasten the screws retaining the wheel cylinder and withdraw the cylinder.

Installation is performed in the reverse order of removal. However, once the hydraulic line has been disconnected from the wheel cylinder, the union seat must be replaced. To replace the seat, proceed in the following manner:

NOTE: This procedure is not required on Corona (1975).

1. Use a screw extractor with a diameter of 0.1 in. and having reverse threads, to remove the union seat from the wheel cylinder.
2. Drive in the new union seat with a $^{5}/_{16}$ in. bar, used as a drift.

Remember to bleed the brake system after completing wheel cylinder, brake shoe and drum installation.

Overhaul

See "General Overhaul" for a description of wheel cylinder overhaul procedures.

Parking Brake

Adjustments

Cressida

1. Release the parking brake fully. Make sure that the light has gone off.
2. Adjust the turnbuckle on the brake cable so that .39 in. (10 mm) of the adjusting rod is through the turnbuckle.
3. Turn the cable adjusting nut so that no slackness exists in the cable.
4. Check the lever travel:
dash mounted: 8-13 notches
floor mounted: 5-7 notches
5. Make sure that both rear wheels turn freely.

FLOOR-MOUNTED LEVER

Corolla, Carina, Celica and Tercel

1. Slowly pull the parking brake lever upward, without depressing the button on the end of it, and while counting the number of notches required until the parking brake is applied.

NOTE: Two "clicks" are equal to one notch.

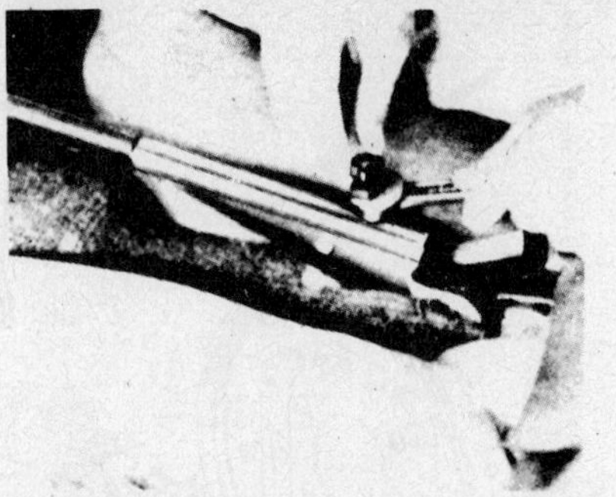

Adjusting the Corolla, Carina and Celica floor mounted parking brake lever

2. Check the number of notches against specifications.
3. If the brake requires adjustment, loosen the cable adjusting nut cap which is located at the rear of the parking brake lever. Hold the cap with an open-end wrench.
4. Take up the slack in the parking brake cable by rotating the adjusting nut with another open-end wrench.
   a. If the number of nitches is *less* than specified, turn the nut *counterclockwise*.
   b. If the number of notches is *more* than specified, turn the nut *clockwise*.
5. Tighten the adjusting cap, using care not to disturb the setting of the adjusting nut.
6. Check the rotation of the rear wheels to be sure that the brakes are not dragging.

1975-76 Mark II

1. Adjust the rear brake shoes.
2. Without depressing the button, pull the parking brake handle up slowly, and count the number of notches before the brake is applied. It should take 3-6 notches; if not, proceed with Step 3.
3. Loosen the locknut on the parking brake equalizer.
4. Screw the adjusting nut *in*, just enough so that the parking brake cables have no slack.
5. Hold the adjusting nut in this position while tightening the locknut.
6. Check the rotation of the rear wheels, with the parking brake off, to be sure that the brake shoes aren't dragging.

DASH-MOUNTED LEVER

Corona and Mark II

1. Loosen the parking brake warning light switch bracket.
2. Push the parking brake lever in until it is stopped by the pawl.

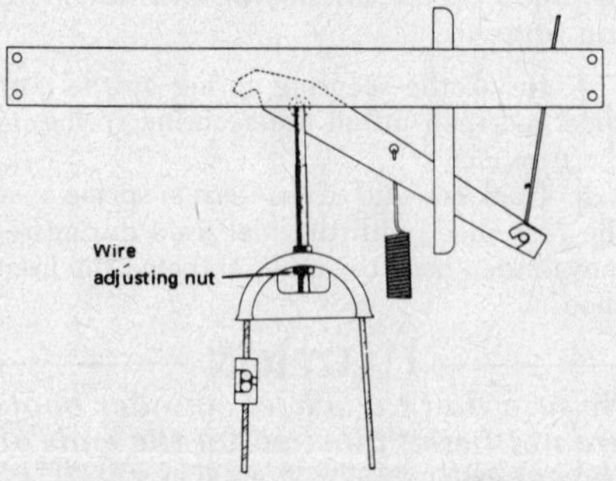

Adjusting the dash mounted or the 1975 floor mounted parking brake from under the car

3. Move the switch so that it will be "off" at this position but "on" when the handle is pulled out.
4. Tighten the switch bracket and push the brake lever in again.
5. Working from underneath the vehicle, loosen the locknut on the parking brake cable equalizer.
6. Screw the adjusting nut *in*, just enough so that the brake cables have no slack.
7. Hold the adjusting nut in this position while tightening the locknut.
8. Check the rotation of the rear wheels to make sure that the brakes are not dragging.
9. Pull out on the parking brake lever, and count the number of notches needed to apply the parking brake. Check the number against the figures given in the chart.

PARKING BRAKE ADJUSTMENT

Model/Year	Range of Adjustment (notches)
Corolla 1200	7-8 ①
Corolla 1600 ('75-77)	2-6
Corolla 1600 ('78-79)	4-12
Tercel	2-5
Celica	3-7
Corona	3-6
Corona	
Console	3-6
Pedal	4-8
Cressida, Supra	5-8
Mark II 1975	3-6
1976	8-12

① 1978-79: 4-12

REMOVAL AND INSTALLATION

Corolla, Celica and Carina–Front Cable

1. Raise and support the rear of the vehicle.
2. Remove the rear console.
3. Remove the parking brake lever adjusting cap.
4. Remove the cable locknut.
5. Remove the parking brake lever.
6. Remove the cable from the underside and disconnect it from the equalizer.
7. Install in reverse of removal.
8. Adjust the brake.

Corolla, Celica and Carina–Rear Cables

1. Remove the front cable.
2. Disconnect the rear cables from the equalizer.
3. Disconnect the cable clamps.
4. Remove the rear brake shoe and pull the cables from the backing plates.
5. Install in reverse of removal.
6. Adjust the brake.

Corona–Floor Lever Type

1. Raise and support the vehicle.
2. Remove the driveshaft.
3. Remove the equalizer from the lever pull rod.
4. Remove the rear brake shoes.
5. Depress the cable retaining claw and remove it from the backing plate.
6. Installation is the reverse of removal.

Corona–Underdash Type

1. Raise and support the vehicle.
2. Remove the driveshaft.
3. Separate the equalizer from the front cable and remove the clip.
4. Remove the return spring.
5. Remove the pin and take off the pulley.
6. Remove the clip and lever pin and take off the front cable.
7. The rear cables are removed as in the floor lever type.
8. Installation is the reverse of removal.

Cressida–Front Cable

1. Raise and support the car.
2. Remove the driveshaft at the transmission.
3. Remove the center bearing support.
4. Remove the retaining clip and disconnect the cable at the equalizer.
5. Disconnect the intermediate lever pin, remove the pulley pin and clip and remove the cable from the intermediate lever.
6. Remove the driver's seat.
7. Remove the scuff plates and roll back the carpeting.
8. Remove the heater ducts on the driver's side.
9. Remove the cable.
10. Installation is the reverse of removal.

Cressida–Rear Cables

1. Raise and support the car.
2. Disconnect the driveshaft at the transmission.
3. Remove the center bearing support.
4. Disconnect the equalizer from the pull rod.
5. Remove the grommet and clamp.
6. Remove the brake drums.
7. Disconnect the cable from the shoes.

Mark II–Front Cable

1. Remove the parking brake signal switch wiring harness and switch bracket.
2. Slightly pull out the parking brake handle and lift the pawl to disengage the ratchet.
3. While holding the pawl, push down on the handle and disconnect the cable from the handle.
4. Remove the pulley, clip and bracket.
5. Remove the upper portion of the brake handle guide and remove the handle.
6. Remove the return spring and cable from the intermediate lever.
7. Remove the cable body clamp clip and remove the front cable.
8. Installation is the reverse of above.
9. Adjust the brake.

Corona Mark II–Rear Cables

1. Remove the equalizer adjusting nut and remove the pull rod.
2. Remove the cables from the equalizer.
3. Remove the retainers and clamps from the cables.
4. Remove the brake drums, disconnect the cables from the shoes and remove them from the backing plates. The retaining claw may be depressed with pliers.
5. Installation is the reverse of removal.

Tercel–Floor Lever Type

1. Jack up your vehicle and support it with jack stands.
2. Disassemble the rear brake shoes.
3. Disconnect the parking brake cable from the rear shoe.
4. Remove the parking brake cable from the backing plate.
5. Remove the cable clamps.
6. Remove the cable.
7. Remove the adjusting nut and the equalizer.
8. Installation is the reverse of removal.

CHASSIS ELECTRICAL

Heater Blower

NOTE: On some models the air conditioner, if so equipped, is integral with the heater, and therefore, heater removal may differ from the procedures detailed below.

REMOVAL AND INSTALLATION

Tercel

1. Disconnect the negative battery terminal.
2. Remove the under tray (if so equipped).
3. Remove the blower duct and air duct.

NOTE: Before removing the air duct remember to remove the two attaching clamps.

4. Remove the glove box.
5. Remove the control cable.
6. Disconnect the electrical connector on the blower motor.
7. Remove the blower motor bolts and remove the motor.
8. Installation is the reverse of removal.

Corolla–1975-81

1. Disconnect the blower wiring harness.
2. Remove the right-hand defroster hose.
3. Remove the three screws which secure the blower motor and lift out the motor.
4. Separate the fan from the motor. Installation is the reverse of removal.

Carina, Celica and Cressida

1. Working from under the instrument panel, unfasten the defroster hoses from the heater box.
2. Unplug the multiconnector.
3. Loosen the mounting screws and withdraw the blower assembly.

Installation is the reverse of removal.

Mark II

1. Remove the center console, after remov-

ing the shift knob (manual), unfastening the wiring, connector, and undoing the console securing screws.

2. Unfasten the heater blower wiring connector.

3. Remove the three bolts which secure the blower motor, complete with fan, from the box.

Installation is the reverse order of removal.

Corona–1975-81

1. Remove the package tray.
2. Remove the trim panel.
3. Disconnect the heater blower motor wiring harness.
4. Loosen the three screws which secure the motor to the housing and remove the motor/blower assembly.

Installation is the reverse of removal.

Heater Core

REMOVAL AND INSTALLATION

Tercel

1. Disconnect the negative battery terminal.
2. Drain the radiator.
3. Remove the ash tray and retainer.
4. Remove the rear heater duct (optional).
5. Remove the left and right side defroster ducts.
6. Remove the under tray (optional).
7. Remove the glove box.
8. Remove the main air duct.
9. Disconnect the radio and remove it.
10. Disconnect the heater control cables and remove them.
11. Disconnect the heater hoses.
12. Remove the front and rear air ducts.
13. Remove the electrical connector.
14. Remove the heater bolts and remove the heater.

NOTE: Slide the heater to the right side of car to remove it.

15. Remove the heater core.
16. Installation is the reverse of removal.

Corolla–1975-81

1. Disconnect the negative battery cable and drain the cooling system.
2. Disconnect the heater hose from the engine compartment side.
3. Remove the knobs from the heater and fan controls.
4. Remove the two securing screws, and take the heater control panel off.
5. Remove the heater control, complete with cables.
6. Disconnect the wiring harness.
7. Remove the three heater assembly securing bolts and remove the assembly.
8. Separate the core from the heater assembly.

Installation is the reverse of removal.

Carina, Celica, Cressida and Mark II

1. Drain the cooling system.
2. Remove the console, if so equipped, by removing the shift knob (manual), wiring connector, and console attaching screws.
3. Remove the carpeting from the tunnel.
4. If necessary, remove the cigarette lighter and ash tray.
5. Remove the package tray, if it makes access to the heater core difficult.
6. Remove the securing screws and remove the center air outlet on the Mark II/6.
7. Remove the bottom cover/intake assembly screws and withdraw the assembly.
8. Remove the cover from the water valve.
9. Remove the water valve.
10. Remove the hose clamps and remove the hoses from the core.
11. Remove the core.

Installation is the reverse of removal.

Corona–1975-81

1. Disconnect the negative battery cable.
2. Drain the cooling system.
3. Disconnect the heater hoses from the engine.
4. Remove the center console, if so equipped.
5. Remove the package tray and disconnect the heater air duct.
6. Unfasten the screws and take the glove compartment out of the dash.
7. Working through the glove compartment opening, remove the rear duct.
8. Detach the ventilation duct.
9. Remove the instrument cluster, as detailed below.
10. Remove the radio, if installed.
11. Remove the heater control assembly.
12. Take the defroster duct assembly out.
13. Tilt the heater assembly to the right and withdraw it from the package tray side.
14. Remove the water valve and outlet hose from the heater assembly.
15. Take off the retaining band and remove the bolt.
16. Take out the core.

Installation is the reverse of removal.

Radio

CAUTION

Never operate the radio without a speaker; severe damage to the output transistors will result. If the speaker must be replaced, use a speaker of the correct impedance (ohms) or else the output transistors will be damaged and require replacement.

REMOVAL AND INSTALLATION

Celica and Cressida

1. Remove the knobs from the radio.
2. Remove the nuts from the radio control shafts.
3. Detach the antenna lead from the jack on the radio case.
4. Remove the cowl air intake duct.
5. Detach the power and speaker leads.
6. Remove the radio support nuts and bolts.
7. Remove the radio from beneath the dashboard.
8. Remove the nuts which secure the speaker through the service hole in the top of the glove box.
9. Remove remainder of the speaker securing nuts from above the radio mounting location.
10. Remove the speaker.

Installation is the reverse of removal.

Corolla–1975-81

1. Remove the two screws from the top of the dashboard center trim panel.
2. Lift the center panel out far enough to gain access to the cigarette lighter wiring and disconnect the wiring. Remove the trim panel.
3. Unfasten the screws which secure the radio to the instrument panel braces.
4. Lift out the radio and disconnect the leads from it. Remove the radio.

Installation is the reverse of removal.

Carina

1. Remove the center air outlet from under the dash.
2. Unfasten the radio control mounting bracket.
3. Remove the radio control knobs and then the securing nuts from the control shafts.
4. Detach the speaker, and the power and antenna leads from the radio.
5. Withdraw the radio from underneath the dashboard.
6. Unfasten the speaker securing nuts and remove the speaker.

Installation is the reverse of removal.

Corona–1975-81 Tercel

1. Disconnect the negative battery terminal.
2. Disconnect the antenna.
3. Disconnect the electrical connector.
4. Remove the radio knobs and remove the face plate.
5. Remove the radio.
6. Installation is the reverse of removal.

INSTRUMENT PANEL-MOUNTED

1. Remove the two screws securing the instrument cluster surround and remove the surround.
2. Remove the knobs from the heater controls and remove the heater control face.
3. Remove the four screws which secure the center trim panel (two are behind the heater control opening).
4. Remove the radio knobs and remove the center trim panel.
5. Remove the four screws which secure the radio bracket.
6. Pull the radio far enough out to remove the antenna, power, and speaker leads.
7. Remove the radio.

Installation is the reverse of removal.

CONSOLE-MOUNTED

1. Remove the screws which secure the console and remove the console, by lowering the armrest rearward and lifting up on the center of the console.
2. Unplug the radio and disconnect the antenna lead.
3. Remove the radio knobs.
4. Remove the radio bracket and then remove the radio.
5. Installation is the reverse of removal.

Mark II–1975-79

1. Remove the instrument cluster housing as detailed in the appropriate section below.

2. Remove the heater control panel assembly.
3. Unfasten the two radio securing bolts.
4. Detach all of the radio leads.
5. Withdraw the radio.

Installation is the reverse of removal.

Windshield Wiper Motor

REMOVAL AND INSTALLATION

Tercel

1. Disconnect the negative battery terminal.
2. Insert a screwdriver between the linkage and the motor.
3. Pry up to separate the linkage from the motor.
4. Disconnect the electrical connector from the motor.
5. Remove the mounting bolts and remove the motor.
6. Installation is the reverse of removal.

Corolla (1975-81), Carina and Corona

1. Disconnect the wiper motor connector.
2. Remove the service cover and loosen the wiper motor bolts.
3. Use a screwdriver to separate the wiper link-to-motor connection.

CAUTION

Be careful not to bend the linkage.

4. Withdraw the wiper motor assembly.

Installation is the reverse of removal.

Celica and Cressida

1. Remove the access hole cover.
2. Separate the wiper and motor by prying gently with a screwdriver.
3. Remove the left and right cowl ventilators.
4. Remove the wiper arms and the linkage mounting nuts. Push the linkage pivot ports into the ventilators.
5. Loosen the wiper link connectors at their ends and with the linkage from the cowl ventilator.
6. Start the wiper motor and turn the ignition key off when the crank is at the position illustrated.

NOTE: The wiper motor is difficult to remove when it is in the parked position. If the motor is turned off at the

Sedan and Wagon

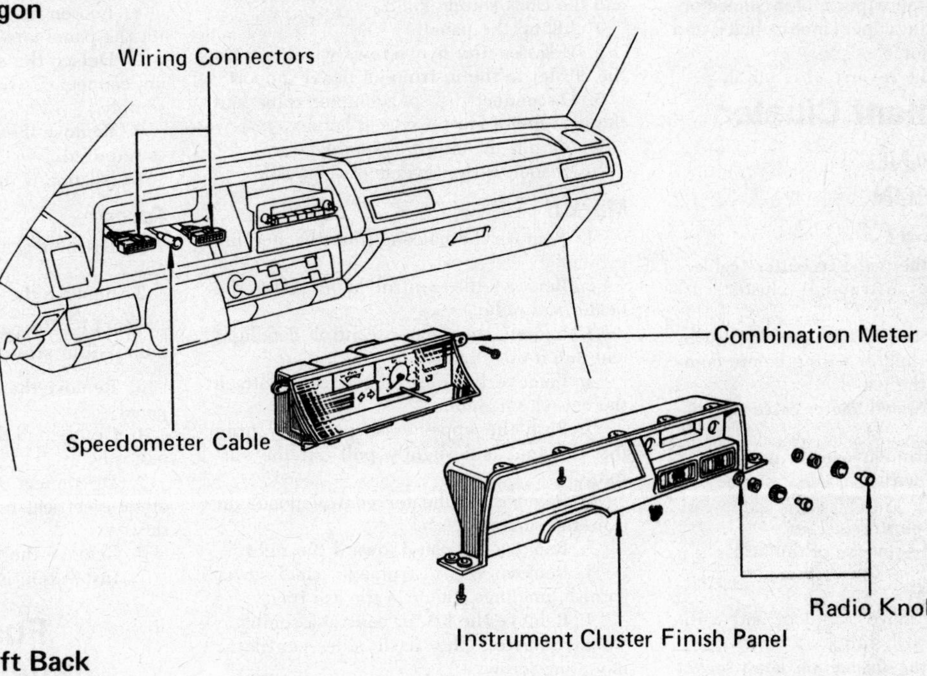

Coupe and Lift Back

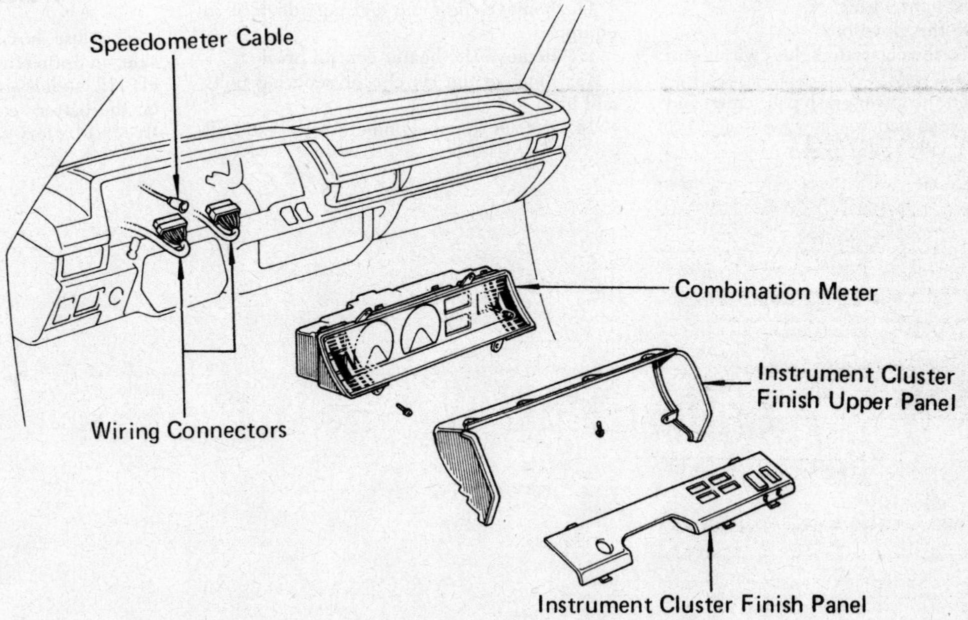

1981 instrument panel layouts, typical for all 1981 models

wiper switch, it will automatically return to this position.

7. Unplug the connector.
8. Loosen the motor bolts and withdraw the motor.

Installation is the reverse of removal. Be sure to install the wiper motor with it in the park position by connecting the multiconnector and operating the wiper control switch. Assemble the crank.

Mark II

1. Remove the cover from the service hole.
2. Set the wiper crank at 180° from park, by turning the wiper switch on and then turning the ignition switch off, once the desired position is reached.
3. Separate the link from the motor crank with a screwdriver.
4. Disconnect the wiper motor connector.
5. Unfasten the wiper motor bolts and withdraw the motor.

Installation is the reverse of removal.

Instrument Cluster

REMOVAL AND INSTALLATION

Corolla–1975-81

1. Disconnect the negative battery cable.
2. Remove the instrument cluster surround.
3. Remove the center trim panel. Disconnect the cigarette lighter wiring before completely removing the panel.
4. Remove the speedometer cable and disconnect it.
5. Pull the instrument cluster out just far enough so that its wiring harness may be disconnected.
6. Remove the cluster.

Installation is the reverse of removal.

Carina

1. Remove the glove box door and withdraw the glove box slightly.
2. Disconnect the inspection lamp socket and glove box light wiring.
3. Remove the glove box.
4. Unfasten the cigarette lighter wiring and remove the ash tray.
5. Unfasten the lower crash pad screws and remove the crash pad.

NOTE: It may be necessary to lower the steering column. Be careful, the column is the collapsible type.

6. Loosen the radio rear screws and detach the heater cable at the heater.
7. Unfasten the instrument retaining screws and tilt the panel toward the rear.
8. Detach the speedometer cable and the wiring connectors. Remove the cluster assembly.

Installation is the reverse of removal.

Corona–1975-81

1. Disconnect the negative (−) battery cable.
2. Remove the two instrument cluster surround.
3. Remove the side air outlet control knob and the clock setting knob.
4. Lift off the panel.
5. Unfasten the five screws which secure the cluster to the instrument panel support.
6. Disconnect the speedometer cable and the instrument cluster wiring harness.
7. Lift out the cluster assembly.

Installation is the reverse of removal.

Mark II

1. Remove the housing from the steering column.
2. Remove the control knobs from the heater and radio.
3. Loosen the heater control floodlight and pull it out slightly.
4. Remove the nine screws which attach the cluster surround.
5. Push the upper crash pad away from the surround and slightly pull out the surround.
6. Remove the heater control floodlight from the surround.
7. Remove the panel toward the right.
8. Remove the instrument panel lower garnish moldings. Remove the ash tray.
9. Remove the heater control assembly.
10. Unfasten the dash side ventilator mounting screws.
11. Remove the radio and tape deck, if so equipped.
12. Remove the heater control bracket.
13. Remove the six cluster securing bolts and lift it our slightly.
14. Detach the speedometer cable and all of the wiring harnesses. Remove the cluster.

Installation is the reverse of removal.

NOTE: Have the heater control floodlight installed in the cluster surround prior to its installation.

Celica and Cressida

1. Disconnect the battery.
2. Detach the heater control cables at the heater box.
3. Loosen the steering column clamping nuts and lower the column.

CAUTION

Be careful when handling the column; it is the collapsible type. Cover the column shroud with a cloth to protect it.

4. Loosen the instrument panel screws and tilt the panel forward.
5. Detach the speedometer cable and wiring connectors. Remove the entire panel assembly.
6. Remove the instruments from the panel as required.

Installation is the reverse of removal.

Tercel

1. Disconnect the negative battery terminal.
2. Remove the steering column cover.

NOTE: Be careful not to damage the collapsible steer column mechanism.

3. Remove the screws from the instrument panel.
4. Gently pull the panel out approximately half way.
5. Disconnect the speedometer and any other electrical connections that are necessary.
6. Remove the panel at this time.
7. Installation is the reverse of removal.

Fuses and Fusible Links

The fuse box is located on the left-hand side, underneath the dashboard, on all models. All models are equipped with fusible links on the battery cables running from the positive (+) battery terminal.

SPECIFICATIONS

INDEX

BEFORE SERVICING, SEE THE SAFETY NOTICE ON THE CONTENTS PAGE

INTRODUCTION

For 1973, the Spitfire engine displacement was increased to 1493 cc, hence the Spitfire 1500. To accommodate the increased torque of the engine, the clutch diameter was increased to 7¼ in.

The TR-6 is identifiable by its full width horizontal grille and its Kammback tail end treatment.

The TR-6 was discontinued after the 1976 model year.

In 1975, the TR-7 was introduced. The car shares few components with former models. New features include the 2 liter overhead cam engine with an aluminum cross-flow cylinder head and an over-square bore-to-stroke ratio; the MacPherson strut front suspension; live rear axle with 4 link coil rear suspension; unitized body/frame construction; electronic ignition; self-adjusting rear drum brakes, sealed cooling system; printed instrument panel electrical circuit; automatic choke (only on California models); and air conditioning.

The TR-8 introduced in 1980 is basically a TR-7 with a 215 cu. in. V8 engine instead of the OHC 4-cylinder engine used through 1979.

SERIAL NUMBER IDENTIFICATION

All Triumphs have the chassis number (commission number) stamped on a plate adjacent to the driver's door striker plate and on another small plate visible through the windshield.

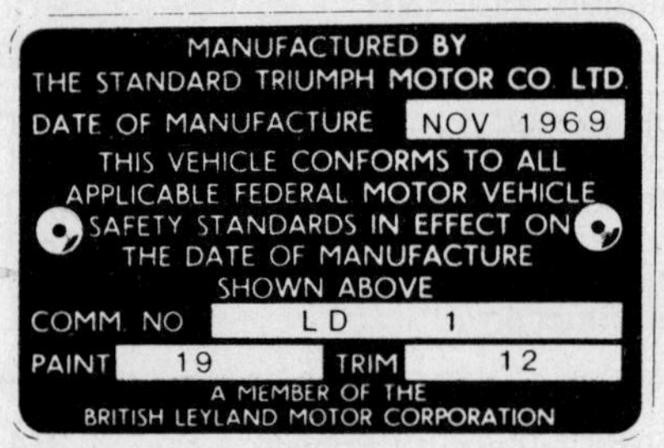

Chassis number plate

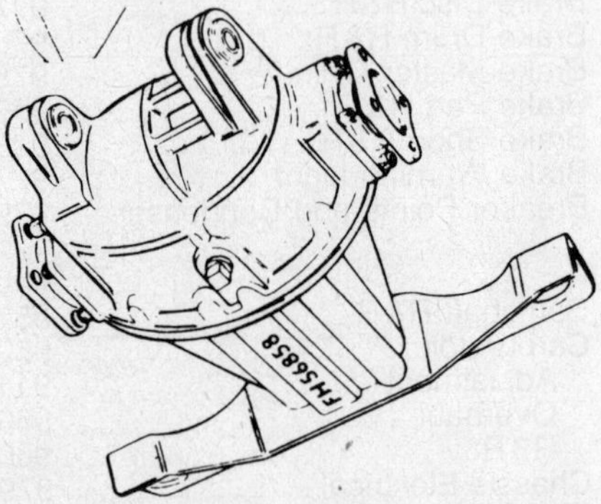

Rear axle number location—Spitfire shown, TR series similar

ENGINE NUMBER

The engine number is stamped on the left side of the engine block on all models.

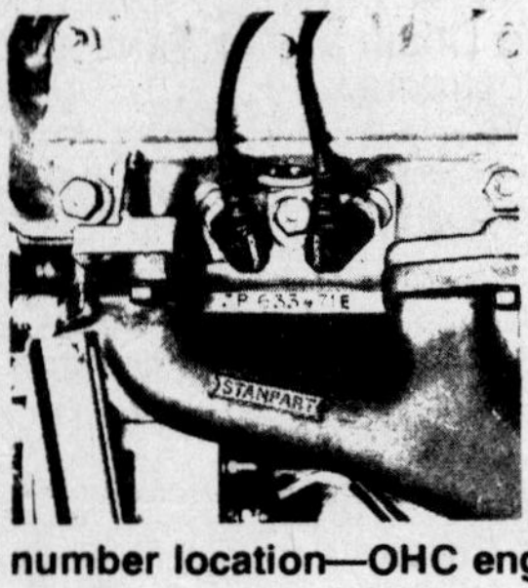

Engine number location—OHC engine

TRANSMISSION NUMBER

The transmission number is stamped on the left side of the clutch housing (TR models), or on the top right side of the transmission case (Spitfire models).

REAR AXLE NUMBER

The rear axle number is stamped on the housing flange on all models.

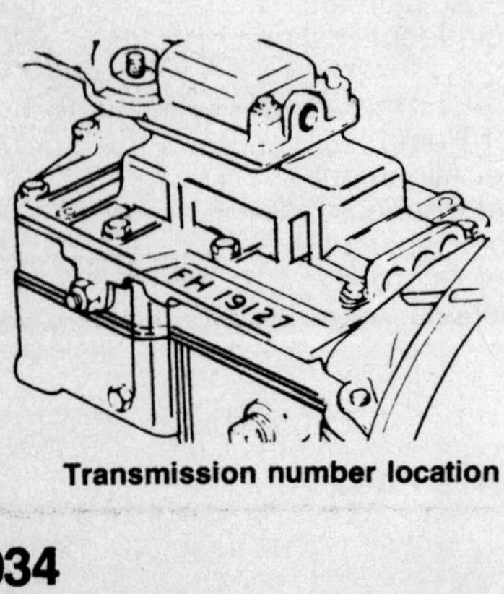

Transmission number location

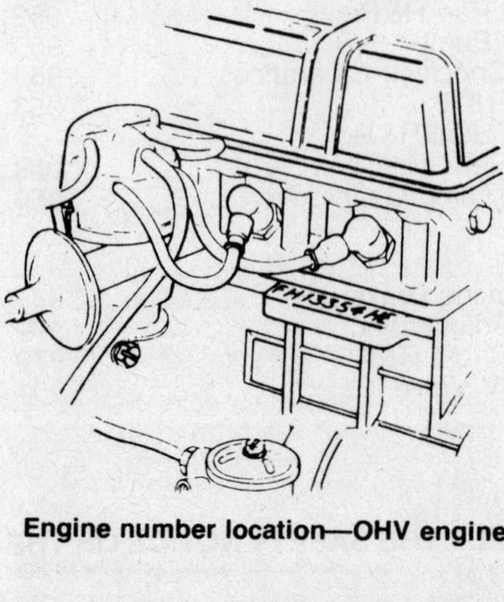

Engine number location—OHV engines

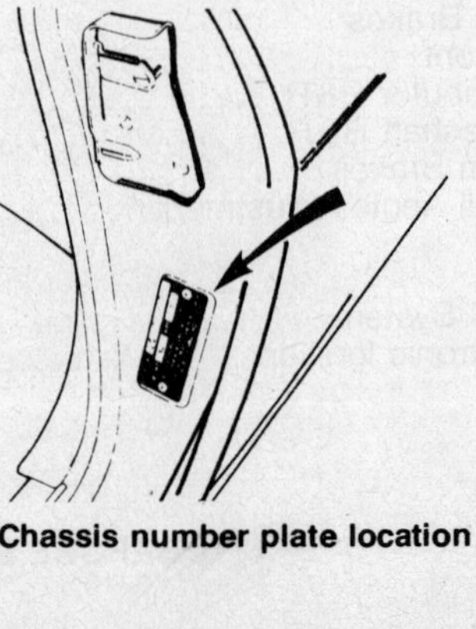
Chassis number plate location

GENERAL ENGINE SPECIFICATIONS

Year	Model	Engine Displacement cu. in. (cc)	Carburetor Type	Horsepower @ rpm	Torque @ rpm (ft. lbs.)	Bore x Stroke (in.)	Compression Ratio	Oil Pressure @ rpm (psi)
1975-77	Spitfire 1500	91.0 (1493)	Single horizontal Zenith-Stromberg 150 CDSE(V)	57 @ 5000	71 @ 3000	2.90 x 3.440	7.5:1	40-60
1978-81	Spitfire 1500	91.0 (1493)	Single horizontal Zenith-Stromberg 150 CD4T	52.5 @ 5000	58.65 @ 2500	2.90 x 3.440	7.5:1	40-60
1975-76	TR-6	152.0 (2498)	Twin horizontal Zenith-Stromberg 175 CDSE(V)	106 @ 4900	133 @ 3000	2.940 x 3.740	7.75:1	70
1975-77	TR-7	122.0 (1998)	Twin horizontal ① Zenith-Stromberg 175 CDSE(V)	90 @ 5000	105 @ 3000	3.56 x 3.07	8.0:1	60
1978-81	TR-7	122.0 (1998)	Twin horizontal Zenith-Stromberg 175 CDFEVX	85.5 @ 5500	102.5 @ 3250	3.56 x 3.07	8.0:1	60
1980-81	TR-8	215 (3528)	Twin horizontal ② Zenith-Stromberg 175 CD Set	133 @ 5000 ③	174 @ 3000	3.50 x 2.80	8.1:1	35

① California: single Zenith-Stromberg 175 CD4TV
② California: Electronic fuel injection
③ California: 148 @ 5000 rpm

TUNE-UP SPECIFICATIONS

When analyzing compression test results, look for uniformity among cylinders, rather than specific pressures

			SPARK PLUGS		DISTRIBUTOR		IGNITION TIMING (deg)		Intake Valve	Fuel Pump	Idle	VALVE CLEAR (in.)	
Year	Model	Engine Displace. (cc)	Type	Gap (in.)	Point Dwell (deg)	Point Gap (in.)	MT	AT	Opens (deg)	Pressure (psi)	Speed (rpm)	In	Ex
1975	Spitfire	1493	N12Y	0.025	38-40	0.014-0.016	8BTDC ①		18BTDC	2.5-3.5	800-850	0.010	0.010
1976-77	Spitfire	1493	N12Y	0.025	Electronic		10BTDC		18BTDC	1.5-2.5	800	0.010	0.010
1978-81	Spitfire	1493	N12Y	0.025	Electronic		10BTDC Fed. ②		18BTDC	2.5-3.5	800	0.010	0.010
1975-76	TR-6	2498	N9Y	0.025	32-38	0.014-0.016	10BTDC		18BTDC	1.5-2.5	800	0.010	0.010
1975-77	TR-7	1998	N12Y ③	0.025	Electronic		10BTDC		16BTDC	2.5-3.5	800	0.008	0.018
1978-81	TR-7	1998	N12Y	0.025	Electronic		10BTDC Fed. ②		16BTDC	2.5-3.5	800	0.008	0.018
1980-81	TR-8	3528	N12Y	0.035 ④	Electronic		TDC	TDC	30BTDC	—	800	Hyd.	Hyd.

NOTE: The underhood specifications sticker often reflects tune-up specification changes made in production. Sticker figures must be used if they disagree with those in this chart.
① 1975 models: 10BTDC
② 2ATDC: Calif.
③ 1977: N-11Y
④ Carbureted engines: 0.030

FIRING ORDERS

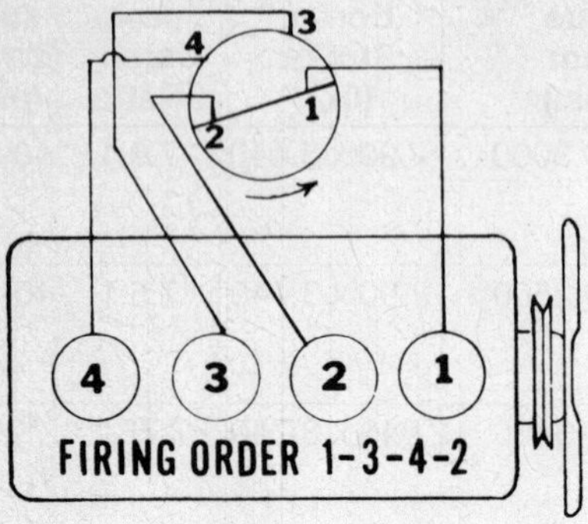

Spitfire

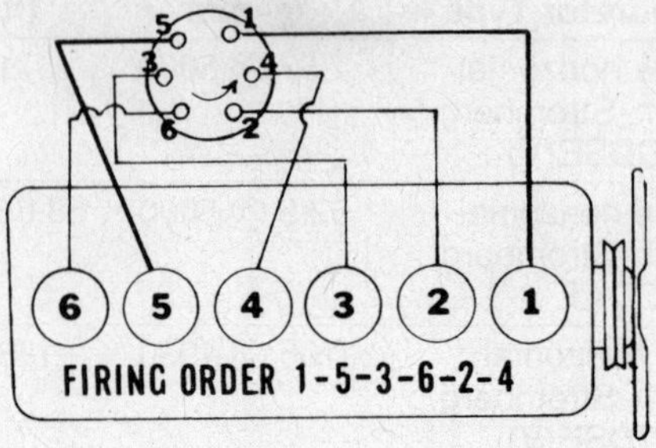

TR-6

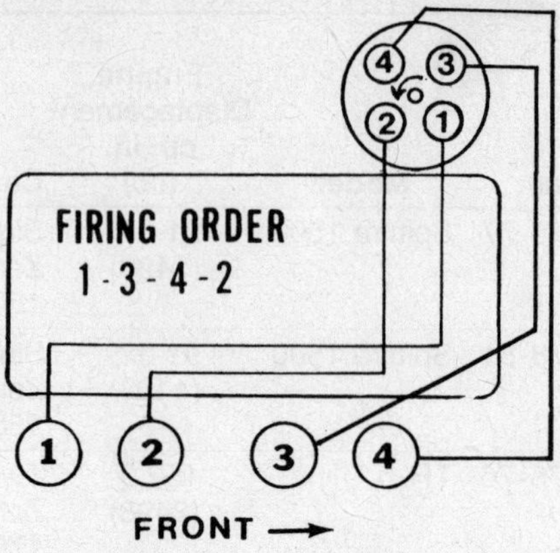

TR-7

CAPACITIES

Year	Model	Engine Displacement (cc)	Engine Crankcase (qts) With Filter	Engine Crankcase (qts) Without Filter	Transmission (pts) 4-Speed	Transmission (pts) With Overdrive	Drive Axis (pts)	Gasoline Tank (gals)	Cooling System (qts) W/AC	Cooling System (qts) W/O A/C
1975-79	Spitfire	1493	4.8	4.2	1.8	3.0	1.2	8.7	—	4.8
1975-76	TR-6	2498	5.4	4.8	2.4	4.2	2.7	11.7	—	6.6
1975-81	TR-7	1998	4.75	4.25	2.5 ①③	—	2.75 ②	14.4	7.75	7.75
1980-81	TR-8	3528	6.2	5.7	3.3 ④	—	2.0	16.8	—	11.7

① 5-speed: 2.7 pts.
② 5-speed option: 1.6 pts.
③ Auto. trans.: 9.5 pts.
④ Auto. trans.: 14.9 pts.

VALVE SPECIFICATIONS

Year	Engine Displacement (cc)	Seat Angle (deg)	Face Angle (deg)	Spring Test Pressure (lbs. @ in.)	Spring (in.) Free Length	Stem to Guide Clearance (in.) Intake	Stem to Guide Clearance (in.) Exhaust	Stem Diameter (in.) Intake	Stem Diameter (in.) Exhaust
1975-81	1493	44.5	45	27-30 @ 1.36	1.61 ①	0.0008-0.0023	0.0015-0.0030	0.3107-0.3112	0.3100-0.3105
1975-76	2498	44.5	46	—	1.14 inner 1.52 outer	0.0013-0.0017	0.0020-0.0024	0.3107-0.3112	0.3101-0.3106
1975-81	1998	44.5	45	—	1.60	0.0017-0.0023	0.0014-0.0030	0.3107-0.3113	0.3100-0.3106
1980-81	3528	46	45	—	②	0.0010-0.0030	0.0050-0.0035	0.3402-0.3412	0.3402-0.3412

① 1975-79: 1.52
② 1.577 in. at 154.35 lbs.
— Not available

CRANKSHAFT AND CONNECTING ROD SPECIFICATIONS

All measurements are given in inches

Year	Engine Displacement cu. in. (cc)	CRANKSHAFT Main Brg. Journal Dia.	Main Brg. Oil Clearance	Shaft End-Play	Thrust on No.	CONNECTING ROD Journal Diameter	Oil Clearance	Side Clearance
1975-79	91.0 (1493)	2.3115-2.3120	—	0.004-0.008	3	1.8750-1.8755	—	—
1975-76	152.0 (2498)	2.3110-2.3115	0.0015-0.0025	0.006-0.008	4	1.8750-1.8755	0.0010-0.0027	0.0070-0.0140
1975-81	122.0 (1998)	2.1260-2.1265	0.0012-0.0022	0.003-0.011	3	1.7500-1.7505	0.0008-0.0023	0.006-0.013
1980-81	215 (3528)	—	0.0006-0.0022	0.004-0.008	4	—	0.0006-0.0022	0.006-0.014

— Not available

PISTON AND RING SPECIFICATIONS

All measurements in inches

Year	Engine Displacement (cc)	PISTON CLEARANCE Crown	Skirt	RING GAP Top Compression	Bottom Compression	Oil Control	RING SIDE CLEARANCE Top Compression	Bottom Compression	Oil Control
1975-81	1493	①	0.0020-0.0030	0.012-0.022	0.012-0.022	(ends butt)	0.0020-0.0025	0.0020-0.0025	0.0028-0.0038
1975-76	2498	0.0038-0.0045	0.0021-0.0028	0.012-0.017	0.008-0.013	②	0.0010-0.0030	0.0010-0.0030	0.0010-0.0030
1975-81	1998	0.0296-0.0350	0.0005-0.0015	0.015-0.025	0.015-0.025	②	0.0019-0.0039	0.0015-0.0025	—
1980-81	3528	0.0296-0.0350	0.0007-0.0013 ③	0.017-0.022	0.017-0.022	0.015-0.055	—	—	—

① Grade F: 0.020-0.024
Grade G: 0.0205-0.0260
② Plain oil rings: 0.015-0.055
Scraper oil ring (ends butt)
③ Skirt bottom
— Not available

TORQUE SPECIFICATIONS

All readings in ft. lbs.

Year	Engine Displace. (cc)	Cylinder Head Bolts	Rod Bearing Bolts	Main Bearing Bolts	Crankshaft Pulley Bolt	Flywheel To Crankshaft Bolts	MANIFOLD Intake	Exhaust	Spark Plug
1975-81	1493	42-46	38-42	50-55	90-110	35-40	20-25	20-25	14-20
1975-76	2498	65-70	38-42	55-60	90-100	55-60	①	①	14-16
1975-81	1998	45-55	40-45	50-65	90-120	40-45	15-20	15-20	14-20
1980-81	3528	②	30-35	65-70	210	60	15	15	12

① TR-6: outer (2)—12-14 ft. lbs., inner—16-18 ft. lbs.

TORQUE SEQUENCES

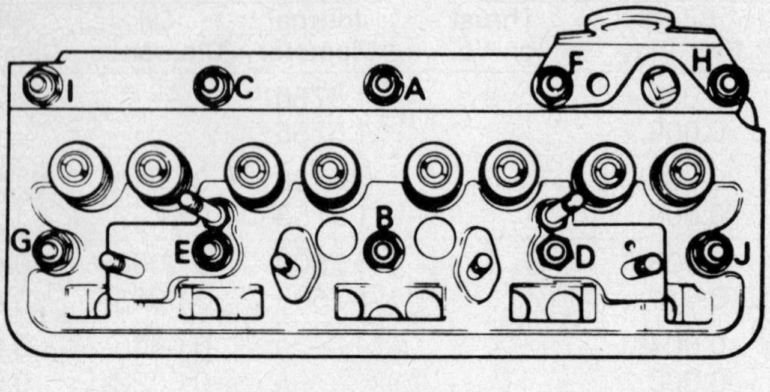

Spitfire cylinder head

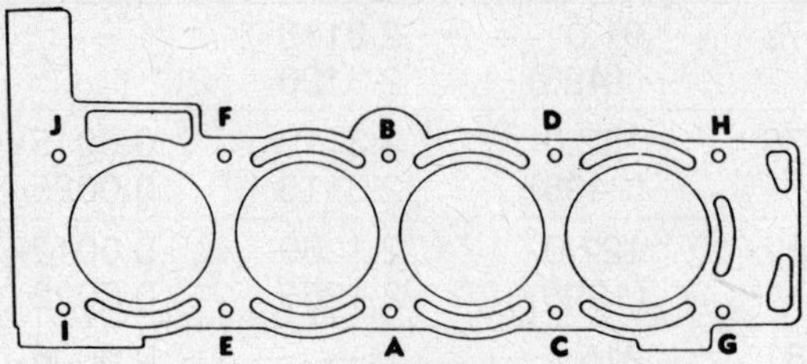

TR-7 cylinder head

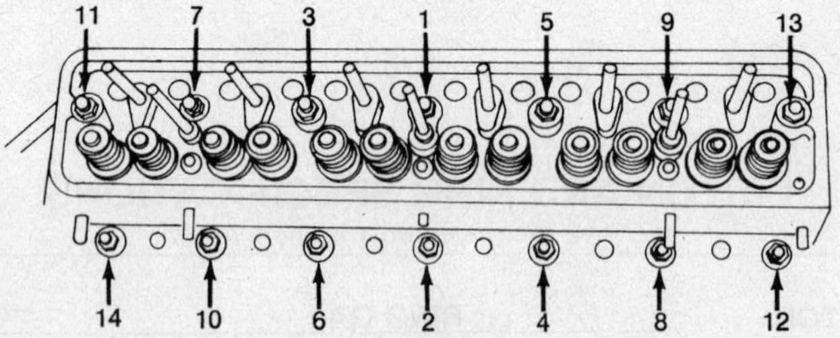

TR-6 cylinder head

ALTERNATOR AND REGULATOR SPECIFICATIONS

		ALTERNATOR			REGULATOR						
						FIELD RELAY			REGULATOR		
Year	Model	Part No. or Manufacturer	Field Current @ 12V	Output (amps)	Part No. or Manufacturer	Air Gap (in.)	Point Gap (in.)	Volts to Close	Air Gap (in.)	Point Gap (in.)	Volts @ 75
1975-81	Spitfire	Lucas 16 ACR	NA	34	NA	Integral regulator					14
1975-76	TR-6	Lucas 18 ACR	NA	43	NA	Integral regulator					14
1975-81	TR-7	Lucas 20 ACR	NA	66	14TR	Integral regulator					14
1980-81	TR-8	Lucas 23 ACR	NA	55	14TR	Integral regulator					14

NA Not available

BATTERY AND STARTER SPECIFICATIONS

All cars use 12 volt, negative ground electrical systems

		BATTERY	STARTER								
			LOCK TEST			NO LOAD TEST					
Year	Model	Amp Hour Capacity	Amps	Volts	Torque (ft. lbs.)	Amps	Volts	rpm	Brush Spring Tension (oz.)	Min. Brush Length (in.)
1975-81	Spitfire	40	350-375	—	7.0	65	12	8000-10000	28	0.500
1975-76	TR-6	57	463	—	14.4	40	12	6000	36	0.710
1975-81	TR-7	50	463	—	14.4	40	12	6000	36	0.710
1980-81	TR-8	66	463	—	14.4	40	12	6000	36	0.710

— Not available

BRAKE SPECIFICATIONS

All measurements given are in. unless noted

Year	Model	Lug Nut Torque (ft. lb.)	Brake Disc Minimum Thickness	Brake Disc Maximum Run-Out	Brake Drum Diameter	Brake Drum Max. Machine O/S	Brake Drum Max. Wear Limit	Minimum Lining Thickness Front	Minimum Lining Thickness Rear
1975-81	Spitfire	48	NA	0.007	7.0	7.03	7.05	1/8	1/16
1975-76	TR-6	70	NA	0.007	9.0	9.03	9.05	1/8	1/16
1975-81	TR-7	72	0.375	0.007	8.0	8.03	8.05	1/8	1/16
1980-81	TR-8	72	—	—	—	—	—	—	—

NOTE: Minimum lining thickness is as recommended by the manufacturer. Due to variations in state inspection laws, the minimum allowable thickness may be different than recommended by the manufacturer.
— Not available

WHEEL ALIGNMENT SPECIFICATIONS

Year	Model	Caster Preferred Setting (deg)	Camber Preferred Setting (deg)	Toe-in (in.)	Steering Axis Inclination (deg)
1975-81	Spitfire	4.0P	2.0P	1/16	6.75
1975-76	TR-6	2.75P	0.25P	1/16	9.25
1975-81	TR-7	3.5P	0.25N	1/16-1/8	11.25
1980-81	TR-8	3.5P	0.25N	1/16-1/8	11.25

P Positive
N Negative
— Not available

TUNE-UP PROCEDURES

Spark Plugs

REMOVAL AND INSTALLATION

Every six months or 6,000 miles, the spark plugs should be removed for inspection. At this time they should be cleaned and regapped. At 12 months or 12,000 mile intervals, the plugs should be replaced.

Prior to removal, number each spark plug with a piece of masking tape bearing the cylinder number. Remove each spark plug wire by grasping its rubber boot and twisting slightly to free the wire from the plug. Using a 13/16 in. spark plug socket, turn the plugs counterclockwise to remove them. Do not allow any foreign matter to enter the cylinder through the spark plug holes.

If the plugs are to be reused, check the porcelain insulator for cracks and the electrodes for excessive wear. Replace the entire set if one plug is damaged. Clean the reusable plugs with a stiff wire brush, or in a sandblasting machine. Uneven wear of the center of ground electrode may be corrected by leveling off the unevenly worn section with a file. The gap must be checked with a feeler gauge. With the ground electrode positioned parallel to the center electrode, a 0.025 in. wire gauge must pass through the opening with a slight drag. If the air gap between the two electrodes is not correct, the ground electrode must be bent to bring it to specifications.

After the plugs are gapped correctly, they may be inserted into their holes and hand tightened. Be careful not to crossthread the plugs. Torque the plugs to their proper specification. Install each numbered plug wire onto its respective plug.

Breaker Points and Condenser

REMOVAL AND INSTALLATION

Remove the distributor cap and rotor, noting their position. Inspect the contacts and replace the points if the contacts are blackened, pitted or worn excessively, if the breaker arm has lost its tension, or if the fiber rubbing block has become worn or loose. Points that appear light gray in color may be cleaned with a point file.

To replace the points and condenser, disconnect the electrical leads at the primary connection, remove the lock screw for the points and lift them straight up. Loosen the condenser retaining bracket and slide out the condenser. While the points are out, lubricate the breaker cam with a very light coating of silicone based grease. Clean the distributor base plate with alcohol to free it of any oil film that might impede completion of the ground circuit. Also clean the contact point surfaces with the solvent. Install the new points and condenser and tighten their retaining screws. Connect the electrical leads for both at the primary connection. If the point contacts are not aligned, bend the stationary arm.

To gap the contact points, turn the engine until the rubbing block on the point assembly is resting on the high point of the cam lobe. Loosen the point holddown screw slightly and

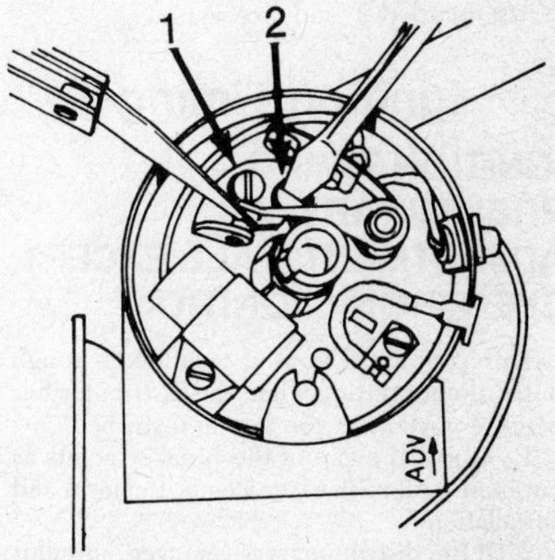

Adjustment of ignition points—typical

insert a feeler gauge of the specified thickness (0.014-0.016 in.) between the point contacts. Fine adjustment is made either by inserting a screwdriver into the eccentric adjusting slot on the stationary arm (late distributors) or by turning the eccentric adjusting screw on the stationary arm (early distributors). When the feeler gauge passes between the point contacts with a slight drag, tighten the holddown screw without disturbing the setting.

If a dwell meter is available, proceed to "Dwell Angle Setting". If the meter is not available, install the rotor and cap, and proceed to "Ignition Timing Adjustment".

Dwell Angle Setting

The dwell angle is the number of degrees of distributor cam rotation through which the breaker points remain fully closed (conducting electricity). Increasing the point gap decreases dwell, while decreasing the point gap increases dwell.

Connect the positive wire of the meter to the distributor primary wire connection on the distributor side of the coil, and the negative wire of the meter to a good ground on the engine (e.g. thermostat housing nut).

The dwell angle may be checked either with the engine running or with the cap and rotor removed and the engine cranking at starter speed. The meter gives a constant reading with the engine running. With the engine cranking, the reading will fluctuate between zero degrees dwell and the maximum figure for that angle. While cranking, the maximum figure is the correct one. Never attempt to change dwell angle while the ignition is on, as touching the point contacts or the primary wire connection with a metal screwdriver may result in a 12 volt shock.

To change dwell angle, loosen the point holddown screw slightly and make the approximate correction. Tighten the holddown screw and test the dwell with the engine cranking. If the dwell appears to be correct, install the rotor and distributor cap and test the dwell with the engine running. Take the engine through its entire rpm range and observe the dwell meter. The dwell should remain within specifications at all times. Great fluctuation of dwell at different engine speeds indicates worn distributor parts.

Following the dwell angle adjustment, the ignition timing must be checked. A 1° increase in dwell results in the ignition timing being retarded 2° and vice-versa.

Ignition Timing

IGNITION TIMING PRELIMINARY ADJUSTMENT—ALL EXCEPT ELECTRONIC IGNITION

This procedure is used to obtain a rough initial timing setting when the distributor has been removed and the timing disturbed.

1. Adjust the gap of the breaker points as outlined under "Breaker Points Removal and Installation."
2. If the distributor was removed, install it in the engine, making sure that the drive gears are engaged. Tighten the clamp bracket.

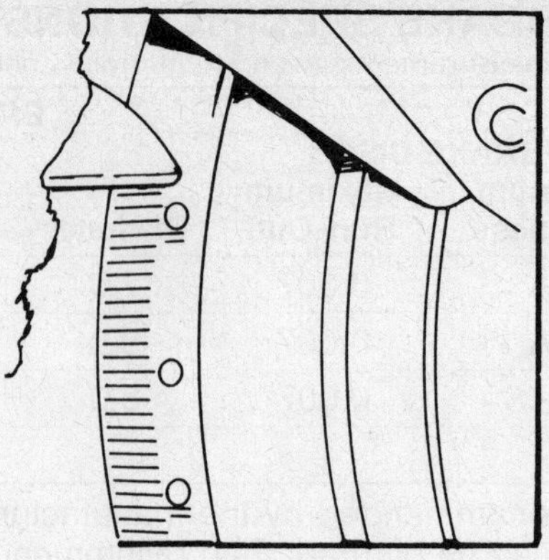

Timing mark—TR-6

3. Disconnect the distributor low tension lead at the coil. Hook up a 12 V test light directly to the disconnected distributor lead and to the positive terminal of the battery.
4. Rotate the engine (crankshaft) manually in the normal direction of rotation (clockwise) until the timing marks nearly coincide with the static timing figure given in the "Tune-Up Specifications" table. The test light should now be illuminated.

CAUTION

Do not rotate the engine counterclockwise.

5. Slowly rotate the crankshaft further in a clockwise direction until the test light just goes out. At this point, the No. 1 piston should be in its compression stroke and the rotor should be pointing at the distributor cap contact for the No. 1 spark plug wire.
6. If the timing is correct, the marks will be aligned at the static timing figure. If the timing proves to be incorrect and the marks do not properly align, loosen the distributor pinch bolt and turn the distributor until the points just open and the test light goes out. Rotate the engine one complete revolution again by hand and make sure that the light goes out at the static timing figure.
7. Disconnect the test light. Reconnect the distributor lead at the coil. Install the distributor cap, if removed.
8. Proceed to final (dynamic) timing adjustment.

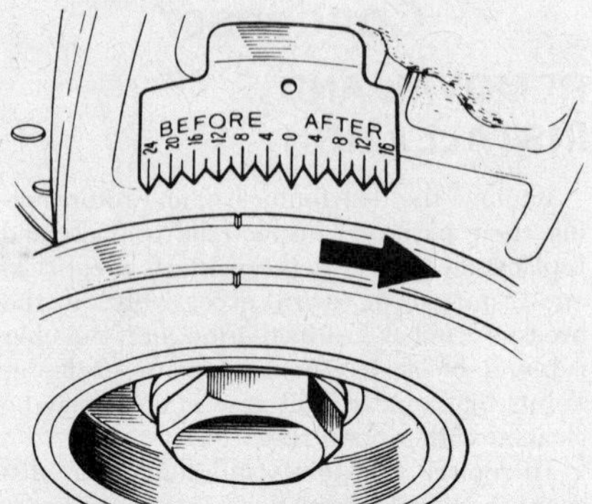

Timing marks—Spitfire, 1500; TR-7 similar

IGNITION TIMING ADJUSTMENT

Clean the crankshaft damper and pointer on the water pump housing. Disconnect the vacuum line(s) from the intake manifold at the distributor and plug the line(s). On breakerless systems, the retard unit pipe should be connected.

Attach a tachometer to the engine and set the idle speed to specifications. Set timing to specifications. As a final check, start the engine once more to make sure that the timing marks do align.

Unplug and reconnect all disconnected hoses. Remove the timing light and tachometer from the engine.

Electronic Ignition

The only adjustment that can be made within the distributor is the pick-up air gap. This adjustment is initially made during assembly and does not have to be changed during the vehicle's accumulated mileage, unless distributor internal problems arise. A brass or plastic feeler gauge should be used when checking the air gap. The clearance should be 0.014 to 0.016 inch.

The ignition timing is adjusted in the conventional manner by rotating the distributor housing in the desired direction.

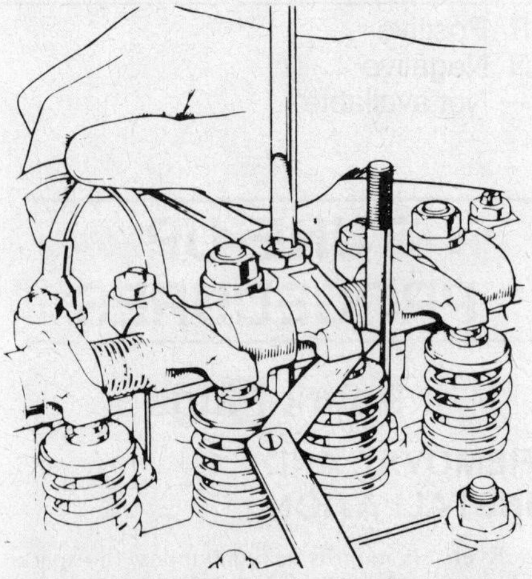

Adjusting valve lash—overhead valve engines

Valve Lash Adjustment

ALL EXCEPT TR-7 AND TR-8

Valve clearances should be as specified with the engine cold. For the four-cylinder engines, adjust the valves as follows: turn the crankshaft until the valve to be adjusted is fully open, then rotate the crankshaft one more revolution to be sure that the valve will be fully closed. Loosen the locking nut and adjust the screw until the specified feeler gauge will just fit between the valve stem and the rocker arm. Tighten the locking nut and recheck the clearance to see that it has not changed.

For the six-cylinder engines, the following sequence of valve clearance adjustments is recommended. Turn the engine clockwise and adjust as follows:

Adjust These Valves	When These Are Fully Open
1 and 3	10 and .2
8 and 11	2 and 5
4 and 6	7 and 9
10 and 12	1 and 3
2 and 5	8 and 11
7 and 9	4 and 6

TR-7

1. Rotate the engine. Check and record each valve clearance. Clearance should be checked with the cam heel facing the tappet.
2. To adjust, remove the camshaft. Remove the shim on each valve which requires adjustment. Keep them in sequence.
3. Using a micrometer, measure and record the thickness of each shim. To determine the thickness required, use the following example and install new shims where necessary.

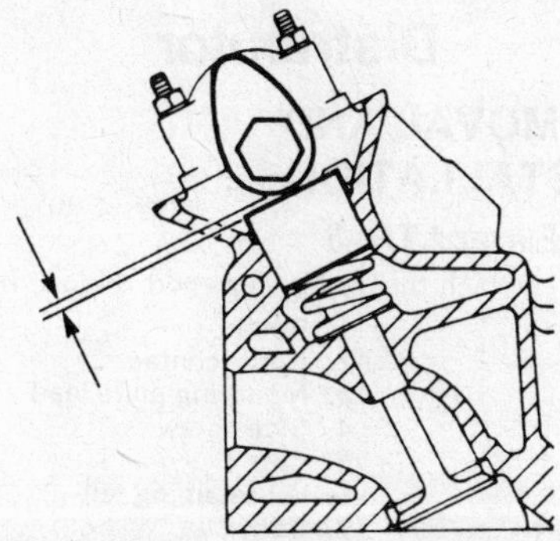

Valve clearance measurement location—TR-7

Carburetor

IDLE SPEED AND MIXTURE ADJUSTMENT

W/Zenith–Stromberg 150 CDSE

Make the following adjustments:
1. Idle speed—screw adjustment.
2. Idle emission—to be used only with a fuel/air ratio meter.
3. Fast idle—simple screw adjustment. Settings are as follows:

1975-79 Spitfire Idle CO level: 0.5-2.5% (warm engine) Equivalent air/fuel ratio: 14.4:1-13.6:1.

1975-76 TR-6 and 1975-79 TR-7 with Twin Carburetors Zenith-Stromberg 175 CDSEV

NOTE: The following procedure requires the use of an air flow meter and a CO analyzer. Since this equipment is expensive and not readily available to the general public, it is suggested that the adjustments be made by a qualified technician.

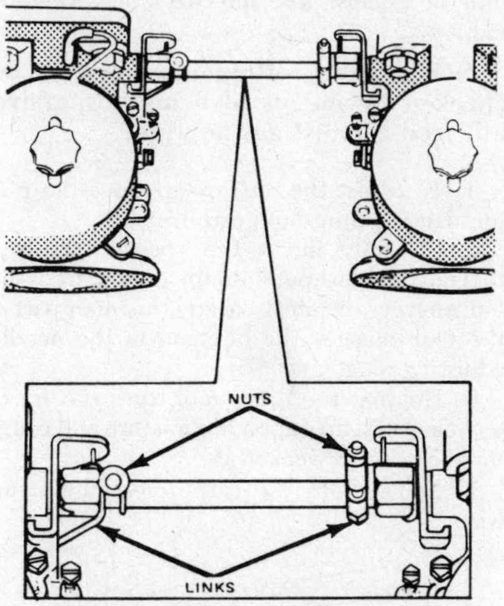

Air flow balance adjustment

1. Check that the fast idle cam is against its stop on each carburetor, and that the fast idle screw is clear of the fast idle cam.
2. Run engine to normal operating temperature.
3. Using an air flow meter check flow on both carburetors.
4. If air flow is not equal, loosen one of the clamping nuts on one of the throttle interconnecting links and loosen the throttle adjusting screws enough to allow the throttles to close, then turn both screws so that they just touch their stops plus ½ turn.
5. Turn both adjusting screws just enough to achieve air flow balance.

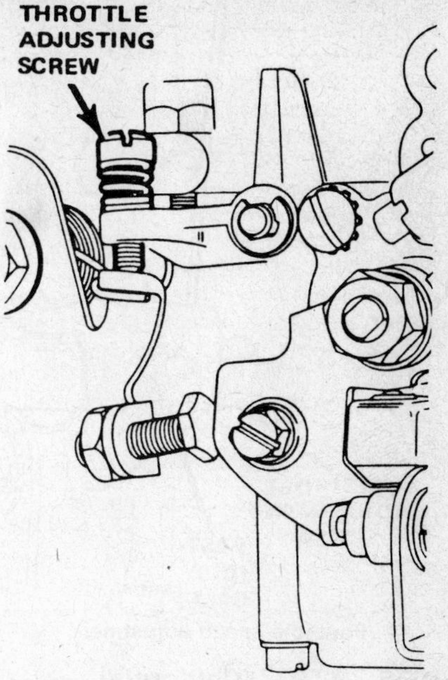

Throttle adjusting screw

6. Tighten the clamping nut on the interconnecting link.
7. If necessary, turn the adjusting screws equally to achieve 800 rpm.
8. Where applicable, disconnect the air pump outlet hose and plug the hose end. Insert the analyzer probe and check the CO reading against the underhood decal.

NOTE: Do not allow the engine to idle for more than 3 minutes without a 1 minute clear-out period at 2000 rpm.

9. If the CO level is above limits, adjust the mixture as follows:
10. Remove the piston dampers and insert a mixture adjusting tool into the dashpot. The tool must be fully engaged and held correctly to prevent tearing the diaphragm.
11. Back out to richen and turn in to lean both carburetors equally until CO is within acceptable limits. Add oil to the dampers if necessary.

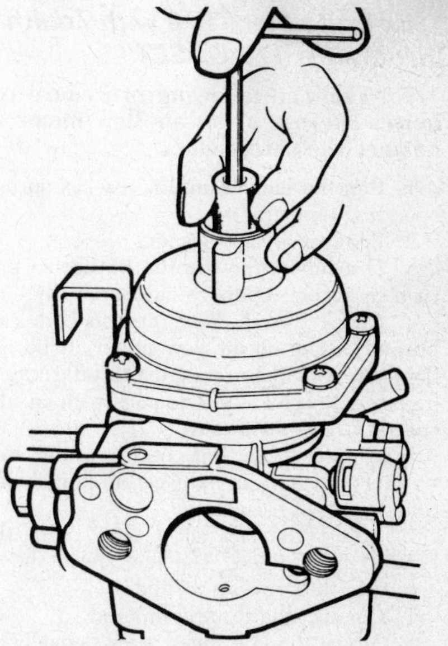

Adjusting the mixture

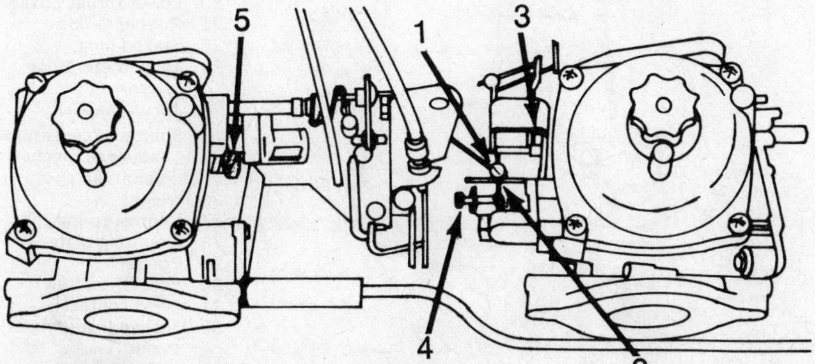

1. Fast idle screws
2. Cam pivots
3. Idling screws
4. Choke cable trunnion
5. Idle trimming screw

Idle speed and mixture adjusting locations—Zenith Stromberg 150 CDE(V) and 175 CDE(V) carburetors

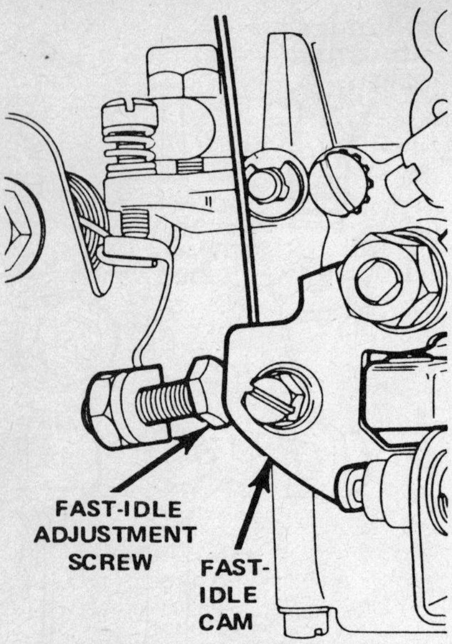

Fast idle speed adjustment

1975-79 TR-7 (California) W/Zenith-Stromberg 175 CD4TV

NOTE: When making adjustments, do not let the engine idle for more than 3 minutes without a 1 minute clear-out period at 2000 rpm.

1. Run engine at normal operating temperature.
2. Set idle to 800 rpm.
3. Disconnect the air pump outlet hose and plug hose end.
4. Insert infrared analyzer probe and check CO readings against the underhood decal.
5. If CO readings are not within specifications, remove damper and insert mixture adjusting tool into dashpot. Tool must be inserted and held properly to avoid tearing the diaphragm.
6. Back off to enrichen and turn in to lean the mixture as required. Add oil, if necessary, to the damper.

IDLE SPEED

1980 and Later TR-8 with Zenith Stromburg 175 CDSET

NOTE: The following procedure requires the use of an air flow meter to balance the carburetors.

1. Run the engine until it reaches normal operating temperature.
2. Remove the air cleaners.
3. Disconnect the throttle linkage so that each carburetor operates independently.
4. Check the air flow through both carburetors using an air flow meter. If the air flows are not equal, rotate the throttle adjusting screw to give equal balance with an idle speed of 750 to 950 rpm.
5. Connect the link between the carburetors. The near side carburetor should then go out of balance.
6. Adjust the anti-rattle screw until the balance is returned. The idle speed should return to the previous setting.
7. Connect the throttle link rod.
8. Adjust the idle speed screws equally on both carburetors.
9. Replace the air cleaners.

MIXTURE ADJUSTMENT

1980 and Later TR-8 with Zenith Stromburg 175 CDSET

NOTE: The following procedure requires the use of an exhaust gas analyzer and a special mixture adjusting tool.

1. Disconnect the air pump diverter valve outlet hose from the valve and plug the hose.
2. Make sure the engine is at the normal operating temperature and that the idle speed is correct.
3. Insert the gas analyzer as far as possible into the exhaust pipe and check the CO reading.

NOTE: The setting must always be checked by means of a non-dispersive infrared exhaust gas analyzer.

4. To adjust the mixture, remove the piston damper from both carburetors.
5. Carefully insert the special adjusting tool into the dashpot until the outer part of the tool engages the air valve and the inner part of the tool engages the hexagon in the needle adjusting plug.
6. Holding the outer tool, turn the inner tool clockwise to enrich the mixture and counterclockwise to weaken it.
7. Adjust both the carburetors the same way.

Fuel Injection

IDLE SPEED ADJUSTMENT

1. Run the engine until it reaches normal operating temperature for at least two minutes.
2. Make sure that the engine timing is correct.
3. Connect a tachometer to the engine according to the manufacturers instructions. The tachometer that comes with the car can be used if necessary.
4. To adjust the idle speed, loosen the locknut and turn the idle adjustment bolt clockwise to decrease the idle speed and counterclockwise to increase the idle speed. After making the adjustment, retighten the locknut.

ENGINE ELECTRICAL

Distributor

REMOVAL AND INSTALLATION

All Except TR-8

1. Detach the spring clips and remove the

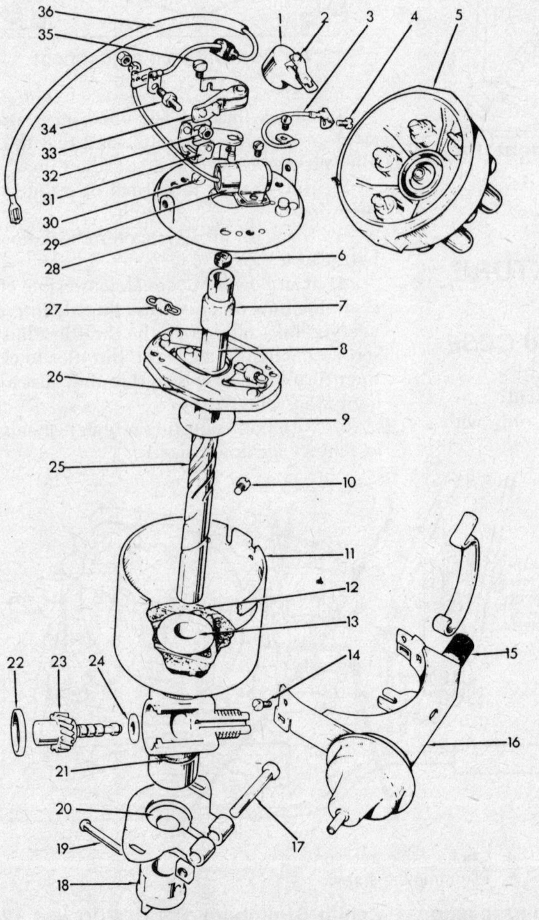

1. Rotor
2. Rotor contact
3. Mounting plate lead
4. Side screw
5. Cap
6. Oil retaining felt
7. Cam
8. Cam spindle
9. Upper thrust washer
10. Short side screw
11. Housing
12. Oil retaining felt
13. Upper sintered iron bearing
14. Side screw
15. Vernier adjustment knob
16. Vacuum advance mechanism
17. Clamp bolt
18. Coupling
19. Coupling pin
20. Lower thrust washer
21. Rubber O-ring
22. Staked plug
23. Tachometer drive gear
24. Thrust washer
25. Shaft and centrifugal advance mechanism unit
26. Weight
27. Control spring
28. Mounting plate
29. Condenser
30. Eccentric screw
31. Fixed contact
32. Terminal stud inner nut
33. Moving contact
34. Terminal stud
35. Lock screw
36. Low tension wire

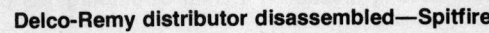

Delco-Remy distributor disassembled—Spitfire

distributor cap, low tension wire, and vacuum connection. Remove the tachometer drive.

2. Release the clamping plate and withdraw the distributor assembly.

NOTE: Do not loosen the pinch bolt unless the ignition timing is to be reset, and note the position of the rotor prior to removal of the assembly.

3. If the pinch bolt has not been loosened, replace the distributor by reversing the installation procedure, and rotate the distributor rotor until it properly engages the driving shaft, then secure the clamping plate.

TR-8

1. Disconnect the negative battery cable.
2. Disconnect all electrical connections and the vacuum advance hose.
3. Remove the distributor cap and rotor.
4. Remove the plastic antiflash cover.
5. Temporarily push on the rotor.
6. Rotate the engine crankshaft so that the rotor is at the No. 1 firing position and the timing pointer is aligned with TDC on the crankshaft pulley scale.
7. Remove the one bolt and the clamp bracket.
8. Remove the distributor assembly.
9. Before installing the distributor, rotate the oil pump shaft with an appropriate tool so that it is in position to accept the slotted end of the distributor shaft.
10. Before installing the distributor, position the body as illustrated and the rotor vertical relative to the engine.
11. Insert the distributor, locating the slotted adapter of the distributor shaft to the oil pump shaft.
12. With the distributor flange against the timing gear cover, the rotor should be pointing as illustrated relative to the engine.
13. Install the retaining clamp and bolt and reconnect all electrical connections and vacuum advance hose.

Alternator

REMOVAL AND INSTALLATION

1. Disconnect the electrical leads.
2. Loosen the main mounting bolt and the adjustment bracket bolts.
3. Remove the drive belt.
4. Remove the outer adjustment bracket bolt and the main mounting bolt and spacer.
5. Installation is the reverse of removal. Adjust the belt tension.

ALTERNATOR PRECAUTIONS

Several precautions must be observed when performing work on alternator equipment.

1. If the battery is removed for any reason, make sure that it is reconnected with the correct polarity. Reversing the battery connections may result in damage to the one-way rectifiers.
2. Never operate the alternator with the main circuit broken. Make sure that the battery, alternator, and regulator leads are not disconnected while the engine is running.
3. Never attempt to polarize an alternator.
4. When charging a battery that is installed

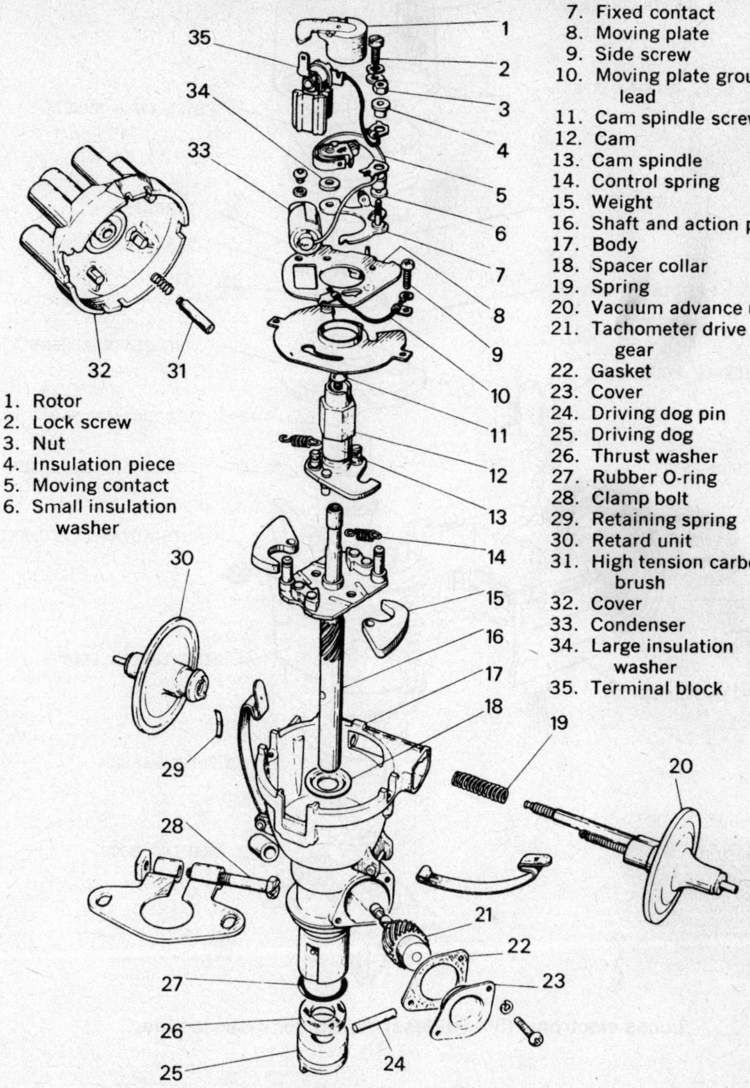

Lucas conventional diaphragm distributor for the TR-6

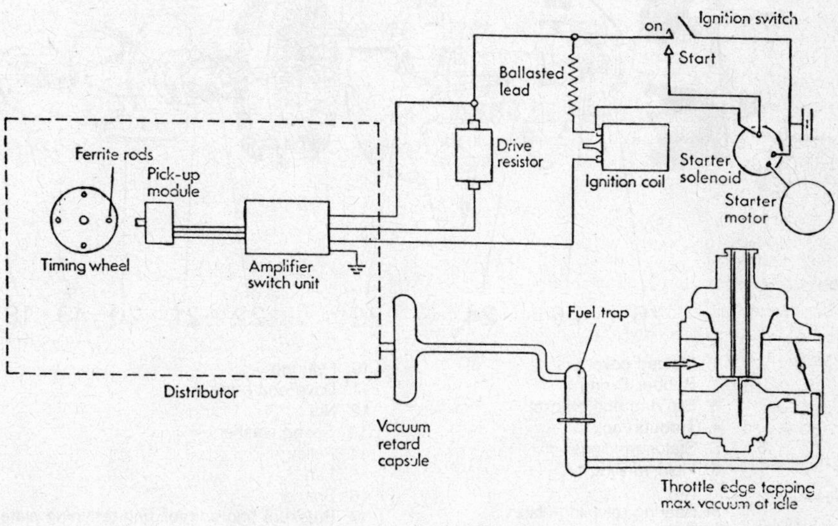

Lucas electronic ignition schematic

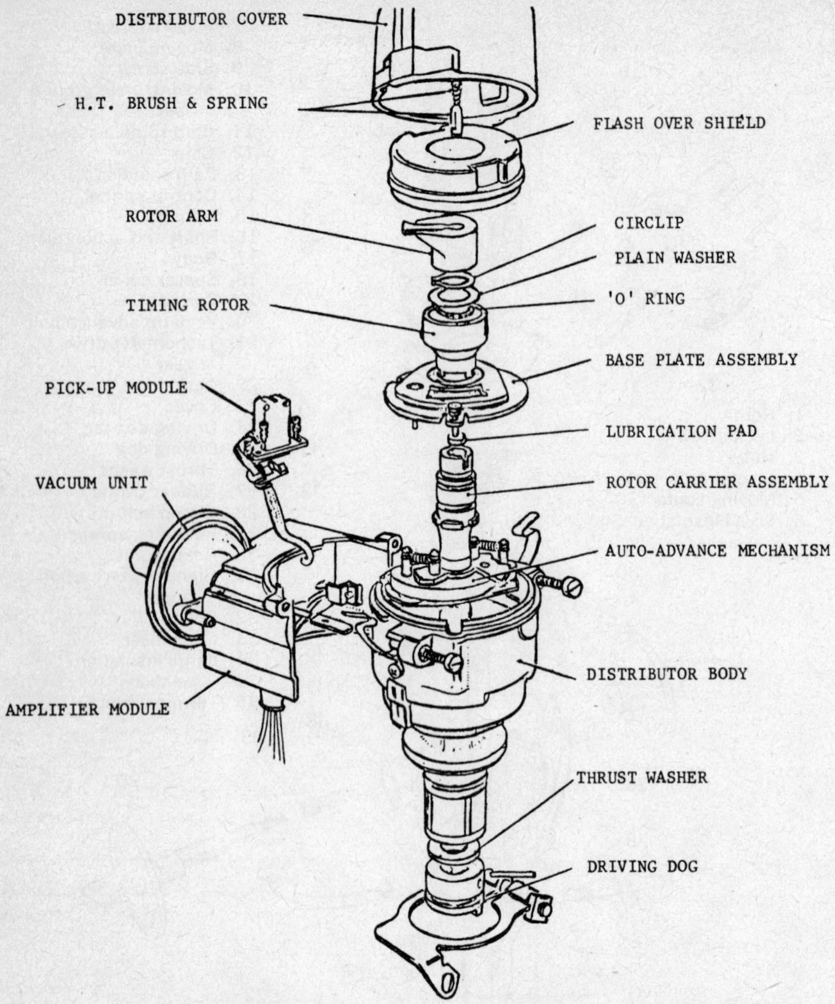

Lucas electronic (breakerless) distributor disassembled

in the vehicle, disconnect the negative battery cable.

5. When utilizing a booster battery as a starting aid, always connect it in parallel; negative to negative, and positive to positive.

6. When arc welding is to be performed on any part of the vehicle, disconnect the negative battery cable, disconnect the alternator leads, and unplug the voltage regulator.

DRIVE BELT ADJUSTMENT

Check the drive belt for cracks and wear. Replace it if its condition is questionable. The belt should be adjusted so that it is possible to depress the belt approximately ¾ in. (all except TR-8), ¼ in. (TR-8), between the pulleys of the longest run. To adjust, loosen the adjusting bolt and alternator mounting bolt, then pivot the alternator until the belt has the correct amount of free movement. Tighten the bolts in this position.

NOTE: Do not use a metal pry bar against the aluminum alternator housing to tension the belt.

Voltage Regulator

The AC voltage regulators are nonadjustable and must be replaced as a unit.

Starter

REMOVAL AND INSTALLATION

1. Removal of the starter requires disconnecting the negative battery cable, all terminal connections and removing bolts and starter.

2. To install the starter, measure the distance between the flywheel ring gear (pinion side) and the starter mounting face.

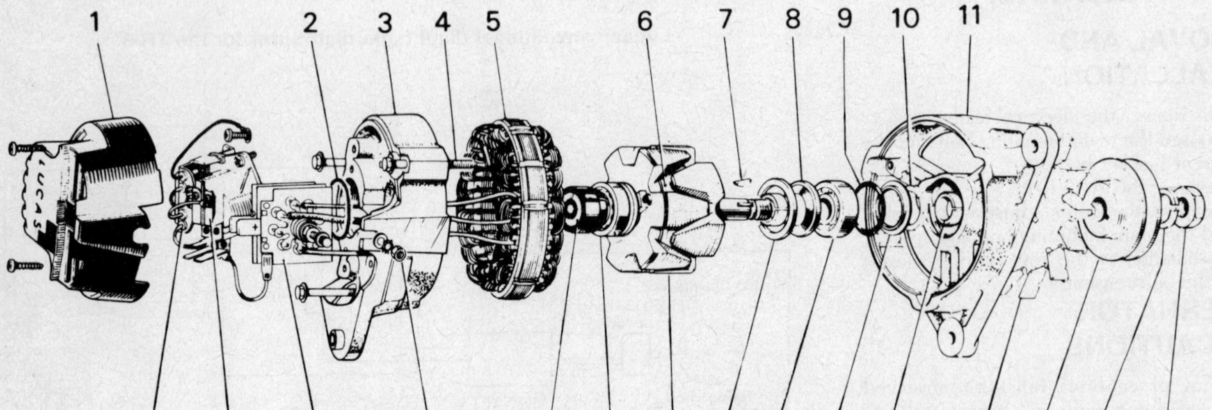

1. Molded cover
2. Rubber O-ring
3. Slip ring end bracket
4. Through bolt
5. Stator windings
6. Field winding
7. Key
8. Bearing retaining plate
9. Pressure ring
10. Felt ring
11. Drive end bracket
12. Nut
13. Spring washer
14. Pulley
15. Fan
16. Spacer
17. Pressure ring and felt ring retaining plate
18. Drive end bearing
19. Circlip
20. Rotor
21. Slip ring end bearing
22. Slip ring moulding
23. Nut
24. Rectifier pack
25. Brushbox assembly
26. Regulator unit

Exploded view—Lucas alternator—typical

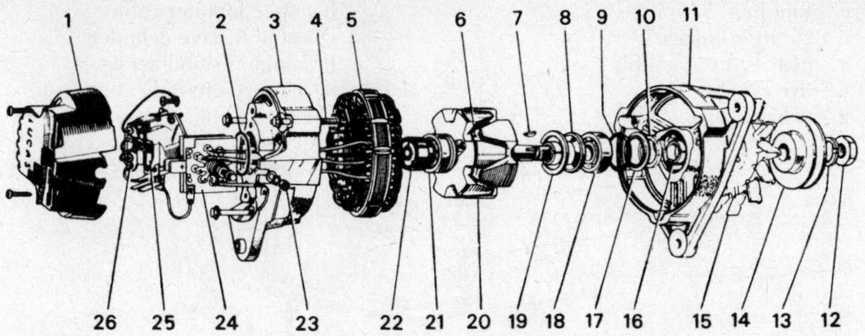

1. Moulded cover
2. Rubber O-ring
3. Slip ring end bracket
4. Through bolt
5. Stator windings
6. Field winding
7. Key
8. Bearing retaining plate
9. Pressure ring
10. Felt ring
11. Drive end bracket
12. Nut
13. Spring washer
14. Pulley
15. Fan
16. Spacer
17. Pressure ring and felt ring retaining plate
18. Drive end bearing
19. Circlip
20. Rotor
21. Slip ring end bearing
22. Slip ring moulding
23. Nut
24. Rectifier pack
25. Brushbox assembly
26. Regulator unit

Lucas 15ACR alternator

3. In addition, measure the distance from the starter face to the pinion end. End clearance from the starter pinion to the flywheel ring gear should be $^3/_{32}$ to $^5/_{32}$ in. (shims are available).

4. Connect all electrical leads.

STARTER DRIVE REPLACEMENT

M35J

1. Remove the starter.
2. Remove the two drive end bracket bolts and lockwashers.
3. Pull the drive end bracket, armature, and inertia drive assembly from the yoke.
4. Remove the four retaining bolts and lay aside the commutator end bracket.
5. Lift out the two field winding brushes and remove the commutator end bracket from the yoke.
6. Compress the main spring and ease the snap-ring from the shaft. Remove the starter drive components.
7. Installation is the reverse of removal. Lubricate the drive end bracket bushing with 10W engine oil.

M-100

The starter drive is not replaceable.

M418G and 2M 100PE

1. Remove the starter.
2. Disconnect the lead from the "STA" terminal.
3. Remove the solenoid, leaving the plunger attached to the engaging lever.
4. Remove the plunger return spring and plunger, from the engaging lever.
5. Loosen the locknut and remove the eccentric pin.
6. Remove the cover band and the brushes.
7. Remove the through bolts. Lightly rap the mounting bracket lugs.

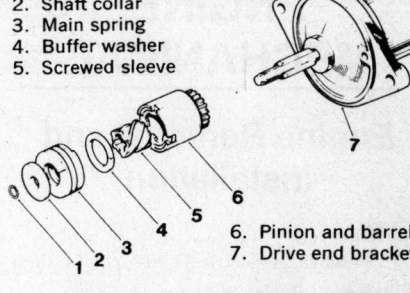

1. Jump ring
2. Shaft collar
3. Main spring
4. Buffer washer
5. Screwed sleeve

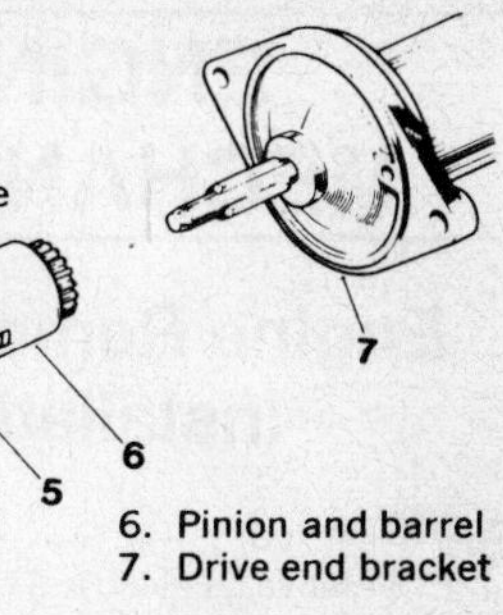

6. Pinion and barrel
7. Drive end bracket

Starter drive components—M35J

8. Separate the commutator end bracket from the yoke.
9. Remove both the steel and fabric thrust washers. Note their placement.
10. Remove the rubber molding. Remove the armature and starter drive assembly.
11. Remove the engaging lever and thrust washer.
12. Using a ⅝ in. I.D. tube, over the shaft end, force the thrust collar of the snap-ring toward the starter drive.
13. Remove the snap-ring.
14. Remove the thrust collar and the starter drive. Replace the entire drive assembly if the roller clutch is defective.

CAUTION

Use a solvent moistened cloth to clean the drive, carefully avoiding the roller clutch.

15. Assembly is the reverse of disassembly. Lubricate the drive sleeve splines and pinion bearing.

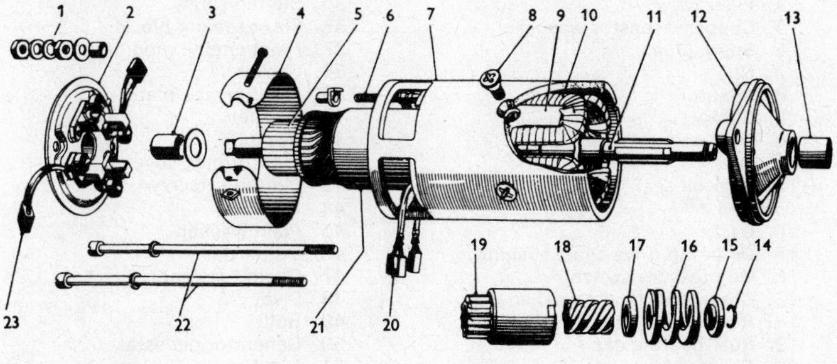

1. Terminal post nuts and washers
2. Commutator end bracket
3. Commutator end bracket bearing bushing
4. Cover band
5. Commutator
6. Terminal post
7. Yoke
8. Pole shoe screw
9. Pole shoe
10. Field winding
11. Shaft
12. Drive end bracket
13. Drive end bracket bearing bushing
14. Ring
15. Shaft collar
16. Main spring
17. Buffer washer
18. Screwed sleeve
19. Pinion and barrel
20. Field winding brush
21. Armature
22. Through bolts
23. Ground brush

Lucas M35G starter; the M35J is similar

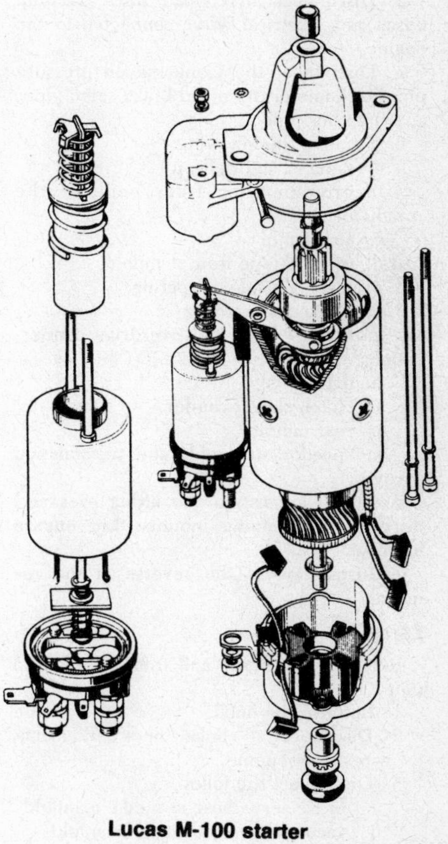

Lucas M-100 starter

ENGINE MECHANICAL

Engine Removal and Installation

Spitfire

1. Remove all electrical wires, coolant lines and vacuum hoses.
2. Remove the hood.
3. Disconnect and plug the fuel intake line.
4. Remove the following:
   a. air cleaners
   b. choke controls
   c. carburetor linkage
   d. exhaust pipe at manifold
   e. radiator
   f. front seats and carpeting
   g. transmission cover
   h. speedometer cable
   i. clutch slave cylinder
   j. overdrive solenoid wires
   k. driveshaft
   l. gearshift extension.
5. Attach a hoist to the lifting eyes, disconnect all mounts and lift the engine and transmission assembly from the car.
6. Installation is the reverse of the removal.

TR-6

1. Remove the battery and hood. Drain the cooling system.
2. Disconnect the choke control, throttle linkage and fuel line.
3. Disconnect all coolant lines, vacuum hoses and electrical wires connected to the engine.
4. Disconnect the crankcase oil pressure pipe, tachometer drive and brake servo pipe, and breather pipe.
5. Remove the following:
   a. radiator and deflector
   b. crossmember from beneath the radiator
   c. air cleaner
   d. exhaust pipe from manifold
   e. seats, console, carpeting
   f. transmission cover
   g. backup light and overdrive connections
   h. driveshaft
   i. clutch slave cylinder
   j. rear mounts
   k. speedometer cable and transmission cover.
6. Attach a hoist to the lifting eyes and disconnect remaining mounts. Lift engine from car.
7. Installation is the reverse of the removal.

TR-7

Remove the engine and transmission as a unit.

1. Remove the hood.
2. Disconnect all coolant lines and electrical wires from engine.
3. Disconnect the following:
   a. brake servo hose at intake manifold
   b. vacuum hoses at intake manifold
   c. fuel line
   d. throttle linkage
   e. gear lever assembly
   f. driveshaft
   g. exhaust pipe
   h. speedometer cable
   i. clutch slave cylinder
   j. engine stabilizer
   k. battery ground
   l. hood lock

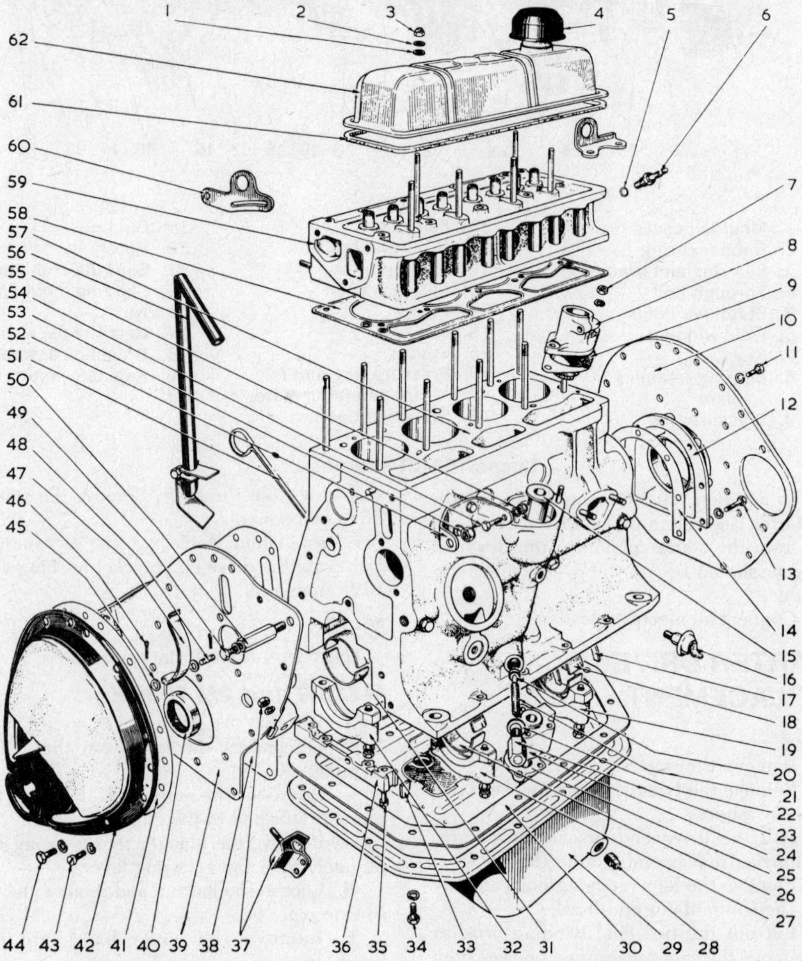

1. Fiber washer
2. Plain washer
3. Nyloc nut
4. Filler cap
5. Copper/asbestos washer
6. Spark plug
7. Nut
8. Adaptor
9. Gasket
10. Rear engine plate
11. Bolt
12. Rear oil seal
13. Bolt
14. Gasket
15. Oil pump drive shaft bushing
16. Oil pressure switch
17. Crankshaft thrust washer
18. Rear bearing shell
19. Rear bearing cap
20. Relief valve
21. Spring
22. Copper washer
23. Cap nut
24. Oil pump body
25. Oil pump end plate
26. Center bearing shell
27. Center main bearing cap
28. Drain plug
29. Oil pan
30. Oil pan gasket
31. Front bearing shell
32. Front main bearing cap
33. Sealing wedges
34. Sump bolt
35. Slotted screw
36. Front sealing block
37. Front engine mounting
38. Gasket
39. Front engine plate
40. Oil seal
41. Gasket
42. Front timing cover
43. Slotted setscrew
44. Bolt
45. Plain washer
46. Cotter pin
47. Chain tensioner
48. Pivot pin
49. Bolt
50. Generator pedestal
51. Dipstick
52. Bracket
53. Nyloc nut
54. Bolt
55. Nyloc nut
56. Breather pipe
57. Cylinder block
58. Cylinder head gasket
59. Cylinder head
60. Generator adjusting link
61. Rocker cover gasket
62. Rocker cover

Stationary components of four cylinder Spitfire engine

m. clutch hydraulic pipe.
4. Discharge the A/C system, if equipped.
5. Raise the rear of the car.
6. Attach a hoist to the lifting eyes, support the engine weight and disconnect the front and rear supports. Lift out the engine and transmission assembly.
7. Installation is the reverse of removal.

TR-8

NOTE: The engine and transmission are removed as a unit from the bottom on these models. Since the removal procedure requires the use of special tools, having this done by a qualified dealer is advisable.

Cylinder Head

REMOVAL AND INSTALLATION

All Models (Except TR-7 and TR-8)

1. Disconnect the battery and drain the cooling system.
2. Remove the air cleaner(s) and the intake and exhaust manifold.
3. Remove the drive belt. Remove the water pump.
4. Remove the rocker arm cover, the rocker assembly, and the pushrods. Be sure that all electrical and hose connections to the cylinder head have been disconnected. Remove the spark plugs.
5. Loosen and remove the cylinder head nuts in reverse order of the tightening sequence. Remove the cylinder head.

NOTE: If the cylinder head does not lift readily, tap each side with a hammer, using a short piece of wood to help absorb the shock. Another method is to reinsert the spark plugs and crank the engine with the starter, using the engine's own compression pressure to supply the force needed to break the seal.

6. Before replacing the cylinder head, be sure that the gasket surfaces of the head and block are perfectly clean and smooth. If any dirt is present, the gasket may leak when the head is installed. Check for the presence of dirt or carbon particles in the stud passages in the head. Also, inspect the valves and guides for wear and damage. Check valve stems for wear and distortion. Any valve with a head thickness less than 1/32 in. (0.8 mm) at the seat edge should be replaced. Valve guide wear may be checked by inserting a new valve into the guide, lifting it 1/8 in. from its seat, and moving it sideways. If the movement of the valve head across the seat exceeds 0.020 in. the guide should be replaced. Valve guides must protrude above the top face of the cylinder head as follows:

Spitfire: 0.749-0.751 in.
TR-6: 0.63 in.

7. To replace the head gasket, note its markings and position it accordingly. Tighten the cylinder head nuts finger tight, then gradually tighten them in the proper order.
8. Replace the valve rocker arm assembly and reverse the cylinder head removal procedure. Check the valve clearances before running the engine, then again after a brief running period when normal temperature is reached. Make a third check after a few hundred miles and at this time check the cylinder head nuts for tightness and tighten them to the specified torque. Although tightening down the cylinder head nuts will affect valve clearances slightly, the differences will not usually be enough to warrant resetting the valves. However, the clearances should be checked.

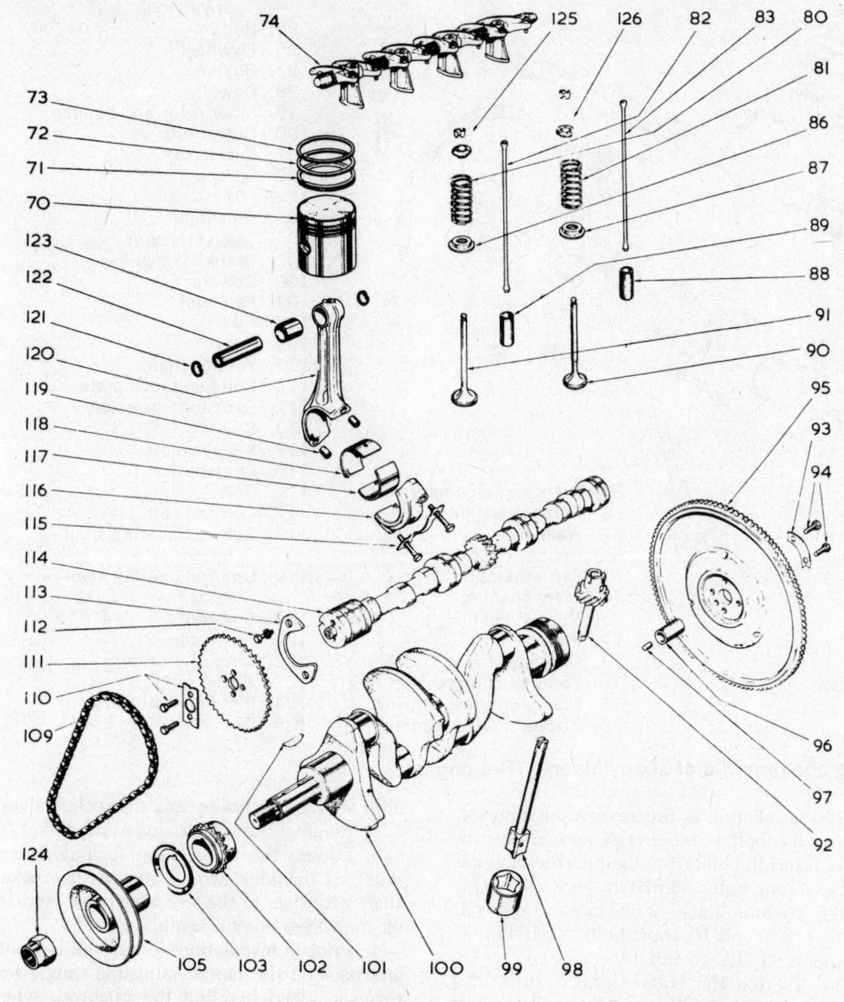

70. Piston
71. Oil control ring
72. Taper compression ring
73. Plain compression ring
74. Rocker assembly
80. Spring—outer
81. Spring—inner
82. Pushrod
83. Pushrod
86. Spring seats
87. Spring seats
88. Tappet
89. Tappet
90. Exhaust valve
91. Intake valve
92. Distributor and oil pump drive gear
93. Lock tab
94. Bolt
95. Flywheel
96. Bush
97. Dowel
98. Inner rotor and spindle
99. Outer rotor
100. Crankshaft
101. Key
102. Sprocket
103. Slinger
105. Crankshaft pulley
109. Timing chain
110. Bolts and lock tab
111. Camshaft sprocket
112. Bolt
113. Keeper plate
114. Camshaft
115. Bolt and locktab
116. Con-rod cap
117. Con-rod bearing shell—lower
118. Con-rod bearing shell—upper
119. Dowels
120. Con-rod
121. Circlip
122. Piston pin
123. Piston pin bushing
124. Nut
125. Retainer and keeper
126. Retainer and keeper

Moving components of four cylinder Spitfire engine

TR-7

1. Disconnect the following:
   a. air cleaner and duct
   b. intake manifold and carburetors
   c. camshaft cover
   d. distributor cap.
2. Turn the crankshaft until the camshaft sprocket bottom bolt is accessible. Remove the bolt.
3. Anchor the sprocket to the support bracket and turn the camshaft so that the flange is in line with the groove on the front bearing cap, and the distributor arm points toward the manifold rear attachment bolt.
4. Remove the camshaft sprocket top bolt.
5. Disconnect the following:
   a. pipe from the check valve
   b. pipe from the water transfer housing
   c. exhaust pipe.

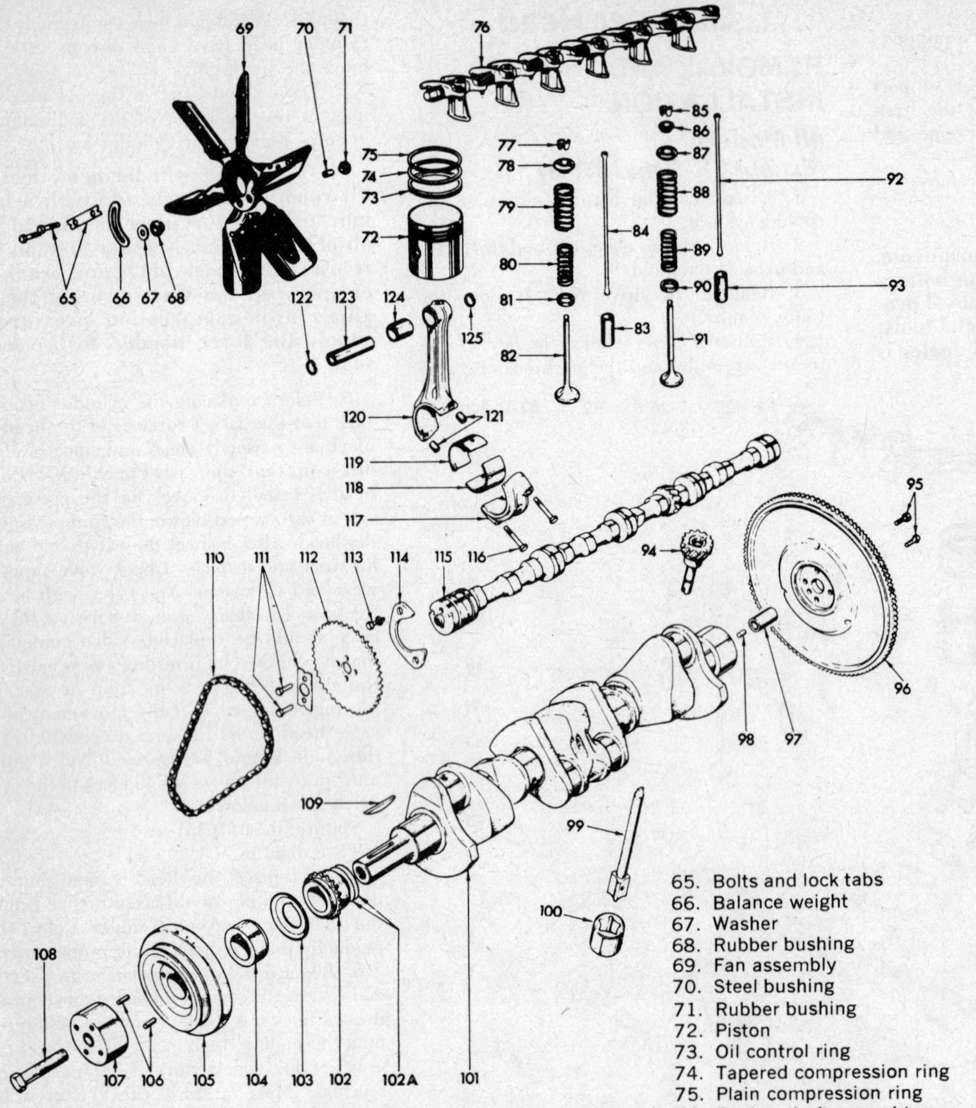

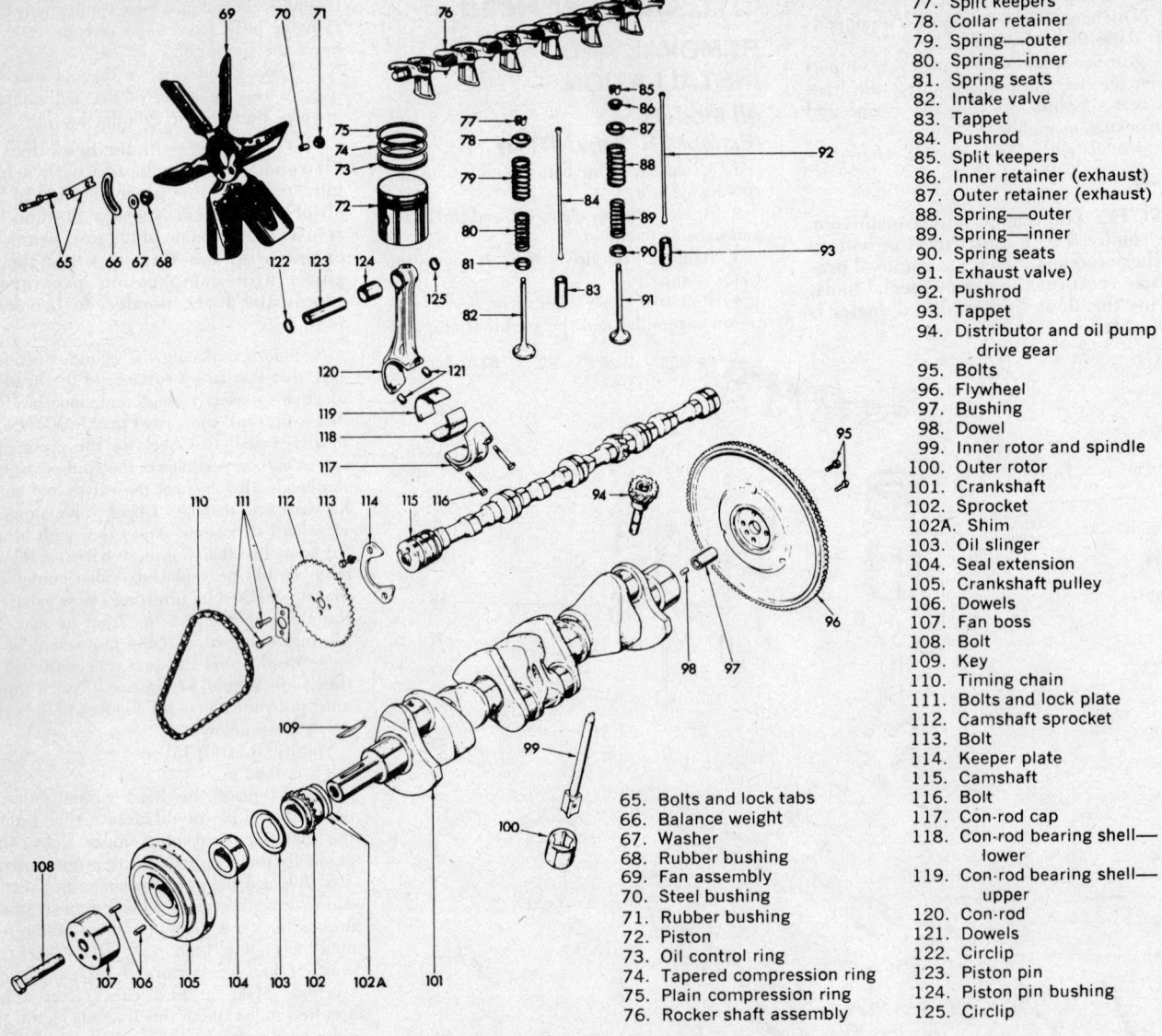

65. Bolts and lock tabs
66. Balance weight
67. Washer
68. Rubber bushing
69. Fan assembly
70. Steel bushing
71. Rubber bushing
72. Piston
73. Oil control ring
74. Tapered compression ring
75. Plain compression ring
76. Rocker shaft assembly
77. Split keepers
78. Collar retainer
79. Spring—outer
80. Spring—inner
81. Spring seats
82. Intake valve
83. Tappet
84. Pushrod
85. Split keepers
86. Inner retainer (exhaust)
87. Outer retainer (exhaust)
88. Spring—outer
89. Spring—inner
90. Spring seats
91. Exhaust valve)
92. Pushrod
93. Tappet
94. Distributor and oil pump drive gear
95. Bolts
96. Flywheel
97. Bushing
98. Dowel
99. Inner rotor and spindle
100. Outer rotor
101. Crankshaft
102. Sprocket
102A. Shim
103. Oil slinger
104. Seal extension
105. Crankshaft pulley
106. Dowels
107. Fan boss
108. Bolt
109. Key
110. Timing chain
111. Bolts and lock plate
112. Camshaft sprocket
113. Bolt
114. Keeper plate
115. Camshaft
116. Bolt
117. Con-rod cap
118. Con-rod bearing shell—lower
119. Con-rod bearing shell—upper
120. Con-rod
121. Dowels
122. Circlip
123. Piston pin
124. Piston pin bushing
125. Circlip

Moving components of six cylinder—TR-6 engine

6. Remove the timing cover from the cylinder head.
7. Unbolt and remove the cylinder head.
8. Installation is the reverse of removal.

TR-8

1. Drain the cooling system.
2. Remove the air cleaner assembly.
3. Remove the intake manifold.
4. Remove the rocker covers.
5. Remove the rocker shaft assemblies.
6. Disconnect the front exhaust pipes from the manifold flanges.
7. Remove the dipstick tube on the left cylinder head on cars equipped with automatic transmission.
8. Remove the engine oil dipstick tube from the left cylinder head.
9. Loosen the alternator link pivot and clamp bolts. Remove the two pivot bolts and nuts securing the alternator to its bracket.
10. Loosen the cylinder head bolts by reversing the tightening sequence.
11. Lift off the cylinder head including the exhaust manifold and separate if needed.
12. Installation is the reverse of removal. Using the bolt tightening sequence illustration, insert the bolts into their correct holes as follows: long bolts—3.820 in.—numbers 1, 3 and 5; medium bolts—2.620 in.—numbers 2, 4, 6, 7, 8, 9 and 10; short bolts—2.160 in.—numbers 11, 12, 13 and 14.
13. Tighten the bolts evenly a little at a time in the sequence shown in the illustration to the following torque figures:
    Bolt numbers 1 thru 10—65-70 ft/lbs.
    Bolt numbers 11 thru 14—40-50 ft/lbs.

CYLINDER HEAD OVERHAUL

See "Engine Rebuilding" section.

Rocker Shaft

REMOVAL AND INSTALLATION

All Models (Except TR-7 and TR-8)

1. Disconnect any PCV hoses and retaining clips for vacuum hoses from the rocker cover.
2. Remove the rocker cover and gasket.
3. Loosen the 4 nuts (four cylinder) or 6 nuts (six cylinder) which secure the rocker shaft pedestals to the cylinder head, and lift off the rocker shaft assembly.
4. Prior to installation, loosen the locknuts and back off the tappet adjusting nuts a few turns to avoid bending the pushrods when tightening the rocker shaft nuts.
5. Install the rocker shaft assembly on the cylinder head, making sure that the pushrods seat correctly on their balls and that the adjusting screws are located correctly. Hand tighten the rocker assembly nuts a few turns.
6. Evenly tighten the rocker shaft pedestal nuts in an order (from the front) of 3-2-4-1 to a torque of 26-32 ft/lbs for 4-cylinder Spitfire engines, and in an order of 4-3-5-2-6-1 to 24-26 ft/lbs for 6-cylinder TR-6 engines.

TR-8

1. Drain the cooling system.
2. Remove the air cleaner and air temperature control.
3. Remove the intake manifold.

4. Remove the rocker covers.
5. Remove the rocker shaft assemblies.
6. Remove the pushrods and tappets and retain in the sequence removed.

NOTE: If a tappet cannot be withdrawn, remove the camshaft and withdraw the tappet from the bottom.

7. Remove the split pin from the one end of the rocker shaft then remove the plain washer, a wave washer, rocker arms, brackets and springs and retain them in the proper sequence for reassembly.
8. Installation is the reverse of removal.

Intake Manifold

REMOVAL AND INSTALLATION

All Except TR-8

1. Drain the cooling system.
2. Remove the air cleaner. Disconnect the throttle linkage spring and the choke cable(s).
3. Disconnect the vacuum lines, the fuel lines, and the water hoses from the induction assembly.
4. Remove the clamps which retain the manifold to the cylinder head and to the exhaust manifold (if so equipped). Remove the manifold.

NOTE: If the intake manifold gasket is in need of replacement, the exhaust manifold must be removed first.

6. Installation is the reverse oif removal. Torque the nuts to specifications.

TR-8

1. Disconnect the negative battery cable.
2. Drain the cooling system.
3. Remove the air cleaner and temperature control assembly.
4. Remove the engine breather pipes.
5. Disconnect the main feed fuel pipe to the carburetors.
6. Disconnect the throttle cable and the mixture control cable.
7. On cars equipped with automatic transmission, remove the kickdown cable bracket.
8. Pull off the carburetor vent pipes.
9. Disconnect the inlet and outlet hoses to the heater.
10. Disconnect the coolant temperature wire.
11. Disconnect the heater return pipe, that connects to the pump, at the manifold connection.
12. Disconnect the thermostat bypass hose at the manifold connection.
13. Disconnect the brake servo hose from the manifold. Disconnect the distributor vacuum hose.
14. Disconnect the vent pipe to the radiator.
15. Disconnect the spark wires and remove the distributor cap.
16. Remove the twelve manifold retaining bolts while noting the location of the different lengths.
17. Lift off the manifold and remove the two gasket clamps.
18. Installation is the reverse of removal. Coat all the retaining bolt threads with a lubricant sealant. Tighten all bolts a little at a time, evenly and alternating sides, working from the center to each end. Torque to 25-30 ft/lbs.

Exhaust Manifold

REMOVAL AND INSTALLATION

All Except TR-8

1. Remove the intake manifold (exc. TR-7).
2. Unbolt the exhaust manifold from the exhaust pipe.
3. Remove the manifold and discard the gasket.
4. Installation is the reverse of removal. Torque nuts to specifications.

TR-8–Without Fuel Injection–L.H.

1. Bend back the locking tabs on the eight manifold retaining bolts.
2. Raise and safely support the front of the car.
3. Remove the three nuts securing the down-pipe to the manifold flange.
4. Lower the car and remove the eight manifold bolts and lock washers.
5. Remove the manifold and discard the two copper O-rings.
6. When installing, use new copper O-rings on the pipe flange and tighten the bolts evenly. Lock the tabs.

TR-8–Without Fuel Injection–R.H.

1. Remove the hot air intake hose.
2. Remove the heat chamber cover.
3. Remove the heat chamber back plate by removing the four bolts.
4. Bend back the locking tabs on the eight manifold retaining bolts.
5. Raise and safely support the front of the car.
6. Remove the three nuts securing the exhaust pipe to the manifold flange.
7. Lower the vehicle and remove the eight manifold bolts and lock washers.
8. Remove the manifold and discard the two copper O-rings.
9. When installing, use new copper O-rings and tighten the eight manifold bolts evenly.

TR-8–With Fuel Injection–L.H.

1. Slacken the air-flow meter to plenum chamber clips.
2. Disconnect one end of the plenum chamber hose and remove the hose.
3. Remove the E.G.R. valve pipe to manifold bolts and remove the pipe.
4. Disconnect the vacuum pipe from the E.G.R. valve.
5. Remove the bolts and strap from the air conditioning compressor.
6. Disconnect the spark plug wires.
7. Remove the exhaust flange nuts.
8. Bend back the locking tabs on the exhaust manifold bolts then remove the bolts.
9. Remove the exhaust manifold.
10. Installation is the reverse of removal.

TR-8–With Fuel Injection–R.H.

1. Remove the windshield washer bottle.
2. Disconnect the spark plug wires.
3. Remove the starter motor heat shield.
4. Remove the exhaust flange nuts.
5. Bend back the lock tabs on the exhaust manifold bolts and remove the bolts.
6. Remove the exhaust manifold.
7. Installation is the reverse of removal.

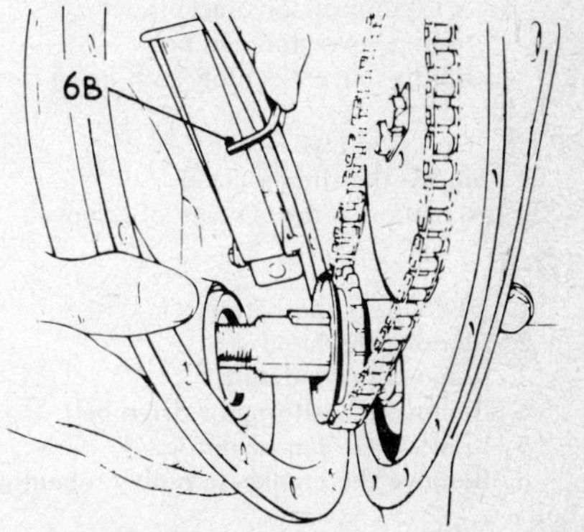

Installing the timing chain cover while holding the tensioner back with a bent rod

Timing Gear Cover

REMOVAL AND INSTALLATION

Spitfire

1. Remove the drive belt.
2. Remove the fan.
3. Remove the crankshaft damper nut (accessible from below), and the damper.

NOTE: It may be necessary to block the flywheel to stop the crankshaft from turning. Replace the nut loosely and pull off the damper with a gear puller.

4. Remove the five screws, six bolts, and one nut which retain the timing gear cover to the engine. Lift off the cover with its gasket, taking care not to damage the seal.
5. Installation is the reverse of removal. To ease installation, hold the chain tensioner back with a bent length of rod until the tensioner clears the chain. When installing the pulley, take care to position the drive key between the pulley and the crankshaft spindle. Tighten the damper nut to specifications. Readjust the drive belt tension.

TR-6

1. Drain the cooling system. Drain the engine oil. Disconnect the overflow pipe and tank, if so equipped.
2. Remove the radiator support(s), radiator valance(s), and radiator.
3. Remove the fan, cross tube and drive belt.
4. On the TR-6, remove the U-bolts from the steering rack and ease the rack forward.
5. Remove the fan adaptor. Using a gear puller, remove the crankshaft pulley.
6. Remove the timing cover, gasket, and spacer.
7. Installation is the reverse of removal. To ease installation, hold the chain tensioner back with a bent length of rod until the tensioner clears the chain. Readjust the drive belt tension.

TR-7

1. Remove the following:
   a. hood
   b. battery ground
   c. alternator and bracket
   d. air pump, diverter and relief valve and bracket
   e. A/C compressor brackets
   f. timing cover-to-head bolts
   g. timing cover center and lower left bolts
   h. fan assembly.
2. Remove the timing cover.
3. Installation is the reverse of removal.

TR-8

1. Disconnect the battery.
2. Remove the hood.
3. Remove the radiator.
4. Remove the alternator drive belt.
5. Remove the fan blade.
6. Remove the crankcase pulley retaining bolt.
7. Turn the crankshaft to TDC number one cylinder firing.
8. Loosen the timing pointer retaining bolts and move the pointer away from the crankshaft pulley assembly.
9. Disconnect the spark plug wires and remove the distributor cap.
10. Remove the crankshaft pulley.
11. Disconnect the vacuum pipe from the distributor.
12. Remove the lower R.H. (viewing from the front of the engine) timing cover bolt and move the transducer to one side.
13. Remove the upper bolt which also releases the power steering pump and vent pipe clip.
14. Remove the power steering pump drive belt and remove the pump to one side.
15. Disconnect the brown wire, at the connector, to the transducer.
16. Disconnect the coolant temperature wire.
17. Remove the timing cover bolts securing the diagnostic socket and move to one side.
18. Disconnect the diagnostic socket leads from the coil.
19. Disconnect the electronic ignition leads from the distributor and coil and remove the plug from the heat-sink.
20. Remove the thermostat bypass and the heater return hoses from the water pump.
21. Disconnect the leads from the oil pressure switch and the oil pressure indicator.

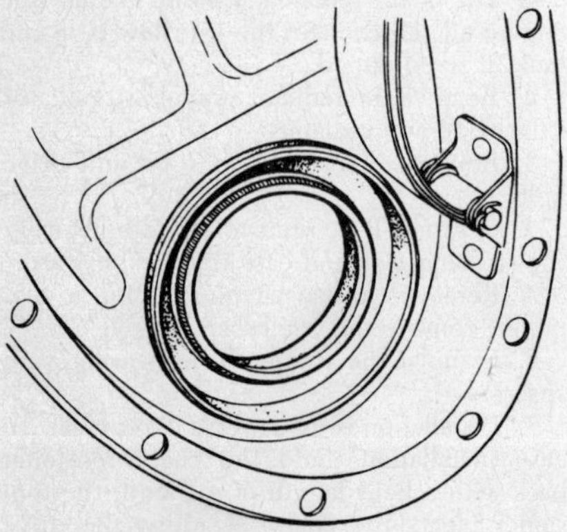

Oil seal installation

22. Remove the two bolts securing the timing cover to the oil pan.
23. Remove the remaining five bolts, one nut and the timing cover from the cylinder block.

NOTE: The timing cover is removed complete with the distributor, oil pump, oil pressure switch, oil pressure indicator transmitter, oil filter and water pump and pulley assembly.

24. To install, clean all gasket contact surfaces.
25. Set the distributor rotor arm approximately 30 degrees before the final position (TDC number one cylinder firing).
26. Position the timing cover and secure with the five bolts and one nut. Install the two sump pump bolts.
27. The rest of the installation is the reverse of removal. When installing the crankshaft pulley assembly, tighten the retaining bolt to 140-160 ft/lbs.

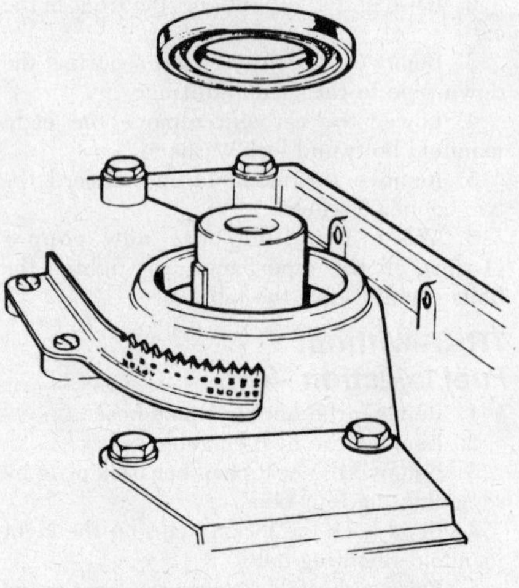

Installation of front oil seal—TR-7

Oil Seal Replacement

All Models (Except TR-7 and TR-8)

1. Remove the timing gear cover.
2. Tap out the old seal.
3. Smear the new seal with engine oil and, making sure that the cavity face of the seal faces the engine, install it into the cover using a drift or wooden block.
4. Install the timing gear cover.

TR-7

1. Remove the pulleys.
2. Pry out old seal.
3. Dip new seal in engine oil and install.

TR-8

1. Remove the crankshaft pulley.
2. Remove the old seal, taking care not to damage the cover.
3. Before installing the new seal, lubricate the outside diameter and position the seal in the housing with the lip facing toward the engine.
4. Using a suitable drift, fit the seal until the back of the seal is flush with the outer face of the seal housing.
5. Install the crankshaft pulley.

Timing Chain

REMOVAL AND INSTALLATION

All Models (Except TR-7 and TR-8)

1. Remove the timing gear cover.
2. Remove the oil thrower.
3. Check timing chain wear by placing a straight edge along the slack length of chain. If the free-play between the straight edge and the chain, at a point midway between the two sprockets, exceeds 0.4 in., the chain must be replaced.
4. Rotate the crankshaft until the crankshaft key is at 12 o'clock and the sprocket dots align.
5. Pry back the locking tabs and remove the bolts which retain the camshaft sprocket to the camshaft.
6. Taking care not to disturb the crankshaft or camshaft, remove both sprockets with the timing chain.
7. To check alignment of the sprockets, remove the crankshaft drive key and temporarily install both sprockets. Place a straight edge across the teeth of both sprockets. Correct any misalignment by placing shims behind the crankshaft sprocket.

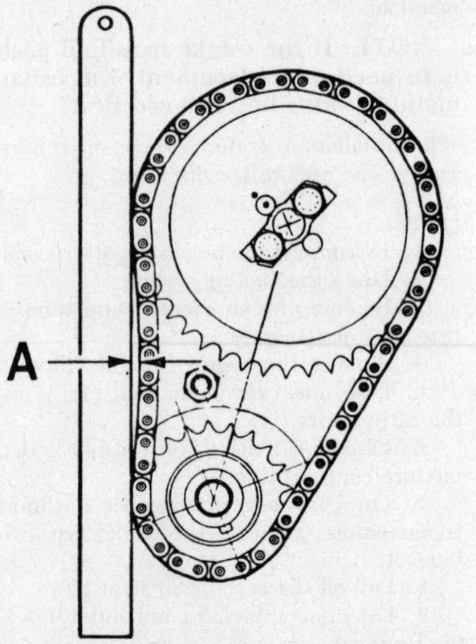

Checking timing chain slack

8. After checking the alignment, remove the sprockets, install the crankshaft drive key, and place the sprocket and chain assembly into position—aligned dot to dot, or line to line. Install the camshaft sprocket retaining bolts using a new lockplate.
9. Install the oil thrower.
10. Install the timing gear cover.

TR-7

1. Remove the timing chain cover, camshaft cover and distributor cap.
2. Turn the crankshaft so that the camshaft timing mark is at the bottom.
3. Remove the exposed camshaft retaining bolt and turn the crankshaft until the mark

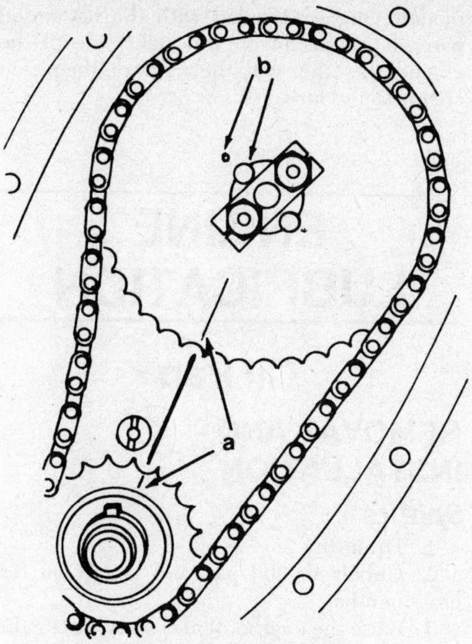

A. Scribed alignment marks
B. Punch mark opposite camshaft groove

Relative position of timing marks on sprockets

is in line with the groove in the front bearing cap.

4. Secure the camshaft sprocket to the support bracket, and remove the last sprocket bolt.
5. Remove the hydraulic tensioner and guide plate as well as the locking bolt from the adjustable chain guide.
6. Remove the common bolt between the adjustable guide and the support and remove the guide.
7. Remove the fixed guide, chain and sprocket.
8. Install the chain over the sprockets and on the engine.
9. Loosely install the fixed guide and support bracket.
10. Loosely install the adjustable guide.
11. Install a guide bolt in the timing cover center bolt hole.
12. Install the camshaft sprocket with one bolt and turn the idler shaft sprocket so that the scribed line is halfway between the guide bolt and the lower adjustable guide bolt.
13. Install and tighten the hydraulic chain tensioner.
14. Remove the nut securing the camshaft sprocket to the support bracket and install the remaining sprocket bolt.
15. Install the distributor cap, camshaft cover and timing cover.

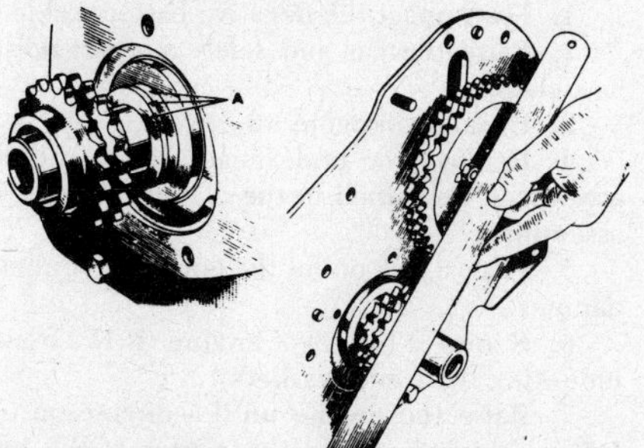

Checking sprocket alignment (right), correcting alignment with shims (A) (left)

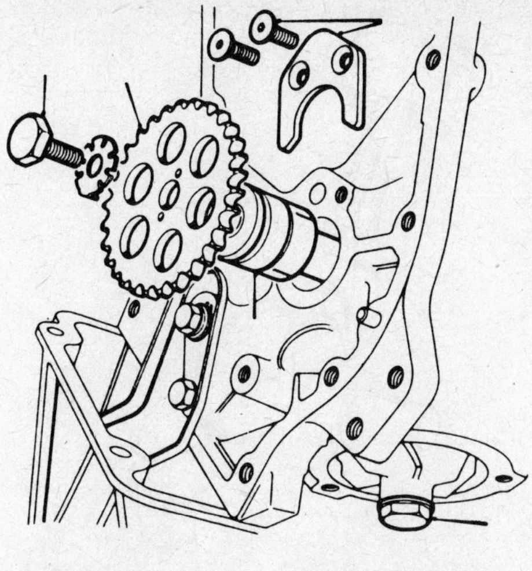

Intermediate shaft and timing chain gear—TR-7

TR-8

1. Set the engine number one piston at TDC.
2. Remove the timing chain cover.
3. Make sure the number one piston is at TDC.
4. Remove the distributor drive gear and the spacer.
5. Remove the gears complete with the chain.

CAUTION

Do not rotate the engine while the rocker shafts are installed, otherwise the valve gear and pistons will be damaged.

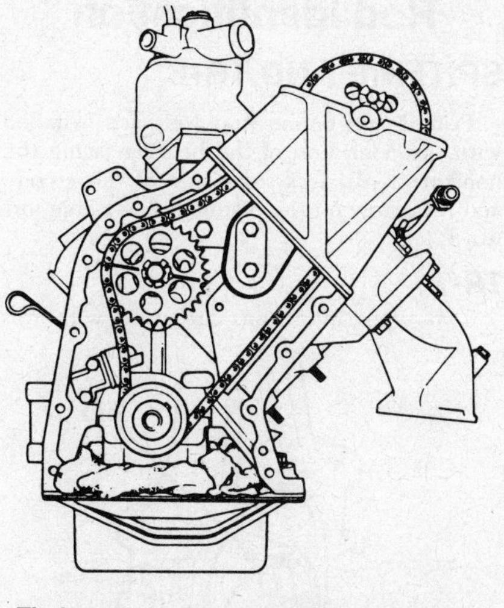

Timing chain and gear location—TR-7

NOTE: If the engine crankshaft and/or camshaft have not been rotated, proceed to step 11. If it is necessary to rotate them, proceed to step 6.

6. Remove the rocker shaft assemblies.
7. Set the engine number one piston at TDC.
8. Temporarily intall the camshaft pulley with the marking "Front" outward.
9. Turn the camshaft until the mark on the camshaft pulley is at the six o'clock position, then remove the pulley without disturbing the camshaft.
10. Locate the pulleys to the chain with the timing marks aligned.
11. Engage the pulleys and chain assembly on the camshaft and crankshaft key locations. Check that the camshaft key is parallel to the shaft axis to ensure adequate lubrication of the distributor drive gear.
12. Make sure the timing marks line up.
13. Install the spacer with the flange to the front.
14. Install the distributor drive gear making sure the annular grooved side is fitted to the rear or towards the spacer.
15. Install the drive gear washer and bolt and tighten to 40-45 ft/lbs.
16. Install the timing chain cover.
17. Install the rocker shaft assemblies.

TIMING CHAIN TENSIONER ADJUSTMENT

The tensioner is non-adjustable. The TR-7 uses a hydraulic tensioner, the others use a spring type. If the chain is not tensioned properly and is not stretched, the tensioner must be replaced. To remove the spring type tensioner, remove the timing chain cover. Spread the tensioner blades apart and slide the tensioner off the anchor pin. The hydraulic type is a simple bolt-on unit.

Installation is the reverse of removal. Make sure that the convex surface of the tensioner faces the timing chain.

Camshaft

REMOVAL AND INSTALLATION

All Models (Except TR-7 and TR-8

1. Drain the cooling system. Remove the radiator valence(s) and the radiator.

On TR-6 models, remove the radiator grille.

2. Remove the timing cover.
3. Remove the timing chain and camshaft sprocket. Remove the fuel pump, the distributor driveshaft, and gear.

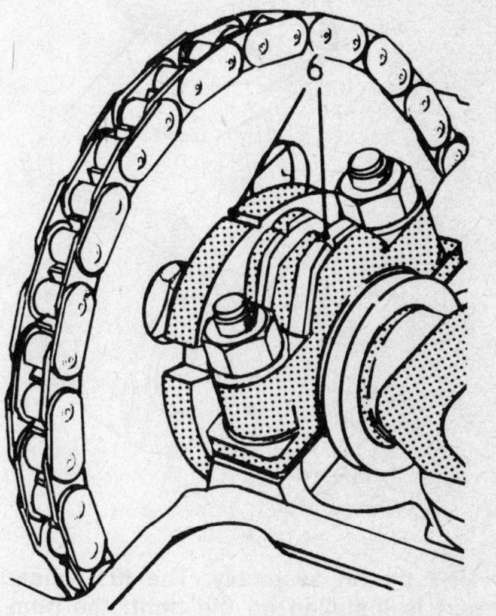

Camshaft timing marks (6)

4. Remove the cylinder head. Remove the pushrods and lifters, keeping them in order.
5. Remove the camshaft keeper plate and slide the camshaft out.
6. Installation is the reverse of removal. Keep the camshaft end play to 0.004-0.008 in. Adjust the valve timing.

TR-7

1. Remove the cover and turn the camshaft so that the timing mark is 180° from the groove in the front bearing cap.
2. Anchor the sprocket to the support bracket and remove the exposed bolt.
3. Align the timing mark and the groove and remove the remaining bolt.
4. Number the bearing caps and remove them. Loosen the nuts evenly.
5. Remove the camshaft.
6. Install in reverse of the above.

NOTE: When installing shaft, make sure that the mark and groove are in alignment. Torque bearing cap nuts to 3-5 ft/lb.

TR-8

1. Remove the timing chain cover as described earlier in this section.
2. Remove the intake manifold complete with carburetors. See Intake Manifold removal and installation.
3. Remove the L.H. and R.H. rocker covers.
4. Remove the eight bolts (four per shaft) and remove the rocker shafts. Identify for reassembly.
5. Remove the eight push rods and identify for reassembly.
6. Remove the camshaft pulley retaining bolt and washer.
7. Remove the camshaft and crankshaft pulleys complete with the chain.
8. Remove the distributor drive gear and spacer.
9. Remove the eight hydraulic lifters and identify for reassembly.
10. Carefully remove the camshaft.

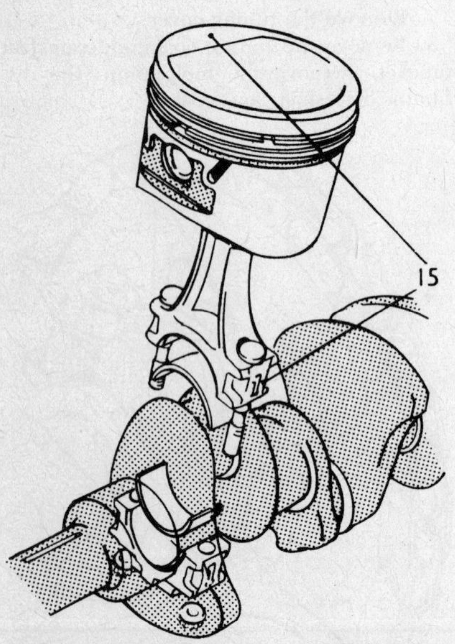

TR-7 piston assembly. The first raised part is installed on the right; the numbered side of the rod (15) goes on the left

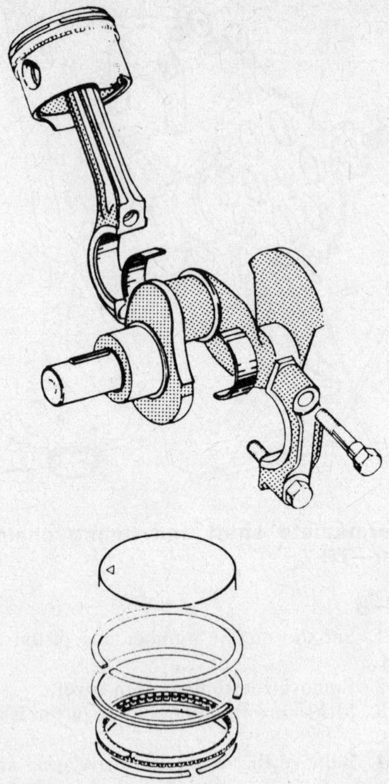

TR-6, Spitfire, GT6 piston and connecting rod

11. Installation is the reverse of removal. Lubricate the five camshaft journals before installing the camshaft.

Piston and Connecting Rod Identification

SPITFIRE AND TR-6

Pistons and connecting rods are installed with the open end of the bearing facing the non-thrust (driver's side) side of the engine and the arrow on the piston crown facing forward.

TR-7

Two types of pistons are used with this model. One is installed with the flat raised part of the piston on the right side of the engine; the other with the arrow on the piston crown facing forward.

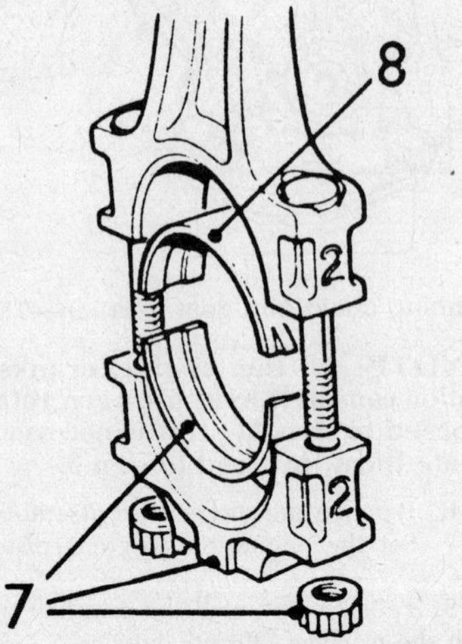

TR-7 connecting rod (7) and bearing caps (8)

ENGINE LUBRICATION

Oil Pan

REMOVAL AND INSTALLATION

Spitfire

1. Drain the engine oil.
2. Unbolt the oil pan and rest it on the crossmember.
3. Raise the engine. If necessary, rotate the crankshaft. Remove the pan.
4. Installation is the reverse of removal. The long bolts go at the rear of the pan.

TR-6

1. Disconnect the negative battery cable.
2. Drain the engine oil. Remove the dipstick.
3. Remove the oil pan bolts and lower out the pan.
4. Using a new gasket and non-drying sealing compound, position the oil pan to the engine and install the retaining bolts. Torque the bolts to specifications.
5. Fill the crankcase to capacity with the proper grade of oil. Install the dipstick.
6. Connect the negative battery cable.

TR-7

1. Remove the air duct, fan guard, coupling plate bolts, and engine stabilizer.
2. Make up a support bracket from angle iron.
3. Remove the alternator support and timing cover lower bolt.
4. Attach the support bracket to the timing cover using these holes.
5. Support the engine under the bracket with a jack.
6. Remove the right engine mount and the left mount-to-frame bolts.
7. Remove the pan bolts and raise the engine far enough to remove the pan, along with the left mount.
8. Installation is the reverse of removal.

TR-8

1. Disconnect the negative battery cable.
2. Raise the car and safely support with jack stands.
3. Drain the engine oil.
4. Remove the underneath panel so that access can be gained to the crankshaft pulley assembly.
5. Place a jack under the crankshaft pulley damper.
6. Remove the two engine L.H. front mounting bolts and washers.
7. Raise the engine until a dimension of 1.5 in. exists between the center of the inboard mounting hole and the corresponding subframe mounting hole.

8. Remove the power steering hose clamp bolt.

9. Remove the fourteen oil pan retaining bolts from both sides and the front.

10. Remove the two rear oil pan retaining bolts together with the reinforcing plate.

11. Remove the two coupling plate bolts and remove the oil pan.

12. Installation is the reverse of removal.

REAR MAIN OIL SEAL REPLACEMENT

All Models (Except TR-7 and TR-8)

1. Remove the transmission.

2. Remove the flywheel. Remove the engine rear transmission adapter plate.

3. On the GT6, lift the engine sufficiently to provide access to the rear main seal bolts.

4. Remove the oil seal housing with gasket. Press out the old seal.

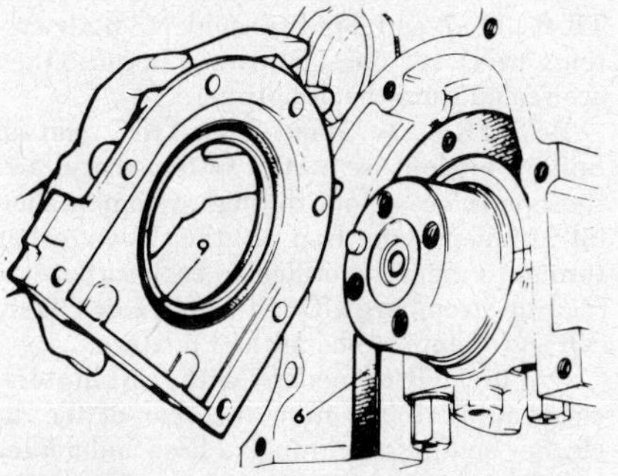

Rear main oil seal correctly positioned in housing

5. Smear the outside diameter of the new oil seal with grease and press it into the housing, lip toward the crankshaft.

6. Coat the crankcase face with sealing compound and smear the crankshaft with oil.

7. Using a new gasket, install the seal housing and hand-tighten the retaining bolts.

8. Position the housing to the crankcase face using a centering sleeve. After the housing is centered, tighten the bolts.

9. Further installation is the reverse of removal.

TR-7

1. Remove the transmission, clutch and flywheel.

2. Remove the two rear pan bolts and loosen the left rear pan bolt.

3. Remove the oil seal housing and pry out the seal.

4. Installation is the reverse of removal.

TR-8

1. On cars equipped with manual transmissions, remove the transmission, clutch and flywheel. On cars equipped with automatic transmissions, remove the transmission, torque converter and drive plate.

2. Remove the oil pan, strainer and baffle plate.

3. Remove the rear main bearing cap and bearing lower half.

4. Remove and discard the rear main bearing cap side seals.

5. Remove and discard the crankshaft rear oil seal.

6. To install, fit the side seals to the grooves each side of the rear main bearing cap.

NOTE: Do not cut the side seals to length. They must protrude approximately 1/16 inch above the bearing cap parting face.

7. Apply a sealing compound to the rearmost half of the rear main bearing cap parting face or to the equivalent area on the cylinder block.

8. Lubricate the bearing half and bearing cap side seals with clean engine oil.

9. Position the bearing cap to the engine and make sure it seats squarely on the cylinder block.

10. Tighten the cap bolts approximately one quarter turn, then back off one complete turn.

11. Position a seal guide, special tool number RO. 1014, on the crankshaft flange.

12. Make sure the oil seal guide and the crankshaft journal are clean. Then coat the seal guide and oil seal journal with clean engine oil.

NOTE: Make sure that the seal guide outer surface is completely coated with lubricant so that the oil seal lip is not turned back during reassembly.

13. Position the oil seal, lipped side towards the engine, on to the seal guide. The seal outside diameter must be clean and dry.

14. Push the oil seal fully by hand into the recess formed in the cap and block until it abuts against the machined step in the recess.

15. Remove the seal guide.

16. Tighten the rear main bearing cap evenly to 65-70 ft/lbs.

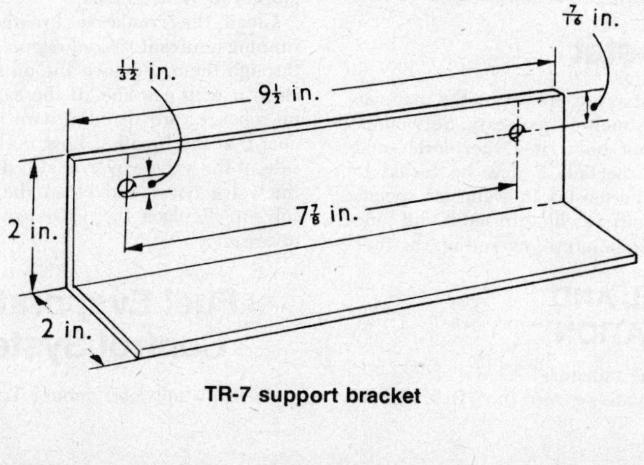

TR-7 support bracket

17. Install the oil pan, strainer and baffle plate.

18. Install the transmission and other related parts.

Oil Pump

REMOVAL AND INSTALLATION

All Models (Except TR-7 and TR-8)

1. Remove the dipstick, drain the oil pan, remove the oil pan and remove the oil pump from the crankcase.

2. With the oil pump assembled except for the top cover, measure the clearances between the inner and outer rotors, the outer rotor and the pump housing, and the inner rotor and the face of the pump housing. Clearances should fall within the specifications.

OIL PUMP CLEARANCES

Model	Inner Rotor to Outer Rotor (in. max.)	Outer Rotor to Pump Housing (in. max.)	Inner Rotor to Housing Face (in. max.)
Spitfire	0.010	0.0075	0.0035 ②
TR-6	0.004 ①	0.0075	0.0040
TR-7	0.004 ①	0.0080	0.0040
TR-8	0.008	0.0070	0.0030

① Min.—0.001 in.
② Min.—0.0015 in.

3. Replace worn components and install the inner rotor in the pump housing, followed by the outer rotor, with its chamfered face leading.

4. Installation is the reverse of removal.

TR-7

1. Remove the clutch slave cylinder, bellhousing nut and bolt, oil pump retaining bolts and pump.

2. Install in reverse of the above using a new O-ring.

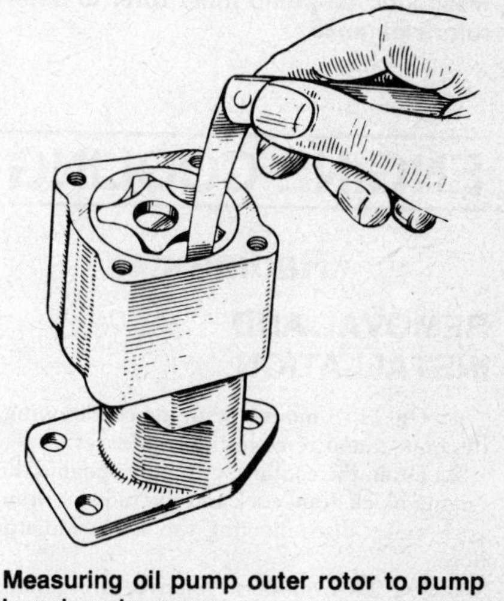

Measuring oil pump outer rotor to pump housing clearance

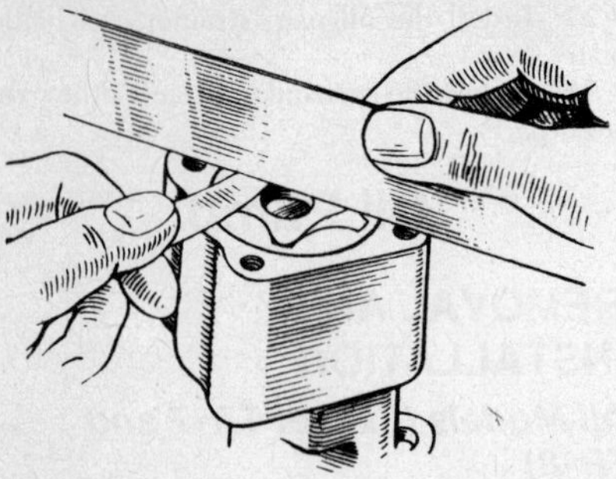

Measuring oil pump rotor end clearance

TR-8

1. Remove the oil filter assembly.
2. Disconnect the electrical lead from the oil pressure switch.
3. Remove the bolts from the oil pump cover and remove the cover and gasket.
4. Remove the oil pump gears.
5. Before installation, pack the oil pump gear housing with petroleum jelly so that the pump will prime itself when the engine is started.
6. Install the oil pump gears and make sure the petroleum jelly is forced into every cavity between the teeth of the gears.
7. Replace the oil pump cover using a new gasket. Tighten the retaining bolts alternately and evenly to 9 ft/lbs.
8. Install the oil filter and the electrical lead to the oil pressure switch.

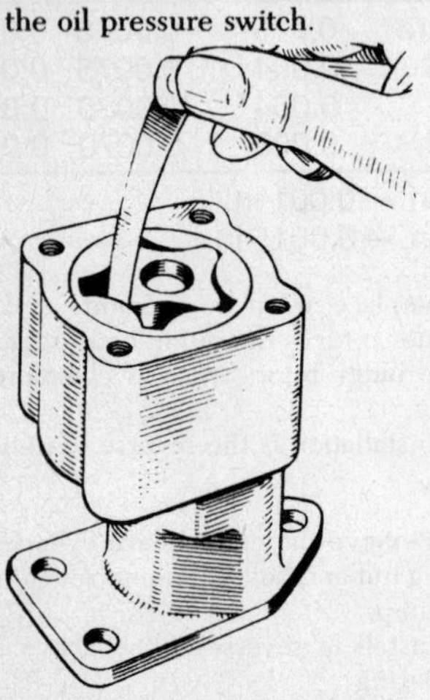

Measuring oil pump inner rotor to outer rotor clearance

ENGINE COOLING

Radiator

REMOVAL AND INSTALLATION

1. On TR-8 models with air conditioning, disconnect and remove the condenser.
2. Drain the cooling system by opening the engine block drain cock and the radiator drain cock or by disconnecting the lower radiator hose.
3. On TR-6 models, remove the radiator valance and position the stay rods to one side. Disconnect the remaining radiator hoses. Disconnect the overflow hose to the expansion tank.
4. On TR-8 models with automatic transmission, remove and clamp the top and bottom fluid hose connections.
5. Remove the radiator retaining bolts and lift out the radiator.
6. Reverse the above procedure to install, making sure that the cooling system is filled to the proper level with a 50% ethylene glycol solution.

Water Pump

REMOVAL AND INSTALLATION

All Models (Except TR-7 and TR-8)

1. Drain the cooling system, and remove the fan belt.
2. Disconnect the radiator and water hoses at the thermostat housing and water pump, and disconnect the fuel supply line at the carburetors and fuel pump.
3. Remove the temperature transmitter connection.
4. Remove the water pump.
5. Installation is the reverse of removal.

TR-7

1. Remove the intake manifold with carburetors.
2. Remove the connecting tube from the water pump cover and the bottom hose from the pump.
3. Remove the pump from the block.
4. Installation is the reverse of removal.

TR-8

1. Disconnect the negative battery cable.
2. Drain the cooling system.
3. Remove the radiator.
4. Remove the fan assembly.
5. Remove the water pump pulley.
6. Remove the alternator belt.
7. Disconnect the diagnostic socket lead at the connector.
8. Remove the two bolts common to the timing cover and water pump and move the diagnostic socket and bracket aside.
9. Remove the two remaining common timing cover and water pump bolts and note that the upper one is longer.
10. Remove the five water pump bolts and remove the water pump and pulley assembly.
11. Use a new gasket and install in reverse of removal.

Thermostat

All thermostats are pre-set by the manufacturer; no adjustment is necessary. Servicing is by replacement only. If a thermostat malfunction is suspected, it may be tested by placing the thermostat in water of specific temperature and watching to see if unit functions at the temperature marked on the thermostat flange.

REMOVAL AND INSTALLATION

1. Drain the radiator.
2. On all models except the TR-8, remove the two bolts securing the elbow to the thermostat housing and lift off the elbow with the top hose attached.
3. On the TR-8, disconnect the radiator top hose from the thermostat housing. Then remove the thermostat housing from the manifold.
4. Remove the thermostat.
5. Installation is the reverse of removal.

EMISSION CONTROLS

Positive Crankcase Ventilation System

Two different systems have been used on TR-6, TR-7 and Spitfire models. Both systems are closed ones, so named because they are sealed from the atmosphere.

1975 TR-6, 1975 and later TR-7, and all Spitfire models use a PCV system that draws the crankcase vapors through a combination oil strainer/flame trap in the valve cover through a metering orifice on each carburetor (Zenith-Stromberg CDSE, CD4VT or CDSE (V)) and then into the air/fuel mixture.

On the TR-8 models with carburetors, clean air is drawn from the rear of the air cleaner and passes through a hose and a filter into the crankcase. The crankcase fumes rise through the pushrod tubes to the right-hand rocker cover and pass up through a flame trap to hoses connected to the depression side of the carburetors. The fumes are finally drawn into the combustion chambers and burned.

To ensure that blow-by gases do not escape from the crankcase to the atmosphere, depression is maintained in the crankcase under all operating conditions on the TR-8 models with fuel injection. This is achieved by connecting the crankcase breathing housing to a point between the air meter flap and the throttle plate. Air is drawn in on the left hand rocker cover through an air filter and restrictor and drawn off from the engine on the right-hand rocker cover. A flame trap is fitted in the draw off housing.

COMPONENT SERVICE

The PCV system is serviced every 12 months or 12,000 miles.

Clean the crankcase breather hoses by running a solvent soaked rag on a coat hanger through them. Remove the oil filler cap and clean it with gasoline. If the cap is gummed up, chances are that the wire screen (flame guard) at the breather hose outlet on the inside of the valve cover is also dirty. Remove the valve cover and clean the screen with solvent. Replace the valve cover gasket, if necessary.

Fuel Evaporative Control System

All 1975 and later model Triumphs have

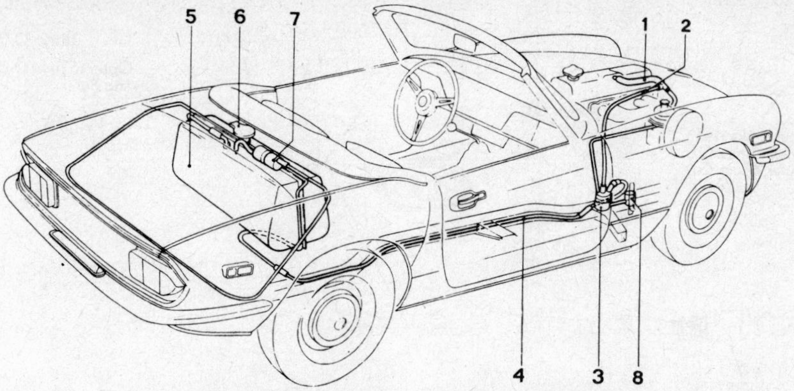

1. Crankcase purge line
2. Canister purge line
3. Canister
4. Vapor feed line
5. Fuel tank (limited fill)
6. Sealed fuel filler cap
7. Vapor separator
8. Anti run-on valve

Spitfire evaporative control system

been equipped with an evaporative control system to prevent unburned fuel vapors in the fuel tank and carburetor float chambers from escaping into the atmosphere. The gas filler cap is sealed from the atmosphere.

All 1975 and later models use a gas filler neck that extends down into the tank, thus preventing complete filling of the tank. This eliminates the need for an expansion tank that would take up much needed trunk space. A small vapor separator, located above the tank, is used instead. The vapor separator contains a restrictor valve which prevents fuel surges from reaching the carbon canister. Those vapors which do not condense and return to the fuel tank are displaced and drawn into an activated charcoal canister located in the engine compartment. The excess fuel vapors in the

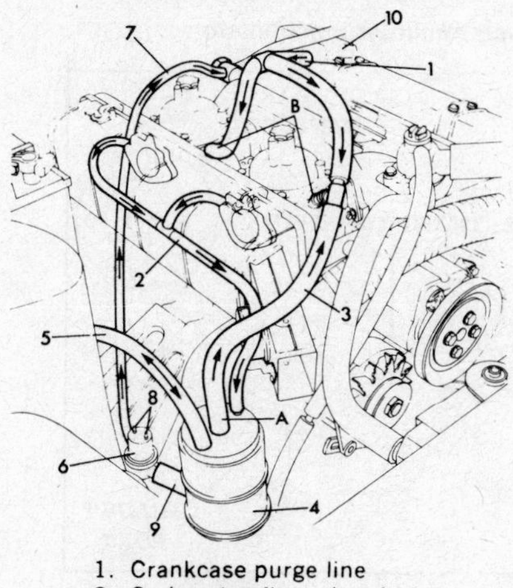

1. Crankcase purge line
2. Carburetor float chamber vent pipe
3. Canister purge line
4. Charcoal canister
5. Fuel tank vent pipe
6. Anti dieseling valve
7. Manifold vacuum line
8. Electrical connections for anti dieseling valve
9. Purge air to canister
10. Flame arrestor

A. 3/32 in. restrictor
B. 5/16 in. restrictor

Crankcase and evaporative control purge system—TR-7 (49 states)

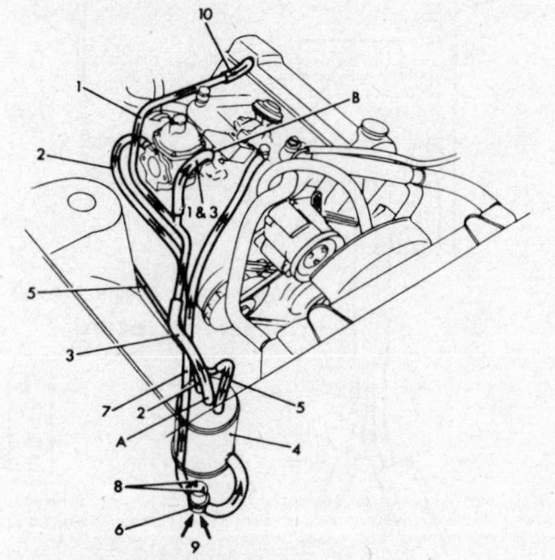

1. Crankcase purge line
2. Carburetor float chamber vent pipe
3. Canister purge line
4. Charcoal canister
5. Fuel tank vent pipe
6. Anti dieseling valve
7. Manifold vacuum line
8. Electrical connections for Anti dieseling valve
9. Purge air to canister
10. Flame arrestor

A. 3/32 in. restrictor
B. 5/16 in. restrictor

Crankcase and evaporative control purge system—TR-7 (Calif.)

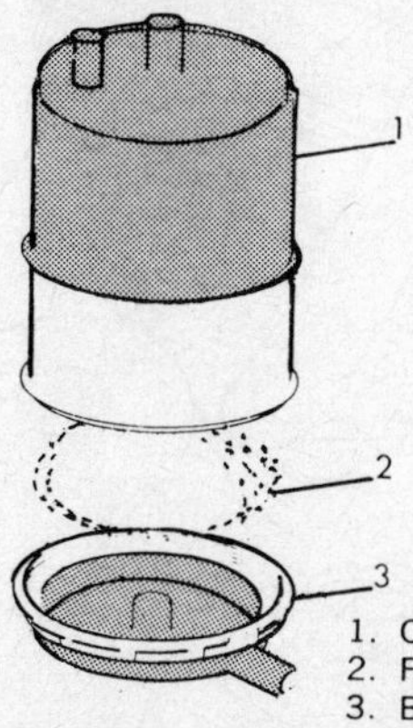

1. Carbon canister
2. Filter gauze
3. Base cap

Evaporation control system carbon canister

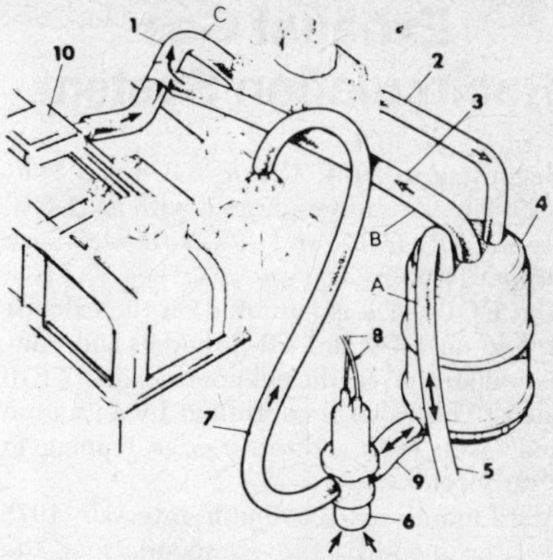

1. Crankcase breather pipe
2. Vent valve connecting pipe(s)
3. Canister purge pipe
4. Evaporative control canister
5. Canister to fuel tank pipe
6. Run-on control valve
7. Vacuum control pipe
8. Solenoid connections
9. Canister to run-on control valve pipe
10. Flame arrestor

A. 1/32 in. restrictor
B. 3/32 in. restrictor
C. 3/16 in. restrictor

Spitfire crankcase and evaporative control emission

carburetor float chambers are also vented to the charcoal canister.

A solenoid actuated anti-run on (anti-dieseling) valve is incorporated into the evaporative control system. When the ignition is switched off, the solenoid is activated, operating a valve that seals off the atmospheric vent at the bottom of the carbon canister. With the vent sealed, the connection to the intake manifold applies a partial vacuum to the canister and subsequently to the float chambers.

The canister is a sealed unit, and must be replaced at 24 month or 24,000 mile intervals.

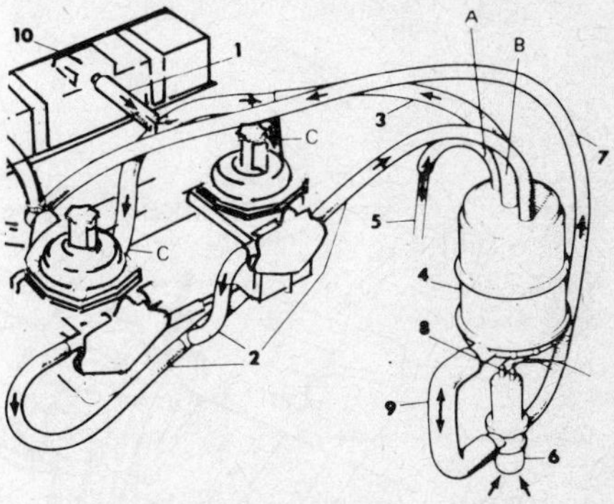

1. Crankcase breather pipe
2. Vent valve connecting pipes
3. Canister purge pipe
4. Evaporative control canister
5. Canister to fuel tank pipe
6. Run-on control valve
7. Vacuum control pipe
8. Solenoid connections
9. Canister to run-on control valve pipe
10. Flame arrestor

A. 1/32 in. restrictor
B. 3/32 in. restrictor
C. 5/16 in. restrictors

TR-6 crankcase and evaporative control emission system details showing anti-run on valve

Exhaust Gas Recirculation System

Beginning in 1974, U.S.A. TR-6 and Spitfire 1500 models are equipped with an (EGR) system. All TR-7 and TR-8 models are equipped with EGR.

The EGR valve is mounted on the exhaust manifold on TR-7 and TR-8 models and Spitfires and located on the cylinder head on TR-6 models. The valve is controlled by a vacuum signal taken from a throttle edge tapping in the carburetor.

At 12 month or 12,500 mile intervals (1975 and later models), the components of the EGR system must be removed for cleaning. Most common EGR valve failures stem from exhaust deposits or a cracked diaphragm. The base of the valve may be cleaned with a wire brush. Clean the valve seat and metering valve with a sand blaster or spark plug cleaning machine. On 1975 and later models, reset the EGR service reminder light (odometer actuated) using the special British Leyland Key at 12,500 mile intervals.

Exhaust Emission Control

AIR INJECTION SYSTEM

All TR-7, TR-8 and Spitfire 1500 models are equipped with an air pump system. A belt driven air pump delivers filtered air under pressure to the exhaust ports. Here, the additional oxygen, supplied by the air pump, reacts with any uncombusted fuel mixture promoting an afterburning effect. To prevent a reverse flow in the air injection manifold when exhaust gas pressure exceeds air supply pressure, a non-return check valve is used. A

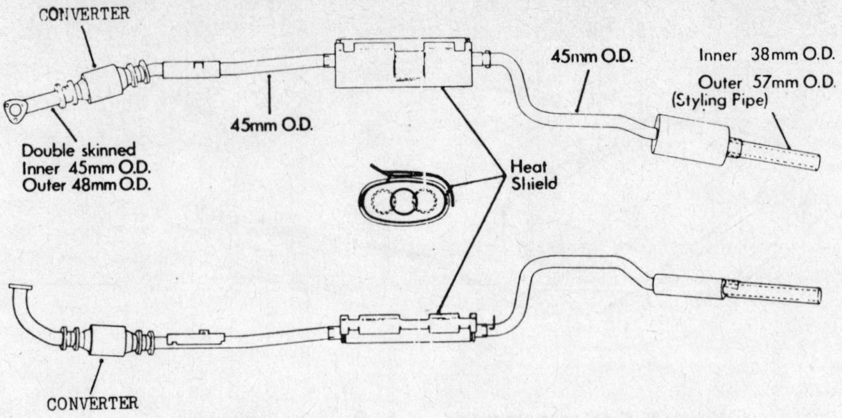

Exhaust system with catalytic converter—TR-7 (California)

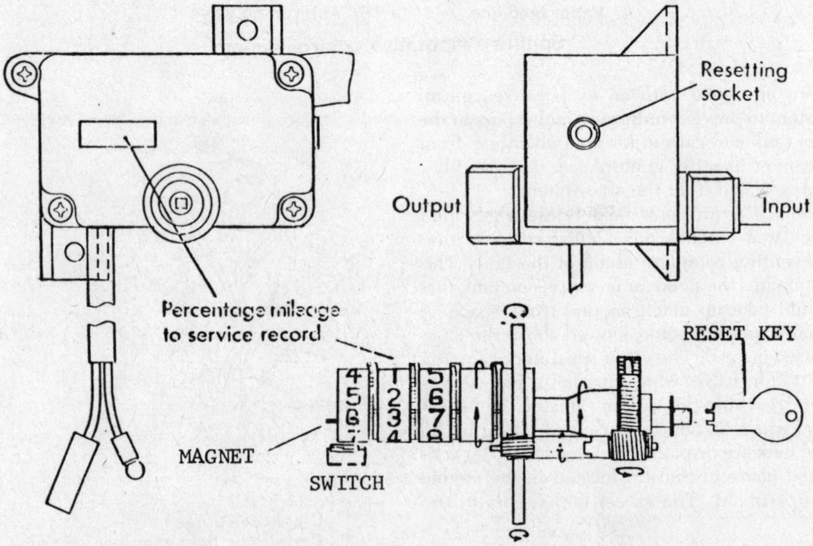

EGR/Catalytic converter service reminder mechanism

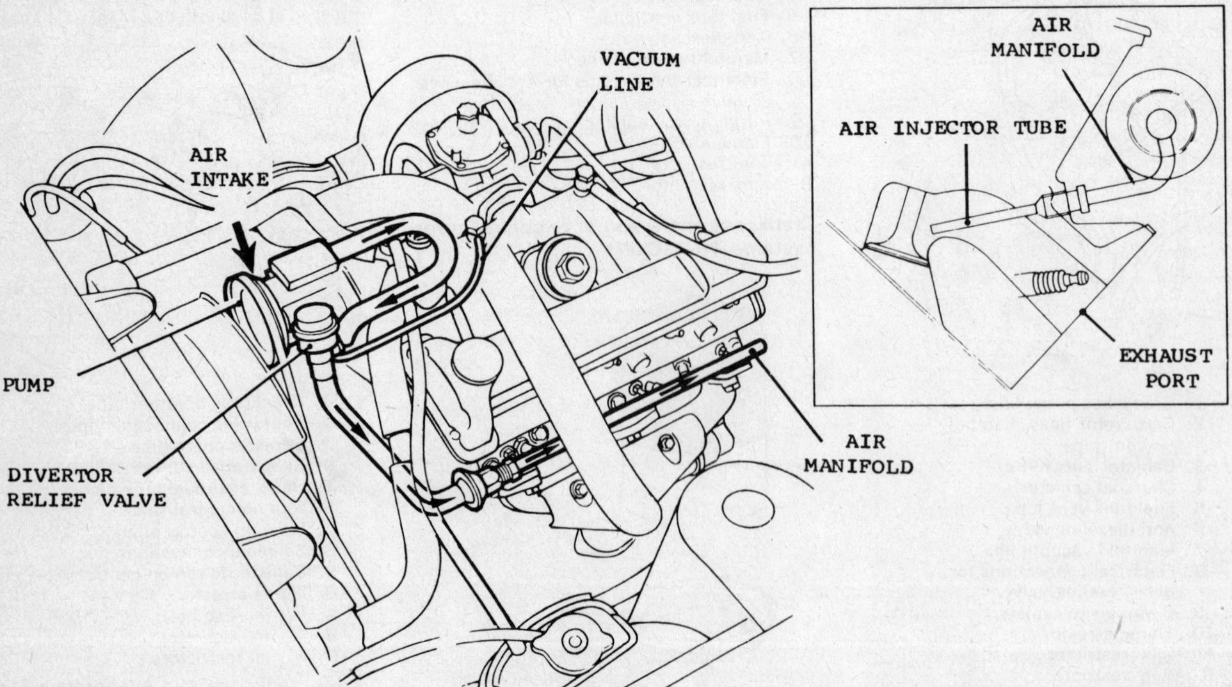

Air injection reactor system—TR-7 (50 states)

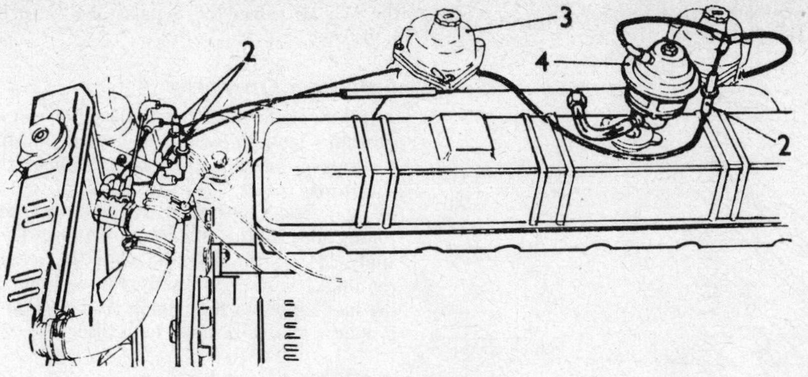

TR-6 EGR system

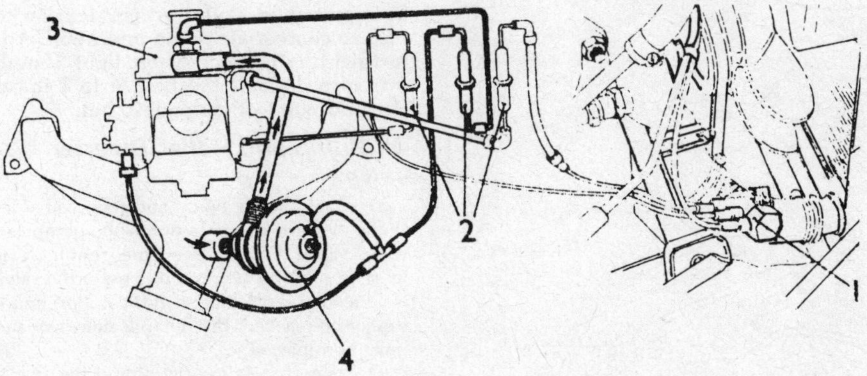

1. Thermostatic vacuum switch
2. Vapor trap
3. Carburetor
4. E.G.R. Valve

Spitfire EGR system

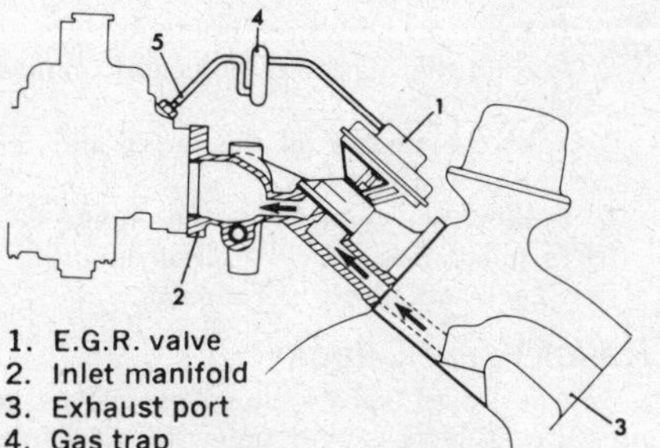

1. E.G.R. valve
2. Inlet manifold
3. Exhaust port
4. Gas trap
5. Vacuum source — throttle edge tapping

Exhaust gas recirculation system—TR-7 (California)

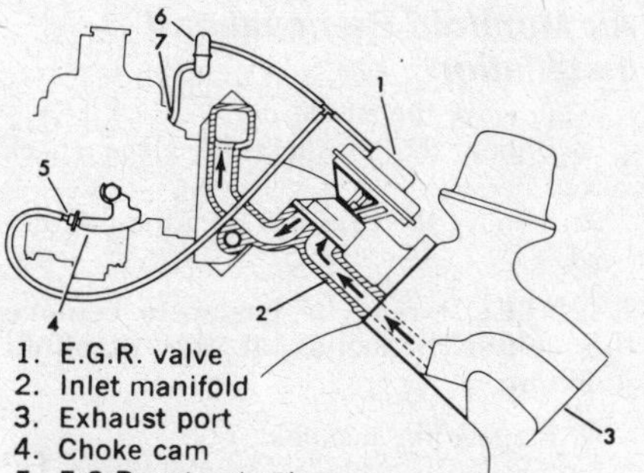

1. E.G.R. valve
2. Inlet manifold
3. Exhaust port
4. Choke cam
5. E.G.R. cut-out valve
6. Gas trap
7. Vacuum source — throttle edge tapping

Exhaust gas recirculation system—TR-7 (49 states)

combination diverter/relief valve is installed to divert air to the atmosphere upon deceleration to prevent backfiring in the system. The diverter/relief valve also vents pump air at high speeds to prevent pump damage.

CATALYTIC CONVERTER

All TR-7 and Spitfire models manufactured for sale in the state of California are equipped with a catalytic converter. The converter is installed in the exhaust system, ahead of the muffler.

ENGINE MODIFICATIONS

Various measures have been taken to limit exhaust emissions resulting from the incomplete combustion of gasoline. Generally speaking, these measures have been designed to provide more efficient combustion of a "leaner" air/fuel mixture. The fuel delivery system has received the most attention in this respect with the use of the Zenith-Stromberg CDSE, CD4VT, and CDSE(V) series carburetors. Features of these carburetors include: a sealed and wired cover to discourage tampering; fixed, non-adjustable fuel jets; a biased metering needle to ensure a consistent air/fuel ratio; free-play built into the throttle linkage permitting a fast idle without disturbing the otherwise closed throttle; a temperature compensator assembly which varies the air supplied to the venturi area to correct the mixture and maintain even running with changing engine temperature; and a throttle bypass valve which is set to open at a predetermined manifold depression to admit air during deceleration.

An intake air temperature control system is used on TR-7 models to maintain the air entering the carburetor(s) at a constant temperature. By blending the engine compartment source air with the exhaust manifold heated air, the intake air is kept at roughly 99° F under all operating conditions. The system is controlled by a temperature sensitive bi-metal strip, which switches intake air sources via a flap valve.

A further reduction of exhaust emissions is gained by the use of ignition distributors that retard the spark during idling and deceleration, on all models. All models utilize distributors with centrifugal advance and vacuum retard.

Other measures taken to reduce the level of exhaust emissions include a modified camshaft that reduces overlap at low engine speeds and a modified cylinder head to promote cleaner burning. Stellite faced exhaust valves are used to maintain effective valve seating over a longer period of time. All models are modified to achieve a lower compression ratio so that regular octane fuels may be used.

Component Testing and Adjustment Temperature Compensator

If the idle speed drops off sharply during extended periods of idling, especially during warm weather, the temperature compensator may be in need of replacement.

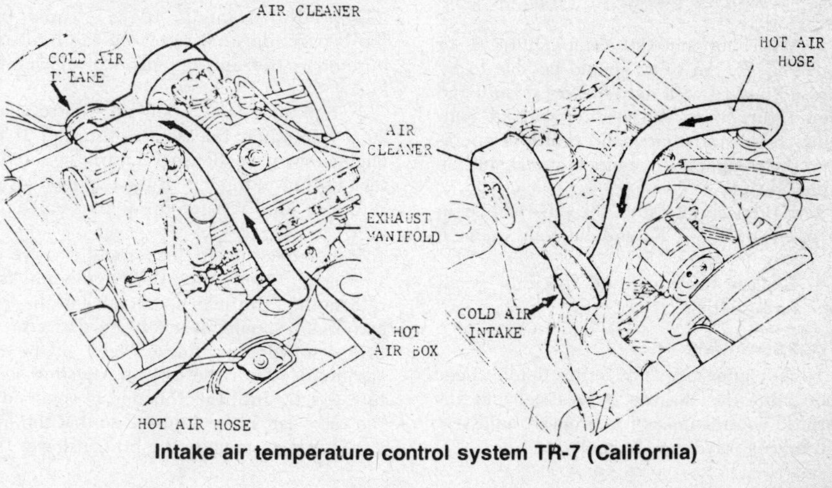

Intake air temperature control system TR-7 (California)

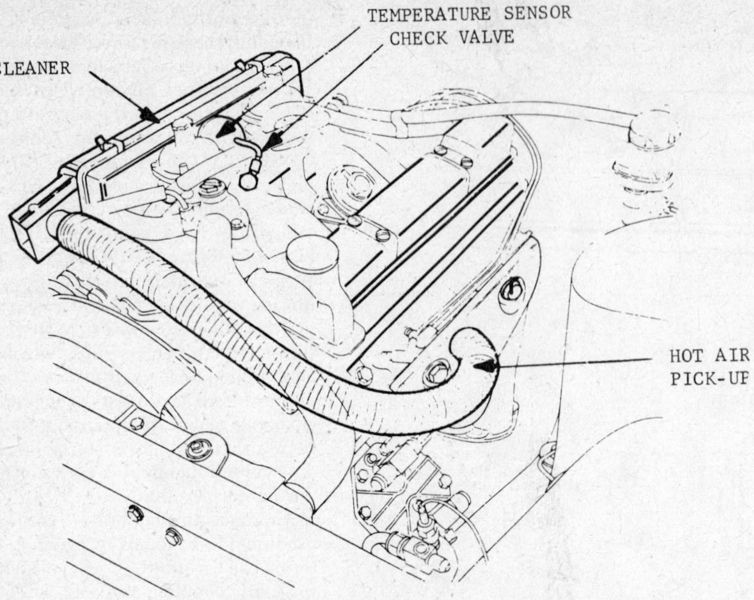

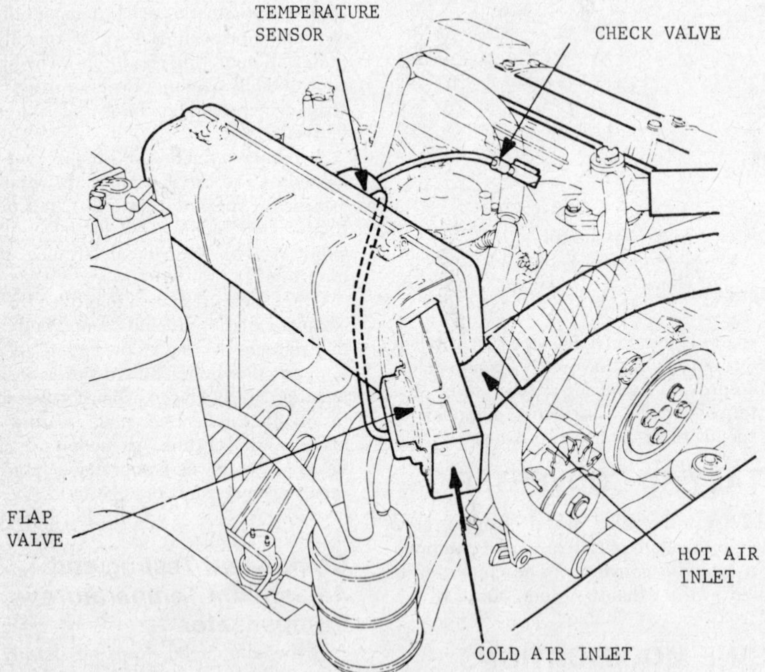

Intake air temperature control system—TR-7 (49 states)

1. Remove the plastic cover from the compensator.
2. With the ambient temperature at or above 85° F, the valve should be able to be pressed inward with light finger pressure and then returned to its position without jamming. If the valve jams and is still in operation, the temperature compensator should be replaced.
3. If properly adjusted, the valve will begin to open at 70-77° F, and be fully open at 85°F.
4. Replace the cover and check its operation during idling.

Bypass Valve

If the engine does not return to idle speed soon after the throttle is released and the throttle control linkage is properly adjusted, the bypass valve may be faulty.

1. If the engine still refuses to return to idle speed when the throttle is released, turn the bypass adjusting screw on the front carburetor to the left and manually lower the idle.
2. Run the engine briefly to approximately 2000 rpm, then release the throttle. If the engine returns to idle speed, turn the screw ½ turn further to the left. If the engine does not return to idle, replace the bypass valve as a unit.
3. Remove the air cleaner and observe the air valves. Briefly race the engine and then release the throttle. The air valve of the front carburetor should normally go down to the bridge slower than the air valve of the rear carburetor. Turn the bypass adjusting screw to the right until this function is obtained. If the valve cannot be adjusted so that the front air valve goes down to the bridge slower than the rear air valve, the bypass valve must be replaced.

Anti-Run On Valve

If the engine continues to diesel or run on after the ignition switch is turned off, the anti-run on valve may be faulty. Check the continuity of the wiring leading to the solenoid and make sure that the electrical connections at the solenoid are tight. Then apply 12V to the solenoid with the engine running. If working properly, this will shut off the fuel supply to the engine. If not working properly, the valve must be replaced.

Air Injection Pump Components

NOTE: The air pump drive belt must be maintained at the proper tension to ensure correct air pump operation. Adjustment is correct when light thumb pressure deflects the belt ¾ to 1 in. at the mid-point of its longest run.

Air Pump and Relief/Diverter Valve

To check the air pump and relief valve install a pressure gauge between the pump and relief valve. With the engine running, air must be relieved at 8.2 to 10.5 psi or the valve is in need of replacement. If the 8.2 psi figure cannot be reached, the pump is defective and must be replaced.

Disconnect the air outlet pipe at the diverter. Make sure that air is dumped on deceleration by opening and closing the throttle quickly while feeling the valve.

Air Pump Removal and Replacement

1. Remove air hose from pump.
2. Loosen the mounting bolts and remove the belt.
3. Take the weight off the pump and remove the mounting bolts.
4. Remove the pump from the engine.
5. Installation is the reversal of removal.
6. Check and adjust belt tension.

Relief Valve Check

1. The relief valve allows excessive air pressure at high engine speed to discharge into the atmosphere.
2. Run the engine at high speeds and check the valve operation.
3. This valve cannot be repaired or adjusted. It must be replaced.

Air Manifold Removal and Installation

1. Remove the air cleaners.
2. Unbolt the manifold from the check valve.
3. Remove the manifold from the cylinder head.

NOTE: It may be easier to remove the center branches at the manifold junction.

4. Remove the manifold.
5. Installation is the reversal of removal.
6. Run engine and check for air leaks.

Check Valve

Remove the valve and blow through it orally. Air should pass from pump to manifold end, but not from the manifold to pump end. Make sure the hose is free of blockage.

Check Valve Removal, Test and Installation

1. Disconnect the air hose from the check valve.
2. Use two open end wrenches to remove the check valve from the air manifold.

NOTE: Do not put excessive force on the air manifold.

3. Blow through the valve orally.
4. Air should pass only through the hose connection end. Should air pass through the valve at the manifold end replace the valve.
5. Installation is the reversal of removal.

EGR Valve

If a sudden loss of idle and full throttle power is noticed when it is known that the ignition, valve and fuel delivery systems are operating properly, the problem may lie in a faulty EGR valve. Warm the engine to operating temperature and make sure that the choke control is fully off. With the engine idling, modulate the throttle and place a finger beneath the EGR valve diaphragm. As the engine rpm changes, you should feel the valve diaphragm moving in conjunction with the changing engine speed. If a vacuum tester is available, make sure that the EGR valve diaphragm retains a vacuum when open. The valve should close immediately when the throttle is closed.

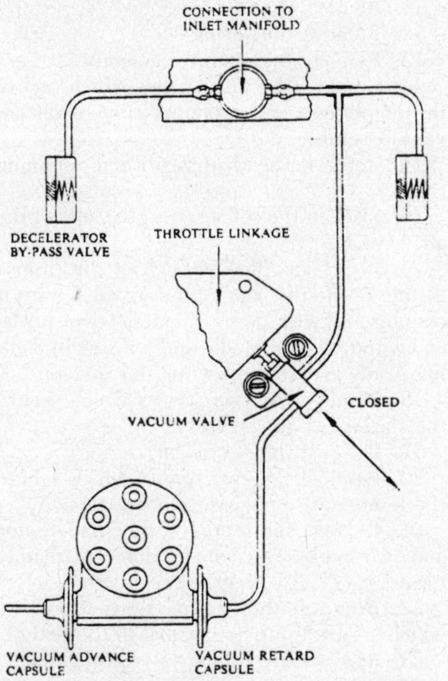

Emission control vacuum circuit—TR-6

COMPONENT REPLACEMENT

Temperature Compensator

1. Remove the compensator.
2. Discard the old rubber seals and replace them with new ones.
3. Install the compensator on the side of the carburetor.
4. Check the operation of the compensator during idle.

Bypass Valve

1. Remove the bypass valve.
2. Discard the old bypass valve-to-carburetor housing gasket.
3. Install a new gasket and bypass valve on the carburetor.
4. Check the operation of the bypass valve.

Anti-Run On Valve

1. Disconnect the electrical connections at the solenoid.
2. Disconnect and plug the evaporative piping from the valve.
3. Lift out the old valve and install the new unit. Connect the vacuum and electrical connections.

FUEL SYSTEM

Fuel Pump

All models are equipped with an AC mechanical diaphragm type fuel pump, located on the left side of the engine, except the TR-8 fuel injected and carburetor model engine.

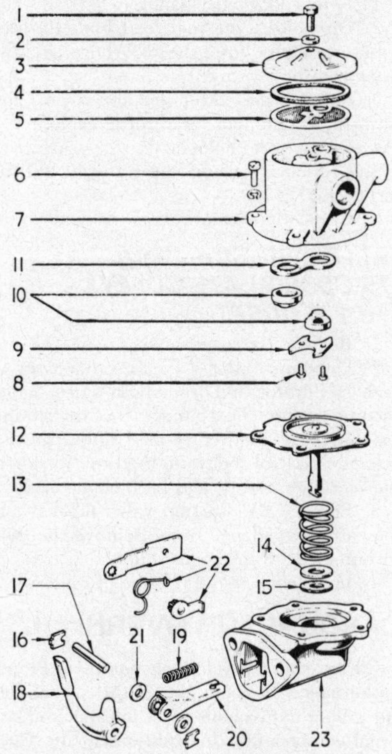

1. Retaining screw
2. Washer
3. Cover
4. Joint
5. Gauze
6. Screw
7. Body
8. Screws
9. Retainer
10. Valves
11. Upper retainer
12. Diaphragm assembly
13. Spring
14. Washer
15. Washer
16. Retainer
17. Spindle
18. Operating lever
19. Return spring
20. Operating fork
21. Distance washer
22. Priming lever assembly
23. Lower body

Spitfire fuel pump assembly

The carbureted engine fuel pump/fuel gauge unit is located in the fuel tank. The fuel injected model is located underneath the car directly in front of the rear.

REMOVAL AND INSTALLATION

Except TR-8

To remove the fuel pump, disconnect the fuel inlet and outlet lines.

Unscrew the attaching nuts and remove the pump.

When installing, make sure that the pump lever (rocker arm) is positioned correctly above its lobe on the cam.

FUEL PUMP CLEANING

Every 12,000 miles the fuel pump should be serviced. This may be accomplished by:

1. Removing the top bolt and domed cover.
2. Removing the gauze filter and thoroughly washing in a safe solvent (denatured alcohol).
3. Cleaning the sediment in the fuel bowl with a small screwdriver. The preferred method for removing loosened sediment is compressed air. Wipe out the interior of the fuel bowl with a soft, clean rag.

CAUTION

The interior of the fuel bowl must be absolutely free of grease or lint.

4. Renewing the cork gasket if cracked or brittle. Fuel pump parts are delicate; use caution. When reassembling, be sure the filter gauze is facing down.

TR-8 Carbureted Engine

1. Disconnect the battery.
2. Fold down the back of the rear seat.
3. Roll luggage compartment carpet toward rear of the car.
4. Roll the left-hand felt strip back.
5. Remove rubber grommet in the floor.
6. Disconnect the electrical plug.
7. Unscrew the pump outlet union.
8. Remove the six screws securing the pump to the tank.
9. Remove the complete assembly.
10. Remove the gasket.
11. Release the pump from the retaining clip.
12. Release the spring clip and pull the pump from the rubber elbow.
13. Remove the terminal cover and disconnect the electrical leads.
14. Installation is the reverse of removal.

NOTE: Electricity is supplied to the fuel pump via the starter solenoid and oil pressure switch. It will only operate when the engine is being started or when there is sufficient oil pressure.

TR-8 Fuel Injected Engine

NOTE: Depressurize the fuel system.

1. Remove the fuel pump ground.
2. Crank the engine for a few seconds.
3. Turn the ignition off and connect the ground.

NOTE: The fuel cut-off inertia switch may be used to disconnect the fuel pump before cranking the engine.

4. Locate the fuel pump beneath the floor in front of the rear axle.
5. Remove the two bolts and nuts on the fuel pump cover. Remove the cover.
6. Remove the fuel line and plug with a ⅜" bolt.
7. Remove the input line and plug with a ⅜" bolt.
8. Remove electrical leads.
9. Remove pump mounting bolts and remove pump from the car.
10. Installation is the reverse of removal.

Electronic Fuel Injection

The electronic fuel injection system is comprised of two parts, a fuel injection system and an electronic control for the fuel system.

Fuel Injection System Components

Fuel is drawn from the tank and pressurized to 2.5 kgf/cm^2 (361bf/in^2) by an electric fuel pump located under the floor. The pump operates only when the ignition and/or the starter is energized. The fuel passes through the filters to a pressure regulator, the spring chamber of which is connected to the intake manifold. This results in the fuel pressure and manifold pressure being held constant, with excess fuel being returned to the tank via an anti-surge pot. A fuel line links the regulator with the injectors. The injectors are programmed to open in banks of four, in unison, twice per cycle. On eight cylinder engines, the two banks operate alternately. The time the injectors are open regulates the amount of fuel to the engine. To assist in cold starts, a cold start injector sprays fuel in the plenum chamber before the fuel is added by the main injectors. The fuel pump is energized independently of the electronic control unit. It is designed not to operate unless the starter motor is energized. The heart of the electronic fuel injection system is the electronic control unit. This unit is sealed, and requires no maintenance. It should not be opened or tampered with. The air flow meter is designed to smooth out air flow fluctuations. The throttle switch provides the electronic control unit with throttle operating conditions. It is located on the plenum chamber. The coolant temperature sensor is located between the cylinder heads. An extra air valve is located in the water passage and registers coolant temperature. Its purpose is to provide additional air to maintain satisfactory idle speed until the engine reaches normal operating temperature. The over-run valve allows air into the manifold via the plenum chamber when vacuum is high and thus maintains combustion during deceleration. This system also has two Lambda sensors in the exhaust system located in front of the catalytic converters. These are designed to pick up the amount of oxygen in the exhaust and thereby regulate the fuel mixture.

FUEL PRESSURE REGULATOR REMOVAL AND INSTALLATION

1. Depressurize the fuel system.

NOTE: See fuel pump removal and installation.

2. Disconnect the battery ground.
3. Remove the bolt in the regulator bracket and pull the regulator and bracket up.

NOTE: Check direction of regulator in the bracket.

4. Clamp inlet and outlet lines on regulator.
5. Remove hose clamps and pull the lines from the regulator.
6. Remove the regulator from the bracket.
7. Installation is the reverse of removal.

Carburetors

REMOVAL AND INSTALLATION

Single Zenith-Stromberg 175 CD4TV

1. Remove the air cleaner.
2. Disconnect the fuel feed line, the distributor vacuum hose, the PCV hose, and the throttle return spring.
3. Remove the cotter pin, clevis pin, and washers. Disconnect the throttle cable.
4. Disconnect choke cable.
5. Remove the flange nuts and lift off the carburetor.
6. Installation is the reverse of removal.

Twin Zenith-Stromberg 175 CDSE(V), 175 CDFEVX and 175 CDSET

1. Remove the air cleaner.
2. Disconnect the vacuum valve lines at each carburetor and from both sides of the vacuum valve. Disconnect the distributor vacuum hose, both fuel feed lines, the accelerator control rod (from the firewall side of the rear carburetor), and both choke cables.
3. Remove the vacuum valve bracket and the carburetor flange nuts. Remove the twin carburetor and linkage assembly.
4. Installation is the reverse of removal.

CARBURETOR OVERHAUL

Carburetors are relatively complex. Proper performance depends upon the cleanliness and proper adjustment of all internal and external components. In addition to the usual adjustments performed at the regular tune-up intervals, it eventually becomes necessary to remove, disassemble, clean, and overhaul the entire carburetor(s), in order to restore its original performance. To overhaul a carburetor, first purchase the proper rebuilding kit. Read the instructions and study the exploded view of the carburetor thoroughly prior to the actual removal and disassembly.

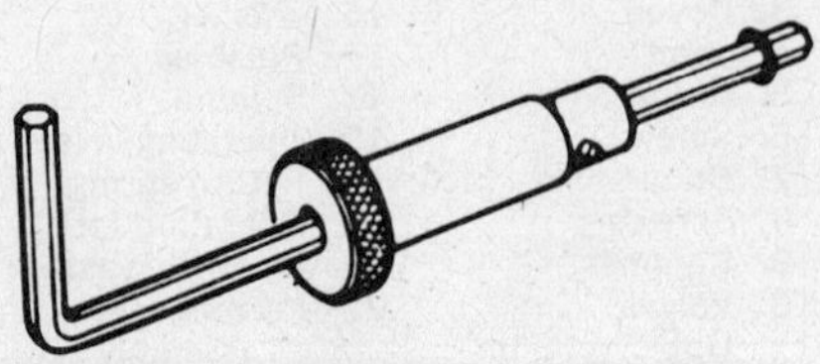

Churchill carburetor adjusting tool no. S.353 for removing and installing spring-loaded metering needles

CARBURETOR DISASSEMBLY AND ASSEMBLY

Zenith-Stromberg 175 CDSE(V) and 175 CDSET

NOTE: Special tool (Churchill) S 353 is needed to remove the spring loaded metering needle from the air valve. If the special tool is not available, an Allen wrench of the proper diameter may be used.

1. Remove the carburetor(s).
2. Remove the damper.
3. Lever out the bottom plug.
4. Drain the carburetor of oil and fuel.
5. Remove the O-ring from its plug.
6. Remove the six screws which secure the float chamber to the body.
7. Remove the float chamber.
8. Remove the float assembly by gently prying the spindle from the clip at each end.
9. Remove the needle valve.
10. Remove the four screws which secure the top cover to the body.
11. Remove the top cover.
12. Remove the spring.
13. Remove the air valve assembly.
14. Remove the four screws which secure the diaphragm and retaining ring to the air valve assembly.
15. Remove the diaphragm and retaining ring.
16. Slacken the set screw in the side of the air valve.
17. Insert an Allen wrench of the proper diameter into the stem of the air valve, turn it counterclockwise approximately two turns, and withdraw the needle and housing by pulling firmly and straight with your fingers.
18. Remove the two screws which secure the starter box to the body.
19. Remove the starter box.
20. Remove the two screws which secure the temperature compensator to the body.
21. Remove the temperature compensator and two rubber washers of different diameters.
22. Remove the three (slotted) screws which secure the bypass valve to the body.
23. Remove the bypass valve and gasket.
24. Remove the two screws which secure the butterfly to the spindle.
25. Turn the spindle return spring.
26. Release the spindle return spring.
27. Withdraw the spindle and spring.
28. Remove the spindle seals from the body by hooking them out with a small screwdriver.
29. Wash all components in clean solvent. Allow them to air dry or use compressed air. Place all components on a clean surface. Discard all seals and gaskets. Scrape all old gasket material from the mating surfaces.
30. Examine the condition of all compo-

nents for wear, paying special attention to the needle and seat and the air valve and diaphragm which should be replaced unless in exceptionally good condition.

31. Use clean compressed air to blow through all ports, needle valve, and starter box.

32. Fit the spindle seals to the body, tapping them gently into position, with the metal casing of the seals flush with the body of the carburetor.

33. Insert the spindle, loading and locating the spindle return spring while doing so.

34. Insert the butterfly with the two protruding spots facing outboard and below the spindle. Tighten the screws.

35. Install the starter box and tighten the screws.

36. Install the bypass valve and gasket and tighten the screws.

37. Install the temperature compensator and tighten the screws.

38. Insert the needle housing assembly into the bottom of the air valve.

39. Install an Allen wrench of the proper diameter, turning it clockwise to engage the threads of the needle valve assembly with the adjusting screw. Then, continue turning until the slot in the needle housing is aligned with the set screw.

40. Tighten the set screw.

NOTE: The set screw does not tighten on the needle housing but locates into the slot. This ensures that during adjustment the needle will remain in its operating position, i.e. biased by a spring in the needle housing toward the air cleaner side of the carburetor.

41. Install the diaphragm, locating the inner tag into the recess in the air valve.

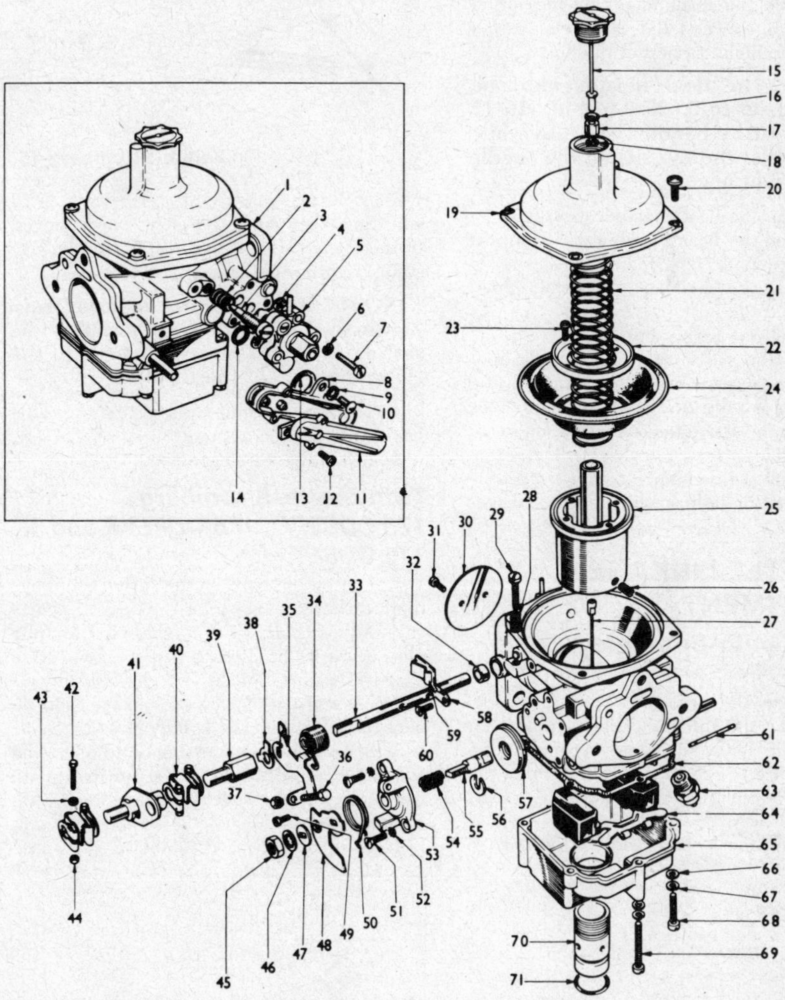

1. Carburetor
2. Spring—idle trimming screw
3. Idle trimming screw
4. Gasket—by-pass valve
5. By-pass valve
6. Lockwasher under (7)
7. Screw—securing (5)
8. Temperature compensator unit
9. Lockwasher under (10)
10. Screw—securing (8)
11. Cover—temperature compensator
12. Screw—securing (11)
13. Seal—on compensator body
14. Seal—inside carburetor
15. Damper rod } damper assembly
16. Washer } damper assembly
17. Spacer sleeve } damper assembly
18. Circlip } damper assembly
19. Cover—air valve
20. Screws—securing (19)
21. Spring—air valve return
22. Ring—diaphragm attachment
23. Screw—securing (22) (24)
24. Diaphragm
25. Air valve
26. Screw—securing (27)
27. Needle assembly
28. Spring—idle adjusting screw
29. Idle adjusting screw
30. Throttle disc
31. Screw—securing (30)
32. Seal—throttle spindle
33. Throttle spindle
34. Spring—throttle return
35. Lever—throttle
36. Screw—fast idle
37. Locknut—securing (36)
38. Lockwasher—retaining (39)
39. Nut—throttle spindle
40. Coupling—throttle spindles
41. Connecting lever assembly
42. Clamping bolt
43. Washer—under (42)
44. Nut—securing (42)

Starter box assembly (45–57):

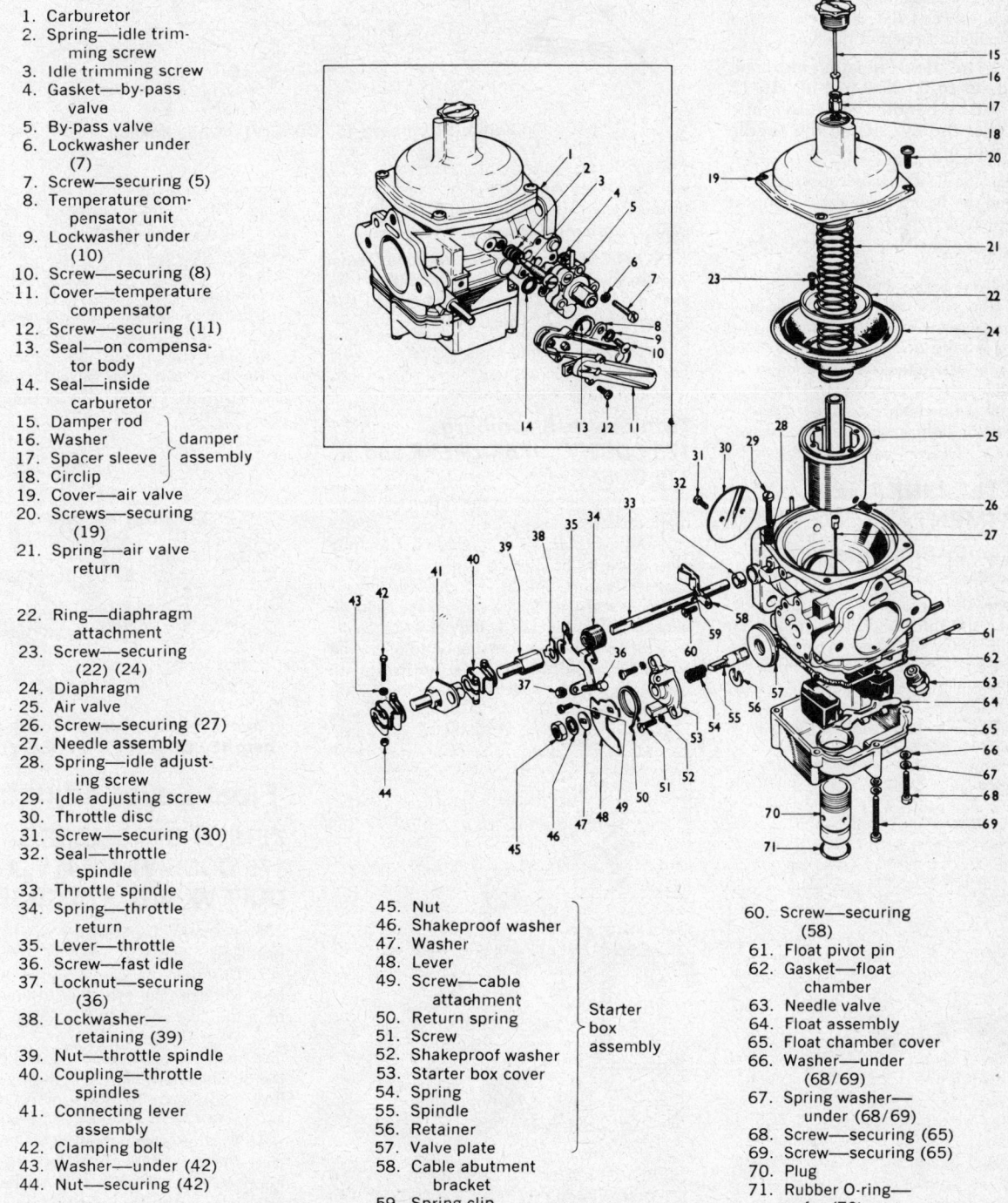

45. Nut
46. Shakeproof washer
47. Washer
48. Lever
49. Screw—cable attachment
50. Return spring
51. Screw
52. Shakeproof washer
53. Starter box cover
54. Spring
55. Spindle
56. Retainer
57. Valve plate

58. Cable abutment bracket
59. Spring clip
60. Screw—securing (58)
61. Float pivot pin
62. Gasket—float chamber
63. Needle valve
64. Float assembly
65. Float chamber cover
66. Washer—under (68/69)
67. Spring washer—under (68/69)
68. Screw—securing (65)
69. Screw—securing (65)
70. Plug
71. Rubber O-ring—for (70)

Zenith-Stromberg 150 CDSE(V), 175 CDSE(V) carburetor assembly

42. Install the diaphragm retaining ring and secure it with four screws.

43. Install the air valve assembly, locating the outer tag and rim of the diaphragm in the complementary recesses in the carburetor body.

44. Install the carburetor top cover with the bulge on the housing neck toward the air intake.

45. Install and evenly tighten the top cover screws.

46. Install the needle valve and sealing washers and tighten them.

47. Install the float assembly by levering the pivot pin gently into the piston.

48. Check the float height by measuring the distance between the carburetor gasket face and the highest point of the floats.

NOTE: The float heights must be equal and set to 0.625-0.672 in. (16-17 mm). Adjust by bending the tabs while ensuring that the tab sits on the needle valve at right angles.

49. Install the float chamber gasket.

50. Install the float chamber and secure it with six screws.

51. Install the O-ring to the bottom plug.

52. Install the bottom plug.

53. Install the carburetor(s).

54. Fill the carburetor damper dashpot with a seasonal grade of engine oil until, using the damper as a dipstick, the threaded plug is 0.25 in. (6 mm) above the dashpot when resistance is felt.

55. Install the damper.

56. Adjust the idle speed, throttle linkage, and choke.

THROTTLE LINKAGE ADJUSTMENT

Single Zenith-Stromberg 175 CD4TV

1. Remove the air cleaner.

2. Loosen the throttle cable nuts. Loosen the fast idle screw to obtain maximum cam clearance. Fully close the throttle. Open the throttle by turning the screw 1½ turns clockwise.

3. Loosen the locknut and set the linkage adjusting screw until the clevis pin is moved to the engine side of the slots in the linkage straps; tighten the locknut.

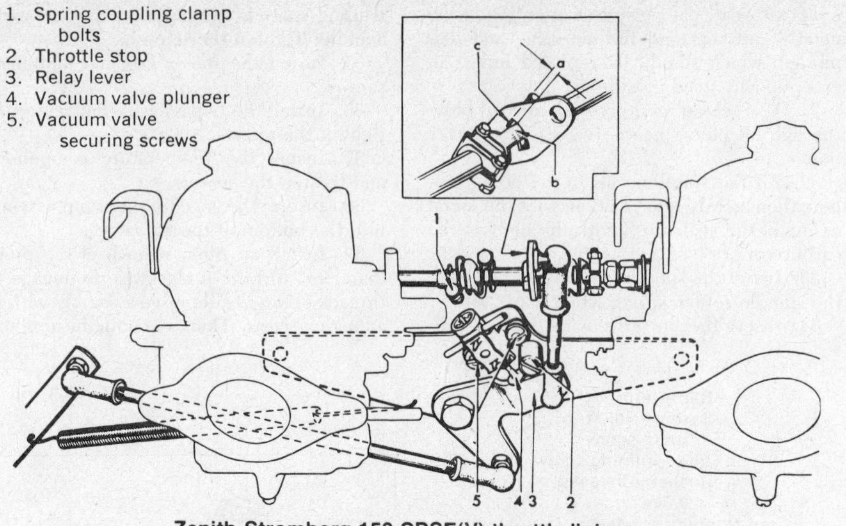

Zenith-Stromberg 150 CDSE(V) throttle linkage

NOTE: It is necessary to have free-play in the linkage to allow for a fast idle setting without interfering with the closed position of the throttle.

4. Tighten the cable nuts so that the cable has no play and is not taut.

5. Install the air cleaner.

Twin Zenith-Stromberg 175 CDSE(V), 175 CDFEVX and 175 CDSET

1. Loosen the bolts on the spring couplings (both carburetor ends).

2. Adjust both idle screws to the fully closed position. Rotate the screws open exactly 1½ turns. Make sure the fast idle adjustment screw is clear of the linkage cam. Be sure the choke linkage is fully closed.

3. Start and warm the engine to operating temperature. Adjust the idle screw to set both carburetors to the specified idle speed. Stop the engine.

4. Place a 3/32 in. drill bit in the space between the lever tongue and the lever slot edge. With the bit in position put pressure on the stop cam and tighten the spring bolts. Remove the bit.

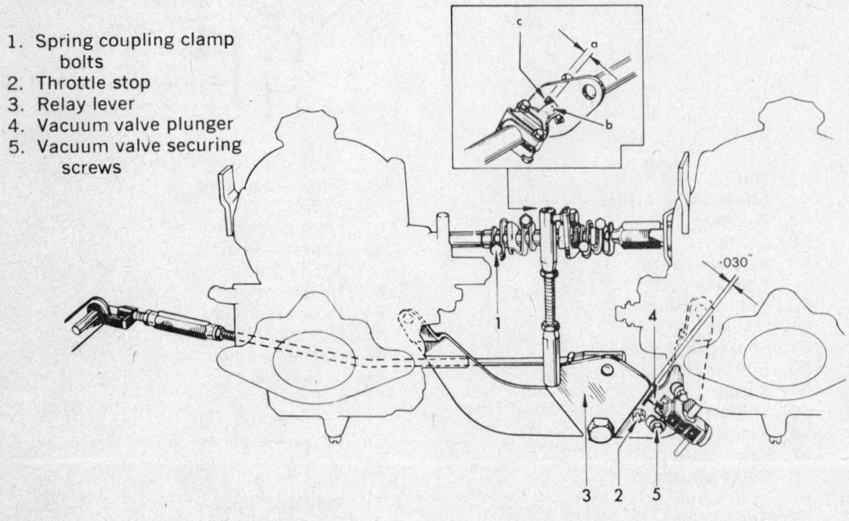

Zenith-Stromberg 175 CDSE(V) throttle linkage

5. Place the relay lever against the stop screw. Loosen the vacuum valve screws. Adjust the valve to 0.030 in. clearance (between the valve and the lever).

6. Move the linkage until the tongue rests in the lever slot. The valve should be fully closed (throttle should be at the point of opening).

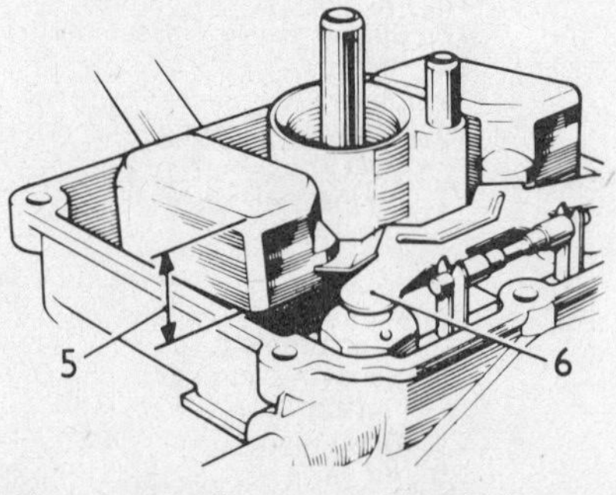

Float level adjustment—Zenith-Stromberg 150 CDSE(V) 175 CDSE(V)

Float Level Adjustment

ZENITH-STROMBERG 175 CDSE(V), CD4TV, 175 CDFEVX AND 175 CDSET

1. Remove the carburetor(s) from the manifold.

2. Unscrew the cap(s) and drain the oil from the damping cylinder(s). Drain the fuel from the float chamber(s).

3. With the carburetor inverted and the float chamber cover removed, make sure that the distance between the highest point of the floats and the carburetor body is 0.625-0.672 in.

4. To adjust, bend the float tang which contacts the needle of the valve assembly. To lower the fuel level, a thin washer may be inserted beneath the needle valve assembly.

5. Install the float chamber cover with a

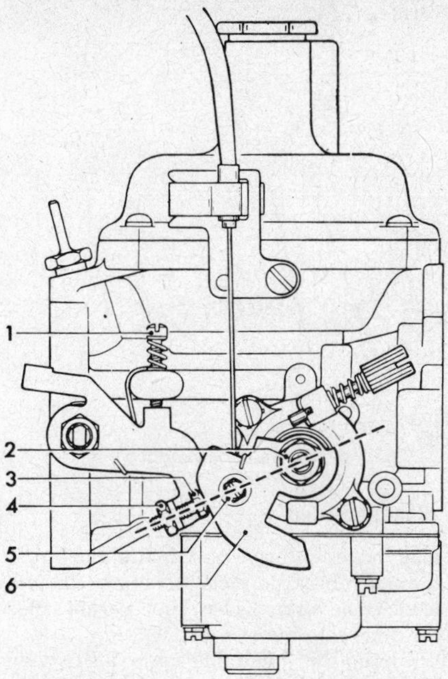

1. Idling screw
2. Starter box
3. Fast-idle screw
4. Locknut
5. Cable trunnion
6. Cam lever

Fast idle adjustment—twin Zenith-Stromberg 150 CDSE(V), 175 CDSE(V)

new gasket. Fill the damping cylinder(s) to ¼ in. from the top with Type A automatic transmission fluid and install the cap(s).

6. Install the carburetor(s).

FAST IDLE AND CHOKE ADJUSTMENT

Twin Zenith-Stromberg 175 CDSE

Make sure that with the choke control knob pushed fully in, the choke lever on each carburetor is against its stop. Adjust the tension of the choke cables as necessary. Pull out the choke control knob until the cable pivot aligns with the center of the fast idle screw and the center of the cam pivot point. Loosen the locknuts and unscrew both idle screws until each is just contacting the cam. Start the engine and, while it is cold (68-86° F), adjust the fast idle screws an equal amount to 1100 rpm. Tighten the locknuts and recheck the fast idle speed.

AUTOMATIC CHOKE

The carburetor models 150 CD4, 175 CDFEVX and 175 CDSET are equipped with automatic chokes to comply with emission control standards. The choke assembly is to be replaced as a unit and the choke mounted carburetor must be removed to accomplish it.

NOTE: The choke assembly is mounted on the front carburetor when dual carburetors are used.

Adjustment

1. Remove the choke cover to expose the fast idle cam.
2. Rotate the fast idle cam high step to position it opposite the fast idle pin.
3. Adjust the fast idle screw until the clearance between the cam step and the fast idle pin is 0.020 inch.
4. Install the choke cover and align the scribed mark of the cover with the scribed mark on the choke housing and tighten the housing/cover screws.

Centering the Jet

The air valve should move freely by raising and allowing the valve to fall. Slow action may indicate the need for cleaning by removing and cleaning both the bore and the air valve with solvent.

If the jet is not centered it may be corrected as follows:

1. Raise the air valve and tighten the jet bushing screw. Tighten the orifice adjusting screw until it is just above the bridge.
2. Loosen the jet bushing screw to release the orifice bushing. Permit the air valve to drop. This will align the bushing. Tighten the bushing screw to secure the bushing and recheck. Repeat until the piston falls freely.
3. Move the adjusting screw until it barely touches the air valve underside when resting on the bridge. Three turns from this position (loose) gives a reasonable figure to use when synchronizing dual carburetors.

MANUAL TRANSMISSION

REMOVAL AND INSTALLATION

Spitfire

1. Raise the vehicle and remove the gear shift knob, overdrive switch and leads, transmission cover, and driveshaft cover plate.
2. Disconnect the driveshaft and speedometer cable.
3. Remove the clutch slave cylinder and drain the transmission.
4. Support the engine, disconnect the exhaust pipe from the support on the transmission and remove the transmission rear mount nuts and washers.
5. Remove the engine restraint cable, bell housing bolts, starter, back-up light, overdrive and seat belt warning leads.
6. Remove the transmission crossmember, remaining bell housing bolts and remove the transmission.
7. Installation is the reverse of removal.

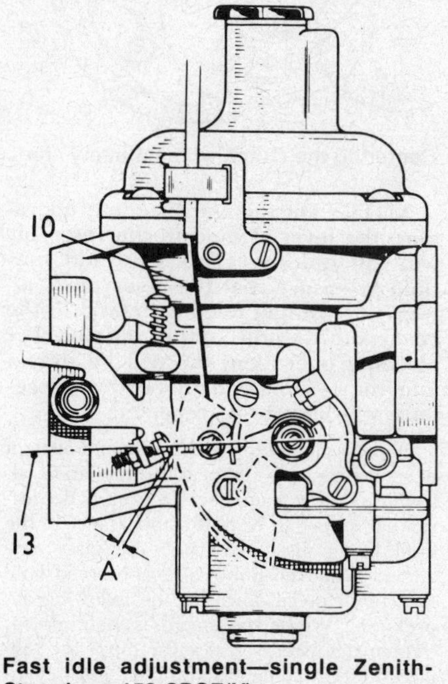

Fast idle adjustment—single Zenith-Stromberg 150 CDSE(V)

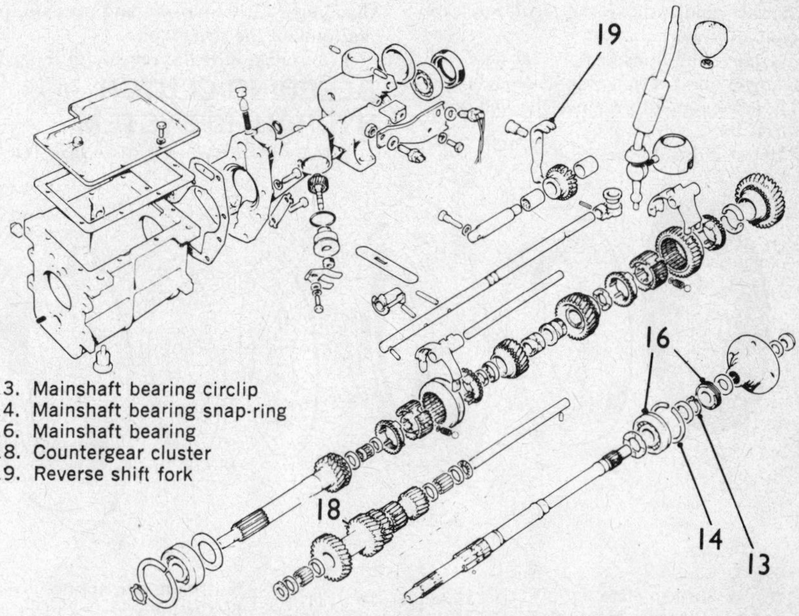

13. Mainshaft bearing circlip
14. Mainshaft bearing snap-ring
16. Mainshaft bearing
18. Countergear cluster
19. Reverse shift fork

Spitfire and TR-7 transmission

TR-6

The transmission is removed, with the engine remaining in position.

1. Disconnect the battery, drain the transmission, and remove the seat cushions and carpets.
2. Disconnect the cables from the heater control switch, the control cable from the heater unit, and the lower left control cable from the center control panel. Remove the dashboard support. Remove the headlight dimmer switch, leaving the electrical connections attached.
3. Remove the center floor cover.
4. Remove the driveshaft.
5. Remove the clutch slave cylinder, allowing it to hang by its flexible hose. Remove the clutch cover plate from the lower part of the clutch housing. Disconnect the speedometer cable and the overdrive connections (if installed).
6. With the block of wood protecting the oil pan, use a jack to support the weight of the engine and transmission. The jack should be placed as far as possible toward the rear of the oil pan.
7. Remove the exhaust pipe bracket next to the hand brake, then detach the rear mounting from the transmission and crossmember.
8. Raise the engine and transmission. Remove the crossmember by sliding it forward.
9. Unbolt the clutch housing flange from the engine.
10. Remove the transmission rearward.
11. Installation is the reverse of removal.

TR-7 and TR-8

1. Remove the shift lever, driveshaft, exhaust pipe-to-bell housing bracket, exhaust pipe-to-rear axle supports, speedometer cable, reverse switch leads, restraint cable, transmission-to-crossmember tie-bar, and support the transmission on a jack.
2. Loosen the engine stabilizer-to-frame nut (lower), and remove the stabilizer from the engine support bracket.
3. Remove the transmission rear mount.
4. Lower the transmission and engine assembly just enough to remove the bell housing top bolts.
5. Remove the starter.

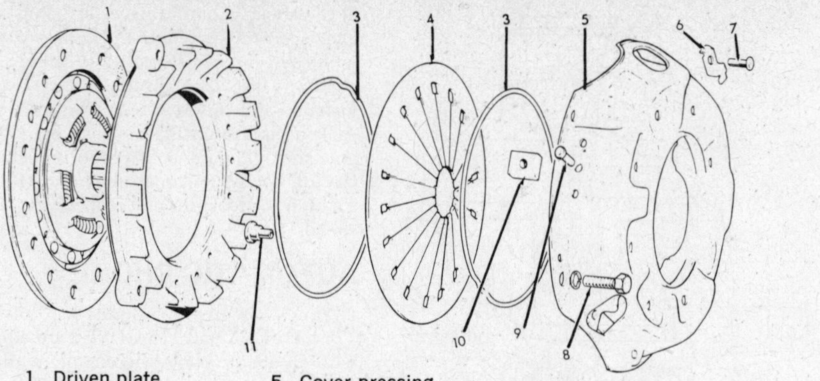

1. Driven plate
2. Pressure plate
3. Fulcrum ring
4. Diaphragm spring
5. Cover pressing
6. Retractor clip
7. Rivet
8. Setscrew
9. Rivet
10. Balance weight
11. Rivet

Borg and Beck clutch disassembled

6. Disconnect the wiring harness and slave cylinder pipe from the bell housing.
7. Unbolt and remove the transmission/bell housing assembly.
8. Installation is the reverse of removal. Adjust the restraint cable as follows:
   a. Fully slack off the front nut at the rear end of the cable.
   b. Tighten the rear nut.
   c. Slack off the rear nut, hold the cable by hand and position the rear nut so that a $^1/_{32}$-$^1/_{16}$'' clearance exists between the nut and the cable bracket.
   d. Tighten the front nut.

CLUTCH

REMOVAL AND INSTALLATION

1. Remove the transmission.
2. In rotation, progressively loosen the bolts which retain the clutch assembly to the flywheel.
3. Lift off the clutch cover assembly (cover, diaphragm, driving plate, and pressure plate) and pull off the driven plate.
4. Installation is the reverse of removal.

BLEEDING CLUTCH HYDRAULIC SYSTEM

If the clutch does not disengage fully, air may have entered the hydraulic system through a break in the system or because the level in the reservoir has fallen too low. Bleed the system to remove the air.

Top up the clutch fluid reservoir to within ¼ in. of the FULL level. Clean the bleed nipple on the slave cylinder and attach to it a short length of tubing. Allow the tubing to hang so that its end is below the fluid level in a clean glass container partially filled with hydraulic fluid. Unscrew the bleed nipple one complete turn.

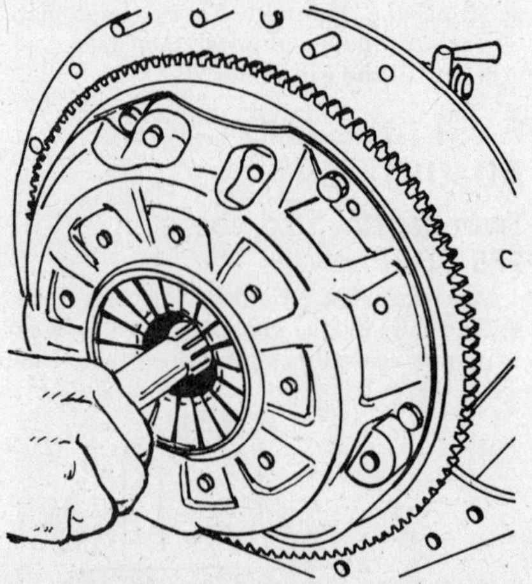

Centering the clutch with a dummy shaft

NOTE: During the bleeding operation, the level of fluid in the reservoir will fall quickly. Constantly add new fluid to ensure that the reservoir is always at least half filled with fluid. If the reservoir should empty during the bleeding operation, air will be drawn into the system and the entire procedure will have to be repeated.

Depress the clutch pedal fully and allow it to return normally. Repeat this operation, allowing a slight pause between each depression of the pedal. Note the appearance of the fluid being discharged into the glass container. When no bubbles are observed hold the clutch pedal down on the following depression. While the pedal is held down, tighten the bleed screw and remove the tubing from the nipple. Top up the master cylinder reservoir with hydraulic fluid.

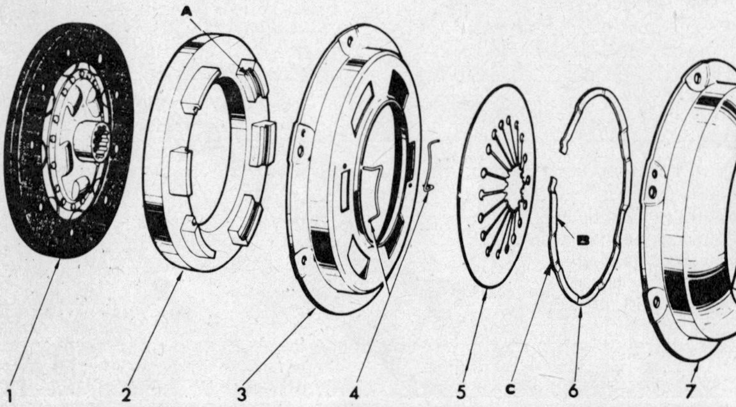

1. Driven plate
2. Pressure plate
3. Inner cover
4. Spring clips
5. Diaphragm spring
6. Circlip
7. Outer cover

Laycock clutch disassembled

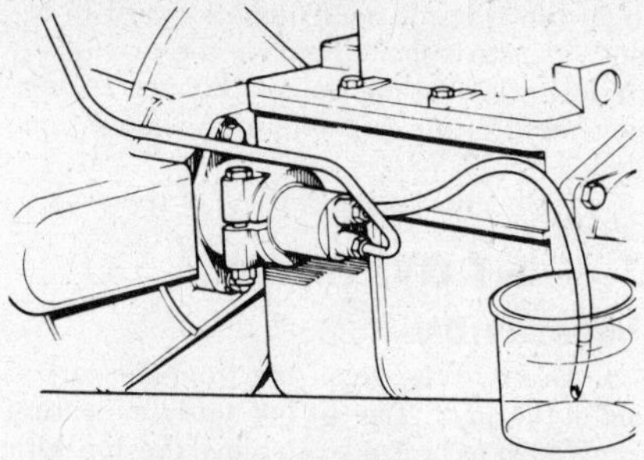

Clutch hydraulic system bleeding—Spitfire shown

Clutch Master Cylinder

REMOVAL AND INSTALLATION

1. Drain the fluid from the master cylinder or pump the fluid from the bleeder nipple on the slave cylinder.
2. Disconnect the fluid pipe from the master cylinder outlet and plug the ends.
3. Pull back the protective dust cover and remove the cotter pin, washer, and clevis pin which retain the master cylinder pushrod to the top of the pedal.
4. Remove the master cylinder from the firewall.
5. Installation is the reverse of removal. Bleed the system.

OVERHAUL

1. Remove the master cylinder as outlined under "Clutch Master Cylinder Removal and Installation."
2. Pull back the rubber dust cover. Lightly press in the pushrod and, with a pair of needle pliers, remove the circlip and withdraw the pushrod and washer.
3. Connect a compressed air line to the outlet connection and, using light pressure, force out the internal parts.
4. Lift the leaf on the spring retainer and pull it free of the plunger.
5. Compress the return spring and slide the valve stem sideways through the larger offset hole of the retainer. Remove the spring, spacer, and spring washer from the valve shank.
6. Using fingers only, remove the two rubber seals and discard them. Replace with new seals. Clean all parts in methylated alcohol or in clean hydraulic fluid meeting SAE 70 R3 specifications. Lay all metal parts out to dry on a clean sheet of paper. Check the cylinder bore for pitting or scoring.
7. Reverse the above procedure to install, taking care to dip each internal part in hydraulic fluid prior to installation. Make sure that the rubber seals are installed with the lips facing the bore.

Clutch Slave Cylinder

REMOVAL AND INSTALLATION

1. Drain the clutch hydraulic system by opening the slave cylinder bleeder nipple ½ turn and pumping on the clutch pedal.
2. Disconnect the hydraulic pipe.
3. Remove the nuts and bolts which retain the cylinder to its bracket on the bellhousing.
4. Remove the dust cover and pull the cylinder forward to clear it from the pushrod. Leave the pushrod attached to the operating shaft lever.
5. Installation is the reverse of removal. Bleed the system.

OVERHAUL

1. Remove the slave cylinder as outlined under "Slave Cylinder Removal and Installation".
2. Remove the rubber dust cover. Depress the piston and, using a pair of needle nose pliers, remove the circlip from the bore.
3. If the internal parts cannot be shaken out, use low pressure compressed air injected into the inlet port to force them out.
4. Remove and discard the rubber seal. Remove the return spring.
5. Clean all metal parts in methylated alcohol or in clean hydraulic fluid meeting SAE 70 R3 specifications. Lay out the parts to dry on a clean sheet of paper. Replace the cylinder body if its bore is pitted or scored. Lubricate the bore and dip each internal part in clean hydraulic fluid.
6. To assemble, insert the internal parts into the cylinder bore, using a new rubber seal. Be careful not to bend back the lips of the seal when installing in the bore. Retain the parts in the bore with the circlip.
7. Install the cylinder as outlined under "Slave Cylinder Removal and Installation".

AUTOMATIC TRANSMISSION

A Borg-Warner, three speed automatic transmission is used in the TR-7 models as an option. A torque converter is used to couple the transmission to the engine.

REMOVAL AND INSTALLATION

1. Place the selector lever in the neutral position.
2. Disconnect the downshift cable from the accelerator linkage.
3. Raise the vehicle and support safely.
4. Remove the front exhaust pipe.
5. Disconnect the transmission dipstick tube from the oil pan and drain the transmission fluid.
6. Disconnect the selector lever breather hose, neutral start switch wire connections and disconnect the speedometer cable.
7. Disconnect the oil cooler lines at the transmission.
8. Remove the driveshaft.
9. Remove the torque converter-to-engine drive plate bolts.
10. Support the engine and transmission with a jack.
11. Remove the rear engine mount center bolt, sway bar, rear cross member, heat shield, radiator lower mounting and the exhaust support bracket.
12. Lower the engine/transmission unit and remove the bellhousing and starter bolts.

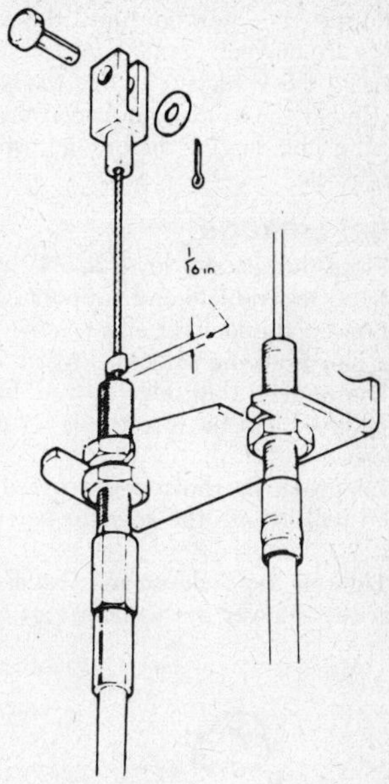

Downshift cable adjustment—Automatic Transmission

13. While supporting the engine, move the transmission rearward and down.

NOTE: While lowering the transmission, clear all wires and pipes from the downward path.

14. Installation is the reverse of removal.

ADJUSTMENTS

Downshift Cable

1. Adjust the idle speed to 750 rpm.
2. Loosen the cable locknut at the carburetor linkage.
3. Adjust the outer cable to $^1/_{16}$ inch from the stop.
4. Remove the transmission oil pan.
5. Be sure the downshift cam is in the idle mode position.
6. With the aid of a helper, fully depress the throttle cable and be sure that the downshift cam is in the kickdown position.
7. If necessary, adjust the outer cable until the idling and kickdown position can be obtained on the downshift cam.
8. Install the transmission oil pan and install the proper level of fluid.

Control Pressure

1. Raise the vehicle and support safely.
2. Remove the pressure line plug from the rear of the transmission and connect a 0-300 psi oil pressure gauge to the pressure line outlet.
3. Lower the vehicle, lock the brakes (both hand and foot), chock the wheels, start the engine and place the selector lever in the "D" position.
4. With the engine idling at 750 rpm, observe the pressure gauge reading.
5. The following is an acceptable reading: 750 rpm—60 to 75 psi 1000 rpm—Pressure increase of 15 to 20 psi.
6. If the pressure increase is less than 15 psi, increase the length of the throttle cable.
7. If the pressure increase is more than 20 psi, decrease the length of the throttle cable.

8. Repeat the operation until the pressure readings are correct.

9. Raise the vehicle, remove the pressure gauge, lower the vehicle and road test. Caution: Stop the engine before adjusting the throttle cable.

Manual Linkage

1. Place the selector lever in "N" position.
2. Raise the vehicle and support safely.
3. Loosen the locknut and remove the retaining clip from the selector lever.
4. Disconnect the selector rod from the selector lever and be sure the lever is in the "N" position.
5. Lengthen or shorten the rod until the rod end will fit into the selector lever with a free fit.
6. Tighten the locknut and install the retaining clip. Lower the vehicle.

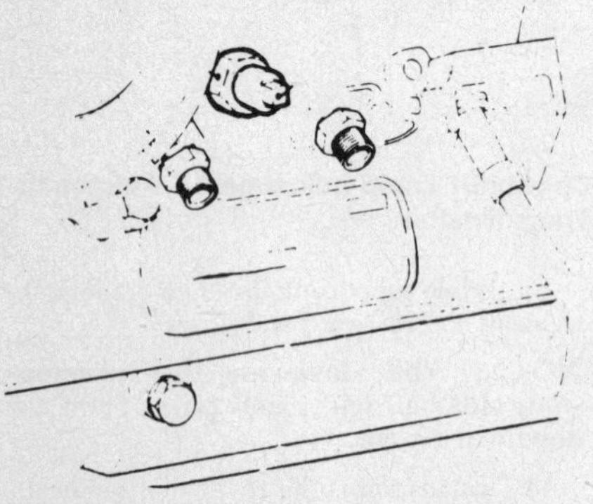

Front transmission band adjusting screw

Front and Rear Bands

1. Raise the vehicle and support safely.
2. Loosen the adjusting screw locknuts.
3. Tighten the adjusting screws to 36 in/lbs and back off exactly ¾ turn.
4. Tighten the locknut to 22 ft/lbs and lower the vehicle.

Stall Test

The stall test is used to determine the satisfactory operation of the torque converter, transmission and/or engine.

1. Check the condition of the engine. Tune if necessary. Bring the engine-transmission to normal operating temperature.
2. Apply the brakes, chock the wheels, install a tachometer on the engine and place the instrument in a place where it can be seen by the operator.
3. Place the selector lever in "1" or "R"

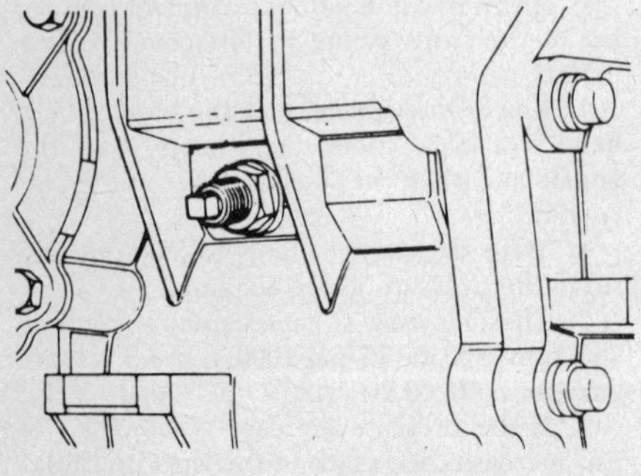

Rear transmission band adjusting screw

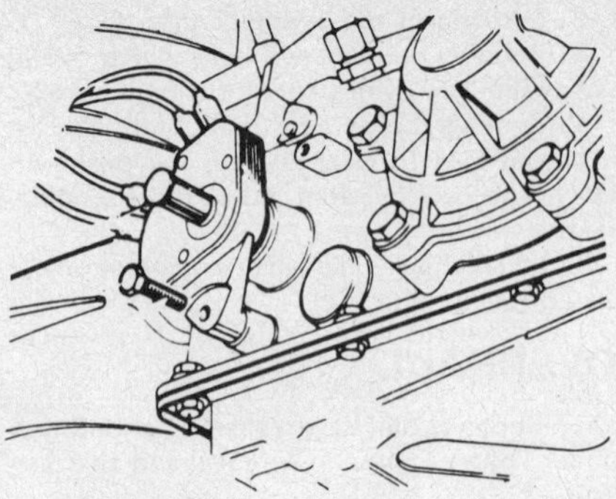

Neutral start/back-up lamp switch

position and depress the accelerator to the kickdown position.

4. Note the rpm reading on the tachometer which should be at 2200 rpm.
5. If the reading is below 1400 rpm, the converter stator is possibly slipping.
6. If the reading is down to 1600 rpm, the engine is not developing full power.
7. If the reading is over 2400 rpm, internal transmission slippage is indicated.

CAUTION

Do not hold the stall test for a longer period than 10 seconds. Place the transmission selector in the neutral position and increase the engine speed to assist in cooling the transmission fluid.

Neutral Start Switch

The neutral start switch is located on the transmission gear selector shaft and is bolted to the transmission case with no adjustment provisions provided. The switch must be replaced if a malfunction occurs.

DRIVE AXLE

Driveshaft and U-Joints

REMOVAL AND INSTALLATION

1. Remove the dashboard supports and transmission cover.
2. Remove the attaching nuts. Gently angle the transmission/engine forward to remove the driveshaft. Remove the driveshaft. Models with sliding splines do not require movement of the engine/transmission assembly.
3. Installation is the reverse of removal.

U-JOINT OVERHAUL

Disassembly

1. Remove the snap-ring from the forked end of the shaft. Tap the lug until the bearing cup is seen to protrude. Remove the cup with pliers.
2. Repeat the operation on the reverse side.
3. Remove the flange.
4. Remove all remaining snap-rings. Rest the shaft on a block and gently tap out the remaining components.

Assembly

1. Place sealing compound on the shoulders of the new spider journals.
2. Fit oil seal retainers over the trunnions with a tubular drift. Fit the oil seals.
3. Place the trunnion into the bearing holes and fit the bearing caps and snap-rings. Make sure they are properly seated.
4. Fit the spider with the lubrication nipple around the driveshaft. Place the other trunnion through the bearing holes in the forked end of the driveshaft and fit the cups and snap-rings.
5. Repeat the procedure on the second universal joint.

CAUTION

Do not disassemble the sliding yoke for any reason.

Outer Axle Shaft and Hub Assembly

REMOVAL AND INSTALLATION

All Models (Except TR-7 and TR-8)

1. Remove the wheel and backing plate. Remove the brake hose, attaching bracket, and brake line. Disconnect the handbrake from the attaching lever.
2. Relieve the shock absorber of load.
3. Release the radius arm.

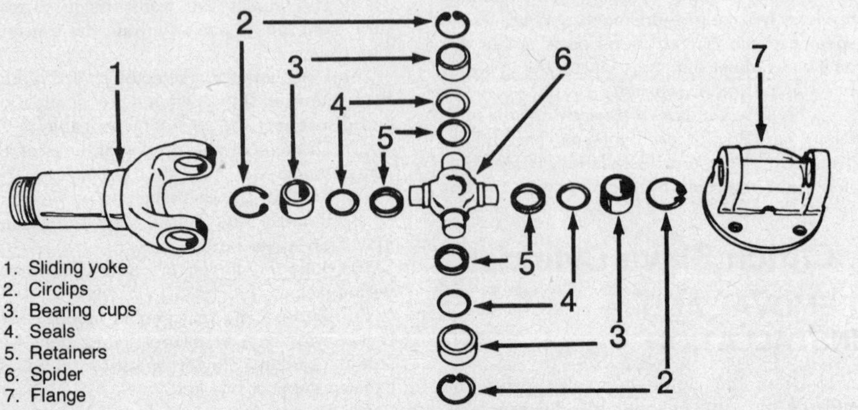

1. Sliding yoke
2. Circlips
3. Bearing cups
4. Seals
5. Retainers
6. Spider
7. Flange

Universal joint disassembled

4. Remove the universal joint coupling bolts.
5. Remove the shock absorber and jack.
6. Remove the spring eye nuts. The hub and axle shafts are now free.
7. Reinstall the vertical link to the spring attaching eye; leave the nut loose.
8. Install the shock absorber and radius arm.
9. Connect the inner and outer axle shafts. Place a load of 300 lbs in the front seats. Tighten the securing nut to the vertical link.
10. Further installation is the reverse of removal.

Inner Axle Shaft

REMOVAL AND INSTALLATION

All Models (Except TR-7 and TR-8)

1. Remove the outer axle shaft.
2. Drain the rear axle.
3. Using a $^{3}/_{16}$ in. Allen wrench, remove the Allen screws from the differential housing and remove the inner axle shaft.
4. Installation is the reverse of removal.

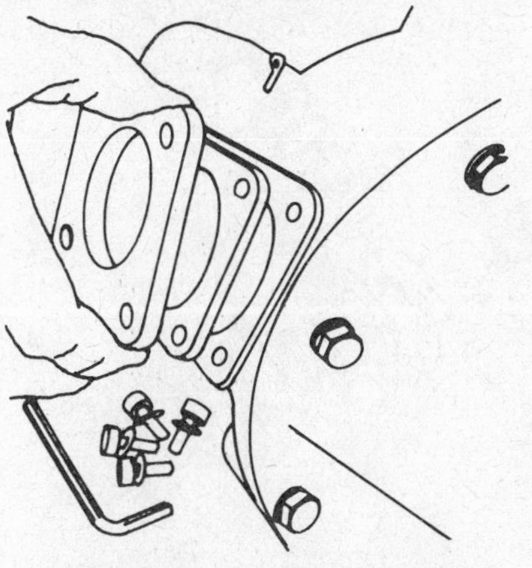

Removing the inner axle shaft

Halfshaft

REMOVAL AND INSTALLATION

TR-7 and TR-8

1. Remove the hub-to-halfshaft nut, brake drum, handbrake cable, brake halfshaft and bearing.
2. Installation is the reverse of removal. Torque the hub nut to 100-110 ft/lbs.

DIFFERENTIAL

REMOVAL AND INSTALLATION

All Models (Except TR-7)

1. Drain the rear axle. Remove the wheels and backing plate.

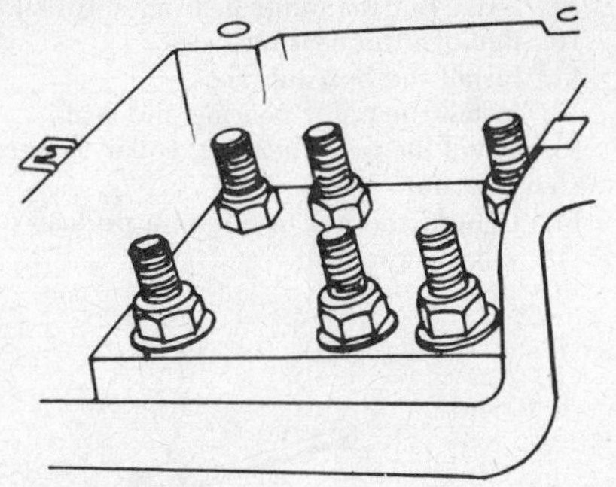

Luggage compartment floor panel removed showing rear leaf spring mounting bolts—Spitfire

2. Support the vertical links and remove the shock absorbers.
3. Remove the resonator and tailpipe.
4. Disconnect the driveshaft.
5. Remove the luggage compartment floor panel; remove the spring access plate. Remove the rear spring attachments.
6. Support the weight of the differential and cautiously release the front mounts.
7. Installation is the reverse of removal.

TR-7 and TR-8

1. Remove the wheels, hub-to-halfshaft nuts, brake drums, handbrake cables, brake pipes, back plate bolts, and halfshafts.
2. Disconnect the driveshaft from the pinion flange.
3. Remove the differential-to-axle nuts and spring washers.
4. Ease the differential out of the axles.
5. Reverse the above to install. Torque the hub nuts to 100-110 ft/lbs.

OVERHAUL

NOTE: Unless one has the experience and the special factory tools, especially the special spreader tool used by Triumph to spread the differential housing sufficiently to free the differential components, the overhaul of the differential assembly should not be attempted. The following specifications, torque figures, and tooth contact conditions are included for reference purposes.

DIFFERENTIAL OVERHAUL

Spitfire and TR-7

1. Remove the differential.
2. Clamp the differential in a vise. Mark and remove the bearing caps. Remove the differential from the housing.
3. Press off the bearings and unbolt and remove the ring gear.
4. Drive out the pinion pin. Remove the side gears.
5. Remove the pinion flange cap and while holding the flange, remove the pinion shaft nut. Remove the flange.
6. Tap out the pinion assembly, and drive out the outer bearing and oil seal.
7. Drive out both bearing races.
8. Install the carrier bearings in the differential with the tapered ends toward the shafts.
9. Lubricate the bearings and install the carrier in the case.
10. Rotate the unit to seat the bearings and push the differential to one side of the case.
11. Install a dial indicator on the ring gear mounting flange and check and run-out. It should not exceed 0.003″.
12. Slide the differential sideways to butt the bearing seats in either direction. Measure the lateral free-play.
13. Remove the differential and bearings. Lubricate and install the side gears.
14. Install the pinion pin. Check and record end-play.
15. Remove the pinion pin, rotate the sun gears to bring the planet gears clear of the case.
16. Lubricate the selected planet thrust washers and slide the thrust washers and planets into position. Install the pinion pin and again check end-play. Zero backlash is required.
17. Install the ring gear assembly. Apply Loctite, or its equivalent, to the ring gear bolts.
18. Install the pinion inner bearing, spacer, washer and nut.
19. Tighten the nut gradually to obtain a 15-18 in/lbs pre-load.
20. Using a dial indicator, check the measurements on the two bearing bores; add the measurements and divide by two. Twenty-two pinion head washers are available in sizes from 0.075-0.096 in.
21. Install the inner bearing. Install the pinion, spacer and bearing in the case.
22. Install a new spacer, oil seal, flange, washer and nut.
23. Gradually tighten the nut checking the bearing preload. Rotate the flange to seat the bearings and check the rotating torque. Tighten the nut to obtain a 13-20 in/lbs reading.
24. Install the ring gear assembly into the case. Mesh the ring and pinion assembly. Move the ring and pinion fully in the opposite direction and check the measurement on the gauge. Check the mesh clearance.
25. To set the backlash, subtract the required backlash (0.005) from the recorded mesh clearance above. To this, add the required bearing preload divided by two.
26. To determine the shims required for ring gear side carrier bearing, subtract the result of Step 25 from the figure recorded in Step 12. To that, add the carrier bearing preload divided by two.
27. Install the necessary carrier bearing shims.
28. Install a spreading tool in the case and carefully stretch the case enough to permit the differential assembly to be installed.
29. Remove the spreader, install the bearing caps, bolts and spring washers.

TR-6

1. Remove ring gear and differential from case.
2. Remove the ring gear.
3. Install the differential in the case and check the flange run-out. This should not exceed 0.003 in.
4. Remove the differential from the case, and press off the bearings.

5. Remove the cross-shaft locking pin and the cross-shaft.
6. Remove the planet and sun gears.
7. Remove the pinion shaft nut and the flange.
8. Remove the front mounting bracket and drive out the pinion shaft, inner bearing, spacer and shim pack.
9. Drive out the outer bearing and seal.
10. Remove the bearing races.
11. Install the bearing races.
12. Install the outer bearing and seal.
13. Install the inner bearing, collar, flange, washer and nut.
14. Tighten the nut to obtain a preload of 15-18 in/lbs of preload.
15. Install a pinion gauge and dummy bearing in the case. Check the free-play to determine necessary shim thickness.
16. Install the mounting flange.
17. Install the pinion shaft and necessary shims.
18. Install the spacer flange washer and nut. Carefully tighten the nut while checking

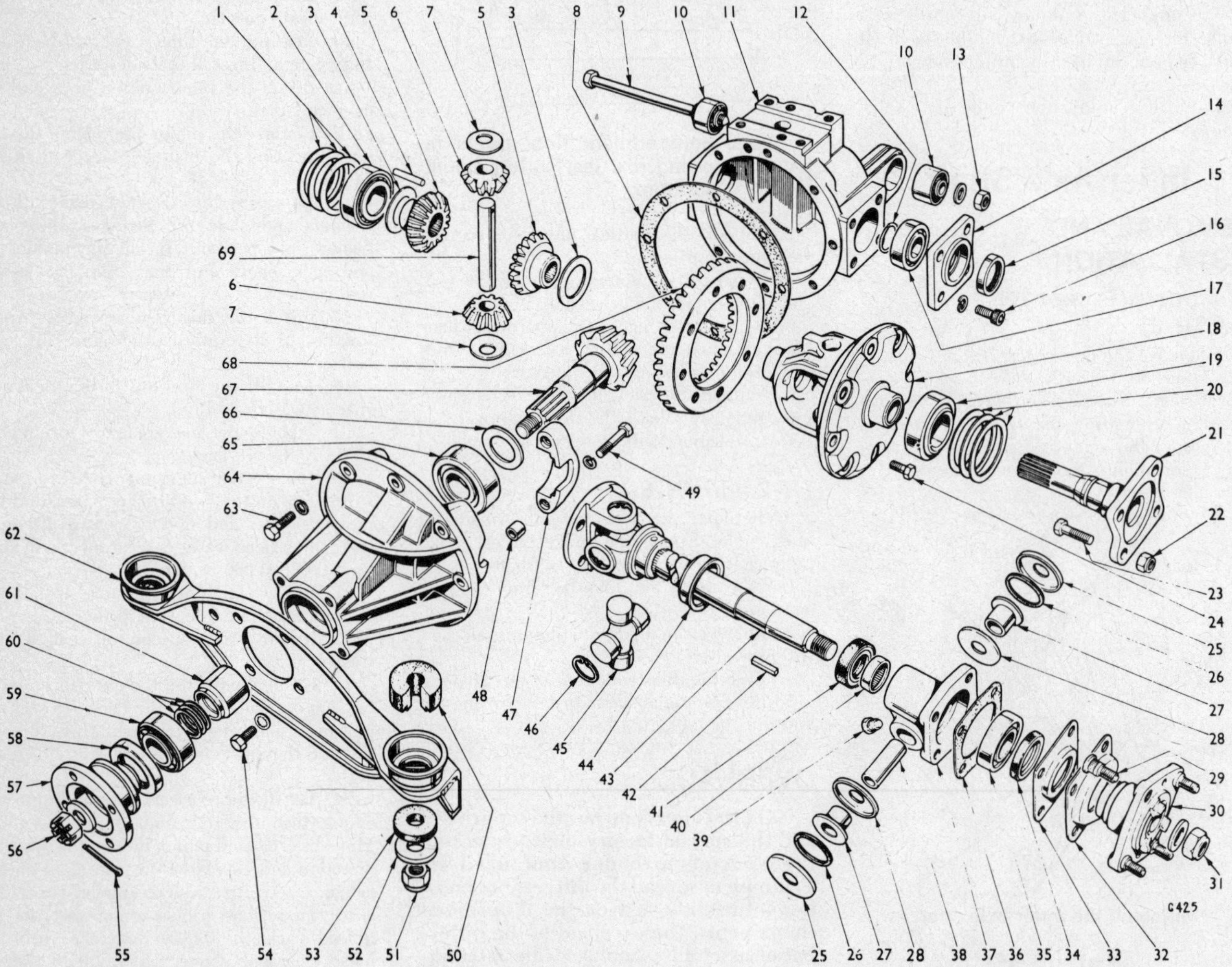

1. Shims
2. Differential side bearing
3. Thrust washer
4. Cross-shaft locking pin
5. Sun gear
6. Planet gear
7. Thrust washer
8. Gasket
9. Rear mounting bolt
10. Bushing
11. Hypoid rear casing
12. Circlip
13. Nyloc nut
14. Seal housing plate
15. Oil seal
16. Hexagon socket screw
17. Ball race
18. Differential carrier
19. Differential side bearing
20. Shims
21. Inner axle shaft
22. Nyloc nut
23. Bolt
24. Bolt
25. Shim
26. Rubber sealing ring
27. Nylon bushing
28. Shim
29. Stud
30. Hub
31. Nyloc nut
32. Grease trap
33. Outer seal housing
34. Seal
35. Ballrace
36. Gasket
37. Trunnion housing
38. Spacer tube
39. Grease plug
40. Needle roller bearing
41. Inner oil seal
42. Key
43. Outer axle shaft
44. Grease flinger
45. Universal joint assembly
46. Circlip
47. Bearing cap
48. Tubular dowel
49. Bolt
50. Mounting rubber
51. Nyloc nut
52. Plain washer
53. Rubber pad
54. Bolt
55. Cotter pin
56. Slotted nut
57. Coupling flange
58. Oil seal
59. Pinion tail bearing
60. Shims
61. Spacer
62. Mounting plate
63. Bolt
64. Hypoid nose piece casing
65. Pinion head bearing
66. Spacer
67. Pinion
68. Ring gear
69. Cross-shaft
70. Bolt
71. Lockplate
72. Brake backplate
73. Bolt
74. Nyloc nut
75. Vertical link

Spitfire, GT6 and TR-7 rear axle

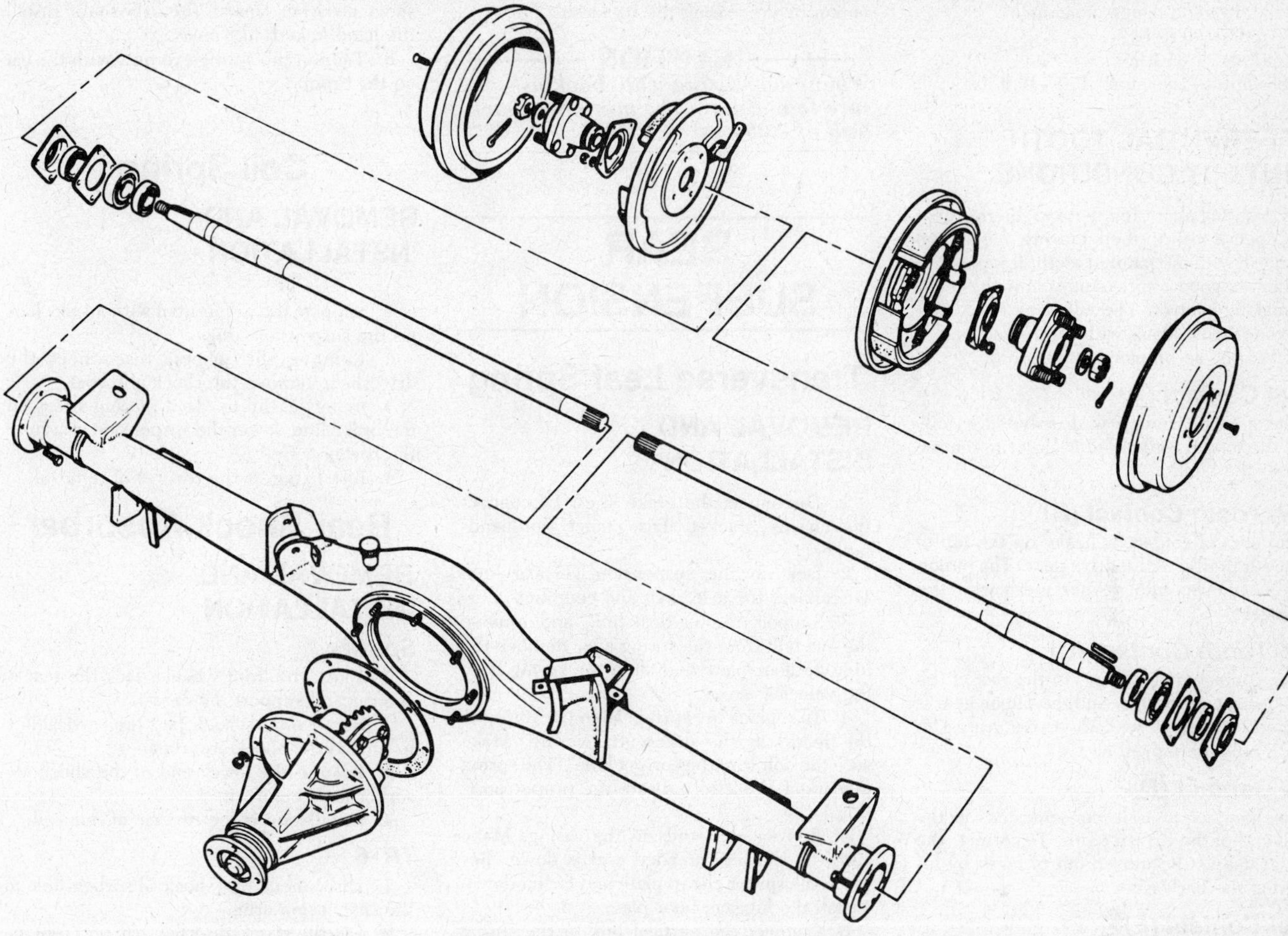

Exploded view of rear axle assembly—TR-7

the preload. Torque the nut to 90-120 ft/lbs to obtain a preload of 15-18 in/lbs.

19. Install the sun gears, planet gears and thrust washers in the housing. Insert the planet gear across shaft and install thrust washers to obtain zero backlash.

20. Install the lock pin and secure by peening.

21. Install the inner carrier bearings, and install the case spreader.

22. Install the outer bearings to the differential and fit the differential in the case. Install a dial indicator and check the axial play of the ring gear flange.

23. Add to this measurement 0.003 in. preload. This figure is the necessary shim total.

24. Remove the differential and install the ring gear.

25. Install the differential.

26. Check the axial movement with a dial gauge.

27. Subtract the correct backlash (0.004-0.006 in.) from this reading.

28. Install the necessary shim pack.

29. Release the spreader, install and tighten the bearing caps. Check the backlash at several points on the ring gear. An average reading of 0.004-0.006 in. should be indicated.

30. Install the rear cover and gasket.

Backlash between pinion and ring gears:
All: 0.004-0.006 in. (0.10-0.15 mm)

Pinion bearing preload, without oil seal:
TR-6: 15-18 in/lbs.
GT6 and Spitfire: 12-16 in/lbs.

Differential bearing preload, measured over both bearings:
All: 0.003 in. (0.076 mm)

Maximum run-out of the ring gear, when bolted to differential carrier:
All: 0.003 in. (0.076 mm)

DIFFERENTIAL TORQUE FIGURES

TR-6, TR-7 and TR-8

Ring gear to differential case: 40-45 ft/lbs

Inner driving flange to inner axle: 100-110 ft/lbs

Driveshaft flange to pinion: TR-6: 90-100 ft/lbs

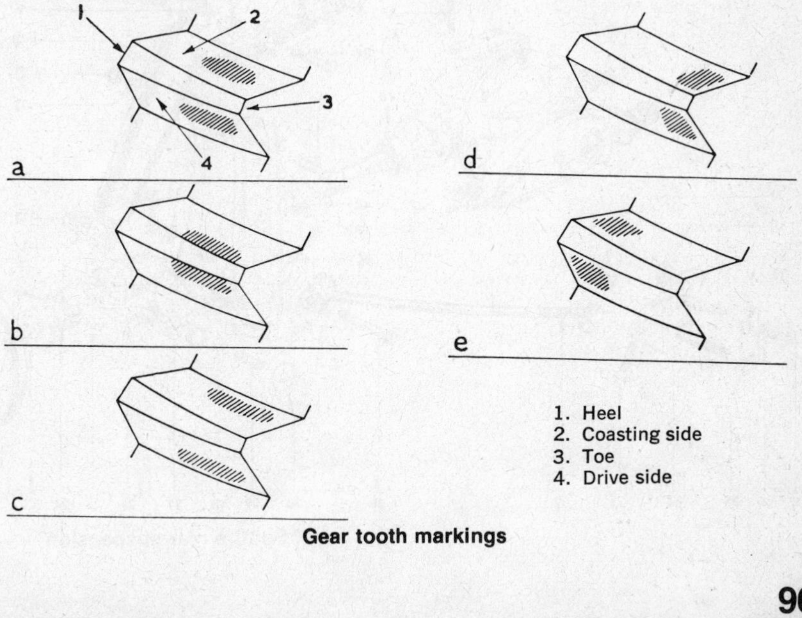

Gear tooth markings

Spitfire

Hypoid pinion flange attachment:
(GT6) 90-100 ft/lbs
(Spitfire) 70-85 ft/lbs
Rear hub to axle shaft: 100-110 ft/lbs

DIFFERENTIAL TOOTH CONTACT CONDITIONS

By painting about ten teeth of the ring gear with special paint, then moving the pinion into mesh with the painted teeth, it is possible to obtain a good impression of how the teeth are making contact. The following tooth contact conditions, along with the remedies, are keyed to the accompanying diagrams:

Ideal Contact (A)

The area of contact is distributed evenly over the tooth profile, and is closer to the toe than to the heel.

High Tooth Contact (B)

The area of contact is heavy on the top of the tooth profile of the drive gear. The pinion must be moved into deeper mesh with the drive gear.

Low Tooth Contact (C)

The contact area is heavy in the root of the drive gear tooth profile, and the pinion gear is meshed too deeply with the drive gear. The pinion must be moved away.

Toe Contact (D)

The contact area is concentrated at the small end of the driven tooth. To correct, the ring gear must be moved out of mesh by increasing the backlash.

Heel Contact (E)

The contact area is concentrated at the large end of the driven tooth. To correct, the ring gear must be moved into closer mesh with the pinion by decreasing the backlash.

CAUTION

When decreasing the backlash, be sure to maintain the minimum backlash of 0.004 in. (0.10 mm).

REAR SUSPENSION

Transverse Leaf Spring

REMOVAL AND INSTALLATION

1. Disconnect the brake lines. Disconnect the chassis bracket. Disconnect the handbrake.
2. Jack up the suspension vertical link. Disconnect the axle shaft and couplings.
3. Support the vertical link, and remove the eye bolt from the spring eye. Remove the luggage floor plate and slide the spring from the vehicle.
4. To replace the spring: align the spring in the recess in the differential casing. Make sure the bolt is in the correct hole. (The spring is marked Front to indicate the proper position.)
5. Replace the studs in the casing. Make sure the shorter threaded end is down. Replace the spring clamp plate and fasten down. Install the luggage floor plate.
6. Connect the vertical link to the spring eyes. Do not tighten the spring eye nut. (Refit the radius arms at this point, if required.)
7. Raise the vertical link and install the shock absorber. Install the axle shaft. Install the handbrake brake lines.
8. Tighten the spring eye nuts with the car on the ground.

Coil Spring

REMOVAL AND INSTALLATION

1. Support the differential with a jack. Jack up the suspension arm.
2. Remove the wheel, disconnect the driveshaft, remove the shock absorber.
3. Being careful to avoid placing stress on the brake line, lower the suspension arm until the spring is free.
4. Installation is the reverse of removal.

Rear Shock Absorber

REMOVAL AND INSTALLATION

Spitfire

1. Block the front wheels. Jack the rear of the car and support the chassis.
2. Remove the wheel. Jack the vertical link to unload the shock absorber.
3. Release the lower end of the shock absorber and remove it.
4. Installation is the reverse of removal.

TR-6

1. Disconnect the shock absorber link to the suspension arm.
2. Lift the shock absorber arm and remove the link from the suspension arm, taking care not to misplace the two rubber buffers and

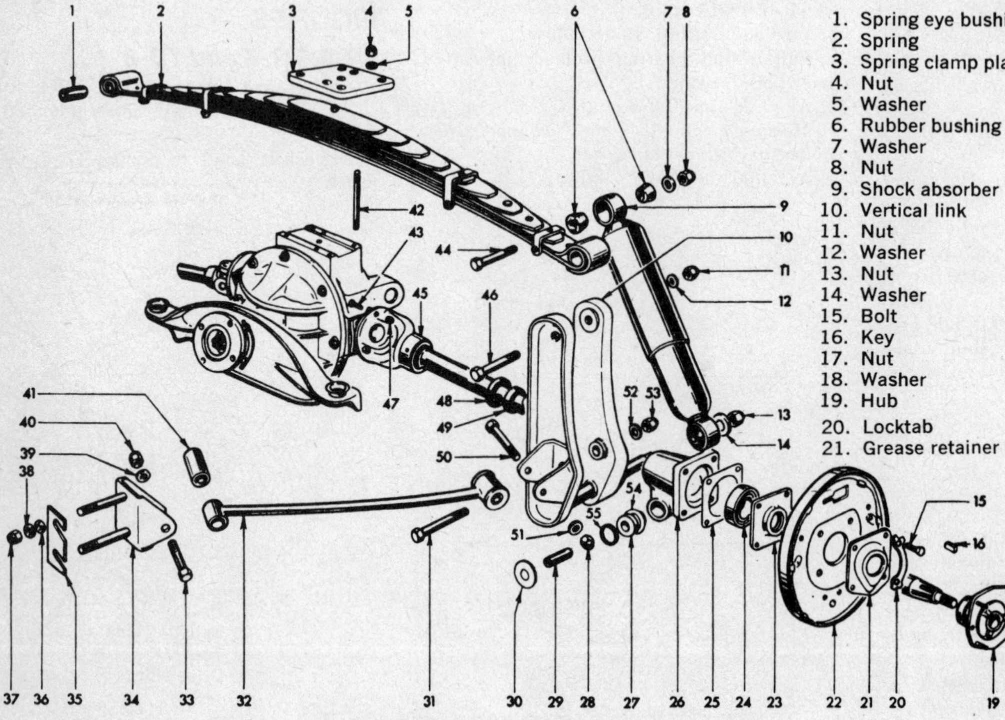

Spitfire rear suspension

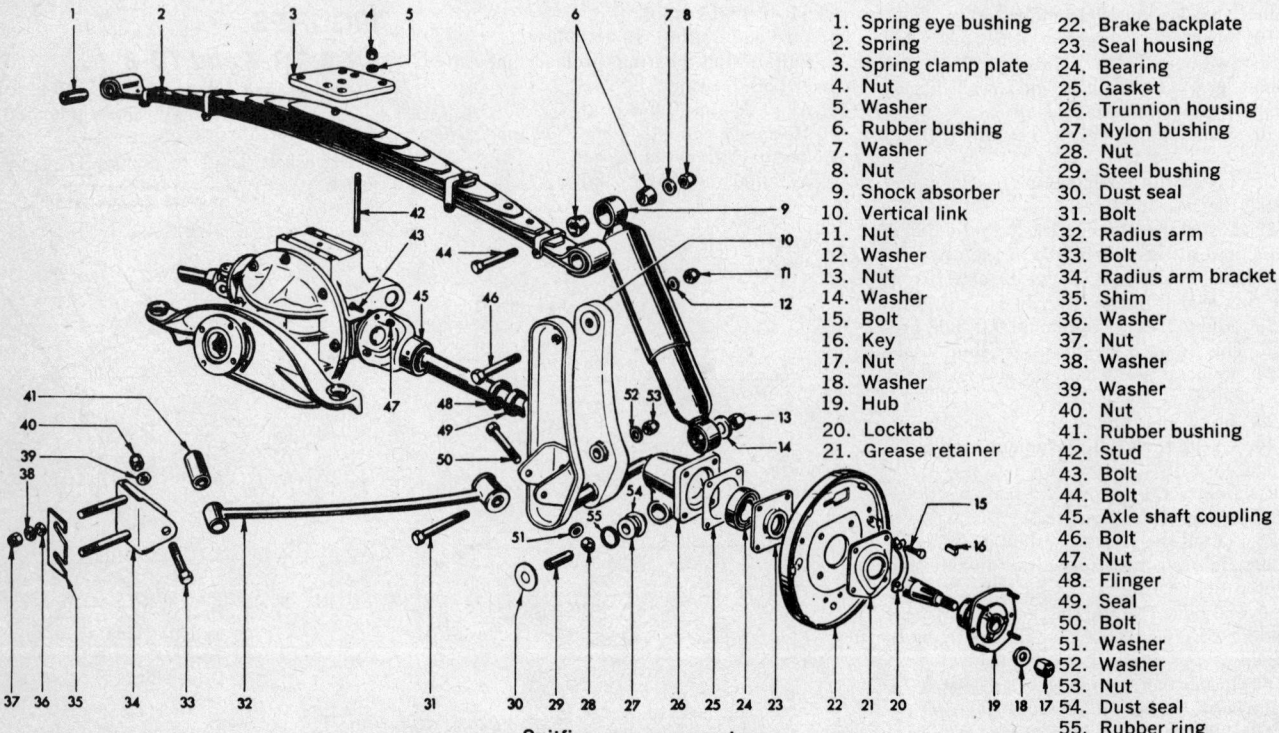

1. Spring eye bushing
2. Spring
3. Spring clamp plate
4. Nut
5. Washer
6. Rubber bushing
7. Washer
8. Nut
9. Shock absorber
10. Vertical link
11. Nut
12. Washer
13. Nut
14. Washer
15. Bolt
16. Key
17. Nut
18. Washer
19. Hub
20. Locktab
21. Grease retainer
22. Brake backplate
23. Seal housing
24. Bearing
25. Gasket
26. Trunnion housing
27. Nylon bushing
28. Nut
29. Steel bushing
30. Dust seal
31. Bolt
32. Radius arm
33. Bolt
34. Radius arm bracket
35. Shim
36. Washer
37. Nut
38. Washer
39. Washer
40. Nut
41. Rubber bushing
42. Stud
43. Bolt
44. Bolt
45. Axle shaft coupling
46. Bolt
47. Nut
48. Flinger
49. Seal
50. Bolt
51. Washer
52. Washer
53. Nut
54. Dust seal
55. Rubber ring

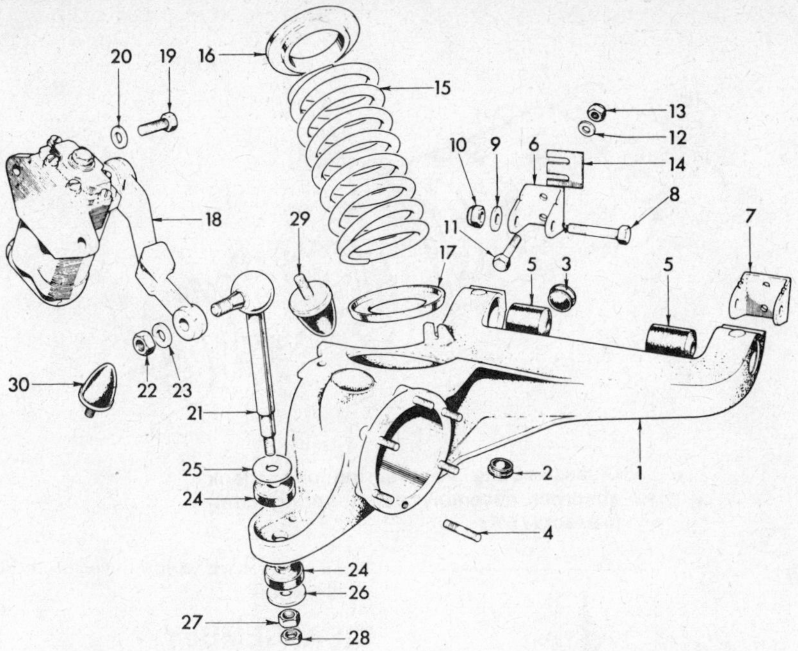

1. Suspension arm
2. Rubber plug
3. Rubber plug
4. Stud
5. Metalastik bushing
6. Fulcrum bracket, inner
7. Fulcrum bracket, outer
8. Bolt
9. Plain washer
10. Nyloc nut
11. Bolt
12. Plain washer
13. Nyloc nut
14. Shim
15. Road spring
16. Rubber insulator
17. Rubber insulator
18. Shock absorber arm
19. Bolt
20. Washer
21. Shock absorber link
22. Nut
23. Washer
24. Rubber buffer
25. Backing plate
26. Backing plate
27. Nut
28. Locknut
29. Bump stop
30. Rebound rubber

TR-6 independent coil spring rear suspension

buffer backing plates. Remove the absorber and link.

3. Clean away any dirt from the filler plug hole. Keeping the shock vertical, unscrew the filler plug and check the level of the fluid. Top-up to the bottom of the filler plug hole with the recommended shock absorber fluid.

CAUTION

Do not overfill the shock as the air space above the fluid is required for the proper operation of the unit. Move the shock absorber arm (lever) up and down a few times to force trapped air to the top of the unit. Recheck the fluid level. Replace the filler plug. Keeping the unit vertical, pump it several times. Discard the unit if it offers pockets of no resistance or if it becomes extremely difficult to move.

4. Installation is the reverse of removal. Transfer the link to the new shock.

TR-7 and TR-8 Right Side

1. Support the car, remove the wheel, gas cap and filler neck.
2. Unbolt and remove the shock absorber.

TR-7 and TR-8 Left Side

1. Support the car, remove the wheel, access plate in the trunk, and unbolt and remove shock absorber.
2. Installation for both left and right side is the reverse of the removal procedure.

Rear Suspension Adjustments

Because special equipment is required to properly adjust the rear suspension alignment, it is not advised that the operation be attempted. The following information is included for reference purposes.

CAMBER

Rear suspension camber angle is nonadjustable. If the camber angle is not within the specifications this indicates a weak or incorrectly set spring or excessive wear in the vertical link bushings (Spitfire), or in the suspension arm bushings (TR-6).

TOE-IN/TOE-OUT

Rear wheel toe-in/toe-out is adjustable by means of shims. Toe-in/toe-out dimensions are influenced by vehicle load, rear spring rate, and wear factors in the vertical link linkage (Spitfire), or in the suspension arm linkage (TR-6). Unlike the front wheels, each rear wheel may be adjusted independently. Adding shims increases toe-out while removing shims decreases toe-out.

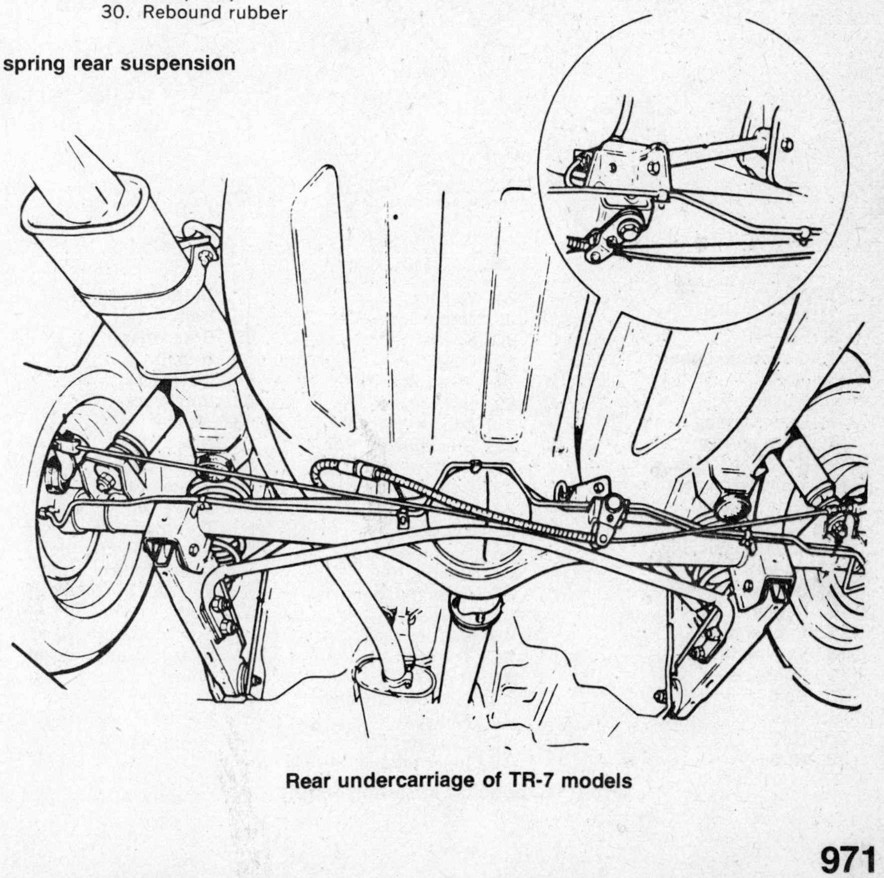

Rear undercarriage of TR-7 models

FRONT SUSPENSION

Front Spring and Shock Absorber

REMOVAL AND INSTALLATION

Spitfire

1. Loosen the bolt and nut which retain the steering trunnion to the lower control arm.
2. Unbolt the shock lower end.
3. Unbolt the front spring pad from its bracket.
4. Remove the spring and shock absorber assembly.
5. Installation is the reverse of removal.

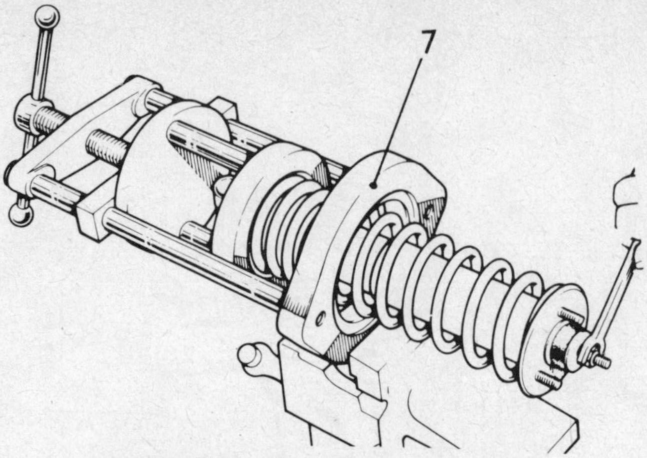

Disassembling front spring and shock absorber assembly using spring compressor (7)

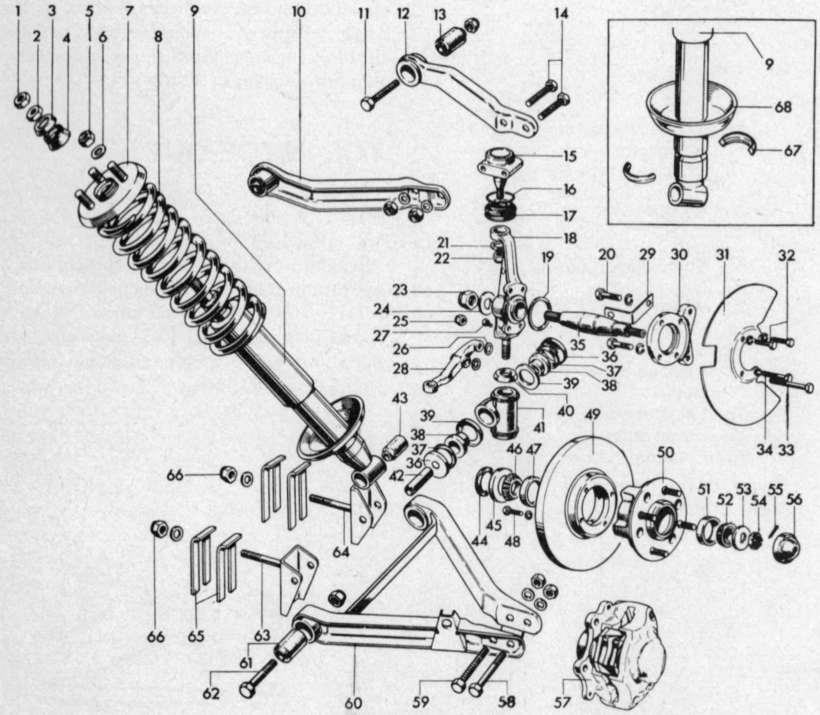

1. Nut
2. Nut
3. Washer
4. Mounting rubber
5. Nut
6. Washer
7. Upper spring pan
8. Road spring
9. Shock absorber
10. Top control arm
11. Fulcrum bolt
12. Top control arm
13. Fulcrum bushing
14. Bolt
15. Ball joint
16. Retainer
17. Rubber seal
18. Vertical link
19. Rubber seal
20. Bolt
21. Washer
22. Nut
23. Nut
24. Washer
25. Nut
26. Spacer
27. Plug
28. Steering arm
29. Bracket
30. Caliper bracket
31. Dust shield
32. Bolt
33. Bolt
34. Bolt
35. Spindle
36. Dust seal
37. Rubber ring
38. Nylon bushing
39. Dust seal
40. Rubber seal
41. Trunnion
42. Bushing
43. Fulcrum bushing
44. Felt seal
45. Seal holder
46. Inner race
47. Outer track
48. Bolt
49. Brake disc
50. Hub
51. Outer track
52. Inner race
53. Washer
54. Nut
55. Cotter pin
56. Grease cap
57. Brake caliper
58. Trunnion bolt
59. Shock absorber bolt
60. Lower control arm
61. Fulcrum bushing
62. Bolt
63. Front fulcrum bracket
64. Rear fulcrum bracket
65. Shim
66. Nut
67. Keeper
68. Lower spring pan

Front suspension assembly—Spitfire

Tighten the shock with the weight of the car on the wheels.

DISASSEMBLY

Spitfire

1. Compress the spring and remove the locknut and nut which retain the shock absorber rod to its mounting flange. Remove the mounting rubbers, mounting rubber seats, and mounting flange from the shock.

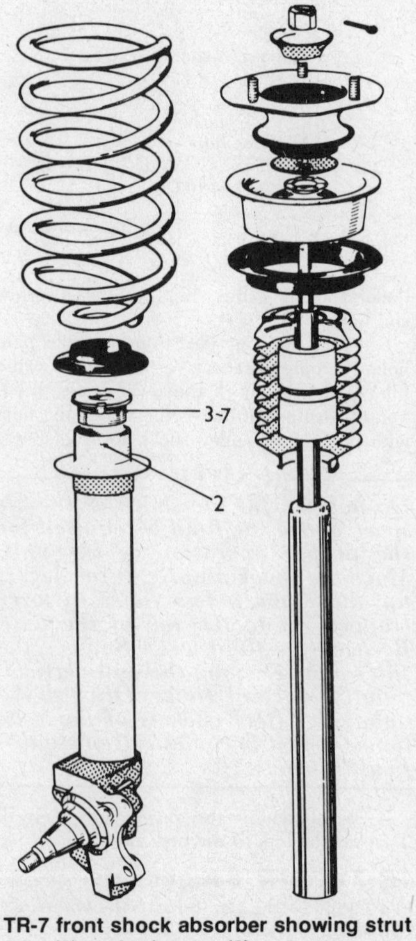

TR-7 front shock absorber showing strut tube (2) and tube cap (3)

2. Remove the spring compressor and remove the shock absorber from the spring.
3. Assembly is the reverse of disassembly.

Front Shock Absorber

REMOVAL AND INSTALLATION

TR-7 and TR-8

1. Remove the spring.
2. Using a 1/8 in. drill, remove the indentation securing the strut tube to the cap nut.
3. Remove the cap nut and lift out the cartridge.
4. Drill a 1/4 in. hole to a depth of 1/16 in. at 90° to the existing notch in the cap nut.
5. Insert the cartridge and tighten the cap nut.
6. Peen the strut at a point locking the cap nut notch.

TR-6

1. Unbolt the shock absorber from the lower attachment plate and remove the plate.
2. Remove the locknut from the top of the shock absorber and remove the shock.
3. Remove the rubber bushing and the inner washer from the top of the shock. Remove the bolts which retain the lower attaching points to the bottom of the shock.
4. Installation is the reverse of removal.

Front Spring

REMOVAL AND INSTALLATION

TR-7 and TR-8

1. Support the car, remove the wheel, detach the steering arm from the stub axle, and loosen the locknut securing the brake hose to the bracket on the strut tube.
2. Remove and support the caliper. Remove the ball joint.
3. Unbolt the strut at the bottom and swing it out of the way.
4. Compress the spring, unbolt the strut at the top and remove it from the car.
5. Installation is the reverse of removal.

TR-6

1. Remove the shock absorber.
2. Jack up the lower control arm until it is clear of the rebound stop. Disconnect the rebound stop and bracket assembly and lower the suspension. Remove the jack.
3. Compress the spring until the lower control arm assembly is horizontal. Use a wooden block between the top of the turret and the upper control arm for support.
4. Unbolt lower control arm from the spring pan. Remove the bump rubber. Replace the front lower control arm-to-spring pan bolt and bump rubber with 3/8x6 in. guide rods.
5. Release the spring compressor, until the spring is loose. Remove the spring pan, rubber collars, front spring, and spacer. Remove the four shock absorber lower attachment bolts.
6. Installation is the reverse of removal.

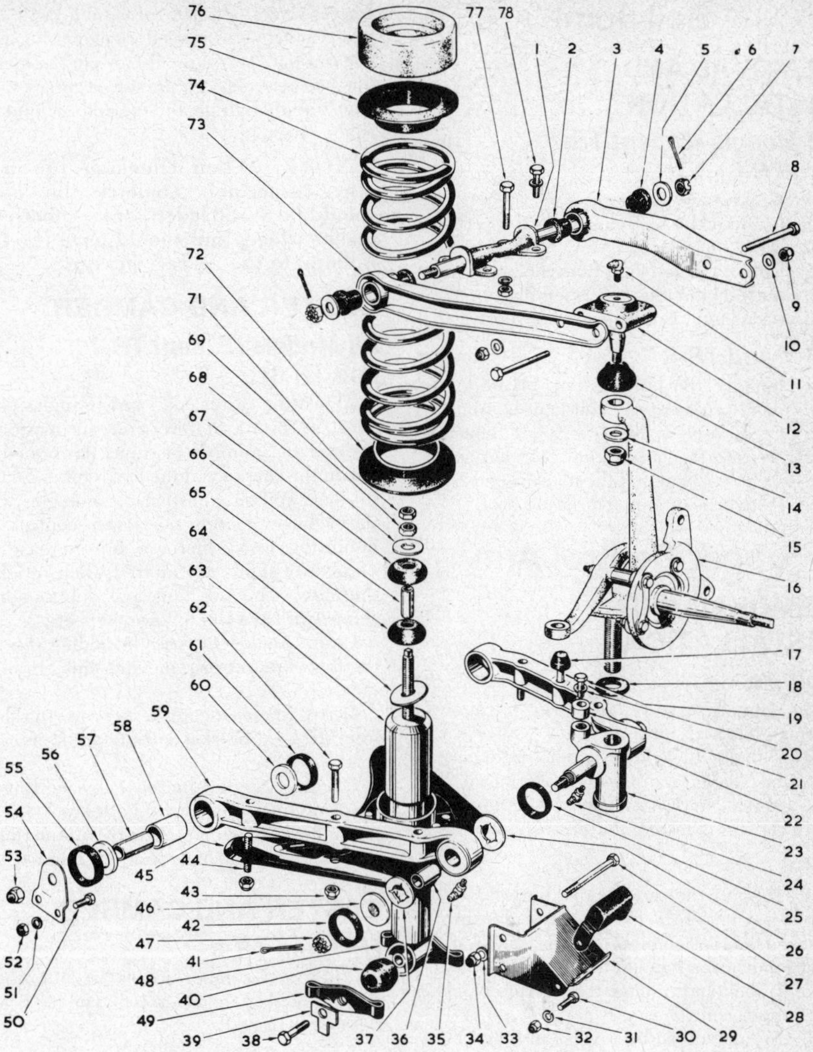

1. Upper inner fulcrum
2. Rubber bushing
3. Upper control arm—rear
4. Rubber bushing
5. Washer
6. Cotter pin
7. Slotted nut
8. Bolt
9. Nyloc nut
10. Plain washer
11. Grease nipple
12. Upper ball joint
13. Rubber seal
14. Plain washer
15. Nyloc nut
16. Caliper bracket and vertical link
17. Bump rubber
18. Rubber seal
19. Bolt
20. Spring washer
21. Lock stop collar
22. Lower control arm—rear
23. Lower trunnion bracket
24. Grease nipple
25. Rubber seal
26. Thrust washer
27. Bolt
28. Rebound rubber
29. Bracket
30. Bolt
31. Spring washer
32. Nyloc nut
33. Plain washer
34. Nyloc nut
35. Grease nipple
36. Bushing—nylon
37. Thrust washer
38. Bolt
39. Tab washer
40. Rubber bushing
41. Cotter pin
42. Rubber seal
43. Nyloc nut
44. Stud
45. Spring pan
46. Serrated washer
47. Slotted nut
48. Shock absorber attachment bracket—rear
49. Shock absorber attachment bracket—front
50. Bolt
51. Spring washer
52. Nut
53. Nyloc nut
54. Fulcrum bracket
55. Rubber seal
56. Thrust washer
57. Steel sleeve
58. Nylon bushing
59. Lower control arm—front
60. Thrust washer
61. Rubber seal
62. Bolt
63. Shock absorber
64. Washer
65. Rubber bushing
66. Sleeve
67. Rubber bushing
68. Washer
69. Nut
71. Locknut
72. Rubber collar
73. Upper control arm—front
74. Spring
75. Rubber collar
76. Spacer
77. Bolt
78. Bolt

Front suspension assembly—TR-6

Ball Joint

REMOVAL AND INSTALLATION

All Models (Except TR-7 and TR-8)

1. Remove the ball joint stud washer and nut. Separate the ball joint from the vertical link.
2. Unbolt the ball joint from the lower control arm. Support the hub assembly.
3. Installation is the reverse of removal.

TR-7 and TR-8

1. Remove the bottom link, plastic boot, circlip and press out the ball joint housing.
2. Press a new ball joint and housing squarely into the bottom link. Do not apply pressure to the center of the housing end cap.
3. Install the circlip and plastic boot.

Upper Control Arm

REMOVAL AND INSTALLATION

Spitfire

1. Support car, remove wheel; remove spring and shock absorber.
2. Unbolt and remove upper control arm.
3. Installation is the reverse of removal. Do not tighten control arm inner fulcrum bolts until the car is resting on the suspension.

TR-6

1. Support the car, remove the wheel, locate a jack under the lower control arm spring pad to take tension off the upper control arm, and remove the ball joint and vertical link.
2. Unbolt and remove the fulcrum bracket and upper control arm.
3. Installation is the reverse of removal.

Lower Control Arm

REMOVAL AND INSTALLATION

Spitfire

1. Support the car, remove the wheel and disconnect the sway bar from the lower control arm.
2. Unbolt the shock absorber at the bottom.
3. Unbolt and remove the control arm.
4. Installation is the reverse of removal.

TR-6

1. Support the car, remove the front wheel and spring.
2. Unbolt and remove the control arm.
3. Installation is the reverse of removal.

Front End Alignment

TOE-IN

With the steering centralized, measure the toe-in. If adjustment is required, loosen the tie rod end locknuts and the outer clip of the rubber seals. Rotate the tie rod ends until the correct alignment is obtained. Note the reading and move the vehicle forward until the wheels rotate one-half turn, then take a second reading. This procedure allows for wheel rim run-out. Adjust the tie rods to the mean of the two readings for greater accuracy. After adjustment, tighten the tie rod locknut and rubber seal clips.

NOTE: When checking toe-in or other suspension geometry, the vehicle should be static laden, on a smooth and level surface, and should have the tires inflated to the correct pressure.

CASTER AND CAMBER

All Models (Except TR-7 and TR-8)

Adjust the caster and camber angles of the TR-6, GT6 and Spitfire front suspension by altering the number of shims positioned between the chassis and the lower inner fulcrum brackets. When adjusting these angles, raise the vehicle, loosen the lower control arm mounting nuts, increase or decrease the number of shims as required, then retighten the nuts. The addition and subtraction of shims will have the following effects:

Caster Angle—increase by adding shims to the front bracket or removing shims from the rear.

Caster Angle—decrease by removing shims from the front bracket and adding shims to the rear.

Camber Angle—increase by adding an equal number of shims to both brackets.

Camber Angle—decrease by subtracting an equal number of shims from both brackets.

CASTER AND CAMBER

TR-7 and TR-8

Caster and camber angles are not adjustable. If angles are incorrect, damaged parts must be replaced.

STEERING

Steering Wheel

REMOVAL AND INSTALLATION

Spitfire

1. Pry off the steering wheel crash pad and the horn button.
2. Remove the horn brush connection.
3. Remove the steering wheel nut and washer.
4. Scribe alignment marks on the steering wheel and column.
5. Being careful not to jar the collapsible column, install a steering wheel puller and remove the wheel.

CAUTION

The use of a knock-off type puller may damage the column.

TR-6

1. Pry off the steering wheel crash pad and the horn button.
2. Remove the six bolts which retain the steering wheel to its support boss.
3. With the front wheels pointing straight ahead, scribe alignment marks on the support boss and steering column.
4. Remove the column nut and carefully pull the support boss from the upper inner steering column.
5. Installation is the reverse of removal.

TR-7 and TR-8

1. Remove the three screws on the underside of the spoke and lift off the pad.
2. Turn the wheels to a straight ahead position and remove the steering wheel nut and washer.
3. Remove the steering wheel.
4. Installation is the reverse of removal.

TURN SIGNAL SWITCH REPLACEMENT

Except TR-7 and TR-8

1. Remove the two screws and the switch fairings.
2. Remove the steering column clamp and harness cover.
3. Disconnect the three snap connectors.
4. Remove the two screws and spring washers.
5. Lift out the switch with its electrical leads.
6. Installation is the reverse of removal.

TR-7 and TR-8

1. Remove the upper and lower switch cover halves.
2. Remove the steering wheel.
3. Remove the wiring harness clip, disconnect the harness plugs and loosen the switch clamp screw.
4. Remove the switch and harness.
5. Installation is the reverse of removal. The arrow on the turn signal handle must align with the center of the column.

Steering Column Ignition Lock Switch

Spitfire and TR-6

1. Remove the steering column.
2. Remove the steering lock shroud and steering column tie-bar.
3. Either unscrew the shear-off bolts with a small chisel, or drill into the bolt heads and remove the bolts with an easy-out.
4. Remove the lock switch.
5. To install, position the lock switch to the column so that the switch dowel locates in the column drilling.
6. Install the steering lock shroud using two new shear-off bolts.
7. Evenly tighten the bolts until the heads shear.
8. Install the steering column.

TR-7 and TR-8

1. Disconnect the battery and remove the upper and lower switch cover halves.
2. Remove the wiring harness clip and disconnect the harness plug.
3. On vehicles with a key warning system, disconnect the single pin harness plug and the correct from below the steering column lock assembly.

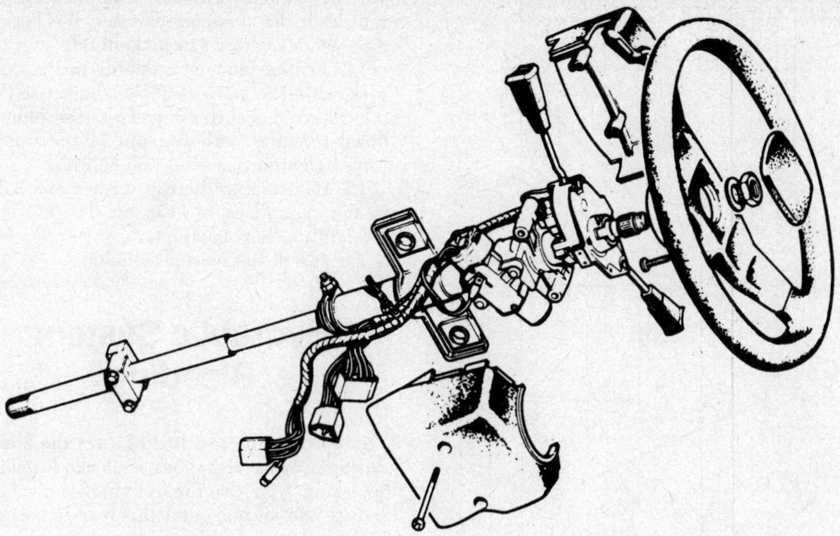

Exploded view of steering column and components—TR-7

4. Unbolt and remove the switch assembly.
5. Installation is the reverse of removal.

Manual Steering Gear

ADJUSTMENT

Adjust the end clearance of the pinion shaft. This should be as little as possible with the pinion still able to rotate freely. There are shims available in thicknesses of 0.004 in. and 0.010 in. to obtain minimal end clearance with free rotation. The second adjustment involves the damper cap. With the pressure pad and cap nut installed to the rack tube, tighten the cap nut to eliminate all end clearance. Measure the clearance between the nut and the housing. Put together a shim package that is equal to the clearance between the cap nut

Measuring clearance between cap nut and housing

and the housing plus 0.004 in. (i.e., pack-clearance + 0.004 in.). Pack the unit with grease and install the cap nut, shim pack, spring, and pressure pad to the housing and tighten the cap nut. When the cap nut is correctly adjusted, a force of 2 lbs on a radius of 8 in. is required to rotate the pinion shaft. Check the unit and readjust if necessary by adding or subtracting shims from beneath the cap nut.

REMOVAL AND INSTALLATION

All Except TR-7 and TR-8

1. Place the vehicle on jack stands and remove the front wheels. Empty the cooling system and remove the bottom radiator hose.

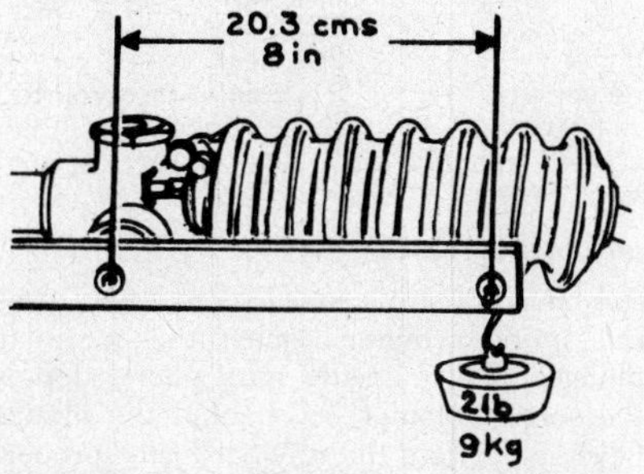

Measuring load required to turn pinion

2. Loosen and remove the bolt from the steering shaft coupling. Remove the steering rod end nuts. Pull the ball joints from the tie rod lever.
3. Remove nuts, U-bolts, and shims. Pull the steering unit forward. Remove the unit by pulling it through the wheel-well.
4. Count the number of pinion shaft turns required to move the gear from lock to lock. Return the shaft to the central position and move the steering wheel to straight ahead. Install the steering unit by placing the splined pinion shaft into the splined coupling.
5. Place the aluminum packing pieces behind the rack and the two front aluminum packing blocks into the dowels. These fit into holes in the rack tube.
6. Replace the U-bolts and nuts. Replace the unit in the car.
7. Place the taper pins of the tie rod ball joints into the steering levers and insert the steering washers and nuts. Replace the bolt and nut.

CAUTION
Check the front end alignment.

TR-7 and TR-8

1. Raise vehicle and set wheels to straight ahead position.
2. Scribe the pinion shaft and lower steering coupling.
3. Disconnect the rack tie rod outer ball joints from the steering arms.
4. Remove the pinch bolt securing the lower steering coupling to the rack pinion.
5. Remove the two bolts, spring washers and plain washers securing the pinion end of the rack to the sub-frame.
6. Remove the two nyloc nuts and washers and remaining bolts securing the rack to the sub-frame.
7. Disconnect the lower coupling from the pinion shaft, and remove the rack from the driver's side.
8. Installation is the reverse of removal.

BRAKE SYSTEM

Adjustment

Disc brakes are inherently self-adjusting and therefore require no adjustments between pad changes. To adjust the rear drum brakes:

1. Block the front wheels. Release the handbrake. Raise the rear of the car so that both rear wheels clear the ground.

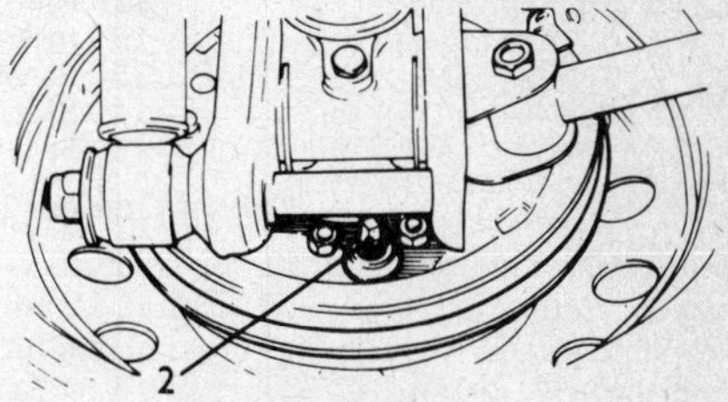

Rear drum brake adjuster (2) Spitfire, GT6 shown; TR-6 similar

2. Turn the square-ended adjuster on the rear of the backing plate clockwise until the wheel is locked.
3. Back-off the adjuster a notch at a time until the wheel may spin freely when turned with one hand.

NOTE: The TR-7 has self adjusting rear brakes.

Master Cylinder

REMOVAL AND INSTALLATION

1. Remove both brake lines. Be careful not to let fluid drip out.
2. Pull out the rubber dust cover. Remove the clevis pin. (This is secured by a cotter pin.)
3. Remove the master cylinder.
4. Installation is the reverse of removal. Bleed the brakes.

OVERHAUL

1. Remove the master cylinder.
2. Drain the master cylinder and discard the old fluid. Remove the screws which hold the reservoir to the body.
3. Press down on the pushrod, remove

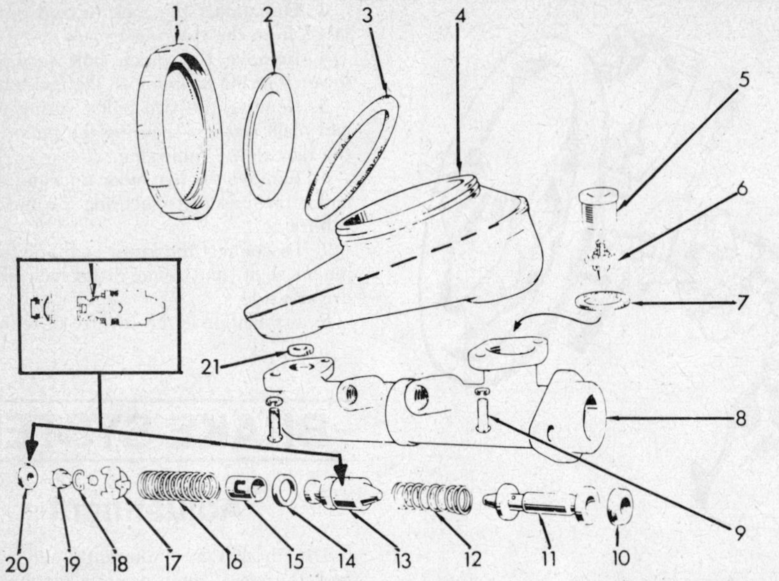

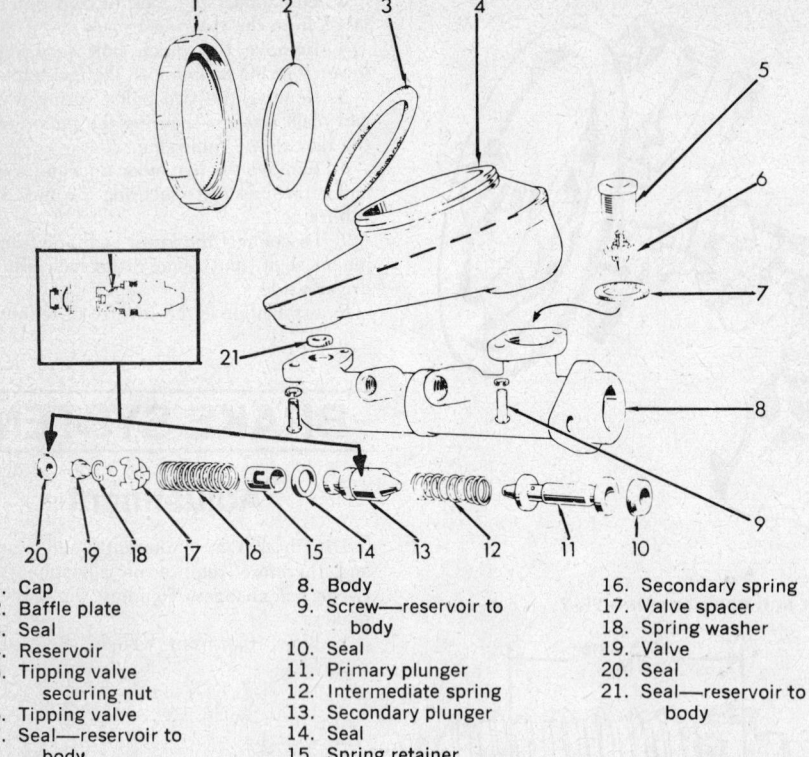

1. Cap
2. Baffle plate
3. Seal
4. Reservoir
5. Tipping valve securing nut
6. Tipping valve
7. Seal—reservoir to body
8. Body
9. Screw—reservoir to body
10. Seal
11. Primary plunger
12. Intermediate spring
13. Secondary plunger
14. Seal
15. Spring retainer
16. Secondary spring
17. Valve spacer
18. Spring washer
19. Valve
20. Seal
21. Seal—reservoir to body

Tandem master cylinder disassembled

the circlip, and pull out the pushrod, abutment plate, and circlip. Using an Allen wrench, remove the tipping valve nut and lift out the seal.

4. Depress the plunger and remove the tipping valve. Lightly shake the body to remove the internal parts. Pull the intermediate spring and plunger apart.

5. Raise the leaf spring of the spring retainer and lift out the valve assembly from the plunger. Remove the spring, valve spacer, and washer spring from the valve stem.

6. Next, take the valve seal from the valve head end. Remove the seals from both plungers. Take the baffle and cap washer from the cap.

7. Replace all seals with new ones from the rebuilding kit. Thoroughly clean all other parts in clean brake fluid. Check the cylinder bore for any imperfections or coarseness. If any doubt exists as to condition, replace the cylinder.

8. Before reassembling, lubricate all parts with clean brake fluid. Place seals on the plungers.

9. Place the valve seals, smaller end leading, on the valve head. Place the spring washer on the stem of the valve. It must be positioned with the flare away from the stem shoulder. Next, fit the valve spacer, legs leading.

10. Place the retainer on the stem, keyway first. Put the spring over the retainer; position the assembly on the plunger.

11. Compress the spring while the retainer is pushed behind the plunger head. To accomplish this, place the subassembly in a vise and place clean paper between each subassembly end and the vise jaws to prevent contamination.

12. Close the vise until the spring is nearly coil bound. Using a small screwdriver, press the spring retainer against the secondary plunger. Using needle nose pliers, depress the spring retainer leaf behind the plunger head. Be certain the retainer leaf is properly aligned (straight) and is firmly located behind the plunger.

13. Place the spring between the plungers. Lubricate the plunger seals and the bore of the cylinder with clean brake fluid.

14. Fit the plunger assembly in the bore. Make sure the valve end is leading. Use caution to avoid seal damage. Press the plunger down into the bore and put in the tipping valve. Tighten the seal to 35-40 ft/lbs.

15. Reassemble the cap washer and baffle to the cap. Place the cap on the reservoir. Assembly is now complete.

16. Install the master cylinder.

Hydraulic System Bleeding

In bleeding the rear brakes, turn the brake adjusters so that the shoes are locked against the drums. Note that the front brakes must be bled as one system, and the rear brakes as another. Attach a tube to the system bleed nipple that is farthest from the master cylinder, allowing the other end of the tube to hang submerged in a jar containing a small amount of clean brake fluid. Unscrew the bleed nipple about half a turn to allow the fluid to be pumped out. Press the brake pedal lightly without pushing through to the end of the stroke. If the pedal is pushed heavily or fully through its stroke, the pressure differential switch could be actuated, causing the brake warning light to glow brightly until the actuating piston is recentralized. Pausing between each depression of the pedal, pump until no bubbles can be seen in the fluid being pumped into the jar. With the pedal depressed, tighten the bleed nipple and repeat on the other brake of the system.

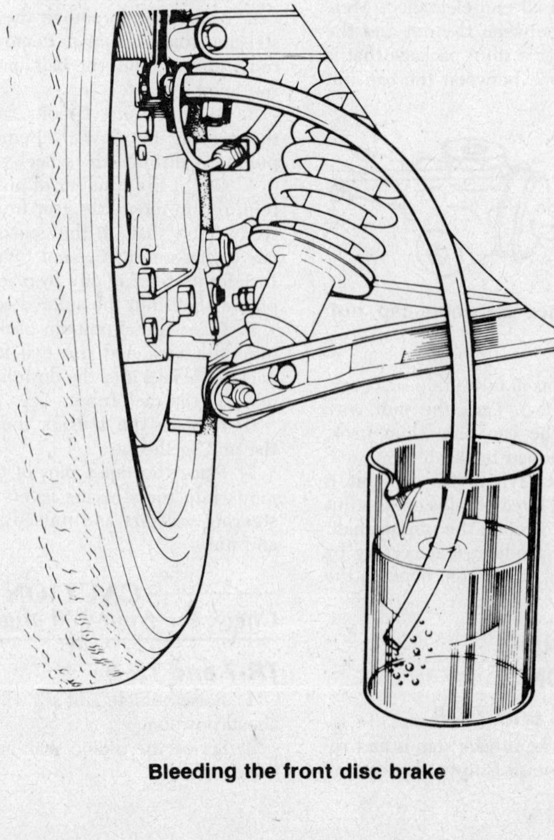

Bleeding the front disc brake

Piston Warning Light Centering

If, by mistake, the brake warning light piston has been pushed off center, causing the brake warning light to glow, the following procedure will have to be followed to recentralize the piston: Attach a rubber tube to a bleed nipple at the opposite end of the car to that which was being bled when the piston was actuated. Open the bleed screw and turn the ignition to the ON position without starting the engine. The brake warning light will glow, but the oil pressure warning light will be out. Push steadily on the brake pedal until the brake light dims and the oil light glows. As the piston returns to mid-position, a click will be felt on the pedal.

NOTE: If the pedal is pushed too hard, the piston will move over to the other side, necessitating the repeat of the preceding operations at the other end of the car.

Tighten the bleed screw.

Front Disc Brakes

DISC PAD REPLACEMENT

1. Remove the spring retainers and pad re-

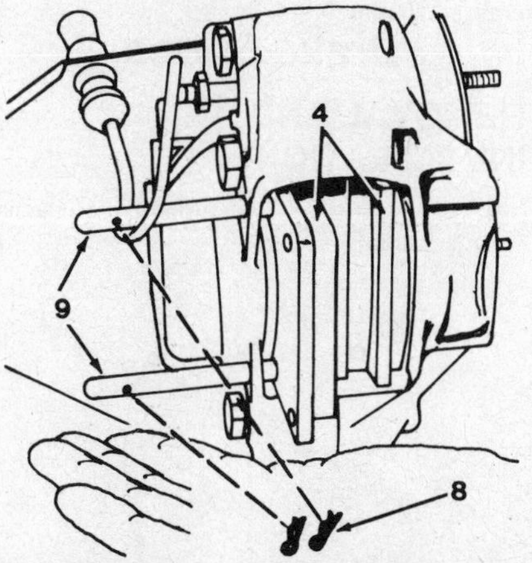

Disc brake pad removal showing pads (4), spring clips (8), and pad retainer pins (9)

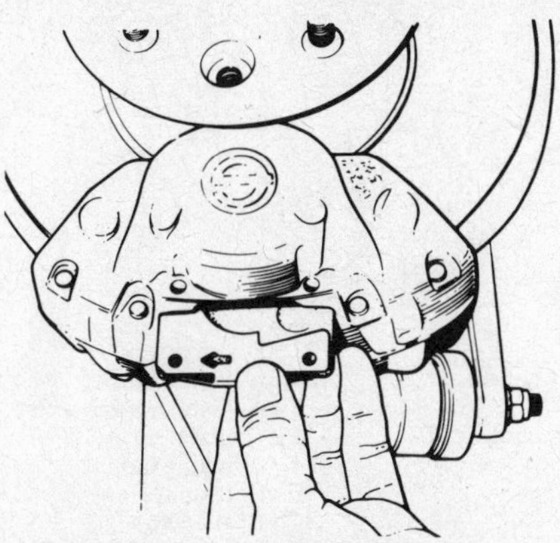

Installing brake pads with damping shim arrows pointing in direction of forward rotation

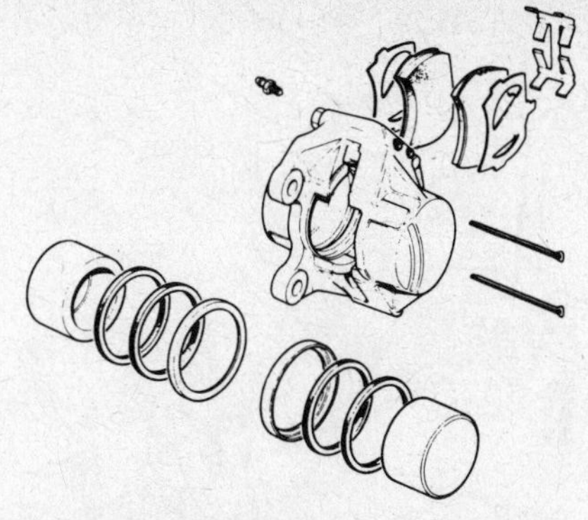

Exploded view of front disc brakes—TR-7

tainer pins. Lift off the pads and the anti-squeal plates.

2. When installing new pads, push the piston all the way back into their cylinders. Place new pads and squeal plates on the wheel; place the arrow in the direction of wheel rotation. Install the retainer pins and secure with clips.

CALIPER

Removal, Installation and Overhaul

1. Remove the line and the locknut at the supporting bracket. Remove the flexible hose.
2. Remove the bolts which hold the caliper to the support bracket; lift off the caliper and take out the pistons.
3. Remove the rubber seals from the recess. Replace all the components as needed; thoroughly clean all others. Oil all parts and the bore with brake fluid.
4. Place the piston seal in the cylinder recess. Locate the lips (projecting) of the dust cover in the cylinder recess. Place the closed end of the piston into the cylinder.

CAUTION

Do not harm the polished surface. Insert the piston to the furthest extent and engage the outer lip of the dust cover with the piston recess.

5. Install the caliper over the disc; place shims between the mounting bracket and the calipers.
6. Replace all hoses and bleed the system.

Brake Disc (Rotor)

REMOVAL AND INSTALLATION

1. Remove the caliper.
2. Remove the grease cap with a screwdriver. Remove the cotter pin, nut, and washer. Pull out the hub with the outer race and part of the inner race.
3. Remove the brake disc from the hub assembly.

NOTE: Bearings, if needed, should only be replaced as a complete set.

4. Install the outer bearing rings (taper outward).

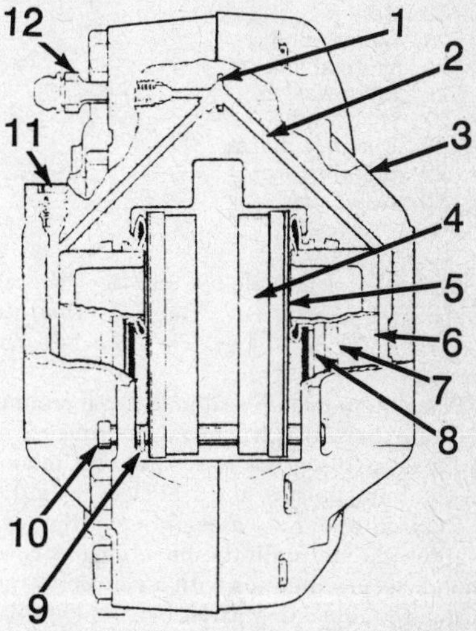

Disc caliper assembly cross-section

5. Replace the discs. Put the inner races together and install the hub with the disc to the stub axle.
6. Install the washer and slotted nut while rotating the hub; finger tighten only. Loosen the nut to the closest cotter pin hole and mark the position by center punching the end of the stub axle and nut. Hub end-play should be 0.003-0.005 in.

If loosening the nut gives excessive play,

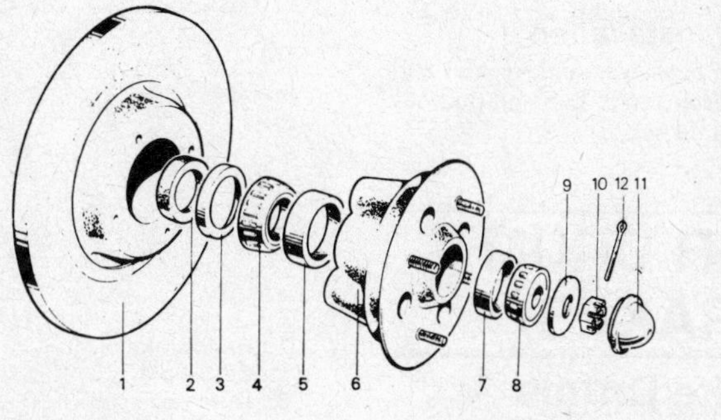

1. Brake disc
2. Oil seal
3. Oil seal cage
4. Taper bearing (inner)
5. Bearing track (inner)
6. Hub casting
7. Bearing track (outer)
8. Taper bearing (outer)
9. "D" washer
10. Slotted nut
11. Grease cap
12. Split pin

Spitfire, GT6 front hub details

1. Bolt
2. Spring washer
3. Nyloc nut
4. Plain washer
5. Dust shield
6. Stub axle
7. Caliper bracket
8. Tab plate
9. Bolt
10. Felt seal
11. Seal retainer
12. Bolt
13. Spring washer
14. Inner tapered race
15. Disc
16. Hub
17. Outer tapered race
18. Washer
19. Slotted nut
20. Cotter pin
21. Hub cap
22. Bolt
23. Bolt
24. Caliper unit
25. Vertical link
26. Plain washer
27. Nyloc nut
28. Distance pieces
29. Steering arm
30. Nyloc nut

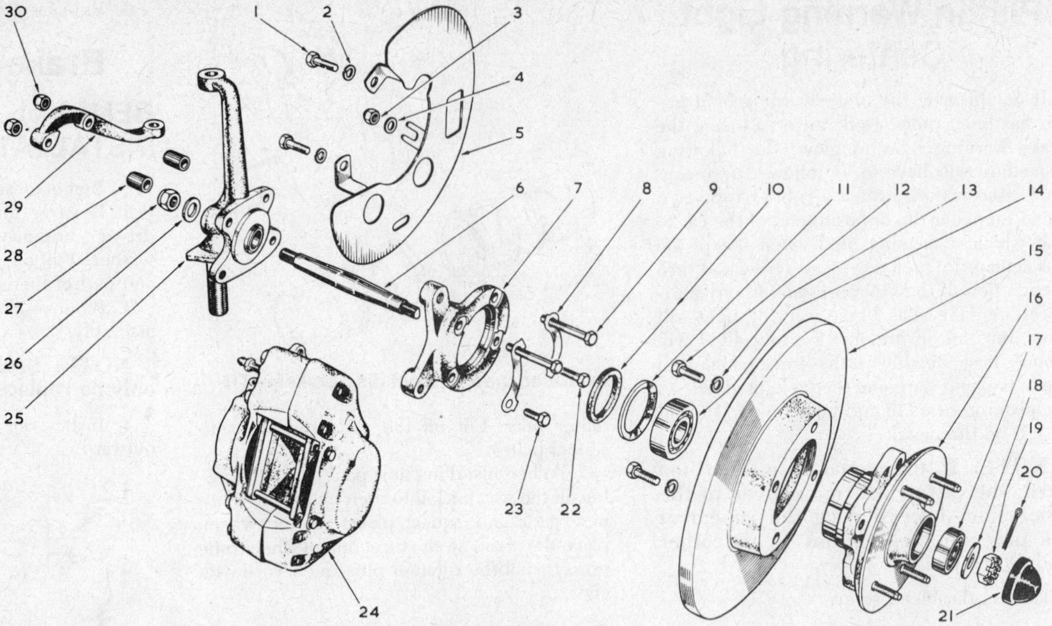

Disc and hub assembly—TR-6

remove the nut and file the rear face. This will correct the problem. Remove the nut, washer, hub, and races. Pack the hub with grease.

Place the new hub seal in the seal retainer. Saturate the seal in engine oil and squeeze out the excess. Place the races and seal retainer on the hub. Be sure the seal faces inward.

Replace the hub assembly on the axle. Tighten the nut until the punch marks correspond; secure the nuts with a new cotter pin. Install the remaining parts. Be sure to replace any shims.

WHEEL BEARING ADJUSTMENT

The end-play of the front wheel bearing should be 0.003-0.005 in. and may be checked by a suitable dial gauge. The front wheel hub nut is provided with slots to accompany a securing cotter pin. In the event that a gauge is not available, rotate the hub, tighten the nut only sufficiently to remove looseness (5 ft/lbs), then loosen the nut by one flat and secure it with a new cotter pin.

Removal and Installation

To remove the bearings, remove hub and outer bearing. Reach inside hub and pull out inner bearing and oil seal.

REAR DRUM BRAKES

Brake Drums

REMOVAL AND INSTALLATION

1. Jack up the rear of the car. Apply the handbrake.
2. Remove the two countersunk screws which retain the rear drum to its hub.
3. Release the handbrake.
4. Lift off the drum. If the drum is difficult to remove, it may be necessary to back off the adjuster a few turns.
5. Installation is the reverse of removal.

INSPECTION

Check the working surface of the drum for scoring. Minor scoring may be removed by having the drum turned on an arbor in a lathe, but deeper scoring may require replacement of the drum.

Check the drum for cracks and replace it if any are evident. A good way to check this is to hang the drum by a wooden handle and tap it with a small metal object. A cracked drum will emit a flat sounding note.

Brake Shoes

REMOVAL AND INSTALLATION

1. Jack up the car and support the chassis with jackstands.

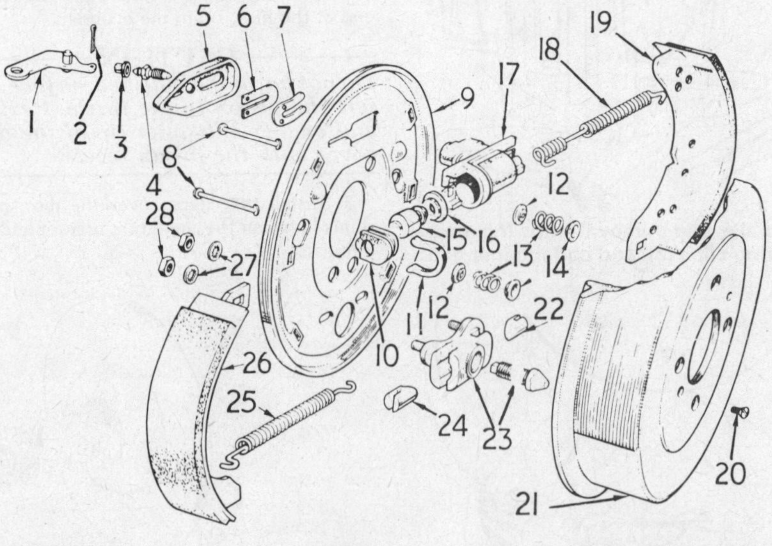

1. Handbrake lever
2. Cotter pin
3. Dust cap
4. Bleed nipple
5. Dust excluder
6. Retaining clip
7. Retaining clip
8. Steady pins
9. Backplate
10. Dust excluder
11. Clip
12. Steady pin cups
13. Springs
14. Steady pin cups
15. Piston
16. Seal
17. Wheel cylinder
18. Return spring
19. Brake shoe
20. Countersunk screw
21. Brake drum
22. Adjuster tappet
23. Adjuster wedge and body
24. Adjuster tappet
25. Return spring
26. Brake shoe
27. Shakeproof washers
28. Nuts

Rear drum brake disassembled—Spitfire

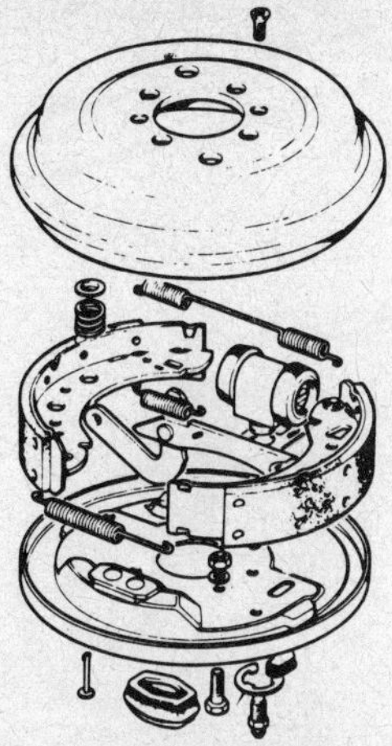

Exploded view of rear brakes—TR-7

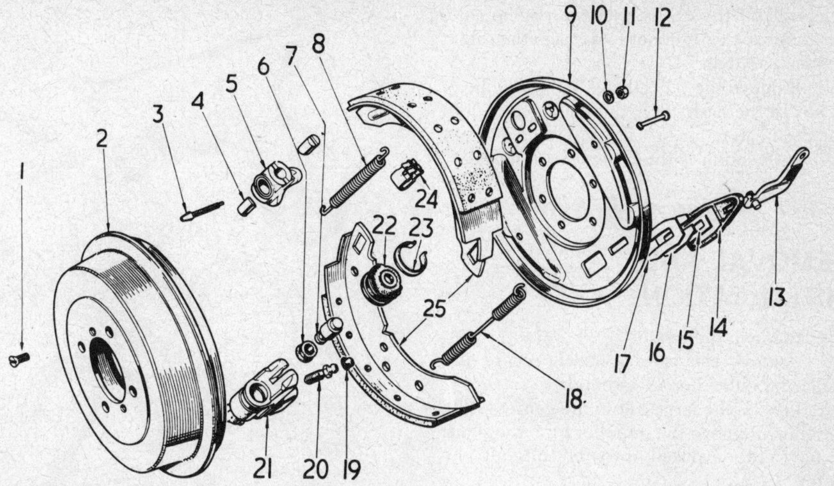

1. Screw
2. Brake drum
3. Tappet
4. Expander-adjuster
5. Adjuster housing
6. Piston seal
7. Piston
8. Spring
9. Backplate
10. Spring washer
11. Nut
12. Steady pin
13. Handbrake lever
14. Dust excluder
15. Abutment plate
16. Spring plate—retaining
17. Spring plate
18. Spring
19. Dust cap
20. Bleed nipple
21. Hydraulic cylinder
22. Dust excluders
23. Clip
24. Spring clip—steady pin
25. Brake shoes

Rear drum brake disassembled—TR-6

2. Remove the brake drum.
3. On Spitfire models only, remove the cotter pin from the handbrake lever. Also remove the brake shoe hold-down pins (shoe-steady pins), caps and springs.
4. On TR-6 models only, remove the spring clips, rotate the shoe-steady pins 90° and remove the pins.
5. Release the lower end of one shoe from the adjuster. Then release the upper end of the same shoe from the wheel cylinder.
6. Remove the brake shoe return springs, and lift off the shoes.
7. Installation is the reverse of removal. Shoe return springs are installed inboard.

Rear Wheel Cylinder

REMOVAL AND INSTALLATION

1. Remove the brake shoes as outlined under "Brake Shoes Removal and Installation."
2. Disconnect and plug the flexible brake hose.
3. Remove the protective rubber shield for the wheel cylinder from the rear of the backing plate and remove the horseshoe clip and spring plate which retain the cylinder.
4. Remove the wheel cylinder and handbrake lever assembly.
5. Reverse the above procedure to install, making sure to bleed the brakes.

OVERHAUL

1. Remove the wheel cylinder as previously described.
2. Remove the clip which retains the rubber boot to the cylinder body.
3. Remove the piston, rubber boot, and seal assembly from the cylinder body. Discard the old boot and seal.
4. Clean the piston and body in methylated alcohol or clean brake fluid meeting SAE 70 R3 specifications. Replace the piston or body if either is corroded or scored.
5. Dip the cylinder bore, the piston, and a new seal in clean brake fluid and insert the piston and seal assembly in the bore.
6. Install the rubber boot and its retaining clip on the cylinder.
7. Install the wheel cylinder as previously described.

Parking Brake

CABLE ADJUSTMENT

Lift the rear wheels from the ground. Lock the brake drums by screwing each adjuster in to its fullest extent. Remove the spring and clevis pin. Adjust the clevis at each cable end by equal amounts to reduce play in the cable. The cable is overly tightened when the clevis pin cannot be inserted without straining the cables. Secure the clevis pin, hook up spring and adjust the cable brackets to give slight spring tension.

Parking Brake Cable

REMOVAL AND INSTALLATION

Spitfire (Front)

1. Remove the handbrake lever and disconnect the cable fork.
2. Disconnect the cable from the relay lever and pull the cable from the car.
3. Installation is the reverse of removal.

Spitfire (Rear)

1. Disconnect the compensator from the relay lever.
2. Unhook the cable return springs and forks from the backplate lever.
3. Remove the cable from the car.
4. Installation is the reverse of removal.

TR-6

1. Remove the clevis pins securing the cable forks to the backplate levers and remove the brake cable supports from the trailing arms.
2. Release the cables from the compensator.
3. Remove the cables.
4. Installation is the reverse of removal.

TR-7 and TR-8

1. Raise the body to allow access to the transmission tunnel.
2. Pull back the rubber boot and release the cable locknut.
3. Unscrew the cable from the operating rod.
4. Back off the nut to release the cable from the bracket and remove the cotter pin, washer and clevis pin retaining the cable to each operating lever.
5. Remove the trunnion nut and bolt, back off the nuts on the compensating levers and remove the cables.
6. Installation is the reverse of removal.

CHASSIS ELECTRICAL

Heater Assembly

REMOVAL AND INSTALLATION

1. Disconnect the battery and empty the cooling system.
2. Remove the heater hoses. Remove the screws which hold the water valve mounting bracket to the dash shelf. Push the bracket and valve assembly away from the dash.
3. Inside the car, remove the dashboard support bracket. Remove the passenger and driver's side parcel shelf. Remove the bracket which holds the choke and heater cable.
4. Disconnect the tachometer and speedometer cables from the back of the

gauges. Pull the cables into the engine compartment. Be careful not to damage the cables or the grommet.

5. Remove the bolts which attach the heater box to the dash. Plug the heater lines. Lift out the heater.

6. Installation is the reverse of removal.

Blower Motor

REMOVAL AND INSTALLATION

1. Remove the heater.
2. Remove the screws which secure the inner and outer heater assembly.
3. Loosen the large nut in the center of the impeller. Remove the impeller from the shaft. Remove the exposed nut and lift out the motor.
4. Installation is the reverse of removal.

Windshield Wipers

REMOVAL AND INSTALLATION

1. Remove all electrical connections.
2. Make a mark on the domed cover and gearbox cover. Remove the four hold down screws. Move the gearbox and cover clear. Remove the exposed spring clip by pulling it sideways.
3. Take off the moving contact limiting switch. Remove the connecting rod.
4. Take the mounting bracket from the firewall. Move the unit to allow the vacuum assembly to be released. Remove the mounting bracket.
5. Installation is the reverse of removal.

ADJUSTING WIPER STOP (PARK POSITION)

Loosen the four holding screws and rotate the domed cover. Rotate the cover either way until the desired stop position is achieved. Replace the cover and tighten down.

Radio

REMOVAL AND INSTALLATION

Radios used in Triumphs are dealer installed or after-market units, therefore, a common procedure is not possible.

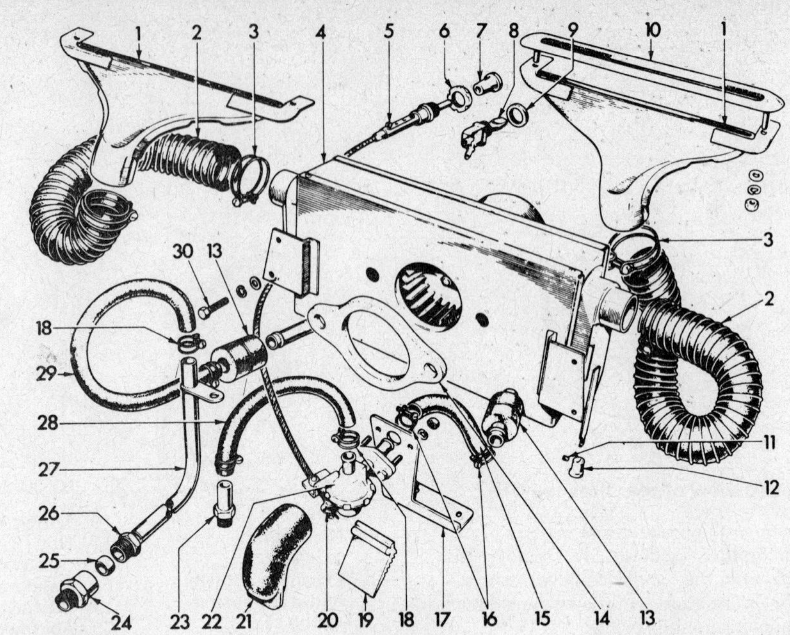

1. Defroster nozzle
2. Air hose
3. Hose clip
4. Heater unit
5. Heat control assembly
6. Bezel
7. Control knob
8. Blower switch
9. Bezel
10. Demister finisher
11. Screw
12. Flap knob
13. Sponge packing
14. Sealing ring
15. Water hose
16. Hose clip
17. Mounting bracket
18. Hose clip
19. Drain flap (from April 1964)
20. Water valve lever
21. Drain elbow (up to April 1964)
22. Water control valve
23. Adapter—cylinder head
24. Adapter—water pump
25. Sealing ring
26. Nut
27. Water return pipe
28. Water hose
29. Water hose
30. Bolt—heater attachment

Typical Spitfire heater assembly

Instruments

REMOVAL AND INSTALLATION

All instruments may be replaced individually from the back of the panel. On some models it may be necessary to loosen the panel screws to get at the instrument. Take care when working behind the panel since in most cases it is a tight fit and wires can be pulled loose without knowing it.

Fuses

A fuse that is burned out may be suspected when all electrical components in the particular circuit refuse to operate. A blown fuse may be identified by merely looking at the glass enclosed metal strip. If it is separated or burned, it must be replaced.

NOTE: It is imperative that a fuse be replaced by one of the same amperage.

If a fuse is replaced and immediately fails, the source of the trouble should be found before the vehicle is operated. Otherwise, serious and costly damage may result.

TR-6

The fusebox is located on the left side of the inner fender panel at the rear of the engine compartment. It contains three 35 amp operating fuses, one fuse for a possible accessory circuit, and two spares.

Fuse one (brown leads) protects the headlamp flasher, dash warning lights, and horn. Fuse two (red/green leads) protects the tail lights, front parking and marker lamp circuits, rear marker, dash board, and license plate lamps. Fuse three (white leads) protects all other electrical components.

Spitfire

The fuse box for all Spitfire models is located under the dashboard on the left side. The unit contains two 35 amp fuses.

SPECIFICATIONS

INDEX

BEFORE SERVICING, SEE THE SAFETY NOTICE ON THE CONTENTS PAGE

INTRODUCTION

In 1932, Ferdinand Porsche produced prototypes for the NSU company of Germany which eventually led to the design of the Volkswagen. The prototypes had a rear mounted, air-cooled engine, torsion bar suspension, and the spare tire mounted at an angle in the front luggage compartment. In 1936, Porsche produced three Volkswagen prototypes, one of which was a 995 cc, horizontally opposed four cylinder automobile. Passenger car development was sidetracked during World War II, when all attention was on military vehicles. In 1945, Volkswagen production began and 1,785 Beetles were built. The Volkswagen convertible was introduced in 1949, the same year that only two Volkswagens were sold in the United States. 1950 marked the beginning of the sunroof models and the transporter series. The Karmann Ghia was introduced in 1956, and remained in the same basic styling format until its demise in 1974. The 1500 Squareback and Fastback were introduced in the United States in 1966 to start the Type 3 series. The Type 4 was imported into the U.S.A. beginning with the 1971 model.

Type numbers are the way Volkswagen designates its various groups of models. The Type 1 group contains the Beetle, Super Beetle, the Karmann Ghia, and the "Thing." Type 2 vehicles are the Delivery Van, the Micro Bus, the Kombi, the Campmobile and the Vanagon. The Type 3 designation is for the Fastback and the Squareback sedans. The Type 4 is for the 411 and 412 sedans and wagon. These type numbers will be used throughout the book when it is necessary to refer to models.

An explanation of the terms suitcase engine and upright fan engine is, perhaps, necessary. The upright fan engine refers to the engine used in the Type 1 (through 1979) and 2 (1970-71) vehicles. This engine has the engine cooling fan mounted on the top of the engine, driven by the generator. The fan is mounted vertically in contrast to a horizontally mounted fan as found on the Chevrolet Corvair engine. The suitcase engine is a comparatively new engine and was designed as a more compact unit to fit in the Type 3, 4 and 1972 and later Type 2 engine compartments. On this engine, the cooling fan is mounted on the crankshaft giving the engine a rectangular shape similar to that of a suitcase.

SERIAL NUMBER IDENTIFICATION

Vehicle (Chassis) Number

The first two numbers are the first two digits of the car's model number and the third digit stands for the car's model year. For example a 0 as the third digit means that the car was produced during the 1970 model year, a 1 would signify 1971, and so forth.

The chassis number is on the frame tunnel under the back seat in the Type 1. In the Type 2, the chassis number is on the right engine cover plate in the engine compartment and behind the front passenger's seat. All models also have an identification plate bearing the chassis number on the top of the instrument panel at the driver's side. This plate is easily visible through the windshield and aids in rapid identification.

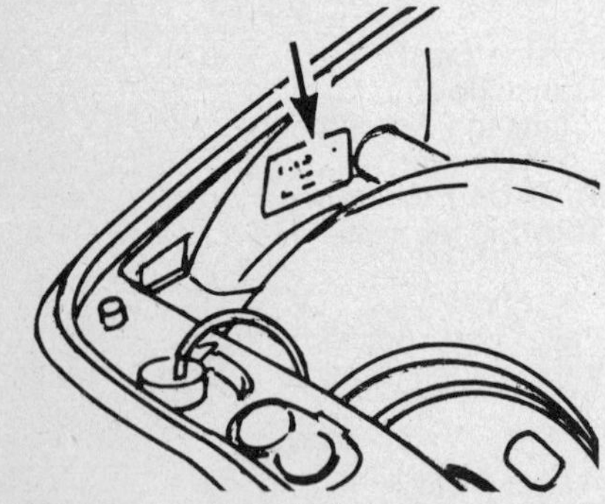

Identification plate in luggage compartment

Another identification plate bearing the vehicle's serial number and paint, body, and assembly codes, is found in the luggage compartment of Types 1.

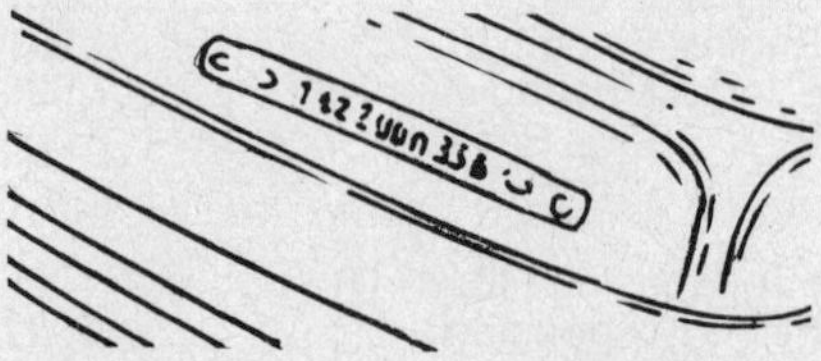

Chassis number location on dashboard

Chassis number location under rear seat

Engine Number

On Type 1 which has the upright engine cooling fan housing, the engine number is on the crankcase flange for the generator sup-

On 1973 and later Type 2 models with the suitcase engine, the number is stamped on the crankcase near the ignition coil and below the crankcase breather. The engine can be identified by the letter or pair of letters preceding the serial number. Engine specifications are listed according to the letters and model year.

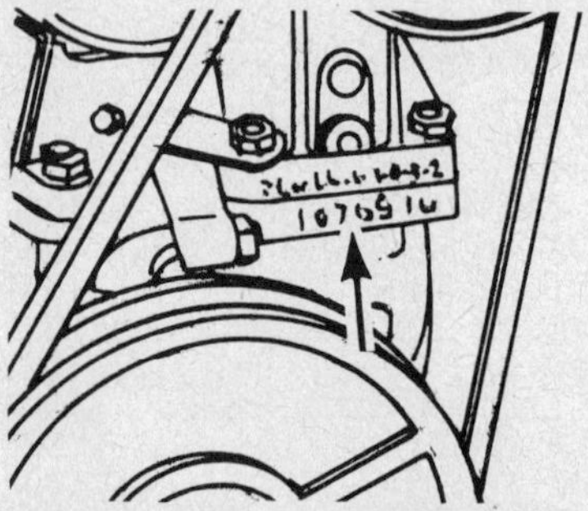

Engine number location on upright fan engine

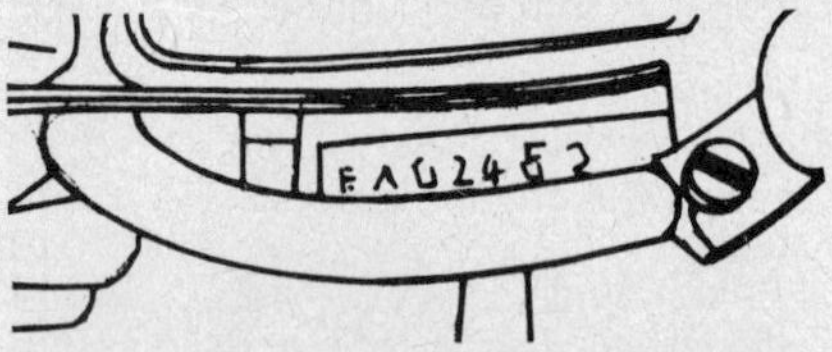

Engine number location on the suitcase engine

Transmission Identification

Transmission identification marks are stamped into the bell housing or on the final drive housing.

ENGINE IDENTIFICATION CHART

Engine Code Letter	Vehicle Type	First Production Year	Last Production Year	Engine Type	Common Designation
AJ	1	1975	1979	Fan driven by generator	1600
ED	2	1975	1975	Fan driven by crankshaft	1800
GD	2	1976	1978	Fan driven by crankshaft	2000
GE	2	1979	1981	Fan driven by crankshaft	2000

CHASSIS NUMBER CHART

Year	Vehicle	Model No.	CHASSIS NUMBER From	CHASSIS NUMBER To
1975	Beetle	11	115 2000 001	115 3200 000
	Beetle Convertible	15	155 2000 001	155 3200 000
	Van	21	215 2000 001	215 2300 000
	Bus	22	225 2000 001	225 2300 000
	Camper, Kombi	23	235 2000 001	235 2300 000
1976	Beetle	11	116 2000 001	—
	Beetle Convertible	15	156 2000 001	—
	Bus	22	226 2000 001	—
	Camper, Kombi	23	236 2000 001	—
1977	Beetle	11	117 2000 001	—
	Beetle Convertible	15	157 2000 001	—
	Bus	22	227 2000 001	—
	Camper, Kombi	23	237 2000 001	—
1978	Beetle Convertible	15	158 2000 001	—
	Bus	22	228 2000 001	—
	Camper	23	238 2000 001	—
1979-81	Beetle Convertible	15	159 2000 001	—
	Bus	22	229 2000 001	—
	Camper	23	239 2000 001	—

GENERAL ENGINE SPECIFICATIONS

Year	Engine Code	Displacement cc	Horsepower @ rpm	Torque @ rpm (ft. lbs.)	Bore x Stroke (in.)	Compression Ratio	Oil Pressure @ rpm (psi)
1975-79	AJ	1584	48 @ 4200	73.1 @ 2800	3.37 x 2.72	7.3:1	42
1975	ED	1795	67 @ 4400	90 @ 2400	3.66 x 2.60	7.3:1	42
1976-81	GD, GE	1970	67 @ 4200	101 @ 3000	3.70 x 2.80	7.3:1	42

TUNE-UP SPECIFICATIONS

Year	Code	Type	Common Designation	SPARK PLUGS Type	SPARK PLUGS Gap (in.)	DISTRIBUTOR Point Dwell (deg)	DISTRIBUTOR Point Gap (in.)	IGNITION TIMING (deg) ① MT	IGNITION TIMING (deg) ① AT	Fuel Pump Pressure (psi) @ 4000 rpm	Compression Pressure (psi)	IDLE SPEED (rpm) MT	IDLE SPEED (rpm) AT	VALVE CLEARANCE (in. cold) In	VALVE CLEARANCE (in. cold) Ex
1975	AJ	1	1600	W145M1 L288	.024	44-50	.016	5ATDC	TDC	28	85-135	875	875	006	.006
	ED	2	1800	W145M2 N288	.024	44-50	.016	5ATDC	5ATDC	28	85-135	900	900	.006	.006
1976	AJ	1	1600	Bosch W145M1 Champ L288	.024	44-50	.016	5ATDC	TDC	28	85-135	875	925	.006	.006
	GD	2	2000	Bosch W145M2 Champ N288	.028	44-50	.016	7½BTDC	7½BTDC	28	85-135	900	950	.006	.006
1977	AJ	1	1600	Bosch M145M1 Champ N288	.028	44-50	.016	5ATDC	5ATDC	28	85-135	800-950	800-950	.006	.006
	GD	2	2000	Bosch M145M2 Champ N288	.028	44-50	.016	7½BTDC	7½BTDC	28	85-135	800-950	850-1000	.006	.006

TUNE-UP SPECIFICATIONS

Year	Code	Type	Common Designation	Spark Plugs Type	Spark Plugs Gap (in.)	Distributor Point Dwell (deg)	Distributor Point Gap (in.)	Ignition Timing (deg) ① MT	Ignition Timing (deg) ① AT	Fuel Pump Pressure (psi) @ 4000 rpm	Compression Pressure (psi)	Idle Speed (rpm) MT	Idle Speed (rpm) AT	Valve Clearance (in. cold) In	Valve Clearance (in. cold) Ex
1978	AJ	1	1600	Bosch W145M1 Champ L288	.028 .028	44-50	.016	5ATDC	5ATDC	28	85-135	800-950	800-950	.006	.006
	GE	2	2000	Bosch W145M2 Champ N288	.028 .028	44-50	.016	7½BTDC	7½BTDC	28	85-135	800-950	900-1000	Hyd.	Hyd.
1979	AJ	1	1600	Bosch W145M1 Champ L288	.028 .028	44-50	.016	5ATDC	5ATDC	28	85-135	800-950	800-950	.006	.006
1979-81	GE	2	2000	Bosch W145M2	.028	44-50	.016	7½BTDC ②	7½BTDC ②	28	85-135	800-950 ③	850-1000 ④	Hyd.	Hyd.

① 1975-77: Carbon canister hose at air cleaner disconnected; at idle; vacuum hose(s) on
② 5ATDC, Calif.
③ Calif.: 850-950
④ Calif.: 850-950

FIRING ORDER

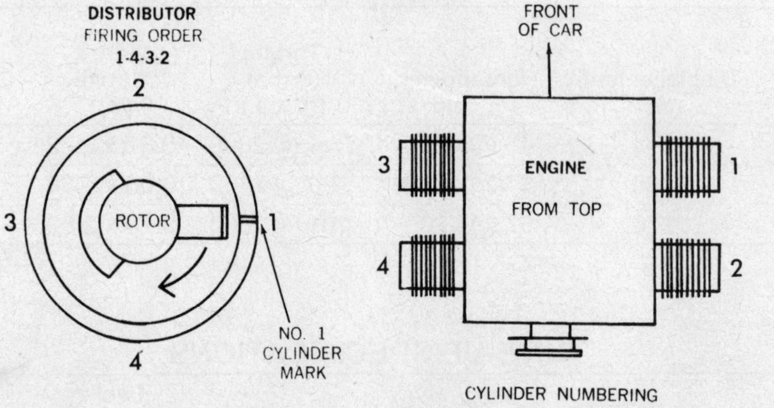

CAPACITIES

Year	Type	Engine Displacement (cc)	Engine Crankcase (qts.) With Filter	Engine Crankcase (qts.) Without Filter	Transaxle (pts.) Manual	Transaxle (pts.) Automatic Conv.	Transaxle (pts.) Automatic Final Drive	Gasoline Tank (gal.)
1975-79	1	1600	—	2.5	6.3	7.6	6.3 ①	10.6 ③
1975-81	2	1800, 2000	3.7	3.2	7.4	12.8 ②	2.6	15.9

① 5.3 when changed
② 6.3 when changed
③ Convertible (11.1)
Conv. = torque converter

CRANKSHAFT AND CONNECTING ROD SPECIFICATIONS

All measurements are given in inches

		CRANKSHAFT									
		MAIN BEARING JOURNAL DIAMETER		MAIN BEARING OIL CLEARANCE					CONNECTING RODS		
Year	Engine	No. 1, 2, 3	No. 4	No. 1, 3	No. 2	No. 4	Crankshaft End-Play	Thrust on No.	Journal Diameter	Oil Clearance	End-Play
1975-79	1600	2.1640-2.1648	1.5739-1.5748	0.0016-0.004	0.001-0.003	0.002-0.004	0.0027-0.005	1 at flywheel	2.1644-2.1653	0.0008-0.0027	0.004-0.016
1975-81	1800, 2000	2.3609-2.3617	1.5739-1.5748	0.002-0.004	0.0012-0.0035	0.002-0.004	0.0027-0.005	1 at flywheel	2.1644-2.1653 ①	0.0008-0.0027	0.004-0.016

① On 1977-79 2000 models, connecting rod journal diameter is 1.968 in.

VALVE SPECIFICATIONS

		SEAT ANGLE (deg)		FACE ANGLE (deg)		VALVE SEAT WIDTH (in.)		Spring Test Pressure	VALVE GUIDE INSIDE DIA (in.)		STEM TO GUIDE CLEARANCE (in.)		STEM DIAMETER (in.)	
Year	Type	Intake	Exhaust	Intake	Exhaust	Intake	Exhaust	(lbs. @ in.)	Intake	Exhaust	Intake	Exhaust	Intake	Exhaust
1975-79	1	45	45	45	45	0.05-0.10	0.05-0.10	117.7-134.8 @ 1.22	0.3150-0.3157	0.353-0.354	0.009-0.010	0.009-0.010	0.3125-0.3129	0.350-0.351
1975-81	2	30	45	30	45	0.07-0.08	0.078-0.098	168-186 @ 1.14	0.3150-0.3157	0.3534-0.3538	0.018-	0.014-	0.3125-0.3129	0.3507-0.3511

PISTON AND RING SPECIFICATIONS

All measurements in inches

			RING GAP			RING SIDE CLEARANCE		
Year	Engine Displacement	Piston Clearance	Top Compression	Bottom Compression	Oil Control	Top Compression	Bottom Compression	Oil Control
1975-79	1600	0.0016-0.0023	0.012-0.018	0.012-0.018	0.010-0.016	0.0027-0.0039	0.002-0.0027	0.0011-0.0019
1975-81	1800, 2000	0.0016-0.0023	0.014-0.021	0.012-0.022	0.010-0.016	0.0023-0.0035	0.0016-0.0027	0.0008-0.0019

TORQUE SPECIFICATIONS

All readings in ft. lbs.

									CRANKCASE HALF NUTS				
Year	Type Vehicle	Cylinder Head Nuts	Rod Bearing Bolts	Generator Pulley	Crankshaft Pulley Bolt	Flywheel to Crankshaft Bolts	Fan to Hub	Hub to Crankshaft	Sealing Nuts	Non-Sealing Nuts	Drive Plate to Crankshaft	Spark Plugs	Oil Strainer Cover
1975-79	1	23	22-25	40-47	29-36	253	—	—	18	14	—	25	5
1975-81	2	23	24	—	—	80 ①	14	23	23	14	61	22	7-9

① Automatic transmission drive plate—14 ft. lbs. (1980 and later Vanagon)

TORQUE SEQUENCES

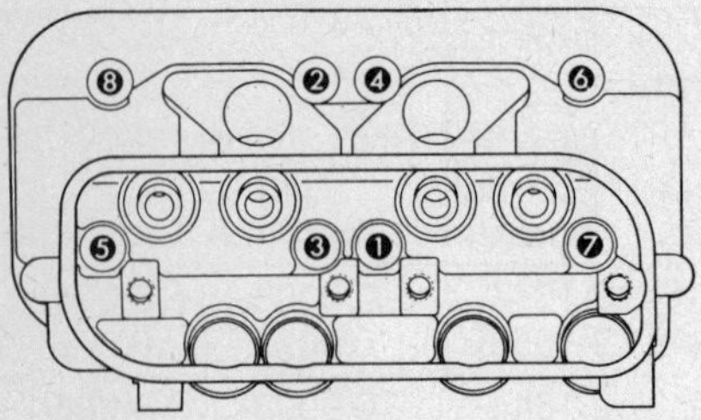

Cylinder head torque sequence—Type 2

I

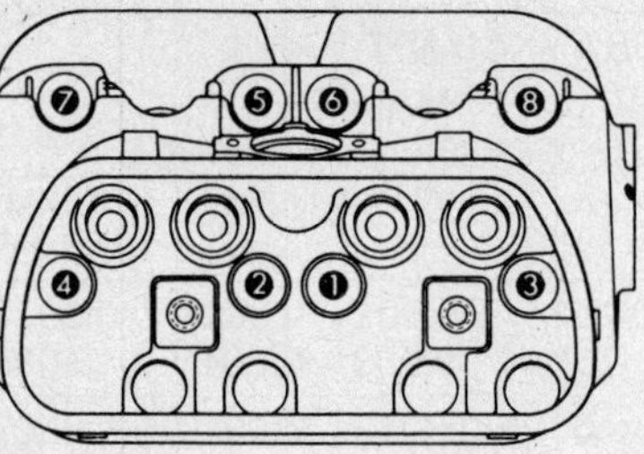

II

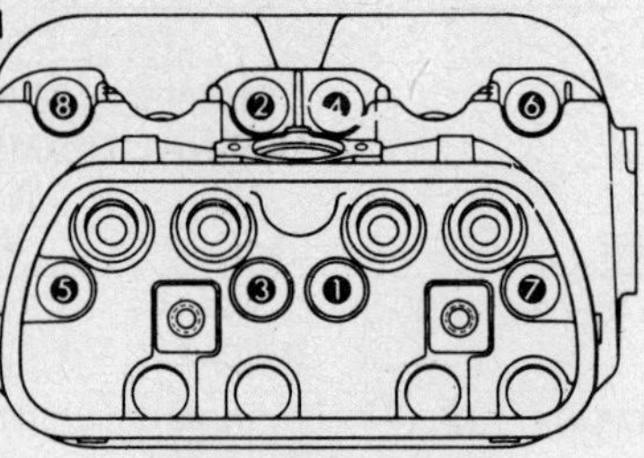

For 1600 cc engines, the cylinder head nuts should initially be tightened to 7 ft. lbs. in order I, then tightened to the recommended torque in order II.

STARTER SPECIFICATIONS

Starter Number	LOCK TEST Amps	LOCK TEST Volts	NO LOAD TEST Amps	NO LOAD TEST Volts	NO LOAD TEST rpm	Brush Spring Tension (oz)
111 911 023A	270-290	6	25-40	12	6700-7800	42
311 911 023B	250-300	6	35-45	12	7400-8100	42
003 911 023A	250-300	6	35-50	12	6400-7900	42

ALTERNATOR AND REGULATOR SPECIFICATIONS

		ALTERNATOR			REGULATOR	
Year	Type	Maximum Output (amps)	Stator Winding Resistance (ohms)	Exciter Winding Resistance (ohms)	Load Current (amps)	Regulating Voltage Under Load (volts)
1975-79	1	50	.13 ± .13	4.0 ± .4	25-30	13.8-14.9 ①
1975-81	2	55	.13 ± .13	4.0 ± .4	25-30	13.8-14.9 ①

① @ 2000 engine rpm's

BRAKE SPECIFICATIONS

All measurements are given in inches

				BRAKE DISC		BRAKE DRUM			MINIMUM LINING THICKNESS	
Year	Type	Lug Nut Torque (ft. lbs.)	Master Cylinder Bore	Minimum Thickness	Maximum Run-Out	Diameter	Max. Machine O/S	Max. Wear Limit	Front	Rear
1975-77	Type 1 (Beetle)	87-94	0.750	—	—	9.059	9.10	9.114	0.100	0.100
1975-79	Type 1 (Super Beetle)	87-94	0.750	—	—	9.768 (fr) 9.059 (rr)	9.80 (fr) 9.10 (rr)	9.823 (fr) 9.114 (rr)	0.100	0.100
1975-81	Type 2 (Bus)	87-94	0.938	0.472 ①	0.0008	9.920	9.97	9.98	0.079	0.100

NOTE: Minimum lining thickness is as recommended by the manufacturer. Due to variations in state inspection regulations, the minimum allowable thickness may be different than recommended by the manufacturer.
① 1981: 0.453
(fr)—front
(rr)—rear
— not applicable

WHEEL ALIGNMENT SPECIFICATIONS

		FRONT AXLE					REAR AXLE		
		Caster		Camber			Camber		
Year	Model	Range (deg)	Pref Setting (deg)	Range (deg)	Pref Setting (deg)	Toe-In (in.)	Range (deg)	Pref Setting (deg)	Toe-In (deg)
1975-77	Type 1	±1°	+3°20′	±20′	+30′	+0.071-+0.213	±40′	−1°	0′±15′
1975-79	Type 1 ①	±35′	+2°	+20′ −40′	+1°	+0.071-+0.231	±40′	−1°	0′±15′
1975-79	Type 2	±40′	+3°	±20′	+40′	0	±30′	−50′	+10′±20′
1980	Type 2	±15′	+7°15′	±30′	+40′	+40′	±30′	−50′	0±10′
1981	Type 2	±15′	+7°15′	±30′	0	+40′	±30′	−50′	0±10′

① Super Beetle

UNLOADED REAR TORSION BAR SETTINGS

Type	Model	Transmission	Setting	Range
1	All	All	20°30′	+50′
2	221, 223, 226	Manual	21°10′	+50′
2	222	Manual	23°	+50′
2 ①	221, 223	All	20°	+50′
2 ②	222	All	23°	+50′

① From chassis 212 2 000 001
② From chassis 212 2 000 001

TUNE-UP PROCEDURES

This section gives specific procedures on how to tune-up your Volkswagen and is intended to be as complete and basic as possible.

CAUTION

When working with a running engine, make sure that the transmission is in Neutral (unless otherwise specified) and the parking brake is fully applied. When the ignition is turned on and the engine running, do not grasp the ignition wires, distributor cap, or coil wire, as a shock in excess of 20,000 volts may result. Whenever working near the distributor, even if the engine is not running, make sure that the ignition is switched off. Always keep hands, clothing, jewelry, and long hair clear of the cooling fan and pulleys. Also, stay clear of the hot exhaust manifolds and catalytic converter (if so equipped).

Spark Plugs

Before attempting any work on the cylinder head, it is very important to note that the cylinder head is cast aluminum alloy. It is extremely easy to damage threads in the cylinder head. Care must be taken not to cross-thread the spark plugs or any bolts or studs. Never overtighten the spark plugs, bolts, or studs.

CAUTION

Always lubricate the spark plug threads with anti-seize compound prior to installation.

To avoid cross-threading the spark plugs, always start the plugs in their threads with your fingers. Never force the plugs into the cylinder head. Do not use a wrench until you are certain that the plug is correctly threaded.

VW spark plugs should be cleaned and regapped every 6000 miles and replaced every 12,000.

REMOVAL AND INSTALLATION

To install the spark plugs, remove the spark plug wire from the plug. Grasp the plug connector and, while removing, do not pull on the wire. Using a 13/16 in. spark plug socket, remove the old spark plugs. Examine the threads of the old plugs; if one or more of the plugs have aluminum clogged threads, it will be necessary to rethread the spark plug hole. See the following section for the necessary information.

Obtain the proper heat range and type of new plug. Set the gap by bending the side electrode only. Do not bend the center electrode to adjust the gap. The proper gap is listed in the "Tune-Up Specifications" chart. Lubricate the plug threads.

Start each new plug in its hole using your fingers. Tighten the plug several turns by hand to assure that the plug is not cross-threaded. Using a wrench, tighten the plug just enough to compress the gasket. Do not overtighten the plug.

RETHREADING SPARK PLUG HOLE

It is possible to repair light damage to spark plug hole threads by using a spark plug hole tap of the proper diameter and thread. Plenty of grease should be used on the tap to catch any metal chips. Exercise caution when using the tap as it is possible to cut a second set of threads instead of straightening the old ones.

If the old threads are beyond repair, then the hole must be drilled and tapped to accept a steel bushing of Heli-Coil. It is not always necessary to remove the cylinder head to rethread the spark plug holes. Bushing kits, Heli-Coil kits, and spark plug hole taps are available at most auto parts stores. Heli-Coil information is contained in the "Engine Rebuilding" section of this book.

Breaker Points and Condenser

REMOVAL AND INSTALLATION

NOTE: 1979-81 California Type 2 vehicles are equipped with an electronic ignition system.

1. Release the spring clips which secure the distributor cap and lift the cap from the distributor. Pull the rotor from the distributor shaft.
2. Disconnect the points wire from the condenser snap connection inside the distributor.
3. Remove the locking screw from the stationary breaker point.
4. To remove the condenser which is located on the outside of the distributor, remove the screw which secures the condenser bracket and condenser connection to the distributor.
5. Disconnect the condenser wire from the coil.
6. With a clean rag, wipe the excess oil from the breaker plate.

NOTE: Make sure that the new point contacts are clean and oil free.

7. Installation of the points and condenser is the reverse of the above; however, it will be necessary to adjust the point gap, (or dwell), and check the timing. Lubricate the point cam with a small amount of lithium or white grease. Set the dwell, or gap, before the ignition timing.

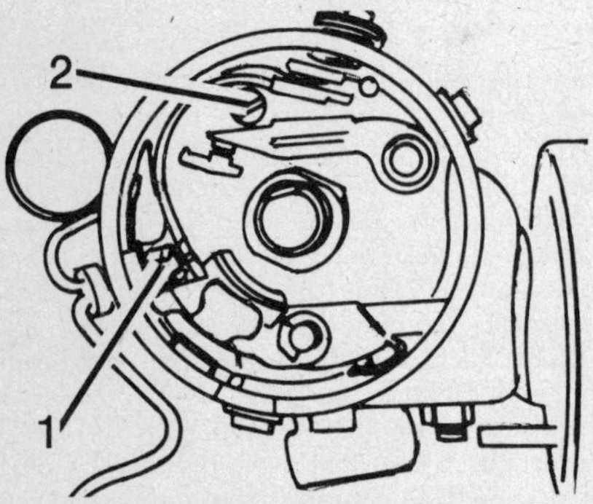

Breaker point removal is accomplished by disconnecting the snap connection (1) and removing the attaching screw (2)

POINT GAP ADJUSTMENT

1. Remove the distributor cap and rotor.
2. Turn the engine by hand until the fiber rubbing block on the movable breaker point rests on a high point of the cam lobe. The point gap is the maximum distance between the points and must be set at the top of a cam lobe.
3. Using a screwdriver, loosen the locking screw of the stationary breaker point.
4. Move the stationary point plate so that the gap is set as specified and then tighten the screw. Make sure that the feeler gauge is clean. After tightening the screw, recheck the gap.

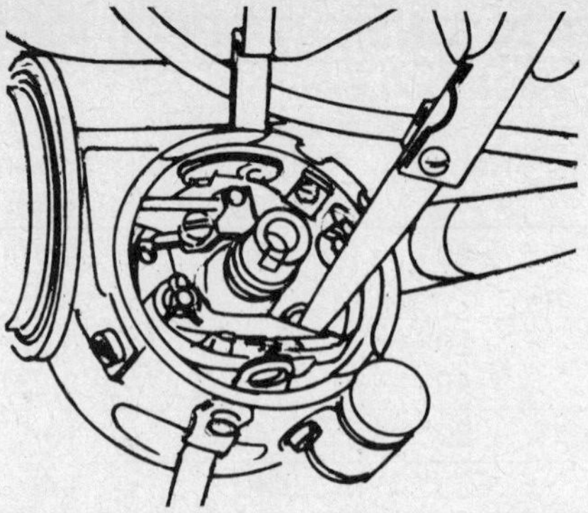

Checking the point gap with a feeler gauge

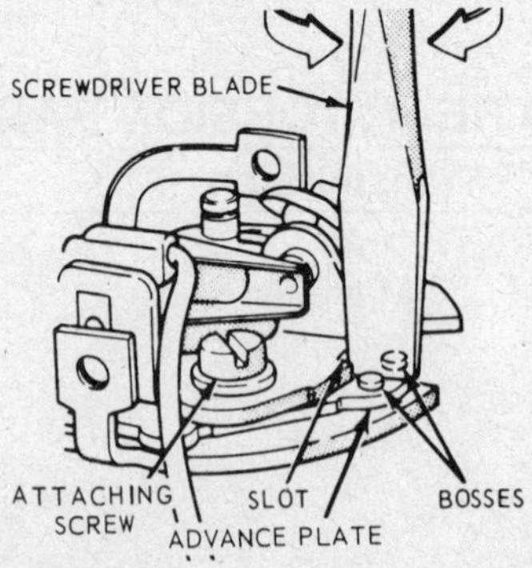

Adjusting point gap by moving stationary arm with a screwdriver

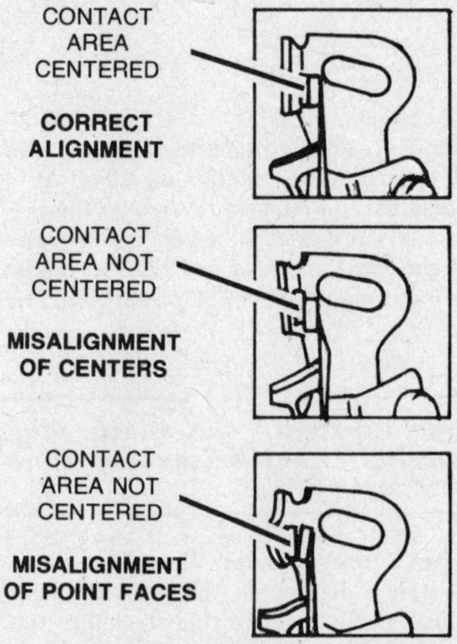

Breaker point alignment guide

Electronic Ignition

All 1979-81 Type 2 vehicles which were made for use in California are equipped with a breakerless, transistorized ignition system. This system consists of a distributor with a "Hall" sender unit, an idle stabilizer, a stronger ignition coil and an electronic control unit to monitor the whole system.

The factory states that there are no adjustments or services to be performed on this system. Any problems which are believed to be originating in the electronic ignition system should be referred to an authorized service technician with access to workshop test equipment.

PRECAUTIONS

1. DO NOT disconnect or connect any wires with the ignition switched "ON".
2. When cranking the engine, without wanting it to start (such as when performing a compression test), always disconnect the high tension wire on the distributor and then connect it to ground.
3. DO NOT install any standard ignition coil (always note the Part no. of the old one).
4. DO NOT connect a condenser to the negative terminal of the ignition coil.
5. DO NOT connect a quick charger (for boost starting) for any longer than 1 minute.

Dwell Angle

NOTE: The dwell angle on all cars with the electronic ignition system is set at the factory and not adjustable.

1. Setting the dwell angle with a dwell meter achieves the same effect as setting the point gap but offers better accuracy.

NOTE: The dwell must be set before setting the timing. Setting the dwell will alter the timing, but when the timing is set, the dwell will not change.

2. Attach the positive the dwell meter to that coil terminal which has a wire leading to the distributor. The negative lead should be attached to a good ground.
3. Remove the distributor cap and rotor. Turn the ignition ON and turn the engine over using a starter or a starter button. Read the dwell from the meter and open or close the points to adjust the dwell.

NOTE: Increasing the gap decreases the dwell and decreasing the gap increases the dwell.

Dwell specifications are listed in the "Tune-Up Specifications" chart.

4. Reinstall the cap and rotor and start the engine. Check the dwell and reset it if necessary.

Ignition Timing

TYPE 1 AND 2 (EXCEPT 1979-81 TYPE 2 CALIF. MODELS)

Dwell or point gap must be set before the timing is set. Also, the idle speed must be set to specifications.

NOTE: The engine must be warmed up before the timing is set (oil temperature of 122° F-158° F).

1. Remove the No. 1 spark plug wire from the distributor cap and attach the timing light lead. Disconnect the vacuum hose if so advised by the "Tune-Up Specifications" chart (and readjust the idle speed if necessary).
2. Start the engine and run it at the specified rpm. Aim the timing light at the crankshaft pulley on upright fan engines and at the engine cooling fan on the suitcase engines. The rubber plug in the fan housing will

have to be removed before the timing marks on the suitcase engine can be seen.

3. Read the timing and rotate the distributor accordingly.

NOTE: Rotate the distributor in the opposite direction of normal rotor rotation to advance the timing. Retard the timing by turning the distributor in the normal direction of rotor rotation.

4. It is necessary to loosen the clamp at the base of the distributor before the distributor can be rotated. It may also be necessary to put a small amount of white paint or chalk on the timing marks to make them more visible.

1979-81 TYPE 2 CALIF. MODELS

1. Run the engine until it reaches normal operating temperature and then turn it off.
2. Bypass the idle stabilizer by pulling the two leads from the unit and connecting them together.
3. Hook up a dwell/tachometer as per the manufacturer's instructions, start the engine and check that the idle is between 850 and 950 rpm.
4. Turn off the engine and follow Steps 1-4 of the previous procedure.
5. Be sure to hook the idle stabilizer back up after the timing has been set.

Valve Lash

NOTE: 1978-81 Type 2 vehicles are equipped with hydraulic valve lifters. No valve adjustment is possible or necessary.

NOTE: The engine must be as cool as possible before adjusting the valves. Adjust the valves as follows:

1. Remove the distributor cap and turn the engine until the rotor points to the No. One spark plug wire post in the distributor cap. To bring the piston to exactly top dead center (TDC) on the compression stroke, align the crankshaft timing marks on TDC.
2. Remove the rocker arm covers. At TDC, the pushrods should be down and there should be clearance between the rocker arms and valve stems of both valves of the subject cylinder.

No. 1 piston at Top Dead Center—Type 1

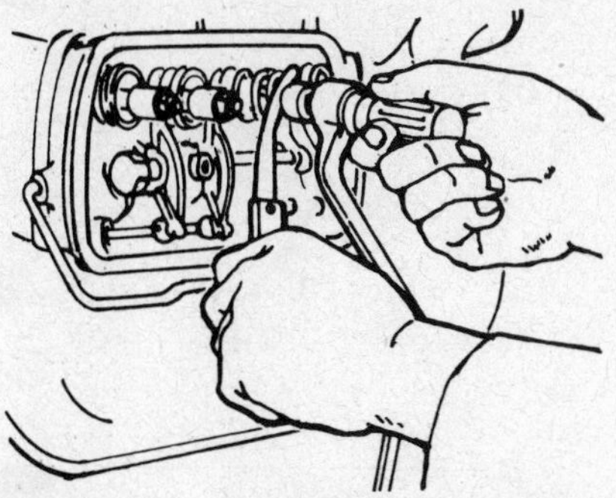

Checking valve clearance with a feeler gauge

3. With the proper feeler gauge, check the clearance between the adjusting screw and the valve stem of both valves for the No. 1 cylinder. If the feeler gauge slides in snugly without being forced, the clearance is correct. It is better that the clearance is a little loose then a little tight.
4. If the clearance is incorrect, the locknut must be loosened and the adjusting screw turned until the proper clearance is obtained. After tightening down the locknut, it is then advisable to recheck the clearance. It is possible to alter the adjustment when tightening the locknut.
5. The valves are adjusted in a 1-2-3-4 sequence. To adjust cylinders 2 through 4, the distributor rotor must be pointed at the appropriate distributor cap post 90° apart from each other. Align the crankshaft timing marks for each cylinder, remembering that the piston must be at TDC on the compression stroke when the valves are adjusted.

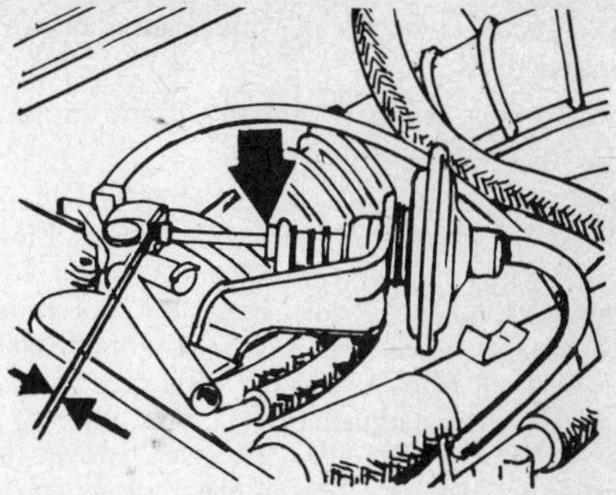

Idle speed regulator adjustment—Type 2 with automatic transmission

NOTE: Always use new valve cover gaskets.

Fuel System Adjustments

FUEL INJECTION IDLE SPEED AND MIXTURE

Idle Mixture

Volkswagen states that the idle mixture should not require adjustment during a tune-up or routine maintenance. The only time that it will require an adjustment is after replacement of the intake air sensor or after extensive engine rebuilding. Due to the requirement of an infrared exhaust gas analyzer to perform this adjustment, we suggest that if in fact the adjustment is needed, the work should be performed by an authorized service facility.

Idle Speed

1. Thoroughly warm up the engine so that the oil will be hot and the auxiliary air regulator will be fully closed.

NOTE: On 1979-81 Type 2 Calif. models the idle stabilizer must be bypassed. Pull the two leads from the stabilizer and connect them together.

2. Turn off the engine and hook up a

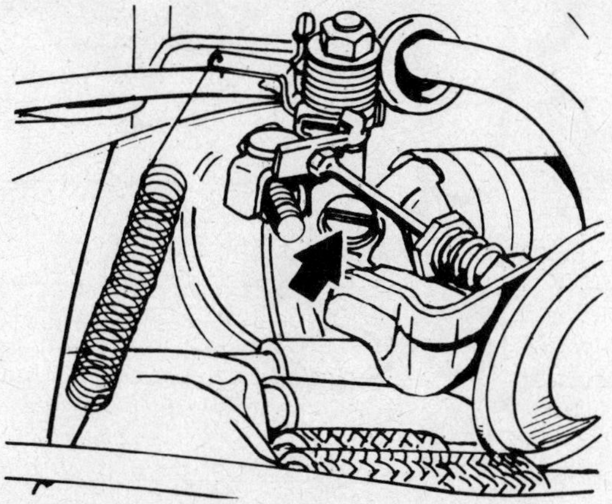

Fuel injection idle speed (by-pass screw) adjustment—Type 1

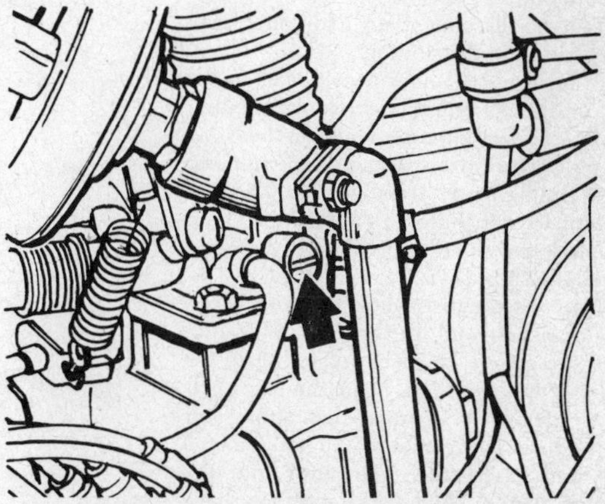

Fuel injection idle speed (by-pass screw) adjustment—Type 2

dwell/tachometer as per the manufacturer's instructions.

NOTE: Don't forget to set the meter to the four cylinder scale.

3. Start the engine, speed it up and then allow it to return to idle. The idle speed for cars with manual transmissions should be 850-950 rpm. The idle speed for cars with automatic transmissions should be 900-1000 rpm. If the idle speed is not within the limits, it will require adjustment.

4. To adjust the idle, use a screwdriver to turn the bypass screw in the throttle valve housing. Turn the screw clockwise to decrease the idle and counterclockwise to increase it.

NOTE: Make sure you reconnect the idle stabilizer if your car is so equipped.

All Type 2 vehicles with an automatic transmission require one further adjustment. When the idle speed has been set properly, set the parking brake, block the front wheels and then put the car in "Drive." The idle should drop between 150-200 rpm. If it drops more than this you will have to adjust the idle speed regulator. To adjust:

1. With the engine idling, place the transmission in "Park" and use a feeler gauge to check the clearance between the end of the plunger and the lever on the throttle valve shaft. It should be between 0.020-0.040 in.

2. If the gap is not within specifications, loosen the locknut on the plunger and screw the plunger in or out until the clearance is correct.

ENGINE ELECTRICAL

Distributor

REMOVAL AND INSTALLATION

1. Take off the vacuum hose(s) at the distributor.
2. Disconnect the coil wire and remove the distributor cap.
3. Tag and disconnect any additional wires leading from the distributor.
4. Bring No. 1 cylinder to top dead center (TDC) on the compression stroke by rotating the engine so that the rotor points to the No. 1 spark plug wire tower on the distributor cap and the timing marks are aligned at 0°. Mark the rotor-to-distributor relationship. Also, matchmark the distributor housing-to-crankcase relationship.
5. Unscrew the distributor retaining screw on the crankcase and lift the distributor out.
6. If the engine has been rotated since the distributor was removed, bring the No. 1 cylinder to TDC on the compression stroke and align the timing marks on 0°. Align the match marks and insert the distributor into the crankcase. If the matchmarks are gone, have the rotor pointing to the No. 1 spark plug wire tower upon insertion.

2. Distributor cap
3. Rotor
6. Points
8. Vacuum unit
9. Condenser
10. Holding spring
16. Ball retaining spring
17. Ball
18. Breaker plate
22. Return spring
23. Distributor cam
25. Flyweight
27. Circlip for drive dog
28. Pin for drive dog
29. Drive dog
30. 0.1 mm compensating washer
32. Distributor shaft
33. Distributor housing
34. Rubber sealing ring
35. Fuel injection trigger contacts

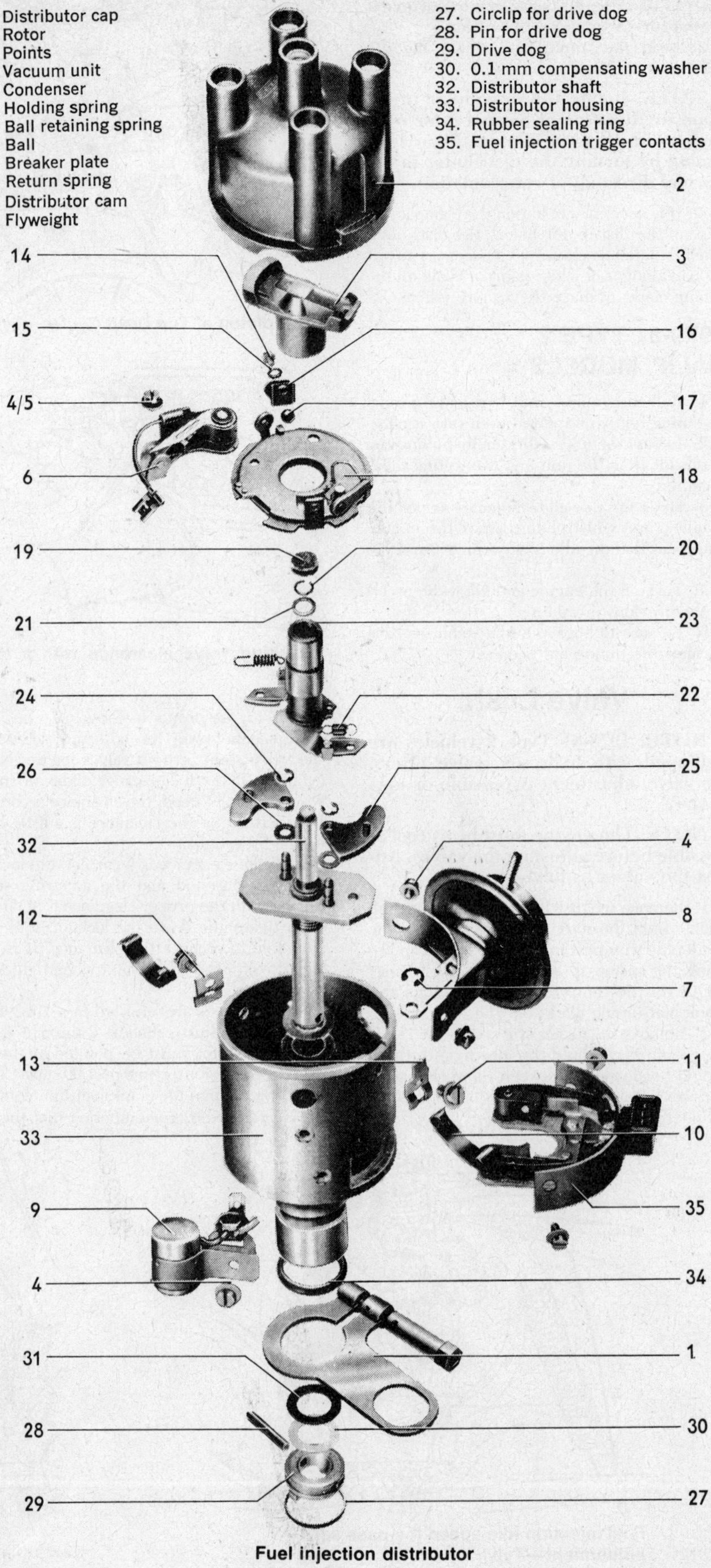

Fuel injection distributor

7. Replace the distributor retaining screw and reconnect the condenser and coil wires. Reinstall the distributor cap.
8. Retime the engine.

Distributor Driveshaft

REMOVAL AND INSTALLATION

1. Bring the engine to TDC on the compression stroke of No. 1 cylinder. Align the timing marks at 0°.
2. Remove the distributor.
3. Remove the spacer spring from the driveshaft.
4. Grasp the shaft and turn it slowly to the left while withdrawing it from its bore.
5. Remove the washer found under the shaft.

CAUTION
Make sure that this washer does not fall down into the engine.

6. To install, make sure that the engine is at TDC on the compression stroke for No. 1 cylinder with the timing marks aligned at 0°.
7. Replace the washer and insert the shaft into its bore.

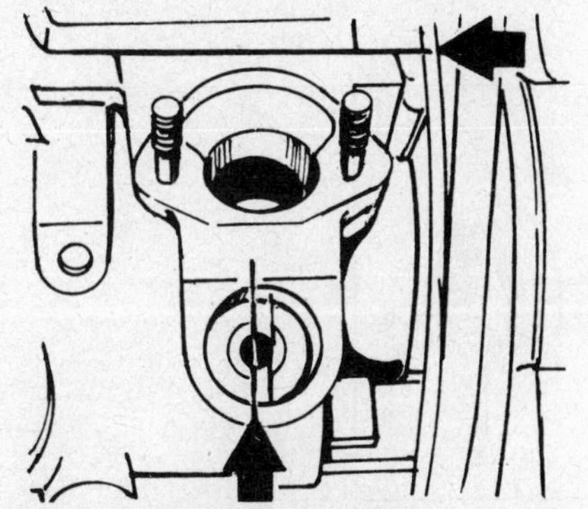

Type 1 distributor driveshaft alignment

NOTE: Due to the slant of the teeth on the drive gears, the shaft must be rotated slightly to the left when it is inserted into the crankcase.

8. When the shaft is properly inserted, the offset slot in the driveshaft of Type 1 engines will be perpendicular to the crankcase joint and the slot offset will be facing the crankshaft pulley. On Type 2/1800 and 2/2000 engines, the slot should be about 12° out of parallel with the center line of the engine and the slot offset should be facing outside the engine.

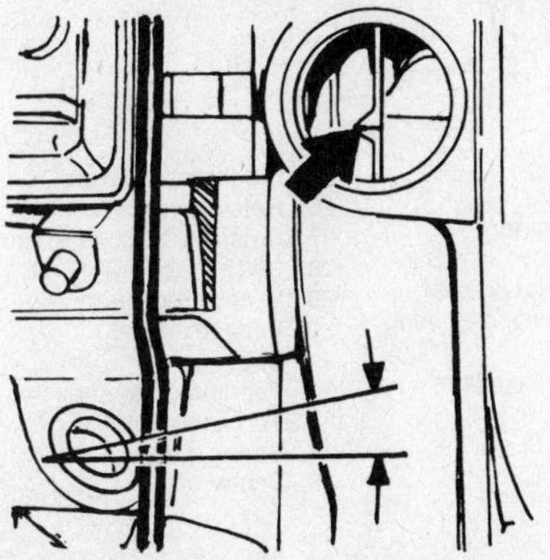

Type 2 distributor driveshaft alignment

9. Reinstall the spacer spring.
10. Reinstall the distributor and fuel pump, if removed.
11. Retime the engine.

Alternator

ALTERNATOR PRECAUTIONS

1. Battery polarity should be checked be-

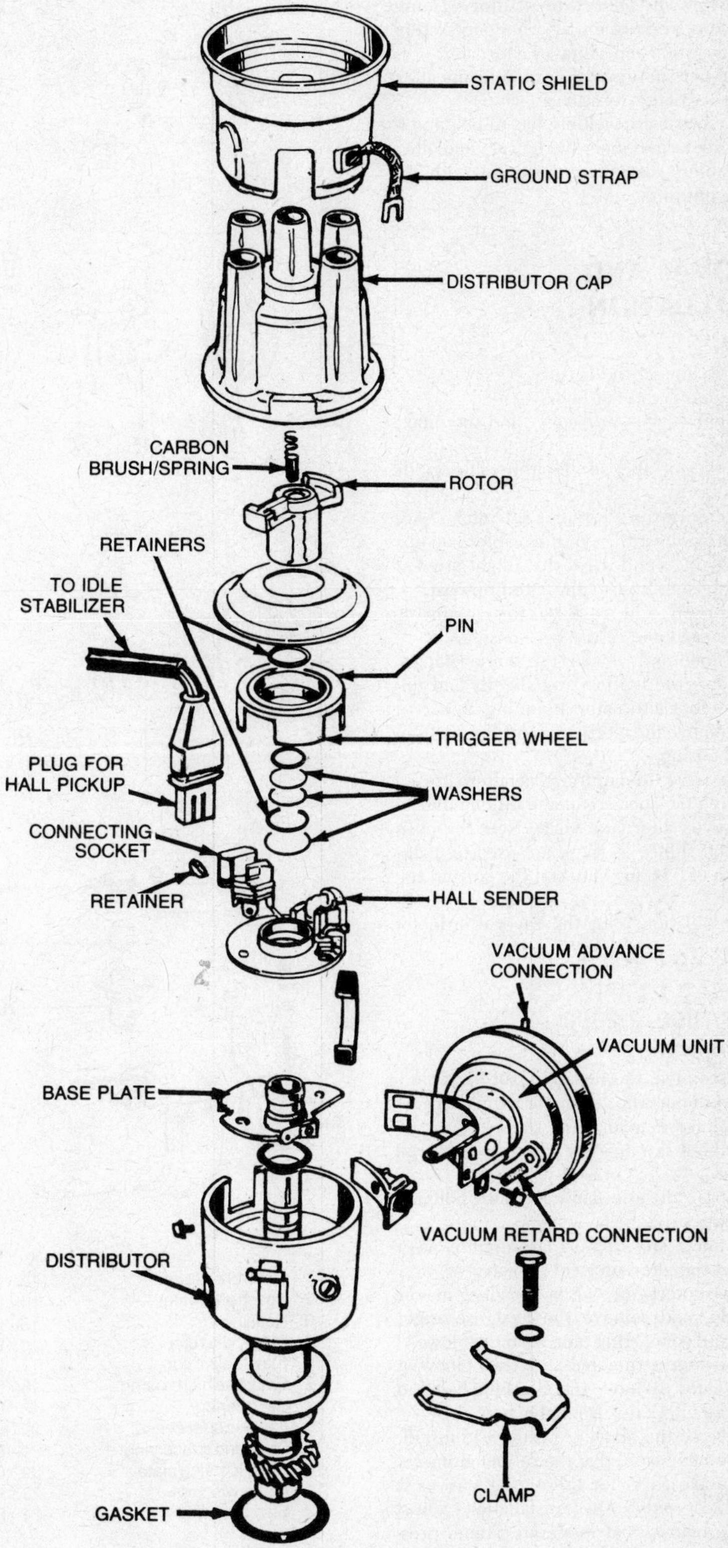

Electronic ignition distributor

fore any connections, such as jumper cables or battery charger leads, are made. Reversing the battery connections will damage the diodes in the alternator. It is recommended that the battery cables be disconnected before connecting a battery charger.

2. The battery must never be disconnected while the alternator is running.

3. Always disconnect the battery ground lead before working on the charging system, especially when replacing an alternator.

4. Do not short across or ground any alternator or regulator terminals.

5. If electric arc welding has to be done to the car, first disconnect the battery and alternator cables. Never start the car with the welding unit attached.

REMOVAL AND INSTALLATION

Type 1

1. Disconnect the battery.
2. Remove the fan belt.
3. Remove the air cleaner and the intake air sensor.
4. Pull out the accelerator cable guide tube.
5. Remove the alternator retaining strap.
6. Disconnect the ignition cables and any hoses, air ducts and wires that might prevent the fan housing from being lifted upward.
7. Loosen and remove the mounting screws at each end of the fan housing.
8. Unbolt and remove the thermostat.
9. Raise the fan housing slightly and unscrew the four alternator mounting bolts.
10. Remove the alternator and the fan from the fan housing.
11. Remove the fan from the alternator by unscrewing the special nut and pulling the fan off the keyed alternator shaft. Note the position of any shims, as these are used to maintain a gap of 0.08 in. between the fan and the fan cover.
12. Installation is in the reverse order of removal.

Type 2/1800, 2/2000 (Fuel Injected)

1. Disconnect the negative battery cable.
2. Disconnect the alternator wiring harness at the voltage regulator and starter.
3. Pull out the dipstick and remove the oil filler neck.
4. Loosen the alternator adjusting bolt and remove the drive belt.
5. Remove the right rear engine cover plate and the alternator cover plate.
6. Disconnect the warm air duct at the right side, and remove the heat exchanger bracket and connecting pipe from the blower.
7. Disconnect the cool air intake elbow at the alternator. Remove the attaching bolt and lift out the alternator from above.
8. Reverse the above procedure to install, taking care to ensure that the rubber grommet on the intake cover for the wiring harness is installed correctly. After installation, adjust the drive belt so that moderate thumb pressure midway on the belt depresses the belt about ½ in.

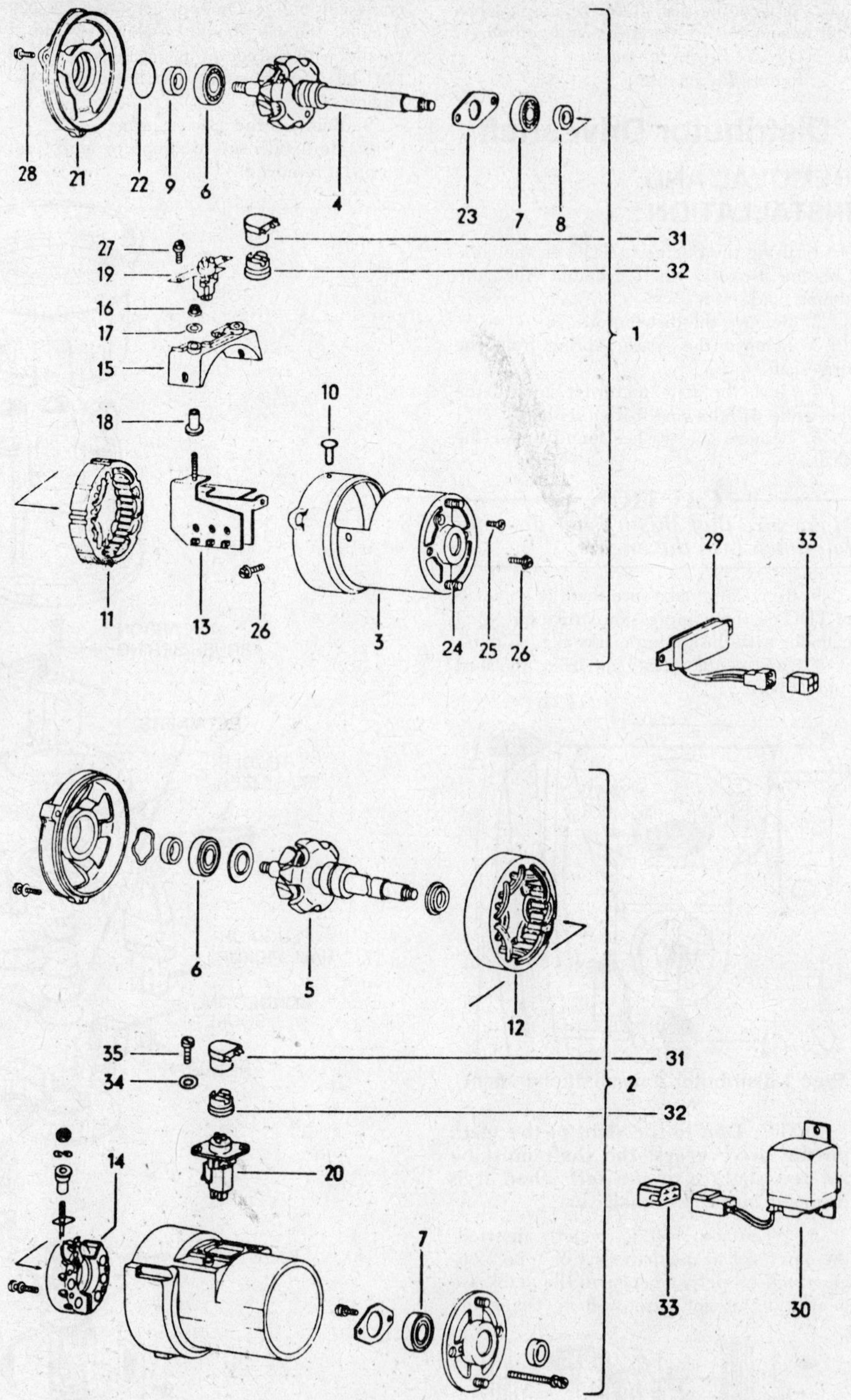

1. Motorola alternator
2. Bosch alternator
3. Housing
4. Claw-pole rotor
5. Claw-pole rotor
6. End plate ball bearing
7. Ball bearing
8. Fan end spacer ring
9. Drive end spacer ring
10. Rotor locating plate
11. Stator winding
12. Stator winding
13. Diode carrier
14. Diode carrier
15. Diode carrier retainer
16. B+ terminal nut
17. B+ terminal insulating washer
18. B+ terminal insulating bushing
19. Brush holder
20. Carbon brush holder plate
21. End plate
22. O-ring
23. Retaining plate
24. Fan cover bolt
25. Diode carrier screw
26. Retaining plate screw
27. Brush holder cover screw
28. End plate screw
29. Voltage regulator
30. Voltage regulator
31. Boot
32. Terminal sleeve housing
33. Terminal pin housing
34. Spring washer
35. Screw

Exploded view of the 50 amp alternator used in Type 1 models

ALTERNATOR BELT ADJUSTMENT

1. Remove the insert in the cover plate and loosen the bolt in the slotted hole.
2. Move the alternator left or right to adjust the tension and then tighten the bolt. Tension is correct if the bolt can be deflected no more than ½ in. at the midpoint of the pulleys.

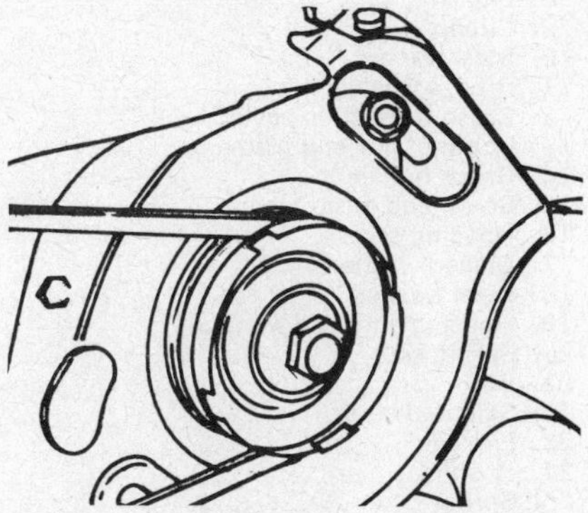

Alternator belt tension adjustment

Voltage Regulator

REMOVAL AND INSTALLATION

Type 1

The regulator is located under the rear seat on the left side. It is secured to the frame by two screws. Take careful note of the wiring connections before removing the wiring from the regulator. Disconnect the battery before removing the regulator.

CAUTION

Interchanging the connections on the regulator will destroy the regulator and generator.

Type 2

Disconnect the battery. The regulator is located in the engine compartment and is secured in place by two screws. Take careful note of the wiring connections before removing the wiring from the regulator.

VOLTAGE ADJUSTMENT

Volkswagen voltage regulators are sealed and cannot be adjusted. A malfunctioning regulator must be replaced as a unit.

Starter

REMOVAL AND INSTALLATION

1. Disconnect the battery.
2. Disconnect the wiring from the starter.
3. The starter is held in place by two bolts. Remove the upper bolt through the engine

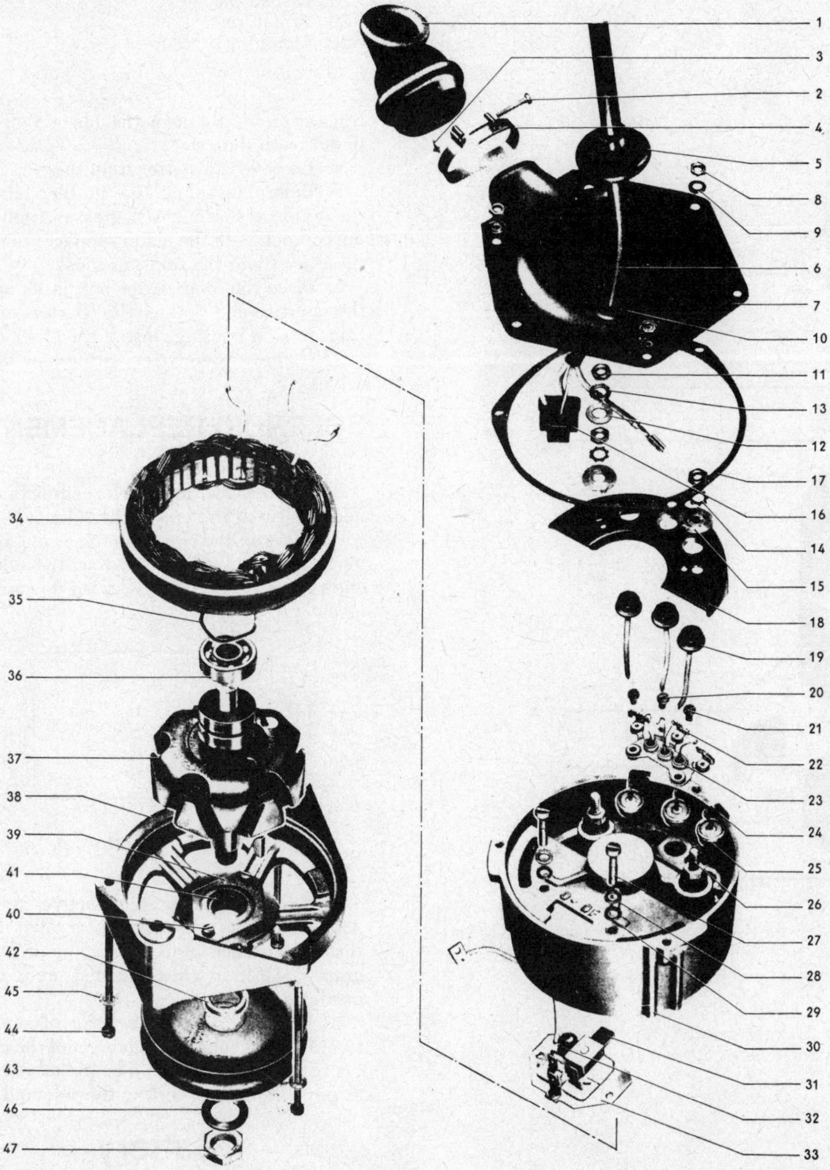

1. Elbow
2. Screw for hose clip
3. Threaded portion for hose clip
4. Cable hose clamp
5. Rubber grommet
6. Alternator wiring harness
7. Intake cover for alternator
8. Hex nut
9. Lockwasher
10. Rubber grommet for intake cover
11. B+ connection hex nut
12. Washer
13. Washer
14. Star washer
15. Contact disc
16. Three pin plug
17. Intake cover gasket
18. Positive diode carrier
19. Positive diodes
20. Screw
21. Stator winding connection screw
22. Exciter diode carrier
23. Exciter diodes
24. Seal
25. Negative diodes
26. Positive diode carrier pin
27. Brush holder screw
28. Washer
29. Spring washer
30. Alternator housing
31. Carbon brush
32. Brush retaining spring
33. Brush holder
34. Stator
35. Spring washer
36. Slip ring ball bearings
37. Claw pole rotor
38. End plate
39. Bearing end plate
40. Screw
41. Drive end ball bearing
42. Intermediate ring
43. Pulley
44. Housing bolt
45. Washer
46. Washer
47. Nut

Exploded view of the 55 amp alternator used in Type 2 models

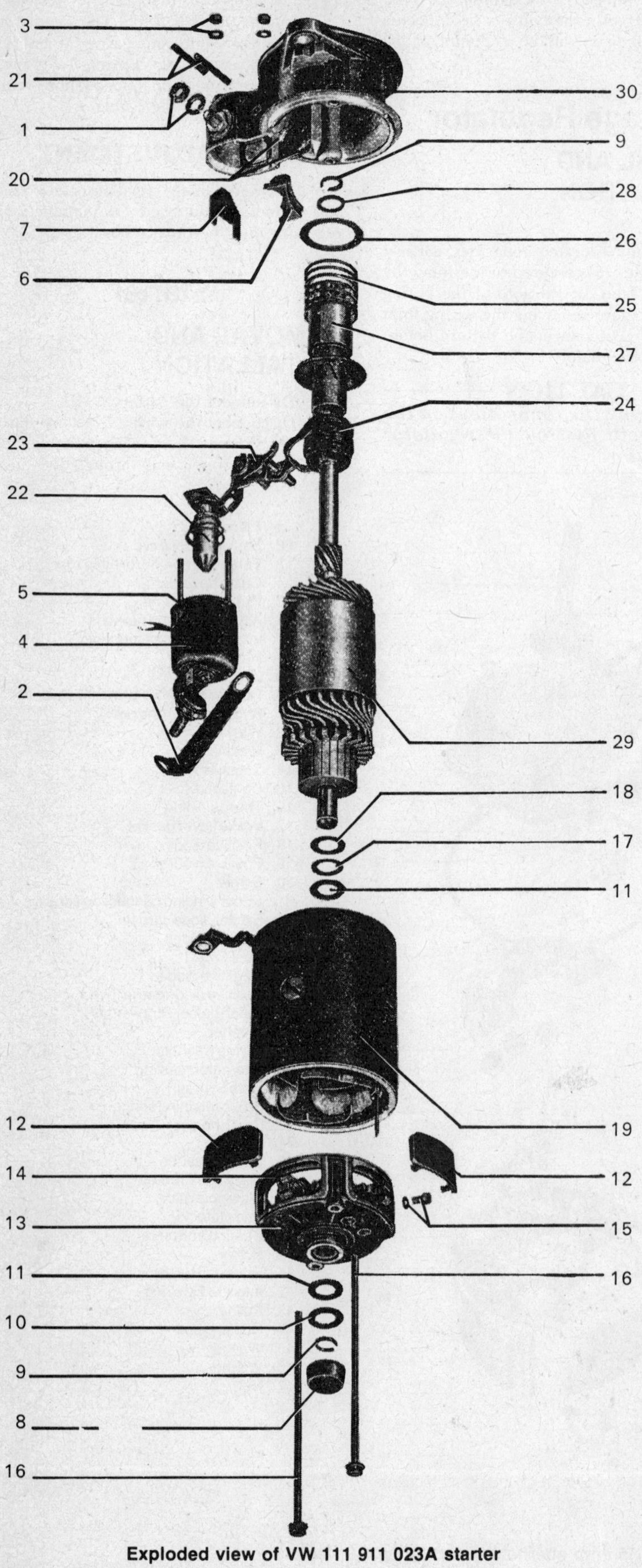

Exploded view of VW 111 911 023A starter

1. Nut and lockwasher
2. Connecting strip
3. Nut and lockwasher
4. Solenoid
5. Insulating disc
6. Seal
7. Insulating plate
8. Cap
9. Circlip
10. Steel washer
11. Bronze washer
12. Brush inspection cover
13. Commutator end plate
14. Brush holder
15. Screw and lockwasher
16. Housing screws
17. Dished washer
18. Steel washer
19. Housing and field windings
20. Spring clip
21. Pin
22. Solenoid core
23. Linkage
24. Bushing
25. Spring
26. Washer
27. Drive pinion
28. Dished washer
29. Armature
30. Mounting bracket

compartment. Remove the lower bolt from underneath the car.

4. Remove the starter from the car.

5. Before installing the starter, lubricate the outboard bushing with grease. Apply sealing compound to the mating surfaces between the starter and the transmission.

6. Place the long starter bolt in its hole in the starter and locate the starter on the transmission housing. Install the other bolt.

7. Connect the starter wiring and battery cables.

SOLENOID REPLACEMENT

1. Remove the starter.

2. Remove the nut which secures the connector strip at the end of the solenoid.

3. Take out the two retaining screws on the mounting bracket and withdraw the solenoid after it has been unhooked from its actuating lever.

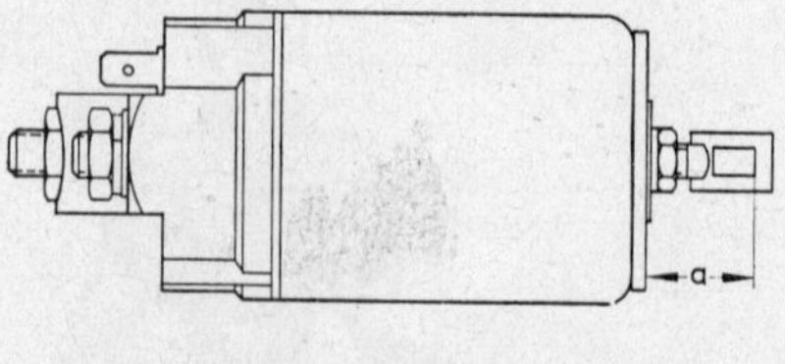

Solenoid adjustment

4. When replacing a defective solenoid with a new one, care should be taken to see that the distance (a) in the accompanying diagram is 19 mm when the magnet is drawn inside the solenoid.

5. Installation is the reverse of removal. In order to facilitate engagement of the actuating rod, the pinion should be pulled out as far as possible when inserting the solenoid.

Battery

The electrical system of the Volkswagen is a

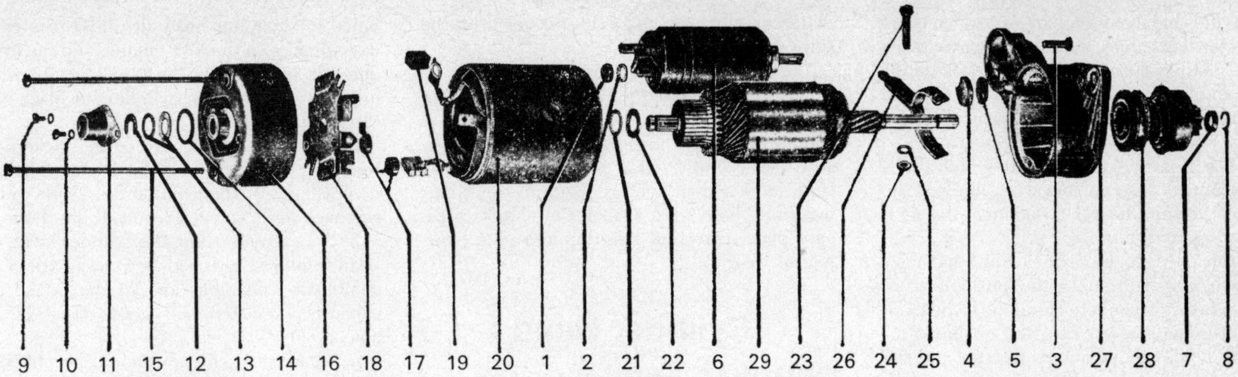

1. Nut
2. Lockwasher
3. Screw
4. Rubber seal
5. Disc
6. Solenoid switch
7. Stop-ring
8. Circlip
9. Screw
10. Washer
11. End cap
12. C-washer
13. Shim
14. Sealing ring
15. Housing screw
16. End plate
17. Spring
18. Brush holder
19. Rubber grommet
20. Housing
21. Insulating washer
22. Thrust washer
23. Pin
24. Nut
25. Lockwasher
26. Operating lever
27. Drive end plate
28. Drive pinion
29. Armature

Exploded view of Bosch 311 911 023B starter

negative grounded type. In most VW models, the battery is located under the right-hand side of the rear seat. In Type 2 models, it is located in the engine compartment.

REMOVAL AND INSTALLATION

1. Disconnect the battery cables. Note the position of the battery cables for installation. The small diameter battery post is the negative terminal. The negative battery cable is usually black.
2. Undo the battery hold-down strap and lift the battery out of its holder.
3. Install the battery in its holder and replace the clamp. Reconnect the battery cables.

ENGINE MECHANICAL

The Volkswagen engine is a flat four cylinder design. This four cycle, overhead valve engine has two pairs of horizontally opposed cylinders. All rear-engined VW models are air cooled.

The Type 1 engine is known as an upright fan engine, that is, the engine cooling fan is mounted in a two piece crankcase. The halves driven by the alternator shaft. The Type 2/1800 and Type 2/2000 engine, although of the same basic design, i.e. flat four, has the cooling fan driven by the crankshaft and is therefore mounted on the front of the engine. This type of engine is known as the suitcase engine.

Because it is air cooled, the VW engine is slightly noisier than a water cooled engine. This is due to the lack of water jacketing around the cylinders which provides sound deadening on water cooled engines. In addition, air cooled engines tend to run at somewhat higher temperatures, necessitating larger operating clearances to allow more room for the expansion of the parts. These larger operating clearances cause an increase in the noise level over a water cooled engine.

The crankshaft of all Volkswagen engines is mounted in a two piece crank case. The halves are machined to very close tolerances and line bored as a pair and, therefore, should always be replaced in pairs. When fitting them, it is necessary to coat only the mating surfaces with sealing compound and tighten them down to the correct torque. No gasket is used.

The pistons and cylinders are identical on any particular engine. However, it is not possible to interchange pistons and cylinders between engines. The four pistons each have three rings, two compression rings and one oil scraper. Each piston is attached to its connecting rod with a fully floating piston pin.

Each pair of cylinders share a detachable cylinder head made of light aluminum alloy casting. The cylinder head contains the valves for both cylinders. Shrunk-in valve guides and valve seats are used.

Engine Removal and Installation

Type 1 and 2

The Volkswagen engine is mounted on the transmission, which in turn is attached to the frame. In the Type 1 and 2 models, there are two bolts and two studs attaching the engine to the transmission.

When removing the engine from the car, it is recommended that the rear of the car be about 3 ft. off the ground. Remove the engine by bringing it out from underneath the car. Proceed with the following steps to remove the engine.

1. Disconnect the battery ground cable.
2. Disconnect the generator wiring.
3. Remove the air cleaner. On Type 1 engines, remove the rear engine cover plate.
4. Disconnect the throttle cable and remove the electrical connections to the automatic choke, coil, electromagnetic cutoff jet, and the oil pressure sending unit.
5. Disconnect the fuel hose at the front engine cover plate and seal it to prevent leakage.
6. Raise the car and support it with jack stands.
7. Remove the flexible air hoses between

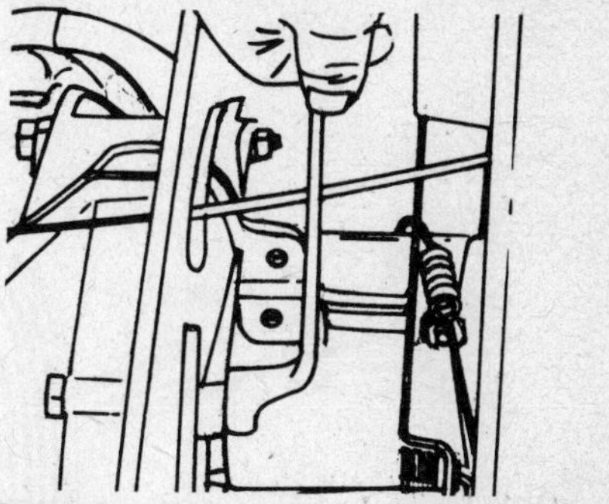

Removing the upper engine mounting bolts

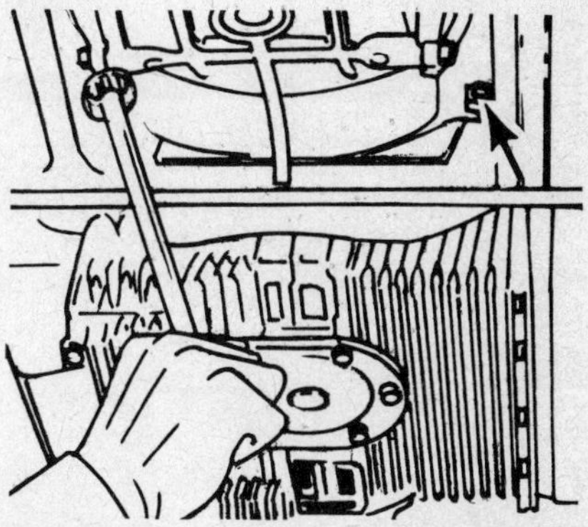

Removing the lower engine mounting bolts

the engine and heat exchangers, disconnect the heater flap cables, unscrew the two lower engine mounting nuts, and slide a jack under the engine. On Type 2 engines, remove the two bolts from the rubber engine mounts located next to the muffler.

8. On Type 1 Automatic Stick Shift models, disconnect the control valve cable and the manifold vacuum hoses. Disconnect the ATF suction line and plug it.

9. On all Automatic Stick Shift and fully automatic models, remove the four bolts from the converter drive plate through the holes in the transmission case. After the engine is removed, hold the torque converter on the transmission input shaft by using a strap bolted to the bellhousing.

10. Raise the jack until it just contacts the engine and have an assistant hold the two upper mounting bolts so that the nuts can be removed from the bottom.

11. When the engine mounts are disconnected and there are no remaining cables or wires left to be disconnected, move the engine toward the back of the car so that the clutch or converter plate disengages from the transmission.

12. Lower the engine out of the car.

13. Installation is the reverse of the above. When the engine is lifted into position, it should be rotated using the generator pulley so that the clutch plate hub will engage the transmission shaft splines. Tighten the upper mounting bolts first. Check the clutch, pressure plate, throwout bearing, and pilot bearing for wear.

Cylinder Head

REMOVAL AND INSTALLATION

In order to remove the cylinder head from either pair of cylinders, it is necessary to lower the engine.

1. Remove the valve cover and gasket. Remove the rocker arm assembly. Unbolt the intake manifold from the cylinder head. The cylinder head is held in place by eight studs. Since the cylinder head also holds the cylinders in place in the VW engine, and the cylinders are not going to be removed, it will be necessary to hold the cylinders in place after the head is removed.

2. After the rocker arm cover, rocker arm retaining nuts, and rocker arm assembly have been removed, the cylinder head nuts can be removed and the cylinder head lifted off.

3. When reinstalling the cylinder head, the head should be checked for cracks both in the combustion chamber and in the intake and exhaust ports. Cracked heads must be replaced.

4. Spark plug threads should be checked. New seals should be used on the pushrod tube ends and they should be checked for proper seating.

5. The pushrod tubes should be turned so that the seam faces upward. In order to ensure perfect sealing, used tubes should be stretched slightly before they are reinstalled.

6. Install the cylinder head. Using new rocker shaft stud seals, install the pushrods and rocker shaft assembly.

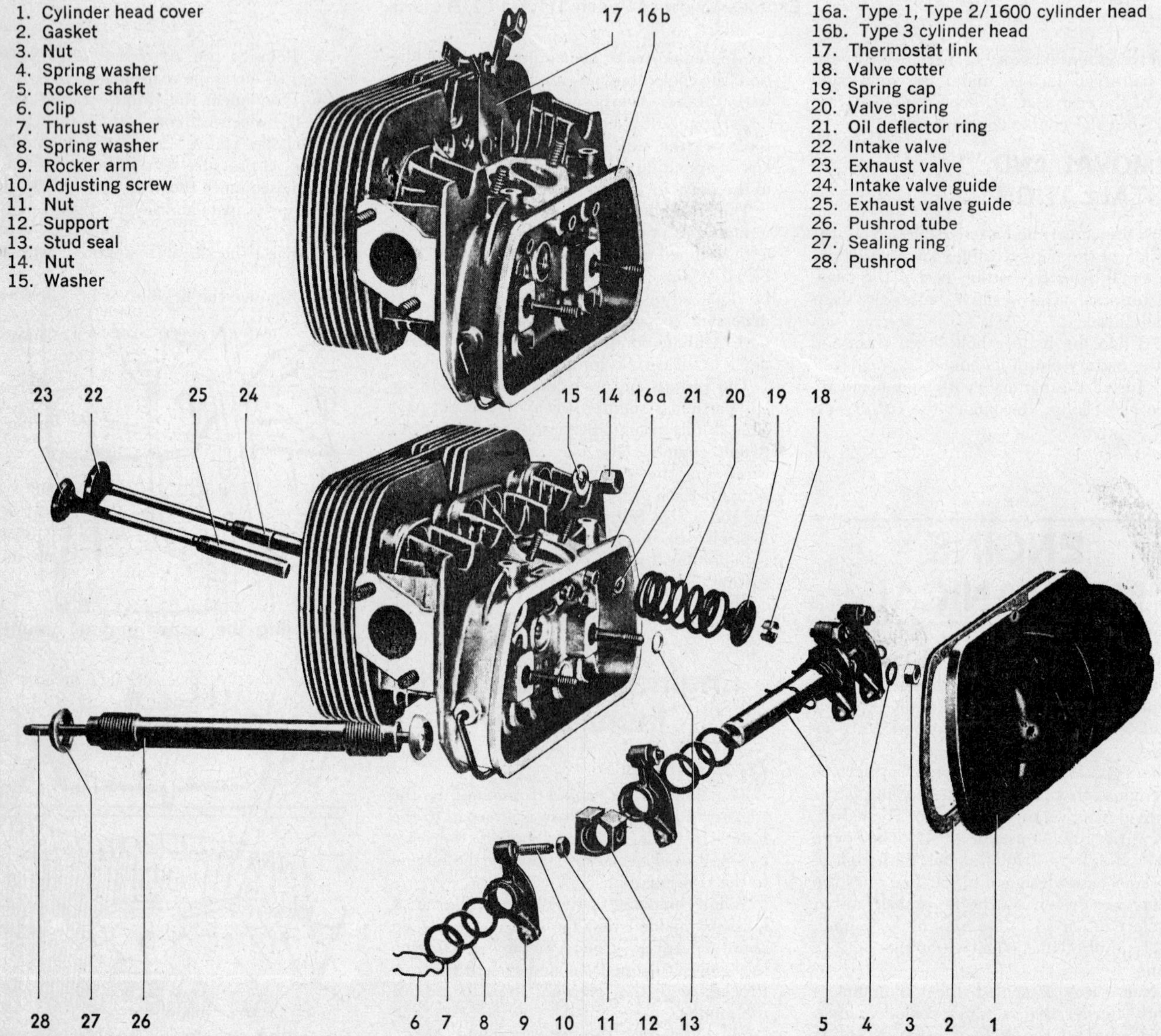

Exploded view of the cylinder head—Type 1

NOTE: Pay careful attention to the orientation of the shaft as described in the "Rocker Shaft" section.

7. Torque the cylinder head in three stages. Adjust the valve clearance. Using a new gasket, install the rocker cover. It may be necessary to readjust the valves after the engine has been run a few minutes and allowed to cool.

Valve Seats

On all air-cooled VW engines, the valve seats are shrunk-fit into the cylinder head. This usually involves freezing the seat with liquid nitrogen or some other refrigerant to about 200° F below zero, and heating up the cylinder head to approximately 400° F. Due to the extreme temperatures required to shrink-fit these items, and because of the extra care needed when working with metals at these extreme temperatures, it is advised that this operation be referred to an experienced repair shop.

CYLINDER HEAD OVERHAUL AND VALVE GUIDE REPLACEMENT

See the "Engine Rebuilding" section at the end of this book.

Rocker Shafts

ROCKER SHAFT REMOVAL AND INSTALLATION

1. Before the valve rocker assembly can be reached, it is necessary to lever off the clip that retains the valve cover and then remove the valve cover.
2. Remove the rocker arm retaining nuts, the rocker arm shaft, and the rocker arms. Remove the stud seals.
3. Before installing the rocker arm mechanism, be sure that the parts are as clean as possible.
4. Install new stud seals. On Type 1, install the rocker shaft assembly with the chamfered edges of the rocker shaft supports pointing outward and the slots pointing upward. On Type 2/1800, 2/2000 models, the chamfered edges must point outward and the slots must face downward, and the pushrod tube retaining wire must engage the slots in the rocker arm shaft supports as well as the grooves in the pushrod tubes.

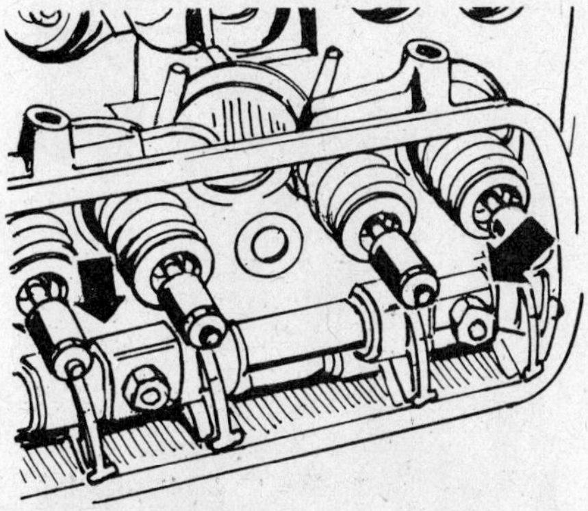

On Type 1 models, install the rocker shaft with the chamfer out and the slot up

On Type 2/1800 models, install the rocker shaft with the chamfer out and the slots down

5. Tighten the retaining nuts to the proper torque. Use only the copper colored nuts that were supplied with the engine.
6. Make sure that the ball ends of the pushrods are centered in the sockets of the rocker arms.
7. Adjust the valve clearance. Install the valve cover using a new gasket.

Intake Manifold

REMOVAL AND INSTALLATION

1. Remove the air cleaner.
2. Remove the pressure switch which is mounted under the right pair of intake manifold pipes. Disconnect the injector wiring.
3. Remove the fuel injectors by removing the two nuts which secure them in place. See Step 7 for proper injector installation.
4. After removing the intake manifold outer cover plate, remove the two screws which secure the manifold inner cover plate.
5. The manifold may be removed by removing the two nuts and washers which hold the manifold flange to the cylinder head.
6. Installation is the reverse of the above. The inner manifold cover should be installed first, but leave the cover loose until the outer cover and manifold are in place. Always use new gaskets.
7. Connect the fuel hoses to the injectors, if removed, after assembling the injector retainer plate in place. Make sure that the sleeves are in place on the injector securing studs. Carefully slip the injectors into the manifold and install the securing nuts. Never force the injectors in or out of the manifold. Reconnect the injector wiring.

Intake Air Distributor

REMOVAL AND INSTALLATION

The intake air distributor is located at the center of the engine at the junction of the intake manifold pipes.

NOTE: It is not necessary to remove the distributor if only the manifold pipes are to be removed.

1. Remove the air cleaner and pressure switch which are located under the right pair of manifold pipes.
2. Push the four rubber hoses onto the intake manifold pipes.
3. Remove the accelerator cable and the throttle valve switch.
4. Disconnect the accelerator cable.
5. Disconnect the vacuum hoses leading to the ignition distributor and the pressure sensor and disconnect the hose running to the auxiliary air regulator.
6. Remove those bolts under the air distributor which secure the air distributor to the crankcase and remove the air distributor.
7. Installation is the reverse of removal.

Mufflers, Tailpipes, Heat Exchangers

REMOVAL AND INSTALLATION

Muffler, Type 1

1. Working under the hood, disconnect the pre-heater hoses.
2. Remove the pre-heater pipe protection plate on each side of the engine. The plates are secured by three screws.
3. Remove the crankshaft pulley cover plate.
4. Remove the rear engine cover plate from the engine compartment. It is held in place by screws at the center, right, and left sides.
5. Remove the four intake manifold preheat pipe bolts. There are two bolts on each side of the engine.
6. Disconnect the warm air channel clamps at the left and right side of the engine.
7. Disconnect the heat exchanger clamps at the left and right side of the engine.
8. Remove the muffler from the engine.
9. Installation is the reverse of above. Always use new gaskets to install the muffler.

Muffler, Type 2/1800, 2/2000

The muffler is secured to the left and right heat exchangers by three bolts. There is a bracket at the left end of the muffler. Always use new gaskets when installing a new muffler.

Heat Exchangers, Type 1

1. Disconnect the air tube at the outlet end of the exchanger.
2. Remove the clamp which secures the muffler to the exchanger.
3. Loosen the clamp which secures the exchanger to the heater hose connection at the muffler.
4. Remove the two nuts which secure the exchanger to the forward end of the cylinder head.
5. Remove the heater flap control wire.
6. Reverse the above to install. Always use new gaskets.

Heat Exchangers, Type 2/1800, 2/2000

1. Disconnect the air hose at the outlet of each exchanger.
2. Disconnect the warm air tube at the outside end of the exchanger.

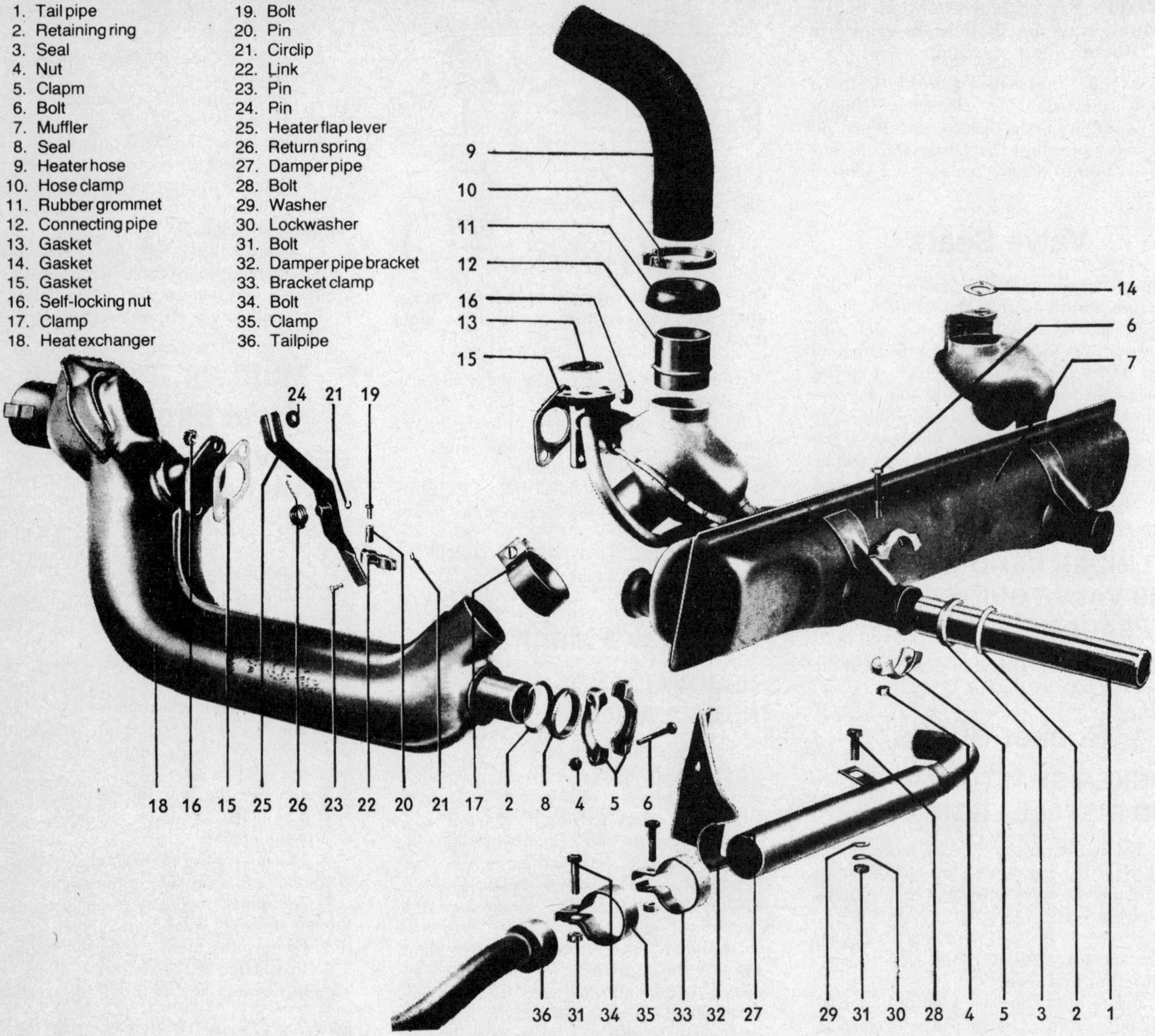

Exhaust system—Type 1

3. Disconnect the three bolts which secure each exchanger to the muffler.

4. Remove the four nuts, two at each exhaust port, which secure the exchanger to the cylinder head.

Installation is the reverse of the above. Always use new gaskets.

Tailpipes, Type 1

Loosen the clamps on the tailpipes and apply penetrating oil. Work the pipe side-to-side while trying to pull the tailpipe out of the muffler.

NOTE: It is often difficult to remove the tailpipes without damaging them.

Tailpipes, Type 2/1800, 2/2000

Remove the bolt which secures the pipe to the muffler. Remove the bolt which secures the pipe to the body and remove the pipe.

Pistons and Cylinders

Pistons and cylinders are matched according to their size. When replacing pistons and cylinders, make sure that they are properly sized.

NOTE: See the "Engine Rebuilding" section for cylinder refinishing.

CYLINDER REMOVAL AND INSTALLATION

1. Remove the engine. Remove the cylinder head, pushrod tubes, and the deflector plate.

2. Slide the cylinder out of its groove in the crankcase and off the piston. Matchmark the cylinders for reassembly. The cylinders must be returned to their original bore in the crankcase. If a cylinder is to be replaced, it must be replaced with a matching piston.

3. Cylinders should be checked for wear and, if necessary, replaced with another matched cylinder and piston assembly of the same size.

4. Check the cylinder seating surface on the crankcase, cylinder shoulder, and gasket, for cleanliness and deep scores. When reinstalling the cylinders, a new gasket, if required, should be used between each cylinder and the crankcase.

5. The piston, as well as the piston rings and pin must be oiled before reassembly.

6. Be sure that the ring gaps are of the correct dimension. Stagger the ring gaps around the piston, but make sure that the oil

Installing a cylinder

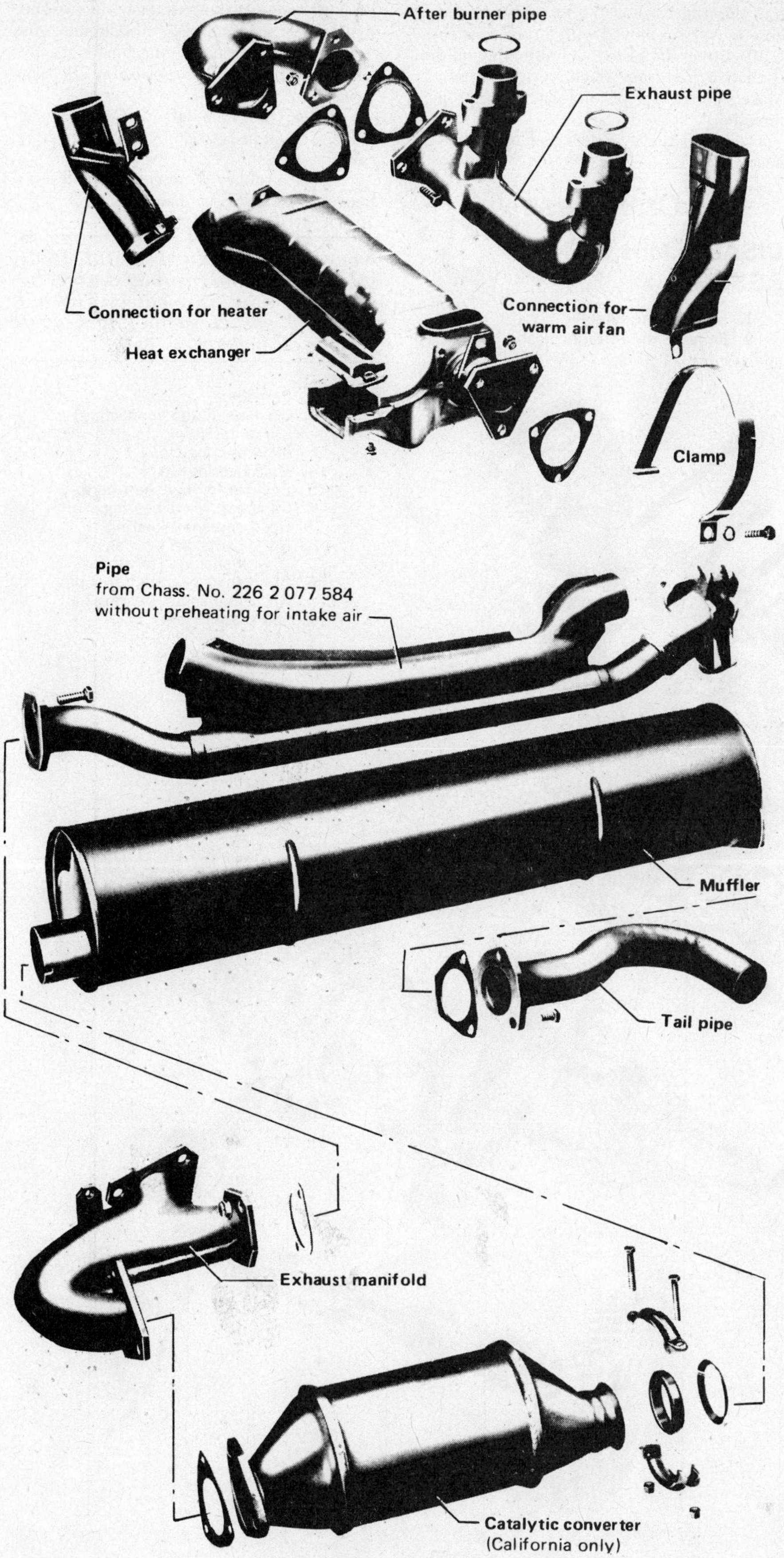

Exhaust system—Type 2

ring gap is positioned up when the pistons are in position on the connecting rods.

7. Compress the rings with a ring compressor, oil the cylinder wall, and slide the cylinder onto the piston. Make sure that the cylinder base gasket is in place.

8. Install the deflector plates.

9. Install the pushrod tubes using new gaskets. Install the pushrods. Make sure that the seam in the pushrod tube is facing upward.

10. Install the cylinder head.

PISTON REMOVAL AND INSTALLATION

1. Remove the engine. Remove the cylinder head and, after matchmarking the cylinders, remove the cylinders.

2. Matchmark the pistons to indicate the cylinder number and which side points toward the clutch.

3. Remove the circlips which retain the piston pin.

4. Heat the piston to 176° F. To heat the piston, boil a clean rag in water and wrap it around the piston. Remove the piston pin after the piston has been heated.

5. Remove the piston from the connecting rod.

6. Before installing the pistons, they should first be cleaned and checked for wear. Remove the old rings. Clean the ring grooves using a groove cleaner or a broken piece of ring. Clean the piston with solvent but do not use a wire brush or sandpaper. Check for any cracks or scuff marks. Check the piston diameter with a micrometer and compare the readings to the specifications. If the running clearance between the piston and cylinder wall is 0.008 in. (0.2 mm) or greater, the cylinder and piston should be replaced by a set of the same size grading. If the cylinder shows no sign of excessive wear or damage, it is permissable to install a new piston and rings of the appropriate size.

7. Place each ring in turn in its cylinder bore and check the piston ring end-gap. If the gap is too large, replace the ring. If the gap is too narrow, file the end of the ring until the proper gap is obtained.

8. Insert the rings on the piston and check

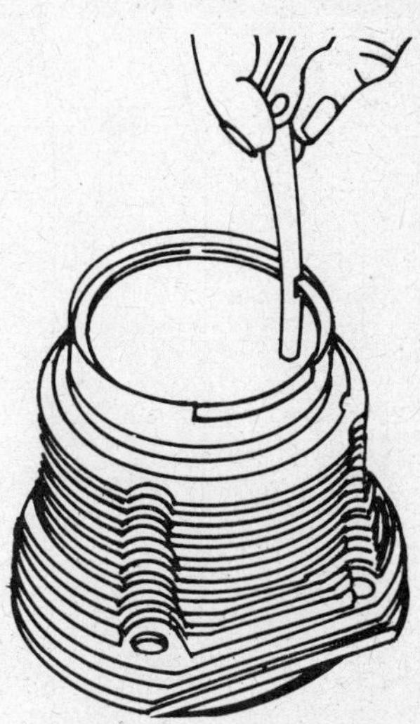

Checking piston ring end gap

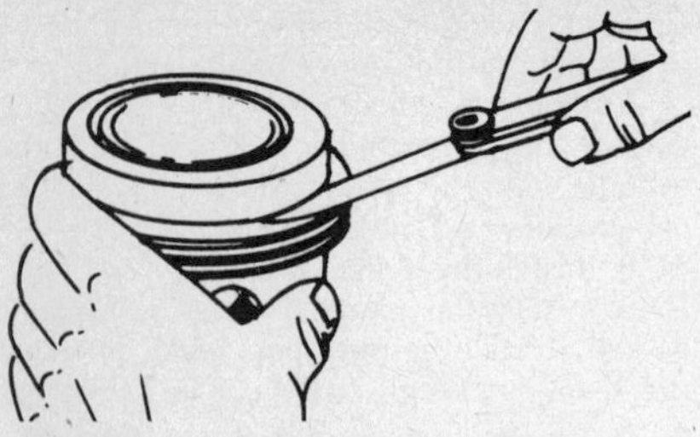

Checking piston ring side clearance

the ring side clearance. If the clearance is too large, replace the piston. Install the rings with the marking "Open" or "Top" pointing upward.

9. If new rings are installed in a used piston, the ring ridge at the top of the cylinder bore must be removed with a ridge reamer.

10. Install the piston and piston pin on the connecting rod from which it originally came. Make sure that the piston is facing the proper direction.

11. Install the cylinders and the cylinder heads.

Crankcase

DISASSEMBLY AND ASSEMBLY

1. Remove the engine.
2. Remove the cylinder heads, cylinders, and pistons.
3. Remove the oil strainer, oil pressure switch, and the crankcase nuts. Remove the flywheel and oil pump. Matchmark the flywheel so that it can be replaced in the same position.
4. Keep the cam followers in the right crankcase half in position by using a retaining spring.
5. Use a rubber hammer to break the seal between the crankcase halves.

CAUTION

Never insert sharp metal tools, wedges, or any prying device between the crankcase halves. This will ruin the gasket surface and cause serious oil leakage.

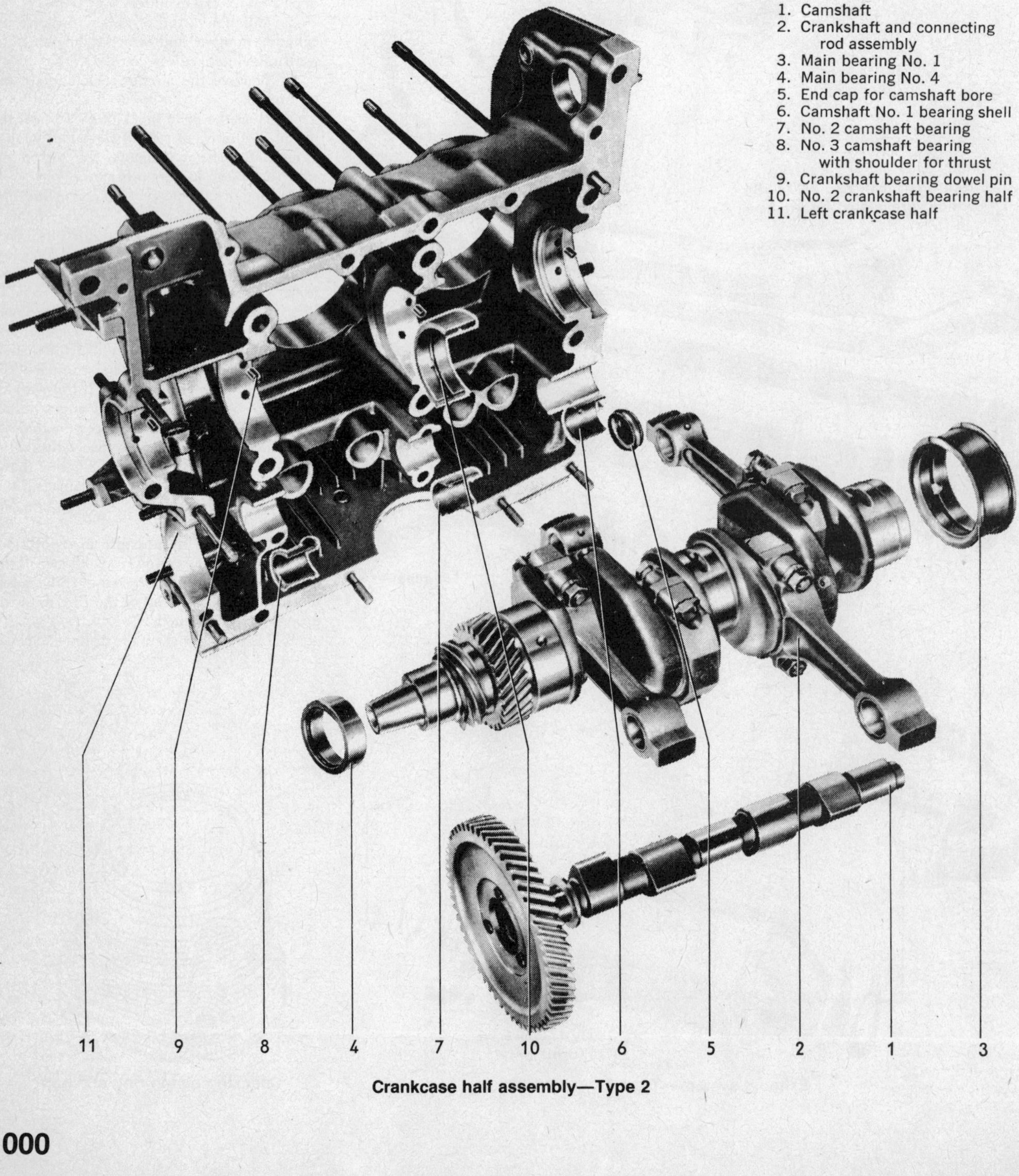

Crankcase half assembly—Type 2

Check the dowel pins for tightness

6. After the seal between the crankcase halves is broken, remove the right-hand crankcase half, the crankshaft oil seal and the camshaft end plug. The camshaft and crankshaft can now be lifted out of the crankcase half.

7. Remove the cam followers, bearing shells, and the oil pressure relief valve.

8. Before starting reassembly, check the crankcase for any damage or cracks.

9. Flush and blow out all ducts and oil passages. Check the studs for tightness. If the tapped holes are worn install a Heli-Coil.

10. Install the crankshaft bearing dowel pins and bearing shells for the crankshaft and camshaft. Make sure that the bearing shells with thrust flanges are installed in the proper journal.

11. Install the crankshaft and camshaft after the bearings have been well lubricated. When installing the camshaft and crankshaft, make sure that the timing marks on the timing gears are aligned.

12. Install the oil pressure relief valve.

13. Oil and install the cam followers.

14. Install the camshaft end plug using sealing compound.

15. Install the thrust washers and crankshaft oil seal. The oil seal must rest squarely on the bottom of its recess in the crankcase. The thrust washers at the flywheel end of the crankshaft are shims used to set the crankshaft end-play.

16. Spread a thin film of sealing compound on the crankcase joining faces and place the two halves together. Torque the nuts in several stages. Tighten the 8 mm nut located next to the 12 mm stud of the No. 1 crankshaft bearing first. As the crankcase halves are being torqued, continually check the crankshaft for ease of rotation.

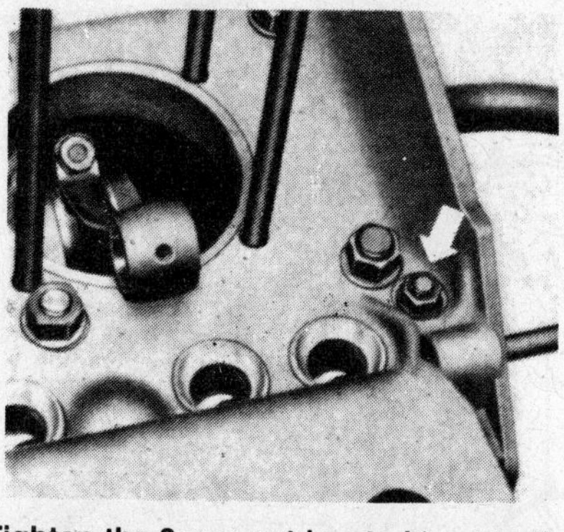

Tighten the 8 mm nut located next to the 12 mm stud of the No. 1 crankcase bearing first on the Type 1

17. Crankshaft end-play is checked when the flywheel is installed. It is adjusted by varying the number and thickness of the shims located behind the flywheel. Measure the end-play with a dial indicator mounted against the flywheel, and attached firmly to the crankcase.

Camshaft and Timing Gears

REMOVAL AND INSTALLATION

1. Removal of the camshaft requires splitting the crankcase. See "Crankcase Disassembly". The camshaft and its bearing shells are then removed from the crankcase halves.

2. Before reinstalling the camshaft, it should be checked for wear on the lobe surfaces and on the bearing surfaces. In addition, the riveted joint between the camshaft timing gear and the camshaft should be checked for tightness.

3. The camshaft should be checked for a maximum run-out of 0.0008 in.

4. The timing gear should be checked for the correct tooth contact and for wear.

5. If the camshaft bearing shells are worn or damaged, new shells should be fitted. The camshaft bearing shells should be installed with the tabs engaging the notches in the crankcase. It is usually a good idea to replace the bearing shells under any circumstances. Before installing the camshaft, the bearing journals and cam lobes should be generously coated with oil.

Aligning valve timing marks on gears

6. When the camshaft is installed, care should be taken to ensure that the timing gear tooth marked (0) is located between the two teeth of the crankshaft timing gear marked with a center punch.

7. The camshaft end-play is measured at the No. 3 bearing. End-play is 0.0015-0.005 in. (0.04-0.12 mm) and the wear limit is 0.006 in. (0.16 mm).

Crankshaft

CRANKSHAFT PULLEY REMOVAL AND INSTALLATION

On the Type 1, the crankshaft pulley can be removed while the engine is still in the car. However, in this instance it is necessary for the rear cover plate of the engine to be removed. Remove the cover plate after taking out the screws in the cover plate below the crankshaft pulley. Remove the fan belt and the crankshaft pulley securing screw. Using a puller, remove the crankshaft pulley. The crankshaft pulley should be checked for proper seating and belt contact. The oil return thread should be cleaned and lubricated with oil. The crankshaft pulley should be installed in the reverse sequence. Check for oil leaks after installing the pulley.

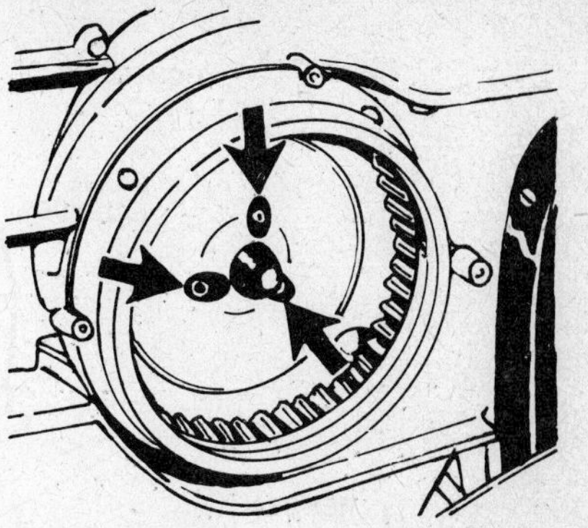

Type 2/1800 engine fan bolts

On the Type 2, the crankshaft pulley can be removed only when the engine is out of the car and the muffler, alternator and cooling air intake housing are removed. After these parts have been removed, take out the plastic cap in the pulley. Unscrew the three socket head screws and the self-locking nut and then remove the pulley.

Installation for Type 2/1800, 2/2000 engines is the reverse of removal. When installing, use a new paper gasket between the fan and the crankshaft pulley. If shims are used, do not forget them. Don't use more than two shims. When inserting the pulley, make sure that the pin engages the hole in the fan. Ensure that the clearance between the generator belt and the intake housing is at least 4 mm and the belt is parallel to the housing.

FLYWHEEL REMOVAL AND INSTALLATION

NOTE: In order to remove the flywheel, the crankshaft will have to be prevented from turning. This may be accomplished on Type 1 models by using a 3 or 4 foot length of angle iron or thick stock sheet steel, such as an old fence post. Drill out two holes in the metal bar that correspond to two of the pressure plate retaining bolt holes. The metal bar is installed as per the accompanying illustration.

Type 1

1. The flywheel is attached to the crankshaft with a gland nut and is located by four dowel pins. An oil seal is recessed in the crankcase casting at No. 1 main bearing. A needle bearing, which supports the main driveshaft, is located in the gland nut. Prior to removing the flywheel, it is necessary to remove the clutch pressure plate and the clutch disc.

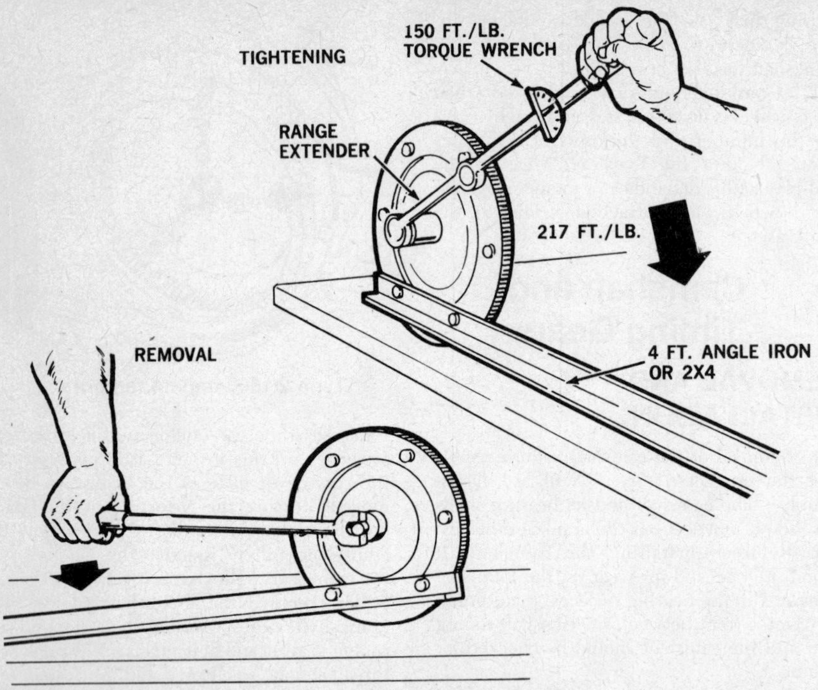

Removing or installing the flywheel on 1600 cc engines using the special bar

2. Loosen the gland nut and remove it, using a 36 mm wrench.
3. Before removing the flywheel, matchmark the flywheel and the crankshaft.
4. Installation is the reverse of removal. Before installing the flywheel, check the flywheel teeth for any wear or damage. Check the dowel pins for correct fit in the crankshaft and in the flywheel.
5. Adjust the crankshaft end-play and check the needle bearing in the gland nut for wear.

Type 2

Removal and installation is similar to the Type 1 except that the flywheel is secured to the crankshaft by five socket head screws.

CRANKSHAFT OIL SEAL (FLYWHEEL END)

Replacement

This seal is removed after removing the flywheel. After the flywheel is removed, inspect the surface on the flywheel joining flange where the seal makes contact. If there is a deep groove or any other damage, the flywheel must be replaced. Remove the oil seal by prying it out of its bore. Before installing a new seal, clean the crankcase oil seal recess and coat it thinly with a sealing compound. Be sure that the seal rests squarely on the bottom of its recess. Make sure that the correct side of the seal is facing outward, that is, the lip of the seal should be facing the inside of the crankcase. Reinstall the flywheel after coating the oil seal contact surface with oil.

NOTE: Be careful not to damage the seal when sliding the flywheel into place.

CRANKSHAFT REMOVAL AND INSTALLATION

NOTE: See the "Engine Rebuilding" section for crankshaft refinishing procedures.

1. Removal of the crankshaft requires splitting the crankcase. See "Crankcase Disassembly."
2. After the crankcase is opened, the crankshaft can then be lifted out.
3. The crankshaft bearings are held in place by dowel pins. These pins must be checked for tightness.
4. When installing the bearings, make sure that the oil holes in the shells are properly aligned. Be sure that the bearing shells are seated properly on their dowel pins. Bearing shells are available in three undersizes. Measure the crankshaft bearing journals to determine the proper bearing size. Place one half of the No. 2 crankshaft bearing in the crankcase. Slide the No. 1 bearing on the crankshaft so that the dowel pin hole is toward the flywheel and the oil groove faces toward the fan. The No. 3 bearing is installed with the dowel pin hole facing toward the crankshaft web.
5. To remove the No. 3 main bearing, remove the distributor gear circlip and the distributor drive gear. Mild heat (176° F) must be applied to remove the gear. Next slide the spacer off the crankshaft.
6. The crankshaft timing gear should now be pressed off the crankshaft after mild heating.
7. When the timing gear is reinstalled, the chamfer must face towards the No. 3 bearing. The No. 3 bearing can then be replaced. When removing and installing the gears on the crankshaft, be careful not to damage the No. 4 bearing journal.
8. When all of the crankshaft bearings are in place, lift the crankshaft and the connecting rod assembly into the crankcase and align the valve timing marks.
9. Install the crankcase half and reassemble the engine.

Connecting Rods

REMOVAL AND INSTALLATION

NOTE: See the "Engine Rebuilding" section for additional information.

1. After splitting the crankcase (See "Crankcase Disassembly"), remove the crankshaft and the connecting rod assembly.
2. Remove the connecting rods, clamping bolts, and the connecting rod caps.
3. Inspect the piston pin bushing. With a new bushing, the correct clearance is indicated by a light finger push fit of the pin at room temperature.
4. Reinsert the new connecting rod bearings after all parts have been thoroughly cleaned.
5. Assemble the connecting rods on the crankshaft, making sure that the rods are oriented properly on the crankshaft. The identification numbers stamped on the connecting rods and connecting rod caps must be on the same side. Note that the marks on the

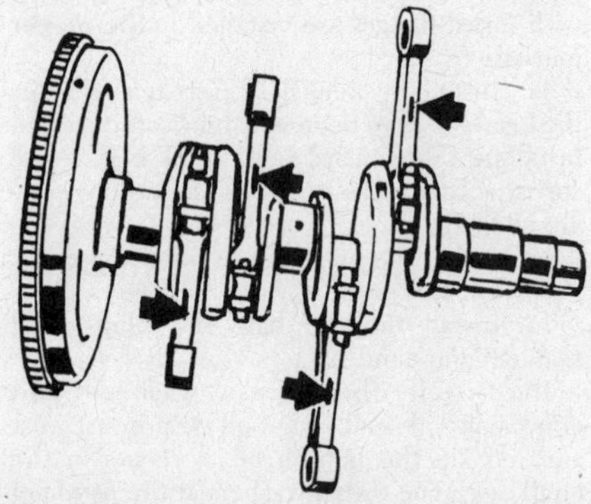

Forge marks on connecting rods must face up

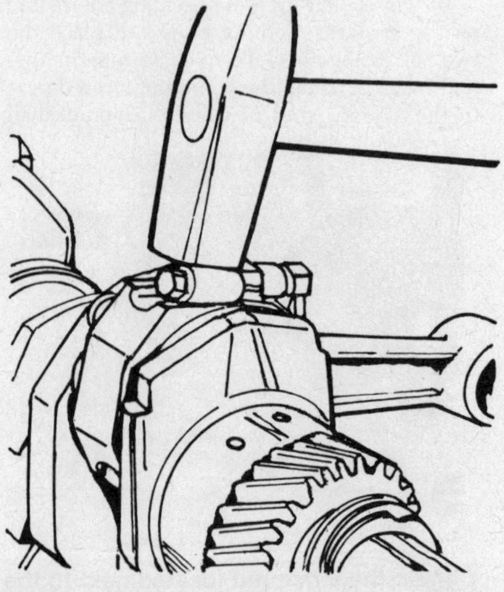

Rapping the connecting rod to relieve pre-tension

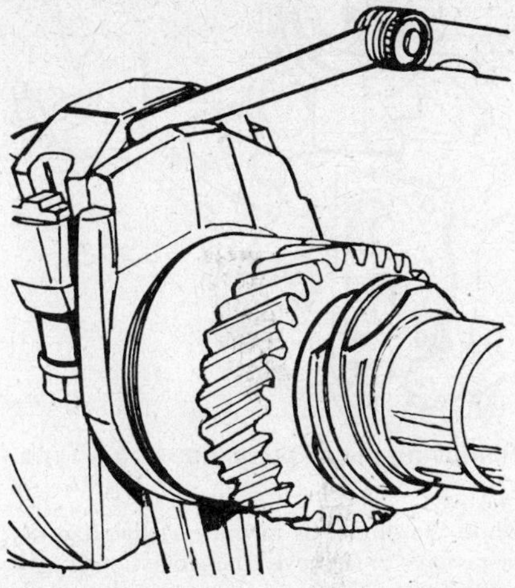

Measuring the connecting rod side clearance

connecting rods are pointing upward, while the rods are pointing toward their respective cylinders. Lubricate the bearing shells before installing them.

6. Tighten the connecting rod bolts to the specified torque. A slight pre-tension between the bearing halves, which is likely to occur when tightening the connecting rod bolts, can be eliminated by gently striking the side of the bearing cap with a hammer.

7. Do not install the connecting rod in the engine unless it swings freely on its journal.

8. Using a peening chisel, secure the connecting rod bolts in place.

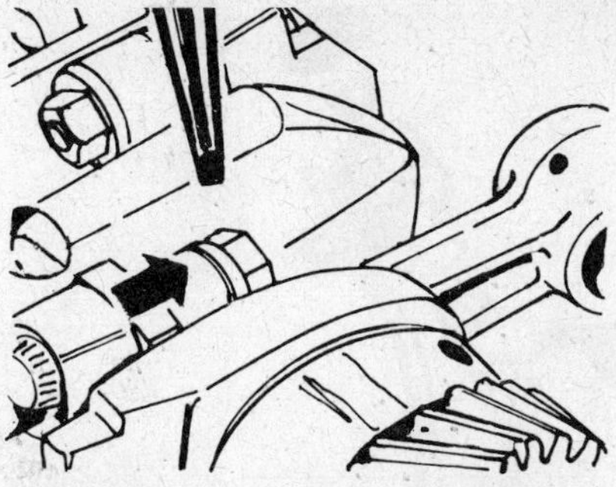

Staking the connecting rod bolt

9. Failure to swing freely on the journal may be caused by improper side clearance, improper bearing clearance, or failure to lubricate the rod before assembly.

ENGINE LUBRICATION

Oil Strainer

REMOVAL AND INSTALLATION

The oil strainer can be easily removed by removing the retaining nuts, washers, oil strainer plate, strainer, and gaskets. The Type 2/1800 and 2/2000 strainer is secured by a single bolt at the center of the strainer. Once taken out, the strainer must be thoroughly cleaned and all traces of oil gaskets removed prior to installing new ones. The suction pipe should be checked for tightness and proper position. When the strainer is installed, be sure that the suction pipe is correctly seated in the strainer. If necessary, the strainer may be bent slightly. The measurement from the strainer flange to the tip of the suction pipe should be 10 mm. The measurement from the flange to the bottom of the strainer should be 6 mm. The cap nuts on Type 1 engines must not be overtightened. The Type 2/1800 and 2/2000 have a spin-off replaceable oil filter as well as the strainer in the crankcase. The oil filter is located at the left rear corner of the engine.

Oil Cooler

REMOVAL AND INSTALLATION

The Type 1 oil cooler is located under the engine cooling fan housing at the left side of the engine. The Type 2/1800 and 2/2000 coolers are mounted near the oil filter, at the left corner of the engine.

The oil cooler may be removed without taking the engine out of the car. On Type 1 models, the engine fan housing must be removed. The Type 2/1800 and 2/2000 cooler is accessible through the left side engine cowl-

1. Oil filter cover
2. Oil filter
3. Nut
4. Spring washer
5. Oil filter seal
6. Oil vent
7. Seal
8. Oil dipstick
9. Dipstick
10. Bellows
11. Nut
12. Spring washer
13. Oil filler
14. Gasket
15. Nut
16. Spring washer
17. Oil pump housing
18. Pump housing seal
19. Locknut
20. Spring washer
21. Oil pump cover
22. Pump cover sealing ring
23. Oil pump gear
24. Driveshaft
25. Oil pressure switch
26. Screw
27. Sealing ring
28. Spring
29. Piston for oil relief valve
30. Screw
31. Sealing ring
32. Spring
33. Piston for oil pressure control valve
34. Nut
35. Sealing ring
36. Oil strainer closing cover
37. Seal
38. Oil strainer
39. Closing screw
40. Sealing ring
41. Nut
42. Spring washer
43. Washer
44. Oil cooler
45. Oil cooler sealing ring
46. Oil filter
47. Nut
48. Spring washer
49. Oil filter intermediate flange
50. Seal

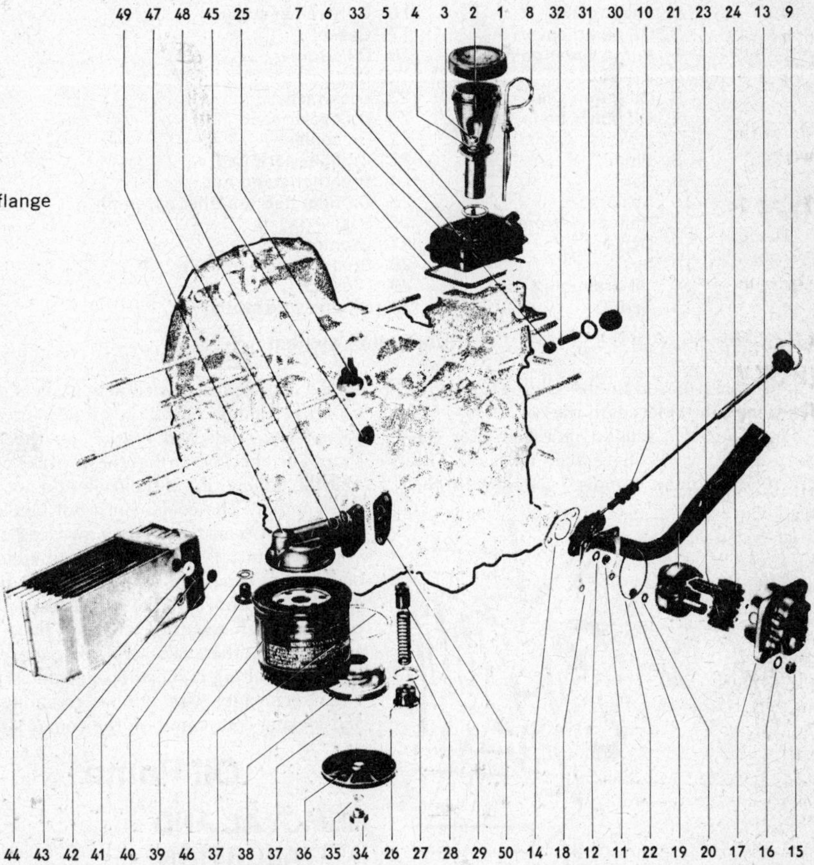

Type 2 lubrication system

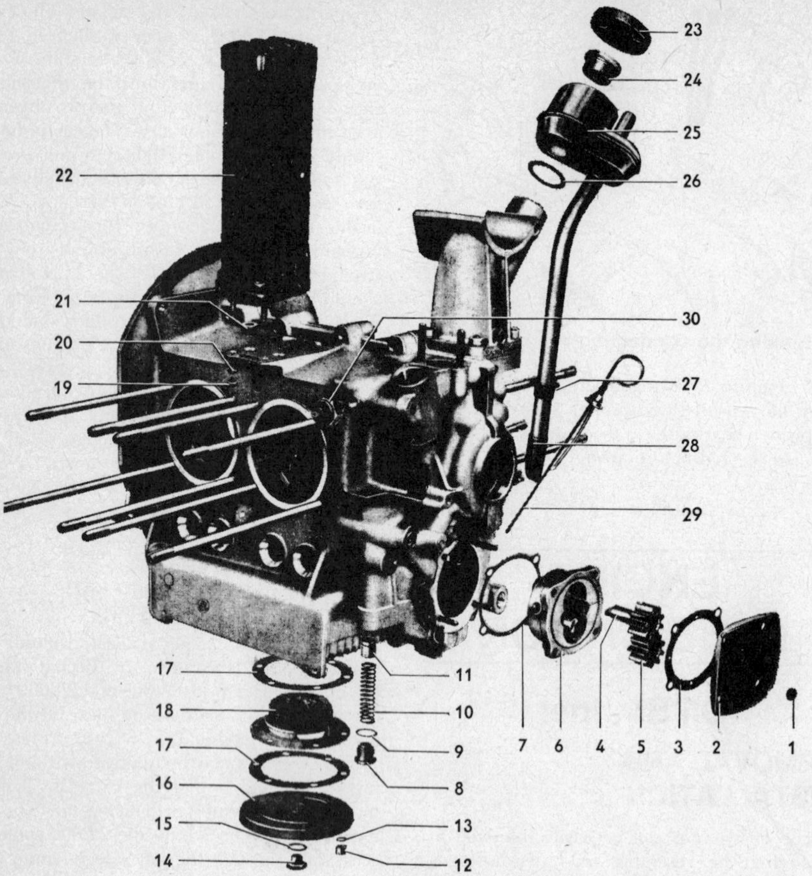

1. Sealing nut
2. Oil pump cover
3. Pump cover gasket
4. Driveshaft
5. Oil pump gear
6. Oil pump housing
7. Housing gasket
8. Plug
9. Seal
10. Spring
11. Relief valve piston
12. Cap nut
13. Seal
14. Oil drain plug
15. Seal
16. Oil strainer cover
17. Gasket
18. Oil strainer
19. Nut
20. Lockwasher
21. Oil cooler seal
22. Oil cooler
23. Oil filler neck cap
24. Breather gland nut
25. Oil filler and breather assembly
26. Seal
27. Grommet
28. Breather rubber valve
29. Dipstick
30. Oil pressure switch

Type 1 lubrication system

ing, working either in the engine compartment or from underneath the car.

The oil cooler can be removed after the three retaining nuts have been taken off. The gaskets should be removed along with the cooler and replaced with new gaskets. If the cooler is leaking, check the oil pressure relief valve. The studs and bracket on the cooler should be checked for tightness. Make certain that the hollow ribs of the cooler do not touch one another. The cooler must not be clogged with dirt. Clean the contact surfaces on the crankcase, install new gaskets, and attach the oil cooler. Types 2/1800 and 2/2000 have a spacer ring between the crankcase and the cooler at each securing screw. If these rings are omitted, the seals may be squeezed too tightly, resulting in oil stoppage and resultant engine damage. Use double retaining nuts and locking compound on the cooler studs.

Oil cooler spacers on suitcase engines

Oil Pump

REMOVAL AND INSTALLATION

1. On Type 1, the pump can be removed while the engine is in the car, but it is first necessary to remove the cover plate, the crankshaft pulley, and the cover plate under the pulley.

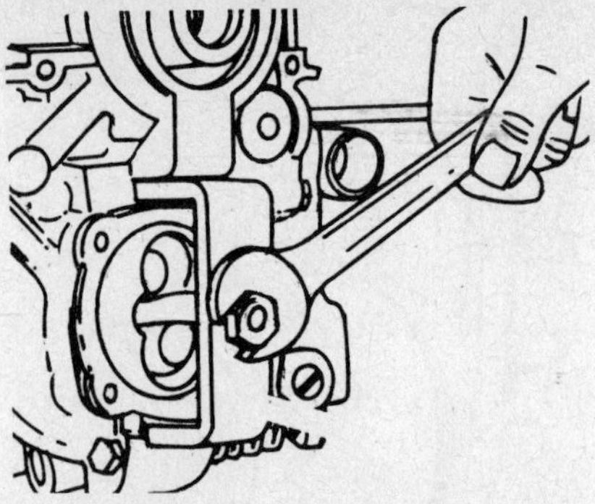

Removing the oil pump housing—Type 1

2. On Types 2/1800 and 2/2000 the oil pump can be taken out only after the engine is removed from the car and the air intake housing, the belt pulley fan housing, and fan are dismantled.
3. On the Automatic Stick Shift models, the torque converter oil pump is driven by the engine oil pump.
4. On Type 1, remove the nuts from the oil pump cover and then remove the cover and its gasket. Remove the gears and take out the pump with a special extractor that pulls the body out of the crankcase. Care should be taken so as not to damage the inside of the pump housing.
5. On Type 2/1800 and 2/2000 engines, remove the four pump securing nuts and, prying on either side of the pump, pry the pump assembly out of the crankcase.
6. To disassemble the pump, the pump cover must be pressed apart.
7. Prior to assembly, check the oil pump body for wear, especially the gear seating surface. If the pump body is worn, the result will be loss of oil pressure. Check the driven gear shaft for tightness and, if necessary, peen it tightly into place or replace the pump housing. The gears should be checked for excessive wear, backlash, and end-play. Maximum end-play without a gasket is 1 mm (0.004 in.). The end-play can be checked using a T-square and a feeler gauge. Check the mating surface of the pump body and the crankcase for damage and cleanliness. Install the pump into the crankcase with a new gasket. Do not use any sealing compound.
8. Turn the camshaft several revolutions

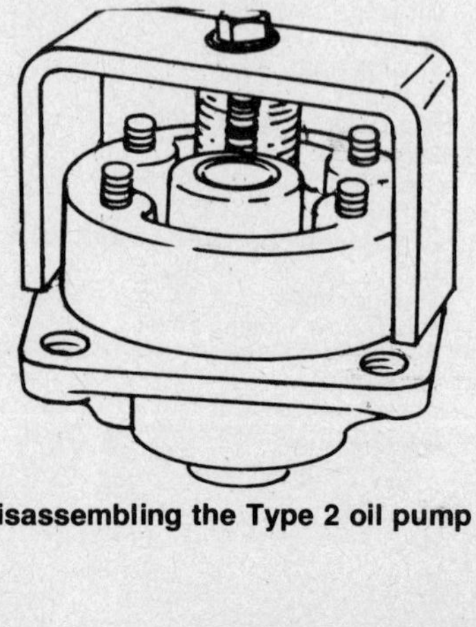

Disassembling the Type 2 oil pump

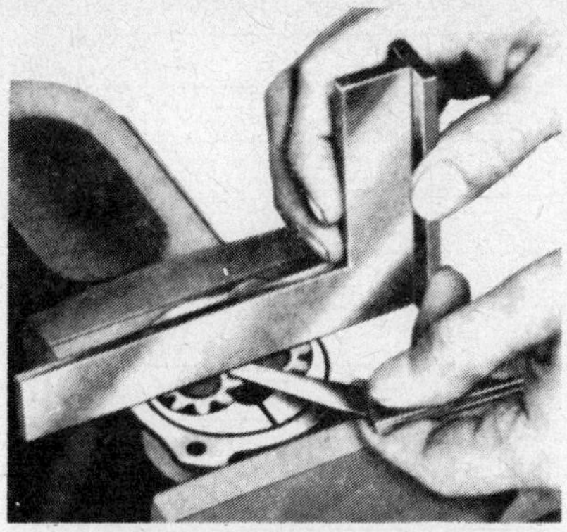

Checking oil pump end play

in order to center the pump body opposite the slot in the camshaft.

9. On Type 1, the cover may now be installed.

10. On Type 2/1800 and 2/2000 models, the pump was installed complete.

11. Tighten the securing nuts.

Oil Pressure Relief Valve

REMOVAL AND INSTALLATION

The oil pressure relief valve is removed by unscrewing the end plug and removing the gasket ring, spring, and plunger. If the plunger sticks in its bore, it can be removed by screwing a 10 mm tap into it.

On 1600 cc engines, the valve is located to the left of the oil pump. On Automatic Stick Shift models, it is located in the oil pump housing. On 1800 and 2000 engines, the valve is located beside the oil filter.

Before installing the valve, check the plunger for any signs of seizure. If necessary, the plunger should be replaced. If there is any doubt about the condition of the spring, it should also be replaced. When installing the relief valve, be careful that you do not scratch the bore. Reinstall the plug with a new gasket.

Type 2/1800 and 2/2000 engines have a second oil pressure relief valve located just to the right of, and below the oil filter.

ENGINE COOLING

FAN HOUSING REMOVAL AND INSTALLATION

Type 1

1. Remove the two heater hoses and the generator strap.

2. Pull out the lead wire from the coil. Remove the distributor cap and take off the spark plug connectors.

3. Remove the retaining screws that are

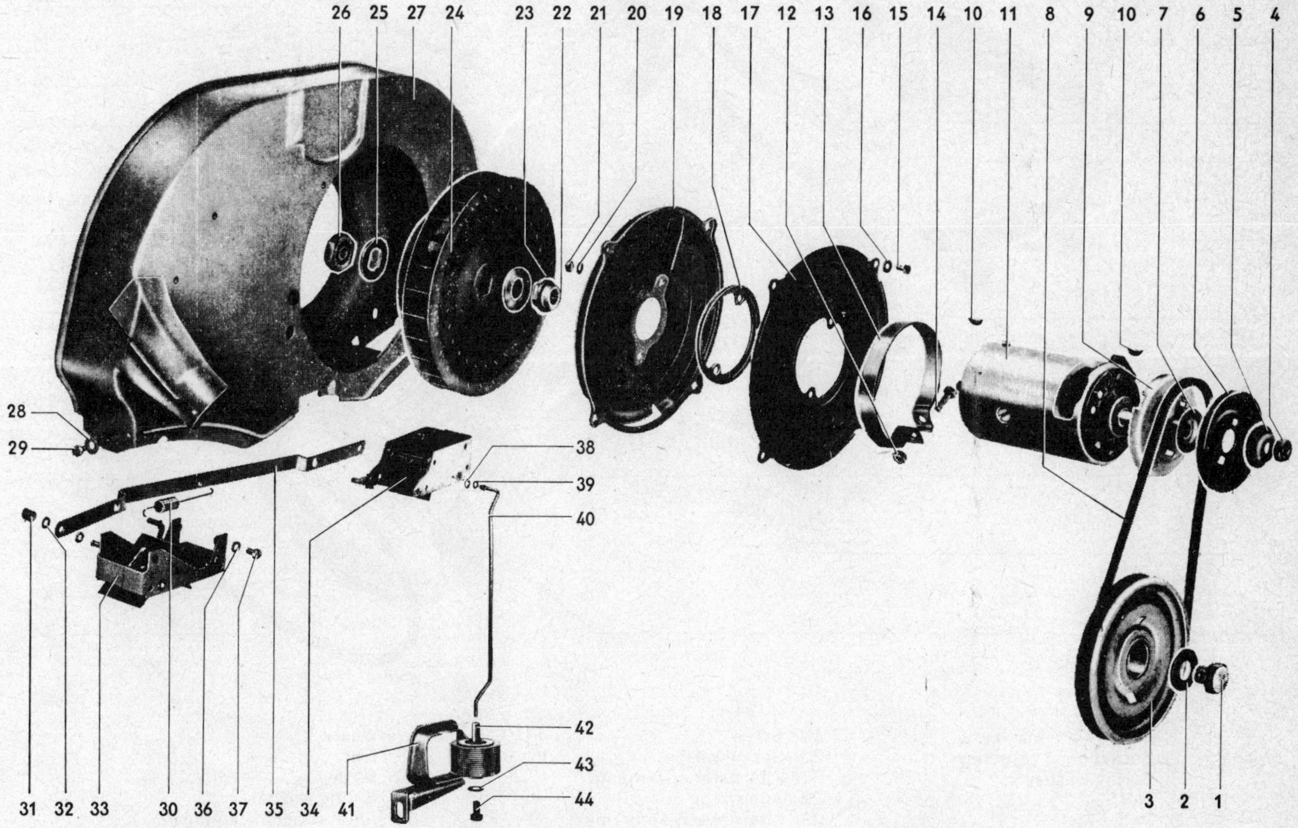

1. Pulley bolt
2. Dished washer
3. Crankshaft pulley
4. Pulley nut
5. Special washer
6. Rear pulley half
7. Spacer washer
8. V-belt
9. Front pulley half
10. Woodruff key
11. Generator
12. Nut
13. Strap
14. Bolt
15. Bolt
16. Lockwasher
17. Outer fan cover
18. Reinforcement flange
19. Inner fan cover
20. Lockwasher
21. Nut
22. Fan hub
23. Shim
24. Fan
25. Lockwasher
26. Special nut
27. Cheese head screw
28. Washer
29. Cheese head screw
30. Return spring
31. Spring
32. Washer
33. Left cooling air regulator
34. Right cooling air regulator
35. Cooling air regulator connecting rod
36. Washer
37. Cheese head screw
38. Lockwasher
39. Washer
40. Connecting rod
41. Thermostat bracket
42. Thermostat
43. Lockwasher
44. Bolt

Type 1 cooling system

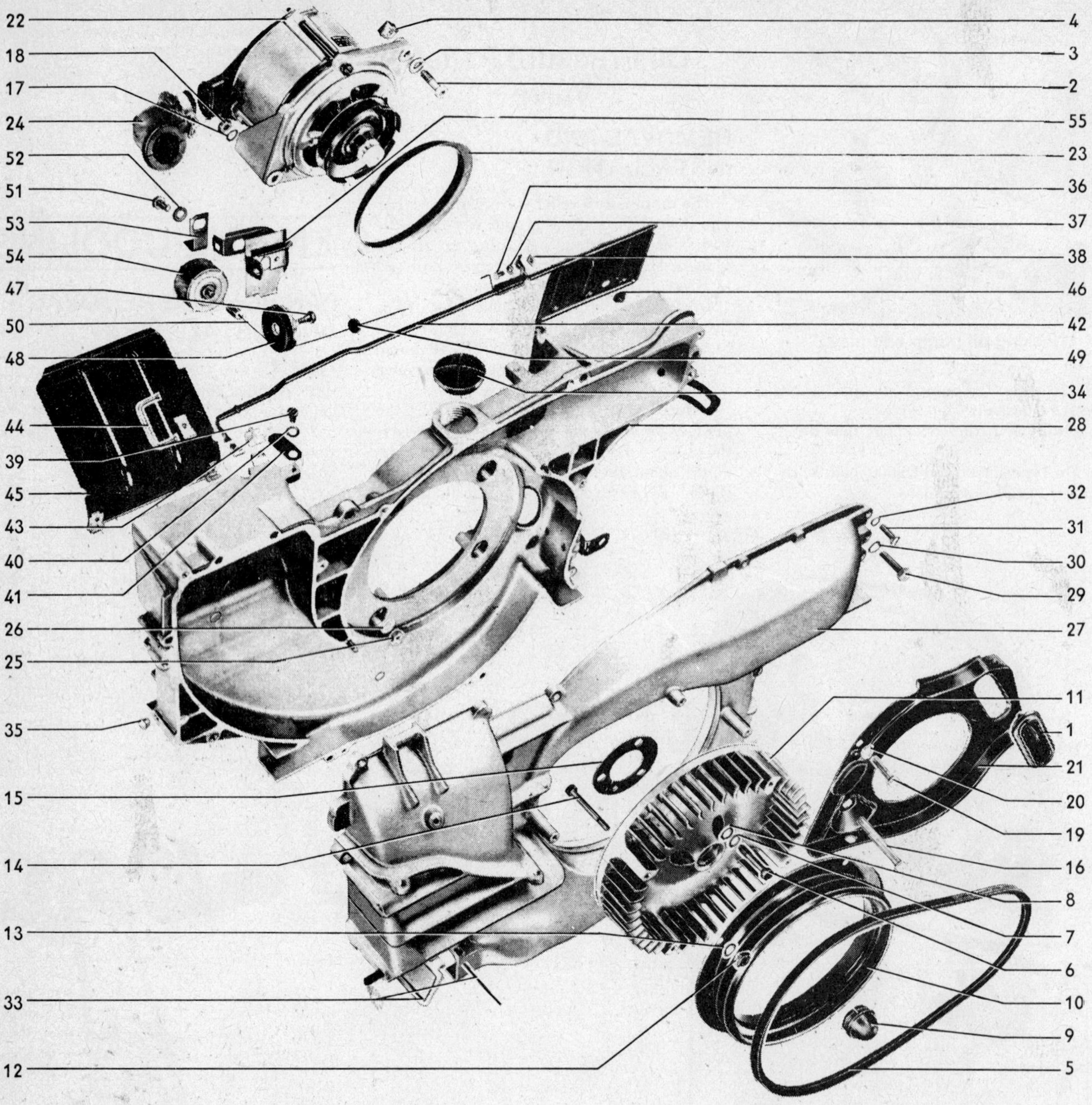

1. Cover plate insert
2. Socket head capscrew
3. Spring washer
4. Nut
5. Belt
6. Socket head capscrew
7. Spring washer
8. Flat washer
9. Cap
10. Crankshaft pulley
11. Fan
12. Nut
13. Spring nut
14. Socket head capscrew
15. Spacer
16. Bolt
17. Spring washer
18. Nut
19. Screw
20. Spring washer
21. Alternator cover plate
22. Alternator
23. Alternator sealing ring
24. Alternator elbow
25. Nut
26. Spring washer
27. Fan housing—rear half
28. Fan housing—front half
29. Bolt
30. Spring washer
31. Screw
32. Spring washer
33. Air non-return flap
34. Inspection hole cover
35. Plug
36. Bolt
37. Washer
38. Nut
39. Screw
40. Spring washer
41. Shaft retaining spring
42. Right flap and shaft
43. Bearing
44. Flap link
45. Left flap
46. Plug
47. Bolt
48. Cooling air control cable roller
49. Sealing washer
50. Cooling air control cable
51. Bolt
52. Washer
53. Thermostat washer
54. Thermostat
55. Thermostat bracket

Type 2 cooling system

located on both sides of the fan housing. Remove the rear hood.

4. Remove the outer half of the alternator pulley and remove the fan belt.

5. Remove the thermostat securing screw and take out the thermostat.

6. Remove the lower part of the carburetor pre-heater duct.

7. The fan housing can now be removed with the alternator. After removal, check the fan housing for damage and for loose air deflector plates.

8. Installation is the reverse of the above.

9. Make sure that the thermostat connecting rod is inserted into its hole in the cylinder head. The fan housing should be fitted properly on the cylinder cover plates so that there is no loss of cooling air.

FAN REMOVAL AND INSTALLATION

Type 1

1. Remove the alternator and fan assembly as described in the "Alternator Removal and Installation" section.

2. While holding the fan, unscrew the fan retaining nut and take off the fan, spacer washers, and the hub.

3. To install, place the hub on the alternator shaft, making sure that the woodruff key is securely positioned.

4. Insert the spacer washers. The clearance between the fan and the fan cover is 0.06-0.07 in. Place the fan into position and tighten its retaining nut. Correct the spacing by inserting the proper number of spacer washers. Place any extra washers between the lockwasher and the fan.

5. Reinstall the alternator and the fan assembly.

FAN HOUSING AND FAN REMOVAL AND INSTALLATION

Type 2/1800 and 2/2000

1. Pry out the alternator cover insert, and, using a 12 point Allen wrench, loosen the alternator adjusting bolt. Remove the alternator drive belt, the ignition timing scale and the grille over the fan. Remove the three socket head screws attaching the fan and crankshaft assembly to the crankshaft and remove the fan and pulley.

2. Disconnect the cooling air control cable at the flap control shaft.

3. On models so equipped, pull out the rubber elbow for the alternator from the front half of the fan housing.

4. Remove the four nuts retaining the fan housing to the engine crankcase. The assembled fan housing may then be removed by pulling it to the rear and off the engine. It is not necessary to separare the fan housing halves or remove the alternator to remove the fan housing.

5. Reverse the above procedure to install.

AIR FLAP AND THERMOSTAT ADJUSTMENT

Type 1

1. Loosen the thermostat bracket securing nut and disconnect the thermostat from the bracket.

2. Push the thermostat upwards to fully open the air flaps.

3. Reposition the thermostat bracket so that the thermostat contacts the bracket at the upper stop, and then tighten the bracket nut.

4. Reconnect the thermostat to the bracket.

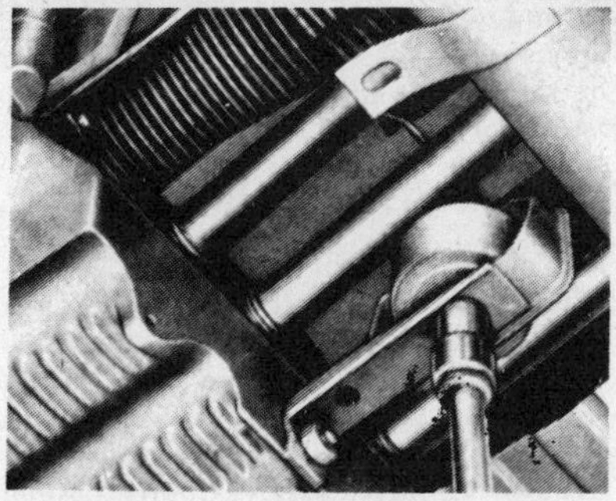

Engine cooling air thermostat

Type 2/1800 and 2/2000

1. Loosen the cable control.
2. Push the air flaps completely closed.
3. Tighten the cable control.

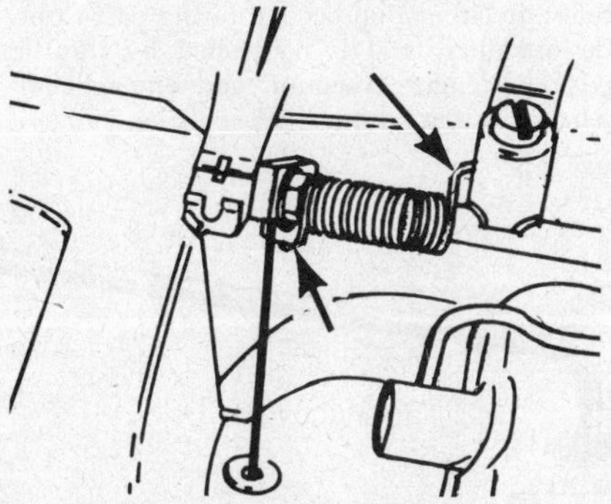

Type 2 air flap cable control

EMISSION CONTROLS

Crankcase Ventilation System

All models are equipped with a crankcase ventilation system. The purpose of the crankcase ventilation system is two-fold. It keeps harmful vapors from escaping into the atmosphere and prevents the buildup of crankcase pressure. Prior to the 1960s, most cars employed a vented oil filler cap and road draft tube to dispose of crankcase vapor. The crankcase ventilation systems now in use are improvements over the old method and, when functioning properly, will not reduce engine efficiency.

Type 1 and 2 crankcase vapors are recirculated from the oil breather through a rubber hose to the air cleaner. The vapors then join the air/fuel mixture and are burned in the engine. Fuel injected cars mix crankcase vapors into the air/fuel mixture to be burned in the combustion chambers. Fresh air is forced through the engine to evacuate vapors and recirculate them into the oil breather, intake air distributor, and then to be burned.

The only maintenance required on the crankcase ventilation system is a periodic check. At every tune-up, examine the hoses for clogging or deterioration. Clean or replace the hoses as required.

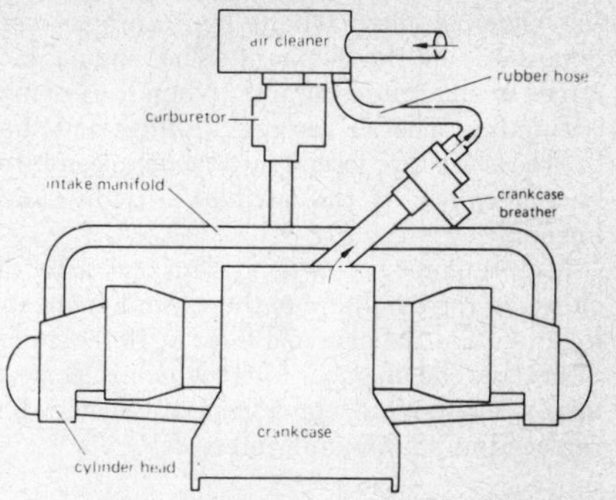

Crankcase ventilation system—Type 1

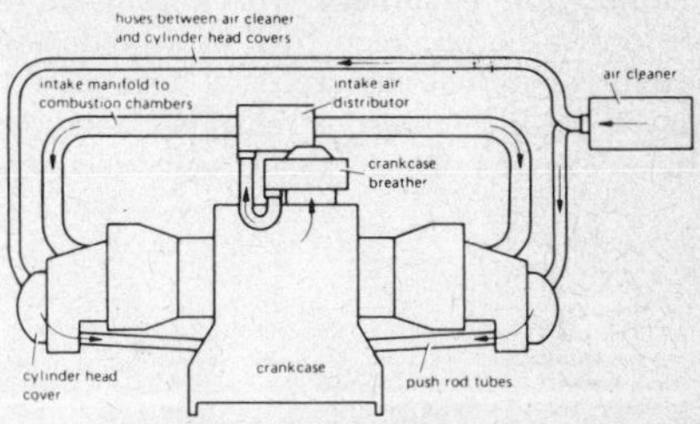

Crankcase ventilation system—Type 2

Evaporative Emission Control System

Required by law since 1971, this system prevents raw fuel vapors from entering the atmosphere. The various systems for different models are similar. They consist of an expansion chamber, activated charcoal filter, and connecting lines. Fuel vapors are vented to

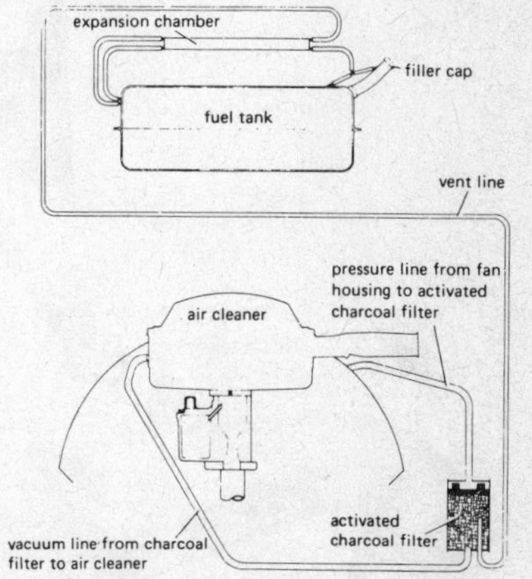

Typical evaporative emission control system

the charcoal filter where hydrocarbons are deposited on the element. The engine fan forces fresh air into the filter when the engine is running. The air purges the filter and the hydrocarbons are forced into the air cleaner to become part of the air/fuel mixture and burned.

Maintenance of this system consists of checking the condition of the various connecting lines and the charcoal filter at 10,000 mile intervals. The charcoal filter, which is located under the engine compartment, should be replaced at 48,000 mile intervals.

Exhaust Gas Recirculation System

In order to control exhaust emissions of oxides of nitrogen (NO_x), an exhaust gas recirculation (EGR) system is employed on all 1973 and later Type 2 models, and on all 1974 and later Type 1 models. The system lowers peak flame temperature during combustion by introducing a small (about 10%) percentage of relatively inert exhaust gas into the intake charge. Since the exhaust gas contains little or no oxygen, it cannot react with nor influence the air/fuel mixture. However, the exhaust gas does (by volume) take up space in the combustion chambers (space that would otherwise be occupied by a heat-producing, explosive air/fuel mixture), and does serve to lower peak combustion chamber temperature. The amount of exhaust gas directed to the combustion chambers is infinitely variable by means of a vacuum operated EGR valve. For system specifics, see the vehicle type breakdown under "General Description."

GENERAL DESCRIPTION

Type 1

EGR is installed on all 1975 and later models. All applications use the element type filter and single stage EGR valve. Recirculations occurs during part throttle applications as before. The system is controlled by a throttle valve switch which measures throttle position, and an intake air sensor which reacts to engine vacuum. Beginning in 1975, an odometer actuated EGR reminder light (on the dashboard) is used to inform the driver that it is time to service the EGR system. The reminder light measures elapsed mileage and lights at 15,000 mile intervals. A reset button is located behind the switch.

NOTE: On 1977 and later Calif. models, the EGR valve is operated mechanically by a rod attached to the throttle valve lever.

Type 2

All 1975 and later Type 2 models utilize an EGR system. A single stage EGR valve and element type filter are used on all applications. Recirculation occurs during part throttle openings, and is controlled by throttle position, engine vacuum, and engine compartment temperature. When the ambient temperature exceeds 54° F, a sensor switch (located above the battery) opens, permitting EGR during part throttle applications. At 15,000 mile intervals, a dash mounted EGR service reminder light is activated to warn the driver that EGR service is now due. A reset button is located behind the switch.

Catalytic Converter

EGR VALVE CHECKING

Type 1 and 2 (except 1977 and later Type 1 Calif. cars)

1. With the engine idling, pull the plug off the EGR valve's vacuum unit. The engine should slow down noticeably or stall, indicating that the EGR gases are being recirculated.
2. If there is no change when the plug is pulled, stop the engine. Turn the ignition key to the running (2) position without starting the engine.
3. Connect a test lamp as shown in the illustration. Now operate the throttle valve by hand, moving the throttle valve shaft from the idle position into the mid-speed range.
4. If the test light goes off when the throttle is moved off the idle position and lights at idle and at or near full throttle, the EGR valve is faulty and should be replaced.

1977 and Later Type 1 Calif. Cars

1. Remove the E-clip that holds the operating rod to the EGR valve.

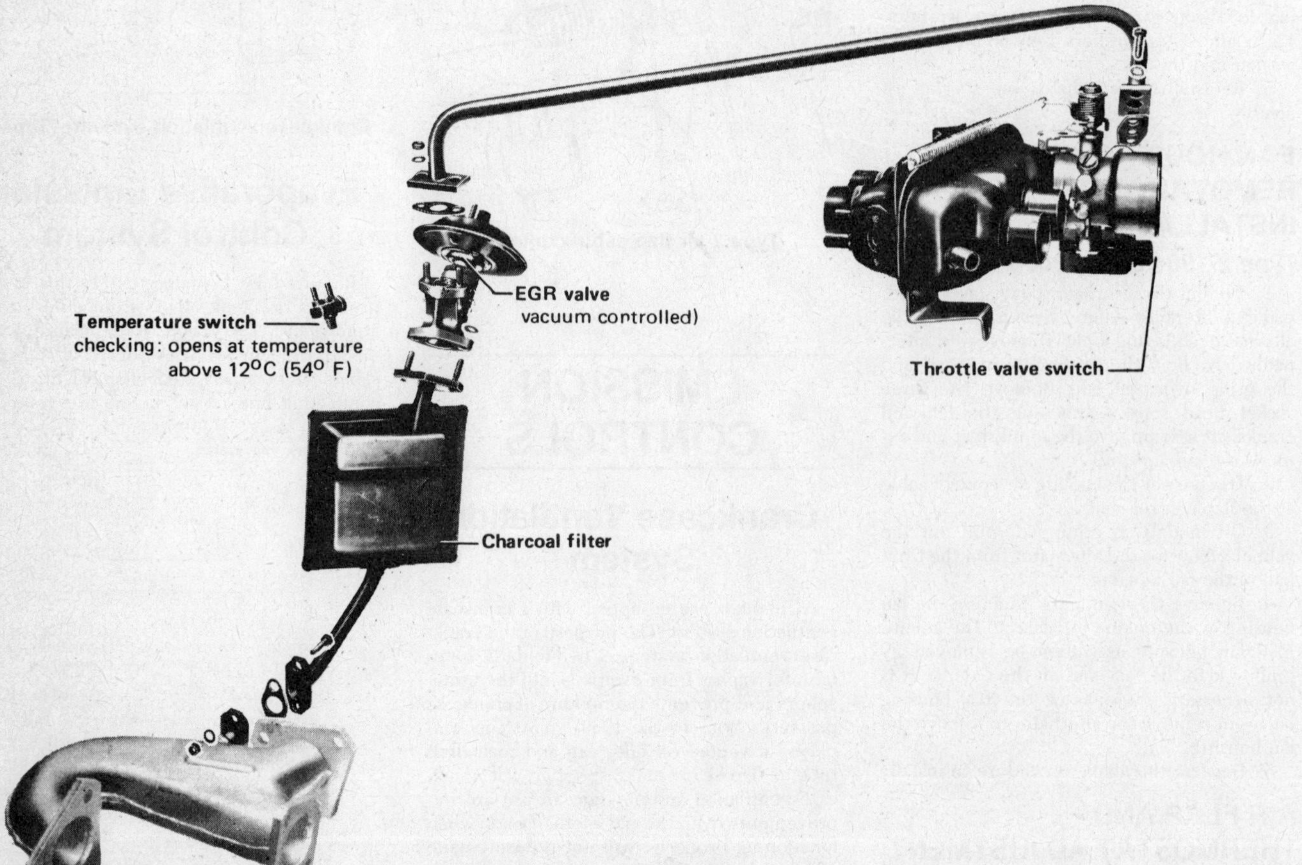

Type 2 EGR system

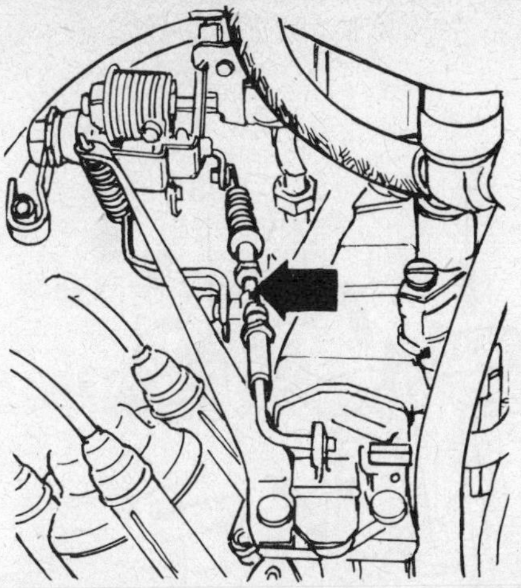

1977 and later Type 1 Calif. EGR linkage; arrow indicates hex-with-pin that is turned to adjust the valve

2. With the engine idling, hand open the EGR valve.

3. The engine should slow down or stall, indicating that the exhaust gases are being recirculated. If not, the EGR valve or the EGR pipe is clogged and will require replacement or cleaning.

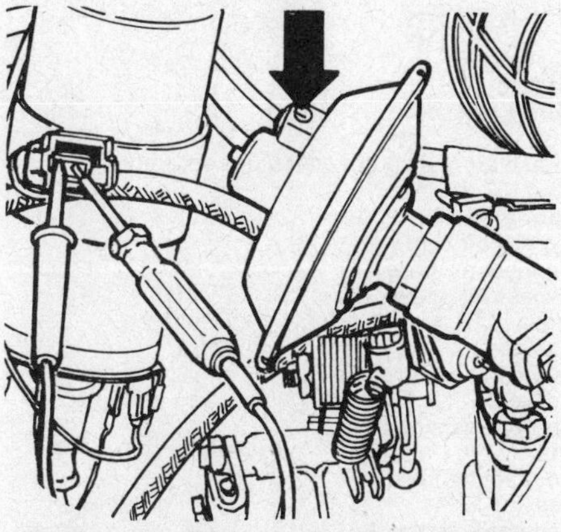

Testing the EGR valve; arrow indicates the location of the plug on the vacuum unit

Catalytic Converter System

All 1975-76 Type 1 and 2 models sold in California and all 1977 and later models are equipped with a catalytic converter. The converter is installed in the exhaust system, upstream and adjacent to the muffler.

Catalytic converters change noxious emissions of hydrocarbons (HC) and carbon monoxide (CO) into harmless carbon dioxide and water vapor. The reaction takes place inside the converter at great heat using platinum and palladium metals as the catalyst. If the engine is operated on lead-free fuel, they are designed to last 50,000 miles before replacement.

Starting in 1980, all Type 2 models made for Calif. utilize a three-way catalytic converter. The three-way converter not only reduces HC and CO emissions but it can also reduce oxides of nitrogen (NO_x).

However, the three-way converter can only achieve this reduction of harmful pollutants with the aid of the Lambda Control System. This system is designed to maintain close control of the air/fuel mixture under all operating conditions.

Lambda Control System

All 1980-81 Type 2 models made for use in Calif. are equipped with the Lambda Control System. Basically, the Lambda Control System is an oxygen sensor which is installed in the exhaust manifold. This oxygen sensor makes it possible to maintain the precise air/fuel mixture required by the three-way catalytic converter. The oxygen sensor continuously senses the oxygen content of the exhaust and signals the information to an electronic control unit. The control unit corrects the fuel injector operating time, so that the engine always receives an accurately metered air/fuel mixture.

The oxygen sensor system is monitored by an indicator light in the instrument panel which will light up every 30,000 miles. This is your signal to take the car to a service facility and get the Lambda Control System checked out.

Deceleration Control

All 1975 and later Type 2 models, as well as those 1975 and later Type 1 models equipped with manual transmission, are equipped with deceleration control to prevent an overly rich fuel mixture from reaching the exhaust. During deceleration, a vacuum valve (manual transmission) or electrical transmission switch (automatic transmission) opens, bypassing the closed throttle plate and allowing air to enter the combustion chambers.

FUEL SYSTEM

Electric Fuel Pump

All 1975 and later Type 1 and Type 2 models have an electric pump. The fuel pump is located near the front axle.

REMOVAL AND INSTALLATION

1. Disconnect the fuel pump wiring. Pull the plug from the pump but do not pull on the wiring.
2. Disconnect the fuel hoses and plug them to prevent any leakage.
3. Remove the two nuts which secure the pump and then remove the pump.
4. Reconnect the fuel pump hoses and wiring and install the pump on the vehicle.

ADJUSTMENTS

Electric fuel pump pressure is 28 psi. Fuel pump pressure is determined by a pressure regulator which diverts part of the fuel pump output to the gas tank when 28 psi is reached. The regulator, located on the engine firewall, has a screw and locknut on its end. Loosen the locknut and adjust the screw to adjust the pressure. Do not force the screw in or out if it does not turn.

Type 2 fuel pump location (1) and filter (2)

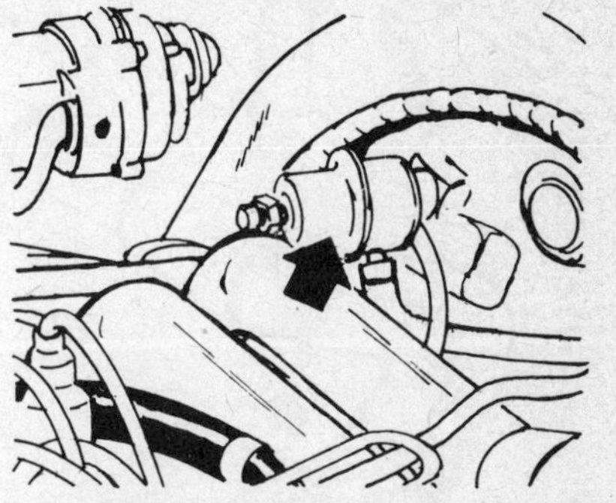

Fuel pressure regulator with locknut and adjusting screw at left end

Electronic Fuel Injection–Air Flow Controlled

All 1975 and later Type 1 and Type 2 models, are equipped with an improved system known as the Air Flow Controlled Electronic Fuel Injection System. With this system, some of the electronic sensors and wiring are eliminated, and the control box is smaller. Fuel is metered according to intake air flow.

The system consists of the following components;

Intake air sensor—measures intake air volume and temperature and sends voltage signals to the control unit (brain box). It also controls the electric fuel pump by shutting it off when intake air stops. It is located between the air cleaner and the intake air distributor.

Ignition contact breaker points—these are the regular points inside the distributor. When the points open, all four injectors are triggered. The points also send engine speed signals to the control unit. No separate triggering contacts are used.

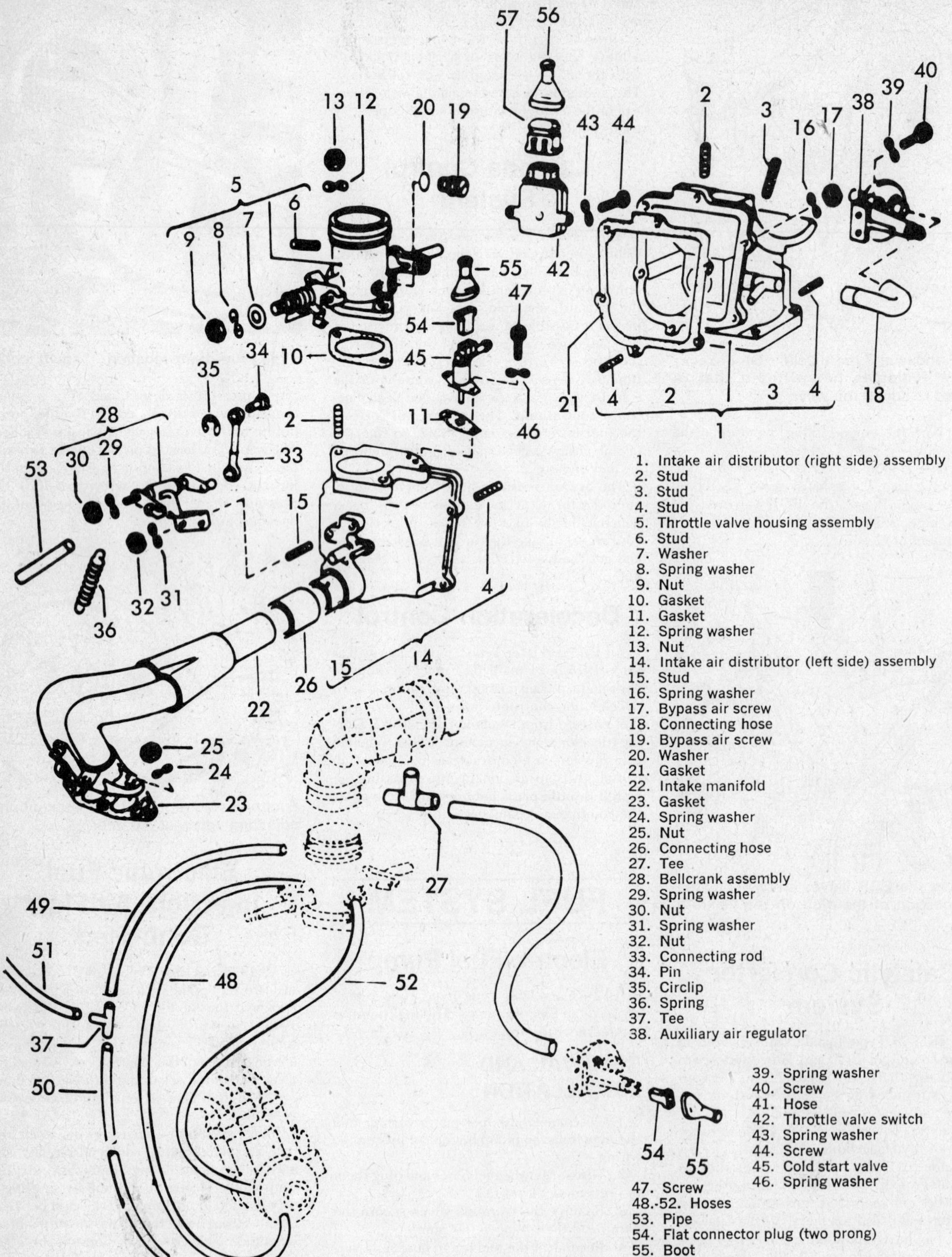

1. Intake air distributor (right side) assembly
2. Stud
3. Stud
4. Stud
5. Throttle valve housing assembly
6. Stud
7. Washer
8. Spring washer
9. Nut
10. Gasket
11. Gasket
12. Spring washer
13. Nut
14. Intake air distributor (left side) assembly
15. Stud
16. Spring washer
17. Bypass air screw
18. Connecting hose
19. Bypass air screw
20. Washer
21. Gasket
22. Intake manifold
23. Gasket
24. Spring washer
25. Nut
26. Connecting hose
27. Tee
28. Bellcrank assembly
29. Spring washer
30. Nut
31. Spring washer
32. Nut
33. Connecting rod
34. Pin
35. Circlip
36. Spring
37. Tee
38. Auxiliary air regulator
39. Spring washer
40. Screw
41. Hose
42. Throttle valve switch
43. Spring washer
44. Screw
45. Cold start valve
46. Spring washer
47. Screw
48.-52. Hoses
53. Pipe
54. Flat connector plug (two prong)
55. Boot
56. Boot
57. Flat connector plug (five prong)

Exploded view of the Type 1 airflow controlled electronic fuel injection system

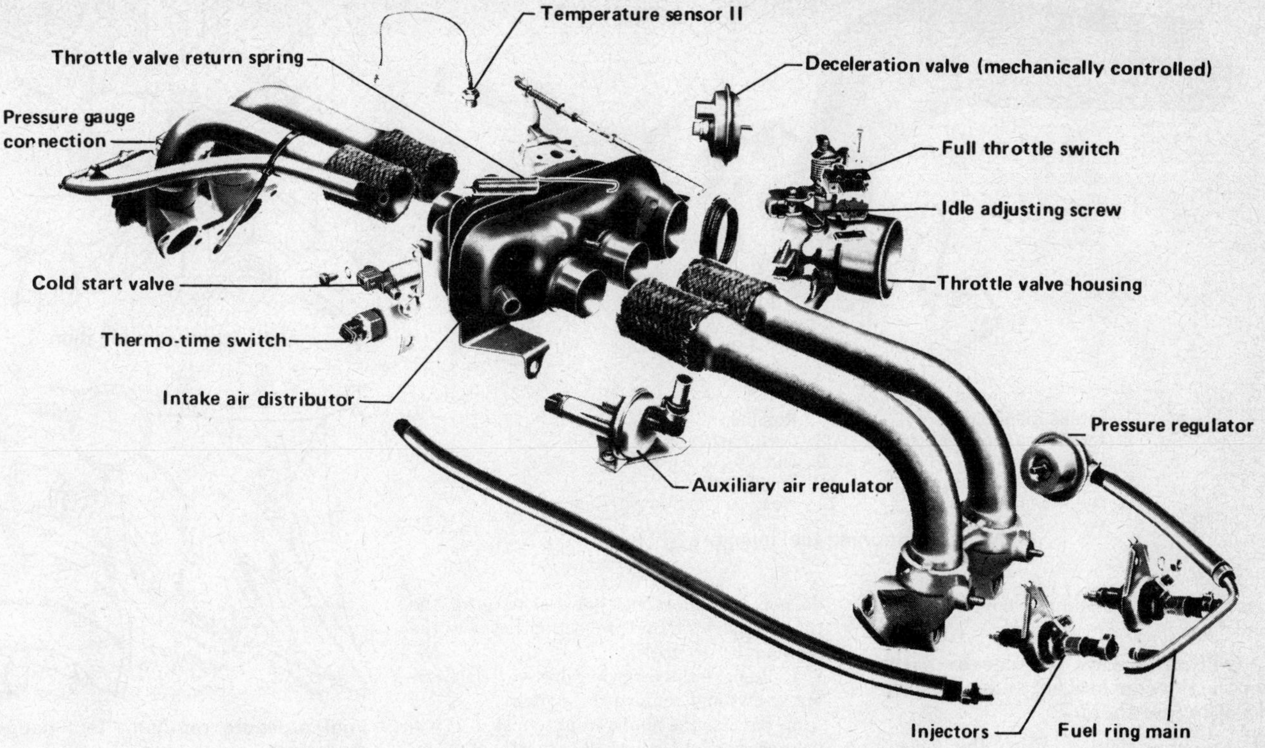

Exploded view of the Type 2 airflow controlled electronic fuel injection system

Throttle valve switch—provides only for full load enrichment. This switch is not adjustable.

Temperature sensor I—senses intake temperature as before. It is now located in the intake air sensor.

Temperature sensor II—senses cylinder head temperature as before.

Control unit (brain box)—contains only 80 components compared to the old system's 300.

Pressure regulator—is connected by a vacuum hose to the intake air distributor and is no longer adjustable. It adjusts fuel pressure according to manifold vacuum.

Auxiliary air regulator—provides more air during cold warmup.

ELECTRONIC CONTROL BOX

All work concerning the control box is to be performed by the dealer. Do not remove the control box and take it to a dealer because the dealer will not be able to test it without the vehicle. Do not disconnect the control box unless the battery is disconnected and the ignition is OFF.

FUEL INJECTORS

There are two types of injectors. One type is secured in place by a ring that holds a single injector. The second type of injector is secured to the intake manifold in pairs by a common bracket.

Removal and Installation

SINGLE INJECTORS

1. Remove the nut which secures the injector bracket to the manifold.
2. If the injector is not going to be replaced, do not disconnect the fuel line. Disconnect the injector wiring.
3. Gently slide the injector bracket up the injector and pull the injector from the intake manifold. Be careful not to damage the inner and outer rubber sealing rings. These sealing rings are used to seal the injector to the manifold and must be replaced if they show any sign of deterioration.
4. Installation is the reverse of removal. Be careful not to damage the injector tip or contaminate the injector with dirt.

PAIRED INJECTORS

1. Disconnect the injector wiring.
2. Remove the two nuts which secure the injector bracket to the manifold. Slide the bracket up the injector. Do not disconnect the fuel lines if the injector is not going to be replaced.
3. Gently slide the pair of injectors out of their bores along with the rubber sealing rings, injector plate, and the inner and outer injector locating bushings. It may be necessary to remove the inner bushings from the intake manifold after the injectors are re-

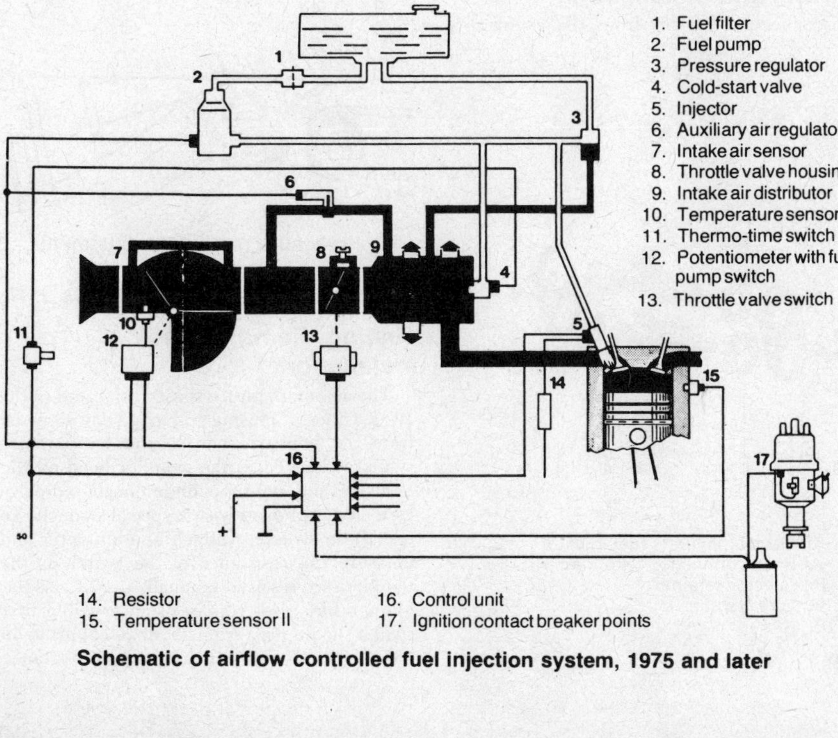

1. Fuel filter
2. Fuel pump
3. Pressure regulator
4. Cold-start valve
5. Injector
6. Auxiliary air regulator
7. Intake air sensor
8. Throttle valve housing
9. Intake air distributor
10. Temperature sensor I
11. Thermo-time switch
12. Potentiometer with fuel pump switch
13. Throttle valve switch
14. Resistor
15. Temperature sensor II
16. Control unit
17. Ignition contact breaker points

Schematic of airflow controlled fuel injection system, 1975 and later

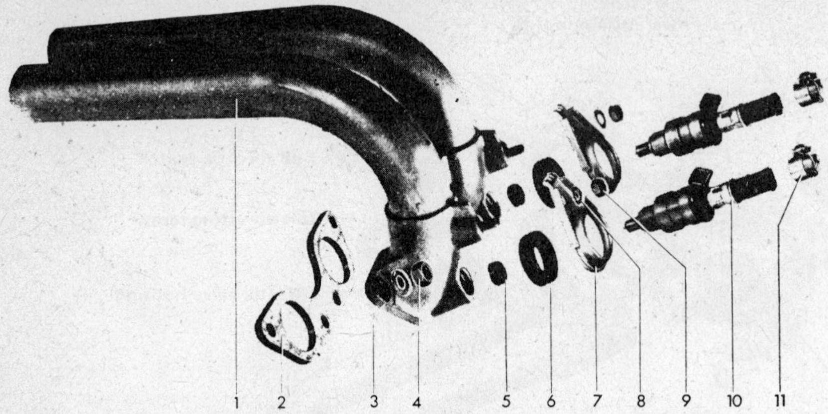

1. Intake manifold
2. Intake manifold gasket
3. Lock washer
5. Inner sealing bushing
6. Outer sealing bushing
7. Retainer
8. Lock washer
9. Nut
10. Fuel injector
11. Hose connection with clamp

Individually mounted fuel injectors

moved since they sometimes lodge within the manifold.

NOTE: There are two sleeves that fit over the injector bracket studs. Be careful not to lose them.

4. Upon installation, place the injector bracket, the outer locating bushings, the injector plate, and the inner locating bushings on the pair of injectors in that order.

5. Gently slip the injector assembly into the manifold and install the bracket nuts. Be careful not to damage the injector tips or contaminate the injectors with dirt.

6. Reconnect the injector wiring.

THROTTLE VALVE SWITCH

Removal and Installation

1. Remove the air filter.

2. The switch is located on the throttle valve housing. Disconnect the throttle valve return spring.

3. Remove the throttle valve assembly but do not disconnect the bowden wire for the throttle valve or the connecting hoses to the ignition distributor.

4. Remove the throttle valve, switch securing screws and remove the switch.

5. Reverse the above steps to install. It will be necessary to adjust the switch after installation.

COLD START VALVE

Removal and Installation

The cold start valve is located near the thermo-switch and is secured to the air intake distributor by two screws. This valve sometimes jams open and causes excessive consumption, rough idle, and low power output.

FUEL PRESSURE REGULATOR

Removal and Installation

Disconnect the hoses from the regulator

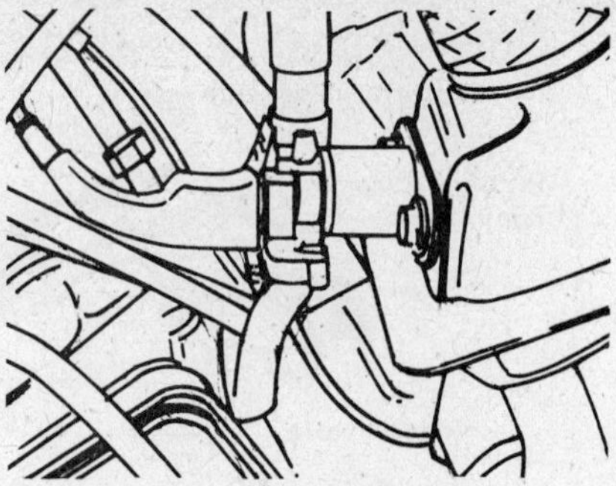

Cold start valve location

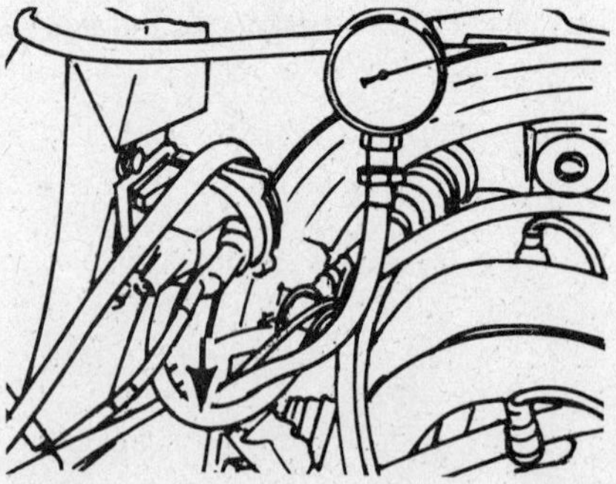

Fuel pressure regulator test gauge installation

and remove the regulator from its bracket. The fuel pump pressure is adjustable; however, lack of fuel pressure is usually due to other defects in the system and the regulator should be adjusted only as a last resort.

Adjustment

1. Remove the air cleaner.
2. Connect a fuel pressure gauge.
3. Start the engine and operate at idle.
4. Loosen locknut "A" and adjust fuel pressure to 35 psi with screw "B".

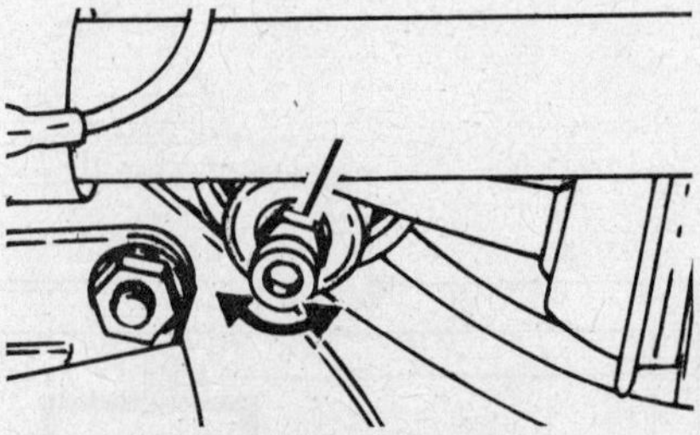

Fuel pressure regulator adjustment

TEMPERATURE SENSOR

Testing, Removal and Installation

The air temperature sensor is located in the air distributor housing and may be unscrewed from the housing. The second temperature switch is located in the cylinder head on the left side and senses cylinder head temperature. It is removed with a special wrench. To test these switches, attach an ohmmeter and measure the resistance of the switch as the temperature is raised gradually to 212°. As the temperature rises, the resistance of the first switch should drop from about 200 ohms to 80 ohms. The cylinder head switch resistance

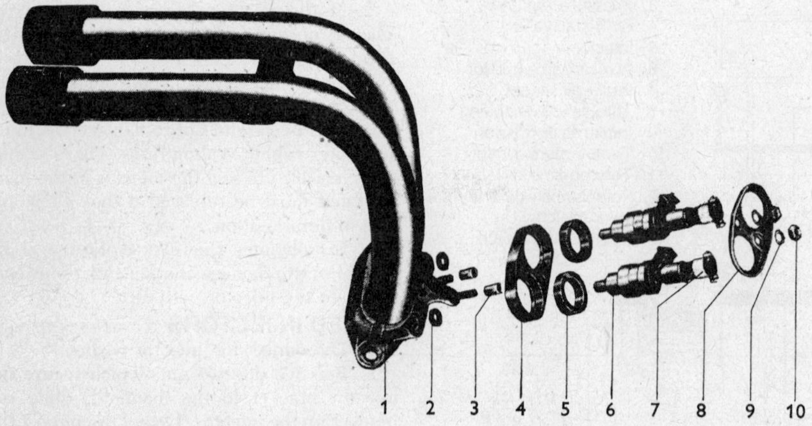

1. Intake manifolds with injector seats
2. Injector inner locating sealing bushings
3. Sleeves
4. Injector plate
5. Injector outer locating bushings
6. Electromagnetic fuel injector
7. Hose connection with clamp
8. Injector retainer
9. Lock washer
10. Nut

Paired fuel injectors

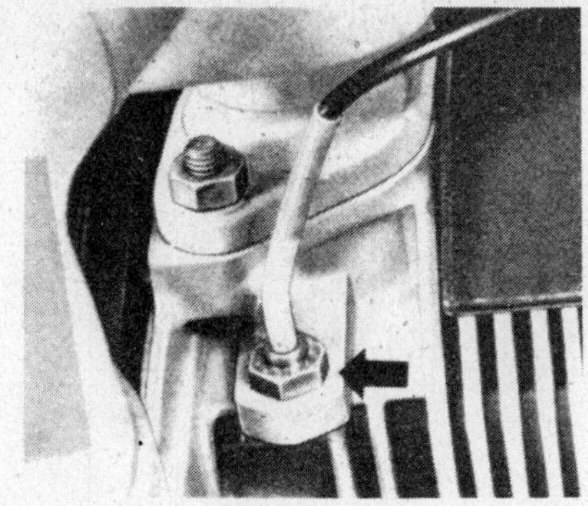

Cylinder head temperature sensing switch

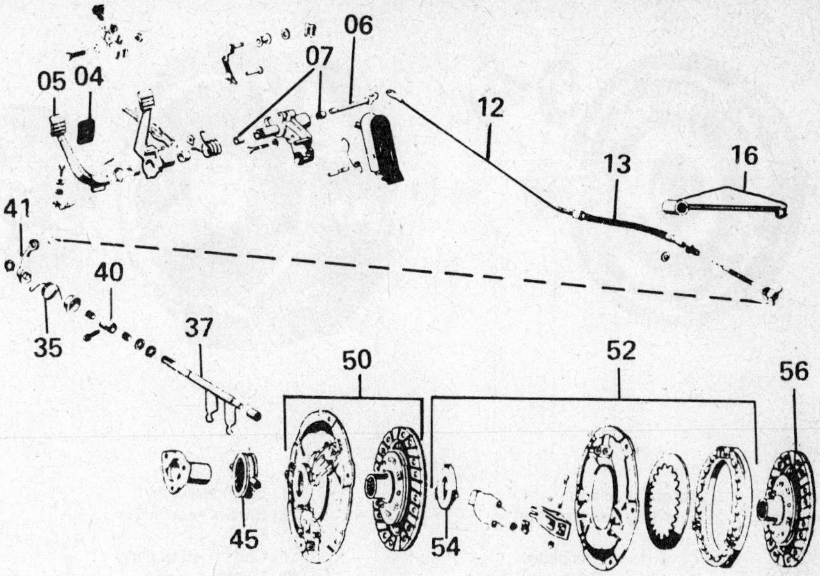

4. Clutch pedal pad
5. Clutch pedal
6. Clutch pedal shaft
7. Bushings for pedal cluster
12. Clutch cable
13. Clutch cable sleeve
16. Angle plate for clutch cable
35. Clutch return spring
37. Clutch cross shaft
40. Bushing—operating shaft
41. Clutch operating lever
45. Clutch release bearing
50. Clutch
52. Pressure plate
54. Clutch release plate
56. Clutch disc

Type 1 clutch components

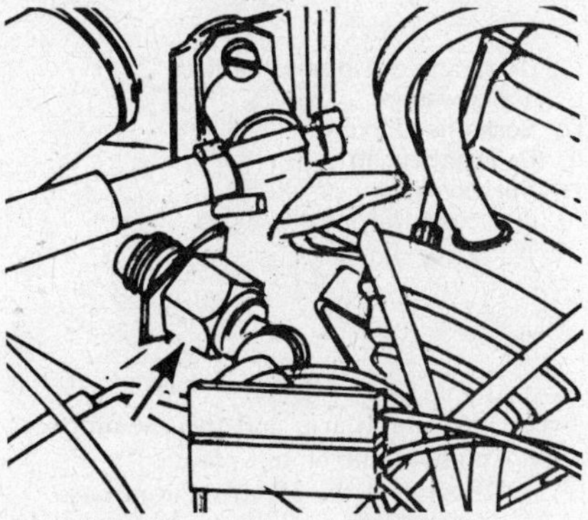

Thermoswitch location

should drop from about 1700 ohms to 190 ohms at 212°.

The third switch is actually a thermoswitch and is an ON/OFF type switch. Below 41° it is ON to activate the cold starting valve. The switch is located next to the distributor and may be removed with a 24 mm wrench.

TROUBLESHOOTING

There are very few items to check without the special tester used by the dealer.

It is possible to check the fuel pressure by inserting a fuel pressure gauge in the line after the pressure regulator. Insert the gauge using a T-fitting. Turn on the key and check the pressure. If the pressure is low, check for leaking injectors, restricted lines, clogged fuel filters, damaged pressure regulator, bad fuel pump, water in the gas and resultant corrosion of the injectors, or a leaking or jammed cold start valve.

CLUTCH

The clutch used in all models is a single dry disc mounted on the flywheel with a diaphragm spring type pressure plate. The release bearing is the ball bearing type and does not require lubrication. On Types 1 and 2 the clutch is engaged mechanically via a cable which attaches to the clutch pedal. The Vanagon, although a Type 2, utilizes a hydraulically engaged clutch. It features a clutch pedal operated master cylinder and a bell housing mounted slave cylinder.

REMOVAL AND INSTALLATION

Manual Transmission

1. Remove the engine.
2. Remove the pressure plate securing bolts one turn at a time until all spring pressure is released.
3. Remove the bolts and remove the clutch assembly.

NOTE: Notice which side of the clutch disc faces the flywheel and install the new disc in the same direction.

4. Before installing the new clutch, check the condition of the flywheel. It should not have excessive heat cracks and the friction surface should not be scored or warped. Check the condition of the throw out bearing. If the bearing is worn, replace it.
5. Lubricate the pilot bearing in the end of the crankshaft with grease.
6. Insert a pilot shaft, used for centering the clutch disc, through the clutch disc and place the disc against the flywheel. The pilot shaft will hold the disc in place.
7. Place the pressure plate over the disc and loosely install the bolts.

NOTE: Make sure the correct side of the clutch disc is facing outward. The disc will rub the flywheel if it is incorrectly positioned.

8. After making sure that the pressure plate aligning dowels will fit into the pressure plate, gradually tighten the bolts.
9. Remove the pilot shaft and reinstall the engine.
10. Adjust the clutch pedal free-play.
11. Bleed the clutch (Vanagon only).

Automatic Stick Shift

1. Disconnect the negative battery cable.
2. Remove the engine.
3. Remove the transaxle.
4. Remove the torque converter by sliding it off the input shaft. Seal off the hub opening.
5. Mount the transaxle in a repair stand or on a suitable bench.
6. Loosen the clamp screw and pull off the clutch operating lever. Remove the transmission cover.
7. Remove the hex nuts between the clutch housing and the transmission case.

NOTE: Two nuts are located inside the differential housing.

8. The oil need not be drained if the clutch is removed with the cover opening up and the gearshift housing breather blocked.
9. Pull the transmission from the clutch housing studs.
10. Turn the clutch lever shaft to disengage the release bearing.
11. Remove both lower engine mounting bolts.
12. Loosen the clutch retaining bolts gradually and alternately to prevent distortion. Remove the bolts, pressure plate, clutch plate, and release bearing.
13. Do not wash the release bearing. Wipe it dry only.
14. Check the clutch plate, pressure plate, and release bearing for wear and damage. Check the clutch carrier plate, needle bear-

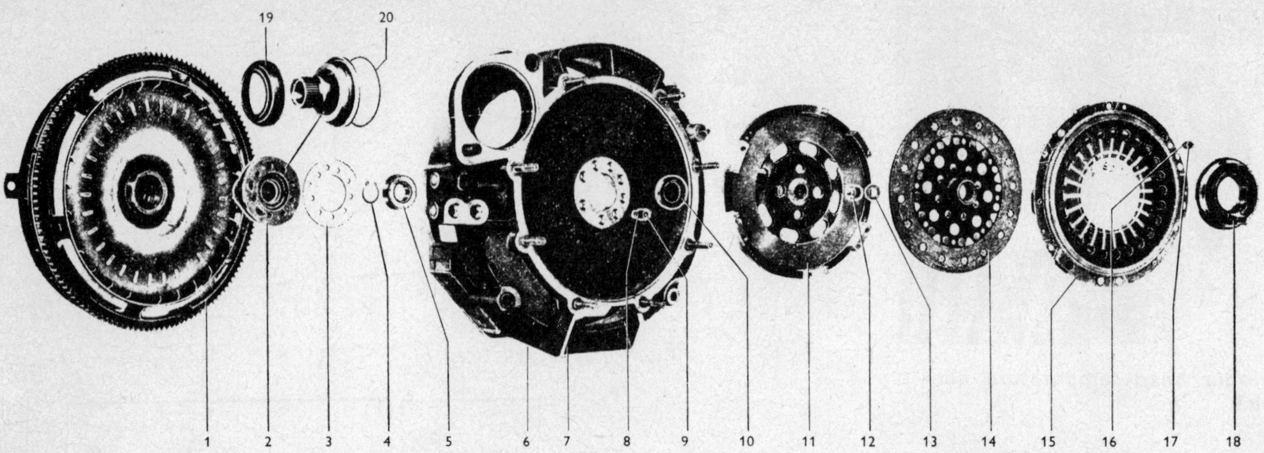

1. Torque converter
2. One-way clutch support
3. Gasket
4. Circlip for carrier plate
5. Ball bearing
6. O-ring for stud
7. Converter housing
8. Spring washer
9. Socket head screw
10. Seal
11. Clutch carrier plate
12. Needle bearing
13. Seal/carrier plate
14. Clutch plate
15. Diaphragm clutch pressure plate
16. Spring washer
17. Socket head screw
18. Release bearing
19. Seal/converter
20. O-ring/one-way clutch support

Automatic Stick Shift clutch assembly

ing, and seat for wear. Replace the necessary parts.

15. If the clutch is wet with ATF, replace the clutch carrier plate seal and the clutch disc. If the clutch is wet with transmission oil, replace the transmission case seal and clutch disc.

16. Coat the release bearing guide on the transmission case neck and both lugs on the release bearing with grease. Insert the bearing into the clutch.

17. Grease the carrier plate needle bearing. Install the clutch disc and pressure plate using a pilot shaft to center the disc on the flywheel.

18. Tighten the pressure plate retaining bolts evenly and alternately. Make sure that the release bearing is correctly located in the diaphragm spring.

19. Insert the lower engine mounting bolts from the front. Replace the sealing rings if necessary. Some units have aluminum sealing rings and cap nuts.

20. Push the transmission onto the converter housing studs. Insert the clutch lever shaft behind the release bearing lugs. Push the release bearing onto the transmission case neck. Tighten the bolts which hold the clutch housing to the transmission case.

21. Install the clutch operating lever.

22. It is necessary to adjust the basic clutch setting. The clutch operating lever should contact the clutch housing. Tighten the lever clamp screw slightly.

23. First adjust dimension (a) to 0.335 in. Adjust dimension (b) to 3.03 in. Finally adjust dimension (c) to 1.6 in. by repositioning the clutch lever on the clutch shaft. Tighten the lever clamp screw.

24. Push the torque converter onto the support tube. Insert it into the turbine shaft by turning the converter.

25. Check the clutch play after installing the transaxle and engine.

CLUTCH CABLE ADJUSTMENT

Manual Transmission—Types 1 and 2

1. Check the clutch pedal travel by measuring the distance the pedal travels toward the floor until pressure is exerted against the clutch. The distance is ⅜ to ¾ in.

2. To adjust the clutch, jack up the rear of the car and support it on jackstands.

3. Remove the left rear wheel.

4. Adjust the cable tension by turning the wing nut on the end of the clutch cable. Turning the wing nut counterclockwise decreases pedal free-play, turning it clockwise increases free-play.

5. When the adjustment is completed, the wings of the wing nut must be horizontal so that the lugs on the nut engage the recesses in the clutch lever.

6. Push on the clutch pedal several times and check the pedal free-play

7. Install the wheel and lower the car.

Automatic Stick Shift—Type 1

The adjustment is made on the linkage between the clutch arm and the vacuum servo unit. To check the clutch play:

1. Disconnect the servo vacuum hose.
2. Measure the clearance between the upper edge of the servo unit mounting bracket and the lower edge of the adjusting turnbuckle. If the clearance (e) is 0.16 in. or more, the clutch needs adjustment.
3. Reconnect the vacuum hose.

To adjust the clutch:

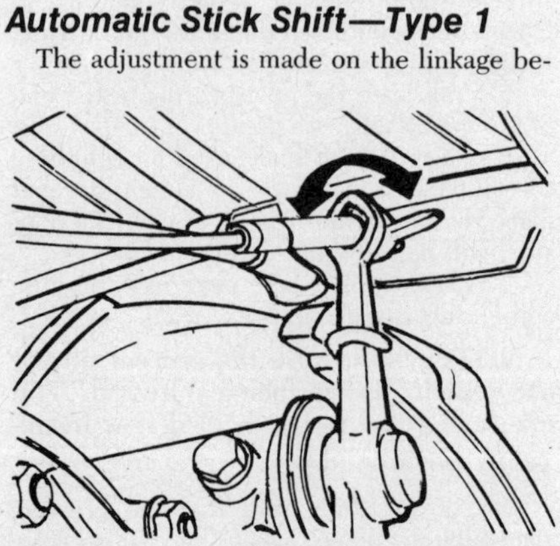

Wing nut for clutch cable adjustment

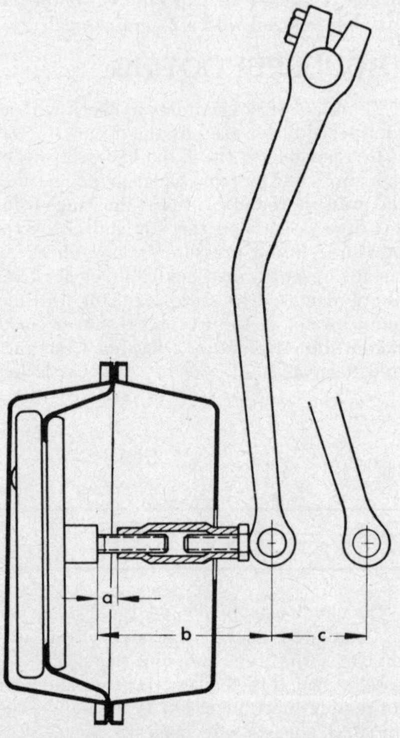

Automatic Stick Shift basic clutch adjusting dimensions

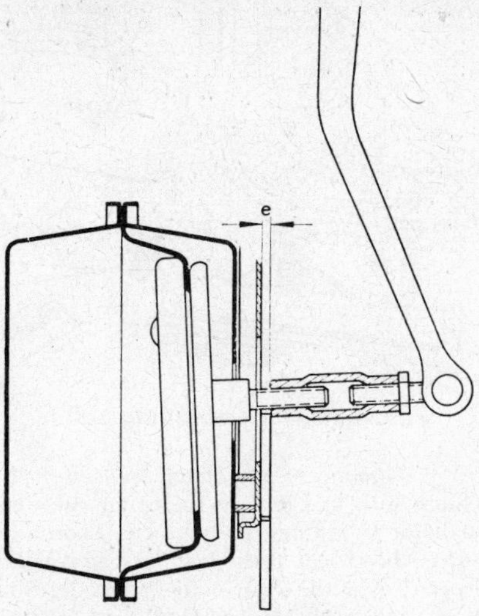

Checking the clutch adjustment on the Automatic Stick Shift

1. Disconnect the servo vacuum hose.
2. Loosen the turnbuckle locknut and back it off completely to the lever arm. Then turn the servo turnbuckle against the locknut. Now back off the turnbuckle 5-5½ turns. The distance between the locknut and the turnbuckle should be 0.25 in.
3. Tighten the locknut against the adjusting sleeve.
4. Reconnect the vacuum hose and road test the vehicle. The clutch is properly adjusted when Reverse gear can be engaged silently and the clutch does not slip on acceleration. If the clutch arm contacts the clutch housing, there is no more adjustment possible and the clutch plate must be replaced.

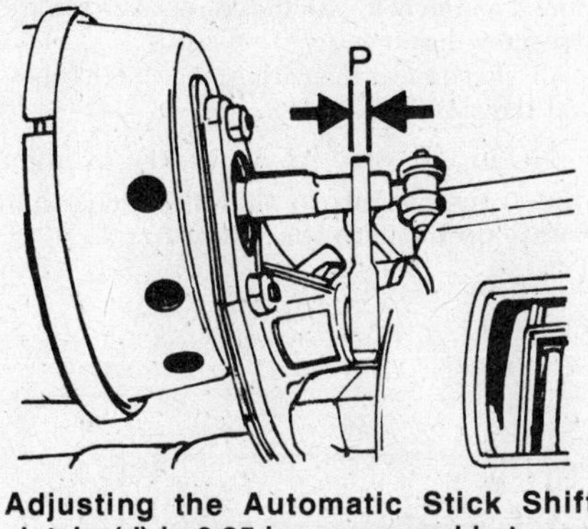

Adjusting the Automatic Stick Shift clutch; (d) is 0.25 in., measured between the locknut and the turnbuckle

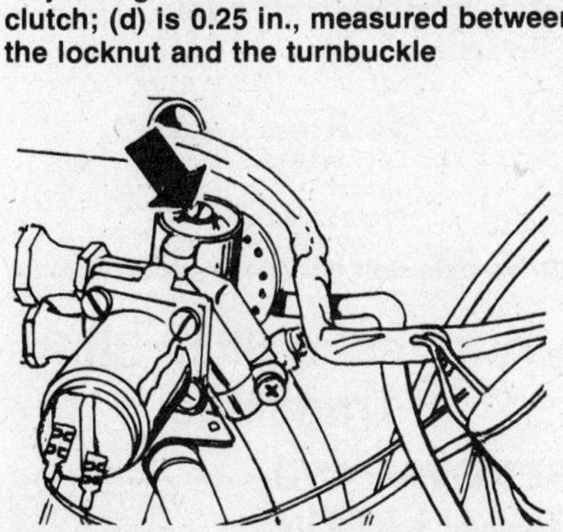

Adjusting screw for speed of engagement

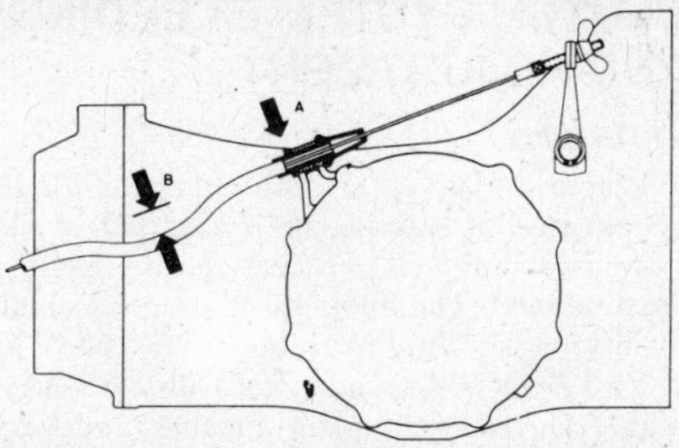

For smooth clutch action, dimension B should be 1.0-1.7 in. Adjust the cable to provide slight sag at point B by installing spacer washers at point A.

The speed of engagement of the Automatic Stick Shift clutch is regulated by the vacuum operated valve rather than by the driver's foot. The adjusting screw is on top of the valve under a small protective cap. Adjust the valve as follows:

1. Remove the cap.
2. To slow the engagement, turn the adjusting screw ¼-½ turn clockwise. To speed engagement, turn the screw counterclockwise.
3. Replace the cap.
4. Test operation by shifting from Second to First at 44 mph without depressing the accelerator. The shift should take exactly one second to occur.

CLUTCH CABLE REPLACEMENT

Types 1 and 2

1. Jack up the car and remove the left rear wheel.
2. Disconnect the cable from the clutch operating lever.
3. Remove the rubber boot from the end of the guide tube and off the end of the cable.
4. On Type 1, unbolt the pedal cluster and remove it from the car. It will also be necessary to disconnect the brake master cylinder push rod and throttle cable from the pedal cluster. On Type 2, remove the cover under the pedal cluster, then remove the pin from the clevis on the end of the clutch cable.
5. Pull the cable out of its guide tube from the pedal cluster end.
6. Installation is the reverse of the above.

NOTE: Grease the cable before installing it and readjust the clutch pedal freeplay.

Clutch Master Cylinder

REMOVAL AND INSTALLATION

Vanagon

1. Siphon the hydraulic fluid from the master cylinder (clutch) reservoir.

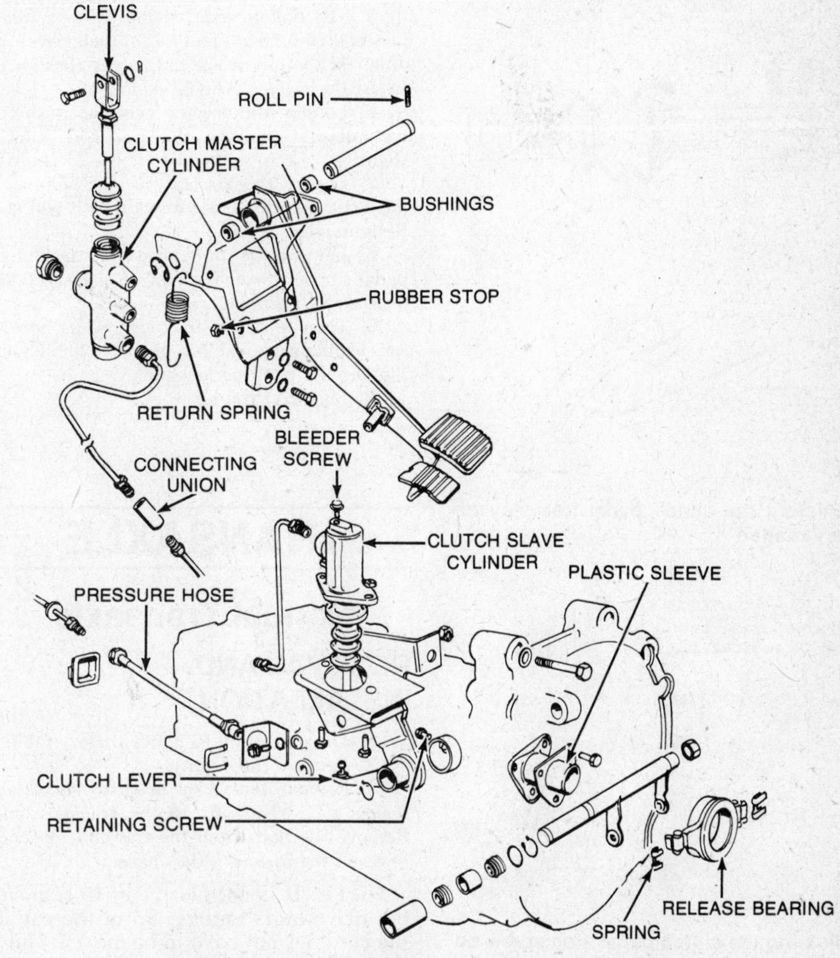

Components of the Vanagon hydraulic clutch system

2. Pull back the carpeting from the pedal area and lay down some absorbent rags.
3. Pull the elbow connection from the top of the master cylinder.
4. Disconnect and plug the pressure line from the rear of the master cylinder.
5. Remove the master cylinder mounting bolts and remove the cylinder to the rear.
6. Reverse the above procedure to install, taking care to bleed the system and adjust pedal free-play.

Clutch Slave Cylinder

REMOVAL AND INSTALLATION

Vanagon

1. Locate the slave cylinder on the bell housing.
2. Disconnect and plug the pressure line from the slave cylinder.
3. Disconnect the return spring from the pushrod.
4. Remove the retaining circlip from the boot and remove the boot.
5. Remove the circlip and slide the slave cylinder rearwards from its mount.
6. Remove the spring clip from the mount.
7. Reverse the above procedure to install, taking care to bleed the system and adjust pedal free-play.

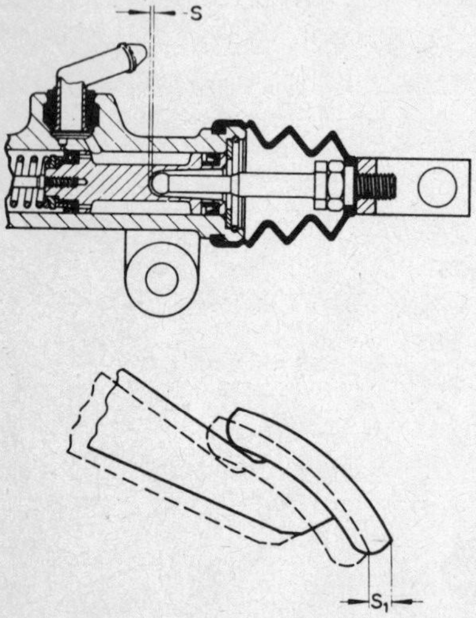

Adjusting the clutch pedal free play on the Vanagon

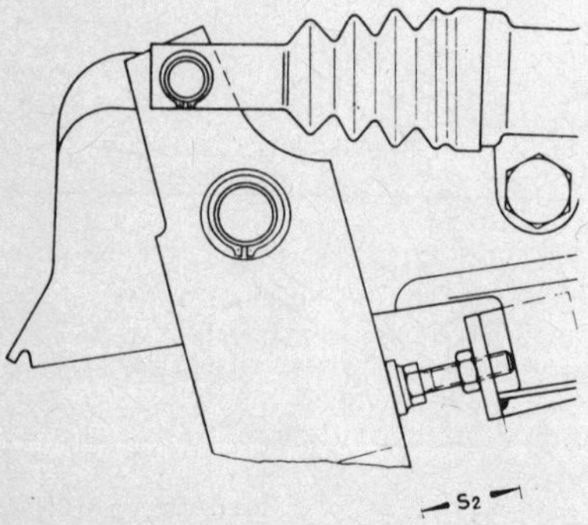

Adjusting the clutch pedal stop screw on the Vanagon

CLUTCH SYSTEM BLEEDING AND ADJUSTMENT

Vanagon

Whenever air enters the clutch hydraulic system due to leakage, or if any part of the system is removed for service, the system must be bled. The hydraulic system uses high quality brake fluid meeting SAE J1703 or DOT 3 or DOT 4 specifications. Brake fluid is highly corrosive to plant finishes and care should be exercised that no spillage occurs. The procedure is as follows;

1. Top up the clutch fluid reservoir and make sure the cap vent is open.
2. Locate the slave cylinder bleed nipple and remove all dirt and grease from the valve. Attach a hose to the nipple and submerge the other end of the hose in a jar containing a few inches of clean brake fluid.
3. Find a friend to operate the clutch pedal. When your friend depresses the clutch pedal slowly to the floor, open the bleeder valve about one turn. Have your friend keep the pedal on the floor until you close the bleeder valve. Repeat this operation several times until no air bubbles are emitted from the tube.

NOTE: Keep a close check on the fluid level in the fluid reservoir. Never let the level fall below the ½ full mark.

4. After bleeding, discard the old fluid and top up the reservoir.
5. The clutch pedal should have a free-play of 0.20-0.28 in., and a 7 in. total travel. If either of the above are not to specifications, adjust the master cylinder as follows.
6. Loosen the master cylinder pushrod locknut and shorten the pushrod length slightly.
7. Loosen the master cylinder bolts and push the cylinder as far forward as it will go. Retighten the bolts.
8. Remove the rubber cap from the clutch pedal stop screw and adjust distance to 0.89 in. Install the rubber cap.
9. Then lengthen the pushrod as necessary to obtain a pedal free-play of 0.20-0.28 in. Tighten the pushrod locknut.
10. Road-test the car.

TRANSAXLE

Manual Transaxle

REMOVAL AND INSTALLATION

1. Disconnect the negative battery cable.
2. Remove the engine.
3. Remove the socket head screws which secure the driveshafts to the transmission. Remove the bolts from the transmission end first and then remove the shafts.

NOTE: It is not necessary to remove the driveshafts entirely from the car if the car does not have to be moved while the transaxle is out.

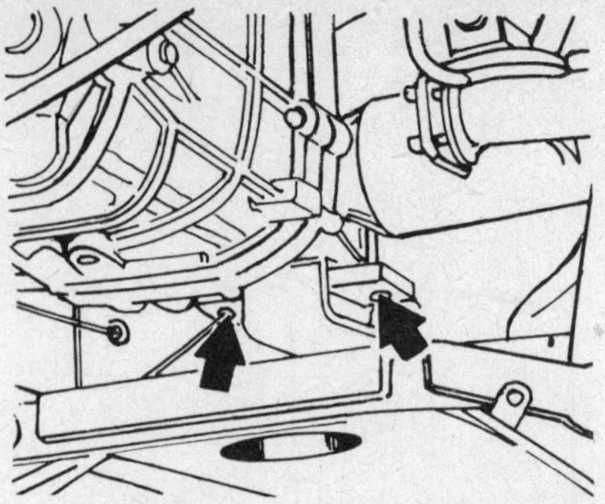

Transaxle front mounting bolts

4. Disconnect the clutch cable from the clutch lever and remove the clutch cable and its guide tube from the transaxle. Loosen the square head bolt at the shift linkage coupling located near the rear of the transaxle. Slide the coupling off the inner shaft lever. There is an access plate under the rear seat to reach the coupling on Type 1. It is necessary to work under the car to reach the coupling on Type 2 models.
5. Disconnect the starter wiring.
6. Disconnect the back-up light switch wiring.
7. Remove the front transaxle mounting bolts.
8. Support the transaxle with a jack and remove the transmission carrier bolts.
9. Carefully lower the jack and remove the transaxle from the car.
10. To install, jack the transaxle into position and loosely install the bolts.
11. Tighten the transmission carrier bolts first, then tighten the front mounting nuts.
12. Install the driveshaft bolts with new lockwashers. The lockwashers should be positioned on the bolt with the convex side toward the screw head.
13. Reconnect the wiring, the clutch cable, and the shift linkage.

NOTE: It may be necessary to align the transmission so that the driveshaft joints do not rub the frame.

14. Install the engine.

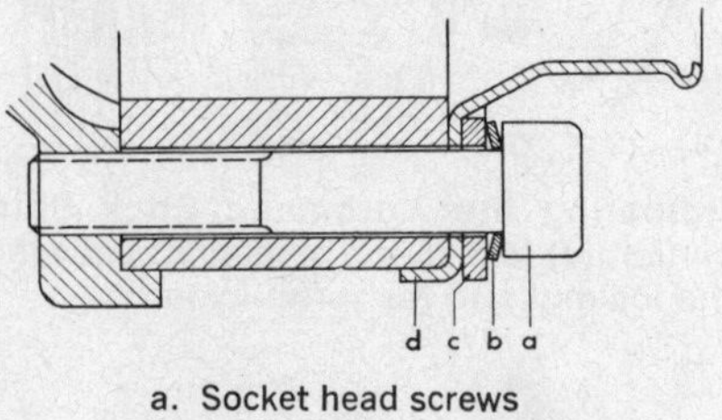

a. Socket head screws
b. Lock washer
c. Spacer
d. Protective cap

Drive axle bolt and washer positioning

Automatic Stick Shift Transaxle

REMOVAL AND INSTALLATION

1. Disconnect the negative battery cable.

2. Remove the engine.

3. Make a bracket to hold the torque converter in place. If a bracket is not used, the converter will slide off the transmission input shaft.

4. Detach the gearshaft rod coupling.

5. Disconnect the driveshafts at the transmission end. If the driveshafts are not going to be repaired, it is not necessary to detach the wheel end.

6. Disconnect the ATF hoses from the transmission. Seal the open ends. Disconnect the temperature switch, neutral safety switch, and the back-up light switch.

7. Pull off the vacuum servo hose.

8. Disconnect the starter wiring.

9. Remove the front transaxle mounting nuts.

10. Loosen the rear transaxle mounting bolts. Support the transaxle and remove the bolts.

11. Lower the axle and remove it from the car.

12. With the torque converter bracket still in place, raise the axle into the car.

13. Tighten the nuts for the front transmission mounting. Insert the rear mounting bolts but do not tighten them at this time.

14. Replace the vacuum servo hose.

15. Connect the ATF hoses, using new washers. The washers are seals.

16. Connect the temperature switch and starter cables.

17. Install the driveshafts, using new washers. Turn the convex sides of the washers toward the screw head.

18. Align the transaxle so that the inner driveshaft joints do not rub on the frame fork and then tighten the rear mounting bolts.

19. Insert the shift rod coupling, tighten the screw, and secure it with wire.

20. Remove the torque converter bracket, and install the engine.

21. After installing the engine, bleed the ATF lines if return flow has not started after 2-3 minutes.

SHIFT LINKAGE ADJUSTMENT

1. The Volkswagen shift linkage is not adjustable. When shifting becomes difficult or there is an excessive amount of play in the linkage, check the shifting mechanism for worn parts. Make sure the shift linkage coupling is tightly connected to the inner shaft lever located at the rear of the transaxle under the rear seat. Worn parts may be found in the shift lever mechanism and the supports for the linkage rod sometimes wear out.

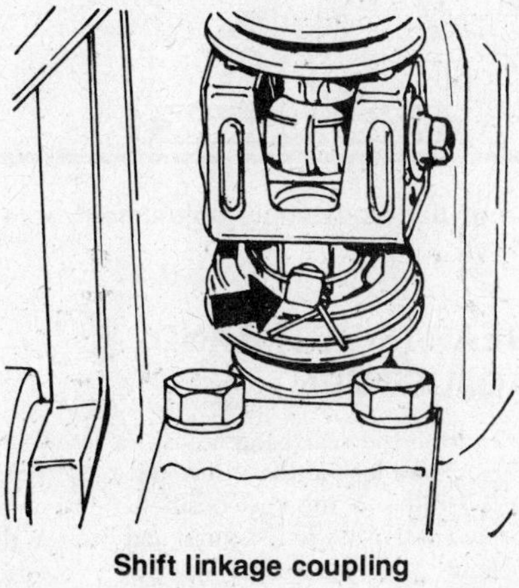

Shift linkage coupling

2. The gear shift lever can be removed after the front floor mat has been lifted.

3. After the two retaining screws have been removed from the gear shift lever ball housing, the gear shift lever, ball housing, rubber boot, and spring are removed as a unit.

CAUTION

Carefully mark the position of the stop plate and note the position of the turned up ramp at the side of the stop plate. Normally the ramp is turned up and on the right hand side of the hole.

4. Installation is the reverse of removal.

5. Lubricate all moving parts with grease.

6. Test the gear shift pattern. If there is difficulty in shifting, adjust the stop plate back and forth in its slotted holes.

Driveshaft and Constant Velocity U-Joint

REMOVAL AND INSTALLATION

1. Remove the bolts which secure the joints at each end of the shaft, tilt the shaft down, and remove the shaft.

2. Loosen the clamps which secure the rubber boot to the axle and slide the boot back on the axle.

3. Drive the stamped steel cover off the joint with a drift.

NOTE: After the cover is removed, do not tilt the ball hub as the balls will fall out of the hub.

4. Remove the circlip from the end of the axle and press the axle out of the joint.

5. Reverse the above steps to install. The position of the dished washer is dependent on the type of transmission. On automatic transmissions, it is placed between the ball hub and the circlip. On manual transmissions, it is placed between the ball hub and the shoulder on the shaft. Be sure to pack the joint with grease.

NOTE: The chamfer on the splined inside diameter of the ball hub faces the shoulder on the driveshaft.

AUTOMATIC TRANSMISSION

REMOVAL AND INSTALLATION

NOTE: The engine and transmission must be removed as an assembly on the Type 2/1800 and 2/2000.

1. Remove the battery ground cable.

2. On the sedan, remove the cooling air intake duct with the heating fan and hoses. Remove the cooling air intake connection and bellows, then detach the hoses to the air cleaner.

3. On the station wagons, remove the warm air hoses and air cleaner. Remove the boot between the dipstick tube and the body and the boot between the oil filler neck and the body. Disconnect the cooling air bellows at the body.

4. Disconnect the wires at the regulator and the alternator wires at the snap connector located by the regulator. Disconnect the auxiliary air regulator and the oil pressure switch at the snap connectors located by the distributor.

5. Disconnect the accelerator cable.

6. Disconnect the right fuel return line.

7. Raise the car.

8. Disconnect the hoses from the heat exchangers.

9. Disconnect the starter wires and push the engine wiring harness through the engine cover plate.

10. Disconnect the fuel supply line and plug it.

11. Remove the heater booster exhaust pipe.

12. Remove the rear axles and cover the ends to protect them from dirt.

13. Remove the selector cable by unscrewing the cable sleeve.

14. Remove the wire from the kickdown switch.

15. Remove the bolts from the rubber transmission mountings, taking careful note of the position, number, and thickness of the spacers that are present.

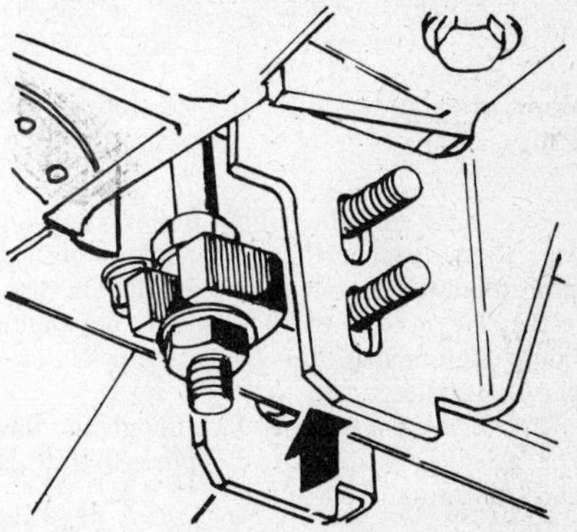

Engine carrier bolts positioned at the top of their elongated holes

CAUTION

These spacers must be reinstalled exactly as they were removed. Do not detach the transmission carrier from the body.

16. Support the engine and transmission assembly in such a way that it may be lowered and moved rearward at the same time.

17. Remove the engine carrier bolts and the engine and transmission assembly from the car.

18. Matchmark the flywheel and the torque converter and remove the three attaching bolts.

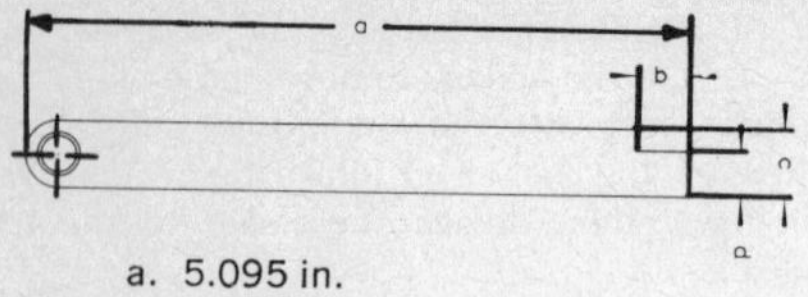

a. 5.095 in.
b. 0.472 in.
c. 0.590 in.
d. 0.393, 0.433, and 0.472 in.

Buffer alignment gauge

19. Remove the engine-to-transmission bolts and separate the engine and transmission.

CAUTION

Exercise care when separating the engine and transmission as the torque converter will easily slip off the input shaft if the transmission is tilted downward.

20. Installation is as follows. Install and tighten the engine-to-transmission bolts after aligning the match marks on the flywheel and converter.

21. Making sure the match marks are aligned, install the converter-to-flywheel bolts.

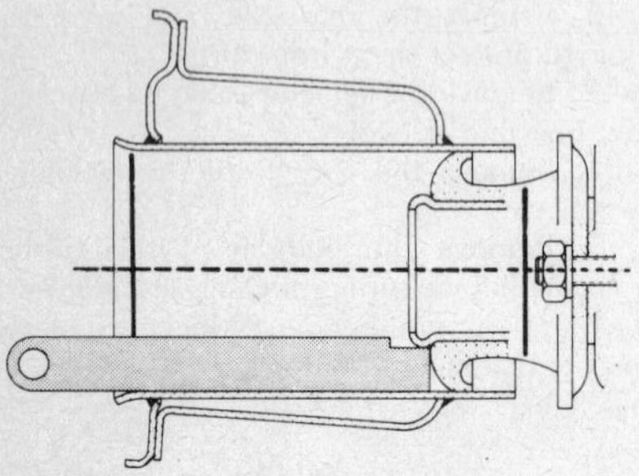

Measuring procedure for centering the buffer

22. Make sure the rubber buffer is in place and the two securing studs do not project more than 0.7 in. from the transmission case.

23. Tie a cord to the slot in the engine compartment seal. This will make positioning the seal easier.

24. Lift the assembly far enough to allow the accelerator cable to be pushed through the front engine cover.

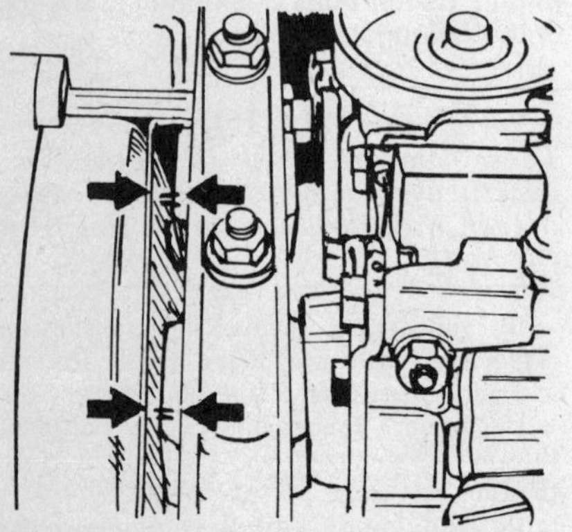

Checking the position of the engine carrier

25. Continue lifting the assembly into place. Slide the rubber buffer into the locating tube in the rear axle carrier.

26. Insert the engine carrier bolts and raise the engine until the bolts are at the top of their elongated slots. Tighten the bolts.

NOTE: A set of three gauges must be obtained to check the alignment of the rubber buffer in its locating tube. The dimensions are given in the illustration as is the measuring technique. The rubber buffer is centered horizontally where the 11 mm gauge can be inserted on both sides. The buffer is located vertically when the 10 mm gauge can be inserted on the bottom side and the 12 mm gauge can be inserted on the top side. See Steps 27 and 28 for adjustment procedure.

27. Install the rubber transmission mount bolts with spacers of the correct thickness. The purpose of the spacers is to center the rubber buffer vertically in its support tube. The buffer is not supposed to carry any weight; it absorbs torsional forces only.

28. To locate the buffer horizontally in its locating tube, the engine carrier must be vertical and parallel to the fan housing. It is adjusted by moving the engine carrier bolts in elongated slots. Further travel may be obtained by moving the brackets attached to the body. It may be necessary to adjust the two rear suspension wishbones with the center of the transmission after the rubber buffer is horizontally centered. Take the car to a dealer or alignment specialist to align the rear suspension.

29. Adjust the selector lever cable.

30. Connect the wire to the kickdown switch.

31. Install the rear axles. Make sure the lockwashers are placed with the convex side out.

32. Reconnect the fuel hoses and heat exchanger hoses. Install the pipe for the heater booster.

33. Lower the car and pull the engine compartment seal into place with the cord.

34. Reconnect the fuel injection and engine wiring. Push the starter wires through the engine cover plate and connect the wires to the starter.

35. Install the intake duct with the fan and hoses, also the cooling air intake.

PAN REMOVAL AND INSTALLATION

1. Some models have a drain plug in the pan. Remove the plug and drain the transmission. On models without the plug, loosen the pan bolts 2-3 turns and lower one corner of the pan to drain.

2. Remove the pan bolts and remove the pan from the transmission.

NOTE: It may be necessary to tap the pan with a rubber hammer to loosen it.

3. Use a new gasket and install the pan. Tighten the bolts loosely until the pan is properly in place, then tighten the bolts fully, moving in a diagonal pattern.

NOTE: Do not overtighten the bolts.

4. Refill the transmission with ATF.

5. At 5 minute intervals, retighten the pan bolts two or three times.

FILTER SERVICE

The Volkswagen automatic transmission has a filter screen secured by a screw to the bottom of the valve body. Remove the pan and remove the filter screen from the valve body.

CAUTION

Never use a cloth that will leave the slightest bit of lint in the transmission when cleaning transmission parts. The lint will expand when exposed to transmission fluid and clog the valve body and filter.

Clean the filter screen with compressed air.

FRONT (SECOND) BAND ADJUSTMENT

Tighten the front band adjusting screw to 7 ft/lbs. Then loosen the screw and tighten it to 3.5 ft/lbs. From this position, loosen the screw exactly 1¾ to 2 turns and tighten the locknut.

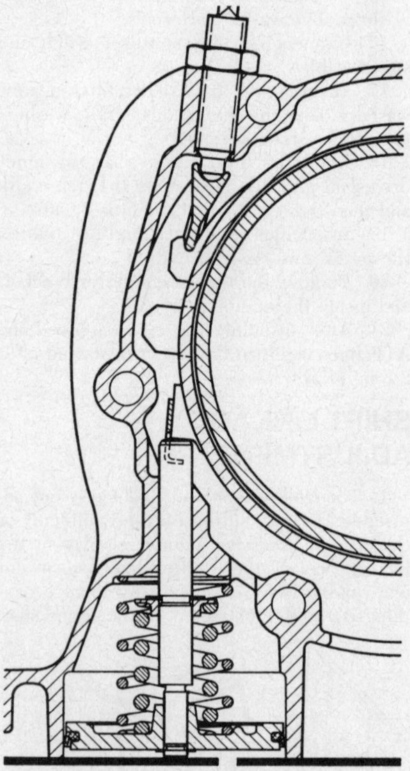

Front band assembly adjustment screw at top

REAR (FIRST) BAND ADJUSTMENT

Tighten the rear band adjusting screw to 7 ft/lbs. Then loosen the screw and retighten it to 3.5 ft/lbs. From this position, loosen the screw exactly 3¼ to 3½ turns and tighten the locknut.

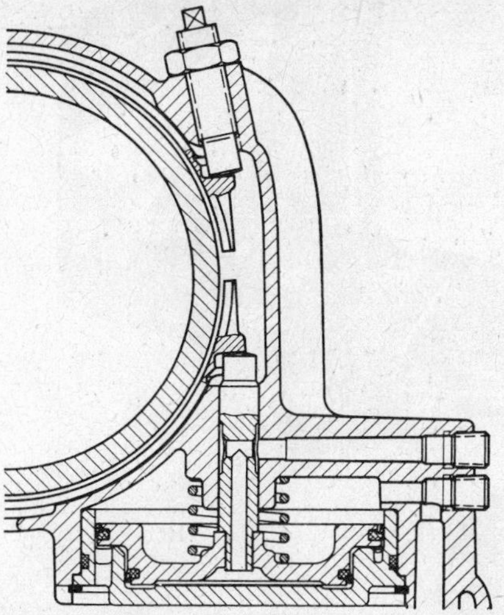

Rear band assembly adjustment screw at top

SHIFT LINKAGE ADJUSTMENT

Make sure the shifting cable is not kinked or bent and that the linkage and cable are properly lubricated.

1. Move the gear shift lever to the Park position.
2. Loosen the clamp which holds the front and rear halves of the shifting rod together. Loosen the clamping bolts on the transmission lever.
3. Press the lever on the transmission rearward as far as possible. Spring pressure will be felt. The manual valve must be on the stop in the valve body.
4. Holding the transmission lever against its stop, tighten the clamping bolt.
5. Holding the rear shifting rod half, push the front half forward to take up any clearance and tighten the clamp bolt.
6. Test the shift pattern.

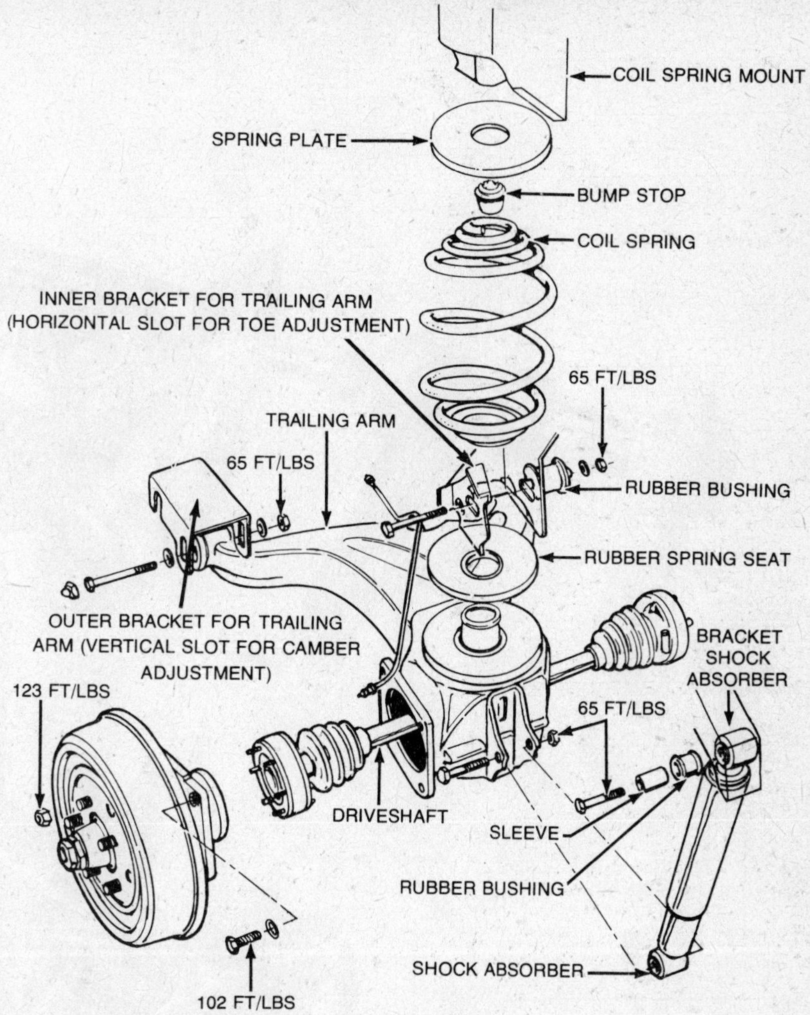

Exploded view of the Vanagon rear suspension

REAR SUSPENSION

Diagonal Arm Suspension—Types 1 and 2 (Except Vanagon)

DIAGONAL ARM REMOVAL AND INSTALLATION

1. Remove the wheel shaft nuts.

CAUTION

Do not raise the car to remove the nuts. They can be safely removed only if the weight on the car is on its wheels.

2. Disconnect the driveshaft of the side to be removed.
3. Remove the lower shock absorber mount. Raise the car and remove the wheel and tire.
4. Remove the brake drum, disconnect the brake lines and emergency brake cable, and remove the backing plate.
5. Matchmark the torsion bar plate and the diagonal arm with a cold chisel.
6. Remove the four bolts and nuts which secure the plate to the diagonal arm.
7. Remove the pivot bolts for the diagonal arm and remove the arm from the car.

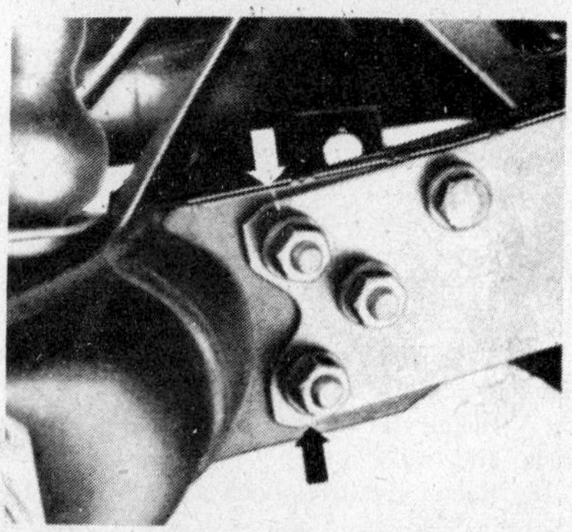

Matchmark the torsion bar and diagonal arm with a cold chisel

NOTE: Take careful note of the washers at the pivot bolts. These washers are used to determine alignment and they must be put back in the same place.

8. Remove the spring plate hub cover.
9. Using a steel bar, lift the spring plate off the lower suspension stop.
10. On Type 1, remove the five bolts at the front of the fender. On all others, remove the cover in the side of the fender.

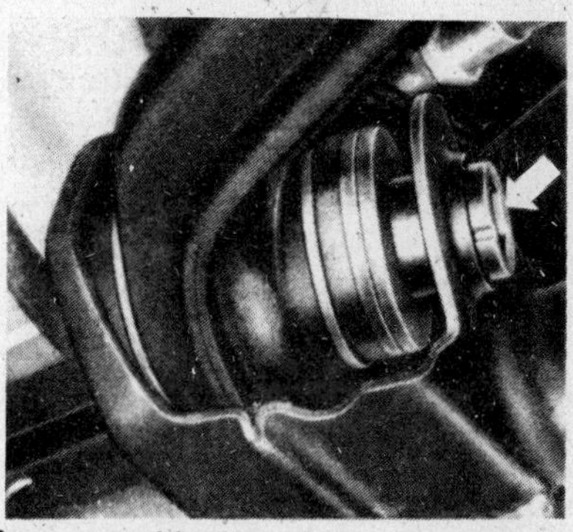

Proper positioning of the diagonal arm pivot bolt with both spacer washers on the outside

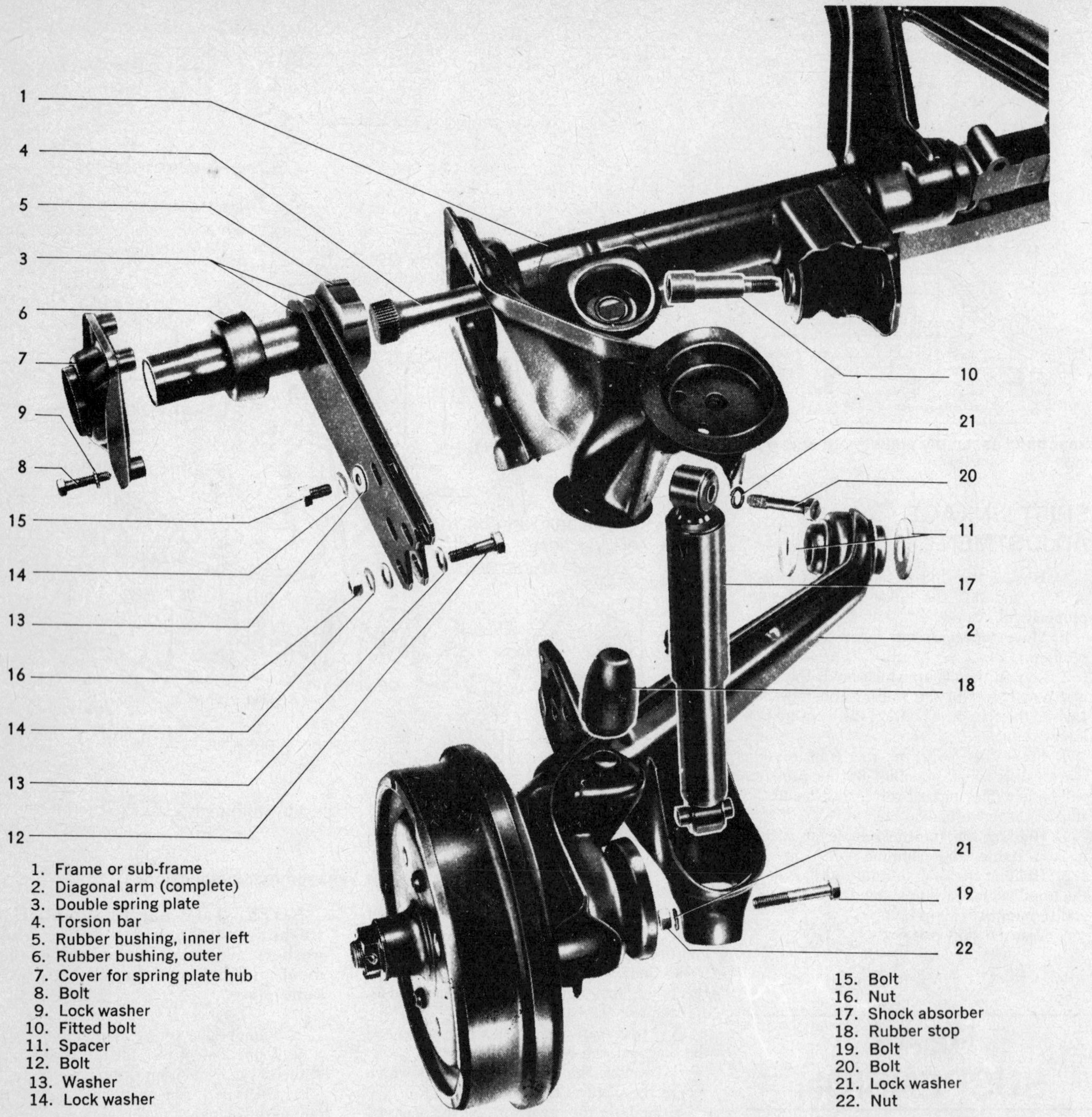

Diagonal arm rear suspension—Type 1 and 2 (except Vanagon)

11. Remove the spring plate and pull the torsion bar out of its housing.

NOTE: There are left and right torsion bars designated by an (L) or (R) on the end face. (Coat any rubber bushings with talcum powder upon installation. Do not use graphite, silicon, or grease.

12. To install, insert the torsion bar, outer bushing, and spring plate. The torsion bar is properly adjusted when the spring plate, with no load, is the specified number of degrees below a horizontal position.

13. Using two bolts, loosely secure the spring plate hub cover. Place a thick nut between the leaves of the spring plate.

14. Lift the spring plate up to the lower suspension stop and install the remaining bolts into the hub cover. Tighten the hub cover bolts.

15. Install the diagonal arm pivot bolt and washers and peen it with a chisel. There must always be at least one washer on the outside end of the bolt.

16. Align the chisel marks and attach the diagonal arm to the spring plate.

17. Install the backing plate, parking brake cable, and brake lines.

18. Reconnect the shock absorber. Install the brake drum and wheel shaft nuts.

19. Reconnect the drive shaft. Bleed the brakes.

20. Install the wheel and tire.

21. Check the suspension alignment.

Trailing Arm Suspension—Vanagon

TRAILING ARM REMOVAL AND INSTALLATION

1. Raise the rear of the car and support it with jack stands.

2. Remove the wheel and then disconnect the brake line from the wheel cylinder.

3. Unbolt the driveshaft at the transaxle side.

4. Unscrew the four wheel hub mounting bolts and remove it along with the driveshaft.

NOTE: Removal of the brake drum may provide better access to the wheel hub mounting bolts.

5. Place a floor jack under the trailing arm to hold its position and then remove the upper and lower shock absorber retaining bolts and remove the shock absorber.
6. Lower the trailing arm until you can remove the coil spring. Note the positioning of the upper spring plate and the lower spring seat.
7. Unscrew the two trailing arm mounting bolts and then remove the trailing arm.
8. Installation is in the reverse order of removal. When installing the coil spring, be sure that the contours for the end of the spring in the seat and the trailing arm are aligned. Also, turn the spring plate so that the end of the spring fits into the depression on the plate.
9. Adjust the camber and toe.

SHOCK ABSORBER REMOVAL AND INSTALLATION

Diagonal Arm Suspension

The shock absorber is secured at the top and bottom by a through bolt. Raise the car and remove the bolts. Remove the shock absorber from the car.

Trailing Arm Suspension

Procedures for removing the shock absorbers are detailed in the "Trailing Arm Removal and Installation" section.

COIL SPRING REMOVAL AND INSTALLATION—VANAGON ONLY

Procedures for removing the coil spring are detailed in the "Trailing Arm Removal and Installation" section.

REAR SUSPENSION ADJUSTMENTS

Type 1, Diagonal Arm Suspension

The only adjustment is the toe-in adjustment. The adjustment is performed by varying the number of washers at the diagonal arm pivot. There must always be one washer located on the outboard side of the pivot.

Type 2, Diagonal Arm Suspension

The transmission and engine assembly position in the vehicle is adjustable. It is necessary that the assembly be correctly centered before the suspension is aligned. It may be adjusted by moving the engine and transmission brackets in their elongated slots.

The distance between the diagonal arms may be adjusted by moving the washers at the A-arm pivots. The washers may be positioned only two ways. Either both washers on the outboard side of the pivot or a single washer on each side of the pivot. To adjust the distance, position the diagonal arms and move the washers in the same manner at both pivots.

The wheel track angle may be adjusted by moving the diagonal arm flange in the elongated slot in the spring plate.

The toe-in may be adjusted by positioning the washers and the diagonal arm pivot.

Type 2–Trailing Arm Suspension

On vehicles with the trailing arm suspension, it is possible to adjust the camber and the toe. To adjust the toe, loosen the INSIDE mounting bolt on the trailing arm and slide it forward or backward in the horizontal slot until the proper toe is achieved. To adjust the camber, loosen the OUTSIDE mounting bolt on the trailing arm and slide it up or down until the proper camber is achieved. Being careful not to move the bolts, tighten them both to 65 ft/lbs after adjustment.

FRONT SUSPENSION

Torsion Bar Suspension–Types 1 and 2 (Except Super Beetle and Beetle Convertible)

TORSION BAR REMOVAL AND INSTALLATION

1. Jack up the car and remove both wheels and brake drums.
2. Remove the ball joint nuts and remove the left and right steering knuckles. A forked ball joint removing tool is available at an auto parts store.

CAUTION

Never strike the ball joint stud.

3. Remove those arms attached to the torsion bars on one side only. To remove the arms, loosen and remove the arm setscrew and pull the arm off the end of the torsion bar.
4. Loosen and remove the setscrew which secures the torsion bar to the torsion bar housing.
5. Pull the torsion bar out of its housing.
6. To install, carefully note the number of leaves and the position of the countersink marks for the torsion bar and the torsion arm.
7. Align the countersink mark in the center of the bar with the hole for the setscrew and insert the torsion bar into its housing. Install the torsion arm.
8. Reverse Steps 1-3 to complete.

TORSION ARM REMOVAL AND INSTALLATION

1. Jack up the car and remove the wheel and tire.

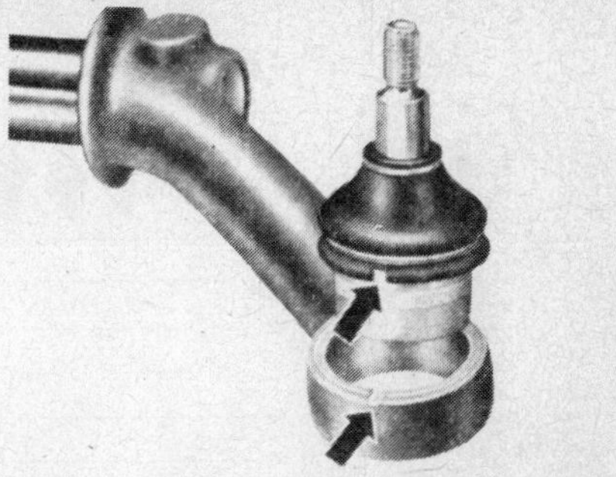

Align the square notch in the ball joint with the notch in the torsion bar upon installation

A notched ball joint on a car with a torsion bar suspension indicates that it is oversized

2. Remove the brake drum and the steering knuckle.
3. If the lower torsion arm is being removed, disconnect the stabilizer bar. To remove the stabilizer bar clamp, tap the wedge shaped keeper toward the outside of the car or in the direction the narrow end of the keeper is pointing.
4. On Type 1 and 2, back off on the setscrew locknut and remove the setscrew.
5. Slide the torsion arm off the end of the torsion bar.
6. Reverse the above steps to install. Check the camber and toe-in settings.

Strut Suspension—Type 1 Super Beetle, Beetle Convertible

SUSPENSION STRUT REMOVAL AND INSTALLATION

1. Jack up the car and remove the wheel and tire.
2. If the left strut is to be removed, remove the speedometer cable from the steering knuckle.
3. Disconnect the brake line from the bracket on the strut.
4. At the base of the strut, bend down the locking tabs for the three bolts and remove the bolts.
5. Push down on the steering knuckle and pull the strut out of the knuckle.
6. Remove the three nuts which secure the

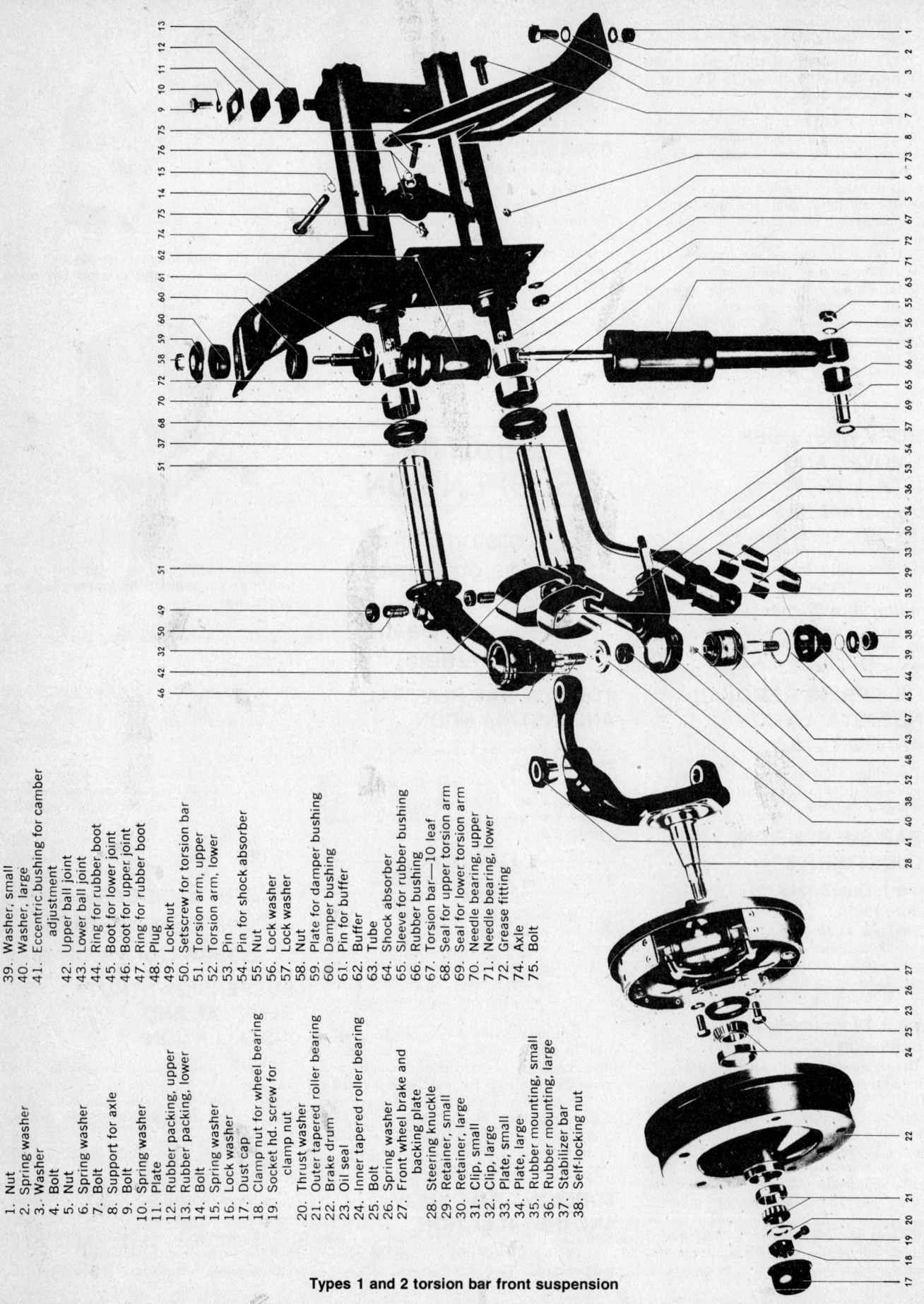

1. Nut
2. Spring washer
3. Washer
4. Bolt
5. Nut
6. Spring washer
7. Bolt
8. Support for axle
9. Bolt
10. Spring washer
11. Plate
12. Rubber packing, upper
13. Rubber packing, lower
14. Bolt
15. Spring washer
16. Lock washer
17. Dust cap
18. Clamp nut for wheel bearing
19. Socket hd. screw for clamp nut
20. Thrust washer
21. Outer tapered roller bearing
22. Brake drum
23. Oil seal
24. Inner tapered roller bearing
25. Bolt
26. Spring washer
27. Front wheel brake and backing plate
28. Steering knuckle
29. Retainer, small
30. Retainer, large
31. Clip, small
32. Clip, large
33. Plate, small
34. Plate, large
35. Rubber mounting, small
36. Rubber mounting, large
37. Stabilizer bar
38. Self-locking nut
39. Washer, small
40. Washer, large
41. Eccentric bushing for camber adjustment
42. Upper ball joint
43. Lower ball joint
44. Ring for rubber boot
45. Boot for lower joint
46. Boot for upper joint
47. Ring for rubber boot
48. Plug
49. Locknut
50. Setscrew for torsion bar
51. Torsion arm, upper
52. Torsion arm, lower
53. Pin
54. Pin for shock absorber
55. Nut
56. Lock washer
57. Lock washer
58. Nut
59. Plate for damper bushing
60. Damper bushing
61. Pin for buffer
62. Buffer
63. Tube
64. Shock absorber
65. Sleeve for rubber bushing
66. Rubber bushing
67. Torsion bar—10 leaf
68. Seal for upper torsion arm
69. Seal for lower torsion arm
70. Needle bearing, upper
71. Needle bearing, lower
72. Grease fitting
74. Axle
75. Bolt

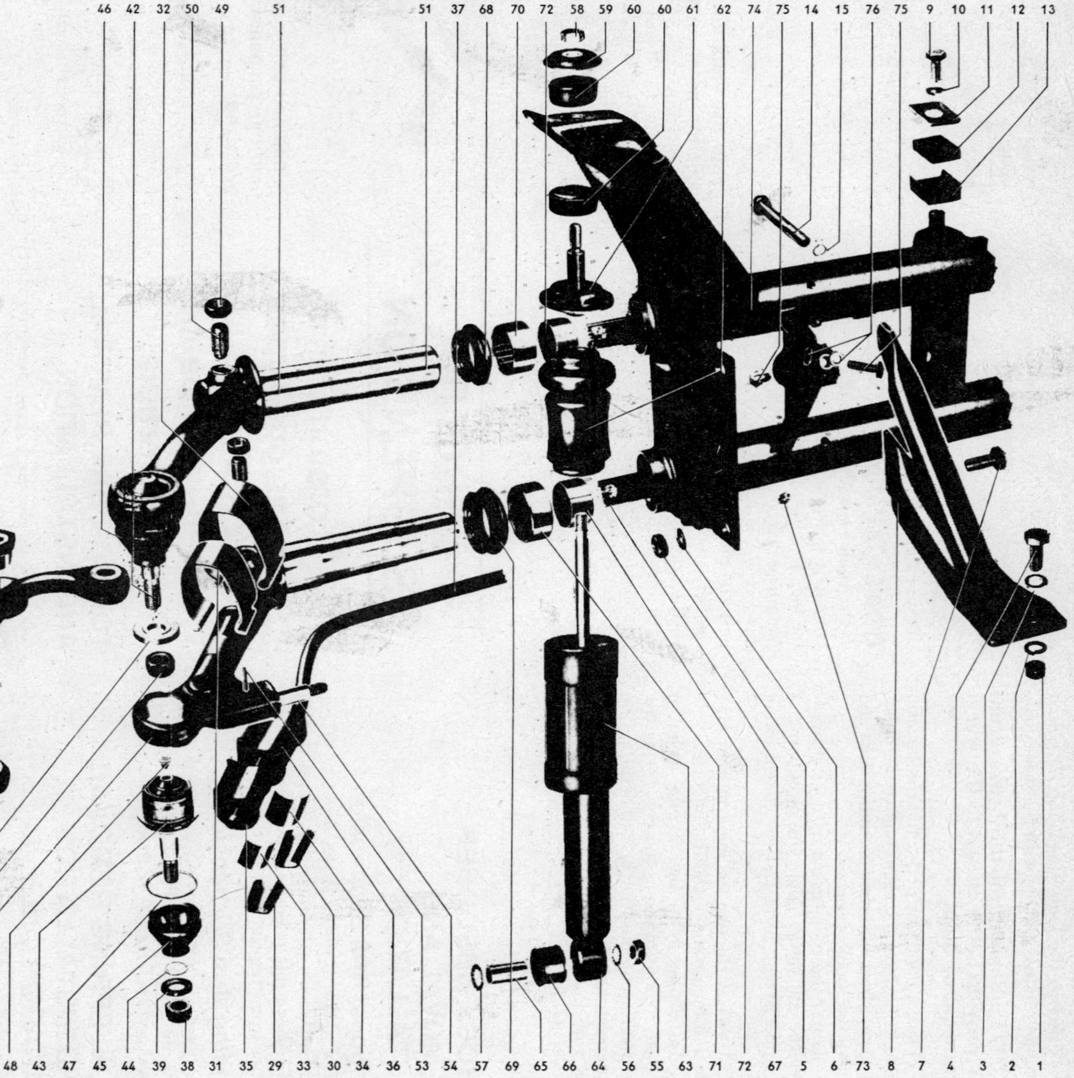
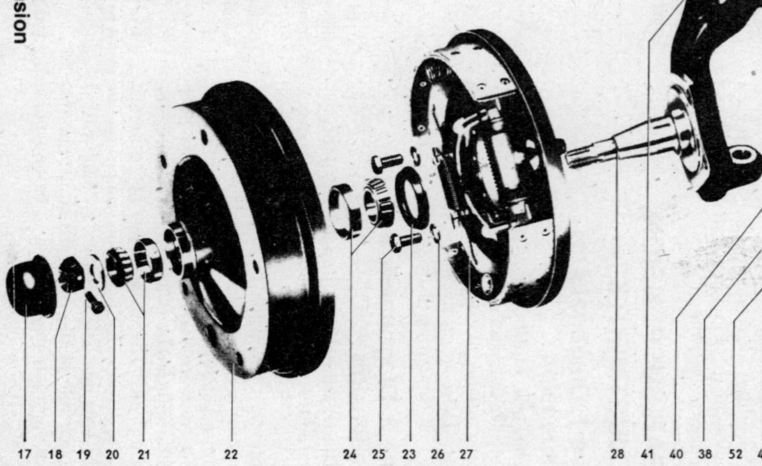

Types 1 and 2 torsion bar front suspension

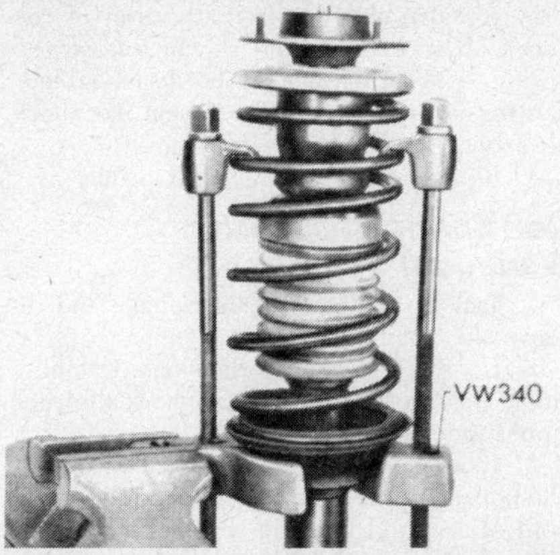

Using a spring compressor to remove the coil spring

top of the strut to the body. Before removing the last nut, support the strut so that it does not fall out of the car.

7. Reverse the above steps to install the strut. Always use new nuts and locking tabs during installation.

TRACK CONTROL ARM REMOVAL AND INSTALLATION

1. Remove the ball joint stud nut and remove the stud from the control arm.
2. Disconnect the stabilizer bar from the control arm.
3. Remove the nut and eccentric bolt at the frame. This is the pivot bolt for the control arm and is used to adjust camber.
4. Pull the arm downward and remove it from the vehicle.
5. Reverse the above steps to install. Make sure the groove in the stabilizer bar bushing is horizontal.
6. Realign the front end.

Coil Spring Suspension–Vanagon

The front suspension consists of upper and lower control arms, a separate upper coil spring/shock absorber mount, steering knuckle and attaching ball joints and a strut arm mounted on the lower control arm for stability.

UPPER CONTROL ARM REMOVAL AND INSTALLATION

1. Jack up the vehicle and remove the front wheel.

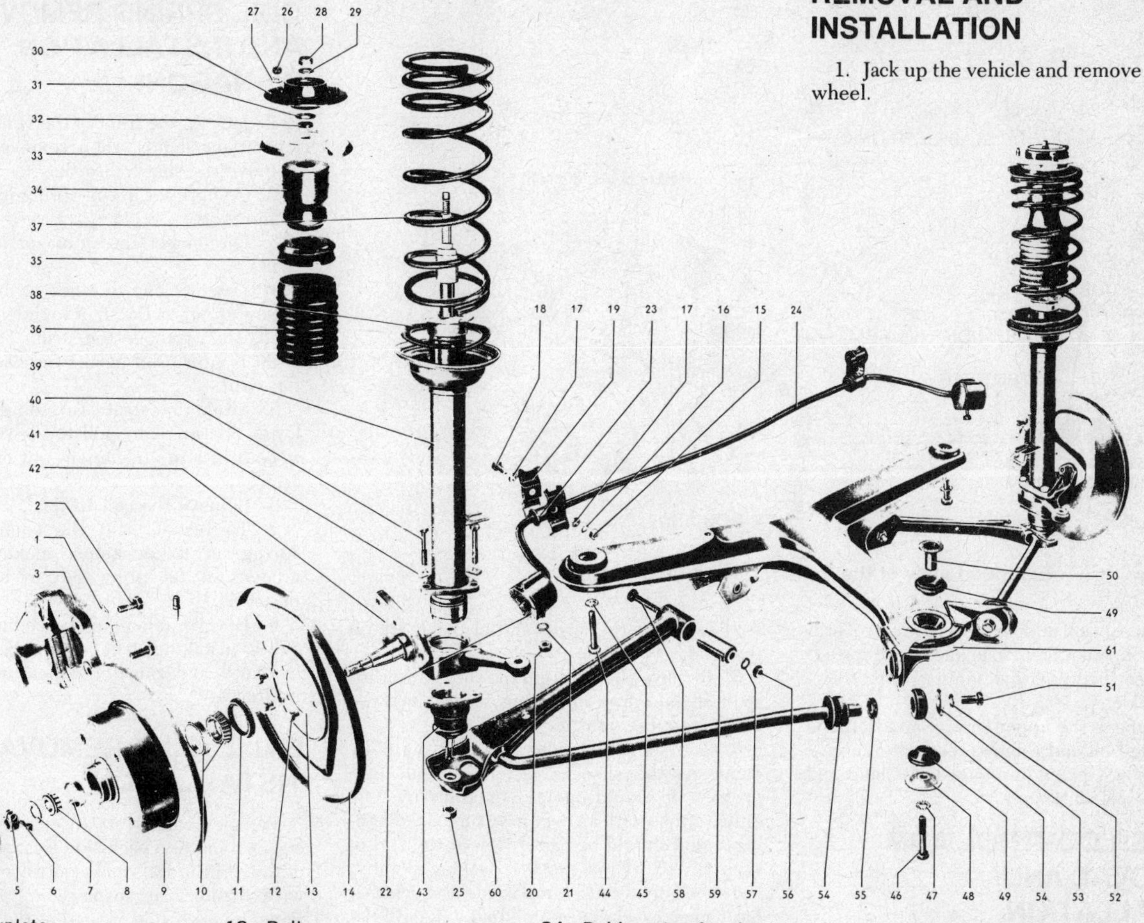

1. Lockplate
2. Bolt
3. Caliper
4. Hub cap
5. Wheel bearing locknut
6. Allen screw for locknut
7. Thrust washer
8. Outer taper roller bearing
9. Brake disc
10. Inner taper roller bearing
11. Oil seal
12. Bolt
13. Spring washer
14. Splash shield for disc
15. Nut
16. Spring washer
17. Washer
18. Bolt
19. Clamp for stabilizer bar
20. Nut
21. Spring washer
22. Stabilizer mounting for control arm
23. Rubber bushing for clamp
24. Stabilizer bar
25. Self-locking nut
26. Self-locking nut
27. Washer
28. Self-locking nut
29. Washer, small
30. Suspension strut bearing
31. Sealing plate
32. Spacer ring
33. Spring plate
34. Rubber stop for shock absorber
35. Retaining ring for protective tube
36. Protective tube for shock absorber
37. Coil spring
38. Damping ring, coil spring
39. Shock absorber
40. Bolt
41. Lock washer
42. Steering knuckle
43. Ball joint
44. Bolt
45. Lock washer
46. Bolt
47. Lock washer
48. Seat for damping ring
49. Damping ring for front axle carrier
50. Spacer sleeve
51. Bolt
52. Spring washer
53. Plate for damping ring
54. Damping ring for radius rod
55. Locating ring for radius rod
56. Nut
57. Spring washer
58. Bolt
59. Bushing for track control arm
60. Track control arm
61. Front axle carrier

Strut type front suspension—Type 1 Super Beetle and Beetle Convertible

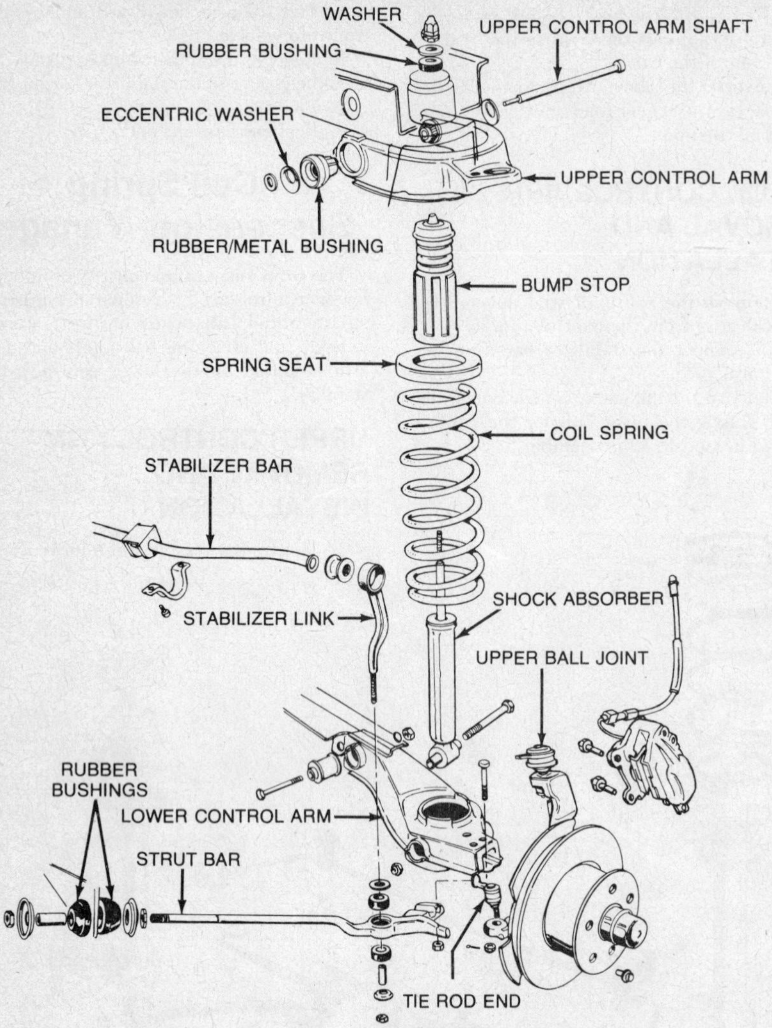

Exploded view of the Vanagon front suspension

2. Place a jack under the lower control arm and raise to put a slight load on the coil spring.
3. Free the upper ball jont from the steering knuckle.
4. Remove the upper control arm to frame mounting bolt and remove the control arm.
5. Reverse procedure to install. Check and adjust wheel alignment.

LOWER CONTROL ARM REMOVAL AND INSTALLATION

1. Jack up the vehicle and remove the wheel.
2. Remove the coil spring.
3. Remove the lower control arm to frame mounting bolt and remove the control arm.
4. Reverse procedure to install.

SHOCK ABSORBER REMOVAL AND INSTALLATION

Torsion Bar Suspension (Types 1 and 2)

1. Remove the wheel and tire.
2. Remove the nut from the torsion arm stud and slide the lower end of the shock off the stud.
3. Remove the nut from the shock absorber shaft at the upper mounting and remove the shock from the vehicle.
4. The shock is tested by operating it by hand. As the shock is extended and compressed, it should operate smoothly over its entire stroke with an even pressure. Its damping action should be clearly felt at the end of each stroke. If the shock is leaking slightly, the shock need not be replaced. A shock that has had an excessive loss of fluid will have flat spots in the stroke as the shock is compressed and extended. That is, the pressure will feel as through it has been suddenly released for a short distance during the stroke.
5. Installation is the reverse of Steps 1-3.

Strut Suspension (Super Beetle)

In this type suspension system, the shock absorber is actually the supporting vertical member.

1. Remove the strut.
2. It is necessary to disassemble the strut to replace the shock absorber. To remove the spring, it must be compressed. The proper type compressor is available at an auto parts store.
3. Remove the nut from the end of the shock absorber shaft and slowly release the spring. The strut can now be disassembled. Testing is the same as the torsion bar shock absorber.
4. Reverse the above steps to install.

Coil Spring Suspension (Vanagon)

1. Jack up the front of the vehicle and remove the front wheel.
2. Loosen and remove the single retaining nut at the top of the coil spring/shock absorber upper mount.
3. Remove the through bolt which retains the bottom of the shock absorber to the lower control arm and pull the shock absorber out through the bottom of the lower control arm.
4. Reverse the procedure to install.

COIL SPRING REMOVAL AND INSTALLATION (VANAGON)

1. Jack up the front of the vehicle and support it on stands, then remove the wheel. Remove the shock absorber.
2. Compress the coil spring using a spring compressor.
3. Disconnect the stabilizer bar from the strut.
4. Measure the distance from the end of the outer nut on the strut to the tip of the strut itself, then remove the strut. This measurement is later used during installation to align the strut.
5. After the strut is removed from the lower control arm, pull the lower ball joint-to-control arm attachment out of the control arm.
6. Remove the coil spring.
7. To install, seat the compressed coil spring on its cushions, making sure the grooves for the spring ends are in the correct positions.
8. Reverse remaining procedures to install. When installing strut, adjust the outside nut so that it conforms to the measurement made in Step 4.

BALL JOINT REMOVAL AND INSTALLATION

Vehicles with strut suspension have only one ball joint on each side located at the base of the strut in the track control arm. Vehicles with torsion bar suspension have two ball joints on each side located at the end of each torsion arm.

Vehicles with coil spring suspension have two ball joints on each side located at the ends of the upper and lower control arms.

Torsion Bar Suspension

1. Jack up the car and remove the wheel and tire.
2. Remove the brake drum and disconnect the brake line from the backing plate.
3. Remove the nut from each ball joint stud and remove the ball joint stud from the steering knuckle. Remove the steering knuckle from the car. A ball joint removal tool is available at an auto parts store. Do not strike the ball joint stud.

4. Remove the torsion arm from the torsion bar.

5. Remove the ball joint from the torsion arm by pressing it out.

6. Press a new ball joint in, making sure that the square notch in the joint is in line with the notch in the torsion arm eye.

NOTE: Ball joints are supplied in different sizes designated by V-notches in the ring around the side of the joint. When replacing a ball joint, make sure that the new part has the same number of V-notches. If it has no notches, the replacement joint should have no notches.

7. Reverse Steps 1-4 to complete the installation.

Strut Suspension

1. Jack up the car and remove the wheel and tire.

2. Remove the nut from the ball joint stud and remove the stud from the track control arm.

3. Bend back the locking tab and remove the three ball joint securing screws.

4. Pull the track control arm downward and remove the ball joint from the strut.

5. Reverse the above steps to install.

Coil Spring Suspension

UPPER BALL JOINT

1. Raise the vehicle and support it on jack stands, then remove the wheel.

2. Place a jack under the lower control arm as close to the steering knuckle as possible and jack up just enough to put a slight load on the coil spring.

3. Loosen the steering knuckle-to-ball joint nut but do not remove completely.

4. Free the ball joint from the steering knuckle using a ball joint removal tool. Then remove the nut.

5. Remove the two upper ball joint to upper control arm bolts and remove the ball joint.

6. Reverse procedure to install. Check wheel alignment.

LOWER BALL JOINT

1. Jack up the front of the vehicle and support it on stands, then remove the wheel.

2. Place a jack under the lower control arm as close to steering knuckle as possible and put a slight load on the coil spring by jacking up the jack.

3. Disconnect the brake caliper hose from the caliper, and remove the brake caliper and rotor if they are in the way.

4. Loosen the upper ball joint to steering knuckle to ball joint nut, but do not remove it. Free the upper ball joint from the steering knuckle and remove the nut.

5. Remove the lower ball joint to lower control arm nut and free the ball joint from the control arm using a ball joint removal tool. Remove the steering knuckle.

6. Press the ball joint off the steering knuckle.

7. Press a new ball joint in place on knuckle, observing any alignment marks on the ball joint and the knuckle.

8. Reverse the procedure to install. Bleed the brakes.

BALL JOINT INSPECTION

Torsion Bar Suspension

1. A quick initial inspection can be made with the vehicle on the ground.

2. Grasp the top of the tire and vigorously pull the top of the tire in and out. Test both sides in this manner.

3. If the ball joints are excessively worn, there will be an audible tap as the ball moves around in its socket. Excess play can sometimes be felt through the tire.

4. A more rigorous test may be performed by jacking the car under the lower torsion arm and inserting a lever under the tire.

5. Lift up gently on the lever so as to pry the tire upward.

6. If the ball joints are worn, the tire will move upward ⅛-¼ in. or more.

7. If the tire displays excessive movement, have an assistant inspect each joint, as the tire is pried upward, to determine which ball joint is defective.

Strut Suspension

1. Raise the car and support it under the frame. The wheel must be clear of the ground.

2. With a lever, apply upward pressure to the track control arm.

3. Apply the pressure gently and slowly; it is important that only enough pressure be exerted to check the play in the ball joint and not compress the suspension.

4. Using a vernier caliper, measure the distance between the control arm and the lower edge of the ball joint flange. Record the reading.

5. Release the pressure on the track control arm and again measure the distance between the control arm and the lower edge of the ball joint flange.

6. Record the reading.

7. Subtract the higher reading from the lower reading. If the difference is more than 0.10 in., the ball joint should be replaced.

NOTE: Remember that even in a new joint there will be measurable play because the ball in the ball joint is spring loaded.

FRONT END ALIGNMENT

Caster Adjustment

Caster is the forward or backward tilt of the spindle. Forward tilt is negative caster and backward tilt is positive caster. Caster is not adjustable on either the torsion bar or the strut suspensions.

Caster on the coil spring suspension is adjusted by moving the strut bar. Loosen the locknut and then turn the adjusting nut clockwise to increase the caster and counterclockwise to decrease the caster.

Camber Adjustment

Camber is the tilt of the top of the wheel, inward or outward, from true vertical. Outward tilt is positive, inward tilt is negative.

TORSION BAR SUSPENSION

The upper ball joint on each side is mounted in an eccentric bushing. The bushing has a hex head and it may be rotated in either direction using a wrench.

STRUT SUSPENSION

The track control arm pivots on an eccentric bolt. Camber is adjusted by loosening the nut and rotating the bolt.

COIL SPRING SUSPENSION

The upper control arm pivots on an eccentric bolt. To adjust the camber, loosen the retaining nut and rotate the bolt.

TOE-IN ADJUSTMENT

Toe-in is the adjustment made to make the front wheels point slightly into the front. Toe-in is adjusted on all types of front suspensions by adjusting the length of the tie rod sleeves.

STEERING

Steering Wheel

REMOVAL AND INSTALLATION

1. Disconnect the negative battery cable.

2. Remove the center emblem. This emblem will gently pry off the wheel, or is attached by screws from the back of the steering wheel.

3. Remove the nut from the steering shaft. This is a right-hand thread.

NOTE: Mark the steering shaft and steering wheel so that the wheel may be installed in the same position on the shaft.

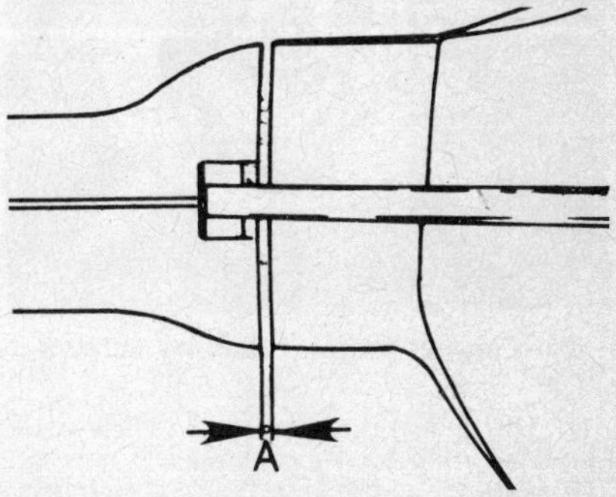

Correct gap (a) between the steering wheel and column

4. Using a steering wheel puller, remove the wheel from the splined steering shaft. Do not strike the end of the steering shaft.

5. Reverse the above steps to install. Make sure to align the matchmarks made on the steering wheel and steering shaft. The gap between the turn signal switch housing and the back of the wheel is 0.08-0.12 in. (0.08-0.159 for Vanagon).

Turn Signal Switch

REMOVAL AND INSTALLATION

1. Disconnect the negative battery cable.

2. Remove the steering wheel.

3. Remove the four turn signal switch securing screws.

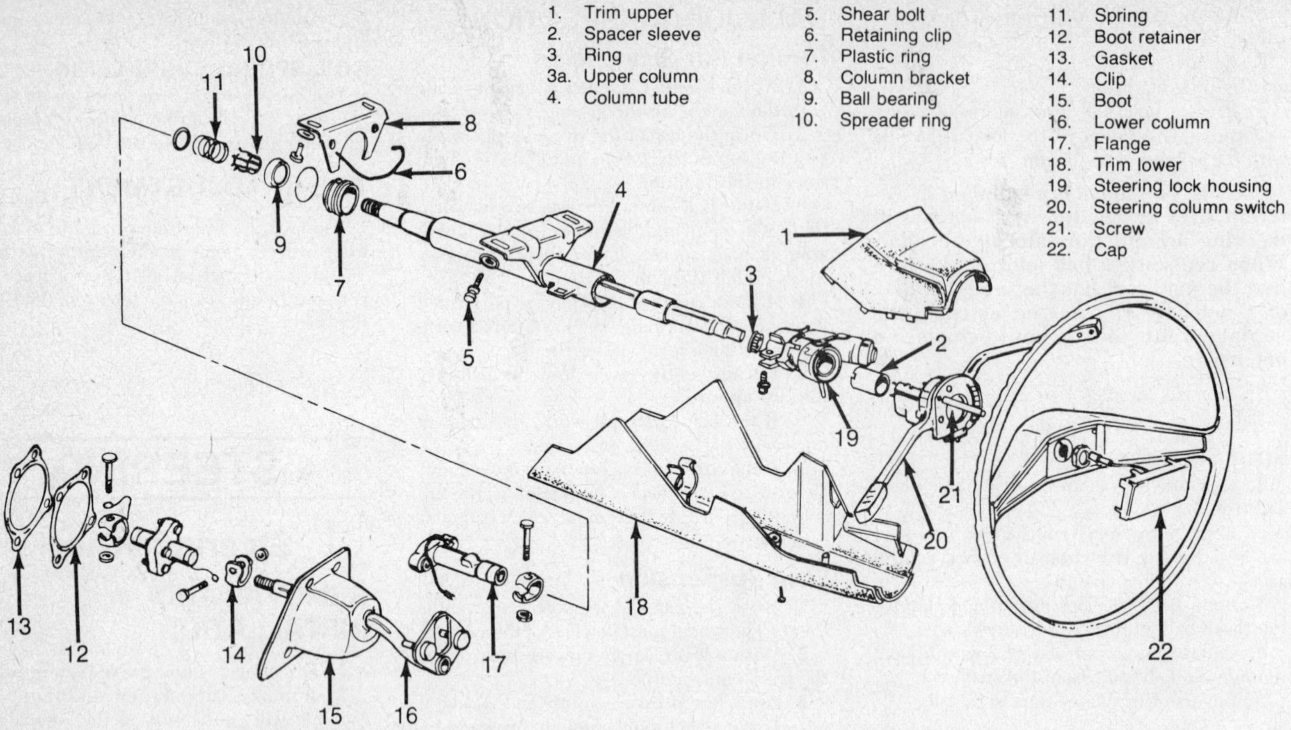

Exploded view of the Vanagon steering column assembly

Turn signal switch retaining screws

4. Disconnect the turn signal switch wiring plug under the steering column.
5. Pull the switch and wiring guide rail up and out of the steering column.
6. Reverse the above steps to install. Make sure the spacers located behind the switch, if installed originally, are in position. The distance between the steering wheel and the steering column housing is 0.08-0.12 in. (0.08-0.159 for Vanagon). Install the switch with the lever on the central position.

Ignition Switch

REMOVAL AND INSTALLATION

Type 1 and 2 (Except Vanagon)

Disconnect the steering column wiring at the block located behind the instrument panel and pull the column wiring harness into the passenger compartment.

1. Remove the steering wheel.
2. Remove the circlip on the steering shaft.
3. Insert the key and turn the switch to the ON position.
4. Remove the three securing screws and slide the switch assembly from the steering column tube.
5. After removing the wiring retainer, press the ignition switch wiring block upward and out of the housing and disconnect the wiring.
6. Remove the lock cylinder and the steering lock mechanism.
7. Remove the ignition switch screw and pull the ignition switch rearward.
8. Reverse the above steps to install.

When reinstalling the turn signal switch, make sure the lever is in the center position.

Vanagon

1. Disconnect the negative battery terminal.
2. Remove the steering wheel.
3. Loosen the mounting screws and then remove the upper and lower steering column trim.
4. Unscrew the four retaining bolts and then pull off the steering column switch.
5. Loosen the steering lock housing clamp bolt and pull the assembly up and out slightly.
6. Disconnect the wiring and remove the steering lock housing.
7. Unscrew the ignition switch screw and pull out the switch.
8. Installation is in the reverse order of removal.

Ignition Lock Cylinder

REMOVAL AND INSTALLATION

1. Remove the ignition switch.
2. With the key in the cylinder and turned to the ON position, pull the lock cylinder out far enough so the securing pin can be depressed through a hole in the side of the lock cylinder housing.
3. As the pin is depressed, pull the lock cylinder out of its housing.
4. To install the lock cylinder, gently push the cylinder into its housing. Make sure the pin engages correctly and that the retainer fits easily in place. Do not force any parts together; when they are correctly aligned, they will fit easily together.

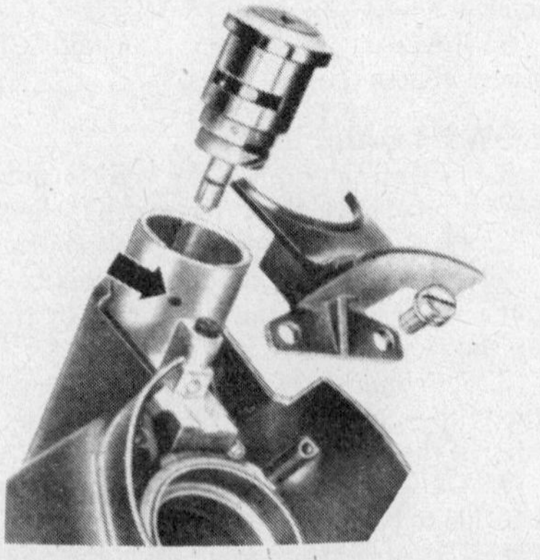

Access hole for depressing lock cylinder retaining pin

Steering Linkage

REMOVAL AND INSTALLATION

1. All tie-ends are secured by a nut which holds the tapered tie rod end stud into a matching tapered hole. There are several

ways to remove the tapered stud from its hole after the nut has been removed.

2. First, there are several types of removal tools available from auto parts stores. These tools include directions for their use. One of the most commonly available tool is the fork shaped tool which is a wedge that is forced under the tie rod end. This tool should be used with caution because instead of removing the tie rod end from its hole it may pull the ball out of its socket, ruining the tie rod end.

3. It is also possible to remove the tie rod end by holding a heavy hammer on one side of the tapered hole and striking the opposite side of the hole sharply with another hammer. The stud will pop out of its hole, usually.

CAUTION

Never strike the end of the tie rod end stud. It is impossible to remove the tie rod end in this manner.

4. Once the tie rod end stud has been removed, turn the tie rod end out of the adjusting sleeve.

5. On the pieces of the steering linkage that are not used to adjust the toe-in, the tie rod end is welded in place and it will be necessary to replace the whole assembly.

6. When reassembling the steering linkage, never put lubricant in the tapered hole.

MANUAL STEERING GEAR ADJUSTMENT

There are two types of steering gear boxes. The first type is the roller type, identified by the square housing cover secured by four screws, one at each corner. The second type is the rack and pinion type used on 1975 Super Beetles, Beelte Convertibles and the Vanagon.

Worm and Roller Type–Type 1 and 2

Disconnect the steering linkage from the pitman arm and make sure the gearbox mounting bolts are tight. Have an assistant rotate the steering wheel so that the pitman arm move alternately 10° to the left and then 10° to the right of the straight ahead position. Turn the adjusting screw in until no further play can be felt while moving the pitman arm. Tighten the adjusting screw locknut and recheck the adjustment.

Rack and Pinion Type–1975 Type 1 Super Beetle and Convertible

The steering gear requires adjustment if it begins to rattle noticeably. First, remove the access cover in the spare tire well. Then, with the car standing on all four wheels, turn the adjusting screw in by hand until it contacts the thrust washer. While holding the screw in this position, tighten the locknut.

The adjustment is correct when there is no binding and the steering self-centers properly.

Rack and Pinion Type–Vanagon

The steering gear on the Vanagon is not adjustable. If problems develop, the gear must be replaced.

BRAKES

Brake Adjustment

Disc brakes are self adjusting and cannot be adjusted by hand. As the pads wear, they will automatically compensate for the wear by moving closer to the disc, maintaining the proper operating clearance.

Drum brakes, however, must be manually adjusted to take up excess clearance as the shoes wear.

1. To adjust drum brakes, both front and rear, it is necessary to jack up the car and support it on a jack stand. The wheel must spin freely.

2. On the backing plate there are four inspection holes with a rubber plug in each hole. Two of the holes are for checking the thickness of the brake lining and the other two are used for adjustment.

NOTE: There is an adjustment for each brake shoe. That means that on each wheel it is necessary to make two adjustments, one for each shoe on that wheel.

3. Remove the adjustment hole plugs and, using a screwdriver or brake adjusting tool, insert the tool into the hole.

4. Turn the star wheel until a slight drag is noticed as the wheel is rotated by hand.

5. Back off on the star wheel 3-4 notches so that the wheel turns freely.

6. Perform the same adjustment on the other shoe.

NOTE: One of the star wheels in each wheel has left-hand threads and the other star wheel has right-hand threads.

7. Repeat the above procedure on each wheel with drum brakes.

Adjusting drum brakes through the access hole in the backing plate; rear brakes shown

Master Cylinder

NOTE: The master cylinder fluid reservoirs on Volkswagens are found in a number of different places. The reservoirs on all Type 1 models can be found in the front luggage compartment. On 1975 and later Type 2 models (except the Vanagon), the reservoir is located underneath the driver's seat, while on the Vanagon, it is underneath the raised portion of the instrument panel.

With the exception of the Vanagon, all Type 2 models, in addition to the refill reservoir mentioned above, also have a twin-chamber reservoir attached directly to the master cylinder.

REMOVAL AND INSTALLATION

Type 1 and 2 (except Vanagon)

1. Drain the brake fluid from the master cylinder reservoir.

CAUTION

Do not get any brake fluid on the paint, as it will dissolve the paint.

2. Pull the plastic elbows out of the rubber sealing rings on the top of the master cylinder.

3. Remove the two bolts which secure the master cylinder to the frame and remove the cylinder. Note the spacers on the Type 1 between the frame and the master cylinder.

4. To install, bolt the master cylinder to the frame. Do not forget the spacers on the Type 1.

5. Lubricate the elbows with brake fluid and insert them into the rubber seals.

6. If necessary, adjust the brake pedal free travel. On Type 1, adjust the length of the master cylinder pushrod so that there is 5-7 mm of brake pedal free-play before the pushrod contacts the master cylinder piston. On Type 2, the free-play is properly adjusted when the length of the pushrod, measured between the ball end and the center of the clevis pin hole, is 4.17 in.

7. Refill the master cylinder reservoir and bleed the brakes.

Vanagon

1. Grasp the two recesses provided on the back of the instrument cluster frame and pull it forward.

2. Tag and disconnect any wiring leading to the back of the instrument cluster and then remove it.

3. Drain the brake fluid from the reservoir.

4. Pull the reservoir out of the master cylinder.

5. Disconnect and plug the brake fluid lines leading from the master cylinder.

6. Unscrew the two mounting bolts and remove the master cylinder.

7. Installation is in the reverse order of removal.

8. Refill the master cylinder reservoir and bleed the brakes.

MASTER CYLINDER OVERHAUL

1. Remove the master cylinder from the car.

2. Remove the rubber sealing boot.

3. Remove the stop screw and sealing ring on the top of the unit.

4. Insert a screwdriver in the master cylinder piston, exert inward pressure, and re-

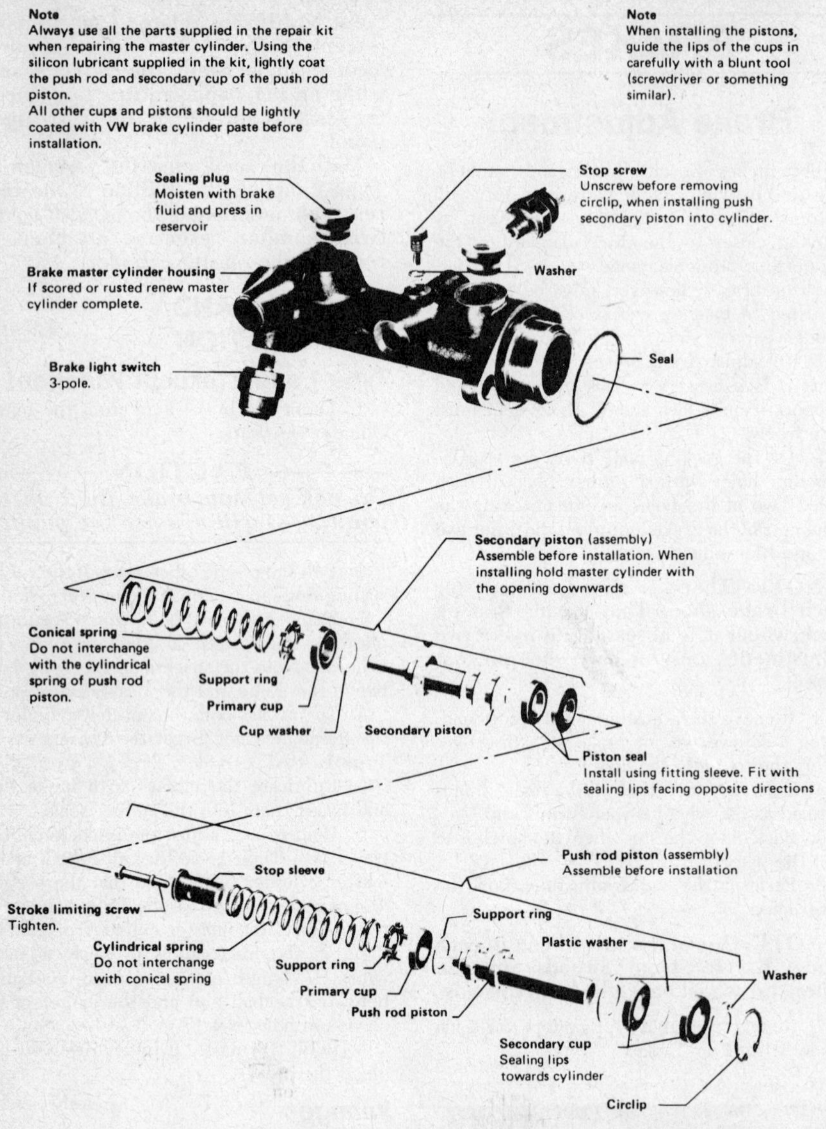
Note
Always use all the parts supplied in the repair kit when repairing the master cylinder. Using the silicon lubricant supplied in the kit, lightly coat the push rod and secondary cup of the push rod piston.
All other cups and pistons should be lightly coated with VW brake cylinder paste before installation.
Note
When installing the pistons, guide the lips of the cups in carefully with a blunt tool (screwdriver or something similar).
Sealing plug
Moisten with brake fluid and press in reservoir
Stop screw
Unscrew before removing circlip, when installing push secondary piston into cylinder.
Washer
Brake master cylinder housing
If scored or rusted renew master cylinder complete.
Brake light switch
3-pole.
Seal
Secondary piston (assembly)
Assemble before installation. When installing hold master cylinder with the opening downwards
Conical spring
Do not interchange with the cylindrical spring of push rod piston.
Support ring
Primary cup
Cup washer
Secondary piston
Piston seal
Install using fitting sleeve. Fit with sealing lips facing opposite directions
Stop sleeve
Push rod piston (assembly)
Assemble before installation
Stroke limiting screw
Tighten.
Cylindrical spring
Do not interchange with conical spring
Support ring
Primary cup
Push rod piston
Support ring
Plastic washer
Washer
Secondary cup
Sealing lips towards cylinder
Circlip

Type 2 master cylinder

move the snap-ring from its groove in the end of the unit. The internal parts are spring loaded and must be kept from flying out when the snap-ring is removed.

5. Carefully remove the internal parts of the unit and make note of their order and the orientation of the internal parts. If parts remain in the cylinder bore, they must be removed with a wire hook or very gentle application of low pressure air to the stop screw hole. Cover the end of the cylinder bore with a rag and stand away from the open end of the bore when using compressed air.

6. Use alcohol or brake fluid to clean the master cylinder and its parts.

7. It may be necessary to hone the cylinder bore, or clean it by lightly sanding it with emery cloth. Clean thoroughly after honing or sanding. Lubricate the bore with brake fluid before reassembly.

8. Holding the master cylinder with the open end downward, place the cup washer, primary cup, support washer, spring retainer, and spring onto the front brake circuit piston and insert the piston vertically into the master cylinder bore.

9. Assemble the rear brake circuit piston, cup washer, primary cup, support washer, spring retainer, stop sleeve, spring, and stroke limiting screw and insert the assembly into the master cylinder.

10. Install the stop washer and snap-ring.

11. Install the stop screw and seal, making sure the hole for the screw is not blocked by the piston. If the hole is blocked, it will be necessary to push the piston further in until the screw can be turned in.

NOTE: Some Type 2 vehicles have a brake servo.

12. Install the master cylinder and bleed the brakes.

Hydraulic System Bleeding

The hydraulic brake system must be bled any time one of the lines is disconnected or air enters the system.

MANUAL BLEEDING

This method requires two people, one to depress the brake pedal and the other to open the bleeder nipples.

1. Remove the reservoir caps and fill the reservoir.

2. Attach a bleeder hose and a clear container as outlined in the pressure bleeding procedure.

3. Have the assistant depress the brake pedal to the floor several times and then have him hold the pedal to the floor. With the pedal to the floor, open the bleeder nipple until the fluid flow ceases and then close the nipple. Repeat this sequence until there are no more air bubbles in the fluid.

NOTE: As the air is gradually forced out of the system it will no longer be possible to force the brake pedal to the floor.

Periodically check the master cylinder for an adequate supply of fluid. Keep the master cylinder reservoir full of fluid to prevent air from entering the system. If the reservoir does run dry during bleeding, it will be necessary to rebleed the entire system.

Front Disc Brakes

NOTE: All Type 2 models are equipped with front disc brakes.

BRAKE PAD

Removal and Installation

1. Loosen but do not remove the reservoir cover.

2. Jack up the car and remove the wheel and tire.

3. Using a punch, remove the two pins which retain the disc brake pads in the caliper.

NOTE: If the pads are to be reused, mark the pads to insure that they are reinstalled in the same caliper and on the same side of the disc. Do not invert the pads. Changing pads from one location to another can cause uneven braking.

4. If the pads are not going to be reused, force a wedge between the disc and the pad and pry the piston back into the caliper as far as possible.

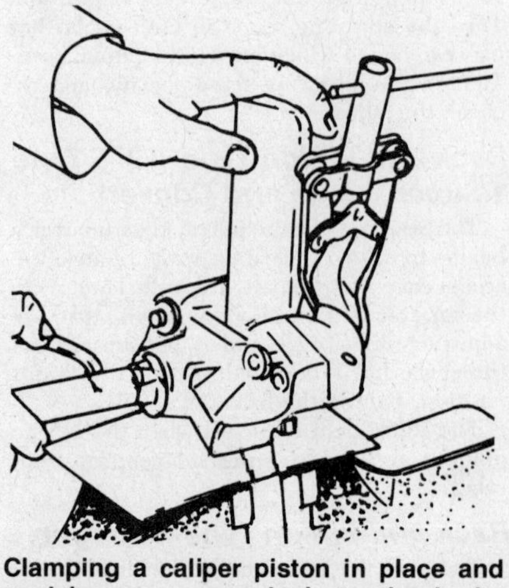

Clamping a caliper piston in place and applying compressed air to the brake hose port

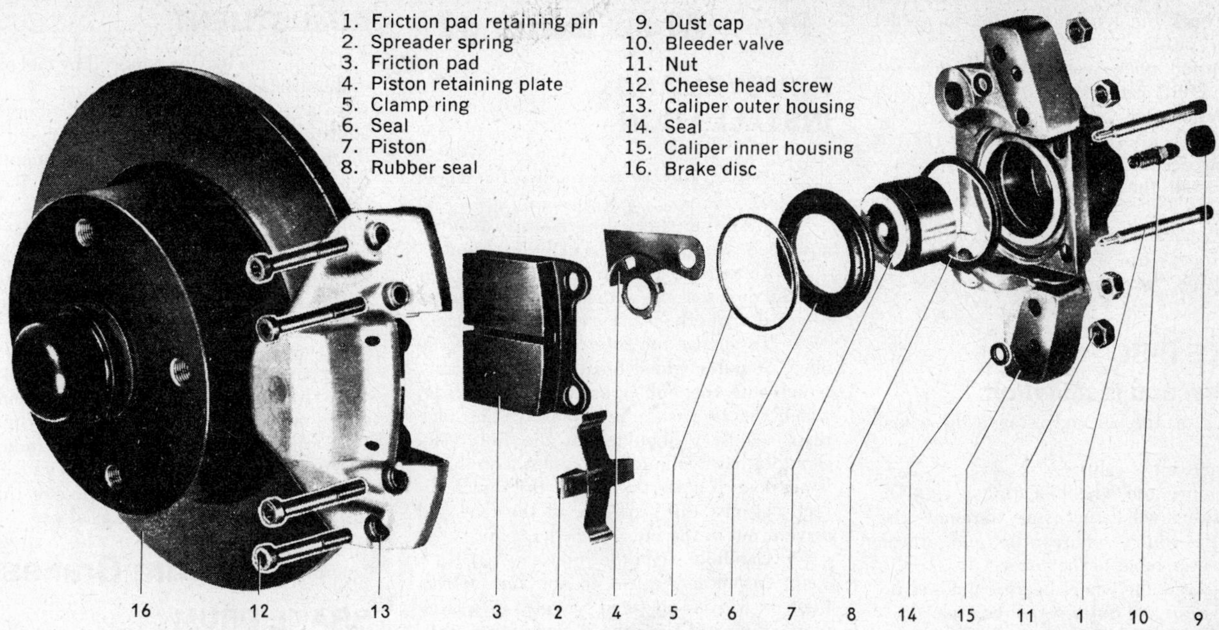

Type 1 front disc brake assembly

5. Using compressed air, blow away the brake dust. Pull the old pad out of the caliper and insert a new one.

6. Now insert the wedge between the disc and pad on the opposite side and force that piston into the caliper. Remove the old pad and insert a new one.

7. If the old pads are to be reused, it is not necessary to push the piston into the caliper. Pull the pads from the caliper and reinstall the pads when necessary.

8. Install a new brake pad spreader spring and insert the retaining pins. Be careful not to shear the split clamping bushing from the pin. Insert the pin from the inside of the caliper and drive it to the outside.

9. Pump the brake pedal several times to take up the clearance between the pads and the disc before driving the car.

10. Install the wheel and tire and carefully road test the car. Apply the brakes gently for 500 to 1000 miles to properly break in the pads and prevent glazing them.

BRAKE CALIPER

Removal and Installation

1. Jack up the car and remove the wheel and tire.
2. Remove the brake pads.
3. Disconnect the brake line from the caliper.
4. Remove the two bolts which secure the caliper to the steering knuckle and remove the caliper from the vehicle.
5. Reverse the above steps to install the caliper and bleed the brakes after the caliper is installed.

OVERHAUL

Clean all parts in alcohol or brake fluid.

1. Remove the caliper from the vehicle.
2. Remove the piston retaining plates.
3. Pry out the seal spring ring using a small screwdriver. Do not damage the seal beneath the ring.
4. Remove the seal with a plastic or hard rubber rod. Do not use sharp edged or metal tools.
5. Rebuild one piston at a time. Securely clamp one piston in place so that it cannot come out of its bore. Place a block of wood between the two pistons and apply air pressure to the brake fluid port.

CAUTION

Use extreme care with this technique because the piston can fly out of the caliper with tremendous force.

6. Remove the rubber seal at the bottom of the piston bore using a rubber or plastic tool.

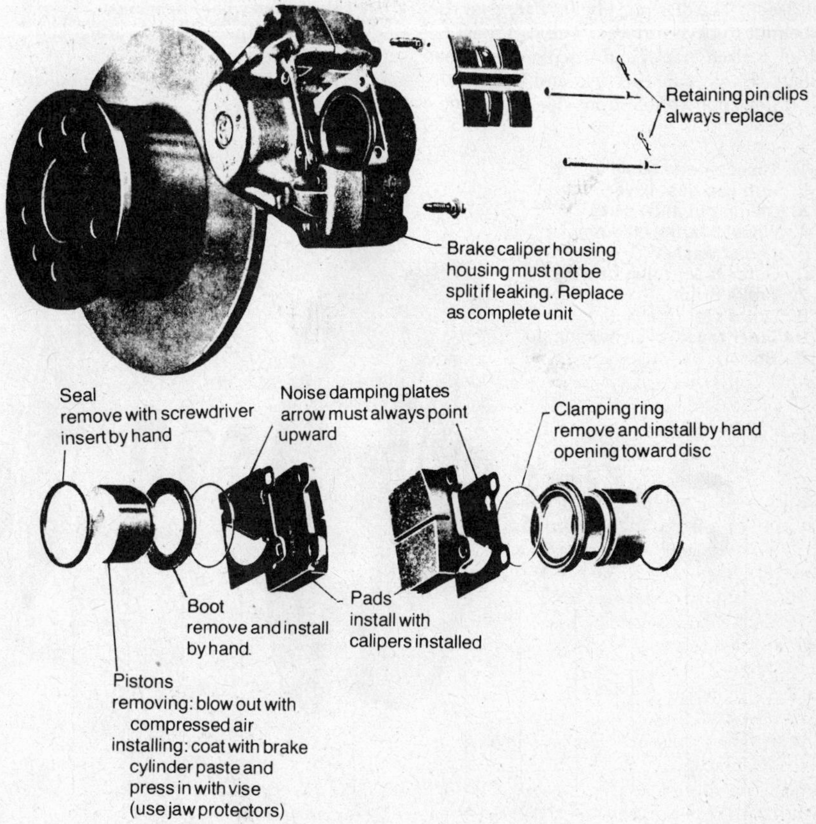

Type 2 front disc brake assembly

7. Check the bore and piston for wear, rust, and pitting.
8. Install a new seal in the bottom of the bore and lubricate the bore and seal with brake fluid.
9. Gently insert the piston, making sure it does not cock and jam in the bore.
10. Install the new outer seal and new spring ring.
11. Install the piston retaining plate.
12. Repeat the above procedure on the other piston. Never rebuild only one side of a caliper.

BRAKE DISC

Removal and Installation

1. Jack up the car and remove the wheel and tire.
2. Remove the caliper.
3. Remove the wheel bearing cover. On the left side it will be necessary to remove the small clip which secures the end of the speedometer cable to the cover.
4. Unscrew the wheel bearing nut and remove the nut and outer wheel bearing.
5. Pull the disc off of the spindle.
6. To remove the wheel bearing races, see the "Wheel Bearing Removal and Installation" procedure.
7. Installation is the reverse of the above. Make sure the wheel bearing is properly adjusted.

Inspection

Visually check the rotor for excessive scoring. Minor scores will not affect the performance; however, if the scores are over 1/32 in., it is necessary to replace the disc or have it resurfaced. The disc must be 0.02 in. over the wear limit to be resurfaced. The disc must be free of surface cracks and discoloration (heat bluing). Hand spin the disc and make sure that it does not wobble from side to side.

Front Wheel Bearings

REMOVAL AND INSTALLATION

1. Jack up the car and remove the wheel and tire.
2. Remove the caliper and disc (if equipped with disc brakes) or brake drum.
3. To remove the inside wheel bearing, pry the dust seal out of the hub with a screwdriver. Lift out the bearing and its inner race.
4. To remove the outer race for either the inner or outer wheel bearing, insert a long punch into the hub opposite the end from which the race is to be removed. The race rests against a shoulder in the hub. The shoulder has two notches cut into it so that it is possible to place the end of the punch directly against the back side of the race and drive it out of the hub.
5. Carefully clean the hub.
6. Install new races in the hub. Drive them in with a soft faced hammer or a large piece of pipe of the proper diameter. Lubricate the races with a light coating of wheel bearing grease.
7. Force wheel bearing grease into the sides of the tapered roller bearings so that all the spaces are filled.
8. Place a small amount of grease inside the hub.
9. Place the inner wheel bearing into its race in the hub and tap a new seal into the hub. Lubricate the sealing surface of the seal with grease.
10. Install the hub on the spindle and install the outer wheel bearing.
11. Adjust the wheel bearing and install the dust cover.
12. Install the caliper (if equipped with disc brakes).

ADJUSTMENT

The bearing may be adjusted by feel or by a dial indicator.

To adjust the bearing by feel, tighten the adjusting nut so that all the play is taken up in the bearing. There will be a slight amount of drag on the wheel if it is hand spun. Back off fully on the adjusting nut and retighten very lightly. There should be no drag when the wheel is hand spun and there should be no perceptible play in the bearing when the wheel is grasped and wiggled from side to side.

To use a dial indicator, remove the dust cover and mount a dial indicator against the hub. Grasp the wheel at the side and pull the wheel in and out along the axis of the spindle. Read the axial play on the dial indicator. Screw the adjusting nut in or out to obtain 0.001-0.005 in. of axial play. Secure the adjusting nut and recheck the axial play.

Front Drum Brakes

BRAKE DRUM

NOTE: All type 1 models are equipped with front drum brakes.

Removal and Installation

1. Jack up the car and remove the wheel and tire.
2. On the left side, remove the clip which secures the speedometer cable to the wheel bearing dust cover. Remove the dust cover.
3. Remove the wheel bearing adjusting nut and slide the brake drum off of the spindle. It may be necessary to back off on the brake shoe star wheels so that there is enough clearance to remove the drum.
4. Installation is the reverse of removal. Adjust the wheel bearings after installing the drum.

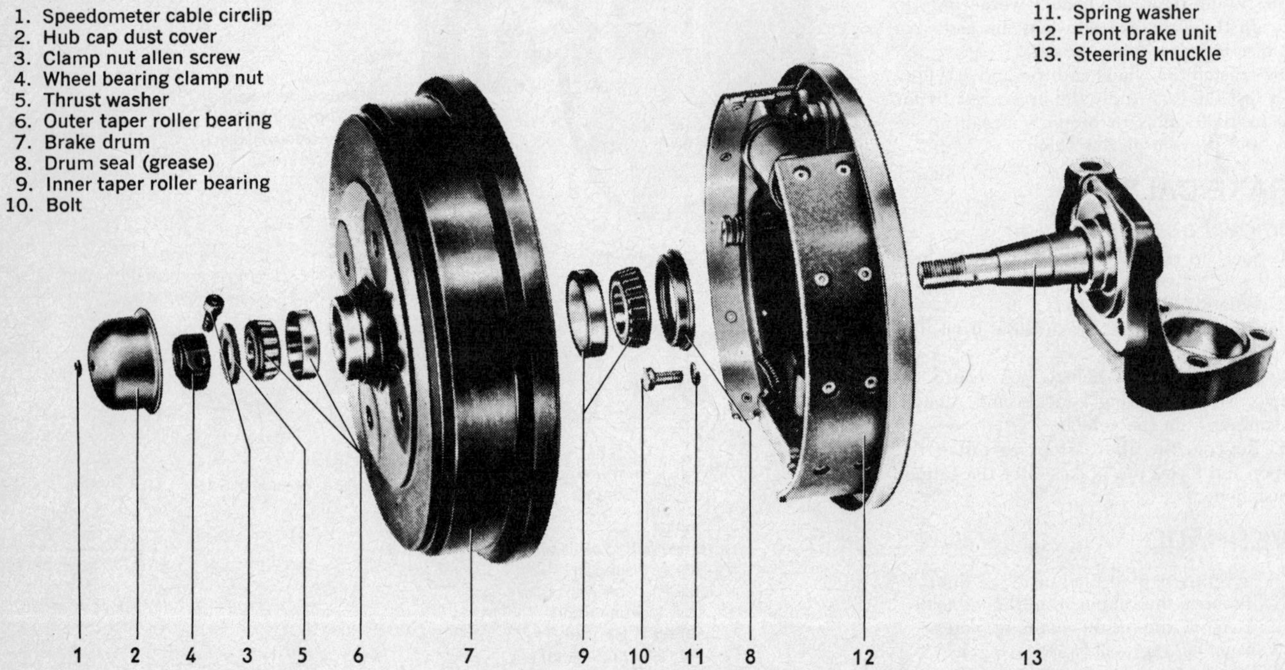

Exploded view of the Type 1 front wheel bearings

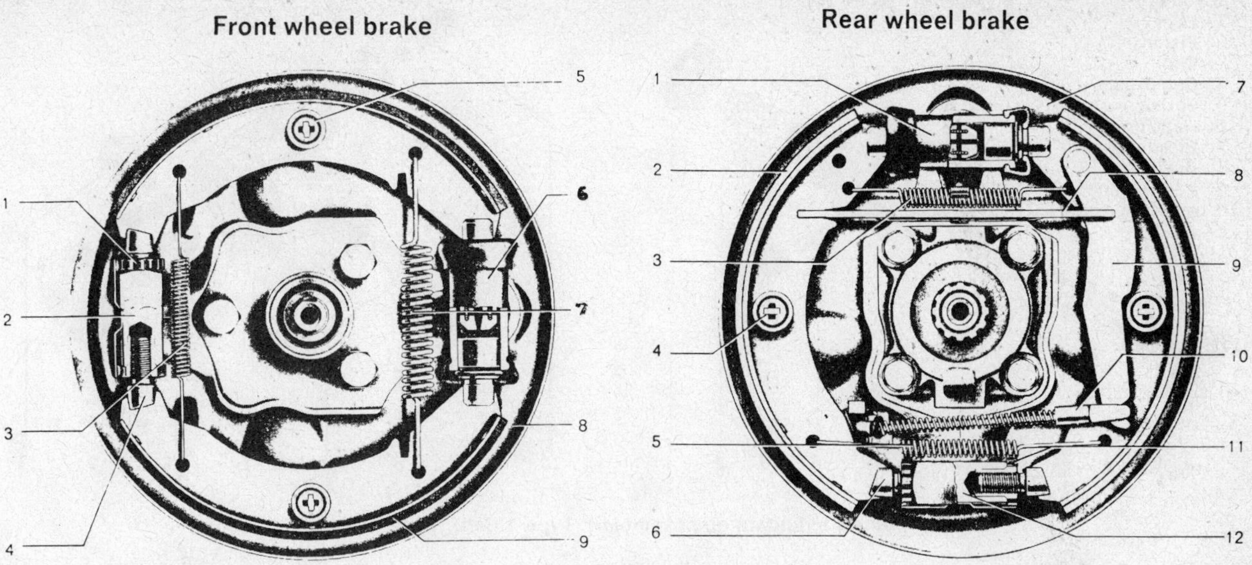

FRONT
1. Adjusting screw
2. Anchor block
3. Front return spring
4. Adjusting nut
5. Guide spring with cup and pin
6. Cylinder
7. Rear return spring
8. Back plate
9. Brake shoe with lining

REAR
1. Cylinder
2. Brake shoe with lining
3. Upper return spring
4. Spring with cup and pin
5. Lower return spring
6. Adjusting screw
7. Back plate
8. Connecting link
9. Lever
10. Brake cable
11. Adjusting nut
12. Anchor block

Type 1 front and rear drum brakes

CAUTION

Do not forget to readjust the brake shoes if they were disturbed during removal.

Inspection

If the brake drums are scored or cracked, they must be replaced or machined. If the vehicle pulls to one side or exhibits a pulsating braking action, the drum is probably out of round and should be checked at a machine shop. The drum may have a smooth even surface and still be out of round. The drum should be free of surface cracks and dark spots.

BRAKE LININGS

Removal and Installation

1. Jack up the car and remove the wheel and tire.

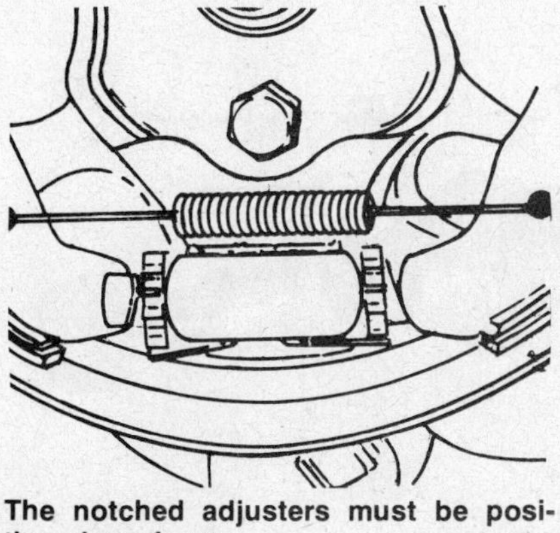

The notched adjusters must be positioned as shown

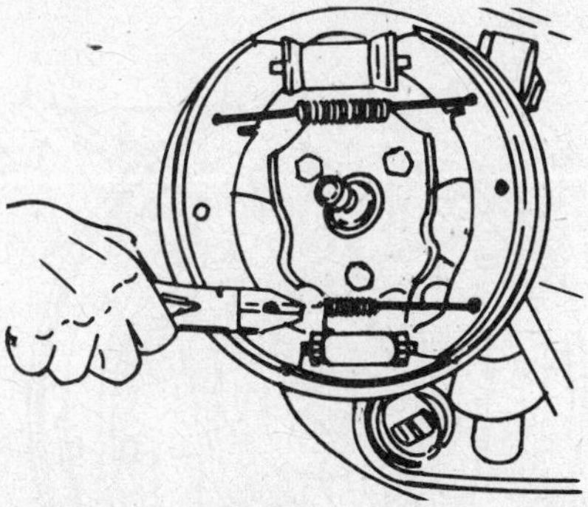

For proper installation, Type 1 brake shoes must have notches in the shoes on the wheel cylinder side

2. Remove the brake drum.
3. Remove the small disc and spring which secure each shoe to the backing plate.
4. Remove the two long springs between the two shoes.
5. Remove the shoes from the backing plate.
6. If new shoes are being installed, remove the adjusters in the end of each wheel cylinder and screw the star wheel up against the head of the adjuster. When inserting the adjusters back in the wheel cylinders, notice that the slot in the adjuster is angled and must be positioned as illustrated.
7. Position new shoes on the backing plate. The slot in the shoes and the stronger return spring must be at the wheel cylinder end.
8. Install the disc and spring which secure the shoe to the backing plate.
9. Install the brake drum and adjust the wheel bearing.

WHEEL CYLINDER

Removal and Installation

1. Remove the brake shoes.
2. Disconnect the brake line from the rear of the cylinder.
3. Remove the bolts which secure the cylinder to the backing plate and remove the cylinder from the vehicle.
4. Reverse the above steps to install and bleed the brakes.

Overhaul

1. Remove the wheel cylinder.
2. Remove the brake adjusters and remove the rubber boot from each end.
3. Push in on one of the pistons to force out the opposite piston and rubber cup.
4. Wash the pistons and cylinder in clean brake fluid or alcohol.
5. Inspect the cylinder bore for signs of pitting, scoring, and excessive wear. If it is badly scored or pitted, the whole cylinder should be replaced. It is possible to remove the glaze and light scores with crocus cloth or a brake cylinder hone. Before rebuilding the cylinder, make sure the bleeder screw is free. If the bleeder is rusted shut or broken off, replace the entire cylinder.
6. Dip the new pistons and rubber cups in brake fluid. Place the spring in the bore and insert the rubber cups into the bore against the spring. The concave side of the rubber cup should face inward.
7. Place the pistons in the bore and install the rubber boot.
8. Install the cylinder and bleed the brakes after the shoes and drum are in place. Make sure that the brakes are adjusted.

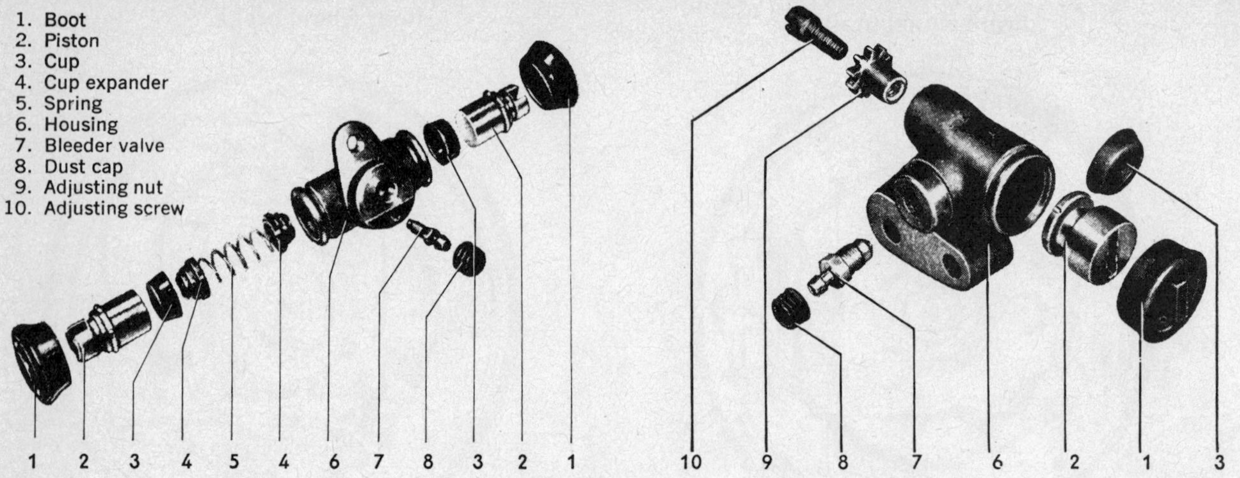

Front wheel cylinders disassembled: Type 1 (left), Type 2 (right)

Rear Drum Brakes

BRAKE DRUM

Removal and Installation

1. With the wheels still on the ground, remove the cotter pin from the slotted nut on the rear axle and remove the nut from the axle.

CAUTION

Make sure the emergency brake is now released.

2. Jack up the car and remove the wheel and tire.
3. The brake drum is splined to the rear axle and the drum should slip off the axle. However, the drum sometimes rusts on the splines and it is necessary to remove the drum using a puller.
4. Before installing the drum, lubricate the splines. Install the drum on the axle and tighten the nut on the axle. Line up a slot in the nut with a hole in the axle and insert a cotter pin. Never loosen the nut to align the slot and hole.

Inspection

Inspection is the same as given in the "Front Drum Brake" section.

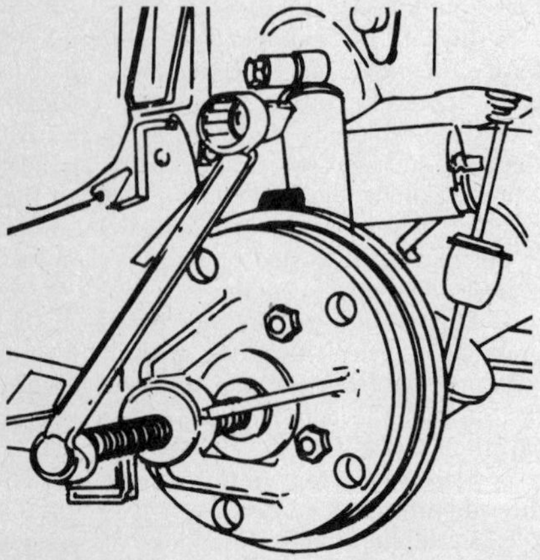

Removing the rear brake drum using a puller

BRAKE LINING

Removal and Installation

1. Remove the brake drum.
2. Remove both shoe retaining springs.
3. Disconnect the lower return spring.
4. Disconnect the hand brake cable from the lever attached to the rear shoe.
5. Remove the upper return spring and clip.
6. Remove the brake shoes and connecting link.
7. Remove the emergency brake lever from the rear shoe.
8. Lubricate the adjusting screws and the star wheel against the head of the adjusting screw.
9. Reverse Steps 1-7 to install the shoes.
10. Adjust the brakes.

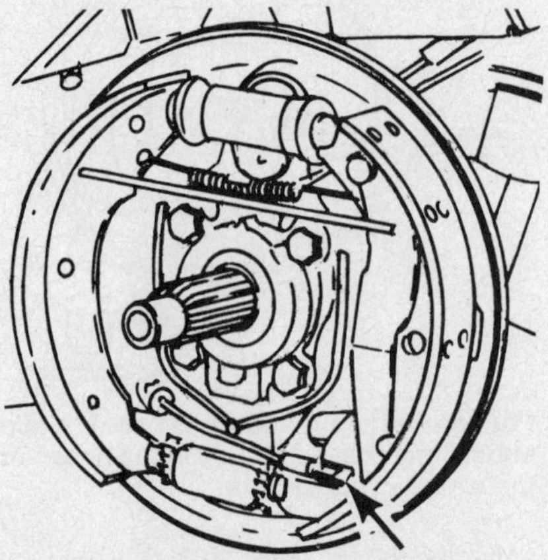

Rear wheel brake assembly, parking brake disconnected

WHEEL CYLINDER

Removal and Installation

Remove the brake drum and brake shoes. Disconnect the brake line from the cylinder and remove the bolts which secure the cylinder to the backing plate. Remove the cylinder from the vehicle.

Overhaul

Overhaul is the same as given in the "Front Drum Brake" section.

NOTE: The Type 2 cylinder has only one rubber boot piston and cup. The rebuilding procedures are the same.

Also, the piston on Type 2 models is removed by blowing compressed air into the brake line hole.

Parking Brake

CABLE ADJUSTMENT

Brake cable adjustment is performed at the handbrake lever in the passenger compart-

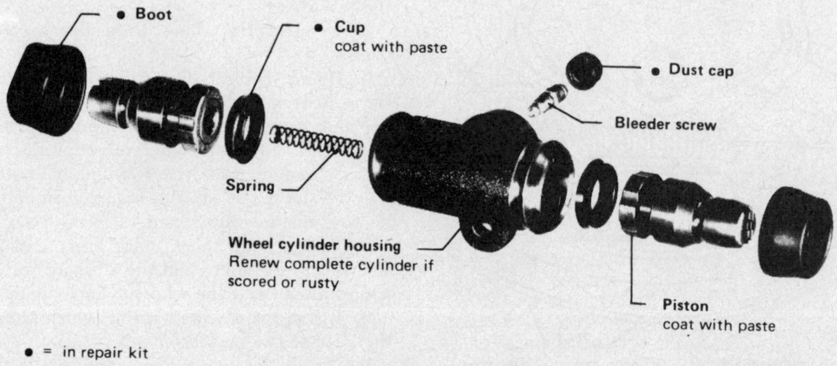

Type 2 rear wheel cylinder

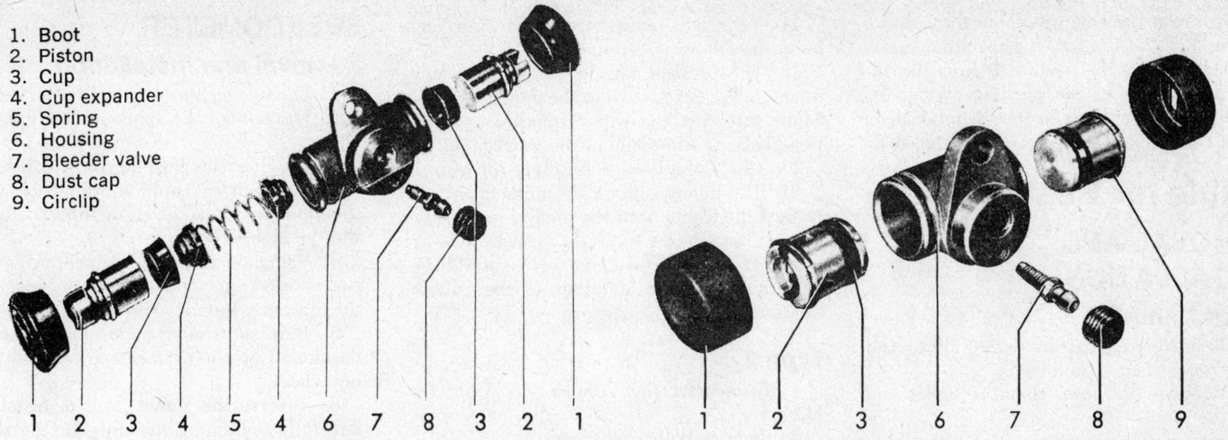

Rear wheel cylinder disassembled; Type 1 (left) and Type 2 (right)

Parking brake cable adjusting nuts

ment. There is a cable for each rear wheel and there are two adjusting nuts at the lever.

To adjust the cable, loosen the locknut. Jack up the rear wheel to be adjusted so that it can be hand spun. Turn the adjusting nut until a very slight drag is felt as the wheel is spun. Then back off on the adjusting nut until the lever can be pulled up three notches.

CAUTION

Never pull up on the handbrake lever with the cables disconnected.

CABLE

Removal and Installation

1. Disconnect the cables at the handbrake lever by removing the two nuts which secure the cables to the lever. Pull the cables rearward to remove that end from the lever bracket.

2. Remove the brake drum and detach the cable end from the lever attached to the rear brake shoe.

3. Remove the brake cable bracket from the backing plate and remove the cable from the vehicle.

4. Reverse the above steps to install and adjust the cable.

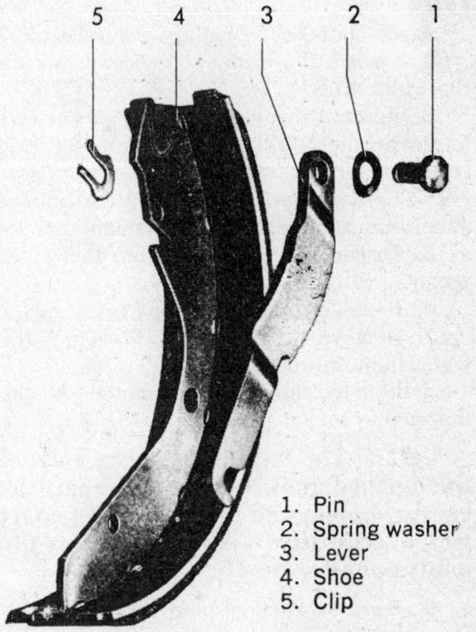

Parking brake hand lever and cable end assembly

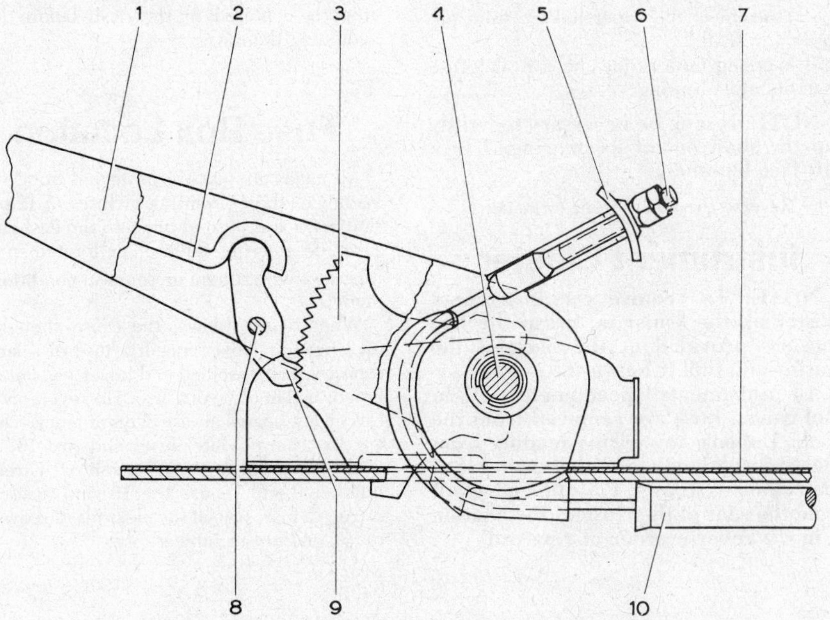

1. Hand brake lever
2. Pawl rod
3. Ratchet segment
4. Lever pin
5. Cable compensator
6. Brake cable
7. Frame
8. Pawl pin
9. Pawl
10. Cable guide tube

Parking brake hand lever and cable end assembly

CHASSIS ELECTRICAL

Heater

The Volkswagen heating system has no electrical blower. The engine cooling fan blows air over the engine and out through the cooling ducts. If the heater flaps are opened, then a portion of the heated air from the engine is diverted to the passenger compartment. An auxiliary gas heater is optional on Types 1 and 2, and standard on the Vanagon.

Cable for Heater Outlet

REMOVAL AND INSTALLATION

Types 1 and 2

1. Remove the rear air outlet, hose, and heater pipe as an assembly.
2. Remove the hose from the outlet and from the pipe.
3. Remove the pin which attaches the cable to the flap in the heater pipe.

NOTE: The pin is push-fit.

4. Remove the heater pipe from the outlet.
5. Bend up the tabs which secure the cable shielding to the outlet.
6. Disconnect the opposite end from the heater controls and remove the cable.
7. Reverse the above steps to install.

Windshield Wipers

MOTOR REMOVAL AND INSTALLATION

Type 1

1. Disconnect the battery ground cable.
2. Loosen the clamp screws and remove the wiper arms.
3. Remove the wiper bearing nuts as well as the washers. Take off the outer bearing seals.
4. Remove the back of the instrument panel from the luggage compartment.
5. Disconnect the cable from the wiper motor.
6. Remove the glove compartment box.
7. Remove the screw which secures the wiper frame to the body.
8. Remove the frame and motor with the linkage.

NOTE: The ball joints at the ends of the linkage may be slipped apart by gently popping the ball and socket apart with a screwdriver. Always lubricate the joints upon reassembly.

9. Remove the lock and spring washers from the motor driveshaft and remove the connecting rod. Matchmark the motor and frame to ensure proper realignment when the motor is reinstalled.
10. Remove the nut located at the base of the motor driveshaft, and the nut at the side of the driveshaft, and remove the motor from the frame.
11. To install, reverse the above steps and heed the following reminders.
12. The pressed lug on the wiper frame must engage the groove in the wiper bearing. Make sure that the wiper spindles are perpendicular to the plane of the windshield.
13. Check the linkage bushings for wear.
14. The hollow side of the links must face toward the frame with the angled end of the driving link toward the right bearing.
15. The inner bearing seal should be placed so that the shoulder of the rubber molding faces the wiper arm.

Type 2

1. Disconnect the ground wire from the battery.
2. Remove both wiper arms.
3. Remove the bearing cover and nut.
4. Remove the heater branch connections under the instrument panel.
5. Disconnect the wiper motor wiring.
6. Remove the wiper motor securing screw and remove the motor.
7. Reverse the above steps to install.

LINKAGE REMOVAL AND INSTALLATION

The windshield wiper linkage is secured at the ends by a ball and socket type joint. The ball and joint may be gently pryed apart with the aid of a screwdriver. Always lubricate the joints with grease before reassembly.

Wiper Arm Shaft

1. Remove the wiper arm.
2. Remove the bearing cover or the shaft seal depending on the type.
3. Remove the large wiper shaft bearing securing nut and remove the accompanying washer and rubber seal.
4. Disconnect the wiper linkage from the wiper arm shaft.
5. Working from inside the car, slide the shaft out of its bearing.

NOTE: It may be necessary to lightly tap the shaft out of its bearing. Use a soft face hammer.

6. Reverse the above steps to install.

Instrument Cluster

NOTE: To remove the instrument cluster on the Vanagon, grasp the two recesses provided at the back of the cluster and pull it forward.

All instruments (speedometer, clock, fuel gauge, etc.) are removed from the back. Unhook any wiring leading from the particular gauge and then remove the retaining screws. Pull the gauge out from the rear of the cluster. Installation is in the reverse order of removal.

SPEEDOMETER

Removal and Installation

1. Disconnect the negative battery cable.
2. Disconnect the speedometer light bulb wires.
3. Unscrew the knurled nut which secures the speedometer cable to the back of the speedometer. Pull the cable from the back of the speedometer.
4. Using a 4 mm allen wrench, remove the two knurled nuts which secure the speedometer brackets. Remove the brackets.
5. Remove the speedometer from the dashboard by sliding it out toward the steering wheel.
6. Reverse the above steps to install. Before fully tightening the nuts for the speedometer brackets, make sure the speedometer is correctly positioned in the dash.
dash.

FUEL GAUGE AND CLOCK ASSEMBLY

Removal and Installation

1. Disconnect the negative battery cable.
2. Disconnect the wiring from the back of the assembly.
3. Remove the knurled nuts and brackets which secure the assembly in the dash. Use a 4 mm allen wrench.
4. Remove the assembly by gently sliding it toward the steering wheel and out of the dash.
5. The fuel gauge is secured into the base of the clock by two screws. Remove the screws and slip the fuel gauge out of the clock.
6. Reverse the above steps to install. Make sure the clock and fuel gauge assembly is properly centered in the dash before fully tightening the nuts.

Fuse Box Location

All major circuits are protected from overloading or short circuiting by fuses. A 12 position fusebox is located beneath the dashboard near the steering column, or located in the luggage compartment on some air conditioned models.

When a fuse blows, the cause should be investigated. Never install a fuse of a larger capacity than specified and never use foil or a bolt or nail in place of a fuse. However, always carry a few spares in case of emergency. There are 10 8 amp (white) fuses and two 16 amp (red) fuses in the VW fusebox. Circuits number 9 and 10 use the 16 amp fuses. To replace a fuse, pry off the clear plastic cover at either end of the subject fuse.

SPECIFICATIONS

INDEX

BEFORE SERVICING, SEE THE SAFETY NOTICE ON THE CONTENTS PAGE

INTRODUCTION

At the time of its introduction, the Dasher was a unique VW. Most of the Dasher's features are the opposite of those traditionally associated with VWs, such as air cooling, rear engine placement, and torsion bar suspension. The Dasher has front wheel drive and a water-cooled, inline, overhead camshaft engine. Suspension is by coil springs, with MacPherson strut spring/shock units at the front. Steering is by rack and pinion, and radial ply tires are standard equipment. The front suspension is designed with negative roll radius. This safety feature keeps the car straight when drag on the front tires is not equal, as would happen with one wheel on wet pavement and one wheel on dry pavement.

The Rabbit, the Jetta, and the Scirocco share most of the Dasher's unique features. The most striking difference is that the engine is mounted transversely. The rear wheels are suspended by trailing arms connected by a torsion beam and shock absorber/strut units.

SERIAL NUMBER IDENTIFICATION

Vehicle Identification Plate

The Dasher vehicle identification plate is riveted to the inner right fender. On the Rabbit, Jetta and Scirocco, the plate is on top of the body crossmember above the grille. On the plate are the date of manufacture and the chassis number.

Chassis Number

The chassis number is located on the driver's side windshield pillar on the Scirocco and Dasher, and on the left front corner of the instrument panel on the Rabbit and Jetta, (visible through the windshield). The Dasher chassis number is also stamped on the firewall over the windshield washer reservoir. The Rabbit, Jetta and Scirocco chassis number is also on top of the right suspension strut mounting. It also appears on the vehicle identification plate.

Engine Number

The Engine number is stamped on the left side (front on the Rabbit, Jetta and Scirocco) of the engine block between the fuel pump and the distributor.

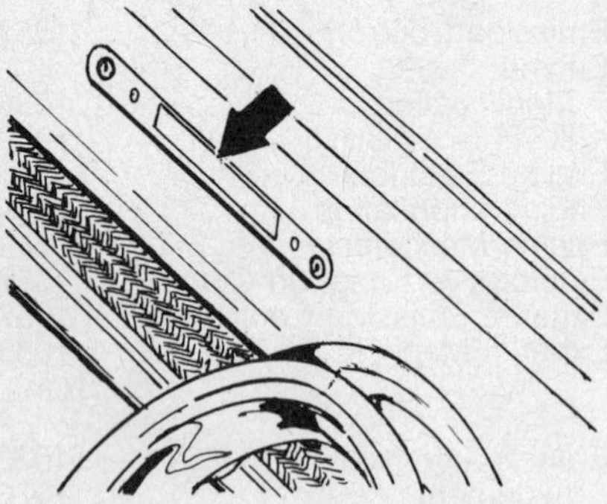

Dasher and Scirocco chassis number

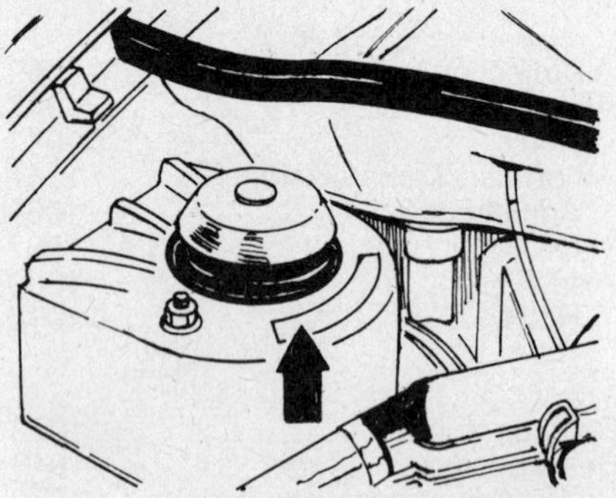

Rabbit, Jetta chassis number

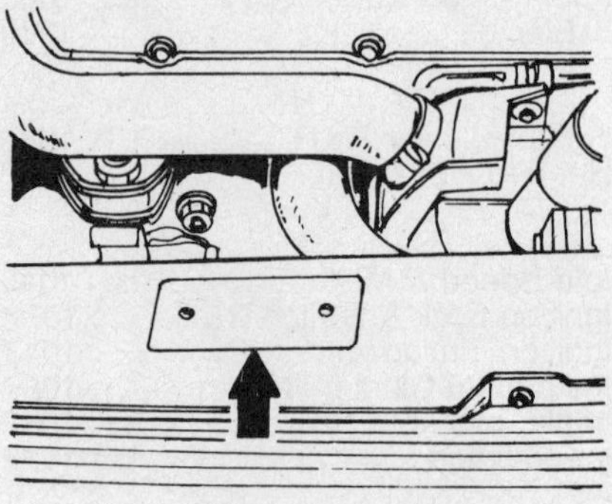

Identification plate

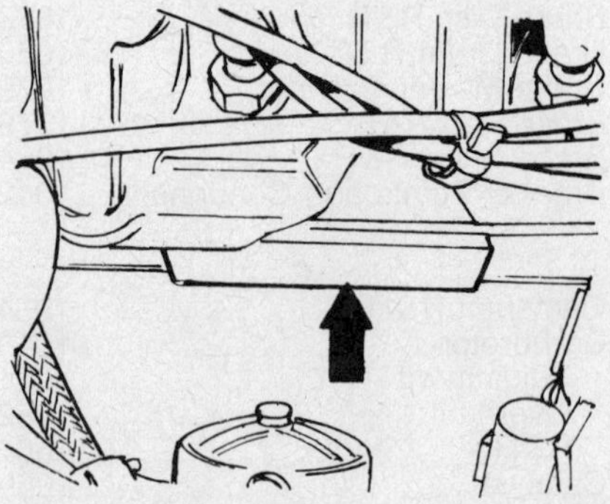

Engine number location

ENGINE CODES

Model	Year	Engine Capacity	Engine Code
Dasher	1975	1.5 liter 1.6 liter	XS, XR YG, YH
Rabbit, Scirocco	1975-78	1.5 liter 1.6 liter	FC, FG CK (diesel) FN, EF EE
Dasher	1976-78	1.6 liter	YK, YH YG
	1979-80	1.6 liter 1.5 liter	YK, YH YG CK (diesel)
Rabbit, Scirocco, Jetta	1979-80	1.5 liter 1.6 liter	EH, CK (diesel) FX EJ

GENERAL ENGINE SPECIFICATIONS

Year/Model	Engine Displacement cu. in. (cc)	Fuel Delivery	Horsepower @ rpm (SAE)	Torque @ rpm ft. lbs. (SAE)	Bore x Stroke (in.)	Compression Ratio	Oil Pressure @ rpm (psi)
1975 Dasher	89.7 (1471)	2-bbl Solex	75 @ 8500	81 @ 4000	3.01 x 3.15	8.5:1	40 @ 2500
1975 Scirocco, Rabbit	89.7 (1471)	2-bbl Zenith	70 @ 6000	91 @ 3500	3.01 x 3.15	9.2:1	40 @ 2500
1976-77 Dasher	96.8 (1588)	CIS Fuel inj.	81 @ 5800	90 @ 3300	3.3 x 3.15	8.0:1	40 @ 2500
1976 Rabbit, Scirocco Scirocco	96.8 (1588)	2-bbl Zenith	71 @ 5600	82 @ 3300	3.13 x 3.15	8.2:1	40 @ 2500
1977 Rabbit, Scirocco	96.8 (1588)	CIS Fuel inj.	81 @ 5800	90 @ 3300	3.13 x 3.15	8.0:1	40 @ 2500
1977-80 Rabbit (Diesel)	89.7 (1471)	Fuel inj.	48 @ 5000	56.5 @ 3000	3.01 x 3.15	23.5:1	27 @ 2000
1978-80 Dasher	97.0 (1588)	Fuel inj.	78 @ 5500 ①	84 @ 3200 ②	3.13 x 3.15	8.0:1	28 @ 2000
1979-80 Dasher (Diesel)	89.7 (1471)	Fuel inj.	48 @ 5000	56.5 @ 3000	3.01 x 3.15	23.5:1	28 @ 2000
1978-80 Rabbit	88.9 (1457)	Fuel ⑤ inj.	71 @ 5800 ③	73 @ 3500 ④	3.13 x 2.89	8.0:1	28 @ 2000
1980-81 Jetta	97.0 (1588)	Fuel inj.	78 @ 5500	84 @ 3200	3.13 x 3.15	8.0:1	28 @ 2000
1978 Scirocco	88.9 (1457)	Fuel inj.	73 @ 5800	73 @ 3500 ④	3.13 x 2.89	8.0:1	28 @ 2000
1979-80 Scirocco	97.0 (1588)	Fuel inj.	78 @ 5500 ①	84 @ 3200 ②	3.13 x 3.15	8.0:1	28 @ 2000
1981 Jetta, Scirocco, Rabbit	105.0 (1715)	Fuel inj.	74 @ 5000 ⑥	90 @ 3000 ⑦	3.13 x 3.40	8.2:1	28 @ 2000
1981 Dasher, Rabbit Diesel	97.0 (1588)	Fuel inj.	52 @ 4800	72 @ 3000	3.01 x 3.40	23.0:1	28 @ 2000

① 76 @ 5000—Calif.
② 83 @ 3200—Calif.
③ 70 @ 5800—Calif.
④ 72 @ 3500—Calif.
⑤ Some 1978 Rabbits are equipped with a Solex 1-bbl carburetor
⑥ Canada: 76 hp
⑦ Canada: 92 ft. lbs.

GASOLINE ENGINE TUNE-UP SPECIFICATIONS

Year, Model	SPARK PLUGS Type	SPARK PLUGS Gap (in.)	DISTRIBUTOR Point Dwell (deg)	DISTRIBUTOR Point Gap (in.)	Ignition Timing (deg)	Intake Valve Opens (deg)	Compression Pressure (psi)	Idle Speed (rpm)	VALVE CLEARANCE (in.) In ⑥	VALVE CLEARANCE (in.) Ex ⑥
1975 Dasher (Canada)	W200 T30 N8Y	0.024-0.028	44-50	0.016	3 ATDC @ Idle	4 BTDC	142-184	850-1000	0.008-0.012	0.016-0.020
1975 Rabbit, Scirocco	W200 T30 N8Y	0.024-0.028	44-50	0.016	3 ATDC @ Idle	4 BTDC	142-184	850-1000	0.008-0.012	0.016-0.020
1976-79 Dasher	W215 T30 N7Y	0.024-0.028	44-50	0.016	3 ATDC @ Idle	4 BTDC	142-184	850-1000	0.008-0.012	0.016-0.020
1976 Rabbit, Scirocco	W200 T30 N8Y	0.024-0.028	44-50	0.016	3 ATDC @ Idle	4 BTDC	142-184	850-1000	0.008-0.012	0.016-0.020

GASOLINE ENGINE TUNE-UP SPECIFICATIONS

Year, Model	Spark Plugs Type	Spark Plugs Gap (in.)	Distributor Point Dwell (deg)	Distributor Point Gap (in.)	Ignition Timing (deg)	Intake Valve Opens (deg)	Compression Pressure (psi)	Idle Speed (rpm)	Valve Clearance (in.) In ⑥	Valve Clearance (in.) Ex ⑥
1977 Rabbit, Scirocco	W215 T30 N7Y	0.024-0.028	44-50	0.016	3 ATDC @ Idle	4 BTDC	142-184	850-1000	0.008-0.012	0.016-0.020
1978 Rabbit, Scirocco	W175 T30 N8Y	0.024-0.028	44-50	0.016	②	4 BTDC	142-184	850-1000	0.008-0.012	0.016-0.020
1979 Rabbit	W175 T30 N8Y	0.024-0.032	44-50	0.016	3 ATDC @ Idle	4 BTDC	142-184	850-1000	0.008-0.012	0.016-0.020
1979 Scirocco	W175 T30 N8Y	0.024-0.032	44-50	0.016	3 ATDC @ Idle	4 BTDC	142-184	850-1000	0.008-0.012	0.016-0.020
1980 Dasher (49 states)	W175 T30 N8Y	0.024-0.032	44-50 ⑦	0.016 ⑦	3 ATDC @ Idle	4 BTDC	142-184	850-1000	0.008-0.012	0.016-0.020
1980 Dasher (California)	WR7DS N8GY	0.024-0.028	Electronic		3 ATDC @ Idle	4 BTDC	142-184	880-1000	0.008-0.012	0.016-0.020
1980 Rabbit ③	W175 T30 N8Y	0.024-0.032	Electronic		7½ BTDC @ Idle	4 BTDC	142-184	850-1000	0.008-0.012	0.016-0.020
1980 Rabbit (California)	WR7DS N8GY	0.024-0.028	Electronic		3 ATDC @ Idle	4 BTDC	142-184	880-1000	0.008-0.012	0.016-0.020
1980-81 Rabbit 49 states and 1981 California ⑤	W175 T30 N8Y	0.024-0.032	44-50 ⑦	0.016 ⑦	3 ATDC @ Idle	4 BTDC	142-184	850-1000 ④	0.008-0.012	0.016-0.020
1980-81 Scirorro, Jetta (49 states)	W175 T30 N8Y	0.024-0.032	44-50 ⑦	0.016 ⑦	3 ATDC @ Idle	4 BTDC	142-184	850-1000	0.008-0.012	0.016-0.020
1980-81 Scirocco, Jetta (California)	WR7DS N8GY	0.024-0.028	Electronic		3 ATDC @ Idle	4 BTDC	142-184	880-1000	0.008-0.012	0.016-0.020

NOTE: The underhood specifications sticker often reflects tune-up specification changes made in production. Sticker figures must be used if they disagree with those in this chart.

① 47°-53° California
② 3 ATDC @ Idle with CIS fuel injection; 7½ BTDC @ Idle with 34 PICT-5 Carburetor
③ Non-California Rabbit with 1 barrel carburetor
④ w/o Idle stabilizer
⑤ With fuel injection
⑥ Valve clearance need not be adjusted unless it varies more than 0.002 in. from specifications.
⑦ 1981 has Electronic Ignition

DIESEL TUNE-UP SPECIFICATIONS

Model	Valve Clearance (cold) ① Intake (in.)	Valve Clearance (cold) ① Exhaust (in.)	Intake Valve Opens (deg)	Injection Pump Setting (deg)	Injection Nozzle Pressure (psi) New	Injection Nozzle Pressure (psi) Used	Idle Speed (rpm)	Cranking Compression Pressure (psi)
Diesel (All Models)	0.008-0.012	0.016-0.020	N.A.	Align marks	1849	1706	800-850 ②	398 minimum

① Warm clearance given—Cold clearance: Intake 0.006-0.010
Exhaust 0.014-0.018

② Volkswagen has lowered the idle speed on early models to this specification.

Valve clearance need not be adjusted unless it varies more than 0.002 in. from specification.

N.A. Not Available

FIRING ORDER

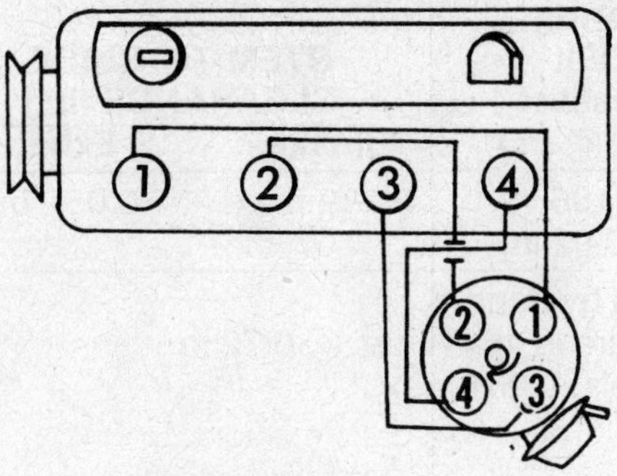

Firing order: 1-3-4-2

CAPACITIES

Year	Model	Engine Crankcase (qts) With Filter	Engine Crankcase (qts) Without Filter	Transmission (pts) Manual	Transmission (pts) Automatic	Drive Axle (pts)	Gasoline Tank (gals)	Cooling System (pts)
1975	Dasher	3.7	3.1	3.4 ①	12.8 ②	3.0	12.1 ③	12.7
1975	Scirocco, Rabbit	3.7	3.2	2.6	12.8 ②	1.6	11.9	13.6
1976	Dasher	3.7	3.2	3.4	12.8 ②	3.0	12.1	12.8
1976	Rabbit, Scirocco	3.7	3.2	2.6	12.8 ②	3.0	12.1	13.8
1977-80	Dasher	3.2	2.6	3.4	12.4 ②	1.6	12.1	12.6
1977	Rabbit, Scirocco	3.7	3.2	2.6	12.8 ②	1.6	12.1	9.8
1977-80	Rabbit Diesel	3.7	3.2	2.6	—	1.6	10.9	12.6
1978-80	Rabbit	3.7	3.2	2.6 ④	12.8 ②	1.6	10.6	9.8
1978	Scirocco	3.7	3.2	3.2 ④	12.8	1.6	10.6	9.8
1979-80	Scirocco	3.7	3.2	3.2 ④	12.8	1.6	10.6	9.8
	Dasher Diesel	3.7	3.2	3.2 ④	—	1.6	11.9	9.8
1980	Jetta	3.7	3.2	3.2 ④	12.8	1.6	10.5	10.2
1981	Scirocco, Rabbit, Jetta	4.5	4.0	3.2 ④	12.8	1.6	10.0 ⑤	9.8
1981	Dasher, Rabbit Diesel	3.7	3.2	3.2 ④	—	1.6	10.0 ⑤	14.3 ⑥

① At change, initial amount 4.2 pts
② Dry refill; normal refill is 6.4 pts
③ Doesn't include 1.3 gal reserve
④ 5-speed—4.2
⑤ Dasher: 12.0
⑥ Dasher: 12.2
— Not applicable

CRANKSHAFT AND CONNECTING ROD SPECIFICATIONS

All measurements are given in inches

Year/Model	Crankshaft Main Brg. Journal Dia.	Crankshaft Main Brg. Oil Clearance	Crankshaft Shaft End-Play	Crankshaft Thrust on No.	Connecting Rod Journal Diameter	Connecting Rod Oil Clearance	Connecting Rod Side Clearance (max.)
1975-81 All	2.126	0.001-0.003	0.003-0.007	3	1.811	0.001-0.003	0.015

NOTE: Main and connecting rod bearings are available in three undersizes

VALVE SPECIFICATIONS

Year/Model	Seat Angle (deg)	Spring Test Pressure (lbs. @ in.)	STEM TO GUIDE CLEARANCE (in.) Intake	Exhaust	STEM DIAMETER (in.) Intake	Exhaust
1975-81 All	45	96-106 ① @ 0.92 in.	0.039 max. ②	0.051 max.	0.314	0.313

NOTE: Exhaust valves must be ground by hand.
① Outer spring, inner spring test pressure is 46-51 lbs. @ 0.72 in.
② 1975-78 Rabbit and all Dasher Diesels: 0.051 max.

TORQUE SPECIFICATIONS

(All readings in ft. lbs.)

Year/Model	Cylinder Head Bolts	Rod Bearing Bolts ④	Main Bearing Bolts	Crankshaft Pulley Bolt	Flywheel To Crankshaft Bolts	MANIFOLD Intake	Exhaust
1975-80 Dasher	54 ①	33	47	58	54	18	18
1975-81 Rabbit, Scirocco, Jetta	54 ①	33	47	58	54 ②	18	18
1977-81 Diesel Rabbit, Dasher	65 ③	33	47	56	54 ②	18	18

① Cold; 61 ft. lbs. warm—1978-79 54 ft. lbs. plus ¼ turn (polygon bolts)
② Pressure plate to crankshaft bolts
③ Cold, 69 ft. lbs. warm
④ Always use new bolts

TORQUE SEQUENCE

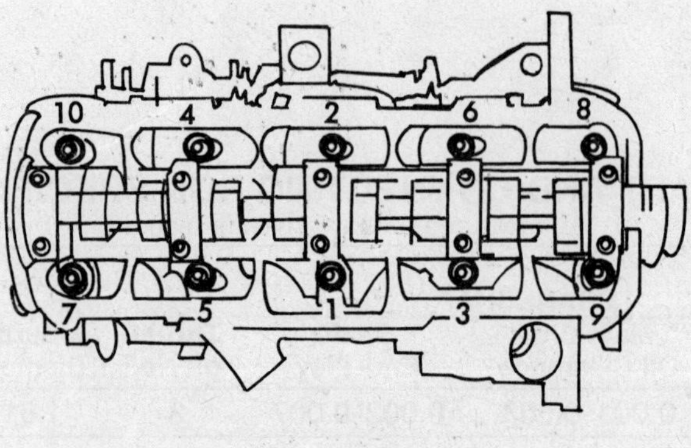

Cylinder head

BRAKE SPECIFICATIONS

Year	Model	Lug Nut Torque (ft. lbs.)	Master Cylinder Bore	BRAKE DISC Minimum Thickness	BRAKE DISC Maximum Run-Out	Diameter	BRAKE DRUM Maximum Machine o/s	BRAKE DRUM Maximum Wear Limit	MINIMUM BRAKE LINING THICKNESS* Front	MINIMUM BRAKE LINING THICKNESS* Rear
1975-80	Dasher	65	0.82	0.41	0.004	7.87	7.90	7.97	0.250	0.098
1975-81	Rabbit, Jetta, Scirocco	65	0.82	0.41	0.004	7.08 ①	7.10 ②	7.12 ③	0.250 ④	0.098

*NOTE: Minimum lining thickness is as recommended by manufacturer. Due to variations in state inspection regulations, the minimum thickness may be different than that recommended by the manufacturer.

① Rabbit front brake drums—9.05-9.06 in.
② Rabbit front brake drums—9.087 in.
③ Rabbit front brake drums—9.106 in.
④ Rabbit front brake drums—0.039 in.

BATTERY AND STARTER SPECIFICATIONS

(All models use 12 volt, negative ground system)

Year	Model	Battery Amp Hour Capacity	LOCK TEST Amps	LOCK TEST Volts	LOCK TEST Torque (ft. lbs.)	NO LOAD TEST Amps	NO LOAD TEST Volts	NO LOAD TEST rpm	Brush Spring Tension (oz.)	Minimum Brush Length (in.)
1975-81	All	45/54 ①	280-370	7.5	2.42	33-55	11.5	6000-8000	35.5	0.5

① w/AC

PISTON AND RING SPECIFICATIONS

(All measurements in inches)

Year/Model	Piston Clearance	RING GAP Top Compression	RING GAP Bottom Compression	RING GAP Oil Control	RING SIDE CLEARANCE Top Compression	RING SIDE CLEARANCE Bottom Compression	RING SIDE CLEARANCE Oil Control
1975-81 All Gasoline Engines	0.001-0.003	0.012-0.018	0.012-0.018	0.010-0.016	0.001-0.002	0.001-0.002	0.001-0.002
1977-81 All Diesel Engines	0.001-0.003	0.012-0.020	0.012-0.020	0.010-0.016	0.002-0.004	0.002-0.003	0.001-0.002

NOTE: Three piston sizes are available to accommodate over-bores up to 0.040 in.

WHEEL ALIGNMENT

Year	Model	CASTER ① Range (deg)	CASTER ① Pref Setting (deg)	CAMBER ② Range (deg)	CAMBER ② Pref Setting (deg)	Toe-In ③ (in.)	Steering Axis Inclination ① (deg)
All	Dasher	0°-1°	0°30′	0-1°	0°30′	0.08	10°30′
All	Rabbit, Scirocco, Jetta	+1°20′-2°20′	+1°50′	−10′-+50′	+20′	0.08	10°30′

① Not adjustable

② Rear wheel camber (not adjustable)
Rabbit (to Ch. No. 176 3 241 690)—1°N ± 30′
Rabbit (from Ch. No. 176 3 261 691)—1¼°N ± 30′
Scirocco (all)—1°N ± 30′
Dasher (all)—½°N ± 30′

③ Rear wheel toe-in (not adjustable)
Rabbit—0° ± 15′
Scirocco (to Ch. No. 536 2 031 722)—10°P ± 30′
Scirocco (from Ch. No. 536 2 031 723)—20′P ± 30′

TUNE-UP PROCEDURES

VW recommends a tune-up, including new points and plugs, at 15,000 mile intervals. The only procedure required for diesel engines in this section is the valve lash adjustment and minimum/maximum engine speed checking and adjustment.

Spark Plugs

The firing order is 1-3-4-2, with No. 1 cylinder at the front (right on the Rabbit, Jetta and Scirocco) of the engine.

1. Grasp the spark plug boot and pull it straight out. Don't pull on the wire. Either number the wires or remove them one at a time to avoid mixups.
2. Place the spark plug socket firmly on the plug and screw the spark plug out.

NOTE: The cylinder head is aluminum alloy, which is easily stripped of threads. Remove the plugs only when the engine is cold.

If removal is difficult, loosen the plug only slightly and drip penetating oil onto the threads.

3. Inspect the plugs and clean or discard them. The recommended spark plug gap is listed in the "Tune-Up Specifications" chart. Use a round wire feeler gauge to check the gap between the plug electrodes. If the gap is incorrect, gently bend the side electrode to correct. Do not bend the center electrode.
4. Torque the new spark plugs to 22 ft/lbs. Install the ignition wire boots firmly.

Breaker Points and Condenser

Snap off the two retaining clips on the distributor cap. Remove the cap and examine it for cracks, deterioration, or carbon tracking. Replace the cap, if necessary, by transferring one wire at a time from the old cap to the new one. Examine the rotor for corrosion or wear and replace it if questionable. Remove the dust shield. Check the points for pitting and burning. Slight imperfections on the contact surface may be filed off with a point file. It is best to replace the breaker point set. Always

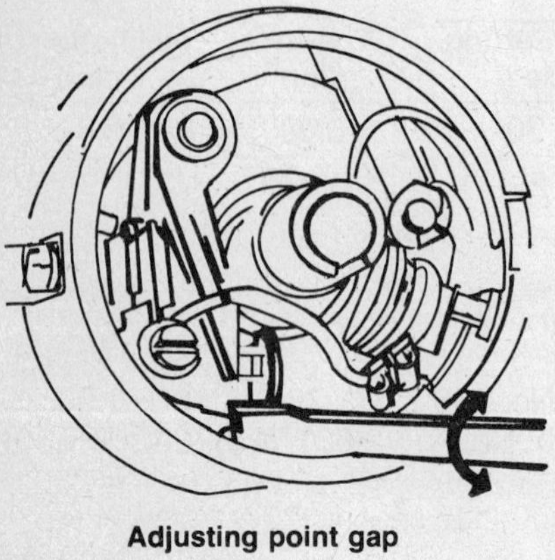

Adjusting point gap

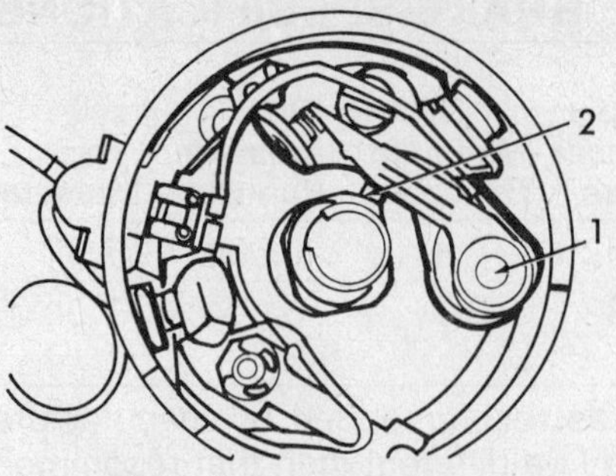

Breaker points and condenser. Lubricate at (1) with a drop of engine oil and at (2) with high melting point grease.

replace the condenser when you replace the point set.

To replace the breaker points:

1. Remove the rotor.
2. Unsnap the point connector from the terminal at the side of the distributor. Remove the retaining screw, and lift out the point set.
3. Install the new point set, making sure that the pin on the bottom engages the hole in the breaker plate.
4. Install the wire connector and the retaining screws (hand-tight).
5. Turn the engine with a wrench on the crankshaft pulley until the breaker arm rubbing block is in the high point of one of the cam lobes. Turn the engine only in the direction of normal rotation to avoid damage to the timing belt.
6. A 0.016 in. feeler gauge should just slip through the points. If the gap is incorrect, pivot a screwdriver in the point set notch and the two projections on the breaker plate to bring it within specifications.
7. When the gap is correct, tighten the retaining screw. Recheck the adjustment.
8. Lubricate the distributor cam with silicone grease.
9. Install the dust cover, rotor and distributor cap.
10. Check the dwell angle and the ignition timing.
11. The condenser is mounted on the outside of the distributor. Undo the mounting screw and the terminal block to replace.

Dwell Angle (Breaker-Point Gasoline Engines Only)

The dwell angle or cam angle is the number of degrees that the distributor cam rotates while the points are closed. There is an inverse relationship between dwell angle and point gap. Increasing the point gap will decrease the dwell angle and vice versa. Checking the dwell angle with a meter is a far more accurate method of measuring point opening than the feeler gauge method.

After setting the point gap to specification with a feeler gauge, check the dwell angle. Attach the dwell meter. The negative lead is grounded and the positive lead is connected to the primary wire, Terminal No. 1 that runs from the coil to the distrubutor. Start the engine, let it idle and reach operating temperature, and observe the dwell on the meter. The reading should fall within the allowable range. If it does not, the gap will have to be reset. Dwell can also be checked with the engine cranking. In this case, dwell will vary between 0° and the dwell figure for that setting.

Hall Effect Electronic Ignition System

The 1980 Dasher, Jetta and Scirocco destined for California, the 1980 Rabbit 1.6 liter (California) and 1.5 liter (49 states) and 1981 Rabbits and Sciroccos are equipped with the Hall effect electronic ignition system.

The distributor contains the Hall Effect pickup assembly which replaces the breaker points assembly in conventional systems.

The "Hall Effect" is a shift in magnetic field caused when one of the rotors on the distributor shaft passes the sensors mounted in the distributor. This shift performs the same function as breaker points, which is to allow the current (coil field) stored in the coil to collapse, causing a spark to run from the coil to the distributor and down to the spark plugs, which make the current jump a gap between the two spark plug electrodes, causing a spark which ignites the air-fuel mixture in the combustion chamber. Since there are no breaker points and condenser to replace, the system should be maintenance free.

ELECTRONIC IGNITION PRECAUTIONS

When working on the Hall ignition, observe the following precautions to prevent damage to the ignition system.

1. Connect and disconnect test equipment only when the ignition switch is OFF.
2. On the carbureted Rabbit, if you use a conventional tachometer, you will have to rig up an adapter. See below for instructions.
3. Do not crank the engine with the starter for compression tests, etc., until the high tension coil wire (terminal 4) is grounded.
4. Do not replace the original equipment coil (Part No. 211 905 115 B) with a conventional coil.
5. Do not install any kind of condenser to coil terminal 1.
6. Do not use a battery booster for longer than 1 (one) minute.
7. On the fuel injected models, do not tow cars with defective ignitions systems without disconnecting the plugs on the idle stabilizer at the ignition control unit.

TACHOMETER ADAPTATION (CARBURETED RABBITS)

An adapter must be used when connecting a conventional tachometer to the Hall Effect ignition system to prevent damage to the ignition components. Use the illustration as a guide. All components will be available to you locally. Connect the positive wire of the tachometer to the adapter and the negative wire to the ground.

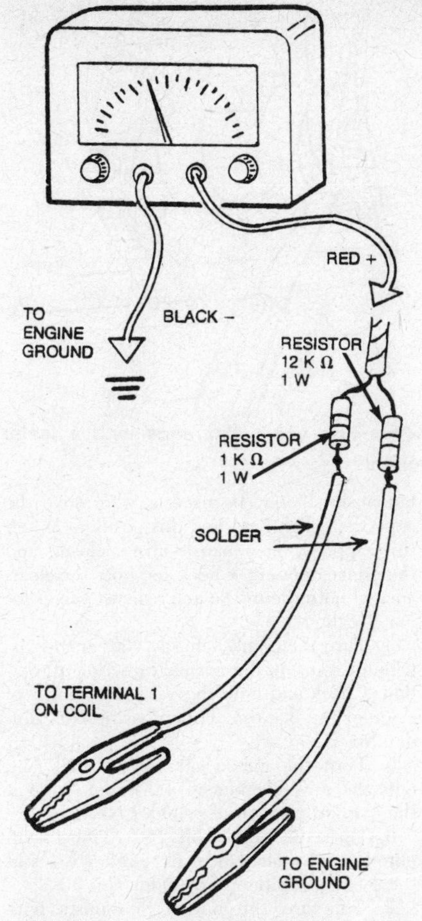

Adapter for hooking a tachometer up to 1980 carbureted Rabbit with electronic ignition

IGNITION COIL TEST

A defective Hall ignition coil cannot be checked with standard coil testing equipment. If there is no high tension current and all other components of the igntion system check out, see if you're getting a spark from the coil wire to the distributor cap by unplugging the coil wire at the distributor, holding the end of it with insulated pliers about ½ in. from ground (engine block, etc.) and turning over the engine. If a weak or no spark is obtained, try replacing the coil.

HALL PICKUP UNIT TEST

1. Check for voltage on terminal 15 (+) of the igntion coil. There should be voltage with the ignition ON.
2. Ground a high tension coil wire.
3. Connect a test light (4 to 24 volts) between terminal 15 (+) and terminal 1 (−).
4. Crank the engine with the starter for approximately 5 seconds, The test light should flicker. If not, replace the ignition distributor.

IGNITION CONTROL UNIT TEST

1. On fuel injected models, disconnect the plugs at the control unit and connect the plugs to each other. Ground high tension coil wire on carbureted Rabbit.

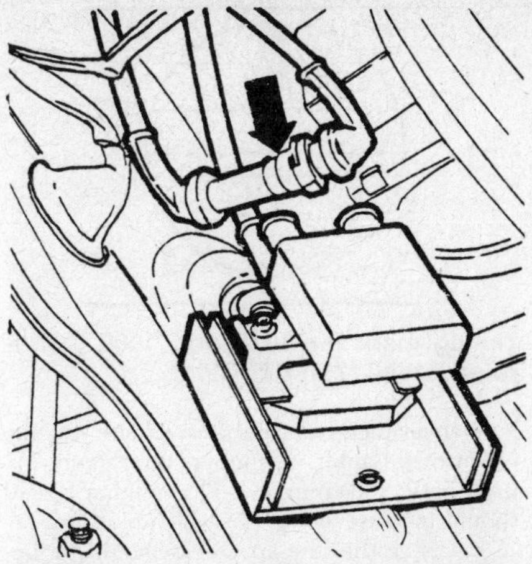

Disconnect the plugs on the idle stabilizer at the control unit and plug them together

2. Turn the ignition switch on and make sure there is current at terminal 15 (−) of the ignition col. Turn the ignition OFF.
3. Disconnect the high tension wire between the ignition coil and the distributor at the distributor on fuel injected models.
4. Disconnect the wire (plug) between the control unit and the distributor at the distributor.
5. Connect the positive (+) terminal of the voltmeter to terminal 1 of the ignition coil and the negative (−) terminal to ground.
6. Turn the ignition ON. There must be a voltage reading of at least 12 volts. If voltage drops below 12 volts in one second, turn off the ignition. The control unit is defective and will have to be replaced.
7. Disconnect the green wire where it connects to the distributor and ground the wire. Turn the ignition switch ON. The voltmeter should read about 12 volts. Disconnect the ground wire. The voltage should drop to 6 volts. If not, replace the control unit. Turn off the ignition.
8. On fuel injected models, connect the terminals of the voltmeter to the outer connector of the control unit. Connect the positive (+) lead to the red wire and the negative (−) lead to the brown wire. Switch on the ignition. The voltmeter should read about 10 volts. If not, replace the control unit.

IDLE STABILIZER

The idle stabilizer is located on top of the ignition control unit. The idle stabilizer controls idle speed by either advancing or retarding the distributor timing in accordance with engine load (air conditioner on, lights on, etc.) If idle speed is erratic or if the engine fails to start, try bypassing the idle stabilizer by disconnecting the two plugs at the idle stabilizer and plugging them together. If idle improves, the idle stabilizer should probably be replaced.

Ignition Timing

BREAKER-POINT IGNITION SYSTEMS

1. Attach the timing light as outlined above or according to the manufacturer's instruc-

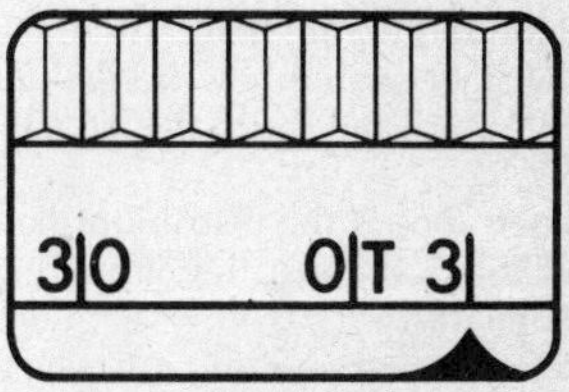

Dasher timing marks aligned at 3°ATDC

ELECTRONIC IGNITION TESTING SPECIFICATIONS

Component Tested	Specification
Rotor resistance	5000 ohms
Plug wire resistance	
With radio	800-1200 ohms
W/O radio	0 ohms
Spark Plug Connector resistance	
Suppressed	4000-6000 ohms
Not suppressed	800-1200 ohms
Air gap ①	0.25 mm (0.010 in.)
Inductive signal resistance ②	890-1285 ohms
Resistance from the coil tower to the negative coil terminal	5500-8000 ohms
Resistance from the coil positive terminal to the coil negative terminal	0.95-1.50 ohms
Vacuum retard	8°-10°
Vacuum advance	4°-8°
Centrifugal advance	6°-12°

① Air gap is adjustable by bending the teeth on the stator (reluctor)
② Measure resistance between the connectors to the control unit on the distributor (connects to the green and white wires)

Timing window for Dasher

tions. Hook-up a dwell/tachometer since you'll need an rpm indication for correct timing.

2. Locate the timing mark opening in the clutch or torque converter housing at the rear of the engine directly behind the distributor. The OT mark stands for TDC or 0° advance. The other mark designates the correct timing position. Mark them with chalk so that they will be more visible. Don't disconnect the vacuum line.

NOTE: Some models do not have an OT mark.

3. Start the engine and allow it to reach the normal operating temperature. The engine should be running at normal idle speed.

4. Shine the timing light at the marks.

5. The light should now be flashing when the timing mark and the V-shaped pointer are aligned.

6. If not, loosen the distributor hold-down bolt and rotate the distributor very slowly to align the marks.

7. Tighten the mounting nut when the ignition timing is correct.

8. Recheck the timing when the distributor is secured.

With ignition timing correctly adjusted, the spark plugs will fire at the exact instant in which the piston is nearing the top of the compression stroke, thus providing maximum power and economy.

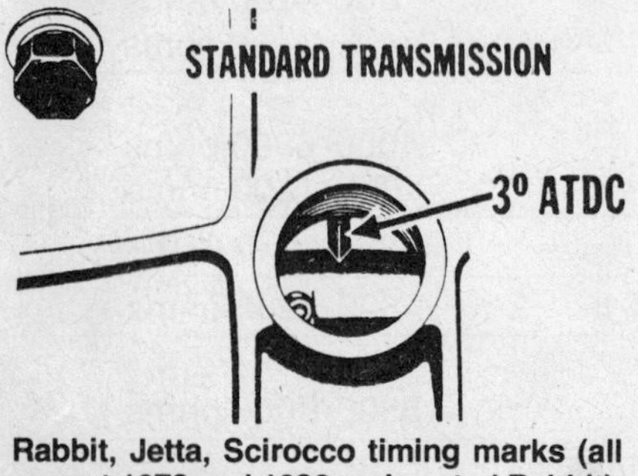

Rabbit, Jetta, Scirocco timing marks (all except 1978 and 1980 carbureted Rabbit). Manual transmission shown

ELECTRONIC IGNITION SYSTEMS

1. Run the engine to operating temperature. Connect tachometer. See "Electronic Ignition Precautions," above.

2. Stop the engine. Disconnect the plugs on the idle stabilizer at the control unit and

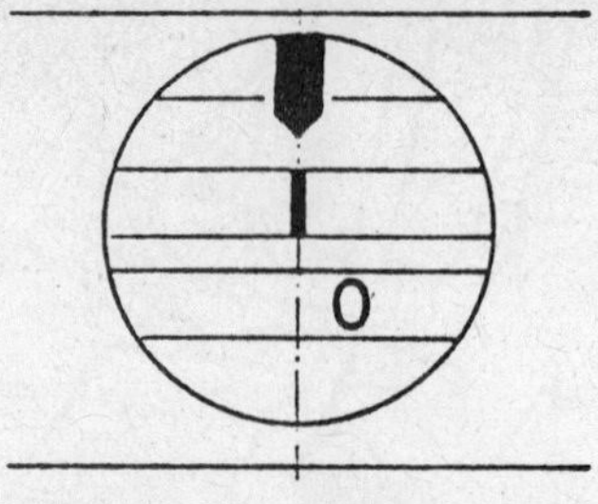

Timing mark for 1978 and 1980 carbureted Rabbit (7½° BTDC)

plug them together (see illustration). On the carbureted Rabbit, disconnect the vacuum retard hose and plug it. The engine speed should increase as the hose is unplugged.

3. Check the idle speed. It should be between 800 and 1000 rpm.

4. With your timing light attached according to manufacturers instructions, and shine to light on the timing hole. The pointer in the hole must line up with the notch in the flywheel. To adjust the timing, loosen the distributor at its base and turn it.

5. On the carbureted Rabbit, reinstall the vacuum retard hose. Idle speed should drop to 600-750 rpm.

6. Stop the engine and reconnect the plugs at the control unit. On the carbureted Rabbit, start the engine and rev it a few times to activate the idle stabilizer. On the carbureted Rabbit, the idle speed should now be 850-950 rpm.

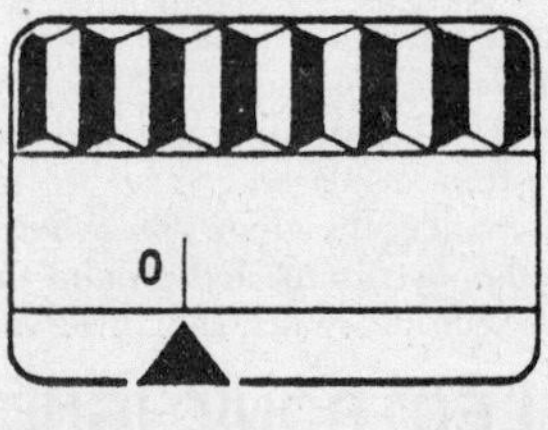

1980 electronic ignition Dashers have only one mark for correct timing (3° ATDC)

Valve Lash

Check the valve clearance every 20,000 miles in firing order, with the engine at normal operating temperature.

1. Remove the camshaft cover and the distributor cap.

2. Set the engine at TDC on No. 1 cylinder by aligning the 0°T mark on the flywheel with the pointer and aligning the distributor rotor with the No. 1 cylinder mark on the rim of the distributor body.

NOTE: Always turn the crankshaft in the normal direction of rotation. There is a hole in the body behind the front license plate through which a wrench can be used on the crankshaft on the Dasher. Do not turn the engine by means of the timing belt (or camshaft bolt), because the belt will stretch or lose teeth.

3. The valve clearances of cylinder No. 1 should be checked when the valves of No. 4 cylinder overlap, i.e. when both No. 4 cylinder valves move in opposite directions simultaneously. It may be necessary to move the crankshaft slightly to find this position. When this happens, the exhaust valve is closing and the intake opening. Check and note the clearance of both the intake and exhaust valves for No. 1 cylinder.

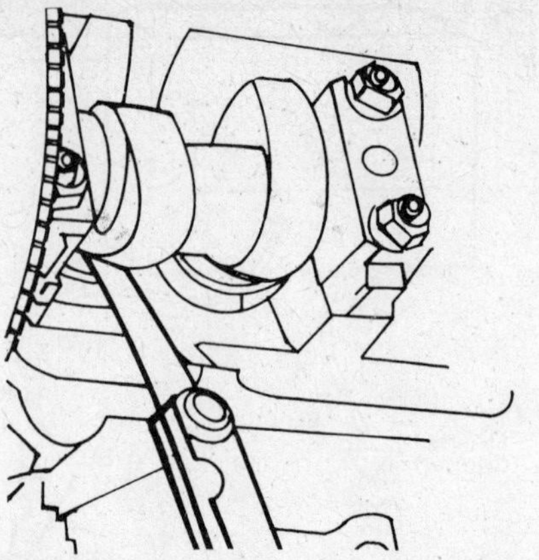

Checking valve clearance with a feeler gauge

4. Turn the crankshaft 180° (90° at the distributor rotor) in the normal direction of rotation. Check and note the valve clearances of cylinder No. 3 at the overlap position of cylinder No. 2.

5. Turn the crankshaft 180°. Check and note the valve clearances of cylinder No. 4 at the overlap position of cylinder No. 1.

6. Turn the crankshaft 180°. Check and note the valve clearances of cylinder No. 2 at the overlap position of cylinder No. 3.

7. Compare the noted clearances with those listed in the Tune-Up Specifications Chart. Adjustment is made by replacing the tappet clearance disc in the top of each tappet. These are available in 26 sizes ranging from 3.0 mm (0.119 in.) to 4.25 mm (0.166 in.) in increments of 0.05 mm (0.002 in.). The thickness of each disc is marked on the bottom.

NOTE: If a valve clearance deviates 0.002 in. or less from the specified clearance, it need not be adjusted.

8. To remove a tappet clearance disc, turn the cylinder to TDC and press down the tappet so that the disc can be lifted out.

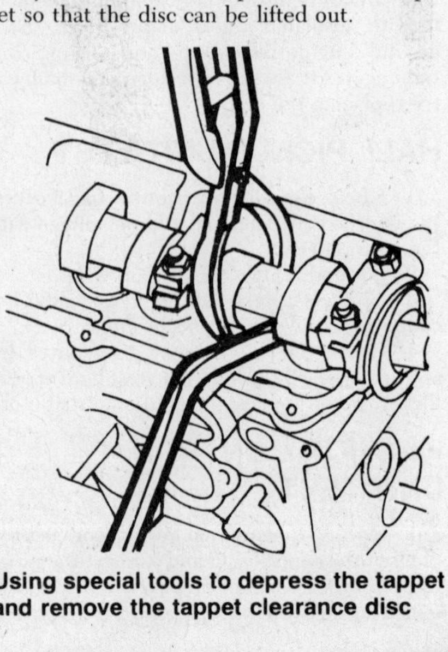

Using special tools to depress the tappet and remove the tappet clearance disc

NOTE: When adjusting clearances on a diesel, the pistons must not be at TDC. Turn the crankshaft ¼ turn past TDC, so that the valves do not contact the pistons when the tappets are depressed.

A special tool is available from VW for this operation. Once the disc is removed, check its size and determine what size will be needed to produce the required adjustment.

9. Install the required disc. When all the clearances have been corrected, recheck valve clearances.

Carburetor

The Dasher carburetor is a Zenith 2B3 in 1975, with a vacuum operated secondary barrel. The 1975-76 Rabbit and Scirocco use a Zenith 32/32-2B2 two barrel carburetor with a vacuum operated secondary barrel and dual floats. Some 1978 and 1980 Rabbits are equipped with the 34 PICT-5 single barrel carburetor.

IDLE SPEED ADJUSTMENT

Solex 32/35 DIDTA Carburetor, Zenith 2B2 And 2B3 Carburetors

1. Start the engine and run it until normal operating temperature is reached.
2. Hook-up a tachometer to the engine and observe the idle speed.
3. If the idle speed is not as specified, turn the curb idle screw to correct it. Make sure that you are turning the correct screw. Do not mistake the idle mixture screw for the curb idle screw.

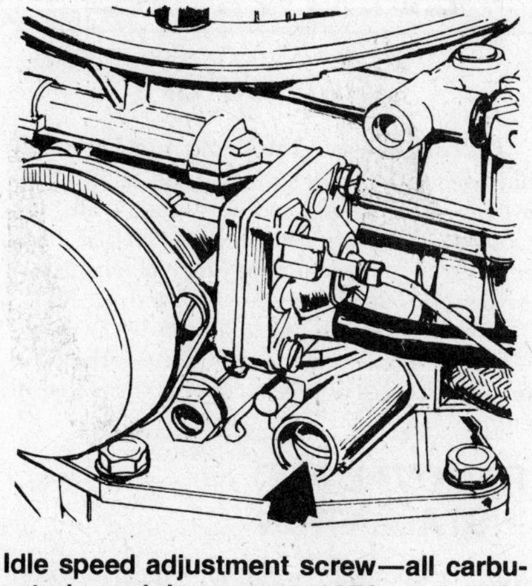

Idle speed adjustment screw—all carbureted models except 1978 and 1980 Rabbit

Solex 34 PICT-5 Carburetor

1978 RABBIT

The choke must be fully open and the engine at normal operating temperature.

1. Remove the hose from the charcoal filter at the air intake elbow. Plug the hose.
2. Remove the air injection hose at the air cleaner. Plug the hose.
3. Make sure no electrical equipment is ON. In particular the cooling fan must be OFF.
4. Connect a tachometer. Adjust the idle speed to specifications at the idle speed adjusting screw (A). The CO content can be adjusted at screw (B) if a CO meter is available.

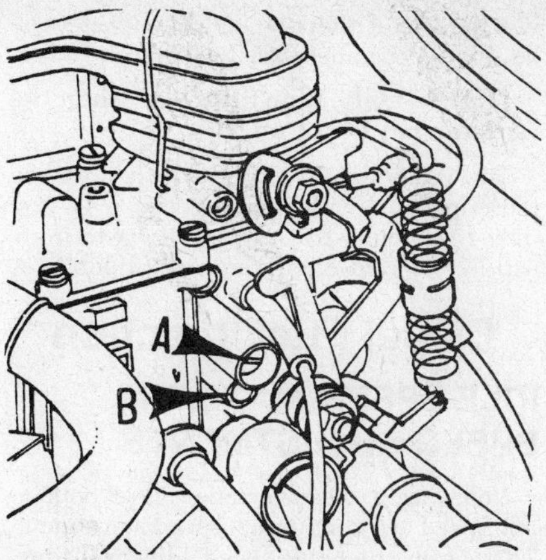

Idle speed screw (A) and idle mixture screw (B)—1978 and 1980 carbureted Rabbit

5. Disconnect the tachometer and reconnect 11 hoses.

1980 RABBIT

1. The engine must be at operating temperature and the choke must be fully open.
2. Remove the two hoses from the carburetor air intake elbow and plug the two hose inlets in the elbow. The air intake elbow sits right on top of the carburetor.
3. Remove both of the air injection hoses at the air injection valves, located side by side in the front middle of the engine. Plug the air injection valves.
4. Shut off all electrical equipment, including the air conditioner (if installed).
5. Connect a tachometer, timing light and CO meter (if available) to the engine.

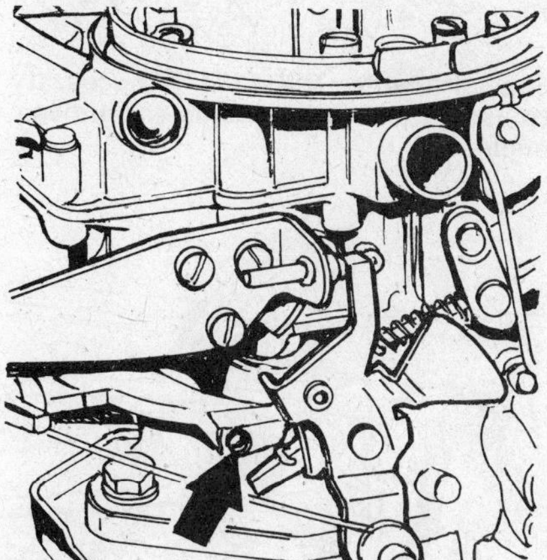

Idle mixture adjustment screw—all except 1978 and 1980 carbureted Rabbit

CAUTION

See "Tachometer Adaptation (Carbureted Rabbits)," under the electronic ignition section, above, for method of connecting tachometer. If you do not follow these instructions, you will damage your ignition system.

6. Start the engine. Rev the engine a few times to start the idle stabilizer.
7. Check the idle; it should be 850-950 rpm. If the idle is not correct, disconnect the plugs at the control unit and plug them together (see electronic ignition system, above).
8. Remove the vacuum advance and retard hoses, then plug the hoses.
9. Adjust the idle speed to 800-1000 rpm at the idle adjustment screw. Check the timing, see above section for procedures.
10. If the timing was off, recheck the idle speed.
11. Reconnect the advance and retard hoses. Adjust the CO lever at the CO adjusting screw to 0.5-1.1%.
12. Reconnect the plugs at the control unit.
13. Rev the engine to reactivate idle stabilizer and check the idle speed and CO. Idle speed should be 850-950 rpm, CO should be 0.5-1.5%.
14. If the idle speed is still not correct, replace the control unit or the idle stabilizer.

IDLE MIXTURE ADJUSTMENT

This adjustment should only be performed with a CO meter.

Rabbit, Scirocco And Dasher

1. Run the engine until it reaches normal operating temperature.
2. Check the ignition timing and idle speed are as specified.
3. Adjust the CO level with the idle mixture screw.

1978 And 1980 Rabbit

Mixture adjustment is contained in the idle speed adjustment procedure, above.

CIS Fuel Injection

IDLE AND CO ADJUSTMENT

All Except 1980 California And 1981 Models

The following adjustments can be made *only* with a CO meter and the CO adjusting tool (VW-P377).

1. Run the engine until it reaches normal operating temperature.
2. Adjust the ignition timing to specification with the vacuum hoses connected and the engine at idle.
3. Adjust the idle speed to specification.
4. Remove the charcoal filter hose from the air cleaner except on Canadian models.
5. Turn on the headlight high beams.
6. Remove the plug from the CO adjusting

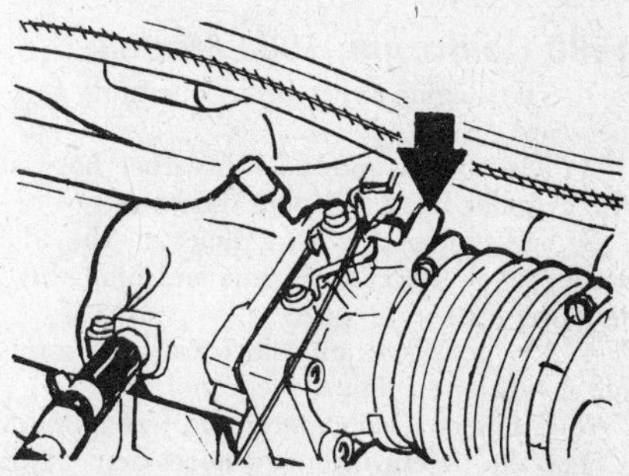

Idle speed adjustment screw—fuel injected Rabbit, Jetta, Scirocco

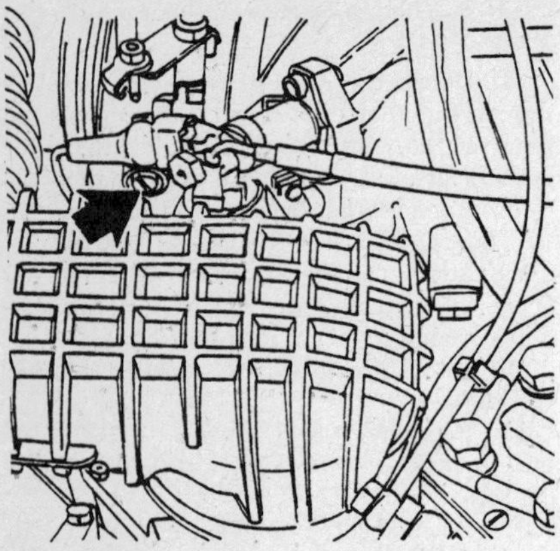

Idle speed adjustment screw—fuel injected Dasher

hole and insert adjustment tool VW-P377. Turn the adjustment screw clockwise to raise the percentage of CO and counterclockwise to lower the percentage of CO.

CAUTION

Do not push the adjustment tool down or accelerate the engine with the tool in place.

7. Remove the tool after each adjustment and accelerate the engine briefly before reading the percentage of CO. The correct CO values are as follows:

49 States: 1976-78 1.5% M/T; 1.0% A/T
1979-80 0.6+0.4%
California: 1976: 0.5%
1977-78: 0.3%
1979: 0.5+0.4%

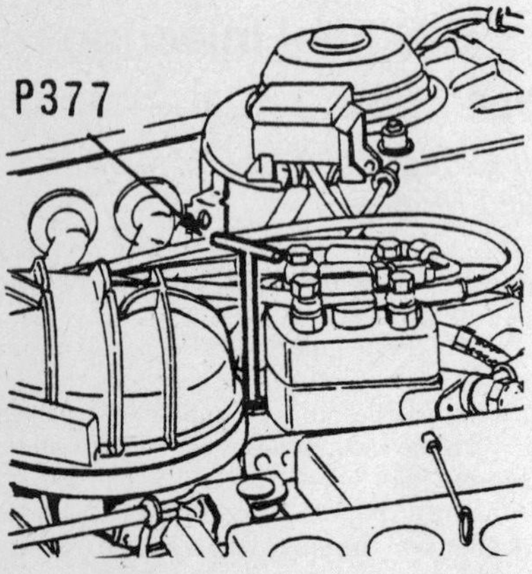

CO adjusting tool installed—CIS fuel injection (Rabbit, Jetta, Scirocco shown)

1980 California, 1981 Models

1. The engine must be at operating temperature.
2. Disconnect crankcase breather hose at the cylinder head and plug the hose.
3. Disconnect the two plugs on the idle stabilizer at the control unit and plug them together.
4. Do not have any electrical accessories (air conditioner, lights, etc.) on.
5. Connect a tachometer and timing light. Check the timing. Adjust if necessary.
6. Check the idle speed against the specifications chart or your underhood sticker. Adjust the idle at the idle adjustment screw on he throttle chamber (880-1000 rpm).

NOTE: Only adjust the idle when the radiator fan is not on.

The only way CO levels can be adjusted on these model is with special dealer tools (frequency counter, CO tester, etc.) which are usually not available to the general public.

Diesel Fuel Injection

IDLE SPEED/MAXIMUM SPEED ADJUSTMENTS

Volkswagen diesel engines have both an idle speed and a maximum speed adjustment. The maximum engine speed adjustment prevents the engine from over-revving and swallowing itself whole. The adjusters are located side by side on top of the injection pump. The screw closest to the engine is the idle speed adjuster, while the outer screw is the maximum speed adjuster.

The idle and maximum speed must be adjusted with the engine warm (normal operating temperature). Because the diesel engine has no conventional ignition, you will need a special adaptor (VW 1324) to connect your tachometer, or use the tachometer in the instrument panel, if equipped. You should check with the manufacturer of your tachometer to see if it will work with diesel engines. Adjust all engines to 770-870 rpm (through 1980) or 800-850 rpm (1981).

Special adapter VW 1324 is necessary to use an external tachometer on diesel engines

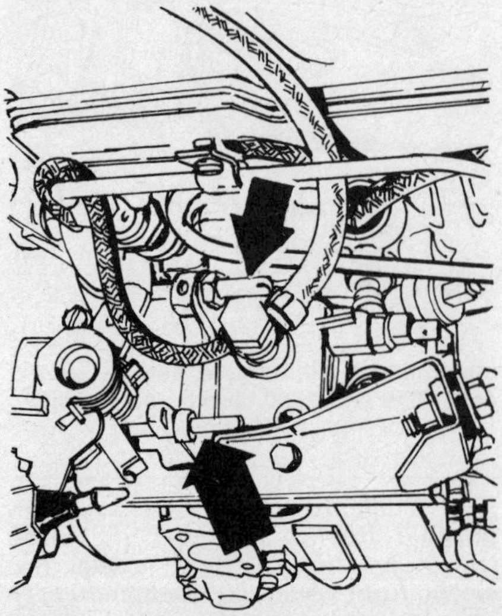

Diesel engine idle speed (upper) and maximum speed (lower) adjustment screws

NOTE: The sticker on your pre-1978 Rabbit may indicate an idle range of 850-950 rpm. This has been altered by Volkswagen to 770-870 rpm.

When adjustment is correct, lock the locknut on the screw and apply a dab of paint or non-hardening thread sealer to prevent the screw from vibrating loose.

The maximum speed for all engines is between 5500 and 5600 rpm (through 1980) or 5300-5400 rpm (1981). If it is not in this range, loosen the screw and correct the speed (turning the screw clockwise decreases rpm). Lock the nut on the adjusting screw and apply a dab of paint in the same manner as you did on the idle screw.

CAUTION

Do not attempt to squeeze more power out of your engine by raising the maximum speed. If you do, you'll probably be in for a major overhaul in the not too distant future.

ENGINE ELECTRICAL

Distributor

The distributor is a single breaker point unit on all 1975-79 models, and some 1980 models. Electronic ignition is used on all 1981 models and some 1980 models. It has both centrifugal and vacuum advance mechanisms. A vacuum retard system works only at idle.

The distributor is gear driven by an intermediate shaft which also drives the fuel pump. The distributor shaft also turns lhe oil pump.

REMOVAL AND INSTALLATION

1. Disconnect the coil high tension wire.

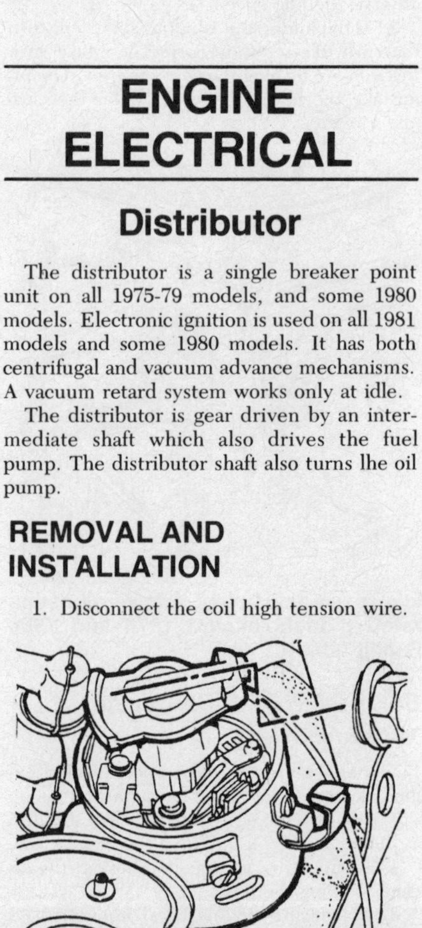

Rotor alignment with the notch for No. 1 cylinder

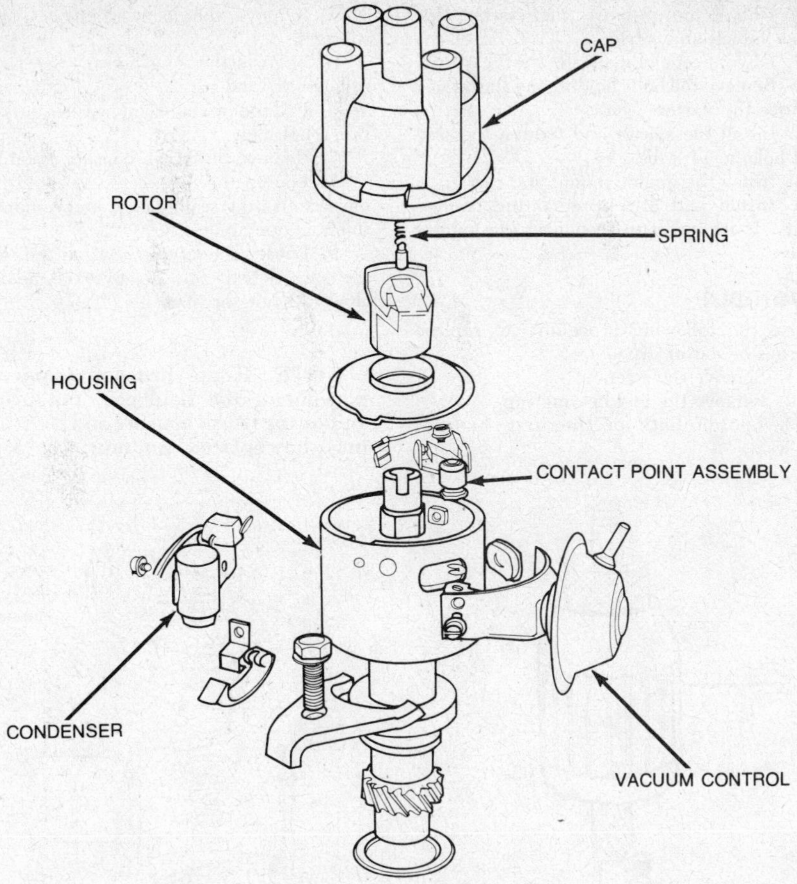

Point type distributor

2. Detach the primary wire.
3. Remove the distributor cap.
4. Turn the engine until the rotor aligns with the index mark on the outer edge of the distributor. This is the No. 1 position. Mark the bottom of the distributor housing and its mounting flange on the engine.
5. Remove the bolt and lift off the retaining flange. Lift the distributor straight out of the engine.

If the engine has not been disturbed while the distributor was out i.e., the crankshaft was not turned, then reinstall the distributor in the reverse order of removal. Carefully align the marks.

If the engine has been rotated while the distributor was out, then proceed as follows:

1. Turn the crankshaft so that No. 1 piston is on its compression stroke and the 0°T timing mark is aligned with the V-shaped pointer.
2. Turn the distributor so that the rotor points approximately 15° before the No. 1 cylinder position on the distributor.
3. Insert the distributor into the engine block. If the oil pump drive doesn't engage, remove the distributor and, using a long screwdriver turn the pump shaft so that it is parallel to the centerline of the crankshaft.
4. Install the distributor, aligning the marks. Tighten the retaining nut.
5. Install the cap. Adjust the ignition timing.

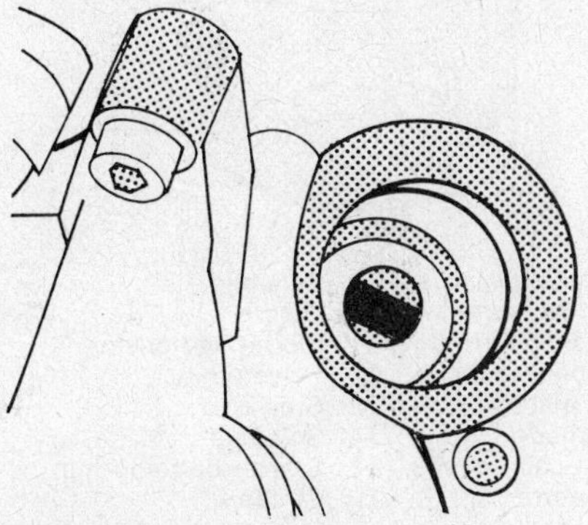

The oil pump drive should be parallel to the crankshaft

Alternator

ALTERNATOR PRECAUTIONS

An alternating current (AC) generator (alternator) is used. Unlike the direct current (DC) generators used in many older cars, there are several precautions which must be strictly observed in order to avoid damaging the unit.

1. Reversing the battery connections will result in damage to the diodes.
2. Booster batteries should be connected from negative to negative, and positive to positive.
3. Never use a fast charger as a booster to start cars with AC circuits.
4. When servicing the battery with a fast charger, always disconnect the car battery cables.
5. Never attempt to polarize an AC generator.
6. Avoid long soldering times when replacing diodes or transistors. Prolonged heat is damaging to AC generators.
7. Do not use test lamps of more than 12 volts (V) for checking diode continuity.
8. Do not short across or ground any of the terminals on the AC generator.
9. The polarity of the battery, generator, and regulator must be matched and considered before making any electrical connections within the system.
10. Never operate the AC generator on an open circuit. Make sure that all connections within the circuit are clean and tight.
11. Disconnect the battery terminals when performing any service on the electrical system. This will eliminate the possibility of accidental reversal of polarity.
12. Disconnect the battery ground cable if arc welding is to be done on any part of the car.

REMOVAL AND INSTALLATION

The alternator and voltage regulator are combined in one housing. No voltage adjustment can be made with this unit. The regulator can be replaced without removing the alternator. Unbolt the regulator and remove from the rear.

1. Disconnect the battery cables.
2. Remove the multi-connector retaining bracket and unplug the connector from the rear of the alternator.
3. Loosen and remove the top mounting nut and bolt.

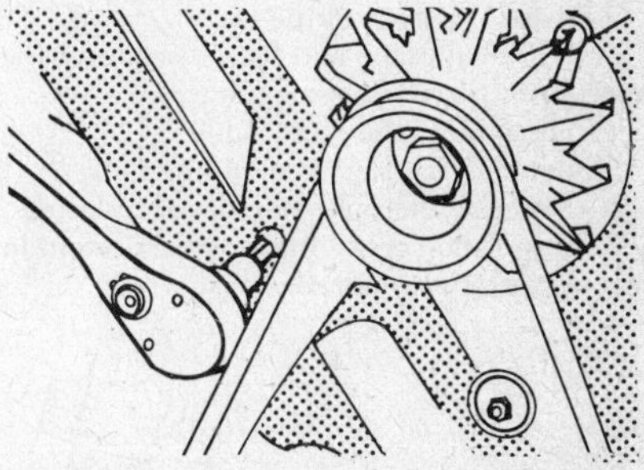

Removing the lower alternator bolt through the timing cover

4. Using a socket inserted through the timing belt cover (it is not necessary to remove the cover), loosen the lower mounting bolt.
5. Swing the alternator over and remove the alternator belt.
6. Remove the lower nut and bolt.
7. Remove the alternator.
8. Install the alternator with the lower bolt. *Do not* tighten it at this point.
9. Install the alternator belt over the pulleys.
10. Loosely install the top mounting bolt and pivot the alternator until the belt is correctly tensioned.
11. Tighten the top and bottom bolts to 14 ft/lbs.
12. Connect the alternator and battery wires.

BELT REPLACEMENT AND TENSIONING

1. Loosen the top alternator mounting bolt.
2. Using a socket inserted through the timing belt cover loosen the lower mounting bolt.
3. Use a wooden hammer handle or a broomstick to lever the alternator over and remove the belt.
4. Slip the new belt over the pulleys.
5. Pry the alternator over until the belt deflection midway between the crankshaft pulley and the alternator pulley is $3/8$-$9/16$ in. (10-15 mm).
6. Securely tighten the mounting bolts.

STARTER

Beginning approximately July 1975, a new type of starter is used on the manual transmission Rabbit and Scirocco which is not interchangeable with the old design. The new starter does not need a rear support bracket. The old type starter is used on all automatic transmission cars up to chassis No. 175 3 439 592 (Rabbit) or 535 2 058 507 (Scirocco).

On the Jetta, all automatic transmission models use the "old" type starter while the manual transmission models use the "new" type.

On the Dasher, all models, both automatic and manual transmission, use the "new" type starter.

REMOVAL AND INSTALLATION

All Models Except Dasher Diesel

1. Disconnect the battery ground cable.
2. Raise the front of the car.
3. Mark with tape and then disconnect the wires from the starter solenoid.
4. Disconnect the large cable.
5. Remove the starter retaining nuts.
6. Unscrew the bolt. Remove the starter.
7. Installation of the starter is carried out in reverse order of removal.

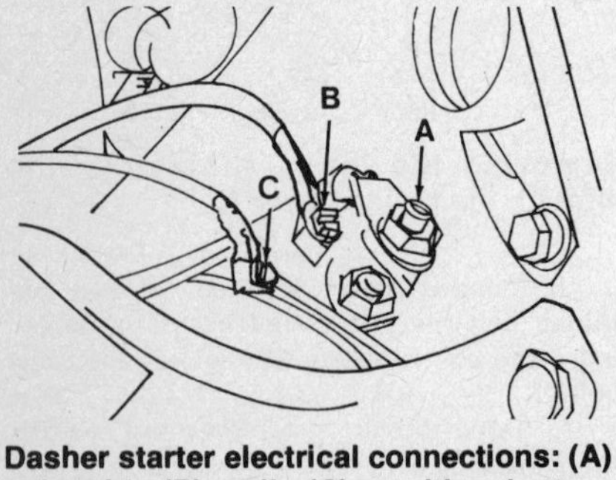

Dasher starter electrical connections: (A) solenoid, (B) coil, (C) positive battery cable

Dasher Diesel

1. Disconnect the battery ground cable.
2. Support the weight of the engine with either Volkswagen special tool 10-222 or use a jack with a block of wood under the oil pan. Don't jack the engine too high, just take the weight off the motor mounts. Be careful not to bend the oil pan.
3. Remove the engine/transmission cover plate.
4. Unbolt and remove the starter side motor mount and carrier.
5. Disconnect and mark the starter wiring.
6. Remove the bolts holding the starter and remove the starter.
7. Install the starter and tighten the nuts and bolts to 14 ft/lbs.
8. Install the engine mount and carrier.
9. Install and attach remaining components. Don't forget to reconnect the battery cable.

Overhaul

Use the following procedure to replace brushes or starter drive.

1. Remove the solenoid.
2. Remove the end bearing cap.
3. Loosen both of the long housing screws.
4. Remove the lockwasher and spacer washers.
5. Remove the long housing screws and remove the end cover.
6. Pull the two field coil brushes out of the brush housing.
7. Remove the brush housing assembly.
8. Loosen the nut on the solenoid housing, remove the sealing disc, and remove the solenoid operating lever.
9. Loosen the large screws on the side of the starter body and remove the field coil along with the brushes.

NOTE: If the brushes require replacement, the field coil and brushes and/or the brush housing and its brushes must be replaced as a unit.

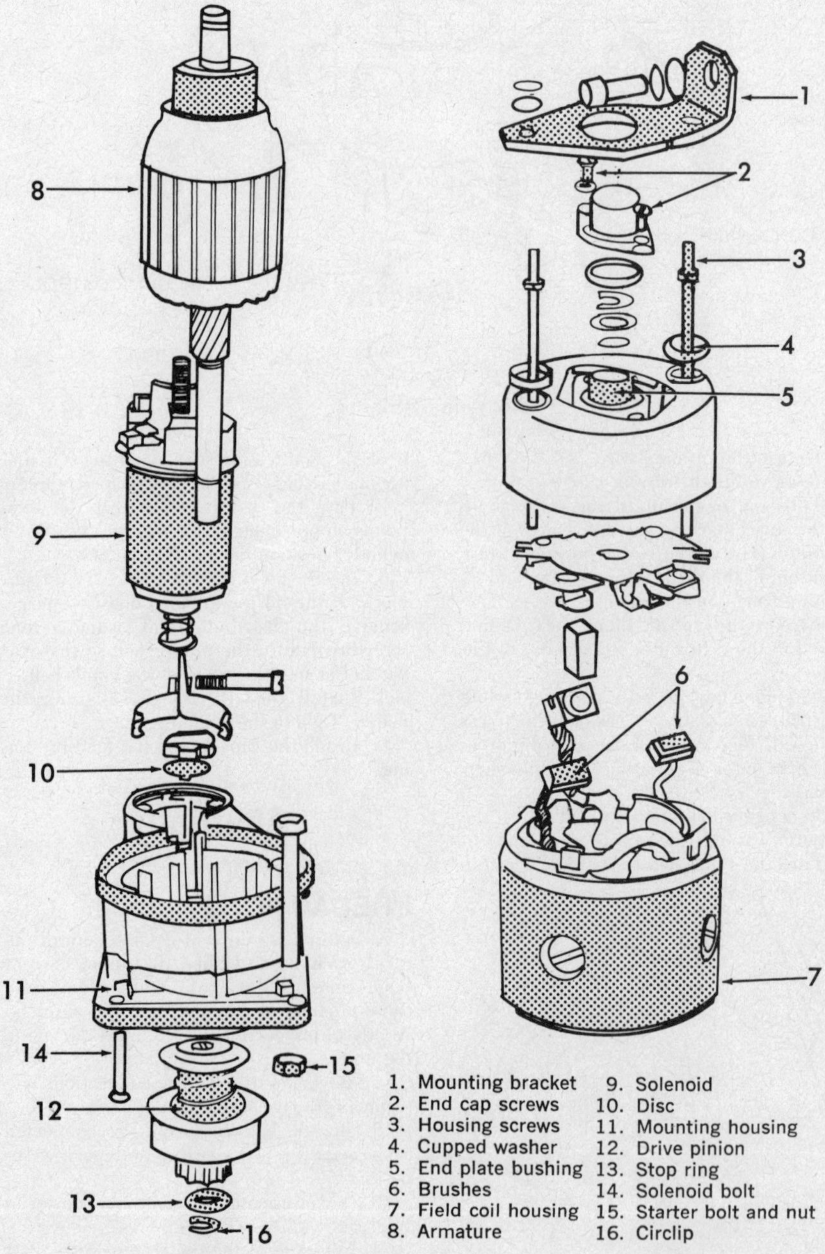

1. Mounting bracket
2. End cap screws
3. Housing screws
4. Cupped washer
5. End plate bushing
6. Brushes
7. Field coil housing
8. Armature
9. Solenoid
10. Disc
11. Mounting housing
12. Drive pinion
13. Stop ring
14. Solenoid bolt
15. Starter bolt and nut
16. Circlip

Exploded view of new type starter

New type
(Part No. 055–911–023B)

Old type
(Part No. 055–911–023)

New and old type starters are not interchangeable. See text for identification

10. If the starter drive is being replaced on all Dasher and Jetta and new type Rabbit and Scirocco starters, push the stop-ring down and remove the circlip on the end of the shaft. Remove the stop-ring and remove the drive.

11. To remove the starter drive on old type Rabbit and Scirocco starters, remove the armature and pull the drive unit off the end.

12. Assembly of the starter is carried out in the reverse order of disassembly. Use a gear puller to install the stop-ring in its groove (on models so equipped). Use a new circlip on the shaft.

SOLENOID REPLACEMENT

1. Remove the starter.
2. Remove the nut which secures the connector strip on the end of the solenoid.
3. Take out the two retaining screws on the mounting bracket and pull out the solenoid after it has been unhooked from the operating lever.
4. Installation is the reverse of removal. In order to facilitate engagement of the lever, the pinion should be pulled out as far as possible when inserting the solenoid.

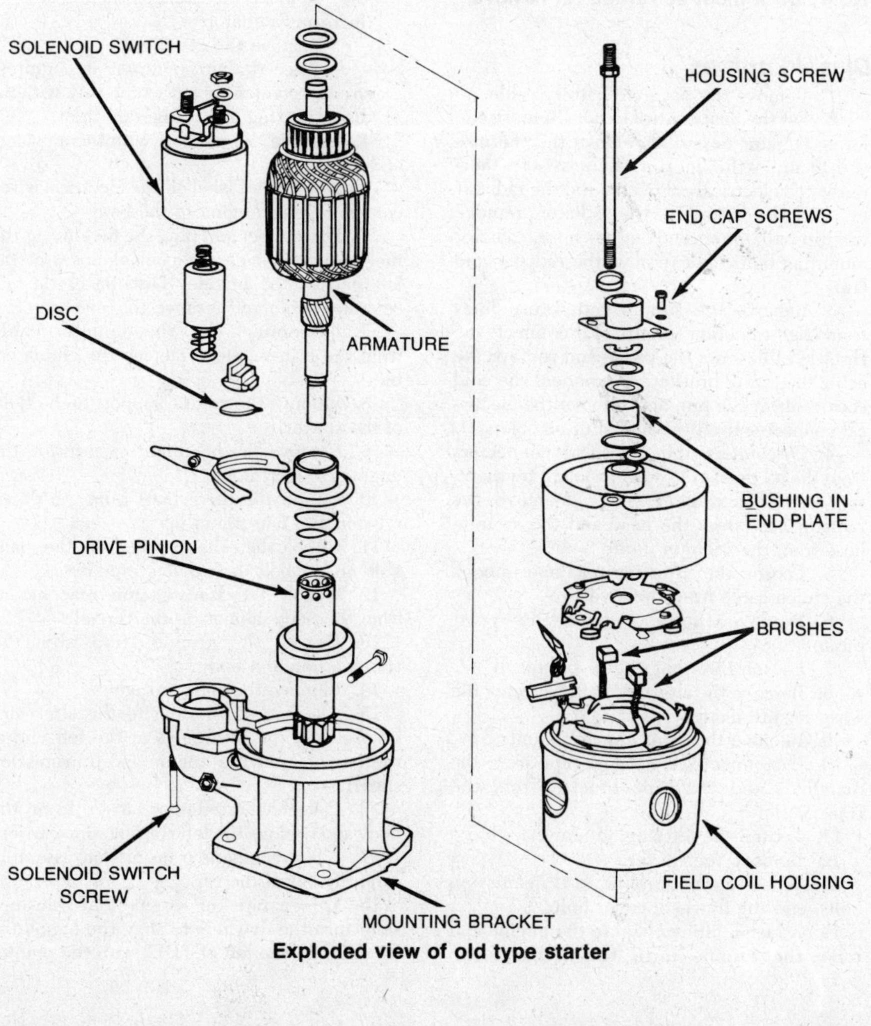

Exploded view of old type starter

ENGINE MECHANICAL

The engine is an inline four cylinder unit with single overhead camshaft. It is inclined 30° to the right (to the rear in the Rabbit and Scirocco). The crankshaft runs in five bearings with thrust taken on the center bearing. The cylinder block is cast iron. A steel reinforced rubber belt drives the intermediate shaft and camshaft. The intermediate shaft drives the oil pump, distributor and fuel pump.

The cylinder head is lightweight aluminum alloy. The intake and exhaust manifolds are mounted on the same side of the cylinder head. The valves are opened and closed by camshaft lobes operating on cupped cam followers which fit over the valves and springs. This design results in lighter valve train weight and fewer moving parts.

VW introduced the diesel engine option on 1977 Rabbit models and 1979 Dashers.

The key difference between the gasoline and diesel engine is that the diesel has no carburetor and no electrical ignition system. There are no plugs, points or coil to replace. Combustion occurs when a fine mist of diesel fuel is sprayed into hot compressed air (1650° F) under high pressure (850 psi). The air is heated by the compression as the piston moves up on the compression stroke. The diesel engine has a compression ratio of 23.5:1 compared to the gasoline engine's compression ratio of 8.2:1.

VW's diesel block, flywheel, bearings and crankshaft are identical to those in the Rabbit gasoline engine. The connecting rod wrist pins were strengthened and new pistons and cylinder head, made of aluminum for lightness, were designed.

Engine Removal and Installation

DASHER

Gasoline Engines

1. Disconnect the battery cables.
2. Remove the exhaust manifold heater hose and breather hose from the air cleaner.
3. Remove the air cleaner assembly.
4. On carbureted models, pull the clip off the accelerator cable and detach the cable. On fuel injected models, disconnect the electrical connector for the fuel injection and detach the control pressure regulator lines.
5. Loosen the upper adjustment nut on the clutch cable and detach it.
6. On carbureted models only, disconnect the fuel line from the fuel pump, plug it, and place it out of the way. On fuel injected models, disconnect the air duct. Remove the cold start valve. Remove the fuel injectors from the head and the accelerator cable. Remove the air flow sensor with the fuel distributor and place out of the way.
7. Detach emission control hoses.
8. On 1974 models, disconnect relay plate fuse box. Bend the harness clip open.
9. Disconnect the wiring from the alternator.

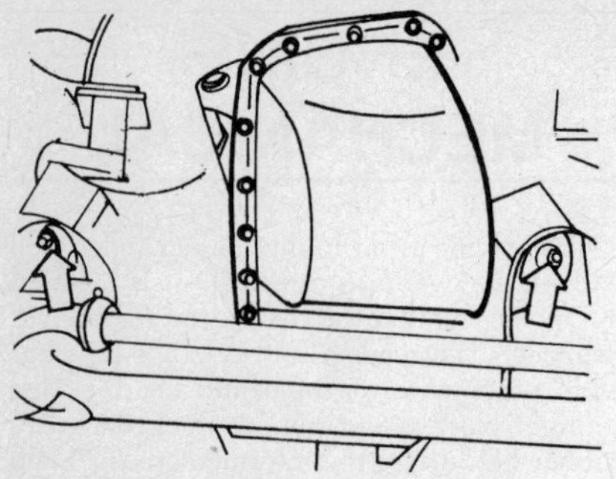

Dasher engine side mounts

10. Detach the clip and remove the heater cable.

CAUTION

Do not disconnect refrigerant lines on cars equipped with air conditioning.

11. On cars with air conditioning:
a. Remove the horn, compressor and condenser assemblies.
b. Move the compressor and condensers out of the way, without disconnecting the refrigerant lines.
c. Disconnect the vacuum hoses and brake booster hose, if equipped.
12. Disconnect the front engine mount and remove the mount bracket.
13. Drain the coolant from the radiator. The plug is located near the lower hose, or remove the hose on models without the drain plug. Drain the cylinder block at the plug near the starter.
14. Disconnect the electrical wire from the coil and distributor, oil pressure and temperature sending units, fan and the thermal switch on the radiator.
15. Disconnect the radiator and heater hoses from the engine. Detach the heater valve cable.
16. Loosen the radiator shroud retainers. Remove the mounting bolts and nuts and lift out the radiator and fan.
17. Raise the front of the car and safely support it.
18. Remove the starter.
19. Disconnect the exhaust pipe from the manifold.
20. Detach the engine side mounts.
21. Loosen the upper engine-to-transmission bolts. Remove the lower bolts. If the car is equipped with an automatic transmission, remove the three torque converter-to-flywheel bolts by working through the starter hole. Use a bar to hold the flywheel. Also disconnect the automatic transmission vacuum hose.
22. Support the transmission with a floor jack.
23. Lower the car until the wheels are on the ground.
24. Attach the hoist to the engine lift points.
25. Raise the engine/transmission until the transmission touches the steering rack.
26. Adjust your jack or support so that the transmission is held firmly.
27. Remove the upper engine-to-transmission bolts.
28. Pry the engine and transmission apart and remove the intermediate plate. Install a bar or cable to the torque converter housing on automatic cars to prevent the converter from falling out.
29. Remove the engine by slowly lifting and turning simultaneously.

CAUTION

Do this very carefully to avoid damaging the driveshafts or transmission.

30. Installation is the reverse of removal. Be careful not to damage the input shaft of the transmission during installation. Install new torque converter mounting bolts. Tighten the torque converter bolts to 25 ft/lbs, engine to transaxle bolts to 40 ft/lbs, and the engine mount bolts to 32 ft/lbs.

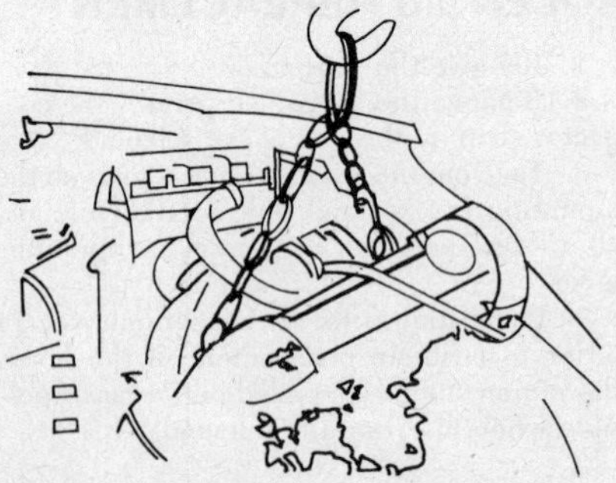

Lifting the Dasher engine out of the car. Note how it must be turned for removal.

Diesel Engines

1. Remove the negative battery cable.
2. Set the heat control to hot. Remove the lower radiator hose and remove the thermostat to drain the coolant. Remove the thermoswitch electrical connector and the radiator brace at the bottom of the radiator, remove the top radiator shroud, upper hose, radiator mounting bolts, and remove the radiator and fan.
3. Remove the supply and return lines from the injection pump. Disconnect the throttle cable from the pump and remove the cable mounting bracket. Disconnect the cold start cable at the pin, and remove the electrical connector from the fuel shut-off solenoid.
4. Disconnect the electrical connectors from the oil pressure switch, coolant temperature sensor and glow plugs. Remove the radiator hose from the head and the vacuum hose from the vacuum pump.
5. Loosen the adjusting nuts and unhook the clutch cable from the lever.
6. Remove the hose from the water pump.
7. Loosen the right engine mount.
8. Remove the alternator after tagging the wires for installation.
9. Remove the front engine mounts.
10. Disconnect the exhaust pipe from the manifold, and the pipe bracket from the transmission.
11. Loosen the left engine mount.
12. Remove the starter.
13. Remove the engine-to-transmission bolts, and the flywheel cover bolts.
14. Attach a lifting chain to the engine and raise the engine until the transmission touches the steering rack. Remove the left engine mount.
15. Support the transmission with a jack and raise and turn the engine at the same time to remove.
16. Installation is the reverse. Tighten the engine-to-transmission bolts to 40 ft/lbs and the engine mount bolts to 29 ft/lbs. After installation adjust the throttle and cold starting cables.

RABBIT, JETTA AND SCIROCCO WITH MANUAL TRANSMISSION

Gasoline Engines

The engine and transmission are removed as an assembly.
1. Disconnect the battery ground cable.
2. Drain the coolant by unbolting the lower water pump flange or by removing the hoses.

CAUTION

Do not disconnect or loosen any refrigerant hose connections during engine removal on cars equipped with air conditioning.

3. On cars equipped with air conditioning:
a. Loosen the compressor support bolts and remove the compressor.
b. Remove the radiator cooling fan, air ducts and radiator.
c. Remove the condenser.
d. Place the air conditioning compressor and condenser out of the way without disconnecting any refrigerant lines.
4. Remove the radiator with the air ducts and fan.
5. Detach and label all the electrical wires connecting the engine to the body.
6. Disconnect and plug the fuel line at the fuel pump. Detach the coolant hoses at the left end of the engine. Disconnect the accelerator cable and remove the air cleaner.
7. Disconnect the speedometer cable from the transmission. Detach the clutch cable.
8. Remove the engine support to the right of the starter.
9. Remove the headlight caps inside the engine compartment.
10. Unbolt the driveshafts from the transmission and wire them up.
11. Unbolt the exhaust pipe from the manifold and unbolt the exhaust pipe brace.
12. Unbolt the transmission rear mount from the body (alongside the tunnel).
13. Detach the ground strap from the transmission and body.
14. Remove the shift linkage.
15. Attach a chain sling to the alternator bracket and the lifting eye at the left end of the engine. Lift the engine and transmission slightly.
16. Detach the engine carrier from the body and remove the left transmission carrier.
17. Lift the engine/transmission assembly carefully out of the car.
18. To separate the engine and transmission, turn the flywheel to align the lug on the flywheel (to the left of TDC) with the pointer

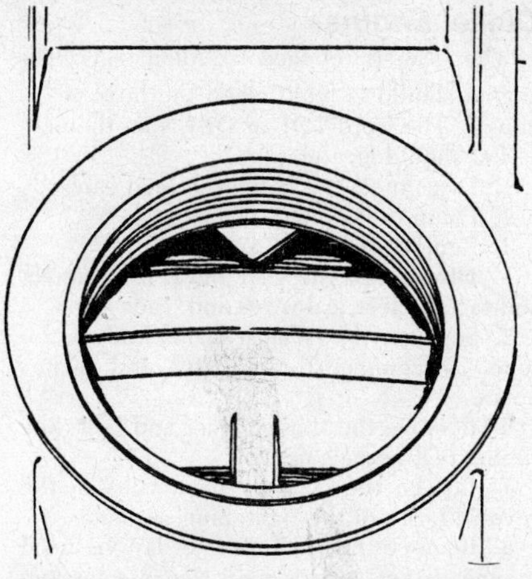

Aligning flywheel for manual transmission and engine separation—Rabbit, Jetta, Scirocco

in the opening. The engine and transmission can only be separated in this position. Remove the cover plate over the driveshaft flange and remove the engine to transmission bolts and the transmission housing cover plate.

To install the engine:

19. To attach the transmission to the engine, the recess in the flywheel edge must be at 3:00 o'clock (facing the left end of the engine). Torque the engine to transmission bolts to 40 ft/lbs. Lift the engine/transmission assembly into place. Loosen the bolts for the engine and transmission mounts. Move the engine assembly from side to side until the rear transmission mount is straight. Center the left and right transmission mounts and tighten all transmission bolts. Push the front mount upward to center the rubber cone, then tighten the mount. Loosen the exhaust pipe clamps, release any strain, then tighten the clamps. Torque the 10 mm bolts to 29 ft/lbs. Torque the driveshaft flange bolts to 32 ft/lbs. Refill the cooling system.

RABBIT, JETTA AND SCIROCCO WITH AUTOMATIC TRANSMISSION

Gasoline Engines

The engine and transmission are removed as an assembly.

1. Shift the transmission into "Park." Disconnect both battery cables.
2. Drain the coolant by unbolting the lower water pump flange or by removing the hoses.

CAUTION

Do not disconnect or loosen any refrigerant hose connections during engine removal on cars equipped with air conditioning.

3. On cars equipped with air conditioning, proceed as follows:
   a. Loosen the compressor support bolts and remove the compressor.
   b. Remove the radiator cooling fan, air ducts, and radiator.
   c. Remove the condenser.
   d. Place the air conditioning components out of the way without disconnecting any refrigerant lines.
4. Remove the radiator with the air ducts and fan.
5. Remove the air cleaner.
6. Detach the speedometer cable from the transmission.
7. Detach and label all electrical wires connecting the engine to the body. Detach the coolant hoses.
8. Remove the screws holding the accelerator cable bracket to the carburetor float bowl (do not disassemble linkage), detach the end of the gearshift selector cable from the transmission, detach the accelerator cable and pedal cable at the transmission, and remove the two bracket bolts behind this linkage on the transmission.
9. Unbolt the exhaust pipe from the manifold.
10. Remove the rear transmission mount. Unbolt the driveshafts and wire them up out of the way.
11. Remove the converter cover plate and remove the three torque converter to drive plate bolts.
12. Attach a chain sling to the alternator bracket and the lifting eye at the left end of the engine. It may be necessary to remove the alternator. Lift the engine and transmission slightly.
13. Detach the engine front mounting support; remove the left transmission carrier and the right engine carrier.
14. Lift the engine/transmission assembly carefully out of the car.
15. The transmission can now be detached from the engine.

To install the engine:

16. The engine to transmission bolts should be torqued to 40 ft/lbs. Lift the engine/transmission assembly into place and install the left transmission carrier, tightening first the body, then the transmission bolts. Lower the assembly to attach the engine carrier to the body, tightening the bolts to 40 ft/lbs. Install the engine mounting support. Check that all mounts and clamps are free of strain. Torque converter bolts should be torqued to 21 ft/lbs and driveshaft bolts to 32 ft/lbs. Refill the cooling system. Check the adjustment of transmission and carburetor linkages.

Diesel Engines

The diesel engine is removed with the transmission attached.

1. Disconnect the battery.
2. Disconnect the radiator hoses and drain the coolant. It can be saved for reuse, if it's not too old.
3. Remove the radiator complete with fan.
4. Remove the alternator.
5. Disconnect the fuel filter and set it aside near the windshield washer reservoir.
6. Detach the supply and return lines from the injection pump.
7. Disconnect the accelerator cable from the lever on the injection pump and remove the injection pump complete with bracket.
8. Disconnect the cold start cable from the pump.
9. Disconnect and label all electrical wires and leads.
10. Remove the front transmission mount.
11. Disconnect the clutch cable.
12. Remove the relay rod and connecting rod from the transmission and turn the relay lever shaft to the rear.
13. Disconnect the selector rod.
14. Unbolt the driveshafts and wire them up out of the way. Remove the rear support.
15. Disconnect the exhaust pipe at the manifold and remove the rear transmission mount.
16. Attach a lifting sling to the engine and take the weight from the engine mounts. Remove the left and right transmission mounts.
17. Carefully guide the engine out of the car while turning it slightly.
18. To separate the engine from the transmission, unscrew the plug from the TDC sensor opening and turn the flywheel to align the mark on the flywheel with the pointer. The engine/transmission can only be separated in this position.
19. Remove the cover plate over the driveshaft flange and remove the engine-to-transmission bolts.
20. Press the engine off the transmission.
21. Installation is the reverse of removal. Turn the flywheel so that the recess in the flywheel is level with the driveshaft flange. Lower the engine into the car and attach the left transmission mount to the transmission first. Align the rear transmission mount, center the engine/transmission and center the front transmission mount. Adjust the accelerator and cold start cables and bleed the injection system.

Cylinder Head

REMOVAL AND INSTALLATION

The engine should be cold before the cylinder head can be removed. The head is retained by 10 socket head bolts. It can be removed without removing the intake and exhaust manifolds.

NOTE: Beginning approximately July 1977, 12 point socket head bolts were used in place of 6 point older version. These should be used in complete sets only and need not be retorqued after the mileage interval.

Carbureted Engines

1. Disconnect the battery ground cable.
2. Drain the cooling system.
3. Remove the air cleaner. Disconnect the fuel line.
4. Disconnect the radiator, heater, and choke hoses.
5. Disconnect all electrical wires. Remove the spark plug wires.
6. Separate the exhaust manifold from the exhaust pipe.
7. Disconnect the EGR line from the exhaust manifold. Remove the EGR valve and filter from the intake manifold.
8. Remove the carburetor.
9. Disconnect the air pump fittings.
10. Remove the timing belt cover and belt.
11. Loosen the cylinder head bolts in the reverse of the tightening sequence.

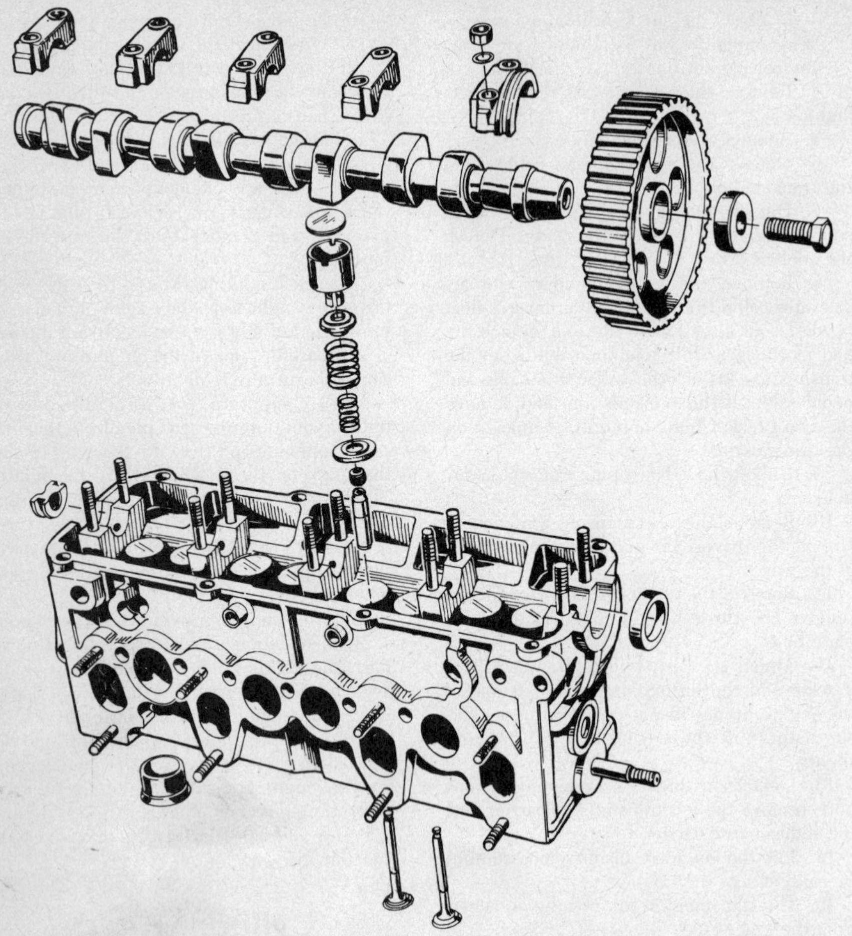

Exploded view of the cylinder head showing the valve train components

12. Remove the bolts and lift the head straight off.
13. Install the new cylinder head gasket with the word TOP or OBEN up.
14. Install bolts No. 10 and 8 first; these holes are smaller and will properly locate the gasket and cylinder head.
15. Install the remaining bolts. Tighten them in three stages in the sequence shown. Cylinder head bolt torque (cold) is 55 ft/lbs, 12 point bolts should be tightened to 55 ft/lbs, then tightened ¼ turn more.

NOTE: After approximately 1000 miles, retighten the cylinder head bolts. Torque them hot to 61 ft/lbs. (six point bolts only).

16. Install the remaining components in the reverse order of removal.

Fuel Injected Engines

1. Disconnect the battery ground cable.
2. Drain the cooling system.
3. Disconnect the air duct from the throttle valve assembly.
4. Disconnect the throttle valve assembly.
5. Remove the injectors and disconnect the line from the cold start valve.
6. Disconnect the radiator and heater hoses.
7. Disconnect the vacuum and PCV lines (label lines for installation).
8. Remove the auxiliary air regulator from the intake manifold.
9. Disconnect all electrical lines and remove the spark plugs (label all lines and wires for installation).
10. Separate the exhaust manifold from the exhaust pipe.
11. Remove the EGR line from the exhaust manifold.
12. Remove the intake manifold.
13. Remove the timing belt cover and belt.
14. Loosen the cylinder head bolts in the reverse of the tightening sequence.
15. Remove the bolts and lift the head straight off.
16. Check the flatness of the cylinder block.
17. Install the new cylinder head gasket with the word TOP or OBEN facing upward.
18. Install bolts No. 10 and 8 first; these holes are smaller and will properly locate the gasket and cylinder head.
19. Install the remaining bolts. Tighten them in three stages using the sequence shown in the illustration. Cylinder head bolts must be torqued cold to 55 ft/lbs. 12 point bolts should be tightened to 55 ft/lbs, then tightened ¼ turn more.

NOTE: After 1000 miles, retighten the cylinder head bolts to 61 ft/lbs hot (six point bolts only).

20. Install the remaining components in the reverse order of removal.

Diesel Engines

The head is retained by Allen bolts. The engine should be cold when the head is removed. The word TOP or OBEN on the new gasket should face up.

1. Disconnect the battery ground cable.
2. Drain the cooling system.
3. Remove the air cleaner.
4. Disconnect the fuel lines. Disconnect and tag all electrical wires and leads.
5. Separate the exhaust manifold from the pipe. Disconnect the radiator and heater hoses.
6. Remove the timing cover and belt (See timing belt replacement).
7. Loosen the cylinder head bolts in the reverse order of the tightening sequence.
8. Remove the head. Do not lay the head on the gasket surface with the injectors installed. Support it at the ends on strips of wood.
9. Install the cylinder head with a new gasket. Be sure the new gasket has the same number of notches and the same identifying number as the old one, unless the pistons were also replaced.

Install bolts 8 and 10 first and torque the bolts to the specification in the proper sequence. After 1000 miles, loosen all bolts ⅓ turn and retorque the bolts.

OVERHAUL

Valve guides are a shrink fit. Always install new valve seals when doing a valve job. Valve seats are not replaceable; the cylinder head should be replaced if the seat width and face angle cannot be maintained.

Refer to general information section under Engine Overhaul.

Intake Manifold

REMOVAL AND INSTALLATION

Carbureted Models

1. Remove the air cleaner. Drain the cooling system.
2. Disconnect the accelerator cable.
3. Disconnect the EGR valve connections.
4. Detach all electrical leads.
5. Disconnect the coolant hoses.
6. Disconnect the fuel line from the carburetor.
7. Remove the vacuum hoses from the carburetor.
8. Loosen and remove the retaining bolts and lift off the manifold.
9. Install a new gasket. Install the manifold and tighten the bolts from the inside out. Tightening torque is 18 ft/lbs.
10. Install the remaining components in the reverse order of removal. Refill the cooling system.

Fuel Injected Models

1. Disconnect the air duct from the throttle valve body. Drain the cooling system.
2. Disconnect the accelerator cable.
3. Remove the injectors and disconnect the line from the cold start valve.
4. Disconnect all coolant hoses.

5. Disconnect all vacuum and emission control hoses (label all hoses for installation).
6. Remove the auxiliary air regulator.
7. Disconnect all electrical lines (label all wires for installation).
8. Disconnect the EGR line from the exhaust manifold.
9. Loosen and remove the retaining bolts and lift off the manifold.
10. Install a new gasket. Install the manifold and tighten the bolts to 18 ft/lbs.
11. Install the remaining components in the reverse order of removal.

Exhaust Manifold

REMOVAL AND INSTALLATION

1. Disconnect the EGR tube from the exhaust manifold.
2. Remove the interfering air pump components if so equipped.
3. Remove the air cleaner hose from the exhaust manifold.
4. Disconnect the intake manifold support.
5. Separate the exhaust pipe from the manifold.
6. Remove the retaining nuts and remove the manifold.
7. Clean the cylinder head and manifold mating surfaces.
8. Install the exhaust manifold using a new gasket.
9. Tighten the nuts to 18 ft/lbs. Work from the inside out.
10. Install the remaining components in the reverse order of removal. Use a new manifold flange gasket.

Timing Belt Cover

REMOVAL AND INSTALLATION

1. Loosen the alternator mounting bolts.
2. Pivot the alternator and slip the drive belt off the sprockets.
3. Unscrew the cover retaining nuts and remove the cover.
4. Reposition the spacers on the studs and then install the washers and nuts.
5. Install the alternator belt and adjust its tension.

Timing Belt

NOTE: The timing belt is designed to last for more than 60,000 miles and does not normally require tension adjustments. If the belt is removed or replaced, the basic valve timing must be checked and the belt retensioned.

REMOVAL, INSTALLATION, AND TENSIONING

Gasoline Engines

Timing belt installation will be easier if the engine is set to TDC prior to belt removal. The 0°T mark will be aligned with the pointer on the bell housing, and the mark on the rear face of the camshaft pulley will align with the camshaft cover gasket on the left. Also, the V-notch in the crankshaft pulley should align with the dot mark on the intermediate shaft, and the distributor rotor should be pointing toward the mark on the rim of the housing.

If the belt has broken and timing is off, remove the belt cover and belt, then set the engine to TDC before installing the belt, as outlined in Steps, 5, 6, and 7.

1. Remove the timing belt cover.
2. While holding the large hex on the tension sprocket, loosen the pulley locknut.
3. Release the tensioner from the timing belt.
4. Slide the belt off the three toothed sprockets and remove it.
5. Turn the crankshaft until No. 1 cylinder is at TDC. At this point, the 0°T mark will be aligned with the pointer on the bell housing.

Camshaft sprocket alignment

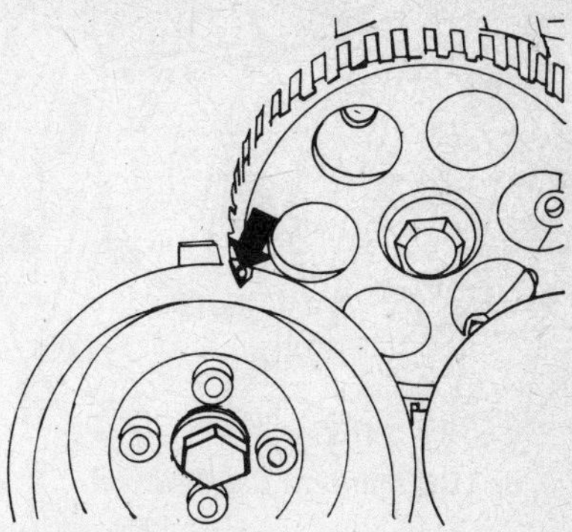

Crankshaft pulley and intermediate shaft sprocket alignment

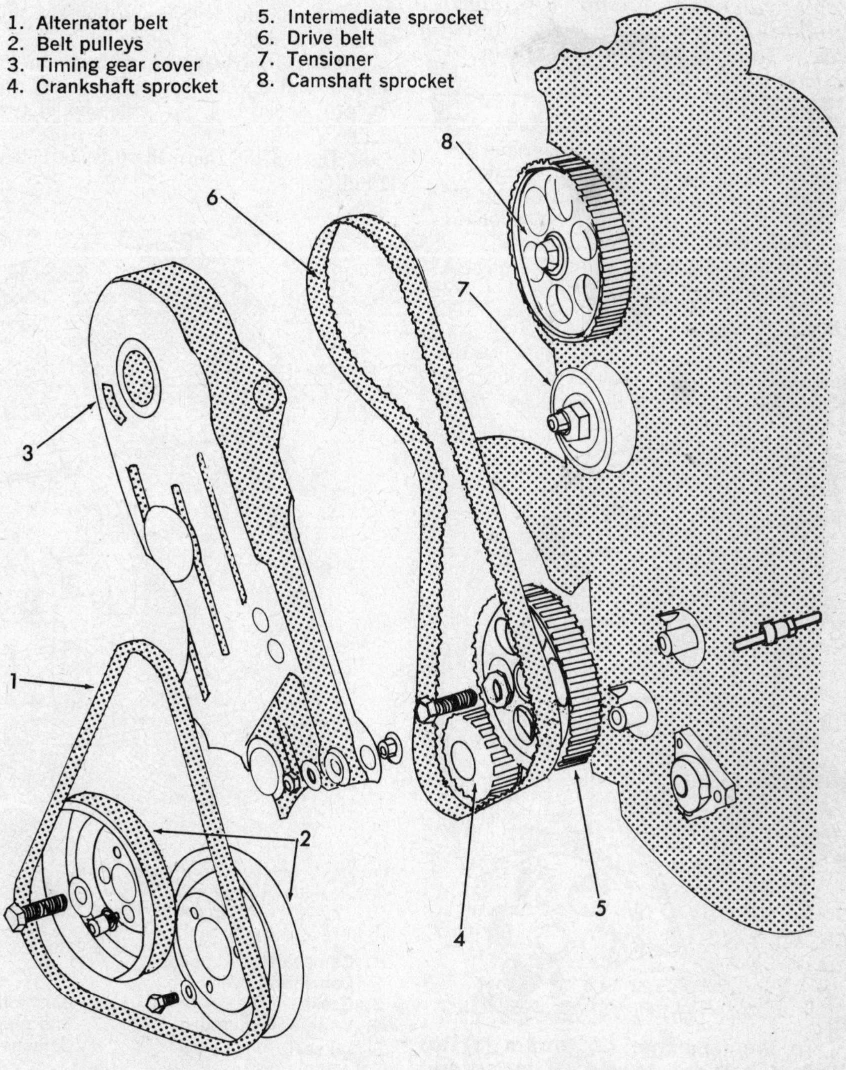

Exploded view of camshaft drive arrangement

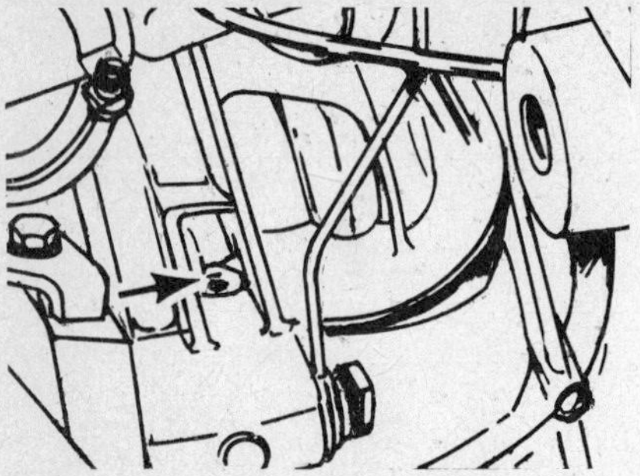

0° T or TDC mark on the flywheel

6. Align the timing mark on the rear face of the camshaft pulley with the camshaft cover gasket on the left.

7. Align the V-notch in the crankshaft pulley with the dot mark on the intermediate shaft. The distributor rotor should be pointing to the No. 1 cylinder mark on the rim of the distributor.

CAUTION

If the timing marks are not correctly aligned, valve timing will be incorrect. Poor performance and serious engine damage can result from improper valve timing. Steps 5, 6, and 7 should not be necessary if the engine was in time and set to TDC prior to belt removal.

8. Install the belt on the sprockets.

9. Adjust the tensioner by turning the large tensioner hex to the right. Tension is correct when you can just twist the belt 90° with two fingers at the midpoint. Tighten the locknut to 32 ft/lbs.

10. Install the timing belt cover and check the ignition timing.

Diesel Engine

The drive belt on the diesel also drives the injection pump. It is necessary that this procedure be followed exactly to ensure proper valve timing and injection pump timing. You will also need special tool VW 210 to properly tension the belt.

1. Remove the alternator belt.
2. Remove the timing belt cover and rocker cover.
3. Set the engine at TDC on No. 1 cylinder. In this position both valves of No. 1 cylinder will be closed and the OT mark on the flywheel will be aligned with the pointer on the bell housing.
4. Use a pin (VW special tool 2064) or suitable bolt to hold the injection pump sprocket and camshaft sprocket in position. The pin or bolt must be exactly the size of the hole. There can be no "slop" in the gears.
5. Loosen the tensioner. Remove the fan belt pulley from the crankshaft.
6. Remove the belt and belt shield from the drive gears.

To install the belt:

7. Check that the TDC mark is aligned with the flywheel mark.
8. Loosen the camshaft sprocket bolt ½ turn and tap the gear loose from the camshaft with a rubber mallet.
9. Install the drive belt and remove the pin from the camshaft and injection pump gears.
10. Tension the belt by turning the tensioner to the right.
11. Check the belt tension between the camshaft and injection pump sprockets. On VW 210 special tool, the scale should read 12-13
12. Tighten the camshaft sprocket bolt to 32 ft/lbs.
13. Turn the crankshaft 2 complete turns in the direction of normal rotation and check the belt tension again.

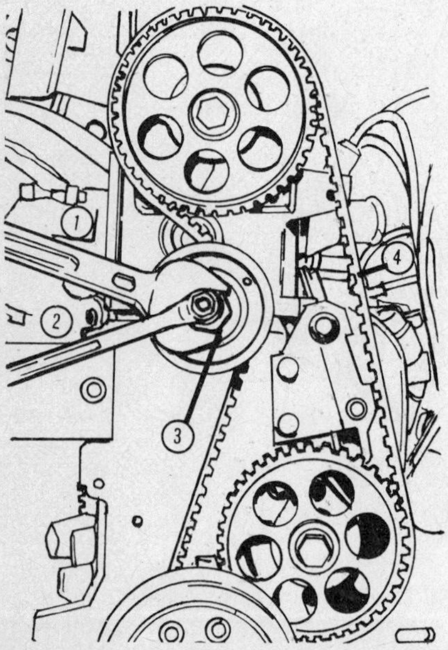

Turn the tensioner (3) toward (1) to tighten belt and toward (2) to loosen. Check tension at (4)

Timing Sprockets

REMOVAL AND INSTALLATION

The camshaft, intermediate shaft, and crankshaft sprockets are located by keys on their respective shafts and each is retained by a bolt. To remove any or all of the pulleys, first remove the timing belt cover and belt.

NOTE: When removing the crankshaft pulley, don't remove the four allen head bolts which hold the outer belt pulley to the timing belt sprocket.

1. Remove the center bolt.
2. Gently pry the sprocket off the shaft. If the gear does not come off easily, use a gear puller. Don't hammer on the sprocket.
3. Remove the sprocket and key.
4. Install in the reverse order of removal.
5. Tighten the center bolt to 58 ft/lbs.
6. Install the timing belt, check the valve timing, tension the belt, and install the cover.

Camshaft

REMOVAL AND INSTALLATION

1. Remove the timing belt.

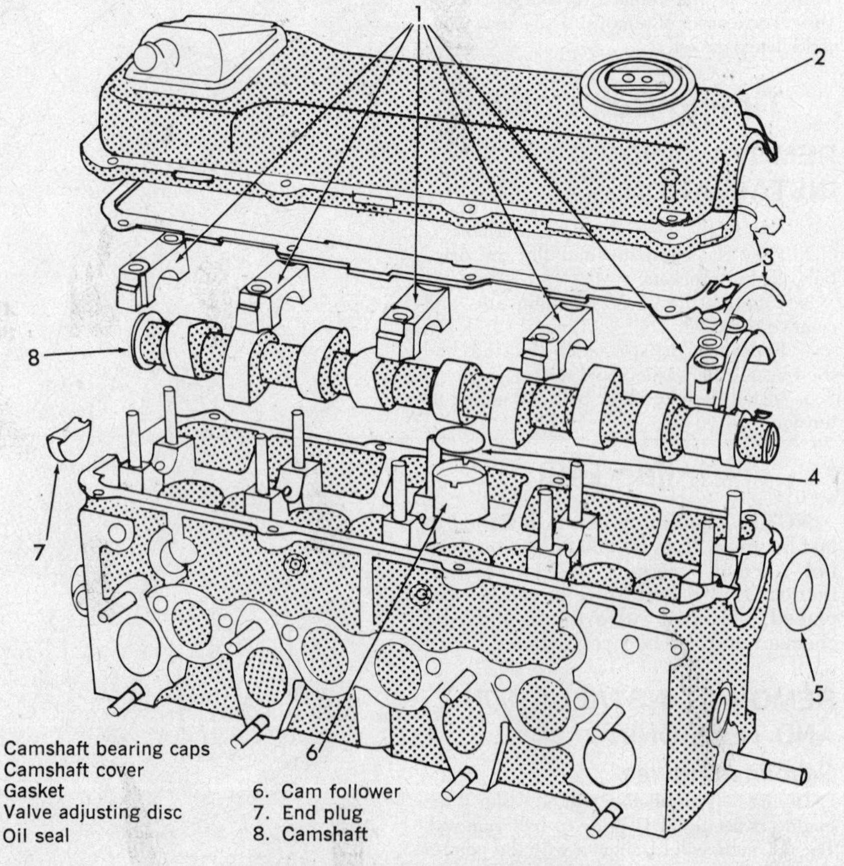

1. Camshaft bearing caps
2. Camshaft cover
3. Gasket
4. Valve adjusting disc
5. Oil seal
6. Cam follower
7. End plug
8. Camshaft

Exploded view of camshaft assembly

2. Remove the camshaft sprocket.
3. Remove the air cleaner.
4. Remove the camshaft cover.
5. Unscrew and remove the No. 1, 3, and 5 bearing caps (No. 1 is at the front).
6. Unscrew the No. 2 and 4 bearing caps, diagonally and in increments.
7. Lift the camshaft out of the cylinder head.
8. Lubricate the camshaft journals and lobes with assembly lube or gear oil before installing it in the cylinder head.
9. Replace the camshaft oil seal with a new one whenever the cam is removed.
10. Install the No. 1, 3, and 5 bearing caps and tighten the nuts to 14 ft/lbs. Note that the bores are offset, and the numbers are not always on the same side.
11. Install the No. 2 and 4 bearing caps and diagonally tighten the nuts to 14 ft/lbs.

NOTE: If checking end play, install a dial indicator so that the feeler touches the camshaft snout. End-play should be no more than 0.006 in. (0.15 mm).

12. Replace the seal in the No. 1 bearing cap. If necessary, replace the end plug in the cylinder head.
13. Install the camshaft cover.
14. Install the camshaft pulley and the timing belt.
15. Check the valve clearance.

Piston and Connecting Rods

GASOLINE ENGINES

The pistons must be installed in the block with the arrow at the edge of the crown facing to the front of the car on Dashers and toward the right front wheel on Rabbits, Sciroccos and Jettas. The connecting rod and cap alignment casting grooves must face the intermediate shaft. New connecting rod bolts must always be used. The pistons must be heated to 140° F in an oven before the piston pins can be pressed in. Three piston oversizes are available to accommodate overbores up to 0.040 in.

There is a piston size code stamped on the cylinder block above the water pump.

NOTE: 1978 and later models have different pistons from 1975-77 models. The parts are not interchangeable.

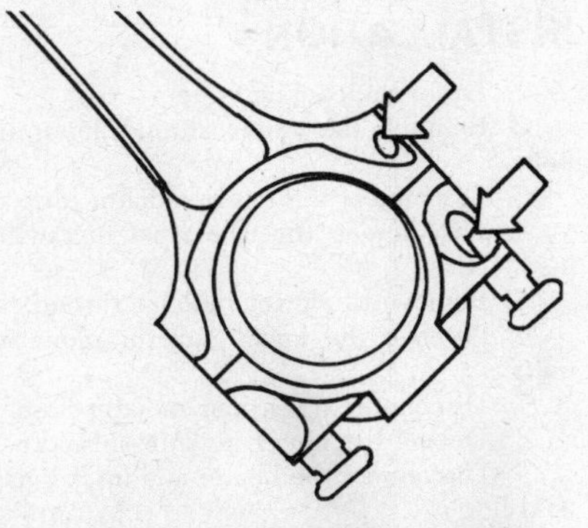

The connecting rod and cap alignmet casting grooves must face the intermediate shaft

DIESEL ENGINES

The same installation procedures apply to the diesel as to the gas engine. However, whenever new pistons or a short block are installed, the piston projection must be checked.

A spacer (VW 385/17) and bar with a micrometer are necessary, and must be set up to measure the maximum amount of piston projection above the deck height. The following chart should be used to select a head gasket of the correct thickness to match piston projection.

Piston Projection (mm)	Gasket Identification No. of Notches	Part Number
0.43-0.63	2	068 103 383
0.63-0.82	3	068 103 383C
0.82-0.92	4	068 103 383G
0.92-1.02	5	068 103 383H

NOTE: 1978 and later models (beginning with engine CK 024 944) have pistons with a new piston height and a thicker cylinder head gasket. These pistons are marked with a "9" next to installation direction arrow. New pistons can be used in earlier cars, but only in sets of 4.

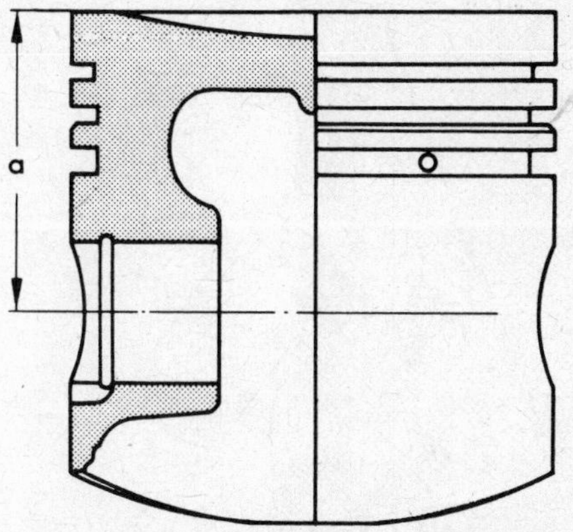

Beginning with Sept., 1977, production, the piston height (A) on diesel engines was increased from 1.759 in. to 1.768 in.

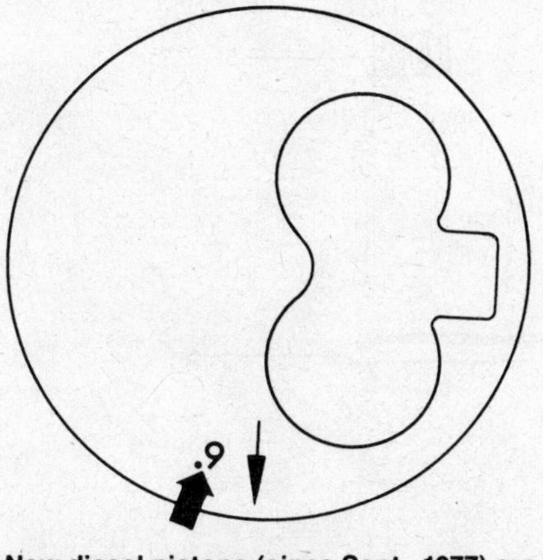

New diesel pistons (since Sept., 1977) are identified by a number "9" next to the arrow denoting installation direction

ENGINE LUBRICATION

The lubrication system is a conventional wet-sump design. The gear type oil pump is driven by the intermediate shaft. A pressure relief valve limits pressure and prevents extreme pressure from developing in the system. All oil is filtered by a full flow replaceable filter. A bypass valve assures lubrication in the event the filter becomes plugged. The oil pressure switch is located at the end of the cylinder head gallery (the end of the system) to assure accurate pressure readings.

Oil Pan

REMOVAL AND INSTALLATION

Dasher

1. Drain the oil pan.
2. Support and slightly raise the engine with an overhead hoist.
3. Gradually loosen the engine crossmember mounting bolts. Remove the left and right side engine mounts.
4. Lower the crossmember very carefully.
5. Loosen and remove the oil pan retaining bolts.
6. Lower the pan from the car.
7. Install the pan using a new gasket and sealer.
8. Tighten the retaining bolts in a crosswise pattern. Tighten hex head bolts to 14 ft/lbs, or Allen head bolts to 7 ft/lbs.
9. Raise the crossmember. Tighten the crossmember bolts to 42 ft/lbs and the engine mounting bolts to 32 ft/lbs.
10. Refill the engine with oil. Start the engine and check for leaks.

Rabbit, Jetta and Scirocco

1. Drain the engine oil.
2. Loosen and remove the bolts retaining the oil pan.
3. Lower the pan from the car.
4. Install the pan using a new oil pan gasket.
5. Tighten the retaining bolts in a crisscross pattern. Tighten hex head bolts to 14 ft/lbs, or Allen head bolts to 7 ft/lbs.
6. Refill the engine with oil. Start the engine and examine the pan for leaks.

Rear Main Oil Seal

REPLACEMENT

The rear main oil seal is located in a housing on the rear of the cylinder block. To replace the seal on the Dasher, it is necessary to remove the transmission and perform the work from underneath the car or remove the engine and perform the work on an engine stand or work bench. See "Transmission Removal and Installation."

On the Rabbit, Jetta and Scirocco, the engine should be removed from the car.

1. Remove the transmission and flywheel.
2. Using a screwdriver, very carefully pry the old seal out of the support ring.

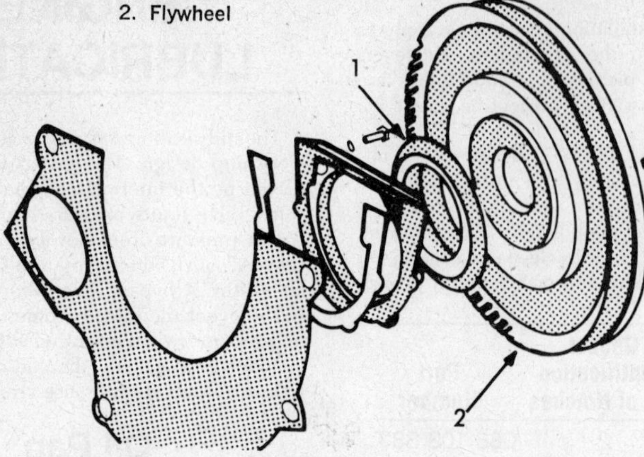

Rear main oil seal assembly

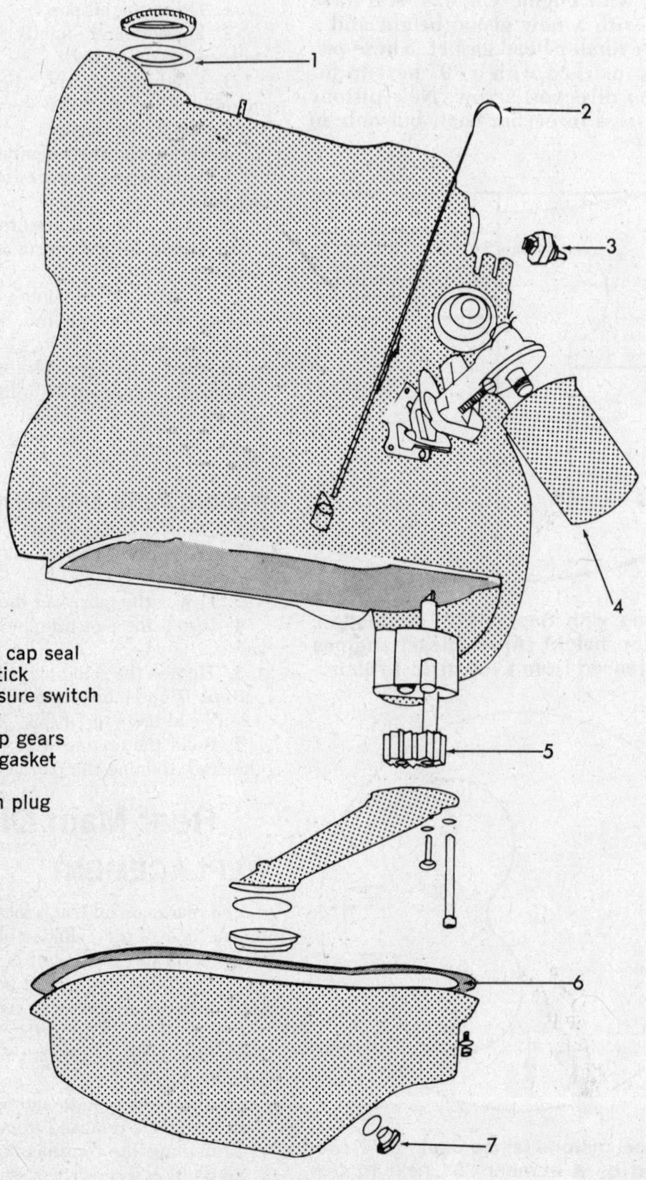

Lubrication system components

3. Remove the seal.
4. Lightly oil the replacement seal and then press it into place using a circular piece of flat metal. Be careful not to damage the seal or score the crankshaft.
5. Install the flywheel and transmission. Flywheel-to-engine bolts are tightened to 36 ft/lbs.

Oil Pump

REMOVAL AND INSTALLATION

1. Remove the oil pan.
2. Remove the two mounting bolts.
3. Pull the oil pump down and out of the engine.
4. Unscrew the two bolts and separate the pump halves.
5. Remove the driveshaft and gear from the upper body.
6. Clean the bottom half in solvent. Pry up the metal edges to remove the filter screen for cleaning.
7. Examine the gears and driveshaft for wear or damage. Replace them if necessary.
8. Reassemble the pump halves.
9. Prime the pump with oil and install in the reverse order of removal.

ENGINE COOLING

The cooling system consists of a belt driven, external water pump, thermostat, radiator, and thermostatically controlled electric cooling fan. When the engine is cold the thermostat is closed and blocks the water from the radiator so the coolant is circulated only through the engine. When the engine warms up, the thermostat opens and the radiator is included in the coolant circuit. The thermostatic switch is in the bottom of the radiator and turns the electrical fan on at 199° F, off at 186° F. This reduces power loss and engine noise.

Radiator and Fan

REMOVAL AND INSTALLATION

1. Drain the cooling system.
2. Remove the inner shroud mounting bolts.
3. Disconnect the lower radiator hose.
4. Disconnect the thermostatic switch lead.
5. Remove the lower radiator shroud.
6. Remove the lower radiator mounting units.
7. Disconnect the upper radiator hose.
8. Detach the upper radiator shroud.
9. Disconnect the heater and intake manifold hoses.
10. Remove the side mounting bolts and lift the radiator and fan out as an assembly.
11. Installation is the reverse of removal.

Thermostat

REMOVAL AND INSTALLATION

The thermostat is located in the bottom radiator hose neck on the water pump.

1. Drain the cooling system.
2. Remove the two retaining bolts from the lower water pump neck.

NOTE: It isn't necessary to disconnect the hose.

3. Move the neck, with the hoses attached, out of the way.
4. Remove the thermostat.
5. Install a new seal on the water pump neck.
6. Install the thermostat with the spring end up.
7. Replace the water pump neck and tighten the two retaining bolts.

Water Pump

REMOVAL AND INSTALLATION

1. Drain the cooling system.
2. Remove the alternator and drive belt.
3. Remove the timing belt cover.
4. Disconnect the lower radiator hose, engine hose, and heater hose from the water pump.
5. Remove the four pump retaining bolts. Notice where the different length bolts are located.
6. Turn the pump slightly and lift it out of the engine block.
7. Installation is the reverse of removal. Use a new seal on the mating surface with the engine.

EMISSION CONTROLS

Crankcase Ventilation

The crankcase ventilation system keeps harmful vapor byproducts of combustion from escaping into the atmosphere and prevents the building of crankcase pressure which can lead to oil leaking. Crankcase vapors are recirculated from the camshaft cover through a hose to the air cleaner. Here they are mixed with the air/fuel mixture and burned in the combustion chamber.

SERVICE

The only maintenance required on the crankcase ventilation system is a periodic check. At every tune up, examine the hoses for clogging or deterioration. Clean or replace the hoses as necessary.

Evaporation Emission Control System

This system prevents the escape of raw fuel vapors (unburned hydrocarbons or HC) into the atmosphere. The system consists of a sealed carburetor, unvented fuel tank filler cap, fuel tank expansion chamber, an activated charcoal filter canister and connector hoses. Fuel vapors which reach the filter deposit hydrocarbons on the surface of the charcoal filter element. Fresh air enters the filter when the engine is running and forces the hydrocarbons to the air cleaner where they join the air/fuel mixture and are burned.

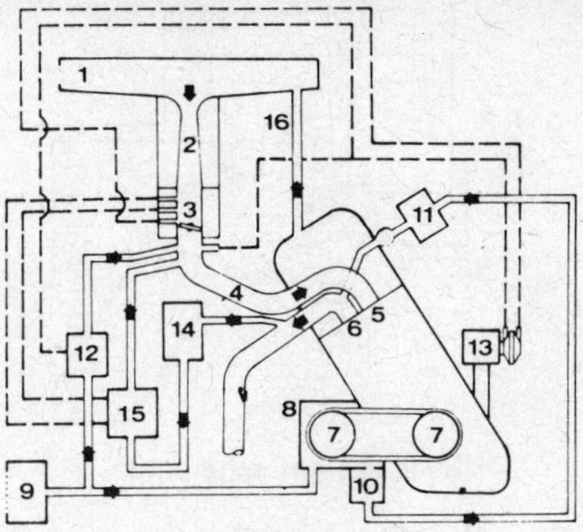

1. Air cleaner
2. Carburetor venturi
3. Throttle valve
4. Intake manifold
5. Cylinder head intake port
6. Cylinder head exhaust port
7. Belt drive for air pump
8. Air pump
9. Air pump filter
10. Pressure relief valve
11. Check valve
12. Diverter valve
13. Distributor
14. EGR filter
15. EGR valve
16. Crankcase ventilation

Carbureted Dasher emission control system. Arrows indicate flow

Many 1979 and later models are equipped with a charcoal filter valve which prevents vapors from escaping from the canister when the engine is not running.

SERVICE

Maintenance of the system requires checking the condition of the various connector hoses and the charcoal filter at 10,000 mile intervals. The charcoal filter should be replaced at 50,000 mile intervals.

Dual Diaphragm Distributors

The purpose of the dual diaphragm distributor is to improve exhaust emissions during one of the engine's dirtier operating modes—idling. The distributor has a vacuum retard diaphragm, in addition to a vacuum advance diaphragm. A temperature valve shuts off vacuum from the carburetor when coolant temperatures are below 130° F.

TESTING

Advance Diaphragm

1. Connect a timing light to the engine. Check the ignition timing.
2. Remove the retard hose from the distributor and plug it. Increase the engine speed. The ignition timing should advance. If it doesn't, then the vacuum unit is faulty and must be replaced.

Temperature Valve

1. Remove the temperature valve and place the threaded portion in hot water.
2. Create a vacuum by sucking on the angled connection.
3. The valve must be open above approximately 130° F.

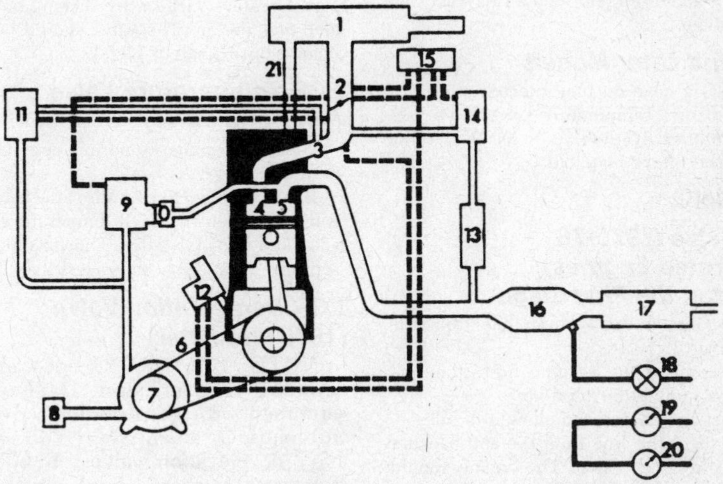

1. Air cleaner
2. Carburetor
3. Intake manifold
4. Intake port
5. Exhaust port
6. Air pump belt
7. Air pump
8. Air pump air filter
9. Diverter valve
10. Pressure valve
11. Anti-backfire valve
12. Distributor
13. EGR filter
14. EGR valve
15. Temperature valve
16. Catalytic converter
17. Muffler
18. Converter temperature light
19. EGR system indicator light
20. Converter indicator light
21. Crankcase ventilation line

Typical carbureted Rabbit, Scirocco emission control system

Exhaust Gas Recirculation (EGR)

To reduce NOx (oxides of nitrogen) emissions, metered amounts of exhaust gases are added to the air/fuel mixture. The recirculated exhaust gas lowers the peak flame temperature during combustion. Exhaust gas from the manifold passes through a filter where it is cleaned. The vacuum operated EGR valve controls the volume of this exhaust gas which is allowed into the intake manifold. There is no EGR at idle, partial at slight throttle and full EGR at mid-throttle.

1975 Models

1974-75 models have an EGR filter and a 2-stage EGR valve. The first stage is controlled by the temperature valve. The second stage is controlled by the microswitch on the carburetor throttle valve. The switch opens the valve when the throttle valve is open between 30°-67° (manual transmission) or 23°-63° (automatic transmission).

1976 Models

The EGR filter was discontinued on 1976 models but the 2-stage EGR valve was retained. On Federal vehicles, only the first stage is connected; California vehicles use both stages.

First stage EGR is controlled by engine vacuum and coolant temperature. The EGR valve is open above approximately 120° F coolant temperature and below approximately 80° F. At idle and during full throttle acceleration (engine hot), there is no EGR since the engine vacuum is too low to open the valve.

The second stage is controlled by temperature, engine vacuum and microswitch on the carburetor throttle valve. Vacuum is always present at the second stage and the valve is opened at about 120° F coolant temperature. When the throttle valve opens between 25° and 67°, the micro-switch activates the 2-way valve and allows engine vacuum to reach the second stage.

1977 and Later Models

The EGR valve on fuel injected models is controlled by a temperature valve and a vacuum amplifier. The valve is located at the front of the intake manifold.

TESTING

EGR Valve (1975-76 Carbureted Engines), Checking the First Stage

1. Disconnect the vacuum line from the EGR valve.
2. Disconnect the vacuum hose from the distributor unit and extend hose.
3. Start the engine and allow it to idle.
4. Connect the line from the anti-backfire valve to the EGR valve. The engine should stumble or stall.
5. If the idle stays even, the EGR line is clogged or the EGR valve is defective, or the filter is clogged.

EGR Valve (1975-76 Carbureted Engines), Checking the Second Stage

The EGR valve second stage is on all 1975

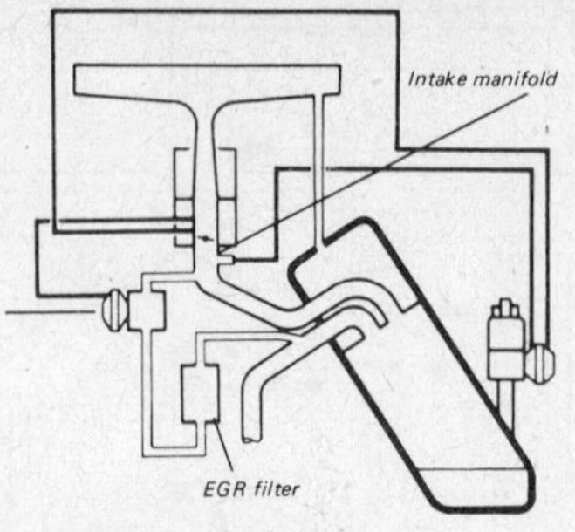

EGR system schematic

USA and California models and on 1976 California Rabbits and Sciroccos only. The system includes a micro-switch located on the side of the carburetor near the throttle valve. To check the system, manually operate the switch with the engine at idle. If the engine speed drops or the engine stalls, the switch is operating correctly. If not, check the micro-switch, the EGR filter and the EGR return lines for blockage.

EGR Valve–Fuel Injected Models

Be sure the vacuum lines are not leaking. Replace any that are leaking or cracked.

1. Warm the engine to normal operating temperature.
2. Run the engine at idle.
3. Remove the vacuum hose from the EGR valve.
4. Connect the line from the brake booster to the EGR valve (this can be done by installing a Tee in the vacuum line to the retard side of the distributor diaphragm and running a separate hose from there to the EGR valve).
5. If the engine speed does not change, the EGR valve is clogged or damaged.

EGR Temperature Valve (1975-76)

1. Remove the temperature valve and place the threaded portion in hot water.
2. Create a vacuum by sucking on the angled connection. The valve should be closed below approximately 120° F.

EGR Temperature Valve (1977 and Later)

Warm the engine to normal operating temperature.

1. With the engine at idle, attach a vacuum gauge between the EGR temperature control valve and the EGR valve. The valve should be replaced if the gauge shows less than 2 in. Hg.

EGR Deceleration Valve (1976 and Later)

NOTE: 1976 USA except California manual transmission Dashers are equipped with deceleration valves. No automatic transmission Volkswagens have deceleration valves. Rabbits and Sciroccos first received deceleration valves in 1977.

1. Remove the hose from the deceleration valve. Plug the hose.
2. Run the engine for a few seconds at 3000 rpm.
3. Snap the throttle valve closed.
4. With your finger, check for suction at the hose connection.
5. Remove the hose from the connector.
6. Run the engine at about 3000 rpm. No suction should be felt.

EGR Vacuum Amplifier (1976 and Later)

NOTE: 1976 Dashers are equipped with EGR Vacuum Amplifiers, while Rabbits and Sciroccos first received them in 1977.

1. Run the engine at idle.
2. Connect a vacuum gauge between the vacuum amplifier and the throttle valve port.
3. The gauge should read 0.2-0.3 in./Hg. If not, check the throttle plate for correct position or check the port for obstruction.
4. Connect a vacuum gauge between the vacuum amplifier and the temperature valve.
5. Replace the vacuum amplifier if the gauge reads less than 2 in./Hg.

MAINTENANCE

The only maintenance is to replace the EGR filter (1975 models only) and to reset the EGR elapsed mileage switch.

Resetting the Elapsed Mileage Switch

The EGR reminder light in the speedometer should light up every 15,000 miles as a reminder for maintenance.

To reset the light switch, press the white button. The speedometer light should go out.

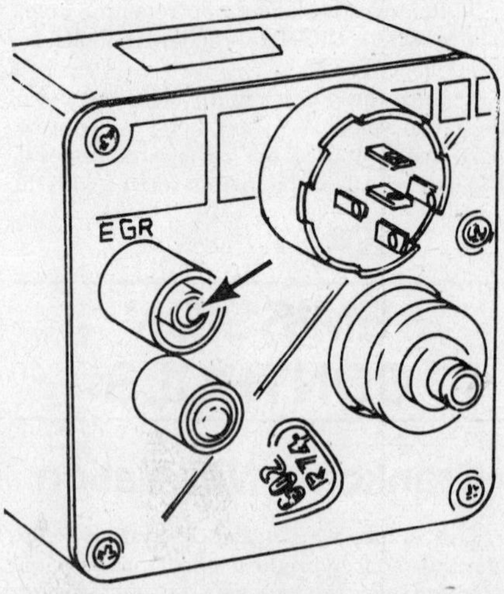

Resetting the EGR elapsed mileage odometer

Filter Replacement

1. Disconnect the filter EGR line fittings.
2. Remove the filter and discard.
3. Install the new filter into the EGR lines and securely tighten fittings.

REMOVAL AND INSTALLATION

EGR Valve

1. Disconnect the vacuum hose from the EGR valve.
2. Unbolt the EGR line fitting on the opposite side of the valve.
3. Remove the two remaining bolts and lift the EGR valve from the intake manifold.

4. Install the EGR valve in the reverse order of removal. Use a new gasket at the intake manifold.

Air Injection

The air injection system used on most carbureted engines, except the 1978 and 1980 Rabbit with 34 PICT-5 carburetor, includes a belt driven air pump, filter, check valve, anti-backfire valve or gulp valve, and connecting hoses and air lines. The system reduces exhaust emissions by pumping fresh air to the exhaust manifold or directly behind the exhaust valves where it combines with the hot exhaust gas to burn away excess hydrocarbons and reduce carbon monoxide.

The air injection systems on the 1978 and 1980 Rabbits with the 24 PICT-5 carburetors do not have air pumps. Instead, air is drawn from the air cleaner through a silencer to two check valves. The valves turn blue when overheated. If the valves are blue, replace them.

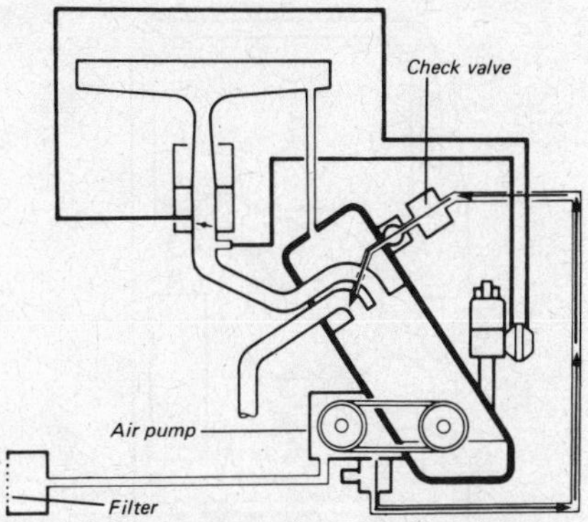

Air injection system schematic. The arrows indicate air flow

MAINTENANCE

Required maintenance on the air pump involves visually checking the pump, control valves, hoses and lines every 10,000 miles. Clean the air pump filter element at this interval. The filter element should be replaced every 20,000 miles or two years.

TESTING AND SERVICE

Air Pump System

1. Remove and clean the air manifold.
2. Blow compressed air into the anti-backfire valve in the direction of the air flow.
3. Clean or replace the air pump filter.
4. Start the engine.
5. Exhaust gas should flow equally from each air inlet.
6. With the engine idling block the relief valve air outlet–only a slight pressure should be felt if the system is operating properly.

Anti-Backfire Valve

1. Disconnect the air pump filter line from the anti-backfire valve.
2. Briefly disconnect the anti-backfire valve vacuum line with the engine running. There should be a noticeable vacuum.
3. Replace the anti-backfire valve if the engine backfires.

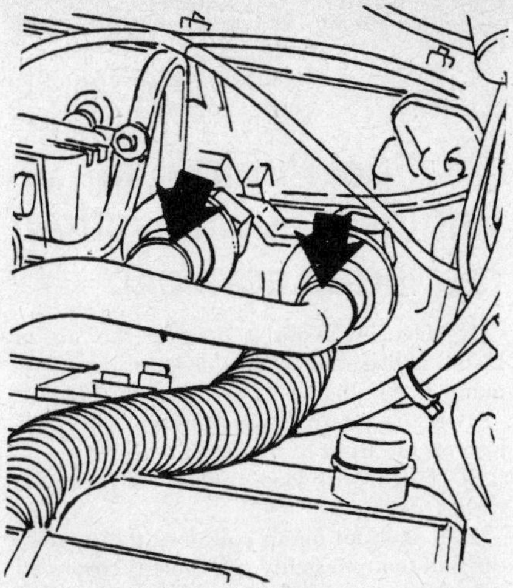
Air injection check valves on the 1978 and 1980 Rabbit (carbureted). If the valves turn blue, replace them

Catalytic Converter

MAINTENANCE

Required maintenance on the catalytic converter involves checking the condition of the ceramic insert every 30,000 miles. As this interval is reached, a indicator light on the dash will glow. Once service to the converter is performed, the odometer must be reset.

TESTING AND SERVICE

CAUTION

Do not drop or strike the converter assembly or damage to the ceramic insert will result.

Damage and overheating of the catalytic converter, indicated by the flickering of the "CAT" warning light, can be caused by the following:

1. Engine misfire caused by faulty spark plug, ignition wires and so on.
2. Improper ignition timing.
3. CO valve set too high.
4. Faulty air pump diverter valve.
5. Faulty temperature sensor.
6. Engine under strain caused by trailer hauling, high speed driving in hot weather, etc.

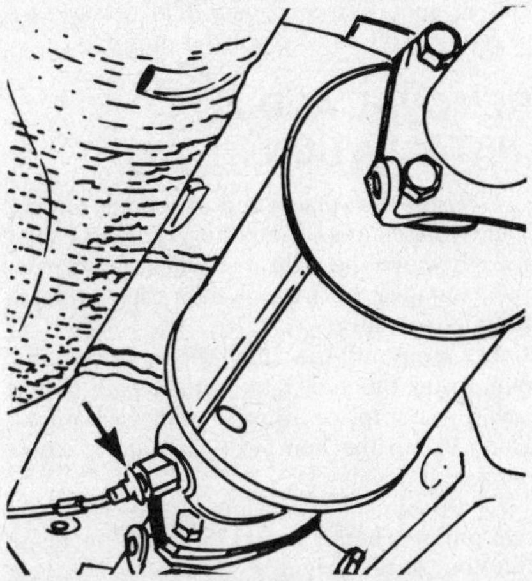
Checking catalytic converter arrow indicates the temperature sensor

A faulty converter is indicated by one of the following symptoms:

1. Poor engine performance.
2. The engine stalls.
3. Rattling in the exhaust system.
4. A CO reading geater than 0.4% at the tail pipe.

Check or replace the converter as follows:

1. Disconnect the temperature sensor.
2. Loosen and remove the bolts holding the converter to the exhaust system and the chassis.
3. Remove the converter.
4. Hold the converter up to a strong light and look through both ends, checking for blockages. If the converter is blocked, replace it.
5. Install the converter in the reverse order of removal.
6. Reset the elapsed mileage odometer by pushing the white button marked "CAT".

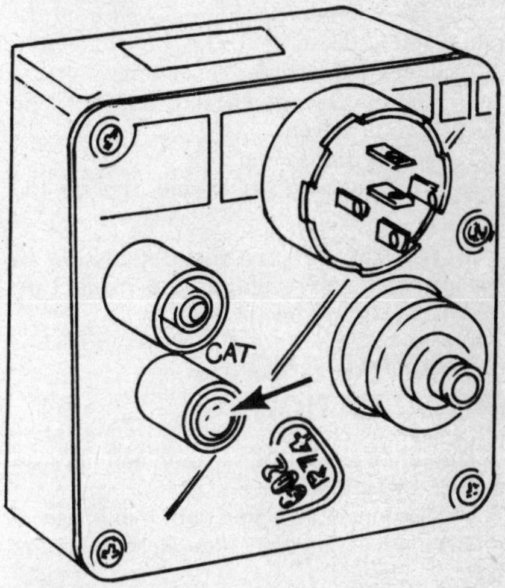

Resetting the catalytic converter elapsed mileage odometer

Oxygen Sensor System (1980 California and 1981 Models)

Many 1980 fuel injected California and 1981 models are equipped with an oxygen sensor system which lowers toxic exhaust emissions while increasing fuel economy. In effect, the sensor system monitors the oxygen content in the exhaust system and, through a control unit and frequency valve, makes adjustments to the air/fuel mixture to achieve maximum fuel efficiency over a wide range of operating conditions. The system consists of the following.

Oxygen Sensor: located in the exhaust manifold. Unscrew to replace.

Control Unit: located behind the glove compartment cover.

Frequency Valve: located next to the fuel distributor.

Thermoswitch: located in the coolant system.

Oxygen Sensor System Relay: white colored relay located in the fuse/relay panel.

Elapsed Mileage Switch: located on the firewall.

Warning Light: marked OXS and located in the instrument panel. Comes on when the oxygen sensor must be replaced (every 30,000 miles).

RESETTING THE ELAPSED MILEAGE SWITCH

After replacing the oxygen sensor, reset the elapsed mileage switch by pushing the white button on the front of the switch.

FUEL SYSTEM

Fuel Pump–Carbureted Engines

CLEANING

The filter screen can be removed from the pump and cleaned.

1. Remove the center cover screw.
2. Remove the screen and gasket. Clean the screen in solvent.
3. Replace the screen.
4. Install a new gasket and replace the cover.

NOTE: Make sure the depression in the pump cover engages the projection on the body of the pump.

REMOVAL AND INSTALLATION

The pump cannot be repaired and must be replaced when defective.

1. Disconnect and plug both fuel lines.
2. Remove the two Allen head retaining bolts.

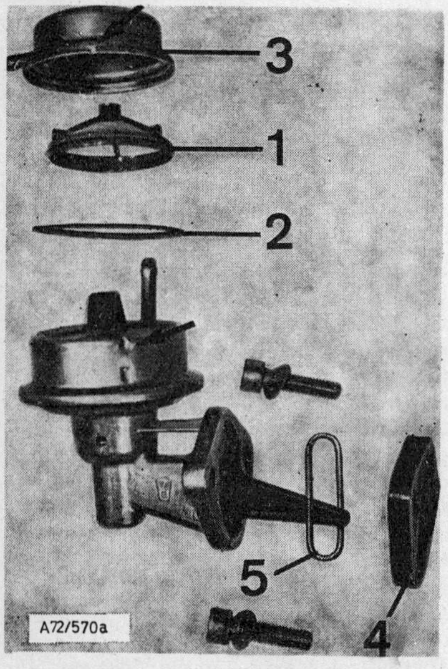

1. Screen
2. Gasket
3. Cover
4. Plastic flange
5. Flange seal

Exploded view of the fuel pump

3. Remove the fuel pump and its plastic flange.
4. Replace the pump in the reverse order of removal. Use a new flange seal.

Fuel Pump–CIS Engines (Fuel Injection)

TESTING–ELECTRICAL

1. Have an assistant operate the starter. Listen at the rear wheel to determine if the pump is running.
2. If the pump is not running, check the fuse on the front of the fuel pump relay.
3. If the fuse is good, replace the fuel pump relay.
4. If the fuel pump still does not operate, the fuel pump is faulty and must be replaced.

TESTING–FUEL PUMP DELIVERY

1. Check the condition of the fuel filter, make sure it is clean.
2. Connect a jumper wire between the #1 terminal on the ignition coil and ground.
3. Disconnect the return fuel line and hold it in a measuring container with a capacity of 1 quart or 1000 cc.
4. Have an assistant run the starter for 30 seconds while watching the quantity of fuel delivered.

The minimum allowable flow for the 1975-78 Rabbit and Scirocco is 750 cc (¾ of a quart) in 30 seconds; 900 cc (9/10 of a quart) in 30 seconds for 1979 and later Rabbits, Jettas and Sciroccos.

For Dashers with the type A fuel pump, identified by the fuel inlet and outlet ports being at opposite ends of the pump, the pump must deliver 1000 cc (1 quart) of fuel in 32 seconds. For Dashers with the type B fuel pump, identified by the inlet and outlet ports forming a 90° angle through the center of the pump, the pump must deliver 1000 cc (1 quart) of fuel in 40 seconds.

NOTE: For the above test, the battery must be fully charged. Also, make sure you have plenty of fuel in the tank.

If the pump fails its specific test, check for a dirty fuel filter, blocked lines or blocked fuel tank strainer (if so equipped). If all of these are in good condition, replace the pump.

REMOVAL AND INSTALLATION

1. Raise the vehicle and support it on jack stands. Disconnect the battery ground cable.
2. Remove the right rear wheel on all cars.
3. Remove the gas tank filler cap to release the fuel pressure.
4. Clamp off the line between the fuel pump and the fuel tank with a pair of soft jawed vise grips or other suitable lock pliers. Don't clamp the line too tightly or you may damage it.
5. Disconnect the clamped line from the fuel pump. There's bound to be a little gas in the line, so be careful.
6. If your vehicle has an accumulator mounted next to the fuel pump, disconnect the fuel lines from the accumulator. Disconnect the wiring from the fuel pump and remove all other lines after marking them for assembly.
7. Loosen and remove the retaining nuts and remove the fuel pump on Dashers and pre-79 Rabbits and Sciroccos. On 1979 and later Rabbits, Jettas and Sciroccos, remove the nuts on the lower bracket, loosen the nut on the upper slotted bracket where it connects to the body and slide the pump out.
8. Install the new fuel pump in the reverse order of removal. Make sure that the new seal washers are installed on the fuel discharge line.

Carburetor

REMOVAL AND INSTALLATION

1. Remove the air cleaner.
2. Disconnect the fuel line.

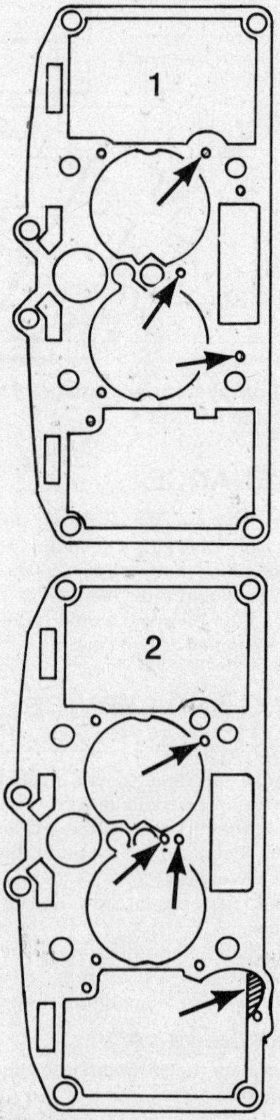

Old (1) and new (2) type carburetor gaskets are not interchangable. Dashers and 1975 Rabbits and Siroccos use old type: 1976 Rabbits and Sciroccos use new type

3. Drain some of the coolant and then disconnect the choke hoses.
4. Disconnect the distributor and EGR valve vacuum lines.
5. Disconnect the electrical lead for the idle cut-off valve.
6. Remove the clip which secures the throttle linkage to the carburetor. Detach the linkage, being careful not to lose any washers or bushings.
7. Unbolt the carburetor from the manifold and remove it.
8. Use a new gasket when replacing the carburetor. Don't overtighten the nuts.

AUTOMATIC CHOKE ADJUSTMENT

The standard adjustment on all versions of the automatic choke is with the two notches aligned with the notch on the housing. To adjust, loosen the three clamping screws and move the outer part of the choke unit.

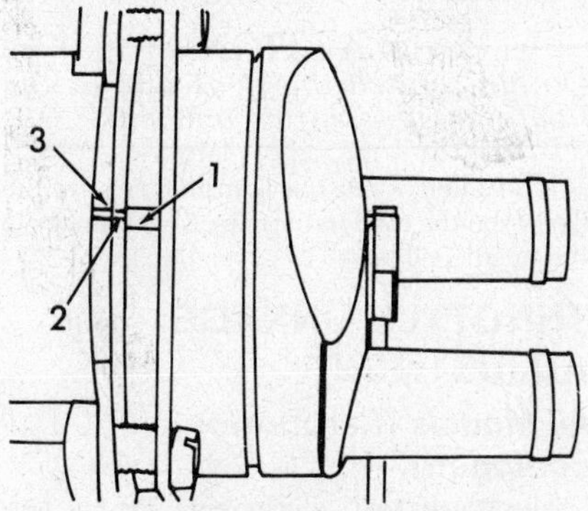

Dasher automatic choke is correctly adjusted when (1) the choke cover, (2) the adjusting ring, and (3) the mark on the carburetor housing are aligned

INTERNAL CHOKE ADJUSTMENT

Dasher

If after performing the automatic choke adjustment, the choke doesn't operate correctly, use the following procedure.
1. Remove the choke cover with the coolant hoses attached and place it out of the way.
2. The control notch should be 180° opposite the adjusting notch. If not turn it with a screwdriver.
3. Reassemble the choke cover and adjust the choke.

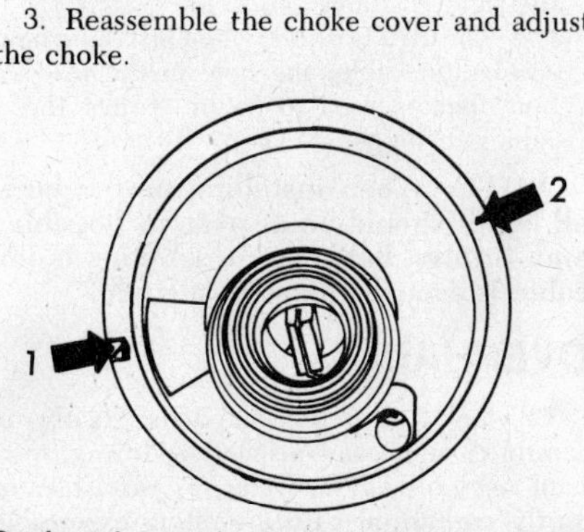

Dasher internal choke adjustment—(1) the adjusting notch, and (2) the control notch

Throttle gap adjusting screw, Rabbit and Scirocco

THROTTLE GAP ADJUSTMENT

All Models Except 1978 and 1980 Rabbit

To adjust first stage throttle gap:
1. The choke must be open and the first stage (primary) throttle closed.
2. Turn the first stage throttle valve stop screw until there is a gap between it and the lever it moves.
3. Turn the screw in until it just touches the lever.
4. Turn screw in ¼ turn more.
5. Adjust the idle speed and CO level.

To adjust the second stage (secondary) throttle gap, proceed as follows.
6. The choke must be open and the first stage throttle must be closed.
7. Turn the second stage (secondary) adjusting screw until there is no clearance in the lever it is mounted on.
8. From this position, turn the screw out ¼ turn. There should be noticeable clearance at the lever.

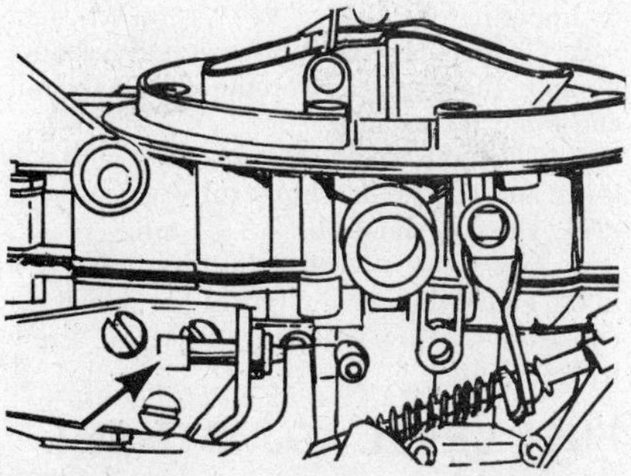

Second stage throttle gap adjustment—all except 1978 and 1980 carbureted Rabbit

1978 Rabbit

You need a vacuum gauge to set the throttle valve. The stop screw (1) is set at the factory, and should not be moved. If the screw is accidentally turned, proceed as follows. Make no adjustment at screw (2).
1. Run the engine at idle.
2. Remove the vacuum advance hose at the carburetor and connect a vacuum gauge.
3. Remove the plastic screw cap and turn the stop screw in until the gauge indicates vacuum.
4. Turn the stop screw out until the gauge indicates no vacuum. Turn the screw an additional ¼ turn and install the plastic cap.
5. Adjust the idle and CO.

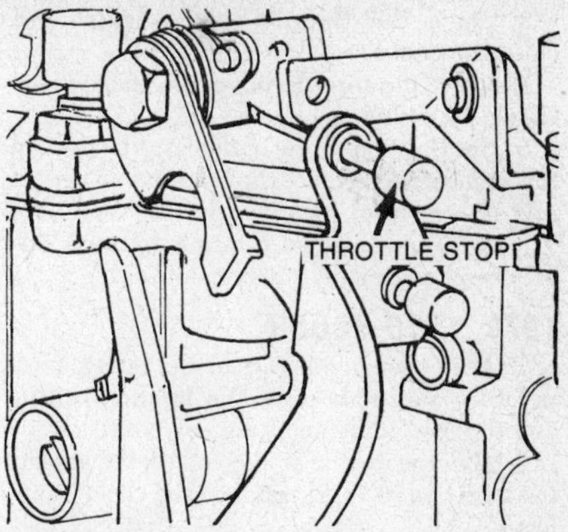

1978 Rabbit throttle gap adjustment (basic)

1980 Rabbit

Throttle gap is set at the factory and should not be tampered with.

FAST IDLE ADJUSTMENT

Dasher, 1975 Rabbit, Scirocco

It will be necessary to remove the carburetor from the engine to perform this procedure.
1. Turn the carburetor upside down and drain the fuel from it.
2. With the carburetor upside down, close the choke tightly and measure the gap between the lower edge of the throttle valve and the housing wall with a drill. The measurement should be: 0.018-0.020 in. (0.45-0.50 mm).
3. Adjust the gap at the adjusting screw (beside the first stage valve) which is facing up when the carburetor is upside down.

1976 Rabbit, Scirocco

On these models it is not necessary to remove the carburetor. The engine must be at normal operating temperature.
1. Set the ignition timing.
2. Disconnect and plug the hose from the choke pull-down unit.

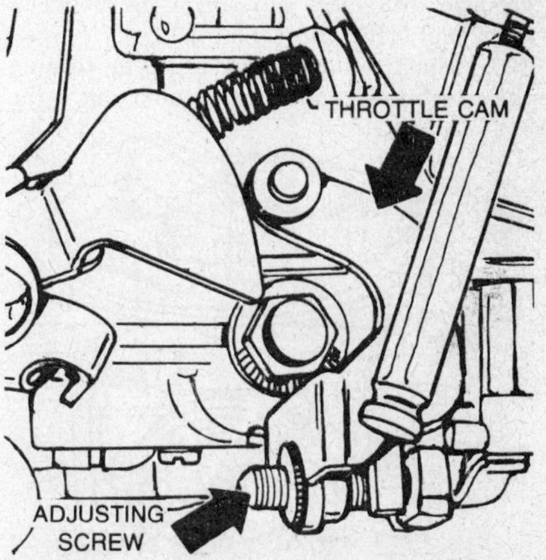

First stage throttle gap adjustment (basic)—all except 1978 and 1980 carbureted Rabbit

3. Open the throttle valve slightly and close the choke valve.
4. Close the throttle valve; the choke valve should be fully open again.
5. Set the stop screw of the fast idle cam on the highest step. Start the engine.
6. Adjust the speed with the screw to: 3150-3250 rpm manual transmission or 3350-3450 rpm automatic transmission.

1978, 1980 Rabbit

1. Run the engine up to operating temperature and make sure the ignition setting and the idle adjustment are correct.
2. Run the engine at idle and set the adjusting screw on its third notch on the choke valve lever.
3. Open the choke valve fully by hand using the choke valve lever.
4. Connect a tachometer and check the rpm, or use the tachometer in the car, if equipped.

CAUTION

See "Electronic Ignition Precaution," above, for warning about connecting tachometers to electronic ignition systems.

5. The fast idle speed should be between 2350-2450 rpm. If not, adjust with fast idle adjustment screw. Lock screw with safety cap after adjustment.
6. On 1978 models, stop the engine, open the choke valve fully and check the gap between the adjusting screw and fast idle cam. It should be 0.008 in.

CHOKE GAP ADJUSTMENT

Dasher

1. Remove the automatic choke cover. You should be able to remove the cover without unfastening the water hoses.
2. Open and close the choke to make sure its internal spring is working. If not, remove the vacuum cover at the side of the choke assembly and check the spring.
3. Push the choke lever to its stop and hold the rod there with a rubber band.
4. Equalize the bushing and lever clearances by pushing the choke valve slightly open.
5. Check the choke gap with an appropriate size drill. The gap should be between 0.152 and 0.168 (3.8-4.2 mm).
6. Adjust the choke valve gap by turning the screw in the end of the vacuum unit at the side of the choke assembly. Lock the adjusting screw by dabbing a little paint over its end.

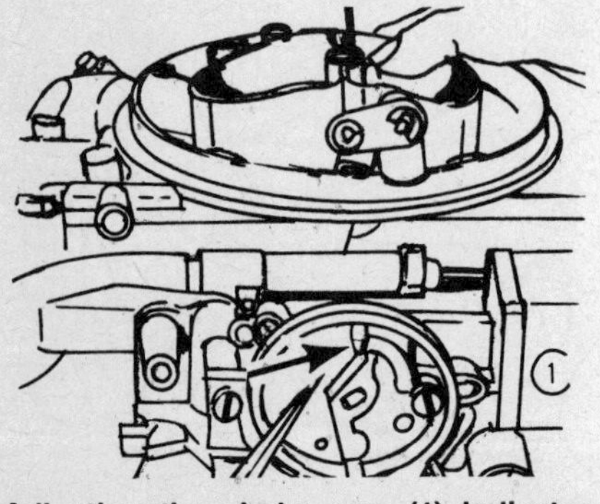

Adjusting the choke gap. (1) indicates vacuum unit which houses the choke valve gap adjusting screw (not shown)

NOTE: When installing the automatic choke cover, the choke lever (protruding part) must fit in the loop on the coiled spring.

1975-76 Rabbit, Scirocco

1. Remove the automatic choke cover.
2. Close the choke valve and push the choke rod to the stop.
3. Hold the choke in position with a rubber band.
4. Push the choke lever down slightly to equalize the clearances.
5. Check the choke gap between the edge of the carburetor wall and the edge of the valve with a drill. It should be:

1975—0.17-0.19 in. with vacuum delay valve
—0.15-0.17 in. without vacuum delay valve
1976—0.14 in. primary activated
—0.20 in. secondary activated

6. Adjust the gap by turning the screw on the choke vacuum unit in to decrease the gap or out to increase the gap.

1978 Rabbit

1. Remove the cover from the automatic choke and fully close the choke.
2. Push the choke rod in the direction of the arrow and check the gap between the choke valve and the air horn wall. It should be 0.11-0.13 in.
3. Adjust the gap with the adjusting screw in the end of the vacuum unit at the side of the choke unit.
4. Reassemble the choke cover. There is an index mark on the choke housing and another on the choke cover.

1980 Rabbit

1. Set the cold idle speed adjuster screw in its upper notch.
2. Connect a manually operated vacuum pump to the connection on the pull-down unit and build up vacuum.
3. Close the choke valve by hand with the lever and check the choke valve gap with a drill. The gap should be 3.3-3.7 mm.
4. Adjust the gap using the adjusting screw in the end of the vacuum unit at the side of the choke unit. After adjusting, lock the screw with sealant.

FUEL LEVEL ADJUSTMENT

Dasher, 1975-76 Rabbit, Scirocco

Remove the top of the carburetor. You should not have to remove the entire carburetor from the engine to perform this operation.

1. With the carburetor top upside down and canted at a 45° angle to prevent the damping ball in the needle valve from settling too deeply due to the weight of the float, measure from the highest tip of the first stage float to the carburetor surface (minus the gasket). The distance for the first stage float should be 1.10 in.±0.02 in. (28 mm±0.5 mm).
2. Adjust the float level by bending the float bracket.
3. Adjust the second stage float in the same manner. The distance for the second stage float should be 1.20±0.02 in. (30 mm±0.5 mm).
4. Adjust the float level by bending the float bracket.

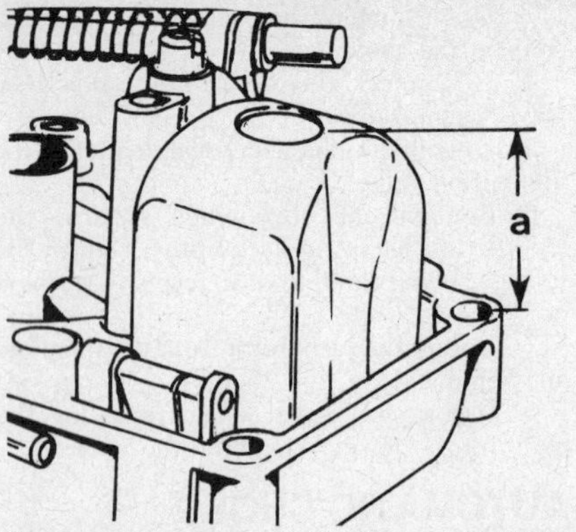

Float adjustment—1975 Dasher, 1975-76 Rabbit, Scirocco

CAUTION

Do not scratch the float skin or the float may absorb fuel and sink.

If float height must be adjusted, remove the float from the carburetor to prevent damage to the needle valve.

THROTTLE LINKAGE ADJUSTMENT

All Models (Carburetor Equipped)

Throttle linkage adjustments are not normally required. However, it is a good idea to make sure that the throttle valve(s) in the carburetor open all the way when the accelerator pedal is held in the wide-open position. Only the primary (first stage) throttle valve will open when the pedal is pushed with the engine off: the secondary throttle on Volkswagen two-barrel carburetors is vacuum-operated.

Make note of the following:

a. Always be careful not to kink or twist the cables during installation or adjustment—this can cause rapid wear and binding.
b. On the Rabbits and Sciroccos, the accelerator cable will only bend one way—make sure you install it with the bends in the right positions.
c. On 1975 Dashers, when installing new accelerator cable, the hole in the firewall must be enlarged to 5/8 in. Adjust these cables at the pedal clamp.

NOTE: When installing new cables, all bends should be as wide as possible, and fittings between which the inner cable is exposed must be aligned.

OVERHAUL

Efficient carburetion depends greatly on careful cleaning and inspection during overhaul since dirt, gum, water, or varnish in or on the carburetor parts are often responsible for poor performance.

Overhaul the carburetor in a clean, dust-free area. Carefully disassemble the carburetor, referring often to a diagram. Keep all similar and look-alike parts segregated during disassembly and cleaning to avoid accidental interchange during assembly. Make a note of all jet sizes.

When the carburetor is disassembled, wash all parts (except diaphragms, electric choke units, pump plunger, and any other plastic, leather, fiber, or rubber parts) in clean carburetor solvent. Do not leave parts in the solvent any longer than is necessary to sufficiently loosen the deposits. Excessive cleaning may remove the special finish from the float bowl and choke valve bodies, leaving these parts unfit for service. Rinse all parts in clean solvent and blow them dry with compressed air or allow them to air dry. Wipe clean all cork, plastic, leather, and fiber parts with a clean, lint-free cloth.

Blow out all passages and jets with compressed air and be sure that there are not restrictions or blockages. Never use wire or similar tools to clean jets, fuel passages, or air bleeds. Clean all jets and valves separately to avoid accidental interchange.

Check all parts for wear or damage. If wear or damage is found, replace the defective parts. Especially check the following:

1. Check the float needle and seat for wear. If wear is found, replace the complete assembly.
2. Check the float hinge pin for wear and the float(s) for dents or distortion. Replace the float if fuel has leaked into it.
3. Check the throttle and choke shaft bores for wear or an out-of-round condition. Damage or wear to the throttle arm, shaft, or shaft bore will often require replacement of the throttle body. These parts require a close tolerance of fit; wear may allow air leakage, which could adversely affect starting and idling.

NOTE: Throttle shafts and bushings are not included in overhaul kits. They can be purchased separately.

4. Inspect the idle mixture adjusting needles for burrs or grooves. Any such condition requires replacement of the needle, since you will not be able to obtain a satisfactory idle.
5. Test the accelerator pump check valves. They should pass air one way but not the other. Test for proper seating by blowing and sucking on the valve. Replace the valve if necessary. If the valve is satisfactory, wash the valve again to remove breath moisture.
6. Check the bowl cover for warped surfaces with a straightedge.
7. Closely inspect the valves and seats for wear and damage, replacing as necessary.
8. After the carburetor is assembled, check the choke valve for freedom of operation.

Carburetor overhaul kits are recommended for each overhaul. These kits contain all gaskets and new parts to replace those that deteriorate most rapidly. Failure to replace all parts supplied with the kit (especially gaskets) can result in poor performance later.

After cleaning and checking all components, reassemble the carburetor, using new parts and referring to the exploded view. When reassembling, make sure that all screws and jets are tight in their seats, but do not overtighten, as the tips will be distorted. Tighten all screws gradually, in rotation. Do not tighten needle valves into their seats; uneven jetting will result. Always use new gaskets. Be sure to adjust the float level when reassembling.

CIS Fuel Injection

AIR FLOW SENSOR-TESTING AND ADJUSTMENT

Sensor Plate Lever and Control Plunger

1. Run the engine for a short time at idle.
2. Remove the air duct from the air flow sensor assembly.
3. Using a magnet, lift the sensor plate. A light even resistance must be felt over the sensor plate entire travel.

NOTE: Make certain that the air sensor plate is centered in the air cone. If adjustment is necessary, proceed as follows:

a. Loosen the centering bolt slightly.
b. Run a 0.004 in. (0.10 mm) feeler gauge around the perimeter of the air gap.
c. Tighten the centering bolt.

4. No resistance must be felt when the sensor plate is moved rapidly up and down. If resistance is felt, the air sensor must be replaced.
5. If the sensor plate is hard to move upward but moves freely down, the control plunger is sticking. Remove the fuel distributor and clean the control plunger in solvent. If after installation the plunger is still sticking, the fuel distributor must be replaced.

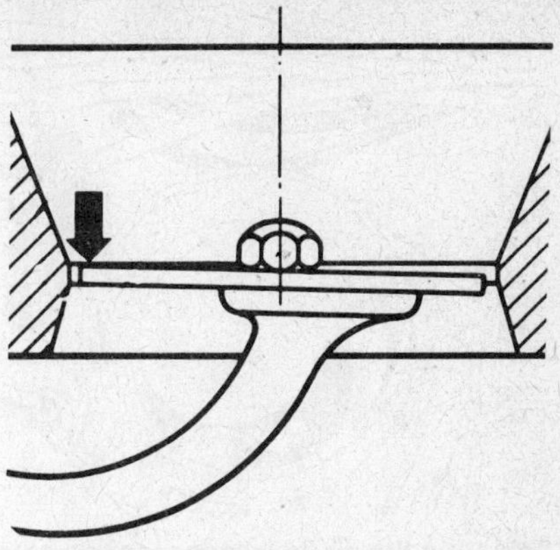

Aligning the air flow sensor plate with the edge of the air cone

Sensor Plate Height Adjustment

The height adjustment of the sensor plate must be checked under fuel pressure. You will also need a bridging adaptor (US 4480/3).

1. Install a pressure gauge in the line between the fuel distributor and control pressure regulator.
2. Remove the rubber elbow from the air flow sensor housing.
3. Remove the fuel pump relay from the fuse panel and install a bridging adaptor (US 4480/3).
4. Switch the adaptor ON and wait until pressure reads 49-54 psi.
5. Switch the bridging adaptor OFF; the pressure should fall to 28-37 psi.
6. The upper edge of the sensor plate must be even with the bottom of the air cone taper

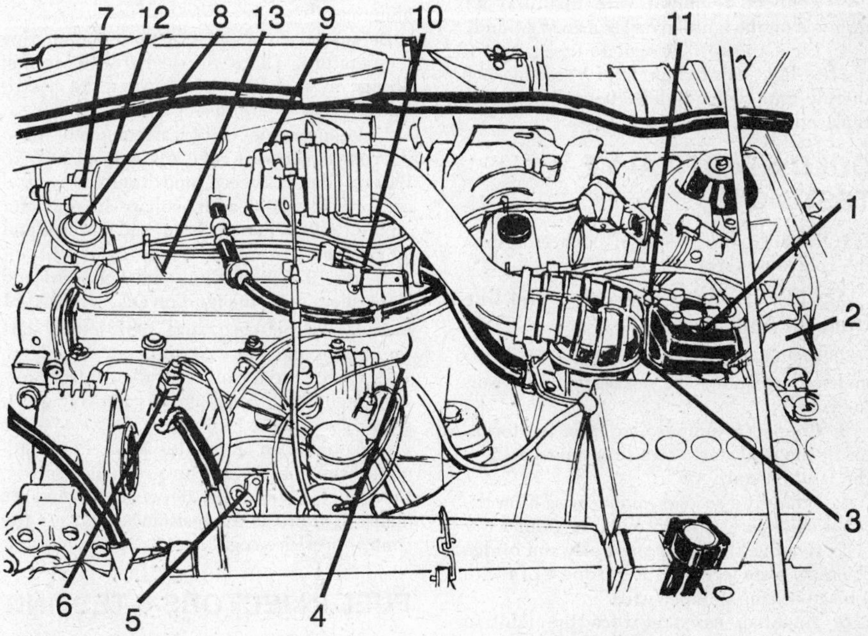

1. Fuel distributor
2. Fuel filter
3. Air flow sensor
4. EGR temperature control valve (not shown)
5. Control pressure regulator
6. Thermo-time switch
7. Cold start valve
8. EGR valve
9. Idle adjust
10. Deceleration valve
11. Plug for CO adjustment
12. Auxiliary air regulator (not shown)
13. Fuel injector

CIS fuel injection components—Rabbit, Jetta, Scirocco shown

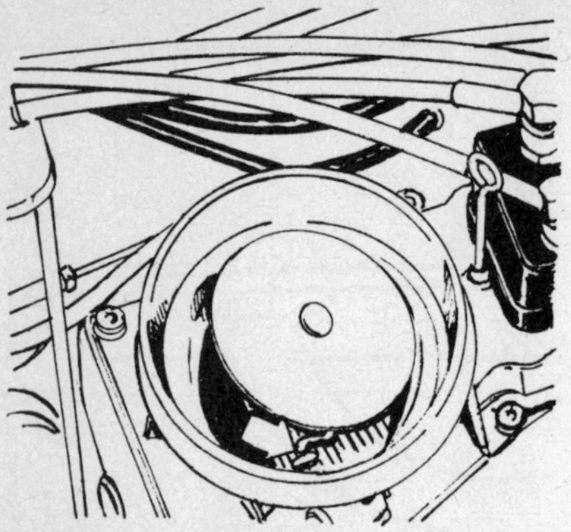

Adjusting the air flow sensor spring stop

or no more than 0.020 in. below the bottom of the taper.

7. Bend the clip to adjust the height.
8. Recheck the pressure readings after adjusting.
9. Remove the pressure gauge, reconnect the fuel lines and install the fuel pump relay.

THERMO-TIME SWITCH-TESTING

NOTE: To properly perform the following tests, the engine must be cold with the water temperature below 95 F (35C).

1. Disconnect the electrical connector from the cold start valve on the end of the intake manifold.
2. Connect a test light across the cold start valve terminals.
3. Connect a jumper wire from the #1 terminal on the ignition coil to a good ground.
4. Have an assistant operate the starter. If the test light fails to light after 8 seconds, the thermo-time switch is defective and should be replaced.

COLD START VALVE—TESTING

1. Remove the electrical connector from the cold start valve.

NOTE: Do not remove the fuel line from the cold start valve.

2. Remove the cold start valve from the manifold and point the nozzle into a measuring container.
3. Connect a jumper wire from one terminal of the cold start valve to terminal #15 on the ignition coil.
4. Connect a second jumper wire from the other cold start valve terminal to ground.
5. Remove the fuel pump relay and bridge the relay plate terminals #L13 and #L14 with a fused (8 amp) jumper wire.
6. Have an assistant turn the ignition switch on while observing the fuel spray pattern from the cold start valve. The spray pattern from the nozzle must be cone-shaped and steady, if not replace the valve.
7. Turn the ignition switch off.
8. Wipe the nozzle dry with a clean rag and check for leakage. If drops form within one minute, the valve is defective and must be replaced.

AUXILIARY AIR REGULATOR—TESTING

1975-78 Rabbits, Sciroccos

NOTE: The engine must be cold to perform this test.

1. Remove the hose from the auxiliary air regulator and plug.
2. Observe gate valve with the aid of a mirror. The valve must be open. If the valve is not open, replace the regulator.
3. Run the engine at idle for 5 minutes. Again check the gate valve, it should be closed. If the valve did not close, replace the auxiliary air regulator.

Dasher, 1979-81 Rabbit, Scirocco, Jetta

NOTE: The engine must be cold to perform this test.

1. Unplug the electrical connector from the auxiliary air regulator.
2. Start the engine and check the idle.
3. Pinch the hose between the auxiliary air regulator and the intake manifold. The engine idle should drop. Reconnect the electrical connector.
4. Repeat the test on the engine at operating temperature. The idle speed should remain constant when the hose is pinched. If not, replace the auxiliary air regulator.

CONTROL PRESSURE REGULATOR—TESTING

The system is under considerable constant pressure. The only practical test that should be attempted by the owner is one using an ohmmeter.

Be sure the engine is at normal operating temperature. There should be no loose fuel fittings or other fire hazards when the electrical connections are disengaged.

1. Remove the electrical connector from the control pressure regulator only on 1975-78 Rabbits and Sciroccos, and from the control pressure regulator and auxiliary air regulator on the 1979-81 Rabbit, Jetta, and Scirocco and all Dashers.
2. On 1975-78 Rabbits and Sciroccos and all Dashers, turn the ignition ON. On 1979-81 Rabbits and Sciroccos and 1981 Jettas, start the engine and run it at idle.
3. Check the terminals of the control pressure regulator wiring harness for voltage. It should be at least 11.5 volts.
4. Connect an ohmmeter across the terminals of the control pressure regulator socket. Resistance should be between 16 and 22 ohms. If there is no resistance, replace the control pressure regulator.

FUEL INJECTORS—TESTING

1. Remove the injector but leave it connected to the fuel line.
2. Point the injector into a measuring container.
3. Remove the fuel pump relay and bridge the relay plate terminals #L13 and L14 with a fused (8 amp) jumper wire.
4. Remove the air duct from the air flow sensor.
5. Have an assistant turn the ignition switch on.
6. Lift the air flow sensor plate with a magnet and observe the injector nozzle spray pattern. The spray pattern must be cone shaped and even, if not replace the injector.
7. Turn the ignition off and hold the injector horizontally. It should not drip.

NOTE: One or more injectors may be checked at the same time.

8. Moisten the rubber seals on the injectors with fuel before installing.
9. Press the injectors firmly into place.

FUEL DISTRIBUTOR—REMOVAL AND INSTALLATION

1. Release the pressure in the system by loosening the fuel line on the control pressure regulator (large connector). Have a rag ready to catch the fuel that escapes.
2. Mark the fuel lines in the top of the distributor so that you will be able to put them back in their correct positions.

NOTE: Using different colored paints is usually a good marking device. When you mark each line, be sure to mark the spot where it connects to the distributor.

3. Clean the fuel lines, then remove them from the distributor. Remove the little looped wire plug (the CO adjusting screw plug). Remove the two retaining screws in the top of the distributor.

NOTE: When removing the fuel distributor be sure the control plunger does not fall out from underneath.

4. If the control plunger has been removed, moisten it with gasoline before installing. The small shoulder on the plunger is inserted first.

NOTE: Always use new gaskets and O-ring when removing and installing fuel distributor. Lock all retaining screws with loctite or its equivalent.

System Pressure Adjustments

The fuel system pressure is present at the factory and is adjusted by either adding or subtracting shims to or from the back of the pressure relief valve spring located in the fuel distributor.

Since special pressure and measuring gauges are needed to adjust system pressure, this job should be left to your Volkswagen dealer.

SUBSTITUTE FOR BRIDGING ADAPTOR 4480/3

The bridging adapter simply connects two terminals of the fuel pump relay socket. To fashion a homemade adapter, attach an 8 amp in-line fuse (the kind commonly used in radios; make sure it's 8 amp, though) between terminals L 13 and L 14 of the fuel pump relay socket in the fuse/relay panel.

Diesel Fuel Injection

The diesel fuel system is an extremely

complex and sensitive system. Very few repairs or adjustments are possible by the owner. Any service other than that listed here should be referred to an authorized VW dealer or diesel specialist. The injection pump itself is not repairable; it can only be replaced.

Any work done to the diesel fuel injection should be done with absolute cleanliness. Even the smallest specks of dirt will have a disastrous effect on the injection system.

Do not attempt to remove the fuel injectors. They are very delicate and must be removed with a special tool to prevent damage. The fuel in the system is also under tremendous pressure (1700-1850 psi), so it's not wise to loosen any lines with the engine running. Exposing your skin to the spray from the injector at working pressure can cause fuel to penetrate the skin.

CHECKING INJECTION PUMP TIMING

Checking the injection pump timing also involves checking the valve timing. To alter the injection pump timing, the camshaft gear must be removed and repositioned. This also changes the valve timing. Special tool (VW 210) is necessary to properly tension the injection pump drive belt on the diesel engine.

1. Set the engine at TDC on No. 1 cylinder. In this position, the TDC mark on the flywheel should be aligned with boss on the bell housing and both valves of No. 1 cylinder should be closed.
2. The marks on the pump and mounting plate should also be aligned.
3. If the valve timing is incorrect, set the valve timing as detailed in the engine section.

ACCELERATOR CABLE ADJUSTMENT

The ball pin on the pump lever should be pointing up and be aligned with the mark in the slot. The accelerator cable should be attached at the upper hole in the bracket. With the pedal in the full throttle position, adjust the cable so that the pump lever contacts the stop with no binding or strain.

COLD START CABLE ADJUSTMENT

When the cold start knob on the dash is pulled out, the fuel injection pump timing is advanced 2.5°. This improves cold starting and running until the engine warms up.

1. Insert the washer on the cable.
2. Insert the cable in the bracket with the rubber housing. Install the cable in the pin.
3. Install the lockwasher.
4. Move the lever to the zero position (direction of arrow). Pull the inner cable tight and tighten the clamp screw.

CHECKING GLOW PLUGS CURRENT SUPPLY

1. Connect a test light between No. 4 cylinder glow plug and ground.
2. Turn the key to the heat position. The test light should light up.
3. If not, check the glow plug relay, ignition switch, or fuse box relay plate.

CHECKING GLOW PLUGS

Make this check after establishing that there is current to the glow plugs.

1. Remove the wire and glow plug bus bar.
2. Connect the test light between the battery positive terminal and each glow plug in turn.
3. If the light lights, the glow plug is OK. If not, the glow plug is defective and must be replaced.

MANUAL TRANSMISSION

TRANSAXLE REMOVAL AND INSTALLATION

Dasher

1. Disconnect the battery ground cable.
2. Disconnect the exhaust pipe from the manifold and its bracket on the transaxle.
3. Remove the square-headed bolt on the shift linkage. Later models have a hex lead bolt.
4. Press the shift linkage coupling off.
5. Disconnect the clutch cable.
6. Disconnect the speedometer cable.
7. Detach the axle shafts from the transaxle.
8. Remove the starter.
9. Remove the inspection plate.
10. Remove the engine-to-transaxle bolts.
11. Remove the transaxle crossmember.
12. Support the transaxle with a jack.
13. Pry the transaxle out from the engine.
14. Lift the transaxle out of the car with an assistant.
15. Installation is the reverse of removal. Observe the following when installing the transaxle.
    a. When installing the transaxle crossmember, do not fully tighten the bolts until the transaxle is aligned and fully installed in the vehicle.
    b. Tighten the engine-to-transaxle bolts to 40 ft/lbs.
    c. Tighten the axle shaft bolts to 33 ft/lbs.
    d. On models with the rubber core rear transaxle mount, the rubber core must be centered in its housing.
    e. Make sure there is a 3/8 in. clearance between the header pipe and the floor of the vehicle.
    f. Adjust the clutch (see below).

Rabbit, Scirocco, Jetta

The engine and transaxle may be removed together as explained under Engine Removal and Installation or the transaxle may be removed alone, as explained here.

1. Disconnect the battery ground cable.
2. Support the left end of the engine at the lifting eye.
3. Remove the left transmission mount (between the transmission and the firewall).
4. Turn the engine until the lug on the flywheel (to the left of the TDC mark) aligns with the flywheel timing pointer.
5. Detach the speedometer drive cable, backup light wire, and clutch cable.
6. Remove the engine to transmission bolts.
7. Disconnect the shift linkage.
8. Detach the transmission ground strap.
9. Remove the starter.
10. Remove the engine mounting support near the starter.
11. Remove the rear transmission mount.
12. Unbolt and wire up the driveshafts.
13. From underneath, remove the bolts for the large cover plate, but don't remove it. Unbolt the small cover plate on the firewall side of the engine. Remove the engine to transmission nut immediately below the small plate.
14. Press the transmission off the dowels and remove it from below the car.

To install the transaxle:

15. The recess in the flywheel edge must be at 3:00 o'clock. Tighten the engine to transmission bolts to 47 ft/lbs. Tighten the engine mounting support bolts to 47 ft/lbs. Tighten the driveshaft bolts to 32 ft/lbs.
16. Check the adjustment of the shift linkage.

SHIFT LINKAGE ADJUSTMENT

Dasher

TO CHASSIS NO. 3-5 2 044 764

1. Shift to Neutral.
2. Remove the round floor cover.
3. Loosen the nuts and move the bearing house so that the shift lever inclines approximately 5° to the rear.
4. Tighten the nuts.
5. Shift into second gear.
6. Loosen the stop plate bolts.
7. Adjust the plate so that the shift lever has 3/8-5/8 in. lateral movement at the shift knob.

NOTE: Moving the plate to the right increases play; moving the plate to the left decreases play.

8. Tighten the bolts. Check the shift pattern and make sure that reverse engages easily.

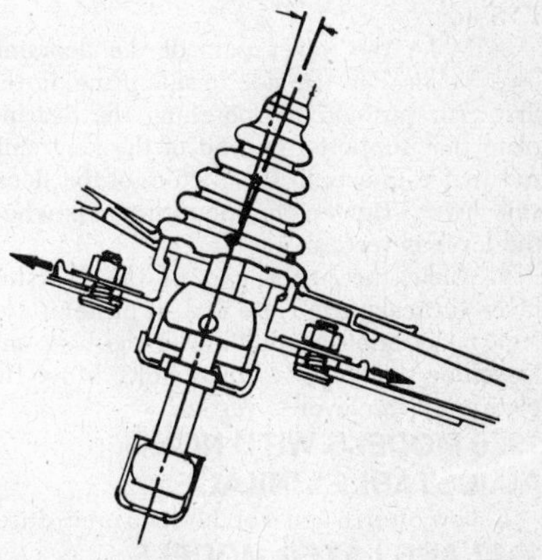

Dasher manual transmission neutral shift lever adjustment

FROM CHASSIS NO. 3-5 2 044 765

An adjusting tool, VW 3014, must be used on these models.

1. Place the lever in Neutral.
2. Working under the car, loosen the clamp nut.
3. Inside the car, remove the gear lever knob and the shift boot. It is not necessary to remove the console. Align the centering holes of the lever housing and the lever bearing housing.
4. Install the tool with the locating pin toward the front. Push the lever to the left side of the tool cutout. Tighten the lower knurled knob to secure the tool.
5. Move the top slide of the tool to the left stop and tighten the upper knurled knob.
6. Push the shift lever to the right side of the cutout. Align the shift rod and shift finger under the car, and tighten the clamp nut. Remove the tool.
7. Place the lever in first. Press the lever to the left side against the stop. Release the lever; it should spring back ¼ to ½ in. If not, move the lever housing slightly sideways to correct. Check that all gears can be engaged easily, particularly reverse.

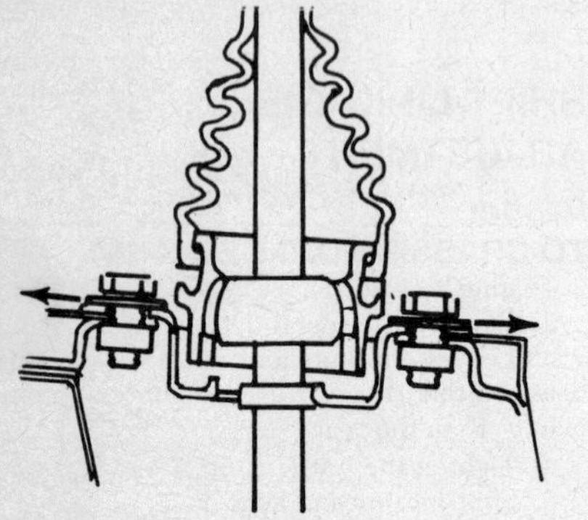

Dasher manual transmission second gear shift lever adjustment

Rabbit, Scirocco, Jetta

1975 MODELS WITH ADJUSTABLE LINKAGE

1. Adjust the long rod over the left driveshaft coupling to a length of 6.42-6.50 in.
2. Adjust the short angled rod that attaches to the final drive housing to a length of 1.18-1.25 in.
3. Make the lower part of the floorshift lever vertical (in the side to side plane) in the first gear position by loosening the bearing plate that supports the end of the long shift rod that connects to the bottom of the floorshift lever. Tighten the mounting nuts when the lever is vertical.
4. Make the lower part of the floorshift lever vertical (in the fore and aft plane) in the Neutral position by pulling up the boot and loosening the two lever plate bolts. Move the plate until the lever is vertical.

1976 MODELS WITH NON-ADJUSTABLE LINKAGE

Follow Steps 3 and 4 of the 1975 procedure.

1977 AND LATER MODELS

This category includes some late 1976 models; it is for Rabbits from chassis No. 176 3 000 001, and Sciroccos from chassis No. 536 2 000 001.

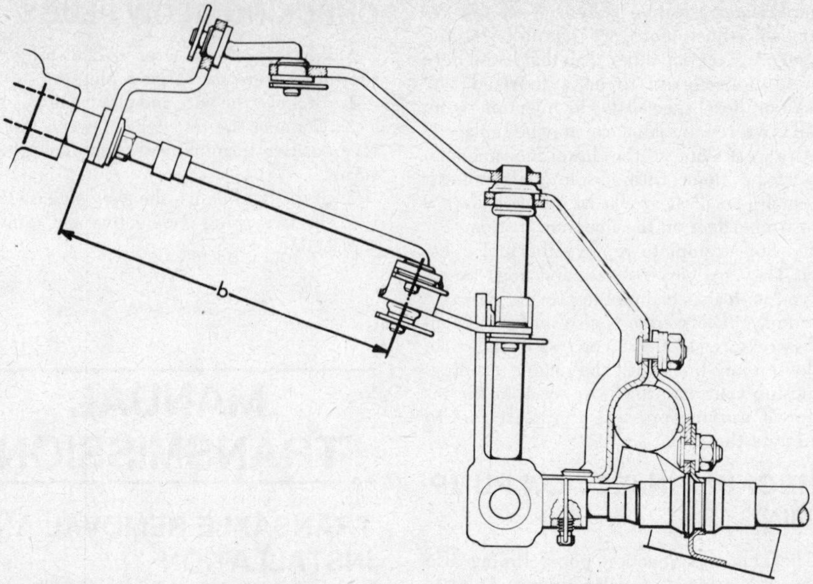

The long rod on the Rabbit and Sirocco shift linkage is to be adjusted to a length (b) of 6.42-6.50 in.

1. Align the holes of the lever housing plate with the holes of the lever bearing plate.
2. Loosen the shift rod clamp. Pull the boot off the lever housing and push it out of the way. It may be necessary to loosen the screws in the cover plate to free the boot.
3. Check that the shift finger is in the center of the stopping plate.
4. Adjust the shift rod end so that it is ¾ in. (9/32 in. for five speed transmissions) from the right side of the lever housing. Tighten the shift rod clamp and check the shifter operation.

Selector Shaft Lockbolt Adjustment

Make this adjustment on Rabbits, Jettas and Sciroccos after linkage adjustment, if the linkage still feels spongy or jams. There are 2 kinds of lockbolts; those with plastic caps (1975) or those with lockrings (1976 and later).

1975 MODELS

1. Remove the linkage from the selector shaft lever and put the transmission in Neutral.

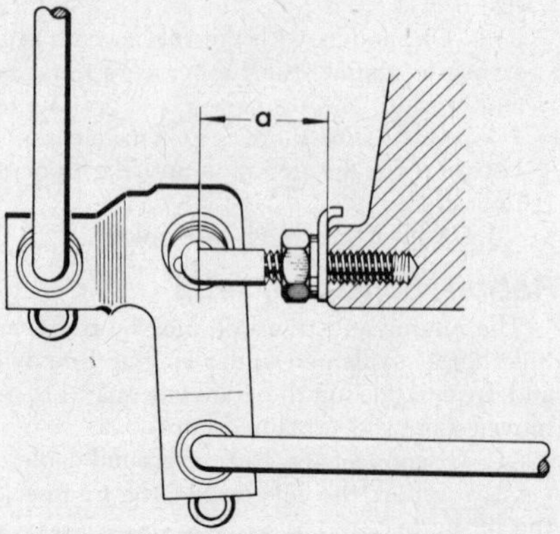

The short angled rod on the Rabbit and Scirocco shift linkage is to be adjusted to a length (a) of 1.18—1.25 in.

2. Turn the slotted plunger until the plunger hits bottom. The nut will start to move out.
3. From here, turn the plunger back ¼ turn and install the plastic cap.
4. Reconnect the linkage.

1976 AND LATER MODELS

1. Disconnect the shift linkage and put the transmission in Neutral.
2. Loosen the locknut and turn the adjusting sleeve in until the lockring lifts off the sleeve.
3. Turn the adjusting sleeve back until the lockring just contacts the sleeve. Tighten the locknut.
4. Turn the shaft slightly. The lockring should lift as soon as the shaft is turned.
5. Reconnect the linkage.

Fifth Gear Lockbolt Adjustment

RABBIT, SCIROCCO, JETTA ONLY

This adjustment is made with the transmission in neutral. The fifth gear lockbolt is located on top of the transmission next to the selector shaft lockbolt. It has a large protective cap over it.

1. Remove the protective cap.
2. Loosen the locknut and tighten the adjusting sleeve until the detent plunger in the center of the sleeve just begins to move up.
3. Loosen the adjusting sleeve ⅓ of a turn and tighten the locknut. Make sure the transmission shifts in and out of fifth gear easily. Replace the protective cap.

CLUTCH

PEDAL FREE PLAY ADJUSTMENT

Clutch pedal free play should be ⅝ in. for all Dashers and pre-1979 Rabbits and Sciroc-

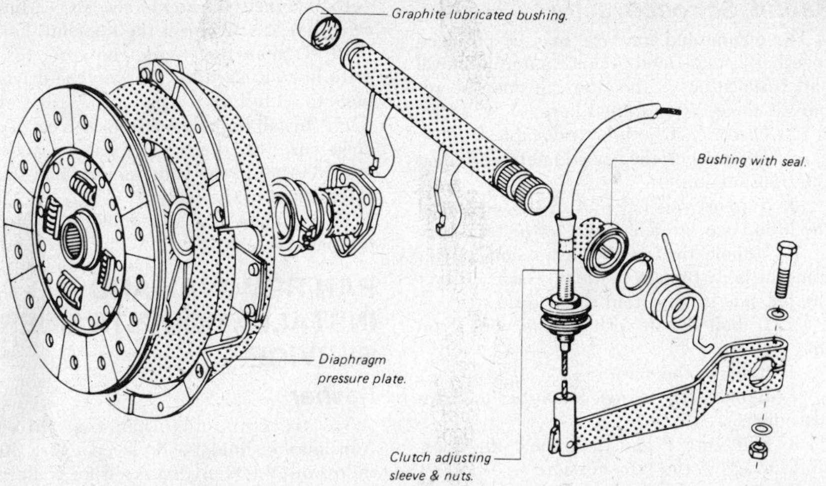

Dasher clutch components; the adjusting sleeve and nuts are adjacent to the oil filter in the engine compartment

cos. 1979 and later Rabbits, Jettas and Sciroccos should have 9/16 in. free play at the pedal. Pedal free play is the distance the pedal can be depressed before the linkage starts to act on the throwout bearing.

1. Adjust the clutch pedal free play by loosening the two nuts on the cable near the oil filter on the Dasher. On the Rabbit, Jetta and Scirocco, the cable adjustment point is on the front of the transmission.
2. After obtaining the correct free play, tighten the adjusting nuts.

REMOVAL AND INSTALLATION

Dasher

1. Remove the transaxle.
2. Match mark the flywheel and pressure plate if the pressure plate is being reused.
3. Gradually loosen the pressure plate bolts one or two turns at a time in a crisscross pattern to prevent distortion.
4. Remove the pressure plate and disc.
5. Check the clutch disc for uneven or excessive lining wear. Examine the pressure plate for cracking, scorching, or scoring. Replace any questionable components.
6. Install the clutch disc and pressure plate. Use a dummy shaft to keep the disc centered.
7. Gradually tighten the pressure-plate-to-flywheel bolts in a crisscross pattern. Tighten the bolts to 18 ft/lbs.
8. Install the throwout bearing.
9. Install the transaxle on the engine.
10. Replace the transaxle.

Rabbit, Scirocco, Jetta

1. Remove the transmission.
2. Attach a toothed flywheel holder and gradually loosen the flywheel to pressure plate bolts one or two turns at a time in a crisscross pattern to prevent distortion.
3. Remove the flywheel and the clutch disc.
4. Use a screwdriver to remove the release plate retaining ring. Remove the release plate.
5. Lock the pressure plate in place and unbolt it from the crankshaft. Loosen the bolts one or two turns at a time in a crisscross pattern to prevent distortion.
6. On installation, use new bolts to attach the pressure plate to the crankshaft. Use a thread locking compound and torque the bolts in a diagonal pattern to 54 ft/lbs.
7. Lubricate the clutch disc splines with multi-purpose grease. Lubricate the release plate contact surface and pushrod socket with multi-purpose grease. Install the release plate, retaining ring, and clutch disc.
8. Install a dummy shaft to align the clutch disc.
9. Install the flywheel, tightening the bolts one or two turns at a time in a crisscross pattern to prevent distortion. Torque the bolts to 14 ft/lbs.
10. Replace the transmission.

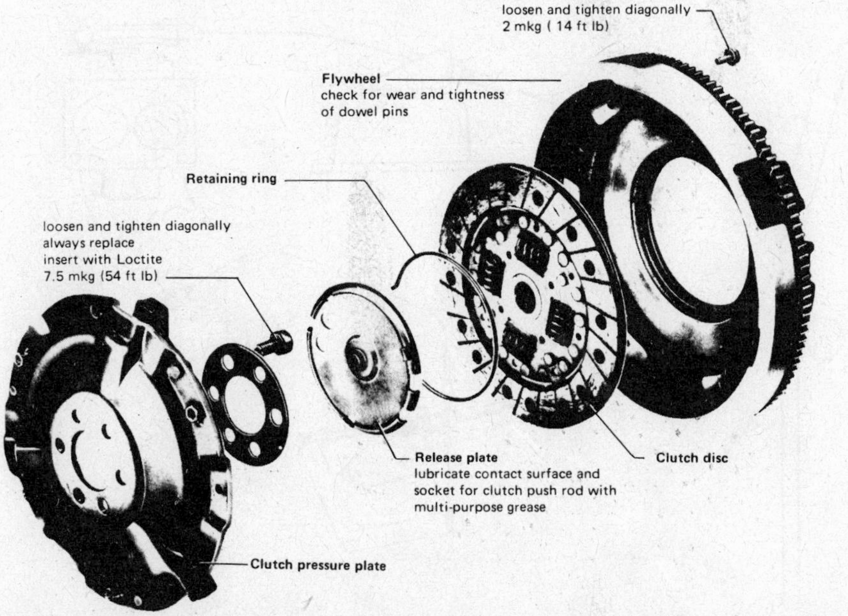

The Rabbit, Jetta and Scirocco clutch; the pressure plate is bolted to the crankshaft and the clutch is actuated by a pushrod working on the release plate

AUTOMATIC TRANSMISSION

TRANSAXLE REMOVAL AND INSTALLATION

Dasher

The following procedures are for both types of Dasher automatic transmissions, the 003 and the 089. The type numbers are visible on the top of the automatic transmission unit (as opposed to the differential unit) of the transaxle. Another way to tell the type 003 transmission from the 089 is the type 003 has a vacuum modulator hose coming from the driver's side front of the transmission above the pan. The type 089 does not. Don't confuse the ATF filler pipe with the above mentioned hose.

1. Disconnect the battery ground strap.
2. Raise the car and place the support stands so that you will have free access to the transaxle and axle shafts.
3. Disconnect the speedometer cable.
4. On the 089, remove the accelerator cable from the throttle valve housing.
5. Remove two of the upper engine/transaxle bolts. On the 089 transmission, support the engine with either special tool 10-222 or an appropriate jack.
6. Disconnect the exhaust pipe.
7. Remove the torque converter cover plate. On the 003 transmission, remove the vacuum modulator hose.
8. Remove the circlip holding the selector lever cable to the lever and remove the cable.
9. Remove the starter.
10. On the 003 disconnect the kickdown switch wires.
11. The torque converter is mounted to the flywheel by three bolts. The bolts are accesi-

ble through the starter hole. You'll have to turn the engine over by hand to remove all three.

12. Remove the axle shaft to transaxle socket head bolts.

13. Matchmark the position of the ball joint on the left control arm and remove the ball joint from the arm. Hold the wheel assembly out away from the arm to provide clearance between the axle shaft and the transmission.

14. Remove the exhaust pipe from the transaxle bracket.

15. Disconnect the remaining transmission controls. Those you cannot reach can be removed when the transaxle is lowered a little.

16. Unbolt the transaxle crossmember and remove it from the transaxle.

17. Support the transaxle on a jack and loosen the lower engine/transaxle bolts.

18. On the 089 transmission, remove all engine/transaxle bolts. Have an assistant pull the left wheel out as far as it will go and slowly lower the transmission, making sure the torque converter does not fall off.

19. On the 003 transmission, loosen the union nut on the ATF filler pipe so that the pipe can be swivelled. Remove the engine/transaxle bolts and lower the unit. You may have to pull the left wheel out a little so that the axle shaft clears the transaxle case. Make sure the torque converter does not fall off.

20. Installation is the reverse of removal with the following notes.

On both transaxles, the torque converter nipple must be about 1³/₁₆ in. from the bell housing face surface. If it sticks out further than this, the oil pump shaft has probably pulled out. You'll have to manipulate the converter and shaft until it goes in again.

Tighten the engine/transaxle bolts to 40 ft/lbs and the torque converter bolts to 20-23 ft/lbs. New torque converter bolts should be used. Torque the axle shaft bolts to 33 ft/lbs, and the ball joint to control arm bolts to 45 ft/lbs.

Check the shift linkage adjustment.

Rabbit, Scirocco, Jetta

The engine and transaxle may be removed together as explained under Engine Removal and Installation or the transaxle may be removed alone, as explained here.

1. Disconnect both battery cables.
2. Disconnect the speedometer cable at the transmission.
3. Support the left end of the engine at the lifting eye. Attach a hoist to the transaxle.
4. Unbolt the rear transmission carrier from the body then from the transaxle. Unbolt the left side carrier from the body.
5. Unbolt the driveshafts and wire them up.
6. Remove the starter.
7. Remove the three converter to drive plate bolts.
8. Shift into P and disconnect the floorshift linkage at the transmission.
9. Remove the accelerator and carburetor cable bracket at the transmission.
10. Unbolt the left side transmission carrier from the transmission.
11. Unbolt the front transmission mount from the transmission.
12. Unbolt the bottom of the engine from the transmission. Lift the transaxle slightly, remove the rest of the bolts, pull the transmission off the mounting dowels, and lower the transaxle out of the car. Secure the converter so it doesn't fall out.

CAUTION

Don't tilt the torque converter.

To install:

13. Be sure the torque converter is fully seated on the one-way clutch support. Push the transmission onto the mounting dowels and install two bolts. Lift the unit until the left driveshaft can be installed and install the rest of the bolts. Torque them to 39 ft/lbs.
14. Tighten the front transmission mount bolts to 39 ft/lbs. Install the left side transmission carrier to the transmission.
15. Connect the accelerator and carburetor cable bracket. Connect the floorshift linkage.
16. Tighten the torque converter to drive plate bolts to 22 ft/lbs. Torque the driveshaft bolts to 32 ft/lbs.
17. Install the rear transmission carrier and make sure that the left side carrier is aligned in the center of the body mount. Bolt the left side carrier to the body.
18. Connect the speedometer cable and the battery cables.

PAN REMOVAL AND INSTALLATION, STRAINER SERVICE

Dasher

VW recommends that the automatic transmission fluid be replaced every 30,000 miles, or 20,000 miles if used for trailer towing, mountain driving, or other severe service.

1. Four (4) quarts of automatic transmission fluid (Type A or Dexron) and a pan gasket are required.
2. Slide a drain pan under the transmission. Jack up the front of the car and support it.
3. Remove the drain plug and allow all the fluid to drain.

NOTE: Some models are not equipped with pan drain plugs. In this case, empty the pan by loosening the pan bolts and allowing the fluid to drain out.

4. Remove the pan retaining bolts and drop the pan.
5. Discard the old gasket and clean the pan with solvent.
6. Unscrew and clean the circular strainer. If it is dirty, it should be replaced.
7. Install the strainer, but don't tighten the bolt too much—specified torque is only 4 ft/lbs.
8. Refill the transmission with about 2¾

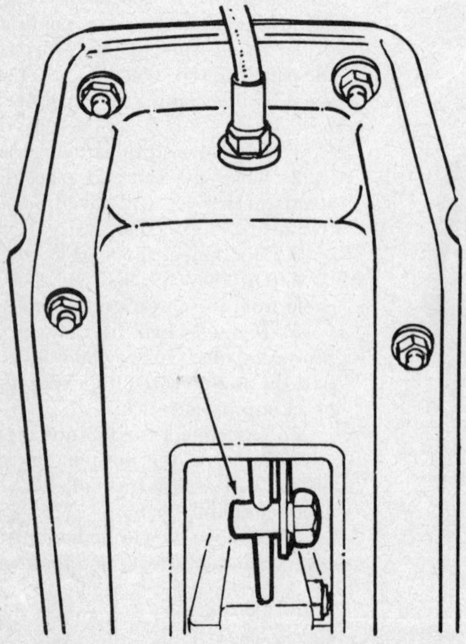

Dasher automatic transaxle linkage adjustment—before chassis no. 3-5 2 044 957

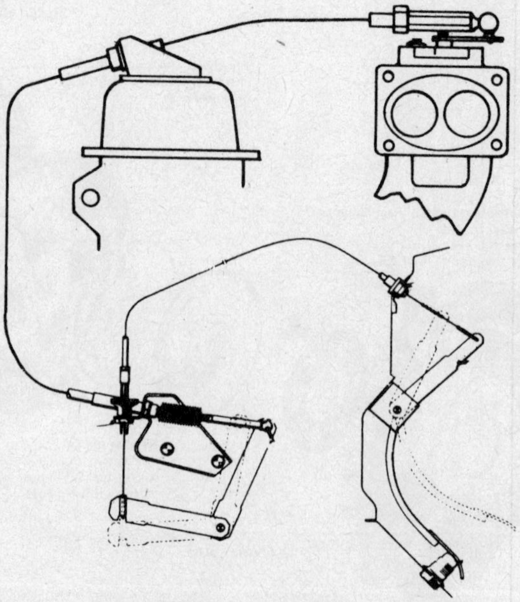

Rabbit, Jetta, Scirocco automatic transmission cable arrangement—fuel injected

qts. of fluid. Check the level with the dipstick. Run the car for a few minutes and check again.

Rabbit, Scirocco, Jetta

NOTE: As of transmission No 09096 a new, cleanable oil filter is used which requires a deeper oil pan. Also beginning with transmission number EQ-15 106, the drain plug was no longer installed in the oil pan.

1. Remove the drain plug and let the fluid drain into a pan. If the pan has no drain plug, loosen the pan bolts until a corner of the pan can be lowered to drain the fluid.
2. Remove the pan bolts and take off the pan.
3. Discard the old gasket and clean the pan out. Be very careful not to get any threads or lint from rags into the pan.
4. The filter needn't be replaced unless the fluid is dirty or smells burnt. The specified torque for the strainer screws is 2 ft/lbs.

NOTE: Beginning with Transmission number 13 03 8, there is an additional strainer under the valve body. When installing it, be sure it fits into the locating lug of the transfer plate.

5. Replace the pan with a new gasket and tighten the bolts, in a crisscross pattern, to 14 ft/lbs.
6. Using a long-necked funnel, pour in 2½ qts of Dextron automatic transmission fluid through the dipstick tube. Start the engine and shift through all the transmission ranges with the car stationary. Check the level on the dipstick with the lever in Neutral. It should be up to the lower end of the dipstick. Drive the car until it is warmed up and recheck the level.

LINKAGE ADJUSTMENT

Check the cable adjustment as follows:

1. Run the engine at 1000-1200 rpm with the parking brake on.
2. Select Reverse—a drop in engine speed should be noticed.
3. Select Park—engine speed should increase. Pull the shift lever against Reverse, the engine speed shouldn't drop (because reverse gear has not been engaged).
4. Move the shift lever to engage Reverse—engine speed should drop as the gear engages.
5. Move the shift lever to Neutral—an increase in engine speed should be noticed.
6. Shift the lever into Drive—a noticeable drop in engine speed should result.
7. Shift into 1—the lever must engage without having to overcome any resistance.
8. To adjust the cable—shift into Park. On Dashers before chassis no. 3-5 2 044 957, remove the cover from the bottom of the shift lever case under the car and loosen the cable clamp. Using pliers, press the lever on the transmission to the rear (against spring tension) until it hits the stop and tighten the clamp.

On Dashers from chassis no. 3-5 2 044 957 and later, the shift cable clamp is loosened from inside the passenbers compartment. Have an assistant under the car press the transmission lever toward the Park position and tighten the clamp.

On the Rabbit, Jetta and Scirocco, shift into Park, loosen the cable clamp at the transmission end of the cable, press the transmission lever all the way to the left and tighten the cable clamp.

TRANSMISSION CABLE ADJUSTMENT

NOTE: Early Dashers with the type 003 automatic transmission (identified by the modulator hose attached to the driver's side front of the transmission above the pan) have a kickdown switch rather than a throttle cable. See below for switch test.

Make sure the throttle is closed, and the choke and fast idle cam are off (carbureted models).

1. Detach the cable end at the transmission.
2. Press the lever at the transmission into its closed throttle position.
3. You should be able to attach the cable end onto the transmission lever without moving the lever.
4. Adjust the cable length to the correct setting.

KICKDOWN SWITCH CHECK

Dasher

NOTE: Early Dashers with the type 003 automatic transmission (identified by the modulator hose attached to the driver's side front of the transmission above the pan) are the only VWs equipped with kickdown switches. All other models have throttle cable kickdowns (see above).

1. Turn the ignition switch ON.
2. Floor the accelerator—you should hear a click from the solenoid on the transmission.
3. Replace the solenoid if no sound is heard. The solenoid is housed in the valve body and is accessible only by removing this unit from the transmission: a job you should depend on a qualified mechanic to perform.

FIRST AND SECOND GEAR (FRONT AND REAR) BAND ADJUSTMENTS

Dasher W/Type 003 Transmission Only

The type 003 transmission is identified by the modulator hose attached to the driver's side front of the transmission above the pan.

NOTE: The transmission must be horizontal when the band adjustments are performed.

The adjustment screws are located at the top of the transmission housing with the first gear band being closest to the front of the unit on the passenger's side of the car. The second gear band adjustment screw is located toward the rear of the unit on the driver's side of the vehicle.

1. To adjust the first gear band, loosen the locknut and tighten the adjusting screw to 7 ft/lbs.
2. Loosen the screw and retighten it to 3.5 ft/lbs.
3. Turn the screw out 3¼-3½ turns and then tighten the locknut.
4. To adjust the second gear band, repeat Steps 1 and 2 on the second gear band adjusting screw, then turn the screw out exactly 2½ turns and tighten the locknut.

SECOND GEAR (REAR) BAND ADJUSTMENT

Dasher W/Type 089 Transmission, Rabbit, Jetta, Scirocco

NOTE: The transmission must be horizontal when band adjustments are performed.

1. Loosen the locknut on the adjusting screw, which is located on the front of the Rabbit and Scirocco transmission and the driver's side on the Dasher.
2. Tighten the adjusting screw to 7 ft/lbs.
3. Loosen the screw and tighten it again to 4 ft/lbs.
4. Turn the screw out exactly 2½ turns and then tighten the locknut.

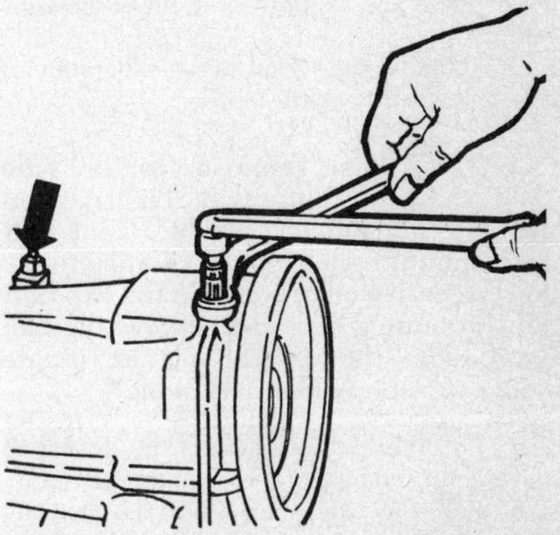

Dasher type 003 transaxle band adjustment—front band (first gear) being adjusted, arrow locates second gear band adjustment screw

NEUTRAL START/BACKUP LIGHT SWITCH

The combination neutral start and backup light switch is mounted inside the shifter housing. The starter should operate in Park or Neutral only. Adjust the switch by moving it on its mounts. The backup lights should only come on when the shift selector is in the Reverse position.

DRIVE AXLES

HALFSHAFT REMOVAL AND INSTALLATION

Dasher

NOTE: When removing the right side axle shaft, you must detach the exhaust

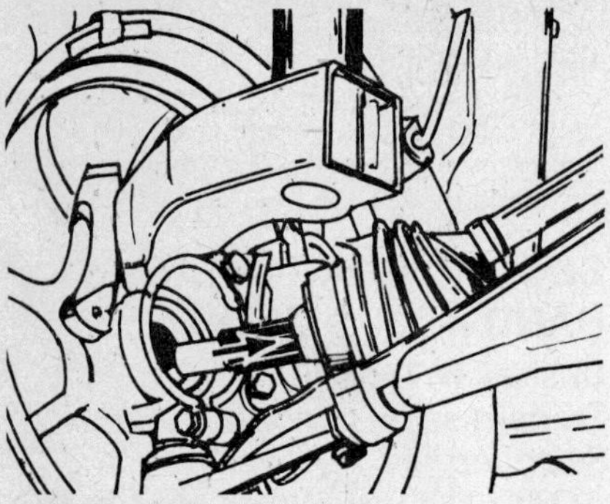

Pulling the Dasher axle shaft from the steering knuckle

pipe from the manifold and the transaxle bracket. Be sure to buy a new exhaust flange gasket.

1. With the car on the ground, remove the front axle nut.

NOTE: Use a longer breaker bar with an extension (length of pipe).

2. Raise and support the front of the vehicle.
3. Remove the socket head bolts retaining the axle shaft to the transaxle.

NOTE: When removing the left side axle shaft on automatic transmission models, matchmark the ball joint (left side) mounting position in relation to the lower control arm. Remove the two ball joint retaining nuts and remove the ball joint from the control arm to create room to remove the axle shaft.

4. Pull the transaxle side of the driveshaft out and up and place it on top of the transaxle.
5. Pull the axle shaft from the steering knuckle.
6. Installation is the reverse of removal. Tighten the transaxle bolts to 25-33 ft/lbs. The axle nut should be tightened to 145 ft/lbs (M 18 nut), or 175 ft/lbs (M 20 nut).

NOTE: Be aware that the axle shafts are two different lengths on automatic transmission models, with the left side axle shaft being slightly longer than the right. Manual transmission and automatic transmission axle shafts are of different lengths and should not be interchanged.

Rabbit, Scirocco, Jetta

1. Complete Steps 1 through 3 under Dasher in this section. Disregard the first NOTE.
2. Remove the bolt holding the ball joint to the steering knuckle and separate the knuckle from the ball joint.
3. Removing the ball joint from the knuckle should give enough clearance to remove the axle shaft. It pulls right out of the steering hub.
4. Installation is the reverse of removal. Tighten the axle shaft to transaxle bolts to 32 ft/lbs, the ball joint bolt to 21 ft/lbs and the axle nut to 173 ft/lbs. Be sure to check the alignment after work is completed.

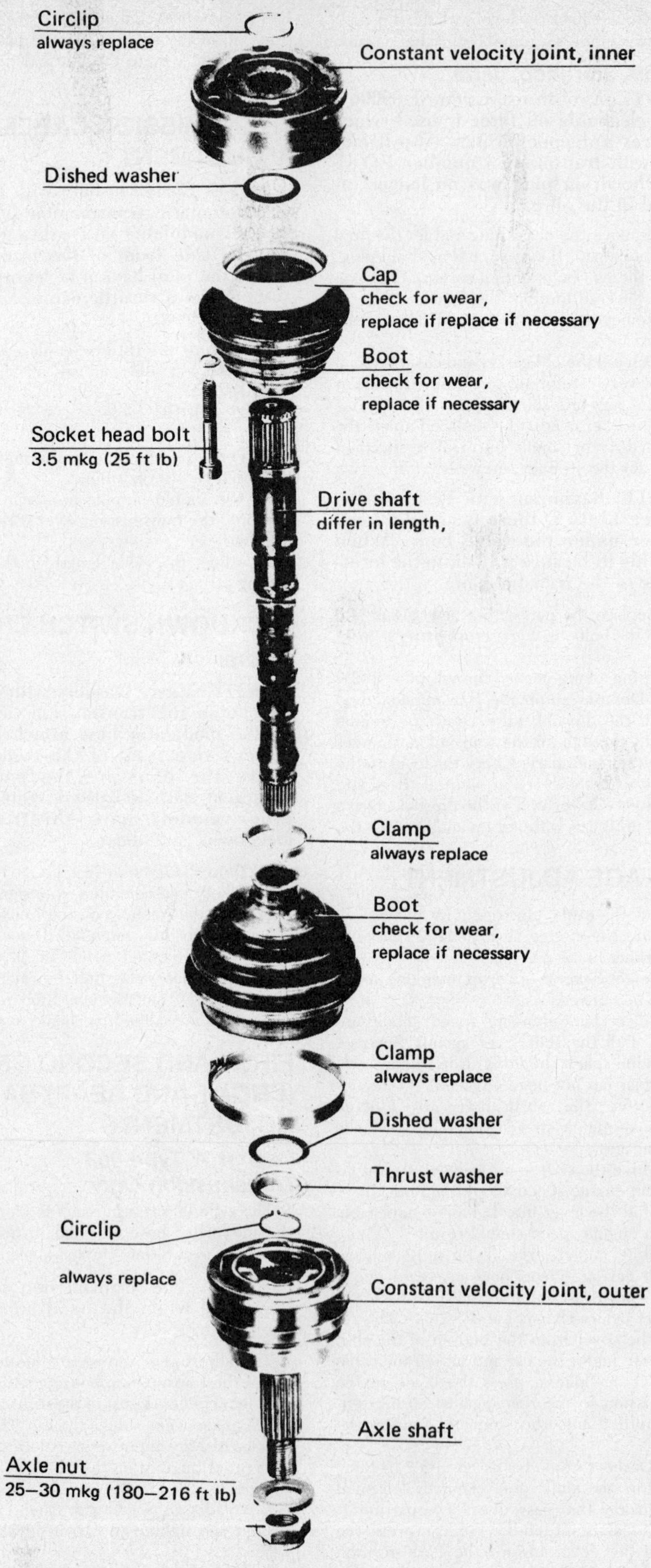

Dasher axle shaft

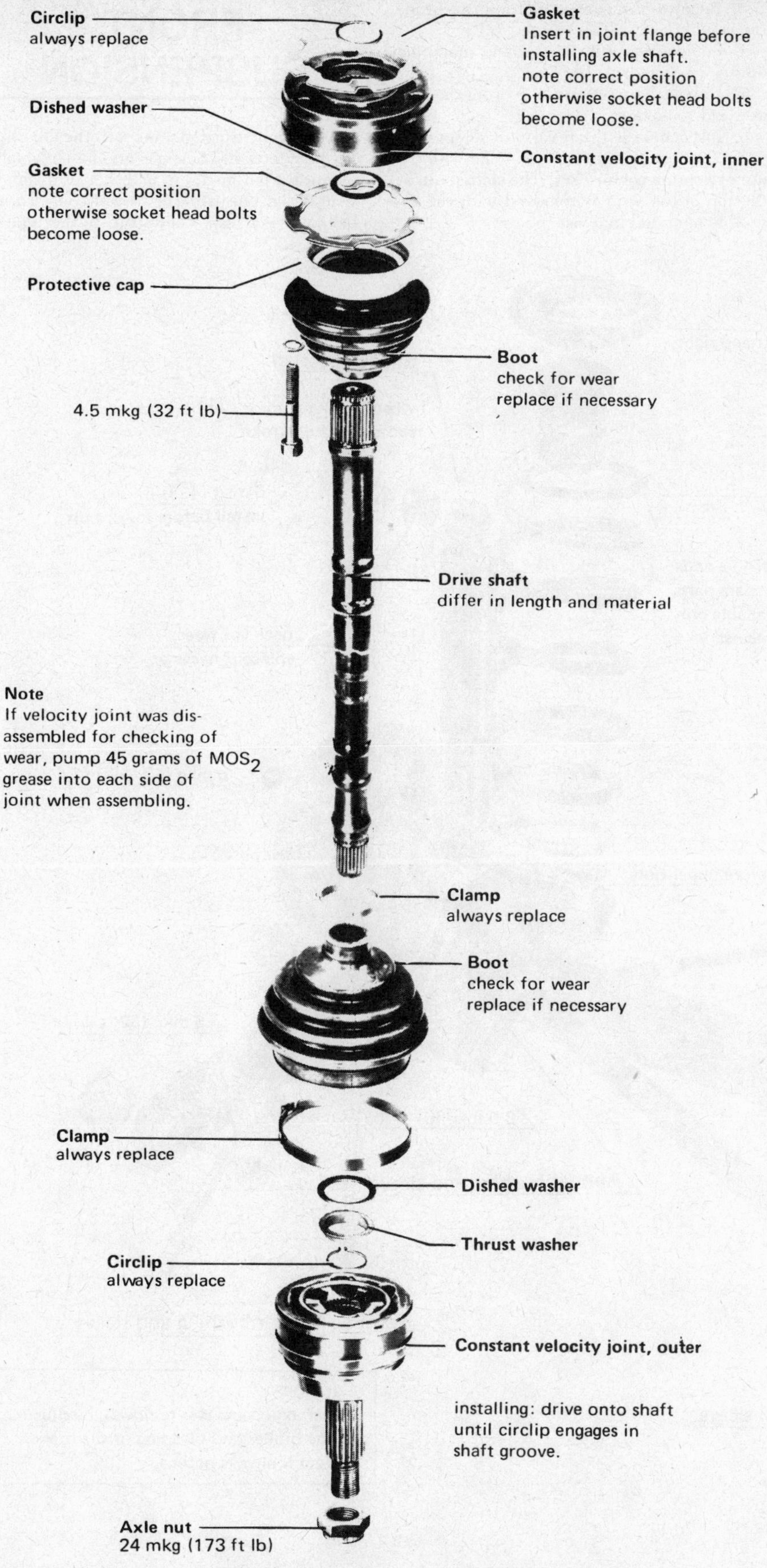

Rabbit, Jetta and Scirocco axle shaft

REAR SUSPENSION

The Dasher rear suspension has a rear axle beam containing a full length torsion bar. A trailing arm is welded to the axle beam tube on each side. The trailing arms mount to the unit body in rubber bushings. A coil spring provides the suspension at each wheel. A Panhard rod locates the axle against side forces.

The Rabbit, Jetta and Scirocco rear suspension includes a torsion beam which connects the two trailing arms. On these models, the coil spring and the shock absorber are combined into a strut.

Coil Springs

REMOVAL AND INSTALLATION

Dasher Only

1. Raise the car on a lift.
2. Support the axle.
3. Install spring compressor on the coil spring, and remove.
4. Installation is the reverse of removal.

NOTE: It is not necessary to replace both springs if only one is damaged.

Shock Absorbers

REMOVAL AND INSTALLATION

Dasher

NOTE: Only remove one shock absorber at a time. Do not allow the rear axle to hang by its body mounts only, as it may damage the brake lines.

This operation requires the use of either special tool VW 655/3 or a suitable spring compressor and floor jack.

1. Raise the car and support it on jack stands. Do not place the jack stands under the axle beam.
2. Remove the wheel.
3. Attach special tool VW 655/3 between the axle beam and a prefabricated hook hung on the body frame above the beam. Jack the tool until you can see the shock absorber compressing. If you are using a spring compressor and a floor jack, compress the spring a little and, placing the floor jack under the beam below the spring, jack it up until you see the shock absorber compress.
4. Unbolt and remove the shock absorber.
5. Installation is the reverse of removal. Tighten the shock absorber bolts to 43 ft/lbs.

NOTE: There are two types of shock absorbers for the Dasher and they have different mounts. Make sure you get the correct type for your vehicle.

Strut Assembly

REMOVAL AND INSTALLATION

Rabbit, Jetta, Scirocco

1. Raise the car on a lift.
2. Support the axle, but do not put any load on the springs.
3. Remove the rubber guard from inside the car.
4. Remove the nut, washer and mounting disc.
5. Unbolt the strut assembly from the rear axle and remove it.
6. Installation is the reverse of removal.
7. The struts can be disassembled with the use of a spring compressor. The slotted nut at the top of the strut is removed with the assembly mounted in a vise.

FRONT SUSPENSION

The front suspensions on the Rabbit, Dasher, Jetta and Scirocco are fundamentally identical from model to model. It is a simple strut design consisting of a lower control arm, ball joint and suspension strut. In this type of

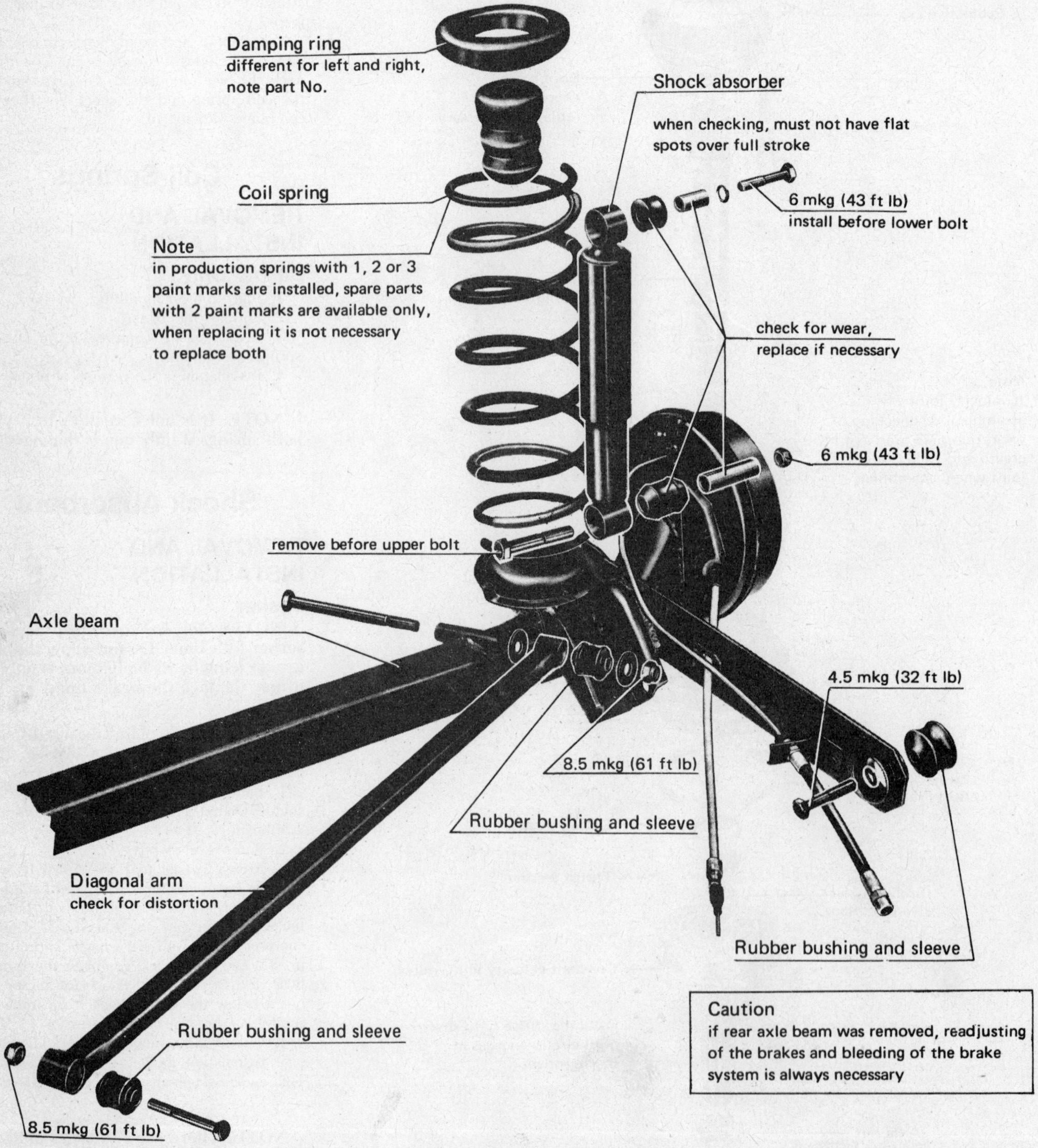

Dasher rear suspension

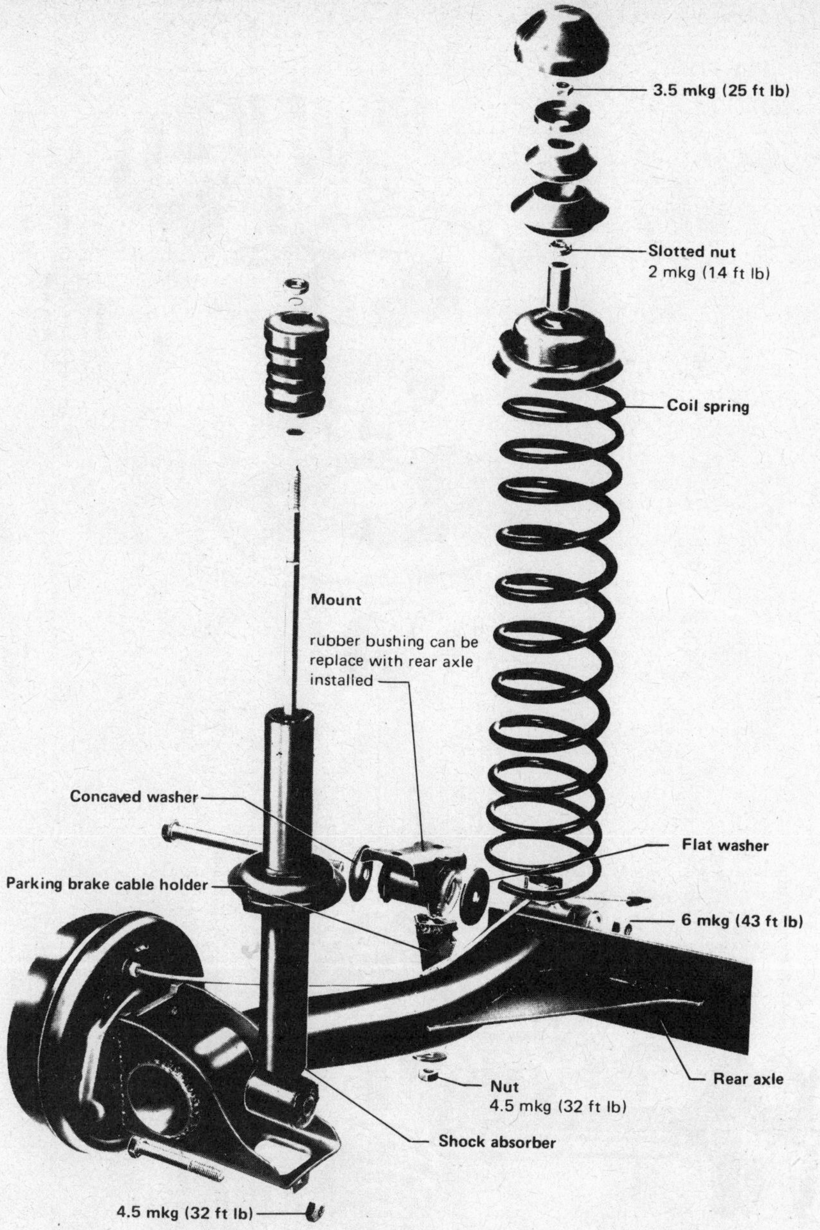

Exploded view of the Rabbit, Jetta and Scirocco rear suspension

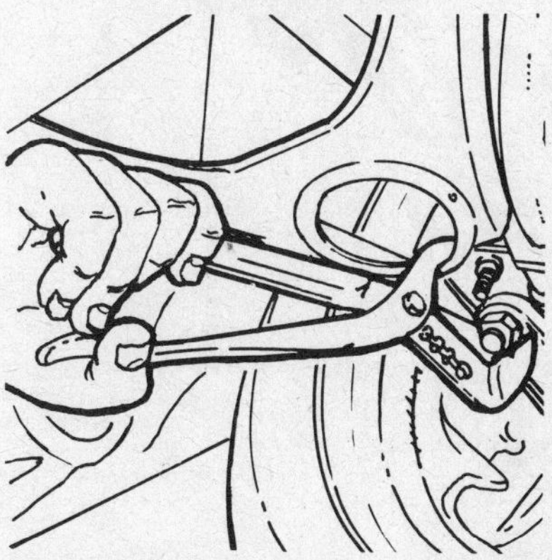

Pulling the Dasher ball joint into alignment on installation

design, known as a MacPherson strut, the shock absorber strut acts as a locating member for the suspension as well as a damper. The shock absorber itself is part of the strut and cannot be removed except on Dashers up to chassis No. 3-5 2 117 398, which have a removable cartridge.

In addition, all Dashers are equipped with a stabilizer bar to reduce front body roll.

Ball Joint

REMOVAL AND INSTALLATION

1. Jack up the front of the car and support it on stands.
2. Matchmark the ball joint-to-control arm position on the Dasher.
3. Remove the retaining bolt and nut from the hub (wheel bearing housing).
4. Pry the lower control arm and ball joint down and out of the strut.
5. Remove the two ball joint-to-lower control arm retaining nuts and bolts on the Dasher. Drill out the rivets on the Rabbit, Jetta and Scirocco; enlarge the holes to $^{21}/_{64}$ in.
6. Remove the ball joint assembly.
7. Install the Dasher ball joint in the reverse order of removal. If no parts were installed other than the ball joint, align the matchmarks made in Step 2. No camber adjustment is necessary if this is done. Pull the ball joint into alignment with pliers. Tighten the two control arm-to-ball joint bolts to 47 ft/lbs and the strut-to-ball joint bolt to 25 ft/lbs (M8 bolt) or 36 ft/lbs (M10 bolt).
8. On the Rabbit, Jetta and Scirocco, bolt the new ball joint in place. Torque the bolts to 18 ft-lbs. Tighten the retaining bolt for the ball joint stud to 21 ft/lbs.

Shock Absorber

REMOVAL AND INSTALLATION

Shock absorber removal and installation is contained in the strut overhaul section, above. Be aware, however, that on all models

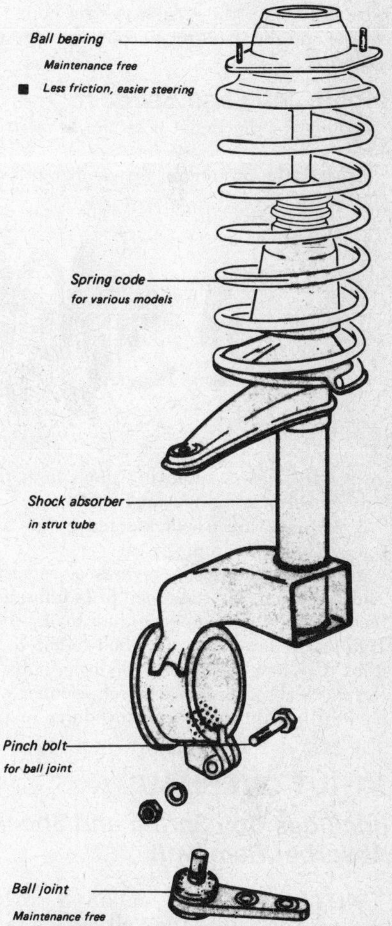

A pinch bolt holds the ball joint to the combination strut and steering knuckle

except Dashers up to chassis No. 3-5 2 117 398, replacing the shock absorber means replacing the strut itself (except for the coil spring and its attaching parts).

Strut

REMOVAL AND INSTALLATION

Dasher

1. With the car on the ground, remove the front axle nut. Loosen the wheel bolts.
2. Raise and support the front of the car. Remove the wheels.
3. Remove the brake caliper from the strut and hang it with wire. Detach the brake line clips from the strut.
4. At the tie rod end, remove the cotter pin, back off the castellated nut, and pull the end off the strut with a puller.
5. Loosen the stabilizer bar bushings and detach the end from the strut being removed.
6. Remove the ball joint from the strut.
7. Pull the axle driveshaft from the strut.
8. Remove the upper strut-to-fender retaining nuts.
9. Pull the strut assembly down and out of the car.
10. Installation is the reverse of removal. The axle nut is tightened to 145 ft/lbs (M 18 nut) or 175 ft/lbs (M 20 nut). Tighten the ball joint-to-strut nut to 25 ft/lbs (M8 nut) or 36 ft/lbs (M10 nut), the caliper-to-strut bolts to 44 ft/lbs and the stabilizer-to-control arm bolts to 7 ft/lbs.

Rabbit, Jetta and Scirocco

1. Remove the brake hose from the strut clip.
2. Mark the position of the camber adjustment bolts before removing them from the hub (wheel bearing housing).
3. Remove the upper mounting nuts and remove the strut from the car.
4. Installation is the reverse of removal. The upper nuts are tightened to 14 ft/lbs, and the adjusting bolt (upper) to hub to 58 ft/lbs. Tighten the lower adjusting bolt-to-hub to 43 ft/lbs. Use new washers on the lower bolts. If the shock absorber was replaced, camber will have to be adjusted. See procedures in this chapter.

STRUT OVERHAUL

(Includes Coil Spring and Shock Absorber Removal)

NOTE: You must obtain a spring compressor, either the Volkswagen type (VW 340/5 and VW 340) or a comparable consumer type.

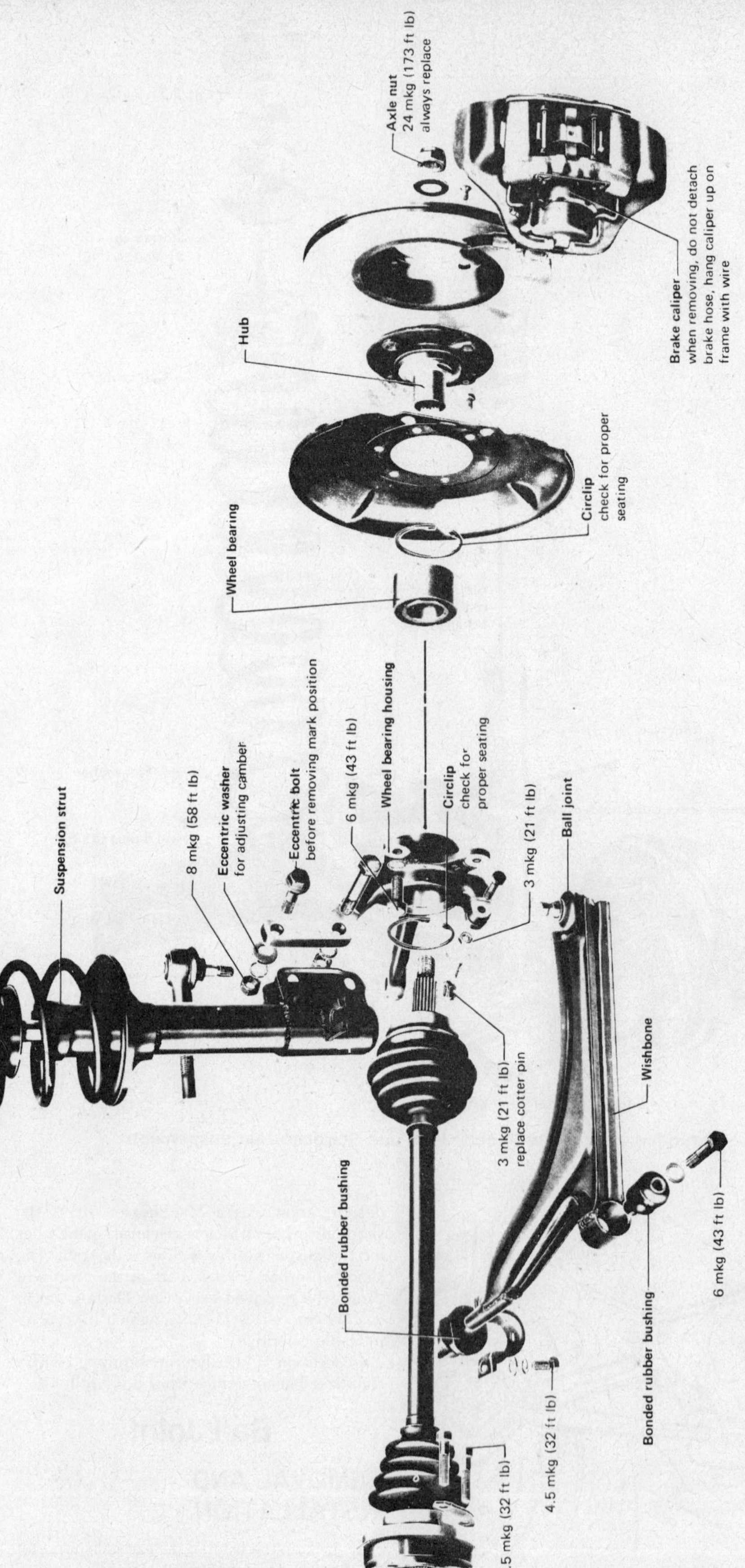

Exploded view of the Rabbit, Jetta and Scirocco front suspension

1. Remove the strut from the vehicle. See above for procedures.

2. Anchor the strut in a vise so it cannot move and attach the spring compressor. Be sure to follow the compressor instructions to the letter. The coil spring is under considerable pressure and has the potential to seriously harm you.

3. Compress the spring and loosen the center nut at the top of the strut assembly. To aid in removing the nut, fit an Allen wrench in the top of the shock absorber rod and loosen the nut with a closed end wrench.

4. Remove the collar parts from the top of the spring and arrange the parts in the order of removal to aid you in reassembly.

5. Slowly release the pressure on the spring and remove the spring from the strut.

NOTE: The springs are color-coded. When replacing, make sure both replacement springs have the same color-code.

Dashers after chassis No. 3-5 2 117 398 and all Rabbits, Jettas and Sciroccos have nonremovable shock absorbers in the struts. If the shock absorbers on these models wear out, you must replace the entire strut assembly (except for the coil spring and its attaching parts).

To replace the removable shock absorber cartridge in Dashers before chassis No. 3-5 2 117 398, proceed as follows:

6. Remove the rubber cap and collar on the shock tube and remove the round, threaded retaining cap. There is a special VW tool (40-201) for this job, but you should be able to loosen the cap with a pipe wrench. Be careful not to bend or dent the cap when removing.

7. Pull the shock absorber cartridge out of the strut. You may have to put the nut back on the shock absorber rod and use it as a stop-point to tap the cartridge out of the strut. When installing, the threaded retaining cap should be tightened to 108 ft/lbs.

8. Installation of the coil spring is the reverse of removal. Tighten the coil spring retaining nut to 43 ft/lbs on the Dasher and 58 ft/lbs on the Rabbit, Jetta and Scirocco.

Make sure the coil spring fits into its grooves in the strut. If the strut has been replaced, the camber must be adjusted. See the section in this chapter.

Coil Spring

REMOVAL AND INSTALLATION

Coil spring removal and installation procedures are contained in the strut overhaul section, above. The coil springs are color-coded and must be matched with other springs of the same color code.

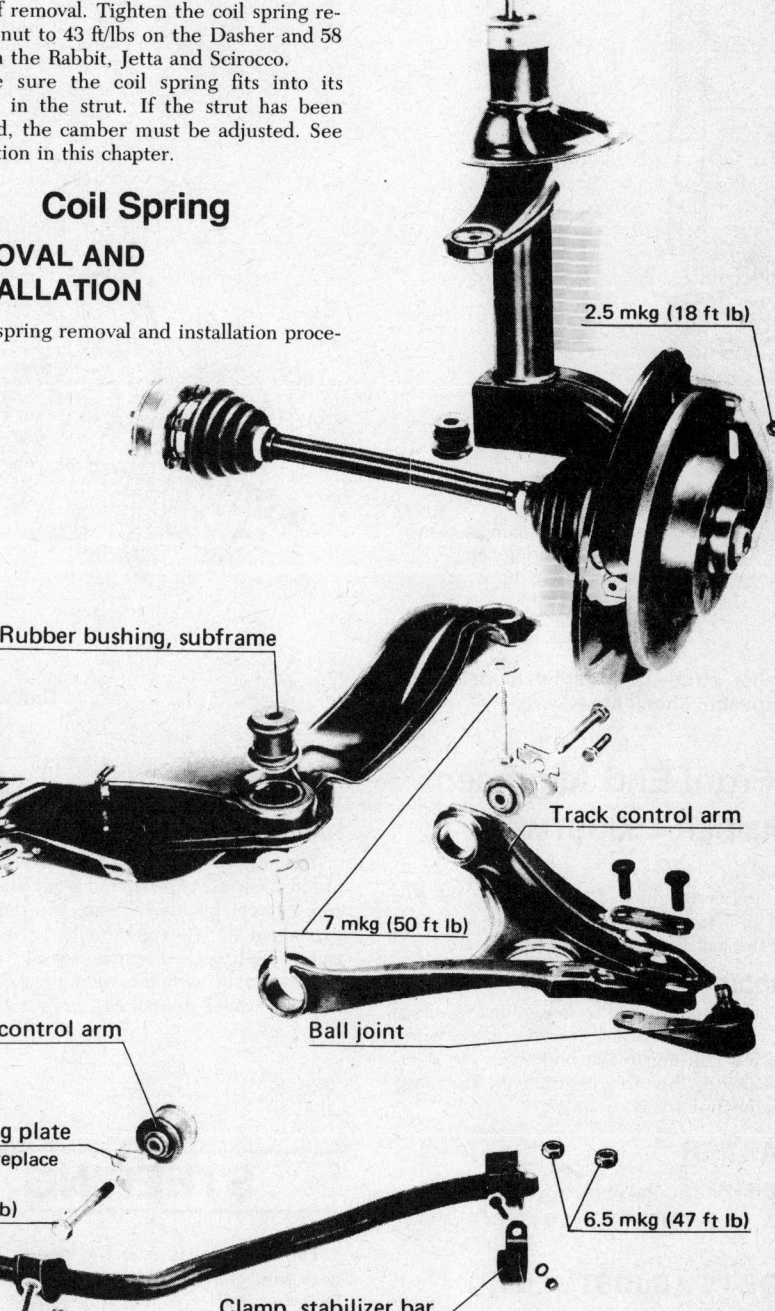

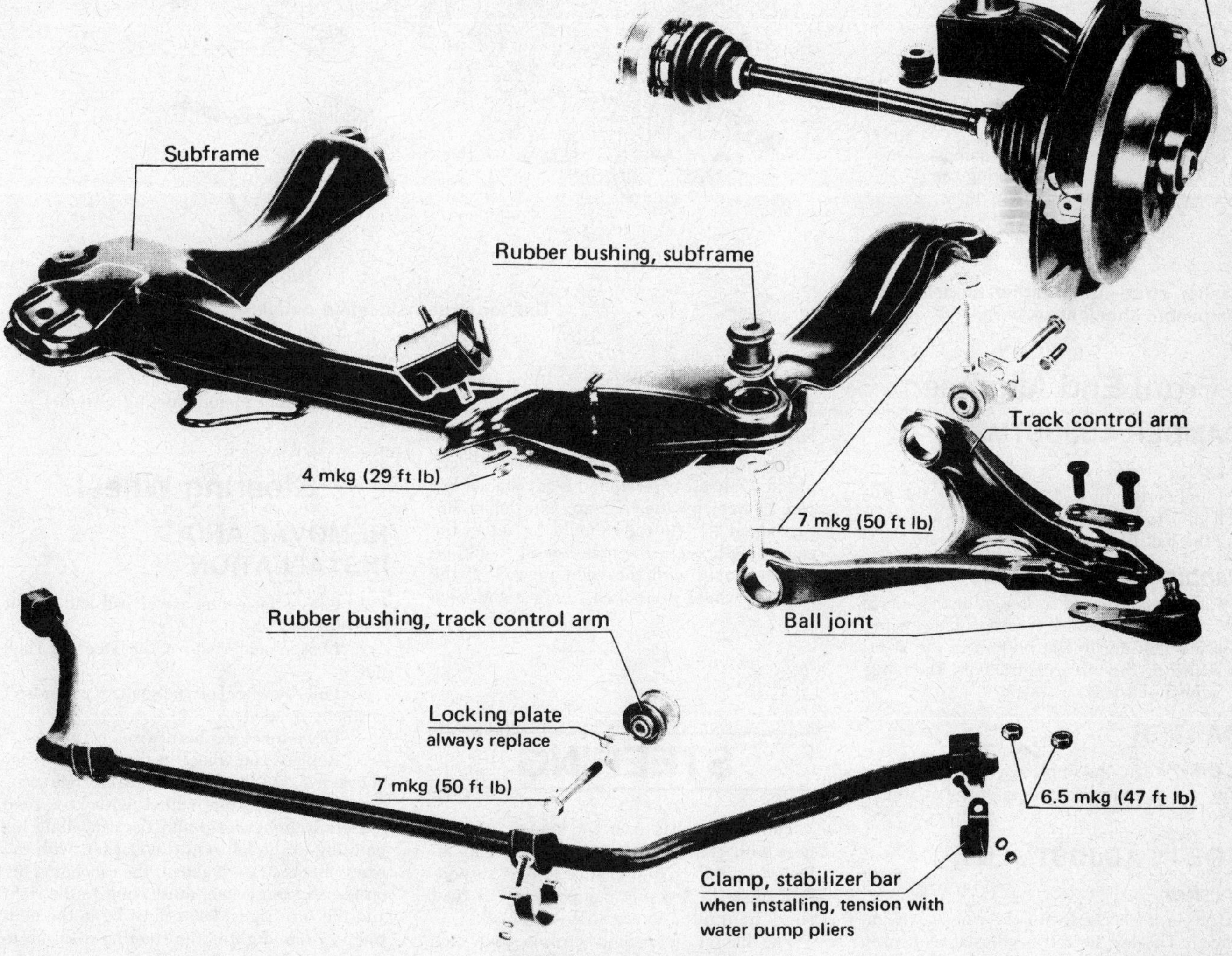

Dasher front suspension

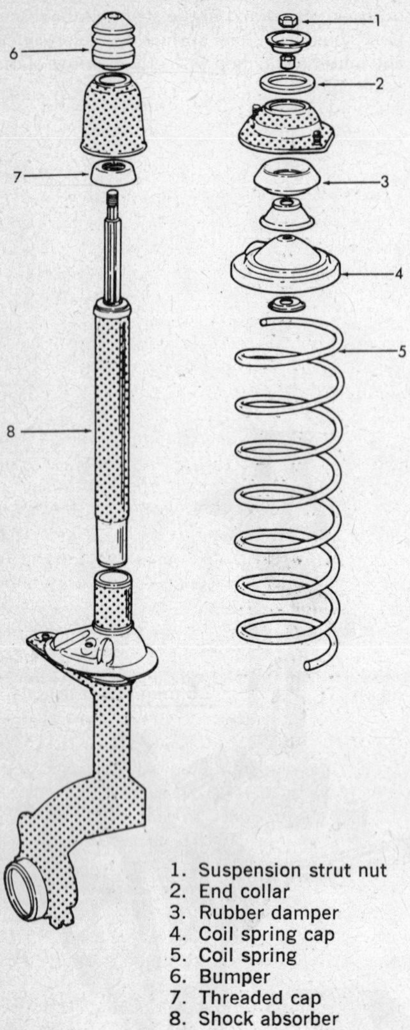

Dasher strut—only earlier models have removable shock absorber

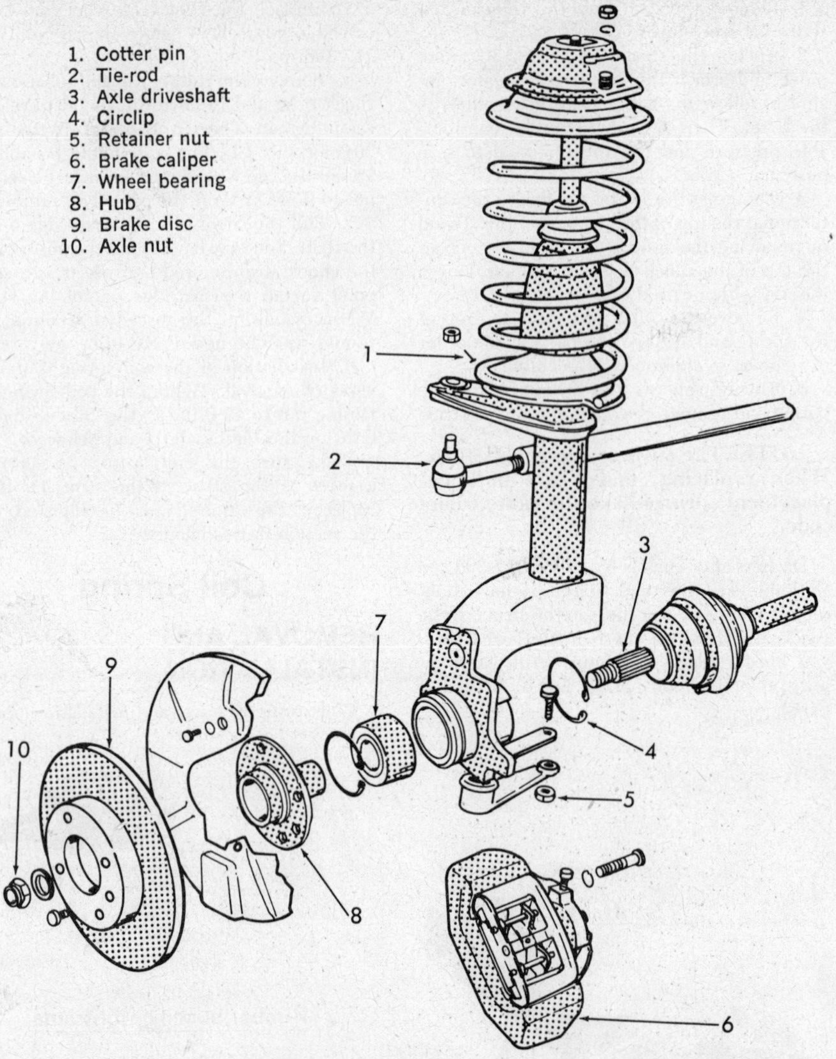

Dasher strut installation details

Front End Alignment

CAMBER ADJUSTMENT

Dasher

Camber is adjusted by loosening the two ball joint-to-lower control arm bolts, and moving the ball joint in or out as necessary.

Rabbit, Scirocco, Jetta

Camber is adjusted by loosening the nuts of the two bolts holding the top of the wheel bearing housing to the bottom of the strut, and turning the top eccentric bolt. The range of adjustment is 2°.

CASTER

Other than the replacement of damaged suspension components, caster is not adjustable.

TOE-IN ADJUSTMENT

Dasher

Toe-in is checked with the wheels straight ahead. The left tie rod is adjustable. Loosen the nuts and clamps and adjust the length of the tie rod for correct toe-out. If the steering wheel is crooked, remove and align it.

Rabbit, Scirocco, Jetta

Toe-in is checked with the wheels straight ahead. Only the right tie rod is adjustable, but replacement left tie rods are adjustable. Replacement left tie rods should be set to the same length as the original. Toe-in should be adjusted only with the right tie rod. If the steering wheel is crooked, remove and align it.

STEERING

The Dasher has rack and pinion steering gear with center-mounted tie rods. This allows very little toe-in change during suspension travel. A steering damper reduces road shock transmittal to the steering wheel.

The Rabbit, Jetta and Scirocco have rack and pinion steering with end-mounted tie rods. No periodic maintenance is required on either rack and pinion steering system.

Steering Wheel

REMOVAL AND INSTALLATION

1. Grasp the center cover pad and pull it from the wheel.
2. Loosen and remove the steering shaft nut.
3. Pull the wheel off the shaft. A puller isn't normally needed.
4. Disconnect the horn wire.
5. Replace the wheel in the reverse order of removal. On the Rabbit, Jetta and Scirocco, install the steering wheel with the road wheels straight ahead and the cancelling lug pointing to the left. On the Dasher, with the road wheels straight ahead, the cancelling lug on the steering wheel must point to the right and the turn signal lever must be in the neutral position. Tighten the steering shaft nut to 36 ft/lbs.

Turn Signal and Headlight Dimmer Switch Replacement

1. Disconnect the battery ground cable.
2. Remove the steering wheel.
3. Remove the switch retaining screws.
4. Pry the switch housing off the column.
5. Disconnect the electrical plugs at the back of the switch.
6. Remove the switch housing.
7. Replace in the reverse order of removal.

Ignition Switch

REMOVAL AND INSTALLATION

The ignition switch is located at the bottom of the ignition key cylinder body. To remove the ignition switch, remove the steering lock body, see below for procedures. On all models except Dashers made before 1978, remove the switch by removing the screw at the bottom of the switch and pulling the switch out. On Dasher made before 1978, the screw is located in the side of the cylinder body.

Installation is the reverse of removal.

Steering Lock

REMOVAL AND INSTALLATION

On some models, the hole in the lock body for removing the steering lock cylinder was not drilled by Volkswagen. To make the hole, use the following measurements in conjunction with the illustrations. Drill the hole where "a" and "b" intersect on the lock body. The hole should be drilled ⅛ in. deep.

1974-77 Dasher
- a = 11.5 mm (0.453 in.)
- b = 8.0 mm (0.315 in.)

1975-76 Rabbit, Scirocco
- a = 11 mm (7/16 in.)
- b = 11 mm (7/16 in.)

1977-81 Rabbit, Jetta, Scirocco, 1978-81 Dasher
- a = 12 mm (0.472 in.)
- b = 10 mm (0.393 in.)

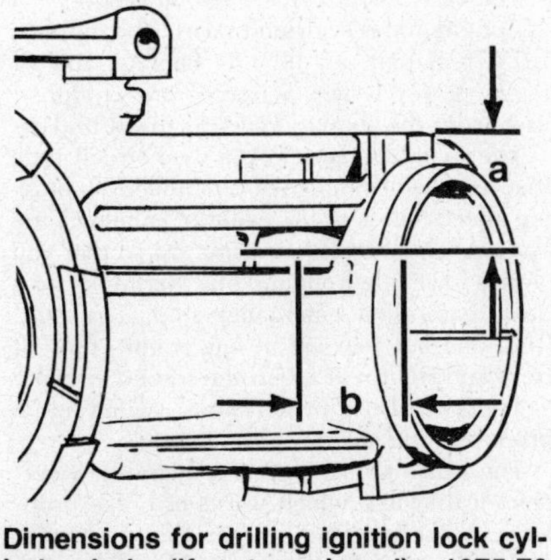

Dimensions for drilling ignition lock cylinder hole (if not equipped)—1975-76 Rabbit, Scirocco

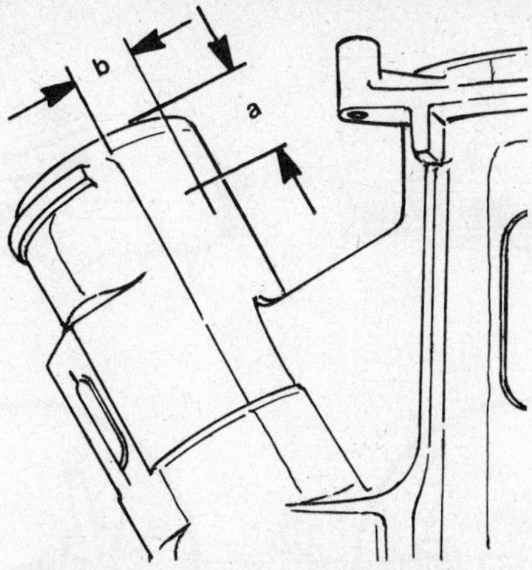

Dimensions for drilling ignition lock cylinder hole (if not equipped)—1977 and later Rabbit, Jetta, Scirocco and 1978 and later Dasher

NOTE: Measurements are given in metric form first because this unit of measurement will be easier to make.

Remove the lock cylinder by pushing a small drill bit or piece of wire into the hole and pulling the cylinder out. It might be easier to insert the ignition key, turn it to the right a little and pull on it.

NOTE: On 1975-76 Rabbits and Sciroccos, the lock cylinder can also be removed by removing the steering and windshield wiper components and removing the locking plate holding the cylinder with a pair of pliers. When installing the plate, peen it slightly to hold it in place.

To remove the lock body, proceed as follows:

1. Remove the steering wheel and turn signal switch. See above for procedures. Remove the steering column shaft covers.
2. The lock is clamped to the steering column with special bolts whose heads shear off on installation. These must be drilled out in order to remove the switch.
3. On replacement, make sure that the lock tang is aligned with the slot in the steering column.

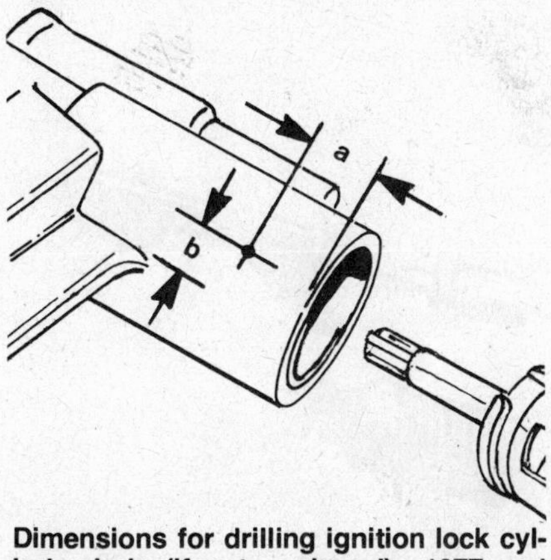

Dimensions for drilling ignition lock cylinder hole (if not equipped)—1977 and earlier Dasher

Steering Gear

REMOVAL AND INSTALLATION

Dasher

1. Pry off the lock plate and remove both tie rod mounting bolts from the steering rack, inside the engine compartment. Pry the tie rods out of the mounting pivot.
2. Remove the lower instrument panel trim.
3. Remove the shaft clamp bolt, pry off the clip, and drive the shaft toward the inside of the car with a brass drift.
4. Remove the steering gear mounting bolts.
5. Turn the wheels all the way to the right and remove the steering gear through the opening in the right wheelhousing.
6. For installation, temporarily install the tie rod mounting pivot to the rack with both mounting bolts. Remove one bolt, install the tie rod, and replace the bolt. Do the same on the other tie rod. Make sure to install a new lockplate. Torque the tie rod bolts to 39 ft/lbs, the mounting pivot bolt to 15 ft/lbs, and the steering gear to body mounting bolts to 15 ft/lbs.

Rabbit, Jetta and Scirocco

1. Disconnect the steering shaft universal joint and wire up out of the way.
2. Disconnect the tie rods at the steering rack and wire up and out of the way.
3. Remove the steering rack and drive.
4. Install the steering rack and drive and torque the attaching hardware to 14 ft/lbs.
5. Set the steering rack with equal distances between the housing on the right side and left side.
6. Install the tie rods and screw both sides to the measurements shown in the illustration.
7. Tighten the steering gear adjusting screw until it touches the thrust washer. Tighten the locknut.
8. Install the steering shaft.
9. Check the front end alignment.

Steering Linkage

TIE ROD REMOVAL AND INSTALLATION

Dasher

1. Raise the car and remove the front wheels.
2. Disconnect the outer end of the steering tie rod from the steering knuckle by removing the cotter pin and nut and pressing out the tie rod end. A small puller or press is required to free the tie rod end.
3. Under the hood, pry off the lockplate and remove the mounting bolts from both tie rod inner ends. Pry the tie rod out of the mounting pivot.
4. First install the mounting pivot to the rack with both mounting bolts. Remove one bolt, install the tie rod, and replace the bolt. Do the same on the other tie rod. Be sure to install a new lockplate. The inner tie rod end bolts should be torqued to 40 ft/lbs.
5. If you are replacing the adjustable left

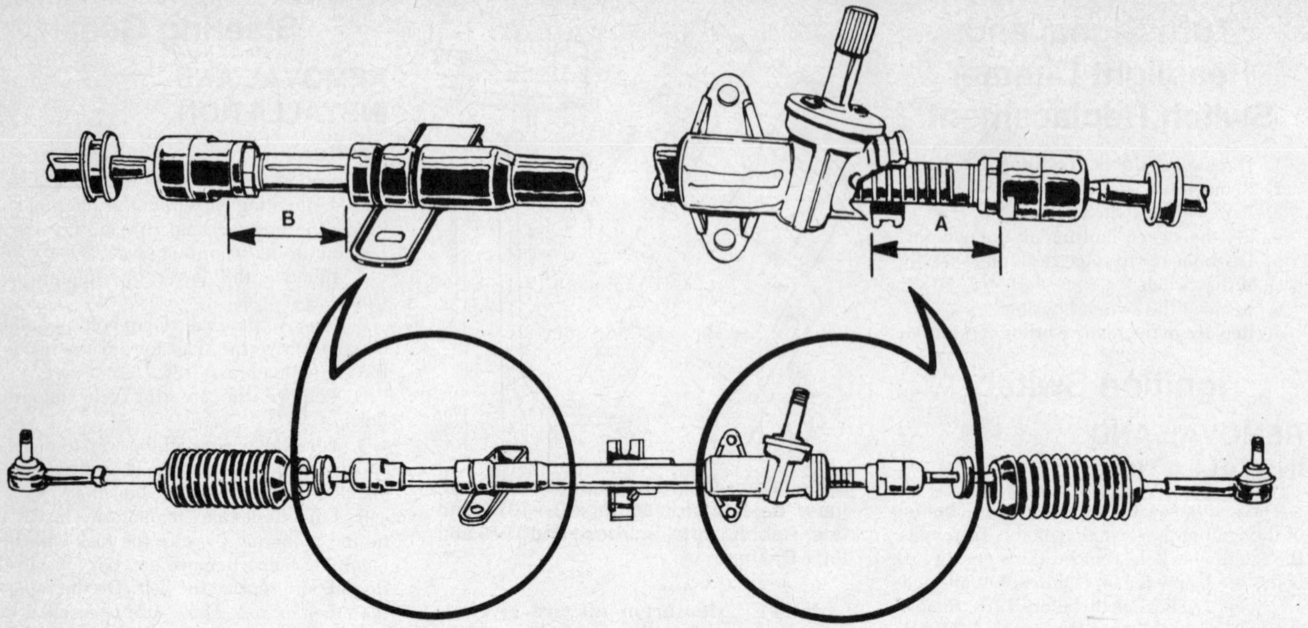

Adjusting Rabbit and Scirocco tie-rod position. b=2.64 in.

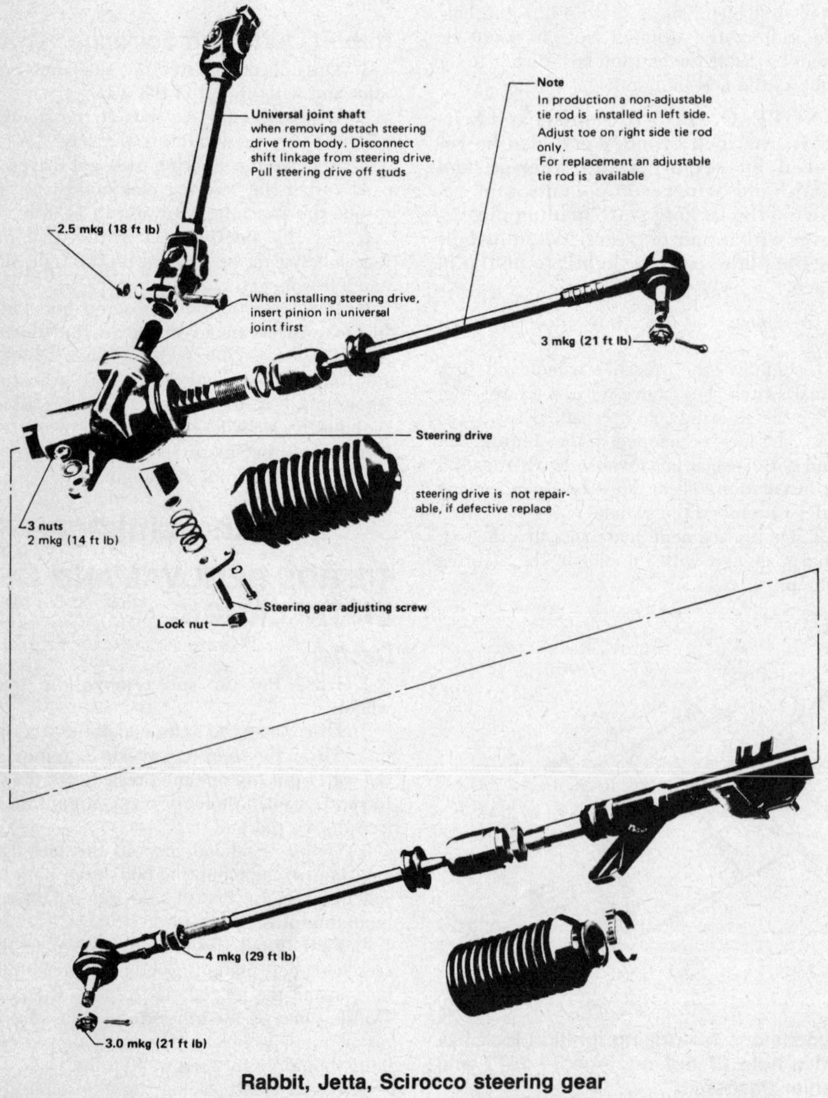

Rabbit, Jetta, Scirocco steering gear

tie rod, adjust it to the same length as the old one. Check the toe-in when the job is done.

6. Use new cotter pins when installing the outer tie rod ends. Torque the nut to 22 ft/lbs.

Rabbit, Jetta and Scirocco

1. Center the steering rack.
2. Remove the cotter pin and nut from the tie rod end.
3. Disconnect the tie rod from the steering rack.
4. If the left side tie rod is being replaced, adjust it to 14.92 in. (379 mm).
5. Adjust the steering rack and tie rods as outlined in Steps 5 and 6 of the Rabbit and Scirocco "Steering Gear Removal and Installation."
6. Tighten the tie rod end retaining nut to 21 ft/lbs and install a new cotter pin.

BRAKES

The base model 1975-78 Rabbit is equipped with front and rear drum brakes. The optional 1975-78 Rabbit, all 1979-81 Rabbits, and all Dashers, Jettas and Sciroccos are equipped with front disc brakes and rear drum brakes.

The hydraulic system is a dual circuit type that has the advantage of retaining 50% braking effectiveness in the event of failure in one system. The circuits are arranged so that you always have one front and one rear brake for a more controlled emergency stop. The right front and left rear are in one circuit; the left front and right rear are in the second circuit.

There is also a brake failure switch and a proportioning valve.

The brake failure unit is a hydraulic valve/electrical switch which warns of brake problems by the warning light on the instrument panel. A piston inside the switch is kept centered by one brake system pressure on one side and the other system pressure on the opposite side. Should a failure occur in one system, the piston would go to the "failed" side and complete an electrical circuit to the warning lamp. This switch also functions as a parking brake reminder light and will go out when the parking brake is released. The proportioning valve, actually two separate valves on manual transmission Dasher sedans, provides balanced front-to-rear braking during hard stops.

Extreme brake line pressure will overcome the spring pressure on the piston within the valve causing it to proportionately restrict pressure to the rear brakes. In this manner, the rear brakes are kept from locking. The proportioner doesn't operate under normal braking conditions.

Adjustment

The front disc brakes require no adjustment, as disc brakes automatically adjust themselves to compensate for pad wear. The drum brakes must be adjusted whenever free travel is one third or more of the total pedal travel. All 1979 and later Dashers, Jettas and Rabbit Pick-ups and many 1979 and later Rabbits and Sciroccos have self-adjusting rear brakes.

FRONT DRUM BRAKES

Rabbit Only

1. Raise and support the front of the car. Block the rear wheels.
2. Remove the rubber plugs covering the adjusters.
3. Insert a screwdriver through the hole and turn the adjuster clockwise until the brake locks.
4. Back off the adjuster until the wheel can be turned. The shoes should drag lightly.
5. Back off the adjuster two notches. The wheel should spin without brake drag. Replace the rubber plugs.

REAR DRUM BRAKES

All Models

NOTE: On all models except manual transmission Dasher sedans, it is necessary to push the brake proportioning lever toward the rear axle to relieve the pressure in the right rear brake line.

1. Raise the rear of the car. Place the jack under the center of the Dasher torsion bar/axle. The jack pad should be at least 4 in. square, otherwise you may damage the axle. Raise the Rabbit and Scirocco on a chassis lift.
2. Block the front wheels and release the parking brake. Step on the brake pedal hard to center the linings.
3. Remove the rubber plug from the rear of the backing plate on each wheel.
4. Insert a brake adjusting tool or wide-bladed screwdriver and turn the adjuster wheel clockwise until the brakes drag as you turn the wheel in the forward direction.
5. Turn the adjuster in the opposite direction until you just pass the point of drag.
6. Repeat on the other wheel.
7. Lower the car and road test. Readjust, if necessary.

Master Cylinder

REMOVAL AND INSTALLATION

1. Disconnect and plug the brake lines.
2. Disconnect the electrical plug from the sending unit for the brake failure switch.
3. Remove the two master cylinder mounting nuts.
4. Lift the master cylinder and reservoir out of the engine compartment being careful not to spill any fluid on the fender. Empty out and discard the brake fluid.

CAUTION

Do not depress the brake pedal while the master cylinder is removed.

5. Position the master cylinder and reservoir assembly onto the studs for the booster and install the washers and nuts. Tighten the nuts to no more than 9 ft/lbs.
6. Remove the plugs and connect the brake lines.
7. Bleed the entire brake system.

OVERHAUL

1. Remove the master cylinder from the booster.
2. Firmly mount the master cylinder in a vise. Use clean rags to protect the cylinder from the vise jaws.
3. Grasp the plastic reservoir and pull it out of the rubber plugs. Remove the plugs.
4. In the center of the cylinder there is a stop screw; remove it. Discard the stop screw seal, there should be a new one in the rebuilding kit.
5. At the end of the master cylinder is a snap-ring (circlip); remove it, using snap-ring pliers.
6. Shake out the secondary piston assembly. If the primary piston remains lodged in the bore, it can be forced by applying compressed air to the open line fitting.
7. Disassemble the secondary piston. The two secondary springs will be replaced with those in the rebuilding kit. Save the washers and spacers.
8. Carefully clamp the secondary piston. Slightly compress the spring and screw out the stroke limiting bolt.
9. Remove the secondary piston stop sleeve bolt, spring, spring seat, and support washer.
10. Replace all the parts with those supplied in the overhaul kit. Be careful not to interchange the piston cups and the piston seals.
11. Clean all metal parts in alcohol and dry them with compressed air.
12. Check every part you are reusing. Pay close attention to the cylinder bores. If there is any scoring or rust, have the master cylinder honed or replace it.
13. Lightly coat the bores and cups with brake fluid. Assemble the cylinder components in the exact sequence shown in the illustration.
14. Install the primary piston assembly; notice that the primary spring is conically shaped. Be sure that you aren't using the secondary spring.

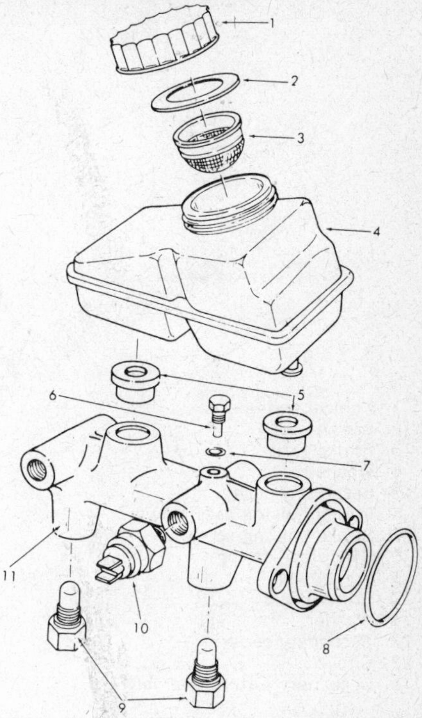

1. Reservoir cap
2. Washer
3. Filter screen
4. Reservoir
5. Master cylinder plugs
6. Stop screw
7. Stop screw seal
8. Master cylinder seal
9. Residual pressure valves
10. Warning light sender unit
11. Brake master cylinder housing

Master cylinder assembly for Rabbit, Jetta and Scirocco (typical)—Dasher similar

NOTE: Since April 1977, the primary clip and piston seal (in Teves master cylinders) have number of small grooves on the lips. The new versions have a groove and chamfer and can be installed in place of earlier versions, identified by a silver strip around the seal.

15. Using a plastic rod or other nonmetallic tool, push the primary piston assembly into the housing until the stop bolt (with a new seal) can be screwed in and tightened.
16. Assemble the secondary piston. Fasten the spring, spring seat, primary cup, and stop sleeve to the piston with the stroke limiting bolt.
17. Assemble the remaining master cylinder components in the reverse order of disassembly. Ensure that the snap-ring is fully seated and that the piston caps are properly positioned. Install the secondary piston with master cylinder opening facing down.
18. Install and tighten the brake failure warning sending unit.

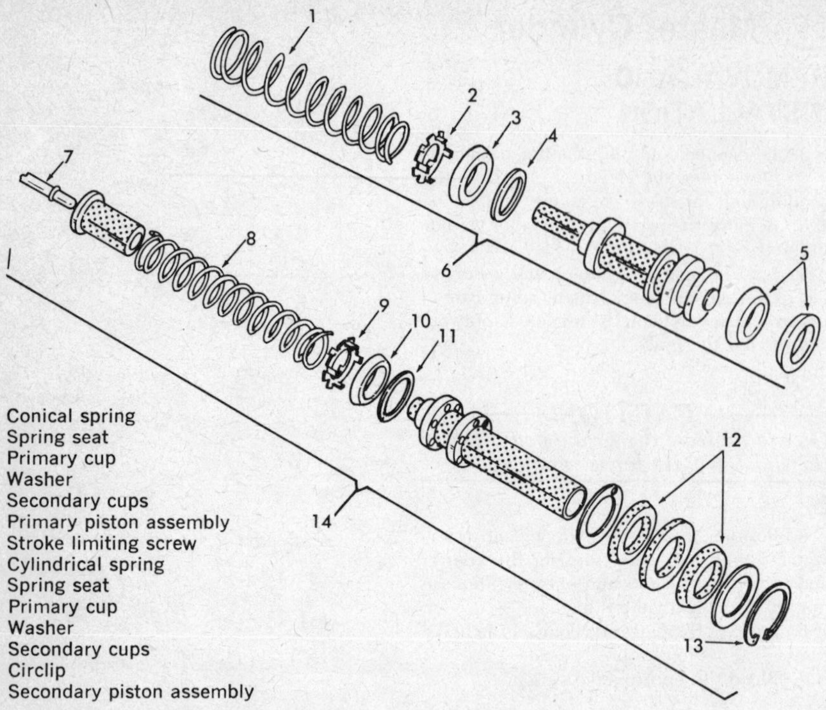

1. Conical spring
2. Spring seat
3. Primary cup
4. Washer
5. Secondary cups
6. Primary piston assembly
7. Stroke limiting screw
8. Cylindrical spring
9. Spring seat
10. Primary cup
11. Washer
12. Secondary cups
13. Circlip
14. Secondary piston assembly

Master cylinder internal components

Bleeding

Anytime a brake line has been disconnected the hydraulic system should be bled. The brakes should also be bled when the pedal travel becomes unusually long ("soft pedal") or the car pulls to one side during braking. The proper bleeding sequence is: right rear wheel, left rear wheel, right front caliper, and left front caliper. You'll need a helper to pump the brake pedal while you open the bleeder valves.

NOTE: If the system has been drained, first refill it with fresh brake fluid. Following the above sequence, open each bleeder valve by ½ to ¾ of a turn and pump the brake pedal until fluid runs out of the valve. Proceed with the bleeding as outlined below.

1. Remove the bleeder valve dust cover and install a clear rubber bleeder hose.
2. Insert the other end of the hose into a container about ⅓ full of brake fluid.
3. Have an assistant pump the brake pedal several times until the pedal pressure increases.
4. Hold the pedal under pressure and then start to open the bleeder valve about ½ to ¾ of a turn. At this point, have your assistant depress the pedal all the way and then quickly close the valve. The helper should allow the pedal to return slowly.

NOTE: Keep a close check on the brake fluid in the reservoir and top it up as necessary throughout the bleeding process.

5. Keep repeating this procedure until no more air bubbles can be seen coming from the hose in the brake fluid.
6. Remove the bleeder hose and install the dust cover.
7. Continue the bleeding at each wheel in sequence.

NOTE: Don't splash any brake fluid on the paintwork. Brake fluid is very corrosive and will eat paint away. Any fluid accidentally spilled on the body should be immediately flushed off with water.

Front Disc Brakes

There are four types of disc brake calipers used on these Volkswagens: Teves, Girling, and Kelsey-Hayes units. There are two types of Girling brakes, one similar to the Teves unit and one (Girling Clam-type) similar to the Kelsey-Hayes unit. All units have the floating caliper, which uses the movement of the caliper in its frame to press the brake pads against the rotor disc. The advantages of the floating caliper are; better heat dissipation, simpler repairs and fewer leaks. Use the illustrations of the disc brake calipers to find which type your vehicle uses.

Many Dashers made in 1978 and later use the Girling clam-type caliper. All other models are equipped with any of the designs except the Girling clam-type caliper, which is used exclusively by the 1978 and later Dasher.

BRAKE PADS

Removal and Installation

ALL EXCEPT GIRLING CLAM-TYPE AND KELSEY-HAYES CALIPERS

Brake pads should be replaced when there is no visible clearance between the pads and the cross-spring or when they are worn to a thickness of ¼ in. (6 mm).

NOTE: Most models are equipped with brake pad wear indicators. When the pad is worn, a lug on the pad contacts the disc causing a pulsation in the brake pedal.

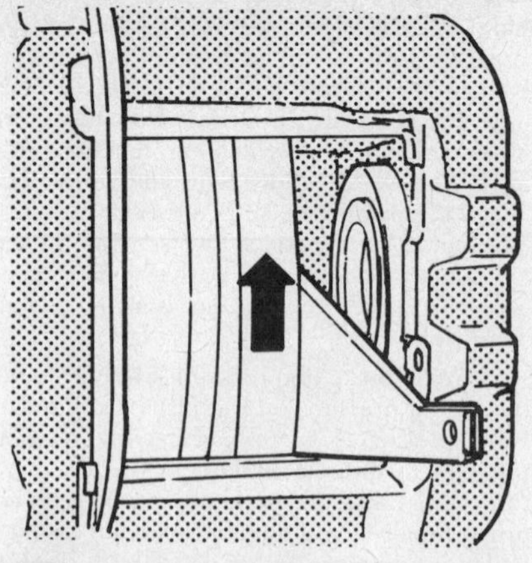

Checking that the piston is at the correct 20° angle—Teves caliper

1. Jack up the front of the car and support it on stands. Remove the wheels.
2. On the Girling caliper, pry off the spring spreader. On the Teves caliper, pry the spring clip out of both retaining pins and while pushing down on the cross spring, drive the pins out with a small punch. On the Girling caliper, remove the bolt and nut holding the pad retainer pins in place and pull the pins out.
3. Reference mark the positions of the brake pads if they are being used again. Switching used pads from their original sides in the caliper can cause uneven braking.
4. On Teves caliper, remove the cross spring from on top of the pads.
5. On the Girling caliper, pull the pads out using a small screwdriver inserted in the pin holes to pry them. On the Teves caliper, pull out the inner pad first. The outer brake pad is positioned in a notch. Use a flat-smooth piece of hardwood or metal to press the floating caliper frame and piston cylinder outward, and pull the pad out. There is a special VW tool (US 1023/3) for pulling the pads out, but you should be able to get by using a screwdriver and a pair of pliers.
6. With a bulb siphon, remove about half of the brake fluid from the master cylinder reservoir to prevent it from overflowing when the piston(s) are pushed in to make room for the thicker replacement pads.

CAUTION

Do not attempt to siphon the brake fluid with your mouth or you may poison yourself.

7. On the Teves caliper, the piston must have its notched surface at a 20° angle to the top of the brake pad.
8. After pressing in the piston, insert the pads. The remaining assembly procedures are the reverse of disassembly. Be sure to fill the master cylinder with fluid. Pump the brake pedal several times before road testing.

GIRLING CLAM-TYPE (1978-81 DASHER ONLY)

Brake pads should be replaced when there is less than ¼ in. of pad thickness.

1. Jack up the front of the car and support it on stands. Remove the front wheels.
2. Siphon some brake fluid from the master cylinder.

CAUTION

Brake fluid is poisonous. Do not siphon by mouth.

3. Press the caliper toward the outside of the car by hand.
4. Remove the lower caliper mounting bolt. Hold the old guide pin head with a wrench while loosening the bolt.
5. Swing the caliper up.
6. If the pads are to be reused, mark their positions so that they can be installed in the same places. Remove the pads; they simply slip out.
7. Installation is the reverse. If new pads are installed, be sure to replace all pads on both front wheels. Mixed pads will cause uneven braking. Install the new self-locking bolt that comes with the repair kit. Tighten the bolt to 25 ft/lbs.

KELSEY-HAYES CALIPER

Brake pads should be replaced when there is less than ¼ in. of pad thickness.

1. Jack up the front of the vehicle and support it on jack stands. Remove the front wheel.
2. Pull out the anti-rattle springs using a pair of needle nosed pliers.
3. Using an Allen wrench, remove the two guide pins which hold the caliper to the caliper support.
4. Swing the caliper out and hang it by a wire, not by its brake hose. You don't have to unhook the brake lines to change the brake pads.
5. Using a bulb siphon, remove some of the brake fluid from the master cylinder reservoir, so that it does not overflow when the piston is pushed in to make room for the thicker brake pads. Don't use your mouth to siphon: brake fluid is poisonous.
6. Insert the pads into the caliper support. The inner pad has chamfered edges. Press the caliper piston in as far as it will go and install the caliper with the guide pins. The long guide pin goes at the top, while the small guide pin goes at the bottom. Torque the pins to 30 ft/lbs.
7. Install the anti-rattle springs.
8. Fill the reservoir with brake fluid and pump the brake pedal several times to set the piston. Check the master cylinder fluid level.

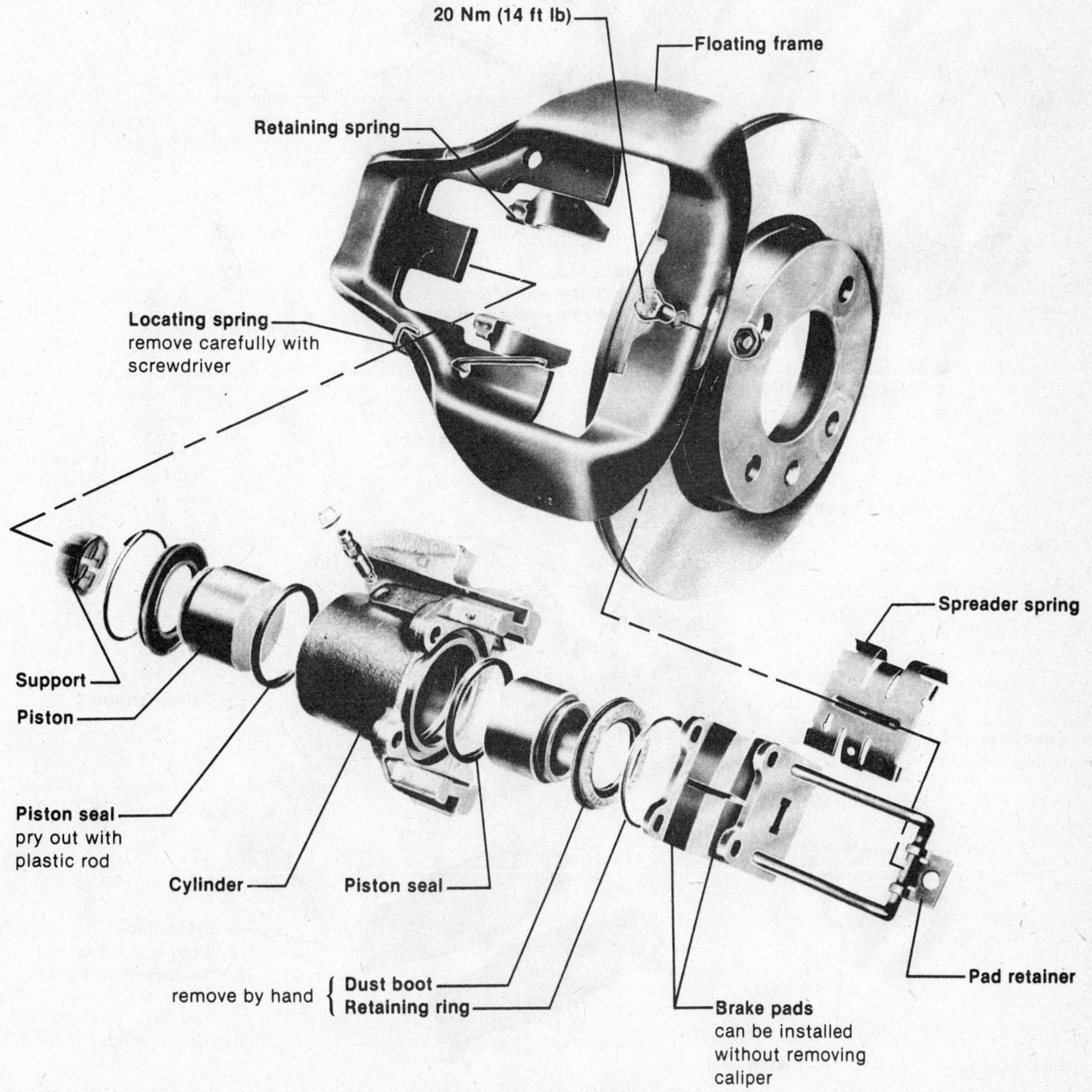

Girling disc brake assembly

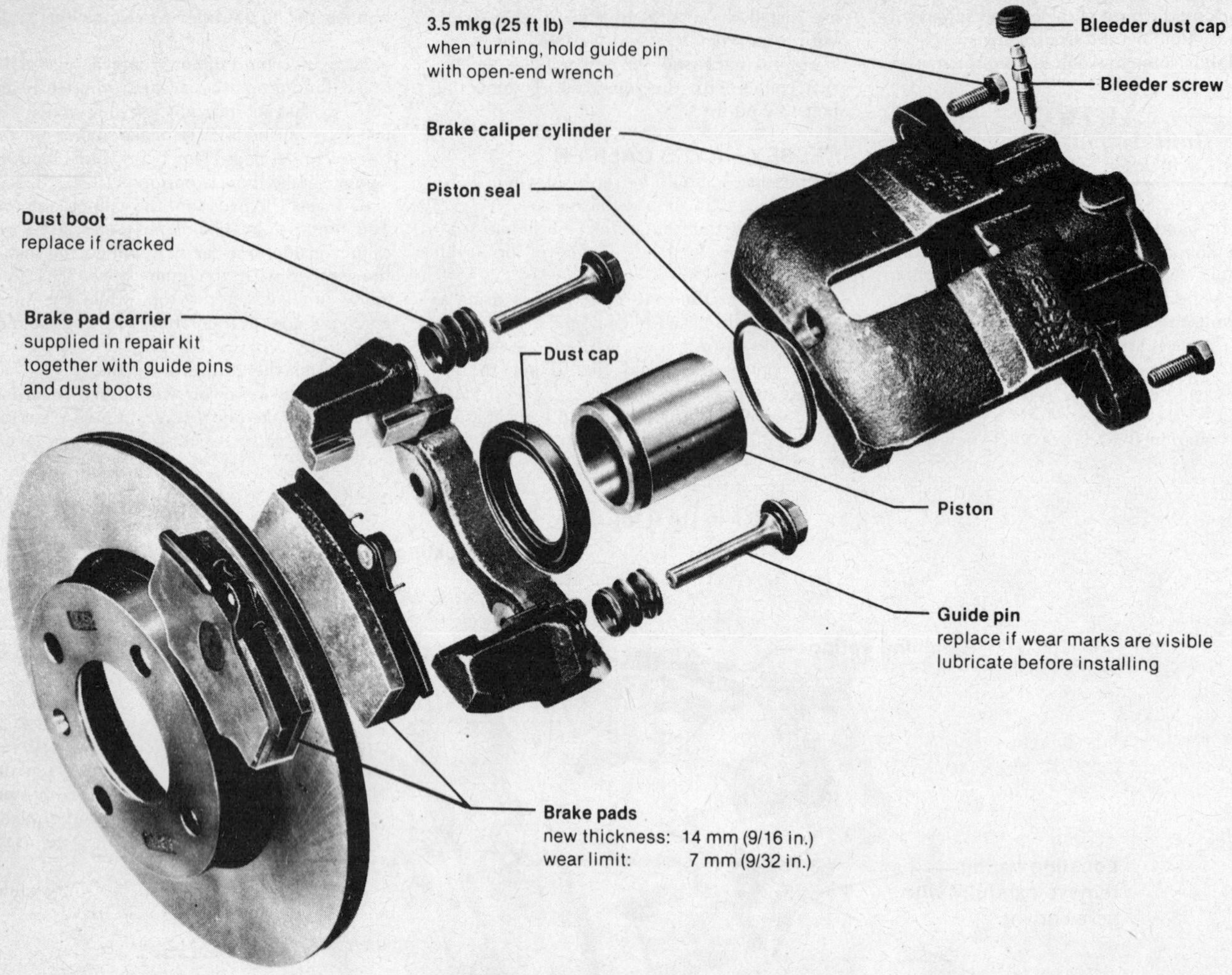

Girling clam-type disc brake assembly

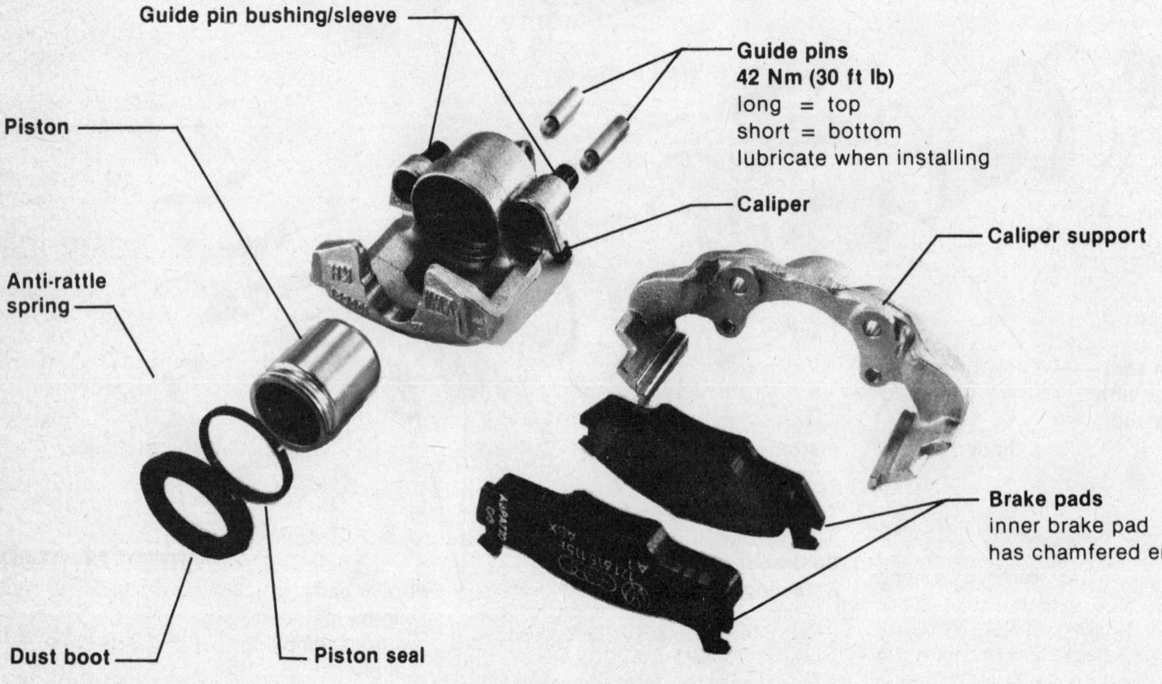

Kelsey Hayes disc brake assembly

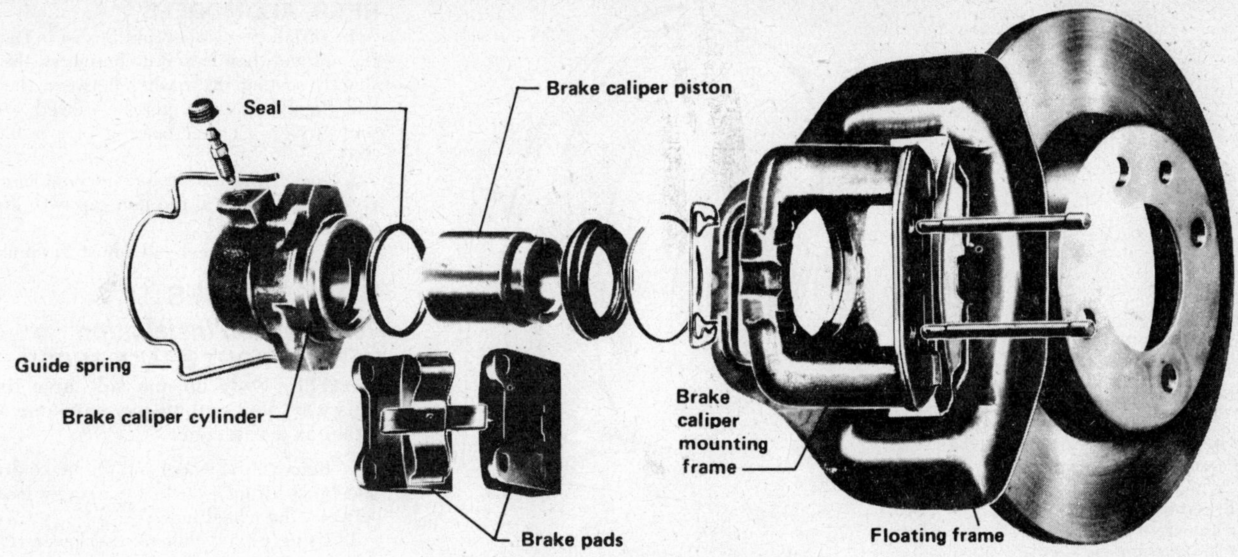

Teves disc brake assembly

CALIPERS

Removal and Installation

1. Jack up and support the front of the car.
2. Remove the brake pads.
3. If you are removing the caliper for overhaul, disconnect and plug the brake line at the caliper. If not, do not remove the hose–hang the caliper by a wire.
4. Remove the two caliper-to-strut retaining bolts and remove the caliper.
5. Install the caliper using the reverse of the removal procedure. Tighten the two retaining bolts to 43 ft/lbs, or 25 ft/lbs for 1978 and later Dashers.
6. Bleed the brakes.

Overhaul

NOTE: Purchase a genuine VW overhaul kit and sufficient brake fluid before starting.

1. Remove the caliper as outlined above. On the Girling clam-type (1978-81 Dasher) and the Kelsey-Hayes calipers, you need only remove the top of the caliper, leaving the support, or carrier, in place.

NOTE: Remove and overhaul one caliper at a time. In this way you can use the other caliper as a reference.

2. Mount the caliper in a soft-jawed vise or place rags over the jaws to protect the caliper.
3. On the Teves, pry the fixed mounting frame off the floating frame.
4. On the Teves and the nonclam-type Girling, drive the caliper cylinder off the floating frame with a brass drift. Do not damage the piston(s).
5. On all models, remove the dust boot(s) and retaining ring(s) from the piston(s) either by hand or using a screwdriver. Some models do not have a retaining ring.
6. Remove the piston(s) from the cylinder. If the piston(s) is stubborn, remove the bleeder screw and use compressed air to force it out.

CAUTION

Hold the piston(s) between blocks of wood when doing this, as they will fly out with considerable force.

7. When the piston pops out of the caliper, remove the rubber seal with a wood or plastic pin to avoid damaging the seal groove.
8. Clean all metal parts in denatured alcohol. Never use a mineral based solvent such as gasoline, kerosene, acetone or the like: these solvents deteriorate rubber parts. Inspect the pistons and their bores. They must be free of scoring and pitting. Replace the cylinder if there is any damage.
9. Discard all rubber parts. The caliper rebuilding kit includes new boots and seals which should be used as the caliper is reassembled.
10. Lightly coat the cylinder bore, piston and seal with brake assembly paste or fresh brake fluid.
11. Install the piston into the cylinder. Fit the dust cover.
12. Installation is the reverse of removal. On the Teves and the nonclamp-type Girling, be sure to install the guide or mounting springs in the correct position.
13. Install the pads and caliper and bleed the brakes.

BRAKE DISC

Inspection

Brake discs may be checked for lateral run-out while on the car. This check will require a dial indicator gauge and stand to mount it on the caliper. VW has a special tool for this purpose which mounts the dial indicator to the caliper, but it can also be mounted on the shaft of a C-clamp attached to the outside of the caliper.

1. Remove the wheel and reinstall the wheel bolts to retain the disc to the hub.
2. Mount the dial indicator securely to the caliper. The feeler should touch the disc about ½-in. below the outer edge.
3. Rotate the disc and observe the gauge. Radial run-out (wobble) must not exceed 0.004 in. (0.002 in., 1978-81 Dasher). A disc which exceeds this specification must be replaced or refinished.
4. Brake discs which have excessive radial run-out, sharp ridges, or scoring can be refinished. Finish grinding must be done on both sides of disc to prevent squeaking and vibrating. Discs which have only light grooves and are otherwise acceptable can be used without refinishing.

The standard disc is 0.47 in. thick. It should not be ground to less than 0.41 in.

Removal and Installation

1. Loosen the wheel bolts. Remove the hub cap.
2. Jack up the front of the car and place it on stands. Remove the wheel(s).
3. Remove the caliper.
4. Remove the disc-to-hub retaining screw.
5. Remove the disc with a sharp pull by hand, or use a puller.
6. The disc is installed in the reverse order or removal. Install the caliper and bleed the brakes.
7. Install the wheel and lower the car. Tighten the wheel bolts diagonally to 65 ft/lbs.

FRONT WHEEL BEARINGS

There is no front wheel bearing adjustment. The bearing is pressed into the steering knuckle. Axle nut torque is 175 ft/lbs. The axle nut should be tightened only with the wheels resting on the ground.

Drum Brakes

BRAKE DRUMS

Removal

FRONT–1975 AND LATER RABBITS

1. Raise and support the car. Remove the wheel.
2. Remove the rubber plug and back off the brake adjuster.
3. Remove the screw securing the drum to the hub. Pull off the drum.

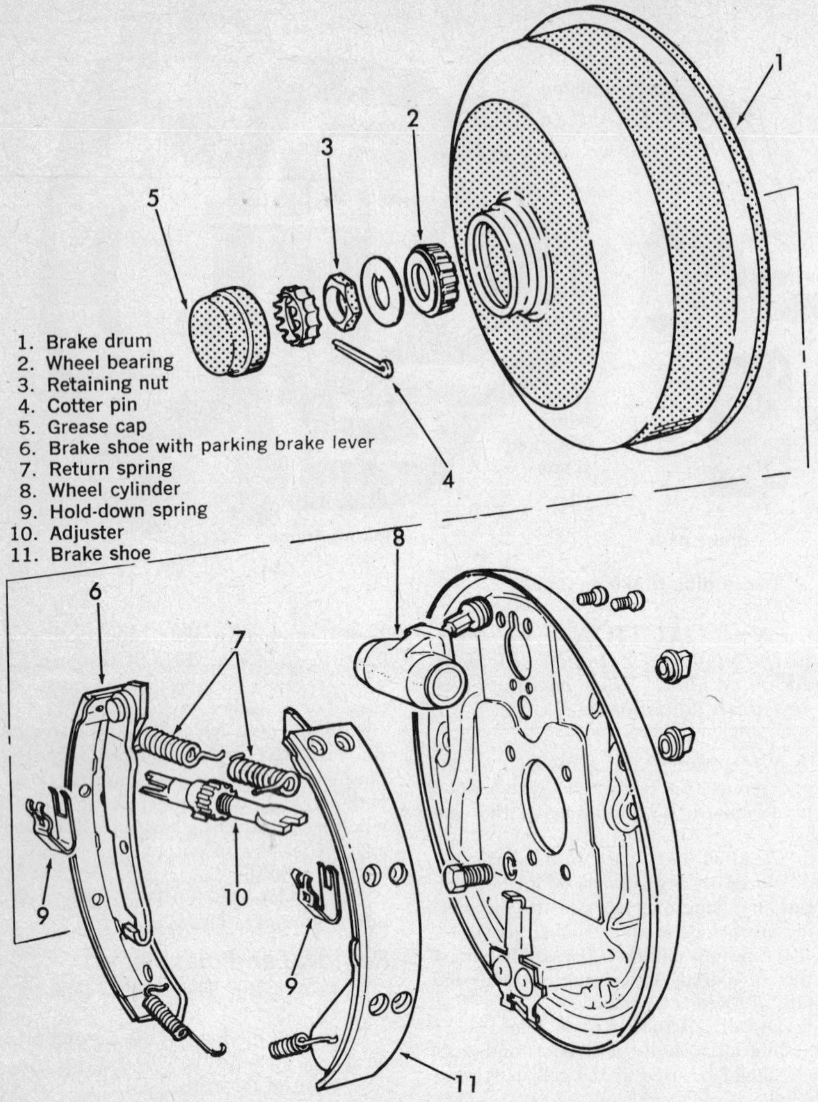

Typical non-self adjusting rear drum brake assembly. On the Rabbit, Jetta and Scirocco there is no inner wheel bearing snap-ring

4. Installation is the reverse. Adjust the brakes after installation. See the Inspection procedure below.

REAR–ALL EXCEPT 1979 AND LATER SELF-ADJUSTING

1. Remove and discard the cotter pin.
2. Remove the castellated nut, hex nut, and washers.
3. Pull of the brake drum. Be careful not to lose the inner race of the outer bearing.

NOTE: If the drum does not come off easily, remove the rubber cover at the backing plate and back off the brake adjuster.

See the Inspection procedure.

REAR–1979 AND LATER SELF-ADJUSTING

1. Remove one wheel bolt.
2. Insert a screwdriver through the wheel bolt hole and push the adjusting wedge upward.
3. Reinstall the wheel bolt and tighten to 65 ft/lbs.
4. Remove the grease cap, axle nut, and cotter pin, and remove the drum. See the Inspection procedure.

Inspection

Check the brake drum for any cracks, scores, grooves, or an out-of-round condition. Replace a drum that shows cracking. Smooth out light scoring with fine emery cloth. If scoring is extensive have the drum turned. Never have a drum turned more than 0.030 in. (0.020 for the Rabbit and Scirocco).

The stub axle bearings in the rear brake drum must be pressed out for replacement. Always use new seals on reassembly. The outer bearing race is retained by a snap-ring (circlip) on the Dasher.

After greasing the bearings and installing them in the drum with new seals, place the drum on the stub axle.

Installation

FRONT

See the Removal procedure.

REAR–ALL MODELS

1. Install the washer and hex nut. Tighten the nut and then loosen it. Retighten the nut slightly so that the washer between the nut and the bearing can just be moved with a screwdriver. Correct bearing play is 0.001-.003 in.
2. Install the castellated nut and insert a new cotter pin. Fill the hub cap with grease and install it.
3 Install the wheel and adjust the brakes.

BRAKE SHOES

Removal and Installation

RABBIT FRONT BRAKE SHOES

NOTE: Only do one side at a time. This way, you will always have one side intact as a reference.

1. Remove the wheel and the brake drum. The brake drum is held by a screw located between the wheel lugs.
2. Using pliers, unhook the lower return springs.
3. Unhook the two spring clips holding the shoes to the backing plate.
4. Pull the lower part of the brake shoe over the wheel hub and unhook the upper retaining spring. Remove the adjuster with the retaining spring.
5. Installation is the reverse of removal.

ADJUSTABLE REAR BRAKES

1. Remove the brake drum.
2. Using pliers, disconnect the lower spring.
3. Disconnect the anchor spring and pins from each shoe.
4. Detach the parking brake cable by pressing back the spring with needle-nosed pliers and then disconnecting the cable at the lever.
5. Remove the second lower spring.
6. Raise one brake shoe from the bottom and remove the adjusting mechanism.
7. Lift the brake shoes and remove the upper springs. Remove both brake shoes.
8. Clean and inspect all brake parts. Spray solvents which do not affect linings are available for brake cleaning. Do not spray rubber parts with solvent.
9. Check the wheel cylinders for boot condition and leaking.
10. Inspect the replacement shoes for nicks or burrs; lubricate the backing plate contact points with Lubriplate, lubricate the brake cable, lever and adjuster, and then assemble.
11. Reverse the removal procedure for assembly. When completed, install the drum and make an initial adjustment by turning the adjuster wheel until a slight drag is felt between the shoes and drum, and back off about ¼ turn. Adjust the brakes.

SELF-ADJUSTING REAR BRAKES

1. Remove the drum.
2. Remove the spring retainers by pressing in and turning ¼ turn.
3. Remove the brake shoes from the supports and the lower return spring.
4. Unhook the parking brake cable on the lever.
5. Use pliers to unhook the spring for the adjusting wedge and the upper return spring.
6. Remove the brake shoes.
7. To remove the self-adjuster pushrod,

place the pushrod in a vise and unhook the tensioning spring.

8. See Steps 8, 9 and 10 of the preceding Rear Brake Shoe Removal procedure for inspection.

9. To install, place the pushrod in a vise, attach the brake shoe to the pushrod to install the tension spring on the rod and shoe.

10. Install the adjusting wedge with the lug toward the backing plate.

11. Attach the brake shoe with the lever to the pushrod. Install the upper return spring.

12. Hook the parking brake cable on the lever. Place the shoes on the cylinder pistons and hook the lower return spring into the shoes.

13. Mount the brake shoes on the support and hook the spring for the adjusting wedge into the wedge and shoe.

14. Install the retaining springs and retainers. Install the drum and adjust the wheel bearings. Apply the brakes firmly to set the self-adjuster.

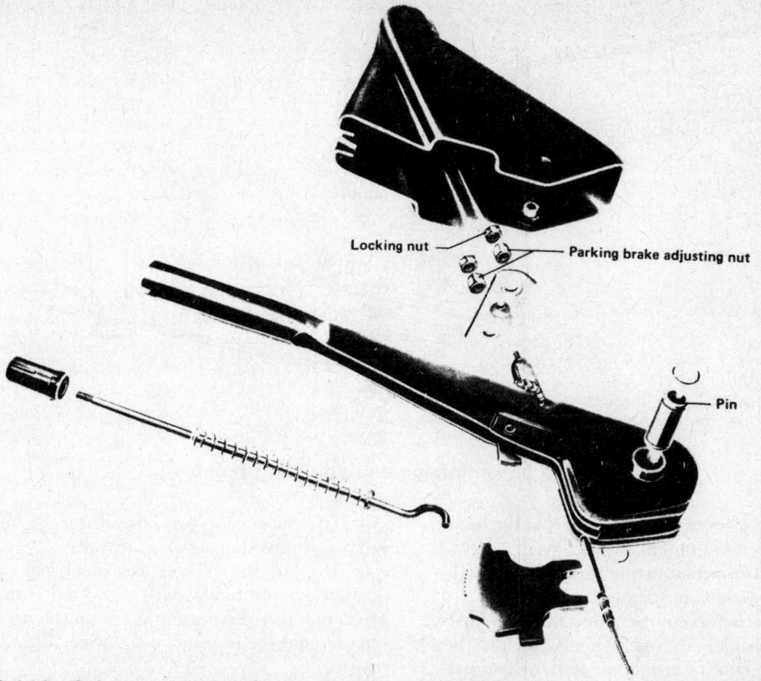

Rabbit, Scirocco parking brake through 1978. 1979 and later Rabbit, Jetta and Scirocco adjusting nuts are located below the brake lever

WHEEL CYLINDERS

Removal and Installation

1. Remove the brake shoes.
2. Loosen the brake line on the rear of the cylinder, but do not pull the line away from the cylinder or it may bend.
3. Remove the bolts and lockwashers that attach the wheel cylinder to the backing plate and remove the cylinder.
4. Position the new wheel cylinder on the backing plate and install the cylinder attaching bolts and lockwashers.
5. Attach the brake line.
6. Install the brakes and bleed the system.

Overhaul

1. Remove the brakes.
2. Place a bucket or some newspapers under the brake backing plate to catch the brake fluid that will run out of the wheel cylinder.
3. Remove the boots from the ends of the wheel cylinders.
4. Push one piston toward the center of the cylinder to force the opposite piston and cup out the other end of the cylinder. Reach in the open end of the cylinder and push the spring, cup, and piston out of the cylinder.
5. Remove the bleeder screw from the rear of the cylinder, on the back of the backing plate.
6. Inspect the inside of the wheel cylinder. If it is scored in any way, the cylinder must be honed with a wheel cylinder hone or fine emery paper, and finished with crocus cloth if emery paper is used. If the inside of the cylinder is excessively worn, the cylinder will have to be replaced, as only 0.003 in. of material can be removed from the cylinder walls. Whenever honing or cleaning wheel cylinders, keep a small amount of brake fluid in the cylinder to serve as a lubricant.
7. Clean any foreign matter from the pistons. The sides of the pistons must be smooth for the wheel cylinders to operate properly.
8. Clean the cylinder bore with alcohol and a lint-free rag. Pull the rag through the bore several times to remove all foreign matter and dry the cylinder.
9. Install the bleeder screw and the return spring in the cylinder.
10. Coat new cylinder cups with new brake fluid and install them in the cylinder. Make sure they are square in the bore or they will leak.
11. Install the pistons in the cylinder after coating them with new brake fluid.
12. Coat the insides of the boots with new brake fluid and install them on the cylinder. Install and bleed the brakes.

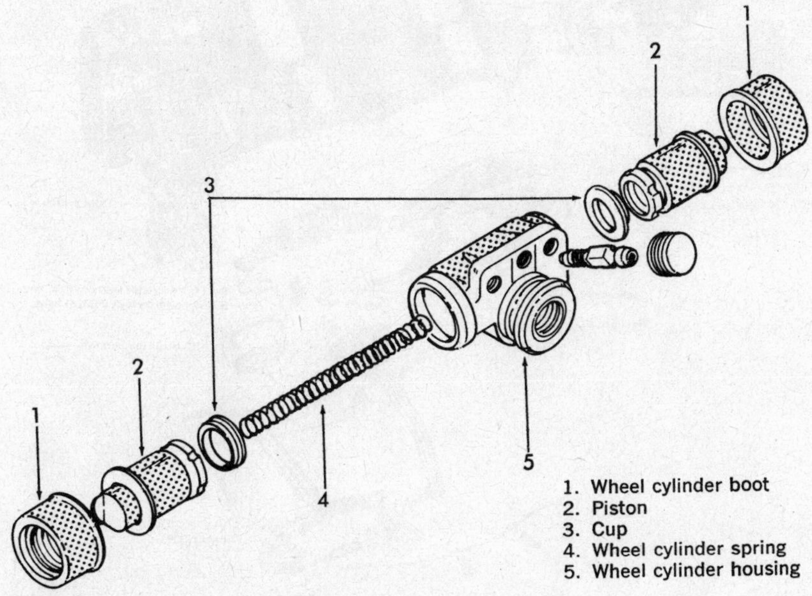

Exploded view of the wheel cylinder

REAR WHEEL BEARINGS

Rear wheel bearing adjustment is covered under Brake Drum Removal and Installation.

Parking Brake

ADJUSTMENT

Dasher parking brake adjustment is made at the cable compensator, which is attached to the lever pushrod underneath the car. On the 1975-78 Rabbit and Scirocco, adjustment is made at the cable end nuts on the top of the handbrake lever. On 1979 and later Rabbits, Sciroccos and Jettas, the position of the cable end nuts has been changed from the top of the handbrake lever to below the front of the lever. Adjustment is performed in the same manner as on 1975-78 Rabbits and Sciroccos.

1. Block the front wheels. Raise the rear of the car.

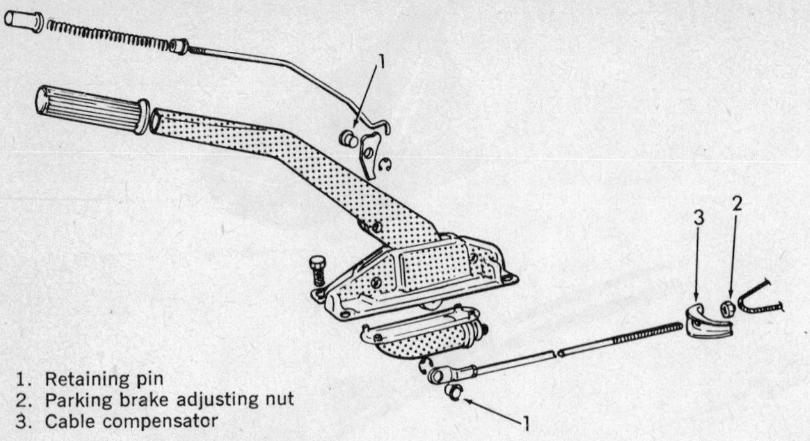

Dasher parking brake linkage and adjusting point

2. Apply the parking brake so that the lever is on the second notch.
3. The Dasher adjustment is made directly under the passenger compartment.
4. Tighten the compensator nut or adjusting nuts until both rear wheels can just be turned by hand. On models with self-adjusting rear brakes, you shouldn't be able to turn them at all.
5. Release the parking brake lever and check that both wheels can be easily turned.
6. Lubricate the Dasher compensator with chassis grease.

CHASSIS ELECTRICAL

Heater

The heater core and blower on all models are contained in the heater box (fresh air housing) located in the center of the passenger compartment under the dashboard. On air conditioned Rabbits, Jettas and Sciroccos, the evaporator is located in the heater box. On air conditioned Dashers, the evaporator is located under the hood separate from the heater box.

The blower fan on non-air conditioned models before 1977 is open bladed, much like an airplane propeller. The blower fan on all air conditioned models and non-air conditioned models after 1977 is of the turbine-type.

CAUTION

When working on air conditioning components, use extreme caution.

REMOVAL AND INSTALLATION

1. Disconnect the battery ground cable.
2. Drain the cooling system.
3. Remove the windshield washer container from its mounts and remove the ignition coil only if they restrict your access to the heater components under the hood.
4. Disconnect the two hoses from the heater core connections at the firewall.
5. Unplug the blower fan electrical connections. Some models are equipped with an external series resistor mounted on the heater box. Do not try to remove the wires from the resistor.
6. Remove the heater control knobs on the dash.
7. Remove the two retaining screws and remove the controls from the dash complete with brackets.
8. Some model Dashers have a cable attached to a lever which is operated by a round knob on the dashboard. Remove the cable from the lever.
9. Remove either the clips or the screws holding the heater box in place and remove the heater box with the heater controls.

Installation is the reverse of removal. Be sure to refill the cooling system.

Heater Blower

REMOVAL AND INSTALLATION

Pre-1977 Models

1. Remove the heater box. See procedure above.
2. On Rabbits and Scirocco, remove the screws holding the heater cover in place and remove the heater cover. Remove the circular cutoff flap by unhooking it from its hinge. On Dashers, remove the heater cover by pulling out its pins.
3. On the Rabbit and Scirocco, the heater blower should pull right out of the assembly.
4. On Dashers, remove the clips holding the heater box halves together and separate the halves. The fan should just pull out.

Installation is the reverse of removal.

NOTE: On the Dasher, when installing the fan in the heater box halves, make sure the wiring connections on the fan face the wiring harness on the heater box. Also, when jointing the housing halves, make sure there is no side to side play in the blower motor.

1977 and Later Models

1. Remove the heater unit from the vehicle. See above for procedures.
2. Remove the screws holding the cover on the heater box and remove the cover. Remove the blower motor cover, if so equipped.
3. Remove the electrical connections from the blower motor after matchmarking them to

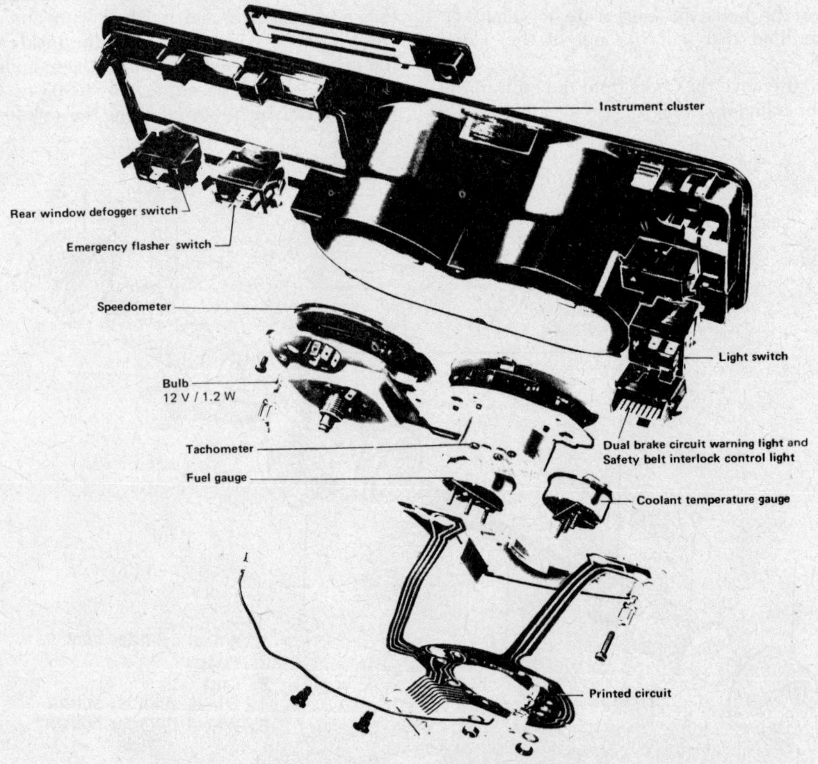

Exploded view of Rabbit and Scirocco instrument cluster

insure that you assemble them in the correct order.

4. Remove the clamp or screws holding the motor in place and remove the motor.

Installation is the reverse of removal.

Heater Core

REMOVAL AND INSTALLATION

NOTE: On some 1977 and later models, it is possible to remove the heater core without removing the heater box. Proceed as follows:

a. Drain the cooling system.

b. Locate and remove the heater core cover in the side of the heater box.

c. Disconnect the heater hoses from the core and pull the core out.

1. Remove the heater box from the vehicle.
2. If the unit has a core cover in its side, remove the screws or unclip the cover and remove it. The core should pull out.
3. On other models, remove the heater box clips that hold the two halves of the heater box together, separate the halves after removing any components that are in the way, and remove the heater core.

Windshield Wiper Motor

REMOVAL AND INSTALLATION

Dasher

1. Unplug the multi-connector from the wiper motor.
2. Remove the three motor-to-linkage bracket retaining screws.
3. Carefully pry the motor crank out of the two linkage arms.
4. Remove the motor from the car.
5. Install the motor in the reverse order of removal. The crank arm should be at a right angle to the motor.

Rabbit, Scirocco, Jetta

When removing the wiper motor, leave the mounting frame in place. On all models with two front wiper arms, do not remove the wiper drive crank from the motor shaft.

On Sciroccos with one front wiper arm, matchmark the drive crank and motor arm and then remove the arm.

NOTE: If, for any reason you must remove the wiper drive crank from the motor shaft on two wiper arm models, matchmark both parts for reassembly.

1. Access is with the hood open. Disconnect the battery ground cable.
2. Detach the connecting rods from the motor crank arm.
3. Pull off the wiring plug.
4. Remove the 4 mounting bolts. You may have to energize the motor for access to the top bolt.
5. Remove the motor. Reverse the procedure for installation.

Instrument Cluster

REMOVAL AND INSTALLATION

1975-78 Dasher

1. Disconnect the battery ground cable.
2. Unscrew the speedometer cable from the rear of the cluster.
3. Using needle-nosed pliers, detach the retaining springs on either side of the cluster.
4. Pivot the instrument cluster out of the dash.
5. Disconnect the multi-connector plug at the rear of the cluster.

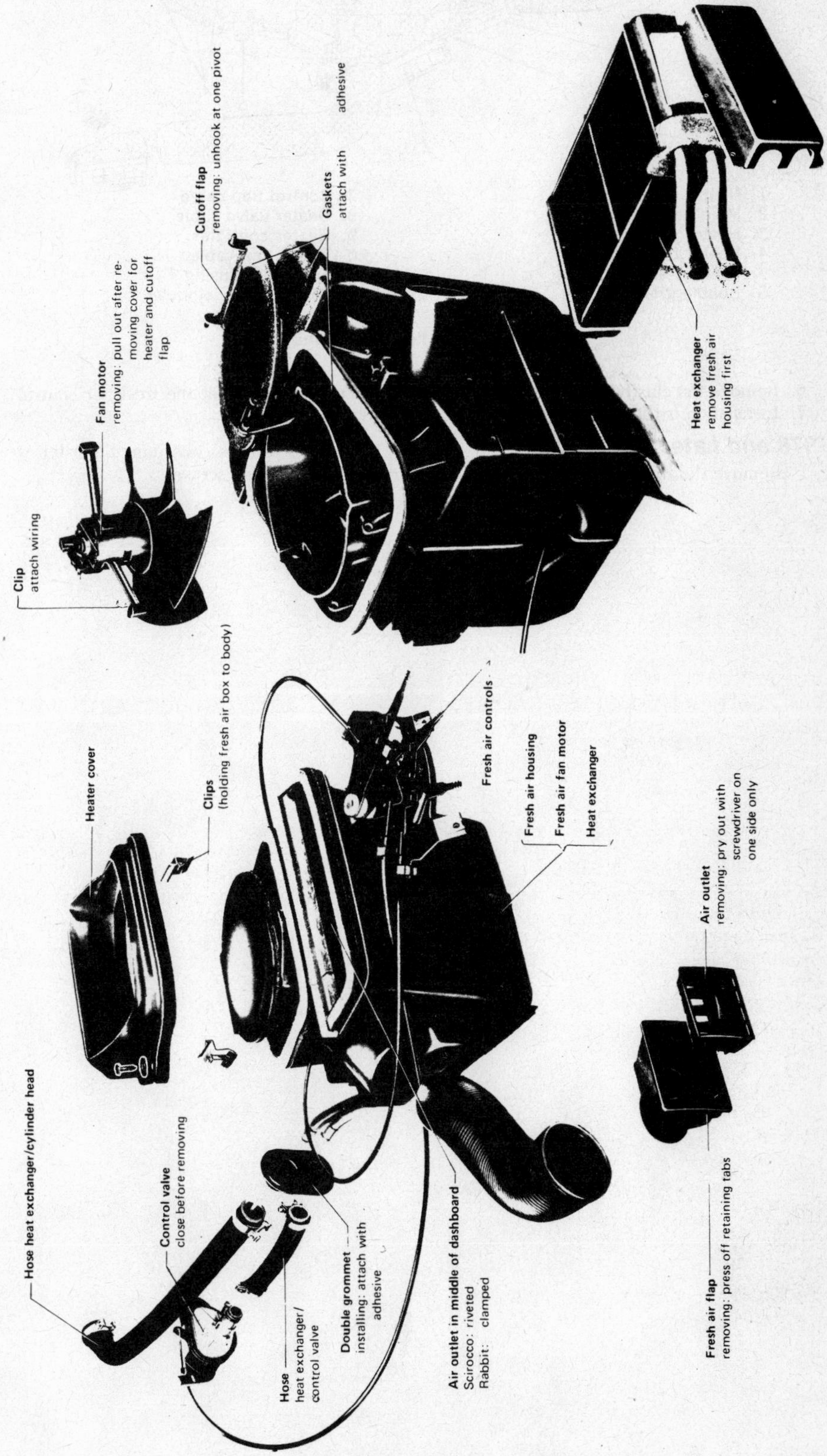

Early Rabbit, Scirocco heater

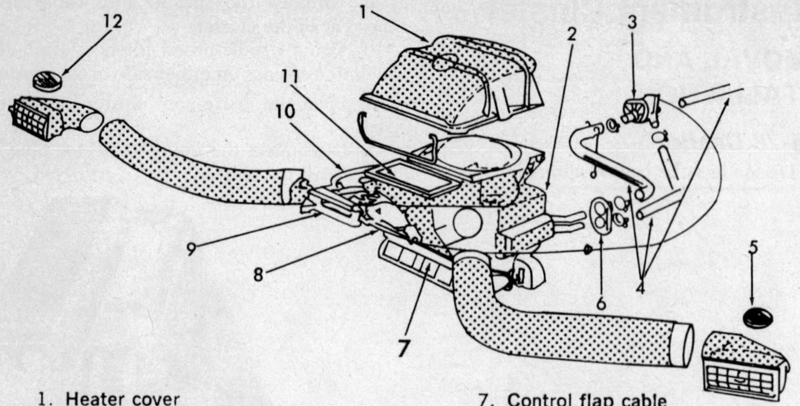

1. Heater cover
2. Main heater assembly
3. Heater valve
4. Heater hoses
5. Vent for side windows
6. Double grommet
7. Control flap cable
8. Heater valve cable
9. Heater controls
10. Cutoff flap cable
11. Fresh air housing
12. Vent for side windows

Early Dasher heater assembly

6. Remove the cluster from the dash.
7. Installation is the reverse of removal.

1978 and Later Dasher

1. Remove the radio or shelf.
2. Pull the knobs off the fresh air control and fan switch.
3. Remove the six instrument cluster to dashboard retaining screws.
4. Snap out the light, emergency flasher and rear window defogger switches.
5. Disconnect the air fan switch electrical connector.
6. Remove the instrument cluster and disconnect the speedometer cable and the multi-point connector from the back of the cluster.

Rabbit, Scirocco, Jetta

1. Disconnect the battery ground cable.
2. Remove the fresh air controls trim plate.
3. Remove the radio or glove box.
4. Unscrew the speedometer drive cable from the back of the speedometer. Detach the electrical plug.
5. Remove the attaching screw inside the radio/glove box opening.
6. Remove the instrument cluster. Reverse the procedure for installation.

Fuses and Relays

The 1974-75 Dasher fuse/relay panel is located under the hood on the driver's side fender. The fuse/relay panel on all other models is located in the lower left side of the dashboard. Use VW ceramic fuses. VW recommends that relays be replaced by your dealer.

SPECIFICATIONS

INDEX

BEFORE SERVICING, SEE THE SAFETY NOTICE ON THE CONTENTS PAGE

INTRODUCTION

Since 1975 seven series of Volvos have been sold in the U.S. The 164 series through 1975. The 240 series: 242, 244 and 245, and the 260 series: 262, 264 and 265.

The 240 series uses inline four cylinder engines. The 164 uses an inline six and the 260 series uses a V6. All engines are fuel injected.

SERIAL NUMBER IDENTIFICATION

Vehicle Type Designation and Chassis Number

Type designation (164, 242, 262, etc.) and chassis number appear at several locations on every Volvo. On all series Volvos, they are stamped into the sheet metal of the right front door pillar. The type designation and the chassis number also appear on a metal plate (1) riveted to the engine side of the firewall. For 1975-79, they appear on the V.I.N. plate (3) located at the foot of the left door post.

For 1980-81, the model designations are DL-GL-GT (formerly 242-244-245), GLE (formerly 264-265), Coupe (formerly 262C). The VIN plate appears on the right side shock absorber housing.

CHASSIS NUMBER CHART

Year	Model	Starting Chassis No.
1975	242	1
	244	1
	245	1
	164	132577
1976	242	53865
	244	82980
	245	54710
	262	1
	264	9675
	265	5

CHASSIS NUMBER CHART

Year	Model	Starting Chassis No.
1977	242	99680
	244	174910
	245	115350
	262	2430
	264	34470
	265	8115
1978	242	122895
	244	274965
	245	163835
	262	2660
	264	46515
	265	10920
1979	242	142125
	244	364650
	245	211325
	262	4330
	264	62105
	265	15735
1980	DL, GT (2 dr.)	165570
	DL, GL (4 dr.)	482505
	Coupe	6450
	GLE	83055
	4 cyl. wgn.	264755
	6 cyl. wgn.	21755

Component Identification

The engine type designation, part number, and serial number are given on the left side of the block (4). The last figures of the part number are stamped on a tab and are followed by the serial number stamped on the block.

The transmission type designation, serial number, and part number appear on a metal plate (5) riveted to the underside of the transmission. The final drive reduction ratio, part number, and serial number are found on a metal plate (6) riveted to the left-hand side of the differential.

Engine, Transmission and Final Drive Identification

Beginning with 1975 models, a component data plate is used to specify the manufacturer of major serviceable components such as the brakes, fuel pump, clutch, alternator, and steering gear. The plate is located on the right front door pillar. Each component manufacturer is assigned a code.

GENERAL ENGINE SPECIFICATIONS

Year		Engine Displacement cu. in. (cc)	Fuel Delivery Type	Horsepower @ rpm	Torque @ rpm (ft. lbs.)	Bore x Stroke (in.)	Compression Ratio	Oil Pressure @ rpm (psi)
1975	B 20 F	122 (1990)	Bosch continuous injection	98 @ 6000 ①	110 @ 3500 ②	3.5008 x 3.150	8.7:1	36-85 @ 2000
1976-78	B 21 F	130 (2127)	Bosch continuous injection	102 @ 5200 ⑤	114 @ 2500 ⑥	3.623 x 3.150	8.5:1	35-85 @ 2000
1979-81	B 21 F	130 (2127)	Bosch continuous fuel injection	107 @ 5250	117 @ 2500 ⑨	3.623 x 3.150	9.3:1	35-85 @ 2000
1976-78	B 27 F	162 (2660)	Bosch continuous injection	125 @ 5500 ⑦	150 @ 2750 ⑧	3.4646 x 2.8740	8.2:1	58 @ 3000
1979-81	B 27 F	162 (2660)	Bosch continuous injection	127 @ 5500	146 @ 2750	3.4646 x 2.8740	8.8:1	58 @ 3000

GENERAL ENGINE SPECIFICATIONS

Year		Engine Displacement cu. in. (cc)	Fuel Delivery Type	Horsepower @ rpm	Torque @ rpm (ft. lbs.)	Bore x Stroke (in.)	Compression Ratio	Oil Pressure @ rpm (psi)
1975	B 30 F	183 (2978)	Bosch electronic fuel injection	130 @ 5250 ③	150 @ 4000 ④	3.501 x 3.150	8.7:1	36-85 @ 2000
1980-81	B 28 F	174 (2849)	Bosch continuous injection	130 @ 5500	153 @ 2750	3.582 x 2.863	8.8:1	60 @ 3000
1980-81	D24	145 (2383)	Diesel	78 @ 4800	102 @ 3000	3.012 x 3.402	23.0:1	28 @ 2000

① 94 @ 6000 w/catalytic converter
② 105 @ 3500 w/catalytic converter
③ 125 @ 5250 w/catalytic converter
④ 145 @ 4000 w/catalytic converter
⑤ 99 @ 5200 in Calif.
⑥ 114 @ 2500 in Calif.
⑦ 121 @ 5500 in Calif.
⑧ 148 @ 2750 in Calif.
⑨ 114 in Calif.

TUNE-UP SPECIFICATIONS

When analyzing compression test results, look for uniformity among cylinders, rather than specific pressures

Year	Engine Displacement cu.in.	Spark Plugs Type	Spark Plugs Gap (in.)	Distributor Point Dwell (deg)	Distributor Point Gap (in.)	Ignition Timing (deg) MT	Ignition Timing (deg) AT	Intake Valve Opens (deg)	Fuel Pump Pressure (psi)	Idle Speed (rpm) MT	Idle Speed (rpm) AT	Valve Clearance (cold) (in.) In	Valve Clearance (cold) (in.) Ex
1975	B 20 F 122	Bosch W200T35	0.030	Electronic		10B ①	10B ①	5.5B	71	900	800	0.016-0.018	0.016-0.018
	B 30 F 183	Bosch W200T35	0.030	Electronic		10B ①	10B ①	TDC	28	900	800	0.020-0.022	0.020-0.022
1976	B 21 F 130	Bosch W175T30	0.030	Electronic		15B ①	15B ①	15B	64-75	900	800	0.014-0.016	0.014-0.016
	B 27 F 162	Bosch WA200T30 Champ BN9Y	0.026	Electronic		10B ①	10B ①	②	64-75	900	900	0.004-0.006	0.010-0.012
1977	B 21 F 130	Bosch WA175T30	0.030	Electronic		12B ①	12B ①	—	64-75	900	900	0.014-0.016	0.014-0.016
	B 27 F 162	Bosch WA200T30	0.026	Electronic		10B ①	10B ①	—	64-75	900	900	0.004-0.006	0.010-0.012
1978	B 21 F 130	Bosch WA175T30	0.030	Electronic		12B ①	12B ①	—	64-75	900	900	0.014-0.016	0.014-0.016
1978-79	B 27 F 162	Bosch WA200T30	0.030	Electronic		10B ①	10B ①	—	64-75	900	900	0.004-0.006	0.010-0.012
1979	B 21 F 130	Bosch W6DC	0.030	Electronic		10B ①③	10B ①③	—	64-75	900	900	0.014-0.016	0.014-0.016
1980-81	B 21 F 130	Bosch WR7DS	0.030	Electronic		8B ①	8B ①	—	64-75	950	950	0.014-0.016	0.014-0.016
1980-81	B 28 F 174	Bosch WR7DS	0.030	Electronic		10B ①④	10B ①④	—	64-75	950	950	0.008-0.010	0.012-0.014

① @ 700 rpm
② 9B—left side; 7B—right side
③ Calif: 8B
④ Vacuum advance disconnected, A/C turned off

DIESEL TUNE-UP SPECIFICATIONS

Year	Model	VALVE CLEARANCE ① Intake (in.)	VALVE CLEARANCE ① Exhaust (in.)	Injection Pump Setting (in.)	Injector Nozzle Opening Pressure (psi)	Idle Speed (rpm)	Compression Pressure (psi)
1980-81	D24	0.006-0.010	0.014-0.018	0.0265-0.0287 ②	1700-1845 ③	720-880 ④	485 ⑤

① Cold
② See text
③ Acceptable range. When servicing set to 1775-1920 psi
④ Maximum safe speed: 5100-5300 rpm

FIRING ORDERS

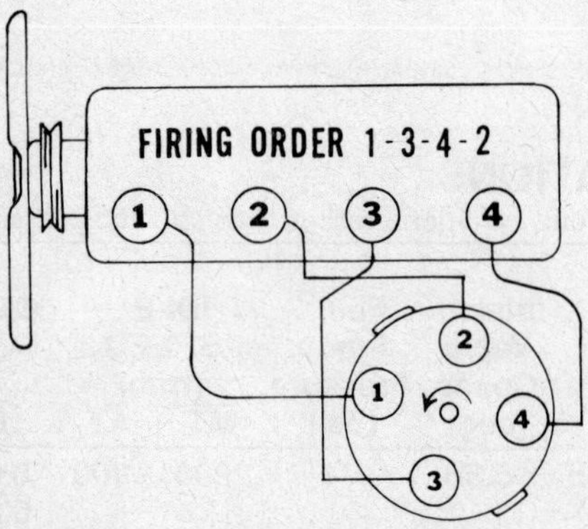

B20F

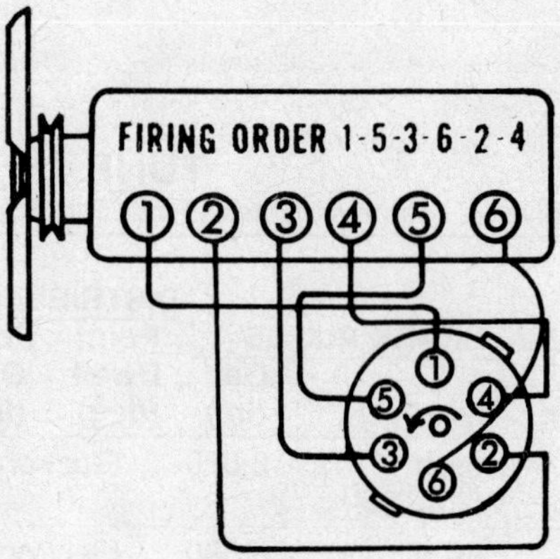

B30F

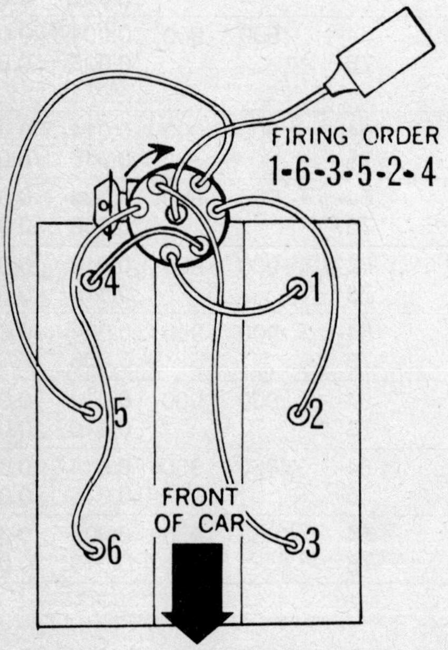

B27F, B28

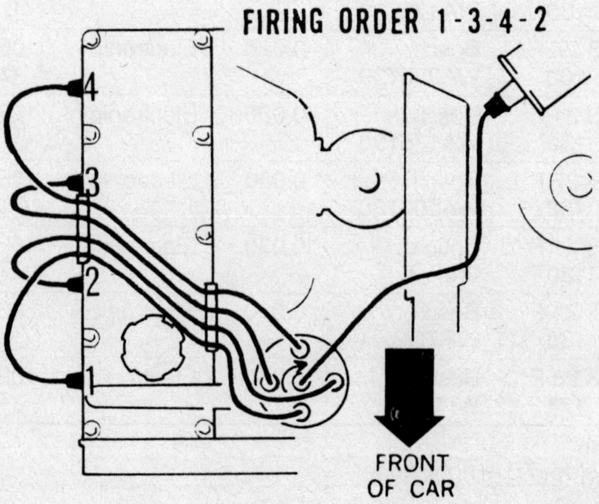

B21F

CAPACITIES

Year	Model	Engine Displacement cu. in. (cc)	Engine Crankcase (qt) With Filter	Engine Crankcase (qt) Without Filter	Transmission (pts) Manual 4-Spd ③	Transmission (pts) Automatic	Drive Axle (pt)	Gasoline Tank (gal)	Cooling System (qt)
1975	242, 244, 245	122 (1990)	4.0	3.4	1.6 (3.4)	13.5	2.7	15.8	10.0
	164	183 (2978)	6.3	5.5	(3.1)	18.0	3.4	15.8	11.0
1976-77	242, 244, 245	130 (2127)	4.0	3.5	1.6 (4.8)	13.8	3.4	15.8	10.0 ①
	262, 264, 265	162 (2660)	7.4	6.8	1.6 (4.8)	13.8	3.4	15.8	12.0
1978	242, 244, 245	130 (2127)	4.0	3.5	1.6 (3.8)	14.0	3.4	15.8	10.0
	262, 264, 265	162 (2660)	6.8	6.3	1.6 (4.8)	14.0	3.4	15.8	11.5
1979	242, 244, 245	130 (2127)	4.0	3.5	1.6 (3.8)	14.0 ②	3.4	15.8	10.0
	262, 264, 265	162 (2660)	6.8	6.3	1.6 (4.8)	14.0 ②	3.4	15.8	11.5
1980-81	DL, GL, GT	130 (2127)	4.0	3.5	1.6 (4.8)	14.6	3.4	15.8	10.0
1980-81	GLE, Coupe	174 (2849)	6.8	6.3	1.6 (4.8)	14.6	3.4	15.8	11.5
1980-81	Diesel	145 (2383)	7.4	6.6	1.6 (4.8)	14.6	3.4	15.8	10.0

① 9.8 qts w/auto trans.
② With extra capacity fluid pan: 14.6
③ Figures in parentheses are for overdrive transmission

VALVE SPECIFICATIONS

Year	Engine and Displacement cu. in. (cc)	Cylinder Head Seat Angle (deg)	Valve Face Angle (deg)	Seat Width (in.)	Spring Test Pressure (lbs. @ in.)	Spring Installed Height (in.)	Stem to Guide Clearance (in.) Intake	Stem to Guide Clearance (in.) Exhaust	Stem Diameter (in.) Intake	Stem Diameter (in.) Exhaust
1975	B 20 F 122 (1990)	44.5	45	0.08	181.5 @ 1.18	1.81	0.0012-0.0026	0.0024-0.0038	0.3132-0.3138	0.3120-0.3126
1976-81	B 21 F 130 (2127)	44.75	45.5	0.08	170 @ 1.06	1.77	0.0012-0.0024	0.0024-0.0035	0.3132-0.3135	0.3128-0.3126
1975	B 30 F 183 (2978)	44.5	45	0.08	181.5 @ 1.18	1.81	0.0012-0.0026	0.0024-0.0038	0.3132-0.3138	0.3120-0.3126
1976-79	B 27 F 162 (2660) B 28 F 174 (2849)	29.5 int 30 exh	29.5 int 30 exh	①	124.3 @ 1.27	1.86	②	②	0.3136-0.3142 to 0.3140-0.3146	0.3128-0.3134 to 0.3136-0.3142
1980-81	B 28 F	29.5 int 30 exh	29.5 int 30 exh	①	143 @ 1.181	1.85	②	②	0.3136-0.3142 to 0.3140-0.3146	0.3128-0.3134 to 0.3136-0.3142

① 0.067-0.083 intake; 0.079-0.094 exhaust
② Tapered; valve guide ID is 0.3150-0.3158

CRANKSHAFT AND CONNECTING ROD SPECIFICATIONS

All measurements are given in inches

Engine Model	Engine Displacement cu. in. (cc)	CRANKSHAFT Main Brg. Journal Dia.	Main Brg. Oil Clearance	Shaft End-Play	Thrust on No.	CONNECTING ROD Journal Diameter	Oil Clearance	Side Clearance
B 20 F	122 (1990)	2.4981-2.4986	0.0011-0.0033	0.0018-0.0054	5	2.1255-2.1260	0.0012-0.0028	0.006-0.014
B 21 F	130 (2127)	2.4981-2.4986	0.0011-0.0033	0.0015-0.0058	5	2.1255-2.1260	0.0009-0.0028	0.006-0.014
B 30 F	183 (2978)	2.4981-2.4986	0.0011-0.0033	0.0018-0.0054	7	2.1255-2.1260	0.0012-0.0028	0.006-0.014
B 27 F B 28 F	162 (2660) 174 (2849)	2.7576-2.7583	0.0015-0.0035	0.0028-0.0106	4	2.0578-2.0585	0.0012-0.0031	0.008-0.015

PISTON AND RING SPECIFICATIONS

Year	Engine Displacement cu. in. (cc)	Piston Clearance	RING GAP Top Compression	Bottom Compression	Oil Control	RING SIDE CLEARANCE Top Compression	Bottom Compression	Oil Control
1975	B 20 F 122 (1990)	0.0004-0.0012	0.016-0.022	0.016-0.022	0.016-0.022	0.0016-0.0028	0.0016-0.0028	0.0016-0.0028
1976-81	B 21 F 130 (2127)	0.0004-0.0012	0.0138-0.0217	0.0138-0.0217	0.010-0.016	0.0016-0.0028	0.0016-0.0028	0.0016-0.0028
1975	B 30 F 183 (2978)	0.0016-0.0024 ①	0.016-0.022	0.016-0.022	0.016-0.022	0.0016-0.0032	0.0016-0.0028	0.0016-0.0028
1976-79 1980-81	B 27 F 162 (2660) B 28 F 174 (2849)	0.0008-0.0016	0.016-0.022	0.016-0.022	0.015-0.055	0.0018-0.0029	0.0010-0.0021	0.0004-0.0092

TORQUE SPECIFICATIONS

All readings in ft. lbs.

Year	Engine	Cyl. Head Bolts	Rod Bearing Bolts	Main Bearing Bolts	Crank-shaft Pulley Bolt	Flywheel-To-Crank-shaft Bolts	MANIFOLD BOLTS Intake	Exhaust	Cam-shaft Nut	Spark Plug	Oil Pan
1975	All	65 ①	51-57	87-&4	69-76 ②	47-51	13-16	13-16	94-108	25-29	6-8
1976-81	B 21 F	76-83 ③	43-48	85-91	107-128	47-54	15	15	32-38	25-29	8
1976-79 1980-81	B 27 F B 28 F	④	33-37	⑤	118-132 ⑥	33-37	7-11	7-11	51-59	13-15	7-11
1980-81	D24	65 ⑦	N.A.	N.A.	330 ⑧	55	18	18	⑩	⑨	N.A.

① Torque head bolts in three stages: first, torque in sequence to 29 ft. lbs., then to 58 ft. lbs., and finally after driving the car for 10 minutes, torque to the final figure of 65 ft. lbs.

② Double pulley: 80-101 ft. lbs.

③ Torque head bolts in two stages; first, tighten in sequence to 43 ft. lbs., then to 76-83 ft. lbs.

④ Torque heads bolts in sequence to 7 ft. lbs., then 22 ft. lbs., then 44 ft. lbs. Wait 10-15 minutes and slacken the bolts ½ turn. Then torque to 11-14 ft. lbs. and then protractor torque to 116-120° (⅓ of a turn). Finally run to operating temperature, shut off and allow to cool for 30 min. Following the sequence, slacken, torque to 11-14 ft. lbs., and protractor torque to 113-117° each bolt.

⑤ Torque main bearing nuts to 22 ft. lbs., in sequence. Then slacken 1st nut ½ turn, tighten to 22-26 ft. lbs., and protractor torque to 73-77°. Repeat for remaining nuts following the sequence.

⑥ 1978-81: 175-200

⑦ Torque in two stages: 30 ft. lbs. then 65 ft. lbs. After 1000 miles torque to 62 ft. lbs. (warm)

⑧ Using regular torque wrench. If Volvo tool 5188 is used, torque to 255 ft. lbs.

⑨ Injector: 50 ft. lbs.

⑩ Front camshaft bolt: 33; Rear: 73

TORQUE SEQUENCES

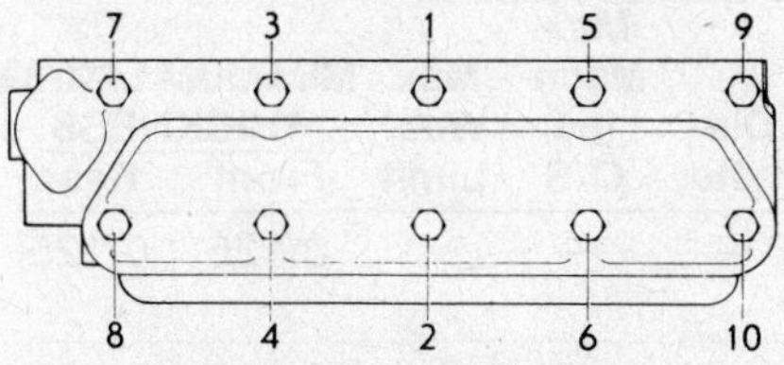

Cylinder head—B20

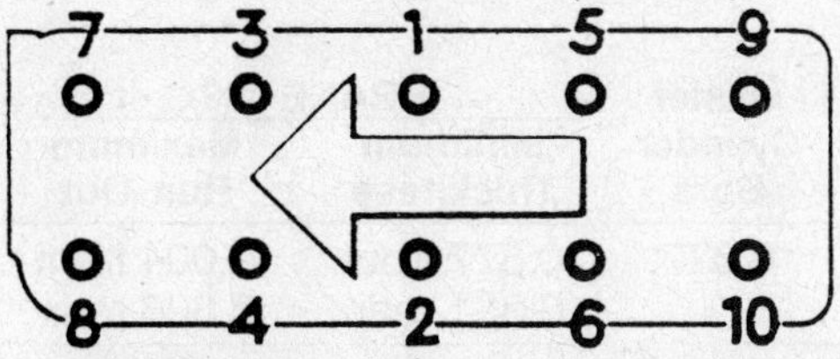

Cylinder head bolt tightening sequence—B21

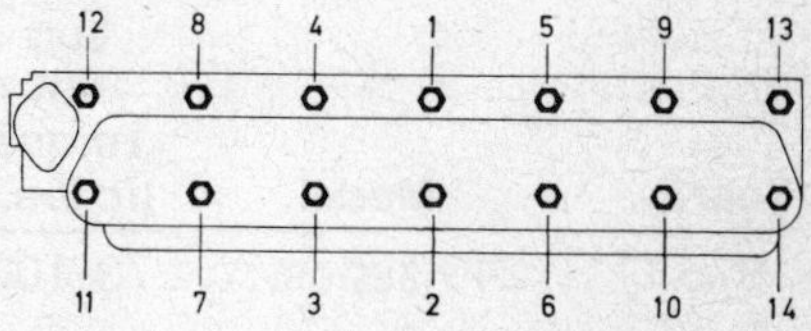

Cylinder head—B30

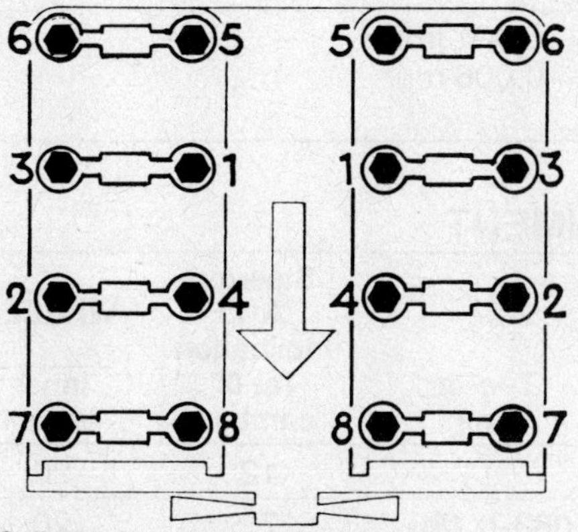

Cylinder head bolt tightening sequence, B27, B28

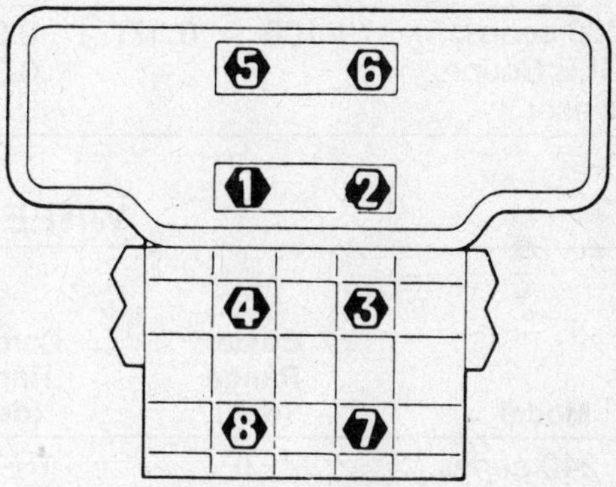

Main bearing nut tightening sequence, B27, B28

ALTERNATOR AND REGULATOR SPECIFICATIONS

		ALTERNATOR			REGULATOR	
Year	Vehicle Model	Part No. and Manufacturer	Output (amps.)	Min. Brush Length (in.)	Part No. and Manufacturer	Volts @ Alternator rpm (cold)
1975	164	S.E.V. Motorola 14V 34833	55	0.20	S.E.V. Motorola 14V 33544	13.1-14.4 @ 4000
1975-81	240, DL, GL, GT	14V 55A20	55	0.20	—	13.5-14.1 @ 4000 ①
1976-81	260 GLE Coupe	S.E.V. Marchal A14/55A 7160410	55 ②	0.20	S.E.V. Marchal 72710502	13.5-14.1 @ 4000 ①

① After driving 10 minutes
② 1979 and later—70

BATTERY AND STARTER SPECIFICATIONS

All cars use 12 volt, negative ground electrical systems

		STARTER							
		LOCK TEST			NO LOAD TEST				
Model	Battery Amp Hour Capacity	Amps	Volts	Torque (ft. lbs.)	Amps	Volts	rpm	Brush Spring Tension (oz.)	Min. Brush Length (in.)
164	60	300-350	6	—	40-50	12	6900-8100	2.53-2.86	0.60
All except 164	60 ① ②	400-490	7	—	30-50	11.5	5800-7800	3.10-3.50	0.52

① 260 series: 70 amp hour battery
② Diesel: 88

BRAKE SPECIFICATIONS

All measurements given are in. unless noted

Year	Model	Lug Nut Torque (ft. lbs.)	Master Cylinder Bore	BRAKE DISC Minimum Thickness	BRAKE DISC Maximum Run-Out	BRAKE DRUM Diameter	BRAKE DRUM Max. Machine O/S	BRAKE DRUM Max. Wear Limit	MINIMUM LINING THICKNESS Front	MINIMUM LINING THICKNESS Rear
1975	240 series,	70-100	0.877	0.577 front 0.331 rear	0.004 front 0.006 rear	—	—	—	0.125	0.125
	164	70-100	0.875	0.900 front 0.331 rear	0.004 front 0.006 rear	—	—	—	0.125	0.125
1976-81	240 series, DL, GL, GT	70-100	0.877	0.557 front 0.331 rear	0.004 front 0.006 rear	—	—	—	0.125	0.125
	260 series, GLE Coupe, Diesel	70-100	0.877	0.900 front 0.331 rear	0.004 front 0.006 rear	—	—	—	0.125	0.125

WHEEL ALIGNMENT

Year	Model	Caster Range (deg)	Camber Range (deg)	Toe-In (in.)	Steering Axis Inclination (at 0° camber)	WHEEL PIVOT RATIO (deg) Inner Wheel	WHEEL PIVOT RATIO (deg) Outer Wheel
1975	240 series	2P-3P	1P-1½P	①	12	20	20.8
1975	164	½P-⅛1½P	¾N-1¼N	0.063-0.188	7.5	20	21.5-23.5
1976-77	240 series, 260 series	2P-3P	1P-1½P	0.18-0.030	12	20	20.8
1978	240, 260 series	2P-3P	1P-1½P	0.12-0.24 ②	12	20	20.8
1979-81	All Models	2P-3P ③	0-1N	0.12-0.24 ②	12	20	20.8

① w/manual steering: 1/8 in. to 1/4 in.
w/power steering: 1/16 in to 3/16 in.
② Power steering: 0.06-0.18
③ Power steering: 3P-4P

TUNE-UP PROCEDURES

CAUTION

When working with a running engine, make sure that there is proper ventilation. Also make sure that the transmission is in neutral, and the parking brake is firmly applied. Always keep hands, clothing, and tools well clear of the radiator fan.

Spark Plug Removal and Installation

Every six months or 6000 miles, the spark plugs should be removed for inspection. At this time they should be cleaned and regapped. At 12-month or 15,000 mile intervals the plugs should be replaced.

Remove each spark plug wire by grasping its rubber boot on the end and twisting slightly to free the wire from the plug. Using a 13/16 in. spark plug socket, turn the plugs counterclockwise to remove them. Do not allow any foreign matter to enter the cylinders through the spark plug holes.

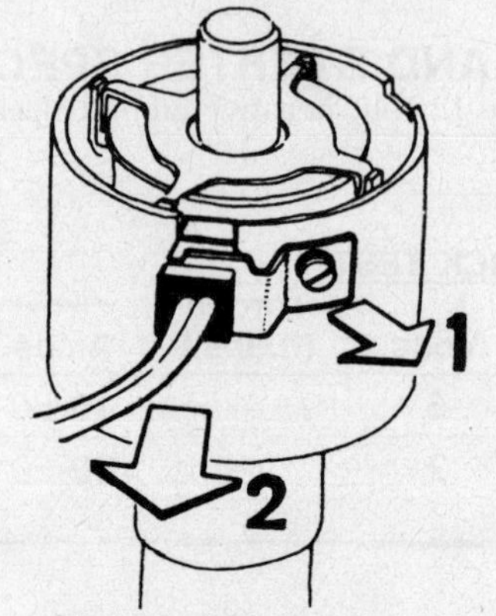

Contact screw removal

The gap must be checked with a feeler gauge before installing the plug in the engine. With the ground electrode positioned parallel to the center electrode, the specified wire gauge must pass through the opening with a slight drag. If the air gap between the two electrodes is not correct, the ground electrode must be bent to bring it to specifications.

After the plugs are gapped correctly, they may be inserted into their holes and hand-tightened. Be careful not to crossthread the plugs. Install each spark plug wire on its respective plug, making sure that each spark plug end is making good metal-to-metal contact in its wire socket.

Electronic Ignition

There are two major differences from the point type systems: First the points and condenser are replaced by an induction type impulse sender. Second, an electronic module has been added to amplify the electrical impulses between the distributor and coil. The impulse sender is located inside the dis-

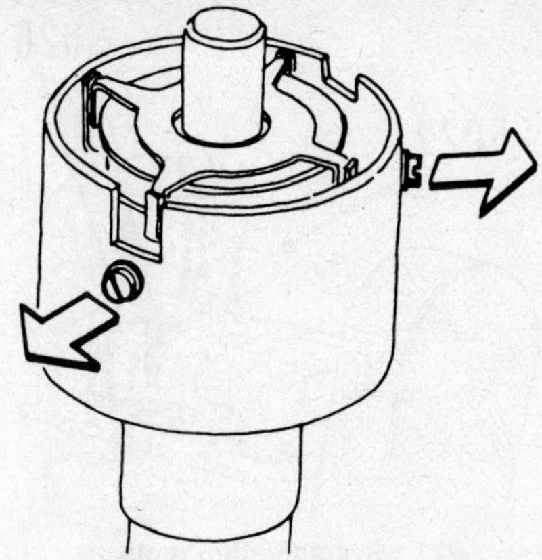

Impulse sender plate removal

tributor where the points used to be. Instead of opening and closing an electrical circuit, the sender opens and closes a magnetic circuit. This induces impulses in a magnetic pick-up. The sender consists of a stator, pick-up, rotor, and permanent magnet. The stator and armature each have the same number of teeth as there are cylinders. The permanent magnet creates a magnetic field which goes through the stator. The circuit is closed when the teeth are opposite each other. This means that the rotor opens and closes the magnetic field while rotating. This generates current pulses in the magnetic pick-up.

The electronic module is a solid state design which is fully transistorized. It amplifies the impulses from the sender and controls the dwell angle.

REPLACING THE IMPULSE SENDER

1. Unsnap the lock clasps.
2. Remove the cap, rotor and dust cover.

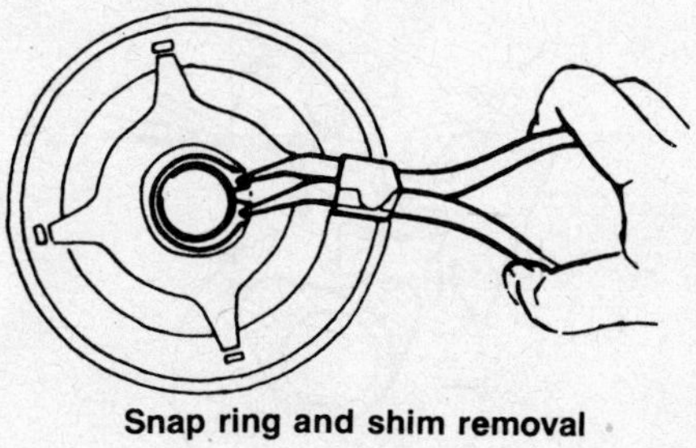

Snap ring and shim removal

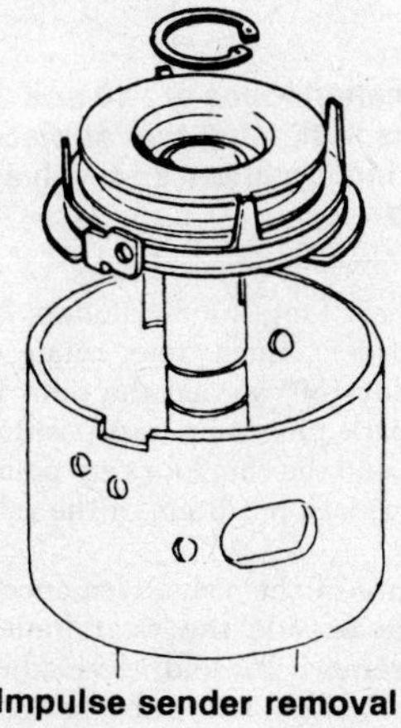

Impulse sender removal

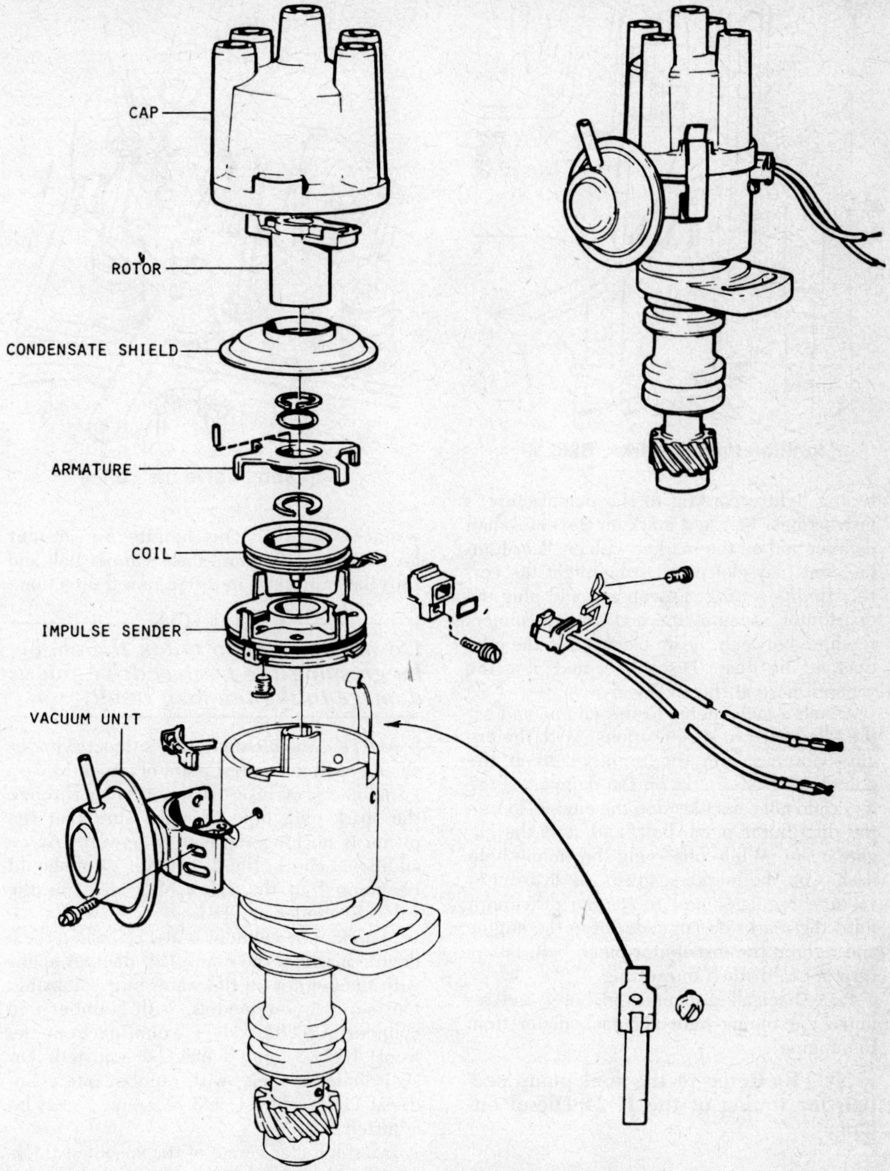

Electronic ignition distributor–240 series

3. Remove the vacuum advance unit and the cap hold-down clips.
4. Remove the screw securing the contact and pull the contact straight out.
5. Remove the impulse sender plate screws.

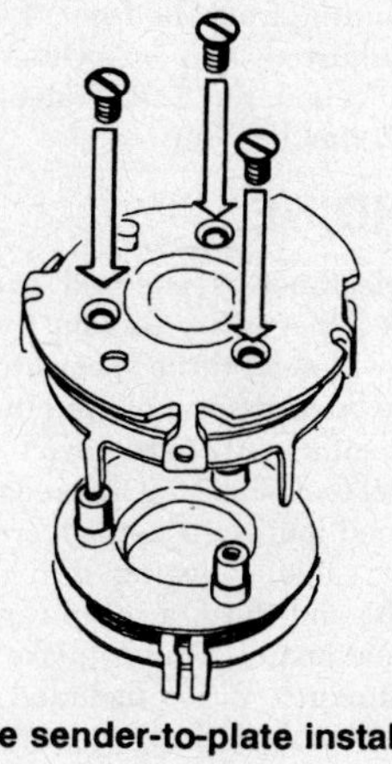

Impulse sender-to-plate installation

6. Remove the snap-ring and shims and pull the rotor straight off along with the small lock pin.
7. Remove the snap-ring retaining the sender and lift off the sender and plate.
8. Installation is the reverse of removal. Note that the screws for the vacuum unit and the hold-down clips are different lengths. When attaching the new sender to the plate, the connector pins should be directly opposite and above the attachment ear on the plate. When installation is completed, rotate the shaft several times to make sure there is no noise or binding.

Ignition Timing Adjustment

Volvo recommends that the ignition timing be checked at 15,000 mile intervals on 1975-81 models.

Clean the crankshaft damper and pointer on the water pump housing with a solvent-soaked rag so that the marks can be seen. Connect a

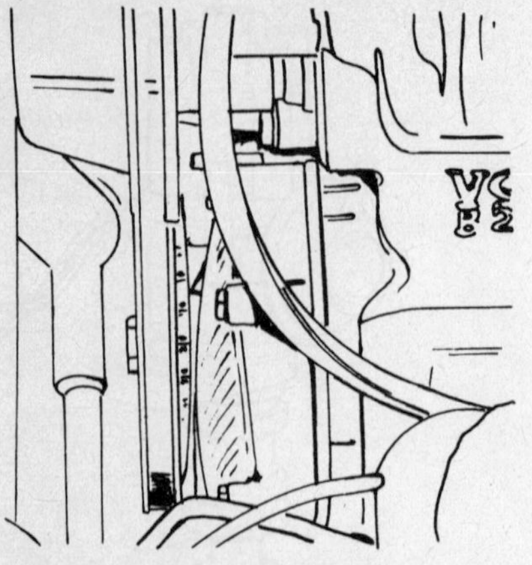

Ignition timing marks, B20, 30

timing light according to the manufacturer's instructions. Scribe a mark on the crankshaft damper and on the marker with chalk or luminescent (day-glo) paint to highlight the correct timing setting. Disconnect and plug the distributor vacuum line and also disconnect the hose between the air cleaner and the inlet duct at the duct. Disconnect and plug the vacuum hose at the EGR valve.

Attach a tachometer to the engine and set the idle speed to specifications. With the engine running, aim the timing light at the pointer and the marks on the damper. If the marks do not coincide, stop the engine, loosen the distributor pinch bolt, and start the engine again. While observing the timing light flashes on the markers, grasp the distributor vacuum regulator and rotate the distributor until the marks do coincide. Stop the engine and tighten the distributor pinch bolt, taking care not to disturb the setting.

Reconnect all disconnected hoses and remove the timing light and tachometer from the engine.

NOTE: Refer to the fuel pump section for timing of the D-24 Diesel engine.

Valve Lash Adjustment

B20 AND B30 ENGINES

The recommended maintenance interval for valve clearance adjustment is 12 months or 15,000 miles on 1975-76 models. The clearance may be checked with the engine *hot* or *cold*.

Remove the valve cover and crank the engine until Number one cylinder is at Top Dead Center (TDC). TDC is the point at which both intake and exhaust valves are fully closed and the piston is on its compression stroke. To find TDC, crank the engine, preferably with a remote starter switch, until the pushrods for both valves on the subject cylinder stop rising (both valves closed). Stop cranking the engine. At this point, it will be easier to find TDC by turning the engine over manually. To accomplish this, remove all of the spark plugs so the compression and resistance to cranking are diminished, and remove the distributor cap so the position of the rotor may be observed. To crank the engine manually, position a socket or closed-end

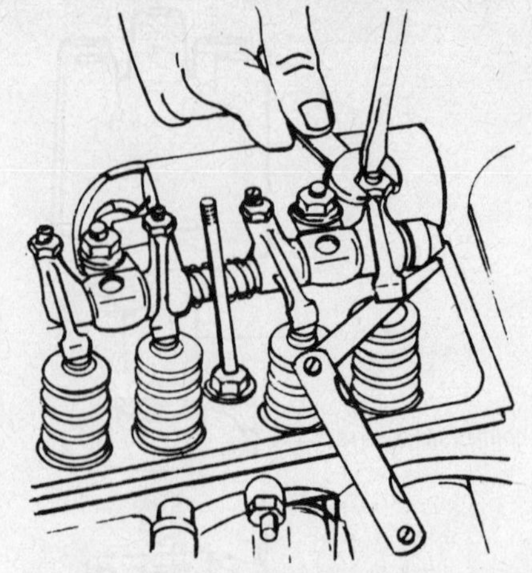

Adjusting valve clearance

wrench—with a long handle for greater leverage—on the crankshaft damper bolt and turn the crankshaft in the required direction.

CAUTION

Do not attempt to crank the engine by grasping the viscous drive fan as damage to the fan may result.

At TDC, the piston for the subject cylinder should be at its highest point of travel. Make a visual check or insert a screwdriver through the spark plug hole to make sure that the piston is no longer traveling upward. As an additional check, the distributor rotor should be pointed to the spark plug wire for the subject cylinder at TDC.

Number one cylinder is at TDC when the 0 degree mark on the crankshaft damper aligns with the pointer on the water pump housing. On four-cylinder models, with Number one cylinder at TDC, valves (counting from the front) 1, 2, 3, and 5 may be adjusted. On six-cylinder models, with number one cylinder at TDC, valves 1, 2, 3, 6, 7, and 10 may be adjusted.

Insert a feeler gauge of the specified thickness between the rocker arm and the valve stem. Adjustment is accomplished by loosening the locknut and turning the adjusting screw and then, without disturbing the adjustment, retightening the locknut.

The remainder of the valves may be adjusted in the following manner. On four-cylinder models, with No. 4 cylinder at TDC, valves (counting from the front) 4, 6, 7, and 8 may be adjusted. On six-cylinder models, with No. 6 cylinder at TDC, valves 4, 5, 8, 9, 11, and 12 may be adjusted.

B21 ENGINE

Valve clearance is checked every 15,000 miles. If it is necessary to adjust valve clearance, you will need three special tools: first, a valve tappet depressor tool used to push down the tappet sufficiently to remove the adjusting disc (Volvo tool #999 5022); second, a specially shaped pliers to actually remove and install the valve adjusting disc (Volvo tool #999 5026); and third, a set of varying thickness valve adjusting discs to make the necessary adjustments. We've included pictures of these special tools so that you might be able to

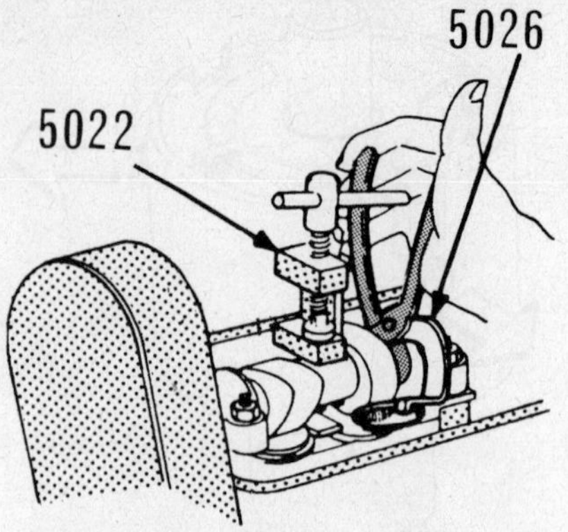

B21 valve adjusting tools

find a suitable substitute. Otherwise, don't attempt the job.

The procedure for checking, and, if necessary, adjusting the valves is as follows:

1. Remove the valve cover. Scribe chalkmarks on the distributor body indicating each of the four spark plug wire leads in the cap. Remove the distributor cap.

2. Crank over the engine with a remote starter switch or with a wrench on the crankshaft pulley center bolt (22 mm hex) until the engine is in the firing position for No. 1 cylinder. At this point, the 0 degree or TDC mark on the crankshaft pulley is aligned with the timing pointer, the rotor is pointing at the No. 1 spark plug wire cap position, and the camshaft lobes for No. 1 cylinder are pointing at the 10 o'clock and 2 o'clock positions. At this point, the clearance between the rocker arm and valve depressor (tappet) may be checked for the intake and exhaust valves of cylinder No. 1, using a feeler gauge. When checking clearance, the wear limit is 0.012-0.018 in. for a cold engine, and 0.012-0.020 in. for a hot one (176° F).

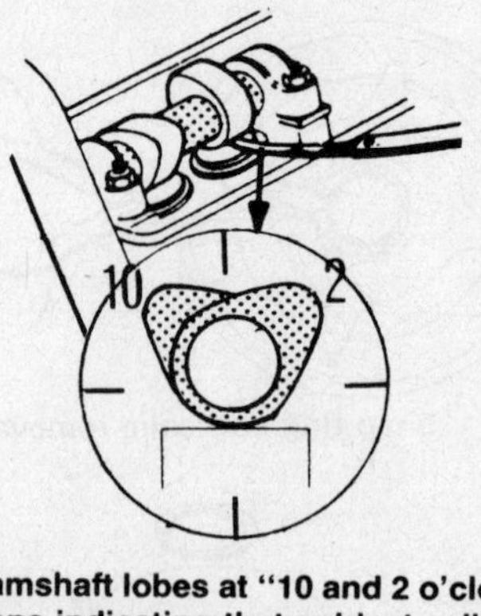

B21 camshaft lobes at "10 and 2 o'clock" positions indicating that subject cylinder is in firing position and valves can be adjusted

3. Repeat Step 2 for cylinders 3, 4, and 2 (in that order). Each time, rotate the crankshaft pulley 180° so that the rotor is pointing to the spark plug wire cap position for that cylinder, and the cam lobes are pointing at the 10 and 2 o'clock positions for the valves of that cylinder.

4. If any of the valve clearance measurements are outside the wear limit, you will have to remove the old valve adjusting disc and install a new one to bring the clearance

within specifications. First, rotate the valve depressors (tappets) until their notches are at a right angle to the engine center line. Attach valve depressor tool 999 5022 to the camshaft and screw down the tool spindle until the depressor (tappet) groove is just above the edge of its bore and still accessible with the special pliers (tool No. 999 5026).

5. Remove the valve adjusting disc and measure with a micrometer. Once you've gone to all this trouble, the valve clearance should be set to these tolerances; 0.014-0.016 in. for a cold engine, and 0.016-0.018 for a hot one. So, if the measured clearance had been 0.019 in. and the desired clearance 0.016 in. (for a net difference of 0.003 in.), then the new valve adjusting disc should be 0.003 in. thicker than the old one to take up the clearance. Valve adjusting discs are available from Volvo in sizes from 0.130 to 0.180 in. (in 0.002 in. increments). Always oil the new disc and install it with the marks facing down.

6. Remove the valve tappet depressor tool. Rotate the engine a few times and recheck clearance. Install the valve cover with a new gasket.

B27 ENGINE AND B28F

Valve clearance is checked every 15,000 miles. No special tools are required.

1. In order to gain access to the valve covers, disconnect or remove the following:

a. Air conditioning compressor from bracket (do not disconnect refrigerant hoses)

b. EGR valve and hoses

c. A/C compressor bracket

d. Fuel injection control pressure regulator

e. Air pump

f. Vacuum pump

g. Hoses and wires from solenoid valve (Calif. only)

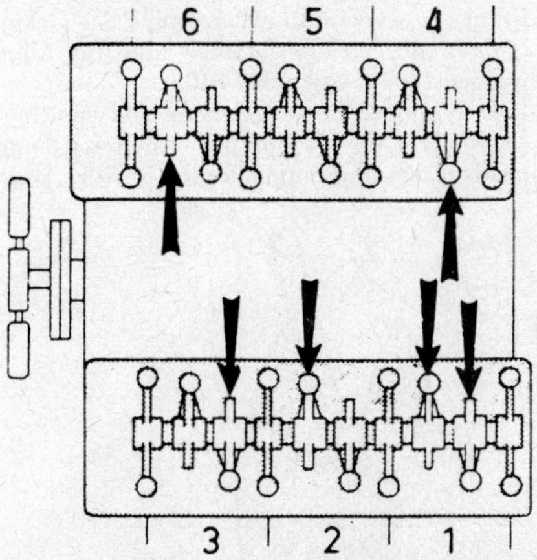

On B27 and 28 with no. 1 cylinder at TDC, adjust these valves (arrows)

2. Using a 36 mm hex socket on the crankshaft pulley bolt, rotate the crankshaft to the No. 1 cylinder TDC position. At this point the "O" mark on the timing plate aligns with the crankshaft pulley notch, the distributor rotor is pointing to the No. 1 cylinder spark plug wire cap position, and both valves for No. 1 cylinder have clearance. At this position, adjust the intake valves of cylinders No. 1, 2 and 4, and the exhaust valves of cylinders No. 1, 3, and 6. Insert a feeler gauge between the rocker arm and valve stem. Loosen the locknut and turn the adjusting screw in the required direction. Tighten the locknut and recheck clearance. Clearance is 0.004-0.006 in. intake and 0.010-0.012 in. exhaust for a cold engine and 0.006-0.008 in. intake and 0.012-0.014 in. exhaust for a hot engine. The B28F cold intake valve adjustment 0.008-0.010 in.; cold exhaust valve adjustment 0.012-0.014 in.

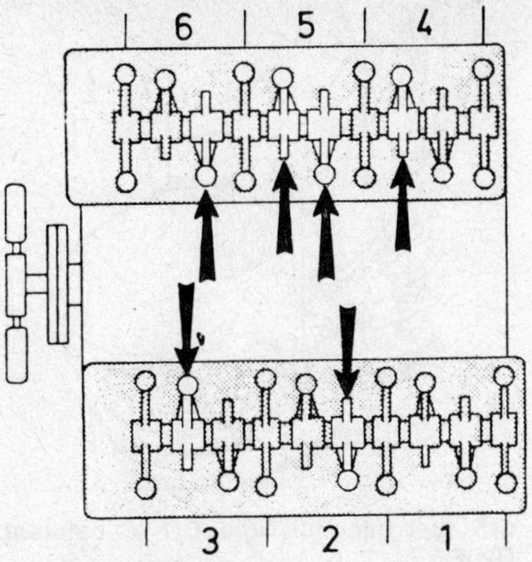

On B27 and 28, rotate the crankshaft 360 degrees and adjust the remaining valves (arrow)

3. Rotate the crankshaft pulley one full 360° turn to adjust the remaining valves. At this point, the "O" mark will again align with the pulley notch, the rotor is pointing 180° opposite its former position, and the No. 1 cylinder rockers contact the ramps of the camshaft. At this position (see illustration), adjust the intake valves of cylinders No. 3, 5, and 6, and the exhaust valves of cylinders No. 2, 4, and 5.

4. Install the valve covers with new gaskets. Connect all disconnected equipment.

D-24 Diesel Engine

1. Remove the valve cover.

2. Use a $1^{1}/_{16}''$ socket on the crankshaft pulley. Turn the pulley until the engine is ready to fire on the No. 1 cylinder. The flywheel timing mark should be at zero.

NOTE: The piston should not be at top dead center when setting the valve clearance.

3. Line up the valve depressors.

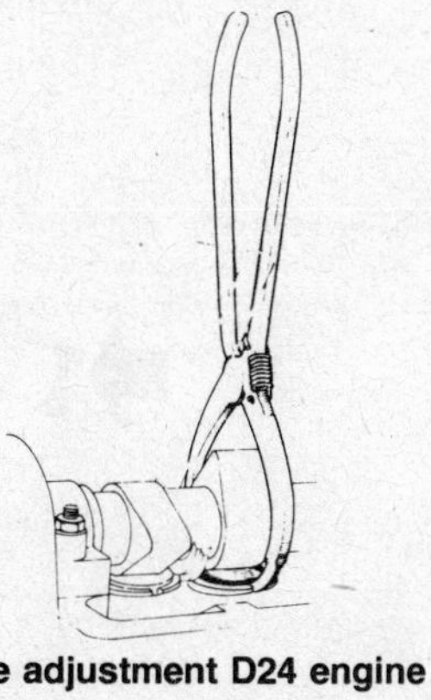

Valve adjustment D24 engine

4. Turn them so that the notches point slightly upward.

NOTE: Use tool #5196 to depress the valve depressors. This tool is available from your Volvo dealer.

5. The depressor groves must be above the face so that the disc can be gripped with pliers. These pliers are available from your Volvo dealer under part #5195.

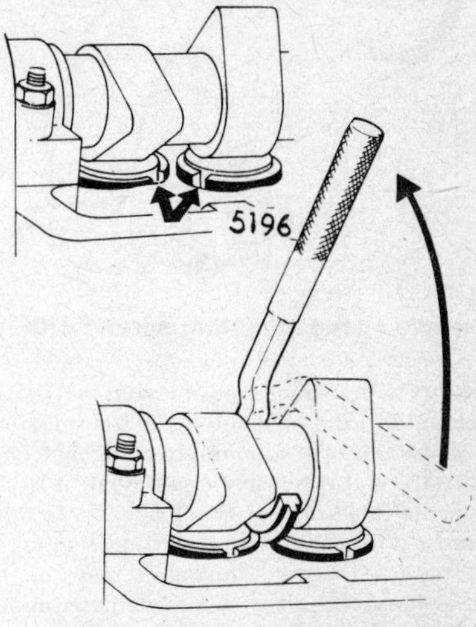

Cam disc removal D24 engine

6. Remove the disc.

7. Calculate the disc thickness, using a micrometer. The discs are available in thicknesses of 0.1299-0.1673 in. with increments of 0.002 in.

8. Cold engine 0.008-intake, 0.016 exhaust. Warm engine 0.010-intake, 0.018 exhaust.

NOTE: Always use new discs when performing this procedure.

9. Oil the new disc and install it with the marked side down.

10. Check the remaining valve clearances.

11. Use the following sequence 1, 5, 3, 6, 2, 4.

NOTE: Always check the valve clearances with the cylinder at top dead center. Turn the engine ¼ turn after top dead center, to set.

12. Recheck the valve clearance for all cylinders.

13. Rotate the engine several times, and recheck the clearance.

14. Install the valve cover with a new gasket.

Bosch Electronic Fuel Injection Adjustments

IDLE SPEED AND MIXTURE

The idle mixture adjustment or CO valve may be set only with the use of a CO meter. This adjustment is made by attaching a CO meter to the exhaust pipe of a vehicle with a warm (176° F) engine, and turning the adjusting screw of the Bosch control unit (beneath the passenger seat) until the correct CO value is obtained. The correct value is 1-1.5 percent

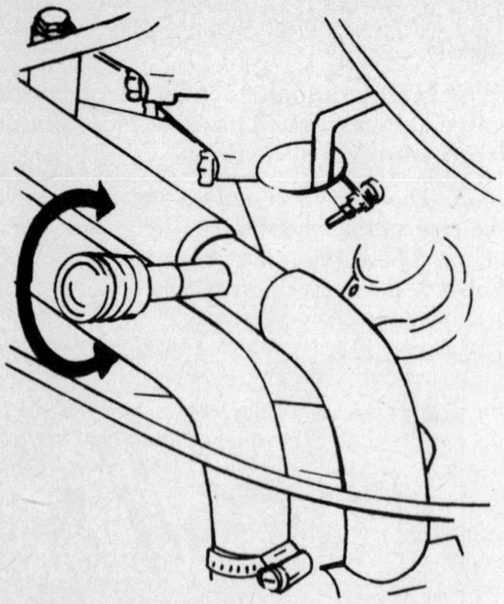

Idle speed adjusting screw, B30F

for cars with manual transmissions and 0.5-1.0 percent for cars with automatic transmissions. Because this operation requires highly technical skills and expensive equipment, it is best referred to a Volvo or Bosch agency. In other words, don't mess with the control unit.

The idle speed adjustment may, on the other hand, be set with a tachometer and an average amount of expertise. The check should be made with the engine idling at operating temperature (176° F). The idle adjusting screw is located on the inlet duct below the air cleaner hose opening on four-cylinder models and inline in the auxiliary air pipe on six-cylinder models (see illustrations).

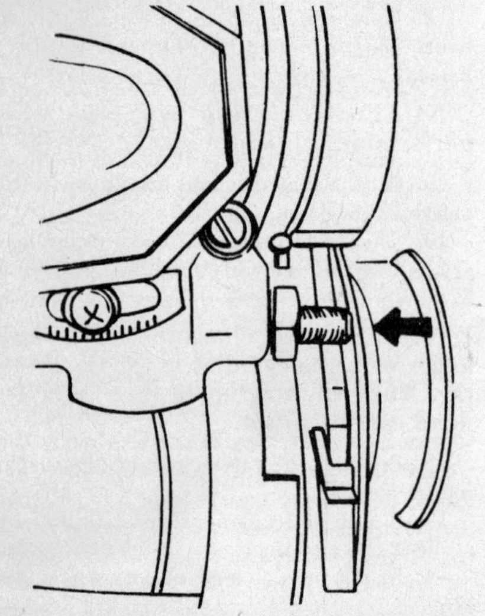

Idle speed adjusting screw, B20F with fuel injection

Bosch Continuous Fuel Injection Adjustments

IDLE SPEED AND MIXTURE

All 240 and 260 series models and 1980-81 models are equipped with the continuous fuel injection system. With this system, the injectors are open all the time, and the amount of fuel injected is directly proportional to the amount of air drawn into the intake.

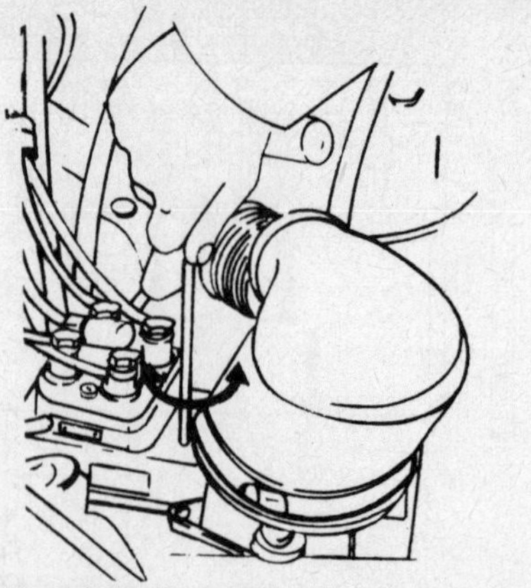

CIS fuel injection idle CO adjustment, B20F

1975-B20F

The idle mixture adjustment or CO value may be set only with the use of a CO meter. Also, a special tapered setscrew tool is needed to turn the mixture adjusting screw. The adjustment is made with the engine idling at curb idle speed and at operating temperature (176° F) and the CO meter attached to the exhaust pipe. 1975 models with air injection require disconnecting and plugging the air pump output hose to prevent an erroneous CO reading. With the special setscrew tool inserted into the small hole between the fuel distributor and the bellows for the air sensor plate, engage the adjusting screw and adjust to a 1.5% CO value.

The idle speed adjustment is a simple matter of rotating the idle adjusting screw located in-line in the auxiliary air pipe. With the engine idling at operating temperature (176° F), and the transmission in Neutral, adjust to 800 rpm on cars with automatic transmission, and 900 rpm on cars with manual transmission.

B21F

Special Tools Required: CO meter and CO idle mixture adjusting Allen wrench (Volvo tool #999 5015).

1. Disconnect and plug the air injection pump output hose and the EGR vacuum hose.
2. With the engine warmed to operating temperature (176° F), check that the idle speed is 900 rpm (manual trans) or 800 rpm (automatic) with the car idling in neutral. Adjust as necessary by rotating the air adjusting screw (knob) located beneath the intake air box.
3. With the engine at specified idle speed, check that the CO value is 2.0% (1.0% 1977-81). Adjust as necessary by inserting special tool #5015 into adjustment hole located between the air intake bellows and the fuel distributor. Recheck the idle speed.

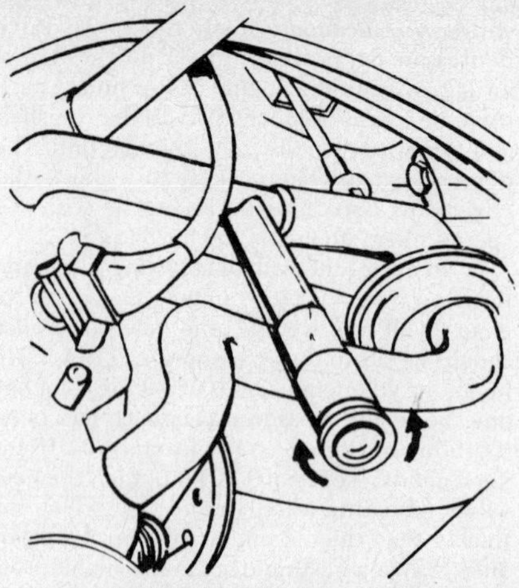

CIS idle adjustment, B20F

CAUTION

Do not race the engine with the tool inserted.

4. Stop the engine. Connect the air pump and EGR hoses.

B27F and B28F

Special Tools Required: CO meter with two position switch capable of isolating left or right cylinder banks, and CO meter plumbing and fittings to screw into exhaust pipe gas pickup points; and CO idle mixture adjusting Allen wrench (Volvo tool #999 5102).

1. Remove the air cleaner and housing. Disconnect the air pump output hose (large hose on rear of pump) and plug it with a large

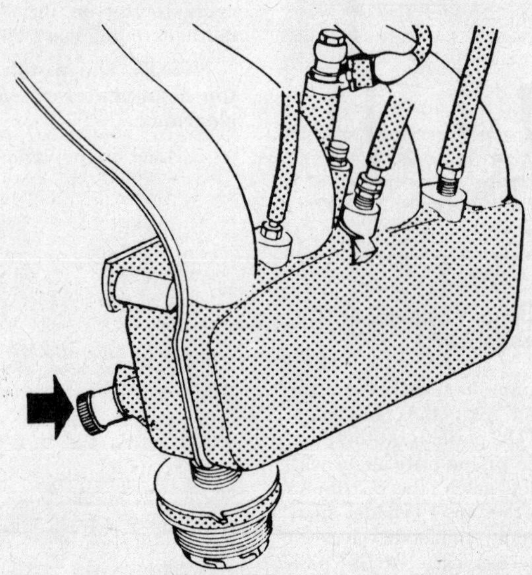

Continuous injection idle speed adjustment—B21F

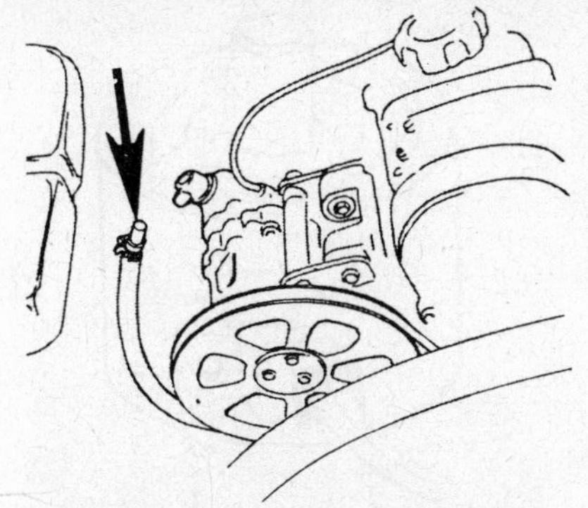

Disconnect the air pump outlet hose to readjust the mixture on B27, 28

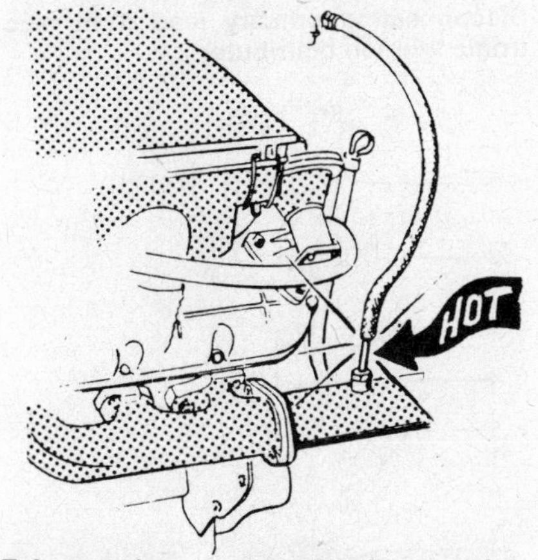

Exhaust pipe gas sample pickup points on B27, 28

diameter screwdriver shaft. Disconnect and plug the vacuum hose at the EGR valve.

2. Set the idle balance screws (#1 and #2) to their basic setting by screwing them in clockwise until they bottom out, and then backing them off counterclockwise 4 full turns each.

3. Start the engine and allow it to reach operating temperature (176° F). Using the idle air adjusting screw (#3), set the idle speed to 900 rpm.

4. Using the CO meter, check that the carbon monoxide level is 1.4-2.0% (1.0% 1977-79) at 900 rpm. The B28F engine CO level is 1.0%±0.3% at 950 rpm. If necessary, adjust

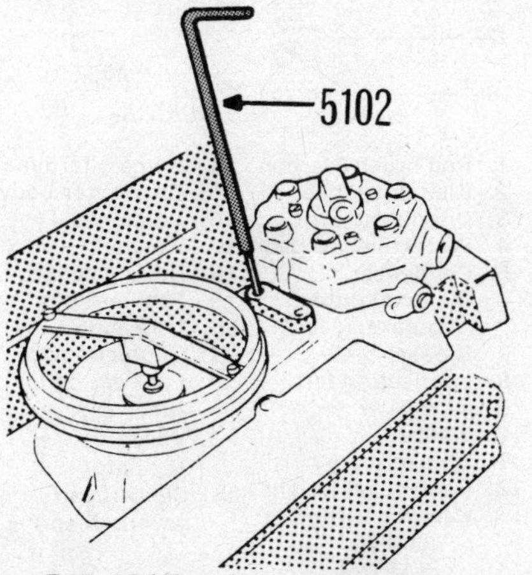

B27, 28 idle mixture adjustment

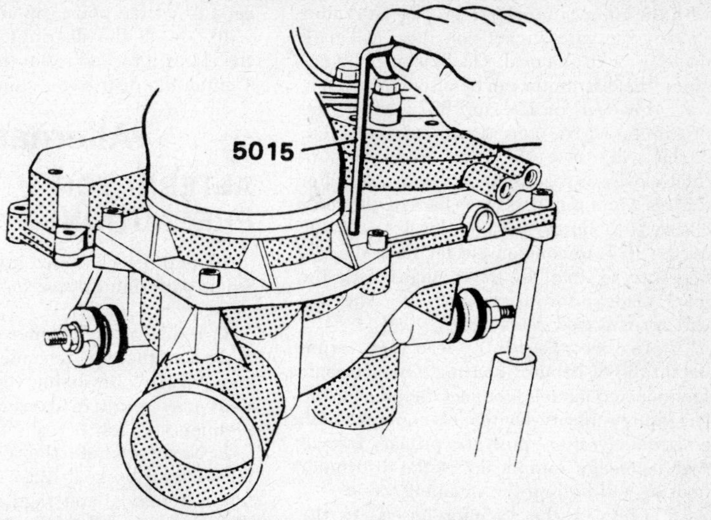

Continuous injection idle mixture (CO) adjustment—B21F

CO level by inserting the special Allen wrench (Volvo tool #5102) into the adjustment hole between the fuel distributor and throttle valve, and turning it clockwise to increase CO and counterclockwise to reduce CO. Before inserting the tool, remove the copper washer and plug convering the hole. Also, between adjustments, remove the tool and plug the hole to prevent a lean mixture and erroneous reading.

CAUTION

Do not race the engine with the tool inserted, as the lever may become damaged.

5. The final step is to check the CO balance between the right and left cylinder banks. Both must have an equal CO value; 1.4-2.0% at 900 rpm, 1980 and later should be 1.0±0.3% at 950 rpm. Air adjusting screw #3 controls the total amount of air bypassing the throttles at idle, whereas idle balance screws #1 and #2 divide this air to the two cylinder banks. Screw #1 is for the right (passenger) side cylinders, and screw #2 for the left (driver) side. If you decrease the airflow past screw #2, it will increase the airflow past screw #1, and vice versa. More air means a leaner mixture, and less air a richer mixture. After balancing the CO value of each cylinder bank, recheck the total CO value at 900 rpm. Stop the engine.

6. Connect the EGR hose, air pump hose, and air cleaner.

ENGINE ELECTRICAL

Distributor

REMOVAL AND INSTALLATION

1. Unsnap the distributor cap clasps and remove the cap.

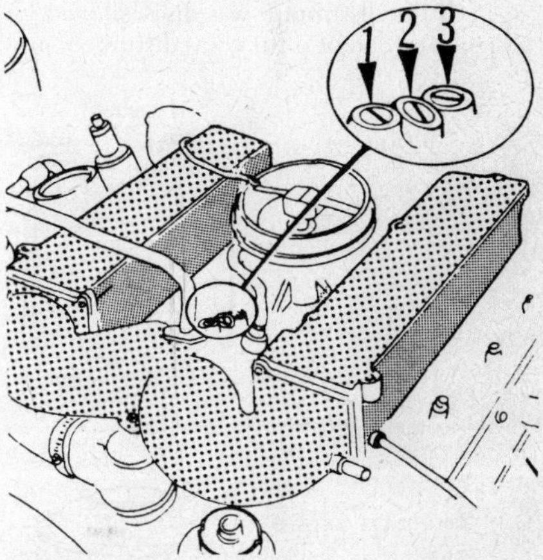

B27, 28 idle balance (nos. 1 and 2), and air adjusting screws (no. 3)

2. Crank the engine until No. 1 cylinder is at Top Dead Center (TDC). At this point, the rotor should point to the spark plug wire socket for No. 1 cylinder, and the 0° timing mark on the crankshaft damper should be aligned with the pointer. For ease of assembly, scribe a chalkmark on the distributor housing to note the position of the rotor.

3. Disconnect the primary lead from the coil at its terminal on the distributor housing. On electronic fuel-injected models, disconnect the plug for the triggering contacts. On models with electronic ignition remove the retaining screw for the primary voltage wire connector and pull it from the distributor housing.

4. Remove the vacuum hose(s) from the regulator. Take care not to damage the bakelite connection during removal.

5. On B20 and B30 engines, slacken the distributor attaching screw and hold-down clamp enough to slide the distributor up and out of position. On B21 and B27 engines, remove the distributor attaching screw and lift out the distributor.

6. When ready to install the distributor, if the engine has been disturbed (cranked), find TDC for No. 1 cylinder as outlined under "Valve Lash Adjustment". If the engine has not been disturbed, install the distributor

with the rotor pointing to the No. 1 cylinder spark plug wire socket, or the chalkmark made prior to removal. On B20 and B30 engines, the distributor can be installed only one way. However, on B21 and B27 engines, the distributor drive gear teeth are bevelled, which will cause the rotor to turn counterclockwise as the distributor is installed. For this reason, it is necessary to back off the rotor clockwise (about 60° and on the B21, and 40° on the B27) to compensate for this. What is necessary is that the rotor aligns with the mark made prior to removal after the distributor is bolted down.

7. Connect the primary lead to its terminal on the distributor housing. On electronic fuel-injected models, connect the plug for the triggering contacts. On models equipped with electronic ignition, push the primary voltage wire connector into its slot in the distributor housing and tighten the retaining screw.

8. Connect the vacuum hose(s) to the bakelite connection(s) on the vacuum regulator, (if so equipped).

9. If the distributor was disassembled, or if the contact point setting was disturbed, proceed to set the point gap and/or dwell angle.

10. Install the distributor cap and secure the clasps. Proceed to set the ignition timing. Tighten the distributor attaching screw.

Alternator

ALTERNATOR PRECAUTIONS

Several precautions must be observed when performing work on alternator equipment.

1. If the battery is removed for any reason, make sure that it is reconnected with the correct polarity. Reversing the battery connections may result in damage to the one-way rectifiers.

2. Never operate the alternator with the main circuit broken. Make sure that the battery, alternator, and regulator leads are not disconnected while the engine is running.

3. Never attempt to polarize an alternator.

4. When charging a battery that is installed in the vehicle, disconnect the negative battery cable.

5. When utilizing a booster battery as a starting aid, always connect it in parallel; negative to negative, and positive to positive.

6. When arc welding is to be performed on any part of the vehicle, disconnect the negative battery cable, disconnect the alternator leads, and unplug the voltage regulator.

DRIVE BELT ADJUSTMENT

Accessory drive belt tension is checked every six months or 6000 miles. On 1980 and later models, no belt adjustment is recommended until 30,000 miles. Loose belts can cause poor engine cooling and diminish alternator output. A belt that is too tight places a severe strain on the water pump, alternator, air injection pumps, or power steering pump bearings.

Accessory drive belt tension is correct when the deflection made with light finger pressure

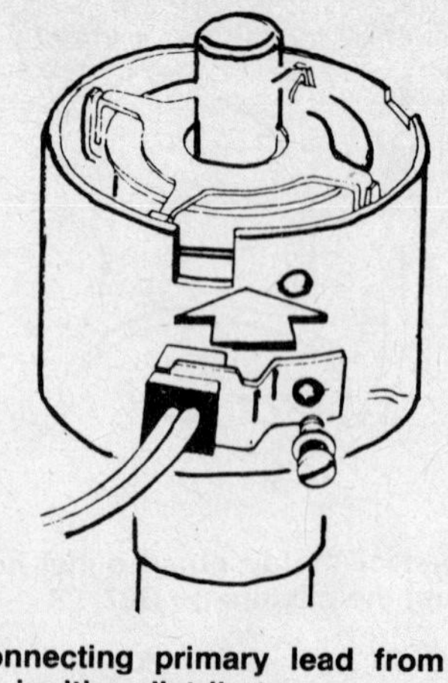

Disconnecting primary lead from electronic ignition distributor

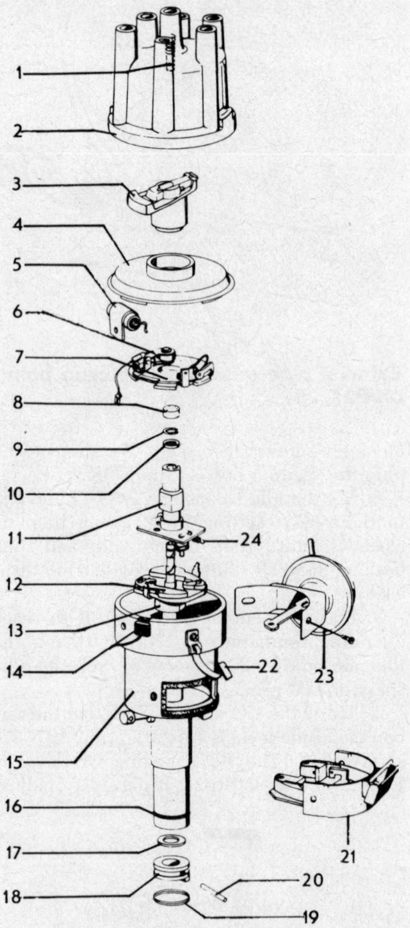

1. Rod brush (carbon)
2. Distributor cap
3. Distributor arm
4. Protective cover
5. Condenser
6. Ignition contact breaker
7. Breaker plate
8. Lubricating felt
9. Circlip
10. Washer
11. Breaker cam
12. Centrifugal weight
13. Cam for triggering contacts
14. Primary terminal
15. Distributor body
16. Rubber seal
17. Washers
18. Driving collar
19. Resilient ring
20. Lock pin
21. Contact device
22. Lock clamp for distr. cap
23. Vacuum regulator
24. Centrifugal governor spring

Distributor assembly—B30F

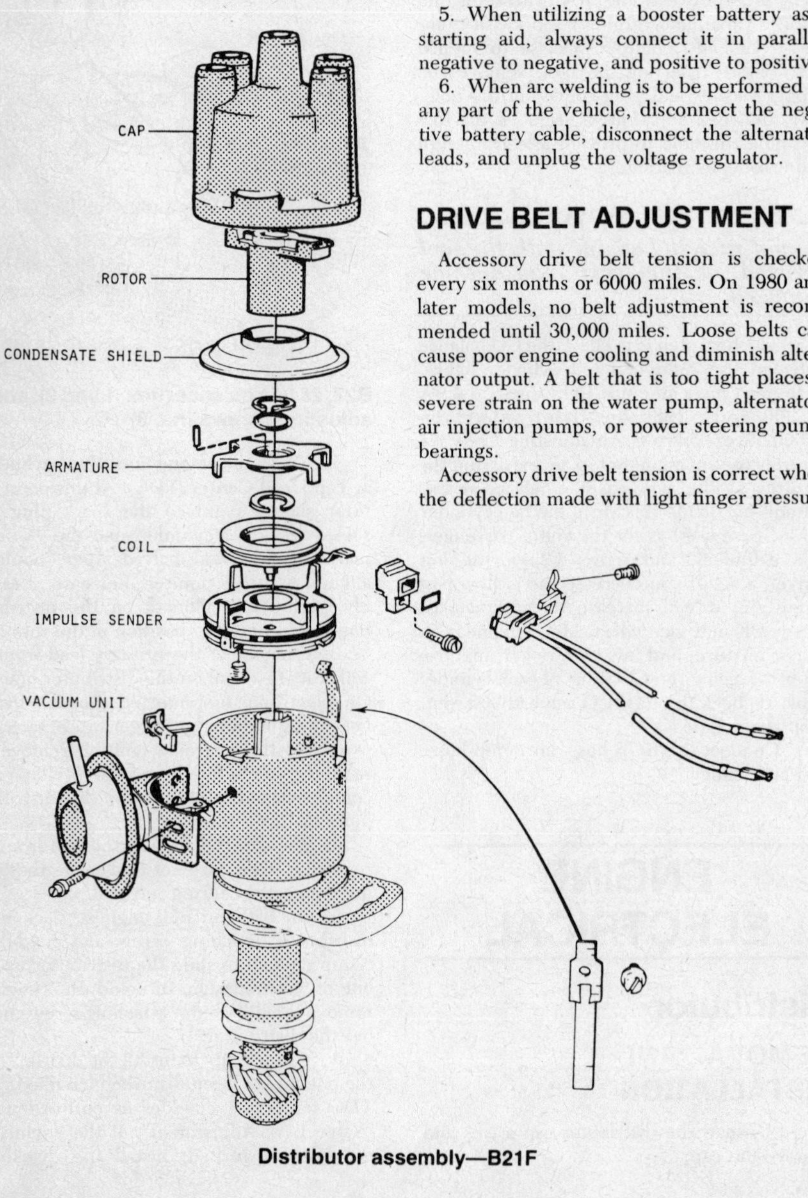

Distributor assembly—B21F

on the belt at a midway point is about ½ in. Any belt that is glazed, frayed, or stretched so that it cannot be tightened sufficiently must be replaced.

Incorrect belt tension is corrected by moving the driven accessory (alternator, air pump, power steering pump or air conditioning compressor) away from or toward the driving pulley. Loosen the mounting and adjusting bolts on the respective accessory and tighten them, once the belt tension is correct. Never position a metal pry bar on the rear end of the alternator, air pump or power steering pump housing; they can be deformed easily.

ALTERNATOR REMOVAL AND INSTALLATION

NOTE: On 1975 models, it will be necessary to remove the air pump and place it to one side, to gain access to the alternator.

1. Disconnect the negative battery cable.
2. Disconnect the electrical leads to the alternator.
3. Remove the adjusting arm-to-alternator bolt and the adjusting arm-to-engine bolt.
4. Remove the alternator mounting bolt.
5. Remove the fan belt and lift the alternator forward and out.
6. Reverse the above procedure to install, taking care to properly tension the fan (drive) belt.

Voltage Regulator

VOLTAGE REGULATOR REMOVAL AND INSTALLATION

1. Disconnect the negative battery cable.
2. Disconnect the leads or plug socket from the old regulator taking note of their (its) location.
3. Remove the hold-down screws from the old regulator and install the new one.
4. Connect the leads or plug socket and reconnect the negative battery cable.

VOLTAGE ADJUSTMENT

Motorola (S.E.V. Marchal) Regulator

If the Motorola A.C. regulator is found to be defective, it must be replaced. No adjustments can be made on this unit.

The following test may be performed on the Motorola regulator to see if it is functioning properly. An ammeter, tachometer, and voltmeter are required.

1. Connect the alternator and regulator as shown in the illustration.
2. Run the engine at 2500 rpm (5000 alternator rpm) for 15 seconds. With no load on the alternator, and the regulator ambient temperature at 77° F, the reading on the voltmeter should be 13.1-14.4 V. For regulator ambient temperatures other than 77° F, consult the voltage-temperature diagram for cold regulator.
3. Load the alternator with 10-15 amps (high-beam headlights) while the engine is running at 2500 rpm. The voltmeter reading

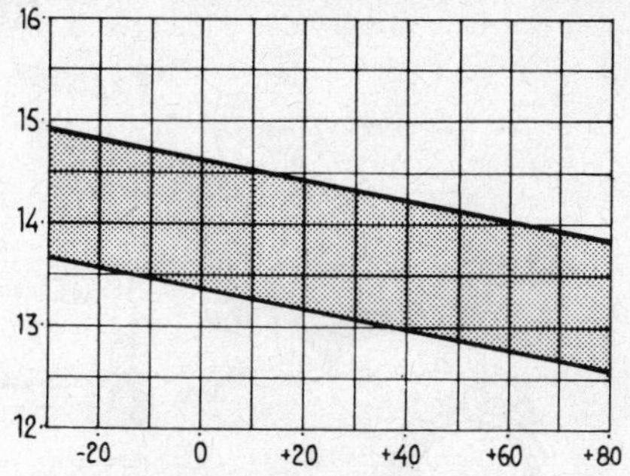

Voltage-temperature diagram for cold regulator—Motorola

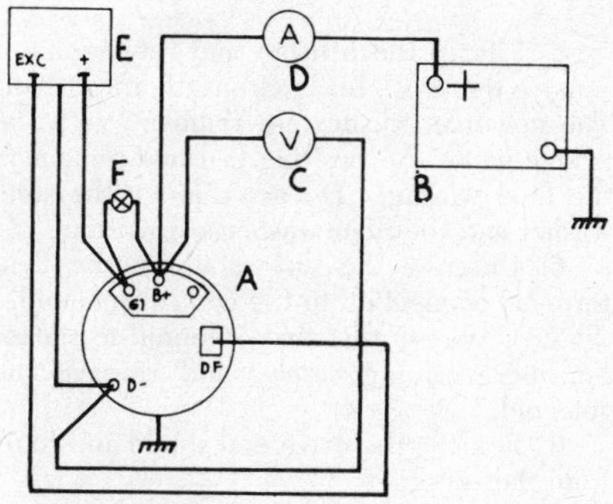

A. Alternator
B. Battery 60 Ah
C. Voltmeter 0—20 amps.
D. Ammeter 0—50 amps.
E. Voltage regulator
F. Warning lamp 12 volts. 2 watts

Wiring diagram for testing Motorola regulator

should again be 13.1-14.4 V. Replace the regulator if it does not fall within these limits.

4. For a more accurate indication of the regulator's performance, drive the vehicle for about 45 minutes at a minimum speed of 30 mph. The regulator will be at the correct working temperature immediately after this drive.
5. With the engine running at 2500 rpm, and the regulator ambient temperature at 77° F, the voltmeter reading should be 13.85-14.25 V. For regulator ambient temperatures other than 77° F, consult the Voltage-temperature diagram for warm regulator.

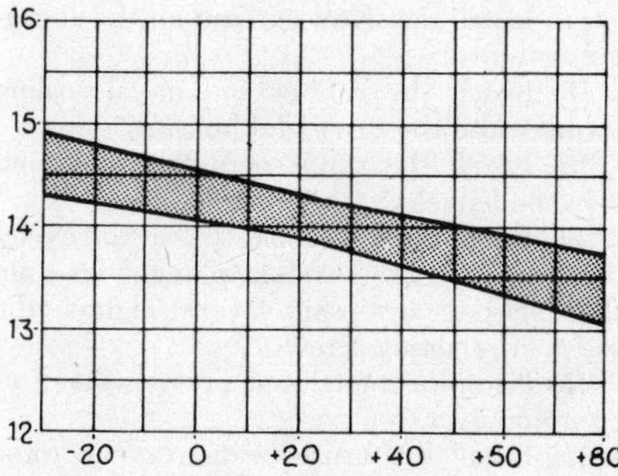

Voltage-temperature diagram for warm regulator—Motorola

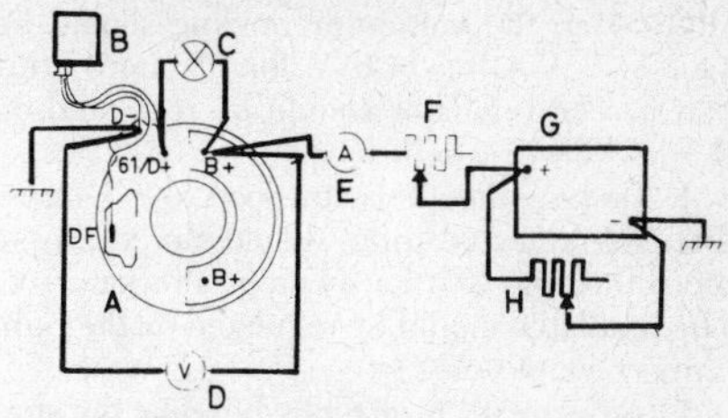

A. Alternator
B. Voltage lamp 12 volts
C. Control lamp 12 volts, 2 watts
D. Voltmeter 0-20 volts
F. Regulator resistance
G. Battery 60 amperehours
H. Load resistance
E. Ammeter 0-50 amps

Wiring diagram for testing Bosch A.C. regulator

Bosch A.C. Regulator (35, 55 and 70 Amp)

The Bosch A.C. regulator is fully adjustable. To determine which adjustments are necessary—if any—perform the following test. (An ammeter, 12 V control lamp, tachometer, and voltmeter are required for this test)

NOTE: Where the numerical values differ for the 35 amp voltage regulator and the 55 amp unit, the figures for the 55 amp regulator will be given in parentheses.

1. Connect the alternator and regulator as shown in the illustration.

NOTE: The first reading must be taken within 30 seconds of beginning of test.

2. While running the engine at 2000 rpm, load the alternator with 28-30 amps (44-46 for 55 amp alternator).
3. Rapidly lower the engine to idle speed or 500 rpm, and then return it to 2000 rpm. With a load of 28-30 amps (44-46 for 55 amp

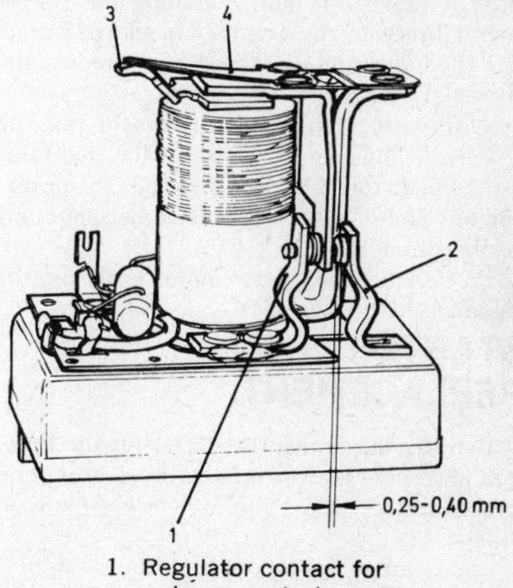

1. Regulator contact for lower control range (lower contact)
2. Regulator contact for upper control range (upper contact)
3. Spring tensioner
4. Spring upper section: Steel spring Lower section: Bimetal spring

Bosch A.C. voltage adjustments

alternator), the voltmeter reading should be 14.0-15.0 V (13.9-14.8 V for 55 amp alternator). The regulator should be regulated on the left (lower) contact.

4. Reduce the alternator load to 3-8 amps. The voltmeter reading should not decrease more than 0.3 (0.4 for 44 amp, alternator) V. The regulator should be regulated on the right (upper) contact.

5. Adjustment is made by bending the stop bracket for the bimetal spring. Bending the stop bracket down lowers the regulating voltage; bending it up raises the voltage. If the voltmeter reading for the low amp alternator load decreased more than 0.3 (0.4 for 55 amp alternator), V, compared to the reading for the high amp alternator load, adjust the regulator by bending the holder for the left (lower) contact and simultaneously adjust the gap between the right (upper) contact and the movable contact. The gap should be adjusted to 0.010-0.015 in. (0.25-0.40 mm). If the holder is bent toward the right (upper) contact, the regulating voltage under high amp alternator load will be lowered.

To avoid faulty adjustments due to residual magnetism in the regulator core, it may be necessary to rapidly lower the engine rpm to idle after each adjustment, and then raise it to 2000 rpm to take a new reading.

NOTE: Warm regulators may be cooled to ambient temperature by directing a stream of compressed air on them. Final readings should be made with the regulator at ambient temperature.

Starter

STARTER REMOVAL AND INSTALLATION

1. Disconnect the negative battery cable at the battery.
2. Disconnect the leads from the starter motor.
3. Remove the bolts retaining the starter motor brace to the cylinder block (B21 only) and the bolts retaining the starter motor to the flywheel housing and lift it off.
4. Position the starter motor to the flywheel housing and install the retaining bolts finger-tight. Torque the bolts to approximately 25 ft/lbs, and apply locking compound to the threads.
5. Connect the starter motor leads and the negative battery cable.

STARTER DRIVE REPLACEMENT

In order to remove the starter pinion drive, it is necessary to disassemble the starter. The procedure for disassembling the starter is as follows:

1. Remove the starter from the car as outlined in "Starter Removal and Installation."
2. Unscrew the two screws and remove the small cover from the front end of the starter shaft.
3. Unsnap the lockwasher and remove the adjusting washers from the front end of the shaft.
4. Unscrew the two screws retaining the commutator bearing shield and remove the shield.

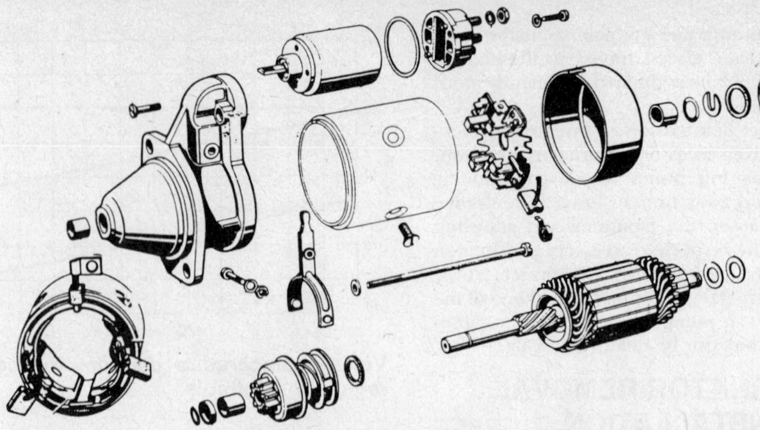

Exploded view of starter motor

5. Lift up the brushes and retainers and remove the brush bridge from the rotor shaft. The negative brushes are removed with the bridge while the positive brushes remain in the field winding. Do not remove the steel washer and the fiber washer at this time.
6. Unscrew the nut retaining the field terminal connection to the control solenoid.
7. Unscrew the two solenoid-to-starter housing retaining screws and remove the solenoid.
8. Remove the drive end shield and rotor from the stator.
9. Remove the rubber and metal sealing washers from the housing.
10. Unscrew the nut and remove the screw on which the engaging arm pivots.
11. Remove the rotor, with the pinion and engaging arm attached, from the drive end shield.
12. Push back the stop washer and remove the snap-ring from the rotor shaft.
13. Remove the stop washer and pull off the starter pinion with a gear puller.

While the starter is disassembled, a few quick checks may be performed. Check the rotor shaft, commutator, and windings. If the rotor shaft is bent or worn, it must be replaced. Maximum rotor shaft radial throw is 0.003 in. If the commutator is scored or worn unevenly, it should be turned. Minimum commutator diameter is 1.3 in. Check the end shield which houses the brushes, for excessive wear. Maximum bearing clearance is 0.005 in.

14. Lubricate the starter.
15. Press the starter pinion onto the rotor shaft. Install the stop washer and secure it with a new snap-ring.
16. Position the engaging arm on the pinion. Install the rotor into the drive end frame.
17. Install the screw and nut for the engaging arm pivot.
18. Install the rubber and metal sealing washers into the drive end housing.
19. Install the stator onto the rotor and drive end shield.
20. Position the solenoid so that the eyelet on the end of the solenoid plunger fits onto the engaging arm (shift lever). Tighten the solenoid retaining screws.
21. Place the metal and fiber washers on the rotor shaft.
22. Install the brush bridge on the rotor shaft and replace the brushes.
23. Fit the commutator bearing shield into position and install the retaining screws.
24. Install the adjusting washers and snap a new lockwasher into position on the end of the shaft. Make sure that the rotor axial clearance does not exceed 0.12 in. If necessary, adjust the clearance with washers, maintaining a minimum clearance of 0.002 in.
25. Replace the small cover over the front end of the shaft and install the two retaining screws.
26. Install the starter in the car as outlined in "Starter Removal and Installation."

SOLENOID REPLACEMENT

Before replacing the solenoid when the starter will not crank, see if the battery has sufficient charge. If the no-crank condition persists when the battery is known to be good, connect a jumper wire between the positive terminal of the battery and the contact screw for the solenoid lead. If the solenoid engages the starter pinion, the starter switch or leads are at fault. If the starter still does not crank, replace the solenoid. To remove the solenoid, remove the starter from the car. The solenoid may be removed from the starter while installed in the car, but then aligning the solenoid is as follows.

1. Remove the starter from the car as outlined in "Starter Removal and Installation."
2. Unscrew the two solenoid-to-starter housing retaining screws and remove the solenoid.
3. As a final test, wipe the solenoid clean and press in the armature. Test its operation by connecting it to a battery. If the solenoid still does not function, replace it with a new unit.
4. Position the new solenoid so that the eyelet on the end of the plunger fits into the engaging arm. Tighten the retaining screws.
5. Replace the starter in the car as outlined in "Starter Removal and Installation."

ENGINE MECHANICAL

Six basic engines are covered here. They are the B20F (1999 cc), a four cylinder engine used through 1975; the B30F (2980 cc), a six cylinder engine used in the 164 through 1975; the B21F (2127 cc), a four cylinder engine used in the 242, 244, and 245 since 1976; the B27F (2664 cc), a V6 engine used in the 262, 264, and 265 since 1976, the B28F, new for 1980-81, and the D24 diesel, also new for 1980-81.

The B20F and B30F are both based on the same in-line, overhead valve design and are of cast iron construction.

The B21F is of overhead camshaft design with a cast iron block and aluminum, cross-flow head. The B27F and B28F are a 90° V6 design with both the block and the heads being of aluminum alloy. The cylinders are equipped with cast iron sleeves. The sleeves are the replaceable, wet type. The overhead camshafts are chain driven.

Engine Removal and Installation

B20 and B30

All Volvo engines and transmissions are removed as a unit. In most cases, a good chain hoist will suffice. Do not attempt to lift the engine with the chain wrapped around either the oil filter or the distributor. Lifting eyes may be fabricated from heavy gauge steel or angle iron.

1. Scribe the outline of the hinges on the hood and remove the hood .
2. Drain the oil from the crankcase. Open the drain plug on the right-hand side of the engine block, disconnect the lower radiator hose at the radiator, and drain the cooling system. On Volvos with automatic transmissions, disconnect and plug the transmission cooler lines.
3. Remove the expansion tank, radiator cover plate, upper radiator hose, radiator, and fan shroud, if so equipped.
4. Remove the positive lead from the battery.
5. Remove the electric cables for the starter, the coil high-tension wires, the distributor lead, alternator wires, water and oil temperature sensors, and the lead for the oil pressure sensor, if so equipped.
6. Remove the vacuum hoses for the distributor advance, and the power brake booster, if so equipped. Remove the positive crankcase ventilation (PCV) hoses, and the oil pressure gauge hose at the pipe connection, if so equipped.

7a. On electric fuel-injected models, remove the air cleaner and intake hoses; pressure sensor hose from the inlet duct; the plug contacts for the temperature sensor, cold start valve, throttle valve switch, fuel injectors, and distributor impulse. In addition, remove the ground wire from the inlet duct, the throttle cable bracket from the inlet duct, the throttle cable from the throttle valve switch, the cold start valve fuel hose from the distribution pipe, the fuel return line from the pressure regulator, and the fuel inlet line from the distribution pipe. Remove the injectors by turning the lock-rings counterclockwise and lifting them out of their bayonet fittings. The injectors should then be fitted with protective covers and plugs to prevent dirt from entering.

b. On continuous (air-flow controlled) fuel-injected models, disconnect the rubber hose to the control pressure regulator, the plastic hose from the pressure regulator to the fuel distributor, the hose at the cold start injector, the fuel filter hose, and the fuel return hose at the fuel distributor. Remove the pipe connecting the air cleaner and the intake manifold. Disconnect the electrical leads from the cold start injector, control pressure regulator, auxiliary air valve, coolant temperature sensor and the thermal time switch (engine side). Disconnect the ground wire for the control pressure regulator. Disconnect and plug the 4 fuel hoses at the injectors. Disconnect the throttle cable from the throttle and intake manifold. Disconnect the brake booster vacuum hose. Remove the thermal time switch.

8. Disconnect the heater pipes from all models. Remove the exhaust pipe flange nuts and disconnect the exhaust pipe from the manifold. Remove the EGR valve pipe from the manifold. On models equipped with power steering, remove the steering pump bolts and place the pump and reservoir to one side.
9. On Volvos with manual transmissions, place the gearshift in Neutral and remove the shifter lever. On Volvos with automatic transmissions, disconnect the control rod from the selector lever, and the ground cable from the start inhibitor switch.
10. Disconnect the wires for the backup lights and overdrive, if so equipped. Remove the speedometer drive cable from the transmission. Remove the clamp for the exhaust manifold and the clamp for the automatic transmission filler tube, if so equipped.
11. Jack up the vehicle and place two jack stands under the front jack attachments and two more in front of the rear jack attachments.
12. Place a hydraulic jack under the transmission. On manual transmission cars, remove the return spring from the throw-out fork, and disconnect the clutch cable.
13. Separate the transmission (or overdrive) from the front universal joint by unbolting the flange. Unbolt the rear crossmember.
14. Disconnect the negative ground cable from the engine.
15. Remove the rear crossmember and rear engine mounts. Remove the lower nuts for the front engine mounts.
16. Install the lifting eyes and lifting crossbar. The lifting eyes are attached by ⅜ x 1¾ x 1 in. bolts. Lift out the engine and set it on an engine stand or rack. The engine is removed by raising its front and lowering it back while pulling forward until it clears the front crossmember, then leveling it and raising the complete unit.
17. Install the lifting apparatus on the engine. Make sure that the jack stands are located beneath the front jack attachments and in front of the rear jack attachments. Place the hydraulic jack beneath the transmission tunnel.
18. Carefully lower the engine into the engine compartment. Place the hydraulic jack under the transmission and guide the unit into place. Be careful not to damage the oil filter, or oil pressure sending unit against the exhaust pipe. Be careful not to damage the distributor against the steering column.
19. Tighten the nuts for the front engine mounts.
20. Connect the wires for the back-up lights, start inhibitor switch (automatic transmission), and overdrive, if so equipped.
21. Install the brackets for the exhaust manifold and the automatic transmission filler tube. Install the rear engine mounts and rear crossmember, then tighten the nuts.
22. Remove the hydraulic jack from the transmission and the lifting apparatus from the engine. Connect the negative ground cable to the engine.
23. Connect the front universal joint to the transmission (or overdrive) flange. Connect the speedometer drive cable.
24. On manual transmission cars, connect the clutch cable and install the return spring. Adjust clutch free-play. On automatic transmission cars, connect the control rod to the selector lever, and the ground cable to the start inhibitor switch.
25. Connect the exhaust pipe to the exhaust manifold with new gaskets and tighten the nuts. Connect the EGR valve pipe.
26. Connect the jack stands from the jack attachments and lower the vehicle.
27. Connect the heater pipes. On models with power steering, install the pump and reservoir to the engine block and adjust the drive belt tension.

28a. On continuous (air-flow controlled) fuel-injected models, install the thermal time switch and connect the hose for the brake booster. Instal the throttle cable and connect the 4 fuel hoses to the injectors. Connect the control pressure regulator ground wire and the cold start injector, control pressure regulator, auxiliary air valve, temperature sensor, and thermal time switch leads. Connect the fuel hoses to the control pressure regulator and fuel distributor. Connect the hoses to the fuel filter, cold start injector, and the fuel return hose to the fuel distributor. Install the pipe between the air filter and the intake manifold.

b. On electronic fuel-injected models, place the injectors in their bayonet fittings with new rubber seals, and turn them clockwise to install. In addition, connect the fuel inlet line and the cold start valve hose to the distribution pipe, and the return line from the pressure regulator. Install the ground wire and the throttle cable bracket to the inlet duct, and connect the throttle cable. Connect the plug contact for the temperature sensor, cold start valve, throttle valve switch, fuel injectors, and distributor impulse. Install the pressure sensor vacuum hose, air cleaner, and intake hoses.

29. On all models, connect the positive crankcase ventilation hoses, and the distributor vacuum advance hose. Connect the vacuum hose for the power brake booster, and the oil pressure gauge hose at the pipe connection, if so equipped.
30. Install the electric cables for the starter, the coil high-tension wire, the distributor lead, alternator wires, water and oil temperature sensors, and the lead for the oil pressure sensor, if so equipped.

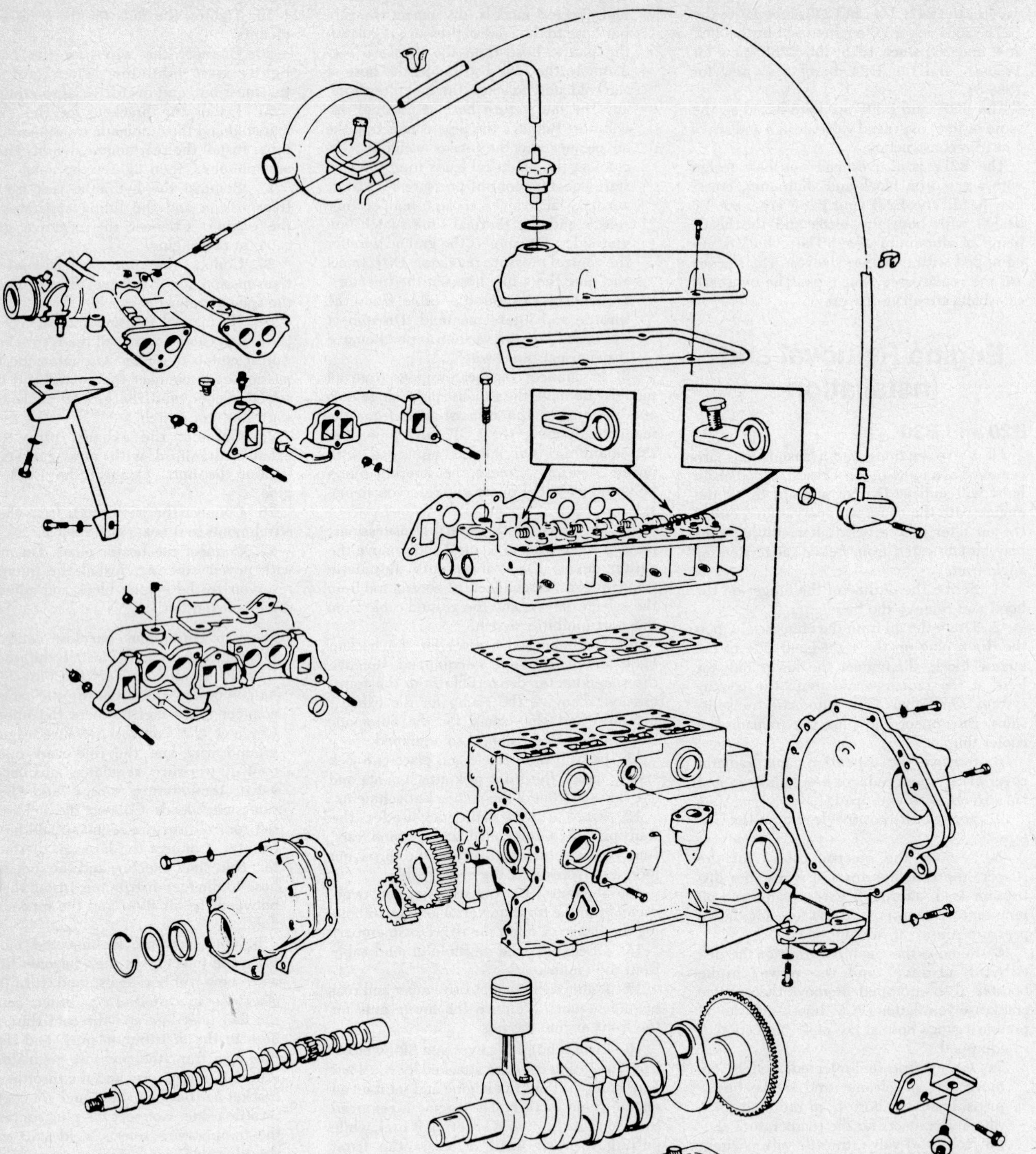

B20 engine (B30 engine similar)

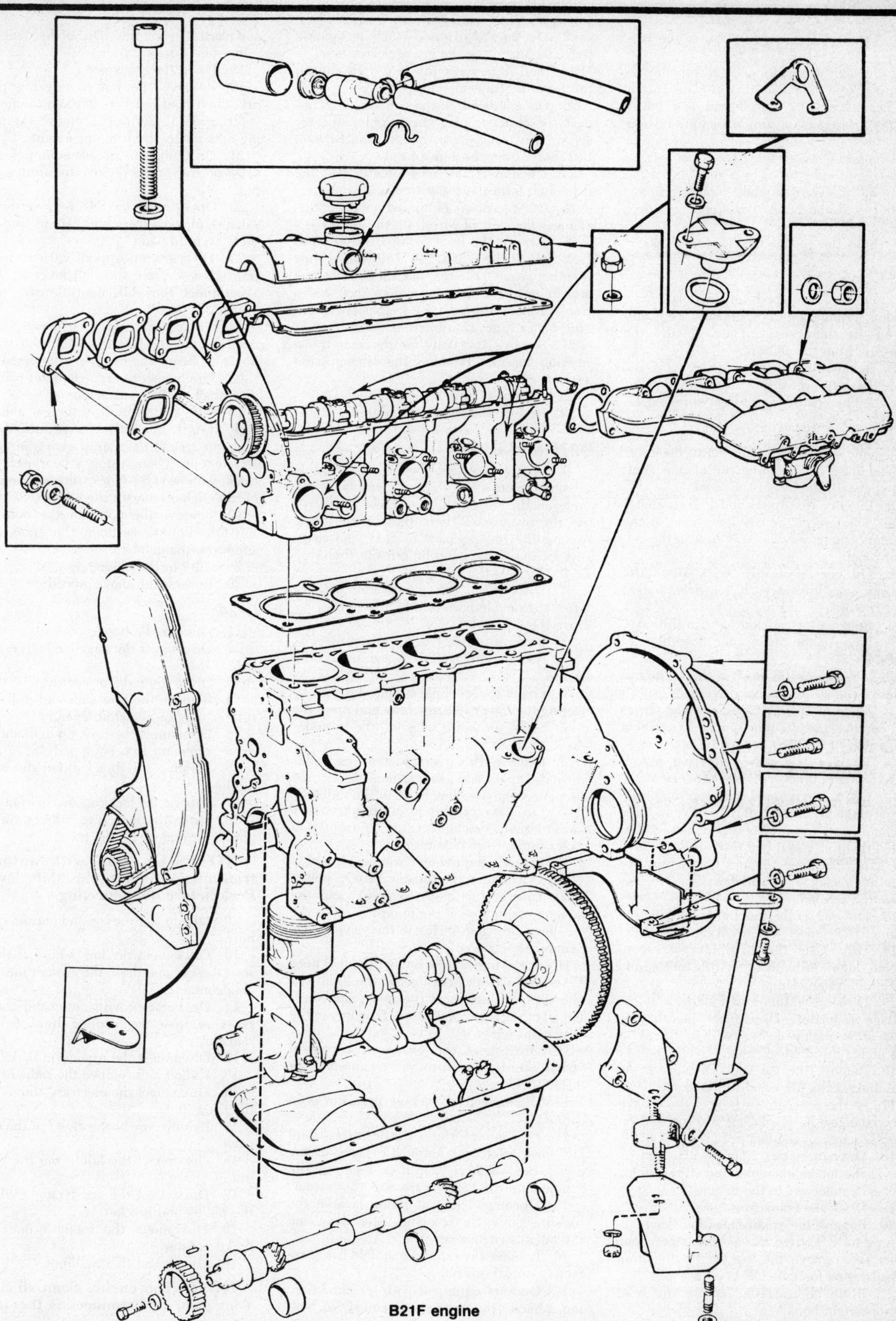

B21F engine

31. Connect the positive lead to the battery.

32. Install the radiator and fan shroud, if so equipped, and the radiator cover plate. Install the expansion tank, the upper and lower radiator hoses, and, on automatic transmission cars, the transmission oil cooler lines. Make sure that the cooler lines clear the engine mounts and brake tubes by a generous ¾ in.

33. Fill the crankcase and cooling system.

34. Install the hood. Install the gearshift lever.

35. Start the engine and check for leaks.

B21F

1. On cars equipped with manual transmission, remove the four retaining clips and lift up the shifter boot. Then, remove the snap-ring from the shifter.

2. Remove the battery.

3. Disconnect the windshield washer hose, engine compartment light wire and remove the hood.

4. Remove the overflow tank cap. Drain the cooling system by disconnecting the lower radiator hose and opening the engine drain cock (beneath the exhaust manifold).

5. Remove the upper and lower radiator hoses. Disconnect the overflow hoses at the radiator. Disconnect the PCV hose at the cylinder head.

6. On cars equipped with automatic transmission, disconnect the oil cooler lines at the radiator.

7. Remove the radiator and fan shroud.

8. Remove the air cleaner assembly and hoses.

9. Disconnect the hoses at the air pump. Remove the air pump and drive belt.

10. Disconnect the vacuum pump hoses and remove the vacuum pump. Disconnect the power brake booster vacuum hose.

11. Remove the power steering pump, drive belt and bracket. Position to one side.

12. On cars equipped with air conditioning, remove the crankshaft pulley (5 mm Allen wrench), and compressor drive belt. Then, install the pulley again for reference. Remove the AC wire connector and the compressor from its bracket and position to one side. Remove the bracket.

13. Disconnect the vacuum hoses from the engine. Disconnect the carbon canister hoses.

14. Disconnect the distributor wire connector, high tension lead, starter cables, and the clutch cable clamp.

15. Disconnect the wiring harness at the voltage regulator. Disconnect the throttle cable at the pulley, and the wire for the AC at the intake manifold solenoid.

16. Remove the gas cap. Disconnect the fuel lines at the filter and return pipe.

17. At the firewall, disconnect the electrical connectors for the ballast resistor, and relays. Disconnect the heater hoses.

18. Disconnect the micro switch connectors at the intake manifold, and all remaining harness connectors to the engine.

19. Drain the crankcase.

20. Remove the exhaust manifold flange retaining nuts. Loosen the exhaust pipe clamp bolts and remove the bracket for the front exhaust pipe mount.

21. From underneath, remove the front motor mount bolts.

22. On cars equipped with automatic transmission, place the gear selector lever in "Park" and disconnect the gear shift control rod from the transmission.

23. On manual transmission cars, disconnect the clutch cable. Then, loosen the set screw, drive out the pivot pin, and remove the shifter from the control rod.

24. Disconnect the speedometer and the driveshaft from the transmission.

25. On overdrive equipped models, disconnect the control wire from the shifter.

26. Jack up the front of the car and place jack stands beneath the reinforced box member areas to the rear of each front jacking attachment. Then, using a floor jack and a wooden block, support the weight of the engine beneath the transmission.

27. Remove the bolts for the rear transmission mount. Remove the transmission support crossmember.

28. Lift out the engine.

29. Reverse the above procedure to install.

B27F and B28F

1. On cars equipped with manual transmission, remove the shifter assembly. From underneath, loosen the set screw and drive out the pivot pin. Then, pull up the boot, remove the reverse pawl bracket, and snapring for the shifter, and lift out the shifter.

2. Remove the battery.

3. Disconnect the windshield washer hose, engine compartment light wire and remove the hood.

4. Remove the air cleaner assembly.

5. Remove the splash guard under the engine.

6. Drain the cooling system by disconnecting the lower radiator hose and open the drain cocks on both sides of the cylinder block.

7. Remove the overflow tank cap. Remove the upper and lower radiator hoses, and disconnect the overflow hoses at the radiator.

8. On cars equipped with automatic transmission, disconnect the transmission cooler lines at the radiator.

9. Remove the radiator and fan shroud.

10. Disconnect the heater hoses, power brake hose at the intake manifold and the vacuum pump hose at the pump. Remove the vacuum pump and O-ring in the valve cover. Remove the gas cap.

11. At the firewall disconnect the fuel lines (**CAUTION: High pressure**) at the filter and return pipe, disconnect the relay connectors and all other wire connectors. Disconnect the distributor wires.

12. Disconnect the evaporative control carbon canister hoses and the vacuum hose at the EGR valve.

13. Disconnect the voltage regulator wire connector.

14. Disconnect the throttle cable (and kickdown cable on automatic transmission cars), the vacuum amplifier hose at the T-pipe, and the hoses at the wax thermostat.

15. Disconnect the air pump hose at the backfire valve, the solenoid valve wire, and the micro switch wire.

16. Remove the exhaust manifold flange retaining nuts (both sides).

17. On cars equipped with air conditioning, remove the compressor and drive belt, and place it to one side. Do not disconnect the refrigerant hoses.

18. Drain the crankcase.

19. Remove the power steering pump, drive belt, and bracket. Position to one side.

20. From underneath, remove the retaining nuts for the front motor mounts.

21. On California models equipped with a catalytic converter, remove the front exhuast pipe.

22. On 49 states models, remove the front exhaust pipe hangers and clamps and allow the system to hang.

23. On cars equipped with automatic transmission, place the shift lever in "Park". Disconnect the shift control lever at the transmission.

24. On manual transmission cars, disconnect the clutch slave cylinder from the bell housing. Leave the cylinder connected.

25. Disconnect the speedometer cable and driveshaft at the transmission.

26. Jack up the front of the car and place jack stands beneath the reinforced box member area to the rear of each front jacking attachment. Then, using a floor jack and a thick, wide wooden block, support the weight of the engine beneath the oil pan.

27. Remove the bolts for the rear transmission mount. Remove the transmission support crossmember.

28. Lift out the engine.

29. Reverse the above procedure to install.

D-24

1. Remove the hood.

2. Disconnect the negative battery terminal.

3. Drain the radiator coolant.

4. Remove the four clips and pull up the rubber boot on the shift lever.

5. Disconnect the back-up light and overdrive connector if so equipped.

6. Remove the bracket for the reverse inhibitor.

7. Release the lock ring on the shift lever.

8. Move the lock ring, rubber ring, and plastic journal up on the lever.

NOTE: On cars with automatic transmissions place the shift lever in Park before disconnecting.

9. Disconnect the top and bottom radiator hoses.

10. Disconnect the lower hose at the cold start device, and drain the coolant into a suitable container.

11. On vehicles with automatic transmissions remove the cooling lines from the radiator.

12. Disconnect the expansion tank hose.

13. Unbolt and remove the radiator.

14. Disconnect the electrical connection at the firewall.

15. Remove the heater hoses at the control valve.

16. Disconnect the hose from the vacuum pump.

17. Disconnect the accelerator cable from the pulley and bracket.

18. Disconnect the vacuum line to the brake booster.

19. Disconnect the fuel lines.

NOTE: Thoroughly clean all connections prior to disconnecting them.

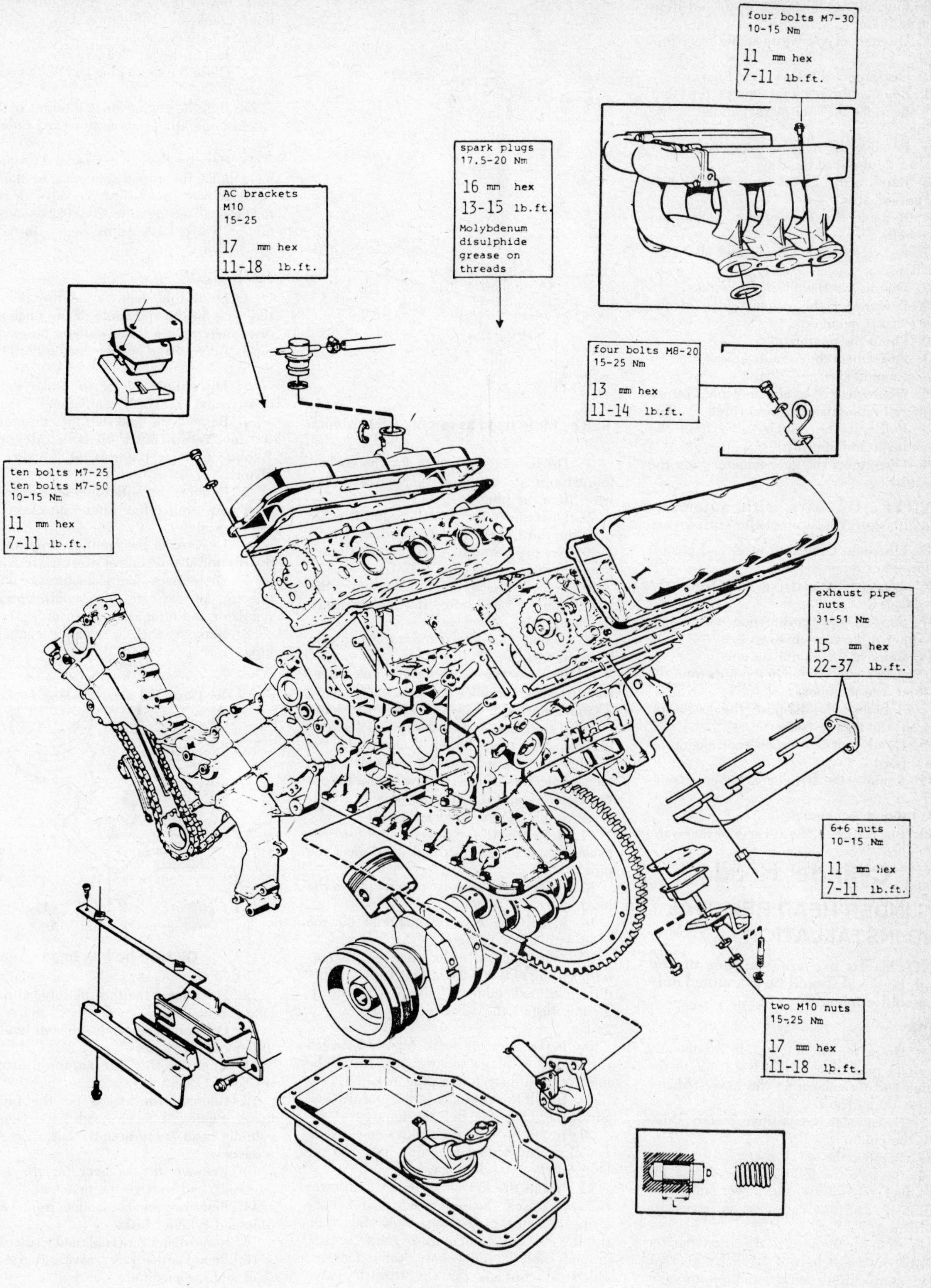

four bolts M7-30
10-15 Nm
11 mm hex
7-11 lb.ft.
spark plugs
17.5-20 Nm
16 mm hex
13-15 lb.ft.
Molybdenum disulphide grease on threads
AC brackets
M10
15-25
17 mm hex
11-18 lb.ft.
four bolts M8-20
15-25 Nm
13 mm hex
11-14 lb.ft.
ten bolts M7-25
ten bolts M7-50
10-15 Nm
11 mm hex
7-11 lb.ft.
exhaust pipe nuts
31-51 Nm
15 mm hex
22-37 lb.ft.
6+6 nuts
10-15 Nm
11 mm hex
7-11 lb.ft.
two M10 nuts
15-25 Nm
17 mm hex
11-18 lb.ft.

B27 and 28 engine

20. Plug all fuel lines to prevent dirt from entering them.

21. Disconnect the wires at the main terminal.

22. Disconnect the glow plug relay.

23. Remove the relay retaining screws and hang the relay and the wire bundle on the engine.

24. Remove the steering pump and brackets, and tie it out of the way.

25. Remove the starter wires and the battery ground strap.

26. Remove the fan, spacer, pulley and drive belts.

27. Remove the air cleaner and all necessary hoses.

28. Disconnect the alternator wires.

29. Disconnect the exhaust pipe at the front exhaust manifold.

30. Drain the engine oil.

31. Disconnect the exhaust pipe at the rear exhaust manifold.

32. Disconnect the clutch cable, return spring, vibration damper, and rubber buffer.

33. Pull out the clutch cable from the clutch lever and housing.

34. Disconnect the speedometer from the transmission.

NOTE: On cars with automatic transmissions disconnect the shift lever.

35. Disconnect the shift lever and push it up into the car.

36. Remove the driveshaft from the transmission.

37. Support the transmission with a jack and remove the rear crossmember.

38. Remove the engine mounts.

  a. Left side: Remove the nuts from the front axle member.

  b. Right side: Remove the lower nut from the rubber pad.

39. Gently put tension on your engine removal hoist.

40. Remove the left engine mount assembly.

41. Remove the engine.

42. Installation is the reverse of removal.

Cylinder Head

CYLINDER HEAD REMOVAL AND INSTALLATION

NOTE: To prevent warpage of the head, removal should be attempted only on a cold engine.

B30F

1. Drain the cooling system by opening the drain plug on the right-hand side of the engine and disconnecting the lower radiator hose at the radiator.

2. Disconnect the positive battery cable from the engine.

3. Remove the air cleaner.

4. Remove the following hoses from the inlet duct, pressure sensor, power brake (if so equipped), distributor advance, and crankcase ventilation.

5. Remove the electrical contacts for the throttle valve switch, cold start valve, thermal timer, temperature sensor, and injectors.

6. Remove the ground cable from the inlet duct and remove the cable harness.

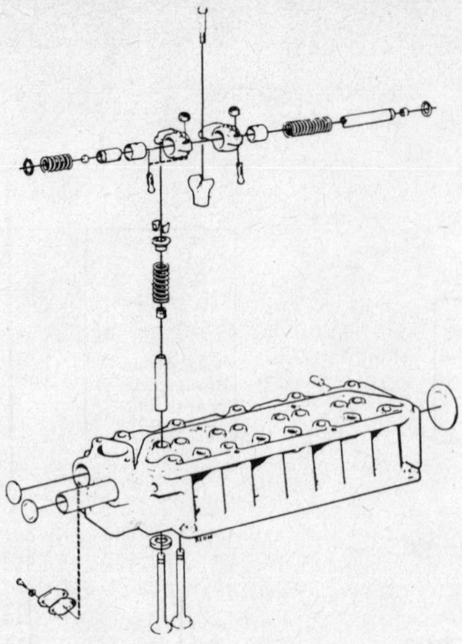

B20 cylinder head assembly—B30 similar

7. Disconnect the sensor for the coolant temperature gauge. Remove the spark plug wires from the plugs.

8. Disconnect the throttle control cable from the throttle valve and inlet duct.

9. Remove and pinch shut the fuel hoses from the distributing pipe.

10. Remove the upper radiator hose, the heater control valve hose, and the clamp for the heater pipe.

11. Unbolt the alternator adjusting arm from the head.

12. Remove the bolts for the inlet duct stay. Remove the inlet duct-to-cylinder head retaining nuts and disconnect the inlet duct.

13. If any cleaning or machine work is to be performed on the cylinder head, remove the fuel injectors beforehand. Turn the lock-rings on the injectors counterclockwise and lift out the injectors and distributing pipe as a unit. Remove the injector holders from the head.

14. Remove the exhaust manifold-to-exhaust pipe flange nuts and disconnect the pipe.

15. Remove the exhaust manifold from the head.

16. Install the exhaust manifold on the head with a new gasket.

17. Adjust the valve clearance to a *preliminary* setting of 0.022-0.024 F. Use the procedure outlined under "Valve Lash Adjustment." Install the valve cover with a new gasket.

18. If the injectors were removed, install the holders with new sealing rings. Install the injectors and distributing pipe as a unit.

19. Install the alternator adjusting arm and adjust the drive (fan) belt tension.

20. Install the inlet duct with a new gasket. Install the inlet duct retaining nuts and the bolts for the inlet duct stay.

21. Install the following: upper and lower radiator hoses, heater hose, heater hose clamp, exhaust pipe flange nuts, fuel line, throttle linkage, temperature gauge sensor, ground cable to inlet duct, cable harness, electrical contacts for the throttle valve switch, cold start valve, thermal timer, temperature sensor and injectors, pressure sensor hose, power brake hose, distributor advance line, crankcase ventilation hoses, and the positive battery cable.

22. Install the air cleaner.

23. Close the drain plug and fill the cooling system.

24. Run the engine for 10 minutes so that it reaches operating temperature and then stop it.

25. Remove the valve cover and torque the head bolts in proper sequence to the final figure of 65 ft/lbs. Adjust the valve clearance to the final setting of 0.020-0.022 as outlined under "Valve Lash Adjustment." Install the valve cover.

1975 B20F

1. Drain the cooling system by removing the plug on the right-side of the engine and disconnecting the lower radiator hose.

2. Remove the positive lead from the battery.

3. Disconnect hoses to brake vacuum booster and crankcase ventilation.

4. Remove the cold start injector hose and the fuel return hoses on both sides of the T-connection (at the control pressure regulator).

5. Remove the outlet fuel hose at the fuel filter and remove fuel filter with clamp from the firewall.

6. Disconnect the fuel hose from the fuel distributor at the control pressure regulator.

7. Disconnect electrical wires at cold start injector, auxiliary air valve, control pressure regulator and temperature sensor.

8. Remove the air cleaner connecting pipe.

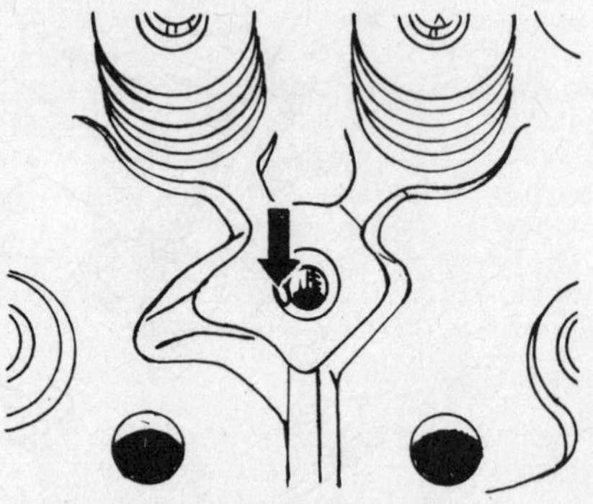

Oil feed hole in head

9. Disconnect the throttle cable at the intake manifold.

10. Disconnect hose for heater and the upper radiator hose.

11. Remove the alternator adjustment bracket.

12. Remove the straps for the injector hoses. Remove injectors with hoses from the cylinder head, by turning the lock rings counterclockwise.

13. Remove the bracket for the intake manifold, and remove the manifold.

14. Remove exhaust manifold from exhaust pipe and cylinder head.

15. Remove ignition leads and spark plugs.

16. Remove the valve cover, rocker arm shaft and the pushrods.

17. Remove the cylinder head bolts and lift off the head. Take off the cylinder head gas-

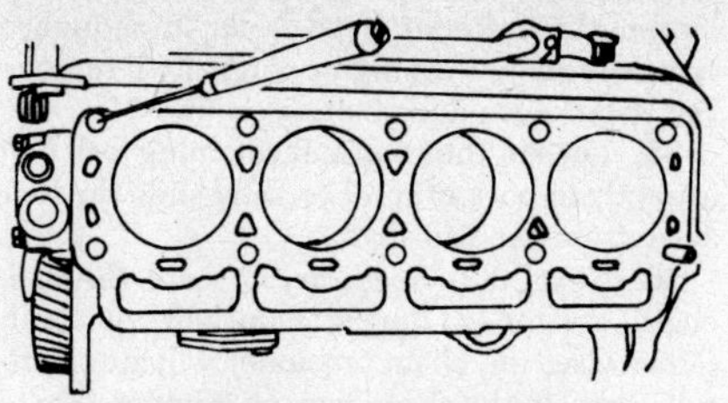

Guide stud installation

ket, the flange gasket and the rubber rings for the water pump.

18. Follow Steps 14, 16, 17, 18, 19 and 20 under "Cylinder Head Removal and Installation" for the B20F.

19. Install pushrods and rocker arm shaft. Adjust the valves to .45-.50 mm (.018-.020 in.) (Not final clearance.)

20. Reverse the removal procedure to install. Then, run the engine for 10 minutes. Retighten the cylinder head bolts to 65 ft/lbs with a torque wrench. Readjust valve clearance as outlined under "Valve Lash Adjustment." Install the valve cover.

B21F

1. Disconnect the battery.
2. Remove the overflow tank cap and drain the coolant. Disconnect the upper radiator hose.
3. Remove the distributor cap and wires.
4. Remove the PCV hoses.
5. Remove the EGR valve and vacuum pump.
6. Remove the air pump, and air injection manifold.
7. Remove the exhaust manifold and header pipe bracket.
8. Remove the intake manifold. Disconnect the manifold brace and the hose clamp to the bellows for the fuel injection air/flow unit. Disconnect the throttle cable, and all vacuum hoses and electrical connectors to the fuel injection unit.
9. Remove the fuel injectors.
10. Remove the valve cover.
11. Loosen the fan shroud and remove the fan. Remove the shroud. Remove the upper belts and pulleys.
12. Remove the timing belt cover. Remove the timing belt cover. Remove the timing belt as described later in this section.
13. Remove the camshaft (if so desired) as outlined later in this section.
14. Remove the cylinder head (10 mm Allen head bolts.
15. To install, reverse the removal procedure. Oil the head bolts. Tighten the head bolts in the prescribed torque sequence first to 44 ft/lbs, then to 81 ft/lbs. After the engine has been run 30 minutes, slacken the bolts to relieve any pretension, and then retorque to 81 ft/lbs. To set the valve timing, follow the steps for timing belt installation later in this section.

B27F and B28F

1. Disconnect the battery. Drain the coolant.
2. Remove the air cleaner assembly and all attaching hoses.
3. Disconnect the throttle cable. On automatic transmission equipped cars, disconnect the kick-down cable.

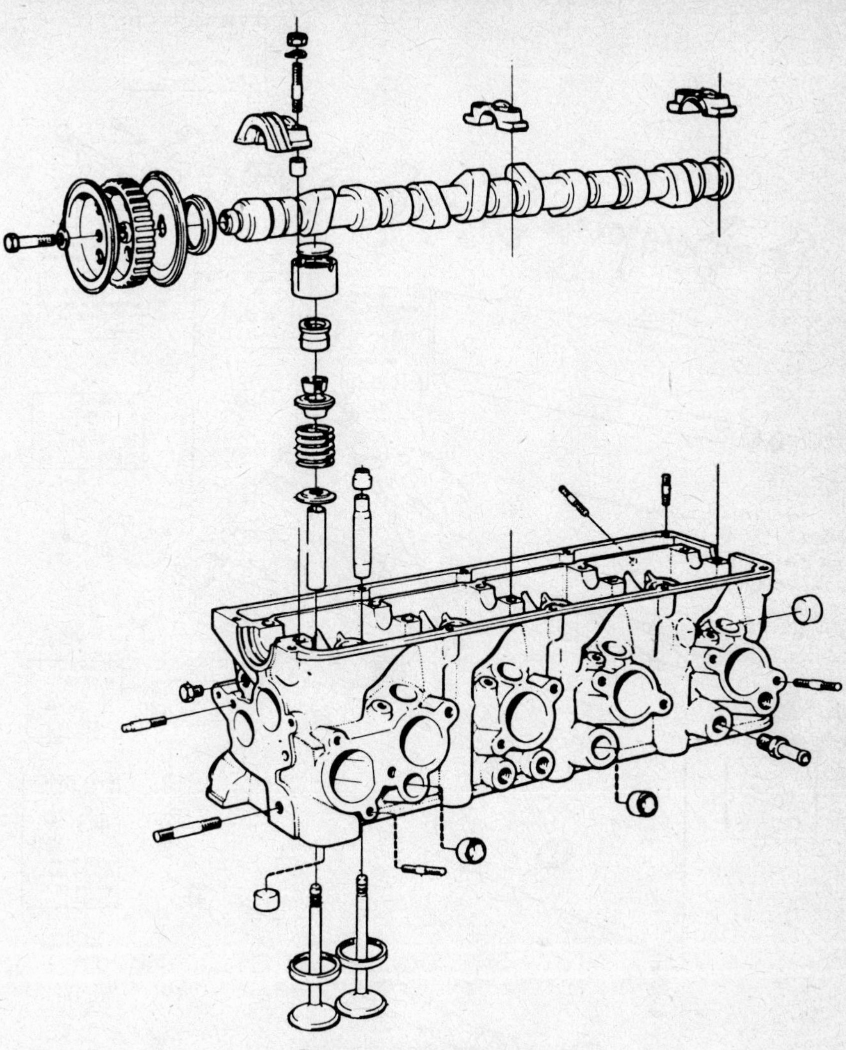

B21 cylinder head assembly

4. Disconnect the EGR vacuum hose and remove the pipe between the EGR valve and manifold.
5. Remove the oil filler cap, and cover the hole with a rag. Disconnect the PCV pipe from the intake manifold.
6. Remove the front section of the intake manifold.
7. Disconnect the electrical connector and fuel line at the cold start injector. Disconnect the vacuum hose, both fuel lines, and the electrical connector from the control pressure regulator.
8. Disconnect the hose, pipe, and electrical connector from the auxiliary air valve. Remove the auxiliary air valve.
9. Disconnect the electrical connector from the fuel distributor. Remove the wire looms from the intake manifolds. Disconnect the spark plug wires.
10. Disconnect the fuel injectors from their holders.
11. Disconnect the distributor vacuum hose, carbon filter hose, and diverter valve hose from the intake manifold. Also, disconnect the power brake hose and heater hose at the intake manifold.
12. Disconnect the throttle control link from its pulley.
13. On cars equipped with an EGR vacuum amplifier, disconnect the wires from the throttle micro switch and solenoid valve.
14. At the firewall, disconnect the fuel lines from the fuel filter and return line.
15. Remove the two attaching screws and lift out the fuel distributor and throttle housing assembly.
16. On cars not equipped with an EGR vacuum amplifier, disconnect the EGR valve hose from underneath the throttle housing.
17. Remove the cold start injector, rubber ring, and pipe.
18. Remove the four retaining bolts and lift off the intake manifold. Remove the rubber rings.
19. Remove the splash guard beneath the engine.
20. If removing the left cylinder head, remove the air pump from its bracket.
21. Remove the vacuum pump and O-ring in the valve cover. Remove the vacuum hoses from the wax thermostat.
22. If removing the right cylinder head, disconnect the upper radiator hose.
23. On air conditioned models, remove the AC compressor and place it to one side. Do not disconnect the refrigerant lines.
24. Disconnect the distributor leads and remove the distributor. Remove the EGR valve, bracket and pipe. At the firewall, dis-

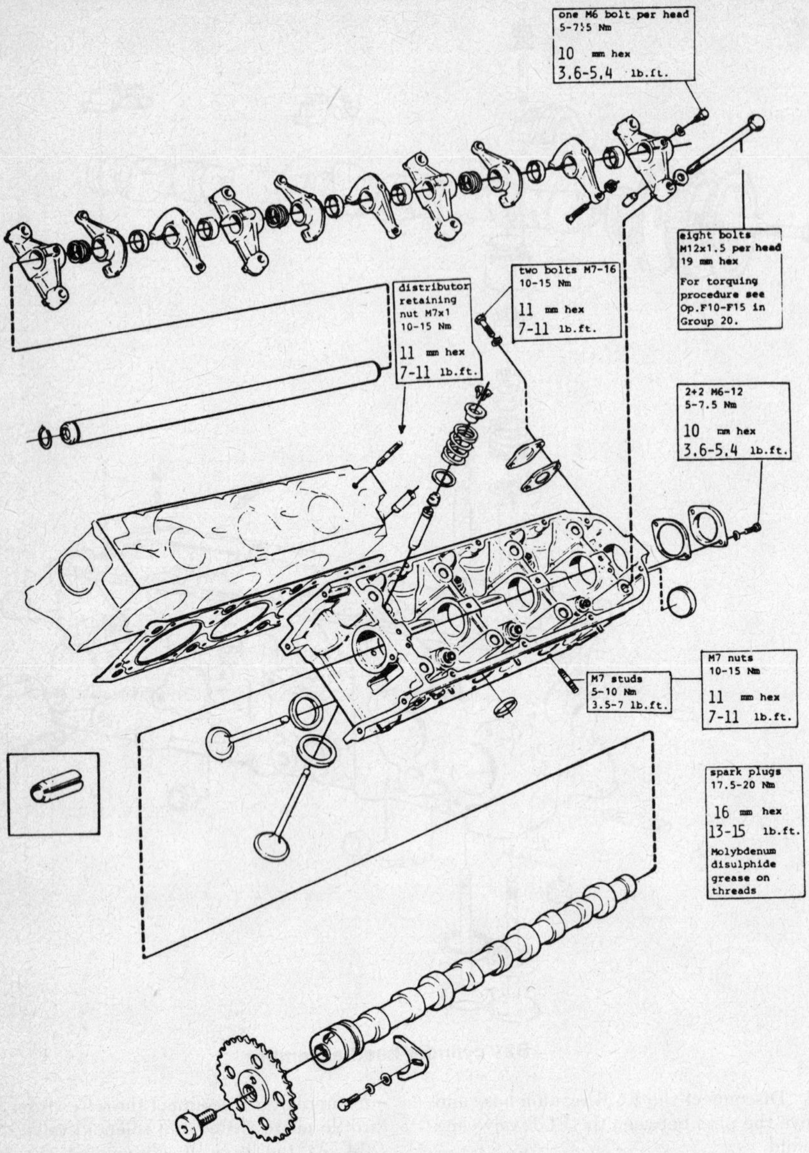

B27, 28 cylinder head assembly

connect the electrical connectors at the relays.

25. On air conditioned models, remove the rear compressor bracket.

26. Disconnect the coolant hose(s) from the water pump to the cylinder head(s). If removing the left cylinder head, disconnect the lower radiator hose at the water pump.

27. Disconnect the air injection system supply hose from the applicable cylinder head. Separate the air manifold at the rear of the engine. If removing the left cylinder head, remove the backfire valve and air hose.

28. Remove the valve cover(s).

29. On the left cylinder head, remove the Allen head screw and four upper bolts to the timing gear cover. On the right cylinder head, remove the four upper bolts to the timing gear cover and the front cover plate.

30. From beneath the car, remove the exhaust pipe clamps for both header pipes.

31. If removing the right cylinder head, remove the retainer bracket bolt and pull the dipstick tube out of the crankcase.

32. Remove the applicable exhaust manifold(s).

33. Remove the cover plate at the rear of the cylinder head.

34. Rotate the camshaft sprocket (for the applicable cylinder head) into position so that the large sprocket hole aligns with the rocker arm shaft. With the camshaft in this position, loosen the cylinder head bolts in sequence (same sequence as tightening), and remove the rocker arm and shaft assembly.

35. Loosen the camshaft retaining fork bolt (directly in back of sprocket) and slide the fork away from the camshaft.

36. Next, it is necessary to hold the cam chain stretched during camshaft removal. Otherwise, the chain tensioner will automatically take up the slack, making it impossible to reinstall the sprocket on the cam without removing the timing chain cover to loosen the tensioner device. To accomplish this, a special sprocket retainer tool (Volvo #999 5104) is installed over the sprocket with two bolts in the top of the timing chain cover. A bolt is then screwed into the sprocket to hold it in place.

37. Remove the camshaft sprocket center bolt and push the camshaft to the rear, so it clears the sprocket.

38. Remove the cylinder head.

NOTE: Do not remove the cylinder head by pulling straight up. Instead, lever the head off by inserting two spare head bolts into the front and rear inboard cylinder head bolt holes, and pulling toward the applicable wheel housing. Otherwise, the cylinder liners may be pulled up, breaking the lower liner seal and leaking coolant into the crankcase. If any do pull up, new liner seals must be used, and the crankcase completely drained.

39. Remove the head gasket. Clean the contact surfaces with a plastic scraper and lacquer thinner.

40. If the head is going to be off for any length of time, install liner holders (Volvo special tool #999 5093) or two strips of thick stock steel with holes for the head bolts, so that the liners stay pressed down against their seals. Install the holders widthwise between the middle four head bolt holes.

41. Reverse the above procedure to install, using the following installation notes:

a. There are a pair of guide dowels at both outboard corners of the head. If they fell down during removal, pull them back out with a puller hammer. They can be propped up with a ⅛ in. drill shank.

b. Remove the liner holders.

c. The right and left head gaskets are different.

d. Check the timing chain cover gasket.

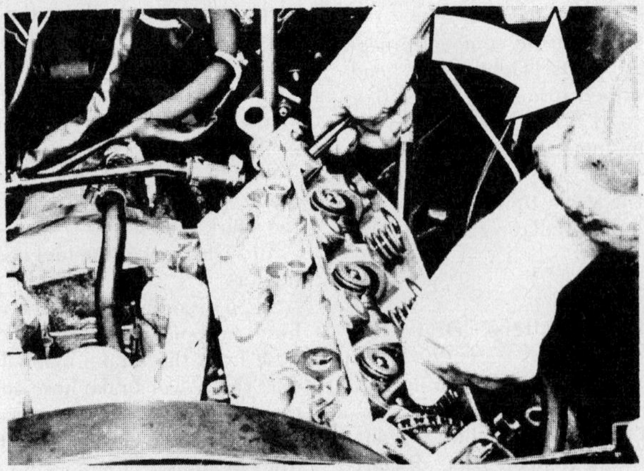

B27, 28 cylinder head removal

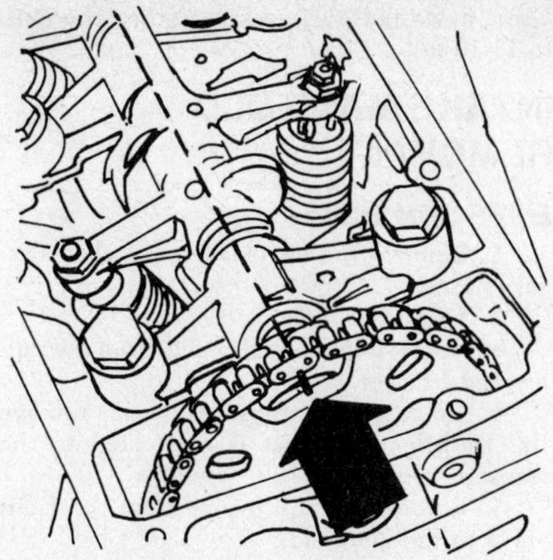

Aligning camshaft for cylinder head removal, B27, 28

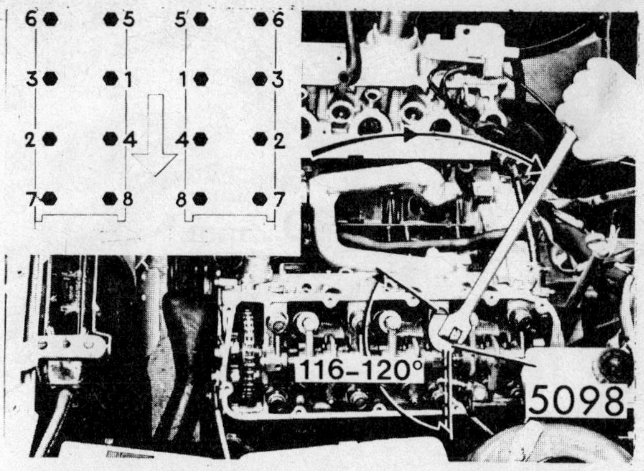

Final step of cylinder head tightening sequence is protractor torquing to 116-120 degrees (1/3 of a full turn)

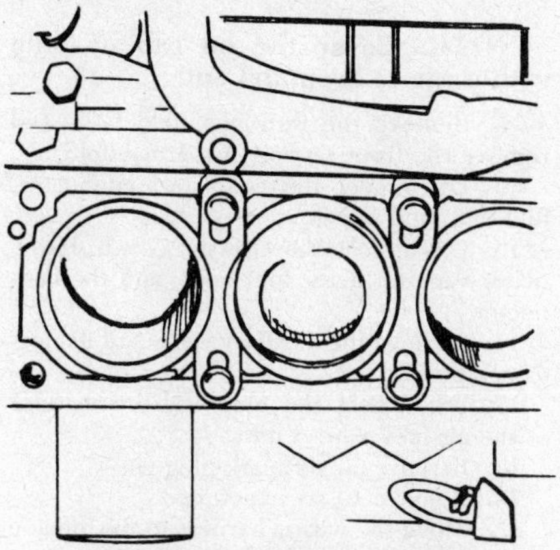

Cylinder liner holders installed

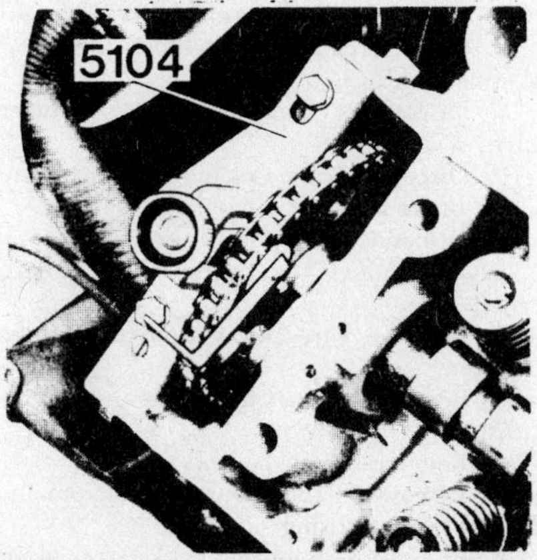

B27, 28 camshaft sprocket retainer tool

If damaged, replace only the upper section.

e. Oil the head bolt threads. Position the head on the dowels and install (hand tight) one center head bolt. Then, slide the camshaft forward into position against the sprocket and install the sprocket center bolts, and remove the retainer tool.

f. Before installing the head bolts, remove the guide dowel drill shanks, if used.

g. Using the correct tightening sequence, tighten the head bolts to 7 ft/lbs, then 22 ft/lbs, and then 44 ft/lbs. Next, slacken the head bolts (in the tightening sequence) to relieve any pre-tension. Now, tighten the bolts to 11-14 ft/lbs. *Finally, tighten the head bolts exactly one-third of a full 360° turn (116-120°) in the tightening sequence. This is critical for proper piston liner O-ring sealing. If necessary, use a protractor to ensure accuracy.*

h. Adjust the valves after completing assembly.

i. After running the engine to operating temperature, allow to cool for 30 minutes, and retorque the head bolts. Following the tightening sequence slacken the bolts to relieve any pre-tension, then tighten to 11-14 ft/lbs *and finally protractor torque them to 113-117° (one-third of a full turn).*

D-24

1. Disconnect the negative battery terminal.
2. Remove the engine splash guard.
3. Disconnect the exhaust pipe from the transmission bracket.
4. Disconnect the exhaust pipe from the rear exhaust manifold.
5. Disconnect the exhaust pipe from the front exhaust manifold.
6. Remove the air cleaner and all necessary hoses.
7. Drain the radiator.
8. Remove the bottom and top radiator hoses.
9. Remove the bottom hose from the cold start device and drain it into a suitable container.
10. Remove the top cold start hose.
11. Remove the vacuum pump and the plunger.
12. Remove all the fuel lines and plug the fuel line connections.

NOTE: Carefully remove all dirt from the fuel line connections to prevent dirt from entering the system.

13. Remove the glow plug wires and temperature sender wire.
14. Remove the rear injector return line hose.
15. Remove the valve cover.
16. Remove the front and rear timing belt covers.
17. Set the engine at top dead center and the fuel pump to the injection position for the Number one cylinder.
18. Remove the timing belt shield from the head.

NOTE: Be careful not to drop the washers or bolts into the lower cover.

19. Loosen the bolts on the water pump and the belt idler pulley.
20. Remove the belt from the camshaft.
21. Use special tool #5199 or a suitable replacement to hold the cam gear steady while removing it. This tool is available from your Volvo dealer.

NOTE: Do not allow the camshaft to turn.

22. Loosen the fuel pump bracket retaining screws to loosen the belt tension.
23. Remove the belt.
24. Remove the rear camshaft gear; see Step #21 for this procedure.
25. Remove the head bolts, and remove the head.
26. Installation is the reverse of removal.

NOTE: Always use a new gasket when replacing the head.

The following special tools are needed for reinstallation of the head: Belt tension gauge #5197, Camshaft position gauge #5190.

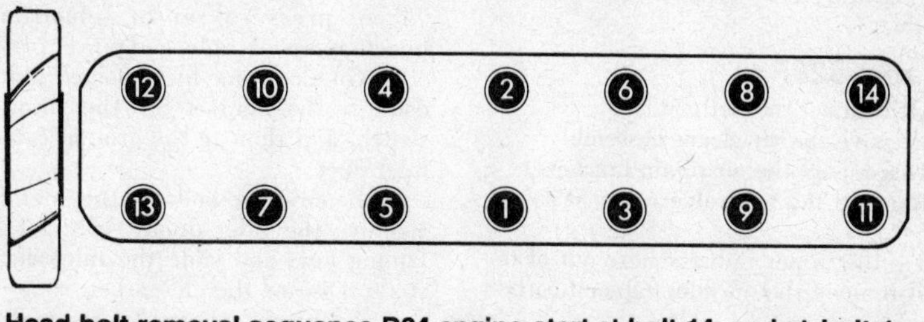

Head bolt removal sequence D24 engine start at bolt 14, end at bolt 1

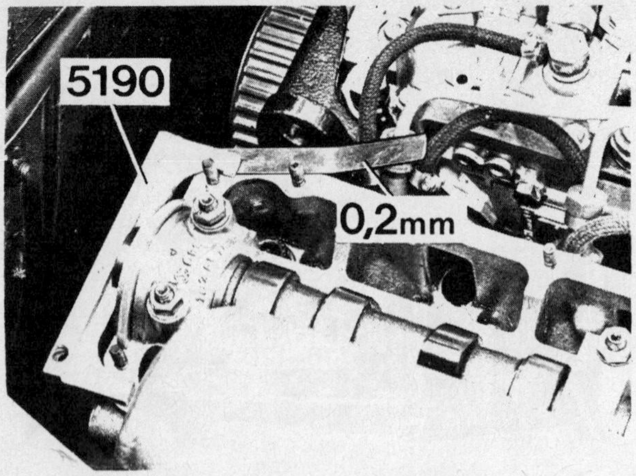

Camshaft position gauge

CYLINDER HEAD OVERHAUL

Refer to "Cylinder Head Reconditioning" in the "Engine Rebuilding" section.

Rocker Shafts

REMOVAL AND INSTALLATION

B20, B30

1. Remove the four retaining screws and the valve cover and gasket.
2. Remove the rocker shaft-to-cylinder head bolts and lift out the shaft and rocker arms as a unit.
3. Lift out the pushrods, keeping them in order, and check them for straightness by rolling them on a flat surface. Replace any bent pushrods.
4. Inspect the rocker shaft and arms. If the shaft and rockers are coated with baked-on sludge, oil may not be reaching them. Clean out the oil feed holes in the rocker shaft with 0.020 in. wire (piano wire). If the clearance between the rocker arms and shaft exceeds 0.004 in., the rocker arm needs to be rebushed. The rocker arm bushings are press fitted, and are removed with a drift. When pressing in a new bushing, make sure that the oil hole in the bushing aligns with the hole in the arm.
5. Position the pushrods on their respective lifters. Install the rocker shaft and arm assembly on the head, and install the retaining bolts. Step-tighten the bolts, moving front to rear, until a torque of approximately 20 ft/lbs is reached.
6. Check to see that valve lash has remained within specifications. Adjust valve lash, if necessary.
7. Install the valve cover and gasket, and snugly tighten the valve cover retaining screws.

B27F and B28F

1. Disconnect the battery.
2. Remove the air cleaner assembly.
3. Disconnect the air pump bracket.
4. Remove the left valve cover (if so desired).
5. Tie the upper radiator hose out of the way and remove the oil filler cap and carbon canister hose.
6. On air conditioned models, remove the AC compressor from its bracket. Do not disconnect the hoses.
7. Remove the EGR valve.
8. Remove the AC compressor rear bracket.
9. Remove the control pressure regulator.
10. Disconnect any hoses or wires in the way. Remove the right valve cover (if so desired).
11. The rocker arm bolts double as cylinder head bolts. When loosening, follow the cylinder head bolt tightening sequence diagram. If removing both rocker shafts, mark them left and right.

NOTE: Do not jar or strike head while rockers and bolts are out, as cylinder liner O-ring seals may break, necessitating teardown of engine to clean coolant out of crankcase and installation of new seals.

12. To install, reverse removal procedure. Follow cylinder head installation procedure for proper torque sequence.

Intake and Exhaust Manifolds

INLET DUCT REMOVAL AND INSTALLATION—FUEL INJECTED IN-LINE ENGINES

1. On B30F engines, remove the air cleaner. On B20F engines, remove the inlet duct-to-air cleaner hose at the inlet duct.
2. Disconnect the negative battery cable (fuel-injection models only).
3. Disconnect the throttle and downshift linkage. Remove from the inlet duct, the positive crankcase ventilation, distributor advance, pressure sensor (electronic fuel-injection models only) and power brake hoses.
4. On electronic fuel-injected models, disconnect the contact for the throttle valve switch, and remove the ground cable for the inlet duct.
5. Remove the bolts for the inlet duct stay. Remove the inlet duct-to-cylinder head retaining nuts and slide the inlet duct off the studs. Discard the old gasket.
6. To install, reverse the above procedure. Use a new inlet duct gasket. Torque the nuts to 13-16 ft/lbs.

INTAKE MANIFOLD REMOVAL

B27F and B28F

1. Remove the air cleaner and all necessary hoses.
2. Drain the radiator coolant.
3. Remove the throttle cable from the pulley and bracket.
4. On automatic transmission cars remove the throttle cable that is connected to the transmission.
5. Remove the EGR pipe from the EGR valve to the manifold.
6. Disconnect the EGR vacuum line.
7. Remove the oil filler cap and PCV valve.

NOTE: Cover the oil cap opening with a rag to keep dirt out.

8. Remove the front manifold bolts and remove the front section of the manifold.
9. Disconnect the cold start connector, fuel line, and injector.
10. Disconnect the pressure control regulator vacuum lines, fuel lines, and the connector.
11. Remove the auxiliary valve and its necessary piping.
12. Disconnect the electrical connections at the air-fuel control unit.
13. Remove all six spark plug wires.
14. Remove all six injectors.
15. Move the wiring harness to the outside of the manifold.
16. Disconnect the vacuum hose at the distributor and the intake manifold.
17. Disconnect the heater hose at the intake manifold.
18. Disconnect the hose to the diverter valve.
19. Disconnect the vacuum hose to the power brake booster.
20. Disconnect the throttle cable link.
21. Disconnect the wires to the micro switch.
22. Pull the wires away from the intake manifold.
23. Remove the fuel filter line and the return line.
24. Remove the air control unit.
25. Disconnect the vacuum hose from the throttle valve housing.
26. Remove the pipe and cold start injector assembly.
27. Remove the intake assembly.
28. Installation is the reverse of removal.

NOTE: Always use new gaskets when reinstalling the manifold.

29. Torque the manifold bolts to 7-11 ft/lbs.

B21F

1. Remove the air cleaner and all necessary hoses.
2. Remove the PCV valve.
3. Remove the connector at the cold start injector.
4. Remove the fuel hose from the cold start injector.
5. Remove the cold start injector.

6. Remove the connector on the auxiliary valve.
7. Disconnect the hoses at the auxiliary valve.
8. Remove the auxiliary valve.
9. Remove the intake manifold brace.
10. Disconnect the distributor vacuum hose at the intake manifold.
11. Loosen the clamp for the rubber connecting pipe on the air-fuel control unit.
12. Remove the manifold bolts and remove the manifold.
13. Installation is the reverse of removal.

NOTE: Remember to install new manifold gaskets before replacing the manifold.

14. Torque the manifold bolts to 15 ft/lbs.

D24 Diesel

1. Disconnect the negative battery terminal.
2. Remove the air cleaner and all necessary hoses.
3. Remove any other necessary vacuum or electrical lines.
4. Remove the intake manifold bolts and remove the manifold.
5. Installation is the reverse of removal.

NOTE: Always use a new gasket when reinstalling the intake manifold.

6. Torque the intake bolts to 18 ft/lbs.

EXHAUST MANIFOLD REMOVAL

B27F and B28F

Depending upon the type of optional equipment your particular vehicle has the exhaust manifolds may be removed from underneath the car.

1. Jack up your vehicle and support it with jack stands.
2. Unbolt the crossover pipe from the left and right side of your exhaust manifolds, (if so equipped).

NOTE: If your car has the "Y" type exhaust pipe disconnect this pipe at the left and right manifolds.

3. Remove any other necessary hardware.
4. Remove the left and right side manifolds.
5. Installation is the reverse of removal.

NOTE: Always use new gaskets when reinstalling the manifolds.

6. Torque the manifold bolts to 7-11 ft/lbs.

B21F

1. Remove the air cleaner and all necessary hoses.
2. Remove the EGR valve pipe from the manifold.
3. Remove the exhaust pipe from the exhaust manifold.
4. Remove the manifold bolts and remove the manifold.

NOTE: Remember to install new manifold gaskets before installing the manifold.

5. Installation is the reverse of removal.
6. Torque the manifold bolts to 10-20 ft/lbs.

D24 Diesel

1. Disconnect the negative battery terminal.
2. Remove the air cleaner and all necessary hoses.
3. Remove the exhaust pipes from the manifolds.

NOTE: the exhaust manifold is made in two separate sections.

4. Remove any other necessary hardware.
5. Remove the intake manifold. See the intake manifold removal section.
6. Remove the exhaust manifold in two sections.
7. Installation is the reverse of removal.

NOTE: Always use new gaskets when reinstalling the exhaust manifold.

8. Torque the bolts to 18 ft/lbs.

Timing Gear Cover

REMOVAL AND INSTALLATION

B 20

1. Loosen the fan (drive) belt. Remove the fan and water pump pulley. Disconnect the stabilizer attachment from the frame.
2. Remove the crankshaft pulley and bolt.
3. Remove the retaining bolts and the timing gear cover. Loosen a few oil pan bolts, being careful not to damage the pan gasket.
4. Remove the circlip, washer, and felt ring from the cover. Replace any gasket in questionable condition. Make sure that the oil drain hole is open and clean.

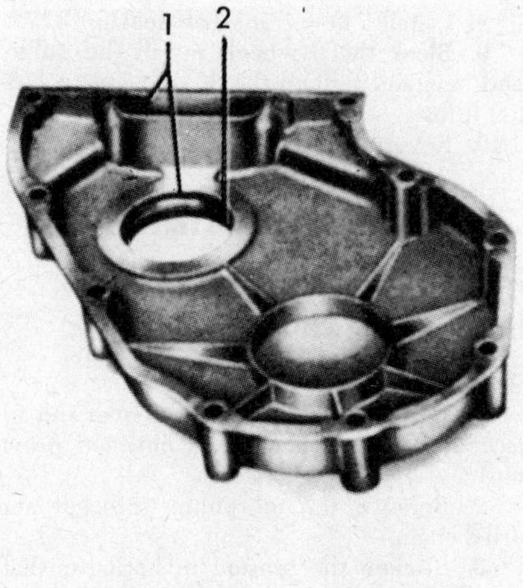

1. Drain holes 2. Sealing ring

Timing gear cover—B20

5. Place the cover in position and install the retaining bolts finger-tight.
6. Center the cover with a sleeve. Turn the sleeve while tightening and adjust the position of the cover so that the sleeve may be easily rotated without jamming.
7. Install a new felt ring, washer, and circlip. Push them into their positions with the engaging sleeve. Check to make sure that the circlip has seated in its groove.
8. Tighten the cover bolts. Install the pulleys and fan. Tension the accessory drive belts. Tighten the stabilizer attachment firmly to the frame.

TIMING GEAR COVER OIL SEAL REPLACEMENT

B 20

1. Remove the fan belt. Loosen the stabilizer attachment at the frame.
2. Remove the crankshaft pulley and bolt.
3. Remove the circlip for the washer retaining the felt ring. Check to make sure that the cover is correctly installed by inserting a 0.004 in. feeler gauge between the casing and the crankshaft hub. If the feeler gauge jams at any point, the cover must be centered.
4. Install a new felt ring. Place the washer in position and install the circlip in its groove.
5. Install the crankshaft pulley and fan. Tension the fan (drive) belt. Tighten the stabilizer attachment at the frame.

B 30

1. Drain the cooling system by opening the engine drain plug and disconnecting the lower radiator hose. On automatic transmission cars, disconnect and plug the transmission oil cooler lines at the radiator. Remove the radiator, fan shroud, and grille.
2. Remove the fan (drive) belt. Remove the bolts for the pulley and crankshaft damper.
3. Remove the center bolt and pull off the hub by hand or, if necessary, with a puller.

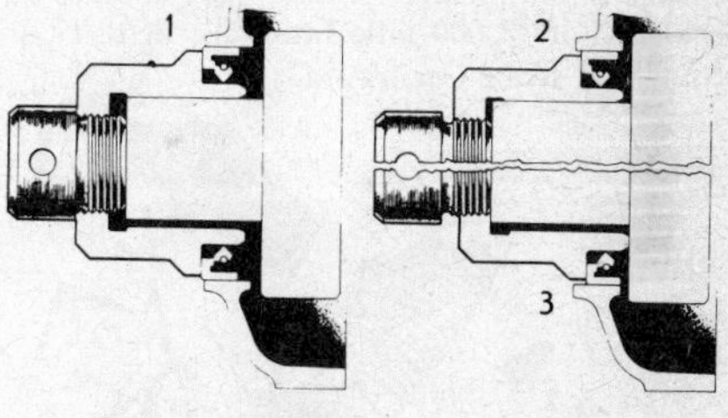

Center spindle position—B30

4. Remove the oil seal. Lubricate the sealing lip on the new seal and install the seal with a drift. The seal may be installed in one of three positions, depending on the amount of wear on the hub. With a new hub, the seal will be installed in its outer position (position 1). With a wear mark on the hub, install the seal in position 2. With two wear marks on the hub, install the seal in position 3. With three wear marks on the hub, you either have a very old engine or you have gone through more than a normal share of oil seals, and it's time to think about replacing that old hub with a new one.
5. Grease the sliding surfaces of the hub and install the hub. Note the center punch marks on the crankshaft end and hub. Install the center bolt and torque it to 50-57 ft/lbs.
6. Install the crankshaft damper and pulley.
7. Install and properly tension the fan (drive) belt. Install the radiator, fan shroud, and grille. Install the lower radiator hose, close the drain plug, and fill the cooling system. On cars with automatic transmissions, connect the transmission oil cooler lines at the radiator.

Timing Belt Cover

REMOVAL AND INSTALLATION

B21F

1. Loosen the fan shroud and remove the fan. Remove the shroud.
2. Loosen the alternator, air pump, power steering pump (if so equipped), and AC compressor (if so equipped) and remove their drive belts.
3. Remove the water pump pulley.
4. Remove the four retaining bolts and lift off the timing belt cover.
5. Reverse the above procedure to install.

Timing Belt

REMOVAL AND INSTALLATION

B21F

1. Remove the timing belt cover as outlined previously.
2. To remove the tension from the belt, loosen the nut for the tensioner and press the idler roller back. The tension spring can be locked in this position by inserting the shank end of a 3 mm drill through the pusher rod.
3. Remove the six retaining bolts and the crankshaft pulley.
4. Remove the belt, taking care not to bend it at any sharp angles. The belt should be replaced at 45,000 mile intervals, or if it becomes oil soaked or frayed.

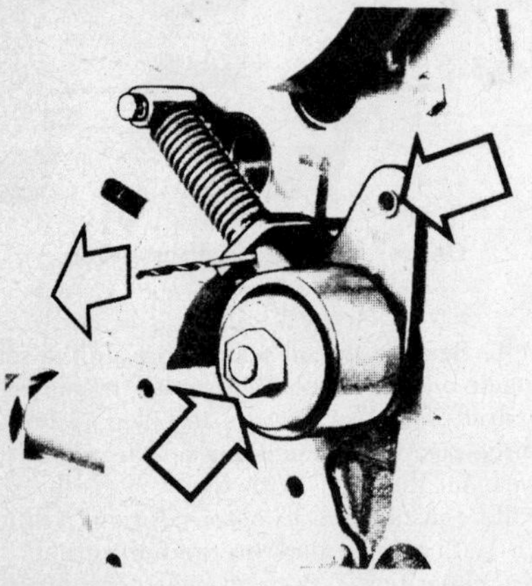

Locking tensioner spring with drill shank

5. If the crankshaft, idler shaft, or camshaft were disturbed while the belt was out, align each shaft with its corresponding index mark to assure proper valve timing and ignition timing, as follows:
   a. Rotate the crankshaft so that the notch in the convex crankshaft gear belt guide aligns with the embossed mark on the front cover (12 o'clock position).
   b. Rotate the idler shaft so that the dot on the idler shaft drive sprocket aligns with the notch on the timing belt rear cover (four o'clock position).
   c. Rotate the camshaft so that the notch in the camshaft sprocket inner belt guide aligns with the notch in the forward edge of the valve cover (12 o'clock position).
6. Install the timing belt (don't use any sharp tools) over the sprockets, and then over the tensioner roller. Loosen the tensioner nut and let the spring tension automatically take up the slack. Tighten the tensioner nut to 37 ft/lbs.
7. Rotate the crankshaft one full revolution clockwise, and make sure the timing marks still align.
8. Reverse Steps 1-3 to install.

Timing Chain Cover

REMOVAL AND INSTALLATION

B27F and B28F

1. Remove the air cleaner and valve covers.
2. Loosen the fan shroud and remove the fan. Remove the shroud.
3. Loosen the alternator, air pump, power steering pump, and AC compressor (if so equipped) and remove their drive belts.
4. Block the flywheel from turning, remove the crankshaft pulley nut (36 mm) and the pulley.

NOTE: Do not drop the pulley key into the crankcase.

5. Remove the power steering pump and place to one side. Remove the pump bracket.
6. Remove the timing chain cover retaining bolts (25 11 mm hex bolts), tap and remove the cover.
7. Clean the gasket contact surfaces. Place the upper gasket on the cover and the lower gasket on the block. Install the cover and tighten to 7-11 ft/lbs. Trim the gaskets flush with the valve cover.
8. Install a new crankshaft seal.
9. Block the flywheel, install the pulley (and key) and tighten the 36 mm nut to 118-132 ft/lbs.
10. Reverse Steps 1-5 to install.

Timing Chain

REMOVAL AND INSTALLATION

B27F

1. Remove the timing chain cover and adjacent engine accessories as outlined previously.
2. Remove the oil pump sprocket and drive chain.
3. Slacken the tension in both camshaft timing chains by rotating each tensioner lock

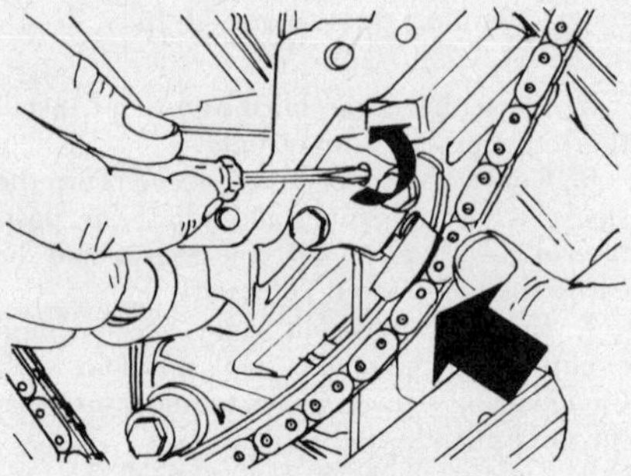

Relieving chain tension

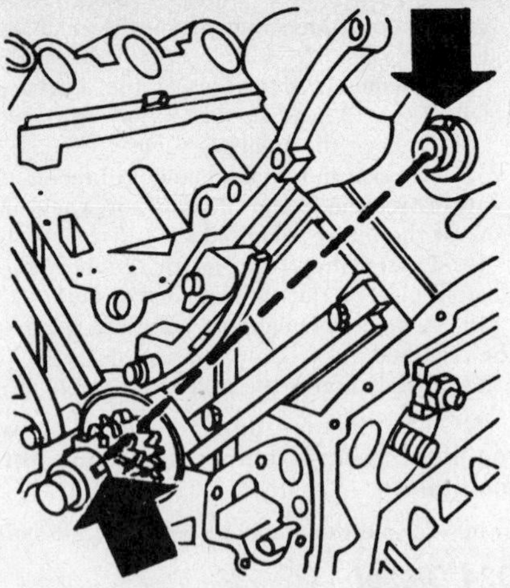

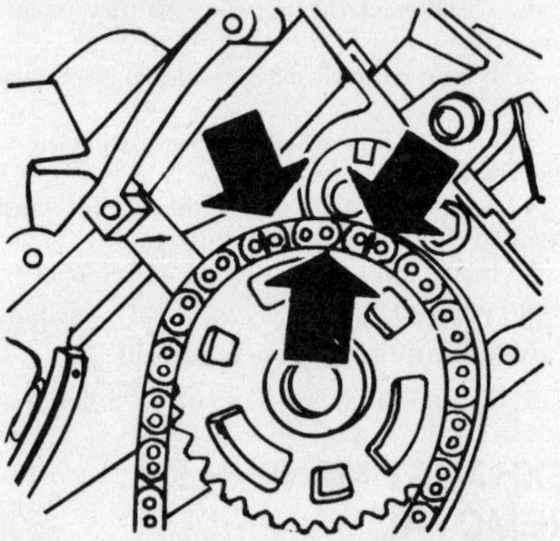

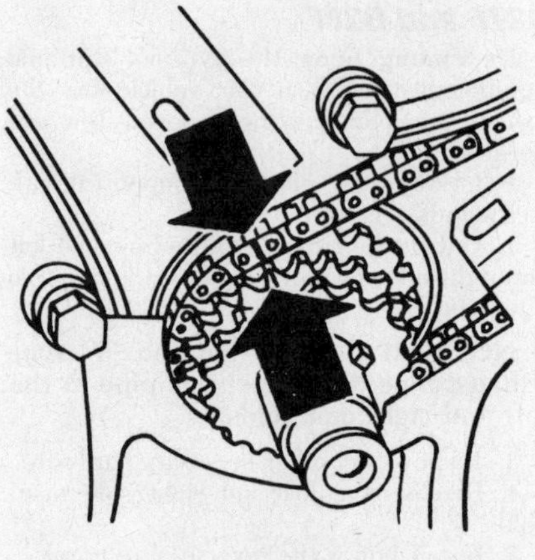

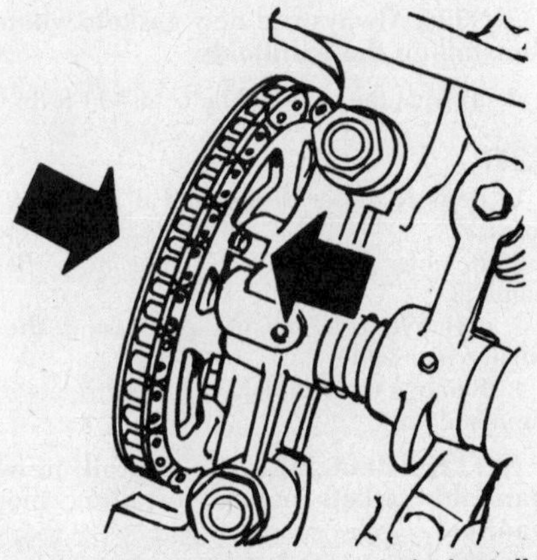

Left side camshaft timing chain installation sequence

¼ turn counterclockwise and pushing the rubbing block piston.

4. Remove both chain tensioners. Remove the two curved and the two straight chain damper/runners.

5. Remove the camshaft sprocket retaining bolt (10 mm Allen head) and the sprocket and chain assembly. Repeat for other side.

6. Install the chain tensioners and tighten to 5 ft/lbs. Install the curved chain damper/runners and tighten to 7-11 ft/lbs. Install the straight chain damper/runners and torque to 5 ft/lbs.

7. First install the left (driver) side camshaft sprocket and chain. Rotate the crankshaft (use crankshaft nut, if necessary) until No. 1 cylinder is at TDC. At this point, the crankshaft key is pointing directly to the left side camshaft, and the left side camshaft key groove is pointing straight up (12 o'clock). Place the chain on the left side sprocket so that the sprocket notchmark is centered precisely between the two white lines on the chain. Then, position the chain on the crank-

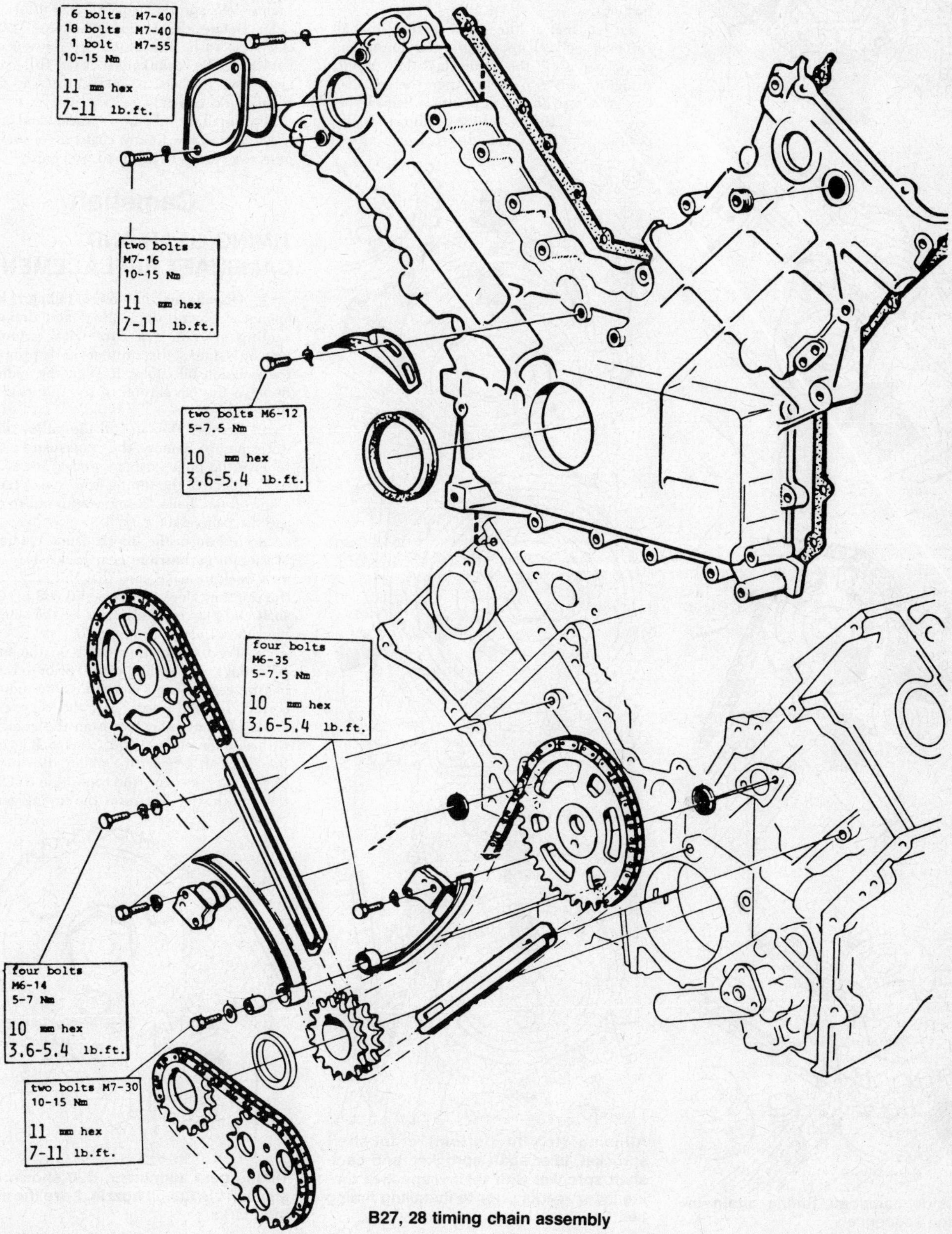

B27, 28 timing chain assembly

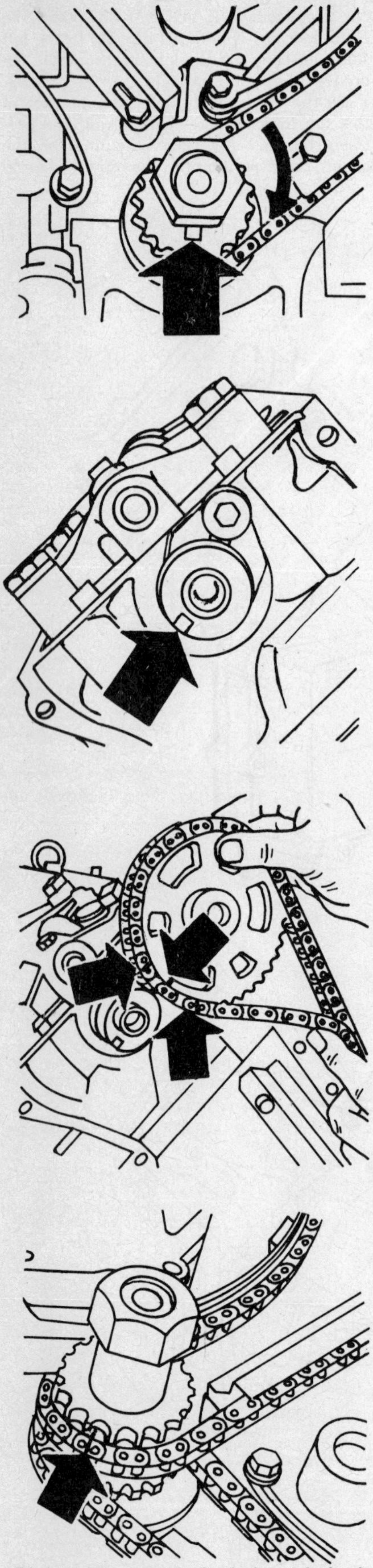

Right side camshaft timing chain installation sequence

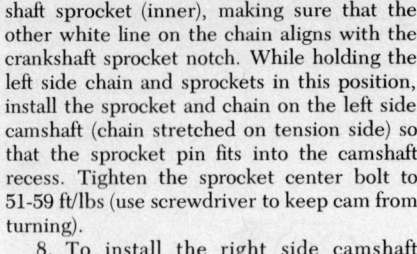

shaft sprocket (inner), making sure that the other white line on the chain aligns with the crankshaft sprocket notch. While holding the left side chain and sprockets in this position, install the sprocket and chain on the left side camshaft (chain stretched on tension side) so that the sprocket pin fits into the camshaft recess. Tighten the sprocket center bolt to 51-59 ft/lbs (use screwdriver to keep cam from turning).

8. To install the right side camshaft sprocket and chain, rotate the crankshaft clockwise until the crankshaft key points straight down (6 o'clock). Align the camshaft key groove so that it is pointing halfway between the 8 and 9 o'clock positions (at this position, the No. 6 cylinder rocker arms will rock). Place the chain on the right side sprocket so that the sprocket notchmark is centered precisely between the two white lines on the chain. Then, position the chain on the middle crankshaft sprocket, making sure that the other white line aligns with the crankshaft sprocket notch. Then, install the sprocket and chain on the camshaft so that the sprocket notch fits into the camshaft recess. Tighten the sprocket nut to 51-59 ft/lbs.

9. Rotate the chain tensioners ¼ turn clockwise eash. The chains are tensioned by rotating the crankshaft two full turns clockwise. Recheck to make sure the alignment marks coincide.

10. Install the oil pump sprocket and chain.

11. Install the timing chain cover and engine accessories as outlined previously.

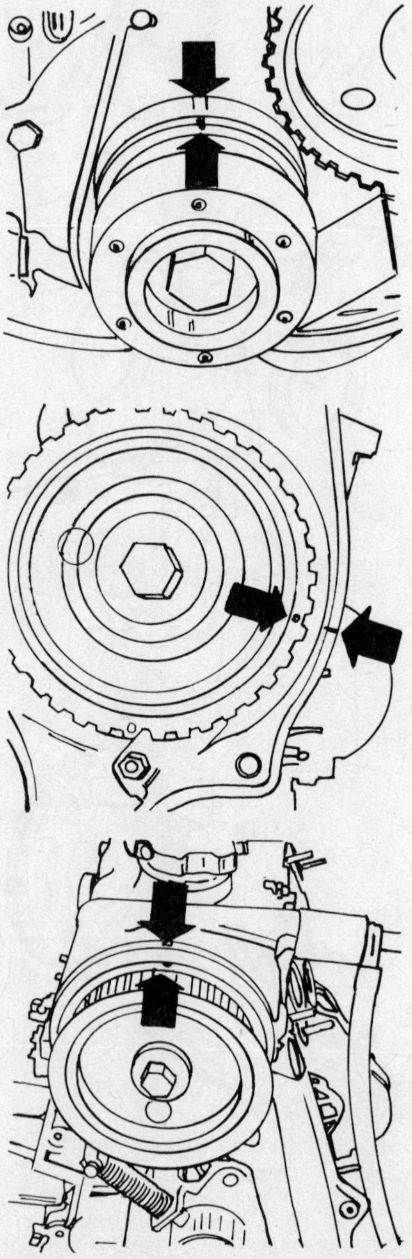

Aligning (top to bottom) crankshaft sprocket, idler shaft sprocket, and camshaft sprocket with their respective timing index marks prior to installing timing belt

Camshaft

TIMING GEAR AND CAMSHAFT REPLACEMENT

1. Disconnect the lower radiator hose, open the engine drain plug, and drain the cooling system. On cars with automatic transmissions, disconnect and plug the transmission oil cooler lines at the radiator. Remove the fan shroud (if so equipped) and the radiator.

2. Remove the fan and the pulley on the water pump. Remove the crankshaft bolt and remove the pulley using a puller.

3. Remove the timing gear cover. Loosen a few oil pan bolts, being careful not to damage the pan gasket.

4. Measure the tooth flank clearance. Maximum permissible gear backlash is 0.005 in. Check to make sure that the end-play of the camshaft does not exceed 0.002 in. Camshaft end-play is determined by the shim behind the camshaft timing gear.

5. Try to align the marks on the timing gears dot to dot (or line to dot) prior to removing the gears. If this is not possible, note the correct relative position of the timing gear marks. Remove the hub from the crankshaft with a puller. Remove the crankshaft gear and the camshaft gear with a puller. Remove the oil jet, blow it clean, and reposition it. Oil fed through this jet lubricates the timing gears.

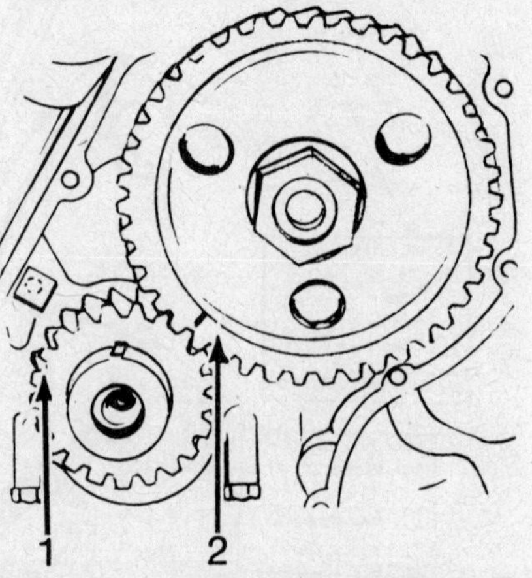

Timing gear alignment, B20 shown, B30 similar. 1 is the oil nozzle, 2 are the aligning marks.

6. If the camshaft is being replaced, it is necessary to remove the distributor (noting its position), the distributor/oil pump driveshaft, fuel pump, valve cover, rocker shaft and arm assembly, pushrods, cylinder head, valve lifters, and the thrust flange. The camshaft may then be pulled out the front.

7. Reverse the above procedure to install. Replace the camshaft if the lobes exhibit excessive or uneven wear. Install the crankshaft and camshaft timing gears, making sure that they align in the correct relative positions. Do not push the camshaft backward, or the seal washer on the rear end may be forced out. Recheck the tooth flank clearance and the camshaft end-play.

8. Bring No. 1 piston to Top Dead Center. Install the distrubutor/oil pump driveshaft so that the offset position of the distributor slot (angle A) is 35° for the B30F engines, and 5° for the B20F engines.

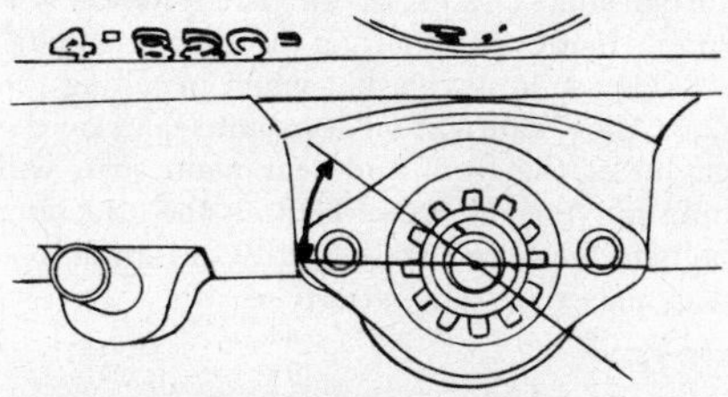

After installing camshaft, bring no. 1 piston to TDC and align the distributor drive shaft angle "A" as outlined in the text.

NOTE: Make sure that the distributor/oil pump driveshaft seats fully in the slot at the top of the oil pump. If necessary , use a long screwdriver to turn the pump manually until the slot aligns.

9. When installing the timing case cover, make sure that the drain holes are open. Center the cover with a sleeve. Install the distributor, making sure the rotor points to the No. 1 cylinder position.

10. Install the pulleys and fan. Install the fan (drive) belt and adjust the tension. Refit the radiator hose, close the drain plug, and fill the cooling system.

11. Adjust the ignition timing.

B21F

1. Remove the timing belt cover and timing belt as outlined in their appropriate sections.

2. Remove the valve cover.

3. Remove the camshaft center bearing cap. Install special camshaft press tool (Volvo #5021) over the center bearing journal to hold the camshaft in place while removing the other bearing caps.

4. Remove the four remaining bearings caps.

5. Remove the seal from the forward edge of the camshaft.

6. Release camshaft press tool, and lift out the camshaft.

7. Reverse the above procedure to install.

B27F and B28F

1. Remove the cylinder head as outlined previously.

2. Remove the camshaft rear cover plate.

3. Remove the camshaft retaining fork at the front of the cylinder head.

B21 camshaft press tool installed

4. Pull the camshaft out the rear of the head.

5. Reverse the above to install.

D24 Diesel

1. Disconnect the negative battery terminal.

2. Drain the radiator.

3. Remove the expansion tank hose.

4. Remove the top and bottom radiator hoses.

5. Remove the fan with the spacer and pulley.

6. Remove all the drive belts.

7. Remove the valve cover.

8. Remove the timing gear belt cover.

9. Set the Number 1 cylinder to top dead center.

NOTE: This is accomplished by turning the crankshaft pulley with an 1$^{1}/_{16}$ socket. The flywheel timing mark should be set at zero.

10. Remove the crankshaft pulley bolt.

11. Remove the four Allen head bolts in the center of the pulley and remove the pulley.

NOTE: The pulley and the crankshaft gear may be stuck together. Gently tap them apart with a hammer.

12. Remove the lower belt shield.

13. Loosen and remove the timing belt.

14. Remove the front camshaft gear.

NOTE: Use tool #5199 available from Volvo or another suitable tool to prevent the camshaft from turning.

15. Remove the rear timing belt cover.

16. Loosen the injection pump bracket to release tension from the injection pump drive belt.

17. Remove the timing belt.

18. Remove the rear camshaft gear.

NOTE: See Step #14 for this procedure.

19. Installation is the reverse of removal.

The following torque specifications are needed: Front camshaft gear 33 ft/lbs., Rear camshaft gear 73 ft/lbs., Crankshaft pulley 330 ft/lbs., Crankshaft pulley Allen bolts 15 ft/lbs.

D24 Diesel

1. Follow the procedure for the camshaft gear removal.

2. Remove the first and fourth bearing caps.

3. Remove the second and third bearing caps.

NOTE: Loosen the bearing cap nuts on an alternating basis to prevent cam distortion.

4. Remove the camshaft and discard the seals.

5. Installation is the reverse of removal, with the following suggestions.

1. When reinstalling the cam you must use special tool #5190 available from your Volvo dealer.

2. Place grease on the oil seal lips before installation. The seals must be driven into place with Volvo tool #5200 or a suitable substitute.

3. Torque the cam bearing caps to 15 ft/lbs.

4. The second and third bearing caps should be installed first.

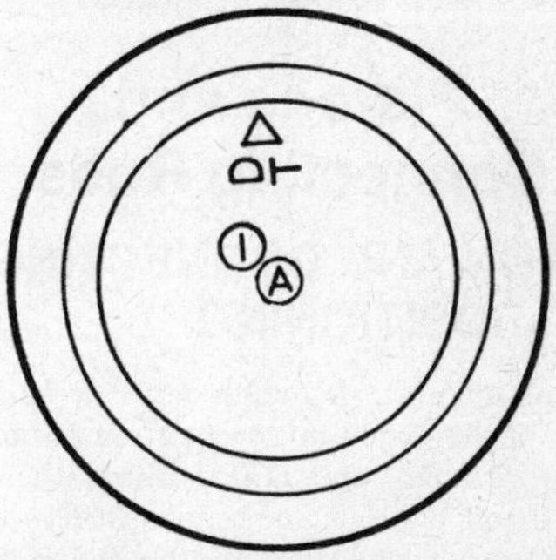

B27, 28 piston positioning. Arrowhead faces forward

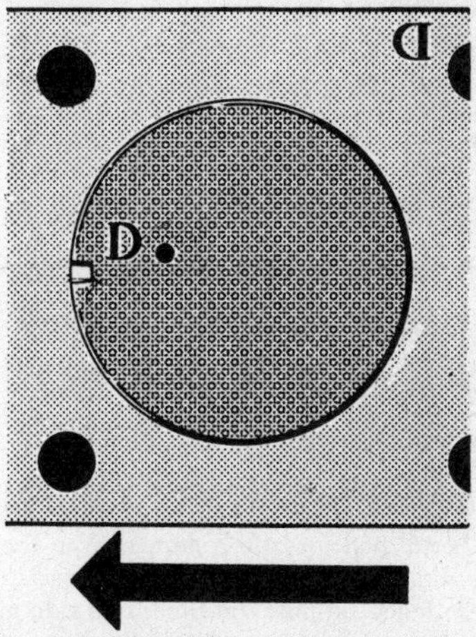

B20, B21, and B30 piston positioning; notch faces forward

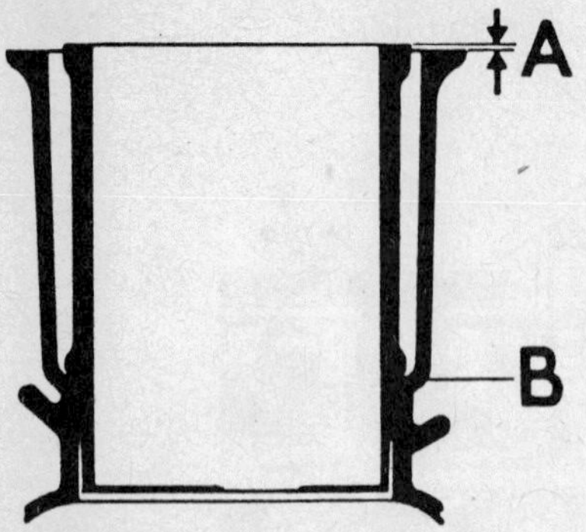

Correct B27, 28 piston liner height "A" above block face is 0.0091 in. Shims are available for installation at point "B" and should be uniform for all cylinders

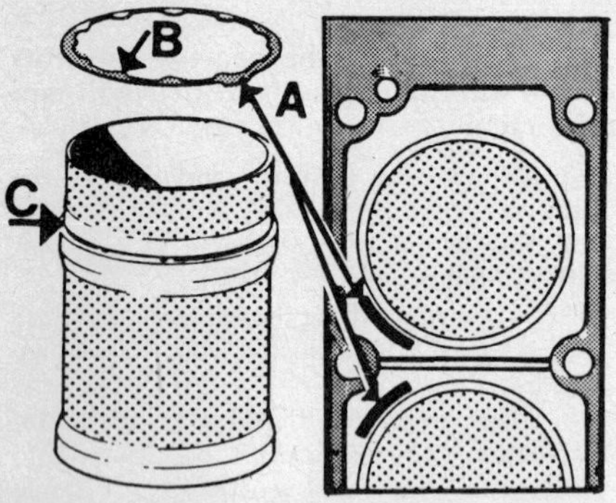

When installing B27 and B28 liner shims, color marking "A" must face up and be positioned where shown. Inside tabs "B" fit into liner groove

Pistons and Connecting Rods

PISTON AND CONNECTING ROD POSITIONING

On all engines, the notch or arrow stamped on top of the piston must face the front of the engine. On B20 and B30 engines, the connecting rod big end marking must face away from the camshaft side, and on the B21 the connecting rod marking must face the front of the engine.

ENGINE LUBRICATION

Oil Pan

REMOVAL AND INSTALLATION

B20 (Except 240 Series) and B30

The oil pan may be removed from the engine while the engine is still in chassis.

1. Place supports on the frame side members. Insert a lifting hook into the lifting plate bolted to the front of the engine. Using the lifting apparatus, raise the engine until there is no weight on the front engine mounts. Remove the oil dipstick.
2. Jack up the vehicle and place jack stands under the front jacking points. Drain the crankcase oil.
3. Remove the lower nuts for the engine mounts. On 140 series models, remove the steering rods from the pitman arm and relay arm with a puller.
4. Place a hydraulic floor jack beneath the front axle member. Remove the rear bolts of the front axle member and replace them with two longer auxiliary bolts (UNC ½-13 x 114). Remove the front bolts for the front axle member and lower the hydraulic jack, allowing the axle member to hang on the auxiliary bolts.
5. Remove the plug for the oil temperature gauge, if so equipped, and the reinforcing bracket at the flywheel.
6. Unscrew the oil pan bolts and lower the pan. Remove the old gasket and clean the surfaces of the cylinder block and oil pan. Remove any sludge or foreign matter that has accumulated at the bottom of the pan.
7. Using a new gasket, position the pan to the cylinder block and install the oil pan bolts. Torque the bolts to 6-8 ft/lbs.
8. Install the plug for the oil temperature guage, if so equipped. Position the reinforcing bracket to the cylinder block and flywheel casing and install the bolts finger-tight. Snugly tighten the bolts for the flywheel casing and then those for the cylinder block.
9. Raise the hydraulic jack, raising the front axle member, and tighten the front bolts. Remove the auxiliary bolts and install the original rear bolts of the front axle member.
10. Install the lower nuts for the front engine mounts. On 140 series models, connect the steering rods at the pitman arm and relay arm, and fit the nuts.
11. Remove the jack stands and hydraulic jack. Lower the vehicle. Remove the lifting apparatus.
12. Insert the dipstick. Fill the crankcase with the proper amount and grade of oil.
13. Start the engine and check for leaks.

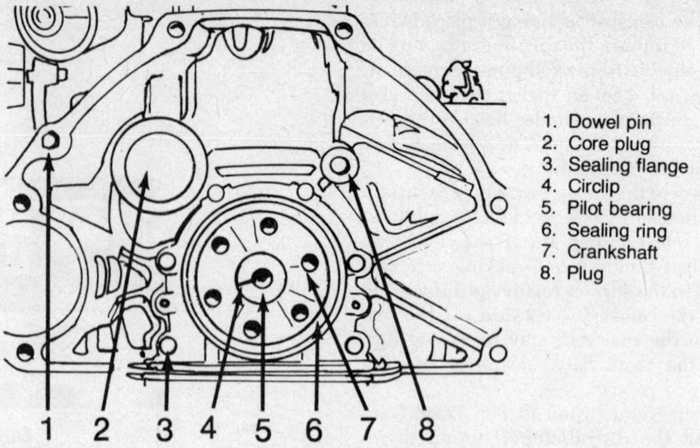

Rear of engine, B20, 30

1975 240 Series (B20)

On these models, the motor mounts are located high in the chassis, permitting more than 2 inches of clearance between the bottom of the oil pan and the steering linkage and suspension. Therefore, oil pan removal is a simple matter of unbolting the attaching bolts. Always use a new gasket when installing the pan. A few daubs of oil resistant sealer on the gasket at the front and rear main seals will help prevent oil leaks. Tighten the attaching bolts to no more than 6-8 ft/lbs of torque in a diagonal criss cross pattern.

B21F

1. Attach a chain/pulley hoist to the lifting eye on the thermostat housing.
2. On air conditioned models, remove the compressor from its bracket to gain access to the motor mount.
3. Remove the retaining bolts for the left (drive side) motor mount at the cylinder block.
4. Drain the crankcase.
5. Remove the splash guard.
6. Raise the engine slightly.
7. Remove the left motor mount from the chassis.
8. Remove the engine-to-clutch housing brace.
9. Remove the oil pan retaining bolts. Tap the pan loose, swivel and remove.
10. Reverse the removal procedure to install.

B21F Late 79-81

A new oil pan was introduced in May 1979. It is deeper with a lowered oil baffle. It is

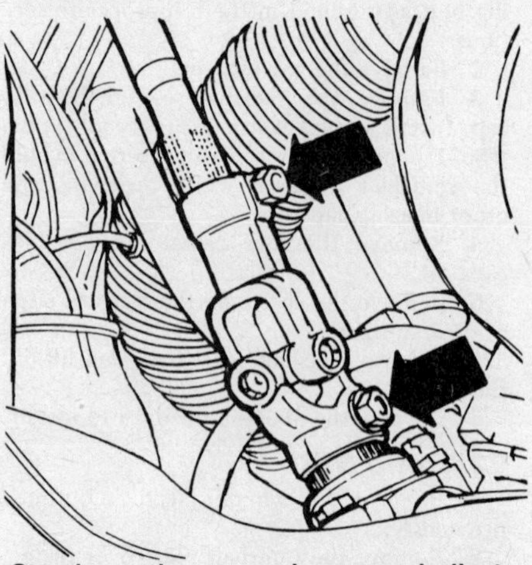

Steering yoke removal; arrows indicate retaining nuts

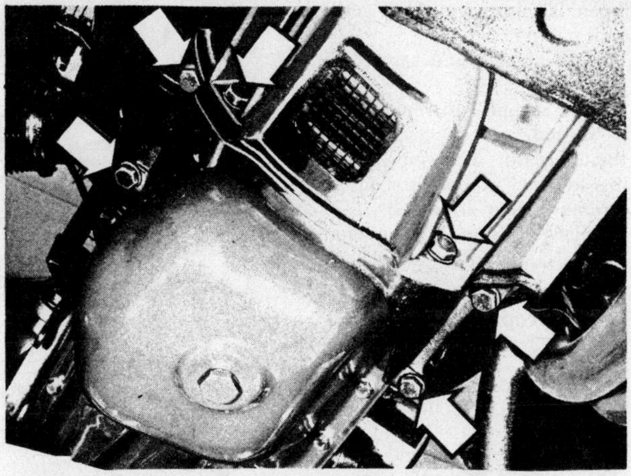

Pan support bracket B21 engine

designed to insure oil supply during rapid acceleration and provide less engine noise.

1. Jack up your vehicle and support it with jack stands.
2. Drain the engine oil.
3. Remove the splash guard.
4. Remove the engine mount retaining nuts.
5. Remove the lower bolt and loosen the top bolt on the steering column yoke.
6. Slide the yoke assembly up on the steering shaft.
7. Jack up the front of the engine.
8. Remove the retaining bolts for the front axle crossmember.
9. Remove the crossmember.
10. Remove the left engine mount.
11. Remove the pan support bracket.
12. Remove the pan bolts and remove the pan.
13. Installation is the reverse of removal.

NOTE: Always use a new pan gasket when reinstalling the pan.

The following torque specifications are needed: Pan bolts 8 ft/lbs. Steering yoke lower bolt, 18 ft/lbs.

B27F and B28F

1. Remove the splash guard.
2. Drain the crankcase.
3. Remove the oil pan retaining bolts. Swivel the pan past the stabilizer bar and remove.
4. Reverse the above to install.

REAR MAIN OIL SEAL REPLACEMENT

1. Remove the transmission, clutch (if so equipped), and flywheel from the engine. Remove the two oil pan bolts from the bottom of the sealing flange, and loosen two more on each side so that the pressure on the sealing flange is reduced.
2. Remove the sealing flange retaining bolts and pull off the sealing flange and old gasket. Press out the sealing ring in the flange with a drift.
3. Make sure that the sealing surfaces of the flange are clean. Also make sure that the oil drain hole is not blocked by the oil pan gasket.
4. Oil the sealing ring. Install the sealing ring, sealing flange, and new gasket to the block, but do not tighten the bolts.
5. Center the flange with special SVO tool 2439 (for B 20), or 2817 (for B 30). Rotate the sleeve while tightening the flange bolts. Adjust the position of the flange if the sleeve should rotate easily if the flange is properly positioned. Make sure that the sealing flange is seated against the underside of the block.
6. Install a new felt ring and replace the washer and circlip. Install the sealing ring into its groove with the centering sleeve.
7. Install and tighten the oil pan bolts. Install the flywheel, clutch (if so equipped), and transmission.

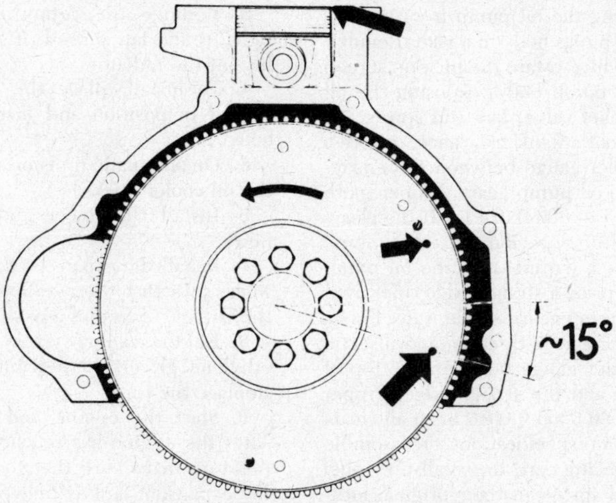

Flywheel installation B21 engine

D24

1. Disconnect the negative battery terminal.
2. Remove the transmission, (see the transmission removal section).
3. Remove all but one starter bolt to keep it from falling out.
4. Remove the clutch and pressure plate assembly (if so equipped).
5. Remove the pilot bearing.
6. Remove the flywheel.

NOTE: Use special tool #5112 or a suitable replacement to keep the flywheel from turning while removing the bolts.

7. Remove the oil seal with a screwdriver.
8. Check the contact surfaces on the seal holder and crankshaft.
9. Installation is the reverse of removal.

When reinstalling a new seal use special tool #5208 available from Volvo or a suitable replacement. Coat the seal with oil before installation. Torque the flywheel bolts to 55 ft/lbs. Use a liquid sealer on the bolts prior to installing them.

B27F and B28F

1. Disconnect the negative battery terminal.
2. Remove the transmission (see the transmission removal section).
3. Remove the clutch and pressure plate (if so equipped).
4. Remove the flywheel (drive plate on automatic transmissions).

NOTE: On automatic transmissions remove the crankshaft spacer.

5. Remove the two rear pan bolts.
6. Remove the bolts in the seal housing and then the housing.

NOTE: Gently remove the housing so as not to damage the oil pan gasket.

7. Use special tool #5107 to remove the old seal and install the new one. This tool is available from Volvo or use a suitable replacement.
8. Installation is the reverse of removal.

The following torque specifications are needed; Flywheel 33-37 ft/lbs, Seal housing 7-11 ft/lbs.

B21F

1. Disconnect the negative battery terminal.
2. Remove the transmission (see the transmission removal section).
3. Remove the clutch and pressure plate (if so equipped).
4. Remove the pilot bearing snap-ring and remove the bearing.
5. Remove the flywheel or driveplate which ever is applicable.

NOTE: Be careful not to press in the activator pins for the timing device.

6. Remove the rear oil pan brace.

7. Remove the two center bolts from the pan that bolt into the seal housing.
8. Loosen two bolts on either side of the two in the seal housing.
9. Remove the six seal housing bolts, and remove the seal housing.

NOTE: Be careful not to damage the oil pan gasket when removing the seal housing.

10. Remove the seal using special tool #2817 or a suitable replacement.
11. Installation is the reverse of removal.

NOTE: Use a new gasket on the seal housing and coat the seal with oil prior to installation.

The following torque specifications are needed: Flywheel 47-54 ft/lbs. When installing the flywheel turn the crankshaft to bring the No. 1 piston to top dead center. The lower flywheel pin should be installed approximately 15° from the horizontal and opposite the starter. Install the bolts.

Oil Pump

REPLACEMENT

B20 and B30

The oil pump must be removed with the engine removed from the car.

1. Crank the engine to TDC at No. 1 cylinder. Remove the distributor.
2. Drain the crankcase and remove the oil pan. Remove the oil pump retaining bolts.
3. Disconnect the oil pump from the delivery tube by unscrewing the connecting flange. Be careful not to discard the rubber sealing rings from the sealing flange.
4. Unscrew the connecting flange and remove the delivery tube from the block.
5. To install, fit the delivery tube with sealing rings to the oil pump, and then to the block. If the tube does not seat properly in the block, it may be tapped lightly with a soft mallet. Tightly screw the connecting flanges.
6. With No. 1 cylinder at TDC, install the oil pump drive and distributor. Make sure that the shaft goes down into its groove in the pump shaft. Tighten the oil pump retaining bolts.
7. Install the oil pan with a new gasket and fill the crankcase.

B21F

1. Remove the oil pan as described previously.
2. Remove the two oil pump retaining bolts, and pull the delivery tube from the block.
3. When installing, use new sealing rings at either end of the delivery tube.

NOTE: On 1980 and later, the oil pump has been redesigned to position the suction pipe and strainer further forward in the oil pan.

B27F and B28F

The oil pump body is cast integrally with the cylinder block. It is chain driven by a separate sprocket on the crankshaft and is located behind the timing chain cover. The pick-up screen and tube are serviced by removing the oil pan. To check the pump gears or remove the oil pump cover:

1. Remove the air cleaner and valve covers.
2. Loosen the fan shroud and remove the fan. Remove the shroud.
3. Loosen the alternator, air pump, power steering pump, and AC compressor (if so equipped) and remove their drive belts.
4. Block the flywhell from turning, and remove the 36 mm bolt and the crankshaft pulley.

NOTE: Do not drop key into crankcase.

5. Remove the timing gear cover (25 bolts).
6. Remove the oil pump drive sprocket and chain.
7. Remove the oil pump cover, and gears.
8. Reverse the removal procedure to install.

D24

The oil pan can not be removed without removing the engine. Refer to the Engine Removal section. This procedure requires quite a few special tools, and without them this job should be left to your Volvo dealer or a professional mechanic.

1. Remove the engine from the car.
2. Remove the oil pan and the oil suction pipe.
3. Remove the front timing belt cover, timing belt, vibration damper, and lower timing belt cover.

NOTE: Do not allow the crankshaft to turn when disconnected from the camshaft. If this should happen the fuel injection timing must be reset.

4. Remove the crankshaft gear and seal with a puller.
5. Remove the timing belt inner shield.
6. Remove the oil pump bolts and remove the pump.

NOTE: The oil pump can not be repaired. It must be replaced as a unit.

7. When installing the oil pump the triangular mark on the pump outer gear must face the oil pump rear cover.
9. Installation is the reverse of removal.

OIL PUMP CLEARANCE

After removing the oil pump from the engine, place the pump body in a vise. Remove the four bolts which retain the pick-up screen housing to the pump body, exposing the oil pump gears, relief valve, ball and spring. To measure the tooth flank clearance, insert a proper size feeler gauge between the engaging teeth of the oil pump gears. Proper tooth flank clearance is 0.006-0.014 in. If the clearance is not within specifications the pump must be replaced. To measure the oil pump gear end-float, place a straightedge ruler over top of the two pump gears so that it lies flat on the pump housing at both ends, and insert a proper size feeler gauge between the top of the pump gear and the straightedge. Proper gear end float is 0.0008-0.0040 in. If all clearances are within specifications, reassemble the oil pump taking care to install the relief valve, ball, and spring in their original locations.

1. Pump body
2. Spring for relief valve
3. Gear
4. Valve ball
5. Hole for oil pipe

Oil pump—B20, 21, 27

ENGINE COOLING

Radiator

REMOVAL AND INSTALLATION

1. Remove the radiator and expansion tank caps, disconnect the lower radiator hose, and drain the cooling system.
2. Remove the expansion tank and hose, and drain the coolant. Remove the upper radiator hose. On cars with automatic transmissions, disconnect and plug the transmission oil cooler lines at the radiator.
3. Remove the retaining bolts for the radiator and fan shroud, if so equipped, and lift out the radiator.
4. To install, place the radiator and fan shroud in position and install the retaining bolts.
5. On automatic transmission cars, connect the oil cooler lines.
6. Install the lower and upper radiator hoses.
7. Install the expansion tank with its hose. Make sure that the overflow hose is clear of the fan and is free of any sharp bends.
8. Fill the cooling system with a 50 percent ethylene glycol, 40 percent water solution. Replace the caps.
9. Start the engine and check for leaks. After the engine has reached operating temperature make sure that the coolant level in the expansion tank is between the maximum and minimum marks.

Water Pump

REMOVAL AND INSTALLATION

B20, B30

1. Drain the cooling system and remove the radiator as previously described.
2. Loosen the fan belt by slackening the alternator adjusting bolt. Remove the fan.
3. Remove the housing bolts from the water pump. Carefully remove the aluminum housing from the engine along with all the old gasket material. Remove the sealing rings.
4. To install, position the water pump assembly to the block, using a new housing gasket and water resistant sealer, and making sure that the sealing rings on the upper side of the pump are seated fully. Press the pump upward against the cylinder head extension to seat the rings.
5. Hand-tighten the housing bolts until snug. Do not tighten the bolts more than ½ turn further to avoid cracking the housing or breaking the bolts.
6. Install the fan and adjust the (drive) belt tension.
7. Install the radiator as previously described. Fill the cooling system.
8. Start the engine and check for leaks.

B21F

1. Remove the overflow tank cap. Drain the cooling system by opening the cylinder block drain cock (beneath the exhaust manifold) and disconnecting the lower radiator hose.
2. Remove the fan and fan shroud.
3. Remove the alternator and air pump drive belts. Remove the water pump pulley.
4. Remove the timing belt cover.
5. Remove the lower radiator hose.
6. Remove the retaining bolt for the coolant pipe (beneath exhaust manifold) and pull the pipe rearward.
7. Remove the six retaining bolts and lift off the water pump.
8. Clean the gasket contact surfaces thoroughly, and use a new gasket and O-rings (especially between the cylinder head and top of water pump).
9. Reverse Steps 1-7 to install.

B27F and B28F

1. Remove the front and main sections of the intake manifold.
2. Remove the overflow tank cap and drain the cooling system.
3. Disconnect both radiator hoses. On automatic transmission cars, disconnect the transmission cooler lines at the radiator. Disconnect the fan shroud. Remove the radiator and fan shroud.
4. Remove the fan.
5. Remove the hoses from the water pump to each cylinder head.
6. Remove the fan belts. Remove the water pump pulley.
7. Loosen the hose clamps at the rear of the water pump.
8. Transfer the thermal time sender and temperature sensor to the new pump.
9. Remove the water pump from the block (three bolts).
10. Transfer the thermostat cover, thermostat, and rear pump cover to the new pump.
11. Reverse the removal procedure to install.

D24

1. Drain the radiator.
2. Remove the splash gear under the engine.
3. Remove the expansion tank.
4. Remove the top and bottom radiator hoses.

NOTE: On cars with automatic transmissions remove the cooler lines from the radiator.

5. Remove the radiator (and shroud if so equipped).
6. Remove all the drive belts.
7. Remove the fan with the spacer and pulley.
8. Remove the front timing gear cover.
9. Disconnect the cold start device.
10. Loosen screw #1 and push the lever forward, rotate the lever 90° and push it backward against the stop.

NOTE: Do not touch the second screw. If it becomes loosened, the cold start device must be reset on a test bench.

11. Remove the injection pump plug and install a dial indicator gauge with a measuring range of 0-.118 in.

NOTE: This gauge must have adapter #5194, available from Volvo attached to it.

12. Set the gauge to approximately .078 in.
13. Set the Number 1 cylinder to top dead center.
14. The marking on the injection pump gear should coincide with the marking on the injection pump bracket.
15. The flywheel timing mark should be at zero.
16. Turn the engine ¼ turn past zero and then back to zero again. This is done in order to place slack in the timing belt on the drive side. Otherwise the engine setting would be incorrect.

NOTE: The gauge must not move during the remainder of the work. If it does the engine must be completely retimed.

17. Loosen the water pump bolts to release the belt tension.
18. Remove the timing bolt from the camshaft gear.
19. Remove the camshaft gear.
20. Remove the vibration damper.
21. Remove the lower belt guard.
22. Loosen the bracket for the fan and alternator.
23. Remove the lower retaining bolt and move the bracket away from the engine.
24. Remove the inner belt shield and water pump.
25. Installation is the reverse of removal.

NOTE: Grease the O-ring before installing it in the water pump.

The following torque specifications are needed; Vibration damper screws 15 ft/lbs, crankshaft center bolt 255 ft/lbs, camshaft gear 33 ft/lbs, pump setting 0.0256-0.0287 in.

Thermostat

REMOVAL AND INSTALLATION

1. Disconnect the lower radiator hose and drain the cooling system.
2. Remove the two bolts securing the thermostat housing to the cylinder head and carefully lift the housing free.
3. Remove all old gasket material from the mating surfaces and remove the thermostat.
4. Test the operation of the thermostat by immersing it in a container of heated water. Replace any thermostat that does not open at the correct temperature.
5. Place the thermostat, with a new gasket, in the cylinder head. Fit the thermostat housing to the head and hand-tighten the two bolts until snug. Do not tighten the bolts more than ¼ turn past snug.
6. Connect the lower radiator hose and replace the coolant.

EMISSION CONTROLS

PCV System

Volvos have been equipped with positive crankcase ventilation (PCV) systems to control crankcase vapors since the early 1960s. The present system is a closed one; it is sealed to the atmosphere. A metal filter located inline

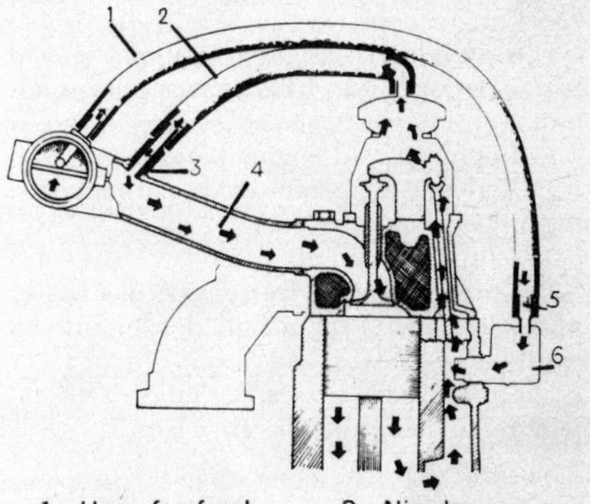

1. Hose for fresh air supply
2. Hose for crankcase gases
3. Nipple
4. Inlet duct
5. Flame guard
6. Oil trap

Positive crankcase ventilation system—B20F

between the fresh air source and the crankcase prevents engine backfire from reaching the crankcase and oil from being drawn into the induction system.

Evaporative Control System

All post-1969 model Volvos have been

equipped with an evaporative control system to prevent unburnt fuel vapors in the fuel tank from escaping into the atmosphere. An expansion tank above the fuel tank provides for thermal expansion of fuel vapors in warm weather.

NOTE: 1975 and later models have the expansion tank inside the fuel tank.

Those vapors which do not condense and return to the fuel tank are displaced and drawn into an activated charcoal canister in the engine compartment. The charcoal canister then absorbs and stores these fuel tank vapors when the engine is shut off or is idling. Throttling the engine causes the vapors to be drawn out of the canister into the inlet duct and then into the combustion chambers where they are burned.

NOTE: All 1980 and later B21F and B28F engines are equipped with a rollover valve. It is designed to close at 45° from horizontal. This valve will prevent a fuel spill through the carbon filter.

Exhaust Emission Control

Various measures have been taken to limit exhaust emissions of hydrocarbons, carbon monoxide, and more recently, oxides of nitrogen. Basic modifications include a distributor which retards the timing from its basic setting during idle, and the installation of a "hotter" 190° F thermostat in the cooling system. Fuel injection, which is inherently cleaner due to its precise regulation of the air-fuel mixture under varying rpm, engine load, and ambient temperature conditions, has been available since 1970.

PRE-HEATING AIR INTAKE

B28F

This system is designed to improve cold engine performance. Its advantages are as follows:

1. Improved cold engine performance.
2. Ambient temperatures do not influence engine performance.
3. Icing has been eliminated.

The pre-heating device consists of a heater on the left side of the manifold, a thermostat controlled air mixer, and hoses.

The thermostat senses the intake air temperature and controls the air mixture.

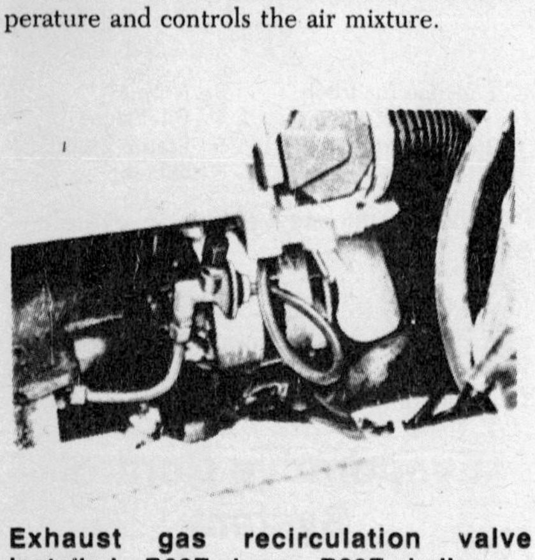

Exhaust gas recirculation valve installed—B20F shown, B30F similar

EXHAUST GAS RECIRCULATION SYSTEM

In order to control emissions of NO_x, 1975-79 models are equipped with an exhaust gas recirculation system.

NOTE: Models equipped with the Lambda Sond oxygen sensor system do not have EGR valves. These include 78-80 California and all 1980 and later vehicles.

The system consists of a metering valve, a tubular pipe running from the exhaust manifold to the valve, another tubular pipe running from the valve to the inlet duct, and a vacuum hose running from the valve's diaphragm to the inlet duct in front of the air regulator shutter. The valve permits a regulated amount of exhaust gases to enter the inlet duct and mix with the incoming intake air when the throttle is partly open. Every 12 months or 15,000 miles (1975-76), the system must be disassembled and cleaned. Fvery 30,000 miles (1975-76), the valve must be replaced with a new one.

On 1975 B20 engines, and 1976 B21 and B27 models sold in California, and all later models with EGR valves, the EGR system is modified to improve cold start driveability by the addition of a venturi vacuum amplifier system. The EGR system with vacuum amplifier works as follows: Venturi vacuum at the air intake is used to measure the total air

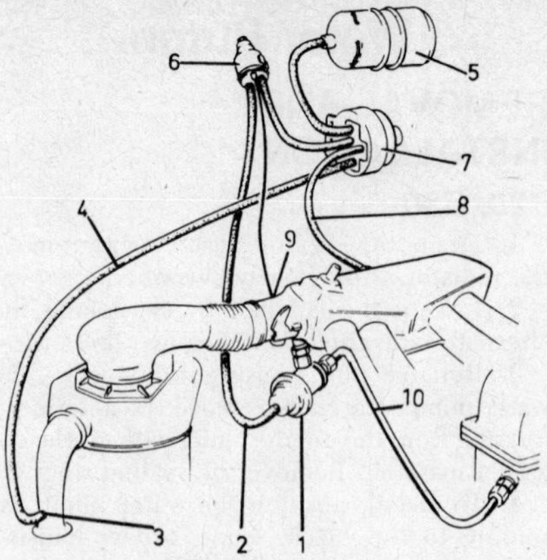

1. EGR valve
2. Vacuum control hose
3. Air venturi
4. Vacuum control hose
5. Vacuum tank
6. Vacuum valve
7. Vacuum amplifier
8. Vacuum supply hose
9. Micro switch
10. EGR-line

B20 EGR system with vacuum amplifier

flow. This weak vacuum signal controls the vacuum amplifier which regulates the EGR valve via a solenoid valve. The vacuum amplifier receives inputs both from the strong intake manifold source which is used as a power source, and from the weak air intake

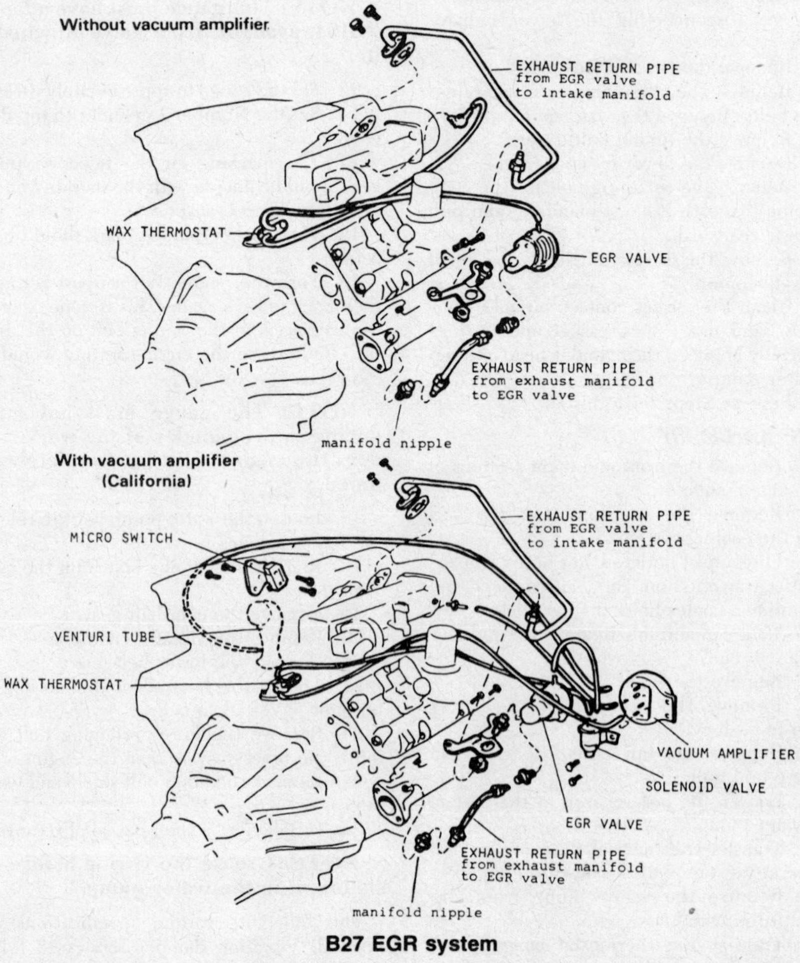

B27 EGR system

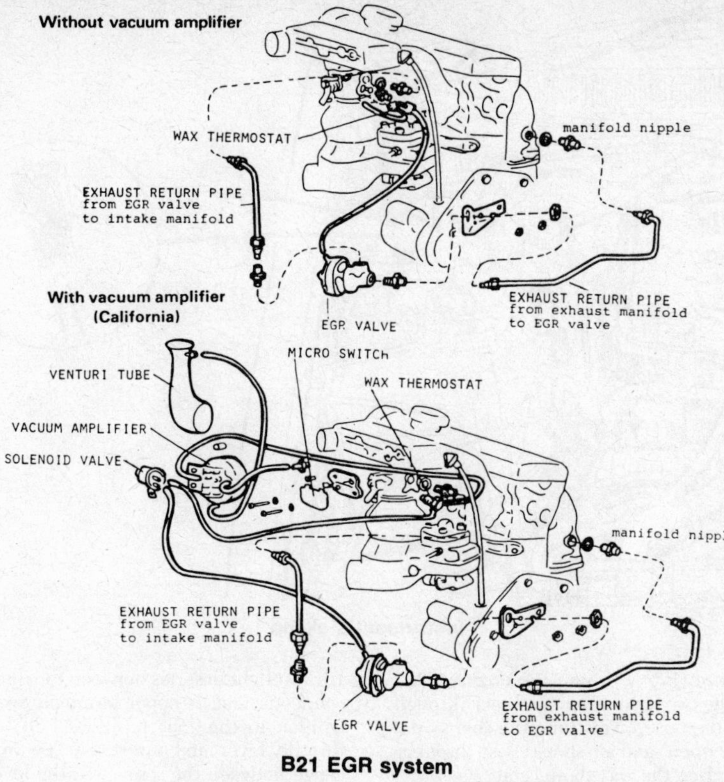

B21 EGR system

EGR, catalytic converter service reminder light reset button

source which is to be amplified. The intake vacuum is stored in the vacuum reservoir and is controlled by a check valve in the amplifier. This allows a generous amount of vacuum on tap regardless of variations in engine manifold vacuum. The amplifier then continues to supply adequate vacuum at higher speeds and moderate throttle openings, when manifold vacuum normally would drop to an insufficient amount. The EGR system functions as before, except that the exhaust gases are prevented from recirculation at idle and full throttle by a throttle angle sensing microswitch and an electrically operated solenoid valve, rather than simple vacuum as in 1973. On 1976 models and later, a wax thermostat blocks exhaust gas recirculation until the engine warms to 140° F.

Beginning with the 1975 model year, all Volvos are equipped with an EGR service reminder light which is actuated by the odometer at 15,000 mile intervals. The light may be reset by pressing a white button at the rear of the odometer.

AIR INJECTION REACTOR SYSTEM

All 1975-81 Volvos are equipped with an air injection reactor system except the diesel. Basically, the system injects filtered air into the exhaust manifold in order to reduce emissions of carbon monoxide and hydrocarbons. The oxygen in the air reacts with the exhaust gas and promotes further combustion in the exhaust manifold.

The system consists of an air pump (belt-driven), a diverter valve, a backfiring valve, and an air manifold which is attached to the exhaust manifold. Under normal conditions, air is pumped from the air pump via the diverter valve, the backfiring valve and the air manifold into the exhaust manifold ports. The air pump takes in filtered air which is then compressed and discharged to the diverter valve. The diverter valve sends the air through to the backfiring valve, except during deceleration. The diverter valve also releases some of the air into the atmosphere if the pressure is too great. The backfiring valve is a

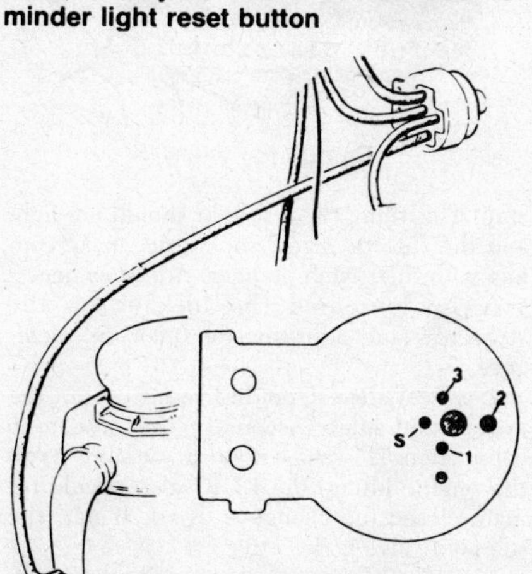

1. To air intake
2. To manifold
3. To vacuum reservoir
S. To solenoid

Vacuum amplifier connections—B20

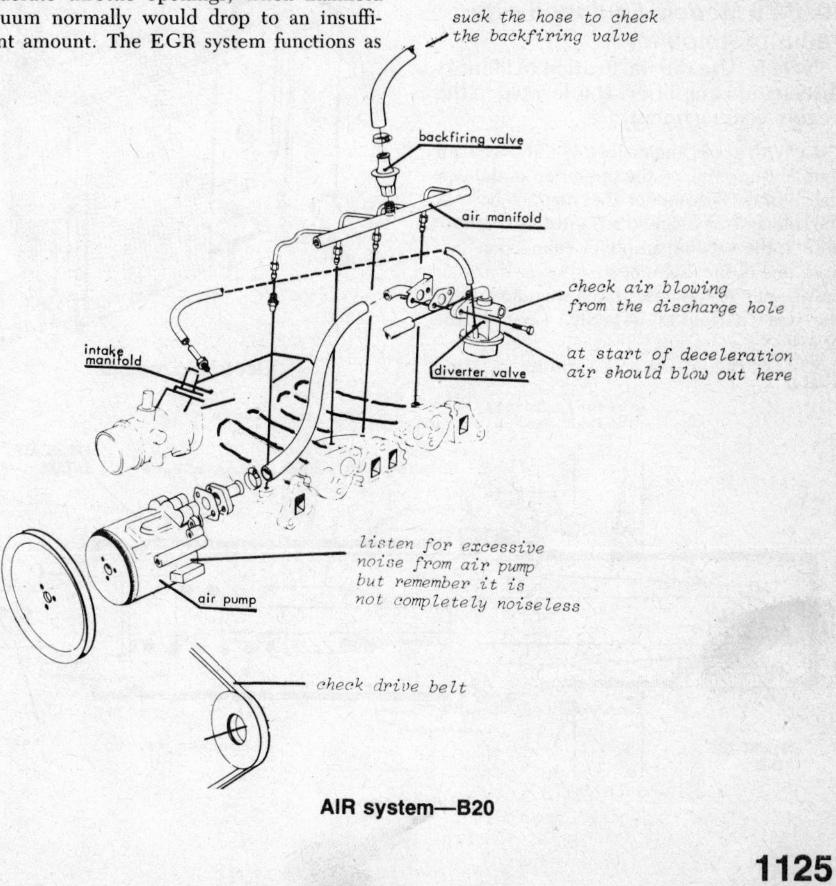

AIR system—B20

one-way valve which prevents the exhaust gases from flowing back towards the air injection components, but allows the pump air to pass into the air manifold and exhaust manifold.

CHECKING THE AIR SYSTEM

Service the AIR system every 15,000 miles. Make sure the drive belt is in good condition on the air pump. If the belt breaks, the backfire valve must be checked.

Make sure all attaching nuts and bolts for the air pump and bracket are secure.

To check the air pump, use the following procedure.

Start the engine and listen for excessive noise from the pump. Remember, though, that the air pump is not normally completely noiseless, and it can make a bit of a racket when its cold. Under normal circumstances, the noise rises in pitch as engine speed increases. Do not attempt to lubricate or repair the pump: it must be replaced.

To check the backfire valve, use the following procedure.

1. Disconnect the hose from the diverter valve.
2. Apply a vacuum to the hose: no air should come through. If it does, replace the backfire valve.

To check the diverter valve, use the following procedure.

1. Disconnect and plug the hose from the diverter valve.
2. Run the engine at idle. Air should only be coming out of point "A" in the illustration.
3. Increase the engine speed to 3000-3500 rpm, then quickly release the throttle. Air should now flow from points "B" in the illustration. If not, replace the diverter valve.

1976-79 Models Equipped with Vacuum Amplifier

NOTE: Use the illustration to identify the vacuum amplifier. It is located in the engine compartment.

1. With a cold engine (below 130° F coolant temperature), check the operation of the wax thermostat. Disconnect the vacuum hose at the solenoid valve and disconnect the vacuum hose at the vacuum amplifier connection "S". Suck one of the disconnected hoses. If any air passes, one of the hoses has a vacuum leak or the wax thermostat is faulty. Connect the hoses.
2. Start the engine and warm to operating temperature (176° F). Stop the engine. Disconnect the two hoses again, and suck through either of the hoses. This time the thermostat should be open, and air should pass through. If not, replace the wax thermostat.
3. Connect the hoses. Check the throttle position sensing micro-switch next. Connect a 12v test light in series between the upper wire connector and its upper terminal. Switch the ignition to the "on" position. Pull back the throttle lever and insert a 0.006 in. feeler gauge between the screw and the lever stop. When the lever is released and the throttle screw makes contact with the switch plunger, the test light should illuminate. This indicates that current is reaching the solenoid valve, the micro-switch is activating, and the fuse is good. Then, repeat by inserting an 0.008 in. feeler gauge between the screw and lever stop. This time, the test light should not light and the throttle screw should not make contact with the switch plunger. Adjust as necessary by loosening the locknut on the stopscrew and adjusting for 0.006 in. clearance.
4. Check the solenoid valve next. Start the engine and idle. Disconnect the hose from connection "1", and create a vacuum. With the engine idling, the EGR valve should remain closed (no change in rpm). If not, the solenoid valve is defective.
5. With the vacuum pump still connected, and engine idling, check that the vacuum reading does not change for 10 seconds. If the reading changes, this indicates a bad amplifier or leaking hoses.

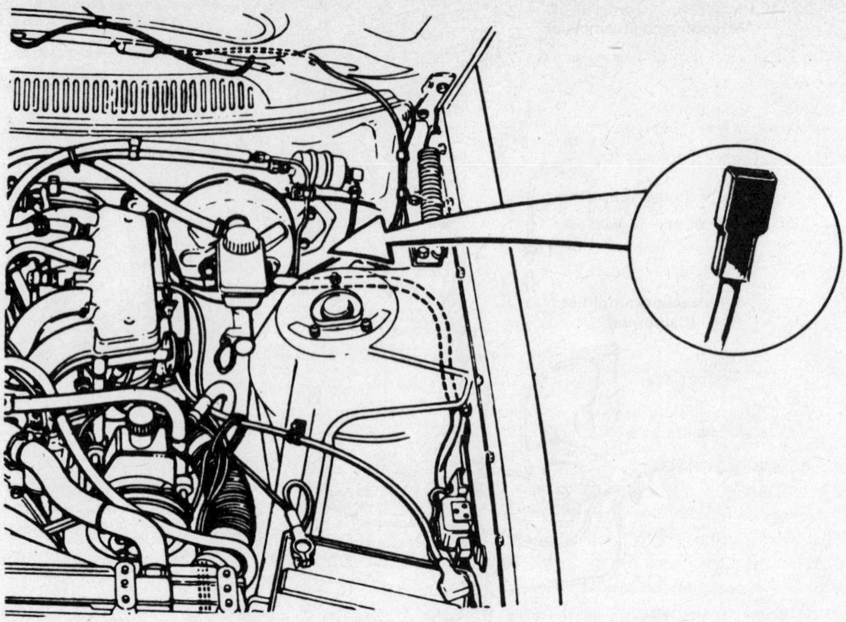

Instrument pick-up

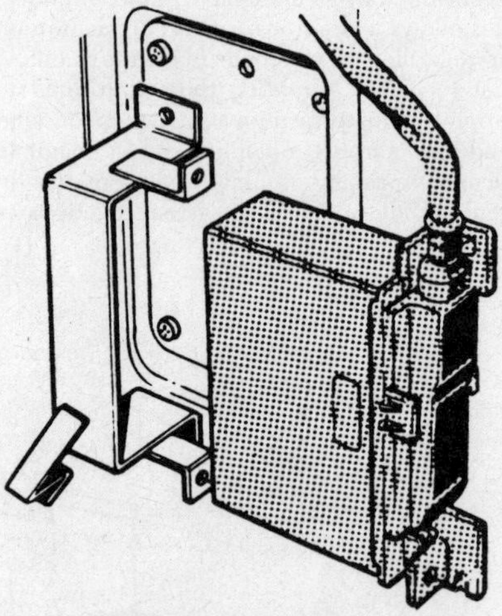

Electronic module

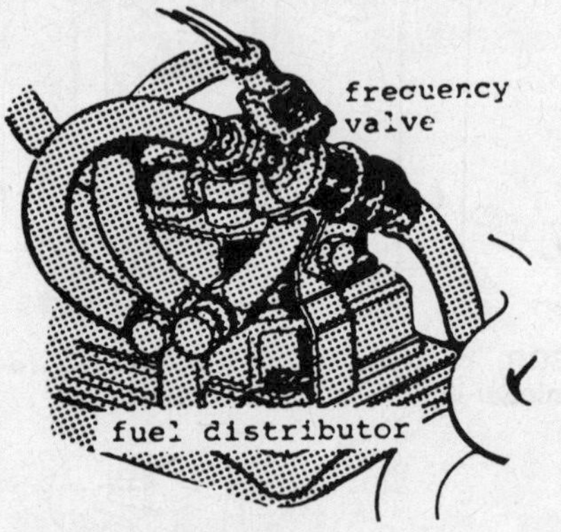

Frequency valve

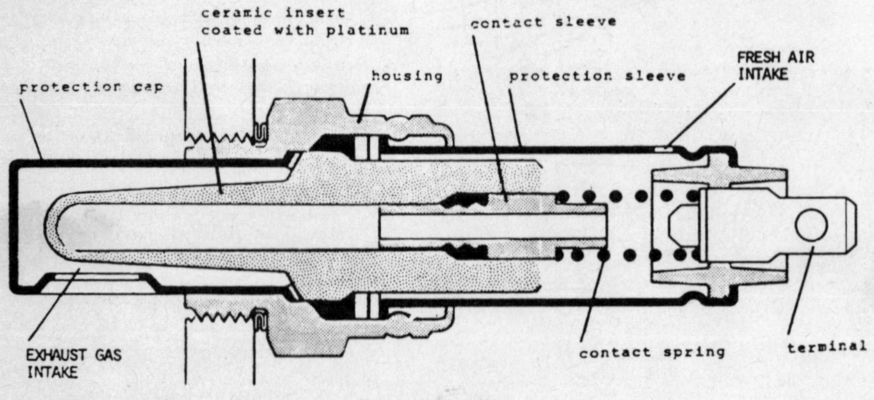

Oxygen sensor

6. Finally, with the engine idling, increase the rpm while observing the EGR valve. If the EGR valve rod does not open, check for a clogged venturi or leaking venturi vacuum hose. Then, suddenly release the throttle and check that the EGR valve rod closes. If not, the solenoid valve is faulty.

CATALYTIC CONVERTER SYSTEM

All 1975-81 Volvos are equipped with a catalytic converter. The converters are installted to further control emissions of carbon monoxide and hydrocarbons which have resisted the treatment of the air injection system.

The converter is installed in the exhaust system ahead of the muffler. The catalytic converter on 1980 and later B28F engines is located closer to the engine compartment. This design allows quicker warm-up and reduced emissions. The converter uses platinum and palladium metals in a substrate or beaded form as the catalyst. The catalyst and the oxygen supplied by the air pump then react with the exhaust gases producing harmless carbon dioxide and water vapor, as well as a minute amount of sulphur dioxide or sulphuric acid.

The 1977 California 240 series, all 1978-80 260 California series, all 1979 49 states 260 series and the 1979 49 states 242 GT are equipped with three way catalytic converters.

NOTE: All 1980 and later models use the three way catalytic converter.

The purpose of the three way catalytic converter is to neutralize carbon monoxide, hydrocarbons and oxides of nitrogen in the exhaust gases. The main difference between this catalytic converter and the oxidation converter is that the three way converter is able to process large amounts of oxides of nitrogen (NO_x), while the oxidation catalyst cannot.

The operating range of the three way catalyst is limited to a narrow band around the

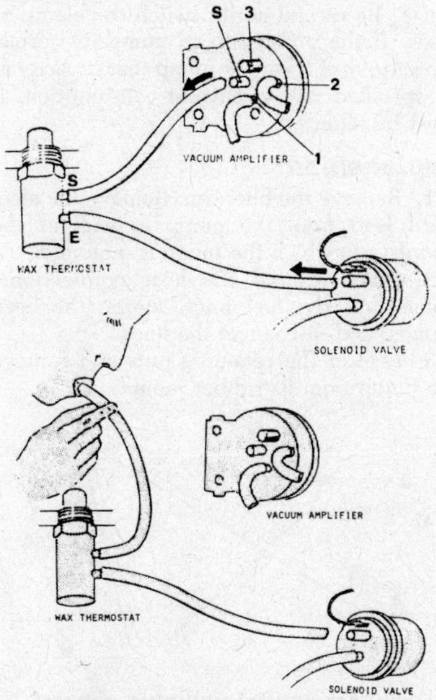

Checking wax thermostat

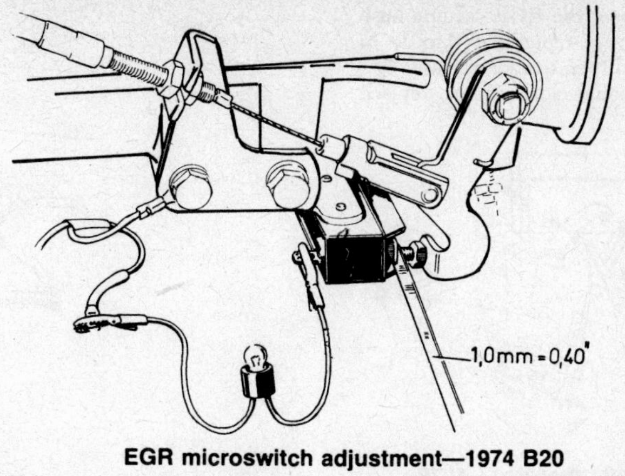

EGR microswitch adjustment—1974 B20

ideal air/fuel mixture for the engine. To keep the mixture within this narrow band, an oxygen sensor is used to monitor the amount of oxygen in the exhaust gases and fine tune the air/fuel mixture. See "Oxygen Sensor Feedback System (Lambda Sond)" for more information on the oxygen sensor system.

The converter is designed, if properly maintained, to last 50,000 miles as long as leaded gasoline is not used. The lead in gasoline will coat the catalytic substrate or beads, thereby preventing the reaction process, rendering the converter ineffective.

At 15,000 mile intervals, the retaining bolts for the converter must be checked for tightness. A service reminder light on the dashboard lights at 15,000 mile intervals. To extinguish the light, press the white reset button at the rear of the odometer.

NOTE: The 1980-81 diesel engine is not equipped with a catalytic converter.

OXYGEN SENSOR FEEDBACK SYSTEM (LAMBDA SOND)

This is a self-tuning engine controlled system, designed to reduce emissions and improve fuel economy. An exhaust gas sensor (oxygen sensor or lambda sensor) located in the exhaust manifold, monitors the composition of the exhaust gases leaving the engine. This analysis is fed into a closed loop feedback system. This continuously adjusts the air-fuel mixture to provide optimum conditions for combustion and efficient breakdown of all three major pollutants by a three-way catalytic converter.

The major components of the system are: the oxygen sensor, the electronic module and the frequency valve. The oxygen sensor is a platinum coated ceramic tube. It is located in the exhaust manifold. The inside is vented to the atmosphere while the outside is connected to the exhaust gas flow. The output from the sensor is fed to the electronic module. This device supplies a control current to the frequency valve. The frequency valve alters the flow of fuel in the CI system by activating a diaphragm in the fuel pressure regulating valve. The frequence valve, so called because it operates on a set frequency, functions during what is called its duty cycle. This duty cycle corresponds to the ratio of closed to open circuit impulses from the electronic module. The cycle can be measured in terms of degrees by using an ordinary ignition system dwell meter. The dwell meter is connected to an instrument pick-up connector located on a wire coming from the electronic module. The pick-up connector is located on the firewall, in the engine compartment to the left of the master cylinder. The duty cycle of the B21F system is 54° while that of the B27F system is 40-50°. The B28F (1980 and later) cycle is 49-59°.

NOTE: 1980 and later B28F engines have a micro-switch at the throttle cable pulley. It closes a circuit at full throttle and grounds the electronic module of the Lambda Sond allowing a richer mixture at full throttle.

All other tests on the system are made with extremely sophisticated equipment and should be performed by trained service men only.

If the oxygen sensor in the manifold is obviously damaged, it can be replaced by simply disconnecting it and unscrewing it from the manifold. When installing a new sensor, the threads must be coated with anti-seize compound. The unit should be torqued to 40 ft/lbs.

NOTE: The oxygen sensor should be replaced every 30,000 miles.

Component Testing and Adjustment

EGR SYSTEM CHECKING

49 States Models–B21, B27

1. With a cold engine, check the operation of the wax thermostat. Start the engine and idle. Manipulate the throttle by hand and check that the EGR valve rod does not move in and out. If it does, the thermostat is faulty. It should not operate the EGR valve until the coolant reaches 130-140° F.

2. With the engine warmed up (176° F), check that the EGR valve rod does move in and out when the throttle is opened and closed. If not, the wax thermostat, hoses or EGR valve may be at fault.

3. Stop the engine. Disconnect the vacuum hose from the EGR valve. Blow through the hose. If no air passes, the wax thermostat is faulty. If air does pass, either the hose is incorrectly installed or the EGR valve is defective.

4. Finally, connect the EGR vacuum hose and start the engine. Open the throttle to 3000-4000 rpm and then quickly release. The EGR valve rod should close. If not, replace the EGR valve.

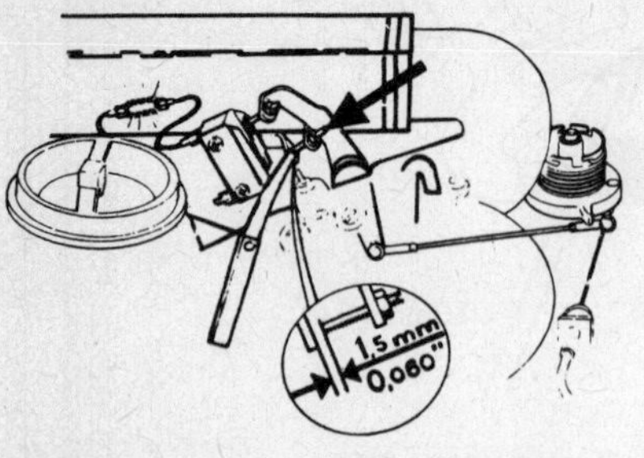

Checking micro-switch—1976

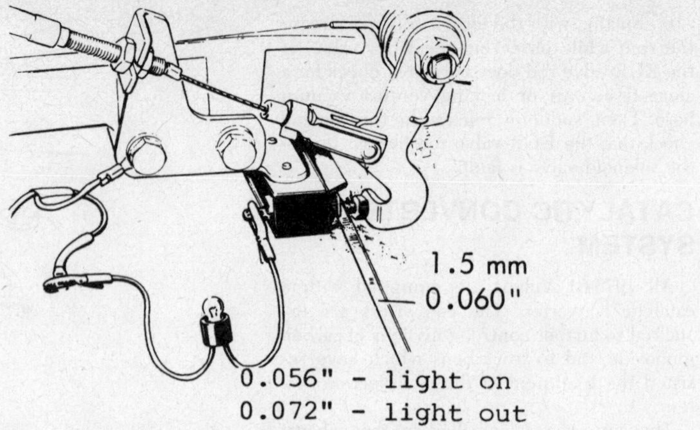

EGR microswitch adjustment—1975 B20

California Models–B21, B27 and B28F

1. With a cold engine (below 130° F coolant temperature), check the operation of the wax thermostat. Disconnect the vacuum hose at the solenoid valve and disconnect the vacuum hose at the vacuum amplifier connection "S". Suck one of the disconnected hoses. If any air passes, one of the hoses has a vacuum leak or the wax thermostat is faulty. Connect the hoses.

2. Start the engine and warm to operating temperature (176° F). Stop the engine. Disconnect the two hoses again, and suck through either of the hoses. This time the thermostat should be open, and air should pass through. If not, replace the wax thermostat.

3. Connect the hoses. Check the throttle position sensing micro-switch next. Connect a 12v test light in series between the upper wire connector and its upper terminal. Switch the ignition to the "on" position. Pull back the

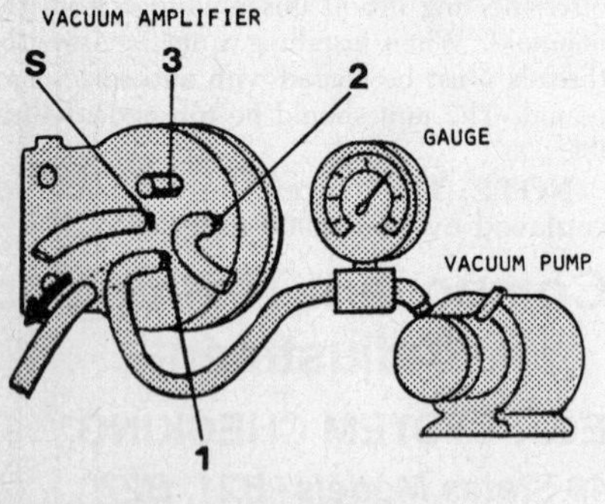

Checking solenoid valve

throttle lever and insert a 0.006 in. feeler gauge between the screw and the lever stop. When the lever is released and the throttle screw makes contact with the switch plunger, the test light should illuminate. This indicates that current is reaching the solenoid valve, the micro-switch is activating, and the fuse is good. Then, repeat by inserting an 0.008 in. feeler gauge between the screw and lever stop. This time, the test light should not light and the throttle screw should not make contact with the switch plunger. Adjust as necessary by loosening the locknut on the stop-screw and adjusting for 0.006 in. clearance.

4. Check the solenoid valve next. Start the engine and idle. Disconnect the hose from connection "1", and create a vacuum. With the engine idling, the EGR valve should remain closed (no change in rpm). If not, the solenoid valve is defective.

5. With the vacuum pump still connected, and engine idling, check that the vacuum reading does not change for 10 seconds. If the reading changes, this indicates a bad amplifier or leaking hoses.

6. Finally, with the engine idling, increase the rpm while observing the EGR valve. If the EGR valve rod does not open, check for a clogged venturi or leaking venturi vacuum hose. Then, suddenly release the throttle and check that the EGR valve rod closes. If not, the solenoid valve is faulty.

Component Service

POSITIVE CRANKCASE VENTILATION SYSTEM

The only service required for the PCV system is the cleaning of the hoses, nipples, and metal filter every 15,000 miles (1975-79), 60,000 miles 1980 and later gasoline engines; 15,000 miles 1980-81 diesel engines.

FUEL EVAPORATIVE CONTROL SYSTEM

The only items requiring service in the evaporative control system are the foam plastic filter in the bottom of the charcoal canister. The canister filter is replaced every 45,000 miles (1975-81).

FUEL SYSTEM

NOTE: All Volvos manufactured for sale in the U.S. since 1975 have been equipped with fuel injection.

Fuel Pump

All pumps are electrical.

NOTE: Volvo states that a no-start condition may occasionally occur when the car has not been started for an extended period of time. This may be due to the fuel pump sticking in one position because of foreign matter entering the pump, or corrosion forming on the rotor shaft or commutator and brushes. It is, therefore, very important to clean the fuel tank pick-up screen every 12 months or 12,000 miles to prevent corrosion causing water condensation and foreign matter from entering the pump. As an additional corrosion prevention measure, add an alcohol solution or "dry gas" to the fuel, especially in winter months. If, however, the pump does become "stuck" in one position for any of the above reasons, it may be "unstuck" by lightly rapping on the pump casing with a length of hardwood such as a hammer handle, while the ignition is switched on.

NOTE: 1980-81 fuel tank filters require replacement at 60,000 miles.

Testing and Adjustment

No adjustments may be made to the fuel pump. If the pump is not functioning properly, it must be discarded and replaced. To check the function of the fuel pump, the pump should be connected to a pressure gauge. Be careful not to switch the electrical leads. If the pump fails to pump its normal capacity, or if it cannot pump that capacity at its specified rate of current consumption, it must be replaced.

Replacement

1. Remove the filler cap. Remove the electrical lead from the pump as well as the template to which the pump is mounted.

2. Clean around the hose connections. Pinch shut the fuel lines, loosen the hose clamps, and disconnect the lines.

3. Loosen the retaining nuts and remove the pump from its rubber mounts.

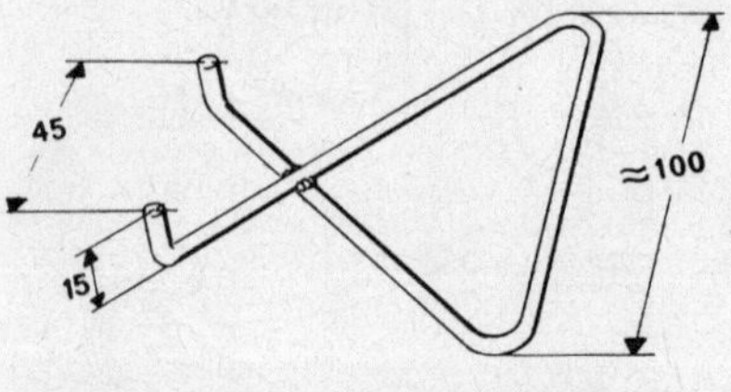

Puller for control unit plug contact

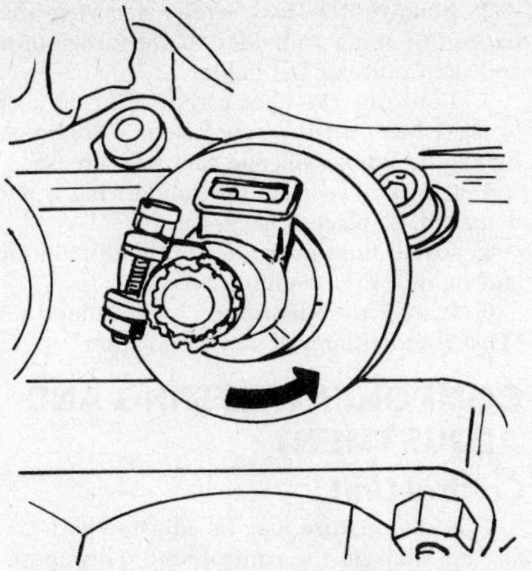

Injector removal, electronic injection

4. Install the new pump on its rubber mounts and tighten the retaining nuts.
5. Reconnect the fuel lines, tighten the hose clamps, and remove the pinchers.
6. Mount the template beneath the car and connect the electrical lead.
7. Start the engine and check for leaks.

Bosch Electronic Fuel Injection

All 1975 164 series are equipped with this system. The complete system contains the following components: electronic control unit (brain), electrical fuel pump, fuel filter, fuel pressure regulator, fuel injectors, cold-start valve, inlet duct (for intake air), throttle valve switch, auxiliary air regulator, intake air temperature sensor, coolant temperature sensor, intake air pressure sensor, and the triggering contacts in the ignition distributor.

FUEL INJECTION SYSTEM PRECAUTIONS

Due to the highly sensitive nature of the Bosch electronic fuel injection system, the following special precautions must be strictly adhered to in order to avoid damage to the system.

1. Do not operate the engine with the battery disconnected.
2. Do not utilize a high-speed battery charger as a starting aid.
3. When using a high-speed battery charger to charge the battery while it is installed in the vehicle, at least one battery cable must be disconnected.
4. Do not allow the control unit to be subjected to temperatures exceeding 185° F, such as when the vehicle is being banked after painting. If there is a risk of the temperature exceeding 185° F, the control unit must be removed.
5. The engine must not be started when the ambient temperature exceeds 158° F, or damage to the control unit will result.
6. The ignition must be in the off position when disconnecting or connecting the control unit.
7. When working on the fuel system, take care not to allow dirt to enter the system. Small dust particles may jam fuel injectors.

COMPONENT REPLACEMENT

The fuel injection system is repaired simply by replacing the defective component. There are adjustments that can be made to the pressure regulator, throttle valve, throttle valve switch, throttle stopscrew, and the fuel mixture. To make resistance checks, use an ohmmeter, and for continuity checks, a 12 V test light. If the control unit is defective, return it to a qualified repair agency and install a new unit.

Control Unit

1. Disconnect the defroster hose, remove the control unit bracket retaining screws, and lower the unit to the floor, move the passenger's front seat all the way back, unscrew the bolt securing the seat's front, move the seat forward while folding the seat bottom to the rear, remove the control unit retaining screws, and draw out the unit.
2. Remove the screw for the cap holding the cable harness to the unit. Pull out the plastic cover strip.

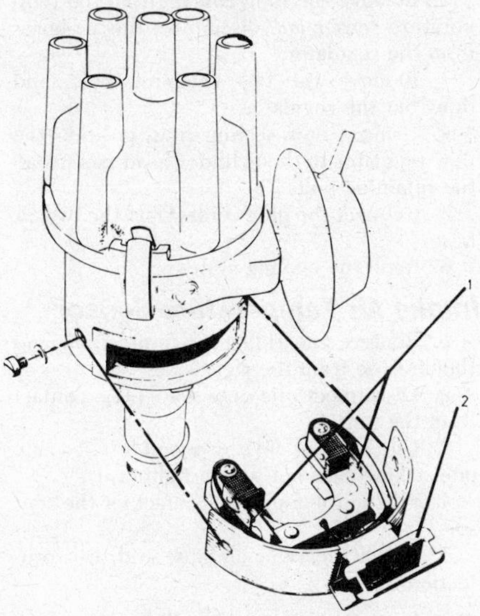

1. Triggering contacts
2. Electrical connection

Distributor with control device—B30F

3. Construct a puller out of $^5/_{64}$ in. welding wire to disconnect the main plug contact. Insert the puller in the rear of the control unit and pull out the plug carefully.
4. Press the plug contact firmly into the new or reconditioned control unit. Fit the plastic cover strip, retaining cap, and screw.
5. Fit the control unit into place and install its retaining screws.

Pressure Regulator

If the pressure regulator cannot be adjusted to 28 psi with its adjusting nut, it must be replaced.

1. Place pinch clamps on the three fuel hoses connected to the regulator.
2. Loosen the hose clamps and remove the hoses.
3. Remove the regulator from its bracket and replace it with a new one.
4. Connect the fuel hoses to the new regulator, tighten the hose clamps, and remove the pinch clamps.
5. Start the engine and check for fuel leaks.

Fuel Injectors

1. Remove the air cleaner.
2. Pinch shut the fuel hose to the header pipe.
3. Loosen the hose clamps for the injectors and lift up the header pipe.
4. Remove the plug contacts from the injectors. Disconnect the cable harness from the distributing pipe.
5. Turn the lock rings on the injectors counterclockwise so that they loosen from their bayonet fittings. Lift out the injectors.
6. Place the new injectors, with new washers and rubber sealing rings, in position and secure them by turning the lock-rings clockwise.
7. Connect the cable harness at the distributing pipe. Connect the plug contacts to the injectors.
8. Place the header pipe in position, and tighten the hose clamps. Remove the pinch clamps.
9. Install the air cleaner.

Cold-Start Valve

1. Remove the air cleaner.
2. Pinch shut the fuel line to the valve.

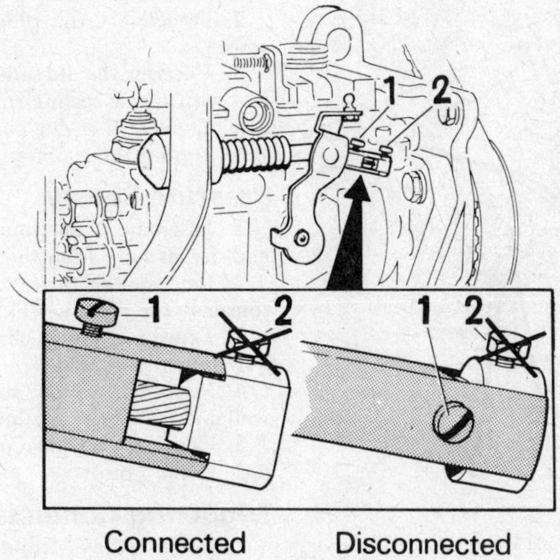

Cold start device

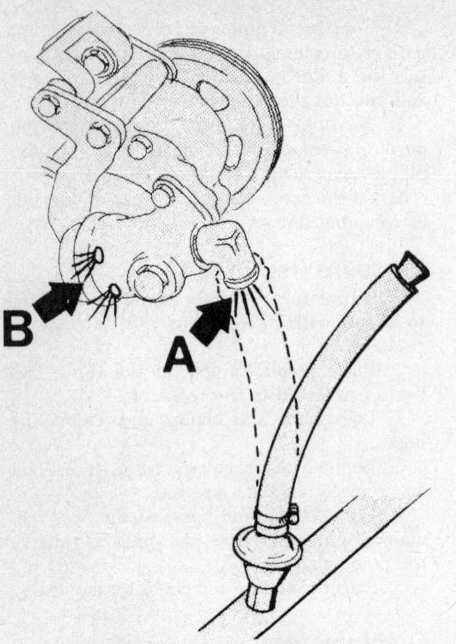

Diverter valve check

3. Remove the plug contact and the fuel hose from the valve.
4. Remove the two retaining screws and the cold-start valve from the inlet duct.
5. Place the new cold-start valve in position with packing and install the retaining screws.
6. Connect the plug contact and fuel hose to the valve. Remove the pinch clamp.
7. Install the air cleaner.

Thermal Timer

1. Drain the cooling system.
2. Disconnect the plug contacts and unscrew the thermal timer from the cylinder head.
3. Install a new timer and connect the plug contacts.
4. Refill the cooling system.

Throttle Valve Switch

1. Disconnect the plug contact from the switch. Remove the two retaining screws and pull the switch straight out of the inlet duct.
2. Fit the new switch to the inlet duct and install the retaining screws. Connect the plug contact.

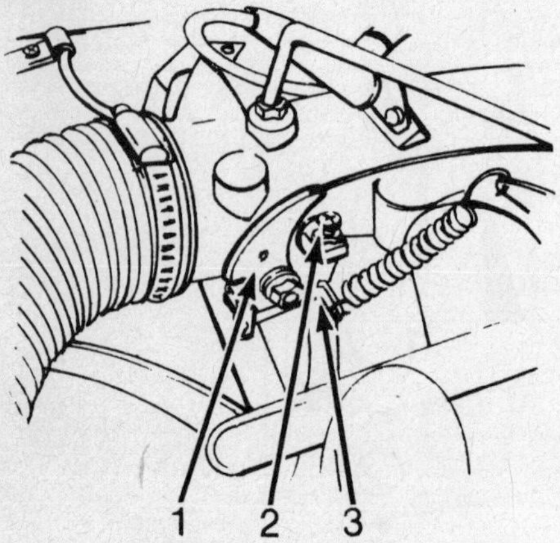

1. Locknut
2. Stop screw
3. Stop on throttle valve spindle

Throttle valve adjustment, B20F

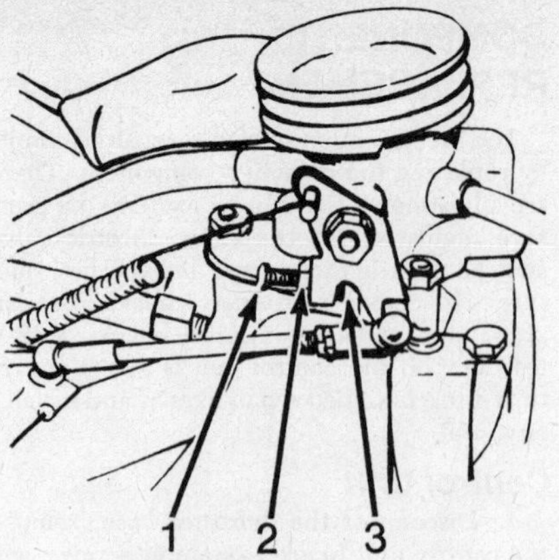

1. Stop screw
2. Locknut
3. Stop on valve spindle

Throttle valve adjustment, B30F

3. Adjust the switch as outlined in "Throttle Valve Switch Adjustment."

Auxiliary Air Regulator

1. Drain the cooling system.
2. Remove the plug contact from the temperature sensor and disconnect the air hoses from the regulator.
3. Remove the two retaining bolts and draw out the regulator.
4. Using a new sealing ring, position the new regulator to the cylinder head and install the retaining bolts.
5. Connect the plug contact and the two air hoses.
6. Refill the cooling system.

Intake Air Temperature Sensor

1. Remove the right drip protection, and the air hose from the right side.
2. Disconnect the four-way plug contact from the sensor.
3. Unscrew the old sensor and install a new one, taking care not to overtighten it.
4. Plug in the four-way contact for the sensor.
5. Install the right air hose and drip protection.

Coolant Temperature Sensor

1. Drain a portion of the cooling system so that the coolant level in the radiator and engine is below the temperature sensor.
2. Disconnect the plug contact from the sensor.
3. Unscrew the old sensor and install a new one with a new sealing ring.
4. Connect the plug contact.
5. Top up the cooling system.

Pressure Sensor

1. Disconnect the four-way plug contact and the air hose from the sensor.
2. Remove the three screws retaining the sensor to the right wheel housing.
3. Transfer the attaching bracket to the new pressure sensor.
4. Position the new sensor to the wheel well and install the retaining screws.
5. Connect the plug contact and the air hose to the sensor.

Triggering Contacts

1. Remove the distributor as oulined under "Distributor Removal and Installation."
2. Remove the two screws securing the triggering contacts holder to the distributor and then pull out the holder.
3. Lubricate the fiber pieces of the contact breaker lever on the new holder with Bosch Ft 1V4 or similar silicone cam lobe grease.
4. Check to see that the rubber ring is not damaged. Replace if necessary.
5. Install the new holder in the distributor and tighten the retaining screws.
6. Install the distributor as outlined in "Distributor Removal and Installation."

COMPONENT TESTING AND ADJUSTMENT

Control Unit

The idle mixture may be adjusted with the slotted knob on the control unit. This operation is best performed with the use of a CO meter. Refer to the "Fuel Injection System Idle Mixture Adjustment" for details.

The control unit may be tested only with the help of sophisticated test equipment available, again, only at the dealer level.

Pressure Regulator

The regulator may be adjusted with its adjusting nut. Pinch and disconnect the flexible fuel hose between the pressure regulator and the header pipe and insert a tee fitting and pressure gauge. Tighten the fuel connections and start the engine. Slacken the locknut and adjust the pressure to 28 psi. If the regulator cannot be adjusted properly, it must be replaced. Remove the tee fitting and gauge, and connect the fuel hoses.

Throttle Valve

The throttle valve may be adjusted with its stopscrew near the mouth of the inlet duct. Release the stopscrew locknut for the throttle valve switch, and back off the screw several turns so that it does not lie against the throttle valve spindle stop. Make sure that the valve is completely closed. Screw in the stopscrew so that it contacts the spindle stop. At this point, turn the stopscrew ¼-⅓ additional turn and tighten the locknut. Check to see that the switch does not jam in the closed position. Proceed to adjust the throttle valve switch as follows.

NOTE: The stopscrew must not be used for idle adjustment.

Throttle Valve Switch

The throttle valve switch may be adjusted with an ohmmeter. Connect the ohmmeter to the control unit (contacts 14 and 17 for four-cylinder, and contacts 9 and 14 for six-cylinder). Loosen the screws slightly so that the switch may be rotated. Scribe a mark at the upper switch screw on the inlet duct if one is not there already. Close the throttle valve by turning the switch clockwise as far as it will go. Then, observing the ohmmeter, carefully turn the switch counterclockwise until the ohmmeter registers 0 (zero). At this point, the switch is turned a further 1° counterclockwise (½ graduation mark at upper screw), and both switch screws are tightened. Check to make sure that the ohmmeter reading rises to infinity when the throttle valve opens approximately 1°.

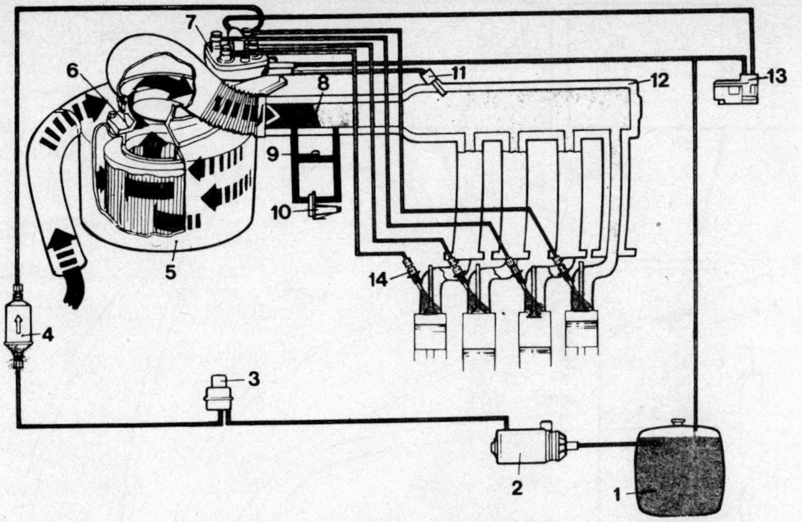

1. Fuel tank
2. Fuel pump
3. Fuel accumulator
4. Fuel filter
5. Air cleaner
6. Air flow sensor
7. Fuel distributor
8. Throttle
9. Idle adjustment screw
10. Auxiliary air valve
11. Cold start injector
12. Intake manifold
13. Control pressure regulator
14. Injector

Continuous injection principle of operation—B20F

Auxiliary Air Regulator

To check the operation of the auxiliary air regulator, start the engine and allow it to reach operation temperature (176° F). Make a note of the idle speed and then disconnect the hose between the inlet duct and the regulator. While covering the hose opening with your hand, check to see that the idle speed does not drop significantly over the first reading. A drop in idle speed indicates a leak in the regulator, requiring its replacement.

Continuous Fuel Injection

Continuous fuel injection is standard on all 240 and 260 models. It differs from electronic fuel injection in that injection takes place continuously; controlled through variation of the fuel flow rate through the injectors, rather than variation of the fuel injection duration. This system has no electronic computer. It is an electro-mechanical system that will provide suitable air/fuel mixtures to accommodate differing driving conditions.

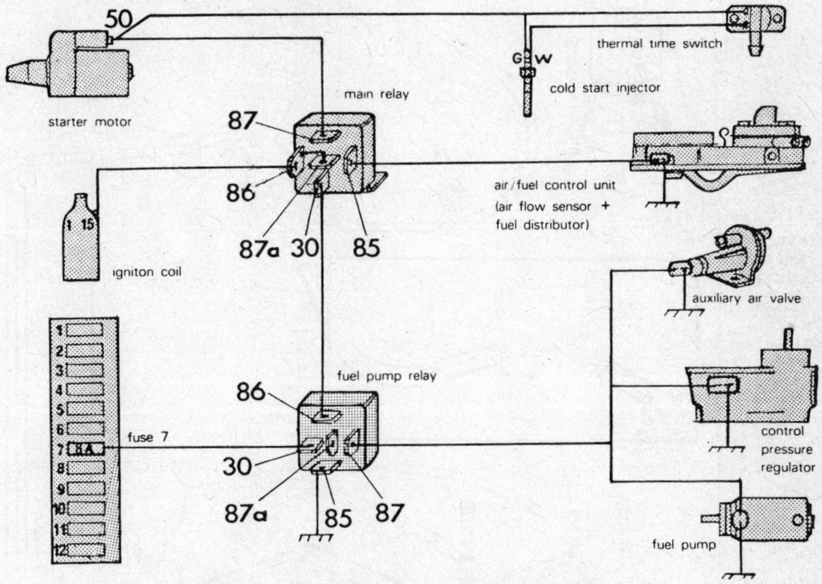

Continuous injection system electrical schematic

1. Injector
2. Auxiliary air valve
3. Idle adjustment screw
4. Cold start injector
5. Intake manifold
6. Air flow sensor
7. Fuel distributor
8. Air cleaner
9. Thermal time switch
10. Control pressure regulator
11. Fuel filter
12-13. Safety relay and pump relay

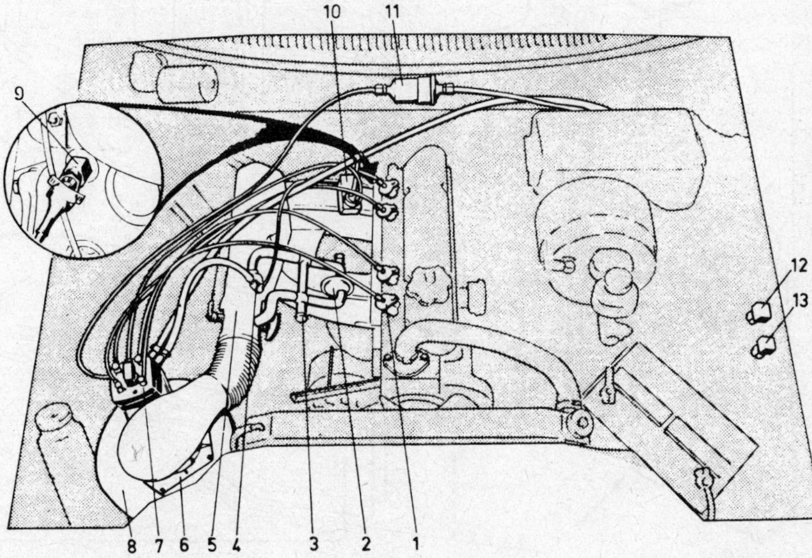

Continuous injection system installation—B20F

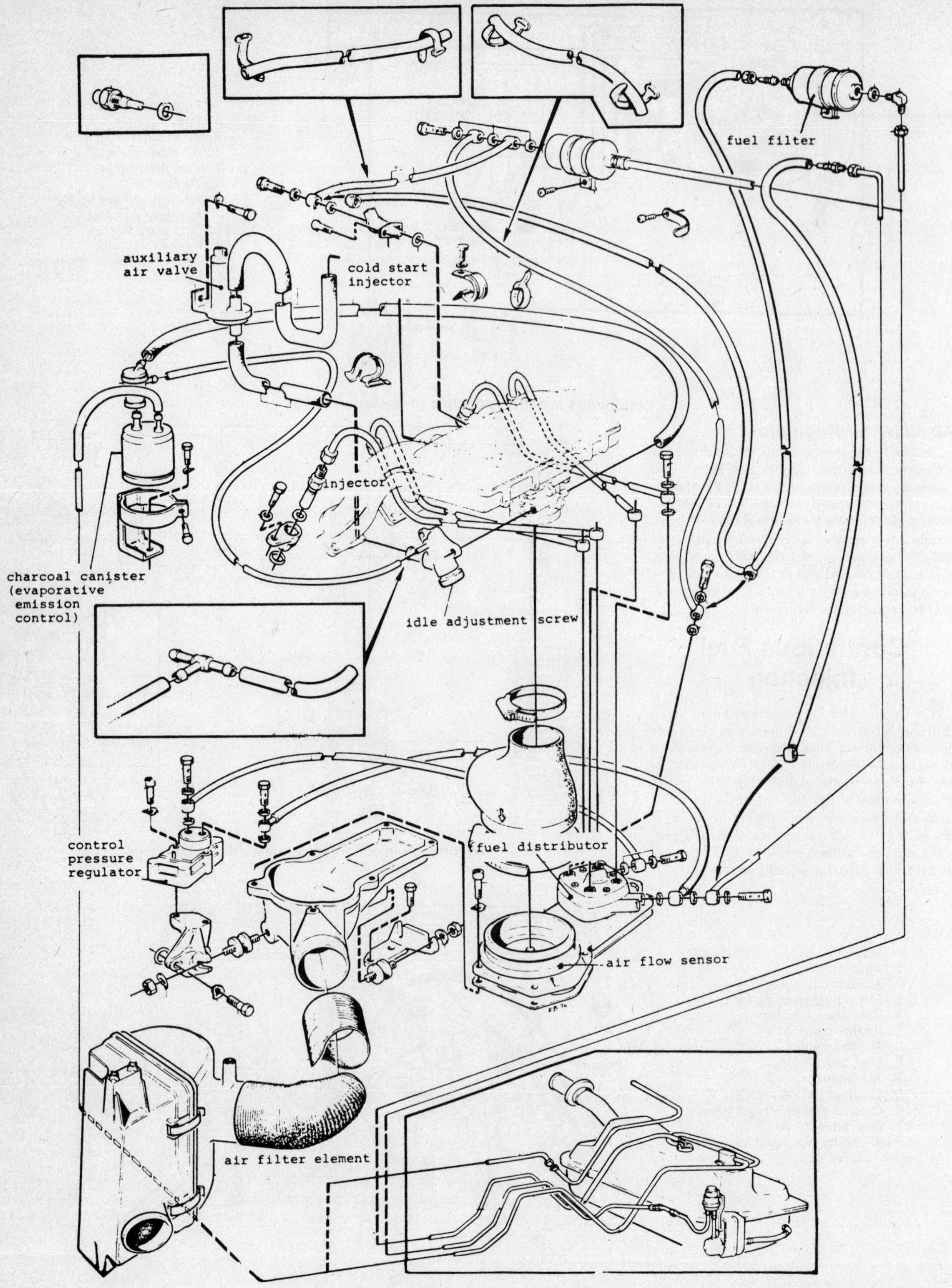

Continuous injection system components—B21

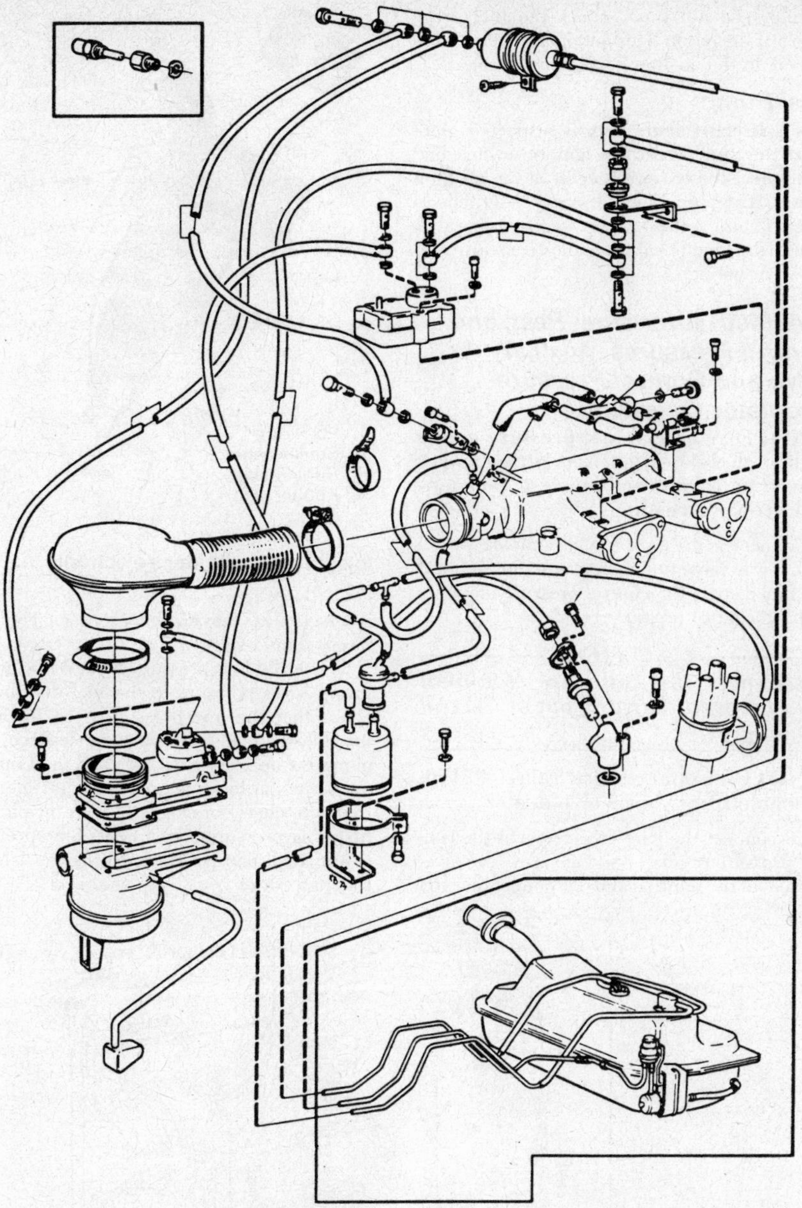

Continuous injection system components—B20

The complete system consists of the following components: air/fuel control unit (housing both air flow sensor and fuel distributor), electric fuel pump (and fuel pressure accumulator), fuel filter, control pressure regulator, continuous fuel injectors, auxiliary air valve, cold-start injector, thermal time switch, main relay, and a fuel pump relay.

The heart of the system is the air/fuel control Unit. It consists of an air flow sensor and a fuel distributor. Intake air flows past the air cleaner and through the air venturi raising (four cylinder) or lowering (V6) the counterbalanced air flow sensor plate. The plate is connected to a pivoting lever which moves the control plunger in the fuel distributor in direct proportion to the intake air flow.

The fuel distributor, which controls and distributes the amount of fuel to the injectors consists of a line pressure regulator, a control plunger, and (4 or 6) pressure regulator valves (one for each injector).

NOTE: There is no CO adjustment on the 1980 and later fuel distributor.

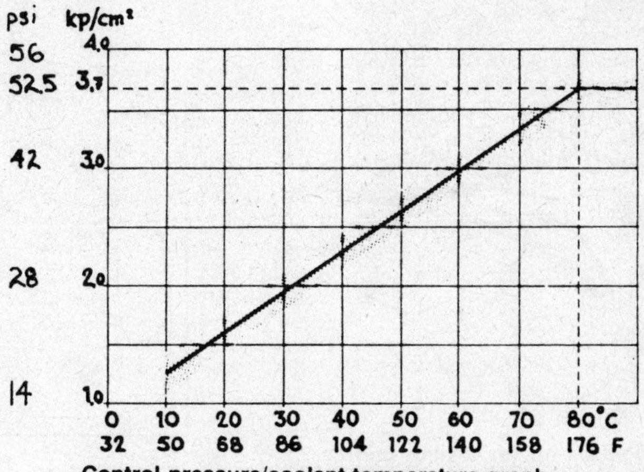

Control pressure/coolant temperature graph

The line pressure regulator maintains the fuel distributor inlet pressure at about 65 psi., and will recirculate fuel to the tank if pressure exceeds this valve. The control plunger, which is connected to the air flow sensor plate, controls the amount of fuel available to each of the pressure regulator valves. The pressure regulator valves maintain a constant fuel pressure differential (1.4 psi) between the inlet and outlet sides of the control plunger. This is independent of the amount of fuel passing through the valves, which varies according to plunger height.

The injectors themselves are spring loaded and calibrated to open at 47-51 psi. They are not electrically operated as on the older electronic fuel injection system.

The control pressure regulator, located on the intake manifold, acts to regulate the fuel/air mixture according to engine temperature. When the engine is cold, the control pressure regulator richens the mixture (4-5 minutes max.). This is accomplished in the following manner; a certain amount of fuel is bled off into a separate control pressure system. The control pressure regulator maintains this fuel at about 52.5 psi. The regulator is connected to the upper side of the fuel distributor control plunger. When the engine temperature is below operating parameters, a bi-metal spring in the regulator senses this and reduces the fuel pressure on top of the plunger. This allows the plunger to rise further and channel more fuel to the regulator valves and injectors, thereby richening the mixture. When the engine warms, the bi-metal spring in the regulator increases the pressure back to 52.5 psi, leaning the mixture back to its normal operation ratio. On V6 models, a vacuum feature is added to the regulator, whereby low vacuum situations, such as acceleration, temporarily lowers the control pressure and richens the mixture. At idle, full throttle, and steady state conditions, the vacuum is high and the mixture returns to normal.

The auxiliary air valve provides extra air to mix with the richer mixture during warm-up, thus raising the engine speed and improving cold-start driveability. The auxiliary air valve, which also has a temperature sensitive bimetal spring, works directly with the control pressure regulator. At cold startup, the valve is fully open. As the engine warms, an electric coil slowly closes the valve (4-5 minutes max.), blocking off the extra air and fast idle speed.

The cold start injector, located on the inlet duct, sprays extra fuel into the intake air stream during starter motor operation when the engine coolant temperature is below 95° F. It has a maximum spraying duration of 12 seconds.

The thermal time switch, located on the cylinder head, actuates the cold start injector. It has a bi-metal spring which senses coolant temperature and an electric coil which limits the cold start injector spray to 12 seconds.

The fuel accumulator, located adjacent to the fuel tank mounted electric fuel pump, has a check valve which keeps residual fuel pressure from dropping below 28 psi when the engine or fuel pump are shut off. Therefore, the system is always pressurized, preventing vapor lock in hot start situations.

COMPONENT TESTING AND ADJUSTING

Air-Fuel Control Unit

The air-flow sensor plate adjustment is critical. The distance between the sensor plate and the plate stop must be 0.002 in. The plate must also be centered in the venturi, and must not contact the venturi walls. Loosen the plate center screw to adjust. The plate should not bind, and although (due to the control pressure) the plate will offer some resistance when depressed, it should return to its rest position when released.

To check the air-flow sensor contact switch, depress the sensor plate by hand. The fuel injectors should buzz, and the fuel pump should activate. If the pump operates, but the injectors do not buzz, check the fuel pressures. If the pump does not operate, check for a short in the air-flow sensor connector.

Fuel Pump

If a defective fuel pump is suspected, perform this test. With the ignition switch on, disconnect the wire connector at the air-flow sensor. The pump should work. If not, check fuse #7, and voltage across auxiliary air valve terminals. Live terminals indicate a faulty fuel pump or wiring.

Fuel Distributor Line, Rest, and Control Pressures, Auxiliary Air Valve and Control Pressure Regulator Operation

NOTE: A special fuel pressure gauge with a three position tee fitting is required to isolate the line, rest, and control pressure readings.

Connect a pressure gauge and tee fitting with 3-way valve in-line between the center of the fuel distributor (control pressure fuel line) and the control pressure regulator.

CAUTION

Disconnect the coil wire (terminal 15) to prevent burning out of the coil windings.

NOTE: Connect test relay #5170, available from your Volvo dealer.

Disconnect the wire connectors at the control pressure regulator and auxiliary air valve. Switch on the ignition and disconnect the wire connector at the air-flow sensor. The fuel pump should start.

Check the line pressure first. With the tee fitting lever pointing to the fuel distributor, check that the line pressure is 64-75 psi. If insufficient, check fuel lines for leakage, fuel pump for delivery capacity (25.3 fluid ounces in 30 sec.), or low line pressure adjustment. If too high, check for clogged fuel return line or high line pressure adjustment. Line pressure is adjusted along with rest pressure later in this procedure.

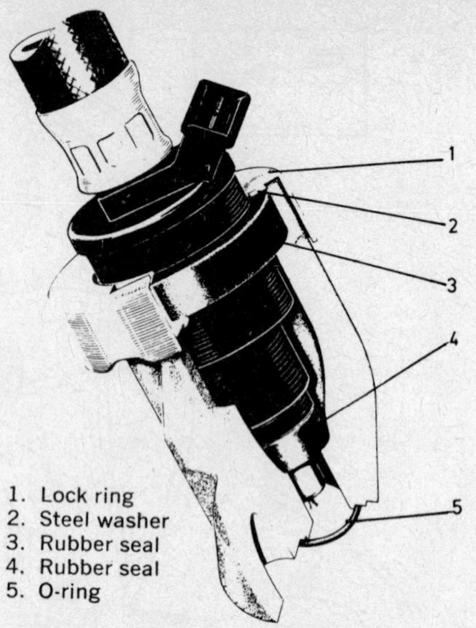

Injector with holder—electronic fuel injection

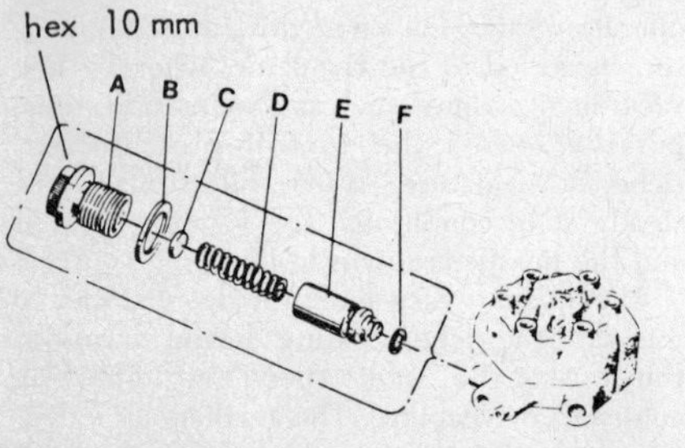

Line and rest pressure regulator plunger is located on side of fuel distributor. Add or remove shims "C" to adjust pressure

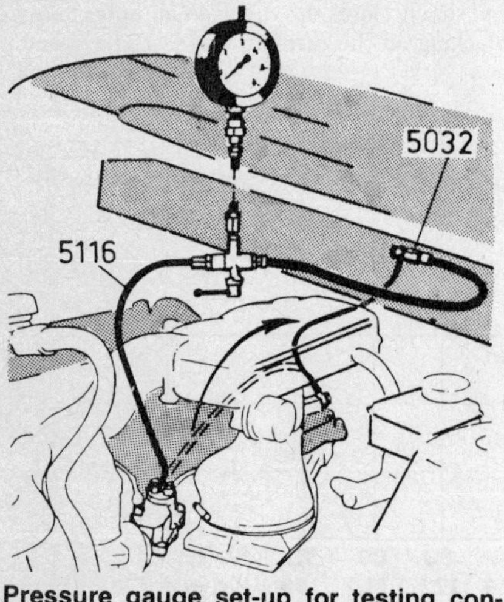

Pressure gauge set-up for testing continuous injection system—B21

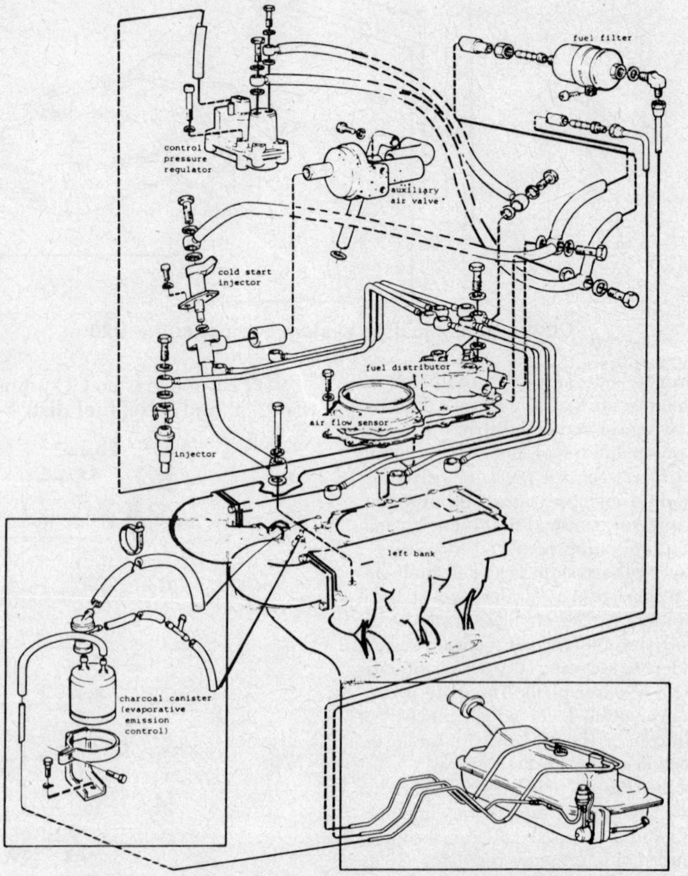

Continuous injection system components—B27

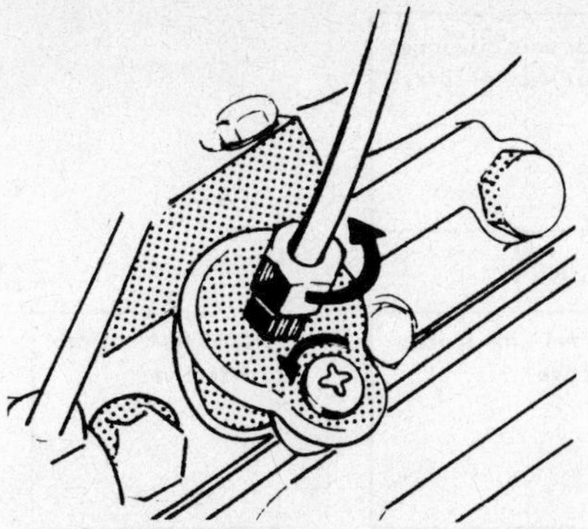

B20F injector removal. Note right-hand threads on pipe fitting

Check the control pressure next. With the tee fitting turned at a right angle to the hoses, check that the control pressure corresponds to those values given in the control pressure/coolant temperature graph. Depending on coolant temperature, the control pressure will be somewhere between 18-55 psi, lower for cool temperatures, higher for warm temperatures. If the control pressure is insufficient, try a new pressure regulator. If the pressure is too high, check for a clogged fuel return line, or try a new control pressure regulator. Reconnect the control pressure regulator electrical connector. After 4-5 minutes, the pressure should decrease to 44-50 psi. If not, disconnect the electrical connector at the control pressure regulator and check with a 12v test light across the terminals. No voltage indicates a defective wire. Voltage indicates a possible faulty regulator. Then, check across the terminals with an ohmmeter. Resistance indicates corroded terminals. No resistance indicates a defective control pressure regulator.

NOTE: The 1980 B28F has two heater resistors wires in parallel in the circuit. Correct resistance 32-38 ohms below 55° F, 16.5-19.5 ohms above 65° F.

The vacuum function of the control pressure regulator on the V6 engine is checked later in this test.

The auxiliary air valve is checked next. Disconnect the auxiliary air valve hoses. Using a dentist's mirror and a flashlight, check that the valve is partly open at room temperature. Then, reconnect the wire connector at the

ENGINE CRANKS BUT DOES NOT START

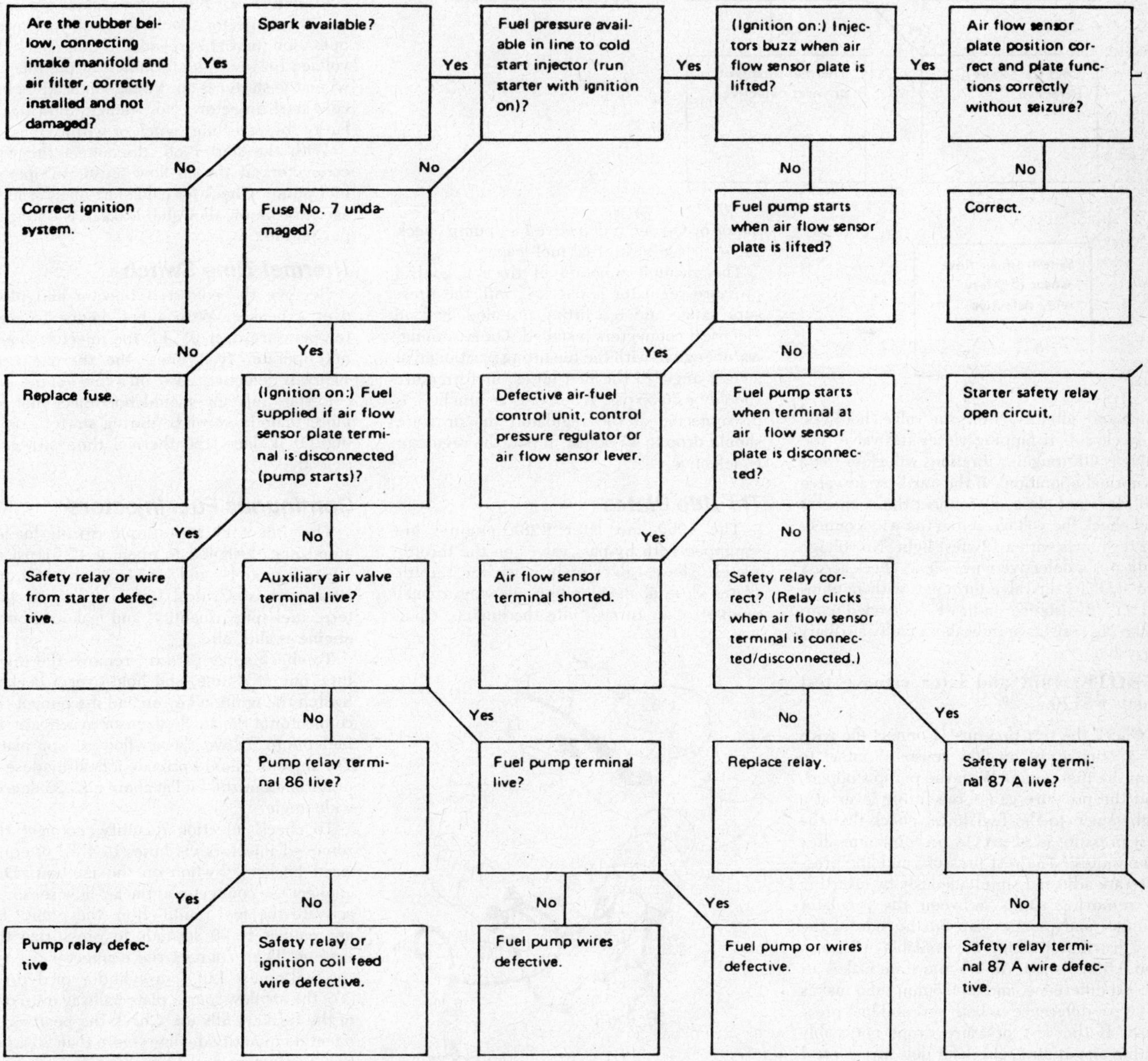

Continuous injection system troubleshcoting guide

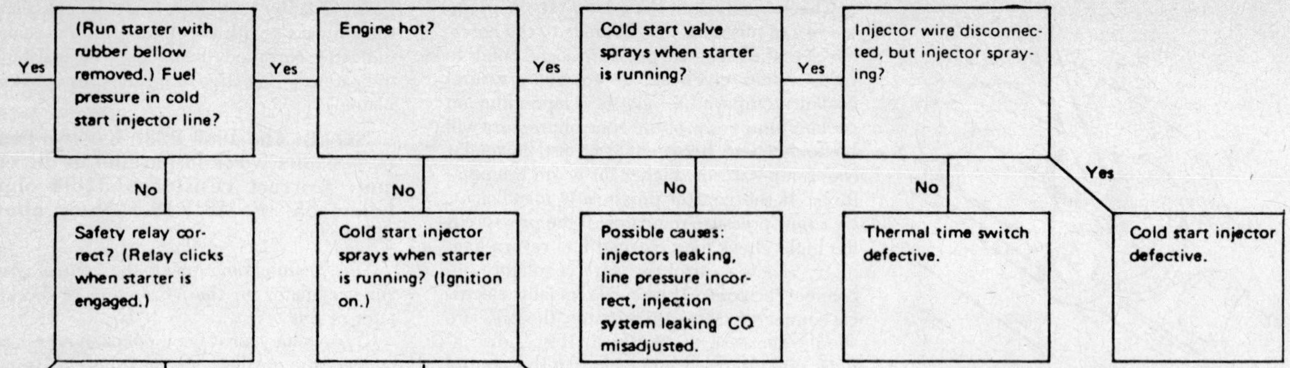
Yes
(Run starter with rubber bellow removed.) Fuel pressure in cold start injector line?
Yes
Engine hot?
Yes
Cold start valve sprays when starter is running?
Yes
Injector wire disconnected, but injector spraying?
No
No
No
No
Yes
Safety relay correct? (Relay clicks when starter is engaged.)
Cold start injector sprays when starter is running? (Ignition on.)
Possible causes: injectors leaking, line pressure incorrect, injection system leaking CO misadjusted.
Thermal time switch defective.
Cold start injector defective.

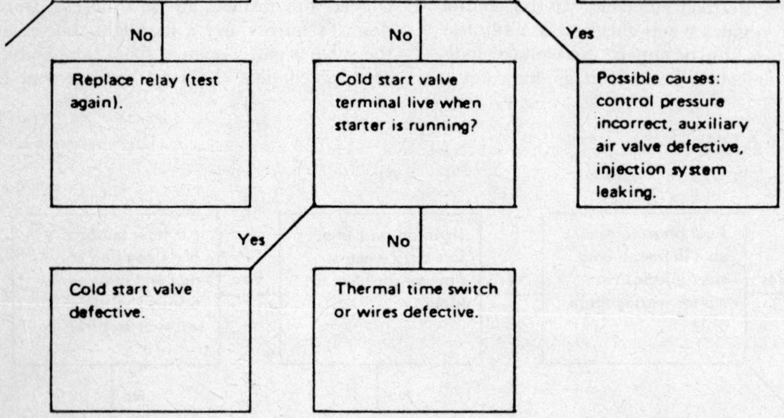
No
No
Yes
Replace relay (test again).
Cold start valve terminal live when starter is running?
Possible causes: control pressure incorrect, auxiliary air valve defective, injection system leaking.
Yes
No
Cold start valve defective.
Thermal time switch or wires defective.

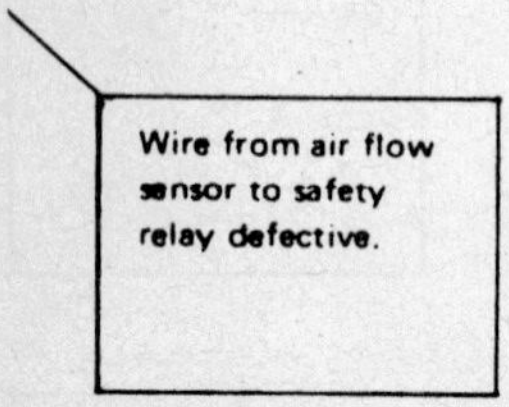
Wire from air flow sensor to safety relay defective.

valve and, after 4-5 min., the valve should be fully closed. If tapping closes the valve, the valve is OK (engine vibrations will close valve in normal operation). If the auxiliary air valve still does not close, disconnect the connector and check the voltage across the wire connector terminals with a 12v test light. No voltage indicates a defective wire. Next, check across the auxiliary air valve terminals with an ohmmeter. Resistance indicates corroded contacts. No resistance indicates a faulty auxiliary air valve.

NOTE: 1978 and later remove test relay #5170.

Check the rest pressure. Connect the wire connector at the air-flow sensor terminal to stop the fuel pump. With the pump stopped, and the pressure gauge tee fitting lever at a right angle to the fuel lines, check that the rest pressure is 24 psi (14 psi minimum after 10 minutes). The rest pressure and line pressure are adjusted simultaneously by inserting or removing shims between the regulator plunger and plunger cap on the side of the fuel distributor. Shims are available in 0.1 mm and 0.5 mm sizes. An 0.1 mm shim makes an 0.8 psi difference, and an 0.5 mm shim makes a 4.3 psi difference in both rest and line pressure. If the rest pressure drops noticeably within one minute, check for defective control pressure regulator, leaky line pressure regulator or O-ring, a defective fuel pump check valve, or some external fuel leak.

The vacuum function of the V6 control pressure regulator is checked with the pressure gauge and tee fitting installed, and all electrical connectors installed. On a running, warm engine, with the tee fitting positioned at a right angle to the fuel hoses, fuel pressure should be 50-55 psi. When the vacuum hose is disconnected at the regulator, the pressure should drop to 44-50 psi. If not, the regulator is defective.

Throttle Plates

The 1980 and later B28F engines are equipped with by-pass valves on the throttle plates. These valves open when the throttle plates close at deceleration allowing a small amount of air to pass into the engine. Combustion is thus more effective and emissions are reduced. Engine deceleration to idle will also be smoother.

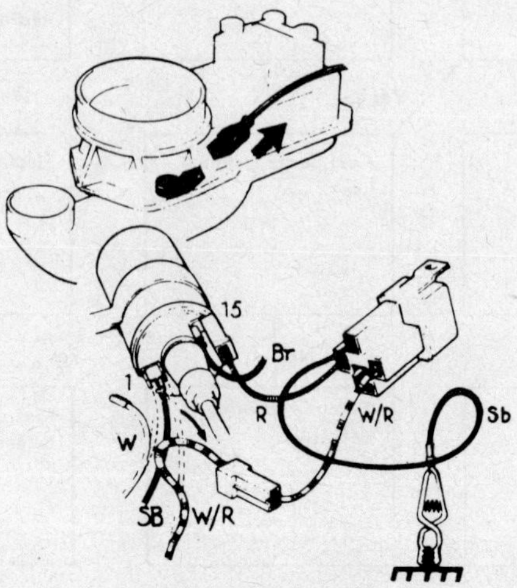
15
Br
1
R
W/R
Sb
W
SB
W/R

Test relay # 5170

Cold-Start Injector

Remove the cold-start injector from the intake manifold and hold over a beaker. With a cold engine (95° F or lower coolant temperature), the injector should spray during starter operation (max. 12 seconds). If not, check the voltage between the terminals of the injector when the starter is on. Voltage indicates a bad cold-start injector. No voltage indicates a faulty thermal time switch or wiring.

With the starter off, disconnect the wire connectors at the air-flow sensor to operate fuel pump. Check for cold-start injector leakage. Maximum allowable leakage is one drop per minute.

Thermal Time Switch

Remove the cold-start injector and place over a beaker. With a hot engine (coolant temperature over 95° F), the injector should not operate. If it does, the thermal time switch is defective. Also, on a cold engine, the cold-start injector should not inject fuel for more than 12 seconds (during starter cranking). If it does, the thermal time switch is defective.

Continuous Fuel Injectors

The injectors are simple spring-loaded atomizers, designed to open at 47-51 psi on 1974-78 models, and 37-54 psi on 1979 and later models. Critical factors are spray pattern, fuel spray quantity, and leakdown after engine is shut off.

To check spray pattern, remove the injectors, one at a time, and hold over a beaker. Switch the ignition key on and disconnect the connector at the air-flow sensor to activate the fuel pump. Move the air-flow sensor plate. The injector should provide a healthy dose of uniform atomized fuel at about a 15-25 degree wide angle.

To check injection quantity, connect the removed injectors via hoses to 4 (or 6) equal sized beakers. Switch on the ignition. Disconnect the connector at the air-flow sensor to activate the fuel pump. Run (the pump) for approximately 30 seconds to pressurize the system. Then connect the connector to stop the fuel pump. Lift (four-cylinder) or depress (V6) the air-flow sensor plate halfway until one of the beakers fills up. Check the beakers. If injection quantity deviates more than 20% between injectors, isolate problem by swapping the lowest and highest (in fuel quantity) injectors and repeating the test. If the same injector still injects less, clean or replace that injector and fuel supply line. If the other injector is now faulty, the fuel distributor is defective.

The check for injector leakdown (when closed) can now be conducted. Injector leakage more than slight seepage may be due to air-flow sensor plate set to incorrect height, seizing of fuel distributor plunger, or internal leaks in the fuel distributor. Connect the air-flow sensor connector to deactivate the fuel pump and switch off the ignition. Check for injector leakage at rest pressure. Depress the sensor plate to open the fuel distributor slots. Maximum permissible leakage is one drop per 15 seconds. If all injectors leak, the problem may be excessive rest pressure.

Diesel Fuel System

The Volvo diesel engine has indirect fuel injection, which means that the fuel is not injected directly into the combustion chamber but rather is fed into a small pre-combustion chamber in the head. During the compression stroke, air is forced up into the swirl chamber, which is connected to the combustion chamber by a narrow channel in the head. The shape of the swirl chamber causes the air to rotate rapidly. This air speed in the swirl chamber promotes even combustion and is the reason the engine can reach fairly high engine speeds.

Fuel is injected into the swirl chamber just before the piston reaches top dead center and the fuel mixes with the turbulent air. As the piston reaches TDC, it compresses the air/fuel mixture to a ration of 23.0:1. This ratio is over twice that of a gasoline engine. The mere act of compressing air to this level generates tremendous heat (1400° F), and it is this heat which ignites the air/fuel mixture.

FUEL PUMP/INJECTION PUMP

The fuel pump is also the injection pump and is located on the left rear side of the engine and is driven by a belt running off the rear of the camshaft. The pump supplies the engine with more fuel than it can use, the excess fuel being returned to the fuel tank through suction-return lines. The system constantly bleeds itself of air. Because the pump constantly moves such large amounts of fuel, it tends to stay cool and this reduces the chances of vapor lock. The pump is lubricated by the fuel passing through it. Do not use fuel additives unless specifically recommended by Volvo for fear of damaging the pump.

The pump contains a single piston which rotates and distributes fuel to each injector in the correct sequence, much in the same way the distributor on a gasoline engine distributes the spark to the spark plugs.

REMOVAL AND INSTALLATION

NOTE: Several special tools are needed to remove and install the pump and to set its timing. If these tools are not available, do not attempt to remove the pump. The tool numbers are given in the procedure.

1. Pinch off and remove the two coolant hoses running to the cold-start device on the fuel pump.
2. Disconnect the accelerator linkage at the pump and disconnect the wire from the stop valve on the top of the pump.
3. Remove the rear timing belt cover and thoroughly clean the fuel lines, and their connections at the injection pump.
4. Disconnect the fuel lines at the pump and plug the open connections to prevent dirt from entering the fuel system.
5. Remove the vacuum pump and its plunger.
6. Clean and remove the delivery lines at the fuel injectors. Plug all connections.
7. Set cylinder No. 1 to TDC injection stroke. At this position, the 0 mark on the flywheel aligns with the pointer and the notch on the injection pump pulley aligns with the notch on the pump housing. Both valves on No. 1 cylinder are closed and their camshaft lobes are pointing up at equally large angles.
8. Loosen the retaining bolts for the injection pump and push the pump up, then remove the pump drive belt. Tighten one bolt to hold the pump in the upper position.
9. Loosen the center bolt in the rear camshaft gear while using wrench 5199 to hold the gear. The bolts will be easily accessible if wrench 5201 is used.

NOTE: The camshaft must not rotate. Loosen the bolt only enough to rotate the gear on the camshaft.

10. Insert pin number 5193 into the injection pump gear to lock it in position and remove the injection pump gear nut.
11. With the pin still in position, use a puller to remove the pump gear.
12. Remove the bolts retaining the front injection pump bracket to the engine, then remove the inhex screws retaining the pump and remove the pump from the engine.
13. Install the pump on the engine and tighten the bolts only fingertight so that pump position can be adjusted.
14. Set the injection pump so that the mark on pump and the pump bracket align, then tighten the retaining bolts.
15. Make sure the shaft key is correctly installed and install the injection pump gear, washer and nut. Use pin 5193 to hold the gear while tightening the nut.
16. Proceed to "Setting the Injection Pump Timing," below.
17. After the injection pump timing is set, fill the pump with clean diesel fuel through the fuel line connection *only* if a new fuel pump is being installed or if the old pump was drained and rebuilt.
18. Install the rear timing gear cover. Connect the fuel lines and fuel delivery pipes. Tighten the fuel delivery line cap nuts and the fuel line banjo bolts to 18 ft/lbs.

When installing the fuel line on the pump, do not mix the banjo bolts: the bolt for the fuel return line has a small hole in it and is marked OUT.

19. Install the vacuum pump and all remaining components in the reverse order of removal. Adjust the accelerator linkage.

SETTING THE INJECTION PUMP TIMING

1. Disconnect the cold-start device on the injection pump by loosening screw "1" in the illustration, pushing the lever forward and rotating the sleeve 90°. Push the lever back against the stop. Do not touch screw "2" in the illustration or the cold-start device will have to be reset on a test bench.
2. Loosen the injection pump retaining screws and turn the pump so that the markings on the injection pump and the pump bracket align.
3. Install lock pin 5193 in the injection pump gear to lock the gear in position. Any pin can be used to lock the gear, however there cannot be any movement of the gear when the pin is installed.

NOTE: At this point the engine should be at TDC of the compression stroke for No. 1 cylinder.

4. Remove the plug in the injection pump distributor and install special holder 5194 and a dial indicator gauge with a measuring range of 0-3 mm. Set the dial gauge at 2 mm. Turn the injection pump using its gear (after removing the stop pin) until the marks on the injection pump gear and the bracket align.
5. Turn the injection pump gear slightly counterclockwise until the dial gauge indicates its lowest reading. In this position set the dial gauge to zero. Turn the injection pump gear clockwise until the marks on the gear and the bracket align again, then refit the lock pin to lock the gear in position.
6. Install the rear camshaft gear (if removed) and tighten its center bolt only hand tight. Install the drive belt.
7. Using the special tension gauge 5197, apply tension to the belt by moving the injection pump and its bracket. Set the tension gauge to 12.5 and apply tension to the belt until the mark on the plunger of the gauge is flush with the gauge sleeve.
8. Depress the belt heavily with your hand, then recheck and adjust the tension.
9. Use wrench 5199 or a suitable substitute to hold the rear camshaft gear in place and install wrench 5201 with a torque wrench attached to it on the center bolt. The torque wrench should be installed at a ninety degree angle to the wrench 5201 to give correct readings. Use wrench 5199 or its substitute to turn the camshaft gear until the dial gauge in the injection pump reads 0.70 mm (0.028 in.). Hold the gear in this position and tighten the center bolt to 73 ft/lbs without moving either the camshaft or the gear.
10. Remove the lock pin and turn the engine over two full turns (one complete four stroke cycle) until the No. 1 cylinder is again on TDC compression stroke. Check the reading on the dial indicator gauge. It should read 0.70 mm (0.028 in.). If the reading is correct, proceed to Step 13.
11. If the reading is less than 0.70 mm, loosen the injection pump retaining screws and turn the pump inward until a reading of 0.70 mm is obtained. Repeat Step 10.
12. If the reading is more than 0.70 mm, loosen the injection pump retaining screws and turn the pump outward until the reading on the gauge is approximately 0.60 mm (0.024

in.). Next, turn the pump inward to obtain a reading of 0.70 mm (0.028 in.) and tighten the retaining bolts. Repeat Step 10.

NOTE: When adjusting, do not tap or knock the pump as this will alter the settings.

13. Remove the dial indicator and its holder and install the plug. Tighten the plug to 6.5 ft/lbs.
14. Attach the cold-start device. Reverse Step 1, above. Install all remaining components.

MANUAL TRANSMISSION

All are fully synchronized four speed transmissions, with all forward gears in constant mesh. The M41, M46 and M410 units are equipped with Laycock-de-Normanville overdrive units, and except for the overdrive engaging switch and push plate, are identical to their M40, M45 and M400 counterparts. The heavy-duty, top cover, Volvo manufactured M40 is installed as standard equipment on 1975 240 series models. The similar M41 overdrive transmission is optional on 1975 240 series models. The extra heavy-duty, top cover, ZF manufactured M400 is standard equipment on 164 models. The similar M410 overdrive transmission is optional on the 164.

The Volvo-made M45 is standard on 1976 and later 240 series models. The similar M46 overdrive transmission is optional on 240 models and standard on the 260 series.

REMOVAL AND INSTALLATION

The transmission or the transmission-overdrive assembly may be removed with the engine installed in the vehicle.

1975 and Later 240 Series

1. If an engine lifting (support) apparatus, such as SVO 2727, is available, install it in the engine compartment. If using an SVO 2727, secure the lifting hook around the exhaust pipe. The purpose of supporting the rear of the engine here is to prevent damage to the viscous fan, radiator, or front engine mounts by limiting the downward travel of the rear of the engine when the transmission support crossmember is removed. If no lifting apparatus is available, place a jack with a protective wooden block beneath the engine oil pan. Do not place the jack under the flywheel (clutch) housing.
2. Lift up the rubber boot, unscrew the protective cover, and remove the gear shift lever from the transmission.
3. Jack up the vehicle sufficiently to allow removal of the transmission. Maintain the car at a level attitude and place jack stands beneath the jack points for support. Remove the lower drain plug from the transmission and drain the oil.
4. Slowly loosen the nuts for the transmission support crossmember. Make sure that the supporting apparatus or the jack prevent the rear of the engine from lowering. Remove the crossmember. Disconnect the front universal joint from the transmission (or overdrive) output shaft flange. Disconnect the speedometer cable. Disconnect the rear engine mount and the exhaust pipe bracket.
5. Allow the rear of the engine to drop 0.8 in. Disconnect the back-up light wires, and the wires for the overdrive, if so equipped.
6. Remove the four bolts which retain the transmission to the flywheel (clutch) housing. It may be necessary to use a universal joint on the wrench to gain access to the two upper bolts. Before removing the transmission, keep in mind that is is quite heavy, and a hydraulic floor jack may offer some support and maneuverability as the box is being removed. To remove the transmission, pull it straight out to the rear.
7. While the transmission is removed, it is a good time to inspect the condition of the clutch and the throwout bearing. Replace the throwout bearing if it is scored or if it has been emitting metal-to-metal noises.

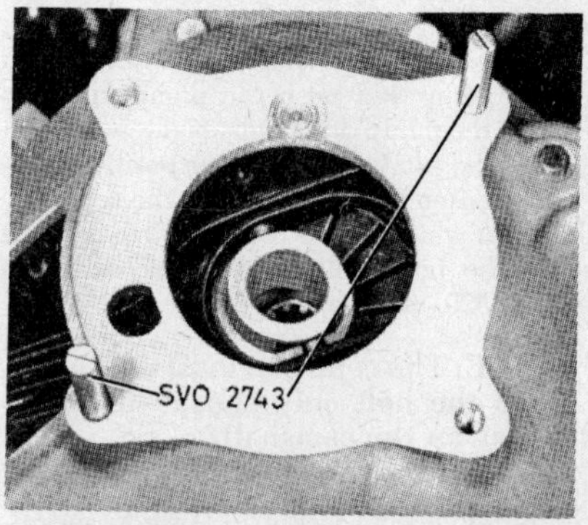

Transmission guide pins installed

8. Reverse Steps 1-6 to install, being careful to install two guide pins in the flywheel (clutch) housing. This will aid in aligning the transmission input shaft with the clutch spline when the transmission is being fitted to the flywheel housing. After two transmission-to-flywheel housing bolts are installed, the guide pins may be removed and the remaining two bolts installed. Torque the transmission-to-flywheel housing bolts to 45 ft/lbs. Fill the transmission to the proper level with oil.

164

1. Follow Steps 1-3 under "Transmission Removal and Installation" for the 140 series.
2. Remove the upper radiator bolts and the exhaust manifold flange nuts. Disconnect the negative battery cable, the throttle shaft and clutch cable from the flywheel (clutch) housing.
3. Slowly loosen the nuts for the transmission support crossmember. Making sure that the rear of the engine remains supported, remove the crossmember. Disconnect the exhaust pipe bracket and the speedometer cable. Disconnect the front universal joint from the transmission (or overdrive) output shaft flange.
4. Lower the rear of the engine approximately 1.8 in. Disconnect the back-up light wires and the wires for the overdrive, if so equipped.
5. Place a hydraulic floor jack beneath the transmission. Remove the bolts which retain the transmission and flywheel (clutch) housing assembly to the engine. Leave the starter connected but position it to one side. Remove the transmission by pulling it straight to the rear.
6. Prior to assembly, inspect the condition of the clutch and throwout bearing. Replace the bearing if it is scored or noisy in operation.
7. Reverse Steps 1-5 to install. Torque the flywheel (clutch) housing-to-engine bolts to 45 ft/lbs and the universal joint-to-output shaft flange bolts to 25-30 ft/lbs. Fill the transmission to the proper level with oil.

1976 and Later 240 and 260 Series

1. Disconnect the battery. At the firewall, disconnect the back-up light connector.
2. Jack up the front of the car and install jack stands. Loosen the set screw and drive out the pin for the shifter rod. Disconnect the shift lever from the rod.
3. Inside the car, pull up the shift boot. Remove the fork for the reverse gear detent. Remove the snap-ring and lift up the shifter. If overdrive-equipped, disconnect the engaging switch wire.
4. On 240 Series models, disconnect the clutch cable and return spring at the throwout fork and flywheel housing. On 260 series models, remove the bolts retaining the slave cylinder to the flywheel housing and tie the cylinder back out of the way (do not disconnect).
5. Disconnect the exhaust pipe bracket(s) from the flywheel cover. Remove the oil pan splash guard.
6. Using a floor jack and a block of wood, support the engine beneath the oil pan. Remove the transmission support crossmember.
7. Disconnect the driveshaft. Disconnect the speedometer cable. If so equipped, disconnect the overdrive wire.
8. Remove the starter retaining bolts and pull free of the flywheel housing.
9. Support beneath the transmission using another floor jack. Remove the flywheel (bell) housing-to-engine bolts and remove the transmission.
10. Reverse Steps 1-9 to install. Tighten the flywheel housing-to-engine bolts to 25-35 ft/lbs.

LINKAGE ADJUSTMENT

Adjustments are not necessary.

OVERDRIVE

The overdrive unit for the M41, M46 and M410 transmissions is a planetary gear type and is mounted on the rear of the transmission. When the overdrive is in the direct drive position (overdrive switched off) and the car is driven forward, power from the transmission mainshaft is transmitted through the freewheel rollers and uni-directional clutch to the overdrive output shaft. When the car is backing up or during periods of engine braking, torque is transmitted through the clutch sliding member which is held by spring pressure against the tapered portion of the output shaft. When the overdrive is actuated, the clutch sliding member is pressed by hydraulic pressure against the brake disc (ring), which locks the sun wheel. As a result, the output shaft of the overdrive rotates at a higher speed than the mainshaft thereby accomplishing a 20° reduction in engine speed in relation to vehicle speed.

REMOVAL AND INSTALLATION

To facilitate removal, the vehicle should first be driven in 4th gear with the overdrive engaged, and then coasted for a few seconds with the overdrive disengaged and the clutch pedal depressed.

1. Remove the transmission from the vehicle as outlined in the applicable "Transmission Removal and Installation" section.
2. Disconnect the solenoid cables.
3. If the overdrive unit has not already been drained, remove the six bolts and the overdrive oil pan.
4. Remove the bolts which retain the overdrive unit to the transmission intermediate flange. Pull the unit straight to the rear until it clears the transmission mainshaft.
5. Reverse the above procedure to install. Install the overdrive oil pan with a new gasket. After installation of the transmission and overdrive assembly, fill the transmission (which automatically fills the overdrive) to the proper level with the correct lubricant. Check the lubricant level in the transmission after driving 6-9 miles.

CLUTCH

All Volvos are equipped with Borg and Beck or Fichtel and Sachs diaphragm spring clutches. The 240, DL, GL and GT Diesel series use an 8½ in. disc, while the carbureted 164 uses a 9 in. disc, and the fuel-injected 164 uses a 9½ in. disc. The 260 uses a 9 in. disc.

REMOVAL AND INSTALLATION

M40 and M41

1. Remove the transmission as outlined in the applicable "Transmission Removal and Installation" procedure.
2. Remove the upper bolt for the starter motor.
3. Remove the throwout bearing. Disconnect the clutch cable at the release lever (fork) and slacken the cable sleeve at its bracket.
4. Remove the bolts which retain the flywheel (clutch) housing to the engine, and lift off the housing.
5. Remove the bolt for the release fork ball joint, and remove the ball and release fork.
6. Scribe alignment marks on the clutch and flywheel. In order to prevent warpage, slowly loosen the bolts which retain the clutch to the flywheel diagonally in rotation. Remove the bolts and lift off the clutch and pressure plate.
7. Inspect the clutch assembly as outlined under "Clutch Inspection."
8. When ready to install, wash the pressure plate and flywheel with solvent to remove any traces of oil, and wipe them clean with a cloth.
9. Position the clutch assembly (the longest side of the hub facing backward) to the flywheel and align the bolt holes. Insert a pilot shaft (centering mandrel), or an input shaft from an old transmission of the same type, through the clutch assembly and flywheel so that the flywheel pilot bearing is centered.
10. Install the six bolts which retain the clutch assembly to the flywheel and tighten them diagonally in rotation, a few turns at a time. After all the bolts are tightened, remove the pilot shaft (centering mandrel).
11. Install the ball and release fork in the flywheel housing.
12. Place the upper starter bolt in the housing. Position the housing to the engine and first install the four upper bolts (7/16 in.), then the lower starter bolt, and finally the two lower bolts (3/8 in.).
13. Insert the cable sleeve in its bracket and install the rear nut. Connect the cable at the release lever (fork), and install the throwout bearing.
14. Install the nut for the upper starter motor bolt.
15. Install the transmission as outlined in the applicable "Transmission Removal and Installation" section.
16. Adjust the clutch pedal free travel.

M45 and M46

1. Remove the transmission as outlined under M45, M46 Removal and Installation.
2. Follow Steps 6, 7, 8, 9, and 10 under "Clutch Removal and Installation" for the M40 and M41.
3. Install the transmission as outlined under M45, M46 Removal and Installation.
4. On the 260 series, bleed the clutch hydraulic system, if necessary.

M400 and M410

1. Remove the transmission as outlined in the applicable "Transmission Removal and Installation" section.
2. Scribe alignment marks on the clutch and flywheel. In order to prevent warpage, slowly loosen the bolts which retain the clutch assembly to the flywheel diagonally in rotation. Remove the bolts and lift off the clutch and pressure plate.
3. Inspect the clutch assembly as outlined under "Clutch Inspection."
4. When ready to install, wash the pressure plate and flywheel with solvent to remove any traces of oil, and wipe them clean with a cloth.
5. Position the clutch assembly (the longest side of the hub facing backward) to the flywheel and align the bolt holes. Insert a pilot shaft (centering mandrel), or an input shaft from an old transmission of the same type, through the clutch assembly and flywheel so that the flywheel pilot bearing is centered.
6. Install the six bolts which retain the clutch assembly to the flywheel, and tighten them diagonally in rotation, a few turns at a time. After all the bolts are tightened, remove the pilot shaft (centering mandrel).
7. Install the transmission as outlined in the applicable "Transmission Removal and Installation" section.

CLUTCH INSPECTION

Check the pressure plate for heat damage, cracks, scoring, or other damage to the friction surface. Check the curvature of the pressure plate with a steel ruler. Place the ruler diagonally over the pressure plate friction surface and measure the distance between the straight edge of the ruler and the inner diameter of the pressure plate. This measurement must not be greater than 0.0012 in. In addition, there must be no clearance between the straight edge of the ruler and the outer diameter of the pressure plate. This check should be made at several points. Replace the clutch as a unit if it proves faulty.

Check the throwout bearing by rotating it several times while applying finger pressure, so that the ball bearings roll against the inside of the races. If the bearing does not turn easily or if it binds at any point, replace it as a unit. Also make sure that the bearing slides easily on the guide sleeve from the transmission.

CLUTCH FORK FREE PLAY ADJUSTMENT (ALL EXCEPT 260 SERIES)

1. Loosen the locknut for the fork on the clutch cable.
2. Make the necessary adjustment and tighten the locknut. The free-play (A) at the

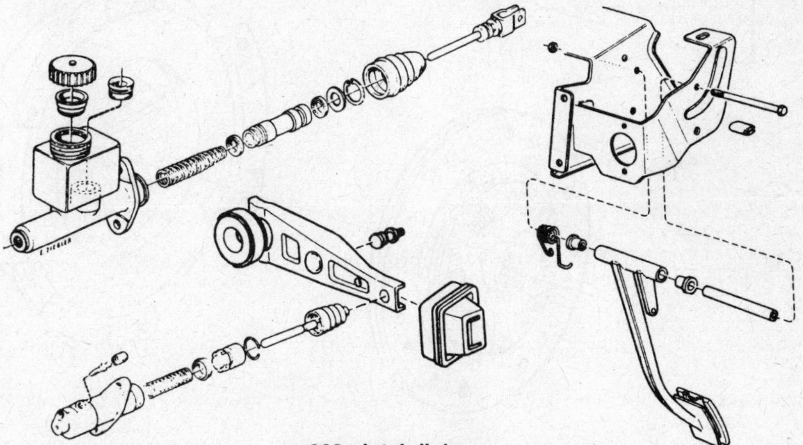

260 clutch linkage

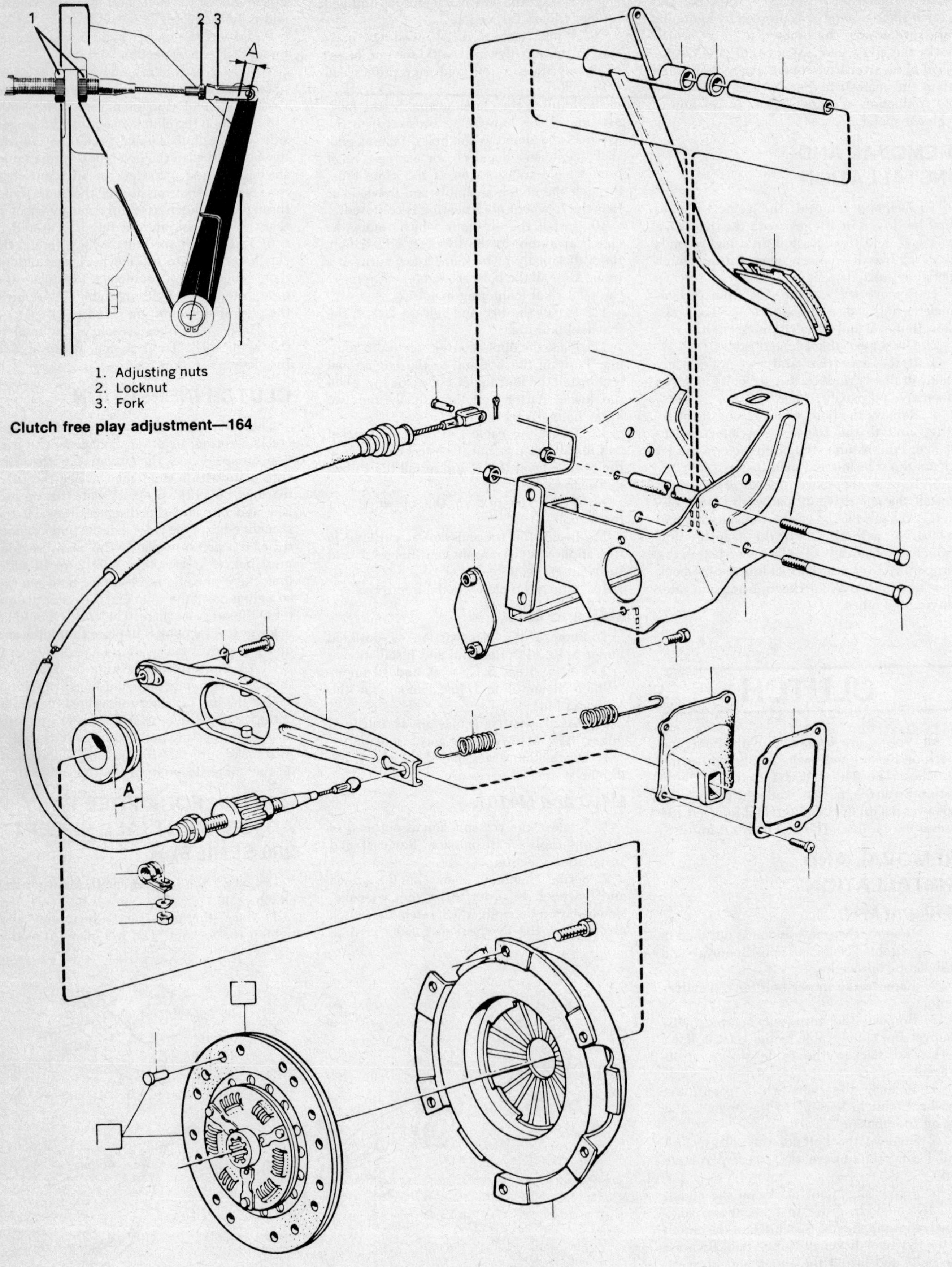

1. Adjusting nuts
2. Locknut
3. Fork

Clutch free play adjustment—164

240 series—clutch linkage

fork should be 0.12 in. for 240 series models, and 0.16-0.20 for the 164.

3. If this adjustment is insufficient, or if a new cable is installed, the sleeve attachment to the flywheel housing should be adjusted with the adjusting nuts.

NOTE: The free-play adjustment on 260 series (GLE and Coupe) should be ⅛″.

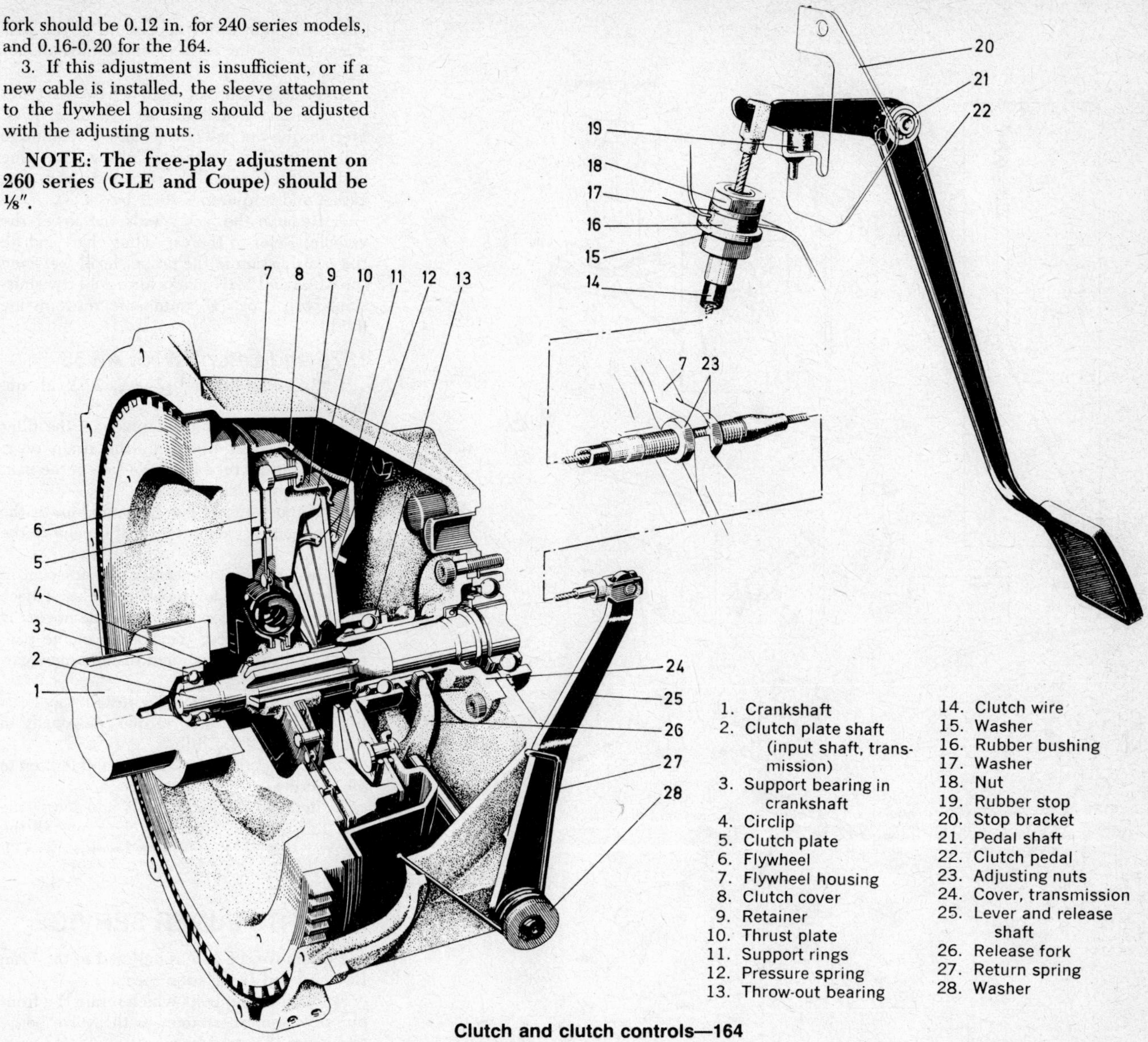

1. Crankshaft
2. Clutch plate shaft (input shaft, transmission)
3. Support bearing in crankshaft
4. Circlip
5. Clutch plate
6. Flywheel
7. Flywheel housing
8. Clutch cover
9. Retainer
10. Thrust plate
11. Support rings
12. Pressure spring
13. Throw-out bearing
14. Clutch wire
15. Washer
16. Rubber bushing
17. Washer
18. Nut
19. Rubber stop
20. Stop bracket
21. Pedal shaft
22. Clutch pedal
23. Adjusting nuts
24. Cover, transmission
25. Lever and release shaft
26. Release fork
27. Return spring
28. Washer

Clutch and clutch controls—164

AUTOMATIC TRANSMISSION

The transmission used on 1975 and earlier models is a three-speed, dual-range, Borg-Warner model 35. The BW 35 consists of a three element torque converter coupling, planetary gear set, and a valve control system. A similar Borg-Warner (BW) 55 or Aisin-Warner (AW) 55 (made in Japan under license) is used beginning in the 1976 and later models.

REMOVAL AND INSTALLATION

164 and 240 Series

1. Remove the dipstick and filler pipe clamp.
2. Remove the bracket and throttle cable from the dashboard and throttle control, respectively.
3. Disconnect the exhaust pipe at the manifold.
4. Raise the car and support it on jack stands at the front and rear axles.
5. Drain the fluid into a clean container.
6. Disconnect the driveshaft from the transmission flange.
7. Disconnect the selector lever controls and remove the reinforcing bracket from the pan.
8. Remove the torque converter attaching bolts.
9. Support the transmission with a jack equipped with a holding fixture.
10. Remove the rear crossmember.
11. Disconnect the exhaust pipe brackets and remove the speedometer cable from the case.
12. Remove the filler pipe.
13. Place a wooden block between the engine and firewall and lower the jack until the engine is against the block.

NOTE: If the battery cable appears to stretch too much, remove it.

14. Disconnect the starter wires, remove the converter housing bolts and pull the transmission backwards to clear the guide pins.
15. Install in the reverse of removal. Torque all 14 mm bolts to 35 ft/lbs.

260 Series

1. Remove air cleaner.
2. Disconnect throttle cable.
3. Remove the two upper converter housing bolts.
4. Remove the filler pipe.
5. Raise the vehicle, support it front and rear with jack stands and drain the transmission into a clean container.
6. Remove the splash shield (8 bolts).
7. Disconnect the front muffler from the rubber suspensor.
8. Disconnect the driveshaft from the transmission flange.
9. Remove the exhaust pipe brackets at the rear of the transmission.

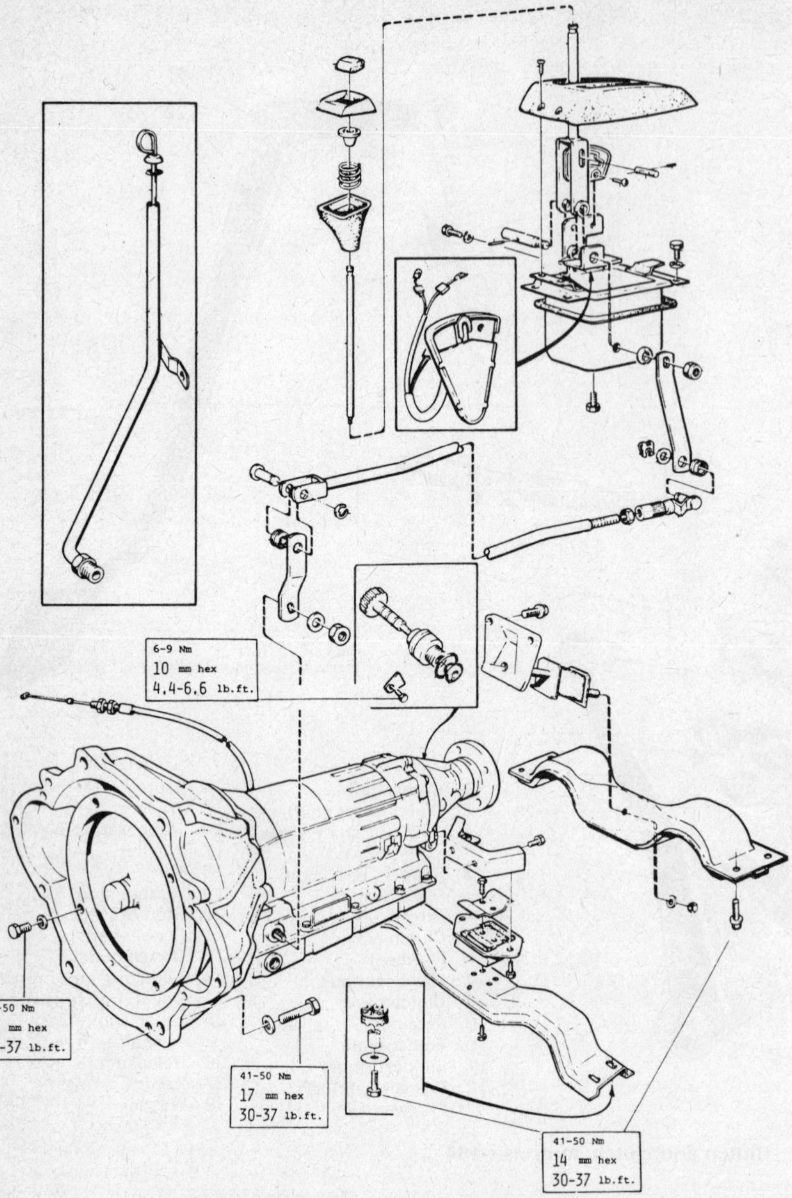

BW55, AW55 mountings and controls

10. Remove the rear crossmember.
11. Remove the rear engine support and exhaust pipe bracket.
12. Remove the speedometer cable.
13. Disconnect the cooler lines at the transmission.
14. Remove the electrical connections from transmission.
15. Remove neutral start switch.
16. Remove shift control rod.
17. Remove the engine-to-transmission cover plate.
18. Remove starter motor and cover.
19. Remove converter-to-drive plate bolts.
20. Position jack, with holding fixture, under transmission.
21. Remove the two lower converter housing bolts.
22. Pull the transmission back and down to clear the guide pins.
23. Installation is the reverse of removal. Torque the converter housing bolts to 35 ft/lbs. Torque filler pipe nut to 70 ft/lbs. Torque converter-to-drive plate bolts to 35 ft/lbs. Adjust control rod so that 1⅛" of thread is visible. Torque crossmember bolts to 35 ft/lbs.

Fluid Pan

REMOVAL AND INSTALLATION

1975 BW35

1. Place the transmission selector in Park.
2. Raise the vehicle and place jack stands underneath.
3. The drain plug is located on the pan. Place a container underneath to catch the fluid. If the vehicle has been driven for any length of time, be careful, as the transmission fluid will be scalding hot.
4. After the fluid has stopped draining, remove the 15 pan retaining bolts, and lower the pan and gasket.
5. Inspect the magnetic element in the pan for metal shavings or chips. Also remove any sludge or gum from the bottom of the pan. Clean the mating surfaces of the transmission case and pan.
6. Position the pan (with a new gasket) to the case and install the 15 retaining bolts. Step torque the bolts diagonally in rotation to 8-13 ft/lbs. Coat the threads of the drain plug with Loctite®. Install the plug and a new plug gasket and torque to 8-10 ft/lbs.
7. Remove the jack stands and lower the vehicle. Refer to the capacities chart and fill the transmission to the proper level (between the MAX and MIN marks for a cold transmission) with type "F" automatic transmission fluid.

1976 and Later BW55, AW55

1. Raise the car and place jack stands underneath.
2. The dipstick tube doubles as the filler tube, and when removed, the drain plug. Disconnect the tube from the side of the pan, and drain the transmission.
3. Remove the 14 pan bolts, and lower the pan and gasket (some fluid will remain in the pan).
4. Inspect the magnet (located adjacent to the filter screen) for metal particles. Check the filter screen for the pump. Remove any gum or sludge from the bottom of the pan. Clean and dry the pan and install a new gasket.
5. Position the pan and install the bolts fingertight. Then, step torque, diagonally in rotation, to 4.4-7.4 ft/lbs.
6. Connect the dipstick tube and tighten to 59-74 ft/lbs.
7. Remove the jack stands and lower the car. Refer to the capacities chart and fill the transmission to the proper level with ATF Type F.

PUMP STRAINER SERVICE

1. Remove the pan as outlined in the "Pan Removal and Installation" section.
2. Remove the bolts which retain the front pump wire-mesh strainer to the valve body, and lower the strainer.
3. Clean the strainers in an alcohol based solvent solution.
4. Position the strainers to the valve body and install the retaining screws and bolts. Torque the bolts to 1.7-2.5 ft/lbs, (BW35) or 3.7-4.4 ft/lbs, (BW55 and AW55).
5. Install the pan with a new gasket as outlined in the "Pan Removal and Installation" section.

FRONT BAND ADJUSTMENT–BW35

1. Remove the pan as outlined in the "Pan Removal and Installation" section.
2. Insert a 0.25 in. gauge block between the adjusting bolt and the servo cylinder. Tighten the bolt with an inch pound torque wrench to a torque of 10 in/lbs.
3. Adjust the position of the adjusting bolt spring. It should be 1-2 threads from the lever.
4. Remove the gauge block and torque wrench. Make sure that the long end of the adjusting bolt spring is inserted in the cam for the front brake band.

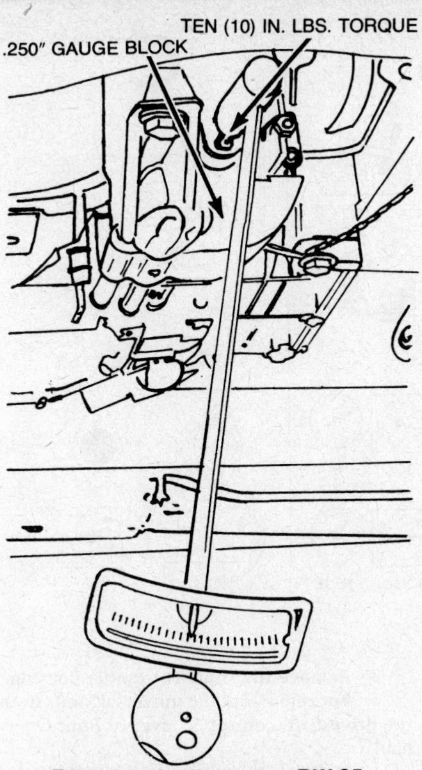

Front band adjustment, BW 35

5. Install the pan as outlined in the "Pan Removal and Installation" section.

REAR BAND ADJUSTMENT–BW35

1. An access hole is provided in the right side of the transmission tunnel. On some 140 series and 164 models, it is necessary to disconnect the right heater duct. Lift up the carpet and position it to one side. Remove the rubber plug from the access hole.
2. Loosen the locknut for the adjusting screw located on the right side of the transmission case.
3. Using a $^5/_{16}$ in. square socket and a foot pound torque wrench, tighten the adjusting screw to a torque of 10 ft/lbs; then back off the adjusting screw one complete turn.
4. Without disturbing the adjustment, tighten the locknut.
5. Install the rubber plug, fit the carpet, and install the heater duct, if removed.

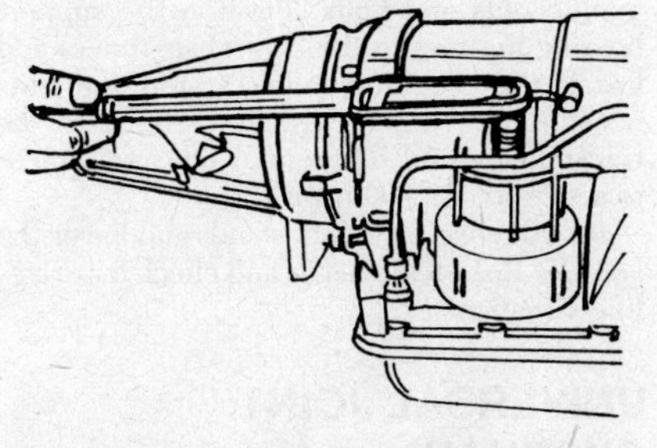

Rear band adjustment—Borg Warner type 35

BAND ADJUSTMENTS–BW55 AND AW55

The BW55 and AW55 transmissions are equipped with a multi-disc brake (band) system which does not require any adjustment. No provision is made for band adjustment, even at overhaul.

NEUTRAL START SWITCH ADJUSTMENT

1975

If a switch is not operating correctly it must be replaced complete with a new spacing washer, as it is not adjustable. The switch serves a dual function: first, it prevents the engine from being started while the gear selector is in any position other than Neutral or Park, and second, it closes the circuit that actuates the back-up lights when the slector is placed in Reverse.

1976 and Later Models

Some early production 1976 models have a nonadjustable neutral start switch located on the side of the case. All subsequent production models have an adjustable switch, located beneath the shifter quadrant on the tunnel. To adjust:

1. Remove the shifter quadrant cover.
2. Place the shifter lever in Park. Check that the round switch contact centers over the indicating line for "P" (park). If not, loosen the two switch mounting screws and align the switch.

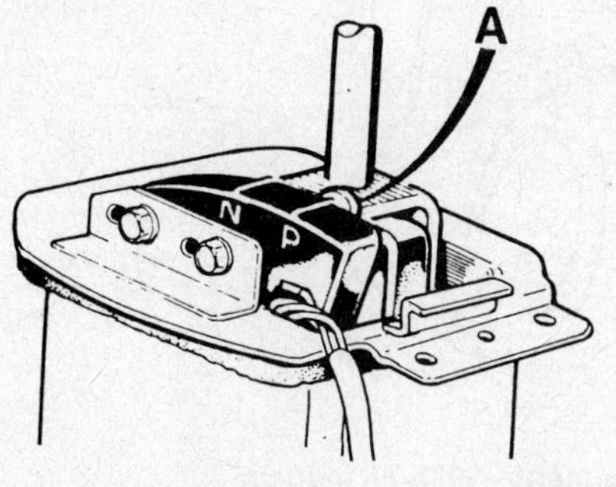

Neutral start switch adjustment—1976-77

3. Place the shifter lever in Neutral. Repeat the check and adjust as necessary.
4. Finally, check that the engine starts only in Park or Neutral, and check that the back-up lights work only in Reverse.

GEAR SELECTOR LINKAGE ADJUSTMENT

164, 240, 260 Series and BW35

1. Disconnect the shift rod from the transmission lever. Place both the transmission lever and the gear selector lever in the "2" position.
2. Adjust the length of the shift control rod so that a small clearance (distance B) of 0.04 in. is obtained between the gear selector lever inhibitor and the inhibitor plate, when the shift control rod is connected to the transmission lever.
3. Position the gear selector lever in Drive and make sure that a similar small clearance (distance A) of 0.04 in. exists between the lever inhibitor and the inhibitor plate. Disconnect the shift control rod from the transmission lever and adjust, if necessary.
4. Lock the control rod bolt with its safety clasp and tighten the locknut. Make sure that the control rod lug follows with the transmission lever.

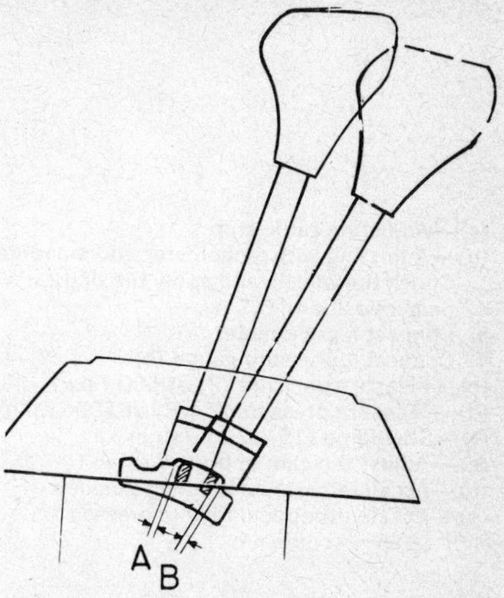

Gear selector adjustments, 1975 models

5. After moving the transmission lever to the Park and "1" positions, make sure that the clearances A and B remain the same. In addition, make sure that the output shaft is locked with the selector lever in the Park position.

1976 AND LATER BW55

1. With the engine off, check that the distance between the "D" position and its forward stop is equal to the distance between the "2" position and its rearward stop, when the gear selector is moved. If you are not sure, remove the gear quadrant cover, and measure.
2. If adjustment is necessary, a rough setting is made by loosening the locknut and rotating the clevis on the control rod to the transmission. A fine adjustment can be made by rotating the knurled sleeve between the control rod locknut and the pivot for the gear selector lever. Increasing the rod length will decrease clearance between the "D" position and its forward stop, and vice versa. Maximum permissable length of exposed thread between the locknut and the control rod is 1.1 in.

THROTTLE AND DOWNSHIFT CABLE ADJUSTMENT

1. First, adjust the throttle plate angle and throttle cable. Disconnect the cable at the control pulley and the linkage rod at the throttle shaft. Set the throttle plate angle by loosening the adjusting screw locknut and backing off the screw. Then, turn in the screw until it just makes contact and then one additional turn. Tighten the locknut. Adjust the linkage rod so that it fits onto the throttle shaft pulley ball without moving the cable pulley. Attach the throttle cable to the pulley and adjust the cable sheath so that the cable is stretched but does not move the cable pulley. Finally, fully depress the gas pedal and check that the pulley contacts the full throttle abutment.
2. With the transmission cable hooked up, check that there is 0.010-0.040 in. clearance between the cable clip and the adjusting sheath. The cable should be stretched at idle.

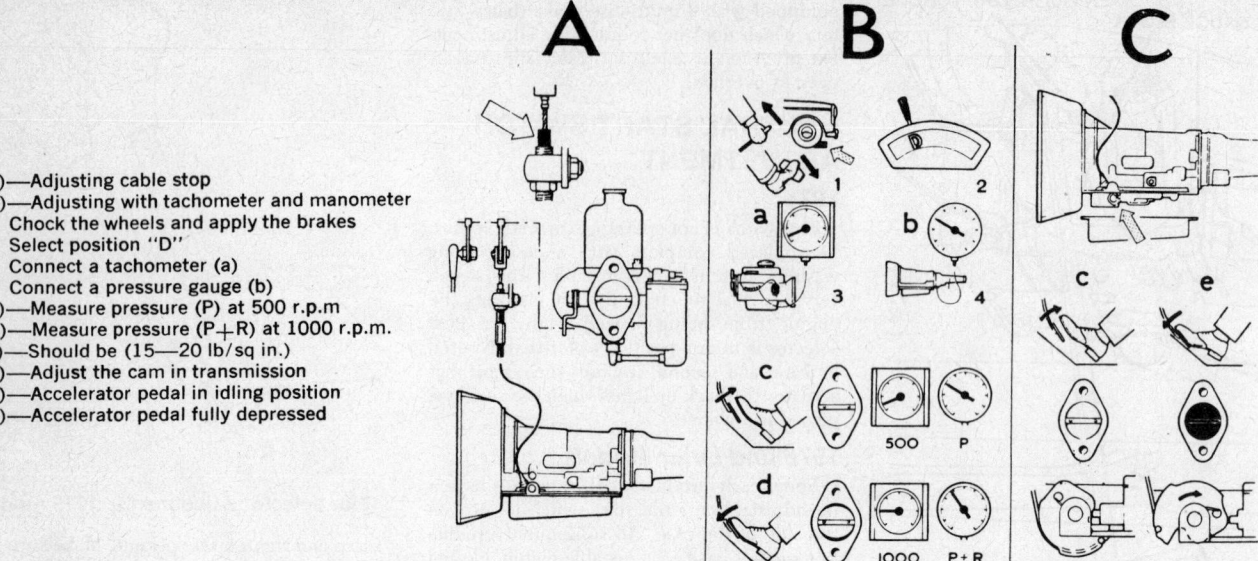

(a)—Adjusting cable stop
(b)—Adjusting with tachometer and manometer
1. Chock the wheels and apply the brakes
2. Select position "D"
3. Connect a tachometer (a)
4. Connect a pressure gauge (b)
(c)—Measure pressure (P) at 500 r.p.m
(d)—Measure pressure (P+R) at 1000 r.p.m.
(r)—Should be (15—20 lb/sq in.)
(c)—Adjust the cam in transmission
(c)—Accelerator pedal in idling position
(e)—Accelerator pedal fully depressed

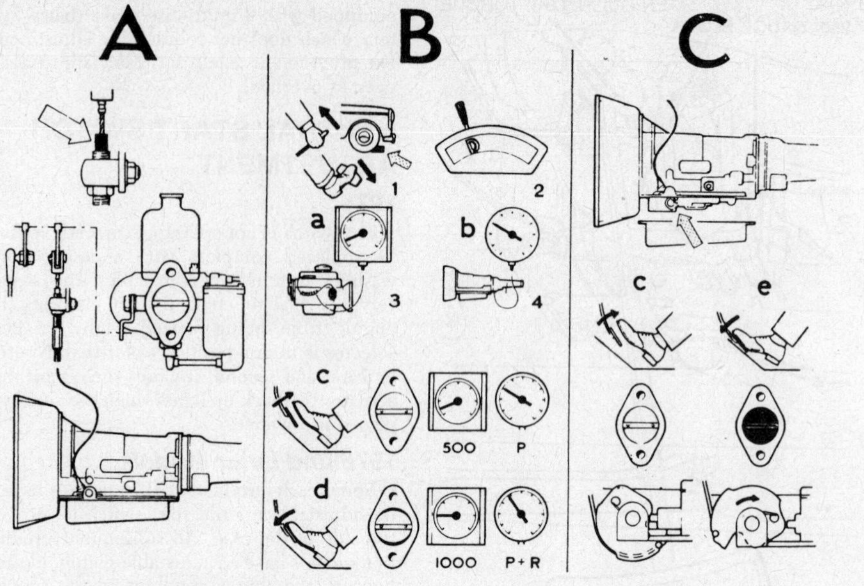

Throttle cable adjustment

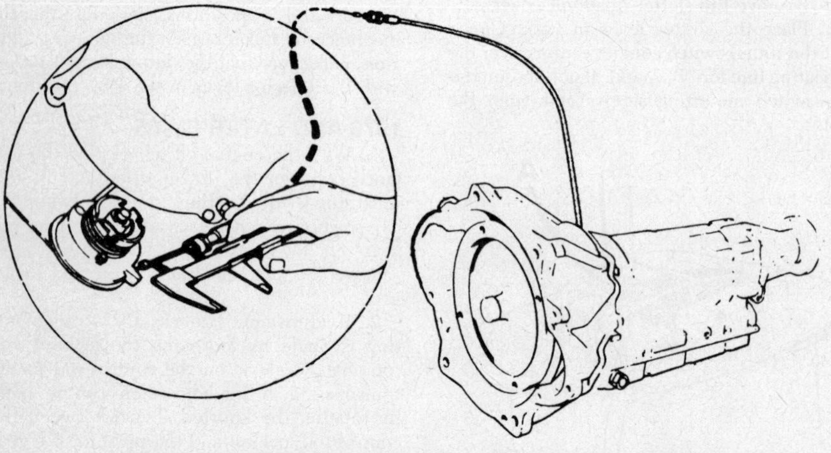

Throttle and downshaft cable adjustment—1976-77 models

Pull out the cable about ½ in. and release. A distinct click should be heard from the transmission as the throttle cam returns to its initial position. Depress the gas pedal again to wide open throttle. Check that the transmission cable moves about 2 in. Adjust as necessary at the adjusting sheath.

DRIVELINE

Driveshaft and U-Joints

The driveshaft is a two-piece, tubular unit, connected by an intermediate universal joint. The rear end of the front section of the driveshaft forms a splined sleeve. A splined shaft forming one of the yokes for the intermediate U-joint fits into this sleeve. The front section is supported by a ball bearing contained in an insulated rubber housing which is attached to the bottom of the driveshaft tunnel. The front section is connected to the transmission flange, and the rear section is connected to the differential housing flange by universal joints. Each joint consists of a spider with four ground trunnions carried in the flange yokes by needle bearings.

DRIVESHAFT AND UNIVERSAL JOINT REMOVAL AND INSTALLATION

1. Jack up the vehicle and install safety stands.
2. Mark the relative positions of the driveshaft yokes and transmission and differential housing flanges for purposes of assembly. Remove the nuts and bolts which retain the front and rear driveshaft sections to the transmission and differential housing flanges, respectively. Remove the support bearing housing from the driveshaft tunnel, and lower the driveshaft and universal joint assembly as a unit.
3. Pry up the lock washer and remove the support bearing retaining nut. Pull off the rear section of the driveshaft with the intermediate universal joint and splined shaft of the front section. The support bearing may now be pressed off the driveshaft.
4. Remove the support from its housing.
5. For removal of the universal joints from the driveshaft, consult "Universal Joint Overhaul."
6. Inspect the driveshaft sections for straightness. Using a dial indicator, or rolling the shafts along a flat surface, make sure that the driveshaft out-of-round does not exceed 0.010 in. Do not attempt to straighten a damaged shaft. Any shaft exceeding 0.010 in. out-of-round will cause substantial vibration, and must be replaced. Also, inspect the support bearing by pressing the races against each other by hand, and turning them in opposite directions. If the bearing binds at any point, it must be discarded and replaced.
7. Install the support bearing into its housing.
8. Press the support bearing and housing onto the front driveshaft section. Push the splined shaft of the front section, with the intermediate universal joint and rear driveshaft section, into the splined sleeve of the front section. Install the retaining nut and lock washer for the support bearing.
9. Taking note of the alignment marks made prior to removal, position the driveshaft and universal joint assembly to its flange connections and install but do not tighten its retaining nuts and bolts. Position the support bearing housing to the driveshaft tunnel and install the retaining nut. Tighten the nuts which retain the driveshaft sections to the transmission and differential housing flanges to a torque of 25-30 ft/lbs.
10. Remove the safety stands and lower the vehicle. Road test the car and check for driveline vibrations.

UNIVERSAL JOINT OVERHAUL

1. Remove the driveshaft and universal joint assembly as outlined in "Driveshaft and Universal Joint Assembly Removal and Installation."
2. Place the driveshaft section in a vise so that the joint being removed comes as close as

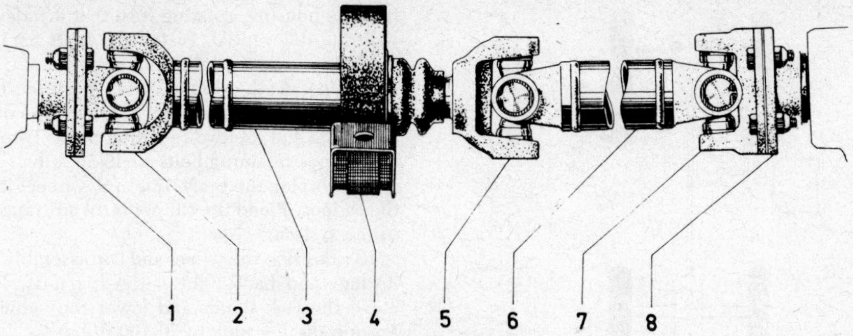

1. Flange on transmission
2. Front universal joint
3. Front section of driveshaft
4. Support bearing
5. Intermediate universal joint
6. Rear section of driveshaft
7. Rear universal joint
8. Flange on rear axle

Driveshaft with support bearing

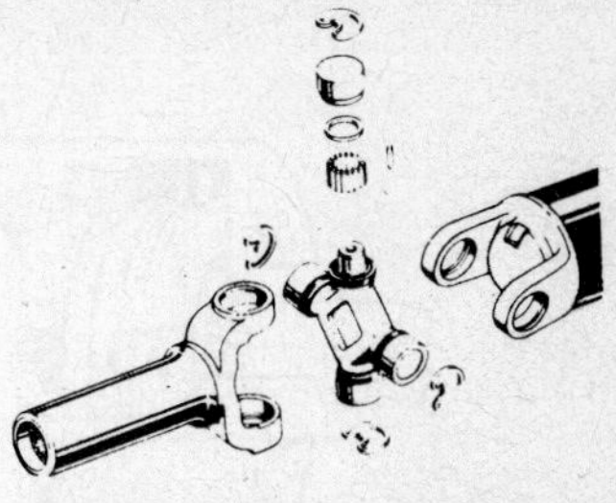

Universal joint disassembled

possible to the vise jaws. Do not tighten the vise any more than is necessary as the driveshaft is of tubular construction, and easily deformed.

3. Remove the snap-rings, which secure the needle bearings in the yokes, with snap-ring pliers.

4. With a hammer and a metal punch, drive the spider as far as it will go in one direction. The needle bearing should come about half-way out. Then, drive the spider as far as it will go in the other direction.

5. Drive out one of the needle bearings with a thinner punch. Remove the spider, and then drive out the other needle bearing.

6. Clean the spider and needle bearings completely. Check the frictional surfaces for wear. Replace any worn or broken parts. If the old needle bearings and spider are to be reused, fill them with molybdenum disulphide chassis grease, and make sure that the rubber seals are not damaged. If new needle bearings are used, fill them half-way with the grease.

7. To install, position the spider in the yoke and push the spider in one direction as far as it will go, so that the needle bearing can be fitted onto the spider trunnion. Then, using a drift of a slightly smaller diameter than the needle bearing sleeve, press the needle bearing in until the bearing sleeve and snap-ring can be fitted.

8. Install the other needle bearing, bearing sleeve, and snap-ring as outlined in Step 7.

9. Remove the driveshaft section from the vise and repeat Steps 2-8 for the other universal joints.

10. Install the driveshaft and universal joint assembly as outlined under "Driveshaft and Universal Joint Removal and Installation."

REAR AXLE

All Volvos utilize a solid rear axle housing carried in two support arms. Two torque rods, connected between the axle shaft tubes and the body, limit the rear axle wind-up. A track bar controls lateral movement of the axle housing. Final drive is of the hypoid design, with the drive pinion lying below the ring gear. Each axle shaft is indexed into a splined sleeve for the differential side gears, and supported at its outer end in a tapered roller bearing. Bearing clearance is not adjustable by use of shims as on earlier model Volvos,

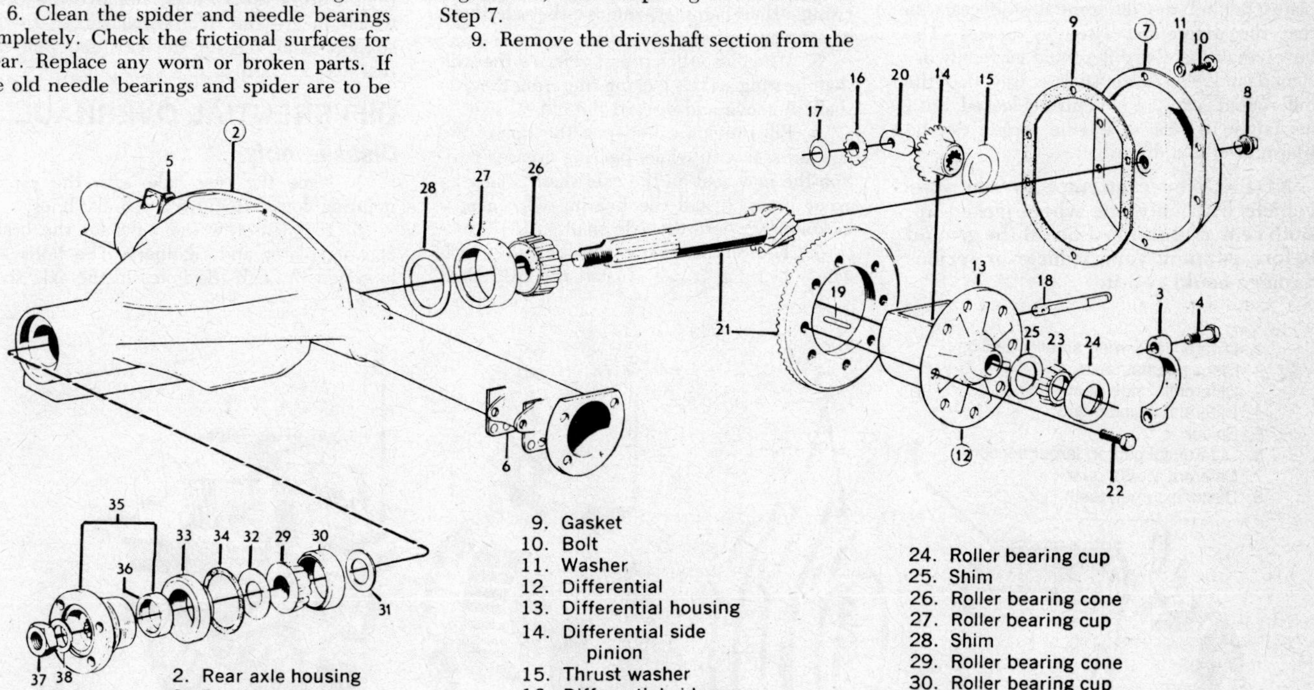

2. Rear axle housing
3. Bearing cap
4. Bolt
5. Anchorage point (track bar)
6. Anchorage point (support arm)
7. Inspection cover
8. Plug
9. Gasket
10. Bolt
11. Washer
12. Differential
13. Differential housing
14. Differential side pinion
15. Thrust washer
16. Differential side gear
17. Thrust washer
18. Pivot pin
19. Lock pin
20. Spacer sleeve
21. Ring and pinion
22. Bolt
23. Roller bearing cone
24. Roller bearing cup
25. Shim
26. Roller bearing cone
27. Roller bearing cup
28. Shim
29. Roller bearing cone
30. Roller bearing cup
31. Shim
32. Oil deflector
33. Oil seal
34. Gasket
35. Flange
36. Mud slinger
37. Nut
38. Washer

Rear axle disassembled

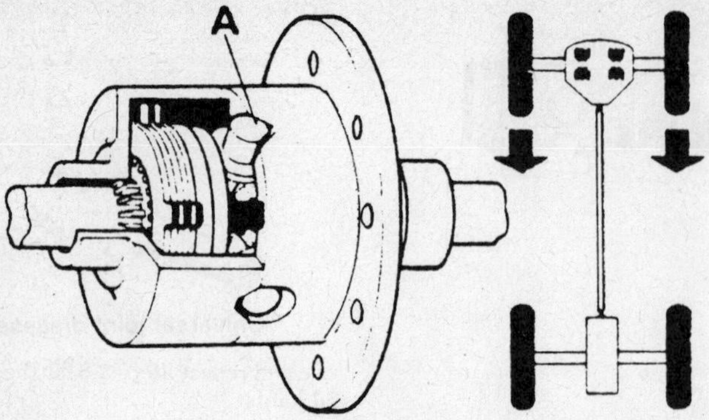

Limited slip differential driving force

but instead is determined by bearing thickness. Both sides of the axles beaings are protected by oil seals.

NOTE: Some Volvos are equipped with a limited slip differential that requires a special type lubricant available from your Volvo dealer.

LIMITED SLIP DIFFERENTIAL

Except for the differential assembly the design is the same as the standard differential.

Two shafts make up the spider for the differential pinion gears. On the side where it is against the differential carrier, each shaft has a V-shaped bevel. The differential carrier is similarily designed. When power from the engine starts to drive the vehicle, the shafts (A) glide up the beveled recess in the differential carrier. This compresses the friction plates behind the differential side gears so that the differential assembly brakes. The bevel angle on the differential carrier is designed and chosen in such a way that the differential gears are not entirely locked, but a maximum of 75% of engine torque can be transmitted to a driveshaft.

NOTE: Never attempt to run your vehicle with only one wheel jacked up. Both rear wheels must be off the ground before running your vehicle or serious damage could result.

AXLE SHAFT REMOVAL AND INSTALLATION, BEARING AND OIL SEAL REPLACEMENT

1. Raise the vehicle and install safety stands.
2. Remove the applicable wheel and tire assembly.
3. Place a wooden block beneath the brake pedal, plug the master cylinder reservoir vent hole, and remove and plug the brake line from the caliper. Be careful not to allow any brake fluid to spill onto the disc or pads. Remove the two bolts which retain brake caliper to the axle housing, and lift off the caliper. Lift off the brake disc.
4. Remove the thrust washer bolts through the holes in the axle shaft flange. Using a slide hammer, remove the axle shaft, bearing and oil seal assembly.
5. Using an arbor press, remove the axle shaft bearing and its locking ring from the axle shaft. Remove and discard the old oil seal.
6. Fill the space between the lips of the new oil seal with wheel bearing grease. Position the new seal on the axle shaft. Using an arbor press, install the bearing with a new locking ring, onto the axle shaft.
7. Thoroughly pack the bearing with wheel bearing grease. Install the axle shaft into the housing, rotating it so that it indexes with the differential. Install the bolts for the thrust washer and tighten to 36 ft/lbs.
8. Install the brake disc. Position the brake caliper to its retainer on the axle housing and install the two retaining bolts. Torque the caliper retaining bolts to 45-50 ft/lbs.
9. Unplug the brake line and connect it to the caliper. Bleed the caliper of all air trapped in the system.
10. Position the wheel and tire assembly on its lugs and hand-tighten the lug nuts. Remove the jack stands and lower the vehicle. Torque the lug nuts to 70-100 ft/lbs.

REAR AXLE HOUSING REMOVAL

1. Block the front wheels. Unscrew the rear wheel nuts. Jack up the rear of the vehicle. Place blocks in front of the rear jack attachments and lower the jack slightly. Remove the rear wheels.
2. Unscrew the upper bolts for the shock absorbers. Disconnect the handbrake cables from the lever arms and brackets on the brake backing plates.
3. Disconnect the driveshaft from the flange (yoke) on the pinion. Remove the brake line union from the differential carrier.
4. Loosen the front attaching bolt for the support arms about 1 turn. Remove the rear screws for the torque rods. Disconnect the track rod from the bracket on the differential carrier. Remove the lower attaching bolts for the springs.
5. Lower the jack until the support arms release from the springs. Remove the bolts which secure the differential carrier to the support arms. Lower the jack and pull the rear axle forward.

DIFFERENTIAL OVERHAUL

Disassembly

1. Place the rear axle with the pinion pointing down. Remove the brake lines.
2. 164: Unscrew the bolts for the brake backing plates and retainers. The bolts are loosened through the holes in the axle shaft

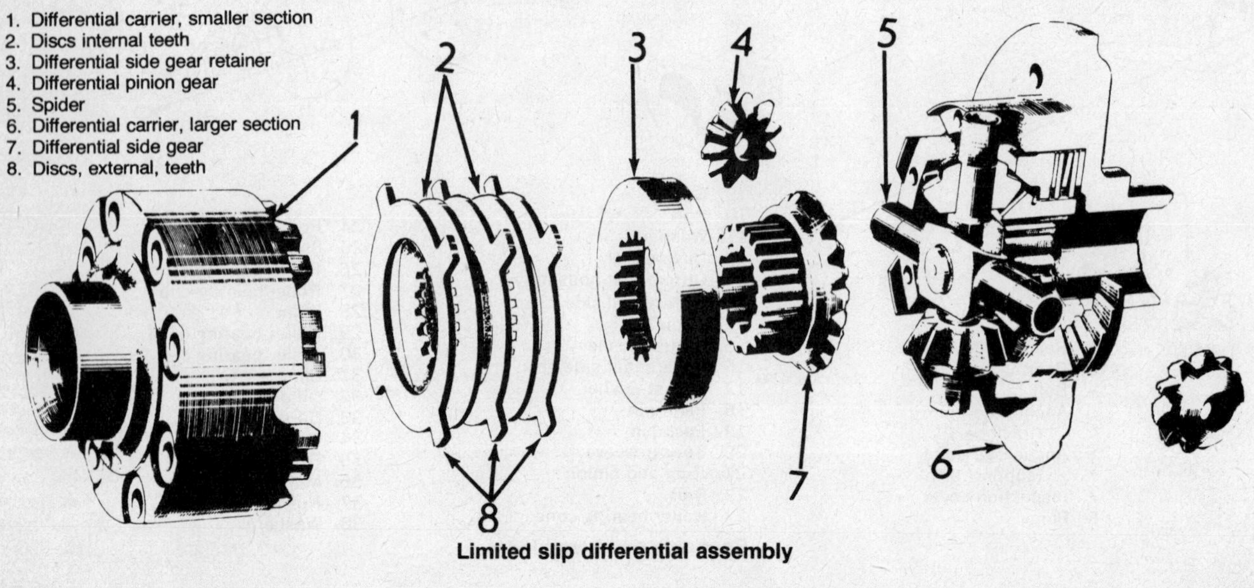

Limited slip differential assembly

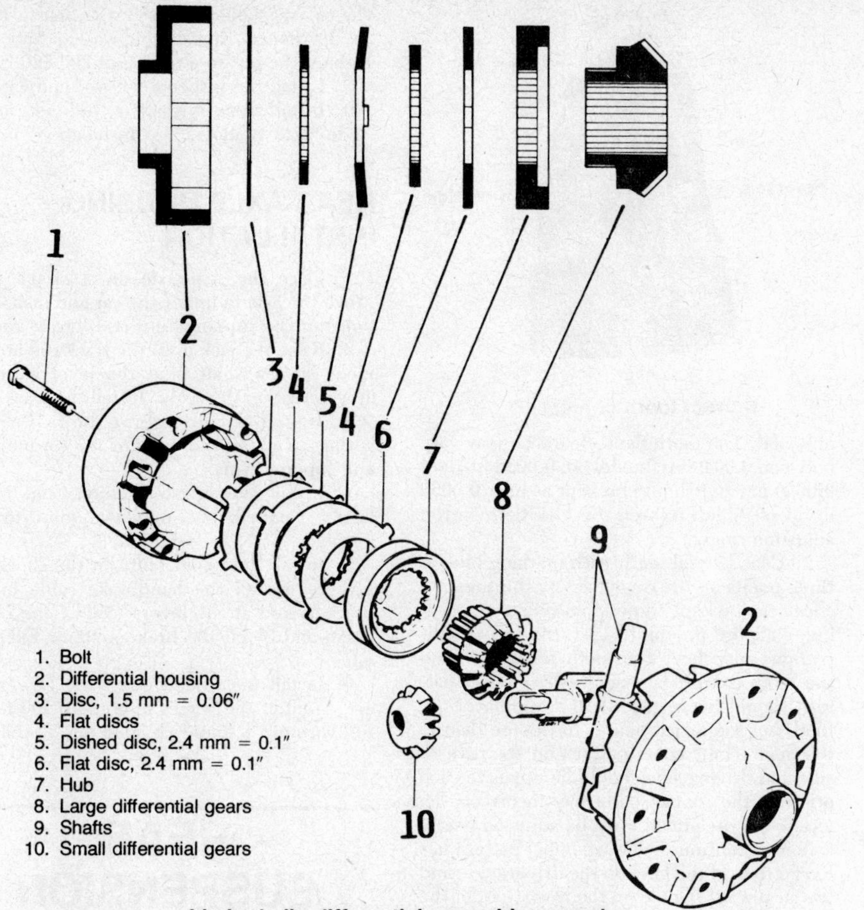

1. Bolt
2. Differential housing
3. Disc, 1.5 mm = 0.06″
4. Flat discs
5. Dished disc, 2.4 mm = 0.1″
6. Flat disc, 2.4 mm = 0.1″
7. Hub
8. Large differential gears
9. Shafts
10. Small differential gears

Limited slip differential assembly procedure

flanges. Pull out the axle shafts with a slide hammer.

3. Remove the inspection cover.
4. If the unit is being overhauled because of noise, the backlash and the gear tooth pattern should be checked before disassembly. Clean the teeth to avoid a misleading tooth pattern.
5. Check the alignment markings on the cap and carrier. If there are no alignment marks, or if they are difficult to see, mark one side with a punch. Remove the cap.
6. Expand the pinion carrier with a special tool. Pull out the differential carrier with ring gear. A special tool is available for this purpose.
7. Turn the assembly and allow the oil to run out. Remove the nuts for the flange. Pull the flange off with a puller. Press out the pinion.
8. Drive out the front pinion bearing, the washer, and oil seal.
9. If necessary, drive out the rear bearing outer ring.
10. Clean the gasket surface. Remove all burrs with a file.
11. If necessary, pull off the rear bearing from the pinion with a puller. Slide the puller down over the rollers and press down the lock ring. Then tighten the puller until the rollers are flush against the edge of the inner race. Tap the lock ring with a hammer.
12. Loosen the ring gear bolts and remove the ring gear.
13. Drive out the lock pin, and the shaft for the differential gears. Remove the thrust block, the differential gears, and the thrust washers.
14. Remove the differential carrier bearings with a puller. Do not lose the shims.

Inspection

Clean all the parts thoroughly. Check all the bearing races and bearings. All damaged bearings and bearing races must be replaced. Check both the pinion drive and ring gear carefully for damage to the teeth. Tooth damage is caused by incorrect break-in, wrong oil, insuficient tooth flank clearance, or faulty tooth contact.

The differential gears should also be examined for tooth damage. They should be placed in the differential carrier together with the shaft and thrust washers. Play should then be checked. If the play exceeds 0.0024 in. install thicker washers. These are available in 0.78 mm, 0.86 mm, and 0.94 mm sizes. Also check to see whether the cylindrical part of the flange which goes into the oil seal is worn or scratched. If it is, replace the flange and the oil seal.

The pinion nut has a locking slit. In time this slit loses its effectiveness. For this reason, the nut should be replaced if it has been removed more than once. The washer under the nut should also be replaced it it is deformed.

Check the oil seals and replace them if they are damaged or worn.

Check for cracks in the rear axle casing. Make sure that the brackets for the support arms and track rod are intact.

NOTE: On limited slip differentials, if the discs are worn all the discs should be replaced at the same time.

Assembly

Great cleanliness should be observed when assembling and adjusting the differential. Dirt in a tapered roller bearing can result in inaccurate measurement. When measuring the bearing clearance or preloading, the bearing should be oiled and rotated several turns loaded.

1. Place the differential side gears and the thrust washers in the differential side gears and the thrust washers in the differential pinions simultaneously with the dished thrust washers.
2. Insert the thrust block and drive in the shaft.
3. Check the differential unit. If the gear play has not been measured, check it as described under "Inspection." If oversize washers are installed, check by turning the gears one turn. The turning torque should not exceed 7.23 ft/lbs. The tool for making this check can be easily made from a shortened axle shaft adapted to a suitable torque wrench. After checking the replacement of the thrust washers, install the lock pin.
4. Install the ring gear. Make sure that the contact surfaces are clean and without burrs. Tighten the bolts to 45-65 ft/lbs, for standard head type, 65-80 ft/lbs flanged head type.

NOTE: Always use new bolts for gears in which the bolts are locked only by thread friction and the contact surface of the screw head.

NOTE: Assemble the limited slip differential in the order of the illustration. Tighten the case bolts to the proper torque, 45-55 ft/lbs.

PINION INSTALLATION

1. Polish the marking surface on the pinion with very fine emery cloth. Place the pinion in the casing so that the screw on the adjusting ring faces the larger part of the casing.
2. The pinion should have a certain nominal measurement to the center line of the ring gear. Due to manufacturing tolerances, there are deviations from the nominal measurement. This is indicated on the pinion.

On differentials made by Volvo, the surface is generally ground down 0.012 in. so that the deviation is always indicated by plus tolerance in hundredths of a millimeter. The plus sign is not indicated. On other units, the deviation is indicated in thousandths of an inch and with a plus or minus sign. If there is a plus sign in front of the figure, the nominal neasurement is to be increased and, in the case of a minus sign, the nominal measurement is to be decreased.

To check the pinion location, use a dial indicator, an indicator retainer (SVO 2284), and a measuring tool (SVO 2393), which consists of two parts: a pinion gauge and an adjuster fixture. Place the pinion gauge on the ground end surface of the pinion and place the adjuster fixture in the differential bearing recesses. Place the indicator retainer on the drive pinion carrier and zero the indicator against the adjuster fixture. Then move the indicator retainer so that the indicator is against the pinion gauge. Read the indicator.

On a Volvo unit on which the pinion is, for example, marked 33, the pinion gauge should be 0.013 in. (0.33 mm) under the adjuster fixture. On other units, if the pinion is marked 0, the adjuster fixture and pinion gauge should be at the same height; if the pinion is marked −, the pinion gauge should be higher than the adjuster fixture; and if it is marked +, the pinion gauge should be lower than the adjuster fixture. The setting is adjusted by turning the cam on the pinion until the gauge dial shows the correct figure, then locking in the adjusting ring with the lock screw. Remove the measuring tool and pinion.

3. Place the rear pinion bearing complete with the outer ring in a measuring fixture (SVO 2600). Install the plate, spring and nut. The flat side of the nut should face upward. The plate (and the bearing) should be turned forward and backward several times so that the rollers take up the correct position. Place the adjusting ring in the measuring fixture. Use an indicator retainer (SVO 2284) and a dial indicator. Place the measuring point on the gauge against the adjusting ring and set the gauge to zero. Then place the point of the gauge against the outer ring of the bearing. The gauge now shows the required size for the shims. Measure the thickness of the shims with a micrometer. It is not always possible to obtain shims with exactly the correct thickness. However, they may not be more than 0.0012 in. thicker than the measured value but may be up to 0.0020 in. thinner.

4. Press the rear bearing on the pinion with a sleeve. The washer under the rear bearing inner ring on a new Volvo unit should not be installed after overhaul. Install the measured shims and press in both the outer rings of the bearings.

5. Install the pinion in the carrier and mount three 0.38 in. thick shims and the front pinion bearing. Tighten the pinion. If a nut remover is used when installing the pinion, the pinion must be pressed forward so that it does not strike against the bearing positions.

6. Install the pinion gauge and indicator retainer. Move the pinion down while turning it forward and backward at the same time. Set the indicator gauge to zero. Then press the pinion forward at the same time. Read the play.

7. Remove the pinion. Remove a sufficient number of shims corresponding to the measured play plus 0.0028 in. Reinstall the pinion.

8. Then check the pinion bearings with a torque gauge. The torque gauge should show a torque of 5-10 in/lbs for used bearings and 10-20 in/lbs for new bearings when the pinion rotates. On new units, turning torque may be higher due to another installation method.

Check the location of the pinion with a dial indicator, an indicator retainer (SVO 2284), and a measuring tool (SVO 2393).

DIFFERENTIAL INSTALLATION

1. Oil the adjusting rings internally and install them on the differential carrier. The ring with the oxidized adjusting ring is placed on the ring gear side. Also oil the bearing seal in the carrier. The differential carrier and adjusting rings are placed in the carrier. Use the dial indicator and adjust the ring so that the correct tooth flank clearance, 0.0060 in. is

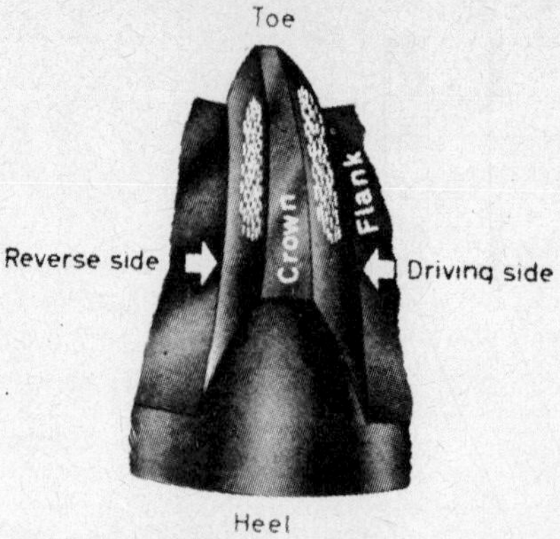

Correct tooth contact

obtained. The tooth flank clearance may vary between 0.0040 in. (model 30: 0.0052 in.) and 0.0080 in., but should be kept as near 0.0060 in. as possible. Tighten the lock bolts in the adjusting rings.

2. Coat several teeth with marking blue at three points on the ring gear. By this means a check can be kept on possible ring gear warping. Pull the pinion 10-12 turns in both directions and check the tooth pattern. When the tooth contact is correct, the contact pattern should be vertical in the middle of the tooth but somewhat nearer to the toe than to the heel. The contact pattern on the reverse side and driving side should lie opposite each other. If the contact pattern is incorrect, the location of the pinion must be adjusted before assembly continues. If the contact pattern lies too far toward the heel on the driving side and too far toward the toe on the reverse side, the pinion should be moved inward. If the contact pattern lies too far toward the toe on the driving side and too far toward the heel on the reverse side, the pinion should be moved outward. Note that the contact pattern will lie somewhat nearer the toe when the adjusting rings are installed than when the bearings are installed.

3. When correct tooth flank clearance and contact pattern are obtained, remove the differential and adjusting ring. Place the center washer on the measuring fixture. Place a bearing in the measuring fixture and fit the plate, spring and nut. The nut should be fitted with the flat side facing downward. Turn the plate forward and backward several times. Install the dial indicator gauge and retainer. Set the gauge to zero against the adjusting ring and then place the pointer facing the bearing. Read the gauge. With a micrometer, measure the shims. The total shim thickness should correspond to the indicator reading plus 0.028 in. Repeat with the other bearing. Keep a careful check on which side the bearing and shim are to be fitted.

4. Install the shims on the differential carrier and press on the bearings. Use a drift. When installing the second bearing, use a drift as a cushioning ring to avoid damage to the first bearing.

5. Expand the pinion carrier with a special tool. Install the differential and outer rings. Remove the tool. Install the bearing caps and tighten the bolts to 35-50 ft/lbs.

6. Check the tooth flank clearance and contact pattern.

7. Install the oil slinger and the oil seal. The oil seal should be fitted with a drift. Press on the flange. Install the washer and nut. Tighten the nut to a torque of 200-220 ft/lbs.

8. Install the inspection cover and gasket.

9. Install the axle shafts as outlined in the "Axle Shaft Removal and Installation" procedure.

REAR AXLE HOUSING INSTALLATION

1. Place the rear axle on a garage jack. Move the axle in under the car and install the bolts for the support arms and torque rods.

2. Raise the jack until the track rod attachment on the shaft is at the level with the attachment on the body. Install the track rod.

3. Install the attaching bolts for the springs. Tighten the nuts for the torque rods and support arms.

4. Install the bracket, union, and brake hoses. Connect the universal joint to the flange.

5. Install the upper bolts for the shock absorbers. Install the handbrake cable in the brackets and at the levers. Adjust the handbrake and bleed the brake system. Fill with oil.

6. Install the wheels and nuts. Lower the car. Tighten the wheel nuts to 70-100 ft/lbs. Fill with oil. Use only hypoid oil, 80w/90.

REAR SUSPENSION

All Volvos use a coil spring rear suspension. The solid rear axle is suspended from the rigid frame member by a pair of support arms and damped by a pair of double-acting telescopic shock absorbers. A pair of torque rods control rear axle wind-up and a track rod limits the lateral movement of the rear axle in relation to the car. A rear stabilizer bar, attached to both rear support (trailing) arms, is installed on 240 and 260 models.

Springs

REMOVAL AND INSTALLATION

1. Remove the hub cap and loosen the lug nuts a few turns. Jack up the car and place jack stands in front of the rear jacking points. Remove the wheel and tire assembly.

2. Place a hydraulic jack beneath the rear axle housing and raise the housing sufficiently to compress the spring. Loosen the nuts for the upper and lower spring attachments.

CAUTION

Due to the fact that the spring is compressed under several hundred pounds of pressure, when it is freed from its lower attachment, it will attempt to suddenly return to its extended position. It is therefore imperative that the axle housing be lowered with extreme care until the spring is fully extended. As an added

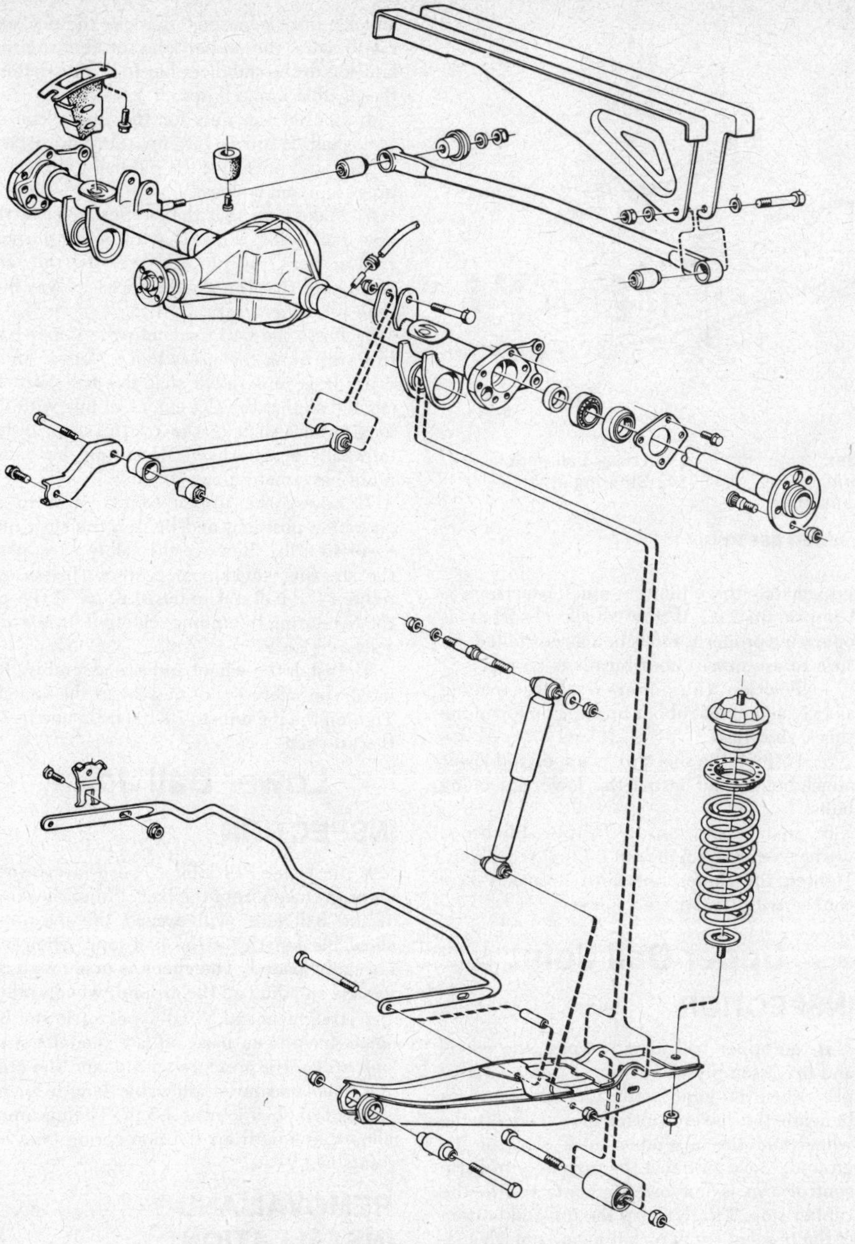

Rear suspension—240,260 series

safety measure, a chain may be attached to the lower spring coil and secured to the axle housing.

3. Disconnect the shock absorber at its upper attachment. Carefully lower the jack and axle housing until the spring is fully extended. Remove the spring.

4. To install, position the retaining bolt and inner washer, for the upper attachment, inside the spring and then, while holding the outer washer and rubber spacer to the upper body attachment, install the spring and inner washer to the upper attachment (sandwiching the rubber spacer), and tighten the retaining bolt.

5. Raise the jack and secure the bottom of the spring to its lower attachment with the washer and retaining bolt.

6. Connect the shock absorber to its upper attachment. Install the wheel and tire assembly.

7. Remove the jack stands and lower the car. Tighten the lug nuts to 70-100 ft/lbs and install the hub cap.

Shock Absorbers

REMOVAL AND INSTALLATION

1. Remove the hub cap and loosen the lug nuts a few turns. Place blocks in front of the front wheels. Jack up the rear of the car and place jack stands in front of the rear jacking points. Remove the wheel and tire assembly.

2. Remove the nuts and bolts which retain the shock absorber to its upper and lower attachments and remove the shock absorber. Make sure that the spacing sleeve, inside the axle support arm for the lower attachment, is not misplaced.

3. The damping effect of the shock absorber may be tested by securing the lower attachment in a vise and extending and compressing it. A properly operating shock absorber should offer approximately three times as much resistance to extending the unit as compressing it. Replace the shock absorber if it does not function as above, or if its fixed rubber bushings are damaged. Replace any leaking shock absorber.

4. To install, position the shock absorber to its upper and lower attachments. Make sure that the spacing sleeve is installed inside the axle support (trailing) arm and is aligned with the lower attachment bolt hole. Install the retaining nuts and bolts. On 240 series models, the shock fits *inside* the support arm. On all 164 models, the shock attaches on the *outboard* side of the support arm.

5. Install the wheel and tire assembly. Remove the jack stands and lower the car. Tighten the lug nuts to 70-100 ft/lbs, and install the hub cap.

FRONT SUSPENSION–MODEL 164

All 164 series model Volvos use a coil spring independent front suspension utilizing a pair of upper and lower control arms bolted to each side of the rigid front frame member. The coil springs and telescopic double-acting shock absorbers are bolted to the lower control arms at the bottom and seat in the crossmember at the top. A pair of steering knuckles are carried in ball joints between the upper and lower control arms. A stabilizer bar is attached to the lower control arms and to the body.

Springs

REMOVAL AND INSTALLATION

1. Remove the hub cap and loosen the lug nuts a few turns.

2. Firmly apply the parking brake and place blocks in back of the rear wheels. Jack up the front of the car and place jack stands in back of the front jacking points. Remove the wheel and tire assembly.

3. Remove the shock absorber as outlined in the applicable "Shock Absorber Removal and Installation" procedure.

4. Remove the cotter pin and ball nut and disconnect the steering rod from the steering knuckle. Loosen the clamp for the flexible brake hoses. Remove the stabilizer attachment from the lower control arm.

5. Place a jack under the lower control arm. Raise the jack to unload the lower control arm. Remove the cotter pins and loosen the nuts for the upper and lower ball joints; then rap with a hammer until they loosen from the spindle. Remove the nuts and lower the jack slightly.

6. Remove the steering knuckle with the

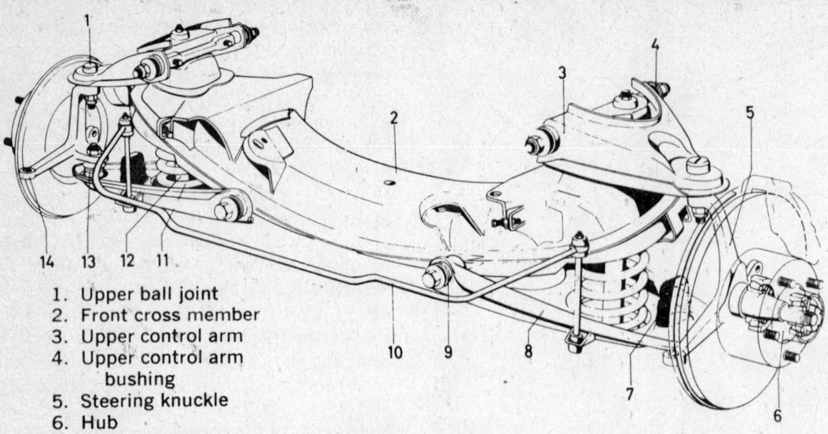

1. Upper ball joint
2. Front cross member
3. Upper control arm
4. Upper control arm bushing
5. Steering knuckle
6. Hub
7. Rubber buffer
8. Lower control arm
9. Lower control arm bushing
10. Stabilizer
11. Coil spring
12. Shock absorber
13. Lower ball joint
14. Steering arm

164 series front suspension assembly

front brake caliper and disc still connected to the brake lines. In order not to stretch the brake lines, place the brake unit on a milk crate or other suitable stand.

CAUTION

Do not attempt to remove the spring until it is fully extended. As an added safety measure, a chain may be attached to the lower spring coil and secured to the frame.

7. Slowly lower the jack and lower control arm to the fullest extent. Remove the spring and rubber spacer.
8. To install the spring place a jack directly beneath the spring attachment to the lower control arm. Place the spring with the rubber spacer in position, and lift up the lower control arm with the jack so that the steering knuckle and brake unit assembly may be installed.
9. Install and tighten the upper and lower ball joint nuts. Connect the stabilizer to its attachment on the lower control arm.
10. Install the shock absorber as outlined in the applicable "Shock Absorber Removal and Installation" section.
11. With the wheels pointing straight ahead, and the lower control arm unloaded, connect the steering rod to the steering knuckle and install the ball nut and cotter pin.
12. Clamp the brake hoses to the stabilizer bolt.
13. Install the wheel and tire assembly. Remove the jack stands and lower the car. Tighten the lug nuts to 70-100 ft/lbs and install the hub cap.

Shock Absorbers

REMOVAL AND INSTALLATION

1. Remove the upper nut, washer and other rubber bushing.
2. Remove the two lower attaching bolts beneath the lower control arm, and pull the shock absorber assembly down and out.
3. Test the damping action of the shock absorber. Extending the unit should offer approximately three times as much resistance as compressing it. If the shock absorber is operating properly and is being reinstalled, be sure to use new rubber bushings on top.
4. Position the inner washer, spacing sleeve, and inner rubber bushing on top of the shock absorber.
5. Position the shock to its upper and lower attachments, and install the lower attaching bolts.
6. Install the outer rubber bushing, washer, and the upper nut on top of the unit. Tighten the upper nut until it makes firm contact with the spacing sleeve.

Upper Ball Joint

INSPECTION

If the upper ball joint is worn, the wheel and tire assembly will exhibit excessive radial play when the joint is offloaded. Place a jack beneath the lower control arm, and lift the wheel and tire assembly until clear of the ground. Make sure that the upper control arm control arm is not making contact with the rubber stop. Firmly grasp the top and bottom of the tire and try to rock it in and out; that is, intermittently push the top of the tire towards the engine compartment, then pull it away from the car, while simultaneously doing the opposite to the bottom of the tire. Replace the upper ball joint if the radial play of the wheel and tire assembly is excessive.

NOTE: Do not confuse possible wheel bearing play with ball joint play. It is advisable that the wheel bearing adjustment procedure in Chapter nine be followed prior to replacing the ball joint.

REMOVAL AND INSTALLATION

1. Remove the hub cap and loosen the lug nuts a few turns.
2. Jack up the front of the vehicle and place safety stands beneath the front jacking points. Remove the wheel and tire assembly.
3. Loosen, but do not remove the nut for the upper ball joint. With a hammer, rap around the ball joint stud on the steering knuckle until it loosens. Remove the nut, and safety wire the upper end of the steering knuckle to the stabilizer bar to avoid straining the flexible brake hoses.
4. Loosen the nuts for the upper control arm shaft ½ turn. Lift up the control arm slightly and press out the old ball joint with a press tool and a sleeve.
5. Make sure that the rubber cover of the new ball joint is filled with multi-purpose grease. Bend the pin end over the slot, and make sure that the grease forces its way out, then fill as necessary.
6. Press the ball joint into the upper control arm using the press tool a sleeve, and a drift. It is imperative that the ball joint be aligned so that the slot comes in line with the longitudinal shaft of the control arm, either internally or externally, as the pin has maximum movement along this line.
7. Lower the upper control arm to its operating position, and tighten the shaft nuts to 40-45 ft/lbs. Remove the safety wire; place the steering knuckle in position; install and tighten the ball nut to 60-70 ft/lbs. If the pin rotates during tightening, clamp it firmly with a screw vise.
8. Install the wheel and tire assembly. Remove the safety stands and lower the vehicle. Tighten the lug nuts to 70-100 ft/lbs and install the hub cap.

Lower Ball Joint

INSPECTION

If the lower ball joint is worn, a measurement (A) taken from the ball stud to the cover of the ball joint will exceed the maximum allowable length for the ball joint when it is normally loaded. The check is made with the vehicle standing on the ground, wheels pointing straight ahead. Two types of lower ball joints have been used on late model Volvos; one utilizing a pressure spring, and the other not. The maximum allowable length for the spring type ball joint is 4.5 in. The maximum allowable length for the non-spring type ball joints is 3.91 in.

REMOVAL AND INSTALLATION

1. Remove the hub cap and loosen the lug nuts a few turns.

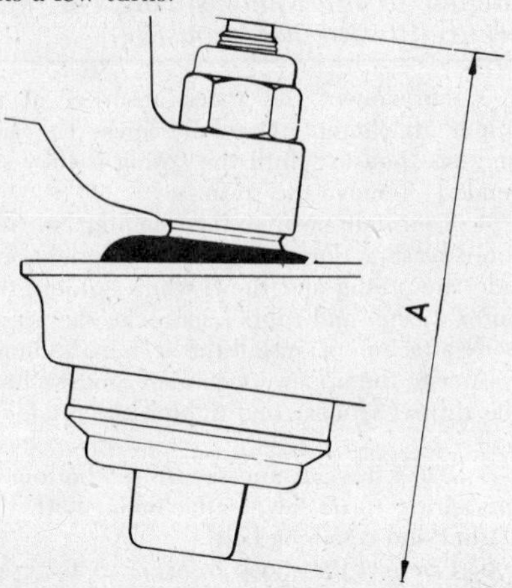

Spring–type lower ball joint maximum allowable length

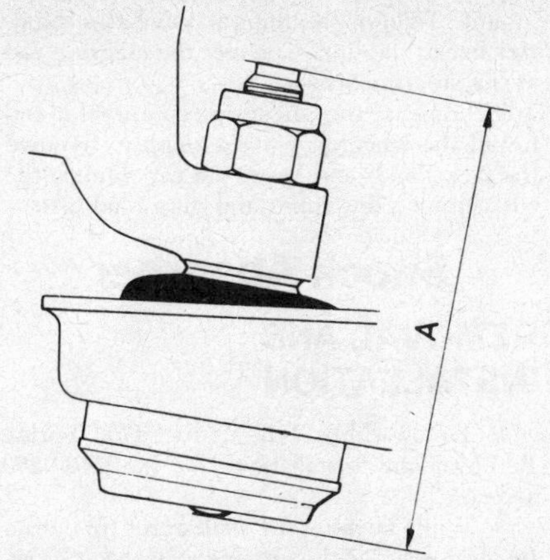

Non-spring type lower ball joint maximum allowable length

2. Jack up the front of the vehicle and place jack stands beneath the front jacking points. Remove the wheel and tire assembly.
3. Remove the cotter pin and ball stud nut, and press the steering rod ball stud from the steering knuckle. Remove the brake lines form their bracket at the stabilizer bolt.
4. Remove the cotter pins and loosen but do not remove the nuts for both the upper and lower ball joints. Rap with a hammer until the ball joints loosen from the spindle. Place a jack beneath the lower control arm and raise it to off-load the control arm. Remove the ball joint nuts.
5. Remove the steering knuckle with the front brake until still connected to the brake lines. In order not to stretch the brake lines, place the brake unit on a milk crate or other suitable stand.
6. Press the lower ball joint out of the lower control arm with a press tool and sleeve.
7. Make sure that the rubber cover of the new ball joint is filled witth multi-purpose grease. Bend the pin end to the side, and make sure that the grease forces its way out, then fill as necessary.
8. To install, press the lower ball joint into its control arm with a press tool, sleeve, and drift. Make sure that the ball joint is not loose in the control arm.
9. Position the steering knuckle and brake unit assembly in between the upper and lower control arms and tighten the ball joint stud nuts to 60-70 ft/lbs (upper ball joint), and 75-90 ft/lbs (lower ball joint). If the pins rotate during tightening, clamp them firmly with a screw vise.
10. Install the steering rod ball stud into the steering knuckle and tighten the stud nut. Lower the jack beneath the lower control arm slightl and with the front wheels pointing straight ahead, attach the brake lines to their bracket at the stabilizer bolt.
11. Install the wheel and tire assembly. Remove the jack stands and lower the vehicle. Tighten the lug nuts to 70-100 ft/lbs and install the hub cap.

Upper Control Arm

REMOVAL AND INSTALLATION

1. Loosen the wheel lugs.
2. Raise and support the front end and remove the wheel.
3. Loosen, but do not remove, the ball joint nut. Tap on the knuckle, around the ball joint pin until the ball joint loosens from the axle.
4. Remove the nut and suspend the axle to avoid straining the brake hose.
5. Disconnect the control arm from the cross shaft. Note the number and location of the shims.
6. Install in reverse of the removal. Torque the cross shaft nuts to 43 ft/lbs.

Lower Control Arm

REMOVAL AND INSTALLATION

1. Loosen wheel lugs, raise and support car and remove wheels.
2. Remove shock absorber.
3. Disconnect the tie rod from the steering arm with a separator tool.
4. Loosen the brake hose clamp and remove the stabilizer.
5. Place a jack under the lower control arm.
6. Loosen the ball joint nuts and tap around the ball joints with a hammer until they loosen from the knuckle.
7. Remove the nuts, lower the jack and remove the knuckle with the front brake unit. Suspend or position this assembly out of the way.
8. Lower the jack slowly and carefully, and when all tension is relieved, remove the spring.

NOTE: The spring is under considerable pressure. It is adviseable to use a spring compressor or safety chain when removing spring.

9. Remove the control arm shaft nut, turn the relay rod with the tie rod and remove the control arm shaft.
10. Remove the control arm.
11. Install in reverse of removal.

FRONT SUSPENSION—240 AND 260 SERIES

All 240 and 260 series Volvos use a coil spring independent front suspension utilizing a pair of MacPherson-type struts located between a sheet metal tower at the top and a lower control arm at the bottom. The MacPherson strut design incorporates the coil spring, shock absorber and wheel spindle into a single assembly, eliminating the need for an upper suspension control arm. The MacPherson strut design provides for generous vertical suspension travel allowing the use of softer springs. The strut design is extremely sensitive to front wheel imbalance; the slightest imbalance often leading to front end wobble.

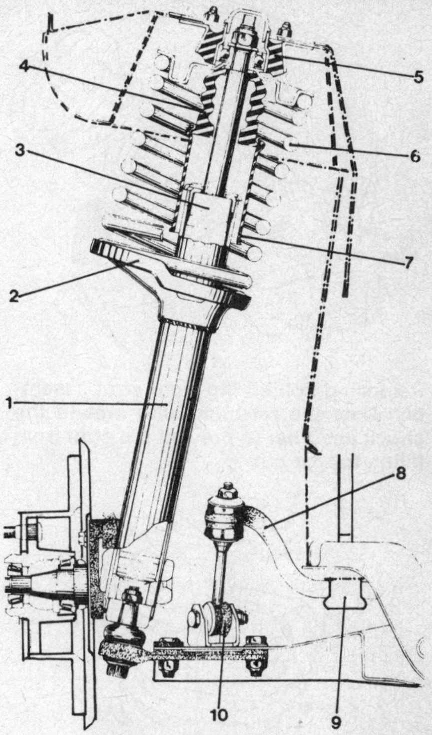

1. Strut assembly
2. Lower spring support
3. Shock absorber
4. Rubber bumper
5. Upper attachment
6. Coil spring
7. Ruber sleeve, protecting the shock absorber
8. Stabilizer bar
9. Stabilizer bar attachment
10. Stabilizer link

Front suspension—240, 260 series

Finally, the caster angle of the front suspension is preset and cannot be adjusted. If the caster angle is not up to specifications, the damaged components must be replaced as a unit.

Coil Spring

REMOVAL AND INSTALLATION

NOTE: In order to perform the following procedure, a special coil spring compressor tool must be available. Under no circumstances should you attempt to lower and disassemble the strut assembly without the proper spring compressor tool, as serious injury could result.

1. Remove the hub cap and loosen the lug nuts a few turns.
2. Firmly apply the parking brake and place blocks in back of the rear wheels.
3. Install the spring compressor on the spring directly beneath the sheet metal tower. Make sure that 3 coils of the spring are free between the tool attachment points. Then tighten the tool and compress the spring.
4. Jack up the front of the car with a hoist or using a floor jack at the center of the front crossmember. When the wheels are 2-3 in. off

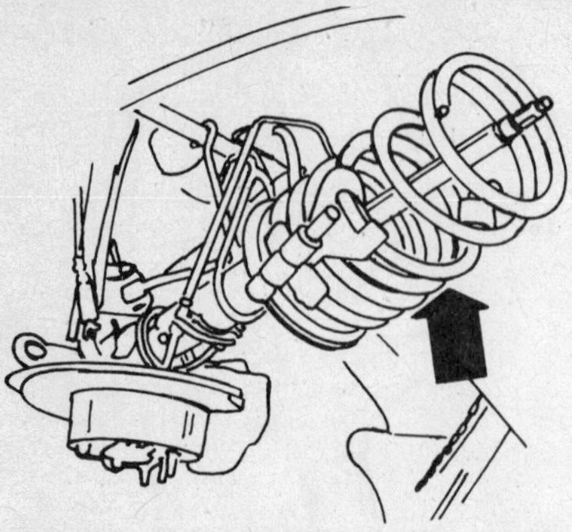

Removing coil spring from strut assembly. Note the retaining wire around the shock absorber to prevent the strut from tilting too far out

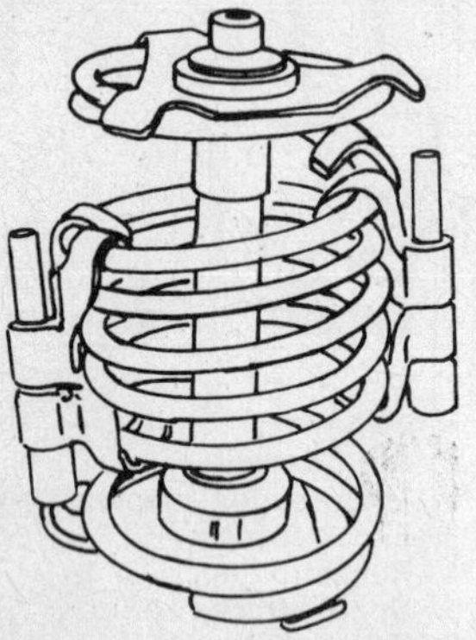

If the claw type spring compressor does not have enough travel to release all of the spring tension, a sandwich type compressor will have to be used to remove the original compressor

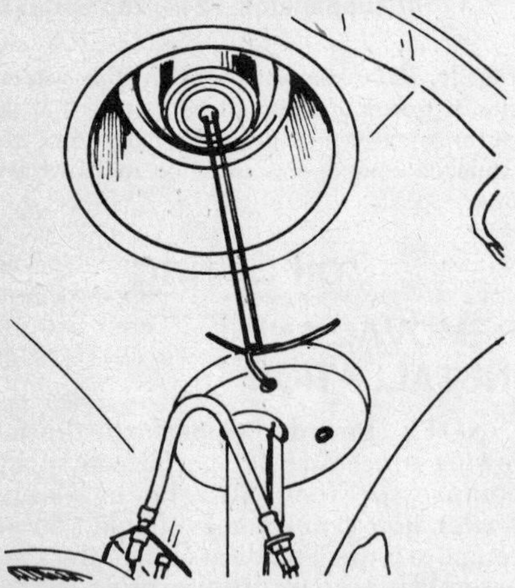

Suspending the top of the strut from the body with a wire while removing the lower ball joint

the ground, the car is high enough. Place jack stands beneath the front jacking points. Then, remove the floor jack from the crossmember (if used), and reposition it beneath the applicable lower control arm to provide support at the outer end. Remove the wheel and tire assembly.

5. Using a ball joint puller, disconnect the steering rod from the steering arm.

6. Disconnect the stabilizer bar at the link upper attachment.

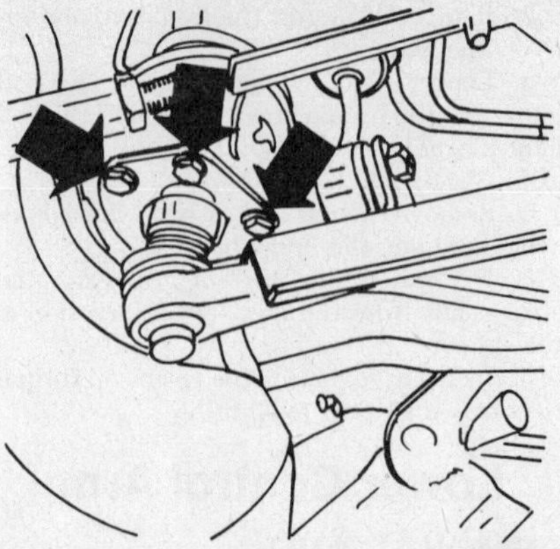

Late production type lower ball joint-to-strut retainint bolts

7. Remove the bolt retaining the brake line bracket to the fender well.

8. Open the hood and remove the cover for the strut assembly upper attachment.

9. While keeping the strut from turning, loosen and remove the nut for the upper attachment.

10. Before lowering the strut assembly, wire or tie the strut to some stationary component, or use a holding fixture such as SVO 5045, to prevent the strut from traveling down too far and damaging the hydraulic brake lines. Then lower the jack supporting the lower arm and allow the strut to tilt out to about a 60 degree angle. At this angle, the top of the strut assembly should just protrude past the wheel well, allowing removal of the strut components from the top.

11. Lift off the spring seat, rubber bumper, and the shock absorber protection. Remove the coil spring and compressor assembly from the strut.

12. Slowly relieve the tension on the compressor and remove it from the spring. Place the compressor on the replacement spring (making sure 3 coils separate the attachment points as before), and compress.

NOTE: If the spring compressor does not have enough travel to fully release the spring tension, it will be necessary to use another "sandwich" type compressor to remove the original compressor once the spring is out of the car.

13. Position the new spring and compressor on the strut assembly. Make sure the spring end is properly aligned with the strut bracket.

NOTE: Make sure that the compressor bolts face downwards.

14. Install the rubber bumper and the shock absorber protection. Position the spring seat on the spring, making sure it is aligned with the spring.

15. Carefully lift and guide the strut assembly into its upper attachment in the spring tower. Connect the stabilizer bar to the stabilizer link. Guide the shock absorber spindle into the upper attachment and raise the jack beneath the lower control arm. Install the washer and nut on top of the shock absorber spindle. While holding the spindle from turning, tighten the nut to 15-25 ft/lbs. Install the cover.

16. Attach the brake line bracket to its mount. Tighten the nut retaining the stabilizer bar to the link. Connect the steering rod at the steering arm.

17. Release the coil spring compressor and install the wheel and tire assembly. Remove the jack stands and lower the car. Jounce the suspension a few times and then road test.

Shock Absorber

REMOVAL AND INSTALLATION

1. Follow Steps 1-11 under "Coil Spring Removal and Installation" for the 240, 260 series.

2. While keeping the strut outer tube from turning, remove the upper shock absorber retaining nut.

3. Pull the shock absorber unit out of the outer tube (casing). On 1979 models, gas type shock absorbers are used. A special tool, Volvo #9995173 must be used to remove and install the unit.

4. Install the new shock absorber unit into the outer tube and install the retaining nut. You can stop the outer tube from turning with the nut by holding the tube at the weld with a pair of channel-lock pliers.

5. Pull the shock absorber spindle to its uppermost position.

6. Follow Steps 13-17 under "Coil Spring Removal and Installation" for the 240 series.

Lower Control Arm

REPLACEMENT

1. Jack up car, support on stands and remove wheels.
2. Remove stabilizer bar.
3. Remove ball joint from control arm.
4. Remove control arm front retaining bolt.
5. Remove control arm rear attachment plate.
6. Remove attachment plate from control arm.
7. Remove stabilizer link from control arm.
8. Install in reverse of removal.

NOTE: Right and left bushings are not interchangeable. The right side bushing should be turned so that the small slots point horizontally when installed. Torque the front retaining bolt to 55 ft/lbs, the rear bushing nut to 4 ft/lbs, and the rear attachment bolts to 30 ft/lbs.

Lower Ball Joint

REMOVAL AND INSTALLATION

Early Production Models

1. Follow Steps 1-11 under "Coil Spring Removal and Installation" for the 240, 260 series.

2. While grasping the strut outer tube (casing) with a pair of locking pliers, loosen and remove the shock absorber retaining nut.

3. Pull the shock absorber unit out of the outer tube.

4. Loosen the ball joint retaining nut. Grasp the outer tube at the weld with a pair of

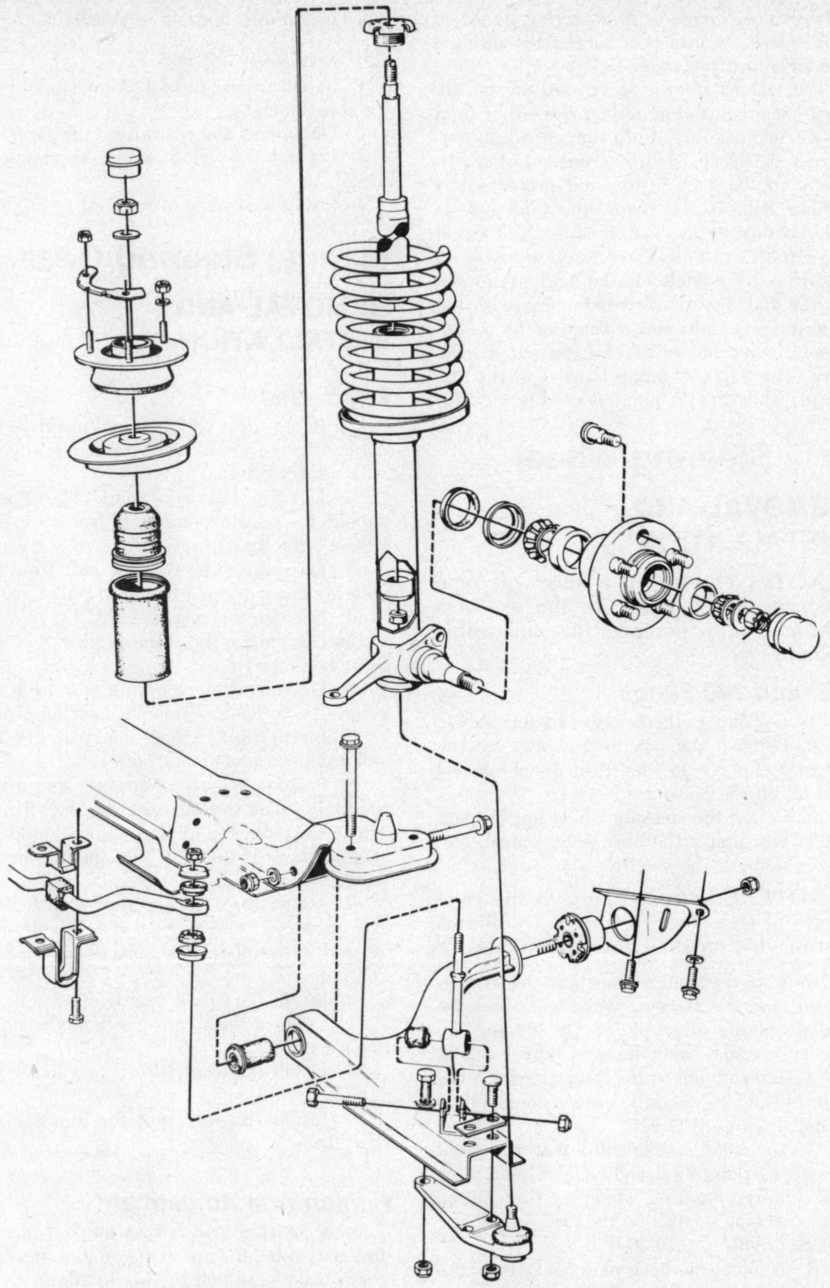

Front suspension strut—240, 260 series

channel-lock pliers and loosen the nut with a 19 mm socket and a long extension, until the joint bracket comes loose.

5. Using a drift and hammer, loosen the conical part of the ball joint from the strut assembly.

6. Using the 19 mm socket coated on the inside with vaseline or wheel bearing grease, remove the ball joint retaining nut. The grease should keep the nut from falling down into the strut tube.

7. Wire the top of the strut assembly to the sheet metal tower, and allow the strut to hang vertically. Disconnect the ball joint from the bottom of the strut assembly. Take care not to damage the brake hoses. Then, disconnect the ball joint from the lower control arm.

8. Attach the new ball joint to the lower control arm.

NOTE: Make sure the new ball joint sutd is free of grease, or the stud could be tightened too far into the cone making the rubber bellows stick to the strut.

9. Remove the securing wire and lift the strut assembly into position. Install the ball joint nut, and torque to 30-50 ft/lbs. Stop the outer tube from turning with locking pliers at the weld.

10. Install the shock absorber and retaining nut. Tighten as in Step 9. Pull the shock absorber spindle to its uppermost position.

11. Follow Steps 13-17 under "Coil Spring Removal and Installation" for the 240, 260 series.

Late Production Models

1. Jack up the front of the car and install jack stands beneath the front jacking attachments.

2. Remove the tire and wheel assembly.

3. Reach in between the spring coils and loosen the shock absorber cap nut a few turns.

4. Remove the four bolts (12 mm) retaining the ball joint seat to the bottom of the strut.

5. Remove the three nuts (19 mm) retaining the ball joint to the lower control arm.

6. Place the ball joint and attachment assembly in a vise and remove the 19 mm nut from the ball joint stud. Then, drive out the old ball joint.

7. Install the new ball joint in the attachment and tighten the stud nut to 35-50 ft/lbs.

8. Attach the ball joint assembly to the strut. Tighten to 15-20 ft/lbs.

9. Attach the ball joint assembly to the control arm. Tighten to 70-95 ft/lbs.

10. Tighten the shock absorber cap nut. Install the wheel and tire. Lower the car and road-test.

NOTE: On 1979 and later models with power steering, the ball joints are different for the left and right side.

Compared to previous years, the ball joint is .393 in. forward in control rod attachment. It is therefore most important that these ball joints are installed on the correct side.

Wheel Alignment

CASTER AND CAMBER ADJUSTMENT

Model 164

The procedures for adjusting caster and camber are grouped together here as they may be peformed at the same time on these Volvos. Both adjustments are made by inserting shims between the upper control arm shaft and the sheet metal of the shock absorber tower. Loosen the bolts which retain the control arm shaft to the shock tower and insert the shims. Before each adjustment is completed, the bolts must be tightened or an erroneous measurement will be obtained. A special SVO tool (No. 2713) is available from dealers for loosening or tightening the control arm shaft bolts on the 140 series and 164 models, because gaining access to these bolts is difficult.

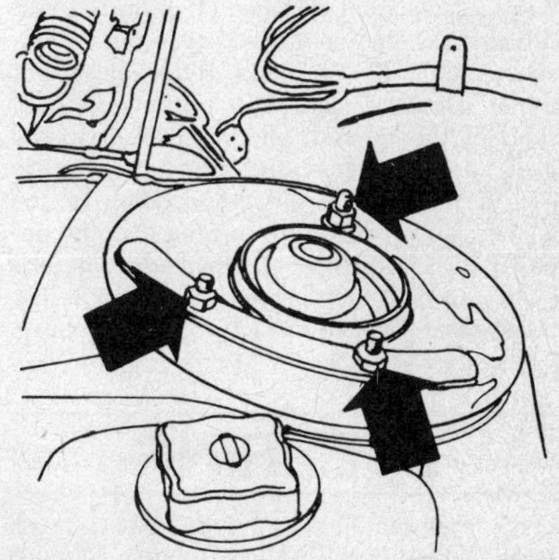

Loosen the upper strut nuts to adjust the camber of 240 and 260 series

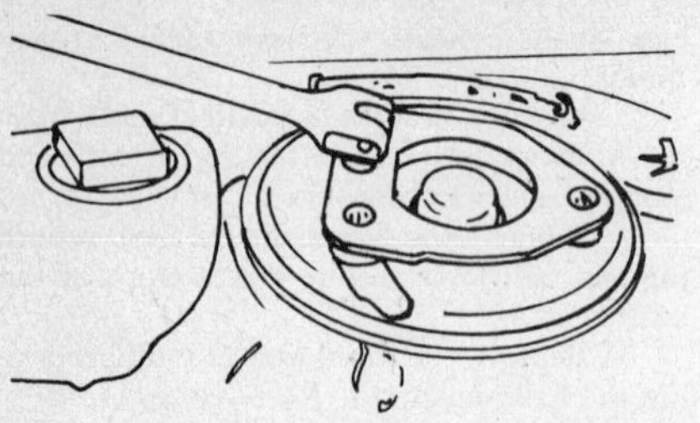

Caster is adjusted by either removing a shim at one of the bolts, adding a shim at the other bolt, or by transferring half of the required shim thickness from one bolt to another. Caster is adjusted to the positive side, for example, by inserting shims at the rear bolt or removing shims at the front bolt.

Camber is adjusted by either removing or adding shims of equal thickness at both bolts. Camber is increased toward the positive by removing shims, and decreased toward the negative by adding shims.

Shims are available in sizes of 0.15, 0.5, 1.0, 3.0, and 6.0 mm (0.006, 0.020, 0.039, 0.12, and 0.24 in.). Remember to torque the control arm shaft bolts to 40-50 ft/lbs after making the adjustment.

240 and 260 Models

Caster angle is fixed by suspension design and cannot be adjusted. If caster is not within specifications, check front end parts for damage and replace as necessary.

Camber angle, however, may be adjusted. At the strut upper attachment to the body, two of the three bolts holes are eccentric, allowing the upper end of the strut to tilt out or in as necessary. A special pivot lever tool SVO #5038, which attaches to the tops of the strut upper attachment retaining bolt threads is recommended for this job. To adjust, loosen the three retaining nuts, install the pivot lever tool, and adjust to specifications. After adjusting, torque the nuts to 15-25 ft/lbs.

Toe-In Adjustment–All Models

Toe-in may be adjusted after performing the caster and camber adjustments. With a wheel spreader, measure the distance (X) between the rear of the right and left front tires, at spindle (hub) height, and then measure the distance (Y) between the front of the right and left front tires, also at spindle (hub) height. Subtract the front distance (Y) from the rear distance (X), and compare that to the specifications table. X−Y = toe-in. If the adjustment is not correct, loosen the locknuts on both sides of the tie rod, and rotate the tie rod itself. Toe-in is increased by turning the tie rod in the normal forward rotation of the wheels, and reduced by turning it in the opposite direction. After the final adjustment is made, torque the locknuts to 55-65 ft/lbs, being careful not to disturb the adjustment.

STEERING

All Volvos use divided steering columns that protect the driver during front end collisions. The 164 uses a telescoping column and a breakaway flange at the steering box. The power steering gear used on the 164 series is the ZF worm and roller type.

The manual steering gear used on the 240 series is a rack and pinion type of either Cam or ZF manufacture. Both units are fully enclosed, with the steering rods attached directly to the rack piston and protected by rubber bellows. However, the Cam unit is filled with steering gear oil while the ZF unit is grease-filled. Power steering is available on all 240 series models and standard equipment on the 260. Power assist is integral with the steering rear unit, and is supplied by an engine driven pump of ZF or Saginaw manufacture. The Saginaw pump is used in the 260 series, while the ZF pump is used in the 240.

Steering Wheel

REMOVAL AND INSTALLATION

NOTE: The use of a knock-off type steering wheel puller, or the use of a hammer may damage the collapsible column.

164 and 240 Series

1. Disconnect the negative battery cable.
2. Remove the retaining screws for the upper half of the molded turn signal housing and lift off the housing.
3. Pry off the steering wheel impact pad.
4. Disconnect the horn plug contact.
5. Remove the steering wheel nut.

NOTE: Due to a change in the cone angle of this steering shaft, a puller is not needed on 1979 and later models.

6. With the front wheels pointing straight ahead, and the steering wheel centered, install a steering wheel puller. On 164 models, use an outside circumference type, such as SVO 5003, and pull off the steering wheel. On 140, 240 and 260 models, use a universal type puller, such as SVO 2263.
7. To install, make sure that the front wheels are pointing straight ahead, then place the centered steering wheel on the column with the plug contact to the left. Install the nut and tighten to 20-30 ft/lbs.
8. Connect the horn plug contact and install the impact pad.
9. Install the upper turn signal housing half.
10. Connect the negative battery cable and test the operation of the horn.

TURN SIGNAL SWITCH REPLACEMENT

See Steering Wheel Removal and Installation.

Ignition Lock and Switch

REPLACEMENT

164 Series

1. Disconnect the wiring from the switch.
2. Remove the attaching screws and lift out switch.
3. Install in reverse of removal.

240 and 260 Series

1. Remove noise insulation panel and center side panel.
2. Disconnect the wires from the switch.
3. Pry out the switch with a short screwdriver.
4. Install in reverse of removal.

Manual Steering Gear

REMOVAL AND INSTALLATION

240 Series

1. Remove the lock bolt and nut from the column flange. Bend apart the flange slightly with a screwdriver.
2. Jack up the front end. The stands should be positioned at the jack supports. Remove the front wheels.
3. Disconnect the steering rods from the steering arms, using a ball joint puller.
4. Remove the splash guard.
5. Disconnect the steering gear from the front axle member.
6. Disconnect the steering gear from the steering gear flange. Remove steering gear.
7. Install rubber spacers and plates for the steering gear attachment points.
8. Position the steering gear, and guide the pinion shaft into the steering shaft flange. The recess on the pinion shaft should be aligned towards the lock bolt opening in the flange.
9. Attach the steering gear to the front axle member. Check that the U-bolts are aligned in the plate slots. Install flat washers and nuts.
10. Install the splash guard.
11. Connect the steering rods to the steering arms.
12. Install the front wheels and lower the vehicle.
13. Install the lock bolt for the steering shaft flange.

Pitman Arm Adjustment

On a steering gear with a marked pitman arm and pitman arm shaft (on the steering gear), make sure that the marks align.

On a steering gear without the marks, lift up the front of the vehicle so that the front wheels are free. Turn the steering wheel to its center position (count the number of turns). Lower the vehicle. If the vehicle is correctly loaded, the wheels should now point straight forward. If the wheels do not, remove the pitman arm from the shaft with a puller. Then set the left wheel straight ahead and replace the pitman arm. The steering wheel should be in its center position. Tighten the pitman arm nut to 100-120 ft/lbs.

Power Steering Gear

REMOVAL AND INSTALLATION

Model 164

1. Jack up the front end.
2. Drain the system.

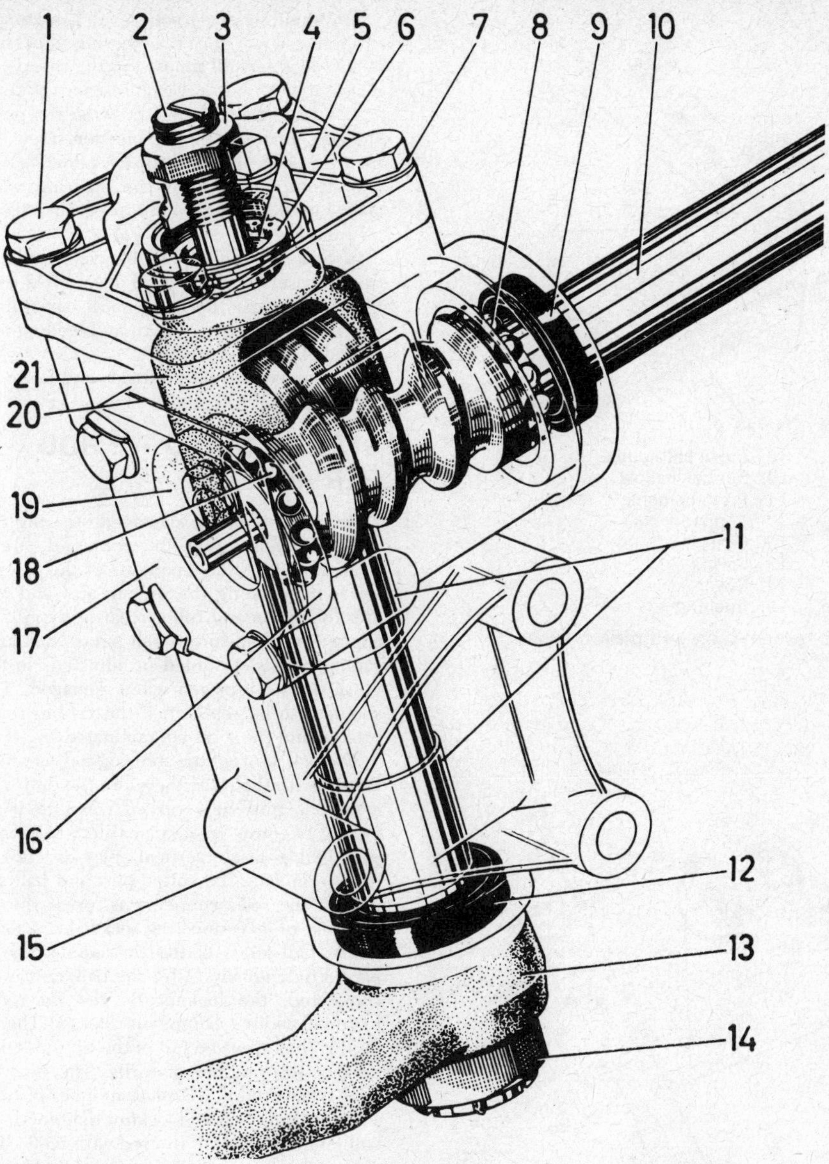

1. Bolt
2. Adjusting screw
3. Locknut
4. Pitman arm shaft bushing
5. Cover
6. Lock ring
7. Tab washer
8. Upper steering cam bearing
9. Oil seal, steering column
10. Steering cam
11. Pitman arm shaft bushing
12. Pitman arm shaft seal
13. Pitman arm
14. Nut
15. Housing
16. Lower bearing cap
17. Steering column cover
18. Lower cam bearing
19. Washer
20. Shims
21. Pitman arm shaft with roller

Manual steering gear—worm and roller

3. Remove the locknut for the pitman arm. Pull the pitman arm off.

4. Disconnect the lines from the steering box after the connections have been cleaned. Loosen the clamp bolt.

5. Remove the attaching bolts and pull the steering box forward.

To replace:

1. Place the steering box in the center positon. A slight increase in resistance should then be felt, the position of the pitman arm shaft lands should be as marked and the alignment marks on the control spindle and housing should conincide.

2. Check to make sure that the steering wheel is straight.

3. Install the steering box spindle in the flange of the lower steering column section. Install and tighten the attaching bolts. Tighten the clamp bolt. Connect the lines. The longer delivery line should run in a curve and be clamped.

4. Point the front wheels straight and install the pitman arm. Tighten the nut to 125-141 ft/lbs.

5. Fill and bleed the system.

240 and 260 Series

1. Loosen the steering column shaft flange from the pinion shaft. Remove the lock bolt and bend apart the flange slightly.

2. Jack up the front end. Position jack stands at the front jack supports. Remove the front wheels.

3. Disconnect the steering rods from the steering arms, with a ball joint puller.

4. Remove the splash guard.

5. Disconnect the hoses at the steering gear. Install protective plugs in the hose connections.

6. Remove the steering gear from the front axle member.

7. Remove the steering gear by pulling down until it is free from the steering shaft flange. Then remove the unit on the left side of the vehicle.

8. Position the steering gear and attach the pinion shaft to the steering shaft flange. Take care to align the recess for the lock bolt.

9. Install rtght side U-bolt and bracket, but do *NOT* tighten the nuts.

10. Install left side retaining bolts, and tighten. Tighten the U-bolt nuts.

11. Connect the steering rods to the steering arms.

12. Install the lock bolt on the steering column flange.

13. Connect the return and pressure hoses to the steering gear.

Power Steering Pump

REMOVAL AND INSTALLATION

1. Remove all dirt and grease from around the suction line connections and from around the delivery line on the pump housing.

2. Using a container to catch any power steering fluid that might run out, disconnect the lines, and plug them to prevent dirt from entering the system.

3. Remove the tensioning bolt and the attaching bolts.

4. Clear the pump free of the fan belt and lift it out.

5. If a new pump is to be used, the old brackets, fittings, and pulley must be transferred from the old unit. The pulley may be removed with a puller, and pressed on the pump shaft with a press tool. Under no circumstances should the pulley be hammered on, as this will damage the pump bearings.

6. To install, place the pump in position and loosely fit the attaching bolts. Connect the lines to the pump with new seals.

7. Place the fan belt onto the pulley and adjust the fan belt tension as outlined in Chapter one.

8. Tighten the tensioning bolt and the attaching bolts.

9. Fill the reservoir with Type "A" automatic transmission fluid and bleed the system as outlined under "Power Steering System Bleeding."

POWER STEERING SYSTEM BLEEDING

1. Fill the reservoir up to the edge with Automatic Transmission Fluid Type "A". Raise the front wheels off the ground, and install safety stands. Place the transmission in neutral and apply the parking brake.

2. Keeping a can of ATF Type "A" within easy reach, start the engine and fill the reservoir as the level drops.

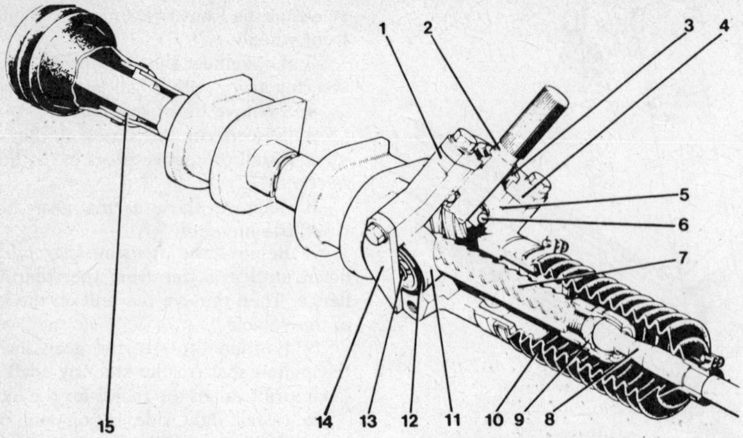

1. Housing
2. Pinion
3. Seal
4. Pinion cover
5. Spacer sleeve
6. Upper Pinion bearing
7. Rack
8. Steering rod
9. Inner ball joint
10. Rubber bellow
11. Pre-tensioning piston
12. O-ring
13. Spring
14. Cover
15. Bushing

Manual steering gear assembly (cam gear)—rack and pinion type

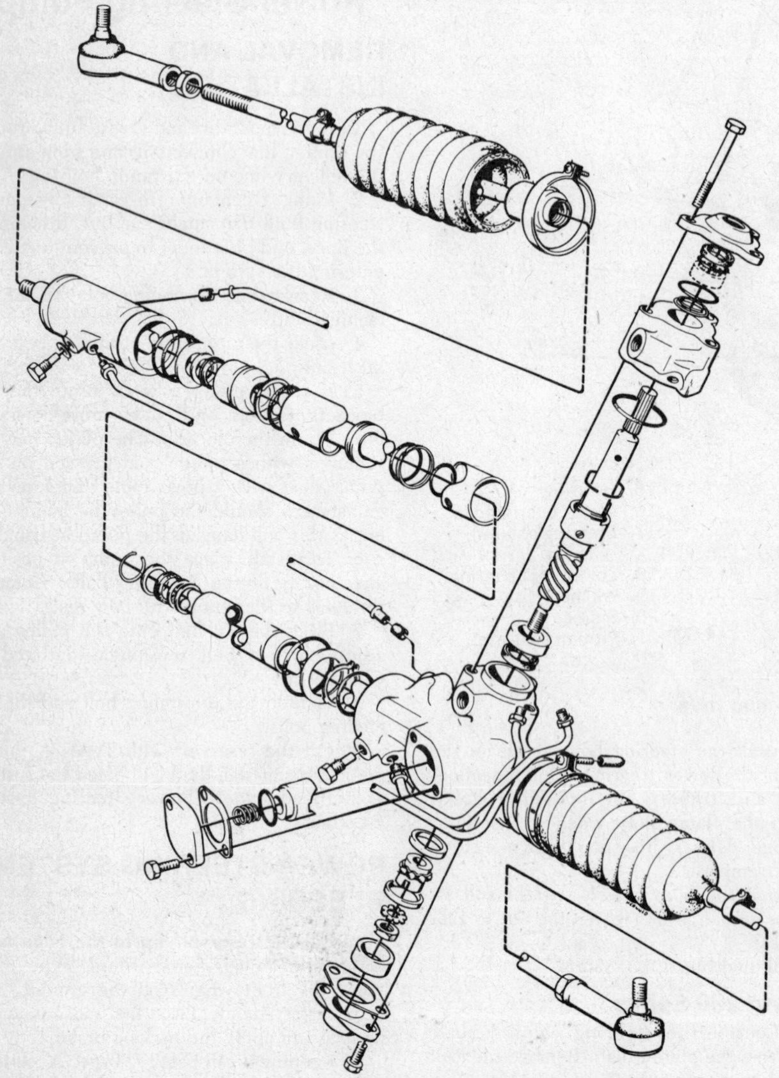

Rack and pinion steering gear disassembled

3. When the reservoir level has stopped dropping, slowly turn the steering wheel from lock to lock several times. Fill the reservoir if necessary.

4. Locate the bleeder screw on the power steering gear. Open the bleeder screw ½-1 turn, and close it when oil starts flowing out.

5. Continue to turn the steering wheel slowly until the fluid in the reservoir is free of air bubbles.

6. Stop the engine and observe the oil level in the reservoir. If the oil level rises more than ¼ in. past the level mark, air still remains in the system. Continue bleeding until the level rise is correct.

7. Remove the safety stands and lower the car.

STEERING AND TIE ROD SERVICE

Bent or otherwise damaged steering rods and tie rods must be replaced, never straightened. All components of the steering linkage, including the pitman arm and idler arm (on worm and roller steering types), are connected by means of ball joints. Ball joints cannot be disassembled or adjusted, so they must also be replaced when damaged. They should also be replaced if the rubber seal is broken and the joint contaminated.

The ball joints of the steering rods are made in unit with the rods, therefore the entire rod assembly must be replaced when their ball joints become unserviceable. Maximum permissible axial (vertical) play is .120 in. After removing the cotter pins and ball stud nuts at the rod's connections, press the ball joint out of its connecting socket.

The ball joints of the tie rod may be replaced individually. After the ball joint is disconnected, the locknut on the tie rod is loosened and the clamp bolt released. The ball joint is then screwed out of the tie rod, taking note of the number of turns. The new ball joint is screwed in the same number of turns, and the clamp bolt and locknut tightened. The ball joint is locked to the rod with 55-65 ft/lbs of torque. The new ball joint is pressed into its connection and the ball stud not tightened to 23-27 ft/lbs.

After reconditioning of the rods and joints, the wheel alignment must be adjusted.

BRAKE SYSTEM

All Volvos are equipped with a four wheel power-assisted disc brake system. The four wheel disc system utilizes a pair of four-piston, fixed calipers at the rear. The calipers are either Girling or ATE manufacture, so when ordering disc pads or caliper rebuilding kits, you must identify which you have. The discs are one-piece castings. 164 models equipped with internally vented discs.

NOTE: All models except DL2/4 door models have ventilated front brake discs.

Whenever adding to or replacing brake fluid, it is imperative that the fluid be of SAE 70 R3 (SAE J 1703) quality or better. Fluid

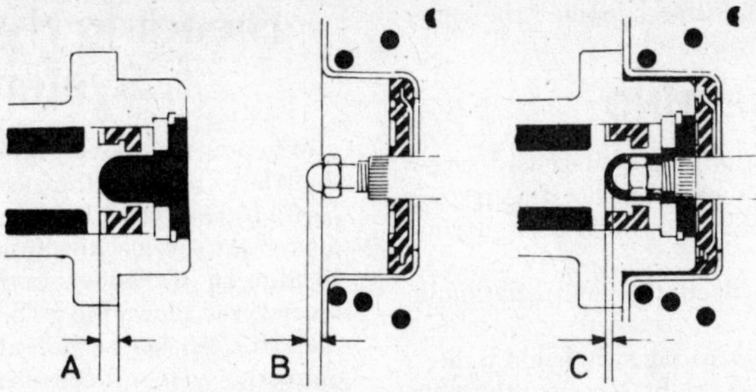

Adjusting thrust rod

meeting DOT 3 or DOT 4 specifications is also acceptable. Avoid mixing brake fluids from different manufacturers and never reuse old brake fluid.

DRUM BRAKE ADJUSTMENT

1. Jack up the car and place supports under the rear axle. Release the hand brake.
2. Remove the rubber seal. Turn the wheel in its normal direction of rotation while bringing the brake shoes into contact with the drum. Use an adjusting tool to turn the adjuster screw. When the wheel can just be turned by using one hand, stop tightening the screw. Then back off the adjuster screw 1-2 notches. Install the rubber seal.
3. Repeat the adjustment procedure on the other brake. Remove the supports and lower the car.

DISC BRAKE ADJUSTMENT

Disc brakes require no adjustment. They should, however, be checked frequently for wear. Consult the specifications table for new pad thickness. Pads should never be allowed to wear down to less than 0.125 in., or disc damage may occur.

Master Cylinder

REMOVAL AND INSTALLATION

240 and 260 Series

1. To prevent brake fluid from spilling onto and damaging the paint, place a protective cover over the fender apron, and rags beneath the master cylinder.
2. Disconnect and plug the brake lines from the master cylinder.
3. Remove the nuts which retain the master cylinder and reservoir assembly to the vacuum booster, and lift the assembly forward, being careful not to spill any fluid on the fender. Empty out and discard the brake fluid.

CAUTION

Do not depress the brake pedal while the master cylinder is removed.

4. In order for the master cylinder to function properly when installed to the vacuum booster, the adjusting nut for the thrust rod of the booster must not prevent the primary piston of the master cylinder from returning to its resting position. A clearance (C) of 0.004-0.04 in. is required between the thrust rod and primary piston with the master cylinder installed. The clearance may be adjusted by rotating the adjusting nut for the booster thrust rod in the required direction. To determine what the clearance (C) will be when the master cylinder and booster are connected, first measure the distance (A) between the face of the attaching flange and the center of the primary piston on the master cylinder, then measure the distance (B) that the thrust rod protrudes from the fixed surface of the booster (making sure that the thrust rod is depressed fully with a partial vacuum existing in the booster). When measurement (B) is subtracted from measurement (A), clearance (C) should be obtained. If not, adjust the length of the thrust rod by turning the adjusting screw to suit. After the final adjustment is obtained, apply a few drops of locking compound, such as Loctite®, to the adjusting nut.
5. Position the master cylinder and reservoir assembly onto the studs for the booster, and install the washers and nuts. Tighten the nuts to 17 ft/lbs.
6. Remove the plugs and connect the brake lines.
7. Bleed the entire brake system.

Model 164

1. Follow Steps 1-3 under "Master Cylinder Removal and Installation" for the 140 series.

CAUTION

Do not depress the brake pedal while the master cylinder is removed.

2. To install, place a new sealing ring onto the sealing flange of the master cylinder. Position the master cylinder and reservoir assembly onto the booster studs, and install the washer and nuts. Tighten the nuts to 8.7-10.8 ft/lbs.
3. Remove the plugs and loosely connect the brake lines. Have a friend depress the brake pedal to remove air from the cylinder. Tighten the nuts for the lines when the brake fluid (free of air bubbles) is forced out.
4. Bleed the entire brake system.

MASTER CYLINDER OVERHAUL

240 and 260 Series

1. Remove the master cylinder from the booster as outlined in the applicable "Master Cylinder Removal and Installation" section.
2. Firmly fasten the flange of the master cylinder in a vise.
3. Position both hands beneath the reservoir and pull it free of its rubber seals. Remove the filler cap and strainer from the reservoir, as well as the rubber seals and nuts (if so equipped) from the cylinder.
4. Remove the stop screw. Using a pair of snap-ring pliers, remove the snap-ring from the primary piston and shake out the piston. If the secondary piston remains lodged in the bore, it may be forced out by blowing air ino the stoplight switch hole.
5. Remove both the seals from the secondary piston, taking care not to damage or score the surfaces of the plunger. The old primary piston should be discarded and replaced.
6. Clean all reusable metal parts in clean brake fluid or methylated alcohol. The parts may be allowed to thoroughly air dry, or compressed air may be used. At any rate, all alcohol must be removed from the parts, as alcohol lowers the boiling temperature of brake fluid. If the inside of the cylinder is scored or scratched, the cylinder must be replaced. Minor pitting or corrosion may be removed by honing. Remember to flush the cylinder clean after honing, and make sure that the passages are clear. Check the piston for damage and proper clearance in the bore.
7. Install new seals on the secondary piston, making sure that they are positioned in the proper direction.
8. Coat the cylinder bore with brake fluid and dip the secondary piston and seals in brake fluid prior to installation. Slide the spring, spring plate, and washer onto the secondary piston and install the assembly in the bore, taking care not to damage the seals. Dip the new primary piston and seal assembly in brake fluid. Press the primary piston assembly into the bore and install a new washer and snap-ring.
9. Make sure that the hole for the stop screw is clear and install the new stop screw and sealing washer. Torque the screw to 7-9 ft/lbs.
10. Check the movement of the pistons and make sure that the flow-through holes are clear. The equilizing hole is checked by inserting a 25 gauge soft copper wire through it and making sure that it is not blocked by the secondary piston seal. If it is blocked, then master cylinder is incorrectly assembled, and you must take it through the numbers once more.
11. Install the nuts (if so equipped), new rubber seal, and washers onto the master cylinder at the reservoir connections. After making sure that the venting hole in the cap is open, install the cleaned strainer and cap. Press the reservoir into the master cylinder by hand. If the stoplight switch was removed, reinstall it.
12. Install the master cylinder as outlined in the applicable "Master Cylinder Removal and Installation" section.

Model 164

1. Remove the master cylinder from he booster as outlined in the applicable "Master Cylinder Removal and Installation" section.
2. Follow Steps 2-4 under "Master Cylinder Overhaul" for the 240, 260 series.
3. Discard both the primary and secondary pistons.
4. Clean all reusable metal parts in clean brake fluid or methylated alcohol. The parts must be thoroughly dried with filtered,

water-free compressed air, or air dried. All cleaning alcohol must be removed from the parts, as it lowers the boiling temperature of brake fluid. If the inside of the cylinder is scored or scratched, the cylinder must be replaced. Minor pitting and corrosion may be removed by honing. Remember to flush the cylinder clean after honing, and make sure that the passages are clear. Check the cylinder bore for excessive wear.

5. Make sure that new rubber seals, a new brass washer and back-up ring are installed on the new secondary piston. Make sure that the rubber seals are pointing in the right direction.

6. Coat the cylinder bore with brake fluid and dip the secondary piston and seals in brake fluid prior to installation. Install the secondary piston and spring in the bore, taking care not to damage the rubber seals.

7. Make sure that the new rubber seals, metal washers, plastic washer, back-up ring, sleeve, and spring are installed on the new primary piston. Make sure that the seals are facing in the right direction.

8. Dip the primary piston assembly in brake fluid and install it in the bore, taking care not to damage the rubber seals. While holding the piston in the bore, install the snap-ring.

9. Check that the hole for the stop screw is clear, and install the new stop screw and sealing washer. Torque the screw to 3.5-5.7 ft/lbs on all 164 series.

10. Check the movement of the pistons and make sure that the flow-through holes are clear. The equalizing hole is checked by inserting a 22 gauge soft copper wire through it and making sure that it is not blocked by the secondary piston seal. If it is blocked, the master cylinder will not function properly and must be reassembled.

11. Install the nuts (if so equipped), new rubber seals and washers onto the master cylinder at the reservoir connections. After making sure that the venting hole in the cap is open, install the cleaned strainer and cap. Press the reservoir into the master cylinder by hand. If the stoplight switch was removed, reinstall it.

12. Install the master cylinder as outlined in the applicable "Master Cylinder Removal and Installation" section.

Brake System Warning Valve

The brake system warning valve is located near the master cylinder in the engine compartment. On 1975-77 models. On 1978 and later models it is located under a bolt on the front axle member. The valve is centered by hydraulic pressure from the primary circuit on one side and the secondary circuit on the other. When a hydraulic imbalance exists, such as a leak in one of the calipers, the valve will move off-center toward the system with the leak and, therefore, the lowest pressure. When the valve moves off-center, it closes a circuit to a warning light on the dashboard, warning the driver of the imbalance. Sometimes, the valve will actuate the warning light when one of the systems is bled during normal maintenance. When this happens, the valve has to be reset.

VALVE RESETTING

1. Disconnect the plug contact and screw out the warning switch so that the pistons inside the valve may return to their normal position.

2. Repair and bleed the faulty hydraulic circuit.

3. Screw in the warning switch and tighten it to a torque of 10-14 ft/lbs. Connect the plug contact.

VALVE REPLACEMENT

1. Placing a rag beneath the valve to catch the brake fluid, loosen the pipe connections, and disconnect the six brake lines. Disconnect the electrical plug contact, and lift out the valve.

2. Connect the new warning valve in the reverse order of removal, and connect the plug contact.

3. Bleed the entire brake system.

Brake System Proportioning Valves

Each of the brake circuits has a proportioning (relief) valve located inline between the rear wheels. The purpose of these valves is to ensure that brake pressure on all four wheels compensates for the change in weight distribution under varied braking conditions. The harder the brakes are applied, the more weight there is on the front wheels. The valves regulate the hydraulic pressure to the rear wheels so that under hard braking conditions, they receive a smaller percentage of the total braking effort. This prevents premature rear wheel lock-up when the brakes are applied in emergency situations.

VALVE REPLACEMENT

Sophisticated pressure testing equipment is required to troubleshoot the dual hydraulic system in order to determine if the proportioning valve(s) are in need of replacement. However, if the car is demonstrating signs of rear wheel lock-up under moderate to heavy braking pressure, and other variables such as tire pressure, tread depth, etc. have been ruled out, the valve(s) may be at fault. The valves are not rebuildable, and must be replaced as a unit.

1. Unscrew, disconnect and plug the brake pipe from the master cylinder, at the valve connection.

2. Slacken the connection for the flexible brake hose to the rear wheel a *maximum* of ¼ turn.

3. Remove the bolt(s) which retain the valve to the underbody, and unscrew the valve from the rear brake hose.

4. To install the valve, place a new seal on it, and screw the valve onto the rear brake hose and hand tighten. Secure the valve to the underbody with the retaining bolt(s).

5. Connect the brake pipe and tighten both connections, making sure that there is no tension on the flexible rear hose.

6. Bleed the brake system.

Bleeding Hydraulic System

Whenever a spongy brake pedal indicates that there is air in the system, or when any part of the hydraulic system has been removed for service, the system must be bled. In addition, if the level in the master cylinder reservoir is allowed to go below the minimum mark for too long a period of time, air may enter the system, necessitating bleeding.

If only one brake caliper or wheel cylinder is removed for servicing, it is usually necessary to bleed only that unit. If, however, the master cylinder, warning valve, or any of the main brake lines are removed, the entire system must be bled.

Be careful not to spill any brake fluid onto the brake disc or pads or drum and linings and, of course, the paintwork. When bleeding the entire system, the rear of the car should be raised higher than the front. Only use brake fluid bearing the designation SAE 1703 (SAE 70 R3), DOT 3, or DOT 4. Never reuse old brake fluid.

1. Check to make sure that there are no mats or other materials obstructing the travel of the brake pedal. During bleeding, the full pedal travel should be 5.5 in. (providing that both circuits are bled simultaneously).

2. Disconnect the plug contact, and unscrew the electric switch from the warning valve.

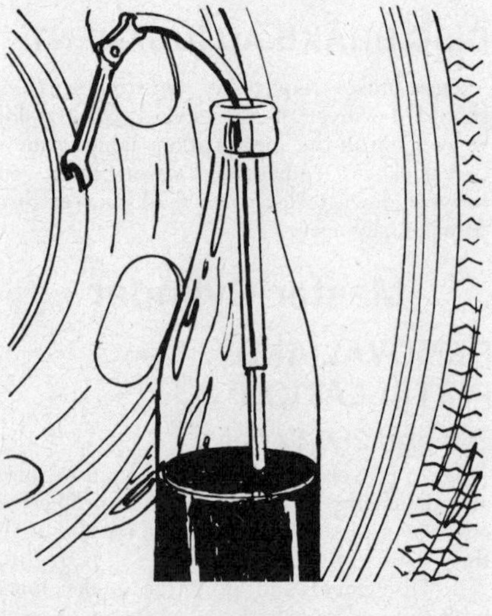

3. Clean the cap and the top of the master cylinder reservoir, and make sure that the vent hole in the cap is open. Fill the reservoir to the maximum mark, if necessary. Never allow the level to dip below the minimum mark during bleeding, as this will allow air into the system.

4. If only one brake caliper or wheel cylinder was removed, it will usually suffice to bleed only that wheel. Otherwise, prepare to bleed the entire system.

5. Remove the protective cap for the bleeder screw, and fit a ⁵/₁₆ in. ring spanner wrench on the nipple. Install a tight fitting plastic hose onto the nipple, and insert the other end of the hose into a glass bottle containing clean brake fluid. The hose must hang down below the surface of the fluid, or air will be sucked into the system when the brake

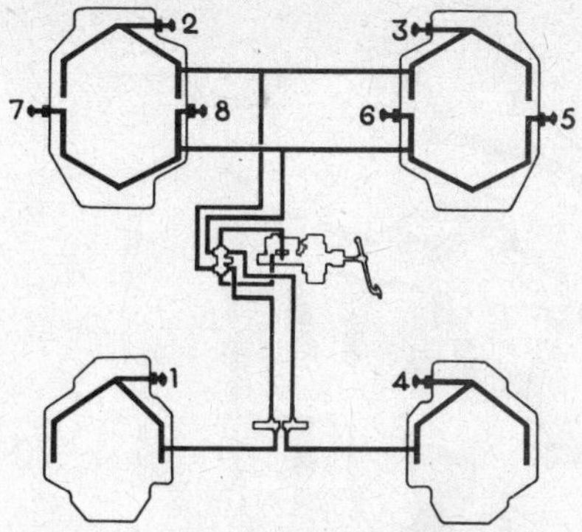

Bleeding sequence, 140 series and 164 series with Girling brakes

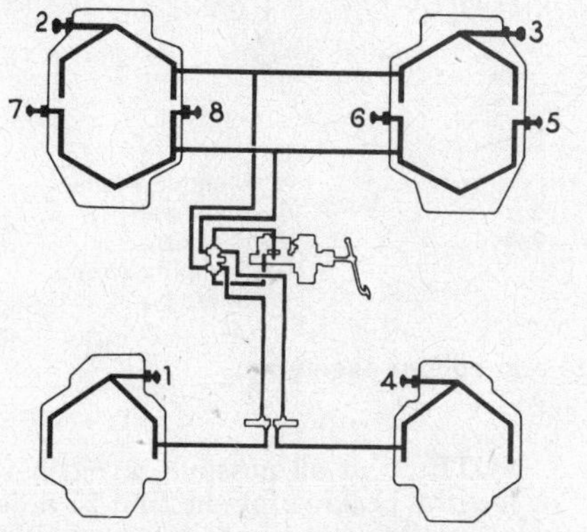

Bleeding sequence, 164 series with Ate brakes

pedal is released. Open the bleeder screw a maximum of ½ turn. Slowly depress the brake pedal until it bottoms, pause a second or two, and then quickly release the pedal. This should be repeated until the fluid flowing into the bottle is completely free of air bubbles. Then have a friend press the pedal to the bottom and hold it there while you tighten the bleeder screw. Install the protective cap.

6. If the entire system is to be bled, follow the above procedure for the remaining nipples. Generally, it is sufficient to bleed each circuit once. However, if the pedal continues to feel spongy, repeat the bleeding sequence. Remember to keep the master cylinder reservoir level above the minimum mark.

7. Fill the reservoir with the specified brake fluid to the maximum mark.

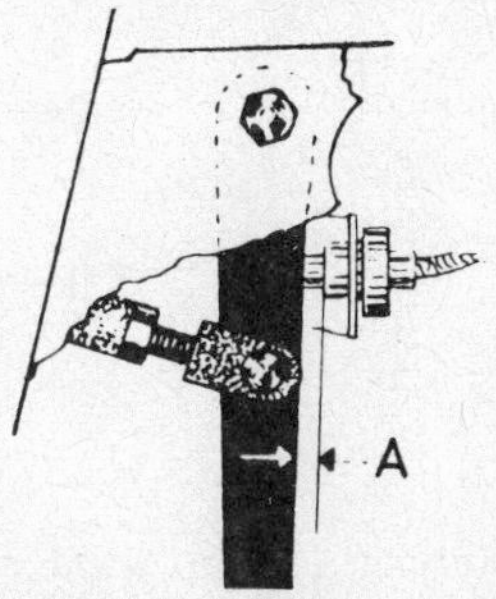

Stoplight switch adjustment

8. Screw the electric switch into the warning valve and connect the plug contact. Tighten the switch to 10-14 ft/lbs. Make sure that the warning light is actuated only when the parking brake is applied.

STOPLIGHT SWITCH ADJUSTMENT

With the brake pedal in the released position, the distance (A) between the brass hub of the switch and the pedal lever should be 0.08-0.24 in. To adjust, loosen the attaching screws for the switch bracket and move the switch in the required direction.

DISC BRAKES

Brake Pads

REMOVAL AND INSTALLATION

Girling Brakes

1. Remove the hub caps and loosen the lug nuts a few turns.

2. Raise the vehicle and place jack stands beneath the rear axle and the front jack attachments. Remove the wheel and tire assemblies.

3. Remove the hairpin-shaped locking clips, one lock pin then the other, together with the damping springs for the brake pads. Pull out the pads. Discard them if they are worn down to a lining thickness of ⅛ in. or less. If they are reusable, mark them for ease of assembly.

4. Carefully clean out the pad cavity. Replace any damaged dust covers. If any dirt has contaminated the cylinders, the caliper must be removed for overhaul. Inspect the brake disc as described under "Brake Discs—Inspection and Replacement."

5. Carefully depress the pistons in their cylinders so that the new pads will fit. This may be done with a screwdriver, but extra care must be exercised not to damage the rubber piston seals, the pistons, or the new pads themselves. A piston depressing tool

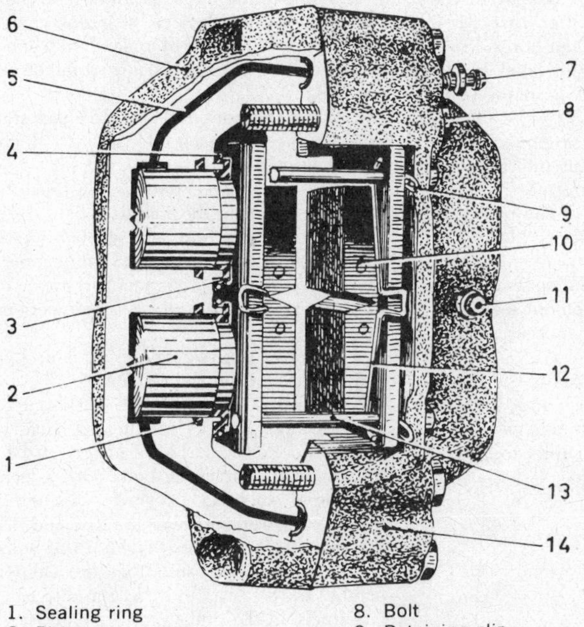

1. Sealing ring
2. Piston
3. Rubber dust cover
4. Retaining ring
5. Channel
6. Outer half
7. Upper bleeder nipple
8. Bolt
9. Retaining clip
10. Brake pad
11. Lower bleeder nipple
12. Damping spring
13. Retaining pin
14. Inner half

Girling front caliper assembly

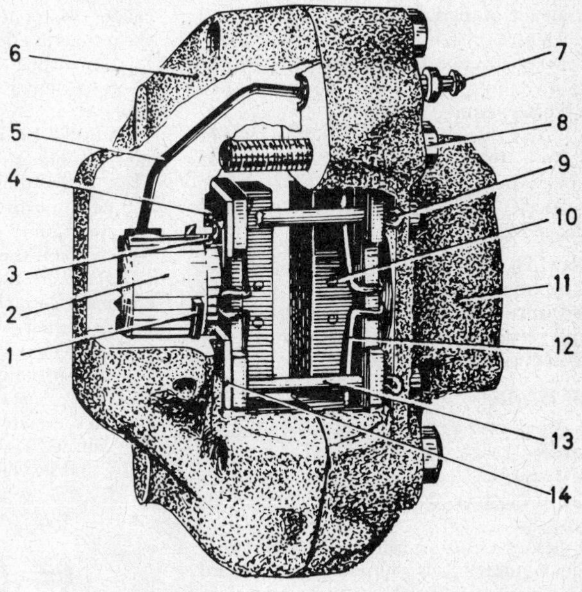

1. Sealing ring
2. Piston
3. Rubber dust cover
4. Retaining ring
5. Channel
6. Outer half
7. Bleeder nipple
8. Bolt
9. Retaining clip
10. Brake pad
11. Inner half
12. Damping spring
13. Retaining pin
14. Washer

Girling rear caliper assembly

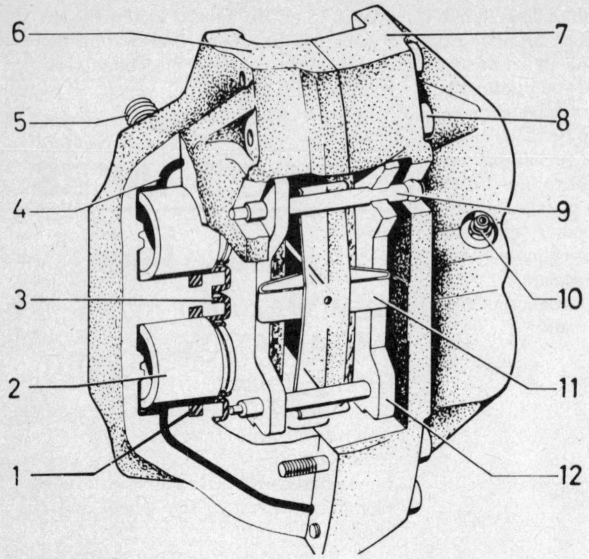

1. Sealing ring
2. Piston
3. Rubber dust cover
4. Channel
5. Upper bleeder nipple
6. Outer half
7. Inner half
8. Bolt
9. Guide pin
10. Inner bleeder nipple
11. Damping spring
12. Brake pad

Ate front caliper assembly

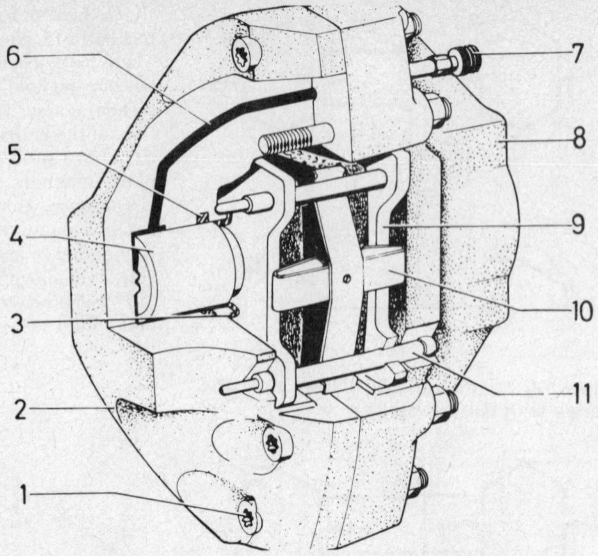

1. Bolt
2. Outer half
3. Rubber dust cover
4. Piston
5. Sealing ring
6. Channel
7. Bleeder nipple
8. Inner half
9. Brake pad
10. Damping spring
11. Guide pin

Ate rear caliper assembly

(SVO 2809) is available from the dealer that accomplishes the job without danger to the caliper components. Remember that when the pistons are depressed in their bores, brake fluid is displaced causing the level in the master cylinder to rise, and perhaps, overflow.

6. Install the new pads and secure them with first one lock pin, then the other pin with the damping springs. Install new locking clips on the lock pins. Make sure that the pads are able to move and that the linings do not project outside of the brake disc.

7. Depress the brake pedal several times and make sure that the movement feels normal. Bleeding is not usually necessary after pad replacement.

8. Clean the contact surfaces of the wheel and hub. Install the wheel and tire assemblies. Remove the jack stands and lower the vehicle. Tighten the lug nuts to 70-100 ft/lbs, and install the hub cap.

NOTE: If at all possible, braking should be moderate for the first 25 miles or so until the new pads seat correctly. Avoid panic stops in the beginning, unless necessary.

ATE Brakes

1. Remove the hub caps and loosen the lug nuts a few turns.

2. Raise the vehicle and place jack stands beneath the rear axle and the front jack attachments.

3. Using a 9/64 in. drift, tap out the upper guide pin for the pads and remove and discard the tensioning spring. Tap out the lower pin. Pull out the pads. Discard them if they are worn down to a lining thickness of 1/8 in. or less. If they are reusable, mark them for ease of assembly.

4. Carefully clean out the pad cavities. Replace any damaged dust covers. If any dirt has contaminated the cylinders, the caliper must be removed for overhaul. Inspect the brake disc as described under "Brake Discs—Inspection and Replacement."

5. Carefully depress the pistons in their cylinders so that the new pads will fit. This may be done with a screwdriver, but extra care must be exercised not to damage the rubber piston seals, the pistons, or the new pads themselves. A piston depressing tool (SVO 2809) is available from the dealer that accomplishes the job without danger to the caliper components. Remember that when the pistons are depressed in their bores, brake fluid is displaced, causing the level in the master cylinder to rise, and perhaps, overflow.

6. Install the new pads. Using only a hammer, tap one of the guide pins into position. Place a new tensioning spring into position, and while pushing it in against the pads, tap the other guide pin into position. Make sure that the pads can move.

7. Depress the brake pedal several times and make sure that the movement feels normal. Bleeding is not normally necessary after pad replacement.

8. Clean the contact surfaces of the wheel and hub. Install the wheel and tire assemblies. Remove the jack stands and lower the vehicle. Tighten the lug nuts to 70-100 ft/lbs, and install the hub cap.

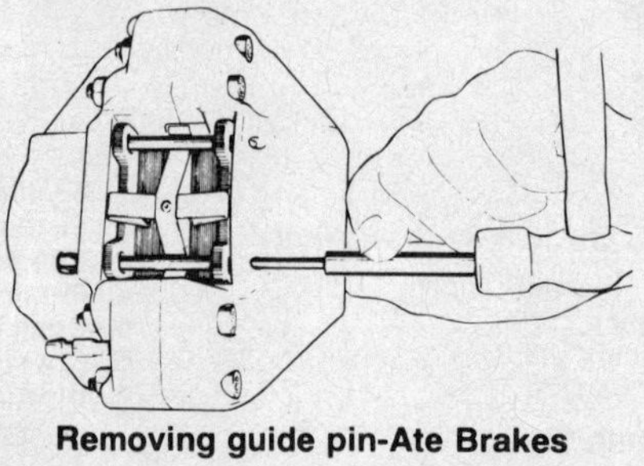

Removing guide pin-Ate Brakes

NOTE: If at all possible, avoid hard or lengthy braking for the first 25 miles or so, until the new pads seat correctly.

Front Brake Caliper

REMOVAL AND INSTALLATION

1. Remove the hub cap and loosen the lug nuts a few turns. Block the reservoir cap vent hole to reduce leakage of brake fluid when the lines are disconnected. Firmly apply the parking brake.

2. Raise the front end and place jack stands beneath the front jack attachments. Remove the wheel and tire assembly.

3. On 164 models, remove the brake hose retaining clip from the stabilizer bar, and disconnect the lower hose and secondary circuit brake pipe from their inboard connection underneath the car. Disconnect the upper hose from the caliper. Plug all brake connections to prevent leakage.

4. Remove the two caliper attaching bolts and lift the unit off the retainer.

5. To install, first check the mating surfaces of the caliper and its retainer to make sure that they are clean and not damaged. Coat the threads of the attaching bolts with a locking compound such as Loctite®. Position the caliper to its retainer over the disc and install the two attaching bolts. Tighten the bolts to 65–70 ft/lbs. Make sure that the caliper is parallel to the disc, and that the disc can rotate freely in the brake pads.

6. On 164 models, connect the lower brake hose and the secondary circuit brake pipe to their inboard connection and install the brake hose retaining clip to the stabilizer bar. Connect the upper brake hose to the caliper.

7. Unplug the reservoir cap vent hole. In-

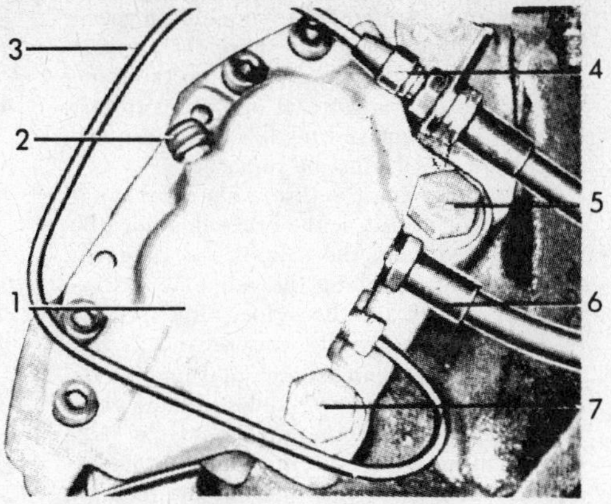

Front caliper installed—Ate

stall the wheel and tire assembly. Remove the jack stands and lower the car. Tighten the lug nuts to 70–100 ft/lbs and install the hub cap.

8. Bleed the brake system as outlined under "Bleeding Hydraulic System."

Rear Brake Caliper

REMOVAL AND INSTALLATION

1. Remove the hub cap and loosen the lug nuts a few turns. Block the reservoir cap vent hole to reduce leakage of brake fluid when the line is disconnected.
2. Place blocks in front of the front wheels. Raise the rear of the car and place jack stand beneath the rear axle. Remove the wheel and tire assembly. Release the parking brake.
3. Disconnect the brake line from the caliper and plug it to prevent leakage.
4. Remove the two caliper attaching bolts and lift the unit off the retainer.
5. To install, first check the mating surfaces of the caliper and its retainer to make sure that they are clean and not damaged. Coat the threads of the attaching bolts with locking compound, such as Loctite® type AV. Position the caliper to its retainer and install the two attaching bolts. Tighten the bolts to 45–50 ft/lbs. Make sure that the caliper is parallel to the disc, and that the disc can rotate freely in the brake pads.
6. Connect the brake line to the caliper. Unplug the reservoir cap hole.
7. Install the wheel and tire assembly. Remove the jack stands and lower the car. Tighten the lug nuts to 70–100 ft/lbs, and install the hub cap.
8. Bleed the applicable rear brake caliper as outlined under "Bleeding Hydraulic System."

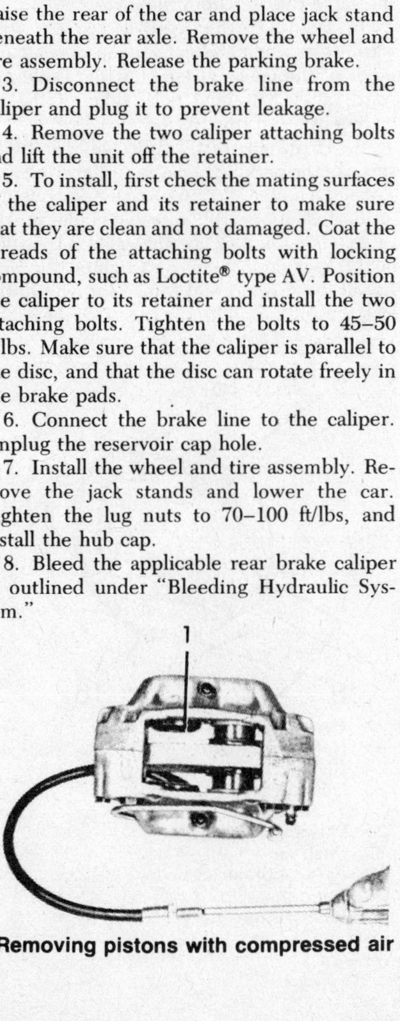

Removing pistons with compressed air

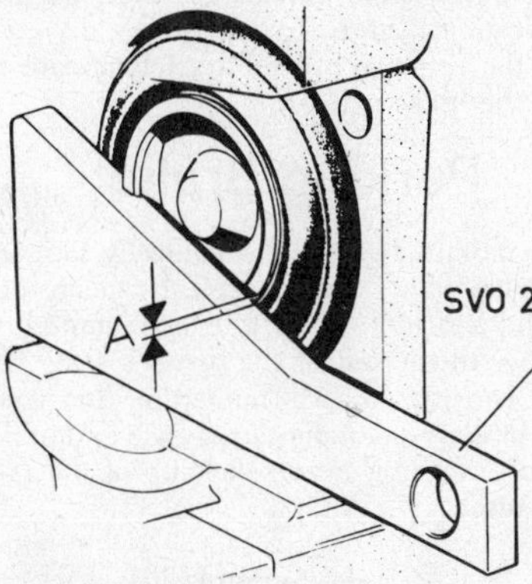

Checking location of rear caliper pistons—Ate

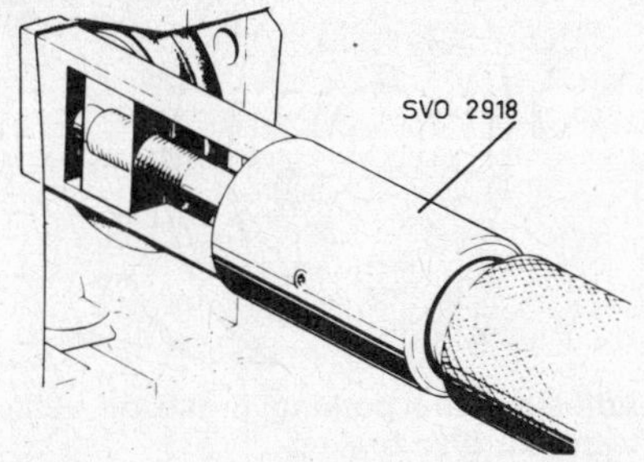

Adjusting location of rear caliper pistons—Ate

CALIPER OVERHAUL

The following procedure applies to front calipers and rear calipers of both Girling and Ate design.

1. Remove the brake caliper from the car as outlined in the applicable "Caliper Removal and Installation" section.
2. Remove the brake pads as outlined in Step 3 of the applicable "Brake Pad Removal and Installation" section.
3. Remove the retaining rings and the rubber dust covers. Place a wooden block (1) between the pistons. Using compressed air applied through the brake line connection, force the pistons toward the wooden block. Remove the pistons from their bores, taking care not to burr or scratch them.
4. Remove the sealing rings with a blunt plastic tool. Be careful not to damage the edges of the grooves. Screw out the bleeder nipple(s), and on front calipers, remove the external connecting pipe.

NOTE: It is not necessary to separate the caliper halves. Assembling the halves would require special pressure testing equipment.

5. Clean all reusable metal parts in clean brake fluid or methylated alcohol. Dry all parts with compressed air or allow to air dry. Make sure that all of the passages are clear. All alcohol must be removed from the parts as alcohol lowers the boiling temperature of brake fluid. If any of the cylinders are scored or scratched, the entire housing must be replaced. Minor scratching may be removed from the pistons by fine polishing. Replace any piston that is damaged or worn.
6. Coat the mating surfaces of the pistons and cylinders with brake fluid.
7. Install new sealing rings in the cylinders.
8. On Girling brakes and Ate front brakes, press the pistons into their bores with the large diameter end facing inward. Make sure that the pistons are installed straight and are not scratched in the process.
9. On Ate rear brakes, check to make sure that the pistons are in the proper postions to prevent brake squeal. The piston recess should incline 20" in relation to the lower guide area on the caliper. Check the location of the piston with template SVO 2919. When the template is placed against the one recess, the distance (A) to the other recess may be no greater than 0.039 in. If the location of the piston needs adjusting, press SVO 2918 against the piston and force out the shoes by screwing in the handle. Turn the piston in the required direction, release the tool, and remeasure with the template. Repeat this operation for the other piston.
10. Place the new rubber dust covers on the pistons and housing. Install the new retaining rings.
11. Install the brake pads as outlined in Step 6 of the applicable "Brake Pad Removal and Installation" section.
12. Screw in the bleeder nipple(s).
13. Install the caliper as outlined in the applicable "Caliper Removal and Installation" section.

Front Wheel Bearings

REPLACEMENT AND ADJUSTMENT

1. Remove the hub cap, and loosen the lug nuts a few turns.
2. Firmly apply the parking brake. Jack up the front of the car and place jack stands beneath the lower control arms. Remove the wheel and tire assembly.
3. Remove the front caliper as outlined in "Front Caliper Removal and Installation."
4. Pry off the grease cap. Remove the cotter pin and castle nut. Use a hub puller to pull off the hub. If the inner bearing remains lodged on the stub axle, remove it with a puller.
5. Using a drift, remove the inner and outer bearing rings.
6. Thoroughly clean the hub, brake disc, and grease cap.
7. Press in the new inner and outer bearing rings with a drift.

8. Press grease into both bearings with a bearing packer. If one is not available, pack the bearings with as much wheel bearing grease as possible by hand. Also coat the outsides of the bearings and the outer rings pressed into the hub. Fill the recess in the hub with grease up to the smallest diameter on the outer ring for the outer bearing. Place the inner bearing in position in the hub and press its seal in with a drift. The felt ring should be thoroughly coated with light engine oil.

9. Place the hub onto the stub axle. Install the outer bearing, washer, and castle nut.

10. Adjust the front wheel bearings by tightening the castle nut to 50 ft/lbs to seat the bearings. Then, back off the nut ⅓ of a turn counterclockwise. If the nut slot does not align with the hole in the stub axle, loosen the nut until the cotter pin may be installed. Make sure that the wheel spins freely without any side play.

11. Fill the grease cap halfway with wheel bearing grease, and install it on the hub.

12. Install the front caliper as outlined in "Front Caliper Removal and Installation."

13. Install the wheel and tire assembly. Remove the jack stand and lower the car. Tighten the lug nuts to 70–100 ft/lbs, and install the hub cap.

Brake Discs

INSPECTION AND REPLACEMENT

Remove the hub cap, loosen the lug nuts, raise the car, and remove the wheel and tire assembly. The friction surface on both sides of the disc should be examined for surface deviations such as scoring or corrosion. Minor radial scratches and small rust spots may be removed by turning or fine polishing the disc. The lateral run-out of the disc must not exceed 0.004 in. for the front, and 0.060 in. for the rear, measured at the outer edge of the disc. Do not mistake a faulty wheel bearing adjustment, or an improperly mounted disc for lateral runout. Actual disc thickness, which varies from model to model (see specifications), should not vary more than 0.0012 in. when taken at several points on the same disc. If the disc is worn at any point to less than the minimum permissible thickness (see specifications), it must be replaced.

When removing the disc, either to have it machined or replaced, the brake line must be disconnected from the caliper and plugged, the two bolts attaching the caliper to its retainer removed, and the caliper lifted off. The disc is then removed by unscrewing its two Philips head retaining screws and rapping on the inside of the disc with a plastic hammer or rubber mallet. Machining should be performed in unit with the hub, and should be equal on both sides. After machining, recheck the disc thickness and compare it to the minimum permissible thickness value on the specifications chart. To install the disc, reverse the removal procedure, taking care to bleed the brake caliper.

Parking Brake

The parking brake is mechanically actuated by a cable which is connected, by means of a pull rod and linkage, to a lever mounted on the floor to the left of the driver's seat. The brake consists of two miniature duo-servo drum brakes, one mounted at each end of the rear axle housing inside the hub of the rear brake discs.

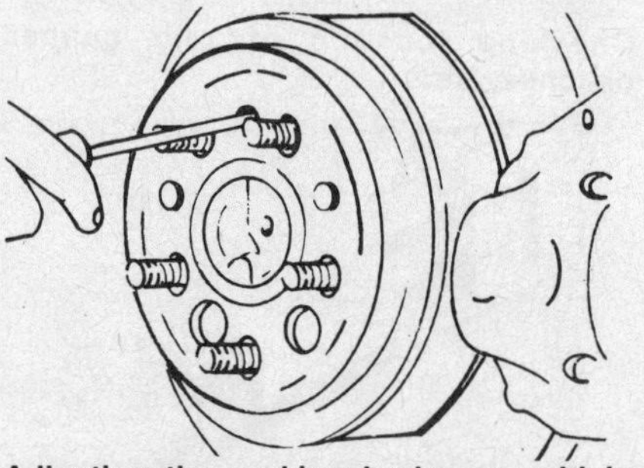

Adjusting the parking brake on vehicle with rear disc brakes

ADJUSTMENT

1. Remove the rear ashtray (between the front seat backs).
2. Tighten the parking brake cable adjusting screw so that the brake is fully applied when pulled up 2-3 notches.
3. If one cable is stretched more than the other, they can be individually adjusted by removing the parking brake cover (2 screws) and turning the individual cable adjusting nut at the front of each yoke pivot.
4. Install the ashtray, and parking brake cover (if removed).

CABLE REPLACEMENT

1. Apply the parking brake. Remove the hub caps for the rear wheels and loosen the lug nuts a few turns.
2. Place blocks in front of the front wheels. Jack up the rear end and place jackstands beneath the rear axle. Remove the wheel and tire assembly. Release the parking brake.
3. Remove the bolt and the wheel from the pulley.
4. Remove the rubber cover for the front attachment of the cable sleeve and nut, as well as the attachment for the rubber suspension ring on the frame. Remove the cable from the other side of the attachment in the same manner.
5. Hold the return spring in position. Pry up the lock and remove the lock pin so that the cable releases from the lever.
6. Remove the return spring with washers. Loosen the nut for the rear attachment of the cable sleeve. Lift the cable forward, after loosening both sides of the attachments, and remove it.
7. To install, first adjust the rear brake shoes of the parking brake as outlined in Steps 3, 4 and 5 under "Parking Brake Adjustment."
8. Install new rubber cable guides for the cable suspension. Place the cable in position in the rear attachment and tighten the nut. Install the washers and return spring. Oil the lock pin and install it, together with the cable,

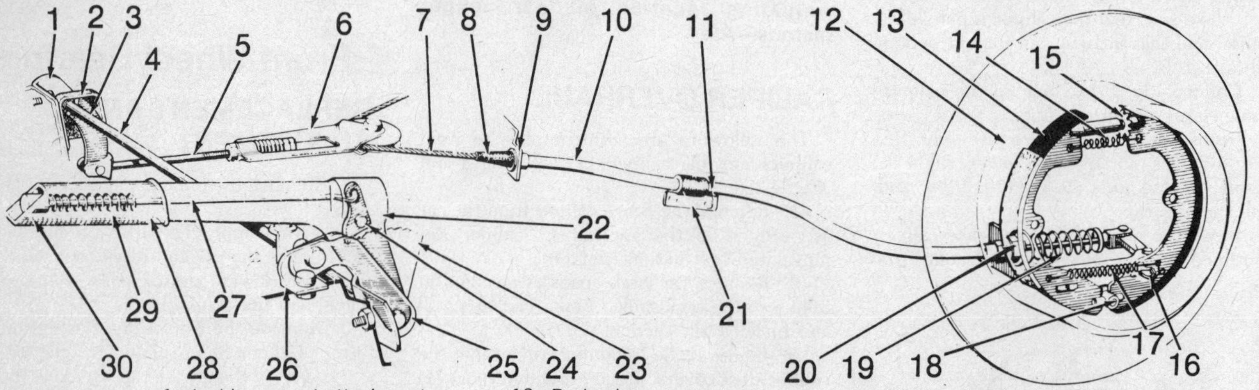

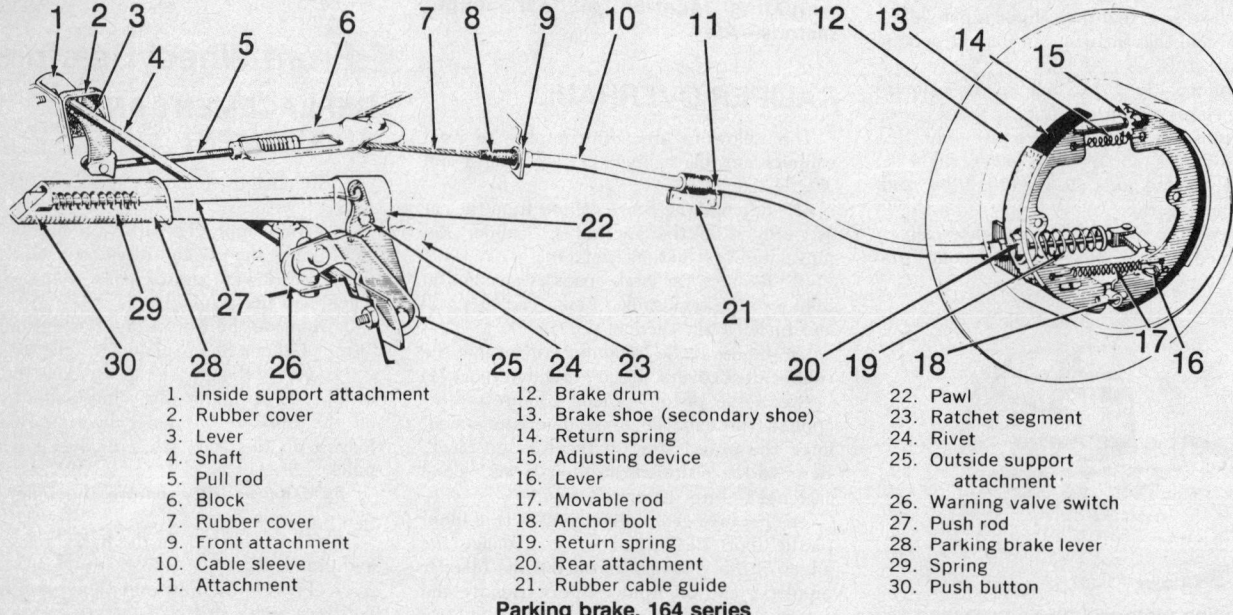

1. Inside support attachment
2. Rubber cover
3. Lever
4. Shaft
5. Pull rod
6. Block
7. Rubber cover
9. Front attachment
10. Cable sleeve
11. Attachment
12. Brake drum
13. Brake shoe (secondary shoe)
14. Return spring
15. Adjusting device
16. Lever
17. Movable rod
18. Anchor bolt
19. Return spring
20. Rear attachment
21. Rubber cable guide
22. Pawl
23. Ratchet segment
24. Rivet
25. Outside support attachment
26. Warning valve switch
27. Push rod
28. Parking brake lever
29. Spring
30. Push button

Parking brake, 164 series

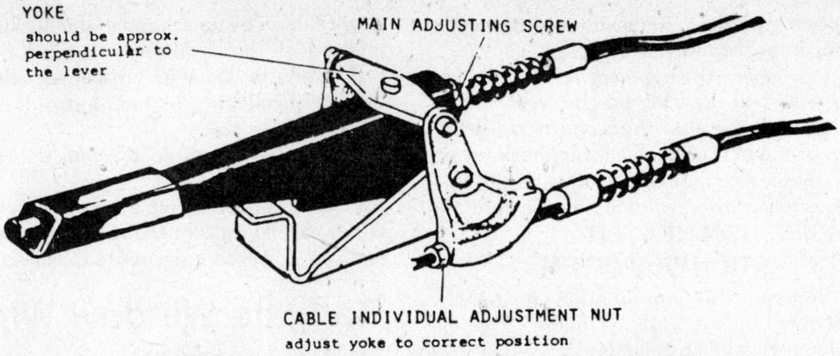

Parking brake cable adjustment, 1975 and later

on the lever. Install the attachment and rubber cable guide on the frame.

9. Install the cable in the same manner on the side of the vehicle.

10. Place the cable sleeve in position in the front attachments and install the rubber covers.

11. Lubricate and install the pulley on the pull rod. Adjust the pulley so that the parking brake is fully engaged with the lever at the third or fourth notch.

12. Install the wheel and tire assemblies. Remove the jack stands and lower the vehicle. Tighten the lug nut to 70–100 ft/lbs and install the hub caps.

PARKING BRAKE SHOE REPLACEMENT

1. Remove the rear ashtray and back off the adjusting screw so that the cable goes slack.
2. Jack up and support the rear end.
3. Remove the wheels.
4. Remove the brake line-to-axle clamp.
5. Remove the caliper retaining bolts and suspend the caliper out of the way.
6. Unbolt and remove the brake drum.
7. Unhook the return springs and remove the shoes.
8. Install in reverse of the above. Adjust the parking brake.

CHASSIS ELECTRICAL

Heater

HEATER UNIT REMOVAL AND INSTALLATION

Model 164 and 240 Series

STANDARD HEATING SYSTEM

1. Remove the lower radiator hose, open the engine drain plug, and drain the cooling system. Disconnect the negative battery cable.
2. Remove the center panel and the left-hand defroster hose.
3. Lift up the driveshaft tunnel mat, disconnect the front and rear attaching screws of the rear seat heater ducts, and then remove the ducts from the heater.
4. Disconnect the heater control valve and air-mix cables from their shutters.
5. Disconnect and plug the pressure hose at the heater. Also plug the heater pipes to prevent residual coolant from spilling onto the carpet.
6. Remove the attaching screws which secure the left-hand upper bracket to the dashboard and the left-hand lower bracket to the transmission tunnel.
7. Remove the glovebox by unscrewing the four attaching screws, removing the glovebox door stop, and disconnecting the wires from the glovebox courtesy light.
8. Disconnect the defroster and floor heating cables from their levers.
9. Disconnect the fan motor wires at the switch contact plate.
10. Remove the attaching screws which secure the right-hand upper bracket to the dashboard and the right-hand lower bracket to the transmission tunnel.
11. Remove the right-hand defroster hose. Disconnect the hose between the heater and the dashboard circular vents. Lift the heater unit to the right, and then out of the vehicle.
12. Reverse the above procedure to install, taking care to ensure that the air vent rubber seal is properly located, and that the fan motor ground cable is attached to the upper right-hand bracket attaching screw.

COMBINATION HEATER–AIR CONDITIONER SYSTEM

1. Remove the lower radiator hose, open the engine drain plug, and drain the cooling system. Disconnect the negative battery cable.
2. Remove the heater hoses from the heater pipes at the engine side of the firewall. Plug the heater pipes.
3. Remove the evaporator hose brackets from their body mounts and disconnect the dryer from its bracket. Position the dryer as close to the firewall as the evaporator hose permits.
4. Remove the instrument cluster by removing the steering column molded casings, removing the bracket retaining screw and lowering it toward the steering column, removing the four instruments cluster retaining screws, disconnecting the speedometer cable, tilting the speedometer out of its snap fitting, moving the electrical plug contacts, then lifting the cluster out of the vehicle.
5. Remove the air hose between the central unit and the left inner air vent. Remove the hose from the vacuum motor for the left defroster nozzle.
6. Remove the left-side panel from the central unit.
7. Lift up the driveshaft tunnel mat and disconnect the rear seat heater duct from the central unit.
8. Remove the heater pipes from the passenger side of the firewall.
9. Remove the upper and lower attaching screws for the left support leg. Remove the attaching screws which secure the upper bracket to the dashboard and the lower bracket to the transmission tunnel.

NOTE: If the upper bracket screw holes are slotted, the screws need only be slackened a few turns.

10. Remove the right-side panel from the central unit.
11. Remove the glovebox by unscrewing the four attaching screws, removing the glovebox door stop, and disconnecting the glovebox courtesy light wires.
12. Remove the right defroster nozzle, and also the air hose between the central unit and the right inner air vent.
13. Lift up the driveshaft tunnel mat and disconnect the rear seat heater duct from the central unit.
14. Remove the upper and lower attaching screws for the right support leg. Remove the lower attaching screws for the control panel.
15. Disconnect the fan motor wires and the ground wires from the control panel.
16. Disconnect the yellow lead cable from its plug contact.
17. Separate the halves of the vacuum hose connector and disconnect the vacuum tank hose at the connector.
18. Position the control panel as far back on the transmission tunnel as the cables permit.
19. Remove the screws which attach the upper brackets to the firewall and the lower brackets to the transmission tunnel.
20. Remove the thermostat clamp from the central unit, and the two evaporator cover retaining clamps.
21. Without disconnecting any of the refrigerant lines, remove the evaporator from the central unit, placing it on the right-hand side of the firewall.
22. Remove the molded dashboard padding from beneath the glovebox.
23. Remove the retaining clamps for the right outer vent duct, and remove the duct. Pry off the locking retainer for the blower, and remove the turbine. Remove the clamps which retain the blower housing (inner end) to the central unit and remove the housing.
24. Remove the passenger's front seat cushion and lift the central unit forward and onto the floor of the vehicle. Be careful not to place undue stress on the connected refrigerant lines.
25. Reverse the above procedure to install, taking care to ensure that the evaporator pipes and thermostat capillary are enclosed in sealing compound, that the drainage tubes are inserted in the respective transmission tunnel holes, and that the ground cables are connected.

BLOWER MOTOR REMOVAL AND INSTALLATION

Model 164 and 240 Series

STANDARD HEATING SYSTEM

1. Remove the heater unit as outlined in "Heater Unit Removal and Installation."

2. Place the unit on its side with the control valve facing upward. Remove the spring clips and separate the housing halves.

3. Lift out the old fan motor and replace it with a new unit, making sure that the support leg without the "foot" points to the output for the defroster channel.

4. Assemble the heater housing halves with new spring clips, and seal the joint without clips with soft sealing compound.

5. Install the heater unit as outlined in "Heater Unit Removal and Installation."

COMBINATION HEATER–AIR CONDITIONER SYSTEM

In order to remove the blower motor, both the right and left blower wheels must first be removed. The heater unit does not have to be removed.

1. Disconnect the negative battery cable.
2. Lift the carpet and remove the central unit side panels.
3. Remove the retaining screws for the control panel and move the panel as far back on the transmission tunnel as the electrical cables will permit.
4. Remove the attaching screws for the rear seat heater ducts and disconnect the ducts from the central unit.
5. Remove the instrument cluster as outlined in "Instrument Cluster Removal and Installation."
6. Remove the glovebox by unscrewing the four attaching screws, removing the glovebox door stop, and disconnecting the wires from the glovebox courtesy light. Remove the molded dashboard padding from beneath the glovebox.
7. Disconnect the vacuum hoses to the left and right defroster nozzle vacuum motors, then remove the nozzles and the left and right air ducts.
8. Remove the air hoses between the left and right inside air vents.
9. Remove the clamps on the central unit outer ends, and remove the ends.
10. Pry off the locking retainer for the turbines (blower wheels), and remove both left and right blower wheels.
11. Position the heater control valve capillary tube to one side.
12. Remove the left inner end (blower housing) from the central unit.
13. Unscrew the three retaining screws and remove the fan motor retainer.
14. Disconnect the plug contact from the fan motor control panel. Release the tabs of electric cables from the plug contact, and, removing the rubber grommet, pull the electrical cables down through the central unit right opening.
15. Remove the fan motor from the left opening.
16. Reverse the above procedure to install.

HEATER CORE REMOVAL AND INSTALLATION

Model 164, 240 Series

STANDARD HEATING SYSTEM

1. Remove the heater unit as outlined in "Heater Unit Removal and Installation."
2. Place the unit on its side with the control valve facing upward. Remove the spring clips and separate the housing halves.
3. Disconnect the capillary tube from the heater core and then lift out the core.
4. Reverse the above procedure to install, being careful to transfer the foam plastic packing to the new heater core, and to install the fragile capillary tube carefully on the core.

COMBINATION HEATER–AIR CONDITIONER SYSTEM

1. Remove the combination heater-air conditioner unit as outlined under "Heater Unit Removal and Installation."
2. Remove the left outer end of the central unit. Remove the locking retainer and the turbine (blower wheel).
3. Remove the two retaining screws for the left transmission tunnel bracket.
4. Remove the lockring for the left intake shutter shaft.
5. Remove the three retaining screws and lift off the inner end.
6. Remove the three retaining screws for the fan motor retainer.
7. Disconnect the heater hoses at the heater core.
8. Remove the clamps which retain the central unit halves together, lift off the left half, and remove the heater core.
9. Reverse the above procedure to install, taking care to transfer the foam plastic packing to the new heater core.

Radio

RADIO REMOVAL AND INSTALLATION

1. Disconnect the negative battery cable.
2. Remove the radio control knobs by pulling them straight out. Remove the control shaft retaining nuts.
3. Disconnect the speaker wires, the power lead (either at the fuse box or the inline fuse connection), and the antenna cable from its jack on the radio.
4. Remove the hardware which attaches the radio to its mounting (support) bracket(s), and slide it back and down from the dash.
5. Reverse the above procedure to install.

Windshield Wipers

MOTOR REMOVAL AND INSTALLATION

1. Disconnect the negative battery cable.
2. Disconnect the drive link from the wiper motor lever by unsnapping the locking tab underneath the dashboard.
3. Open the hood and disconnect the plug contact from the motor, located on the firewall.
4. Remove the three attaching screws and lift out the motor.
5. Reverse the above procedure to install, taking care to transfer the rubber seal, rubber damper, and spacer sleeves to the new motor.

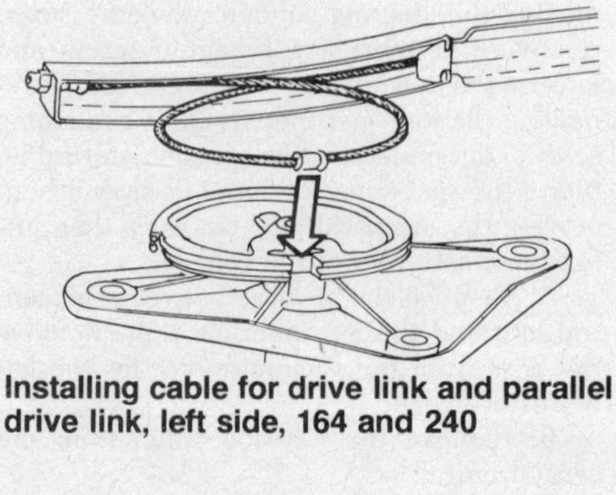

Installing cable for drive link and parallel drive link, left side, 164 and 240

Tailgate Window Wiper

MOTOR REMOVAL AND INSTALLATION

1. Disconnect the negative battery cable.
2. Remove the upholstered finish panel on the inside of the tailgate.
3. Remove the screws which retain the reinforcing bracket beneath the wiper motor.
4. Disconnect the wiper link arm. Bend the reinforcing bracket to one side and lower the wiper motor until it is clear of the bracket.
5. Disconnect the electrical wires from the motor and remove the motor.
6. Reverse the above procedure to install.

Instruments

INSTRUMENT CLUSTER REMOVAL AND INSTALLATION

A voltage stabilizer feeds a 10 V current to both the temperature and the fuel gauges. Electrical malfunctions in these gauges must be checked with an ohmmeter, not a 12 V test light. If malfunctions occur simultaneously in all three of the gauges that are fed by the stabilizer, the stabilizer itself is probably malfunctioning. When replacing the voltage stabilizer, the new unit must fit in the same position as the old one. If the stabilizer is not located correctly in the dash, the voltage output may be altered.

1. Disconnect the negative battery cable.
2. Remove the molded plastic casings from the steering column.
3. Remove the bracket retaining screw and lower the bracket toward the steering column.
4. Remove the cluster attaching screws.
5. Disconnect the speedometer cable.
6. Tilt the cluster out of its snap fitting and disconnect the plug contact. On vehicles equipped with a tachometer, disconnect the tachometer sending wire.
7. Lift the cluster out of the dashboard.
8. Reverse the above procedure to install.

Fuses

On 240, 260 series, and 164 models, the fuse box is located beneath a protective cover, below the dashboard, in front of the driver's door.

On electronic fuel-injected models, an additional fuse box is located in the engine compartment on the left wheel well. It houses a single fuse protecting the electrical fuel pump.

UNIT REPAIR SECTION

Tools and Equipment

The service procedures in this book presuppose a familiarity with hand tools and their proper use. However, it is possible that you may have a limited amount of experience with the sort of equipment needed to work on an automobile. This section is designed to help you assemble a basic set of tools that will handle the majority of jobs you may undertake.

In addition to the normal assortment of screwdrivers and pliers, automotive service work requires an investment in wrenches, sockets and the handles needed to drive them, and various measuring tools such as torque wrenches and feeler gauges.

The best approach to gathering the required equipment is to proceed slowly, buying high-quality tools as they are needed. An initial investment should be made in a set of quality wrenches, ranging in size from 1/4 inch to one inch, if your car has standard bolts, or from 5 mm to 19 mm if your car has metric fasteners. High quality forged wrenches are available in three styles: open end, box end, and combination open/box end. The combination tools are generally the most desirable as a starter set; the wrenches shown in the illustration are of the combination type.

The other set of tools inevitably required is a ratchet handle and socket set. This set should have the same size range as your wrench set. The ratchet, extension, and flex drives for the sockets are available in many sizes; it is advisable to choose a 3/8 inch drive set initially. One break in the inch/metric sizing war is that metric-sized sockets sold in the U.S. have inch-sized drive (1/4, 3/8, 1/2, etc.). Sockets are available in six and twelve point versions; six point types are generally cheaper and are a good choice for a first set. The choice of a drive handle for the sockets should be made with some care. If this is your first set, take the plunge and invest in a flex-head ratchet; it will get into many places otherwise accessible only through a long chain of universal joints, extensions and adapters. An alternative is a flex handle; such a tool is shown, in the illustration, below the ratchet handle. In addition to the range of sockets mentioned, a rubber-lined spark plug socket should be purchased. Spark plugs have either a 13/16 or a 5/8 inch hex; get the correct socket for the plugs in your car.

The most important thing to consider when purchasing hand tools is quality. Don't be misled by the low cost of "bargain" tools. Forged wrenches, tempered screwdriver blades, and fine tooth ratchets are a much better investment than their less expensive counterparts. The skinned knuckles and frustration inflicted by poor quality tools make any job an unhappy chore. Another consideration is that quality tools sold by reputable firms come with an on-the-spot replacement guarantee—if the tool breaks, you get a new one, no questions asked.

The tools needed for basic maintenance jobs, in addition to those just mentioned, include:

1. Jackstands, for support;
2. Oil filter wrench;
3. Oil filler spout or funnel;
4. Grease gun;
5. Battery hydrometer;
6. Battery post and clamp cleaner;
7. Container for draining oil;
8. Many rags for the inevitable spills.

In addition to these items there are several others which are not absolutely necessary, but handy to have around. These include a transmission funnel and filler tube, a drop (trouble) light on a long cord, an adjustable wrench (crescent wrench), and slip joint pliers.

A more extensive list of tools, suitable for tune-up work, can be drawn up easily. While the tools involved are slightly more sophisticated, they need not be outrageously expensive. For example, there are several inexpensive tach/dwell meters on the market that are every bit as good for the average mechanic as a $100.00 professional model. The key to these purchases is to make them with an eye towards adaptability and wide range. Using the tach/dwell meter example again, if the

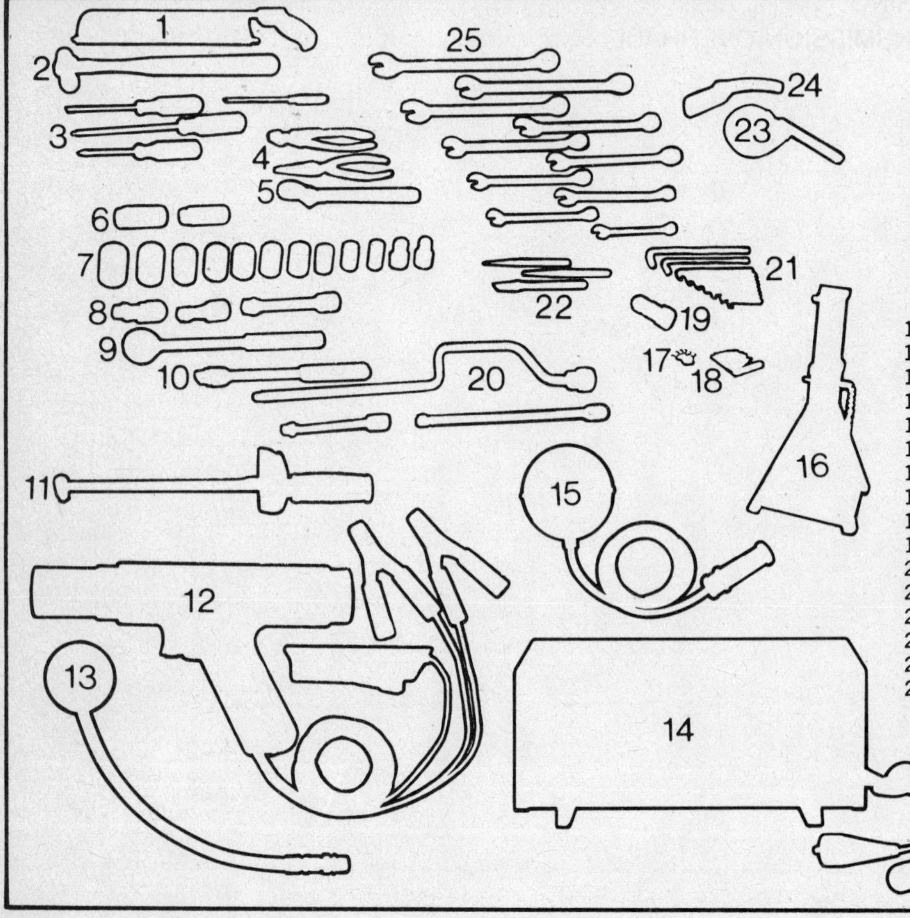

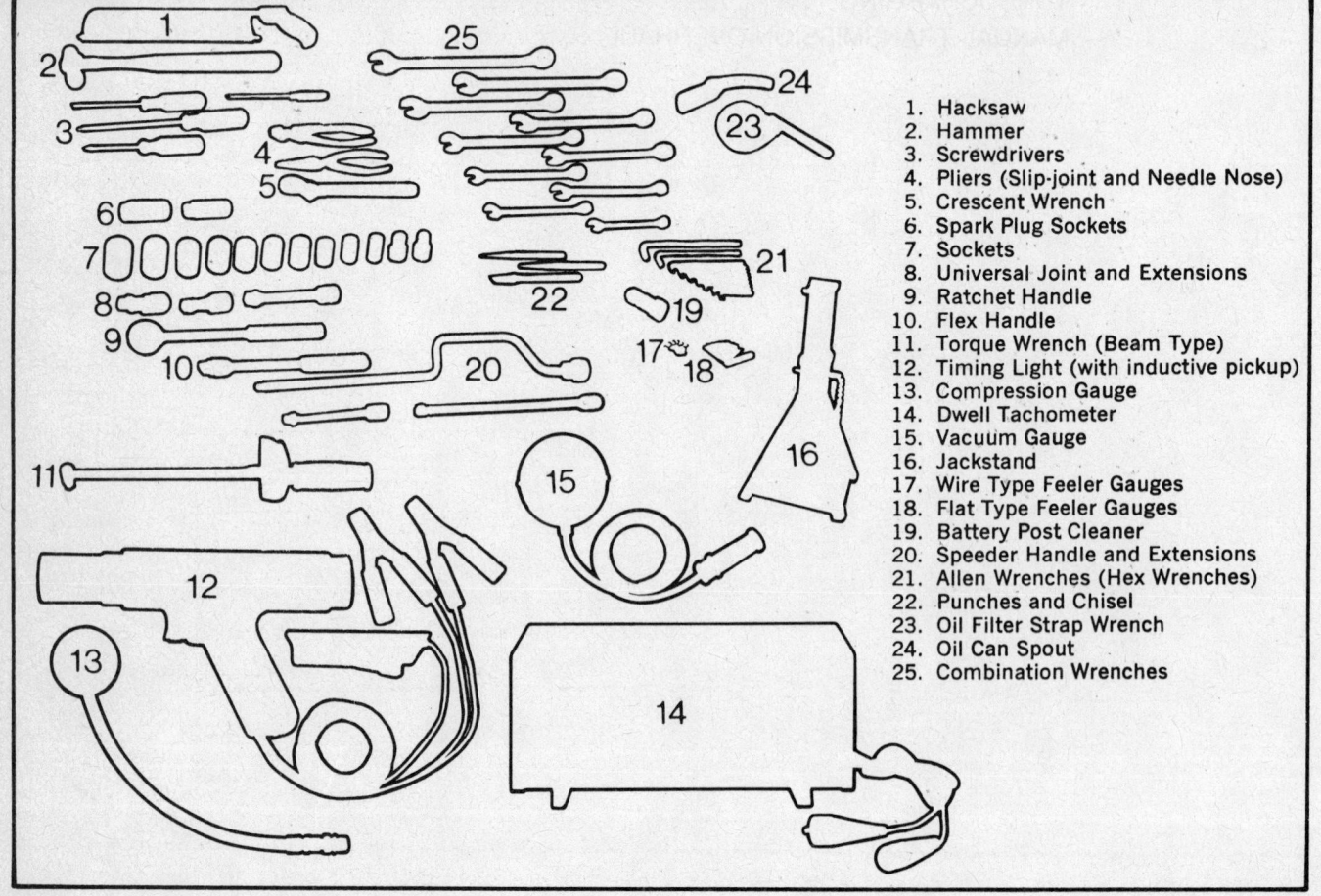

1. Hacksaw
2. Hammer
3. Screwdrivers
4. Pliers (Slip-joint and Needle Nose)
5. Crescent Wrench
6. Spark Plug Sockets
7. Sockets
8. Universal Joint and Extensions
9. Ratchet Handle
10. Flex Handle
11. Torque Wrench (Beam Type)
12. Timing Light (with inductive pickup)
13. Compression Gauge
14. Dwell Tachometer
15. Vacuum Gauge
16. Jackstand
17. Wire Type Feeler Gauges
18. Flat Type Feeler Gauges
19. Battery Post Cleaner
20. Speeder Handle and Extensions
21. Allen Wrenches (Hex Wrenches)
22. Punches and Chisel
23. Oil Filter Strap Wrench
24. Oil Can Spout
25. Combination Wrenches

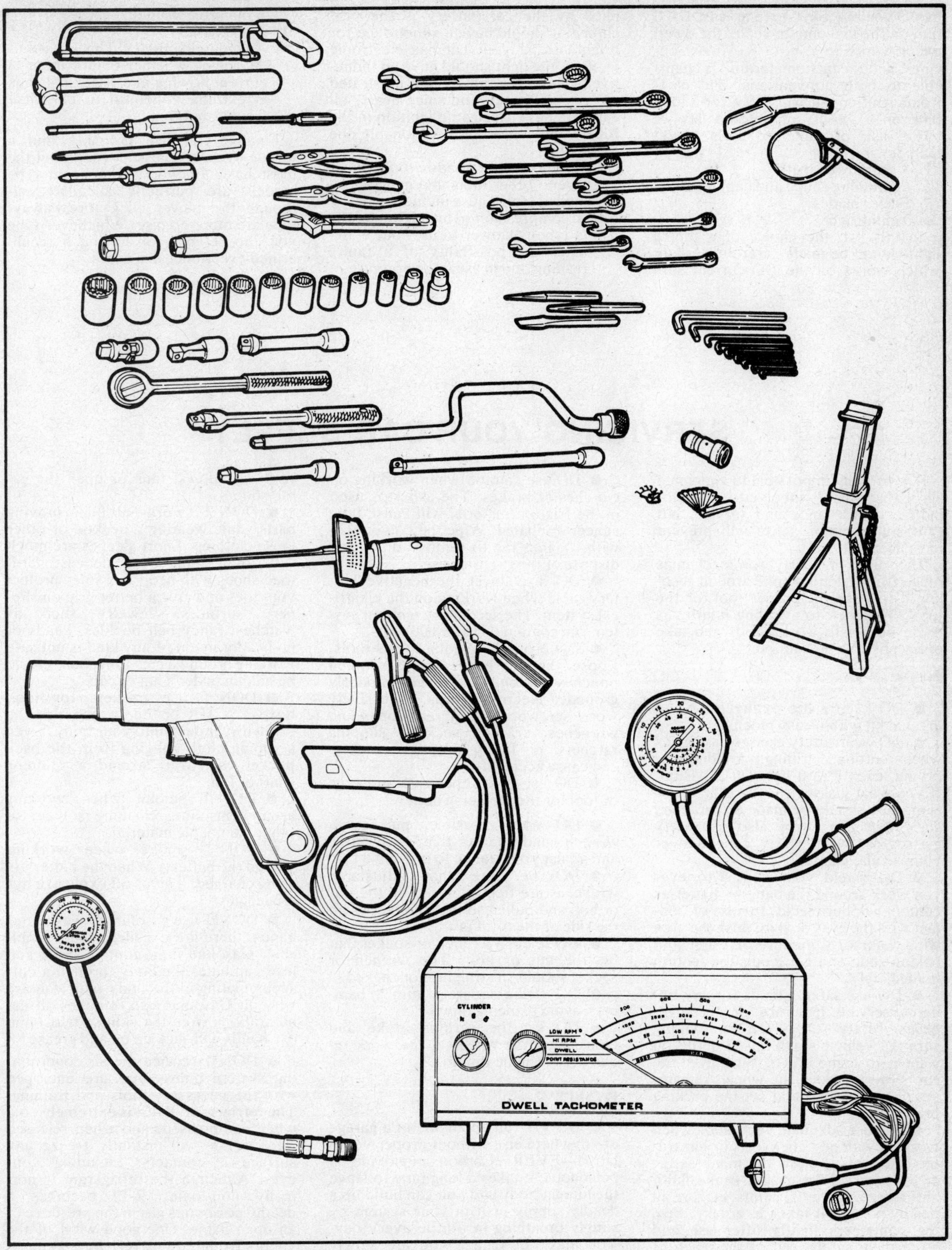

A basic tool collection will handle almost any automotive repair work

model you buy runs up to at least 1,500 rpm on the tachometer scale, the dwell meter works on 4, 6, or 8 cylinder engines, and the tachometer unit is adaptable to both conventional and electronic ignitions, it will serve for a long time on a variety of automobiles. A basic list of tune-up tools could include:

1. A tach/dwell meter;
2. Spark plug gauge and gapping tool;
3. Feeler blades;
4. Timing light.

In this list, the choice of a timing light should be made carefully. A light which works on the DC current supplied by the car battery is the best choice: it should have a xenon tube for brightness. If your car has electronic ignition, the light should have an inductive pick-up (the timing light illustrated has one of these), and since nearly all cars will have electronic ignition in the future, this feature is a reasonable one to look for.

In addition to these basic tools, there are several other tools and gauges you may find useful. These include:

1. A compression gauge. The screw-in type is slower to use, but eliminates the possibility of a faulty reading due to escaping pressure.
2. A manifold vacuum gauge.
3. A test light.
4. An induction meter. This is used to determine whether or not there is current flowing in a wire, and thus is extremely helpful in electrical troubleshooting.

Finally, you will probably find a torque wrench necessary for all but the most basic of work. The beam type models are perfectly adequate, although the newer click (breakaway) type are more precise. Whichever type you choose, plan on having it recalibrated every once in a while.

SERVICING YOUR CAR SAFELY

It is virtually impossible to anticipate all of the hazards involved with automotive maintenance and service, but care and common sense will prevent most accidents.

The rules of safety for mechanics range from "don't smoke around gasoline," to "use the proper tool for the job." The trick to avoiding injuries is to develop safe work habits and take every possible precaution.

DO'S

- DO keep a fire extinguisher and first aid kit within easy reach.
- DO wear safety glasses or goggles when cutting, drilling, grinding or prying, even if you have 20-20 vision. If you wear glasses for the sake of vision, they should be made of hardened glass that can serve also as safety glasses, or wear safety goggles over your regular glasses.
- DO shield your eyes whenever you work around the battery. Batteries contain sulphuric acid. In case of contact with the eyes or skin, flush the area with water or a mixture of water and baking soda and get medical attention immediately.
- DO use safety stands for any undercar service. Jacks are for raising vehicles: safety stands are for making sure the vehicle stays raised until you want it to come down. Whenever the car is raised, block the wheels remaining on the ground and set the parking brake.
- DO use adequate ventilation when working with any chemicals or hazardous materials. Follow the manufacturer's directions for usage. Brake fluid, anti-freeze, solvents, paints, etc. are all deadly poisons if taken internally. Seal the containers tightly after use and store them safely, out of the reach of children.
- DO use caution when working on clutches or brakes. The asbestos used in the friction material will cause lung cancer if inhaled. Wipe the component with a damp rag to remove dust, and dispose of the rag after use.
- DO disconnect the negative battery cable when working on the electrical system. The secondary ignition system can contain up to 40,000 volts.
- DO properly maintain your tools. Loose hammerheads, mushroomed punches and chisels, frayed or poorly grounded electrical cords, excessively worn screwdrivers, spread open-end wrenches, cracked sockets, slipping ratchets, or faulty droplight sockets can cause accidents.
- DO use the proper size and type of tool for the job being done.
- DO when possible, pull on a wrench handle rather than push on it, and adjust your stance to prevent a fall.
- DO be sure that adjustable wrenches are tightly closed on the nut or bolt and pulled so that the face is on the side of the fixed jaw.
- DO select a wrench or socket that fits the nut or bolt. The wrench or socket should sit straight, not cocked.
- DO strike squarely with a hammer: avoid glancing blows.
- DO set the parking brake and block the drive wheels if the work requires the engine running.

DONT'S

- DON'T run an engine in a garage or anywhere else without proper ventilation—EVER! Carbon monoxide is poisonous: it takes a long time to leave the human body and you can build up a deadly supply of it in your system by simply breathing in a little every day. You may not realize you are slowly poisoning yourself. Always use power vents, windows, fans or open the garage doors.
- DON'T work around moving parts while wearing a necktie or other loose clothing. Short sleeves are much safer than long, loose sleeves: hard-toed shoes with neoprene soles protect your toes and give a better grip on slippery surfaces. Jewelry such as watches, fancy belt buckles, beads or body adornment of any kind is not safe working around a car. Long hair should be hidden under a hat or cap.
- DON'T use pockets for toolboxes. A fall or bump can drive a screwdriver deep into your body. Even a wiping cloth hanging from the back pocket can wrap around a spinning shaft or fan.
- DON'T smoke when working around gasoline, cleaning solvent or other flammable material.
- DON'T smoke when working around the battery. When the battery is being charged, it gives off explosive hydrogen gas.
- DON'T use gasoline to wash your hands: there are excellent soaps available. Gasoline may contain lead, and lead can enter the body through a cut, accumulating in the body until you are very ill. Gasoline also removes all the natural oils from the skin so that bone dry hands will suck up oil and grease.
- DON'T service the air conditioning system unless you are equipped with the necessary tools and training. The refrigerant, R-12, is extremely cold when compressed, and when released into the air will instantly freeze any surface it contacts, including your eyes. Although the refrigerant is normally non-toxic, R-12 becomes a deadly poisonous gas in the presence of an open flame. One good whiff of the vapors from burning refrigerant can be fatal.

INTRODUCTION

Routine maintenance is probably the most important part of automobile care and the easiest to neglect. A regular program aimed at monitoring essential systems ensures that all components are in good and safe working order, and can prevent small problems from developing into major headaches. Routine maintenance also pays big dividends in keeping major repair costs at a minimum and extending the life of the car.

The owner's manual that came with your car includes a maintenance schedule, indicating service intervals in numbers of months or thousand of miles. This schedule should always be followed. We have provided, in each section, a guide to service intervals based on an averaging of manufacturer's recommendations. In most cases, the suggested interval offered here will be close to that given by the manufacturer of your car, but the manufacturer's schedule should always take precedence.

We have divided the maintenance work to be done into three categories: Under Hood, Under Car, and Exterior. The checks in each section require only a few minutes of attention every few weeks; the services to be performed can be easily accomplished in a morning. The most important part of any maintenance program is regularity. The few minutes or occasional morning spent on these seemingly trivial tasks will forestall or eliminate major problems later.

UNDER HOOD

Automatic Transmission, Automatic Transaxle

The fluid level in the automatic transmission or transaxle should be checked every three months or 6000 miles. All automatic transmissions have a dipstick for fluid level checks.

1. Drive the car until it is at normal operating temperature. The level should not be checked immediately after the car has been driven for a long time at high speed, or in city traffic in hot weather; in those cases, the transmission should be given a half hour to cool down.

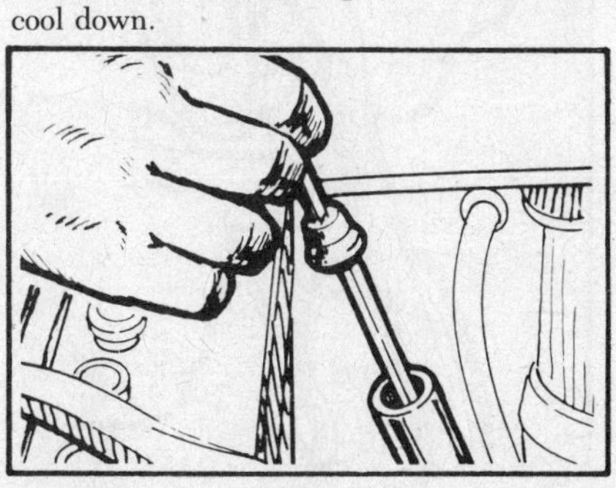

Check the automatic transmission fluid level with the dipstick provided

2. Stop the car, apply the parking brake, then shift slowly through all gear positions, ending in Park. Leave the engine running.
3. Remove the dipstick, wipe it clean, then reinsert it, pushing it fully home.
4. Pull the dipstick again and, holding it horizontally, read the fluid level.
5. Cautiously feel the end of the dipstick to determine the temperature. Most dipsticks are marked with both cool and hot levels. If the fluid is not up to the correct level, more will have to be added.
6. Fluid is added through the dipstick tube. You will probably need the aid of a spout or a long-necked funnel. Be sure that whatever you pour through is perfectly clean and dry. Fluid recommendations can be found in the owner's manual.

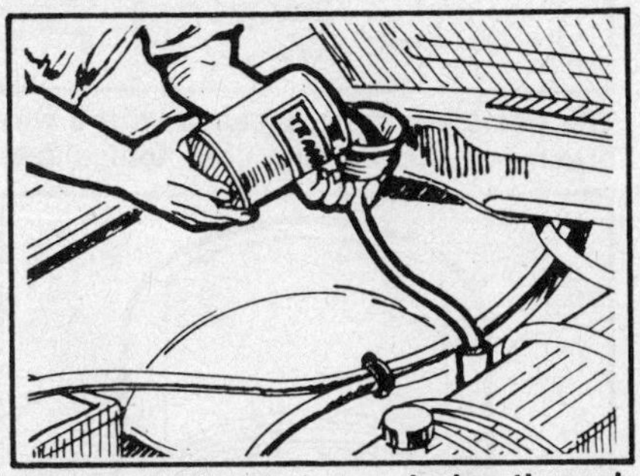

Fill the automatic transmission through the dipstick tube

Add fluid slowly, and in small amounts, checking the level frequently between additions. Do not overfill, which will cause foaming, fluid loss, slippage, and possible transmission damage.

Battery

FLUID LEVEL (EXCEPT "MAINTENANCE FREE" BATTERIES)

Check the battery electrolyte level at least once a month, or more often in hot weather or during periods of extended car operation. The level can be checked through the case on translucent polypropylene batteries; the cell caps must be removed on other models. The electrolyte level in each cell should be kept filled to the split ring inside, or the line marked on the outside of the case.

If the level is low, add only distilled water, or colorless, odorless drinking water, through the opening until the level is correct. Each cell is completely separate from the others, so each must be checked and filled individually.

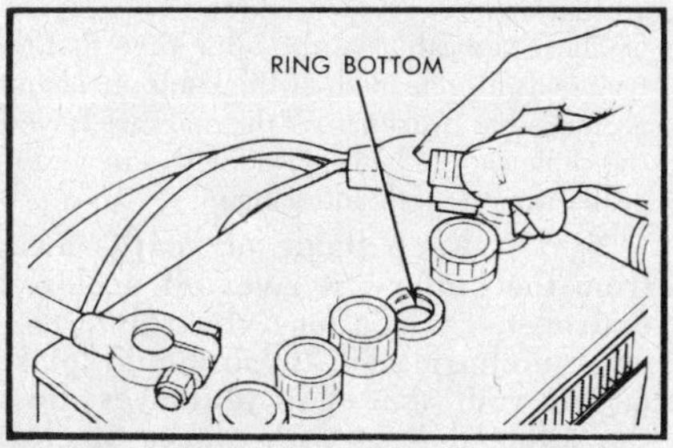

Fill the battery cell to the bottom of the split ring

If water is added in freezing weather, the car should be driven several miles to allow the water to mix with the electrolyte. Otherwise, the battery could freeze.

SPECIFIC GRAVITY (EXCEPT "MAINTENANCE FREE" BATTERIES)

While not technically exact, a practical measurement of the chemical condition of the battery is indicated by measuring the specific gravity of the acid (electrolyte) contained in each cell. The electrolyte in a fully charged battery is usually between 1.260 and 1.280 times as heavy as pure water at the same temperature (80° F). Variations in the specific gravity readings for a fully charged battery may differ. Therefore, it is most important that all battery cells produce an equal reading.

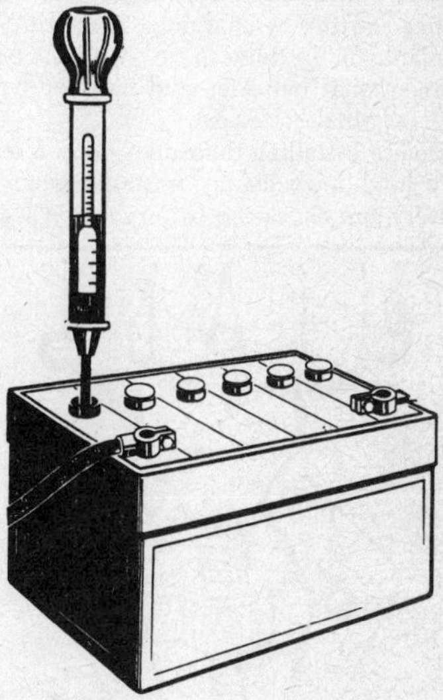

Testing battery specific gravity

As a battery discharges, a chemical change takes place within each cell. The sulfate factor of the electrolyte combines chemically with the battery plates, reducing the weight of the electrolyte. A reading of the specific gravity of the acid, or electrolyte, of any partially charged battery, will therefore be less than that taken in a fully charged one.

The hydrometer is the instrument used for determining the specific gravity of liquids. The battery hydrometer is readily available from many sources, including local auto replacement parts stores. The following chart gives an indication of specific gravity value, related to battery charge condition. If, after charging, the specific gravity between any two cells varies more than 50 points (.050), the battery is probably bad.

Specific Gravity Reading	Charged Condition
1.260-1.280	Fully charged
1.230-1.250	Three-quarter charged
1.200-1.220	One-half charged
1.170-1.190	One-quarter charged
1.140-1.160	Just about flat
1.110-1.130	All the way down

CABLES AND CLAMPS

Once a year, the battery terminals and the cable clamps should be cleaned. Loosen the clamps and remove the cables, negative cable first. On batteries with posts on top, the use of a puller specially made for the purpose is recommended. These are inexpensive, and available in auto parts stores. Side terminal battery cables are secured with a bolt.

Clean the cable clamps and the battery terminal with a wire brush, until all corrosion, grease, etc. is removed and the metal is shiny. It is especially important to clean the inside of the clamp thoroughly, since a small deposit of foreign material or oxidation there will prevent a sound electrical connection and inhibit either starting or charging. Special tools are available for cleaning these parts, one type for conventional batteries and another type for side terminal batteries.

Before installing the cables, loosen the battery hold-down clamp or strap, remove the battery and check the battery tray. Clear it of any debris, and check it for soundness. Rust should be wire brushed away, and the metal given a coat of anti-rust paint. Replace the battery and tighten the hold-down clamp or strap securely, but be careful not to overtighten, which will crack the battery case.

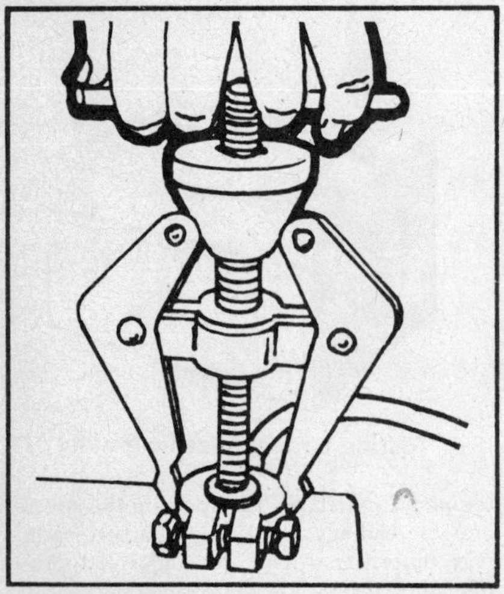

Use a puller to remove the clamp on post-type batteries

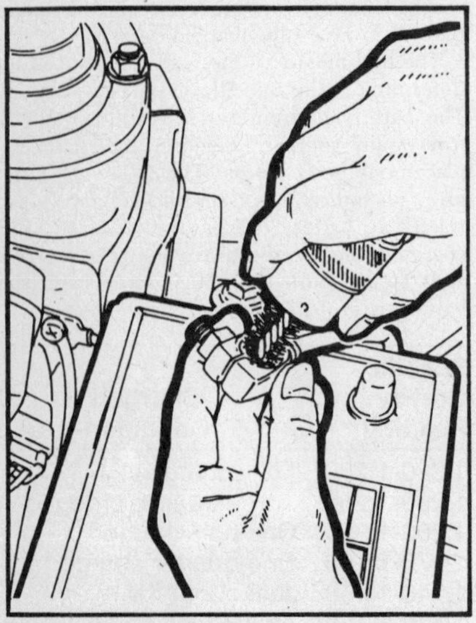

Clean the clamp with a wire brush

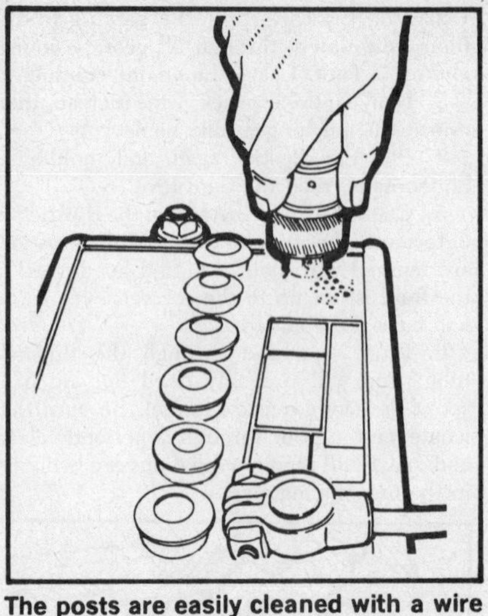

The posts are easily cleaned with a wire brush, or the battery post tool shown

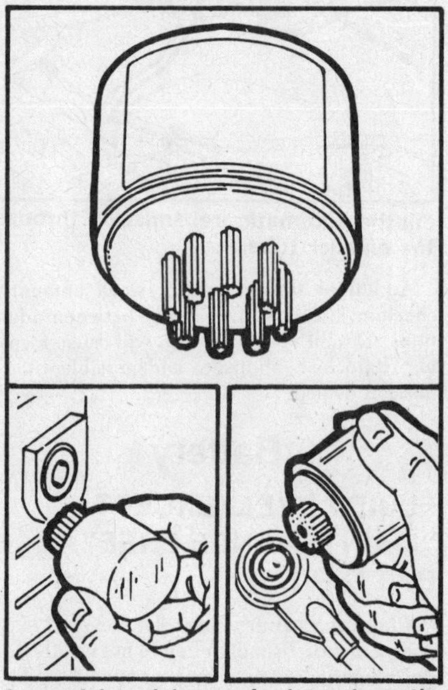

A special tool is required to clean the terminals and clamps on side terminal batteries

After the clamps and terminals are clean, reinstall the cables, negative cable last; do not hammer on the clamps to install. Tighten the clamps securely, but do not distort them. Give the clamps and terminals a thin external coat of grease after installation, to retard corrosion.

Check the cables at the same time that the terminals are cleaned. If the cable insulation is cracked or broken, or if the ends are frayed, the cable should be replaced with a new cable of the same length and gauge.

NOTE: Keep flame or sparks away from the battery; it gives off explosive hydrogen gas. Battery electrolyte contains sulphuric acid. If you should splash any on your skin or in your eyes, flush the affected area with plenty of clear water; if it lands in your eyes, get medical help immediately.

Brake Fluid

Once a month, the fluid level in the brake master cylinder should be checked.

1. Park the car on a level surface.
2. Clean off the master cylinder cover before removal. Some covers are retained by a bolt. Some of the newer master cylinders with plastic reservoirs have screw caps. Remove the cover, being careful not to drop or tear the rubber diaphragm which will probably be underneath. Be careful also not to drip any brake fluid on painted surfaces; the stuff eats paint.

NOTE: Brake fluid absorbs moisture from the air, which reduces effectiveness and will corrode brake parts once in the system. Never leave the master cylinder or the brake fluid container uncovered for any longer than necessary.

3. The fluid level should be about ¼ inch below the lip of the master cylinder well.
4. If fluid addition is necessary, use only extra heavy duty disc brake fluid meeting DOT 3 or DOT 4 specifications. The fluid should be reasonably fresh, because brake fluid deteriorates with age.
5. Replace the cover, making sure that the diaphragm is correctly seated.

If the brake fluid is constantly low, the system should be checked for leaks. However, it is normal for the fluid level to fall gradually as the disc brake pads wear; expect the fluid level to drop about ⅛ inch for every 10,000 miles of wear.

Belt Tension

Every six months or 12,000 miles, check the water pump, alternator, power steering pump, air pump, and air conditioning compressor drive belts for proper tension. Also look for signs of wear, fraying, separation, glazing and so on, and replace the belts as required.

Belt tension should be checked with a gauge made for the purpose. If a gauge is not available, tension can be checked with moderate thumb pressure applied to the belt at its longest span midway between pulleys. If the belt has a free span less than twelve inches, it should deflect approximately ⅛-¼ inch. If the span is longer than twelve inches, deflection can range between ⅛ and ⅜ inches.

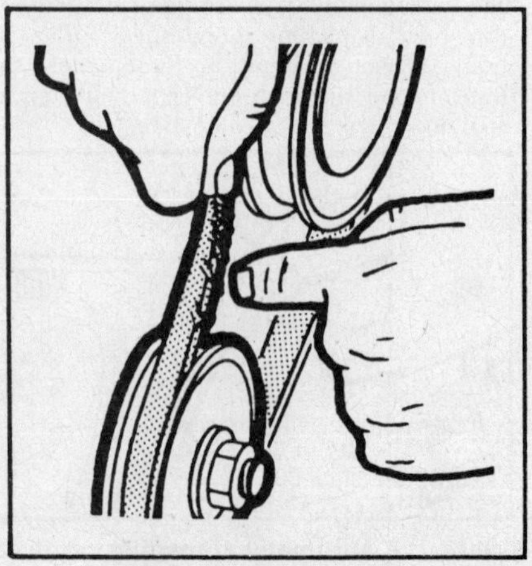

Check the belts for wear

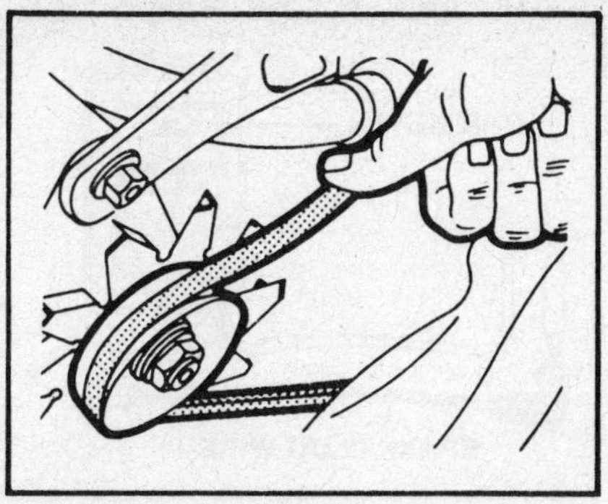

Check the belt tension at the middle of the longest span between pulleys

To adjust or replace belts:

1. Loosen the driven accessory's pivot and mounting bolts. Some air conditioning compressor belts are tensioned by an idler pulley; in this case, loosen the idler pulley and use a ½ in. drive ratchet in the square hole provided to lever the idler pulley up or down.
2. Move the accessory toward or away from the engine until the tension is correct. You can use a wooden hammer handle or broomstick as a lever, but do not use anything metallic.
3. Tighten the bolts and recheck the tension. If new bolts have been installed, run the engine for a few minutes, then recheck and readjust as necessary.

NOTE: If the driven component has two drive belts, the belts should be replaced in pairs to maintain proper tension.

It is better to have belts too loose than too tight, because overtight belts will lead to bearing failure, particularly in the water pump and alternator. However, loose belts place and extremely high impact load on the driven components due to the whipping action of the belt.

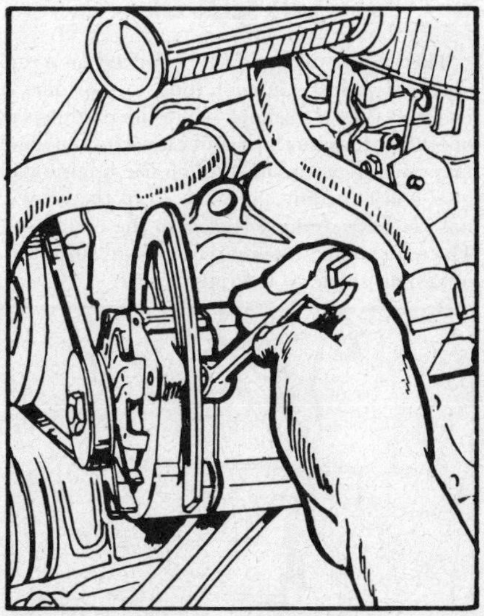

To either adjust or remove a belt, loosen the driven component's adjusting bolt

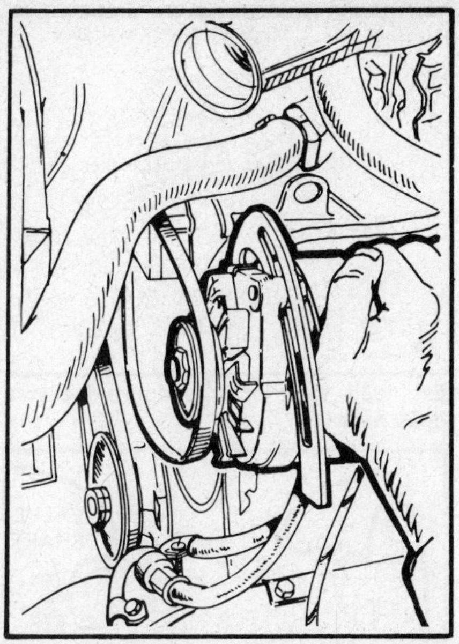

Push the component toward the engine to remove the belt

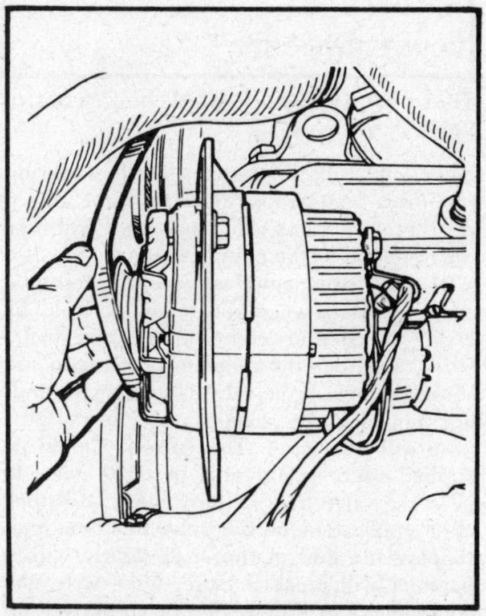

Slip the replacement belt over the pulley

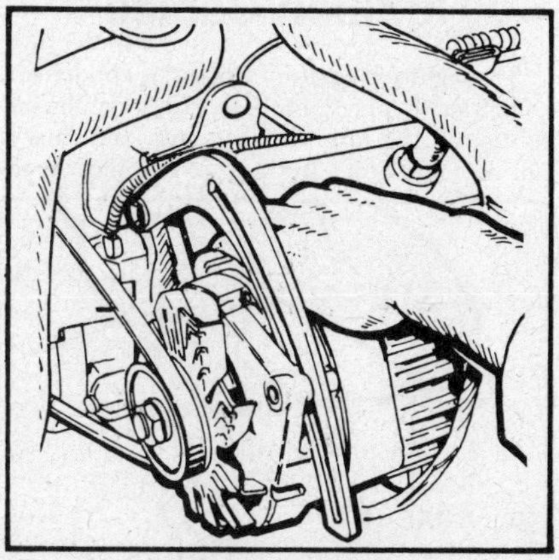

Pull outwards on the component to tension the belt, then tighten the bolts; recheck the belt tension after tightening

Carburetor and Choke Linkage

Every 12 months or 6000 miles, examine the carburetor linkage and choke plate for free movement. The choke plate action can generally be freed, if necessary, with the application of a solvent made for the purpose to the ends of the choke shaft. This solvent will also clean grease and dirt from the throttle linkage.

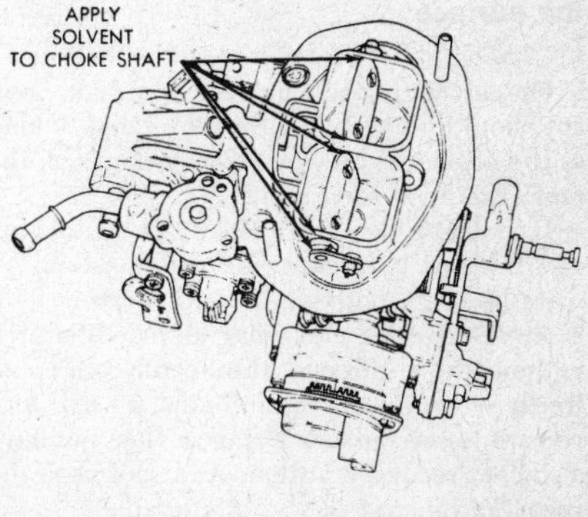

Use a spray solvent on the choke shaft, but do not apply any lubricants

Cooling System

Once a month, the engine coolant level should be checked. On cars without a coolant recovery system, this should only be done when the engine is cold. Remove the radiator cap; the coolant level should be about one inch below the radiator filler neck.

CAUTION

To avoid injury when working with a hot engine, cover the radiator cap with a thick cloth. Wear a heavy glove to protect your hand. Turn the radiator cap slowly to the first stop, and allow all the pressure to vent (indicated when the hissing noise stops). When the pressure has been released, remove the cap the rest of the way.

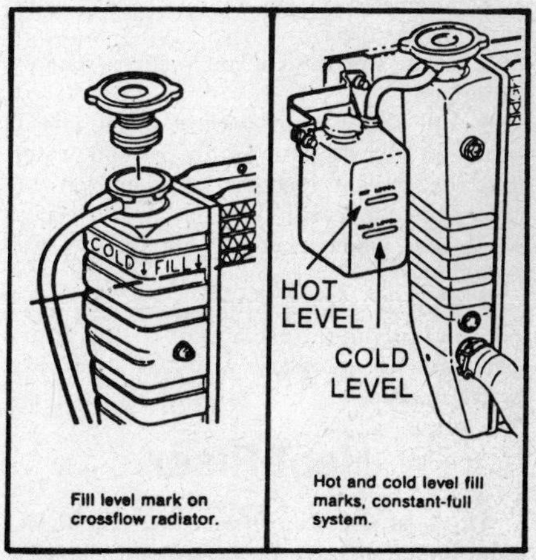

Proper coolant level is about one inch below the radiator neck, or between the lines on the recovery tank

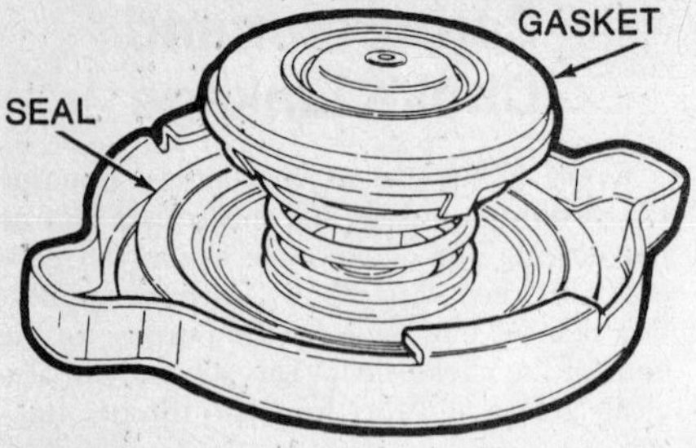

Check the radiator cap gasket and sealing surface

On cars with a coolant recovery tank, coolant should be visible within the tank; as long as the coolant is between the markings on the tank, the level is correct.

If coolant is needed, a 50/50 mix of ethylene glycol-based antifreeze and water should always be used, both winter and summer. This is imperative on cars with air conditioning; without the antifreeze, the heater core could freeze when the air conditioning is used. Add coolant to the radiator if the car does not have a coolant recovery system. Add coolant to the recovery tank on cars so equipped.

The radiator hoses and clamps and the radiator cap should be checked at the same time as the coolant level. Hoses which are brittle, cracked, or swollen should be replaced. Clamps should be checked for tightness (screwdriver tight only—do not allow the clamp to cut into the hose or crush the fitting). The radiator cap gasket should be checked for any obvious tears, cracks or swelling, or any signs of incorrect seating in the radiator neck.

The cooling system should be drained, flushed and refilled after the first 24 months or 24,000 miles, and every year thereafter.

1. Drain the radiator by opening the drain cock at the bottom. Some radiators do not have these; the lower radiator hose must be disconnected at the radiator instead. If the engine block has drain plugs, they should be opened to speed draining.
2. Close the drain cocks and fill the system with clear water. A cooling system flushing additive can be used, if desired.
3. Run the engine until it is hot. The heater should be turned on to its maximum heat position so that the core is flushed out.
4. Drain the system, then flush with water until it runs clear.
5. Clean out the coolant recovery tank, if equipped.
6. Fill the system with a 50/50 mix of ethylene glycol-based antifreeze and water. Fill the coolant recovery tank midway between the marks with this mixture also (except G.M. cars, which should be filled to the "Full Cold" mark).
7. Run the engine until it is hot, then let it cool and top up the radiator or coolant recovery tank as necessary with the antifreeze/water mixture.

Heat Riser

The heat riser is a thermostatically or vacuum operated valve in the exhaust manifold. (Not all cars have one.) It closes when the engine is warming up, in order to preheat the incoming fuel/air mixture. If it sticks open,

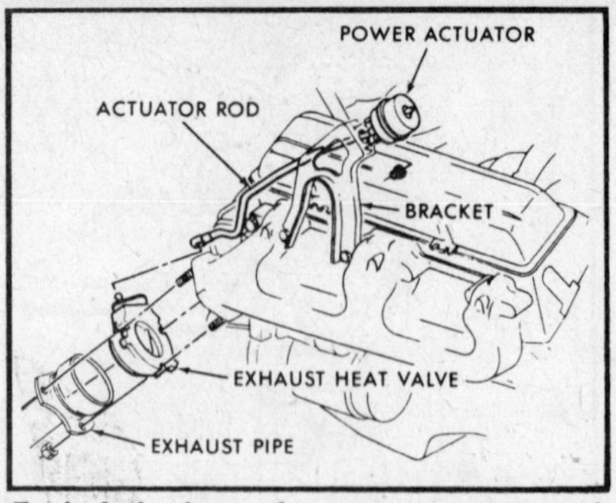

Exploded view of a vacuum-operated heat riser

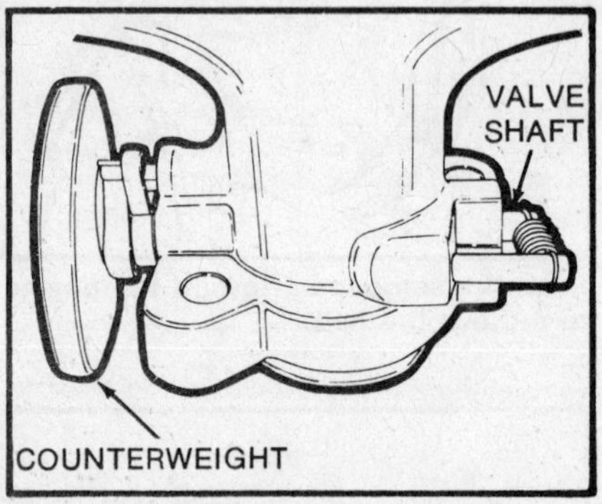

Thermostatically-operated heat control valve

the result will be frequent stalling during warmup, especially in cold and damp weather. If it sticks shut, the result will be a rough idle after the engine is warm.

The heat riser should move freely. It can be checked easily when the engine is cold by giving the counterweight on the valve shaft a twirl, or pulling the vacuum rod to open and shut the valve. If the valve is sticking or binding, a quick shot of solvent made for the purpose will free it up. This solvent should be applied every six months or 6000 miles to keep the valve free. If the valve is still stuck after application of the solvent, sometimes rapping the end of the shaft lightly with a hammer will break it loose. Otherwise, the components will have to be removed for further repairs.

Ignition Cables

The ignition system (points, condenser, rotor, spark plugs, etc.) receives regular attention in the form of a tune-up, and thus is not covered here. But one of the most commonly overlooked components is the ignition cable, or spark plug wire.

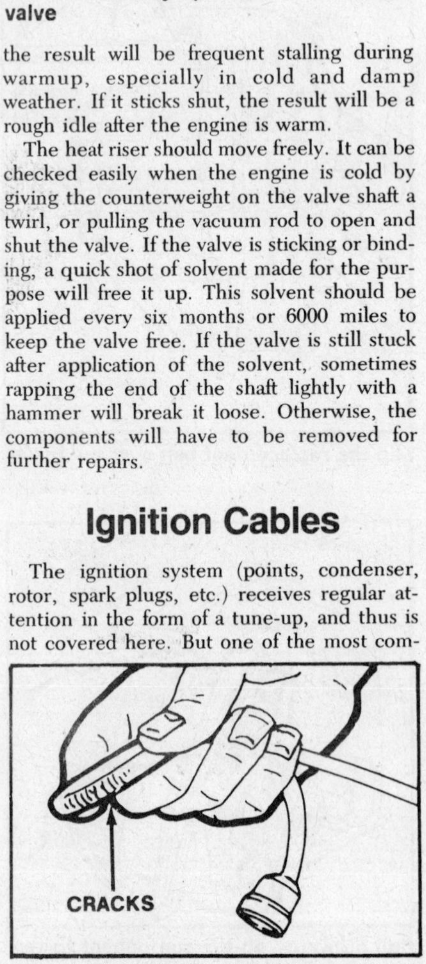

Inspect the ignition cables for cracks or breaks in the insulation

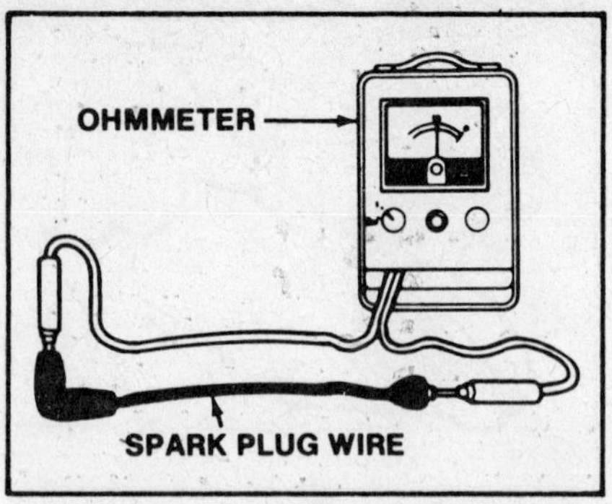

Test the ignition cables with an ohmmeter. Conventional ignition cables should be removed from the distributor cap, but electronic ignition wires should first be tested through the cap

Although they rarely show any visible signs of deterioration, the ignition cables should be checked at every tune-up, and replaced every 50,000 miles. Cracking and embrittlement are of course obvious signs of wear, but most newer cables have silicone insulation and thus are not prone to display these conditions.

The most reliable way to check the cables is with an ohmmeter. On conventional ignitions, the resistance should be less than 7,000 ohms per foot (wire removed). On cars with electronic ignitions, it is generally recommended to leave the wire attached to the distributor cap; test with one lead from the ohmmeter connected to the corresponding terminal in the distributor cap, the other lead touched to the disconnected end of the cable at the spark plug. Then, if resistance seems close to the limit, remove the wire from the cap and retest. In general, the spark plug wires on electronic ignitions should be replaced if the total resistance is over 36,000 ohms.

Always replace the cables with new ones of the same type. Replace the wire one at a time, working from the longest to the shortest.

Oil Level

The engine oil should be checked on a regular basis, ideally at each fuel stop, or once a week. It is best to check when the engine is at operating temperature, but checking the level immediately after shutting off the engine will give a fast reading, because all of the oil will not yet have drained back into the crankcase. The car should be parked on a level surface to obtain an accurate reading.

Check the engine oil level with the dipstick

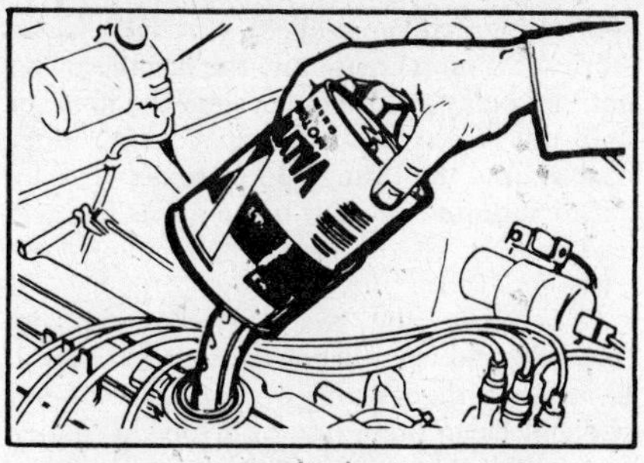

Add oil through the valve cover

1. Remove the oil dipstick. Wipe it clean, then replace it, seating it firmly.

2. Remove the dipstick again and hold it horizontally to prevent the oil from running. The level should be between the "Add" and "Full" marks on the dipstick. The dipstick may be marked "Add" and "Full", "Add" and "Safe", or may have lines scribed on it; in any case, the oil level should be above the lower marking.

3. If the oil is below the lower mark, enough oil should be added to the engine to raise the level to the upper mark. The markings are usually spaced so that one quart of oil will raise the level from the "Add" mark to the "Full" mark. Oil is added through the capped opening in the valve cover. Only oils labeled SE (gasoline engines) or CC (diesel engines) should be used; select a viscosity that will be compatible with the temperatures expected until the next drain interval.

4. Replace the dipstick, then check the level again after any additions of oil. Be careful not to overfill, which will lead to leakage and seal damage.

Power Steering

The power steering fluid level is checked with a dipstick inserted into the pump reservoir. The dipstick may be attached to the reservoir cap, or inserted into a tube on the pump body. The level should be checked at every oil change. On some models, the power steering reservoir is translucent, allowing the

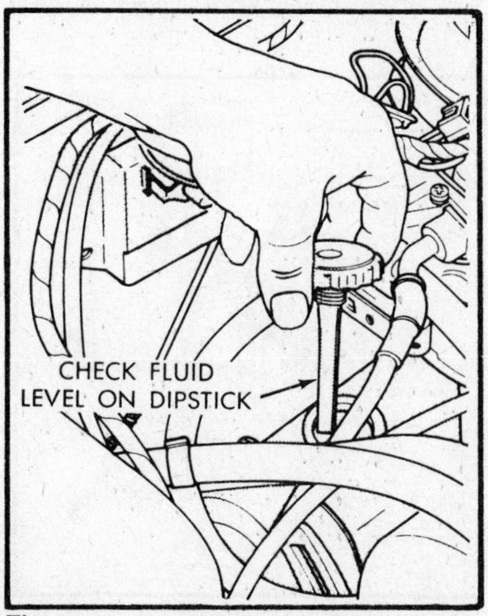

The power steering level is checked with the dipstick installed in the reservoir

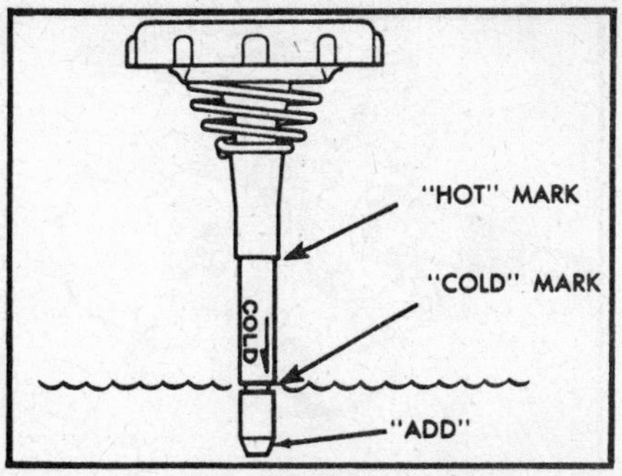

Power steering dipstick markings, typical of all types except Ford

level to be checked through the sides of the container without removing the cap. On others, the reservoir is a metal canister with a wingnut attached cap. After the cap is removed, the level is checked with the scribed lines on the inside of the container.

On most models, the fluid level may be checked with the fluid either warm or cold. If checked with the fluid cold, the level will be slightly lower than with the fluid warm. If doubts arise about the specific procedures for the car being checked, consult the owner's manual.

1. On all models, with the engine off, remove the dipstick, remove the cap or check the level through the side of the reservoir. If warm, the level should be between the "Hot" and "Cold" marks or even with the scribed line in the reservoir. If the fluid is cold, the level should be slightly lower.

NOTE: On some Volvos and other makes the level should be checked with the engine running. Consult the owner's manual.

2. If the level is low, add power steering fluid until the correct level is reached. Do not overfill the reservoir.

Windshield Washer Fluid

Check the fluid level in the windshield washer tank at every oil level check. The fluid can be mixed in a 50% solution with water, if desired, as long as temperatures remain above freezing. Below freezing, the fluid should be used full strength. Never add engine coolant antifreeze to the washer fluid, because it will damage the car's paint.

UNDER CAR

Axle

The fluid level in the rear axle should be checked every 12 months or 12,000 miles.

1. With the car parked on a level surface, remove the filler plug. The plug can be found either in the rear cover of the differential, or on the front of the pinion housing.

2. If lubricant dribbles out when the plug is removed, the level is correct. Otherwise, stick in your finger (watch out for sharp threads); the fluid should be even with the filler hole.

3. If lubricant is needed, use SAE 80W-90 GL-5 gear oil (SAE 80W GL-5 in very cold climates) to fill standard axles. Limited slip axles require a special lubricant, available in auto parts stores.

4. When the level is correct, install the plug to tighten until snug. Do not overtighten.

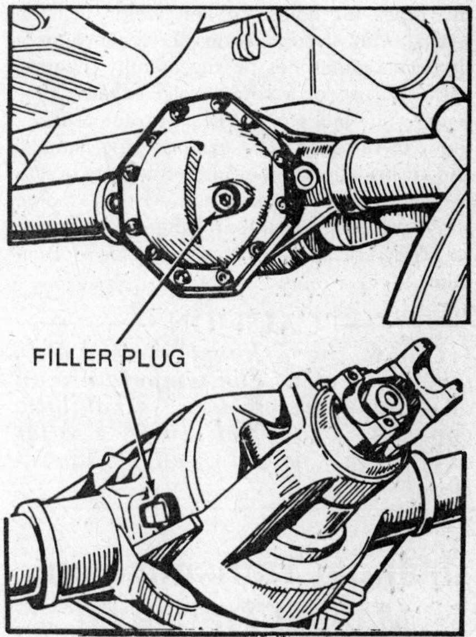

Rear axle filler plug locations

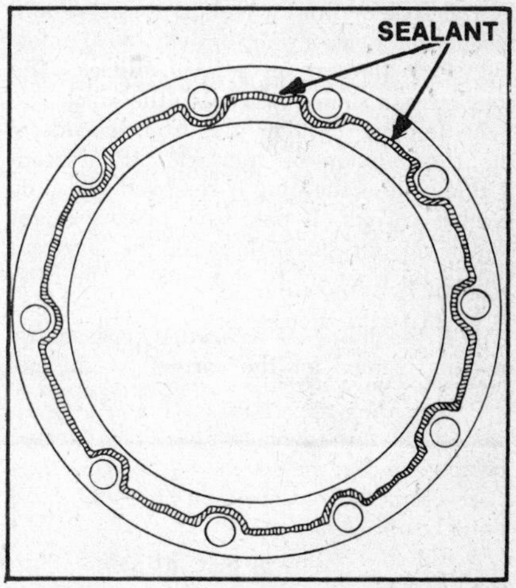

Apply a bead of silicone sealer to the rear cover if no gasket is used

Standard axles should be drained and refilled with fresh lubricant every 15,000 miles when the car is used to pull a trailer. Limited slip axles should be drained and refilled at the first 7500 miles; the limited slip lubricant should be changed every 7500 miles when the car is used for trailer pulling. The axle may be drained by removing the drain plug at the bottom of the differential housing, if present. Otherwise, the rear cover must be removed, or a suction gun used through the filler hole. When installing a rear cover which does not use a gasket, apply a thin bead of silicone sealer to the cover, running the bead around the inside of the bolt holes. Install the cover, then tighten the bolts a few turns at a time in a crisscross pattern.

NOTE: On many later models, the rear axle is filled for life and fluid does not have to be replaced.

Exhaust System

The exhaust system should be checked twice a year for general soundness. Inspect the pipes for holes, broken welds, leaking seams, or loose connections. Leaks at connections can sometimes be successfully repaired with the use of a commercial exhaust pipe sealer, but holes or brakes warrant replacement of the part. The exhaust pipe hangers and straps should be examined for any breaks or cracks; replace these as necessary. Some slight cracking or rubber hangers is normal, but deep cracks or cuts are cause for replacement.

CAUTION

Check the exhaust system only when it is cold. The temperature on an exhaust system using a catalytic converter can reach 1000° F after only a short period of engine operation.

Manual Transmission, Manual Transaxle

The fluid level in the manual transmission (or transaxle on front wheel drive cars) should be checked twice a year, or every 6000 miles.

1. Park the car on a level surface. The transmission should be cool to the touch.
2. Remove the filler plug from the side of the transmission or transaxle. If lubricant trickles out as the plug is removed, the fluid level is correct. If not, stick in your finger (watch out for sharp threads); the lubricant should be right up to the edge of the filler hole.
3. If the lubricant is needed, consult the owner's manual for the correct weight and type of fluid.

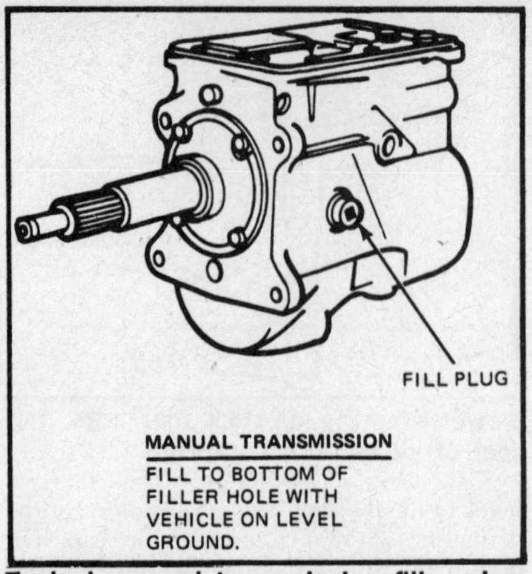

FILL PLUG
MANUAL TRANSMISSION
FILL TO BOTTOM OF FILLER HOLE WITH VEHICLE ON LEVEL GROUND.

Typical manual transmission filler plug location

NOTE: Some manual transmission/transaxle assemblies are filled with automatic transmission fluid rather than gear oil. Consult the owner's manual for lubricant information.

4. When the level is correct, install the filler plug and tighten until snug.

Parking Brake Linkage

The parking brake cable assembly should be inspected twice a year for fraying, kinks, and binding. A smooth white waterproof lubricant should be applied at the same time to all pivot points and areas in sliding contact.

Suspension Lubrication

Depending on the year of manufacture, there may be as many as twelve grease fittings on the suspension parts, or as few as two. Typical locations for grease nipples are on the ball joints, control arm pivot points, steering linkage, and the tie rod ends.

Lubricate these fittings with a small hand operated grease gun filled with EP chassis lubricant. Pump grease into the fitting slowly, until it begins to ooze out around the joint, or until the grease begins to expand the rubber boot around the fitting. Be extremely careful not to rupture any seals or boots, as this will lead to lubricant loss and contamination of the parts involved.

Ocassionaly, the grease nipples may become clogged with dirt or hardened grease. If so, unscrew them with a wrench of the proper size and clean them out with solvent. When reinstalled, they may be covered with plastic caps made for the purpose, or a piece of aluminum foil.

The chassis and suspension parts should be lubricated once a year, or every 7500 miles, whichever comes first.

EXTERIOR

Drain Holes and Underbody

Most cars have drain holes spaced along the lower edge of the rocker panels and doors. These holes should be cleared of any debris or rust twice a year. A small screwdriver can be used to open plugged drain holes.

Every spring, the underbody should be flushed with clear water to remove deposits of mud, road salt, and debris. It is advisable to loosen any packed-in sediment before flushing to assure a more thorough cleaning.

Hinges and Locks

Once a year, the door, hood, and trunk hinges, and all locks should be lubricated to ensure smooth operation. The hinge points should be lightly oiled. Lock cylinders may be easily lubricated with a shot of silicone spray directed into the keyhole. Silicone lubricant also works well on the door latch mechanisms, and keeps the door, trunk, and window weatherseals pliable when applied in a light film.

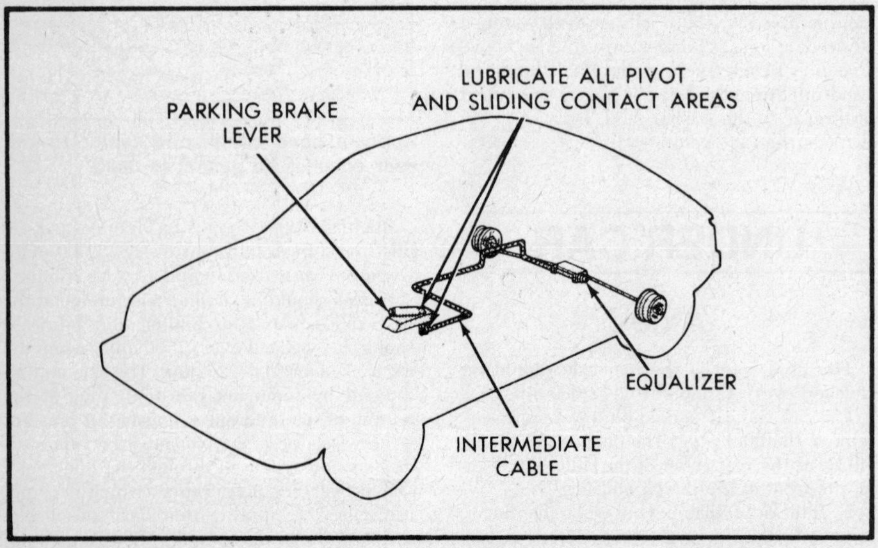

Lubricate the parking brake cable with white waterproof grease

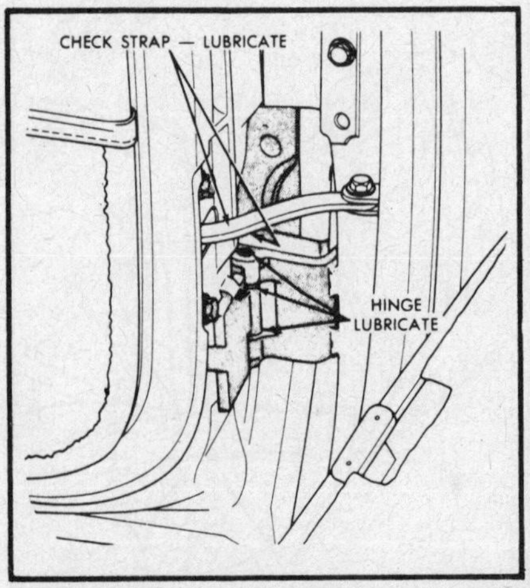

Use engine oil to lubricate the door, hood, and trunk hinges

Tires

Tires should be checked weekly for proper air pressure. A chart, located either in the glove compartment or on the driver's or passenger's door, gives the recommended inflation pressures. Maximum fuel economy and tire life will result if the pressure is maintained at the highest figure given on the chart. Pressures should be checked before driving since pressure can increase as much as six pounds per sqaure inch (psi) due to heat buildup. It is a good idea to have your own accurate pressure gauge, because not all gauges on service station air pumps can be trusted. When checking pressures, do not neglect the spare tire. Note that some spare tires require pressures considerably higher than those used in the other tires.

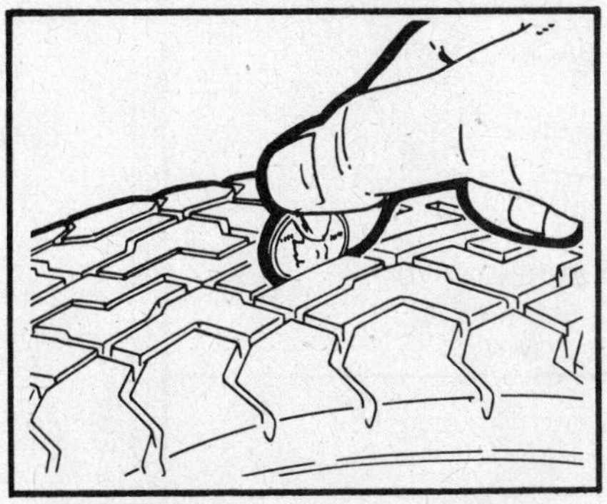

Tire tread depth can be checked with a penny. If the top of Lincoln's head is visible, the tires are due for replacement

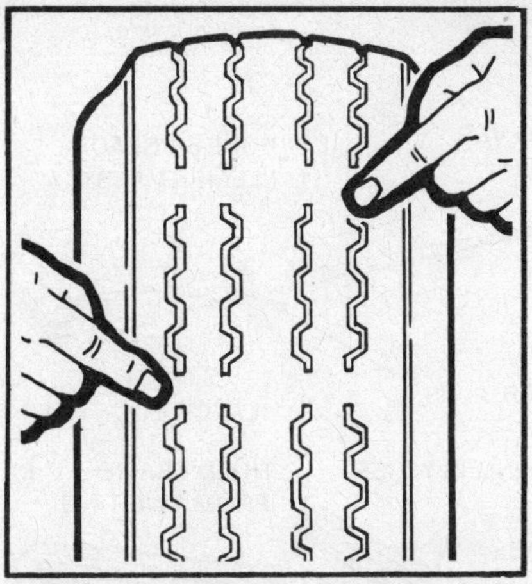

Tread wear indicators will appear as a band across the tire when the tread has worn out.

While you are about the task of checking air pressure, inspect the tir treads for cuts, bruises and other damage. Check the air valves to be sure that they are tight. Replace any missing valve caps.

Check the tires for uneven wear that might indicate the need for front end alignment or tire rotation. Tires should be replaced when a tread wear indicator appears as a solid band across the tread.

When buying new tires, give some thought to the following points, especially if you are considering a switch to larger tires or a different profile series:

1. All four tires must be of the same construction type. This rule cannot be violated. Radial, bias, and bias-belted tires must not be mixed.
2. The wheels should be the correct width for the tire. Tire dealers have charts of tire and rim compatibility. A mismatch will cause sloppy handling and rapid tire wear. The tread width should match the rim width (inside bead to inside bead) within an inch. For radial tires, the rim width should be 80% or less of the tire (not tread) width.
3. The height (mounted diameter) of the new tires can change speedometer accuracy, engine speed at a given road speed, fuel mileage, acceleration, and ground clearance. Tire manufacturers furnish full measurement specifications.
4. The spare tire should be usable, at least for short distance and low speed operation, with the new tires.
5. There shouldn't be any body interference when loaded, on bumps, or in turns.

TIRE ROTATION

Tire rotation is recommended every 6000 miles or so, to obtain maximum tire wear. The pattern you use depends on whether or not your car has a usable spare. Radial tires should not be cross-switched (from one side of the car to the other); they last longer if their direction of rotation is not changed. Snow tires sometimes have directional arrows molded into the side of the car-cass; the arrow shows the direction of rotation. They will wear very rapidly if the rotation is reversed. Studded tires will lose their studs if their rotational direction is reversed.

NOTE: Mark the wheel position or direction of rotation on radial tires or studded snow tires before removing them.

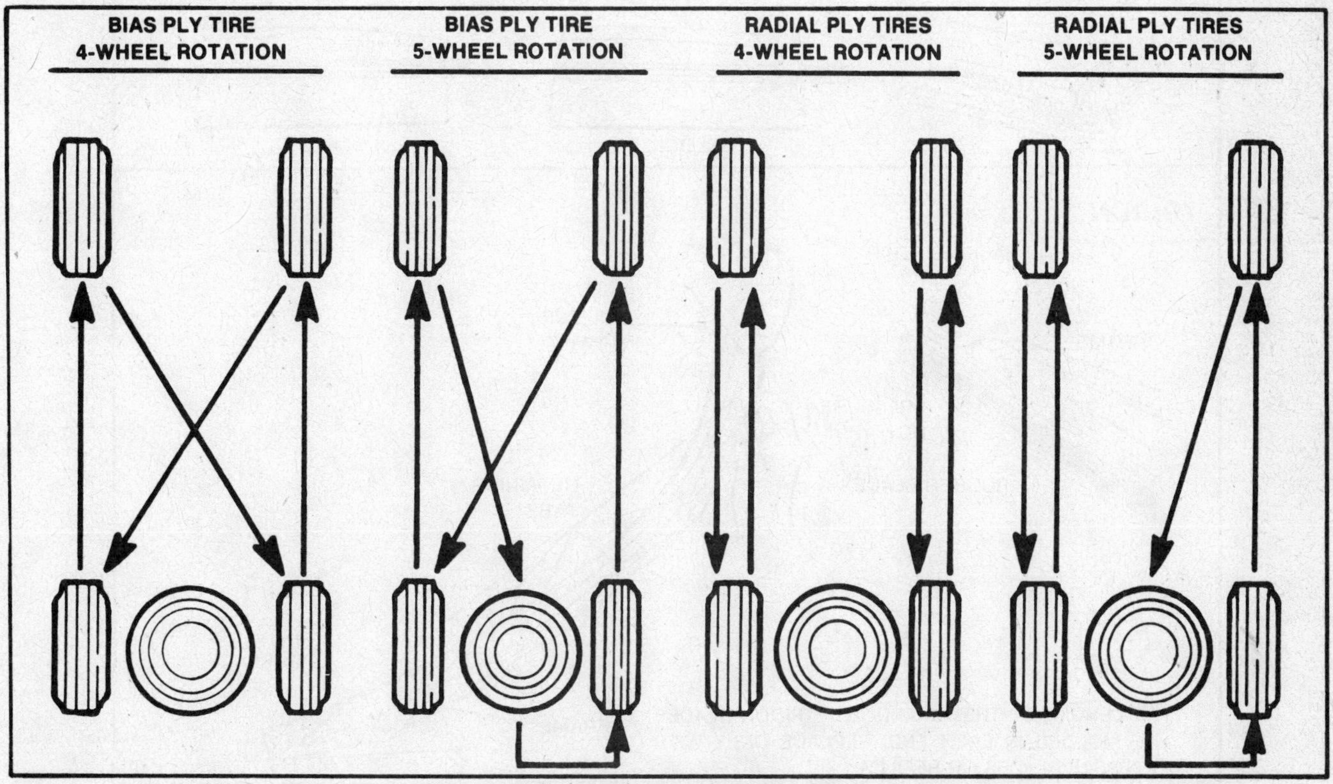

Tire rotation diagrams

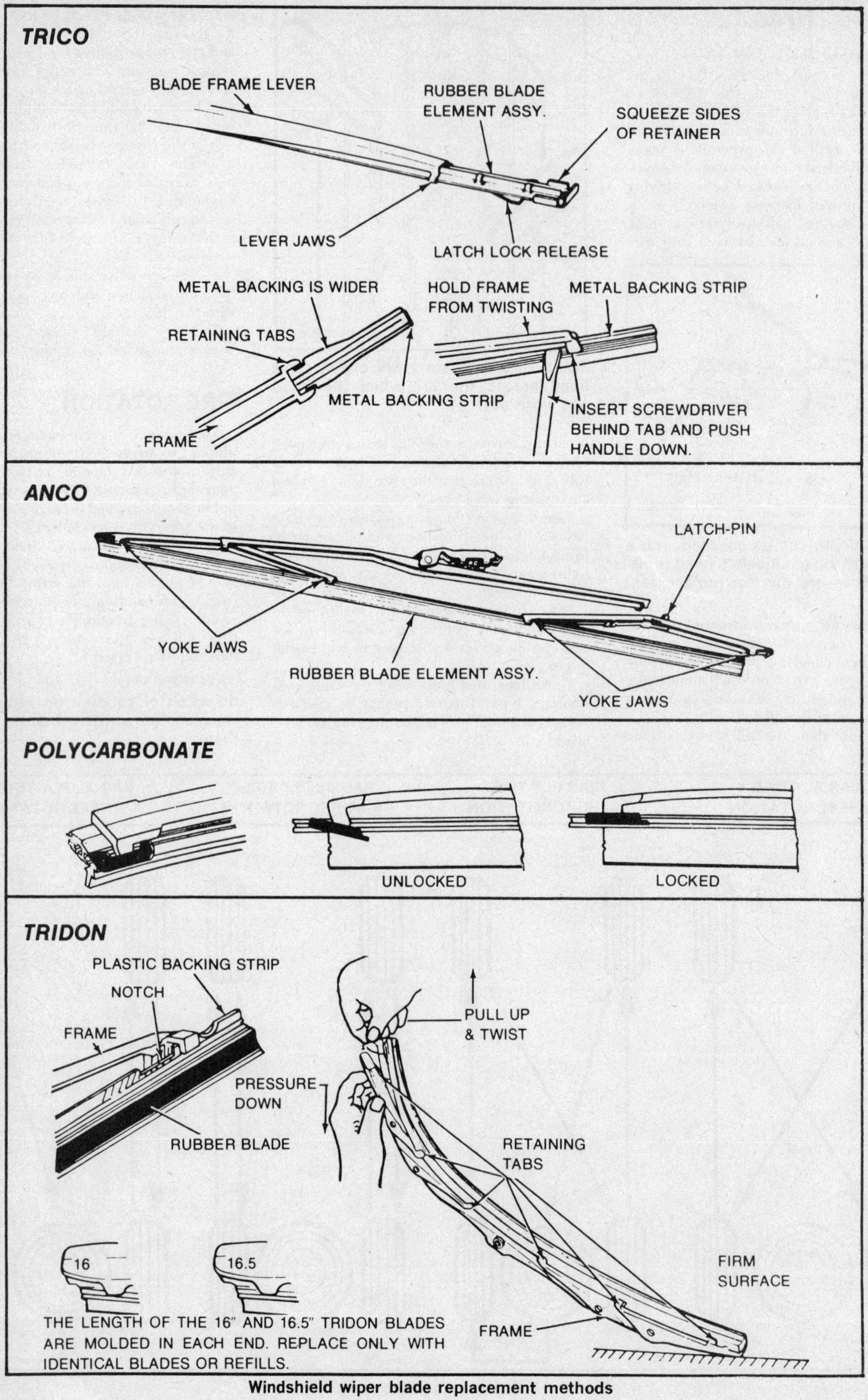

Windshield wiper blade replacement methods

STORAGE

Store the tires at proper inflation pressure if they are mounted on wheels. Keep them in a cool dry place, laid on their sides. If the tires are stored in the garage or basement, do not let them stand on a concrete floor; set them on strips of wood.

Windshield Wipers and Washers

For maximum effectiveness, and longest element life, the windshield and wiper blades should be kept clean. Dirt, tree sap, road tar and so on will cause streaking, smearing and blade deterioration if left on the glass. It is advisable to wash the windshield carefully with a commercial glass cleaner at least once a month. Wipe off the rubber blades with the wet rag afterwards. For access to the blades on wiper systems which park below the hood line, turn the ignition key to "On" and run the wipers to the center of the windshield. Shut the wipers off with the ignition key, not the wiper switch. Do not attempt to move the wipers by hand; damage to the motor and drive mechanism will result.

If the blades are found to be craked, broken or torn, they should be replaced immediately. Replacement intervals will vary with usage, although ozone deterioration usually limits blade life to about one year. If the wiper pattern is smeared or streaked, or if the blade chatters across the glass, the elements should be replaced. It is easist and most sensible to replace the elements in pairs.

There are basically three different types of refills, which differ in their method of replacement. One type has two release buttons, approximately one-third of the way up from the ends of the blade frame. Pushing the buttons down release a lock and allows the rubber filler to be removed from the frame. The new filler slides back into the frame and locks in place.

The second type of refill has two metal tabs which are unlocked by squeezing them together. The rubber filler can then be withdrawn from the frame jaws. A new refill is installed by inserting the refill into the front frame jaws and sliding it rearward to engage the remaining frame jaws. There are usually four jaws; be certain when installing that the refill is engaged in all of them. At the end of its travel, the tabs will lock into place on the front jaws of the wiper blade frame.

The third type is a refill made from polycarbonate. The refill has a simple locking device at one end which flexes downward out of the groove into which the jaws of the holder fit, allowing easy release. By sliding the new refill through all the jaws and pushing through the slight resistance when it reaches the end of its travel, the refill will lock into position.

Regardless of the type of refill used, make sure that all of the frame jaws are engaged as the refill is pushed into place and locked. The metal blade holder and frame will scratch the glass if allowed to touch it.

WASHER NOZZLE ADJUSTMENT

Centered Single Post–Non-Adjustable Nozzles

This type is usually located on the rear center of the hood panel, directly in front of the windshield. By loosening the body retaining nut from under the hood, the nozzle body can be turned to provide the best spray discharge to cover the windshield. Tighten the retaining nut while holding the nozzle in position.

Centered Single Post–Adjustable Nozzles

This nozzle is adjusted with a wrench, screwdriver, or pliers. If the nozzle has no gripping area, the adjustment is made by inserting a stiff wire into the nozzle opening and moving the nozzle in the direction desired. When using the wire as an adjuster tool, do not force the nozzle; the wire can be broken within the nozzle opening.

Individual Nozzles

A tab is usually fastened to the nozzle stem to assist in turning the nozzle in the desired direction. If a tab is not present, use a pair of pliers to gently move the nozzle.

Wiper Arm Nozzles

No adjustment is necessary on this type of nozzle, because the opening is centered on the wiper arm and moves along with the arm.

INDEX

Group		Topic
1	*	Battery
2	*	Cranking system
3	*	Primary electrical system
4	*	Secondary electrical system
5	*	Fuel system
6	*	Engine compression
7	**	Engine vacuum
8	**	Secondary electrical system
9	**	Valve train
10	**	Exhaust system
11	**	Cooling system
12	**	Engine lubrication

*—The engine need not be running. **—The engine must be running.

The following section is designed to aid in the rapid diagnosis of engine problems. The systematic format is used to diagnose problems ranging from engine starting difficulties to the need for engine overhaul. It is assumed that the user is equipped with basic hand tools and test equipment (tach-dwell meter, timing light, voltmeter, and ohmmeter).

Troubleshooting is divided into two sections. The first, *General Diagnosis*, is used to locate the problem area. In the second, *Specific Diagnosis*, the problem is systematically evaluated.

NOTE: ***Troubleshooting fuel injection systems is covered in a separate section in this manual. Consult the index.***

SPECIFIC DIAGNOSIS

This section is arranged so that following each test, instructions are given to proceed to another, until a problem is diagnosed.

General Diagnosis

PROBLEM: Symptom	*Begin diagnosis at Section Two, Number ———*
Engine won't start:	
Starter doesn't turn	1.1, 2.1
Starter turns, engine doesn't	2.1
Starter turns engine very slowly	1.1, 2.4
Starter turns engine normally	3.1, 4.1
Starter turns engine very quickly	6.1
Engine fires intermittently	4.1
Engine fires consistently	5.1, 6.1
Engine runs poorly:	
Hard starting	3.1, 4.1, 5.1, 8.1
Rough idle	4.1, 5.1, 8.1
Stalling	3.1, 4.1, 5.1, 8.1
Engine dies at high speeds	4.1, 5.1
Hesitation (on acceleration from standing stop)	5.1, 8.1
Poor pickup	4.1, 5.1, 8.1
Lack of power	3.1, 4.1, 5.1, 8.1
Backfire through the carburetor	4.1, 8.1, 9.1
Backfire through the exhaust	4.1, 8.1, 9.1
Blue exhaust gases	6.1, 7.1
Black exhaust gases	5.1
Running on (after the ignition is shut off)	3.1, 8.1
Susceptible to moisture	4.1
Engine misfires under load	4.1, 7.1, 8.4, 9.1
Engine misfires at speed	4.1, 8.4
Engine misfires at idle	3.1, 4.1, 5.1, 7.1, 8.4

PROBLEM: Symptom	*Probable Cause*
Engine noises: ①	
Metallic grind while starting	Starter drive not engaging completely
Constant grind or rumble	*Starter drive not releasing, worn main bearings
Constant knock	Worn connecting rod bearings
Knock under load	Fuel octane too low, worn connecting rod bearings
Double knock	Loose piston pin
Metallic tap	*Collapsed or sticky valve lifter, excessive valve clearance, excessive end play in a rotating shaft
Scrape	*Fan belt contacting a stationary surface
Tick while starting	S.U. electric fuel pump (normal), starter brushes
Constant tick	*Generator brushes, shreaded fan belt
Squeal	*Improperly tensioned fan belt
Hiss or roar	*Steam escaping through a leak in the cooling system or the radiator overflow vent
Whistle	*Vacuum leak
Wheeze	Loose or cracked spark plug

①—It is extremely difficult to evaluate vehicle noises. While the above are general definitions of engine noises, those starred (*) should be considered as possibly originating elsewhere in the car. To aid diagnosis, the following list considers other potential sources of these sounds.

Metallic grind:
Throwout bearing; transmission gears, bearings, or synchronizers; differential bearings, gears; something metallic in contact with brake drum or disc.

Metallic tap:
U-joints; fan-to-radiator (or shroud) contact.

Scrape:
Brake shoe or pad dragging; tire to body contact; suspension contacting undercarriage or exhaust; something non-metallic contacting brake shoe or drum.

Tick:
Transmission gears; differential gears; lack of radio suppression; resonant vibration of body panels; windshield wiper motor or transmission; heater motor and blower.

Squeal:
Brake shoe or pad not fully releasing; tires (excessive wear, uneven wear, improper inflation); front or rear wheel alignment (most commonly due to improper toe-in).

Hiss or whistle:
Wind leaks (body or window); heater motor and blower fan.

Roar:
Wheel bearings; wind leaks (body and window).

SAMPLE SECTION

Test and Procedure	*Results and Indications*	*Proceed to*
4.1—Check for spark: Hold each spark plug wire approximately 1/4" from ground with gloves or a heavy, dry rag. Crank the engine and observe the spark.	If no spark is evident:	**4.2**
	If spark is good in some cases:	**4.3**
	If spark is good in all cases:	**4.6**

DIAGNOSIS

1.1—Inspect the battery visually for case condition (corrosion, cracks) and water level.	If case is cracked, replace battery:	**1.4**
	If the case is intact, remove corrosion with a solution of baking soda and water (CAUTION: *do not get the solution into the battery*), and fill with water:	**1.2**
1.2—Check the battery cable connections: Insert a screwdriver between the battery post and the cable clamp. Turn the headlights on high beam, and observe them as the screwdriver is gently twisted to ensure good metal to metal contact.	If the lights brighten, remove and clean the clamp and post; coat the post with petroleum jelly, install and tighten the clamp:	**1.4**
	If no improvement is noted:	**1.3**

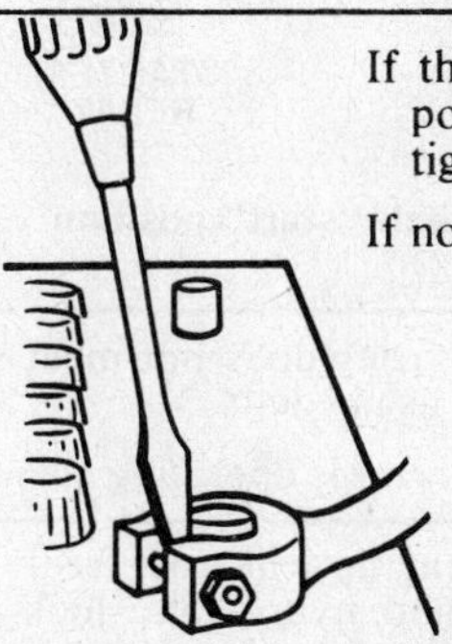

Testing battery cable connections using a screwdriver

1.3—Test the state of charge of the battery using an individual cell tester or hydrometer.	If indicated, charge the battery. NOTE: *If no obvious reason exists for the low state of charge (i.e., battery age, prolonged storage), the charging system should be tested:*	**1.4**

Spec. Grav. Reading	*Charged Condition*
1.260-1.280	Fully Charged
1.230-1.250	Three Quarter Charged
1.200-1.220	One Half Charged
1.170-1.190	One Quarter Charged
1.140-1.160	Just About Flat
1.110-1.130	All The Way Down

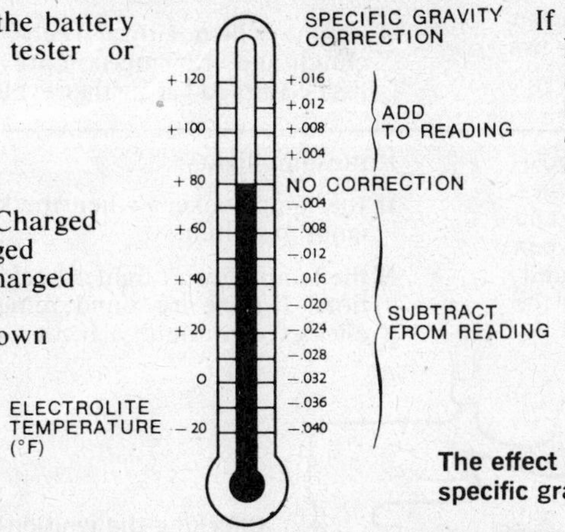

The effect of temperature on the specific gravity of battery electrolyte

1.4—Visually inspect battery cables for cracking, bad connection to ground, or bad connection to starter.	If necessary, tighten connections or replace the cables:	**2.1**

Tests in Group 2 are performed with coil high tension lead disconnected to prevent accidental starting.

2.1—Test the starter motor and solenoid: Connect a jumper from the battery post of the solenoid (or relay) to the ignition switch post of the solenoid (or relay).	If starter turns the engine normally:	**2.2**
	If the starter buzzes, or turns the engine very slowly:	**2.4**
	If no response, replace the solenoid (or relay).	**3.1**
	If the starter turns, but the engine doesn't, ensure that the flywheel ring gear is intact. If the gear is undamaged, replace the starter drive.	**3.1**
2.2—Determine whether ignition override switches are functioning properly (clutch start switch, neutral safety switch), by connecting a jumper across the switch(es), and turning the ignition switch to "start".	If starter operates, adjust or replace switch:	**3.1**
	If the starter doesn't operate:	**2.3**

Test and Procedure	*Results and Indications*	*Proceed to*
2.3—Check the ignition switch "start" position: Connect a 12V test lamp between the starter post of the solenoid (or relay) and ground. Turn the ignition switch to the "start" position, and jiggle the key.	If the lamp doesn't light when the switch is turned, check the ignition switch for loose connections, cracked insulation, or broken wires. Repair or replace as necessary:	**3.1**
	If the lamp flickers when the key is jiggled, replace the ignition switch.	**3.3**

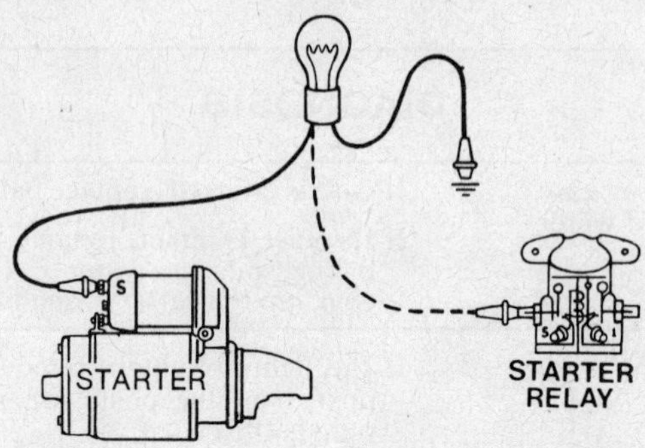

Checking the ignition switch "start" position

Test and Procedure	*Results and Indications*	*Proceed to*
2.4—Remove and bench test the starter.	If the starter does not meet specifications, repair or replace as needed:	**3.1**
	If the starter is operating properly:	**2.5**
2.5—Determine whether the engine can turn freely: Remove the spark plugs, and check for water in the cylinders. Check for water on the dipstick, or oil in the radiator. Attempt to turn the engine using an 18" flex drive and socket on the crankshaft pulley nut or bolt.	If the engine will turn freely only with the spark plugs out, and hydrostatic lock (water in the cylinders) is ruled out, check valve timing:	**9.2**
	If engine will not turn freely, and it is known that the clutch and transmission are free, the engine must be disassembled for further evaluation.	
3.1—Check the ignition switch "on" position: Connect a jumper wire between the distributor side of the coil and ground, and a 12V test lamp between the switch side of the coil and ground. Remove the high tension lead from the coil. Turn the ignition switch on and jiggle the key.	If the lamp lights:	**3.2**
	If the lamp flickers when the key is jiggled, replace the ignition switch:	**3.3**
	If the lamp doesn't light, check for loose or open connections. If none are found, remove the ignition switch and check for continuity. If the switch is faulty, replace it:	

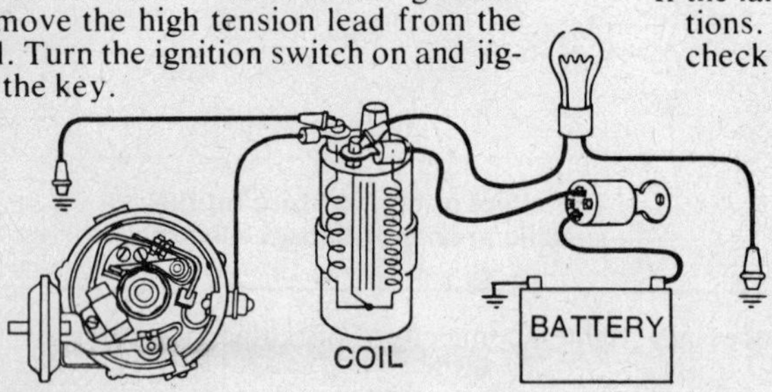

Checking the ignition switch "on" position

Test and Procedure	*Results and Indications*	*Proceed to*
3.2—Check the ballast resistor or resistance wire, if used, for an open circuit, using an ohmmeter.	Replace the resistor or the resistance wire if the resistance is zero.	**3.3**
3.3—Visually inspect the breaker points for burning, pitting, or excessive wear. Gray coloring of the point contact surfaces is normal. Rotate the crankshaft until the contact heel rests on a high point of the distributor cam, and adjust the point gap to specifications.	If the breaker points are intact, clean the contact surfaces with fine emery cloth, and adjust the point gap to specifications. If pitted or worn, replace the points and condenser, and adjust the gap to specifications: NOTE: *Always lubricate the distributor cam according to manufacturer's recommendations when servicing the breaker points.*	**3.4**
On electronic ignitions with adjustable pick-up coils, use non-magnetic feeler gauges to check the air gap.	Set gap to specifications.	**3.4**
Make sure the timing rotor is tight on the shaft, and rotates when engine is cranked.	Repair as necessary.	**3.4**

Test and Procedure	Results and Indications	Proceed to
3.4—Connect a dwell meter between the distributor primary lead and ground. Crank the engine and observe the point dwell angle. On electronic ignitions test the pick-up coil according to the manufacturer's specifications.	If necessary, adjust the point dwell angle: NOTE: *Increasing the point gap decreases the dwell angle, and vice-versa.* If dwell meter shows little or no reading: Replace as necessary.	3.6 3.5 3.6

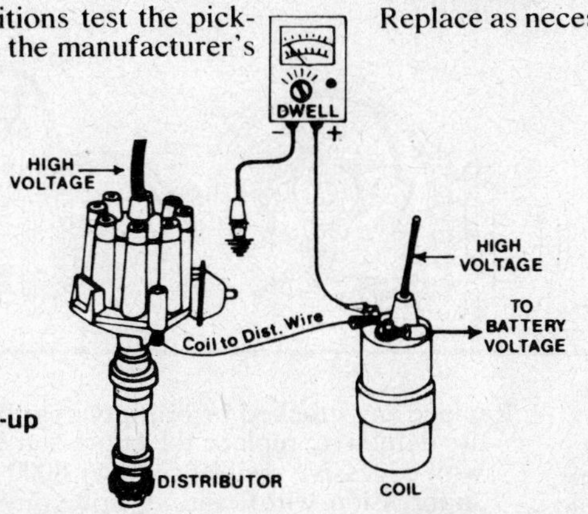

Dwell meter hook-up

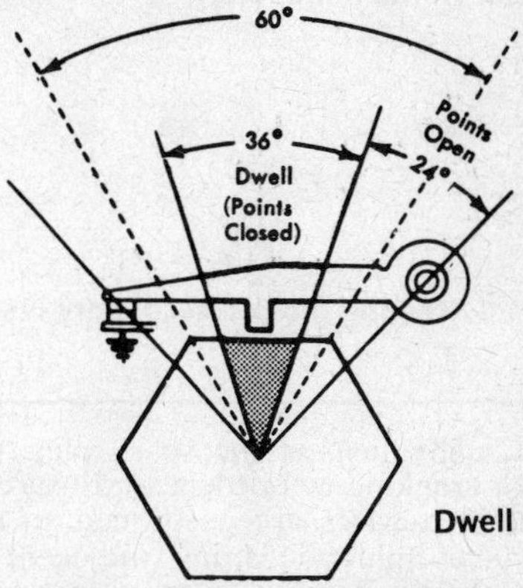

Dwell angle

Test and Procedure	Results and Indications	Proceed to
3.5—Check the condenser for short: Connect an ohmmeter across the condenser body and the pigtail lead.	If any reading other than infinite resistance is noted, replace the condenser:	3.6

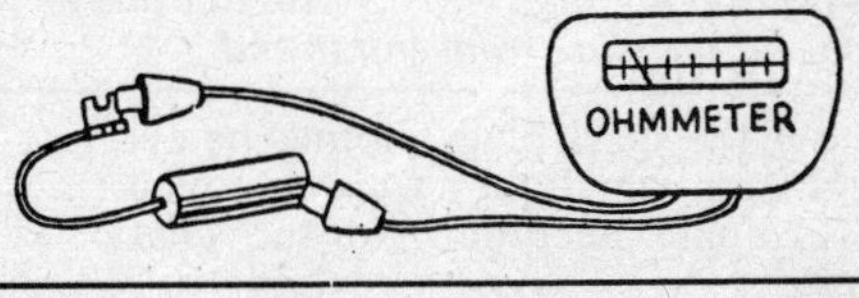

Checking the condenser for short

Test and Procedure	Results and Indications	Proceed to
3.6—Test the coil primary resistance: Connect an ohmmeter across the coil primary terminals, and read the resistance on the low scale. Note whether an external ballast resistor or resistance wire is utilized.	Coils utilizing ballast resistors or resistance wires should have approximately 1.0-2.0 ohms resistance; coils with internal resistors should have approximately 4.0 ohms resistance. If values far from the above are noted, replace the coil:	4.1
4.1—Check for spark: Hold each spark plug wire approximately 1/4" from ground with gloves or a heavy, dry rag. Crank the engine, and observe the spark. NOTE: *On some electronic ignitions, this test must not be performed on certain cylinders.*	If no spark is evident: If spark is good in some cylinders: If spark is good in all cylinders:	4.2 4.3 4.6
4.2—Check for spark at the coil high tension lead: Remove the coil high tension lead from the distributor and position it approximately 1/4" from ground. Crank the engine and observe spark. CAUTION: *This test should not be performed on cars equipped with transistorized ignition.*	If the spark is good and consistent: If the spark is good but intermittent, test the primary electrical system starting at 3.3: If the spark is weak or non-existent, replace the coil high tension lead, clean and tighten all connections and retest. If no improvement is noted:	4.3 3.3 4.4
4.3—Visually inspect the distributor cap and rotor for burned or corroded contacts, cracks, carbon tracks, or moisture. Also check the fit of the rotor on the distributor shaft (where applicable). If silicone grease is used on the contacts, check for correct application.	If moisture is present, dry thoroughly, and retest per 4.1: If burned or excessively corroded contacts, cracks, or carbon tracks are noted, replace the defective part(s) and retest per 4.1: If the rotor and cap appear intact, or are only slightly corroded, clean the contacts thoroughly (including the cap towers and spark plug wire ends) and retest per 4.1: If the spark is good in all cases: If the spark is poor in all cases:	4.1 4.1 4.6 4.5

Test and Procedure	*Results and Indications*	*Proceed to*
4.4—Check the coil secondary resistance: Connect an ohmmeter across the distributor side of the coil and the coil tower. Read the resistance on the high scale of the ohmmeter.	The resistance of a satisfactory coil should be between 4K ohms and 12K ohms. If the resistance is considerably higher (i.e., 40K ohms) replace the coil, and retest per 4.1: NOTE: *This does not apply to high performance coils.*	**4.1**

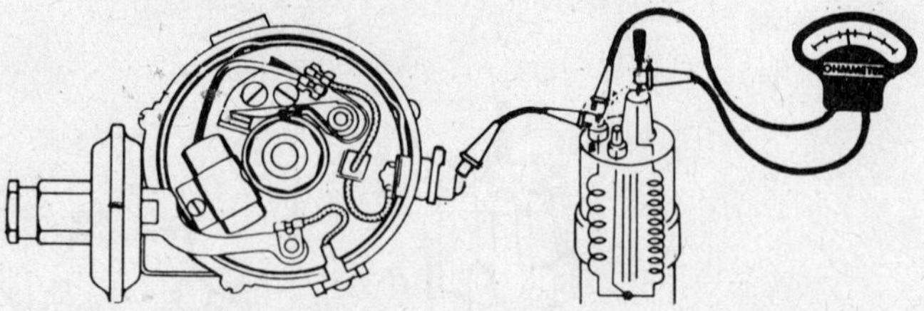

Testing the coil secondary resistance

Test and Procedure	*Results and Indications*	*Proceed to*
4.5—Visually inspect the spark plug wires for cracking or brittleness. Ensure that no two wires are positioned so as to cause induction firing (adjacent and parallel). Remove each wire, one by one, and check resistance with an ohmmeter. NOTE: *Do not pierce wires with a probe to check; measure from end to end.*	Replace any cracked or brittle wires. If any of the wires are defective, replace the entire set. Replace any wires with excessive resistance (over 8000 ohms per foot for suppression wire), and separate any wires that might cause induction firing.	**4.6**
4.6—Remove the spark plugs, noting the cylinders from which they were removed, and evaluate according to the chart below.	See below.	**See below.**

Condition	*Cause*	*Remedy*	*Proceed/to*
Electrodes eroded, light brown deposits.	Normal wear. Normal wear is indicated by approximately .001″ wear per 1000 miles.	Clean and regap the spark plug if wear is not excessive: Replace the spark plug if excessively worn:	**4.7**

Condition	*Cause*	*Remedy*	*Proceed/to*
Carbon fouling (black, dry, fluffy deposits).	If present on one or two plugs:		
	Faulty high tension lead(s).	Test the high tension leads:	**4.5**
	Burnt or sticking valve(s).	Check the valve train: (Clean and regap the plugs in either case.)	**9.1**
	If present on most or all plugs: Overly rich fuel mixture, due to restricted air filter, improper carburetor adjustment, improper choke or heat riser adjustment or operation.	Check the fuel system:	**5.1**

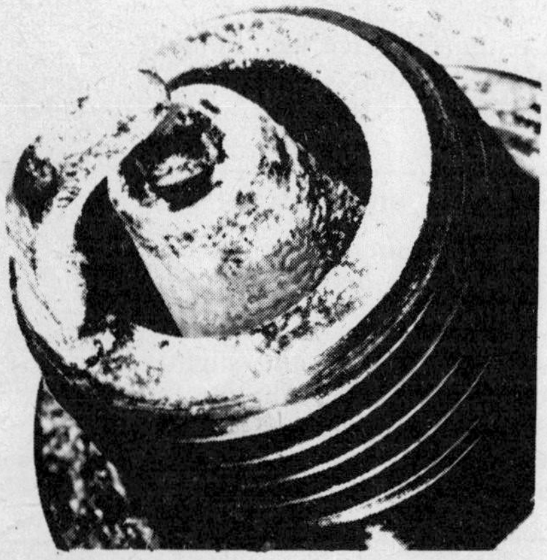

Test and Procedure	Results and Indications		Proceed to
Oil fouling (wet black deposits)	Worn engine components. NOTE: *Oil fouling may occur in new or recently rebuilt engines until broken in.*	Check engine vacuum and compression: Replace with new spark plug.	6.1

Test and Procedure	Results and Indications		Proceed to
Lead fouling (gray, black, red, green, tan, or yellow deposits, which appear glazed or cinderlike).	Combustion by-products.	Clean and regap the plugs: (Use plugs of a different heat range if the problem recurs.)	4.7

Test and Procedure	Results and Indications		Proceed to
Gap bridging (deposits lodged between the electrodes).	Incomplete combustion, or transfer of deposits from the combustion chamber.	Replace the spark plugs.	

Test and Procedure	Results and Indications		Proceed to
Overheating (burnt electrodes, and extremely white insulator with small black spots).	Ignition timing advanced too far.	Adjust timing to specifications:	8.2
	Overly lean fuel mixture.	Check the fuel system:	5.1
	Spark plugs not seated properly.	Clean spark plug seat and install a new gasket washer: (Replace the spark plugs in all cases.)	4.7

Pre-ignition (melted or severely burned electrodes, blistered or cracked insulators, or metallic deposits on the insulator).	Incorrect spark plug heat range.	Replace with plugs of the proper heat range:	4.7
	Ignition timing advanced too far.	Adjust timing to specifications:	8.2
	Spark plugs not being cooled efficiently.	Clean the spark plug seat, and check the cooling system:	11.1
	Fuel mixture too lean	Check the fuel system:	5.1
	Poor compression.	Check compression:	6.1
	Fuel grade too low.	Use higher octane fuel:	4.7

4.7—Determine the static ignition timing: Using the flywheel or crankshaft pulley timing marks as a guide, locate top dead center on the *compression* stroke of the No. 1 cylinder. Remove the distributor cap.	Adjust the distributor so that the rotor points toward the No. 1 tower in the distributor cap, when the points are just opening on conventional ignitions, or when a trigger wheel spoke is aligned with the pick-up coil on electronic ignitions:		4.8
4.8—Check coil polarity: Connect a voltmeter negative lead to the coil high tension lead, and the positive lead to ground (NOTE: *reverse the hook-up for positive ground cars*). Crank the engine momentarily.	If the voltmeter reads up-scale, the polarity is correct:		5.1
	If the voltmeter reads down-scale, reverse the coil polarity (switch the primary leads):		5.1
5.1—Determine that the air filter is functioning efficiently: Hold paper elements up to a strong light, and attempt to see light through the filter.	Clean permanent air filters in solvent (or manufacturer's recommendation), and allow to dry. Replace paper elements through which light cannot be seen:		5.2

Checking coil polarity

Test and Procedure	Results and Indications	Proceed to
5.2—Determine whether a flooding condition exists: Flooding is identified by a strong gasoline odor, and excessive gasoline present in the throttle bore(s) of the carburetor.	If flooding is not evident:	5.3
	If flooding is evident, permit the gasoline to dry for a few moments and restart. If flooding doesn't recur:	5.6
	If flooding is persistant:	5.5
5.3—Check that fuel is reaching the carburetor: Detach the fuel line at the carburetor inlet. Hold the end of the line in a cup (not styrofoam), and crank the engine.	If fuel flows smoothly:	5.6
	If fuel doesn't flow (NOTE: *Make sure that there is fuel in the tank*), or flows erratically:	5.4
5.4—Test the fuel pump: Disconnect all fuel lines from the fuel pump. Hold a finger over the input fitting, crank the engine (with electric pump, turn the ignition or pump on), and feel for suction.	If suction is evident, blow out the fuel line to the tank with low pressure compressed air until bubbling is heard from the fuel filler neck. Also blow out the carburetor fuel line (both ends disconnected):	5.6
	If no suction is evident, replace or repair the fuel pump: NOTE: *Repeated oil fouling of the spark plugs, or a no-start condition, could be the result of a ruptured vacuum booster pump diaphragm, through which oil or gasoline is being drawn into the intake manifold (where applicable).*	5.6
5.5—Check the needle and seat: Tap the carburetor in the area of the needle and seat.	If flooding stops, a gasoline additive (e.g., Gumout) will often cure the problem:	5.6
	If flooding continues, check the fuel pump for excessive pressure at the caruburetor (according to specifications). If the pressure is normal, the needle and seat must be removed and checked, and/or the float level adjusted:	5.6
5.6—Test the accelerator pump by looking into the throttle bores while operating the throttle.	If the accelerator pump appears to be operating normally:	5.7
	If the accelerator pump is not operating, the pump must be reconditioned. Where possible, service the pump with the carburetor(s) installed on the engine. If necessary, remove the carburetor. Prior to removal:	5.7
5.7—Determine whether the carburetor main fuel system is functioning: Spray a commercial starting fluid into the carburetor while attempting to start the engine.	If the engine starts, runs for a few seconds, and dies:	5.8
	If the engine doesn't start:	6.1
5.8—Uncommon fuel system malfunctions: See below:	If the problem is solved:	6.1
	If the problem remains, remove and recondition the carburetor.	

Condition	Indication	Test	Usual Weather Conditions	Remedy
Vapor lock	Car will not restart shortly after running.	Cool the components of the fuel system until the engine starts.	Hot to very hot	Ensure that the exhaust manifold heat control valve is operating. Check with the vehicle manufacturer for the recommended solution to vapor lock on the model in question.
Carburetor icing	Car will not idle, stalls at low speeds.	Visually inspect the throttle plate area of the throttle bores for frost.	High humidity, 32-40 F.	Ensure that the exhaust manifold heat control valve is operating, and that the intake manifold heat riser is not blocked.
Water in the fuel	Engine sputters and stalls; may not start.	Pump a small amount of fuel into a glass jar. Allow to stand, and inspect for droplets or a layer of water.	High humidity, extreme temperature changes.	For droplets, use one or two cans of commercial gas line anti-freeze. For a layer of water, the tank must be drained, and the fuel lines blown out with compressed air.

Test and Procedure	Results and Indications	Proceed to
6.1—Test engine compression: Remove all spark plugs. Insert a compression gauge into a spark plug port, crank the engine to obtain the maximum reading, and record.	If compression is within limits on all cylinders:	7.1
	If guage reading is extremely low on all cylinders:	6.2
	If gauge reading is low on one or two cylinders: (If gauge readings are identical and low on two or more adjacent cylinders, the head gasket must be replaced.)	6.2

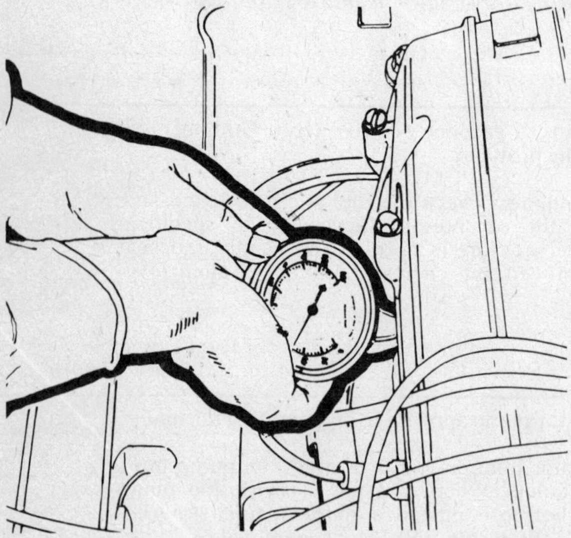

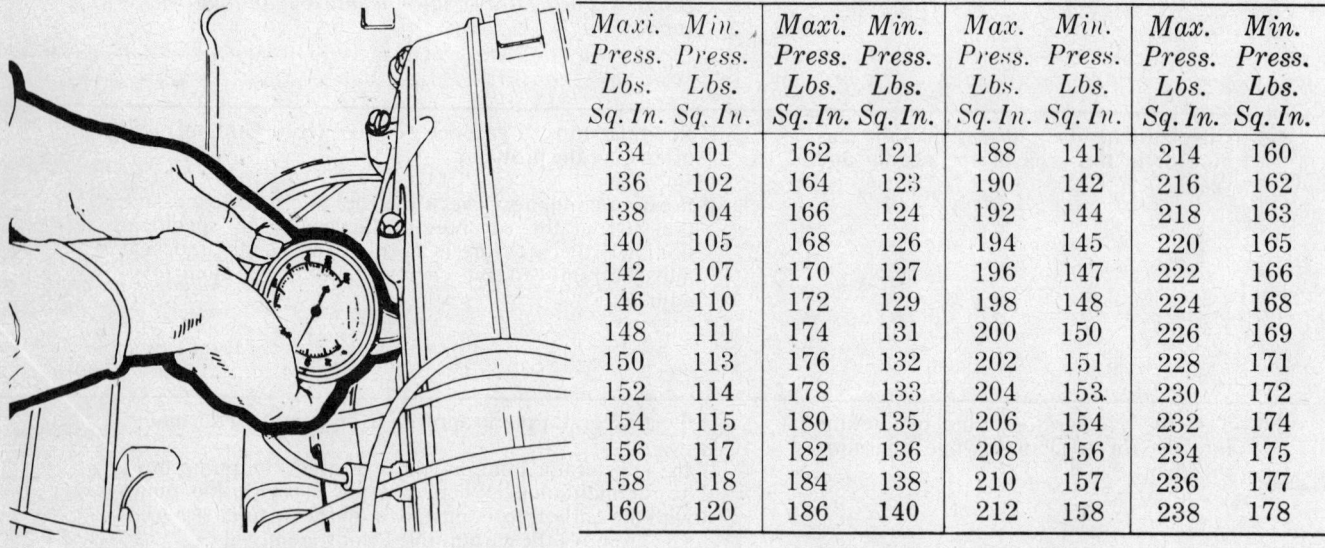

Testing compression

Maxi. Press. Lbs. Sq. In.	Min. Press. Lbs. Sq. In.	Maxi. Press. Lbs. Sq. In.	Min. Press. Lbs. Sq. In.	Max. Press. Lbs. Sq. In.	Min. Press. Lbs. Sq. In.	Max. Press. Lbs. Sq. In.	Min. Press. Lbs. Sq. In.
134	101	162	121	188	141	214	160
136	102	164	123	190	142	216	162
138	104	166	124	192	144	218	163
140	105	168	126	194	145	220	165
142	107	170	127	196	147	222	166
146	110	172	129	198	148	224	168
148	111	174	131	200	150	226	169
150	113	176	132	202	151	228	171
152	114	178	133	204	153	230	172
154	115	180	135	206	154	232	174
156	117	182	136	208	156	234	175
158	118	184	138	210	157	236	177
160	120	186	140	212	158	238	178

Compression pressure limits

Test and Procedure	Results and Indications	Proceed to
6.2—Test engine compression (wet): Squirt approximately 30 cc. of engine oil into each cylinder, and retest per 6.1.	If the readings improve, worn or cracked rings or broken pistons are indicated:	
	If the readings do not improve, burned or excessively carboned valves or a jumped timing chain are indicated: NOTE: *A jumped timing chain or belt is often indicated by difficult cranking.*	7.1
7.1—Perform a vacuum check of the engine: Attach a vacuum gauge to the intake manifold beyond the throttle plate. Start the engine, and observe the action of the needle over the range of engine speeds.	See below.	**See below**

	Reading	*Indications*	*Proceed to*
	Steady, from 17-22 in. Hg.	Normal.	**8.1**
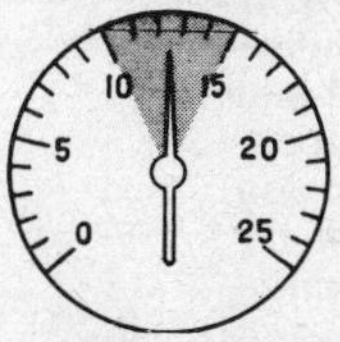	Low and steady.	Late ignition or valve timing, or low compression:	**6.1**
	Very low.	Vacuum leak:	
	Needle fluctuates as engine speed increases.	Ignition miss, blown cylinder head gasket, leaking valve or weak valve spring:	**6.1, 8.3**
	Gradual drop in reading at idle.	Excessive back pressure in the exhaust system:	**10.1**
	Intermittent fluctuation at idle.	Ignition miss, sticking valve:	**8.3, 9.1**
	Drifting needle.	Improper idle mixture adjustment, carburetors not synchronized (where applicable), or minor intake leak. Synchronize the carburetors, adjust the idle, and retest. If the condition persists:	**7.2**
	High and steady.	Early ignition timing:	**8.2**
	7.2—Attach a vacuum gauge per 7.1, and test for an intake manifold leak. Squirt a small amount of oil around the intake manifold gaskets, carburetor gaskets, plugs and fittings. Obsserve the action of the vacuum gauge.	If the reading improves, replace the indicated gasket, or seal the indicated fitting or plug:	**8.1**
		If the reading remains low:	**7.3**

Reading	Indications	Proceed to
7.3—Test all vacuum hoses and accessories for leaks as described in 7.2. Also check the carburetor body (dashpots, automatic choke mechanism, throttle shafts) for leaks in the same manner.	If the reading improves, service or replace the offending part(s):	**8.1**
	If the reading remains low:	**6.1**
8.1—Check the point dwell angle: Connect a dwell meter between the distributor primary wire and ground. Start the engine, and observe the dwell angle from idle to 3000 rpm.	If necessary, adjust the dwell angle. NOTE: *Increasing the point gap reduces the dwell angle and vice-versa.* If the dwell angle moves outside specifications as engine speed increases, the distributor should be removed and checked for cam accuracy, shaft endplay and concentricity, bushing wear, and adequate point arm tension (NOTE: *Most of these items may be checked with the distributor installed in the engine, using an oscilloscope):*	**8.2**
8.2—Connect a timing light (per manufacturer's recommendation) and check the dynamic ignition timing. Disconnect and plug the vacuum hose(s) to the distributor if specified, start the engine, and observe the timing marks at the specified engine speed.	If the timing is not correct, adjust to specifications by rotating the distributor in the engine: (Advance timing by rotating distributor opposite normal direction of rotor rotation, retard timing by rotating distributor in same direction as rotor rotation.)	**8.3**
8.3—Check the operation of the distributor advance mechanism(s): To test the mechanical advance, disconnect the vacuum advance, and observe the timing marks with a timing light as the engine speed is increased from idle. If the mark moves smoothly, without hesitation, it may be assumed that the mechanical advance is functioning properly. To test vacuum advance and/or retard systems, alternately crimp and release the vacuum line, and observe the timing mark for movement. If movement is noted, the system is operating.	If the systems are functioning:	**8.4**
	If the systems are not functioning, remove the distributor, and test on a distributor tester:	**8.4**
8.4—Locate an ignition miss: With the engine running, remove each spark plug wire, one by one, until one is found that doesn't cause the engine to roughen and slow down. NOTE: *Certain cylinders must not be disconnected on some electronic ignitions.*	When the missing cylinder is identified:	**4.1**
9.1—Evaluate the valve train: Remove the valve cover, and ensure that the valves are adjusted to specifications. A mechanic's stehoscope may be used to aid in the diagnosis of the valve train. By pushing the probe on or near push rods or rockers, valve noise often can be isolated. A timing light also may be used to diagnose valve problems. Connect the light according to manufacturer's recommendations, and start the engine. Vary the firing moment of the light by increasing the engine speed (and therefore the ignition advance), and moving the trigger from cylinder to cylinder. Observe the movement of each valve.	See below	**See below**

Observation	Probable Cause	Remedy	Proceed to
Metallic tap heard through the stethoscope.	Sticking hydraulic lifter or excessive valve clearance.	Adjust valve. If tap persists, remove and replace the lifter:	**10.0**
Metallic tap through the stethoscope, able to push the rocker arm (lifter side) down by hand.	Collapsed valve lifter.	Remove and replace the lifter:	**10.1**
Erratic, irregular motion of the valve stem.*	Sticking valve, burned valve.	Recondition the valve and/or valve guide:	**Next Chapter**
Eccentric motion of the pushrod at the rocker arm.*	Bent pushrod.	Replace the pushrod:	**10.1**
Valve retainer bounces as the valve closes.*	Weak valve spring or damper.	Remove and test the spring and damper. Replace if necessary:	**10.1**

*—When observed with a timing light.

Test and Procedure	Results and Indications	Proceed to
9.2—Check the valve timing: Locate top dead center of the No. 1 piston, and install a degree wheel or tape on the crankshaft pulley or damper with zero corresponding to an index mark on the engine. Rotate the crankshaft in its direction of rotation, and observe the opening of the No. 1 cylinder intake valve. The opening should correspond with the correct mark on the degree wheel according to specifications.	If the timing is not correct, the timing cover must be removed for further investigation:	
10.1—Determine whether the exhaust manifold heat control valve is operating: Operate the valve by hand to determine whether it is free to move. If the valve is free, run the engine to operating temperature and observe the action of the valve, to ensure that it is opening.	If the valve sticks, spray it with a suitable solvent, open and close the valve to free it, and retest.	
	If the valve functions properly:	**10.2**
	If the valve does not free, or does not operate, replace the valve:	**10.2**
10.2—Ensure that there are no exhaust restrictions: Visually inspect the exhaust system for kinks, dents, or crushing. Also note that gases are flowing freely from the tailpipe at all engine speeds, indicating no restriction in the muffler or resonator.	Replace any damaged portion of the system:	**11.1**
11.1—Visually inspect the fan belt for glazing, cracks, and fraying, and replace if necessary. Tighten the belt so that the longest span has approximately 1/2″ play at its midpoint under thumb pressure.	Replace or tighten the fan belt as necessary:	**11.2**

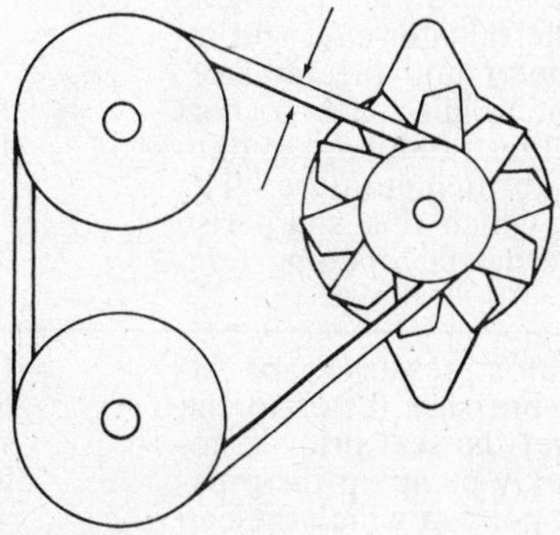

Checking the fan belt tension

Test and Procedure	*Results and Indications*	*Proceed to*
11.2—Check the fluid level of the cooling system.	If full or slightly low, fill as necessary:	**11.5**
	If extremely low:	**11.3**
11.3—Visually inspect the external portions of the cooling system (radiator, radiator hoses, thermostat elbow, water pump seals, heater hoses, etc.) for leaks. If none are found, pressurize the cooling system to 14-15 psi.	If cooling system holds the pressure:	**11.5**
	If cooling system loses pressure rapidly, reinspect external parts of the system for leaks under pressure. If none are found, check dipstick for coolant in crankcase. If no coolant is present, but pressure loss continues:	**11.4**
	If coolant is evident in crankcase, remove cylinder head(s), and check gasket(s). If gaskets are intact, block and cylinder heads(s) should be checked for cracks or holes.	
	If the gasket(s) is blown, replace, and purge the crankcase of coolant:	**12.6**
	NOTE: *Occasionally, due to atmospheric and driving conditions, condensation of water can occur in the crankcase. This causes the oil to appear milky white. To remedy, run the engine until hot, and change the oil and oil filter.*	
11.4—Check for combustion leaks into the cooling system: Pressurize the cooling system as above. Start the engine, and observe the pressure gauge. If the needle fluctuates, remove each spark plug wire, one by one, noting which cylinder(s) reduce or eliminate the fluctuation. NOTE: *Certain cylinders must not be disconnected on some electronic ignitions.*	Cylinders which reduce or eliminate the fluctuation, when the spark plug wire is removed, are leaking into the cooling system. Replace the head gasket on the affected cylinder bank(s).	

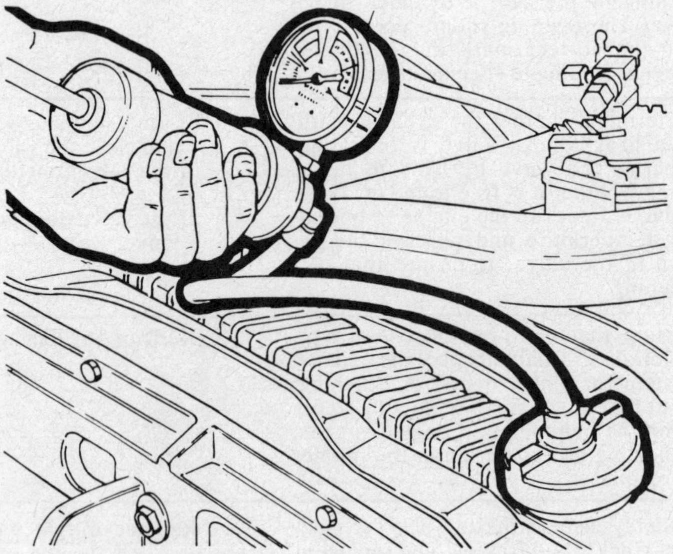

Radiator pressure tester

Test and Procedure	*Results and Indications*	*Proceed to*
11.6—Test the thermostat: Start the engine cold, remove the radiator cap, and insert a thermometer into the radiator. Allow the engine to idle. After a short while, there will be a sudden, rapid increase in coolant temperature. The temperature at which this sharp rise stops is the thermostat opening temperature.	If the thermostat opens at or about the specified temperature:	**11.7**
	If the temperature doesn't increase: (If the temperature increases slowly and gradually, replace the thermostat.)	**11.7**
11.5—Check the radiator pressure cap: Attach a radiator pressure tester to the radiator cap (wet the seal prior to installation). Quickly pump up the pressure, noting the point at which the cap releases.	If the cap releases within ± 1 psi of the specified rating, it is operating properly:	**11.6**
	If the cap releases at more than ± 1 psi of the specified rating. It should be replaced:	**11.6**

Test and Procedure	*Results and Indications*	*Proceed to*

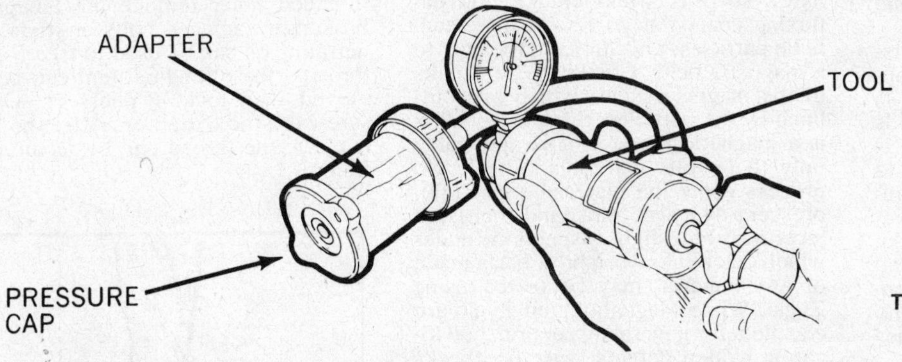

Testing the radiator pressure cap

Test and Procedure	*Results and Indications*	*Proceed to*
11.7—Check the water pump: Remove the thermostat elbow and the thermostat, disconnect the coil high tension lead (to prevent starting), and crank the engine momentarily.	If coolant flows, replace the thermostat and retest per 11.6:	**11.6**
	If coolant doesn't flow, reverse flush the cooling system to alleviate any blockage that might exist. If system is not blocked, and coolant will not flow, recondition the water pump.	
12.1—Check the oil pressure gauge or warning light: If the gauge shows low pressure, or the light is on, for no obvious reason, remove the oil pressure sender. Install an accurate oil pressure gauge and run the engine momentarily.	If oil pressure builds normally, run engine for a few moments to determine that it is functioning normally, and replace the sender.	
	If the pressure remains low:	**12.2**
	If the pressure surges:	**12.3**
	If the oil pressure is zero:	**12.3**
12.2—Visually inspect the oil: If the oil is watery or very thin, milky, or foamy, replace the oil and oil filter.	If the oil is normal:	**12.3**
	If after replacing oil the pressure remains low:	**12.3**
	If after replacing oil the pressure becomes normal:	
12.3—Inspect the oil pressure relief valve and spring, to ensure that it is not sticking or stuck. Remove and thoroughly clean the valve, spring, and the valve body.	If the oil pressure improves:	
	If no improvement is noted:	**12.4**
12.4—Check to ensure that the oil pump is not cavitating (sucking air instead of oil): See that the crankcase is neither over nor underfull, and that the pickup in the sump is in the proper position and free from sludge.	Fill or drain the crankcase to the proper capacity, and clean the pickup screen in solvent if necessary. If no improvement is noted:	**12.5**
12.5—Inspect the oil pump drive and the oil pump:	If the pump drive or the oil pump appear to be defective, service as necessary and retest per 12.1:	**12.1**
	If the pump drive and pump appear to be operating normally, the engine should be disassembled to determine where blockage exists.	
12.6—Purge the engine of ethylene glycol coolant: Completely drain the crankcase and the oil filter. Obtain a commercial solvent, designated for this purpose, and follow the instructions precisely. Following this, install a new oil filter and refill the crankcase with the proper viscosity oil. The next oil and filter change should follow shortly thereafter (1000 miles).		

This section describes, in detail, the procedures involved in rebuilding a typical engine. The procedures are basically identical to those used in rebuilding engines of nearly all design and configurations.

The section is divided into two parts. The first, Cylinder Head Reconditioning, assumes that the cylinder head is removed from the engine, all manifolds are removed, and the cylinder head is on a workbench. The camshaft should be removed from overhead cam cylinder heads. The second section, Cylinder Block Reconditioning, covers the block, pistons, connecting rods and crankshaft. It is assumed that the engine is mounted on a work stand, and the cylinder head and all accessories are removed.

Procedures are identified as follows:

Unmarked—Basic procedures that must be performed in order to successfully complete the rebuilding process.

Starred (*)—Procedures that should be performed to ensure maximum performance and engine life.

Double starred (**)—Procedures that may be performed to increase engine performance and reliability.

In many cases, a choice of methods is also provided. Methods are identified in the same manner as procedures. The choice of method for a procedure is at the discretion of the user.

The tools required for the basic rebuilding procedure should, with minor exceptions, be those included in a mechanic's tool kit. An accurate torque wrench, and a dial indicator (reading in thousandths) mounted on a universal base should be available. Special tools, where required, all are readily available from the major tool suppliers. The services of a competent automotive machine shop must also be readily available.

When assembling the engine, any parts that will be in frictional contact must be pre-lubricated, to provide protection on initial start-up. Any product specifically formulated for this purpose may be used. NOTE: *Do not use engine oil.* Where semi-permanent (locked but removable) installation of bolts or nuts is desired, threads should be cleaned and coated with Loctite or a similar product (non-hardening).

Aluminum has become increasingly popular for use in engines, due to its low weight and excellent heat transfer characteristics. The following precautions must be observed when handling aluminum engine parts:

—Never hot-tank aluminum parts.

—Remove all aluminum parts (identification tags, etc.) from engine parts before hot-tanking (otherwise they will be removed during the process).

—Always coat threads lightly with engine oil or anti-seize compounds before installation, to prevent seizure.

—Never over-torque bolts or spark plugs in aluminum threads. Should stripping occur, threads can be restored using any of a number of thread repair kits available (see next section).

Magnaflux and Zyglo are inspection techniques used to locate material flaws, such as stress cracks. Magnafluxing coats the part with fine magnetic particles, and subjects the part to a magnetic field. Cracks cause breaks in the magnetic field, which are outlined by the particles. Since Magnaflux is a magnetic process, it is applicable only to ferrous materials. The Zyglo process coats the material with a fluorescent dye penetrant, and then subjects it to blacklight inspection, under which cracks glow brightly. Parts made of any material may be tested using Zyglo. While Magnaflux and Zyglo are excellent for general inspection, and locating hidden defects, specific checks of suspected cracks may be made at lower cost and more readily using spot check dye. The dye is sprayed onto the suspected area, wiped off, and the area is then sprayed with a developer. Cracks then will show up brightly. Spot check dyes will only indicate surface cracks; therefore, structural cracks below the surface may escape detection. When questionable, the part should be tested using Magnaflux or Zyglo.

REPAIRING DAMAGED THREADS

Several methods of repairing damaged threads are available. Heli-Coil® (shown here), Keenserts® and Microdot® are among the most widely used. All involve basically the same principle —drilling out stripped threads, tapping the hole and installing a pre-wound insert —making welding, plugging and oversize fasteners unnecessary.

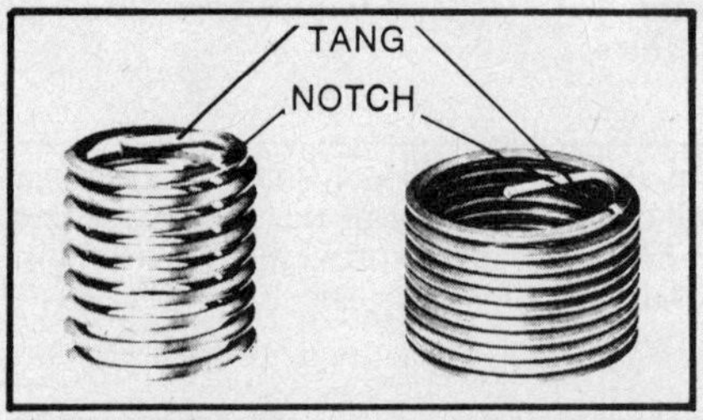

Standard thread repair insert (left) and spark plug thread insert (right)

Two types of thread repair inserts are usually supplied—a standard type for most Inch Coarse, Inch Fine, Metric Coarse and Metric Fine thread sizes and a spark plug type to fit most spark plug port sizes. Consult the individual manufacturer's catalog to determine exact applications. Typical thread repair kits will contain a selection of prewound threaded inserts, a tap (corresponding to the outside diameter threads of the insert) and an installation tool. Most manufacturers also supply blister-packed thread repair inserts separately and a master kit with a variety of taps and inserts plus installation tools.

Before effecting a repair to a threaded hole, remove any snapped, broken or damaged bolts or studs. Penetrating oil can be used to free frozen threads; the offending item can be removed with locking pliers or with a screw or stud extractor. After the hole is clear, the thread can be repaired as follows:

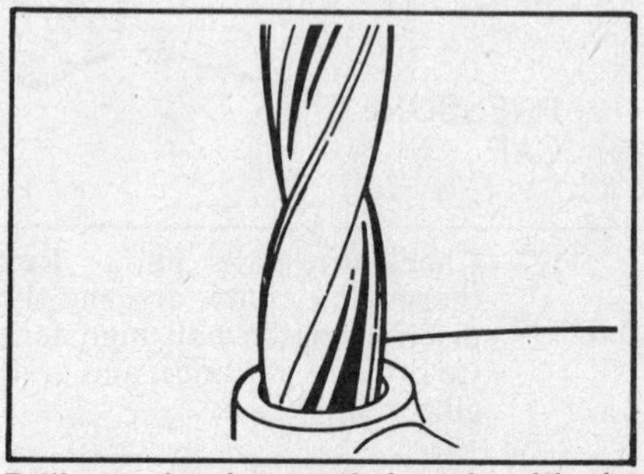

Drill out the damaged threads with the specified drill. Drill completely through the hole or to the bottom of a blind hole.

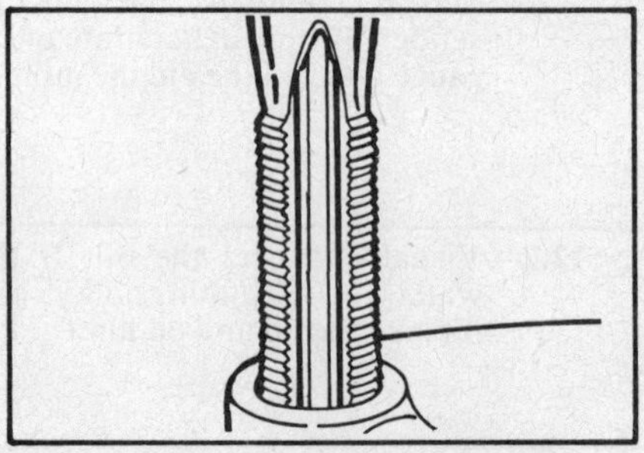

With the tap supplied, tap the hole to receive the threaded insert. Keep the tap well oiled and back it out frequently to avoid clogging the threads.

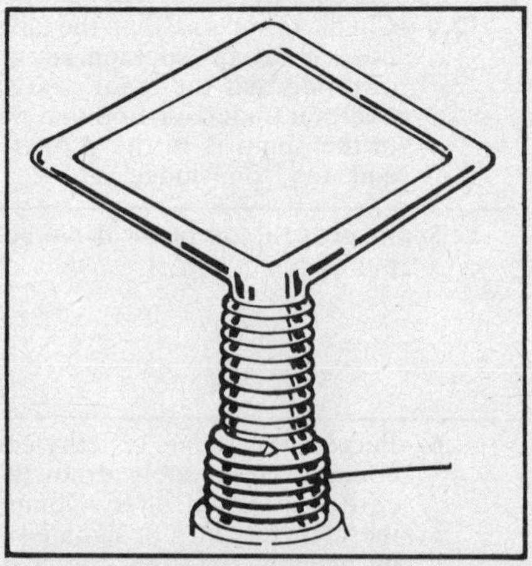

Screw the threaded insert onto the installation tool until the tang engages the slot. Screw the insert into the tapped hole until it is ¼-½ turn below the top surface. After installation, break the tang off with a hammer and punch.

STANDARD TORQUE SPECIFICATIONS AND CAPSCREW MARKINGS

Newton-Meter has been designated as the world standard for measuring torque and will gradually replace the foot-pound and kilogram-meter torque measuring standard. Torquing tools are still being manufactured with foot-pounds and kilogram-meter scales, along with the new Newton-Meter standard. To assist the repairman, foot-pounds, kilogram-meter and Newton-Meter are listed in the following charts, and should be followed as applicable.

U.S. BOLTS

SAE Grade Number	1 or 2			5			6 or 7			8		
Capscrew Head Markings Manufacturer's marks may vary. Three-line markings on heads below indicate SAE Grade 5. 	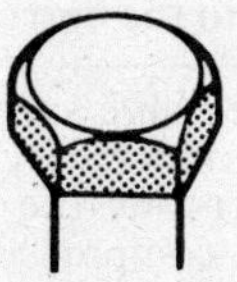						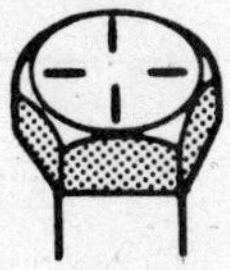			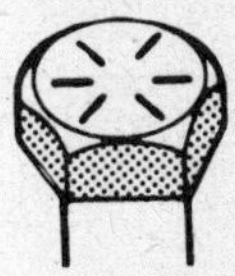		
Usage	Used Frequently			Used Frequently			Used at Times			Used at Times		
Quality of Material	Indeterminate			Minimum Commercial			Medium Commercial			Best Commercial		
Capacity Body Size	**Torque**			**Torque**			**Torque**			**Torque**		
(inches)-(thread)	Ft-Lb	kgm	Nm	Ft-Lb	kgm	Nm	Ft-Lb	kgm	Nm	Ft-Lb	kgm	Nm
1/4-20	5	0.6915	6.7791	8	1.1064	10.8465	10	1.3630	13.5582	12	1.6596	16.2698
-28	6	0.8298	8.1349	10	1.3830	13.5582				14	1.9362	18.9815
5/16-18	11	1.5213	14.9140	17	2.3511	23.0489	19	2.6277	25.7605	24	3.3192	32.5396
-24	13	1.7979	17.6256	19	2.6277	25.7605				27	3.7341	36.6071
3/8-16	18	2.4894	24.4047	31	4.2873	42.0304	34	4.7022	46.0978	44	6.0852	59.6560
-24	20	2.7660	27.1164	35	4.8405	47.4536				49	6.7767	66.4351
7/16-14	28	3.8132	37.9629	49	6.7767	66.4351	55	7.6065	74.5700	70	9.6810	94.9073
-20	30	4.1490	40.6745	55	7.6065	74.5700				78	10.7874	105.7538
1/2-13	39	5.3937	52.8769	75	10.3725	101.6863	85	11.7555	115.2445	105	14.5215	142.3609
-20	41	5.6703	55.5885	85	11.7555	115.2445				120	16.5860	162.6960
9/16-12	51	7.0533	69.1467	110	15.2130	149.1380	120	16.5960	162.6960	155	21.4365	210.1490
-18	55	7.6065	74.5700	120	16.5960	162.6960				170	23.5110	230.4860
5/8-11	83	11.4789	112.5329	150	20.7450	203.3700	167	23.0961	226.4186	210	29.0430	284.7180
-18	95	13.1385	128.8027	170	23.5110	230.4860				240	33.1920	325.3920
3/4-10	105	14.5215	142.3609	270	37.3410	366.0660	280	38.7240	379.6240	375	51.8625	508.4250
-16	115	15.9045	155.9170	295	40.7985	399.9610				420	58.0860	568.4360
7/8-9	160	22.1280	216.9280	395	54.6285	535.5410	440	60.8520	596.5520	605	83.6715	820.2590
-14	175	24.2025	237.2650	435	60.1605	589.7730				675	93.3525	915.1650
1-8	236	32.5005	318.6130	590	81.5970	799.9220	660	91.2780	894.8280	910	125.8530	1233.7780
-14	250	34.5750	338.9500	660	91.2780	849.8280				990	136.9170	1342.2420

METRIC BOLTS

Description	Torque ft-lbs. (Nm)			
Thread for general purposes (size x pitch (mm))	**Head Mark 4**		**Head Mark 7**	
6 x 1.0	2.2 to 2.9	(3.0 to 3.9)	3.6 to 5.8	(4.9 to 7.8)
8 x 1.25	5.8 to 8.7	(7.9 to 12)	9.4 to 14	(13 to 19)
10 x 1.25	12 to 17	(16 to 23)	20 to 29	(27 to 39)
12 x 1.25	21 to 32	(29 to 43)	35 to 53	(47 to 72)
14 x 1.5	35 to 52	(48 to 70)	57 to 85	(77 to 110)
16 x 1.5	51 to 77	(67 to 100)	90 to 120	(130 to 160)
18 x 1.5	74 to 110	(100 to 150)	130 to 170	(180 to 230)
20 x 1.5	110 to 140	(150 to 190)	190 to 240	(160 to 320)
22 x 1.5	150 to 190	(200 to 260)	250 to 320	(340 to 430)
24 x 1.5	190 to 240	(260 to 320)	310 to 410	(420 to 550)

CAUTION: Bolts threaded into aluminum require much less torque

NOTE: This engine rebuilding section is a guide to accepted rebuilding procedures. Typical examples of standard rebuilding procedures are illustrated.

CYLINDER HEAD RECONDITIONING

Procedure	*Method*
Identify the valves:	Invert the cylinder head, and number the valve faces front to rear, using a permanent felt-tip marker.
Remove the rocker arms (OHV engines only):	Remove the rocker arms with shaft(s) or balls and nuts. Wire the sets of rockers, balls and nuts together, and identify according to the corresponding valve.
Remove the valves and springs:	Using an appropriate valve spring compressor (depending on the configuration of the cylinder head), compress the valve springs. Lift out the keepers with needlenose pliers, release the compressor, and remove the valve, spring, and spring retainer.
Check the valve stem-to-guide clearance: 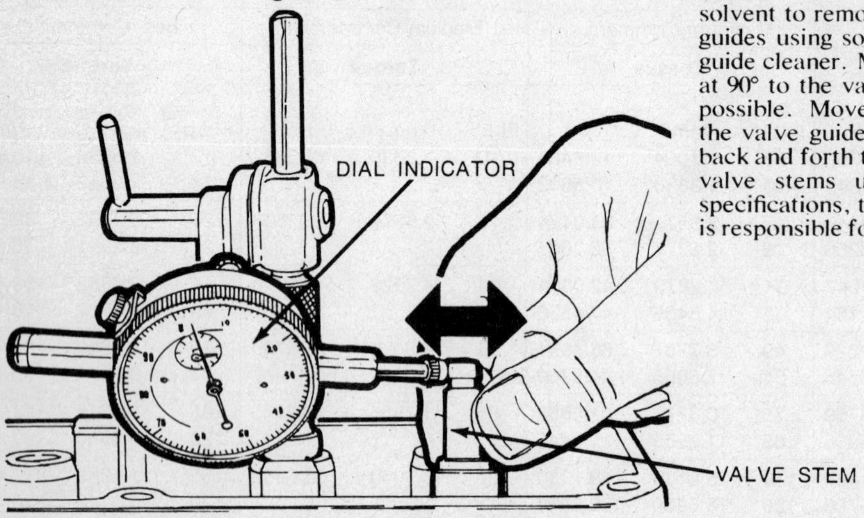 **Checking the valve stem-to-guide clearance**	Clean the valve stem with lacquer thinner or a similar solvent to remove all gum and varnish. Clean the valve guides using solvent and an expanding wire-type valve guide cleaner. Mount a dial indicator so that the stem is at 90° to the valve stem, as close to the valve guide as possible. Move the valve off its seat, and measure the valve guide-to-stem clearance by rocking the stem back and forth to actuate the dial indicator. Measure the valve stems using a micrometer, and compare to specifications, to determine whether stem or guide wear is responsible for excessive clearance.
De-carbon the cylinder head and valves: 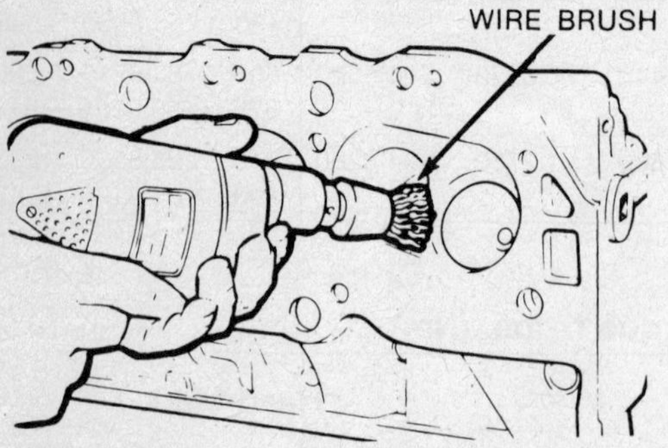 **Removing carbon from the cylinder head**	Chip carbon away from the valve heads, combustion chambers, and ports, using a chisel made of hardwood. Remove the remaining deposits with a stiff wire brush. NOTE: *Ensure that the deposits are actually removed, rather than burnished.*
Hot-tank the cylinder head (cast iron heads only): CAUTION: *Do not hot-tank aluminum parts.*	Have the cylinder head hot-tanked to remove grease, corrosion, and scale from the water passages. NOTE: *In the case of overhead cam cylinder heads, consult the operator to determine whether the camshaft bearings will be damaged by the caustic solution.*
Degrease the remaining cylinder head parts:	Using solvent (i.e., Gunk), clean the rockers, rocker shaft(s) (where applicable), rocker balls and nuts, springs, spring retainers, and keepers. Do not remove the protective coating from the springs.

CYLINDER HEAD RECONDITIONING

Procedure	*Method*
Check the cylinder head for warpage: 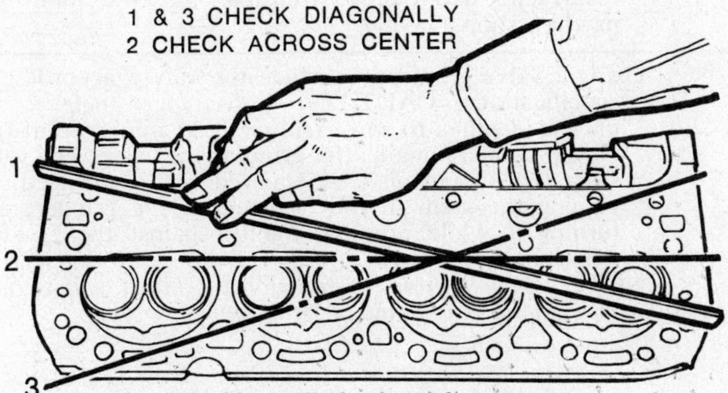 **Checking cylinder head for warpage**	Place a straight-edge across the gasket surface of the cylinder head. Using feeler gauges, determine the clearance at the center of the straight-edge. Measure across both diagonals, along the longitudinal centerline, and across the cylinder head at several points. If warpage exceeds .003″ in a 6″ span, or .006″ over the total length, the cylinder head must be resurfaced. NOTE: *If warpage exceeds the manufacturer's maximum tolerance for material removal, the cylinder head must be replaced.* When milling the cylinder heads of V-type engines, the intake manifold mounting position is altered, and must be corrected by milling the manifold flange a proportionate amount.
** Porting and gasket matching:	** Coat the manifold flanges of the cylinder head with Prussian blue dye. Glue intake and exhaust gaskets to the cylinder head in their installed position using rubber cement and scribe the outline of the ports on the manifold flanges. Remove the gaskets. Using a small cutter in a hand-held power tool gradually taper the walls of the port out to the scribed outline of the gasket. Further enlargement of the ports should include the removal of sharp edges and radiusing of sharp corners. Do not alter the valve guides. NOTE: *The most efficient port configuration is determined only by extensive testing. Therefore, it is best to consult someone experienced with the head in question to determine the optimum alterations.*
* Knurling the valve guides: 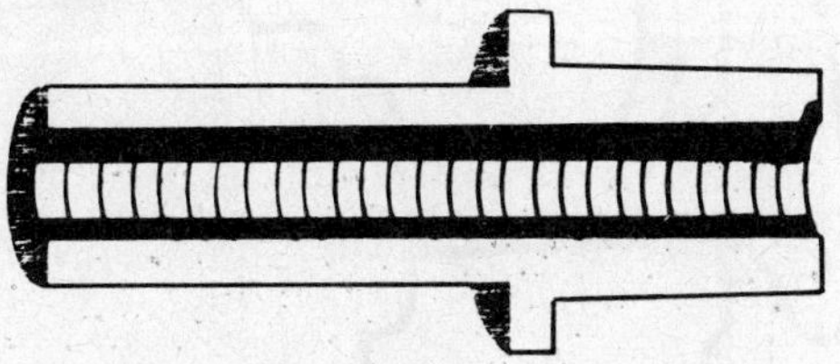 **Cut-away view of a knurled valve guide**	* Valve guides which are not excessively worn or distorted may, in some cases, be knurled rather than replaced. Knurling is a process in which metal is displaced and raised, thereby reducing clearance. Knurling also provides excellent oil control. The possibility of knurling rather than replacing valve guides should be discussed with a machinist.
Replacing the valve guides: NOTE: *Valve guides should only be replaced if damaged or if an oversize valve stem is not available.* 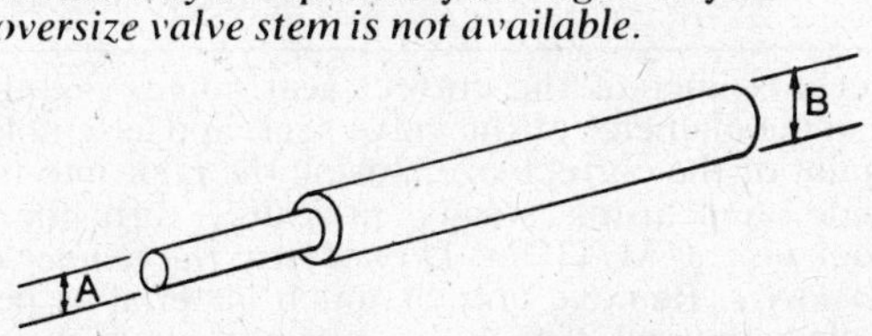 A—VALVE GUIDE I.D. B—LARGER THAN THE VALVE GUIDE O.D. **Valve guide removal tool** 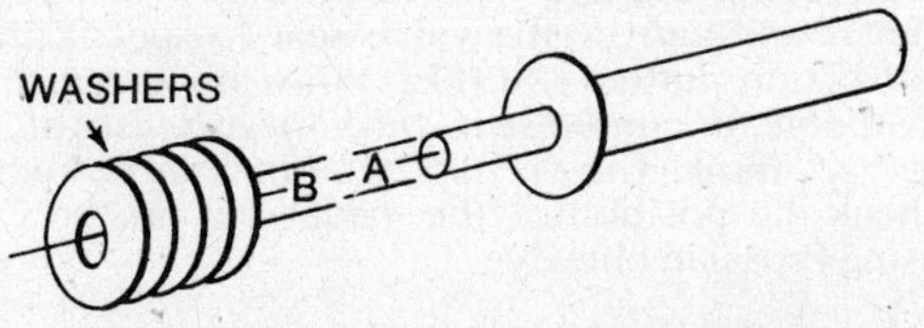 A—VALVE GUIDE I.D. B—LARGER THAN THE VALVE GUIDE O.D. **Valve guide installation tool (with washers used for installation)**	Depending on the type of cylinder head, valve guides may be pressed, hammered, or shrunk in. In cases where the guides are shrunk into the head, replacement should be left to an equipped machine shop. In other cases, the guides are replaced as follows: Press or tap the valve guides out of the head using a stepped drift (see illustration). Determine the height above the boss that the guide must extend, and obtain a stack of washers, their I.D. similar to the guide's O.D., of that height. Place the stack of washers on the guide, and insert the guide into the boss. NOTE: *Valve guides are often tapered or beveled for installation.* Using the stepped installation tool (see illustration), press or tap the guides into position. Ream the guides according to the size of the valve stem.

CYLINDER HEAD RECONDITIONING

Procedure	*Method*
Replacing valve seat inserts:	Replacement of valve seat inserts which are worn beyond resurfacing or broken, if feasible, must be done by a machine shop.
Resurfacing (grinding) the valve face:	Using a valve grinder, resurface the valves according to specifications. CAUTION: *Valve face angle is not always identical to valve seat angle.* A minimum margin of 1/32″ should remain after grinding the valve. The valve stem top should also be squared and resurfaced, by placing the stem in the V-block of the grinder, and turning it while pressing lightly against the grinding wheel. NOTE: *Do not grind sodium filled exhaust valves on a machine. These should be hand lapped.*

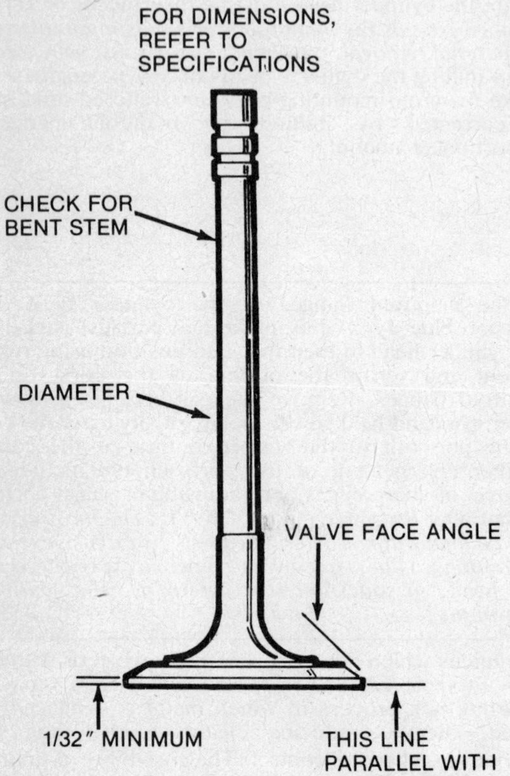

Critical valve dimensions

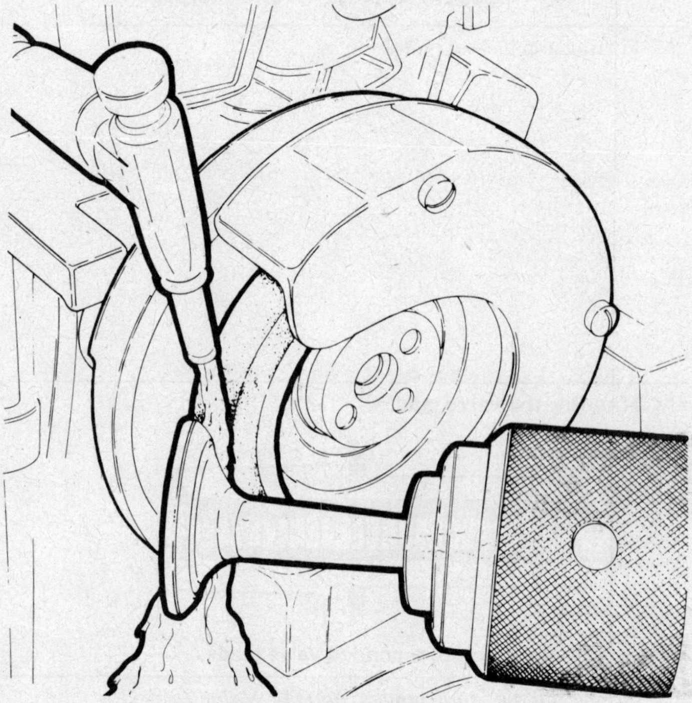

Valve grinding by machine

Procedure	*Method*
Resurfacing the valve seats using reamers:	Select a reamer of the correct seat angle, slightly larger than the diameter of the valve seat, and assemble it with a pilot of the correct size. Install the pilot into the valve guide, and using steady pressure, turn the reamer clockwise. CAUTION: *Do not turn the reamer counter-clockwise.* Remove only as much material as necessary to clean the seat. Check the concentricity of the seat (see below). If the dye method is not used, coat the valve face with Prussian blue dye, install and rotate it on the valve seat. Using the dye marked area as a centering guide, center and narrow the valve seat to specifications with correction cutters. NOTE: *When no specifications are available, minimum seat width for exhaust valves should be 5/64″, intake valves 1/16″.* After making correction cuts, check the position of the valve seat on the valve face using Prussian blue dye.

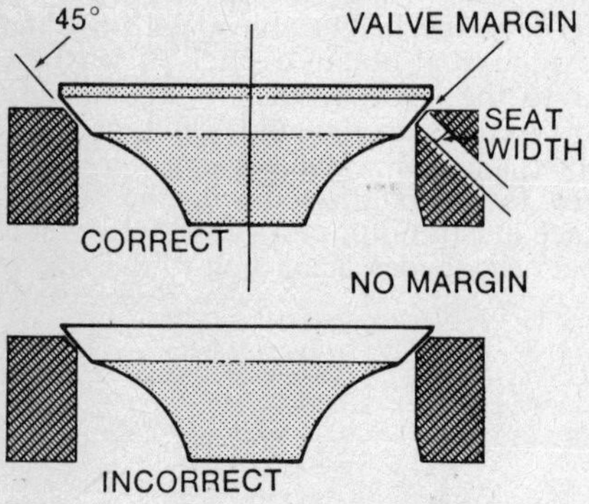

Valve seat width and centering

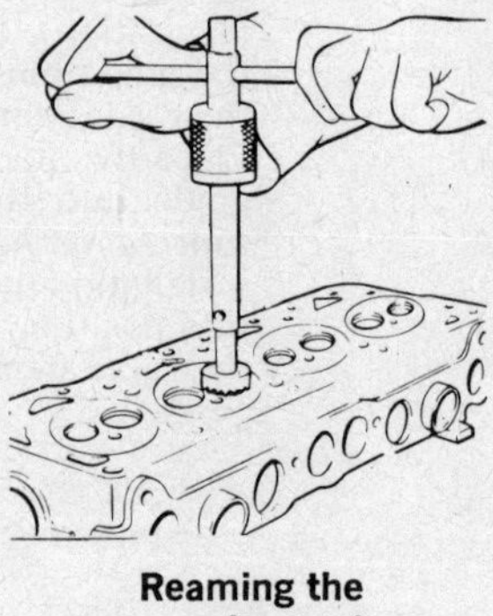

Reaming the valve seat

CYLINDER HEAD RECONDITIONING

Procedure — *Method*

* Resurfacing the valve seats using a grinder:

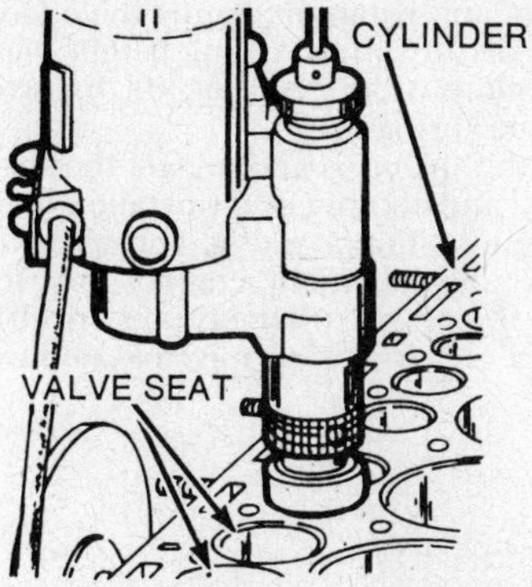

Grinding a valve seat

Select a pilot of the correct size, and a coarse stone of the correct seat angle. Lubricate the pilot if necessary, and install the tool in the valve guide. Move the stone on and off the seat at approximately two cycles per second, until all flaws are removed from the seat. Install a fine stone, and finish the seat. Center and narrow the seat using correction stones, as described above.

Checking the valve seat concentricity:

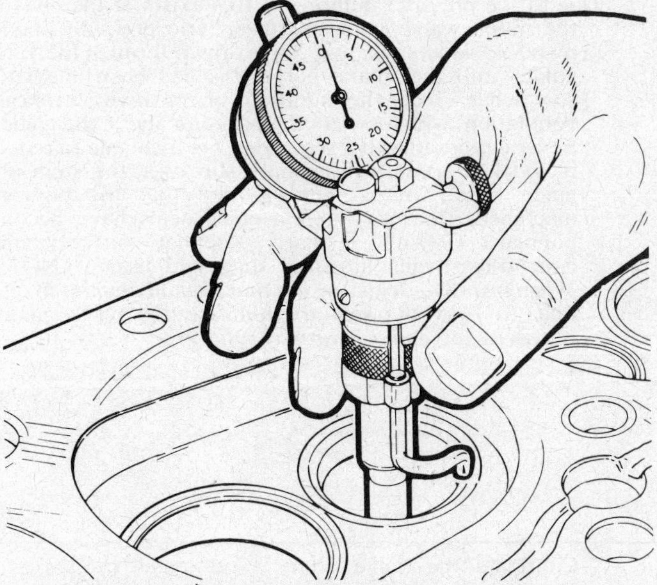

Checking valve seat concentricity using a dial gauge

Coat the valve face with Prussian blue dye, install the valve, and rotate it on the valve seat. If the entire seat becomes coated, and the valve is known to be concentric, the seat is concentric.

* Install the dial gauge pilot into the guide, and rest of the arm on the valve seat. Zero the gauge, and rotate the arm around the seat. Run-out should not exceed .002″.

* Lapping the valves: NOTE: *Valve lapping is done to ensure efficient sealing of resurfaced valves and seats.*

Hand lapping the valves

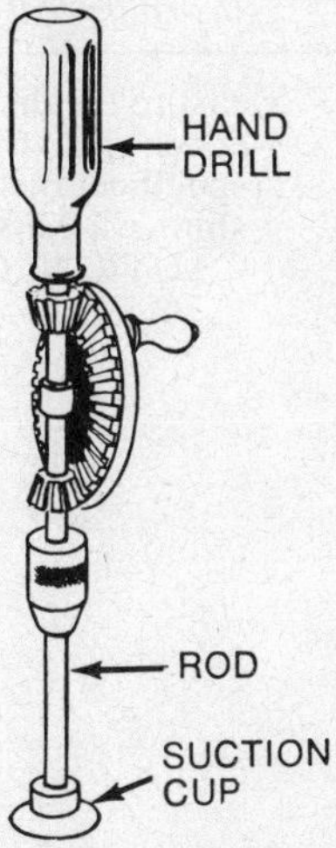

Home made mechanical valve lapping tool

* Invert the cylinder head, lightly lubricate the valve stems, and install the valves in the head as numbered. Coat valve seats with fine grinding compound, and attach the lapping tool suction cup to a valve head (NOTE: *Moisten the suction cup*). Rotate the tool between the palms, changing position and lifting the tool often to prevent grooving. Lap the valve until a smooth, polished seat is evident. Remove the valve and tool, and rinse away all traces of grinding compound.

** Fasten a suction cup to a piece of drill rod, and mount the rod in a hand drill. Proceed as above, using the hand drill as a lapping tool. CAUTION: *Due to the higher speeds involved when using the hand drill, care must be exercised to avoid grooving the seat.* Lift the tool and change direction of rotation often.

CYLINDER HEAD RECONDITIONING

Procedure	*Method*
Check the valve springs:	Place the spring on a flat surface next to a square. Measure the height of the spring, and rotate it against the edge of the square to measure distortion. If spring height varies (by comparison) by more than $^1/_{16}$" or if distortion exceeds $^1/_{16}$", replace the spring. ** In addition to evaluating the spring as above, test the spring pressure at the installed and compressed (installed height minus valve lift) height using a valve spring tester. Springs used on small displacement engines (up to 3 liters) should be ∓ 1 lb. of all other springs in either position. A tolerance of ∓ 5 lbs. is permissible on larger engines.
* Install valve stem seals:	* Due to the pressure differential that exists at the ends of the intake valve guides (atmospheric pressure above, manifold vacuum below), oil is drawn through the valve guides into the intake port. This has been alleviated somewhat since the addition of positive crankcase ventilation, which lowers the pressure above the guides. Several types of valve stem seals are available to reduce blow-by. Certain seals simply slip over the stem and guide boss, while others require that the boss be machined. Recently, Teflon guide seals have become popular. Consult a parts supplier or machinist concerning availability and suggested usages. NOTE: *When installing seals, ensure that a small amount of oil is able to pass the seal to lubricate the valve guides; otherwise, excessive wear may result.*
Install the valves:	Lubricate the valve stems, and install the valves in the cylinder head as numbered. Lubricate and position the seals (if used, see above) and the valve springs. Install the spring retainers, compress the springs, and insert the keys using needlenose pliers or a tool designed for this purpose. NOTE: *Retain the keys with wheel bearing grease during installation.*
Check valve spring installed height:	Measure the distance between the spring pad and the lower edge of the spring retainer, and compare to specifications. If the installed height is incorrect, add shim washers between the spring pad and the spring. CAUTION: *Use only washers designed for this purpose.*

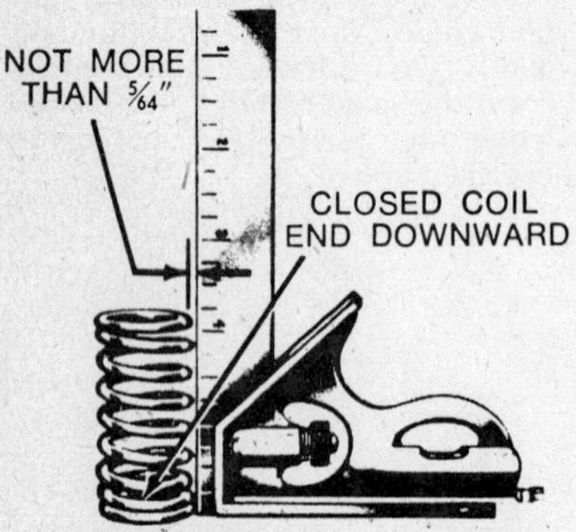

Checking valve spring free length and squareness

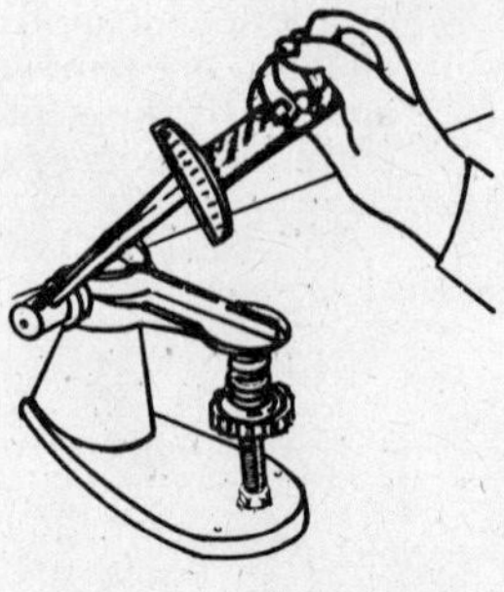
Measuring valve spring test pressure

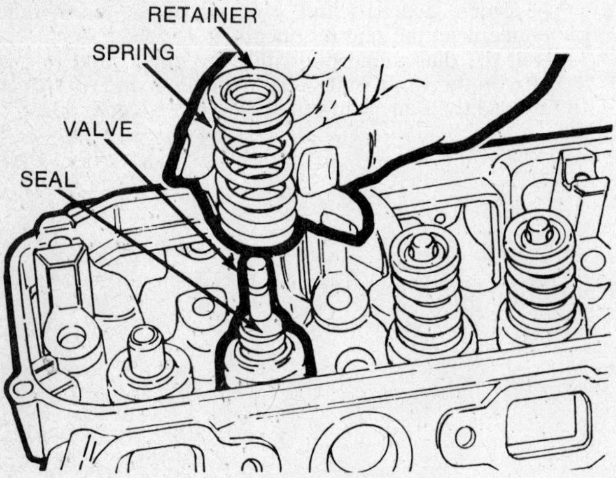

Valve stem seal installation

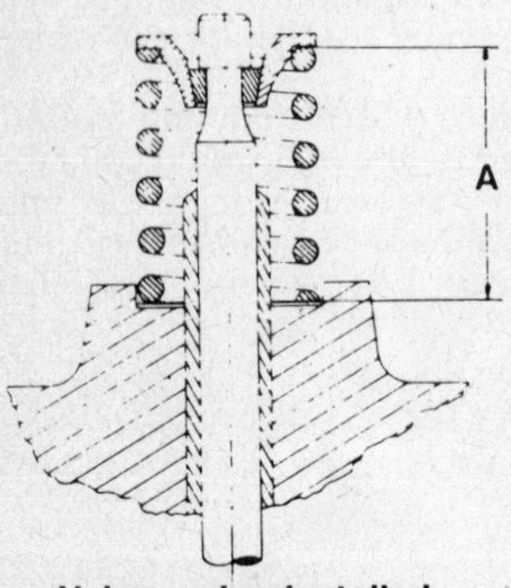

Valve spring installed height dimension

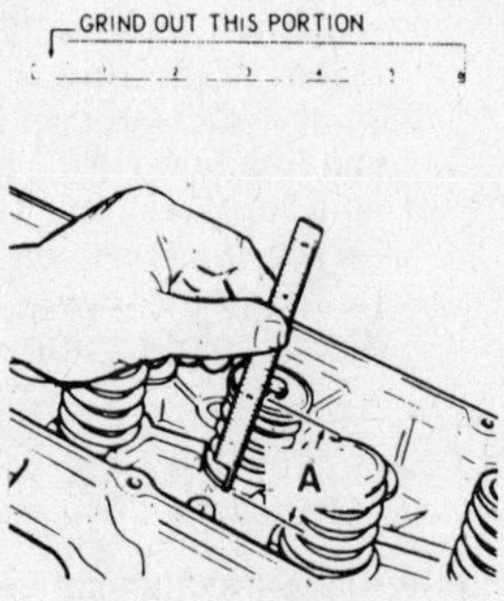

Measuring valve spring installed height

CYLINDER HEAD RECONDITIONING

Procedure	*Method*
Inspect the rocker arms, balls, studs, and nuts (where applicable):	Visually inspect the rocker arms, balls, studs, and nuts for cracks, galling, burning, scoring, or wear. If all parts are intact, liberally lubricate the rocker arms and balls, and install them on the cylinder head. If wear is noted on a rocker arm at the point of valve contact, grind it smooth and square, removing as little material as possible. Replace the rocker arm if excessively worn. If a rocker stud shows signs of wear, it must be replaced (see below). If a rocker nut shows stress cracks, replace it. If an exhaust ball is galled or burned, substitute the intake ball from the same cylinder (if it is intact), and install a new intake ball. NOTE: *Avoid using new rocker balls on exhaust valves.*

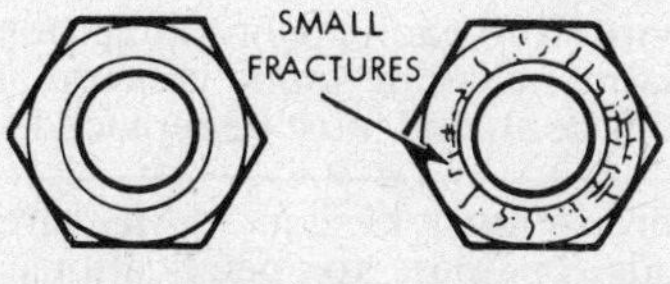

Stress cracks in the rocker nuts

Replacing rocker studs:	In order to remove a threaded stud, lock two nuts on the stud, and unscrew the stud using the lower nut. Coat the lower threads of the new stud with Loctite, and install. Two alternative methods are available for replacing pressed in studs. Remove the damaged stud using a stack of washers and a nut (see illustration). In the first, the boss is reamed .005-.006" oversize, and an oversize stud pressed in. Control the stud extension over the boss using washers, in the same manner as valve guides. Before installing the stud, coat it with white lead and grease. To retain the stud more positively drill a hole through the stud and boss, and install a roll pin. In the second method, the boss is tapped, and a threaded stud installed. Retain the stud using Loctite Stud and Bearing Mount.

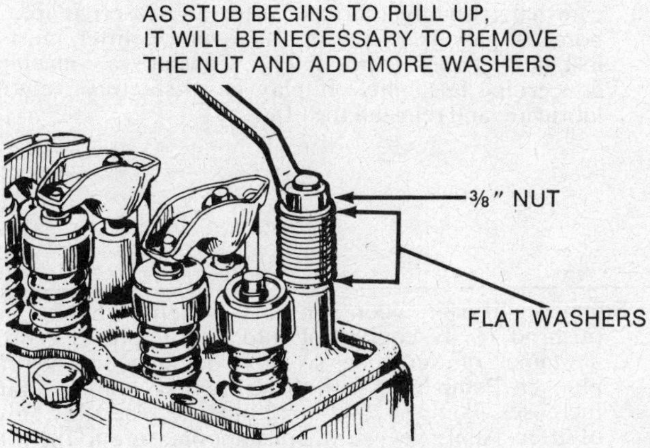

Extracting a pressed-in rocker stud

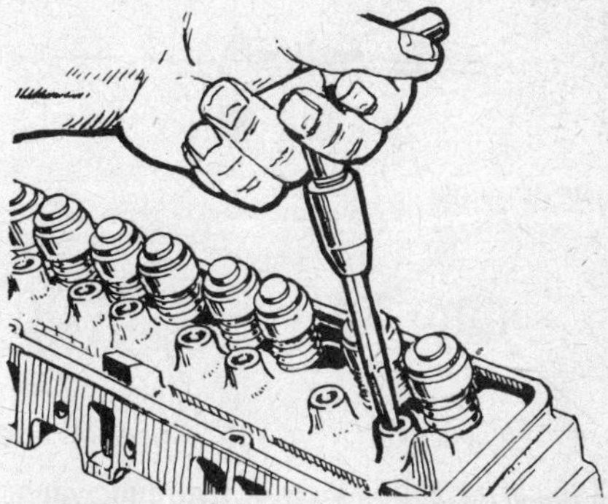

Reaming the stud bore for oversize rocker studs

Inspect the rocker shaft(s) and rocker arms (where applicable):	Remove rocker arms, springs and washers from rocker shaft. NOTE: *Lay out parts in the order as they are removed.* Inspect rocker arms for pitting or wear on the valve contact point, or excessive bushing wear. Bushings need only be replaced if wear is excessive, because the rocker arm normally contacts the shaft at one point only. Grind the valve contact point of rocker arm smooth if necessary, removing as little material as possible. If excessive material must be removed to smooth and square the arm, it should be replaced. Clean out all oil holes and passages in rocker shaft. If shaft is grooved or worn, replace it. Lubricate and assemble the rocker shaft.

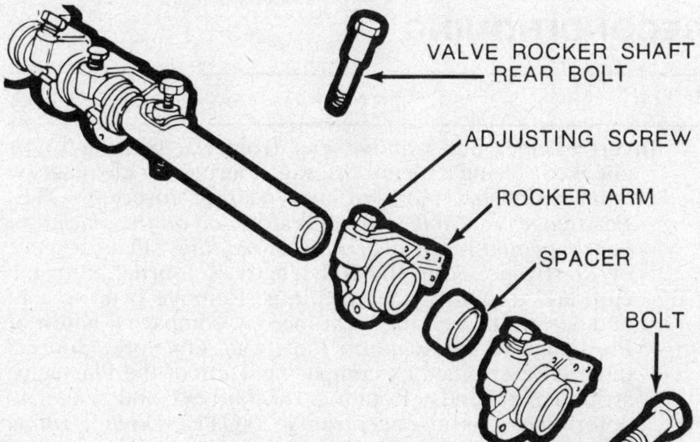

Disassemble the rocker shaft for inspection

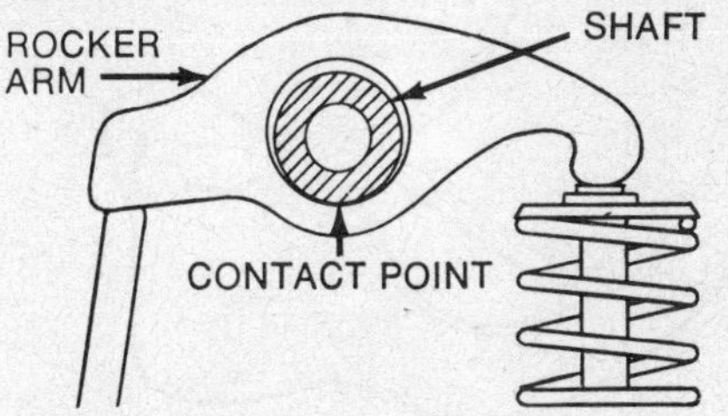

Rocker arm-to-rocker shaft contact area

CYLINDER HEAD RECONDITIONING

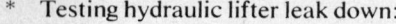

Procedure	*Method*
Inspect the camshaft bushings and the camshaft (overhead cam engines):	See next section.
Inspect the pushrods (OHV engines only):	Remove the pushrods, and, if hollow, clean out the oil passages using fine wire. Roll each pushrod over a piece of clean glass. If a distinct clicking sound is heard as the pushrod rolls, the rod is bent, and must be replaced.
	* The length of all pushrods must be equal. Measure the length of the pushrods, compare to specifications, and replace as necessary.
Inspect the valve lifters (OHV engines only):	Remove lifters from their bores, and remove gum and varnish, using solvent. Clean walls of lifter bores. Check lifters for concave wear as illustrated. If face is worn concave, replace lifter, and carefully inspect the camshaft. Lightly lubricate lifter and insert it into its bore. If play is excessive, an oversize lifter must be installed (where possible). Consult a machinist concerning feasibility. If play is satisfactory, remove, lubricate, and reinstall the lifter.
* Testing hydraulic lifter leak down:	Submerge lifter in a container of kerosene. Chuck a used pushrod or its equivalent into a drill press. Position container of kerosene so pushrod acts on the lifter plunger. Pump lifter with the drill press, until resistance increases. Pump several more times to bleed any air out of lifter. Apply very firm, constant pressure to the lifter, and observe rate at which fluid bleeds out of lifter. If the fluid bleeds very quickly (less than 15 seconds), lifter is defective. If the time exceeds 60 seconds, lifter is sticking. In either case, recondition or replace lifter. If lifter is operating properly (leak down time 15-60 seconds), lubricate and install it.

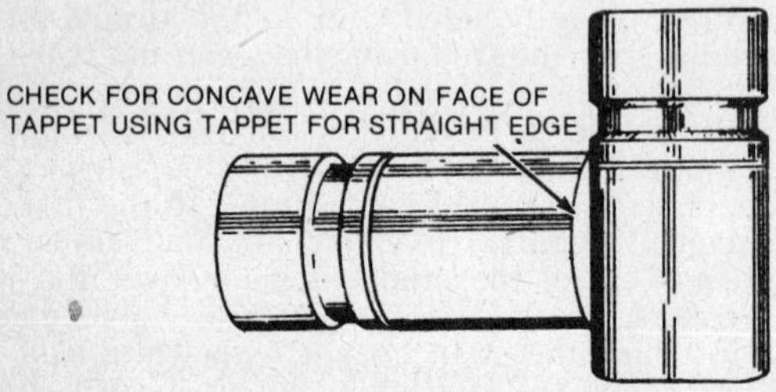

Checking the lifter face

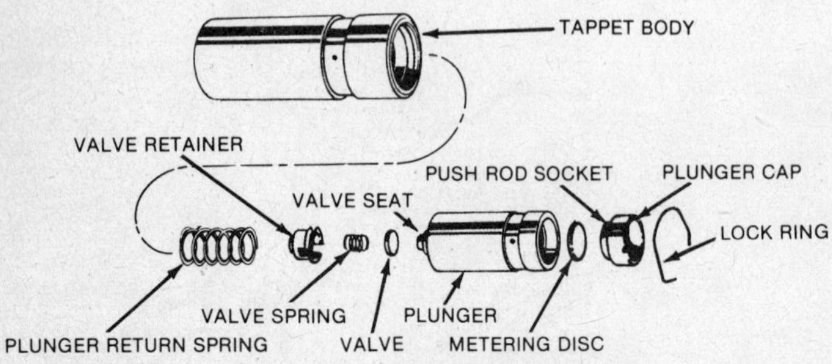

Typical exploded view of hydraulic valve lifter

CYLINDER BLOCK RECONDITIONING

Procedure	*Method*
Checking the main bearing clearance:	Invert engine, and remove cap from the bearing to be checked. Using a clean, dry rag, thoroughly clean all oil from crankshaft journal and bearing insert. NOTE: *Plastigage is soluble in oil; therefore, oil on the journal or bearing could result in erroneous readings.* Place a piece of Plastigage along the full length of journal, reinstall cap, and torque to specifications. Remove bearing cap, and determine bearing clearance by comparing width of Plastigage to the scale on Plastigage envelope. Journal taper is determined by comparing width of the Plastigage strip near its ends. Rotate crankshaft 90° and retest, to determine journal eccentricity. NOTE: *Do not rotate crankshaft with Plastigage installed.* If bearing insert and journal appear intact, and are within tolerances, no further main bearing service is required. If bearing or journal appear defective, cause of failure should be determined before replacement.

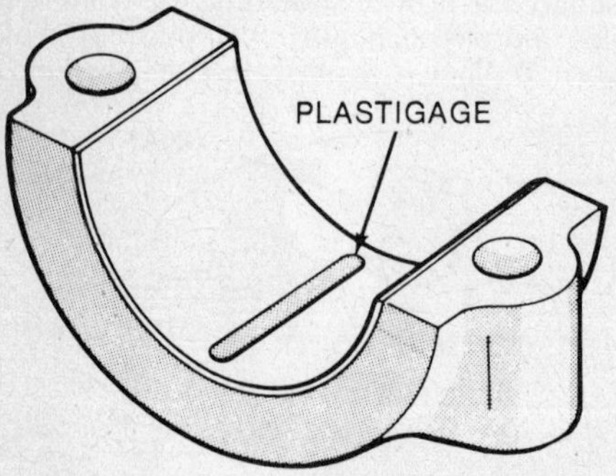

Plastigage® installed on the lower bearing shell

CYLINDER BLOCK RECONDITIONING

Procedure	Method

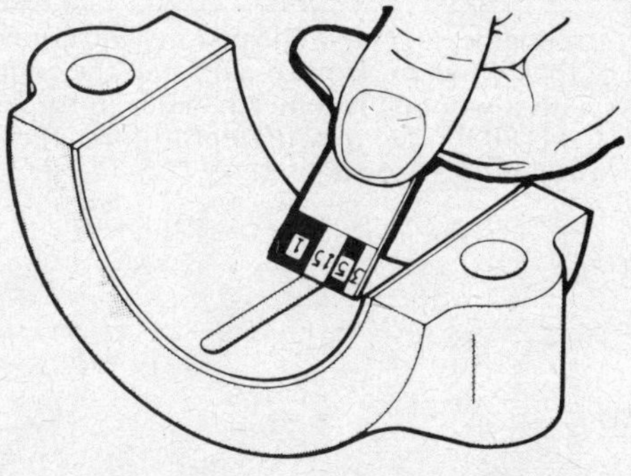

Measuring Plastigage® to determine bearing clearance

* Remove crankshaft from block (see below). Measure the main bearing journals at each end twice (90° apart) using a micrometer, to determine diameter, journal taper and eccentricity. If journals are within tolerances, reinstall bearing caps at their specified torque. Using a telescope gauge and micrometer, measure bearing I.D. parallel to piston axis and at 30° on each side of piston axis. Subtract journal O.D. from bearing I.D. to determine oil clearance. If crankshaft journals appear defective, or do not meet tolerances, there is no need to measure bearings; for the crankshaft will require grinding and/or undersize bearings will be required. If bearing appears defective, cause for failure should be determined prior to replacement.

Checking the connecting rod bearing clearance:

Connecting rod bearing clearance is checked in the same manner as main bearing clearance, using Plastigage. Before removing the crankshaft, connecting rod side clearance also should be measured and recorded.

* Checking connecting rod bearing clearance, using a micrometer, is identical to checking main bearing clearance. If no other service is required, the piston and rod assemblies need not be removed.

Removing the crankshaft:

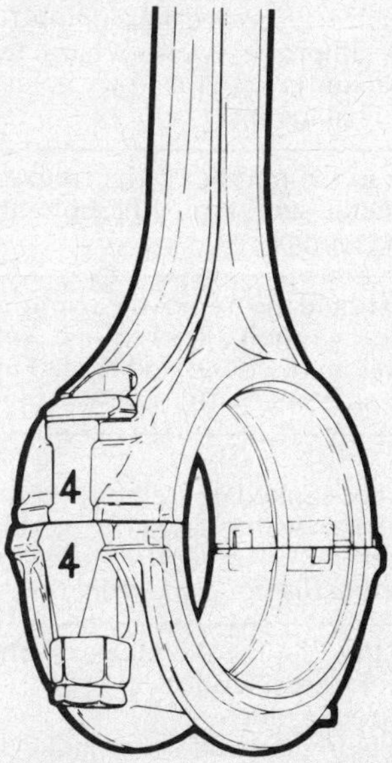

Connecting rod matched to cylinder with a number stamp

Using a punch, mark the corresponding main bearing caps and saddles according to position (i.e., one punch on the front main cap and saddle, two on the second, three on the third, etc.). Using number stamps, identify the corresponding connecting rods and caps, according to cylinder (if no numbers are present). Remove the main and connecting rod caps, and place sleeves of plastic tubing over the connecting rod bolts, to protect the journals as the crankshaft is removed. Lift the crankshaft out of the block.

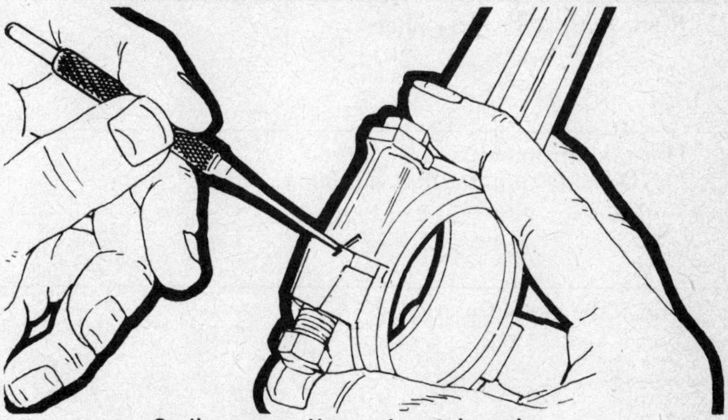

Scribe connecting rod matchmarks

Remove the ridge from the top of the cylinder:

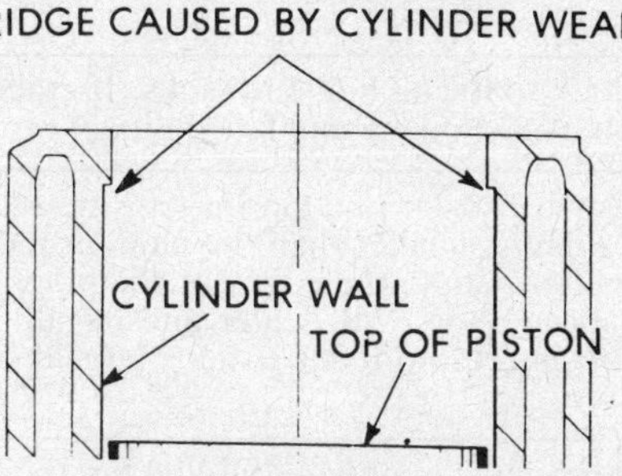

Cylinder bore ridge

In order to facilitate removal of the piston and connecting rod, the ridge at the top of the cylinder (unworn area; see illustration) must be removed. Place the piston at the bottom of the bore, and cover it with a rag. Cut the ridge away using a ridge reamer, exercising extreme care to avoid cutting too deeply. Remove the rag, and remove cuttings that remain on the piston. CAUTION: *If the ridge is not removed, and new rings are installed, damage to rings will result.*

CYLINDER BLOCK RECONDITIONING

Procedure	*Method*
Removing the piston and connecting rod: 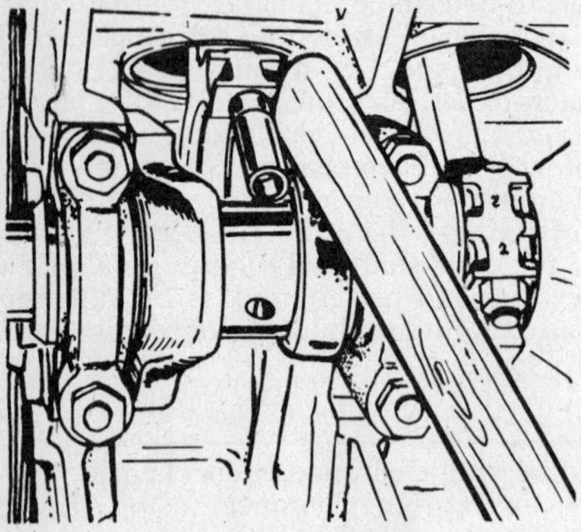 **Removing the piston**	Invert the engine, and push the pistons and connecting rods out of the cylinders. If necessary, tap the connecting rod boss with a wooden hammer handle, to force the piston out. CAUTION: *Do not attempt to force the piston past the cylinder ridge* (see above).
Service the crankshaft:	Ensure that all oil holes and passages in the crankshaft are open and free of sludge. If necessary, have the crankshaft ground to the largest possible undersize.
	** Have the crankshaft Magnafluxed, to locate stress cracks. Consult a machinist concerning additional service procedures, such as surface hardening (e.g., nitriding, Tuftriding) to improve wear characteristics, cross drilling and chamfering the oil holes to improve lubrication, and balancing.
Removing freeze plugs:	Drill a small hole in the middle of the freeze plugs. Thread a large sheet metal screw into the hole and remove the plug with a slide hammer.
Remove the oil gallery plugs:	Threaded plugs should be removed using an appropriate (usually square) wrench. To remove soft, pressed in plugs, drill a hole in the plug, and thread in a sheet metal screw. Pull the plug out by the screw using pliers.
Hot-tank the block: NOTE: *Do not hot-tank aluminum parts.*	Have the block hot-tanked to remove grease, corrosion, and scale from the water jackets. NOTE: *Consult the operator to determine whether the camshaft bearings will be damaged during the hot-tank process.*
Check the block for cracks:	Visually inspect the block for cracks or chips. The most common locations are as follows: Adjacent to freeze plugs. Between the cylinders and water jackets. Adjacent to the main bearing saddles. At the extreme bottom of the cylinders. Check only suspected cracks using spot check dye (see introduction). If a crack is located, consult a machinist concerning possible repairs.
	** Magnaflux the block to locate hidden cracks. If cracks are located, consult a machinist about feasibility of repair.
Install the oil gallery plugs and freeze plugs:	Coat freeze plugs with sealer and tap into position using a piece of pipe, slightly smaller than the plug, as a driver. To ensure retention, stake the edges of the plugs. Coat threaded oil gallery plugs with sealer and install. Drive replacement soft plugs into block using a large drift as a driver.
	* Rather than reinstalling lead plugs, drill and tap the holes, and install threaded plugs.

CYLINDER BLOCK RECONDITIONING

Procedure	*Method*
Check the bore diameter and surface:	Visually inspect the cylinder bores for roughness, scoring, or scuffing. If evident, the cylinder bore must be bored or honed oversize to eliminate imperfections, and the smallest possible oversize piston used. The new pistons should be given to the machinist with the block, so that the cylinders can be bored or honed exactly to the piston size (plus clearance). If no flaws are evident, measure the bore diameter using a telescope gauge and micrometer, or dial guage, parallel and perpendicular to the engine centerline, at the top (below the ridge) and bottom of the bore. Subtract the bottom measurements from the top to determine taper, and the parallel to the centerline measurements from the perpendicular measurements to determine eccentricity. If the measurements are not within specifications, the cylinder must be bored or honed, and an oversize piston installed. If the measurements are within specifications the cylinder may be used as is, with only finish honing (see below). NOTE: *Prior to submitting the block for boring, perform the following operation(s).*

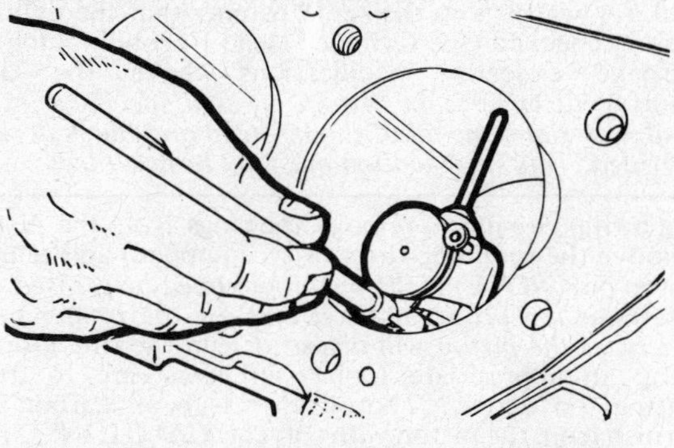

Measuring the cylinder bore with a dial gauge

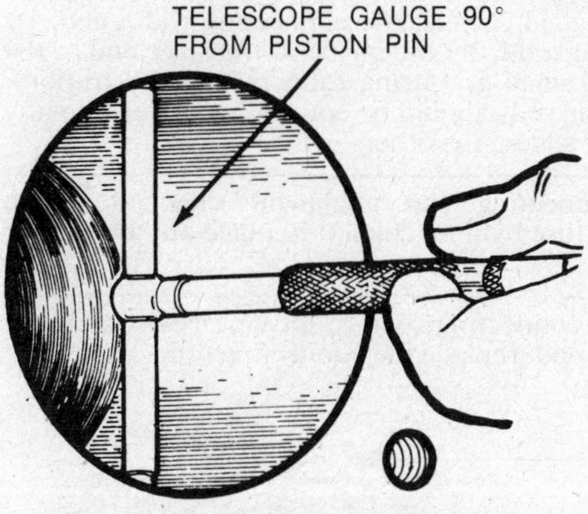

Measuring cylinder bore with a telescope gauge

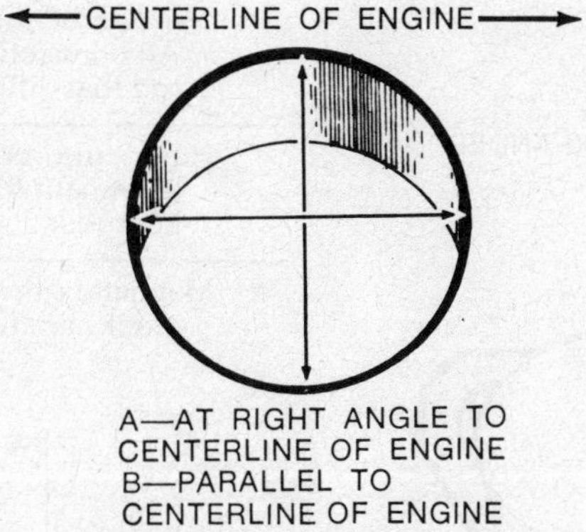

Cylinder bore measuring points

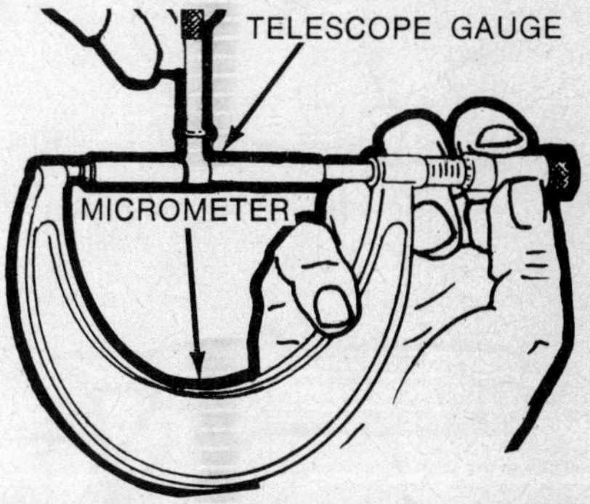

Determining cylinder bore by measuring telescope gauge with a micrometer

Check the cylinder block bearing alignment:	Remove the upper bearing inserts. Place a straightedge in the bearing saddles along the centerline of the crankshaft. If clearance exists between the straightedge and the center saddle, the block must be alignbored.

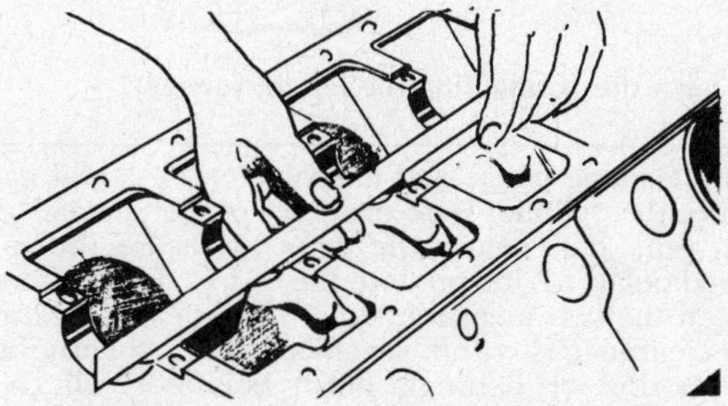

Checking main bearing saddle alignment

* Check the deck height:	The deck height is the distance from the crankshaft centerline to the block deck. To measure, invert the engine, and install the crankshaft, retaining it with the center main cap. Measure the distance from the crankshaft journal to the block deck, parallel to the cylinder centerline. Measure the diameter of the end (front and rear) main journals, parallel to the centerline of the cylinders, divide the diameter in half, and subtract it from the previous measurement. The results of the front and rear measurements should be identical. If the difference exceeds .005", the deck height should be corrected. NOTE: *Block deck height and warpage should be corrected at the same time.*

CYLINDER BLOCK RECONDITIONING

Procedure	*Method*
Check the block deck for warpage:	Using a straightedge and feeler gauges, check the block deck for warpage in the same manner that the cylinder head is checked (see Cylinder Head Reconditioning). If warpage exceeds specifications, have the deck resurfaced. NOTE: *In certain cases a specification for total material removal (Cylinder head and block deck) is provided. This specification must not be exceeded.*
Clean and inspect the pistons and connecting rods:	Using a ring expander, remove the rings from the piston. Remove the retaining rings (if so equipped) and remove piston pin. NOTE: *If the piston pin must be pressed out, determine the proper method and use the proper tools; otherwise the piston will distort.* Clean the ring grooves using an appropriate tool, exercising care to avoid cutting too deeply. Thoroughly clean all carbon and varnish from the piston with solvent. CAUTION: *Do not use a wire brush or caustic solvent on pistons.* Inspect the pistons for scuffing, scoring, cracks, pitting, or excessive ring groove wear. If wear is evident, the piston must be replaced. Check the connecting rod length by measuring the rod from the inside of the large end to the inside of the small end using calipers (see illustration). All connecting rods should be equal length. Replace any rod that differs from the others in the engine.
	* Have the connecting rod alignment checked in an alignment fixture by a machinist. Replace any twisted or bent rods.
	* Magnaflux the connecting rods to locate stress cracks. If cracks are found, replace the connecting rod.

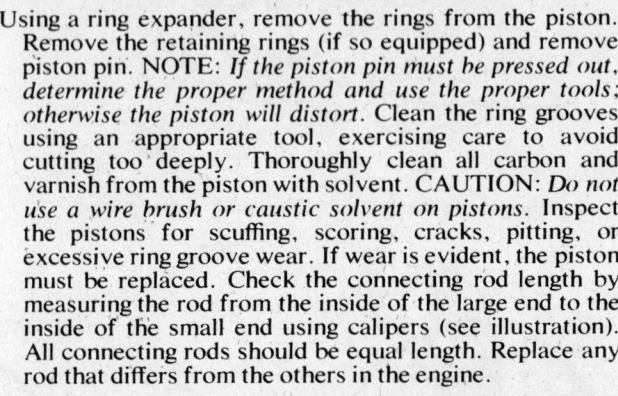

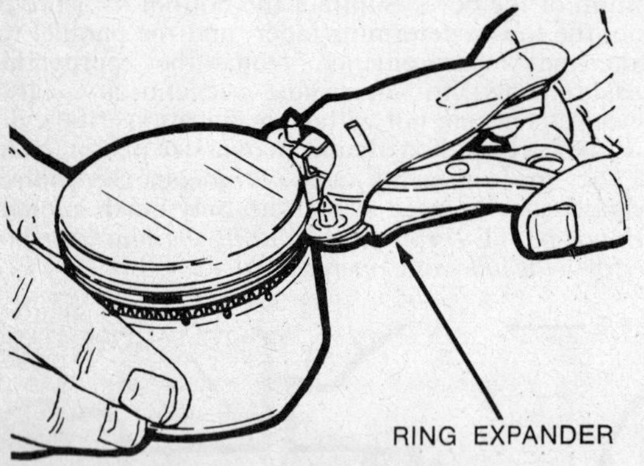

Removing the piston rings

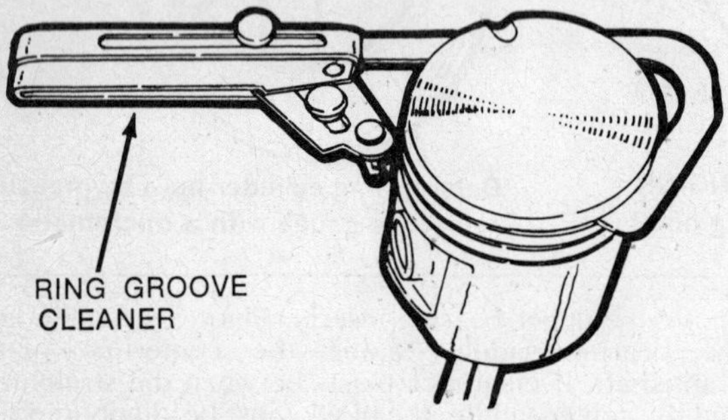

Cleaning the piston ring grooves

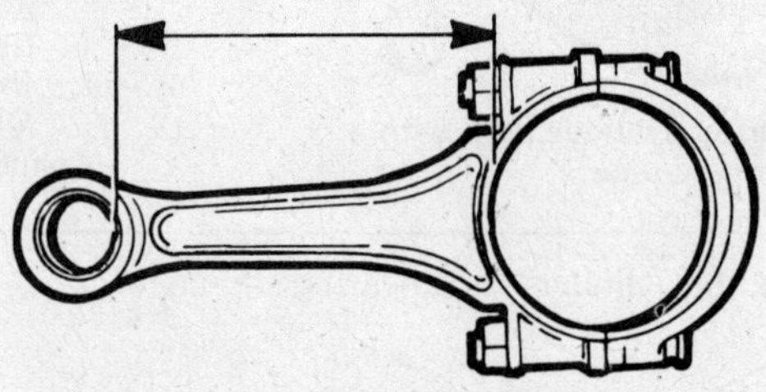
Check the connecting rod length (arrow)

Procedure	*Method*
Fit the pistons to the cylinders:	Using a telescope gauge and micrometer, or a dial gauge, measure the cylinder bore diameter perpendicular to the piston pin, 2½" below the deck. Measure the piston perpendicular to its pin on the skirt. The difference between the two measurements is the piston clearance. If the clearance is within specifications or slightly below (after boring or honing), finish honing is all that is required. If the clearance is excessive, try to obtain a slightly larger piston to bring clearance within specifications. Where this is not possible, obtain the first oversize piston, and hone (or if necessary, bore) the cylinder to size.

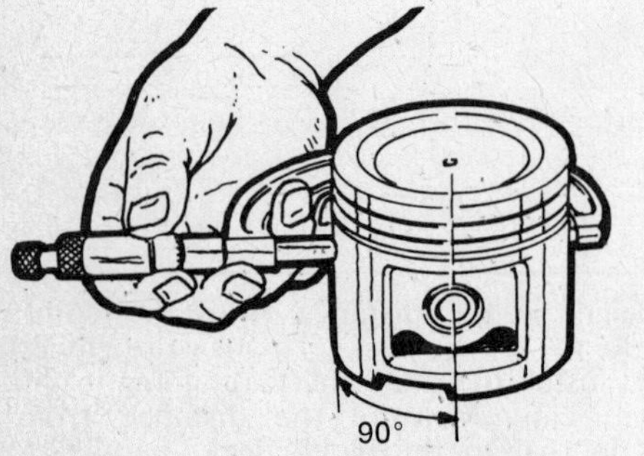

Measuring the piston prior to fitting

Procedure	*Method*
Assemble the pistons and connecting rods:	Inspect piston pin, connecting rod small end bushing, and piston bore for galling, scoring, or excessive wear. If evident, replace defective part(s). Measure the I.D. of the piston boss and connecting rod small end, and the O.D. of the piston pin. If within specifications, assemble piston pin and rod. CAUTION: *If piston pin must be*

CYLINDER BLOCK RECONDITIONING

Procedure	*Method*

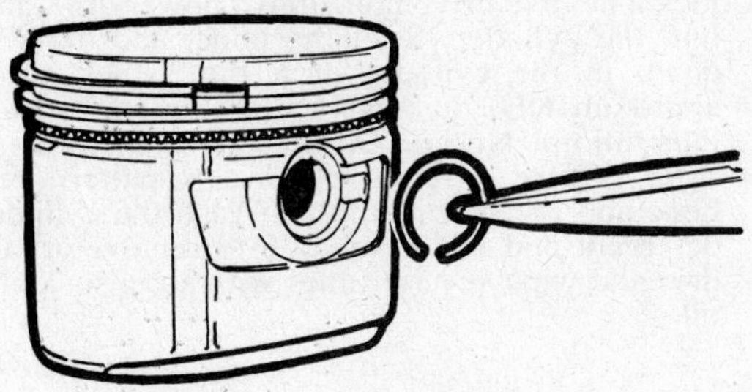

Installing piston pin lock rings

pressed in, determine the proper method and use the proper tools; otherwise the piston will distort. Install the lock rings; ensure that they seat properly. If the parts are not within specifications, determine the service method for the type of engine. In some cases, piston and pin are serviced as an assembly when either is defective. Others specify reaming the piston and connecting rods for an oversize pin. If the connecting rod bushing is worn, it may in many cases be replaced. Reaming the piston and replacing the rod bushing are machine shop operations.

Clean and inspect the camshaft:

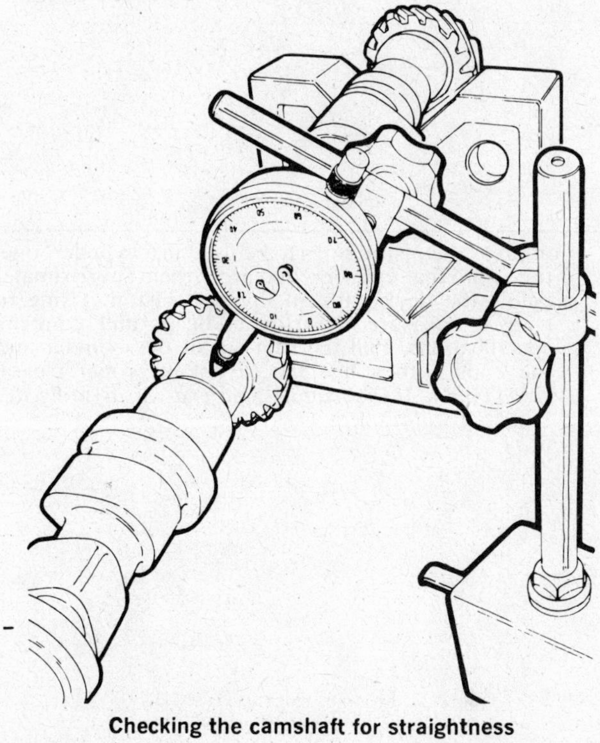

Checking the camshaft for straightness

Degrease the camshaft, using solvent, and clean out all oil holes. Visually inspect cam lobes and bearing journals for excessive wear. If a lobe is questionable, check all lobes as indicated below. If a journal or lobe is worn, the camshaft must be reground or replaced. NOTE: *If a journal is worn, there is a good chance that the bushings are worn.* If lobes and journals appear intact, place the front and rear journals in V-blocks, and rest a dial indicator on the center journal. Rotate the camshaft to check straightness. If deviation exceeds .001", replace the camshaft.

* Check the camshaft lobes with a micrometer, by measuring the lobes from the nose to base and again at 90° (see illustration). The lift is determined by subtracting the second measurement from the first. If all exhaust lobes and all intake lobes are not identical, the camshaft must be reground or replaced.

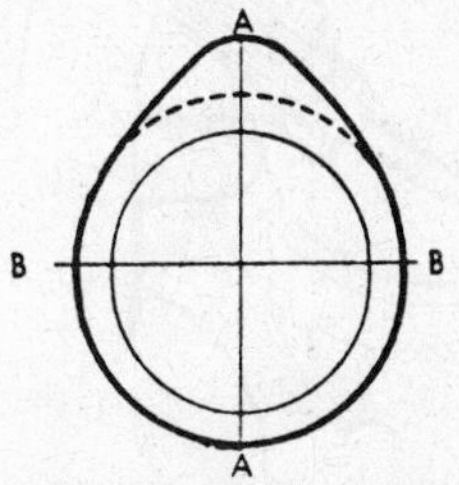

Camshaft lobe measurement

Replace the camshaft bearings:

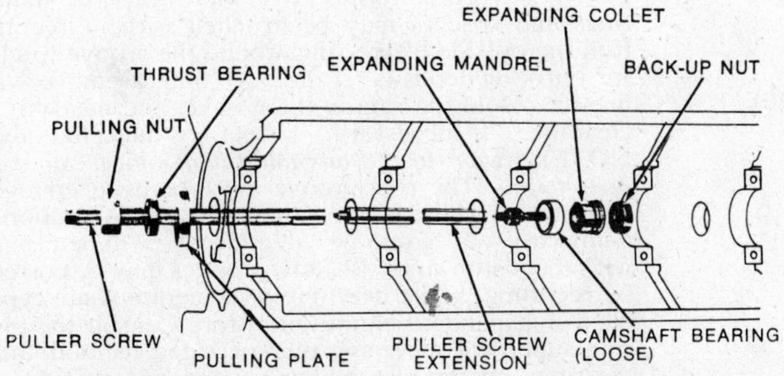

Camshaft removal and installation tool (typical)

If excessive wear is indicated, or if the engine is being completely rebuilt, camshaft bearings should be replaced as follows: Drive the camshaft rear plug from the block. Assemble the removal puller with its shoulder on the bearing to be removed. Gradually tighten the puller nut until bearing is removed. Remove remaining bearings, leaving the front and rear for last. To remove front and rear bearings, reverse position of the tool, so as to pull the bearings in toward the center of the block. Leave the tool in this position, pilot the new front and rear bearings on the installer, and pull them into position: Return the tool to its original position and pull remaining bearings into position. NOTE: *Ensure that oil holes align when installing bearings.* Replace camshaft rear plug, and stake it into position to aid retention.

CYLINDER BLOCK RECONDITIONING

Procedure	*Method*
Finish hone the cylinders:	Chuck a flexible drive hone into a power drill, and insert it into the cylinder. Start the hone, and move it up and down in the cylinder at a rate which will produce approximately a 60° cross-hatch pattern (see illustration). NOTE: *Do not extend the hone below the cylinder bore.* After developing the pattern, remove the hone and recheck piston fit. Wash the cylinders with a detergent and water solution to remove abrasive dust, dry, and wipe several times with a rag soaked in engine oil.

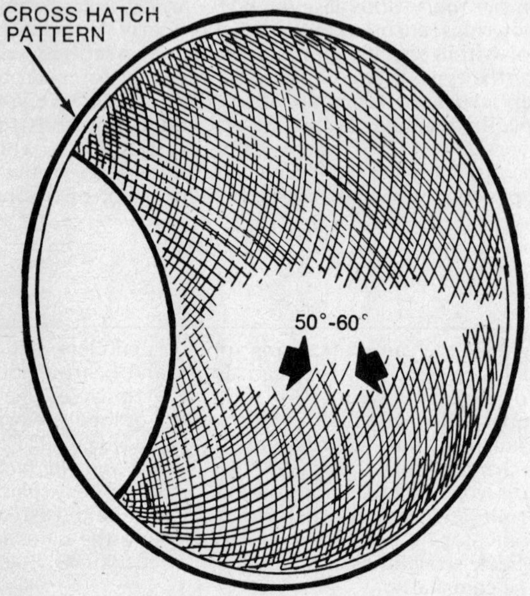

Check piston ring end-gap:	Compress the piston rings to be used in a cylinder, one at a time, into that cylinder, and press them approximately 1" below the deck with an inverted piston. Using feeler gauges, measure the ring end-gap, and compare to specifications. Pull the ring out of the cylinder and file the ends with a fine file to obtain proper clearance. CAUTION: *If inadequate ring end-gap is utilized, ring breakage will result.*

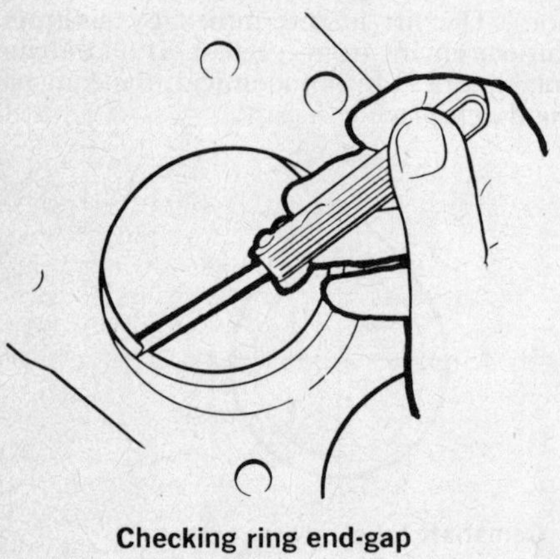

Checking ring end-gap

Install the piston rings:	Inspect the ring grooves in the piston for excessive wear or taper. If necessary, recut the groove(s) for use with an overwidth ring or a standard ring and spacer. If the groove is worn uniformly, overwidth rings, or standard rings and spacers may be installed without recutting. Roll the outside of the ring around the groove to check for burrs or deposits. If any are found, remove with a fine file. Hold the ring in the groove, and measure side clearance. If necessary, correct as indicated above. NOTE: *Always install any additional spacers above the piston ring.* The ring groove must be deep enough to allow the ring to seat below the lands (see illustration). In many cases, a "go-no-go" depth gauge will be provided with the piston rings. Shallow grooves may be corrected by recutting, while deep grooves require some type of filler or expander behind the piston. Consult the piston ring supplier concerning the suggested method. Install the rings on the piston, lowest ring first, using a ring expander. NOTE: *Position the ring markings as specified by the manufacturer (see car section).*

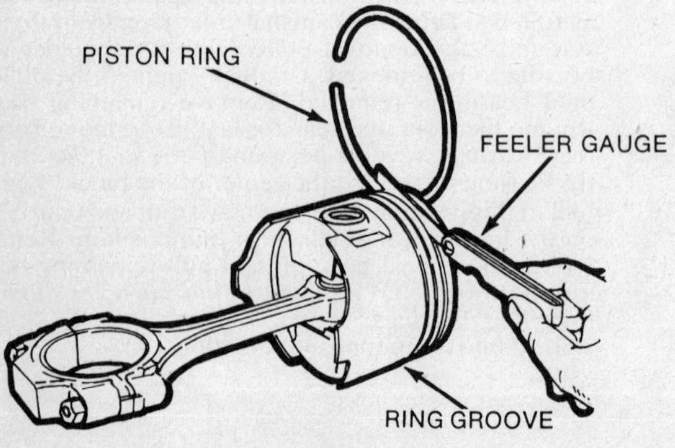

Checking ring side clearance

CYLINDER BLOCK RECONDITIONING

Procedure — *Method*

Install the camshaft:

Liberally lubricate the camshaft lobes and journals, and install the camshaft. CAUTION: *Exercise extreme care to avoid damaging the bearings when inserting the camshaft.* Install and tighten the camshaft thrust plate retaining bolts.

See the appropriate procedures for each individual engine.

Check camshaft end-play:

Checking camshaft end-play with a feeler gauge

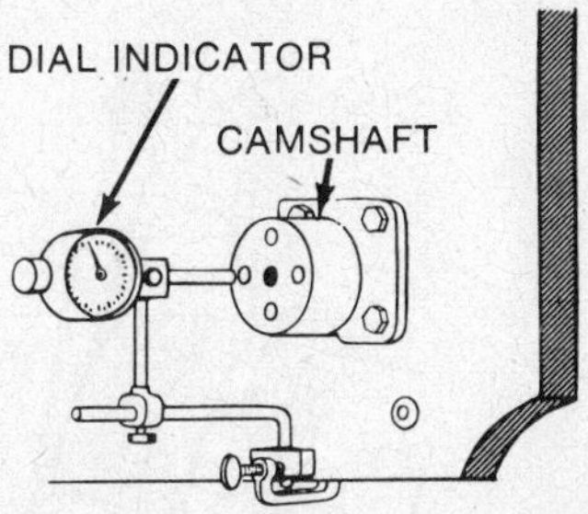

Checking camshaft end-play with a dial indicator

Using feeler gauges, determine whether the clearance between the camshaft boss (or gear) and backing plate is within specifications. Install shims behind the thrust plate, or reposition the camshaft gear and retest end-play. In some cases, adjustment is by replacing the thrust plate.

* Mount a dial indicator stand so that the stem of the dial indicator rests on the nose of the camshaft, parallel to the camshaft axis. Push the camshaft as far in as possible and zero the gauge. Move the camshaft outward to determine the amount of camshaft endplay. If the end-play is not within tolerance, install shims behind the thrust plate, or reposition the camshaft gear and retest.

Install the rear main seal (where applicable):

See the appropriate procedures for each individual engine.

Install the crankshaft:

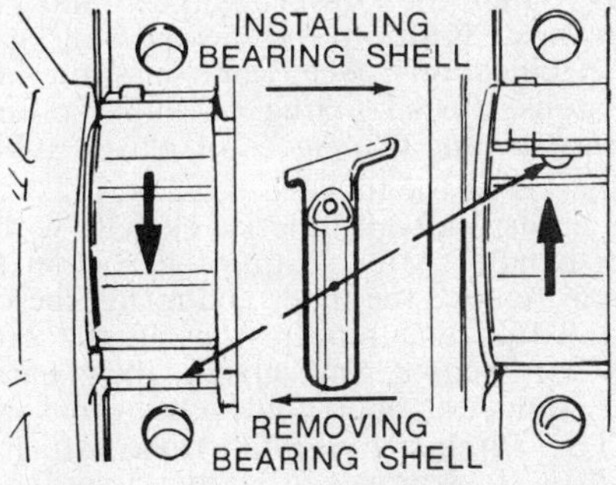

Removal and installation of upper bearing insert using a roll-out pin

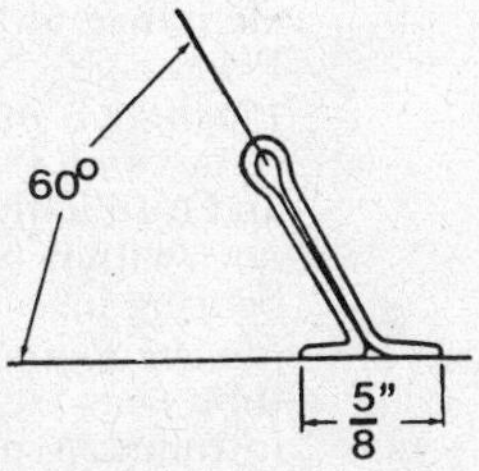

Home-made bearing roll-out pin

Thoroughly clean the main bearing saddles and caps. Place the upper halves of the bearing inserts on the saddles and press into position. NOTE: *Ensure that the oil holes align.* Press the corresponding bearing inserts into the main bearing caps. Lubricate the upper main bearings, and lay the crankshaft in position. Place a strip of Plastigage on each of the crankshaft journals, install the main caps, and torque to specifications. Remove the main caps, and compare the Plastigage to the scale on the Plastigage envelope. If clearances are within tolerances, remove the Plastigage, turn the crankshaft 90°, wipe off all oil and retest. If all clearances are correct, remove all Plastigage, thoroughly lubricate the main caps and bearing journals, and install the main caps. If clearances are not within tolerance, the upper bearing inserts may be removed, without removing the crankshaft, using a bearing roll out pin (see illustration). Roll in a bearing that will provide proper clearance, and retest. Torque all main caps, excluding the thrust bearing cap, to specifications. Tighten the thrust bearing cap finger tight. To properly align the thrust bearing, pry the crankshaft the extent of its axial travel several times, the last movement held toward the front of the engine, and torque the thrust bearing cap to specifications. Determine the crankshaft end-play (see below), and bring within tolerance with thrust washers.

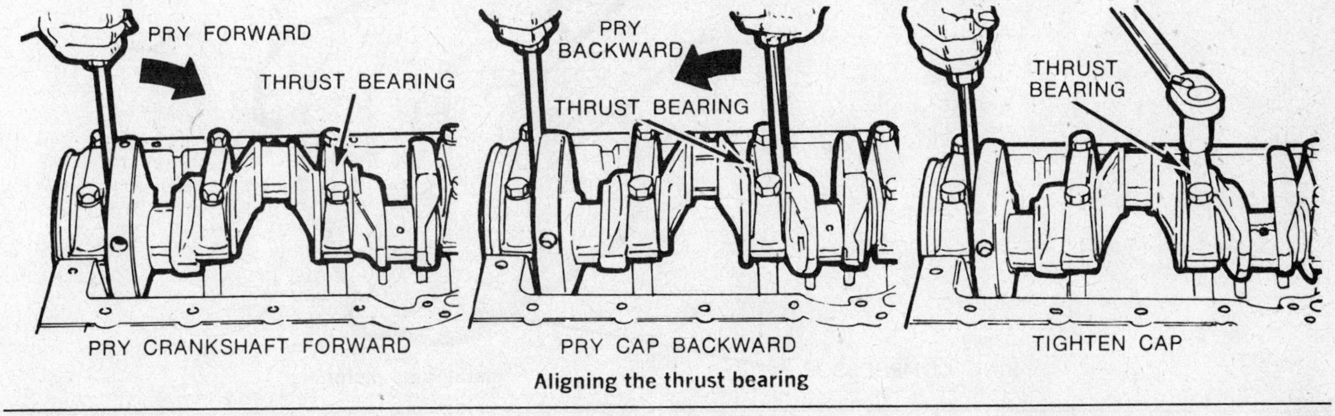

Aligning the thrust bearing

CYLINDER BLOCK RECONDITIONING

Procedure	*Method*
Measure crankshaft end-play:	Mount a dial indicator stand on the front of the block, with the dial indicator stem resting on the nose of the crankshaft, parallel to the crankshaft axis. Pry the crankshaft the extent of its travel rearward, and zero the indicator. Pry the crankshaft forward and record crankshaft end-play. NOTE: *Crankshaft end-play also may be measured at the thrust bearing, using feeler gauges* (see illustration).

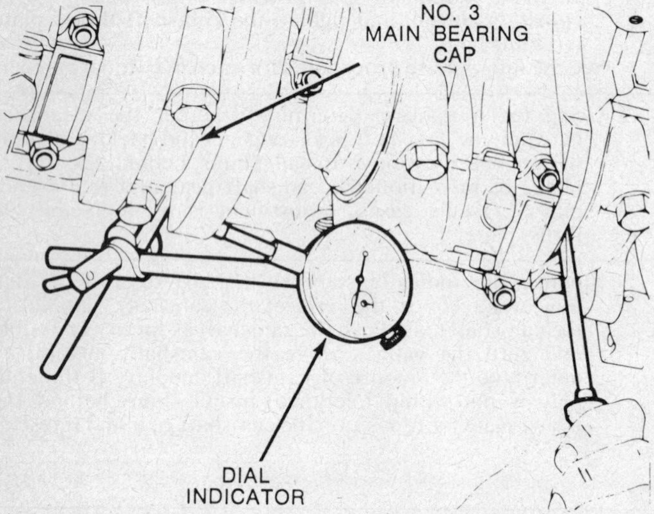

Checking crankshaft end-play with a dial indicator

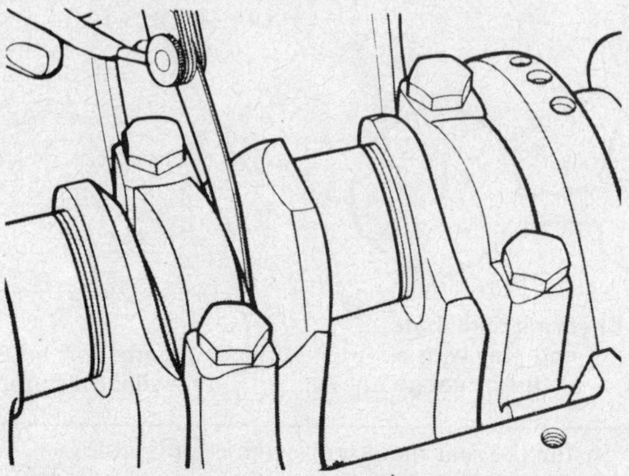

Checking crankshaft end-play with a feeler gauge

Procedure	*Method*
Install the pistons:	Press the upper connecting rod bearing halves into the connecting rods, and the lower halves into the connecting rod caps. Position the piston ring gaps according to specifications (see car section), and lubricate the pistons. Install a ring compresser on a piston, and press two long (8") pieces of plastic tubing over the rod bolts. Using the tubes as a guide, press the pistons into the bores and onto the crankshaft with a wooden hammer handle. After seating the rod on the crankshaft journal, remove the tubes and install the cap finger tight. Install the remaining pistons in the same manner. Invert the engine and check the bearing clearance at two points (90° apart) on each journal with Plastigage. NOTE: *Do not turn the crankshaft with Plastigage installed.* If clearance is within tolerances, remove *all* Plastigage, thoroughly lubricate the journals, and torque the rod caps to specifications. If clearance is not within specifications, install different thickness bearing inserts and recheck. CAUTION: *Never shim or file the connecting rods or caps.* Always install plastic tube sleeves over the rod bolts when the caps are not installed, to protect the crankshaft journals.

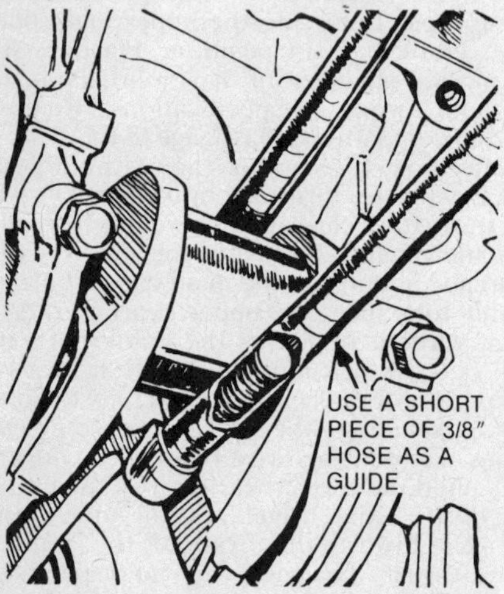

Tubing used to protect crankshaft journals and cylinder walls during piston installation

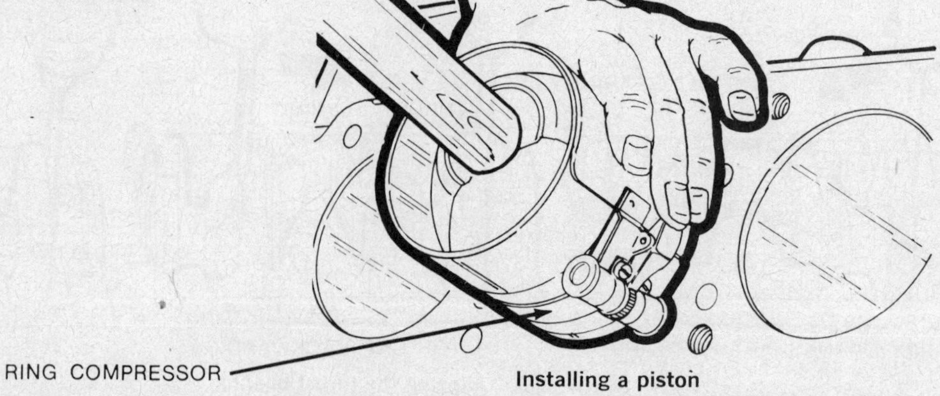

Installing a piston

CYLINDER BLOCK RECONDITIONING

Procedure	*Method*
Check connecting rod side clearance: 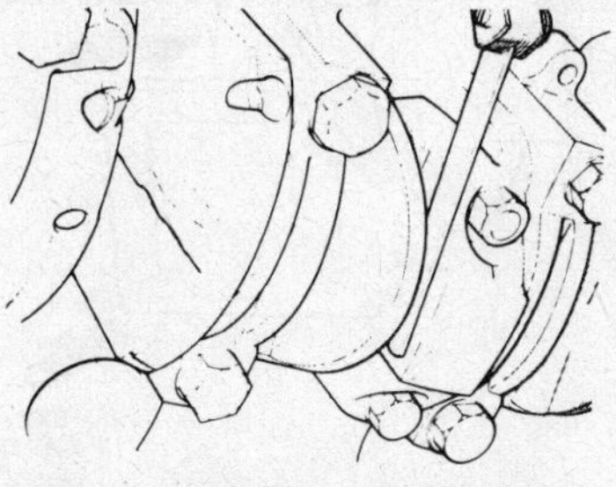 **Checking connecting rod side clearance**	Determine the clearance between the sides of the connecting rods and the crankshaft, using feeler gauges. If clearance is below the minimum tolerance, the rod may be machined to provide adequate clearance. If clearance is excessive, substitute an unworn rod, and recheck. If clearance is still outside specifications, the crankshaft must be welded and reground, or replaced.
Inspect the timing chain (or belt):	Visually inspect the timing chain for broken or loose links, and replace the chain if any are found. If the chain will flex sideways, it must be replaced. Install the timing chain as specified. Be sure the timing belt is not stretched, frayed or broken. NOTE: *If the original timing chain is to be reused, install it in its original position.*
Check timing gear backlash and runout (OHV engines): 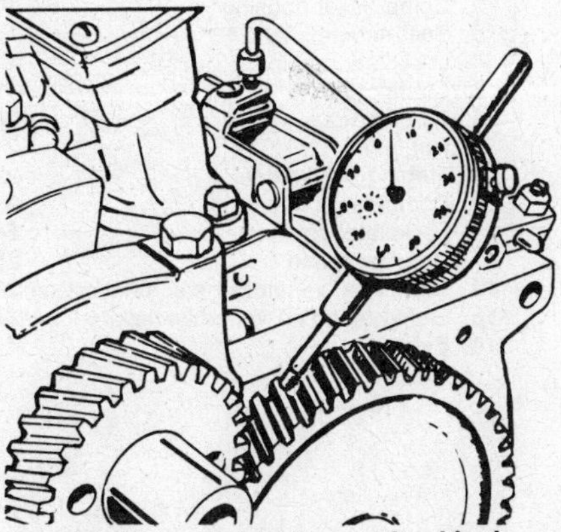 **Checking camshaft gear backlash**	Mount a dial indicator with its stem resting on a tooth of the camshaft gear (as illustrated). Rotate the gear until all slack is removed, and zero the indicator. Rotate the gear in the opposite direction until slack is removed, and record gear backlash. Mount the indicator with its stem resting on the edge of the camshaft gear, parallel to the axis of the camshaft. Zero the indicator, and turn the camshaft gear one full turn, recording the runout. If either backlash or runout exceed specifications, replace the worn gear(s).  **Checking camshaft gear runout**

Completing the Rebuilding Process

Following the above procedures, complete the rebuilding process as follows:

Fill the oil pump with oil, to prevent cavitating (sucking air) on initial engine start up. Install the oil pump and the pickup tube on the engine. Coat the oil pan gasket as necessary, and install the gasket and the oil pan. Mount the flywheel and the crankshaft vibration damper or pulley on the crankshaft. NOTE: *Always use new bolts when installing the flywheel.* Inspect the clutch shaft pilot bushing in the crankshaft. If the bushing is excessively worn, remove it with an expanding puller and a slide hammer, and tap a new bushing into place.

Position the engine, cylinder head side up. Lubricate the lifters, and install them into their bores. Install the cylinder head, and torque it as specified. Insert the pushrods (where applicable), and install the rocker shaft(s) (if so equipped) or position the rocker arms on the pushrods. Adjust the valves.

Install the intake and exhaust manifolds, the carburetor(s), the distributor and spark plugs. Adjust the point gap and the static ignition timing. Mount all accessories and install the engine in the car. Fill the radiator with coolant, and the crankcase with high quality engine oil.

Break-in Procedure

Start the engine, and allow it to run at low speed for a few minutes, while checking for leaks. Stop the engine, check the oil level, and fill as necessary. Restart the engine, and fill the cooling system to capacity. Check the point dwell angle and adjust the ignition timing and the valves. Run the engine at low to medium speed (800-2500 rpm) for approximately 1/2 hour, and retorque the cylinder head bolts. Road test the car, and check again for leaks.

Follow the manufacturer's recommended engine break-in procedure and maintenance schedule for new engines.

DESCRIPTION

A turbocharger is an exhaust-driven turbine which drives a centrifugal compressor wheel. The compressor is usually located between the air cleaner and the engine's intake manifold, while the turbine is located between the exhaust manifold and the muffler. Primarily, the turbocharger compresses the air entering the engine, forcing more air into the cylinders. This allows the engine to efficiently burn more fuel, thereby producing more horsepower.

All of the exhaust gases pass through the turbine housing. The expansion of these gases, acting on the turbine wheel, causes it to turn. After passing through the turbine the exhaust gases are routed to the atmosphere through the exhaust system. On some non-automotive applications, the turbocharger provides sufficient muffling of the exhaust noises to eliminate the need for a muffler.

The turbine also functions as a spark arrester. For example, the US Department of Agriculture recognizes the turbocharger as an adequate spark arrester for forestry operations.

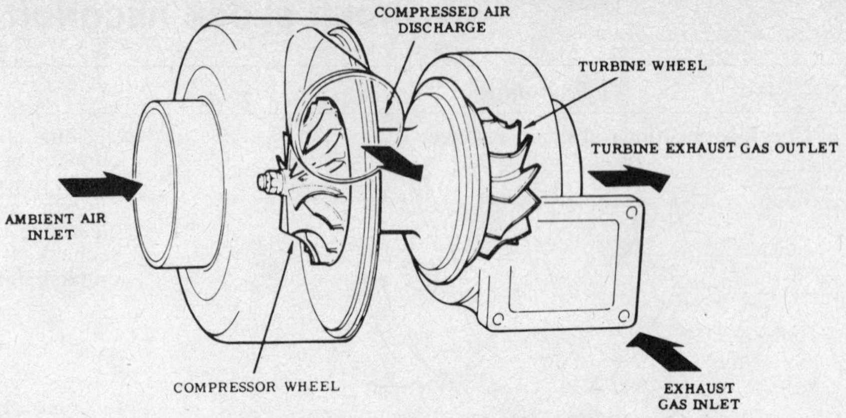

Typical turbocharger air flow schematic

OPERATION

The compressor and turbine are each enclosed in their own housings and are directly connected by a shaft. The housings are constructed of light alloy and are designed for maximum heat dissipation. The only power loss from the turbine to the compressor is the slight friction of the shaft journal bearings. Air is drawn in through the filtered intake system, compressed by the compressor wheel and discharged into the intake manifold. The extra charge of air provided by the turbocharger allows more fuel to be burned, providing more power.

As engine speed increases, the length of

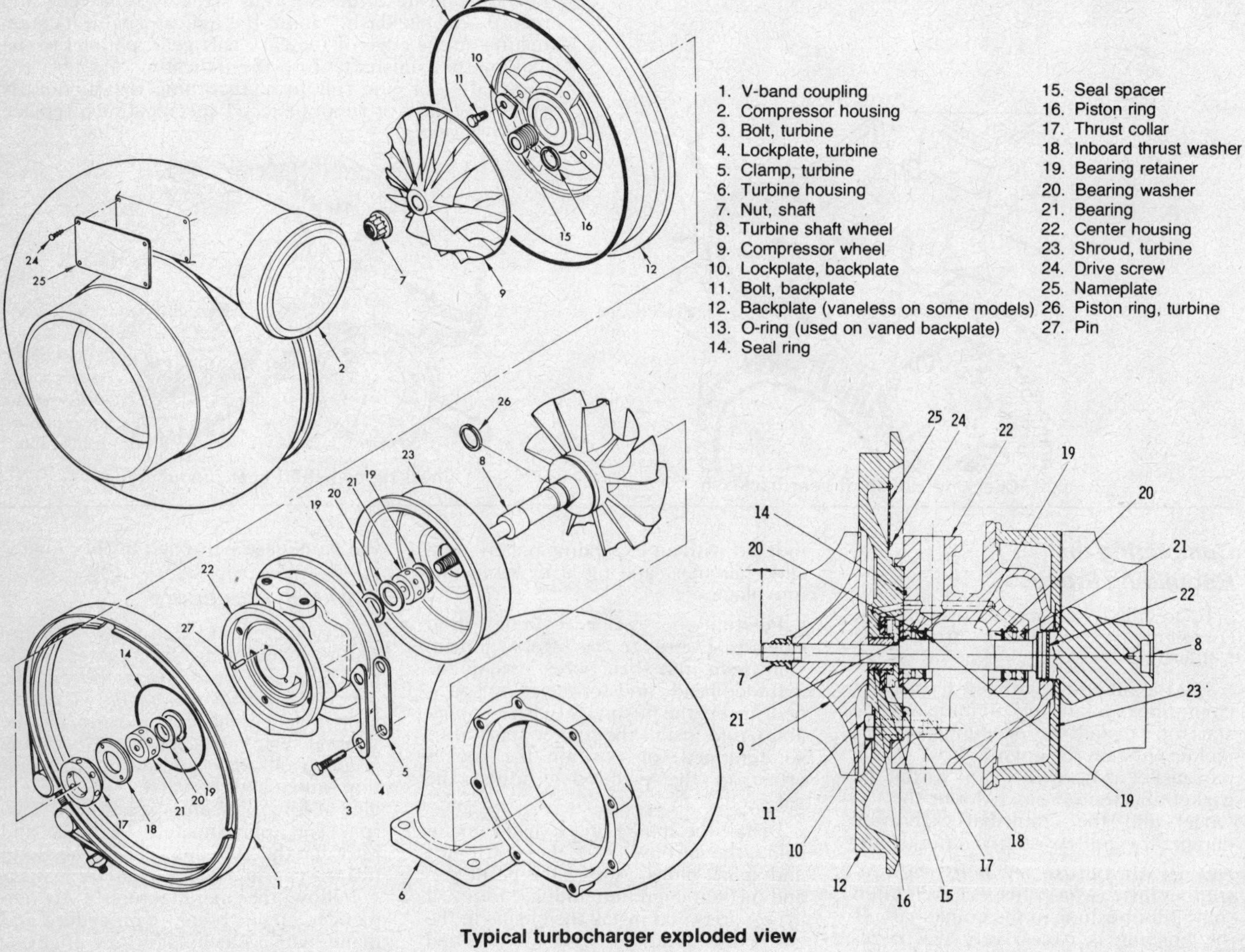

1. V-band coupling
2. Compressor housing
3. Bolt, turbine
4. Lockplate, turbine
5. Clamp, turbine
6. Turbine housing
7. Nut, shaft
8. Turbine shaft wheel
9. Compressor wheel
10. Lockplate, backplate
11. Bolt, backplate
12. Backplate (vaneless on some models)
13. O-ring (used on vaned backplate)
14. Seal ring
15. Seal spacer
16. Piston ring
17. Thrust collar
18. Inboard thrust washer
19. Bearing retainer
20. Bearing washer
21. Bearing
22. Center housing
23. Shroud, turbine
24. Drive screw
25. Nameplate
26. Piston ring, turbine
27. Pin

Typical turbocharger exploded view

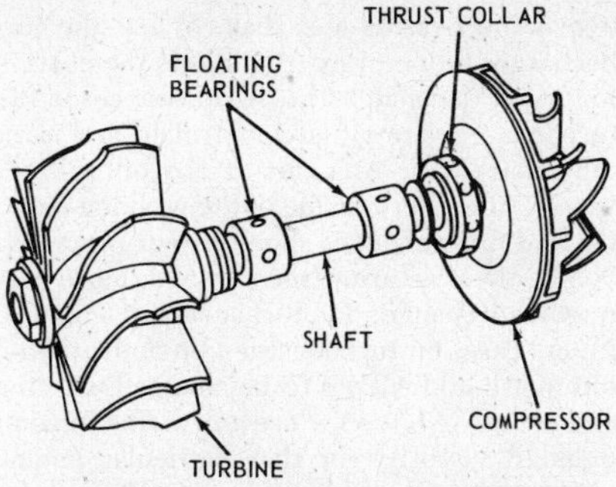

Basic parts of the turbocharger

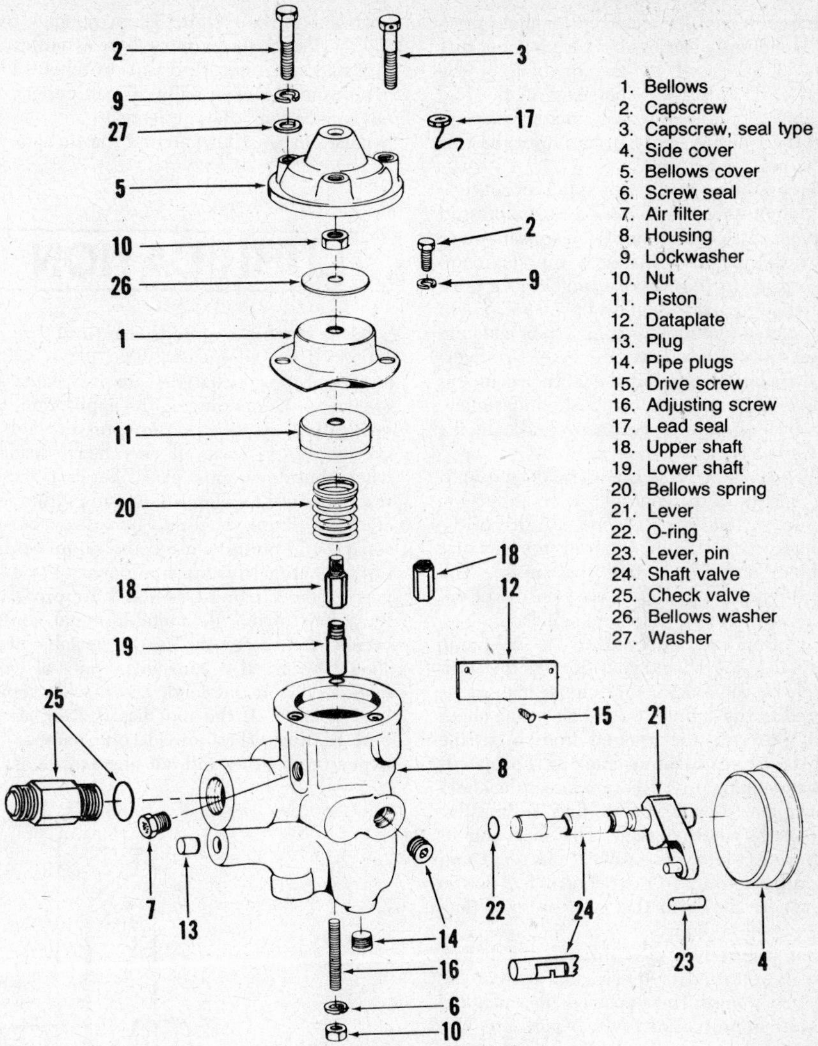

Aneroid exploded view

time the intake valves are open decreases, giving the air less time to fill the cylinders. On an engine running at 2500 rpm, the intake valves are open less than 0.017 second. The air drawn into a naturally aspirated engine's cylinder is less than atmospheric pressure. Turbochargers pack air into the cylinder at greater than atmospheric pressure at all speeds. The flow of exhaust gas from each cylinder occurs intermittantly as the exhaust valve opens. This results in fluctuating gas pressures, also known as pulse energy, at the turbine inlet. With a conventional turbine housing, only a small amount of pulse energy is used.

To better utilize these impulses, one design has an internal division in the turbine housing and the exhaust manifold which directs these exhaust gases to the turbine wheel. There is a separate passage for each half of the engine cylinder exhaust.

On some four and six cylinder engines built to accommodate turbochargers, there is a separate passage for the front two or three cylinders and another for the rear half.

By using a fully divided exhaust system combined with a dual scroll turbine housing, the result is a highly effective nozzle velocity. This produces higher turbine speeds and manifold pressures than can be obtained with an undivided system.

At high altitudes, a naturally aspirated engine drops 3% in horsepower per 1000 feet elevation due to a 3% decrease in air density per 1000 feet.

With a turbocharged engine, an increase in altitude also increases the pressure drop across the turbine. Inlet turbine pressure remains the same, but the outlet pressure decreases as the altitude increases. Turbine speed also increases as the pressure difference increases. The compressor wheel turns faster, providing approximately the same inlet pressure as at sea level, even though the incoming air is less dense.

There are, however, limitations to the actual amount of compensation for altitude provided by the turbocharger. These limitations are primarily a result of varying amounts of boost pressure and turbocharger-to-engine match. To make up for the difference in altitude compensation, an altitude compensator is added to the system. During rapid acceleration or rapid engine load changes, the tur-

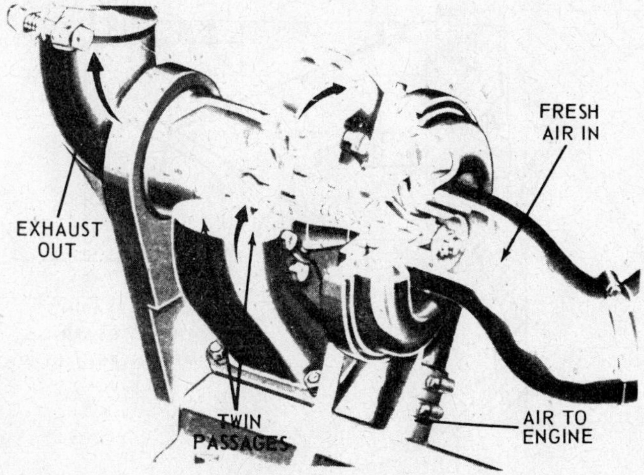

Twin passage turbine

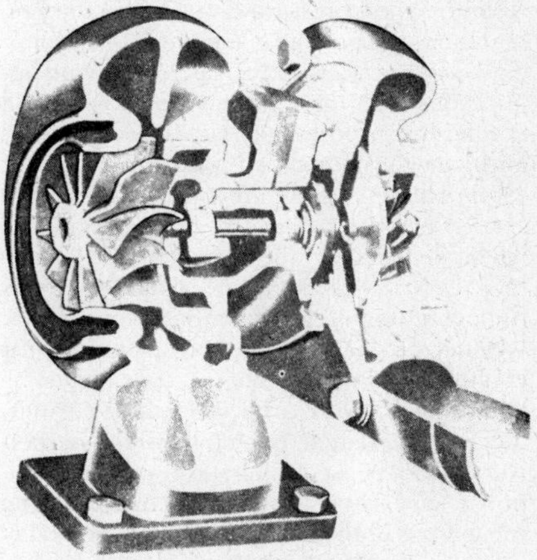
Altitude compensator

bocharger speed, reflected in manifold pressure, inherently lags behind the power or fuel demand exercised by the opening of the throttle. This lag does not exist in the fuel system, so an overly rich mixture accompanied by heavy smoke occurs until the turbocharger catches up.

On diesel engines, two types of altitude compensators are used. One is a compressed air type which is very similar in appearance to the turbocharger. This type supplies compressed air to the intake manifold at a pressure about equal to sea level pressure. There is no increase of fuel for combustion and consequently no horsepower increase. However, the extra air provided by the altitude compensator usually increases combustion efficiency, thereby increasing fuel economy and reducing smoke levels.

The second type is the aneroid type unit. The function of the aneroid is to create a lag in the fuel system response equal to that of the turbocharger, thereby control the mixture problem and eliminating the smoke. The aneroid system is widely used on diesel engines and on some gasoline engines.

Fuel from the outlet side of the fuel pump enters the aneroid and goes through the starting check valve area. On others, it must be located in the supply line. The starting check valve prevents the aneroid from bypassing fuel at the engine during cranking. For speeds above cranking, fuel pressure forces the check valve open, allowing fuel to flow to the valve port of the aneroid shaft. The shaft and its bore form the bypass valve. This shaft and bore allow passage or restriction of fuel flow in a manner similar to that of a pressure/time type injection pump.

Fuel allowed to pass through the bypass valve is returned to the suction side of the injection pump. The bypassed fuel manifold pressure in proportion to the bypass rate. The shaft and sleeve are bypassing fuel when the control arm on the aneroid is resting against the adjusting screw. The amount of fuel bypassed is regulated by this screw which is located at the bottom of the aneroid body. The control lever, which is connected to a piston in the aneroid body by an actuating shaft, rotates the shaft closing the valve port. The lever is actuated by manifold pressure against the piston and diaphragm. Anytime the manifold pressure is above a present air actuating pressure, the aneroid is effectively out of the system. When pressure drops below the preset figure, the aneroid comes into the system.

In modern automotive gasoline engine applications with their stricter emission control standards, turbocharger lag is compensated for by means of modified spark control and/or an enrichment vacuum regulator system. The spark control system changes the ignition timing on demand and the vacuum regulator system regulates vacuum flow at the carburetor through a remote power enrichment port.

Some engines, particularly passenger car applications, in which boost pressure must be held at low levels, utilize a wastegate unit. Since turbocharger operation is self-perpetuating, unchecked operation will increase boost pressure beyond the operating capabilities of these engines. Some method of limiting this boost increases must be used. The principle means is by the inclusion of a wastegate in the system. The wastegate, usually located in the outlet elbow assembly, is activated when boost pressure reaches a predetermined level (usually 3-7 psi depending on application). The wastegate opens and bypasses exhaust flow around the turbine.

LUBRICATION

Since turbine speeds routinely reach 140,000 rpm, adequate lubrication is vitally important. Turbochargers are lubricated by engine oil. Depending on the application, the lubrication may be either pressure-fed or gravity-fed. In areas of very heavy load or when shut-down after peak operation is routine, pressure feeding, sometimes with a separate oil pump, is used. In cases where a separate oil pump is used, the pump continues operating during spin-down. Since all parts of the rotating assemblies are protected by a film of oil, no metal-to-metal contact occurs. Consequently, no appreciable wear should occur. If a constant supply of clean engine oil is maintained, bearing life should be indefinite. If the unit has floating sleeve type bearings, they provide oil clearance between the bearing and housing as well as between the bearing and shaft. When the turbocharger is operating, this allows the bearing to turn as the shaft turns. All clearances in the turbocharger are closely controlled and carefully machined. Any dirt in the oil will adversely affect service life of the working parts. Oil and filter changes should occur regularly. Some manufacturers recommend more frequent oil changes for turbocharged engines. In any case, on turbocharged engines, the oil filter(s) should ALWAYS be changed with the engine oil. ALWAYS use oil of the recommended viscosity for that particular engine application. Check the owner's manual for your engine or vehicle for recommended intervals and proper viscosity.

TWO-CYCLE APPLICATIONS

Turbochargers may be used in addition to the regular scavenging process. In these cases, the air is drawn into the blower or scavenging pump and then transferred to the turbocharger where it is compressed and forced into the engine.

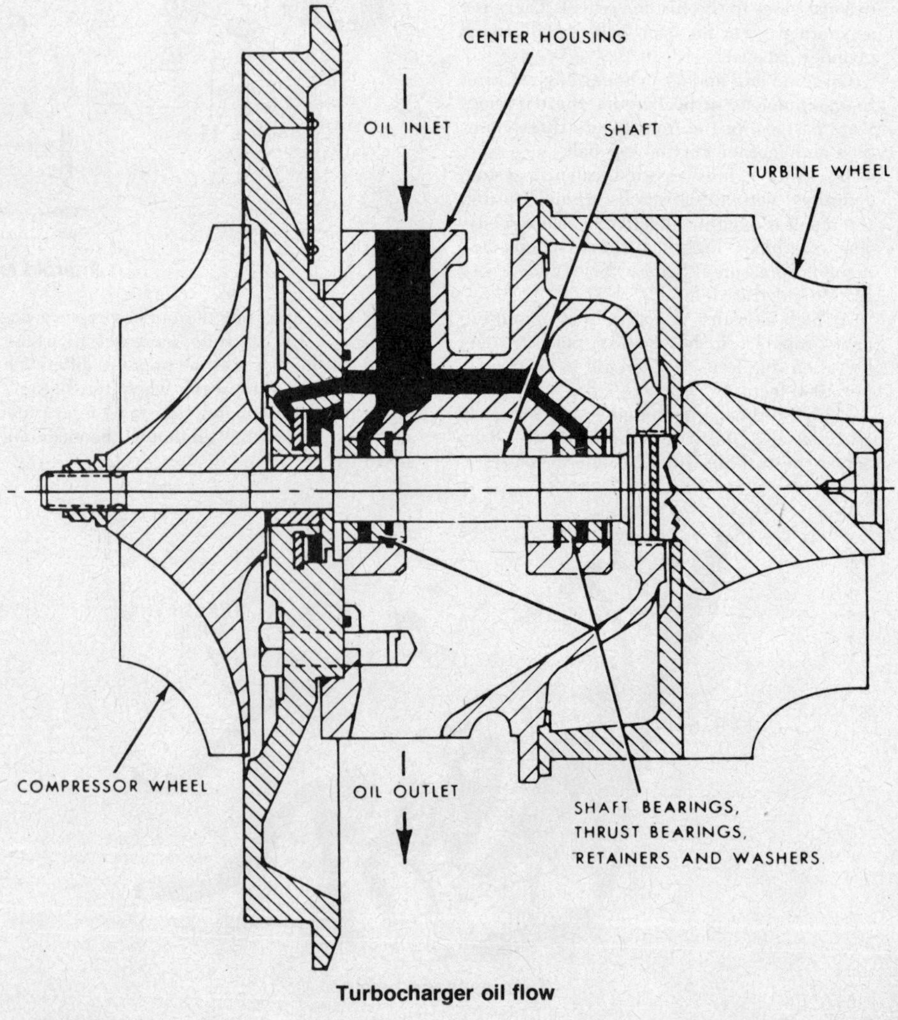

Turbocharger oil flow

At light loads, there is little energy available to drive the turbocharger. The mechanically driven blower alone supplies scavenging air to cylinders. At increased loads, the turbocharger speeds up and takes in a sufficient amount of additional air to allow the inlet pressure to drop to atmospheric levels, causing the blower check valve to open. At this engine speed, the blower becomes unloaded, saving engine power, and the turbocharger enters the load range where it alone can provide scavenging and turbocharging. Under ideal conditions, the engine starting air contains enough energy to start the turbocharger and also supply enough air for combustion. In some applications, however, turbochargers can be equipped with additional methods for supplying necessary scavenging air while the engine is being started. This can be accomplished either mechanically by coupling the turbocharger to the crankshaft in such a manner that it is mechanically driven during starting and automatically disconnects when exhaust pressure is high enough or by jet air starting, where air is blown through jets into the turbocharger turbine or compressor. The air passing through the compressor also aids in scavenging during starting.

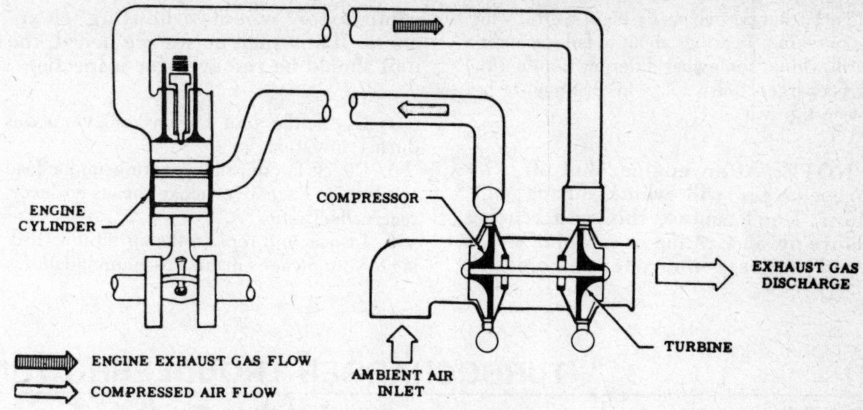

Two cycle air flow

INTERCOOLERS

When the air passing through the compressor is compressed it becomes heated and expands. Expanding air is less dense, therefore less air is forced into the engine. This helps defeat the turbocharging process. To overcome this condition, some engine applications use a heat exchanger, also known as an intercooler or after cooler. The intercooler reduces intake air temperature by as much as 90° F.

Located between the turbocharger and the intake manifold, the intercooler is a series of connected tubes, finned to provide dissipation, through which engine coolant is circulated. The carrying off of heat from the air makes the air denser, allowing more air to be forced into the engine. This provides more power, greater economy and quieter combustion.

GENERAL OPERATING INSTRUCTIONS FOR TURBOCHARGED ENGINES

1. After starting the engine, make sure there is sufficient oil pressure before accelerating or applying load.
2. When starting in cold weather, allow the engine to run a sufficient length of time (up to five minutes for diesel engines in extreme cold) before applying load or accelerating. This will insure adequate lubrication.
3. Should the engine stall at normal operating temperature, restart it immediately. This will prevent a rapid rise in the turbocharger known as "temperature soaking". Also, the turbocharger, running hot during operation, may experience coking due to hot oil build-up in the center section. This coking will cause a blockage of the oil passages leading to failure of the unit.
4. Before stopping the engine, allow it to run for a short length of time (up to two or three minutes for some diesels) to allow internal engine temperatures to normalize or equalize. Failure to allow temperature normalization can lead to heat fatique and/or blockage of oil passages due to coking.

CAUTION

When transporting an engine equipped with a turbocharger, always cover the exhaust outlet. This will prevent entrance of foreign material and/or the rotation of the turbine. Turbine rotation on a stopped engine could lead to bearing failure since no lubricating oil will be provided.

PREVENTIVE MAINTENANCE

1. Inspect all mountings and connections regularly to make sure they are secure and no leakage is present.
2. Make certain that there is no restriction in air flow at the crankcase ventilation system.
3. Run the engine at various, normal operating speeds and listen for unusual noises at the turbocharger.

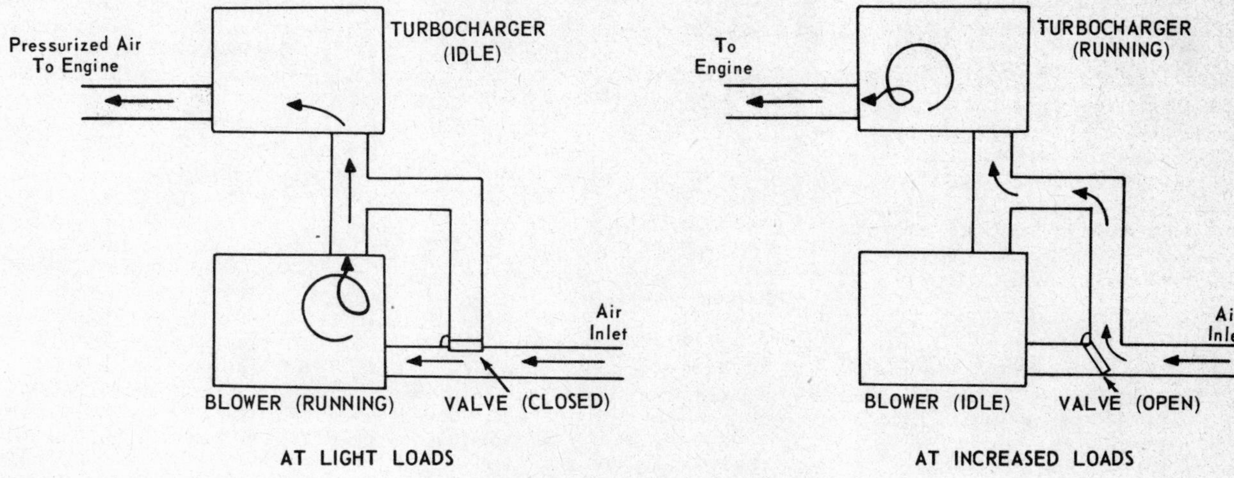

Scavenging pump and turbocharger

Turbochargers normally emit a shrill whistle or whine. Bearings about to fail also emit a shrill whine, somewhat different from normal turbocharger noise. Try to distinguish between the two.

NOTE: After engine shut-off, the turbocharger will whine during rundown. Don't confuse this with bearing failure noise. Grating or scraping noises could indicate improper turbine or compressor wheel-to-housing clearances. If any such noises are heard, the unit should be removed for inspection.

4. Check the unit for unusual vibrations during operation.
5. Check for unusual smoking under load conditions. Excessive smoke means an incorrect air/fuel ratio.
6. Inspect and replace the air filter according to your owner's manual recommendations.

TROUBLE-SHOOTING

The turbocharger is a relatively simple unit. Most problems occur in other parts of the engine such as the lubrication system or the fuel system. With proper routine maintenance, the unit should give troublefree operation.

TURBOCHARGER TROUBLESHOOTING CHART

Trouble	Possible Cause	Remedy
Noisy operation or vibration.	Bearings not being lubricated.	Supply required oil pressure. Clean or replace oil line. If trouble persists, overhaul the turbocharger.
	Leak in engine intake or exhaust manifold.	Tighten loose connections or replace manifold gaskets.
Engine will not deliver rated power.	Clogged manifold system.	Clear all ducting.
	Foreign matter lodged in compressor, impeller, or turbine.	Disassemble and clean.
	Excessive buildup in compressor.	Thoroughly clean compressor assembly. Clean air cleaner and check for leaks.
	Leak in engine intake or exhaust manifold.	Tighten loose connections or replace manifold gaskets.
	Rotating assembly bearing seizure.	Overhaul turbocharger.
Oil seal leakage.	Failure of seal.	Overhaul turbocharger.
	Restriction in air cleaner or air intake creating suction.	Remove the restriction.

INDEX

TRANSAXLES

BEFORE SERVICING, SEE THE SAFETY NOTICE ON THE CONTENTS PAGE

TYPE 1

4 Speed Transmission–Model KM 110 (Mitsubishi)

1975-78 Colt
1976-78 Arrow

DISASSEMBLY

1. Using a 3/16 in. punch, drive out the clutch spring pins. Remove the clutch shaft with release fork and springs.
2. Remove the speedometer gear assembly and the lockplate. Remove the clutch and the back-up light switches.
3. The extension housing can be removed by tapping lightly with a hammer.
4. With the transmission inverted remove the bottom cover.
5. Remove the speedometer drive snap-rings, and gear. Remove the main drive gear retainer. Remove the countershaft stopper.
6. Remove the countershaft rearward. Remove the countergear, 40 roller bearings, spacers, and front and rear washers.
7. Lift out the thrust washer, rear idler gear, needle bearings, and spacer located on the reverse idler gear shaft.
8. Withdraw the gear shaft bolt and pull the shaft from the case. Remove the front idler gear.
9. Locate the three plugs on the left case side. Remove them and the poppet springs and balls.
10. Loosen the reverse shift bar and reverse locking bolt. Pull out the reverse shift bar. Remove the reverse shaft fork and spacer.
11. Using a 3/16 in. punch, drive the fork spring pins and shift bar from the mount. Remove the shift bar and the shaft fork. Do not disassemble the shift bar.
12. Remove the reverse gear from the case.
13. Remove the mainshaft and the main drive gear synchronizer ring.
14. Pull the main drive gear assembly from the case front. Remove all snap-rings.
15. Remove the shifter assembly.

TRANSMISSION SPECIFICATIONS:

Helical gear backlash: 0.002-0.006 in.

Shift fork to sleeve clearance: 0.004-0.008 in.

Spur gear backlash: 0.004-0.008 in.

Gear change lever-selector groove clearance: 0.004-0.012 in.

Reverse shift fork-reverse gear groove clearance: 0.004-0.012 in.

ASSEMBLY

1. Press the bearing onto the main drive gear.
2. Secure it with the snap-ring of appropriate thickness to give an end-play of 0.002 in.

Snap-Ring Code (in.):
White 0.091
None 0.093
Red 0.094
Yellow 0.098

3. Assemble the hub and synchronizer ring.

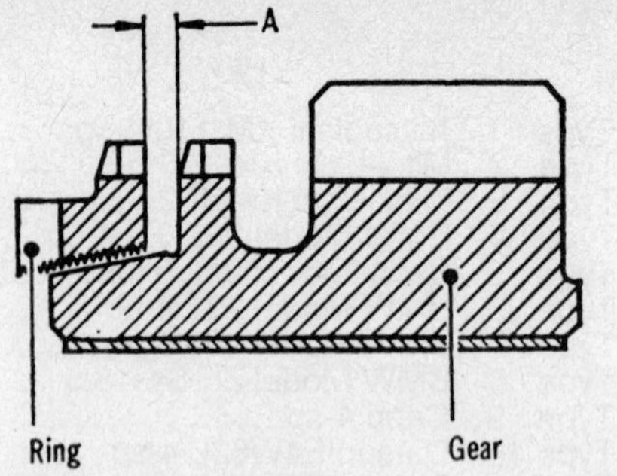

Synchronizer inspection—Dimension A = 0.059 in.

4. Place the front and rear springs on the shaft in opposite directions.
5. Assemble the second gear synchronizer hub with the stepped gear end (narrow toothed side rearward).
6. Install the needle bearings and third gear onto the mainshaft from the front end.
7. Install the snychronizer assembly.
8. Assemble the first-second synchronizer in the same direction it was removed.
9. Fit the snap-rings to give a proper end-play of 0.0012-0.0075 in. Third-fourth gear hub end-play is 0.00-0.0043 in.

Snap-Ring Code (in.):
None 0.085
Yellow 0.087
Green 0.090
Blue 0.093

10. Place the needle bearings and the second gear on the mainshaft from the rear.
11. Install the synchronizer assembly.

1. Flywheel
2. Transmission case
3. Main drive gear
4. Synchronizer sleeve (for third-fourth speed)
5. Third-speed gear
6. Second-speed gear
7. Synchronizer sleeve (for first-second speeds)
8. First-speed gear
9. Rear bearing retainer
10. Reverse gear
11. Control shaft
12. Gearshift lever assembly
13. Pressure plate assembly
14. Counter gear
15. Under cover
16. Mainshaft
17. Reverse idler gear
18. Extension housing
19. Shift fork (reverse)
20. Speedometer drive gear

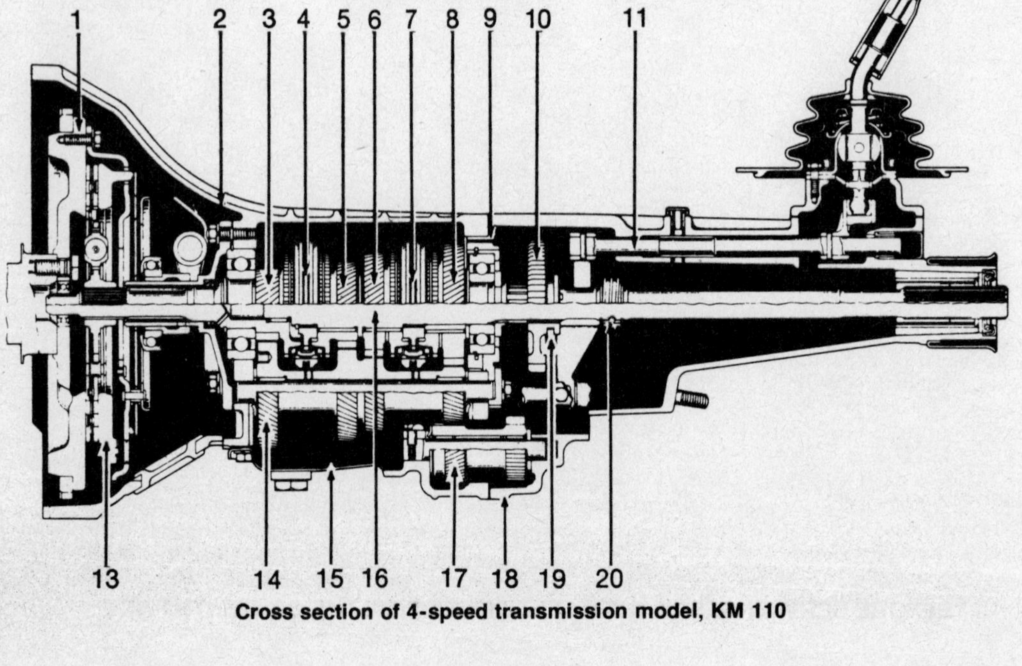

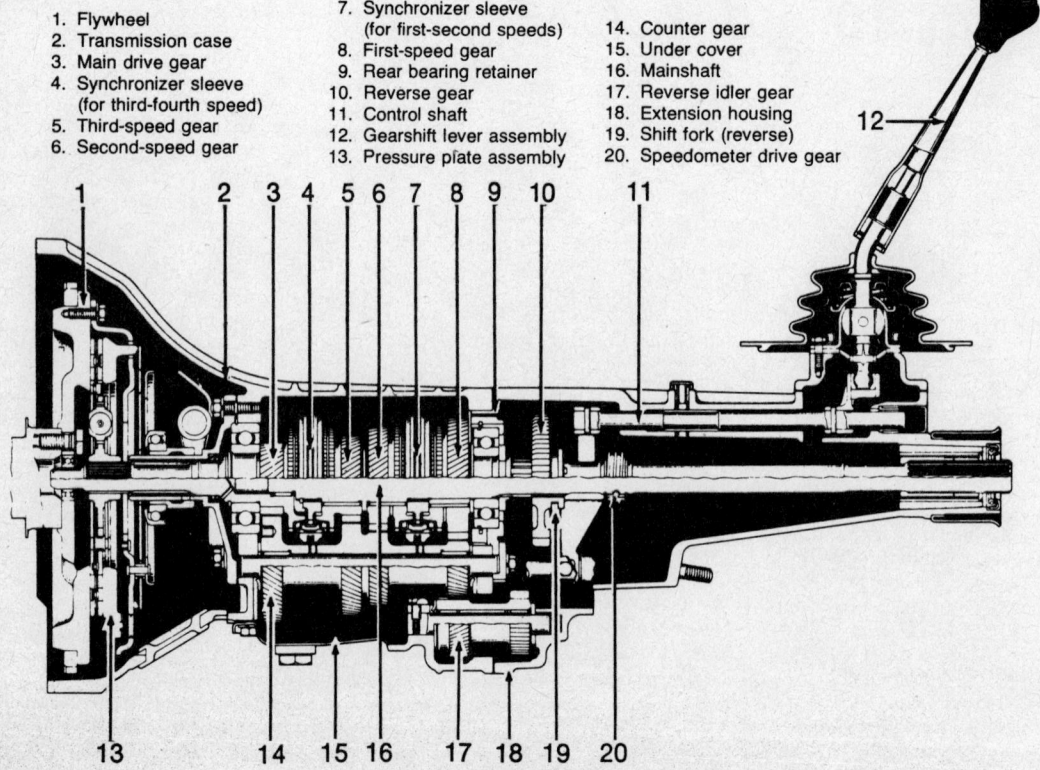

Cross section of 4-speed transmission model, KM 110

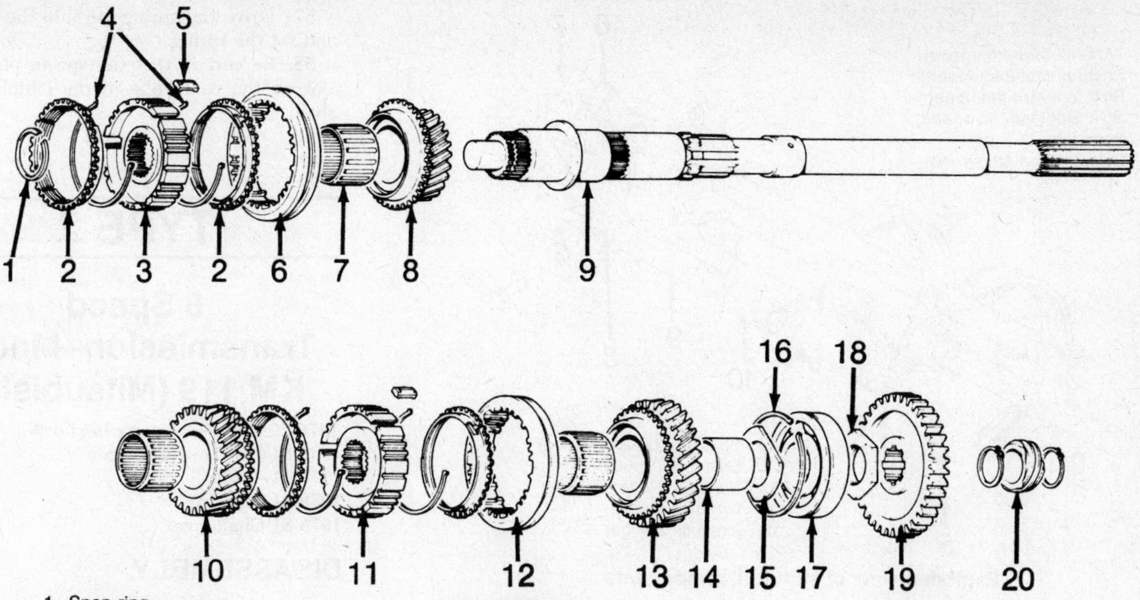

1. Snap-ring
2. Synchronizer ring
3. Synchronizer hub (3rd-4th speeds)
4. Synchronizer spring
5. Synchronizer piece
6. Synchronizer sleeve (3rd-4th speeds)
7. Needle bearing
8. 3rd-speed gear
9. Mainshaft
10. 2nd-speed gear
11. Synchronizer hub (1st-2nd speeds)
12. Synchronizer sleeve (1st-2nd speeds)
13. Low-speed gear
14. Spacer bushing
15. Spacer
16. Snap-ring
17. Ball bearing
18. Locknut
19. Reverse gear
20. Speedometer drive gear

Exploded view of mainshaft components

12. Check and adjust the end-play to 0.0012-0.0075 in.

13. Place the first gear spacer, middle bearings, synchronizer, and first gear on the shaft.

14. Adjust end-play to 0.0012-0.0075 in.

15. Spacer must be installed with the I mark in the direction of the ball bearing.

16. Install the mainshaft bearing with a suitable driver and tighten the locknut.

17. Install the snap-ring and retainer.

18. Adjust to give a mainshaft bearing end-play of 0.00-0.006 in.

Snap-Ring Code (in.):
None 0.057
Red 0.060
White 0.064
Yellow 0.067
Blue 0.071

19. Invert the transmission case.

20. Install the main drive gear assembly into the transmission case.

21. Place the needle bearings on the main drive gear front end.

22. Install the synchronizer ring.

23. Be certain that all synchronizer rings are in proper mesh.

24. Install the rear bearing retainer in the case.

25. Place the reverse gear in position on the mainshaft. Install the shift fork into the shift fork groove in the synchronizer sleeve. While holding the forks, place the third-fourth shift bar assembly into the case through the lower rear hole.

26. Insert the first interlock plunger in the case; drive the plunger into position with the use of an appropriate driver.

27. Place the first-second gear shift bar assembly into the case. Position the shift forks so that the pin holes are aligned with the shift bar holes. Secure the shift forks to the shift bars with spring pins into position with the slot of the centerline of the shift bar.

28. Insert the second interlock plunger into the case.

29. Place the reverse shift fork ends in the reverse gear groove. Insert the reverse gear bar into the fork. Install the spacer on the shift bar and place the reverse shift bar assembly into the case. Secure the fork to the bar with a locking bolt.

30. Position the poppet balls and springs. Insert the plugs with commercial sealant. Be certain to install the tapered end of the poppet spring toward the poppet balls.

To install the reverse idler gear:

Place the needle bearings and spacers in position on the rear reverse idler gear. Insert the assembly into the rear of the case. Place the front idler gear with the thrust washer onto the rear shaft end. Insert the gear shaft in the case and secure with a bolt.

31. Measure the size from the rear surface of the transmission case to the rear of the reverse idler gear.

32. Measure the depth from the extension housing end to the idler gear shaft end. Add 0.004 in. This figure is the extension housing packing thickness.

33. Subtract NO. 2 from NO. 1. Subtract 0.009-0.012 in. (thrust washer clearance) from the result. (This figure is the thickness of the thrust washer required.)

Thrust Washer Identification (in.):
A-0.078
B-0.085
C-0.093
D-0.100

To install the countergear:

34. Insert the needle roller bearings (20 front, 20 rear) and spacers in the front and rear holes of the countergear.

35. Be sure the spacers are installed on the outside of the roller bearings.

36. Install a 1.378 in. OD thrust washer on the rear end.

37. Install a 1.181 in. ID thrust washer on the rear end.

38. Holding the countergear cluster inside the case, install the countergear shaft from the rear and properly mesh the gears.

39. Select a tear thrust washer to give 0.002-0.007 in. countergear end-play.

40. Secure the rear shaft end with a stopper plate.

41. Place the front bearing retainer in position and install the front bearing.

42. Bearing-to-retainer clearance should be 0.002-0.0012 in.

43. Place the speedometer drive gear on the mainshaft.

44. There should be no clearance between the speedometer gear and the snap-ring.

45. Shim if necessary.

46. Connect the extension housing to the transmission case.

47. When installing the washers, install with the bulged side toward the bolt head.

48. Install the transmission and backup light switch.

49. Next, install the locking plate and the transmission driven gear.

50. Finally, secure the under-cover to the transmission.

51. Place the gear lever in the first gear gate.

52. Be sure the nylon bushing is in the vertical position.

1. Shift rail (3rd-4th speed)
2. Shift rail (1st-2nd speed)
3. Shift fork (3rd-4th speed)
4. Shift fork (1st-2nd speed)
5. Spring pin
6. Selector (3rd-4th speed)

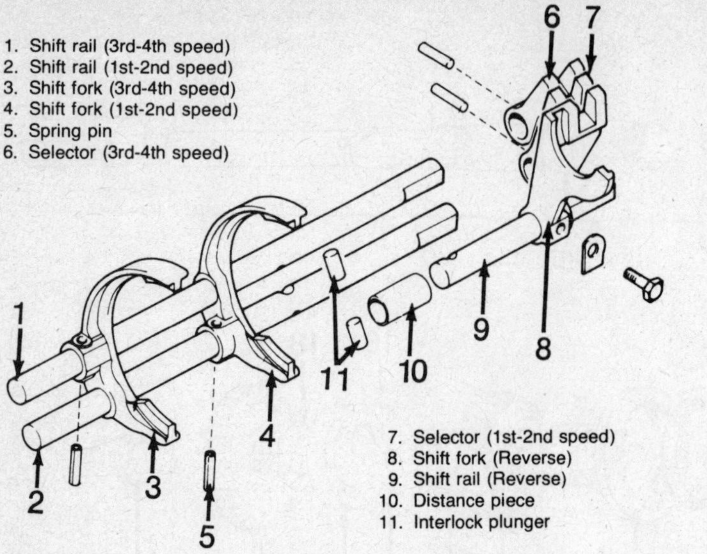

7. Selector (1st-2nd speed)
8. Shift fork (Reverse)
9. Shift rail (Reverse)
10. Distance piece
11. Interlock plunger

Exploded view of shift rail components

53. With the transmission in the car, apply sealant to the packings and grease bushings.

54. Insert the clutch control shaft into the transmission from the left-hand side.

55. Assemble the shift fork and springs onto the shaft.

56. Align the shift fork with the clutch control shaft.

57. Drive the spring pin into the pin hole and set the spring.

58. Be certain that the spring pin has its slot on the centerline of the clutch control shaft.

TYPE 2

5 Speed Transmission–Model KM 119 (Mitsubishi)

1976-79 Colt exc. front wheel drive
1980-81 Colt Station Wagon
1976-81 Arrow
1978-81 Sapporo
1978-81 Challenger

DISASSEMBLY

1. Remove the clutch assembly.
2. Remove the under cover.
3. Remove the backup lamp switch. Remove the steel ball from the extension housing.
4. Remove the extension housing assem-

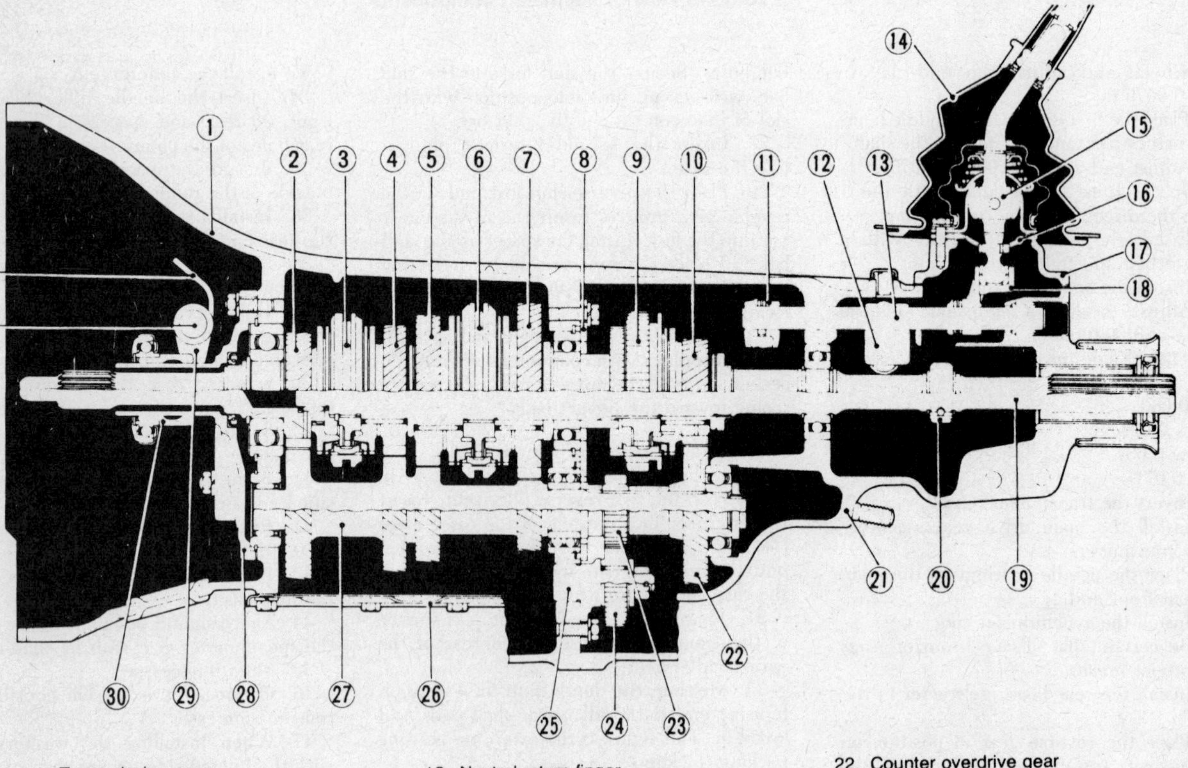

1. Transmission case
2. Main drive pinion
3. Synchronizer assy (3-4 speed)
4. 3rd speed gear
5. 2nd speed gear
6. Synchronizer assy (1-2 speed)
7. 1st speed gear
8. Rear bearing retainer
9. Synchronizer assy (overdrive)
10. Overdrive gear
11. Control finger
12. Neutral return finger
13. Control shaft
14. Control level cover
15. Control lever assy
16. Stopper plate
17. Control housing
18. Change shifter
19. Mainshaft
20. Speedometer drive gear
21. Extension housing
22. Counter overdrive gear
23. Counter reverse gear
24. Reverse idler gear
25. Reverse idler gear shaft
26. Under cover
27. Counter gear
28. Front bearing retainer
29. Clutch shift arm
30. Release bearing carrier
31. Clutch control shaft
32. Return spring

Cross section of 5-speed transmission, model KM 119

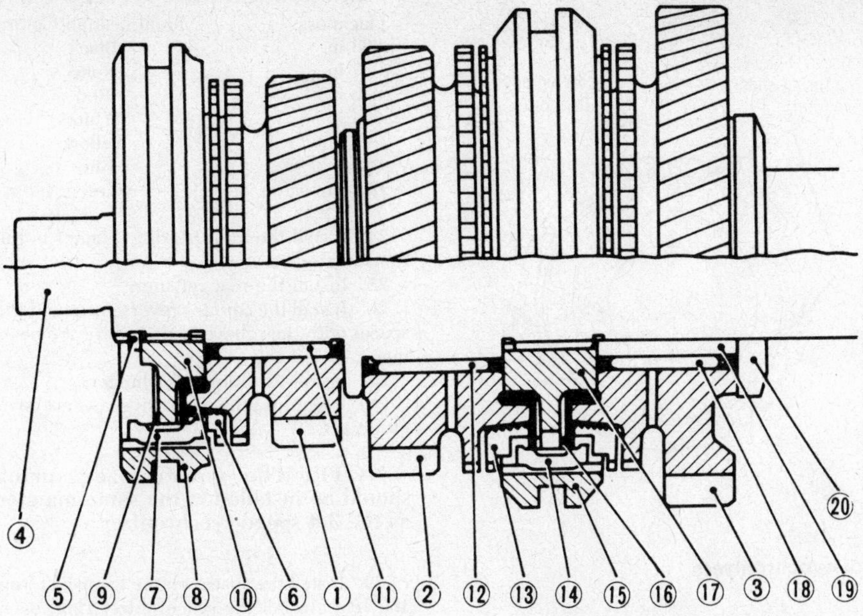

1. 3rd speed gear
2. 2nd speed gear
3. 1st speed gear
4. Mainshaft
5. Snap ring
6. Synchronizer ring (3-4 speed)
7. Synchronizer piece
8. Synchronizer sleeve (3-4 speed)
9. Synchronizer spring (3-4 speed)
10. Synchronizer hub (3-4 speed)
11. Needle bearing (3rd speed gear)
12. Needle bearing (2nd speed gear)
13. Synchronizer ring (1-2 speed)
14. Synchronizer piece
15. Synchronizer sleeve (1-2 speed)
16. Synchronizer spring (1-2 speed)
17. Synchronizer hub (1-2 speed)
18. Needle bearing (1st speed gear)
19. 1st gear bearing sleeve
20. Bearing spacer

Assembled view of mainshaft

bly, with the gearshift lever placed in the reverse and overtop position.

5. Remove the snap-ring. Remove the speedometer drive gear and the steel ball. Also remove the gear front snap-ring.

6. Remove the mainshaft rear bearing. Remove the bearing front snap-ring.

7. Remove the reverse idler gear and related parts.

8. Loosen and remove the mainshaft intermediate locknut and the countershaft gear rear end locknut. The mainshaft intermediate locknut cannot be removed and therefore is to be loosened only.

9. Remove the three poppet springs from the right-hand side of the transmission case, and then remove three poppet springs and three balls.

10. Remove the cotter pin retaining the 1-2 and 3-4 speed shift forks.

11. Pull the 1-2 speed shift rail toward the rear of the case. Remove the counter overdrive gear and the ball bearing simultaneously with the rail.

12. Pull the 3-4 speed shift rail out toward the rear of the case.

13. Remove the mainshaft nut.

14. Remove the overdrive-reverse synchronizer assembly, the overdrive gear, and the overdrive-reverse shift rail and shift fork at the same time. Pull off the spacer also.

15. Remove two interlock plungers.

16. Remove the spacer and the counter reverse gear.

17. Remove the rear retainer.

18. Remove the front bearing retainer and spacer.

19. Insert rear stopper plate special tool between the clutch gear and synchronizer ring of the 3rd speed gear, and the front stopper plate between the clutch gear and the synchronizer ring of the main drive gear.

NOTE: The front and rear stopper plates inserted are special tools used to prevent the 3-4 speed synchronizer from damage by the main drive gear bearing when these bearings are removed or installed.

20. Remove the mainshaft bearing snap-ring. Remove the ball bearing. After removal of the bearing, slide special tool Mainshaft Support in place of the bearing over the mainshaft to support the mainshaft.

21. Remove the main drive gear bearing snap-rings. Pull off the bearing.

22. Remove special tools.

23. Remove the countershift gear front bearing snap-ring, of the countershaft gear front bearing.

24. Remove the countershaft gear rear bearing snap-ring, and remove the countershaft rear bearing.

25. Remove mainshaft adapter special tool. Lower the mainshaft assembly and at the same time take the 1st speed gear rear bearing spacer out of the case.

Shift the 3-4 speed synchronizer sleeve to the 3rd speed side to permit easy removal of the countershaft gear without interference with the sleeve.

26. Remove the countershaft gear.

27. Remove the 1-2 speed and 3-4 speed shift forks.

28. Remove the main drive gear.

29. Remove the mainshaft. Disassemble the mainshaft related parts. The synchronizer hub, sleeve, piece and spring, and the bearings for the 3-4 speed should be so laid as to prevent confusion with the 1-2 speed parts.

ASSEMBLY

1. Slide the 3rd speed gear and the needle bearing over the mainshaft from the front.

2. Install the synchronizer ring.

3. Assemble the 3-4 speed synchronizer hub and sleeve. Insert the synchronizer pieces, then install the synchronizer springs.

4. Install the assembled 3-4 speed synchronizer assembly on the mainshaft, with the synchronizer piece fitted into the ring groove in the synchronizer. Install a selected snapring so that the synchronizer hub will have end-play of 0-.003 in.

Thickness:	Identification Color:
.085 in.	Blue
.087 in.	None
.090 in.	Brown
.093 in.	White

5. Slide the 2nd speed gear and needle bearing over the mainshaft from the rear end.

6. Install the synchronizer ring.

7. Assemble the 1-2 speed synchronizer hub and sleeve. Insert the synchronizer piece and install the synchronizer spring. The synchronizer spring should be installed in the same manner as the 3-4 speed synchronizer spring.

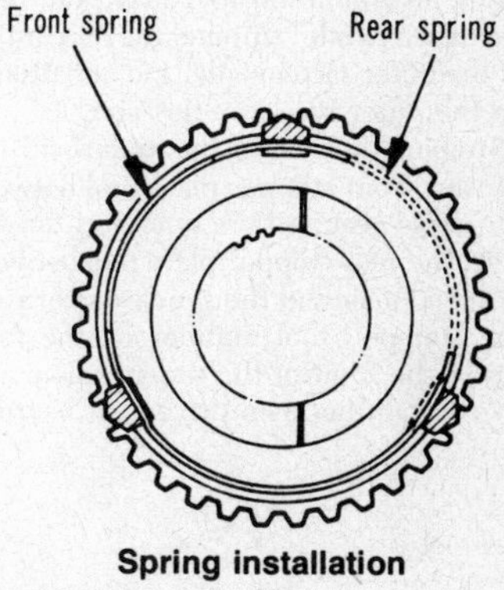

Spring installation

8. Install the assembled 1-2 speed synchronizer assembly on the mainshaft, fitting the synchronizer piece into the groove in the synchronizer.

9. Install the synchronizer ring. Install the 1st speed gear, needle bearing and sleeve.

10. Install the bearing spacer. Check to see if, when the bearing spacer is pressed firmly forward, the 1st and 2nd speed gears have an end-play in excess of 0.001-0.007 in. Check the gear and hub ends for wear.

11. Install the mainshaft.

12. Install the synchronizer ring and the needle bearing to the main drive gear, and install the main drive gear.

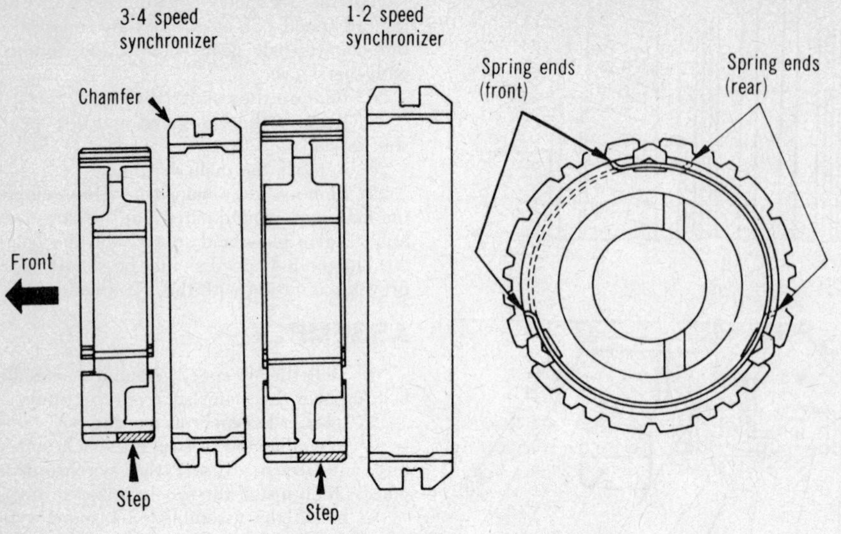

Assembled view of synchronizers

13. Install the 1-2 speed and 3-4 speed shift forks. Shift the 3-4 speed synchronzier sleeve to 3rd speed side until the 1st speed gear rear bearing spacer is out of the case.

14. Install the countershaft gear.

15. Insert countershaft gear support special tool into the case to support the countergear.

16. After installing the snap-ring, install the countershaft gear bearing.

17. To install the countershaft gear front bearing, first install the outer race only into the transmission case and then install the needle bearing. The outer race and needle bearing, if assembled before installation, will damage the countershaft at the time of installation. To install the countershaft gear bearing, attach the snap-ring to the outer race and, using an aluminum rod, drive the bearing into place while tapping the circumference of the outer race evenly. Do not attempt to force the outer race into position.

18. Support the rear of the mainshaft.

19. Insert front stopper plate tool between the main drive gear and the synchronizer ring and insert the rear stopper plate tool between the 3rd speed gear and the synchronizer ring, with the stamped tool number on the tools directed to the front of the transmission.

20. To install the main drive gear bearing, first install the snap-ring to the bearing, and then using a bearing installer, drive the bearing into position. Subsequently, install the snap-ring (small) on the main drive gear. This snap-ring must be selected and installed to obtain 0-.002 in. clearance between the bearing inner race and the snap-ring.

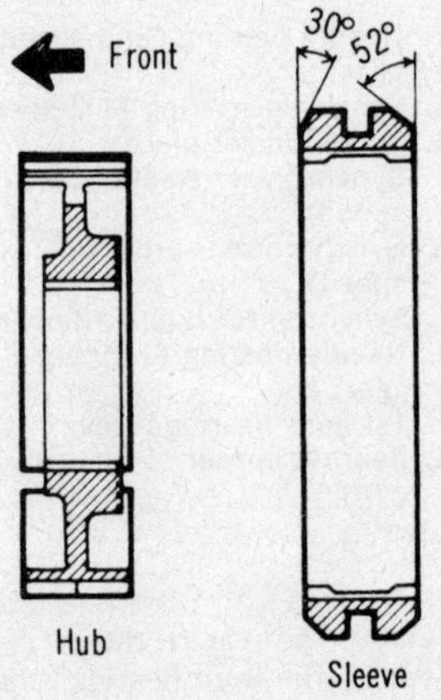

3-4-speed synchronizer

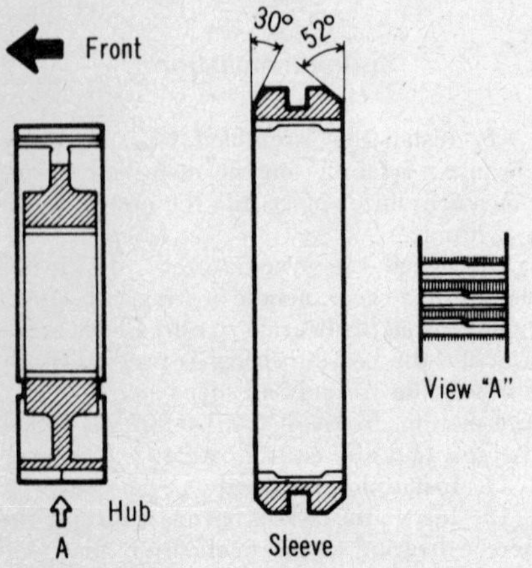

1-2-speed synchronizer

Thickness:	Identification Color:
.087 in.	Dark Blue
.089 in.	Brown
.090 in.	Orange
.092 in.	Blue
.093 in.	Green

21. Install the snap-ring to the mainshaft bearing. Drive the bearing into proper position. Remove front and rear stopper plates.

22. Install the oil seal in the front bearing retainer.

23. Before installing the front bearing retainer, check the clearance between front bearing retainer and main drive gear. Select and install a spacer to obtain 0-0.004 in. To measure the clearance, check the amount of bearing projection (A) from the front end of the case and the depth (B) of the retainer. The thickness of the spacer to be installed can be obtained from the formula (B + .3 (thickness of gasket) − A = Clearance). (0-.004 in.)

Thickness:	Identification Color:
.033 in.	Black
.037 in.	None
.040 in.	Red
.044 in.	White
.047 in.	Yellow
.051 in.	Blue
.054 in.	Green

24. Install the front bearing retainer in the transmission case.

25. Install the rear retainer.

26. Install the counter reverse gear and the spacer with the relieved side toward the bearing.

27. Install two interlock plungers.

28. Assemble the overdrive-reverse synchronizer.

NOTE: The synchronizer spring should be installed in the same manner as the 3-4 speed synchronizer.

29. Install the spacer on the mainshaft from the rear. Install the synchronizer ring, overdrive gear, needle bearing and sleeve to the synchronizer assembly assembled above.

30. Install the mainshaft locknut.

31. Insert the 3-4 speed shift rail into the case from the rear and further into the 1-2 speed and 3-4 speed shift forks.

32. Insert the 1-2 speed shift rail into the case from the rear and further into the shift forks. At the same time, align the counter-overdrive gear with the relieved portion of the shift rail and install both parts simultaneously since they cannot be installed individually.

33. Install the spring pins into the holes. In this case the pin must not project out of the fork, and the slit of the pin must be in the direction of the axis of the shift rail.

34. Install the poppet balls and springs. Install the plugs until their heads are flush with the case surface and then apply sealant to them. The springs must be installed with their tapered ends directed inside (on the ball side).

35. Tighten the mainshaft and countershaft gear nuts.

36. Insert the reverse idler shaft into the case. Install the spacer bushing, gear, needle bearing and thrust washer. The thrust washer must be installed with the ground side on the gear side.

37. Install the rear ball bearing on the mainshaft. Install the snap-ring. There should be 0-0.007 in. clearance.

Thickness:	Identification Color:
.0591 in.	Red
.0630 in.	White

38. Install the speedometer drive gear and snap-ring.

39. Assemble the extension housing.

40. Install the extension housing assembly in the case.

When installing the extension housing, tilt the change shifter fully down to the left and install the change lever in the groove provided in the selector. Install the back-up light switch.

41. Install neutral return plungers A and B, springs and steel ball, and spring.

42. Install the under cover and gasket.

43. Install the transmission control lever.

TYPE 3

5 Speed Transmission—Model KM 132 (Mitsubishi)

1975-79 Colt exc. front wheel drive
1980-81 Colt Station Wagon
1976-81 Arrow
1978-81 Challenger
1978-81 Sapporo

DISASSEMBLY

1. Remove the clutch release bearing and carrier.
2. Remove the spring pin and the clutch control shaft. Remove the felt, return spring and clutch shift arm.
3. Remove the case cover.
4. Remove the back-up light switch.
5. Remove the extension housing.
6. Remove the speedometer drive gear.
7. Remove the ball bearing from the mainshaft rear end.
8. Loosen three poppet spring plugs, then remove three poppet springs and three balls.
9. Remove the 3-4 and 1-2 speed shift fork spring pins. Pull off each shift rail toward the rear of the transmission case, then remove the shift fork. Remove the interlock plunger.
10. Remove the overdrive and reverse shift forks spring pins, shift rails and forks.
11. Loosen the locknuts (mainshaft and countershaft rear ends).
12. Pull off the counter overdrive gear and the ball bearing at the same time using a puller. Remove the spacer and the counter reverse gear.
13. Remove the overdrive gear and sleeve from the mainshaft. Remove the overtop synchronizer assembly and spacer.
14. Remove the reverse idler gear.
15. Remove the rear bearing retainer.
16. Drive the reverse idler gear shaft from inside the case.
17. Remove the front bearing retainer.
18. With the countergear pressed to the rear, remove the rear bearing snap-ring. Remove the counter rear bearing.
19. Remove the counter front bearing.
20. Remove the countergear from the inside of the case.
21. Remove the main drive pinion from the front of the case. Remove the main drive pinion bearing.
22. Remove the mainshaft bearing snap-ring. Remove the ball bearing.
23. Pull the mainshaft assembly from the case.
24. Disassemble the mainshaft in the following order:
   a. Remove the 1st gear, the 1-2 speed synchronizer and the 2nd speed gear toward the rear of the mainshaft.
   b. Remove the snap-ring from the forward end of the mainshaft. Remove the 3-4 speed synchronizer and the 3rd gear.
25. Disassemble the extension housing.
   a. Remove the lock plate and the speedometer driven gear.
   b. Remove the plug, spring and neutral return plunger.
   c. When removing the control shaft assembly, pull off the lock pin locking the gear shifter. To remove the lock pin, press the gear shifter forward and pull it off.

ASSEMBLY

1. Install the ball bearing on the main drive pinion. Install a selective snap-ring so that there will be 0-0.002 in. clearance between the snap-ring and the bearing.

Thickness of Snap-Ring:	Identification Color:
.0906 in.	White
.0925 in.	None
.0945 in.	Red

1. Transmission case
2. Main drive pinion
3. Synchronizer assy (3-4 speed)
4. 3rd speed gear
5. 2nd speed gear
6. Synchronizer assy (1-2 speed)
7. 1st speed gear
8. Rear bearing retainer
9. Synchronizer assy (overtop)
10. Overtop gear
11. Control finger
12. Neutral return finger
13. Control shaft
14. Control lever cover
15. Control lever assy
16. Stopper plate
17. Control housing
18. Change shifter
19. Mainshaft
20. Speedometer drive gear
21. Extension housing
22. Counter overtop gear
23. Counter reverse gear
24. Reverse idler gear
25. Reverse idler gear shaft
26. Case cover
27. Counter gear
28. Front bearing retainer
29. Clutch shift arm
30. Release bearing carrier
31. Clutch control shaft
32. Return spring

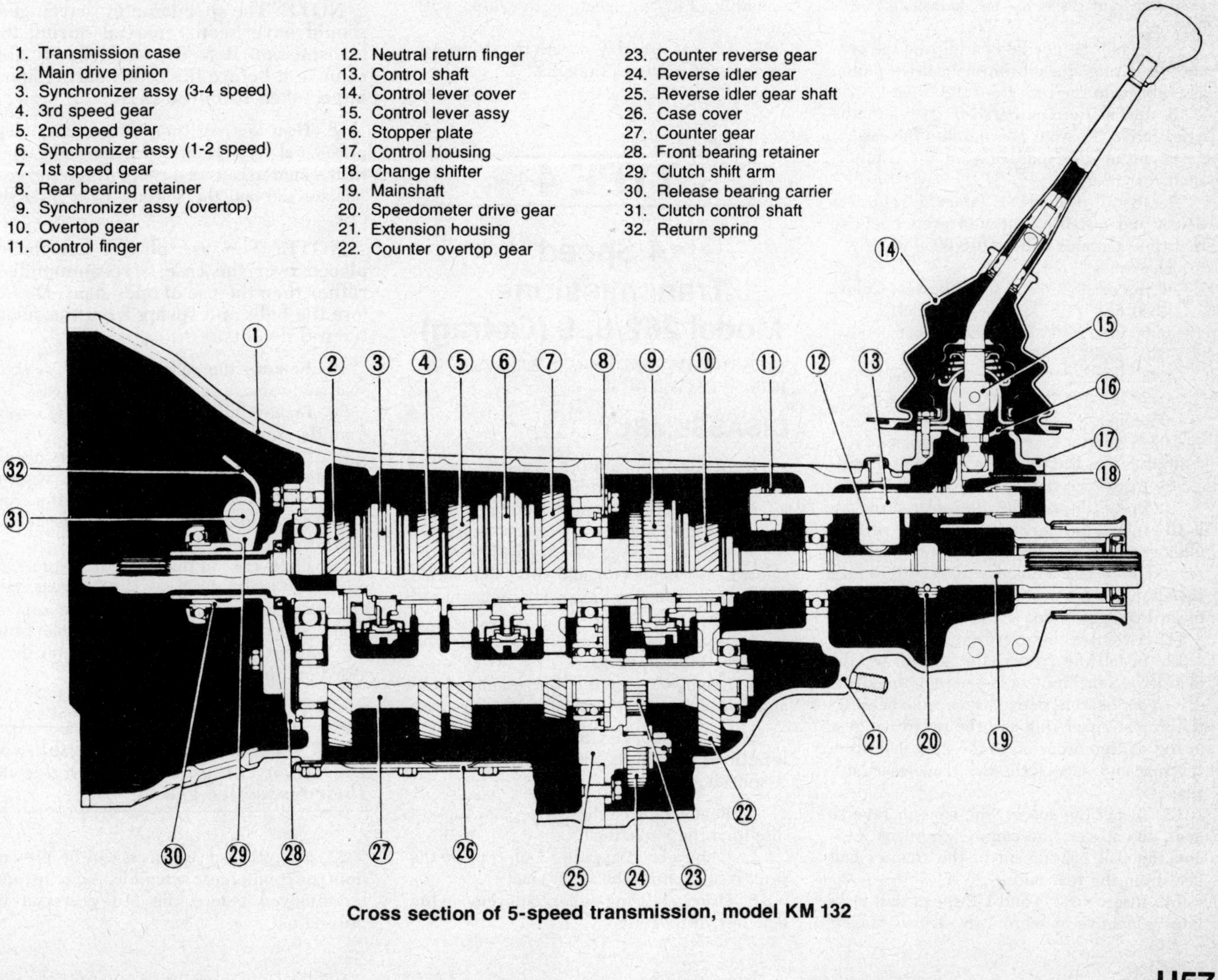

Cross section of 5-speed transmission, model KM 132

.0965 in.	Blue
.0984 in.	Yellow

2. Install the mainshaft in the following order:

a. Assemble the 3-4 speed and 1-2 speed synchronizers. The front and rear ends of the synchronizer sleeve and hub can be identified as shown. The synchronizer spring can be installed as shown.

b. Install the needle bearing, the 3rd speed gear, the synchronizer ring, and the 3-4 speed synchronizer assembly on to the mainshaft from the front end. Select and install a snap-ring of proper size so that the 3-4 speed synchronizer hub end-play will be 0-0.003 in.

Thickness of Snap-Ring:	Identification Color:
.0846 in.	None
.0874 in.	Yellow
.0902 in.	Green
.0929 in.	White

c. Check the 3rd gear end-play (.0016-0079 in.)

d. Install the needle bearing, the 2nd speed gear, the synchronizer assembly, the bearing sleeve, the needle bearing, the 1st speed gear, and the bearing spacer on the mainshaft from the rear. With the bearing spacer pressed forward, check the 2nd and 1st gear end-play (0.0016-0.0079 in.).

3. Install the mainshaft into the transmission case and drive in the mainshaft center bearing.

4. Install the needle bearing and the synchronizer ring. Install the main drive pinion assembly into the case from the front.

5. Install the countershaft gear into the case. Drive the front bearing into the case.

6. Install the snap-ring on the countershaft rear bearing.

7. Install the front bearing retainer. Select and install a spacer of proper size so that the clearance will be 0-0.0039 in.

Thickness of Spacer:	Identification Color:
.0030 in.	Black
.0366 in.	None
.0402 in.	Red
.0437 in.	White
.0472 in.	Yellow
.0508 in.	Blue
.0543 in.	Green

Replace the front bearing retainer oil seal.

8. Install the rear bearing retainer.

9. Install the reverse idler gear shaft.

10. Install the needle bearing, the reverse idler gear and the thrust washer. Check the reverse idler gear end-play (.0047-.0110 in.). Install the thrust washer with the ground side toward the gear side.

11. Assemble the overdrive synchronizer.

12. Install the spacer, the stop plate, the overdrive synchronizer assembly, the overdrive gear bearing sleeve, the needle bearing, the synchronizer ring and the overdrive gear in the written order on to the mainshaft from the rear end. Check the overdrive gear end-play.

13. Install the spacer, the counter reverse gear, the spacer, the counter overdrive gear and the ball bearing on to the countershaft gear from the rear end.

14. Insert the 3-4 and 1-2 speed shift forks into respective synchronizer sleeves. Insert each shift rail from the rear of the case. Lock the shift forks and rails with spring pins. Install an interlock plunger between shift rails. The pin should be installed with the slit in the axial direction of the shift rail.

15. Insert the ball and poppet spring into each shift rail. Install the poppet spring with the small end on the ball side.

16. Install the ball bearing on to the rear end of the mainshaft.

17. Install the speedometer drive gear.

18. Install the extension housing. Turn the change shifter fully down to the left. Make sure the forward end of the control finger is snugly fitted in the slot of the shift lug.

19. Install the neutral return plungers (A) and (B), the spring, and resistance spring and ball. Tighten each plug till its top is flush with the boss top surface.

20. Install the speedometer driven gear sleeve into the extension housing and into mesh with the drive gear.

21. Install the back-up light switch. Remember the steel ball.

22. Install the under cover.

23. Insert the clutch control shaft. Install the packing (felt), the return spring and the clutch shift arm. The spring pin should be installed in such a manner that the slip will be at right angles with the axis of the control shaft.

24. Install the transmission control level assembly. Fill the gear shifter area with grease.

25. After reassembly, rotate the drive pinion to see if it rotates smoothly.

TYPE 4

4 Speed Transmission-Model 262/8, 9 (Getrag)

1977-81 BMW 530i, 630CSi, 633i, 733i
1975-76 BMW 3.0CSi

DISASSEMBLY

1. Remove the console bracket from the rear of the transmission housing.

2. Remove the rear crossmember and the exhaust system bracket.

3. Slide the spring sleeve cover from the selector rod nonnector and drive the round pin from the coupler. Remove the selector rod connector.

4. Mount the transmission securely and drain the lubricating oil.

5. Remove the front cover retaining bolts and remove the cove with shims.

NOTE: Observe the difference in the length of the bolts and mark them for assembly.

6. Remove the circlip, spacer and support disc from the input shaft.

7. Using a bearing puller tool, remove the front bearing from the input shaft.

8. Using a bearing puller tool, remove the countershaft bearing.

9. Remove the selector lever lockpin cover, the lockpin and spring from the upper front side of the transmission case.

10. Remove the back-up light switch from the left front side of the transmission case.

11. Remove the front transmission case retaining bolts and remove the case from over the gear train.

12. Loosen the reverse gear selector lever holding bolt from outside the rear surface of the case, far enough so that the lever can be removed.

13. Using a pin punch, remove the lockpins from the 3rd-4th and reverse selector rods and forks.

14. Pull the reverse gear selector rod from the rear case. Do not lose the detent balls.

15. Turn the selector shaft so that the 3rd-4th gear selector rod can be pulled from the rear case. Do not lose the detent balls.

16. Install an output flange holding tool or equivalent on the output shaft flange, straight the retaining nut lock-washer and remove the retaining nut from the shaft.

NOTE: Certain transmissions will have a collared nut without a lock washer and will require the use of a thread-lock compound.

17. Remove the rear bearing cover retaining bolts and remove the cover.

NOTE: The speedometer driven gear should have been removed during the transmission R & R procedure. If not, remove it before the rear bearing housing is taken from the case.

18. Heat the rear transmission case to approximately 175° F (80° C). Remove the input shaft, countershaft, reverse gear, 1st-2nd gear selector rod and the selector forks from the case.

NOTE: The use of wet hot towels placed over the case is recommended, rather than the use of open heat. Do not lose the balls and spring from the selector rod detents.

19. Remove the rollers from the selector shaft and remove the shaft from the case.

20. Remove all selector rod sealing covers from the case.

21. Remove the input shaft and its needle bearing cage. Remove the circlip, support disc, synchronizer assembly with the synchronizer (baulk) rings attached, the needle bearing cage and the 3rd gear.

22. Place the output shaft in a press or equivalent tool and remove the 2nd gear, synchronizer assembly with the synchronizer (baulk) rings, 1st gear, support ring, ball bearing, support disc and the speedometer drive gear from the shaft.

CAUTION

Mark the synchronizer assemblies so that they can be reassembled with their respective gears.

23. The 4th and 3rd gears can be pressed from the countergear assembly. A circlip must be removed before the 3rd gear can be pressed off.

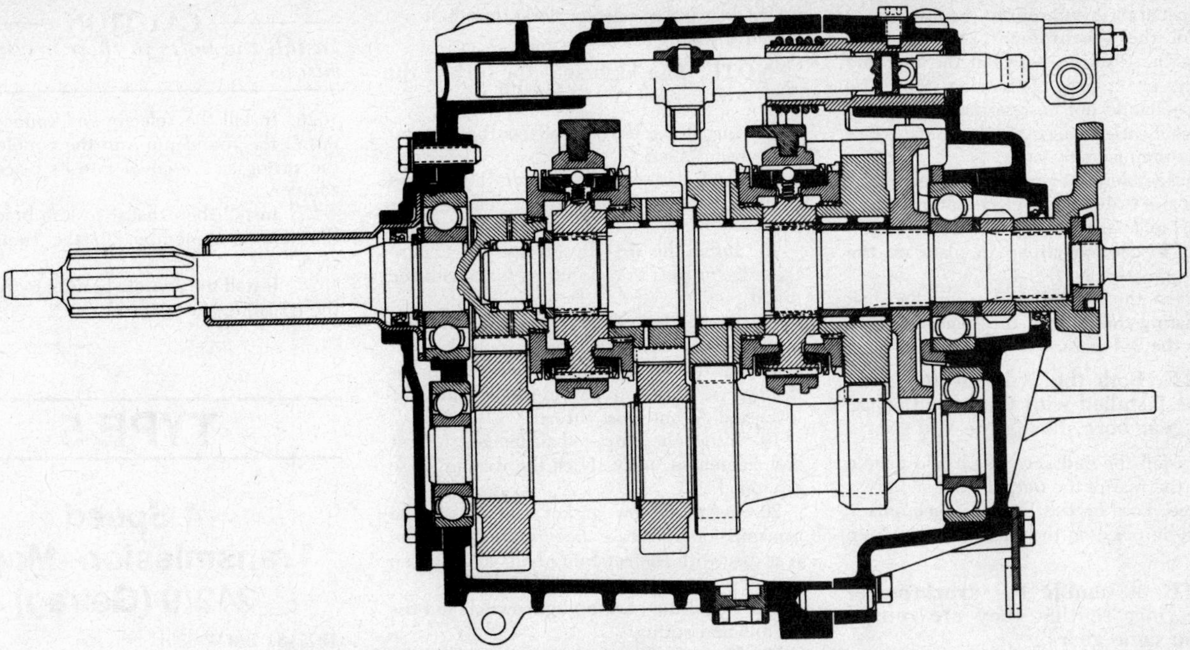

Cross section of 4-speed transmission, model 262/8, 9 (Getrag)

CAUTION

Note the direction of the gears during the removal.

24. Remove the sliding sleeve from the synchronizer hub. Do not lose the balls, springs and pressure pads from the hub.

25. The seals, gaskets, necessary replacement parts should be renewed in preparation for assembly.

ASSEMBLY

1. Assemble the synchronizer sliding sleeve to the synchronizer hub, halfway, and install the springs, pressure pads and the balls in their positions on the hub. Press the balls in until the sleeve can be slid over the hub completely.

NOTE: The convex face of the pressure pads must face the sliding sleeve.

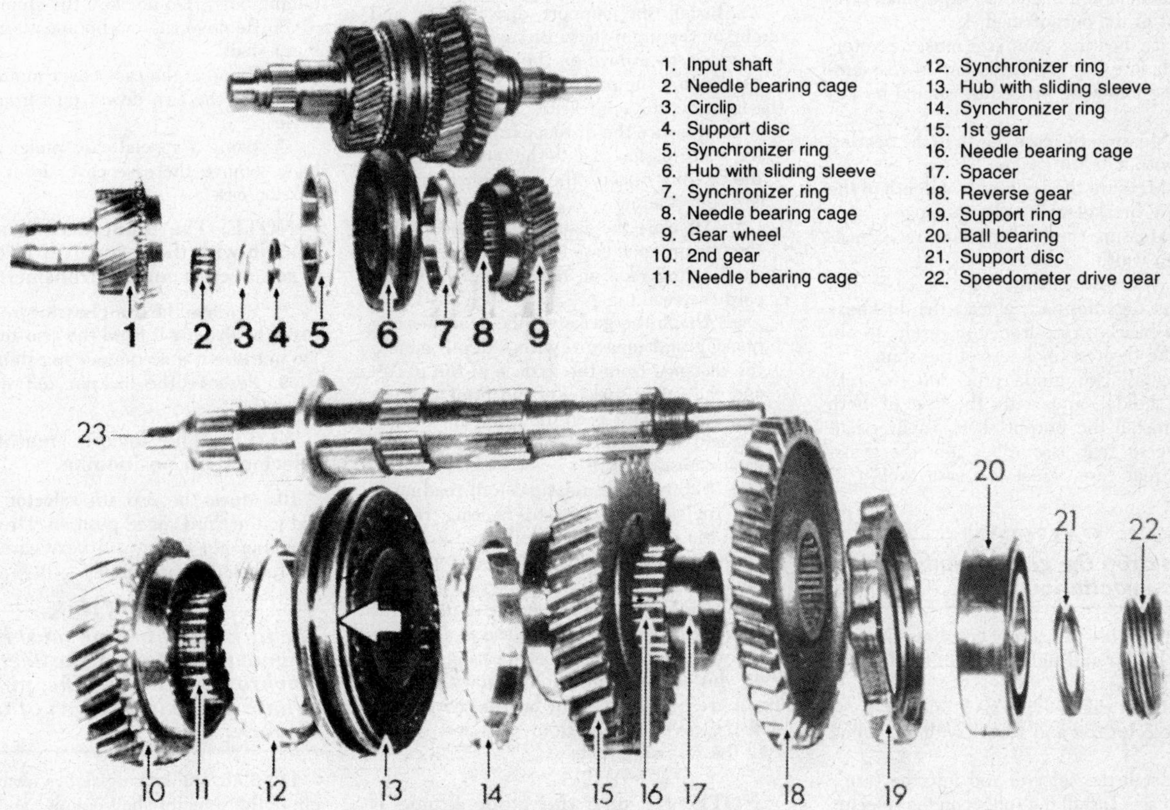

1. Input shaft
2. Needle bearing cage
3. Circlip
4. Support disc
5. Synchronizer ring
6. Hub with sliding sleeve
7. Synchronizer ring
8. Needle bearing cage
9. Gear wheel
10. 2nd gear
11. Needle bearing cage
12. Synchronizer ring
13. Hub with sliding sleeve
14. Synchronizer ring
15. 1st gear
16. Needle bearing cage
17. Spacer
18. Reverse gear
19. Support ring
20. Ball bearing
21. Support disc
22. Speedometer drive gear

Input and mainshaft components

2. Install the synchronizer (baulk) rings in place on the synchronizer assembly and measure the distance between the ring and the body, in the area of the ring stops. The clearance should not be less than 0.031 inch (0.8 mm) for used rings, nor less than 0.039 inch (1.0 mm) for new rings.

3. Assemble the countergear assembly by pressing the 3rd gear in place, after heating the gear to approximately 250-300° F (120-150° C). Install the circlip in place on the shaft.

4. Press the 4th gear in place on the shaft after heating the gear to the same temperatures as the 3rd gear.

NOTE: Both the 3rd and 4th gears must be installed with the raised collar on the gear bore, facing the 2nd gear.

5. Install the 2nd speed gear and needle cage on the rear of the output shaft and press into place. Position the 1st/2nd synchronizer assembly in place on the shaft and press into place.

NOTE: Assemble the synchronizer (baulk) rings so that they are reused with the same gears.

6. Install the 1st gear, the needle cage, spacer, reverse gear, support ring, ball bearing, support disc and the speedometer gear in place on the shaft.

7. Install the 3rd gear, needle cage, synchronizer assembly, support disc and circlip in place on the front of the output shaft.

NOTE: Assemble the synchronizer (baulk) rings so that they are reused with the same gears.

8. Install the needle bearing in the bore of the input shaft and install the input shaft onto the front of the output shaft.

The rear bearing shim size must be determined before the transmission is reassembled. The following procedure should be followed:

a. Measure the case depth to the bearing seat with a depth gauge.

b. Measure the bearing seat depth of the bearing bracket with a depth gauge.

c. Measure the bearing outer race thickness in width.

d. Add the results of the case and bracket together and subtract the thickness of the bearing race from the results to obtain the desired thickness of the shim.

9. Install two guide pins into the rear bearing holder and with the use of both hands, install the output shaft, countershaft and reverse gear assemblies into the transmission rear case. Heat the case to 175° F (80° C).

CAUTION

Do not drop the gear assemblies during the installation.

10. Install the remaining bolts into the rear bearing holder and tighten securely. Remove the guide pins.

11. Mount the reverse gear selector lever to the selector rod and secure with the rolled pin.

12. Install the selector rod into the transmission case. Install the rollers on the selector shaft.

13. Place the selector forks on their respective sliding sleeves.

NOTE: The high selector fork is the 3rd-4th.

14. Install the detent balls as the selector rods are installed.

15. Turn the selector shaft to the reverse position and install the 1st-2nd gear selector shaft.

16. Install the 3rd-4th selector rod. Secure the selector rods to the shifting forks with the rolled pins.

17. Install the shifting rod covers in the case and seal with a sealing compound.

18. Install and secure the selector lever for the reverse gear arm. Install the bolt into the lever and do not cross thread.

19. Install the output shaft flange, the nut and tighten securely. Lock the washer, if so equipped.

20. Install a new gasket and install the transmission front case. Secure the case to the rear case with the retaining bolts and tighten securely.

21. Install the back-up light switch and the lockpin and spring.

22. Heat the grooved inner races of the countershaft and input shaft bearings and install them on their respective shafts with a bearing installing tool.

NOTE: Heat the inner races to approximately 175° F (80° C).

CAUTION

Be sure the bearings are seated to the shafts tightly.

23. Install the support disc, spacer and circlip on the input shaft. Be sure the circlip is engaged in its groove on the shaft.

24. To find the proper shims to be used on the front bearings, measure as outlined:

a. Measure the distance from the front of the transmission case to the outer surface of the bearing race on the input shaft and record the reading.

b. Measure the distance from the front of the transmission case to the outer surface of the bearing race on the countershaft. Record the reading.

c. Attach the gasket to the front bearing housing and measure with a depth gauge, the distance from the surface of the gasket and the inner surface of the front bearing housing seat, for both the input shaft bearing and the countershaft bearing. Record each measurement.

d. Subtract the measurement reading of the transmission case to bearing results from the results of the depth measurement of the bearing seats in the front bearing housing.

e. The difference is the size of the shims needed to properly control the end-play of the input and countershaft bearings.

25. Install the shims and retain with a coating of grease, in the front bearing cover. Install the cover on the front case and secure with the retaining bolts.

NOTE: Be sure the guide flange is installed with the front cover.

CAUTION

Install the bolts in their original positions.

26. Install the selector rod connector and install the round pin into the coupler. Slide the spring sleeve cover into its place on the coupler.

27. Install the exhaust system bracket and the rear crossmember to the transmission case.

28. Install the console bracket to the rear of the transmission case.

TYPE 5

4 Speed Transmission–Model 242/9 (Getrag)

1977-81 BMW 320i

DISASSEMBLY

1. Remove the crossmember and exhaust system bracket from the rear of the transmission.

2. Mount the transmission securely and drain the lubricating oil from the unit. Remove the console from the transmission.

3. Remove the clutch release bearing assembly and release lever from the front of the transmission.

4. Remove the front guide sleeve and retaining bolts. Do not lose the shims.

5. Remove the circlip and shim from the input shaft.

6. Remove the case cover mounting bolts and drive the two dowel pins from the case cover.

7. Using a special case puller or equivalent, remove the case cover from the transmission case.

NOTE: The input shaft bearing will remain with the case cover as the cover is removed from the transmission case.

8. Remove the front bearing from the case cover by driving it from the rear to the front. Do not lose the accompanying shim.

9. Remove the lockpin and spring from the case.

NOTE: The lockpin maintains the selector shaft positioning.

10. Move the 3rd/4th selector lever and rod to the third speed position. Drive the fork retaining pin downward very carefully until the rod can be pulled out.

CAUTION

The fork retaining pin must be driven downward between the teeth of the synchronizer body. The pin should remain in the lower part of the selector fork.

11. Slide the locking sleeve away from the pin of the selector shaft coupler and drive the pin from the coupler.

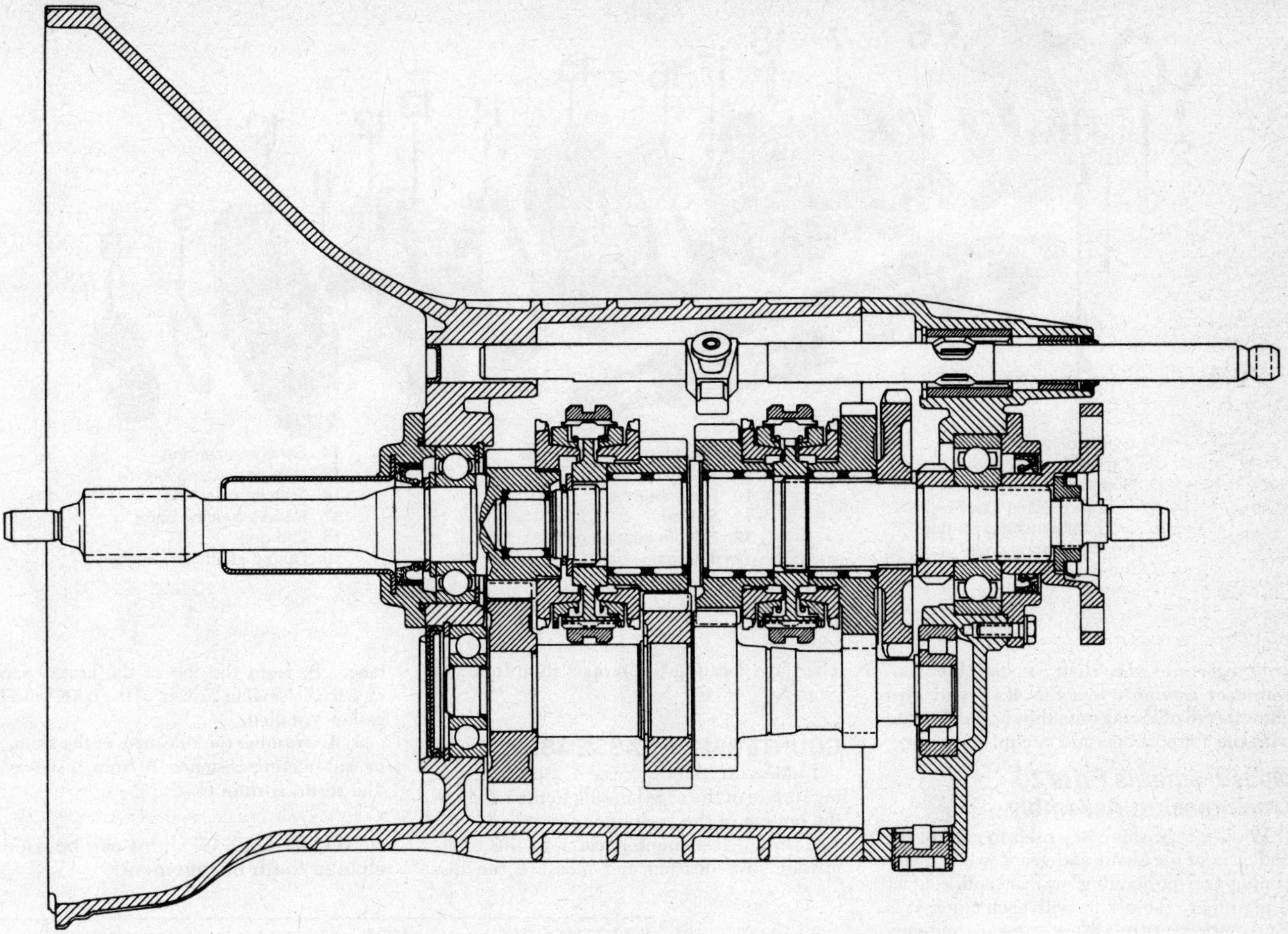

Cross section of 4-speed transmission, model 242/9 (Getrag)

12. Remove the selector rod by pulling it forward and out of the shifting fork.

13. Move the gear sleeve back to the neutral position and remove the selector fork.

14. Remove the bushing and the speedometer driven gear.

15. Straighten the bend in the lockplate on the output flange retaining nut. Install a flange holding tool and remove the locknut. Pull the flange from the output shaft.

16. Remove the rear bearing support ring and shims.

17. Using a special bearing puller or equivalent, remove the rear bearing from the transmission cover.

NOTE: A 0.078 inch (2.0 mm) metal strip must be placed between the 2nd and 3rd gears to prevent the pressing off of the 2nd gear synchronizer body during the removal of the rear bearing from the shaft and cover.

18. Lift the input and output shaft assemblies slightly and remove the countergear assembly from the end bearing and out of the cover.

19. Pull the selector fork, the reverse gear and the selector rod from the transmission cover. Do not lose the detent balls.

20. Remove the input and output shaft assemblies, along with the 1st/2nd selector rod and fork, from the transmission cover. Do not lose the detent balls.

21. Remove the back-up lamp switch and the end cap for the 1st/2nd selector shaft.

22. Remove the input shaft from the output shaft and remove the 4th speed synchronizer (baulk) ring.

23. Remove the circlip from the front of the output shaft and remove the support disc, synchronizer body assembly, 3rd gear synchronizer (baulk) ring, needle bearing race and the 3rd gear from the shaft.

24. Place the output shaft into a press or equivalent, and remove the speedometer drive gear, washer, reverse gear, spacer, needle bearing race, 1st gear, synchronizer (baulk) ring, synchronizer body with the sliding sleeve, synchronizer (baulk) ring, needle bearing race and the 2nd speed gear from the shaft.

25. The 3rd and 4th gears can be pressed from the countershaft gear assembly, along with the roller bearing.

26. The pilot bearing can be removed from the bore of the input shaft.

27. The synchronizer unit can be disassembled by sliding the sleeve off the hub. The pressure pads will drop from the unit as the sleeve is removed.

28. Replace all worn, damaged or broken parts, along with new gaskets and seals.

ASSEMBLY

1. Install the synchronizer springs onto the hub with the hooked ends of the springs in different pressure pads.

2. Install the pressure pads in place and slide the sleeve, with the flat teeth locations, over the pressure pads.

3. If the 3rd and 4th gears have been removed from the countershaft, reinstall or replace the gears back on to the shaft. Heat the gears to 250 to 300° F (120 to 150° C) and install. The high collar on the bore of the 3rd and 4th gears should face the 2nd gear. Install the bearing and race onto the shaft.

4. Place the output shaft in an upright position with the rear of the shaft up. Place the 2nd speed gear and needle bearing assembly onto the shaft. Install the 1st/2nd synchronizer assembly with the two synchronizer (baulk) rings onto the shaft, followed by the 1st speed gear, needle bearing, spacer, reverse gear wheel, washer and complete the assembly by pressing the speedometer gear onto the shaft.

NOTE: The end-play of the gear train should be 0.003 inch (0.09 mm). Adjust by changing the selective washer between the speedometer gear and the reverse gear.

5. Invert the output shaft and install the

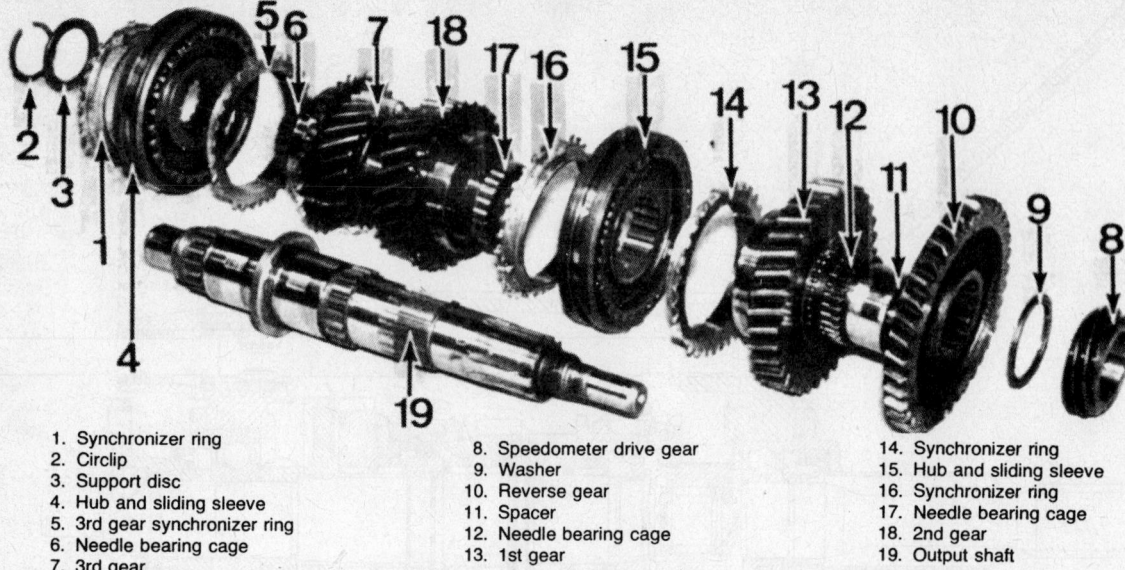

1. Synchronizer ring
2. Circlip
3. Support disc
4. Hub and sliding sleeve
5. 3rd gear synchronizer ring
6. Needle bearing cage
7. 3rd gear
8. Speedometer drive gear
9. Washer
10. Reverse gear
11. Spacer
12. Needle bearing cage
13. 1st gear
14. Synchronizer ring
15. Hub and sliding sleeve
16. Synchronizer ring
17. Needle bearing cage
18. 2nd gear
19. Output shaft

Output shaft components

3rd gear onto the shaft. Install the synchronizer assembly less the 4th speed synchronizer (baulk) ring onto the shaft and retain with the support disc and circlip.

Measurements Prior to Transmission Assembly

Washer type shims are used to control the end-play of the shafts and gears, while maintaining gear positioning, so that tooth contact is in proper relationship with each other. It is most important to inspect, measure and correct the shim packs to obtain the necessary preloads and clearances.

INPUT SHAFT

1. Install a 0.039 inch (1.0 mm) shim and the ball bearing into the case bore.
2. With a depth gauge, measure the distance, A, from the sealing surface of the case to the surface of the bearing race.
3. A numerical figure is electrically engraved on the input shaft and represents column B in the accompanying chart.
4. The thickness of the shim, X, needed on the input shaft can be determined by corresponding the measurements A and B to the chart and locating the proper shim from column X.

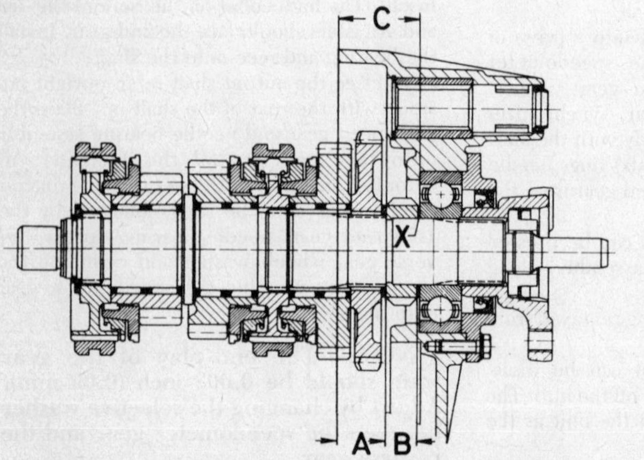

Measurement of extension case and gear assembly to determine shim "X" thickness

COUNTERSHAFT ASSEMBLY

1. Measure the distance, A, from the sealing surface of the case housing to the circlip in the bottom of the housing.
2. Install the countershaft into the transmission case bearing and measure the distance, B, from the top of the large bearing race to the sealing surface of the case, with the gasket installed.
3. Determine the thickness of the shim, C, by subtracting distance B from distance A. The result is shim C.

NOTE: The "C" shims can be used to change tooth engagement.

"A"	"B"	"X"
153.9 mm 6.059″	45 . . . 50 mm 1.772 . . . 1.968″	0.5 mm / 0.020″
	35 . . . 40 mm 1.378 . . . 1.575″	0.6 mm / 0.024″
	25 . . . 30 mm 0.984 . . . 1.181″	0.7 mm / 0.027″
153.8 mm 6.055″	45 . . . 50 mm 1.772 . . . 1.968″	0.4 mm / 0.016″
	35 . . . 40 mm 1.378 . . . 1.575″	0.5 mm / 0.020″
	25 . . . 30 mm 0.984 . . . 1.181″	0.6 mm / 0.024″
153.7 mm 6.051″	45 . . . 50 mm 1.772 . . . 1.968″	0.3 mm / 0.012″
	35 . . . 40 mm 1.378 . . . 1.575″	0.4 mm / 0.016″
	25 . . . 30 mm 0.984 . . . 1.181″	0.5 mm / 0.020″
153.6 mm 6.047″	45 . . . 50 mm 1.722 . . . 1.968″	0.2 mm / 0.008″
	35 . . . 40 mm 1.378 . . . 1.575″	0.3 mm / 0.012″
	25 . . . 30 mm 0.984 . . . 1.181″	0.4 mm / 0.016″

Location of shim "X" and engraved measurement "B".

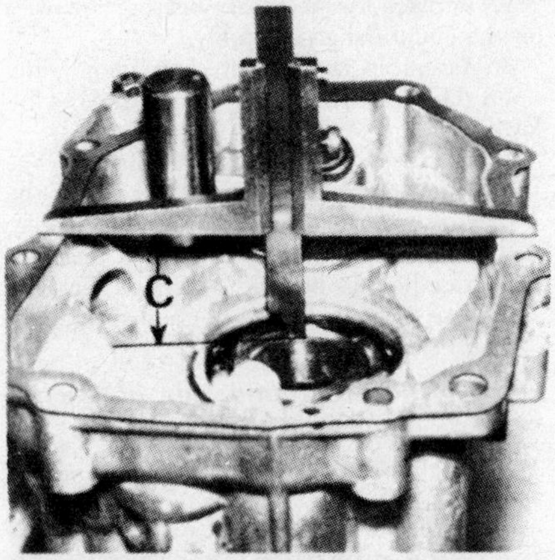

Measurement of distance between extension case edge and ball bearing. "C" equals distance.

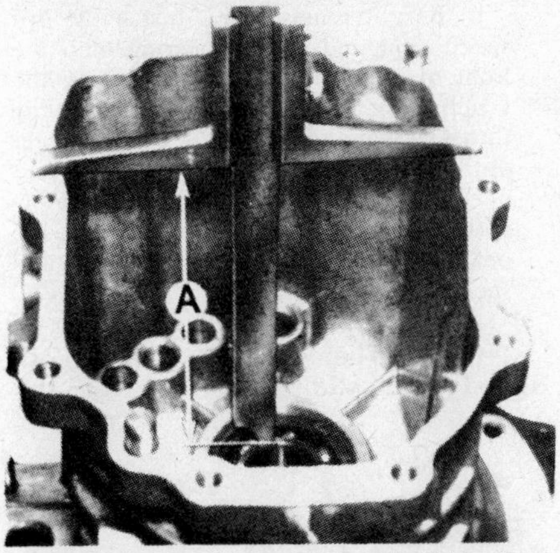

Measurement of case edge to ball bearing . . . "A" equals distance.

SPEEDOMETER GEAR TO TRANSMISSION CASE

1. Measure the thickness, B, of the speedometer gear.
2. Press the ball bearing into the transmission case and measure the distance, C, from the sealing surface of the case to the race of the bearing, without the gasket installed.
3. The nominal distance, A, is a predetermined distance and is used to arrive at the proper sized shim.
4. Subtract distance B from the nominal distance A. Subtract the result of A minus B from distance C, which is the proper sized shim, X, to be used between the speedometer gear and the ball bearing of the case.
5. An example is as follows;

Example:	A	22.0 mm (0.866″) nominal distance
	+ B	14.8 mm (0.582″)
		36.8 mm (1.488″)
	C	37.0 mm (1.456″)
	−	36.8 mm (1.448″)
	X	0.2 mm (0.008″)

Transmission Assembly After Basic Measurements

1. Have the transmission case in a secure support.
2. Insert the selector rod detent balls and springs. Install the reverse gear selector rod with the reverse gear, into the case until the 1st lock is engaged.
3. Install the countershaft into the roller bearing, mounted in the case.
4. Install the input shaft on the output shaft and install the assembly into its position on the transmission case.
5. Install the predetermined shim between the speedometer gear and the ball bearing. Install the bearing into the case, but do not seat completely.
6. Using a special bearing installer tool or equivalent, seat the bearing on the output shaft and into the transmission case.
7. Check the tooth engagement of the input, output and countergear assemblies. Tooth engagement can be changed by movement of shims.
8. Install the speedometer bushing and driven gear.
9. Set the transmission assembly in the upright position with the output shaft pointing upward. Measure the distance A, from the case to the ball bearing race.
10. Measure the distance B, from the shoulder height of the sealing cover, to the surface of the gasket on the cover.
11. Subtract distance B from distance A and the result is the thickness of the needed shim between the ball bearing and the sealing cover.

CAUTION

There should be no end-play between the ball bearing race and the sealing cover. Remeasure and remove play with shims.

12. Secure the sealing cover and install the output flange. Install the locknut and washer. Jam the lockplate washer into the groove of the flange.
13. Install the 1st-2nd gear selector rod and fork into place. Insert the locking detent balls and springs. Secure the fork to the rod with the rolled pin.
14. Install the 3rd-4th selector fork into place on the sliding sleeve. Install the main selector rod. Install the lockpin and spring into the tapered bushing. Install the locking detent balls and springs.
15. Install the 3rd-4th gear selector rod and secure to the fork with the rolled pin. (Remove pin and reinstall from the top of the fork.)
16. Install the back-up lamp switch and the selector rod cap.
17. Install the gasket on the mating surfaces of the transmission case and housing. Install the predetermined shims on their respective locations and install the transmission housing over the gear assembly.
18. Bolt the housing to the case securely.

NOTE: It may be necessary to heat the transmission area of the input shaft to install the front bearing.

19. Install the shim and bearing onto the input shaft and housing. Install washer and circlip.
20. Install the clutch release guide sleeve and install a shim to eliminate any existing play between the guide and the bearing.
21. Measure the distance between the case and the ball bearing. This distance is A. Measure the distance from the top of the shoulder of the guide sleeve to the mating surface, with the gasket installed. This distance is B.
22. Subtract distance B from distance A and the result is the thickness of shim needed to remove the existing play between the guide and the bearing.
23. Install the selector rod coupler and secure with the pin. Slide the sleeve over the pin location.
24. Install the console onto the transmission case.
25. Fill the unit with the proper level of lubricating oil.
26. Install the clutch release bearing assembly and the operating lever.
27. Install the crossmember and the exhaust system bracket.

TYPE 6

4 Speed Transmission—Model 232

1975-76 BMW 2002

DISASSEMBLY

1. Remove the exhaust system bracket from the rear of the transmission.

2. Mount the transmission securely and drain the lubricating oil.

3. Remove the clutch release bearing guide sleeve, the ball bearing circlip retainer and the shim(s).

4. Using a special puller, remove the front ball bearing from the input shaft and housing.

NOTE: Should a ball bearing with a plastic cage be encountered that would restrict the use of the special bearing puller, it would be necessary to remove the transmission housing with the use of a special housing removal tool or equivalent.

5. Remove the retaining bolts from the transmission housing and drive the dowel pins from the housing.

6. Heat the housing in the area of the countershaft bearing so that when the housing is removed, the countershaft bearing will slide from the housing easily.

CAUTION

It is recommended to use hot, wet towels instead of an open flame to heat the transmission housing.

7. Carefully remove the transmission housing from the cover assembly.

8. Remove the locking pin, spring and retaining cap from the cover.

9. Move the 3rd/4th selector rod to the 4th gear position. Rotate the guide sleeve until the rolled pin can be driven from the fork and rod. Pull the selector lever from the cover assembly.

CAUTION

Do not drop or lose the detent balls.

10. Turn the main selector rod until the selector bar is up and remove the selector rod from the cover assembly.

CAUTION

Do not drop or lose the detent balls and sleeve.

11. Move the 3rd/4th selector fork to the neutral position and remove the fork from the sliding sleeve.

12. Move the 1st/2nd selector fork and rod into the 2nd gear position. Remove the roll pin from the selector fork and slide the rod from the cover assembly. Remove the fork from the sleeve and push the sliding sleeve into the neutral position.

CAUTION

Do not drop or lose the detent balls.

13. Remove the speedometer driven gear and bushing.

14. Straighten the output flange locking plate and with the use of special holding tools or equivalent, remove the nut and flange from the output shaft.

15. Remove the rear bearing support ring and the shim(s) from the rear of the cover assembly.

16. Install a metal strip between the 2nd and 3rd gears to prevent the synchronizer assembly from being forced off when the rear ball bearing is removed. The metal strip size should be 0.079 inch (2.0 mm).

17. Using a special bearing remover or equivalent, remove the rear bearing from the cover and output shaft.

18. Remove the input and output shaft assembly by moving the assembly away from the selector rod and pulling the unit from the cover.

19. Relieve the weight of the countergear assembly and drive the unit from the cover with a plastic hammer.

NOTE: Two types of bearings are used in the cover for the countershaft. If the shaft is equipped with a ball bearing, it will come out of the cover with the shaft. If the shaft is equipped with a roller bearing, the roller bearing will remain in the cover and must be removed separately.

20. Pull the selector rod with the lever from the cover, along with the reverse gear pinion.

CAUTION

Do not drop or lose the detent balls.

NOTE: Observe the reverse gear and pinion for a groove around the outer face of the gears. If the groove is present, the gears are of a later design with a 15° mesh angle, instead of an earlier mesh angle of 20°. The gears are not to be interchanged. The new designed mesh angle was incorporated when the synchronizer assemblies were changed from the Porsche type to the Borg-Warner type.

21. Separate the input shaft from the output shaft by pulling the two assemblies apart. The needle roller cage will remain on the output shaft.

22. Remove the circlip from the output shaft, along with the support disc, shim, sliding sleeve and the 3rd speed gear with the synchronizer assembly. Remove the needle bearing cage.

23. Place the output shaft into a press or equivalent tool and press the shaft from the gear train.

CAUTION

Mark the sequence of gear and bearing removal from the shaft and the type of synchronizer unit used.

24. The 4th and 3rd gears can be pressed from the countershaft. Remove the circlip from the 3rd speed gear location before the 3rd speed gear is pressed off.

25. Replace all necessary gears, bearings, seals and gaskets.

ASSEMBLY

1. If the counter 3rd and 4th gears were removed, heat the replacement gears to 248 to 302° F (120 to 150° C) and press the gears onto the shaft. Install the bearings.

CAUTION

After pressing the 3rd speed gear on the countershaft, be sure to install the circlip.

2. Replace the necessary bearings or races on the countershaft assembly.

3. Assemble the output shaft, depending upon the type synchronizer unit used, as follows.

a. Porsche Type—Place the needle cage bearing and the 2nd speed gear onto the rear of the shaft. Install the guide sleeve, the selector sleeve, the distance bushing, the needle cage bearing, 1st speed gear, the reverse gear, thrust washer and the speedometer drive gear.

NOTE: The ground side of the reverse gear must face the 1st gear.

Install the 3rd speed gear with the needle bearing onto the front of the input shaft, followed by the guide sleeve, the thrust washer and the circlip. Determine the gap between the thrust washer and the guide sleeve with a feeler gauge and change the shim until zero clearance is obtained.

b. Borg Warner Type—Install the 3rd speed gear and needle bearing onto the front of the input shaft, followed by the synchronizer assembly with rings, the thrust washer and the circlip. From the rear of the shaft, install the 2nd speed gear and needle bearing, the synchronizer assembly with rings, the 1st speed gear and needle bearing, the reverse gear, washer and speedometer drive gear.

NOTE: When installing the 3rd/4th speed gear sliding sleeve, face the

1. Speedometer drive gear
2. Thrust washer
3. Reverse gear
4. 1st gear
5. Needle bearing cage
6. Spacer
7. Selector sleeve
8. Guide sleeve
9. 2nd Gear
10. Needle bearing cage

Output shaft components—Porsche type synchronizer units

groove in the sleeve towards the 3rd gear.

Measurements Prior to Assembly

OUTPUT SHAFT ASSEMBLY (PORSCHE TYPE SYNCHRONIZERS)

1. After the synchronizer assemblies are installed on the output shaft, determine the actual distance from the machined surface of the guide sleeve on the front of the shaft, to the face of the reverse gear hub on the rear of the shaft.

2. The nominal distance should be 5.433 ± 0.039 inch (138.0 ± 0.1 mm). Subtract the actual measured distance from the nominal distance and install a shim behind the reverse gear to provide the correct clearance.

MAINSHAFT END CLEARANCE IN COVER

1. Measure the thickness of the speedometer drive gear.

2. Install the ball bearing into the transmission cover and measure the distance from the face of the bearing race to the top of the cover's mating surface, with the sealing gasket in place. This distance is known as C.

3. Using the nominal measurement A, representing 5.433 inch (138.0 mm), add the measurement B, representing the thickness of the speedometer gear, to measurement A. Subtract the measurement C from the results of A + B, which represents the actual measurement of the gear train above the mating surface of the cover with the gasket installed. This measurement is considered to be D. The nominal measurement of D is 4.567 inch (116.0 mm). To find the thickness of the shim X, subtract the actual measurement D from the nominal measurement D. Shim X is installed between the speedometer drive gear and the ball bearings in the transmission cover.

4. An example is given to assist the repairman in determining shim X thickness.

Nominal
Measurement A = 5.433 inch (138.0 mm)
Add
Measurement B = 0.583 inch (14.8 mm)
Results = 6.016 inch (152.8 mm)
Subtract
Measurement C = 1.457 inch (37.0 mm)
Results = 4.559 inch (115.8 mm)
Nominal
Measurement D = 4.567 inch (116.0 mm)
Subtract Actual
Measurement D = 4.559 inch (115.8 mm)
Results
(Shim X Thickness)= 0.008 inch (0.2 mm)

NOTE: Nominal measurements represent theoretical measurements, determined by the manufacturer at time of design.

COUNTERSHAFT END-PLAY

1. Measure the distance, A, from the mating surface of the housing to the top of the bearing bore circlip in the base of the housing.

2. Place the assembled countergear assembly into the cover and measure the distance, B, from the mating surface of the cover, with the gasket in place, to the top of the bearing race on the countergear assembly.

3. Subtract distance B, from distance A and the result is the width of the shim, C, needed to control the end-play of the countergear.

NOTE: The tooth engagement of the output shaft and the countershaft gears can be altered by splitting the shim C, between the front and the rear bearing seats.

CAUTION

When rotating the gear train and a noise is heard, check the reverse gear teeth and the support disc on the countershaft for signs of contact. If necessary, the points of contact can be ground down no more than 0.051 inch (1.3 mm) on the support disc and no more than 0.055 inch (1.4 mm) on the reverse gear teeth.

Transmission Assembly After the Basic Measurement

1. Install the detent ball and spring, insert the reverse gear selector rod with the reverse pinion gear into the cover, while holding the detent ball downward and engage the ball to detent groove.

2. Place the predetermined shim C, into the housing and install the countershaft assembly.

3. Assemble the input shaft to the output shaft while engaging the 4th speed synchronizer (baulk) ring grooves to the lugs of the guide sleeve (Porsche Type), or on the pressure plates (Borg Warner Type).

4. Install the input-output shaft assembly into the cover and install the predetermined shim X on the output shaft and install the rear bearing until it seats.

5. Check the tooth engagement of the output shaft and the countershaft gears.

NOTE: The tooth engagement can be altered with shim C.

6. Measure the distance, A, from the housing cover to the grooved ball bearing race.

7. Measure the flange height, B, of the sealing cover with the gasket in place.

8. Subtract distance B from distance A and the result is the width shim needed to reduce the end-play to zero. Install the shim, the sealing cover and secure the cover with retaining bolts.

9. Install the output flange and secure it to the output shaft.

10. Install the gear selector fork into 1st/2nd sliding sleeve. Install the detent ball and spring. Install the selector rod into the fork and the cover. Push the detent ball downward and engage the ball with the detent groove on the rod. Install the retaining roll pin in the selector fork to rod.

11. Install the 3rd/4th gear selector fork into the sliding sleeve.

12. Install the primary selector shaft into the housing. Note the position of the tapered bushing. Install the locking pin, spring and the threaded retainer.

13. Install the detent ball and spring. Install the 3rd/4th selector rod and secure it to the fork with a rolled pin.

14. Fit the sealing cap into the selector rod hole and install the back-up lamp switch. Install the speedometer driven gear assembly.

15. Install the circlip into the input bearing bore groove of the housing and from the front, seat a 0.039 inch (1.0 mm) shim and ball bearing on the circlip.

16. Invert the housing and measure the distance, A, from the housing mating surface to the inner race of the input shaft bearing.

17. Distance B is electrically engraved on the input shaft. Locate and record.

18. From the following chart, determine the size of the shim needed to control the input-output shaft end-play.

19. Place the required shim, X, on the output shaft and the shim C, on the bearing of the countershaft.

20. Install the gasket on the housing and install the housing over the gear assembly.

21. Use a special pressure tool or equivalent, to force the housing into place on the cover assembly.

22. Secure the housing with the retaining bolts.

23. Measure the thickness of the circlip needed to retain the front bearing on the input shaft. This measurement is considered A. Install the circlip into its groove.

24. Determine the distance, B, from the circlip to the face of the ball bearing. This distance is the size of the shim, C, needed to remove the end-play from between the circlip and the ball bearing.

25. Install the shim and the circlip in their respective places on the input shaft.

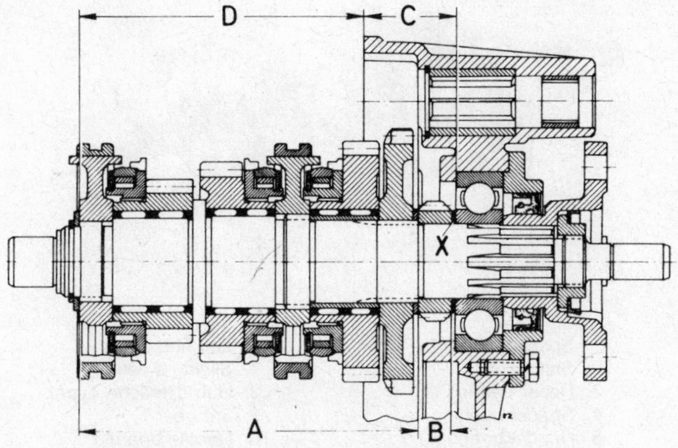

Measurement points to determine shim "x"

A	B	ins.	X mm
153.9	45-50	(0.0196)	0.5
(6.059)	35-40	(0.0236)	0.6
	25-30	(0.0276)	0.7
153.8	45-50	(0.0157)	0.4
(6.055)	35-40	(0.0196)	0.5
	25-30	(0.0236)	0.6
153.7	45-50	(0.0118)	0.3
(6.051)	35-40	(0.0157)	0.4
	25-30	(0.0196)	0.5
153.6	45-50	(0.0078)	0.2
(6.047)	35-40	(0.0118)	0.3
	25-30	(0.0157)	0.4

26. Install the guide sleeve for the clutch release bearing.
27. Install the exhaust system bracket to the rear of the transmission assembly.

TYPE 7

5 Speed Transmission–Model 235/5 (Getrag)

1975-76 BMW 2002

DISASSEMBLY

1. Remove the exhaust system support, the gear lever coupler and the bracket from the rear of the transmission.
2. Mount the transmission securely and drain the lubricating oil.
3. Compress the clutch release lever retaining spring and remove the lever assembly from the pivot ball stud.
4. Remove the clutch release bearing guide sleeve from the front of the transmission.
5. Remove the circlip and shim from the input shaft, retaining the front bearing.
6. Remove the retaining bolts from the transmission cover, freeing the intermediate housing and the front housing.
7. Mount a special pressing tool on the front housing, contacting the input shaft, and press the front housing away from the intermediate housing.

NOTE: Do not lose the shims from the input and countershafts.

8. Lift the locking plate from the output shaft flange. Using a special holding tool or equivalent, remove the retaining nut and the output flange.
9. Remove the rear bearing support ring and the retaining bolts.

NOTE: Do not lose the bolts.

10. Hold the cover assembly and the intermediate housing together with two bolts and nuts.
11. With a special bearing remover or equivalent, remove the rear ball bearing and bushing.
12. Place the transmission in the neutral position and remove the locking pin threaded cap, spring and the locking pin.
13. Remove the speedometer driven gear from the cover assembly.
14. Place the transmission in the 5th gear and turn the guide sleeve until the roll pin can be removed.
15. Remove the 4th/5th gear selector rod from the fork and the intermediate housing and cover assembly.

CAUTION

During the removal of the selector rods from the intermediate housing and the cover assembly, do not lose the detent balls and springs.

16. Engage the third gear and turn the guide sleeve until the rolled pin can be driven out of the 2nd/3rd fork and rod.
17. Remove the 2nd/3rd selector rod from the intermediate housing and cover assembly.
18. Position the selector sleeve in the neutral position and drive the dowel pins from the intermediate housing. Remove the two retaining bolts and nuts.
19. Pull the gear assembly with the intermediate housing, selector shaft and selector rod of the 1st/reverse gear, from the transmission cover.

CAUTION

Do not lose the ball bearing from the cover.

20. Place the intermediate housing in a vise or other holding tool and remove the speedometer drive gear and the reverse gear with the needle bearing cage.

NOTE: Mark the speedometer drive gear before removal.

21. Remove the rolled pins from the fork for the 1st and reverse gears.
22. Pull the 1st/reverse selector rod from the intermediate housing, toward the rear.
23. Remove the selector forks of the 2nd/3rd and 4th/5th gears from the sliding sleeves.
24. Move the output shaft towards the rear until it is to the stop in the housing. Pull the selector hinion of the 1st gear with the guide sleeve and spacer bushing.

NOTE: Use a puller with extra long arms to grip gear.

25. Move the output shaft carefully forward until the synchronizer unit of the 3rd speed contacts the 3rd gear of the countershaft.
26. From the rear of the intermediate housing, remove the Allen headed screws and the retaining keys.

NOTE: Shims are used to obtain a good fit on the keys, as necessary. Do not lose them.

27. Position the gear and housing assembly into a press. Position a long tube on the countershaft so that it is even with the output shaft end. Lay a flat bar, horizontally on the output shaft and the extension for the countershaft, and press the two shafts from the housing with the gear assemblies attached.
28. Separate the input shaft from the output shaft assembly, along with the selector sleeve and the needle bearing.
29. Remove the circlip from the front of the

1. Spacer bushing
2. Shim
3. Roller bearing
4. Spacer bushing
5. Needle bearing
6. 2nd Gear
7. Sliding sleeve
8. Hub (Porsche Type)
9. 3rd gear
10. Needle bearing

Output shaft components from the machined collar to the rear of the shaft

output shaft and remove the support disc, the shim, sliding sleeve and the 4th gear with the needle bearing cage.

30. Invert the output shaft and press the spacer bushing, shim, roller bearing, spacer bushing, needle bearing 2nd gear, selector sleeve, 3rd gear and the needle bearing from the shaft.

CAUTION

Do not drop the gears.

31. The 5th and 4th gears may be pressed from the countershaft, if necessary. If the 1st gear and or bearing must be replaced on the countershaft, the retaining screw, support disc and shim must be removed.

32. Replace any bearings, seals, broken or worn gears, as required.

Synchronizer Assembly Overhaul

PORSCHE TYPE

1. Remove the lock washer, the synchronizer baulk ring, the baulk strap, the block and the stop.

NOTE: The synchronizer ring for the 1st speed is more oval in shape than the rings for the second, third and fourth gears.

Identification marks for these are as follows; 1st gear—white spot of paint, 2nd, 3rd and 4th—blue spot of paint.

2. Examine the synchronizer and replace the defective parts.

3. Install the synchronizer ring into the selector sleeve. Install the stop, the block, the baulk strap and install the lock washer.

4. The synchronizer ring must be able to easily turn.

Borg-Warner Type

1. Press the selector sleeve from the synchronizer hub. Catch the pressure plates as the sleeve is removed.

2. Remove the synchronizer springs from the hub. Note the installed position.

3. Measure the synchronizer rings to the hub.

Service limit—0.032 inch (0.8 mm).
New limit —0.039 inch (1.0 mm)

4. Reassemble the synchronizer springs to the hub in a staggered manner. Attach the pressure plates to the springs.

5. Press the selector sleeve over the hub assembly, with the flat teeth of the selector sleeve in line with the pressure plates.

NOTE: The teeth in the selector sleeves are recessed for 1st, 2nd and 3rd speeds. When assembling, the groove in the selector sleeve for the 3rd speed, must be visible.

ASSEMBLY

1. From the rear of the output shaft, install the needle bearing and 3rd gear, the selector sleeve, 2nd gear pinion and needle bearing, the spacer bushing, roller bearing, shim and spacer bushing.

NOTE: A press will have to be used on certain parts during the installation.

2. From the front of the output shaft, install the 4th gear and needle bearing, the sliding sleeve, shim and the support disc. Install the circlip.

3. Check output shaft end-play as follows:

a. Front of shaft: Check the clearance between the support disc and the guide sleeve with a feeler gauge. Replace the shim with one of proper thickness to eliminate end-play.

b. Rear of shaft: Install the guide sleeve for the 1st speed and determine the end-play between the spacer bushing and the guide sleeve. Adjust the size of the shim to remove the end-play. Remove shim, spacer bushing and guide sleeve.

4. Assemble the 4th and 5th speed gears on the countershaft, if removed. The 1st speed gear should be removed before the shaft is installed in the housing.

5. Install the roller bearings of the output and countershafts into the intermediate housing. Install the retaining keys and Allen headed screws to retain the output shaft bearing.

NOTE: Do not tilt the retaining keys. Use shims to obtain a parallel fit to the bearing and housing.

6. Install the output and countershaft into the roller bearings. Install the 1st speed gear onto the countershaft and install the support disc and bolt. Measure the distance between the gear and the support disc and install a shim of the proper size between the support disc and the 1st speed gear. Secure the bolt with a locking substance.

7. Install the previously determined shim on the output shaft and press the spacer bushing into place.

8. Install the 1st speed gear and the guide sleeve, with the long bars of the sleeve towards the gear.

9. Install the selector forks on the selector sleeves for the 2nd/ 3rd and 4th/5th gears.

10. Push the selector rod for the 1st/ reverse gear, along with the selector, into the intermediate housing.

11. Install the selector sleeve into the selector fork, install on the selector rod and slide the selector sleeve onto the guide sleeve for the 1st/reverse gear.

12. Install the rolled pins into the selector fork and the selector rod.

13. Install the reverse gear pinion onto the output shaft and adjust the tooth engagement of the output and countershaft with shims between the speedometer drive gear and the ball bearing. To accomplish this measurement, proceed as follows:

a. Place the roller bearing into the transmission cover bore and set the speedometer gear on top of the bearing inner race. Measure the distance, C, from the cover sealing surface to the top of the speedometer drive gear.

b. The tooth engagement is set correctly when the distance C, is 0.866 ± 0.0039 inch (22.0 ± 0.1 mm). Remove the ball bearing from the cover.

14. Remove the back-up lamp switch and the selector sealing cap, if not already done.

15. Install the double pinion gear and the thrust washer onto the shaft in the cover. Place the sealing gasket on the cover.

16. Fit the intermediate housing and gear assemblies to the cover. Loosely secure the housing to the cover with two bolts.

17. Install the detent balls and springs in their respective bores, holding them down while installing the selector rods.

NOTE: The locking balls have to be installed as the selector rods are installed in the housing and cover.

18. Install the 5th gear locking ball and detent ball in the bore, with the 1st/reverse selector rod in the Neutral position.

19. Install the 2nd/3rd selector rod through the fork and into the housing. Install the rolled pin through the fork and rod.

20. Position the selector sleeve of the 4th/5th gear to the neutral position and install the locking and detent balls. Install the selector rod and secure it to the fork with the rolled pin.

21. Install the back-up light switch and the sealing cap into their respective bores.

22. Install the dowel pins into the bores of the intermediate housing.

23. Fit the locking pin and the speedometer driven gear assembly.

24. Install the bushing onto the output shaft and drive the ball bearing on the shaft until it is fully seated.

25. Determine distance A, which is the dis-

1. Correct installation
2. Incorrect installation
3. Shim

Proper use of retaining keys and shims

Measuring from intermediate housing to top of countershaft for dimension "D"

A	B	C
150.6	23.6 (0.9291)	0. (0)
(5.929)	23.5 (0.9252)	0.1 (0.0039)
	23.4 (0.9212)	0.2 (0.0078)
150.7	23.6 (0.9291)	0.1 (0.0039)
(5.933)	23.5 (0.9252)	0.2 (0.0078)
	23.4 (0.9212)	0.3 (0.0118)
150.8	23.6 (0.9291)	0.2 (0.0078)
(5.937)	23.5 (0.9252)	0.3 (0.0118)
	23.4 (0.9212)	0.4 (0.0157)
150.9	23.6 (0.9291)	0.3 (0.0118)
(5.941)	23.5 (0.9252)	0.4 (0.0157)
	23.4 (0.9212)	0.5 (0.0196)
151.0	23.6 (0.9291)	0.4 (0.0157)
(5.945)	23.5 (0.9252)	0.5 (0.0196)
	23.4 (0.9212)	0.6 (0.0236)
151.1	23.6 (0.9291)	0.5 (0.0196)
(5.949)	23.5 (0.9252)	0.6 (0.0236)
	23.4 (0.9212)	0.7 (0.0275)
151.2	23.6 (0.9291)	0.6 (0.0236)
(5.953)	23.5 (0.9252)	0.7 (0.0275)
	23.4 (0.9212)	0.8 (0.0315)
151.3	23.6 (0.9291)	0.7 (0.0275)
(5.957)	23.5 (0.9252)	0.8 (0.0315)
	23.4 (0.9212)	0.8 (0.0315)

Example: A = 150.90 mm (5.941 in.)
B = 0.42 mm (0.017 in.)

C = 0.50 mm (0.020 in.)

tance from the outer face of the ball bearing and the face of the transmission cover.

26. Install the gasket on the sealing bearing cover and measure the distance B, from the top of the seal to the bearing contact surface of the cover.

27. Determine the thickness of the shim by subtracting distance B from distance A. The result is the size of the shim needed between the bearing cover and the bearing to obtain zero end-play.

28. Install the shim and the sealing cover. Install the retaining bolts. Install the output shaft flange.

29. Rotate the transmission assembly so that the gears are in an upright position. Remove the retaining bolts from the intermediate housing to the cover. Install the gasket on the intermediate housing mating surface and measure the distance from the gasket area to the top of the countershaft gear. This distance is considered D.

30. Measure the distance, known as E, from the mating surface of the front housing to the surface of the countershaft ball bearing, in its bore of the housing.

31. Determine the thickness of the shim, known as F, that is needed on the end of the countershaft, to allow 0.0079 inch (0.2 mm) end-play between the end of the shaft and the front housing.

32. Determine distance A, from the front housing mating surface to the input ball bearing, seated in its bore.

33. Install the input shaft, needle bearing and selector sleeve onto the output shaft. Locate the electrically engraved number on the machined surface of the input shaft. This number represents distance B. Locate the proper shim from the following chart.

NOTE The engraved number always denotes the digit after 23, as taken from the accompanying chart.

34. Install the proper shim on the input shaft. Carefully install the front housing over the gear assembly. Install a pulling tool or equivalent, and pull the input shaft into the ball bearing and the front housing to the mating surface of the intermediate housing. Secure the housings with the retaining bolts.

35. After the front bearing and housing are pulled into position, measure the distance, E, from the circlip to the ball bearing.

36. Measure the thickness, D, of the circlip.

37. Select a shim to provide the needed zero clearance between the circlip and the bearing, with the support disc in place.

38. Install the guide sleeve gasket and install the guide to the transmission housing. Retain with the retaining bolts.

39. Install the clutch release lever and bearing, the exhaust support, the gear lever, stay and the bracket assembly.

40. Fill the transmission to the proper level with lubricating oil.

TYPE 8

4 Speed Transmission–Model ZF-S4-18/3

1975-76 BMW 3.0Si

DISASSEMBLY

1. Mount the transmission securely and drain the lubricating oil.

2. Remove the gearshift upper housing with the torsion spring and centering spring, mounted on the shift plate.

3. Remove the shift control housing from the rear of the transmission.

4. Remove the vibration damper, located between the shift control housing and the transmission case.

5. Slide the shifting bars guide piece from the shifting bars.

6. Remove the front bearing cover from the front of the transmission.

NOTE: Do not lose the shims.

7. Remove the small circlip from the input shaft and remove the shims.

8. With the aid of a bearing puller or equivalent, remove the front bearing from the input shaft.

NOTE: Do not lose the shims between the bearing and the shaft.

9. Remove the bearing pins from the 3rd/4th selector fork. The pins are retained by bolts on the left and right sides of the front housing.

10. Remove the front housing retaining bolts and separate the front housing from the rear housing.

11. Remove the shift rails for the 3rd/4th and 1st/2nd gears towards the front of the transmission.

12. Remove the reverse shift rail from the rear of the transmission.

Removing the reverse gear by pressing the 1st/2nd gear against notch

Removing the 1st/2nd shift forks bearing bolts

NOTE: The deep shift rail cutouts should be towards the shift lever side.

13. Engage the 1st speed gear and remove the 3rd/4th selector fork.
14. Remove the output shaft flange locking plate, the locking nut and remove the flange from the shaft.
15. Remove the rear bearing cover and shims from the rear of the transmission.
16. Remove the speedometer drive gear and washer.
17. Using a special bearing puller or equivalent, remove the countershaft ball bearing.
18. Remove the input shaft and the countershaft gear assemblies from the rear housing.
19. Engage 2nd gear and remove the bearing pins from the 1st/2nd selector fork.
20. Remove the bearing pin for the reverse selector fork and remove the fork from the housing.
21. Press the 1st/2nd selector fork against the notch in housing and pull the reverse gear out.
22. Remove the rear output shaft bearing by either pulling the bearing from the shaft or pressing the shaft from the bearing. Remove the bearing from the housing, if remaining. Do not lose the shim from under the large circlip.
23. Remove the output shaft gear assembly from the housing and remove the 1st/2nd selector fork from the sliding sleeve.
24. Press the 1st and reverse gears from the output shaft. Remove the needle bearing and remove the snap-ring. Remove the synchronizer ring.
25. Press the synchronizer assembly and the 2nd speed gear from the shaft and remove the needle bearing.
26. Remove the front snap-ring and remove the synchronizer assembly and the 3rd gear from the shaft.
27. If necessary, the 3rd and 4th countershaft gears can be replaced, by removing the circlip and pulling the ball bearing from the shaft to expose the gears. Remove the circlip from between the gears.
28. Replace any worn or defective parts, seals and gaskets, in preparation for the reassembly.

ASSEMBLY

1. Check the synchronizer rings to the clutch body gap and renew the rings if the gap is less than 0.0157 inch (0.4 mm).

Removing or installing input, output and countershaft assemblies from transmission rear housing

2. Assemble the synchronizer assembly with the springs and pressure plates in position. Install the sliding sleeve over the hub assembly.

NOTE: The sliding sleeve for the 1st/2nd gears has equal serrations all around. The sliding sleeve for the 3rd/4th gears has interrupted serrations. The hub for the 1st/2nd gears is equal on both sides while the hub for the 3rd/4th gears is lower on the side facing the 4th gear.

3. Install the needle bearing and the 3rd gear onto the front of the output shaft. Install the 3rd/4th synchronizer assembly on the shaft with the higher side towards the 3rd gear. Install the circlip of a size that no end-play is present.
4. Install the needle bearing and the 2nd gear onto the rear of the output shaft. Assemble the 1st/2nd synchronizer assembly and install on the shaft. Install the retaining snap-ring of a size to prevent end-play.

NOTE: Be sure the synchronizer rings are in place on the synchronizer hub.

5. Install the needle bearing and the 1st gear onto the shaft and press the reverse gear in place with its thicker hub side facing to the outside.
6. Measure the distance, A, from the hub of the front synchronizer, less snap-ring, to the machined surface on the rear of the reverse gear.
7. Install the rear bearing into the rear housing and measure the distance, B, from the housing mating surface, less gasket, to the ball bearing inner race.
8. Add distance A and B together and the result is the actual measurement, C, from the face of the inner race of the ball bearing to the front of the synchronizer hub. A theoretical measurement is given for this distance and is noted as 2.106 inch (53.5 mm).

NOTE: The theoretical measurement is obtained at time of transmission design and the difference is in the machining of the various internal part, which represents the actual measurement.

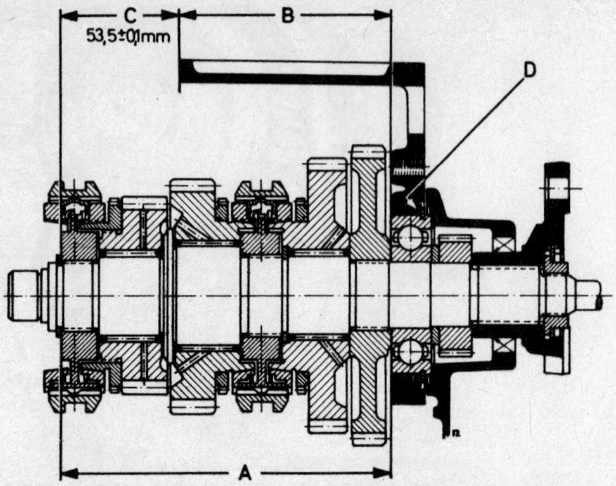

Measurement locations to determine shim "D"

9. Subtract the theoretical measurement, C, from the actual measurement, C, and the result is the size shim needed, known as D, between the rear bearing and the transmission case for the output shaft. Remove the rear bearing and install the shim D, and reinstall the bearing in its bore.

10. Place the 1st/2nd selector fork into the sliding sleeve of the 1st/2nd synchronizer assembly.

NOTE: Play between the fork follower and the sliding sleeve should be 0.0629 inch (1.6 mm) so as to avoid vibration of the shift lever.

11. Position and press the output shaft into the rear bearing, seated in the rear housing.

12. Engage the 2nd gear and press the selector fork against the stop. Position the reverse gear pinion with the relieved tooth face side towards the housing and install on the shaft.

13. Install the reverse gear selector fork and secure with the bearing pin.

14. Secure the 1st/2nd selector fork with the bearing pins. Place the gear train into the Neutral position.

15. Place the transmission gear train in the upright position and install the 3rd/4th sliding sleeve and synchronizer ring, if not previously done. Position the roller bearing on the front of the output shaft and install the input shaft. Be sure the synchronizer rings fit into their respective notches.

16. Install the countershaft assembly and support the assembly until the rear bearing can be pressed on to the shaft and into the housing. Allow the bearing to project from the face of the housing, 0.196 inch (5.0 mm) and is known as dimension D.

17. Install the gasket on the rear of the housing and measure the distance A, from the face of the gasket to the height of the output shaft bearing.

18. Measure the distance B, from the surface of the bearing cover to the seat of the bearing bore within the cover.

19. Determine the thickness of shim C by subtracting distance A from distance B.

NOTE: The shimming accuracy should be ± 0.002 inch (0.06 mm).

20. Install the washer and the speedometer drive gear onto the output shaft.

21. Hold shim C with grease to the bearing cover and install the cover to the rear of the transmission case. Install the retaining bolts and secure. Install the output shaft flange, the locking nut and the locking plate.

22. Install the selector fork to the 3rd/4th sliding sleeve. Install the shift rails, reverse from the rear of the transmission and the 1st/2nd or 3rd/4th from the front of the transmission.

23. Install the front housing to the rear housing and secure. Install the 3rd/4th bearing pins, vibration damper and shift arm.

24. Measure the distance A, from the front face of the housing to the contact face on the input shaft for the front bearing.

25. Measure the distance from the ball bearing edge (facing inward), to the lock-ring on the ball bearing. This measurement is known as distance B.

26. Subtract distance A from distance B. The result is known as C. Subtract 0.019 inch (0.5 mm) from distance C and the results are the thickness of shim D.

NOTE: A range of 0.019 to 0.031 inch (0.5 to 0.8 mm) is given to subtract from distance C.

27. Install shim D on the input shaft and press the bearing into place on the shaft and into the bore of the housing.

28. Shim the clearance between the ball bearing inner race and the circlip to zero by adding the proper sized shim.

29. Install the gasket on the front of the transmission.

30. Measure the distance between the top of the countershaft bearing and the gasket surface. This distance is known as A.

31. Distance B is the known end-play of the countershaft, 0.004 to 0.008 inch (0.1 to 0.2 mm). Subtract distance B from distance A to obtain the thickness of shim C.

32. Measure distance D between the mating face and the machined bore bottom of the guide sleeve. (Input shaft).

33. Measure the distance E from the ball bearing top face to the gasket on the housing. (Input shaft.)

34. Subtract distance E from distance D and the result is shim size F, ± 0.002 inch (± 0.05 mm).

35. Install the shims on the respective bearings and install the guide sleeve and secure it with the retaining bolts.

36. Fill the transmission with lubricating oil to its proper level.

TYPE 9

4 Speed Transmission

1975-77 Capri and Capri II

DISASSEMBLY

1. Remove the retaining clips and the flat washers from the shift rods at the shift levers. Remove the rods.

2. Remove the shift linkage cover. Remove the shifter forks from the gear box.

3. Remove the bolts which hold the tailshaft to the gear box and twist the tailshaft until the countershaft becomes fully visible.

4. Remove the countershaft by driving it from the front of the gear box toward the rear using a brass drift. The countershaft should just clear the front of the case. Push the countershaft out the rest of the way with a dummy shaft. Lower the cluster gear to the bottom of the gear box.

5. Remove the snap-ring which secures the input shaft bearing and press off the bearing.

6. Remove the tailshaft and the output shaft assembly from the gear box.

7. Disassemble the cluster gear by allowing the dummy countershaft to fall out. Remove the needle bearings and the spacers from the cluster gear.

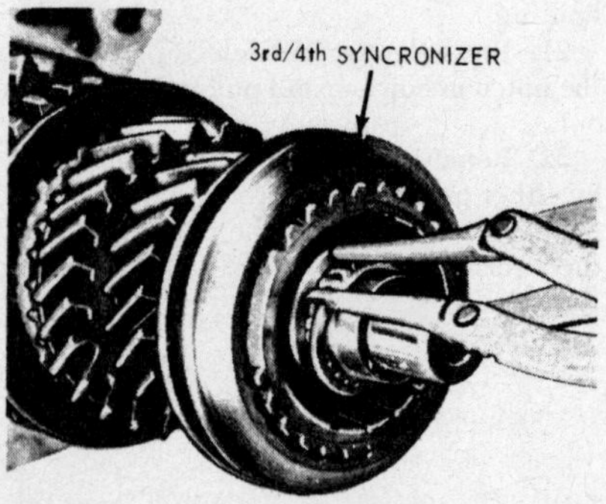

Removing third gear snap-ring—2000, 2300, and V6 transmissions

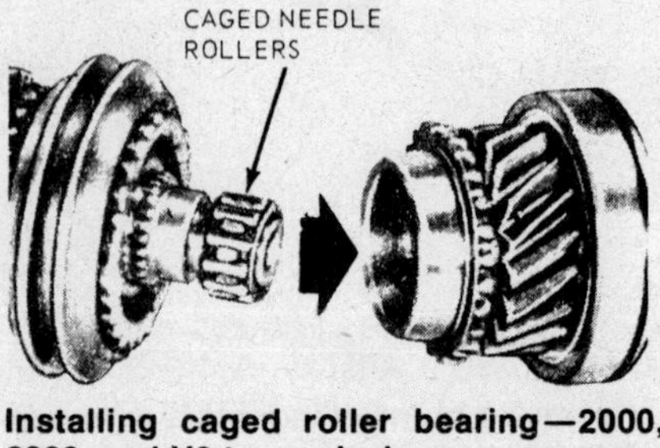

Installing caged roller bearing—2000, 2300, and V6 transmissions

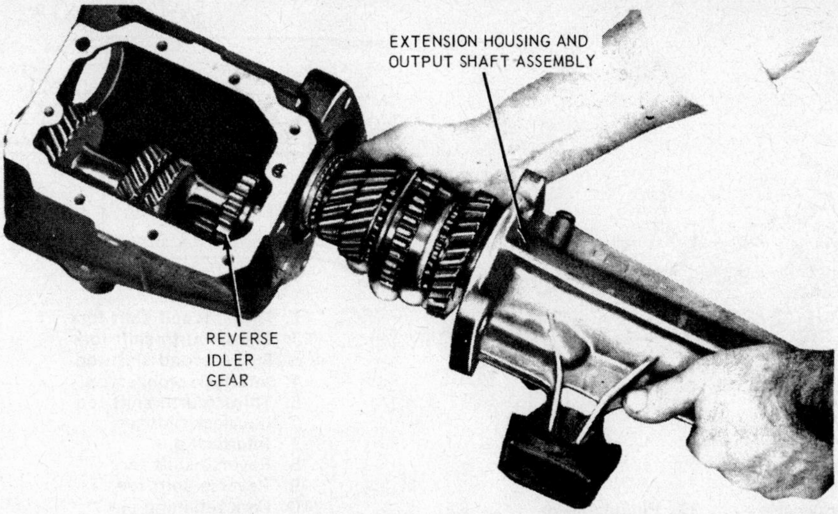

Removing tailshaft—2000, 2300, and V6 transmission

8. Drive out the reverse idler gear shaft toward the rear of the gear box.

9. Remove the snap-ring in front of the third and fourth gear synchronizer, from the output shaft assembly. Remove the synchronizer assembly including third gear.

10. Remove the snap-ring and the thrust washer in front of the second gear. Remove second gear and the blocking ring.

11. Remove the first and second gear synchronizer sleeve and remove the synchronizer inserts.

12. Remove the speedometer drive gear.

13. Remove the snap-ring which retains the output bearing in the tailshaft.

14. Remove the output shaft from the tailshaft.

15. Remove the snap-ring from the output shaft and press off the bearing using an arbor press. Remove the spacer and first gear with the blocking ring and insert spring.

ASSEMBLY

1. Slide the insert spring, blocking ring, first gear, and the spacer onto the rear of the output shaft. Make sure that the broad side of the spacer is pointing toward the shaft bearing.

2. Install a new snap-ring on the tailshaft output shaft.

When installing a new bearing on the tailshaft, a new snap-ring should be selected as follows: Place a dummy bearing into the tailshaft and determine the distance between the top face of the bearing and the outer edge of the retaining groove, using a feeler gauge.

The thickness of the dummy bearing (0.688 in.) plus the feeler gauge blades is the total width between the stop for the bearing, and the outer edge of the snap-ring retaining groove. Measure the width of the new bearing and subtract that number from the total width just obtained. This figure is the thickness that the new snap-ring should be.

3. Install the speedometer gear along the output shaft by pressing it into place.

4. Position the first and second gear synchronizer springs in the synchronizer hub by placing one end of each spring into the same groove.

5. Position the inserts in their grooves and then slide the first and second gear synchronizer sleeve onto the synchronizer hub.

6. Slide the blocking ring, second gear and the thrust washer onto the output shaft. Install the snap-ring.

7. Heat the tailshaft. A pan of hot water is recommended. Install the output shaft and bearing into the tailshaft.

8. Install the snap-ring which you had previously measured in the tailshaft.

9. Position the synchronizer springs as described in Step 4. Install the inserts in their groove. Slide the third and fourth gear synchronizer sleeve onto the hub.

10. Install the third and fourth gear synchronizer assembly by sliding it onto the output shaft and install the snap-ring.

11. Press the input shaft bearing onto the input shaft and install a snap-ring that gives the least possible end-play.

12. Install the input shaft and gear to the gear box using a brass drift.

13. Install the front bearing retainer to the gear box with the gasket in place. The oil groove in the retainer should be in line with the oil passage in the gear box.

14. Install the reverse idler gear, with the collar for the selector fork facing rearward, then drive the idler gear shaft into position until it is flush against the case.

15. With a dummy pinion installed in the bottom of the gear box, install the countershaft. Position the thrust washers in the gear box.

16. Install the tailshaft using sealer on both ends. Slide the tailshaft and the output shaft into position.

17. Using cords, raise the cluster gear into mesh with the main gear train and install the countershaft. The offset lug on the rear of the countershaft must be positioned to allow final installation of the tailshaft.

18. Use a sealer and install the tailshaft bolts. Install the speedometer driven gear.

19. Install the shifter forks for first/second and third/fourth gears so that the numbers stamped on the forks face the front of the transmission. Install the reverse fork with the number facing the rear.

20. Install the retaining clips and the flat washers on the shift levers and install the shift rods to the shift levers.

TYPE 10

4 Speed Transmission–Model F4W63L

1978-81 Datsun 510
1975-77 Datsun 610
1975-81 Datsun 710

DISASSEMBLY

The reverse and reverse idler drive gears are contained in the extension housing of this transmission. On late units, the cast, ribbed bottom cover is replaced by a stamped steel cover. Virtually all of these transmissions imported to the U.S. have a modified extension housing incorporating a floorshift mechanism.

1. Drain the transmission.

2. Remove the clutch throughout lever and release bearing.

3. Remove the clevis pin which connects the striker rod to the shift lever.

4. Remove the speedometer drive pinion assembly.

5. Unbolt and remove the extension housing, disengaging the striker rod from the shift rod gates.

6. Remove the bottom and front covers.

7. Remove the three detent plugs, springs and balls.

8. Drive out the shift fork retaining pins. Remove the rods and forks.

9. Move the first/second and third/fourth coupling sleeves into gear at the same time to lock the mainshaft.

10. Pull out the countershaft and countergear with the two needle roller bearings and spacers.

11. Remove the snap-ring, reverse idler gears, and shaft.

12. Unbolt the mainshaft rear bearing retainer.

13. Pull out the mainshaft assembly to the rear. Pull out the clutch shaft to the front.

14. To disassemble the mainshaft, remove the snap-ring, third/ fourth synchronizer hub and coupling sleeve. Remove third gear, with the roller bearing. Remove the mainshaft nut, lock-plate, speedometer drive gear, and steel ball. Take off reverse gear, and the hub. Press off the bearing and retainer.

ASSEMBLY

1. Assembly procedures are generally the reverse of disassembly, however the following special instructions are required.

2. On the clutch shaft, there should be no end-play between the bearing and the snap-ring. Snap-rings are available in sizes from 0.0598 in. (1.52 mm) to 0.0697 in. (1.77 mm).

3. Some of these transmissions use a servo type synchronizer which utilizes brake bands. To assemble these synchronizers, place each

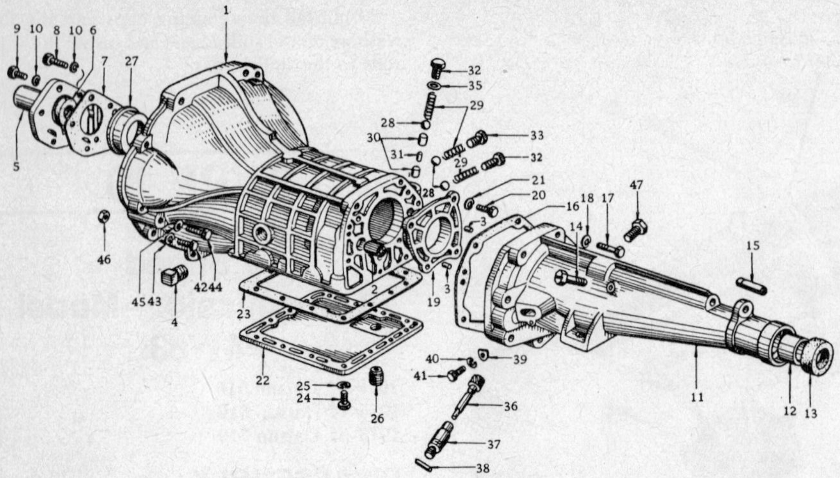

1. Case
2. Needle bearing
3. Dowel pin
4. Plug assembly
5. Front cover
6. Oil seal
7. Gasket
8. Bolt
9. Bolt
0. Lockwasher
11. Extension housing
12. Bushing
13. Oil seal
14. Breather
15. Striker bushing
16. Gasket
17. Bolt
18. Lockwasher
19. Bearing retainer
20. Bolt
21. Lockwasher
22. Bottom cover
23. Gasket
24. Bolt
25. Lockwasher
26. Drain plug
27. Bearing retainer
28. Detent ball
29. Detent spring
30. Interlock plunger
31. Interlock pin
32. Detent plug
33. Detent plug
34. Not used
35. Washer
36. Speedometer pinion
37. Pinion sleeve
38. Pin
39. Lockplate
40. Lockwasher
41. Bolt
42. Bolt
43. Lockwasher
44. Bolt
45. Lockwasher
46. Nut
47. Plug for backup light switch

Transmission case components, model F4W63L

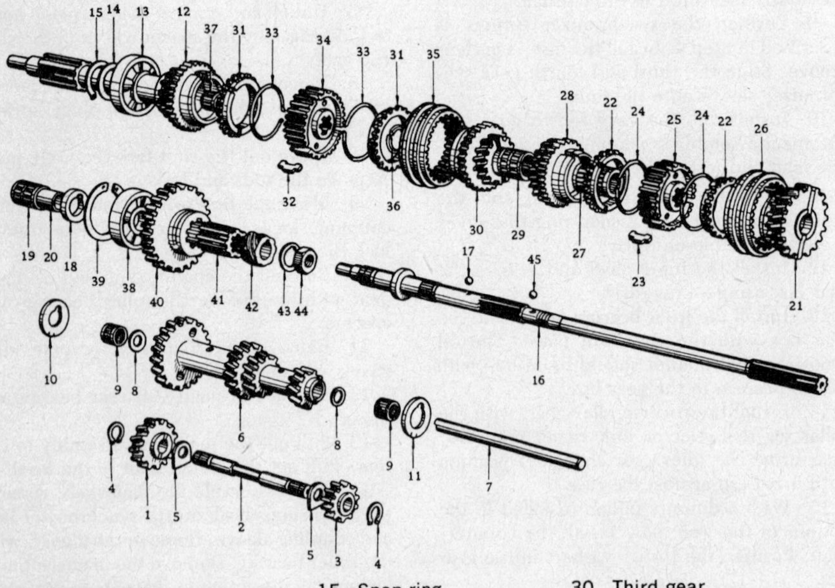

1. Reverse idler gear
2. Reverse idler shaft
3. Main reverse idler gear
4. Snap-ring
5. Thrust washer
6. Countergear
7. Countershaft
8. Spacer
9. Needle bearing
10. Front countershaft thrust washer
11. Rear countershaft thrust washer
12. Main drive gear
13. Main drive gear bearing
14. Washer
15. Snap-ring
16. Mainshaft
17. 5/32" steel ball
18. Thrust washer
19. Needle bearing
20. First gear bushing
21. First gear
22. Baulk ring
23. Shifting insert
24. Spreader ring
25. First/second synchro hub
26. Coupling sleeve
27. Needle bearing
28. Second gear
29. Needle bearing
30. Third gear
31. Baulk ring
32. Shifting insert
33. Spreader ring
34. Third/fourth synchro hub
35. Coupling sleeve
36. Snap-ring
37. Pilot bearing
38. Bearing
39. Snap-ring
40. Reverse gear
41. Reverse gear hub
42. Speedometer drive gear
43. Lockwasher
44. Nut
45. Steel ball

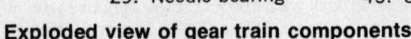

Exploded view of gear train components

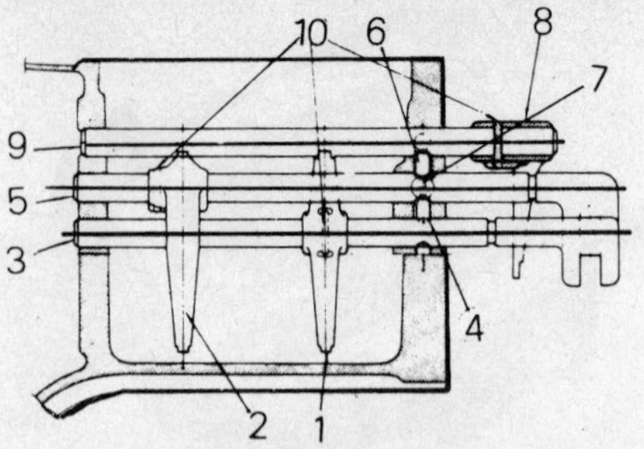

1. First/second shift fork
2. Third/fourth shift fork
3. First/second shift rod
4. Interlock plunger
5. Third/fourth shift rod
6. Interlock plunger
7. Interlock pin
8. Reverse shift fork
9. Reverse shift rod
10. Fork retaining pin

Shift rod and fork details, four speed bottom cover transmission

gear on a flat surface. Install the synchronizer ring into the clutch gear. Place the thrust block and anchor block and install the circlip into the groove.

4. Third gear should be adjusted to give an end-play of 0.0020-0.0059 in. Snap-rings for adjustment are available in sizes from 0.0551 in. to 0.0630 in.

5. Install the reverse idler driving gear on the reverse shaft and fasten with a snap-ring. Install the shaft and gear into the case, placing a thrust washer between the gear and case. Place a thrust washer, idler gear, and snap-ring on the inside end of the shaft. Idler gear end-play should be 0.0039-0.0118 in. Snap-rings are available in sizes from 0.0433 in. to 0.0591 in.

6. Countergear end-play should be 0.0020-0.0059 in. Thrust washers for adjustment are available from 0.0945 in. to 0.1024 in.

7. To assemble the shift mechanism, place the first/second and third/fourth forks onto their sleeves. Insert the first/second shift rod. Install an interlock plunger and then the third/forth shift rod with the interlock pin. Install the other interlock plunger and then

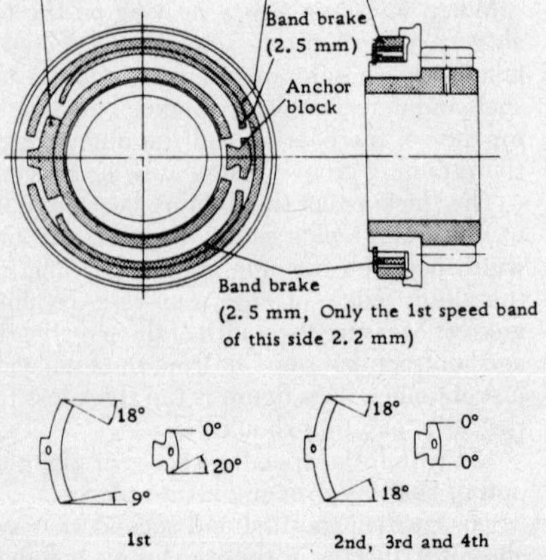

Servo type synchronizer assembly details

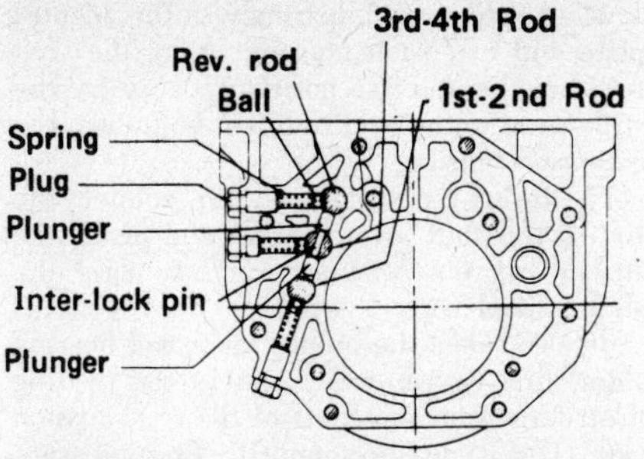

Shift rod interlock details for four speed bottom cover transmission

the reverse shift fork and rod. Place a detent ball and spring into each detent hole. Use sealant on the plug threads.

8. Install the extension housing, engaging the striker rod with the shift rod.

TYPE 11

4 Speed Transmission–Model F4W71B

1975-79 Datsun 280Z, 280ZX
1978-81 Datsun 810

DISASSEMBLY

This transmission is constructed in three sections: clutch housing, transmission housing and extension housing. There are no case cover plates. There is a cast iron adapter plate between the transmission and extension housings.

1. Remove the clutch housing dust cover. Remove the retaining spring, release bearing sleeve, and throwout lever.
2. Remove the backup light/neutral safety switch.
3. Unbolt and remove the clutch housing, rapping with a soft hammer if necessary. Remove the gasket, mainshaft bearing shim, and countershaft bearing shim.
4. Remove the speedometer pinion sleeve.
5. Remove the striker rod pin from the rod. Separate the striker rod from the shift lever bracket.
6. Unbolt and remove the rear extension. It may be necessary to rap the housing with a soft hammer.
7. Remove the mainshaft bearing snap-ring.
8. Remove the adapter plate and gear assembly from the transmission case.
9. Punch out the shift fork retaining pins. Remove the shift rod snap-rings. Remove the detent plugs, springs and balls from the adapter plate. Remove the shift rods, being careful not to lose the interlock balls.
10. Remove the snap-ring, speedometer drive gear and locating ball.
11. Remove the nut, lockwasher, thrust washer, reverse hub and reverse gear.
12. Remove the snap-ring and countershaft reverse gear. Remove the snap-ring, reverse idler gear, thrust washer and needle bearing.
13. Support the gear assembly while rapping on the rear of the mainshaft wih a soft hammer.
14. Remove the setscrew from the adapter plate. Remove the shaft nut, spring washer, plain washer and reverse idler shaft.
15. Remove the bearing retainer and the mainshaft rear bushing.
16. To disassemble the mainshaft (rear section), remove the front snap-ring, third/fourth synchronizer assembly, third gear and needle bearing. From the rear, remove the thrust washer, locating ball, first gear, needle bearing, first gear bushing, first/second synchronizer assembly, second gear, and needle bearing.
17. To disassemble the clutch shaft, remove the snap-ring and bearing spacer and press off the bearing.
18. To disassemble the countershaft, press off the front bearing. Press off the rear bearing, press off the gears and remove the keys.
19. Remove the retaining pin, control arm pin and shift control arm from the rear of the extension housing.

ASSEMBLY

1. Place the O-ring in the front cover. Install the front cover to the clutch housing with a press. Put in the front cover oil seal.
2. Install the rear extension oil seal.
3. Assemble the first/second and third/fourth synchronizer assemblies. Make sure that the ring gaps are not both on the same side of the unit.

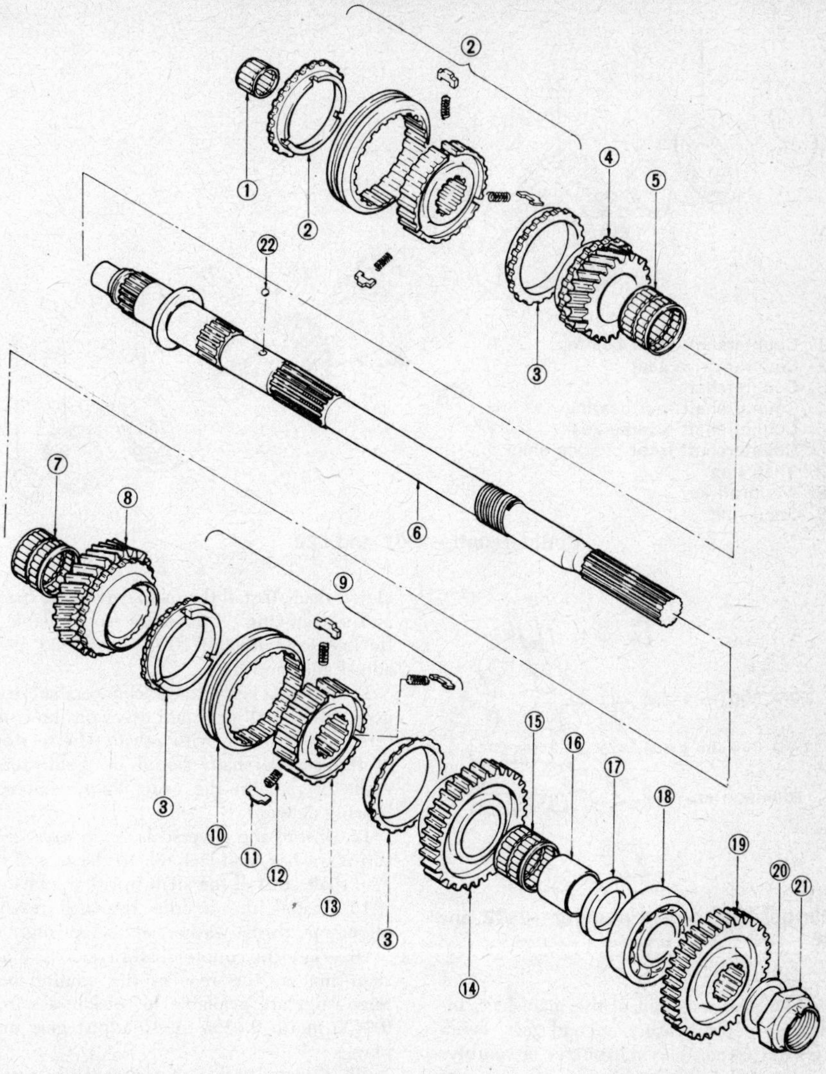

1. Pilot bearing
2. 3rd & 4th synchromesh assembly
3. Baulk ring
4. 3rd gear, mainshaft
5. Needle bearing
6. Mainshaft
7. Needle bearing
8. 2nd gear, mainshaft
9. 1st & 2nd synchromesh assembly
10. Coupling sleeve
11. Shifting insert
12. Spread spring
13. Synchronizer hub
14. 1st gear, mainshaft
15. Needle bearing
16. Bushing, 1st gear
17. Thrust washer, mainshaft
18. Mainshaft bearing
19. Reverse gear, mainshaft
10. Thrust washer
21. Nut
22. Steel ball

Mainshaft—280Z

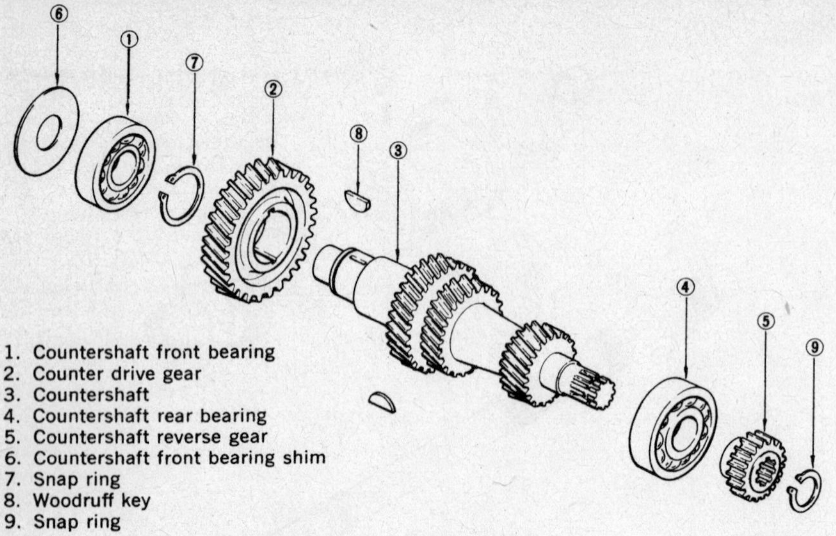

1. Countershaft front bearing
2. Counter drive gear
3. Countershaft
4. Countershaft rear bearing
5. Countershaft reverse gear
6. Countershaft front bearing shim
7. Snap ring
8. Woodruff key
9. Snap ring

Countershaft—280Z and 620

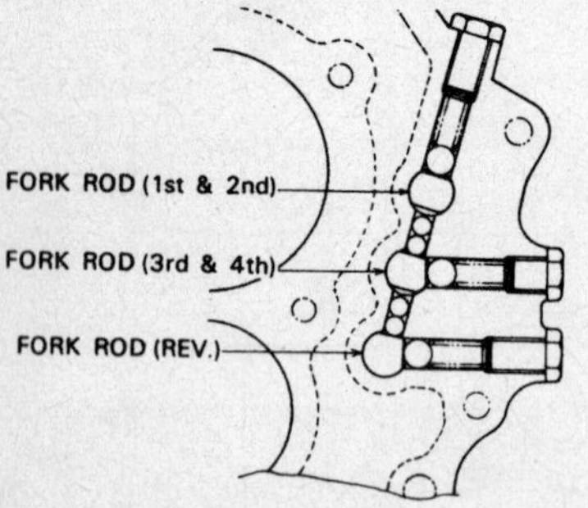

Interlock and detent plunger—280Z and 620

4. On the rear end of the mainshaft, install the needle bearing, second gear, baulk ring, first/second synchronizer assembly, baulk ring, first gear bushing, needle bearing, first gear, locating ball and thrust washer.

5. Drive or press on the mainshaft rear bearing.

6. Install the countershaft rear bearing to the adapter plate. Drive or press the mainshaft rear bearing into the adapter plate until the bearing snap-ring groove comes through the rear side of the plate. Install the snap-ring. If it is not tight against the plate, press the bearing back in slightly.

7. Insert the countershaft bearing ring between the countershaft rear bearing and bearing retainer. Install the bearing retainer to the adapter plate. Stake both ends of the screws.

8. Insert the reverse idler shaft from the rear of the adapter plate. Install the spring washer and plain washer to the idler shaft.

9. Place the two keys on the countershaft and oil the shaft lightly. Press on third gear and install a snap-ring.

10. Install the countershaft into its rear bearing.

11. From the front of the mainshaft, install the needle bearing, third gear, baulk ring, third/fourth synchronizer assembly and snap-ring. Snap-rings are available in thicknesses from 0.0561 in. to 0.0640 in. to adjust gear end-play.

12. Press the main drive bearing onto the clutch shaft. Install the main drive gear spacer and a snap-ring. Snap-rings are available in thicknesses from 0.0710 in. to 0.0820 in. to adjust gear end-play.

13. Insert a key into the countershaft drive gear with fourth gear and drive on the countershaft fourth gear with a drift. The rear end of the countershaft should be held steady while driving on the gear, to prevent rear bearing damage.

14. Install the reverse hub, reverse gear, thrust washer, and lock tab on the rear of the mainshaft. Install the shaft nut temporarily.

15. Install the needle bearing, reverse idler gear, thrust washer, and snap-ring.

16. Place the countershaft reverse gear and snap-ring on the rear of the countershaft. Snap-rings are available in thicknesses from 0.0433 in. to 0.0590 in. to adjust gear end-play.

17. Engage both first and second gears to lock the shaft.

18. On the rear of the mainshaft, install the snap-ring, locating ball, speedometer drive gear, and snap-ring. Snap-rings are available in thicknesses from 0.0433 in. to 0.0590 in.

19. Recheck end-play and backlash of all gears.

20. Place the reverse shift fork on the reverse gear and install the reverse shift rod. Install the detent ball, spring and plug. Install the fork retaining pin. Place two interlock balls between the reverse shift rod and the third/fourth shift rod location. Install the third/fourth shift fork and rod. Install the detent ball, spring and plug. This plug is shorter than the other two. Install the fork retaining pin. Place two interlock balls between the first/second shift rod location and the third/fourth shift rod. Install the first/second shift fork and rod. Install the detent ball, spring and plug.

21. Install the shift rod snap-rings.

22. Apply sealant sparingly to the adapter plate and transmission housing. Install the transmission housing to the adapter plate and bolt it down temporarily.

23. Drive in the countershaft front bearing with a drift. Place the snap-ring in the mainshaft front bearing.

24. Apply sealant sparingly to the adapter plate and extension housing. Align the shift rods in the neutral positions. Position the striker rod to the shift rods and bolt down the extension housing.

25. Insert the striker rod pin, connect the rod to the shift lever bracket and install the striker rod pin retaining ring. Replace the shift control arm.

26. To select the proper mainshaft bearing shim, first measure the amount the bearing protrudes from the front of the transmission case. This is measurement (B). Then measure the depth of the bearing recess in the rear of the clutch housing. This is measurement (A). Required shim thickness is found by subtracting (B) from (A). Shims are available in thicknesses of 0.0551 in. and 0.0630 in.

27. To select the proper countershaft front bearing shim, measure the amount that the bearing is recessed into the transmission case. Shim thickness should equal this measurement. Shims are available in thicknesses from 0.0157 in. (.4 mm) to 0.0394 in. (1.0 mm).

28. Apply sealant sparingly to the clutch and transmission housing mating surfaces.

29. Replace the clutch operating mechanism.

30. Install the shift lever temporarily and check shifting action.

TYPE 12

5 Speed Transmission–Model FS5W71B

1977-81 Datsun 280Z
280ZX
710
810

This transmission is similar to the 4 speed transmission, model F4W71B and the overhaul can be accomplished by following the outline for the disassembly and assembly of the model F4W71B transmission.

Servo type synchromesh is used, instead of the Borg-Warner type in the four speed. Shift linkage and interlock arrangements are the same, except the reverse shift rod also operates fifth gear. Most service procedures are identical to those for the four speed unit. Those unique to the five-speed follow.

DISASSEMBLY

To disassemble the synchronizers, remove the circlip, synchronizer ring, thrust block, brake band, and anchor block. Be careful not to mix parts of the different synchronizer assemblies.

ASSEMBLY

1. The synchronizer assemblies for second, third, and fourth are identical. When assembling the first gear synchronizer, be sure to install the 0.0866 in. thick brake band at the bottom.

2. When assembling the mainshaft, select a third gear synchronizer hub snap-ring to minimize hub end-play. Snap-rings are available in thicknesses of 0.061-0.630 in. 0.0591-0.0610 in. and 0.0571-0.0591 in. The synchronizer hub must be installed with the longer boss to the rear.

3. When reassembling the gear train, install the mainshaft, countershaft, and gears to the adapter plate. Hold the rear nut and force the front nut against it to a torque of 217 ft/lbs. Select a snap-ring to minimize end-play of the fifth gear bearing at the rear of the mainshaft. Snap-rings are available in thicknesses from 0.0433 in. to 0.0551 in.

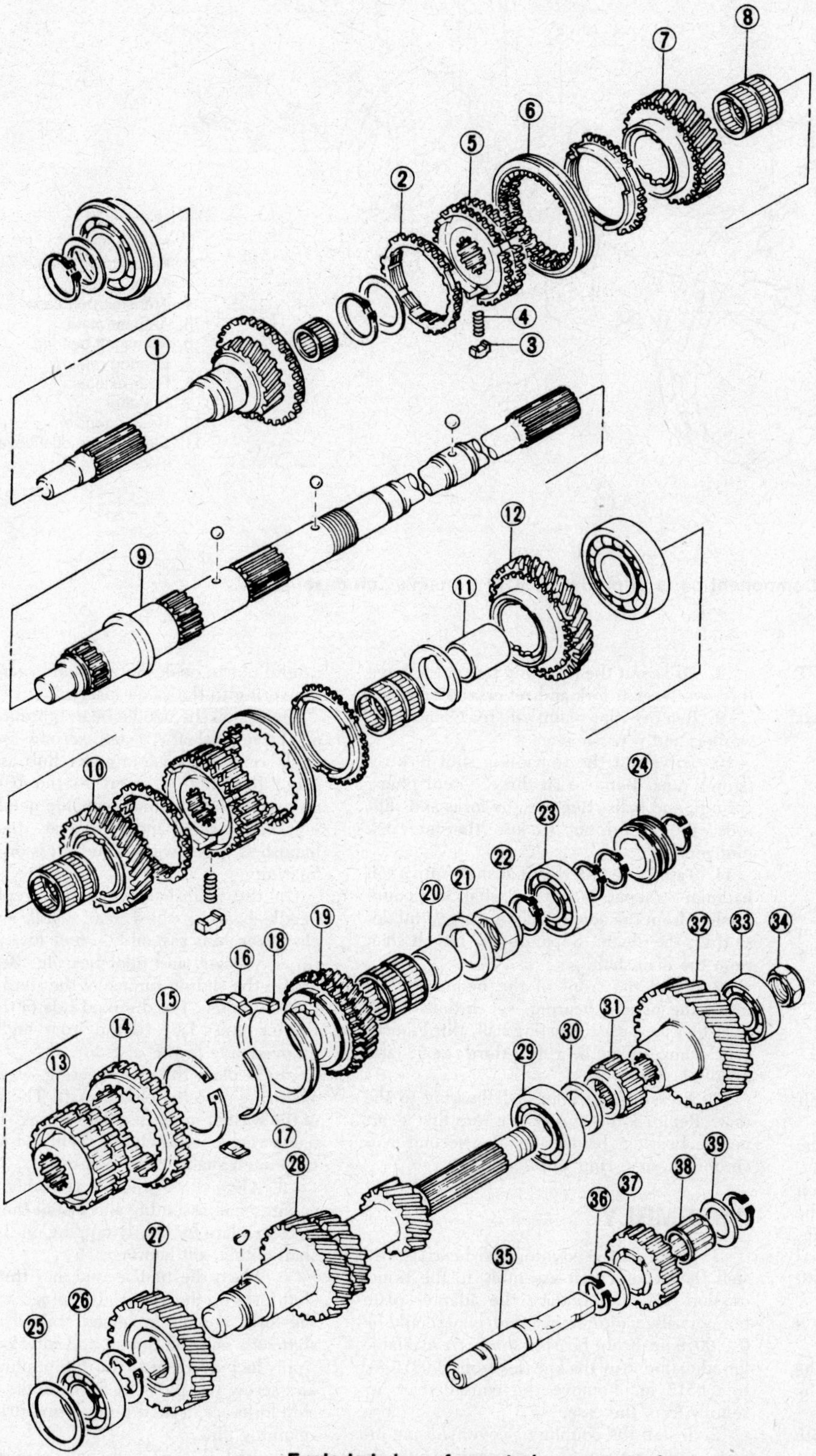

1. Main drive gear
2. Baulk ring
3. Shifting insert
4. Shifting insert spring
5. Synchronizer hub
6. Coupling sleeve
7. 3rd main gear
8. Needle bearing
9. Mainshaft
10. 2nd main gear
11. Bushing
12. 1st main gear
13. OD-reverse synchronizer hub
14. Reverse gear
15. Circlip
16. Thrust block
17. Brake band
18. Synchronizer ring
19. Overdrive main gear
20. Overdrive gear bushing
21. Washer
22. Mainshaft nut
23. Overdrive mainshaft bearing
24. Speedometer drive gear
25. Countershaft front bearing shim
26. Countershaft front bearing
27. Countershaft drive gear
28. Countershaft
29. Countershaft bearing
30. Reverse counter gear spacer
31. Reverse counter gear
32. Overdrive counter gear
33. Countershaft rear bearing
34. Countershaft nut
35. Reverse idler shaft
36. Reverse idler thrust washer
37. Reverse idler gear
38. Reverse idler gear bearing
39. Reverse idler thrust washer

Exploded view of gear train components

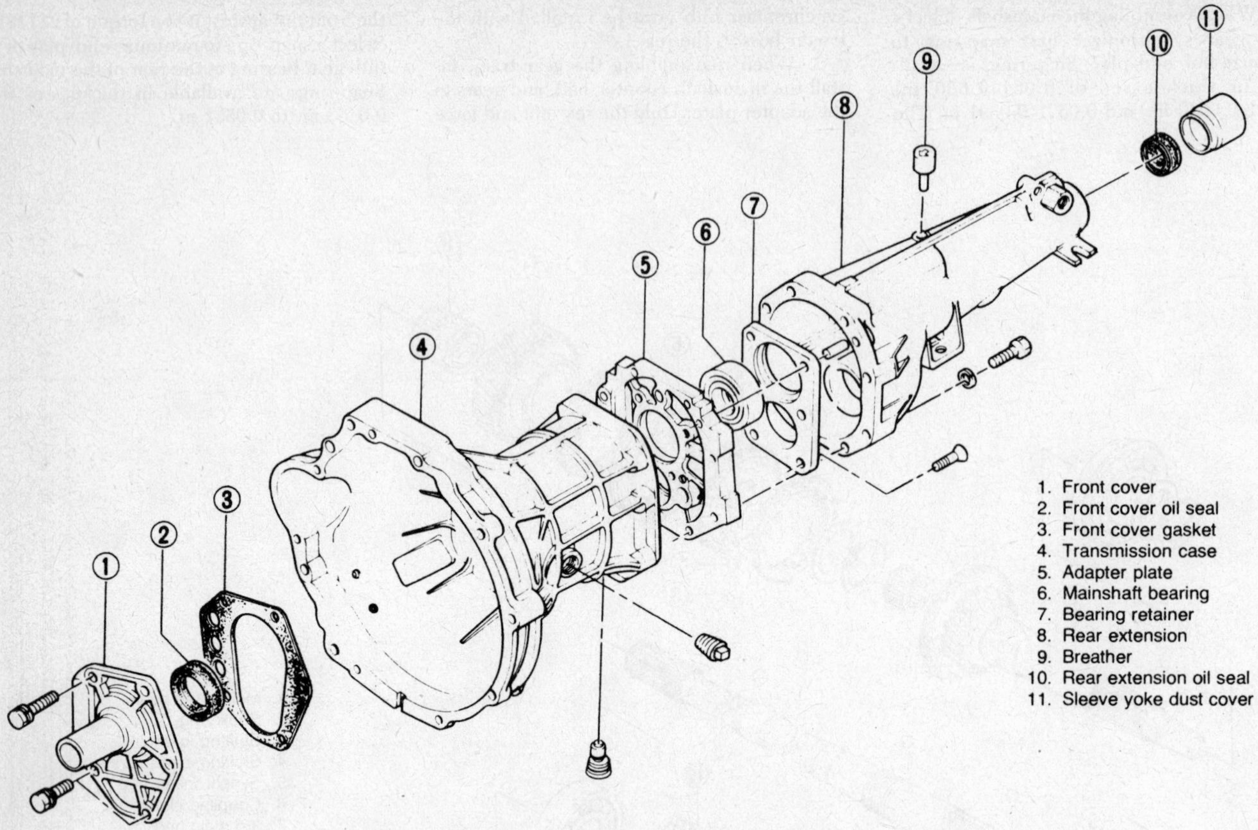

Component parts of model FS5C71 transmission case

TYPE 13

4 Speed Transmission–Model F4W56A

1980-81 Datsun 210

This transmission is constructed in two sections: a combined clutch and transmission housing, and an extension housing. There is a cast iron adapter plate between the housings. There are no case cover plates.

DISASSEMBLY

1. Drain the oil.
2. Remove the dust cover, spring, clutch throwout lever, and release bearing.
3. Remove the front cover from inside the clutch housing.
4. Remove the speedometer drive pinion from the extension housing. Remove the striker rod return spring plug, spring, plunger, and bushing. Remove the striker rod pin and separate the striker rod from the shift lever bracket.
5. Remove the extension housing. Tap it with a soft hammer, if necessary.
6. Separate the adapter plate from the transmission case, being careful not to lose the countershaft bearing washer.
7. Clamp the adapter plate in a vise with the reverse idler gear up.
8. Drive out the retaining pin and remove the reverse shift fork and reverse idler gear.
9. Remove the mainshaft rear snap-ring, washer, and reverse gear.
10. Drive out the remaining shift fork retaining pins. Remove all three detent plugs, springs, and balls. Remove the forks and shift rods. Be careful not to lose the interlock plungers.
11. Tap the rear of the mainshaft with a soft hammer to separate the mainshaft and countershaft from the adapter plate. Be careful not to drop the shafts. Separate the clutch shaft from the mainshaft.
12. From the front of the mainshaft, remove the needle bearing, synchronizer hub thrust washer, steel locating ball, third/fourth synchronizer, baulk ring, third gear, and needle bearing.
13. Press off the mainshaft bearing to the rear. Remove the thrust washer, first gear, needle bearing, baulk ring, first/second synchronizer, snap-ring and bearing.

ASSEMBLY

1. Press on the countershaft bearings. Install the countershaft assembly to the transmission case and replace the adapter plate temporarily. Countershaft end-play should be 0-0.0079 in. Front bearing shims are available for adjustment in thicknesses from 0.0315 in. to 0.0512 in. Remove the countershaft assembly from the case.
2. Install the coupling sleeve, shifting inserts, and spring on the synchronizer hub. Be careful not to hook the front and rear ends of the spring to the same insert.
3. Install the needle bearing from the rear of the mainshaft. Install second gear, the baulk ring, and synchronizer hub assembly. Align the shifting insert to the baulk ring groove. Install the first gear side needle bearing, baulk ring, and first gear. Install the mainshaft thrust washer and press on the rear bearing.

   On the mainshaft front end, replace the needle bearing, third gear, baulk ring, synchronizer hub assembly, steel locating ball, thrust washer, and pilot bearing. Be sure to grease the sliding surface of the steel ball and thrust washer. The dimpled side of the thrust washer must face to the front and the oil grooved side to the rear.
4. Replace the main bearing, washer, and snap-ring onto the clutch shaft. The web side of the washer must face the bearing. Place the baulk ring on the clutch shaft and assemble the clutch shaft to the mainshaft.
5. Align the mainshaft assembly with the countershaft assembly and install them to the adapter plate by lightly tapping on the clutch shaft with a soft hammer.
6. Place the first/second and third/fourth shift forks on the shift rods, being careful that the forks are not reversed. Install all three shift rods and the detent and interlock parts. Apply locking agent to the detent plug threads and screw the plugs in flush. Make sure the shift forks are in their grooves and drive in the retaining pins.
7. Install the mainshaft reverse gear,

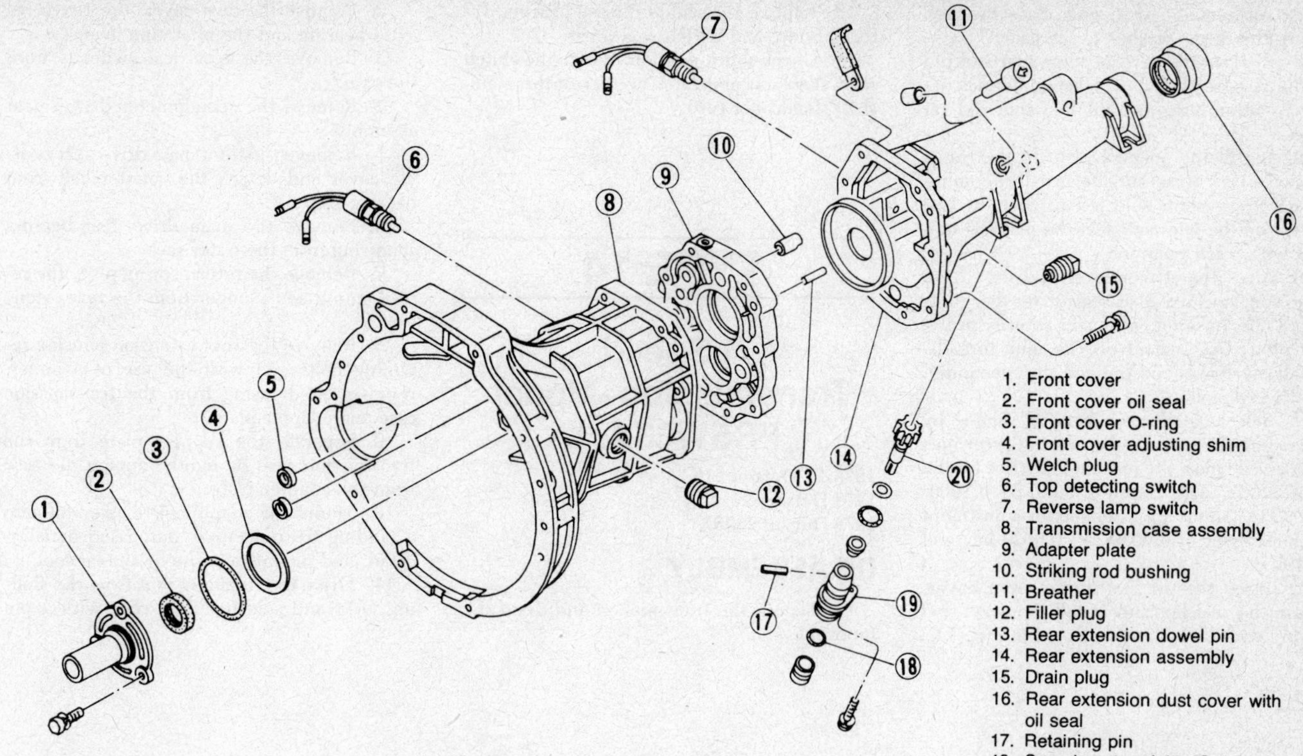

1. Front cover
2. Front cover oil seal
3. Front cover O-ring
4. Front cover adjusting shim
5. Welch plug
6. Top detecting switch
7. Reverse lamp switch
8. Transmission case assembly
9. Adapter plate
10. Striking rod bushing
11. Breather
12. Filler plug
13. Rear extension dowel pin
14. Rear extension assembly
15. Drain plug
16. Rear extension dust cover with oil seal
17. Retaining pin
18. Speedometer pinion O-ring
19. Speedometer sleeve
20. Speedometer pinion

Transmission case components—model F4W56A

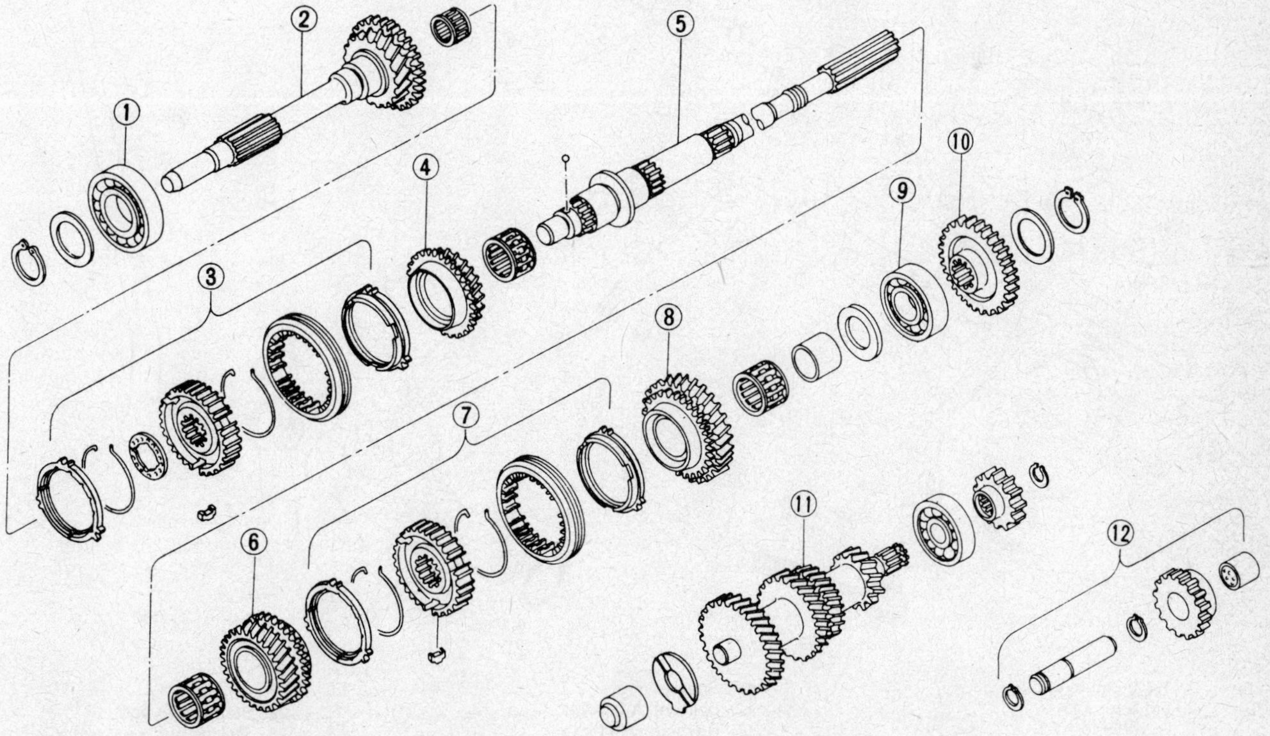

1. Main drive bearing
2. Main drive gear
3. 3rd & top synchronizer
4. 3rd gear, mainshaft
5. Mainshaft
6. 2nd gear, mainshaft
7. 1st & 2nd synchronizer
8. 1st gear, mainshaft
9. Mainshaft bearing
10. Reverse gear, mainshaft
11. Counter gear assembly
12. Idler gear assembly

Exploded view of the gear train components

thrust washer, and snap-ring. Face the web side of the thrust washer to the gear.

8. Replace the reverse idler gear and pin on the reverse shift fork. Check interlock action by attempting to shift two shift rods at once.

9. Install the adapter plate to the transmission case. Make sure to install the countergear front shim selected in Step 1. Use sealant on the joint and seat the plate by tapping with a soft hammer.

10. Align the striker lever and install the extension housing. Use sealant on the joint. Install the bushing, plunger, return spring, and plug. Use sealant on the plug threads. Install the striker rod pin and the speedometer drive pinion.

11. Select clutch shaft bearing shim(s) by measuring the amount the bearing outer race is recessed below the machined surface for the front cover. The depth should be 0.1969-0.2028 in. Shims are available for adjustment in thicknesses of 0.0039 in., 0.0079 in., and 0.0197 in.

12. Place the oil seal in the front cover, grease the seal lip, and install the cover and O-ring with the shim(s) selected in Step 11.

13. Replace the clutch release bearing, return spring, and withdrawal lever.

14. Check shifting action. Rotate the clutch shaft slowly in neutral. The rear of the mainshaft should not turn.

TYPE 14

5 Speed Transmission–Model FS5W63A, L

1978-81 Datsun 510
1978 Datsun B210
1979 Datsun 200SX

DISASSEMBLY

1. Secure the transmission and drain the lubricant.

2. Remove the dust cover, the clutch release bearing and the operating lever.

3. Remove the electrical switches from the case.

4. Remove the speedometer driven gear assembly.

5. Remove the front main drive gear bearing cover and detach the countershaft front bearing shim.

6. Remove the main drive gear bearing snap-ring from the outer race.

7. Remove the return spring plug, the return spring and plunger from the rear extension.

8. Remove the rear extension housing retaining bolts and with the use of a puller, remove the housing from the transmission case and adapter plate.

9. Separate the adapter plate from the transmission case by lightly tapping the case from the adapter plate.

10. Mount the adapter plate assembly into a holding fixture, either purchased or fabricated, and mount in a vise or similar tool.

11. Drive the retaining pins from the shifting forks and selector shaft rods with a pin punch.

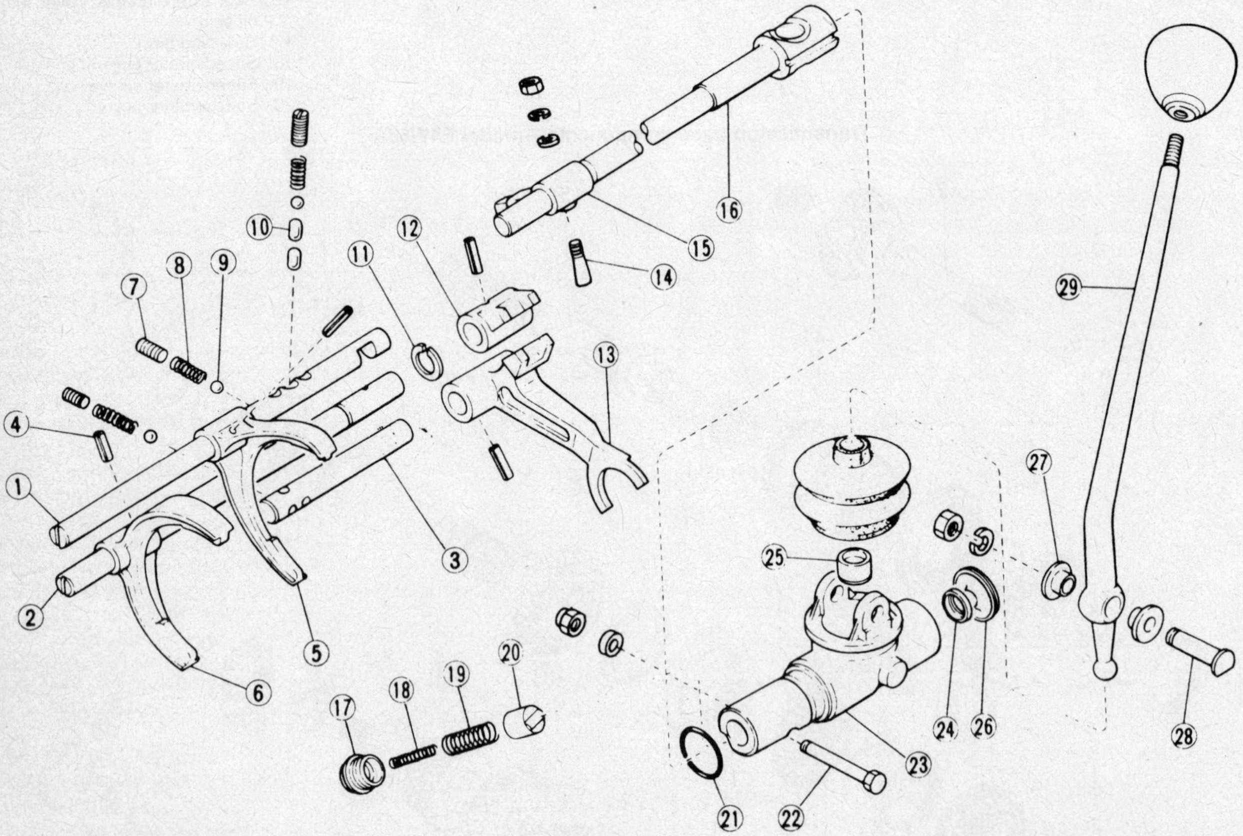

1. 1st & 2nd fork rod
2. 3rd & top fork rod
3. Reverse fork rod
4. Retaining pin
5. 1st & 2nd shift fork
6. 3rd & top shift fork
7. Checking ball plug
8. Check ball spring
9. Check ball
10. Interlock plunger
11. Stopper ring
12. Shift rod A bracket
13. Reverse shift fork
14. Lock pin
15. Striking lever
16. Striking rod
17. Return spring plug
18. Reverse check spring
19. Return spring
20. Plunger
21. O-ring
22. Stopper pin bolt
23. Striking guide assembly
24. Striking guide oil seal
25. Control lever bushing
26. Expansion plug
27. Control pin bushing
28. Control arm pin
29. Control lever

Exploded view of shift selector rod and fork components

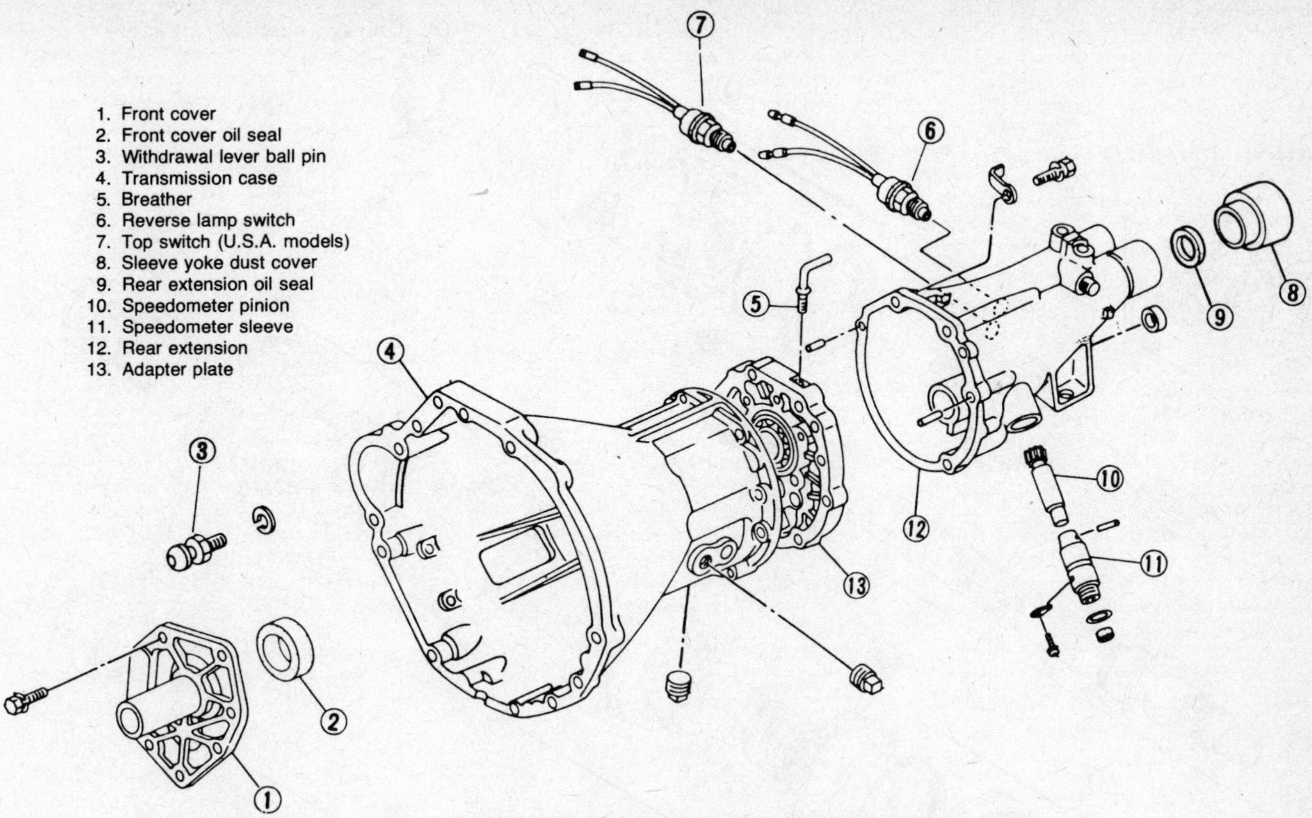

Transmission case components, model FS5W63A

12. Remove the three selector rod check ball plugs. Remove the check balls and springs.

13. Remove the selector rods from the front to the rear by lightly tapping on the rods with a soft-faced hammer. Remove the interlock plungers.

14. Remove the mainshaft bearing snap-ring and with the aid of a puller, remove the mainshaft bearing from the shaft. Remove the second snap-ring from the mainshaft.

15. Engage two gears to lock the gear train and remove the mainshaft locking nut, from the rear extension side.

16. After the nut has been removed, remove the speedometer drive gear and steel ball, the synchronizer hub with reverse gear, 1st gear with the needle bearing and the bushing, the idler gear and needle bearing. Remove the thrust washer and the second steel ball.

17. From the rear extension housing end of the adapter plate, remove the snap-ring and thrust washer, 1st gear using a puller tool, from the countershaft.

18. Attaching a special pushing tool or equivalent, to the adapter plate and push the mainshaft approximately 0.39 inch (10 mm) from the adapter plate. Remove the main drive gear and the countergear. Holding the mainshaft gear assembly by hand, remove the mainshaft and mainshaft gears as an assembly.

19. After the mainshaft has been removed, take the thrust washer, the steel ball, 2nd gear and the needle bearing from the mainshaft.

20. Using a press or similar tool, remove the 2nd gear mainshaft bushing, 3rd gear and the 2nd/3rd synchronizer assembly from the mainshaft.

21. Remove the snap-ring on the front end of the mainshaft and remove the 4th/5th speed synchronizer and the 5th gear.

22. The bearing can be removed from the maindrive gear by the removal of the snap-ring and spacer. The bearing should be pressed from the shaft.

23. Remove the front and rear bearings from the countergear by using a press or similar tool.

24. To disassemble the synchronizers, remove the spread springs and the shift inserts. Separate the coupling sleeve from the hub.

25. With the adapter plate still in the holding fixture, remove the bearing retainer bolts with an appropriate tool. Remove the bearing from the rear extension side of the adapter plate. The outer race of the counter gear rear bearing can be removed from the adapter plate with the aid of a brass punch.

26. The rear extension housing can be disassembled by the removal of the lock pin from the striking lever and the main selector shift rod (striking rod). The rod can then be removed from the housing.

27. Replace all necessary parts, seals and gaskets.

ASSEMBLY

1. With the adapter plate in the holding fixture and locked in a vise or appropriate tool, install the countergear bearing outer race. Install the mainshaft bearing. Install the bearing retainer and screws. Torque the screws to 5.8 to 9.4 ft/lbs (0.8 to 1.3 Kg-m). Stake each screw head to the retainer at two points.

2. Assemble the synchronizers by placing the hubs into the coupling sleeves. Fit the inserts into their respective grooves and install the spread springs so that the ends of the springs are not in the same insert.

3. Install the 5th speed needle bearing, 5th gear, synchronizer (baulk) ring and the 4th/5th speed synchronizer assembly on the front of the mainshaft.

4. Install a selective snap-ring onto the mainshaft so that the minimum clearance exists between the end face of the hub and the snap-ring. The snap-ring can be selected from the following list:

	Thickness	
No.	mm	(in.)
1	1.40 to 1.45	(0.0551 to 0.0571)
2	1.45 to 1.50	(0.0571 to 0.0591)
3	1.50 to 1.55	(0.0591 to 0.0610)
4	1.55 to 1.60	(0.0610 to 0.0630)
5	1.60 to 1.65	(0.0630 to 0.0650)

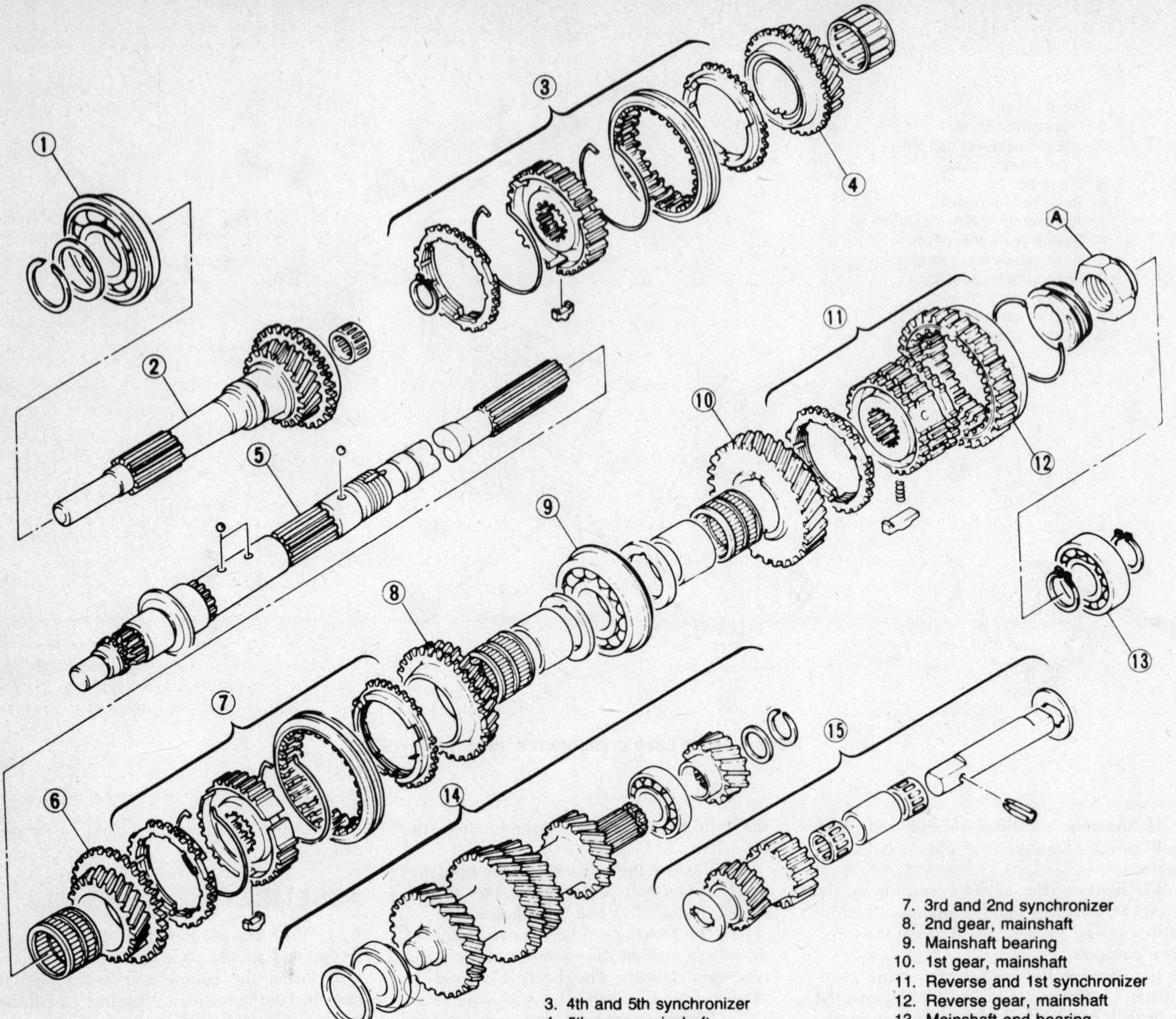

1. Main drive bearing
2. Main drive gear
3. 4th and 5th synchronizer
4. 5th gear, mainshaft
5. Mainshaft
6. 3rd gear, mainshaft
7. 3rd and 2nd synchronizer
8. 2nd gear, mainshaft
9. Mainshaft bearing
10. 1st gear, mainshaft
11. Reverse and 1st synchronizer
12. Reverse gear, mainshaft
13. Mainshaft end bearing
14. Counter gear assembly
15. Idler gear assembly

Exploded view of gear train components

5. Install the 3rd gear needle bearing, 3rd gear, 3rd gear synchronizer (baulk) ring, 2nd/3rd gear synchronizer, fit the 2nd gear bushing to the mainshaft, along with the mainshaft bearing thrust washer.

6. Install the 2nd speed synchronizer (baulk) ring, needle bearing, 2nd gear, steel ball and the thrust washer.

7. Press the main drive gear bearing on to the main drive gear and install the spacer and secure with a snap-ring that will eliminate end-play between the spacer and the snap-ring. A selective snap-ring can be selected from the following list:

No.	Thickness mm	(in.)
1	1.49 to 1.55	(0.0587 to 0.0610)
2	1.56 to 1.62	(0.0614 to 0.0638)
3	1.62 to 1.68	(0.0638 to 0.0661)
4	1.68 to 1.74	(0.0661 to 0.0685)
5	1.74 to 1.80	(0.0685 to 0.0709)
6	1.80 to 1.86	(0.0709 to 0.0732)
7	1.86 to 1.92	(0.0732 to 0.0756)

8. Press the front and rear bearings onto the countergear with appropriate tools.

9. Place the mainshaft assembly into the adapter plate and place the mainshaft nut onto the shaft.

10. Using a puller type tool, move the mainshaft into the adapter plate until the thrust washer to bearing clearance is approximately 0.39 inch (10. mm).

11. Install the pilot bearing into the main drive gear bore and install the main drive gear and the synchronizer (baulk) ring onto the mainshaft assembly.

12. Assemble the countergear assembly to the mainshaft gear assembly.

13. Continuing the pulling effort, move the mainshaft and countergear assemblies into the adapter plate.

14. Place the 1st countergear on the countergear assembly and press into position. Install the spacer on the rear of the 1st countergear and secure it with a new snap-ring.

15. Install the steel ball and the thick thrust washer on the end of the mainshaft, install the synchronizer with the reverse gear, 1st gear along with the needle bearing and bushing, the idler gear and the needle bearing.

16. Install the mainshaft nut and tighten it snugly. Lock two gears at the same time to lock the gear train, and tighten the locknut to 101 to 123 ft/lbs (14 to 17 Kg-m). Stake the nut to the groove of the mainshaft with a punch.

17. Check the gear end-play, which should conform to the following specifications:

1st gear
 0.27 to 0.37 mm
 (0.0106 to 0.0146 in.)
2nd gear
 0.20 to 0.30 mm
 (0.0079 to 0.0118 in.)
3rd gear
 0.05 to 0.15 mm
 (0.0020 to 0.0059 in.)
5th gear
 0.05 to 0.20 mm
 (0.0020 to 0.0079 in.)
Reverse idler gear
 0.15 to 0.40 mm
 (0.0059 to 0.0157 in.)

18. Fit a 0.043 inch (1.1 mm) thick snap-ring to the front side of the mainshaft end bearing. Install the mainshaft end bearing and fit another snap-ring to the mainshaft on the rear side of the bearing, to eliminate end-play. A list of selective snap-rings are available as follows:

No.	Thickness mm	(in)
1	1.1	(0.043)
2	1.2	(0.047)
3	1.3	(0.051)
4	1.4	(0.055)

19. Place the 1st/reverse selector rod into the adapter plate, position the 1st/reverse fork into its gear position, and slide the selector rod into the fork.

20. Place the 1st/reverse selector rod in the neutral position and install the interlock plunger into the adapter plate.

21. Insert the 2nd/3rd selector rod into the adapter plate, position the 2nd/3rd and 4th/5th forks in their respective gear grooves and slide the 2nd/3rd selector rod through the 2nd/3rd and 4th/5th forks.

22. Place the 2nd/3rd selector rod in the neutral position and insert the interlock plunger in the adapter plate.

23. Install the 4th/5th selector rod into the adapter plate and through the 4th/5th fork.

24. Secure the forks to the selector rods with the retaining pins.

25. Install the check balls and springs in their respective bores of the adapter plate.

26. Apply sealer to the check ball plugs and install the plugs in the adapter plate.

NOTE: The check ball plug for the 1st/reverse selector rod is longer than the other plugs.

27. To insure that the interlock plungers are operating properly, slide the 2nd/3rd selector rod into gear and attempt to move the other selector rods into gear. The gears should not mesh. Continue to check the remaining selector rods.

28. Remove the adapter plate from the holder tool. Apply sealer to the mating surfaces of the transmission case and the adapter plate.

29. Slide the transmission case onto the adapter plate by lightly tapping on the case with a soft hammer until the case and the adapter plate meet. Be sure the dowel pin is properly aligned.

30. As the case is being installed to the adapter plate, the front drive gear bearing and the countergear front bearing must be aligned to the transmission case.

31. Install the front drive gear bearing snap-ring into the bearing groove.

32. Assemble the main selector rod to the rear extension housing in the reverse of its removal. Apply sealer to the mating surfaces of the extension housing and the transmission case. Place the transmission gear train in the

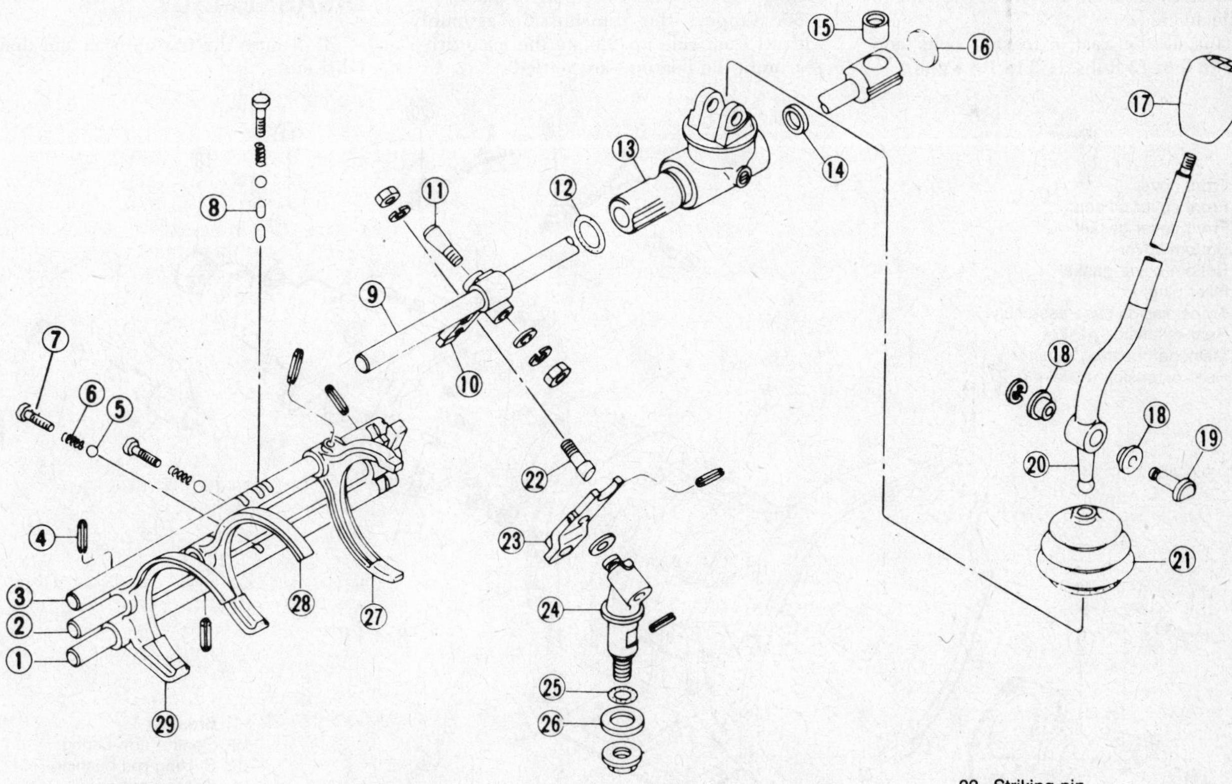

1. 4th and 5th fork rod
2. 2nd and 3rd fork rod
3. 1st and reverse fork rod
4. Retaining pin
5. Checking ball
6. Check ball spring
7. Check ball plug
8. Interlock plunger
9. Striking rod
10. Striking lever
11. Lock pin
12. O-ring
13. Striking guide
14. Striking guide oil seal
15. Control lever bushing
16. Expansion plug
17. Control lever knob
18. Control pin bushing
19. Control arm pin
20. Control lever
21. Control lever boot
22. Striking pin
23. Shift arm
24. Shift arm bracket
25. Arm bracket O-ring
26. Arm bracket plain washer
27. 1st and reverse shift fork
28. 2nd and 3rd shift fork
29. 4th and 5th shift fork

Exploded view of shift selector rod and fork components

No.	"H" mm	(in)	Thickness of countershaft front bearing shim mm	(in)
1	1.200 to 1.225	(0.0472 to 0.0482)	1.350	(0.0531)
2	1.225 to 1.250	(0.0482 to 0.0492)	1.375	(0.0541)
3	1.250 to 1.275	(0.0492 to 0.0502)	1.400	(0.0551)
4	1.275 to 1.300	(0.0502 to 0.0512)	1.425	(0.0561)
5	1.300 to 1.325	(0.0512 to 0.0522)	1.450	(0.0571)
6	1.325 to 1.350	(0.0522 to 0.0531)	1.475	(0.0581)
7	1.350 to 1.375	(0.0531 to 0.0541)	1.500	(0.0591)
8	1.375 to 1.400	(0.0541 to 0.0551)	1.525	(0.0600)
9	1.400 to 1.425	(0.0551 to 0.0561)	1.550	(0.0610)
10	1.425 to 1.450	(0.0561 to 0.0571)	1.575	(0.0620)
11	1.450 to 1.475	(0.0571 to 0.0581)	1.600	(0.0630)
12	1.475 to 1.500	(0.0581 to 0.0591)	1.625	(0.0640)
13	1.500 to 1.525	(0.0591 to 0.0600)	1.650	(0.0650)
14	1.525 to 1.550	(0.0600 to 0.0610)	1.675	(0.0659)
15	1.550 to 1.575	(0.0610 to 0.0620)	1.700	(0.0669)
16	1.575 to 1.600	(0.0620 to 0.0630)	1.725	(0.0679)
17	1.600 to 1.625	(0.0630 to 0.0640)	1.750	(0.0689)
18	1.625 to 1.650	(0.0640 to 0.0650)	1.775	(0.0699)

5th gear and install the rear extension into place.

33. During the installation of the rear extension housing, align the striking lever into the selector rods.

34. Install the rear extension bolts and torque to 9 to 13 ft/lbs. (1.3 to 1.8 Kg-m).

35. Install the plunger into the rear extension. Install the reverse check spring and the return spring. Apply sealer to the return spring plug and install the plug in place.

36. Support the transmission assembly with its front side up. Rotate the main drive gear until the bearings are settled.

37. Using a special measuring tool or equivalent, measure the clearance between the measuring tool, mounted on the countergear, and the transmission case, using a thickness gauge.

38. When the correct shim is selected, install the front cover. Apply sealant to the threads of the bolts and torque to 9 to 13 ft/lbs (1.3 to 1.8 Kg-m).

39. Install the speedometer driven gear assembly, install the electrical switches that were removed during the disassembly.

40. Install the operating lever, the clutch release bearing and the return spring.

41. Install the dust cover, fill the transmission to the proper level with lubricant.

TYPE 15

4 Speed Transmission–Model F4W63L

1978-81 Datsun 510
1980-81 Datsun 710

DISASSEMBLY

1. Secure the transmission and drain the lubricant.

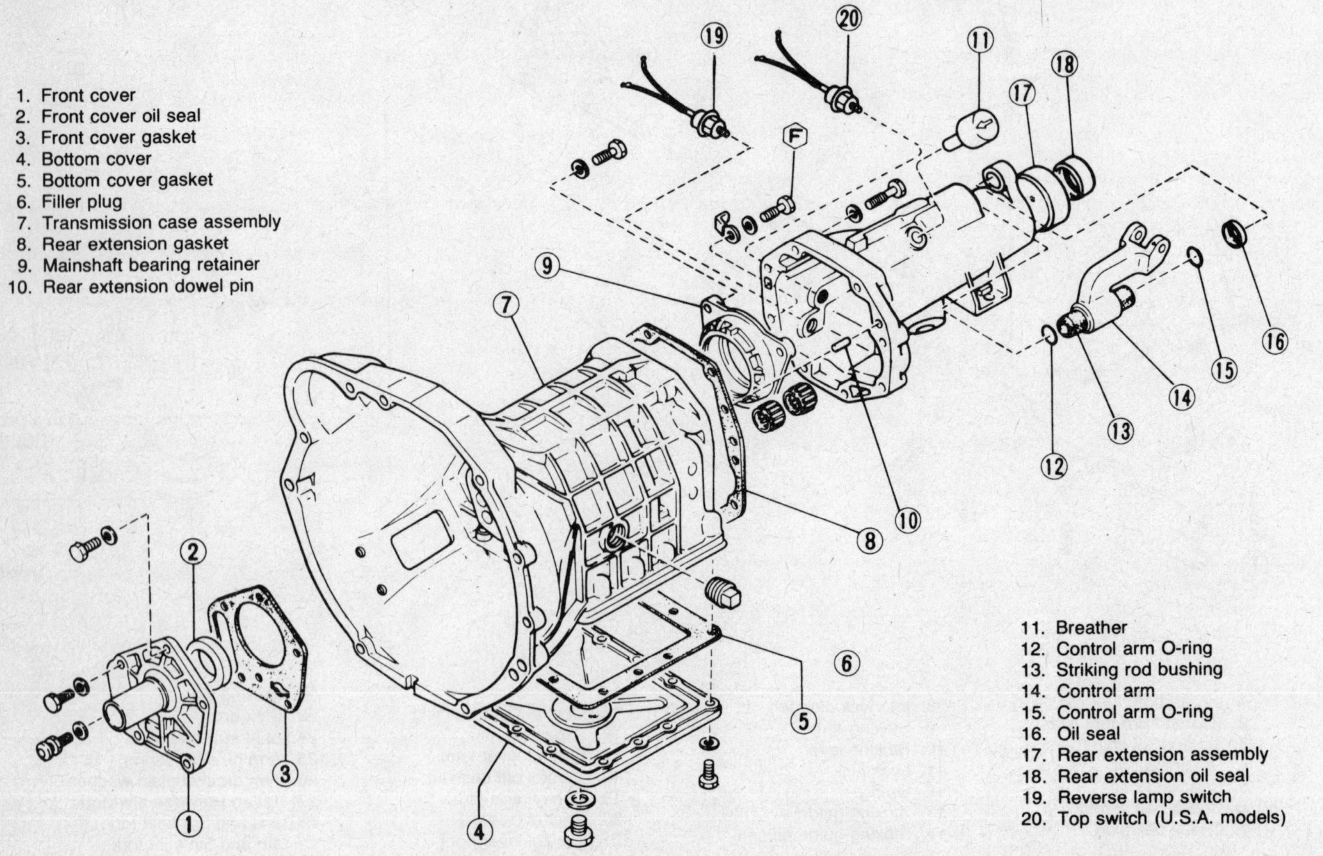

Transmission case components, model F4W63L

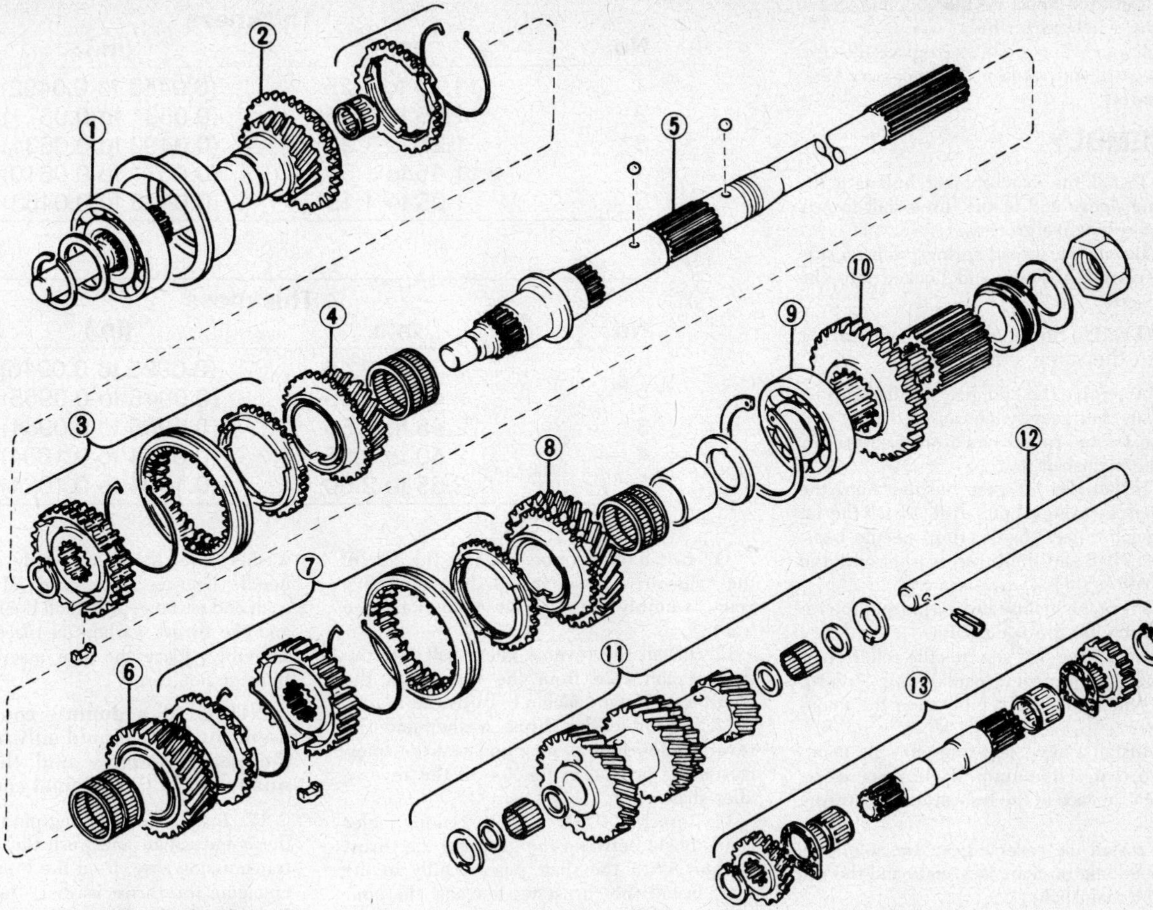

1. Main drive bearing
2. Main drive gear
3. 3rd & 4th synchronizer
4. 3rd gear, mainshaft
5. Mainshaft
6. 2nd gear, mainshaft
7. 1st & 2nd synchronizer
8. 1st gear, mainshaft
9. Mainshaft bearing
10. Reverse gear, mainshaft
11. Counter gear assembly
12. Countershaft
13. Idler gear assembly

Exploded view of gear train components

2. Remove the dust cover from the transmission case.
3. Remove the release bearing and the operating lever. Remove the electrical switches from the case.
4. Remove the speedometer driven gear assembly.
5. Remove the front cover and the bottom cover from the transmission assembly.
6. Position the gearshift into the neutral position and pull out the striking rod (main shift control rod) pin bolt.
7. Remove the rear extension housing retaining bolts and tap the housing with a soft hammer to remove it from the transmission case.
8. Remove the striking rod (main shift control rod).
9. Drive the shifting fork retaining pins from the forks and selector shafts.
10. Remove the three check ball plugs. Do not lose the check balls and springs. Remove the two interlock plungers.
11. Remove the selector rods and shifting forks from the transmission. Keep in their proper order for installation.
12. Lock the gear train by meshing two gears at the same time. Straighten the lock washer and loosen the nut on the mainshaft. Place the gear train back in the neutral position.
13. Use a dummy countershaft tool or equivalent, and push the countershaft from the transmission case, from the rear to the front. Do not drop the needle bearings or thrust washers into the transmission.
14. Remove the counter gear assembly from the case.
15. Remove the snap-ring retaining the reverse idler counter gear in place and remove the shaft from the rear of the case. Do not remove the needle bearing.
16. Remove the mainshaft bearing retainer and bolts. Remove the mainshaft assembly from the rear of the transmission case. Remove the loose synchronizer (baulk) ring from the front of the mainshaft.
17. Remove the pilot bearing located between the main drive gear and the mainshaft.
18. Using a wooden shaft, drive the main drive gear and bearing from the transmission case. Do not allow the gear to drop.
19. The main drive gear bearing can be removed after the retaining snap-ring is removed. A press or bearing puller should be used.
20. Remove the front retaining snap-ring from the mainshaft and remove the 3rd/4th synchronizer assembly, the 3rd gear and mainshaft needle bearing from the shaft.
21. Remove the locknut from the mainshaft and remove the reverse gear, reverse gear hub and the speedometer drive gear.

NOTE: Do not lose the steel ball locating the speedometer drive gear to the mainshaft.

22. Install a suitable puller or set in a press and remove the 1st speed gear, along with the bearing and retainer.

CAUTION

Do not attach pulling or press tool to the 2nd gear as damage to the 1st gear mainshaft bushing can result. Do not remove the needle bearing with the 1st gear bearing as the needle bearing could be damaged by the second steel ball on the mainshaft.

23. Remove the second steel ball on the mainshaft and install a puller or set in a press and remove the 1st gear bushing, along with the 1st/2nd synchronizer assembly and the 2nd gear.
24. To disassemble the synchronizers, remove the spread springs and take out the

shifting inserts. Separate the coupling sleeve from the synchronizer hub.

25. Clean the assemblies, replace the necessary parts and replace the necessary seals and gaskets.

ASSEMBLY

1. Install the synchronizer hub into the coupling sleeve and fit the three shift inserts in their respective grooves.

2. Install the spread springs on each side of the coupling sleeve and hooked into the shift inserts.

NOTE: Do not hook the spread spring ends in the same shift insert.

3. Assemble the 2nd gear needle bearing, 2nd gear, 2nd gear synchronizer (baulk) ring and the 1st/2nd speed synchronizer assembly onto the mainshaft.

4. Install the 1st gear bushing onto the mainshaft by using a brass drift. Install the 1st gear synchronizer (baulk) ring, needle bearing, steel ball and the thrust washer onto the mainshaft.

5. Press the mainshaft bearing and the reverse hub onto the mainshaft.

6. Install the 3rd gear needle roller bearing, 3rd synchronizer (baulk) ring, 3rd/4th speed synchronizer assembly onto the mainshaft.

7. Install a new snap-ring onto the mainshaft so that a minimum of clearance exists between the face of the hub and the snap-ring groove.

8. Install the reverse gear, the steel ball, the speedometer gear, lock plate and the nut onto the mainshaft.

9. Install the mainshaft assembly into the rear of the transmission case and install the mainshaft bearing retainer plate and bolts. Torque to 5.8 to 7.2 ft/lbs (7.8 to 9.8 Nm).

10. Install the main drive gear bearing in place, using a press or bearing installer. Install the spacer and the retaining selector snap-ring, so that a mimimum of clearance exists between the spacer and the snap-ring. Available selections are as follows:

No.	Thickness mm	(in.)
1	1.40 to 1.45	(0.0551 to 0.0571)
2	1.45 to 1.50	(0.0571 to 0.0591)
3	1.50 to 1.55	(0.0591 to 0.0610)
4	1.55 to 1.60	(0.0610 to 0.0630)
5	1.60 to 1.65	(0.0630 to 0.0650)

No.	Thickness mm	(in.)
1	1.49 to 1.55	(0.0587 to 0.0610)
2	1.56 to 1.62	(0.0614 to 0.0638)
3	1.62 to 1.68	(0.0638 to 0.0661)
4	1.68 to 1.74	(0.0661 to 0.0685)
5	1.74 to 1.80	(0.0685 to 0.0709)
6	1.80 to 1.86	(0.0709 to 0.0732)
7	1.86 to 1.92	(0.0732 to 0.0756)

No.	Thickness mm	(in.)
1	1.15 to 1.25	(0.0453 to 0.0492)
2	1.35 to 1.45	(0.0531 to 0.0571)
3	1.25 to 1.35	(0.0492 to 0.0531)
4	1.45 to 1.55	(0.0571 to 0.0610)
5	1.05 to 1.15	(0.0413 to 0.0453)

No.	Thickness mm	(in.)
1	2.35 to 2.40	(0.0925 to 0.0945)
2	2.40 to 2.45	(0.0945 to 0.0965)
3	2.45 to 2.50	(0.0965 to 0.0984)
4	2.50 to 2.55	(0.0984 to 0.1004)
5	2.55 to 2.60	(0.1004 to 0.1024)

11. Install the pilot bearing into the bore of the main drive gear. Install the main drive gear assembly into the transmission case front.

12. Install the reverse idler shaft into the transmission case from the rear, with the identification mark facing towards the rear.

13. Assemble the thrust washer and the reverse idler (helical) gear and seat the snap-ring in its groove in the top of the reverse idler shaft.

14. Insert a 0.004 inch (0.1 mm) feeler gauge blade between the gear and the thrust washer. With the shaft pushed fully to the rear, install the thrust washer and the spur gear and fit the snap-ring, selected to obtain the proper end-play for the reverse idler gear.

15. The reverse idler gear end-play is 0.0039 to 0.0118 inch (0.10 to 0.30 mm).

NOTE: Install the thrust washers so that the grooved sides are facing towards the gears.

16. Install a dummy shaft or equivalent into the countergear and install the inner washers into the gear. Apply grease to the needle bearings and install 21 bearings on each end of the gear. Install the outer washers and the thrust washers in place on the gear assembly. Place the gear assembly into the transmission case.

NOTE: If a dummy countershaft is used, the shaft should only be as long as the gear assembly and the diameter smaller than the original countershaft.

17. Install the retaining pin in the front of the countershaft and push the shaft into the transmission case, from the front to the rear, engaging the thrust washer, the countergear and forcing the dummy shaft (if used) out through the hole in the back of the case.

18. The rear thrust washer is used to determine the countergear end-play. The end-play is 0.0020 to 0.0059 inch (0.05 to 0.15 mm).

19. After the end-play has been determined, locate the countershaft pin in its indent at the front of the transmission case.

20. Mesh two gears so that the transmission gear train is locked. Tighten the mainshaft locknut to 58 to 80 ft/lbs (8.0 to 11.0 Kg-m). Secure the mainshaft locknut washer by bending over the nut.

21. Align the 1st/2nd shift fork and the 3rd/4th shift fork with the grooves of the coupling sleeves.

22. Install the 1st/2nd selector shift rod into the case and through the selector fork. Install the retaining pin through the fork and rod.

23. Place the 1st/2nd shift fork and gear in the Neutral position. Install the interlock plunger and install the 3rd/4th selector shift rod into the case and the 3rd/4th shift fork. Install the retaining pin in the fork and rod.

24. Place the 3rd/4th selector rod in the Neutral position and install the interlock plunger.

25. Install the reverse shift selector rod through the reverse shift fork and install the retaining pin.

26. Install the check balls and the check ball springs. Install sealer on the plugs and install them into their respective bores.

NOTE: The check ball plug for the

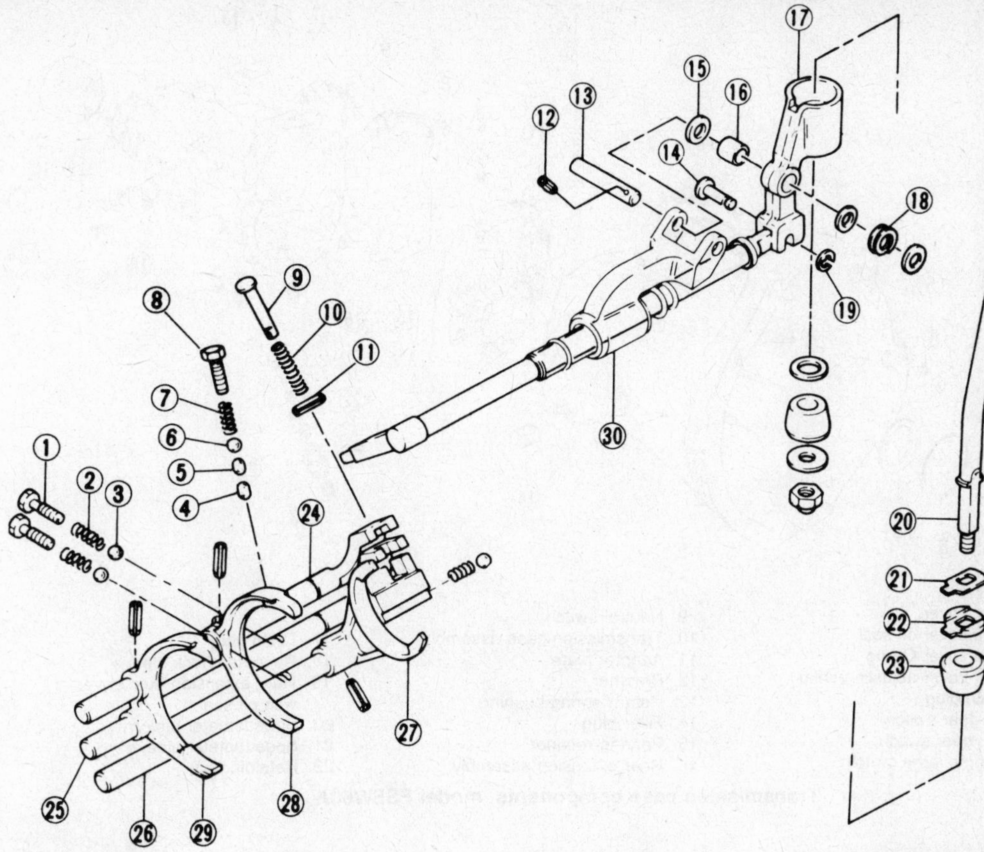

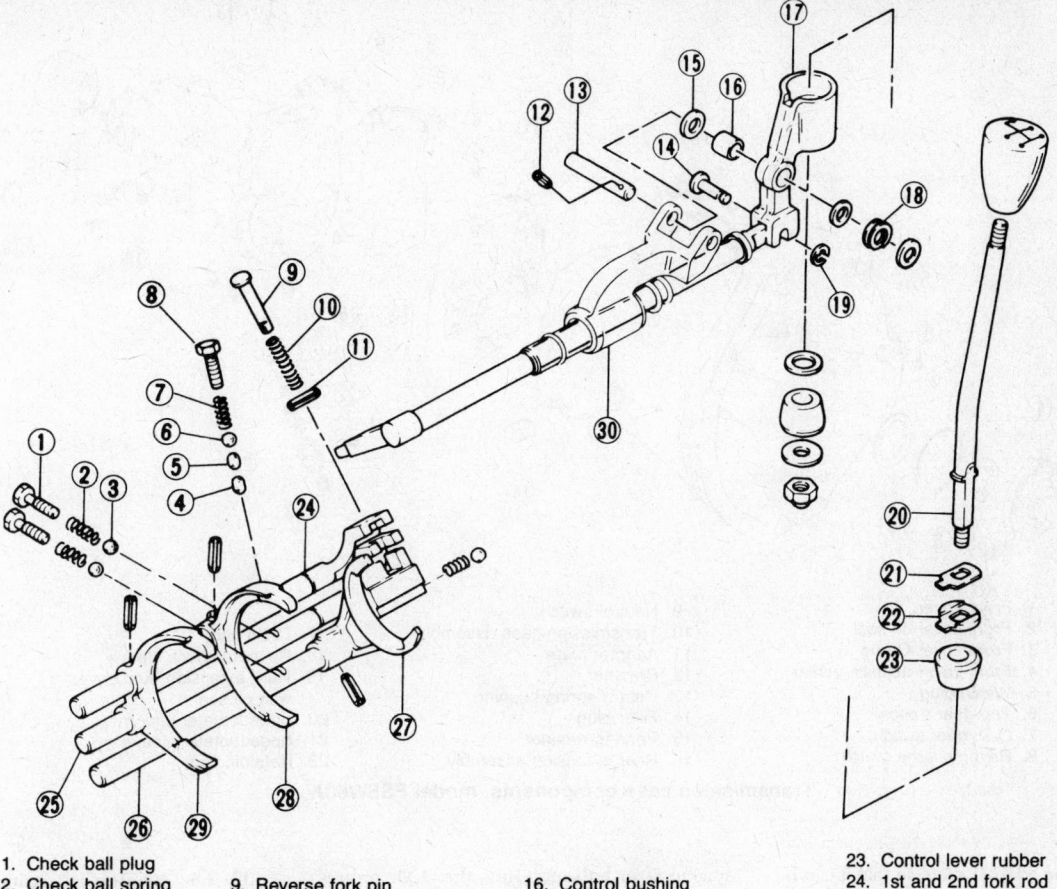

1. Check ball plug
2. Check ball spring
3. Check ball
4. Interlock plunger
5. Interlock plunger
6. Check ball
7. Check ball spring
8. Check ball plug
9. Reverse fork pin
10. Reverse pin return spring
11. Roller pin
12. Retaining pin
13. Control arm pin
14. Striking rod pin
15. Thrust washer
16. Control bushing
17. Control lever bracket
18. Control spring
19. Striking pin C-ring
20. Control lever
21. Control lever upper washer
22. Control lever upper washer
23. Control lever rubber
24. 1st and 2nd fork rod
25. 3rd and 4th fork rod
26. Reverse fork rod
27. Reverse shift fork
28. 1st and 2nd shift fork
29. 3rd and 4th fork rod
30. Control arm

Exploded view of shift selector rod and fork components

3rd/4th fork and shift rod is shorter than those for the reverse and 1st/2nd fork and shift rods.

CAUTION

To insure that the interlock plungers are properly installed, slide the 3rd/4th fork selector rod into gear and try to operate the other selector rods. All other gears should not mesh. Operate the other selector rods and check in the same manner.

27. Place all gears in the Neutral position and install the rear extension to the transmission case, using sealer on the mating surfaces.
28. As the rear extension housing is being installed, align the striking lever to the shift rod brackets.
29. Install the front main shaft cover. Apply sealer to the threads of the bolts and torque to 5.8 to 7.2 ft/lbs (0.8 to 1.0 Kg-m).
30. Install the clutch release bearing and the operating shaft to the front of the case. Install the dust cover.
31. Install the electrical switches that were removed during the disassembly.
32. Install the speedometer driven gear assembly.
33. Install the bottom cover to the case and fill the unit with the proper level of lubricant.

TYPE 16

5 Speed Transmission–Model FS5W60A, L

1979-81 Datsun 210

DISASSEMBLY

1. Secure the transmission and drain the lubricating oil.
2. Remove the dust cover from the transmission case.
3. Remove the clutch release bearing and withdraw the pivot lever.
4. Remove the electrical switches from the case.
5. Remove the speedometer driven gear assembly.
6. Remove the shift selector stopper pin bolt and nut from the boss of the rear extension housing.
7. Remove the shift selector return spring plug, return spring and plunger from the rear extension.
8. Remove the reverse check sleeves assembly.
9. Remove the front bearing cover, O-ring and front cover adjusting shim.
10. Remove the main bearing snap-ring from the groove in the bearing outer race.
11. Remove the rear extension retaining bolts and turn the shift selector rod clockwise.
12. Using a special puller, remove the rear extension housing from the output shaft.
13. Separate the transmission case from the adapter plate by tapping evenly around the transmission case.

NOTE: Do not pry the units apart with a prybar. Damage can occur to the mating surfaces.

14. A special type holding tool should be

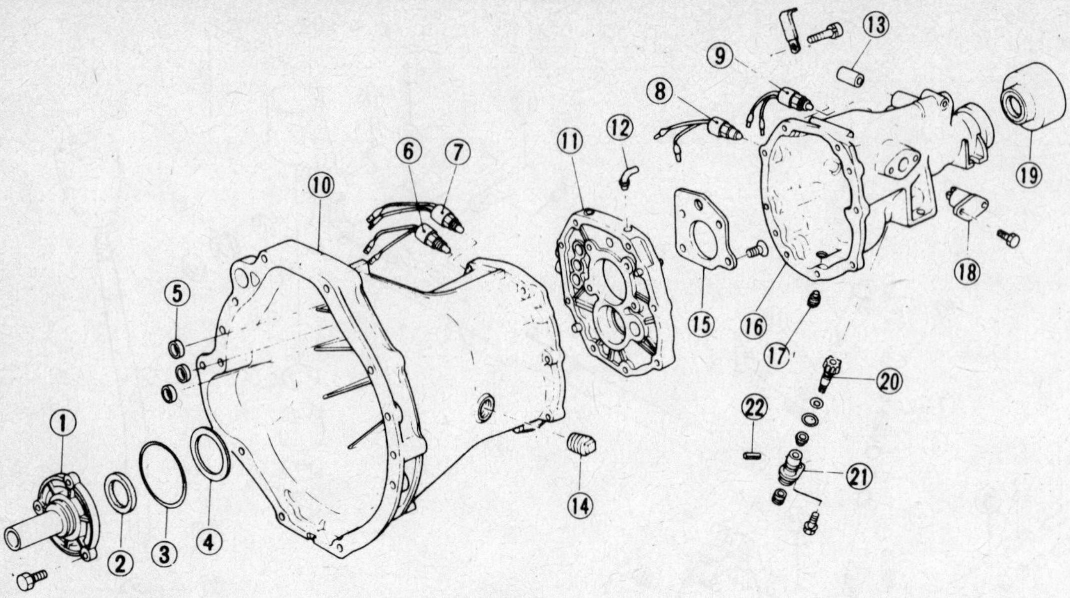

1. Front cover
2. Front cover oil seal
3. Front cover O-ring
4. Front cover adjusting shim
5. Welch plug
6. Top gear switch
7. O.D. gear switch
8. Reverse lamp switch
9. Neutral switch
10. Transmission case assembly
11. Adapter plate
12. Breather
13. Return spring bushing
14. Filler plug
15. Bearing retainer
16. Rear extension assembly
17. Drain plug
18. Reverse check sleeve
19. Rear extension dust cover with oil seal
20. Speedometer pinion
21. Speedometer sleeve
22. Retaining pin

Transmission case components, model FS5W60A

used to hold the adapter plate so that it can be held in a vise or other holding tool. This plate can be purchased or fabricated.

15. Mount the unit in the holding tool and remove the countergear thrust washer.

16. Using a pin punch, remove the retaining pins from the forks and selector rods.

17. Remove the check ball plugs (3).

18. Remove the selector rods from the adapter plate and detach the forks from the rods.

CAUTION

Do not lose the check balls, springs and the two interlock plungers.

NOTE: Each gear and shaft can be removed from the adapter plate independently of the other shaft and without the removal of the selector rods and forks.

19. Remove the outer snap-ring of the mainshaft end bearing with a bearing puller. Remove the second bearing snap-ring from the shaft.

20. Engage the 1st and reverse speeds so that the gear train is locked in two gears at the same time. Remove the countergear nut after releasing the staking.

21. From the rear extension side of the adapter plate, remove the mainshaft holding snap-ring, C-ring holder, C-ring and the thrust washer.

22. Remove the O.D. main gear with the needle bearings and the O.D. countergear together.

23. Remove the synchronizer (baulk) ring, the coupling sleeve, the O.D. and reverse synchronizer hub snap-ring, the O.D. and reverse synchronizer hub and the reverse gear together with the needle bearing and bushing, and the reverse countergear at one time.

24. Remove the bearing retainer screws from the adapter plate. Remove the bearing retainer.

25. Remove the snap-ring from the mainshaft rear bearing and remove the mainshaft assembly together with the countergear by lightly tapping on the rear shaft while holding the front of the mainshaft and countergear assembly by hand to avoid dropping the assembly.

26. Remove the snap-ring and spacer from the reverse idler shaft and tap the idler shaft outward slightly.

27. Using a pin punch, remove the retaining pin from the reverse idler shaft and remove the shaft. Remove the thrust washers, spacer and reverse idler gear with the needle bearing.

28. Disassemble the mainshaft assembly by removing the snap-ring from the shaft front end. Remove the 3rd/4th synchronizer assembly, synchronizer (baulk) rings, 3rd gear and the mainshaft needle bearing toward the front side.

29. Remove the mainshaft bearing with a puller.

30. Remove the thrust washer and 1st gear, together with the needle bearing and bushing, synchronizer (baulk) rings, coupling sleeve, 1st/2nd synchronizer hub and the 2nd gear with the needle bearing.

31. Remove the snap-ring and spacer from the maindrive gear and remove the bearing with a press or puller.

32. The countershaft rear bearing can be removed with the use of a press.

33. The synchronizers can be disassembled for repairs by removing the spread spring and removing the shifting insert. Separate the coupling sleeve from the synchronizer hub.

ASSEMBLY

1. Replace any bearings, seals or worn parts as required.

2. Install the synchronizer hub into the coupling sleeve and fit the shifting inserts into their respective grooves on the assembly.

3. Install the spread springs to the inserts so that the insert is securely attached to the inner side of the coupling sleeve.

CAUTION

Do not hook the ends of the spread springs to the same insert. The hub and sleeve should operate smoothly when moved by hand.

4. Install the 2nd gear needle bearing, 2nd gear, synchronizer (baulk) ring, 1st/2nd speed synchronizer assembly, 1st gear synchronizer (baulk) ring, 1st gear bushing, needle bearing, 1st gear and thrust washer onto the mainshaft.

5. Press the bearing onto the mainshaft, using a pressor bearing installer.

6. Install the 3rd gear needle bearing, 3rd gear, synchronizer (baulk) ring, 3rd/4th synchronizer assembly on the front side of the mainshaft.

7. Install a selective snap-ring on the mainshaft so that a minimum clearance exists between the face of the hub and the ring.

CAUTION

Be sure the snap-ring is fully seated in its groove.

8. Install the main drive gear bearing onto the shaft. Install the main drive bearing spacer on the main drive bearing and secure the bearing with a proper sized snap-ring that will eliminate any end play.
9. Install the countergear thrust washer and countergear into the transmission case and select the countergear thrust washer of proper thickness, by using a straightedge, from the countergear face to the transmission case, allowing for standard end play of 0.0039 to 0.0079 inch (0.10 mm to 0.20 mm).
10. Remove the countergear from the transmission and keep the thrust washer with the gear.
11. Install the thrust washers, needle bearing, reverse idler gear and inner thrust washer in place on the reverse idler shaft. Install a new retaining pin in the reverse idler shaft.
12. Install the reverse idler shaft into the adapter plate. Position a thrust washer and install a new snap-ring so that the minimum clearance exists between the adapter plate and the thrust washer.
13. Install a synchronizer (baulk) ring on the main drive gear and place with the mainshaft to complete this portion of the assembly.

	Thickness	
No.	**mm**	**(in)**
1	1.55-1.60	(0.0610-0.0630)
2	1.60-1.65	(0.0630-0.0650)
3	1.65-1.70	(0.0650-0.0669)

	Thickness	
No.	**mm**	**(in)**
1	1.34-1.40	(0.0528-0.0551)
2	1.40-1.46	(0.0551-0.0575)
3	1.46-1.52	(0.0575-0.0598)
4	1.52-1.58	(0.0598-0.0622)
5	1.58-1.64	(0.0622-0.0646)
6	1.64-1.70	(0.0646-0.0669)
7	1.70-1.76	(0.0669-0.0693)

	Thickness	
No.	**mm**	**(in)**
1	2.20-2.25	(0.0866-0.0886)
2	2.25-2.30	(0.0886-0.0906)
3	2.30-2.35	(0.0906-0.0925)
4	2.35-2.40	(0.0925-0.0945)
5	2.40-2.45	(0.0945-0.0965)
6	2.45-2.50	(0.0965-0.0984)
7	2.50-2.55	(0.0984-0.1004)
8	2.55-2.60	(0.1004-0.1024)

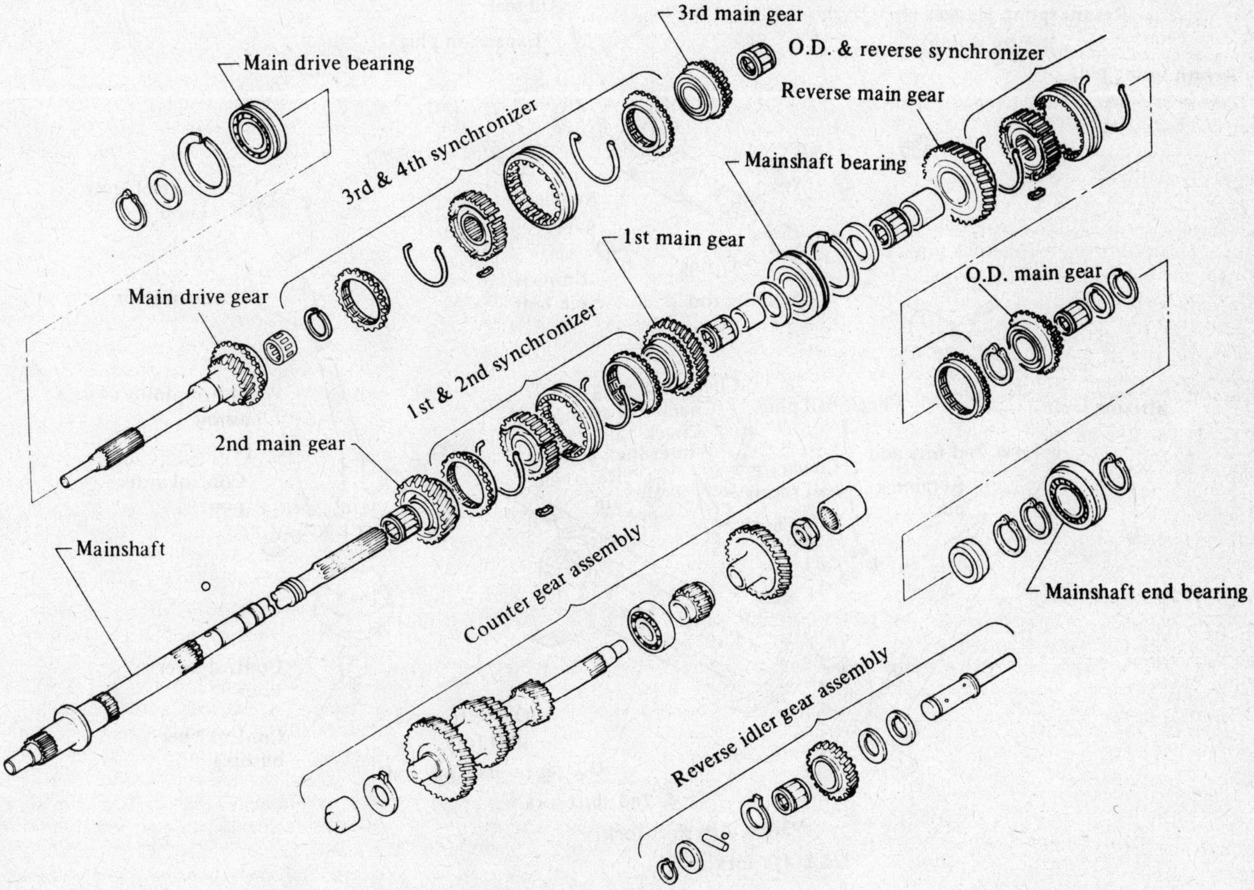

Exploded view of gear train components

NOTE: Install the pilot bearing in place before coupling the main drive gear to the mainshaft.

14. Combine the mainshaft assembly with the countergear assembly and place them into the adapter plate as a unit.

NOTE: Use a puller tool to move the mainshaft into the adapter plate. Carefully hold the gears to avoid dropping them until in position.

CAUTION

Be sure the snap-ring groove on the mainshaft rear bearing clears the adapter plate.

15. Install the rear bearing snap-ring into its groove. Install the bearing retainer and install the retaining screws. Torque to 5.1 to 7.2 ft/lbs (6.9 to 9.8 Nm).

IMPORTANT: Stake each screw at two points with a center punch.

The selective snap-rings are as follows:

No.	Thickness mm	(in)
1	1.1	(0.043)
2	1.2	(0.047)

16. Place the thrust washer, reverse gear bushing, needle bearing and the reverse main drive gear on the end of the mainshaft.
17. Install the reverse countergear on the end of the countershaft.
18. Install the O.D. and reverse synchronizer assembly and install a new snap-ring so that the minimum amount of clearance exists between the end face of the hub and the snap-ring.

The selective snap-rings are as follows:

No.	Thickness mm	(in)
1	1.32	(0.0520)
2	1.38	(0.0543)
3	1.46	(0.0575)
4	1.54	(0.0606)
5	1.62	(0.0638)

19. Position the synchronizer (baulk) ring, O.D. gear needle bearing and the O.D. main gear on the end of the mainshaft.
20. Install the O.D. countergear on the end of the mainshaft.
21. Place the thrust washer in place so that a minimum of clearance exists between the C-holder and the ring. Position the C-ring and the C-ring holder and fit a new mainshaft holder snap-ring.

The selective snap-rings are as follows:

No.	Thickness mm	(in.)
1	7.87	(0.3098)
2	7.94	(0.3126)
3	8.01	(0.3154)
4	8.08	(0.3181)
5	8.15	(0.3209)
6	8.22	(0.3236)

22. Engage the 1st and reverse gears and tighten the countershaft nut to 36 to 43 ft/lbs (49 to 59 Nm).
23. Stake the countershaft nut to the groove in the countershaft with a punch.
24. Measure the gear end-play. The measurements are as follows:

1st main gear
0.15-0.25 mm
(0.0059-0.0098 in.)
2nd main gear
0.30-0.40 mm
(0.0118-0.0157 in.)
3rd main gear
0.15-0.35 mm
(0.0059-0.0138 in.)
O.D. (5th) main gear
0.30-0.40 mm
(0.0118-0.0157 in.)

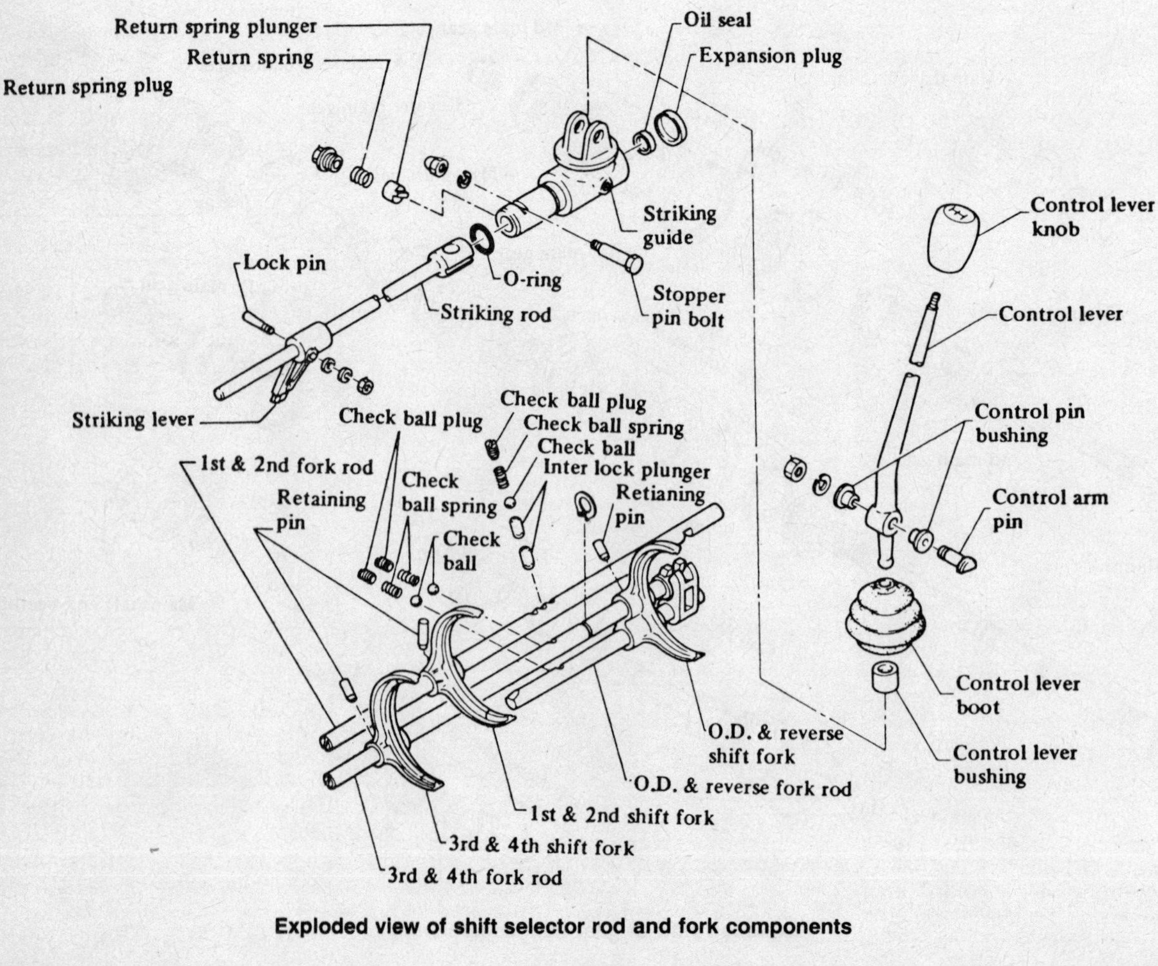

Exploded view of shift selector rod and fork components

Reverse main gear
0.30-0.55 mm
(0.0118-0.0217 in.)
Countergear
0.10-0.20 mm
(0.0039-0.0079 in.)
Reverse idler gear
0-0.20 mm
(0-0.0079 in.)

25. Place a snap-ring to the front of the mainshaft end bearing, measuring 0.0453 inch (1.15 mm).

26. Install the mainshaft end bearing using a bearing installer. Fit a snap-ring to the rear side of the bearing to eliminate any end-play. The available snap-rings are as follows:

No.	Thickness mm	(in.)
1	1.15	(0.0453)
2	1.02	(0.047)

27. Install the O.D. and reverse fork and selector rod into the adapter plate. Place the rod in the neutral position and install the interlock plunger into its bore in the adapter plate.

28. Install the 3rd/4th selector rod into the fork and install a new snap-ring. Install the selector rod and fork into the adapter plate.

29. Insert the interlock plunger into the adapter plate with the selector rods in the neutral position.

30. Install the 1st/2nd selector rod into the fork and install both into the adapter plate.

31. Secure all the selector rods and forks with new retaining pins.

IMPORTANT: Properly align the groove in the assembled selector rod with the interlock plunger, during the assembly. Align the shift forks with their respective coupling sleeves before installing.

32. Install the check balls and springs into the proper bores. Seal and install the check ball plugs.

33. Align the center notch in each fork selector rod with the check balls, as required.

NOTE: The selector rod for the 1st/2nd gear is longer than the 3rd/4th or the O.D./Reverse selector rods.

CAUTION

To make sure the interlock plunger is installed properly, slide the 1st/2nd selector rod into gear and operate the other selector rods. All other gears should not mesh. Check all other rods in the same manner.

34. Prepare the adapter plate and transmission case by installing a sealer to the mating surfaces.

35. Apply grease to the sliding surface of the thrust washer for the countergear, that was selected previously. The oil groove should face to the front while the dimpled side should face towards the thrust side.

36. Place the clutch housing end of the transmission case flat on a surface and level the housing. Position the adapter plate assembly into the transmission housing and tap the plate into the transmission housing. Line the dowel pin to its proper position.

37. Carefully install the main drive bearing and countergear front needle bearing.

NOTE: Be sure the mainshaft rotates freely.

38. Install the main drive bearing snap-ring in its groove in the bearing.

39. Apply sealant to the mating surfaces of the adapter plate and the rear extension housing.

40. Place the selector rods in the O.D. position on the transmission, while placing the main selector rod in the neutral position. Turn the striking guide clockwise and then adjust the main selector rod and the shift arm. Align the shift arm pin with the groove in the selector rods and assemble the rear extension housing to the adapter plate. Install the retaining bolts and torque to 12 to 16 ft/lbs (16 to 22 Nm).

41. Install grease to the plunger and install it into the rear extension. Install the return spring, apply sealer to the return spring plug and install it.

42. Turn the transmission assembly so that the front is up. Measure the distance from the front end of the transmission case to the main drive bearing outer race with a depth gauge. Select a shim to correspond to the dimension or thickness "A". The front cover adjusting shim can be one of seven shims.

No.	"A" mm	(in.)	Adjusting shim mm	(in.)
1	6.05-6.09	(0.2382-0.2398)	0.50	(0.0197)
2	6.10-6.14	(0.2402-0.2417)	0.55	(0.0217)
3	6.15-6.19	(0.2421-0.2437)	0.60	(0.0236)
4	6.20-6.24	(0.2441-0.2457)	0.65	(0.0256)
5	6.25-6.29	(0.2461-0.2476)	0.70	(0.0276)
6	6.30-6.34	(0.2480-0.2496)	0.75	(0.0295)
7	6.35-6.39	(0.2500-0.2516)	0.80	(0.0315)

43. Install the front cover with the adjusting shim and the O-ring in place.

44. Install the speedometer driven gear and install the securing bolt and nut.

45. Install a new O-ring in the groove of the reverse check sleeve and tighten the bolts.

46. Replace the electrical switches that were removed during the disassembly.

47. Install the pivot lever, the release bearing and sleeve. Connect the holding spring and install the dust cover.

TYPE 17

4 Speed Transmission–Model F4W60L

1979-81 Datsun 210
1975-78 Datsun B210

DISASSEMBLY

1. Secure the transmission and drain the lubricating oil.

2. Remove the dust cover from the transmission case.

3. Remove the clutch release bearing and the pivot lever.

4. Remove the electrical switches from the transmission case.

5. Remove the speedometer driven gear assembly from the rear extension housing.

6. Remove the stopper pin bolt and nut from the rear extension housing. Remove the return spring plug, the return spring, reverse check spring and the plunger from the rear extension housing.

7. Remove the front cover along with the O-ring and the front cover adjusting shim.

8. Remove the main drive bearing snap-ring from the bearing groove.

9. Remove the rear extension housing retaining bolts and rotate the striking rod (main shift control shaft) clockwise.

10. Drive the rear extension housing rearward by lightly tapping on the housing to separate the housing from the transmission.

11. Separate the transmission case from the adapter plate by lightly tapping the case from the plate.

CAUTION

Do not pry the transmission assembly apart with a pry bar. The mating surfaces can be damaged.

12. A special type holding tool should be used to hold the adapter plate so that it can be held in a vise or other holding tool. The plate can be purchased or fabricated.

13. Remove the countergear thrust washer and drive the shift fork retaining pins from the selector shafts.

14. Remove the reverse gear shift fork and the reverse idler gear.

15. Remove the three check ball plugs. The check balls and the springs will be exposed for removal. Visually check the spring lengths for proper installation and mark accordingly.

16. Drive the selector rods from the adapter plate by tapping on the front end of the rods. Do not lose the interlock plungers from between the selector shift rods. Remove the shifting forks as necessary.

IMPORTANT: Measure the end-play of the mainshaft before disassembly of the shaft. Measure between the end face of the 3rd/4th synchronizer hub and the snap-ring. Record the clearance.

17. Remove the reverse gear snap-ring from the rear of the shaft and remove the thrust washer and mainshaft reverse gear.

18. Remove the four bearing retainer at-

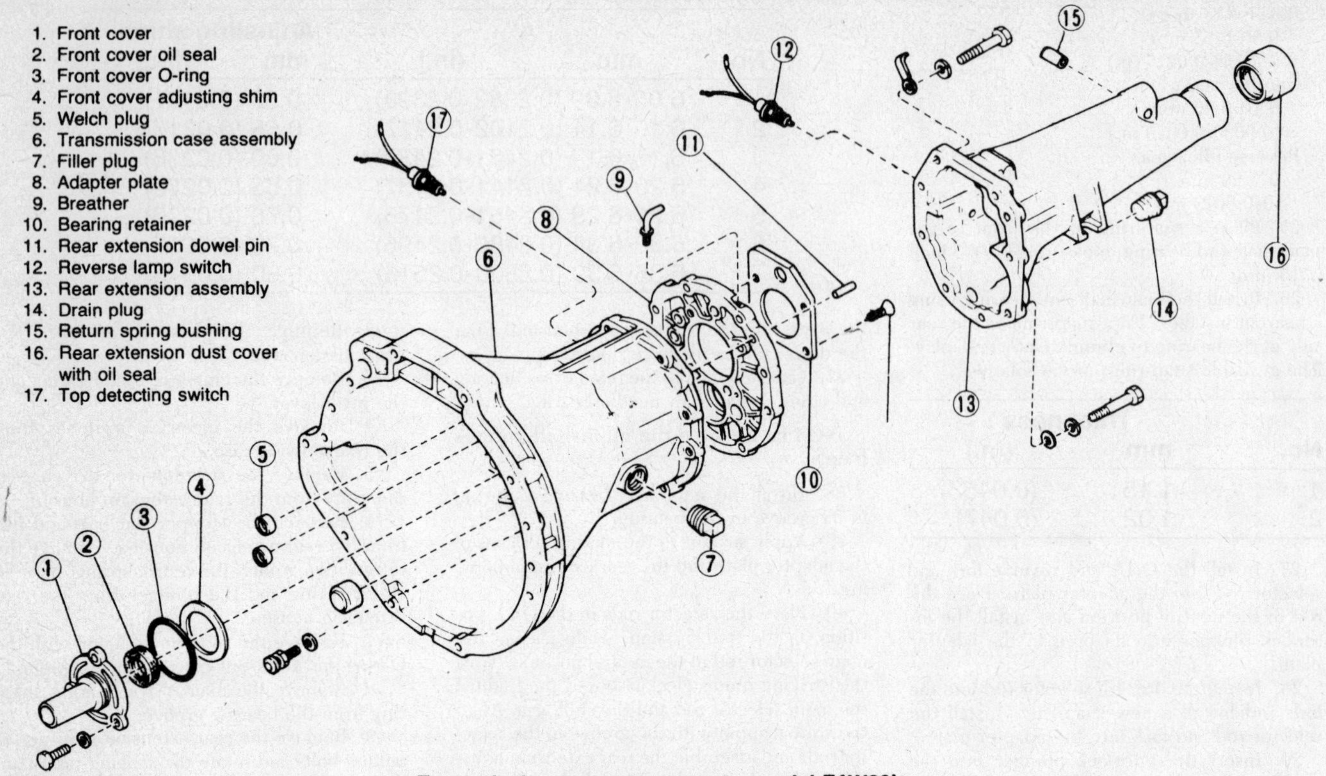

Transmission case components, model F4W60L

taching screws and remove the bearing retainer.

19. Remove the snap-ring from the mainshaft rear bearing.

20. Remove the mainshaft gear assembly along with the countergear assembly by lightly tapping on the rear of the shafts with a soft hammer while holding the gears by hand to avoid their dropping to the floor.

21. Separate the countergear, main drive gear and mainshaft assembly.

22. The mainshaft gear assembly can be disassembled by removal of the retaining snap-ring from the front of the shaft.

23. The mainshaft bearing must be pressed from the shaft and the remaining gears and hubs can be removed.

IMPORTANT: Observe the sequence and direction of the gear and hubs during the disassembly. Mark as required.

24. The main drive gear bearing can be pressed from the shaft after the removal of the retaining snap-ring. The pilot bearing can be removed from the shaft bore.

25. Remove the snap-ring from the rear of the countershaft and press out the counter reverse gear, using a suitable puller.

26. Remove the countergear rear bearing by the use of the bearing puller.

27. The synchronizers can be disassembled by removing the spread springs and removing the shifting inserts. Remove the coupling sleeves from the synchronizer hubs.

IMPORTANT: Note the direction of the coupling sleeves in relation to the hubs.

28. The reverse idler shaft snap-ring is removed and the shaft is removed from the adapter plate by lightly tapping on the shaft with a soft hammer.

29. The rear extension housing can be disassembled by removing the lock pin nut and lock pin from the striking lever (main shift control shaft). Remove the lever and the shaft can be removed from the housing.

30. Replace the necessary parts, clean the assembly, install new seal and prepare to reassemble.

ASSEMBLY

1. Assemble the rear extension housing by installing the striking lever shaft (mainshaft control shaft) into the housing. Fit the striking lever to the shaft and install the retaining pin.

2. Install the reverse idler shaft into the adapter plate and install the retaining snap-ring.

3. Assemble the synchronizers by installing the coupling sleeves over the synchronizer hubs. Install the shifting inserts and the spread springs, being careful not to connect the spread spring ends to the same insert.

4. Assemble the mainshaft by installing the 2nd gear needle bearing, 2nd gear, the synchronizer (baulk) ring, 1st-2nd speed synchronizer assembly, the 1st gear synchronizer (baulk) ring, 1st gear bushing, needle bearing, 1st gear and the thrust washer.

5. Press the mainshaft bearing in place with a bearing instalter.

6. Position the 3rd gear needle bearing, 3rd gear, synchronizer (baulk) ring and the 3rd-4th synchronizer assembly onto the front side of the mainshaft.

7. Fit a new snap-ring in place on the shaft so that a minimum of clearance exists between the end face of the hub and the snap-ring.

8. Install the main drive gear bearing in place on the shaft by the use of a bearing installer tool or press. Install the bearing spacer and a snap-ring to provide a minimum of clearance between the snap-ring and the bearing spacer.

9. Using a bearing press, install the countergear bearing onto the countergear.

10. Install a countergear thrust washer and the countergear with bearing into the transmission case and with a special height gauge or equivalent, select a thrust washer from the accompanying chart to provide a standard end-play of 0.0039 to 0.0079 inch (0.10 to 0.20 mm).

	Thickness	
No.	mm	(in.)
1	1.55 to 1.60	(0.0610 to 0.0630)
2	1.60 to 1.65	(0.0630 to 0.0650)
3	1.65 to 1.70	(0.0650 to 0.0669)

No.	Thickness mm	(in.)
1	1.34 to 1.40	(0.0528 to 0.0551)
2	1.40 to 1.46	(0.0551 to 0.0575)
3	1.46 to 1.52	(0.0575 to 0.0598)
4	1.52 to 1.58	(0.0598 to 0.0622)
5	1.58 to 1.64	(0.0622 to 0.0646)
6	1.64 to 1.70	(0.0646 to 0.0669)
7	1.70 to 1.76	(0.0669 to 0.0693)

No.	Thickness mm	(in.)
1	2.20 to 2.25	(0.0866 to 0.0886)
2	2.25 to 2.30	(0.0886 to 0.0906)
3	2.30 to 2.35	(0.0906 to 0.0925)
4	2.35 to 2.40	(0.0925 to 0.0945)
5	2.40 to 2.45	(0.0945 to 0.0965)
6	2.45 to 2.50	(0.0965 to 0.0984)
7	2.50 to 2.55	(0.0984 to 0.1004)
8	2.55 to 2.60	(0.1004 to 0.1024)

10. Remove the countergear assembly from the transmission and press the counter reverse gear onto the countergear assembly, using a press or equivalent tool.

11. Install a new snap-ring into the groove at the end of the countergear.

12. Install a synchronizer (baulk) ring on the main drive gear and install it onto the mainshaft to complete the mainshaft assembly.

NOTE: Be sure to install the pilot bearing into the main drive gear bore.

13. Place the adapter plate in the holding device and assemble the mainshaft and countershaft and place them into the adapter plate as a unit. Hold the gears by hand so as not to drop them.

14. A puller should be used to pull the mainshaft into the adapter plate. The countershaft can be installed at the same time by tapping lightly with a soft hammer.

IMPORTANT: Make sure the snap-ring groove on the mainshaft clears the adapter plate.

15. Install the snap-ring on to the mainshaft.

16. Install the bearing retainer plate on the adapter plate and install the retaining screws.

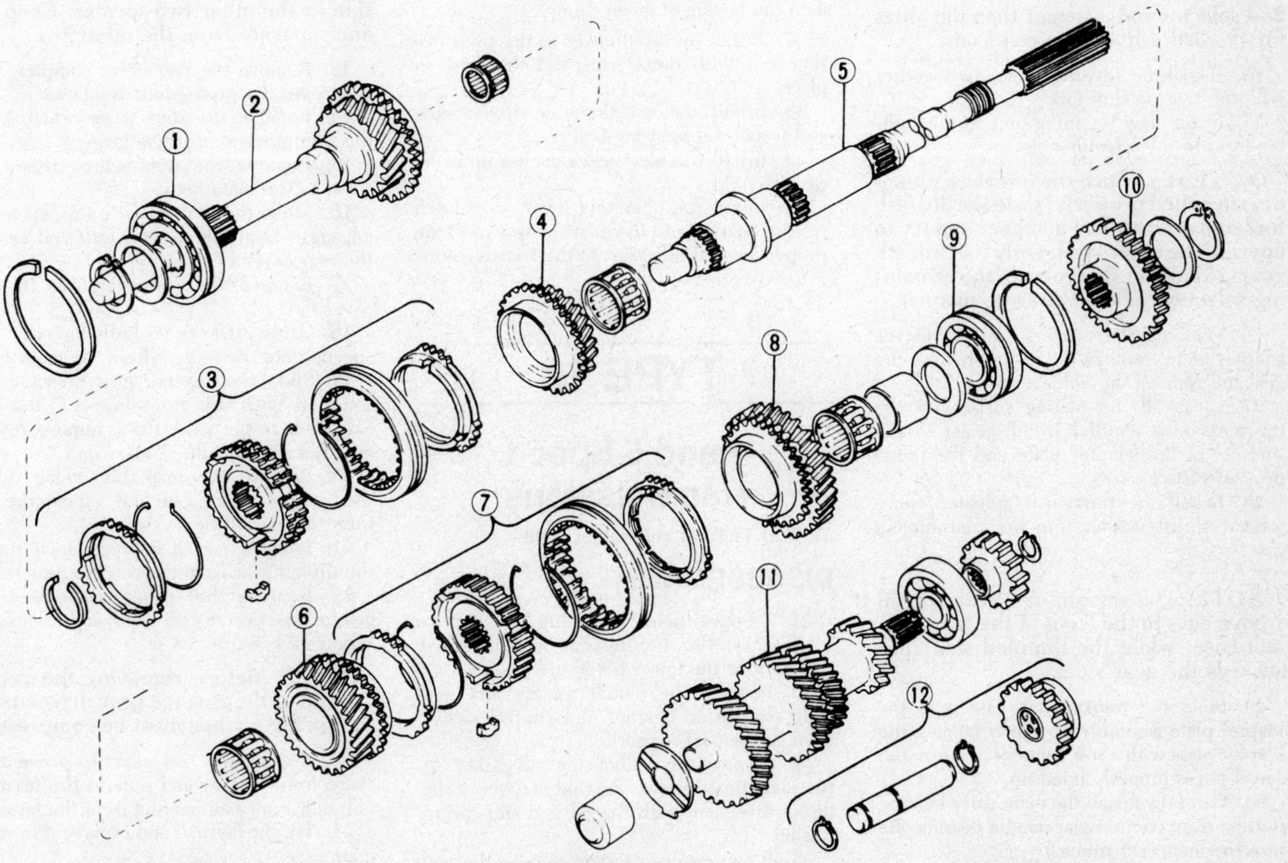

1. Main drive bearing
2. Main drive gear
3. 3rd & top synchronizer
4. 3rd gear, mainshaft
5. Mainshaft
6. 2nd gear, mainshaft
7. 1st & 2nd synchronizer
8. 1st gear, mainshaft
9. Mainshaft bearing
10. Reverse gear, mainshaft
11. Counter gear assembly
12. Idler gear assembly

Exploded view of gear train components

No.	"A" mm	(in.)	Adjusting shim mm	(in.)
1	6.05 to 6.09	(0.2382 to 0.2398)	0.50	(0.0197)
2	6.10 to 6.14	(0.2402 to 0.2417)	0.55	(0.0271)
3	6.15 to 6.19	(0.2421 to 0.2437)	0.60	(0.0236)
4	6.20 to 6.24	(0.2441 to 0.2457)	0.65	(0.0256)
5	6.25 to 6.29	(0.2461 to 0.2476)	0.70	(0.0276)
6	6.30 to 6.34	(0.2480 to 0.2496)	0.75	(0.0295)
7	6.35 to 6.39	(0.2500 to 0.2516)	0.80	(0.0315)

Torque the screws to 5.1 to 7.2 ft/lbs (6.9 to 9.8 Nm) and stake each screw in two places with a center punch.

17. Install the mainshaft reverse gear and thrust washer on the rear of the mainshaft and secure with a new snap-ring.

NOTE: Install the thrust washer with its concave side towards the mainshaft reverse gear.

18. Install the 1st/2nd selector rod into the adapter plate and install the shifting fork onto the rod.
19. Place the 1st/2nd selector rod in the neutral position and install the interlock plunger into the adapter plate.
20. Insert the 3rd/4th selector rod into the adapter plate and install the shifting fork.
21. Set the 3rd/4th selector rod in the neutral position and install the interlock plunger into the adapter plate.
22. Install the reverse selector rod into the adapter plate.

NOTE: Be sure to install the interlock plungers into the adapter plate between each adjacent selector rod. Align the shifting forks with the sliding sleeves before installation.

23. Install the check balls and springs in their respective bores in the adapter plate. Install sealer to the check ball plugs and install in place.

NOTE: The check ball plug for 1st/2nd selector rod is longer than the plugs for the 3rd/4th and reverse rods.

24. Install the reverse idler gear together with the reverse shift fork.
25. Install new retaining pins in the shifting forks to the selector rods.

NOTE: To insure the interlock plunger is installed properly, slide the 3rd/4th fork and selector rod into gear and try to operate the other rods. Only the 3rd/4th gears should mesh. Operate the remaining selector rods in the same manner.

26. With all the gears assembled to the adapter plate, remove the assembly from the vise and remove the holder.
27. Clean all the mating surfaces of the transmission assembly. Install sealer to the surfaces of the adapter plate and the transmission surfaces.
28. Install the previously selected countergear thrust washer into the transmission case.

NOTE: The smooth side with the oil groove goes to the front of the transmission case, while the dimpled side goes towards the gear side.

29. Slide the transmission case onto the adapter plate assembly by lightly tapping the adapter plate with a soft hammer. Be sure the dowel pin is properly lined up.
30. Carefully install the main drive bearing and the front countergear needle bearing. Be sure the mainshaft rotates.
31. Install the main drive bearing snap-ring into its groove on the bearing outer race.
32. Apply sealant to the rear extension housing and the adapter plate. Place the selector rods in the neutral position and turn the striking rod (main shift selector rod) clockwise and gradually slide the rear extension onto the adapter plate, being sure the striking lever engages the fork rod brackets correctly.
33. Install the retaining bolts and tighten to 12 to 16 ft/lbs (16 to 22 Nm).
34. Install the stopper pin bolt into the rear extension and tighten to 3.6 to 5.8 ft/lbs (4.9 to 7.8 Nm).
35. Lubricate the plunger and install it into the rear extension. Install the reverse check spring and return spring. Apply sealer to the return spring plug and install it in place.
36. Turn the transmission assembly so that the front is up. Measure the distance from the front end of the transmission case to the main drive bearing outer race with a depth gauge. Select a shim to correspond to the dimension or thickness "A". The front cover adjusting shim can be one of seven shims.
37. Install the front cover to the transmission case with the O-ring and the shim in place.
38. Install the speedometer driven gear and install the securing bolt.
39. Install the electrical switches onto the case assembly.
40. Install the operating lever, the clutch release bearing and the dust cover. Install the proper level of lubricant to the transmission.

TYPE 18

4 and 5 Speed Transmissions

1975-81 Fiat 124 and Spider 2000

DISASSEMBLY

1. Remove the oil filler plug.
2. Place the transmission upside down and remove the lower cover and gasket.
3. Remove the clutch release fork and slide the thrust bearing and control sleeve from the central support.
4. Remove the bellhousing and gasket. At the same time remove the center cover of the direct driveshaft with the oil seal and spring washer.
5. It may be necessary to remove the seal on the bench.
6. Remove the bolts which secure the 3rd and 4th gear selector forks.

NOTE: When the bolts have been removed the fork can be removed along the bar and the two gears can be engaged simultaneously.

7. Slide the rubber dust cover from the end of the mainshaft.
8. Remove the snap-ring and flexible coupling ring.
9. Lock the mainshaft by proceeding according to the note above, and remove the spider from the mainshaft.
10. Remove the speedometer drive support and gasket from the rear transmission cover.
11. Remove the selector rod detent ball spring cover plate from the main casing.
12. Remove the springs from the recesses, followed by the detent balls.

NOTE: The reverse gear selector rod ball spring is not of the same compression as the other two springs. Keep this one separate from the other two.

13. Remove the rear cover complete with gear lever, by proceeding as follows:
14. Remove the stop screw which limits the side movement of the lever.
15. Remove the nuts which retain the cover to the main body.
16. Move the gear lever to the left to disengage it from the selector rods and remove the rear cover.
17. Remove the gear lever from the rear cover.
18. Slide the rear ball bearing and speedometer drive gear from the mainshaft.
19. Slide the reverse gear selector rod, complete with fork, from its seat in the main case and, at the same time, remove reverse gear from its spindle.
20. Remove the snap-ring which retains the reverse driving gear and remove the gear from the end of the layshaft.
21. Remove the snap-ring which retains the driven gear from the reverse gear train.
22. Remove the spring washers, driven gear of the reverse gear train, and remove the Woodruff key from its seat.

NOTE: Before removing the retaining clip of the reverse gear driven train, the spring washer must be compressed.

23. Engage the two gears to prevent the shafts from turning and remove the retaining bolt and front ball bearing from the layshaft.
24. Tilt the layshaft and remove it from the main case.
25. Remove the 3rd and 4th gear selector rods from the case and remove the bolt and spring washer holding the 1st and 2nd gear selector forks to the rod.
26. Remove the rod, followed by the 1st/

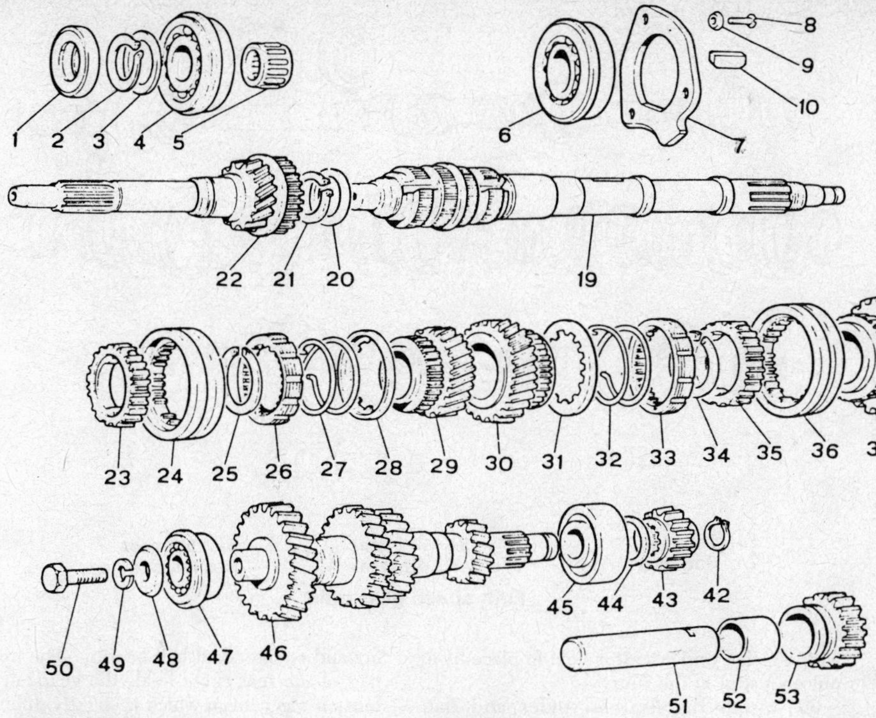

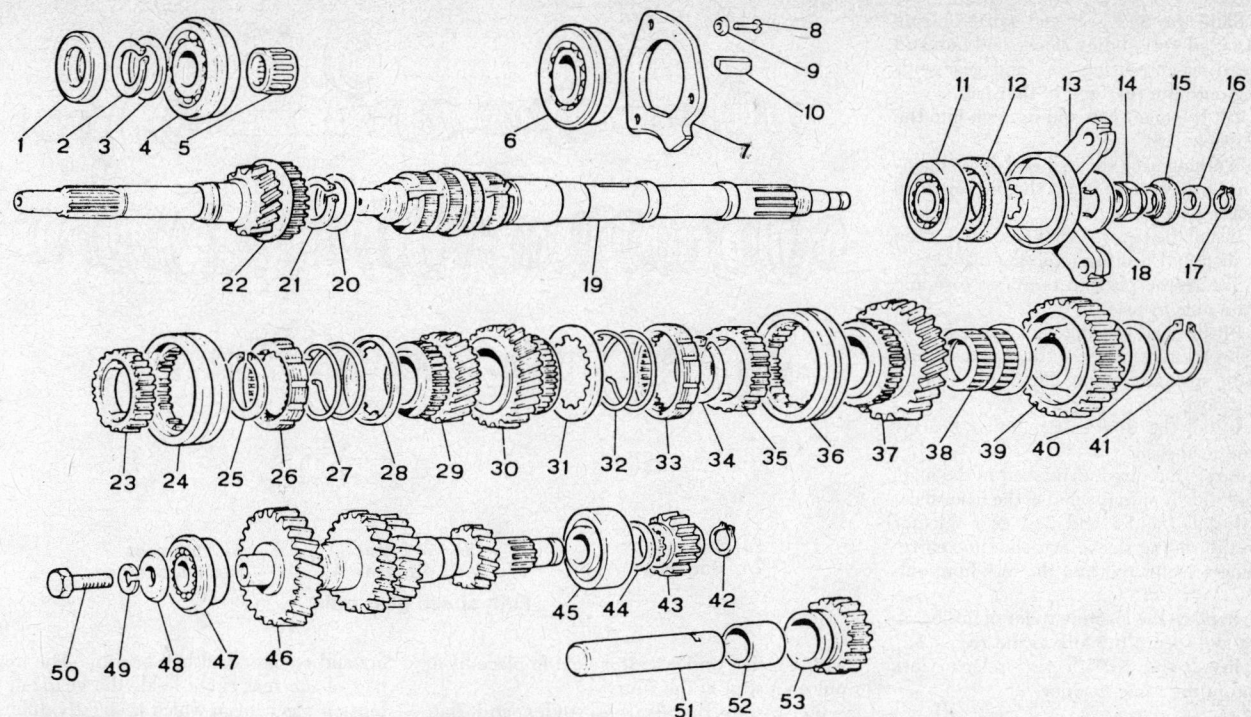

1. Inner cover seal
2. Bearing snap-ring
3. Spring washer
4. Direct drive shaft bearing
5. Needle roller bearing
6. Mainshaft intermediate bearing
7. Bearing retaining plate
8. Retaining screw
9. Retaining screw washer
10. Key
11. Mainshaft rear bearing
12. Rear cover oil seal
13. Flexible coupling
14. Retaining nut
15. Sealing ring
16. Centering ring
17. Snap-ring
18. Lock washer
19. Mainshaft
20. Spring washer
21. Retaining snap-ring
22. Direct drive and 4th gear shaft
23. 3rd/4th gear sliding sleeve hub
24. Sliding sleeve
25. Lock ring
26. Synchronizer ring
27. Synchronizer spring
28. Cup
29. 3rd speed driven gear
30. 2nd speed driven gear
31. Cup
32. Synchronizer spring
33. Synchronizer ring
34. Lock ring
35. 1st/2nd gear sliding sleeve hub
36. Sliding sleeve
37. 1st speed driven gear
38. 1st gear bushing
39. Reverse driven gear
40. Spring washer
41. Retaining snap-ring
42. Snap-ring
43. Reverse driving gear
44. Spring washer
45. Countershaft rear roller bearing
46. Countershaft with 1st, 2nd and 3rd speed gears
47. Countershaft front double row bearing
48. Flat washer
49. Spring washer
50. Countershaft front bearing
51. Reverse idler gear spindle
52. Reverse idler gear bushing
53. Reverse idler gear

Exploded view of gear train components, 4-speed transmission without intermediate housing

2nd and 3rd/4th gear forks. The three safety rollers will be released as the selector rods are removed.

27. Remove the plate which retains the mainshaft intermediate ball bearing.
28. Withdraw the bearing from its housing.
29. Withdraw the reverse gear spindle from the main case.
30. Remove the direct drive and 4th gear shaft from the mainshaft, complete with ball bearing and 4th gear synchronizing ring.
31. Tilt the mainshaft and remove it from the case, complete with gears, hubs, sliding sleeves and synchronizing rings.
32. Remove the following parts from the mainshaft: 1st gear with synchronizer and bushing. 1st and 2nd gear hub and sliding sleeve, 2nd gear and synchronizer assembly.
33. Remove the snap-ring from its seat in the front end of the mainshaft and remove the following parts: spring washer, 3rd/4th gear hub, 3rd gear, and synchronizer assembly.
34. Remove the snap-ring from the direct drive and 4th gear shaft and remove the spring washer and ball bearing.

ASSEMBLY

1. Assemble the following parts on the front of the mainshaft, in the order given: 3rd gear and synchronizing ring, 3rd/4th gears and spring washer.
2. Insert the snap-ring in the groove, securing the parts listed above to the front of the mainshaft.

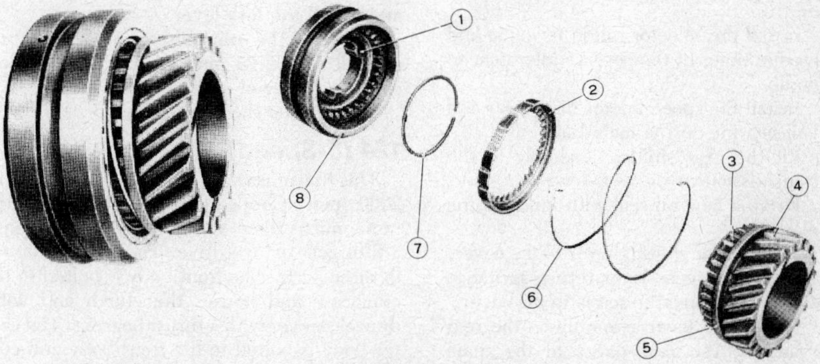

1. Hub
2. Synchronizing ring
3. Blocker ring
4. 3rd gear pinion
5. Cup ring
6. Spring
7. Circlip
8. Sliding sleeve

Third gear synchronizer—4 and 5-speed

3. Slide the 2nd gear and synchronizing ring, 1st/2nd gear sliding sleeve and hub and 1st speed synchronizing ring and gear with bushing onto the rear end of the shaft.

4. Tilt the mainshaft and insert it into the transmission case.

5. Working from the rear end of the mainshaft, use a driver and insert the intermediate ball bearing.

6. Install the reverse idler gear shaft, then fit the shaft and bearing retaining plate.

7. Secure the plate to the main case and stake the nuts in place.

8. Fit the ball bearing and spring washer to the direct driveshaft and 4th gear shaft, and insert the spring retaining clip of the bearing in the groove.

9. Install the direct drive roller bearing onto the mainshaft.

10. Insert the direct driveshaft in the main case and slide it onto the end of the mainshaft.

11. Install the 1st and 2nd gear selector fork to the sliding sleeve and slide the corresponding selector rod into the fork from outside.

12. Replace the locating roller of this bar to its seat and secure the fork to the rod.

13. Install the 3rd/4th gear selector fork and rod in the same manner.

NOTE: Do not lock the fork to the rod at this point, since it will be necessary to use this fork to lock the transmission at a later time.

14. Insert the layshaft into the main case.

15. Replace the front ball bearing and rear ball bearing of the layshaft.

16. Lock the shafts by engaging two gears at the same time.

17. Use the flat washer, spring washer and bolt to secure the front bearing to the layshaft.

18. Fit the key to the mainshaft and install the reverse driving gear and spring washer.

19. Retain these with a snap-ring.

NOTE: When installing the reverse driven gear snap-ring, center the spring washer so that the snap-ring cannot snap into the groove of the shaft. Fit the spring washer and reverse driving gear to the rear end of the layshaft and secure them with a snap-ring.

20. Insert the reverse selector rod locating roller in its seating, and fit the selector fork to the rod.

21. Retain this with a bolt and spring washer.

22. Install the selector rod in its guide and at the same time, fit the reverse idler gear to its spindle.

23. Install the speedometer drive gear and rear ball bearing on the mainshaft.

24. Fit the gear shifting assembly to the rear transmission cover, as follows.

25. Drive a new oil seal with inner spring into place.

26. Fit the gear shifting lever to the cover.

27. Attach the gear lever return spring to the lever and replace the screw in the cover.

28. Mount the lever assembly on the rear cover and fit the rear cover to the main transmission case. Be sure to fit a gasket between the two cases. Install the back-up light switch.

29. Replace the speedometer drive support with a gasket under it. It is held in place by a nut on a stud in the cover.

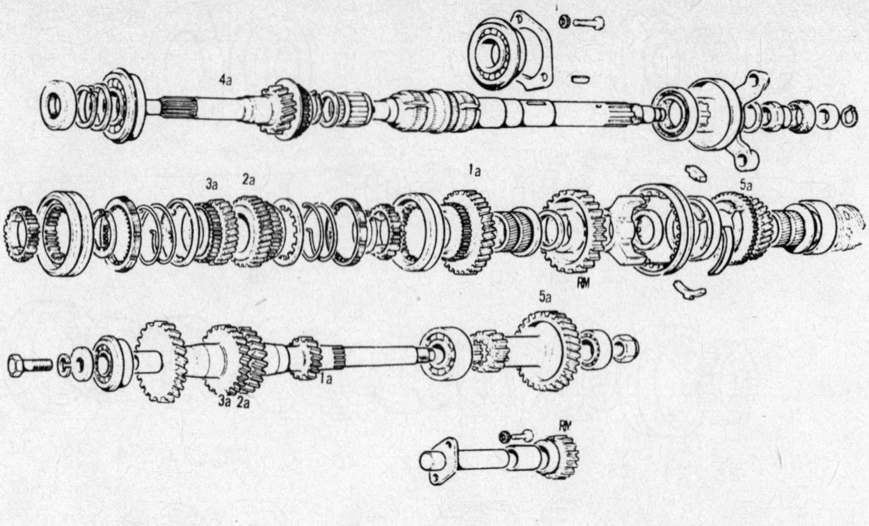

1A. 1st gear
2A. 2nd gear
3A. 3rd gear
4A. 4th gear
5A. 5th gear
RM. Reverse gear

Fifth speed gear train

30. Install the flexible spider and flat washer on the tail of the mainshaft.

31. Lock the gears and tighten the nut, bending up the tab washer.

32. Install the dust cover on the mainshaft and drive the coupling centering ring into place and insert the snap-ring in the groove.

33. Drive an oil seal into the cover of the direct drive and 4th gear shaft and attach this cover to the front of the transmission body (bellhousing).

34. Insert a sealing ring between them.

35. Install the spring washer of the cover and fit the bellhousing to the main case, with a gasket.

36. Fit the 3rd and 4th gear selector fork to the selector rod and secure with a bolt and washer.

37. Replace the three selector rod detent balls and springs in their proper bores. Note that the reverse spring is different from the other two.

38. Fit the lower cover and gasket to the main case.

39. Install the oil drain plug.

40. Fit the clutch release sleeve and thrust bearing to the cover of the direct driveshaft and install the fork lever.

41. Turn the transmission right side up, and fill with 2.75 pints of oil. The oil must come to the brim of the filler hole.

42. Replace the filler plug.

124 (5-Speed)

This transmission is used on 124 Spider and 2000 Spider Coupe models. Basically, it is the same unit as the 4-speed, with the addition of a fifth gear or overdrive. The transmission is in three parts. The front body is bolted to the crankcase and houses the clutch and withdrawal sleeve, with a thrust bearing. The center body is bolted to the front body and contains the 1st, 2nd, 3rd and 4th gears. The rear cover is bolted to the center body and carries 5th and reverse gears, along with the selector bars. It also contains the mainshaft roller bearing and countershaft ball bearing. The upper part of the rear cover holds the gearshift extension mechanism which is slightly different from the 4-speed unit.

Disassembly and assembly are basically the same procedures as those outlined for the 124 (4-speed). Specifications remain identical to those for the 4-speed unit.

When assembling a synchronizer, be sure that the returned ends of the spring are inserted in the slots in the blocker ring, without distorting the normal diameter of the spring. This should be done before the circlip is fitted.

TYPE 19

5 Speed Transmission

1975-81 Fiat 131, Brava

DISASSEMBLY

1. Pull the output yoke off of the output shaft.

2. Remove the speedometer driven gear retainer and gasket.

3. Remove the gearshift support and gasket from the rear housing.

4. Remove the seven bolts and washers retaining the rear housing to the main case. Tap lightly with wooden or plastic hammer and pull off to the rear.

5. Disconnect clutch release lever from ball joint pivot. Remove release bearing support and release lever.

6. Inside bellhousing, remove the seven bolts retaining bellhousing to main case. Tap lightly and remove bellhousing.

7. Remove snap-ring for speedometer drive gear and slide gear off output shaft.

8. Remove snap-ring in front of input shaft bearing.

9. Apply pressure to spring washer behind snap-ring at rear of output shaft and remove snap-ring. Remove spring washer.

10. Remove bolt retaining reverse shifting fork to shifting rod, and remove fork and reverse idler gear. Remove shifting rod spacer. Remove reverse gear from the mainshaft.

11. Remove bolt retaining extension for 3rd and 4th gear shifting rod. Remove extension.

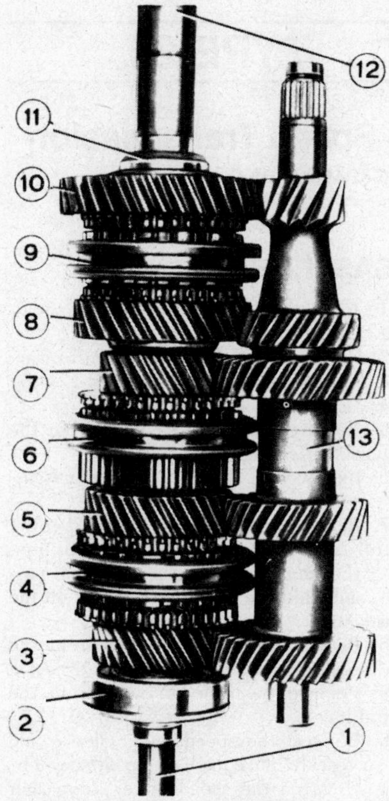

1. Input shaft
2. Bearing
3. 4th gear
4. 3rd and 4th gear synchronizer
5. 3rd gear
6. 5th gear synchronizer
7. 5th gear
8. 2nd gear
9. 1st and 2nd gear synchronizer
10. 1st gear
11. Bearing outer race
12. Main shaft
13. Auxiliary shaft

Main and auxiliary shafts—131 and Brava 5-speed transmission

12. Remove snap-ring retaining reverse drive gear onto auxiliary shaft, and remove the gear.

13. Remove two bolts retaining detent ball cover. Remove cover, springs and balls.

14. Remove Woodruff key from output shaft. Slide main case off of shafts. Remove magnet for front housing slot.

15. Remove bolt retaining fork to shifting rod, and remove rod. Assemble fork to rod for reference. Repeat for other shifting rods.

16. Remove mainshaft and auxiliary shaft from housing.

17. Disconnect input shaft from mainshaft. Remove bearing from inside input shaft.

18. Position mainshaft in vise with protective jaws. Using two screwdrivers, pry outer bearing race off of shaft. Then, slide 1st gear, outer race for thrust bearing, thrust bearing, inner race, and thrust washer off of mainshaft.

19. Remove roller bearing (122 rollers) and separator for bearings.

20. Remove snap-ring retaining 1st and 2nd gear synchronizer hub. Place mainshaft in press with block beneath 2nd gear. Press off hub, synchronizer ring, gear, and washers. Remove roller bearing (134 rollers) from shaft.

21. Invert mainshaft. Depress spring washer and remove snap-ring and washer from other end. Pull the 3rd and 4th gear synchronizer hub from shaft. Remove 3rd gear.

22. Remove snap-ring retaining 5th gear synchronizer hub. Pull off hub. Remove 5th gear.

23. Depress spring washer and remove snap-ring. Pull bearing from mainshaft.

ASSEMBLY

1. Press bearing on input shaft. Position spring washer and snap-ring on shaft. Depress spring washer and install snap-ring in groove.

2. Place 5th gear and synchronizer ring on mainshaft. Tap hub for 5th gear synchronizer down with brass drift until ring seats correctly in hub. Secure with snap-ring. Position sliding sleeve on hub with beveled teeth facing 5th gear.

3. Place 3rd gear and synchronizer on mainshaft. Tap hub down with brass drift. Install sliding sleeve on hub with grooved side down. Position spring washer and snap-ring on shaft. Depress spring washer and install snap-ring in groove.

4. Invert mainshaft. Position two rows of 67 roller bearings on shaft and retain with clean wheel bearing grease.

5. Place 2nd gear and synchronizer ring and hub for 1st and 2nd gear on mainshaft.

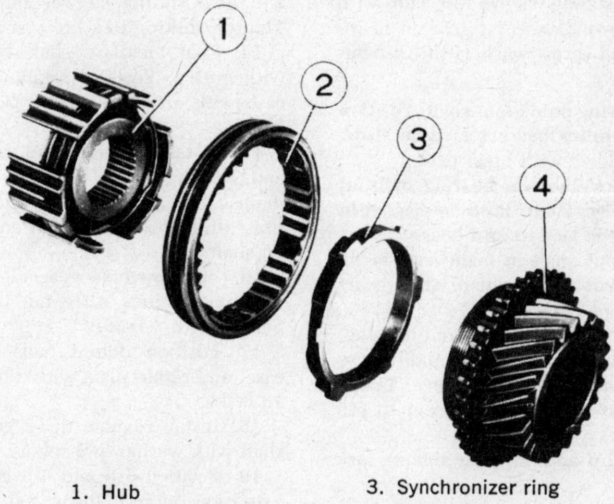

1. Hub
2. Sliding sleeve
3. Synchronizer ring
4. 5th gear

Third gear and synchronizer—131 and Brava

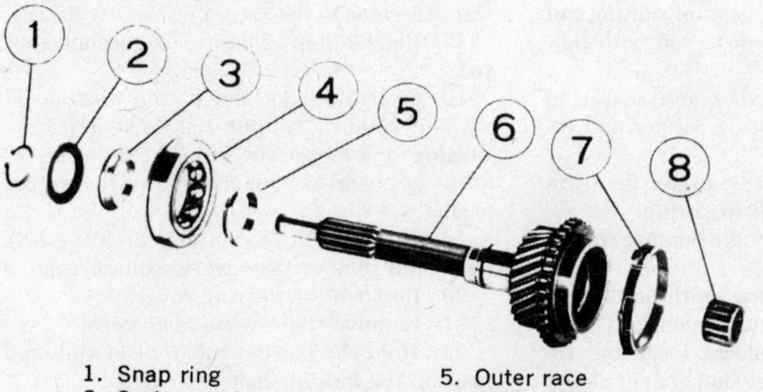

1. Snap ring
2. Spring washer
3. Outer race
4. Bearing
5. Outer race
6. Input shaft
7. Synchronizer ring
8. Bearing

Input shaft—131 and Brava

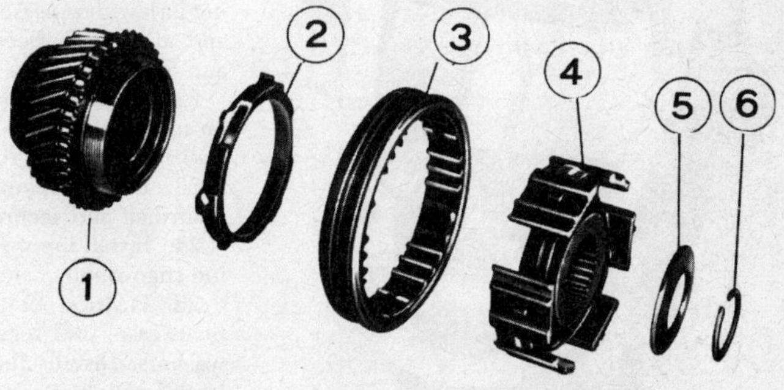

1. 3rd gear
2. Synchronizer ring
3. Sliding sleeve
4. Hub
5. Spring washer
6. Snap ring

Fifth gear synchronizer—131 and Brava

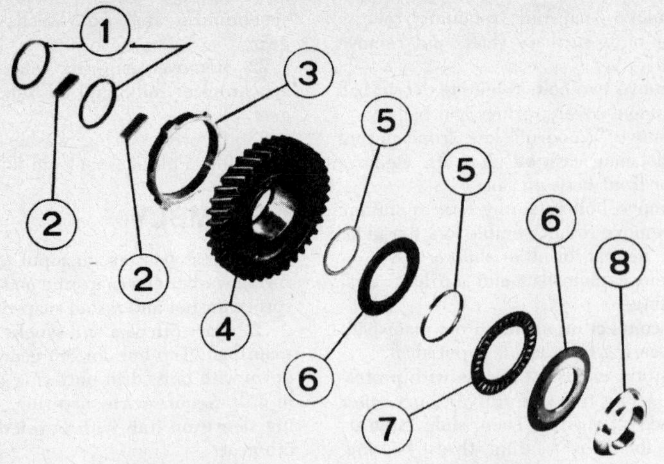

1. Spacer
2. Roller bearings
3. Synchronizer ring
4. 1st gear
5. Flat washer
6. Thrust washer
7. Thrust bearing
8. Outer race

First gear and synchronizer—131 and Brava

Tap hub down with brass drift. Retain with snap-ring.

6. Position flat washer on mainshaft. Place a row of 61 roller bearings on the shaft, install a spacer, and then a second row of 61 bearings, forming a ring. Retain with grease.

7. Position sliding sleeve on hub with grooved side down. Place 1st gear on mainshaft, then install thrust washer, thrust bearing and washer.

8. Press bearing onto input shaft. Position flat washer and outer bearing race on shaft. Tap outer race down with brass drift.

9. Place lockwasher on bearing in front housing for auxiliary shaft. Position magnet in case with magnetic face toward gears.

10. Install input shaft in mainshaft. Mesh together mainshaft and auxiliary shaft gears and install in front housing.

11. Remove Allen bolt from front housing. Position 5th gear shifting fork on rod in case with fork on 5th gear sliding sleeve. Install detent ball in front housing adjacent to 5th gear shifting rod.

12. Position 3rd and 4th gear shifting fork on rod. Install rod in case with fork on 3rd and 4th gear sliding sleeve. Install detent ball in front housing adjacent to 3rd and 4th gear shifting rod.

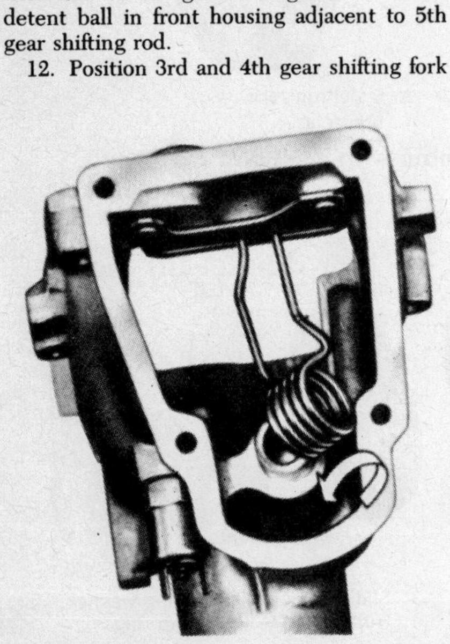

Installing shifter spring—131 and Brava

13. Position 1st and 3rd gear shifting fork on rod. Install rod in case with fork on 1st and 2nd gear sliding sleeve. Install Allen bolt. Tighten shifting fork bolts to 14.5 ft/lbs.

14. Coat auxiliary shaft bearing retainer with grease. Position retainer on bearing in case with grooved surface facing away from bearing.

15. Install main case and gasket over shafts and shifting rods. Position outer race for mainshaft bearing on shaft, and tap down with brass drift. Position washer and retainer plate on shaft.

16. Place reverse gear idle shaft in case. Position retainer plate tab in shaft groove. Secure with 4 bolts.

17. Position detent balls and springs in case, and retain plate with 2 bolts. Tighten to 18 ft/lbs.

18. Install reverse drive gear on auxiliary shaft with washer and secure with snap-ring.

19. Position 3rd and 4th gear shifting rod extension on rod. Install extension retaining bolt and lockwasher and tighten.

20. Install Woodruff key in mainshaft.

21. Install reverse gear on mainshaft. Place spacer on reverse shifting rod. Position shifting fork with reverse idler gear on shifting rod and idler shaft. Secure fork to rod with bolt and lockwasher.

22. Position spring washer and snap-ring on mainshaft. Depress spring washer and install snap-ring in groove.

23. Install speedometer drive gear on mainshaft and secure with snap-ring.

24. Install input shaft outer bearing retaining snap-ring.

25. Position bellhousing with gasket to main case, and secure with seven bolts and washers. Install clutch release lever and release bearing on input shaft and connect lever to ball joint pivot.

26. Position rear housing with gasket to main case and secure with seven bolts and washers.

27. Place both ends of shifter spring in rear housing slotted plate. Then, flip spring over and install over spring support boss.

28. Install gearshift support with gasket on rear housing. Install retaining bolts and check shifting action.

29. Install speedometer driven gear housing and gasket.

30. Slide output shaft yoke onto shaft.

TYPE 20

4 Speed Transmission

1975-81 Mazda RX-3
RX-4
808

DISASSEMBLY

1. Install the transmission on a workstand.
2. Drain the oil.
3. Remove the fork and throwout bearing from the housing.
4. Remove the bellhousing.
5. Remove the adjusting shim from the bellhousing bearing bore.
6. Remove the shift lever tower and gasket.
7. Remove the extension housing. Set the control lever end in the neutral position, presss the control lever end as far left as possible, and slide the extension housing off the transmission.
8. Remove the neutral switch from the transmission (models with seat belt interlock).
9. Remove the gearshift yoke from the central lever.
10. Remove the speedometer sleeve and driven gear. Remove the back-up light switch.
11. Unfasten the speedometer drive gear snap-ring, slide the drive gear off of the output shaft, and remove the lockball.
12. Remove the bottom cover and gasket.
13. Remove the cap bolts, the detent springs, and detent balls.
14. Remove the blind covers and gaskets from the transmission case.
15. Remove the reverse shift rod and idler gear from the rear of the transmission case. Remove the reverse shift fork.
16. Unfasten third/fourth shift fork securing bolt and remove the third/fourth shift rod from the rear of the case.
17. Repeat Step 16 for the first/second shift rod.
18. Straighten out the output shaft lockwasher. Hold the output shaft to keep it from turning, and loosen the locknut. Slide the reverse gear and key off the end of the output shaft.
19. Remove the countershaft snap-ring (rear) and remove the reverse countergear.
20. Remove the bearing cover.
21. Remove the reverse idler gear.
22. Hold the fourth synchronizer ring and gear on the output shaft.
23. Remove the countershaft front bearing snap-ring. Remove the front bearing. Remove the adjusting shim from the case bearing bore.
24. Remove the countershaft rear bearing.

Remove the adjusting shim from the case bearing bore.

25. Remove the input shaft bearing snap-ring and remove the bearing with the puller.

26. Lift the countershaft out.

27. Separate the input and output shafts. Remove the input shaft. Remove the fourth synchronizer ring and needle bearing from the input shaft.

28. Remove the output shaft gear assembly.

29. Remove first/second and third/fourth shift forks from the case. Withdraw the shift interlock pins.

30. Remove the third/ fourth clutch hub snap-ring, then slide the clutch hub sleeve, third synchronizer ring and third gear off the front of the output shaft. Be careful not to mix up the synchronizer rings.

31. Slide the first gear and synchronizer ring off the rear of the output shaft.

32. Slide the first gear sleeve, second gear, second synchronizer ring and first/ second clutch hub/sleeve assembly off the output shaft.

ASSEMBLY

1. Install the first/second clutch hub on its sleeve, place the three shift keys in the clutch hub key slots, and install the key springs. Be sure to keep the open ends of the key springs 120° apart.

2. Repeat Step 1 for the third/fourth synchronizer assembly.

3. Place the synchronizer ring on second gear and then slide second gear on the output shaft, so that the synchronizer ring faces the rear of the shaft.

4. Slide the first/second clutch hub and sleeve on the output shaft so that the clutch oil grooves face forward. Be sure that the three synchronizer keys engage the notches on the second gear synchronizer ring.

5. Install the first gear sleeve in the output shaft.

6. Install the synchronizer ring in the first gear and install the gear on the output shaft so that the ring faces the front of the shaft.

7. Install the same thrust washer on the output shaft that was removed.

8. Repeat Step 6 for third gear.

9. Install the third/fourth clutch hub and sleeve on the output shaft, being sure to engage the three synchronizer keys with the notches in the ring.

NOTE: The larger boss on the third/ fourth clutch hub goes toward the front.

10. Install the snap-ring on the front of the output shaft. Install the output shaft/gear set assembly in the case. Fit the needle bearing on the front of the output shaft.

11. Place the synchronizer ring on the input shaft gear (fourth) and install the gear on the front of the output shaft. Be sure that the synchronizer keys engage the notches in the synchronizer ring.

12. Position the first/ second and third/ fourth shift forks in groove on the clutch hub/sleeve assembly.

13. Install the countergear assembly in the case, being careful to engage each countergear with its respective output shift gear.

14. Check the output shaft bearing endplay as follows:

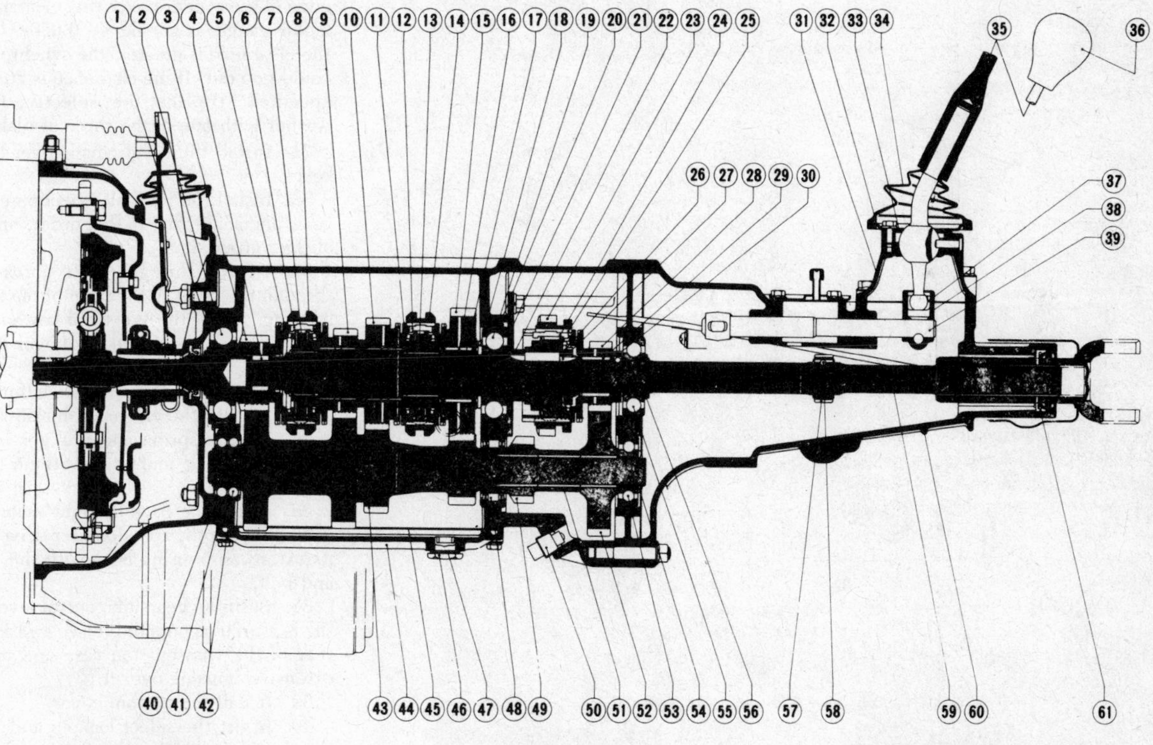

1. Adjusting shim
2. Main driveshaft bearing
3. Main driveshaft and gear
4. Needle bearing
5. Synchronizer ring
6. Third-and-fourth clutch hub
7. Synchronizer key
8. Clutch sleeve
9. Third gear
10. Second gear
11. Synchronizer ring
12. Synchronizer key
13. First-and-second clutch hub
14. Clutch sleeve
15. First gear
16. First gear sleeve
17. Thrust washer
18. Mainshaft bearing
19. Adjusting shim
20. Bearing cover plate
21. Key
22. Gearshift lever retainer
23. Cover
24. Shim
25. Boot
26. Gearshift lever
27. Gearshift lever knob
28. Bush
29. Control lever end
30. Gearshift control lever
31. Adjusting shim
32. Transmission case
33. Countershaft front bearing
34. Gasket
35. Transmission under cover
36. Countershaft
37. Drain plug
38. Gasket
39. Countershaft rear bearing
40. Counter reverse gear
41. Reverse gear
42. Lock washer
43. Locknut
44. Mainshaft
45. Speedometer drive gear
46. Lock ball
47. Extension housing
48. Mainshaft oil seal

Cross section of Mazda 4-speed transmission without intermediate housing

a. Measure the depth of the transmission case output shaft bearing bore.

b. Measure the height of the bearing.

c. The difference between these two measurements indicates the correct thickness of the adjusting shim to be used. The amount of end-play permitted is 0-0.0039 in.

d. Shims are available in thicknesses of 0.0039 or 0.0118 in.

15. Hold the fourth synchronizer ring off the input shaft synchronizer gear.

16. Install the input and output shaft bearings in their respective bores with a press.

17. Install the input shaft bearing snap-ring.

18. Check the countershaft bearing end-play, as outlined in Step 14 for the input shaft. The amount of end-play allowed and available shim size are the same for both bearings.

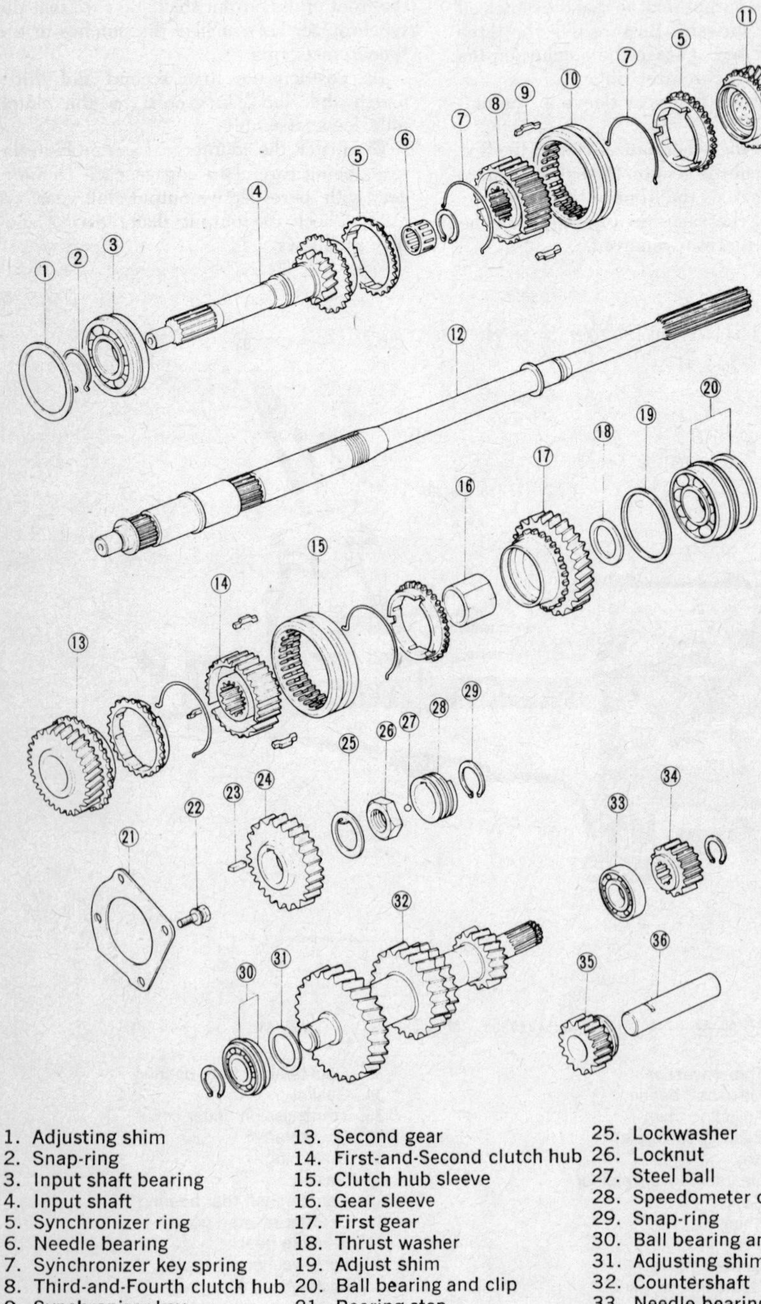

1. Adjusting shim
2. Snap-ring
3. Input shaft bearing
4. Input shaft
5. Synchronizer ring
6. Needle bearing
7. Synchronizer key spring
8. Third-and-Fourth clutch hub
9. Synchronizer key
10. Clutch hub sleeve
11. Third gear
12. Output shaft
13. Second gear
14. First-and-Second clutch hub
15. Clutch hub sleeve
16. Gear sleeve
17. First gear
18. Thrust washer
19. Adjust shim
20. Ball bearing and clip
21. Bearing stop
22. Bolt
23. Key
24. Reverse gear
25. Lockwasher
26. Locknut
27. Steel ball
28. Speedometer drive gear
29. Snap-ring
30. Ball bearing and clip
31. Adjusting shim
32. Countershaft
33. Needle bearing
34. Reverse countergear
35. Reverse idler gear
36. Reverse idler gear shaft

Exploded view of gear train components—Mazda 4-speed transmission without intermediate housing

19. Repeat Step 15.

20. Press the countershaft front and rear bearings into their respective bores. Install the snap-ring on the front bearing.

21. Install the reverse countergear on the rear of the countershaft.

22. Install the reverse gear idler shaft in the transmission case.

23. Install the bearing cover on the case.

24. Secure the reverse gear on the output shaft with its key.

25. Hold the output shaft to keep it from turning and tighten to 150-180 ft/lbs.

26. Install the first/second shift rod into the case and secure it to the shift fork with the lockbolt. Place the shift rod in Neutral. Drive the interlock pin into its bore.

27. Repeat Step 26 for the third/fourth shift rod.

28. Slide the reverse shift rod, complete with the reverse idler gear, in from the rear of the case. Secure the shift rod to the reverse fork with its lockbolt.

29. Install the detent balls and springs in their bores and secure them with their cap bolts.

30. Check the synchronizer key-to-exposed edge of the synchronizer ring clearance with a feeler gauge; it should be 0.026-0.079 in. If the clearance is greater, the synchronizer key could pop out. If the clearance is greater than specified, replace the selective-fit thrust washer with one of the three available sizes.

31. Install the blind covers over their gaskets.

32. Install the lockball, speedometer drive gear, and snap-ring, in that order, on the rear of the output shaft.

33. Install the gearshift control lever through the holes in the front of the extension housing. Install the Woodruff key on the control lever and install the yoke over it. Secure the yoke with its setbolt.

34. Thread the Neutral switch (for seat belt interlock) into the extension housing.

35. Fit the spring and plunger in the extension housing and secure them with the capbolt.

36. Install the back-up light switch.

37. Secure the speedometer driven gear in its extension housing bore with the lockplate and bolt.

38. Push the gearshift control lever over to the left as far as possible. Place a gasket on the rear of the transmission case and install the extension housing over it.

39. Install the bottom cover.

40. Insert the select lockpin and spring in the shift tower. Align the slot in the pin with the lockball bore. Drop the lockball and spring into the bore; secure with the capbolt.

41. Install the shift tower on the extension housing and secure it with its bolts.

42. Repeat Step 14 for the input shaft bearing and clutch housing bore. The end-play and shim thickness are the same as in Step 14.

43. Lubricate the lip of the bellhousing oil seal.

44. Put a gasket on the front of the transmission case, and install the bell housing.

45. Install the throwout bearing, release fork and boot in the bellhousing.

TYPE 21

4 and 5 Speed Transmission

1975-81 Mazda GLC
626

The 4 and 5 speed transmissions are basically the same, with an added housing located between the adapter plate and the rear extension housing, to carry the 5th and reverse gears. Added roller bearings are used in the housing to prevent shaft misalignment.

DISASSEMBLY

1. Remove the throwout bearing return spring, throwout bearing, and the release fork.
2. Remove the bearing housing.
3. Remove the input shaft and countershaft snap-rings.
4. Remove the floorshift lever retainer, complete with gasket.
5. Unfasten the cap bolt and withdraw the spring, steel ball, select lock pin and spring from the retainer.
6. Remove the extension housing. Turn the control lever as far left as it will go and slide the extension housing off the output shaft.
7. Remove the spring seat and spring from the end of the shift control lever.
8. Loosen the spring cap and withdraw the spring and plunger from their bore.
9. Remove the control rod and boss from the extension housing.
10. Remove the speedometer driven gear. Remove the back-up light switch.
11. Remove the speedometer drive gear.
12. Tap the front ends of the input shaft and countershaft with a plastic hammer; then remove the intermediate housing assembly from the transmission case.
13. Remove the three cap bolts; then withdraw the springs and lockballs.
14. Remove the reverse shift rod, reverse idler gear, and shift lever.
15. Remove the setscrews from all the shift forks and push the shift rods rearward to remove them. Remove the shift forks.
16. Withdraw the reverse shift rod lockball, spring, and interlock pins from the intermediate housing.
17. Remove reverse gear and key from the output shaft.
18. Remove the reverse countergear.
19. Remove the countershaft and output shaft from the intermediate housing.
20. Remove the bearings from the intermediate housing and transmission case.
21. Remove the snap-ring from the output shaft.
22. Slide the third/fourth clutch hub, sleeve, synchronizer ring, and third gear off the output shaft.
23. Remove the thrust washer, first gear, sleeve, synchronizer ring, and second gear from the rear of the output shaft.

ASSEMBLY

1. Install the third/fourth synchronizer clutch hub on the sleeve. Place the three synchronizer keys in the clutch hub key slots. Install the key springs with their open ends 120° apart.
2. Install third gear and the synchronizer ring on the front of the output shaft. Install the third/fourth clutch hub assembly on the output shaft. Be sure that the larger boss faces the front of the shaft.
3. Secure the gear and synchronizer with the snap-ring.
4. Repeat Step 1 for the first/second synchronizer assembly.
5. Position the synchronizer ring on second gear. Slide second gear on the output shaft so that the synchronizer ring faces the rear of the shaft.
6. Install the first/second clutch hub assembly on the output shaft so that its oil grooves face the front of the shaft. Engage the keys in the notches on the second gear synchronizer ring.
7. Slide the first gear sleeve onto the output shaft. Position the synchronizer ring on first gear. Install the first gear on the output shaft so that the synchronizer ring faces frontward. Rotate the first gear as required to engage the notches in the synchronizer ring with the keys in the clutch hub.
8. Slip the thrust washer on the rear of the output shaft. Install the needle bearing on the front of the output shaft.
9. Install the synchronizer ring on fourth gear and install the input shaft on the front of the output shaft.
10. Press the countershaft rear bearing and shim into the intermediate housing, then press the countershaft into the rear bearing.

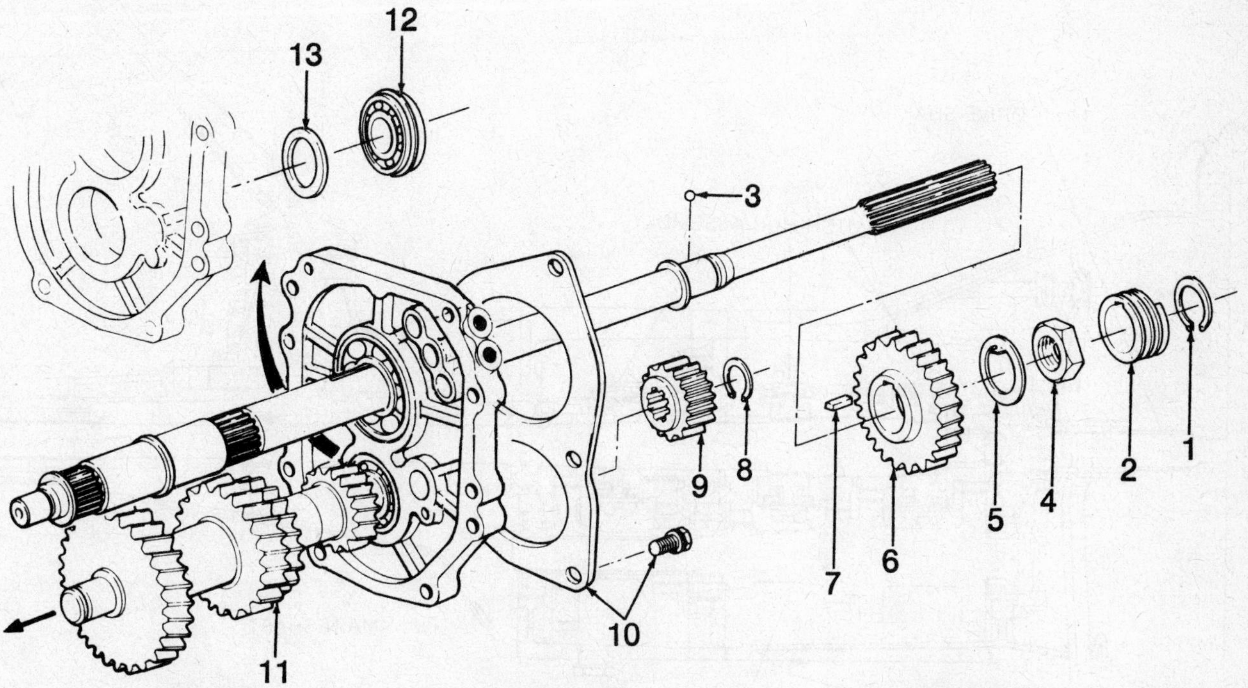

1. Snap-ring
2. Speedometer drive gear
3. Ball
4. Locknut
5. Lock washer
6. Reverse gear
7. Key
8. Snap-ring
9. Counter reverse gear
10. Bolt/bearing cover
11. Countershaft
12. Countershaft rear bearing
13. Shim

Gear train position in 4-speed transmission with intermediate housing

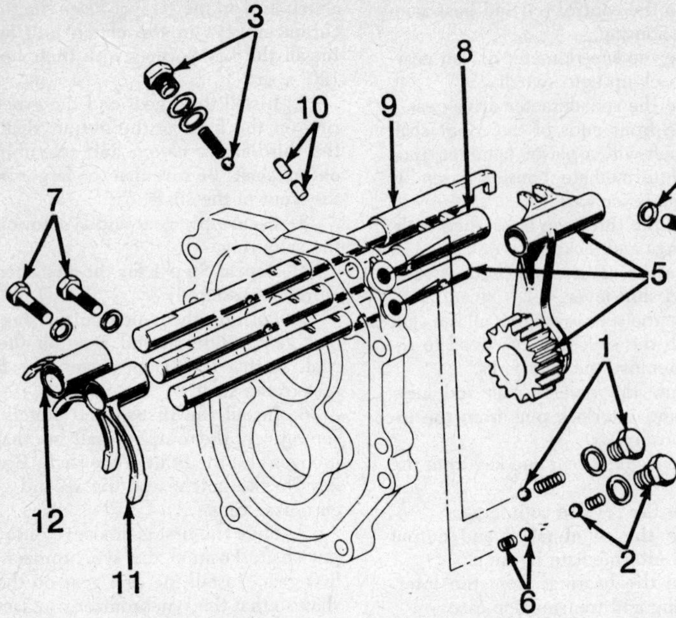

1. Spring cap bolt/packing/spring/locking ball
2. Spring cap bolt/packing/spring/locking ball
3. Spring cap bolt/packing/spring/locking ball
4. Bolt/washer
5. Shift fork (Reverse)/rod/reverse idler gear
6. Spring/locking ball
7. Bolt/washer
8. Shift rod (3rd & 4th)
9. Shift rod (1st & 2nd)
10. Interlock pin
11. Shift fork (3rd & 4th)
12. Shift fork (1st & 2nd)

Exploded view of shift selector rods and forks, 4-speed with intermediate housing

11. Keep the thrust washer and first gear from falling off the output shaft by supporting the shaft. Install the output shaft on the intermediate housing. Be sure that each output shaft gear engages with its opposite number on the countershaft.

12. Tap the output shaft bearing and shim into the intermediate housing with a plastic hammer. Install the cover.

13. Install reverse gear on the output shaft and secure it with its key.

NOTE: The chamfer on the teeth of both the reverse gear and the reverse countergear should face rearward.

14. Install the reverse countergear.

15. Install the lockball and spring into the bore in the intermediate housing. Depress the ball with a screwdriver.

16. Install the reverse shift rod, lever, and idler gear at the same time. Place the reverse shift rod in the neutral position.

17. Align the bores and insert the shift interlock pin.

18. Install the third/fourth shift rod into the intermediate housing and shift bores. Place the shift rod in Neutral.

19. Install the next interlock pin in the bore.

20. Install the first/second shift rod.

21. Install the lockballs and springs in their bores. Install the cap bolt.

22. Install the speedometer drive gear and lockball on the output shaft, and install its snap-ring.

23. Apply sealer to the mating surfaces of

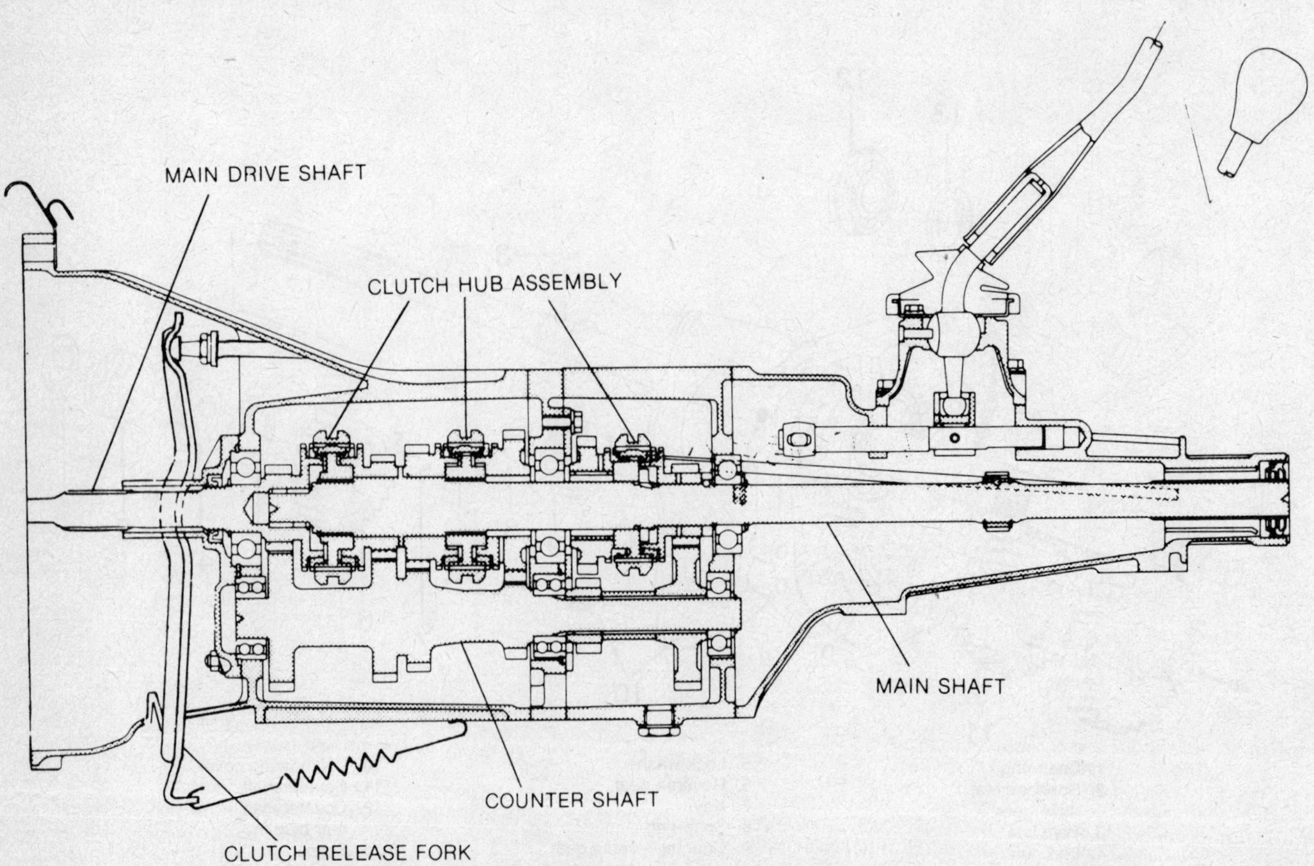

Cross section of 5-speed transmission showing added housing

the intermediate housing. Install the intermediate housing in the transmission case.

24. Install the input shaft and countershaft front bearings in the transmission case.

25. Secure the speedometer driven gear.

26. Install the control rod through the holes in the front of the extension housing.

27. Align the key with the keyway and install the yoke on the end of the control rod. Install the yoke lockbolt.

28. Fit the plunger and spring into the extension housing bore and secure with the spring cap.

29. Turn the control rod all the way to the left and install the extension housing on the intermediate housing.

30. Insert the spring and select lockpin inside the gearshift retainer. Align the steel ball and spring with the lockpin slot, and secure it with the spring cap.

31. Install the spring and spring seat in the control rod yoke.

32. Install the gearshift lever retainer over its gasket on the extension housing.

33. Lubricate the lip of the front bearing cover oil seal and secure the cover on the transmission case.

34. Check the clearance between the front bearing cover and bearing. It should be less than 0.006 in. If it is not within specifications insert additional adjusting shims. The shims are available in 0.006 in. or 0.012 in. sizes.

35. Install the throwout bearing, return spring and release fork.

5 Speed

The disassembly and assembly of the rear extension housing, selector levers and forks are completed in the same manner as the 4 speed transmission. After this has been done, the added housing can be removed by taking out the retaining bolts. The housing will have to be lightly tapped with a soft-faced hammer. The removal of the housing exposes the 5th/reverse synchronizer assembly, the reverse countergear, the countershaft and mainshaft bearings. The bearings are pulled from the shafts and then the gears can be removed. The assembly is in the reverse of the removal procedure.

TYPE 22

5 Speed Transmission

1975-81 Mazda RX-4
808
Cosmo

DISASSEMBLY

1. Pull the release fork outward until the

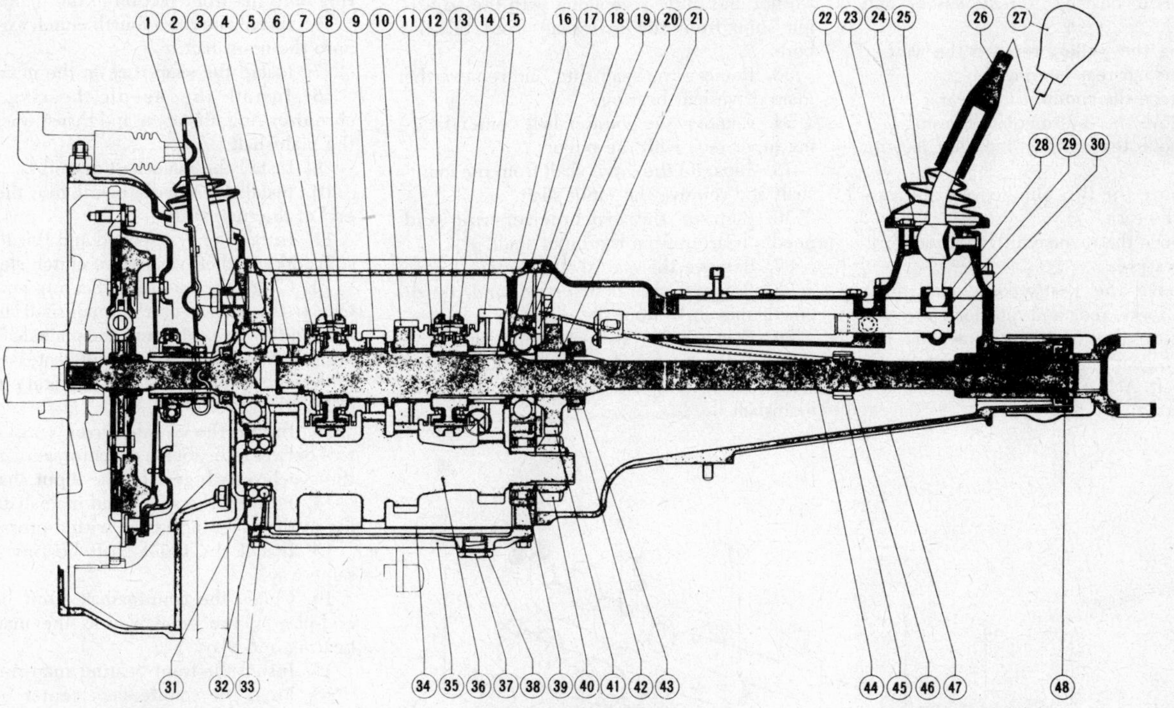

1. Adjusting shim
2. Main driveshaft bearing
3. Main driveshaft gear
4. Needle bearing
5. Synchronizer ring
6. Synchronizer key
7. 3rd-and-4th clutch hub
8. Clutch sleeve
9. 3rd gear
10. 2nd gear
11. Synchronizer ring
12. Synchronizer key
13. 1st-and-2nd clutch hub
14. Clutch sleeve
15. 1st gear
16. Needle bearing
17. Needle bearing inner race
18. Thrust washer
19. Mainshaft front bearing
20. Adjusting shim
21. Bearing cover plate
22. Spacer
23. Reverse gear and clutch sleeve assembly
24. Synchronizer key
25. Synchronizer ring
26. Lock washer
27. Locknut
28. 5th gear
29. Needle bearing
30. Thrust washer
31. Gearshift lever retainer
32. Cover
33. Gasket
34. Boot
35. Gearshift lever
36. Gearshift lever knob
37. Bush
38. Gearshift control lever end
39. Gearshift control lever
40. Adjusting shim
41. Transmission case
42. Countershaft front bearing
43. Countershaft
44. Transmission under cover
45. Gasket
46. Drain plug
47. Gasket
48. Countershaft center bearing
49. Counter reverse gear
50. Drain plug
51. Spacer
52. Counter 5th gear
53. Countershaft rear bearing
54. Thrust washer
55. Mainshaft rear bearing
56. Thrust washer
57. Speedometer drive gear
58. Lock ball
59. Mainshaft
60. Extension housng
61. Mainshaft oil seal

Cross section of Mazda 5-speed transmission

spring clip of the fork releases from the ball pivot.

2. Remove the fork and release bearing.
3. Remove the clutch housing shim and gasket.
4. Remove the gearshift lever retainer and gasket.
5. Remove the spring and steel ball, select lock spindle and spring from the gearshift lever retainer.
6. Remove the extension housing with the control lever end down to the left as far as it will go.
7. Remove the control lever end, key and control rod.
8. Remove the lock plate and speedometer gear.
9. Remove the back-up light switch.
10. Remove the snap-ring and slide the speedometer drive gear from the mainshaft.
11. Remove the bottom cover and gasket.
12. Remove the shift rod ends.
13. Remove the rear bearing housing.
14. Remove the snap-ring and remove the mainshaft rear bearing, thrust washer and race.
15. Using the puller, remove the washer and countershaft rear bearing.
16. Remove the counter fifth gear.
17. Remove the intermediate housing.
18. Remove the springs and shift locking balls.
19. Remove the two blind covers and gaskets from the case.
20. Remove the reverse/fifth shift rod, fork and interlock pin.
21. Remove the first/second and third/fourth shift forks, rods and interlock pins.
22. Remove the snap-ring and slide the washer, fifth gear and synchronizer ring from the mainshaft. Also, remove the steel ball and needle bearing.
23. Lock the rotation of the mainshaft with second and reverse.
24. Remove the locknut and slide the reverse/fifth clutch hub and sleeve assembly, synchronizer ring, reverse gear and needle bearing from the mainshaft.
25. Remove the spacer and counter reverse gear from the countershaft.
26. Remove the reverse idler gear, thrust washers and shaft from the transmission case.
27. Remove the bearing rear cover plate.
28. Remove the snap-ring from the front end of the countershaft and install Mazda tool number 49 0839 445 synchronizer ring holder or its equivalent between the fourth synchronizer ring and the synchromesh gear on the main driveshaft.
29. Remove the countershaft front bearing.
30. Remove the adjusting shim from the countershaft front bearing bore.
31. Remove the countershaft center bearing outer race.
32. With a special puller and attachment, remove the mainshaft front bearing, thrust washer and inner race along with the adjusting shim from the mainshaft front bearing bore.
33. Remove the snap-ring, and remove the main driveshaft bearing.
34. Remove the countershaft center bearing inner race with the puller.
35. Separate the input shaft from the mainshaft and remove the input shaft.
36. Remove the synchronizer ring and needle bearing from the input shaft.
37. Remove the mainshaft assembly.
38. Remove the first/second and third/fourth shift forks from the case.
39. Remove the snap-ring and slide the third/fourth clutch hub and sleeve assembly, synchronizer ring and third gear from the mainshaft.

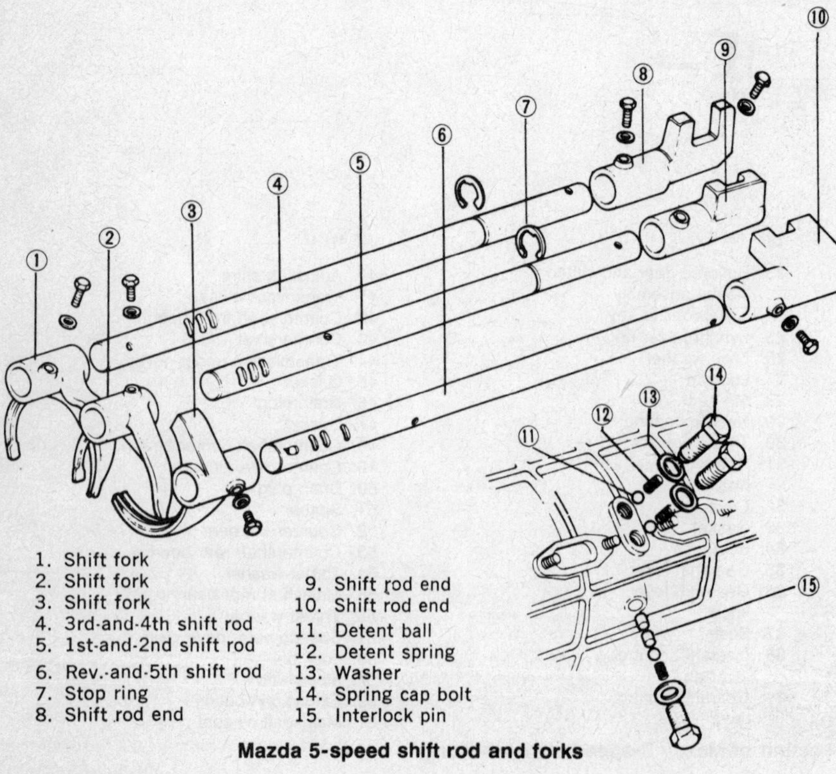

1. Shift fork
2. Shift fork
3. Shift fork
4. 3rd-and-4th shift rod
5. 1st-and-2nd shift rod
6. Rev.-and-5th shift rod
7. Stop ring
8. Shift rod end
9. Shift rod end
10. Shift rod end
11. Detent ball
12. Detent spring
13. Washer
14. Spring cap bolt
15. Interlock pin

Mazda 5-speed shift rod and forks

40. Remove the thrust washer, first gear and needle bearing from the rear of the mainshaft.
41. Press out the needle bearing inner race, synchronizer ring, first and second clutch hub, sleeve assembly, synchronizer ring and second gear from the mainshaft.

ASSEMBLY

1. Install the third/fourth clutch hub into the sleeve, place the three keys into the clutch hub slots and install the springs onto the hub.
2. Assemble the first/second and reverse/fifth clutch hub and sleeve as described in Step 1.
3. Install the needle bearing, second gear, synchronizer ring, and first/second clutch assembly on the rear section of the mainshaft.
4. Press on the first gear needle bearing inner race.
5. Install the third gear and synchronizer ring onto the front section of the mainshaft.
6. Install the third/fourth clutch assembly onto the mainshaft.
7. Install the snap-ring on the mainshaft.
8. Install the needle bearing, synchronizer ring, first gear and thrust washer on the mainshaft.
9. Install the mainshaft assembly.
10. Install the needle bearing on the front end of the mainshaft.
11. Install the first/second and third/fourth shift forks in their respective clutch sleeves.
12. Check the mainshaft bearing end-play. Check the depth of the mainshaft bearing bore in the case. Measure the mainshaft bearing height. The difference indicates the required adjusting shim to give a total end-play of less than 0.0039 in.
13. Install the synchronizer ring holder tool between the fourth synchronizer ring and the synchromesh gear on the input shaft.
14. Position the shims and mainshaft bearing in the bore and install with a press.
15. Install the input shaft bearing in the same way.
16. Check the countershaft front bearing end-play in the same way as the mainshaft bearing end-play.
17. Install the front bearing snap-ring.
18. Press the countershaft center bearing into position.
19. Install the bearing cover plate.
20. Install the reverse idler gearshaft, thrust washers and reverse idler gear.
21. Install the counter reverse gear and spacer on the rear end on the countershaft.
22. Install the thrust washer and press the needle bearing inner race of the reverse gear on the mainshaft.
23. Install the needle bearing, reverse gear, synchronizer ring, reverse/fifth clutch assembly and new mainshaft locknut on the mainshaft.
24. Lock the mainshaft with the second and reverse gears. Tighten the locknut.
25. Install the needle bearing, synchronizer ring and fifth gear on the mainshaft.
26. Install the thrust washer, steel ball and snap-ring on the mainshaft.
27. Check the thrust washer-to-snap-ring clearance. It should be 0.0039-0.0118 in.

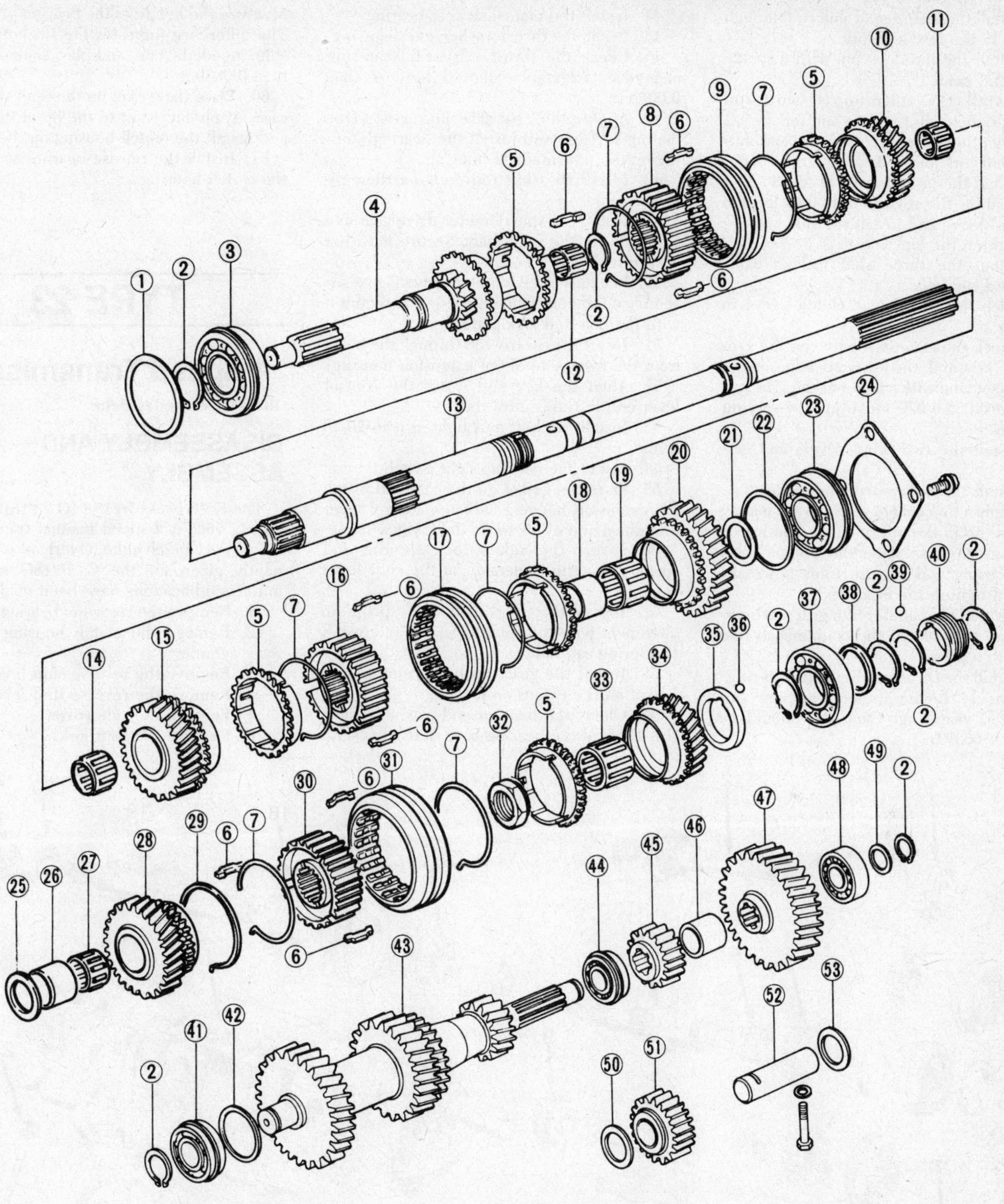

1. Shim
2. Snap ring
3. Main drive shaft bearing
4. Main drive shaft gear
5. Synchronizer ring
6. Synchronizer key
7. Synchronizer key spring
8. 3rd-and-4th clutch hub
9. Clutch sleeve
10. 3rd gear
11. Needle bearing
12. Needle bearing
13. Main shaft
14. Needle bearing
15. 2nd gear
16. 1st-and-2nd clutch hub
17. Clutch sleeve
18. Bearing inner race
19. Needle bearing
20. 1st gear
21. Thrust washer
22. Shim
23. Main shaft front bearing
24. Bearing cover
25. Thrust washer
26. Bearing inner race
27. Needle bearing
28. Reverse gear
29. Stop ring
30. Rev.-and-5th clutch hub
31. Clutch sleeve
32. Main shaft lock nut
33. Needle bearing
34. 5th gear
35. Thrust washer
36. Lock ball
37. Main shaft rear bearing
38. Thrust washer
39. Lock ball
40. Speedometer drive gear
41. Counter shaft front bearing
42. Shim
43. Counter shaft
44. Counter shaft center bearing
45. Counter reverse gear
46. Spacer
47. Reverse gear
48. Counter shaft rear bearing
49. Thrust washer
50. Thrust washer
51. Reverse idler gear
52. Idler gear shaft
53. Thrust washer

Mazda 5-speed gear train

28. Install the first/second shift rod through the holes in the case and fork.
29. Install the interlock pin with a special installer and guide.
30. Install the third/fourth shift rod through the holes in the case and fork.
31. Align the holes and install the lockbolts of each shift fork and rod.
32. Install the interlock pin as above.
33. Position the reverse/fifth shift fork on the clutch sleeve and install the shift rod.
34. Tighten the lockbolt.
35. Install the three shift locking balls, springs and cap bolts.
36. Place the third/fourth clutch sleeve in third gear.
37. Check the clearance between the synchronizer key and the exposed edge of the synchronizer ring with a feeler gauge. The gap should be 0.026-0.079 in. Adjust by varying thrust washers.
38. Install the two blind covers and gaskets.
39. Install the undercover and gasket.
40. Apply a thin coat of sealer to the mating edges and install the intermediate housing on the transmission case. Align the lockbolt holes of the housing and reverse idler gearshaft, install and tighten the lockbolt.
41. Position the counter fifth gear and bearing to the rear end of the countershaft and install with a press.
42. Install the thrust washer and snap-ring.
43. Check the clearance between the washer and snap-ring. Clearance should be less than 0.0039 in.
44. Install the mainshaft rear bearing.
45. Install the thrust washer and snap-ring.
46. Check the thrust washer-to-snap-ring clearance. Clearance should be less than 0.0059 in.
47. Apply a thin coat of sealing agent to the mating surfaces and install the bearing housing on the intermediate housing.
48. Install the shift rod ends on their respective rods.
49. Install the speedometer drive gear and steel ball on the mainshaft. Secure it with a snap-ring.
50. Install a speedometer driven gear assembly on the extension housing and secure it with the bolt and lock plate.
51. Insert the control rod through the holes from the front side of the extension housing.
52. Align the key and insert the control lever end in the control rod.
53. Install the bolt and tighten it to 20-30 ft/lbs.
54. Install the back-up light switch.
55. Place the gasket on the case and install the extension housing with the control lever end down and as far to the left as it will go.
56. Insert the select lock spindle and spring from the underside of the shift lever retainer.
57. Install the steel ball and spring in alignment with the spindle groove and install the spring cap bolt.
58. Install the gearshift lever retainer and gasket on the extension housing.
59. Check the bearing end-play. Measure the depth of the bearing bore in the housing. Measure the height of the bearing protrusion. The difference indicates the thickness of the shim needed. The end-play should be less than 0.0039 in.
60. Place the gasket on the front side of the case. Apply lubricant to the lip of the oil seal and install the clutch housing on the case.
61. Install the release bearing and fork on the clutch housing.

TYPE 23

4 Speed Transmission

1975-81 Mercedes-Benz

DISASSEMBLY AND ASSEMBLY

The G 76/18, G 76/18A, G 76/18B, G 76/27 end G 76/27A 4-speed manual transmissions are all very much alike. Overhaul is predominantly given for the G 76/18C since only minor modifications have been made.

1. Remove the throwout bearing and fork.
2. Remove the clutch housing with the slave cylinder.
3. Remove the reverse shift lever clamp.
4. Remove the reverse shift lever.
5. Remove the side cover.
6. Remove the shift forks.

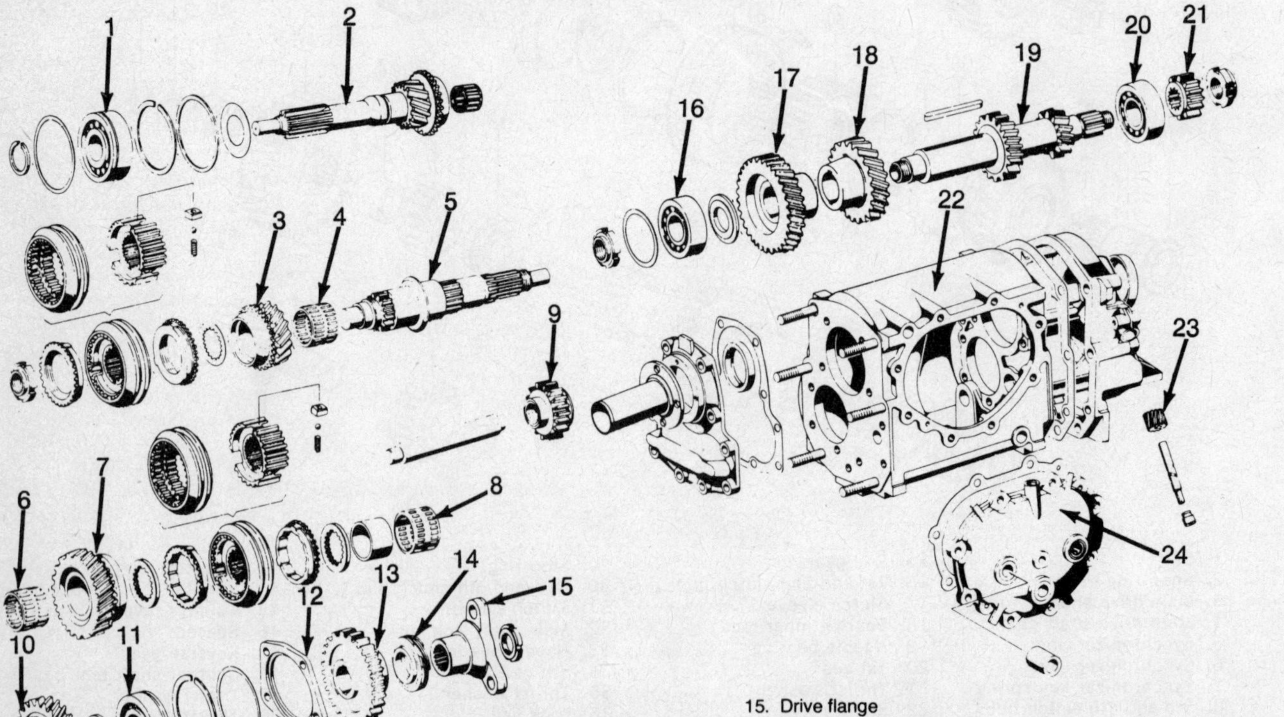

1. Input shaft bearing
2. Input shaft
3. 3rd gear
4. 3rd gear needle bearing
5. Mainshaft
6. 2nd gear needle bearing
7. 2nd gear
8. 1st gear needle bearing
9. Reverse slide gear
10. 1st gear
11. Rear bearing
12. Rear bearing holder
13. Reverse gear, mainshaft
14. Speedometer drive gear
15. Drive flange
16. Countershaft front bearing
17. Countershaft gear, constant speed
18. Countershaft gear, 3rd speed
19. Countershaft gear, 2nd and 1st speed
20. Countershaft rear bearing
21. Countershaft gear, reverse
22. Transmission case
23. Speedometer driven gear
24. Side cover

Exploded view of typical Mercedes-Benz 4-speed

7. Disassemble the side cover and forks.
8. Unbolt and remove the transmission front cover.
9. Remove the bearing housing.
10. Remove the rear transmission cover.
11. Press out the speedometer drive gear.
12. Remove the tachometer drive seal.
13. Remove the reverse gear from the mainshaft.
14. Remove the reverse sliding gear shaft from the housing while holding the sliding gear.
15. Unlock the nut on the rear of the countershaft.
16. Remove reverse gear from the countershaft.
17. Knock the pin from reverse shifter shaft and move the shaft as far forward as possible.
18. Remove the shift rod from the housing.
19. Unlock the slotted nut.
20. Remove the front countershaft bearing. On G 76/27A transmissions, the bearing is beveled and is removed toward the inside of the case.
21. Remove the rear countershaft bearing.
22. Lift the mainshaft at the rear and pull the input shaft out of the housing.
23. Push the mainshaft completely rearward and remove it at an angle.
24. Remove the countershaft from the housing.
25. Disassemble the mainshaft, if necessary.
26. If necessary, disassemble the countershaft.
27. Assembly is basically the reverse of disassembly. Try to obtain 0 end-play on the main and input shafts.

TYPE 24

4 Speed Transmission–British Leyland Model

1975-80 MGB

DISASSEMBLY

1. Remove the driveshaft flange.
2. Remove the shift linkage housing.
3. Withdraw the selector interlock arm and plate assembly.
4. Remove the extension and mainshaft shims.

At this point, if it is desired to rebuild the shift linkage, the extension components can be disassembled.

5. Remove the snap-ring and oil seal from the rear of the extension and press the bearing out if it is to be replaced.
6. Remove the shift lever locating bolt.
7. Remove the retaining cap, damper and spring at the base of the shift lever.
8. Remove the shift lever.
9. Remove the linkage shaft.
10. Remove the clutch release bearing and release lever.
11. Remove the front cover and bearing shims.
12. Remove the side cover.
13. Remove the selector detent plunger plugs and springs.
14. Remove the selector fork and selector lever retaining bolts.
15. Remove the selector rods and selector forks.
16. Remove the reverse shaft and gear.
17. Carefully drive the countershaft out of the case.
18. Drive the input shaft assembly forward out of the case, making sure it is clear of the clustergear.
19. Remove the spacer and shims from the mainshaft.
20. Remove the rear extension mounting studs from the rear of the transmission case.
21. Check that the mainshaft components are clear of the clustergear teeth, and press the mainshaft assembly out the back of the transmission. Remove the clustergear.

ASSEMBLY

1. Transmission assembly is in reverse order of disassembly. The following points should be noted:
2. When the rear extension housing or any mainshaft components have been replaced, the shim thickness for the rear extension must be checked. Temporarily install the extension with the gasket, to allow the gasket to be compressed. Remove the extension and measure the amount that the bearing is recessed from the transmission case mating surface, and add to this the thickness from the extension bearing surface. Use the number of shims required to make the second distance equal to or 0.001 in. less than the first distance.
3. If the front cover or any of the input shaft components have been replaced, the shim thickness for the front cover must be checked. Temporarily install the cover with the gasket, to allow the gasket to be compressed. Measure the amount that the bearing protrudes from the transmission case. Measure the distance from the cover mating surface to the face of the cover bearing surface and add to this the thickness of the gasket. Use the number of shims required to make the second distance equal to or 0.001 in. less than the first distance.

TYPE 25

4 Speed Transmission–British Leyland Model

1975-80 MG Midget (Top Cover)

DISASSEMBLY

1. Remove the top cover from the transmission.
2. Twist and release the cap at the base of the gearshift lever. Remove the nyloc nut and bolt to release the shaft from the gearshift lever.
3. Lift the gearshift lever assembly from the rear extension and remove the cups along with the outer spring.
4. Remove the snap-ring from the gearshift lever, then remove the inner spring and the nylon ball.
5. Remove the reverse stop plate.
6. Remove the reverse stop bolt from the gearshift lever.
7. Remove the threaded and tapered locking pin and extract the shaft from the extension housing and selector.
8. Remove the rubber O-rings from the bores of the extension housing.
9. Remove the retaining nut and withdraw the pivot bolt from the coupling fork. Extract the shaft and fiber washers from the coupling. Remove the steel pin, releasing the coupling fork from the shaft.
10. Disassemble the selector shaft and fork assemblies.
11. Remove the threaded, tapered locking pins from the selector shafts and forks. Release the 1st/2nd selector fork, spacer washer and sleeve by pushing the 1st/2nd selector shaft out of the cover.
12. Remove the two interlock balls and plunger.
13. Release the 3rd/4th selector fork by pushing the 3rd/4th selector shaft out of the cover.
14. Release the reverse selector by pushing the reverse selector shaft out of the cover. Remove the detent plungers and springs from the cover.
15. Disassemble the clutch housing. Remove the release lever from its pivot pin and remove the lever and bearing. Remove the retaining bolts, releasing the clutch housing, and remove the springs.
16. Disassemble the rear extension. Remove the retaining nut and extract the driving flange from the mainshaft. Remove the retaining bolts and carefully withdraw the extension from the transmission. The operation may be facilitated by lightly tapping the mounting lugs with a soft-headed hammer.
17. Remove the paper washer and spacer washer from the mainshaft.
18. Remove the bolt and extract the reverse spindle and spacer.
19. If necessary, withdraw the ball bearing and oil seal from the extension.
20. Withdraw the countershaft, retaining the needle roller bearing. Using a special tool, withdraw the input shaft assembly from the transmission case. Shake out the roller bearing and remove the baulk ring.
21. Remove the circlip and snap-ring and use the special tool and adaptor to extract the ball race and oil thrower.
22. With an abutment plate installed, remove the snap-ring, circlip, and spacer washer. Withdraw the ball bearing and speedometer gear, using the special tool and adaptors used for the first ball race.
23. Remove the abutment plate, tilt the mainshaft assembly and remove it from the transmission case.
24. Disassemble the mainshaft as follows: Remove the 3rd/4th synchronizer unit, 3rd

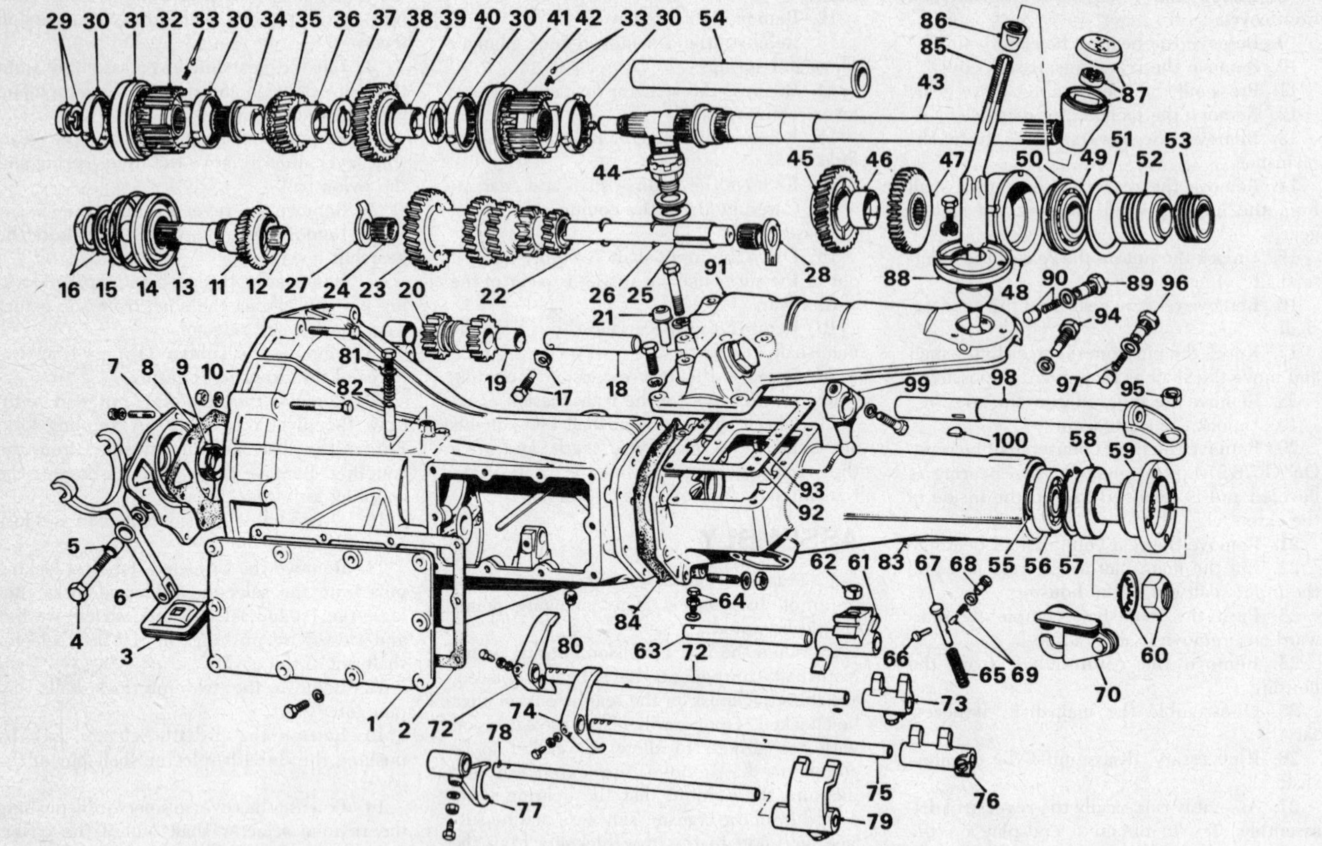

1. Side cover
2. Gasket
3. Dust cover
4. Pivot bolt for clutch withdrawal lever
5. Bush for clutch withdrawal lever
6. Clutch withdrawal lever
7. Front cover
8. Gasket
9. Oil seal
10. Gearbox case
11. First motion shaft
12. Spigot bearing
13. Bearing
14. Circlip for bearing
15. Shim
16. Nut and lock washer
17. Locking screw and lock washer
18. Reverse shaft
19. Bush for reverse wheel
20. Reverse wheel
21. Breather
22. Layshaft
23. Laygear
24. Bearing for laygear
25. Distance tube
26. Circlip for laygear
27. Front thrust washer for laygear
28. Rear thrust washer for laygear
29. Third motion shaft front nut and lock washer
30. Baulk ring
31. Third/fourth synchronizer coupling
32. Third/fourth synchronizer hub
33. Synchronizer ball and spring
34. Sleeve for third speed gear
35. Third speed gear
36. Bush for third speed gear
37. Thrust washer for third speed gear
38. Second speed gear
39. Bush for second speed gear
40. Thrust washer for second speed gear
41. First/second speed synchronizer coupling
42. First/second speed synchronizer hub
43. Third motion shaft
44. Reverse light switch
45. First speed gear
46. Bush for first speed gear
47. Reverse gear
48. Bearing housing
49. Roller bearing
50. Circlip for bearing
51. Shim
52. Distance piece
53. Speedometer drive gear
54. Distance tube
55. Shim
56. Bearing
57. Circlip for bearing
58. Oil seal
59. Drive flange
60. Nut and lock washer
61. Selector lever
62. Bush for selector lever
63. Selector lever shaft
64. Locking screw and lock washer
65. Spring for reverse plunger
66. Locating pin
67. Reverse plunger
68. Detent plug and washer
69. Detent spring and plunger
70. Interlock arm
71. First/second speed selector fork
72. First/second speed selector rod
73. First/second speed selector
74. Third/fourth speed selector fork
75. Third/fourth speed selector rod
76. Third/fourth speed selector
77. Reverse selector fork
78. Reverse selector rod
79. Reverse selector
80. Drain plug
81. Detent plug and washer
82. Detent spring and plunger
83. Rear extension
84. Gasket
85. Change speed lever
86. Seating cone
87. Change speed lever knob and retaining nut
88. Change speed lever retainer
89. Retaining cap for plunger
90. Damper plunger and spring for change speed lever
91. Remote control housing
92. Gasket
93. Dowel
94. Locating pin for change speed lever
95. Bush for change speed lever
96. Retaining cap for plunger
97. Damper plunger and spring for remote control shaft
98. Remote control shaft
99. Selector lever
100. Key for selector lever

Exploded view of MGB transmission

gear baulk ring, thrust washer, 1st gear and 1st gear baulk ring. Remove the circlip, washer, 3rd gear, bushing, thrust washer, 2nd gear, bushing, thrust washer, 2nd gear baulk ring, 1st/2nd synchronizer unit, and split collars.

25. Disassemble each synchronizer unit by pressing the hub through the sleeve. During this operation, the synchronizer unit should be placed in a container to prevent the loss of the spring-loaded balls.

26. Withdraw the countershaft assembly from the case and lift out the thrust washers. The countershaft may be further disassembled by removing the needle rollers and the retaining rings.

27. Disassemble the reverse idler gear and actuator by taking out the idler gear, removing the securing nut, and removing the actuator and pivot pin.

ASSEMBLY

1. Replace the needle rollers, smearing them with grease, and insert the retaining tube.

2. With the steel face of the front thrust washer smeared with grease, locate the washer in the transmission case. The tag should engage the recess provided.

3. Insert the end of the countershaft spindle through the case to centralize the thrust washer.

4. With the countershaft gear cluster assembly lowered into the case, install the rear thrust washer and insert the spindle.

5. Measure the end clearance of the countershaft and adjust if necessary to 0.007-0.013 in. by using thrust washers of selected thick-

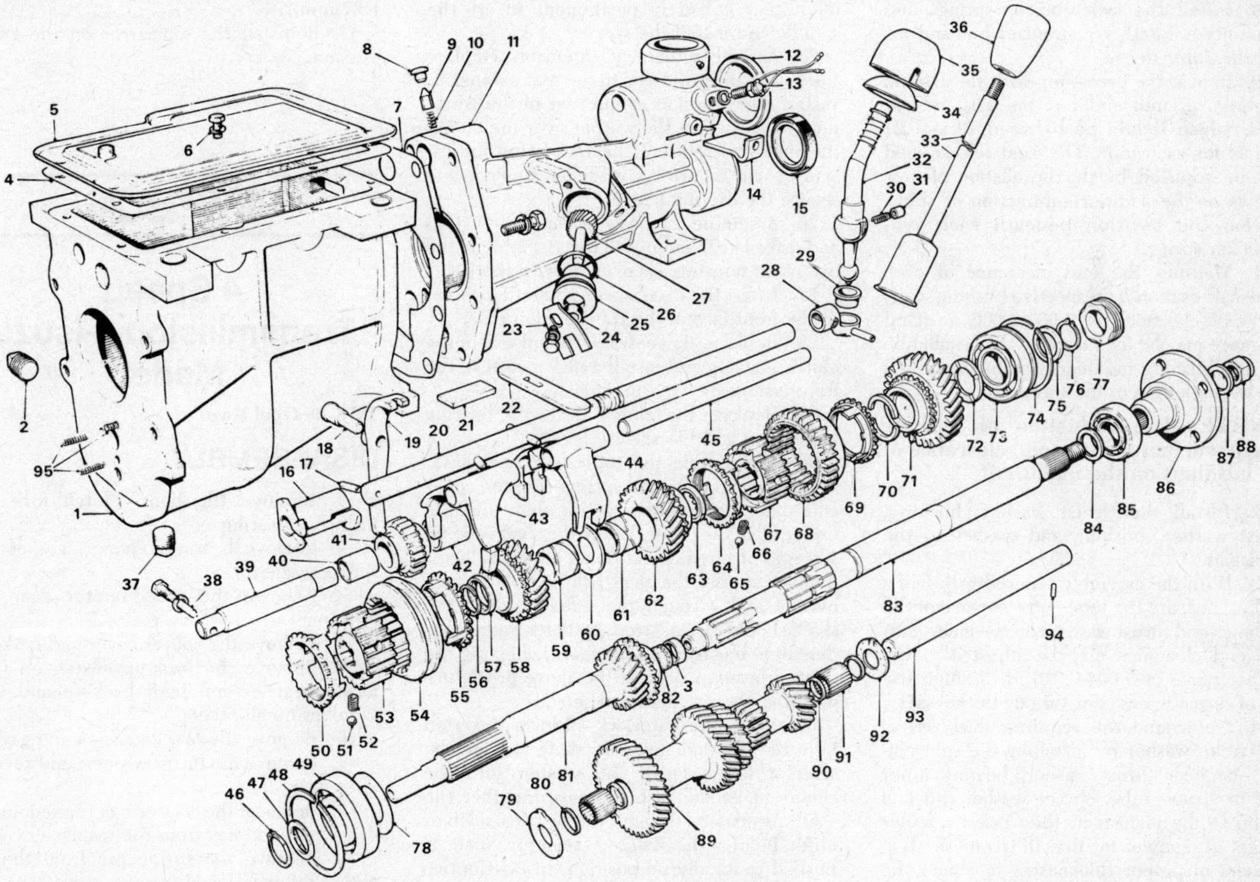

1. Gearbox case
2. Oil filter level plug
3. Spacer
4. Joint gaskets
5. Top cover
6. Top cover bolt
7. Joint gasket
8. Plug
9. Detent plunger
10. Detent spring
11. Rear extension
12. End cover
13. Reverse light switch
14. Reverse lift plate
15. Oil seal
16. Interlock spool
17. Selector shaft roll pin
18. Reverse operating lever pin
19. Reverse operating lever
20. Gear selector shaft
21. Magnet
22. Interlock spool plate
23. Retaining clip
24. Seal
25. Housing
26. "O"-ring
27. Speedometer pinion
28. Gear lever yoke
29. Seat
30. Spring
31. Anti-rattle plunger
32. Lower gear-change lever
33. Upper gear-change lever
34. Dust cover washer
35. Dust cover
36. Knob
37. Drain plug
38. Reverse idler spindle locating screw
39. Reverse idler spindle
40. Reverse idler gear bushing
41. Reverse idler gear
42. Reverse idler spacer
43. 3rd and 4th speed selector forks
44. 1st and 2nd speed selector forks
45. Selector fork shaft
46. Circlip
47. Backing washer
48. Snap-ring
49. Ball bearing
50. Synchromesh cup
51. Ball
52. Spring
53. 3rd and 4th speed synchromesh hub
54. 3rd and 4th speed operating sleeve
55. Synchromesh cup
56. Mainshaft circlip
57. 3rd speed gear thrust washer
58. 3rd speed gear
59. Gear bushing
60. Selective washer
61. Gear bushing
62. 2nd speed gear
63. Thrust washer
64. Synchromesh cup
65. Ball
66. Spring
67. 1st and 2nd speed operating sleeve
68. Mainshaft reverse gear
69. Synchromesh cup
70. Split collar
71. 1st speed gear
72. Thrust washer
73. Mainshaft center bearing
74. Snap-ring
75. Selective washer
76. Circlip
77. Speedometer wheel
78. Oil flinger
79. Front thrust washer
80. Bearing outer retaining ring
81. 1st motion shaft
82. Needle-roller bearing
83. Mainshaft
84. Washer
85. Ball bearing
86. Drive flange
87. Washer
88. Self-locking nut
89. Countershaft gear cluster
90. Bearing inner retaining ring
91. Needle rollers
92. Rear thrust washer
93. Layshaft
94. Layshaft dowel
95. Laygear pre-load springs

MG Midget 4-speed case and gear train

ness. If the thickness of a thrust washer must be reduced, do not remove metal from the bronze face.

6. Insert the needle roller retaining tube and remove the countershaft spindle. Allow the gear cluster assembly to drop to the bottom of the transmission case.

7. Assemble the reverse idle gear mechanism by screwing the pivot pin into the actuator until a thread protrudes through the boss of the lever. Install it into the transmission case and secure it with a nut and washer.

8. Position the reverse idler gear in the case.

9. Install the synchronizer springs and balls to the 3rd/4th synchronizer hub and install the outer sleeve.

10. Repeat the preceding with the 1st/2nd synchronizer unit and test the axial release loads, which should be between 19 and 21 pounds for each unit. The axial release load may be adjusted by the installation of new springs or the addition/subtraction of shims to/from the position beneath each synchronizer spring.

11. Measure the end clearance of each mainshaft gear on its respective bushing. Correct end clearance is 0.002-0.006 in. End clearance may be increased by the installation of a new bushing and decreased by the reduction of the length of the bushing.

NOTE: The reduction of bushing length will increase the end clearance of the bushings on the mainshaft.

12. Install the thrust washer, bushing, thrust washer, bushing and washer to the mainshaft.

13. With the assembly secured with half a circlip, measure the total end clearance of the bushings and thrust washers on the mainshaft. The end clearance may be adjusted to the correct range of 0.004-0.010 in. through the use of thrust washers of various thicknesses.

14. Determine the required thickness of the circlip washer by installing the split collars, 1st gear thrust washer, bearing inner race or spacer tube, spacer washer and half circlip to the mainshaft, then insert a feeler gauge as shown in the illustration. Use washers of proper thicknesses to obtain the correct clearance of 0.000-0.002 in.

15. Install the following components on the mainshaft: 1st/2nd synchronizer unit, and washer. Use a special tool to install the circlip, and install the 3rd/4th synchronizer unit, split collars, 1st gear baulk ring, and 1st gear.

16. Position the mainshaft assembly in the transmission case, install an abutment plate tool or its equivalent, and install the thrust washer.

17. With the transmission positioned vertically, and the abutment plate held in a vise, install the snap-ring to the ball bearing and position the ball bearing over the mainshaft.

18. Being sure that the mainshaft is correctly located in the abutment plate, drive the ball bearing into position, using the special tool and adapter or their equivalents.

19. Install the speedometer drive gear and remove the abutment plate from the transmission.

20. Assemble the input shaft components: Position the 4th gear baulk ring into the 3rd/4th synchronizer unit.

21. Using the special tool and adapter or their equivalents, press the ball bearing and oil thrower onto the input shaft and secure the ball bearing with the circlip.

22. Install the snap-ring onto the ball bearing and place the roller bearing in the bore of the input shaft.

23. Ensuring that the baulk ring is correctly located, drive the input shaft assembly into the transmission case.

24. Assemble the countershaft by inverting the transmission, lining up the countershaft thrust washers and gearcluster, and inserting the spindle from the rear. With the reverse idler gear correctly positioned, insert the spindle and install the spacer.

25. Assemble the rear extension. Replace the ball bearing and seal to the rear extension. Install a new gasket at the rear of the transmission and place the washer over the end of the mainshaft. Install the rear extension assembly and secure it with bolts. Replace and secure the driving flange.

26. Assemble the bearing, oil seal, O-rings and driven gear and install the assembly to the extension housing, securing it with the bolt.

27. Insert the three springs into their holes in the front face of the transmission case.

28. Replace, if necessary, the oil seal in the clutch housing and install a new gasket to the front face of the transmission.

29. Replace the clutch throwout bearing and sleeve and the release lever.

30. Reassemble the top cover as follows. Insert the plungers and springs into the cover and slide the 3rd/4th selector shaft into the front end of the cover. While the shaft is being slid into position, press down on the selector plunger so that the shaft will be able to pass over it and through the selector fork. The shaft should be inserted until its middle indentation engages the plunger, achieving the neutral position. Repeat the above procedure with the reverse shaft and selector.

31. With the interlock plunger inserted into the 1st/2nd selector shaft, install the selector fork, sleeve and washer into the comer in similar fashion, ensuring that the shaft also passes through the 3rd/4th selector fork. Before the 1st/2nd selector shaft is pushed to its neutral position, insert the two interlock balls into the transverse bore which connects the shaft bores at the rear of the casting and then push the shaft further into the cover until the selector plunger engages the middle identation and the balls and plunger are retained by the shafts.

32. Use new tapered locking pins to secure the selector and forks to the shafts.

33. Use sealing compound around the edges of the plugs before driving them into the ends of the selector shaft bores.

34. Use a new pin to secure the fork to the shaft. If necessary, replace the "Metalistik" bushing in the shaft. Using new fiber washers, secure the shaft to the fork with the bolt and nut.

35. Install new O-rings to the case and install the shaft through the bores of the case and through the selector.

36. Use a new tapered locking pin when securing the selector to the shaft.

37. Install the reverse stop bolt, locknut, nylon ball, spring and snap-ring to the gearshift lever.

38. Install the reverse stop plate to the cover and secure with the retaining screws. With the gearshift lever assembly positioned in the cover, install two new bushings to the lever, install the spacer tube, and secure the lever to the shaft with the retaining bolt and nut.

39. Install the spring, cups, and cap over the gearshift lever.

40. Adjust the reverse stop plate and bolt with the gearshift lever in the neutral position of the 1st/2nd gate. The clearance between the reverse stop plate and bolt should be, as shown in the diagram, 0.010-0.050 in. (0.26-1.27 mm).

41. Reinstall the top cover on the transmission.

TYPE 26

4 Speed Transmission—Isuzu Model

1976-80 Opel Isuzu

DISASSEMBLY

1. Remove the boot, clutch fork and throwout bearing.

2. Remove bearing retainer, gasket and spring washer.

3. Remove the speedometer gear and bushing.

4. Remove the shifter cover and gasket.

5. Remove the back-up switch on California vehicles and both back-up and CRS switches on all others.

6. Remove the rear extension and gasket.

7. Remove the thrust washers and reverse idler gear.

8. Remove the snap-rings, speedometer drive gear and key from the mainshaft.

9. Remove the spring pin from the reverse shifter fork and reverse gear.

10. Remove the snap-ring from the outer circumference of the clutch gear shaft ball bearing.

11. Remove the center support assembly from the transmission case.

12. Drive out the spring pins from the third and fourth and first and second shift forks.

NOTE: When removing the spring pin, hold a round bar against the end of the shifter rods to prevent damage.

13. Remove the detent spring plate from the center support, then remove the detent springs and balls.

14. Remove the first and second and the third and fourth shifter rods from the center support, then remove the shifter forks.

15. Remove the reverse shifter rod forward as it is fitted with a stopper pin.

NOTE: Be careful not to loose the detent interlock plugs located between the shifter rods in the center support.

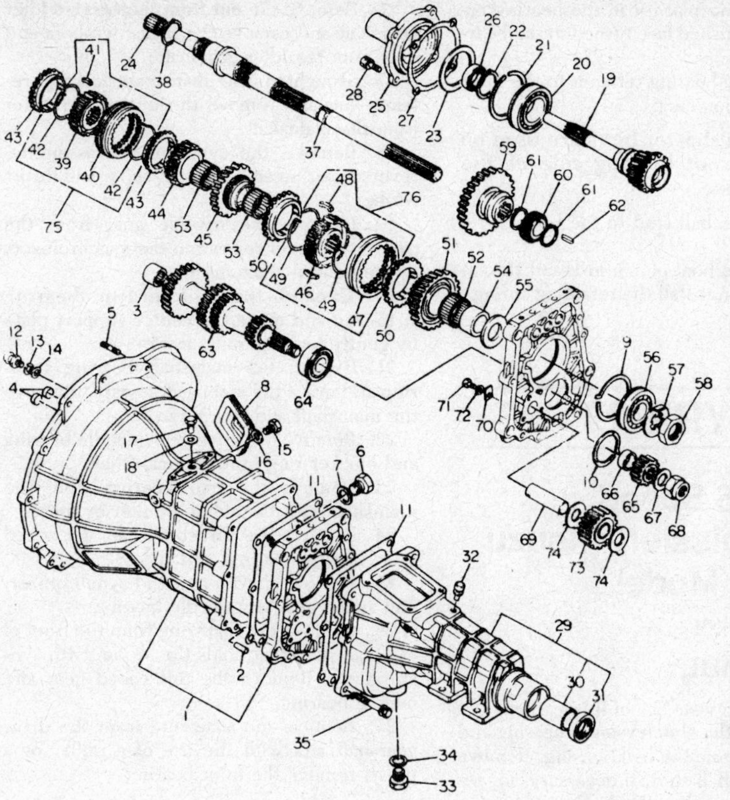

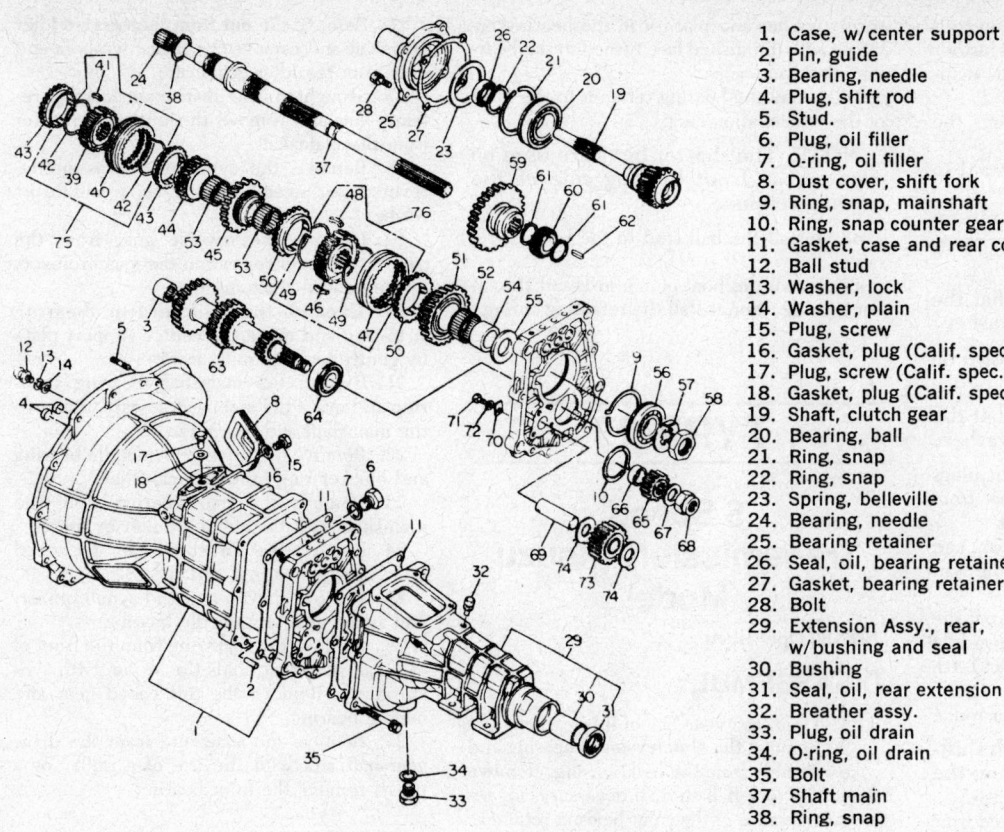

1. Case, w/center support
2. Pin, guide
3. Bearing, needle
4. Plug, shift rod
5. Stud.
6. Plug, oil filler
7. O-ring, oil filler
8. Dust cover, shift fork
9. Ring, snap, mainshaft
10. Ring, snap counter gear
11. Gasket, case and rear cover
12. Ball stud
13. Washer, lock
14. Washer, plain
15. Plug, screw
16. Gasket, plug (Calif. spec.)
17. Plug, screw (Calif. spec.)
18. Gasket, plug (Calif. spec.)
19. Shaft, clutch gear
20. Bearing, ball
21. Ring, snap
22. Ring, snap
23. Spring, belleville
24. Bearing, needle
25. Bearing retainer
26. Seal, oil, bearing retainer
27. Gasket, bearing retainer
28. Bolt
29. Extension Assy., rear, w/bushing and seal
30. Bushing
31. Seal, oil, rear extension
32. Breather assy.
33. Plug, oil drain
34. O-ring, oil drain
35. Bolt
37. Shaft main
38. Ring, snap
39. Hub, synchronizer, 3rd-4th
40. Sleeve, synchronizer
41. Key, synchronizer
42. Spring, synchronizer
43. Ring, blocker
44. Gear assy., 3rd
45. Gear assy., 2nd
46. Hub, synchronizer, 1st-2nd
47. Sleeve, synchronizer
48. Key, synchronizer
49. Spring, synchronizer
50. Ring blocker
51. Gear assy., 1st
52. Bearing, needle, 1st
53. Bearing, needle, 2nd
54. Collar, needle bearing
55. Washer, thrust, 1st
56. Bearing, mainshaft
57. Washer, lock, mainshaft
58. Nut, mainshaft
59. Gear, reverse
60. Gear, speed drive
61. Ring, snap, drive gear
62. Key
63. Gear, counter
64. Bearing, angular ball
65. Gear, counter reverse
66. Spacer
67. Washer, plain
68. Nut, self lock
69. Shaft, reverse idle
70. Plate, lock
71. Bolt, lock
72, Washer, spring
73. Gear, reverse idle
74. Washer, thrust
75. Synchronizer assy., 3rd-4th
76. Synchronizer assy., 1st-2nd

Isuzu 4-speed manual transmission

16. Move both synchronizers rearward to prevent turning of the mainshaft.

NOTE: It may be necessary to tap the synchronizers with the hammer handle to get them engaged.

17. Remove the locknut and washer from the mainshaft.
18. Remove the nut, washer, countershaft reverse gear and collar from the rear of the countergear.
19. Remove the center support countergear bearing snap-ring.
20. Remove the center support.
21. Separate the clutch gear, needle bearings and blocker ring from the mainshaft assembly.
22. Press the rear bearing from the mainshaft.
23. Remove the thrust washer, 1st speed gear, needle roller bearing, a collar and blocker ring.
24. Remove the 1st and 2nd gear synchronizer assembly.
25. Remove the 2nd gear, blocker ring and needle roller bearing from the mainshaft.
26. Remove the snap-ring, 3rd and 4th synchronizer assembly and blocker ring from the mainshaft.
27. Remove the 3rd gear and needle bearings.
28. Remove the snap-ring and press off the clutch bearing and countergear bearing from the shaft.

ASSEMBLY

1. Stand the front of the mainshaft upward and install the 3rd speed gear and needle roller bearing with the tapered side of the gear facing the front of the mainshaft.
2. Install a blocker ring with the clutching teeth upward over the synchronizing surface of the 3rd speed gear.
3. If it is necessary to reassemble the synchronizer assembly turn the face of the synchronizer hub with the heavy boss to the face of the sleeve with the light chamfering on the outer rim.
4. Fit the keys into the key groove and position the synchronizer springs into the hole in the side face of the hub.
5. Install the 3rd and 4th synchronizer assembly on the mainshaft with the face of the sleeve with the light chamfer rearward.
6. Turn the rear of the mainshaft upward and install the 2nd speed gear and needle roller bearing on the mainshaft with the tapered surface of the gear facing the rear of the mainshaft.
7. Install a blocker ring with the clutching teeth downward over the synchronizing surface of the 2nd speed gear.
8. Install the 1st and 2nd synchronizer assembly with the chamfer on the sleeve facing the front of the mainshaft.
9. Install a blocker ring with the clutching teeth rearward.
10. Install the colllr, needle roller bearing and 1st speed gear on the mainshaft.

NOTE: The tapered side of the gear should be facing the front of the mainshaft.

11. Install the 1st speed gear thrust washer on the mainshaft with the grooved side facing 1st gear.
12. Press the rear bearing on the mainshaft with the snap-ring groove facing the front of the mainshaft.
13. If removed, press the ball bearing on the clutch gearshaft with the snap-ring groove on the bearing facing the front of the transmission. Install the snap-ring on the clutch gear shaft.
14. Assemble the needle roller bearing, blocker ring and clutch gear to the front of the mainshaft.
15. If removed, press on the countergear ball bearing with the snap-ring groove facing the rear of the transmission.
16. If removed, install the snap-rings in the inner circumference of the mainshaft and countergear holes of the center support.
17. If removed, insert the idler gear shaft with the lock plate groove side into the center support from the rear, then install the lock plate.
18. Mesh the countergear with the mainshaft assembly and install a holding tool on the mainshaft and countergear.
19. Install the center support.
20. Press the center support onto the shaft until the countergear bearing is brought into contact with its snap-ring.

21. Expand the countergear bearing snap-ring and press the center support further until the mainshaft and countergear snap-rings are fitted into their grooves.

22. Remove the holding tool from the mainshaft and countergear.

23. Move both synchronizers rearward to prevent turning of the mainshaft.

24. Install the collar, countershaft reverse gear, washer and nut on the rear of the countergear.

NOTE: Install the locknut so that the chamfered side if facing the lockwasher.

25. Install the locknut and lock washer on the mainshaft.

NOTE: Install the locknut so that the chamfered side is facing the lockwasher.

26. Apply grease to the two detent plugs and insert them into their detent holes from the middle hole of the center support.

27. Install the 1st and 2nd shifter forks and the 3rd and 4th into their grooves in the synchronizer assembly.

28. Install 3rd and 4th shifter rod from the rear of the center support through the middle hole and into the 1st and 2nd, 3rd and 4th shifter forks. Align the spring pin hole in the shifter fork with the hole in the shifter rod.

NOTE: Identify the 3rd and 4th shifter rod by the two detent grooves on the side of the rod.

29. Install the 1st and 2nd shifter rod from the rear of the center support through the 1st and 2nd shifter fork and align the hole in the rod to the hole in the shifter fork.

30. If removed, install the stopper pin in the reverse shifter rod and the front of the center support.

31. Install the two spring pins in the 1st/2nd and 3rd/4th shifter forks.

32. Install the detent balls, spring, gasket and retainer on the center support.

33. Install the center support assembly and gasket.

34. Assemble the reverse shifter fork to the reverse gear and install these parts into position from the rear side of the mainshift, then connect them to the reverse shifter rod.

35. Install the spring pin in the reverse shifter fork.

36. Install the thrust washer and reverse idler gear on the idler shaft.

NOTE: The reverse idler gear should be installed with undercut teeth forward.

37. Install the speedometer drive gear snap-ring and key on the mainshaft.

38. Install a new oil seal in the rear extension.

39. Apply grease to the outer thrust washer of the reverse idler shaft and insert it in the rear extensions.

40. Install the rear extension and gasket.

41. Install the back-up lamp switch and CRS switch.

42. Install the shifter cover and gasket.

43. Install the oil O-ring to the speedometer drive gear and install the gear.

44. Install the front bearing retainer seal.

45. Install a snap-ring in the outer circumference of the clutch gear bearing.

46. Apply grease to the bearing retainer spring washer and place it in the bearing retainer with the dished face turned to the bearing outer race.

47. Install the bearing retainer to the front of the transmission case.

NOTE: The shorter bolts are used on countergear front bearing side of the bearing retainer.

48. Install the ball stud to the bearing retainer.

49. Install the boot clutch fork and throwout bearing, then install the retaining spring.

TYPE 27

5 Speed Transmission—Isuzu Model

1977-80 Opel Isuzu

DISASSEMBLY

1. Drain the gear box of lubrication.

2. Remove the clutch release bearing and yoke assembly from the bell housing. Remove the clutch fork ball stud, if necessary, for removal clearance of the front bearing retainer.

3. Remove the front bearing retainer and Belleville spring.

4. Remove the speedometer driven gear and shift lever quadrant from the extension housing.

NOTE: Remove the Coasting Richer System switch from the quadrant on California models.

5. Remove the back-up lamp switch and the extension housing from the gear box.

6. Remove the snap-rings, speedometer drive gear, key, spacer and bearing from the mainshaft.

7. Remove the snap-ring, thrust washer and lock ball from the fifth gear on the mainshaft.

8. Remove the large snap-ring from the front bearing.

9. Remove the center support plate from the transmission case, with the mainshaft, countergear and drive gear as an assembly.

10. Support the ends of the 1st and 2nd, 3rd and 4th and 5th and reverse shift forks and drive the retaining pins from the forks.

11. Remove the detent spring plate from the center support plate and remove the three springs and balls.

12. Remove the shifter shafts from the center support plate and remove the shift forks and interlock pins.

13. To prevent the turning of the mainshaft and countergear while removing the locking nuts from the gear assembly, engage the synchronizers in 1st and 3rd gears.

14. Remove the nut and washer retaining the countergear and by using a puller, remove the ball bearing and the fifth gear from the rear of the countershaft.

15. Remove the fifth gear, blocker ring and needle bearing from the mainshaft.

16. Remove the nut from the reverse idler gearshaft and remove the thrust washers and gear from the idler gearshaft.

17. Straighten the mainshaft locking retainer tab and remove the nut and retainer from the mainshaft.

18. Remove the synchronizer assembly, reverse gear, needle bearing, collar and thrust washer.

19. Remove the reverse gear from the countergear and reposition the synchronizers to the neutral position.

20. Expand the countergear bearing snap-ring and move the center support plate by gently tapping on its front.

21. Expand the mainshaft bearing snap-ring and move the mainshaft inward. Remove the mainshaft and countergear.

22. Remove the drive gear, needle bearing and blocker ring from the mainshaft.

23. Remove the rear bearing from the mainshaft with the aid of a puller or press.

24. Remove the thrust washer, 1st speed gear, needle bearings and spacer.

25. Remove the 1st and 2nd synchronizer, 2nd speed gear and needle bearing.

26. Remove the snap-ring from the front of the mainshaft that holds the 3rd and 4th synchronizer. Remove the 3rd speed gear and needle bearing.

27. Remove the snap-ring from the drive gearshaft and with the use of a puller or a press, remove the front bearing.

ASSEMBLY

1. Place the coned side of the 3rd speed gear towards the front of the transmission and install it and the needle bearing on the front of the mainshaft.

2. Install the 3rd and 4th synchronizer on the mainshaft with the chamfered end towards the front of the transmission. Retain with a snap-ring.

3. Install the 2nd speed gear and needle bearing on the rear of the mainshaft with the coned end of the gear towards the rear of the transmission.

4. Install the 1st and 2nd synchronizer on the mainshaft with the large chamfered end towards the rear on the transmission.

5. Install the spacer, needle bearings and 1st speed gear on the mainshaft, with the coned end of the gear towards the front of the transmission.

6. Install the first gear thrust washer with the slots towards the gear.

7. Press the rear bearing onto the mainshaft with the snap-ring groove towards the front of the transmission.

8. Install the center support plate snap-rings and reverse idler shaft. Torque bolts to 14 ft-lbs.

9. Install the drive gear on the front of the mainshaft and engage with the countergear to install the center support plate.

10. Install countergear and mainshaft bearings into the center support plate and while expanding the snap-rings, move the bearings into place on the support plate and engage the snap-rings in the bearing grooves.

11. Engage the gears in 1st and 3rd to prevent turning and install the reverse gear on the countergear.

12. Install the thrust washer on the main-

1. Drive gear
2. Release bearing
3. Drive gear bearing retainer
4. Shift fork
5. Drive gear bearing
6. Shifter shaft
7. 3rd & 4th shift fork
8. 1st & 2nd shift fork
9. Mainshaft bearing
10. Center support
11. Shift lever quadrant
12. Shift lever
13. 5th & reverse shift fork
14. Mainshaft rear bearing
15. Extension housing
16. Rear seal
17. Speedometer drive gear
18. 5th gear assy
19. Counter gear rear bearing
20. 5th counter gear
21. Needle bearing
22. Reverse counter gear
23. Reverse idler shaft
24. Reverse idler gear
25. Counter gear bearing
26. Needle bearing
27. Counter gear
28. Mainshaft
29. Counter gear front bearing
30. Needle gearing

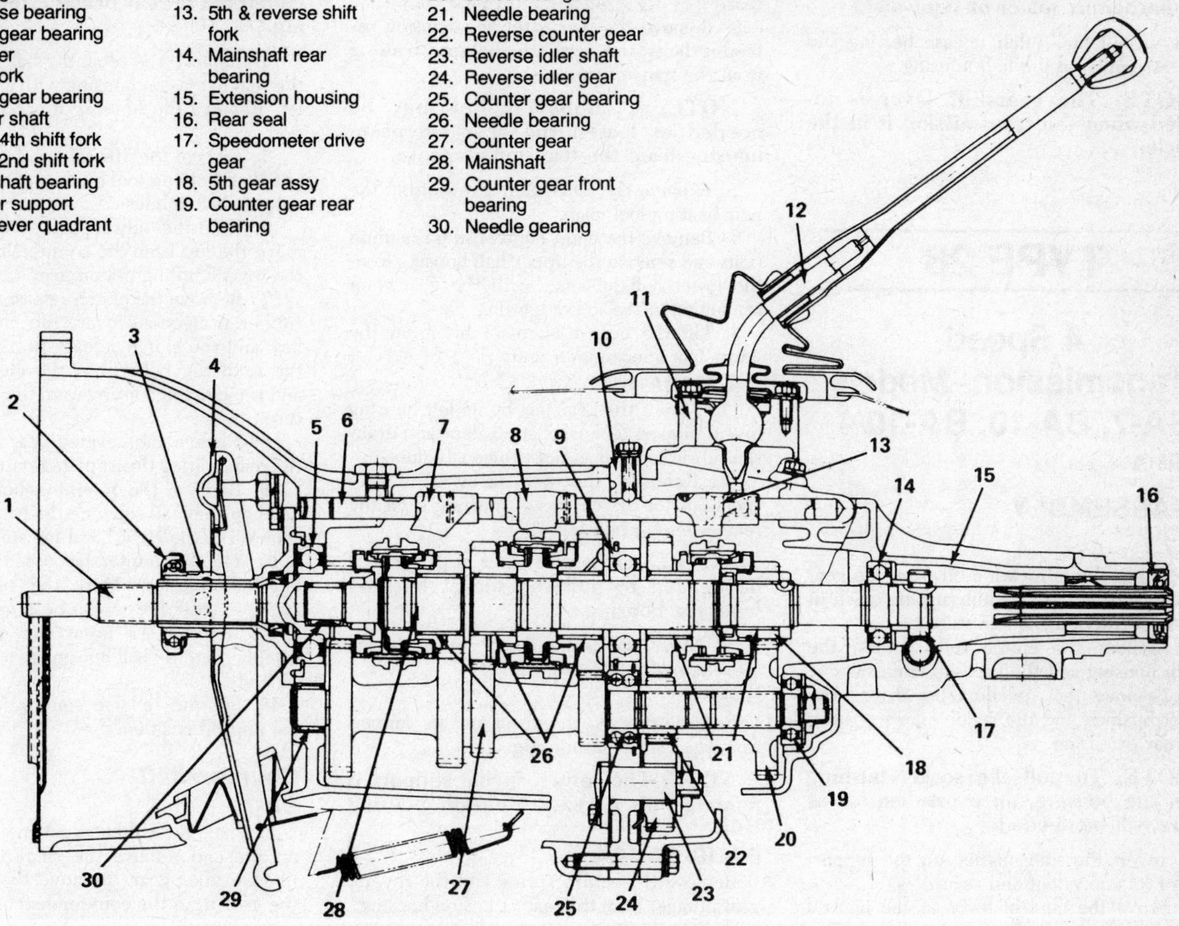

Cross section of Opel Isuzu 5-speed transmission

shaft with the oil grooves turned towards the reverse gear. Install the collar, needle bearings and reverse gear on the mainshaft.

13. Install the synchronizer assembly so that the face of the clutch hub boss is turned to the reverse gear side.

14. Install the locking retainer and nut on the front of the mainshaft. Torque the nut to 94 ft/lbs. Bend the retainer tab to lock the nut in place.

15. Install the thrust washers and reverse idler gear on the reverse idler shaft and tighten the nut to 80 ft/lbs.

NOTE: Install new self-locking nut on countergear.

16. Install the blocker ring, needle bearing and 5th gear on the mainshaft.

17. Install the countergear 5th gear, ball bearing, washer and selflocking nut on the rear of the countergear. Torque the nut to 80 ft/lbs.

NOTE: Install new self-locking nut on countergear.

18. Reposition the synchronizers to the neutral position.

19. Lubricate the interlock pins and install in the center support plate.

20. Place the shift forks on the synchronizer sleeves and install the 3rd and 4th shifter shaft through the center support plate and into the shift fork for 3rd and 4th gear.

21. Install the 1st and 2nd shifter shaft through the center support plate and through the 1st and 2nd shift fork.

22. Install the reverse and 5th shifter shaft through the center support plate and into the reverse and 5th shifter fork.

23. Install the three detent balls and springs in the center support plate and retain with the detent plate and gasket. Torque the bolts to 14 ft/lbs.

24. Install the retaining pins in the shifter forks to the shifter shafts while supporting the ends of the shaft with a bar or block of wood.

25. Install the countergear needle bearing in the front of the transmission case.

26. Install a new gasket on the transmission case and install the center support plate assembly into the transmission case.

27. Install the large snap-ring on the front bearing of the mainshaft.

28. Install the lock ball and thrust washer on the mainshaft and retain with a snap-ring.

29. Measure the clearance between the 5th gear and the thrust washer on the mainshaft. The clearance should be 0.010 to 0.016 in.

30. If the clearance is out of specifications, replace the thrust washer with one of the following:

Part Number	Thickness (inches)	(Millimeters)
94025579	0.3014	7.656
94025580	0.3073	7.805
94025581	0.3132	7.955
94025582	0.3191	8.105

31. Install the speedometer drive gear front snap-ring, ball bearing and key onto the mainshaft.

32. Align the groove in the speedometer drive gear with the key on the mainshaft and install the gear. Retain with a snap-ring.

33. Install the rear extension housing with a new gasket on to the center support plate. Torque the bolts to 27 ft/lbs.

34. Install the shift lever quadrant with gasket on the extension housing. Torque the bolts to 14 ft/lbs.

35. Install the speedometer driven gear and torque the retaining bolt to 14 ft/lbs.

36. California Models only: Install the CRS switch on the extension housing.

37. Install the Belleview washer with the dished side towards the drive gear bearing and install the bearing retainer and gasket. Torque the bolts to 14 ft/lbs.

NOTE: Seal the lower left bolt with a non-hardening sealer or equivalent.

38. Install the clutch release bearing and yoke assembly on the bell housing.

NOTE: The gearshift lever is installed when the transmission is in the vehicle.

TYPE 28

4 Speed Transmission–Models BA-7, BA-10, BA-10/4

1975-81 Peugeot

DISASSEMBLY

BA-7

1. Drain the lubricating oil from the gear box and mount the assembly upside down in the support tool or its equivalent.
2. Remove the clutch release fork, the clutch housing and the back-up lamp switch.
3. Remove the speedometer drive gear socket bushing and the retaining screw from the rear extension.

NOTE: To pull the socket bushing from the housing, an expanding set of pliers will be needed.

4. Invert the transmission on the support tool or its equivalent and secure.
5. Move the control lever to the neutral position and pull the selector lever fully to the rear.
6. Remove the rear extension housing retaining bolts and separate the rear housing from the transmission case.

NOTE: A rubber mallet may be needed to loosen the rear extension housing from the transmission case.

7. Remove the four Allen screws from the rear bearing lock plate.
8. Remove the eight half housing retaining bolts and remove the upper half housing from the lower half housing, with the gear train remaining in the lower housing.
9. Lift the gear train assembly from the lower half housing as a unit.

BA-10, BA-10/4

1. Mount the gear box by its left housing in the support tool or its equivalent and drain the lubricating oil, if not previously done.
2. Remove the set screw and the speedometer driven socket bushing from the rear extension housing.

NOTE: An expanding set of pliers will be needed to pull the socket bushing from the housing.

3. Move the selector and control levers into the neutral position.

BA-7

Remove the return spring and its support from the extension housing.

NOTE: The return spring support is mounted on a rear extension housing bolt.

BA-10, BA-10/4

Remove the return spring and the reverse gear plunger from the rear extension housing.

NOTE: The return spring support is bolted to the rear of the extension housing.

4. Remove the retaining bolts and loosen the rear extension housing with a rubber mallet. Remove the housing from the transmission.
5. Engage the 4th gear and place an output shaft holding tool or its equivalent on the output shaft splines.
6. Hold the output shaft securely and remove the nut from the countershaft. Remove the reverse idling pinion gear.
7. Remove the clutch release bearing fork rubber protection cover, the clutch release fork and the clutch release bearing. Remove the retaining bolts from the clutch housing and remove the housing from the transmission case.
8. Engage the reverse gear and remove the rear bearing thrust plate retaining screws.
9. Remove the retaining bolts from the half housings and separate the two halfs by the removal of the right hand housing.
10. Lift the countershaft assembly from the left half housing. Mark the bearing outer races, in case they are to be reused.
11. Remove the input and mainshaft assembly from the half housing as a unit. Do not separate.
12. Set the reverse semi-synchronizer to the neutral position.

Countershaft

BA-7

1. Place the countershaft in a holding tool or vise and remove the snap-ring from the reverse idler gear. Remove the washer and the gear from the countershaft.

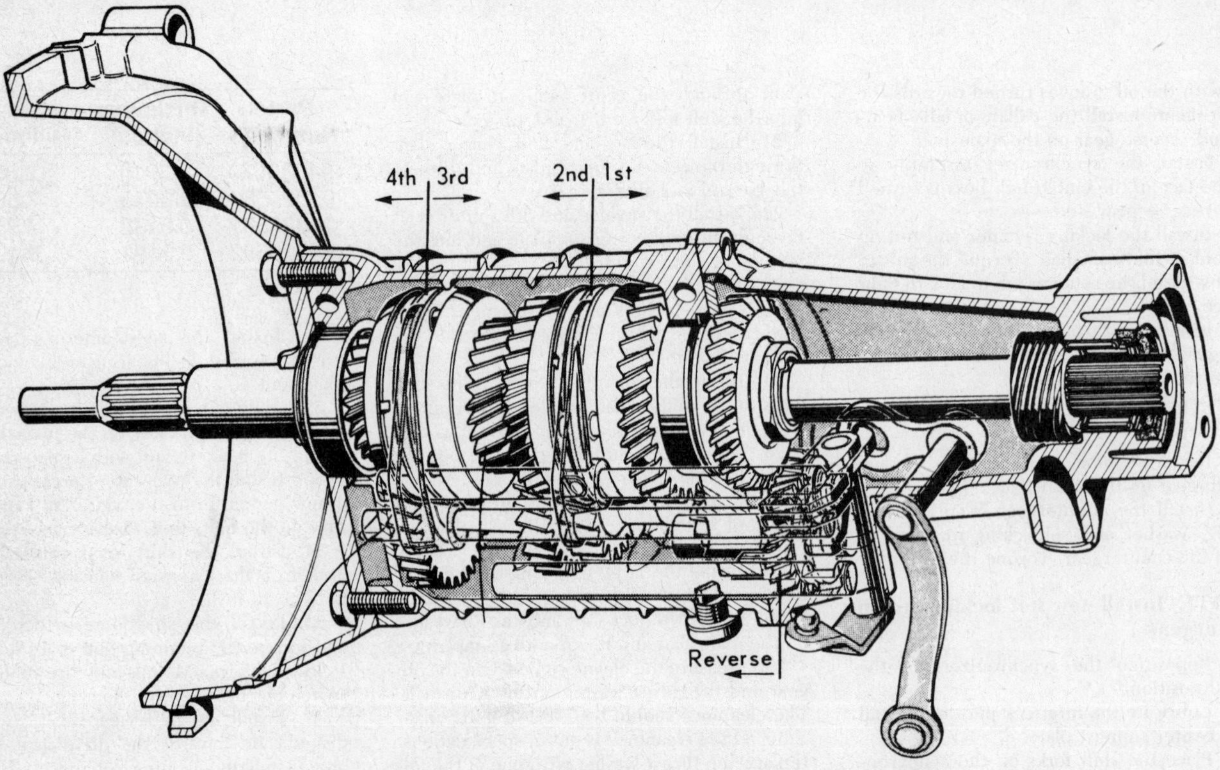

Gear train position and shift direction of synchronizers—Model BA-7

Gear train position in half housing and shift direction of synchronizers—Model BA-10

2. Remove the outer race from the bearing and with the use of a press, remove the front and rear bearings.

NOTE: Do not lose the adjusting shim located behind the front bearing.

BA-10, BA-10/4

1. Place the countershaft in a press and remove the front bearing and adjusting shim.
2. Invert the countershaft and press the rear bearing from the shaft.

Separation of Input and Mainshaft—All Models

1. Place the 3rd/4th synchronizer assembly in the 3rd speed position and pull the input

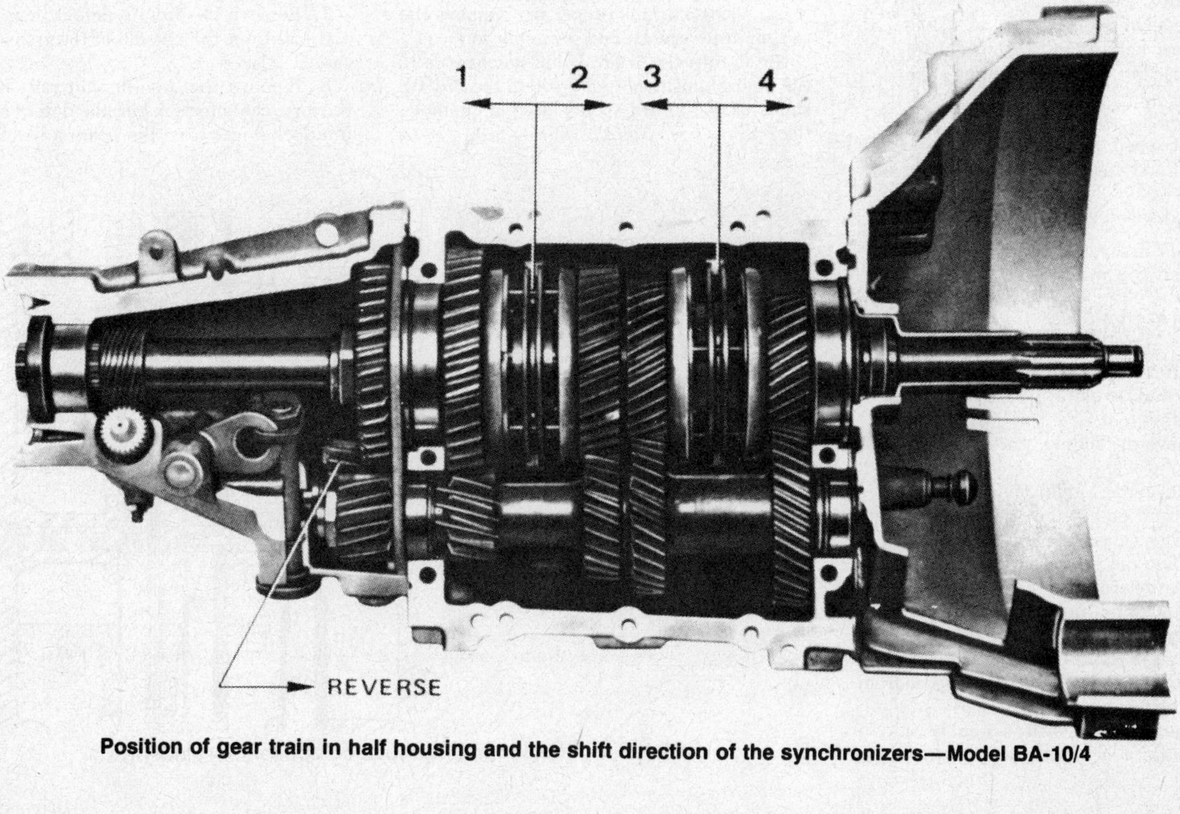

Position of gear train in half housing and the shift direction of the synchronizers—Model BA-10/4

shaft from the mainshaft. Do not lose the needle bearing from the input shaft bore.

Mainshaft

BA-7

1. Remove the grease from the 3rd/4th synchronizer assembly. Place the mainshaft assembly in a holding tool or vise.
2. Mark the position of the 3rd/4th sliding gear on the 3rd/4th hub, using a sharp brass rod or its equivalent. Remove the sliding gear.
3. Remove the snap-ring and spring washer retaining the 3rd/4th speed hub to the mainshaft.
4. While holding the reverse pinion with a holding tool or equivalent, and the mainshaft still in the vise or holding tool, fully unscrew the reverse pinion retaining nut from the mainshaft threads.

NOTE: The nut is retained on the shaft by the speedometer gear.

5 .Remove the 3rd/4th synchronizer hub and 3rd speed gear from the mainshaft. A puller or a press may have to be used.
6. Place the mainshaft assembly into a press and press the mainshaft downward to free the rear bearing from its seat on the mainshaft.

CAUTION

Be sure the retaining nut is free of its threads on the mainshaft, before the press pressure is applied.

7. Continue the downward pressure on the mainshaft and remove the speedometer drive gear from the mainshaft.
8. Remove the assembly from the press and remove the parts from the mainshaft in the following order:
   a. Speedometer drive gear
   b. Nut
   c. Reverse pinion gear
   d. Rear bearing and retainer plate
   e. Rear bearing and adjusting shims
   f. 1st speed gear spacer bushing
   g. Needle bearing cage
   h. 1st speed gear
   i. 1st/2nd speed gear synchronizer and hub.
   j. 2nd speed gear.

NOTE: Observe the direction of gear position on the mainshaft.

BA-10, BA-10/4

1. Degrease the 3rd/4th synchronizer assembly and mark the positioning of the sliding gear to the hub assembly with a sharp piece of brass welding rod.
2. Remove the sliding gear from the mainshaft.
3. Remove the circlip and spring washer from the front end of the mainshaft, holding the 3rd/4th synchronizer hub in place.
4. Holding the mainshaft in a vise or other holding fixture, remove the reverse gear nut from its threads on the mainshaft, while holding the reverse gear stationary.
5. Using a press or a puller, remove the 3rd gear synchronizer hub and the 3rd gear from the mainshaft.
6. Place the mainshaft assembly into a press with the rear of the mainshaft pointing upward. Using press pressure, force the mainshaft downward to unseat the rear bearing from its seat on the mainshaft.

CAUTION

Be sure the nut is free of its threads on the mainshaft, before the press pressure is applied.

7. Continue the downward pressure of the press on the mainshaft and remove the speedometer drive gear from the mainshaft.
8. Remove the assembly from the press and remove the parts from the mainshaft in the following order:
   a. Speedometer drive gear
   b. Retaining nut
   c. Reverse gear driven pinion
   d. Rear bearing thrust plate
   e. Rear bearing and adjusting shims
   f. 1st gear spacer collar
   g. Needle bearing
   h. 1st gear driven pinion
   i. 1st/2nd synchronizer assembly with hub.
   j. 2nd gear driven pinion
   k. Needle bearing

NOTE: Observe the direction of gear position on the mainshaft.

Input Shaft

ALL MODELS

1. Remove the large and small circlips from the bearing and the shaft. Remove the spring washer from under the small circlip.
2. Using a press, force the input shaft from the bearing. Do not lose the oil defector or the adjusting shims.

Shifting Rails and Forks

BA-7

1. Place the 1st/2nd shifting mechanism in the 2nd speed position.
2. Using a drift of proper size, remove the roll pin from the 1st/2nd gear shift fork.
3. Return the 1st/2nd shift mechanism to the neutral position, and position the 3rd/4th shift rail to the 4th speed location. Remove the roll pin from 3rd/4th shifting fork.
4. Return the 3rd/4th shift rail to the neutral position.
5. Remove the detent ball locking plug from the outside of the transmission case. An Allen key type tool is used.
6. Remove the 1st/2nd gear shift rail and the 3rd/4th gear shift rail from the transmission case.
7. Invert the transmission case and remove the reverse shifting detent ball locking plug with the Allen key tool.
8. Remove the shift rail and fork with the countershaft pinion from the transmission case.
9. Locate and remove from the case, the three locking springs, four balls and the one locking finger.

NOTE: If the balls are stuck in the passages, use a long rod to free them.

10. Remove the locking needle from the 3rd/4th speed shifting rail.
11. Using a drift, remove the roll pin from the reverse pinion shaft and move the shaft towards the inside of the case and remove.

BA-10

1. Place the 1st/2nd shift fork in the neutral position and remove the roll pin with a proper sized drift.
2. Move the 3rd/4th shift rail into the 4th speed position and remove the roll pin from the fork.
3. Remove the 1st/2nd locking spring plug and remove the spring and ball from the outside of the transmission case.
4. Remove the shift rail and the shift fork.
5. Remove the reverse detent spring plug, the spring and the ball. If not done previously, remove the back-up light switch.
6. Remove the reverse shift fork and idler gear assembly. Remove the indent and spring (Operating spigot).
7. Remove the 3rd/4th detent plug, spring and ball from the outside of the transmission case.
8. Remove the 3rd/4th shift rail. Remove the fork, the interlock pin, the detent ball and interlock finger from the bearing block.

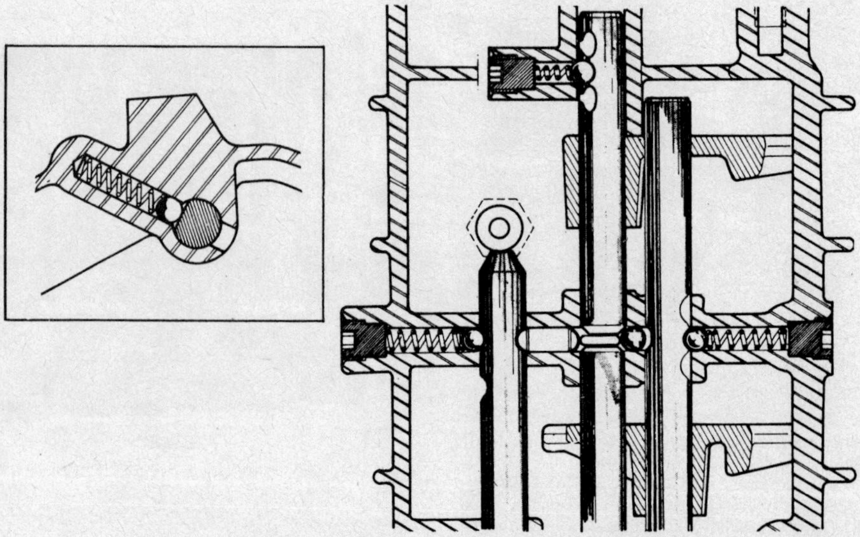

Diagram of detent and interlock components—Model BA-7

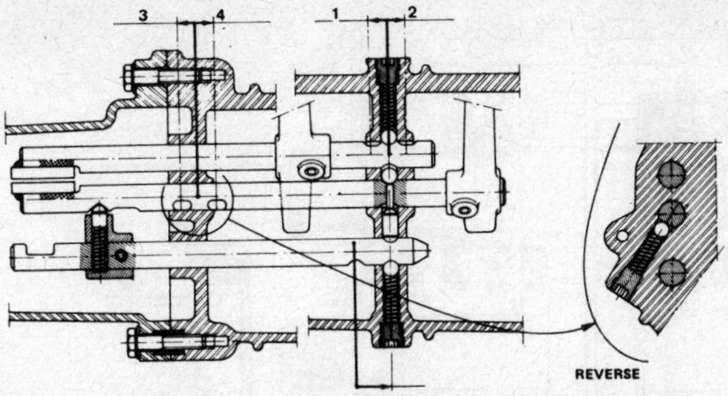

Diagram of detent and interlock components—Model BA-10

9. Using a drift, remove the roll pin from the reverse shaft and push the shaft towards the outside of the housing.

BA-10/4

1. Remove the 3rd/4th detent spring from the hole in the bearing seat at the rear of the transmission half housing.
2. Place the selector rail into 4th gear and remove the roll pins from the 1st/2nd and 3rd/4th rails and forks.
3. If not done previously, remove the back-up light switch from the case.
4. Remove the 1st/2nd detent ball plug and spring from the outside of the case.
5. Remove the 1st/2nd shift rail and the 1st/2nd shift fork.
6. Remove the 3rd/4th shift rail and fork. Remove the detent balls and recover the interlock pins.
7. Remove the roll pin from the reverse gearshaft.
8. Remove the remaining detent plugs and springs from the outside of the case.
9. Remove the reverse gear assembly, consisting of the gear, shaft, fork and shifting rail and the semi-synchronizer bushing.
10. Obtain the detent balls and the interlock pins from the passages in the transmission case.

Neutral Ball Detent-Rear Extension Housing

ALL MODELS

1. Check the operation of the neutral position ball detent by pushing and pulling the selector lever in and out of the housing.
2. If the detent is found to be defective, remove the detent plug and check the condition of the spring and ball. Replace the necessary parts.

ASSEMBLY

General

1. When reassembling the gearboxes, replace the following parts as standard procedure.
   a. Shaft circlips
   b. Spring washers
   c. Roll pins
   d. Mainshaft nut
   e. Output shaft oil seal
   f. Input shaft oil seal
   g. Speedometer driven socket bushing
   h. Thrust washers
2. Oil the various gears, shafts and components before installation.
3. When joining the housings, apply a thin coat of jointing compound to seal the units.
4. Inspect the clutch housing to be sure the front and rear surfaces are parallel to each other. If a difference of more than 0.004 inch (0.10 mm) exists, the housing should be replaced.
5. Replace the thrust guide in the clutch housing by removing the oil seal, the circlip and pressing the guide from the housing.
6. Replace the thrust guide by applying a grease to the tube and pressing it into place in the housing. Install the circlip and the oil seal.

NOTE: To avoid damage to the seal, do not install it into the clutch housing until the adjustment operations are made during the assembly of the unit.

7. Remove the rear oil seal in the extension housing by prying it from the housing bore. Remove the needle bearing with the aid of a press.
8. Install the needle bearing with the aid of a press and install the seal in its bore.

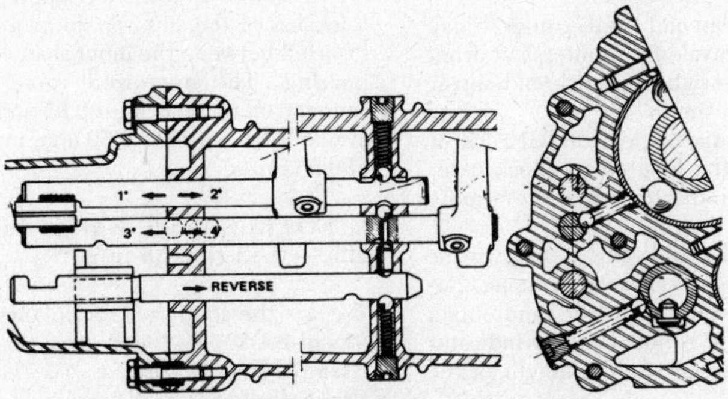

Diagram of detent and interlock components—Model BA-10/4

NOTE: The needle bearing assembly and seal should be replaced any time the transmission is disassembled.

When installing the needle bearing, position the bearings wih the markings on it towards the outside.

Installation of Shift Rails, Forks and Detents

BA-7

1. Place the left hand transmission housing in the holding tool or equivalent.
2. Install the reverse pinion shaft and align the roll pin holes. Install the roll pin into the pre-aligned holes.
3. Turn the housing on its side so that the drain plug is upward and install the reverse gear along with the shifting fork.

NOTE: The shift fork collar on the gear should be towards the rear.

4. Install the ball and the spring detent into its passage, from the outside of the case. Install a sealer on the plug threads and install the plug into the case. Torque to 9.4 ft/lb. Locate the reverse shift rail to the neutral position.
5. Rotate the housing to the opposite side to expose the lock ng passage and install the 3rd/4th locking finger (indent) into the passage.
6. Install the locking needle on the 3rd/4th shifting rail and hold with grease. Install the rail into its respective bore.
7. Rotate the housing until it is in its upright position and install the 1st/2nd shift fork into the case and 3rd/4th shift fork onto the shift rail. Push the rail inward until it is flush with the ball lock hole in the front of the case.

NOTE: The 1st/2nd shift fork will be along side the shift rail.

8. Insert a ball and spring into the hole and compress the spring and ball. Push the rail forward and over the ball and spring.
9. Set the shaft into the neutral position and secure the 3rd/4th shifting fork to the shift rail with a new roll pin.
10. Rest the housing on its side and install a locking ball into the passage to rest against the 3rd/4th shift rail.
11. Install the 1st/2nd shift rail into its respective bore until the neutral position is reached, and entering the 1st/2nd shift fork.
12. Install the locking ball and spring into its bore, sealing the plug and installing it into the housing. Torque to 9.4 ft/lb. Secure the 1st/2nd shifting fork with a new roll pin.

BA-10

1. Install the reverse gear shaft and align the pin holes. Install a new roll pin into the pre-aligned holes.
2. Install the reverse gear, the shift fork and the shifting rail into the transmission case.

NOTE: The shifting fork collar of the reverse gear should face to the rear.

3. Install the ball and spring into the reverse lock hole and install the locking plug, after coating it with a sealer, into the transmission case.
4. Position the shifting shaft into the neutral position.
5. Place the 3rd/4th and reverse indent

pin into the passage to contact the reverse shift rail.

6. Lubricate the interlock pin and place it in its position on the 3rd/4th shift rail.

7. Place the operating indent and spring on the reverse shift fork.

NOTE: The indent is commonly called "spigot".

8. Position the 3rd/4th shift fork rail into the case with the operating clevis horizontal and pointing to the left. Engage the rail by compressing the drive interlock pin (spigot) until the locking flat is opposite the indent.

9. Place the 3rd/4th shift fork in position with its collar towards the rear and engage the rail into the fork. Secure the shifting fork to the rail with a new roll pin.

IMPORTANT: Be assured that the interlock pin is in its proper position in the passage, located in the strut of the case.

10. Rotate the transmission case and install the detent ball in the passage to locate the ball between the 3rd/4th and the 1st/2nd shift rails.

11. Install the 1st/2nd shift rail and the 1st/2nd shift fork into the transmission case, with the shift collar of the gear towards the front. Engage the shift rail into the shift fork and install a new roll pin.

12. Install a ball and spring into the 1st/2nd speed detent passage and after coating the plug with sealer, install the plug into the passageway. Torque to 9.4 ft/lb.

13. Install the ball and spring into the 3rd/4th detent passage.

14. Coat the plug with a sealer and install into the transmission case. Torque to 9.4 ft/lb.

BA-10/4

1. Install the reverse gear assembly consisting of the gear, shaft, fork and rail and the semi-synchronizer ring, into the transmission housing.

2. Align the holes in the reverse gear shaft and the transmission case strut and install a new roll pin.

3. Install the detent balls and springs into the detent passages in the following order.
Rear passage—A detent ball and the 50 mm long spring.
Intermediate passage—A detent ball and a 30 mm long spring.

4. Coat the plugs with a sealer and install in the case. Torque to 9.4 ft/lbs. Set the reverse rail to neutral position.

5. Install the interlock pin into the passage towards the front of the case.

6. Install the interlock pin into the hole in the 3rd/4th shift rail and hold in position with grease.

7. Place the 3rd/4th shifting fork in the case with the boss to the rear. Slide the 3rd/4th shifting rail into position, through the case and into the shifting fork.

8. Install a detent ball into the open passage, towards the front of the case.

9. Install the 1st/2nd shifting fork with the boss towards the front of the case. Install the 1st/2nd shifting rail into the case and the fork.

10. Install a detent ball and a 30 mm long spring into the open detent passage, closest to the front, and coat the plug with sealer and install it into the case. Torque to 9.4 ft/lbs.

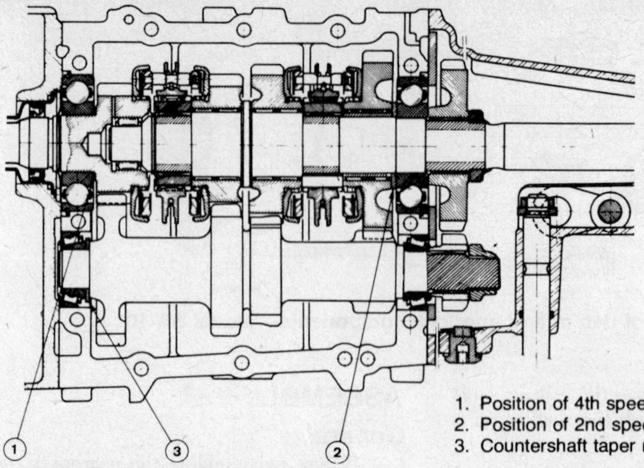

Location of adjusting shims needed during the transmission assembly—Models BA-7, BA-10, BA-10/4

11. Align the holes in the 1st/2nd and 3rd/4th shifting forks and rails and install new roll pins to secure them.

Adjustment Prior to Assembly

Three major adjustments should be made prior to the assembly of the gear box components. The adjustments are as follows.

a. Position of the 4th speed synchronizer cone.

b. Position of the 2nd speed synchronizer cone.

c. Countershaft taper roller bearing preload.

Special tools are needed for the adjustments and should be attained prior to transmission repairs.

An explanation of the adjustments are outlined, with the use of the special tools included in the outline.

ADJUSTMENT OF THE 4TH SPEED SYNCHRONIZER CONE

1. Install the input shaft and bearing, less shims and oil deflector, into the clutch housing, inverted on a flat surface.

2. Install the right hand half of the transmission housing to the clutch housing and install two bolts. Torque the bolts to 14.5 ft/lbs.

CAUTION

Be sure the bearing is properly seated in the clutch housing bore and in the right transmission housing bore.

3. Seat the special tool gauge block (8.0314 G or equivalent) countershaft front bearing bore of the right transmission housing and the clutch housing.

4. Install the dial indictor (8.0310 FZ or equivalent), into the hole on its block base. Retain the dial indicator with the thumb screw.

5. Align the dial indicator stem with the edge of the 4th speed synchronizer cone. Rotate the shaft and cone, one turn, and obtain an average reading. Adjust the dial indicator to zero at the average reading height of the cone.

6. Reposition the dial indicator base to the tool gauge block so that the stem is resting on the gauge block surface. Record the measurement.

Position of dial indicator, input shaft and bearing, clutch housing and half housing during 4th speed synchronizer cone measurement

7. The measurement result represents the thickness of the shim or shims needed to be inserted between the input shaft and the front bearing. The measured value should be rounded off to the nearest 0.05 mm. Shims are available from 0.15 to 0.50 mm, in increments of 0.05 mm.

NOTE: Model BA-7, shims available—0.15 to 0.35 mm.

Prepare the shim stacks as follows;
Model BA-7
Example

Dial indicator reading	0.58 mm
Total shim pack needed (rounded off)	0.60 mm

Use—Oil deflector washer (constant size)	0.15 mm
Shim	0.20 mm
Shim	0.25 mm
Total	0.60 mm

Model BA-10 (Synchronizer cone diameter—91. mm)

Example	
Dial indicator reading	0.43 mm
Total shim thickness needed (rounded off)	0.45 mm

NOTE: Remove the oil deflector washer and discard. Do not include it in the shim pact measurement.

Model BA-10/4 (Synchronizer cone diameter—96. mm)

Example	
Dial indicator reading	0.87 mm
Subtract from obtained reading (constant)	0.50 mm
Result	0.37 mm
Shim required (rounded off)	0.35 mm

NOTE: Remove the oil deflector washer and discard. Do not include it in the shim pack measurement.

ADJUSTMENT OF THE 2ND SPEED SYNCHRONIZER CONE

1. With the input shaft and bearing in the same position as in the 1st measurement procedure, install a needle bearing into the bore of the input shaft.
2. Install the mainshaft, with the 2nd speed gear and needle bearing, the 1st/2nd speed synchronizer hub and the spacer. Be sure the 2nd speed gear is seated properly.
3. Install the rear bearing temporarily to steady the mainshaft.
4. Install the tool gauge block, (8.0314 K or equivalent) in the countershaft front bearing bore.
5. Place the dial indicator and block base, on the upper part of the transmission half case housing. Using a long dial indicator stem, place the end on the surface of the tool gauge block and set the dial indicator to zero.
6. Position the long dial indicator stem on the rim of the 2nd speed synchronizer cone and record the measurement.
7. The dial indicator reading represents the thickness of the shim or shims needed between the spacer and the rear bearing. Round the results off to the nearest 0.05 mm.

Prepare the shim pack as follows;

Model BA-7

Example	
Dial indicator reading	0.47 mm
Shims required (rounded off)	0.45 mm

NOTE: Shim available from 0.15 to 0.50 mm in increments of 0.05 mm.

Model BA-10

Example	
Dial indicator reading	2.82 mm
Shim required (rounded off)	2.80 mm

Model BA-10/4

Example	
Dial indicator reading	2.91 mm
Add to obtained reading (constant)	0.50 mm
Result	3.41 mm
Shim required (rounded off)	3.40 mm

NOTE: Shims are available for models BA-10 and BA-10/4 in steps of 0.05 mm, from 2.35 to 3.65 mm.

8. Remove the dial indicator unit, the mainshaft, the right hand housing and the input shaft.

ADJUSTMENT OF THE COUNTERSHAFT TAPERED ROLLER BEARING PRELOAD

1. Place the left hand half housing in the holding stand or its equivalent.
2. Install the countershaft with its bearings and the thrust plate into the housing. Engage the reverse position.
3. Place the right hand half housing on the left housing, with the dowel pins in position, and install two bearing center bolts and four thrust plate bolts. Hand-tighten only.
4. Position the gearbox housing in an upright position, with the front pointing up.
5. With tool number 8.0314 or equivalent, apply pressure to the countershaft bearings. Rotate the shaft to seat the bearings properly.
6. Tighten the previously hand-tightened bolts to a torque of 7.2 ft/lb. (Bearing center bolts and the thrust plate bolts.)
7. Place the dial indicator and its base on the countershaft end, with the indicator stem contacting the front bearing outer race. Turn the indicator and base in a complete circle and record the average measurement.
8. Move the dial indicator and base to have the stem contact the face of the half housing and again turn the indicator and base in a complete circle. Record the average measurement.
9. The difference between the two measurements is the run-out between the outer race and the front of the half housings. This measurement should not exceed 0.003 mm.
10. Should the measurement of the run-out exceed specifications, tap gently with a mallet on the outer bearing race, be sure the effort to turn the countershaft has not increased, and recheck the run-out.
11. If necessary, loosen and retighten the front bearing center bolt.
12. Position the dial indicator on the countershaft end with the stem resting on the bearing race. Set the dial indicator hands on 2 and 0.
13. Move the dial indicator so that the stem moves from the race to the front face of the housings. Note and record the dial indicator movement.
14. Add 0.10 mm to this measurement to provide for the bearing preload, and round off to the nearest 0.05 mm.

Example	
Measurement to housing	4.27 mm
Preset measurement on race	2.00 mm
Difference	2.27 mm
Add preload	0.10 mm
Necessary shim	2.37 mm
Round off to nearest 0.05 mm	2.35 mm

NOTE: Available shims for the Model BA-7 range from 2.25 to 3.25 mm in increments of 0.05 mm. Available shims for the models BA-10 and BA-10/4 range from 2.15 to 3.30 mm in increments of 0.05 mm.

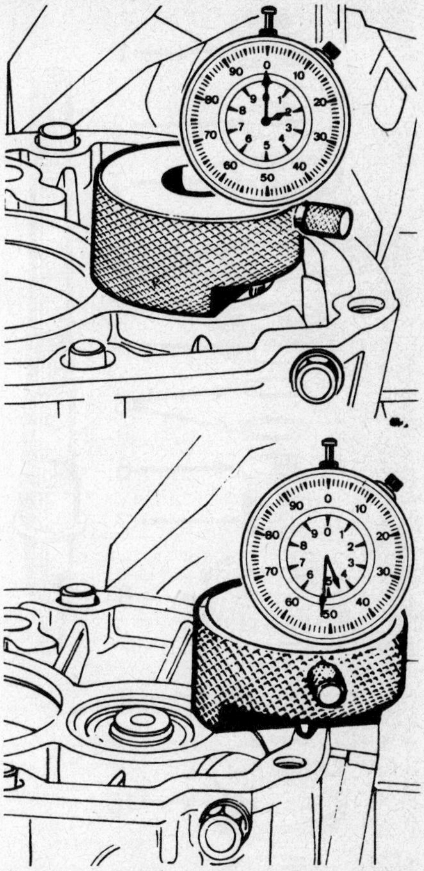

Position of dial indicator and base for measuring preload of countershaft tapered roller bearing

15. Remove the retaining bolts from the thrust plate and the bearing areas of the half housings and separate the two housings. Remove the countershaft and bearings.
16. Remove the front bearing from the countershaft and install the shim of proper thickness, as determined in the previous adjustment procedure, between the bearing and the gear. The shim chamfer should be facing the gear. Press the bearing in place on the countershaft.

Mainshaft Assembly

BA-7

1. Install the following components in order, aligning the previously marked reference points, made during the disassembly, on the mainshaft, from rear to front.
   a. 2nd gear
   b. Synchronizer hub and sliding sleeve
   c. 1st gear
   d. Needle bearing
   e. Spacer
   f. Adjusting shims
   g. Rear bearing with snap-ring groove towards the rear

NOTE: The bearing should be pressed on the shaft, not to exceed 3 tons with the parts bottomed.

   h. The thrust plate with the machined surface towards bearing

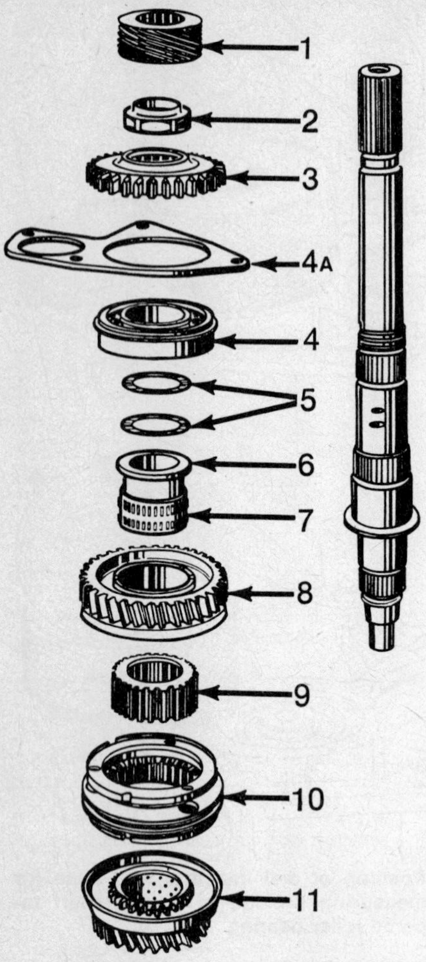

1. Speedometer drive gear
2. Nut
3. Reverse gear
4A. Rear bearing thrust plate
4. Rear bearing
5. Adjusting shim pack
6. 1st speed spacer bushing
7. Needle bearing
8. 1st speed gear
9. Synchronizer cage
10. Synchronizer hub
11. 2nd speed gear

Main shaft components—Model BA-7

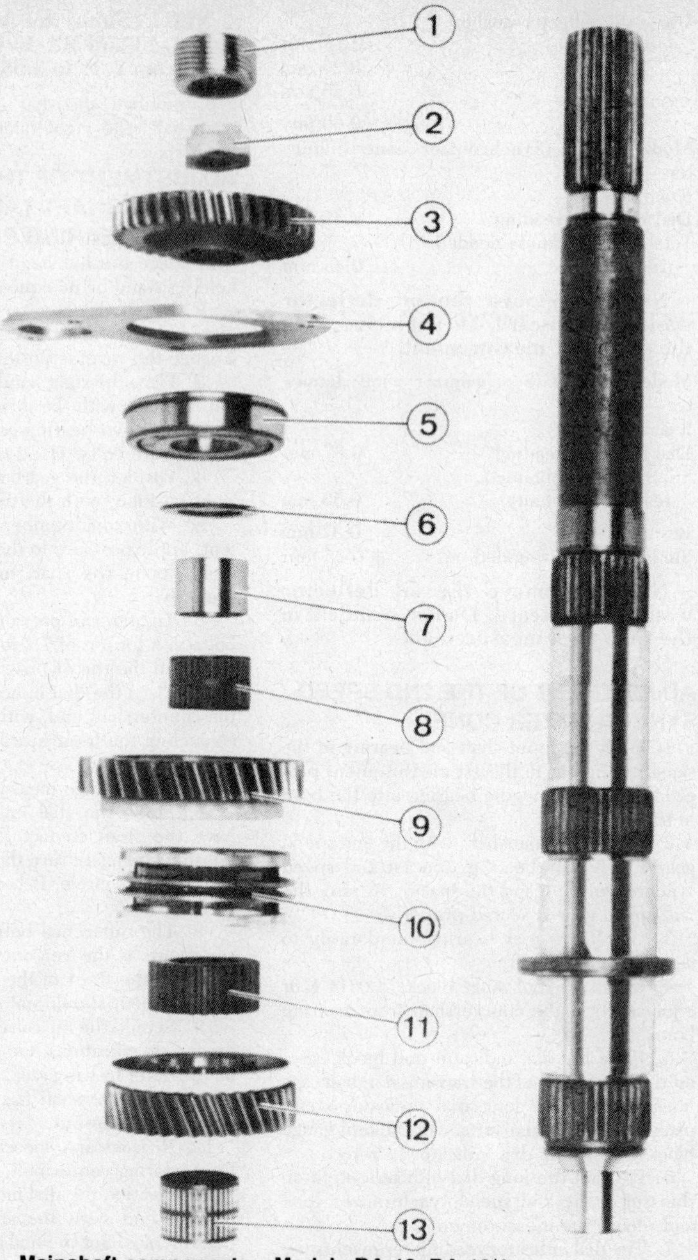

1. Speedometer drive gear
2. Nut
3. Reverse gear
4. Rear bearing thrust plate
5. Rear bearing
6. Shim washer
7. 1st gear spacer collar
8. Needle bearing
9. 1st gear
10. Synchronizer cage
11. Synchronizer hub
12. 2nd gear
13. Needle bearing

Mainshaft components—Models BA-10, BA-10/4

i. Reverse gear with chamfered edge of teeth towards the rear

j. A new nut. Tighten to 40 ft-lbs and lock

k. Press speedometer drive gear onto mainshaft

2. Install the following components in order, onto the mainshaft from front to rear, following the reference marks made previously.

a. 3rd gear

b. 3rd/4th gear synchronizer hub (press if necessary)

c. Spring washer

d. Snap-ring

e. 3rd/4th sliding gear and engage 3rd gear

BA-10, BA-10/4

1. Install the following components on the mainshaft from rear to front, following the reference marks made during the disassembly.

a. 2nd speed gear with needle bearing (length—31 mm)

b. 1st/2nd synchronizer hub and cage, with the marking groove towards the 1st gear

c. 1st speed gear

d. Needle bearing (length—29 mm)

e. Spacer ring

f. Adjustment shims

g. Rear bearing. Press the bearing onto the shaft and do not exceed 3 tons of pressure when bearing bottoms.

h. Thrust plate

i. Reverse drive gear with the flat face towards the rear

j. New nut, torque to 39 ft/lbs and lock in place

k. Speedometer drive gear. Press on shaft with the undercut towards the front

2. Install the following components on the front of the mainshaft, following the reference marks made during the disassembly.

a. 3rd speed gear and needle bearing

b. 3rd/4th synchronizer hub. Press on if necessary

c. Spring washer

d. Snap-ring (Install with components under pressure, if necessary)

Input Shaft

ALL MODELS

1. Install the predetermined shims (with oil deflector on model BA-7) on the input shaft.

2. Position the bearing with the outer snap-ring groove facing the front of the shaft, and press the bearing into place on the shaft.

3. Install a new spring washer and snap-ring while the pressure is on the bearing.
4. Install the outer snap-ring in the outer bearing race groove.
5. Install the needle bearing in the bore of the input shaft.
6. Position the 3rd/4th synchronizer cage to the reference marks, made during the disassembly, on the mainshaft.
7. Install the input shaft to the mainshaft, again aligning the reference marks made during the disassembly.
8. Set both synchronizers to the neutral position.

Assembly of Components to the Half Housings

BA-7

1. Secure the half housing with the shifting forks to the support base or equivalent.
2. Install the countershaft assembly to the mainshaft/input shaft assembly by passing the reverse gear on the countershaft through the opening in the thrust plate Mesh the gear teeth together and install the assembly into the left hand housing, aligning the shifting forks to the synchronizer sliding sleeves.
3. Install the countershaft front bearing outer race to the bearing.
4. Apply sealer to the housing mating surfaces and install the right housing to the left housing.
5. Install the four housing retaining bolts and torque to 3.6 ft/lbs. (Two bolts at the rear and two bolts at the front.)
6. Apply sealer to the rear face of the clutch housing and install on the transmission case.
7. Secure the housing with the six bolts and torque to 20 ft/lbs.
8. Install the four Allen screws and secure the rear bearing thrust plate. Torque to 7.2 ft/lbs.
9. Loosen the four housing retaining bolts and strike the housings with a rubber mallet while turning the mainshaft. Retighten and torque the bolts to 11 ft/lbs.
10. Use a dial indicator and base block to check the "out of Flush" of the two half housings at their rear mating surfaces. The housings should not be out of flush more than 0.02 mm.
11. Install the four assembly bolts and nuts to the half housings and torque to 7.2 ft/lbs.
12. Apply sealer to the rear housing mating surface and install the housing to the transmission.
13. Tighten the seven studs and bolts to 11 ft/lbs after pulling the selector lever fully rearward.
14. Install the speedometer drive socket bushing with a lubricated O-ring. Install the stop screw and locknut.
15. Install the clutch release bearing and fork. Install the back-up lamp and fill with lubricant.

BA-10, BA-10/4

1. Place the left hand housing in the support tool or equivalent.
2. BA-10/4—Install a detent ball and a 30 mm long spring in the detent passage of the rear bearing seat.
3. Set the reverse gear semi-synchronizer to the neutral position. Set the assembled input and mainshaft synchronizers to the neutral position.
4. Install the gear trains into the half housing while engaging the shifting forks to their respective synchronizer sleeves.
5. Install the outer races to the countershaft bearings and install the countershaft into the housing. Mate the gears of the countershaft and the mainshaft.
6. Coat the half housing mating surfaces with sealer and install the right housing to the left, being sure the dowel pins are properly located.
7. Install the six end housing retaining bolts and torque to 3.5 ft/lbs.
8. Engage the reverse gear and install the four thrust plate bolts. Torque to 9.4 ft/lbs.
9. Fit the reverse idler gear to the countershaft with the boss of the gear to the front. Install a new nut.
10. Engage 4th gear, hold the mainshaft with a special holding tool or equivalent, and tighten the nut to 18 ft/lbs.
11. Lock the skirt of the nut to the countershaft by crimping the skirt with a pair of lock pliers.

CAUTION

Never hammer the nut to lock the skirt.

12. Install the oil seal in the clutch housing if not previously done. Coat the clutch housing mating surface with sealer and install on the transmission case. Tighten the seven securing nuts to a torque of 20 ft/lbs.

NOTE: Turn the mainshaft while tightening the clutch housing bolts.

13. Loosen the six bolts at the front and the rear of the transmission case. Tap the housing with a rubber mallet while turning the mainshaft. Retighten the six bearing bolts to a torque of 10 ft/lbs.
14. Install the remaining six bolts in the flanges of the assembled housings. Tighten to a torque of 7 ft/lbs.
15. Reset the reverse gear synchronizer to the neutral position. Apply sealer to the rear extension housing mating surface.
16. Turn the selector lever to the left (counterclockwise) as far as it will go and fit the rear housing to the transmission assembly. Tighten the bolts and nut to 10 ft/lbs.
17. Install the shift control return spring bracket and attach the spring.
18. BA-10/4—Install special tool 8.0310 V or equivalent between the jack lever and the housing. Install the reverse gear plunger until it touches the selector lever. Tighten the two bolts and connect the spring. Remove the gauge tool.
19. Install the speedometer driven gear socket bushing and a lubricated O-ring. Install the set screw and tighten.
20. Install the clutch release fork and bearing assembly, along with the rubber protector.
21. Install the back-up light switch and fill the transmission with lubricant.

TYPE 29

5 Speed Transmission–British Leyland Models

1977-81 Triumph TR-7, TR-8

DISASSEMBLY

1. Secure the transmission and drain the lubricating oil from the unit.
2. Remove the clutch release lever pivot bolt and remove the clutch release lever complete with the pivot bolt and the bearing slippers.
3. Remove the release bearing and the slippers from the clutch release bearing, as required.
4. Remove the bell housing retaining bolts and carefully remove the bell housing from the transmission case.
5. Remove the nut and connecting pin that connects the selector shaft to the remote control shaft.
6. Remove the remote control housing from the transmission rear extension.
7. Remove the nut and washer securing the drive flange to the output shaft. Remove the flange.

NOTE: It is necessary to hold the input shaft while the transmission gear train is in gear, during the removal of the nut and washer from the output shaft.

8. Remove the speedometer driven gear and housing.
9. Remove the two locating boss bolts for the selector rear spool and remove the selector boss.
10. Remove the retaining bolts and remove the rear extension housing from the transmission case.
11. Remove the oil pump driveshaft from the countergear assembly.
12. Remove the 5th gear selector fork and bracket by the removal of the two retaining bolts.
13. Remove the circlip from the selector shaft and remove the 5th gear selector spool.

NOTE: The longer cam of the selector spool is positioned towards the bottom of the transmission.

14. Remove the circlip retaining the 5th gear synchronizer assembly to the output shaft and remove the assembly, the 5th gear (driven) and the spacer from the shaft.
15. Remove the circlip retaining the 5th gear (drive) from the countershaft. Remove the gear and spacer from the countershaft.
16. Remove the front cover and gasket from the transmission, along with the input shaft selective washer, bearing race, countershaft selector washer and the bearing race.
17. Remove the retaining bolts for the locating boss of the selector shaft front spool and withdraw the locating boss.
18. Remove the selector plug, spring and ball from the center plate.
19. Support the gearbox assembly on the

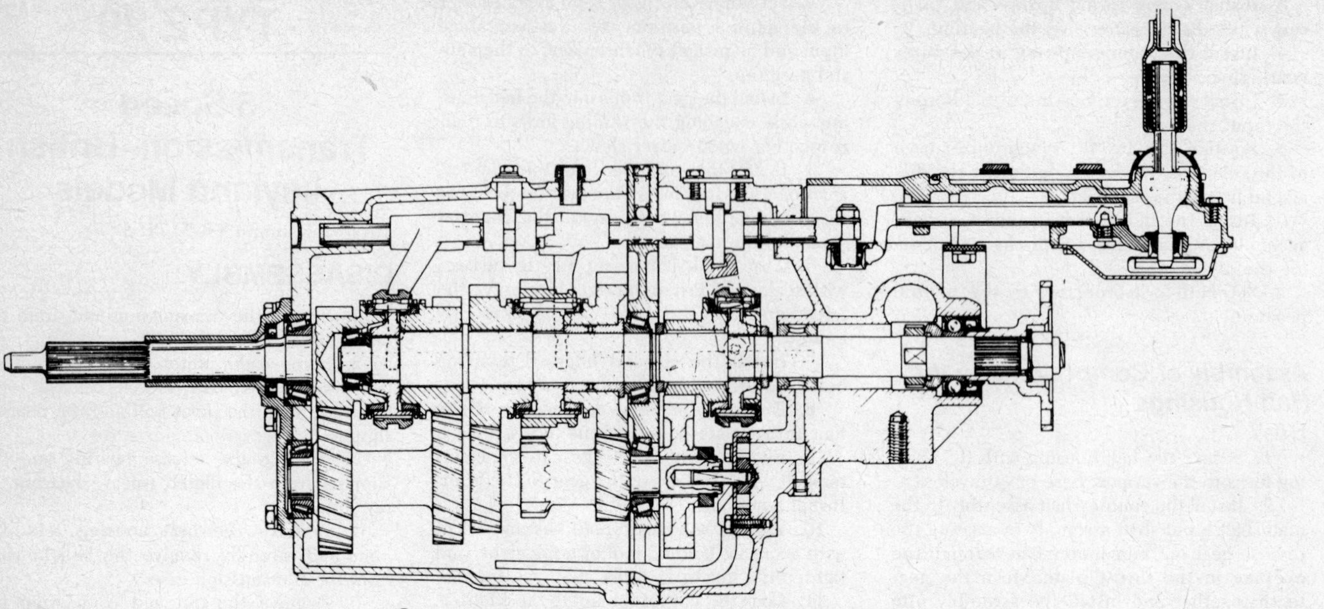

Cross section of Triumph 5-speed transmission

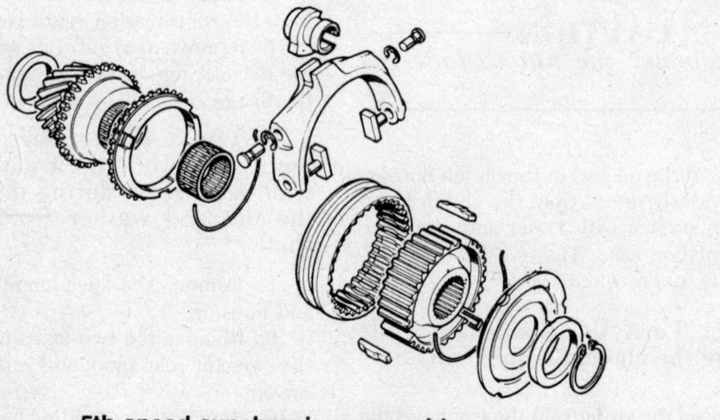

5th speed synchronizer assembly

center plate and remove the case assembly upward from the center plate and gear assembly.

20. Remove the input shaft and the 1st gear synchronizer cone.

21. Remove the countergear assembly from the center plate.

22. Place the center plate assembly in a vise with protected jaws or in a similar holding tool.

23. Remove the reverse lever pivot pin circlip and the pivot pin.

24. Remove the reverse lever and the slipper pad.

25. Slide the reverse shaft towards the rear and remove the reverse gear spacer, the mainshaft, the selector shaft, selector shaft fork and spool in a forward direction to clear the center plate.

26. Remove the selector shaft fork and spool.

NOTE: The shorter cam of the spool is fitted towards the bottom of the transmission.

27. Remove the retaining nut for the reverse gear pivot shaft and remove the pivot shaft, if replacement of the pivot shaft and/or the center plate is necessary.

28. With an appropriate bearing puller, remove the bearings from the input shaft and the race from the front cover assembly. Remove the oil seal from the front cover.

29. Remove the countershaft bearings, using a bearing puller as required.

30. Remove the following from the mainshaft;

a. Remove the pilot bearing and spacer.

b. Remove the 3rd/4th speed synchronizer hub and sleeve.

c. Remove the 3rd speed gear.

d. Remove the circlip securing the mainshaft bearing and remove the bearing, 1st gear and bushing, 1st and 2nd speed hub, sleeve and synchronizer cones and the 2nd gear.

31. Remove the oil seal, bearing, speedometer drive gear, circlip, sleeve and the oil sleeve from the rear extension housing. Remove the oil pump drive, pump cover and gears.

32. Replace the necessary parts, seals and gaskets as required.

ASSEMBLY

1. Install the bearings on the countershaft with an appropriate bearing installer.

2. Install the 2nd gear, synchronizer (baulk) ring and the 1st/2nd speed synchronizer sleeve and hub on the rear of the mainshaft.

NOTE: Assembly the 1st/2nd speed synchronizer so that the short splines on the inner member are towards the 2nd speed gear and the sleeve fork groove is towards the rear of the transmission.

3. Install the synchronizer (baulk) ring, the 1st speed gear, the selective bushing (collars of different thicknesses), the bearing and a new circlip on the mainshaft.

NOTE: End play of from 0.0002 to 0.002 inch (0.005 to 0.055 mm) should exist between the selective bushing and the assembled gear train.

4. Install the 3rd gear, synchronizer (baulk) ring and the synchronizer hub and sleeve onto the front of the mainshaft.

NOTE: The longer boss of the synchronizer hub should be towards the front of the transmission.

5. Install the spacer and the bearing to the front of the mainshaft.

6. Install the bearing race into the centerplate for the countershaft bearing.

7. Install the countergear assembly into the center plate and install the 5th gear onto the shaft. Install the spacer and a new circlip.

8. Install the mainshaft bearing race into the center plate. Place the center plate into a vise with soft jaws or into a similar holding tool.

9. Assemble the selector shaft with the 1st/2nd and 3rd/4th forks and spool and place the assembly onto the mainshaft in their respective synchronizer sleeves.

10. Install the mainshaft and selector shaft

assembly into the center plate. Install the spacer, the 5th gear, the synchronizer (baulk) ring, the synchronizer hub and sleeve, end plate, the selective spacer and a new circlip.

NOTE: The end play for the 5th gear should be from 0.0002 to 0.002 inch (0.005 to 0.055 mm).

11. Install the reverse gear, with the lip for the slipper pad to the front of the transmission, the front and rear spacers and the reverse shaft.
12. Install the reverse lever, slipper pad, pivot pin and circlip.
13. Remove the center plate assembly from the holding vise or other tool and set the assembly in an upright position with the front of the mainshaft up.
14. Install the centerplate gasket. Install the external bearing and the internal bearing race onto the input shaft.
15. Install the input shaft into the transmission case.
16. Carefully slide the transmission case and input shaft over the gear assembly. Be sure that the center plate dowels and the selector shaft are both engaged in their respective locations.
17. Install the countershaft and input shaft bearing races in place.
18. Evenly draw the transmission case into position with seven bolts and *flat* washers, to avoid damage to the rear face of the center plate.
19. Install a countershaft spacer of a thickness of 0.040 inch (1.02 mm) on the countershaft bearing race and install the front cover and gasket. Secure the cover with bolts.
20. Check the end play of the countershaft with a dial indicator gauge. The required end play is 0.0002 to 0.002 inch (0.005 to 0.050 mm).
21. Remove the front cover and the provisional spacer. The spacer thickness required is the provisional spacer thickness plus the end play obtained, minus 0.002 inch (0.055 mm).
22. Select the correct spacer and reinstall the front cover and retaining bolts. Recheck the countershaft end play to be certain it is correct.
23. Place a ball bearing into the center of the input shaft and mount a dial indicator with the stylus resting on the bearing. Zero the gauge.
24. Check the mainshaft and output shaft end play combined by lifting the rear of the mainshaft until all play is measured. Total should be 0.0002 to 0.002 inch (0.005 to 0.055 mm).

NOTE: Care must be exercised when checking end play that only the end play is measured and not side play.

25. When the end play measurement is taken, the selective washer can be determined as follows; End play measurement minus 0.002 inch (0.055 mm). Remove the front cover and install the spacer, reinstall the cover and recheck the mainshaft and input shaft endplay. Remove the front cover again.
26. Install the front seal in the front cover and lubricate the seal lips. Protect the seal lips from the input shaft splines and reinstall the front cover and bolt into place.
27. Place the gearbox assembly on a flat surface and remove the seven bolts and flat washers from the center plate to the transmission case.
28. Install the 5th gear spool and circlip to the selector shaft.

NOTE: The longer cam of the spool is fitted towards the bottom of the transmission.

29. Install the 5th gear selector fork and bracket. Renew the selector shaft O-ring in the rear cover and install the oil ring bushing.
30. Install the rear center plate gasket in place and install the oil pump driveshaft in place on the countershaft.
31. Install the oil pump gears and the cover in place on the rear extension housing.
32. Install the rear extension housing over the output shaft and make sure the oil pump driveshaft engages the oil pump gears.
33. Install the selector shaft ball, spring and plug to the center plate.
34. Install the spool locating bosses (2) to the 1st/2nd spool and the 5th gear spool. Install the speedometer drive gear to engage the mainshaft flats.
35. Install the bell housing with the clutch release bearing and operating lever, with the pivot bolt in place.
36. Install the shifting mechanism to the transmission.
37. Install the proper lubrication to the level and secure the fill plug.

TYPE 30

4 Speed Transmission–British Leyland Model

Triumph Spitfire 1500, TR-7, TR-8

DISASSEMBLY

1. Remove the transmission.
2. Remove the bellhousing and clutch lever.
3. Take out the top cover retaining bolts.
4. Lift off the top cover and extension and the joint washer.
5. Unscrew the output flange nut and remove the washer.
6. Withdraw the output flange.
7. Unscrew the bolts retaining the rear extension to the case.
8. Remove the rear extension and joint washer.
9. Unscrew the retaining bolt, for the reverse idler spindle.
10. Withdraw the reverse idler spindle and spacer.
11. Insert the needle-roller retaining tube and remove the layshaft spindle to the rear. Allow the layshaft cluster to drop to the bottom of the transmission.
12. Remove the constant pinion assembly.
13. Remove the top gear baulk ring.
14. Remove the circlip retaining the speedometer drive gear.
15. Remove the speedometer drive gear and ball.
16. Remove the snap-ring from the mainshaft ballrace.
17. Remove the circlip from the mainshaft ballrace.
18. Withdraw the ballrace using special tools S4221A and S4221A—19/1.
19. Tilt the mainshaft and remove it from the transmission.
20. Remove the 3rd/top synchro unit.
21. Remove the 3rd gear baulk ring.
22. From the rear of the mainshaft; remove the thrust washer.
23. Remove the 1st speed gear.
24. Remove the 1st gear baulk ring.
25. Remove the circlip.
26. Withdraw the washer.
27. Remove the 3rd speed gear and bushing.
28. Remove the thrust washer.
29. Remove the 2nd speed gear and bushing.
30. Remove the 2nd gear baulk ring.
31. Remove the thrust washer.
32. Remove the 1st/2nd synchro unit.
33. Remove the split collars.
34. Lift out the jackshaft cluster.
35. Take out the jackshaft thrust washer.
36. Remove the reverse idler gear.
37. Unscrew the nut retaining the reverse actuator.
38. Remove the reverse actuator and pivot pin.

ASSEMBLY

1. Screw the pivot pin into the reverse actuator until one full thread protrudes through the lever boss.
2. Install the actuator and pivot pin into the gear casing.
3. Install the plain washer and tighten the nut.
4. Smear the front face of the jackshaft front thrust washer with grease and stick it in position in the gear casing. Insert one end of the jackshaft spindle through the casing to centralize the washer.
5. Lower the jackshaft cluster assembly into the transmission.
6. Install the rear thrust washer in position.
7. Insert the jackshaft spindle and eject the needle-roller retaining tube.
8. Measure the jackshaft cluster end-play. Adjust the layshaft end-float to 0.007 to 0.013 in. (0.18 to 0.33 mm), by selective use of thrust washers.
9. Insert the needle-roller retaining tube, eject the layshaft spindle and allow the cluster to drop to the bottom of the transmission.
10. Install the split collars to the mainshaft.
11. Slide the 1st/2nd synchro unit onto the shaft.
12. Reinstall the thrust washer.
13. Fit the 2nd gear baulk ring.
14. Check the end-play of the second gear on the bushing, which if correct will be 0.002 to 0.006 in. (0.0508 to 0.1524 mm). Reduce the length of the bushing to reduce the end-play.

13. Mainshaft bearing circlip
14. Mainshaft bearing snap-ring
16. Mainshaft bearing
18. Countergear cluster
19. Reverse shift fork

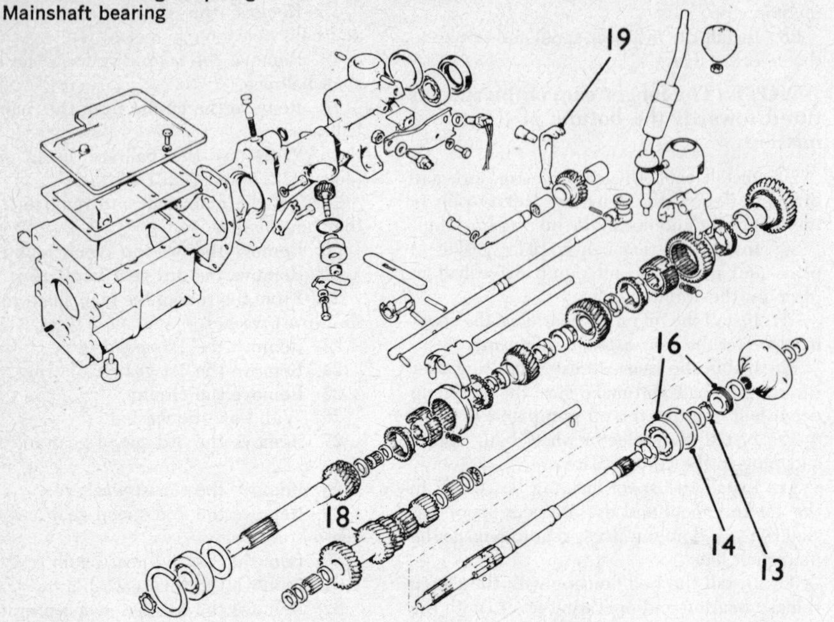

Triumph manual transmission—typical

15. Install the second gear bushing to the shaft.
16. Reinstall the thrust washer.
17. Check the end-play of the 3rd gear on the bushing, which if correct will be 0.002 to 0.006 in.
18. Install the 3rd gear bushing to the shaft.
19. Install the washer.
20. Secure the assembly using a discarded half circlip.
21. Measure the end-play of the bushing on the mainshaft and adjust by selective use of thrust washers until an end-play of 0.000 to 0.006 in. is obtained. Dismantle the mainshaft.
22. Install the split collars to the mainshaft.
23. Install the 1st speed gear.
24. Install the thrust washer.
25. Install a discarded bearing inner race to spacer 0.784 to 0.750 in. long.
26. Measure the thickness of the circlip washer and assemble to the shaft.
27. Install a discarded half circlip.
28. Measure the 1st gear end-play and determine the thickness of the circlip washer required to provide an end-play of 0.000 to 0.002 in.
29. Dismantle the mainshaft. Assemble components to the mainshaft as follows:
    - First/second synchro unit
    - Second gear baulk ring
    - Thrust washer
    - Second speed gear and bushing
    - Thrust washer
    - Third speed gear and bushing
    - Washer
    - Circlip, offset outermost
    - Split collars
    - First gear baulk ring
    - First speed gear
    - Third/top synchro unit
30. Position the reverse idler gear in the casing.
31. Place the mainshaft assembly in the transmission.
32. Install the abutment plate on the case and mount in a vise.
33. Install the thrust washer over the mainshaft.
34. Assemble the snap-ring to the ball race.
35. Place the ball race over the mainshaft and drive into position.
36. Install the circlip washer selected. (See Step 28.)
37. Install a new circlip.
38. Install the speedometer drive gear, ball and circlip.
39. Remove the transmission from the vise and take off the abutment plate.
40. Place the top gear baulk ring in the 3rd/top synchro unit.
41. Install the constant pinion assembly using Tool No. S314/1 and adapter S4221A—19/3.
42. Invert the transmission and align the jackshaft cluster and thrust washer.
43. Insert the jackshaft spindle from the gear and remove the needle-roller retaining tube.
44. Position the reverse idler gear and fit the spindle and spacer. Install the locating bolt.
45. Locate the washer on the end of the mainshaft.
46. Refit the rear extension assembly and a new joint washer.
47. Install the bolts and washers.
48. Replace the drive flange.
49. Install and tighten the nut and washer and secure the cotter pin.
50. Refit the bellhousing assembly and a new joint washer. Install the clutch lever.
51. Install and tighten the bottom bolt and copper washer.
52. Select 1st gear on the top cover and the transmission.
53. Install the top cover and a new washer.

TYPE 31

4 Speed Transmission–British Leyland Model

Triumph TR-6

DISASSEMBLY

1. Disassemble the top cover. Remove the bolts, washers, top cover, and paper gasket. Remove the nut, cross pin, cover, and withdraw the gear shift lever assembly from the top cover. With the cover inverted, remove the plugs, spacer, springs, plunger, and balls. Detach the peg bolts. With the selector shafts in the neutral position, withdraw the 3rd/4th gear selector shaft, being careful to remove the interlock plunger and balls as they are released. Remove the 3rd/4th selector fork and spacer tube from the top cover. Repeat the preceding operation for the 1st/2nd and reverse gear selector shifts. Remove the retaining screws and take out the retaining plate. Remove the sealing rings from their recesses. If necessary, remove the peg bolts and remove the selectors from their shafts.
2. Disassemble the front cover. Remove the tapered bolt, bolt, and spring washer. Withdraw the cross-shaft along with the release spring, release bearing, sleeve and fork. Remove the retaining bolts and remove the front cover, bolts, and plate.
3. Disassemble the rear extension. Remove the peg bolt and withdraw the speedometer drive gear assembly. Remove the cotter pin, slotted nut, and withdraw the flange. Remove the retaining bolts and detach the rear extension, using an extractor.
4. Remove the countershaft and reverse pinion shaft by removing the retaining screw and plate.
5. Withdraw the input shaft assembly from the transmission.
6. Remove the circlips, spacer washer, and withdraw the bearing.
7. Detach the disc and, if necessary, remove the needle roller bearing.
8. Remove the circlip, spacer washer, and circlip, and remove the mainshaft rear bearing.
9. After maneuvering the mainshaft assembly through the transmission top cover opening, lift out the countershaft assembly, thrust washers, and reverse gear.
10. Remove the countershaft gears from the hub and, if necessary, remove the needle roller assemblies from the hub bore.
11. Remove the circlip by driving a special tool beneath the circlip and then levering the 3rd gear forward to remove the circlip from its groove.
12. Remove all mainshaft components and remove the 1st/2nd and 3rd/4th synchronizer inner hubs from the outer sleeves (being careful not to catch the springs and balls).

ASSEMBLY

1. Install the reverse gear in the transmission, with the selector groove to the rear.

2. Install the reverse gear shaft, securing it with string to prevent it from sliding into the transmission.

3. Use a stepped drift to drive a new needle roller bearing (with lettered face outward) into each end of the countershaft hub.

4. Install the gears, spacer, and gear to the countershaft hub.

5. Using grease to retain the countershaft thrust washers, install the washers into the transmission and lower the gear cluster into position. With the countershaft temporarily installed, measure the cluster gear end-play, which should be 0.007-0.012 in. End clearance may be adjusted to within this range through the use of thrust washers of larger or smaller thickness. Remove the countershaft and drop the gear cluster to the bottom of the transmission case.

6. Assemble the synchronizer springs, balls and shims to the 3rd/4th synchronizer hub. Install the outer sleeve. Repeat the preceding operations with the 1st/2nd synchronizer unit. Check the axial release loads. The points of release should be as follows:

3rd/4th: 19/21 lbs.
1st/2nd: 25/27 lbs.

If the actual release loads observed are greater or less than those specified above, the correct loading may be achieved by adjusting the number of shims beneath each synchronizer spring.

7. Using a straightedge and a feeler gauge, measure the end clearance of each mainshaft gear on its bushing. The end clearance measured should be 0.004-0.006 in., and may be increased by installing a new bushing and decreased by reducing bushing length. In the preceding adjustments, take care, as reduction of bushing length will cause the end clearance of the bushings on the mainshaft to increase.

8. Install the thrust washer, bushings and thrust washer to the mainshaft, secure the assembly and measure the total end clearance of the bushings and thrust washers on the mainshaft. This measurement should be 0.003-0.009 in. (0.08-0.23 mm), and may be adjusted by using thrust washers available.

9. Install the thrust washer, bushing, and thrust washer to the mainshaft.

10. Using a special tool, assemble the race into position and install the washer and circlip. The race should be driven toward the rear to ensure that it is firmly against the circlip.

11. Measure the 1st gear end clearance by gauging the distance between the washer and bushing. The end clearance should be 0.003-0.009 in. and is adjustable by use of the various thrust washers (Step 8).

12. Prior to final assembly, all components should be removed from the mainshaft.

13. Assemble the mainshaft as follows. With the components placed in their proper relative positions, install them in the following order: thrust washer, gear and bushing, gear and bushing, thrust washer, a new circlip, 3rd/4th synchronizer unit with baulk ring at each side. Install a baulk ring to each side of the 1st/2nd synchronizer unit, slide the unit over the rear of the mainshaft and onto the larger splines. Install the washer, gear and bushing, and washer to the rear of the mainshaft.

14. Pass the rear of the mainshaft through the rear bearing housing and position the shaft.

15. With the mainshaft in position, a special tool is installed in place of the front cover. This tool consists of a plate that holds the front of the mainshaft in position.

16. Install the circlip to the bearing and drive the bearing into position. Install the washer and cirlip.

17. Tap the rear of the mainshaft with a soft-headed mallet to take up the clearance between the circlip, washer, and bearing.

18. Install the disc, bearing (with circlip groove to the front), washer, and circlip to the input shaft. If necessary, a new bearing should be installed to the bore of the input shaft, with the lettered face of the bearing facing outwards.

19. Install the circlip to the bearing and install the assembly.

20. Install the front cover as follows. With the lip of the seal toward the gears, use a special tool to drive a new seal into the front cover.

21. With a seal protector protecting the oil seal, install the gasket and cover and secure with the retaining washers and bolts.

22. With a tapered pilot tool inserted to align the countershaft gears and thrust

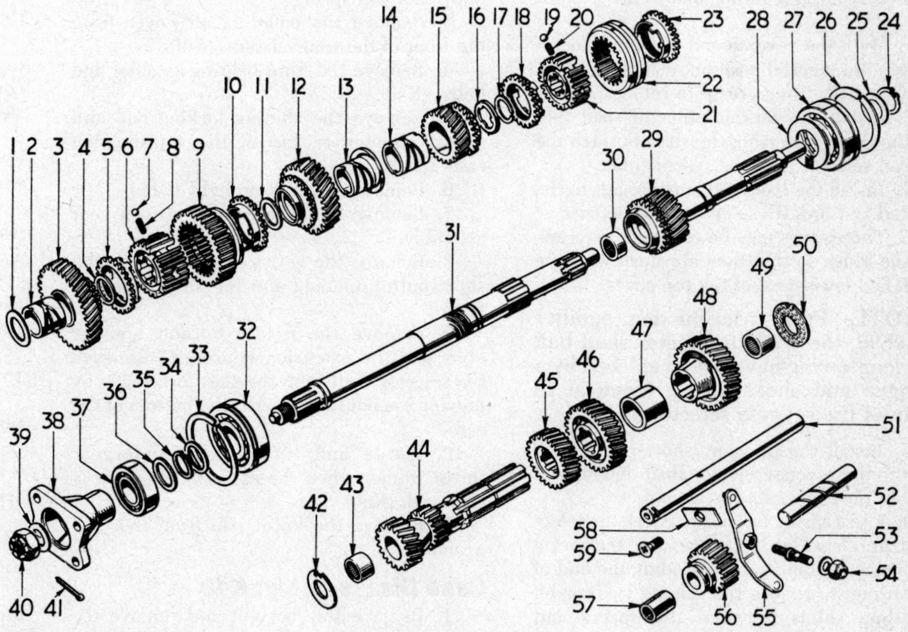

1. Thrust washer
2. Bushing—1st speed gear
3. 1st speed gear
4. Thrust washer
5. 1st speed synchro cup
6. 1st/2nd speed synchro hub
7. Synchro ball
8. Spring
9. Reverse mainshaft gear and synchro outer sleeve
10. 2nd speed synchro cup
11. Thrust washer
12. 2nd speed gear
13. Bushing—2nd speed gear
14. Bushing—3rd speed gear
15. 3rd speed gear
16. Thrust washer
17. Circlip
18. 3rd speed synchro cup
19. Synchro ball
20. Spring
21. 3rd/top synchro hub
22. Synchro sleeve
23. Top gear synchro cup
24. Circlip
25. Spacer washer
26. Circlip
27. Ball race
28. Oil deflector plate
29. Input shaft
30. Needle roller bearing
31. Mainshaft
32. Ball race
33. Circlip
34. Spacer washer
36. Spacer washer
37. Rear ball race
38. Flange
39. Plain washer
40. Slotted nut
41. Cotter pin
42. Rear thrust washer
43. Needle roller bearing
44. Countershaft hub
45. 2nd speed countershaft gear
46. 3rd speed countershaft gear
47. Spacer piece
48. Countershaft gear
49. Needle roller bearing
50. Front thrust washer
51. Countershaft
52. Reverse gear shaft
53. Pivot stud
54. Nyloc nut and washer
55. Reverse gear operating lever
56. Reverse gear
57. Reverse gear bushing
58. Locating plate
59. Screw

TR-6 transmission components

washers, insert the countershaft, pushing out the pilot tool.

23. With the ends of the countershaft and reverse gear shafts engaged at the retaining plate, secure with the Phillips head screw.

24. Install and secure the countershaft cover gasket and cover plate.

25. Assemble the rear extension as follows. Install a new gasket and the rear extension to the transmission and secure with the retaining bolts.

26. Install a spacer washer to the mainshaft and drive the extension ball bearing into position. With its sealing face forward, install a new oil seal.

27. With the driving flange positioned on the mainshaft, install the washer and slotted nut.

28. Install the speedometer drive gear assembly, and secure with a retaining bolt.

29. Reassemble the top cover. Install the selectors to their shafts and secure with the retaining bolts.

30. Install the new O-rings to the recesses in the rear of the top cover and install the retaining plate and secure it.

31. With the interlock plunger positioned in the 3rd/4th selector shaft, insert the shaft into the top cover.

32. Install the selector fork, spacer tube, and retaining bolt.

33. Install the interlock ball between the bores of the reverse and 3rd/4th selector shafts, using grease to retain the ball. Slide the reverse selector shaft into the top cover and engage it with the reverse selector fork and spacer.

34. Install the retaining bolt to the selector fork.

35. With the reverse and 3rd/4th selector shafts in the neutral position, install the other interlock ball, using grease to retain it.

36. Install the 1st/2nd selector shaft into the top cover, inserting the shaft through the 1st/2nd selector fork and spacer tube.

37. Install the balls and long springs to the 1st/2nd and 3rd/4th selector shaft detents.

38. The springs may be retained by screwing the plugs so that they are flush with the machined lower face of the top cover.

NOTE: From transmission number CT.9899, the 3rd/4th selector shaft ball and long spring have been replaced by a plunger and short spring identical to those of the reverse selector shaft.

39. Install the plunger, short spring, and shim to the reverse selector shaft detent, and use the plug to retain the assembly.

40. Use a spring balance to check the selector shaft release loads. If necessary, the spring loads may be adjusted by grinding the end of the spring (to reduce the release load) or by installing shims between the spring and plunger (to increase the load).

41. Replace the spring and plunger to the gearshift lever.

42. Assemble the gearshift lever, spring and plate to the top cover, pressing the plunger with a screwdriver as the end of the gearshift lever engages the selectors.

43. Retain the gearshift lever with the cap, cross pin, and nut.

44. Install a new gasket and replace the top cover assembly to the transmission. Be sure that the reverse selector fork engages the actuating lever. Install the strap beneath the head of the rear mounting bolt.

NOTE: With the modified gearshift lever installed in TR-6 models, the position of the gearshift lever is adjusted as follows: With the gearshift lever positioned into the 1st and 2nd gate, screw the locating pin clockwise until it just causes the gearshift lever to move, then turn the locating pin one-half turn in the counterclockwise direction and tighten the locknut. Move the gearshift lever into the reverse gate position and adjust the other locating pin in the same manner.

TYPE 32

4 and 5 Speed Transmissions—Models K40, K50

1975-79 Toyota Corolla (1200)
(Chassis—KE)

DISASSEMBLY

1. Secure the transmission and drain the lubricant from the unit.

2. Remove the clutch release bearing, fork, boot and spring.

3. Remove the countershaft cover from the front of the transmission. (K40).

4. Remove the front bearing retainer and bolts. (K40).

5. Remove the shifting locking ball and spring retainer on top of the transmission case. (K40).

6. Remove the back-up light switch.

7. Remove the speedometer driven gear assembly.

8. Remove the restricting pins from the shift control opening and the shift lever retainer.

9. Remove the rear extension housing bolts and the extension housing. Disengage the selector shaft from the shift fork shafts by moving the housing towards the bottom of the case.

10. Locate and retain the countergear thrust washer when the extension housing is removed. (K50).

11. Remove the lower pan from the case assembly.

Case Disassembly: K40

1. Remove the lockbolt and remove the reverse idler gear and shaft.

2. Remove the countershaft by driving it from the front to the rear.

3. Remove the countergear, bearings and thrust washers from the case.

4. Shift the number one shift fork shaft to the neutral position and using a pin punch, remove the slotted spring pins from the shift forks and shafts.

5. Set each fork shaft to the neutral position and pull the shaft from the case.

6. Shift the number one clutch hub sleeve into 2nd gear and remove the shift fork from inside the case.

7. Arrange the three interlock pins and slotted spring pins and lay aside for the assembly.

8. Remove the output shaft from the rear of the transmission with the gear intact. Remove the input shaft and bearing.

9. Remove the snap-rings at the speedometer drive gear and remove the gear from the shaft.

10. Release the staked parts of the locknut on the mainshaft and remove the nut from the shaft with a holding tool and special wrench.

11. Remove the rear bearing and housing from the mainshaft.

12. Remove the 1st gear, bushing, needle bearing and locking ball from the shaft.

13. Remove the synchronizer (baulk) ring, 1st/2nd clutch hub and sleeve, synchronizer (baulk) ring and the 2nd speed gear from the shaft.

14. Remove the snap-ring from the front of the shaft and remove the 3rd/4th synchronizer assembly and the 3rd speed gear, with spacer.

Case Disassembly: K50

1. Remove the snap-rings and speedometer drive gear from the output or mainshaft.

2. Remove the 5th gearshift arm bracket, arm and the number 3 shift fork.

3. Remove the snap-ring and the shifting key retainer from the mainshaft.

4. Remove the number three clutch hub and sleeve, the synchronizer (baulk) ring and the 5th gear with its needle roller bearing.

5. Remove the snap-ring from the countergear and remove the counter 5th gear, the countergear rear bearing and sleeve. The sleeve is retained with a snap-ring.

6. Remove the locking bolt and pull the reverse idler shaft from the case. Remove the reverse idler gear.

7. Remove the countergear, thrust washer and the front bearing from the case as a unit.

8. Remove the locking balls and springs cover from the top of the transmission case. Remove the springs and balls.

9. Using a pin punch, drive the slotted spring pins from the forks and shafts.

10. Place each shaft into the neutral position and remove from the case.

11. Arrange the slotted spring pins, the interlock pins, and locking ball for easier assembly.

12. Shift the number one clutch into 2nd gear and remove the shift fork from inside the case.

13. Remove the input shaft and front bearing retainer from the front of the case.

14. Secure the pilot bearing rollers and the 4th speed synchronizer (baulk) ring.

15. Spread the expanding snap-ring on the rear bearing and remove the output shaft assembly from the front of the transmission case.

16. Disassemble the mainshaft by removing the rear snap-ring and removing the rear bearing, bushing, needle roller bearing and locating ball. Continue by removing the 1st gear, synchronizer (baulk) ring, number one

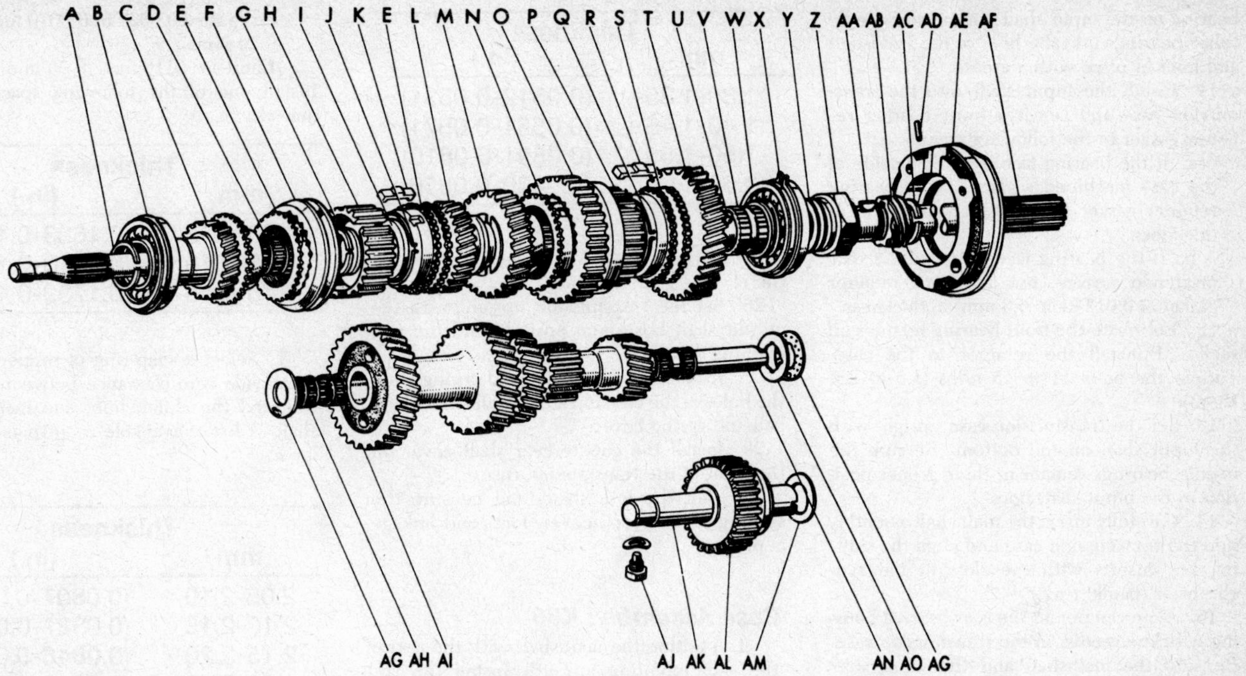

(a)—Shaft snap-ring
(b)—Bearing (transmission front)
(c)—Input shaft
(d)—Needle roller bearing
(e)—Synchronizer ring No. 3
(f)—Transmission hub sleeve
(g)—Shaft snap-ring
(h)—Transmission clutch hub No. 2
(i)—Clutch hub spacer
(j)—Synchromesh shifting key spring No. 2
(k)—Synchromesh shifting key No. 2
(l)—Side gear
(m)—Second gear
(n)—Synchronizer ring No. 2
(o)—Reverse gear
(p)—Transmission clutch hub No. 1
(q)—Synchromesh shifting key spring No. 1
(r)—Synchromesh shifting key No. 1
(s)—Synchronizer ring No. 1
(t)—First gear
(u)—Ball
(v)—First gear bushing
(w)—Bearing (transmission rear)
(x)—Shaft snap-ring
(y)—Shim
(z)—Nut
(aa)—Woodruff key
(ab)—Speedometer drive gear
(ac)—Shaft snap-ring
(ad)—Slotted split pin
(ae)—Output shaft rear retainer
(af)—Output shaft
(ag)—Countergear thrust washer (case side)
(ah)—Needle roller bearing
(ai)—Countergear
(aj)—Shaft retaining bolt
(ak)—Reverse idler gear shaft
(al)—Reverse idler gear
(am)—Spacer
(an)—Counter shaft
(ao)—Countergear thrust washer (gear side)

Corolla 1200 transmission components

clutch hub, sleeve, synchronizer (baulk) ring and the second gear.

17. Remove the front snap-ring, the number two clutch hub, sleeve, synchronizer (baulk) ring and the second gear.

NOTE: During the disassembly and assembly of the K40 and K50 transmissions, the need to press bearings or gears from and back onto the shafts will exist. Govern the disassembly and assembly procedures accordingly.

INSPECTION

Inspect the gears, shafts, bearings and other internal components and replace or repair the necessary parts. Install new seals and gaskets during the reassembly.

ASSEMBLY

Case Assembly K40

1. Place the mainshaft in an upright position with the rear of the shaft pointing up. Place the 2nd speed gear and the synchronizer (baulk) ring onto the shaft, followed by the number one clutch hub and sleeve. Ring identification: Narrow insert gap for 1st gear and wide insert gap for 2nd gear.

2. Install the second synchronizer (baulk) ring, the 1st gear, the locking ball, the needle roller bearing and the bushing.

3. Install the rear bearing and housing onto the shaft and retain it with a washer and locknut. Tighten the locknut to a torque of 33 to 72 ft/lbs (4.5 to 10.0 Kg-m) with the special wrench and the shaft holding tool. Stake the nut to the shaft.

4. Measure the thrust clearance of the 1st and 2nd speed gears:

1st gear—0.0071 to 0.0110 inch (0.18 to 0.28 mm)

2nd gear—0.0039 to 0.0098 inch (0.10 to 0.25 mm)

5. Install the 3rd gear on the front of the shaft. Line up the shifting key inserts with the insert slots in the synchronizer (baulk) ring and install the number two clutch hub and sleeve.

6. Push the number two clutch hub inward as far as it will go and measure the 3rd gear thrust clearance:

3rd gear—0.0020 to 0.0079 inch (0.05 to 0.20 mm)

Limit—0.0018 inch (0.30 mm)

7. When the 3rd gear thrust clearance is not within specifications, select a spacer from the following list;

Thickness mm	Thickness (in.)
4.30-4.35	(0.1693-0.1713)
4.35-4.40	(0.1713-0.1732)
4.40-4.45	(0.1732-0.1752)

8. Select a snap-ring that will control the clearance to zero between the snap-ring and the clutch hub, from the following list:

Thickness mm	Thickness (in.)
2.05-2.10	(0.0807-0.0827)
2.10-2.15	(0.0827-0.0846)
2.15-2.20	(0.0846-0.0866)
2.20-2.25	(0.0866-0.0886)
2.25-2.30	(0.0886-0.0906)
2.30-2.35	(0.0906-0.0925)
2.35-2.40	(0.0925-0.0945)
2.40-2.45	(0.0945-0.0965)

9. Install the snap-ring in place on the mainshaft.

10. If not previously done, install the front

bearing on the input shaft. Install the needle roller bearings into the bore of the mainshaft and hold in place with a grease.

11. Install the input shaft into the transmission case and select a front bearing retainer gasket in the following manner.

a. If the bearing face extends outside of the case machined surface, use a bearing retainer gasket of 0.020 inch (0.5 mm) in thickness.

b. If the bearing face is below the case machined surface, use a bearing retainer gasket of 0.012 inch (0.3 mm) in thickness.

12. Lubricate the front bearing retainer oil seal and install the retainer to the case. Torque the bolts 11 to 15 ft/lbs (1.5 to 2.2 Kg-m).

13. Set the transmission case upright with the input shaft on the bottom. Be sure the needle bearings remain in their proper position in the input shaft bore.

14. Carefully insert the mainshaft assembly into the transmission case and align the shifting key inserts with the slots in the synchronizer (baulk) ring.

15. Align the pin on the rear bearing housing with the groove in the transmission case. Be sure the mainshaft and the input shaft rotate freely.

16. Temporarily, install a holding tool over the rear bearing retainer so that the gear train is held securely. Place the transmission with the bottom up.

17. Shift the synchronizer assembly sleeve into the 2nd speed position. Install the reverse shift fork, the 1st/2nd shift fork and the 3rd/4th shift fork in their respective sleeve grooves.

18. Insert the shift shafts into the transmission case and through their respective shifting forks. Place the center shaft in the neutral position, along with the reverse shifting shaft in the neutral position.

19. Install the 1st-2nd shifting shaft to the point where the shaft dummy hole and the case hole line up.

20. Insert a probe into the case hole and be sure the outer two shaft holes line up and the probe touches the inner shaft.

21. Install the interlock pins and push the inner shaft to the neutral position. Move the center shift shaft to the third speed position. The other shafts should not move.

22. Align the forks to the holes in the shafts and install the slotted spring pins.

23. Coat the countergear thrust washers with a grease and place them on the inner walls of the transmission case. Insert the countershaft from the rear of the case until the shaft end is even with the rear thrust washer.

24. Carefully install the countergear and push the countershaft into the transmission case and the countergear bearings. Measure the thrust clearance and correct by selecting a proper sized thrust washer. The thrust clearance should be 0.0020 to 0.0098 inch (0.05 to 0.25 mm).

25. Install the reverse idler gear and shaft. An adjustment can be made to prevent the gear from contacting the case surface. A spacer can be installed between the gear and the case. A clearance of 0.039 to 0.079 inch (1.0 to 2.0 mm) should exist between the teeth of the reverse gear and the teeth of the countergear. A pivot screw and locknut are pro-

Thickness mm	(in.)
1.30-1.35	(0.0512-0.0531)
1.40-1.45	(0.0551-0.0571)
1.50-1.55	(0.0591-0.0610)
1.60-1.65	(0.0630-0.0650)

vided on the case to help in the adjustment of the reverse gear clearance.

26. Set the transmission upright with the output shaft horizontal position and the pan opening down.

27. Install the three balls and springs into the holes in the case top and install the locking ball and spring cover.

28. Install the countergear shaft cover on the front of the transmission case.

29. Shift the fork shafts and be sure the shifting of the gear sleeves, forks and linkage is proper.

Case Assembly: K50

1. Position the mainshaft with the rear of the shaft pointing upward. Install the 2nd speed gear and the synchronizer (baulk) ring onto the shaft, followed by the number one clutch hub and sleeve.

Ring identification: Narrow insert gap for 1st gear and the wide insert gap for the 2nd gear.

2. Install the second synchronizer (baulk) ring, the 1st gear, the locking ball, the needle roller bearing and the bushing.

3. Install the rear bearing and select a selective snap-ring that will allow zero thrust clearance. The snap-ring thicknesses are as follows:

Thickness mm	(in.)
2.05-2.10	(0.0807-0.0827)
2.10-2.15	(0.0827-0.0846)
2.15-2.20	(0.0846-0.0866)
2.20-2.25	(0.0866-0.0886)
2.25-2.30	(0.0886-0.0906)
2.30-2.35	(0.0906-0.0925)
2.35-2.40	(0.0925-0.0945)
2.40-2.45	(0.0945-0.0965)
2.45-2.50	(0.0965-0.0984)
2.50-2.55	(0.0984-0.1004)

Install the snap-ring on the mainshaft in its groove.

4. Check the thrust clearances of the 1st and 2nd gears. The clearances should be as follows:

1st gear—0.0071 to 0.0110 inch (0.18 to 0.28 mm)
2nd gear—0.0039 to 0.0098 inch (0.10 to 0.25 mm)
Limit—0.0118 inch (0.30 mm)

5. Install the 3rd gear onto the front of the shaft and install the synchronizer hub and sleeve, along with the inner synchronizer (baulk) ring in place on the gear unit.

6. Push inward on the number two clutch hub and measure the 3rd gear thrust clearance. The clearance should be as follows:

3rd gear—0.0020 to 0.0079 inch (0.05 to 0.20 mm)
Limit—0.0118 inch (0.30 mm)

Install one of the following spacers as required:

Thickness mm	(in.)
4.30-4.35	(0.1693-0.1713)
4.35-4.40	(0.1713-0.1732)
4.40-4.45	(0.1732-0.1752)

7. Select a snap-ring of proper thickness to provide zero clearance between the snap-ring and the clutch hub, and install on the shaft. A list of available snap-rings are as follows:

Thickness mm	(in.)
2.05-2.10	(0.0807-0.0827)
2.10-2.15	(0.0827-0.0846)
2.15-2.20	(0.0846-0.0866)
2.20-2.25	(0.0866-0.0886)
2.25-2.30	(0.0886-0.0906)
2.30-2.35	(0.0906-0.0925)
2.35-2.40	(0.0925-0.0945)
2.40-2.45	(0.0945-0.0965)

8. Install the mainshaft assembly into the transmission case from the front. Stand the case assembly upright and pull the mainshaft assembly upward, seating the bearing into the case bore, while having the bearing snap-ring expanded in the case. Secure the bearing in the case with the snap-ring.

9. Install the roller bearing and housing on the input shaft, if not previously done. Install the needle bearings in the bore of the input shaft, holding them in place with grease. Place the synchronizer (baulk) ring on the input shaft and install the shaft assembly into the front of the case. Align the shifting key insert slots properly during the installation.

10. Install the front bearing retainer bolts and torque to 11 to 15 ft/lb.

11. Shift the transmission gear train into the 2nd gear. Install the shift forks in their respective sleeve grooves.

12. Install the reverse shift shaft and fork. Install the interlock ball (coated with grease) into the hole in the reverse shift fork. Push it into position into the shaft groove.

13. Position the three shafts into their respective bores in the transmission case and position in the neutral mode, having entered the bores of the shifting forks. Move the 1st/2nd speed shaft until the dummy hole on the shaft is lined up with the case hole. Insert a probe in the hole to be sure the shafts are aligned.

14. Install the grease coated interlock pins and push them into position with a probe. Move the three fork shafts in the neutral position. Shift the number two or center shaft into the 3rd gear position and check that the remaining shafts do not move.

15. Align the pin holes in the shift forks and shift fork shafts and secure with the slotted spring pins.

16. Assemble the countergear and shaft with the thrust washer oil groove facing the countergear side, and install into the transmission case. Install the rear bearing and outer race into position in the case. The outer snap-ring must be expanded during this operation.

17. Install the reverse idler gear and shaft. Have the shift arm engaged with the hub of the reverse idler gear.

18. Install the 5th gear on the countershaft with the stepped side of the gear hub facing the case. Secure the gear to the shaft with a snap-ring of a selected size to provide zero clearance, as taken from the following list:

Thickness mm	(in.)
2.25-2.35	(0.0886-0.0925)
2.35-2.45	(0.0925-0.0965)
2.45-2.55	(0.0965-0.1004)

19. Select a countergear thrust washer by installing a thrust washer in place on the countergear and installing the rear extension housing and torquing the retaining bolts 22 to 32 ft/lbs (3.0 to 4.5 Kg-m) and measuring the thrust clearance of the countergear to case.

NOTE: Position the thrust washer with the oil groove facing the 5th gear.

20. The thrust clearance should be 0.0031 to 0.0157 inch (0.08 to 0.40 mm). Select the proper sized thrust washer from the following list:

Thickness mm	(in.)
1.71-1.81	(0.0673-0.0713)
1.83-1.93	(0.0720-0.0760)
1.95-2.05	(0.0768-0.0807)

21. Remove the extension housing and install the proper thrust washer in place on the counter 5th gear.

22. Align the shifting key insert slots and install the 5th gear and the 5th synchronizer assembly onto the output shaft. Tap the output shaft to the front of the transmission and with a snap-ring retainer pressed against the hub, select a snap-ring to provide a thrust clearance of 0.008 to 0.012 inch (0.2 to 0.3 mm) between the 5th gear hub and the rear bearing face.

23. Install the snap-ring and recheck the thrust clearance. Push up on the reverse idler gear until the fork shaft is in a position with the groove above the case.

24. Install the 5th gearshift arm bracket in place on the rear of the case and engage the bracket in the reverse shaft fork. Position the fork claw in the hub sleeve groove and the

Thickness mm	(in.)
2.05-2.10	(0.0807-0.0827)
2.10-2.15	(0.0827-0.0846)
2.15-2.20	(0.0846-0.0866)
2.20-2.25	(0.0866-0.0886)
2.25-2.30	(0.0886-0.0906)
2.30-2.35	(0.0906-0.0925)
2.35-2.40	(0.0925-0.0945)
2.40-2.45	(0.0945-0.0965)
2.45-2.50	(0.0965-0.0984)
2.50-2.55	(0.0984-0.1004)
2.55-2.60	(0.1004-0.1024)
2.60-2.65	(0.1024-0.1043)
2.65-2.70	(0.1043-0.1063)
2.70-2.75	(0.1063-0.1083)
2.75-2.80	(0.1083-0.1102)

shift arm shaft in the gearshift head 1st groove.

25. Install the three locking balls and springs in the bores of the case. Install the cover and the retaining bolts.

26. Install the inner snap-ring, the speedometer drive gear and the outer snap-ring on the mainshaft. Be sure the locking ball is placed between the gear and the shaft.

27. Adjust the reverse idler gear position so that a clearance of 0.039 to 0.079 inch (1.0 to 2.0 mm) exists between the gear teeth of the countergear and the reverse idler gear teeth by the adjustment of the pivot bolt and locknut, located on the outside of the case.

28. Adjust the 5th speed synchronizer sleeve position so that the bottom of the sleeve groove is 0.039 to 0.059 inch (1.0 to 1.5 mm) above the rear face of the counter 5th gear.

K40, K50

1. Install the thrust washer on the counter 5th gear with the oil groove towards the gear side. (K50). Install the rear gaskets.

2. Align the shifting fork shafts in the neutral position and install the rear extension housing. Engage the selector shaft to the shift fork shafts. Install the housing retaining bolts and torque to 22-32 ft/lbs.

3. Install the shift control restricting pins and torque to the following values:

K40—Black = 1st and 2nd
White = Reverse
K50—Black = 1st and 2nd
White = 5th and Reverse
All—27 to 31 ft/lbs (3.7 to 4.3 Kg-m)

4. Install the speedometer driven gear assembly.

5. Install the back-up light switch.

6. Install the clutch release bearing, fork, boot and spring.

7. Install the bottom cover and gasket. Fill the transmission with lubricant to its proper level.

8. Attach the shift lever and make sure the shifting of the gear train is proper.

TYPE 33

4 and 5 Speed Transmissions–Models T-40, T-50

1975-81 Toyota Corolla

DISASSEMBLY

CAUTION

The clutch housing, split transmission case, and extension housing are all made of aluminum.

1. Drain the oil.
2. Remove the clutch housing, bearing retainer, release bearing, and release fork.
3. Remove the speedometer shaft sleeve and driven gear.
4. Remove the extension housing.
5. Remove the back-up light switch.
6. Separate the case halves. Do not pry apart.
7. Measure gear backlash. The backlash for all gears should be 0.004-0.008 in.
8. Remove the countergear set from the right-hand half of the case.
9. Use a magnet to remove the ball from the second countergear bearing.
10. Withdraw the input and the output shafts as a unit.
11. Use a punch to drive the three slotted spring pins out of the shift forks and shift fork shafts.

NOTE: The slotted pin cannot always be fully removed from the first/second shift fork; however, the shift fork can still be withdrawn. Do not try to force the pin out, as damage to the transmission case could result.

12. Remove the case cover and the three detent balls and springs.
13. Remove the shift fork shafts in the following order:
    a. First/second shaft
    b. Pin
    c. Reverse shift fork shaft
    d. Third/fourth shaft
    e. Pin
14. Measure the thrust clearance of the reverse idler gear. The specified clearance is 0.002-0.020 in.
15. Remove the idler shaft. Remove the gear and washer.
16. Measure the thrust clearance of the gears on the output shaft.

1st, 2nd, 5th	0.006-0.010 in.
3rd	0.006-0.012 in.
Reverse	0.008-0.012 in.

5th gear is optional

17. Disassemble the components of the output shaft. Five-speed transmissions have an extra gearset and related parts.

Replace the front bearing, if it is rough or noisy. Use a drift and a press. Remove the snap-ring first.

For bearing installation, replacement snap-rings are available in a range of sizes (0.0925-0.1024 in.) to obtain *minimum* axial play between the input shaft and the bearing.

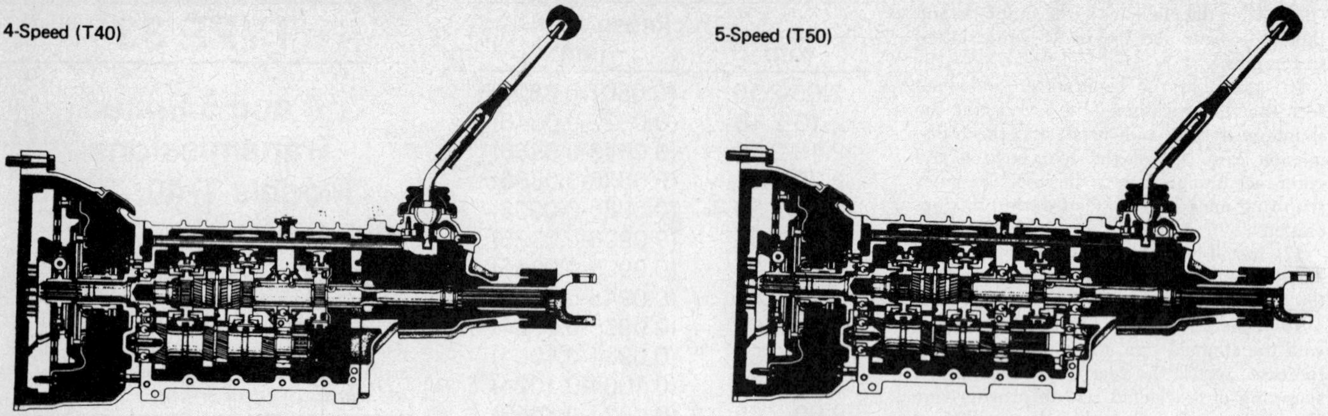

Cross section of models T 40 and T 50 transmissions

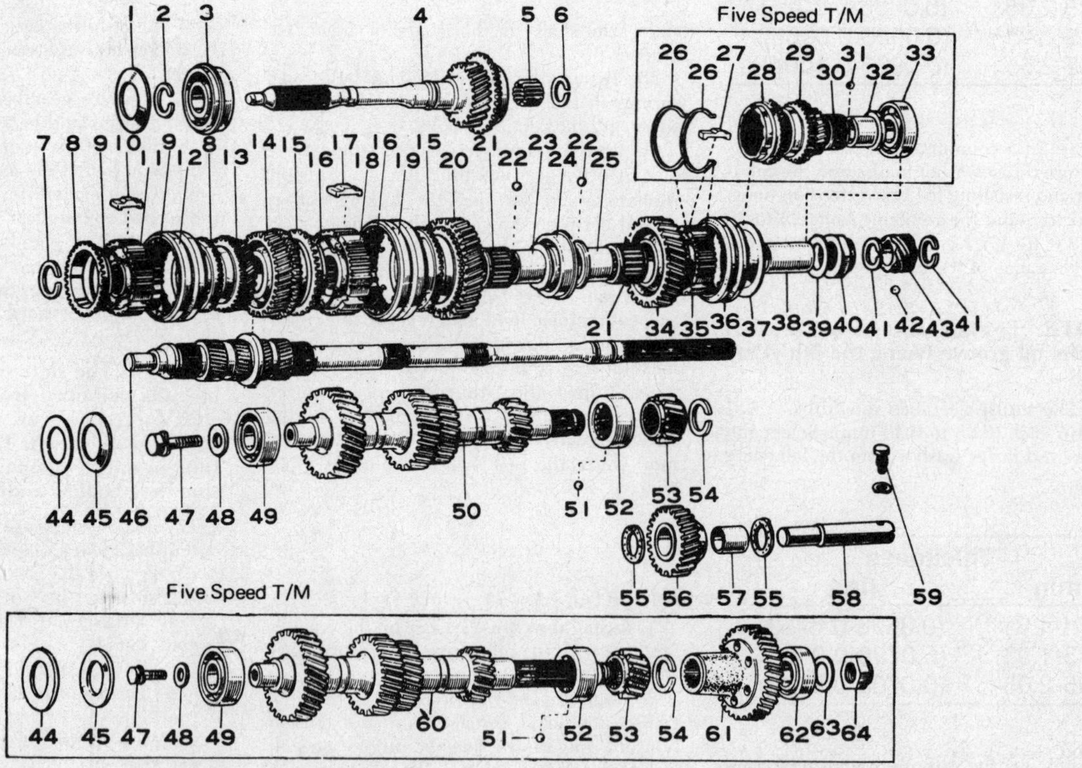

1. Conical spring
2. Shaft snap-ring
3. Ball bearing
4. Input shaft
5. Roller
6. Snap-ring
7. Shaft snap-ring
8. Synchronizer ring
9. Shift-key spring
10. Shift-key
11. Clutch hub
12. Hub sleeve
13. Third gear assembly
14. Second gear assembly
15. Synchronizer ring
16. Shift-key spring
17. Shift-key
18. Clutch hub
19. Hub sleeve
20. First gear assembly
21. Needle roller bearing
22. Ball
23. First gear bushing
24. Ball bearing
25. Reverse gear bushing
26. Shift-key spring*
27. Shift-key*
28. Synchronizer ring*
29. Fifth gear assembly*
30. Needle roller bearing*
31. Ball*
32. Fifth gear bushing*
33. Ball bearing*
34. Reverse gear
35. Clutch hub
36. Hub sleeve
37. Spacer
38. Spacer (long)
39. Shim
40. Nut
41. Shaft snap-ring
42. Ball
43. Speedometer drive gear
44. Shim
45. Conical spring
46. Output shaft
47. Bolt and washer
48. Plate washer
49. Ball bearing
50. Countergear
51. Ball
52. Roller bearing
53. Reverse countergear
54. Snap-ring
55. Thrust washer—reverse idler gear
56. Reverse idler gear
57. Bushing
58. Reverse idler gear shaft
59. Shaft retaining bolt
60. Countergear*
61. Fifth-speed countergear*
62. Ball bearing*
63. Shim*
64. Nut*

* Five-speed transmission only

Corolla and Carina 4 and 5-speed transmission components

ASSEMBLY

1. Assemble the components of the synchronizer hubs, and the output shaft.
2. Install the rear bushing on the output shaft, being careful to install it in the proper direction.
3. Install the ball into the groove of the bushing and slide the bushing over the shaft.
4. Install the needle roller bearing, reverse gear, the ball and the reverse gear synchronizer hub.
5. Install the following items on the output shaft of the four-speed transmission, in the order indicated:
    a. Large-diameter reverse gear spacer
    b. Long spacer
    c. Shims
6. Install the following items on the output shaft of the five-speed transmission in the order indicated:
    a. Ball
    b. Fifth gear synchronizer ring
    c. Fifth gear
    d. Needle roller bearing
    e. Bushing
    f. Rear support ball bearing.
7. Install the shims and the nut on the end of the output shaft.

NOTE: If the original nut is being used, change the number of shims to alter the locking portion of the nut.

8. Check the thrust clearance of each gear.
9. Working from the rear of the output shaft, install 3rd gear, synchronizer, spacer, and 3rd/4th synchronizer hub (should face forward).
10. Select a snap-ring to obtain a thrust clearance of less than 0.002 in. for the 3rd/4th synchronizer hub.
11. Assemble the following from the rear of the output shaft:
    a. Snap-ring
    b. Key
    c. Speedometer drive gear
    d. Snap-ring
12. Check thrust clearance of gears.
13. Install the fork and shaft assembly in the transmission case.
14. Insert the straight pins in the grooves on either side of the third/fourth shift shaft.
15. Assemble the first/second gear shaft and fork.
16. Perform Step 11 for the reverse shift fork shaft.
17. Insert the three detent balls, followed by their springs.
18. Place the cover gasket on the case and install the cover.
19. Use a punch to drive a slotted spring pin into each shift fork to secure it.
20. Assemble the input and output shafts.
21. Install the shift forks into their respective grooves on the input/output shaft assembly.
22. Install the shaft assembly in the right-hand half of the transmission case, so that the snap-ring is positioned firmly against the front surface of the transmission case.
23. Apply grease to the countergear rear bearing lockball. Insert the ball into the hole in the rear bearing outer race.
24. Place the countergear assembly into the right-hand half of the transmission case. Mate the lockball with the hole in the transmission case. Place the bearing snap-ring firmly against the front surface of the transmission case.
25. Install the reverse idler gear.
26. Install the washers, so that their protrusions align with the grooves in the transmission case.
27. Install the shaft into the case and through the gears and washers.
28. Align the grooves in the idler shaft with the hole in the shaft boss. Install the retaining bolt and washer into the boss.
29. Apply a light coating of liquid sealer over the joint surfaces of the transmission case halves.

CAUTION

Do not apply sealer to the ½ in. hole for the back-up light switch.

30. Align the transmission case locating pins with their holes and assemble the halves of the case.

NOTE: There are four different bolt lengths, do not install the wrong bolt in the wrong hole.

31. Insert the ball, spring, and washer in the back-up light switch hole. Screw in the switch assembly.
32. Install the gasket and bolt the extension housing to the rear of the transmission.
33. Install the speedometer shaft sleeve and drive gear.
34. Apply grease to the conical springs. Install one spring over the input shaft bearing and the other over the countershaft bearing. Install the spacer over the countershaft bearing spring, after coating the spacer with grease.
35. Install the gasket and the clutch housing.

TYPE 34

4 Speed Transmission–Model W-40

1975-81 Toyota Celica
1975-81 Toyota Corona

DISASSEMBLY

1. Drain the oil.
2. Remove the clutch housing, with the release fork, bearing and hub still attached.
3. Remove the back-up light switch.
4. Remove the gearshift lever retainer.
5. Rotate the shift rod housing counterclockwise (viewed from behind) and then disconnect the rod from the shift fork shafts.
6. Unbolt and remove the extension housing.
7. Drive out the slotted pin and separate the shift rod, housing and spring.
8. Remove the front bearing retainer.
9. Take off both of the front countershaft covers and the spacer.
10. Remove the snap-rings from the input and countershaft bearings.
11. Remove the intermediate plate.
12. When removing the intermediate plate, leave all of the gears and other parts attached.
13. Remove the speedometer driven gear.
14. Punch the slotted pin out of the reverse shift arm bracket bolt and remove the bracket, complete with the shift arm.
15. Remove the reverse idler shaft stop and withdraw the idler gear and shaft assembly away from the intermediate plate.
16. Remove the output shaft rear bearing retainer.
17. Remove the screw plug and spring from each shift fork and shaft.
18. Drive the slotted interlock pins out of each shaft.
19. Remove the shift fork shafts in the following order:
    a. Reverse
    b. First/second
    c. Third/fourth

Once the shafts have been removed, slide the shift forks off them.

20. Remove the snap-ring from the output shaft rear bearing. Push the output shaft and countershaft out as an assembly, working from the rear side of the plate.
21. Separate the input shaft and the front synchronizer ring from the output shaft.
22. Remove the hub and synchronizer ring, followed by third gear.
23. Press off the rear bearing.
24. Remove the following items from the output shaft, in the order listed:
    a. First gear
    b. Roller bearing with inner race
    c. Synchronizer ring
    d. Reverse gear
    e. Clutch hub
    f. Second gear
    g. Synchronizer ring

ASSEMBLY

1. Apply a thin coating of gear oil to all rotating or sliding surfaces, prior to assembly.
2. Assemble the 3rd/4th synchronizer hub:
    a. Install key springs in the hub.
    b. Place the 3 keys in the hub slots.
    c. Install the 2nd clutch hub in the sleeve.

To maintain uniform spring pressure, keep the open end of the key springs 120° apart.

3. Assemble the synchronizer ring to third gear, and fit both of them on the output shaft.
4. Insert the third/fourth synchronizer hub on the output shaft, until it contacts the shoulder of the shaft.
5. Select a snap-ring to provide 0.002 in. axial play for the synchronizer hub and fit it onto the shaft. Snap-rings are available in a range of sizes.
6. Measure third gear thrust clearance with a feeler gauge. The clearance should be 0.004-0.010 in. Replace third gear if the clearance exceeds the limit of 0.012 in.
7. Install the synchronizer ring for second gear to the gear and install the assembly on the output shaft.

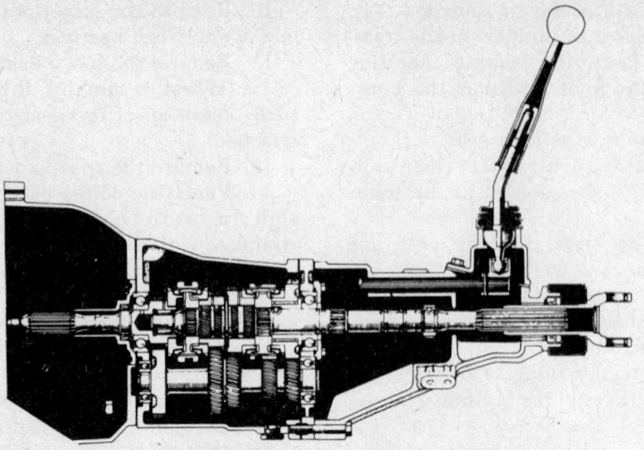

Cross section of model W 40 transmission

8. Install the reverse gear over its clutch hub.

9. Install the reverse gear and hub on the output shaft so that they contact the shoulder.

10. Measure second gear thrust clearance; it should be between 0.004-0.010 in. Replace the gear if the clearance is more than 0.012 in.

11. Coat the locking ball with grease. Insert it, and the roller bearing inner race, on the output shaft.

12. Assemble first gear with its synchronizer ring, bearing and bearing inner race. Install them on the output shaft, so that the end of the inner race contacts the clutch hub and the groove on the inner race aligns with the locking ball.

13. Press the rear bearing onto the output shaft.

14. Measure first gear thrust clearance; it should be 0.004-0.010 in. Replace the gear if the clearance exceeds 0.012 in.

15. Select a snap-ring for the rear output shaft bearing that will provide 0.002 in. axial play for it.

16. Use a press to insert the straight pin into the intermediate plate, until it protrudes ¼-5/16 in. from the cover front side.

17. Coat the roller bearing with grease and install it over the input shaft.

18. Apply gear oil to the front synchronizer ring on the output shaft.

19. Assemble the output shaft and the input shaft.

20. Assemble the output shaft and countergear, then fit them through the holes in the intermediate plate. Push them in until the snap-ring sticks out beyond the plate. Install the snap-ring and then push the shafts back until the snap-ring is flush with the intermediate plate.

21. Install the shaft through the reverse idler gear. Insert the end of the shaft into the end of the intermediate plate.

22. Install the spacer on the idler shaft and secure it with a snap-ring.

23. Install the idler shaft stop.

24. Install the first/second and third/fourth shift forks into the grooves on the hub sleeves, so that the longer parts of their bosses face each other.

25. Assemble the ends of the three shift fork shafts and insert them into the intermediate plate. Install the interlock pins, after coating them with grease.

26. Install the shafts through the forks and drive in the slotted spring pins to secure them.

27. Insert the lockballs, followed by their springs.

28. Install the output shaft rear bearing retainer.

NOTE: There should be zero clearance between the rear bearing snap-ring and the surface of the intermediate plate.

29. Assemble the reverse shift arm to its bracket. Install on the intermediate cover.

30. Drive the slotted mounting pin in, so that it protrudes 0.08-0.16 in. beyond the intermediate cover.

31. Shift the gears so that reverse is selected. Check the gear contact. If the gears are meshing properly, the front face of the idler gear will align with the front face of the reverse gear.

32. If necessary, adjust the gear mesh at the pivot.

NOTE: When the gears are meshing properly, the slot in the pivot should be perpendicular to the intermediate plate.

33. Tighten the pivot nut and install the lockpin. Be careful not to change gear contact.

34. Install the shift rod from the front end of the extension housing. Install the spring and housing onto the end of the shift rod.

35. Clean the gasket surfaces of the rear

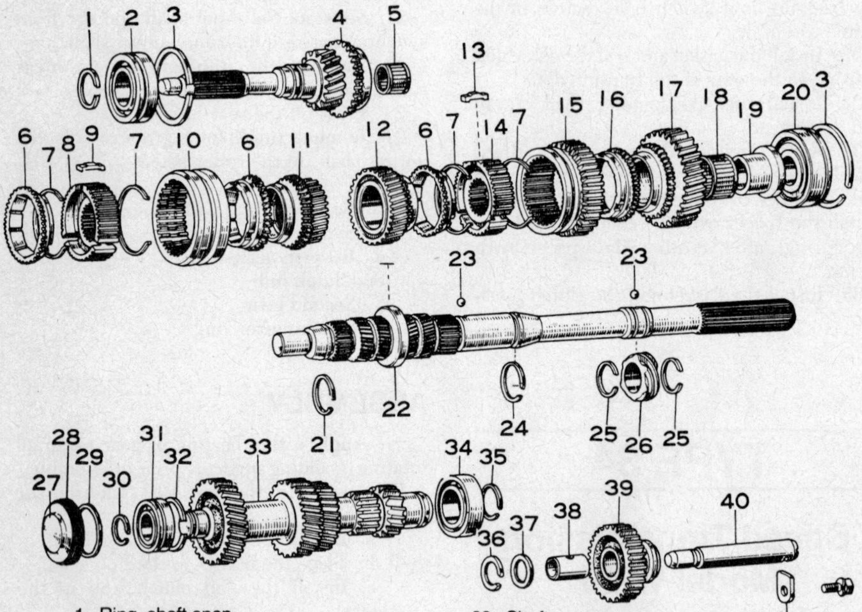

1. Ring, shaft snap
2. Bearing, radial ball
3. Ring, shaft snap
4. Shaft subassy., input
5. Bearing, needle roller
6. Ring, synchronizer, No. 2
7. Spring, synchromesh shifting key
8. Hub, transmission clutch, No. 2
9. Key, synchromesh shifting, No. 2
10. Spring, transmission hub, No. 2
11. Gear subassy., third
12. Gear subassy., second
13. Key, synchromesh shifting, No. 1
14. Hub, transmission clutch, No. 1
15. Gear, reverse
16. Ring, synchronizer, No. 1
17. Gear subassy., first
18. Bearing, needle roller
19. Race, first gear bearing inner
20. Bearing, radial ball
21. Ring, shaft snap
22. Shaft, output
23. Ball, reverse shaft restrict
24. Ring, shaft snap
25. Ring, shaft snap
26. Gear, speedometer drive
27. Cover, counter shaft, No. 1
28. Cover, counter shaft, No. 2
29. Spacer
30. Ring, shaft snap
31. Bearing, radial ball
32. Ring, shaft snap
33. Gear, counter
34. Bearing, radial ball
35. Ring, shaft snap
36. Ring, shaft snap
37. Spacer
38. Bushing, bimetal formed
39. Gear, reverse idler
40. Shaft, reverse idler
41. Stopper, reverse idler gear shaft

Exploded view of model W 40 gear train

cover and transmission case. Install the intermediate plate.

36. Install the input shaft and countergear front bearing snap-rings.

37. Install the extension housing and gasket over the intermediate cover, after cleaning both gasket mounting surfaces.

38. Screw the securing bolts through the extension housing, the intermediate cover and into the transmission case.

39. Install the reverse restrictor pin and gasket.

40. Push the countergear rearward, as far as it will go and measure the distance (E) in the illustration. Select a spacer to yield the *minimum* clearance which is closest to the measurement obtained.

41. Install the spacer and then the countershaft end covers.

42. Align the front bearing retainer gasket with the oil holes. Install the bearing retainer over the gasket.

43. Bolt the clutch housing onto the front of the transmission case.

44. Attach the shift lever retainer to the extension housing.

45. Install the speedometer driven gear.

46. Install the back-up light switch.

TYPE 35

5 Speed Transmission–Model W-50 Model P-51

1975-81 Toyota Celica
1975-81 Toyota Corona
1975-76 Toyota Celica (RA-28)

DISASSEMBLY

NOTE: The Model P-51 transmission disassembly and assembly, is basically the same as the W-50 transmission, with only minor variations.

1. Drain the oil.

2. Remove the clutch housing, with the release fork, bearing and hub still attached.

3. Remove the back-up light switch.

4. Remove the gearshift lever retainer.

5. Rotate the shift rod housing counterclockwise (viewed from behind) and then disconnect the rod from the shift fork shafts.

6. Unbolt and remove the extension housing.

7. Drive out the slotted pin and separate the shift rod, housing and spring.

8. Remove the front bearing retainer.

9. Take off both of the front countershaft covers, and the spacer.

10. Remove the snap-rings from the input and countershaft bearings.

11. Remove the intermediate plate.

12. When removing the intermediate plate, leave all the gears and other parts attached.

13. Remove the speedometer driven gear.

NOTE: There are two reverse restrictor pins. The pins are located underneath plugs on the extension housing.

14. Remove the straight screw plugs from the shift forks and withdraw the springs.

15. Drive the slotted spring pins out of each shift fork.

16. Slide the gear shift fork shafts back and remove the forks.

17. Remove the speedometer drive gear snap-ring and remove the drive gear.

18. Remove the output shaft bearing.

19. Remove the countershaft bearing.

20. Remove the fifth and reverse gears from the countershaft.

21. Remove the snap-ring, fifth gear, its synchronizer ring, needle roller bearing, and fifth gear bearing inner race from the output shaft.

22. Remove the reverse gear and clutch hub from the output shaft.

23. Loosen the bolt and remove the reverse idler gear stop from the rear cover. Withdraw the reverse idler shaft from the rear; remove the reverse idler gear and spacer.

24. Remove the output shaft rear bearing retainer. Remove the rear bearing snap-ring.

25. Push the countergear bearing outer race rearward, and remove the bearing. Separate the countergear from the intermediate plate.

26. Separate the input shaft and synchronizer ring from the output shaft.

27. Remove the output shaft from the intermediate plate.

28. Remove the hub and synchronizer ring, followed by third gear.

29. Press off the rear bearing.

30. Remove the following items from the output shaft, in the order listed:

  a. First gear
  b. Roller bearing with inner race
  c. Synchronizer ring
  d. Reverse gear
  e. Clutch hub
  f. Second gear
  g. Synchronizer ring

ASSEMBLY

1. Install the sleeve over the third gear synchronizer hub. Insert the three shift keys into the hub and sleeve keyways install the hub two springs.

2. Assemble the synchronizer ring to third gear, and fit both of them on the output shaft.

3. Insert the third/fourth synchronizer hub on the output shaft, until it contacts the shoulder of the shaft.

4. Select a snap-ring to provide 0.002 in. axial play for the synchronizer hub and fit it onto the shaft. Snap-rings are available in a range of sizes.

5. Measure third gear thrust clearance with a feeler gauge. The clearance should be 0.004-0.010 in. Replace third gear if the clearance exceeds the limit of 0.010 in.

6. Install the synchronizer ring for second gear to the gear and install the assembly on the output shaft.

7. Install the reverse gear over its clutch hub.

8. Install the reverse gear and hub on the output shaft so that they contact the shoulder.

9. Measure second gear thrust clearance; it should be between 0.004-0.010 in. Replace the gear if the clearance is more than 0.010 in.

10. Coat the locking ball with grease. Insert it, and the roller bearing inner race, on the output shaft.

11. Assemble first gear with its synchronizer ring, bearing and bearing inner

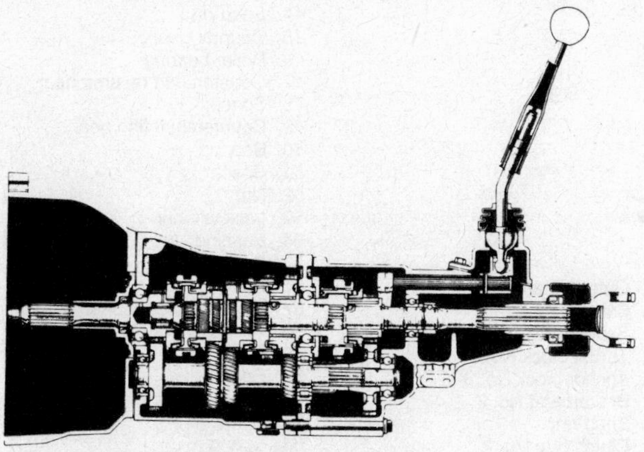

Cross section of model W 50 transmission

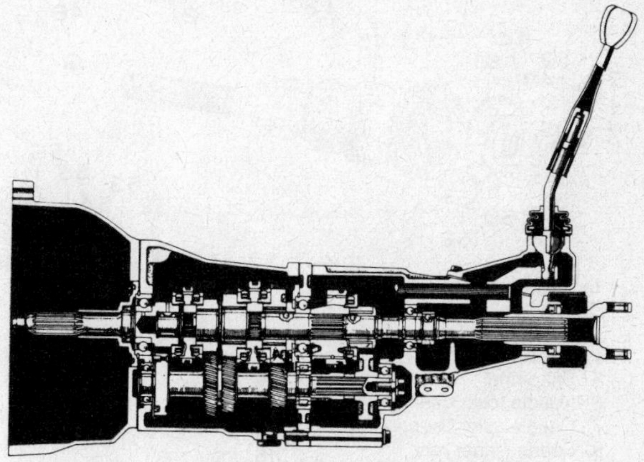

Cross section of model P-51 transmission

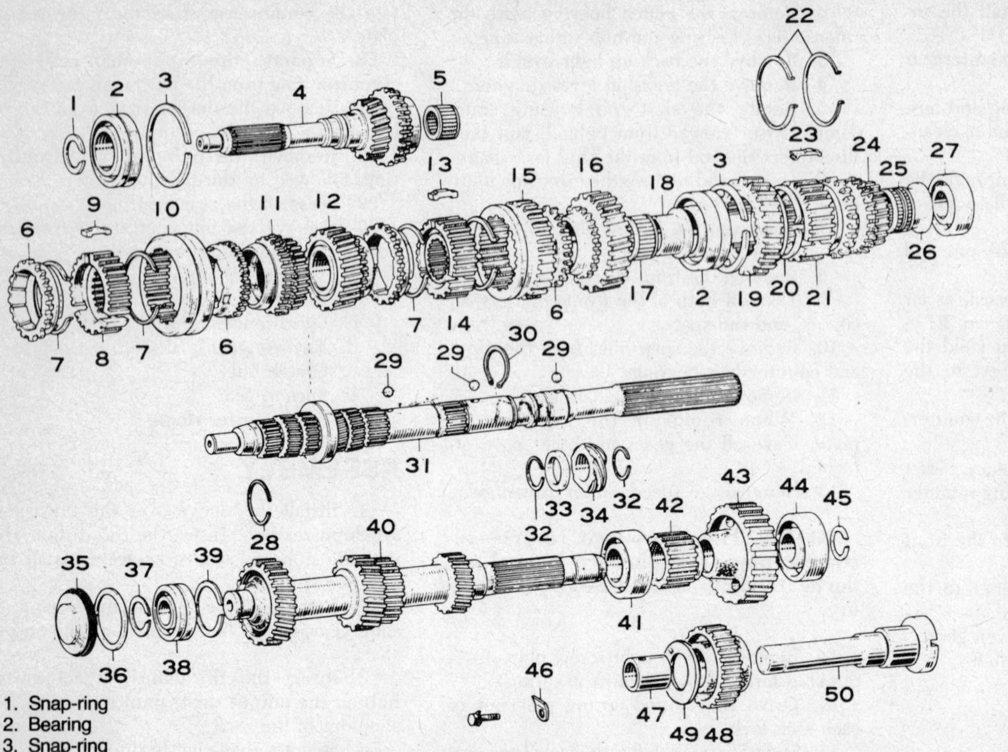

1. Snap-ring
2. Bearing
3. Snap-ring
4. Input shaft
5. Bearing
6. Synchronizer ring, No. 2
7. Synchromesh shifting key spring
8. Transmission clutch hub, No. 2
9. Synchromesh shifting key, No. 2
10. Transmission hub sleeve, No. 2
11. Third gear
12. Second gear sub-assembly
13. Synchromesh shifting key, No. 1
14. Transmission clutch hub, No. 1
15. Reverse gear
16. First gear
17. Bearing
18. First gear bearing inner race
19. Reverse gear
20. Snap-ring
21. Transmission clutch hub, No. 3
22. Synchromesh shifting key spring
23. Synchromesh shifting key, No. 3
24. Fifth gear
25. Bearing
26. Fifth gear bushing
27. Bearing
28. Snap-ring
29. Ball
30. Snap-ring
31. Output shaft
32. Snap-ring
33. Spacer
34. Speedometer drive gear
35. Countershaft cover
36. Spacer
37. Snap-ring
38. Bearing
39. Snap-ring
40. Counter gear
41. Bearing
42. Countershaft reverse gear
43. Countershaft fifth gear
44. Bearing
45. Snap-ring
46. Stopper
47. Bimetal formed bushing
48. Reverse idler gear
49. Reverse idler gear shaft spacer
50. Reverse idler gear shaft

Exploded view of gear train, model W 50 transmission

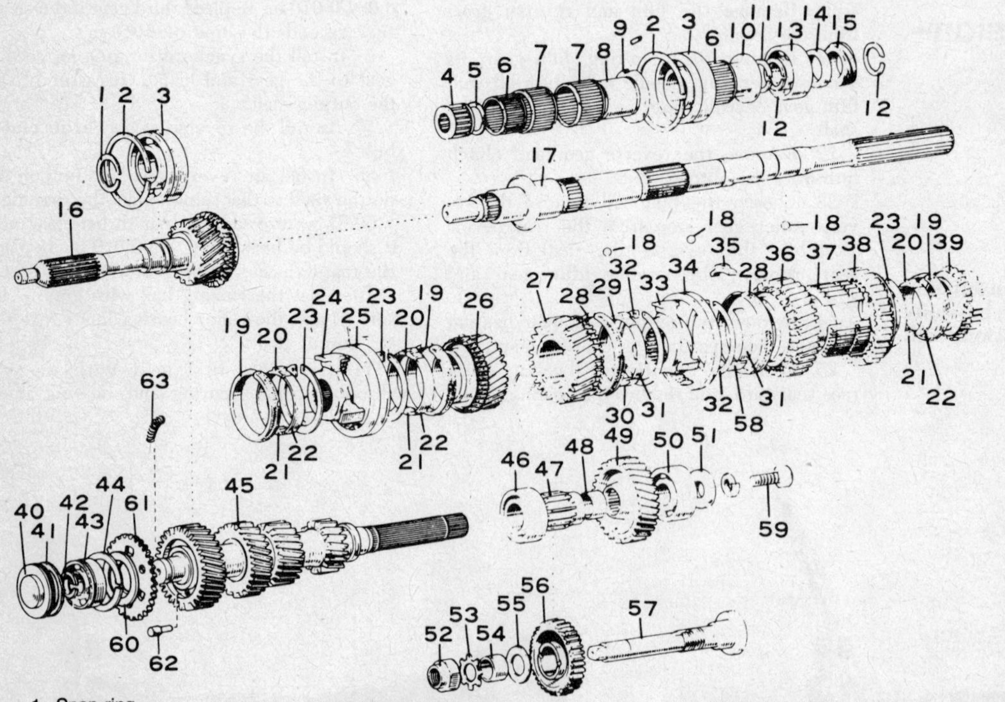

1. Snap-ring
2. Snap-ring
3. Bearing
4. Needle roller bearing
5. Snap-ring
6. Needle roller bearing
7. Needle roller bearing
8. Bearing inner race
9. Thrust washer
10. Bearing inner race
11. Snap-ring
12. Snap-ring
13. Bearing
14. Spacer
15. Speedometer drive gear
16. Input shaft
17. Output shaft
18. Ball
19. Synchronizer ring No. 2
20. Thrust block No. 3
21. Anchor block No. 3
22. Brake band No. 2
23. Snap-ring
24. Clutch hub No. 2
25. Hub sleeve No. 2
26. Third gear
27. Second gear
28. Synchronizer ring No. 1
29. Thrust block No. 2
30. Anchor block No. 2
31. Brake band No. 1
32. Snap-ring
33. Clutch hub No. 1
34. Hub sleeve No. 1
35. Thrust block No. 1
36. First gear
37. Clutch hub No. 3
38. Reverse gear
39. Fifth gear
40. Countershaft cover
41. Spacer
42. Snap-ring
43. Bearing
44. Snap-ring
45. Counter gear
46. Roller bearing
47. Countershaft reverse gear
48. Spacer
49. Countershaft fifth gear
50. Bearing
51. Spacer
52. Nut
53. Lock washer
54. Bushing
55. Spacer
56. Reverse idler gear
57. Reverse idler gear shaft
58. Anchor block No. 1
59. Bolt
60. Spacer
61. Counter gear plate
62. Pin
63. Spring

Exploded view of gear train, model P-51 transmission

race. Install them on the output shaft, so that the end of the inner race contacts the clutch hub and the groove on the inner race aligns with the locking ball.

12. Press the rear bearing onto the output shaft.

13. Measure first gear thrust clearance.

NOTE: The thrust clearance of all gears in the W-50 5-speed transmission should be between 0.006-0.010 in.; the thrust clearance limit for all gears is 0.012 in.

14. Use a press to insert the straight pin into the intermediate plate, until it protrudes $1/4$-$5/16$ in. from the cover front side.

15. Install the output shaft on the intermediate plate.

16. Coat the roller bearing with grease and install it over the input shaft.

17. Apply gear oil to the front synchronizer ring on the output shaft.

18. Assemble the output shaft and the input shaft.

19. Install the countergear on the intermediate plate.

20. Install the cylindrical roller bearing into the intermediate plate, and then install the spacer.

21. Assemble the output shaft and countergear, then fit them through the holes in the intermediate plate. Push them in until the snap-ring sticks out beyond the intermediate plate. Install the snap-ring and then push the shafts back until the snap-ring is flush with the intermediate plate surface.

22. Install the shaft through the reverse idler gear. Insert the end of the shaft into the end of the intermediate plate.

23. Install the spacer on the idler shaft and secure it with a snap-ring.

24. Lock the reverse idler shaft on the intermediate plate with its stop. Check the reverse idler gear thrust clearance, it should be 0.006-0.010 in.

25. Install the reverse clutch hub on the reverse gear.

26. Install the three shift keys into the hub keyways and secure them with the two springs and a snap-ring.

27. Slide the reverse gear hub over the output shaft until it registers against the inner race of the intermediate plate bearing.

28. Insert the inner race lockball into the output shaft bore, after greasing it so that it can't fall out.

29. Assemble fifth gear, its synchronizer ring, needle roller bearing, and race. Slide the assembly onto the output shaft until the inner bear face rests against the reverse clutch hub. Be sure that the inner race groove is aligned with the lockball.

30. Secure fifth gear with a snap-ring.

31. Measure fifth gear thrust clearance; it should be 0.004 to 0.010 in. The thrust clearance limit is 0.012 in.

32. Install the countershaft reverse gear so that it just rests against the bearing inner race. Install the countershaft fifth gear and then install the countershaft bearing with a brass drift.

33. Install a snap-ring on the countershaft; select a snap-ring from one of the four available sizes.

34. Install a snap-ring on the output shaft, and drive its bearing into place with a brass drift. Coat the bearing with grease first.

35. Install the spacer, ball, and speedometer drive gear on the output shaft.

36. Install the three shift forks in their hub sleeve grooves. Install the first and third shift fork shafts and secure them with their interlock pins. Install the second shift fork shaft next.

NOTE: Place each shift fork shaft in Neutral during assembly.

37. Secure the shift fork shafts to the end cover by inserting the lockballs into their bores, followed by the lockball springs.

38. Use a new gasket between the transmission case and the intermediate plate. Slide the case into place.

39. Fit snap-rings on the input shaft and countershaft front bearings.

40. Install the shift lever housing on the end of the shifter shaft. Slide the shifter shaft into the extension housing and secure it with a slotted spring pin.

41. Install a new gasket and slide the extension housing into place, until there is about an inch of clearance between it and the intermediate plate.

42. Rotate the shift lever housing clockwise (as viewed from the rear) to engage the shifter

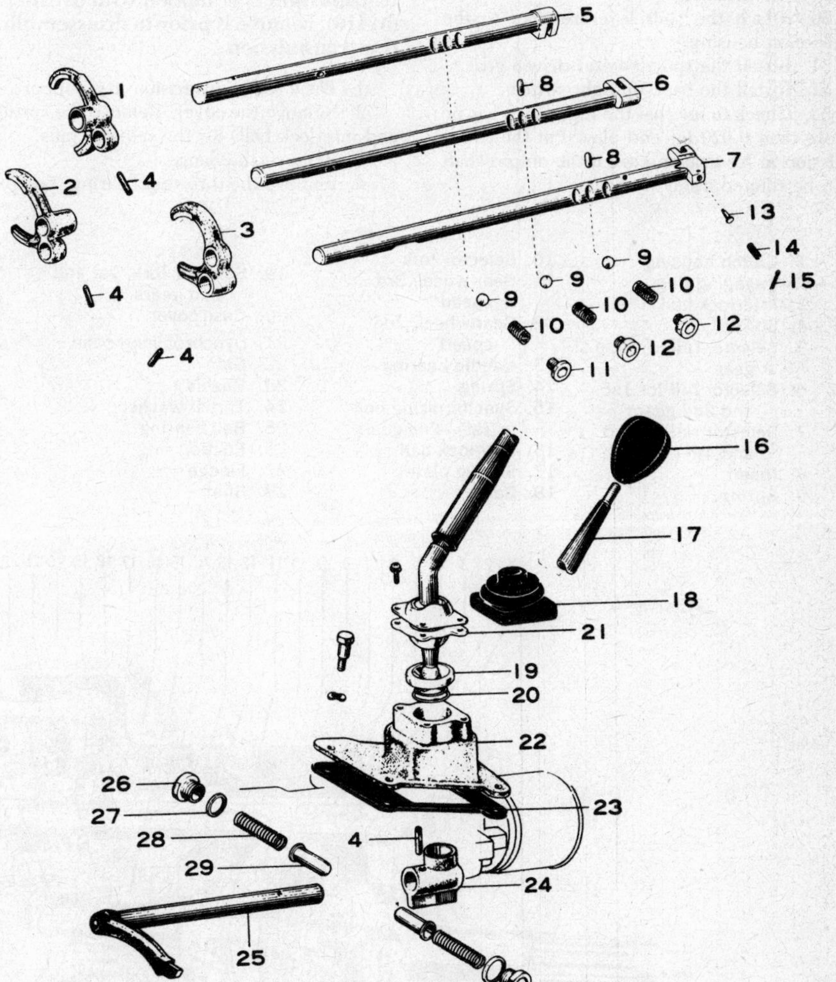

1. Gear shift fork, No. 2
2. Gear shift fork, No. 1
3. Gear shift fork, No. 3
4. Slotted spring pin
5. Gear shift fork shaft, No. 1
6. Gear shift fork shaft, No. 2
7. Gear shift fork shaft, No. 3
8. Shift interlock pin
9. Ball
10. Compression spring
11. Plug
12. Plug
13. Reverse restrict pin
14. Compression spring
15. Cotter pin
16. Shift lever knob sub-assembly
17. Shift lever
18. Shift and select lever boot
19. Transmission shift lever ball seat
20. Conical spring
21. Control shift lever retainer gasket, No. 2
22. Control shift lever retainer
23. Extension housing oil baffle
24. Shift lever housing
25. Shift lever shaft, No. 1
26. Plug
27. Gasket
28. Compression spring
29. Restrict pin

Exploded view of model W 50 shift linkage—typical of model P-51

shaft with the selector lever and the shift fork shaft.

43. Slide the extension housing the rest of the way.

44. Install the spacer and then the countershaft end covers.

45. Align the front bearing retainer gasket with the oil holes. Install the bearing retainer over the gasket.

46. Bolt the clutch housing onto the front of the transmission case.

47. Fit the restrictor pins and springs into their extension housing bores.

48. Install the shift lever retainer over the oil baffle on the extension housing.

49. Install the shift lever conical spring, large side down, and install the ball seat in the shift lever retainer.

50. Attach the shift lever retainer to the extension housing.

51. Install the speedometer driven gear.

52. Install the back-up light switch.

53. Check to see that the input shaft has no more than 0.020 in. end-play. Put the transmission in Neutral and see if the output shaft can be rotated freely by hand.

TYPE 36

4 Speed Transmission–Models M-400 (4 spd.) M-410 (4 spd. w/OD)

1975 Volvo 164

DISASSEMBLY

NOTE: The following procedure applies to units without overdrive. If the transmission is equipped with overdrive (M410), remove it prior to disassembling the transmission.

1. Place the transmission in a support.
2. Remove the cover. Remove the springs and interlock balls for the selector rails.
3. Remove the flange.
4. Remove the throwout bearing. Remove the cover for the input shaft. Remove the clutch housing.
5. Turn the transmission upside down. Using an internal, expanding bearing puller, pull out the front bearing for the intermediate shaft. Remove the rear cover, and pull out the rear bearing for the intermediate shaft.
6. Return the transmission to its normal position, taking care not to damage the teeth of the intermediate shaft as the shaft drops to the bottom of the transmission.
7. Remove the bolts for the selector forks. Push the selector rails backward and drive out the tensioning pin in the flange of the selector rails. Push out the selector rails, taking care not to jam them onto the selector forks. Remove the forks.
8. Remove the speedometer gear. Remove the rear bearing for the mainshaft on the M400 transmission with internal, expanding puller SVO 2828. If the bearing remains lodged in the case, push the mainshaft forward until the drive and synchronizers are positioned against the intermediate shaft drive. For the overdrive (M410) transmission, remove the bolt in SVO 2828 and install puller

1. Clutch housing
2. Engaging ring
3. Interlock ball
4. Spring
5. Selector rail, reverse gear
6. Selector rail for 1st and 2nd gears
7. Selector rail for 3rd and 4th gears
8. Insert
9. Spring
10. Selector fork
11. Gear wheel, 3rd speed
12. Gear wheel, 2nd speed
13. Needle bearing
14. Spring
15. Synchronizing hub, 1st—2nd gears
16. Interlock ball
17. Sliding plate
18. Gate
19. Selector fork, 1st and 2nd gears
20. Case cover
21. Synchronizing cone
22. Gate
23. Bushing
24. Thrust washer
25. Ball bearing
26. Friction ring
27. Flange
28. Shaft
29. Bushing
30. Gear lever knob
31. Gear lever, upper section
32. Rubber bushing
33. Rubber bushing
34. Gear lever, lower section
35. Washer
36. Cover
37. Spring
38. Protective casing

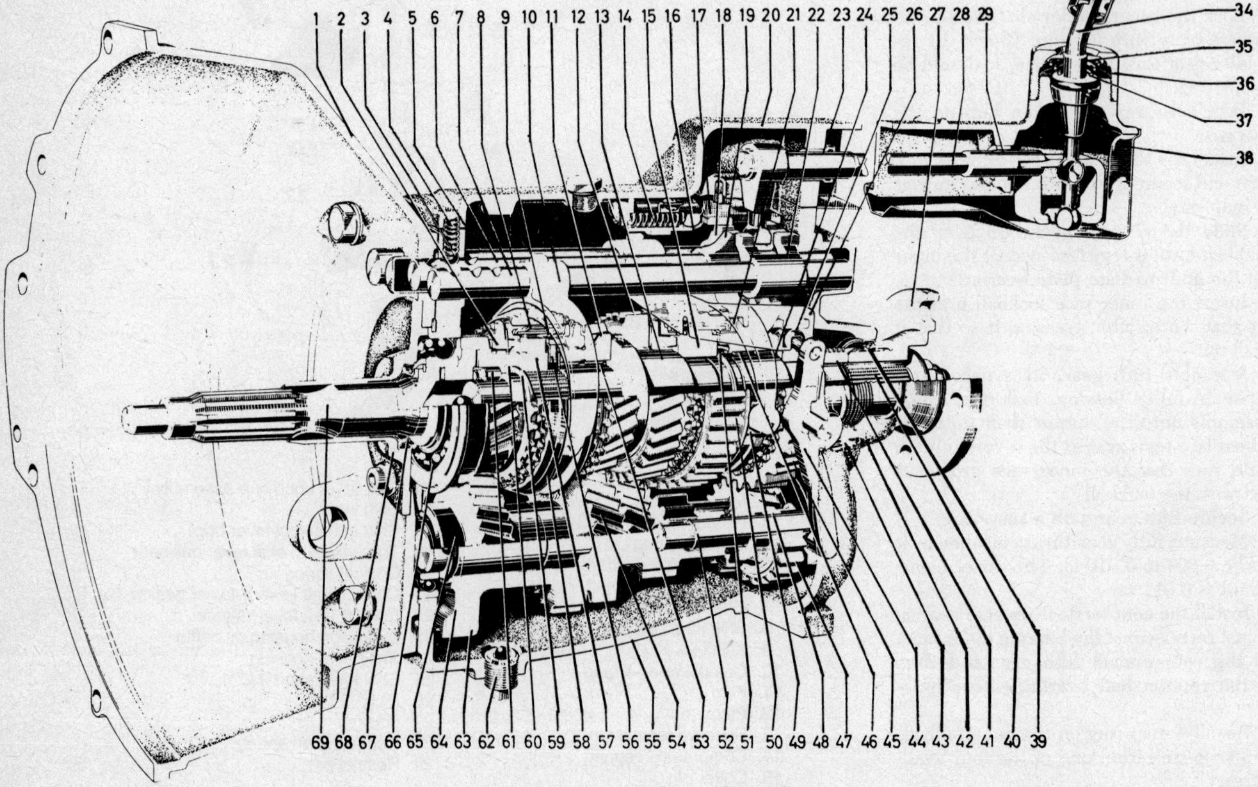

Volvo M400 transmission—M410 similar

SVO 2832 in place of the bolt. Using both tools in conjunction, pull out the rear mainshaft bearing.

9. Pull out the input shaft and remove the synchronizing ring. Remove the thrust washer from the rear of the mainshaft. Push the 1st and 2nd speed engaging sleeve rearward. Lift out the mainshaft.

10. Pull out the reversing shaft and remove the reverse gear. Remove the front and rear cover oil seals with a drift.

11. If a lifting tool was used to remove the mainshaft from the case, remove it. Remove the 1st speed gear wheel, the needle bearing and the synchronizing cone.

12. Remove the engaging sleeves and the flanges for the synchronizers. Remove the synchronizing hub circlips.

13. Place the mainshaft in a press and support it under the 1st speed synchronizing hub. Press off the 2nd speed gear wheel and the 1st and 2nd speed synchronizing hub.

14. Invert the mainshaft and press off the 3rd speed gear wheel and the 4th speed synchronizing hub.

ASSEMBLY

1. Assemble the 1st/2nd and 3rd/4th speed synchronizers, taking care to fit the snap-rings according to the illustration. Position the snap-ring in the hub for the 3rd/4th speed synchronizers.

2. Position the 3rd/4th speed synchronizer, synchronizing cone, 3rd speed gear wheel and needle bearing on top of a ring type support, and after making sure that the synchronizing flange locates correctly into the synchronizing cone grooves, and that the snap-ring fits properly on the 3rd speed gear wheel, press the mainshaft into the synchronizing hub. While pressing in the mainshaft, rotate the 3rd speed gear wheel to make sure that it and the needle bearing are fitted correctly. Install the snap-ring.

3. Position the 1st/2nd speed synchronizer, synchronizing cone, 2nd speed gear wheel, and needle bearing on top of a ring type support, making sure that the engaging sleeve gear ring comes forward and the flanges fit correctly in the synchronizing cone grooves. While pressing in the mainshaft, rotate the 2nd speed gear wheel to prevent it from seizing on the shaft. Install the snap-ring.

4. Install the 1st speed gear wheel, with needle bearing and synchronizing cone, onto the mainshaft. If a lifting tool is needed to lower the mainshaft into the case, install it now.

5. Press the oil seals into the front and rear covers with a drift. Press the ball bearing onto the input shaft with a drift and cushioning ring. Install a snug fitting snap-ring into the groove.

6. Position the reverse shaft gear lever onto the bearing pin in the case. Install the reverse gear and reverse gear shaft, taking care to ensure that the reverse gear shaft lies level or is a maximum of 0.08 in. below the rear end of the case.

7. Place the intermediate shaft in the bottom of the case. Install the mainshaft. Remove the lifting tool, if used, and place the thrust washer on the mainshaft.

8. Press the rear ball bearing onto the mainshaft. If the bearing does not seat correctly in the case, the spindle on SVO tool 2831 can be screwed out and a flat iron piece placed between this and the front end of the case, then the bearing pressed in.

9. Fit the needle bearing into the input shaft. Install the loose synchronizing cone in the synchronizer for the 3rd/4th speeds, taking care to insert the flanges in the grooves. Push the input shaft into the case and onto the mainshaft pin.

10. Turn the transmission upside down. Press on the front and rear bearings for the intermediate shaft. Install the clutch housing with a new gasket.

11. Install the selector forks, flanges, and selector rails. Make sure that the flange for the reverse gear fits correctly in the gear lever. Install the bolts and new tensioning pins.

12. Position the transmission with the rear end facing upward. Drive the intermediate shaft forward until its front bearing contacts the clutch housing. Install shims for the intermediate shaft bearing so that they lie flush or within a maximum of 0.002 in. of the rear end.

13. Install the speedometer gear. Install the rear cover with a new gasket, taking care to compress the gasket. Make sure that the intermediate shaft has 0.008-0.010 in. clearance.

14. Press on the rear flange. Install the washer and nut and torque to 80-110 ft/lbs.

15. Position the interlock balls and springs and install the case cover with a new gasket. Install the input shaft cover. Install the throwout bearing.

TYPE 37

4 Speed Transmission–Models M-45 (4 spd.) M-46 (4 spd. w/OD)

1976-79 Volvo 240
1980-81 Volvo DL, GL, GLE, GT
1976-81 Volvo 260

DISASSEMBLY

1. Remove the transmission.

2. Remove the gearshift bracket extension assembly. Remove the gearshift joint sleeve. Drive out the front pin for the gearshift joint and remove the rear gearshift extension rod.

3. On the M45, block the output shaft flange from turning, and remove the rear flange.

4. On the M46, unbolt the overdrive unit. Attach a slide hammer to the output shaft of the overdrive unit and disconnect and remove the overdrive. Unbolt the intermediate housing.

5. On the M45, remove the speedometer driven gear. Remove the transmission rear cover, noting placement of bearing shims (if so equipped). Remove the speedometer drive gear.

6. Remove the back-up light switch.

7. Remove the top cover and gasket. Use a magnet to remove the spring detent balls.

8. Knock out the lockpins for the shift forks and shift rails.

NOTE: The forward gear shifters should be separated so that the pins do not damage the gears when driven out.

9. Remove the shift rails, shift forks and shifters for all forward speeds.

10. On the M46, remove the snap-ring and oil pump eccentric for the overdrive from the output shaft. Remove the eccentric retaining key.

11. Remove the mainshaft (output shaft) bearing inner and outer snap-rings. Before removing the mainshaft bearing, place a metal spacer (guard plate Volvo #2985) between the input shaft and the front synchronizer ring to prevent damage to the ring during bearing removal. Remove the mainshaft bearing ring and pull off the bearing. Remove the bearing thrust washer.

12. Remove the flywheel (bell) housing.

13. Remove the snap-ring and spacer rings retaining the input shaft bearing. With the front synchronizer ring protective spacer still in place, pull out the input shaft bearing. Remove the protective plate.

14. Knock the intermediate shaft back and remove the rear outer race for the intermediate shaft. Then, knock the shaft forward and remove the front intermediate shaft outer race.

15. Remove the input shaft.

16. Lift out the 4th gear synchronizer ring.

17. Lift out the mainshaft.

18. Lift out the intermediate shaft.

19. Drive back the reverse gear sliding shaft and remove the gear shift rail, unhook and remove the reverse gear shift fork. Remove the reverse gear shift rail.

20. Pull off the intermediate shaft bearing.

21. Remove 1st gear and its synchronizer ring from the mainshaft. Remove the snap-ring for the 1-2 synchronizer hub. Press off the synchronizer hub and gear. Remove the 3-4 synchronizer hub snap-ring and press off that gear and hub.

22. If the shift mechanism needs repair, unhook the detent plate spring, remove the three retaining bolts, and remove the detent plate. Remove the shifter shaft. If necessary, remove the shaft seal at the rear of the cover.

23. If leaking, remove the bell housing seal and the rear cover seal.

24. Push the two synchronizer hubs out of their sleeves and inspect for wear.

ASSEMBLY

1. Install new seals in the bell housing, shift cover and rear cover as required. Install the shifter assembly in the cover. The detent plate is installed with the flat washers between the plate and C-clips.

2. Connect the 3rd and 4th gear synchronizer hubs. The dogs must be positioned in the grounded slots in the hub. The sleeve end

with the turned groove must face in the same direction as the hub flat end.

3. Assemble the mainshaft: install the 3rd gear and synchronizer ring, 3rd/4th synchronizer hubs, and snap-ring; install the 2nd gear and synchronizer ring, 1st/2nd synchronizer hubs, and snap-ring; install the 1st gear and synchronizer ring.

4. Press on the two intermediate shaft bearings.

5. Press on the input shaft bearing, and install its snap-ring.

NOTE: Do not install the spacer ring yet.

6. Install the reverse gear shift rail (without lockpin), shift fork and shifter. Install the reverse gear and shaft. Check that the reverse gear shaft aligns flush with the outside of the case. Also, check that the clearance between the reverse gear and shift fork is 0.004 0.08 in. Adjust as necessary by knocking the shift fork pivot in axially with a punch.

7. Lay the intermediate shaft at the bottom of the case. Slip the thrust washer, ball bearing and positioning ring over the output end of the mainshaft. Press the mainshaft bearing into place, taking care not to damage the reverse gear. When the bearing seats properly, the positioning ring will butt against the case.

8. Grease and install the input shaft inner roller bearing.

9. On the M46, install the snap-ring for the mainshaft bearing. Install the Woodruff key, overdrive oil pump eccentric and snap-ring on the mainshaft extension.

10. Position the 4th gear synchronizer ring in its hub.

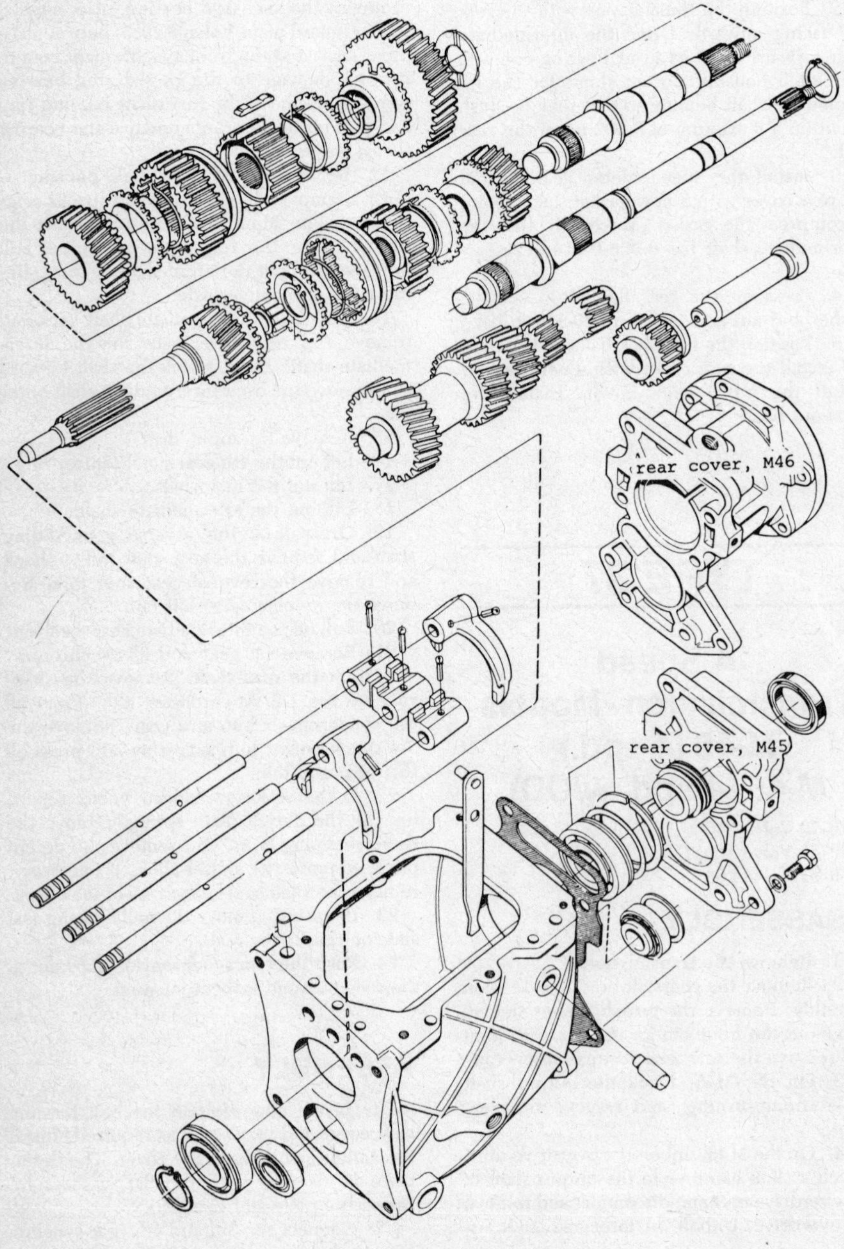

Volvo M45, M46 gear train

11. Push the input shaft into the case all the way, so it makes contact with the mainshaft.

12. Lift up the intermediate shaft so that both bearings locate in the case.

13. Pull out the input shaft slightly to install the spacer ring. Then push the input shaft back in so that the spacer rings contact the case.

14. Install the intermediate shaft outer bearing races.

15. Determine the shim thickness required between the bell housing and the input shaft bearing. Measure how much the input shaft bearing protrudes from the case, and measure the depth of the bearing seat in the bell housing. Subtract bell housing seat depth and bell housing gasket thickness (0.25 mm) from the input shaft bearing protrusion height, and then subtract from this the allowable clearance (0.01-0.15 mm), and you have your required shim clearance. Shims come in 0.10, 0.15 and 0.20 mm sizes.

16. Install the bell housing.

17. Install the shift forks on the synchronizer hubs (the forks are identical). Install the forward shift rails and shifters (not interchangeable) and secure with the lock pins. Drive in the pins until flush.

18. Determine the shim thickness required between the rear cover and the intermediate shaft outer race, and the shim thickness between the rear cover and the mainshaft bearing. Allowable clearance is 1.98 mm for the intermediate shaft outer race, and 0.24 mm for the mainshaft bearing. Gasket thickness is 0.25 mm. When measuring, turn the transmission case vertical with the input shaft facing down, to take any slack out of the intermediate or mainshafts.

19. On the M45, install the speedometer drive gear.

20. Install the rear cover (or intermediate housing on the M46) with shims and a new gasket.

21. On the M45, install the output shaft flange. Install the speedometer driven gear and new O-ring. Install the gear retainer and bolt.

22. Position the top cover gasket with shifter detent balls and springs. Install the cover. Install the back-up light switch. Check gear operation by inserting a punch through the shift rod eye and rotating the mainshaft.

23. On the M46, install the overdrive assembly.

24. Install a new rubber O-ring in the gearshift rod joint. Connect the gearshift rod and drive in the locking pin. Install the cover sleeve.

25. Install the gearshift bracket extension assembly with the spacers, rubber washers, and flat washers as shown to eliminate vibration. First install the two upper bolts flush with the spacer sleever, and then the two lower bolts. Then, tighten all four bolts to 15-18 lbs.

26. Fill the transmission with 0.8 qts. (2.4 qts. with overdrive M46) of 80W/90 hypoid gear oil. Install the plug(s).

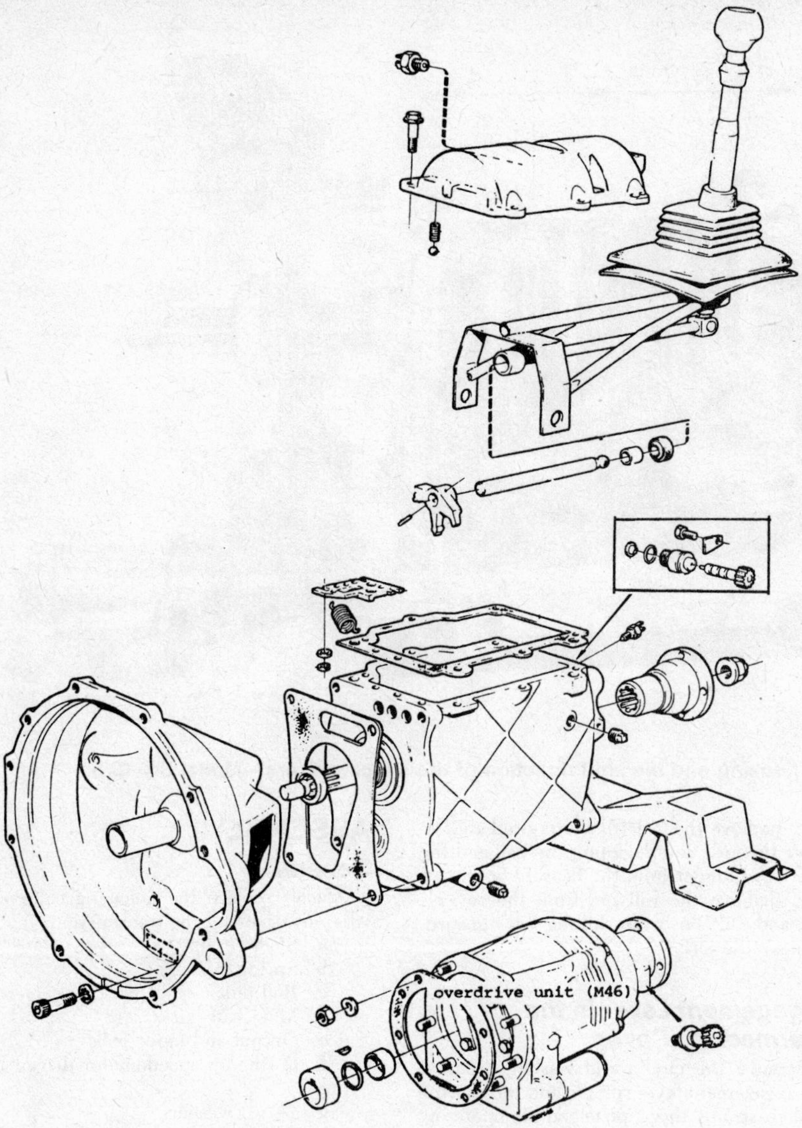

Volvo M45, M46 case and overdrive

TYPE 38

5 Speed Transmission–Model BA-10/5

1977-81 Peugeot

DISASSEMBLY

1. Mount the transmission in a holding fixture or equivalent and drain the lubricant.
2. Remove the speedometer driven gear socket set screw and remove the driven gear socket from the rear extension housing.
3. Position the transmission in the vertical position with the rear upward. Set the gear selectors in the neutral position. Remove the selection lever return spring.
4. Remove the 5th gear cover plate and its gasket. Remove the extension housing bolts.
5. Place an extractor plate tool or equivalent to the rear housing, using the three bolts of the cover plate. Remove the rear housing from the transmission.
6. Remove the 5th speed gear from the mainshaft with an appropriate puller. The rear bearing will be removed as part of the 5th speed gear.
7. Remove the 5th speed drive gear shim washer, the spacer washer, the 5th gear and its needle bearing from the 5th gear stub shaft.
8. Mark the direction of rotation of the 5th/reverse synchronizer and the position of the cage and hub, in relation to each other.
9. Engage the 5th gear and drive the 5th/reverse selector fork roll pin from the fork and rail.

CAUTION

Do not damage the mating surface of the housing.

10. Reset the rail to the neutral position and remove the 5th/ reverse synchronizer cage and selector fork assembly, the synchronizer hub and the 5th gear subshaft.
11. Disengage the selection lever finger from the selector forks spindles. Remove the intermediate housing and retaining bolts.
12. Place the transmission in a horizontal position with the right side up. Remove the clutch fork and release bearing assembly from the front of the transmission. Remove the clutch housing and bolts.
13. Remove the six Allen headed screws from the rear bearing thrust plate. Remove the right hand housing retaining bolts and the housing.
14. Remove the countershaft from the exposed left hand housing.

NOTE: Mark and set aside the bearing races, if to be used again.

15. Lift the input and mainshaft assembly from the case as a unit. Do not separate while removing.
16. Separate the input and the mainshaft when the assembly is on a work bench. Remove the needle bearing from the bore of the input shaft. Hold the mainshaft in the 3rd gear position.
17. To disassemble the input shaft, remove the circlips, the spring washer and press the bearing from the shaft. Do not lose the adjusting shims.
18. To disassemble the mainshaft, mark the direction of rotation of the 3rd/4th synchronizer cage in relation to the synchronizer hub.

NOTE: Mark the components with a sharp piece of brass welding rod.

19. Remove the front synchronizer ring, the circlip and the spring washer from the front of the mainshaft.
20. Remove the 3rd/4th gear synchronizer hub and 3rd gear with an appropriate puller.
21. Invert the mainshaft and lock in a holding device such as a vise. Unscrew the reverse driven gear locknut from the mainshaft. Remove the reverse gear from the shaft.
22. Position the mainshaft and the remaining gears on a press bench and press the mainshaft through the rear bearing. Remove the gear components from the mainshaft in the following order;
    a. Rear bearing
    b. Bearing spacer
    c. Adjustment shim washer
    d. 1st speed driven gear
    e. Needle bearing
    f. 1st gear bushing
    g. 1st/2nd gear synchronizer and hub
    h. 2nd speed driven gear
    i. Needle bearing
23. Using a press, remove the front bearing and the shim adjusting washers. Remove the rear bearing.
24. To disassemble the rear housing, the ball bearing, the oil seal and the bearing race is pressed from the housing. Locate the shim washer in the race bore.

CAUTION

The press ram should be no bigger than 24 mm in diameter.

Position of the gear train in the half housing and the shift direction of the synchronizers—Model BA-10/5

Selector Forks and Shift Rail Removal

1. Remove the spring and the 4th speed locking ball from the rear bearing bore of the half case.
2. Move the 4th gearfork and rail to the engaged position and drive the roll pins from the 1st/2nd and 3rd/4th selector forks. Return the 3rd/4th shift rail to the neutral position.
3. Remove the 1st/2nd locking ball plug, spring and ball from the passage on the center of the outer side of the case.
4. Pivot the 3rd/4th selector rail and remove the 1st/2nd rail from the case. Remove the fork.
5. Remove the reverse gear locking ball plug, spring and ball from the opposite side from the 3rd/4th locking ball passage.
6. Disengage the reverse fork and rail assembly and withdraw it from the case.
7. Remove the 3rd/4th shifting rail and remove the fork, interlock pin, the ball and the interlock plunger from the bearing bore.
8. Remove the roll pin from the reverse fork and rail. Push the shifting rail outward. Remove the fork.

Engagement Lever in the Intermediate Cover

Remove the circlip and washer. Remove the engagement lever spindle and recover the washer, spring, thrust plate and the operating fingers from the inside of the housing.

Clutch Housing

The thrust guide sleeve can be pressed from the housing after the oil seal has been removed.

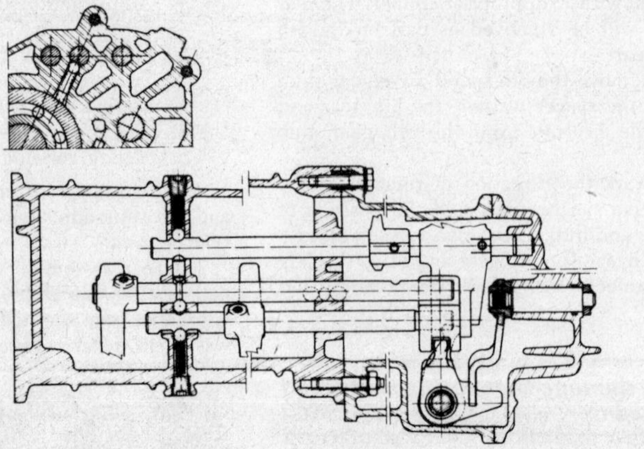

Diagram of the detent and interlock components—model BA-10/5

ASSEMBLY

General

Always replace the following components when overhauling the transmission:

a. Shaft circlips
b. Spring washers
c. Roll pins
d. Mainshaft nut
e. Output and input seals
f. O-ring on speedometer driven bushing
g. Thrust washers
h. Necessary gaskets
i. Sealing compound to mating surfaces

Engagement Levers

Install the lever spindle while fitting the operating fingers, the spring thrust plate, the spring and the washer. Install the washer and the circlip on the lever spindle, exposed on the side of the intermediate housing.

Forks, Shift Rails and Interlocks

1. Install the reverse gear sliding shift rail into the case and into the bracket. Align the roll pin holes and install a new roll pin.
2. Install the reverse sliding gear with the 5th/reverse fork and shifting rail into the case.
3. Install in the reverse interlock passage on the outside of the case, a ball and spring. Coat the plug with a sealer and install it into the passage. Torque to 9.5 ft/lbs. Move the shift rail to the neutral position.
4. Install the 3rd/4th and 5th/reverse interlock plunger into its passage in the case.
5. Install an interlock pin in the 3rd/4th shift rail and retain with grease. Install the shifting rail into the case. Align the holes in the fork and the rail. Be sure the interlock pin

is in the correct position and install a new roll pin.

6. Install an interlock ball in the passage between the 3rd/4th and the 1st/2nd fork rails. Install the 1st/2nd gear fork in the case with the boss towards the front. Install the shifting rail and engage the shifting fork. Align the holes in the fork and the shifting rail and install a new roll pin.

7. Install an interlock ball and spring in the 3rd/4th/2nd/1st interlock passage. Coat the plug with sealer and install it in the passage. Torque to 9.5 ft/lbs.

8. Install the ball and spring in the passage of the rear bearing bore, for the 3rd/ 4th shifting rail.

Preparing the Input Shaft and Mainshaft for Adjustment

INPUT SHAFT

Press the front bearing on the input shaft with the snap-ring groove to the front. Do not install any shims.

MAINSHAFT

1. Install the 2nd speed gear and its needle bearing, the 1st/2nd synchronizer hub, the 1st speed gear spacer and washer. Install the rear bearing along with a new circlip.

NOTE: The bearing will have to be pressed on the shaft.

Do not exceed 3 meteric tons pressure after the bearing is seated.

2. Install the adjustment shim removed during the disassembly, the spacer and a new nut on the shaft following the rear bearing. Tighten the nut to 39 ft/lbs.

COUNTERSHAFT

Press the new bearings onto the countershaft, beginning with the rear bearing and then the front.

CLUTCH HOUSING

1. Install the thrust guide sleeve and new circlip in its groove.

NOTE: Do not install an oil seal in the housing until all adjustments are completed.

2. Verify the front and rear faces of the clutch housing are parallel with the use of a dial indicator. If out of parallel more than 0.10 mm, replace the housing.

Adjustments Prior to Assembly

Five adjustments are necessary, prior to the complete assembly of the transmission. The adjustments are as follows.

1. Position of the 4th gear synchronizer cone (prior to assembly).
2. Position of the 2nd gear synchronizer cone (prior to assembly).
3. Preload of the countershaft tapered roller bearings (prior to assembly).
4. Preload of the mainshaft tapered roller bearings (during assembly).
5. End play of the 5th/reverse sub-shaft (during assembly).

Special tools are available through the manufacturer and other sources for the measurement procedures needed during the adjustment phases. References will be made to the special tools needed.

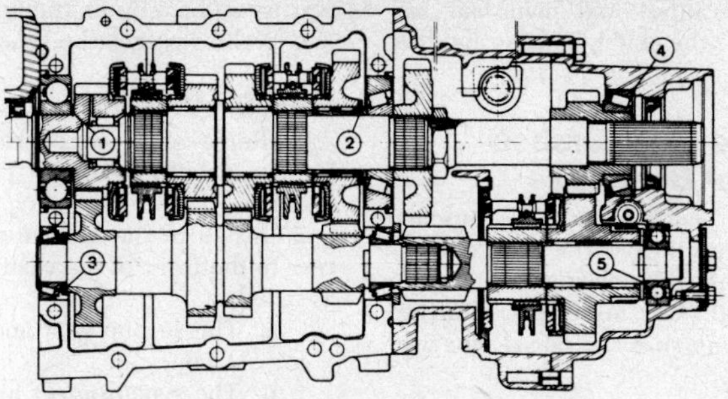

1. Position of 4th gear synchro cone
2. Position of 2nd gear synchro cone
3. Preloading of countershaft taper roller bearings
4. Preloading of mainshaft taper roller bearings
5. End float of 5th/R sub-shaft

Location of the adjustment shims needed during the assembly

Position of the 4th Gear Synchronizer Cone

1. Place the clutch housing, front down on a flat surface, and install the input shaft and bearing.

2. Install the right hand housing onto the clutch housing and secure with two bolts. Tighten to 14 ft/lbs.

CAUTION

Be sure the bearing fits into the bore of the clutch housing and the half housing.

3. Install the special setting gauge tool, 80314G or equivalent, into the clutch housing, in place of the countershaft front bearing.

4. Place the dial indicator and the special tool base, 80310FZ or equivalent, on the top of the setting tool.

5. Align the dial indicator stem on the edge of the synchronizer cone and rotate the input shaft one complete turn and obtain an average reading. Adjust the indicator to zero at the average reading point on the cone edge.

6. Reposition the dial indicator and base on the setting gauge block and record the measurement.

Position of dial indicator and special tools for the measurements of the 4th gear synchronizer cone

7. The measurement obtained represents the thickness of shims needed between the input shaft and the front bearing, minus 0.5 mm and rounded off to the nearest 0.05 mm.

Example:

Indicator reading	1.12 mm
Minus	0.50 mm
Result	0.62 mm
Rounded off to nearest 0.05 mm	0.60 mm

Therefore, a shim pack of 0.60 mm is needed between the input shaft and the front bearing to properly position the 4th speed synchronizer cone, in this hypothetical example.

NOTE: Shims are available in steps of 0.05 mm, from 0.15 to 0.50 mm.

Position of the 2nd Gear Synchronizer Cone

1. Install the needle bearing into the bore of the input shaft. Install the mainshaft and prepared components into the input shaft, with the rear bearing seated in its bore on the right hand housing.

NOTE: Be sure the bearing circlip is installed in the half housing groove.

2. Install the larger setting tool, 80314K or equivalent, into the countershaft front bearing bore of the clutch housing.

3. Install a longer stem, 80310 J or equivalent, onto the dial indicator. Place the dial indicator and special base on the top of the right hand half housing, in a position to touch both the setting tool and the 2nd synchronizer cone.

4. With the dial indicator set to zero, position the stem on the top of the setting tool.

5. Reposition the indicator stem to the edge of the 2nd synchronizer cone and record the measurement reading. The amount of movement noted, represents the thickness of shims needed between the 1st gear spacer and the rear bearing, plus 0.50 mm, rounded off to the nearest 0.05 mm.

Example:

Indicator reading	2.51 mm
Plus	0.50 mm
Result	3.01 mm
Rounded off to nearest 0.05 mm	3.00 mm

6. Remove the input and mainshaft assemblies. Separate the clutch housing and the half housing.

Preload of the Countershaft Tapered Roller Bearings

1. Place the left half housing in the support stand or equivalent. Install the countershaft and its bearings into the housing.
2. Place the right housing in place on the left housing, making sure the dowel pins are in position.
3. Install two bearing center bolts into the housings and hand tighten the bolts. Install bolts into the rear bearing thrust plate and hand tighten the bolts.
4. Position the transmission with the front of the housings upward. Apply a downward pressure to the countershaft front bearing while rotating the countershaft, in order to seat the bearings.
5. Tighten the bearing center bolts and the bearing thrust plate bolts to 7 ft/lb.
6. By placing the dial indicator on the end of the countershaft and rotating it one complete turn with the stem contacting the housings, the run-out between the outer race and the face of the half housings must not exceed 0.03 mm.
7. Should the run-out exceed the specifications, the race must be realigned by tapping with a mallet. Should the countershaft be difficult to turn, the bearing center bolts and the bearing thrust plate bolts must be loosened and retightened and the run-out rechecked.
8. If the run-out is within specifications, set the dial indicator with a short stem, to number 2 and zero, with the stem resting on the side of the outer race. Move the indicator until the stem is contacting the face of the housing and record the measurement of the movement. Add 0.10 mm to the results for the preload of the bearings and round the results to the nearest 0.05 mm.

Example:

Housing reading	4.27 mm
Bearing reading (preset)	2.00 mm
Result	2.27 mm
Plus preload	0.10 mm
Shim pack needed	2.37 mm
Rounded off to nearest 0.05 mm	2.35 mm

NOTE: Shims are available from 2.15 to 3.30 mm, in increments of 0.05 mm.

9. Remove the countershaft and the front bearing from the countershaft. Install the predetermined shim with the chamfer facing the gear, between the gear and the bearing. Press the bearing in place.

NOTE: The 4th and 5th adjustments are made during the assembly of the transmission as noted in the adjustment list.

Final Assembly

INPUT SHAFT

1. Remove the bearing from the shaft and install the predetermined shim pack between the shaft and the bearing.
2. Reinstall the bearing, with the groove for the large circlip to the front. Press the bearing into position and install the spring washer and circlip on the input shaft. Be sure the circlip engages the groove completely.

MAINSHAFT

1. Remove the rear bearing and shims from the mainshaft, used in the measurement check.
2. Install in the following order, from the rear to the front of the shaft, the components as listed;
   a. The second gear and its needle bearing (31 mm wide).
   b. The synchronizer hub and cage.
   c. The 1st gear and needle bearing (29 mm wide).
   d. The spacer and adjusting shim (from measurement check).
   e. The bearing spacer.
   f. Press the bearing onto the shaft with the circlip to the rear.
   g. Install the reverse driven gear with the plain face to the rear.
   h. Install a new nut and tighten to 39 ft/lbs and lock the collar to the shaft.
3. Invert the mainshaft and install the following in order.
   a. 3rd gear along with its needle bearing (31 mm wide).
   b. 3rd-4th synchronizer hub.
4. Install a new spring washer and circlip on the end of the mainshaft. Be sure circlip is in the groove.
5. Insert the needle bearing in the bore of the input shaft, fit the 3rd-4th synchronizer cage and assemble the input and mainshaft together. Set the synchronizers to neutral positions.

INSTALLING GEAR TRAINS INTO TRANSMISSION CASES

1. Be sure the reverse synchronizer is in the neutral position and the 3rd-4th gear locking ball and spring is in position in the bearing bore.
2. Install the input and mainshaft assembly into the left half housing, engaging the selector forks with the synchronizer cages.
3. Install the outer races to the countershaft and install the countershaft into the housing. Be sure the teeth of both gear trains mate properly.
4. Be sure the alignment dowel pins are in place. Coat the mating surfaces of the half housings with sealer and position the right hand housing onto the left. Position the rear bearing thrust plate.
5. Install the six bearing bolts and tighten to 3 ft/lbs. Install the two thrust plate bolts and tighten to 7 ft/lbs.
6. Be sure the oil seal is installed in the clutch cover and install the clutch cover in place on the transmission housing.
7. Tighten the seven securing bolts to 19 ft/lbs. Rotate the input shaft during the clutch cover retaining bolt tightening.
8. Loosen the six bearing bolts in the housings and tap the half housings with a rubber mallet while rotating the input shaft. Retighten the six bearing bolts to 11 ft/lbs.
9. Install the six assembly bolts in the housing and torque to 7 ft/lbs.
10. Invert the transmission with the rear of the mainshaft upward. Be sure the alignment dowels are in place, coat the mating surfaces of the transmission housing and the intermediate housing with sealing compound and install the intermediate housing in place, while engaging the finger in the selector fork detents.
11. Tighten the five nuts and two bolts to 13 ft/lbs. Place the 5th/reverse spindle to the 5th gear position.
12. Install the 5th/reverse stub shaft and the 5th/reverse synchronizer hub.

NOTE: If a new hub is used, the marking groove should be towards the reverse gear.

13. As a unit, install the 5th/reverse synchronizer cage and the selector fork, bringing together the marks on the synchronizer hub and the cage.
14. Align the holes and install a new roll pin. Set the unit to the neutral position.
15. Install the 5th gear and needle bearing, along with the spacer.

5TH GEAR ASSEMBLY AND PREPARATION FOR MEASUREMENTS 4TH AND 5TH

1. Press the bearing on to the gear pinion.

CAUTION

When new parts are used, match the pinion gear to the mainshaft by green or yellow color.

2. Place the 5th gear pinion with the bearing fitted, on a hot plate and place a small piece of solder on the pinion. When the solder melts, place the pinion gear onto the shaft.

NOTE: A drift may have to be used to seat the gear.

3. Remove the alignment dowels from the rear housing and set them aside for later use. Install a shim pack, 4.0 mm thick and the bearing race, into the rear housing.

PRELOAD OF THE MAINSHAFT TAPERED ROLLER BEARING (NUMBER 4 MEASUREMENT)

1. Place the rear housing in position on the transmission case. Fit three bolts to hold housing and hand tighten.
2. Rotate the mainshaft, loosen the three bolts of the rear housing and retighten hand tight only.
3. A gap will exist between the two housings. Measure the gap to check for parallelism and to calculate the shim thickness needed to preload the mainshaft bearing.

Example

Thickness of basic shim	4.00 mm
Measurement of gap	1.85 mm
Difference	2.15 mm
Plus preload	0.10 mm
Shim thickness required	2.25 mm

NOTE: Shims are available in increments of 0.05 mm from 1.5 mm to 2.95 mm.

4. Remove the rear housing and remove the rear bearing outer race and the basic 4.00 mm shim pack.

TRANSAXLES

TYPE 1

4 Speed Transaxle

Audi 100, 5000

DISASSEMBLY

1. Mount the transaxle in a holding fixture.
2. Block the drive flange with a drift and remove the center bolt. Remove both drive flanges.
3. Remove the differential cover and O-ring. Remove the differential.

CAUTION

If the tapered roller bearings on the pinion shaft are to be replaced, it is necessary to measure the pinion position before the transaxle is disassembled. Both pinion shaft bearings must be replaced at the same time with bearings of the same make. The pinion must be set to its original position when the transaxle is assembled.

4. Remove the bolts holding the gear carrier to the final drive housing.
5. Remove the dowel pin from the gear carrier.
6. Remove the selector shaft spring and cap. Push the selector shaft into the final drive housing.
7. Separate the gear carrier and the final drive housing.
8. Remove the end cap from the gear carrier. Remove the mainshaft bolt and washer.
9. Remove the shift rod stop-screws, springs, and interlock plungers.
10. Drive the spring pin out of the third/fourth gear shaft fork.
11. Pull the third/fourth gear selector rod out of the gear carrier. The shift fork will stay on the mainshaft.
12. Press the mainshaft out of the bearing. Guide the mainshaft and pinion shaft with the selector rod and fork for first/second gear.
13. Remove the main and pinion shafts together with the selector rod and shift forks. Swing the pinion shaft slightly to clear the reverse sliding gear.
14. Remove the speedometer drive gear.
15. Pry the oil seal from the differential cover.
16. Remove the bearing race from the differential cover. Remove the shim and record the size.
17. Remove the drive flange oil seal.
18. Pull the differential bearing outer race out of the final drive housing. Remove the shim and record the size.
19. Remove the selector shaft and oil seal.
20. Remove the clutch release shaft, bearing springs, and bushings. Remove the clutch bearing guide sleeve.
21. Remove the mainshaft oil seal.
22. Remove the pinion shaft needle bearings from the final drive housing.
23. Remove the mainshaft needle bearings.

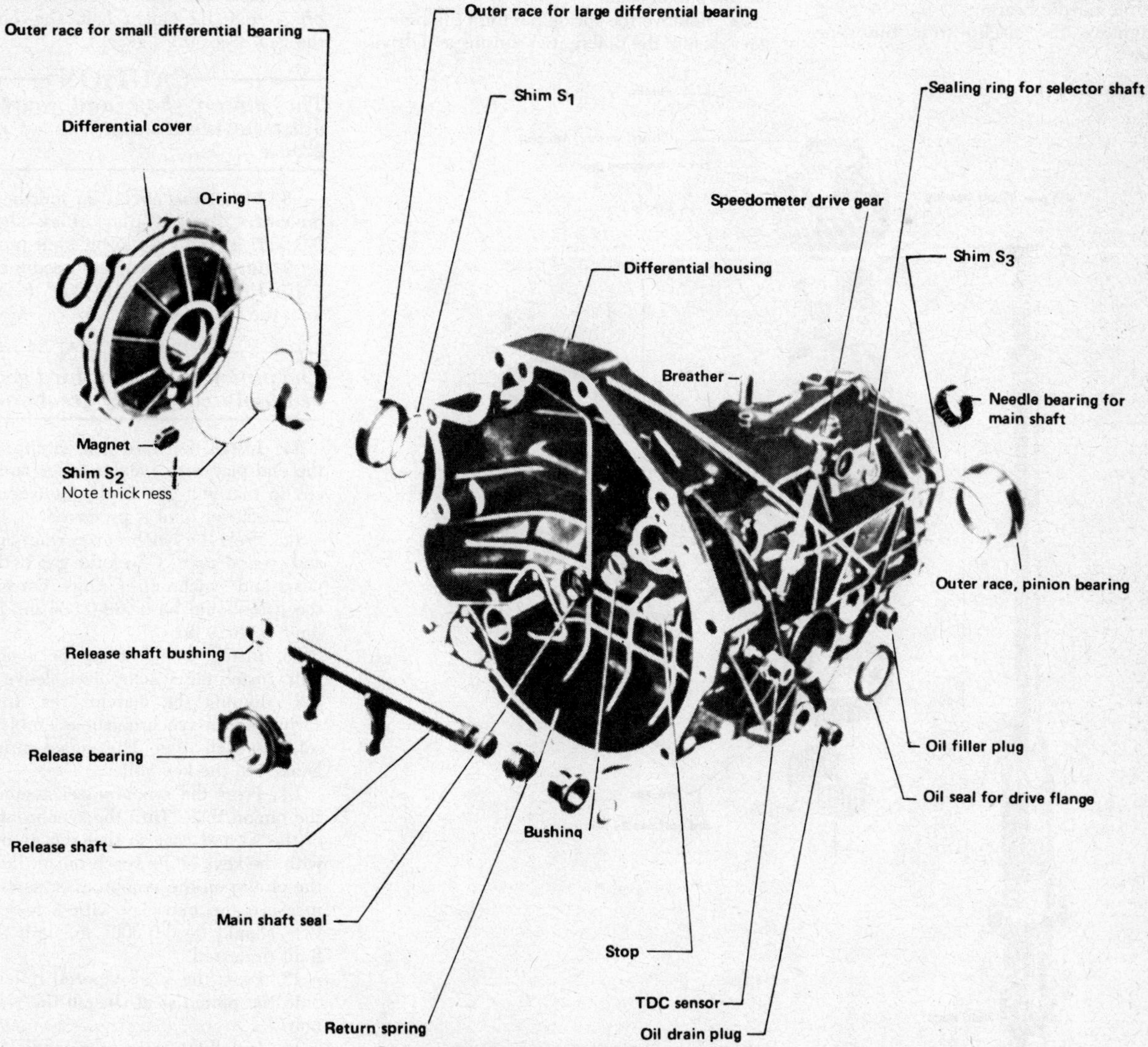

Components of the final drive housing

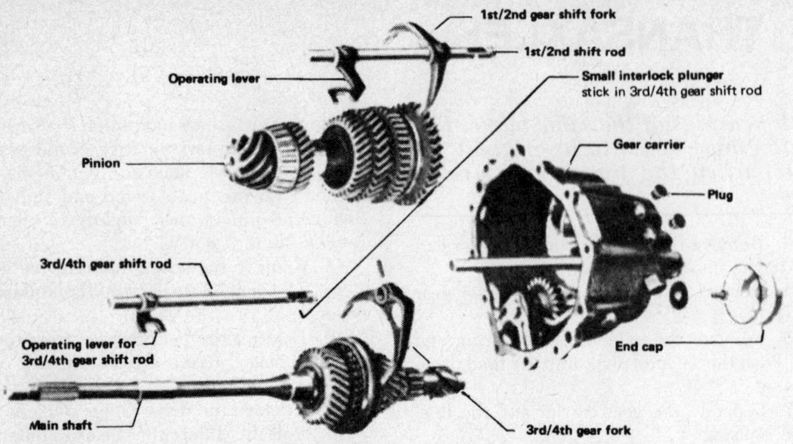

Gear carrier with gear train and selector components

24. Remove the reverse gear relay lever and the reverse selector rod.
25. Remove the reverse shaft and gear.
26. Press the synchronizer assembly (with third gear) off the mainshaft. Remove the needle bearings.
27. Remove the pinion shaft bolt.
28. Press the bearing (along with first gear and synchronizer ring) off the pinion shaft. Remove the needle bearings.
29. Remove the circlip from the synchronizer.
30. Press the synchronizer assembly (along with second gear and synchronizer ring) off the pinion shaft. Remove the needle bearings.
31. Remove the third gear circlip and press third gear off the pinion shaft.
32. Remove the circlip from fourth gear and press it off the pinion shaft.
33. Press the large tapered roller bearing off the pinion shaft.
34. Remove the spring pin from the pinion gear shaft in the differential housing and drive the shaft out. Remove the thrust washers and pinion gears.
35. Remove the side gears, threaded washers, and shims. Record the shim size.
36. Remove the differential bearings and speedometer drive gear.
37. Remove the ring gear.

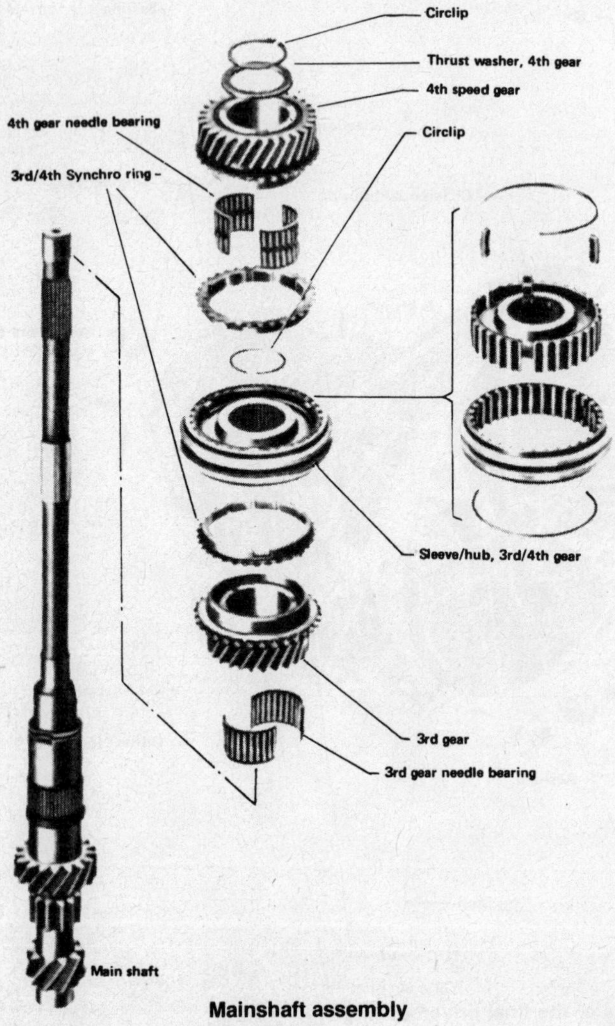

Mainshaft assembly

ASSEMBLY

1. Heat the ring gear to 212° F. and install it.
2. Heat the differential housing bearings to 212° F and press them on. Install the speedometer drive gear.
3. Install the side gears with a 0.5 mm shims. Install the pinion gears and thrust washers.
4. Press the small gears outward and check the side gear play. Insert shims for the side gears until the play does not exceed 0.003 in. Install the threaded washers.

NOTE: The adjustment is correct when no play can be felt and the gears turn easily by hand without jamming.

5. Install the pinion gear shaft.
6. Press the large tapered roller bearing onto the pinion shaft.
7. Heat the fourth gear to 250° F and press it onto the pinion shaft. The shoulder on the gear faces third gear.

CAUTION

The pinion shaft and fourth gear must be absolutely free of oil and grease.

8. Install the circlip on fourth gear and measure the end-play. Play should be 0-0.0007 in. with the lower limit preferred.
9. Install the third gear needle bearings.
10. Heat third gear to 250° F and press onto the pinion shaft.

CAUTION

The pinion shaft and third gear must be absolutely free of grease or oil.

11. Install the third gear circlip. Measure the end-play with a feeler gauge and install a circlip that will give a play between 0-0.001 in. The lower limit is preferred.
12. Press the synchronizer rings on the first and second gears. Check the gap between the gears and synchronizer rings. On new parts the gap should be 0.039-0.066 in. The wear limit is 0.019 in.
13. Install the keys on the synchronizer hub. Install the synchronizer sleeve over the hub aligning the matchmarks. Install the springs on the synchronizer assembly 120° offset from each other. The angled spring end is hooked in the key hollow.
14. Press the synchronizer assembly onto the pinion shaft. Turn the synchronizing ring of the second gear so that the grooves align with the keys in the synchronizer hub. Install the circlip on the synchronizer assembly and measure the end-play with a feeler gauge. Play should be 0-0.0007 in. with the lower limit preferred.
15. Press the small tapered roller bearing onto the pinion shaft. Install the washer and bolt.
16. Install the third gear needle bearings.

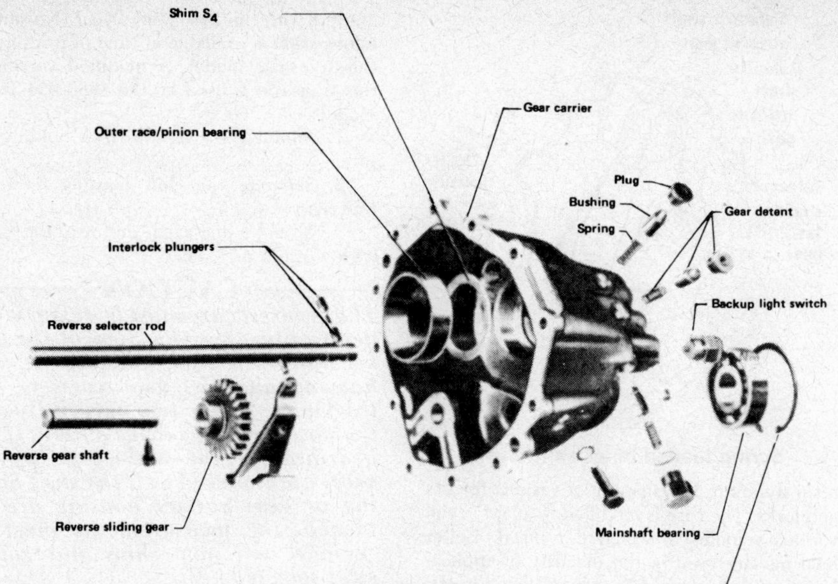

Gear carrier housing

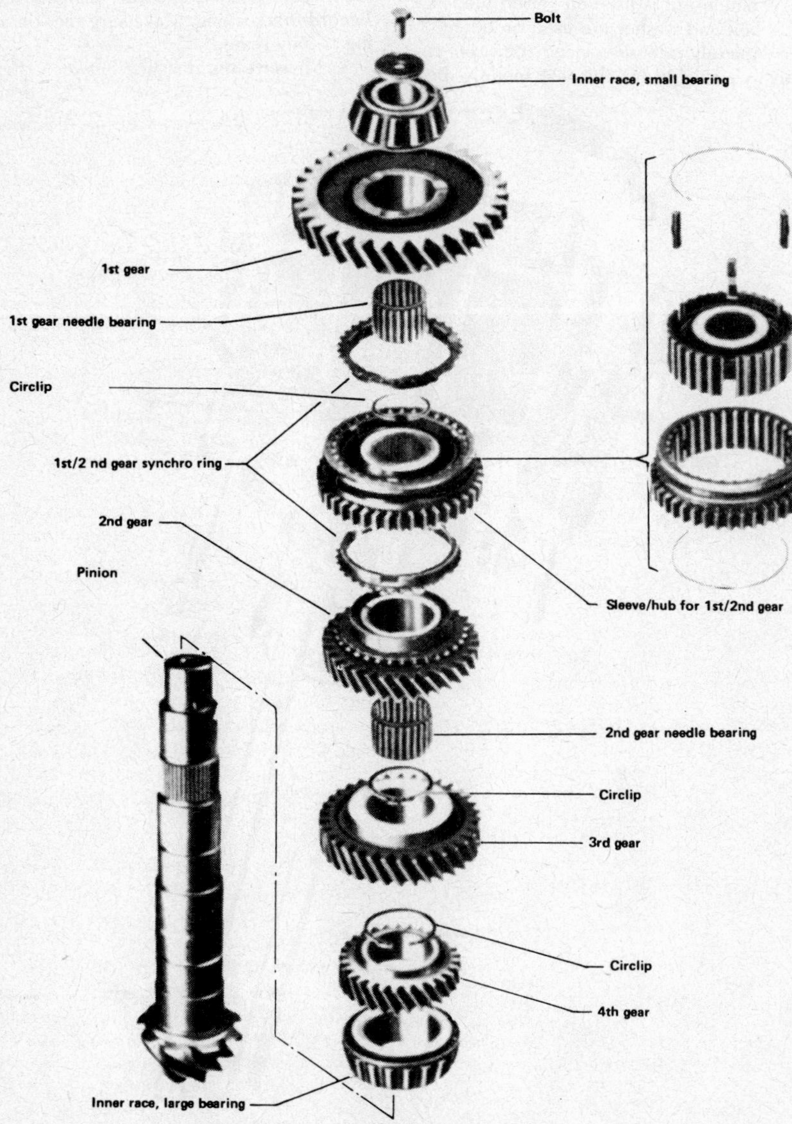

Pinion shaft assembly

17. Install the synchronizer rings on third and fourth gears. The gap between new gears should be 0.039-0.066 in.
18. Assemble the third/fourth synchronizer.
19. Align the grooves in the synchronizer ring for third gear with the keys in the synchronizer hub. Press the synchronizer assembly, synchronizer ring, and third gear onto the mainshaft.
20. Install the synchronizer assembly circlip and measure the end-play. End-play should be 0-0.001 in.
21. Install the fourth gear bearings.
22. Install fourth gear and thrust washer on the mainshaft. Play should be 0.007-0.013 in.
23. Drive the mainshaft bearing into the gear carrier (closed side out).
24. Install the shim and pinion bearing outer race.
25. Install reverse gear shaft and reverse gear.
26. Install the interlock plungers in the gear carrier. Install the reverse selector shaft. Install the reverse relay lever through the gear carrier and into the threaded portion of the lever. Press the lever toward the center of the carrier and tighten the bolt in until it touches the relay lever. Press the lever against the bolt and turn back until the thread starts to engage.
27. Install the interlock plungers, bushings, springs and plugs.
28. Install the differential bearing shim and outer race.
29. Install the mainshaft needle bearings. The lettering on the bearing should be toward the drift.
30. Heat the final drive housing *completely* to 212° F and press the pinion bearing outer race and shim into the housing. Hold the pressure on the race for 1-2 minutes until heat transfer has taken place.
31. Install the mainshaft bushing. The bushing should be driven in 0.452 in. from the surface of the clutch bearing guide sleeve flange.
32. Install the mainshaft oil seal.
33. Drive the selector shaft oil seal into the final drive housing. Install the selector shaft.
34. Install the clutch bearing guide sleeve, the clutch release shaft bushings, spring, shaft, oil seal, and release bearing.
35. Drive the drive flange oil seals into the differential cover and the final drive housing.
36. Install the main and pinion shafts along with the shift forks and first/second gear selector rod. These components must be installed as an assembly. Hook the hole in web of third/fourth gear fork over the reverse selector rod.

NOTE: Make sure the interlock plungers engage the shift selector rod.

37. Pull the mainshaft into the bearing with an 8 mm bolt. When fully seated install the mainshaft bolt.
38. Move the selector rods for first/second and reverse into neutral.
39. Slide the third/fourth selector rod into the shift fork and gear carrier. Make sure that the interlock plungers engage. Secure the shift fork to the rod with a new spring pin.
40. Install the shift rod stop screws.
41. Press the mainshaft cap and O-ring into

the gear carrier. The recess in the cap points toward the oil drilling in gear carrier.

42. Install the gear carrier.
43. Assemble the measuring bar and measure the pinion location.

NOTE: Refer to Differential and Rear Axle section.

If the measurement is not the same as previously recorded, proceed as follows:

a. If the reading is smaller, a thinner shim must be installed between the pinion shaft outer race and final drive housing.

b. If the reading is the same or very close to the original reading, proceed to the next step.

c. If the reading is larger, a thicker shim must be installed between the final drive housing. Install new shim if necessary.

44. Install the dowel pin between the final drive housing and gear carrier.
45. Install the differential.
46. Install the differential cover.
47. Install the drive flanges.
48. Install the selector shaft spring and cover.

TYPE 2

4 Speed Transaxle

VW Dasher
Audi Fox
Audi 4000
Porsche 924

DISASSEMBLY

Certain variations are used in the application of this basic transaxle. The gear arrangement remains the same, the shifting mechanism differs in the shaping of various fingers and forks. The case is modified to adapt to the various vehicles in which it is used. Roller bearings are used in the majority of applications, while tapered bearings are used in the remainder. Needle caged bearings may be found as split, one piece or with a foldable cage. A pinion nut is used on varied models, while a bolt and washer are used on others.

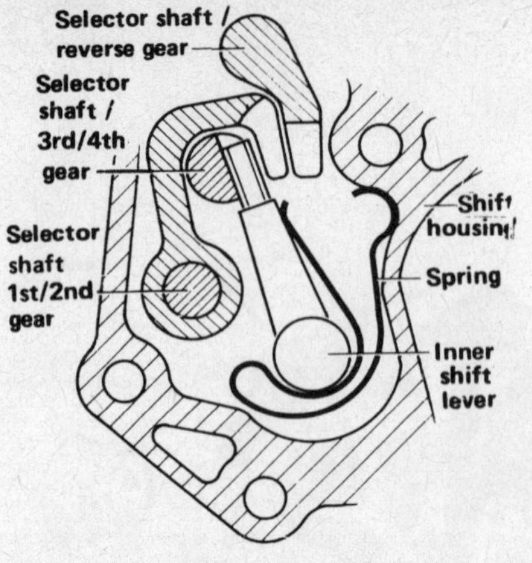

Spring loaded inner shift lever

A completely new five speed transaxle assembly is available for the 924 models, beginning with the 1980 model year. No service information is available at time of printing on this transaxle model. A modified version of this transaxle is used on the 1980 924 Turbo models.

1. Mount the transaxle in a holding fixture.
2. Separate the shift housing from the transaxle.
3. Mount a dial gauge and zero the gauge with a 3 mm preload.

CAUTION

The greatest care must be taken when determining the thickness of the gasket and shim used between the shift housing and the gear carrier. The thickness of these two parts influence the position of the drive pinion. If the bearings for the mainshaft, pinion shaft are replaced or if the shift housing or gear carrier housing are replaced, the measurements must be remade and new shim and gasket sizes selected.

4. Measure the distance between the main shaft bearing and the gear carrier (a). Record this reading. Make sure that the bearing is fully seated.
5. Measure the distance between the pin-

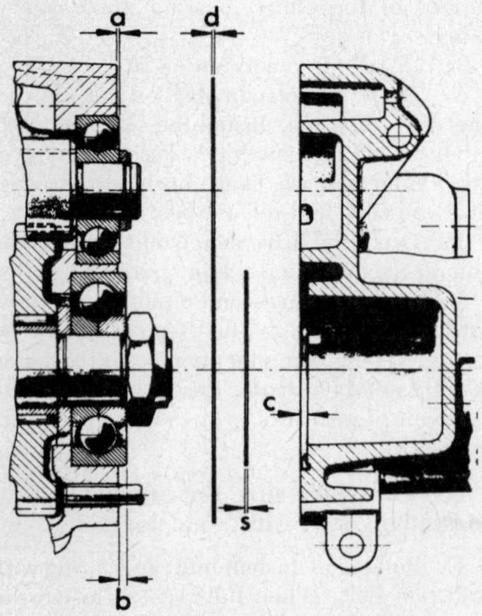

a – between main shaft bearing and gear carrier
b – between pinion bearing and gear carrier
c – between end face of gearshift housing and shim contact in gearshift housing
d – gasket thickness
s – shim thickness

End cover gasket and shim dimensions

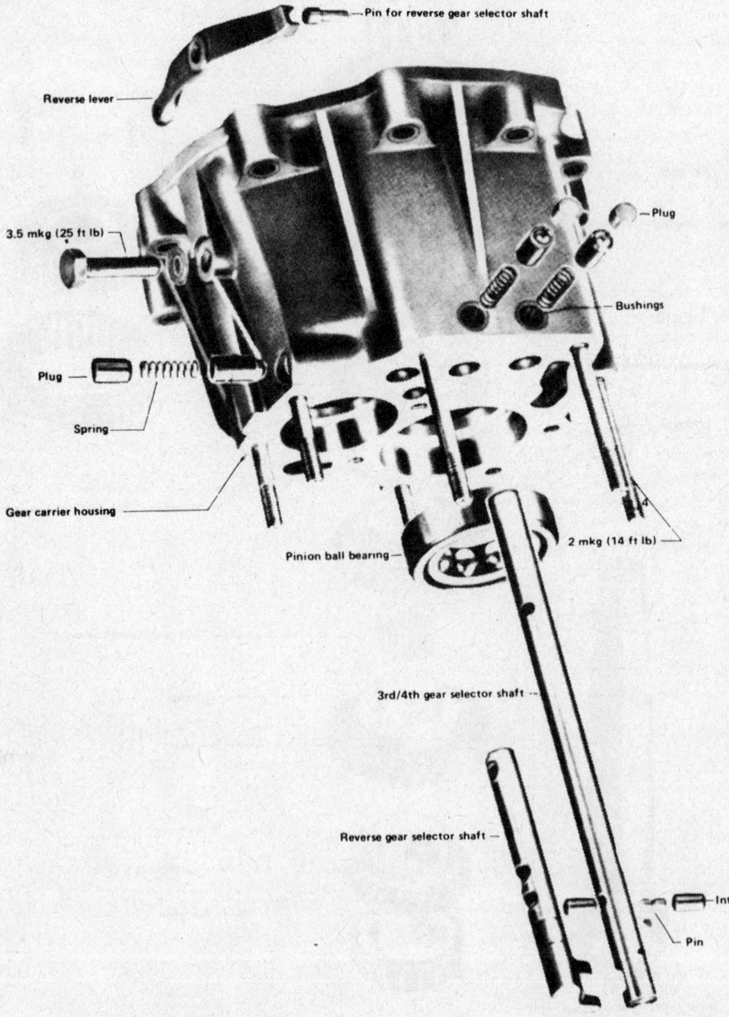

Gear carrier housing and shift rod interlock components

ion bearing and the gear carrier (b). Record the reading. Make sure that the bearing is fully seated.

6. Measure the distance between the end face and the shim contact surface on the gear carrier (c). Record the reading.

7. Determine the shim thickness as follows; add the measurements from Step 4 (a) and 6 (c), then subtract step 5 (b). This will give the shim thickness required.

8. (Fox only.) The gasket thickness is determined by the mainshaft bearing projection obtained in step 4.

Bearing projection (mm)	Gasket size (mm)
0.20-0.26	0.30
0.27-0.32	0.40

NOTE: When replacing the transmission housing, gear carrier, first gear needle bearing or the pinion bearing the exact location of the pinion must be determined before disassembly. Once the new parts have been installed, it will be necessary to set the pinion to its original position.

9. Block the drive flange and remove the bolt.

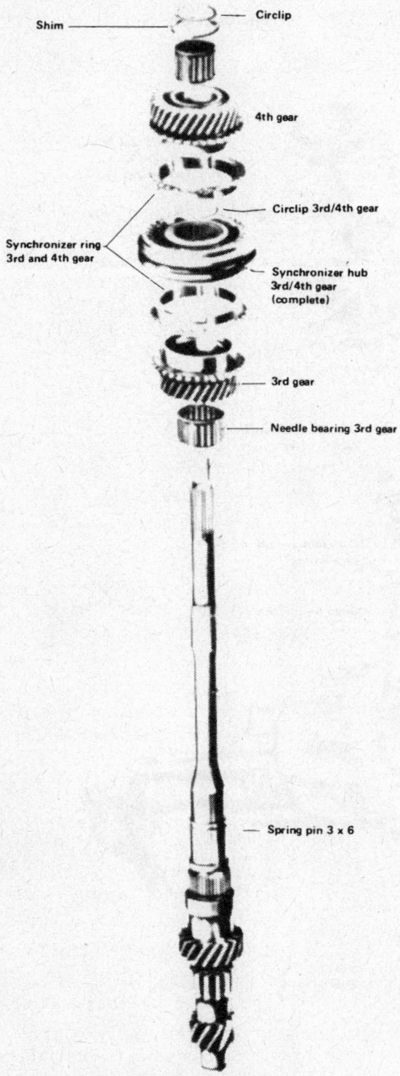

Mainshaft assembly

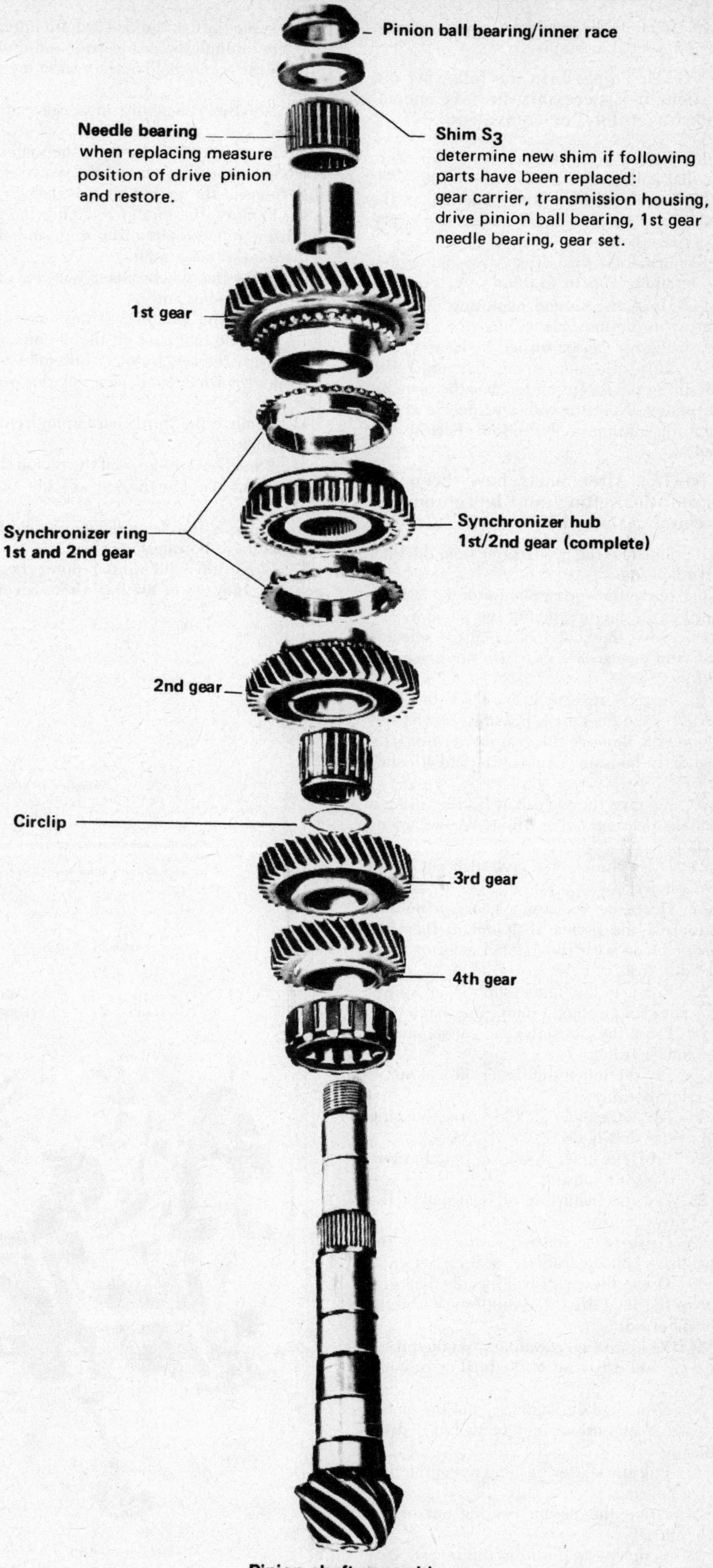

Pinion shaft assembly

10. Remove the final drive cover. Remove the differential assembly.

NOTE: To perform the following operation, it is necessary to have special Volkswagen tools or equivalent.

11. Assemble the tool universal bar. Zero the dial indicator with a 2 mm preload.

12. Install the measuring plate tool on the pinion and install the measuring bar in the final drive housing.

13. Install the final drive cover and tighten the retaining nuts to 18 ft/lbs.

14. Move the second centering disc outward with the movable setting ring until the measuring bar can be turned by hand.

15. Turn the measuring bar until the measuring pin extension touches the plate on the pinion. Note the indicator needle at the point of maximum deflection. Record the reading.

NOTE: After parts have been replaced, this setting must be reproduced as closely as possible.

16. Separate the gear carrier from the final drive housing.

17. Drive the spring pin out of the 3rd/4th shift fork in the direction of the pinion.

18. Move the shift fork along the selector shaft and engage 3rd gear. *Do not move the shaft.*

19. Engage reverse gear. Place the gear carrier in the final drive housing. Loosen the pinion nut. Remove the gear carrier from the final drive housing. Remove the 3rd/4th shift fork.

20. Remove the mainshaft bearing using a suitable bearing puller. Remove the mainshaft.

21. Drive the reverse gear shaft out of the gear carrier.

22. Place the remaining gears in neutral and press the pinion shaft out of the gear carrier along with the 1st/2nd selector shaft and shift fork.

23. Remove the inner shift lever spring from the shift housing, remove the shift lever.

24. Press the transmission rear mount off the shift housing.

25. Pry the inner shift lever oil seal out of the shift housing.

26. Drive the inner shift lever rear bushing out of the shift housing.

27. Press the inner shift lever front bushing out of the shift housing.

28. Pry the mainshaft oil seal out of the final drive housing.

29. Drive the mainshaft sleeve out of the final drive housing from the gear carrier end.

30. Drive the mainshaft needle bearings out of the final drive housing from the front (flywheel side).

31. Remove the dowel pin from the pinion bearing and drive out of the final drive housing.

32. Using a slide hammer, pull the clutch release shaft bushing out of the final drive housing.

33. Pull the starter bushing out of the final drive housing.

34. Drive the pinion bearing out of the gear carrier.

35. Remove the pin from the reverse gear selector shaft.

36. Drive the 1st/2nd and 3rd/4th interlock plungers through the gear carrier and remove through the access hole in the rear of the gear carrier.

37. Tap the remaining interlock plunger plug out.

38. Remove the circlip from the mainshaft which holds the 4th gear and the synchronizer ring. Remove the parts from the shaft.

39. Remove the circlip retaining the synchronizer hub, synchronizer ring, and third gear from the main shaft.

40. Press the synchronizer hub and third gear off the mainshaft.

41. Press the pinion bearing inner race along with the first gear off the pinion shaft.

42. Press the synchronizer hub for 1st/2nd gear along with second gear off the pinion shaft.

43. Remove the third gear circlip from the pinion shaft.

44. Press the third gear off the pinion shaft.

45. Press the fourth gear off the pinion shaft.

46. Remove the drive flange oil seal from the final drive housing by prying.

47. Drive the differential outer bearing race and shim out of the final drive cover.

48. Using a suitable puller, remove the differential bearing inner race/cage from the side opposite the ring gear.

49. Pull the bearing from the ring gear side of the differential assembly, along with the speedometer drive gear and bushing.

50. Remove the bolts holding the ring gear to the differential housing and drive the housing and gear apart.

51. Remove the circlip from the pinion gear shaft. Slide the shaft out of the differential housing.

52. Remove the pinion gears, side gears and the drive flange nuts.

ASSEMBLY

1. Insert the side gears and drive flange nuts. Bolt the drive flanges to the side gears.

2. Insert the pinion gears and move the drive flange until the pinion gears are aligned. Install the pinion shaft. Remove the drive flanges.

NOTE: The drive pinion and the ring gears are matched units and can be replaced only as a matched set.

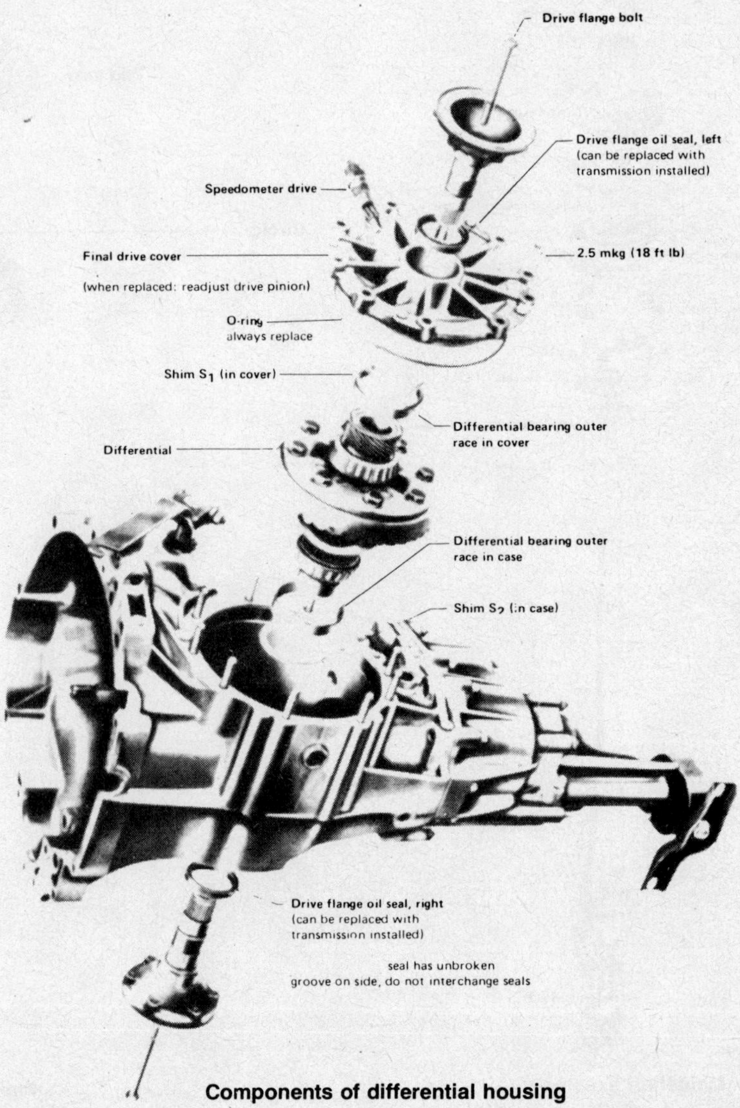

Components of differential housing

Exploded view of 1st/2nd synchronizer

3. Heat the ring gear to approximately 212° F and center on the differential housing with a drift.
4. Install the bearing opposite to the ring gear by heating to 212° F and pressing onto the differential housing.
5. Install the bearing on the ring gear side of the differential housing by heating to 212° F and pressing onto the differential housing.
6. Insert 1.8 mm shim onto differential housing and press drive gear bushing on.
7. Insert the shim into the final drive cover and drive the outer bearing race into place and insert the shim in the final drive housing.
8. Drive the right side drive flange oil seal into place in the final drive housing.
9. Press the 4th gear onto the pinion shaft while holding the bearing with the wide shoulder facing the pinion head.
10. Press the third gear onto the pinion shaft.
11. Measure with a feeler gauge the space between the third gear and the pinion shaft. Install a circlip of the correct size.
12. Position the three keys in the slots in the 1st/2nd gear synchronizer hub.
13. Place the synchronizer sleeve over the synchronizer hub and align marks.
14. Install the springs 120° offset with the angled ends engaged in the hollow of a key.
15. Position the shift fork slot and the groove in the synchronizer hub so that they face the first gear and press the synchronizer assembly onto the pinion shaft.
16. Press the synchronizer ring onto the first gear and measure the gap between the parts with a feeler gauge. New parts should be between 0.042-0.066 in. and a used part should be no more than 0.023 in.
17. Install the first gear on the pinion shaft, slide on bearing and shim.
18. Press the inner race onto the pinion shaft.
19. Assemble the 3rd/4th gear synchronizer in the same way as the 1st/2nd synchronizer.
20. Press the synchronizer rings onto the third and fourth gears. Check the gap between the synchronizer rings and the gears. New parts should measure 0.053-0.075 in. and used parts should be no more than 0.023 in.
21. Install needle bearing on mainshaft.
22. Press the synchronizer hub along with the third gear onto the mainshaft. The chamfer on the synchronizer hub inner splines faces third gear.
23. Install the circlip on the mainshaft for the synchronizer assembly.
24. Install the needle bearing.
25. Install the spring pin in the mainshaft and align the pin with the slot in the 4th gear.
26. Install the fourth gear and shim, secure with the circlip.

CAUTION

Before measuring end-play, press the synchronizer and third gear against the circlip located against the synchronizer hub.

27. Measure the end-play between the shim and fourth gear. If the measurement is not between 0.10-0.40 mm remove the circlip and install a shim that will bring the measurement within limits.
28. Install the plunger and spring for the first second shift selector shaft. Install the interlock plunger (between the 1st/2nd and the 3rd/4th shafts) from the top of the case.
29. Install the plunger and spring for the 3rd/4th selector shaft. Hold down the plunger and install the 3rd/4th shift selector shaft.
30. Install the pin for the reverse gear selector shaft.
31. Install the second interlock plunger from the top of the gear carrier.
32. Install the reverse gear selector shaft. Install the remaining spring and plunger. Install the reverse lever pin in selector shaft.

NOTE: The first/second shift selector shaft is not installed until the gear train is in place.

33. Install the plugs in the interlock plunger bores.
34. Install the reverse sliding gear. Insert the reverse lever with the shift segment.
35. Install the bolt and washer and press the reverse lever toward the center of the gear carrier.
36. Turn the bolt in until it touches the reverse lever. Press the lever against the bolt and make certain that the threads engage smoothly. Continue until the bolt is seated in the gear carrier. Tighten the bolt to 25 ft/lbs.
37. Check the operation of the reverse selector several times. Make sure that the lever moves easily in all positions. Remove the reverse sliding gear.
38. Press the pinion bearing into the gear carrier.
39. Drive a new starter bushing into the final drive housing.
40. Drive a new clutch release shaft bushing into the final drive housing.
41. Align the pinion bearing outer race with the hole in the final drive housing drive into place. The groove on the side must be toward the gear carrier. Install the dowel pin.
42. Drive the mainshaft needle bearings into place in the final drive housing.
43. Drive the mainshaft sleeve into position in the final drive housing.
44. Drive the mainshaft oil seal into position.
45. Install the clutch bearing guide sleeve, the clutch release shaft and spring and the clutch release bearing.
46. Press the inner shift lever rear bushing into the shift lever housing until it is flush with shoulder.
47. Press the shift lever oil seal into the shift lever housing until it is flush with the housing.
48. Press the transmission rear mount onto the shift housing.
49. Press the inner shift lever front bushing into the housing until it is flush.
50. Install the inner shift lever and install the spring.
51. Press the pinion shaft assembly into the ball bearing in the gear carrier.
52. Drive the mainshaft bearing into the gear carrier assembly.
53. Position the 1st/2nd selector shaft and fork on the assembled pinion shaft assembly.
54. Press the pinion shaft assembly into the gear carrier assembly. Guide the shift selector shaft into the operating sleeve. Make sure that the selector shaft does not jam.
55. Place the pinion shaft in a vise and tighten the pinion nut to 14-21 ft/lbs. Install the gear carrier in the final drive housing and secure with four nuts.
56. Repeat the measurements from Steps 11 thru 15 of disassembly. If the measurements are not the same as previously recorded, proceed as follows:
   a. If the second measurement is smaller, a thinner shim must be installed (between the pinion shaft inner bearing race and needle bearing on the pinion shaft).
   b. If the measurement is the same or very close to the original reading proceed to the next step.
   c. If the measurement is larger, a thicker shim must be installed.
57. Remove the gear carrier from the final drive housing, install new shim if needed.
58. Place the mainshaft assembly in the gear carrier. Install the shim and circlip.
59. Install the 3rd/4th shift fork with the wider shoulder facing toward fourth gear. Secure the shift fork with a new spring pin.
60. Block the gear train and tighten the pinion nut to 72 ft/lbs.
61. Install the first/second gear selector dog.
62. Install the gear carrier assembly on the final drive housing. Install the dowel pins before tightening the nuts or bolts.
63. Install the differential assembly into the final drive housing.
64. Install the final drive cover.
65. Install the drive flanges and block with suitable drift.
66. Repeat the measurements from Steps 3 thru 8 of Disassembly. Select the proper shim and gasket to be installed between the gear carrier and shift housing.
67. Install the shift housing on the gear carrier assembly.

TYPE 3

4 Speed Transaxle–Model KM 160
4 Speed Transaxle w/Twin Stick–Model KM 165

1980-81 Colt, Champ

DISASSEMBLY

1. Mount the transaxle securely and drain the lubricating oil.
2. Remove the clutch operating bracket and the transaxle mounting bracket.
3. Remove the backup lamp switch and the steel ball from inside the transaxle case.
4. Remove the rear cover from the transaxle case. Remove the two spacers from the rear of the tapered roller bearings.
5. Remove the transaxle case, exposing the gear train assembly.
6. Locate all the shift rails in the neutral position.

NOTE: The shift rails would be locked if any one of the shift rails are in a position other than neutral.

7. Remove the three poppet plugs and remove the springs and balls (three each).
8. Remove the reverse idler shaft and the reverse idler gear.

NOTE: The reverse idler shaft sometimes will come off with the removal of the transaxle case.

9. Remove the reverse shift lever assembly.
10. Remove the reverse shift rail and the 3rd/4th speed shift rail spacer collar.
11. Using a pin punch and light hammer, remove the spring pins from the 1st/2nd and 3rd/4th speed shift forks.

CAUTION
Support the shift forks before attempting to remove the spring pins.

12. Pull the 1st/2nd speed shift rail upward from the case, sliding the rail through the fork.

NOTE: The 1st/2nd speed shift rail and fork cannot be removed until after Step 13.

13. Pull the 3rd/4th speed shift rail from the case and remove the 1st/2nd and 3rd/4th speed shift rails and forks together.
14. Move the 3rd/4th speed synchronizer into the 4th speed position and remove the output shaft assembly.
15. Remove the differential assembly from the case.
16. **KM 165 models:** Remove the plug, poppet and spring for the two-speed shift rail and fork.
17. Remove the bolts from the input shaft bearing retainer and remove the input shaft assembly.
18. **KM 165 models:** Remove the shift rail and fork, along with the intermediate shaft assembly, when the input shaft is removed.
19. Remove the shift shaft spring retainer and pull out the spring pin with pliers.
20. Move the shift shaft towards the outside of the case by using a pin punch in the pin

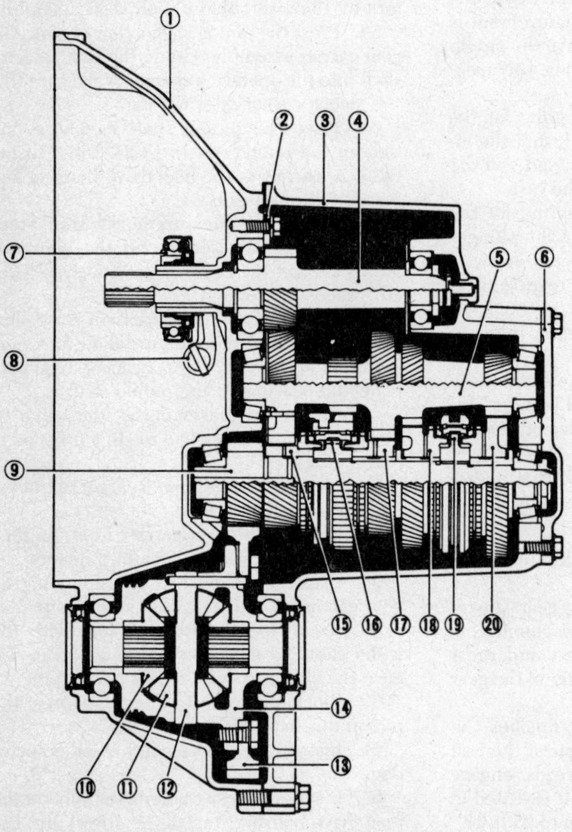

1. Clutch housing
2. Bearing retainer
3. Transaxle
4. Input shaft
5. Intermediate gear
6. Rear cover
7. Clutch release bearing
8. Clutch release fork
9. Output shaft
10. Differential side gear
11. Differential pinion
12. Pinion shaft
13. Differential drive gear
14. Differential case
15. 4th speed gear
16. 3rd and 4th speed synchronizer assembly
17. 3rd speed gear
18. 2nd speed gear
19. 1st and 2nd speed synchronizer assembly
20. 1st speed gear

Cross section of model KM 160 transaxle

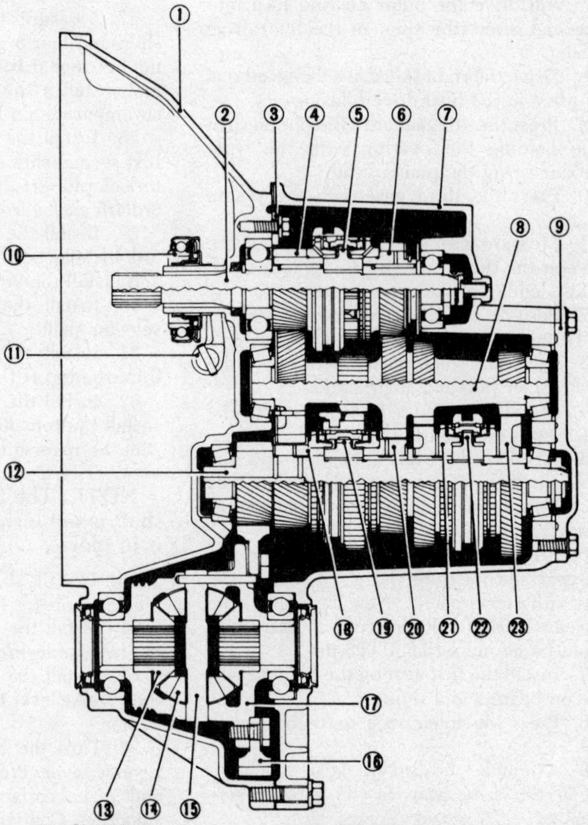

1. Clutch housing
2. Input shaft
3. Bearing retainer
4. Input low gear
5. Synchronizer assembly
6. Input high gear
7. Transaxle case
8. Intermediate gear
9. Rear cover
10. Clutch release bearing
11. Clutch release fork
12. Output shaft
13. Differential side gear
14. Differential pinion
15. Pinion shaft
16. Differential drive gear
17. Differential case
18. 4th speed gear
19. 3rd and 4th speed synchronizer assembly
20. 3rd speed gear
21. 2nd speed gear
22. 1st and 2nd speed synchronizer assembly
23. 1st speed gear

Cross section of model KM 165 transaxle (twin-stick)

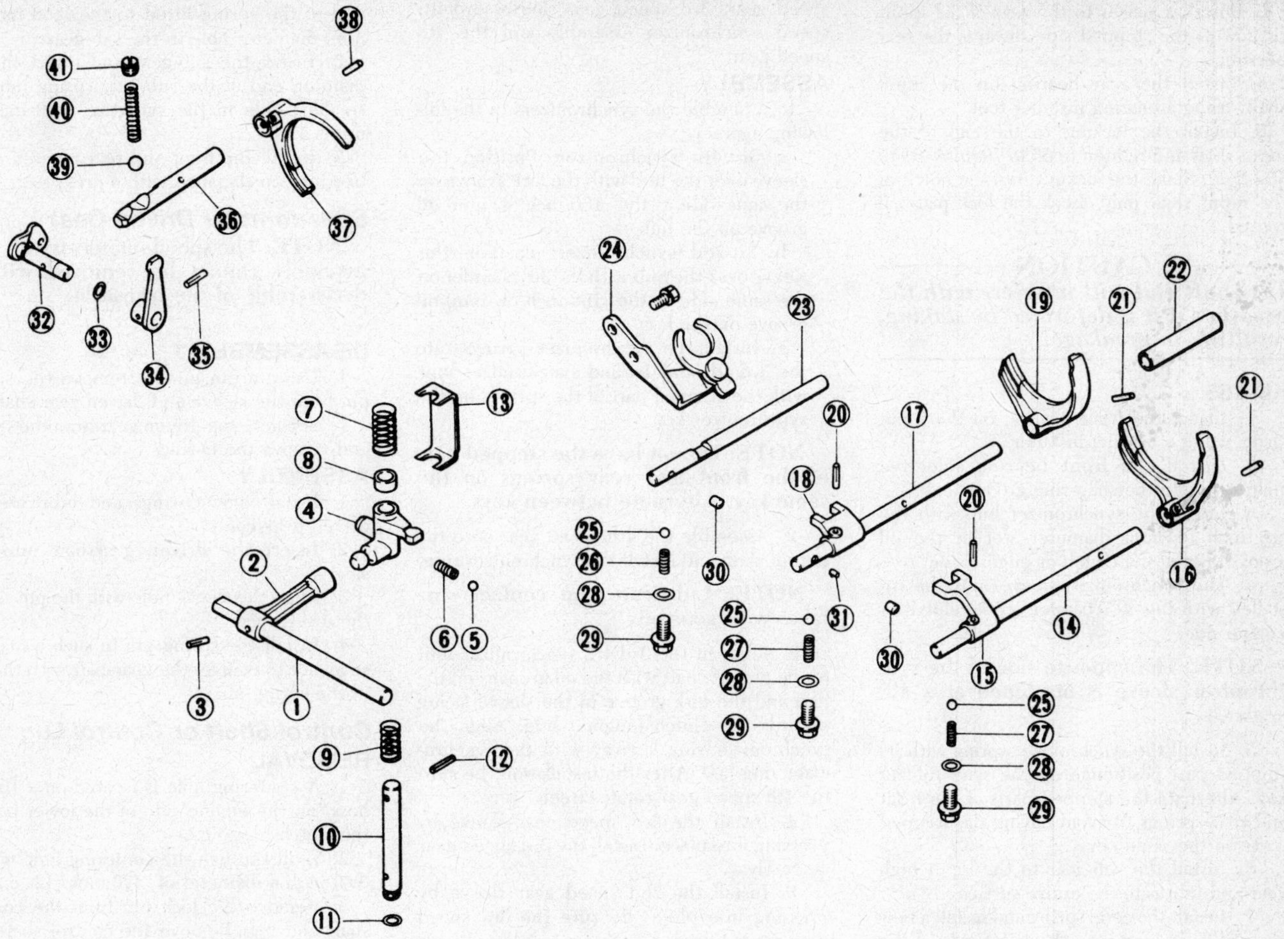

1. Control shaft
2. Control lug
3. Lock pin
4. Control finger
5. Steel ball
6. Spring [Length; 18.9 mm (.74 in.)]
7. Neutral return spring
8. Spacer collar
9. Reverse restrict spring
10. Shift shaft
11. O-ring
12. Spring pin
13. Spring retainer
14. 1st and 2nd speed shift rail
15. Shift lug
16. Shift fork
17. 3rd and 4th speed shift rail
18. Shift lug
19. Shift fork
20. Lock pin
21. Spring pin
22. Spacer collar
23. Reverse shift rail
24. Reverse shift lever assembly
25. Steel ball
26. Reverse spring [Length; 16.6 mm (.65 in.)]
27. Spring [Length; 18.9 mm (.74 in.)]
28. Gasket
29. Plug
30. Interlock plunger A
31. Interlock plunger B
*32. Selector shaft
*33. O-ring
*34. Selector finger
*35. Lock pin
*36. Shift rail
*37. Shift fork
*38. Lock pin
*39. Steel ball
*40. Spring
*41. Plug

NOTE: Part marked * is applicable to KM165.

Exploded view of shift mechanism

hole. Pull the shaft from the case and remove the control finger, two springs, spacer collar, poppet spring and ball.

CAUTION

During removal of the shift shaft from the case, the poppet ball will jump out of the control finger hole. Close the hole with an object of finger tip to prevent loss of the ball.

21. Put an identifying mark on the tapered roller bearing outer race and remove it from the case.

22. Remove the lock and the speedometer driven gear assembly.

Input Shaft

KM 160

1. Remove the front bearing snap-ring and using a special puller, remove the front bearing from the input shaft.
2. Straighten the locking washer and remove the locknut at the rear of the input shaft.
3. Using a press or a special puller, remove the rear bearing from the shaft.

KM 165

1. Remove the front bearing snap-ring and emove the front bearing with a special puller.
2. Straighten the locking washer and remove the locknut at the rear of the input shaft.
3. Using a press and supporting the low gear of the input shaft, press on the rear of the input shaft and remove the input high gear, gear sleeve, synchronizer assembly, input low gear and the rear bearing.

NOTE: To remove the rear bearing only, use a special puller. The input high gear will come off with the rear bearing.

ASSEMBLY

KM 160

1. Install the front bearing on the input shaft, using a bearing installer tool.
2. Install the front bearing selective snap-ring into the snap-ring groove.

3. Install a spacer to the rear of the input shaft with the stepped side towards the rear bearing.

4. Install the rear bearing on the input shaft, using a bearing installer tool.

5. Install the locknut to the end of the input shaft and tighten to 66 to 79 ft/lbs (89 to 107 Nm). Stake the locknut into the notch of the input shaft only. Lock the lock plate, if reused.

CAUTION

The shaft end will interfere with the breather if it is deformed by staking, resulting in breakage.

KM 165

1. Install the front bearing on the input shaft, using a bearing installer.

2. Install the front bearing selective snap-ring into the snap-ring groove.

3. Install the synchronizer hub with the .16 inch (4 mm) diameter slot in the oil groove, facing the clutch or engine side.

4. The synchronizer sleeve must be installed with the 30° chamfer on the clutch or engine side.

NOTE: The opposite side of the synchronizer sleeve is machined at a 45° angle.

5. Install the synchronizer spring with its stepped part positioned on the synchronizer key. Alternate the stepped parts of the front and rear springs to avoid having the stepped parts on the same key.

6. Install the sub-gear to the input high gear and lubricate the entire surface.

7. Install the cone spring and install a new snap-ring, making sure the inner side of the cone spring is not in the snap-ring groove.

8. Install the input low gear and the needle bearing on the input shaft.

9. Install the synchronizer ring.

10. Using a special installer tool, press fit the synchronizer assembly onto the input shaft with the synchronizer key correctly aligned with the synchronizer ring keyway.

11. Install the input high gear sleeve with a special installer tool. The input low gear should rotate smoothly. Install the synchronizer ring, the input high gear and needle bearing.

12. Install the spacer with the stepped side facing the rear bearing side.

13. Install the rear bearing with a special nstaller tool.

14. Install and tighten the input shaft rear nut to 66 to 79 ft/lbs (89 to 107 Nm.) and stake in place into the notch on the input shaft. Should the lockplate be reused, bend the plate over a shoulder of the locknut.

Output Shaft

DISASSEMBLY

1. Unlock the rear locknut plate and remove the locknut from the shaft.

2. Remove the front and rear tapered bearings from the output shaft, using special bearing puller tools.

3. Using a puller tool, remove the 1st speed gear, gear sleeve, 1st and 2nd speed synchronizer assembly and the 2nd speed gear.

4. Remove the 2nd speed gear sleeve, 3rd speed gear, 3rd speed gear sleeve, 3rd/4th speed synchronizer assembly and the 4th speed gear.

ASSEMBLY

1. Assemble the synchronizers in the following manner;

a. 3rd/4th synchronizer: Position the sleeve over the hub with the fork groove on the same side as the .160 inch (4. mm) oil groove on the hub.

b. 1st/2nd synchronizer: Position the sleeve over the hub with the 30° chamfer on the same side as the .160 inch (4. mm) oil groove on the hub.

c. Install the synchronizer springs into the 3rd/4th and 1st/2nd synchronizer unit with the stepped part of the springs on the synchronizer key.

NOTE: Do not have the stepped part of the front and rear springs on the same key. Alternate between keys.

2. Assemble the 4th speed gear onto the output shaft and install the synchronizer ring.

NOTE: Lubricate the contact surfaces with gear oil.

3. Press fit the 3rd/4th synchronizer unit to the output shaft with the oil grooves on the hub and the fork groove in the sleeve facing towards the clutch (engine) side. Align the synchronizer ring keyway with the synchronizer ring key. After the installation, be sure the 4th speed gear rotates freely.

4. Install the 3rd speed gear sleeve by pressing into place. Install the 3rd speed gear assembly.

5. Install the 2nd speed gear sleeve by pressing into place. Be sure the 3rd speed gear rotates freely.

6. Install the 2nd speed gear and the 1st/2nd synchronizer ring.

7. Install the 1st/2nd speed synchronizer assembly onto the output shaft by pressing with the proper tools. Be sure the 2nd speed gear rotates freely.

8. Install the 1st/2nd synchronizer ring. Press the 1st/2nd speed synchronizer assembly into place on the output shaft. Be sure the 2nd speed gear rotates freely.

9. Install the 1st/2nd speed synchronizer ring with the keyways properly aligned with the keys.

10. Install the 1st gear to the gear sleeve and press the unit onto the output shaft. Be sure the 1st speed gear rotates freely.

11. Install the front and rear tapered bearings on the front and the rear of the shaft.

12. Install the locknut on the rear of the shaft and torque to 66 to 79 ft/lbs. (89 to 107 Nm). Lock the locking plate to the nut, if used. Stake the locknut securely to the output shaft.

Intermediate Shaft

DISASSEMBLY

1. Remove the front tapered bearing with a press unit.

2. Remove the sub-gear and the spring assembly.

3. Remove the rear tapered bearing with the use of a press.

ASSEMBLY

1. Assemble the sub-gear spring assembly to the intermediate shaft gear with the longer end of the spring fitted to the .160 inch (4. mm) diameter hole in the sub-gear.

2. Install the sub-gear and insert the remaining end of the sub-gear spring into the smallest hole in the sub-gear, .160 inch (4. mm).

3. Install the front and rear tapered roller bearings on the shaft with a press tool.

Speedometer Driven Gear

NOTE: The speedometer driven gear assembly cannot be removed without disassembly of the transaxle.

DISASSEMBLY

1. Using a pin punch, remove the spring pin from the sleeve and driven gear shaft.

2. Separate the driven gear from the sleeve and remove the O-rings.

ASSEMBLY

1. Install new O-rings and lubricate the driven gearshaft.

2. Insert the driven gearshaft into the sleeve.

3. Align the sleeve hole with the pin slot in the driven gear.

4. Install the spring pin in such a manner so as not to contact the gearshaft with the slit in the spring pin.

Control Shaft or Control Lug

REMOVAL

1. A centering hole is located on a 16 mm boss, on the engine side of the lower part of the clutch housing.

2. Drill through the centering hole with a drill with a diameter of .470 inch (12. mm).

3. Remove the lock pin from the control shaft and lug. Remove the control shaft and lug.

INSTALLATION

1. Install the control shaft and lug. Install a new lock pin through the control lug and shaft.

2. Install a .470 inch (12. mm) cup plug in the drilled hole and seal the plug with a bonding sealant.

Differential

The overhaul of the differential assembly is confined to the replacement of the side bearings, ring gear and the differential and pinion gears. The replacement is done in the conventional manner. Necessary measurements during the assembly is given in the transaxle assembly procedures.

ASSEMBLY OF TRANSAXLE

NOTE: Lubricate all seals and O-rings during the assembly.

1. Prepare the transaxle case for component assembly by replacing all oil seals and case internal small parts that were removed during the disassembly.

2. Install the speedometer driven gear assembly into the clutch housing. Install the locking plate into the groove cur into the sleeve.

3. **Model KM 165:** Install an O-ring onto the selector shaft and lubricate the ring and the bore in the case. Install the shaft into the case and install the selector finger. Install the

lock pin so that it is flush on the clutch housing side of the selector finger.

4. Install the poppet spring and steel ball into the control finger and with the use of a special tool, force the poppet ball into its bore. Leave the tool in position.

5. Install a new O-ring onto the shift shaft and install the shaft into the clutch housing and engage the reverse restrict spring and the control finger.

6. Press the shift shaft inward until the special tool, used to hold the poppet ball and spring, is forced out. Recover and lay aside. Install the spacer collar and the neutral return spring and force the shift shaft to its bore in the opposite side of the case opening.

7. Align the spring pin holes and install the spring pins.

8. Install the spring retainer in place over the control finger assembly.

9. Install the differential gear assembly into the clutch housing. Adjust the differential case end-play as follows:

a. Place two pieces of plastic type gauge material, approximately ¾ inch in length, on the differential ball bearing outer race, 180° apart.

b. Install the transaxle case and gasket. Tighten the mounting bolts to 26 to 30 ft/lbs. (35 to 41 Nm). Remove the bolts and the transaxle case. Lay the case aside for later installation.

c. Measure the thickness of the plastic type gauge material and select a spacer of the proper thickness to provide the standard end-play. The end-play should range between 0.000 to 0.0059 inch (0.0 to 0.15 mm).

d. Spacer thicknesses are as follows:

Inch	MM	I.D. Mark
0.0516	1.31	E
0.0551	1.40	None
0.0587	1.49	C
0.0622	1.58	B
0.0657	1.67	A
0.0693	1.76	F

10. Turn the sub gear in the direction of the embossed arrow to align the .310 inch (8 mm) hole in the intermediate gear with that in the sub-gear. Insert a bar or bolt in the holes to maintain alignment.

11. Install the input shaft assembly and the intermediate shaft assembly into the clutch housing as a unit.

NOTE: KM 165 models—Install the selector shift rail and fork assembly at the same time.

12. Install the selector shaft poppet ball, poppet spring and plug. Apply a sealer to the plug and seat it flush with the housing surface.

13. Install the input shaft bearing retainer and remove the bar or bolt used to retain the alignment of the sub-gear to the intermediate gear.

14. Install the output shaft assembly.

15. Install the interlock plungers into the housing. Reassamble the 1st/2nd and 3rd/4th speed shift rails and forks in the reverse order of removal, into the housing.

16. Align the holes in the shift rail and the shift fork and install the pin. The pin must have its slit on the shift rail center line. Even the spring pin protrusion on both sides.

17. Install the reverse shift rail and install the three poppet balls, springs and plugs.

NOTE: The poppet spring with the white paint I.D. must be installed in the poppet hole of the reverse shift rail. Install the small diameter ends of the springs towards the steel balls.

18. Install the reverse shift lever assembly, the reverse idler gear and shaft and apply lubricate to the gear and shaft.

19. Measure the height of the reverse idler gear. The height from the face of the case to the upper flat of the gear should be 1.4429 to 1.5374 inch (37.85±1.2 mm). If less than specified, replace the reverse shift lever assembly.

20. Apply a sealer to the gasket and install on to the clutch housing.

21. Install the selected spacer on the differential side bearing and install the transaxle case. Install the bolts and torque to 26 to 30 ft/lbs (35 to 41 Nm).

22. Install the intermediate and output shaft rear tapered bearing outer races and press them in by hand.

23. Install the oil seal into the axle output shaft case hole, if not previously done.

NOTE: The oil seal hole must be chamfered before the seal is installed into the case, to prevent periphery damage to the seal and to cause leakages.

24. To select the outer race end spacer, use the following procedure:

a. Seat the outer races properly and measure the depths of the transaxle case to the races, using a depth micrometer.

b. Select a spacer for each race 0.004 inch (0.4 mm) thicker than the measured value.

c. Install the spacers in their respective bores and install the rear cover. Torque the bolts to 14 to 16 ft/lbs (19 to 22 Nm).

d. Using the special tool seal installer or equivalent, shift the transaxle to any desired gear, while rotating the input shaft.

NOTE: The input shaft may turn hard and the installation of the clutch plate may be necessary to assist in turning the shaft.

e. Remove the rear cover after setting the transaxle in a position with the rear cover up.

f. Remove the spacers and remeasure the depth as was done in Step a.

g. Reselect spacers of proper thickness so that an end-play of 0.000 to 0.0020 inch (0.0 to 0.05 mm) exists at the tapered roller bearing outer races.

h. Spacer thicknesses are as follows:

Inch	MM	I.D. Mark
.0724	1.84	84
.0736	1.87	87
.0748	1.90	90
.0760	1.93	93
.0772	1.96	96
.0783	1.99	99
.0795	2.02	02
.0807	2.05	05
.0819	2.08	08
.0831	2.11	11
.0843	2.14	14
.0854	2.17	17
.0866	2.20	20
.0878	2.23	23
.0890	2.26	26
.0902	2.29	29
.0913	2.32	32
.0925	2.35	35
.0937	2.38	38
.0949	2.41	41
.0961	2.44	44
.0972	2.47	47
.0984	2.50	50
.0996	2.53	53
.1008	2.56	56
.1020	2.59	59
.1031	2.62	62
.1043	2.65	65
.1055	2.68	68

25. Apply sealer to the gasket and reinstall the rear cover. Torque the bolts to 14 to 16 ft/lbs (19 to 22 Nm).

26. Install the back-up lamp switch with washer and steel ball in place.

27. Verify the transaxle shifts and the internal gear rotate smoothly.

TYPE 4

4 and 5 Speed Transaxle–Models F4WF60A, F5WF60A

Datsun F-10 and B310

DISASSEMBLY

1. Remove the reverse light switch and drain the transmission.

2. Remove the bearing housing and primary gear as a unit.

3. Remove the primary gear cover.

4. Take the bottom cover off the transmission. Put reverse and 1st gears into position (to keep the shaft from turning) and remove the main gear locknut.

5. Remove the primary gear cover.

6. Remove the clutch housing.

7. If necessary, drive out the drive and idler bearing with a puller. Then press the bearing out of the main drive input gear.

8. Remove the differential side flanges.

9. Remove the speedometer pinion gear.

1. Primary drive gear
2. Primary idler gear
3. Sub gear
4. Main drive input gear
5. Main drive gear
6. Baulk ring
7. Spread spring
8. Coupling sleeve
9. Shifting insert
10. Synchronizer hub
11. 3rd main gear
12. Main gear bushing
13. Main gear spacer
14. 2nd main gear
15. 1st main gear
16. Reverse main gear
17. Main shaft
18. Final gear
19. Counter gear
20. Thrust washer
21. Thrust spring
22. Counter shaft
23. Reverse idler gear
24. Reverse idler shaft
25. Bearing retainer

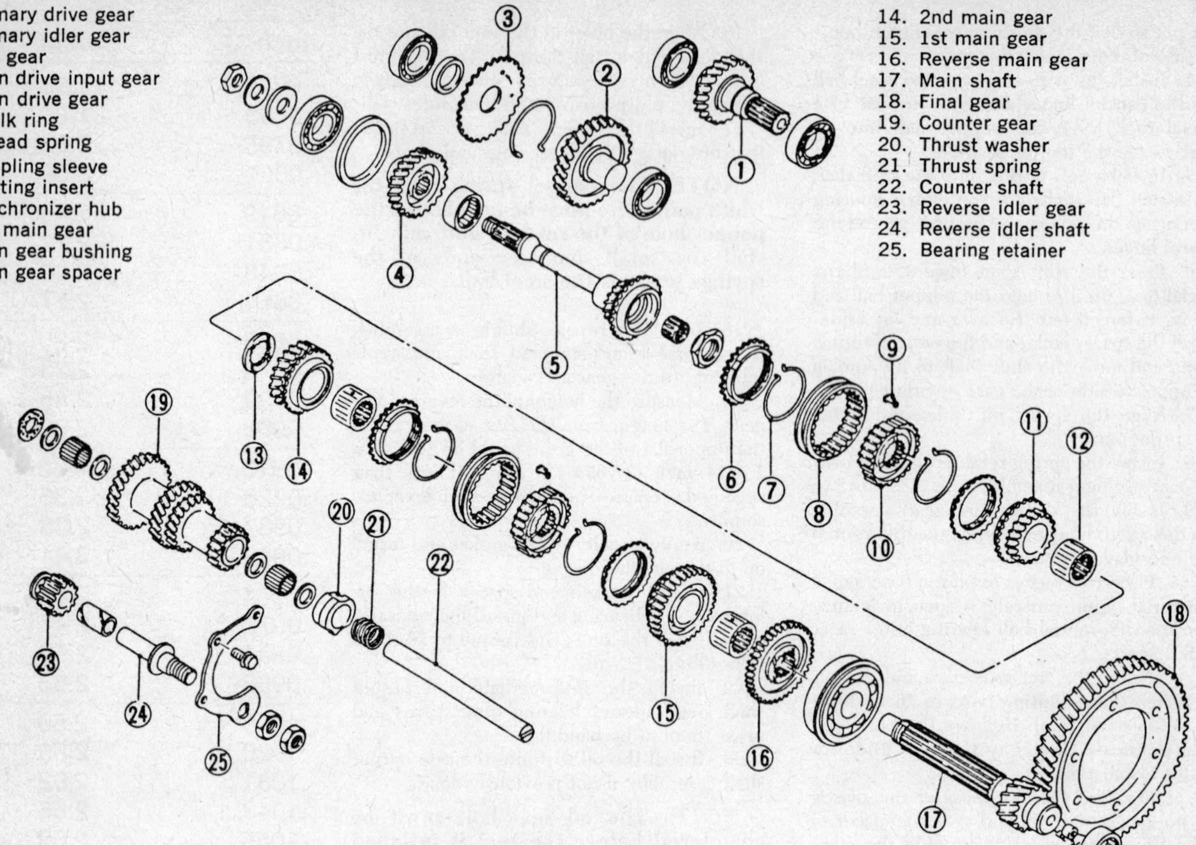

4-speed gear components

1. Bearing housing
2. Primary gear cover
3. Clutch housing
4. Transmission case
5. Transmission case cover
6. Bottom cover

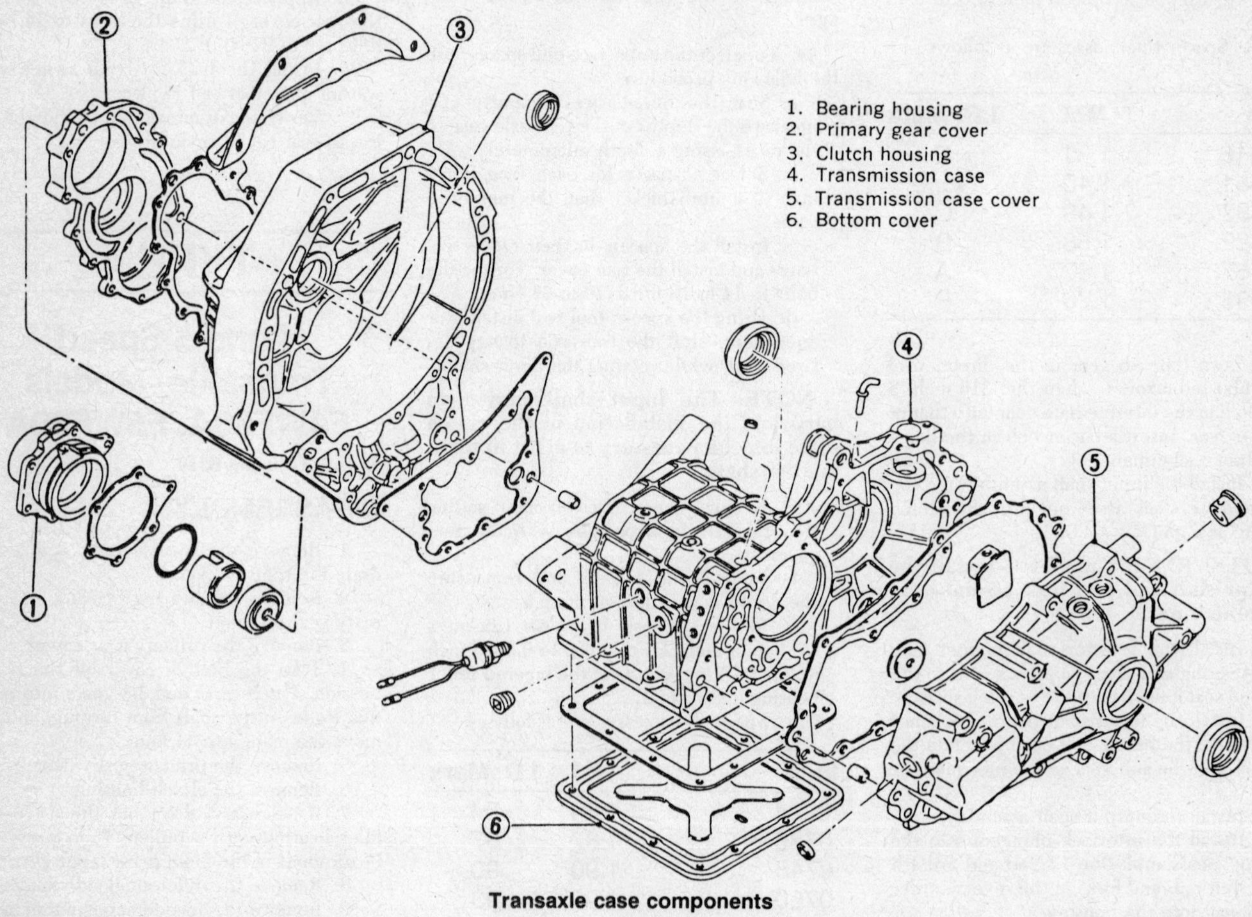

Transaxle case components

10. Remove the differential case as a unit.

11. Pull the differential side bearings and remove the ring gear mounting bolts.

12. Remove the differential case and withdraw the pinion shaft and remove the side gear and pinion mate.

13. Loosen bolts D1 and D2 and remove the reverse fork lever and bracket. Loosen double nuts E1 and bolts D3 and remove the bearing retainer.

NOTE: Double nuts E1 should be loosened before bolts D3.

14. Remove the reverse idler gear and shaft and drive out the countergear and countershaft guide.

NOTE: Needle bearing on countergear is not a retainer type. When removing gear, do not allow the bearing to come off.

15. Remove the transmission case service plug. This will allow access to the roll pin on the 1st/2nd shift fork.

Using a punch drive the roll pins out of the shift forks. Withdraw the fork rods and remove the shift forks.

NOTE: When driving out the roll pin from the 3rd/4th shift fork, shift the rod to 3rd gear before starting. Also be careful of the placement of the interlock plungers.

16. Remove the mainshaft gear assembly and the main drive gear toward the final drive gear side.

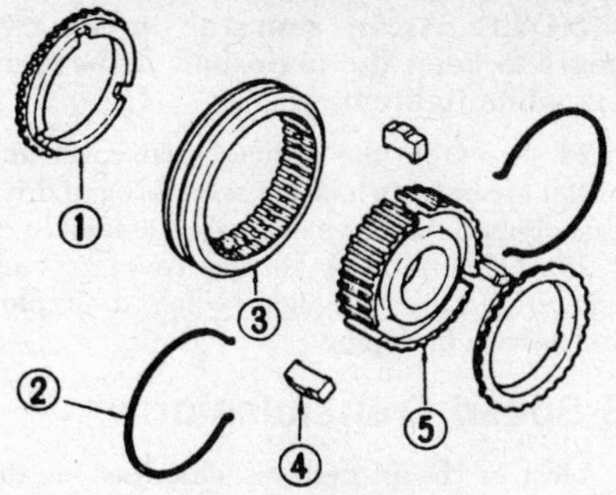
1. Baulk ring
2. Spread spring
3. Coupling sleeve
4. Shifting insert
5. Synchronizer hub

Exploded view of synchronizer unit

NOTE: The locknut is caulked, but you do not have to remove the caulking for loosening.

17. Remove the mainshaft components in this order: 3rd/4th synchronizer, 3rd gear, main gear bushing, main gear spacer, 2nd gear, main gear bushing, 1st/2nd synchronizer, 1st gear, main gear bushing and reverse gear.

NOTE: The 3rd main gear bushing and mainshaft are press-fit. Remove the bushing with the main gear spacer and the 2nd main gear with a puller.

18. Press out the bearing from the mainshaft.

19. To disassemble a synchronizer, remove the spread springs and the shifting inserts, then separate the coupling sleeve from the synchro-hub.

ASSEMBLY

Generally, the procedures for assembly are the reverse of removal. However, there are certain steps you must observe.

1. Slide the synchro-hub into the coupling sleeve and fit the shifting inserts into their grooves.

2. Put one spread spring on the lower side of the shifting inserts to hold them to the inner side of the coupling sleeve. Put the other spread spring on the opposite side of the synchro-hub.

NOTE: Make sure the spread springs are opposite each other.

3. Press ball bearing onto the mainshaft and assemble reverse gear. Assemble the main gear bushing and 1st gear.

NOTE: Be sure to align the oil hole in the bushing with the one on the mainshaft.

4. Assemble baulk ring, synchronizer, main gear bushing, baulk ring, 2nd gear, main gear spacer, main gear bushing, 3rd gear, baulk ring, synchronizer and locknut on the mainshaft.

5. Put the spacers and needles into both sides of the countergear. Be sure to grease the needles before inserting.

1. Primary drive gear
2. Primary idler gear
3. Sub gear
4. Main drive input gear
5. Main drive gear
6. Baulk ring
7. Spread spring
8. Coupling sleeve
9. Shifting insert
10. Synchronizer hub
11. 4th main gear
12. 4th gear bushing
13. Main gear spacer
14. 3rd main gear
15. 2nd main gear
16. Reverse main gear
17. Main shaft
18. Final gear
19. 1st main gear
20. Counter gear
21. 1st-reverse counter gear
22. Reverse idler gear
23. Reverse idler input gear

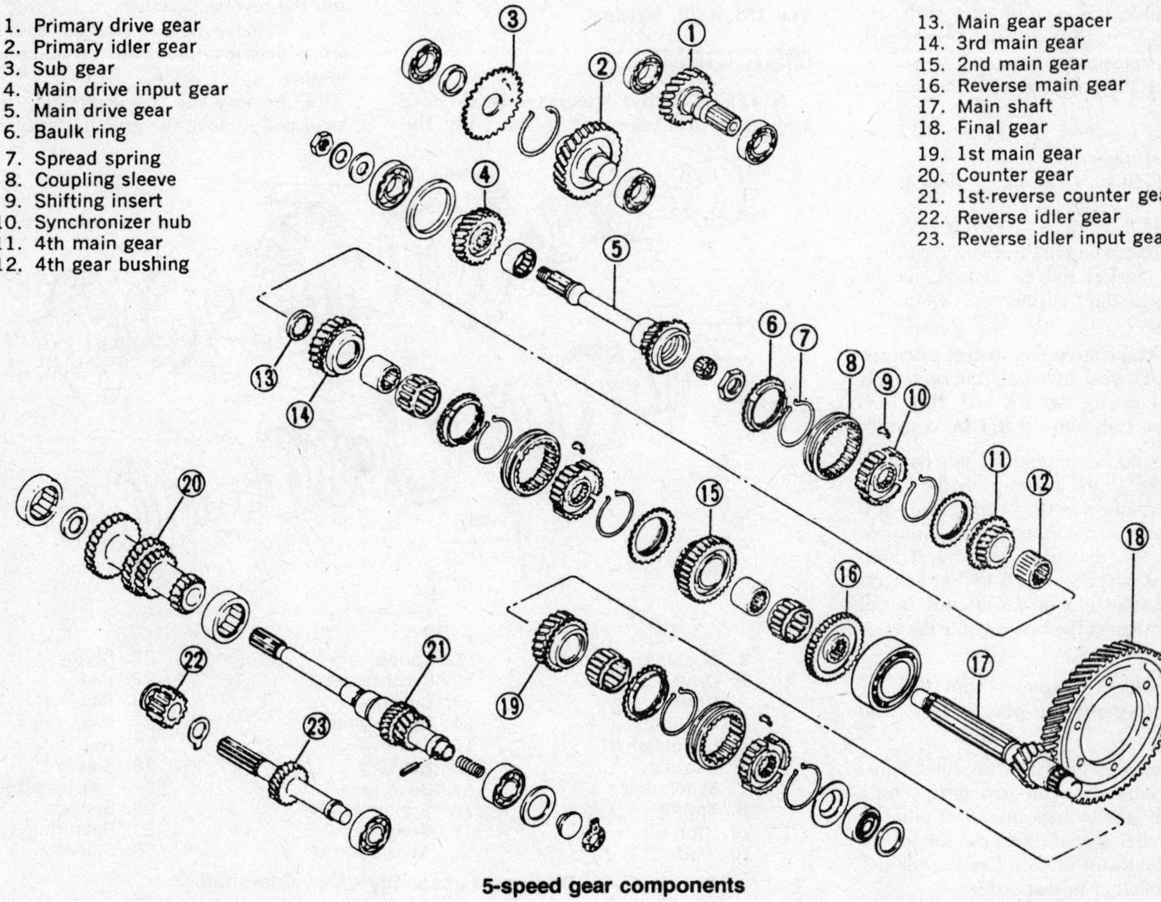

5-speed gear components

6. Insert a countershaft guide into the countergear.

7. Press the differential side bearing into the differential case.

8. Put the pinion mates, side gears, thrust washers and pinion shaft in the case.

9. Select the proper thrust washer to adjust side gear end-play to 0.008 in., then apply oil to gear teeth and thrust surfaces.

10. Put the ring gear onto the differential case.

11. Press in the differential side flange oil seals after lubricating their lips with grease.

12. Assemble the main drive gear and mainshaft in the transmission case.

13. Put in the 1st/2nd shift fork and the 3rd/4th fork. Make sure they are into their grooves in the coupling sleeves.

14. Slide the 3rd/4th fork rod through the transmission case and the 3rd/4th shift fork. Secure it with a new retaining pin.

15. Assemble the check ball, spring and check ball plug. Before tightening, apply sealer to the plug. Be sure to align the notch in the 3rd/4th rod with the check ball. Place the unit in Neutral. Assemble the 1st/2nd and reverse fork rod similarly.

16. With the countershaft guide in place in the countergear, install the countergear, thrust washers and thrust spring on the transmission case. Insert countershaft into countergear and drive out the guide.

NOTE: Pay attention to the direction of thrust washer assembly. Align the cut out portion of the countershaft with the bearing retainer.

17. Assemble the reverse idler shaft, reverse idler gear, bearing retainer, reverse fork and fork bracket with the cutout portion of the reverse idler shaft aligned with the bearing retainer.

18. Before installing the differential case, measure bearing height "H".

If it is 4.720 to 4.730 in., a shim is not needed.

If it is 4.715 to 4.719 in., use a 0.0078 shim.

If it is 4.710 to 4.714 in., use a 0.0118 shim.

19. With the fork rods in Neutral, put the case cover onto the transmission.

NOTE: Make sure the shifter engages with the fork rod brackets correctly. If the resin-coating comes off the bolt threads, the bolt should not be reused.

20. Assemble the differential side flanges.

21. Put the clutch housing on the transmission case and press the bearings onto primary and main drive input gears. Assemble the sub-gear on the idler gear. Insert both ends of the ring spring into 0.197 in. hole on the primary idler gear and sub-gear. Install the spacer and press the bearing onto the idler gear.

NOTE: Select a spacer that will insure the sub-gear end-play is less than 0.004 in.

22. Put the idler gear into the clutch housing and assemble the main drive gear, setting the idler sub-gear by inserting a bar into the hole in the idler gear through the sub-gear.

23. Put the thrust washer, lock washer and drive gear together in that order.

NOTE: As in removal, mesh two gears to keep the mainshaft from turning while tightening.

24. Assemble the primary gear cover and install the bearing housing assembly and drive gear. Rotate the drive gear while assembling.

25. Assemble the bottom cover, speedometer gear, reverse light switch, drain plug and service hole plug.

5-Speed Transmission

Most of the procedures described in the 4-speed section apply to the 5-speed, with the following exceptions:

When removing the mainshaft and drive gear, you may have to tap the end of the mainshaft with a hammer.

When assembling the 3rd main gear bushing, make sure the claw is lined up with the main gear spacer and that the thinner spline tooth side of the 2nd/3rd synchro-hub must point towards 3rd gear.

When installing the main gear spacer, make sure that the uneven side is pointed toward 4th gear. The 4th gear bushing is the same as the 4-speed main gear bushing.

TYPE 5

4 and 5 Speed Transaxle

Fiat 128, X1/9, Strada

DISASSEMBLY

NOTE: The five speed transaxle case and gear arrangement is basically the same as the four speed transaxle, except the rear extension housing is extended to include the fifth gear on the input and output shafts and shift forks are controlled by the fifth and reverse selector rail.

1. Remove the drain plug and drain the lubricant from the transmission/differential.

2. Remove the screws securing the oil boots and remove the axle shafts together with the oil boots.

3. Remove the nuts retaining the cover and remove the cover and gasket.

4. Remove the snap-ring from the mainshaft bearing.

5. Compress the spring washer in the countershaft and remove the snap-ring from the countershaft.

6. Remove the detent ball spring cover and gasket for the shift control rods. Remove the three ball spring and balls.

7. Remove the two ball bearings from the mainshaft and countershaft.

8. Remove the nuts attaching the transmission housing to the main case and lift the case off of the studs.

9. Remove the screws retaining the gearshift forks and dogs to the rods. Remove the rods, forks, and dogs from their seats in the housing.

10. Remove the gear selector and engagement lever support.

11. Remove the gasket between the maincase and the housing.

12. Remove the nut securing the reverse gearshaft retaining plate and remove the plate and the reverse gearshaft.

13. Remove the mainshaft and countershaft assemblies together with the differential assembly.

14. Remove the screw retaining the shift lever and remove the gear shift control rod.

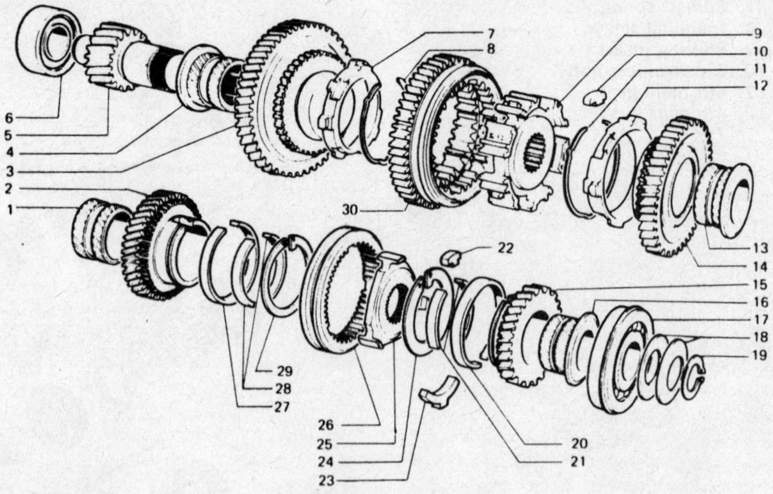

1. Bushing
2. Driven gear
3. Driven gear
4. Bushing
5. Countershaft
6. Bearing
7. Synchronizer
8. Spring
9. Hub
10. Pad
11. Spring
12. Synchronizer
13. Bushing
14. Driven gear
15. Gear
16. Bushing
17. Bearing
18. Spring washer
19. Snap ring
20. Synchronizer
21. Spring
22. Pad
23. Pad
24. Snap ring
25. Hub
26. Sleeve
27. Synchronizer
28. Spring
29. Snap ring
30. Sleeve

Drive gear assembly on countershaft

ASSEMBLY

1. Clean all of the parts with solvent and check the maincase, housing, and cover for cracks and wear or damage to the bearing seats. Check all of the seals for deterioration or wear. Check all shafts for chipping or excessive wear. Check the splines for wear or damage.

Check and make sure that the sliding sleeve hubs for the engagement of first/second and third/fourth gears are not nicked. Check the sleeve sliding surface.

Check the synchronizer rings for signs of deterioration on the inside surface and on the teeth that mesh with the sliding sleeves. The rings must not be loose in its gear seat.

If splined parts do not slide easily and smoothly, remove the cause with a very fine file or replace the defective parts.

2. Install the bearing for the countershaft into the clutch cover end of the transmission case.

3. Install the outer bearing race for the differential bearing onto the case.

4. Install the gear shift control rod in the housing with the spring, gasket, cover, and boot. Next install the control lever.

5. Install the differential assembly in the housing.

6. Install the countershaft assembly in the housing.

7. Install the mainshaft assembly in the housing.

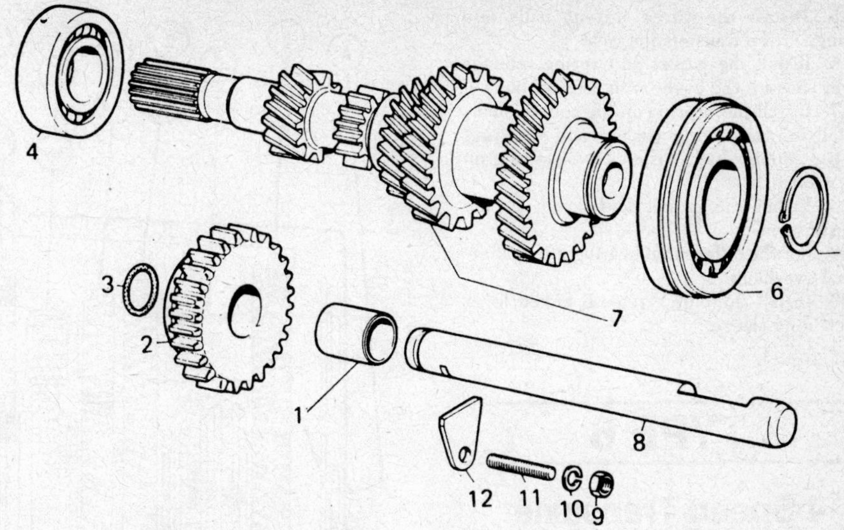

1. Bushing
2. Gear
3. Seal
4. Bearing
5. Snap ring
6. Bearing
7. Mainshaft
8. Shaft
9. Nut
10. Lockwasher
11. Stud
12. Plate

Mainshaft and reverse and reverse idler gear

8. Install the reverse gearshaft with its gasket in the housing. Secure the reverse gear shaft assembly with the plate and nut.

9. Install the gasket onto the housing mating surface.

10. Make sure that the gear selector and engagement lever is sealed on the control lever attached to the gear control rod. Install the support for the selector and engagement lever on the housing. Secure the support with the nut.

11. Install the rod detent rollers in their seats on the support.

12. Install the gear selector rods, forks, and dogs.

13. Install the transmission case on the housing.

14. Secure the two halves of the transmission case together with the washers and nuts.

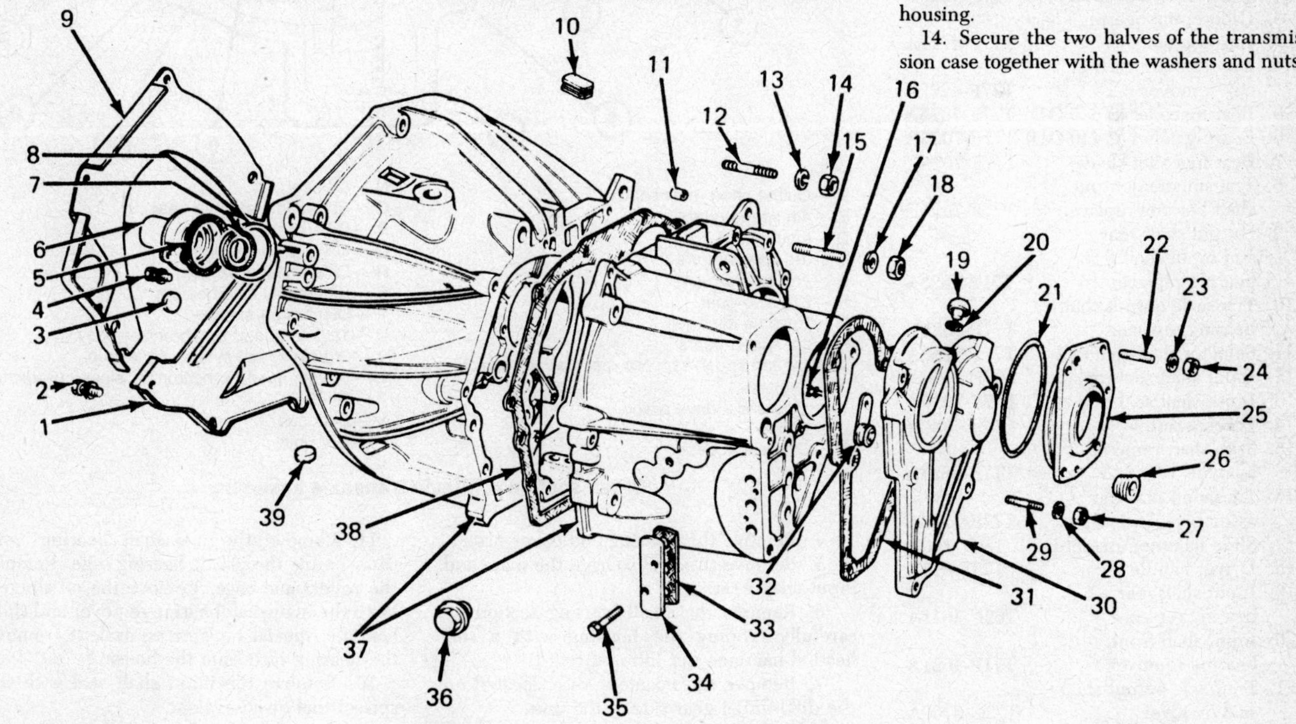

1. Cover
2. Bolt and washer
3. Plug
4. Bolt and washer
5. Gasket
6. Cover
7. Seal
8. Plug
9. Cover
10. Plug
11. Dowel
12. Stud
13. Lockwasher
14. Nut
15. Stud
16. Bolt and washer
17. Lockwasher
18. Nut
19. Vent
20. Gasket
21. Seal
22. Stud
23. Lockwasher
24. Nut
25. Flange
26. Plug
27. Nut
28. Lockwasher
29. Stud
30. Cover
31. Gasket
32. Magnet
33. Gasket
34. Cover
35. Bolt
36. Plug
37. Case
38. Gasket
39. Plug

Transaxle case assembly

15. Install the three detent balls and springs in the transmission case.

16. Install the gasket and spring retainer cover. Secure the cover with the two bolts.

17. Install the bearing on the countershaft. Install the two spring washers and snap-ring on the countershaft. Install the snap-ring on the mainshaft.

18. Install the gasket and cover on the transmission.

19. Set the differential bearing. (See differential overhaul).

20. Install the clutch release forked lever and sliding sleeve.

TYPE 6

4 Speed Transaxle

1978-81 Fiesta

Special tools are needed in the overhaul of the transaxle gear box.

It would be most advantageous for the repairman to obtain the special tools or their equivalent before the overhaul work is begun.

A list of special tools needed and their reference numbers are given for the convenience of the repairman.

1. Differential bearing cone replacer — T77F-4220
2. Differential bearing cone remover and adapter — T77F-4220B
3. Differential bearing cup installer — T77F-4222A
4. Differential bearing cup remover — T77F-4222B
5. Bearing collet (2.675 OD) — T77F-7025A
6. Bearing collet (2.440 OD) — T77F-7025B
7. Bearing collet sleeve — T77F-7025C
8. Transmission output shaft bearing replacer — T77F-7025E
9. Output shaft rear and input shaft front bearing replacer — T71P-7025A
10. Transaxle output shaft bearing replacer — T77F-7025E
11. Selector shaft seal tool — T77F-7288A
12. Input shaft seal replacer — T77F-7050A
13. Input shaft seal remover — T77F-7050B
14. Forcing screw — T75L-7025J
15. Stub shaft remover adapter — T77F-3617A
16. Threaded drawbar assembly — T77F-1176A
17. Slide hammer assembly — T50T-100A
18. Driver handle — T73T-815A
19. Input shaft rear bearing replacer — T62F-4621A
20. Input shaft front bearing remover — T71P-4621B
21. Transaxle output shaft seal remover — T73C-6700A

TRANSAXLE

Disassembly

1. Mount the removed transaxle on a work stand and drain all oil from the unit.

2. Remove the clutch release lever, fork and release bearing.

3. Remove the selector shaft locking retainer nut with the locking pin and spring.

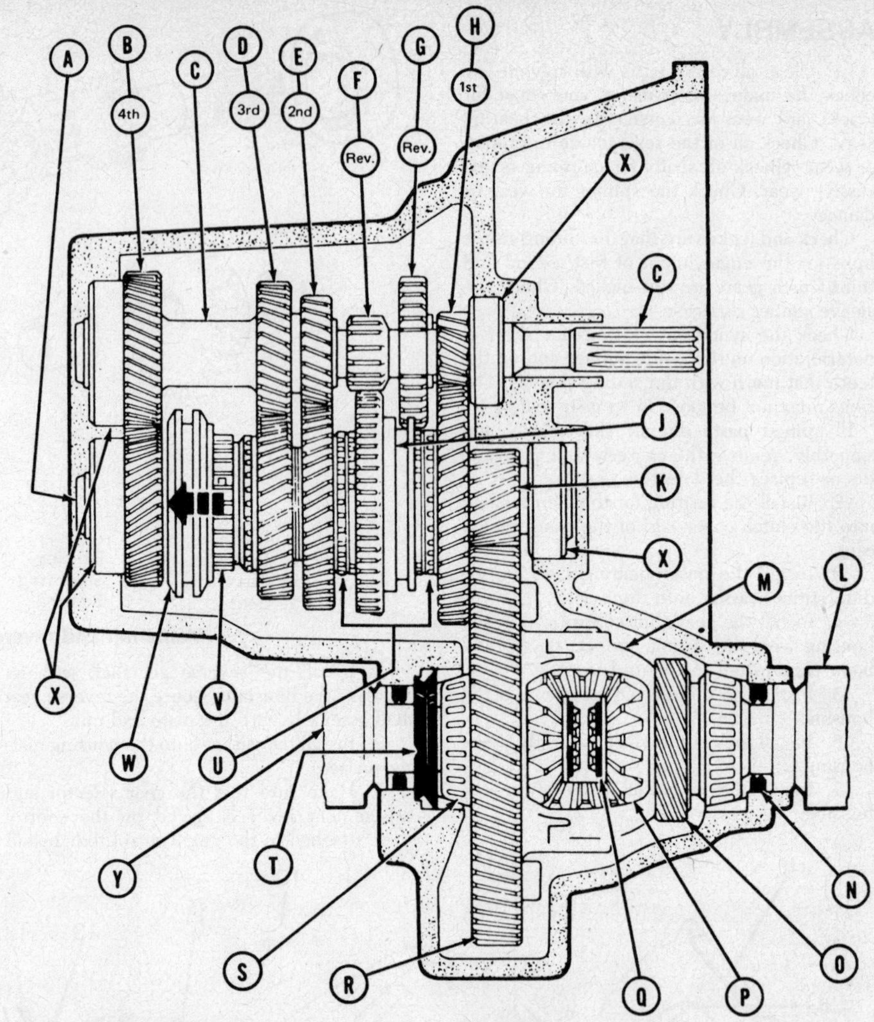

A —Output shaft (mainshaft)
B —4th speed gears
C —Input shaft
D —3rd speed gears
E —2nd speed gears
F —Reverse gear
G —Reverse idler gear
H —1st speed gears
J —1st/2nd speed synchronizer sleeve (Selector ring)
K —Differential drive pinion
L —U-joint
M —Differential case
N —Oil seal
O —Speedometer drive gear
P —Differential side gear
Q —C.V. joint snap ring
R —Differential drive gear
S —Differential side bearing
T —Diaphragm springs
U —1st/2nd speed synchronizer assy
V —3rd/4th speed synchronizer hub
W—3rd/4th speed synchronizer sleeve (Selector Ring)
X —Bearings
Y —C.V. joint

Cross section of Fiesta transaxle assembly

4. Remove the housing end cover plate.

5. Remove the C-clips from the main and input shaft bearings.

6. Remove the small housing section by carefully tapping the housing with a soft headed hammer and lifting upward.

7. Remove the magnetic disc, located on the differential gear side of the unit.

NOTE: Do not drop the disc, as breakage will occur.

8. Remove the selector fork guide shaft, the fork, shift locking plate and spring.

9. Remove the complete mainshaft assembly from the housing, including input shaft and reverse gear.

10. Lift the differential gear from the housing.

11. Remove the mainshaft bearings and disassemble the plastic bearing cage. Remove the rollers and cage. Remove the oil slinger. With the mainshaft bearing remover and slide hammer special tools or equivalent, remove the bearing race from the housing.

12. Remove the input shaft seal with the special tool or equivalent.

NOTE: During the removal of the seal, do not damage the housing.

13. Remove the stubshaft seal from the large housing with the output shaft seal remover or equivalent.

14. Remove the differential gear bearing race from the large housing.

15. Remove the stubshaft from the small

Removing or installing transaxle gears

housing with the stubshaft remover or equivalent.

16. Remove the differential bearing race and cup springs (large and small) from the small housing, with the use of a suitable driver.

TRANSMISSION MAINSHAFT

Disassembly

1. Remove snap-ring from mainshaft end and reinstall the C-clip into the bearing outer race groove. Use a puller and remove the bearing from the shaft, using the C-clip as a pulling base.
2. Remove the fourth gear from the shaft.
3. Remove the retaining ring and remove the third gear synchronizer unit from the shaft.
4. Remove the second speed gear after removing the support ring and locking plate halves.
5. Remove the retaining ring and remove the first/second synchromesh clutch assembly, complete with the first gear.
6. To disassemble the synchronizer clutches, remove the retaining springs with the blocker bars and withdraw the selector ring from the hub.

Assembly

1. Install the first/second gear clutch assembly, complete with the first gear, onto the shaft and secure with the retaining ring.

NOTE: The selector groove of the clutch assembly must face towards the first gear.

2. Slide the second gear on to the shaft and fit the locking plate halves and secure with a retaining clip.
3. Install the third/fourth synchronizer clutch assembly, complete with third gear and secure with a retainer.
4. Install the fourth gear and install the mainshaft bearing with the groove facing upward, with a suitable press tool and secure with a retaining clip.

COUNTERSHAFT CLUSTER

Disassembly and Assembly

1. Remove the input shaft bearing retainer and reinstall the C-clip in the bearing outer groove to use as a pulling base and remove the bearing with a suitable puller.
2. Remove the small input shaft bearing from the shaft, using a suitable puller.
3. The assembly of the countershaft is the installation of the bearings. Use a suitable installer to press the bearings in place.

DIFFERENTIAL GEAR

Disassembly

1. Remove both differential side gears from the case by turning the side gears laterally.
2. Remove the retaining clip from the differential pinion shaft and push the shaft from the housing. The differential pinions can then be removed.
3. With the aid of a puller, remove the differential tapered roller bearings from the gear housing. Remove the speedometer drive gear from the housing.
4. Remove the axle drive gear (ring gear) from the differential gear housing. Use a soft faced hammer to tap the gear from the housing, after the bolts are removed.

Assembly

1. Position the axle drive gear with the chamfered edge of the gear ring towards the differential gear location. Align the axle drive gear bolt holes with the threaded bolt holes in the housing and tighten the new bolts securely.
2. Press the speedometer drive gear on the differential housing.
3. Press the differential taper roller bearings on the housing with the special tool or equivalent.
4. Install the differential pinions and insert the pinion shaft through the pinions and the housing. Install the retaining clip on the pinion shaft.
5. Install the differential side gears by fitting the side gears into the teeth of the pinion gears and turning the gears simultaneously to position the side gears at the axle openings of the housing.

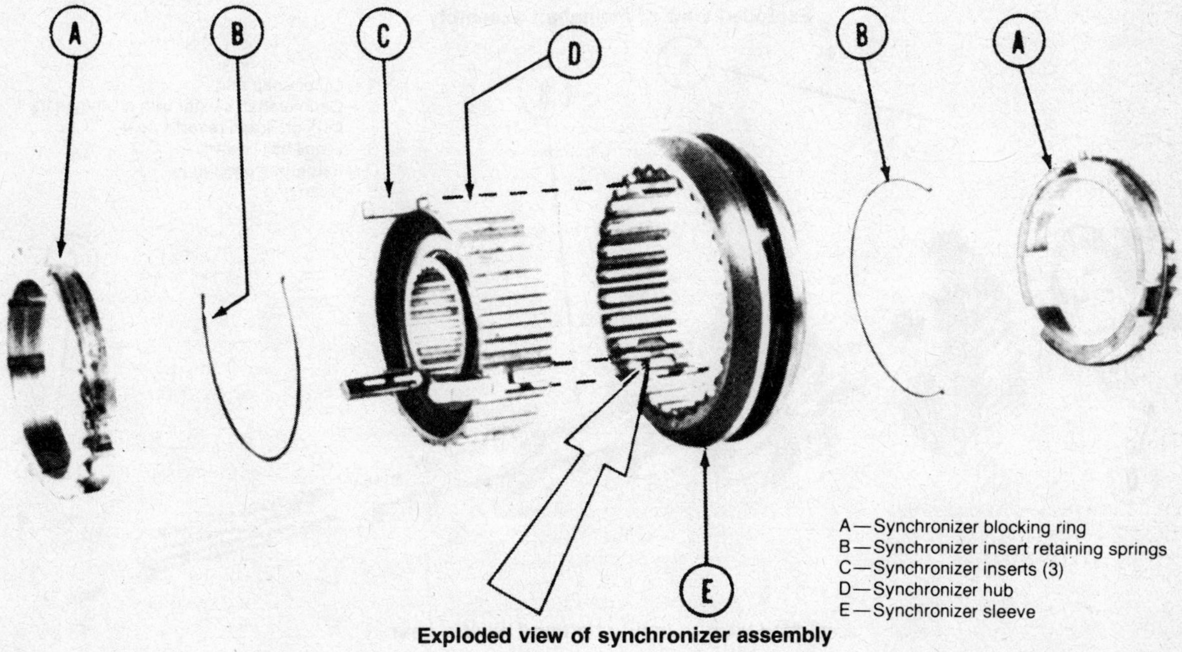

A—Synchronizer blocking ring
B—Synchronizer insert retaining springs
C—Synchronizer inserts (3)
D—Synchronizer hub
E—Synchronizer sleeve

Exploded view of synchronizer assembly

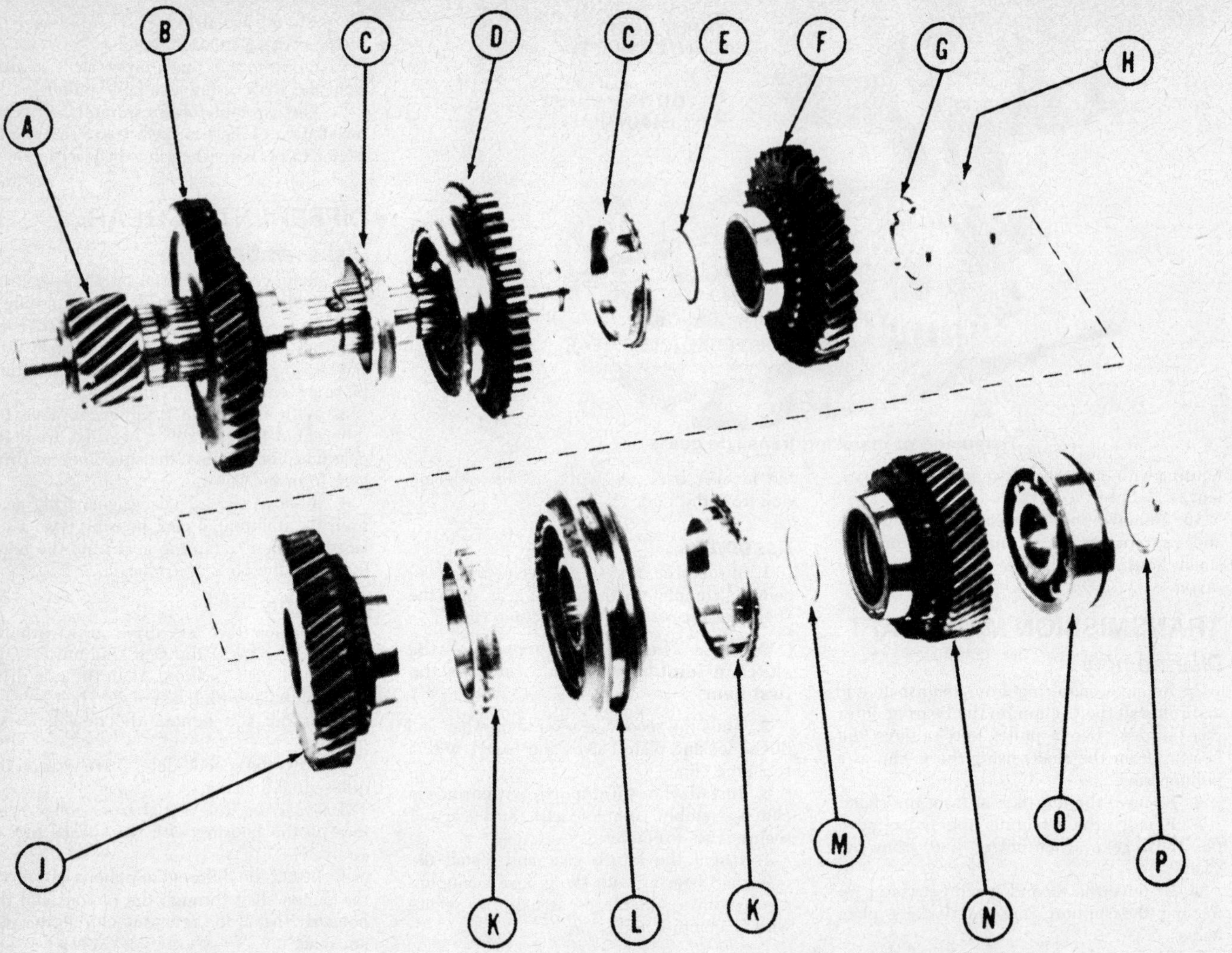

A — Output shaft with drive gear
B — 1st speed gear
C — 1st/2nd speed blocking rings
D — 1st/2nd speed synchronizer sleeve with reverse gear
E — Retaining (snap) ring
F — 2nd speed gear
G — Locking plate halves (2)
H — Locking plate support ring
J — 3rd speed gear
K — 3rd/4th speed blocking rings
L — 3rd/4th speed synchronizer sleeve
M — Retaining (snap) ring
N — 4th speed gear
O — Output shaft bearing (ball)
P — Snap ring

Exploded view of mainshaft assembly

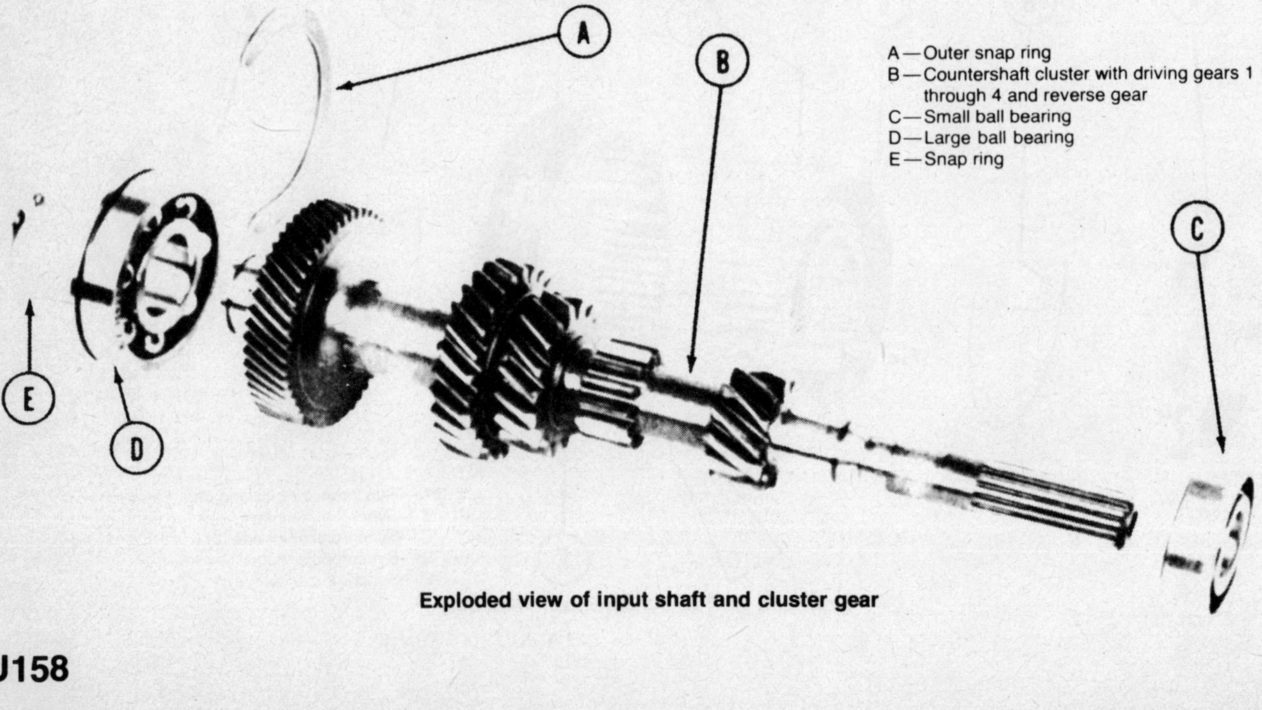

A — Outer snap ring
B — Countershaft cluster with driving gears 1 through 4 and reverse gear
C — Small ball bearing
D — Large ball bearing
E — Snap ring

Exploded view of input shaft and cluster gear

TRANSAXLE

Assembly

1. Seat the tapered roller bearing cup into the large housing section with the aid of the cup installer tool or equivalent.
2. Install the bearing cup with the large and small springs into the small housing section.

Shifting locking plate in position

NOTE: Install the small spring with the outside diameter facing the housing and then insert the large spring.

3. Secure the bearing race with a center punch mark on the housing to avoid having the bearing race drop out during the assembly of the two housings.
4. Install a new input shaft seal with the special seal installer tool or equivalent.
5. Install the mainshaft bearing into the housing and install a new oil slinger.
6. Install the roller bearing with the rear of the cage facing downward with the special installer tool or equivalent.
7. Install the differential assembly with the axle drive gear into the large housing.
8. Slide the reverse idler gear onto the shaft and at the same time, insert the selector lever into the selector groove.

NOTE: Raise the selector lever with the idler gear and support on the selector shaft detent for better installation of the mainshaft and input shaft.

9. Install the mainshaft and input shaft cluster simultaneously and carefully into the housing by pairing up the mainshaft and input shaft gears.
10. Install the selector lever and the reverse idler gear.

CAUTION

During the installation of the input and mainshaft, do not damage seals.

11. Install the selector lock plate and fit the selector forks, (first/ second gear with a short actuating lever, third/fourth gear with a long actuating lever).
12. Install the springs in the housing bore and install the selector fork guide shaft with the long pin pointing downward.

NOTE: Engage fourth gear for later selector lever adjustment.

13. Install the magnetic disc into the housing recess.
14. Install the small housing onto the large housing, using new gasket and install the bolts.
15. Raise the shafts slightly with a screwdriver and install the C-clip in the outer bearing race grooves.

NOTE: The C-clips are available in three different sizes. Select the one that just fits into the groove of the bearing race.

16. Install the cover and new gasket on the housing and install the bolts.
17. Install the detent pin with spring and the retaining nut for the selector shaft detent.
18. Install the stubshaft seals into the large and small housing halves with the seal installer special tool or equivalent.
19. Install the clutch release shaft and link with the release bearing on the housing.

SELECTOR MECHANISM

Removal (Transmission Disassembled)

1. Remove the retainer and remove the reverse gear selector from the shaft.
2. Remove the selector lever retaining plate complete with the lever and remove the guide shaft.
3. Remove the guide lever from the retainer plate by removal of two clips.
4. Remove the rubber collar from the control shaft and unscrew the selector gate from the control shaft and press out the shaft.
5. Remove the shaft seal with the seal remover special tool or equivalent.

Installation

1. Install the seal with the special seal installer or equivalent.
2. Install the control shaft and attach the gearshift gate. Install the rubber boot.
3. Attach the guide lever with clips to the retainer plate.
4. Install the guide shaft and fit retainer plate complete with the guide lever.
5. Install the reverse selector lever on the shaft and install the retainer clip.

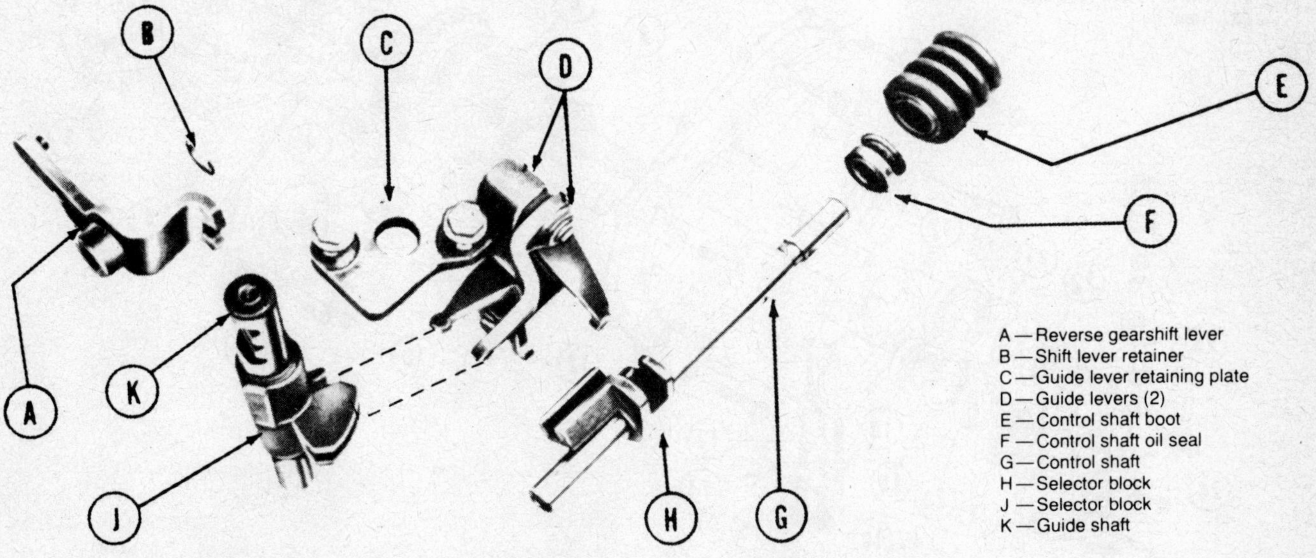

Exploded view of internal shift linkage

TYPE 7

4 and 5 Speed Transaxle

1975-81 Honda

DISASSEMBLY

1. Remove the transmission end cover. Check the transmission mainshaft and countershaft end-play. End-play should be between 0.002-0.003 in. If the clearance is excessive, inspect the ball bearings after transmission disassembly.

2. Remove the locking tab from the mainshaft locknut. The mainshaft locknut has left hand threads. Place the transmission in gear and place the proper size wrench on countershaft to keep it from moving. Remove the mainshaft locknut.

3. Remove the mainshaft bearing and the large snap-ring.

4. Loosen the three shift detent lock ball screws. Remove the screws, springs and balls.

5. Remove the transmission case bolts. Lightly tap the case with a hammer and drift and separate case. Do not pry case apart with a screwdriver.

6. Remove the reverse idler gear and shaft. Remove the reverse shift fork.

7. Remove the shift selector assembly. If repair to the shift selector is necessary, disassemble as follows:

a. Remove two screws and retaining plate. Stake screws when reinstalling.

b. Push the shift arm into the reverse position (towards the large spring). Then release it.

c. The pivot shaft holds a spring loaded detent. Do not lose the detent ball and spring when removing. Remove the pivot shaft.

d. Remove the interlock bar and shift arms.

e. During reassembly, insert a screwdriver into the reverse side (large spring end) of the arm assembly to hold down the detent ball, while inserting the pivot shaft.

8. Remove the shift fork retaining bolts and pull the shift shafts up until they clear the case. Remove the forks and shafts.

NOTE: When reinstalling the fork retaining bolts turn the shaft so the threaded portion of the hole is facing away from the bolt.

9. Remove the mainshaft and countershaft at the same time by holding the two shafts and lightly tapping the flywheel end of the mainshaft.

10. Remove the shift rod boot, shift arm, lock washer and bolt. Remove the shift rod and shift arm.

NOTE: During installation of the shift arm retaining bolt, turn the shaft so that the threaded portion of the hole is facing away from the bolt.

11. Measure the side clearance of the low gear with a feeler gauge, if the clearance is excessive, replace the thrust plate. Perform the same measurement on the remaining gears, if the clearance is beyond the service limit, replace the bearing race (spacer). See chart for specifications.

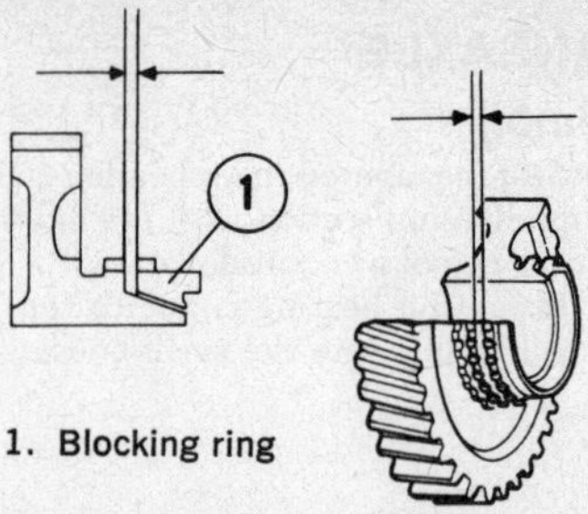

Measuring the clearance between the synchronizer ring and gear hub

12. If the countershaft must be disassembled to adjust clearances, or replace gears, remove the locknut by installing the shaft in the case and holding the differential securely.

NOTE: Place the end lugs of the holder in the case and center the lug in the hole of the differential carrier.

13. Remove the two screws and retaining plate which hold the countershaft bearing. Remove the countershaft bearing with a bearing puller.

14. Clean all component parts thoroughly in the proper solvent.

15. Inspect the surfaces of each gear and blocking ring for roughness or damage. Apply a thin coat of oil to the tapered surfaces of each gear and push them together with a rotating motion. Measure the distance between the ring and gear. Replace all necessary parts. Clearance should be between 0.120-0.139 in.

16. Measure the clearance between the

1. Needle roller bearing set plate
2. Needle roller bearing
3. Clutch case
4. Reverse gear shaft
5. Reverse idle gear
6. Reverse shift fork
7. Shift selector assembly
8. Countershaft gear assembly
9. Main shaft
10. First/second fork shaft
11. Reverse fork shaft
12. Third/fourth fork shaft
13. Steel ball
14. Ball set spring
15. Drain plug washer
16. Set ball spring screw
17. Ball bearing
18. Needle roller bearing
19. 48 mm snap ring
20. Ball bearing
21. 62 mm snap ring
22. 23 mm lock nut
23. 20 mm lock nut
24. Transmission rear cover
25. Speedometer gear

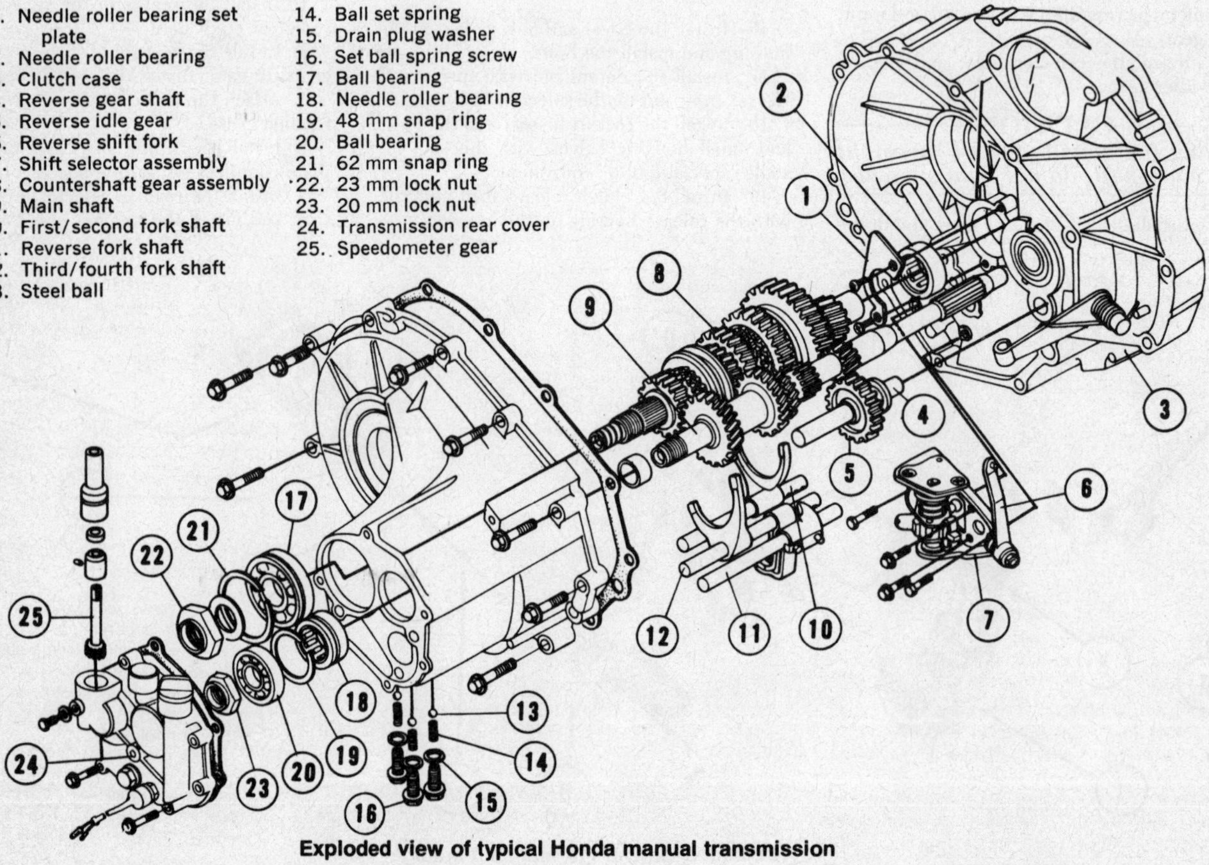

Exploded view of typical Honda manual transmission

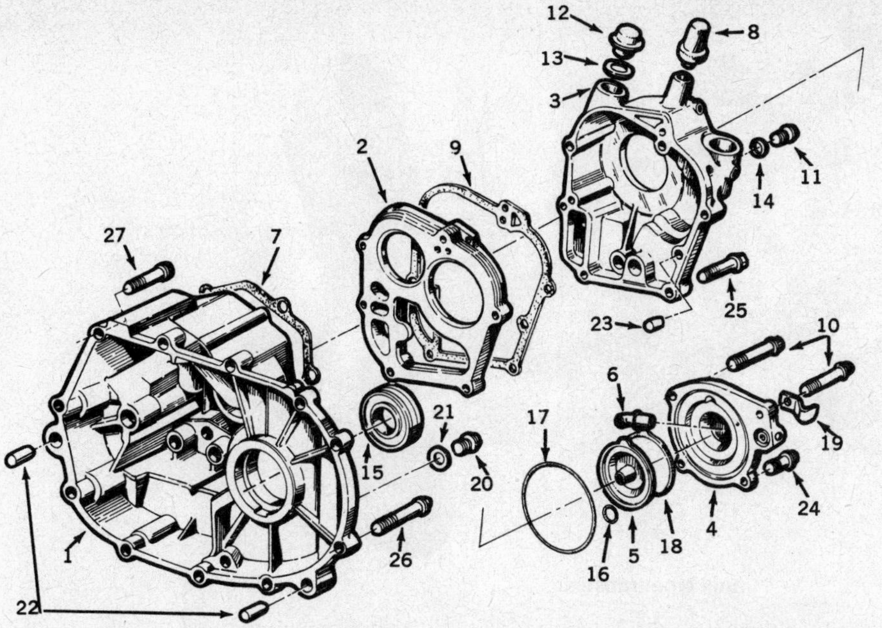

1 Housing, transmission
2 Spacer, transmission housing
3 Cover, transmission
4 Cover, right side
5 Plate, oil barrier
6 Tube, breather
7 Gasket, transmission housing
8 Cap, breather
9 Gasket, transmission case
10 Bolt, flanged, 6 x 85 mm
11 Bolt, oil check
12 Bolt, plug 25 mm
13 Washer, sealing, 25 mm
14 Washer, 8 mm
15 Oil seal, 35 x 56 x 9 mm
16 O-ring, 9.4 x 2.4
17 O-ring, 64.5 x 3
18 O-ring, 42 x 2.4
19 Bracket, wire harness
20 Bolt, drain plug, 14 mm
21 Washer, drain plug, 14 mm
22 Pin, dowel, 14 x 20 mm
23 Pin, dowel, 8 x 14 mm
24 Bolt, flanged, 6 x 20 mm
25 Bolt, flanged, 6 x 45 mm
26 Bolt, flanged, 8 x 40 mm
27 Bolt, flanged, 8 x 45 mm

Exploded view of housing and cover assemblies

shift forks and synchronizer sleeves. The clearance should be between 0.039-0.018. If clearances are excessive, replace the shift forks, synchronizers or both.

17. Ensure that there are no restrictions in the oil holes on the countershaft. Check the splines for wear.

18. Inspect the condition of the mainshaft and countershaft bearing surfaces. Check run-out, gear tooth and spline condition.

19. Check the condition of all the gears. Check the condition of all bearing surfaces.

20. Inspect the bearing race (spacer) of each gear.

21. Replace all questionable parts.

ASSEMBLY

1. Transmission should be assembled in the reverse order of disassembly. During assembly, note the following points.

2. Check the differential bearing clearance.

3. Apply a thin coat of oil to all parts before they are installed.

4. Be certain that hub and synchronizer teeth match when they are assembled.

5. The mainshaft and countershaft must be installed at the same time. Next, install the third/fourth shift fork and shaft, first/second shift fork and shaft, and then the reverse shaft.

6. When the shift selector assembly is installed, there are two special bolts which must be inserted first. These bolts locate the assembly.

7. Lock the mainshaft and countershaft locknuts with a punch.

8. Make sure that the mainshaft and countershaft turn smoothly and that all gears engage freely. Check and be certain that all bolts are properly torqued.

TYPE 8

4 and 5 Speeds Transaxle

Porsche 911, 912, 914

NOTE: Turbo (930) transaxle similar.

When disassembling and assembling a four speed transaxle, the procedures described in the five speed overhaul should be followed. The gear arrangement, 1st through 4th, on the pinion shaft in the four speed transaxle, is the same as the gear arrangement, 2nd through 5th, in the five speed unit, with the front cover housing only the reverse gear.

Because of the reverse action of the 1st speed synchronizer in the four speed unit, as compared to the five speed unit, the synchronizer components have to be installed directly opposite each other. When installing the synchronizer components for the 1st speed in the four speed transaxle, it should be remembered to insert only one brake band.

The Sportomatic transaxle unit is not covered in the manual transaxle section.

External shifting controls have been relocated from the front of the transaxle to the side on one model and the case has been modified from a tunnel type to a removable gear housing type on an other model. The gear trains remain basically the same in all models.

DISASSEMBLY

1. Mount the transaxle securely and drain the lubricating fluid.

2. Remove the starter assembly and the center caps from the drive flanges.

3. Remove the retaining bolts from the drive flanges and remove the flanges from the inner axle stub shafts.

NOTE: Place the transaxle in gear and block the input shaft to prevent turning.

4. Remove the side cover assembly and withdraw the differential assembly.

5. Remove the crossmember from the front cover, if not previously done, and remove the front cover assembly.

CAUTION

During the front cover removal, the reverse gear components may drop. Prevent from falling to the floor.

6. Remove the 1st/reverse selector fork retaining screw and remove the gear with the fork.

7. Remove the retaining bolt from the pinion shaft.

8. Remove the roll pin from the castled nut on the input shaft. Remove the castle nut and the 1st speed gear.

9. Place the transaxle gears in the neutral position and remove the retaining nut from the plate of the inner shift rod guide fork and remove the guide fork.

10. Remove the inner shift rod through the rear access hole. Shift the gears into the 5th speed position with a suitable bar and remove the intermediate plate with the gear clusters.

NOTE: A plastic hammer may be needed to lightly tap the plate loose.

CAUTION

The gear cluster can be installed or removed from the housing only when the transaxle gears are in the 5th speed gear position.

Intermediate Plate and Gear Cluster

DISASSEMBLY

1. Install the intermediate plate assembly in a vise or similar holder and remove the 1st/reverse hub gear, using two suitable prybars.

2. Remove the gear Number two of the 1st speed, along with the needle bearing cage.

3. Shift the gear assembly into neutral position. Remove the selector shaft detent plug and remove the detent spring.

4. Remove the 1st/reverse selector shaft, along with the detent ball.

NOTE: Mark all selector forks and rails during the disassembly to avoid assembly problems.

5. Remove the 2nd/3rd selector fork retaining screw. Remove the selector shaft, fork and detent.

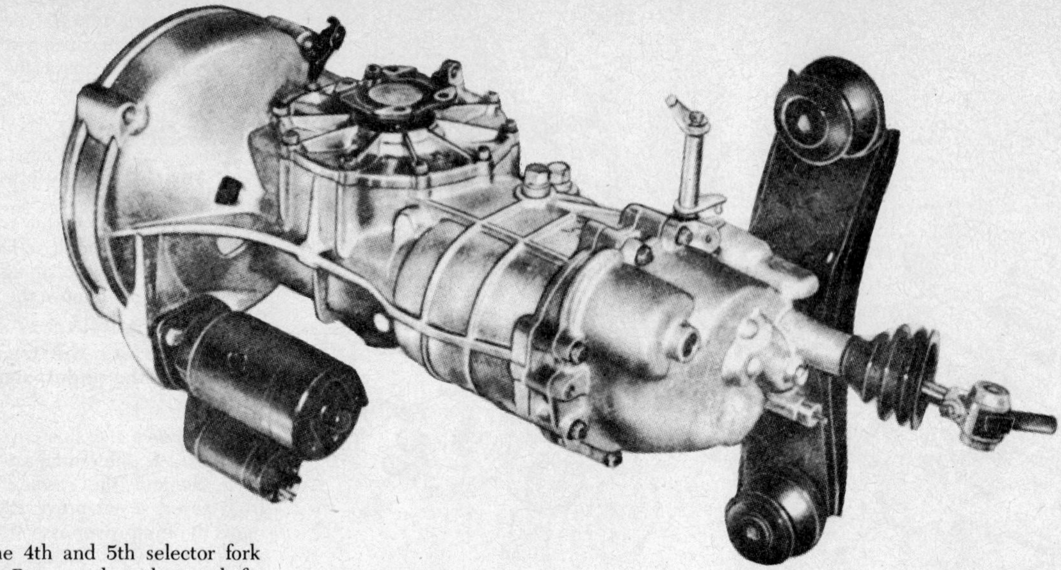

Tunnel type transaxle

6. Remove the 4th and 5th selector fork retaining screw. Remove the selector shaft, fork and detent ball.

7. Remove the detent ball, spring and detent.

8. The input and pinion shafts must be pressed from the intermediate plate.

NOTE: To allow the intermediate plate to lay flat on the press, drive the aligning dowels into the plate and remove the throttle linkage.

9. Remove the bearing plate assembly. Heat the intermediate plate to 248° F (120° C) and press the bearings from the plate. Remove the detent bushings as necessary.

ASSEMBLY

1. Install the detent bushings, if removed.

CAUTION

Do not allow the bushings to protrude into the selector shaft bores.

2. Heat the intermediate plate to 248° F (120° C) and press the two bearings into place.

3. Install the bearing brace plate assembly. Torque the retaining bolts to 18 ft/lbs (2.5 Mkp) and lock the bolt heads in place with the lock plates.

4. Insert the input shaft and pinion shaft assemblies into the intermediate plate assembly.

5. Reposition the aligning dowels and the throttle linkage.

Housing Assembly

DISASSEMBLY AND ASSEMBLY

1. Before any attempt is made to install the bearing races, heat the housing to 248° F (120° C).

2. The bearing races can be installed with installer tools and a hammer. Replace the necessary seal or seals.

3. To prevent damages to the housing, install the bearing races squarely in to the housing.

Pinion Shaft

DISASSEMBLY AND ASSEMBLY

1. Remove the retaining bolt with the

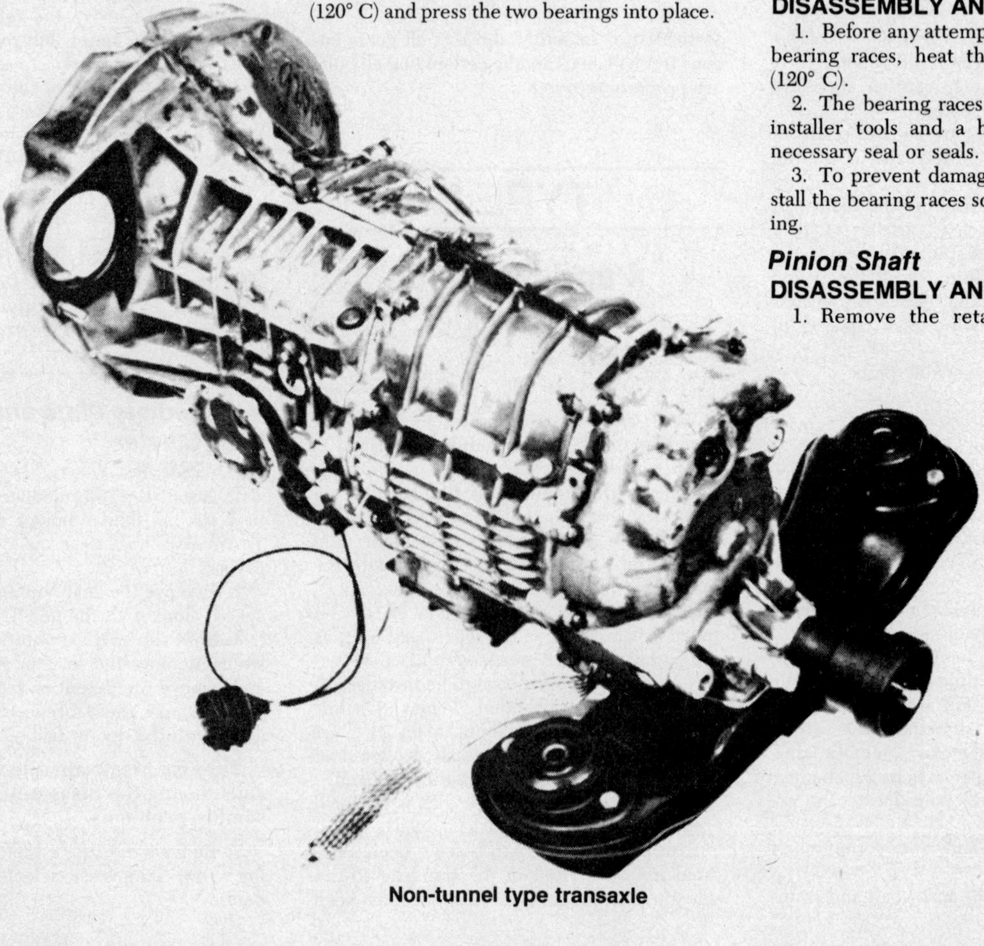

Non-tunnel type transaxle

Side shift type transaxle

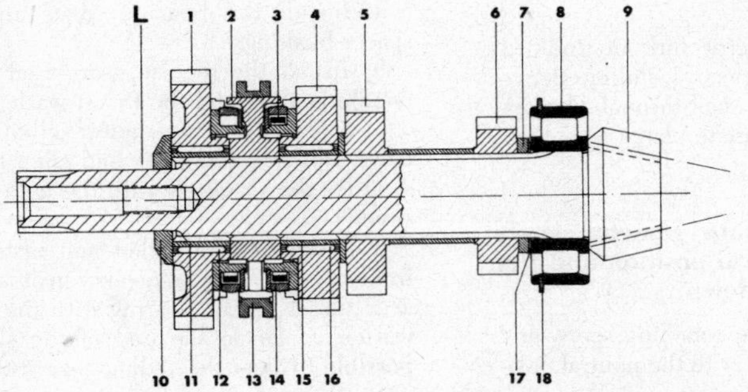

L. Four-point ballbearing
1. Gear II for 1st speed (Freewheeling)
2. Spider
3. Brake band
4. Gear II for 2nd speed (Freewheeling)
5. Gear II for 3rd speed (Fixed)
6. Gear II for 4th speed (Fixed)
7. Spacer
8. Roller bearing
9. Pinion shaft
10. Thrust washer (6.6 mm thickness)
11. Needle bearing inner race (gear speeds 1 thru 4)
12. Needle bearing cage (gear speeds 1 thru 4)
13. Sliding sleeve
14. Synchronizing ring
15. Needle bearing inner race
16. Needle bearing cage
17. Spacers
18. Retaining ring

Cross section of 4-speed pinion shaft assembly

Correct assembly of 1st speed synchronizer for the 5-speed gear train

Correct assembly of 1st speed synchronizer for the 4-speed gear train

speedometer gear attached, from the pinion shaft.

2. The gear assemblies are removed by pressing the shaft from the gears.

3. Mark and identify all components so as to maintain proper assembly sequence.

CAUTION

Note the number and thickness of spacers between the roller bearings and thick spacers to avoid recomputing spacer thickness during reassembly.

NOTE: Later transaxles have the thrust washer and spacer replaced with a single, beveled thrust washer.

Input Shaft

DISASSEMBLY AND ASSEMBLY

1. Straighten the locking tabs from the hex nut. Remove the retaining hex nut from the shaft, using the necessary special tools.

2. Press the roller bearing from the shaft, using special tools as necessary.

3. Remove the gears and components from the input shaft.

NOTE: Mark the needle bearing cages to properly install them during the installation procedure.

4. To remove the inner half of the ball bearing race from the stub end of the shaft, drive the race away from its seat with a drift punch or similar tool, and remove with a puller.

5. The reassembly of the shaft and components should be done in the reverse of the removal procedure.

6. The locknut should be torqued to 72 to 86 ft/lbs (10 to 12 Mkp). Be sure to secure the nut with the locking tabs of the lock plate edge.

Differential Assembly

The differential assembly is overhauled in the conventional manner. Special measuring tools are needed to measure the preload, tooth contact and to determine the thickness of necessary shims and spacers.

TRANSAXLE REASSEMBLY

1. Having the transaxle case overhauled as required and the intermediate plate assembled, place the gears in the 5th speed and prepare to install the assembly into the case.

2. Guide the intermediate plate assembly into the case and lightly tighten at four housing studs.

3. Install gear one of 1st speed on the input shaft. Install the spacer and tighten the castellated nut to a torque of 43 to 47 ft/lbs (6.0 to 6.5 Mkp). Secure the nut with a spiral pin.

4. Install the thrust washer on the pinion shaft with the small collar facing the bearing. Guide the needle bearing in place with a suitable tool.

5. Install the needle bearing and gear two of 1st speed. Install the spider wheel of the 1st/reverse gear.

6. Tighten the pinion shaft bolt (with extension for tachometer) to 80 to 86 ft/lbs (11 to 12 Mkp). Block the gear train to prevent turning.

7. Remove the intermediate plate assembly from the case assembly. Place the intermediate plate assembly into a holder so that the selector shafts can be installed.

8. Install the shafts in the following order:

a. Place the selector sleeve of the 4th/5th speed onto its respective slide and position the 4th/5th speed selector shaft through the fork and through the intermediate plate. Tighten the fork retaining screw.

b. Install into the detent bore, one ball, detent pin, one long spring and one more ball.

c. Place the selector fork of 2nd/3rd speeds onto the respective sliding sleeve and push the selector shaft through the fork and into the intermediate plate.

NOTE: The 4th/5th selector shaft must be in the neutral position and the detent ball pressed down.

d. Tighten the fork retaining screw and move the selector lever to the neutral position. Insert the detent.

e. Install the 1st/reverse selector shaft into the intermediate plate and install the detent ball and short spring. Tighten the detent cap screw to 18 ft/lbs (2.5 Mkp).

f. Slide the selector fork and the sliding gear for the 1st/ reverse speed together onto the spider wheel and selector shaft. Install and tighten the fork retaining screw.

NOTE: The sliding sleeves must be adjusted to a position in the exact center in relation to the synchronizer rings when in the neutral position. The forks can be moved by loosening the retaining bolts. A special gauge block is available for this operation, but normally not available to the average repair shop.

g. When the adjustment of the forks are completed, torque the retaining bolts to 18 ft/lbs (2.5 Mkp).

9. Install the inner shift rod into the transaxle housing, after having installed the shift finger onto the shaft and securing it with the retaining pin and cotter pin.

10. Guide the intermediate plate assembly into the transaxle housing with gaskets attached, carefully to avoid damage to the input shaft seal.

NOTE: The gear train assembly must be in the 5th speed position.

11. Shift the gear train into Neutral. Guide the inner shift rod into its proper position at the selector shaft tabs and into the rear rod bore.

12. Install the guide fork of the inner shift rod, using a new gasket and be sure the inner shift rod enters the guide fork.

13. Assemble the front cover and install on the transaxle assembly.

a. Install the bearing cages and the spacer bushings.

b. Install the reverse gear, axial thrust needle bearing and the thrust washer.

c. Install the tachometer elbow unit drive unit into the cover and align the indent for the set screw with the hole in the cover.

d. Install a new gasket and install the front cover. Pull the reverse gear and its axial thrust needle bearing with the thrust washer as far to the end of the shaft as possible to clear the sliding gear of the 1st/reverse speed gear.

NOTE: The machined recess in the thrust washer must align with the outer collar of the pinion shaft bearing.

14. Install the retaining nuts and torque to 15.2 to 16.6 ft/lbs (2.1 to 2.8 Mkp).

15. Install the transaxle support.

Location of 1st/reverse sliding gear with selector fork in place—5-speed

Gear train assembled in the intermediate plate—typical

TYPE 9

5 Speed Transaxle (Model G 28.03)

Porsche 928

DISASSEMBLY

1. Mount transaxle assembly securely and drain the lubricating oil.
2. Remove the rear cover and top cover from the transaxle case.
3. Remove the right and left axle flange retaining bolts and remove the axle flanges.
4. Remove the right and left side cover retaining bolts and carefully separate the side covers, with shims, from the transaxle case. Carefully remove the differential carrier assembly.
5. Drive the main shift rod pin from the shift finger with a pin punch or other suitable tool. Remove the lockout spring and pin from the shaft. Remove the shaft from the transaxle case.
6. Remove the shift shaft interlock mechanism by removing the screw plugs, located on the left and right sides of the case, near the front upper sides.
7. Drive the pins from the shift fingers and shift forks with a pin punch or other suitable tool. Remove the shafts to the rear of the transaxle case, being careful not to exert undue force. Remove the interlock detents and springs as the shafts are removed. Remove the shift fingers and forks from the case.
8. Remove the input shaft oil seal holder by pulling outward while turning.
9. Remove the countershaft retaining circlip from the transaxle case. From the rear of the case, tap the countershaft forward and out of the case.

NOTE: The pinion shaft bearing plate may have to be loosened.

CAUTION

To avoid damage to the case or gears, hold the countergears from falling into the case with wire as a support.

10. With the use of a special puller to maintain straightness, remove the input shaft from the case.
11. Remove the pinion shaft bearing retainer plate bolts and remove the pinion shaft assembly by using a puller.
12. Lift the countergear assembly from the case.
13. Using an appropriate driver, remove the reverse idler shaft from the gear and case.
14. Remove shift shaft oil seals from the case.

Input Shaft

DISASSEMBLY

1. Remove the synchronizer ring, shift band, stop and thrust block from the input shaft.
2. Remove the front ball bearing circlip and press the bearing from the input shaft.
3. With an appropriate puller, remove the two needle bearings and spacer from the input shaft.

ASSEMBLY

1. Install one needle bearing into the input shaft, followed by the spacer and the second needle bearing.
2. Heat the ball bearing assembly to 212° F (100° C) and drive it on to the input shaft. Install the retaining circlip.
3. Install the thrust block, stop, shift band

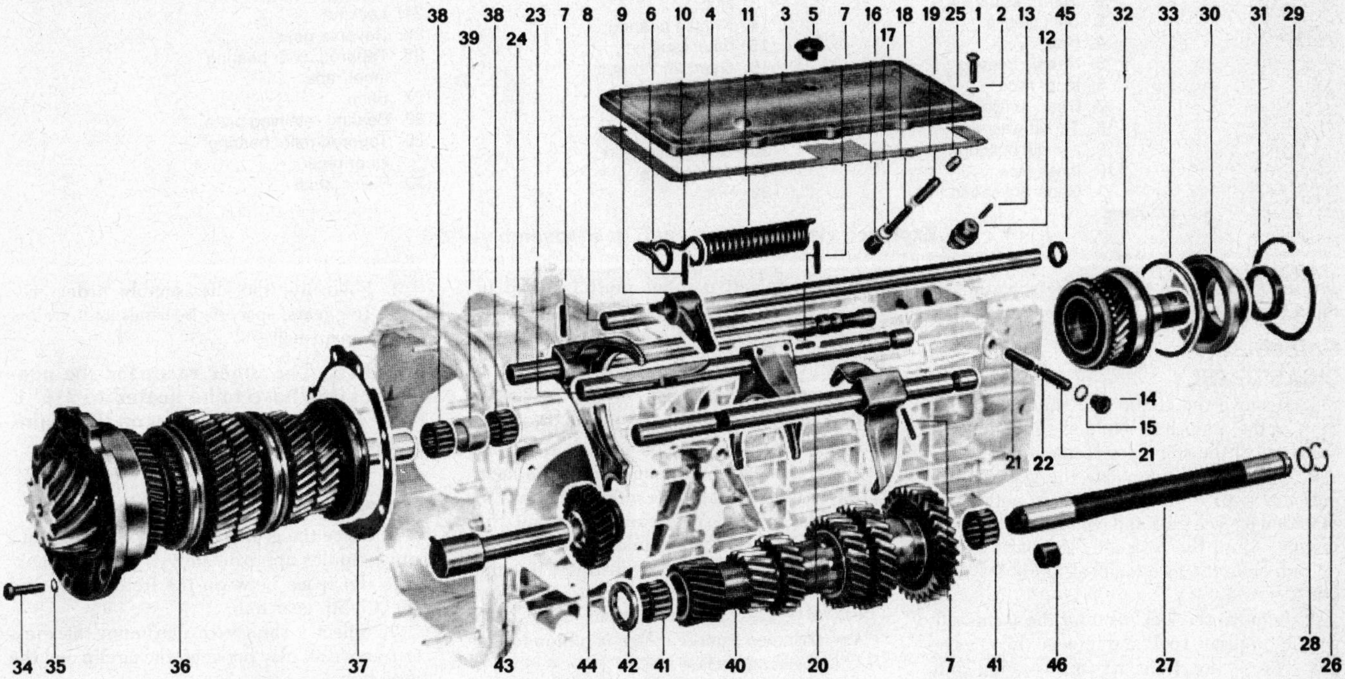

1. Bolt
2. Washer
3. Upper cover
4. Gasket
5. Vent
6. Roll pin
7. Split pin
8. Main shift rod
9. Shift finger
10. U-spring
11. Lockout spring
12. Backup light switch
13. Plunger
14. Plug
15. Seal
16. Plug
17. Seal
18. Spring
19. Detent plunger
20. Shift rod with shift fork for 4th and 5th gear
21. Detent/interlock plungers
22. Spring
23. Shift rod with shift fork for 2nd and 3rd gear
24. Shift rod with shift fork for 1st and reserve gear
25. Interlock pin
26. Circlip
27. Countershaft
28. O-ring
29. Circlip
30. Input shaft oil seal holder
31. Oil seal
32. Input shaft
33. O-ring
34. Bolt
35. Serrated lock washer
36. Pinion shaft assembly
37. Shim
38. Needle bearing
39. Spacer
40. Countershaft hub/gears
41. Needle bearing
42. Thrust washer
43. Reverse idler shaft
44. Reverse idler gear
45. Oil seal
46. Magnetic drain plug

Exploded view of shifting mechanism and gear train—928

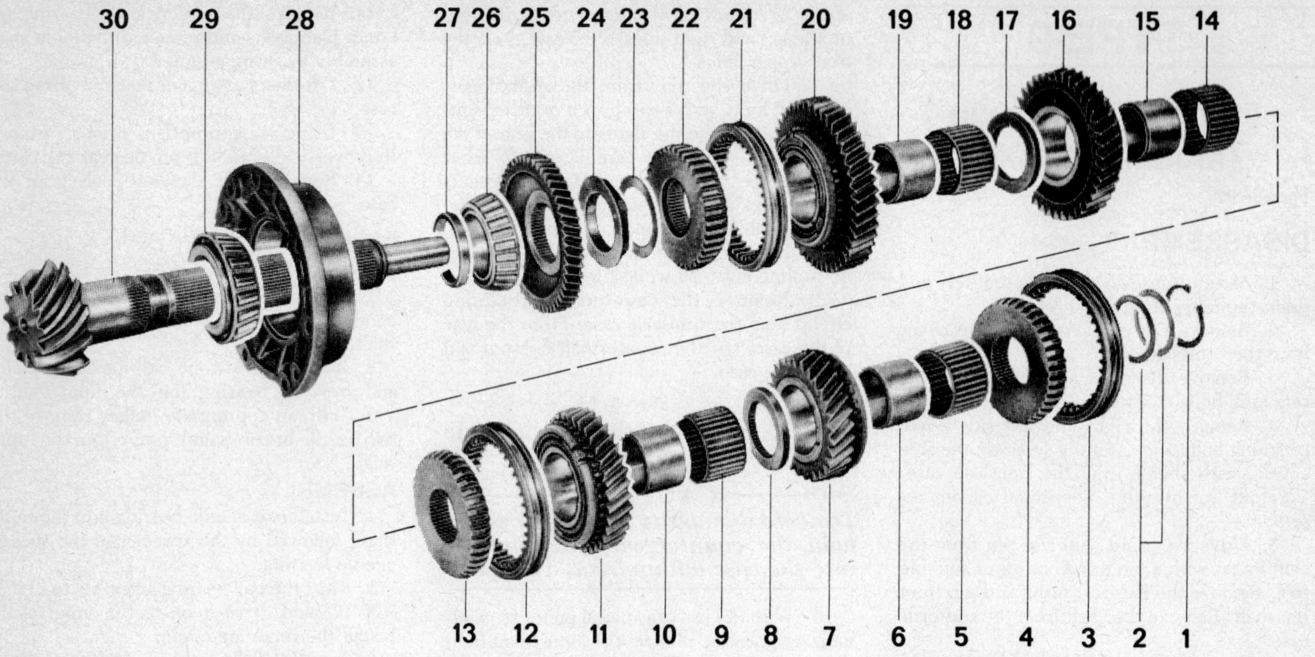

1. Circlip
2. Shim (distance y)
3. Shift sleeve
4. Hub
5. Needle bearing
6. Inner race
7. Gear, 4th speed
8. Thrust washer
9. Needle bearing
10. Inner race
11. Gear, 3rd speed
12. Shift sleeve
13. Hub
14. Needle bearing
15. Inner race
16. Gear, 2nd speed
17. Thrust washer
18. Needle bearing
19. Inner race
20. Gear, 1st speed
21. Shift sleeve
22. Hub
23. Shim (distance x)
24. Locknut
25. Reverse gear
26. Tapered roller bearing inner race
27. Shim
28. Bearing retaining plate
29. Tapered roller bearing inner race
30. Pinion shaft

Exploded view of pinion shaft gear assembly—928

and secure with the synchronizer ring on the input shaft.

Mainshaft

DISASSEMBLY

1. Remove the circlip and shims from the front of the mainshaft. Note the number and thickness of the shims for reassembly.

2. Using a press, remove the gears, bearings and races from the mainshaft, noting the direction of each gear and component for reassembly. Mark the disassembled parts as required. Note the location of all shims for reassembly.

3. Remove the locknut from the mainshaft with appropriate tools and remove the reverse gear. Press the front tapered bearing and bearing retaining plate from the mainshaft. Press the rear tapered bearing from the mainshaft.

ASSEMBLY

1. Heat the rear tapered bearing to 212° F (100° C) and drive on to the mainshaft.

2. Place the bearing retaining plate on the mainshaft and heat the front tapered bearing as was done to the rear bearing, and drive the front bearing on to the mainshaft.

3. Install the reverse gear with the small depression on the hub towards the front of the mainshaft. Install the locknut and torque to 109 to 130 ft/lbs (15 to 18 Mkg). Stake the locknut collar to the small depression in the reverse gear hub.

4. To properly position the gears on the mainshaft, selective shims must be used in conjunction with the locknut. To obtain the proper specification, the following formula must be used.

Measuring Formula

The design specification is 108.80 mm from the rear face of the pinion gear to the front face of the selective shim and should be measured with a sliding caliper or micrometer. To obtain the proper specifications without the needed shim, use the formula by substituting the resulting readings, as illustrated by the example.

108.80 = Design specifications
A = Distance from rear face of pinion to the locknut bearing surface.
B = Distance A + r
X = Shim thickness required
r = Pinion shaft and gear deviation during manufacture

Example
Distance A = 106.90 mm
Distance B = A+r
A = 106.90 mm
r = +0.12 mm
B = 107.02 mm
Distance X = 108.80 mm—B
108.80 mm
107.02 mm
1.78 mm is the thickness of the selective shim needed (Distance X)

5. Following the disassembly order, replace the gears, spacers, bearings and circlips on the mainshaft.

NOTE: The inner races for the needle bearing have to be heated to 212° F (100° C) before installation on the mainshaft.

Determining Shim Thickness

1. Place the gear train of the mainshaft in a press, under approximately 5 ton, and measure the space between the front circlip and the 4th/5th gear hub.

2. Select a shim with maximum thickness to remove all play between the circlip and the gear hub.

3. Remove the unit from the press, remove the circlip and install the shim. Reinstall the circlip.

Determining Input Shaft Clearance (During Assembly)

1. The clearance between the input shaft and the 4th/5th gear hub can be determined by inserting a feeler gauge between the shaft end and the gear hub. The clearance should be 0.2 to 0.3 mm.

2. Should this clearance not be obtained, the mainshaft will have to be disassembled and the shim thickness at the locknut be rechecked and corrected.

3. Reassemble the mainshaft and recheck the clearance, again under pressure, between

the circlip and the 4th/5th gear hub. Correct as required.

4. Recheck the clearance between the input shaft and the 4th/5th gear hub.

Synchronizer Component Identification

1ST GEAR

Synchronizer ring—One groove on face.
Thrust block—Two beveled sides.
Shift band—Uneven shift bands.
Stop—Two straight sides.
Installation note: Short side of shift band must be to the right of the thrust block.

2ND GEAR

Synchronizer ring—Two grooves on the face or a red dot.
Thrust block—Two beveled sides.
Shift band—Even shift bands.
Stop—One straight and one beveled side.
Installation note: Beveled side of stop must be faced to the right as seen from the top view.

3RD GEAR

Synchronizer ring—Two grooves on the face or a red dot.
Thrust block—Two beveled sides.
Shift band—Two separate shift bands.
Stop—Beveled sides.

4TH GEAR

Synchronizer ring—No grooves.
Thrust block—Two beveled sides.
Shift band—Two separate shift bands.
Stop—Beveled sides.

5TH GEAR

Synchronizer ring—No grooves (0.6 mm wider).
Thrust block—Two beveled sides.
Shift band—Two separate shift bands.
Stop—Beveled sides.

NOTE: All synchronizers should have an installed diameter of 86.0 ±0.24 mm, measured at the highest point of the ring.

Countershaft

DISASSEMBLY

1. Remove the circlip from the countershaft hub.
2. Press the 3rd, 4th and 5th gears from the countershaft hub.

INSTALLATION

1. Heat the gears to approximately 212° F (100° C) and press them into their proper position.
2. Install the circlip on the countershaft hub.

TRANSMISSION ASSEMBLY

1. Place the assembled countershaft assembly into the transmission case with lift wires attached.
2. Install the mainshaft into the case and install the bolts in the bearing retaining plate to case.
3. Install the input shaft assembly in the front of the transmission case.
4. With the lifting wire, raise the countershaft hub assembly in place and insert the countershaft from the front of the transmission case and towards the rear, engaging the notched portion of the shaft into the slot provided by the installation of the mainshaft bearing retainer plate.

NOTE: The bearing retaining plate may have to be loosened to allow the entry of the countershaft into its position in the rear of the case. Retighten the bearing retaining plate.

5. Check the gear train for freeness of rotation and proper clearances.
6. Install the shift rods, forks and finger in their proper locations and install the retaining pins through the forks and fingers to engage the shift rods. Install the necessary detent plungers and springs during the shift rod installation.
7. Install the detent plugs, necessary circlips and the input shaft oil seal holder.
8. Install the main shift rod and shift finger. Install the retaining pin into the finger and through the shaft.
9. Install the differential carrier assembly and the side covers with the removed shims.

NOTE: Should the differential need to be adjusted, refer to the individual car section.

10. Install the left and right axle flanges and retain with the retaining bolts.
11. Install the top and rear cover, using new gaskets.
12. Fill the transmission and the differential with hypoid type oil, 90 weight. Each must be filled separately.

TYPE 10

4 Speed Transaxle

Renault LeCar

DISASSEMBLY

1. Mount the transaxle assembly securely and drain the lubricating oil.
2. Remove the clutch housing assembly.
3. Remove the locking washers and bolts from the differential adjusting ring nuts and with the use of a special wrench or equivalent, remove the adjusting ring nuts.
4. Release the clutch shaft roll pin retaining spring and remove the pin. Remove the clutch shaft and the differential assembly.
5. Remove the top cover retaining bolts and the cover.
6. Remove the selector fork shaft springs and the locking balls.
7. Remove the front cover retaining bolts and the top cover.
8. Remove the primary shaft adjusting shims.
9. Remove the primary shaft rear bearing retaining plate and bolts.
10. Using a pin punch, remove the two roll pins holding the reverse gear pinion shaft. Remove the reverse gear selector shaft and the locking disc between the shifting shafts.
11. Engage the gears in one speed, unlock and remove the speedometer end nut from the final drive pinion, along with the rubber washer.
12. Move the gears to the neutral position, move the final drive pinion in towards the differential and remove the tapered bearing. Remove the final drive pinion.
13. Push the primary shaft towards the differential and free the rear bearing cage.
14. Remove the front bearing (freefitting), the primary shaft, the reverse gear shaft and the reverse gear.
15. Remove the 1st/2nd and 3rd/4th gear fork roll pins, using a pin punch. Remove the shafts and selector forks.
16. Remove the lock plate for the secondary bearing adjusting nut and remove the nut.
17. Remove the 4th speed gear thrust washer and push out the primary shaft front bearing assembly.
18. Lift the secondary shaft and the synchronizer assembly from the transaxle.

Differential

The differential assembly is overhauled in the conventional manner. Special tools are needed to measure the bearing preload, tooth contact and to determine the thickness of various shims, when used. To aid the repairman when differential repairs do not need to be done, all necessary measurements should be made of the differential assembly before disassembly and providing no internal parts were installed that would affect the differential measurements, reassemble to the original measurements.

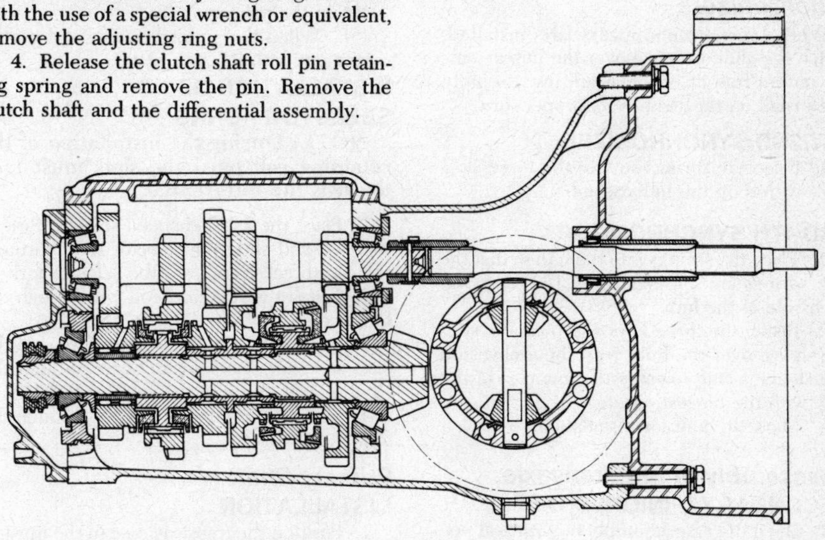

Cross section of Renault 4-speed transaxle

Bearings and Races

REMOVAL AND INSTALLATION

A press and puller is needed to remove and replace the transaxle bearings and races from the case, adjusting ring nuts and the shafts. Caution must be exercised when removing the races because of a lip on varied races. Do not press in the wrong direction. Replace all seals during the overhaul of the transaxle assembly.

Primary Shaft

The disassembly and assembly of the primary shaft is limited to the replacement of the bearings, which should be pressed on and off as necessary.

Secondary Shaft (Pinion)

DISASSEMBLY

1. Mark the position of each sliding gear in relation to its hub, before disassembly.
2. Move each gear, hub and bearing from the shaft, keeping each in its proper order.
3. Remove the pinion gear end bearing by pressing the shaft from the bearing.

ASSEMBLY

1. Install the pinion gear end bearing onto the shaft.
2. Install the gears, hubs and bearings onto the shaft in the order of their removal.

Top Cover

DISASSEMBLY

1. Remove the reverse gear selector and the two roll pins securing the selector finger.
2. Remove the control shaft assembly. Mark the location of the springs, stops and bellows.
3. If necessary, remove the bushing and the seal from the cover.

ASSEMBLY

1. Install the bushing and the seal, if removed.
2. Install the control shaft assembly. Position the spring, spring stops and the bellows.
3. Install the roll pins securing the selector finger.
4. Install the reverse gear selector and retaining bolt.

Synchronizers

When new synchronizers are installed, match the sliding sleeve over the hub assembly until a free fit is felt. Mark the assembly and install on the shaft in its proper turn.

1ST/2ND SYNCHRONIZER

1. Place the springs so that the three slots are covered on the hub assembly.

3RD/4TH SYNCHRONIZER

1. Place the springs into the hub so that the two springs are approximately 180° apart on each side of the hub.
2. Install the three keys and push the sliding sleeve over the hub, with the grooves on the sleeve facing towards the low part of the hub with the biggest offset.
3. Mark the unit for installation.

Reassembly of the Transaxle

SECONDARY (PINION) SHAFT

1. Have the case assembly in a vertical position and place the secondary gear stack, less the 4th speed driven gear, in the transaxle case.
2. Slide the final drive pinion shaft into the casing, mating the shaft splines to the 1st/2nd and 3rd/4th speed synchronizer hubs.

NOTE: A block can be used to hold the pinion shaft in the upright position while completing the assembly of the gear train.

3. Install the 4th speed gear and gear ring onto the shaft. Install the caged two needle bearing and the 4th gear sleeve.
4. Place the 4th speed thrust washer with the large diameter facing the gear and screw the bearing ring adjusting nut into place until snug.
5. Install the tapered roller bearing on the final drive pinion, hand tight.
6. Hold the sliding gear in place with a special wrench or equivalent tool and tighten the speedometer drive pinion with a properly fitted wrench, so that the tapered roller bearing is drawn into position.
7. Remove the speedometer drive pinion and insert the spring washer. Reinstall the drive pinion and torque to 75 to 90 ft/lbs (10 to 12 Nm). Lock the pinion into position.

PINION SHAFT BEARING ADJUSTMENT

1. Unscrew the adjusting ring nut until the race touches the rollers.
2. When using original bearings, no end-play should exist between the rollers and the race and no preload is required. When adjusted, install the lock plate.
3. When installing new bearings, a preload must be obtained. Perform the following operation.
   a. Unscrew the ring nut while turning the secondary (pinion) shaft by hand.
   b. When the shaft becomes hard to turn, preload has developed. Continue to rotate the shaft several times to seat the bearings.
   c. Tie a piece of string around the 3rd/4th sliding sleeve groove and wrap it several times around the sleeve.
   d. Using a spring scale, pull the string and measure the rotating force. The torque preload should be 1 to 3½ lbs (0.5 to 1.7 N).
   e. Adjust the ring nut as necessary to obtain the proper preload.
   f. When the preload is correct, lock the ring nut with the lock plate.

INSTALLATION OF SELECTOR FORKS

NOTE: During the installation of the retaining roll pins, the slots must face towards the differential.

1. Place the 1st/2nd speed selector fork in the case and slide the selector shaft through the case bracket and into the selector fork.
2. Install the retaining roll pin through the fork and shaft.
3. Install the 3rd/4th selector fork into the case and slide the selector shaft through the case bracket and into the selector fork.
4. Install the retaining roll pin through the fork and shaft.

Primary Shaft

INSTALLATION

1. Position the transaxle case in the upright with the differential housing on top.
2. Place the primary shaft into the case with the 4th speed gear setting on the transaxle case.
3. From the differential side, install the tapered roller bearing, using a length of pipe stock, fitted to the inner race of the bearing.
4. Position the reverse gear in the case, with the groove facing towards the differential housing. Install the reverse shaft and secure with a roll pin.

NOTE: The roll pin should protrude equally from both sides of the shaft.

5. Install the primary shaft bearing race onto the rear of the shaft and install the race retaining plate and lockplate.
6. Tighten the lockplate bolts and bend the lockplate tabs over the bolt heads.
7. Install the primary shaft front bearing. The bearing should slide onto the shaft.
8. Install the outer race onto the shaft until it is flush with the case.

PRIMARY SHAFT BEARING ADJUSTMENT

NOTE: The end-play of the primary shaft should be adjusted to 0.001 to 0.005 inch (0.02 to 0.12 mm). Shims are used to adjust the end-play.

1. Mount a dial indicator gauge on the speedometer drive pinion end of the case. Push the bearing race inward to reduce the end-play of the shaft, measured by the dial indicator on the shaft end.
2. When the proper amount of end-play has been obtained, place the adjusting shims in position on the bearing race, so that the last shim extends beyond the gasket face by 0.012 inch (0.30 mm).

Front Cover

INSTALLATION

1. Install the locking disc between the selector shafts and slide the reverse gear shaft in place.
2. Install the lock balls and springs into the bores in the transaxle case.

NOTE: The longest spring is for the 1st/2nd gear selector shaft.

3. Install the speedometer gear sleeve in position, with its O-ring in place.
4. Install the speedometer driven gear, the primary shaft adjusting shims and the paper gasket.
5. Install the front cover and secure it with the retaining bolts.

Top Cover

INSTALLATION

1. Place the transaxle gear train in the neutral position. Slide the reverse gear on the shaft until it rests on the 4th speed gear of the primary shaft.
2. Invert the top cover and space the long end of the selector lever ⅜ inch (10 mm) from the center line of the stop on the top cover.
3. Again, invert the cover and with its sealing gasket, place it onto the transaxle.
4. Move the cover so that the ends of the gear lever engages in the selector fork notches and the ends of the reverse selector lever engages the notch on the selector shaft and the groove in the gear.

5. Secure the cover with the retaining bolts.

Differential
INSTALLATION

1. Install the differential assembly into the housing. Install the clutch shaft and secure with a roll pin. Install the retaining spring.
2. Seal the threads of the differential adjusting nuts and install into the housing, matching the disassembly marks.
3. The backlash is adjusted by the movement of the adjusting ring nuts and should measure 0.005 to 0.010 inch (0.12 to 0.25 mm).
4. Install the lock plates to lock the adjusting rings.

Clutch Housing
INSTALLATION

1. Install the oil seal in the clutch housing and install the gasket.
2. Install a seal protector tool over the clutch shaft and install the clutch housing.
3. Install the retaining bolts for the clutch housing. Torque to 30 ft/lbs (4 Nm).
4. Remove the seal protector tool from the clutch shaft.

TYPE 11

4 Speed Transaxle

Renault R12, R15, R17, R17TS

DISASSEMBLY

NOTE: The shifting control linkage arm can be located at either the top or bottom of the front cover, depending upon the transaxle model.

1. Mount the transaxle securely and drain the lubricating oil.
2. Remove the clutch housing retaining bolts and remove the cover assembly.
3. Remove the back-up light switch and the front cover assembly. Remove the spacer and the primary shaft bearing adjusting shims. Measure the ring and pinion backlash and mark the differential adjusting locknuts for installation purposes.
4. Remove the right and left differential bearing adjusting locknuts, using the appropriate tools.
5. Remove the half housing assembly retaining bolts and separate the half housings.
6. Lift the pinion shaft assembly from the half housing, along with the stop peg which is used to lock the double tapered roller bearing outer cage.
7. Lift the primary shaft and the differential from the half housing.
8. Using a drift, remove the roll pin from the 3rd/4th speed fork. Remove the fork and shaft, while retaining the locking ball and spring. Remove the locking disc located between the shafts.
9. Move the selector lever into the 1st gear position and slide the reverse gear shaft as far as possible back on the control rod side.
10. Using a drift, remove the roll pin from the 1st/2nd gear fork. Remove the fork and shaft while retaining the locking ball and spring.
11. Unscrew the reverse gear swivel lever bolt and remove the swivel lever.
12. Using a drift, remove the reverse gear positioning shaft roll pin. Remove the shaft and fork.

NOTE: The roll pin will touch the housing and must be turned and the pin removed completely with a pair of pliers.

Remove the circlip from the reverse idler gear and shaft. Remove the shaft, the gear, thrust washer and the guide. Retain the locking ball and spring.

14. Necessary replacement of half housing parts and seals can now be accomplished.

Primary Shaft
DISASSEMBLY

1. Separate the clutch shaft from the primary shaft by removal of the roll pin with a drift.
2. Remove the bearings from the shaft, using appropriate pullers.

ASSEMBLY

1. Using a press or its equivalent, install the tapered bearing onto the primary shaft.
2. Install the clutch shaft onto the primary shaft, using a new roll pin.

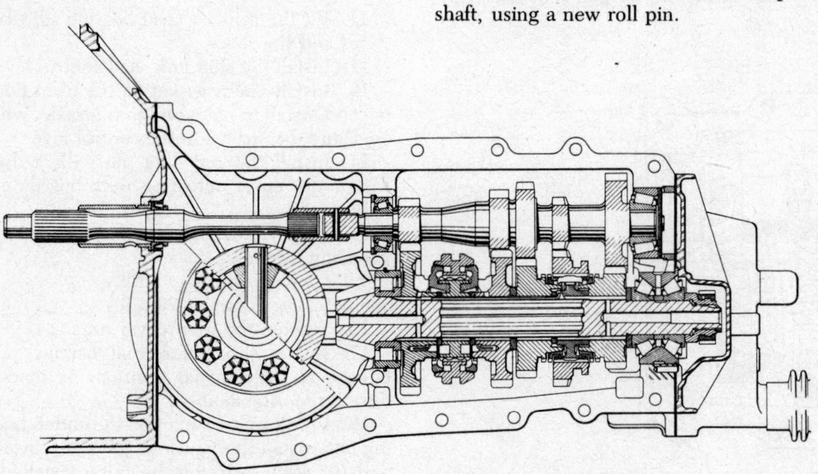

Cross section of Renault split case transaxle

Pinion Shaft (Secondary)
DISASSEMBLY

1. Place the pinion shaft assembly in a vise and secure on the 1st speed gear. Place the 1st/2nd synchronizer in the 1st speed position.
2. Release the speedometer drive gear locking tabs and unscrew the gear from the shaft.
3. Remove the double tapered roller bearing, the adjusting washer, the 4th speed gear and ring, along with the 3rd/4th speed synchronizer sliding sleeve and keys.

CAUTION

Mark the position of the sliding sleeve with reference to its position on the hub.

.4 Using a press and appropriate tools, remove the 3rd/4th speed synchronizer hub from the shaft.

5. Remove the 3rd gear stop washer and retaining key. Remove the 3rd gear and synchronizer ring.
6. Remove the 2nd speed gear stop washer, the 2nd speed gear and synchronizer ring. Remove the 1st/2nd synchronizer sliding gear.

CAUTION

Mark the position of the sliding sleeve with reference to its position on the hub.

7. Remove the stop washer from the shaft for the 1st/2nd synchronizer hub.
8. Using a press or equivalent tool, remove the 1st/2nd gear synchronizer hub from the shaft.
9. Remove the 1st gear synchronizer ring, the stop washer and the 1st speed gear.
10. Install a retaining clip onto the strengthen crown wheel and pinion assemblies to prevent the tapered roller bearing from falling out. This clip is supplied with new crown wheel and pinion assemblies.

NOTE: The bearing inner track (race) is bonded to the final drive pinion shaft and cannot be replaced.

ASSEMBLY

1. Install a new crown wheel and pinion assembly, if required.
2. Install the 1st speed gear, the stop washer and the 1st speed gear onto the shaft.
3. The 1st/2nd synchronizer hub should be heated to 482° F (250° C) maximum, when installed on the pinion shaft.
4. Install the 1st/2nd gear synchronizer stop washer, the 1st/ 2nd synchronizer sliding gear to its original position in reference to the hub, the 2nd speed gear and its ring and the 2nd speed gear stop washer.
5. Install the 3rd speed gear and synchronizer ring, the 3rd speed gear stop washer and the stop washer retaining key.
6. Install the 3rd/4th speed synchronizer hub.

NOTE: The hub can be heated or pressed onto the shaft.

7. Install the 3rd/4th speed synchronizer

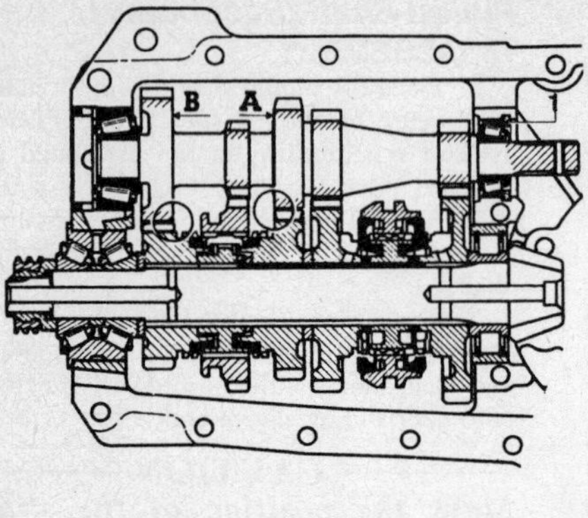

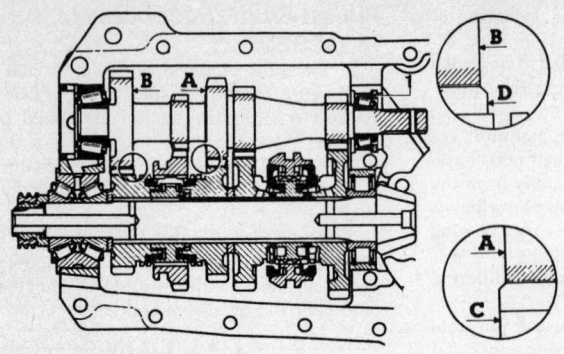

Positioning of the gears on the primary shaft

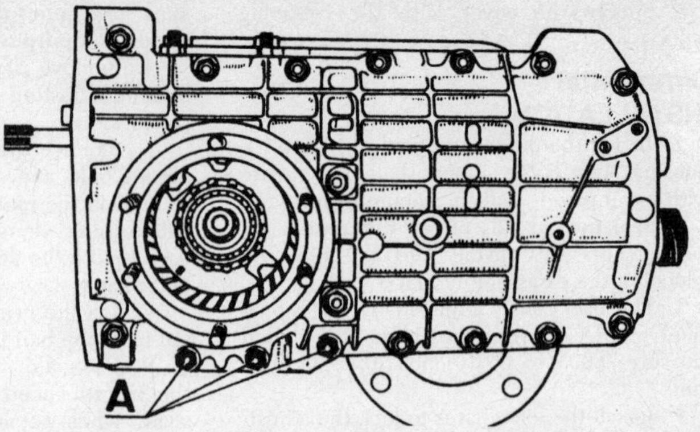

Position (A) of the three reversed nuts for clutch control clearance

sliding gear and keys to their original positions as per the previous marks.

8. Install the 4th speed gear and synchronizer ring, the pinion sleeve adjusting washer and the double tapered roller bearing.

9. Install the speedometer drive gear and screw it on to the shaft. Place the pinion shaft in a vise, and secure the 1st speed gear. Place the synchronizer sliding sleeve into the 1st speed position.

10. Tighten the speedometer drive gear to 75 to 85 ft/lbs. Lock the tabs of the locking ring unless the pinion depth adjustment is to be made.

Differential

The differential assembly is overhauled in the conventional manner. Refer to the general instruction in the rear axle repair unit section. Special measuring tools are needed to measure the pinion depth, ring gear backlash adjustment and differential bearing preload adjustment.

Positioning the Primary and Pinion Shaft

1. Place the primary and the pinion (secondary) shafts into the left half housing.

2. The position of the 3rd speed gear on the primary shaft should be offset with reference to the 3rd speed gear of the pinion (secondary) shaft, by the same amount as the 4th speed gear on the primary shaft in reference to the 4th speed gear on the pinion (secondary) shaft.

3. To achieve the proper distance, the positioning is accomplished by using adjusting washers in selective sizes on the primary shaft.

Adjusting Primary Shaft Bearings

1. Place the primary shaft assembly into the left half housing and fit the right half housing in place, but do not secure it.

2. Fit the spacer and shim pack into the 4th gear side bearing bore.

3. The shaft should turn freely, without any end-play and the spacer should project past the housing 0.008 inch (0.2 mm), which represents the thickness of the front housing paper gasket.

4. Should the clearance be wrong, increase or decrease the shim sizes by selecting one of proper size.

5. Upon obtaining the proper clearance, remove the right half housing and the primary shaft.

ASSEMBLY

1. Install the reverse shaft and position the fork on the shaft. Retain the fork to the shaft by the roll pin.

2. Place the reverse shaft swivel lever in position and retain with the bolt. Torque to 20 ft/lbs.

3. Install the 1st/2nd shaft locking ball and spring. Insert the 1st/2nd speed selector shaft. Fit the reverse end fitting and retain it with a roll pin. Install the 1st/2nd speed gear fork and retain it with a roll pin.

4. Position the locking disc in place between the shafts and install the 3rd/4th selector shaft locking ball and spring.

5. Install the shaft and fit the 3rd/4th gear fork with the hub towards the differential end and retain it with a roll pin.

6. Install the locking ball and spring, the reverse idler shaft and gear, (with the hub towards the differential end) and the thrust washer into the right half housing. The thrust washer bronze face should be against the gear.

7. Install the guide from inside the bore and push the shaft fully into place. Install the gear retaining circlip.

8. Place the differential, the primary shaft with the clutch shaft in place and the secondary shaft assembly into the left half housing.

9. Install a sealing compound on the joint faces of the half housings and fit the right housing to the left housing, being sure the end of the reverse idler lever enters the slot in the reverse gear shaft.

10. Install the retaining bolts and nuts.

CAUTION

The nuts are located on the right half housing, except three under the differential assembly, reversed to allow clearance for the clutch controls.

11. Fit the primary shaft bearing adjusting shims and the spacer.

12. Install the shift fork shaft control lever.

13. Install a new gasket on the front housing and install in place on the transaxle, while engaging the shaft into the control lever.

14. Install the retaining pin with a drift. Install the cover retaining nuts but do not tighten.

15. Tighten the half housing bolts to the following torque;

0.276 inch (7 mm)—15 ft/lbs
0.315 inch (8 mm)—20 ft/lbs

16. Tighten the front cover nuts.

17. Install the differential carriers and tighten to the original positions as marked during the disassembly.

18. Install a new gasket on the clutch housing and install the housing. Fill the transaxle with lubricating oil after the unit is installed in the vehicle.

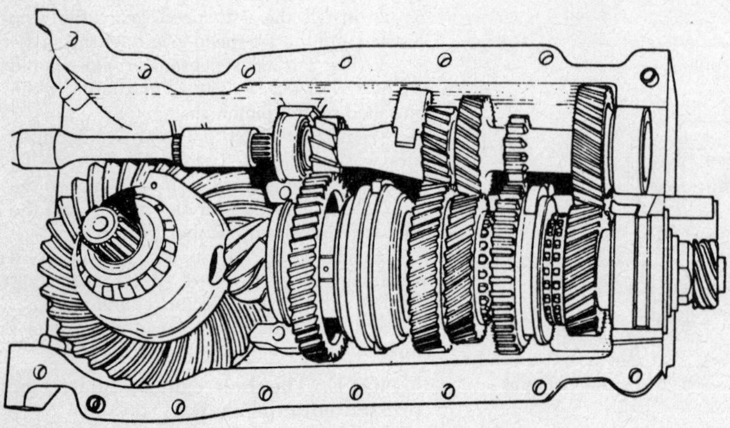

Positioning of gear train in the half case

TYPE 12

4 Speed Transaxle

Saab Models 99, 900

DISASSEMBLY

NOTE: The disassembly and assembly of the transaxle gear train can be accomplished without separating the engine and gearbox. However, the engine flywheel must be removed.

CAUTION

Before the transaxle disassembly is begun, measure the backlash of the differential ring and pinion gears, so that the same backlash is obtained during the reassembly, providing no affected components for the differential are replaced. Upon removal of the differential bearing seats, measure and mark the shims for later installation.

1. Secure the transaxle and drain the lubricating oil. Remove the side and end plates from the case.
2. Remove the differential bearing seat retaining bolts and with the aid of a puller type tool, remove the left and right seats. Remove the spring and plunger on each end of the inner driveshaft, along with the adjusting shims.

NOTE: The inner driveshafts will be removed with the seats as an assembly.

3. Remove the differential assembly from the housing.
4. Remove the lock plate that holds the intermediate and reverse gear shafts in place.
5. Using a special pulling tool or equivalent, pull the intermediate gear shaft from the housing and allow the intermediate gear set to drop downward.
6. Remove the primary gear housing retaining bolts and separate the primary gear housing from the transaxle housing.
7. With the primary gear housing separated from the transaxle housing, the intermediate gear set can be removed from the transaxle.
8. Remove the transaxle side cover, if not already removed, and take out the spring and ball catch for the gear selector rod.
9. Remove the reverse gear selector shaft retaining screw, turn the gear selector rod so the driver is detached from the reverse gear shift and pull out the shaft.
10. Remove the shift shaft for the 1st/2nd gear, 3rd top gear and shift forks. Remove the shift fork and the sliding sleeve for the 3rd speed gear.

NOTE: The reverse lever does not need to be removed from the gear shift shaft when the shaft is removed.

11. Remove the reverse gear shaft and lift the reverse idler gear from the housing.
12. Remove the needle bearing from the pinion shaft and install a special holding tool or equivalent, as a lock on the reverse gear of the pinion shaft. Remove the pinion nut from the shaft.
13. Remove the gear holding tool and remove the 3rd/4th gear synchronizer hub and 3rd gear.
14. Remove the four pinion shaft bearing housing screws. Install a special pushing tool or equivalent, and remove the pinion shaft from the housing. Remove the gears, sleeves, washers and shims from the housing, noting each component's location.

Pinion Shaft and Housing

DISASSEMBLY

1. To remove the pinion shaft from the pinion shaft housing, the pinion bearing nut must be removed. The pinion shaft can then be pressed from the housing and the front bearing removed.
2. Place the pinion shaft and rear bearing in a press and remove the rear bearing from the shaft.
3. Remove the outer races from the pinion shaft housing as required, with a press and the necessary special tools.

ASSEMBLY

1. Install the outer races in the pinion shaft housing and seat firmly.
2. Press the rear bearing onto the pinion shaft. Fit the spacer and bearing housing onto the shaft.

NOTE: The bearings should be lightly oiled before assembly.

3. Place the shaft assembly in a press or equivalent tool, install the front bearing and force into place on the shaft, while turning the housing until a resistance is felt.
4. Install a "locking" substance on the shaft threads and install the locking nut.
5. Wrap a cord around the pinion housing and attach a pull scale to the cord.
6. Tighten the locking nut until a pull torque of 10 to 15 lbs. (47 to 71 N-4.7 to 7.0 kp) is attained for new bearings, or a pull torque of 4.2 to 9.2 lbs. (19 to 43 N-1.9 to 4.3

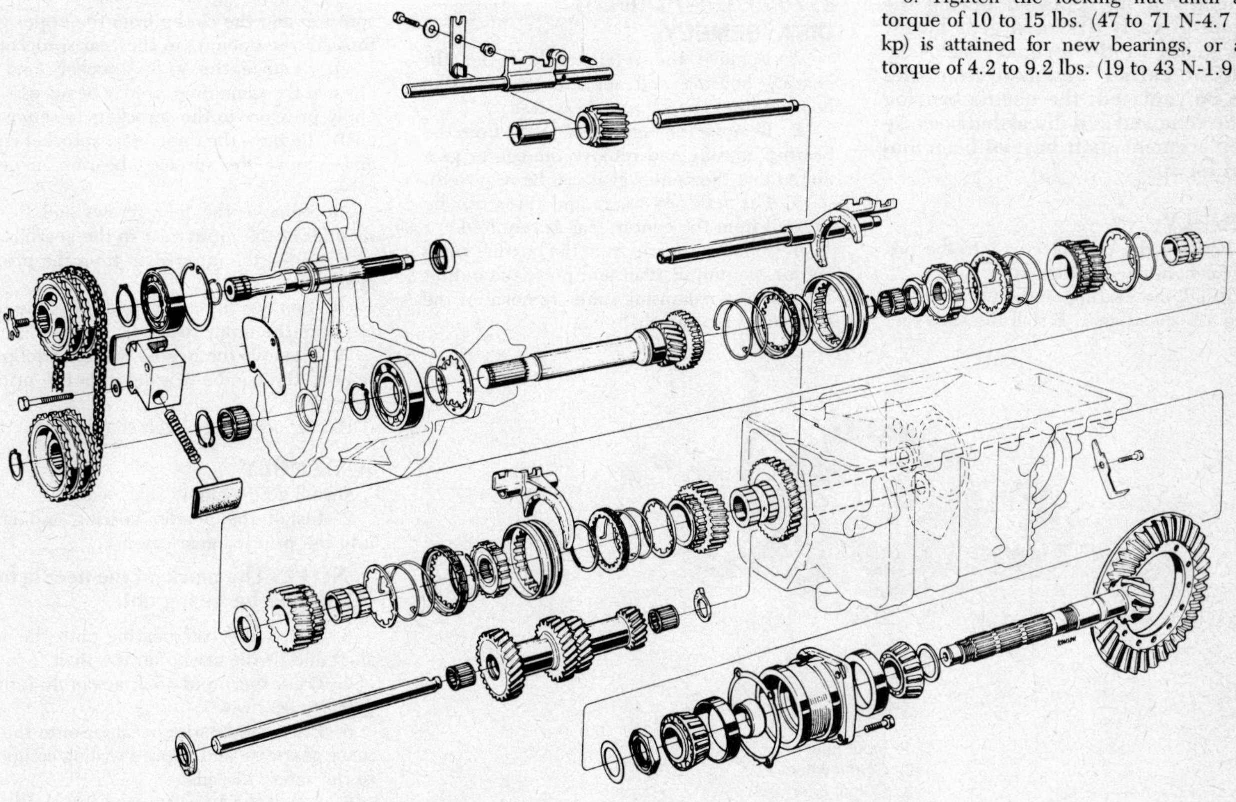

Exploded view of transaxle, chain driven primary gear train

kp) is reached for bearings having more than 1200 miles (2,000 KM), considered to be used bearings.

7. When the bearing pull torque is correct, lock the pinion nut in place on the shaft with a center punch or drift.

Primary Gear Case (Up to and Including Transaxle Number 817000, Gear Driven)

DISASSEMBLY

1. Remove the retaining bolts for the bearing housing and separate the bearing housing from the primary gear case.
2. Remove the center gear shaft from the bearing housing and remove the center gear nut so that the center gear can be removed.
3. The roller bearings and races can be pressed from the center gear as required.
4. Remove the cap from the bearing housing for the output shaft and press the output shaft from the housing, after removal of the snap-ring from the shaft.
5. Press the input gear assembly from the bearing housing, complete with the bearing.
6. Remove the snap-ring and press the bearing from the input shaft.
7. Remove the bearing support that retains the 4th speed input gear with the bearing.
8. Press the primary gear housing 4th speed input gear out of the housing. Remove the snap-ring and remove the bearing from the shaft.
9. If necessary, remove the oil collector and the needle bearing from the primary gear housing.

NOTE: The needle bearing in the primary gear housing has been discontinued from the 1976 and later models and need not be replaced during the overhaul of early designed gear boxes. When gears in the primary gear assembly of earlier designed transaxles are to be replaced, the needle bearing must be removed and discarded because the replacement shaft has not been machined for it.

ASSEMBLY

1. Position the oil collector into the primary gear housing, if removed.
2. Install the bearing on the primary gear housing 4th speed gear. Install the snap-ring and press the 4th speed gear assembly into the primary gear housing.
3. Mount the support for the bearing of the primary gear housing input shaft to the primary gear housing and secure the bolts with a locking substance.
4. Install the bearing onto the input gear and install the snap-ring.
5. Press the primary input gear and bearing into the bearing housing. The bearing must be flush with the mating surface of the bearing housing.
6. Press the output gear ball bearing into the bearing housing, and then press the output gear into the bearing. Install the washer and spring.
7. Install the roller bearing races, bearings and the shaft into the center gear. Install the locknut and snug.
8. Position the gear in a holding device and wrap a cord around the gear teeth so that the gear can be rotated on the bearings.
9. Pull the cord and cause the gear to rotate with a spring scale attached to the cord. A turning torque reading of 1.3 to 1.8 lbs. (6 to 8 N-0.6 to 0.8 kp). Obtain the correct reading by adjusting the locknut. Secure the locknut to the shaft with center punch of drift.
10. Fit the center gear into the bearing housing and secure with the attaching bolt.
11. Install the primary input gear bearing into the primary housing, if previously removed.
12. Install the bearing housing onto the primary gear housing and secure with the retaining bolts.

Primary Gear Case (Up to and Including Transaxle Number 817000, Gear Driven)

DISASSEMBLY

1. Remove the retaining bolts for the bearing housing and separate the bearing housing from the primary gear case.
2. Remove the center gear shaft from the bearing housing and remove the center gear nut so that the center gear can be removed.
3. The roller bearings and races can be pressed from the center gear as required.
4. Remove the cap from the bearing housing for the output shaft and press the output shaft from the housing, after removal of the snap-ring from the shaft.
5. Press the input gear assembly from the bearing housing, complete with the bearing.
6. Press the primary input gear and bearing into the bearing housing. The bearing must be flush with the mating surface of the bearing housing.
7. Press the output gear ball bearing into the bearing housing, and then press the output gear into the bearing. Install the washer and spring.
8. Install the roller bearing races, bearings and the shaft into the center gear. Install the locknut and snug.
9. Position the gear in a holding device and wrap a cord around the gear teeth so that the gear can be rotated on the bearings.
10. Pull the cord and cause the gear to rotate with a spring scale attached to the cord. A turning torque reading of 1.3 to 1.8 lbs (6 to 8 N-0.6 to 0.8 kp). Obtain the correct reading by adjusting the locknut. Secure the locknut to the shaft with center punch of drift.
11. Fit the center gear into the bearing housing and secure with the attaching bolt.
12. Install the primary input gear bearing into the primary housing, if previously removed.
13. Install the bearing housing onto the primary gear housing and secure with the retaining bolts.

1. Input gear
2. Center wheel
3. Output gear

Primary gear train using gears to drive transaxle

Primary Gear Case (From Transaxle Numbers 900001 and S00001, Chain Driven)

DISASSEMBLY

1. Remove the retaining bolts and separate the cover from the primary gear housing.
2. Remove the chain tensioner assembly.
3. Remove the circlip from the lower gear sprocket and the circlip from the upper gear, through the opening in the gear sprocket.
4. Remove the gear sprockets and the chain at the same time. It may be necessary to apply pressure to the sprockets to remove.
5. Remove the upper gear sprocket circlip and remove the sprocket bearing, if necessary.
6. Remove the four screws and bearing retainer at the input gear to the gearbox.
7. Press the input shaft from the primary gear case.
8. Remove the circlip and press the bearing from the input shaft.
9. Remove the needle bearing circlip and remove the needle bearing from the primary gear case.
10. Remove the clutch shaft seal.

ASSEMBLY

Install a new clutch shaft seal.

2. Install the needle bearing and circlip into the primary gear case.

NOTE: The mark on the needle bearing should be facing out.

3. Install the ball bearing onto the input shaft and fit the circlip on the shaft.
4. Press the input shaft assembly into the primary gear case.
5. Place the bearing retainer onto the primary gear case and apply a sealing compound to the screw threads.
6. Install the bearing, race and circlip into the upper gear sprocket.

NOTE: The chamfer of the circlip must face outward when the gear is installed.

Install the chain on the sprocket gears and install onto the splines and stud in the primary gear case. Install the two circlips.

8. Install the chain tensioner with the oil passage at the top and place the backing plate so that its top edge is in line with the top edge of the chain tensioner housing. Apply thread sealant to the chain tensioner bolts and install.

9. Install the primary gear cover and new gasket.

ASSEMBLY OF TRANSAXLE

1. Install the guide studs into the transaxle housing and install the pinion assembly into the case, with the original shims between the bearing housing and the transaxle housing.

NOTE: Should new components be installed that would change the pinion depth, special tools would have to be used to correct the components to the proper pinion depth setting.

2. Remove the guide studs and install the four retaining bolts into the bearing housing.

NOTE: Any measurement operations and adjustments must be done before the bolts are secured with a "locking" substance.

3. The distance between the connecting surface for the primary gear housing and the pinion shaft nut should be checked before installing the reverse gear on the pinion shaft. The distance should be 7.677 to 7.681 inches (195.0 to 195.1 mm). Adjust a depth gauge to the measurement and measure the clearance with a feeler gauge. Install the necessary shims to close the clearance, between the pinion nut and the reverse gear.

NOTE: If the pinion shaft depth was not changed, the original shims can be reused.

4. After the necessary shims have been selected and installed on the pinion shaft, install the reverse gear on the shaft.

NOTE The gears will have to be driven on the pinion shaft with a sleeve and a plastic tipped hammer.

5. Install the 1st gear on the bearing sleeve of the reverse gear.

6. Install the 1st/2nd synchronizer hub in place on the pinion shaft. Place the 1st/2nd gear shift fork into the sliding sleeve and mount on the synchronizer hub.

7. Install the 2nd gear sleeve and mount the 2nd gear onto the sleeve.

8. Install the spacer and sleeve for the 3rd gear. Install the 3rd gear on the sleeve.

9. Install the 3rd/4th synchronizer hub. Place the 3rd/4th shifting fork into the sliding sleeve of the 3rd/4th gear and install on the synchronizer hub.

10. Lock the reverse gear so that the pinion shaft does not turn. Install and torque the pinion shaft nut to 30 to 45 ft/lbs. (40 to 60 Nm—4 to 6 KPM).

11. Secure the nut to the pinion shaft.

12. Install the pinion shaft needle bearing and its locking ring. Remove the shaft locking tool.

13. Locate the sliding sleeves in the neutral position and install the shift shaft for the 1st, 2nd, 3rd and 4th gear shift forks.

14. Turn the gear selector shaft clockwise to gain clearance to install the reverse gear shift shaft. Install the shaft and lock with the stop screw.

15. Mount the needle bearings into the intermediate gear assembly, using grease to hold them in place. Install the gear set into the bottom of the gear box housing.

16. Have the thrust washer located in the correct position for the intermediate gear assembly, on the primary gear housing. Be sure the connecting tube is fitted to the output shaft of the primary gear.

17. Seal the mating surface of the primary gear housing and mount it to the transaxle case.

NOTE: Do not tighten the primary gear housing screws until the intermediate gear shaft is installed.

18. Insert the intermediate gear shaft into position. Move the intermediate gear assembly in order that the shaft can be installed. Align the thrust washer so the shaft can be installed through it. Tighten the primary gear housing retaining screws.

19. Install the reverse gear and shaft. Be sure the reverse lever is fitted into the groove on the reverse gear. Install the lock plate over the reverse gear and the intermediate gear shaft ends. Secure the screw.

20. Install the spring and lock ball for the gear selector rod and fit the housing cover in place and secure with the retaining bolts.

21. Install the differential assembly into the housing.

22. Using the shims that were removed during the disassembly, install the inner drive shaft assemblies in place on the housing. Measure the differential gear backlash and adjust to the measurements obtained before the disassembly.

23. Complete the assembly by installing the cover onto the housing and filling the unit with lubricating oil to the specified level.

TYPE 13

4 Speed Transaxle

Subaru Except 4/WD Models

DISASSEMBLY

1. Disconnect the return springs from the release bearing holder and remove the clutch fork and release bearing holder.

2. Remove the transmission cover.

3. Wind vinyl tape on the spline of the right and left axle drive shafts to prevent the oil seals from being damaged when separating the case.

4. Separate the transmission case by removing the seventeen bolts.

NOTE: The case will separate easily if the two areas around the knock pins are tapped upward with a plastic hammer.

5. Use a shank of a hammer and remove the drive pinion.

6. Remove the transmission mainshaft.

7. Remove the differential.

8. Remove the three shifter rail spring plugs.

9. Remove the shifter forks and rails.

NOTE: When pulling out a rail, keep the other rails placed in Neutral. Pull the rail for the 4th/3rd by turning 90°.

10. Remove the one screw on the right and left side of the transmission case and remove the oil seal holder lock plate. Using a special oil seal holder wrench remove the oil seal holder and O-rings.

11. Remove the speedometer driven gear. Knock the speedometer shaft outside the case by tapping lightly.

12. Pull the knock pins out and then pull out the reverse idler gear shaft, reverse idler gear and shifter lever.

13. Disassemble the transmission mainshaft.

   a. Remove the snap-ring.

   b. Press off the ball bearing, main shaft collar, 4th drive gear, synchronizer hub, 4th drive gear bushing and the 3rd drive gear.

NOTE: The 3rd drive gear bushing may be left installed but if replacement is necessary, cut a groove with a grinder and drive it off with a chisel. When the bushing moves a little remove it with a press.

14. Disassemble the drive pinion.

   a. Unscrew the drive pinion locknut.

   b. Remove the ball bearing and the 4th/3rd driven gear with a press then remove the 2nd gear and needle bearing by hand.

   c. Remove the 1st driven gear, needle bearing race, synchronizer hub and needle bearing by using a press.

   d. Remove the needle bearing race, drive pinion spacer and roller bearing by using a press.

15. Disassemble the transmission cover.

   a. Remove the back-up light switch and remove the reverse accent spring, ball and straight pin.

   b. Remove the plug in the upper part of the cover and then remove the reverse accent shaft and reverse return spring.

16. Disassemble the differential assembly.

   a. Remove the right and left snap-rings and then remove the two axle driveshafts.

   b. Remove the ring gear.

   c. Drive out the straight pin toward the ring gear.

   d. Pull out the differential pinion shaft, and then remove the differential pinion, side gear and washer.

   e. Remove the roller bearing by using a puller.

ASSEMBLY

1. Reassemble the transmission mainshaft.

1. Reverse idle gear complete
2. Reverse idler gear bushing
3. Reverse idler gear shaft
4. Knock pin
5. Reverse shifter rail
6. Shifter fork rail
7. Shifter fork rail 2
8. Shifter rail plunger 2
9. Shifter rail plunger
10. Shifter fork
11. Shifter fork set screw
12. Reverse shifter rail arm
13. Reverse shifter lever complete
14. Shifter fork 2
15. Transmission main shaft collar 2
16. Snap-ring (outer)
17. Ball bearing
18. Transmission main shaft collar
19. Gear set
20. Synchronizer ring
21. 4th drive gear bushing
22. Synchronizer sleeve
23. Synchronizer hub spring
24. Synchronizer hub
25. Synchronizer hub insert
26. Third drive gear bushing
27. Transmission main shaft
28. Needle bearing
29. Oil seal
30. Drive pinion lock nut
31. Drive pinion lock washer
32. Ball bearing
33. Bolt
34. Spring washer
35. Drive pinion shim
36. Second driven gear
37. Synchronizer ring 2
38. Needle bearing
39. Needle bearing inner race
40. Reverse driven gear
41. Synchronizer hub spring 2
42. Synchronizer hub 2
43. Synchronizer hub insert 2
44. Low (1st) driven gear
45. Drive pinion spacer
46. Roller bearing
47. Key

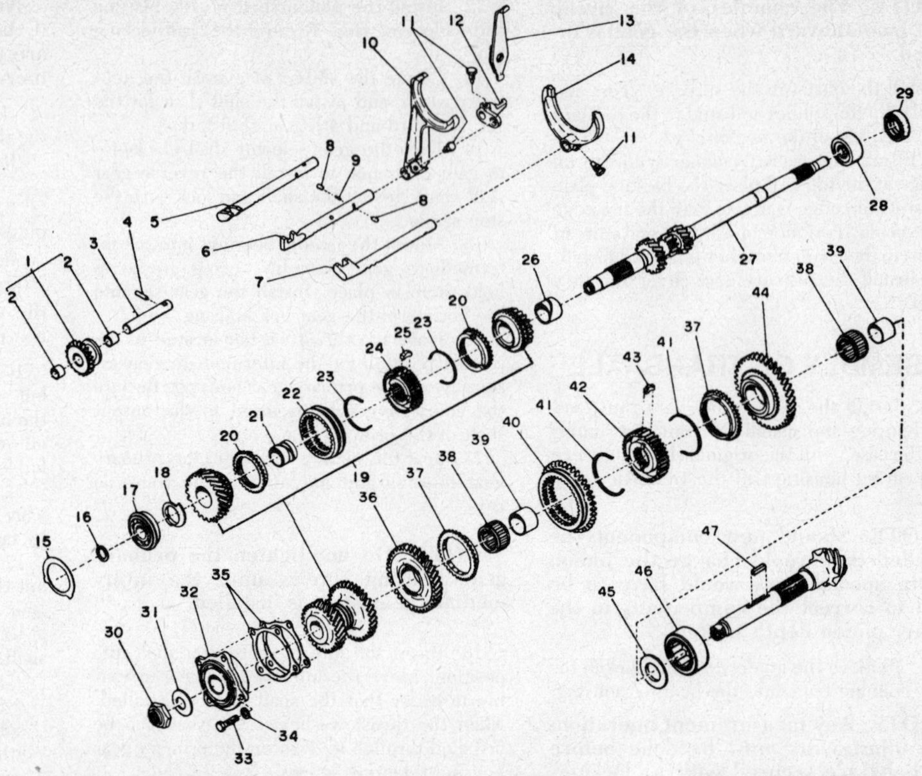

Exploded view of 4-speed transaxle gear assemblies

NOTE: Install the hub so that the end of the spline having the narrower tooth width is on the 3rd gear side. The shorter insert is for the 4th/3rd synchronizer and the longer insert is for the 1st/2nd synchronizer.

2. Reassemble the drive pinion.

a. Install the roller bearing in the drive pinion and press on the spacer.

b. Install the three synchronizer inserts, reverse driven gear and the two springs on the hub.

NOTE: Install the reverse driven gear so that its toothed side and the side of the synchronizer hub has its lower boss face in the same direction.

c. Install the needle bearing race with a press.

d. Install the needle bearing. 1st driven gear, synchronizer rings and hub which was sub-assembled in (c).

e. Install the needle bearing race with a press.

f. Install the 2nd driven gear and insert a key into the groove on the drive pinion.

g. Install the 4th/3rd driven gear with a press.

h. Install the ball bearing with a press.

i. Install the drive pinion lockwasher.

NOTE: Stake the locknut in two places.

3. Reassemble the differential.

a. Install the side and pinion gears on the case and then insert the pinion shaft.

b. Measure the backlash between the gear and pinion and make adjustment using the proper washers.

c. Align the differential pinion shaft with the holes on the differential case and drive the straight pin in from the ring gear side. Drive it in until it falls in about 0.039 in. then stake the pin.

d. Press on the roller bearing on the differential case.

e. Using new lockwashers, clamp the ring gear on the case.

f. Install the axle driveshafts and lock it with snap-rings.

g. Measure the clearance between the pinion shaft and the tip of the axle drive shaft. Clearance should be 0-0.0079 in. Make adjustment by selecting the proper snap-ring.

NOTE: The figure of the lower three digits marked on the drive pinion end face is the match number for combining it with the ring gear. The upper figure is for the shim adjustment. The first three digits on the ring gear indicates a number for combination with the drive pinion. The following digits indicates a value of appropriate backlash.

h. Adjust the drive pinion shim, place the drive pinion on the transmission case without a shim and tighten the pinion.

i. Press on the oil seal into the axle shaft oil seal holder.

4. Position the transmission case on the stand and screw the axle shaft oil seal holder into the case using the special wrench.

NOTE: Make sure the holder marked "R" is installed on the right side and holder marked "L" is installed on the left side.

5. Install the outer snap-ring and washer on the speedometer shaft, then install them into the transmission case. Install the speedometer driven gear on the shaft. Install oil seal.

NOTE: Install the outer snap-ring on the speedometer driveshaft from the driven gear side.

6. Install the reverse shifter lever into the transmission case. Install the reverse idler gear and shaft.

7. Install the reverse shifter rail arm to the end of the reverse shifter lever. Install the reverse shifter rail.

8. Install the shifter fork rail spring, ball and gasket in the case and tighten the shifter rail spring plug.

9. Shift the reverse shifter rail and select the reverse shifter rail arm so that the clearance between the reverse idler gear and the wall of the case is 0.059-0.079 in.

10. Install the shifter rail plunger into the hold of the case.

11. Wind tape around the splines of the axle driveshafts of the differential assembly to prevent damage to the oil seals.

12. Install the differential on the axle shaft oil seal holder.

13. Install the needle bearing on the tranmission mainshaft and install the case.

NOTE: Make sure the knock pin of the case is fitted into the hole in the needle bearing outer race. To prevent damage to the roller bearing place the open end of the roving plunger on the bearing.

14. Install the shifter fork. Install the shifter rail plunger in the shifter fork rail.
15. Install the shims in the drive pinion selected in Step "k" under reassembling the differential assembly, and then install into the transmission case.
16. When installing the roller bearing outer race knock hole to the knock pin of the case, position the knock hole to the edge of the transmission case and put a mark on top of the outer race. Turn the outer race so that the mark comes to the edge of the transmission case while slightly up the drive pinion, then slightly move the outer race right and left and front and rear until the knock pin fits into the knock hole.
17. Install the shifter rail plunger.
18. Install the shifter fork and shifter fork rail.
19. Install the shifter fork rail spring, ball and gasket into the case.
20. Select the shifter forks so that the synchronizer sleeve and reverse driven gear come to the center of the gears when the mainshaft and drive pinion are placed in the normal position (both the shaft and drive pinion are forced against the forward side without any clearance).
21. Check clearance A at the end of each rail. If dimension A is not within the range of 0.012 to 0.063 in., replace the rail, fork and set screw so that the proper dimension is obtained.
22. Install the mainshaft oil seal with its end surface A as shown in the illustration.

NOTE: When joining the cases from above be careful not to let the oil seal tilt. Apply liquid gasket to the case surfaces, remove the outer race of the roller bearings and make sure the speedometer gear tooth is meshed.

23. Clamp the clutch cable bracket, and back-up lamp wire clip together.
24. Install the drive pinion onto the case.
25. Install the outer race of the roller bearing.
26. Check and adjust the backlash of the ring gear and check the adjustment of preload on the roller bearing. Special tools are necessary unless it is done by trial-and-error. Backlash is as specified between 0.0039 to 0.0059 in.
27. Check the tooth contact of the hypoid gear as follows. To reduce backlash, loosen the holder on the upper case side and turn in the holder on the lower case side by the same amount. To increase backlash, loosen the lower and turn in the upper.

The drive pinion shim selected earlier may be too thick or thin. Increase or reduce its thickness.

28. Remove the lock plate (driveshaft holder). Loosen the driveshaft holder until the O-ring groove appears, install the O-ring into the groove and tighten the holder into position where the holder has been tightened in. Do this on both upper and lower heads.
29. Tighten the lock plate. Remove the protective vinyl tape wound on the axle shafts.
30. Reassemble the transmission cover.
31. Install the transmission cover.

a. Adjust the bearing side clearance 0-0.0118 in. using collar (transmission mainshaft). For adjustment, insert collar if required.

b. Install the shifter arm in the cover (and install the cover to the thransmission).

c. Adjust the transmission cover by inserting a bar through the hole of the shifter arm and shift the gear into 4th. Move the shifter arm from 4th position to 2nd and reverse position. The arm will move lightly toward 2nd side but heavy to reverse side because of the function of the return spring, and the arm will come into contact with the stopper at the end. To adjust, remove the plug on the cover and change the thickness of the aluminum gasket, so that the light stroke and heavy stroke become the same.

32. Install the clutch release fork and release bearing holder and secure them with return springs.

NOTE: Fill the internal groove of the holder with grease.

TYPE 14

5 Speed Transaxle

Subaru Except 4/WD Models

DISASSEMBLY

1. Remove the transmission.
2. Remove the clutch release fork and release bearing holder.

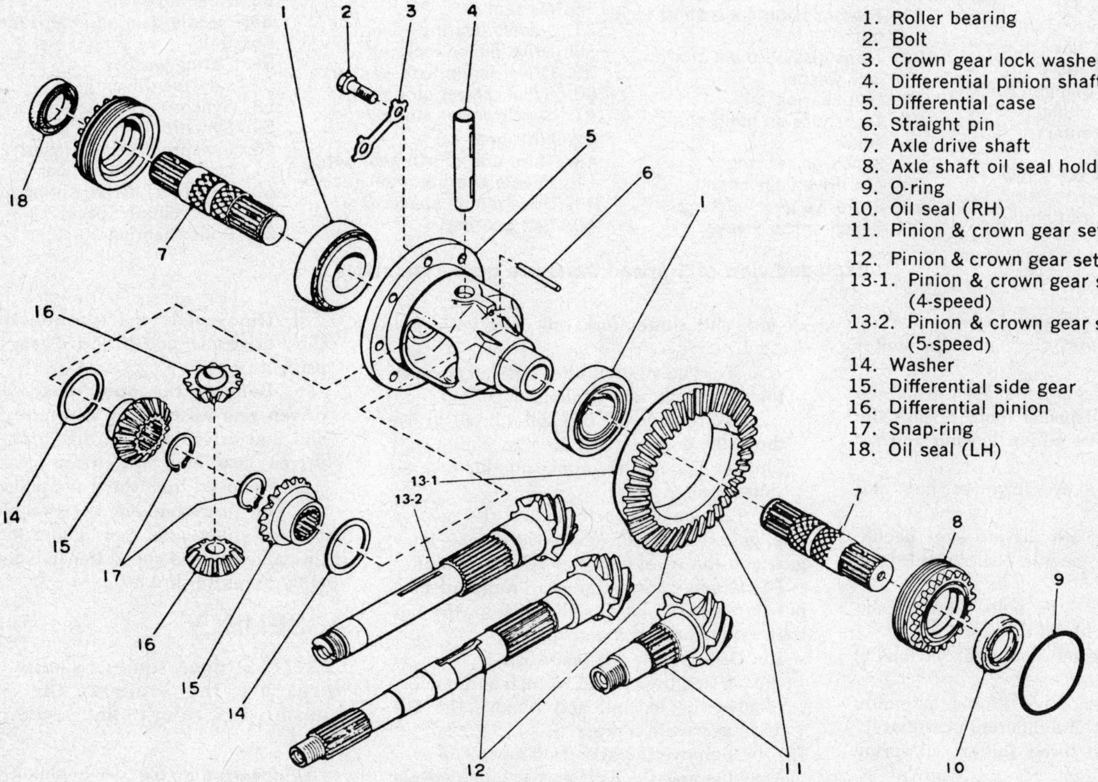

1. Roller bearing
2. Bolt
3. Crown gear lock washer
4. Differential pinion shaft
5. Differential case
6. Straight pin
7. Axle drive shaft
8. Axle shaft oil seal holder
9. O-ring
10. Oil seal (RH)
11. Pinion & crown gear set (AT)
12. Pinion & crown gear set (4WD)

13-1. Pinion & crown gear set (4-speed)

13-2. Pinion & crown gear set (5-speed)

14. Washer
15. Differential side gear
16. Differential pinion
17. Snap-ring
18. Oil seal (LH)

Exploded view of differential assembly and the three pinion gear lengths

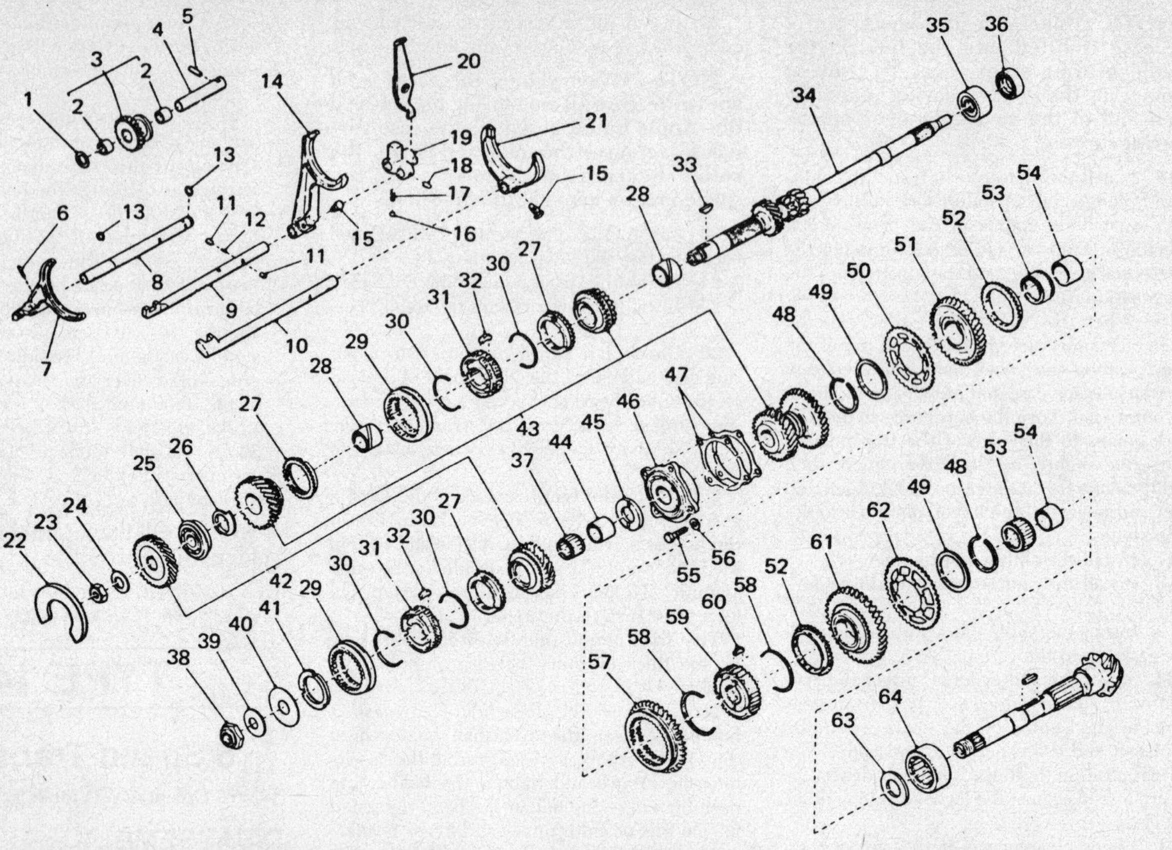

1. Washer
2. Reverse idler gear bushing
3. Reverse idler gear complete
4. Reverse idler gear shaft
5. Knock pin
6. Spring pin
7. Shifter fork 3
8. Reverse shifter rail
9. Shifter fork rail
10. Shifter fork rail 2
11. Shifter rail plunger 2
12. Shifter rail plunger
13. Snap ring (outer)
14. Shifter fork
15. Shifter fork set screw
16. Ball
17. Shifter fork rail spring 2
18. Shifter rail plunger 2
19. Reverse shifter rail arm
20. Reverse shifter lever complete
21. Shifter fork 2
22. Transmission main shaft collar 2
23. Transmission main shaft lock nut
24. Transmission main shaft lock washer
25. Ball bearing
26. Transmission main shaft collar
27. Synchronizer ring
28. 4th drive gear bushing
28. 3rd drive gear bushing
29. Synchronizer sleeve
30. Synchronizer hub spring
31. Synchronizer hub
32. Synchronizer hub insert
33. Woodruff key
34. Transmission main shaft
35. Needle bearing
36. Oil seal
37. Needle bearing
38. Drive pinion lock nut
39. Drive pinion lock washer
40. Synchronizer stopper 2
41. Synchronizer stopper
42. Fifth gear set
43. Third and fourth gear set
44. Needle bearing inner race 5
45. Drive pinion spacer 2
46. Ball bearing
47. Drive pinion shim
48. Snap ring
49. Low (1st) driven gear washer
50. Second driven spring gear
51. Second driven gear
52. Synchronizer ring 2
53. Needle bearing
54. Needle bearing inner race
55. Bolt
56. Spring washer
57. Reverse driven gear
58. Synchronizer hub spring 2
59. Synchronizer hub 2
60. Synchronizer hub insert 2
61. Low (1st) driven gear
62. Low (1st) driven spring gear
63. Drive pinion spacer
64. Roller bearing

Exploded view of 5-speed transaxle gear assemblies

3. Remove the transmission rear cover.
4. Drive out the spring pin on the shifter fork.
5. Shift the gears into first gear, install the mainshaft stopper (special tool), release the staking on the drive pinion locknut and remove the nut.
6. Remove the synchronizer hub and shifter fork together.
7. Remove the 5th driven gear, needle bearing inner race, needle bearing and drive pinion spacer.
8. Remove the three bolts retaining the drive pinion assembly to the case.
9. Separate the left and right sections of the transmission case.
10. Remove the drive pinion assembly mainshaft assembly and differential assembly.
11. Remove the three shifter rail spring plugs.
12. Remove the shifter fork setscrew, shifter fork and shifter fork rail of 3rd/4th and 1st/2nd.
   a. To remove the shifter fork rail position the rest of the rails in neutral.
   b. To remove the 3rd and 4th rails, turn them 90 degrees and let the shifter rail plunger fall in the groove of the reverse shifter rail.
13. Take out the lock pin and the reverse idler gear shaft then, remove the reverse idler gear and the reverse shifter lever as a unit.
14. Remove the outer snap-ring and take out the reverse shifter rail arm from the rail then remove the ball and spring.
15. Disassemble the mainshaft.
   a. Using the special wrench and holder, remove the locknut and remove the 5th drive gear with a press.
   b. Remove the Woodruff key.
   c. Remove the ball bearing and 4th drive gear using a press.
   d. Disassemble the synchronizer hub, third drive gear and 4th drive gear bushing using a press.
   e. Remove the outer snap-ring, 1st driven gear washer, 1st driven gear spring and 2nd driven gear spring, from the 1st driven gear and 2nd driven gear which were removed from the drive pinion.
16. The procedure for disassembling the main shaft differential gear, shifter fork, etc., is the same as the 4 speed transmission disassembly Steps 14 thru 16.

ASSEMBLY

NOTE: Since some assembly procedures are the same as the 4-speed transmission, refer to that section where noted.

1. Reassemble the drive pinion component parts following the procedure in the four

speed transmission section until the ball bearing, then install the spacer, needle bearing race, needle bearing, fifth driven gear, synchronizer hub, stopper, lockwasher and nut. Tighten the locknut to 60 ft-lbs.

2. Select a drive pinion shim (see Step 3—4 speed assembly procedures).

3. Put the shifter rail spring and ball in the reverse shifter rail arm. Insert the reverse shifter rail.

4. Install the outer snap-ring.

5. Put the shifter fork rail spring, ball and gasket in the case.

6. Select the reverse shifter lever so that the gap between the reverse idler gear and the case wall becomes 0.06 to 0.118 in. by shifting the reverse shifter rail.

7. Shift it to the neutral position, then select the right size washer so that the gap between the case wall becomes 0 to 0.02 in.

8. Put the shifter rail plunger into the grooves of the case and the reverse shifter rail arm.

9. Install the 1st driven gear spring (subgear) with the outer snap-ring and 1st driven gear washer to the 2nd driven gear.

NOTE: The clearance between the tooth tops of the gear and spring (subgear) is 0.0039-0.0197 in.

10. Reassemble the transmission mainshaft as given in Step 1 under assembly of 4 speed transmission. Then install a key, 5th drive gear, lock washer and locknut to the mainshaft.

11. Fit the differential assembly into the case.

12. Attach the mainshaft assembly.

13. Insert a shifter rail plunger and install a shifter fork and rail.

14. Install the adjustment shim selected before with the drive pinion assembly and then install them to the case.

15. Insert the shifter rail plunger.

16. Install the shifter fork and shifter rail.

17. Install the shifter fork rail spring and ball in the case.

18. Select the shifter fork so that the synchronizer sleeve comes to the center of the 3rd and 4th drive gears.

19. Select the next shifter fork so that the reverse driven gear comes to the center of the 1st and 2nd driven gears.

20. Apply a liquid gasket to the mating surfaces of the case halves and put them together.

21. Tighten the drive pinion on to the transmission case.

22. Inspect the ring gear backlash and the tooth contact as described under 4 speed transmission assembly Steps 26 and 27.

23. Remove the locknut of the drive pinion assembly to remove the lockwasher, stoppers and hub.

24. Install the hub, fork and rail using the spring pin.

25. Install the synchronizer stoppers and drive pinion lockwasher. Using the mainshaft stopper tool tighten the pinion locknut to 58 ft/lbs.

NOTE: Shift the gear to 1st position when tightening the drive pinion locknut.

26. Select the last shifter fork so that the clearance between the sleeve and the 5th driven gear becomes 0.008 to 0.020 when the gear is in the 5th position.

27. Stake the drive pinion locknut.

28. Check the clearance between the edges of each rail. If the clearance is not within 0.012-0.063 in. replace the rail, fork and setscrew as necessary.

29. Select the correct mainshaft collar.

30. Install the rear cover.

TYPE 15

4 Speed Transaxle

Subaru with 4/WD

DISASSEMBLY

NOTE: Since some of the overhaul procedures are the same as the 4 speed transmission refer to that section when noted.

1. Remove the transmission.
2. Drive out the straight pin and pull out the shifter fork rail, fork, ball and spring.
3. Remove the case assembly.
4. Shift the gear to the 1st position, release the staked part of the nut, then using a main shaft stopper, remove the locknut and take out the rear shaft drive gear from the drive pinion.
5. Remove the case assembly.
6. Remove the race, needle bearing collar and washer from the drive pinion.
7. Shift the sleeve into the drive position and using a holder, remove the mainshaft locknut.
8. Remove the ball bearing assembly.
9. Remove the mainshaft spacer, rearshaft driven gear, sleeve, synchronizer hub and rear drive spacer from the rear driveshaft.
10. Remove the snap-ring from the case.
11. Punch out the rear driveshaft and using a press, remove the ball bearing.
12. Take out the O-ring from the shifter arm and remove the shifter arm.
13. Remove the back-up lamp switch from the case and the reverse accent spring ball and straight pin.
14. Remove the plug from the case and

1. Shifter fork rail 2
2. Shifter fork rail
3. Reverse shifter rail
4. Transmission main shaft lock nut
5. Transmission main shaft lock washer
6. Ball bearing
7. Transmission main shaft collar
8. Rear shaft driven gear
9. Synchronizer ring
10. Rear shaft driven gear bushing
11. Synchronizer sleeve
12. Synchronizer hub spring
13. Synchronizer hub
14. Synchronizer hub insert
15. Rear drive spacer
16. Snap ring
17. Ball bearing
18. Rear drive shaft
19. Washer
20. Drive pinion collar
21. Needle bearing race 5
22. Rear shaft drive gear

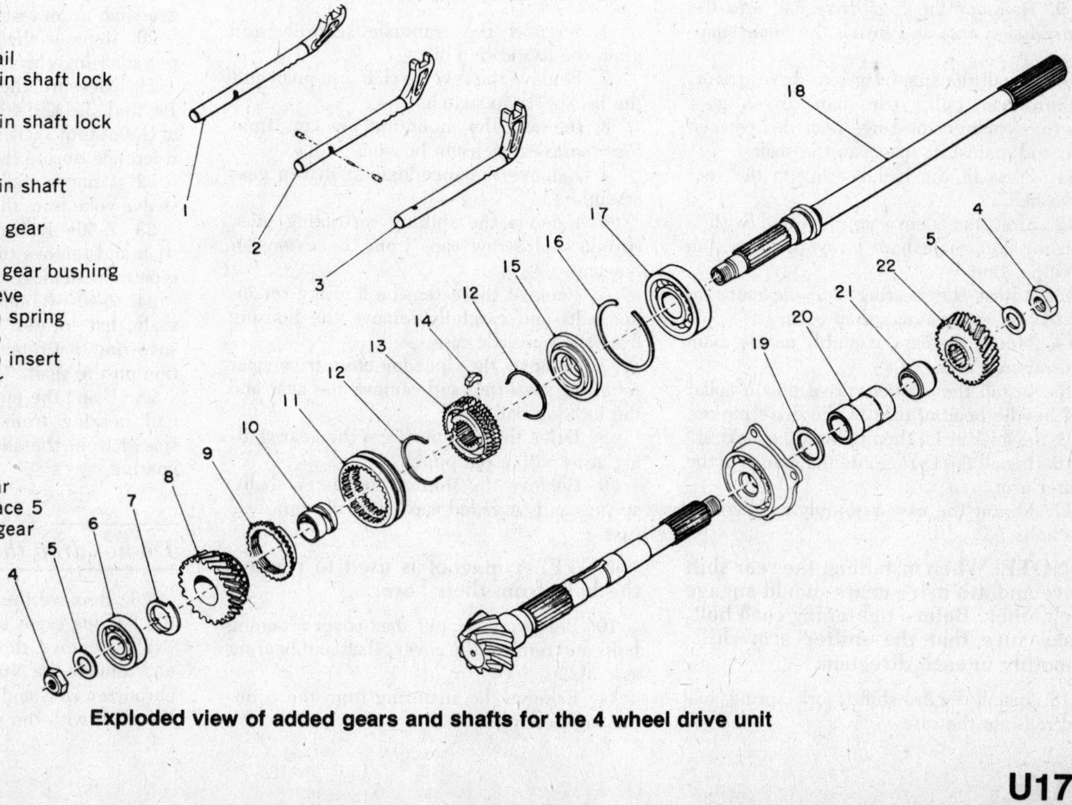

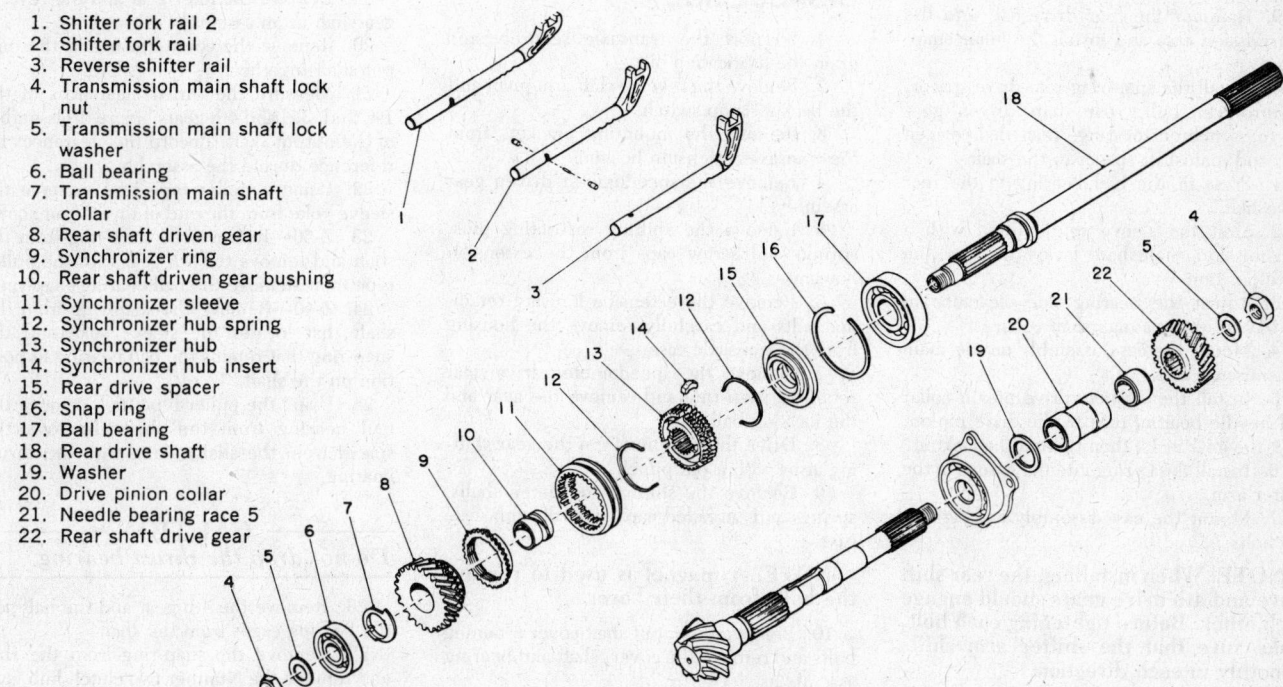

Exploded view of added gears and shafts for the 4 wheel drive unit

take out the reverse accent shaft and turn spring.

15. Remove the needle bearing from the case.

16. Remove the rear extension oil seal.

17. For the remainder of the transmission disassembly procedures refer to the 4 speed transmission section.

ASSEMBLY

1. Assemble the main transmission unit.

a. The drive pinion assembly is assembled by fitting the ball bearing, washer collar, needle bearing inner race, rear drive shaft gear, lockwasher and locknut. Do not stake the nut at this time.

2. Assemble the transmission case without the transfer system.

NOTE: After assembling, remove the locknut, lockwasher and rear shaft drive gear from the drive pinion.

3. Press fit the needle bearing into the case.

4. Insert the reverse return spring and the reverse accent shaft into the case. Install an adjusting aluminum gasket on the plug.

5. Set the ball reverse accent spring, straight pin and aluminum washer on the back-up lamp switch.

6. Install the shifter arm on the transmission case.

7. Assemble the three synchronizer inserts, sleeve and two springs on the synchronizer hub.

NOTE: Make sure the hub is installed so that the spline with the smaller width is on the rear drive spacer side.

8. Press fit the ball bearing to the rear driveshaft.

9. Hammer the rear driveshaft into the transmission case and install the inner snap-ring.

10. Install the snap-ring rear drive spacer, synchronizer hub, rear shaft driven gear sleeve, synchronizer ring, rear shaft driven gear and mainshaft spacer to the shaft.

11. Press fit the ball bearing to the rear driveshaft.

12. Shift the sleeve to be fitted with a transmission mainshaft lockwasher to the drive position.

13. Adjust the bearing side clearance to 0-0.012 in. using a mainshaft collar.

14. Mount the case assembly on the main transmission unit.

15. Install the washer, drive pinion collar and needle bearing race to the drive pinion. Shift the gear in 1st then tighten the locknut.

16. Install the O-ring into the groove of the shifter arm.

17. Mount the case assembly and tighten the bolts.

NOTE: When installing, the rear shift drive and 4th drive gears should engage each other. Before tightening each bolt, make sure that the shifter arm shifts smoothly in each direction.

18. Install the 3rd shifter fork, spring, ball and rail into the case.

NOTE: To install the ball, press it down by using the end of the shifter fork rail while forcing the rail into the case with the round side down. Rotate the rail by 180° to its proper position.

19. Drive in the straight pin, then move the shifter fork rail and check the accent.

20. Install the transmission case cover.

21. Adjust the selecting direction and position of the shifter arm shaft.

a. Install the gear shift system.

b. Shift the gear into 4th.

c. Shift the shifter arm from the 4th/3rd position to the 1st and reverse position.

d. The arm moves lightly to the 1st position while it moves heavily to the reverse position and hits the stopper as the force of the return spring is applied.

e. Adjust so that the light travel becomes the same as the heavy travel by removing the plug on the top of the transmission case and change the thickness of aluminum gasket.

22. When mounting the transmission on the car body, the gearshift system should be removed first.

23. For reassembly of the remaining transmission parts refer to the 4 speed transmission section.

TYPE 16

4 and 5 Speed Transaxle–Models Z-40 and Z-50

1980-81 Toyota Tercel

DISASSEMBLY

1. Support the transaxle securely and drain the lubricating oil.

2. Remove the reverse shift arm pivot and the backup lamp switch.

3. Remove the mounting brackets from the transaxle extension housing.

4. Remove the speedometer driven gear assembly.

5. Remove the shifting restricting pins, springs and screw caps from the extension housing.

6. Remove the extension housing retaining bolts and carefully remove the housing from the transaxle case.

7. Remove the speedometer drive gear retaining snap-ring and remove the gear and the locating ball.

8. Drive the roll pins from the gear shifting arms with a pin punch.

9. Remove the shifting rod detent balls, springs and threaded caps from the transaxle case.

NOTE: A magnet is used to remove the balls from their bores.

10. Remove the input shaft cover retaining bolts and remove the cover, shaft and bearing assemblies.

11. Remove the snap-ring from the countershaft bearing.

12. Remove the extension housing retaining bolts and carefully tap the housing loose from the intermediate plate.

13. Remove the case from the intermediate plate and remove the reverse shift arm from the pivot shaft.

14. Remove the rolled pins from the gear shift head and the shift forks. Pull the Number three shift rod from the intermediate plate. Remove the Number three shift fork from the coupling sleeve.

15. Remove the interlock pin and pull the Number two shift rod from the intermediate plate. Remove the shift fork from the coupling sleeve.

16. Remove the interlock pin and pull the Number one rod from the intermediate plate. Remove the Number one shift fork from the coupling sleeve. Remove the reverse shift fork.

17. To remove the gear assemblies from the intermediate plate, perform the following procedures as applies to each transaxle.

a. Z-50—Measure the 5th gear thrust clearance which should be 0.0059 to 0.0128 inch (0.15 to 0.325 mm), and with a service limit of 0.016 inch (0.4 mm). Remove the retaining snap-ring and remove the 5th gear, clutch hub and synchronizer ring with a puller type tool. Remove the roller bearing cage, the spacer and the steel locater ball.

b. Z-40—Remove the countergear plate, bolt and lock washer.

18. Remove the output shaft bearing retainer and bolts from the intermediate plate. Remove the two ball bearing snap-rings and with a plastic hammer or equivalent, force the output shaft, the reverse gearshaft and idler gear halfway out from the plate.

CAUTION
Support the shafts by hand.

19. Remove the idler gear and the reverse gearshaft as an assembly.

20. Remove the countergear and the output shaft together.

21. Measure the thrust clearances of the 1st, 2nd, 3rd and 4th gears before disassembly of the output shaft. Record the clearances for reference during the assembly.

22. Using a puller type tool, remove the sleeve yoke from the end of the output shaft.

23. Z-50—Remove the snap-ring from the shaft and remove the 5th gear with the puller type tool. Remove the ball bearing snap-ring.

24. Z-40—Remove the snap-ring from the shaft that locates the sleeve yoke and the snap-ring that retains the ball bearing in position on the shaft.

25. Using the puller type tool, remove the ball bearing from the shaft. Remove the spacer from the shaft, along with the thrust bearing.

CAUTION
Do not drop the thrust bearing.

26. Remove the 4th gear and the half needle bearing cages from the shaft.

27. Remove the snap-ring from the shaft and remove the Number two clutch hub, synchronizer ring and the 3rd speed gear from the shaft with the puller type tool.

Z50

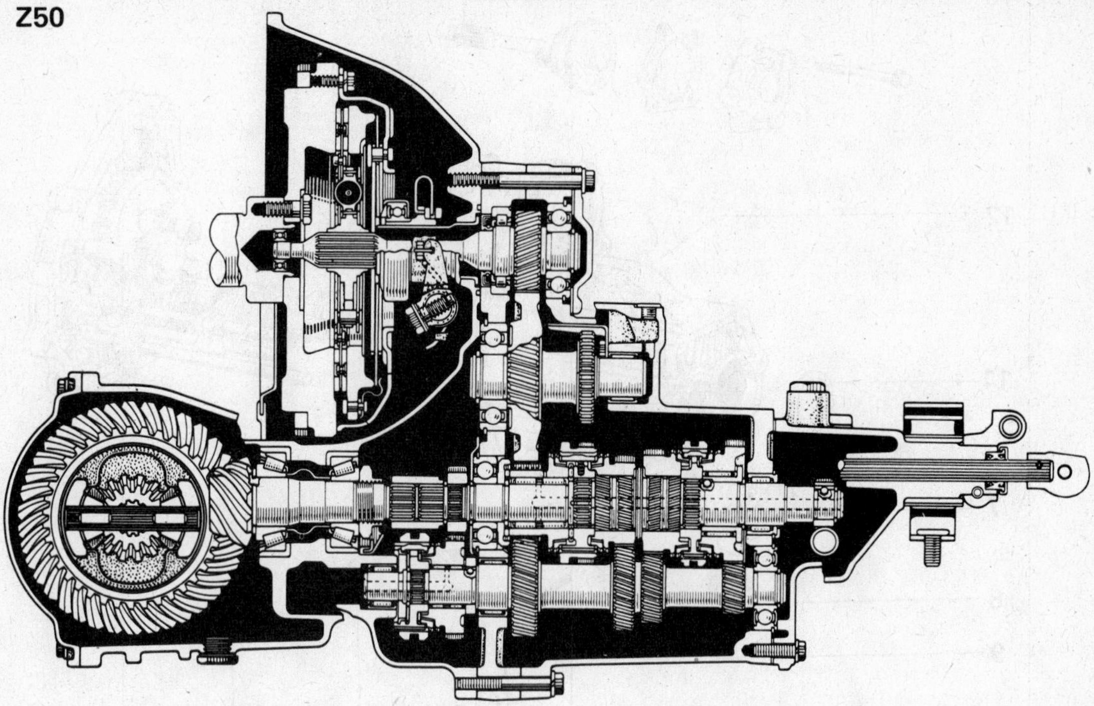

Z40

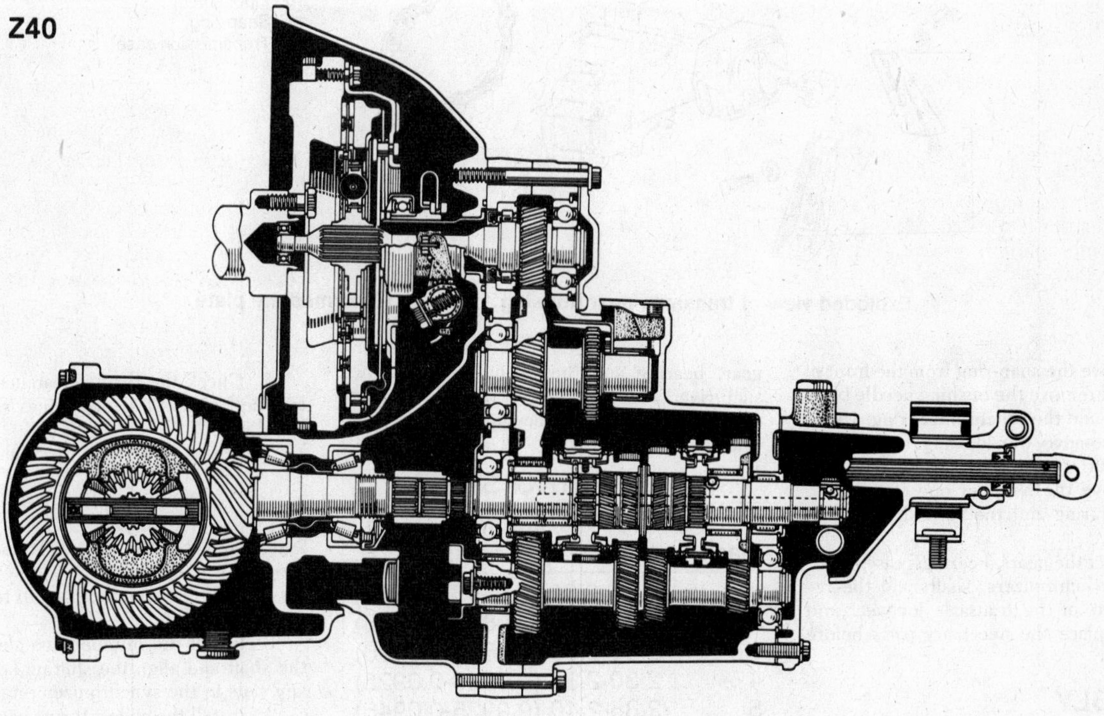

Cross section of models Z50 and Z40 transaxles

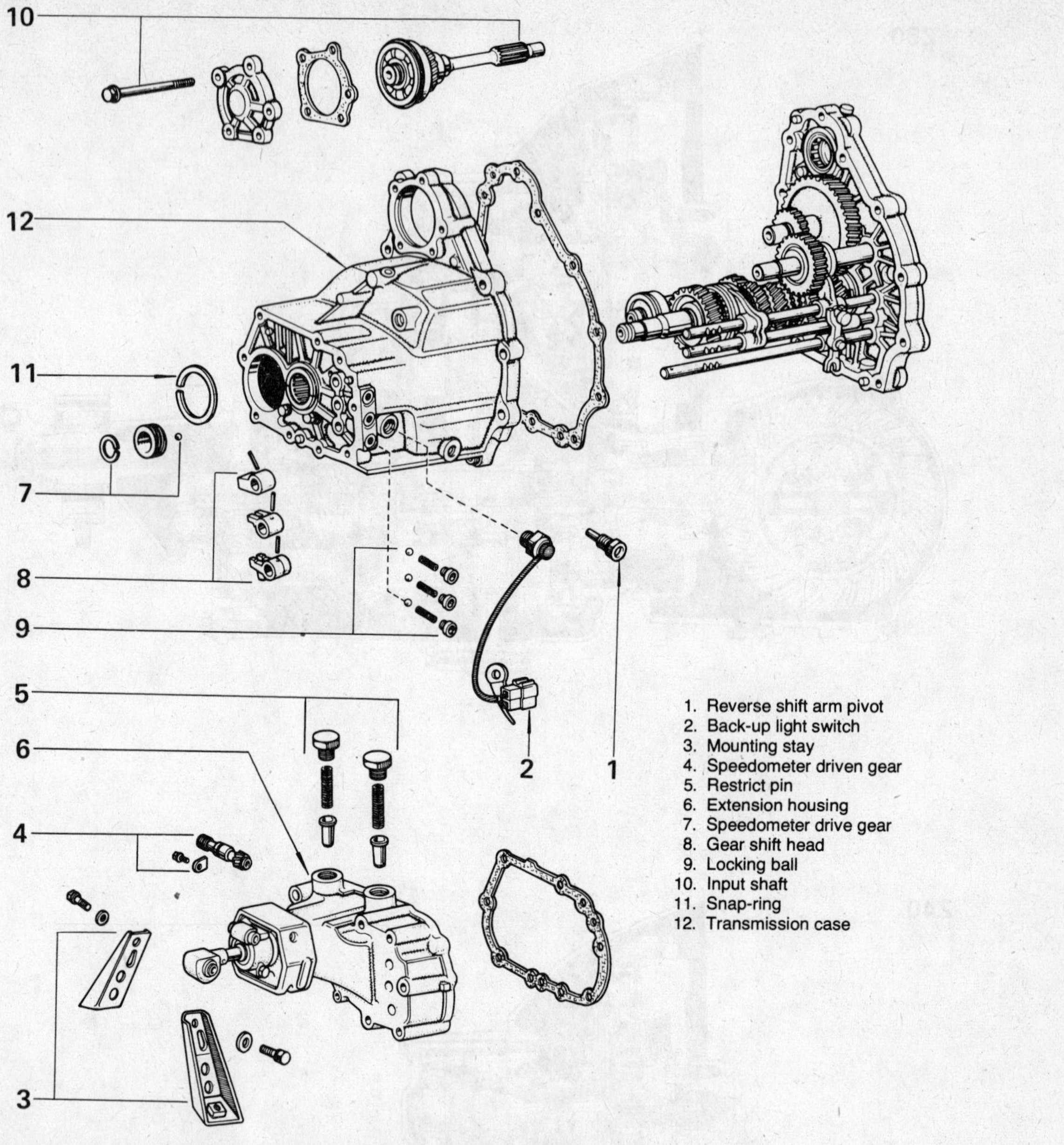

1. Reverse shift arm pivot
2. Back-up light switch
3. Mounting stay
4. Speedometer driven gear
5. Restrict pin
6. Extension housing
7. Speedometer drive gear
8. Gear shift head
9. Locking ball
10. Input shaft
11. Snap-ring
12. Transmission case

Exploded view of transaxle gear housing, cover and intermediate plate

28. Remove the snap-ring from the front of the shaft and remove the bushing needle bearing, 1st gear and the synchronizer ring. Using a magnet, remove the locating locking ball from the shaft.

29. Remove the Number one clutch hub, synchronizer ring and the second gear from the shaft.

30. Inspect the gears, bearings, case, housing, plate, synchronizers, shafts and the remaining parts of the transaxle for wear and damage. Replace the necessary parts before the assembly.

ASSEMBLY

1. Begin the assembly by placing the 2nd gear on the output shaft, followed by the synchronizer ring and the Number one clutch hub. Install the locking ball in place on the shaft and install the synchronizer ring, the 1st gear, bearing and the bushing. Install the snap-ring of a thickness to obtain a thrust clearance of zero. The following snap-rings are available.

SNAP-RING SIZES

Mark	Thickness mm	Thickness (in.)
1	2.15-2.20	(0.0846-0.0866)
2	2.20-2.25	(0.0866-0.0886)
3	2.25-2.30	(0.0886-0.0906)
4	2.30-2.35	(0.0906-0.0925)
5	2.35-2.40	(0.0925-0.0945)
6	2.40-2.45	(0.0945-0.0965)
7	2.45-2.50	(0.0965-0.0984)
8	2.50-2.55	(0.0984-0.1004)
9	2.55-2.60	(0.1004-0.1024)

2. Check the thrust clearances of the 1st and 2nd gears. The clearances should be as listed.

1st gears—0.0059 to 0.0108 inch (0.15 to 0.275 mm)
Service limit—0.0118 inch (0.30mm)

2nd gears—0.0059 to 0.0004 inch (0.15 to 0.25 mm)
Service limit—0.0118 inch (0.30 mm)

3. Install the number two clutch hub on the shaft and align the shifting keys with the key slots in the synchronizer rings.

4. Install the widest thrust bearing against the number two clutch hub. Install the half needle bearing cages, synchronizer ring and the 4th speed gear.

5. Install the spacer and the snap-ring to the front side of the 4th gear.

6. Install the smaller thrust washer into the spacer and install the assembly onto the shaft with the thrust washer facing the 4th speed gear.

NOTE: The spacer will have to be pressed onto the shaft.

7. Press the ball bearing onto the shaft with the groove on the bearing facing towards the front.

8. Select a snap-ring of a thickness to obtain a thrust clearance of zero from the following list of available snap-rings.

SNAP-RING SIZES

Mark	Thickness mm	(in.)
2	2.10-2.15	(0.0827-0.0846)
3	2.15-2.20	(0.0846-0.0866)

SNAP-RING SIZES

Mark	Thickness mm	(in.)
4	2.20-2.25	(0.0866-0.0886)
5	2.25-2.30	(0.0886-0.0906)
6	2.30-2.35	(0.0906-0.0925)
7	2.35-2.40	(0.0925-0.0945)
8	2.40-2.45	(0.0945-0.0965)
9	2.45-2.50	(0.0965-0.0984)
10	2.50-2.55	(0.0984-0.1004)

9. With the selected snap-ring installed, measure the thrust clearance of the 3rd and 4th gears.

The clearance should be as follows.

3rd gear—0.0059 to 0.0098 inch (0.15 to 0.25 mm)
Service limit—0.0118 inch (0.30 mm)

4th gear—0.0008 to 0.0094 inch (0.02 to 0.24 mm)
Service limit—0.0118 inch (0.30 mm)

10. Z-50—Install the 5th gear and select a snap-ring of a thickness to obtain a clearance of zero from the following list of snap-rings.

SNAP-RING SIZES

Mark	Thickness mm	(in.)
2	2.10-2.15	(0.0827-0.0846)
3	2.15-2.20	(0.0846-0.0866)
4	2.20-2.25	(0.0866-0.0886)
5	2.25-2.30	(0.0886-0.0906)
6	2.30-2.35	(0.0906-0.0925)

11. Z-40—Install the snap-ring in the groove on the shaft near the end.

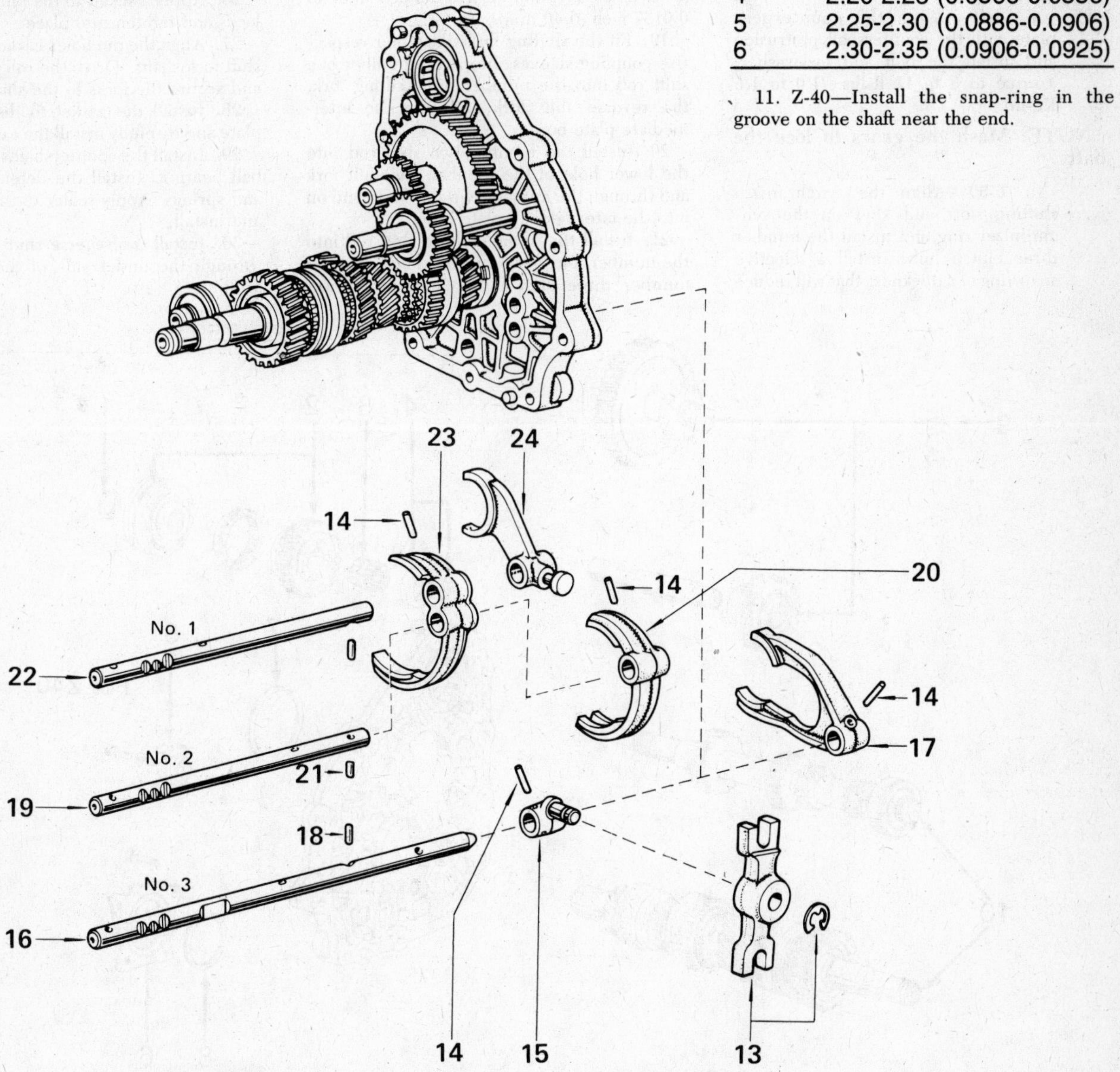

13. Reverse shift arm
14. Slotted spring pin
15. Gear shift head
16. No. 3 shift fork shaft
17. No. 3 shift fork
18. Interlock pin
19. No. 2 shift fork shaft
20. No. 2 shift fork
21. Interlock pin
22. No. 1 shift fork shaft
23. No. 1 shift fork
24. Reverse shift fork

Exploded view of shift mechanism, typical of models Z50 and Z40 transaxles

12. Press the sleeve yoke onto the shaft until the yoke touches the first snap-ring and that zero clearance exists between the snap-ring and the shaft groove.
13. Place the intermediate plate in a holder and place the assembled output shaft and the countershaft gear assembly into the intermediate plate, approximately half-way.
14. Align the idler gear with the notched portion of the reverse idler gearshaft. Tap the idler gearshaft bearing approximately half way into the intermediate plate.

NOTE: Be sure the idler gear and the output shaft spacers are not in contact with each other.

15. Tap each gearshaft until the bearings are seated in the intermediate plate. Install the retaining snap-rings on the bearings.
16. Install the bearing retainer and secure the retaining bolts.
17. a. Z-40—Align the countergear plate with the countershaft protrusion and install the bolt and lockwasher. Torque to 8 to 11 ft-lbs. (1.0 to 1.6 Kg-m).

NOTE: Mesh the gears to lock the shaft.

b. Z-50—Align the synchronizer shifting slots and keys on the synchronizer ring and install the number three clutch hub. Install a selective snap-ring of a thickness that will reduce the thrust clearance to zero, selected from the following chart.

SNAP-RING SIZES

Thickness mm	(in.)
1.80-1.85	(0.0709-0.0728)
1.85-1.90	(0.0728-0.0748)
1.90-1.95	(0.0748-0.0768)
1.95-2.00	(0.0768-0.0787)
2.00-2.05	(0.0787-0.0807)
2.05-2.10	(0.0807-0.0827)
2.10-2.15	(0.0827-0.0846)

18. Measure the 5th gear thrust clearance. The clearance should be 0.0059 to 0.0128 inch (0.15 to 0.325 mm), with a service limit of 0.0157 inch (0.40 mm).
19. Fit the shifting forks into their respective coupling sleeves. Insert the number one shift rod into the number one shifting fork, the reverse shift fork and into the intermediate plate bore.
20. Install the number two shift rod into the lower hole of the number one shift fork and through the number two shift fork, and on into the intermediate plate bore.
21. Install the number three shift rod into the number four gear shift head and into the number three shift fork. Continue inward with the shifting rod until the pin hole of the number three shift fork is aligned with the interlock pin hole.
22. Insert a piece of wire into the interlock pin hole to a length of 4.7 inches (120 mm) from the ouside of the intermediate plate.
23. Assemble the interlock pins so that a long pin is inserted first, followed by the small pin and then the same sized pin as the first one, for a total of three. Push the pins inward with a piece of wire and verify the distance is 3.1 inches (80 mm) from the outside of the intermediate plate.
24. In the transaxle of the Z-50, install the number three shaft into the fork controlling the 5th speed synchronizer.
25. Place the shift rods in the neutral position. Move the number two shift rod into the 3rd gear position and the number one and two shafts should not move.
26. Apply a sealer to the plug for the interlocks and tighten into place.
27. Align the pin holes in the shift forks and shift fork shafts. Drive the roll pins into place and secure the forks to the shafts.
28. Install the gasket to the intermediate plate and carefully install the case to the plate.
29. Install the countershaft snap-ring to the ball bearing. Install the detent locking balls and springs. Apply sealer to the detent plugs and install.
30. Install the reverse shift arm pivot bolt through the under side of the reverse shift arm.

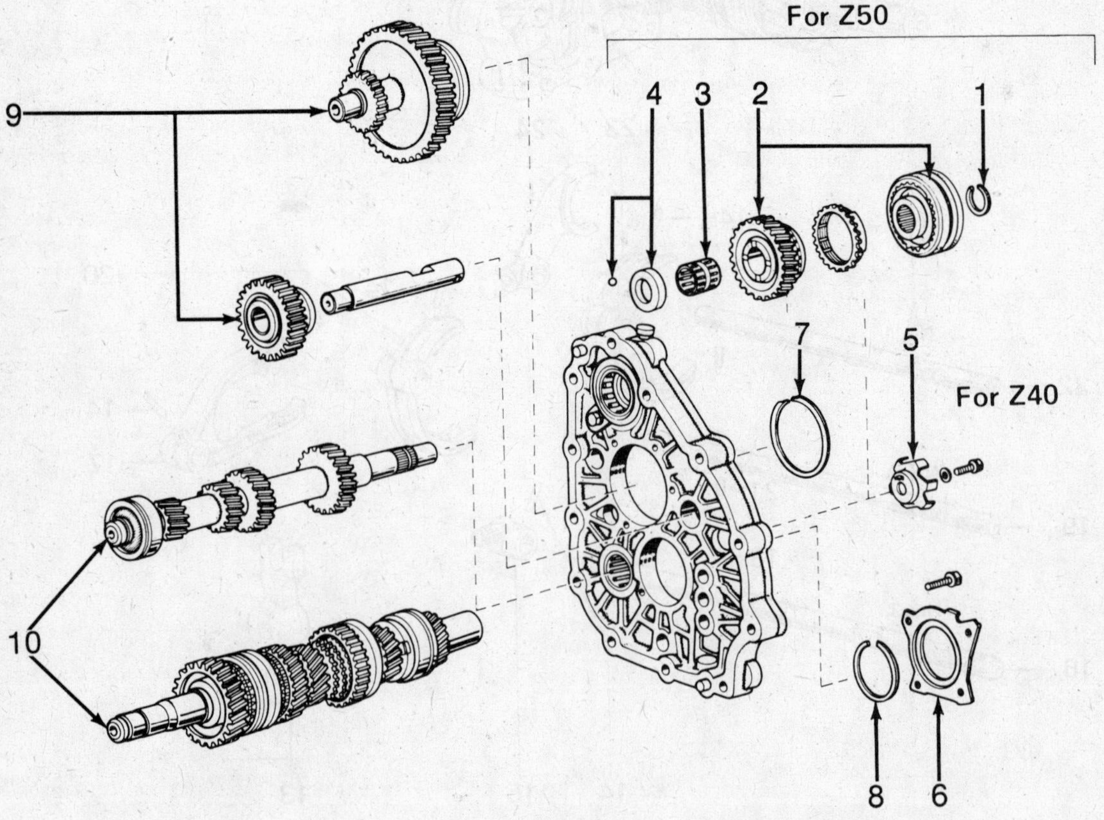

1. Snap-ring
2. No. 3 clutch hub, synchronizer ring and 5th gear
3. Bearing
4. Spacer & steel ball
5. Counter gear plate
6. Bearing retainer
7. Snap-ring
8. Snap-ring
9. Idler gear & reverse idler gear
10. Output gear & counter gear

Exploded view of intermediate plate and gears—model Z40 and Z50 parts illustrated

31. Install the gear shift heads to the shift rods and install the roll pins to retain the heads.
32. Install the locating ball, the speedometer drive gear and the snap-ring.
33. Apply the gasket and sealer to the mating surface of the case and engage the end of the shift lever shaft and the number two shift head, on the extension housing. Install the retaining bolts and secure.
34. Install the restricting pins in their proper positions as follows.
Green—1st and 2nd gears
Red—5th and reverse
35. Install the mounting brackets to their marked positions.
36. Fill the transaxle with lubricating oil to its proper level.
37. Be sure the transaxle gear shifts smoothly in all positions.
38. Install the input shaft, gasket and retainer. Secure with the retaining bolts.
39. Install the speedometer driven gear assembly and electrical switch.

TYPE 17

4 and 5 Speed Transaxle

VW Rabbit, Scirocco, Jetta

DISASSEMBLY

NOTE: A five speed transaxle is available for use in later vehicles. The disassembly and assembly procedures remain basically the same and the same precautions and care should be exercised during the overhaul procedure as is done in the overhaul of the four speed unit.

1. Mount the transaxle assembly in a holding fixture.
2. Remove the end cover and gasket.
3. Remove the circlips from the clutch release shaft. Slide the shaft out of the gear carrier and remove the clutch lever and return spring.
4. Remove the clutch release bearing and clutch pushrod.
5. Mount a bar with a locknut and spacer across the final drive housing to support the mainshaft.
6. Remove the selector shaft cover. Remove the interlock plunger springs, and the selector shaft.
7. Remove the circlip from the gear carrier side drive flange. Install the special tool with two bolts on the drive flange. Remove the drive flange.
8. Remove the plastic caps covering the clamping screws. Remove the clamping screw nuts.
9. Remove the reverse shaft retaining bolt.
10. Mount the special tool on the gear carrier assembly and lift the gear carrier off the final drive assembly while threading the special tool bolt in.
11. Drive the drive flange oil seal out of the gear carrier housing.
12. Pry the clutch operating shaft oil seal out of the carrier housing.
13. Pull the pinion shaft needle bearing out of the gear carrier.
14. Remove the shift fork assembly and the mainshaft from the final drive housing.
15. Remove the remaining drive flange as outlined in Step 7.
16. Remove the needle bearing stop and the first circlip from the pinion shaft. Lift fourth gear off the shaft.

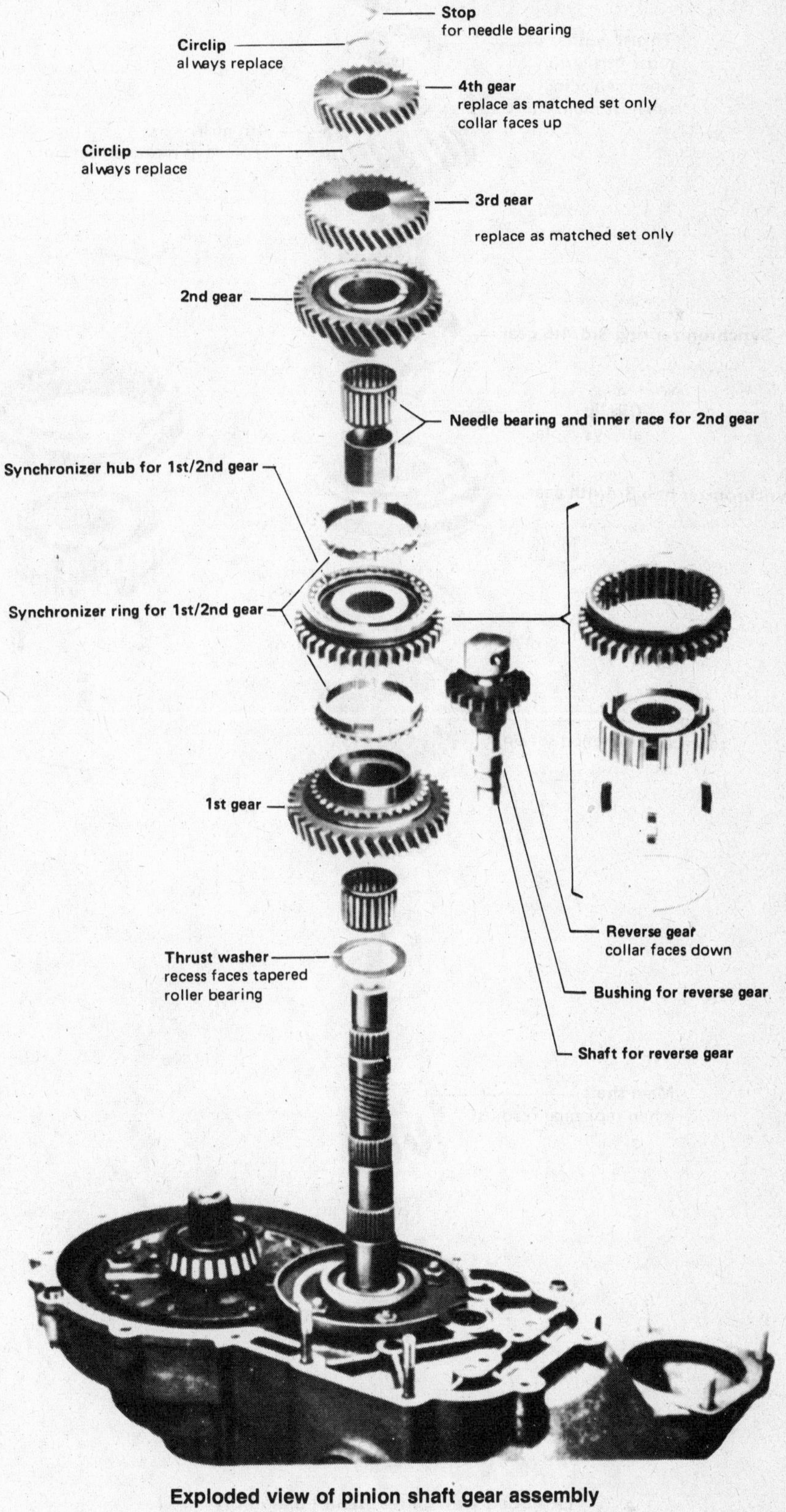

Exploded view of pinion shaft gear assembly

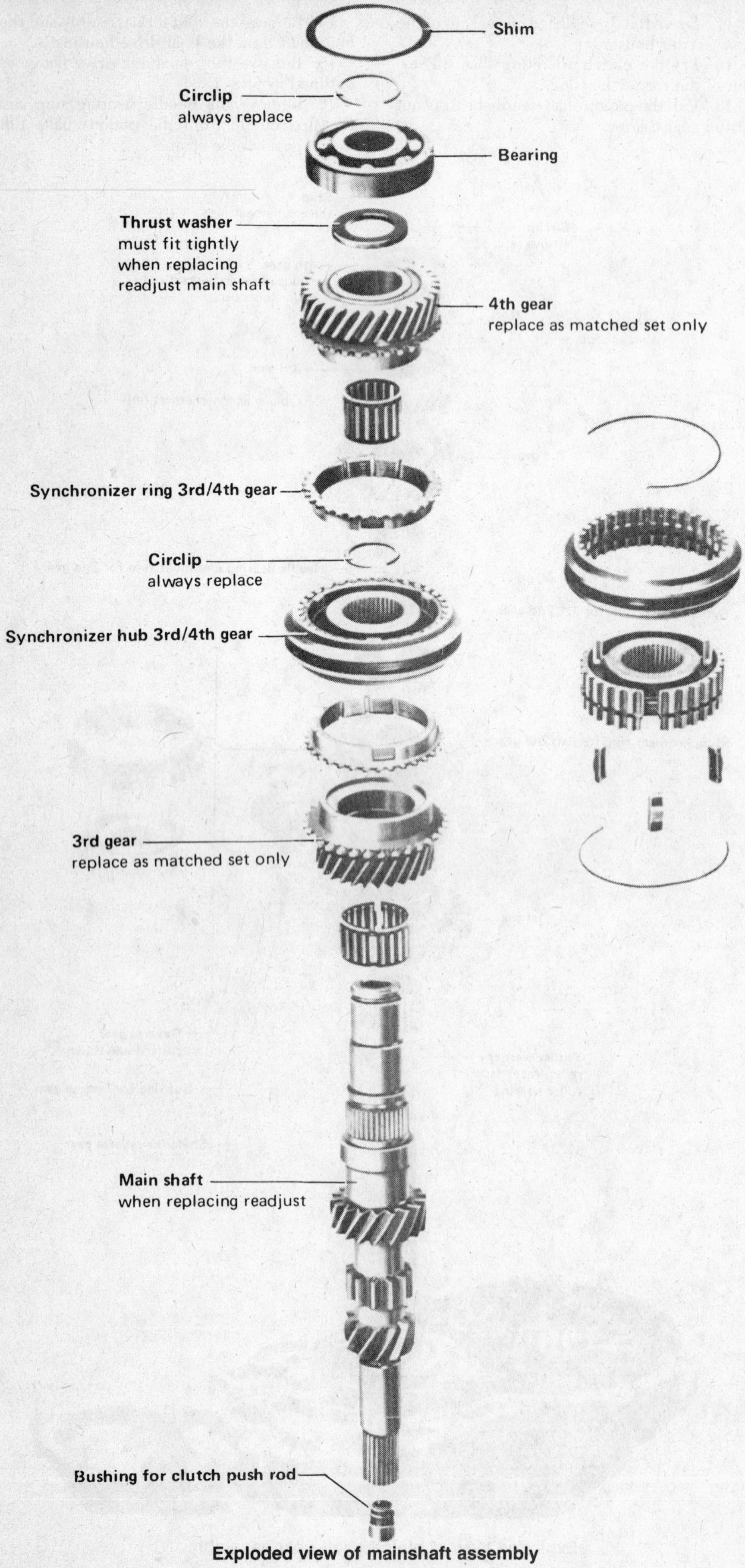

Exploded view of mainshaft assembly

17. Remove the second circlip from the pinion shaft. Lift third gear, second gear, second gear inner race and needle bearing off the shaft.
18. Remove the reverse shaft and gear.
19. Using a gear puller, remove the synchronizer hub and first/second gear from the pinion shaft.
20. Remove the pinion bearing cover and outer bearing race. Remove the pinion shaft.
21. Remove the differential assembly.
22. Pry the mainshaft oil seal out of the final drive housing.
23. Drive the drive flange oil seal out of the final drive housing.
24. Pull the starter bushing out of the final drive housing.
25. Pull the pinion outer bearing race out of the final drive housing.
26. Drive the differential outer bearing race out of the final drive housing.
27. Pull the mainshaft needle bearing out of the final drive housing.
28. Remove the two circlips from the shift fork shaft and slide the components off the shaft.
29. Remove the first circlip from the mainshaft and discard. Press the bearing off the shaft.
30. Mount the separator assembly on fourth gear and press the gear off the mainshaft. Remove the needle bearings.
31. Remove the second circlip from the mainshaft and discard. Press third gear and the synchronizer assembly off the shaft. Remove the needle bearings.
32. Slide a ⅜ in. rod in the mainshaft and drive the clutch pushrod out.
33. Press the two tapered roller bearings off the pinion shaft.
34. Remove the circlips from the differential pinion shaft and drive out.
35. Remove the differential pinion gears and thrust washers.
36. Remove the circlips from the drive flange shafts. Remove the side gears and thrust washers.
37. Press the tapered roller bearing off the housing side of the differential.
38. Remove the tapered roller bearing from the ring gear side of the differential.
39. Remove the ring gear. On 1976-77 models, the ring gear is riveted in place. Drill out rivets and replace with special bolts.

ASSEMBLY

NOTE: The ring gear and pinion shaft can be replaced only as a matched set.

1. Heat the pinion shaft small tapered bearing to 212° F and press onto the shaft.
2. Heat the pinion shaft large tapered bearing to 212° F and press onto the shaft.
3. Place a 0.75 mm shim in the pinion bore in the final drive housing and press the small bearing outer position.
4. Install the pinion shaft and cover.
5. Assemble the pinion adjustment fixture tools. Place the end plate on the pinion shaft. Attach the dial indicator and zero with a 1 mm preload.

CAUTION

Do not turn the pinion shaft while measuring because the bearings will settle and give incorrect reading.

6. Move the pinion shaft up and down and note the reading.

7. Specified bearing preload is obtained by adding the constant figure of 0.20 mm to the measured reading and the shim thickness (0.75 mm).

Example:

Shim installed	0.75 mm
reading	0.30 mm
preload (constant figure)	+0.20 mm
shim size	1.25 mm

8. Remove the pinion shaft cover and the pinion shaft. Pull the pinion shaft small bearing outer race of the final drive housing.

9. Install the correct shim and press the pinion shaft small bearing outer race into the final drive housing.

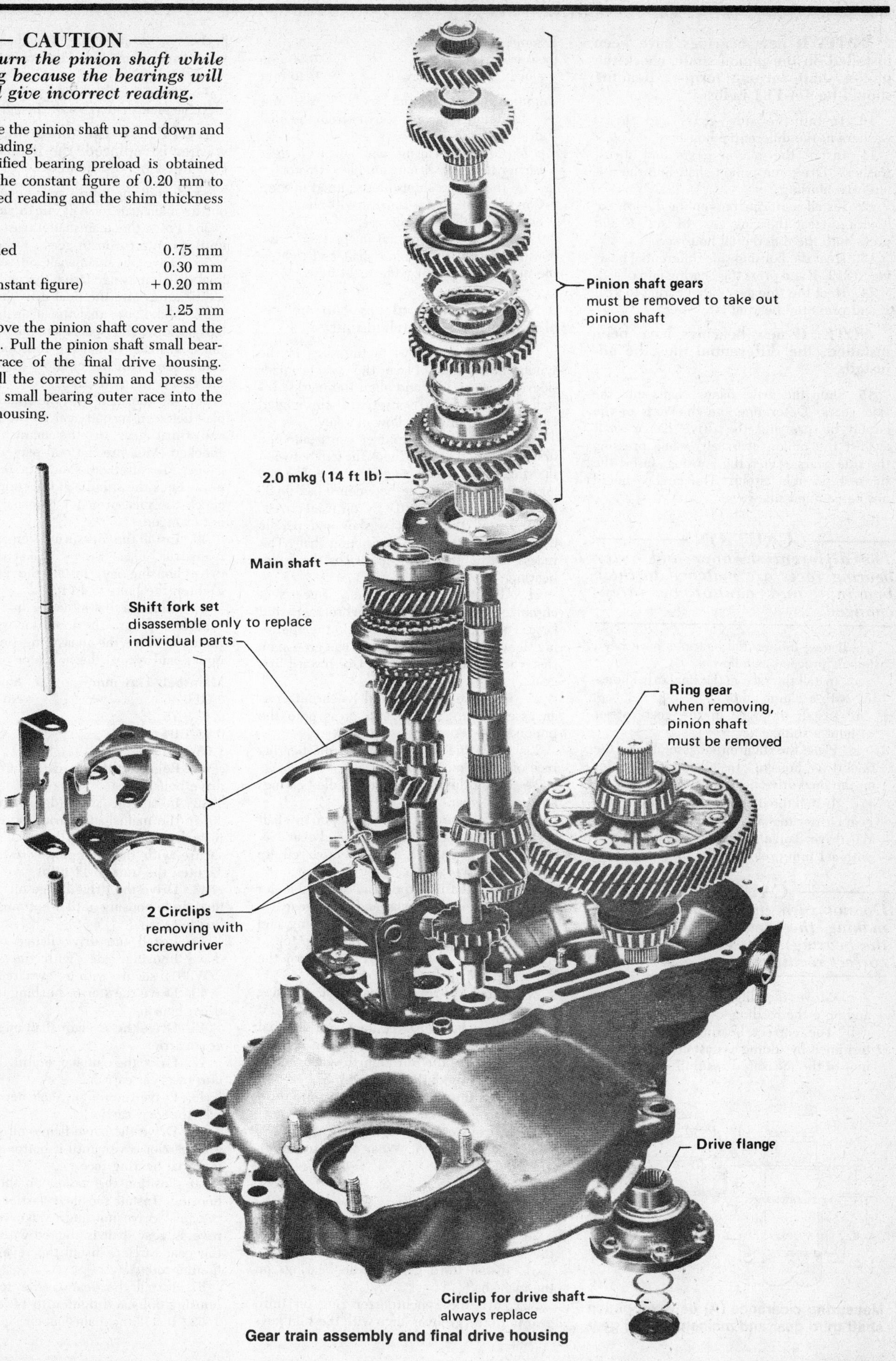

Gear train assembly and final drive housing

NOTE: If new bearings have been installed on the pinion shaft, check the pinion shaft turning torque. Reading should be 4.4-13.1 in/lbs.

10. Install the side gears and thrust washers in the differential housing.

11. Install the pinion gears and thrust washers. Drive the pinion shaft into the differential housing.

12. Install centering pins on the differential housing. Heat the ring gear to 212° F and press onto the differential housing.

13. Heat the housing side differential bearing to 212° F and press the bearing into place.

14. Heat the ring gear side bearing to 212° F and press the bearing into place.

NOTE: If new bearings have been installed, the differential must be adjusted.

15. Slide the drive flange shafts into the side gears. Determine the thickness of the circlip by pressing the drive flange shaft against the pinion gearshaft, while pressing the side gears against the housing. Insert the thickest possible circlip. The circlip should not be jammed sideways.

CAUTION

The differential inner and outer bearing races are matched to their bearings and cannot be interchanged.

16. If new differential bearings have been installed, proceed as follows:

a. Install the race in the final drive housing with a 1 mm shim.

b. Install the race in the gear carrier without a shim.

c. Place the differential assembly in the final drive housing. Install the gear carrier on the final drive housing, with the gasket.

d. Install the dial indicator fixture on the gear carrier tool and place the end plate on the drive flange. Install the dial indicator with a 1 mm preload.

CAUTION

Do not turn the differential when making the measurements because the bearings will settle and give incorrect readings.

e. Move the differential up and down and note the reading.

f. The correct bearing preload is determined by adding a constant figure or .40 mm to the measured reading.

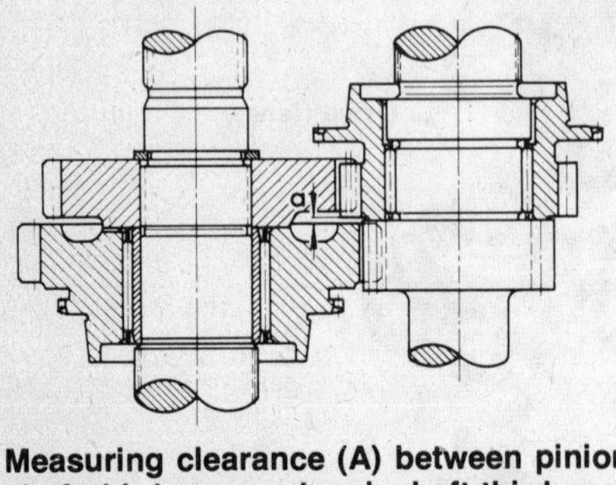

Measuring clearance (A) between pinion shaft third gear and mainshaft third gear

Example:

measured reading	0.90 mm
preload (constant figure)	+0.40 mm
shim (for gear carrier side)	1.30 mm

g. Remove the gear carrier from the final drive housing.

h. Pull the bearing race out of the gear carrier housing with a suitable extractor.

i. Install the shims (determined in Step f) in the gear carrier starting with the thickest. Install the bearing race.

17. With the differential in the final drive housing, install the pinion shaft and tighten the nuts on the cover plate to 14 ft/lbs.

NOTE: Synchronizers can be replaced only as a matched unit.

18. Position the keys in the slots in the synchronizer hub. Place the synchronizer sleeve over the hub and align the marks. Install the springs 120° offset with the angled ends engaged in the hollow of a key.

19. Press the synchronizer rings onto the first and second gears. Check the gap between the ring and gear with a feeler gauge. The gap on new parts should be between 0.042-0.066 in. and no less than 0.019 in. on used parts.

20. Install the thrust washer and needle bearing for first gear on the pinion shaft. The recess in the thrust washer faces the roller bearing.

21. Align the grooves in the first gear synchronizer ring with the synchronizer shift keys. Position the shift fork slot in the operating sleeve toward second gear. The groove on the synchronizer hub should face toward first gear.

22. Heat the first gear and synchronizer as an assembly to 250° F and press onto the pinion shaft.

23. Drive the second gear needle bearing race onto the pinion shaft.

24. Install the second gear needle bearings and second gear.

25. Install third gear on the pinion shaft with the collar facing toward second gear. Secure third gear with the selective circlip which will give an axial play between 0.00-0.20 mm. Measure the play with a feeler gauge between the circlip and third gear.

26. Warm the reverse gear bushing and press it on the reverse shaft until the top of the bushing is 41 mm (1.614 in.) from the bottom of the shaft.

27. Install the reverse gear shaft retaining bolt in the shaft. Center the shaft and drive it in until the collar makes contact with the final drive housing. Remove the retaining bolt.

28. Assemble the third/fourth synchronizer in the same way outlined in Step 57.

29. Press the synchronizer rings onto third and fourth gear. The gap between the gear and synchronizer ring should be as follows.

	New Part in. (mm)	Wear Limit in. (mm)
Third	0.045-0.068	0.019
	(1.15-1.75)	(0.5)
Fourth	0.051-0.074	0.19
	(1.3-1.9)	(0.5)

30. Press the clutch pushrod bushing into the mainshaft until it is flush.

31. Install third gear needle bearings on the mainshaft.

32. Turn the synchronizer ring on third gear until the grooves align with the shift keys in the synchronizer hub. The chamfer on the synchronizer hub inner splines must face toward third gear.

33. Press the third gear and synchronizer onto the mainshaft as a unit. Install the circlip.

NOTE: If the mainshaft thrust washer is replaced, the mainshaft position must be readjusted.

34. Install the fourth gear needle bearings on the mainshaft. Install fourth gear.

35. Press the mainshaft thrust washer on until it contacts fourth gear.

36. Drive the mainshaft oil seal into the final drive housing. Drive the mainshaft needle bearings into the final drive housing.

37. Make sure that the mainshaft support bar, locknut and spacer are in place. Insert the mainshaft. Install the shift fork assembly and secure with the circlips. Make sure that the gears are in Neutral.

38. Lift the shaft with the spindle until the play between second gear on the pinion shaft and third gear on the mainshaft can be checked. Measure the end-play with a feeler gauge. Measurement should be 0.039 in. (1.0 mm). Lock the spindle at the support bar and check the measurement to make sure it has not changed.

39. Install the measuring sleeve tool on the mainshaft. Place a new gasket on the final drive housing and install the gear carrier. Tighten the bolts to 14 ft/lbs.

40. Mount a dial indicator in a holding assembly and zero the indicator with a 3 mm preload. Move the measuring sleeve up and down, and record the indicator reading.

Mainshaft Play mm	Shim Size mm
0.00-0.46	No Shim Used
0.47-0.75	0.30
0.76-1.04	0.60
1.05-1.45	0.90

41. Remove the gear carrier from the final drive housing.

42. Install the shim (determined in Step 40) in the mainshaft bearing bore. Press the mainshaft bearing into the gear carrier, and secure with the clamping screws and nuts. Tighten the nuts to 11 ft/lbs.

43. Drive the drive flange oil seal into the final drive housing until it bottoms against the bearing race.

44. Install the drive flange on the final drive housing side, with the special tool (VW391), secure with a new circlip.

45. Drive the starter bushing into the final drive housing.

46. Drive the selector shaft oil seal into the gear carrier.

47. Drive the clutch operating lever oil seal into the gear carrier.

48. Drive the pinion shaft needle bearings into the gear carrier.

49. Drive the drive flange oil seal into the gear carrier cover until it bottoms on the differential bearing race.

50. Position the gasket on the final drive housing. Install the gear carrier housing on the final drive housing. Make sure that the reverse gear shaft is aligned with the hole in the gear carrier, install the reverse shaft retaining screw.

51. Install the gear carrier to final drive housing bolts and tighten to 14 ft/lbs.

52. Install the mainshaft circlip through the

clutch release bearing opening in the gear carrier.

53. Install the remaining driveshaft flange and circlip using special tools.

54. Remove the mainshaft support bar. Insert the clutch pushrod.

55. Insert the clutch release bearing assembly. Insert the clutch operating lever through the spring and clutch bearing lever. The bent end of the spring must contact the gear carrier. The center part of the spring is hooked over the end of the clutch bearing lever. Install the two circlips. Install the gasket and cover.

56. Insert the selector shaft and springs into the selector opening in the gear carrier assembly. Lubricate the selector with a multi-purpose grease before assembly. Install the selector shaft cover.

57. Install the interlock plunger assembly in the gear carrier assembly. Adjust the interlock plunger as follows:

a. Turn the slotted screw (interlock plunger) in until the nut starts to move out (bottoms).

b. Back the slotted screw out ¼ turn.

c. Install the plastic cap.

58. Install the plastic caps over the bearing clamping screws.

TYPE 18

4 Speed Transaxle–Models 002 and 091

VW Types 1 and 2

NOTE: Many special tools are required in the overhaul procedures of these transaxles. Use only recommended or equivalent tools to prevent personal injury or damage to the units.

DISASSEMBLY

MODELS 002 AND 091

1. Mount the transaxle securely and drain the lubricating oil from the unit.

2. Pry the caps from the center of the left and right drive flanges and remove the circlips from the stub axles. Using a puller, remove the drive flanges.

3. Mark the positions of the differential adjusting rings and measure the distance or depth to which the rings are screwed into the transaxle case. Record the readings for the assembly references.

4. Loosen the left differential adjusting ring to relieve the tension within the transaxle housing and remove the clutch housing assembly. Remove the rear driveshaft by unscrewing the shaft from the front drive or mainshaft. Remove the reverse drive gear.

5. Remove the left and right differential adjusting rings and lift the differential assembly from the case.

6. Remove the pinion gear assembly retaining ring from the differential side of the transaxle case.

NOTE: The retaining ring is peened, so that extra effort must be used to remove the ring.

7. Remove the gear shift housing from the gear carrier housing carefully to avoid damaging the housing mating surfaces.

8. Remove the gear carrier housing from the transaxle case and press the gear train from the transaxle case.

NOTE: Locate the shims from between the tapered roller bearing and the transaxle case for reuse during the reassembly.

9. The pinion and mainshaft must be pressed from the gear carrier housing.

CAUTION

Remove the circlips before attempting press work.

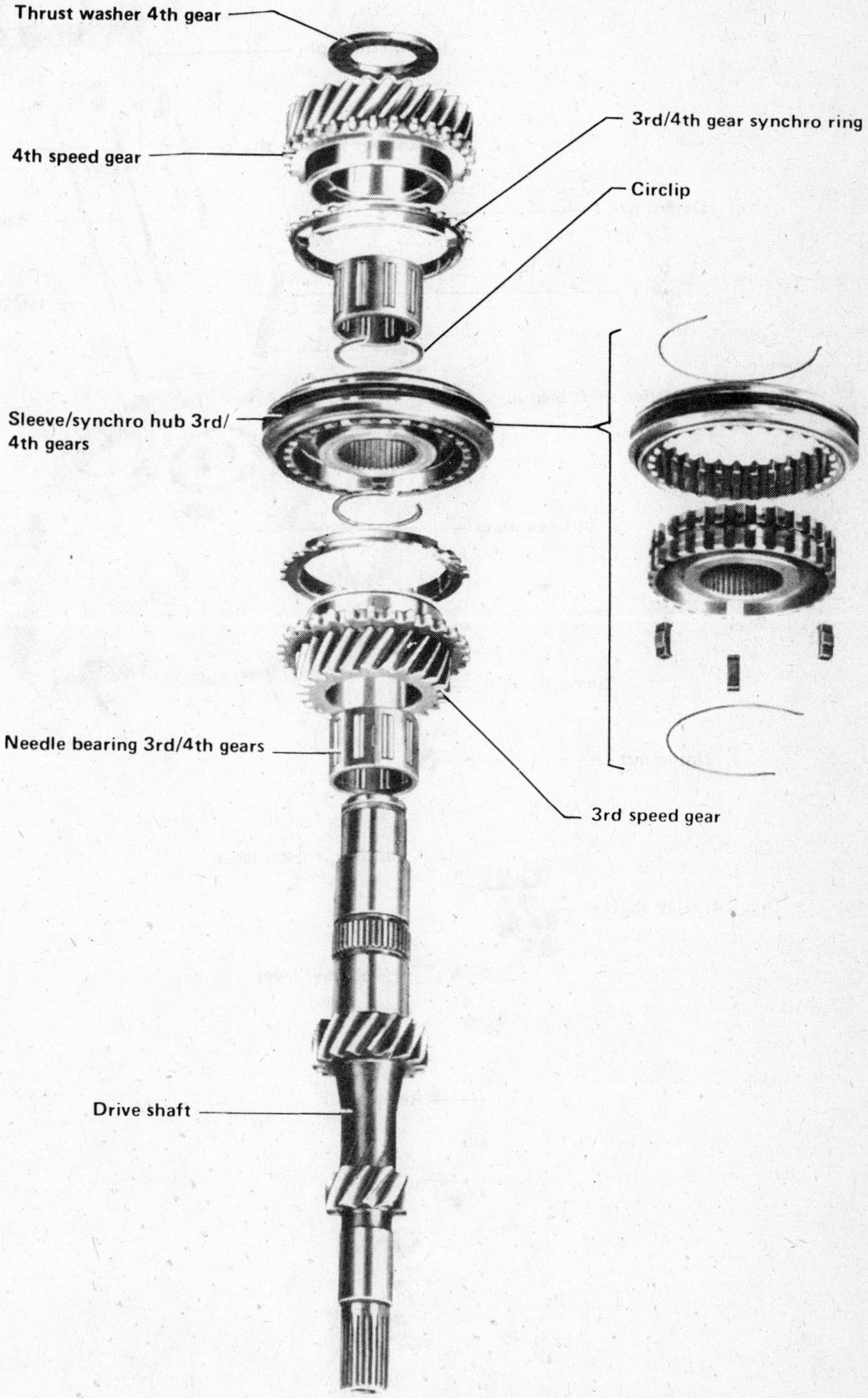

Exploded view of driveshaft (mainshaft) assembly—model 002

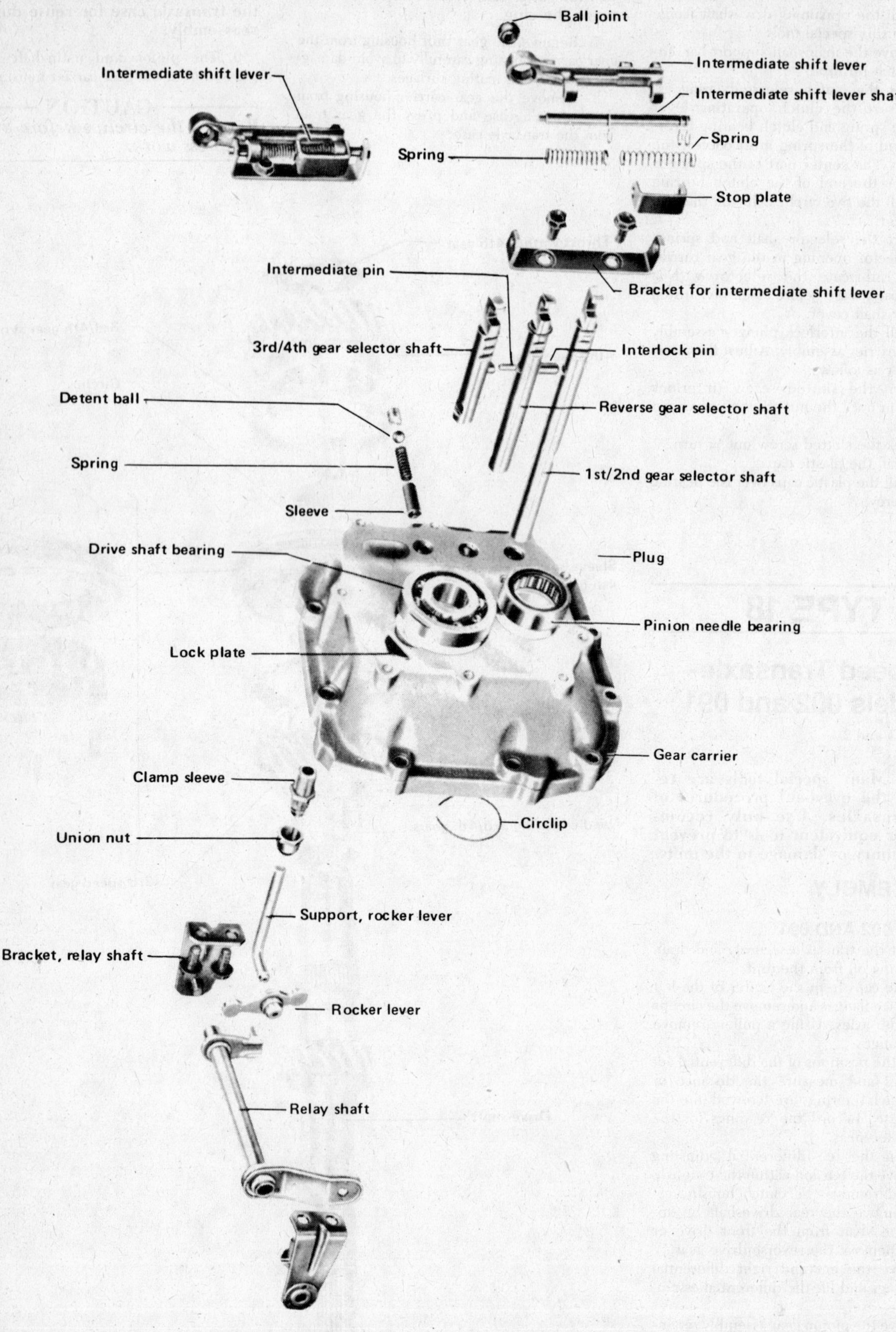

Exploded view of model 091 gear carrier housing and shift mechanism—typical of model 002

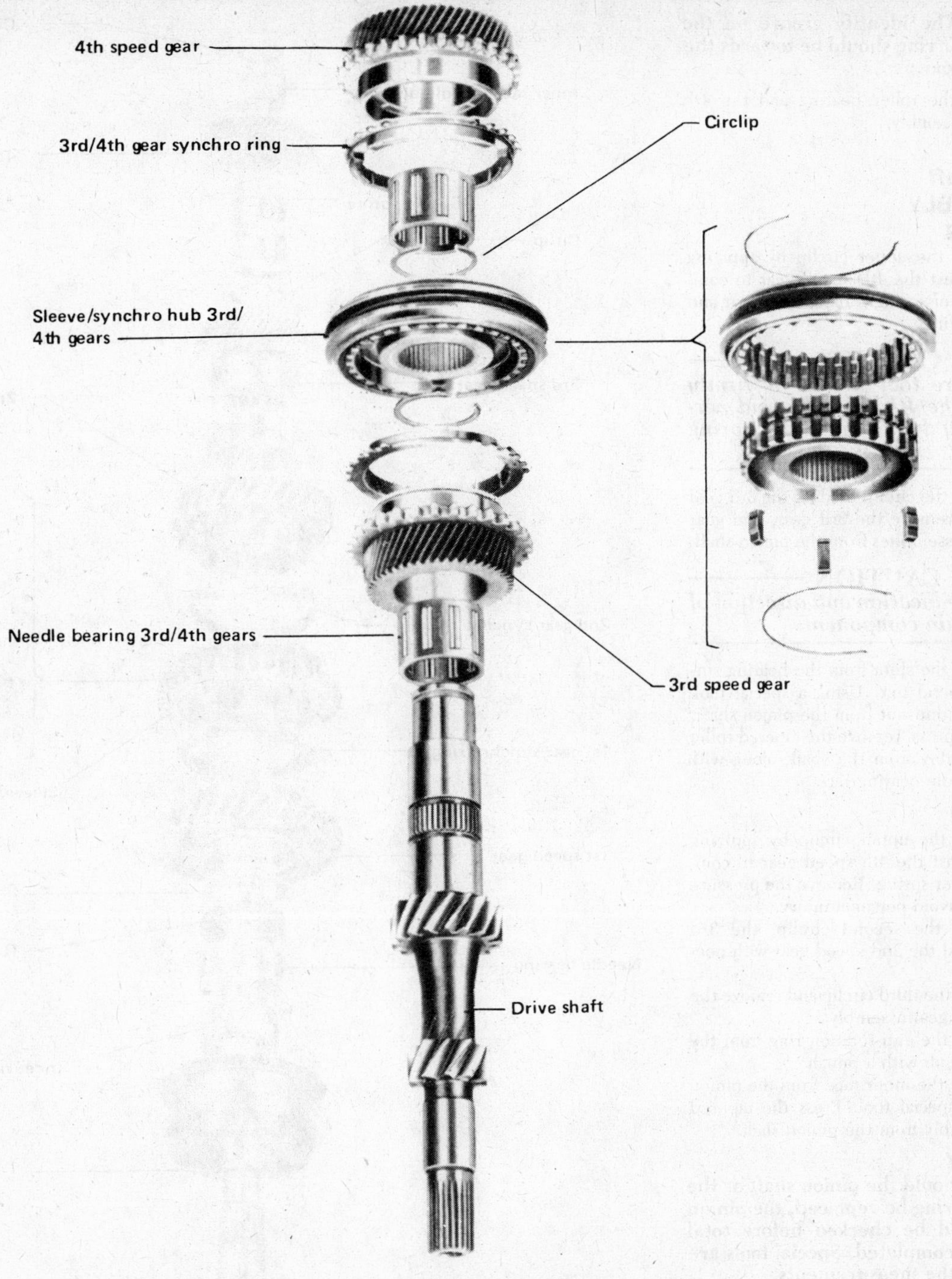

Exploded view of driveshaft (mainshaft) assembly—model 091

Mainshaft (Driveshaft)

DISASSEMBLY

MODEL 002

1. Press the 4th gear and thrust washer from the mainshaft.
2. Remove the caged roller bearing and the circlip.
3. Press the synchronizer hub from the shaft and remove the lower circlip.
4. Remove the 3rd speed gear and the split caged bearing.

MODEL 091

1. Remove the 4th speed gear and roller bearing.
2. Remove the circlip and press the 3rd/4th synchronizer hub from the shaft. Remove the lower circlip.
3. Remove the 3rd speed gear and the caged needle bearing from the shaft.

ASSEMBLY

MODEL 002

1. Install the split caged roller bearing and the 3rd speed gear.

NOTE: Use only the split caged bearings with the needle bearings in pairs.

2. Install the lower circlip in its groove on the shaft.
3. Press the 3rd/4th gear assembly into position on the shaft. Install the upper circlip.
4. Install the roller bearing and the 4th speed gear on the shaft.
5. Heat the thrust washer to 212° F (100° C) and press it on to the shaft with the oil grooves towards the 4th gear.

MODEL 091

1. Install the caged needle bearing on to the shaft and install the 3rd speed gear. Install the circlip.
2. Install the sleeve and hub for the 3rd and 4th gears. Install the second circlip.

NOTE: The identify groove on the synchronizer ring should be towards the 4th speed gear.

3. Install the roller bearing and the 4th speed gear assembly.

Pinion Shaft
DISASSEMBLY
MODEL 002

1. Remove the upper circlip by applying pressure against the 4th speed gear to compress the spacer spring. Remove the gear and the spacer spring.

CAUTION

The pressure tool should be firmly seated on the 4th gear to avoid personal injury due to the spacer spring tension.

2. Remove the circlip holding the 3rd gear in place and remove the 3rd gear, 2nd gear and 1st gear assemblies from the pinion shaft.

CAUTION

Observe the location and direction of the gear train components.

3. Remove the shim from the bearing surface of the round nut. Using a special tool, remove the round nut from the pinion shaft.
4. Using a press, remove the tapered roller bearing assembly from the shaft, along with the inner needle bearing race.

MODEL 091

1. Remove the upper circlip by applying pressure against the 4th speed gear to compress the spacer spring. Remove the pressure cautiously to avoid personal injury.
2. Remove the second circlip, the 3rd speed gear and the 2nd speed gear with needle bearing.
3. Remove the third circlip and remove the 1st/2nd speed gear assembly.
4. Remove the anti-rotation ring from the synchronizer hub with a punch.
5. Unscrew the inner race from the pinion shaft with a special tool. Press the tapered bearing assembly from the pinion shaft.

ASSEMBLY

NOTE: Should the pinion shaft or the tapered bearing be replaced, the pinion depth should be checked before total assembly is completed. Special tools are needed for the measurements.

MODEL 002

1. Heat the tapered bearing assembly to 212° F (100° C) and press into place on the pinion shaft.
2. Oil the bearing with hypoid oil and install the pinion and bearing assembly into the transaxle case. Install the retaining ring and torque to 159 ft/lbs (22 mkg).
3. Install an inch/pound torque wrench or equivalent on to the end of the pinion shaft and turn the shaft in both directions, approximately 15 to 20 turns and read the turning torque. The torque should be between 2.7 to 18.2 in/lbs (3.0 to 21.0 cmkg) for new bearings and 2.7 to 6.1 in/lbs (2.7 to 7.0 cmkg) for used bearings or for bearings that have been run at least 30 miles (50 km).

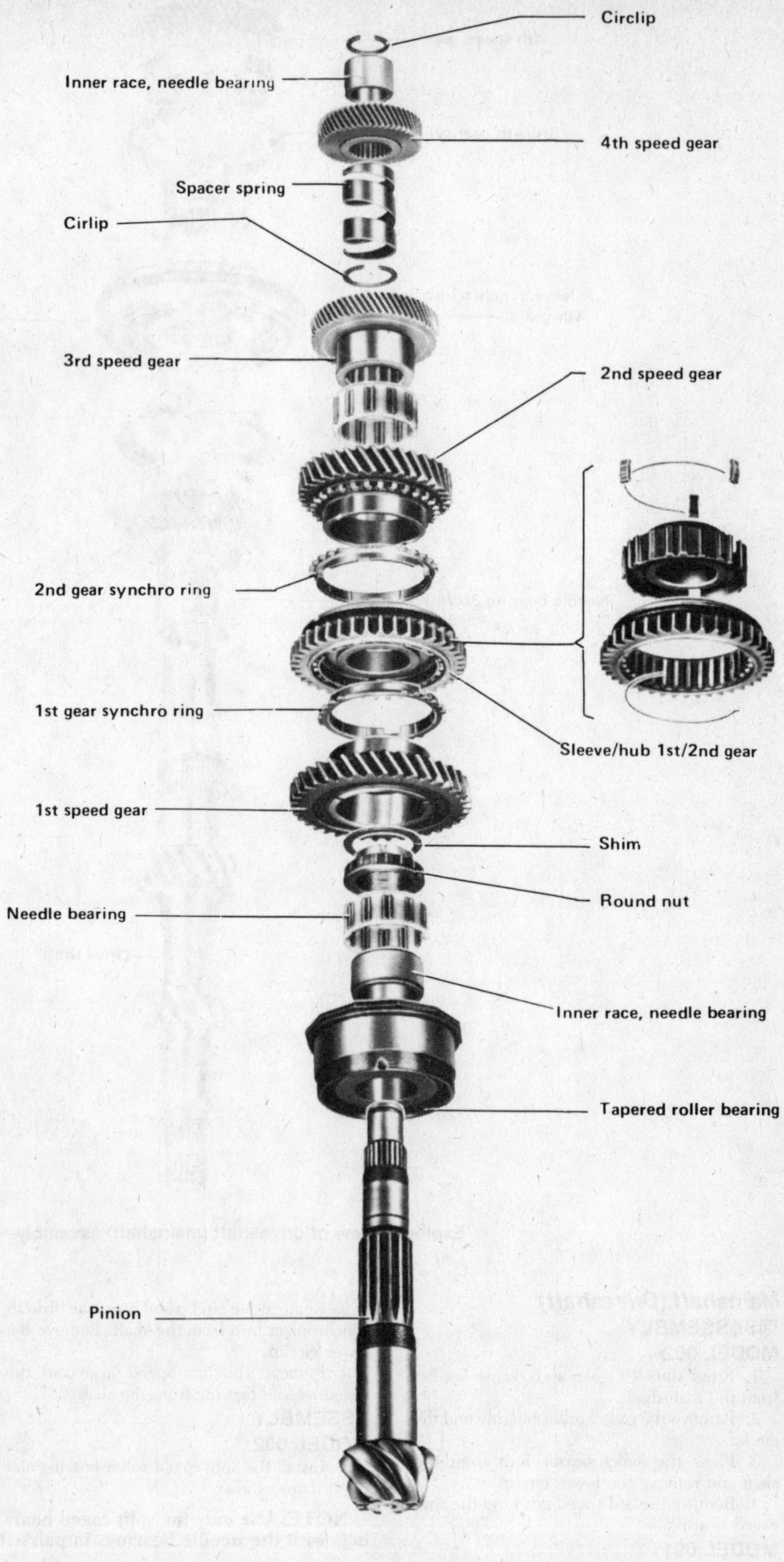

Exploded view of pinion shaft assembly—model 002

4. Remove the tapered bearing assembly and pinion shaft from the case and continue the assembly.

5. Install the needle bearing inner race and the needle bearing assembly. Install the round nut and torque it to 144 ft/lbs (20 mkg). Peen locking shoulder into spline.

6. Install the shim and the 1st gear and preassembled synchronizer as a unit, on the shaft and measure the axial play with a feeler gauge between the tapered bearing and the gear. The play should be 0.004 to 0.010 inch (0.10 to 0.25 mm). Adjust with selective shims.

7. Assemble the 2nd and 3rd speed gears to the shaft and install the circlip. Measure the clearance between the 3rd gear and the circlip. The clearance should be 0.004 to 0.010 inch (0.10 to 0.25 mm). Adjust by installing selective sized circlips.

8. Install the spacer spring, 4th gear and securely press downward with a press.

9. Heat the inner race to 212° F (100° C) and install on the shaft. Install the circlip on the shaft end.

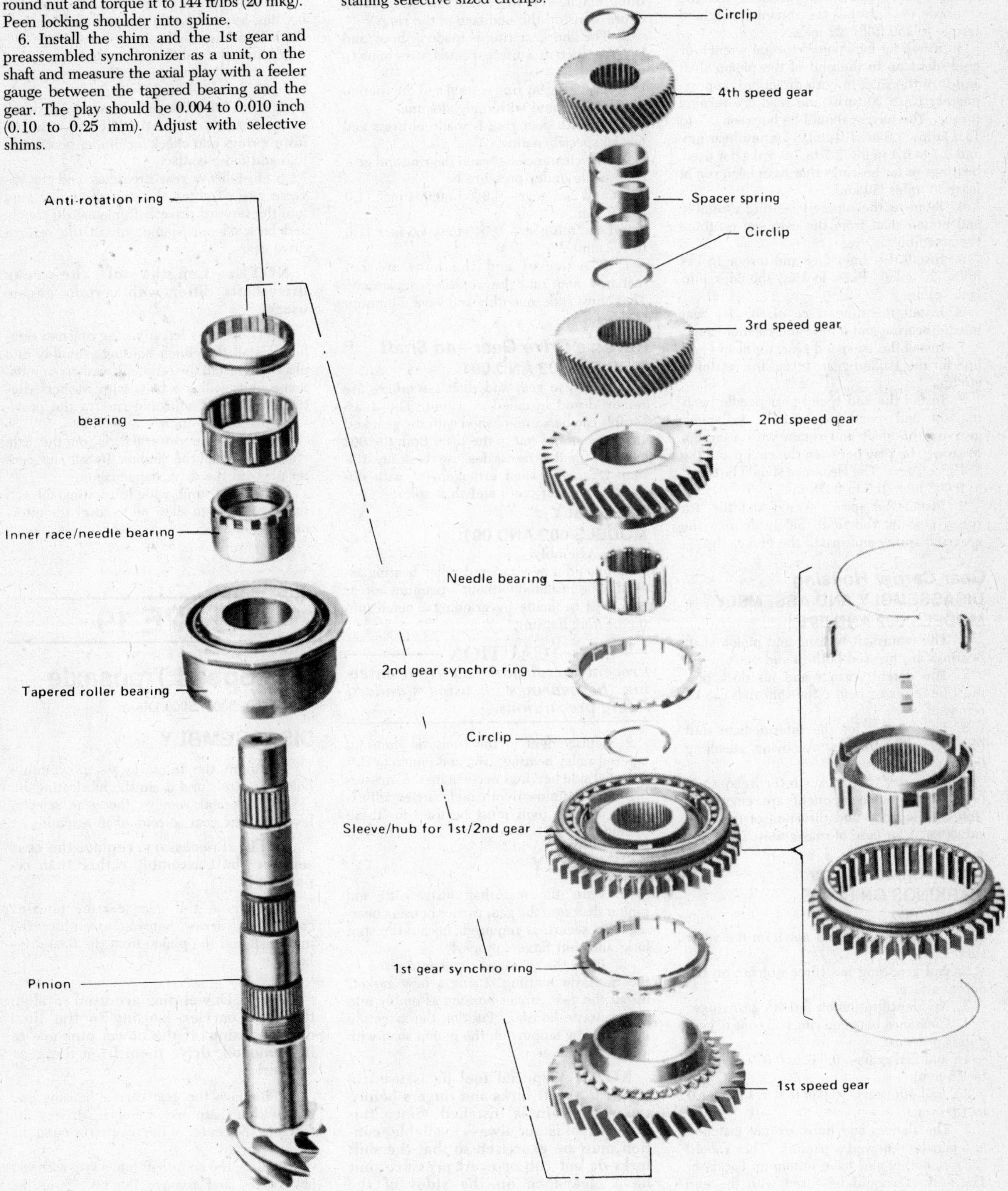

Exploded view of pinion shaft assembly—model 091

MODEL 091

1. Heat the tapered bearing assembly to 212° F (100° C) and press into position on the pinion shaft.

2. Oil the bearing with hypoid oil and install the pinion and bearing assembly into the transaxle case. Install the retaining ring and torque to 159 ft/lbs (22 mkg).

3. Install an inch/pound torque wrench or equivalent on to the end of the pinion shaft and turn the shaft in both directions, approximately 15 to 20 turns and read the turning torque. The torque should be between 2.7 to 18.2 in/lbs (3.0 to 21.0 cmkg) for new bearings and 2.7 to 6.1 in/lbs (2.7 to 7.0 cmkg) for used bearings or for bearings that have been run at least 30 miles (50 km).

4. Remove the tapered bearing assembly and pinion shaft from the case and continue the assembly.

5. Install the inner race and torque to 144 ft/lbs (20 mkg). Peen locking shoulder into gear spline.

6. Install the inner race of the 1st gear needle bearing and a new anti-rotation ring.

7. Install the 1st speed gear, the sleeve and hub for the 1st/2nd gear. Install the retaining circlip.

8. Install the 2nd speed gear needle bearing, the 2nd speed gear and the 3rd speed gear on the shaft and retain with a circlip. Measure the play between the circlip and the 3rd speed gear. The clearance should be 0.002 to 0.008 inch (0.5 to 0.20 mm).

9. Install the spacer spring and the 4th speed gear on the shaft. Safely depress the gear and spring and install the end circlip.

Gear Carrier Housing

DISASSEMBLY AND ASSEMBLY

MODELS 002 AND 091

1. The mainshaft bearing and pinion shaft bearings are pressed both in and out.

2. The detent springs and interlock pins must be removed before the shift rods can be removed.

3. The bracket for the intermediate shift lever is removable by removing attaching bolts.

4. The relay rod, rocker lever, relay shaft bracket and small components are removable. Note the location and direction of the individual parts for ease of reassembly.

Synchronizer Rings

MARKINGS ON RINGS

MODEL 002

1. 1st gear ring has no notch on the outer surface.

2. 2nd gear ring has three notches on the outer surface.

3. No identification on 3rd/4th gear rings.

4. Clearance between ring and cone of gear under pressure.

1st and 2nd gears—0.042 to 0.070 inch (1.1 to 1.8 mm).

3rd and 4th gears—0.039 to 0.074 inch (1.0 to 1.9 mm).

5. The sleeves and hubs are not matched and may be renewed separately. They should slide smoothly and have minimum backlash. The springs should be fitted with the end offset at 120° with the angled ends fitted over the keys.

MODEL 091

1. 1st gear ring has no notch on the outer surface, is made of brass and the friction surface is treated with molybdenum.

2. The 2nd, 3rd and 4th gear rings have three notches on the outer surface or three depressions on the end face of the rings.

3. The 2nd gear ring is made of brass and has the friction surface coated with molybdenum.

4. The 3rd gear ring is steel and the friction surface is treated with molybdenum.

5. The 4th gear ring is made of brass and has no special coating.

6. The clearance between the ring and gear cone while under pressure is:

1st and 2nd gear—0.040 to 0.064 inch (1.0 to 1.6 mm).

3rd and 4th gear—0.040 to 0.066 inch (1.0 to 1.7 mm).

7. The sleeves and the hubs are not matched and may be replaced separately. They must slide smoothly and have minimum backlash.

Reverse Drive Gear and Shaft

MODELS 002 AND 091

The reverse gear and shaft assemblies are removed and installed as a unit. The disassembly can be accomplished with the gear and shaft assemblies out of the case. Both the 002 and 091 model transaxles use basically the same gear and shaft arrangement with differences in gear teeth and shaft splines.

ASSEMBLY

MODELS 002 AND 091

Before Assembly

1. Should a new tapered roller bearing assembly be installed without a peening notch, one must be made by grinding a notch into the bearing housing.

CAUTION

Prevent metal particals from entering the bearings by using standard safety precautions.

2. Replacement of the transaxle housing, tapered roller bearing, ring and pinion or differential side bearings necessitate the measuring of the pinion depth and carrier adjustment. Special tools must be used for these operations.

ASSEMBLY

1. Press the mainshaft (driveshaft) and pinion shaft into the gear carrier housing bearings and secure as required. Locate the shift forks and shift fingers properly.

2. Place the removed shims into place on the transaxle housing. Using a new gasket, install the gear carrier housing assembly into the transaxle housing. Position the assembly into place by tapping on the pinion shaft with a plastic hammer.

NOTE: A special tool jig is used to adjust the shift forks and fingers before the gear train is installed. Since this type of tool is not always available, caution must be exercised so that the shift forks do not rub or exert pressure, but have clearance on the sides of the grooves in the operating sleeves, when in Neutral or while engaged in gear.

3. Install the tapered bearing retaining ring and torque to 159 ft/lbs (22 mkg), back off and retighten to 159 ft/lbs.

4. Peen the retaining ring into the notch on the tapered bearing housing.

5. Using a new gasket, install the gearshift housing by guiding the inner shift lever into the ball joint on the intermediate lever.

6. Install the differential into the case and install the adjusting rings and necessary spacers with new seals and O-rings.

7. Using the disassembly marks and depth measurements, adjust the left and right adjusting rings and check for proper gear backlash and tooth contact.

8. Install the rear driveshaft and the reverse gear. Tighten the rear driveshaft stud into the forward driveshaft (mainshaft) snugly and back off one spline. Install the reverse drive gear.

NOTE: Lengths of the rear driveshafts differ with certain engine usage.

9. Loosen the left adjusting ring and carefully install the clutch housing assembly into place and install the retaining washers or nuts. Some units will use bolts with washers. Retighten the left adjusting ring to the previously marked position.

10. Install the drive flanges on the axle stubs and install the circlips. Install new center plugs in the drive flange centers.

11. Fill the unit with lubricating oil and rotate by hand to allow oil to cover the internal components.

TYPE 19

5 Speed Transaxle

Audi 4000, 5000, 5000 Diesel

DISASSEMBLY

1. Mount the transaxle assembly into a holder securely and drain the lubricating oil.

2. Mark and remove the gear selector lever and the gear selector shaft assembly.

NOTE: If necessary, replace the gear selector shaft assembly rather than repairing it.

3. Remove the gear carrier housing cover/gear carrier housing assembly, the mainshaft and the pinion from the final drive housing.

NOTE: Dowel pins are used to align the gear carrier housing to the final drive housing. If the dowel pins are to be removed, drive them from the gear carrier.

4. Remove the gear carrier housing end plug with a sharp ended tool, by driving the tool into the center of the plug and prying the cover outward.

5. Place the mainshaft into a vise with soft jaw covers and remove the bolt from the mainsahft, in the cover cap opening.

6. Reposition the gear carrier housing so

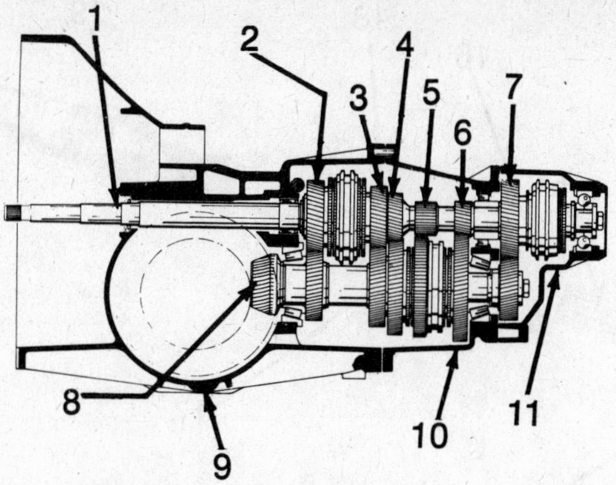

1. Main shaft
2. 4th gear
3. 3rd gear
4. 2nd gear
5. Reverse gear
6. 1st gear
7. 5th gear
8. Pinion
9. Final drive housing
10. Gear carrier housing
11. Gear carrier housing cover

Cross section of 5-speed Audi transaxle

that the vise soft jaws are holding the housing instead of the mainshaft.

7. Remove the twelve retaining bolts from the gear carrier housing cover and separate the cover from the gear housing.

8. Remove the mainshaft bearing inner race from gear carrier housing.

9. Remove the 5th gear clutch hub and mainshaft bearing inner race from the cover end of the mainshaft.

10. Remove the 5th gear synchronizer ring.

11. Drive the 5th gear shift fork roll pin from the fork with a pin punch.

CAUTION

Support the selector rod and fork to avoid damage to the gear carrier housing.

12. Remove the circlip, the 5th speed gear with the synchronizer hub, needle bearing and the 5th speed gear shift fork.

NOTE: The 5th/reverse gear selector rod will remain in the gear carrier housing.

13. Remove the selector rod stop screws from the outside of the gear carrier housing.

14. Reposition the gear carrier housing assembly in the jaws of the vise, with the soft jaw covers, and clamp the 4th speed gear in the vise.

15. Remove the bolt from the pinion shaft and remove the 5th gear and the adjustment shim.

16. Reposition the gear carrier housing in the soft jawed vise and drive the 1st/2nd gear selector fork roll pin from the fork.

CAUTION

Support the selector rod and fork to avoid damage to the gear carrier housing.

17. Remove the 3rd/4th gear selector fork roll pin.

CAUTION

Support the selector rod and fork to avoid damage to the gear carrier housing.

18. Remove the 3rd/4th selector rod from the gear carrier housing. The shifting fork should remain in the synchronizer hub.

NOTE: Do not lose the indent or interlock pin.

19. Remove the relay lever bolt from the reverse gear relay lever.

20. Pull the pinion and mainshaft partially from the gear carrier housing and remove the mainshaft with the 3rd/4th gear shift fork on the synchronizer hub.

21. Pull the pinion from the housing, far enough so that the selector rod and shift fork of the 1st/2nd gears can be removed, after the reverse gear spring clip on the pinion side is unhooked and turned.

22. Remove the pinion from the housing.

23. Inspect the transaxle components, replace all seals and gaskets, gears that are damaged or worn, and bearings, both needle and ball.

Mainshaft and Pinion Shaft

The mainshaft and pinion shaft gears can be disassembled by the removal of the end bearings or circlips. Certain gears will have to be removed either with a puller or a press. Mark the gears before the removal to avoid backward installation. The synchronizers are of the Borg Warner type and should be matchmarked before disassembly.

During the reassembly of the shafts, the following clearances should be observed.

MAINSHAFT

3rd/4th Synchronizer Rings to Hub Clearance

New rings—0.039 to 0.067 inch (1.0 to 1.7 mm)

Wear limit—0.020 inch (0.5 mm)

5th Gear Synchronizer Ring to Hub Clearance

New ring—0.039 to 0.075 inch (1.0 to 1.9 mm)

Wear limit—0.020 inch (0.5 mm)

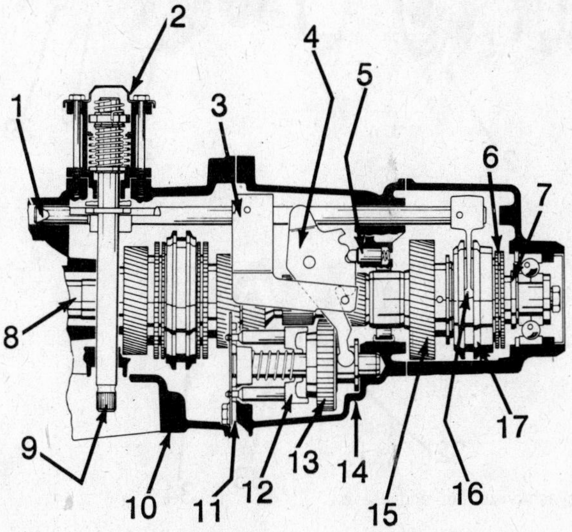

1. 5th and reverse gear selector rod
2. Selector shaft assembly
3. Reverse gear shift fork
4. Relay lever
5. Reverse gear interlock
6. 5th gear synchronizer ring
7. 5th gear clutch sleeve
8. Main shaft
9. Selector shaft
10. Final drive housing
11. Mounting plate
12. Reverse gear synchronizer
13. Reverse gear
14. Gear carrier housing
15. 5th gear
16. 5th gear shift fork
17. 5th gear synchronizer hub

5th and reverse shift linkage viewed from the top

1. Bolt
2. Main shaft bearing outer race
3. Main shaft bearing
4. Circlip
5. Baffle plate
6. Main shaft bearing inner race
7. 5th gear clutch hub
8. 5th gear synchronizer ring
9. Circlip

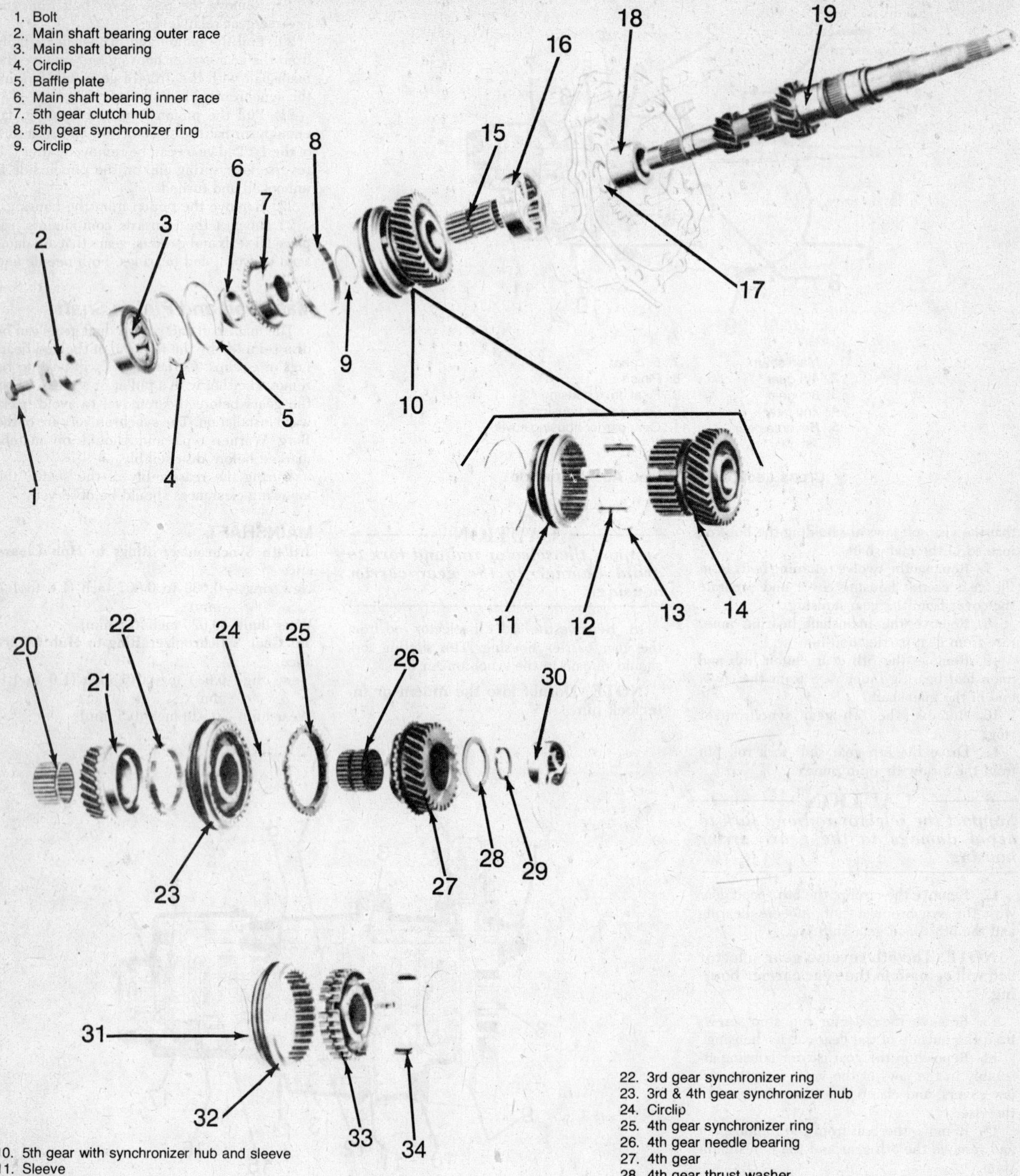

10. 5th gear with synchronizer hub and sleeve
11. Sleeve
12. Hollow key
13. Spring
14. 5th gear with synchronizer hub
15. 5th gear needle bearing
16. Main shaft bearing
17. Circlip
18. Mainshaft bearing inner race
19. Mainshaft
20. 3rd gear needle bearing
21. 3rd gear
22. 3rd gear synchronizer ring
23. 3rd & 4th gear synchronizer hub
24. Circlip
25. 4th gear synchronizer ring
26. 4th gear needle bearing
27. 4th gear
28. 4th gear thrust washer
29. Circlip
30. Main shaft needle bearing
31. Spring
32. Sleeve
33. Hub
34. Hollow key

Exploded view of mainshaft assembly

3rd/4th Synchronizer Hub End-Play
0.000 to 0.002 inch (0.00 to 0.05 mm)
Correct by selective circlips

4th Gear End-Play
0.008 to 0.013 inch (0.20 to 0.35 mm)

PINION SHAFT

4th Gear End-Play
Limit—0.0008 (0.02 mm)
Correct by selective circlip

3rd Gear End-Play
0.000 to 0.0016 inch (0.00 to 0.04 mm)

1st/2nd Synchronizer Rings to Hub Clearance
New rings—0.039 to 0.067 inch (1.0 to 1.7 mm)
Wear limit—0.020 inch (0.5 mm)

1st/2nd Synchronizer Hub End-Play
0.000 to 0.0016 inch (0.00-0.04 mm)
Correct by selective circlip

Reverse Gear Synchronizer Clearance
New ring—0.029 to 0.090 inch (0.75 to 2.3 mm)
Wear limit—0.007 inch (0.2 mm)

Differential Assembly

The differential assembly is removed from the final drive housing after removal of the drive flange and the final drive cover. Methods of repairs are found in the Unit Overhaul section.

ASSEMBLY

1. Have the reverse gear engaged and the spring clip is unhooked on the one side and turned away from the pinion bore.
2. Install the pinion shaft assembly partially into the carrier housing. Install the 1st/2nd gear shift rod and press the pinion into the housing until it is fully seated.
3. Connect the unhooked spring clip and disengage the reverse gear.
4. Install the 3rd/4th gearshift fork with the slot into the 5th/ reverse gearshift rod.
5. If the mainshaft bearing inner race is on the mainshaft, it must be removed before the shaft is installed into the gear carrier.
6. Install the mainshaft partially into the housing and insert the 3rd/4th shift fork into the sliding sleeve and install the mainshaft until fully seated.
7. Move all the shifting rods to the neutral position and check for the correct position of the interlock pins.
8. Install the 3rd/4th gear shift rod into

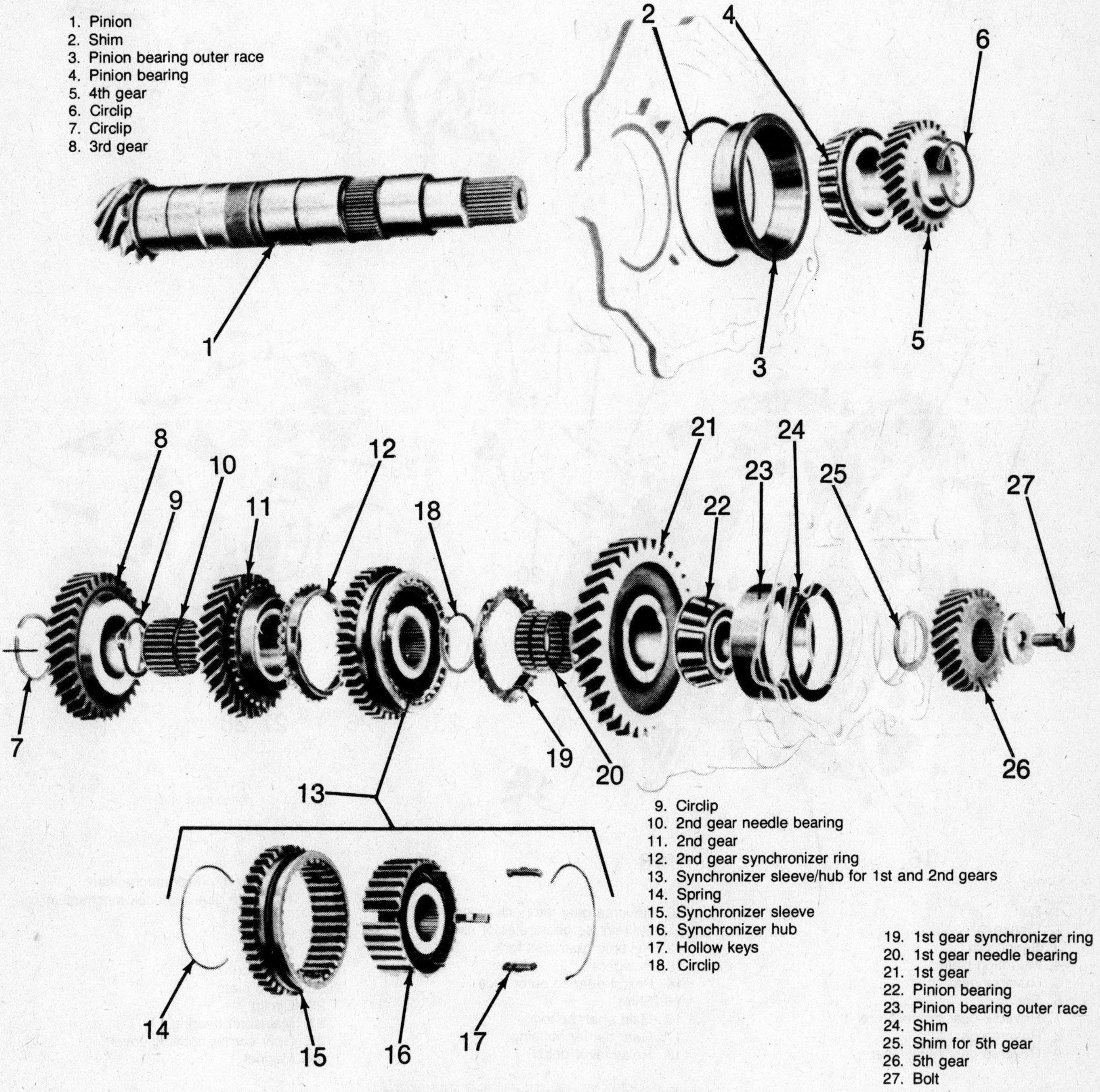

Exploded view of pinion shaft assembly

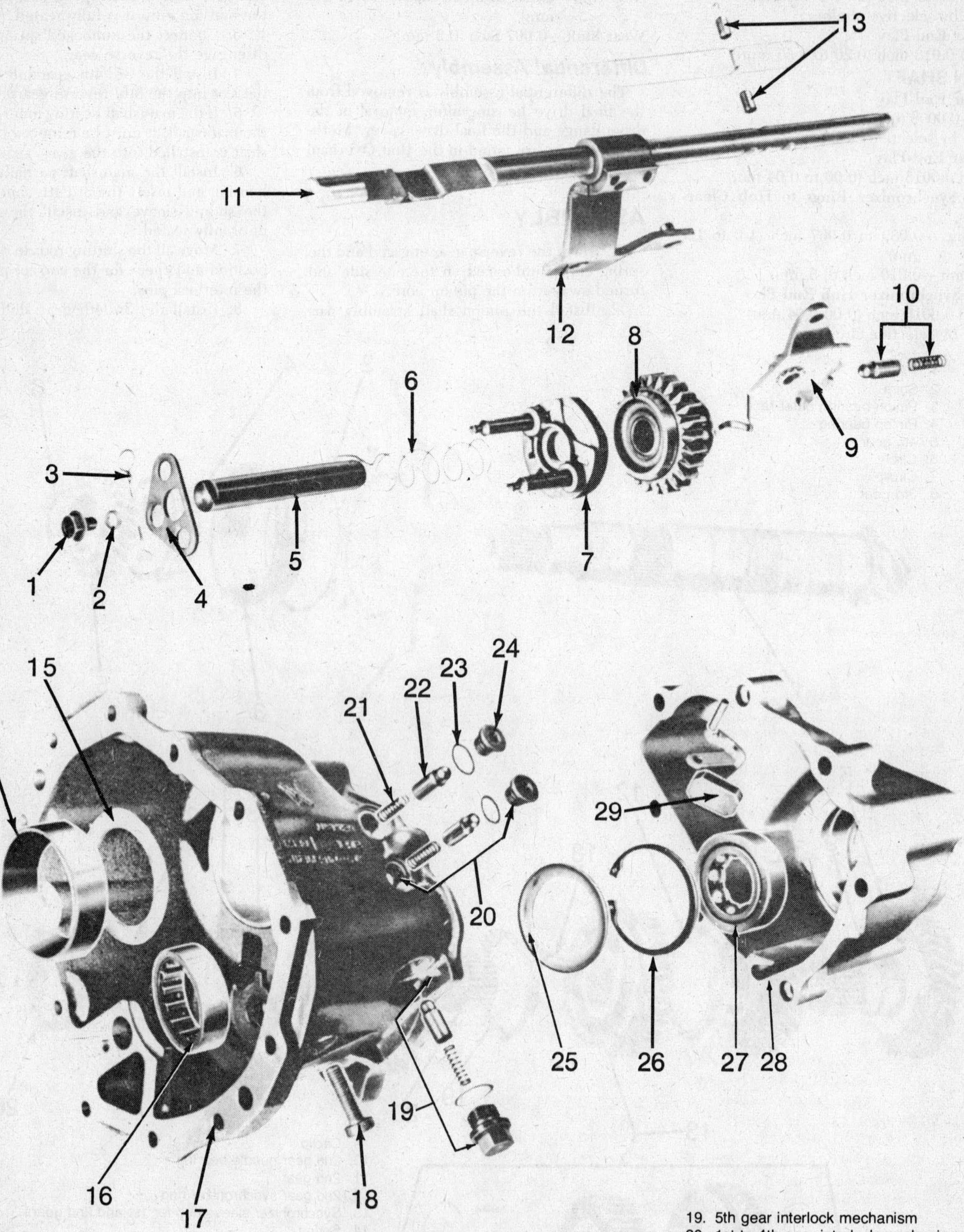

1. Bolt
2. Sleeve
3. Spring clip
4. Mounting plate
5. Reverse gear shaft
6. Spring
7. Reverse gear synchronizer
8. Reverse gear
9. Reverse gear relay lever
10. Reverse gear interlock plunger
11. 5th/reverse gear selector rod
12. Reverse gear shift fork
13. Plungers
14. Pinion bearing outer race
15. Shim
16. Main shaft bearing
17. Gear carrier housing
18. Relay lever bolt
19. 5th gear interlock mechanism
20. 1st to 4th gear interlock mechanism
21. Spring
22. Plunger
23. Gasket
24. Stop screw
25. Baffle plate
26. Circlip
27. Mainshaft bearing
28. Gear carrier housing cover
29. Magnet

Exploded view of gear carrier housing and cover components

the gear carrier housing and the shift fork. Install the interlock pin and secure the fork to the rod with the roll pin.

CAUTION
Support the shift rod and fork when installing the roll pin.

9. Install the roll pin into the 1st/2nd gear selector rod and fork.

CAUTION
Support the shift rod and fork when installing the roll pin.

10. Install the detent balls and springs. Place new gaskets on the stop screws and install them into the housing.
11. Clamp the 4th gear of the pinion shaft into a vise with soft jaw covers.
12. With the gear carrier housing/cover mating surface facing upward, measure the distance from the housing surface to the top of the pinion bearing outer race or to the shim. Selective shims are available as follows.

NOTE: Measurements are in mm. Convert to inches as required.

Depth (mm)	Shim Thickness (mm)
8.35-8.64	1.1
8.65-8.94	1.4
8.95-9.24	1.7
9.25-9.54	2.0
9.55-9.84	2.3

13. Heat the 5th gear to 250° F (120° C) and drive on the pinion shaft until seated on the selected shim.

NOTE: Be sure the collar of the gear faces the pinion head.

14. Install the washer and bolt and torque to 36 ft/lbs (50 Nm).
15. Heat the main bearing inner race to 250° F (120° C) and drive on the mainshaft. Select a circlip of proper thickness to fit tightly in the groove on the mainshaft.
16. Install the 5th gear with the synchronizer hub, needle bearing and shift rod. Support the shift rod and install the roll pin.
17. Install the retaining circlip and install the 5th gear synchronizer ring.
18. Heat the 5th gear clutch hub to 250° F (120° C) and drive on the mainshaft. Drive on the mainshaft inner bearing race with a driving sleeve type tool.
19. Install the dowel pins and a new gasket to the mating surface.
20. Carefully install the gear carrier housing cover, and drive the second mainshaft inner bearing race onto the shaft.
21. Install the washer and bolt onto the mainshaft and tighten to 36 ft/lbs (50 Nm).
22. Install the cover retaining bolts and tighten to 18 ft/lbs (25 Nm).
23. Install a new cover cap into the end of the gear carrier housing cover.
24. Assemble the gear carrier housing/cover assembly to the final drive housing and install the retaining bolts. Tighten to 18 ft/lbs (25 Nm).
25. Install the selector shaft housing into the final drive housing and retain with the retaining bolts. Tighten to 7 ft/lbs (10 Nm).
26. Install the selector shaft lever, flush with the toothed end of the selector shaft. Tighten the clamping bolt.
27. Fill the unit to its proper level with lubricating oil and check for proper shifting of the internal gears.

TYPE 20

4 And 5 Speed Transaxle

Mazda GLC

DISASSEMBLY AND ASSEMBLY

NOTE: The procedures described are for both the four speed and the five speed transaxle. The five speed unit has a rear cover which easily distinguishes it from the other unit.

Disassembly (Fifth Gear)

1. Remove the rear cover. Remove the roll pin that secures the fifth gear shift fork to the selector shaft. Shift the transaxle unit into either first or second gear.

NOTE: Do not shift into fourth gear as, by doing this you may cause damage to the gears.

2. Move the fifth gear clutch sleeve, to engage fifth gear and double lock the transmission.
3. Straighten the tab of the locknut on both the primary and secondary shafts. Remove the locknuts from the shafts.
4. Pull the fifth gear clutch hub assembly out along with the shift fork.

NOTE: Remove the fork to gain access to the primary shaft locknut.

5. Reinstall the fifth gear clutch hub and move the sleeve to the fifth gear position in order to lock the transmission.

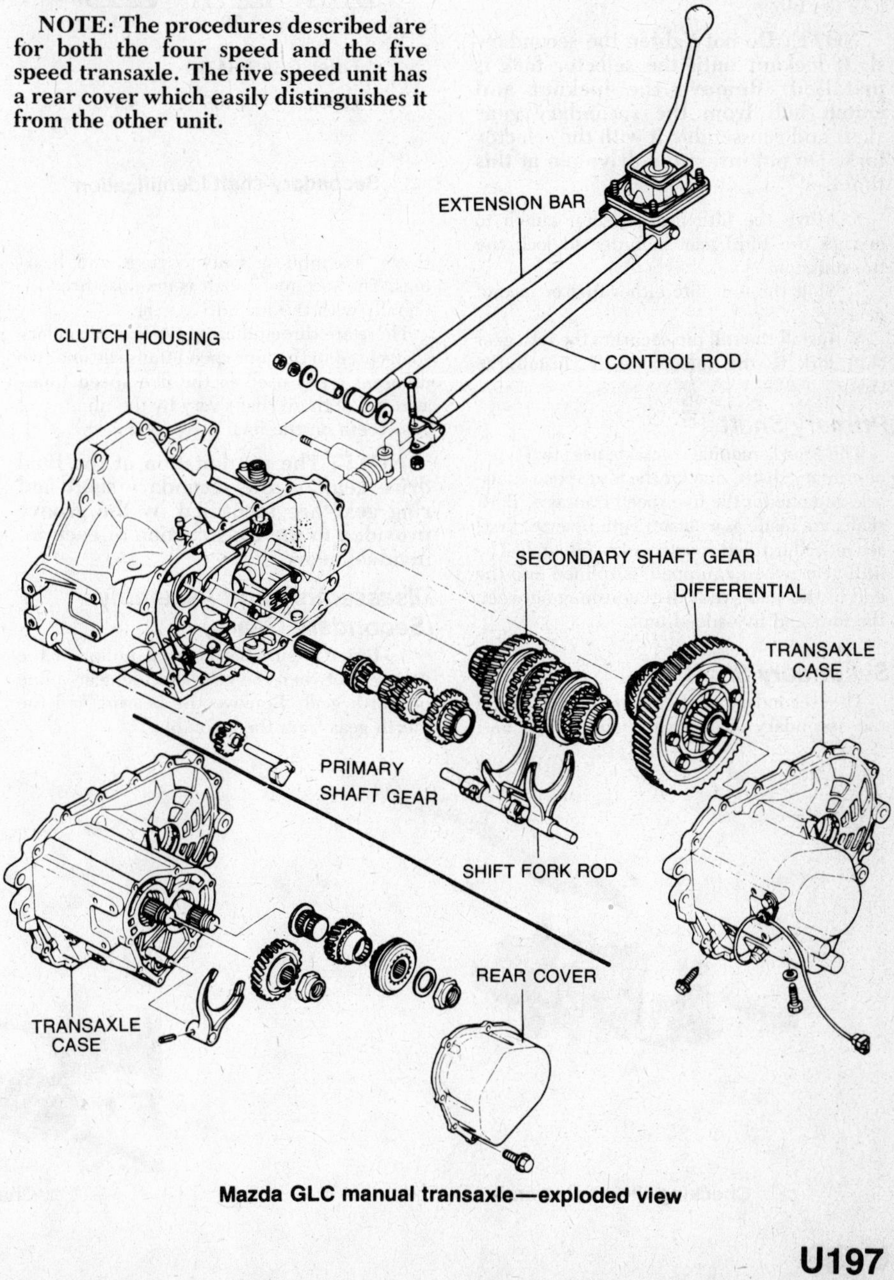

Mazda GLC manual transaxle—exploded view

6. Remove the primary shaft locknut and remove the fifth gear from the transmission case.

Assembly (Fifth Gear)

1. Install the fifth gear on the primary shaft. Be sure that the marked boss is facing toward the locknut. Install the bush and the fifth gear on the secondary shaft.
2. Install the synchronizer ring and clutch hub and the selector fork. Do not install the shift fork pin.

NOTE: The stop washer or plate for the clutch hub must be installed between the locknut and clutch hub to prevent overtravel of the clutch when shifting into reverse gear to prevent the synchronizer keys from falling out.

3. Install the locknuts on both shafts and tighten them slightly.
4. Shift into first or second gear only, using the control rod. Shift into fifth gear to double lock the transmission.
5. Tighten the primary shaft locknut and lock the tub.

NOTE: Do not tighten the secondary shaft locknut until the selector fork is installed. Remove the locknut and clutch hub from the secondary gear shaft and reassemble it with the selector fork. Do not insert the drive pin at this time.

6. Move the fifth gear selector clutch to engage the fifth gear in order to lock the transmission.
7. Shift the unit into either first or second gear.
8. Install the roll pin securing the fifth gear shift fork to the selector shaft. Install the cover.

Primary Shaft

The Mazda manual transaxle uses two types of primary shafts, one for the four speed transaxle and one for the five speed transaxle. Both shafts are made as a cluster with reverse, first, second, third and fourth gears integral. The fifth gear (when equipped) is splined into the end of the shaft, thus distinguishing between the four and five speed unit.

Secondary Shaft

The secondary shaft assembly consists of the secondary shaft, gears, clutch hub and

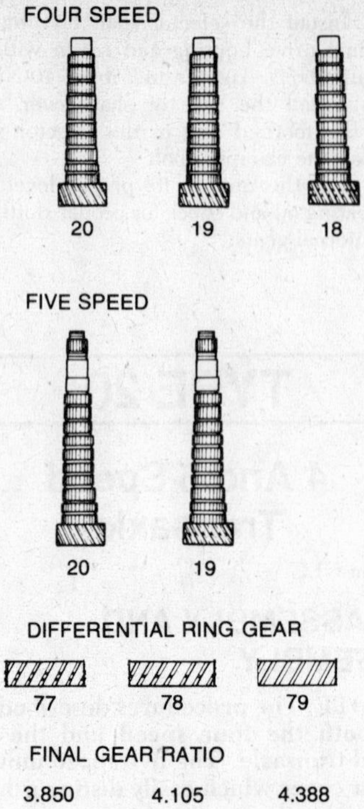

Secondary shaft identification

sleeve assemblies, synchro rings and bearings. The secondary shaft is manufactured integrally with the final drive gear.

There are three different types of secondary shafts used in the four speed transaxle and two different types used in the five speed transaxle. All of these shafts vary by the number of gear teeth on the final drive gears.

NOTE: The combination of the final drive gear on the secondary shaft and ring gear are identified by the groove provided in the construction of each individual gear.

Disassembly and Assembly (Secondary Gears)

1. Install a suitable bearing puller in the grooves between the gear and the gear spline of fourth gear. Remove the bearing and the fourth gear from the assembly.
2. Remove the snap-ring on the third and fourth clutch hub. Slide out the clutch hub and the sleeve assembly.
3. Remove the third gear, the thrust washer and the second gear.
4. Remove the snap-ring, and slide out the clutch hub and reverse gear assembly and first gear.
5. Install the bearing remover tool under the rollers and press out the shaft.
6. Assembly is the reverse of disassembly.

Synchronizer Rings

Bridge type synchronizer rings are used in the Mazda transaxle. There are three different synchronizer rings; one for second, third and fourth speed, another for first and third speed and one for fifth speed if the vehicle is so equipped. The first speed synchro ring can be identified from the other two because it has less teeth.

Thrust Clearance

The thrust clearance of each gear is checked by using a feeler gauge. The specification for thrust clearance is .5 mm (.020 in.).

Reverse Idler Shaft and Shift Rod

The reverse idler shaft has an integral mounting post which is secured to the case with a bolt. When installing the idler shaft, align the holes of the shaft with the notch in the transaxle case. When installing the reverse shift rod to the shift gate, be sure that the screw holes are aligned and that the hole of the shift rod is not 180 degrees out of phase.

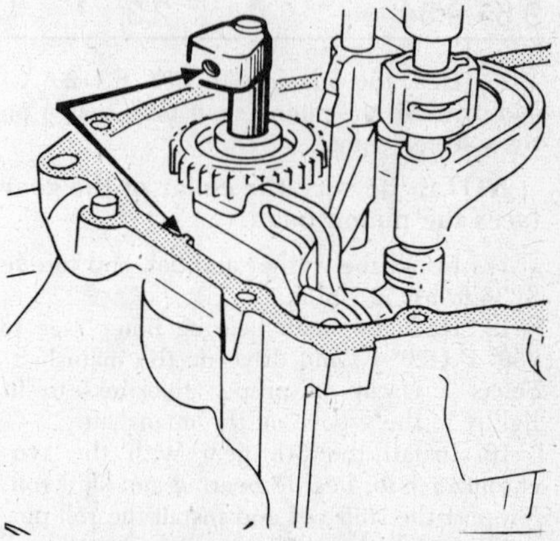

Reverse idler shaft alignment

Checking thrust clearance

Checking thrust clearance—fifth gear

Bearing Preload Adjustment

NOTE: When the clutch housing, transaxle case, primary shaft, secondary shaft, bearings or differential case are replaced the bearing preload should be checked and adjusted.

1. Remove the oil seal and the differential bearing outer race. Adjust the shim from the transaxle case.
2. Remove the bearing outer races from the primary and secondary shafts. Adjust the shims from the transaxle case and the clutch housing.
3. Reinstall the outer races to the transaxle case.
4. Install the outer races (removed in Step 2) to their respective selectors. Install the selectors, primary shaft assembly and the secondary shaft assembly to the clutch housing.
5. Install the transaxle case and place the ten collars between the transaxle case and the clutch housing.

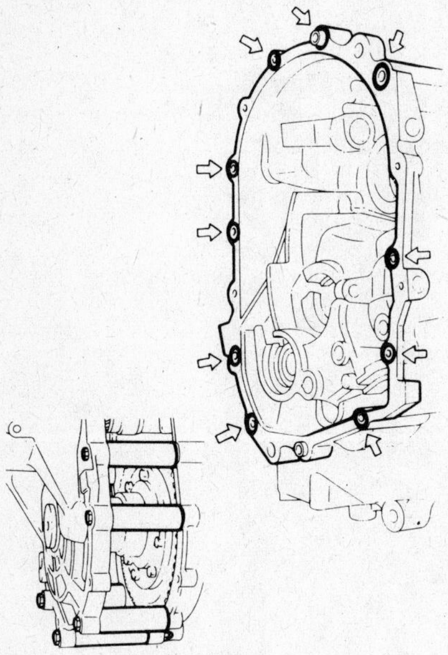

Collar positioning

NOTE: The collars should be positioned as shown in the illustration.

6. To properly settle each bearing, using the tool turn the selector in a direction where the gap is widened until it cannot be turned by hand. Then turn the selector in the opposite direction until the gap is eliminated. Manually turn the selector to a direction where the gap becomes wider until the selector cannot be turned.

NOTE: Make sure that the shaft turns smoothly.

7. Measure the gap of the selector with a feeler gauge.

NOTE: This measurement should be taken at several places along the circumference of the selector.

8. Take the maximum reading and determine the shim to be used as follows.
9. For the primary shaft bearing, first subtract 1.00 mm (thickness of the diaphragm spring) from the gap (determined in Step 7).

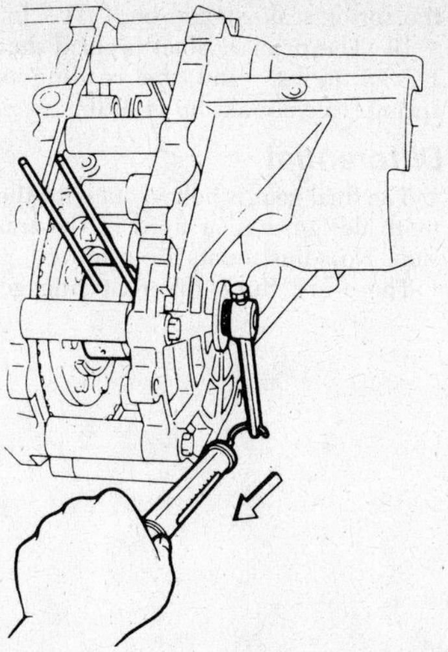

Checking differential bearing preload

e.g.: Measurement 1.39 mm minus 1.00 mm equals .39 mm, so you select the next larger and closer shim which would be .40 mm.

NOTE: Do not use more than two shims.

10. For the secondary shaft bearing, select a shim which has a thickness that is larger and closer to the gap (determined in Step 7).

e.g.: Measurement .42 mm, so you select the next larger and closer shim which would be .45 mm.

NOTE: Do not use more than two shims to accomplish this task.

11. For the differential bearing, set the preload adapters (tool # 49-0180-510A and # 49-FT01-515 or equivalent) to the pinion shaft through the hole for the driveshaft of the transaxle case. Hook a spring scale to the adapter and check the bearing preload.

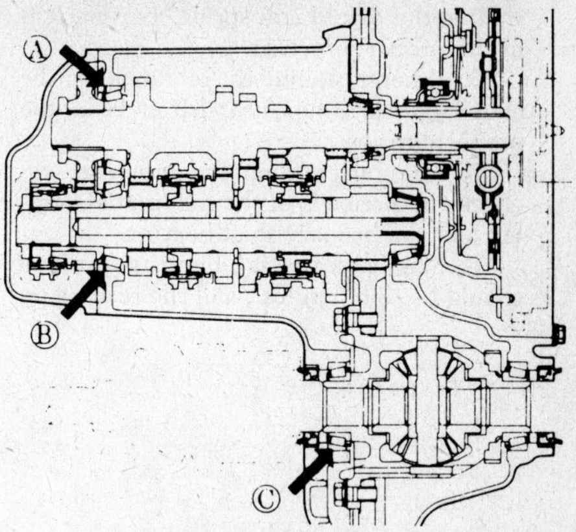

Selected shim installation

NOTE: While checking the preload, turn the selector until the reading of the spring scale becomes 1.1-1.5 lb.

12. Then measure the gap of the selector on the differential using a feeler gauge.

NOTE: This measurement should be taken in several places along the circumference of the selector.

13. Select a shim that has a thickness larger and closer to the maximum reading that was taken in the previous step.

e.g.: Measurement .54 mm, so you select the next larger and closer shim which would be .60 mm.

NOTE: Do not use more than three shims to accomplish this task.

14. Remove the shim selectors and each bearing outer race. Install the shims selected in previous steps between the transaxle case and bearing outer race.
15. A diaphragm spring is used to keep the bearing preload as specified and also to maintain low level gear noise. So when in-

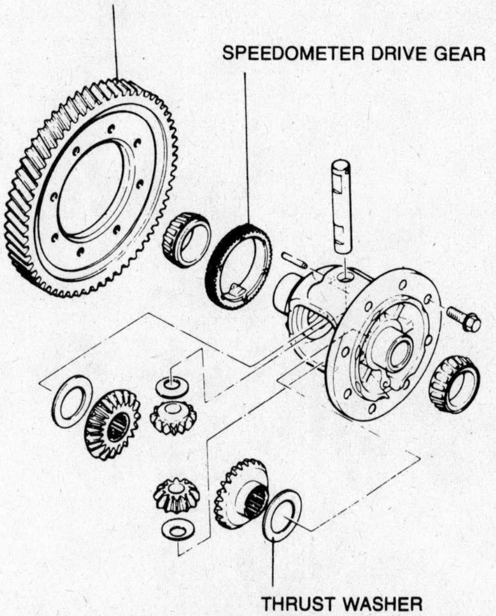

Manual transaxle differential—exploded view

stalling the diaphragm spring, be sure it is in the proper direction.

16. When installing the oil funnel on the clutch housing, be sure that it is in the proper position.

17. After assembling the transaxle, recheck the preloads of the differential bearing and the primary shaft bearing.

18. The differential bearing preload should be .3-6.6 in/lbs., and the reading on the spring scale should be .07-1.7 lb.

19. The primary shaft preload should be 1.7-3.5 in/lbs., and the reading on the spring scale should be .4-.9 lb.

Differential

The final gear is helical cut with the same tooth design as that used in the transmission. No adjustments are required.

There are three different ring gears in numbers of gear teeth on the manual transaxle. They are identified by the marks (grooves) provided on the gear outer surface.

The backlash between the differential side gear and pinion gear is adjusted by the thrust washer installed behind the side gear teeth. There are three different thicknesses of thrust washers available.

When checking the backlash, insert both driveshafts into the side gears.

SI METRIC TABLES

The following tables are given in SI (International System) metric units. SI units replace both customary (English) and the older gravimetric units. The use of SI units as a new worldwide standard was set by the International Committee of Weights and Measures in 1960. SI has since been adopted by most countries as their national standard.

These tables are general conversion tables which will allow you to convert customary units, which appear in the text, into SI units.

The following are a list of SI units and the customary units, used in this book, which they replace:

To measure:	Use SI units:	Which replace (customary units):
mass	kilograms (kg)	pounds (lbs)
temperature	Celsius (°C)	Fahrenheit (°F)
length	millimeters (mm)	inches (in.)
force	newtons (N)	pounds force (lbs)
capacities	liters (l)	pints/quarts/gallons (pts/qts/gals)
torque	newton-meters (N-m)	foot pounds (ft lbs)
pressure	kilopascals (kPa)	pounds per square inch (psi)
volume	cubic centimeters (cm^3)	cubic inches (cu in.)
power	kilowatts (kW)	horsepower (hp)

If you have had any prior experience with the metric system, you may have noticed units in this chart which are not familiar to you. This is because, in some cases, SI units differ from the older gravimetric units which they replace. For example, newtons (N) replace kilograms (kg) as a force unit, kilopascals (kPa) replace atmospheres or bars as a unit of pressure, and, although the units are the same, the name Celsius replaces centigrade for temperature measurement.

If you are not using the SI tables, have a look at them anyway; you will be seeing a lot more of them in the future.

ENGLISH TO METRIC CONVERSION: MASS (WEIGHT)

Current **mass** measurement is expressed in pounds and ounces (lbs. & ozs.). The metric unit of mass (or weight) is the kilogram (kg). Even although this table does not show conversion of masses (weights) larger than 15 lbs, it is easy to calculate larger units by following the data immediately below.

To convert ounces (oz.) to grams (g): multiply th number of ozs. by 28
To convert grams (g) to ounces (oz.): multiply the number of grams by .035

To convert pounds (lbs.) to kilograms (kg): multiply the number of lbs. by .45
To convert kilograms (kg) to pounds (lbs.): multiply the number of kilograms by 2.2

lbs	kg	lbs	kg	oz	kg	oz	kg
0.1	0.04	0.9	0.41	0.1	0.003	0.9	0.024
0.2	0.09	1	0.4	0.2	0.005	1	0.03
0.3	0.14	2	0.9	0.3	0.008	2	0.06
0.4	0.18	3	1.4	0.4	0.011	3	0.08
0.5	0.23	4	1.8	0.5	0.014	4	0.11
0.6	0.27	5	2.3	0.6	0.017	5	0.14
0.7	0.32	10	4.5	0.7	0.020	10	0.28
0.8	0.36	15	6.8	0.8	0.023	15	0.42

ENGLISH TO METRIC CONVERSION: TEMPERATURE

To convert Fahrenheit (°F) to Celsius (°C): take number of °F and subtract 32; multiply result by 5; divide result by 9

To convert Celsius (°C) to Fahrenheit (°F): take number of °C and multiply by 9; divide result by 5; add 32 to total

Fahrenheit (F)		Celsius (C)		Fahrenheit (F)		Celsius (C)		Fahrenheit (F)		Celsius (C)	
°F	°C	°C	°F	°F	°C	°C	°F	°F	°C	°C	°F
−40	−40	−38	−36.4	80	26.7	18	64.4	215	101.7	80	176
−35	−37.2	−36	−32.8	85	29.4	20	68	220	104.4	85	185
−30	−34.4	−34	−29.2	90	32.2	22	71.6	225	107.2	90	194
−25	−31.7	−32	−25.6	95	35.0	24	75.2	230	110.0	95	202
−20	−28.9	−30	−22	100	37.8	26	78.8	235	112.8	100	212
−15	−26.1	−28	−18.4	105	40.6	28	82.4	240	115.6	105	221
−10	−23.3	−26	−14.8	110	43.3	30	86	245	118.3	110	230
−5	−20.6	−24	−11.2	115	46.1	32	89.6	250	121.1	115	239
0	−17.8	−22	−7.6	120	48.9	34	93.2	255	123.9	120	248
1	−17.2	−20	−4	125	51.7	36	96.8	260	126.6	125	257
2	−16.7	−18	−0.4	130	54.4	38	100.4	265	129.4	130	266
3	−16.1	−16	3.2	135	57.2	40	104	270	132.2	135	275
4	−15.6	−14	6.8	140	60.0	42	107.6	275	135.0	140	284
5	−15.0	−12	10.4	145	62.8	44	112.2	280	137.8	145	293
10	−12.2	−10	14	150	65.6	46	114.8	285	140.6	150	302
15	−9.4	−8	17.6	155	68.3	48	118.4	290	143.3	155	311
20	−6.7	−6	21.2	160	71.1	50	122	295	146.1	160	320
25	−3.9	−4	24.8	165	73.9	52	125.6	300	148.9	165	329
30	−1.1	−2	28.4	170	76.7	54	129.2	305	151.7	170	338
35	1.7	0	32	175	79.4	56	132.8	310	154.4	175	347
40	4.4	2	35.6	180	82.2	58	136.4	315	157.2	180	356
45	7.2	4	39.2	185	85.0	60	140	320	160.0	185	365
50	10.0	6	42.8	190	87.8	62	143.6	325	162.8	190	374
55	12.8	8	46.4	195	90.6	64	147.2	330	165.6	195	383
60	15.6	10	50	200	93.3	66	150.8	335	168.3	200	392
65	18.3	12	53.6	205	96.1	68	154.4	340	171.1	205	401
70	21.1	14	57.2	210	98.9	70	158	345	173.9	210	410
75	23.9	16	60.8	212	100.0	75	167	350	176.7	215	414

ENGLISH TO METRIC CONVERSION: LENGTH

To convert inches (ins.) to millimeters (mm): multiply number of inches by 25.4

To convert millimeters (mm) to inches (ins.): multiply number of millimeters by .04

Inches	Decimals	Milli-meters	Inches to millimeters inches	mm	Inches	Decimals	Milli-meters	Inches to millimeters inches	mm
1/64	0.051625	0.3969	0.0001	0.00254	33/64	0.515625	13.0969	0.6	15.24
1/32	0.03125	0.7937	0.0002	0.00508	17/32	0.53125	13.4937	0.7	17.78
3/64	0.046875	1.1906	0.0003	0.00762	35/64	0.546875	13.8906	0.8	20.32
1/16	0.0625	1.5875	0.0004	0.01016	9/16	0.5625	14.2875	0.9	22.86
5/64	0.078125	1.9844	0.0005	0.01270	37/64	0.578125	14.6844	1	25.4
3/32	0.09375	2.3812	0.0006	0.01524	19/32	0.59375	15.0812	2	50.8
7/64	0.109375	2.7781	0.0007	0.01778	39/64	0.609375	15.4781	3	76.2
1/8	0.125	3.1750	0.0008	0.02032	5/8	0.625	15.8750	4	101.6
9/64	0.140625	3.5719	0.0009	0.02286	41/64	0.640625	16.2719	5	127.0
5/32	0.15625	3.9687	0.001	0.0254	21/32	0.65625	16.6687	6	152.4
11/64	0.171875	4.3656	0.002	0.0508	43/64	0.671875	17.0656	7	177.8
3/16	0.1875	4.7625	0.003	0.0762	11/16	0.6875	17.4625	8	203.2
13/64	0.203125	5.1594	0.004	0.1016	45/64	0.703125	17.8594	9	228.6
7/32	0.21875	5.5562	0.005	0.1270	23/32	0.71875	18.2562	10	254.0
15/64	0.234375	5.9531	0.006	0.1524	47/64	0.734375	18.6531	11	279.4
1/4	0.25	6.3500	0.007	0.1778	3/4	0.75	19.0500	12	304.8
17/64	0.265625	6.7469	0.008	0.2032	49/64	0.765625	19.4469	13	330.2
9/32	0.28125	7.1437	0.009	0.2286	25/32	0.78125	19.8437	14	355.6
19/64	0.296875	7.5406	0.01	0.254	51/64	0.796875	20.2406	15	381.0
5/16	0.3125	7.9375	0.02	0.508	13/16	0.8125	20.6375	16	406.4
21/64	0.328125	8.3344	0.03	0.762	53/64	0.828125	21.0344	17	431.8
11/32	0.34375	8.7312	0.04	1.016	27/32	0.84375	21.4312	18	457.2
23/64	0.359375	9.1281	0.05	1.270	55/64	0.859375	21.8281	19	482.6
3/8	0.375	9.5250	0.06	1.524	7/8	0.875	22.2250	20	508.0
25/64	0.390625	9.9219	0.07	1.778	57/64	0.890625	22.6219	21	533.4
13/32	0.40625	10.3187	0.08	2.032	29/32	0.90625	23.0187	22	558.8
27/64	0.421875	10.7156	0.09	2.286	59/64	0.921875	23.4156	23	584.2
7/16	0.4375	11.1125	0.1	2.54	15/16	0.9375	23.8125	24	609.6
29/64	0.453125	11.5094	0.2	5.08	61/64	0.953125	24.2094	25	635.0
15/32	0.46875	11.9062	0.3	7.62	31/32	0.96875	24.6062	26	660.4
31/64	0.484375	12.3031	0.4	10.16	63/64	0.984375	25.0031	27	690.6
1/2	0.5	12.7000	0.5	12.70					

ENGLISH TO METRIC CONVERSION: TORQUE

To convert foot-pounds (ft. lbs.) to Newton-meters: multiply the number of ft. lbs. by 1.3

To convert inch-pounds (in. lbs.) to Newton-meters: multiply the number of in. lbs. by .11

in lbs	N-m	in lbs	N-m	in lbs	N-m	in lbs	N-m	in lbs	N-m
0.1	0.01	1	0.11	10	1.13	19	2.15	28	3.16
0.2	0.02	2	0.23	11	1.24	20	2.26	29	3.28
0.3	0.03	3	0.34	12	1.36	21	2.37	30	3.39
0.4	0.04	4	0.45	13	1.47	22	2.49	31	3.50
0.5	0.06	5	0.56	14	1.58	23	2.60	32	3.62
0.6	0.07	6	0.68	15	1.70	24	2.71	33	3.73
0.7	0.08	7	0.78	16	1.81	25	2.82	34	3.84
0.8	0.09	8	0.90	17	1.92	26	2.94	35	3.95
0.9	0.10	9	1.02	18	2.03	27	3.05	36	4.07

ENGLISH TO METRIC CONVERSION: TORQUE

Torque is now expressed as either foot-pounds (ft./lbs.) or inch-pounds (in./lbs.). The metric measurement unit for torque is the Newton-meter (Nm). This unit—the Nm—will be used for all SI metric torque references, both the present ft./lbs. and in./lbs.

ft lbs	N-m	ft lbs	N-m	ft lbs	N-m	ft lbs	N-m
0.1	0.1	33	44.7	74	100.3	115	155.9
0.2	0.3	34	46.1	75	101.7	116	157.3
0.3	0.4	35	47.4	76	103.0	117	158.6
0.4	0.5	36	48.8	77	104.4	118	160.0
0.5	0.7	37	50.7	78	105.8	119	161.3
0.6	0.8	38	51.5	79	107.1	120	162.7
0.7	1.0	39	52.9	80	108.5	121	164.0
0.8	1.1	40	54.2	81	109.8	122	165.4
0.9	1.2	41	55.6	82	111.2	123	166.8
1	1.3	42	56.9	83	112.5	124	168.1
2	2.7	43	58.3	84	113.9	125	169.5
3	4.1	44	59.7	85	115.2	126	170.8
4	5.4	45	61.0	86	116.6	127	172.2
5	6.8	46	62.4	87	118.0	128	173.5
6	8.1	47	63.7	88	119.3	129	174.9
7	9.5	48	65.1	89	120.7	130	176.2
8	10.8	49	66.4	90	122.0	131	177.6
9	12.2	50	67.8	91	123.4	132	179.0
10	13.6	51	69.2	92	124.7	133	180.3
11	14.9	52	70.5	93	126.1	134	181.7
12	16.3	53	71.9	94	127.4	135	183.0
13	17.6	54	73.2	95	128.8	136	184.4
14	18.9	55	74.6	96	130.2	137	185.7
15	20.3	56	75.9	97	131.5	138	187.1
16	21.7	57	77.3	98	132.9	139	188.5
17	23.0	58	78.6	99	134.2	140	189.8
18	24.4	59	80.0	100	135.6	141	191.2
19	25.8	60	81.4	101	136.9	142	192.5
20	27.1	61	82.7	102	138.3	143	193.9
21	28.5	62	84.1	103	139.6	144	195.2
22	29.8	63	85.4	104	141.0	145	196.6
23	31.2	64	86.8	105	142.4	146	198.0
24	32.5	65	88.1	106	143.7	147	199.3
25	33.9	66	89.5	107	145.1	148	200.7
26	35.2	67	90.8	108	146.4	149	202.0
27	36.6	68	92.2	109	147.8	150	203.4
28	38.0	69	93.6	110	149.1	151	204.7
29	39.3	70	94.9	111	150.5	152	206.1
30	40.7	71	96.3	112	151.8	153	207.4
31	42.0	72	97.6	113	153.2	154	208.8
32	43.4	73	99.0	114	154.6	155	210.2

ENGLISH TO METRIC CONVERSION: FORCE

Force is presently measured in pounds (lbs.). This type of measurement is used to measure spring pressure, specifically how many pounds it takes to compress a spring. Our present force unit (the pound) will be replaced in SI metric measurements by the Newton (N). This term will eventually see use in specifications for electric motor brush spring pressures, valve spring pressures, etc.

To convert pounds (lbs.) to Newton (N): multiply the number of lbs. by 4.45

lbs	N	lbs	N	lbs	N	oz	N
0.01	0.04	21	93.4	59	262.4	1	0.3
0.02	0.09	22	97.9	60	266.9	2	0.6
0.03	0.13	23	102.3	61	271.3	3	0.8
0.04	0.18	24	106.8	62	275.8	4	1.1
0.05	0.22	25	111.2	63	280.2	5	1.4
0.06	0.27	26	115.6	64	284.6	6	1.7
0.07	0.31	27	120.1	65	289.1	7	2.0
0.08	0.36	28	124.6	66	293.6	8	2.2
0.09	0.40	29	129.0	67	298.0	9	2.5
0.1	0.4	30	133.4	68	302.5	10	2.8
0.2	0.9	31	137.9	69	306.9	11	3.1
0.3	1.3	32	142.3	70	311.4	12	3.3
0.4	1.8	33	146.8	71	315.8	13	3.6
0.5	2.2	34	151.2	72	320.3	14	3.9
0.6	2.7	35	155.7	73	324.7	15	4.2
0.7	3.1	36	160.1	74	329.2	16	4.4
0.8	3.6	37	164.6	75	333.6	17	4.7
0.9	4.0	38	169.0	76	338.1	18	5.0
1	4.4	39	173.5	77	342.5	19	5.3
2	8.9	40	177.9	78	347.0	20	5.6
3	13.4	41	182.4	79	351.4	21	5.8
4	17.8	42	186.8	80	355.9	22	6.1
5	22.2	43	191.3	81	360.3	23	6.4
6	26.7	44	195.7	82	364.8	24	6.7
7	31.1	45	200.2	83	369.2	25	7.0
8	35.6	46	204.6	84	373.6	26	7.2
9	40.0	47	209.1	85	378.1	27	7.5
10	44.5	48	213.5	86	382.6	28	7.8
11	48.9	49	218.0	87	387.0	29	8.1
12	53.4	50	224.4	88	391.4	30	8.3
13	57.8	51	226.9	89	395.9	31	8.6
14	62.3	52	231.3	90	400.3	32	8.9
15	66.7	53	235.8	91	404.8	33	9.2
16	71.2	54	240.2	92	409.2	34	9.4
17	75.6	55	244.6	93	413.7	35	9.7
18	80.1	56	249.1	94	418.1	36	10.0
19	84.5	57	253.6	95	422.6	37	10.3
20	89.0	58	258.0	96	427.0	38	10.6

ENGLISH TO METRIC CONVERSION: LIQUID CAPACITY

Liquid or fluid capacity is presently expressed as pints, quarts or gallons, or a combination of all of these. In the metric system the liter (l) will become the basic unit. Fractions of a liter would be expressed as deciliters, centiliters, or most frequently (and commonly) as milliliters.

To convert pints (pts.) to liters (l): multiply the number of pints by .47
To convert liters (l) to pints (pts.): multiply the number of liters by 2.1
To convert quarts (qts.) to liters (l): multiply the number of quarts by .95

To convert liters (l) to quarts (qts.): multiply the number of liters by 1.06
To convert gallons (gals.) to liters (l): multiply the number of gallons by 3.8
To convert liters (l) to gallons (gals.): multiply the number of liters by .26

gals	liters	qts	liters	pts	liters
0.1	0.38	0.1	0.10	0.1	0.05
0.2	0.76	0.2	0.19	0.2	0.10
0.3	1.1	0.3	0.28	0.3	0.14
0.4	1.5	0.4	0.38	0.4	0.19
0.5	1.9	0.5	0.47	0.5	0.24
0.6	2.3	0.6	0.57	0.6	0.28
0.7	2.6	0.7	0.66	0.7	0.33
0.8	3.0	0.8	0.76	0.8	0.38
0.9	3.4	0.9	0.85	0.9	0.43
1	3.8	1	1.0	1	0.5
2	7.6	2	1.9	2	1.0
3	11.4	3	2.8	3	1.4
4	15.1	4	3.8	4	1.9
5	18.9	5	4.7	5	2.4
6	22.7	6	5.7	6	2.8
7	26.5	7	6.6	7	3.3
8	30.3	8	7.6	8	3.8
9	34.1	9	8.5	9	4.3
10	37.8	10	9.5	10	4.7
11	41.6	11	10.4	11	5.2
12	45.4	12	11.4	12	5.7
13	49.2	13	12.3	13	6.2
14	53.0	14	13.2	14	6.6
15	56.8	15	14.2	15	7.1
16	60.6	16	15.1	16	7.6
17	64.3	17	16.1	17	8.0
18	68.1	18	17.0	18	8.5
19	71.9	19	18.0	19	9.0
20	75.7	20	18.9	20	9.5
21	79.5	21	19.9	21	9.9
22	83.2	22	20.8	22	10.4
23	87.0	23	21.8	23	10.9
24	90.8	24	22.7	24	11.4
25	94.6	25	23.6	25	11.8
26	98.4	26	24.6	26	12.3
27	102.2	27	25.5	27	12.8
28	106.0	28	26.5	28	13.2
29	110.0	29	27.4	29	13.7
30	113.5	30	28.4	30	14.2

ENGLISH TO METRIC CONVERSION: PRESSURE

The basic unit of pressure measurement used today is expressed as pounds per square inch (psi). The metric unit for psi will be the kilopascal (kPa). This will apply to either fluid pressure or air pressure, and will be frequently seen in tire pressure readings, oil pressure specifications, fuel pump pressure, etc.

To convert pounds per square inch (psi) to kilopascals (kPa): multiply the number of psi by 6.89

Psi	kPa	Psi	kPa	Psi	kPa	Psi	kPa
0.1	0.7	37	255.1	82	565.4	127	875.6
0.2	1.4	38	262.0	83	572.3	128	882.5
0.3	2.1	39	268.9	84	579.2	129	889.4
0.4	2.8	40	275.8	85	586.0	130	896.3
0.5	3.4	41	282.7	86	592.9	131	903.2
0.6	4.1	42	289.6	87	599.8	132	910.1
0.7	4.8	43	296.5	88	606.7	133	917.0
0.8	5.5	44	303.4	89	613.6	134	923.9
0.9	6.2	45	310.3	90	620.5	135	930.8
1	6.9	46	317.2	91	627.4	136	937.7
2	13.8	47	324.0	92	634.3	137	944.6
3	20.7	48	331.0	93	641.2	138	951.5
4	27.6	49	337.8	94	648.1	139	958.4
5	34.5	50	344.7	95	655.0	140	965.2
6	41.4	51	351.6	96	661.9	141	972.2
7	48.3	52	358.5	97	668.8	142	979.0
8	55.2	53	365.4	98	675.7	143	985.9
9	62.1	54	372.3	99	682.6	144	992.8
10	69.0	55	379.2	100	689.5	145	999.7
11	75.8	56	386.1	101	696.4	146	1006.6
12	82.7	57	393.0	102	703.3	147	1013.5
13	89.6	58	399.9	103	710.2	148	1020.4
14	96.5	59	406.8	104	717.0	149	1027.3
15	103.4	60	413.7	105	723.9	150	1034.2
16	110.3	61	420.6	106	730.8	151	1041.1
17	117.2	62	427.5	107	737.7	152	1048.0
18	124.1	63	434.4	108	744.6	153	1054.9
19	131.0	64	441.3	109	751.5	154	1061.8
20	137.9	65	448.2	110	758.4	155	1068.7
21	144.8	66	455.0	111	765.3	156	1075.6
22	151.7	67	461.9	112	772.2	157	1082.5
23	158.6	68	468.8	113	779.1	158	1089.4
24	165.5	69	475.7	114	786.0	159	1096.3
25	172.4	70	482.6	115	792.9	160	1103.2
26	179.3	71	489.5	116	799.8	161	1110.0
27	186.2	72	496.4	117	806.7	162	1116.9
28	193.0	73	503.3	118	813.6	163	1123.8
29	200.0	74	510.2	119	820.5	164	1130.7
30	206.8	75	517.1	120	827.4	165	1137.6
31	213.7	76	524.0	121	834.3	166	1144.5
32	220.6	77	530.9	122	841.2	167	1151.4
33	227.5	78	537.8	123	848.0	168	1158.3
34	234.4	79	544.7	124	854.9	169	1165.2
35	241.3	80	551.6	125	861.8	170	1172.1
36	248.2	81	558.5	126	868.7	171	1179.0

ENGLISH TO METRIC CONVERSION: PRESSURE

The basic unit of pressure measurement used today is expressed as pounds per square inch (psi). The metric unit for psi will be the kilopascal (kPa). This will apply to either fluid pressure or air pressure, and will be frequently seen in tire pressure readings, oil pressure specifications, fuel pump pressure, etc.

To convert pounds per square inch (psi) to kilopascals (kPa): multiply the number of psi by 6.89

Psi	kPa	Psi	kPa	Psi	kPa	Psi	kPa
172	1185.9	216	1489.3	260	1792.6	304	2096.0
173	1192.8	217	1496.2	261	1799.5	305	2102.9
174	1199.7	218	1503.1	262	1806.4	306	2109.8
175	1206.6	219	1510.0	263	1813.3	307	2116.7
176	1213.5	220	1516.8	264	1820.2	308	2123.6
177	1220.4	221	1523.7	265	1827.1	309	2130.5
178	1227.3	222	1530.6	266	1834.0	310	2137.4
179	1234.2	223	1537.5	267	1840.9	311	2144.3
180	1241.0	224	1544.4	268	1847.8	312	2151.2
181	1247.9	225	1551.3	269	1854.7	313	2158.1
182	1254.8	226	1558.2	270	1861.6	314	2164.9
183	1261.7	227	1565.1	271	1868.5	315	2171.8
184	1268.6	228	1572.0	272	1875.4	316	2178.7
185	1275.5	229	1578.9	273	1882.3	317	2185.6
186	1282.4	230	1585.8	274	1889.2	318	2192.5
187	1289.3	231	1592.7	275	1896.1	319	2199.4
188	1296.2	232	1599.6	276	1903.0	320	2206.3
189	1303.1	233	1606.5	277	1909.8	321	2213.2
190	1310.0	234	1613.4	278	1916.7	322	2220.1
191	1316.9	235	1620.3	279	1923.6	323	2227.0
192	1323.8	236	1627.2	280	1930.5	324	2233.9
193	1330.7	237	1634.1	281	1937.4	325	2240.8
194	1337.6	238	1641.0	282	1944.3	326	2247.7
195	1344.5	239	1647.8	283	1951.2	327	2254.6
196	1351.4	240	1654.7	284	1958.1	328	2261.5
197	1358.3	241	1661.6	285	1965.0	329	2268.4
198	1365.2	242	1668.5	286	1971.9	330	2275.3
199	1372.0	243	1675.4	287	1978.8	331	2282.2
200	1378.9	244	1682.3	288	1985.7	332	2289.1
201	1385.8	245	1689.2	289	1992.6	333	2295.9
202	1392.7	246	1696.1	290	1999.5	334	2302.8
203	1399.6	247	1703.0	291	2006.4	335	2309.7
204	1406.5	248	1709.9	292	2013.3	336	2316.6
205	1413.4	249	1716.8	293	2020.2	337	2323.5
206	1420.3	250	1723.7	294	2027.1	338	2330.4
207	1427.2	251	1730.6	295	2034.0	339	2337.3
208	1434.1	252	1737.5	296	2040.8	240	2344.2
209	1441.0	253	1744.4	297	2047.7	341	2351.1
210	1447.9	254	1751.3	298	2054.6	342	2358.0
211	1454.8	255	1758.2	299	2061.5	343	2364.9
212	1461.7	256	1765.1	300	2068.4	344	2371.8
213	1468.7	257	1772.0	301	2075.3	345	2378.7
214	1475.5	258	1778.8	302	2082.2	346	2385.6
215	1482.4	259	1785.7	303	2089.1	347	2392.5